STANDARD CATALOG OF

AMERICAN CARS

1805-1942

Beverly Rae Kimes, Historian and Author

Henry Austin Clark, Jr., Chief of Research

Consultants to the Author
Ralph Dunwoodie, Keith Marvin

Marque Researchers
Robert C. Ackerson, Dr. William Bell, Jim Benjaminson, Arch Brown, Dennis Casteele, Phil Dumka, John A. Gunnell, Gary Hoonsbeen, Bruce McCally, M.C. "Pinky" Randall.

Cover Design
Paul Tofte

Second Edition

krause publications

IOLA, WISCONSIN 54990

FOREWORD

The *Standard Catalog of American Cars 1805-1942* provides historical, technical and current pricing information about thousands of automobiles built in the United States prior to World War II. It is the companion volume to Krause Publication's award-winning *Standard Catalog of American Cars 1946-1975*.

The scope of coverage in this catalog's more than 1,500 pages ranges from steam, electric, spring and gasoline powered automobiles to high-wheelers and cycle cars. It covers marques built by both large and small manufacturers.

Historian and Author Beverly Rae Kimes compiled the majority of information in the catalog. Henry Austin Clark, Jr. served as Chief of Research. Ralph Dunwoodie and Keith Marvin were Consultants to the Author. Countless other historians, hobbyists, collectors and photographers made significant contributions to the catalog.

Four basic types of formats were used to catalog different brands and types of automobiles. Information on page 7 explains how to read the long form listings used in the case of 16 more popular makes of cars. Introductions for these marques were written by Beverly Rae Kimes and the data compilations were done by eleven Marque Research Specialists shown on the title page. Their individual specialty areas are noted on page 9. The gathering of all current pricing information was supervised by Ken Buttolph, the Research Editor of *Old Cars Price Guide,* a periodical published quarterly by Krause Publications.

Three different formats were used to catalog other brands and types of automobiles, depending upon the size of the manufacturer and the amount of detailed information available on a particular make. Information on page 8 explains how to use these short form listings.

Chester L. Krause, publisher of *Old Cars Weekly,* is responsible for the overall concept of creating the "Standard Catalog" series covering American automobiles. David V. Brownell, editor of *Special Interest Autos* undertook preliminary work on the concept while serving as editor of *Old Cars Weekly* in the 1970s. Editor John A. Gunnell assumed the project in 1978. The first *Standard Catalog,* covering postwar models, was published in 1982, while Beverly Rae Kimes continued her writing and research for this prewar edition.

The two-volume set provides students of automotive history with a comprehensive, easy to use reference source that can be used as a guide for the direction of their efforts. The two *Standard Catalogs* set forth, at the same time, a great deal of detailed information that car collectors, hobbyists and restorers will not find in any other one place.

These *Standard Catalogs* are not perfect books. Perfection is a goal which we can strive for, but never obtain. They are, rather, intended as a contribution to the pursuit of greater knowledge about the many wonderful automobiles built in the United States over 171 years.

We hope that you will find either or both of the *Standard Catalogs* informative, useful and entertaining. We sincerely believe that they answer thousands of questions which are frequently asked of the editors of *Old Cars Weekly* and *Old Cars Price Guide.* At the same time, we expect they will raise new questions and bring forth new facts that deserve inclusion in future editions.

Should you have access to expanded information that you wish to share, please don't hesitate to contact the editors, in care of: Krause Publications, 700 East State St., Iola, WI 54990.

CONTENTS

Staff 4
Abbreviations 4
Introduction 5
How to Use Catalog:
    Major Marque Listings 7
    Minor Marque Listings 8
Marque Research Specialists 9
Photo Sources 9
1-5 Condition Code Chart 10
Body Popularity Trend 1919-1941 10
Standard Catalog of American Cars 11

Acknowledgments 1532
Archives, Libraries, Museums, Societies
.... 1534
Bibliography 1540
Index: Alternate Power Cars 1542
Index: Cyclecars 1544
Index: Highwheelers 1545
Index: Makers by State and City 1546
Historian and Author Biography 1558
Chief of Research Biography 1559
Catalog Awards 1560
Museums in America 1561

ABBREVIATIONS

A.L.A.M.	Assoc. of Licensed Automobile Manufacturers
A.S.	Auxiliary seat
A.W. or A/W	All-Weather
Amb.	Ambassador
Aero	Aerodynamic
BHP	Brake Horsepower
B x S	Bore x Stroke
B.T.	Boattailed
BerL.	Berline
Blk. Hwk.	Black Hawk
Brdcl.	Broadcloth
Brn.	Brunn
Brou. or Brgm.	Brougham
C.C.	Close-coupled
Cabr.	Cabriolet
Carb.	Carburetor
Car. Sed.	Carryall Sedan
Clb.	Club
Clpsl. or Coll.	Collapsible
C'ml. Rds.	Commercial Roadster
Conv.	Convertible
Conv. Sed.	Convertible Sedan
Cpe.	Coupe
Cpe. P.U.	Coupe Pickup
Crw. or Crwn.	Crown
Ctry. Clb.	Country Club
Cus. or Cust.	Custom
D.C. or D/C	Dual Cowl
D.W. or D/W	Dual Windshield
Darr.	Darrin
Dr. (2-dr.)	Door (two-door)
DeL.	Deluxe
Demi. T.C.	Demi Tonneau Covered
Dep. Hk.	Depot Hack
Der.	Derham
Div.	Division Window
Dtrch.	Dietrich
Dict.	Dictator
Disp.	Displacement
Drhm.	Derham
Dup. or Dupl.	Duplex
E.D.	Enclosed Drive
E.W.B.	Extended Wheelbase
Eight	Eight-Cylinder
Encl.	Enclosed
Est. Wag.	Estate Wagon
F (3F)	Forward (three forward speeds)
FP	Factory Price
Fam.	Family
FmL.	Formal
Fordor	Four-door sedan
Four	Four-Cylinder
Frsm.	Foursome
Frt.	Front
FsBk.	Fastback
G.R.	Gear Ratio
H.	Height
HdTp.	Hardtop
Holb. or Hol.	Holbrook
Imp.	Imperial
J.S. or J/S	Jump Seats
Jud.	Judkins
L.B. or Lthr. Bk.	Leather Back
L.T. or Lthr. Tp.	Leather Top
L.W.B.	Long Wheelbase
Lan.	Landau
Lan'let.	Landaulet
LeB.	LeBaron
Lke.	Locke
Limo.	Limousine
Lthr. Trm.	Leather Trim
M.B. or Mtl. Bk.	Metal Back
MPG	Miles per Gallon
MPH	Miles per Hour
Mast.	Master
Metro.	Metropolitan
Mhr.	Mohair
Mstr.	Master
Mur.	Murphy
Murr.	Murray
N.A.C.C.	National Automobile Chamber of Commerce
N.C.	Non-Collapsible
N & M	Nordyke & Marmon
Nwpt.	Newport
O.L.	Overall Length
O.S. or O/S	Opera Seat
OSRV	Outside Rear View
O.W. or O/W	Opera Window
Oxf.	Oxford
P (2P)	Passengers (two-pass.)
Pat.	Patrician
Phae.	Phaeton
Pres.	President
R. (1R)	Reverse (one reverse speed)
R.P.M.	Revolutions Per Minute
R.S. or R/S	Rumbleseat
Rbt.	Runabout
Rds.	Roadster
Reg.	Regal
Rex	Rex All-Weather Top
Rlstn.	Rollston
Roy. or Ryl.	Royal
S.C.	Semi-Collapsible
S.M.	Side Mount
S-R	Sunroof
S.W.B.	Short Wheelbase
Sal.	Salon
Sed.	Sedan
Sed. Dly.	Sedan Delivery
Six	Six-Cylinder
Spdbt.	Speedabout
Spds.	Speedster
Spec. or Spl.	Special
Spt.	Sport(s)
Sptman.	Sportsman
Sta. Wag.	Station Wagon
Std.	Standard
St. Reg. or St. R.	St. Regis
Strom.	Stromberg
Sub.	Suburban
T.C. or T/C	Tonneau Cowl
T & C	Town & Country
Taxi	Taxicab
Torp.	Torpedo
Tour.	Tourist(er)
Tr.	Touring
Trans.	Transformable
Trk.	Trunk
Tudor	Two-door sedan
T. Wis.	Tonneau Windshield
Twn.	Town
Twn.C.	Town Car
Univ.	Universal
Utl.	Utility
Vic.	Victoria
W (2W)	Window (two window)
W.B.	Wheelbase
W.P. or W/P	With Partition
W.S.W.	White Sidewall
W.W.	Whitewalls
W.T.	Winter Top
Wan.	Wanderer
Wd. Whl.	Wood Wheel
W. Whl.	Wire Wheel
Wlby.	Willoughby
Woodie	Wood-bodied Car

STAFF

Publisher: Chester L. Krause
Editor: John A. Gunnell
Research Editor: Ken Buttolph

INTRODUCTION

Preparing this second edition has been a case of *deja vu*. After nearly four years, I couldn't recall everything that I had said in the introduction to the first edition but, even without rereading, I remembered mentioning that volume was a start and that preparation of subsequent ones would undoubtedly be just as spirited an adventure. What follows in the next fifteen-hundred-plus pages is a continuation — and it has been enormously exciting to compile.

The wealth of new material that publication of the first edition brought to light has been simply staggering. Particularly rewarding for me was the enthusiasm and dedication with which historians dug deeper into cars produced in their regions, invariably ferreting out fascinating new data and sometimes hilarious anecdotes. In many cases I had provided only a clue, and they solved the mystery. Devotees of specific marques were likewise generous in offering fresh information and setting me right where I went wrong. All of these additions — and they run into the thousands — have been incorporated in this second edition. This edition benefits, too, from hundreds of new photographs — cars for which no illustration was available for the first edition, as well as a more representative sampling for the prominent and long-lived marques.

It's rather a pity that Madison Avenue usurped, and long ago relegated to banality, the phrase "new and improved." Because that's what this second edition is. All those who helped make it so are acknowledged elsewhere in this book. But it should be emphasized that in no way is this volume regarded as the final word on the American automobile prior to 1942. Thankfully, there may never be one. Among the most compelling aspects of American automobile history is its vitality — there is always something new to discover.

And so we shall ever continue....

--Beverly Rae Kimes
October, 1988

Were he alive today, Benjamin Franklin might say it differently. Back in 1789, commenting to a friend that although the new U.S. Constitution was in operation whether it would last was another matter, he observed that the only certainties were death and taxes. To them may be added another: We shall never know the exact number of cars built in this country.

The history of the American automobile is a can of worms that would make any self-respecting bilateral invertebrate blanche. This is not meant as a pejorative, however; in fact, it is the sublime disorderliness of the saga of the American car that is among its chief charms, and doubtless shall ever hold the fascination of those who pursue its history.

That automobile history would ever remain untidy was preordained at the turn of the century when Gardner D. Hiscox printed his "List of Automobile Manufacturers in the United States, With Their Addresses" in the book *Horseless Vehicles, Automobiles, Motor Cycles.* This was followed nine years later by "MoToR's Historical Table of the Motor Car Industry" published in that magazine's March

1909 issue — and a positive deluge of car rosters ever since. As the industry grew up, so did the publications serving it, with trade directories routinely printing up lists of the cars being built in this country in their annual, biannual or tri-monthly editions.

After the Second World War, by which time natural attrition and the Great Depression had dwindled the ranks of manufacturers from the many to the few, the tantalizing notion of just how many different cars had been built in this country gained new force. Prior to 1950 the Antique Automobile Club of America published a list totaling 1525, the Eaton Manufacturing Company a roll call numbering 1876. In the next two decades magazines as diverse as the *Saturday Evening Post* and *Esquire* took up the question and came up with rosters numbering 2726 and 1690 respectively. Meanwhile American automobile historians were compiling their own lists and finding many more cars than had appeared on any of the others. It all turned into a wonderful free-for-all, with numbers quickly surmounting three thousand and no end in sight.

Every list compiled was important, certainly, because every new list brought new cars to light. The pioneering efforts of such historians as Stanley K. Yost, W.E. Miller, Dr. Alfred Lewerenz, Ralph Dunwoodie and Frank T. Snyder on all-America lists, together with the many historians tackling list making on a regional basis, and culminating in the "5000 Marques" roster, the annotated compilation of all earlier lists, plus some more, that was published in 1971 in the Automobile Quarterly Publications book *The American Car Since 1775* — all these efforts should be applauded as providing guideposts for further research.

A factor inherent in any list, of course, is that it is quantitative, and by its nature does not for the most part judge qualitatively. Compounding of error is thus inevitable. A car incorrectly indicated to have been built on a 1908 car roster, for example, may be perpetuated as a bona-fide entry for decades thereafter. A typo appearing in a list from the 1950's might continue to be entered as a legitimate car on lists in the 1980's. And to further muddy things, some historians (myself and Ralph Dunwoodie among them) are convinced that a few list compilers inserted bogus cars in their own efforts just to determine if other list compilers were indulging in plagiarism. There is something perversely delightful about that, but it does nonetheless present a dilemma.

The result of all this is that can of worms mentioned earlier, and the problem of how to approach the presentation of this volume. Early on, we decided to go with the whole can, or as much of it anyway that was fathomable at all. Only in this way could we avoid the otherwise inevitable "hey, but you forgot. . ." by replying in effect, no, we didn't forget, it was simply a mistake, or we don't believe anything was built.

Vis-a-vis American car compilations of the past, it should be noted that research for this volume revealed there were both more American cars built than previously believed, and there were less. Among the reasons for the latter is that during the early days a projected new car might be announced under one name, by the time the pilot model was built and promoted it had acquired another, and when finally it arrived on the marketplace it was called something else yet again. Thus the same car could have led three different lives before a single exam- ple was sold. But for every two cars which fell by the way- side this way, it seemed that another two were discov- ered and documented which had never before even been known about. Incredibly, new old cars are still being found, even as this is written.

Differentiation should be made between cars that were built and cars that were manufactured. Although on the face of it, this appears easy, it is not because a fine line exists even when both quantitative and qualitative judg- ments are brought to bear. Is an officially organized com- pany that barely made it to a pilot assembly line any more properly regarded as a manufacturer than the small unin- corporated machine shop that put together cars for a number of years whenever someone in the neighborhood asked for one? The answer to that could be endlessly and provocatively debated, though any conclusions drawn would probably veer toward the existential.

For the purpose of this volume, the simple matter of a car having been built was the criterion. Recognizing the efforts of those early pioneers who made their own cars, if only in a single example, is important for an overall under- standing of what this country was like during the dawn of the horseless age. The American automobile did not arise full-grown onto an assembly line. Its borning years and its puberty were experienced in hundreds of villages and towns from coast to coast, as small machine shops, bicy- cle builders and carriage makers — even doctors, jewel- ers and florists — used a few tools and varying talent to put themselves automotively on the road. Some of these early pioneers built their cars with the glorious hope of full-fledged manufacture, others because they thought they could do better than what was available to them on the market, which often they could, as witnessed by some of the admirable one-off efforts which remain in existence to this day. Other attempts were less successful, of course, and some were downright bizarre, but all of these pioneer vehicles deserve to be woven into the fabric of this nation's automotive heritage because they were undeniably part of it.

Undeniably part of that heritage too were the frauds and stock swindles. It was inevitable that the automobile would attract its share of charlatans and get-rich-quick schemers who produced vast quantities of stock certifi- cates and enticing brochures, and very little else. Since most of these flim-flam artists were adroit in promotion, their ventures were frequently and lavishly reported in the trade press, their companies were included in trade direc- tories, and ever after they have been listed as manufac- turers of cars, though their total production may have been just one, or none at all.

In addition, of course, to those whose intentions were nefarious from the beginning were the untold others who legitimately launched ventures for the purpose of manu- facturing cars, but who seem not to have managed to fol- low through. Again, these companies announced their presence to the trade press, were duly listed at the time as bona-fide manufacturers, and have continued to be thought so since — though the only documentation extant of their activity was the notice of intent to manu- facture. This is not to suggest that there was never an automobile built of such ventures, only that we have not discovered any evidence of one thus far. But if one lesson has been learned in this project, it is not to give up easily. On numerous occasions when all hope was about to be abandoned regarding the reality of a particular automo- bile, likely as not evidence of it turned up almost immedi- ately somewhere. This sort of thing tends to keep an automobile historian humble, and reluctant to use the word never.

incorporation notice and a trade directory listing have been included here, with the disclaimer that manufacture is doubted, though we will very happily stand corrected whenever documentation otherwise is forthcoming. The interesting curiosity of automobile history is that one can- not facilely make assumptions regarding the viability of projected automobile ventures. A goodly number which were incorporated with a capital stock of $5000 or less proceeded into production, while others incorporated for millions did not. Indeed, some of the latter are not repre- sented in this book, what might be called the Croteau law being exercised here. During the years surrounding the World War I era, one T.L. Croteau enjoyed membership in that phalanx of attorneys and official incorporators who took care of the paperwork for a veritable multitude of unnamed automobile entrepreneurs launching ventures under the lenient laws of such states as Delaware and Maine. Never — and that word being operative in this case — heard of again, there remains nothing upon which any further research could be undertaken in these cases, and it is virtually unquestionable that no automobile activ- ity followed.

Likewise not included here are those cars which have appeared previously in name only, because more often than not the automobile indicated was nothing more than a misspelling of another one. The Durgen of pre-World War I was a convolution of the Duryea, for example, the Bar- clay of the early Twenties was in reality the Barley; what the Pitcher listed in AC Spark Plug ads about the same time hasn't been deciphered with certainty yet, but a Pitcher most probably it wasn't. The uppermost factor in the mention of a questionable car in this volume is that there be something upon which subsequent research might be based — a place where the car was to have been built and the names of those involved in its proposed building.

This indicates of course that this book does not pretend to be the final word on the subject of the American car. Automobile history is not static, it is alive, ongoing and ever changing as more is learned and documented. There are more cars presented here than ever before, but with- out the presumption that the result is complete. Errors

Therefore, automobiles and automobile ventures for which no further evidence has been discovered than an which have been perpetuated through the years regard- ing many cars are corrected here, though it is acknow- ledged that unquestionably there will be mistakes in this book.

But this is a start, and that one has to start somewhere is both a cliche and a fact. This volume does not close the book on American cars, instead it opens it wider. In over two decades there has not been one of the hundreds of car histories I've written which did not generate new information from sources one could not possibly have known about previously. There are thousands of Ameri- can automobiles here — steamers, electrics, gasoline cars, high-wheeled motor buggies, cyclecars, light cars, touring cars, taxis, assembled cars, grand classics, juve- niles, racytype roadsters, streamlined experimentals, Doctor's specials, stanhopes, dual cowl phaetons, cars of one cylinder, two, three, four, five, six, eight, nine, twelve, sixteen . . . cars that are magnificent, cars that are ungodly, cars that are, well, just cars. It is positively mind- boggling to consider the new information and lore that will arise about them from the publication of this book. Pre- paring subsequent editions promises to be an even more spirited adventure than this one was.

--Beverly Rae Kimes
January, 1985

APPEARANCE AND EQUIPMENT: Word descriptions help identify prewar cars down to details such as styling features, trim and even paint colors. A list of technical equipment features is provided when available. Information is given according to series, with separate series covered in separate data blocks.

VEHICLE I.D. NUMBERS: Most listings explain the basic serial numbering system used by each auto-maker. These codes can help determine where, when and in what order your car was built. They sometimes provide a hint of how many were produced.

SPECIFICATIONS CHART: The first chart column gives series, model or body style numbers used on prewar cars. The second column gives the number of doors, body type and passenger capacity. It may also reveal if a car has deluxe equipment, a rumbleseat, etc. The first 1917 Dodge listing seen here is for a Model 30 two-door roadster of two-passenger style. The third column gives the factory delivered price of the car when it was new, in this case $835. The fourth column gives the car's original shipping weight; 2,200 pounds for the 1917 Dodge Model 30 roadster. The sixth column tells how many cars of the same type were made or makes reference to additional notes about production found directly under the specifications chart. Production records may be according to calendar year (January to January), model year (production startup to finish) or series. Many prewar cars were part of a series carried over for several full or partial model years.

ENGINE DATA: According to year and make of car, engine data will be found either below the 'Specifications Chart' or near the 'Chassis' data block. It depends on whether different series had different engines. Typical specifications for power plants include type of configuration, block material, bore and stroke, displacement, horsepower rating and carburetor data.

CHASSIS: Information compiled here generally includes the wheelbase and tire sizes. Where available, overall length, tread width, body dimensions such as width and height, and wheel sizes are given.

TECHNICAL: This data block gives available information on type of transmission, number of forward and reverse speeds, gearshift location, type of clutch, the drive mechanism, overall gear ratio, type of axle, brake system and wheel construction. The information is general, covering all models, with exceptions noted in parenthesis. Data about technical equipment options is also given in many cases.

OPTIONS: Information about optional equipment for prewar cars is limited. We have listed accessories described in sales literature and seen in old photos, some of which may have been standard features. Some aftermarket ''period'' accessories may also be included. In some cases, complete lists and prices were found.

HISTORICAL: Data presented in this block includes introduction dates or production startup dates, styling and mechanical innovations, calendar and/or model year production information, corporate history, industry sales rankings, racing facts, special informative notes and other types of automotive historical trivia. The amount of available information varies.

'BALLPARK' PRICES: Charts give a list of models and 'ballpark' prices they bring in the collector's market today. Five values are given, one for each of the five numbered condition classes (see page 9 for a chart giving word descriptions of each class).

1917

DODGE — MODEL 30 — FOUR: According to the contemporary sources used for our research, the 1917 Dodge was referred to as the Dodge Model 30. It was rated at 35 advertised horsepower. These cars had a longer 114 inch wheelbase. There were four new models, in addition to the roadster and touring. Two of these were simply ''Rex'' top models. This term referred to a type of removable hardtop fitted with snap-on glass windows and detachable side panels. Built by the Rex Manufacturing Co. of Connersville, Ind., these tops allowed the owner to ''convert'' his roadster or touring car into a variety of configurations: open car, open-side hardtop or fully enclosed. The other models were a permanently enclosed center door sedan coupe with lowerable windows. Mechanically, a multiple disc clutch was used in place of the leather-faced cone type. Cars built after approximately Oct. 1, 1916 (for model year 1917) also had higher radiators, headlights mounted ahead of the radiator, splash aprons on the inner sides of the fenders and a rear cross bar (inside the spare tire carrier) supporting the rear license plate bracket and an electric taillamp.

I.D. DATA: Serial numbers were in the same location. Starting: 116,339. Ending: 210,000. Engine numbers were in the same location. Engine numbers are not available.

Model No.	Body Type & Seating	Price	Weight	Prod. Total
30	2-dr. Rds.-2P	835	2200	Note 1
30	4-dr. Tr.-5P	835	2200	Note 1
30	2-dr. Rex Rds.-2P	1000	2500	Note 1
30	4-dr. Rex Tr.-5P	1000	2700	Note 1
30	2-dr. C/D Sed.-5P	1265	2795	Note 1
30	2-dr. Cpe.-2P	1265	2520	Note 1

Note 1: Total series production was 90,000.

ENGINE: Same as 1914-16 engines. See previous specifications.

CHASSIS: W.B.: 114 in. Tires: 33 x 4.

1917 Dodge Brothers Custom, limousine

TECHNICAL: Selective sliding transmission. Speeds: 3F/1R. Floor shift controls. Multiple dry disc clutch. Shaft drive. Two-wheel mechanical brakes. Wood spoke wheels.

OPTIONS: Spare tire. Side curtains. Tool kit. Running board luggage rack. Horn. Wind wings. Motometer. Windshield wiper. Spotlight. Wire wheels.

HISTORICAL: Introduced July, 1916. Innovations: Longer wheelbase. Multiple dry disc clutch. Four new body styles. New hood styling. Repositioned headlights and taillights. New splash aprons. Calendar year production: 90,000. Dodge entered the commercial vehicle field in 1917, building both civilian and military trucks. Dodge dropped to fifth sales rank in the American auto industry.

1917 DODGE

	5	4	3	2	1
Rds.	2100	2600	4400	6500	9000
Tr.	2000	2500	4300	6400	8800
Rex Rds.	2200	2700	4500	7000	9500
Rex Tr.	2100	2600	4400	6800	9200
C/D Sed.	1200	2100	3500	4700	6500
Cpe.	1100	2000	3100	4500	6000

SHORT FORM LISTING, TYPE 1: The first type of short form listing in the *Standard Catalog of American Cars 1805-1942* is used to present facts about cars that were in series production, by a relatively well-established manufacturer, for a number of years. Examples would range from the Barley Model 6-50 shown to the right, to Pierce-Arrow. As you can see, the Barley was built in Kalamazoo, Mich. for only two years — 1923 and 1924. In contrast, Pierce-Arrows were built in Buffalo, N.Y. from 1909 to 1938. Unfortunately, we did not have sufficiently detailed research on all marques at this time, to treat them with a long form type listing. It is our hope that most of the larger companies listed in short form style can be converted to long form listings in future editions of this catalog. This will depend upon filling gaps that exist in currently available research. Keeping this in mind, you will see that the Type 1 listing consists chiefly of two or three elements. The first is a data block listing the name of the car, city of manufacture and dates of manufacture in bold-face type. This is followed by a paragraph giving general information about the marque. Included here are historical facts and, in some cases, a physical description of the car and/or technical details. The second element in most Type 1 listings is one or more photos of cars being described in the text. Photo captions give the year, make and model and a photo credit code. The final element in the Type 1 listing is a chart that combines specifications with 'ballpark' pricing information. Bold-face column heads on the chart show the year, make, model, type of engine, horsepower rating, wheelbase and the codes "FP" for factory price and "1-5" for conditions. The first column (left-hand side) gives a list of models noting passenger capacity. The second column — under "FP" — gives factory prices for each model. The remaining columns list 'ballpark' prices in each of five condition classes. The five different condition classes are fully explained in a chart on page 9 of this catalog. Due to limitations upon factual research, some Type 1 listings are more extensive than others.

SHORT FORM LISTING, TYPE 2: The second type of short form listing is used for very obscure autos about which only sketchy information exists. Bold-face type shows the name of the car and, sometimes, the city and date information. This is followed by text giving historical data. No attempt has been made to give a list of models and prices as such details are unavailable. In most cases, production may never have started.

SHORT FORM LISTING, TYPE 3: The third type of short form listing is used in the case of relatively obscure autos that were actually built on either a one-of-a-kind or limited production basis. Again, bold-face type shows the name of the car and the dates of manufacture. This is followed by a paragraph presenting background information about the company's history and, possibly, some styling and technical details. Where available, captioned photos of the car are included. Below the text will be found an abbreviated form of the Type 1 chart giving all applicable information that is currently available. This includes a list of models, but note that slashes are used in the six columns where factory prices and 'ballpark' prices normally go. This form is being used because it seemed improper to place estimated values on cars that probably no longer exist today, as well as cars which have never been offered or approximated in the general marketplace.

NOTE: Because automotive history is a inexact-exact science, variations upon the above formats may appear in the *Standard Catalog*. However, a basic understanding of the three formats presented above will serve as a guide to all listings herein.

BARLEY — Kalamazoo, Michigan — (1923-1924) — In a speech before the Kalamazoo Exchange Club on August 7th, 1922, George Hopkins announced that a new, smaller, medium-priced automobile was forthcoming from the Barley Motor Car Company — and he took pains to emphasize that the car would not be a model of the prestigious and high-priced Roamer which the firm had been building since 1916. The company took pains to insure that the Barley did not look like it either. The most noticeable area in which to do that was radiator configuration; the Barley's was straight sided with a sharp flare at the top. Its engine was Continental's L-head six, and standard components were used throughout. Touring and sedan models were introduced in September of 1922, with a sport sedan and touring sedan later to follow for the '23 model year. The 1924 model year was the Barley's last. The name was thereafter dropped, and the car ultimately became what the company had earlier insisted it was not: a Roamer, Model 6-50. Interestingly, a taxicab carrying the Barley badge was available from the beginning, though in 1923 its name was changed to Pennant. The Pennant taxi was produced into 1925, a year longer than the Barley passenger car.

1923 Barley, 5-pass. touring, WLB

1923 BARLEY
Model 6-50 — 6-cyl., 50 hp, 118" wb

	FP	5	4	3	2	1
Tour.-5P	1395	3200	4300	6500	11,000	23,000
Sed.-5P	1850	2700	3600	5300	8800	19,000
Spt. Sed.-5P	1495	2900	3700	5600	9100	20,000
Tour. Sed.-5P	2250	2950	3900	5800	9300	20,500

1924 BARLEY
Model 6-50 — 6-cyl., 50 hp, 118" wb

	FP	5	4	3	2	1
Phae.-5P	1395	3200	4300	6500	11,000	23,000
Spt. Sed.-5P	1495	2900	3700	5600	9100	20,000
Spec. Spt.-5P	1685	3000	4000	6000	9500	21,000
Tour. Sed.-5P	1695	2700	3600	5300	8800	19,000
Sed.-5P	1850	2500	3500	5000	8500	18,000

BARLOW — The Barlow Motors Corporation has been cited as the manufacturer of an automobile in 1924 in Philadelphia, Pennsylvania. City directory references for that year and those preceding and succeeding indicate no Barlow automobile company in town.

BARLOW STEAM — Detroit, Michigan — (1917-1922) — The Barlow was a steam car that spent a half decade in the experimental stage. The first one was on the road during the fall of 1917, the third prototype was finished and ready to undergo a series of experimental tests in the spring of 1922. It was in late March that year that the Barlow Steam Engineering Syndicate was formed, its members including an impressive roster of engineers and executives from the Ford Motor Company, Timken Axle, Detroit Lubricator and Penberthy Injector, among other prominent Motor City concerns. About fifty people were involved in this venture to promote and manufacture the vehicle designed by Lester P. Barlow, the most enthusiastic being Fred Ball who had built his own car at the turn of the century and who was now manager of the Ball and Ball carburetor department of Penberthy. Initial press releases indicated a $300,000 incorporation and a $3000 selling price for the car, with promotional emphasis to be placed on its boiler construction which was said to be uniquely different from any other contemporary steam car. Apparently, undue optimism was the actual not-uniquely-different feature of this manufacturing venture. Preliminary announcements in late 1921 spoke of the eminent start-up of production at the Commercial Manufacturing Company in Detroit, with the car to be on the market early in 1922. Early in 1922 the date was moved up to June. By November the Barlow company was said to be preparing to manufacture a steam-generating device invented by Lester Barlow, and that Barlow looked forward to building steam-driven buses in Cleveland. The entire venture died soon after that.

1917-1922 BARLOW STEAM

	FP	5	4	3	2	1
Barlow Steam Car prototypes	—	—	—	—	—	—

MARQUE RESEARCH SPECIALISTS

Buick ....Robert C. Ackerson
Cadillac ....Philip S. Dumka
Chevrolet ........................M.C. ''Pinky'' Randall
Chrysler ....John A. Gunnell
DeSoto ....John A. Gunnell
Dodge ....John A. Gunnell
Essex ....Robert C. Ackerson
Ford ....Robert C. Ackerson
Model T Ford ....Bruce McCally
Hudson ....Robert C. Ackerson

LaSalle ....Philip S. Dumka
Lincoln ....Robert C. Ackerson
Nash ....Arch Brown
Oldsmobile ....Dennis Casteele
Curved Dash Oldsmobile ....Gary Hoonsbeen
Packard ....Dr. William Bell
Plymouth ....Jim Benjaminson
Pontiac ....John A. Gunnell
Studebaker ....John A. Gunnell
Terraplane ....Robert C. Ackerson

PHOTO SOURCES

AA	Applegate & Applegate
AB	Arch Brown
BC	Briggs Cunningham
CCC	Classic Car Club of America
CG	Catherine Gunnell
CHC	Chrysler Historical Collection
CP	Crestline Publishing
CX	Car Exchange
DAB	Donald A. Bougher
DC	Dennis Casteele
DFR	Durant Family Registry
DJK	D.J. Kava
FP	Frank Potter
FR	Fred Roe
GMI	GMI Alumni Historical Collection
GR	George Risley (now NAHC)
HAC	Henry Austin Clark, Jr.
HC	Harrah Collection
HET	Hudson-Essex-Terraplane Club / Jack Miller
HFM	Henry Ford Museum
HJE	Helen J. Earley / Oldsmobile Division
HS	Hayden Shepley
IB	Ira Brichta / Stern Walters / Earle Ludgin Inc.
IMS	Indianapolis Motor Speedway
JAC	John A. Conde
JB	Jim Benjaminson
JC	Jeff Canning
JDE	Joe D. Ersland
JG	Jeff Gillis
JHC	James H. Cox
JHV	J.H. Valentine
JMP	John M. Peckham
KCHSM	Kalkaska County Historical Society Museum
KFG	Kennth F. Gypson
KM	Keith Marvin

LC	Library of Congress
LPL	Lansing (Michigan) Public Library
MC	Michael Carbonella
MCHS	Michigan City Historical Society
MVMA	Motor Vehicle Manufacturers Association of the United States, Inc.
NAHC	National Automotive History Collection, Detroit Public Library
NOPL	New Orleans Public Library
NSHS	Nebraska State Historical Society
OCW	Old Cars Weekly
PAW	Philip A. Weibler
PH	Phil Hall
RBB	Richard B. Brigham
RD	Ralph Dunwoodie
RER	Richard E. Riegel, Jr.
SI	Smithsonian Institution
SIA	Special Interest Autos
SKY	Stanley K. Yost
SM	Sloan Museum
SR	Steve Richmond
SS	Sam Shields
TM	Thomas Mercer
TP	Tommy Protsman
TVB	Terry V. Boyce
WES	William E. Swigart, Jr.
WFOR	W.F.O. Rosenmiller
WJL	William J. Lewis
WLB	William L. Bailey
WNBC	Woburn (Massachusetts) National Bank Collection
WRG	Wayne R. Graefen
WSH	Wallace Spencer Huffman
WTC	William T. Cameron

BODY STYLE POPULARITY TREND 1919-1941

Year/Body	% Total
1919	
Open	89.70
Closed	10.30
1920	
Open	83.00
Closed	17.00
1921	
Open	77.90
Closed	22.10
1922	
Open	70.00
Closed	30.00
1923	
Open	66.00
Closed	34.00
1924	
Open	57.00
Closed	43.00
1925	
Open	43.50
Closed	56.50
1926	
Roadster	8.60
Phaeton	17.40
Closed	74.00
1927	
Open	15.10
Closed	84.90
1928	
Open	11.50
Closed	88.50
1929	
Open	10.60
Closed	89.40
1930	
Open	9.60
Closed	90.40
1931	
Roadster	5.45
Touring	1.62
Conv. Cpe.	3.25
Conv. Sed.	.94
Coupe	21.50
2-dr. Sedan	25.71
4-dr. Sedan	37.57
Other closed	3.23
Chassis	.73
1932	
Roadster	3.04
Touring	.96
Conv. Cpe.	2.81
Conv. Sed.	.74
Coupe	21.70
2-dr. Sedan	30.57
4-dr. Sedan	37.27
Other closed	1.45
Chassis	1.46
1933	
Roadster	.73
Touring	.65
Conv. Cpe.	1.30
Conv. Sed.	.10
Coupe	19.99
2-dr. Sedan	32.80
4-dr. Sedan	42.20
Other closed	1.41
Chassis	.82
1934	
Roadster	.57
Touring	.65
Conv. Cpe.	1.58
Conv. Sed.	.13
Coupe	15.93
2-dr. Sedan	36.58
4-dr. Sedan	42.38
Other closed	.26
Chassis	1.92
1935	
Rds./Trg.	.70
Coupe	15.90
2-dr. Sedan	38.40
4-dr. Sedan	42.90
Chassis	2.10
1936	
Rds./Trg.	.70
Coupe	13.90
2-dr. Sedan	38.40
4-dr. Sedan	42.90
Chassis	2.10
1937	
Rds./Trg.	.50
Coupe	15.30
2-dr. Sedan	38.40
4-dr. Sedan	44.20
Chassis	1.60
1938	
Rds./Trg.	.50
Coupe	16.20
2-dr. Sedan	35.70
4-dr. Sedan	45.60
Chassis	1.60
1939	
Rds./Trg.	.30
Coupe	17.70
2-dr. Sedan	36.70
4-dr. Sedan	43.90
Chassis	1.40
1940	
Rds./Trg.	.30
Coupe	18.50
2-dr. Sedan	35.20
4-dr. Sedan	44.20
Chassis	1.80
1941	
Rds./Trg.	.20
Coupe	19.10
2-dr. Sedan	37.80
4-dr. Sedan	41.90
Chassis	1.00

Sources:
Automotive Industries
N.A.C.C. ''Statistics of the Automobile Industry''
Wards Automotive Yearbook

CONDITION CODE CHART

VEHICLE CLASSES

1) EXCELLENT: Restored to current professional standards of quality in every area; or original with all components operating and appearing as new.

2) FINE: Well-restored; or combination of superior restoration and excellent original; or extremely well-maintained original showing very minimal wear.

3) VERY GOOD: Completely operable original or older restoration showing wear; or amateur restoration; all presentable and serviceable inside and out. Also combinations of well-done restoration and good operable components; or partially restored car with all parts to complete/or valuable NOS parts.

4) GOOD: A driveable vehicle needing no or only minor work to be functional; or a deteriorated restoration; or a very poor amateur restoration. All components may need restoration to be EXCELLENT, but mostly usable "as is."

5) RESTORABLE: Needs complete restoration of body, chassis, interior. Not driveable, but is not weathered, wrecked or stripped to the point of being useful only for parts salvage.

A AUTOMOBILE — The A Automobile Company was the firm's name, the firm's automobile was called the Blue & Gold. Refer to Blue & Gold.

ABBOTT-AKIN — Early in 1914, in Johnsonville, New York, the Abbott-Akin Company was incorporated with a capital stock of $10,000 for the manufacture and sale of automobiles. The incorporators were Ernest H. Abbott, John Slade and Howard V. Akin, all of Johnsonville. No Abbott-Akin automobile is believed to have followed.

1910 Abbott-Detroit, model A, touring, HAC

ABBOTT-DETROIT — Detroit, Michigan — (1909-1916)/ABBOTT — Cleveland, Ohio — (1917-1918) — Abbott was a victim of overenthusiasm and overreach. Established in Detroit in 1909, the Abbott Motor Car Company produced cars combining both company name and city of manufacture for seven years. Engines were always proprietary: Continental fours and sixes, later a Herschell-Spillman eight. The car was completely conventional, but some of the things it did were not. Among these was the 100,000-mile trek of the Abbott-Detroit "Bull Dog" which Dr. Charles G. Percival, the editor of *Health Magazine*, drove around the borders of the United States and from coast to coast three times "over the vilest roads the country possesses." Although the company said it never built a race car, it did enter numerous events in the stock category, taking the Philadelphia Trophy at Fairmount Park in 1910, winning the Algonquin (Illinois) hill climb in 1911, and putting up a commendable showing as the lowest-powered car in a field of racing behemoths in the 1911 Vanderbilt and Grand Prize events. Probably the most eye-catching Abbott-Detroit was the $1250 Battleship Roadster introduced for 1913. It had a sharp vee radiator and a steel metal body with rows of rivet heads showing for dramatic effect. According to the company, the entire year's output was sold from blueprints before the first car had made its appearance. From the beginning, however, the life of the Abbott-Detroit was checkered. Founding president Charles Abbott elected to retire a year after starting the business; he turned up later in Detroit in a stamping plant. When creditors complained in 1913, they were mollified initially by being made stockholders, and the company was purchased that December by Edward F. Gerber who paid $237,500 for the plant and the entire business, paid off the creditors at fifteen cents on the dollar, and vowed to continue manufacture. He was out two years later, and R.A. Palmer (former manager of Cartercar) was in. Though slogans like "The One Perfect Car" and "Built for Performance and Guaranteed for Life" may have been overdoing it even for that age of gross exaggeration in advertising, production rose to a healthy fifteen to twenty units a day — and it was this salubrious fact which prompted Abbott to overdo with a vengeance. The company name had been changed to Consolidated Car Corporation with Palmer's entrance on the scene, and in 1916 the decision was made to consolidate manufacture in a huge and expensive plant in Cleveland which was leased for ten years. Most cars built there by the again-renamed Abbott Corporation were called simply Abbotts, though the name Abbott-Detroit continued to be used occasionally. Any confusion resulting was short-lived, however, because sales couldn't pay the rent on the pricey new factory, and after a merger attempt with the Hal Motor Car Company failed in October 1917, the company proceeded into bankruptcy the following January.

1909-1910 ABBOTT-DETROIT

Model A — 4-cyl., 30 hp, 110" wb

	FP	5	4	3	2	1
Tour.-5P	1500	4500	5800	9500	18,000	32,000

1911 Abbott-Detroit, model B, touring, HAC

1911 ABBOTT-DETROIT
Model B — 4-cyl., 30 hp, 110" wb

	FP	5	4	3	2	1
Demi-Tonneau	1650	4200	5500	9000	17,000	30,000
Rds.	1500	4500	5800	9500	18,000	32,000
Tour.	1500	4200	5500	9000	17,000	30,000
Demi-Tour.	1550	4000	5200	8500	16,000	29,000
Cpe.	2350	3000	4000	6000	9500	21,000

1912 Abbott-Detroit, model 30, roadster, WLB

1912 ABBOTT-DETROIT
Model B — 4-cyl., 30 hp, 110" wb

	FP	5	4	3	2	1
4-dr Rds.	1275	4500	5800	9500	18,000	32,000
4-dr Tour.	1350	4600	5900	9600	18,300	32,500
4-dr Demi-Tonneau	1350	4600	5900	9600	18,300	32,500
Cpe.	2150	3000	4000	6000	9500	21,000

1912 Abbott-Detroit, model 44, 7 pass. fore-door touring, WLB

Model C — 4-cyl., 44 hp, 120" wb

	FP	5	4	3	2	1
Demi-Tonneau	1775	4700	6000	10,000	18,500	33,000
Tour.-7P	1800	4500	5800	9600	18,300	32,500
Limo.-7P	3000	4000	5200	8500	16,000	29,000

1913 Abbott-Detroit, model 44-50, touring, HAC

1913 ABBOTT-DETROIT
Model 34-40 — 4-cyl., 40 hp, 116" wb

	FP	5	4	3	2	1
Rds.	1700	4500	5800	9500	18,000	32,000
Tour.-5P	1700	4200	5500	9000	17,000	30,000
Col. Cpe.	2000	3000	4000	6000	9500	21,000

1913 Abbott-Detroit, model 44-50, Battleship roadster, HAC

Model 44-50 — 4-cyl., 50 hp, 121" wb

Demi-Tonneau	1975	4700	6000	9700	18,500	33,000
Tour.-7P	2000	4800	6200	10,000	19,000	34,000
Battleship Rds.	2150	5000	6500	10,500	19,500	35,000
Limo.	3050	4500	5800	9500	18,000	32,000

1914 Abbott-Detroit, model F, touring, HAC

1914 ABBOTT-DETROIT
Model K — 4-cyl., 34/40 hp, 116" wb

Tour.-5P	1785	4200	5500	9000	17,000	30,000
Rds.-2P	1785	4500	5800	9500	18,000	32,000
Cpe.	2250	3500	4500	7000	13,000	25,000

Model L — 4-cyl., 44/50 hp, 121" wb

Tour.-7P	2085	4500	5800	9500	18,000	32,000
Demi-Tonneau	2085	4500	5800	9500	18,000	32,000
Rds.	2085	4700	6000	9700	18,500	33,000
Limo.	3150	4200	5500	9000	17,000	30,000

Model F — 6-cyl., 50/60 hp, 130" wb

Tour.-7P	2290	4700	6000	9700	18,500	33,000
Rds.	2290	5000	6500	10,500	19,500	35,000
Limo.	3500	4500	5800	9500	18,000	30,000

1915 Abbott-Detroit, model F, touring, HAC

1915 ABBOTT-DETROIT
Model L — 4-cyl., 44/50 hp, 121" wb

Tour.-7P	2085	4500	5800	9500	18,000	32,000

Model F — 6-cyl., 50/60 hp, 130" wb

Tour.-7P	2290	4700	6000	9700	18,500	33,000
Rds.	2190	5000	6500	10,500	19,500	35,000
Tour.-5P	2190	4900	6200	10,000	19,000	34,000

1916 Abbott-Detroit, model 8-80, roadster, HAC

1916 ABBOTT-DETROIT
Model 6-44 — 6-cyl., 44 hp, 122" wb

	FP	5	4	3	2	1
Tour.-7P	1195	4000	5000	8000	15,000	28,000
Spds.-2P	1195	4500	5500	9000	16,000	30,000
Rds.-4P	1250	4800	6000	9500	17,000	31,000
Coach-4P	1495	2500	3500	5000	8500	18,000
Tour. Sed.-5P	1795	2500	3500	5000	8500	18,000

Model 8-80 — 8-cyl., 80 hp, 121" wb

Tour.-7P	1950	4500	5500	9000	16,000	30,000
Racy Rds.	1950	5000	6500	11,000	22,000	35,000

1917 Abbott, touring, WLB

1917-1918 ABBOTT
Model 6-44 — 6-cyl., 44 hp, 122" wb

Rds.-4P	1250	4800	6000	9500	17,000	31,000
Tour.-7P	1195	4000	5000	8000	15,000	28,000
Rbt.-2P	1195	4500	5500	9000	16,000	30,000
Tour. Sed.-5P	1820	2500	3500	5000	8500	18,000
Tour. Sed.-7P	1870	2500	3500	5000	8500	18,000
Coach-3P	1475	2500	3500	5000	8500	18,000

A.B.C. — The initials represent American Bicycle Company, the huge and ill-fated trust engineered by Colonel Albert Pope. Many of its member companies produced cars (the three-wheelers of Crescent and Cleveland, the Rambler from Gormully & Jeffery, for example), and the American Bicycle Company itself, under affiliate organizations, manufactured the Waverley electric and the Toledo steamer. An A.B.C. steamer competed in the Nelson Hill Climb in Poughkeepsie, New York in 1901, and the initials were used sporadically in other motor sport events at the turn of the century, probably accounting for the presence of this A.B.C. on various car rosters. Neither the American Bicycle Company nor any of its member organizations ever marketed an automobile under the A.B.C. initials, however.

1906 A.B.C., runabout, NAHC

A.B.C. — St. Louis, Missouri — (1905-1910) — Amedee B. Cole, an erstwhile electrical engineer, had the perfect name for a highwheeler producer. It allowed him legitimate use of a marque designation and an accompanying slogan regarding how easy his product was, though he did play it rather too preciously by declaring "as simple as you can guess to operate." Still, he was pretty much right. The A.B.C. was one of the most primeval of highwheelers. It had an air-cooled engine, friction transmission with drive to a divided rear axle by single chain, and it rode on solid 36-inch (initially 40-inch) tires. Initially too, A.B. Cole organized as the Auto Buggy Manufacturing Company, but late in 1908 when he decided to offer more cylinders and water-cooled, pneumatic-tired models somewhat more complicated than his initials, he changed the firm's name to A.B.C. Motor Vehicle Manufacturing Company. Probably his sale of 183 vehicles during 1908 prompted this unwise decision to expand his line. A few days before Christmas in 1910 suppliers to whom A.B. Cole owed $1070 filed an involuntary petition in bankruptcy against him.

1907 A.B.C., runabout, NAHC

1905-1907 A.B.C.
1-cyl., 10 hp, 72" wb

	FP	5	4	3	2	1
Rbt.-2P	300	2000	3000	4200	6500	14,000

1908 A.B.C.
2-cyl., 16/18 hp, 90" wb

Rbt.-2P	600	2000	3000	4300	6500	14,500
Rbt.-3P	650	2100	3100	4400	6700	14,600
Surrey-4P	850	2200	3200	4900	6800	15,000
Deliv. Wag.	700	1900	2800	4000	6500	14,000

1909 A.B.C., model I, touring, NAHC

1909 A.B.C.
2-cyl., 16/18 hp, 90" wb

Model PD Rds.-3P (a/c)	725	2200	3200	4900	7000	15,000
Model PD Rds.-3P (w/c)	775	2200	3200	4900	7000	15,000
Model C Rbt.-2P (a/c)	600	2000	3000	4400	6700	14,500
Model C Rbt.-2P (w/c)	650	2000	3000	4400	6700	14,500
Model PE Surrey-4P (a/c)	775	2500	3500	5000	7500	15,500
Model PE Surrey-4P (w/c)	825	2500	3500	5000	7500	15,500
Model PC Rbt.-2P (a/c)	690	2000	3000	4500	7000	15,000
Model PC Rbt.-2P (w/c)	740	2000	3000	4500	7000	15,000
Model E Surrey-4P (a/c)	700	2500	3500	5000	7500	15,500
Model E Surrey-4P (w/c)	750	2500	3500	5000	7500	15,500

Note 1: "P" in designation indicates pneumatic tires.
Note 2: (w/c) - water cooled, (a/c) - air cooled.

4-cyl., 30/35 hp, 112" wb

Model G Rbt.-2P	1100	2300	3300	5300	7300	16,000

	FP	5	4	3	2	1
Model H Rdst.-3P	1200	2500	3500	5500	7500	16,200
Model I Tour.-4P	1250	2700	3700	5700	7700	16,400

1910 A.B.C.
2-cyl., 16/18 hp, 90" wb

Model C Rbt.-2P	690	2400	3000	4500	7000	15,000
Model D Rds.-3P	690	2400	3000	4500	7000	15,000
Model E Surrey-4P	750	2500	3500	5000	7500	15,500

4-cyl., 30/35 hp, 112" wb

Model G Rbt.-2P	1250	2500	3500	5500	7900	17,000
Model H Rds.-4P	1400	2600	3700	5600	8000	17,500
Model I Tour.-5P	1400	2600	3700	5600	8000	17,500

A.B.C. — Albany, New York — (1921-1922) — Following the First World War, a number of budding entrepreneurs in America harbored the notion that quick and substantial profits might be realized by building an automobile in the United States and exporting it to Europe where war had ravaged many of the existing car factories. In Albany two fellows by the names of Lee Arthur and George Boynton joined together in 1921 as the Arthur-Boynton Corporation for the building of such a car to be known as the A.B.C. It was planned as an air-cooled four on a 104-inch wheelbase to be available in touring and roadster variations, both priced at $300. Possibly a prototype was built, but the partners very soon realized that profits from the enterprise were neither quick nor substantial, nor was the venture as easy as they had envisioned. The 1923 Albany City Directory indicates Boynton's occupation as "automobiles," which probably means he was now a salesman, and Arthur's occupation as "tracer."

ABEL — Fond du Lac, Wisconsin — (1901) — The Abel Brothers ran a machine shop at the corner of Portland and First streets in Fond du Lac, and in mid-May of 1901 completed a steam carriage which they built at a cost somewhere between $700 and $800. The car was equipped with a two-cylinder 5 hp engine, and was given a trial run around town during which it performed admirably. Production of the car was not contemplated, a fact which Henry and Otto Abel emphatically announced. "The owners of the vehicle state that it was manufactured merely for pleasure purposes and is not for sale," commented the *Fond du Lac Daily Reporter* in its May 18th, 1901 edition.

ABENAQUE — Westminster Station, Vermont — (1900) — The Abenaque Machine Works was established by the Colgate family of Westminster Station in 1883 for the purpose of manufacturing gasoline engines, gasoline tractors, pumping plants, building contractors' machinery, in addition to saw mill and farm machinery. In 1900 Abenaque built an experimental gasoline automobile, but quickly decided to forego production to concentrate instead on the company's lucrative farm machinery program. That phase of its business remained lucrative until just before the First World War, when the firm moved to Marlborough, New Hampshire. Abenaque proceeded into bankruptcy there in August 1915. Abenaque gasoline engines are highly prized by collectors today.

ABENDROTH & ROOT — The company was Abendroth & Root, but the product was called a Frontenac, a car manufactured in Newburgh, New York from 1906 to 1913. Refer to Frontenac.

ABERDEEN — The Aberdeen Automobile Company was organized during the late spring of 1909 in Aberdeen, Mississippi, for the manufacture of motor vehicles. The people involved were J.L. Shell, A.A. Friers, E.A. Stinson, J.W. Bowling and L. Porter. No Aberdeen automobile resulted.

ABLE EIGHT — The name refers to the Able V-8 engine which was used in the Vernon car built in Mt. Vernon, New York from 1918 to 1921. Refer to Vernon.

ABRESCH — Milwaukee, Wisconsin — (1899 et seq.) — During the fall of 1889, Charles Abresch, proprietor of the Abresch Carriage Company which had been in business in Milwaukee since 1871, announced his intention to "form a $5,000,000 trust to control the manufacture of automobiles." He was beaten to the punch, however, by the Electric Vehicle Company people on the East Coast who acquired the Selden patent that year. At this point, Charles Abresch seems to have built just one car. It was a heavy brake seating seven passengers, powered by a two-cylinder 10 hp water-cooled engine and driven by a belt from the engine to a differential gear and thence by chain to the rear wheels. A very substantial looking car, the Abresch weighed 2300 pounds and was capable of 12 mph on level road. In April of 1900, *The Automobile Review* announced Abresch's plans "to go extensively into the building of self-propelling heavy trucks and delivery wagons, with pleasure carriages as a side issue later." This does not appear to have happened immediately. The Abresch horsedrawn wagon and carriage business remained a thriving one, but motorized vehicles built during the next few years were minimal. Abresch is known to have supplied the coachwork for the first Ramblers and the Fawick Flyer/Silent Sioux, in addition to building bodies for commercial vehicles. In 1908 the firm became the Milwaukee agent for the Kissels. In February of 1910 announcement was made of the incorporation of the Abresch-Cramer Auto Truck Company in Milwaukee. Abresch's partner in this venture was a man named Kremers, who possibly changed the spelling of his last name for reasons of euphony or marketability. Complete trucks were produced by this company for about a year and a half. Charles Abresch died April 28th, 1912, and though his wagon and body-building business survived him, his truck venture did not.

A-C — Although sometimes advertised as the A-C, the product of the Alter Motor Car Company more often carried the firm's name. The car was produced in Plymouth and Grand Haven, Michigan from 1915-1917. Refer to Alter.

A.C. — New Orleans, Louisana — (1914) — Arthur B. LeCour and George E. Dicks were the men behind the Autocycle Company of New Orleans. Their plan was to build the A.C. cyclecar with two engines (a twin and a four), two chassis and three body types (tandem, roadster and light delivery). They announced that their factory on Girod Street was "fully equipped for a production capacity of ten machines a day." From their sales offices at 811 St. Charles Street, they also announced that agency contacts had been closed for 100 cars and further orders were expected for another 100. That would have provided the Autocycle Company with twenty days of work at production capacity. Doubtless the company never worked at full peak. More than likely, the A.C. cyclecar never proceeded beyond the prototype stage.

1903 Acadia, runabout, NAHC

ACADIA — Wilmington, Delaware — (1903-1904) — Ernest R. Kelly was a general machinist and a repairer of bicycles in Wilmington. In 1903, after "several years' experience in automobile work," as he put it, Kelly placed a little single-cylinder 5 hp runabout on the market. It had a Renault-type hood, right-hand wheel steering, chain drive and a high-backed single bench seat. The car was sold without fenders, lamps or horn, though Kelly would make these available as accessories. The figures for the car's weight and price were the same: 600 pounds, $600. Obviously production fell far short of expectations, because Kelly never did incorporate a company for the sale of his Acadia. Sometime during 1904 he left Wilmington for Philadelphia. His activities there could not be determined.

1903-1904 ACADIA
1-cyl., 5 hp, 62" wb

	FP	5	4	3	2	1
Rbt.	600	2000	3000	4200	6500	14,000

1909 A Car Without A Name, toy tonneau, NAHC

CAR WITHOUT A NAME — Chicago, Illinois — (1909) — A name, the advertisements said, was all the car was lacking. It was the product of a company which identified itself only as Department C at 19 North May Street in Chicago. Producing an automobile in a nameless state was not unusual during the early years of the industry, this allowing potential dealers to affix their own names to the car and to get into the automobile game with a minimum of fuss. The car in this case had a 30 hp engine, three-speed sliding gear transmission, shaft drive, and three body styles (toy tonneau, roadster and touring) priced at $1650 apiece. Within months, however, the people behind A Car Without a Name decided they would prefer giving the vehicle a pedigree. It became the F.A.L., the initials representing backers T.S. Fauntleroy, H.R. Averill and E.H. Lowe.

ACCESSIBLE — Although sometimes shortened to Accessible, this car is more properly designated by its full name: Hobbie Accessible. It was built in Hampton, Iowa from 1908-1910. Refer to Hobbie Accessible.

ACE — Ypsilanti, Michigan — (1920-1922) — The Ace was born of the proverbial necessity. In this case, the mother of invention was the shortage of automobiles following World War I. In the summer of 1919, Seattle (Washington) dealer F.E. Earnest traveled to Detroit to secure contracts for new cars for his dealership. When he couldn't be supplied, he decided

1921 Ace, coupe, MVMA

to finagle manufacture instead and happened upon Fred M. Guy, an engineer, and O.W Heinz, his collaborator. While chief engineer for Hackett, Guy had devised a new type of powerplant, the Guy Disc-Valve Motor in which the overhead valves were driven by a master gear in the head, thus eliminating camshaft, valve spring, et al. Both he and Heinz would have preferred more time for further development work, but were persuaded by Earnest to build a complete car immediately with Guy serving as chief engineer, Heinz as president of the venture. Ground for the factory of the new Apex Motor Car Company was broken in Ypsilanti in October of 1919. Construction was completed three months later. Three months and ten days following that, the first carload of Ace cars was on its way to the West Coast. In September of 1920 the Ace with Guy Disc-Valve Motor was shown at the Michigan State Fair. In January 1921 the car was exhibited at the Commodore Hotel in New York, and among the models on display was a finely wrought coupe with a coachbuilt look, quite unusual for a production car of this period. But something went wrong somewhere. In April Guy and Heinz left Apex to form the Guy-Disc-Valve Motor Company late that year for the development and manufacture of the Guy engine, though earlier Heinz had flirted with the idea of bringing out another car under his own name. Meanwhile H.T. Hanover took over the Apex company, and all subsequent Aces carried conventional engines, the Herschell-Spillman six usually. The Ace from Apex now was distinguished mainly by Hanover's penchant for World War I nostalgia in naming the models. The venture fell apart quickly. In May of 1922 the Saxon Motor Car Company took over part of the Apex plant; in September of 1923 the entire factory was sold to Commerce Motor Truck Corporation. Where Earnest turned to secure automobiles for his dealership after the Ace failed is not known. H.T. Hanover immediately joined Frank Klingensmith in Detroit to promote a new taxi called the Diamond.

1920 ACE
Six — 6-cyl., 57 hp, 115" wb

	FP	5	4	3	2	1
Model T Tour.	2050	2500	3500	5000	8500	18,000

1921 ACE
Six (Rotary) — 123" wb

	FP	5	4	3	2	1
Model G Tour.		2000	3000	4500	8000	17,000
Model G Cpe.	—	1500	2500	4000	7500	15,000

Six (Herschell-Spillman) — 64 hp, 117" wb

	FP	5	4	3	2	1
Model H Touring		2000	3000	4500	8000	17,000

1922 Ace, Pup, touring, WLB

1922 Ace, Combat, roadster, WLB

14

1922 ACE
Model F — 4-cyl., 43 hp, 114" wb

	FP	5	4	3	2	1
Pup Tour.-5P	1295	2000	3000	4500	8000	17,000
Pup Rds.-2P	1295	2000	3000	4500	8000	17,000

Model C — 6-cyl., 77 hp, 120" wb

	FP	5	4	3	2	1
Combat Tour.-5P	2975	3300	4400	6700	12,000	24,000
Combat Rds.-2P	2975	3500	4500	7000	13,000	25,000
Combat Spds.-3P	3150	4600	9150	15,250	21,350	30,500

1922 Ace, custom dual cowl landau, WLB

Model L — 6-cyl., 59 hp, 117" wb

	FP	5	4	3	2	1
Scout Tour.-5P	2260	3100	6150	10,250	14,350	20,500
Scout Rds.-2P	2260	3100	6150	10,250	14,350	20,500

ACE SIX — The Ace Six was one of the three models produced by Continental Motors Corporation of Grand Rapids, Michigan in 1933. Refer to Continental.

ACETYLENE — This 1899 car from New York City is properly designated by its full name. Refer to Auto-Acetylene.

ACKERMAN — Detroit, Michigan — (1897-1899) — Prior to the turn of the century, W.K. Ackerman of Detroit built his first automobile. This was strictly an experimental car, and Ackerman did not market it. Subsequently, he found work in the engineering department of Cadillac, and in late 1903 joined with fellow Cadillac employee E.O. Abbott to design and build the Reliance car which was produced in Detroit through 1906.

ACKERMAN & BAIRD — Ackerman & Baird, Inc. was organized in Brooklyn, New York with a capital stock of $10,000 early in 1913 for the manufacture of automobiles, motors and internal combustion engines. Raymond P. Ackerman and Andrew D. Baird were the partners involved. No car is believed to have resulted.

A.C.M. — Flint, Michigan — (1913) — The initials represented Arthur C. Mason, the engineer whom William C. Durant had hired away from Cadillac in 1903 when he was promoting Buick and who remained with Durant through Billy's formation of General Motors in 1908 and those stormy days in 1910 when Billy was about to be kicked out of the company he had started. On July 31, 1911 — following Durant's ouster from GM and with Durant's backing — the Mason Motor Company was organized in Flint. Its purpose was to build the engines for Durant's two new motorcars: the Little and the Chevrolet. To this task, Arthur Mason immediately applied himself, and when Durant approached him in November 1912 with another job to do, Mason got on it right away. It seemed that for some reason gasoline fuel had abruptly come into short supply. Durant asked Mason to design a vehicle to be powered by kerosene, and issued a press release noting the "growing difficulties in the fuel situation" and the wisdom of being "independent of gasoline." Arthur Mason designed the kerosene-powered car, which bore the code name A.C.M. By the time it was completed in 1913, however, the gasoline crisis had abated. The A.C.M. was promptly forgotten, and Arthur Mason returned to his original job of building engines.

ACME — Acme Roadster was the designation used only in 1908 for the car produced by the Motor Buggy Manufacturing Company of Minneapolis. Refer to M.B.

Although Acme appeared in a 1914 trade press reference as the name to be used by the Hawkins Cyclecar Company of Xenia, Ohio to designate its new product, the car was never marketed as such. Refer to Xenia.

The Acme Auto Appliance Company was organized with a capital stock of $5000 during the fall of 1910 in Joliet, Illinois for the manufacture of automobiles and supplies. Harvey Wood, Maurice Lennon and John Garnsey were the incorporators. No Acme car is believed to have resulted.

The Acme Automobile Company was organized in Chicago, Illinois early in 1905 with a capital stock of $30,000 to manufacture and deal in vehicles. The incorporators were George N. Lyman, William R. Keene and Frank H. Lyman. No Acme car is believed to have resulted.

The Acme Electric Auto Works was a Los Angeles, California incorporation from early 1913. Its capital stock was $10,000, its incorporators were F.W. Jackman, E.E. Mason and F.C. Morgan. The partners planned to manufacture and sell electric automobiles, and to operate a garage and charging station. Manufacture is doubted to have followed.

The Acme Electric Garage was organized early in 1909 in New York City with a capital stock of $5000 to manufacture, store and deal in motorcars.

The Illeh brothers — A.G., H.H. and H.C. — were the people involved. Manufacture did not follow.

The Acme Engine Company of Lansing, Michigan built the 1914 car which was planned to be marketed in Saginaw as the Thomas. Refer to Thomas.

The Acme Motor Car Company was organized with a capital stock of $12,000 in New York City early in 1905 to make automobiles. The incorporators were J.D. Maguire, R.L. Julian and G.H. Strout. There is no indication that manufacture followed.

1905 Acme, type VI, light touring, WLB

ACME — Reading, Pennsylvania — (1903-1911) — James C. Reber founded his Acme Bicycle Manufacturing Company in 1892. In 1900 he built his first two-cylinder gasoline car. When he decided to go into manufacture two years later, he named the vehicle after himself, but quickly concluded that the name of his bicycle had more cachet. The Reber survived for just one year; on June 9th, 1903 the Acme Motor Car Company was incorporated. Initially, the Acme was merely the Reber reborn, but meanwhile Reber had imported engineer Victor Jakob from Daimler in Germany, and Jakob designed cars of four cylinders (with automatic intake valves) and, later, six cylinders (with ball-bearing transmissions) which featured integral splined key shafts and laminated frames as well. "From steel bar to finished car" was the slogan of the Acme, and the man charged with selling it was Frederick E. Moskovics who became the company's sales manager late in 1904, but who would go on to greater things with Stutz a number of years later. Whether it was Moskovics who suggested that the Acme was so sturdily built that a "perpetual guarantee" should be offered is not known. What is known is that perpetuity was not enjoyed by the company. Acme survived its first receivership in 1906. When it was in trouble again in 1911, the company was sold for $250,000 to the Messrs. Sternberg, Graham and Van Tine who would use the factory to build their S.G.V.

1904 ACME
2-cyl., 16 hp, 84" wb

	FP	5	4	3	2	1
Tour.-5P	1650	2000	3000	4200	6500	14,000

1905 Acme, type VI, opera bus, WLB

1905 ACME
2-cyl., 16 hp, 78-1/2" wb

	FP	5	4	3	2	1
Racing Rbt.	1000	2500	3500	4500	7000	15,000

Type VI — 2-cyl., 16 hp, 89" wb

	FP	5	4	3	2	1
Tonneau	1650	2100	3100	4300	6600	14,500

Type VIII — 4-cyl., 30 hp, 102-1/2" wb

	FP	5	4	3	2	1
Tonneau	2750	2500	3500	4500	7000	15,000

1906 ACME
Type XIV — 4-cyl., 30/35 hp, 102" wb

	FP	5	4	3	2	1
Tour.-5P	2750	2600	3600	4700	7500	15,500

Type XV — 4-cyl., 45/50 hp, 114" wb

	FP	5	4	3	2	1
Limousine-7P	3500	2400	3400	4500	7000	14,500

1907 Acme, type 18, touring, WLB

1907 ACME
Type 16 — 4-cyl., 50 hp, 102" wb

	FP	5	4	3	2	1
Rbt.-3P	3250	3200	4200	6400	10,000	22,000

Type 18 — 4-cyl., 50 hp, 115-1/2" wb

Tour.-7P	4000	4050	8100	13,500	18,900	27,000

1908 ACME
Four — 30 hp, 102-1/2" wb

Type 16 Rbt.	3500	2600	3600	5800	9000	19,500

Four — 30 hp, 115-1/2" wb

Type 18 Tour.	4000	2800	3800	6000	9400	20,000
Type 21 Rbt.	4250	2900	4000	6200	9600	20,500

Four — 30 hp, 126" wb

Type 20 Tour.	4500	4000	5000	8000	15,000	28,000

1909 Acme, type 20, limousine, HAC

1909 ACME
Type 19 — 4-cyl., 28 hp, 110" wb

		5	4	3	2	1
Special Rbt.-2P	2500	3500	4500	6600	9700	18,700

Type 21 — 6-cyl., 48 hp, 115" wb

Model B Rbt.-3/4P	4500	4000	5000	8100	15,000	28,000

Type 20 — 6-cyl., 48 hp, 126" wb

Model A Tour.-7P	4500	4000	5000	8000	15,000	28,000
Model C Limo.-7P	4500	3800	4800	7500	12,000	25,000

Type 25 — 6-cyl., 60 hp, 126" wb

Model A Tour.-7P	6000	4500	5800	9500	18,000	32,000
Model B Rbt.-3P	6000	4600	6000	9700	18,500	32,500

Type 26 — 4-cyl., 30 hp, 102" wb

Model A Tour.-5P	3250	3000	4000	6000	9000	18,000
Model B Rds.-3P	3250	3200	4200	6500	9500	18,500

Type 28 — 4-cyl., 40 hp, 115" wb

Model A Tour.-4P	3750	3400	4400	6500	9500	18,500
Model B Rds.-3P	3750	3600	4600	6700	9800	19,000

1910-1911 ACME
Type 26 — 4-cyl., 30 hp, 102" wb

Rds.	3500	3000	4000	6000	9000	18,000
Tour'abt.-5P	3500	2900	3900	5900	8900	17,900
Toy Tonneau-5P	3500	3000	4000	6000	9000	18,000

Type 27 — 4-cyl., 40 hp, 115-1/2" wb

Tour.-5P	3750	3200	4200	6300	9500	18,500
Tour.-7P	3750	3000	4000	6000	9200	18,300

Type 21 — 6-cyl., 48 hp, 118" wb

Rds.-2/3P	4250	4000	5000	8000	15,000	28,000
Tour'abt.-4P	4250	3800	4800	7800	14,700	27,800

Type 20 — 6-cyl., 48 hp, 126" wb

Tour'abt.	4750	4000	5000	8000	15,000	28,000
Baby Tonneau	4750	4000	5000	8000	15,000	28,000

Type 25 — 6-cyl., 60 hp, 130" wb

Tour.-5P	5000	4500	5800	9500	18,000	32,000
Tour.-5P	5000	4500	5800	9500	18,000	32,000

ACME — Spokane, Washington — (1907) — Levi Rhodes, B.W. Woolverton and A.E. Gallagher, amongst a virtual regiment of others, were the principals behind the million-dollar incorporation of the Acme Engine Company in Spokane in February 1907. The Messrs. Rhodes, Woolverton and Gallagher are mentioned specifically because these self-same men had three years earlier tried to "revolutionize the automobile industry" with the Spokane car. According to a March 1907 issue of *Motor Field*, the Acme company proposed to "at once begin to manufacture for business purposes, automobiles and traction cars." The firm had taken over the plant and patents of the Motor Traction Company in Spokane, but this venture appears to have stalled at the prototype stage.

ACME — Spokane, Washington — (1907) — Levi Rhodes, B.W. Woolverton and A.E. Gallagher, amongst a virtual regiment of others, were the principals behind the million-dollar incorporation of the Acme Engine Company in Spokane in February 1907. The Messrs. Rhodes, Woolverton and Gallagher are mentioned specifically because these self-same men had three years earlier tried to "revolutionize the automobile industry" with the Spokane car. According to a March 1907 issue of *Motor Field*, the Acme company proposed to "at once begin to manufacture for business purposes, automobiles and traction cars." The firm had taken over the plant and patents of the Motor Traction Company in Spokane, but this venture appears to have stalled at the prototype stage.

ACME — Worcester, Massachusetts — (1912) — The Acme Motor Car Company of Worcester was headed by Ernest Wheeler as general manager and William Vincent as sales manager. The firm was a dealership for Knox and Velie automobiles, delivery wagons, trucks, fire apparatus and tractors — and was also the exclusive owner and manufacturer of Wheeler's Screw Press. Although not a manufacturer of automobiles, the company did in 1912 occasionally custom outfit a Velie or Knox for a local client and attach the Acme name to it. The company had been organized late in 1911 with a capital stock of $40,000. This was not Ernest Wheeler's first automotive venture, incidentally. At the turn of the century in Marlboro, he and his father, O.D. Wheeler, had dreams of manufacture, though the reverie ended after the building of just three Wheelers.

ACORN — Cincinnati, Ohio — (1910-1912) — The Acorn Automobile Company was in business in Cincinnati from 1910 into 1912, and although an occasional runabout or touring car might have been built to special custom order, a passenger car was not marketed. Instead the company focused manufacture on a two-cylinder 18/20 hp delivery wagon with a 1000-pound capacity.

ACTON — The Acton Garage, Inc. was organized with a capital stock of $10,000 in New York City late in 1906 for the manufacture of motors, engines, cars and carriages. William C. Strange, Robert G. Strange and William C. Strange, Jr., all of New York City, were the people involved. No manufacture is believed to have followed.

ADAMS — The Adams Automobile Company of Hiawatha, Kansas preferred using a slogan rather than a name for its 1906 car. Refer to Average Man's Runabout.

The Adams Garage Company was organized in Trenton, New Jersey during the summer of 1909 by W. Eldridge, C.E. Wilson and C.F. Adams. The capital stock was $25,000, and the plan was to manufacture motorcars and to operate a garage. There is no indication of a sustained manufacture.

The Adams Repair Company of New York City was organized with a capital stock of $10,000 early in 1908 to engage in the manufacture and repairing of motorcars. The incorporators were C.W. Adams, C.A. Post and Robert P. Kernan. No Adams automobile was marketed.

The Adams Vehicle Company was a $5000 incorporation in New York City late in 1905 to manufacture and deal in automobiles. The incorporators were Levi C. Weir, Basil W. Rowe and Horatio H. Gates, all of New York City. Manufacture is not believed to have followed.

The R. Adams Brothers Company was incorporated in Chicago late in 1910 by C.R. Horns, Walter D. Tuff and J.B. Diebler. Capital stock was $10,000, and the plan was to manufacture and deal in motorcars. This venture is not believed to have produced an automobile.

1911 Adams, model C, touring, WLB

ADAMS — Findlay, Ohio — (1910-1911) — The Adams Brothers Company of Findlay was incorporated in 1910 to build a four-cylinder 30 hp car with a Renault-type hood and an enclosed driving compartment. The vehicle was designed by Joseph Borovitz and was put into production later in 1910. Then Borovitz had another idea. As the foreword to the company's 1911 catalog stated, "The demand for a dependable commercial vehicle has influenced the Adams Brothers . . . to add this type of car to the pleasure car of their manufacture." After 1911 the company built trucks only, undergoing a friendly receivership in mid-1914 ("we are doing a good business but need cash to go ahead") and continuing in manufacture until mid-1916 when the Adams brothers announced the discontinuation of their commercial vehicles and the concentration of their company henceforth on foundry and machine shop work.

1910-1911 ADAMS
Thirty — 4-cyl., 30 hp, 118" wb

	FP	5	4	3	2	1
Model C Tour.-5P	—	3100	4200	6300	10,500	22,000

Series 6 — 5-cyl., 40/45 hp, 90" wb

	FP	5	4	3	2	1
Tour.-5P	2500	3700	4700	7200	13,400	25,600
Land'et.-7P	3000	3200	4200	6300	9700	21,500
Extension Brgm. (94" wb)	4000	3500	4500	6500	10,000	22,000

Model 7-A — 5-cyl., 40/45 hp, 108" wb

	FP	5	4	3	2	1
Tour.-7P	3000	3700	4700	7200	13,400	25,600

Model 8-A — 5-cyl., 40/45 hp, 86" wb

	FP	5	4	3	2	1
Gentleman's Speed Rds.	4000	3900	5000	8000	14,000	26,000

1907 ADAMS-FARWELL
Model 7-A — 5-cyl., 40/45 hp, 120" wb

	FP	5	4	3	2	1
Tour.-7P	3250	4000	5000	8000	15,000	28,000

1908 ADAMS-FARWELL
Model 9 — 5-cyl., 50 hp, 120" wb

	FP	5	4	3	2	1
Tour.-7P	3500	4000	5000	8000	15,000	28,000
Rds.-3P	3000	4200	5200	8400	15,500	28,500
Cpe.-3P	4000	3500	4500	6500	10,000	22,000

1905 Adams-Farwell, model 6, brougham, NAHC

1909 Adams-Farwell, model 9, roadster, WLB

1909-1912 ADAMS-FARWELL
Model 9 — 5-cyl., 50 hp

	FP	5	4	3	2	1
Tour.-7P (128" wb)	3500	4700	9450	15,750	22,000	31,500
Rds.-4P (120" wb)	3000	4600	9150	15,250	21,300	30,500

ADAMS-FARWELL — Dubuque, Iowa — (1905-1913) — The Adams Company was founded in 1883 by Herbert and Eugene Adams for the manufacture of grave markers and park benches, soon branching into milling and general foundry equipment. Fay Oliver Farwell joined the company as superintendent several years later, but by 1895 was bored with its activity and began experimenting with internal combustion engines. The most effective one he came up with was radial (an idea he got from a steam-powered hoist), rotary (in order to forego the ponderous weight of a fly-wheel) and air cooled (the rotating engine itself nicely effecting cooling). Around a fixed shaft, cylinders and crankcase revolved horizontally, with power transmitted by bevel gears to the gearbox and hence by single chain to the rear axle. In 1898 he put his first three-cylinder engine between the front wheels of an iron-tired express wagon, the following year he moved the engine to the rear in his bicycle-wheeled Model 2 runabout. All subsequent cars had rear engines. The Model 3 of 1901 sported wooden artillery wheels, the Model 4 was sold to a resident in Dubuque, the Model 5 was the production prototype shown at the Chicago Automobile Show in February 1905, after which the company began taking orders. For 1906 the Adams-Farwell was available as either a three-or five-cylinder car. The company slogan was "it spins like a top." The Model 8A Gentleman's Speed Roadster offered in 1906 weighed but 1400 pounds and was capable of 75 mph. It was frameless, a very early, albeit ingenuous, example of unit body construction. Other unusual features offered through the years included foot pedal and steering controls which could be removed from the front seat and inserted in slots of the floor of the rear-seat compartment so the motorist could literally become a "back seat driver"; a "side sliding steering wheel" which at a moment's notice could change the car from left to right hand drive; and a double-clutch (one for second and fourth, the other for first, third and reverse) operated by a single clutch lever with a steering-column-mounted shift lever provided for each set of gears. (Among its advantages, this allowed forward/backward maneuvering without the bother of shifting gears; one simply put one shift lever in second and the other in reverse and then swung the clutch lever back and forth.) Despite such ingenuity, or perhaps because of it, the Adams-Farwell never was widely regarded as more than a novelty. By 1913 Herbert and Eugene Adams decided that the foundry and gear-cutting business was a much more lucrative, and easier, proposition than motorcar manufacture. Fay Farwell stayed on awhile, but left in 1921 to travel the carnival circuit and try to sell a merry-go-round he had patented. Total production of the marque, including Models 1 through 5 of which only a single example each was made, is estimated at fifty-two cars. Only one is known to exist, and it is in Harrah's Automobile Collection.

1905 ADAMS-FARWELL
Model 6 — 3-cyl., 20/25 hp, 84" wb

	FP	5	4	3	2	1
Conv. Brougham	2500	3000	4000	6000	9500	21,000

1906 Adams-Farwell, series 6 (5-cyl.), convertible runabout, HAC

1906 ADAMS-FARWELL
Series 6 — 3-cyl., 20/25 hp, 90" wb

		5	4	3	2	1
Model A Tour.-5P	2000	3500	4500	7000	13,000	25,000
Model B Land'et.-7P	2500	3000	4000	6000	9500	21,000

ADE — Ade (for the humorist George Ade) was among the names considered for the new car planned in Brook, Indiana in 1909. Refer to Brook.

ADELPHIA — Philadelphia, Pennsylvania — (1920) — Adelphia was the droll name given to the car built for export by the Winfield Barnes Company of Philadelphia. It was put into production "only after a tremendous financial outlay in experimental work and road tests." The Adelphia featured right-hand drive and a Herschell-Spillman four-cylinder engine, and its debut was announced during the summer of 1920. A few months later, in October, there was the notice of its demise because of "insufficient capital to continue" — which was something of an understatement since the company's available cash was only $757. Its assets, listed as $609,960, must have been virtually all on paper; its $208,806 in liabilities was probably real. Promotional photographs indicate the Adelphia to be a quite ordinary touring car with a square Rolls-Royce-like radiator. (The Amco and the Alsace looked much like it.) Doubtlessly many more Adelphia brochures were printed up than Adelphia cars ever saw the assembly line. The real estate and personal property of the Winfield Barnes Company went to the auction block in July 1921. The first sale of the plant was set aside by the court as being too low; in 1922 the factory was finally sold for $86,000.

1920 Adelphia, touring

1920 ADELPHIA
Model 4B — 4-cyl., 39 hp, 115" wb

	FP	5	4	3	2	1
Tour.-5P	1695	1800	2800	4200	7000	14,500

ADMIRAL/ADMIRALTY — The Admiral Motor Car Company was organized in St. Louis, Michigan early in 1913 with a capital stock of $50,000 and the plan to manufacture motorcars. No Admiral automobile followed.

The Admiralty Power Company was organized in Port Richmond, Staten Island, New York early in 1910 for the manufacture and sale of motors, engines and automobiles. The capital stock was $80,000. C.L. Straub (Plainfield, New Jersey), J.H. Davidson (West New Brighton, Staten Island) and G.H. Bates (Cranford, New Jersey) were the people involved. No manufacture is believed to have followed.

17

ADREM — In New Castle, Indiana, late in 1909, the Adrem Motor Company was organized with a capital stock of $5000 for the manufacture of automobiles. Among the people involved were J.D. Smith, H.E. Jennings, H.C. Yauky, W.C. Bond, H.F. Burk, D.W. Kinsey, H.C. Chase. No manufacture is believed to have followed.

Strikingly Beautiful

Price $1495

1921 Adria, model A-1, touring, KM

ADRIA — Batavia, New York — (1921-1922) — The Adria Motor Car Corporation was in trouble almost as soon as it began. Although its product was an assembled car with a four-cylinder Supreme engine, the company widely ballyhooed the "radical departures from conventional design" it represented. These departures included a chassis made up in four pieces and put together like the sides of a box; a body made in three main sections and built up in appropriate jigs so as to be interchangeable; and a unique design of cross springs and non-loading axles both front and rear. Unfortunately, this last-named novelty was not as legally unique as Adria thought, which the company quickly found out when Parenti Motors Corporation of Buffalo sued for patent infringement in October of 1921, and the Adria factory was ordered shut down. In his argument on the injunction, Adria president Louis F. Vremsak claimed that when he and Joseph Parenti had been associated in 1911, Parenti knew nothing at all about automobiles and it "required a painstaking effort to make of him a workman of even average ability." The New York State Supreme Court vacated the Parenti injunction and allowed Adria to resume manufacture pursuant to a trial on the merits of the case. A short while later Adria experienced a cash flow problem, which closed the factory again, but this was solved by early March of 1922 when the company paid its creditors in full. How many cars had been produced prior to the Parenti injunction is not known. Between the quashing of the Parenti injunction and the cash-flow problem, fifteen cars had been assembled, and seventeen others were in the process before the second shutdown. Presumably not many more than that were put together when the factory opened for the third time. The company's cash flowed the wrong way for the last time later that year, and Adria gave up altogether. The Parenti vs Adria case never came to trial. And Louis Vremsak left town.

1921-1922 ADRIA
Model A-1 — 4-cyl., 39 hp, 120" wb

	FP	5	4	3	2	1
Tour.-5P	1495	1500	2500	3600	5600	10,500
Sedanette-5P	1995	1400	2300	3400	5500	10,000

ADRIAN — The Adrian Motor Works has frequently been represented as an automobile producer in Adrian, Michigan from 1902-1903. This is in error. There was a "motor works" in Adrian at that time, but neither the car nor the company bore the name Adrian. The firm was the Church Manufacturing Company, and the car was called the Murray. Refer to Murray.

ADVANCE — The 1899 car built in the shops of the Advance Manufacturing Company of Hamilton, Ohio is more correctly designated by its inventor's name. Refer to Ritchie.

The car produced by the Advance Motor Vehicle Company of Miamisburg, Ohio from 1909-1912 was called the Kauffman. Refer to Kauffman.

The Advance Auto & Machinery Company was organized early in 1911 in Evansville, Indiana to manufacture, buy and sell automobiles. Capital stock was $10,000, with Henry Kollker, Walter Wheeler and John Diers the men behind this venture. No manufacture is believed to have resulted.

The Advance Engine & Manufacturing Company was a $25,000 incorporation from Jersey City, New Jersey during the fall of 1907. Incorporators were H.O. Coughlin, A.C. Bear and John R. Turner, and the plan was the manufacture of automobiles and motors. No Advance car resulted.

The Advance Garage Company was organized in Chicago late in 1914 to manufacture and deal in, store and repair motor vehicles. Capital stock was $2500. Manufacture did not follow.

ADVIS — This frequent typographical error on car rosters was in actuality the Davis, a cyclecar built in Detroit in 1914. Refer to Davis.

A.E.C. (ANGER) — Milwaukee, Wisconsin — (1913-1915) — The Anger Engineering Company was organized in April 1912 by Walter A. Anger, who was described as "a well-known auto tradesman." He could not make up his mind as to his preference between T-head or L-head engines so he offered each, a 38 hp six-cylinder L-head and a 43 hp T-head six, and he threw in a smaller four for good measure. Whether to name his car after himself or the initials of his company also apparently perplexed him, because it was known as both during its short life. Most of the cars appear to have been built on a custom basis to buyer's specifications. Walter Anger's first automobile venture had been the Brendel-Anger Company in Milwaukee in 1908, but it appears to have produced no cars at all.

1913-1915 A.E.C. (ANGER)
Model 4-40 — 4-cyl., 26 hp, 120" wb

	FP	5	4	3	2	1
Tour.-5P	1800	—	—	—	—	—
Rds.-2P	1750	—	—	—	—	—

Model 6-50 — 6-cyl., 38 hp, 134" wb

	FP	5	4	3	2	1
Tour.-5P	2550	—	—	—	—	—
Rds.-2P	2550	—	—	—	—	—

Model 6-60 — 6-cyl., 43 hp, 140" wb

	FP	5	4	3	2	1
Tour.-5P	2750	—	—	—	—	—
Rds.-2P	2750	—	—	—	—	—

AERIAL — The manufacture of aeroplanes and automobiles was the plan of the Aerial Manufacturing and Supplies Company which was a $50,000 incorporation in New York City during the fall of 1910. S. Shethar (Great Neck, Long Island), J. Loughran (Long Island City) and C.H. Stoll (New York City) were the people involved. No Aerial automobile followed.

AERO — The Aero and Aero Type are more properly considered as models of the car best known as the Victor Page, which was produced in Stamford, Connecticut from 1921-1924. Refer to Victor Page.

Aero Auto-Bob was an occasional designation for the juvenile car built by Jack Hickman in 1914-1915 in East Pittsburgh, Pennsylvania. More frequently the car was called simply the Auto-Bob. Refer to Auto-Bob.

Aero-Car was the abbreviated designation which even Sheldon F. Reese himself used to refer to the car he built in Huron, South Dakota in 1921. Its full name is the more appropriate, however. Refer to Reese Aero-Car.

The Aerocar Company was a $10,000 incorporation to manufacture automobiles and parts emanating from Cleveland, Ohio in the spring of 1906. D.C. Westhover, F.C. Howe, James C. Brooks, W. J. Rudolph and Al Welch were the people involved. No manufacture is indicated.

The Aeroplane Motor Company of Detroit noted in 1910 the plan to include automobiles in its manufacture. The incorporators of this $100,000 firm were Henry J. Galarneau, Mary A. Galarneau, Thaddeus E. Smith and Ezra P. Beechler. No automobile, however, ever resulted.

1906 Aerocar, touring, NAHC

AEROCAR — Detroit, Michigan — (1906-1908) — According to the Aerocar Company, the superior merit of its product was due to its engine, an air-cooled unit designed by Milton O. Reeves of the Reeves Pulley Company. In the Chicago Economy Contest of 1906, an Aerocar finished the 57-mile run, held in a driving rain, in about two hours and consumed only two gallons and one quart of gasoline. In 1907 the "Practical Car Built by Practical Men" was also offered with a water-cooled engine designed by Leo Melanowski, who earlier had been chief engineer for Dragon. Meantime the company had fallen into financial trouble — and by 1908 was out of business. The two most interesting pieces of history regarding the Aerocar have nothing to do with the automobile itself. The company's chief investor was coal baron Alexander Y. Malcomson who previously had been one of the principal financial angels in Henry Ford's early automotive efforts. And, after the Aeorcar was no more, its factory was utilized to build the first Hudson cars.

1906 AEROCAR
Model A — 4-cyl., 24 hp, 104" wb

Tour.-5P	2800	3500	4500	7000	13,000	25,000

1907 Aerocar, model C, runabout

1907 AEROCAR
Model D — 4-cyl., 20 hp, 104" wb

	FP	5	4	3	2	1
Tour.-5P	2000	3200	4200	6500	12,500	24,000

Model C — 4-cyl., 20 hp, 104" wb

Rbt.-2P	2000	3300	4300	6700	12,700	24,500

Model F — 4-cyl., 40 hp, 115" wb

Tour.-5P	2750	3500	4500	7000	13,000	25,000

1908 Aerocar, model F, touring, WLB

1908 AEROCAR
Model D — 4-cyl., 20 hp, 104" wb

Tour.-5P	1500	3200	4200	6500	12,500	24,000

Model E — 4-cyl., 20 hp, 104" wb

Tour. Rbt.-3P	1500	3300	4300	6700	12,700	24,500

Model F — 4-cyl., 40 hp, 115" wb

Tour.-5P	2200	3500	4500	7000	13,000	25,000

1936 Aerocoupe, MVMA

AEROCOUPE — East Haven, Connecticut — (1936) — Richard Crossley of East Haven built a three-wheeled speedster using parts from both used airplanes and used automobiles in 1936. He claimed the car had a speed of 75 mph. Although he never built another, his single Aerocoupe received a good deal of attention, including a picture syndicated by Wide World, which is probably the reason the vehicle has appeared on various lists as a manufactured car.

AETNA — Detroit, Michigan — (1910) — In the spring of 1910 the Aetna Investment Company was organized in Detroit by Malcom T. Faulkner (president), Dr. L.C. Moore (vice-president), M.W. Allen (secretary-treasurer), and John A. Stuart and F. Stephem Kratzett as directors. Initial capital stock was $5000, raised almost immediately to $20,000 for the purpose of building a five-passenger touring car of torpedo type. Organized by these same people at the same time was the Huron Radiator Company, which was in operation by that summer. The Aetna passenger car built as a prototype remained just that, however, a prototype. Ultimately, Aetna did move into commercial vehicle production, as the Aetna Motor Truck Company.

AGONTZ — The Agontz was simply the Ogontz misspelled. Refer to Ogontz.

1913 Ahrens-Fox, model E-C, battalion roadster, KM

AHRENS-FOX — Cincinnati, Ohio — (1913) — John P. Ahrens and Charles P. Fox had been building horse-drawn steam pumpers in Cincinnati since 1868. In 1911 they completed their first motorized fire engine, and by the end of 1912 the Ahrens-Fox Fire Engine Company had gone automotive completely. Like rival American LaFrance, Ahrens-Fox decided to produce automobiles as well, envisioning a likely market among the fire chiefs of the larger cities to whom the company sold its traditional products. Unlike American LaFrance, Ahrens-Fox provided some fire-fighting equipment onboard its Model E-C Battalion Roadster. The engine was a 44 hp six, with transmission a selective four-speed. Fire chiefs were guaranteed they could go to blazes at speeds "upwards to 50 miles an hour." But a blaze of orders did not result. Just a half-dozen Battalion Roadsters were built in 1913 and all of them remained in Cincinnati.

1850 Aiken, auto buggy, NAHC

AIKEN — Baltimore, Maryland — (circa 1850) — William A.E. Aiken was a professor of chemistry at the University of Maryland Medical School. Around 1850 he built a steam carriage with two seats, high wheels, and its engine and smokestack to the rear. The car was strictly experimental, and Aiken never built another. Accounts of this steamer contemporary to the period appear lacking, but it remained extant as late as 1939. What happened to the Aiken vehicle subsequently is not known.

AIRLAND — The Airland Motor Company was organized in Greensburg, Pennsylvania during the late spring of 1919 for the manufacture of automobiles, trucks and accessories. Capital stock was $75,000. Benjamin Ratner and T.A. Gilligan of Latrobe were among the incorporators. The others, all of Pittsburgh, were Emma Baer, Samuel Osgood and M. Harry Cuff. An Airland automobile was never marketed.

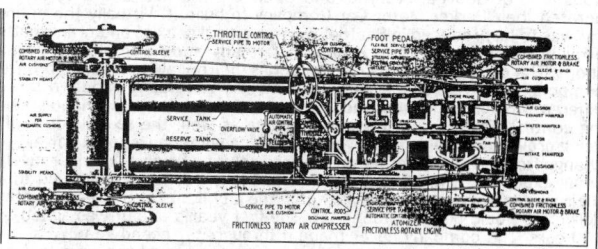

1914 Airmobile, four wheel air drive car, JHV

AIRMOBILE — Los Angeles, California — (1914) — The car produced by the Rotary Air Brake Company of Los Angeles remains a mystery. The firm advertised Airmobile five-passenger touring cars and roadsters at $1000, and a seven-passenger touring at $2000, in the program for the 1914 Santa Monica Road Races. No photograph appeared, but there was a complex drawing of the Airmobile chassis showing the firm's specialized equipment in place. The text noted that output for 1914 had been sold already, and the car was "Revolutionizing the Motor Vehicle Business." The Los Angeles Automobile Show program that year included the Rotary Air Brake Company among its exhibitors. But 1914 was the last one heard of the Airmobile. By 1915 the Rotary Air Brake people were touting the advantages of their multi-function air / steam / gas / water engines, which are known to have gone into production. Involved in this company were Edward D. Foster and Herbert C. Steele. Engines remained their specialty for the next several years. Compressed air driven units for industrial use became their product in 1920. At some point during the First World War the firm's name was changed to Rotary Products Company.

AIROMOBILE — With a capital stock of $500,000, the Airomobile Company of America was organized late in 1910 "to manufacture, buy, sell and deal in aeroplanes and vehicles to be operated in the air, automobiles and motor carriages." The venture was a Delaware incorporation; the incorporators were E.J. Forham, H.P. Jones and G.F. Martin, all of New York City; and one reference indicates the plan to locate near Philadelphia. No Airomobile automobile is believed to have resulted of this venture.

19

1937 Airomobile, coupe, OCW

1925 Ajax, touring, WLB

AIROMOBILE — Denver, Colorado & Syracuse, New York — (1937) — The Airomobile was a streamlined three-wheeler that was the idea of Paul M. Lewis who lived in Denver. In 1935 he incorporated Lewis-American Airways and then traveled East to find production facilities. Meanwhile, in Syracuse, the H.H. Franklin Company had gone to the wall, and two of its top engineers, Carl Doman and Ed Marks, had gone into partnership as freelance engineers and prototype builders. The three men got together and the four-cylinder 60 hp Airomobile prototype was built. It was on the road on April 19th, 1937, and so was Paul Lewis in what the press described as a "novel" method for financing an automobile venture in its early stages. This involved the sale of county and state franchises to dealers on a three-payment basis, one-third down, a second third when a demonstrator was delivered, and the third payment when production was established. Production never was established, however, nor were any demonstrators delivered. Unlike so many car ventures that never got off the ground, the Airomobile was a financial loss ($250,000) only for its promoter. A Securities and Exchange Commission investigation revealed that no one had complained or been bilked. Lewis had envisioned selling the car for $300, which should have made it an attractive proposition. But a streamlined three-wheeler, even if capable of 80 mph, was considered bizarre at the time. With the approach of the Second World War, Lewis gave up on the project. (After the war, the VW Beetle with basically the same concept and the addition of one more wheel found ready public acceptance.) The four-cylinder 60 hp air-cooled engine Doman and Marks developed for the Airomobile was later used with modification in such light aircraft as the Piper, the Aeronica and the Taylorcraft. Their Doman-Marks Engine Company was bought out by Republic Aircraft prior to the war. When peace came, Republic sold the company to Preston Tucker who had plans to build his own automobile. The Airomobile prototype remains extant.

1937 AIROMOBILE
Four — 60 hp, 126" wb

	FP	5	4	3	2	1
Prototype	—	—	—	—	—	—

AJAX — Seattle, Washington — (1914-1915) — This Ajax was the ambitious idea of George, Frank L. and Charles L. Parker, and they incorporated their Parker Motor Car Company to build it. Virtually the entire car was to be produced in Seattle, with gear blanks, axles and crankshafts arriving rough-forged from Krupp in Germany and finished in the Ajax shops. The company built its own foundries for iron, aluminum and bronze components. Diversity was the Ajax aim. The car was provided in three different wheelbase lengths and with the choice of left or right hand steering control. There was a choice of engine as well, the six-cylinder unit being provided as either a sleeve valve or a conventional poppet-valve, the change from one to the other on the assembly line being a "comparatively small expense." On February 28th, 1914, the Parkers announced that their new factory would be built within the city limits of Seattle and that deliveries would begin October 1st. The first year's output was slated at 100 cars. The company never made it through its second year. At some point, there appears to have been a name change of the firm to Ajax Motors Company.

1914-1915 AJAX
Ajax Six

		5	4	3	2	1
Rds. (120" wb)	—	4700	6000	10,000	18,500	32,500
Tour. (133" wb)	—	4500	5800	9500	18,000	32,000
Limo. (136" wb)	—	4000	5000	8000	15,000	28,000

AJAX — Boston, Massachusetts — (1920-1921) — Ajax Motors Corporation was organized in 1920 for the manufacture of both cars and trucks, some references indicating the factory in Hyde Park. The Ajax car was a six-cylinder 55 hp (Continental engine) five-passenger touring on a 116-inch wheelbase. Production was limited, perhaps to just pilot models. In 1921 Ajax was taken over by the Walker-Johnson Truck Company of Woburn, which produced only trucks, under the tradename of W-J, into 1924. Conceivably, Ajax Motors Corporation may have evolved from the Lenox Motor Car Company which had enjoyed some success with its Lenox car from 1911 until 1917.

1920-1921 AJAX
Six — 55 hp, 116" wb

		5	4	3	2	1
Tour.-5P	—	3500	4500	7000	13,000	25,000

AJAX — Racine, Wisconsin — (1925-1926) — Because he liked the mythological significance of the name, Charles W. Nash decided to call his "entirely new idea of motor car purchasing power in the $1000 field" the Ajax. Early in 1924 he had outbid the Hupmobile people for the huge plant of the defunct Mitchell Motors Company in Racine in which to build it, and

he assigned its design to engineer Earl G. Gunn who had time on his hands since the LaFayette he had designed for Nash had just folded in Milwaukee. The machinery from the old LaFayette plant was quickly dispatched to Racine for the building of the new Ajax. Stationery for the new Ajax Motors Company was just as quickly ordered; the success of the enterprise was virtually assured, motoring journalists said, because of the Ajax's backing by its prestigious parent organization, Nash Motors of Kenosha. Motoring journalists were also very impressed with the Ajax when it debuted. Its seven-bearing crankshaft was most unusual for the car of its size and price: its 170-cubic-inch L-head six provided for a genuine 60 mph. The Ajax sold well in its first year, some 22,122 units, but this was about a quarter of the Nash production in Kenosha. Since the mythological reference wasn't providing heroic sales, Charlie Nash concluded he might better call the car what in fact it really was. On the Ajax's first anniversary, it became the Nash Light Six. New nameplates and hubcaps were made available to Nash dealers for updating any Ajaxes on hand — and that was that. This was probably the industry's first example of one car becoming another so easily.

1925 Ajax, sedan, JAC

1925-1926 AJAX
Six — 40 hp, 109" wb

	FP	5	4	3	2	1
Tour.-5P	865	1600	3000	4000	6500	10,000
Sed.-5P	995	800	1400	2100	3400	5000

AJAX CYCLECAR — Ajax had been its name in France, but when Benjamin Briscoe brought the car to America to be built in Jackson, Michigan, the name was changed to Argo. Refer to Argo.

1903 Ajax Electric, runabout, NAHC

AJAX ELECTRIC — New York, New York — (1901-1903) — The Ajax Motor Vehicle Company had its factory on West 36th Street in Manhattan, a few blocks north of Macy's department store. The venture was apparently a family affair, the company's incorporators being S.L., A.L. and Walter Simpson of New York. The firm was incorporated for $10,000 in July 1901. The most memorable aspect of the Simpsons' product, perhaps, was its trademark: a drawing of biceps and clenched fist that renders the famous Arm & Hammer logo a muscular alsoran. It was also a bit incongruous for a little two-seater runabout on scrawny bicycle wheels. "The Honest Automobile at an Honest Price" was priced initially at $1100 and subsequently was made considerably more honest at $250 less. Late in 1902 A.L. Simpson announced that he was seeking sales for the Ajax Electric outside New York City. He never found them.

1901-1902 AJAX ELECTRIC

	FP	5	4	3	2	1
Ajax Electric Rbt.	1100	2000	3000	4200	6500	14,000
1903 AJAX ELECTRIC						
Ajax Electric Rbt.	850	2000	3000	4200	6500	14,000

A-K — A-K was the popular nickname of the Allen-Kingston. Refer to Allen-Kingston.

1901 Akron, stanhope, NAHC

AKRON — Akron, Ohio — (1899-1901) — F.E. Smith was the president, E.W. Hull the secretary-treasurer, and M.J. Gilbo the general manager of the Akron Machine Company which manufactured mower knives, binder sickles, sections, guards, guard plates and drop forgings "of every description" — and in 1899 built the first automobile in town. The car was completed and tested during the summer of 1899. It was wonderfully described in the July 26th edition of the *Akron Beacon Journal:* "The vehicle is a natty affair and of compact form. It is equipped with the gasoline system of motive power, with storage battery attachment. The 'mobile has a way of working well on a straightway course, but when an attempt is made to turn around there is still a constant hitch somewhere in the construction of the machinery. It also makes too much noise. These two defects are being overcome gradually, and will eventually be eliminated." There were definite plans for manufacture and a number of wealthy men in Akron (who refused to disclose their names) were said to be on the verge of organizing a company for production. "There Is Money In It," the newspaper headline commented regarding the nascent automobile industry. The Akron Motor Carriage Company was announced to the automotive press during 1900, as well as the forthcoming production of a single-cylinder gasoline stanhope. Several sample vehicles were built, but the car was never placed on the market. Possibly the problem of noise and turning corners was never completely eliminated. In July of 1901 the S.M. York Machinery Company of Cleveland bought out the entire equipment of the Akron factory. It was rumored at the time that the Woodruff brothers, who were described as the "mechanical heads" of the machine company, would go into the business themselves — which they did, with their Woodruff automobile.

AKRON — Akron, Ohio — (1905) — Following the death of his brother George, and the failure of their Woodruff car in Akron, Albert M. Woodruff relocated in a small shop at 65 West Market Street and announced to the trade press that he was now organizing the Akron Two-Cycle Automobile Company for the manufacture of his two-stroke engines. A car called the Akron, using one of Woodruff's two-strokes as well as his own transmission, was also to be built. Four touring cars were, but then Woodruff decided to confine his efforts to engine production only. He died in 1909.

1905 AKRON

	FP	5	4	3	2	1
Touring Car	—	2000	3000	4200	6500	14,000

ALAMEDA — Early in 1906, in Oakland, California, the Alameda Garage was organized with a capital stock of $20,000 to manufacture, sell and repair automobiles. The organizers were Paul K. Buckley, Frank Smith, E.K. Taylor, William E. Keene and John F. Buttrick. An Alameda automobile was never marketed.

ALAMO — A capital stock of $75 million and the plan to manufacture and deal in motorcars, supplies, parts and accessories was announced by the Alamo Automobile Corporation early in 1917. F.H. Larsen and John Armstrong were behind this venture, which was based in Phoenix, Arizona. No automobile resulted, but possibly some stock was sold.

ALAMOBILE — Hillsdale, Michigan — (1902) — The Alamo Manufacturing Company of Hillsdale was established in 1901 with a capital stock of $15,000 and a workforce of five men. Its purpose was the manufacture of gasoline engines. By 1902 capitalization was increased to $75,000, business was booming, and the company had outgrown its original premises. Construction of a new factory was begun, and the Alamo people decided to expand their product line. "A trial automobile has been built and tried and proved very satisfactory," the *Hillsdale Leader* reported on July 18th, 1902, "but the manufacture of these will be deferred until they move into their new factory building." According to the press release the company provided automotive trade publications, the name decided upon for the car was Alamobile. But after moving into the new factory, Alamo decided not to manufacture it. Most probably this was because of the pressures of the Alamo engine-building business, which was thriving. Alamo gasoline engines were sold worldwide. By 1915 capitalization had been increased to $350,000, the workforce was over 300 men, and annual sales surpassed a half-million dollars. The Great Depression killed the Alamo Manufacturing Company in 1934. Its factory today is owned by Essex Wire Corporation.

1917 Aland, Four, 5-pass., touring, WLB

ALAND — Detroit, Michigan — (1916-1917) — The Aland was the very ambitious idea of engineer R.C. Aland, and the Aland Motor Car Company was incorporated in Michigan with a total capital of $500,000 to build it. Its "racing type aluminum engine," as referred to by the press, featured a single overhead camshaft and four overhead valves for each of the four cylinders. Although the horsepower rating was 14, Aland stated his 155 cubic inch engine would develop more than 65 hp at 3200 rpm, or one horsepower for every 2.39 cubic inches of displacement, which for that era was high efficiency indeed. Unusual too were the diagonally-connected internal expanding brakes on all four wheels. Probably the Aland was a bit too avant-garde for its era. Deliveries began around Christmas time of 1916. The car had failed by the holiday season of 1917. Few were built.

1916-1917 ALAND
Four — 14 hp, 122" wb

	FP	5	4	3	2	1
Tour.-5P	1500	3200	4300	6500	11,000	23,000
Rds.-2P	1500	3300	4400	6700	12,000	24,000

ALBANUS — Albanus was the second half of the partnership which produced the Roach & Albanus car in Ft. Wayne, Indiana at the turn of the century. Refer to Roach & Albanus.

ALBANY — The Albany Garage Company was a late 1905 incorporation to "manufacture, purchase, use, lease, sell and store self-propelling vehicles of all descriptions." The place was Albany, New York, and the capital stock was $50,000. E. Palmer Gavit, W.L.L. Peltz, Frederick W. Rockwell, Matthew Van Alstyne, William L. Visscher, Gerrit Y. Lansing and Francis C. Huyck, Jr. were behind this venture. No car is believed to have resulted.

The Albany Vulcanizing Works of Albany, New York indicated its plan to increase capital stock by $2000 in order to manufacture automobiles and bicycles in early 1909. Henry T. Martin, J. Edward Brooks and William T. Martin were the directors of this firm. No manufacture is believed to have followed.

ALBANY — Albany, Indiana — (1907-1908) — In 1905, John L. Lulley designed a highwheeler with a single-cylinder engine mounted under the seat, tiller steering, steel buggy wheels and no fenders. Local businessmen backed him in the formation of the Albany Automobile Company late in 1906; production began in the spring of the following year. Almost immediately, the Albany backers asked for a few refinements over the original which Lulley provided with a wheel for steering, solid rubber tires, fenders, and a false hood to make the Albany look more like a proper motorcar. Obviously even more was needed. For 1908 Lulley provided another cylinder, again air cooled, mounted the twin upfront and thus made the false hood a real one. But still it was not enough. By August 1908, after the production of about 850 cars, the company was bankrupt. The Albany assets were sold the following month to the Union Automobile Company of Seymour, Indiana, which may have continued production for a short while, though no documentation of that survives. J.S. Tully, James P. McNary, William S. Cory and Walter Bryan were indicated as among the Albany businessmen who had backed this venture.

1907 ALBANY
Model B — 1-cyl., 6/7 hp, 62" wb

	FP	5	4	3	2	1
Rbt.	325	1500	2500	3600	5500	11,000
Model C — 1-cyl., 10/12 hp, 62" wb						
Rbt.	350	1500	2500	3700	5600	11,200

1907 Albany, runabout, NAHC

1908 ALBANY
Model G — 2-cyl., 18/20 hp, 96" wb

	FP	5	4	3	2	1
Surrey	525	1500	2500	3600	5500	11,000

Model F — 2-cyl., 18/20 hp, 96" wb

Rbt.	500	1400	2400	3500	5300	10,000

1939 Albatross, four-place racing convertible, HRS

ALBATROSS — **New York, New York** — **(1939)** — By the mid-Thirties, Peter Arno was among the most popular illustrators whose work enlivened the pages of *The New Yorker.* He was certainly the most debonair, fond of executing his next "Whoops Sisters" cartoon while dressed in dinner jacket and opera pumps, and fond of fast sporting cars too. It was perhaps inevitable that one day he would design one himself. And it was probably his wont as well that the car would be steeped in mystery, as it has remained to this day. Among the legends growing up about it was that it had been built in Europe and was fitted with platinum fenders which, once safely past customs, were replaced with steel, the platinum then reaping a grand profit. In fact, the car was built in New York by Inskip at the Brewster Aeronautics plant on Long Island. It was based on a 1939 Mercury chassis, stretched out to a 137-inch wheelbase. But its look was strictly European, strongly suggestive of the 540-K Mercedes by Erdmann & Rossi. Interestingly, in the one advertisement prepared for the car, which noted 1780 Broadway at 57th Street as headquarters, it was referred to as a "137 K." Four-place racing convertible was Arno's quite apt designation for the coachwork. Interestingly, too, one month after the advertisement — in December 1939 — a press release was issued indicating that the car was to be manufactured by the new Albatross Motor Car Company. Now, three body styles (a convertible cabriolet carrying five, a town car and a two-seater speedster) were projected. None of these cars were built. But the one "four-place racing convertible" definitely was. Peter Arno used it as his personal transportation. No one has yet determined how serious Peter Arno really was about going into manufacture of his Albatross. The car was deliciously named. And it remains extant. In 1982, after an arduous search, historian Keith Marvin discovered it in a Midwest collection.

ALBAUGH — The company's name was Albaugh-Dover. The company's car, a highwheeler produced in Chicago in 1910, was the Aldo. Refer to Aldo.

ALBERTSON — The Albertson Company was incorporated with a capital stock of $25,000 in late 1913 for the purpose of manufacturing and dealing in automobiles. F.R. Hansell (Philadelphia, Pennsylvania) and George H.B. Martin (Camden, New Jersey) were the partners behind this venture, and they planned to locate near Philadelphia. No manufacture is believed to have followed.

ALBION — The Albion was produced in Glasgow, Scotland from the turn of the century until shortly before the First World War. It was imported into this country, but never built here, despite its presence on various car rosters.

ALBRECHT — In February of 1900 announcement was made in a trade press publication of forthcoming car production by the Milwaukee, Wisconsin firm of Charles Albrecht & Company. This was simply a typographical error, which has been repeated on car rosters ever since. Refer to Abresch.

ALL-BRIGHT — The All-Bright Auto Company was organized in New York City during the summer of 1909 to manufacture cars, wagons, boats and engines. R.J. and V.R. Welch, in association with Fred Edwards, backed this venture. No manufacture is believed to have resulted.

1910 Alco, touring, OCW

ALCO — **Providence, Rhode Island** — **(1909-1913)** — Having produced the American Berliet under license from France for three years, the American Locomotive Company felt sure it could build a better car — and one that would be as financially lucrative as the steam locomotives for which the firm was renowned. The result was the Alco which, the company said, combined "power, strength, weight and simple construction . . . to give it perfect balance and fitness for conquest of all roads." It was available in a welter of factory body styles, and any custom-built variations desired. William K. Vanderbilt "designed" his own rakish sportster. And Harry Grant won both the 1909 and 1910 Vanderbilt Cups in an Alco. By the latter year the company had branched into taxicab and truck manufacture as well, but it was the production Alco in which the most pride — and almost absurdly painstaking care — was taken. Alco boasted that one year and seven months were required to build a single motorcar, six months alone to build the rear axle. Doubtless it was the firm's locomotive-building background which made it adamant on building so well. Early Alco catalogs made only passing reference to anything other than the vehicle's chassis, drivetrain and engine. The engines were huge: 453 cubic inches for the four in 1911, 579 cubic inches for the six. By 1912, however, convinced that the Alco could not be made better, efforts turned to making it more beautiful. Body styling was given careful attention, and the Alco became as noteworthy for its elegant coachwork as its sterling engineering qualities. A white stripe around the body at the top of the doors became a feature of distinction. American Locomotive also proudly claimed that its cars, in the $6000-$7500-plus range, were the most expensive in America. Then, on August 22nd, 1913, *The New York Times* reported rumors that the Alco was to be discontinued. The industry was aghast. The Alco plant was among the best equipped in America, the Alco product was among the most respected in the nation, the American Locomotive Company had just revealed gross earnings for the fiscal year of $34 million. Unfortunately, none of the profit accruing was from the automobile division. The Alco people apparently had been unaware that while locomotives are bought, automobiles have to be sold. When the time was taken to total up and analyze the figures, they revealed that thus far 5000 Alcos in 54 different models had been built, and the company had lost an average of $460 on each one of them. Almost immediately, American Locomotive announced its desire "to sever as completely and as soon as possible all connections with the automobile branch of the business." Fortunately, a handful of Alco cars survive today as testimony to how a motorcar can be built too well for its own good.

1909 ALCO
4-cyl., 22 hp, 112" wb

	FP	5	4	3	2	1
Limo.-6P	4500	3500	4500	7000	13,000	25,000
Land'et.-6P	4500	4000	5000	8000	15,000	28,000

4-cyl., 40 hp, 126" wb

Tour. 7-P	5000	4000	5000	8000	15,000	28,000

6-cyl., 60 hp, 134" wb

Tour. 7-P	6000	5000	6500	11,000	22,000	35,000

1910 ALCO
Model 40 — 4-cyl., 40 hp, 126" wb

	FP	5	4	3	2	1
Tour.-7P	4750	5000	6500	11,000	22,000	35,000
Toy Tonneau	4750	4500	5800	9500	18,000	32,000
Rbt.	4750	4700	6000	10,000	20,000	33,000
Limo.	5500	4000	5000	8000	15,000	28,000
Land'et.	5500	4000	5000	8000	15,000	28,000

Six — 6-cyl., 60 hp, 134" wb

Tour.-7P	6000	6000	12,000	20,000	28,000	40,000
Rbt.	6000	5900	11,800	19,750	27,600	39,500
Toy Tonneau	6000	5800	11,500	19,250	27,000	38,500
Land'et.	6750	4000	5000	8000	15,000	28,000
Limo.	6750	4000	5000	8000	15,000	28,000

Model 16 — 4-cyl., 16 hp, 104" wb	FP	5	4	3	2	1
Land'et. taxi	3350	3400	4400	6900	12,000	24,000
Model 22 — 4-cyl., 22 hp, 112" wb						
Town Car-5P	4350	4500	5800	9500	18,000	32,000

1911 Alco, runabout, WLB

1911 Alco, touring, HAC

1911 ALCO
Sixteen — 4-cyl., 16 hp, 104" wb

	FP	5	4	3	2	1
Land'et taxi	3350	3400	4400	6700	12,000	24,000
Forty — 6-cyl., 40 hp, 126" wb						
Toy Tonneau	4500	4400	5700	9400	17,000	28,000
Tour.-7P	4500	4700	6000	9500	18,000	29,000
Land'et.	5500	4000	5000	8500	16,000	27,000
Sixty — 6-cyl., 60 hp, 134" wb						
Limo.	6750	4000	5000	8500	16,000	27,000
Tour.-7P	6000	6000	12,000	20,000	28,000	40,000
Rbt.	6000	4400	5700	9400	17,000	28,000
Land'et.	6750	4000	5000	8500	16,000	27,000
Toy Tonneau	6000	4400	5700	9400	17,000	28,000

1912 Alco, runabout, JAC

1912 Alco, six, touring, WLB

1912 ALCO
Four — 4-cyl., 40 hp, 126" wb

	FP	5	4	3	2	1
Tour.	4500	4400	5700	9500	17,000	28,000
Toy Tonneau	4500	4200	5500	9000	16,500	27,500
Rbt.	4500	4400	5700	9400	17,000	28,000
Limo.	5500	3700	4700	7500	13,500	26,000
Land'et.	5500	3700	4700	7500	13,500	26,000
Ber.	6000	4000	5000	8500	16,000	27,000
Six — 6-cyl., 60 hp, 134" wb						
Tour.	6000	6000	12,000	20,000	28,000	40,000
Toy Tonneau	6000	4700	6000	9500	18,000	29,000
Rbt.	6000	5000	6500	11,000	22,000	35,000
Limo.	6750	4000	5000	8500	16,000	27,000
Land'et.	6750	4000	5000	8500	16,000	27,000
Ber.	7250	4500	5500	9000	16,500	27,500

1913 Alco, limousine, JAC

1913 ALCO
Six — 6-cyl., 60 hp, 133-1/2" wb

Tour.-7P	6000	6200	12,500	22,000	30,000	42,000
Colonial Limo.	6750	4000	5000	8500	16,000	27,000
Ber. Limo.	7250	4500	5500	9000	16,500	27,500
Tour.-5P	6000	5000	6500	11,000	22,000	35,000

1904 Alden Sampson, type 3A, touring, NAHC

ALDEN SAMPSON — Pittsfield, Massachusetts — (1904) — Although generally believed not to have produced motorcars, and certainly not under the full company name, there was indeed an automobile called the Alden Sampson — and fortuitous circumstance was responsible for its building. When the Rye (New York) factory of the Moyea Automobile Company was delayed in completion, the building of the prototype for its 1904 model was entrusted to the Alden Sampson Machine Company in Pittsfield, Massachusetts. Alden Sampson was so impressed with the car that, when the opportunity arose, he bought out Moyea and brought out a slightly revised version as the Alden Sampson in 1904. It was a four-cylinder touring car with a King of Belgium body from Springfield and a $3750 price tag. Phaeton, limousine, "Tapissiere" and "coupe diligence" bodies were available on special order, and the "chassis nu" could be had for $3250 for the mounting of whatever coachwork a purchaser might desire. These were high-quality cars, and Alden Sampson might well have been on the way to making a big name for himself in the prestige car field — except that he decided to build a truck called the Sampson instead. The Alden Sampson automobile was discontinued immediately; Sampson trucks became widely known in the years following. In 1909 Alden Sampson died, and by 1911 his widow had sold the Alden Sampson Manufacturing Company for a reported $200,000 to the United States Motor Company, the ill-fated conglomerate that Benjamin Briscoe was attempting to put together along General Motors lines. Interestingly, United States Motor, which had removed the Alden Sampson factory to Detroit, decided that the company should again produce a passenger car — but this one was marketed as a Sampson. Both it and the Sampson truck died with the collapse of United States Motor in 1912. How many Alden-Sampson touring cars had been built is not known. California records indicate one being registered in that state in 1916. Its serial number was U50265.

1904 ALDEN SAMPSON
Alden Sampson — 4-cyl., 16 hp, 88" wb

Type 3A Tour.-5P	3750	3500	4500	7000	13,000	25,000

ALDO — Chicago, Illinois — (1910) — If highwheeler country could be said to have a capital, it was Chicago. No fewer than twenty companies went into the motor buggy business in the Windy City, the example of one prompting another down the street that here was an easy road to maximum profit with minimum effort because a highwheeler was, after all, the simplest of conveyances to build. The Messrs. Albaugh and Dover were typical. (Albaugh was Gilbert R., who had designed the Star from Cleveland in 1902, and the Wolverine produced in Michigan from 1903 to 1906; Dover's previous automotive background is not known.) In 1910 they

1910 Aldo, auto-buggy, NAHC

formed the Albaugh-Dover Company, combined their last names into Aldo, came up with a two-cylinder 12 hp air cooled buggy which was easy enough, then found that selling it, even at the low price of $395, was the hard part. They were out of the automobile business by the end of the year, but apparently stayed alive in other Chicago ventures. A press report from 1916 announced the building of a new $30,000 Albaugh-Dover machine shop "to take care of the increased volume of business on cream separators and gear cuttings." A reference from 1917 indicates the company was then marketing a tractor. In 1924 a syndicate composed of former stockholders purchased the entire assets of the firm, reincorporated at $200,000 as the Albaugh-Dover Manufacturing Company, and continued in the manufacture of gears and cream separators.

1910 ALDO
2-cyl., 12 hp, 76" wb

	FP	5	4	3	2	1
Motor Buggy	395	2000	3000	4000	6200	13,000

1898 Aldrich, auto-buggy, GSA

ALDRICH — Millville, Massachusetts — (1897-1898) — Robert Aldrich was an engineer residing on Quaker Street in Millville and employed by the American Steel & Wire Company of nearby Worcester. From 1897-1898 he built a small 475-pound single-cylinder gasoline runabout which successfully negotiated Massachusetts roads. *The Horseless Age* indicated that he had several orders for the vehicle, and a mechanic from Worcester named C. H. Thurston indicated his plans to produce the car in 1898. Surviving family members recall only the one vehicle being built, however. Subsequently, during 1898, Robert Aldrich designed a carburetor ("Just What Engine Makers and Users Have Been Waiting For," the brochure headlined) that was manufactured for some years thereafter.

ALENA STEAM — Indianapolis, Indiana — (1922) — The Alena Steam Products Company of Indianapolis launched itself into the commercial vehicle field in 1922. In addition to trucks and tractors, it produced two examples of a two-cylinder 115-cubic-inch touring car set on a 126-inch wheelbase. Because the car was announced for sale at $2750, doubtless Alena envisioned entry into the passenger car field as well. Only the pair of cars was built, however. Alena's automotive venture was a short one. The company ceased building trucks and tractors the following year.

1922 ALENA STEAM

	FP	5	4	3	2	1
Alena Steam	2750	3000	4000	6000	9500	21,000

ALGER — Detroit, Michigan — (1902) — In 1902 Russell A. Alger, Jr. and his brother Fred, whose family was a wealthy and prominent one in Michigan and whose father had served as Secretary of War under President McKinley, had a gasoline automobile built after their own design. Although they indicated their intention to the trade press during the summer that manufacture was contemplated, probably the building of this particular car was more a whim on the part of the brothers, for already they had begun to involve themselves with another automobile company. On April 26th, 1902, James Ward Packard noted in his diary that he had met with Henry B. Joy and Russell A. Alger, Jr. at the exclusive Grosse Pointe Country Club. Henry Joy was the first Detroit investor in the Packard Motor Car Company of Warren, Ohio; Russell Alger was the second, his brother Fred the third, followed by other moneyed Detroit friends and associates of Joy's. By October 13th, 1902 the Detroit investors had controlling interest in the Packard company. One year later Packard moved from Warren to Detroit.

ALLEGHENY — The Allegheny Motor Vehicle Company was organized in Trenton, New Jersey late in 1906 for the manufacture and sale of automobiles. Capital stock was $50,000, and the incorporators were E.L. Kerns, W. Harry Williams and Walter G. Reinman. No manufacture is believed to have followed.

1905 Allegheny, touring, WLB

ALLEGHENY — Warren, Pennsylvania — (1904-1906) — Although total production was just two automobiles, the Allegheny was a technically progressive car for the period, albeit with a homemade look. It was designed by James A. Viele, secretary of the Allegheny Foundry Company in Warren. The first Allegheny was a 24 hp four-cylinder air-cooled roadster with planetary transmission, shaft drive and left-hand wheel steering. The building of its engine and body was farmed out to other shops in Warren, the wooden wheels came from Salisbury in Jamestown (New York), and the car was assembled in the Allegheny Foundry, the completion date being December 1904. The second car Viele designed was a 68 hp four, also air-cooled, with a touring car body purchased from Buffalo (New York). Both engine and chassis were built in the Allegheny Foundry this time, and the car was finished during the winter of 1905-1906. Sometime during 1906 James Viele bought a Chadwick and sold his Allegheny touring car to a local Warren resident. His roadster had apparently been after the tourer was completed. He never built another car.

1896 Allen Motor Wagon, auto-buggy, NAHC

ALLEN — Hueneme, California — (1896) — In 1895 Charles F. Allen designed and built a motor wagon powered by a 4-1/2 hp gasoline engine. From Hueneme, California, Allen wrote to *The Horseless Age* in New York and described the vehicle enticingly. One lever only was required for operation, a slight pressure to the right or left being sufficient to turn the vehicle, with the wheels locked firmly in position until any change of direction was desired. No sprocket chains, ratchets or "other noisy gearing" was fitted. Odor was said to be eliminated and the noise of the exhaust effectively muffled by devices which Allen did not describe. A few months later, Allen wrote *The Horseless Age* again indicating that so overwhelmed had he been by correspondence following the initial article that he had been compelled to print a circular answering the many questions asked. He also indicated that he was forming a company to manufacture his carriage. It does not appear that he was able to finalize those plans, however, though apparently he did continue to involve himself in the automotive industry. In 1901 he was granted a patent for steel-clad pneumatic tire.

1899 Allen, gasoline runabout, OCW

ALLEN — New York, New York — (1895-1900) — G. Edgar Allen was a carriagebuilder from Englewood, New Jersey who located his shop at 304 West 53rd Street in New York City. That he also built automobiles there was noted in the Hiscox book *Horseless Vehicles, Automobiles, Motor Cycles* published in 1900, with further references indicating that he began doing so as early as 1895. His total production is unknown, but no doubt was small. One Allen car remains extant, a beguiling little tiller-steered runabout. Its engine is a single-cylinder 7-1/2 hp Aster, its transmission a friction disc, its final drive by chain. Interestingly, in 1899, the 300 block of West 53rd in Manhattan was abuzz with automobile activity, the International Motor Wheel Company moving in at 302 and the Safety Three Wheel and Vehicle Company establishing itself at 306. Possibly G. Edgar Allen was involved in these ventures as well.

ALLEN — Adams, Massachusetts — (1901) — In March of 1901 *The Motor Vehicle Review* reported that the Allen Iron Works of Adams was "experimenting with motor vehicles." Further details are lacking, but the experimentation did not lead into manufacture.

1902 Allen, gasoline car, WLB

ALLEN — New Bedford, Massachusetts — (1902) — George C. Allen was a gasfitter and a tinsmith, and the proprietor of a piping shop in New Bedford, in which he built an automobile in 1902. With the exception of its engine (a 3 hp marine launch unit), the body (old packing crates) and wheels, the Allen was made entirely of gas and steam piping. The car cost George Allen very little to build, and he used only his spare time to do it. "It is expected to prove a serviceable wagon for Mr. Allen's business," *Motor Review* reported in May 1902, "and natives of New Bedford are anticipating a sensation when it appears in the streets."

ALLEN — New Bedford, Massachusetts — (1902) — George C. Allen was a gasfitter and a tinsmith, and the proprietor of a piping shop in New Bedford, in which he built an automobile in 1902. With the exception of its engine (a 3 hp marine launch unit), the body (old packing crates) and wheels, the Allen was made entirely of gas and steam piping. The car cost George Allen very little to build, and he used only his spare time to do it. "It is expected to prove a serviceable wagon for Mr. Allen's business," *Motor Review* reported in May 1902, "and natives of New Bedford are anticipating a sensation when it appears in the streets."

1914 Allen, model 40, 5-pass., touring, JAC

ALLEN — Fostoria & Columbus, Ohio — (1913-1922) — The brothers E.W. and W.O. Allen began business with a neat automobile featuring a 221-cubic-inch four-cylinder L-head engine designed by L.A. Sommer (formerly of Hammer-Sommer), a full-floating rear axle of which they were especially proud, and a top they boasted as being "of genuine 'Neverleek' (sic)." Having done all this, they decided to rest on their laurels. As home for their venture the Allens had secured the Peabody Buggy Company works in Fostoria and the three buildings of the old Columbia Buggy Company at 400 Dublin Avenue in Columbus. Initially, Sommer produced the Allen engines in his plant at Bucyrus, but by 1916 the Allen brothers had bought him out so they could manufacture their engines themselves. Allen car production was at the 2000-per-annum mark; 7150 cars were built during war years 1917-1918. The postwar era appeared promising, but appearances deceived. Although engineering improvements remained virtually nil, styling was given a vigorous nod in 1921. Since "everyone agrees that the color of automobiles has been altogether too sombre," the company said, Allen Artcraft bodies were now available in colors named for precious stones: to wit, Sapphire, Garnet, Turquoise, Amethyst. Unfortunately, the color of the ink in the company financial ledgers was red as a ruby. Already the firm was in receivership, with claims against it totaling about $2,000,000 (assets were somewhat less). In 1920 Allen had sold the Fostoria factory to Willys Corporation, which used it to produce farm lighting powerplants during this era before rural electrification. (Subsequently, AutoLite, then a Willys subsidiary, took over that plant.) Meanwhile the brothers Allen struggled to continue production and to secure more capital. Their efforts were unavailing. The remainder of the Allen property in Columbus and Bucyrus went to the auction block in 1922. L.A. Sommer tried to buy back his old plant but is believed to have not succeeded. Altogether an estimated 20,000 Allen cars had been produced.

1913-1914 ALLEN
4-cyl., 27 hp, 118" wb

	FP	5	4	3	2	1
Model 40 Tour.-5P	1395	2500	3500	5000	8500	18,000
Model 38 Rds.-2P	1395	2700	3700	5500	9000	18,500

1915 ALLEN
4-cyl., 21 hp, 110" wb

Model 34 Tour.-5P	895	2000	3000	4500	8000	17,500
Model 32 Rds.-2P	875	2200	3200	4800	8300	17,800
Model 35 Tour.-5P	1095	2500	3500	5000	8500	18,000

4-cyl., 27 hp, 118" wb

Model 40 Tour.-5P	1395	2500	3500	5000	8500	18,000

1916 ALLEN
Model 37 — 4-cyl., 23 hp, 112" wb

Tour.-5P	795	2300	3300	4700	8300	17,800
Rds.-2P	795	2400	3400	4800	8400	17,900

1917 Allen, model 37, 5-pass., touring, WLB

1917 ALLEN
Classic — 4-cyl., 22.5 hp, 112" wb

Tour.-5P	850	2300	3300	4700	8300	17,800
Rds.-4P	875	2400	3400	4800	8400	17,900

Model 37 — 4-cyl., 22.5 hp, 112" wb

Sed.-5P	1195	1900	2900	4100	6500	13,500
Cpe.-3P	1175	2000	3000	4500	7500	14,000
Tour.-5P	795	2400	3400	4800	8400	17,900
Rds.-2P	795	2500	3500	5000	8500	18,000

1918 ALLEN
Model 41 — 4-cyl., 22.5 hp, 112" wb

	FP	5	4	3	2	1
Tour.-5P	1095	2400	3400	4800	8000	17,000
Sed.-5P	1395	2000	3000	4500	7500	14,000
Rds.-4P	1095	2500	3500	5000	8500	18,000

1919 ALLEN
Model 41 — 4-cyl., 22.5 hp, 112" wb

Tour.-5P	1195	2400	3400	4800	8000	17,000
Sed.-5P	1695	2000	3000	4500	7500	14,000

1920 ALLEN
Model 43 — 4-cyl., 37 hp, 110" wb

Tour.-5P	1495	2400	3400	4800	8000	17,000
Sed.-5P	2145	2000	3000	4500	7500	14,000
Rds.-3P	1495	2500	3500	5000	8500	18,000

1921 Allen Artcraft Combination

1921 ALLEN
Model 43 — 4-cyl., 37 hp, 110" wb

Tour.-5P	1595	2600	3600	5400	8900	18,300
Rds.-3P	1595	2700	3700	5500	9000	18,500
Sed.-5P	2395	2000	3000	4500	7500	14,000
Artcraft Combination-5P	2045	2400	3400	4800	8400	17,000

1922 ALLEN
Model 43 — 4-cyl., 37 hp, 110" wb

Tour.-5P	1195	2500	3500	5000	8500	18,000
Rds.-3P	1195	2700	3700	5500	9000	18,500
Sed.-5P	1845	2000	3000	4500	7500	14,000
Artcraft Tour.-5P	1595	2600	3600	5400	8900	18,400
Artcraft Rdst.-3P	1495	2800	3800	6000	9500	19,000

1914 Allen Light Car, roadster, NAHC

ALLEN — Philadelphia, Pennsylvania — (1914) — Phillip M. Maloney of the Allen Iron & Steel Company announced the completion of his cyclecar prototype in early spring of 1914. It featured a four-cylinder water-cooled 20 hp engine, friction transmission, double belt drive, and electric lights. The wheelbase was 108 inches, the tread 44, the seating side by side, and the projected price tag $450, which included a one-piece top. Tests around Philadelphia, Maloney averred, indicated a top speed of 50 mph and fuel economy of 30-35 mpg. The Allen Iron & Steel Company, which was located at the corner of Third and Venago streets, was expected to produce the cyclecar "in considerable quantity" during 1914, but the evidence suggests this did not happen. Late in 1914 Maloney indicated his plans to try a shaft-drive car next, but doubtless that one did not proceed beyond prototype. There had been a small production of the belt-drive Allen, however.

1914 ALLEN

Light Car	—	1500	2500	3600	5500	11,000

ALLEN & CLARK — This was the name of the company promoted by Albert F. Clark in Toledo in 1909. The car was called the Clark Electric. Refer to Clark Electric.

ALLEN-KINGSTON — Kingston, New York — (1908-1910)/Bristol, Connecticut — (1910) — New York City foreign car importer Walter C. Allen wholeheartedly believed in two things: first, that racing improved the breed and, second, that plagiarism was not a bad idea so long as credit

was given where due. In the summer of 1906 he began building three experimental four-cylinder cars, the year following he put two of them to the test of New York City streets, the third he took racing. The few 1907 cars marketed were built by the New York Car & Truck Company of Kingston and were called New Yorks. That firm had failed by March of 1908, however, at which time Walter Allen moved his Allen-Kingston Motor Car Company into its factory and the former New York became the new Allen-Kingston, or A-K as it was popularly nicknamed. By year's end, Allen had produced 100 cars to sell in the $4000 range and had put up an admirable competition record on the East Coast, including victory in the Meadowbrook Sweepstakes over the Vanderbilt Cup course on Long Island. He proudly advertised that Robert Guggenheim had purchased on the spot the little A-K which had vanquished the Guggenheim entry in the Independence Day races in Long Beach, New Jersey. For 1909 Walter Allen offered two four-cylinder models the engines for which were patterned after Isotta, the front axles after Fiat, and the shaft drive after Mercedes. "In fact," Allen said, "the whole transmission and running gear is designed on Mercedes lines." There were more references to the Mercedes than mentions of Allen-Kingston in the 1909 catalog, which may have been carrying the flattery of imitation too far. The smaller Allen-Kingston Junior model, introduced for 1910, was built for the company by George J. Grossman in White Plains, and was a virtual copy of the small G.J.G. In 1910 the Allen-Kingston Motor Car Company moved to Bristol, Connecticut, with a financial assist from Bristol Engineering Company, a subsidiary of the New Departure ball bearing combine. Apparently no further financial assistance ensued. Fred Moskovics had worked for Allen-Kingston for a while, incidentally, before transferring allegiance to the Bristol Engineering team for whom he assisted in the design of the Rockwell taxi.

1908 Allen-Kingston, touring, WLB

1908 ALLEN-KINGSTON
Model D — 4-cyl., 40/45 hp, 121" wb

	FP	5	4	3	2	1
Rbt.	3900	3600	4600	7900	13,800	25,500

Model C — 4-cyl., 40/45 hp, 126" wb

Tour.-7P	4000	3700	4700	8000	14,000	26,000

Model E — 4-cyl., 40/45 hp, 126" wb

Limo.	5000	3500	4500	7000	13,000	25,000

1909-10 Allen-Kingston, runabout, HAC

1909 ALLEN-KINGSTON
Four — 17 hp, 106" wb

Town Car	3300	3300	4300	6300	12,500	20,700

Four — 48 hp, 125" wb

Tour.	4400	3500	4500	7000	13,000	25,000
Rbt.	4250	3600	4600	7200	13,300	25,500
Meadowbrook	3990	3000	4000	6000	12,000	20,000
Gunboat	4500	3600	4600	7200	13,300	25,500
Baby Tonneau	4300	3500	4500	7000	13,000	25,000
Limo.	5200	3200	4200	6200	12,200	20,500

1910 ALLEN-KINGSTON
Junior — 36 hp, 120" wb

Baby Tonneau	2500	3400	4400	6800	12,500	24,500
Rds.	2500	3500	4500	7000	13,000	25,000

Four — 48 hp, 125" wb

Rds.	4250	3500	4500	7000	13,000	25,000
Racer	3090	3600	4600	7200	13,300	25,500
Tour.	4400	3400	4400	6800	12,500	24,500
Gunboat	4500	3600	4600	7200	13,300	25,500
Town Car	5200	3300	4300	6500	12,000	24,000

ALLENTOWN — The Allentown Motor Company was a 1917 Delaware incorporation with a capital stock of $100,000. Three brothers named Mettler — Franklin L., M.E. and L.F. — were behind this venture the plan for which was the manufacture of automobiles in Pennsylvania. The plan was not realized.

ALLIANCE — In 1895 the Alliance Carriage Company of Cincinnati, Ohio built an automobile to the design of Walter MacLeod, a British mechanical engineer based in New York City. Refer to MacLeod.

The Alliance Motor Car Company was organized in Alliance, Ohio with a capital stock of $50,000 early in 1913 for the manufacture of automobiles and other vehicles. Among the incorporators were C.C. Mummert, Morris W. Geigle, G.K. Pritchard, R.M. Scranton, J.O. Ellis, C.G. Kline and Edward P. Kinney. No manufacture is believed to have followed.

The Alliance Motorcar Sales Company was a $50,000 Delaware incorporation of early 1918 for the manufacture of automobiles, engines, motors, machinery and supplies. C.L. Rimlinger, M.M. Clancy and F.A. Armstrong were the incorporators. No manufacture followed.

ALLIED — Elkhart, Indiana — (1932-1935) — This taxi venture, which was variously styled the Allied Cab Manufacturing Company and the Allied Products Manufacturing Company, was an attempt to put to good, and hopefully profitable, use the facilities of Elcar in Elkhart. Taxi production had been a dominant factor in Elcar Motor Company fortunes from the early Twenties until 1931 when the firm's irrevocable receivership arrived. Some of the former Elcar taxi people — including Jules Martin — stayed on as the newly organized Allied company. Taxis carrying the Allied name were built in 1932-1934, with the Super Allied following in 1935. In addition, there was another cab in 1933 that was marketed under the name of Prosperity, an optimistic designation for the depths of the Great Depression. And the optimism, unfortunately, was ill founded. Only twelve Prosperity taxis were built. The number produced under the Allied name is not known.

ALLITH — There never was an Allith automobile, despite its appearance on numerous automobile rosters. The Allith had presumably been built by the Allen & Clark Company, but this was simply a clerical error made in a listing compiled in the early 1960's and perpetuated on automobile rosters ever since. The only car ever made by Allen & Clark was the Clark Electric of Toledo in 1909.

ALL-STEEL — The car produced in Macon, Missouri from 1915-1917 by the All-Steel Motor Car Company was marketed under the tradename Macon. Refer to Macon.

ALLYN — In April of 1909 the *New England Automobile Journal* announced the organization in Portland, Maine of the Allyn Automobile Company for the manufacture and sale of motor vehicles. Ten thousand dollars was the capital stock, and Frederic L. Jeine of Portland was indicated as Allyn's president and treasurer. No manufacture followed.

ALLYNE-ZEDER — A car called the Allyne-Zeder was the initial plan, but when that project fell through in 1922, the venture was carried on and ultimately resulted in the Rollin automobile of 1923-1925. Refer to Rollin.

ALMA STEAM — West Newton, Massachusetts — (1938) — Alma Steam Motors of Newton was the last-gasp prewar effort to convince Americans that a steam car was still the best way to motor on a highway. The Alma was not a car per se, but rather a steam powerplant (a double-acting opposed unit consisting of four small two-cylinder engines geared to a central main-shaft) which could readily convert one's gasoline automobile into a steamer. Alma Steam Motors was organized in April 1938. Its chief engineer was Eric H. Delling, whose impressive credits in the industry included the Stanley, Mercer, Brooks and Delling. Reportedly only one Alma steam powerplant was built. Headquarters for this venture was the American Steam Car Company plant.

1911 Alpena Flyer, touring, WLB

ALPENA — Alpena, Michigan — (1911-1914) — The town of Alpena, Michigan was anxious to carve a niche for itself in the automobile world. Early in 1910 the Chamber of Commerce offered one Thomas F. Ahern ten acres of land and $50,000 in cash if he would bring automobile manufacture to town. Ahern, a Detroit mechanical engineer, approached a friend, Daniel D. Hanover, who liked the deal too. Thus, in June of 1910, the Alpena Motor Car Company was established, the following month absorbed what was left of the defunct Wolverine Motor Car Company of Mt. Clemens, Michigan — and all parties and removable property were in Alpena by August. "Let it be borne in mind that we do not make cheap runabouts nor luxurious limousines," the company's first ad read. "But we have the greatest value in a five-passenger car offered anywhere in America for less than $2000 at $1450 f.o.b. Alpena, Michigan." Things went well initially, but in the midst of the first selling season, Daniel Hanover, who had taken the position of Alpena's president, had to relinquish it because of ill health. Richard Collins, a native of Alpena, took over in late June of 1911. Only in 1911 was the car called the Alpena Flyer, thereafter it was simply the Alpena. Fours only were offered through 1912, a six (Rutenber engine) being added for 1913. Models for 1914 were announced but were not in production long, bankruptcy being petitioned

in February that year. High bidder at the receivers' auction was the Besser Manufacturing Company. For a sale price of $5200, Besser moved its foundry business into the Alpena automobile plant, reputedly one of the finest structures in Northern Michigan at the time. Besser still owns and uses the building.

1911 ALPENA
Flyer — 4-cyl., 30 hp, 112" wb

	FP	5	4	3	2	1
Model A Tour.-5P	1450	3100	4200	6300	10,500	22,000
Model B Tour.-4P	1450	3100	4200	6300	10,500	22,000
Model C Fore-Door Tour.	1600	3200	4300	6500	11,000	23,000
Model D Torpedo Rds.	1450	3200	4300	6500	11,000	23,000

1912 Alpena, touring, WLB

1912 ALPENA
Four — 30 hp, 112" wb

Model J Fore-Door Tour.	1200	3000	4000	6000	9500	21,000
Model L Det. Tonneau	1200	3100	4200	6300	10,500	22,000
Model K Rds.	1100	3200	4300	6500	11,000	23,000
Model M Tour.	1175	3100	4200	6300	10,500	22,000

Four — 40 hp, 120" wb

Model F Fore-Door Tour.	1600	3100	4200	6300	10,500	22,000
Model G Rds.	1600	3200	4300	6500	11,000	23,000
Model H Det. Tonneau	1600	3250	4400	6600	11,500	23,500

1913-1914 ALPENA
Four — 44 hp, 124" wb

Model X Rds.	1800	3500	4500	7000	13,000	25,000

Four — 40 hp, 124" wb

Model P-40 Rbt.-2P	1750	3300	4400	6700	12,000	24,000
Model P-40 Torpedo-4P	1800	3500	4500	7000	13,000	25,000
Model O-38 Tour.-5P	1800	3300	4400	6700	12,000	24,000

Six — 50 hp, 135" wb

Model N-50 Rds.-2P	2200	4000	5000	8000	15,000	28,000
Model N-50 Trbt.-4P	2250	4000	4900	7900	14,700	27,500
Model N-50 Tour.-5P	2250	3700	4700	7300	13,700	26,000
Model N-50 Tour.-7P	2390	3700	4700	7300	13,700	26,000

1903 Alpha, runabout, NAHC

ALPHA — New York, New York — (1903) — R.E. Jarrige of New York City built a light runabout with a three-speed progressive transmission, a one-cylinder vertical engine mounted under the hood, and a divided seat to carry two passengers. The car featured a honeycomb radiator, and in general configuration resembled a Renault or Panhard. Although its wheelbase and weight were not indicated, both the dimension and poundage of Jarrige's car must have been minimal. A surviving photograph of the inventor beside his invention indicates that the vehicle was quite small. Because the car was the first of what he hoped would be a series, Jarrige called it Alpha. Alas, he could not find sufficient capital to proceed to Beta. Later in 1903 Jarrige joined with several other New Yorkers in organizing the American de Dietrich Motor Car Company for importation of that French car into the United States. In 1904 he also put himself into the automobile supply business.

ALPINE — To manufacture and deal in automobiles was the announced plan of the Alpine Motor Company during the spring of 1912. This Pittsburgh, Pennsylvania venture was capitalized at $25,000 by James F. Sweeney, H.F. Bott and C.Z. Pote. No manufacture is believed to have followed.

1920 Alsace, touring, NAHC

ALSACE — New York, New York — (1920-1921) — In essence, the Alsace was a Piedmont that was sent overseas by the Automotive Products Company of New York City. It was never marketed as other than an export car, and it was built for Automotive Products by the Piedmont Motor Car Company in Lynchburg, Virginia. Changes from the standard Piedmont included conversion to right-hand drive, the installation of a magneto, a redesigned hood line and radiator that was a steal from the Rolls-Royce and a triangular radiator emblem reading "Alsace" that was entirely its own. At least one Alsace sedan would appear to have been built according to photographs extant, which is interesting because Piedmont never built a closed car for its own market. The Alsace touring car was the only model advertised, however, and the first one off the line in Lynchburg was sent to the 1920 Automobile Show at Olympia (London). *The Autocar* gave it a fine review: ". . . it will doubtless attract much attention if only on the score of the excellent value offered." The attention attracted, alas, didn't result in sufficient sales for the venture to survive.

1920-1921 ALSACE
4-cyl., 30 hp, 116" wb

	FP	5	4	3	2	1
Tour.-5P	1485	—	—	—	—	—

ALSOP — The Alsop Motor Company was incorporated with a capital stock of $5000 during the summer of 1913 for the manufacture and sale of automobiles in Richmond, Virginia. J.B. Alsop was president and treasurer, C. Armentrout the secretary. No manufacture followed.

ALSTEL — Although trade press references from 1915 indicate the name Alstel for the product of the All-Steel Motor Car Company of Macon, Missouri, the official tradename under which the car was marketed was Macon. Refer to Macon.

ALTENBERG — Cincinnati, Ohio — (1906) — During the early summer of 1906, George P. Altenberg announced the ongoing testing of his 24/32 hp gasoline car prototype which he said was patterned after the French Richard-Brasier, was "absolutely silent when running" and was particularly "well adapted to hill work." At the time he was making arrangements to move his automobile venture into an existing factory in Cincinnati, pursuant to a later relocation in a factory of his own in Norwood where he would also construct a test track in order to run each new Altenberg 150 miles before delivery to dealers. George Altenberg never made it to Norwood, however, and the total Altenberg production seems to have been the one prototype car.

1915 Alter, 5-pass. touring, WLB

ALTER — Plymouth, Michigan — (1915-1916)/Grand Haven, Michigan (1916-1917) — Guy Hamilton was the president, C.A. Alter the vice-president, and R.A. Skinner the secretary and general manager — and in April of 1914 they announced that the capital stock of their Alter Motor Car Company had been increased from $10,000 to $75,000 and that their new two-story factory in Plymouth was well underway. By August they had moved in and were employing fifty workmen to assemble the new Alter fours and sixes. Early in 1916 they contemplated the building of a V-8 as well, but plans for it were sidelined when the decision was made to move the entire company to Grand Haven where a new one-story factory was being built. That move was completed just about the time the company declared bankruptcy in January 1917, after a total production of about 1000 cars, some of the last of which were advertised as the A-C. Although the Alter venture seems to have soured everyone else involved, Guy Hamilton remained sweet on cars. Prior to the Alter, he had tried with the Gaylord. Now he would try again with a new car named for himself.

1915 ALTER
Model C — 4-cyl., 23 hp, 106" wb

	FP	5	4	3	2	1
Tour.-5P	600	2700	3600	5300	8800	19,000
Rds.-2P	600	2800	3700	5500	9000	19,500

Model F — 6-cyl., 28 hp, 114" wb

	FP	5	4	3	2	1
Tour.-5P	850	4000	5000	8000	15,000	28,000

1916 ALTER
Model C — 4-cyl., 23 hp, 108" wb

	FP	5	4	3	2	1
Tour.-5P	685	2700	3600	5300	8800	19,000

Model F — 6-cyl., 28 hp, 114" wb

	FP	5	4	3	2	1
Tour.-5P	850	2900	3700	5600	9100	20,000

1917 ALTER
Model E — 4-cyl., 18 hp, 106" wb

	FP	5	4	3	2	1
Tour.-5P	675	2700	3600	5300	8800	19,000

Model C — 4-cyl., 23 hp, 108" wb

	FP	5	4	3	2	1
Tour.-5P	735	2800	3700	5500	9000	19,500

Model F — 6-cyl., 28 hp, 114" wb

	FP	5	4	3	2	1
Tour.-5P	850	2900	3700	5600	9100	20,000

ALTHA ELECTRIC — Dover, Delaware — (1905) — Inclusive manufacturing dates for the Altha Electric have frequently been listed as 1900 to 1905. This would seem to indicate manufacture in some quantity. But, more than likely, the quantity was one. In June of 1900 the Altha Automobile & Power Company was incorporated in New York City with a capital stock which was announced at $500,000, all of which must have been on paper. Five years later a site for manufacture was located in Dover, Delaware but whether Altha ever moved into it is problematical. It would appear, however, that at least a prototype had been put together by 1905.

1898 Altham Motor Carriage, auto-buggy, NAHC

ALTHAM — Fall River, Massachusetts — (1897-1899) — In November of 1896, the Boston *Herald* carried the news that Fall River inventor George J. Altham had "perfected the hydrocarbon motor on which he has been engaged for several years past." By August of 1897 he had devised a carriage in which to put it, though he termed the new vehicle "purely experimental." By October of 1898, however, he was ready for manufacture, and rather grandly so, establishing his Altham International Motor Car Company with head office in Boston and factory in Fall River. By now he had refined his engine into an air-cooled two-cylinder unit developing 6 hp and variable in speed from 200 to 1000 rpm. "This variation in speed is obtained by means of a small lever at the end of the steering handle," Altham said, "and the response to the touch of the operator is instantaneous, like that of a horse to the crack of a whip." Transmission of power was purportedly seen to without the use of friction, belts or chains, and was "simplicity itself," although Altham refused to divulge any details. Apparently Altham built several of these carriages, but serious manufacture was never forthcoming. George Altham was a better tinkerer than he was a businessman.

ALTMAN — Cleveland, Ohio — (1901) — Henry J. Altman of 11 Pier Street in Cleveland finished his automobile in 1901 after two years of hard work in which Mrs. Altman assisted by helping to put together the radiator in her kitchen. The result was a good-looking car, with its two-cylinder opposed engine (which had been hand-built to order) suspended midship under the seat. Top speed was 20 mph, and the Altmans used the car frequently for pleasure trips in the area. Originally its body style was a rear-entrance tonneau, but around 1909 Henry Altman revised the car into a sporty roadster. He sold it a few years later to a local paperhanger for $200.

ALUMINUM — The car produced during the early Twenties under the aegis of the Aluminum Company of America (that firm's name later shortened to Alcoa) is more justly named for its designer. Refer to Pomeroy.

The Aluminum Motor Vehicle Company of Chicago was the organization which promoted the electric car designed by Clinton E. Woods in 1897. Refer to Clinton E. Woods.

A & M — These initials were occasionally used to designate the automobile built from 1901-1902 in Camden, New Jersey by the Automobile & Marine Power Company. The car's name, however, was New Era. Refer to New Era.

AMALGAMATED STEAM — Chicago, Illinois — (1919) — The Amalgamated Machinery Corporation of 72 West Adams Street in Chicago had come to prominence during the First World War through its design and manufacture of shell-turning and gun-boring machinery. When the Armistice dictated finding other work to do, Amalgamated launched itself into the automobile business. During the summer of 1919 the company announced that it had secured all manufacturing rights to patented steam car features owned by the General Engineering Company, the Doble-Detroit Steam Motor Company and other firms in the field. In essence, the Amalgamated was an amalgam of several steam cars on the market. James L. Breese, Jr., former chief engineer of the Alco, was Amalgamated's chief engineer of this venture. "An experimental machine which has already been constructed consumes but one gallon of kerosene every fourteen miles," the company said. Among the purported advantages of the Amalgamated was its ability to burn a nonvolatile fuel without vaporization and to control combustion without the use of a pilot light. Something went wrong somewhere. The company began construction on a five-story addition to its plant at 37th Street and Racine in Chicago, but before it was completed Amalgamated had run out of steam. The only steam which rose out of Amalgamated Machinery thereafter was in the cars it built for Abner Doble.

1921 Ambassador, model R, touring, WLB

AMBASSADOR — Chicago, Illinois — (1921-1925) — When John Hertz took over control of the Walden W. Shaw Livery Corporation of Chicago, he made two decisions about the Weidely twelve-cylinder engined production car that the company had been marketing variously as a Shaw or a Colonial. The first was that it would not carry a Weidely engine, the second that it would be called neither a Shaw nor a Colonial. Instead Hertz contracted for enough six-cylinder Continental engines for the remaining Shaw/Colonial chassis/bodies on hand, fitted a different emblem and called the result Ambassador. He did not allude to any of this in his advertising. "Backed by a mighty American institution" (the Yellow Cab Manufacturing Company which he also headed) and with the experience of "fourteen years of building motor vehicles for heavy duty service" (Shaw Livery had long been a taxicab builder), the "new Ambassador stands out prominently in the field of the world's finest cars." These large Ambassa-

1925 Ambassador, model D-1, sedan, WLB

dors featured a full-leather trunk equipped with two silk-lined, rawhide cases as standard equipment. The car made its formal debut at the Drake Hotel during Chicago Automobile Show week in February 1921. Interestingly, one of the show cars did carry the Weidely engine, and a couple of further Ambassadors may have been fitted with the same unit, although this obviously was simply utilizing the few Weidely engines on hand. Even more interesting, there was announcement in October of a small $700 four-cylinder Ambassador on a 109-inch wheelbase, but it appears this one never arrived at all. Instead the big Ambassador Six remained in production until the Shaw stock ran out. By that time John Hertz had another idea, described in *Automobile Topics* as "a system designed after the old livery stable plan . . . where a man might go hire a 'rig' for a day's pleasure or business traveling." A smaller six-cylinder Ambassador was designed for this "system" which was introduced in late October of 1924. The car was offered both for sale and for lease. John Hertz soon renamed it for himself.

1922 Ambassador, model R, 7-pass. touring, JAC

1921-1923 AMBASSADOR
Model R — 6-cyl, 75 hp, 136" wb

	FP	5	4	3	2	1
Tour.-7P	4500	4500	9000	15,000	21,000	30,000
Rds.-2P	4500	4500	9000	15,000	21,000	30,000
Spt.-4P	4500	4400	8850	14,750	20,650	29,500
Ber. Sed.-7P	6500	2000	3000	4200	6500	14,000
Ber. Limo.-7P	6500	2500	3500	5000	8500	18,000

1924-1925 AMBASSADOR
Model D-1 — 6-cyl, 25 hp, 114" wb

Amb. Drive-It-Yourself Sed.	1675	2000	3000	4200	6500	14,000
Amb. Drive-It-Yourself Tour.	1675	2500	3500	5000	8500	18,000

AMBLER — A cyclecar called the Ambler was announced in 1914 by the King Cyclecar Company of Cleveland, Ohio. That even a prototype was built has not been documented. Certainly manufacture did not follow.

1919 A.M.C., touring, HAC

A.M.C. — Chicago, Illinois — (1919) — Yet another mystery. In 1919 the A.M.C. Truck Company of 130 North Wells Street in Chicago advertised that "A.M.C. Passenger and Commercial Cars Are Now Ready for Dealers in Quantities." The quantity mentioned was a proposed production of 6000 units for 1919. The automobile pictured was a standard assembled touring car. "For 9 years A.M.C. passenger cars have been storing up fame for themselves," the ad read. But one wonders where. Probably these automobiles were built to order for use by sales, service or supervisory personnel of those companies purchasing A.M.C. trucks. Further details are lacking.

1920 Amco, touring, WLB

29

AMCO — New York, New York — (1917-1922) — American Motors, Inc. of New York City produced a $1600 car for export only. Designed by D.M. Eller, the Amco was powered by a four-cylinder engine, was provided with either left or right hand drive, and sported a radiator that could stand up to torrid climes. It was described in the trade press of the day as "a mainly British car" combining the "finest grade American components" with British bodies. Engines were Rutenber, GB & S or Herschell-Spillman fours. Production initially was in Norwalk, Connecticut, but apparently moved soon to Stamford following a merger with Springfield Motors Company and the John Davenport Foundry in that city.

1917-1922 AMCO
Four — 35 hp, 114" wb

	FP	5	4	3	2	1
Tour.-5P	1600	2400	3400	5800	8000	17,000

1911 America, model 40, touring, WLB

AMERICA — New York, New York — (1911) — Also known as the America 40 for the developed horsepower of its four-cylinder engine, this product of the Motor Car Company of America, which was located at 2100 Broadway in upper Manhattan, was available in four body styles. Its most distinctive feature was the fitting of an auxiliary gallon-and-a-half fuel tank for emergencies. Almost immediately after — or possibly before — production began, the company was taken over by W.H. McIntyre of Auburn, Indiana. McIntyre was a highwheeler producer anxious to add standard cars to his line; the America was thereafter produced and marketed in Auburn as the McIntyre Special.

1911 AMERICA
Model 40 — 4-cyl, 40 hp, 118" wb

Model H Torpedo-4P	2250	1500	2500	3600	5500	11,000
Model W Rds.-2P	2100	1600	2600	3700	5900	11,500
Model S Tour.-5P	2250	1500	2500	3600	5500	11,000
Model F Lan.-5P	2450	1400	2400	3500	5200	10,500

AMERICAN — The American or, alternatively, the American Voiturette was the designation used only in 1899 for the car produced in New York City by the Automobile Company of America. Thereafter it was referred to as the Gasmobile. Refer to Gasmobile.

The American Aeroplane Manufacturing Company was a $100,000 New York City incorporation from September 1910 organized to manufacture and deal in motorcars, aeroplanes, gliders and motors. The incorporators were B.E. Freed and S.J. Leback. No American automobile followed from this venture.

The American Auto Appliance Company was organized in Chicago in early 1919 to manufacture and deal in vehicles. The capital stock was $200,000, and the incorporators were E.A. Garvey, C.A. Garvey and F.R. Belt. Manufacture did not follow.

The American Auto Rim Company of New York City, incorporated for $100,000 in early 1908, announced its intention to manufacture motorcars. William E. Burroughs, J.W. Cavanagh and J.N. Axt were behind this venture, which is not believed to have produced a single car.

The American Automobile Company which is indicated as a manufacture in Portland, Maine in the Hiscox book *Horseless Vehicles, Automobiles, Motor Cycles* published in 1900 is undoubtedly an error, possibly confused with the company of that same name which was then in manufacture in New York City but which may have been incorporated in Maine.

The American Automobile Company of Cleveland, which was incorporated with a capital stock of $50,000 early in 1904 for the purpose of manufacturing automobiles and parts, is not believed to have done either. Behind this venture were Carl Dautel, Charles W. Demory, V.F. Bonhard, G.D. Rudd and J.H. Van Deven.

The American Automobile Company "of St. Paul," so the incorporation notice read, was organized with a capital stock of $250,000 in Huron, South Dakota during the fall of 1903. Manufacture does not appear to have followed.

The American Automobile Company was organized in Springfield, Illinois during the summer of 1907 for the manufacture and repair of motorcars. Capital stock was $10,000, and the incorporators were L.W. Thompson, J.T. Tyrrell and P. Steele. Manufacture did not follow.

The American Automobile Company was organized in Hackensack, New Jersey with a capital stock of $50,000 during the fall of 1911 for the purpose of manufacturing motorcars. Ralph D. Earle, George M. Brewster, John R. Ramsey and Wendell J. Wright were the people involved. Manufacture did not follow.

The American Automobile Front Company was a $500,000 Maine incorporation from 1903 which was organized "to make and sell power carriages." President was Horace Mitchell of Kittery; treasurer was A.M. Meloon of Newcastle, New Hampshire. No automobile is believed to have resulted.

The American Automobile Manufacturing Company was announced in the spring of 1911 as "a corporation of Arizona, with $1,000,000, admitted to do business in Indiana," with New Albany chosen as the factory site. Behind this venture were H.K. Cole, Powell McRoberts, A.C. Davis and Berton B. Bales. Manufacture has not been documented.

The American Automobile & Power Company was organized in Sanford,

Maine with a capital stock of $500,000 during late 1903. This venture did proceed into manufacture of a car called the American Populaire. Refer to American Populaire.

The American Automobile Specialty Company was a $2500 Chicago incorporation of early 1914 to manufacture and deal in automobiles. Thomas Lindskog, Peter Ewerts and Orpheus A. Harding were behind this venture. Manufacture did not result.

The American Automobile Vehicle Company of Detroit was listed as a car manufacturer in a 1907 trade publication. There is no evidence, however, that this firm ever produced an automobile. Possibly the name was an error for the American Machine Manufacturing Company of Detroit, the builders that year of the Commerce car.

The American Bicycle Company, more popularly referred to at the turn of the century as the "bicycle trust," was the overall sponsoring organization for a steamer called Toledo and an electric called Waverley. Refer to Toledo and Waverley.

The American Body Company was organized for the manufacture of automobiles in Buffalo, New York in April of 1909. Capital stock was $10,000, and the incorporators were E.J. Freitas, J.W. Kelly and Edward W. Selkirk. Manufacture of an automobile did not follow.

The American Box Ball Company of Indianapolis has been indicated on rosters to have produced a car called the Holcomb in 1913. Refer to Holcomb.

The American Brass Company of Waterbury, Connecticut has been reported to have built an automobile in 1907-1908. This was not so. American Brass apparently did have plans for producing a truck, but manufacture of it remains unsubstantiated.

The American Dynamic Company was organized in New York City late in 1906 with a capital stock of $50,000 for the manufacture of automobiles and motorboats. S.D. McComb, T.H. Fulton and W.M. Finkenauer were the people involved. Automobile manufacture did not follow.

The American Electric Car Company was the result of the January 1914 merger of the firms producing the Argo, Borland and Broc electric cars. Refer to those specific vehicles.

The American Electric Manufacturing & Power Company was a $1,000,000 Delaware incorporation announced in May 1899. Henry E. Cain, William M. Baldwin and Howard L. Mendenhall (all of Philadelphia) were behind this venture, with the plan to "make motor vehicles of all kinds" at 20th and Washington Avenues in Philadelphia. This company was listed as a manufacturer in the Hiscox book *Horseless Vehicles, Automobiles, Motor Cycles* produced in 1900, but actual manufacture has not been documented.

The American Electric Vehicle Company at 134 West 38th Street in New York City was also indicated in the 1900 Hiscox book as a manufacturer, as was another company of that same name at 1545 Michigan Avenue in Chicago. In neither case has manufacture been substantiated.

An American Electric has been reported to have been built in 1897 in Boston by the American Motor Wagon Company. City directories of the period for that Massachusetts city do not reveal the existence of such a company.

The American Garage and Maintenance Company was organized in New York City during the spring of 1904 for the manufacture of motor vehicles. Capital stock was $100,000, and the incorporators were John T. Rainier, P.N. Lineberger and H.V. Kibbe. Automobile manufacture did not follow, though in 1905 Rainier organized another company which did move into production of the Rainier car.

The American Generator Company was a $100,000 New York City incorporation of late 1909 for the manufacture of vehicles and motors. H.C. Cryder, Townsend Morgan and W.M. Seabury were the directors of this firm, which is not believed to have produced an automobile.

The American Machine Manufacturing Company of Detroit produced an automobile called the Commerce in 1907-1908. Refer to Commerce.

The American Machine & Manufacturing Company of Boulder, Colorado produced an automobile called the Linace in 1909. Refer to Linace.

The American Manufacturing Company was the name of the firm which, *Motor Field* revealed in July 1905, would "soon build a plant" and begin the manufacture of automobiles in Denver, Colorado. H.C. Carterfi, described as a "patentee of many improvements in automobile construction," was behind this venture of which no further word was heard.

The American Metal Wheel and Auto Company of Toledo, Ohio introduced its juvenile car in November 1906. Although occasionally referred to as the American, American Juvenile was the more usual reference. Refer to American Juvenile.

The American Motive Power Company was a late 1904 incorporation "to build automobiles, boats, carriages and motors" in New Haven, Connecticut. The incorporators of this $100,000 venture were Charles E. Graham, J.J. Hogan and Andrew H. Smith. Manufacture is not believed to have followed.

The American Motor Company was a late 1903 Maine incorporation for the purpose of making and selling cycles and automobiles. The president was H.C. Houston, the treasurer was G.M. Holmes, and P.I. Larrabee was a director. All three of these people were residents of Portland, Maine. Of the $150,000 capital stock, a grand total of $15 was reported paid in. Manufacture did not follow.

The American Motor Company of Brockton, Massachusetts produced a small runabout from 1905-1906 which was marketed as a Marsh. In addition to this venture, the Marsh brothers of Brockton built or promoted a variety of further cars, including the Lima Roadster, the Eastern, the Vulcan, the Caesar, the Sterling, and yet another Marsh in 1920.

The American Motor Company of Eau Claire, Wisconsin was a $15,000 incorporation from late 1906. C.T. Bundy, Roy P. Wilcox and Hanna F. Johnson announced their plan "to build motor cars," but apparently never followed through on it.

Yet another American Motor Company was the $25,000 incorporation from late 1908 in Greensboro, Virginia. Again, manufacture did not follow.

The American Motor Car Company of St. Louis, Missouri has been frequently indicated on car rosters as a manufacturer in 1903. This seems to have been an error perpetuated that year by *Cycle and Automobile Trade Journal* in reporting on the model line of the St. Louis Motor Car Company.

The American Motor Car Company was incorporated with a $25,000 stock in Indianapolis in late 1905. William A. Moore, William E. Barton and

Clifton R. Cameron were the people involved, and the plan was the manufacture of "all kinds of motor vehicles." This did not happen, though this venture may have evolved into the American Motors Company which subsequently became famous for the American Underslung.

The American Motor Car Company was incorporated with a capital stock of $100,000 in Canton, Ohio during the summer of 1917 for the purpose of manufacturing automobiles. Among the incorporators were Clyde A. Volzer, William E. Patterson, Adolph S. Vance, Clotilda Volzer, Jacob M. Glaser and Moritz Glaser. Manufacture is not believed to have followed.

The American Motor Carriage Company on Glen Avenue in Newton Center, Massachusetts was indicated as a manufacturer in the Hiscox book *Horseless Vehicles, Automobiles, Motor Cycles* published in 1900. Actual manufacture has not been substantiated.

The American produced by the American Motor Carriage Company of Cleveland from 1902-1904 was more familiarly known by its nickname of American Gas. Refer to American Gas.

The American Motor Cycle Company was a $15,000 Chicago incorporation from late 1908 for the manufacture and sale of motorcycles and automobiles. William H. Hess, O.W. Frischkorn and A.J. Musselman were the people involved. An automobile did not follow.

The American Motor League was organized in Syracuse, New York early in 1910 with a capital stock of $25,000 for the manufacture and sale of engines, motors and motor vehicles. The incorporators were A.A. Schlachter, J.J. Barrett and S.G. Schlachter. An automobile was never forthcoming.

The American Motor Sales Company of St. Louis, Missouri was organized to "manufacture, buy, sell and deal in automobiles" early in 1912. Capital stock was $5000, and the incorporators were C.T. Strauss, F.B. Nelsen and C.W. Wanghop. No car is believed to have resulted.

The American Motor Sales Company of Mason City, Iowa is known to have attempted the building of a cyclecar in 1913. In January of the year following *The American Cyclecar* reported that "the car is now going through the experimental stage, but will not be placed upon the market for some time." It never was.

The American Motor Traffic Company was an early 1913 incorporation "to operate and manufacture motor vehicles for all uses" in Washington, D.C. The incorporators were E.S. Alford, S.J. McFarren, W.J. Moore, A.L. Kley, J.C. Muncaster and J.C. Mencher. No manufacture followed.

The American Motor & Vehicle Company at 145 Broadway in New York City was listed as a manufacturer in the Hiscox book *Motor Vehicles, Automobiles, Motor Cycles* published in 1900. No company of that name existed in Manhattan prior to or following the turn of the century, according to the city directories of the period.

The American National Sales Company was a $100,000 Delaware incorporation to manufacture and sell automobiles that was announced during the summer of 1917. F.R. Hansell of Philadelphia and J. Vernon Pimm and S.C. Seymour of Camden, New Jersey were the principals involved. Manufacture did not follow.

The American Silent Motors Company of Los Angeles, California promoted an automobile called the Silent in 1915. Refer to Silent.

The American Standard Motor Company was organized in Indianapolis early in 1915 for the manufacture of automobiles and trucks. Capital stock was $100,000, and the incorporators were Harry B. Gardner, James P. Gardner and Leo A. Gardner. Subsequent manufacture is not indicated.

Another American Standard Motor Company was a late 1918 Delaware incorporation with a capital stock of $2 million, again for the manufacture of cars and trucks. The incorporators were C.L. Rimlinger, M.M. Clancy and P.B. Drew. Again, manufacture does not appear to have followed.

The American Steam Motor Company was a $400,000 incorporation emanating from Milwaukee, Wisconsin early in 1904. Subsequent manufacture has not been established.

The American Taxameter Cab Company was organized in New York City during the summer of 1908. The taxis which it put into service were built by the Bristol Engineering Company of Bristol, Connecticut, Bristol also designing the Rockwell and W.C.P. cabs of this period.

The American Touring Car Company was organized in the late summer of 1903 "to make automobiles" in New York City. Capital stock was $100,000, and the incorporators were John H. Fogarty, Daniel Fogarty, Margaret E. Flaherty and William H. Flaherty, all of Brooklyn. A factory in Brooklyn was planned, but for the moment offices were taken at 62 West 43rd Street in Manhattan. Two months later the company was sold to G.L. Henry, whose plans for it apparently did not include manufacture.

The American Vehicle Company of New York City was incorporated in West Virginia in early 1900 "to use and apply air as motive power for operating vehicles and engines." Refer to American Pneumatic.

The American Wheelock Engine Company of Worcester, Massachusetts was indicated as an automobile manufacturer in the Hiscox book *Horseless Vehicles, Automobiles, Motor Cycles* published in 1900. Actual manufacture has not been substantiated.

AMERICAN — New York, New York — (1896) — In March of 1896 the American Carriage Motor Company was reported to be being organized "by prominent carriage and business men of New York City." The company was headquartered at 414 East 125th Street, the heart of present-day East Harlem. The company's engine was regarded at the time as "novel" — a two-stroke four with paired cylinders and its flywheel constructed as a dynamo which charged a storage battery. The engine was placed in a chassis of 75-inch wheelbase and 60-inch tread, which was regarded as extraordinarily substantial. There was something unsubstantial, however, about either the car or the company prepared to produce it. American Carriage announced plans to enter one of its vehicles in the Cosmopolitan race to take place Memorial Day weekend in May 1896. The car never made it to the starting line, and American Carriage Motor Company never made it into production.

AMERICAN — New York, New York — (1897-1898) — The American Motor Company of New York City had been building De Dion-type engines since 1895. Early in 1896 company officials announced that they had secured the services of "competent draftsmen and mechanics" and were "prepared to work out for inventors any ideas they may have in the application of motor to vehicles." The following year they decided to work out

some of those ideas themselves. In the spring of 1898 the firm ballyhooed the completion of 100 tricycles and three quadricycles which would be marketed in the East. That fall there was further ballyhooing with regard to continuing production in lots of 100 or more, the company's progress toward making all parts interchangeable (sic), and its development work on a new but undescribed transmission which would be tested in two four-wheel carriages then under construction. Then all announcements stopped. It would seem the firm was better at ballyhooing than producing. The American Motor Company, whose offices were in the Havemeyer Building in New York with a factory in Hoboken (New Jersey), certainly did build a number of vehicles, though probably not the hundreds claimed. There is also reference to the firm building the prototype of the Barrows Electric for C.H. Barrows. After discontinuing production of the American Tricycle and Quadricycle, the American Motor Company remained in business awhile as suppliers of engines to the Automobile Company of America, producers of the Gasmobile.

1899 American, style No. 4, auto-buggy, WLB

AMERICAN — New York, New York — (1899-1901) — The American Automobile Company had its offices in the Commercial Cable Building at 20 Broad Street in the Financial District of Manhattan. The location of its factory remains a mystery. The highly touted features of this American were its three-cylinder hydro-carbon engine, and the fact that the motor could be started while the driver was seated in the carriage. Although it was not so widely touted, the vehicle had been designed by J. Frank Duryea who by this time had quarreled with his brother Charles E. This American was J. Frank's first independent venture following the break-up of their partnership. Apparently he conducted most of his experimental work at his home in New England. There is a record that one of the cars ran from Springfield (Massachusetts) to Providence (Rhode Island), a distance of 105 miles, in six hours and ten minutes. Another of the Americans outran "three noted horsemen" during a run through Prospect Park in Brooklyn. Apparently, J. Frank Duryea's role in the American venture was as designer only. In September of 1900 he established his own company in Massachusetts and proceeded to build the Hampden, a car very similar to the American, though there is no evidence of any connection between the two companies. Meanwhile, the American Automobile Company had been succeeded by the United Power Vehicle Company.

AMERICAN — Brooklyn, New York — (1900) — The American Automobile, Motor & Power Company of Brooklyn built a car in 1900 following patents provided by one George Rothenbucher. The vehicle had a two-cylinder engine and a steering wheel. In cornering, the inside wheel was automatically thrown out of gear by means of a clutch, with the outer wheel only being driven. This was accomplished without either a differential gear or driving the wheels from separate motors, and was seen by the makers as an ingenious boon that would allow the vehicle's drivetrain to be attached to any ordinary wagon or carriage. But the real novelty was in the engine. "Two carbonic acid gas cylinders, such as are to be found at soda water fountains, are used," *The Automobile* reported in February 1900. "These are placed in the wagon box lying at the outer side. The pressure of this gas is lowered by a reducing valve and passes through a coil over a gasoline flame before going to the engine." This American fizzled out during the prototype stage. One car was definitely built, but the American Automobile, Motor & Power Company concluded thereafter that its most profitable course was to simply sell the engine and drive unit for application to horsedrawn wagons and carriages. There is no evidence the company ever made a profit doing this, although it offered a compressed air version for anyone who might be apprehensive about the seltzer principle.

AMERICAN — Alexandria, Virginia — (1904) — The American Manufacturing Company was the idea of Frank L. Carter. His main office was in Washington, D.C., his factory in Alexandria. He seemed willing to build just about anything, and in 1904 that included an automobile. In advertisements in the trade press that year, he showed a photo of a car with shaft drive and front-mounted engine and proposed to manufacture it in touring, runabout and commercial form. Whose idea the car was is not known, but it was certainly not Frank L. Carter's. His *modus operandi* was to manufacture the inventions of others on a royalty basis. The evidence suggests that no meaningful production of an automobile ever resulted, but several other products of American Manufacturing — an air-and-oil vapor burner, a fire extinguisher and a device to make French fries out of potatoes — may have enjoyed some success during this period. Frank Carter does not

1904 American, tonneau, GR

seem to have been involved with his brother Howard in the two engine Carter automobile venture, though he was part of the organization founded by another brother, A. Gary Carter, which produced the Washington from 1909 to 1912.

1906 American, King of Belgium, touring, WLB

AMERICAN — AMERICAN (UNDERSLUNG) — Indianapolis, Indiana — (1906-1914) — The product of the American Motors Company of Indianapolis is most familiarly known today as the American Underslung, although this description was seldom used then, the company preferring to go with varying model designations, i.e. "American Scout," "American Tourist," "American Traveler," "American Roadster." Offering a variety of derivative or proprietary four- and six-cylinder engines during its history, the company also usually offered a conventional chassis in addition to the underslung model. The frame that hung below the axles, however, was the focus of most American advertising. Company propagandists noted that the average car "would turn turtle" at 43° whereas theirs could tilt safely at 55°; and ground clearance was not sacrificed, the usual "overhead" car's being 10-1/4 inches which was bettered by an inch in the American's underslung chassis. Boston agent W.A. Frederick put up a straightaway mile in 45 seconds at Lowell, Massachusetts in 1907 in one of these cars. Harry Stutz had designed the conventional chassis American but not the underslung model, popular legend to the contrary. The underslung chassis was designed by Fred I. Tone. By 1907 Harry Stutz had left American for Marion. By 1911 the American was offered in 50 and 60 hp versions with $4000-plus pricetags as "A Car for the Discriminating Few." Unfortunately there weren't enough such people to keep the company in business long. Fred Tone left in 1913 to pursue his own automotive venture, and by spring 1914, after the production of 45,000 cars, American Motors Company was bankrupt. Fifty cars remained unsold; they were acquired by Auto Parts Company of Chicago and bargain-basement priced at $600 for a Scout and $900 for an Underslung roadster. Doubtless these cars found ready discriminating buyers. Meanwhile, American president J.I. Handley was not without a job, since he also happened to be the president of Marion in Indianapolis too.

1906 AMERICAN
Four — 35/40 hp, 106" wb

	FP	5	4	3	2	1
Tour.-5P	3000	6600	13,200	22,000	30,800	44,000

1907 American, Roadster, HAC

1907 AMERICAN
Four — 40 hp, 116" wb

American Tourist-5P	3250	6600	13,200	22,000	30,800	44,000
Four — 40 hp, 106" wb						
American Rds.-2P	3250	6600	13,200	22,000	30,800	44,000

1908 American, Roadster, HAC

1908 AMERICAN
Forty — 4-cyl., 40 hp, 116" wb

	FP	5	4	3	2	1
Tourist	3250	6000	8500	13,000	30,000	42,000
Rds.	3250	6200	8700	13,500	31,000	45,000
Fifty — 4-cyl., 50/60 hp, 124" wb						
Tourist	2000	6500	9500	15,000	34,000	46,000
Rds.	3750	6700	9700	16,000	35,000	49,000

1909 American, Tourist, HAC

1909 AMERICAN
Underslung — 4-cyl., 50/60 hp, 124" wb

Rds.-3P	3750	15,000	25,000	40,000	85,000	120,000
Trav.-4P	4000	14,000	24,000	38,000	80,000	110,000
Regular chassis — 4-cyl., 50/60 hp, 124" wb						
Tourist-7P	4000	10,000	20,000	30,000	60,000	80,000
Gadabout-5P	3750	11,000	22,000	32,000	62,000	82,000
Wayfarer-5P	3750	11,000	22,000	32,000	62,000	80,000

1910 American, Tourist, WLB

1910 AMERICAN
Underslung — 4-cyl., 50 hp

Amer. Rds. (110" wb)	4000	15,000	25,000	40,000	85,000	120,000
Amer. Trav. (122" wb)	4000	16,000	26,000	42,000	87,000	125,000
Amer. Tour. (124" wb)	4000	18,000	28,000	45,000	90,000	130,000
Regular chassis — 4-cyl., 50 hp						
Amer. Limo. (124" wb)	5000	14,000	24,000	38,000	80,000	110,000

1911 American, Traveler, coupe, HAC

1911 AMERICAN
Underslung — 4-cyl., 50 hp, 112" wb

	FP	5	4	3	2	1
Amer. Rds.	4250	15,000	25,000	40,000	85,000	120,000
Amer. Rds. Cpe.	5250	16,000	26,000	41,000	86,000	121,000

Underslung — 4-cyl., 60 hp, 112" wb

Amer. Rds. Spec.	5000	17,000	28,000	45,000	90,000	130,000
Amer. Spdstr.	5000	18,000	30,000	47,000	92,000	135,000

Underslung — 4-cyl., 50 hp, 124" wb

Amer. Trav.	4250	15,000	25,000	40,000	85,000	120,000
Amer. Tour.	4250	16,000	26,000	42,000	87,000	123,000
Amer. Trav. Cpe.	5250	14,000	24,000	35,000	80,000	110,000

Underslung — 4-cyl., 60 hp, 124" wb

Amer. Trav. Spec.	5000	19,000	32,000	50,000	95,000	140,000

Regular Chassis — 4-cyl., 50 hp, 124" wb

Amer. Limo.	5250	13,000	23,000	34,000	78,000	100,000

1912 American, type 34, Tourist, touring, WLB

1912 American, type 22, Scout, 2 pass. roadster, WLB

1912 American, type 56, Traveler, touring, WLB

1912 AMERCIAN
American Scout — 4-cyl., 20 hp, 102" wb

Model 22 Tour.-5P	1250	5500	7500	12,000	26,000	39,000
Model 22 Rds.-2P	1250	6000	8500	13,000	30,000	42,000

American Tourist — 4-cyl., 30 hp, 118" wb

Model 34 Tour.-5P	2250	6500	9500	15,000	34,000	46,000
Model 34 Rds.-2P	2250	7000	11,000	17,000	37,000	49,000

American Traveler — 4-cyl., 50 hp

Model 54 Tour. (124" wb)	4250	18,000	30,000	47,000	92,000	135,000
Model 56 Tour. (140" wb)	4500	19,000	32,000	50,000	95,000	140,000

1913 American, type 56-A, Traveler, touring, HAC

1913 American, type 22-B, Scout, roadster, HFM

1913 AMERICAN
American Scout — 4-cyl., 30 hp, 105" wb

	FP	5	4	3	2	1
Model 22-B Rds.-2P	1475	7000	11,000	17,000	37,000	49,000
Model 22-B Col. Cpe.-3P	2000	5500	7500	12,000	26,000	39,000

American Tourist — 4-cyl., 50 hp, 118" wb

Model 34-A Tour.-4P	2350	6500	10,000	16,000	36,000	48,000
Model 32-A Runabout-2P	2350	7000	11,000	17,000	38,000	50,000
Model 34-A Cpe.-5P	3500	6000	8500	13,000	30,000	42,000

American Traveler — 4-cyl., 60 hp, 140" wb

Model 56-A Tour.-6P	4500	18,000	30,000	48,000	90,000	135,000
Model 54-A Tour.-4P	4250	19,000	32,000	50,000	95,000	140,000
Model 56-A Limo.-6P	6000	13,000	23,000	34,000	78,000	100,000

1914 American Underslung, touring, OCW

1914 AMERICAN
Underslung — 4-cyl., 26 hp, 105" wb

Model 422 Rds.-2P	1550	18,000	30,000	48,000	92,000	130,000

Underslung — 6-cyl., 49 hp, 140" wb

Model 666 Tour.-6P	4500	20,000	35,000	55,000	100,000	150,000

Underslung — 6-cyl., 43 hp, 132" wb

Model 642 Rds.-2P	4500	19,000	32,000	50,000	95,000	140,000

Underslung — 6-cyl., 43 hp, 140" wb

Model 646 Tour.-6P	2950	19,000	32,000	50,000	95,000	140,000

1917-18 American Six, touring, HAC

AMERICAN — AMERICAN BALANCED SIX — AMERICAN SIX — Plain-field, New Jersey — (1917-1924) — The American Motors Corporation of Plainfield built the "Smile Car," the company having earned the right to this designation, it said in 1920, because of the millions of miles of happy motoring it had provided owners for the three years previous. The vehicle offering this mirth was an assembled car in the medium-price range known variously as an American, American Six or American Balanced Six, the designation changing sporadically through the years. Production began in February 1917. Initially, Louis Chevrolet was associated with the company as vice-president and chief engineer, although the six-cylinder unit he engineered was simply an uprated Rutenber, and he soon returned to his Frontenac adventures. An "O.K. Chevrolet" plaque was fitted on the dash of those cars produced during his tenure. Production was said to be 1500 units annually by 1920, during which year a more powerful Herschell-Spillman six was added. That year, too, an affiliated company, American Southern Motors, was established in Greensboro, North Carolina to assemble Americans for distribution in Dixie — and also to produce a new top-market car called the Vaughn. In 1921 American survived receivership and early in 1922 was reported to be "coming along nicely" under a reorganization that brought Carl H. Page to the presidency. Page, whose credits included sales and distribution for such diverse cars as White, Mitchell, Chalmers, Jordan, Saxon and Roamer, was widely viewed as the tonic the ailing company needed — but Page's plans were followed by an unwelcome chaser: merger. Following consolidation with the Bessemer Truck Corporation in 1923, American continued production as the Passenger Car Division of Bessemer-American Motors Corporation for some months. But after the truck-building companies of Winther, Krebs and Northway were added that October to form Amalgamated Motors, the Smile Car was phased out before the spring of 1924.

1917 AMERICAN
Six — 45 hp, 122" wb

	FP	5	4	3	2	1
Model A Tour.-5P	1285	2500	3500	5000	8500	18,000

1918 AMERICAN
Six — 45 hp, 122" wb

Model B Tour.-5P	1375	2500	3500	5000	8500	18,000
Model B Rds.-2P	1465	2600	3600	5200	8700	18,500
Model B Cloverleaf Rds.-4P	1465	2700	3700	5500	9000	19,000

1919 AMERICAN
Six — 45 hp, 122" wb

Model G Tour.-5P	1765	2500	3500	5000	8500	18,000
Model G Rds.-2P	1835	2600	3600	5200	8700	18,500
Model G Tour. Sd.-5P	2875	2000	3000	4200	6500	14,000

1920 American Balanced Six, touring, HAC

1920 AMERICAN
Model Six-B — 45 hp, 122" wb

Rds.-3P	1895	2600	3600	5200	8700	18,500
Tour.-5P	1865	2500	3500	5000	8500	18,000
Tour.-7P	1965	2400	3400	4800	8000	17,500
Sed. Sextet	2950	2000	3000	4200	6500	14,000

Note: The Model Six C-60 was introduced mid-model year.

1921 American, roadster, WLB

1921 AMERICAN
Model Six C-60 — 58 hp, 127" wb

Tour.-5P	2395	3000	4000	6000	9500	21,000
Rds.-2P	2395	3200	4200	6500	10,000	24,000
Tour.-7P	2495	2900	3900	5900	9400	20,500
Spt.-4P	2595	3200	4200	6500	10,000	24,000
Cpe.-3P	3295	3000	4000	5500	9000	18,500
Sed.-5P	3495	2500	3500	5000	8500	18,000

1922 AMERICAN
Model Six C-60 — 58 hp, 125" wb

Tour.-5P	2395	3000	4000	6000	9500	21,000
Rdstr.-2P	2395	3200	4200	6500	10,000	24,000
Tour.-7P	2495	2900	3900	5900	9400	20,500
Sport-4P	2595	3200	4200	6500	10,000	24,000
Cpe.-3P	3295	3000	4000	5500	9000	18,500
Sed.-5P	3495	2500	3500	5000	8500	18,000

1921 American, 5 pass. touring, WLB

1923 American, touring, WLB

1923 AMERICAN
Model D-66 — 6-cyl., 66 hp, 127" wb

Tour.-5P	1785	3000	4000	6000	9500	21,000
Tour.-7P	1850	3100	4100	6100	9600	22,000
Spt.-4P	1885	3200	4200	6200	9700	23,000
Rds.-2P	1885	3300	4300	6300	9800	24,000
Sed.-7P	2485	2500	3500	5500	8500	18,000

1924 AMERICAN
Model D-66 — 6-cyl., 66 hp, 127" wb

Tour.-5P	1695	3000	4000	6000	9500	21,000
Rds.-2P	2050	3300	4300	6300	9800	24,000
Brougham	2195	2600	3600	5600	8600	18,500
Spt. Phaeton	1850	3200	4200	6200	9700	23,000
Sed.-5P	2350	2400	3400	5400	8400	17,500
Del. Sed.-5P	2550	2500	3500	5500	8500	18,000

1930 American Austin, roadster, AA

AMERICAN AUSTIN — Butler, Pennsylvania — (1930-1934) / AMERICAN BANTAM — (1938-1941) — In 1929 the American Austin Car Company was incorporated in Delaware, with factory facilities in Butler, Pennsylvania, and in the decade following proved that America, despite the Great Depression which seemingly might have dictated otherwise, was not ready for a small car. The first American Austins were 1930 models built on the English Austin Seven chassis with coachwork which can only be described as adorable, courtesy of Alexis de Sakhnoffsky and Hayes Body Company of Detroit. Sixteen inches narrower and twenty-eight inches shorter than any other car in America, the American Austin may have been the first U.S. production car to carry its battery under the hood. Its water-cooled four-cylinder engine displaced a fraction over 45 cubic inches and developed a fraction under 15 hp. At $445, the car cost five dollars more than the Model A Ford, which probably was one of its prob-

1930 American Austin, coupe, HAC

lems. It guaranteed 40 miles per gallon of gasoline, which wasn't regarded as very important then. The American Austin did not lack for attention, Al Jolson, Buster Keaton and the Ernest Hemingways, among other celebrities, buying one. Our Gang loved the car, and so did cartoonists and radio comedians. Instead of being regarded as a viable motorcar, the American Austin became something of a joke. Instead of production in the hundreds of thousands, fewer than 10,000 American Austins were built in its first two years of production. In 1932 the company went into receivership. It survived for two years thereafter through the herculean efforts of a super salesman by the name of Roy Evans, but by June of 1934 a petition of bankruptcy was filed. Production ceased in Butler during 1935 and 1936, but by 1937 Roy Evans was back with a new company and a new car. In June of the year previous he had seen to the formation of the American Bantam Car Company. In September of 1937 the American Bantam made its debut in the Hotel Roosevelt in New York. Its engine was Austin-like but sufficiently changed to avoid royalty payments to England. (Harry Miller worked some on the manifolding.) Alexis de Sakhnoffsky helped out on new styling, charging Evans only $300, his expenses. Former race driver Lee Oldfield also assisted. The Boulevard Delivery was a particularly comely model, and model names like Riviera and Hollywood were designed to lend chic to what was undeniably a shoestring operation. It didn't work. Although Willys and Ford would garner the huge military contracts and a good deal of the fame, history must record that American Bantam designed and built the first successful Jeep for the United States Army in 1940. The year following the last few American Bantam cars left the Butler factory.

1930-1931
4-cyl., 15 hp, 75" wb

	FP	5	4	3	2	1
Rds	445	2800	5700	9500	13,300	19,000
Cpe	465	1400	4200	7000	9800	14,000
DeL Cpe	550	1500	4350	7250	10.150	14,500

1932
4-cyl., 15 hp, 75" wb

	FP	5	4	3	2	1
Rbt	395	2800	5700	9500	13,300	19,000
Bus Cpe	330	1400	4200	7000	9800	14,000
Cabr	475	2300	5400	9000	12,600	18,000
Std Cpe	395	1450	4250	7150	10,000	14,300
DeL Cpe	495	1500	4350	7250	10,150	14,500

1933 American Austin, sedan delivery, AA

1933
4-cyl., 15 hp, 75" wb

Rds	305	2800	5700	9500	13,300	19,000
Bus Cpe	275	1400	4200	7000	9800	14,000
Spl Cpe	295	1550	4500	7500	10,500	15,000
Cpe	315	1000	2400	5000	7000	10,000

1934
4-cyl., 15 hp, 75" wb

	FP	5	4	3	2	1
Bus Cpe	295	1400	4200	7000	9800	14,000
Std Cpe	345	1500	4350	7250	10,150	14,500
DeL Cpe	365	1550	4500	7500	10,500	15,000

1935
4-cyl., 15 hp, 75" wb

Bus Cpe	295	1400	4200	7000	9800	14,000
Std Cpe	345	1500	4350	7250	10,150	14,500
DeL Cpe	385	1550	4500	7500	10,500	15,000

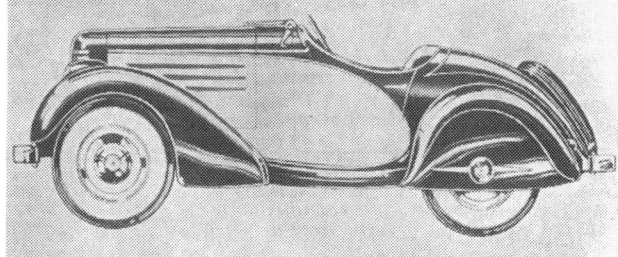

1938 American Bantam, roadster, WLB

1938
Model 60 — 4-cyl., 19 hp, 75" wb

Rds	479	2000	5100	8500	11,900	17,000
Cpe	469	1150	3600	6000	8400	12,000

1939
Model 60 — 4-cyl., 20 hp, 75" wb

Std Cpe	399	900	1900	4500	6300	9000
Std Rds	399	1650	4650	7750	10,850	15,500
Spl Cpe	439	950	2100	4750	6650	9500
Spl Rds	479	1750	4800	8000	11,200	16,000
Spds	497	1800	4950	8250	11,550	16,500
DeL Cpe	469	975	2300	4900	6850	9800
DeL Rds	525	2000	5100	8500	11,900	17,000
DeL Spds	549	2200	5250	8750	12,250	17,500
Sta Wag	565	1000	2400	5000	7000	10,000

1940 American Bantam, station wagon, HAC

1940-1941
Model 65 — 4-cyl., 22 hp, 75" wb

Std Cpe	399	900	1900	4500	6300	9000
Master Cpe	449	950	2100	4750	6650	9500
Master Rds	449	2000	5100	8500	11,900	17,000
Conv Cpe	525	1800	4950	8250	11,550	16,500
Conv Sed	549	1800	4950	8250	11,550	16,500
Sta Wag	575	1400	4200	7000	9800	14,000

AMERICAN BEAUTY — For the 1918 through 1920 model years, American Beauty was the advertised name of the car produced by the Pan-American Motors Corporation of Decatur, Illinois. More practically, it was the model designation. Refer to Pan-American. Interestingly, American Motors Corporation of Plainfield, New Jersey initially planned to call its car an American Beauty as well — but by the time the first models rolled off the assembly line in February 1917 the decision had been made for simply American.

AMERICAN BEAUTY — **Jonesville, Michigan** — **(1916)** — ''American Beauty Will Bloom Soon,'' *Automobile Topics* headlined in July 1916. Fresh from the failure of his electric cyclecar the year previous, William E. Storms was trying again. This time his car would be a standard electric priced at $1485, and he promised a light electric truck too. Storms' cyclecar had been made in Detroit. For the new American Beauty, he ventured first to Adrian, Michigan but got nowhere there, and then traveled to Jonesville where he interested local capitalists in supporting him. The Colonial Car Company was organized, with Storms as president, Elmer H. Oversmith as vice-president and John B. Drew as secretary-treasurer. The firm was out of business practically as soon as it began. Possibly the American Beauty never passed the prototype stage.

AMERICAN BENHAM — Trade press references occasionally called the car built in 1913-1914 in Detroit the American Benham, but there is no evidence that George W. Benham ever did. Refer to Benham.

1907 American Berliet, landaulette, OCW

AMERICAN BERLIET — Providence, Rhode Island —(1906-1908) —

Sometime during the spring of 1905, the American Locomobile Company of Providence, Rhode Island concluded arrangements with Automobiles Berliet of Lyons, France to manufacture the famed Berliet automobile in this country. The collaboration was a logical one, the two companies having had previous business dealings in the railroad locomotive field. Production began in 1906, and in November that year three four-cylinder chain-drive models were shown at Grand Central Palace in New York City. A 60 hp six-cylinder shaft-drive car was offered in 1908, and all smaller fours in the line were also provided shaft drive that year. There was a good deal of confusion during this period as to precisely which models the company was offering, and a bit more about just what they were called. Officially, the car was the American Locomotive Motor Car, which was unwieldy, and the trade press took to referring to it variously as the American Locomotive (Berliet), the American Berliet, or just Berliet. By September 1908, it would appear the company had begun to prefer the American Berliet designation, but by then it was obsolete anyway. Having learned everything necessary to know to design their own car, the company's engineers persuaded the front office they should be allowed to do just that. The Berliet license was discontinued, the word "Automobile" was dropped from the firm's name, and the American Locomotive Company carried forth on its own to build the renowned and mighty Alco.

1906 AMERICAN BERLIET
4-cyl., 40/50 hp, 118" wb

	FP	5	4	3	2	1
Touring -5/7P	8500	8000	14,000	21,000	45,000	65,000
4-cyl., 40/50 hp, 126" wb						
Land'et.-5/7P	8500	7500	9500	18,000	40,000	60,000
4-cyl., 24/30 hp, 112" wb						
Tour.-5/7P	5500	7900	13,000	20,000	44,000	64,000

1907 American Berliet, limousine, WLB

1908 American Berliet, touring, WLB

1907 AMERICAN BERLIET
4-cyl., 24/30 hp, 112" wb

	FP	5	4	3	2	1
Land'et.	6500	6200	7200	13,000	33,000	53,000
Tour.-5/7P	6500	6500	8500	15,000	35,000	55,000
Limo.	6500	6000	7000	12,000	30,000	50,000
4-cyl., 40/50 hp, 126" wb						
Land'et.	8500	6600	8600	16,000	36,000	56,000
Tour.-7P	8500	7500	9500	18,000	40,000	60,000
Limo.	8500	6500	8500	15,000	35,000	55,000
4-cyl., 60 hp, 126" wb						
Land'et.	10,000	7500	9500	18,000	40,000	60,000
Tour.	10,000	8000	14,000	21,000	45,000	65,000
Limo.	10,000	7000	9000	16,000	38,000	59,000

AMERICAN BORLAND/BROC — In 1914 the electric-car-producing companies of Argo, Borland and Broc were merged into a new firm called the American Electric Vehicle Company. Ostensibly, the Borland thus became the American Borland, the Broc the American Broc. As often as not, however, the cars were referred to by their former designations. Refer to Borland and Broc.

AMERICAN CARBONIC ACID — Carbonic acid describes the motive force of this unusual turn of the century vehicle, but the car of the American Automobile, Motor & Power Company of Brooklyn is more properly referred to simply as an American. Refer to American.

AMERICAN CARRIAGE — The American Carriage Motor Company of New York City produced an automobile in 1896 that is more properly designated simply as the American. Refer to American.

1903 American C.G.V., MVMA

AMERICAN C.G.V. — New York, New York — (1902-1903) — Smith & Mabley of New York City were importers of the motorcar built in France by Charron, Girardot & Voigt. For a short period during 1902-1903, the company produced the car here as well under license. "The Only Authorized French Machine Made in this Country," advertising headlined during this era of blatant plagiarism. The Charron, Girardot & Voigt Company of America was casually organized. Only seven cars resulted apparently, with bodies supplied by the coachbuilding house of J.M. Quinby & Sons (Newark, New Jersey), and assembly seen to by the Rome Locomotive Works (Rome, New York). The price as a five-passenger tonneau was $5500. After this short production run, Smith & Mabley returned to the importation of the C.G.V., including a model custom-built in France for an American customer who requested bathroom facilities in the back seat. In 1904, A.D. Proctor Smith and Carlton R. Mabley decided to build an all-American car, and the S & M Simplex was the result.

1903 AMERICAN C.G.V.

Tonneau	5500	5000	6500	11,000	22,000	35,000

AMERICAN CHOCOLATE — Although the car designed by William Walter was built in the factory of his American Chocolate Machinery Company in New York City from 1902-1906, it never carried the name American Chocolate. Refer to Walter.

AMERICAN CYCLECAR — Although a number of companies producing cyclecars during the 1913-1915 period bore the name American, the cars were marketed under other designations.
    The American Cyclecar Company of Seattle, Washington called its car the Columbia.
    The American Manufacturing Company of Chicago, Illinois called its car the Pioneer.
    The American Cyclecar Company of Detroit, Michigan was absorbed into the Trumbull Motor Car Company which produced the Trumbull.

AMERICAN DARRACQ — Early in 1902 the Kensington Automobile Company of Buffalo, New York began negotiations with Societe A. Darracq of Suresnes, France for production of the Darracq under license in the United States. The negotiations fell through, however, and though a subsequent Kensington had a French look, it was not an American-built Darracq. The Darracq was imported into this country by another firm altogether, the American Darracq Automobile Company, headed by F.A. La Roche.

AMERICAN DE DIETRICH — The American de Dietrich Motor Car Company was organized in New York City in the fall of 1903 by R.E. Jarrige, Louis Frankel and Albert le Maitre. The capital stock was $100,000, and the firm's purpose was the importation of the French de Dietrich automobile to the United States. The presence of the American de Dietrich on rosters of American-built cars is in error; the car was never manufactured here. Earlier in 1903, however, R.E. Jarrige had built an automobile of his own in New York which he called the Alpha. When that venture failed, apparently, he decided automobile importation might be a better route to go.

1900-01 American De Dion Motorette, Doctor's Coupe, HAC

AMERICAN DE DION — Brooklyn, New York — (1900-1901) — Although the French De Dion-Bouton was imported by a number of firms at the turn of the century, there was but a single attempt to manufacture the car in the United States. This was the De Dion-Bouton Motorette Company organized in 1900 by Fred C. Cocheu, James C. Church, P.H. Flynn, C. J. Field and A.A. Halsey, who set themselves up in business at the corner of 37th Street and Church Lane in Brooklyn and secured the necessary license from Kenneth A. Skinner who controlled the U.S. patents for the French organization. "The main talking feature around the display of the Brooklyn company," reported *The Motor Age* in its automobile show edition of 1900, "is the statement that its manufacturing operations are along lines which have been given a thorough test on the other side of the Atlantic and that its mechanical contingency is not merely experimenting." Three models were produced, the Brooklyn Motorette with a single two-passenger seat, the New York Motorette with two facing seats, and "an extremely nobby brougham especially adapted for use by doctors and which is unique because of its neat littleness and lowness in comparison with the large electric brougham." Although C.G. Wridgeway, a former motorcycle racing champion from England, drove one of the prototype American-built De Dions successfully from Brooklyn to Chicago in 1900, obviously similar care in construction was not taken with the production cars, three owners demanding their money back in 1901. The sheriff helped them get it. By January 1902 Kenneth Skinner was advising the trade press that the De Dion-Bouton Motorette Company had violated its contract and that he was now prepared to sell rights for manufacture to anyone "who may wish to take them up." No one did.

1900-1901 AMERICAN DE DION
Brooklyn — 1-cyl., 3-1/2 hp

	FP	5	4	3	2	1
Motorette	850	—	—	—	—	—
New York — 1-cyl., 3-1/2 hp						
Motorette	—	—	—	—	—	—
Doctor's — 1-cyl., 3-1/2 or 5 hp						
Brougham	—	—	—	—	—	—

AMERICAN EAGLE — The car produced by the Eagle Automobile Company of St. Louis, Missouri in 1909 was occasionally called an American Eagle, but more often the Eagle. Refer to Eagle.

AMERICAN ELECTRIC — Chicago, Illinois — (1896-1900)/Hoboken, New Jersey — (1900-1902) — The common assumption has long been that the American Electric Vehicle Company of Chicago was established in 1899. Its first catalog, however, was issued in May 1896, and it was an aggressive sales piece asserting that the American Electric could be run for one-third the cost "per annum of that of horse flesh" because the "cost of attention is greatly reduced," the space it occupied was less, and there was no expense involved when it was standing idle, not being required "to be supplied with oats." The company was making plans for charging stations around Chicago where owners could have their vehicles tended "in the same manner they now have their horses boarded." A letter to a potential customer dated March 31st, 1897 and signed by general manager O.E. Corrigan noted "Montgomery Ward & Co. of this city as one

1899 American Electric, runabout, NAHC

of the most prominent parties who have purchased and used one of our carriages for over a year." The car was offered as a two-seater at $900 and a four-seater at $1250, its range between charges being five hours at a 12 mph pace. Some of the early American Electrics were built for the firm by the Elgin Sewing Machine and Bicycle Company in suburban Chicago. In 1900 the American Electric Vehicle Company was the only U.S. manufacturer to receive a Gold Medal at the Paris Exposition. Unfortunately, the company made a tactical mistake that year, president J. Herbert Ballantine electing to move to New York City (with factory in Hoboken) "to find more wealthy buyers." The line was expanded to include twenty-one body styles (from a "golf trap" to nine varieties of delivery wagon) priced from $1500 to $3500. This ambitious program drove the firm into quick oblivion. By October of 1902 a receiver had been appointed, and in November the American factory was sold for $15,000.

1896-1899 AMERICAN ELECTRIC

	FP	5	4	3	2	1
Two-Seater Runabout	900	1500	2500	3500	5500	9500
Four-Seater Runabout	1250	1600	2600	3600	5600	9600

1900 American Electric, runabout, WLB

1900-1902 AMERICAN ELECTRIC

Road Buggy	1500	1800	2800	3800	5800	9800
Stanhope	1800	1500	2500	3500	5500	9500
Golf Trap	1800	1200	2400	3400	5400	9400
Surrey	2500	2100	3000	4000	6000	10,000
Four-Seater Brake	2500	1800	2800	3800	5800	9800
Six-Seater Brake	3000	1800	2800	3800	5800	9800
Victoria	2500	1600	2600	3600	5600	9600
Four-Seater Brougham	3000	1500	2500	3500	5500	9500
Six-Seater Brougham	3500	1500	2500	3500	5500	9500
Hansom	3000	1400	2400	3400	5400	9400
Eight-Seater Omnibus	3500	1500	2500	3500	5500	9500
Emergency	2500	1100	2200	3300	5300	9300
Light Delivery	1650	1200	2400	3400	5400	9400

AMERICAN ELECTRO-MOBILE — Detroit, Michigan — (1906-1907) — The American Electro-Mobile Company was organized in the East as a combination of small electric firms for the manufacture of an electric car featuring a new storage battery which would provide a traveling radius of 125 miles between charges. The principals involved were W.L. Woodrow as president, C.W. Beaumont as secretary/treasurer, and Frank P. Ray, who claimed to have worked for Thomas Edison, as chief engineer. In November of 1905, Beaumont announced that the recently incorporated concern would build its new factory the following spring, and it seems to have been completed at 1571 River Street in Detroit that summer. No meaningful production ever occurred there, however, in fact the evidence suggests the American Electro-Mobile was built in pilot models only.

1912 American Fiat, model 54, touring, WLB

AMERICAN FIAT — Poughkeepsie, New York — (1910-1918) — The renowned Fiat of Italy was initially imported into this country by O.H. Keep of New York City, followed soon by the firm of Hollander & Tangeman which traded under the name of Hol-Tan Company and also marketed a car under that designation in 1907-1908. Not until 1909 was the idea of manufacturing Fiats in the United States broached, however, and Hol-Tan was not involved. Indeed, Hol-Tan's contract for Fiat importation was abruptly cancelled that year. The new Fiat Automobile Company was financed by Wall Street money and staffed by prominent East Coast automobile men. President was a diamond importer named Ben J. Eichberg, though day-to-day operation would be seen to by vice-president J.S. Josephs. General manager was Albert E. Schaaf from Pope-Toledo; factory superintendent T.C. Collings and his assistant E.J. Gale were from Lozier; chief draftsman Stanley W. Mills was from E.R. Thomas. American Fiat treasurer John Laurie Treas was on the board of directors of *The Horseless Age* magazine in New York, which helped assure a good press for the new car although the Italian Fiat had never suffered a bad U.S. review. Ground was broken for the U.S branch factory in Poughkeepsie, the plant was completed by spring of 1910, and the first American Fiats rolled out shortly thereafter. The four-cylinder Types 54, 55 and 53 were joined by the new six-cylinder 8.6-liter L-head Type 56 which was a U.S. car exclusively, never made or marketed in Europe. The U.S. company held patent rights to all the Italian company's designs; the Italian company received royalties on every American Fiat built. Virtually all parts for the American Fiat were manufactured in Poughkeepsie. Fiat in Italy was calling some of the shots, however. No Poughkeepsie Fiats produced were ever other than big cars; any smaller Fiats desired by an American clientele had to be imported from Italy. And, theoretically, no Poughkeepsie Fiats were allowed to be exported out of the United States because this would impinge upon the Italian Fiat's lucrative markets in England and on the Continent. (One says "theoretically" because a decade ago a Fiat with a Poughkeepsie chassis was discovered in Argentina; and a batch of fifty armored car Type 55 U.S. chassis intended for Csarist Russia but waylaid because of the Revolution were retained in England, rebodied and sold there in 1920 as the new 40/50 Fiat.) Italian Fiats were imported into the U.S. throughout this period, from 1910 to 1914 27% of the Fiats in this country were imported. Most probably the greatest penetration by Fiat into the marketplace was enjoyed during the glory days of its racing, when David Bruce-Brown was America's most daring and mysteriously romantic race driver. In 1915 the Fiat company in Poughkeepsie sued S.G.V., Daniels and Oldsmobile for infringement of its radiator design. In 1917 Fiat in Italy took over the American operation entirely, although some of the larger U.S. stockholders were allowed to retain their interests, vice-president J.S. Josephs among them. By now, however, the war in Europe was raging; Fiat manufacture in the U.S. was discontinued well before the Armistice. In February 1918 the Fiat plant in Poughkeepsie was purchased by Duesenberg Motors Corporation. But the Duesenberg brothers had no plans to manufacture there; they had purchased the plant solely for its machinery which they moved to Elizabeth, New Jersey. Following the Armistice, Fiats continued to be imported into the U.S., though they were never again manufactured in this country.

1910-1911 AMERICAN FIAT
Type 54 — 4-cyl., 30 hp 124" wb

	FP	5	4	3	2	1
Tour.-5P	4000	3500	4500	7000	13,000	25,000

1912 AMERICAN FIAT
Type 54 — 4-cyl., 30 hp, 124" wb

Tour.-5P	4000	4500	5800	9500	18,000	32,000

Type 56 — 6-cyl., 45 hp, 135" wb

Tour.-7P	5100	5400	7300	18,800	25,000	38,000

1913 American Fiat, model 56, touring, HAC

1913 AMERICAN FIAT
Type 54 — 4-cyl., 30 hp, 124" wb

	FP	5	4	3	2	1
Tour.-7P	4000	4500	5800	9500	18,000	32,000
Phae.-5P	4000	4700	6100	9900	19,000	33,000
Limo.	5000	4400	5600	9200	17,300	31,000
Land'et.	5100	4500	5800	9500	18,000	32,000

Type 55 — 4-cyl., 42 hp, 128" wb

Tour.-7P	4500	5000	6500	11,000	22,000	35,000
Phae.-5P	4500	5200	6800	11,300	23,000	36,000
Limo.	5500	4900	6300	10,300	21,000	34,000
Land'et.	5600	5000	6400	10,700	21,500	34,500

Type 56 — 6-cyl., 45 hp, 135" wb

Tour.-7P	5000	5400	7300	11,800	25,000	38,000
Phae.-5P	5000	5800	8000	12,500	28,000	40,000
Limo.	6000	5200	6800	11,300	23,000	36,000
Land'et.	6100	5300	6900	11,400	23,500	36,500

1914 American Fiat, model 55, limousine, HAC

1914 AMERICAN FIAT
Type 53 — 4-cyl., 25 hp, 116" wb

Tour.-5P	4000	2000	3000	5500	11,500	22,000
Rds.	4000	2000	3000	5500	11,500	22,000
Rbt.	4000	2000	3000	5500	11,500	22,000
Limo.	5100	2000	3000	5000	10,000	19,000
Berline	5200	2500	3500	6000	12,000	23,000
Toy Tonneau	4000	2500	3500	6000	12,000	23,000
Cpe.	5100	2000	3000	5000	10,000	19,000
Sed.	5100	2500	3500	4500	9500	18,000
Town Car	4900	2500	3700	5700	9700	18,500

Type 55 — 4-cyl., 42 hp, 128" wb

Tour.-7P	4500	4500	5800	9500	18,000	32,000
Rbt.	4500	4300	5400	8700	16,500	30,000
Limo.	5500	4200	5200	8400	15,700	29,000
Rds.	4500	4700	6100	9900	19,000	33,000
Land'et.	5600	4300	5400	8700	16,500	30,000
Berline	5800	4400	5600	9200	17,300	31,000

Type 54 — 4-cyl., 30 hp, 124" wb

Land'et.	5100	3800	5000	7500	14,000	26,000
Tour.	4000	3800	5000	7500	14,000	26,000
Phae.	4000	4000	5500	8000	16,000	27,000
Rbt.	4000	3800	5000	7500	14,000	26,000
Limo.	5000	3000	4000	5000	11,000	21,000
Berline	5200	4000	5500	8000	16,000	27,000

Type 56 — 6-cyl., 45 hp, 135" wb

Limo.	6000	4300	5400	8700	16,500	30,000
Phae.-5P	5000	5400	7300	11,800	25,000	38,000
Tour.	5000	5300	7000	11,500	24,000	37,000
Rbt.	5000	5400	7200	11,700	24,500	37,500
Land'et.	6100	4500	5800	9500	18,000	32,000
Berline	6300	4700	6100	9900	190,000	33,000

1915 American Fiat, model 55, limousine, HAC

1915 AMERICAN FIAT
Type 53 — 4-cyl., 25 hp, 116" wb

Tour.-5P	4000	2000	3000	5500	11,500	22,000
Rds.	4000	2000	3000	5500	11,500	22,000
Rbt.	4000	2000	3000	5500	11,500	22,000
Limo.	5100	—	—	5000	10,000	19,000
Berline	5200	2500	3500	6000	12,000	23,000
Toy Tonneau	4000	2500	3500	6000	12,000	23,000
Cpe.	5100	2700	3700	4700	9700	19,000
Sed.	5100	2500	3500	4500	9500	17,000
Town Car	4900	2600	3600	4600	9600	18,000

Type 55 — 4-cyl., 42 hp, 128" wb

Tour.-5P	4650	3500	4500	7000	13,000	25,000
Tour.-7P	4650	3500	4500	7000	13,000	25,000
Rds.-2P	4650	3800	5000	7500	14,000	26,000
Rbt.-3P	4650	3800	5000	7500	14,000	26,000

	FP	5	4	3	2	1
Limo.-7P	5650	2500	3500	4500	10,000	20,000
Berline-7P	5950	3500	4500	7000	13,000	25,000
Toy Tonneau-4P	4650	3500	4500	7000	13,000	25,000
Land'et.-7P	5750	3800	5000	7500	14,000	26,000

Type 56 — 6-cyl., 45 hp, 135" wb

	FP	5	4	3	2	1
Tour.-7P	5150	5300	7000	11,500	24,000	37,000
Tour.-5P	5150	5400	7200	11,700	24,500	37,500
Rds.-2P	5150	5400	7300	11,800	25,000	37,000
Rbt.-3P	5150	5300	7000	11,500	24,000	37,000
Limo.-7P	6150	4400	5600	9200	17,300	31,000
Berline-7P	6450	4500	5800	9500	18,000	32,000
Toy Tonneau-4P	5150	5200	6800	11,300	23,000	36,000
Land'et.-7P	6250	5000	6500	11,000	22,000	35,000

1916 American Fiat, model 55, Riviera Touring, HAC

1916 AMERICAN FIAT
Type 56 — 6-cyl., 46 hp, 135" wb

	FP	5	4	3	2	1
Tour.-7P	5350	5400	7300	11,800	25,000	38,000
Rbt.-3P	5350	5200	6800	11,300	23,000	36,000
Limo.-7P	6150	4400	5600	9200	17,300	31,000
Berline-7P	6400	4500	5800	9500	18,000	32,000
Land'et.	6250	4700	6100	9900	19,000	33,000

Type 55 — 4-cyl., 42 hp, 128" wb

	FP	5	4	3	2	1
Land'et.-7P	5750	4700	6100	9900	19,000	33,000
Tour.-7P	4850	5200	6800	11,300	23,000	36,000
Tour.-5P	4850	5300	7000	11,500	24,000	37,000
Rbt.-3P	4850	5200	6800	11,300	23,000	36,000
Limo.-7P	5650	4400	5600	9200	17,300	31,000
Berline-7P	5900	4500	5800	9500	18,000	32,000

1917-1918 AMERICAN FIAT
Type 55 — 4-cyl., 42 hp, 140" wb

	FP	5	4	3	2	1
Land'et.-7P	5750	5000	6500	11,000	22,000	35,000
Tour.-7P	4850	5400	7300	11,800	25,000	38,000
Tour.-5P	4850	5500	7500	12,000	26,000	39,000
Rbt.-3P	4850	5400	7300	11,800	25,000	38,000
Limo.-7P	5650	4500	5800	9500	18,000	32,000
Berline-7P	5900	4700	6100	9900	19,000	33,000

1902 American Gas, runabout, WLB

AMERICAN GAS — Cleveland, Ohio — (1902-1904) — This American from Cleveland was nicknamed the American Gas, and that name appears to have stuck. It was a thousand-pound runabout which featured a single-cylinder water-cooled engine mounted under the seat, planetary transmission, a seven-gallon gas tank good for 150 miles, and a one-inch roller chain providing drive to the rear wheels. It was a neat machine with leather upholstery, body painted "french carmine" and running gear "valentine red." George F. McKay was president, F.D. Dorman vice-president and general manager; J.F. Morris secretary-treasurer; George W. Dunham the engineer; and George H. Wadsworth the superintendent. The company they organized to build the car was incorporated in August of 1901, and was in receivership two summers later. The car's quick demise was due probably to a price far too high ($1000) for the vehicle it bought, a less-than-forward-thinking name for the firm itself (American Motor Carriage Company), and the fact that its factory was a former interior decorating studio, which undoubtedly didn't convert well to automobile manufacture. In late September of 1903 the management of the firm's affairs was turned over to the Prudential Trust Company as receiver, with engineer George W. Dunham being put in charge of the factory to complete the machines on hand, pending a reorganization which never arrived. At the time, a certain claim for distinction was made for the firm in the automotive press; American Motor Carriage was said to be the first automobile company in Cleveland to go broke. It wasn't, but it was the first substantial one to go under. The factory's annual capacity was reported to be 200

cars, though production never reached that lofty realm. The cars for 1904 were slashed to $750, and they sold more readily. But by then it was too late. A new venture called the American Automobile Company moved into the American Motor Carriage studio-cum-factory in April 1904 but no further production ensued.

1902-1903 AMERICAN GAS
1-cyl., 7 hp, 72" wb

	FP	5	4	3	2	1
Rbt.	1000	3500	4500	7000	13,000	25,000

1904 AMERICAN GAS
1-cyl., 7 hp 72" wb

	FP	5	4	3	2	1
Rbt.	750	3500	4500	7000	13,000	25,000

1917 American Junior, WLB

AMERICAN JUNIOR — Lafayette, Indiana — (1916-1920) — The American Motor Vehicle Company of Lafayette couldn't quite make up its mind about what it was building. It had a 70-inch wheelbase with single-cylinder Davis Motor Wheel (widely used to motorize bicycles as well) at the rear of a spartan two-seater body that weighed only 225 pounds. Although the product was ostensibly designed for children (a brochure from 1917 was written in first person by the car), the company took pains to insist that its $160 vehicle was not a toy ("I'm a 'sure-enough' automobile . . .") and was perfectly suited to adults, too. It is doubtful, however, that many motorists past the age of puberty ever drove an American Junior. The American Motor Vehicle Company also planned to produce an invalid car for the domestic market and to give rickshaws a run for their money in China, but most likely did neither before going under. In 1916 the company had designed a small buckboard called the Red Bug using the Smith Motor Wheel, but almost immediately after placing it on the market, sold rights to the design to the A.O. Smith Company which subsequently produced it, as the Smith Flyer. For the 1918 model year the American Motor Vehicle Company did attempt to market a four-cylinder 10/12 hp, 100-inch wheelbase $385 two-passenger roadster into which adults might comfortably fit themselves, as well as a 1000-pound panel truck, for light delivery work. The former was called the Greyhound, the latter the Dumore, but probably by that time the company was too well-known as a builder of juvenile vehicles for anyone older to pay much attention. Neither the Greyhound nor the Dumore was continued in 1919, and the American Junior itself was out of production by the end of 1920.

1916-1917 AMERICAN

	FP	5	4	3	2	1
Junior	—	600	750	1000	1500	2500

1918 AMERICAN

	FP	5	4	3	2	1
Junior	—	600	750	1000	1500	2500
Greyhound	—	600	750	1000	1500	2500
Dumore	—	600	750	1000	1500	2500

1919-1920 AMERICAN

	FP	5	4	3	2	1
Junior	—	600	750	1000	1500	2500

1907 American Juvenile Electric, HAC

AMERICAN JUVENILE — Toledo, Ohio — (1906-1907) — Among the smaller vehicles on display at the National Automobile Show in New York City's Grand Central Palace in November of 1906 was the product of the American Metal Wheel & Auto Company of Toledo. It was a child's electric car with a box body, left-hand tiller steering, a 41-inch wheelbase, and guarantees of 20 miles to a charge and speeds up to 10 mph. It was cute, but it was expensive. Eight hundred dollars was a lot to pay for a child's toy in those days, and was probably the reason American Metal Wheel & Auto Company didn't make it to the show at the Palace the following year.

1906-1907 AMERICAN JUVENILE

	FP	5	4	3	2	1
Juvenile Electric-2S	800	750	1000	1500	2500	3500

1909 American-La France, touring, HAC

AMERICAN-LA FRANCE — Elmira, New York — (1907-1914) — The number of automobiles produced by the American-La France Fire Engine Company is unknown but the activity was strictly extracurricular. At no time did the famous Elmira firm envision realtering its priorities and concentrating on anything other than the production of vehicles for getting to and putting out fires. Interestingly, among the reasons behind the earliest cars — built in 1903 when the company name was International and the cars were called La France — may have been to provide ''training wheels'' for the

1911 American-La France, roadster, JHC

firm which would not motorize its first apparatus until 1907. The La France cars were marketed by Sidney Bowman in New York City. American-La France cars were built to order beginning at approximately the same time the company entered the motorized apparatus field. These passenger vehicles were familiarly called ''chief's cars,'' although probably the ''chiefs'' in whose garages they were housed were often executives of the company. Genuine passenger cars they were, however, and mighty fast. (American-La France contracted with Simplex in New York for the design of its first four-cylinder engine.) No automobiles have been produced by American-La France since World War I. A shaft-drive sport roadster built in 1911 remains in existence and is owned today by Figge International, the parent company of American-La France. Another roadster is owned by a collector in Ohio.

AMERICAN LIQUID AIR — The American Liquid Air Company which was headquartered in New York City at the turn of the century was a flim-flam operation. Refer to Liquid Air.

AMERICAN LOCOMOTIVE — Although several designations were used to refer to the product of the American Locomotive Automobile Company of Providence, Rhode Island, the cars produced from 1906-1908 were most frequently called American Berliets. Refer to American Berliet.

AMERICAN LOCOMOTOR — American Locomotor Manufacturing Company was, for a brief period at the turn of the century, the name of the firm building the Baldwin steam car of Connellsville, Pennsylvania. Refer to Baldwin.

AMERICAN MATHIS — The U.S. version of the French Mathis, planned for 1931 and promoted by a company called American Mathis, Inc., was referred to in brochures as the Mathis and not the American Mathis. Refer to Mathis.

1905 American Mercedes, touring, WLB

AMERICAN MERCEDES — Long Island City, New York — (1905-1907) — William Steinway, who manufactured pianos in New York City, was probably the first American to see the gasoline automobile invented by Gottlieb Daimler. While in Europe in 1888, he learned of Daimler's experimentation in Cannstatt, paid him a visit and secured patent rights to the German inventor's engines and vehicles. Steinway returned home and set up the Daimler Motor Company to produce engines under license in Hartford, Connecticut, but did not proceed to vehicle manufacture because he believed American roads were not suited for automotive travel. When Steinway died in 1896, the company was reorganized as Daimler Manufacturing Company of Long Island City and it engaged in the production of motors, launches and a few commercial vehicles, in addition to importation of the European cars. In 1905, by which time the product of the Daimler company in Germany had changed its name to Mercedes, Daimler Manufacturing in the United States undertook the assembly of an exact reproduction of the 45 hp Mercedes model. The car sold well. A disastrous fire in the Long Island City factory in February 1907 was the reason for its discontinuation. The Mercedes car was among the most stellar in America during this period, and also was widely emulated by a number of American manufacturers anxious to garner a segment of the chic and sporting luxury car market. All Mercedes since the 1907 fire have been imported.

1906 American Mercedes, touring, WLB

1905-1906 AMERICAN MERCEDES
4-cyl., 45 hp, 127'' wb

	FP	5	4	3	2	1
Tour.-7P	7500	9900	19,800	33,000	46,200	66,000

1907 American Mercedes, demi-limousine, HAC

1907 AMERICAN MERCEDES
4-cyl., 45 hp, 127'' wb

	FP	5	4	3	2	1
Tour.-7P	7500	9900	19,800	33,000	46,200	66,000
Demi-Limo.-7P	10,000	8250	16,500	27,500	38,500	55,000

1907 American Mors, touring, WLB

AMERICAN MORS — St. Louis, Missouri — (1906-1909) — The St. Louis Car Company, long famous as the builder of railroad cars, decided to get into the automobile field in 1906 by building a car already famous in France, as well as the more sophisticated automobile circles in the United States. This was the Missouri firm's third try at automobile manufacture, having been preceded in 1905 by a small runabout called the St. Louis, and earlier in 1906 by a Mors-lookalike named for the company president George J. Kobusch. Now, rather than a carbon copy, the St. Louis Car Company decided to produce the real thing. The U.S. license for Mors manufacture in the United States was secured from Paris, together with necessary blueprints and plans, and the American Mors was in production in Missouri later in 1906. Three years following that, the St. Louis Car Company felt equipped to try again with a car of its own design and did so under a new marque name: Standard Six.

1906-1908 AMERICAN MORS
Model A — 4-cyl., 14/18 hp, 103" wb

	FP	5	4	3	2	1
Tour.-5P	3000	3700	4700	7300	13,700	26,000

Model B — 4-cyl., 23/32 hp, 106" wb

Limo.-7P	5500	3100	4200	6300	10,500	22,000

Model C — 4-cyl., 40/52 hp, 120" wb

Tour.-7P	6250	3500	4500	7000	13,000	25,000

1909 American Mors, limousine, HAC

1909 AMERICAN MORS
Model L — 4-cyl., 30 hp, 110" wb

Tour.-5P	2000	3300	4400	6700	12,000	24,000

Model F — 4-cyl., 24/32 hp, 106" wb

Tour.-7P	3250	3100	4200	6300	10,500	22,000
Limo.-7P	3250	2900	3700	5600	9100	20,000

Model K — 4-cyl., 40/50 hp, 120" wb

Tour.-7P	4000	3700	4700	7300	13,700	26,000

AMERICAN MOTOR SLEIGH — Boston, Massachusetts — (1905) — The American Motor Sleigh Company of Boston thought it had the answer to the problem presented by the dismal roads and the dastardly winters of New England, and it was an "ordinary type of gasoline automobile, except that it is on runners." The invention of a "successful Boston lawyer" whose name was not mentioned, the vehicle was sold without an engine, its makers suggesting that any air-cooled unit the purchaser preferred would do. The Motor Sleigh was advertised as "The Novelty of the Year" in 1905, which perhaps it was. The novelty had apparently worn off by 1906.

1905 American Motor Sleigh, HAC

AMERICAN MOTORETTE — Although planned to be called the American Motorette, by the time this cyclecar from Detroit reached the market in early 1914, its name had been changed to Lincoln. Refer to Lincoln Highway.

AMERICAN NAPIER — Boston, Massachusetts — (1904-1905)/Jamaica Plain, Massachusetts — (1905-1912) — The Napier Motor Company of America was a Boston firm which imported the famed English Napier into the United States and, beginning late in 1904, began assembling these cars as well under license from Great Britain. Initially, production was in a small shop in Boston, but it moved to a large factory in Jamaica Plain in mid-1905. Early in 1906 American Napier employees struck the Jamaica Plain factory, citing grievances and aggravation caused by the English superintendent. There were 200 workers in the factory at that time. The strike was settled, and the company got back to work for a time. On the

1904 American Napier, touring, HAC

1906 American Napier, roadster, OCW

standard Napier chassis were offered either British bodies which were imported and priced at $1500 and up, or special American-made bodies at $1000 and up. Despite the attractive price differential provided under the "Buy American" plan, Napier Motor was in trouble again in April of 1907. This time it was financial, and although reorganization was tried that June, it would appear that U.S. assembly had been stopped. In March of 1909, however, production resumed in the same factory by the American Napier Company, a new organization which superseded Napier Motor and secured the same licensing arrangement with the English firm. This venture lasted a year. It was followed in 1911 by another new firm, the British Napier Motor Company of Boston which endured but a year as well in the same Jamaica Plain factory. Of all the American Napiers built in this country, probably the Nike model was the most distinctively American, with some features unakin the British product.

1907 American Napier, roadster, WLB

1904-1907 AMERICAN NAPIER
Model D-45 — 4-cyl., 18 hp, 104" wb

	FP	5	4	3	2	1
Chassis	6000					
Model L — 6-cyl., 30 hp, 108" wb						
Chassis	11,000	—	—	—	—	—
Model H-70 — 4-cyl., 28 hp						
Chassis	7100	—	—	—	—	—
Model D-50 — 4-cyl., 40 hp						
Chassis	10,000	—	—	—	—	—
"Nike" — 4-cyl., 18 hp, 90" wb						
Rbt.-2P	2250	3500	4500	7000	13,000	25,000

1909 American Napier "Nike", runabout, HAC

1909 American Napier, touring, HAC

1909-1910 AMERICAN NAPIER
"Nike" — 4-cyl., 20 hp, 92" wb

	FP	5	4	3	2	1
Victoria-2P	2000	3150	6300	10,500	14,700	21,000
Rbt.-2P	2000	3500	4500	7000	13,000	25,000

Four — 40 hp, 116" wb

	FP	5	4	3	2	1
Toy Tonneau	3500	5250	10,500	17,500	24,500	35,000
Tourbout	3500	5250	10,500	17,500	24,500	35,000
Rbt.	3500	5200	10,000	17,000	24,000	34,000
Six — 60 hp, 126" wb						
Tour.-7P	6000		3700	4700	7300	13,800	25,800

1911-1912 AMERICAN NAPIER
Four — 15/24 hp, 106" wb

	FP	5	4	3	2	1
Model A Rbt.	3200	11,000	22,000	37,000	52,000	74,000
Model B Tour. (118" wb)	3500	2600	3600	5600	8900	19,900
Model 6-30 Tour.	4600	5400	10,800	18,000	25,200	36,000
Six — 75 hp, 134" wb						
Model 6-50 Tour. (134" wb)	6000	11,000	22,000	37,000	52,000	74,000
Model A Land'et.	7000	2600	3600	5200	8700	19,000
Model A Limo.	7000	2000	3000	4500	8000	18,000

AMERICAN PEUGEOT — The American Peugeot was imported from France by the American Peugeot Automobile Company. The car was exhibited at the Regiment Armory Show in New York City in January 1906, which probably accounts for its erroneous appearance on numerous rosters of American-built cars. There was no plan at that time to manufacture the Peugeot in the United States. Interestingly, in 1921 *Automotive Industries* reported that a Peugeot Company of America was planned for the production of Peugeot cars "somewhere in the New England states," but nothing came of that. Six years later, *Automobile Trade Journal* announced that a Peugeot American Corporation had been formed which would bring the cars to this country in the white, the cars to be painted here and given U.S. wheels and tires. Nothing came of this venture either.

AMERICAN PNEUMATIC — The American Vehicle Company was a million-dollar West Virginia incorporation backed by J. Acken, E.F. Slocum, R.H. Hungerford, A.H. Cooke and J.D. Campbell. In February of 1900 the firm announced its intention to build automobiles powered by compressed air. Probably hot air was the company's principal product. Evidence is lacking that even a prototype of the American Pneumatic was built.

AMERICAN POPULAIRE — Sanford, Maine — (1904-1905) The American Automobile and Power Company was incorporated with a capital stock of $500,000 on December 9th, 1903. Eight people were involved in this venture, three of them from Boston, the others residents of Sanford. Ernest M. Goodall, a Sanford man, was president; Henry D. Long, a Bostonian, was treasurer. The company's car was designed by Edward O. Mosher of Boston, the prototype was built in a small shop in Lawrence (Massachusetts) and it was given its public debut at the Boston Automobile Show in March of 1904. The Mosher engine was of decidedly novel construction. "In its design the use of poppet valves to secure admission and exhaust has been discarded and piston valves adopted in their stead," *The Horseless Age* explained. "The valve stems are tubular, and provision is made to automatically circulate air through them in order to keep them cool." Undoubtedly, the car's coachwork was more successful. Its tonneau version was neither side nor rear entrance, niftily doing away with the need for a door at all by the simple expedient of having one-half of its front seat tilt outward to provide entry to the rear compartment. "We could sell one thousand cars in three months if we could make them," treasurer Long enthused to a reporter for the *Sanford Tribune*. It was late March 1904. Already the company had built and equipped a fine factory in Sanford. But the American Populaire was not built there long. In April 1905 the plant was bought by the Maine Alpaca Company and it was thereafter converted into a shed for weaving.

1904 American Populaire, touring, NAHC

1904-1905 AMERICAN POPULAIRE
Twin — 12 hp, 84" wb

Rbt.	850	1500	2500	3600	5500	11,000
Tonneau	950	1800	2800	4000	6200	13,000
Cape Cod Tour.	1000	1900	3000	4300	6500	13,500

AMERICAN POWER — Boston, Massachusetts — (1899-1900) — The American Power Carriage Company of Boston was organized in 1899 and was testing its first motor carriage as the century turned. A single-cylinder gasoline runabout weighing 350 pounds, the American Power had a minimum speed of 25 mph and could reportedly be geared down to a "snail's pace" while the engine was turning at 750 rpm. "This company is a firm advocate of 'carriages on the road' before spreading itself publicly," *Motor Age* reported in January 1900, "and, as there is no stock for sale, the indications are that it is not troubled by the need of money." Apparently it soon was. Available indications are that the company built few more than fifteen cars before going under.

AMERICAN POWER — Boston, Massachusetts — (1899-1900) — The American Power Carriage Company of Boston was organized in 1899 and was testing its first motor carriage as the century turned. A single-cylinder gasoline runabout weighing 350 pounds, the American Power had a minimum speed of 25 mph and could reportedly be geared down to a "snail's pace" while the engine was turning at 750 rpm. "This company is a firm advocate of 'carriages on the road' before spreading itself publicly," *Motor Age* reported in January 1900, "and, as there is no stock for sale, the indications are that it is not troubled by the need of money." Apparently it soon was. Available indications are that the company built fewer more than fifteen cars before going under.

1899-1900 AMERICAN POWER

	FP	5	4	3	2	1
American Power	—	2700	3600	5300	8800	19,000

AMERICAN ROTARY — In the late fall of 1899, the American Rotary Engine Company of 113 Devonshire Street in Boston announced its intention to build an automobile using its gas rotary engine. "The engine may be run at 5000 revolutions per minute resting on a packing box without the slightest vibration," the company said. "The 28-pound engine develops plenty of power to propel any wagon." The boast seems highly exaggerated. By the time the car was put into production, however, the firm had changed its name to Rotary Motor Vehicle Company. Refer to Rotary.

AMERICAN SCOUT — The American Scout was produced in 1912-1913 and was a model of the car manufactured by the American Motors Company of Indianapolis. Refer to American/American Underslung.

1909 American Simplex, 7-pass. touring, WLB

AMERICAN SIMPLEX — Mishawaka, Indiana — (1906-1910) / AMPLEX — (1910-1913) — The Simplex Motor Car Company of Mishawaka was organized in late 1904 by E.J. Gulick and Harry L. Bell. Their first car was put on the road in September of 1905, and was ready for market by the end of the year. The American Simplex was distinguished by three-point suspension of its chassis and a subframe for the running gear which was rigidly fixed to the rear axle, pivoting on the forward spring. The absence of universal couplings was said to permit a permanent and fixed alignment of all working parts. The engine was a four-cylinder two-stroke, which initially developed 40 hp, ultimately 50 hp at 900 rpm. (Advertised horsepower higher than that was grossly exaggerated.) "The American Simplex has no valves because it doesn't need them," the company boasted. "Valves are the bugbear of every owner of any four-cycle automobile, for the reason that they are a constant source of trouble and expense." The trade press was captivated: "Much interest attached to these large and speedy cars," *Cycle & Automobile Trade Journal* said of the 1909 line, following the New York Automobile Show, "because they are the first elaborate and heavy cars to be driven by two-cycle motors." By 1910, however, the people of American Simplex recognized a problem. It was called simply the Simplex, and the New York firm manufacturing that car was considerably better known. In order to gain admission to the Association of Licensed Automobile Manufacturers (of which Simplex was already a member), the American Simplex shortened its name to Amplex in 1910. Both a Simplex and an Amplex entered the first Indianapolis 500 the following year, the former finishing sixth, the latter eighth. The firm itself was reorganized into the Amplex Motor Car Company in 1912, reorganized once more into the Amplex Manufacturing Company in 1914. In the meantime the firm had changed its mind yet again, about the bugbear of a four-stroke, offering one in six cylinders for 1913. Future plans also

1909 American Simplex, limousine, WLB

called for a new model with a sleeve-valve engine, but this was never produced. After 1913 the only cars built were those put together from parts on hand, because Amplex had decided to call it quits. Wrapping up its affairs took some time. William Wrigley of chewing gum fame bought the company in 1914, but he became disenchanted soon after and would remain uninterested in cars until 1919 when attractive overtures came from the Auburn people in Indiana. In 1916 the Amplex plant was purchased by William Gillette of razor renown who remained interested little longer than had Wrigley.

1906-1907 AMERICAN SIMPLEX
Model A — 2-cyl., 40 hp, 106" wb

	FP	5	4	3	2	1
Tour.-5P	2500	3500	4500	7000	13,000	25,000

1908 AMERICAN SIMPLEX
Model 30-50 — 4-cyl., 50 hp, 117" wb

Tour.	4000	5700	11,400	19,000	26,000	38,000
Close-Coupled Tour. Car	4000	5700	11,400	19,000	26,600	38,000
Rds.	4000	5800	11,700	19,500	27,300	39,000
Limo.	5300	2500	3500	5000	8500	18,000
Land'et.	5400	2600	3600	5200	8800	19,000

1909 American Simplex, runabout, WLB

1909 AMERICAN SIMPLEX
Model D-50 — 4-cyl., 50 hp, 117" wb

Tour.-7P	4000	5700	11,400	19,000	26,600	38,000
Tour.-5P	4000	5500	11,000	18,500	26,000	37,500
Limo.	5000	2500	3500	5000	8500	18,000
Rbt.	3800	4000	5000	8000	15,000	28,000

1910 American Simplex, limousine, WLB

1910 AMERICAN SIMPLEX/AMPLEX
Model 35 — 4-cyl., 50 hp, 117" wb

Tour.-7P	4000	6000	12,000	20,000	28,000	40,000
Close-Coupled Tour.-5P	4000	6000	12,000	20,000	28,000	40,000
Rds.	4000	6000	12,000	20,000	28,000	40,000
Limo.	5300	5000	10,000	16,750	23,500	34,000
Land'et.	5400	5000	10,000	16,750	23,500	34,000

1911 Amplex, 5-pass. toy tonneau, WLB

1911 Amplex, 7-pass. touring, WLB

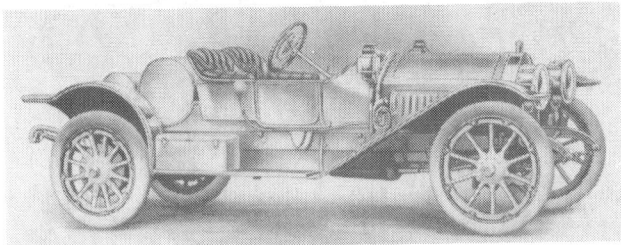

1911 Amplex, roadster, HAC

1911 AMPLEX
Model H — 4-cyl., 50 hp, 128" wb

	FP	5	4	3	2	1
Tour.-7P	4500	6400	9300	14,500	33,000	45,000
Toy Tonneau	4500	6500	9500	15,000	34,000	46,000
Close-Coupled Tour.	4500	6700	9900	15,500	34,800	47,000
Rds.	4500	6800	10,100	15,800	35,200	47,500
Limo.	5650	5800	8000	12,500	28,000	40,000
Land'et.	5650	6300	9000	14,000	32,000	44,000

1912 Amplex, touring, JAC

1912 AMPLEX
Model M — 4-cyl., 30/40 hp, 120" wb

Tour.		2250	4500	5800	9500	18,000	32,000
Rds.		2250	4500	5800	9500	18,000	32,000
Limo.		4000	3500	4500	7000	13,000	25,000
Land'et.		4000		5000	8000	15,000	28,000

Model K — 4-cyl., 50 hp, 128" wb

Tour.		4500	6000	8500	13,000	30,000	42,000
Rds.		4500	6200	8800	13,500	31,000	43,000
Limo.		5800	5800	8000	12,500	28,000	40,000
Land'et.		6000	5900	8300	12,800	29,000	41,000

1913 AMPLEX
Little Six — 6-cyl., 40 hp, 128" wb

Tour.		4500	5000	6500	11,000	22,000	35,000

Baby Amplex — 4-cyl., 40 hp, 120" wb

Tour.		2250	4700	6000	9700	18,500	33,000

AMERICAN SOUTHERN — In 1920 American Southern Motors was organized in Greensboro, North Carolina as an affiliate of the American Motors Corporation of Plainfield, New Jersey to assemble the American Balanced Six for distribution in Dixie — and to build a top-market new car called the Vaughn. Refer to American and Vaughn.

AMERICAN STANDARD — Edwardsville, Missouri — (1914) — "Edwardsville Exploiting New Car" read the headline from October 15th, 1914. The American Standard Automobile Company had just been incorporated with a capital stock of $100,000, of which $50,000 had been paid in. A new factory was being erected on the south side of town, and when finished would see the production of 5000 cars a year. Henry Trares, Jr.,

Judge John E. Hillskotter and Peter Bernhardt of Edwardsville were directors of the new company, along with H.B. Gardner of Chicago. "Six types of cars, to retail at $1375, $1000 and $750, will be manufactured and known as American Standards," the company said. Prototypes only, if that, were built — and the company went under by 1915.

AMERICAN STEAM — In 1853 John Kenrick Fisher established the American Steam Carriage Company in New York City and offered what was perhaps the first automobile for sale to the general public in America. Refer to Fisher.

Although briefly called the American Steam Buggy, the car produced 1898-1899 by the American Waltham Manufacturing Company of Waltham, Massachusetts was predominantly called by the firm's name. Refer to American Waltham.

1936 American Steam Car, MVMA

AMERICAN STEAM CAR — West Newton, Massachusetts — (1926-1942) — A graduate of Harvard and M.I.T., Thomas Derr as a prolific inventor with a proclivity for steam. The service, repair and rebuilding of Stanleys paid most of the rent on his American Steam Car Company plant in West Newton (Alma assisted in 1938 by leasing part of the space), but that was rather unexciting work. Building automobiles was more fulfilling. Derr completed his first American Steam Car (a rebuilt Stanley engine in a Hudson chassis/body) in 1926, and produced more of them whenever anyone asked. Meanwhile he designed his own V-4 poppet valve steam engine and boiler, which represented phase two in his American Steam Car venture. In 1939 historian William J. Lewis (then "an 18-year-old car nut") visited the inventor at the West Newton plant. There he saw two Hudson Eight chassis being converted to Derr steam engines, with raw castings for eight more V-4 steam engines on a nearby pallet. Their internal parts were being machined "on rather ancient lathes and milling machines." The firm's test bench was most unusual: an early 1920's Stanley coupe set on blocks and chained to the floor, with a large cylindrical vertical boiler (about three feet in diameter and five feet high) fitted into the rear deck and a smoke stack rising a foot (folded) or 2½ feet (unfolded) above the roof. This old Stanley was also used for out-of-doors testing and made for a rather remarkable sight on the road. Via this 1939 visit, Bill Lewis could account for twelve Derr V-4 steam engines and estimates that perhaps a half-dozen American Steam Cars were built in the years following to 1942. Thereafter Tom Derr turned his inventive talent to the war effort and helped the Army develop an artificial fog. He died in 1948.

1922 American Steamer, 5-pass. touring, WLB

AMERICAN STEAMER — Chicago & Elgin, Illinois — (1922-1924) — "We have overcome every kink and objectionable feature of the steam car," the company said. "It has taken twenty years of continual experimentation by our engineers to achieve this." One may safely assume neither of those statements to be correct. The American Steam Truck Company was headed by R.R. Howard who launched himself into business first with a steam truck during April of 1922, followed by a passenger car in May. Initially available only as a $1650 touring car, the American Steamer was subsequently also offered as a roadster, coupe and sedan. The car's condenser looked rather Lincoln-like, its engine was a two-cylinder compound double-acting type. An experimental car had been built and tested in 1918, with pictures of it released to the trade press in 1920, five production cars were completed by the end of May 1922, and eleven more followed before year's end. Subsequent production is not known, but the numbers must have been small. The head office of the company was in Chicago, the factory in the western suburb of Elgin. In April of 1924 a petition in bankruptcy was filed against the American Steam Truck Company on claims totaling $15,784. Though the company fought the involuntary receivership, it quickly succumbed. In August American Steam Truck was declared insolvent. Assets were listed at $75,000, liabilities at $141,000.

1922 AMERICAN STEAMER	FP	5	4	3	2	1
Touring	1650	3750	7500	12,500	17,500	25,000
1923-1924 AMERICAN STEAMER						
Touring	1650	3800	8000	13,000	18,000	26,000
Rds.	—	3800	8000	13,000	18,000	26,000
Cpe.	—	2200	3200	4500	7000	14,500
Sed.	—	2000	3000	4000	6500	14,000

AMERICAN TOURIST — The American Tourist was a model produced from 1907-1912 of the American manufactured by the American Motors Company of Indianapolis. Refer to American/American Underslung.

AMERICAN TRAVELER — The American Traveler was a model produced from 1909-1913 of the American manufactured by the American Motors Company of Indianapolis. Refer to American/American Underslung.

The little roadster with tent included which was built by Commonwealth Motors Corporation of Joliet, Illinois from 1919-1922 was called the American Traveler model. Refer to Commonwealth.

1912 American Tri-Car, runabout, WLB

AMERICAN TRI-CAR — Denver, Colorado — (1912) — This automobile from Denver is one of the few cars in American history to boast rear-wheel drive with one-wheel braking. The American Tri-Car was a three-wheeler, with two wheels in front flanking a Renault-type hood that shrouded a two-cylinder air-cooled engine, and one wheel in the rear where all the driving action was. The transmission was planetary. The Tri-Car Company of America introduced its Model A into the marketplace early in 1912. The company went under before the end of the year.

1912 AMERICAN TRI-CAR						
Model A — 2-cyl., 10/12 hp, 82" wb						
Two-Seater Rbt.	385	1000	1800	2800	4200	7000

AMERICAN VOITURETTE — The car produced by the Automobile Company of America in New York City bore the name American Voiturette (or, alternatively, simply American) in the year 1899 only. Thereafter, it was referred to as the Gasmobile. Refer to Gasmobile.

The car produced from 1912-1915 by the American Voiturette Company of Detroit carried the tradename Car-Nation. Refer to Car Nation.

AMERICAN WALTHAM — Waltham, Massachusetts — (1898-1899) — Waltham, Massachusetts lay about ten miles west of Boston, a town famous as the home of the American Watch Company, manufacturers of the celebrated Waltham watch. No doubt, the American Waltham Manufacturing Company was so named to take advantage of the good will of both names. The firm produced the Comet bicycle, and in 1898 built its first steam car which it named the American Waltham. The engine was a two-cylinder, the tubular boiler generated 100 pounds of steam from cold water in less than five minutes. The four-wheel carriage showed American Waltham's bicycle origins. The entire vehicle weighed but 500 pounds; the wheels were thirty inches in diameter, with two-inch pneumatic tires. The gasoline tank held five gallons, the water tank twelve. There were two levers in the driver's compartment, one for steering, the other for starting and changing speed. The company probably built only a handful of these American Waltham steam carriages before electing to return full time to the manufacture of Comet bicycles. This firm, incidently, should not be confused with the Waltham Manufacturing Company, producers of the Orient bicycle, which subsequently built automobiles under both the Orient and Waltham names. Nor with the Waltham Steamer built by two former employees of Waltham Manufacturing.

1898-1899 AMERICAN WALTHAM						
Steam Carriage	—	4000	5000	8000	15,000	28,000

AMERICAN-ZUST — The American-Zust Motor Company was organized in New York City during the spring of 1908 for the manufacture of motorcars, boats, airships and motors. The capital stock was $50,000, and the incorporators were W.F. Sykes, W.F. Sykes, Jr., and L.L. Weber. None of these lofty aims seem to have been realized. The Zust, which was built in Brescia, Italy, was imported into this country for a number of years, but was never manufactured here.

AMERICAR — This was a model of the Willys produced just prior to America's entrance into World War II. Refer to Willys.

AMES — Owatonna, Minnesota — (1895) — On October 11, 1895 the Ames gasoline vehicle was demonstrated on the streets of Owatonna. It was designed by D.J. Ames, president of the Owatonna Manufacturing Company, in collaboration with his partner Frank LaBare, and it featured two cylinders of six-inch bore producing a total of two horsepower. Ames recommended rubber tires for city use, steel tires for the country, and contemplated going into manufacture. Apparently, however, he soon decided against that, purportedly selling the patent rights to his machine to Chicago interests. What may have dissuaded him from entering the motor vehicle industry was the invention of Reuben Disbrow, an employee of the Owatonna Manufacturing Company. This was the famous "Disbrow Combined Churn and Butter Worker" which revolutionized the dairy industry, and which the Owatonna company had begun manufacturing in 1893. Interestingly, another motor vehicle named Ames had also been built in Owatonna in 1895 but it was a steamer built by a local mechanic for one A.C. Ames of Chicago. That D.J. Ames of Owatonna apparently continued to enjoy diversion from the dairy business was indicated by the presence of a four-wheel electric vehicle called the Owatonna Motocycle which was displayed by the Owatonna Manufacturing Company at an 1896 bicycle show in the Minneapolis Exposition Building. Like the gasoline car, however, this electric never was put into production.

AMES — Owatonna, Minnesota — (1895) — A.C. Ames of Chicago, had his heart set on entering the famed Chicago Times-Herald Contest of November 1895. Unfortunately, his car wasn't quite ready on time. The Ames was a singularly unattractive vehicle, with a decided look of having been put together in a backyard. Which it was, built for Ames by a mechanic named Nichols in Owatonna, Minnesota. Inbetween two bicycle frames, Nichols had inserted a simple box, mounting two steam engines of the oscillating type on the lower bars of each bicycle frame and coupling them to the pedal shaft by means of ball-bearing crank pins. The use of ball bearings throughout, and tires that were pneumatic, marked the forward-thinking features of this pram-on-wheels. Conceivably the drive to the rear wheels was the vehicle's undoing; pictures indicate the car might have been happiest driving in circles. Nonetheless, in December 1895 Ames announced from Chicago that he was in the process of organizing the Ames Motor Cycle Company for $100,000 in order to proceed into manufacture. He was not heard from again.

1895 Ames, auto-buggy, NAHC

AMES — Lowell, Massachusetts — (1904) — During the fall of 1904 a gentleman who was described by *Automobile Review* as the "Hon. Butler Ames" was driving the 30 hp car he had designed and built himself in Lowell. Aside from the fact that, according to the magazine, the car attracted a "great deal of attention," nothing further is known about it.

AMES — Owensboro, Kentucky — (1910-1915) — Frederick A. Ames moved from Washington (Pennsylvania) to Owensboro in 1887 and opened a carriage repair shop which by 1904 had grown into the Carriage Woodstock Company, a thriving buggy manufacturing business with factories in two locations. The Ames motorcar was introduced in 1910 and was offered with just one chassis, one engine and two body styles. Vincent Bendix saw the new car at the Chicago Automobile Show and persuaded F.A. Ames to hire him to handle the company's automobile division and to improve its product. How long Bendix remained with Ames is not known.

With a fresh infusion of capital in 1912, the Carriage Woodstock Company was revamped into the Ames Motor Car Company, and the line was expanded into three wheelbases and three engines, though the body styles offered remained the same two. Shortly thereafter, the company returned to its one-chassis/one-engine philosophy, but had a difficult time figuring out which engine it should be. That the Ames was a most meritorious vehicle is indicated by the fact that after a test ride a Texas automobile dealer ordered a lot of fifty because the Ames was the "best $1500 car" in the entire country. During most of its production life, output was fifty units monthly. The last models were called Kentucky Thoroughbred, which *The Automobile* found appropriate: "The car lives up to its nickname . . . by its smooth lines, clean running board and general racy appearance." The schizophrenic life of the Ames motorcar was over in 1915. But the company continued. From that year through 1925, as the Ames Body Corporation, it made replacement bodies for Model T Fords. In 1922 Ames dropped the Body from its name because Ames Corporation switched gears, and began manufacturing upholstered living room furniture. Ames survived in this business until about 1970 when its machinery and assets were acquired by Whitehall Furniture.

1910 AMES
Thirty — 4-cyl., 30 hp, 108" wb

	FP	5	4	3	2	1
Model No. 4 Touring	1500	2500	3500	5000	8500	18,000
Model No. 5 *	1500	3000	4000	6000	9500	21,000

* Gentleman's Rds.

1911 Ames, roadster, WLB

1911 AMES
Thirty — 4-cyl., 30 hp, 108" wb

Tour.	1575	2500	3500	5000	8500	18,000
Rds.	1475	3000	4000	6000	9500	21,000

Forty — 4-cyl., 40 hp, 119" wb

Tour.	2000	3500	4500	7000	13,000	25,000

1912 AMES
Model No. 32 — 4-cyl., 30 hp, 112" wb

Tour.	1250	3000	4000	6000	9500	21,000
Rds.	1250	3200	4200	6400	9800	21,500

Model No. 42 — 4-cyl., 40 hp, 116" wb

Tour.	1600	3500	4700	6700	10,500	23,000
Rds.	1600	3700	5000	7000	11,000	24,000

Model No. 52 — 6-cyl., 50 hp, 124" wb

Tour.	2000	3800	5200	7500	11,500	25,000

1913 AMES
Forty — 4-cyl., 40 hp, 118" wb

Model 45 Tour.	1785	3500	4700	6700	10,500	23,000
Model 44 Rds.	1745	3700	5000	7000	11,000	24,000

1914 Ames, touring, WLB

1914 Ames, Kentucky Thoroughbred, roadster, WLB

1914-1915 AMES
Model 45 — 4-cyl., 40 hp, 118" wb

	FP	5	4	3	2	1
Kentucky Tour.*	1785	3000	4000	6000	9500	21,000
Kentucky Rds.*	1745	3300	4500	6500	10,000	22,000

* Thoroughbred

AMES DEAN — Jackson, Michigan — (1909-1910) — The Ames-Dean was a highwheeler produced alongside the horsedrawn buggies of the Ames-Dean Carriage Company of Jackson. Production began during the fall of 1909, at which time the firm indicated its intention to build 200 motor buggies. Whether indeed that many were produced before their manufacture was discontinued the following year has not been documented.

1909-1910 AMES DEAN

Ames Dean	—	1500	2500	3600	5500	14,000

AMESBURY — Although occasionally referred to as the Amesbury in 1902-1903, the product of the Boston & Amesbury Manufacturing Company of Amesbury, Massachusetts was officially designated the Boston-Amesbury. Refer to Boston-Amesbury.

The Amesbury Auto Company of Amesbury, Massachusetts has frequently been cited as a manufacturer in 1915. City directories from 1913 through 1917 indicate the presence of no company by that name in Amesbury.

AMESBURY — Amesbury, Massachusetts — (1899) — At the turn of the century, Amesbury was among the leading carriage-manufacturing centers in the United States. Organized in the fall of 1899, with a capital stock of $150,000, was the Amesbury Automobile Company. Involved in the venture were a number of local carriage builders, including J.T. Clarkson, C.F. Worthen and Edward R. Briggs. Chief engineer was C.J. Bagley, a well-known electrician in town, who had designed an electric motor which was claimed to be "the lightest and most efficient appliance yet built." Prospects bode well for this venture. "There are no better carriages in the world than those built in Amesbury," *The Motor Review* stated, "and its high reputation will give to the new company a prestige that a town of lesser reputation cannot acquire for years." It appears that the Amesbury Automobile Company proceeded no further than the building of a prototype or two, however, before the carriage makers involved returned to their horsedrawn efforts and Bagley to his general electrical work.

AMPER — The Amper Electric Company was incorporated with a capital stock of $25,000 in Lockport, New York early in 1913. The organizers were T.D. Robinson, E.W. Jones and C.L. Nichols. Initially the partners indicated their plans to include the manufacture of an electric automobile; within a month, however, they decided instead to confine their efforts to dealing in same, and also to electric auto locks and switches.

AMPLEX — The Amplex was a continuation of the American Simplex, the name change effected in 1910 in order for the Simplex Motor Car Company of Mishawaka, Indiana to gain admission to the Association of Licensed Automobile Manufacturers. The car was produced into 1913. Refer to American Simplex/Amplex.

1917 Ams-Sterling, roadster, WLB

AMS-STERLING — Amston, Connecticut — (1917) — Charles W. Ams manufactured food processing equipment as president of the Max Ams Machinery of Bridgeport, Connecticut. His sideline into automobiles began in the fall of 1916 when he bought out the Sterling Automobile Manufacturing Company, erstwhile producers of the Sterling-New York. Several years earlier Ams had acquired F.W. Turner's silk mills in Hebron, Connecticut, and it was into this facility that Ams moved his automotive venture. The mill village, which had previously been called Turnersville, was now renamed Amston. And the new car would be called the Ams-Sterling. A Le Roi four-cylinder engine powered Charles Ams' car, as it had the Sterling-New York, but Ams had the wheelbase lengthened from 102 to 110 inches, made detail changes in the body, and raised prices twenty-five percent. He assumed that all bugs in the car had been ironed out during its Sterling-New York days, but such was not the case. His chief engineer, H.P. Arndt, perpetually revised production schedules as he attempted to make things right. In March 1917 estimates were for an output of 15 cars a month, with ten times that number by September. How unalloyed was that optimism. Probably no more than thirty fully-completed Ams-Sterlings were ever produced in Amston. One potential customer saw the car at the New York Automobile Show, ordered one for a contemplated transcontinental trip (which would have been fine publicity), but then cancelled when delivery could not be made on time. Perhaps he was lucky because the evidence suggests that those who did take delivery of Ams-Sterlings had problems aplenty. One disgruntled owner, returning his car to the factory for repairs, appended a sarcastic P.S. to his letter: "If you are able to dispose of my wonderful roadster, please do so as I would gladly part with same." Another wrote that his doctor had informed him that he'd best sell the car "as it is ruining my health and, incidentally, my pocketbook." On another occasion an Ams-Sterling owner was advised that no wiring diagram existed since each car was wired differently, however, "if you made the connection on the new coil the same as was on the old coil, we see no reason why this coil should not work properly as the old coil was working all right when it left here after we had done considerable work on your car." It would appear that all of the Amstons built by June 1917 had to be recalled by the factory to correct one ailment or another. An internal memo hoped that "the 1918 line would catch on." In September 1917 the firm was officially named the Amston Motor Car Company. Hope sprang eternal with grandiose plans for a luxury car to be called the Royal Amston for which Charles Ams had a sterling silver nameplate designed, but that was as far as the luxury Ams-Sterling idea went. In January 1918 *Motor Age* listed the Ams-Sterling as "among those whose names are not included in the rolls for 1918." Charles Ams sold his Amston factory to a Meriden, Connecticut silversmith and returned to his Bridgeport food processing equipment business completely. Another Sterling automobile arrived in Connecticut in 1920 but whether it rose out of the ashes of Charles Ams' venture is not known.

1917-1918 AMS-STERLING
Four — 28 hp, 110" wb

	FP	5	4	3	2	1
Tour.	845	1500	2500	3600	5500	11,000
Rds.	825	1800	2800	3800	5800	11,800

AMSTERDAM — Amsterdam, New York — (1902) — The Amsterdam Automobile Works announced its incorporation in the New York State city of that same name in mid-summer of 1902. Timothy H. Pettengill, who was described as a former General Electric employee, was vice-president. "A sample vehicle is being made, which will use many of Mr. Pettengill's patents," *The Automobile and Motor Review* reported. Undoubtedly it was the only car built. The company was not further heard from.

AMSTUTZ-OSBORN — Cleveland, Ohio — (1900-1902) — "A gasoline carriage of original design is nearing completion in the shops of the Amstutz-Osborn Company," *The Horseless Age* reported in October of 1900. This would be the first of several cars built by the machine shop for budding automobile inventors of Cleveland. Amstutz-Osborn did not build a car of its own complete design until 1902, a gasoline runabout which was planned to be marketed under the name of Durabile. The company was also developing a steam generator at that time for a firm in London, England named Dawson. Machine work, rather than automobile manufacture, remained the primary focus of Amstutz-Osborn.

AMUSEMENT — The Amusement Company was a $22,000 Delaware incorporation from the summer of 1906. George M. Harton, W.F. Henninger and T.M. Harton of Pittsburgh were among the organizers of this venture, joined by C. MacKalip of Wilkinsburg, Pennsylvania. The partners' plan was "to manufacture and deal in automobiles, nickelodeons, carousels and other amusements." Early on, automobiles were deleted.

ANAHUAC — Indianapolis, Indiana — (1922) — The Anahuac was an attempt by the Frontenac Motor Company of Indianapolis to enter the export field. Four examples of a four-cylinder touring car on a 115-inch wheelbase were produced for Compania Automobiles Anahuac de Mexico of Mexico City. Ultimately, manufacture was planned for Mexico, but the Anahuac venture never left Indianapolis. Curiously, the car was purported to have been based upon the design of an unidentified automobile then being built in Poland.

ANCHOR — Cincinnati, Ohio — (1910-1911) — The Anchor Motor Car Company was the automotive branch of the Anchor Carriage Company of Cincinnati. Unlike most Midwest builders of horse-drawn vehicles, Anchor was a late entry in the automotive field. Its first product did not betray any buggy origins, but was a "touring car of modern design" with a 35 hp four-cylinder T-head engine and attractive styling. Since its first product was also its last, the company might have been wiser to have started earlier and easier.

1910-1911 ANCHOR

Anchor Thirty-Five Tour.	1850	4400	8700	14,500	20,300	29,000

1910 Anchor, touring, GR

ANDERSON — Bedford, Indiana — (1906) — By the time the trade press became aware of the Anderson from Bedford, it was already on its way to becoming something else. A two-cylinder air-cooled runabout with high wheels and solid tires, the car was sold for about six months in small quantities by the Anderson Machine Company. The first published references to the car were in October 1906. The second public references were in November and recorded its demise. The company and its assets were subsequently taken over by Fred Postal who manufactured another highwheeler under his own name in the same factory.

1906 ANDERSON
2-cyl., 12 1/2 hp

	FP	5	4	3	2	1
High Wheel Rbt.	450	2000	3000	4200	6500	14,000

1909 Anderson, Model A, highwheeler auto-buggy, WLB

ANDERSON — Anderson, Indiana — (1907-1910) — Truth in advertising was well served by the Anderson Carriage Manufacturing Company in Indiana. "The Anderson is a motor buggy. It isn't meant to be anything else," the brochure said. "It is not offered as something to take the place of a touring car, or a racing machine. It is built to fill a certain want." This meritorious little example of the highwheeler genre had a two-cylinder air-cooled engine and featured friction drive, wheel steering, 36-inch diameter wheels with solid rubber tires. Offered in Models A (straight dash, no lights) and B (angle dash, with lights), Anderson also reluctantly made available a Model C "with low wheels and pneumatic tires, simply as a concession to a tradition of the trade." History has proven the company's reluctance was ill advised. A 1909 Anderson is on display at the Frederick C. Crawford Auto-Aviation Museum in Cleveland, Ohio.

1909 Anderson, Model B, highwheeler auto-buggy, WLB

1907-1909 ANDERSON
2-cyl., 12 hp, 72" wb

Model A Motor Buggy	500	2500	3500	5000	8500	18,000
Model B Motor Buggy	525	2500	3500	5000	8500	18,000
Model C Motor Buggy	650	2500	3500	5000	8500	18,000

1910 ANDERSON
2-cyl., 14 hp, 72" wb

	FP	5	4	3	2	1
Model E Motor Buggy	575	2500	3500	5000	8500	18,000
Model H Motor Buggy	600	2500	3500	5000	8500	18,000
Model G Limo. Motor Buggy	600	2600	3800	5500	9000	19,000

ANDERSON — Los Angeles, California — (1908) — The Anderson from Los Angeles was short-lived. In March of 1908, *The Motor World* reported that N.M. and Fred Anderson had recently completed a test run of their prototype motor buggy from Southern California into Mexico, and were now "making arrangements for . . . manufacture." Possibly those arrangements were completed and a few Anderson motor buggies were produced in Los Angeles, but no company was ever incorporated for manufacture, nor does it appear the Andersons continued their automotive venture into 1909.

1908 ANDERSON

Anderson Motor Buggy	—	1500	2500	3600	5500	11,000

1916 Anderson, Six-40, touring, HAC

ANDERSON — Rock Hill, South Carolina — (1916-1925) — "A Little Bit Higher in Price, but Made in Dixie!" was a slogan of the company and a succinct summation of the marque. The Anderson was among the best built, and the most successful and long-lived, of all the cars built in the South. Its origins dated back to 1889 when the Holler and Anderson Buggy Company was established in the back of a furniture store in Rock Hill. The furniture store belonged to the Holler family, and John Gary Anderson had married one of the Holler girls. Initially repair and rebuilding of carriages and wagons occupied the firm but by the turn of the century, the Rock Hill Buggy Company was founded for the manufacture of horse-drawn vehicles. And Rock Hill was the name given to the company's first automotive effort, a toy tonneau produced in 1910 which was not successful, the company returning exclusively to its horsedrawn business for the next two years. In 1913, however, a line of commercial bodies for horseless vehicles (adaptable especially to the Model T Ford) was introduced — and by 1916 John Gary Anderson believed himself ready to give the automobile industry another try. He imported Joseph Anglada from New York City as his chief engineer. Anglada was available because the cyclecar he had designed in 1914 called the Liberty had failed within a year. He would be much more successful with the Anderson, which he designed as a typical assembled car (Continental six-cylinder engine) but an especially good one. What Anderson added was the coachwork, and it was exemplary in quality of finish and the quite unusual array of color combinations offered during this generally drab era in the industry. The Anderson automobile was announced in March of 1916, and the Anderson Motor Company was incorporated that December. Initial acceptance of the car was excellent, and profitable government contracts helped the company ride out the difficult war years. In 1920 Anderson had its best year thus far, 1180 units produced; in 1923 it surpassed that with an output of 1875 cars. A new offering during the latter year was the Model 41 "Coachbilt (sic) Anderson Aluminum Six," base priced at $1195, which the company advertised as the world's lowest-priced aluminum-bodied car. But Anderson faltered thereafter. Too many special or gimmicky bodies during the firm's later years were among the problems. Engine failures in the Model 41 and the oppressive competition being dealt out by the Model T were further contributing factors. A factory fire in 1924 resulted in $40,000 in damages and a damaging production shutdown. Sometime during 1925, after Anderson produced its 6300th car, the company breathed its last.

1918 Anderson, Six-40, touring, HAC

1916 ANDERSON
Six-40 — 6-cyl., 25 hp, 118-1/2" wb

	FP	5	4	3	2	1
Tour.-5P	1250	3500	4500	7000	13,000	25,000
Racer-2P	1250	3800	4800	7500	13,500	26,000
Rds.-2P	1235	3800	4800	7500	13,500	26,000

1917-1918 ANDERSON
Six-40 — 6-cyl., 25 hp, 120" wb

	FP	5	4	3	2	1
Tour.-5P	1250	3800	4800	7500	13,500	26,000
Tour.-6P	1250	3800	4800	7500	13,500	26,000
Rds.-4P	1275	4000	5000	8000	15,000	28,000

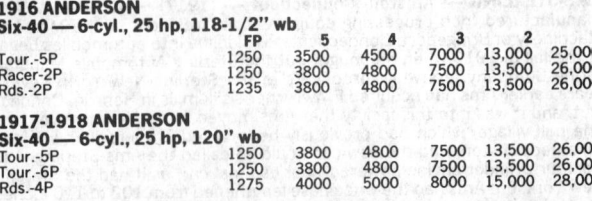

1919 Anderson Ultra, convertible sport, HAC

1919 ANDERSON
Six — 6-cyl., 25 hp, 120" wb

	FP	5	4	3	2	1
Conv. Spt.	1675	4000	5000	8000	15,000	28,000
Tour.-7P	1675	4000	5000	8000	15,000	28,000
Tour.-5P	1675	4000	5000	8000	15,000	28,000
Conv. Sed.	2550	4000	5000	8000	15,000	28,000
Ultra-Conv. Sed.	2450	4200	5300	8500	15,500	28,500
Spt. Tour.-4P	2450	4500	5500	8700	15,800	29,000

1920 ANDERSON
Model S-30 — 6-cyl., 55 hp, 120" wb

	FP	5	4	3	2	1
Tour.-5P	1775	4000	5000	8000	15,000	28,000
Tour.-7P	1850	4000	5000	8000	15,000	28,000
Spt.-4P	1835	4500	5500	8500	15,500	28,500
Conv. Rds.	1775	4200	5200	8200	15,300	28,400
Sed.-5P	2650	3000	4000	6000	9500	21,000
Cpe.-4P	2550	3500	4500	7000	13,000	25,000

1921 Anderson, model D, roadster, WLB

1921 Anderson, model B, coupe, WLB

1922 Anderson, model G, 4-pass., sport touring, WLB

1921 ANDERSON
Model S-40 — 6-cyl., 55 hp, 120" wb

	FP	5	4	3	2	1
Tour.-5P	1245	4000	5000	8000	15,000	28,000
Rds.-4P	2175	4200	5300	8500	15,500	28,500
Tour.-7P	2195	4000	5000	8000	15,000	28,000
Rds.-2P	2195	4100	5200	8300	15,300	28,300
Cpe.-4P	3200	3500	4500	7000	13,000	25,000
Sed.-5P	3200	3000	4000	6000	9500	21,000

1922 ANDERSON
Model S-40 — 6-cyl., 55 hp, 120" wb

Tour.-5P	1650	4200	5300	8500	15,500	28,500
Conv. Rdstr.	1650	4500	5500	8700	16,000	29,000
Tour.-7P	1795	4000	5000	8000	15,000	28,000
Sport-4P	1750	4200	5400	8600	15,800	28,800
Sport Special-4P	1850	4500	5500	8700	16,000	29,000
Speedster-2P	2195	4600	5700	9000	16,500	29,500
Ultra Sport-4P	2395	5000	6500	10,000	17,000	30,000
Coupe-4P	2450	3500	4500	7000	13,000	25,000
Sedan-5P	2550	3000	4000	6000	9500	21,000

1923 Anderson, touring, WLB

1923 ANDERSON
Aluminum Six — 50 hp, 114" wb

Tour.-5P	1195	4000	5000	8000	15,000	28,000
Coach-4P	1450	2000	3000	4200	6500	14,000
Cpe.-2P	1325	2500	3500	5000	8500	18,000
Sed.-5P	1595	2200	3200	4500	7000	14,500

Big Six — 60 hp, 122" wb

Tour.-7P	1395	4200	5300	8500	15,500	28,500
Spt. Tour.-4P	1945	4500	5500	9000	16,000	29,000
Sed.-5P	1995	2500	3500	5000	8500	18,000

1924 Anderson, model 41, sedan, HAC

1925-26 Anderson, model 50, sedan, HAC

1924 ANDERSON
Model 41 — 6-cyl., 50 hp, 114" wb

	FP	5	4	3	2	1
Tour.-5P	1195	4000	5000	8000	15,000	28,000
Cpe.-2P	1425	2500	3500	5000	8500	18,000
Coach-4P	1495	2000	3000	4200	6500	14,000
Sed.-5P	1695	2200	3200	4500	7000	14,500

1925-1926 ANDERSON
Model 50 — 6-cyl., 60 hp, 122" wb

Tour.-5P	1195	4200	5300	8500	15,500	29,000
Spec. Tour.-4P	1445	4500	5500	9000	16,000	29,500
Cpe.-2P	1425	2500	3500	5000	8500	18,000
Sed.-5P	1695	2200	3200	4500	7000	14,500
Spec. Sed.-5P	1895	2500	3500	4700	7500	15,000
Tour.-7P	1595	4200	5300	8500	15,500	29,000
Sed.-7P	1945	2500	3500	4500	7000	14,500

ANDERSON ELECTRIC — In 1907 the Anderson Carriage Company of Detroit began building an electric car, and in 1911 the firm's name was changed to Anderson Electric Car Company. Its car, however, was never known as the Anderson Electric; Detroit Electric was its name from the beginning. Finally, in 1919, the company name changed to Detroit Electric Car Company too. Refer to Detroit Electric.

ANDERSON STEAM CARRIAGE — **Anderson, Indiana** — **(1901-1902)** — J.Q. and A.C. Shimer were the proprietors of the Anderson Steam Carriage Company and the designers of the Anderson Steam Carriage which, they said, had many novel features. Its marine-type engine was claimed to be "the only slide valve engine of this class that has only one throttle valve answering the purpose of reversing and manipulating the throttle." The boiler was the usual water-tube type, though it was so constructed as to allow cleaning without the removal of the pipes. In the spring of 1901 the Shimers advised *The Motor Vehicle Review* that they had passed the experimental stage and were booking orders. How many orders were filled before the company went under in 1902 is not known.

ANDERSON STEAMER — **Painesville, Ohio** — **(1873)** — Leonard Anderson of Painesville was reported to have built a steam car in 1873. He very well might have, though this has not been substantively documented. Anderson is known to have been an inventor, and he operated a machine shop. At his death at age seventy-six in 1903, however, his obituary in the local newspaper did not mention his building of an automobile.

ANDERSON STEAMER — **South Boston, Massachusetts** — **(1899)** — In 1899 Albert and J.M. Anderson of 289 A Street in South Boston announced their plans to produce a steam car under the Whitney patents. A single car appears to have been completed. The presence of their Anderson Manufacturing Company in the Hiscox book *Horseless Vehicles, Automobiles, Motor Cycles* published in 1900 was a case of undue optimism. There is no evidence that the Anderson steamer ever moved into production.

ANDOVER — **Andover, Massachusetts** — **(1915-1917)** — That a 1 1/2-ton electric truck was produced in Andover from 1915 to 1917 has been documented, but any electric cars built were experimental and never marketed. The venture was apparently a rather unstable one, since the firm began as the Andover Motor Vehicle Company and metamorphosed into the Andover Electric Truck Company as well as the Joly & Lambert Electric Company during its short sojourn in the industry.

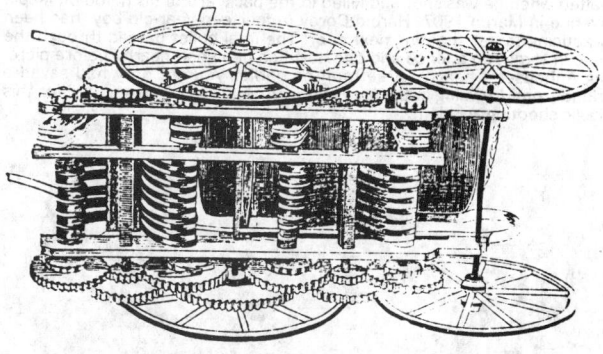

1895 Andrews Spring Motor Car, WLB

ANDREWS — **Center Point, Iowa** — **(1895)** — A.B. Andrews designed and built a baby carriage powered by a spring motor. He envisioned this method of propulsion as eminently suitable to any vehicle. It was described thusly: "The device is attached under the hind axle, one piece on each side. These pieces for a wagon are six feet in length. At each end are two main driving shafts which mesh with cog wheels. The springs are wound with levers. By throwing on the winding gear the mechanism will wind itself up while going down hill, or by setting it into combination it will wind itself up. It winds up six times as fast as it runs down. The amount of power Mr. Andrews says he secures is six horse, 2 1/2 horse to wind up, and 2 1/2 horse to draw the load. There is one spring to wind all the time, and five to wind one up and pull the load." A.B. Andrews announced his plans to build a full-size vehicle for entry in the Chicago Times-Herald Contest in November of 1895. But his spring motor carriage never made it to the starting line.

ANDREWS — San Diego, California — (1899) — In 1899 W.W. Andrews of San Diego produced an air motor which he immediately applied to a carriage. When the vehicle was tested, according to a local report, the expansion of air in the motive unit produced such intense cold that "the engine was at once covered with ice and the pipes were frozen solid." W.W. Andrews remained undeterred, however, though his efforts met with some derision in the East Coast press. Commenting on the Andrews' plan in October 1899, *The Motor Age* noted sarcastically, "The inventor will now apply a coil heater to overcome the cold, and by the time when he shall have learned the common phenomena of latent heat (and cold) will probably have a motor as complicated and unsatisfactory as that which was recently discarded on the street railway cars on Twenty-ninth and Thirty-first streets in New York City." The *Motor Age* judgment was harsh, but probably correct.

ANGELES — Although referred to occasionally in the trade press as an Angeles, (sometimes Angelus) this cyclecar built by L.E. French was never formally called that. Instead it was initially the California, and was renamed Los Angeles when fresh financial backing was found and the Los Angeles Cycle Car Company was established in 1913 in Compton, California. Refer to Los Angeles.

ANGELUS — Angelus was the name given by the Mission Motor Car Company of Los Angeles for the roadster model it planned to manufacture in 1914. Refer to Mission.

ANGER — From 1913 to 1915, Walter A. Anger built four- and six-cylinder automobiles in Milwaukee, Wisconsin. Whether to name the cars after himself or the initials of his Anger Engineering Company seems to have confounded him — and he called the cars both. Refer to A.E.C.

ANGHEIN — Bourbon, Indiana — (1899) — According to a December 1899 issue of *The Autobain*, the man's name was M.J. Anghein and he was a "mechanical genius." His car weighed 910 pounds and cost $350 to build; it would accommodate five passengers and travel at a speed of 18 mph. Manufacture, its inventor said, would begin soon. Another trade reference *(The Motor Vehicle Review)* from that same month alludes to his genius but indicates the man's name to be Anglin and his car's weight to be 900 pounds. Whoever he was, and however weighty his automobile, he did not proceed into manufacture.

ANGLADA — Anglada was the name of its designer. The cyclecar that Joseph Anglada built in 1914 in New York was called the Liberty. Refer to Liberty.

ANGLO-AMERICAN — The Anglo-American Rapid Vehicle Company was established in New York City in 1900 with the declared intention of manufacturing cars in the Barnes bicycle plant in Syracuse. The man behind Anglo-American was Edward Joel Pennington, one of the greatest con artists in American automobile history. Refer to Pennington.

ANHEUSER — Green Bay, Wisconsin — (1905) — Early in 1905 Mathias Anheuser, who was employed as a mechanic in the machine works of C.A. Straubel in Green Bay, completed what *Cycle and Automobile Trade Journal* referred to as "the first model of a two-cylinder gasoline runabout which he has designed." Its wheelbase was 58 inches, and its total weight 650 pounds. "Three and a half gallons of gasoline will run the car 100 miles," the magazine said, and its top speed was 20 mph. Any future plans Anheuser might have had with regard to manufacture were tragically halted when he was shot and killed in the backyard of his home on Maple Avenue in March 1907. Harold Corey, a fourteen-year-old boy, had been practicing target shooting next door. The fatal bullet passed through the tin can target on a fence and one partition of a shed nearby before piercing Anheuser's heart. Three months earlier young Corey had saved a friend from drowning in the icy Fox River. He was not prosecuted for this tragic shooting accident.

© 1925 Anheuser-Busch "Bevo-Boat," JAC

ANHEUSER-BUSCH — St. Louis, Missouri — (1917 et seq.) — In 1903 the Anheuser-Busch Brewing Association of St. Louis experimented with the idea of delivering beer by horseless carriage. The two trucks ordered built that year were electrically powered and said to be the largest of the kind in the world. Twenty-four feet long and ten feet wide, they had a capacity of 30,000 pounds worth of brew, and didn't work out at all well. Subsequently, Anheuser-Busch did go automotive with a better idea for delivery, and inaugurated a vehicle department itself which designed and manufactured truck and bus bodies. This was a particularly advantageous activity during those years when the company's principal product was not legal. During World War I, with the arrival of Prohibition, Anheuser-Busch also marketed a new non-alcoholic concoction of barley malt, rice, hops,

yeast and water called Bevo (from the Bohemian word "pivo" for beer). To promote this beverage, the company had a special automobile built on a Pierce-Arrow chassis, an unusual vehicle with a distinct mariner appearance which was dubbed the Bevo Boat. During the war, the Bevo Boat was used to promote the sale of war bonds. After the Armistice, two further versions were produced, the last during the mid-Twenties. With the repeal of Prohibition in 1933, Bevo the beverage was discontinued and the Bevo Boat was rechristened "the Budweiser car."

1910 Anhut, roadster, HAC

ANHUT — Detroit, Michigan — (1909-1910) — The man behind the Anhut was Michigan State Senator John Anhut, and Detroit's Mayor Breitmeyer was apparently also involved. The Anhut Motor Car Company was incorporated in October of 1909, the pilot model of its light six was on the road that same month, and the first units were off the production line in Detroit as the year ended. These were assembled cars with Brownell engines, but they were very favorably reviewed in the press. Reporter C.E. Morris of *Cycle & Automobile Trade Journal* took an Anhut for a test drive and was most impressed by its "smooth, sweet action . . . At slow speeds especially, the motor is notably sweet in performance, and there is an absence of that pounding and vibration typical of the four on very slow speed." Early sales were so encouraging that in April of 1910, the com-

1910 Anhut, roadster, WLB

pany increased its capital stock from $150,000 to $300,000, and took over the erstwhile Chatham Motor Company in Ontario in order to enter the Canadian market. The next news from Anhut came later that summer, an inquiry by company stockholders and a rumor that Senator Anhut had disappeared. Actually, he had not disappeared; he had simply taken off for Europe for a rest before beginning his fall campaign for re-election. By now, having undoubtedly decided that politics and automobiles didn't mix, the senator had turned over the business anyway to H.C. Barnes, the former Overland factory superintendent who had taken on the same job at Anhut in February. The reorganization of Anhut into the Barnes Motor Car Company was completed by September, with Barnes announcing his plan to manufacture a six at $2250 and a four at $1400. He was bankrupt by November. A brass stamping with a "Barnes Six" logo is known to have been produced, but if any cars with the emblem left the assembly line, the

1910 Anhut, touring, WLB

press was not made aware of it. By January of 1911, everything that remained of the Anhut and the Barnes was sold to Autoparts Company of Detroit, a firm specializing in buying up the quick and the dead in the auto industry.

1909-1910 ANHUT
Six — 36 hp, 110" wb

	FP	5	4	3	2	1
Rds.-2P	1700	4500	9000	15,000	21,000	30,000
Toy Tonneau-4P	1800	4500	9000	15,000	21,000	30,000
Rumble Seat Rds.-4P	1800	4500	9000	15,000	21,000	30,000

ANN ARBOR — "Ann Arbor, Michigan is to have a new automobile factory," *The Automobile Review* announced in May 1903. "The announced intention is to turn out machines which can be sold for $1250." Intention seems to be as far as this venture proceeded. The evidence is lacking that the Ann Arbor Automobile Company ever proceeded into manufacture.

1911 Ann Arbor, touring, NAHC

ANN ARBOR — Ann Arbor, Michigan — (1911-1912) — The Ann Arbor was produced by the Huron River Manufacturing Company and was designed for the one-car family of a farmer or small merchant. Designated as a Convertible Touring Car, it was a go-to-meetin' or go-to-market conveyance. Its rear-seat section was easily removable for the substitution of a delivery box or platform. With two seats and sideboards the price was $950; for three seats and sideboards, $975. A canopy top with side curtains and transparent storm front was a $50 extra. Twenty-five miles an hour was the vehicle's top speed. The Ann Arbor was produced for two years only. Late in 1912 the Star Motor Car Company moved into the Ann Arbor factory. Its product, announced in mid-summer of 1913, would be commercial vehicles exclusively.

1912 Ann Arbor, convertible touring car, NAHC

1911-1912 ANN ARBOR
2-cyl., 100" wb

Convertible Tour.	950	1500	2500	3600	5500	11,000

ANNA — Anna, Illinois — (1912) — The specifications as listed in the January 4th, 1912 issue of *The Automobile* indicate the Anna as featuring a two-cylinder 22 hp L-head water-cooled engine, planetary transmission, chain drive, a 100-inch wheelbase, a two-seater "Democrat" body and a $950 price tag. For years the Anna was considered an orphan, her manufacturer unknown; a number of states have towns named Anna, but none of them claimed her. Trade journals of the period, however, reveal that this little orphan Anna was the product of the Anna Motor Car Company of Anna, Illinois, a shoestring venture ($2500 capital stock) organized by J.J. Corzine, Roy Rinehart and Ernest Lawson. The number of cars they built must have been very small. The Records of Corporations in Anna, Illinois during these years do not reveal automobile manufacturing in town. The incorporation notice for the company, as released to the automotive trade press, stated that the firm would also deal in automobiles, which doubtless came to be the mainstay of the venture.

1912 ANNA
Two — 22 hp, 100"

Rbt.	950	1500	2500	3600	5500	11,000

ANNESLEY — Detroit, Michigan — (1899, 1914) — Charles G. Annesley made two attempts to enter the automobile industry with a car bearing his name. In 1899 he built four electric carriages and three gasoline cars which his friend Walter L. Marr (who built the Marr car and was an engineer for Buick) pronounced most meritorious, but Annesley could not find the backing to go into production. Thereafter he left for the East Coast to work for the Buffalo Gas Engine Company. He was back in Detroit by 1914, however, with the second Annesley, this one a light car designed in collaboration with C.A. Gonolay. It had a four-cylinder engine, a 102-inch wheelbase and a 44-inch tread, though Annesley and Gonolay stood ready to make the car in standard tread "if the demand arises." It never did. Most likely this car never passed the prototype stage, because a company was not forthcoming for its manufacture. It was a rather appealing car, however, with wire wheels, full fenders and a nicely swept-up hood-windshield line. Two passengers sat side by side in a body made of sheet metal. Lighting equipment included two electric headlamps with dimmers, a tail and dash lamp. During tests, the car put up 50 mph and 35 mpg. At $500, which was the projected price, the Annesley would have been an attractive buy. Because both Annesley attempts at automobile manufacture failed Charles G. Annesley remains known today only as the man who bought Henry Ford's first car for $200 in 1896.

ANSONIA — Early in 1904 the Ansonia Motor Car Company was organized with a capital stock of $10,000 in New York City for the manufacture of "vehicles and carriages." F.C. Armstrong and T.B. Townley of Elizabeth, New Jersey, and C.I. Scott of New York City, were the promoters of this venture which seems not to have produced a single car.

In February of 1909 the Ansonia Auto Service Company of New York City was incorporated by H.H. Gordon, F.H. Beard and S.S. Gordon with a capital stock of $15,000 and the announced intention of manufacturing and operating motor vehicles. A car was never built, however; what financial success the company enjoyed was in the livery business only.

ANSTED — Connersville, Indiana — (1921, 1926) — Around the turn of the century, E.W. Ansted was selling about 1200 tons of his Swan Loop Buggy Springs every year. Almost as soon as the carriage went automotive, he began making Ansted Vehicle Springs. He was quick to spot a trend. And he soon became more involved. In 1913 Ansted bought the Lexington Motor Car Company in Connersville and in the years that followed he brought his son F.B. into the company, and produced the

1921 Ansted, roadster, KM

Howard and Lexington automobiles. Engines were the principal product of his subsidiary Ansted Engineering Company, however. (William C. Durant used an Ansted in his Durant Six car.) The cars which bore the Ansted marque name on two occasions in the Connersville company's history were a case of badge engineering. Probably the ego of the company's president was a *raison d'etre*. The 1921 Ansted was a Lexington T Series roadster with a new radiator grille, emblem, hubcaps and such luxurious niceties as seasoned ash body, walnut dashboard, walnut and mahogany interior trim, a cabinet at the rear of the seat with panastote lining and wood lid. Moreover, a completely equipped tool drawer featured an automatic switch and built-in lighting for easy access, and a nickel-plated glove compartment and ladies vanity were standard equipment. The car sold for $4500; the Lexington T range was $2985-$4250. The second Ansteds which arrived a half decade later weren't nearly so grand. They were simply 1926 Lexingtons which were rebadged for sale as Ansteds for the Chicago agency. On August 26th that year, the Ansted engine plant was bought for $40,000 by Errett Lobban Cord, who had ideas of his own. Both the Ansted and the Lexington were gone by 1927.

1921 ANSTED
Six — 65 hp, 119" wb

	FP	5	4	3	2	1
Rds.	4500	3000	4000	6000	9500	21,000

1926 ANSTED
Six — 65 hp, 119" wb

	FP	5	4	3	2	1
Sed.-5P	3425	2500	3500	5000	8500	18,000

ANTHONY — During the summer of 1913 the Anthony Auto Repair Company was organized in New York City with a capital stock of $10,000 and the plan to manufacture and deal in automobiles. J. Yandramitch, F.M. Struckhausen, and H. Struckhausen were the principals involved. The building of even a single Anthony car has not been documented.

ANTHONY — Los Angeles, California — (1897) — In 1897 in Los Angeles a young man built an electric car that was a contraption. Its half-horsepower motor was connected to the rear wheels, its transmission was adapted from a wheelchair, its body was a wagon-type box mounted on

1897 Anthony Electric, runabout, GR

bicycle forks on four bicycle wheels, and its top speed was 8 mph. Fortunately, with the turn of the century and maturity, the young man realized his future in the automobile business lay in other areas. In later years, Earle C. Anthony would claim to have opened the world's first gasoline station (in late 1903 or early '04 he installed pumps on a curb in Los Angeles and called the result the Red and White Filling Station), but it was as a peripatetic automobile dealer in Los Angeles, for Packard particularly, that he gained his fame. Through his efforts Packards appeared in many vintage films of the Thirties, and purportedly it was Anthony who imported the first illuminated signs to this country. After meeting Claude Neon in Paris, he ordered three, one of them reading "Packard," of course.

ANTHONY — **Colorado Springs, Colorado** — **(1899-1900)** — In October of 1899, *The Motor Age* announced the intention of W.O. Anthony of Colorado Springs to manufacture gasoline vehicles in a variety of styles, including phaeton, runabout and delivery wagon. Anthony had been experimenting for three-and-a-half years already, the article said, and he planned as well to manufacture vehicle parts, "especially a new steering gear designed to overcome vibration of the steering lever on rough roads." Although his total output could not have been more than a few vehicles, W.O. Anthony was probably Colorado's first automobile manufacturer. His Anthony Motor and Manufacturing Company (subsequently Anthony Motor and Cycle Company) continued to manufacture motors, steering gear and accessories for the automotive trade after the cessation of automobile manufacture around the turn of the century. In August 1904 W.O. Anthony was killed in an automobile accident. In 1906 his business was sold to the Western Automobile & Supply Company.

ANTHONY-HATCHER — **Grand Rapids, Michigan** — **(1908)** — The Anthony-Hatcher Company was an attempt to pick up the pieces of two defunct ventures in Grand Rapids; the Harrison Motor Company which had produced the Harrison car from 1906-1907 and the Soules Motor Car Company which had produced the Soules delivery truck from 1905-1908. Involved in this resuscitation attempt was George E. Anthony and William A. Hatcher, who incorporated their venture with a capital stock of $20,000 for the purpose of "manufacturing" motor cars, trucks and parts, general machinery tools and to buy and sell all kinds of personal property." Leftover parts of the Harrison and Soules may have been assembled under the Anthony-Hatcher name, but no further production ensued.

APEX — The Apex Motor Company of Bergen, New Jersey was organized early in 1906 for the manufacture of engines and automobiles. Capital stock was $15,000, and the principals involved were A.A. Sands and G.E. Parish of Bergen, and F.O. Bullis of Rochester. Subsequent manufacture is not indicated.
   The Apex Motor Car Company of Ypsilanti, Michigan produced a car called the Ace from 1920 to 1922. Refer to Ace.

APEX — A full line of motor vehicles with price tags not to exceed $500 was the announced plan of the Apex Wheel Company of Rochester, New York. In January 1900, *The Motor Vehicle Review* reported: "Gasoline will be used, the motor being the invention of a lad from Lisbon, Ohio, who has something entirely new in a motor. Experiments have been going on for some time with success. A number of capitalists are reported as back of the venture." Most probably, the capitalists involved soon changed the firm's name to Apex Manufacturing Company, which went nowhere as well. This cannot be proved, but seems likely.

APEX — **Rochester, New York** — **(1901)** — "The Apex Manufacturing Company of Rochester has been experimenting on a rotary motor for the past year and state that they have at last succeeded in producing an engine that runs perfectly," *The Motor Age* reported in March of 1900. Only a few minor changes were necessary before the engine would be ready for a motor vehicle, it was said. These changes were completed by January of 1901, and at that time *The Motor Vehicle Review* noted that

"runabouts, surreys and delivery wagons will be turned out as fast as ordered." The orders apparently were few, and the Apex rotary engine not quite as perfect as reported, because the company was out of the automobile business by year's end.

APOLLO — **Waukegan, Illinois** — **(1906-1907)** — The Apollo is one of a number of examples representing proof positive that during the dawning years of the industry few businesses thought themselves incapable of building an automobile. A shaft-drive water-cooled 35 hp four with three-speed sliding gear transmission, the Apollo was produced by the Chicago Recording Scale Company. It was offered in a single body style, a five-passenger King of Belgium touring, at $2500. One reference indicates it also carried the name Waukegan Apollo.

1906-1907 APOLLO

	FP	5	4	3	2	1
Tour.-5P	2500	2000	3000	4200	6500	14,000

APPEAL — L.M. Passmore, Gideon Haynes, Elsie L. Hamrick, B.L. Vickery and O.A. Vickery were the people behind the Appeal Manufacturing and Jobbing Company which was incorporated in Sacramento, California in early 1902 for the manufacture of "bicycles, automobiles, wagons and boats." Capital stock was $100,000 with Los Angeles indicated as the proposed manufacturing site. There is no documentation that an automobile actually was produced, though the Appeal company did settle in Los Angeles. In 1910 the firm was operating as a dealership for bicycles and Harley-Davidson motorcycles.

APPEL — The Appel car from 1916 which has appeared on numerous car rosters was instead merely the Apple of Dayton, Ohio misspelled. Refer to Apple.

1902 Apperson, model A, touring, HAC

APPERSON — **Kokomo, Indiana** — **(1902-1926)** — In 1889 Elmer Apperson and his younger brother Edgar opened their Riverside Machine Works on Main Street in Kokomo and soon gained a reputation as the best mechanics in town. In 1893 a fellow townsman named Elwood Haynes paid them a visit and offered them a proposition: He owned a one-cylinder two-cycle Sintz marine engine and he wanted help in building a car. The Apperson brothers provided it, and on the Fourth of July in 1894 the car had its maiden test run. Although it wasn't America's first gasoline automobile, it would be claimed as such in promotion of the Haynes-Apperson Automobile Company which was established in 1898. The Appersons split from Haynes in 1901, and the parting was not amicable. Subsequently, Haynes dropped all mention of the Appersons whenever referring to the 1894 car; eventually, the Appersons responded in kind, forgetting the existence of Haynes. The Apperson Brothers Automobile Company was formerly established in November 1901, and the first Apperson car (with Sintz engine) was delivered in July of 1902. The early two-cylinder Appersons were followed by a four in 1903, with all cars fours the following year. Although the company produced a six as early as 1908, it did not formally enter the six-cylinder ranks on a regular production basis until late 1914. The most famous of the early Appersons was the Jack Rabbit which was introduced in 1907 as a racy runabout with round gas tank on the rear deck and a

1904 Apperson, model A, touring, HAC

guaranteed top speed of 75 mph. Though never winning a major race, hopped-up Jack Rabbits did finish in the money in such premiere events as the Briarcliff and the Vanderbilt and at Fairmount Park. In 1907 the company even offered a racer as a limited production car, and the Apperson presence in the 1914 Grand Prize and Vanderbilt represented the last appearance of any chain-drive car in a major U.S. event. Later the Jack Rabbit (company promotion also spelled it "Jackrabbit" on occasion) was extended into a model series of its own, and included tourers as well as roadsters. Vee radiators arrived late in 1914, and a V-8 engine for 1916, during which year the fours were dropped from the line. All models for 1917 were called Roadaplanes. The Apperson-built V-8 remained the company's mainstay into the Twenties; when a new six was introduced late in 1923, it carried a Falls engine; a straight-eight by Lycoming augmented the V-8 line in 1925. During the early Twenties, too, a remote control shifter device was offered although Apperson didn't build it (Kurtz of Cleveland did). Probably the loveliest Appersons in the company's history were the specials with long, lithe lines, bullet headlamps and oval radiators that were designed by New York dealer C.T. Silver. These cars carried the Silver name in 1918 only, but the styling continued on production model Appersons into the Twenties. On March 27th, 1920 Elmer Apperson died of a heart attack at age fifty-eight while attending an automobile race in Los Angeles. It was the partnership of the two Appersons which had made the company strong, and its strength had been abruptly halved. Apperson production had always enjoyed a consistent good health — the company's peak year being 1916 with 2000 units — but now the downhill slide began. In 1923 Apperson had to secure outside capital for the first time in its history. In 1924 the firm was reorganized as the Apperson Automobile Company. Interestingly, Apperson had initially filed a petition to change its name to the Pioneer Automobile Company, believing perhaps that a reminder of the firm's origins in the field might restore confidence and spur sales. Front wheel brakes were introduced to the 1926 Apperson cars. These cars were the company's last. "Apperson Goes Under the Hammer" was the sad headline announcing the receiver's sale to be held beginning July 20th, 1926, in Kokomo. The company of Elwood Haynes had died the year before.

1902 APPERSON
Model A — 2-cyl., 16 hp, 102" wb

	FP	5	4	3	2	1
Tour.-4P	2500	3000	4000	6000	9500	21,000

1903 APPERSON
Model A — 2-cyl., 25 hp, 102" wb

		5	4	3	2	1
Tour.-6P		3000	4000	6000	9500	21,000

Model B — 2-cyl., 20 hp, 102" wb

		5	4	3	2	1
Tour.-4P		3000	4000	6000	9500	21,000

Note: A four was added in March.

1904 APPERSON
Model B — 4-cyl., 24 hp, 102" wb

	FP	5	4	3	2	1
Tour.-5P	3500	3300	4400	6700	12,000	24,000

Model A — 4-cyl., 40 hp, 114" wb

	FP	5	4	3	2	1
Tour.-6/7P	5000	3500	4500	7000	13,000	25,000

1905 Apperson, model B, touring, HAC

1905 APPERSON
Model B — 4-cyl., 24 hp, 102" wb

Tour.-5P	3650	3300	4400	6700	12,000	24,000

Model A — 4-cyl., 40 hp, 108" wb

Tour.-7P	4150	3200	4300	6500	11,000	23,000

Special — 4-cyl., 50 hp, 114" wb

Tour.-7P	5150	3500	4500	7000	13,000	25,000
Limo.-7P	6500	2900	3700	5600	9100	20,000

1906 APPERSON
Model B — 4-cyl., 40/45 hp, 112" wb

Tour.-7P	4500	4900	6300	10,300	21,000	34,000

Model C — 4-cyl., 30/35 hp, 104" wb

Tour.-5P	3500	4500	5800	9500	18,000	32,000
Limo.-5P	5200	4300	5400	8700	16,500	30,000

Model A — 4-cyl., 50/55 hp, 116" wb

Spec. Tour.-7P	5500	5000	6500	11,000	22,000	35,000

1907 APPERSON
Model B — 4-cyl., 40/45 hp, 114" wb

Tour.-7P	4000	6750	13,500	22,500	31,500	45,000
Limo.	6000	4200	5200	8400	15,700	29,000

Model A — 4-cyl., 50/55 hp, 115" wb

Tour.-7P	4700	7000	14,000	23,000	32,000	47,000
Limo.	6700	8250	16,000	27,500	38,000	55,000

Jack Rabbit (60 hp, 100" wb)

	8500	17,000	28,500	40,000	58,000

Special — 4-cyl., 96 hp, 110" wb

Jack Rabbit Racer	15,000	5500	7500	12,000	26,000	39,000

1906 Apperson, model B, touring, WLB

1907 Apperson, Jack Rabbit, roadster, HAC

1908 Apperson, touring, WLB

1908 Apperson, 4-pass. runabout, WLB

1908 APPERSON
Model M — 4-cyl., 35 hp, 106-1/2" wb

Rds.-4P	2750	6750	13,500	22,500	31,500	45,000

Model K — 4-cyl., 50/55 hp, 114" wb

Tour.-7P	4200	6800	14,000	23,000	32,000	48,000
Rbt.	4000	6750	13,500	22,500	31,500	45,000

Jack Rabbit (60 hp, 105" wb)

	5000	7000	14,000	24,000	33,900	47,000

Model S — 6-cyl., 55 hp, 114" wb

Tour.-7P	5000	7000	14,000	24,000	33,900	47,000
Rbt.-3P	5000	6800	13,500	23,600	32,500	46,000

1909 Apperson, model O, runabout, WLB

1909 Apperson, model O, touring, WLB

1909 Apperson, Jack Rabbit, runabout, WLB

1909 APPERSON
Model O — 4-cyl., 30 hp, 119'' wb

	FP	5	4	3	2	1
Tour.-5P	2400	6750	13,500	22,500	31,500	45,000
Rbt.-3P	2250	6800	13,700	23,000	31,800	46,000
Rdstr.-4P	2250	6850	14,000	24,000	34,000	47,000
Model M — 4-cyl., 35/40 hp, 119'' wb						
Tour.-5P	3350	6800	13,500	23,600	32,500	46,000
Rds.-2P/3P	3000	6850	14,000	24,000	33,000	47,000
Model I — 4-cyl., 35/40 hp, 128'' wb						
Tour.-5P	3900	6900	14,500	24,500	34,000	48,000
Rbt.-3/4P	3900	7000	15,000	25,000	35,000	49,000
Model K Jack Rabbit — 4-cyl., 50/55 hp						
Rbt. (105'' wb)	5000	6800	13,500	23,600	32,500	46,000
Tour.-7P (123'' wb)	4700	6900	14,500	24,500	34,000	48,000

1910 Apperson, model 4-30, baby tonneau, HAC

54

1910 APPERSON
Model 4-30 — 4-cyl., 30 hp, 119'' wb

	FP	5	4	3	2	1
Baby Tonneau	2100	6800	13,500	23,600	32,500	46,000
Model 4-40 — 4-cyl., 40 hp, 122'' wb						
Tour.-5P	3000	6850	14,000	24,000	33,000	42,000
Model 4-50 — 4-cyl., 50 hp, 128'' wb						
Tour.-7P	4200	9000	15,000	25,000	34,000	48,000
Model 6-40 — 6-cyl., 50 hp, 128'' wb						
Tour.-7P	4200	7500	15,500	26,000	35,000	49,000
Jack Rabbit — 4-cyl., 50 hp, 116'' wb						
Rdstr.-2P	4250	7700	16,000	26,500	35,000	50,000

1911 Apperson, model 4-30, touring, HAC

1911 APPERSON
Model 4-30 — 4-cyl., 32.4 hp, 114'' wb

	FP	5	4	3	2	1
Jack Rabbit Tour.-5P	2000	5400	7300	11,800	25,000	38,000
Jack Rabbit Fore-Dr. Tour.	2250	5500	7500	12,000	26,000	39,000
Model 4-40 — 4-cyl., 40 hp, 122'' wb						
Jack Rabbit Tour.-5P	3000	5500	7500	12,000	26,000	39,000
Model 4-50 — 4-cyl., 50 hp, 128'' wb						
Jack Rabbit Tour.-7P	4200	6000	8500	13,000	30,000	42,000

Note 1: Although in previous years, touring models carried the Jack Rabbit name intermittently in promotion, 1911 was the first year all Apperson were so designated.

1912 Apperson, Jack Rabbit, 4-45, roadster, WLB

1912 Apperson, Jack Rabbit, 4-55, touring, WLB

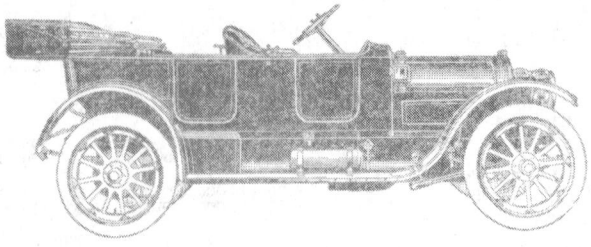

1913 Apperson, Jack Rabbit, touring, OCW

1912 APPERSON
Model 4-45 — 4-cyl., 45 hp, 114" wb

	FP	5	4	3	2	1
Jack Rabbit Tour.-5P	1600	5000	6500	11,000	22,000	35,000
Jack Rabbit Rds.	1750	5200	6800	11,300	23,000	36,000
Jack Rabbit Town Car	2250	4500	5800	9500	18,000	32,000

Model 4-55 — 4-cyl., 55 hp, 118" wb

	FP	5	4	3	2	1
Jack Rabbit Tour.-5P	2000	5200	6800	11,300	23,000	36,000
Jack Rabbit Spec. Tour.*	3000	5500	7500	12,000	26,000	39,000

*(122" wb)

Model 4-65 — 4-cyl., 65 hp, 128" wb

	FP	5	4	3	2	1
Jack Rabbit Tour.-7P	4200	6000	8500	13,000	30,000	42,000

1913 APPERSON
Model 4-45 — 4-cyl., 45 hp, 114" wb

	FP	5	4	3	2	1
Jack Rabbit Tour.-5P	1600	5000	6500	11,000	22,000	35,000
Jack Rabbit Rds.-2P	1600	5200	6800	11,300	23,000	36,000
Jack Rabbit Cpe.-4P	2100	4400	5600	9200	17,300	31,000

Model 4-55 — 4-cyl., 55 hp, 118" wb

	FP	5	4	3	2	1
Jack Rabbit Tour.-5P	2000	5200	6800	11,300	23,000	36,000
Jack Rabbit Tour.-7P*	2250	5400	7300	11,800	25,000	38,000

*(122" wb)

1914 Apperson Light, model 4-45, roadster, HAC

1914 APPERSON
Light 4-45 — 4-cyl., 32 hp, 116" wb

	FP	5	4	3	2	1
Tour.-5P	1600	4500	5800	9500	18,000	32,000
Turtle-Back Rds.	1600	4700	6100	9900	19,000	33,000
Cpe.-4P	2350	4000	5000	8000	15,000	28,000

Model 4-45 — 4-cyl., 32 hp, 120" wb

	FP	5	4	3	2	1
Tour.-5P	1785	5000	6500	11,000	22,000	35,000
Sed. Limo.-5P	2500	4300	5400	8700	16,500	30,000

Model 6-45 — 6-cyl., 38 hp, 128" wb

	FP	5	4	3	2	1
Tour.-5P	2200	5300	7000	11,500	24,000	37,000
Rds.-2P	2200	5400	7300	11,800	25,000	38,000

Model 6-55 — 6-cyl., 43 hp, 128" wb

	FP	5	4	3	2	1
Tour.-5P	2350	5400	7300	11,800	25,000	38,000
Rds.-2P	2350	5800	8000	12,500	28,000	40,000

1915 Apperson, model 6-45, touring, HAC

1915 APPERSON
Model 4-40 — 4-cyl., 26 hp, 116" wb

	FP	5	4	3	2	1
Tour.-5P	1350	4700	6100	9900	19,000	33,000

Model 4-45 — 4-cyl., 32 hp, 120" wb

	FP	5	4	3	2	1
Tour.-5P	1685	5000	6500	11,000	22,000	35,000
Rds.-2P	1685	5200	6800	11,300	23,000	36,000
Cpe.-4P	2350	4200	5200	8400	15,700	29,000

Model 6-45 — 6-cyl., 29 hp, 122" wb

	FP	5	4	3	2	1
Tour.-5P	1485	5200	6800	11,300	23,000	36,000

Model 6-48 — 6-cyl., 29 hp, 126" wb

	FP	5	4	3	2	1
Tour.-5P	—	5400	7300	11,800	25,000	38,000

1916 APPERSON
Model 6-16 — 6-cyl., 29 hp, 128" wb

	FP	5	4	3	2	1
Light Six Tour.-7P	1550	5200	6800	11,300	23,000	36,000
Light Six Tour.-5P	1485	5000	6500	11,000	22,000	35,000
Light Six Rds.-4P	1550	5300	7000	11,500	24,000	37,000

Model 8-16 — V-8, 31 hp, 128" wb

	FP	5	4	3	2	1
Light Eight Tour.-7P	1850	5400	7300	11,800	25,000	38,000
Light Eight Rdstr.-4P	1850	5500	7500	12,000	26,000	39,000

1917 Apperson, touring, WLB

1917 APPERSON
Model 6-17 — 6-cyl., 29.4 hp, 130" wb

	FP	5	4	3	2	1
Roadaplane Chy. Rds.-4P	1750	4500	5800	9500	18,000	32,000
Roadaplane Tour.-7P	1750	4300	5400	8700	16,500	30,000

Model 8-17 — V-8, 31 hp, 130" wb

	FP	5	4	3	2	1
Roadaplane Tour.-7P	2000	5200	6800	11,300	23,000	36,000
Roadaplane Chy. Rds.-4P	2000	5400	7300	11,800	25,000	38,000

1918 Apperson, 7-pass. touring

1918 Apperson, 4-pass., Chummy roadster, WLB

1918 APPERSON
Model 6-18 — 6-cyl., 29.4 hp, 130" wb

	FP	5	4	3	2	1
Chummy Roadster-4P	1990	4500	5800	9500	18,000	32,000
Tour.-7P	1990	4300	5400	8700	16,500	30,000

Model 8-18 — V-8, 33.8 hp, 130" wb

	FP	5	4	3	2	1
Chummy Rds.-4P	2550	5200	6800	11,300	23,000	36,000
Tour.-7P	2550	5000	6500	11,000	22,000	35,000
Silver Spec. Tour.	3500	5400	7300	11,800	25,000	38,000

1919 Apperson Eight, tourster, HAC

1919 APPERSON
Model 8-19 — V-8, 33.8 hp, 130'' wb

	FP	5	4	3	2	1
Tourster-4P	4000	4500	5800	9500	18,000	32,000
Anniversary Tour.-7P	4000	4900	6300	10,300	21,000	34,000

1920 Apperson, Eight, touring, HAC

1920 APPERSON
Model 1920 — V-8, 60 hp, 130'' wb

Tour.-7P	2950	4500	5800	9500	18,000	32,000
Sptstr.-4P	2950	4900	6300	10,300	21,000	34,000
Ace-2P	2950	4500	5800	9500	18,000	32,000
Sed.-7P	4000	3000	4000	6000	9500	21,000
Sedan'et.-4P	4000	3000	4000	6000	9500	21,000
Cpe.-4P	4000	3500	4500	7000	13,000	25,000
Berlin-7P	4000	3300	4400	6700	12,000	24,000

Anniversary Model — V-8 — 60 hp, 130'' wb

Tour.-7P	4000	4700	6100	9900	19,000	33,000
Tourster-4P	4000	5000	6500	11,000	22,000	35,000
Sed.-7P	5500	3200	4300	6500	11,000	23,000
Cabriolet-4P	5500	4500	5800	9500	18,000	32,000
Cpe.-4P	5500	3700	4700	7300	13,700	26,000

1921 Apperson, touring, WLB

1921 APPERSON
Model 8-21 — V-8, 70 hp, 130'' wb

Open Sptstr.-4P	3500	5000	6500	11,000	22,000	35,000
Open Tour.-7P	3500	4500	5800	9500	18,000	32,000
Anniversary Tour.-7P	4250	5000	6500	11,000	22,000	35,000
Tourster-4P	4250	4500	5800	9500	18,000	32,000
Sedanet-4P	4500	3500	4500	7000	13,000	25,000

1922 Apperson, Beverly sportster, HAC

56

1922 APPERSON
Beverly Model — V-8, 70 hp, 130'' wb

	FP	5	4	3	2	1
Sptstr.	2620	5000	6500	11,000	22,000	35,000
Tour.	2645	4500	5800	9500	18,000	32,000
Tourster	2995	4700	6100	9900	19,000	33,000
Sedanet	3895	3500	4500	7000	13,000	25,000
Sedan	3995	3300	4400	6700	12,000	24,000
Limo.-Sed.	4195	4000	5000	8000	15,000	28,000
Sptstr., Tourequipt	2995	4300	5400	8700	16,500	30,000
Tourster, Tourequipt	3245	4300	5400	8700	16,500	30,000

1923 APPERSON
Model 6-23 — 6-cyl., 46 hp, 120'' wb

Tour.-5P	1535	4300	5400	8700	16,500	30,000

Model 8-23S — V-8, 70 hp, 130'' wb

Spt.	2645	5000	6500	11,000	22,000	35,000
Tour.-7P	2620	4500	5800	9500	18,000	32,000
Tour. Sed.-7P	3625	4200	5200	8400	15,700	29,000
Sed.-4P	3695	4000	5000	8000	15,000	28,000

1924 Apperson Six, phaeton, HAC

1924 APPERSON
Model 6-24 — 6-cyl., 46 hp, 120'' wb

Phaeton-5P	1535	4000	5000	8000	15,000	28,000
Sed.-5P	2200	3200	4500	6500	11,000	30,000

Model 8-24 — V-8, 70 hp, 130'' wb

Phaeton-5P	2800	4500	5800	9500	18,000	32,000
Phaeton-7P	2800	4400	5600	9200	17,300	31,000
Sed.-5P	3750	3500	4500	7000	13,000	25,000
Sed.-7P	3950	3300	4400	6700	12,000	24,000

1925 Apperson, coupe, WLB

1925 Apperson, sport phaeton, WLB

1925 APPERSON
Six — 46 hp, 120'' wb

Phaeton-5P	1695	4400	5600	9200	17,300	31,000
Cpe.-2P	1985	3100	4200	6300	10,500	22,000
Sed.-5P	2095	2500	3500	5000	8500	18,000
Spt. Sed.-5P	2295	2700	3600	5300	8800	19,000

Straightaway Eight — 60 hp, 120'' wb

Sport Phaeton-5P	2550	4500	5800	9500	18,000	32,000
Cpe.-2P	2800	3300	4400	6700	12,000	24,000
Four-Door Brougham	2800	3100	4200	6300	10,500	22,000
Sed.-5P	2850	3000	4000	6000	9500	21,000

V-Type Eight — 60 hp, 130" wb

	FP	5	4	3	2	1
Phaeton-5P	2485	5000	6500	11,000	22,000	35,000
Spt. Phaeton-5P	2800	5300	7000	11,500	24,000	37,000
Phaeton-7P	2535	4900	6300	10,300	21,000	34,000
Spt. Phaeton-7P	2900	5200	6800	11,300	23,000	36,000
Sed.-5P	3485	2900	3700	5600	9100	20,000
Spt. Sed.-5P	3750	3000	4000	6000	9500	21,000
Sed.-7P	3585	2700	3600	5300	8800	19,000
Spt. Sed.-7P	3850	2900	3700	5600	9100	20,000

1926 Apperson Eight, coupe, HAC

1926 APPERSON

Six — 46 hp, 120" wb

Phaeton-5P	1575	4400	5600	9200	17,300	31,000
Sport Phaeton-5P	1650	4900	6300	10,300	21,000	34,000
Cpe.-4P	2050	3100	4200	6300	10,500	22,000
Brougham-5P	2050	2900	3700	5600	9100	20,000
Sed.-5P	2100	2700	3600	5300	8800	19,000

Eight — 65 hp, 130" wb

Phaeton-5P	1995	4900	6300	10,300	21,000	34,000
Brougham-5P	2450	3300	4400	6700	12,000	24,000
Cpe.-5P	2450	3500	4500	7000	13,000	25,000
Sed.-5P	2595	3200	4300	6500	11,000	23,000

APPERSON-TOLEDO — In January 1909, Richard D. Apperson announced his ongoing negotiations with the receivers for the bankrupt Pope Motor Car Company of Toledo, Ohio and his intention to continue the Pope-Toledo in production as the Toledo. Refer to Toledo.

1915 Apple 8, touring, KM

APPLE — Dayton, Ohio — (1915-1917) — At an automobile show in Dayton in October of 1915, W.A. Apple exhibited an eight-cylinder 44 hp car on a 118-inch wheelbase which he said he intended to manufacture and sell for $1150. His sales undoubtedly were small. The last reference in the trade press to his Apple Motor Car Company was in January 1917. Most probably, W.A. Apple was a progeny of one of the storage-battery-manufacturing Apple brothers — H.V., O.D. or V.G. — who had organized their Apple Electric Company in Dayton in 1908.

1915-1917 APPLE

Apple Eight	1150	2000	3000	4200	6500	14,000

APPLETON — The Appleton Manufacturing Company of Batavia, New York has appeared on numerous rosters as a car producer during the early 1920's. There is no evidence of such a company in Batavia at that time, according to local city history; the only Appleton in town was an office employee at a local railway company.

APTHORP — The name Apthorp, a prominent one in New York City since Revolutionary War days, was used by two ventures, neither of which seem to have produced a single automobile.

The Apthorp Motor Car Company was a $50,000 incorporation from 1908 announcing the unrealized plan to manufacture "horseless vehicles, motors and engines" in Manhattan.

The Apthorp Garage Company followed in 1910 with a capital stock of $10,000 for the manufacture, sale and renting of automobiles. Incorporators were Samuel Marion, Roger M. Drury and William Rekersdress, all of New York City.

ARABIAN — Waterloo, Iowa — (1915-1917) — The Arabian was produced by William Galloway, who earlier had built a high-wheeler under his own name in Waterloo. Initially, this car was said to have been called a Galloway too, but by the time it was put on the market, the decision had been made for Arabian. Actually, the car was an Argo parading under another name.

From 1915 into 1916, the Arabian was built for Galloway by Benjamin Briscoe's Argo Motor Company in Jackson, Michigan. When Briscoe sold out his business to Mansell Hackett later in 1916, the cars were produced under license in Galloway's own Waterloo factory. Although the Arabian was listed as a current production in the 1919 Chilton Trade Directory, actual manufacture seems to have ceased by the end of 1917.

1915 ARABIAN
Four — 12 hp, 90" wb

	FP	5	4	3	2	1
Rds.	385	1000	1800	3000	4200	7000

1916-1917 ARABIAN
Four — 22 hp, 96" wb

Rds.-2P	385	1000	1800	3000	4000	7000

Four — 22 hp, 103" wb

Tour.-5P	435	1000	1800	2800	4000	6800

1911 ArBenz, model C, touring, HAC

ARBENZ — Chillicothe, Ohio — (1911-1918) — Fred C. Arbenz, and his brother N.J., named their car after themselves and used their defunct furniture company for its manufacture. Initially they named their venture after the river that runs through Chillicothe, but changed their minds about that in 1912 and the Scioto Car Company became the ArBenz (the marque was usually spelled in that manner in promotion) Car Company. Fred was the ArBenz president, N.J. the designer of the cars. As chief engineer, the company hired C.O. Snyder, who claimed to have built an eight-cylinder engine in 1906. The only cars from ArBenz, however, were fours, in the medium-price range through 1915. In December that year, Snyder resigned from the company — and the new ArBenz for 1916 was a smaller Lycoming-built four which was priced three times less than the ArBenz norm. It was also the last ArBenz. In March of 1916 the firm was taken over by the National United Service Company which was in the process of gathering other automotive firms into its fold in yet another industry attempt to emulate General Motors. National United announced plans to continue the ArBenz in production and it may have done so until late 1917. By 1918, however, the only ArBenz production was assembly of cars from parts on hand. Meantime, N.J. Arbenz had joined the army, and was over there with the Allied Expeditionary Forces. The Arbenz family also owned the Florentine Pottery Company in Chillicothe.

1911 ARBENZ
Four — 30/40 hp, 120" wb

Model A Rds.-2P	1675	3000	4000	6000	9500	21,000
Model B Torpedo-4P	1700	2500	3500	5500	9000	20,000
Model C Fore-Dr. Tour.-5P	1725	3000	4000	6000	9500	21,000

1912 ArBenz, model C, touring, HAC

1914 ArBenz, model F, touring, WLB

1914 ArBenz, model H, roadster, WLB

1914 ARBENZ
Four — 27 hp, 120" wb

	FP	5	4	3	2	1
Model G Tour.-4P	1885	2000	3000	4500	8000	17,000
Model F Tour.-5P	1885	2000	3000	4500	8000	17,000
Model H Rds.-2P	1825	2500	3500	5000	8500	18,000

1915 ARBENZ
Model 40 — 4-cyl., 27 hp, 120" wb

	FP	5	4	3	2	1
Rds.-2P	1825	2500	3500	5000	8500	18,000
Tour.-5P	1885	2000	3000	4500	8000	17,000

1916 Arbenz, model 25, touring, HAC

1916-1918 ARBENZ
Model 25 — 4-cyl., 17 hp, 108" wb

	5	4	3	2	1
Tour.-5P	625	2000	3000	4200	6500	14,000

ARCADIA — The Arcadia of 1903 was a typographical error on car rosters. Ernest R. Kelly of Wilmington, Delaware did build a car that year, and the year following, but it was called the Acadia. Refer to Acadia.

ARCHER — Rutland, Vermont — (1910) — The Archer was a four-cylinder two-stroke 30 hp roadster designed by W.L. Archer of Rutland that was probably built as a prototype only. References from 1910 issues of the *New England Automobile Journal* indicate an intention for manufacture, and as late as August of 1911 *The Horseless Age* carried news that the businessmen of Rutland were still discussing the idea of locating an automobile factory there. But the Archer Automobile Association, which was to be a $100,000 incorporation, seems never to have left the discussion stage. This venture is not to be confused with Archer & Company of New York City which produced the De Leon in 1905-1906.

ARCHIBALD — In 1917 the Russell Archibald Company was organized with a capital stock of $5000 and the announced plan of manufacturing automobiles and trucks in Delhi, New York. This venture seems to have been completely a family affair, with Russell Archibald, Carrie M. Archibald and Sloan Archibald involved. And it seems to have gone nowhere.

ARDERY-HOLLIDAY — The manufacture and repair of automobiles was the announced plan of the Ardery-Holliday Motor Car Company which was organized with a capital stock of $10,000 in St. Joseph, Missouri in the fall of 1912. Involved in the venture were J.W. Ardery, J.W. Holliday, W.S. Thompson, Charles Ardery and W.H. Watson. Manufacture seems not to have followed.

1905 Ardsley, touring, WLB

ARDSLEY — Yonkers, New York — (1905-1906) — The Ardsley Motor Car Company was organized by a group of Yonkers businessmen headed by Frederik P. Fuller and A. Everett Hunt, Jr. to produce a car designed by William S. Howard, who had already built a car under his own name in the same city. "Made in New York by New Yorkers for New Yorkers" was the company's slogan, and the product was described as "a Foreign Type car without the usual improvements. A car so perfect in workmanship . . . that two machines could be taken apart and with their parts form a third." The Ardsley had a four-cylinder 35/40 hp engine, 100-inch wheelbase, three-speed sliding gear transmission, shaft drive, and a cut-out device for "energetic muffling." The January 7th, 1905 issue of *The Automobile* advised that twenty-five cars were already under construction, to be followed quickly by another lot of fifty. Probably no more Ardsleys than that were built. The car's price was slashed from $4000 to $3500 in 1906. Although official dissolution of the company was May 16th, 1907, the Ardsley had ceased to exist in reality by the end of 1906. In October that year William S. Howard organized the Howard Motor Works in Yonkers for the manufacture of engines initially and another Howard car subsequently.

1905 ARDSLEY
Four — 35/40 hp — 100" wb

	FP	5	4	3	2	1
King of Belgium Tour.	4000	2000	3000	4200	6500	14,000

1906 Ardsley, touring, WLB

1906 ARDSLEY
Four — 35/40 hp, 100" wb

	5	4	3	2	1
King of Belgium Tour.	3500	2000	3000	4200	6500	14,000

1914 Argo Cyclecar, roadster, NAHC

ARGO — Jackson, Michigan — (1914-1918) — Initially, the product of the Argo Motor Company was a $295 cyclecar with a neat specification: four-cylinder L-head water-cooled engine, shaft drive, sliding gear transmission, 12 hp, 90-inch wheelbase, 44-inch tread, 750 pounds. It had been called the Ajax in France when Benjamin Briscoe ventured there to estab-

1915 Argo roadster, WLB

lish Briscoe Freres in Neuilly on the Seine to add to his budding empire. It returned to the United States with only the Ajax friction drive and the name being changed. Sometimes the U.S. version was referred to as the Argo Motor Vique to sound a little more Frenchified. Although Briscoe envisioned a New York City site for the Argo's manufacture at the time of company incorporation in March 1914, by September he had moved the entire business to Jackson, Michigan when the plant of the erstwhile Standard Electric became available. With the quick death of the cyclecar genre, the Argo became a larger conventional assembled car with standard tread in 1916, by which time Benjamin Briscoe was bored with it, and sold the whole works to Mansell Hackett who reorganized as the Hackett Motor Car Company in the fall of 1916. In addition to producing the new Hackett, the new firm also continued assembly of Argos from parts on hand until as late as January 1918.

1914-1915 ARGO
Four — 12 hp, 90" wb

	FP	5	4	3	2	1
Rds.	295	1500	2500	3600	5500	11,000

1916 Argo, roadster, HAC

1916-1918 ARGO
Four — 22 hp, 96" wb

Rds.-2P	385	1500	2500	3600	5500	11,000
Tour.-5P	435	1450	2400	3500	5300	10,500

ARGO ELECTRIC — Saginaw, Michigan — (1912-1916) — The Argo Electric Vehicle Company claimed that its 100-inch wheelbases were the longest for any electric car on the market. Gemmer wheel steering was also rather avant-garde for a battery-powered car, and shaft drive and the Cutler-Hammer interlocking foot control were also featured. The company was a rather late entry to electric ranks, organized July 6th, 1910 by Fred Buck, Theodore Huss, Benton Hanchett and Otto Schupp of Saginaw, and Albert M. Marshall of Duluth, Minnesota. The old Sommer Brothers Match Company plant at Jefferson and Atwater in Saginaw was secured for manufacture, and Argo moved in during September. To being late, Argo now added being delayed. Apparently some problems arose in preparing the car for production because prototype testing did not begin until 1911, advertising did not commence before that fall, and the official debut of the new Argo Electric followed at the New York Automobile Show in January 1912. The only body style offered that year was a five-passenger brougham. A roadster and limousine, as well as two express truck models, were added for 1913. First indications were that the Argo Electric would find a ready acceptance; as a 1913 ad declared, within ninety days of announcement, 300 Argo Electrics had found "a dignified and careful ownership." But already signs were everywhere present that the electric car as a genre was on the wane in the industry. In January 1914 Argo joined with the Broc and Borland electric companies to become the American Electric Car Company, with each party to the merger being allowed three directors on the board of the new corporation, which was capitalized at $1.5 million. Fred Buck and Theodore Huss were a vice-president and secretary-treasurer respectively of the new combine. Economy of selling and distribution was the purpose of the merger, and it was announced that all three factories would be operated and all three cars produced under their own names. Soon, however, operations were consolidated into the Argo factory in Saginaw, though each car retained its own name. In 1916 they all died. In November that year, Columbia Motors

1912 Argo Electric, brougham, NAHC

Company of Detroit purchased the Argo assets in order to obtain its National Automobile Chamber of Commerce license which was necessary to exhibit at the national automobile shows. The Argo factory was acquired by the Saginaw Motor Car Company, and the Yale 8 was subsequently produced there. Later the same factory saw Jumbo truck production by the Nelson Motor Truck Company.

1912 ARGO
Model A — 110" wb

	FP	5	4	3	2	1
Brougham	3000	2500	3500	5500	9000	18,000

1913-1914 ARGO
Model A — 108 1/2" wb

Brougham	2800	2500	3500	5500	9000	18,000

Model B — 108 1/2" wb

Rds.	2500	3300	4500	6500	10,000	20,000

Model C — 110" wb

Limo.	3100	3000	4000	6000	9500	19,000

1915-1916 ARGO
Model A — 108 1/2" wb

Brougham	2650	2500	3500	5500	9000	18,000

Model B — 108 1/2" wb

Rds.	2350	3300	4500	6500	10,000	20,000

Model C — 110" wb

Limo.	2800	3000	4000	6000	9500	19,000

ARGONAUT — The steam car built by J.W. Wilkins of San Francisco in 1877 was referred to as the Argonaut by its inventor. Because of the complexity of the Wilkins' story, it is more properly designated by its inventor's name. Refer to Wilkins.

1919 Argonne, roadster, JAC

ARGONNE — Jersey City, New Jersey — (1919-1920) — The Argonne, named for the forest in France which had been the scene of one of the most spectacular battles of World War I, was designed by Otto R. Bieler (who had previously been a designer for Biddle) and Harold E. Porter (who had previously plied his trade with Bliss). Initially the venture was sponsored through the Automotive & Machinery Engineering Company of Long Island City which Bieler had established in 1918, but very soon the Argonne Motor Car Company was formed instead, with the cars to be built for the firm by the Jersey City Machine Company. Initially, too, the Argonne was to be a six, but early on Bieler decided on a four-cylinder engine from Buda. Advertisements during the summer of 1919 declared "Power & Speed with Economy" — 20 mpg and 70 mph were guaranteed. The car's transmission was a four-speed. At the Argonne's formal debut at the Hotel Commodore during New York National Automobile Show week in January 1920, *Motor World* noticed that the "general makeup . . . has a decided European tinge to it." Most noticeable was the radiator design, which borrowed liberally from the Austro-Daimler. An altogether handsome car, the Argonne was introduced as the postwar recession took

1920 Argonne, Special, roadster, WLB

hold. This was followed by the sudden death of Otto Bieler. Charles S. Singer took over as general manager and, learning of the availability of the more puissant Rochester-Duesenberg engine, had the chassis revamped to carry it. The Argonne was produced into March 1920; its liabilities estimated at $65,000, the company proceeded into involuntary receivership in July. Probably no more than twenty-four cars had been built. Interestingly, at the sheriff's sale, the remaining parts of the Argonne were bought by Brisk & Beckelman, a dress-making company located on 31st Street in New York City's Garment Center. Purportedly, this inventory was later resold to another garment merchant who also owned a garage in the Bronx and who assembled about ten further Argonnes. These were all closed cars — sedans and at least one coupe — with aluminum coachwork by the Harvard Body Company in the Bronx. All previous Argonnes had been open cars.

1919 ARGONNE
Argonne Four

	FP	5	4	3	2	1
Rds. (119" wb)	4000	4000	5000	8000	15,000	28,000
Tour. (132" wb)	4200	3500	4500	7500	13,000	26,000

1920 ARGONNE
Argonne Four

	FP	5	4	3	2	1
Sport Rds.-2P (118" wb)	4500	3500	4500	7500	13,000	26,000
Sport Rds.-4P (118" wb)	4700	3600	4700	8000	14,000	27,000

1905 Ariel, touring, WLB

ARIEL — Massachusetts, New Jersey, et al. — (1905-1907) — The dilemma of the Ariel Motor Company was that its founders could not settle on a single location to build the product. The Ariel founders were Charles B. Lamont, Charles J. Palmer and Joseph P. Allcott, all of Boston. The product was a rather advanced motorcar whose designer went unheralded, though most probably it was not one of the three gentlemen aforementioned since history does not record any of them as having been mechanics, let alone engineers. And the Ariel had to have been designed by an engineer, since it featured the very early use of an overhead camshaft. The Ariel's engine could be had with either air or water cooling. Both three- and four-cylinder versions were ready by the time of the Boston Automobile Show in March 1905. The Ariel had a distinctively-shaped cast aluminum dash which was most becoming, its round hood and radiator configuration resembled the French Delaunay-Belleville, and the firm seems to have had some affiliation with the British Ariel venture. "Look for the Oval Front" was the company's slogan, but the problem was where to look for it. The Ariel people had begun production in a leased factory in

1905 Ariel, roadster, NAHC

Boston, but suffered landlord problems almost immediately. In January 1906 came the announcement that Ariel production had moved to Nutley (New Jersey), but by April it had changed to Bridgeport (Connecticut), and by fall the Ariel was in yet another factory in Baltimore (Maryland). Less than a year later the Ariel was still in Baltimore but by now it had been renamed the Maryland and was being built by the Sinclair-Scott Company. It would appear that Ariel's continuing landlord problem was the inability of its founders to pay the rent.

1905 ARIEL
Type III — 3-cyl., 15 hp, 88" wb

Rbt.	2000	2000	3000	4200	6500	14,000

Type IV — 4-cyl., 25 hp., 100" wb

Tour.	2500	2200	3200	4500	7000	15,000

60

1906 Ariel, touring, NAHC

1906-1907 ARIEL
Type IV — 4-cyl., 30 hp, 100" wb

	FP	5	4	3	2	1
Tour.	2500	2200	3200	4500	7000	15,000

ARISTOCRAT — Hagerstown, Maryland — (1927-1931) — The Aristocrat was built by the Moller organization of Hagerstown, that company also producing the Dagmar private passenger car as well as no fewer than seven further makes which, like the Aristocrat, were cars for hire. Like most of the Moller-sponsored taxis, the Aristocrat was Buda-engined, and differed from the other Moller taxi varieties (Astor, Blue Light, Five-Boro, Luxor, Paramount, Super Paramount, Twentieth Century) only in radiator configuration or details.

ARISTON — Chicago, Illinois — (1906) — In January of 1906, L.D. Sheppard, who gave his address as 52 South Morgan Street in Chicago, announced that he had a four-cylinder touring car called the Ariston ready for marketing. He must have built a few of them because the March 1916 *List of Automobiles* published by the Saint Paul Fire and Marine Insurance Company in Minnesota indicate a 40/50 hp Model O and 30/35 hp Model S Ariston as having been built, with an asterisk indicating that Saint Paul wouldn't insure them for collison. Neither Sheppard nor the Ariston were heard from again in 1907.

ARISTOS — The Aristos Company of New York City produced a variety of automotive-related products under the brand name of Mondex. In 1913 the company secured license for U.S. manufacture of the slide-valve Magic engine invented by Martin Fischer of Switzerland, and from 1914-1915 produced six-cylinder motorcars called Mondex-Magic. Refer to Mondex-Magic.

ARKANSAS — Arkadelphia, Arkansas — (1912) — In May of 1913 an advertisement in the *Automobile Trade Journal* offered for sale a used 1912 two-cylinder 12 hp two-seater roadster called the Arkansas. The price was $425. The seller was the W.L. Fodrea Garage Company of Arkadelphia. Possibly Fodrea's foray into automotive manufacture never proceeded beyond this one car, and the company was anxious to forget the experience. Possibly the car had been built for a client who reneged. Possibly the car had not even been built by Fodrea at all, but had somehow found its way into the garage. Documentation is lacking. There was a Fodrea-Malott Manufacturing Company in Indiana which produced a car to order called the Beetle Flyer, but there is no evidence of any connection. In 1919 the Arkadelphia Motor Comany was organized in Arkadelphia, but it operated as a dealership only and W.L. Fodrea seems not to have been involved.

ARMAC — Chicago, Illinois — (1905-1906) — Archie McCullen founded the Armac Motorcycle Company in St. Paul, Minnesota in 1903. In 1905 announcement was made that the firm would move to Chicago on August 15th and relocate in a new factory at 464 Carroll Avenue. Capital had been increased to $50,000, the firm's name had been changed to Armac Motor Company, and it now proposed to add side and fore-car attachments to its motorcycle and to produce a 6 hp runabout as well. The latter vehicle was a belt-driven buckboard type powered by one of the company's motorcycle engines. It was built in very small numbers and for a very short period. By 1907, Armac had returned to motors and motorcycles exclusively, in which business it remained into 1908.

1905

Armac	—	900	1500	2500	3600	5500

ARMOND — In Fayetteville, North Carolina, early in 1921, the Armond Motor Company was organized with a capital stock of $100,000 and announced plan to establish "an automobile manufacturing plant in that city this year." Subsequent references indicate that an automobile was not the planned product, but automobile accessories instead. G.D. Gravely was the Armond manager.

ARMSTRONG — In the spring of 1909 the Armstrong Buggy Company of Atlanta, Georgia announced a capitalization of $25,000 and the plan to manufacture high-wheeled motor buggies. D.D. Armstrong, R.K. King and

Thomas Scrutchen were behind this venture, and their plans included the construction of a "two-story factory of fireproof construction containing 25,000 square feet." There is no evidence Armstrong subsequently embarked upon the sustained manufacture of automobiles.

Wayne Armstrong was the man behind a venture in 1910 for the manufacture of gasoline motor cars in Laurelville (Athens County), Ohio. Although $150,000 was indicated as the capital stock, nothing further was heard regarding automobile manufacture in Laurelville.

In Cincinnati, Ohio in 1913, the Armstrong Motors Company was organized with a $10,000 capital stock to manufacture and deal in motor cars and parts. J.H. Armstrong, L.S. Armstrong, C.M. Eggers, C.S. Stewart and H. Bronsworth were the principals involved. Manufacture is not indicated.

1901 Armstrong Electric, MVMA

ARMSTRONG ELECTRIC — Connecticut — (1896, 1901-1902) — The two electric cars bearing the Armstrong name were made in very small numbers in Connecticut, and it is not known whether any connection existed between the two. The 1896 car was built by the Armstrong Manufacturing Company in Bridgeport. The 1901-1902 car was produced by M. Armstrong & Company of New Haven. The latter car was equipped with two Eddy motors and a Willard battery and was capable of speeds of 3-1/2, 7 and 14 mph, either forward or backward. "It has not as yet been given a test on hard, level roads," its makers advised *Cycle and Automobile Trade Journal* in July 1901, "but under the test of a twenty-mile run over country roads it was found that the batteries were not nearly exhausted, however." The financial resources of the company were rather quickly, however.

1896 ARMSTRONG ELECTRIC

	FP	5	4	3	2	1
Armstrong Electric	—	2500	3500	5000	8500	18,000

1901-1902 ARMSTRONG ELECTRIC

	FP	5	4	3	2	1
Armstrong Electric	—	2500	3500	5000	8500	18,000

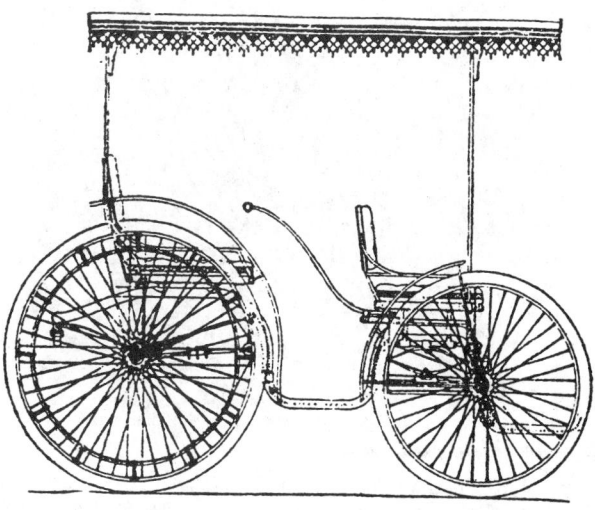

1895 Arnold, WLB

ARNOLD — Chicago, Illinois — (1895) — B.J. Arnold of Chicago has been frequently cited as the builder of an automobile in Chicago in 1895. And he did plan to build a car as early as 1894. His design included the mounting of batteries under the body and steering from the back rather than from the front seat. Arnold was employed as an electrical engineer in Chicago. According to *The Horseless Age* of November 1895, "owing to press of other business, Mr. Arnold has been unable to put his design into practical shape." How practical the vehicle proved to be has not been documented.

ARROW — In 1904 the name Arrow was applied to the cars built by the George N. Pierce Company of Buffalo, New York. Earlier the cars had been called simply Motorette. This Upstate New York car subsequently became famous as the Pierce-Arrow. Refer to Pierce-Arrow.

The Arrow Motor Vehicle Company was a $2500 incorporation from Jefferson City, Missouri announced during the early summer of 1907. August and H.O. Ross were the principals involved, and the plan was the manufacture and sale of motor vehicles and the operation of a general machine shop business. Manufacture of an Arrow car has not been established.

The Arrow Motor Car Company of Long Island City, New York has been indicated on car rosters as an automobile manufacturer in 1912-1913. No firm of that name appears in local city directories.

In July of 1922 Arrow Motors was the company established by A.C. Burch to take over the assets of the defunct Maibohm. In August Arrow was reorganized as Courier Motors and the former Maibohm was refined into the new Courier. Refer to Courier.

The Arrow Taxicab Company of Chicago was organized during the summer of 1909 "to engage in the business of manufacturing and operating motor cars." Capital stock was $5000, William A. Jennings of 171 Washington Street was the man behind the project. Manufacture has not been established.

1907 Arrow, runabout, GR

ARROW — St. Louis, Missouri — (1907) — The Arrow Motor Buggy Company of St. Louis produced a highwheeler that was priced at $250 and which promotion indicated was so simple that a child could operate it. Certainly the car was simple. It probably also was not much good.

1914 Arrow Cyclecar, runabout, OCW

ARROW — Dayton, Ohio — (1914) — The M.C. Whitmore Company of Dayton produced a cyclecar on an ash frame with shaft and bevel gear drive and available as a one-seater, a two-seater, and a light delivery. Further specifications were the usual for vehicles of this genre — 12 hp Spacke vee-twin, two-speed planetary transmission, 100-inch wheelbase, 36-inch tread — but the view from the radiator was interesting. No front axle was used, triple transverse springs serving instead. For the short time the Arrow cyclecar was in production, it was sold through the National United Service Company of Detroit.

1914 ARROW
Model A — 2-cyl., 12 hp, 100" wb

	FP	5	4	3	2	1
Tandem Rdstr.-2P	385	1600	2600	3700	6000	12,000

Model B — 2-cyl., 12 hp, 100" wb

	FP	5	4	3	2	1
Side by Side Rds.-2P	385	1600	2600	3700	6000	12,000
Light Delivery	425	1500	2500	3600	5500	11,000

ARROW — Detroit, Michigan — (1914) — The Arrow cyclecar from Detroit perched high on spindly wire wheels and was suspended on quarter-elliptic springs in front and full cantilever in the rear. It was powered by a four-cylinder 18 hp water-cooled engine. The wheelbase was 100 inches, the tread 40; a left-hand steering wheel was fitted. The transmission was friction, and final drive double belt. The car sold for $395 equipped with two headlamps and one taillight, in addition to horn, top, side curtains and very high windshield. A kit of tools was thrown in for good measure. The Arrow cyclecar was produced in Detroit by the National United Service Company which also handled the Mayer carburetor, the M & P tire air pump, the United spark plug and the Miller storage battery. After the quick failure of the Arrow cyclecar, National United Service no doubt returned full-time to dealing in those other products. In 1914 National United Service also produced another cyclecar which it marketed under the name of United, and served as the distributing agency for the Arrow produced in Dayton (Ohio) and the Beisel produced in Monroe (Michigan).

1914 ARROW
Cyclecar — 4-cyl., 18 hp, 100" wb

	FP	5	4	3	2	1
Rds.-2P	395	1500	2500	3500	5500	11,000

ARROW — Minneapolis, Minnesota — (1914) — M.B. Gilman announced his plans to build a cyclecar called Arrow on November 23rd, 1913. He spent the winter putting together a prototype, and by the following spring he reported test runs had resulted in a fuel economy of 40-50 mpg. The Arrow was powered by a two-cylinder 13 hp engine. The wheelbase was 90 inches, with a 45-inch tread; the axles were tubular with ball bearing hubs, semi-elliptic springs were fitted front and rear, and the transmission was a friction type. The frame was channel steel, the body of wood and steel, finished in "a lead color." The car's price was $395. Earlier in the year the Arrow Cyclecar Company had been incorporated with $500,000 capital stock "under the lenient laws of Maine," as *Automobile Topics* put it. The incorporators were all residents of Augusta who perhaps were in the business of filing the papers for desirous out-of-state ventures. There is no evidence that any viable production resulted in Minnesota, however, and the company was out of business before the end of 1914.

1914 ARROW
Cyclecar — 2-cyl., 13 hp, 90" wb

Rds.-2P	395	—	—	—	—	—

ARROWBILE — Santa Monica, California — (1937) — Waldo D. Waterman was one of the first Californians to learn to fly, and aviation remained the absorbing interest of his life. By the early Thirties he was considered an authority in his field. His organization was rather cleverly named Waterman Arrowplane Corporation. The Arrowbile that he built was, as its name suggests, part aeroplane, part automobile. Removal of the single wing and propeller saw to the easy conversion to land vehicle. Drive to the rear wheels was provided by a system of vee-belt pulleys; the powerplant was a modified Studebaker Dictator six-cylinder engine. In 1937 Waterman traveled to South Bend to interest Studebaker in his vehicle, and the automobile makers were indeed interested. "Studebaker has purchased five of the machines and will demonstrate them in principal cities of the country this summer," *MoToR* reported in July. "They have a top speed of 125 mph and a landing speed of 45 mph. As automobiles they have a top speed of 75 mph." Only the prototype had thus far been built, and it was demonstrated at a national dealership meeting at Studebaker's proving grounds in August. Unfortunately, during that demonstration, the Arrowbile was forced into an emergency landing in the field of a nearby farm. The only injuries suffered were to the plane, and to Studebaker's interest in the project. The corporation decided against accepting any further Arrowbiles, though Waldo Waterman did proceed to build five Arrowbiles himself. The Studebaker price for the vehicle would have been $3000; Waterman found they cost $7000 each to build. After Studebaker reneged, he tried to find other backing but could not.

1936 Arrowhead, three-wheeler, WLB

ARROWHEAD — Los Angeles, California — (1936) — The Arrowhead was designed by W. Everett Miller and was built by the Advance Auto Body Works of Los Angeles as a promotional car for the Arrowhead Spring Water Company. Just the one vehicle was produced, at a cost of $8000. It carried a V-8 engine which was mounted at the rear, with a standard transmission and torque tube drive. A three-wheeler, the Arrowhead was similar to the Dymaxion built by Buckminster Fuller several years previously. The car drove through the two front wheels, and was steered through the single one at the rear. When introduced, it was referred to as the "car of 1960." The car reportedly remains extant.

1936 ARROWHEAD

Arrowhead Three-Wheeler	—	2000	3000	4200	6500	14,000

ARROW LOCOMOTOR — Buffalo, New York — (1896) — Early in 1896 Adolph Moesch & Company of Buffalo completed a very perky motor phaeton powered by a single-cylinder 3 1/2 hp engine of its own design. A top speed of 15 mph was claimed. That Moesch was anxious for production was indicated by the news story appearing in *The Horseless Age* in March that year: "Ball bearings are not used, but the makers are prepared to put them in if desired. Solid rubber tires are fitted on the wheels, and the

whole construction is very strong, so as to be adapted to our rough country roads." How many buyers were enticed by that ringing endorsement is not known. The company was not heard from again in the automotive field.

1896 Arrow Locomotor, auto-buggy, NAHC

ARROW PLANE — Chicago, Illinois — (1932) — The Arrow Plane was a rear-engined teardrop of a car built in 1932 for a wealthy Chicagoan named Lyman Voelpel by the Hill Auto Body Metal Company of Cincinnati. The car, which remains extant, was one of a number built by the Hill company during this period. The McQuay-Norris which followed in 1933 resembled the Arrow Plane, most specifically in its window design. The Hill company specialized in streamlined equipment for airplanes but made periodic forays into the automotive field with race cars and streamlined bodies.

ARTER — Cleveland, Ohio — (1912) — The Arter Auto Carriage Company was organized in Cleveland during the early summer of 1912 with a capital stock of $20,000 and the plan to manufacture, sell and repair automobiles. James G. Arter, C.A. Chapman, James B. Ruhl and C.M. Lemmon were the people involved. Most probably only a prototype, if that, followed of any Arter car. During the summer of 1913 the firm was reorganized for the manufacture of automobile bodies only.

ARTICMOBILE — In late 1911 the Articmobile Company was organized with a capital stock of a million dollars for the manufacture and sale of automobiles in Seattle, Washington. F.G. Horner and S.B. McCrea were among the people involved. Manufacture does not seem to have followed.

1904 Artzberger, steamer, NAHC

ARTZBERGER STEAM — Allegheny, Pennsylvania — (1904) — During the summer of 1904, in a hill climbing contest at Highland Park in Allegheny, W.H. Artzberger drove his steam car to a resounding victory over several Stanleys and Whites, and all other steamers on hand. This was but one of several convincing demonstrations — including first place in the 100-mile run from Rochester to Buffalo — that the Artzberger put up that year. Moreover, as the Artzberger Automobile Company boasted, its competition car was not "stripped, as some of the competing cars were, but was used just as it is used on the road." What the company did not mention in its brochure was that the Artzberger was really a Foster, the steam car which had been built in Rochester, New York since 1901 and which the Pennsylvania company took over in 1904. In trade press interviews, W.H. Artzberger couldn't avoid reference to his car's origins, though he emphasized the vast improvements he had made which seem to have been largely confined to a lengthening of the wheelbase. Production did not continue into 1905.

1904 ARTZBERGER

	FP	5	4	3	2	1
Rds. (76" wb)	900	2500	3500	5000	8500	18,000
Surrey (78" wb)	1000	2600	3600	5500	9000	18,500
Tour. (78" wb)	800	2500	3500	5000	8500	18,000
Light Delivery	1000	2000	3000	4500	8000	17,000

ASBURY PARK — In early 1910 the Asbury Park Automobile Company was organized in New Jersey with a capital stock of $50,000 and the announced plan to "manufacture motor cars, conduct garages, etc." Behind this venture were D. Havens, F.T. Weeden and L.P. Croce, and they may have proceeded to operate a garage, but they did not manufacture an automobile.

ASCOT — The Ascot Vehicle Company at 1 Montgomery Street in Jersey City, New Jersey was indicated to be an automobile manufacturer in the Hiscox book *Horseless Vehicles, Automobiles, Motor Cycles* published in 1900. Manufacture has not been otherwise substantiated.

1915 Asheville Light Car, runabout, WLB

ASHEVILLE — Asheville, North Carolina — (1914) — E.C. Merrell established the Asheville Light Car Company in 1914 for production of a vehicle that, the name notwithstanding, was nothing more than a cyclecar, and a rather flimsy looking one at that. A side-by-side two-seater with a stark metal body and no passenger amenities, the Asheville was powered by an air-cooled 7 hp Indian twin, with two-speed transmission and final drive by a one-inch belt. Suspension was by cantilever springs, the wheelbase was 94 inches, the steering wheel was on the left side, and the entire vehicle weighed but 450 pounds. *Carette*, a magazine established in 1914 to promote the cyclecar cause, captioned its picture of the Asheville, "side view, showing the long bonnet over the motor, giving the impression of a small six." The magazine also noted that it was "the intention of Mr. Merrell to manufacture in quantities as soon as this model has been perfected." Neither the *Carette* magazine nor the Asheville car survived long.

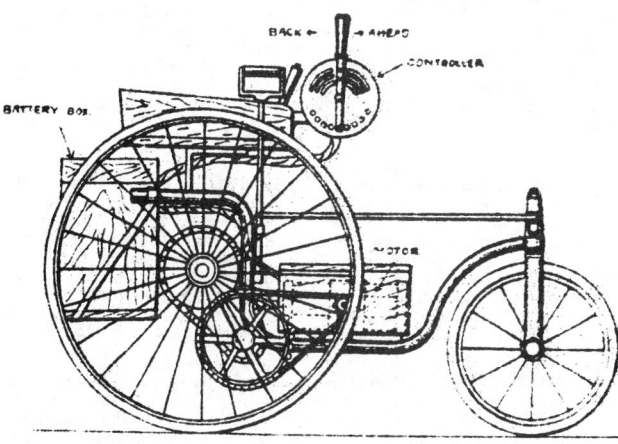

1892 Aspinwall Electric, WLB

ASPINWALL ELECTRIC — Washington, D.C. — (1892) — In 1892 L.M. Aspinwall built an electric vehicle with a 30-volt battery in a chassis that was devised from a large tricycle. The resulting three-wheeler was capable of speeds reaching as high as 10 mph, and the Aspinwall Electric did indeed run. In a letter to the editor of *Cycle and Automobile Trade Journal* published in 1911, L.M. Aspinwall noted with becoming modesty, "It was operated on the streets of Washington on a number of trips, and while it would not at the present time be considered a 'howling success' nevertheless it operated and can probably claim the distinction of being one of the first self propelled pleasure vehicles in this country." Aspinwall never considered manufacture.

ASPROOTH-LEONI ELECTRIC — Philadelphia, Pennsylvania — (1926-1927) — In 1924 A.M. Leoni of Philadelphia designed and built a prototype of an electric truck chassis, and in late 1926 he completed a passenger car chassis which he hoped to market as a taxicab. Its motor was incorporated in the rear axle, with drive through planetary gearing, and both independent service and emergency brakes provided. Although the chassis was designed along conventional lines, it was supported on Hofmann air springs front and rear, this because Leoni did not believe balloon tires practical for electric vehicles due to their greater frictional losses, the use of the air spring compensating for the loss in resiliency of high

pressure to low pressure tires. Because of the nature of taxicab service, provision was made in the Asprooth-Leoni car for a quick (five-minute) interchange of batteries. "The operating company would keep two batteries for each vehicle, one battery being at all times in the vehicle and the other on charge," explained *Automotive Industries*. Undoubtedly, the Asprooth of this Asprooth-Leoni venture provided the capital for the building of the prototype. Soon thereafter, the money flow stopped, because this taxi did not go into production.

1901 Asquith, NAHC

ASQUITH — Waterloo, Iowa — (1901) — By the fall of 1901, S.A. Asquith finally had his car on the road. "I started it two years ago this summer when little wanted in the line could be bought," he explained in a letter published in *The Motor Age*. "The engine is of the double-cylinder balanced type, cranks set at 180 degrees, 3-3/4 inch bore and stroke and 4-inch stroke; water cooled and all of my own making except one cylinder, which I bought." The rest of the vehicle, save for the tires and rims, was also of Asquith's own devising. "Should I build another, it would be a great improvement," he stated, "yet this works finely, and you cannot feel the least vibration when riding." Asquith's principal line of endeavor was as a jeweler and in association with his brother F.R. Asquith, he ran a jewelry business in Waterloo. In 1903 he also became Waterloo's first automobile dealer, taking on the agency for Oldsmobile which he operated under the name of S.A. Asquith Runabout Company for a short period before deciding, as the Waterloo *Courier* later reported, that "the combination of diamonds and motorcars was not a good business proposition." That being so, Asquith decided to stick with diamonds.

ASSOCIATED — Associated Auto Mechanics was the name of the $100,000 venture incorporated in New York City early in 1913 to manufacture motorcars and parts. C. Tichener, H. Barnes and J. Hoover were indicated as the incorporators. Manufacture does not appear to have followed.

The Associated Motors Corporation produced the Sperling car during the early Twenties in New York City. Refer to Sperling.

ASTER — The Aster has appeared on numerous lists of American-built cars. The car was sold in this country in 1906 and 1907 by Aster & Company of New York City, but it was not produced here. It was a French-built car (built by Aries with an Aster engine) that was imported to these shores.

ASTON — Bridgeport, Connecticut — (1908 et seq.) — The Aston Motor Car Company was incorporated during the fall of 1908 by F.R. Aston, M.A. Hall and G.E. Morton. Capital stock was $10,000, and the purpose of the company, which was located at 1103 State Street, was the manufacture of automobiles to custom order. The number of cars thusly produced, and for how long, remains a mystery. It is known that two Aston cars — one a 25 hp, the other a 40 hp — were registered in the state of Connecticut in 1915. The Aston company also served as a dealership for the Chalmers.

ASTOR — Hagerstown, Maryland — (1925-1927) — The Astor was one of a flurry of taxicabs produced by the M.P. Moller Motor Company of Hagerstown. The car's wheelbase was 118 inches, its engine a Buda four. A vee radiator and an unusual paint scheme — beige lower body with black top, running boards and fenders, complemented by a bright orange belt line and disc wheels — were the Astor's most distinctive features. The car was available as a $2295 limousine or $2345 landaulet, the price tags including "finance charges, war tax, fire and theft insurance, delivery expenses and all standard equipment." The Astor Cab Sales Company, Inc. of New York City marketed these cars, though interestingly most of the actual sales were to Philadelphia.

	FP	5	4	3	2	1
Taxi	—	2000	3000	4200	6500	14,000

1920 Astra, touring, WLB

ASTRA — St. Louis, Missouri — (1920) — The Astra was the idea of Associated Motors Corporation of New York City, it was designed by New York engineer Andre Mertzanoff, and it was slated to be built in St. Louis, Missouri. There the Astra Motors Corporation was organized with B.R. Parrott (who formerly had built the farm tractor of that name) as president and treasurer, A.J. Kessinger (vice-president of the Newsom Valve Company) as secretary, and V.C. Kloepper as chief engineer. Kloepper's job promised to be an easy one, since the car had already been designed, and it was an assembled vehicle with a four-cylinder 25 hp LeRoi engine in any case. A radiator that looked like a shark's nose was the car's only real distinguishing feature. Astra's agreement with Associated Motors included a production contract based on cost plus twenty-five percent, in addition to a commitment to produce 300 cars in the next eighteen months. The formation of the Astra company was announced on December 15th, 1919. Rumor floated about that it was the grand plan of Associated Motors Corporation to gain control of Dorris Motors Corporation in St. Louis. Instead, it was Dorris which gained control of Astra late in January of 1920. In mid-February Dorris exhibited several of the completed Astra touring cars at the St. Louis Automobile Show. In March Dorris indicated that it would henceforth produce the Astra car. In June it indicated that it would not. Probably the show cars were the only Astras built. Perhaps, too, the only reason Dorris bought the company was to render a potential St. Louis competitor asunder.

1920 ASTRA
Astra — 4-cyl., 25 hp, 108" wb

Tour. Car		1325	—	—	—	—

ATHENS — The Athens Motor Car Company was organized in Athens, Georgia "with $10,000 capital and privilege to increase this to $50,000" for the manufacture and sale of "all kinds of motor vehicles, supplies and accessories." Walter H. Bishop and Lucien B. Flatow, both of Athens, were the people involved. Manufacture of an automobile is doubted.

ATKIN — This was one-half of the partnership producing the Hughes & Atkin steam carriage in Olneyville, Rhode Island at the turn of the century. Refer to Hughes & Atkin.

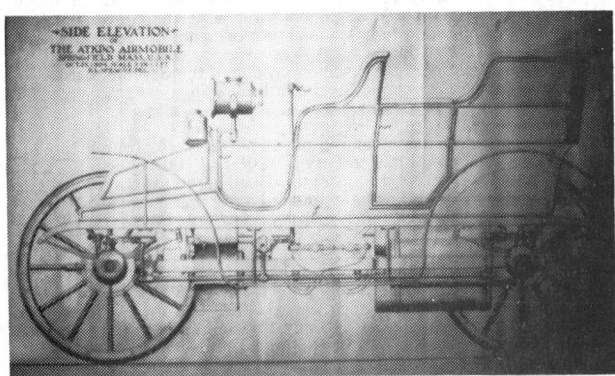

1904 Atkins Airmobile, touring, RNT

ATKINS AIRMOBILE — Springfield, Massachusetts — (1904) — Charles H. Atkins was a mechanical engineer in Springfield who turned himself into an automobile designer in 1904. All that remains of his car is the drawing done of it that year by H.L. Sprague, a local draftsman. How much further than paper this automotive venture proceeded is not known.

ATLANTA — Atlanta, Georgia — (1908) — "Revolutionizer Coming from Georgia" was the trade press headline in August 1908 when the Atlanta Motor Company was announced. A $100,000 incorporation, the firm was the idea of William Knox Cleveland, who said his new invention for a four-wheel-drive car would "revolutionize automobile manufacture." Asso-

ciated with him in this venture were Herbert L. Wiggs, Eugene Callaway and V.L. Smith. Whether the Atlanta prototype was successful is not known, but obviously no "revolution" ever took place. The Atlanta Motor Company was dead by the end of 1908. The year following a new firm came to town called the Atlanta Motor Car Company. None of the same principals were involved, and its product was called the White Star, which was marketed from 1909 to 1911.

ATLANTA — Atlanta Motors Corporation was a $2 million Delaware incorporation for the manufacture of automobiles and trucks which was announced in the motor press from Atlanta, Georgia in May of 1917 and went nowhere fast.

ATLANTIC — The Atlantic Company was organized in Augusta, Maine early in 1905 for the manufacture of automobiles and boats. The announced officers were W.H. Simmons as president, and E.F. Whitten as treasurer, both of Augusta. Capital stock was $50,000. Very shortly thereafter the firm reported that dealing in automobiles would be its only activity.

The Atlantic Auto Service Association was a $40,000 Delaware incorporation for the manufacture of automobiles which was announced in March 1919. Arthur Sellers, Harry G. Gooden and David McGinn were the principals involved. Manufacture did not follow.

The Atlantic Automobile Company was organized with a capital stock of $50,000 late in 1905 for the manufacture of automobiles. Incorporators were Louis H. Hooper, Frank A. Broadhead and Clarence L. Cole. No manufacture is indicated.

The Atlantic Automobile Company of Council Bluffs, Iowa was incorporated by C.L. Herring, J.C. Herring and B.A. Spinney early in 1909. Capital stock was $25,000, with the founders at that time serving as agents for Reo and Ford cars in southwestern Iowa. Although their company's articles of incorporation included provision for the manufacture of motorcars in the future, Atlantic never followed up on that provision. No Atlantic cars were built.

The Atlantic Electric Vehicle Company of Camden, New Jersey was indicated to be an automobile manufacturer in the Hiscox book *Horseless Vehicles, Automobiles, Motor Cycles* published in 1900. Further substantiation of manufacture has not been discovered.

The Atlantic Rim Company of Baltimore, Maryland announced a $20,000 capitalization and the plan to manufacture automobiles and automobile supplies during the fall of 1907. Involved in this venture were Thomas H. Gaither, Jr., Joseph B. McMullen, Dysert McMullen, George R. Gaither and Edward M. Hammond. Subsequent manufacture is not indicated.

The Atlantic States Sales Company was a $25,000 incorporation from Philadelphia for the manufacture and sale of automobiles and accessories that was announced in April of 1914. No car was ever manufactured.

The Atlantic Vehicle Company of Jersey City, New Jersey was a $25,000 incorporation for the manufacture of engines and automobiles that was announced in February of 1907. T.H. Keck and E.T. Gould were among the people involved. Manufacture is doubted.

The Atlantic Vehicle Company announced during the fall of 1911 from New York City for the manufacture and sale of motor vehicles was capitalized at $10,000 and headed by Philip A. Carroll, Joseph D. Dempsey and Eugene A. Donahue. Manufacture did not follow.

The Atlantic Vehicle Company announced in April 1912 from Jersey City, New Jersey had a capitalization of $340,000 and the plan "to manufacture vehicles of all kinds." The incorporators included J.R. Turner of Basking Ridge and M. Black and L.R. Jillson of New York City. An automobile was never produced.

ATLANTIC — Newark, New Jersey — (1912-1914) — The Atlantic Vehicle Company was organized early in 1912 to manufacture electric commercial vehicles and by summer had moved into the former home of the Royal Machine Company in Newark. Atlantic electric trucks followed, the company remaining in business until shortly before the Armistice. During its early years, production of an electric gasoline car was also contemplated but seems not to have proceeded beyond the prototype stage. Likewise an Atlantic electric taxicab was a stillborn. The firm's name was changed to Atlantic Electric Vehicle Company following reorganization in 1915.

ATLANTIC STEAMER — Brockton, Massachusetts — (1899) — In 1899 the Marsh brothers of Brockton built a steam car which they had thoughts of producing. The Atlantic Automobile Manufacturing Company was organized for that purpose, but the brothers quickly decided to build motorcycles instead. The first car put into production by the Marshes was the gasoline-powered Marsh Runabout of 1905-1906.

ATLAS — The Atlas Automobile Company of Newark, New Jersey has been cited as producing an automobile in 1902. No substantiation for this has been uncovered.

The Atlas Motor Company of New York City was organized in 1906 with a capital stock of $1200 and the plan to manufacture engines and automobiles. A.M. Bullows and H.B. Pruser were the men involved. No manufacture seems to have followed.

The Atlas Taxi Company of Brooklyn, New York was an early 1911 incorporation with a capital stock of $10,000 for the manufacture, sale and operation of taxicabs. Charles H. Hohorst and his brother Claus, together with John B. Haff, were the promoters of this venture. That this firm actually manufactured any vehicles itself is doubted.

ATLAS — Pittsburgh, Pennsylvania — (1906-1907) — The Atlas was offered as both a touring car and runabout powered by a four-cylinder 25/30 hp engine in a chassis featuring a three-speed sliding gear transmission and shaft drive. This short-lived venture began in the "new fireproof garage" of the Atlas Automobile Company on College Avenue, East End in Pittsburgh late in 1906 and ended sometime during 1907. W.H. La Fountain, William G. Hughes and Alfred F. Bennett had been the men behind this Atlas.

1907 Atlas, model R, runabout, HAC

1909 Atlas, model S, runabout, HAC

ATLAS — Springfield, Massachusetts — (1907-1911) / ATLAS KNIGHT — (1912-1913)

When Harry A. Knox left the Knox Automobile Company that had been building his air-cooled Knox cars since the turn of the century in Springfield, he set up shop across town as the Knox Motor Truck Company. Though he called the two-tonner he introduced in 1905 the Atlas, his use of the Knox name in his company's designation was annoying to his former partners, and they took him to court on the matter. Meanwhile, Harry Knox had another idea, and that was to produce under license the little two-stroke runabout built by the Sunset Automobile Company in San Francisco. The Sunset people were initially reluctant but following the earthquake in April 1906 which destroyed their factory, they were happy to comply since the money realized from the Knox deal would help in their rebuilding efforts. Thus it was that the Atlas runabout with its "Perfected Two-Cycle Engine" was introduced in Springfield in 1907. The same two-cylinder two-stroke unit was introduced to Atlas delivery vans in 1908, as well as a new Atlas taxicab. Harry Knox, betimes, was developing further the two-stroke principle. Subsequently a three-cylinder ("the continuous power of the ordinary six-cylinder engine . . . with only seven moving parts") touring model proved popular, as did a big 60 hp four-cylinder version. In the 1909 Vanderbilt Cup, Harry Knox entered an Atlas in order to take promotional advantage of being the first two-stroke entrant in a major long-distance road race. He finished a very respectable fifth. But the two-stroke engine was soon finished too — in the marketplace. Consequently, for 1912, a new wrinkle was added: the Knight sleeve-valve engine, made available in five and seven-passenger touring cars in the $3500 range. Initial Atlas automobile production had been under the aegis of the Knox Motor Truck Company. Not until late 1907, and the court decision barring his use of the name, was the Atlas Motor Car Company organized. When it went into bankruptcy early in 1913, purportedly because of difficulty in securing engines, Harry Knox simply packed his bags and left for Indianapolis where he joined the Lyons brothers in producing the Lyons-Knight.

1907 ATLAS
Model R — 2-cyl., 20 hp, 90" wb

	FP	5	4	3	2	1
Rbt.	1250	1500	2000	3000	5000	10,000

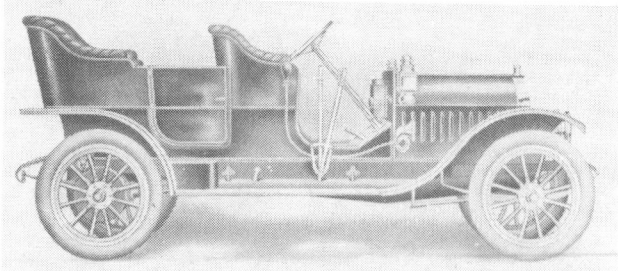

1909 Atlas, model F, touring, WLB

1910 Atlas, model T, taxi, HAC

1908 Atlas, model D, touring, HAC

1908 ATLAS
Model R — 2-cyl., 22 hp, 90" wb

	FP	5	4	3	2	1
Rbt.	1400	1500	2000	3000	5000	10,000
Town Car	2600	1100	1800	2800	4800	9500
Model D — 3-cyl., 34 hp, 106" wb						
Rmblst. Rbt.	1800	2000	3000	4000	6000	12,000
Tour.	2000	1500	2500	3600	5500	11,000
Model E — 4-cyl., 46 hp, 114" wb						
Tour.	2400	2500	3500	4500	6500	15,000

1909 ATLAS
Model S — 2-cyl., 20 hp, 96" wb

	FP	5	4	3	2	1
Rbt. (sliding gear)	1400	1500	2500	4000	7500	16,000
Rbt. (planetary)	1250	1000	2000	3000	6000	15,000
Town Car	2500	1000	1800	2500	4500	10,000
Delivery Car	1800	1000	1500	2000	4000	9000
Model F — 3-cyl., 30 hp, 110" wb						
Tour.	1850	2000	3000	4500	8000	17,000
Rbt.	1800	2500	3500	5000	8500	18,000

1910 ATLAS
Model T — 2-cyl., 20 hp, 102" wb

	FP	5	4	3	2	1
Land'et. Taxi	2400	3200	4500	6000	9500	19,500
Model F — 3-cyl., 30 hp, 110" wb						
Tour.	2000	2500	3500	5000	5800	18,000
Rbt.	1950	3000	4000	5500	9000	19,000
Model G — 4-cyl., 60 hp, 122" wb						
Toy Tonneau	2500	3000	4200	5700	9300	19,500
Model H — 4-cyl., 60 hp, 128" wb						
Tour.-5P	2500	3500	5000	6500	10,000	20,000
Tour.-7P	2600	3000	4000	5500	9000	19,000

1911 Atlas, model N, runabout, HAC

65

1911 ATLAS

Model K — 2-cyl., 20 hp, 102" wb

	FP	5	4	3	2	1
Land'et. Taxi	2400	1500	2500	4000	7500	16,000

Model N — 2-cyl., 20 hp, 106" wb

	FP	5	4	3	2	1
Rbt.		1250	2500	3500	5000	8500	18,000

Model O-3 — 4-cyl., 40 hp, 106" wb

	FP	5	4	3	2	1
Rbt.		2000	3000	4000	6000	9500	21,000

Model O-2 — 4-cyl., 40 hp, 120" wb

	FP	5	4	3	2	1
Toy Tonneau		2250	3000	4000	6000	9500	21,000

Model O — 4-cyl., 40 hp, 128" wb

	FP	5	4	3	2	1
Fore-Door Tour.		2400	3500	4500	7000	13,000	25,000

1912 Atlas-Knight, touring, NAHC

1912 ATLAS-KNIGHT

Knight, Model 12 — 4-cyl., 32.4 hp

Tour.-5P (130" wb)	3500	3500	4500	7000	13,000	25,000
Phaeton-7P (140" wb)	3750	3700	5000	8000	14,000	27,000

1913 Atlas-Knight, 7-pass. touring, WLB

1913 ATLAS-KNIGHT

Knight, Model 12 — 4-cyl., 50 hp, 130" wb

Tour.-5P	3500	3500	4500	7000	13,000	25,000
Tour.-7P	3750	3200	4400	6800	12,500	24,500

ATLAS MOTOR BUGGY — Indianapolis, Indiana — (1909) — The Atlas Motor Buggy was an aborted attempt by the Atlas Engine Works of Indianapolis to manufacture a highwheeler in 1909. Only a prototype resulted, whereupon the company reverted back to its principal business of producing two-stroke gasoline engines and diesel stationary units. Manufacture of an automobile in the Atlas works did follow, however, in 1913 when the Lyons brothers bought out the business and began production of the Lyons-Knight.

ATTERBURY — The Atterbury was a huge ten-passenger touring car produced in 1911. It was the second car built by the firm which had begun business in Buffalo, New York in 1904 as the Auto Car Equipment Company and which, in addition to commercial vehicles, produced a passenger Auto Car in 1907. In 1909 the firm's name was changed to Atterbury Motor Car Company, to avoid confusion with the Autocar from Pennsylvania. Trucks remained the company's principal focus of attention. Refer to Auto Car.

ATTICA — Attica, Indiana — (1909) — "Attica, Indiana is in the throes of local celebration over the appearance of the first automobile to emanate from a local factory," *The Motor World* reported during the summer of 1909. "The Attica Automobile Company is responsible for the machine, which if found satisfactory, is to be the model for the company's intended 1910 production." Apparently satisfaction was not realized, because the intended production does not seem to have been realized.

AUBRY — New Haven, Connecticut — (1900) — The Lee J. Aubry Carriage Company of 139 Park Street in New Haven was indicated as an automobile manufacturer in the Hiscox book *Horseless Vehicles, Automobiles, Motor Cycles* published in 1900. What automobiles may have been produced has not been documented. The New Haven city directory for 1903 reveals that by that year the firm (which had been misspelled Aubrey in the Hiscox list) was in the manufacture of carriages and carriage parts only.

AUBURN — Auburn, Indiana — (1900-1936) — Charles Eckhart was a wheelwright who worked awhile for the wagon-building Studebaker brothers in South Bend, moving to Auburn in 1874 to establish his own Eckhart Carriage Company. He retired in 1893, leaving the business to his sons Frank and Morris. In 1900 the Eckhart brothers built their first single-cylinder, solid-tired, tiller-steered automobile and started the Auburn Automobile Company. The firm was capitalized at $2500. Though the Eckharts

1902 Auburn, runabout, A-C-D

affixed an $800 price tag to their efforts, it does not appear they sold many, if any, of them. In-house experimentation continued for two years. Following the Chicago Automobile Show of 1903 the brothers went into manufacture in earnest. The car remained the same chain-drive runabout, but now with pneumatic tires, and tonneau and touring variations. In 1905 a two-cylinder touring followed; in 1909 there was an Auburn four, in 1912 a six. Through the World War I years, things looked very good for Auburn, on the outside. The Eckharts boasted that their secret of success was the fact there "had been no change in ownership or officers" in their company since its inception, but the truth was they were not very successful, and that secret was out in 1919 when the Eckharts sold controlling interest in Auburn to a group of Chicago businessmen, including William Wrigley, Jr., who made chewing gum. The immediate result was the Auburn Beauty-SIX introduced in 1919, which any beholder could see was a prettier car than its predecessors. But it hit the postwar recession head-on, and in the four years following just 15,717 were sold. By 1924 Auburn was producing six units a day which was more than meeting the demand. Hundreds of unsold touring cars stood forlornly in the company parking lot the day Errett Lobban Cord visited Auburn to see what he could do. Cord, who cheerfully admitted to having made and lost $50,000 three times in a variety of businesses on the West Coast, all before reaching age twenty-one, had become the hotshot salesman of Moon cars for Chicago's Quinlan Motor Company, subsequently acquiring an interest in the firm and a nestegg of $100,000 which was now burning a hole in his pocket. In 1924 he became Auburn's general manager, at modest salary and with the option of buying control if he could save the company. A little stylish nickel plating and some flashy repainting, and the unsold Auburns began to sell.

1903 Auburn, runabout, A-C-D

In 1925 Cord contracted for some Lycoming straight-eight engines, had chief engineer James Crawford fit them into the old six-cylinder Auburn chassis, and introduced the result to the Auburn range as the Auburn 8-63 and 8-88. Two-tone color schemes and a beltline gracefully sweeping over the top of the hood distinguished these Auburns, styling so modish that it would be effectively retained until 1930. In three consecutive years Cord doubled sales, and by the middle of the third one — 1926 — he was president of the Auburn Automobile Company. In 1927, because the demise of Mercer had left Stutz without any apparent challenger, Cord took his Auburn 8-88 racing and record-breaking, renting the Atlantic City Speedway in July so three Auburns could break all speed marks for fully equipped stock cars from 5 to 5000 miles. In 1928 the more powerful 8-115 had hydraulic instead of the former mechanical four-wheel brakes and Bijur lubrication, a rarity for a car in the medium-price class. And it was given a boattail speedster variation styled by Al Leamy that was Cord's answer to the famous Stutz Black Hawk. That year Wade Morton drove an Auburn 8-115 speedster 108.46 mph over the measured mile at Daytona, 2033 miles in 24 hours for a record 84.7 mph average at Atlantic City, and set a new record at Pikes Peak. Though the Stutz Black Hawk admittedly

1904 Auburn, model A, A-C-D

was a slightly faster car, its Bearcat speedster sold for almost $5000. An Auburn 8-115 speedster could be had for about $2000. The 8-120 Auburn followed in 1929, the 8-125 in 1930. Prior to Cord, Auburn dealers had been mostly garage owners with perhaps one demonstration car; with Cord's arrival, a vast distribution network was set up, with carloads of Auburns systematically being sent to dealers. In 1929 Auburn stock on hand averaged a car and a half per showroom; dealers couldn't get Auburns fast enough. By now, with Auburn doing nicely, Cord had begun to build his empire. He acquired Ansted Engine Company, Lexington Motor Car Company, Central Manufacturing and a lot of property in nearby Connersville; he bought Lycoming (Williamsport, Pennsylvania), Limousine Body (Kalamazoo, Michigan) and Duesenberg Motors (Indianapolis). Nineteen twenty-nine was Cord's best year yet. The aerodynamic Auburn Cabin Speedster was the sensation of the New York Automobile Show, he introduced the Model J Duesenberg, as well as a new front-wheel-drive Cord L-29, he gathered all of the diverse companies he had bought into a new one called Cord Corporation, he barely noticed that the stock market crashed. Though Auburn sales fell in the immediate wake of the Great Depression, they more than doubled for '31; profit that year equalled the previous peak of 1929. And there were a thousand new Auburn dealers, most of them abandoning the franchises of other marques to join up.

1904 Auburn, model A, rear entrance tonneau, A-C-D

Auburn production was concentrated on a single straight-eight, the 8-98, with engine by Lycoming, the first center X-bracing ever offered in a rear-drive car, Lovejoy hydraulic shock absorbers, Bijur lubrication, semi-elliptic suspension front and rear, and the L.G.S. Free Wheeling unit. At $1195-$1395 ($945-$1195 less freewheeling), the new Auburn was reported by *Fortune* magazine to be "the biggest package in the world for the price," by *Business Week* as "more car for the money than the public has ever seen." In 1932 Cord outdid even himself with a new V-12 by Lycoming which sold for less than a thousand dollars, certainly the cheapest twelve-cylinder automobile ever marketed. New that year, too, on all Auburns was the two-speed rear axle of the Columbia Axle Company, that firm yet another Cord acquisition for his empire. A fully equipped Auburn Twelve speedster put up a flurry of records at Muroc dry lake that summer, many of which would stand until after World War II. But now things began falling apart. The slight business upswing the nation had enjoyed was followed by the "depression within the depression," and Auburn sales plummeted. The V-12 and eight-cylinder lines were reduced, a cheaper six-cylinder line reinstated. Cord's automotive interests now included Checker Cab, and he was into shipbuilding and aviation too. Auburn was being neglected, and it was in trouble. There was a final blaze of glory, and it was the Auburn 851, with Lycoming straight-eight engine supercharged by Kurt Beier of Schwitzer-Cummins, and boattail speedster body conjured largely from parts on hand by Duesenberg designer Gordon Buehrig. A hundred miles an hour was guaranteed, and the speedster driven by Ab Jenkins at Bonneville became the first fully equipped American stock car to exceed 100

mph for a twelve-hour period. About 500 speedsters were built and sold at $2245, Auburn losing money on each one. The car's purpose was to attract showroom traffic and sales for the bread-and-butter 851 eights and the cheaper sixes. Sales did rise twenty percent, but not enough for a profit. A diesel-powered Auburn airport limousine was rumored for 1936, but it was lost amid the excitement of a brand-new car called the Cord 810. The Auburn line for '36 was virtually unchanged from '35. No Auburns appeared at all at the beginning of '37, though they were announced to be on the way. They never arrived. In August, under heavy scrutiny by both the Bureau of Internal Revenue and the Securites and Exchange Commission for his business dealings, Errett Lobban Cord sold out his holdings. In October of 1937 "informed Wall Street sources" reported that the Auburn, Cord and Duesenberg automobiles would be discontinued. The sources were well informed.

1904
Model A

	FP	5	4	3	2	1
Tr	—	4050	8100	13.500	18.900	27.000

1905 Auburn, model B, touring, A-C-D

1905
Model B, 2-cyl.

Tr	—	3900	7800	13,000	18,200	26,000

1906 Auburn, model C, touring, WLB

1906
Model C, 2-cyl.

Tr	—	3900	7800	13,000	18,200	26,000

1907 Auburn, model D, touring, WLB

1907
Model D, 2-cyl.

Tr	—	3900	7800	13,000	18,200	26,000

1908
Model G, 2-cyl., 24 hp

Tr	—	3900	7800	13,000	18,200	26,000

	FP	5	4	3	2	1
Model H, 2-cyl.						
Tr	—	4050	8100	13,500	18,900	27,000
Model K, 2-cyl.						
Rbt	—	4200	8400	14,000	19,600	28,000

1909 Auburn, model B, touring, HAC

1909

	FP	5	4	3	2	1
Model G, 2-cyl., 24 hp						
Tr	—	4050	8100	13,500	18,900	27,000
Model H, 2cyl.						
Tr	—	4200	8400	14,000	19,600	28,000
Model K						
Rbt	—	4050	8100	13,500	18,900	27,000
Model B, 4-cyl., 25-30 hp						
Tr	—	4050	8100	13,500	18,900	27,000
Model C, 4-cyl.						
Tr	—	4350	8700	14,500	20,300	29,000
Model D, 4-cyl.						
Rbt	—	4500	9000	15,000	21,000	30,000

1910

	FP	5	4	3	2	1
Model G, 2-cyl., 24 hp						
Tr	—	3900	7800	13,000	18,200	26,000
Model H, 2-cyl.						
Tr	—	4050	8100	13,500	18,900	27,000
Model K, 2-cyl.						
Rbt	—	4200	8400	14,000	19,600	28,000
Model B, 4-cyl., 25-30 hp						
Tr	—	4200	8400	14,000	19,600	28,000
Model C, 4-cyl.						
Tr	—	4050	8100	13,500	18,900	27,000
Model D, 4-cyl.						
Rbt	—	4200	8400	14,000	19,600	28,000
Model X, 4-cyl., 35-40 hp						
Tr	—	4200	8400	14,000	19,600	28,000
Model R, 4-cyl.						
Tr	—	4350	8700	14,500	20,300	29,000
Model S, 4-cyl.						
Rds	—	4350	8700	14,500	20,300	29,000

1911 Auburn, model M, roadster, WLB

1911

	FP	5	4	3	2	1
Model G, 2-cyl., 24 hp						
Tr	—	3900	7800	13,000	18,200	26,000
Model K, 2-cyl.						
Rbt	—	4050	8100	13,500	18,900	27,000
Model L, 4-cyl., 25-30 hp						
Tr	—	4050	8100	13,500	18,900	27,000
Model F, 4-cyl.						
Tr	—	4050	8100	13,500	18,900	27,000
Model N, 4-cyl., 40 hp						
Tr	—	4200	8400	14,000	19,600	28,000
Model Y, 4-cyl.						
Tr	—	4050	8100	13,500	18,900	27,000
Model T, 4-cyl.						
Tr	—	4050	8100	13,500	18,900	27,000
Model M, 4-cyl.						
Rds	—	4200	8400	14,000	19,600	28,000

1912

	FP	5	4	3	2	1
Model 6-50, 6-cyl.						
Tr	—	4350	8700	14,500	20,300	29,000
Model 40H, 4-cyl., 35-40 hp						
Tr	—	4050	8100	13,500	18,900	27,000
Model 40M, 4-cyl., 35-40 hp						
Rds	—	4050	8100	13,500	18,900	27,000
Model 40N, 4-cyl., 35-40 hp						
Rds	—	4200	8400	14,000	19,600	28,000
Model 35L, 4-cyl., 30 hp						
Tr	—	3900	7800	13,000	18,200	26,000

1912 Auburn, model 35-L, touring, A-C-D

Model 30L, 4-cyl., 30 hp

	FP	5	4	3	2	1
Rds	—	4050	8100	13,500	18,900	27,000
Tr	—	3900	7800	13,000	18,200	26,000

1913 Auburn, model 33-L, touring, HAC

1913

	FP	5	4	3	2	1
Model 33M, 4-cyl., 33 hp						
Rds	—	4200	8400	14,000	19,600	28,000
Model 33L, 4-cyl., 33 hp						
Tr	—	3900	7800	13,000	18,200	26,000
Model 40A, 4-cyl., 40 hp						
Rds	—	4200	8400	14,000	19,600	28,000
Model 40L, 4-cyl.						
Tr	—	4050	8100	13,500	18,900	27,000
Model 45, 6-cyl., 45 hp						
Tr	—	4200	8400	14,000	19,600	28,000
Model 45B, 6-cyl., 45 hp						
Rds	—	4200	8400	14,000	19,600	28,000
TwnC	—	4050	8100	13,500	18,900	27,000
Cpe	—	3900	7800	13,000	18,200	26,000
Model 50, 6-cyl., 50 hp						
Tr	—	4350	8700	14,500	20,300	29,000

1914 Auburn, model 6-46, touring, HAC

1914

	FP	5	4	3	2	1
Model 4-40, 4-cyl., 40 hp						
Rds	—	4200	8400	14,000	19,600	28,000
Tr	—	4200	8400	14,000	19,600	28,000
Cpe	—	3900	7800	13,000	18,200	26,000
Model 4-41, 4-cyl., 40 hp						
Tr	—	4350	8700	14,500	20,300	29,000
Model 6-45, 6-cyl., 45 hp						
Rds	—	4350	8700	14,500	20,300	29,000
Tr	—	4500	9000	15,000	21,000	30,000
Model 6-46, 6-cyl., 45 hp						
Tr	—	4500	9000	15,000	21,000	30,000

1915

	FP	5	4	3	2	1
Model 4-36, 4-cyl., 36 hp						
Rds	—	4200	8400	14,000	19,600	28,000
Tr	—	4050	8100	13,500	18,900	27,000
Model 4-43, 4-cyl., 43 hp						
Rds	—	4200	8400	14,000	19,600	28,000
Tr	—	4200	8400	14,000	19,600	28,000

1915 Auburn, model 4-36, touring, HAC

Model 6-40, 6-cyl., 50 hp

	FP	5	4	3	2	1
Rds	—	4350	8700	14,500	20,300	29,000
Tr	—	4300	8550	14,250	19,950	28,500
Cpe	—	3900	7800	13,000	18,200	26,000
Model 6-47, 6-cyl., 47 hp						
Rds	—	4350	8700	14,500	20,300	29,000
Tr	—	4350	8700	14,500	20,300	29,000

1916 Auburn, model 4-38, roadster, HAC

1916
Model 4-38, 4-cyl., 38 hp

Rds	—	4350	8700	14,500	20,300	29,000
Tr	—	4200	8400	14,000	19,600	28,000
Model 6-38						
Rds	—	4350	8700	14,500	20,300	29,000
Tr	—	4350	8700	14,500	20,300	29,000
Model 6-40, 6-cyl., 40 hp						
Rds	—	4500	9000	15,000	21,000	30,000
Tr	1550	4500	9000	15,000	21,000	30,000
Model Union 4-36, 6-cyl., 36 hp						
Tr	895	4300	8550	14,250	19,950	28,500

1917 Auburn, model 6-39, touring, HAC

1917
Model 6-39, 6-cyl., 39 hp

Rds	1345	4500	9000	15,000	21,000	30,000
Tr	1345	4500	9000	15,000	21,000	30,000
Model 6-44, 6-cyl., 44 hp						
Rds	1685	4650	9300	15,500	21,700	31,000
Tr	1685	4500	9000	15,000	21,000	30,000
Model 4-36, 4-cyl., 36 hp						
Rds	—	4500	9000	15,000	21,000	30,000
Tr	—	4350	8700	14,500	20,300	29,000
1918						
Model 6-39, 6-cyl.						
Tr	1345	4500	9000	15,000	21,000	30,000
Rds	1345	4500	9000	15,000	21,000	30,000
Spt Tr	1345	4500	9000	15,000	21,000	30,000

1918 Auburn, 6-39, sport touring, WLB

Model 6-44, 6-cyl.

	FP	5	4	3	2	1
Tr	1685	4500	9000	15,000	21,000	30,000
Rds	1685	4500	9000	15,000	21,000	30,000
Spt Tr	—	4650	9300	15,500	21,700	31,000
Sed	—	2800	5700	9500	13,300	19,000

1919 Auburn, model 6-39, touring, HAC

1919
Model 6-39

Tr	—	4500	9000	15,000	21,000	30,000
Rds	—	4500	9000	15,000	21,000	30,000
Cpe	—	3000	6000	10,000	14,000	20,000
Sed	—	2300	5400	9000	12,600	18,000

1920 Auburn, model 6-39K, touring

1920
Model 6-39, 6-cyl.

Tr	—	4500	9000	15,000	21,000	30,000
Spt Tr	—	4650	9300	15,500	21,700	31,000
Rds	—	4650	9300	15,500	21,700	31,000
Sed	—	2800	5700	9500	13,300	19,000
Cpe	—	3000	6000	10,000	14,000	20,000

1921 Auburn Beauty-SIX, model 6-39, sedan, HAC

Model 6-39

	FP	5	4	3	2	1
Tr	—	4500	9000	15,000	21,000	30,000
Spt Tr	—	4800	9600	16,000	22,400	32,000
Rds	—	4800	9600	16,000	22,400	32,000
Cabr	—	4800	9600	16,000	22,400	32,000
Sed	—	2800	5700	9500	13,300	19,000
Cpe	—	3000	6000	10,000	14,000	20,000

1922 Auburn Beauty-SIX, model 6-51, roadster, HAC

1922
Model 6-51, 6-cyl.

Tr	—	4800	9600	16,000	22,400	32,000
Rds	—	4950	9900	16,500	23,100	33,000
Spt Tr	—	4950	9900	16,500	23,100	33,000
Sed	—	3000	6000	10,000	14,000	20,000
Cpe	—	3150	6300	10,500	14,700	21,000

1923
Model 6-43, 6-cyl.

Tr	—	4950	9900	16,500	23,100	33,000
Sed	—	2800	5700	9500	13,300	19,000

Model 6-63, 6-cyl.

Tr	—	5100	10,200	17,000	23,800	34,000
Spt Tr	—	5250	10,500	17,500	24,500	35,000
Brgm	—	3000	6000	10,000	14,000	20,000
Sed	—	2800	5700	9500	13,300	19,000

Model 6-51, 6-cyl.

Phae	—	5250	10,500	17,500	24,500	35,000
Tr	—	5100	10,200	17,000	23,800	34,000
Spt Tr	—	5400	10,800	18,000	25,200	36,000
Brgm	—	3150	6300	10,500	14,700	21,000
Sed	—	3000	6000	10,000	14,000	20,000

1924 Auburn, model 6-43, rumble seat convertible, IMS

1924 Auburn, model 6-43, sport touring, WLB

1924
Model 6-43, 6-cyl.

Tr	—	4950	9900	16,500	23,100	33,000
Spt Tr	—	5100	10,200	17,000	23,800	34,000
Sed	—	2800	5700	9500	13,300	19,000
Cpe	—	3000	6000	10,000	14,000	20,000
2 dr	—	2800	5700	9500	13,300	19,000

Model 6-63, 6-cyl.

	FP	5	4	3	2	1
Tr	—	5100	10,200	17,000	23,800	34,000
Spt Tr	—	5400	10,800	18,000	25,200	36,000
Sed	—	3000	6000	10,000	14,000	20,000
Brgm	—	3150	6300	10,500	14,700	21,000

1925 Auburn, model 6-43, sport phaeton, HAC

1925
Model 8-36, 8-cyl.

Tr	—	5850	11,700	19,500	27,300	39,000
2 dr Brgm	—	2800	5700	9500	13,300	19,000
4 dr Sed	—	2800	5700	9500	13,300	19,000

Model 6-43, 6-cyl.

Phae	—	5550	11,100	18,500	25,900	37,000
Spt Phae	1395	5700	11,400	19,000	26,600	38,000
Cpe	—	3150	6300	10,500	14,700	21,000
4 dr Sed	1595	3000	6000	10,000	14,000	20,000
2 dr Sed	1945	2800	5700	9500	13,300	19,000

Model 6-66, 6-cyl.

Rds	1495	5550	11,100	18,500	25,900	37,000
Brgm	1595	2800	5700	9500	13,300	19,000
4 dr	1795	2800	5700	9500	13,300	19,000
Tr	1395	5550	11,100	18,500	25,900	37,000

Model 8-88, 8-cyl.

Rds	1975	5550	11,100	18,500	25,900	37,000
4 dr Sed 5P	2250	3000	6000	10,000	14,000	20,000
4 dr Sed 7P	—	3000	6000	10,000	14,000	20,000
Brgm	2350	2800	5700	9500	13,300	19,000
Tr	1975	5550	11,100	18,500	25,900	37,000

1926 Auburn 8-88, touring, JAC

1926
Model 4-44, 4-cyl., 42 hp

Tr	1145	5400	10,800	18,000	25,200	36,000
Rds	1175	5550	11,100	18,500	25,900	37,000
Cpe	1145	3000	6000	10,000	14,000	20,000
4 dr Sed	1195	2800	5700	9500	13,300	19,000

Model 6-66, 6-cyl., 48 hp

Rds	1395	6000	12,000	20,000	28,000	40,000
Tr	1395	5850	11,700	19,500	27,300	39,000
Brgm	1495	2800	5700	9500	13,300	19,000
4 dr Sed	1695	3000	6000	10,000	14,000	20,000
Cpe	1445	3150	6300	10,500	14,700	21,000

Model 8-88, 8-cyl., 88 hp, 129" wb

Rds	1695	6300	12,600	21,000	29,400	42,000
Tr	2045	6150	12,300	20,500	28,700	41,000
Cpe	1695	3150	6300	10,500	14,700	21,000
Brgm	1795	3000	6000	10,000	14,000	20,000
5P Sed	1995	3000	6000	10,000	14,000	20,000
7P Sed	2495	3000	6000	10,000	14,000	20,000

Model 8-88, 8-cyl., 88 hp, 146" wb

7P Sed	—	3150	6300	10,500	14,700	21,000

1927 Auburn, model 8-77, Sport sedan, HAC

1927

Model 6-66, 6-cyl., 66 hp

	FP	5	4	3	2	1
Rds	1095	6300	12,600	21,000	29,400	42,000
Tr	1095	6150	12,300	20,500	28,700	41,000
Brgm	1195	2800	5700	9500	13,300	19,000
Sed	1295	3000	6000	10,000	14,000	20,000

Model 8-77, 8-cyl., 77 hp

Rds	1395	6450	12,900	21,500	30,100	43,000
Tr	1395	6300	12,600	21,000	29,400	42,000
Brgm	1495	3000	6000	10,000	14,000	20,000
Sed	1695	3000	6000	10,000	14,000	20,000

Model 8-88, 8-cyl., 88 hp, 129" WB

Tr	1695	6450	12,900	21,500	30,100	43,000
Rds	1695	6600	13,200	22,000	30,800	44,000
Cpe	1745	3150	6300	10,500	14,700	21,000
Brgm	1795	3000	6000	10,000	14,000	20,000
Sed	2495	3000	6000	10,000	14,000	20,000
Spt Sed	2095	3150	6300	10,500	14,700	21,000

Model 8-88, 8-cyl., 88 hp, 146" wb

7P Sed	2595	3150	6300	10,500	14,700	21,000
Tr	—	6600	13,200	22,000	30,800	44,000

1928 Auburn, model 115, club coupe, AA

1928

Model 6-66, 6-cyl., 66 hp

	FP	5	4	3	2	1
Rds	1095	6450	12,900	21,500	30,100	43,000
Cabr	1295	6300	12,600	21,000	29,400	42,000
Sed	1295	2800	5700	9500	13,300	19,000
Spt Sed	1195	3000	6000	10,000	14,000	20,000

Model 8-77, 8-cyl., 77 hp

Rds	1395	6600	13,200	22,000	30,800	44,000
Cabr	1595	6450	12,900	21,500	30,100	43,000
Sed	1695	3000	6000	10,000	14,000	20,000
Spt Sed	1495	3150	6300	10,500	14,700	21,000

Model 8-88, 8-cyl., 88 hp

Rds	1995	6750	13,500	22,500	31,500	45,000
Tr	2295	6600	13,200	22,000	30,800	44,000
Cabr	2095	6600	13,200	22,000	30,800	44,000
Sed	2195	3150	6300	10,500	14,700	21,000
Spt Sed	2095	3300	6600	11,000	15,400	22,000

Model 8-88, 8-cyl., 88 hp, 136" wb

7P Sed	2595	3400	6900	11,500	16,100	23,000

SECOND SERIES

Model 76, 6-cyl.

Rds	1195	8100	16,200	27,000	37,800	54,000
Cabr	1395	7650	15,300	25,500	35,700	51,000
Sed	1395	3150	6300	10,500	14,700	21,000
Spt Sed	1295	3300	6600	11,000	15,400	22,000

Model 88, 8-cyl.

Spds	1695	13,800	27,600	46,000	73,500	92,000
Rds	1495	9000	18,000	30,000	42,000	60,000
Cabr	1695	7800	15,600	26,000	36,400	52,000
Sed	1695	3150	6300	10,500	14,700	21,000
Spt Sed	1595	3300	6600	11,000	15,400	22,000
Phae	1895	6900	13,800	23,000	32,200	46,000

Model 115, 8-cyl.

Spds	2195	14,700	29,400	49,000	78,000	98,000
Rds	1995	9300	18,600	31,000	43,400	62,000
Cabr	2195	8550	17,100	28,500	39,900	57,000
Sed	2195	3400	6900	11,500	16,100	23,000
Spt Sed	2095	3600	7200	12,000	16,800	24,000
Phae	2395	7050	14,100	23,500	32,900	47,000

1929 Auburn Cabin Speedster, coupe, WLB

1929

Model 76, 6-cyl.

Rds	1195	8550	17,100	28,500	39,900	57,000
Tr	1395	8100	16,200	27,000	37,800	54,000
Cabr	1395	7800	15,600	26,000	36,400	52,000
Vic	1395	5100	10,200	17,000	23,800	34,000
Sed	1395	3300	6600	11,000	15,400	22,000
Spt Sed	1295	3400	6900	11,500	16,100	23,000

Model 88, 8-cyl.

	FP	5	4	3	2	1
Spds	1695	14,700	29,400	49,000	78,000	98,000
Rds	1495	8550	17,100	28,500	39,900	57,000
Tr	1495	8250	16,500	27,500	38,500	55,000
Cabr	1695	8100	16,200	27,000	37,800	54,000
Vic	1695	5700	11,400	19,000	26,600	38,000
Sed	1595	3300	6600	11,000	15,400	22,000
Spt Sed	1595	3400	6900	11,500	16,100	23,000
Phae	1895	8400	16,800	28,000	39,200	56,000

Model 115, 8-cyl.

Spds	2195	15,000	30,000	50,000	80,000	100,000
Rds	1995	10,200	20,400	34,000	47,600	68,000
Cabr	2195	9300	18,600	31,000	43,400	62,000
Vic	2195	5850	11,700	19,500	27,300	39,000
Sed	2195	3400	6900	11,500	16,100	23,000
Spt Sed	2095	3600	7200	12,000	16,800	24,000
Phae	2395	9600	19,200	32,000	44,800	64,000

1929 Auburn, model 6-80, cabriolet, AA

Model 6-80, 6-cyl.

Tr	995	8550	17,100	28,500	39,900	57,000
Cabr	1095	8850	17,700	29,500	41,300	59,000
Vic	1095	5100	10,200	17,000	23,800	34,000
Sed	1095	3150	6300	10,500	14,700	21,000
Spt Sed	995	3300	6600	11,000	15,400	22,000

Model 8-90, 8-cyl.

Spds	1495	15,000	30,000	50,000	80,000	100,000
Tr	1395	8850	17,700	29,500	41,300	59,000
Cabr	1495	9000	18,000	30,000	42,000	60,000
Vic	1495	6000	12,000	20,000	28,000	40,000
Sed	1495	3150	6300	10,500	14,700	21,000
Spt Sed	1395	3600	7200	12,000	16,800	24,000
Phae	1695	9600	19,200	32,000	44,800	64,000

Model 120, 8-cyl.

Spds	1895	15,700	30,600	51,000	81,000	102,000
Cabr	1895	9300	18,600	31,000	43,400	62,000
Vic	1895	6300	12,600	21,000	29,400	42,000
Sed	1895	3400	6900	11,500	16,100	23,000
Spt Sed	1795	3900	7800	13,000	18,200	26,000
Phae	2095	9600	19,200	32,000	44,800	64,000
7P Sed	2145	4050	8100	13,500	18,900	27,000

1930 Auburn, model 125, 4-dr. sport sedan, AA

1930

Model 6-85, 6-cyl.

Cabr	1095	7800	15,600	26,000	36,400	52,000
Sed	1095	3150	6300	10,500	14,700	21,000
Spt Sed	995	3300	6600	11,000	15,400	22,000

Model 8-95, 8-cyl.

Cabr	1295	8100	16,200	27,000	37,800	54,000
Sed	1295	3300	6600	11,000	15,400	22,000
Spt Sed	1195	3400	6900	11,500	16,100	23,000
Phae	1395	9600	19,200	32,000	44,800	64,000

Model 125, 8-cyl.

Cabr	1595	8550	17,100	28,500	39,900	57,000
Sed	1595	3400	6900	11,500	16,100	23,000
Spt Sed	1495	3600	7200	12,000	16,800	24,000
Phae	1695	10,200	20,400	34,000	47,600	68,000

1931 Auburn, boattail speedster, AA

1931 Auburn, convertible coupe, OCW

1931
Model 8-98, 8-cyl., Standard, 127" wb

	FP	5	4	3	2	1
Spds	945	10,800	21,600	36,000	50,500	72,000
Cpe	995	3600	7200	12,000	16,800	24,000
Cabr	1045	7800	15,600	26,000	36,400	52,000
Brgm	945	3300	6600	11,000	15,400	22,000
5P Sed	995	3400	6900	11,500	16,100	23,000
Phae	1145	10,200	20,400	34,000	47,600	68,000

Model 8-98, 8-cyl., 136" wb
7P Sed	1195	3600	7200	12,000	16,800	24,000

Model 8-98A, 8-cyl., Custom, 127"wb
Spds	1395	11,700	23,400	39,000	58,000	78,000
Cpe	1195	3750	7500	12,500	17,500	25,000
Cabr	1245	8550	17,100	28,500	39,900	57,000
Brgm	1145	3400	6900	11,500	16,100	23,000
Sed	1195	3400	6900	11,500	16,100	23,000
Phae	1345	10,800	21,600	36,000	50,500	72,000

Model 8-98, 8-cyl., 136" wb
7P Sed	1395	3750	7500	12,500	17,500	25,000

1932 Auburn, 8-100, convertible cabriolet, AA

1932 Auburn, 12-160A, speedster, AA

1932
Model 8-100, 8-cyl., Custom, 127" wb
Spds	845	14,700	29,400	49,000	78,000	98,000
Cabr	795	9300	18,600	31,000	43,400	62,000
Cpe	675	3900	7800	13,000	18,200	26,000
Brgm	725	3400	6900	11,500	16,100	23,000
Sed	775	3600	7200	12,000	16,800	24,000
Phae	845	10,800	21,600	36,000	50,500	72,000

Model 8-100, 8-cyl., 136" wb
7P Sed	875	3750	7500	12,500	17,500	25,000

Model 8-100A, 8-cyl., Custom Dual Ratio, 127" wb
Spds	975	15,000	30,000	50,000	80,000	100,000
Cpe	805	4050	8100	13,500	18,900	27,000
Cabr	925	8550	17,100	28,500	39,900	57,000
Brgm	855	3600	7200	12,000	16,800	24,000
Sed	905	3750	7500	12,500	17,500	25,000
Phae	975	11,700	23,400	39,000	58,000	78,000

Model 8-100A, 8-cyl., 136" wb
7P Sed	1005	3900	7800	13,000	18,200	26,000

Model 12-160, 12-cyl., Standard
Spds	1145	19,200	33,600	56,000	89,000	112,000
Cpe	975	4800	9600	16,000	22,400	32,000
Cabr	1095	12,300	24,600	41,000	62,000	82,000
Brgm	1025	3750	7500	12,500	17,500	25,000
Sed	1075	3900	7800	13,000	18,200	26,000
Phae	1145	13,800	27,600	46,000	73,500	92,000

Model 12-160A, 12-cyl., Custom Dual Ratio
Spds	1275	21,300	35,400	59,000	92,000	118,000
Cpe	1105	5100	10,200	17,000	23,800	34,000
Cabr	1225	15,700	30,600	51,000	81,000	102,000
Brgm	1155	3900	7800	13,000	18,200	26,000
Sed	1205	4050	8100	13,500	18,900	27,000
Phae	1275	17,800	32,400	54,000	86,000	108,000

1933 Auburn, convertible sedan, OCW

1933
Model 8-101, 8-cyl., Standard, 127" wb
	FP	5	4	3	2	1
Spds	945	13,800	27,600	46,000	73,500	92,000
Cpe	745	3750	7500	12,500	17,500	25,000
Cabr	895	10,200	20,400	34,000	47,600	68,000
Brgm	795	3400	6900	11,500	16,100	23,000
Sed	845	3600	7200	12,000	16,800	24,000
Phae	945	10,800	21,600	36,000	50,500	72,000

Model 8-101, 8-cyl., 136" wb
7P Sed	945	3750	7500	12,500	17,500	25,000

Model 8-101A, 8-cyl., Custom Dual Ratio, 127" wb
Spds	1095	14,400	28,800	48,000	76,000	96,000
Cpe	895	3900	7800	13,000	18,200	26,000
Cabr	1045	10,800	21,600	36,000	50,500	72,000
Brgm	945	3600	7200	12,000	16,800	24,000
Sed	995	3600	7200	12,000	16,800	24,000
Phae	1095	11,700	23,400	39,000	58,000	78,000

Model 8-101A, 8-cyl., 136" wb
7P Sed	1095	3750	7500	12,500	17,500	25,000

Model 8-105, 8-cyl., Salon Dual Ratio
Spds	1345	14,700	29,400	49,000	78,000	98,000
Cabr	1295	10,800	21,600	36,000	50,500	72,000
Brgm	1195	3400	6900	11,500	16,100	23,000
Sed	1245	3500	7050	11,750	16,450	23,500
Phae	1345	11,700	23,400	39,000	58,000	78,000

Model 12-161, 12-cyl., Standard
Spds	1345	15,000	30,000	50,000	80,000	100,000
Cpe	1145	4050	8100	13,500	18,900	27,000
Cabr	1295	11,700	23,400	39,000	58,000	78,000
Brgm	1195	3600	7200	12,000	16,800	24,000
Sed	1245	4050	8100	13,500	18,900	27,000
Phae	1345	12,300	24,600	41,000	62,000	82,000

Model 12-161A, 12-cyl., Custom Dual Ratio
Spds	1495	19,200	33,600	56,000	89,000	112,000
Cpe	1295	4200	8400	14,000	19,600	28,000
Cabr	1445	12,300	24,600	41,000	62,000	82,000
Brgm	1345	3750	7500	12,500	17,500	25,000
Sed	1395	3800	7650	12,750	17,850	25,500
Phae	1495	13,200	26,400	44,000	68,000	88,000

Model 12-165, 12-cyl., Salon Dual Ratio
Spds	1845	21,300	35,400	59,000	92,000	118,000
Cabr	1795	15,700	30,600	51,000	81,000	102,000
Brgm	1695	3900	7800	13,000	18,200	26,000
Sed	1745	4050	8100	13,500	18,900	27,000
Phae	1848	17,800	32,400	54,000	86,000	108,000

1934 Auburn, sedan, A-C-D

1934
Model 652X, 6-cyl., Standard
Cabr	795	8250	16,500	27,500	38,500	55,000
Brgm	695	2000	5100	8500	11,900	17,000
Sed	745	2300	5400	9000	12,600	18,000

Model 652Y, 6-cyl., Custom
Cabr	895	8550	17,100	28,500	39,900	57,000
2 dr Brgm	795	2300	5400	9000	12,600	18,000
Sed	845	2800	5700	9500	13,300	19,000
Phae	945	9600	19,200	32,000	44,800	64,000

Model 850X, 8-cyl., Standard
Cabr	1045	8550	17,100	28,500	39,900	57,000
Brgm	945	2300	5400	9000	12,600	18,000
Sed	995	2800	5700	9500	13,300	19,000

Model 850Y, 8-cyl., Dual Ratio
Cabr	1175	9300	18,600	31,000	43,400	62,000
2 dr Brgm	1075	2800	5700	9500	13,300	19,000
Sed	1125	3000	6000	10,000	14,000	20,000
Phae	1225	10,200	20,400	34,000	47,600	68,000

Model 1250, 12-cyl., Salon Dual Ratio
Cabr	1495	15,700	30,600	51,000	81,000	102,000
2 dr Brgm	1395	2800	5700	9500	13,300	19,000
Sed	1445	3000	6000	10,000	14,000	20,000
Phae	1545	17,800	32,400	54,000	86,000	108,000

1935 Auburn, 653, coupe, AA

1935 Auburn, 851, phaeton, AA

1935

Model 6-653, 6-cyl., Standard

	FP	5	4	3	2	1
Cpe	835	2600	5500	9250	12,950	18,500
Cabr	945	8100	16,200	27,000	37,800	54,000
2 dr Brgm	745	2300	5400	9000	12,600	18,000
Sed	795	2800	5700	9500	13,300	19,000
Phae	995	9900	19,800	33,000	46,200	66,000

Model 6-653, 6-cyl., Custom Dual Ratio

Cpe	942	2700	5600	9350	13,100	18,700
Cabr	1052	8250	16,500	27,500	38,500	55,000
2 dr Brgm	852	2800	5700	9500	13,300	19,000
Sed	902	3000	6000	10,000	14,000	20,000
Phae	1102	9900	19,800	33,000	46,200	66,000

Model 6-653, 6-cyl., Salon Dual Ratio

Cpe	990	3150	6300	10,500	14,700	21,000
Cabr	1100	8400	16,800	28,000	39,200	56,000
2 dr Brgm	932	2800	5700	9500	13,300	19,000
Sed	982	3000	6000	10,000	14,000	20,000
Phae	1182	9900	19,800	33,000	46,200	66,000

Model 8-851, 8-cyl., Standard

Cpe	1085	3150	6300	10,500	14,700	21,000
Cabr	1225	8550	17,100	28,500	39,900	57,000
2 dr Brgm	995	2800	5700	9500	13,300	19,000
Sed	1095	3000	6000	10,000	14,000	20,000
Phae	1275	9900	19,800	33,000	46,200	66,000

Model 8-851, 8-cyl., Custom Dual Ratio

Cpe	1173	3300	6600	11,000	15,400	22,000
Cabr	1313	8700	17,400	29,000	40,600	58,000
2 dr Brgm	1088	3000	6000	10,000	14,000	20,000
Sed	1188	3150	6300	10,500	14,700	21,000
Phae	1368	10,500	21,000	35,000	49,000	70,000

Model 8-851, 8-cyl., Salon Dual Ratio

Cpe	1221	3400	6900	11,500	16,100	23,000
Cabr	1361	9300	18,600	31,000	43,400	62,000
2 dr Brgm	1168	3150	6300	10,500	14,700	21,000
Sed	1268	3300	6600	11,000	15,400	22,000
Phae	1448	10,800	21,600	36,000	50,500	72,000

Model 8-851, 8-cyl., Supercharged Dual Ratio

Spds	2245	13,800	27,600	46,000	73,500	92,000
Cabr	1675	12,300	24,600	41,000	62,000	82,000
Cpe	1545	3600	7200	12,000	16,800	24,000
2 dr Brgm	1445	3150	6300	10,500	14,700	21,000
Sed	1545	3300	6600	11,000	15,400	22,000
Phae	1725	11,100	22,200	37,000	52,000	74,000

1936 Auburn, 852, 4-dr. sedan, AA

1936

Model 6-654, 6-cyl., Standard

Cpe	835	3000	6000	10,000	14,000	20,000
Cabr	945	8100	16,200	27,000	37,800	54,000
2 dr Brgm	745	3000	6000	10,000	14,000	20,000
Sed	795	3150	6300	10,500	14,700	21,000
Phae	995	10,200	20,400	34,000	47,600	68,000

Model 6-654, 6-cyl., Custom Dual Ratio

	FP	5	4	3	2	1
Cpe	942	3300	6600	11,000	15,400	22,000
Cabr	1052	11,400	22,800	38,000	56,000	76,000
2 dr Brgm	852	3000	6000	10,000	14,000	20,000
Sed	902	3150	6300	10,500	14,700	21,000
Phae	1102	10,500	21,000	35,000	49,000	70,000

Model 6-654, 6-cyl., Salon Dual Ratio

Cpe	990	3300	6600	11,000	15,400	22,000
Cabr	1100	11,700	23,400	39,000	58,000	78,000
2 dr Brgm	932	3150	6300	10,500	14,700	21,000
Sed	982	3300	6600	11,000	15,400	22,000
Phae	1182	10,500	21,000	35,000	49,000	70,000

Model 8-852, 8-cyl., Standard

Cpe	1085	3600	7200	12,000	16,800	24,000
Cabr	1225	11,400	22,800	38,000	56,000	76,000
2 dr Brgm	995	3150	6300	10,500	14,700	21,000
Sed	1095	3300	6600	11,000	15,400	22,000
Phae	1275	10,800	21,600	36,000	50,500	72,000

Model 8-852, 8-cyl., Custom Dual Ratio

Cpe	1173	3900	7800	13,000	18,200	26,000
Cabr	1313	11,700	23,400	39,000	58,000	78,000
2 dr Brgm	1088	3300	6600	11,000	15,400	22,000
Sed	1188	3400	6900	11,500	16,100	23,000
Phae	1368	11,100	22,200	37,000	52,000	74,000

Model 8-852, 8-cyl., Salon Dual Ratio

Cpe	1221	4050	8100	13,500	18,900	27,000
Cabr	1361	12,300	24,600	41,000	62,000	82,000
2 dr Brgm	1168	3400	6900	11,500	16,100	23,000
Sed	1268	3600	7200	12,000	16,800	24,000
Phae	1448	11,400	22,800	38,000	56,000	76,000

Model 8, 8-cyl., Supercharged Dual Ratio

Spds	2245	14,700	29,400	49,000	78,000	98,000
Cpe	1545	4200	8400	14,000	19,600	28,000
Cabr	1675	12,600	25,200	42,000	64,000	84,000
Brgm	1445	3600	7200	12,000	16,800	24,000
Sed	1545	3900	7800	13,000	18,200	26,000
Phae	1725	11,700	23,400	39,000	58,000	78,000

1912 Auburn, auto-buggy, NAHC

AUBURN — Auburn, Indiana — (1912-1915) — The Auburn Motor Chassis Company produced a variety of air and water-cooled vehicles with one thing in common. They were all highwheelers. Most of them were delivery wagons with prices calculated to the penny for a fair profit; the 800-pound capacity model, for example, could be had for $365.62. The Handy Wagon, at $487.50, was so called because "it may be used by the owner as a runabout, as a family carryall for the weekend church going, or it can be used as a business vehicle in hauling produce to market." Prices of Auburn highwheelers that were strictly for passengers were generally rounded off to the dollar. There were fewer of them offered, perhaps, because there was another Auburn in town that presented more pleasant motoring possibilities.

1912-1915 AUBURN
2-cyl., 12/14 hp

Air Cooled Buggy (65" wb)	293	2500	3500	5000	8500	18,000
Air Cooled Rbt. (77" wb)	390	2500	3500	5000	8500	18,000
Handy Wagon (77" wb)	487	2500	3500	5000	8500	18,000
AC Del. (800 lb/86" wb)	365	2300	3300	4400	6900	14,500
AC Del. (1500 lb/86" wb)	562	2200	3200	4300	6700	14,200
Water Cooled Del. (1000 lb)	650	2000	3000	4200	6500	14,000

AUBURN-CUMMINS — Auburn, Indiana — (1935) — Auburn-Cummins was the unofficial name given to a nine-passenger airport limousine which was displayed at the New York Automobile Show in November 1935. It was the product of the Auburn Automobile Company, and was powered by a Cummins diesel engine. Although rumors of its impending manufacture were floated about, they were quickly dispelled. Principal attention that year focused instead on a new car from the automotive empire controlled by Errett Lobban Cord. It was called the Cord 810.

AUBURN-MOORE — Cleveland, Ohio — (1906) — The Auburn-Moore was a special one-of-a-kind car that was shown at the Cleveland Automobile Show in February 1906 and which had been built for one Harry S. Moore of that same city. It was a five passenger side entrance tonneau mounted on a two-cylinder 24 hp Auburn chassis, and was quite handsome. Moore has occasionally been cited as a manufacturer of an automobile named for himself. But this is not the case. In October of 1903 he did purchase the assets and good will of the faltering Star Automobile Company of Cleveland, and he continued building that car under the Star name for about six months. Moore's principal livelihood at the time, and the activity to which he returned after his Star quickly eclipsed, was as an automobile repair garage owner. Subsequently he also was a dealer for the Orient, Queen and Stoddard-Dayton. Perhaps he ordered the Auburn-Moore to be built

1906 Auburn-Moore, Special, touring, NAHC

because although he was content to sell the cars of other manufacturers, he preferred to drive something else himself.

1906 AUBURN-MOORE

	FP	5	4	3	2	1
Special Tour.	—	1000	1800	2800	4200	7000

AUDREY — L.H. Solomon was the man behind the half-million-dollar incorporation of the Audrey Motors Corporation of New York City. This venture to manufacture automobiles was announced early in 1920, and died soon after.

AUGUSTA — The Augusta Steam Wagon Company was organized during the late fall of 1901. J. Walter Inman and Joseph S. Hall were among the people involved, and their plan was the manufacture of steam vehicles in Augusta, Georgia. The plan was not realized.

1901 Aultman Steam Carriage, auto-buggy, NAHC

AULTMAN STEAM — Canton, Ohio — (1901-1905) — Henry J. Aultman built his first experimental steam carriage in Cincinnati in 1898 and moved to Canton in 1901 to establish the Aultman Company for its manufacture. By March he was putting the finishing touches on his first ten steam cars, which had already been pre-sold in the local area. By September he was experimenting with a small tiller-steered gasoline buggy, but apparently soon decided to stick with steam. Further experimentation ensued with a four-wheel-drive steam truck, its boiler located up front, following British practice. Commercial vehicle production, however, was moved to the back burner in order to concentrate attention upon the passenger car, which was a piquant little carriage with attractive lines. His company was in trouble in October of 1902, but apparently Aultman revived it and continued production on a small scale for several years thereafter. Irrevocable receivership arrived in September 1905.

1901-1905 AULTMAN STEAM

Aultman Steam Carriage	—	2500	3500	5000	8500	18,000

AURORA — The Aurora Automatic Machinery Company produced the Thor motorcycle in Aurora, Illinois as well as an automobile of that name from 1907-1909. Refer to Thor.

The Aurora Vulcan Company of Bridgeport, Connecticut announced a $250,000 capitalization during the fall of 1913 for the purpose of embark-

ing upon the manufacture of automobiles. S. Sherwood Day, H.N. Billings and R.K. Hall were the people involved. Manufacture is doubted.

1905 Aurora, touring, NAHC

AURORA — Aurora, Illinois — (1905-1906) — A.J. Jeffrey, J.M. Spiker and E.D. Pinney knew a lot about building tops for carriages, either horseless or horsedrawn, but they knew nothing about mechanics. Thus, during late spring of 1905, when they decided to revise their Aurora Carriage Top Company into the Aurora Automobile Company, they imported W.H. Howe from the Chicago Automobile Company. He designed the new Aurora for them. It was a four-cylinder 30 hp touring car on a 100-inch wheelbase, employing shaft drive and a special friction transmission of Howe's own design. The body was presumably also of Howe's design, and conventional from the dash back, peculiar from the dash forward. The Aurora was in production for only a year. This conveniently left the name free for another company to grab on to use for its car in 1907.

1905-1906 AURORA
Four — 30 hp, 100" wb

	FP	5	4	3	2	1
Tour.-5P	—	2500	3500	5000	8500	18,000

1907 Aurora, runabout, GR

AURORA — Aurora, Illinois — (1907-1909) — The Aurora Motor Works believed that "for the service of the average man there is nothing to exceed the two-cylinder, horizontal type of motor." This the company was happy to serve a waiting public. And it did so, beginning in 1907. Then, late in 1908, when it appeared the average man wanted more than the Aurora provided, the company officers abruptly sold their factory to the Black highwheel producers of Chicago. They soon reconsidered and got themselves together again in a new firm called the Emancipator Automobile Company for the production of a four-cylinder car alternately called the Aurora Emancipator or simply the Emancipator. Nomenclature was not long a problem, however, because having already rid themselves of their factory, the Aurora-Emancipator people found they could not easily secure a new one and quickly decided to give up altogether. Not many Aurora runabouts were built, and even fewer of the four-cylinder Emancipator models. (The Aurora had been designed by Dr. D.D. Culver, who earlier had built a car under his own name; the Emancipator designer is not known.) Interestingly, the men behind the Aurora Motor Works were Dr. James Selkirk, William George and A.B. McCord. Neither Selkirk nor George were happy with McCord's performance as production manager, though for some reason they ended up suing each other instead of McCord. About the same time as the Aurora was being produced, George and McCord were allied as well in the Monarch Automobile Company, also located in Aurora. Dr. Selkirk had no part in this enterprise, nor did George and McCord have any part in the venture that saw Selkirk reverse the syllables of his name and produce another automobile in Aurora called the Kirksel.

1907 AURORA
Model A — 2-cyl., 14 hp, 80" wb

		5	4	3	2	1
Rbt.-3P		700	1500	2500	3600	5500	11,000

1908 AURORA

Model A — 2-cyl., 14 hp, 80" wb

	FP	5	4	3	2	1
Rbt.-3P	700	1500	2500	3600	5500	11,000

Model B — 2-cyl., 20 hp, 80" wb

Rbt.-3P	775	1600	2700	3800	5900	11,500

1909 AURORA

Emancipator — 4-cyl., 20 hp, 100" wb

Tour.-5P	1100	1500	2500	3600	5500	11,000
Tonneau-4P	1100	1500	2500	3600	5500	11,000

Aurora — 2-cyl., 16 hp, 80" wb

Rbt.-2P	700	1500	2500	3600	5500	11,000

AUSTEN/AUSTENIUS — These were two names under which carnival man W.W. Austen exhibited the steam cars built by S.H. Roper at fairs and race tracks along the East Coast during the 1860's. Refer to Roper.

AUSTIN — The Austin Agency, Inc. was the designation of a $10,000 company incorporated in Boston, Massachusetts in early 1907, for the manufacture and sale of motorcars. F.E. Litchfield and E.S. Litchfield were the men behind this venture. Manufacture did not follow, only an automobile dealership did.

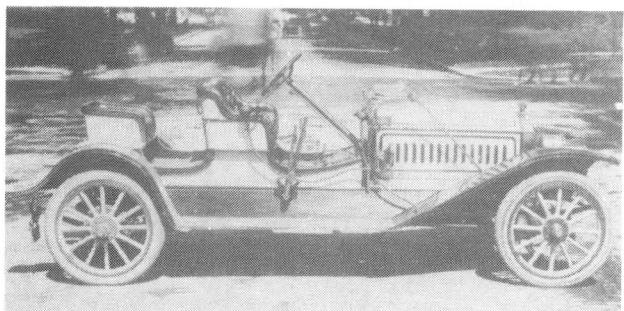

1908 Austin, 3-pass. runabout, WLB

AUSTIN — Grand Rapids, Michigan — (1903-1920) — "Known as the most beautiful car in the world" was the quoted claim of the Austin Automobile Company of Grand Rapids. Precisely who knew it as that was not cited, and the claim was patently untrue. Still, for almost two decades, the Austin was an exemplary automobile, "full of original effects," as Hugh Dolnar noted in *Cycle & Automobile Trade Journal*. It was a father-son collaboration. James E. Austin was a Grand Rapids lumberman who bought the Michigan Iron Works in 1900 for investment purposes and a place in which his mechanically-minded son Walter S. might tinker. The son tinkered, had his first car on the road in December 1902, and sold thirteen of them the following year. The father then consented to a serious foray into automobile manufacture. The first Austin had been a big two-cylinder vehicle on a 90-inch wheelbase, and the car became bigger and more powerful with each passing year. By 1907 the line included four- and six-cylinder models of 60 and 90 hp. Electric lights and left-hand steering were featured by 1911, and two years later a two-speed axle providing two gear ratios, for city and country driving, became an exclusive feature. (Austin's pioneering with this device was verified by a court decision in 1915 which upheld the company's priority over the Cadillac two-speed axle introduced in July of 1913.) Austin's slogan "The Highway King" seemed particularly appropriate for the touring car that stretched over a 142-inch wheelbase with its passenger snugly riding between the axles. By 1914 approximately 230 Austins had been built. During the World War I years, the company attacked in two directions — attempting to market a smaller and less expensive line of cars initially, and then plunging headlong with a lavish twelve-cylinder model. Among the celebrity purchasers of the more grand Austins were publisher William Randolph Hearst and boxing star Jack Johnson. No more than a thousand Austins had been produced in all when the company fell victim to the postwar depression. Although Walter Austin continued tinkering with his automotive ideas (he patented a hydraulic transmission in 1950), father and son turned to real estate development after the demise of their Austin. Their partnership was lifelong. They had lived together seventy years when James Austin died in 1936. Walter Austin died in Grand Rapids in 1965, shortly before his 100th birthday.

1903 AUSTIN

Model XXV — 2-cyl., 25 hp, 90" wb

Tour.	2000	2500	3500	5000	8500	18,000

1905 Austin, 50 h.p., touring, WLB

1904 AUSTIN

Model XXV — 2-cyl., 25 hp, 93" wb

	FP	5	4	3	2	1
Tour.	2500	2500	3500	5000	8500	18,000

Model XVI — 2-cyl., 16 hp, 93" wb

Tour.	2000	2300	3300	4600	7500	16,000

Model XXXV — 4-cyl., 35 hp, 100" wb

Tour.	3500	2700	3600	5300	8800	19,000

Model L — 4-cyl., 50 hp, 100" wb

Tour.	4500	2900	3700	5600	9100	20,000

1905 AUSTIN

Model XXXV — 4-cyl., 35 hp, 108" wb

Tour.	3000	2700	3600	5300	8800	19,000

Model L — 4-cyl., 50 hp, 108" wb

Tour.	3500	2900	3700	5600	9100	20,000

1906 Austin, model LX, limousine, HAC

1906 AUSTIN

Model LX — 4-cyl., 60 hp, 109" wb

Tour.-5P	4500	2900	3700	5600	9100	20,000
Folding Rear Seat Rbt.-4P	4100	3000	4000	6000	9500	21,000
Limo.-7P (114" wb)	6000	2700	3600	3600	8800	19,000

1907 Austin, model LX, touring, HAC

1907 AUSTIN

Model LX — 4-cyl., 60 hp, 116" wb

Tour.-8P	4500	4500	5800	9500	18,000	32,000
Limo.-8P	4500	3500	4500	7000	13,000	25,000

Model XC — 6-cyl., 90 hp, 130" wb

Tour.-8P	6000	5000	6500	11,000	22,000	35,000
Limo.-8P	6000	3900	4800	7700	14,300	27,000

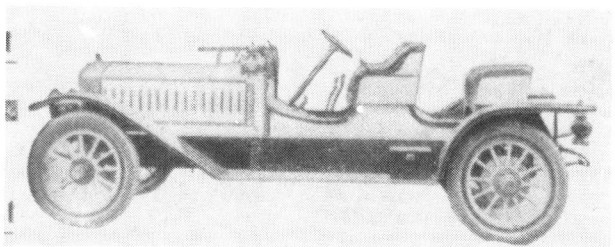

1908 Austin, model XC, roadster, HAC

1908 AUSTIN

Model LX — 4-cyl., 60 hp, 124" wb

Combination Rds.	4500	4500	5800	9500	18,000	32,000
Tour.	4500	4400	5600	9200	17,300	31,000
Detachable Top Limo.	5500	3300	4400	6700	12,000	24,000

Model XC — 6-cyl., 90 hp, 134" wb

Combination Rds.	6000	5000	6500	11,000	22,000	35,000
Tour.	6000	4900	6300	10,300	21,000	34,000
Detachable Top Limo.	7000	3500	4500	7000	13,000	25,000

1909 Austin, model 45, touring, HAC

1909 AUSTIN
Model 45 — 6-cyl., 45/60 hp, 126" wb

	FP	5	4	3	2	1
Tour.	3000	5200	6800	11,300	23,000	36,000
Rds.	2850	5300	7000	11,500	24,000	37,000
Limo.	4000	3700	4700	7300	13,700	26,000

Model 50 — 4-cyl., 60 hp, 124" wb

Tour.	4000	5000	6500	11,000	22,000	35,000
Rds.	4000	5200	6800	11,300	23,000	36,000
Limo.	5000	3500	4500	7000	13,000	25,000

Model 60 — 6-cyl., 60/90 hp, 147" wb

Tour.	5000	6300	9000	14,000	32,000	40,000
Rds.	5000	6000	8500	13,000	30,000	42,000
Limo.	6000	5000	6500	11,000	22,000	35,000

1910 AUSTIN
Model 45 — 6-cyl., 45/60 hp, 126" wb

Tour.-5P	3000	5200	6800	11,300	23,000	36,000

Model 50 — 6-cyl., 50/70 hp, 138" wb

Tour.-5/7P	4500	5400	7300	11,800	25,000	38,000

Model 60 — 6-cyl., 60/90 hp, 147" wb

Tour.-7P	6000	5800	8000	12,500	28,000	40,000

1911 Austin, model 60, touring, FR

1911 AUSTIN
Model 45 — 6-cyl., 45/60 hp, 126" wb

Tour.-5P	3000	5200	6800	11,300	23,000	36,000

Model 50 — 6-cyl., 50/70 hp, 135" wb

Tour.-5/7P	3850	5400	7300	11,800	25,000	38,000
Limo.	5000	4000	5000	8000	15,000	28,000

Model 60 — 6-cyl., 60/90 hp, 147" wb

Tour.-7P	6000	5800	8000	12,500	28,000	40,000

1912 Austin, model 70, touring, HAC

1912 AUSTIN
Model 45 — 6-cyl., 45/55 hp, 126" wb

Tour.-5P	3600	5000	6500	11,000	22,000	35,000

Model 50 — 6-cyl., 48/66 hp, 135" wb

Tour.-7P	4400	5200	6800	11,300	23,000	36,000

Model 70 — 6-cyl., 49 hp, 141" wb

Tour.-7P	6000	5400	7300	11,800	25,000	38,000

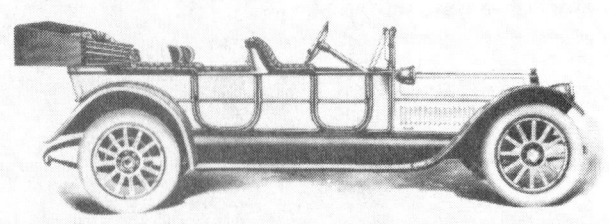

1913 Austin, model 77, touring, HAC

1913 AUSTIN
Model 55 — 6-cyl., 55 hp, 141" wb

	FP	5	4	3	2	1
Tour.-4P/5P/7P	4000	5200	6800	11,300	23,000	36,000
Tour.-9P	4150	5000	6500	11,000	22,000	35,000
Limo.-5P/7P	5000	3500	4500	7000	13,000	25,000

Model 66 — 6-cyl., 66 hp, 141" wb

Tour.-4P/5P/7P	5000	5300	6900	11,500	23,400	36,500
Tour.-9P	5150	5300	6800	11,400	22,500	35,500
Limo.-5P/7P	6000	3600	4600	7200	13,300	25,500

Model 77 — 6-cyl. 77 hp, 141" wb

Tour.-4P/5P/7P	6000	5300	7000	11,500	24,000	37,000
Tour.-9P	6150	5200	6800	11,300	23,000	36,000
Limo.-5P/7P	7000	3700	4700	7300	13,700	26,000

1914 Austin, model 66, touring, HAC

1914 AUSTIN
Model 66 — 6-cyl., 66 hp, 141" wb

Tour.-5P/7P	4000	5200	6800	11,200	23,500	36,500
Rbt.-4P	4000	5300	7000	11,500	24,000	37,000
Limo.	5000	3500	4500	7000	13,000	25,500

Model 77 — 6-cyl., 77 hp, 141" wb

Tour.-7P	6000	5300	7300	11,800	25,000	38,000

1915 Austin, model 66, roadster, WLB

1915 AUSTIN
Model 66 — 6-cyl., 66 hp, 141" wb

Tour.-4P	3600	5200	6800	11,300	23,000	36,000
Rbt.-3P	3600	5300	7000	11,500	24,000	37,000
Close-Coupled Rds.	3600	5400	7300	11,800	25,000	38,000
Tour.-5P/6P	3600	5300	7000	11,500	24,000	37,000
Enclosed Limo.-4P	4200	3500	4500	7000	13,000	25,000
Enclosed Limo.-5P	4250	3600	4600	7200	13,300	25,500
Limo.-7P	4700	3700	4700	7300	13,700	26,000

1916 Austin Highway King, roadster, HAC

1916 AUSTIN
Highway King — 6-cyl., 36.04 hp, 142" wb

	FP	5	4	3	2	1
Tour.-6P	2800	4500	5800	9500	18,000	32,000
Rds.-4P	2800	4700	6100	9900	19,000	33,000
Sed.	3800	3200	4300	6500	11,000	23,000
Vestibule Brougham	4000	3700	4700	7300	13,700	26,000

1917 Austin Highway King, touring, HAC

1917 AUSTIN
Highway King — 12-cyl., 39.68 hp, 142" wb

Tour.-6P	3750	4700	6100	9900	19,000	33,000
Rds.-2P	3750	4900	6300	10,300	21,000	34,000
Rds.-4P	3750	5000	6500	11,000	22,000	35,000
Tour.-7P	3750	4900	6300	10,300	21,000	34,000
Cpe.	4550	4000	5000	8000	15,000	28,000
Sed.	4950	3300	4400	6700	12,000	24,000
Limo.	5250	3700	4700	7300	13,700	26,000

1918 Austin Highway King, limousine, HAC

1918 AUSTIN
Highway King — 12-cyl., 39.68 hp, 142" wb

Tour.-6P	3750	4900	6300	10,300	21,000	34,000
Rds.-4P	3750	5000	6500	11,000	22,000	35,000
Sed.-7P	4950	3300	4400	6700	12,000	24,000
Limo.-7P	5250	4000	5000	8000	15,000	28,000

1919-1920 AUSTIN
Highway King — 12-cyl., 39.68 hp, 142" wb

Tour.-6P	4250	5000	6500	11,000	22,000	35,000
Rds.-4P	4250	5200	6800	11,300	23,000	36,000
Sed.-7P	5500	3500	4500	7000	13,000	25,000
Limo.-7P	5750	4200	5200	8400	15,700	29,000

AUSTIN-BANTAM — This has been a very common error in American automobile history. There never was an Austin-Bantam. The tiny cars produced in Butler, Pennsylvania during the 1930's were called the American Austin and subsequently the American Bantam. Refer to American Austin.

AUSTIN-HUTCHESON — The entire Hutcheson family — Howard B., Louis C. and Carol F. — were involved in the incorporation of the Austin-Hutcheson Company in New York City in early 1907. The manufacture of automobiles and carriages was the Hutcheson's plan, but their $5000 capital stock didn't take them very far in realizing it. Instead, they turned the quarters they had leased at 1964 Broadway into a dealership.

AUSTIN-LYMAN — The Austin-Lyman Company has been indicated on numerous rosters as an automobile producer in 1909 in Buffalo, New York. No firm of that name was listed in the Buffalo city directories from 1907 through 1911.

AUSTIN-WESTERN — There was an Austin-Western built in 1906 by the Austin-Western Engine Works of Chicago, but it was not a car. Instead it was, purportedly, America's first motor-driven street sweeper.

AUTO — The following ventures using the word "Auto" to lead off their company designations were incorporated with the intention of building automobiles. That any of these firms did indeed produce a car has not been documented.

Auto Appliance Company, 525 Main Street, East Orange, New Jersey, incorporated in late 1906 by Charles L. Beck, C.O. Geyer and F.O. Ferguson, all of East Orange. Capital stock was $150,000, and the manufacture of motor vehicles and appliances was the plan.

Auto-Armor Company, incorporated in late 1906 with a capital stock of $100,000, in New York City to build automobiles and carriages. Frank P. Hayes, Everett H. Converse and Madeline M. Mills were the incorporators.

Auto Association, to manufacture, deal in and rent automobiles, in New York City with a capital stock of $10,000 in the fall of 1905. Incorporators were Frank J. Griffin, William A.R. Welcke and Patrick F. Griffin, all of New York.

Auto Car Service Company of New Jersey, in Camden during the summer of 1909, to "manufacture, sell and operate automobiles and other vehicles and to establish a public garage." Capital stock was $10,000, and the incorporators were E.A. Fitts, David S. Ludlum and John O. Clark.

Auto-Coach Company, with $300,000 capital stock, to manufacture automobiles and taxicabs. This was a Delaware corporation, with "dummy directors," as *Automobile Topics* noted in December 1913.

Auto Construction Company, organized during January of 1906 with $50,000 capital stock in Minneapolis, Minnesota. The incorporators were J.M. Murphy, W.C. Hartson, C.E. Evans and G.A. Hughes. According to *The Horseless Age*, this venture had "equipped a factory at Hennepin Avenue and 10th Street and will engage in the manufacture of automobiles." Nothing further was heard of it, however.

Auto Cushioned Hub Company of Jersey City, New Jersey, early in 1906, with $100,000 capital stock by W.M. Lawyer of Brookline, Massachusetts, J.C. Warner of Lancaster, Pennsylvania and Robert Head of New York City. Capital stock was $100,000, and the plan was manufacture of automobiles.

Auto Distributers Limited Company, with $200,000 capital stock, during the summer of 1912 to "manufacture, buy and sell automobiles and other vehicles." Incorporators were Frank R. Hansell, J.C. Clow and John A. McPeak.

Auto Engine Works, a $200,000 venture organized in Minneapolis, Minnesota in the fall of 1904 by Charles H. Scholer, William T. Rogers and William J. West for the manufacture of "engines, automobiles, launches, inspection cars, speeders and similar products." The vehicles were to be powered by an engine patented by Roger.

Auto Export Company, organized in New York City early in 1909 by S.K. Lichtenstein, Henry M. Wise and William F. Ashley. Capital stock was $1000, and the plan was manufacture of "motor cars, motors and self-propelled vehicles."

Auto Import Company, in New York City late in 1903 to manufacture and deal in automobiles. Capital stock was $60,000, with Max S. Hamburger, Royal E. D'Orville and Hyman M. Wise incorporating.

Auto Lock Company, in Chicago with a capital stock of $50,000 early in 1909 to manufacture and deal in automobiles and accessories. Robert W. Dunn, Charles J. Monahan and L.A. Wisner were the incorporators.

Auto Machine Company, a $10,000 incorporation to "make and repair automobiles" in Marion, Indiana late in 1911. G.D. Lindsay, B.A. Tong and R.E. Breed, Jr. were the incorporators.

Auto Machine Company, early in 1911, to manufacture motor cars and motorcycles in Millville, New Jersey. Capital stock was $125,000, and the incorporators were Theodore C. Wheaton, Ivan Shull and Howard A. Gray.

Auto Owners' & Operators' Protective Association, in New York City, during the spring of 1910 with $25,000 capital stock. Incorporators were P.J. McGarth, F.J. Hagen and H. Miller who indicated a plan "to manufacture and deal in automobiles, sundries, automobile insurance, etc."

Auto-Ped Company, in New York City, late in 1913, with a $1 million capital stock to "manufacture, sell and deal in and with cars, carriages, boats and motor vehicles of all kinds." Incorporators were Joseph F. Curtin and Clarence E. Eaton.

Auto Protective League, during the summer of 1905 in New York City, with $25,000 capital stock to "make automobiles, launches, etc." Incorporators were Stefan Kjeldieu, Louis Frankel and Andrew C. Knoeller.

Auto-Quadricycle, a car purported to have been built by the Auto-Cycle Carriage Company in Chicago in 1903. No such company was listed in the Chicago city directory during this period.

Auto Rapid Transit Company, in Buffalo, New York during the summer of 1905, with a capital stock of $5000 to manufacture "automobiles, boats and vehicles." John M. and Catherine L. Campbell and Michael F. Dirnberger were the incorporators, all of Buffalo.

Auto Renewal Company, organized with a capital stock of $2500 in Chicago during the summer of 1910 to "deal in and manufacture motor cars and parts of same." The incorporators were James S. McClellan, Leo Klein and Jerome J. Cermak.

Auto Repair Company, Limited, a $5000 Delaware incorporation during the fall of 1904 for the purpose of manufacturing and dealing in "automobiles and other like vehicles and to repair the same" in Pittsburgh, Pennsylvania. Incorporators were indicated as Rex Remerston of Pittsburgh, Jefferson D. Thompson of Crafton, Pennsylvania and Truman W. Campbell of Wilmington. "Remerston" may have been a misprint for Rex Reinertson who had built the Rex Buckboard in Pittsburgh the year previous.

Auto-Service Company, with a capital stock of $50,000 to "manufacture and deal in automobiles" in New York City during the spring of 1906. Incorporators were Elmer Stouffer, David Hyams, F.L. Creamer, R. Bolshaw and Arthur Low, all of New York.

Auto Shop Company, of Paterson, New Jersey, with a capital stock of

AUTO ACETYLENE — New York, New York — (1899) — In the story on the new Auto-Acetylene Company appearing in its November 7th, 1899 issue, the *Motor Vehicle Review* noted that the company, which was located at 15 Park Row in New York City, had been experimenting for two years, had made "no exceptional claims and has no large stock organization" and planned to concentrate on the production of commercial vehicles, offering one acetylene-fueled automobile only — a runabout, which was pictured and featured wheel steering. The article also indicated that negotiations were ongoing for a plant in Green Point, New York State as well as one in Hyde Park, Massachusetts. The negotiations were never completed. Among the reasons may have been the guilt by association which resulted from the lamentable decision of this new company to call itself Auto-Acetylene. Precisely one year earlier another firm by that name had been incorporated in New York City by one Walter K. Freeman for the manufacture of engines using acetylene instead of gasoline. Freeman had advertised in the New York press for capital and succeeded in raising $5000. Thereupon he left town. As *The Horseless Age* had reported indignantly in a January 1899 issue, Walter K. Freeman "never had any patents, knew nothing about motors, and when his schemes had ripened, and a considerable sum had been realized from his advertisements in part

1899 Auto Acetylene, runabout, LC

payment for acetylene carriages, which neither he nor anybody else had ever succeeded in building, he took train for other parts, leaving his pretentious offices and his dupes behind him.'' Why this new New York City company elected to call itself Auto Acetylene is something of a mystery. Conceivably its founders were unaware of the earlier Auto Acetylene swindle.

AUTO-BI — The Auto-Bi was a motorized bicycle built at the turn of the century by Erwin Ross Thomas of Buffalo, New York. His Buffalo Automobile & Auto-Bi Company also produced the Auto-Two, Auto-Tri and Auto-Quad. Refer to Buffalo.

AUTO-BOB — **East Pittsburgh, Pennsylvania — (1914-1915)** — Jack Hickman began advertising in August of 1914. His little 3-5 hp juvenile car was ready for market, and he would offer it via mail order for $130 in pieces or $150 fully assembled. And he was anxious to establish dealerships too, offering one agent per county, with a check for twenty-five dollars to guarantee the franchise. Jack Hickman was out of business in early 1915.

1914-1915 AUTO-BOB

	FP	5	4	3	2	1
Auto-Bob Juvenile Car	150	600	750	1000	1500	2500

1909 Auto-Bug, auto-buggy, WLB

AUTO-BUG — **Norwalk, Ohio — (1909-1910)** — The Auto-Bug Company built ''The Machine without the Usual Hubub (sic).'' It was a highwheeler with a stationary rear axle to which the engine and related machinery were fitted, and featured sleeves with bearings upon which the wheels turned. Arthur E. Skadden, formerly superintendent of the Pressed Radiator Company (New Castle, Pennsylvania), was the man behind this venture. He organized his Auto-Bug Company in March of 1909, began production in June, and took three Auto-Bugs to the Cleveland Automobile Show in February 1910. Business was good, but Skadden quickly recognized that most automobile purchasers wanted a standard car. Consequently, in April 1910, he introduced the Norwalk. And he revised the name of his firm to Norwalk Motor Car Company. For a while he continued to produce his Auto-Bug alongside his new car, but by 1911 the highwheeler was discontinued.

1909-1910 AUTO-BUG
Model C — 2-cyl., 22 hp
Rbt.

	850	2000	3000	4200	6500	14,000

Model F — 2-cyl., 22 hp
Surrey

	850	2000	3000	4200	6500	14,000

Model E — 2-cyl., 22 hp

	FP	5	4	3	2	1
Tour.	850	2000	3000	4200	6500	14,000

Model 5-24 — 2-cyl., 22 hp

Dly.	850	1500	2500	3600	5500	11,000

AUTO BUGGY — The generic term Auto Buggy was often used during the early years of the American industry by companies producing highwheelers. Refer to A.B.C., International (I.H.C.) and Success.

AUTOCAR — Manufacture of an automobile operated by compressed air was the purported plan of the Autocar Company of Hartford, Connecticut in 1900, according to trade publications of that era. The motive power was right, the name was wrong. Refer to Autocrat.

1901 Autocar, phaeton, JAC

AUTOCAR — **Ardmore, Pennsylvania — (1901-1912)** — The Autocar was the result of a collaboration among Lewis S. Clark, his brothers John S. and James K., his father Charles (for financial support), and a mutual friend, William Morgan — all of Pittsburgh. They formed the Pittsburgh Motor Vehicle Company in 1897, and began production of a modest number of trikes and four-wheelers marketed under the tradename of Pittsburgh. In April 1900 Clark and company moved to nearby Ardmore and established the Autocar Company. Twenty-seven Autocars were produced by year's end 1901, and the next year saw introduction of a two-cylinder model generally believed to be the first American car of more than a single cylinder to have shaft drive. Legend has it that this was the result of the company's experience in the Automobile Club of America's New York to Buffalo Endurance Run of 1901. Two factory Type VI cars had been entered and suffered continual chain breakage. Thereafter Lewis Clark went back to the drawing board, and Autocars had shaft drive in two-and-a-half months. An exceedingly well-made vehicle, the Autocar was adver-

1901 Autocar, runabout, HAC

78

tised initially for the negative reasons that it "cannot blow up or burn up." Ease of control was another touted feature; by 1905 gearshift, clutch, spark and accelerator all fell to hand under the steering column. Autocar's diversification was its passenger car's undoing. Commercial vehicles had been added to the company's output during 1907, an immediately and immensely successful venture. Although the 1911 catalog espoused "continued interest in the manufacture of pleasure cars," Autocar changed its mind about that the following year.

1902 Autocar, runabout, JAC

1901 AUTOCAR
Type V — 2-cyl., 6 hp

	FP	5	4	3	2	1
Rbt.	800	2500	3500	5000	8000	18,000
Phaeton	900	2700	3600	5300	8800	19,000

1902 AUTOCAR
Type VI — 2-cyl., 8 1/2 hp

Rbt.	1100	2500	3500	5000	8500	18,000
Canopy Rbt.	1200	2700	3600	5300	8800	19,000
Dos-a-Dos	1300	2900	3700	5600	9100	20,000

1903 Autocar, touring, HAC

1903 Autocar, runabout, WLB

1903 AUTOCAR
Type VII — 2-cyl., 10 hp

	FP	5	4	3	2	1
Tonneau	1700	2500	3500	5000	8500	18,000

1904 Autocar, touring, WLB

1904 Autocar, type VIII, tonneau, HAC

1904 AUTOCAR
Type X — 2-cyl., 10/12 hp, 70" wb

Rbt.	900	2700	3600	5300	8800	19,000

Type VIII — 2-cyl., 12/14 hp, 76" wb

Tonneau	1700	2900	3700	5600	9100	20,000

1905 Autocar, type VIII, touring, HAC

1905 AUTOCAR
Type X — 2-cyl., 10/12 hp, 70" wb

Rbt.	900	2500	3500	5000	8500	18,000

Type VIII — 2-cyl., 12 hp, 76" wb

Rear Entrance Tonneau	1400	2700	3600	5300	8800	19,000

Type XI — 4-cyl., 16/20 hp, 96" wb

Side Entrance Tonneau	2000	2800	3700	5500	9000	19,500

1906 AUTOCAR
Type X — 2-cyl., 12 hp, 76" wb

Rbt.	1000	2500	3500	5000	8500	18,000

Type XII — 4-cyl., 24 hp, 100" wb

Tour.	2600	2700	3600	5300	8800	19,000
Limo.	3500	2400	3400	4800	8000	17,000

1906 Autocar, type XII, touring, HAC

1907 Autocar, type XV, runabout, HAC

1907 Autocar Taxicab, type RC, JAC

1907 AUTOCAR
Type XV — 2-cyl., 12 hp, 80 1/2" wb

	FP	5	4	3	2	1
Rbt.	1200	2700	3600	5300	8800	19,000
Type XIV — 4-cyl., 30 hp, 109" wb						
Tour.	3000	2900	3700	5600	9100	20,000
Type XII — 4-cyl., 24 hp, 100" wb						
Limo.	3500	2500	3500	5000	8500	18,000
Land'et.	3500	2700	3600	5300	8800	19,000

1908 Autocar, type XV, runabout, HAC

1908 AUTOCAR
Type XV — 2-cyl., 12 hp, 80 1/2" wb

	FP	5	4	3	2	1
Rds.	1200	2900	3700	5600	9100	20,000
Type XIV — 4-cyl., 30 hp, 112" wb						
Tour.	2750	2900	3700	5600	9100	20,000
Limo.	3500	2700	3600	5300	8800	19,000
Rds.	2750	3000	4000	6000	9500	21,000
Type XII — 6-cyl., 60 hp, 128" wb						
Limo.-10P	6500	2700	3600	5300	8800	19,000
Limo.-16P	7000	2700	3600	5300	8800	19,000

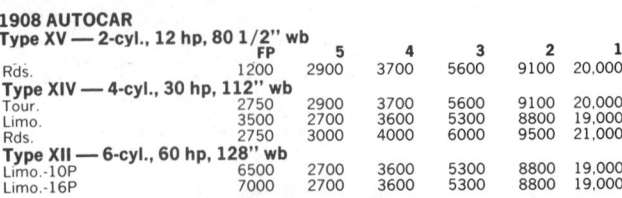

1909 Autocar, type XX, victoria, HAC

1909 AUTOCAR
Type XX — 4-cyl., 26/30 hp, 102 1/4" wb

	FP	5	4	3	2	1
Tourabout-2P/3P/4P	1750	3000	4000	6000	9500	21,000

1910 Autocar, type XXII, touring, HAC

1910 AUTOCAR
Type XXII — 4-cyl., 26/30 hp, 102" wb

	FP	5	4	3	2	1
Tour.	1800	3000	4000	6000	9500	21,000

1911 Autocar, type XXIV, touring, JAC

1911 AUTOCAR
Type XXIV — 4-cyl., 30 hp, 117" wb

	FP	5	4	3	2	1
Tour.	2250	2900	3700	5600	9100	20,000
Foredoor Tour.	2350	3000	3900	5800	9300	20,500
1912 AUTOCAR						
Type XXIV-B — 4-cyl., 30 hp, 117" wb						
Tour.	2650	—	—	—	—	—
Foredoor Tour.	2750	—	—	—	—	—

1908 Auto Car, limousine, NAHC

AUTO CAR — Buffalo, New York — (1907) — ATTERBURY — (1911) — The Auto Car Equipment Company was incorporated by John B. Corcoran, George W. Atterbury and Elmer B. Olmstead in 1904 for the purpose of building commercial vehicles. In 1907, in addition to its line of delivery wagons, trucks, buses and sightseeing cars, Auto Car offered a six-cylinder 60 hp limousine that was stretched over a commercial chassis of unspecified length. It was gargantuan, seating seven to ten passengers, and was advertised (probably without fear of contradiction) as the largest limousine in the United States. Although a "Limousine Department" was set up in Buffalo for its marketing apparently it quickly became a lonely place because Auto Car discontinued the car after only a year to return fulltime to the business it knew best. At some point, the firm name had changed to Auto Car Manufacturing Company, and in December 1909 it changed again, to Atterbury Motor Car Company. The reason given was to avoid confusion with the Autocar from Pennsylvania. In 1911 a ten-passenger Atterbury touring car was offered, but again this venture into the passenger car market was one season only. In May 1912 the Atterbury Motor Car Company changed its name to the Atterbury Motor Truck Company, and commercial vehicle production was the company's sole emphasis.

AUTOCARETTE — Washington, D.C. — (1900-1901) — Two distinct companies were involved in this ill-starred venture. The first was the Autocarette Company which was organized early in 1900 by O.G. Staples and W.E. Schneider "to build and operate motor vehicles in Washington, D.C." Within weeks, however, Staples and Schneider decided to confine themselves to the "operating" part of the business and contacted the Schaum Automobile and Motor Manufacturing Company of Baltimore for the "building" part. The word Autocarette carries a connotation of smallness, but these vehicles were big. Their seating capacity was twenty passengers, purportedly "the first of their kind in the country." The Baltimore firm was contracted to build ten of them for $40,000. The cars were built and delivered, and the trouble began almost immediately. In September 1900 it was reported that Autocarette service had been temporarily discontinued because changes were necessary in the electric motor equipment. In February 1901 a report followed that District of Columbia residents objected strenuously to the vehicles because they were "unsightly in the extreme" and made "an unholy din." The whole affair ended badly. Autocarette, charging defective equipment, refused to pay the balance due on the $40,000 purchase price. As *Cycle and Automobile Trade Journal* explained in January 1902, "This led to counter suits, one company suing for the money paid on account and the other company suing for the balance due on the vehicles." How it all ended does not appear to have been recorded.

AUTO-CARRIAGE — From 1905 to 1906, the cars produced by the Johnson Service Company of Milwaukee, Wisconsin were known simply as Auto-Carriages. Other model designations followed through 1912 when the Johnson Service Company discontinued its automobile department. Refer to Johnson.

AUTOCART — The Autocart Company was a $15,000 venture organized under the lenient laws of Maine during the summer of 1911. Charles H. O'Brien and Lewis A. Burleigh were the incorporators and the manufacture of automobiles and trucks was their plan. No production resulted.

AUTOCRAFT — The manufacture and repair of motor vehicles was the announced plan of the Autocraft Company of Boston, Massachusetts. This early 1913 venture was capitalized at $75,000 by C.M. Jones, G.G. Hinsdale and W.E. Duncanson. No manufacture is indicated.

AUTOCRAT — Hartford, Connecticut — (1899) — Early in 1899 a group of mechanics in Hartford got together as the Autocrat Manufacturing Company to build a car that operated on compressed air. As explained to the press, "the compressed air is stored in cylinders placed in a false bottom in the body of the carriage . . . There are three stages of compression. The first cylinder takes the air at atmospheric pressure and it is compressed to the second cylinder, where it is again compressed up to 700 pounds per square inch. It is then passed to a third cylinder, where the pressure is raised to 3000 pounds if necessary. When the carriage needs recharging all that is necessary is to back up to the power plant and a sufficient quantity of air is taken in about three seconds after the connection is made." Purportedly, the carriage could travel for forty to fifty miles between charges. Its top speed was 10 mph. The Autocrat company planned to establish a complete compressed air plant somewhere in Hartford where all vehicles could be charged. The severe limitations on mobility that the Autocrat represented was probably the reason the car never went into production.

AUTOCRAT STEAM — Salt Lake City, Utah — (1905) — This steam car from Utah was unusual for its feature of front wheel drive, its transmission covered by a patent issued to one George R. Boulding. "Autocrat probably will be the name" read the announcement in the trade press in June 1905, which indicated that the prototype was being built and that the Monarch Motor Company of Salt Lake City was being organized. The desert mining camp district of Nevada was indicated as the venture's prime marketing area. Monarch manager Edgar S. Darling reported that the company expected to "commence regularly the manufacture of automobiles." This did not happen. The only Autocrat produced was the prototype. Whether the Autocrat Company which was organized late in 1911 in Augusta, Georgia with a capital stock of $150,000 was yet another attempt by Boulding to get into manufacture is not known, but it went nowhere too.

AUTOCYCLE — Among the three models produced by the Keystone Motor Company of Philadelphia in 1900 was a three-seated gasoline car called the Autocycle. Refer to Keystone.

In late 1913 the Toledo Auto-Cycle Car Company was organized in Toledo, Ohio for the manufacture of a cyclecar. Refer to Toledo.

The Autocycle Company built a cyclecar in New Orleans, Louisiana in 1914 which was marketed under the initials A.C. Refer to A.C.

AUTOCYCLE — Philadelphia, Pennsylvania — (1906-1907) — The Vandegrift Automobile Company was organized in Philadelphia during the summer of 1906. Among the incorporators were Pedro Salom and Henry G. Morris, the pioneer builders of the Morris & Salom Electrobats. The new Autocycle to be built by Vandegrift was a gasoline-powered vehicle, however, and a most unusual one. Basically, it was a combination of a motor cycle frame with a wheel each front and aft, supplemented by two parallel side wheels which looked like the sort affixed to help train a young bicyclist. "The balance wheels carry little or no weight under normal conditions," reported *Cycle and Automobile Trade Journal*, "and as the speed of the vehicle increases, the demands upon them for maintaining equilibrium naturally decrease." Forty-five miles an hour was said to be the top speed. The Autocycle's engine was an air-cooled 6 hp twin. The complete weight of the vehicle was 380 pounds, its turning radius was seven feet, and its price tag was $400. The Vandegrift factory was located at 13th and Cumberland streets in Philadelphia. Production there ended sometime late in 1907.

1907 Autocycle, NAHC

1906-1907 AUTOCYCLE
Autocycle — 2-cyl., 6 hp, 75" wb

	FP	5	4	3	2	1
Rbt.-2P	400	2000	3000	4200	6500	14,000

AUTO-CYCLECAR — A one-passenger vehicle called the Auto-Cyclecar was announced to be the product of the new Automobile Cycle Car Company of Detroit in December 1913. When the car arrived on the market the following June, however, it had room for two or more passengers and had been renamed the Tiger. Refer to Tiger.

1900 Auto-Dynamic, NAHC

81

AUTO-DYNAMIC — New York, New York — (1900-1902) — The product of the Auto-Dynamic Company of New York City was a small electric that was offered as a trap, hansom, brougham and light delivery wagon. Frank Tilford was president, Thomas W. Stevens treasurer, and Arthur L. Stevens general manager of this company, which manufactured its own batteries and which had patented its controller and other electric devices. "They promise to become an important factor in the automobile business," *The Motor Age* said in October 1900 in a prediction which did not come true. The Auto-Dynamic factory was located at 140 West 39th Street, five blocks north of Macy's on Herald Square.

AUTOETTE — Manistee, Michigan — (1912-1913) — The Manistee Auto Company had one of the earliest cyclecars on the market, and also one of the smallest. Its single-cylinder water-cooled engine, developing a carefully calculated 4.9 horsepower, was placed under the hood of a small 72-inch wheelbase chassis with friction transmission, vee-belt drive and side-by-side seating for two passengers. The price tag was $300. The company had been organized in March of 1912 with a capital stock of $51,000. Its president and general manager was Charles Elmendorf, its secretary-treasurer George N. Burr. The Manistee factory was at River and Fifth streets. Although the company's car was named the Autoette, it was also sometimes referred to as the Manistee during its second year in the marketplace.

1913 Autoette, roadster, WLB

1912-1913 AUTOETTE

	FP	5	4	3	2	1
Autoette Cyclecar	300	2000	3000	4200	6500	14,000

AUTO-ETTE — Chrisman, Illinois — (1913) — The cyclecar from the Auto-Ette Company of Chrisman differed from the Manistee Autoette in offering one more cylinder (for a total of two), nearly twice the horsepower (the horses numbered 9) and two feet more in wheelbase (for a total of 96 inches). Its Spacke engine was air cooled, its chassis shaft drive, its price $368. The Chrisman Auto-Ette and the Manistee Autoette were similar, however, in not surviving long in the marketplace. These two cars should not be confused, incidentally, with the Autoette built in Detroit in 1910 by Allen Horton and J.J. Chapin, that car correctly being called a Horton.

1913 AUTO-ETTE
Two — 9 hp, 96" wb

Rds.-2P	368	1200	2000	3000	4500	8000

AUTO FORE CARRIAGE — This turn of the century kit for turning a horse-drawn carriage into a horseless one is more properly designated by its full name. Refer to Automobile Fore Carriage.

AUTO FRONT-DRIVE — During 1905 the Auto Front Drive-Manufacturing Company of St. Louis was organized for the production of a front-drive axle and a car to be called the Front-Drive. Refer to Front-Drive.

AUTOGO — This was the designation which C.H. Metz used for his Orient tricycles and quadricycles produced from 1900 to 1901. Refer to Orient.

AUTO KING — During the summer of 1900, two companies were incorporated in Portland, Maine by a consortium of businessmen including T. King, D. King, W.E. Burke, H. Talman, E. Knapshoff, W.H. Hastings and W.M. Payson. The first was the New England Auto-King Company, with a capital stock of $1.2 million, to manufacture motor vehicles. The second was the Auto-King Vehicle Company, with a capital stock of $500,000, to deal in motor vehicles. Most probably, the real purpose of both ventures was to sell stock. Nothing further was heard of either company after 1900.

AUTOLET — Autolet was the proposed name for the car which A.B. Holson of Chicago, Illinois planned to build in 1904. Refer to Holson.

AUTOLYTE — The Autolyte Manufacturing Company was organized in Albany, New York late in 1906 for the production of "machinery appliances and motor cars." Additionally, a garage was to be operated. Behind this $6000 venture were W.H. Schleicher of Flushing, New York; Thomas M. Debevoise of Summit, New Jersey and Edward S. Paine of Brooklyn. No automobile manufacture resulted.

AUTOMATIC — Automatic Sturtevant was an occasional designation used for the car produced by the Sturtevant Mill Company in Boston from 1906-1907. Refer to Sturtevant.

The Automatic Appliance Company was organized with a $5000 capital stock in Chicago during the summer of 1911 to "manufacture and deal in automobiles, motorcycles, bicycles, etc." The incorporators were Stephen Velie, Samuel Breakstone and Sarah Procktor. No automobile is believed to have resulted of this venture. Probably Stephen Velie was related to the Velies of downstate Moline who were in successful production of their Velie car during this period.

AUTOMATIC AIR — Albany, New York — (1899) — On June 12th, 1899, the Automatic Air Carriage Company was incorporated with a capital stock of $600,000 in Albany for the manufacture of automobiles propelled by compressed air or gas, or a combination of the two. The men behind this venture were Edward A. Willard, Robert R. Blood, Charles J. Hensley and Seymour L. Husted, Jr., all of New York City. "The system of the company is different from any yet proposed by compressed air experts," the trade press reported, "and is claimed to be a decided improvement over all preceding compressed air locomotion." Apparently not. The Automatic Air Carriage did not proceed beyond prototype.

1921 Automatic Electric, runabout, WLB

AUTOMATIC ELECTRIC — Buffalo, New York — (1921) — The Automatic Transportation Company claimed to be the world's largest manufacturer of electric industrial trucks and tractors. This is doubtful. The little two-seater runabout the company marketed was claimed to "surpass anything the engineering world" had thus far produced in the electric vehicle field. This is doubtful as well. Still, the Automatic Electric was a high class little car: 65-inch wheelbase, 95 inches overall, 900 pounds. Up to 60 miles between charges was promised, the top speed was 18 mph, and the car could be parked in a 4-by-8-foot space. But $1200 was a steep price to pay for all this, and few people did. A company photograph shows about a dozen Automatic Electrics on the road; how many more than that might have been produced is unknown. "Colonel" E.R. (Teddy) Green is known to have bought one. A reference from 1927 indicates that the Automatic Transportation Company was acquired by the Walker Vehicle Company (producer of electric trucks) that year.

1921 AUTOMATIC ELECTRIC

	FP	5	4	3	2	1
Electric Rbt.-2P	1200	2000	3000	4200	6500	14,000

AUTOMOBILE — The Automobile Company of America produced the Gasmobile in New York City and Marion, New Jersey from 1899-1901. Refer to Gasmobile.

The Automobile Company of Philadelphia was organized with a capital stock of $50,000 late in 1906 to "manufacture motor cars, carriages, etc., and to operate a garage and livery." The incorporators were F.A. Hensell, J.A. McPeak and W.T. Nidell, all of Camden, New Jersey. No automobile is believed to have been built.

The Automobile Air Carriage Company was indicated as a manufacturer in New York City in the Hiscox book *Horseless Vehicles, Automobiles, Motor Cycles* published in 1900. No company of that name was listed in the New York City directory for 1899-1901.

The Automobile Boat Manufacturing Company built the Hydromotor in Seattle, Washington during the World War I years. Refer to Hydromotor.

The Automobile Buyers Association was organized with a $10,000 capital stock during the fall of 1905 in New York City. Manufacturing and dealing in automobiles was the company's plan, its incorporators being Samuel C. Meer, Eugene C. Harding and Clarence E. Mandy. There is no evidence of a car having been built.

The Automobile Carriage Supply Company of 411 Euclid Avenue in Cleveland, Ohio is indicated as a manufacturer in the Hiscox book *Horse-Vehicles, Automobiles, Motor Cycles* published in 1900. No such company is listed in the Cleveland city directories of the period.

The Automobile Construction Company of Chicago was organized to "manufacture gasoline commercial and pleasure vehicles" in Chicago during the summer of 1911. Incorporators were Harry M. Wells, Albert T. Graham, William E. Fuller. Subsequent automobile manufacture has not been documented.

The Automobile Cooperative Association was organized with a capital stock of $40,000 in Halfmoon, New York during the summer of 1908. F.B.

Roues, William C. Dickerman and H.H. Williams were the people behind this venture to manufacture automobiles and motor boats. Subsequent automobile manufacture is not indicated.

The Automobile Development Company of Camden, New Jersey was organized by H.B. Martin, S.C. Seymour and J.F. Cotter during the fall of 1913. Capital stock was $10,000, and the plan was to manufacture and deal in automobiles and parts. No automobile is believed to have been produced.

The Automobile Equipment Company was a Cincinnati, Ohio venture of early 1914 incorporated with a capital stock of $100,000 by G.W. Platt, Arno Merkle, Edward H. Maffey, Marion L. Freeman and Alice DeCharmes. The firm announced its plan to "manufacture and deal in motor trucks and automobiles and to do repairing for all motor driven vehicles." No automobile is believed to have been produced of this venture.

The Automobile Equipment Company of early 1917 was a $50,000 Delaware incorporation for the manufacture of automobiles and the conduct of a garage business. Charles Topkis, James N. Ginns and Matthew Finer were the incorporators. Manufacture of an automobile is doubted.

The Automobile Exchange was organized in Chicago early in 1904 by J.H. Holmes and Otto B. Schmidt to "manufacture and deal in automobiles and other vehicles." Capital stock was $8000, and no automobile is believed to have resulted.

The Automobile Exchange from 1906 was another Chicago incorporation, this one with a capital stock of $2500 for the manufacture of automobiles and accessories. Incorporators were Frank Schoenfeld, Milton L. Thackberry and Emil F. Link. No manufacture is believed to have followed.

Yet another Automobile Exchange was the $100,000 incorporation from late 1907 in Bayonne, New Jersey by E.D. Cronin, F. Knowlton and E.A. Monfort to manufacture and deal in automobiles. Manufacture is doubted.

The Automobile Hire and Sales Company of New York City was organized during the fall of 1905 to "manufacture and sell automobiles, motor vehicles and accessories." William N. Balto and John T. Evans were president and secretary respectively of this venture which is not believed to have produced a car.

The Automobile League of New York City was organized with a capital stock of $5000 early in 1908 "to engage in the manufacture of motor vehicles of all kinds." Frank J. Griffin, Nicholas Fancher and William T. Conville were the backers of this venture, which probably did not result in the production of a single automobile.

The Automobile Maintenance Company of Chicago was a $2000 incorporation from the summer of 1903 for the purpose of "manufacturing, repairing and dealing in automobiles." Gail Dray, Herbert R. Lloyd and George C. Madison were the incorporators. No automobile is believed to have resulted.

The Automobile Maintenance Company of America was a New York City incorporation of early 1906 for the manufacture of automobiles. Behind this $200,000 venture were Frank Van Orden, William Wieck and Joseph M. Ayer. There is no evidence of an automobile having been produced.

The Automobile Manufacturing & Engineering Company was organized in Detroit, Michigan during the summer of 1910 by C.M. Miller, H.L. Booth and S.S. Allen, all of Plattsburgh, New York. Capital stock was $1000 and the plan was manufacture of automobiles and self-propelled vehicles "both on land, water and air, or either of them." The rudiments of good grammar obviously eluded the people behind this venture, as apparently did any manufacture.

The Automobile Manufacturing Company of Newark, New Jersey was an early 1911 incorporation with a $500,000 capital stock to manufacture and deal in motor cars. A.E. Egner, W.E. Brown, Jr. and C. English were behind this venture, which did not apparently produce a car.

The Automobile & Marine Power Company of Camden, New Jersey produced the New Era car from 1901-1902. Refer to New Era.

The Automobile Owner's Association was organized under the laws of Delaware during the spring of 1910 with a $250,000 capital stock. Incorporators were J.C. and F.J. Niles, W. Wilson, Alan Carson and H.J. Kunkle, all of Philadelphia, and the manufacture of and dealing in automobiles was the announced plan. It does not appear to have been realized.

The Automobile Owners' Protective Association of early 1909 was a $100,000 incorporation of Camden, New Jersey "to engage in the manufacture of motor cars and . . . also to protect owners." F.J. Curran, J.U. Clarke and T.F. Curley were behind this venture which did not apparently produce an automobile.

The Automobile Owners' Manufacturing Company of Goshen, New York was organized by W. Phillipson, F.H. Vehrenkamp and G.F Munds, Jr. early in 1911 with a capital stock of $1 million and the announced plan of motor vehicle manufacture. This venture was a consolidation of Coates-Goshen and the Dayton Rubber Manufacturing Company for the production of a three-wheeler delivery car. Refer to Coates-Goshen.

The Automobile Realization Company was a $90,000 incorporation from Chicago during the fall of 1913 to "make automobiles, automobile parts and accessories." The incorporators were Frank T. Righeimer, Mark W. Bigelow and Frank T. Murray. No automobile is believed to have resulted.

The Automobile Realty Company was organized in New York City late in 1905 to manufacture automobiles. Capital stock was $6000, and the incorporators were Albert W. Pross, George Maurer and George J. Thompson is doubted.

The Automobile Supply Company of Virginia City, Nevada was the sponsoring organization for the automobile built in 1902 by Frank C. Holmes. Refer to Holmes.

The Automobile Supply Company was organized during the fall of 1905 to "make, deal in and repair automobiles" in St. Louis, Missouri. Incorporators were William Mulford, E.A. Sluder and Freeman Wright. Manufacture has not been documented.

The Automobile Vehicle Corporation was a $20,000 incorporation from Buffalo, New York during the summer of 1912. A.L. Kenyon, Frank H. O'Neill, Otto A. Hegelm and James C. Fox were behind this venture, which is not documented to have produced a single car.

Automobile Voiturette was the name occasionally referred to in the press for the car built by the Automobile Company of America at the turn of the century, which by 1900 became known as the Gasmobile. Refer to Gasmobile.

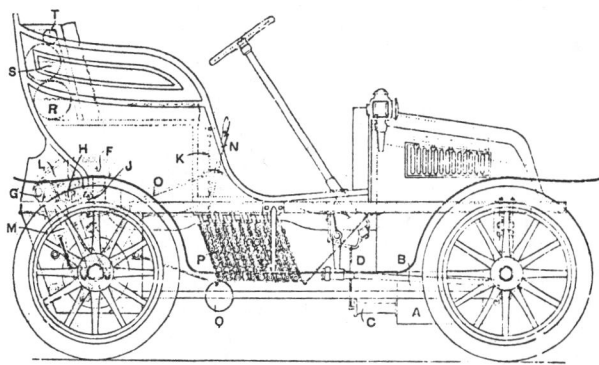

1899 Automobile, steamer, WLB

AUTOMOBILE — Baltimore, Maryland — (1899-1900) — The Automobile Manufacturing Company of Baltimore produced a steam car with two double-acting cylinders and a flash-type boiler heated by petroleum. The car appeared to have been very solidly constructed, though total production of it is not known. One of the company's vehicles did, however, serve as a test case in Baltimore. In the fall of 1899, when W.W. Donaldson attempted to enter the city park with the vehicle, he was stopped by a policeman who threatened his arrest. Donaldson complained to higher authorities, and motor vehicles were thereafter allowed to join horseless carriages on the park drives.

AUTOMOBILE BATTERY — Santa Cruz, California — (1904) — "A project toward establishing an automobile factory in Santa Cruz has been launched," *Motor Field* revealed in December 1904, "and articles of incorporation have already been filed." Henry F. Kron was president, Edward C. Lilly secretary, W.H. Lamb vice-president and Philip Trapp superintendent of the new Automobile Battery Company in Santa Cruz. Trapp was a Chicagoan and the inventor of a process for making electric car batteries. The manufacture of the batteries themselves, in addition to electric cars, was planned in Santa Cruz. It is known that several prototypes were built in Chicago and tested on the streets there. But this venture does not seem to have proceeded into manufacture in California.

AUTOMOBILE CONSTRUCTION — Milwaukee, Wisconsin — (1901-1902) — Actually, it was as much invitation as advertisement. "Recognizing the fact that many people cannot pay the high price asked for some Automobiles," Herman C. Mueller, the manager of the Automobile Construction Company of Milwaukee wrote, "we are inviting propositions to make Automobiles of any design to order on contract plan." Unlike many firms offering cars on a non-marketing basis, Mueller's Automobile Construction Company did not focus on potential dealers for its trade but rather the single owner who wanted a car for himself. Mueller was willing to build such cars from parts furnished by the client, or from stock designs of his own, with pictures of some furnished on request to prospective customers. The cars built by the Automobile Construction Company sold for $350 and up. Mueller's car-building venture seems to have survived about two years. Subsequently, Herman Mueller became a Milwaukee automobile dealer, returning to manufacture briefly in 1909 with a highwheeler produced under his own name.

1914 Automobile Construction

AUTOMOBILE CONSTRUCTION — Philadelphia, Pennsylvania — (1914) — Another of the companies offering a nameless car during the early years of the industry was the Automobile Construction and Engineering Company of 3322 Ludlow Street in Philadelphia. Some cars of this type were offered complete; this one was made available in parts — its engine together, but the rest of the vehicle to be assembled by the dealer, the components guaranteed to "positively fit." The car offered by the Automobile Construction and Engineering Company was claimed to have put up a mile in 41 seconds at Philadelphia's Point Breeze track in September 1913. Components provided potential dealers in this offer included a four-cylinder Continental engine, three-speed selective transmission, shaft drive, a 110-inch wheelbase chassis, and a "first-class" body. The price for all this was $675. "It's a mighty natty and attractive-looking car . . .," the company advertised. "Start selling this under your own name and it will keep you busy the year round. It's a big money-making proposition for any energetic dealer." The company offered this proposition only in 1914.

1900 Automobile Fore-Carriage, phaeton, HAC

1900 Automobile Fore-Carriage, runabout, HAC

AUTOMOBILE FORE CARRIAGE — New York, New York — (1900) — The Automobile Fore Carriage Company was organized in New York City to purchase the U.S. patent rights to the Kullstein-Vollmer gasoline fore-carriage system which had been developed in Germany. This was an attachment cunningly tailored to fit any animal-drawn vehicle and instantly turn it into a horseless carriage. In February 1900 Automobile Fore Carriage announced its incorporation in the State of West Virginia with a capital stock of $5,000,000. Incorporators included H. Bergholtz of Ithaca; J.W.S. Langeman of Paris, France; W. Haxelton and F.H. Rosse of New York City; E.J. Paterson of Plainfield, New Jersey. Two demonstrators are known to have been built, but how many other Automobile Fore Carriages were turned into cars is not known.

1913 Automobilette, (WLB)

AUTOMOBILETTE — The Automobilette was one of myriad cyclecars which burst onto the American scene in 1913 and disappeared soon thereafter. This one's tenure was so abbreviated that the company promoting it does not appear to have ever been revealed. A prototype was built, however, incorporating a two-cylinder water-cooled engine, force-feed lubrication, thermo-syphon cooling, shaft drive from motor to countershaft, with final drive by vee-section belt. The frame was wood, with its outer members curved slightly from the dashboard to the rear section "to give the necessary width for the body without having to bend the main frame to receive the powerplant."

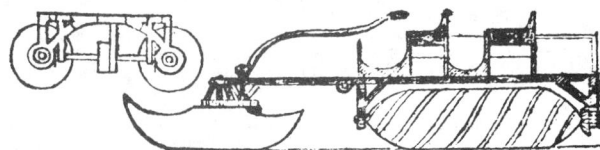

1900 Automosled, WLB

AUTOMOSLED — Bangor, Maine — (1900) — The name was the invention of Ira Peavey, as was every part of the vehicle itself. This motor sled was powered by a 20 hp gasoline engine and its building occupied Ira Peavey's time for more than five years, or so he said. Frustrations he had aplenty, as revealed in *The Motor Vehicle Review* in November 1900: "The mechanism seemed simple enough until he came to adjust the revolving runners. He found that if both the spirals were put on high-handed the sled would go to the right, while it would go the other way if the spirals were left hand. After he had made one left and the other right-handed there was a lot more figuring to do. By putting the coils of the spirals close together he could develop great pulling power, but could develop a very low rate of speed. Spirals put on at wider distances apart gave speed without power. To meet both conditions, he has constructed two sets of runners, one for work on the level or down hill, and the other for hill climbing." When finally he finished his Automosled, Ira Peavey declared that it could not be improved "unless an entirely new model shall be adopted." Doubtless he didn't care to tackle that, since this single example is the only one known to have been built. According to the *Bangor News*, Ira Peavy's plan was to ferry passengers, mails and supplies across Moosehead Lake as soon as it froze over and through the Bangor countryside as soon as the snow fell.

AUTOMOTE — Although Automote was the model designation, this 1900 car from Brooklyn more properly carried the name of the company which built it. Refer to Schaap.

AUTOMOTIVE — The Automotive Company of Philadelphia, Pennsylvania was a $100,000 incorporation from the fall of 1918 for the manufacture of tractors and automobiles. C.L. Rimlinger, M.M. Clancy and F.A. Armstrong were the incorporators. No automobile appears to have been produced.

The Automotive Development Corporation of Stamford, Connecticut has been purported to have produced an automobile called the Fairfield in 1926. Actually, the vehicle was a truck and the corporation a latterday incarnation of Victor Page's automotive venture of the period. The Automotive Development Corporation, which had been incorporated in Delaware, was officially dissolved in 1939, according to the *Marvyn Scudder Manual of Extinct or Obsolete Companies*.

AUTOMOTOR — Automotor was the name of the car purportedly produced by the Lowell Model Company of Lowell, Massachusetts in 1902. Refer to Lowell.

The Automotor Company of Columbus, Ohio was a $30,000 incorporation from early 1911 for the manufacture and sale of automobiles, motor trucks and accessories. A.F. Dickerson, F.W. Dickerson, William F. O'Gara, H.S. Bobo and Frank Lowenan were the people behind this venture. Manufacture is doubted.

The Automotor Corporation of New York City was organized during the fall of 1920 to manufacture automobiles and parts. Capital stock was $275,000; the incorporators were U. Thompson, Jr., D.F. Sullvan and H.P. Swanton. Manufacture is doubted.

1901 Automotor, runabout, WLB

AUTOMOTOR — Springfield, Massachusetts — (1901-1904) — The Automotor Company of Springfield evolved from the Springfield Cornice Works which, at the turn of the century, had built the Springfield Spring Motor and Meteor cars. The Automotor provided purchasers the choice of either planetary or sliding gear transmission, which was not unusual, and with one body that was: it was made of aluminum supplied by the Springfield Metal Body Company. Among the car's documented achievements was a first-class certificate in the Automobile Club of America's 500-mile endurance contest from New York to Boston and back, and 100 miles without a stop in the Long Island Endurance Contest. The company claimed a 45 mph top speed for its product, which cannot be documented. In addition to its larger car, Automotor offered a runabout powered by a choice of single-cylinder De Dion engines. The man behind the Automotor, incidentally, was Hinsdale Smith who later associated himself with Stevens-Duryea and was the designer of the Stevens-Duryea six.

1902 Automotor, runabout, HAC

1903 Automotor, tonneau, NAHC

1901-1904 AUTOMOTOR

	FP	5	4	3	2	1
King of Belgian Tonneau (4-cyl., 16/20 hp)	3000	3500	4500	7000	13,000	25,000
Rbt. (1-cyl., 3 1/2 hp)	850	2500	3500	5000	8500	18,000
Rbt. (1-cyl., 5 hp)	1000	2700	3700	5200	8700	18,500

AUTOMOTORETTE — This was the designation given to one of the several kit cars produced by A.L. Dyke in St. Louis, Missouri at the turn of the century. Refer to Dyke.

1910 Auto Parts, touring, NAHC

AUTO PARTS — Chicago, Illinois — (1907-1914) — Inclusive dates for the Automobile Parts & Equipment Company (later Auto Parts Company) on West Jackson Boulevard in Chicago are difficult to determine. The firm, which was organized during the summer of 1906 by Horace W. Book, Arthur B. Pease and Albert H. Fry, seems to have begun advertising in 1907. Its cars were called Chicago Flyer and Touraine that year. In October of 1909 the company announced a 23 hp shaft-drive touring car "assembled complete with two lamps (and) windshield" for $700. In November it was reported that the firm had bought up the stock of the bankrupt Harrison Motor Car Company, the Logan Construction Company, and the Monarch Motor Car Company. This Chicago enterprise gave all-new meaning to the phrase "assembled car." The vehicles offered under the Auto Parts name were precisely that, part one auto, part another. Its 1910 highwheeler was doubtless mostly Monarch, but the specifications for its $650 Model 4-30 Toy Tonneau of 1912 indicate a Harrison-Logan composite. By 1914 Auto Parts was offering a vehicle that was the epitome of its name: everything necessary to put one of the defunct Michigans together — a complete set of parts for $585. A run-about kit of 1911 was called the Oswald. Occasionally, Auto Parts made up more imaginative names for its automobiles, like Square Deal (for a $385 two-cylinder 14 hp highwheeler on an 82-inch wheelbase in 1910) and Yankee (for a $275 four-cylinder 18 hp cyclecar kit on a 102-inch wheelbase in 1914) — but these remained "parts cars" like all the others.

AUTO PARTS — Chicago, Illinois — (1907-1914) — Inclusive dates for the Automobile Parts & Equipment Company (later Auto Parts Company) on West Jackson Boulevard in Chicago are difficult to determine. The firm, which was organized during the summer of 1906 by Horace W. Book, Arthur B. Pease and Albert H. Fry, seems to have begun advertising in 1907. Its cars were called Chicago Flyer and Touraine that year. In October of 1909 the company announced a 23 hp shaft-drive touring car "assembled complete with two lamps (and) windshield" for $700. In November it was reported that the firm had bought up the stock of the bankrupt Harrison Motor Car Company, the Logan Construction Company, and the Monarch Motor Car Company. This Chicago enterprise gave all-new meaning to the phrase "assembled car." The vehicles offered under the Auto Parts name were precisely that, part one auto, part another. Its 1910 highwheeler was doubtless mostly Monarch, but the specifications for its $650 Model 4-30 Toy Tonneau of 1912 indicate a Harrison-Logan composite. By 1914 Auto Parts was offering a vehicle that was the epitome of its name: everything necessary to put one of the defunct Michigans together — a complete set of parts for $585. A run-about kit of 1911 was called the Oswald. Occasionally, Auto Parts made up more imaginative names for its automobiles, like Square Deal (for a $385 two-cylinder 14 hp highwheeler on an 82-inch wheelbase in 1910) and Yankee (for a $275 four-cylinder 18 hp cyclecar kit on a 102-inch wheelbase in 1914) — but these remained "parts cars" like all the others.

AUTOPLANE — This car that attempted to fly in California during the mid-Twenties to early-Thirties is more properly designated by its full name. Refer to Moore Autoplane.

AUTO-QUAD — The Auto-Quad four-wheeler was one of three models produced by Erwin Ross Thomas who established his Buffalo Automobile & Auto-Bi Company in Upstate New York at the turn of the century. In 1902 he changed the name of his cars to Buffalo. Refer to Buffalo.

The Auto-Quadricycle was a model of the Canda built at the turn of the century in Cartaret, New Jersey. Refer to Canda.

1919 Auto Red Bug, runabout, OCW

AUTO RED BUG — Auto Red Bug was one of several names used to designate a small buckboard which began life as the Red Bug in Layayette (Indiana) in 1916, subsequently became the Smith Flyer, then the Briggs & Stratton in Milwaukee (Wisconsin), and later was continued in manufacture from 1924-1930 in North Bergen (New Jersey) as the Red Bug or Auto Red Bug. Refer to Red Bug.

AUTO SUPPLY — New York, New York — (1901) — In 1901 the Auto Supply Company of 310 Mott Avenue in New York City built an automobile composed entirely of components it manufactured. It was a steamer fitted with a 5 hp engine and a 16-inch boiler. The car was fueled by gasoline, and its water tank held 34 gallons. The steam was superheated, the company said, "and shows little exhaust. The safety valve blows off into the water tank and lessens the danger of frightening horses." A wire-wheeled runabout, this one car was presumably the only example built. According to a press report, "The Auto Supply Company have rejected a number of orders for carriages on similar lines, as their specialty is manufacturing parts, and they would consider it unfair to their patrons to market a complete vehicle."

1901 Auto Supply, runabout, MVMA

AUTOTRI — The Autotri of 1898 was the first car built by Cadwallader Washburn Kelsey. It was not put into manufacture, though Kelsey did subsequently enter the automobile industry. Refer to Kelsey and Motorette.

The Auto-Tri tricycle was one of three models produced by Erwin Ross Thomas who established his Buffalo Automobile & Auto-Bi Company in Upstate New York at the turn of the century. In 1902 he changed the name of his cars to Buffalo. Refer to Buffalo.

The Auto-Tri Manufacturing Company was a Buffalo, New York incorporation from the summer of 1909. The capital stock was $200,000, the incorporators were G.R. Bidwell, W.S. Bull and W.M. Bowen, the plan was the "manufacture, repair, rental and sale of automobiles." Manufacture apparently did not result.

AUTO-TRICAR — New York, New York — (1914) — That it was a three-wheeler and a variation of a car he had built under his own name eight years before were the most interesting factors of the cyclecar produced by A.E. Osborn of 2058 Valentine Avenue in New York City. The single wheel was in the front, and power was provided by either a single- or double-cylinder water-cooled Prugh side-valve engine. A two-speed planetary transmitted the drive to a chain operating on the front wheel. The single-cylinder models had two tread dimensions, 30 inches for the tandem, 42 inches for the side-by-side two-seater and the delivery, all three cars on a 96-inch wheelbase. The two-cylinder Auto-Tricars were on a 108-inch wheelbase. The comparatively large number of models he offered also distinguished A.E. Osborn as a cyclecar manufacturer. His short life in the automotive field was absolutely typical, however.

1914 AUTO-TRICAR
1-cyl., 96" wb

	FP	5	4	3	2	1
Tandem Rbt.	250	2500	3500	5000	8500	18,000
Side-by-Side Rbt.	250	2500	3500	5000	8500	18,000
Light Dly.	250	2000	3000	4200	6500	14,000

2-cyl., 108" wb

	FP	5	4	3	2	1
Surrey	400	2500	3500	5000	8500	18,000
Side-by-Side Rbt.	350	2500	3500	5000	8500	18,000

AUTO-TWO — The Auto-Two tricycle was one of three models produced by Erwin Ross Thomas who established his Buffalo Automobile & Auto-Bi Company in Upstate New York at the turn of the century. In 1902 he changed the name of his cars to Buffalo. Refer to Buffalo.

AUTO-VEHICLE — The firm's name was the Auto-Vehicle Company. Its car was called the Tourist, built in Los Angeles, California from 1902-1910. Refer to Tourist.

AUTOWA — Boston, Massachusetts — (1920) — The Autowa was the short-lived idea of Will-Hall-Sutherland Motors, Inc. of 388 Newbury Street in Boston. The car made its debut at the Boston Automobile Show in 1920. Reported *The Automobile Journal*: "The Autowa is a Ford chassis with various changes of equipment and a specially designed body that attracted no end of attention." But not enough apparently to carry this prettified Model T into 1920. Other Ford-based hopefuls of this era were the Victory and the Mayfair, both of which enjoyed no more enduring commercial success than did the Autowa.

AUTO WAGON — This simple designation was occasionally used circa 1909 to designate the highwheeler produced by the International Harvester Company of America. Refer to International (I.H.C.)

1906 Average Man's Runabout, NAHC

AVERAGE MAN'S RUNABOUT — Hiawatha, Kansas — (1906) — The Adams Automobile Company of Hiawatha produced a vehicle of "the latest runabout type" and chose to give it a slogan in place of a name. The slogan was apt, because the Adams product was average. Its two-cylinder horizontally opposed 10 hp engine was placed under the hood up front. It featured friction drive to the jackshaft, with single chain to the rear axle. Stopping the vehicle was described thusly: "One foot pedal operates the emergency brakes, while another applies the friction wheel and also applies the brake most used under regular conditions when entirely released, but releases its grip on brake when pressure is again applied. When held at any point between those mentioned the machine is allowed to coast." George Adams offered his car to the public only during the 1906 model year. He built a few more from 1907 to 1909, but these were for his personal use only.

1906 AVERAGE MAN'S RUNABOUT
2-cyl., 10 hp, 76" wb

	FP	5	4	3	2	1
Rbt.-2P	500	2400	3400	5300	8700	19,000

AVERY — Chicago, Illinois — (1914) — That Avery Stalnaker of Chicago built a cyclecar in 1914 has been purported and such a car indicated in the 1915 *Blue Book*. Further documentation is lacking. An Avery Stalnaker is not listed in the Chicago city directories of the period.

AVERY & JENNIS — Chicago, Illinois — (1899-1901) — The Avery & Jennis Company of 28 West Washington Street in Chicago reported its completion of an experimental gasoline car in 1899. The firm had previously been in the bicycle trade, and in 1900 decided to go automotive too. Among its products were gasoline engines, a carburetor "which is ahead of anything yet turned out," and a muffler "that completely silences the explosions of a gasoline engine." Complete cars also were built, either to designs furnished by a customer or, if a customer preferred, to one of the in-house designs. Avery & Jennis declared themselves adept to handle either steam or gasoline cars. In 1901 the partners announced their plans to "equip a repair department and put a thoroughly experienced man in charge." It was in automobile repair that the firm focused thereafter.

AVIAUTO — The Aviauto Manufacturing Company was organized in New York City early in 1915 for the production of motor cars, aeroplanes and radiators. The incorporators were B.A. Law, M. Baier and S.F. Miller. Capital stock was a mere $5000. Manufacture of an automobile did not follow.

AXELRAD — Axelrad & Baron, Inc. was the designation of an early 1918 venture from New York City for the manufacture of wagons, trucks and automobiles. Louis Axelrad, Solomon Baron and Joseph Held were the people involved. Capital stock was $10,000; manufacture is doubted.

AYRES — Saginaw, Michigan — (1902-1905) — Unable to accept Horace Greeley's advice to "go west, young man," William F. Ayres, a machinist from San Francisco, decided to head the other way. In 1900 he traveled to Michigan where he first set up shop in Bay City, then moved to Saginaw and the corner of Bristol and North Hamilton. There he formally organized as the Ayres Gasoline Engine & Automobile Works, incorporating with a capital stock of $20,000. It was the former product which was the principal focus of his activity but in 1902 Ayres also began building moderately-priced gasoline automobiles, mostly to customer order. By about 1905 his automobile building ceased, and his automobile work became focused on repair. In 1907 the firm moved to Rochester, Michigan where business was continued for two years. The Michigan charger of the Ayres company was forfeited, and dissolution filed May 3rd, 1909. Shortly thereafter the Ayres factory in Rochester was reported to have been taken over by the new Michigan Motor Car Manufacturing Company, Ltd., though this venture was later revealed to be a stock-selling scheme, with no cars apparently produced.

1910 Babcock, model 30, gasoline, touring, WLB

BABCOCK — Watertown, New York — (1909-1913) — The H.H. Babcock Company had been building horsedrawn vehicles for nearly sixty years in Watertown by April of 1908 when its automobile department was established. Its first car was tested for 5000 miles that winter in the snow, ice and mud for which Upstate New York is well known. The car went to market in the spring, and that summer Babcock absorbed the Watertown Carriage Company. The first Babcocks were highwheelers but, as the company was careful to point out, "the Babcock gasoline machine is not to be classed with motor buggies but is, in all respect, an automobile, although fitted with 36-inch wheels carrying solid rubber tires." Indeed Babcock did not betray its buggy origins, even in its highwheeler, and the company began offering conventional-wheeled vehicles soon after. Commercial vehicles also were produced. In December of 1913 George H. Babcock announced the discontinuation of his automobile department. Thereafter the company built bodies only, and mostly for trucks, a venture that was quite successful. During World War I, Babcock was employing about 800 people in the building of ambulance bodies for the government.

1909 BABCOCK
Model A — 2-cyl., 18 hp, 83" wb

	FP	5	4	3	2	1
High Wheel Buggy Rbt.	1050	2000	3000	4200	6500	14,000
Model B — 2-cyl., 18 hp, 96" wb						
High Wheel Surrey	1250	2200	3200	4400	7000	15,000
1910 BABCOCK						
Model A — 2-cyl., 18 hp, 83" wb						
High Wheel Buggy Rbt.	1050	2000	3000	4200	6500	14,000
Model B — 2-cyl., 18 hp, 96" wb						
High Wheel Surrey	1250	2300	3300	4600	7000	16,000
Model 30 — 4-cyl., 35 hp, 114" wb						
Tour.-5P	2750	2500	3500	5000	8500	18,000
1911 BABCOCK						
Model D — 4-cyl., 35 hp, 114" wb						
Tour.-5P	2500	2500	3500	5000	8500	18,000
Model F — 4-cyl., 40 hp, 120" wb						
Fore-Door Touring-5P	3000	2700	3600	5300	8800	19,000
Limo.-7P	3000	2200	3200	4400	7000	15,000
1912 BABCOCK						
Model H — 4-cyl., 32 hp, 114" wb						
Tour.-7P	3000	2400	3400	4800	8000	17,000
Model F — 4-cyl., 32 hp, 120" wb						
Tour.-7P	2000	2500	3500	5000	8500	18,000
Model K — 4-cyl., 32 hp, 120" wb						
Tour.-7P	3000	2500	3500	5000	8500	18,000

1906 Babcock Electric, special runabout, WLB

BABCOCK ELECTRIC — Buffalo, New York — (1906-1912) — In 1906 Frank A. Babcock took his 1600-pound electric car, fitted with batteries of his own manufacture, from New York to Philadelphia, claiming this 100-mile trip on one charge to be a world's record. The Babcock was said to have a 30 mph top speed and the ability to climb any hill at better than 20 mph. "When you build right, it is right and works right," F.A. Babcock said. Unfortunately, Babcock was not nearly so efficient in managing a business right. He started his Babcock Electric Carriage Company by taking over the plant of the Buffalo Electric Carriage Company which he had also headed and which had built a car called the Buffalo Electric from 1901 to 1906. Subsequently, when Babcock couldn't make a go of it alone, he allied his company with the Clark Motor Company and the Buffalo Automobile Station Company to form the Buffalo Electric Vehicle Company which would build yet another Buffalo from 1912 to 1915. How many Babcocks were built in the factory in the half-dozen years between the two Buffalos is unknown. Frank Babcock died in February 1921 following a long illness.

1906 BABCOCK ELECTRIC

	FP	5	4	3	2	1
Model 1						
Stanhope (63" wb)	1650	2300	3300	4600	7500	16,000
Model 5						
"Babcock Special" (72" wb)	1250	2200	3200	4400	7000	15,000
Model 3						
Rbt. (72" wb)	2000	2400	3400	4800	8000	17,000
Model 4						
Rbt. (72" wb)	2250	2500	3500	5000	8500	18,000
1907 BABCOCK ELECTRIC						
Model 1						
Stanhope (63" wb)	1650	2300	3300	4600	7500	16,000
Model 1						
Spec. Stanhope (66" wb)	1800	2400	3400	4800	8000	17,000
Model 7						
Brougham (72" wb)	4000	2500	3500	5000	8500	18,000
Model 5						
Rbt. (78" wb)	1400	2500	3500	5000	8500	18,000
Model 6						
Rbt. (78" wb)	1600	2500	3500	5000	8500	18,000
Model 8						
Cpe. (65" wb)	2500	2300	3300	4600	7500	16,000

1908 Babcock Electric, model 7, brougham, HAC

1908 BABCOCK ELECTRIC

Model 5						
Rbt. (72" wb)	1500	2200	3200	4400	7000	15,000
Model 6						
Victoria (78" wb)	1700	2300	3300	4600	7500	16,000
Model 7						
Brougham (72" wb)	4000	2200	3200	4400	7000	15,000
Model 10						
Cpe. (65" wb)	2100	1800	2800	4000	6200	13,000
Model 1						
Spec. Stanhope (66" wb)	1800	—	—	—	—	—

1909 Babcock Electric, model 10, coupe, HAC

1909 BABCOCK ELECTRIC

	FP	5	4	3	2	1
Model 10						
Cpe. (65'' wb)	2100	1800	2800	4000	6200	13,000
Model 6						
Victoria (78'' wb)	1700	2000	3000	4200	6500	14,000
Model 15						
Rbt. (72'' wb)	1700	2200	3200	4400	7000	15,000
Model 12						
Rdstr. (94'' wb)	2000	2300	3300	4600	7500	16,000
Model 11						
Town Car (100'' wb)	3250	2200	3200	4400	7000	15,000

1910 Babcock Electric, model 6, victoria, HAC

1910 BABCOCK ELECTRIC

Model 12						
Rdstr. (94'' wb)	2200	2300	3300	4600	7500	16,000
Model 14						
Cpe. (86'' wb)	2600	1800	2800	4000	6200	13,000
Model 5						
Rdstr. (72'' wb)	1500	2200	3200	4400	7000	15,000
Model 6						
Victoria (78'' wb)	1700	2000	3000	4200	6500	14,000
Model 11						
Town Car (100'' wb)	3250	2200	3200	4400	7000	15,000

1911 Babcock Electric, model 12, roadster, HAC

1911 BABCOCK ELECTRIC

	FP	5	4	3	2	1
Model 6						
Victoria (78'' wb)	900	2000	3000	4200	6500	14,000
Model 12						
Rdstr. (94'' wb)	2400	2300	3300	4600	7500	16,000
Model 14						
Cpe. (86'' wb)	2600	1800	2800	4000	6200	13,000

1912 Babcock Electric, model 17, coupe, HAC

1912 BABCOCK ELECTRIC

Model 6						
Victoria (78'' wb)	1900	2200	3200	4400	7000	15,000
Model 12						
Rdstr. (94'' wb)	2400	2400	3400	4800	8000	17,000
Model 18						
Fore-Door Rdstr. (100'' wb)	2600	2300	3300	4600	7500	16,000
Model 14						
Cpe. (86'' wb)	2600	1800	2800	4000	6200	13,000
Model 17						
Large Cpe. (86'' wb)	2900	1900	2900	4100	6400	13,500

BABY MOOSE — St. Paul, Minnesota — (1914) — This cyclecar from Minnesota presents something of a conundrum. Initially it was called the Continental and was announced by the Continental Engine Manufacturing Company of Chicago whose factory was purportedly in Minneapolis, though the factory address given was that of the Dispatch Motor Company. Possibly Dispatch built a few Continental cyclecars under contract, but within months the venture had metamorphosed into the Continental Engineering Company with the cyclecar revised somewhat and renamed the Ceco. That whole operation moved soon to Chicago, the home of the man who had put up the money. The man who designed the car, John E. Pfeffer of Minneapolis, apparently stayed home in Minnesota. Subsequently, late in 1914, the car he had designed as the Continental and which had become the Ceco in Chicago was revised into another car to be produced in St. Paul. This was the Baby Moose, manufactured by the Bull Moose-Cutting Automobile Company. Its specification was typically cyclecar: four-cylinder air-cooled engine, friction drive, 92-inch wheelbase, tandem two-seater and delivery models. The price was $360, the same as the Continental. Occasionally this car has been referred to as the Bull Moose, which was another automobile altogether. A more inappropriate name for a cyclecar can scarcely be imagined.

1914 BABY MOOSE
4-cyl., 92'' wb

Tandem Two-Seater	360	1400	2400	3500	5300	10,000
Light Delivery	360	1100	2200	3200	4900	9000

BACHELLE ELECTRIC — Chicago, Illinois — (1900-1903) — Otto von Bachelle was an electrical engineer from Chicago whose brother was a noted bicycle racer with whom he was often confused. In the fall of 1900, when his first electric carriage was completed and tested and he made this fact known to the world, he was careful to insist that it was his brother ''who shone as a pedal pusher.'' Von Bachelle did shine as an electric car builder, however, if only aesthethically. His little stanhope was compact and neat, and he patented its running gear. He built his car in small numbers through 1902 and then made what was probably a strategic mistake in thinking bigger. Early in 1903, he loftily incorporated the Bachelle Automobile Company for $100,000. It did not survive to 1904. Subsequently, von Bachelle served as a consulting engineer to the E.R. Thomas Company in Buffalo (New York) and with the Hupp Motor Car Company in Detroit. When last heard from, in 1915, he was about to join the A.A. Crumley Company which had just been organized as a dealership to handle the King and the Dort automobiles in Detroit.

1902 Bachelle Electric, auto buggy, NAHC

BACK BAY — At the turn of the century, W.T. McCullough of the Back Bay Cycle & Motor Company of Boston, Massachusetts built an automobile. Refer to McCullough.

The Back Bay Garage Company was organized in Augusta, Maine in late 1907 to manufacture and deal in automobiles. Its president was L.A. Ingalls, its treasurer A.M. Currier. The capital stock of the venture was $25,000, of which nothing was paid in initially, or possibly ever. No Back Bay automobile followed.

BACKUS — **Newark, New Jersey** — **(1903-1904)** — The automobile of the Backus Water Motor Company — which had been building engines in Newark since the 1880's — was exhibited for the first time in February 1903 in New York City. It was a single-cylinder 10 hp runabout with a twenty-two-inch flywheel and sixteen bronze rings shrunk on the cylinder. The car was started from the seat and steered by a tiller. An asking price of $1100 was outrageous for such a primeval vehicle. This was undoubtedly the reason the Backus did not survive 1904.

BACON — **Omaha, Nebraska** — **(1901)/New Castle, Pennsylvania** — **(1919/1920)** — In 1901 a young man by the name of Frank W. Bacon built a gasoline car in his machine shop in Omaha, Nebraska. Although he was able to sell seven examples of this vehicle, he could not secure the necessary financing to proceed into proper manufacture. Subsequently he hired himself out as an engineer to a variety of Omaha automobile builders, ending with Douglas Motor Corporation in 1917. When that company folded the following year, Bacon returned to his first idea: becoming an automobile manufacturer. His car was a light six, and Bacon Motors Corporation was established in New Castle, Pennsylvania the first week of December 1919 to build it. During the second week in December, Frank Bacon was killed in an automobile accident. Plans to proceed with production despite Bacon's death were announced immediately by company president Frederick C. Van Derhoff. A further announcement followed in April of 1920 indicating that production had just begun on a 107-inch wheelbase, $750 roadster with 35 hp Herschell-Spillman engine, and a daily output of twenty-five units was envisioned by October. Doubtless this was either wishful thinking or a brave front. The Bacon was not heard from again.

BADEKER — **Omaha, Nebraska** — **(1901-1902)** — "A year ago the Badeker Gas Engine Company was organized at Omaha to make automobiles under patents issued to Dalton Risley," *The Motor Age* reported in November 1901. "The intervening time has been spent in developing the machine but it is announced that the company will be ready to commence the manufacture of vehicles for the market within a week or two." Trade directories for 1902 indicate Dalton Risley as a manufacture of automobiles in Omaha, but whether the few vehicles built were referred to as Badekers or Risleys is not known.

BADEN — **Baden, Missouri** — **(1916-1919)** — Baden is a suburb of St. Louis, and precisely what the company name was is not known, but the firm did indeed build cars. The Baden was never advertised nor exhibited at automobile shows. Sales were strictly by word of mouth, and one purchased the car directly from the factory. Needless to say, few Badens left Baden. Its gasoline engine was in-house built, the castings having been made in a St. Louis foundry. An ordinary looking touring car, the Baden was noteworthy for being an extraordinarily bad automobile. An old-timer in town who owned one told historian William J. Lewis that the car was a bear to start and that, when it did run, crankshafts were broken with alacrity. When his car digested its fourth crank within a year, the old-timer got rid of it. Apparently between thirty and fifty Badens were produced before word of mouth turned sour. It was said that when Badens found their way to used car lots around St. Louis they were more often scrapped than they were resold. The company turned to the accessory business next.

BADGER — In 1909 in Clintonville, Wisconsin the Badger Four Wheel Drive Automobile Company was organized for the manufacture of vehicles utilizing the Zachow-Besserdich patents. These cars were called Badger or Badger F.W.D. in 1910 only, the name shortened to simply F.W.D. for 1911. Refer to F.W.D.

In early 1915 S.E. Badger of Niles, Michigan announced his formation of the Badger Motor Car Company to build automobiles to order and also to produce "one model, a touring car, selling at about $1000." That any automobiles at all followed has not been documented.

1861 Badger, Thomas Crane Public Library, Quincy, MA

BADGER STEAM — **Quincy, Massachusetts** — **(1861)** — The Badger was the first automobile in Quincy, and it was built by Louis Badger, a local machinist and granite dealer. It was a steamer, powered by two engines, one connected to each of the rear wheels, with the boiler mounted directly behind the driver's seat. Badger built it principally to transport granite, but it hauled passengers on occasion as well. An eyewitness reported one such episode: "I was standing by the Town Pump when my ears were assailed by an infernal racket from the Granite Street bridge. A huge monster without a name and undefinable in shape was seen moving towards the center of the town. It was a large wagon carrying a boiler and engine, trimmed with flags and bunting, and having for passengers some of the members of the West Quincy brass band, who made most of the noise, the rest being furnished by the exhaust from the engine and rattle and clank of machinery." It was the consensus of townspeople that this curiosity could never replace a good ox team.

BADGER STEAM — **Kenosha, Wisconsin** — **(1901)** — In 1901 an experimental steam car was built in the shops of the Badger Brass Manufacturing Company of Kenosha. Its engine had been designed by Joseph Hill, a local machinist; R.H. Welles, Badger Brass treasurer, collaborated on the final design. The engine developed 9 hp, and the car was completely successful. Two examples were produced in the Badger Brass shops, though entering the automobile industry was not contemplated at that time. Instead the cars were built to advertise the company's automobile lamps. "One of these wagons is now making a trip to New York," Badger Brass announced in late summer of 1901, where R.H. Welles and L.J. Keck "will endeavor to demonstrate the superiority of Solar Lamps to the general automotive public." Apparently, they were successful because business boomed. In 1904 the Packard Motor Car Company sent Badger Brass a ringing testimonial letter alluding to the contribution made by the company's lamps in the 1000-mile non-stop test run Charles Schmidt had just completed in the new Model L Packard. By 1910 Badger Brass was employing nearly 400 workers and was one of the largest industries in Kenosha. Briefly, in 1913, the firm tried the automotive field again, with a cyclecar called the True.

1910 Badger, toy tonneau, WLB

BADGER — **Columbus, Wisconsin** — **(1910-1911)** — "An automobile designer and all around automobile man" was the way the *Columbus Journal-Republican* described E.W. Arbogast following his visit to town in early March 1909. Arbogast was the son-in-law of a wealthy grain merchant in nearby Watertown, but had failed to persuade anyone there that he could build a high-powered, high-priced sort of car to sell in the medium-price range. In Columbus he offered to build one example, test it and sell it, provided that if he was successful the town would come up with money for manufacture. "I think the Columbus crowd are framed up all right as to capital," an interested lawyer wrote a few weeks later, "if they have the desire to go ahead and push the proposition.'' By late May the test car was ready, it was successfully demonstrated, and it had a name. Almost immediately it had a company as well, the Badger Motor Car Company being incorporated with A.M. Bellack (a local clothier) as president, Charles E. Fowler (a local grocer) as vice-president, J.R. Wheeler (a local banker) as treasurer, and George C. Holtz (a local lumberman) as secretary. A factory was completed by November, and production began. By February 1910 it was apparent that storage space was necessary for cars completed but not yet delivered, and the third floor of the Columbus Canning Company (most of that firm's directors were Badger stockholders) was secured. Trade press reaction to the introduction of the Badger was uniformly flattering. Typical was the review in *MoToR* which allowed that ''while it may be argued that cars of this class and price necessarily cramp the designer, in that not so much freedom in selection of design and materials is allowed him, as in the case of larger and more expensive cars, such does not seem to be the case'' in the Badger of E.W. Arbogast. ''Pleasing in Color, Classy in Outline, a Hill Climber with Power to Burn'' enthused the press in Columbus. That last quality was amply demonstrated a few months later when the first batch of Badgers drove up to the third floor of Columbus Canning. Then the problems began. The nationwide network of dealers that was envisioned was not realized, and those brought into the fold were not always satisfied. ''Motors too small and torsion rod weakness not improved'' was the word from the Los Angeles agency. The motor was a 30 hp Northway four, and every new car has its teething period. In April 1911 Badger stockholders decided to hedge their bets, however, by getting into real estate, authorizing the trade of ten Badger cars for two parcels of land near Broken Bow, Nebraska and 2200 acres of grazing fields in Cherry County, Wisconsin. That fall, when it appeared that an assessment against stockholders would be required in order to pay the company's debts, the decision was made to liquidate. Two Badger men were dispatched to Broken Bow to sell off the Nebraska acreage; the 2300 acres of grazing land in Cherry County, some of which was discovered to be blow sand, was sold off as well. Columbus Canning bought the Badger factory and turned it into a feed grinding and mixing plant. A grand total of 237 Badgers had been built, not nearly as many as would have had Badger stockholders exercised a little patience and given E.W. Arbogast's car a better chance.

1910 BADGER
4-cyl., 30 hp, 112'' wb

	FP	5	4	3	2	1
Model A Tonneau	1500	2300	3300	4600	7500	16,000
Model B Tour.	1500	2400	3400	4800	8000	17,000
Model C Rds.	1500	2500	3500	5000	8500	18,000

1911 Badger, touring, NAHC

1911 BADGER
4-cyl., 30 hp, 110'' wb

Model B Tour.	1250	2200	3200	4400	7000	15,000
Model C Rds.	1250	2300	3300	4600	7500	16,000
Model D Fore-Door Tour.	1500	2350	3350	4700	7700	16,500

BAGNALL — In St. Louis, Missouri in late 1905, the Bagnall Automobile Company was organized with a capital stock of $10,000 for the manufacture of automobiles. W.F. Bagnall, James E. Morse and Henry B. Graham, all of St. Louis, were the people behind this venture. Any subsequent manufacture has not been documented.

BAILEY — The G.D. Bailey Manufacturing Company has been indicated on car rosters as the producer of an automobile in Detroit in 1912. City directories for the period indicate the presence of no such company in town, although there was a George D. Bailey at 804 Trumbull Avenue who gave his occupation as ''designer.'' If he built an automobile that year, it was obviously for experimental purposes. By 1917 Bailey had relocated to Chicago where his George D. Bailey Company engaged itself in manufacture of the ''Bailey ball thrust bearing, which is made to replace the flat thrush washer used as standard equipment at the left (gear) side of the differential on the Ford and Chevrolet 490 cars.''

References from 1913 indicate the incorporation that year of the F.O. Bailey Carriage Company under the laws of Maine, with a capital stock of $50,000, to manufacture and deal ''in vehicles of every description.'' No Bailey automobile followed of this venture.

BAILEY ELECTRIC — Manheim, Pennsylvania — (1902) — The Bailey from Manheim was an electric built in a barn on South Wolf Street in 1902 by F.E. Bailey, who was president of the Manheim Electric Light Company. According to local historians, the vehicle was a ''contraption'' which its maker took out of the barn about once a week to run up and down Wolf Street. Eventually Bailey sold his electric, and the indications are that he never built another.

BAILEY — Springfield, Massachusetts — (1907-1910) — In Springfield — not far from where the first Duryea was built — two brothers named Perkins had a machine shop and an idea. What they didn't have was money to see it through. After two years in development, Julian L. and James A. Perkins did, however, produce the prototype of their two-cycle, four-cylinder rotary-engined runabout which they called a Perkins. Then their money ran out. Bertram Bailey subsequently was convinced to finance their operation in exchange for use of his name on the car. He put up $20,000 in 1906 to establish the Bailey-Perkins Motor Company. The Perkins brothers quickly spent the money and still didn't have a car in production. More investors were convinced — among them Henry G. Whitman and Willis L. Van Sicklin — and more money followed on February 12th, 1907 when the Bailey Automobile Company was capitalized at $500,000. Promotional material was printed up and the press was informed that a runabout with a 100-inch wheelbase and a 22 hp rotary engine was being manufactured. This was followed a year later by a bigger and more powerful model and additional body styles, followed by a retrenchment in 1910 to just one offering, as Bailey and the Perkins brothers wondered what went wrong. Any unknown administrative problems notwithstanding, surviving photographs indicate that among the Bailey's biggest problems may have been its appearance. It was ungainly and abnormally tall. The running board was a couple of feet off the ground, and brochures do not indicate a stepladder as standard equipment.

1907 BAILEY
4-cyl., 22 hp, 100'' wb

	FP	5	4	3	2	1
Rbt.-2P	2000	3000	4000	6000	9500	21,000

1908 BAILEY
4-cyl., 30/35 hp, 112'' wb

Tour.-5P	2500	2900	3700	5600	9100	20,000
Spdstr.	2500	3000	4000	6000	9500	21,000

1909 BAILEY
4-cyl., 30/35 hp, 112'' wb

Tour.-5/7P	2500	2900	3700	5600	9100	20,000
Rds.-3/4P	2500	3100	4200	6300	10,500	22,000
Baby Tonneau-5P	2500	3000	4000	6000	9500	21,000

1910 BAILEY
4-cyl., 30/35 hp, 114'' wb

Olympic Tour.	2500	3100	4200	6300	10,500	22,000

1912 Bailey Electric, roadster, HAC

BAILEY ELECTRIC — Amesbury, Massachusetts — (1907-1916) — S.R. Bailey & Company, Inc. well knew the value of name-dropping. The Bailey victoria phaeton — the only body style initially available — was said to be the first car designed specifically for the Edison Storage Battery, the collaboration ''with the great inventor and his engineers'' throughout the development period resulting in the ''most nearly perfect motor car of its type.'' The Bailey Electric was capable of 80-100 miles at a 15-16 mph average on a single battery charge. The battery was carried underneath the body, ''getting rid of the boxes usually seen at front and rear'' and vastly improving the usual electric car appearance. The Bailey's wheel steering was unusual for an electric as well. It was a beguiling little car as a victoria phaeton, and in later roadster variations its styling was quite *nouveau* for the period. But its cost was less appealing, and rather pricey even for an electric. In March 1916 the company declared bankruptcy.

1908-1908 BAILEY ELECTRIC

Queen Vict. Phae. (76'' wb)	2000	2700	3600	5300	8800	19,000

1910-1911 BAILEY ELECTRIC

Queen Vict. Phae. (79'' wb)	2000	2900	3700	5600	9100	20,000

1912-1913 BAILEY ELECTRIC

Queen Vict. Phae. (82'' wb)	2600	3100	4200	6300	10,500	22,000
Rds. (106'' wb)	2500	3200	4300	6500	11,000	23,000

1914 BAILEY ELECTRIC

Model F Rds.-2P (112'' wb)	2900	3100	4200	6300	10,500	22,000
Model F Rds.-4P (132'' wb)	3300	3200	4300	6500	11,000	23,000
Model EVP Vict.-2P (82'' wb)	2600	2500	3500	5000	8500	18,000
Model E Rds.-2P (82'' wb)	2305	2900	3700	5600	9100	20,000

1913 Bailey Electric, roadster, model F, JAC

1915 BAILEY ELECTRIC

	FP	5	4	3	2	1
Model F Rds.-2P (112" wb)	2900	3100	4200	6300	10,500	22,000
Model F Tour.-4P (132" wb)	3300	3300	4400	6700	12,000	24,000
Model F Cabr.-3P (82" wb)	3100	3200	4300	6500	11,000	23,000

1916 BAILEY ELECTRIC

	FP	5	4	3	2	1
Model F Rds.-2P (112" wb)	2900	3200	4300	6500	11,000	23,000
Model F Rds.-4P (132" wb)	3300	3300	4400	6700	12,000	24,000

BAILEY-KLAPP — Elwood, Indiana — (1915) — The Bailey-Klapp was one of two cars whose forthcoming manufacture was announced in February 1915 by the Elwood Iron Works. A V-8 engine was the most noteworthy feature of the Bailey-Klapp, which was to be offered as a five- or seven-passenger touring car on a 116-inch wheelbase. The unfortunate bankruptcy of the Elwood Iron Works a few months later called a halt to the Bailey-Klapp at the prototype stage, however. Rights to the other car Elwood was planning to produce, a small four called the Elco, were acquired by the Bimel Buggy Company of Sidney, Ohio — and that one did make it into production.

BAIRD-BANKS — The Baird-Banks Manufacturing & Supply Company was organized in New York City early in 1907 to build motor cars and motor boats. Capital stock was $25,000; behind this venture were Milan E. Baird, George B. Banks and William James. Manufacture has not been documented.

BAKER — One J.C. Baker of Oakland, California was indicated as the manufacturer of an automobile in the Hiscox book *Horseless Vehicles, Automobiles, Motor Cycles* published in 1900. A James C. Baker was employed by the Oakland Iron Works at that time, which also reputedly was an automobile manufacturer. Refer to Oakland.

J.L. Baker was a carriage maker at the corner of 4th and St. Clair in Dayton, Ohio who indicated himself also as a producer of automobiles on occasion during the years prior to the First World War. Reference to any cars built has not been discovered.

The Baker-Cormerais Motor Car Company was organized in Boston with a capital stock of $10,000 late in 1905 to manufacture and deal in motor vehicles. A.E. Baker of Boston and H.D. Cormerais of Newtonville, Massachusetts were the partners behind this venture. Manufacture does not seem to have followed.

The Baker Manufacturing Company of Middletown, Connecticut was organized during the spring of 1902 to "manufacture, sell and deal in all kinds of motors, motor vehicles, boats, engines, tools and machinery." Behind this $10,000 incorporation were Joseph Merriam, J.H. Hale, Frank Brainard, T.M. Russell, L.O. Davis and E.H. Williams. No automobile appears to have arrived of this venture.

The Baker Motor Vehicle Company of New York City was a $20,000 incorporation from the fall of 1907 for the manufacture of motor cars and parts. N. Platt, G.H. Kelly and J.B. Laying were the incorporators. The Baker Vehicle Company followed in early 1909 in New York City as a $1000 incorporation by the same N. Platt, together with F.N. White and R.C. Norton. From neither of these ventures does an automobile appear to have resulted.

BAKER — Southbridge, Massachusetts — (1896) — After studying the motor vehicle question for five years, and trying a steam engine first, Nelson M. Baker decided that internal combustion was the answer, and built a gasoline car in 1896. Its engine had four water-jacketed cylinders and poppet valves. "The valve mechanism is so arranged that one, two, three or four cylinders can be thrown out of work at will," explained *The Horseless Age,* "while the spark ceases when the charge of gasoline and air is cut off, thus saving the battery." Nelson Baker is not known to have built another car.

BAKER — Tarentum, Pennsylvania — (1899) — The Baker Manufacturing Company was incorporated with a capital stock of $100,000 early in 1899 for the manufacture of motor vehicles. Behind this venture were James H. Baker (formerly of the Baker Chain and Baker Forge companies), Henry M. Breckenridge and James D. Wilson (of the Tarentum Glass Company), and John W. Hemphill and O.C. Camp. The company also planned to manufacture heavy forgings for wagons, which it may well have done, but the Baker automobile never proceeded beyond the prototype stage.

BAKER — Hartford, Connecticut — (1897-1899)/Worcester, Massachusetts — (1902) — This Baker represented one of the earliest instances of foreign capital being invested in the American automobile industry. In 1896 Herbert C. Baker of Hartford entered into arrangements with English capitalists who provided him the money to establish a business for the manufacture of motor carriages and marine engines. That was the plan anyway, and the plant selected was the erstwhile Mather Electric Company factory. In December 1896 Baker announced that a "force of men" was at work in the Mather facility on "the first model of the Baker motor carriage, which, it is hoped, will be completed within three months." Nothing further was heard of this venture until 1899 when *The Motor Age* reported that Baker was working on a three-cylinder car to be built by the National Machine Company in Hartford. Doubtless by this time the interest of the English capitalists had cooled. Herbert C. Baker plunged ahead without them, though not very successfully. By 1902 he had established himself in a spot in the Worcester Cycle Company factory in Massachusetts and announced that $75,000 in capital stock had already been pledged to his efforts. Two examples of his three-cylinder car were built "to make a complete test of the motor." And that appears to have been the final end of the Baker venture.

1922 Baker Steam, 7-pass. touring, WLB

BAKER STEAM — Denver & Pueblo, Colorado — (1918-1922; 1925) — Hartley O. Baker was born in Chicago and trekked west to Colorado in the midst of the Indian Wars. Orphaned at age eight, the lad largely supported himself thereafter and ultimately worked his way through medical school, establishing a practice in Denver. An amateur enthusiast of steam power, he used a steam car to make house calls and served as editor of *Steam Motor Journal,* one of the few magazines devoted to steam vehicles. Naturally, he was soon convinced he could do better. The heart of his invention was the Baker-designed steam generator, a burner fired by coal oil which was said to generate considerably more heat. Initially, Baker set up a lucrative sideline business to his doctoring by providing Colorado Stanley owners with replacement burners and boilers — but then he was fired with ambition. The Baker Steam Motor Car & Manufacturing Company was the result, and in April of 1918 the *Pueblo Chieftain* reported the purchase of eighty acres of land in Pueblo as a manufacturing site. Joining Dr. Baker in this venture were a good many prominent Pueblo citizens: a former mayor and retail grocer, an attorney and state representative, a utility superintendent and a druggist, an ex-county superintendent of schools and a professor of psychology. Dr. Baker seemed to have all bases covered. And he and his associates seemed anxious to produce anything which could possibly utilize either oil heat or steam power: oil burners for homes, steam units for factories, engines for motorboats, powerplants for dairies and portable saw mills, tractors, trunks and cars — and the Dobbins Puncture Proof Pneumatic Wheel. This manufacturing diversity was loudly ballyhooed in the Baker brochure for 1921, and was probably among the reasons there was no Baker brochure in 1922. At least one prototype each of the Baker Steam touring car and roadster was built, and photographs in the brochure indicate that three trucks were put together before the good doctor and the people of Pueblo called it quits. Dr. Baker was heard from again in the fall of 1925 by which time he had built another steam car prototype in which he took local newsmen for a spin. Another company, Baker Motors, Inc., (later the Steam Appliance Corporation) resulted, and so did at least one steam bus — the base of operations this time being Cleveland, Ohio, where White steam cars had chuffed to fame and fortune two decades previous. In the mid-Twenties, however, neither fame nor fortune greeted any new steam car venture. This Baker enterprise may have survived as long as 1928, but no meaningful production ever resulted. Indeed it may well be that the prototypes from the Baker days in Pueblo were the only Baker Steam automobiles ever produced. Interestingly, an article in the June 4th, 1918 edition of the *Pueblo Chieftain* had indicated the delays in the appearance of the demonstrator on the streets of town as owing to the company's policy "of doing all things just right or not at all."

BAKER-BELL — Philadelphia, Pennsylvania — (1913) — The Baker-Bell Motor Company was established to produce a small and light four-cylinder roadster which carried the delightful model name of Hummingbird. It was introduced early in 1913. Later that year Baker-Bell launched into the manufacture of small and light delivery vehicles. This venture was continued into 1914; the Hummingbird survived one season only. In 1913 Baker-

Bell had become an agent for the Commerce truck, and the firm remained as vehicle dealers at least as late as 1916.

1913 Baker-Bell, Hummingbird, 2-pass. roadster, WLB

1913 BAKER-BELL
Hummingbird — 4-cyl., 22.5 hp, 90" wb

	FP	5	4	3	2	1
Rds.-2P	675	2400	3400	4800	8000	17,000

1895 Baker & Elberg, electric runabout, LC

BAKER & ELBERG ELECTRIC — Kansas City, Missouri — (1894-1895) —
This pioneer electric car was named for its inventors, Dr. H.C. Baker and J.R. Elberg, who patented it in 1894 and sold it in 1895 to a Texas banker by the name of Stone. Stone in turn shipped the vehicle to New York City and "a well known electrical engineer of the metropolis" by the name of J.A. Barrett. Barrett's partner was one A. Frank Perret, and it was their assignment to see to the custom modifications that Stone desired be made to the vehicle. Although perhaps not the first, this was certainly a very early example of the formidable aftermarket business that would grow up around the automobile.

1894-1895 BAKER & ELBERG ELECTRIC

Baker & Elberg Electric	—	2700	3600	5300	8800	19,000

BAKER ELECTRIC — Cleveland, Ohio — (1899-1916) — "It outsells all other Electrics because it outclasses them," the company said in 1910. "More than three times as many Baker Electrics are sold each year than of any other one make." The popularity of the Baker had a great deal to do with the peripatetic energy of its inventor and promoter. Walter C. Baker graduated from the Case School of Applied Science in Cleveland in 1891, assisted Morris & Salom in the building of their Electrobat for the World's Columbian Exposition in 1893, joined the Cleveland Machine Screw Company in 1894, and soon after organized the American Ball Bearing Company in that same city in 1898. With the help of Fred R. White and Rollin C. White who would begin building White steam and gasoline cars in Cleveland after the turn of the century, he established the Baker Motor Vehicle Company for the manufacture of electric cars. The safety of an electric vis-a-vis "the uncertainties of the Explosive Motor or Steam-Driven Vehicles" was the company's selling tack initially, and only a runabout with stanhope variation was offered. The car was formally introduced at the first National Automobile Show held at Madison Square Garden in New York City in 1900. Among its early purchasers was Thomas Edison; his first car was a Baker. These early production Bakers were capable of two speeds of six and twelve miles an hour, but in 1902 Walter Baker decided to prove that electrics could be very quick too. He designed a submarine-like racer powered by a 12 hp Elwell-Parker Motor (some four times more powerful than Baker production powerplants) which was built for him by the Electric Vehicle Company in Hartford, Connecticut. In June 1902, on a speedway at Staten Island (New York), Baker covered a mile in 47.0 seconds, and then crashed into the crowd, killing two spectators. The follow-

1901 Baker, runabout, HAC

ing year he tried again with the Torpedo Kid, this racer powered by the same 3/4 hp motor as the production Baker. The wheels were fitted with "two-inch Special Goodrich thread-type tires" — Baker may have been the earliest manufacturer to use a cord tire, on his production car in 1900. The wire wheels were also covered with oil cloth to lessen wind resistance. Unlike the first racer which was a two-seater, the Torpedo Kid was monoplace — and at Cleveland in September 1903 Walter Baker drove it to record-breaking speeds for two to ten mile distances, but in a race for electrics later that day he crashed after colliding with a Waverley and thereafter hung up his racing goggles and gloves. The number of body styles available on production Bakers proliferated through the years. Bevel gear shaft drive was adopted in 1910, and this became the soul of Baker promotion thereafter. In 1911 Baker sued Rauch & Lang and Broc for infringement on the shaft drive principle. By June 1915 Baker had merged with Rauch & Lang, and that December the new Baker, Rauch & Lang Company concluded arrangements with R.M. Owen to manufacture his Owen Magnetic. "The Aristocrat of Motordom," as Baker referred to his Electric, was continued in production into 1916. Latterday purchasers of Bakers included "Diamond Jim" Brady and the King of Siam. Later production from Baker included electric industrial trucks, and a successful foray into coachbuilding, the famous Raulang body being featured on such diverse marques as Reo, Franklin, Wills Sainte Claire, Jordan, Lexington, Stanley and Biddle.

1904 Baker, stanhope, HAC

1900-1903 BAKER

	FP	5	4	3	2	1
Imperial Rbt.	850	2200	3200	4400	7000	15,000
Phae. Stanhope	1600	2300	3300	4600	7500	16,000

Note: The Stanhope price was lowered to $1200 for 1903

1904 BAKER

Imperial Rbt.	1200	2200	3200	4400	7000	15,000
Std. Rbt.	850	2000	3000	4200	6500	14,000
Phae. Stanhope	1200	2300	3300	4600	7500	16,000
Physician's Chapalete	1200	2350	3350	4700	7700	16,500

1907 Baker, roadster, WLB

1905 Baker, depot carriage, WLB

1905 BAKER

Imperial Rbt.	1200	2200	3200	4400	7000	15,000
Std. Rbt.	1050	2000	3000	4200	6500	14,000
Phae. Stanhope	1600	2300	3300	4600	7500	16,000
Depot Carriage	3000	2200	3200	4400	7000	15,000
Surrey	2650	2000	3000	4200	6500	14,000

1906 Baker, brougham, HAC

1906 BAKER

Imperial Rbt. (68'' wb)	1200	2200	3200	4400	7000	15,000
Stanhope (68'' wb)	1600	2300	3300	4600	7500	16,000
Suburban (70'' wb)	2000	2400	3400	4800	8000	17,000
Surrey (86-1/2'' wb)	2650	2200	3200	4400	7000	15,000
Inside Drive Brgm.*	3500	2400	3400	4800	8000	17,000
Outside Drive Brgm.*	4000	2500	3500	5000	8500	18,000
* (86-1/2'' wb)						
Depot Carriage	3000	2300	3300	4600	7500	16,000
* (92-1/2'' wb)						

1907 BAKER

Stanhope (68'' wb)	1600	2200	3200	4400	7000	15,000
Imperial (68'' wb)	1200	2300	3300	4600	7500	16,000
Victoria (86-1/2'' wb)	3000	2200	3200	4400	7000	15,000
Queen Victoria (70'' wb)	1800	2300	3300	4600	7500	16,000
Rbt. (70'' wb)	1800	2000	3000	4200	6500	14,000
Inside Drive Cpe. (95' wb)	2000	2200	3200	4400	7000	15,000
Rdstr. (95' wb)	2250	2300	3300	4600	7500	16,000
Suburban (82'' wb)	2000	2400	3400	4800	8000	17,000
Surrey (86-1/2'' wb)	2650	2300	3300	4600	7500	16,000
Extension Front Brgm.*	4000	2500	3500	5000	8500	18,000
* (89'' wb)						
Land'et. (89'' wb)	4000	2400	3400	4800	8000	17,000
Brgm. (89'' wb)	3000	2400	3400	4800	8000	17,000
Depot Carriage	3000	2300	3300	4600	7500	16,000
* (92-1/2'' wb)						
Cpe. (92-1/2'' wb)	3000	2200	3200	4400	7000	15,000

1908 Baker, brougham, HAC

1908 BAKER

	FP	5	4	3	2	1
Model M Rdstr.	2500	2200	3200	4400	7000	15,000
Model L Queen Vic.	1800	2400	3400	4800	8000	17,000
Model L Extension Cpe.	1800	2300	3300	4600	7500	16,000
Baker Cpe.	3000	2200	3200	4400	7000	15,000
Baker Victoria	3000	2300	3300	4600	7500	16,000
Baker Surrey	2600	2400	3400	4800	8000	17,000
Baker Stanhope	1600	2300	3300	4600	7500	16,000
Baker Depot Carriage	3000	2400	3400	4800	8000	17,000
Baker Imperial	1200	2300	3300	4600	7500	16,000
Baker Suburban	2000	2400	3400	4800	8000	17,000
Model I Brougham	4000	2400	3400	4800	8000	17,000
Model I Land'et.	4000	2450	3450	4900	8300	17,500

1909 Baker, runabout, JAC

1909 BAKER

Model S Rbt. (95'' wb)	1850	2300	3300	4600	7500	16,000
Model P Queen Vic.*	1850	2400	3400	4800	8000	17,000
* (71'' wb)						
Model I Land'et. (89'' wb)	3500	2450	3450	4900	8300	17,500
Model P Exten. Cpe. (71'' wb)	2500	2250	3250	4500	7300	15,500

	FP	5	4	3	2	1
Model M Rdstr. (95" wb)	2500	2300	3300	4600	7500	16,000
Model C Stanhope (68" wb)	1000	2200	3200	4400	7000	15,000
Model H Rbt. (82" wb)	1500	2250	3250	4500	7300	15,500
Model F Cpe. (92-1/2" wb)	2500	2100	3100	4300	6700	14,500
Model D Surrey	2200	2300	3300	4600	7500	16,000
* (86-1/2" wb)						

1910 Baker, runabout, HAC

1910 BAKER

(SD) Victoria	2000	2400	3400	4800	8000	17,000
(SD) Extension Cpe.	2600	2300	3300	4600	7500	16,000
(SD) Straight-Front. Cpe.	2400	2200	3200	4400	7000	15,000
(SD) Rbt.	2000	2200	3200	4400	7000	15,000
(SD) Rbt. Cpe.	2400	2250	3250	4500	7300	15,500
(CD) Victoria	1850	2300	3300	4600	7500	16,000
(CD) Extension Cpe.	2500	2300	3300	4600	7500	16,000
(CD) Rbt. Cpe.	2250	2250	3250	4500	7300	15,500
(CD) Straight Front Cpe.	2240	2200	3200	4400	7000	15,000
(CD) Rbt.	1185	2200	3200	4400	7000	15,000
(CD) Stanhope	1000	2000	3000	4200	6500	14,000
(CD) Imperial	850	1800	2800	4000	6200	13,000
(SD) Brougham	3500	2300	3300	4600	7500	16,000
(SD) Land'et.	3500	2350	3350	4700	7700	16,500
(SD) Depot Wagon	2200	2300	3300	4600	7500	16,000
(SD) Formal Cpe.	2200	2300	3300	4600	7500	16,000
(SD) Rdstr.	2500	2350	3350	4700	7700	16,500
(SD) Rear-Driven Vic.	2000	2400	3400	4800	8000	17,000
(SD) Surrey	2200	2300	3300	4600	7500	16,000
(SD) Suburban	1500	2000	3000	4200	6500	14,000

Note: (SD) = Shaft Drive; (CD) = Chain Drive.

1911 Baker, runabout, HAC

1911 BAKER

Queen Victoria	2000	2400	3400	4800	8000	17,000
Extension Cpe.	2600	2300	3300	4600	7500	16,000
Rbt.	2000	2200	3200	4400	7000	15,000
Rbt. Cpe.	2700	2250	3250	4500	7300	15,500
Special Extension Cpe.	2700	2300	3300	4600	7500	16,000
Stanhope	1000	2000	3000	4200	6500	14,000
Suburban	1500	2200	3200	4400	7000	15,000
Brougham	3500	2250	3250	4500	7300	15,500
Land'et.	3500	2250	3250	4500	7300	15,500
Surrey	2200	2100	3100	4300	6700	14,500
Depot Wagon	2200	2100	3100	4300	6700	14,500

1912 BAKER

Rbt. (80" wb)	2000	2400	3400	4800	8000	17,000
Victoria (80" wb)	2000	2450	3450	4900	8300	17,500
Extension Cpe. (80" wb)	2700	2300	3300	4600	7500	16,000
Extension Brgm. (88" wb)	3500	2350	3350	4700	7700	16,500

1913 BAKER

Cpe.-4P (88" wb)	2850	2450	3450	4900	8300	17,500
Brgm.-5P (88" wb)	3200	2500	3500	5000	8500	18,000
Vic.-2P (80" wb)	2000	2300	3300	4600	7500	16,000

1914 BAKER

Model VAE Cpe. (88" wb)	2800	2400	3400	4800	8000	17,000
Model WA Rdstr. (88" wb)	2300	2450	3450	4900	8300	17,500
Model ZFZ Brgm. (88" wb)	3000	2500	3500	5000	8500	18,000

1912 Baker, brougham, HAC

1913 Baker, brougham, HAC

1915 Baker, coupe, HAC

1915 BAKER

	FP	5	4	3	2	1
Model DA Cpe. (90" wb)	2800	2400	3400	4800	8000	17,000
Model WA/WB Rdstr. (90" wb)	2300	2500	3500	5000	8500	18,000
Model BBD Brgm. (100" wb)	3250	2700	3600	5300	8800	19,000

1916 BAKER

Model DA6 Cpe. (90" wb)	2475	2400	3400	4800	8000	17,000
Model BBD6 Brgm. (100" wb)	3000	2450	3450	4900	8300	17,500

BAKER, RAUCH & LANG/BAKER-RAULANG — Although these designations were occasionally used in the trade press following the merger of the Baker and Rauch & Lang companies of Cleveland, Ohio during the summer of 1915, the cars to which they referred were more properly designated under their individual names. Refer to Baker and Rauch & Lang.

BALANCE — During the summer of 1910 the Balance Gear Light Vehicle Company was organized in New York City with a capital stock of $30,000 for the manufacture of "vehicles, motors, engines of all kinds." Behind this venture were Walter E. McDonnell, Thomas Spalding and Michael J. McDonnell. No automobile appears to have been produced.

1925 Balboa, sports brougham, WJL

1925 Balboa, entire production, WJL

1902 Baldner, auto-buggy, NAHC

BALBOA — Fullerton, California — (1924-1925) — "Having undergone over eight years of preparation and experiment," as its makers said from their headquarters in Fullerton in mid-October 1924, the Balboa was at last ready for production. Its makers were Otto W. Heinz (president), William H. Radford (vice-president and chief engineer), J.C. Bliss (secretary), Fred G. Mott (vice-president and sales manager). The factory of their Balboa Motor Car Company was under construction in Pomona, the first models were slated to leave the assembly line at the beginning of 1925, and plans called for an output of 1000 cars the first year. None of this happened, but stock in the new company was sold. The Balboa was powered by an overhead cam straight-eight of 178 cubic inches, which was supercharged "by compressing the charge in a special pocket in the crankcase on the downstroke of the piston," as promotion explained. The engine had been designed during Radford's days with Kessler. The Balboa's streamlined body design was to be available as a touring car to sell for $2900 and in sedan and sports brougham styles at higher prices. A prototype touring car, brougham and one chassis were exhibited at the California Hotel in Fullerton in March of 1924 and at the Ambassador Hotel in Los Angeles that August. The cars were shown again in March 1925 at the Orange County Automobile Show in Santa Ana, by which time Continental engines had been substituted for the supercharged straight-eight, which was offering problems even after the much ballyhooed (and much exaggerated) "eight years of preparation and experiment." Production of the prototypes had taken place in a former wire-manufacturing plant in an orange grove secured by Balboa secretary Bliss. Balboa never did have a proper factory. The failure of the car was a pity, because its engine was so progressive for the period. Had the ballyhoo been subdued, and the Balboa investors been patient enough to allow a teething period, the Balboa would have been quite a motorcar. As it was, it died in the prototype stage, amidst stock promotion fraud charges, and after the building of the two complete cars and one chassis. There appears to have been an attempt by the Balboa people to begin anew with a gasoline-electric car called the Dual, but it proceeded no where as well.

1924-1925 BALBOA
Eight — 100 hp, 127" wb

	FP	5	4	3	2	1
Balboa prototypes						

BALDNER — Xenia, Ohio — (1900-1903) — Jacob Baldner got his start in the automobile business working with Charles Duryea in Peoria (Illinois) in 1896. Shortly before the turn of the century he returned home to Xenia where he and his brother Fred built their first automobile. Both brothers were mechanics, who had predominantly worked as maintenance men and operators of cordage machinery before becoming interested in horse-less carriages. "The first automobile on the streets of Xenia made its appearance Monday afternoon," reported the Xenia *Gazette* on April 24th, 1900. This wasn't precisely true, since Isaac Jones had experimented the year previously with a gasoline car in Xenia, though he was not able to develop his idea further than a single prototype. The Baldners' car was more successful in operation, and it was also the first automobile in Xenia to be manufactured on a production basis. Among the adventures Jacob Baldner had with the Baldner prototype, which apparently was a two-cylinder car, was a test drive which saw his father-in-law tossed out of the seat as they traversed a railway crossing. Following subsequent experimentation, the Baldners' began marketing a three-cylinder car in 1902, after the establishment of the Baldner Motor Vehicle Company late that year. *Cycle and Automobile Trade Journal* was impressed by the Baldner automobile's heavy parts throughout, strength and durability having been given much attention." Roy E. King, a native Xenian who later headed the mechanical engineering department of Georgia Tech, believed it was the difficulty "of balancing a vehicle using a single three-cylinder engine" which was the reason for the Baldners' downfall. They discontinued their vehicle late in 1903 after the building of nine units. Subsequently, Jacob Baldner sued Henry Ford for infringement of a transmission design he had patented in 1902; the case dragged through the courts and ultimately, in the mid-Twenties, Jacob Baldner lost. In 1906 Jacob Baldner built a four-cylinder car which was never marketed. In 1914 his brother Fred was involved with the Xenia cyclecar venture of the Hawkins Cyclecar Company.

1902 BALDNER
Three — 8 hp, 72" wb

	FP	5	4	3	2	1
Rbt.	1000	2700	3600	5300	8800	19,000

1903 BALDNER
Three — 20 hp, 76" wb

	FP	5	4	3	2	1
Tour.	1800	2700	3600	5300	8800	19,000
Light Dly.	2000	2200	3200	4400	7000	15,000
Rbt. (12 hp)	1200	2500	3500	8500	18,000	

BALDWIN — The Baldwin-Day Company was organized in Brooklyn, New York early in 1901 with the capital stock of $6000 and the plan to manufacture motor vehicles. J.E. Baldwin of East Williston and A.V.T. Day of Brooklyn were the partners behind this venture, which seems not to have produced a car.

The Baldwin Motor Service Company was organized in Hackensack, New Jersey during the summer of 1910 to manufacture and deal in automobiles. T.H. Baldwin of Hackensack was joined in this venture by Ferdinand Kaegebelm and G. Charles Norwood of New York City. Capital stock was $250,000. Manufacture of an automobile has not been established.

BALDWIN STEAM — Providence, Rhode Island — (1896-1901) — Although this marque boasted three companies in Providence, it is possible that only one steam car and one delivery wagon were built there. The commercial vehicle was first, a steam van completed in 1896 for the use of Shepard & Company, a local department store. The van had been designed by L.F.N. Baldwin and was built in the Cruickshank Steam Engine Works, where Baldwin was employed as superintendent. In 1897 Baldwin superintended the building of the engines for the Cross steam car at Cruickshank. And the following year he began building his own steam car. Its two-cylinder vertical engine was fired by kerosene or gasoline lamps, with power transmitted to the rear axle by an enclosed sprocket chain. Accommodations were provided for four passengers, and the vehicle's top speed was said to be 25 mph. Completed in 1899, the vehicle was scheduled to be placed on the market forthwith by the newly coined Baldwin Automobile Company. In mid-1900 the firm's name changed to Baldwin Automobile Manufacturing Company. The next news from L.F.N. Baldwin was his reorganization late in 1901 as the Baldwin Motor Wagon Company. It does not appear that production followed any of these organizations. In 1899, however, L.F.N. Baldwin sold rights to his steam car patents to a group of entrepreneurs from Connellsville, Pennsylvania who did manage to get a Baldwin car into production there. L.F.N. Baldwin would subsequently take on agencies in Providence for the White and Stanley steam cars.

95

1901 Baldwin Steamer, (Connellsville), WLB

BALDWIN STEAM — Connellsville, Pennsylvania — (1899-1901) — The Baldwin from Connellsville rose, literally, from the ashes of the largest lock factory in the world. In the fall of 1898 the plant of the Slaymaker-Bary Company burned to the ground. In rebuilding, the managers of Slaymaker-Bary decided to become a producer of steam automobiles instead, and the Baldwin Automobile Company was the result. Built under patents secured from L.F.N. Baldwin of Rhode Island, the Baldwin had a two-cylinder double-acting vertical engine, with its condenser mounted up front, and a straightforward body design with accommodations for two passengers. This venture never did get up a good head of steam, although about 160 men were employed and a dozen cars were built during the company's occasional spurts of financial good health. The first Baldwin steam cars were on the road in 1899, but all operations were halted in mid-1900 when the money ran out. Operations were resumed in December of 1900, but the company reported financial difficulties again in March 1901. A few more cars were put together that summer, but by September the factory was closed again, this time forever. As reported in the *Centennial History of the Borough of Connellsville, Pennsylvania 1806-1906*, "The manufacture of automobiles was a little premature as the business was still in the experimental stage and the owners becoming disappointed in the returns discontinued the business." In January 1902 *Motor Review* stated the Baldwin's assets as $100,298, its liabilities as $98,105. Cash on hand was less than $100. On April 19th, the company was sold at public auction to J.C. Kurtz, who planned to begin anew with the Baldwin in Morgantown, West Virginia. His plans were never realized. At some point in the Baldwin firm's varying existence, there was a change of company name to American Locomotor Manufacturing Company, with the car marketed for a brief period as the Locomotor, this doubtless at the behest of the Baldwin receiver. Among the Baldwin purchasers, incidentally, was Queen Liliuokalani from the Hawaiian Islands.

BALL — The Ball Brothers — J.J. and I.M. — of East Main Street in Bushnell, Illinois indicated themselves as manufacturers of an automobile in 1908. Documentation other than a trade directory listing has not been discovered.

BALL — A.A. Ball of the Thomson-Houston Company of Lynn, Massachusetts was reported to be "testing a new design of steam carriage" in 1903. Conceivably, this may have been at the instigation of Prof. Elihu Thomson who is known to have been experimenting with steam cars in Lynn at the turn of the century. Refer to Thomson.

1902 Ball Steamer, touring, NAHC

BALL STEAM — Paterson, New Jersey — (1868, 1902) — Charles A. Ball was a locomotive designer who built his first road-going steam car in 1868 in Paterson, New Jersey, a vehicle he drove regularly around Rockland County until, as he said, "the citizens made me cease because the machine frightened their horses." The turn of the century found him in

Middletown, Ohio to supervise the construction of a new steam car he had designed which was built for him by the Miami Cycle and Manufacturing Company. He named the car the Ramapaugh Steamer and following completion in late February 1902 began testing it on the streets of Middletown until April 12th when he struck down and killed a local boy. Townspeople were outraged, and Ball left Ohio immediately, taking his Ramapaugh Steamer with him. Undoubtedly, the accident was partly responsible for his quick departure from town, but Ball had already presold the car in any case, to the Waldorf-Astoria Hotel in New York City which planned to use it for the touring pleasure of its guests. The Ramapaugh was a huge vehicle, perhaps the biggest American steam car on the road in 1902, weighing two tons and having passenger accommodations for eight people. In returning to the New York City area, Ball commented only upon his desire to be where the steam automotive action was. He set up shop across the Hudson in Paterson again. Two further steam cars, very much like the Ramapaugh and costing about $10,000 apiece to build, are known to have been designed by Charles Ball. References from the period conflict as to whether these cars were built for him by Miami in Middletown or at the New York Gear Works in New York City. It is known that New York Gear Works produced a two-speed transmission invented by Charles Ball.

1903 Ball, touring, NAHC

BALL — New York, New York — (1902) — In 1902 Frederick A. Ball designed a quite substantial two-cylinder gasoline touring car on an 80-inch wheelbase. It featured a honeycomb radiator mounted in front of the hood, and a starting crank mounted on the dashboard. The vehicle was built at the New York Gear Works in Brooklyn, where Ball was employed. Manufacture of the car apparently was never contemplated. Frederick Ball thereafter moved into the carburetor business, returning to the automobile manufacturing field more than a decade later as one of the prime movers behind the Barlow steam car. Whether Frederick Ball was any relation to Charles Ball whose steam car may have been built at New York Gear Works in 1902 is not known.

BALLARD — Oshkosh, Wisconsin — (1894 et seq.) — A.W. Ballard was a gunsmith who also repaired bicycles in his shop on Harrison, just off Main Street, in Oshkosh. In 1894 he built his first gasoline automobile, a two-seater buggy with two-cylinder motor mounted over the rear axle, chain drive to the rear wheels, and a wheel for steering. He built another the year following, with a tiller for steering, which he exhibited — for a fee of $50 — at the nearby Chilton Fair. The Ballard was also pitted against a man on horseback there in a race around Lake Winnebago — and the car handily won. A Wausau physician by the name of Dr. Sauerherring learned of the Ballard car and ordered one but with four seats and kerosine headlamps so the doctor could find his way home following after-dark house calls. Local Oshkosh historians believe A.W. Ballard regarded automobile building as a hobby, but it would seem that he at least contemplated giving the automobile industry a whirl shortly after the turn of the century. The February 1901 issue of *Cycle and Automobile Trade Journal* reported that the firm of H.C. Ballard & Son at 51 Harrison Street in Oshkosh was in the automobile business and described the Ballard product fully. It was a four-passenger dos-a-dos, like Dr. Sauerherring's car, with a tubular running gear curved over the rear wheels. The motor was placed on the rear axle and geared to it by chain and sprocket. A power lever and a steering lever controlled the car, with a foot pedal for braking. "The exhaust is discharged beneath the gasoline tank," the description read, "which is hung under the body near the engine, thus serving to aid in vaporizing." The Ballard was said to be capable of speeds ranging "from mere motion up to about fourteen miles an hour." Whatever production might have followed was no doubt modest. References to Ballard's automobile venture disappear after March 1902. A.W. Ballard died in 1922 at the age of seventy-seven.

BALLOU — The F.A. Ballou Company was organized in Buffalo, New York early in 1910 with a capital stock of $25,000 and the plan to "manufacture and deal in boats, bicycles, motorcars and other vehicles." In addition to Ballou himself, C.H. Phillips and H.J. Harris were involved in this venture. Manufacture is not indicated.

BALTIMORE — The Baltimore Motor Car Company was organized in that Maryland city during the fall of 1903 for the manufacture and sale of automobiles. George L. Deichman, Christopher R. Wattenscheidt and three Lipps — Rudolph, Christopher and Edward — were the people behind this venture. Manufacture is doubted.

The Baltimore Motor Carriage Company was a $10,000 Maryland incorporation from early 1906 for the manufacture and sale of automobiles. G.F. Buchholz, Wallace C. Hood, H.M. Benzinger, James S. Calwell, E.R. Stringer and Walter E. Collier were the people behind this venture which does not seem to have proceeded into manufacture.

BALTIMORE — Baltimore, Maryland — (1899) — During the summer of 1899, the Baltimore Automobile & Manufacturing Company was organized with $100,000 capital stock to build, operate and sell electric vehicles in Maryland. General offices were taken in the Equitable Building, and Joseph M. Zamoiski was in charge. Delivery wagons were announced to be the firm's specialty, although a taxicab service was also to be introduced. A central charging station was planned to be built, together with a repair shop where vehicles of patrons could be tended to. The plans were grand, but there is no evidence they were ever fulfilled. Possibly a prototype was built.

BALTON — Buffalo, New York — (1919) — "The new car is to be built for speed and power," the Charles A. Balton Engineering Corporation of Buffalo said in late 1919. "It will have a four-cylinder motor of 187 (sic) horsepower, 3300 rpm, with a rated horsepower of 28.7. It will weigh 3100 pounds without body or accessories and will develop in its sport model a speed of 100 miles an hour." Charles A. Balton was the former chief engineer of Luverne in Minnesota, he planned to call his new car the New Era, and there is no evidence it ever happened.

BALZER — Bronx, New York — (1894-1900) — Just how many cars were built by Stephen M. Balzer of the Bronx will probably forever remain a mystery. Fortunately, one of them is extant, the prototype built in 1894, which is on display at the Smithsonian Institution in Washington, D.C. It has a rotary engine, the crankcase and three radial cylinders revolving in a vertical plane around a fixed crankshaft. The constant-mesh transmission provides three speeds forward but no reverse. The tiller-steered voiturette is less than six feet long and three feet wide, with 17-inch wheels in front, 26-inch in the rear. According to references from 1897, Balzer had by then built three cars and was expecting to complete 100 more by spring of the following year. In 1898 the Balzer Motor Carriage Company was established in the Bronx. Further references to Balzer's automobile manufacturing remain inconclusive, but it is known that he proceeded for some time in the building of his three-cylinder rotary engines, and developed a rotary five as well. The latter powerplant was used in the Carey automobile that was produced in New York City during 1906. Balzer also apparently furnished Samuel Langley with a larger radial engine for aeronautical use.

1894 Balzer, voiturette, SI

1897 Balzer, voiturette, NAHC

BALZER — New York, New York — (1910-1917) — The Gus Balzer Company was organized with a capital stock of $25,000 early in 1910 for the purpose of manufacturing and dealing in automobiles. In addition to Balzer, the company incorporators included Charles E. Miller (a prominent figure in the automobile accessory business) and C.S. Zimmerman. The company was located at 1777-79 Broadway in Manhattan. Although the firm may have served as a dealership for a full-size car manufacturer, the only vehicles it produced itself were for children. Some references suggest that the Balzer juvenile car was built as late as 1917. Prior to manufacture of a child's car, Gus Balzer was in the automobile accoutrement business, producing "bouquet holders" for limousines among other accessories.

BANGS & BUTLER — Everett, Massachusetts — (1908) — This wonderfully-named backyard effort was the result of a collaboration between Calvin Bangs of Everett and William Butler of Boston. Their car was a steamer upon which they had spent about $800, and its first outing was a disaster. "Home-Made Automobile a 'Scorcher'," *The Motor World* punned in describing the explosion of the copper boiler: "Butler was sitting in the seat at the time, while Bangs was 'firing-up.' In a twinkling the $800 and their labor 'went to hell' as one of the men expressed it." The partners are not known to have tried again.

BANKER — Chicago, Illinois — (1905) — A.C. Banker of Chicago built an L-head four-cylinder shaft-drive car on a 100-inch wheelbase which he made available as a five-passenger side-entrance tonneau with wood body ($2250) or aluminum body ($2500), and as a $3000 limousine with the buyer's choice of either. He placed his Banker on the market early in 1905 as "A Chicago Car for Chicago People" and announced plans to build 100 of them that year. Whether he did or not is moot, but Banker definitely did not survive into 1906.

1905 BANKER

	FP	5	4	3	2	1
Wood						
Side Entrance Tonneau	2250	2000	3000	4200	6500	14,000
Aluminum						
Side Entrance Tonneau	2500	2000	3000	4200	6500	14,000
Wood or Aluminum						
Limo.	3000	2100	3100	4300	6700	14,500

1905 Banker, touring, WLB

BANKER JUVENILE — Pittsburgh, Pennsylvania — (1905) — The Banker Brothers were bicycle dealers in Pittsburgh who built their first car, with a 2 hp engine of the Kane-Pennington type, in 1895. Thereafter they seemed to dabble betimes in building other gasoline vehicles, brother Arthur even declaring in mid-1902 that they would have a race car ready the year following. None of this, however, paid the rent. Instead, the Bankers enjoyed prosperity as automobile dealers for such diverse marques as Crestmobile, Waverley Electric, St. Louis, Toledo and Daimler, claiming themselves as the "largest dealers in America," with showrooms in Pittsburgh, Philadelphia and New York. In 1905, when they did go into production with a car of their own, it was with an electric for children. Its motor was a 1-1/2 hp Westinghouse; its wheelbase was 52 inches, its tread 39 inches, or approximately three-quarters the dimensions of the standard runabout on the market. Two very good sized children could sit side by side on the seat and drive the Banker Juvenile at speeds up to 12 mph if allowed to. A governor to assure lower speeds was available at the purchaser's request. Apparently not enough purchasers requested the Banker Juvenile, because it was not offered again in 1906, the brothers returning full time to dealing in other manufacturer's full-size cars.

1905 Banker Juvenile, runabout, NAHC

1905 BANKER JUVENILE

Banker Juvenile Electric	600	250	600	1500	3000	5000

BANKS — Stanton, Delaware — (1900) — Robert Banks was described in *The Motor Vehicle Review* as "an enterprising and ingenious blacksmith" from Stanton. In 1900 he completed a steam carriage for his own use, which he declared had been "thoroughly tested and gave entire satisfaction." Banks is not known to have built another car.

BANKS-LUNDWALL — The Banks-Lundwall Auto Corporation was organized by Florence Banks and Eric W. Lundwall early in 1919 in New York City. The manufacture of automobiles was their plan, the initial capital stock was $5000, and it does not appear this venture proceeded much further than that.

BANNER — St. Louis, Missouri — (1910, 1915) — The Banner Buggy Company of St. Louis was one of the largest horse-drawn vehicle manufacturers in the country, and it is rather surprising that it was not until 1910 that the firm began to contemplate embarking upon automobile manufacture. Contemplation, and a few prototypes, proved to be as far as the company proceeded at this time. In July of 1910, Banner president Russell E. Gardner had announced the formation of the subsidiary Banner Automobile Company. Joining him in this venture were Hugh Cartwright, Banner Buggy vice-president; and Elmer L. Roginger, a department manager of Banner Buggy. Gardner stated that this new company would not commence "active manufacturing for some time," but that ultimately a plant would be built with a capacity of 20,000 machines a year. This was quite true, but when the automobile from this new plant arrived at the end of the First World War, it would not be called a Banner, but a Gardner instead. For a few years previous, the Banner Buggy people operated as a Chevrolet assembly plant, and also built Chevrolet bodies. An automobile called the Banner never did see production.

BANTAM — From 1938 to 1941, the American Bantam Car Company of Butler, Pennsylvania produced the second-generation version of the little British Austin-based car which had been known as the American Austin from 1930 to 1934. Refer to American Austin.

1914 Bantam, cyclecar-roadster, WLB

BANTAM — Boston, Massachusetts — (1914) — This little cyclecar from the Bantam Motor Company of 755 Boylston Street in Boston was produced "to meet the demands from all over the world wherever civilized man lives." Designed by Frank J. Tyler, a veteran of Maxwell-Briscoe, it had a two-cylinder air-cooled 14 hp engine (of the type, its makers said, being used in the more than 300,000 motor bicycles in the United States), employed a friction transmission, and set its two-passenger open body (door on right side only) on an 86-inch wheelbase with 46-inch tread. Better than 40 mpg was claimed, and the price was $395. Bostonians quickly discovered that the Bantam was not a civilized way to travel in the Massachusetts wintertime. Production of the car, which was minimal, took place in a rented corner of the Lenox Motor Company.

1914 BANTAM
Cyclecar — 2-cyl, 14 hp, 86" wb

	FP	5	4	3	2	1
Rds.-2P	395	1500	2500	3600	5500	11,000

BARAUF — Port Jefferson, New York — (1920) — A Barauf was displayed at an automobile show in the Greater New York area in February of 1920. It was a five-passenger touring car with a $1495 price tag, four-cylinder 27 hp Le Roi engine, 108-inch wheelbase, and wood wheels. The car was intended for export, and was convertible into a utility vehicle. Whether the Barauf Motor Company ever moved into production in Port Jefferson is not known, but interestingly it indicated its "Brooklyn Office" as 21 Lenox Road which was the address into which the Barbarino moved a few years later.

BARBARINO — Brooklyn, New York — (1923-1925) — Salvatore Barbarino made cement blocks in Brooklyn and was a sometime automobile racer who served as relief driver for Louis Chevrolet in the 1920 Indianapolis 500. In 1923, when the Richelieu company of Asbury Park (New Jersey) folded, he acquired what was left there, and set himself up in business as an automobile manufacturer at 21 Lenox Road in Brooklyn. He said at the time that he had already spent six years developing his "Car in a Class by Itself." The Barbarino was powered by a four-cylinder 137-cubic-inch Le Roi engine which Barbarino revised to his own design. But he was most proud of his four-wheel brakes, which were equalized by cables, not the usual tie-rods: "This does away with oiling, wearing parts and last, but not least, rattle." The wheelbase was 110 inches with bodies built to individual order by Chupudy Auto Coach in New York. There is some confusion regarding the company backing this enterprise. The brochure shows Barbarino Motor Car Corporation; trade press references indicated that another company called Advance Motors (which succeeded Richelieu) was behind the Barbarino, though apparently not very reputably because

an injunction restricting it from the sale of any more stock was handed down late in 1923. When the smoke cleared, and the injunction was lifted, Salvatore Barbarino resigned as president and was succeeded first by Buell Alvord, then Walter L. Adams. Production finally got underway in Brooklyn early in 1925 at the reported rate of three cars per day. Exactly when production stopped is not known, but it must not have been long thereafter since the total number of Barbarinos built has never been estimated at more than ten. Salvatore Barbarino later operated an auto repair shop in the Flatbush section of Brooklyn.

1925 BARBARINO
Four — 28 hp, 110" wb

	FP	5	4	3	2	1
Rds.-2P	950	2500	3500	5000	8500	18,000
Tour.-4P	950	2450	3450	4900	8300	17,500
Sed.-4P	1500	2300	3300	4600	7500	16,000
Twn. Car	1500	2400	3400	4800	8000	17,000

Note 1: A 90 hp straight-eight seven-passenger touring car at $2000 was projected but never arrived.

BARBER — The Barber Auto-Cab & Repair Company was organized in Brooklyn, New York during the summer of 1909. Capital stock was $15,000, the manufacture of automobiles was the plan, and A.S. Barber, William Barber and R.A. Rendich were the incorporators. Production is doubted.

BARBER — Danbury, Connecticut — (1899) — William H. Barber was a carriage maker whose shop was at 81 Railroad Avenue in Danbury. In 1899 he built a small gasoline runabout for his own amusement, turning his attention thereafter to the building of horse-drawn vehicles only, from which business he retired following the First World War.

BARBOUR — South Boston, Virginia — (1916) — The Barbour Buggy Company of South Boston had been in the carriage-making business for thirty years when, in 1916, it announced plans to abandon that activity completely and switch to the automobile field. Two cars were slated to be produced on identical chassis: a four priced at $750 and an eight at $950. Detroit engineer R.A. Skinner designed the prototypes, which apparently were built in Detroit. It does not appear the cars went into production in South Boston, Virginia however.

BARCLAY — The Barclay which appeared in the specifications chart of the January 25th, 1923 issue of *Motor Age* was not an automobile but instead a typographical error for the Barley which was built in Kalamazoo, Michigan that year.

BARCUS — Columbus, Ohio — (1895) — Nemo Barcus lived at 550 East Tawas Street in Columbus and in 1895 submitted his entry for the Chicago Times-Herald Contest. The car he was building for the contest, however, never made it to the starting line — and whether or not it was ever successfully tested has not been documented.

BARD — Two cars to carry the name Bard were announced, but that a single example of either was built has not been documented.
The Bard Automobile Company from late 1909 was a Camden, New Jersey incorporation with $250,000 in capital stock. F.N. Hansell, G.B.H. Martin and J.A. McPeak were the incorporators.
The Bard Motor Car Company from the spring of 1916 was a $500,000 incorporation in Pittsburgh, Pennsylvania backed by K.G. Small, W.E. Harris and W.A. McCoy.

1901 Bardwell, runabout, WLB

BARDWELL — Flint, Michigan — (1901) — Although doubtless there were others who followed the same course during this period, Hiram H. Bardwell of Flint was the first automobile builder to admit that he had designed his car strictly by the book. The book in this case was the renowned *Horseless Vehicles, Automobiles and Motor Cycles* written by

Gardner D. Hiscox and published in 1900. Bardwell, who was a former State legislator and a practicing physician, bought a copy immediately and finished his vehicle in 1901. A two-seater with a substantial hood in front and parcel deck in the rear, the Bardwell was a reasonably attractive car for the period, without the ''paint-by-numbers'' look that might have been the logical result of its book-derived design. Dr. Bardwell built the vehicle strictly for his own pleasure. Upon completing it, he returned to his medical practice and such other sideline inventions as a pill-making machine. Although he has been occasionally credited with building the first automobile in Flint, that honor correctly belongs to Charles H. Wisner who finished his automobile in 1900. Wisner was a circuit court judge.

1900 Bar Harbor, surrey, WLB

BAR HARBOR — Bar Harbor, Maine — (1900-1901) — Precisely why this company from Maine preferred to refer to itself as the Boston Automobile Company tends to perplex, because both its offices and factory were in Bar Harbor. The choice of Bar Harbor was explained by company manager Paul Hunt, however: ''Bar Harbor is noted the country over,'' he said. ''Each summer brings just the class of people to the town who can afford to indulge in the automobile luxury.'' E. Shirley Goddard was president of the company, George P. Billings was superintendent. Initially, in 1900, the cars were referred to as Standards, then as Bostons, but by early 1901 the name of Bar Harbor for the Boston Automobile Company product was finally and irrevocably decided upon. The cars were exhibited as Bar Harbors at the Boston Automobile Show that February. ''The engine used is the latest improved ball bearing, two-cylinder type, with double bearing cross heads,'' *The Motor Vehicle Review* reported. ''. . . The boiler has 370 one-half inch copper tubes, is 17 inches in diameter and 18 inches high . . . The speed is regulated entirely by a throttle lever. It varies from 1 to 46 miles an hour.'' Two and four-passenger models were produced, priced at $700 and $1000 respectively. A reporter from the *Bar Harbor Record* visited the factory and wrote afterward of seeing numerous cars in the course of construction, including two ordered by an engineer from Lancashire, England and a single-seater for someone from Bombay, India. The place was bustling. ''Indeed at the present time there are not men enough to be had for certain work,'' he reported, ''and the superintendent has been looking elsewhere for a supply.'' Why this company failed by 1902 is not known.

1900-1901 BAR HARBOR

	FP	5	4	3	2	1
Std./Boston Rbt.	700	2300	3300	4600	7500	16,000
Std./Boston Surrey	1000	2350	3350	4700	7700	16,500

BARHOFF — Hartford, Connecticut — (1900) — Frederick W. Barhoff was a Cleveland engineer who trekked East before the turn of the century ostensibly to take charge of an automobile factory planned for Germany by the Pope Manufacturing Company of Hartford. The German deal fell through while Barhoff was still in Hartford, however, but he remained in town where his developments in the storage battery field came to the attention of Halsey B. Philbrick, the secretary of the Hartford Accumulator Company. Barhoff's storage battery system was considerably lighter than the norm during this period, which provided for an electric carriage less cumbersome than most. A prototype car was built, which alternatively carried Barhoff's and Philbrick's name in articles about it in the trade press. Although the Hartford Accumulator Company announced its plans to manufacture the car, the firm did not follow through on this, although there was some subsequent production of the Barhoff-designed storage battery.

BARLEY — Kalamazoo, Michigan — (1923-1924) — In a speech before the Kalamazoo Exchange Club on August 7th, 1922, George Hopkins announced that a new, smaller, medium-priced automobile was forthcoming from the Barley Motor Car Company — and he took pains to emphasize that the car would not be a model of the prestigious and high-priced Roamer which the firm had been building since 1916. The company took pains to insure that the Barley did not look like it either. The most noticeable area in which to do that was radiator configuration; the Barley's was

straight sided with a sharp flare at the top. Its engine was Continental's L-head six, and standard components were used throughout. Touring and sedan models were introduced in September of 1922, with a sport sedan and touring sedan later to follow for the '23 model year. The 1924 model year was the Barley's last. The name was thereafter dropped, and the car ultimately became what the company had earlier insisted it was not: a Roamer, Model 6-50. Interestingly, a taxicab carrying the Barley badge was available from the beginning, though in 1923 its name was changed to Pennant. The Pennant taxi was produced into 1925, a year longer than the Barley passenger car.

1923 Barley, 5-pass. touring, WLB

1923 BARLEY
Model 6-50 — 6-cyl., 50 hp, 118'' wb

	FP	5	4	3	2	1
Tour.-5P	1395	3200	4300	6500	11,000	23,000
Sed.-5P	1850	2700	3600	5300	8800	19,000
Spt. Sed.-5P	1495	2900	3700	5600	9100	20,000
Tour. Sed.-5P	2250	2950	3900	5800	9300	20,500

1924 BARLEY
Model 6-50 — 6-cyl., 50 hp, 118'' wb

	FP	5	4	3	2	1
Phae.-5P	1395	3200	4300	6500	11,000	23,000
Spt. Sed.-5P	1495	2900	3700	5600	9100	20,000
Spec. Spt.-5P	1685	3000	4000	6000	9500	21,000
Tour. Sed.-5P	1695	2700	3600	5300	8800	19,000
Sed.-5P	1850	2500	3500	5000	8500	18,000

BARLOW STEAM — Detroit, Michigan — (1917-1922) — The Barlow was a steam car that spent a half decade in the experimental stage. The first one was on the road during the fall of 1917, the third prototype was finished and ready to undergo a series of experimental tests in the spring of 1922. It was in late March that year that the Barlow Steam Engineering Syndicate was formed, its members including an impressive roster of engineers and executives from the Ford Motor Company, Timken Axle, Detroit Lubricator and Penberthy Injector, among other prominent Motor City concerns. About fifty people were involved in this venture to promote and manufacture the vehicle designed by Lester P. Barlow, the most enthusiastic being Fred Ball who had built his own car at the turn of the century and who was now manager of the Ball and Ball carburetor department of Penberthy. Initial press releases indicated a $300,000 incorporation and a $3000 selling price for the car, with promotional emphasis to be placed on its boiler construction which was said to be uniquely different from any other contemporary steam car. Apparently, undue optimism was the actual not-uniquely-different feature of this manufacturing venture. Preliminary announcements in late 1921 spoke of the eminent start-up of production at the Commercial Manufacturing Company in Detroit, with the car to be on the market early in 1922. Early in 1922 the date was moved up to June. By November the Barlow company was said to be preparing to manufacture a steam-generating device invented by Lester Barlow, and that Barlow looked forward to building steam-driven buses in Cleveland. The entire venture died soon after that.

BARNES — The Barnes-Curtiss Company, Inc. was organized with a capital stock of $25,000 in New York City early in 1909 to ''manufacture, rent and deal in automobiles.'' The incorporators were H.B. Barnes, Jr. and A.L. Curtiss. Manufacture is not indicated.

The Barnes Motor Sales Company was organized with a capital stock of $5000 in Rockford, Illinois during the summer of 1911 to both manufacture and deal in automobiles, motorcycles and parts. The incorporators were W.F. Barnes (Sr. and Jr.) and H.S. Hicks. Manufacture does not appear to have followed.

BARNES — Burlington, Iowa — (1900) — C.E. Barnes was a physician from Burlington who designed a car for himself which was built for him by the Autocar company in Pittsburgh. ''The grades of Burlington are generally considered quite heavy,'' *The Autobain* reported in December 1899, ''but any of the modern and up-to-date types of autobain will have no difficulty in negotiating them.'' Apparently, the car, which was delivered in 1900, served Dr. Barnes well for a number of years thereafter.

BARNES — Clemson, South Carolina — (1902) — In January 1902, Professor Albert Barnes of Clemson College announced the completion of an automobile which he had built for his own use, most probably with a little help from his students. ''The machine weighs only 750 pounds,'' reported *The Horseless Age*, ''and nearly all the metal work was done at the college.''

BARNES — Sandusky, Ohio — (1907 et seq.) — The Barnes was one of two new cars introduced by the Barnes Manufacturing Company in 1907. The other was the Servitor, which was produced that year only. Both were air-cooled four-cylinder roadsters. Although some references indicate the cars to have been continued in production through 1910 or 1912, this has not been substantively documented. Possibly the Barnes behind this Barnes was the same H.C. Barnes who took over the Anhut Motor Car Company of Detroit in 1910.

BARNES — Detroit, Michigan — (1910) — H.C. Barnes had been the factory superintendent for the Anhut Motor Car Company in 1909, and in 1910 took over the firm and reorganized it into the Barnes Motor Car Company. A brass stamping with a "Barnes Six" logo is known to have been made, but how many Barnes cars were marketed is problematical. In November 1910 the Barnes Motor Company proceeded into bankruptcy, with assets of $143,540.25, liabilities of $64,242.33, and a total of $10.32 in cash on hand.

BARNES STEAM TRAP — Syracuse, New York — (1899) — George M. Barnes was the president of the bicycle-producing Frontenac Manufacturing Company in Syracuse, and a stockholder with E.C. Stearns in several other bicycle companies in town. In 1899 he built a small steam carriage in his company shops, which received some attention in the automobile press. The car was not marketed as a Barnes, however, although it was marketed. In the fall of 1900, Barnes joined with E.C. Stearns and a number of other Syracuse businessmen in the formation of the Stearns Steam Carriage Company. The Barnes car was put into manufacture at the Barnes factory at Levenworth and Spruce streets in 1901, but it was sold as a Stearns.

BARNHARD-BRIGGS — Woodville, Massachusetts — (1906) — The Barnhard-Briggs Automobile Company was established in Boston in late 1906 and secured an old shoe factory in nearby Woodville with plans to remodel it for the manufacture of a diverse line of four-cylinder automobiles to be priced from one to four thousand dollars. The company also staged a contest, offering a one hundred dollar prize for the person submitting the best name for the new car which was slated to be produced in 1907. There was no new car from Barnhard-Briggs in 1907. One would suspect that the reason was other than that a suitable name had not been forthcoming from the contest. More probably, A.H. Barnhard and J.L. Briggs had simply not been able to make a go of their venture.

BARNHART & BETTS — Warren, Pennsylvania — (1897-1899) — In 1897 H.F. Barnhart built his first gasoline car in partnership with his father-in-law C.D. Betts, who was a mechanic. They neglected to fit the vehicle with brakes, however, and its first test run was completed against the wall of the Wallace livery-stable. Young Barnhart graduated from dental school later that year, began his practice and experimented with automobiles on the side, completing another car in association with his father-in-law in 1899. In 1905 Dr. Barnhart built a car on his own, which he considered worthy of manufacture and named it after the town in which he practiced dentistry. The Warren Automobile Company was short-lived.

BARRETT — S.H. Barrett was one of two inventors backed by ten Springfield businessmen in the building of an experimental steam carriage, the successful operation of which led to the organization of the Springfield Motor Vehicle Company in the fall of 1900. Refer to Springfield.

1896 Barrett & Perret, electric dos-a-dos, HAC

BARRETT & PERRET — New York, New York — (1896) — In 1895 J.A. Barrett and A. Frank Perret, electrical engineers in New York City, were contracted by a Texas banker to customize the Baker & Elberg electric car he had recently purchased. This experience behind them, Barrett and Perret designed their own electric in 1896 which was built for them in the shops of J. Curley in Brooklyn. A handsome vehicle with coachwork purportedly courtesy of Brewster, the Barrett & Perret was laden with the heavy storage batteries necessary for a car of that carrying capacity, and although it operated successfully Perret particularly was disturbed by the cumbersomeness of the machine. The car was not marketed. The Barrett-Perret partnership fell apart some time thereafter; Perret began experimentation in his own storage battery design and in 1900 built another car under his own name.

100

1897 Barrows Electric, auto-buggy, NAHC

BARROWS ELECTRIC— New York, New York — (1895-1899) — The Barrows Vehicle Company resulted from a collaboration among Frederick W. Dunton, Charles H. Barrows and William H. Boynton, who set up their factory on West 53rd Street, off Broadway, in Manhattan. Their product was an electric with the drive components fitted between the two closely-spaced front wheels. "We have what is practically a mechanical horse," the company said. One-passenger to four-passenger bodies were available, and completely interchangeable. Charging batteries was pronounced "simple as feeding a horse, a mistake less possible." Three speeds forward (4, 8 and 12 mph) were provided, and the Barrows could travel 4 mph in reverse. A bicycle handlebar arrangement was fitted for steering, with an ordinary bicycle bell attached as a warning signal. For $10 a pair of steel runners was available, "and you have the prettiest sleigh outfit imaginable." Economy of operation was stressed ("against this vehicle you could not afford to take the horse as a gift"), and a stable was deemed unnecessary ("simply provide vehicle room on ground floor of house or store"). The Barrows was named for the man who had invented it and who had built the prototype in his hometown of Willimantic, Connecticut. In 1896 Charles Barrows licensed the Lengert company of Philadelphia to produce his vehicles, but whether he planned to share his ten percent royalty with his partners is not known. Lengert apparently never proceeded into manufacture anyway. Some Barrows-designed three-wheelers were built at the turn of the century by the New England Electric Vehicle Company, however.

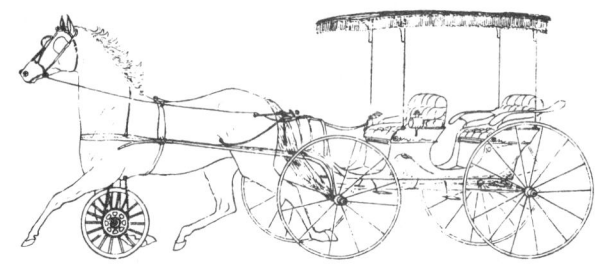

1897 Barsaleaux

BARSALEAUX — Sandy Hill, New York — (1897) — Joseph Barsaleaux was a blacksmith from Sandy Hill and after three years of constant experimentation, he came up with an automotive idea that was both horsedrawn and horseless. This vehicular concept is best described as it was reported in the August 1897 issue of *The Horseless Age:* "The horse does not move on legs, but on a single wheel about two feet in diameter. This wheel is attached to shafts, just as the live horse is. Over the mechanism constructed on an oblong support covering the top of the wheel is the frame of a horse. The reins are attached to the mouth of the horse, and when pulled cause the animal to turn in whatever direction the driver may desire . . . The single front wheel is 27 inches in diameter and has a tire 4 inches wide. On this wheel is mounted an American gasoline motor . . . Six gear wheels operated by one shaft regulate the speed of the machine. At pres-

BARTH-KEITH — During the summer of 1919 the Barth-Keith Motor Car Company was organized in Indianapolis, Indiana with a capital stock of $600,000 and the plan to manufacture automobiles. Jacob S. Barth, Charles A. Barth and J. Ellis Keith were behind this venture. Within a week they had changed their firm's name to Excel Motor Car Company. Manufacture does not seem to have followed.

BARTHEL — Detroit, Michigan — (1903-1904) — At the turn of the century Oliver E. Barthel was a young man who was already an old hand in the automotive field. In 1896 he had assisted Charles B. King of Detroit in building and testing that city's first gasoline automobile. Subsequently he allied himself with Henry Ford in the Detroit Automobile Company and assisted Ford during his early racing days. Ultimately, however, the backers of the Detroit Automobile Company wearied of Ford's penchant for producing racing and not production cars and brought in Henry M. Leland who promised to build a car for the road instead of the track, which he did and called the Cadillac. Both Ford and Barthel were now out of a job, and prepared to strike out on their own. Initially, several local drugstore tycoons came through with financing for Barthel, and the Mohawk Auto Company was organized. Its name was quickly changed to Lafayette Auto Company, however, when it was discovered there was already a Mohawk in Indianapolis. All this happened in September of 1903. Precisely what happened next is not known, but by November the Lafayette venture had ended, without the production of a single car. Now the Davis brothers of Detroit offered financial backing, and the Barthel Motor Company was organized with a capital stock of $400,000. James E. Davis was president, Charles Davis secretary, Oliver Barthel consulting engineer. One prototype of a two-cylinder 14 hp car to sell in the popular price range was ready by November of 1903, while others were "in process of construction" for exhibit at the Chicago and New York shows, and the company was looking for a suitable site for its factory. Only two Barthel cars had been completed by January 1904, however, and the venture died soon thereafter. Meanwhile, Barthel's old racing colleage had organized his Ford Motor Company with considerably more lasting success.

BARTHOLOMEW — The first experimental car built by J.B. Bartholomew of Peoria, Illinois in 1901 was known simply as a Bartholomew. When the Bartholomew Company proceeded into manufacture of the car in 1903, however, its name was changed to Glidemobile, and soon to Glide. Refer to Glide.

BARTLETT — **Philadelphia, Pennsylvania** — **(1915)** — J.C. Bartlett was the operator of a chain of garages in Philadelphia and the inventor of a car called the Bartlett Regenerator Electric, its name derived, as *Automobile Topics* noted, "from the characteristic of the shunt-wound motor becoming a generator when driven instead of driving. Thus, the motor (which was a Diehl) is used as a brake, and in addition charges the battery." The chassis for the Bartlett was designed by F.G. Peck, who had formerly been associated with the Buffalo Electric. An initial run of 100 of these vehicles was slated to be built under the aegis of the new Electric Taxicab Company of New York City, a million-dollar venture organized by E.P. McDowell. Bartlett was to take care of chassis manufacture in his main Philadelphia garage, with bodies to be built by the Blue Ribbon Auto & Carriage Company at 1790 Broadway in New York City. Coachwork was to be of limousine type "with no suggestion of the usual electric lines," but a hood of the Renault type instead shrouding most of the battery equipment. That 100 Bartletts were ultimately built is to be doubted.

BARTON — **Chicago, Illinois** — **(1903)** — The Barton Boiler Company of Chicago mainly built boilers but also offered to produce "special steam tonneau cars" to order. Two such cars were ordered and built. They featured the Barton flash boiler, of course, in conjunction with a Mason two-cylinder slide valve engine and Burnell paraffin burner.

BARY — The Bary which has been indicated on car rosters was in reality the Bray built by James B. Bray of Waverly, New York in 1897. Refer to Bray.

BASSETT — In Holyoke, Massachusetts, during the summer of 1903, the Bassett Motor Vehicle Company was organized with a capital stock of $2 million. Behind this venture were R.S. Couch, Linton T. Bassett, Hatley R. Walker and B.C. Burington. "A new patent is said to be the basis of the concern," *The Horseless Age* reported, "and its first activities will be the sale of stock." Further activities have not been documented.
In Bridgewater, Massachusetts, late in 1911, the William H. Bassett Company was organized with a capital stock of $20,000 for the manufacture of automobiles. J. Gardner Bassett was also involved. Manufacture seems not to have followed.

BATCHELDER & WRITNER STEAM — **Manchester, New Hampshire** — **(1868)** — James S. Batchelder and William H. Writner were employees of the Amoskeag Machine Shop, which manufactured steam fire engines in Manchester. In 1868 they built a steam car at a reported cost of $500. Its boiler was attached to the back of a common democrat wagon and had a tall smokestack on top. Its single-acting engine, calculated to be 8 hp, was underneath the center section of the body. The vehicle ran, and ran well. Its principal problem seemed to be that it didn't run far at a single stretch; every two or three miles it was necessary for the driver to leave his seat and fire the boiler. "It seems to us that although it is an ingenious contrivance, it can never supersede horse flesh anywhere," *The Manchester Union* reported on July 11th, 1868. "People who take short journeys for pleasure prefer live stock in harness and long journeys will follow the iron tracks built expressly for steam carriages of another sort, viz: locomotives . . . A hod full of coal will run it two or three hours . . . two or three hods may be carried. We don't see exactly who has use and need for a carriage of this sort in New England." The paper was quite right. But Batchelder & Writner had the right idea too, though they didn't pursue it further. They returned to their steam fire engine work, and died before the turn of the century and the advent of the automotive age.

1925 Batchelor, NAHC

BATCHELOR — **Savannah, Georgia** — **(1925)** — Many automobiles in America were built in a backyard. The Batchelor's birthplace was a junkyard. All components of the car built by J.H. Batcheler of Savannah were acquired from a scrap heap, and the result looked scarcely the worse for it. Apparently, the car served its owner well. He is known to have driven it to Miami, Florida and back.

BATEMAN — Although the Bateman Manufacturing Company subsidized its manufacture, the car built from 1917 to 1918 in Greenloch, New Jersey was known as the Frontmobile. Refer to Frontmobile.

1897 Bates, gasoline runabout, JAC

BATES — **Chicago, Illinois** — **(1897)** — John W. Bates was working for the Western Wheel Works in Chicago when he designed and built his first experimental gasoline car in 1897. Most probably other automobiles followed, all of them experimental, but word of Bates' talent traveled north to Wisconsin. When William Lewis entered the automobile field in Racine with the Mitchell, he hired John Bates, as his chief engineer.

1904 Bates, touring, WLB

101

BATES — Lansing, Michigan — (1904-1905) — M.F. Bates of Lansing said he built the first internal combustion engine in the State of Michigan in 1889, and his claim seems to have gone unchallenged. His Bates & Edmonds Motor Company was well known for the manufacture of high quality hydrocarbon engines, and it was perhaps inevitable that he would choose one day to build a complete car. In July of 1903 his Bates Automobile Company was incorporated with a capital stock of $60,000, and a two-cylinder 16 hp Bates was in production by the end of that year. A three-cylinder 18 hp followed for the 1905 season, and so did financial trouble for the company. Initially, Bates considered a move to Madison, Wisconsin but ultimately decided to discontinue manufacture. The slogan "Buy a Bates and Keep Your Dates" was heard no more. Today the old Bates factory in Lansing is the home of the R.E. Olds Museum.

BATH — The Bath Automobile and Gas Engine Company was organized in Bath, Maine during the summer of 1906 to manufacture and deal in motor vehicles and boats. E.W. Hyde was president and Scott R. Frye was treasurer. Of the $10,000 capital stock, $5000 was paid in. Manufacture did not follow.

The Bath Beach Garage and Machine Company was organized in Brooklyn, New York early in 1909 to manufacture and deal in motor cars and to maintain a garage. G.E. Reuners and I.L. Carroll backed this $2500 venture. No automobile followed.

BATTEY & CRICKLER STEAM — Springfield, Massachusetts — (1900) — The steam wagon built by the team of Battey & Crickler of Springfield utilized a 12 hp four-cylinder compound engine and water-tube boiler. Its special features included the mounting of a radiator under the floorboard, the casing of the water pipes so they would not freeze in winter, and a steam condenser "so that no steam shows when running." In November of 1900 Battey & Crickler announced the completion of their car, and the fact that it would be ready for the market in about six weeks. There is no evidence, however, that viable manufacture was embarked upon. In 1903 when Frank E. Battey filed a petition in bankruptcy — with liabilities of $1618.55 and no assets — he indicated his occupation as bicycle repairer. The occupation and the fate of Mr. Crickler is not known.

BATTIN STEAM — Newark, New Jersey — (1861) — Undoubtedly Newark's first car was this steamer owned and driven by Joseph Battin, a well-known hydraulic engineer of the period. Precisely who was responsible for the vehicle's building is not known, but its existence and use were affirmed by an eyewitness, Joseph E. Ralph, and the car was documented in both *Scientific American* and *The Autocar* in 1897. "Mr. Ralph says that . . . Mr. Battin had got rid of the horses which he had been accustomed to use, and had replaced them with a carriage driven by steam," noted *The Autocar*. "It had two seats, and the engineer, who always went out with the machine, occupied the rear seat. The front seat was for the owner, and he did the steering with a round hand wheel in front, something like the grip wheel on a Broadway cable car. The wheel had below it a cog-wheel, and this engaged with a toothed half circle segment that was bolted to the fifth wheel of the front axle. Mr. Ralph says he remembers the steering gear very well, because it took several turns of the steering wheel to bring the wheels around enough to turn a sharp corner, and it required lively work to get the wheels back again in line quickly enough to straighten the course of the carriage before it ran up on the sidewalk. This peculiarity was apt to make a new hand at steering the carriage lose his head." Joseph Battin used the vehicle frequently near his home on Broad Street in Newark, and often drove it around Elizabeth to follow the progress on the waterworks and dam he was building there.

BATTLESHIP — The Battleship was the nickname given to the second experimental four-wheel drive automobile built in Clintonville, Wisconsin by Otto Zachow and William Besserdich in 1908. It was the forerunner of the F.W.D. Refer to F.W.D.

BATTON-DAYTON — The Batton-Dayton Motor Company was organized with a capital stock of $125,000 in December of 1910 for the manufacture and sale of automobiles. W.C. Dayton, M.A. Dayton and E.S. Carr were the incorporators of this venture, which seems never to have gotten off the ground.

BAUER STEAM — Beaver Falls, Pennsylvania — (1901) — Edward H. Bauer was a machinist from Beaver Falls who built a steam car at the turn of the century. One-lever control seems to have been its single distinguishing feature, and little more is known about it than that — and the fact that Edward Bauer never built another.

BAUER — Kansas City, Missouri — (1914-1916) — The Bauer Machine Works Company thought it had the answer. Although the Caps and the Kansas City and the Gleason had all been born and quickly died in the factory into which Bauer moved in 1913, the company was convinced this was because those people had not known the automobile business well and did not plan effectively for the future. This Bauer would do, and proceeded forthwith to build a cyclecar. It lasted a year, and the company then made a valiant try in standard car manufacture but were quickly out of business. There is no record that this Missouri factory was ever used again for the manufacture of automobiles. Bauer decided to stick to machine work thereafter. The Bauer truck which the company also built during it's automotive days appears to have been simply a case of using up Gleason truck parts which had been left behind.

1925 Bauer Taxicab, NAHC

BAUER — Chicago, Illinois — (1925-1927) — The Bauer Taxicab Manufacturing Company of Chicago was organized in 1925 by Price E. Hertz, Perry Bauer and A.L. Belle Isle, the last named described as a taxicab operator from Atlanta, Georgia. Perhaps it was his experience which gave rise to the special features of the Bauer. The cab was referred to as "wreck-proof," this owing to its rigid body construction — and the arrangement of passenger doors was unusual. One was in the usual position, but not openable from the inside. The other door was mounted in the front of the body, hinged to a pillar directly behind the driver's seat. This door opened forward and was said to allow a passenger's entrance and egress without disturbing other occupants of the taxi. Westinghouse supplied air brakes and an emergency electric brake for the car. Otherwise the Bauer was quite conventional, with a four-cylinder Buda engine and 115-inch wheelbase. It was produced for a little over two years. In February 1927 the Chicago Title & Trust Company was appointed the Bauer receiver. The firm's liabilities were about $600,000, though its assets — *Motor Vehicle Monthly* revealed — were sufficient "to pay all creditors in full and leave a balance for stockholders."

1925-1927 BAUER

	FP	5	4	3	2	1
Bauer taxi	—	2700	3600	5300	8800	19,000

1906 Bauman, touring, WFOR

BAUMAN — Dillsburg, Pennsylvania — (c. 1908) — J.A. Bauman was a blacksmith and upholsterer who also did general repair work around Dillsburg and about 1908 completed the car he had begun to build for himself a half decade earlier. Its engine was a 6 hp one-lunger, and its body was a five-passenger touring, and very nicely upholstered. An unusual, and rather dubious, feature was the arrangement for directing the car. A steering wheel was provided, but when it was turned one way, the wheels themselves turned the opposite. Why Bauman built the car thusly is not known, though getting used to it must have taken some doing. On one occasion, a relative he allowed to take the wheel ended up on a front porch.

BAUROTH — The Bauroth of 1899 was simply a misspelling of the New York City-based Blaurock Carriage Company which did build an automobile prior to the turn of the century. Refer to Blaurock.

BAY CITIES — Oakland, California — (1906) — The Bay Cities Automobile Company was organized in Oakland in late 1906 with a capital stock of $25,000 of which $15,000 was subscribed and with the announced plan to "buy, sell, rent, operate, repair and manufacture automobiles, motor cycles and carriages and to conduct a general automobile livery and garage business." The principals behind this venture were W.H. Chapman, Fred S. Jacks, O.B. McKay, E.N. Hartman and Alfred Groves. Fred Jacks had produced a car under his own name at the turn of the century in Napa, California. No manufacture is believed to have resulted from Bay Cities, however.

BAYER — Leavenworth, Kansas — (1905) — The Bayer was a three-wheeler designed by Charles Boyle and built in the shops of the Bayer Brothers Carriage Works in Leavenworth. It was powered by a two-cylinder gasoline engine mounted under the seat and was steered by a tiller. Four examples were produced for a total expenditure of $7000. Of these, one was sold to a carnival company and subsequently shipped overseas, another was purchased by a buyer in Los Angeles, California who paid $350 for it, the third was bought for an undisclosed figure by the Hease Motor Company of Kansas City (Missouri), and the fourth was retained by Henry Bayer. By the end of 1905, Henry Bayer decided that the automobile business was not nearly so easy as he had initially thought, and returned exclusively to the buggy business in which his family had prospered since 1857. Interestingly, when Henry Ford was establishing his museum in Dearborn, Michigan more than two decades later, he offered Harry Bayer $1000 and a new Ford sedan for the Bayer automobile. Harry Bayer refused the offer.

BAYERLINE — At various times between 1912 and 1916. J.F. Bayerline announced impending manufacture of an automobile of his own design. No automobile called the Bayerline ever resulted, however. From 1913 to 1915 Bayerline was instead sitting high up on the corporate ladder at the King Motor Car Company, a perch he vacated that year together with King executive W.L. Daly to begin a venture which ultimately resulted in the Columbia car of Detroit.

BAYERSDORFER — Omaha, Nebraska — (1899) — Otto Bayersdorfer repaired bicycles and was the proprietor of the Bicycle Hospital on North Sixteenth Street in Omaha. In 1899 he built a gasoline automobile weighing only 265 pounds which he sometimes called his Otto-Mobile but which he never had plans to manufacture.

BAYLES — The Bayles Sales Company was organized with a capital stock of $10,000 late in 1911 to make and sell automobiles in New York City. Harry T. Bayles, Halsey K. Smith and Ansela P. Anderson backed this venture. Manufacture is doubted.

BAYLESS — The Bayless Motor Car Company was organized in Lexington, Kentucky late in 1909 with a capital stock of $6500 and the announced plan "to manufacture and deal in automobiles and to conduct a livery and garage business." E.B. Chenault and three people — W.K., T.C. and E.B. — named Bayless were involved. There is no indication that manufacture followed.

BAY STATE — In 1896 in Springfield, Massachusetts, the Bay State Motive Power Company was organized for the manufacture of vehicles designed by L.E. Walkins. Refer to Walkins.
The Bay State Automobile & Engine Company of Boston, Massachusetts was indicated as a manufacturer in the Hiscox book *Horseless Vehicles, Automobiles, Motor Cycles* published in 1900. According to the Boston city directory that year, the firm was headquartered in Room 29 at 7 Exchange Place. Obviously no cars were manufactured there, and details regarding anywhere else they might have been built are lacking. The company is listed in neither the 1899 nor 1900 city directory.
In 1901 the Bay State Automobile and Supply Company was incorporated with a $200,000 capital stock at Brookings, South Dakota. Louis N. Fuller, T. Arthur Fuller and Philo Hall were behind this venture, which is not believed to have produced a car.

1907 Bay State Forty, 7-pass. touring, WLB

BAY STATE — Boston, Massachusetts — (1907-1908) — This car which carried the nickname of the Commonwealth of Massachusetts was a 40 hp $3750 four produced by the Bay State Automobile Company of 112 Norway Street in Boston. Two Bostonians — Rossell Drisko and George Temple — organized the firm in January of 1906 and had their first car on the road precisely one year later. Press reports indicate the Bay State was a well thought out and well finished vehicle. But creditors began pressing for payments in December 1907, and the company did not survive long into 1908.

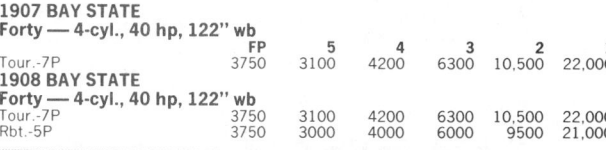

1907 BAY STATE
Forty — 4-cyl., 40 hp, 122" wb

	FP	5	4	3	2	1
Tour.-7P	3750	3100	4200	6300	10,500	22,000

1908 BAY STATE
Forty — 4-cyl., 40 hp, 122" wb

	FP	5	4	3	2	1
Tour.-7P	3750	3100	4200	6300	10,500	22,000
Rbt.-5P	3750	3000	4000	6000	9500	21,000

1923 Bay State, touring, JAC

1923 Bay State, roadster, JAC

1924 Bay State, brougham, JAC

BAY STATE — Framingham, Massachusetts — (1922-1926) — Richard H. Long, who had made his fortune as a shoe manufacturer and canvas/leather goods supplier to the government during World War I, was also a politician. Espousing pet causes was his favored activity, and although he was not always successful, he had a good time doing it. After losing his second gubernatorial race in Massachusetts to Calvin Coolidge, he elected to become an automobile builder. If the question was begged, why? — Richard Long would have replied, why not? He was willing to try just about anything once. The Bay State which resulted was a very fine assembled car designed by Herbert C. Snow, who had previously been an engineer with Peerless, Willys-Overland and Winton. Although usually powered by Continental's Red Seal six-cylinder engine, a Lycoming straight-eight later became available. The Bay State was aimed at a regional market — "Made in Massachusetts" and "A New England Product" were typical slogans. A total of 710 cars were built in 1923. The car enjoyed a modest success for a while thereafter, which was all Richard Long had wished for, but since his R.H. Long Motors Corporation had been undercapitalized at the beginning, the venture couldn't last long. After approximately 2500 units had been built — and 1925 and 1926 cars were simply surplus '24's — he lost everything except one of his factories. In it he established the R.H. Long Motor Sales Company in 1927. This General Motors dealership survives to this day as a family business. The factory in which the Bay State had been built was acquired by the taxicab company which had been building the Luxor there since 1924.

1922 BAY STATE
Model 1 — 6-cyl., 58 hp, 121" wb

	FP	5	4	3	2	1
Cpe.-4P	2400	2500	3500	5000	8500	18,000
Sed.-5P	2500	2300	3300	4600	7500	16,000

1923 BAY STATE
Model 1 — 6-cyl., 58 hp, 121" wb

Tour.-5P	1800	2900	3700	5600	9100	20,000
Rds.-3P	1800	3000	4000	6000	9500	21,000
Cpe.-4P	2400	2700	3600	5300	8800	19,000
Sed.-5P	2500	2300	3300	4600	7500	16,000
Brgm.-5P	2500	2400	3400	4800	8000	17,000
Sed.-7P	2750	2350	3350	4700	7700	16,500

1924-1926 BAY STATE
Model 1 — 6-cyl., 58 hp, 121" wb
Model 2 — 8-cyl., 60 hp, 121" wb

Rds.-3P	1800	3100	4200	6300	10,500	22,000
Tour.-5P	1800	3100	4200	6300	10,500	22,000
Spt. Tour.-5P	2100	3200	4300	6500	11,000	23,000
Cpe.-4P	2500	2700	3600	5300	8800	19,000
Sed.-5P	2500	2300	3300	4600	7500	16,000
Brgm.-5P	2550	2400	3400	4800	8000	17,000
Spt. Sed.-5P	2750	2450	3450	4900	8300	17,500
Sed.-7P (128" wb)	2750	2350	3350	4700	7700	16,500

B.C.K. — The B.C.K. Motor Company was established in 1909 to build an automobile known as the Kline Kar. Refer to Kline Kar.

B.D.A.C. — The initials refer to the Black Diamond Automobile Company which bought out the Buckmobile Company of Utica, New York and continued production of its car in 1904. Although Black Diamond may have built an experimental steam car in 1903, it never marked an automobile under its own name. Refer to Buckmobile.

BEACH — The Beach Motor Vehicle Company has been cited on car rosters as an automobile producer in Everett, Massachusetts in 1900. Everett city directories for the years 1899-1901 reveal the existence of no such company in town.

BEACON — The Beacon Motor Traction Company at 206 Exchange Building in Boston, Massachusetts was listed as an automobile manufacturer in the Hiscox book *Horseless Vehicles, Automobiles, Motor Cycles* published in 1900. This firm, which was a Delaware incorporation, seems to have been a hopeful only. It is not listed in the Boston city directories of this period.
The Beacon was a model of the Continental built in Grand Rapids, Michigan during the early Thirties. Refer to Continental.

BEACON — Beacon, New York — (1917) — In June 1917 Morgan Potter of Beacon decided to go automotive, and in July he decided not to. For over thirty years previous, the Morgan Potter Manufacturing Company had been engaged in manufacturing accessories for the carriage trade; its name was changed to Morgan Potter Motor Company when the decision was made to go horseless. Trucks and truck attachments were to be the new Potter products, with a sideline business of medium-priced, four-cylinder, five-passenger touring cars, all to carry the name Beacon. Whether prototypes of the vehicles were completed is not known, but within a month Morgan Potter had announced his change of plans. Now brakes for trucks were to be the closest the company would come to the automobile field.

1923 Beamer, touring, NAHC

BEAMER — Oakland, California — (1923) — F.C. Beamer was a ship's captain from Oakland who had a rather unusual automobile built for himself in 1923. Its body was a cabin-like construction which could be converted into sleeping quarters by removing the seats. Doubtless he found the boat-like ambience reassuring during his hours away from the sea.

BEAN — Boston, Massachusetts — (1902) — According to the 1901 city directory, Albert E. Bean was a teamster in Boston that year. Apparently he established a little auto shop at 6 Winter Street later that year, because in 1902 he was styling himself the A.E. Bean Automobile Company and announced himself as an automobile manufacturer. Probably by 1903 he was a teamster again.

BEAN-CHAMBERLAIN — Though the Bean-Chamberlain Manufacturing Company was the producing organization behind this steam car built in Hudson, Michigan from 1901-1902, the automobile was marketed under the name of Hudson Steamer. Refer to Hudson Steamer.

1914 Beardsley Electric, coupe & roadster, WLB

BEARDSLEY — Los Angeles, California — (1914-1915)/Culver City, California — (1915-1917) — Volney S. Beardsley was born in the Midwest and entered the automobile field in Ohio as a partner in the Beardsley & Hobbs company which produced the Darling automobile at the turn of the century. Late in 1901, however, Beardsley sold out his interest and headed west, taking on a job with the Auto Vehicle Company, rising to general sales manager by 1906 and becoming president of the firm which succeeded it late in 1909, the California Automobile Company. California was in the manufacturing business only in 1910, continuing parts shortages for the non-Selden-licensed firm being the principal reason that the company functioned as a dealership only beginning in 1911. Among the cars offered was the Columbus Electric. During the summer of 1913 Beardsley decided to become a manufacturer again, of an electric this time. John T. Shannon was hired to design the car, and in October the Beardsley Electric Company was organized, with Beardsley as president and general manager, Watt Moreland (an Auto Vehicle alumnus and now producer of the Moreland truck) as first vice-president. "A somewhat novel spirit seems to have prompted the conception and materialization of this new electric," noted *Automobile Trade Journal* in its introductory article on the Beardsley. And there did seem to be a California flair to the vehicle. California money and California labor produced the car, and it was aimed at a California clientele. A Hollywood-style panache was also seen in its promotion, exemplified by the demonstration run of 1500 miles in 14 consecutive days on 14 battery charges during the summer of 1915. The test driver was Volney Beardsley's wife, and the local press appointed ten observers, all women, to accompany the car on each day of its run. Mrs. Beardsley drove an average of 107.5 miles a day. The Beardsley electric made further news that year as one of the official cars used for transportation within the grounds of the Panama-Pacific Exposition. Commercial vehicles were also introduced, though this venture was absorbed into Moreland's truck company early on. By the fall of 1915, the Beardsley Electric Company had outgrown its original premises, and the factory moved to nearby Culver City. The workforce stood at forty employees, and the firm was prospering. Again, parts shortages (caused by World War I this time) proved troublesome, and combined with the waning popularity of electric cars in general to ultimately result in the Beardsley's demise. The firm's last advertisement appeared in February 1917. Shortly thereafter the Beardsley Electric Company was quietly absorbed into the Moreland Motor Truck Company. California car registrations, and other data, indicate that 160-165 Beardsleys had been built in all.

1914 Beardsley Electric, brougham, NAHC

1915-1916 BEARDSLEY

	FP	5	4	3	2	1
Model 100-B Brgm.-5P	3000	—	—	—	—	18,000
Model 300-B Vic.-5P	2750	—	—	—	—	17,000
Model 200-B Rdstr.-2P	2500	—	—	—	—	18,000

1917 BEARDSLEY

	FP	5	4	3	2	1
Model 100 Brgm.-5P	2650	—	—	—	—	18,000
Model 200 Rdstr.-3P	2250	—	—	—	—	18,000
Model 400 Brgm.-4P	2000	—	—	—	—	17,000
Model 500 Light Rbt.-4P	1285	—	—	—	—	16,500

BEASLEY — The Beasley Company was organized in New York City with a capital stock of $150,000 during the fall of 1911 to both manufacture and deal in automobiles. Incorporators were Robert F. Pratt of Jersey City, and Thomas Moynan and A.E. Beasley of New York City. Manufacture is doubted.

BEATTIE — The Beattie Motor & Wagon Manufacturing Company was organized in Seattle, Washington during the fall of 1912 for the purpose of producing "motor and horsedrawn vehicles." Capital stock was $20,000, and the partners behind the venture were W.J. Beattie and C.W. Burdick. Automobile manufacture has not been established.

BEAU BRUMMEL — Detroit, Michigan — (1917) — The Beau Brummel was built to demonstrate the wares of the Universal Car Equipment Company of Detroit. Details regarding it are lacking; manufacture was never intended. The Universal company was located at 1305 Bellevue Avenue, and William J. Decker was the manager.

BEAVER — Milwaukee, Wisconsin — (1905) — The Beaver Manufacturing Company of Milwaukee was a prominent producer of gasoline engines for the automotive industry. In 1905 the company installed one of its engines in a motor vehicle, but this was strictly for demonstration purposes, and the firm did not proceed into automobile manufacture.

1912 Beaver, touring, WLB

BEAVER — Portland, Oregon — (1912) — "Our first model car, the 'Beaver Six' appeared on the streets of Portland in October 1912," the prospectus to potential investors stated. "It is a high class car with beautiful lines and is a very satisfactory machine." The Beaver State Motor Company had high hopes when earlier that year it was capitalized at $300,000. The man behind it was P.A. Combs, a native of Portland who had been in the automobile supply business in the Beaver State for some time and who believed his fellow Oregonians would snap up his cars by the thousands because of the freight savings afforded by their local production. A factory was being erected in nearby Gresham, and its superintendent would be E.T. "Tom" Fetch, a veteran of twelve years with the Packard Motor Car Company who had become nationally famous as the man who had driven "Old Pacific" from San Francisco to New York in 61 days to establish the transcontinental record for Packard in 1903. That the Beaver may have been as "high class" a car as its makers claimed is indicated by the pro-

spectus photograph of it as well as the fact that it was equipped with the highly regarded Lanchester worm drive, imported from Coventry, England. The company's belief that the Beaver was the first American pleasure car to use the Lanchester worm drive may well have been true, though obviously it was a mixed blessing since problems ensued in obtaining the units in quantity from England. That, other materials shortages and a subsequent lawsuit by Overland for patent infringement, finished the Beaver before it ever saw the assembly line. Interestingly, various motor-car rosters since have listed the company producing another car called the Oregon in 1916, as well as the Beaver as late as 1920. And the factory in Gresham was indeed in operation at least that long, but its products were castings, rail car wheels, sewer pipe, drag saws, cement mixers and gasoline engines. The Beaver automobile never proceeded beyond the prototype stage, and just two examples were built in 1912. The factory wasn't completed before late 1914. Bankruptcy proceedings required nearly a dozen years to complete which is why the Beaver lifespan has heretofore been erroneously lengthened. The two prototypes were sold, and subsequently showed up on California registration lists. One of the cars disappeared during the bankruptcy hassle, the other was burned in a bonfire in 1929.

BECK — C.W. Beck lived at 2572 Lakewood Avenue in Chicago and in 1895 he entered the Chicago Times-Herald Contest with a car of his own design. Alas, he did not make it to the starting line, and documentation has not been discovered indicating the successful completion of his car.

In February of 1908 news reports indicated the Beck & Clausel Company of Memphis, Tennessee was planning to produce the Menges car the prototype for which Albert C. Menges had built the year before in Grand Rapids, Michigan. The deal seems to have fallen through. Refer to Menges.

The Beck Company was incorporated in Rockville Center, Long Island, New York during April of 1910 for the manufacture and sale of cars and motors. Capital stock was $150,000, and the firm's incorporators were W.H. Smith and J.I. Scott of Brooklyn. Manufacture of an automobile has not been established.

BECRAFT — San Francisco, California — (1910) — That A.T. Becraft was engaged in the automobile manufacturing business in San Francisco in 1910 is indicated both in the San Francisco city directory and in the Ware yearbook of the automobile industry published that year. Details regarding the vehicle produced are lacking, but the company's officers included Becraft as president, T. Pilgrim as treasurer, F. Brett as secretary and W.H. Selmidt as general manager.

BEDFORD — The Bedford Automobile Company was organized in Brooklyn, New York during the spring of 1905 with a capital stock of $5000 and the plan to manufacture automobiles. The incorporators were George Shields, F.P.C. Forbes, Jr. and J.C. Forbes, all of Brooklyn. Manufacture is doubted.

Bedford was the proposed name for a light gasoline runabout which was planned to be built in Bedford, Indiana in 1906. E.B. Thornton, W.N. Urmey and J.N. Stron were the president, secretary and superintendent of the automobile company that was in the process of organization that September. Plans apparently fell through shortly thereafter.

The Bedford-Bergen Auto Exchange was organized with a capital stock of $25,000 in Brooklyn, New York late in 1911 to "manufacture automobiles, machinery and motor supplies." M. Keve and R. Brown of Brooklyn, together with C. Goldstein of Manhattan, were the incorporators. Manufacture is doubted.

BEEBE — Chicago, Illinois — (1905-1906) — The Western Motor Truck & Vehicle Company of Chicago began experimenting with horseless carriages at the turn of the century. A few cars may have been sold during this period under the Western name, but the company did not move into manufacture in earnest until 1905 by which time the tradename Beebe had been selected for the product. Two models were built, both powered by a two-cylinder two-stroke Wats engine. Friction transmission was featured, and a 40 mph top speed was claimed for the larger Beebe. What was most unusual about these cars was the method of starting them. A "crankless automatic valve engine starter" was fitted; it was a push-button on the floor of the car which, with a press of the foot, got the Beebe going. What kept it moving smoothly and efficiently, according to the company, was the Beebe's tubular carburetor with a single valve. It was described, almost lyrically, as follows: "The gasoline flows around a special material which absorbs the liquid and effuses from millions of little pores a light gaseous vapor. The air passing of this gas-laden surface pro-

1906 Beebe, runabout, WLB

duces a mixture of great volume, strength and combustible power.'' Neither of these novel features worked well, apparently. The Beebe was out of production by 1907. Interestingly, despite the company's name, it would appear that Western did not build a commercial vehicle until 1906, and its truck fared even more dismally than the Beebe, not proceeding beyond the prototype stage.

1905-1906 BEEBE
Model E — 2-cyl., 30 hp, 100'' wb

	FP	5	4	3	2	1
Side Entrance Tonneau	1250	—	—	—	—	—
Issue No. 3 — 2-cyl., 14 hp, 80'' wb						
Rbt.	650	—	—	—	—	—

BEEBE — St. Clair, Michigan — (1910) — This Beebe's name was John and he was a partner with M.L. Baldwin in the St. Clair machine shop trading under the name of Baldwin & Beebe. In 1910 Beebe completed his design of a car incorporating a transmission of his own invention which the partners said they were building for ''a firm in Detroit.'' The completion and testing of the prototype was to be followed by construction of five more cars, for which Beebe said he already had orders, and he indicated that ''manufacture on a more extensive scale'' might follow. Apparently it did not.

BEEMAN — Valley City, North Dakota — (1900) — O.A. Beeman of Valley City built himself a car in 1900. Its 4½ hp gasoline engine was purchased in Michigan, but the best of the vehicle was his own. Manufacture was not contemplated.

BEETLE FLYER — Noblesville, Indiana — (1909) — In 1909 the Fodrea-Malott Manufacturing Company of Noblesville announced that it would build automobiles to order. Beetle Flyer was the designation given for the car, but other than that it was a motor buggy and with high wheels, specifications are lacking. Orders had apparently stopped coming in for the car by 1910.

1921 Beggs, touring, NAHC

BEGGS — Kansas City, Missouri — (1919-1923) — The Beggs people were long-time buggy and horsedrawn-vehicle builders from Kansas City whose specialty seems to have been ornate and elaborately carved circus wagons. Probably only waning profits from its usual products finally moved Beggs into the automobile industry in 1919. The Beggs Motor Car Company was incorporated that year to build a six powered by the Continental Red Seal engine. The car was ready for the 1920 model year and was introduced in touring and roadster body styles. Sport and closed variations followed for 1921. In July that year several disgruntled stockholders brought suit against Beggs and pressed for receivership. The court, upon hearing the case, decided that on the showing made the company was not insolvent. The receivership was denied. Two years later it was not. Production ceased immediately, though the Beggs case was still in litigation as late as 1926.

1920 BEGGS
Model 20T — 6-cyl., 56 hp, 120'' wb

Tour.-5P	1835	2900	3700	5600	9100	20,000
Rdstr.-4P	1835	3000	4000	6000	9500	21,000

1921-1923 BEGGS
Model 20T — 6-cyl., 56 hp, 120'' wb

Tour.-5P	1520	2900	3700	5600	9500	20,000
Rdstr.-4P	1520	3000	4000	6000	9500	21,000
Spt.-5P	1800	3100	4200	6300	10,500	22,000
Cpe.-3P	2200	2500	3500	5000	8500	18,000
Sed.-5P	2320	2300	3300	4600	7500	16,000

BEGUELIN-BUSCHART — In early July of 1906 the Beguelin-Buschart Motor Car Company moved into the building at 4390 Olive Street in St. Louis, Missouri announcing that it would ''begin business at once, entering directly into the manufacture of automobiles.'' The firm's reins were pulled in a little a few weeks later when word came from St. Louis that Beguelin-Buschart instead would serve as a dealership for the Selden car and would conduct a general repair shop. Most probably the firm never did produce a car of its own.

BEHLEN — Cincinnati, Ohio — (1909) — Charles Behlen Sons' Company of Cincinnati had been long-time carriage builders when, in 1909, the firm decided to add automobiles to its product line. The Behlen was a four-cylinder 24/30 hp, shaft-drive runabout on a 102-inch wheelbase with a $1500 price tag. According to a June issue that year of *The Motor World*, the Behlens' automotive effort was ''well advanced.'' This must have been stretching the truth, since the company was not heard from again in the automotive field.

1909 BEHLEN
Four — 24/30 hp, 102'' wb

	FP	5	4	3	2	1
Rbt.	1500	2500	3500	5000	8500	18,000

1914 Beisel Motorette, roadster, NAHC

BEISEL — Monroe, Michigan — (1914) — The Beisel was a cyclecar powered by a four-cylinder Prugh engine of 95-cubic-inch displacement and undisclosed, though obviously modest, horsepower. It had friction transmission, belt drive, and side-by-side seating for two. In April of 1914 the Beisel Motorette Company announced that its car would be sold through the National United Service Company of Detroit, which had contracted for two years' output. In July the designer of the Beisel, Frank McPhillips, asked for receivership and a dissolution of partnership, claiming he was frozen out of the company. His request was granted.

1914 BEISEL
Motorette — 4-cyl., 96'' wb

Rdstr.-2P	385	2200	3200	4400	7000	15,000

B.E.L. — Middlefield, Connecticut — (1920) — The initials represent Bert E. Lazaro, and the car was one of two produced by Lazaro and his partners who operated under the corporate name of Consolidated Motor Car Company. The other car, called the Sterling, was a $1185 Le Roi-engined four offered as touring and roadster. The B.E.L. carried a 12.1 hp overhead valve four of in-house manufacture and was touted as the company's ''Sport Model.'' Probably one couldn't be very sporting with such a modestly powered car, but this runabout's $495 price tag was modest enough for Consolidated to assume it might be a sure-fire seller. It wasn't. Some trade press directories continued to list the B.E.L. into 1923, but it seems more likely that this venture had come to a swift end earlier.

1921 B.E.L.
B.E.L. — 4-cyl., 12.1 hp, 90'' wb

Rbt.-2P	495	2000	3000	4200	6500	14,000

1909 Belden, tourabout, NAHC

BELDEN — Pittsburgh, Pennsylvania — (1907-1911) — The Belden Motor Car Company of Pittsburgh evolved from the Belden Automobile Transmission Company which had been organized in 1905 by E.H. Belden to exploit a transmission he had patented. When he discovered he didn't have anything new to exploit there, he tried next with a car. The Belden four was launched in 1907 though only a prototype was built that year, and turned into a six for 1908 though full production did not begin until 1909. Early in 1909 *Motor World* rumored a possible involvement of U.S. Steel Corporation with the Belden enterprise, but this never came to pass. Belden's production schedule for 1909 was 100 cars. Although the company also declared itself ready to produce a variety of luxury cars, including a convertible limousine, laudaulette limousine and ''grand limousine,'' it would appear that Belden had enough trouble simply selling his regular line. Finally, in 1911, bargain prices were affixed to two limousines, probably to unload bodies on hand since 1909. The company failed later that year.

1907 BELDEN Four — 30 hp, 124" wb	FP	5	4	3	2	1
Tour.-7P	4500					
1908 BELDEN						
Model A — 6-cyl., 40/50 hp, 127" wb						
Tour.-5P	4800	—	—	—	—	—
Twn. Car-7P	5000	—	—	—	—	—
Model B — 6-cyl., 40/60 hp, 120" wb						
Rds.-3P	4700	—	—	—	—	—
1909 BELDEN						
Model A — 6-cyl., 40/60 hp, 132" wb						
Tour.-7P	6000	3000	4000	6000	9500	21,000
Overland Tour.-5P	5800	2900	3700	5600	9100	20,000
Model B — 6-cyl., 40/60 hp, 120" wb						
Rds.-3P	5700	3100	4200	6300	10,500	22,000
1910 BELDEN						
Model A — 6-cyl., 70 hp, 136" wb						
Tour.-7P	6000	3100	4200	6300	10,500	22,000
Model B — 6-cyl., 50 hp, 132" wb						
Rds.-2/4P	4500	3200	4300	6500	11,000	23,000
1911 BELDEN						
Model A — 6-cyl., 70 hp, 136" wb						
Tour.-7P	6000	3100	4200	6300	10,500	22,000
Limo-7P	6000	2900	3700	5600	9100	20,000
Model B — 6-cyl., 50 hp, 132" wb						
Tour. Rds.-4P	4500	3000	4000	6000	9500	21,000
Tour. Tonneau-5P	4500	2900	3700	5600	9100	20,000
Limo.-6P	4500	2700	3600	5300	8800	19,000

BELFIELD — The Belfield Automobile & Implement Company was organized with a capital stock of $50,000 during the spring of 1911 for the manufacture of "automobiles, parts and farming machinery and implements" in Belfield, North Dakota. L.P. Albrecht, M.A. Dempsey and Fred Weyman were the incorporators. Subsequent manufacture of an automobile is doubted.

BELGER & BOWKER — Natick, Massachusetts — (1900) — At last, the people of Natick thought, their town would be famous for more than just shoes. The reason was the new steam car built by James E. Belger, the baggage master at the Natick railroad station, and Samuel Bowker, a local mechanic. "It makes 1000 revolutions a minute with no more noise than a palm leaf fan," *The Motor Vehicle Review* reported in January of 1900. "The whole mechanism is automatic and there is no necessity of opening the box and lighting a match in a gale of wind in order to start the engine." Francis Bigelow was so impressed with the car that he bought the first one before it was even completed, and it was in his factory off North Main Street that manufacture was expected to begin. But it did not. What happened is not clear, but possibly there was a falling out between Belger and Bowker. Later that year, in September, Harry G. Sleeper of Natick announced the formation of the Bowker Automobile & Machine Company, a Maine incorporation with a capital stock of $10,000 and the plan to manufacture automobiles. But the Bowker without Belger venture does not appear to have produced even a prototype. In 1905 Belger built a gasoline car called the Goodnow.

BELKNAP — Although built in the shops of the Belknap Motor Company of Portland, Maine, this turn of the century electric car was not marketed under the firm's name but rather that of the man who had designed it. Refer to Chapman Electric.

In 1917, in Newark, New Jersey, A.C. Belknap, Inc. was organized with a capital stock of $100,000 for the manufacture of automobiles, engines and boats. Frank and Harold Van Syckle (both of Perth Amboy) and A.C. Belknap of East Orange were the incorporators. Manufacture is doubted.

BELL — In August of 1901 *The Motor Age* reported the building of an automobile by Carl Bell of Greencastle, Indiana. Further details are lacking.

W.L. Bell was one-half of the partnership which produced the Croesus car in Kansas City, Missouri in 1906. Refer to Croesus.

The Bell Locomotive Works in Yonkers, New York announced a capitalization of $20,000 for the manufacture of automobiles during the summer of 1913. H.W. Bell, J.H. Bell, Francis W.G. Bellows were the people involved. Manufacture is doubted.

1916 Bell, touring, MVMA

BELL — York, Pennsylvania — (1916-1921) — The Bell Motor Car Company was organized in June of 1915 and moved into the factory of the former Baily Manufacturing Company in York. Among the people involved in the Bell venture was Ernest T. Gilliard, who had been associated with both the Pullman and Sphinx, also built in York. Gilliard designed the new Bell, which was ready for the 1916 model year. "A four-cylinder car of many attractions," *MoToR* said, and with "remarkably full equipment at the moderate price of $775." An assembled car with GB&S and Continen-

tal engines initially, Herschell-Spillmans from 1919, the Bell sold pleasantly well. In 1918 the company moved into the Pullman factory, when that firm went out of business. But Bell was soon in trouble as well; the company's modest capitalization of $50,000 going in was far too small to allow for any growth potential. Already two different men had occupied the Bell presidential chair, and in June of 1921 there was a third. Charles E. Riess announced that month that he was organizing Riess Motors, Inc. to take over Bell for the production of a new car to be known as the Riess Royal. It was to carry a Herschell-Spillman engine, but otherwise was to be a Bell. The Riess deal fell through, however, and the Bell four tolled for the last time in the early fall of 1921.

1916 BELL Model 16 — 4-cyl., 20 hp, 112" wb	FP	5	4	3	2	1
Tour.-5P	775	2000	3000	4200	6500	14,000
Rds.-2P	775	2100	3100	4300	6800	14,500
1917 BELL						
Model 17 — 4-cyl., 20 hp, 112" wb						
Tour.-5P	875	2000	3000	4200	6500	14,000
Rds.-2P	875	2100	3100	4300	6800	14,500
1918-1919 BELL						
Models 18/19 — 4-cyl., 22.5 hp, 114" wb						
Tour.-5P	995	2200	3200	4400	7000	15,000
Rds.-4P	995	2250	3250	4500	7300	15,500

1921 Bell, touring, WLB

1920-1921 BELL Models 20/21 — 4-cyl., 36 hp, 114" wb						
Tour.-5P	1395	2200	3200	4400	7000	15,000
Rds.-4P	1395	2250	3250	4500	7300	15,500

BELL — New York, New York — (1917) — In April of 1917 the Bell Automobile Corporation was organized as a New York City company with a half-million-dollar capital stock. Its product was to be a car featuring a brand-new powerplant idea. "The engine is of a unique rotary type, the cylinders not rotating in the accepted sense, but preserving their vertical position as they oscillate," *Automobile Topics* reported. "The normal throw of the crankshaft is divided between it and the cylinder oscillations, so that the connecting rods are vertical at all times." Apparently at least a couple of prototypes resulted, because there is evidence that these cars may be extant.

BELLAIRE — The Bellaire Automobile Company was organized in Bellaire, Ohio early in 1913 with a capital stock of $65,000 and the plan to manufacture and deal in automobiles, trucks and gasoline engines. George D. Spragg, J.F. Johnson, George Hill, J.R. Greenlee and W.H. Morris were the people involved. Manufacture has not been documented.

BELLEFONTAINE — Columbus, Ohio — (1900) — Whether the Bellefontaine Carriage Body Company carried through completely with its plans is not known, but possibly a few prototypes resulted. During the summer of 1900, news releases from Columbus revealed that the firm had been purchased by local capitalists to be "utilized as a motor vehicle factory where complete machines will be turned out. The new factory will employ about forty hands at first, but in case of success will increase the force as needed." Apparently the need never arose.

1908 Bellefontaine, touring, NAHC

BELLEFONTAINE — Bellefontaine, Ohio — (1908) — The Bellefontaine of 1908 was successor to the Traveler of 1907, and was built in the same factory by the Bellefontaine Automobile Company. A slightly larger and more expensive car than the Traveler, the Bellefontaine was fitted with a four-cylinder 32 hp engine, selective sliding gear transmisson and shaft drive. A King of Belgium tonneau was the only body style offered, and the price was $2500. The Bellefontaine appears to have been built in 1908 only. Thereafter the company occupied itself as a garage and agency for the cars of other manufacturers until late 1916 when the company was reorganized to again enter the manufacturing field. A.J. Miller was the president, J.H. Welles the vice-president and E.P. Humphreys the secretary-treasurer at that time, and they offered a prize to the person suggesting the best name for their new car. Conceivably a prototype may have been built, but it was never marketed. Instead, by January 1917, Bellefontaine had reentered manufacturing ranks more conveniently by simply merging with the Economy Motor Company of Tiffin, a firm already in manufacture with the Economy Car.

1908 BELLEFONTAINE
Model B-8 — 4-cyl., 32 hp, 112" wb

	FP	5	4	3	2	1
Tour.-5P	2500	—	—	—	—	—

BELLEFONTE — Bellefonte, Pennsylvania — (1913) — During the summer of 1913 ground was broken for a new automobile factory in Bellefonte. The building was to be two stories high, 60 by 384 feet in dimension, and constructed of "native limestone, with a structural steel roof, hence will be almost absolutely fireproof." It was to house the Bellefonte Automobile Manufacturing Company which had just been incorporated with Ernest Blakely as president, William P. Sieg as treasurer and sales manager, L.E. Rice as secretary, Joseph P. Harbold as chief designer and factory manager. Sieg and Harbold were the prime movers behind the project. Earlier Sieg had been involved with the B.C.K. Motor Company, the makers of the Kline Kar in York, Pennsylvania. When that company moved to Richmond, Virginia, Sieg moved with it, but soon decided to return to Pennsylvania and start his own automotive venture. He brought Joe Harbold, who had been B.C.K.'s chief mechanic, back with him. The plan was for the production of 240 cars during Bellefonte's maiden year. But the car died aborning. Possibly a few more pilot models of the Bellefonte Six were built in the company's temporary machine shop before the money ran out. But Bellefonte never did move into its "almost absolutely fireproof" factory. Subsequently Sieg and Harbold were employed awhile at the Lingle Machine Shops producing the Lingle Power Hammer. After the First World War, William P. Sieg began the Titan Metal Manufacturing Company, which became a thriving success.

1912 Belmobile, model A, roadster, WLB

BELMOBILE — Detroit, Michigan — (1912) — The Bell Motor Car Company was organized late in 1911 in Detroit, with offices taken in the Chamber of Commerce Building. Its founders were W.D. Bell, who had spent three years with the Peerless Motor Car Company in Cleveland, and H.R. Fordyce, who had resigned his position as assistant manager of the Buffalo branch of the E-M-F company to join Bell in the venture. The Belmobile was fitted with a two-cylinder 20 hp engine built in unit with a two-speed selective sliding gear transmission. Final drive was by shaft, and the suspension by semi-elliptics in the front, full elliptics in the rear. The Belmobile was offered only as a low, racy semi-torpedo with a fifteen-gallon oval gasoline tank placed behind the seat. Wide fenders joined with the running-boards, and the steering wheel was set at a jaunty angle from its mounting in the dash. There were doors on both sides. The price was $750. The body was finished in blue, the chassis and hood in gray, "a very effective combination," *The Automobile* said. Obviously there had been something ineffective in the company's organization, because the first Belmobile was rushed to completion for exhibition at the Detroit Automobile Show in January 1912, and then quietly faded from the scene thereafter.

BELMONT — New York & Connecticut — (1909-1910) — The Belmont was a four-cylinder $1650 car which, *Cycle and Automobile Trade Journal* said at its introduction, "represents at that price all that any purchaser could expect, and a little more." It was a very finely made car. The problem was in the front office. Dr. C. Baxter Tiley of Tiley Pratt was one of the car's backers, amongst a virtual regiment of others who never could get the Belmont act together. Organized as the Belmont Automobile Manufacturing Company in New Rochelle (New York) in May 1909, the venture had become the Belmont Motor Vehicle Company of Castleton (New York) by late summer. Presumably this was because Arthur C. Cheney offered his

1910 Belmont 30, model B, touring, NAHC

piano action factory as a manufacturing site in exchange for becoming Belmont's secretary-treasurer. Something went wrong there, however, because by early 1910 the venture had become the Belmont Automobile Manufacturing Company again and had moved to New Haven (Connecticut). Brochures indicate the office staff was perhaps kept busiest rubber-stamping new company names and addresses on promotional material. Another problem which might ultimately have led to the Belmont's demise was the unfailing belief that so mechanically perfect was the product "we will replace, at any time, any defective part, except tires, at our own expense." A new model to be called the Liberty was projected for 1910. But time ran out. The company was reported to be bankrupt in New Haven in August of 1910. In September it was reported to be trying a comeback in Castleton. There were no further reports.

1909-1910 BELMONT
Thirty — 4-cyl., 30 hp, 110" wb

	FP	5	4	3	2	1
Model A Tonneau-4P	1650	—	—	—	—	17,000
Model B Tour.-5P	1650	—	—	—	—	17,000

BELMONT — Wyandotte, Michigan — (1916) — Whose idea the Belmont Electric Automobile Company was has not been determined, but the venture appears to have been begun even without the proverbial shoestring. In March of 1916, several months after the initial announcement of the firm, it was revealed that J.H. Bishop, described as a "wealthy citizen of Wyandotte," had come to the rescue with a fresh infusion of capital — and the Belmont presidential chair was his. The Belmont was a gas-electric offered as a limousine and a light delivery, either of which was claimed to travel seventy-five miles between charges. The price range was a modest $985-$1600, and a "charging plant" was also available for $150. The Belmont was not continued in 1917. Its place of manufacture was said to have been the Murphy Machine Shop in Wyandotte.

1916 BELMONT

Limo.-4P	1400	2500	3500	5000	8500	18,000
Limo.-6P	1600	2600	3700	5200	8700	18,500
Light Delivery	985	—	—	—	—	—

BELMONT — Lewiston, Pennsylvania — (1919) — The Belmont Motors Corporation (later Belmont Motor Company) of Lewiston has been indicated on various rosters as having produced an automobile from 1919-1922. This does not seem to have been the case. In the fall of 1918 the firm did purchase the defunct Dile Motor Car Company of Reading, and briefly considered the manufacture of an automobile. Possibly a few Dile-like prototypes were assembled from leftover Dile parts. But in March of 1920, when Belmont was reported to be searching for additional working capital in order to get into production on a quantity scale, its product was indicated to be a truck only. Later that year the company's factory burned down which left Belmont without a home until the summer of 1922 when the North American Tannery in Lewistown was remodeled for that purpose. Again, trucks were indicated as the firm's sole product.

BELMONT SIX — Toledo, Ohio — (1917) — With a capitalization of $125,000, A.T. Wilson and R.W. Beaschler organized the Belmont Motor Company of Toledo in 1917. Andrew A. Lehr, formerly of Pope-Toledo, was installed as president and general manager. He was also the designer of the new Belmont Six, which carried a Buda engine, and featured Hotchkiss drive and was expected to be priced at $1750. "The two final experimental jobs are running over the roads in the South at the present time," the company announced in March 1917, "and matters are being cleared away preliminary to a campaign to obtain dealers and a final selection of all the component parts in the car." An advertisement followed in May. Because nothing further was heard from Belmont, it is probable only those two prototypes were ever built.

BELT — Fredonia, Kansas — (1904-1909) — Precisely when P.P. Belt built his automobile is not known, but this machinist and bicycle repairman from Fredonia was listed in the *State Gazetteer* between the years 1904 and 1909, so undoubtedly his vehicle was built during that period. The Belt car was gasoline powered, wagon-like in appearance, used a wheel for steering, and rode on wooden wheels shod with solid rubber tires. P.P. Belt is also known to have built a single-seater airplane.

BELVIDERE — Belvidere was the name of the bicycle produced by the National Sewing Machine Company of Belvidere, Illinois. The automobile produced by the firm beginning in 1903 was not a Belvidere, however. Instead it was named for the company's president. Refer to Eldredge.

1919 Bender Special, MVMA

1934 Bendix, model SWC, 4-dr. sedan, NAHC

BENDER SPECIAL — Chicago, Illinois — (1919) — The Ahlberg Bearing Company had been regrinding annular ball bearings in Chicago since about 1910, and in 1919 built a car to advertise its service. A two-seater roadster dubbed the Bender Special and fitted with a Buda four-cylinder engine, it was claimed capable of a 70 mph speed along Chicago's boulevards, and carried the legend "We Make Old Ones New" on its side-mounted spare-wheel cover. As noted in the trade press, "the machine is fitted throughout with Ahlberg remade ball bearings, which demonstrates the mechanical value of the restoration processes of the Ahlberg company."

BENDIX — Benton Harbor, Michigan — (1934) — Vincent Bendix's second car was built as a "traveling showcase" for his company's products. It traveled a good deal, throughout the United States in 1934 and on a tour of Europe in 1935. With streamlined Airflow-like styling, the car featured an electric vacuum gearshift, built-in ventilation system, front wheel drive, four-wheel hydraulic brakes, a clock in the steering wheel hub, and distinctive hubcaps which a generation later would have been called "mag" wheels. With the coming of the Second World War, the car was put into storage from which it was retrieved in 1974 to be put on display at the Bendix Automotive Development Center near New Carlisle, Indiana.

1934 BENDIX

Bendix "Traveling Showcase"	FP	5	4	3	2	1
	—	—	—	—	—	—

1909 Bendix, gentleman's roadster, JAC

1914 Benham Six, roadster, WLB

BENDIX — Chicago & Logansport, Indiana — (1908-1909) — Vincent Bendix was born in Moline, Illinois in 1883, left home at age sixteen to become an elevator operator in New York City, joined aircraft pioneer Glenn Curtiss in a motorcycle manufacturing venture in 1901, and in 1905 returned to the Midwest to become sales manager for the Holsman Automobile Company in Chicago. Two years thereafter, he and a Holsman colleague joined together to establish the Bendix Company. In addition to purchasing the plant and assets of the Triumph Motor Car Company of Chicago and continuing that car in production, Vincent Bendix built two new cars beginning in 1908. The first was called the Duplex. The second carried his name. Bendix designed a double disc friction transmission for it the change speed mechanism of which could also be used for braking. A variation of this principle was used in the Duplex too. In November 1908 the Bendix Company located its factory in Logansport and added a line of Hi-Lo models (high wheels, low center of gravity). Approximately 7000 cars were built before both the Bendix and the Duplex were discontinued in 1909. In 1910 Vincent Bendix joined F.A. Ames in his automobile venture in Owensboro, Kentucky — and thereafter went on to considerable fame and fortune, with the Bendix name appearing on magnetos, generators and braking systems for both automotive and aviation use, in addition of course to laundry machines. A second Bendix car was built as a showcase for Bendix automotive products in 1934. Vincent Bendix died in 1945.

1908 BENDIX
Four — 20/24 hp, 103" wb

	FP	5	4	3	2	1
No. 4 Gentleman's Rds.	1250	2400	3400	4800	8000	17,000
No. 5 Surrey	1350	2450	3450	4900	8300	17,500

1909 BENDIX
Four — 30 hp, 102" wb

No. 4 Gentleman's Rds.	1400	2400	3400	4800	8000	17,000
No. 5 Surrey	1500	2450	3450	4900	8300	17,500

Hi-Lo — 4-cyl., 40 hp, 102" wb

No. 9-H Rds.-3P	1500	2400	3400	4800	8000	17,000
No. 9-L Rds.-2P	1500	2400	3400	4800	8000	17,000

BENHAM — Detroit, Michigan — (1914) — The Benham was a revival of the S & M. In January of 1914 the assets of the bankrupt S & M Motor Company of Detroit were purchased by George Benham. Although Benham was stated to be a mechanical and electrical engineering graduate of the University of Michigan (class of '97), he does not appear to have engineered much in the new Benham. Its specifications were the same as the former S & M, with a new radiator badge and detail changes. In September of 1914, after assembling nineteen of these cars, Benham asked the circuit court in Detroit for permission to dissolve his Benham Manufacturing Company. Its assets, which included leftover steering gears which Benham had also produced, totaled $109,452. Its liabilities, which could not be verified, were at least $76,889. Benham remained in the automobile field, although never again as a manufacturer. During the Second World War, although now well into his sixties, he worked as a Navy inspector in the Hudson factory. In later years he alluded to the building of sixty automobiles, although this total undoubtedly included the forty S & M's upon which his Benham was based. Five Benhams were registered in California during the World War I years.

1914 BENHAM
Model 6-48 — 6-cyl., 48 hp, 130" wb

Rds.-2P	2485	2900	3700	5600	9100	20,000
Tour.-5P	2485	2700	3600	5300	8800	19,000
Twn. Car-7P	2535	2400	3400	4800	8000	17,000

BEN HUR — The Ben Hur Motor Company was organized in Chicago during the fall of 1906 with a capital stock of $50,000 and the plan to manufacture and deal in automobiles and motor boats. Incorporators were J. Herbert Hopp, Albert A. Barrett and C. Glenn Moats. Subsequent manufacture has not been established.

BEN HUR — Willoughby, Ohio — (1917-1918) — L.L. Allen elected for a name more dramatic than his own for his motorcar and his Ben Hur Motor Company had its first cars on the road for the 1917 model season. In February of 1918 Allen announced that between thirty and forty cars had already been shipped, and that present plans called for five to ten cars per week for the time being, owing to the "difficulty in securing bodies." The factory had a twenty-car-per-day capacity, however, and a stockholders meeting was scheduled to be held in March to vote upon a proposed increase in capitalization from one million dollars to six — and to get things moving. Whether that meeting was ever held is not known. The company was in the hands of the receiver by May. Meantime, B.P. Bagby, who had designed the Ben Hur, moved to Missouri to design the Kay-See.

1917 Ben Hur, 7-pass. touring, WLB

1917 BEN HUR
Six — 29 hp, 126" wb

	FP	5	4	3	2	1
Rds.-2P	1875	2600	3550	5200	8700	18,500
Cloverleaf Rds.-4P	1875	2700	3600	5300	8800	19,000
Tour.-7P	1875	2500	3500	5000	8500	18,000
Tour. Sed.-7P	2750	1800	2800	4000	6200	13,000

BENJAMIN — C. Arthur Benjamin, Inc. of Syracuse, New York was organized early in 1909 to manufacture, sell and rent automobiles. Capital stock was $5000, and the incorporators in addition to Benjamin were Forman Wilkinson and Alvie G. Williams. A Benjamin automobile does not seem to have resulted from this venture, although C. Arthur Benjamin had been involved earlier in other enterprises in Syracuse which did produce automobiles, the Syracuse Automobile Company among them.

1909 Benner, Six, roadster, NAHC

BENNER — New York, New York — (1909) — R.P. Benner was a machinist who took hundreds of engines apart in his little auto repair shop in New York City and after eight years of studying them came up with something he thought was better. It was an overhead valve 25-30 hp six that he put into a commodious four-passenger touring car. He incorporated the Benner Motor Car Company in May 1908 with a capital stock of $40,000, and was into production by October. "This car comes into a market that is already pretty well crowded," he said. "It puts forth its claim for public attention in a small but earnest voice among a large and confused chorus making similar claims." In addition to being a well-built car, the Benner claim for attention seemed reasonable. Marketing was confined entirely to the New York City area; all cars were sold from the factory at 1677 Broadway, there were no showrooms or agencies. The absence of middlemen made for an attractive selling price of $1750 for the Benner Six. Approximately 200 units were built.

1909 BENNER
Six — 25/30 hp, 100" wb

Model A Rbt.-2P	1750	2500	3500	5000	8500	18,000
Model B Rdstr.-3P	1750	2500	3500	5000	8500	18,000
Model C Tourabout-4P	1800	2600	3550	5200	8700	18,500

BENNETT — Findlay, Ohio — (1898) — Harry Bennett of Findlay motorized a bicycle in 1896 and followed with a four-wheeler in 1898. This was his first and only automobile. Subsequently Bennett established an agency in Toledo for the Elmore which was built in Clyde, and in 1911 organized Bennett Electric, Inc. in Norwalk which sold and repaired magnetos and batteries for automobiles and which he operated until his death, at age eighty-two, in 1960.

BENNETT-BIRD — The Bennett-Bird Company was organized in late 1904 in Chicago with a capital stock of $10,000 and the announced intention of manufacturing automobiles. Arthur G. Bennett and George H. Bird were the principals involved, but despite their intention manufacture did not follow. Almost immediately, the company took over quarters at 1404-1406 Michigan Avenue and there a Premier dealership was established. Subsequently, the firm also handled the Corbin and Dolson. There never was a Bennett-Bird automobile.

BENNETT-HUTCHINS — Los Angeles, California — (1906) — Old bicycle and motorcycle parts were the components of this car built in 1906 by Ernest Bennett and G.C. Hutchins of Los Angeles. Its 2 hp engine was an air-cooled Thor tweaked a bit for better performance. It was placed on the frame between the front wheels. Pulley and belt drive was used, with a coaster brake on the rear wheels. There was no differential on the rear axle. Springs were provided on the rear wheels only, and steering was by tiller. The car was said to be a particularly effective hillclimber. So far as is known, it was the only example built.

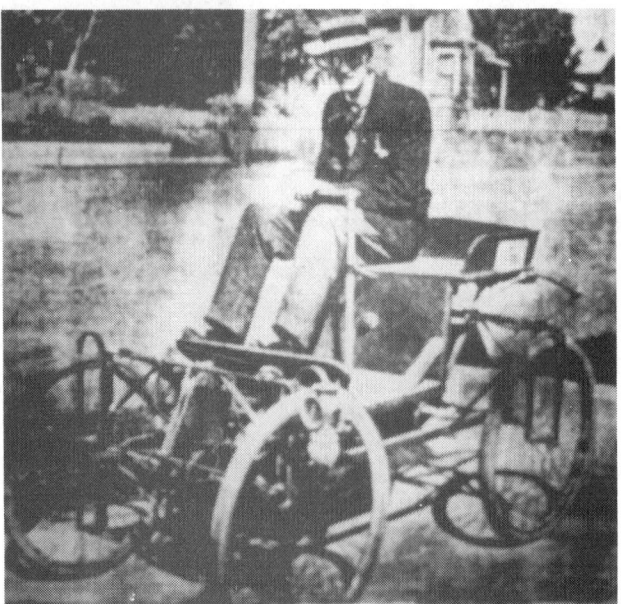
1906 Bennett-Hutchins, runabout, JHV

BENNINGHOF — The Benninghof-Nolan Company was organized in Evansville, Indiana during the fall of 1904 for the manufacture of automobiles. Ten thousand dollars was the capital stock, and B.P. Benninghof and the brothers Nolan — J.J. and V.F. — were the people involved. Subsequent manufacture has not been established.

BENOIT — Benson, Minnesota — (1902) — Although he may have built as many as twenty stationary gasoline engines, it appears that J.B.A. Benoit built just one car in Benson, Minnesota. It was the first automobile in Swift County and Benoit put the runabout together in his general repair shop. In a race against an automobilist from Appleton during the 1902 Fourth of July celebration in Benson, J.B.A. Benoit won handily.

BENSON — The Benson Automobile Company of Cleveland was organized in March of 1901 to take over the steam car department of the Eastman Automobile Company, Henry F. Eastman having decided to confine all future efforts to the building of all metal bodies only. The transfer was completed by May with A.M. Benson (a manufacturer of stave machinery) joined in this new enterprise by L.P. McLouth (a former Eastman official) and Edward F. Hamm and H.P. Shupe (old bicycle men). A factory at 102 Canal Street in Cleveland was outfitted for manufacture of the former Eastman, which was modified only in detail to become the new Benson. It featured a semi-flash boiler, a Kelly burner, an Eastman all-steel body, and a $750 price tag. The first Benson was being tested on Cleveland streets later in May, and at least a dozen more were built before year's end. The venture does not seem to have survived into 1902, however.

1901 BENSON

	FP	5	4	3	2	1
Benson	—	2000	3000	4200	6500	14,000

1901 Benson, (Chicago), runabout, MVMA

110

BENSON — Chicago, Illinois — (1901) — Andrew and John B. Benson were the designers of a small gasoline runabout which was "amply protected by patents," they said, and "thoroughly practical." Its one distinguishing feature was the use of a single lever to do just about everything. As described by Benson, "a detachable spade handle is used, which, when inserted into the lever and given a one-fourth turn, automatically sets in motion the entire mechanism, including the engine, gas feeder and igniters, while the carriage remains motionless. The power is then transmitted to the rear axle by moving the lever down . . . the carriage is run backward by giving the rung of the spade handle a one-fourth turn, which instantly reverses the engine and all the mechanism." This ingenuity attracted the attention of R.P. Price & Company of 156 East Washington Street in Chicago. In July of 1901, Price stated that he planned to form another company for manufacture of the Benson car. Those plans fell through. In 1902 the Snell Cycle Fitting Company of Toledo, Ohio indicated interest in the Benson, but again production did not follow, and by 1903 Snell had allied with another bicycle builder in Toledo in manufacture of the Yale car. Probably the only Benson built was the prototype.

BENTEL — Pittsburgh, Pennsylvania — (1900-1901) — The Theodore F. Bentel Company, Ltd. was the grand title for one of the largest bicycle houses in Pittsburgh. In 1900 the firm negotiated with an inventor of a steam car "designed with a view to adaptability to the heavy roads and steep hills of Western Pennsylvania." Theodore Bentel oversaw the testing of the machine and following that made a trip through East Coast cities, as he said, "with a view to picking up any other good vehicle I can find." According to *The Motor Vehicle Review* in June 1900, "His new store at Sixth Street and Duquesne Way was selected with the view of providing a fine motor vehicle theater." Early in 1901, with his wife, Annie T. Bentel and Thomas J. and Lillie B. Jones as incorporators, Bentel was granted a charter to manufacture motor vehicles. Some production of a steam car called the Bentel did follow, but it would appear the company operated principally as a dealership for other manufacturers' cars.

$10,000 car was built

1919 Bentel, touring, WLB

BENTEL — Los Angeles, California — (1916-1919) — George R. Bentel was the Los Angeles distributor for the Mercer, and beginning late in 1916 he began offering specially-designed Mercers himself. Rather like C.T. Silver on the East Coast, Bentel's cars had a distinctly sporting and rakish flavor. He did away with running boards in most of them, and provided a disappearing top in open cars. The brass or nickel finish disc wheels he designed were a particular point of pride, and adaptable over wood or wire spokes. "The disc is not a part of the wheel, but simply a plate that is attached, one on each side," explained *Motor Age*. "Besides keeping out dirt and grime, the highly polished finish gives a decidedly scintillating effect to the wheels, when in motion." When the First World War brought materials shortages to the industry, Bentel made a fortune devising new cars out of old ones, selling the results for as high as $10,000. By early 1918 he had ceased being a seller of automobiles and was a custom builder exclusively instead. Among other agencies he had acquired in the meantime were Simplex and Jordan, and many of his new creations were on their chassis. According to *Motor World* in late 1918, Bentel "introduced wire wheels to the Pacific Coast, was first to build Victoria tops, was first to put disks on wheels, first to make tonneau windshields, first to make a roller curtain top." That Bentel's taste in motorcars was a refined one was indicated as early as 1907 when he handled the agency on the West Coast for the American Mercedes. And that he was a sporting blade was indicated by his specially-disguised Mercers which, circa 1915-1916, were campaigned under the name of California, as the fourth car when race regulations limited a team's entry to three.

BENTON — Benton, Illinois — (1913) — The Benton of 1913 was the Stuyvesant of 1912. This car, which presumably was to present a marvelous new industry for the town of Benton, Illinois, was promoted by Harry Stotlar, W.S. Cantrell and A.H. Fraunfelder, who incorporated the Benton Motor Car Company with a capital stock of $65,000 in October 1912. Which member of this trio appeared in Benton is not known, but as local legend has it, he was not there long. Brochures for the new Benton were printed (using Stuyvesant Six photographs), and a Stuyvesant Six touring car was paraded through town as a "Made in Benton" automobile. Stock in this new venture was sold, naturally. Then, as the *Benton Evening News* later remarked "the promoter and his car drove off in the sunset, never to be seen again."

BENTON — Athol, Massachusetts — (1904) — In 1904 George Benton was described as a "hermit automanufacturer who has erected a small cabin and workshop in the deep woods on Chestnut Hill" in Athol. The quotation is from the February 11th edition that year of the *New York American*, and how word of this recluse in Massachusetts reached a Manhattan newspaper is something of a mystery. In any case, several New York reporters visited Benton in his cabin in the woods, where his only companion was a big yellow dog and his pride and joy was an automobile he had built. The newsmen were allowed to see the car which they subsequently described as resembling "an antique Roman chariot." Benton made every piece of the vehicle himself, including its water-cooled 6 hp gasoline engine, He whittled the wood for the wheel spokes, and made the tires out of newspapers clamped and chiseled into shape. He planned to place the car on the market for $600. But this "hermit automanufacturer's" dream died with him. Only the one car was built. He spent the remainder of his life tinkering with other automotive inventions and seeing to his few material necessities with blacksmith work for farmers in the area.

1896 Benton Harbor Motor Carriage, auto-buggy, NAHC

BENTON HARBOR — Benton Harbor, Michigan — (1896) — A. Baushke and his brothers rather grandly claimed to have been experimenting with horseless carriages since 1884. Their Benton Harbor Motor Carriage Company did build a center-tiller-steered two-seater buggy powered by a 7 1/2 hp hydro-carbon motor in 1896. They may also have built an electric. It would appear the brothers never proceeded beyond the experimental stage with any of their vehicles, however.

1900 Benz Spirit, MVMA

BENZ SPIRIT — Columbus, Ohio — (1900) — The Columbus Automobile Company was located at 32 South Front Street in Columbus. At the turn of the century the firm built a version of the German Benz one model of which bore the Frenchy designation "Le Duc." Its engine was a 5 hp one-lunger, its coachwork was a good-looking runabout style, and its price was $1700. Deviations from the Benz norm were minimal, though the car's tiller steering was of the Columbus company's own design. "The Columbus Company say that they are in a position to deliver anything from a light racing carriage to a heavy truck within 60 days after receipt of order, and at prices ranging from $1000-$5000," reported *Cycle and Automobile Trade Journal*. Despite such heady ambition, or possibly because of it, the Columbus Automobile Company didn't remain a factor in Ohio industry circles long.

BERG — The Berg Carriage of Dallas City, Illinois was reported to be "making ready to build automobiles" in the summer of 1909. That reference from *The Motor World* was correct except for the typographical error in the firm's name. Refer to Burg.

111

1903 Berg, limousine, WLB

BERG — Cleveland, Ohio — (1903-1905) — In the fall of 1902 Hart O. Berg of New York City announced that he would soon be placing two cars "of foreign type" on the market. The first one to arrive was the Berg. It was built in Ohio by the Berg Automobile Company which was set up in Cleveland following the building of pilot models by the Cleveland Machine Screw Company. Among the company's investors were John Wylie, August Treadwell and J.E. Hays; the firm was capitalized at $400,000, and the new car was introduced at the New York Automobile Show in January 1903. Early Bergs sported gilled tube radiators and double chain drive; vertical honeycomb radiators and shaft drive followed on later models. Seldom has imitation been more unabashedly acknowledged; a Berg advertisement referred to its product as "almost an exact copy of the Panhard." That this was perfectly acceptable to the French company is indicated by the fact that on a trip to France in 1904 Berg received the Legion of Honor. It was in 1904, too, that Berg introduced his second car, built also in Cleveland, and called the Euclid. Apparently, Robert Jardine, who designed the Berg, designed the Euclid as well. That same year Berg sold out to the Worthington Automobile Company of New York which continued to build the Berg into early 1905, and also produced the Meteor and Worthington cars. Robert Jardine went on to design the Royal Tourist car in Cleveland; Hart Berg became a subsequent financial backer, and partner, of the Wright brothers.

1903 BERG
2-cyl., 8 hp, 78" wb

	FP	5	4	3	2	1
Rbt.	1750	1800	2800	4000	6200	13,000
4-cyl., 15 hp, 90" wb						
Tour.	2750	2000	3000	4200	6500	14,000

Pric

1904 Berg, touring, JAC

1904 BERG
4-cyl., 24 hp, 96" wb

Tour.	3500	2200	3200	4400	7000	15,000
1905 BERG						
4-cyl., 24 hp, 96" wb						
Side Entrance Tonneau	3000	2200	3200	4400	7000	15,000
Rear Entrance Tonneau	2750	2200	3200	4400	7000	15,000

BERG ELECTRIC — New York, New York — (1920-1921) — "The Last Word in Automotive Efficiency," as the Berg Electric Car Company called its product, was introduced at the New York Electrical Exposition in October of 1920. Although a town car was to be offered to the general public, Berg was convinced its real success would result from its new idea in taxicabs. "Charging stations will be provided by the central station, electric light companies, at all public cab stands and hotels," the company said,

"where a plug will be inserted into the batteries while the cab is idle, so that the batteries can be kept at practically full charge at all times." Moreover, Berg proposed to supply a taxi operating company's garage with a battery changing device capable of removing an exhausted battery and inserting a "fresh sixty-mile" battery in two minutes time. Although very sophisticated market research had been carried out prior to the Berg's introduction, the company still did not last out a year.

1920-1921 BERG ELECTRIC

	FP	5	4	3	2	1
Berg Electric Twn. Car	2650	2400	3400	4800	8000	17,000
Berg Electric Taxicab	—	2300	3300	4600	7500	16,000

BERGDOLL — The Bergdoll, Ambler Company was organized with a capital stock of $100,000 for the manufacture of automobiles during the spring of 1906. Incorporators were J.A. McPeak, F.R. Hansell and G.H.B. Martin of Camden, New Jersey, who undoubtedly were fronting for the Bergdoll brothers and a Mr. or Messrs. Ambler. No manufacture seems to have resulted of this venture, though the Bergdoll brothers did subsequently enter the automobile field in 1910.

BERGDOLL — Philadelphia, Pennsylvania — (1910-1913) — The Bergdoll brothers were from Main Line Philadelphia society and had the wherewithal to buy the best European cars available, which they did and which they raced, Erwin Bergdoll to more prominent success than Louis J. or Grover Cleveland. The Louis J. Bergdoll Motor Company became the middle brother's pet project, and he produced some of the finest high-quality automobiles in America prior to the First World War. The downtown Philadelphia factory at 16th and Callowhill streets was splendid, a seven-story reinforced concrete and steel structure with over 100,000 square feet of floor space. From there came the four-cylinder Models 30 and 40 guaranteeing 50 and 60 mph respectively. Annular ball bearings throughout, a full floating rear axle and extremely large brakes were featured in the Model 30; the Model 40 had a self-starter in 1912. Building the Bergdoll well apparently proved easier than administering its business affairs. The company went into receivership in March 1913, and its magnificent factory and everything inside was sold to an undisclosed party in mid-May for $45,062. There was a try by Louis Bergdoll at reorganizing, which included a projected move to Trenton, New Jersey. This never materialized. Possibly the last few Bergdolls were assembled in 1913-1914 at the brothers' Erwin Motor & Machine Company elsewhere in Philadelphia.

1910 BERGDOLL
Thirty — 4-cyl., 30 hp, 112" wb

Tour.-5P	1500	2500	3500	5000	8500	18,000

1911 Bergdoll, touring, HAC

1911 BERGDOLL
Thirty — 4-cyl., 30 hp, 115" wb

Tour.-5P	1500	2500	3500	5000	8500	18,000
Toy Tonneau-4P	1600	2600	3550	5200	8700	18,500
Rds.-3P	1500	2700	3600	5300	8800	19,000
Louis J. Rds.-2P	1600	2700	3600	5300	8800	19,000
Limo.-7P	2500	2300	3300	4600	7500	16,000
Land'et.-7P	2600	2400	3400	4800	8000	17,000
Cpe.-2P	2000	2200	3200	4400	7000	15,000
Colonial Cpe.-3P	2500	2250	3250	4500	7300	15,500
Fore-Door Tour.-5P	1600	2300	3300	4600	7500	16,000

1912 Bergdoll, Louis J, roadster, HAC

1912 BERGDOLL
Thirty — 4-cyl., 30 hp, 115" wb

	FP	5	4	3	2	1
Tour.	1500	2300	3300	4600	7500	16,000
Toy Tonneau	1500	2350	3350	4700	7700	16,500
Louis J. Rds.	1500	2400	3400	4800	8000	17,000

Forty — 4-cyl., 40 hp, 115" wb

Tour.	1900	2300	3300	4600	7500	16,000
Torpedo	1900	2300	3300	4600	7500	16,000
Limo.	3000	2200	3200	4400	7000	150,000
Cpe.	2500	2000	3000	4200	6500	14,000

1913 BERGDOLL
Thirty — 4-cyl., 30 hp, 115" wb

Tour.-5P	1600	2300	3300	4600	7500	16,000
Torpedo-4P	1600	2300	3300	4600	7500	16,000

Forty — 4-cyl., 40 hp, 115" wb

Tour.-5P	1800	3000	5900	9900	13,800	19,800
Rds.-2P	1800	2500	3500	5000	8500	18,000
Torpedo Tour.-5P	2500	2400	3400	4800	8000	17,000
Fairmount Tour.-7P	2000	2400	3400	4800	8000	17,000
Fairmount Rds.-2P	2000	2400	3400	4800	8000	17,000
Fairmount Colonial Cpe.-4P	3250	2200	3200	4400	7000	15,000

BERGEN — Two ventures with the Bergen name were organized in Jersey City, New Jersey neither of which seems to have produced a car, despite the announced intention of doing so.

The Bergen and West Side Automobile Company of late 1905 incorporated with a capital stock of $9000 by Walter G. Russell, Albert Lanly and Miniford Green.

The Bergen and West Side Motor Car Company incorporated with a capital stock of $100,000 in the fall of 1909 by Charles E. Collard, Martha L. Collard and Beverly D. Sparks.

BERGER — The Berger Taxicab Company was organized with a capital stock of $25,000 early in 1909 to manufacture and rent "automobiles, wagon trucks, carriages, etc." H.A. Berger, W. Wing and P. Wilds were behind this venture. Manufacture is doubted.

BERGER — Canton, Ohio — (1899) — Early in 1899 J.A. Berger of the Berger Manufacturing Company in Canton began experimenting with a gasoline carriage. By that fall, the vehicle was almost ready for a trial run; "much is expected of it by Mr. Berger," reported *The Autobain*. Expectation apparently led to disappointment, however, because J.A. Berger does not seem to have built another car. His manufacture of automobile specialties and sheet metal work prospered, to Berger's personal good fortune, and in 1909 he again gave brief thoughts to becoming an automobile manufacturer, announcing an increase of his company's stock from $2 million to $5 million for that purpose. Again, the expectation was not fulfilled. Today the Berger company is a division of Republic Steel.

1932 Bergholt, sedan, SIA

BERGHOLT — Minneapolis, Minnesota — (1932) — It was elegant and sleek, and the perfect car to use to publicize his cosmetics business, but most probably Fred Bergholt built his car principally because he wanted to. Seven aspects of its design were patented, and the one car produced used a 1932 Ford V-8 chassis as its basis. The coachwork, however, was purely Bergholt, and as streamlined as the 1933 Pierce Silver Arrow. The car required nearly five months and $3000 to build, and was used extensively to promote the products of Bergholt Laboratories. "At one time I took the car to Detroit and visited several auto manufacturers," Fred Bergholt told *Special Interest Autos* in 1971. "A lot of big Detroit men rode in the car, and most were interested, but they said it was too far ahead of its time — to come back in four to five years. Meanwhile, they infringed on some of my patents, so we sued for $1.5 million and finally settled for a token amount, but it's okay because we've had a lot of fun with that car." The Bergholt remains extant.

BERGSTROM — Minneapolis, Minnesota — (circa 1896) — Oscar Bergstrom of Minneapolis had been a spectator at the Chicago Times-Herald Contest of 1895 which inspired him to build one of the first cars in the state of Minnesota. Exactly when he completed it is not certain, but a surviving photograph indicates that bicycle parts were largely used in its construction. Though Oscar Bergstrom believed the result to be "a wonderful machine," he did encounter some problems in operating it, none of them the car's fault. As he explained to reporters later, "after I made a couple of test runs, it became necessary for me to push the car away from home several blocks as my neighbors threatened to lynch me if I continued to make so much noise, and I was always careful to take a new direction, seeking new victims each time."

1904 Berkeley, tonneau, WLB

BERKELEY — The Berkeley was one of a number of kit cars produced by the Neustadt-Perry Company of St. Louis, Missouri during 1903-1904. Refer to Neustadt.

1906 Berkshire, model B, touring, HAC

BERKSHIRE — Pittsfield, Massachusetts — (1905-1911) / Cambridge, Massachusetts — (1912) — "Made and tested in the Berkshire hills" was the company slogan, with the accompanying claim that any vehicle to negotiate those grades would "do good work anywhere." Although the first Berkshire was completed in 1903, production did not begin until late 1904 after sufficient capital had been secured by company founders Dr. William J. Mercer, Frank V. Whyland, Fred A. Cooley and Clarence P. Hollister. The Messrs. Whyland and Hollister had formerly worked for the Stanley Electric Company; Mercer was a physician, Cooley an insurance agent. (Hollister would also be involved with the Stilson car built in Pittsfield beginning in 1907.) Life for the Berkshire was uphill most of the time. During the first three years of the firm's existence, it was known as the Berkshire Motor Company, then Berkshire Automobile Company, then Berkshire Motor Car Company. Under one of these firm names, a transmission designed to prevent stripping of gears was patented and installed on the Berkshire — and it proved a disaster. The factory was shut down in December 1907, and the Messrs. Mercer, Whyland, Cooley and Hollister declared that operations would not resume "unless local capital is offered." It was not. Undaunted, Berkshire tried again late in 1909 with the Berkshire Auto-Car Company in Pittsfield, building approximately thirty cars for 1910, and threatening to relocate in Hartford, Connecticut. Still, local capital did not materialize. By early 1912 the "shot in the arm" the Berkshire company said it needed was believed to have arrived. From Cambridge, Massachusetts came James Addison, S.H. Clapp and E.B. Belcher of the Belcher Engineering Company. They bought up all the parts Berkshire had on hand and built three additional cars in Cambridge. Final liquidation came in early October 1912. Total production of the "Unequalled Hill Climber" has been said to be 150 units. Frank V. Whyland went on to further automobile ventures of his own, including the Whyland-Nelson of Buffalo, New York.

1905 BERKSHIRE
Model A — 4-cyl., 18 hp, 86" wb

	FP	5	4	3	2	1
Side Entrance Tonneau	1750	2700	3600	5300	8800	19,000

Model B — 4-cyl., 30 hp, 109" wb

Side Entrance Tonneau	2400	2700	3600	5300	8800	19,000

Model D - 4-cyl., 50 hp, 108 & 120" wb

Side Entrance Tonneau						

1906 BERKSHIRE
Model A — 4-cyl., 20 hp, 98" wb

Tour.-5P	2500	3100	4200	6300	10,500	22,000

Model B — 4-cyl., 30 hp, 115" wb

Tour.-5P	3000	3200	4300	6500	11,000	23,000

Model C — 6-cyl., 50 hp, 122" wb

Tour.-7P	4500	4800	9600	16,000	22,400	32,000

1907 BERKSHIRE
Model D — 4-cyl., 35 hp, 118" wb

Tour.-5P	3500	3500	4500	7000	13,000	25,000

1907 Berkshire, model D, 5-pass. touring, WLB

1910 Berkshire, model E, touring, JAC

1910 BERKSHIRE
Model E — 4-cyl., 35 hp, 106" & 119" wb

	FP	5	4	3	2	1
Toy Tonneau-4P	2800	3100	4200	6300	10,500	22,000
Tour.-5P	2900	3000	4000	6000	9500	21,000
Rbt.-2/3P (106" wb)	2650	3200	4300	6500	11,000	23,000

1911 Berkshire, model E, roadster, HAC

1911 BERKSHIRE
Model E — 4-cyl., 35 hp, 119" wb

Tour.-5P	2000	4000	5000	8000	15,000	28,000
Land'et.-6P	3500	3900	4800	7700	14,300	27,000
Limo.-6P	3600	3500	4500	7000	13,000	25,000
Rds.-2/4P	2800	4300	5400	8700	16,500	30,000
Toy Tonneau-4/5P	2800	4000	5000	8000	15,000	28,000
Gunboat-5P	2960	4200	5200	8400	15,700	29,000

1912 Berkshire, model E, touring, HAC

114

1912 BERKSHIRE
Model E — 4-cyl., 35 hp, 124" wb

	FP	5	4	3	2	1
Rbt.	2800	4200	5200	8400	15,700	29,000
Toy Tonneau	2800	4300	5400	8700	16,500	30,000
Torpedo	3000	4500	5800	9500	18,000	32,000
Tour.	3000	4400	5600	9200	17,300	31,000

Model F — 6-cyl., 58 hp (SAE), 134" wb

Tour.	3500	4700	6100	9900	19,000	33,000

BERLIET — The French Berliet built under license by the American Locomotive Automobile Company of Providence, Rhode Island from 1906-1908 is properly referred to as the American Berliet. Refer to the American Berliet.

BERLO — Boston, Massachusetts — (1900) — Boston bicycle man Peter Berlo built two gasoline automobiles in 1900, and apparently he did so modestly. "There are so many going to be revolutionizing motor vehicles that it is refreshing to meet a man that claims to be doing nothing more than what is human," *The Motor Vehicle Review* commented. Details regarding Berlo's cars are lacking, though obviously his building of them convinced him that four wheels were not his forte. He continued in the bicycle business, adding motors to many of his two-wheelers.

BERNARD — The Bernard Automobile Company was organized in Troy, New York with a capital stock of $5000 early in 1908 to "manufacture and deal in motor cars and supplies." Incorporators were W.C. DeVoe of Watervliet, and P. Bullock and E.G. Bernard of Troy. Manufacture is doubted.

BERRY — The John Berry Automobile Company was organized in St. Louis, Missouri early in 1913 with a capital stock of $20,000 and the plan to manufacture and repair motor cars. In addition to Berry, the incorporators were A. Sommer and L.J. Koenigstein. Manufacture has not been established.

BERTELLI — During the spring of 1906, R. Bertelli & Company was organized in New York City with a capital stock of $75,000 to manufacture engines, machinery and automobiles. R.R. Bertelli, E. Paladina and Celestina Piva, all of New York City, were among the incorporators. The firm settled into quarters at 144 West 39th Street in Manhattan, and exhibited at the automobile show at year's end. The car on the Bertelli stand was an Italian Zust, however. The company is not believed to have produced any automobiles itself.

1908 Bertolet, touring, NAHC

BERTOLET — Reading, Pennsylvania — (1908-1910) — Dr. J.M. Bertolet of Reading joined the automotive ranks in 1908 by offering a convertible touring/runabout, a rear deck being furnished to substitute for the rear seat when a more sporting effect was desired. "The body is so ingeniously designed and constructed," *Cycle and Automotive Trade Journal* said, "that its interchangeability is not perceptible in either touring car or runabout form." The touring car alone was available for $150 less. Initial sales were so encouraging that the doctor incorporated Bertolet Motor Car Company in 1909. By the end of 1910, however, production ceased, though a few more cars may have been assembled from parts on hand into late 1911.

1908-1909 BERTOLET
Type X — 4-cyl., 40 hp, 102" wb

Tour./Rbt.	2400	2700	3600	5300	8800	19,000
Tour.-7P	2250	2600	3550	5200	8700	18,500

1910 BERTOLET
Model 40 — 4-cyl., 40 hp, 110" wb

Tour.-5P	2500	2700	3600	5300	8800	19,000

BERTZCHY — Council Bluffs, Iowa — (1909) — Though his Desert Flyer venture had ended with the building of a single prototype, A.J.P. Bertzchy was somehow able to convince the Council Bluffs Commercial Club of his good and potentially profitable intentions. Deciding against establishing a stage line between that town and Omaha, Bertzchy's new notion for his newly organized Bertzchy Motor Company was the manufacture of traction engines, freight trucks, fire engines and a 50 hp convertible vehicle for "hauling gang plows in the fields" during the week and taking "the family to church on Sunday." These cars were to carry the tradename of Bertzchy, and material for 25 units was ordered in 1909 with a factory secured at Washington Avenue and North Main Street — all via the help of the Council Bluffs Commercial Club. Certainly no more than 25 of the Bertzchy cars were ever built; the Bertzchy Motor Company seems to have made most of its money by handling the Kisselkar agency in town. Bertzchy also developed a system of autogenous welding which made money too. His Bertzchy Motor Company was in business in Council Bluffs into 1912. Then A.J.P. Bertzchy returned to Omaha and opened a garage there.

BERWICK — Elizabeth, New Jersey — (1903) — O.F. Ferris, S.W. Dickson, Duval Dickson, Frank Corkins and C.C. Evans were among those anxious to get the Berwick Automobile Company off the ground. They organized their venture with a capital stock of $10,000 in Elizabeth during the summer of 1903, and ordered a sample automobile to be built by a machine shop in town. Apparently, the car was completed, though it proved unsatisfactory, and the venture ended then and there.

1904 Berwick Electric, runabout, WLB

BERWICK ELECTRIC — Grand Rapids, Michigan — (1904) — The Berwick Auto Car Company was organized in Hastings, Michigan in June 1903, and was forced to reorganize in Grand Rapids that December without yet having built one car. That this did not bode well for the future of the venture was quickly proved when the company was out of business within a year. Some Berwicks were manufactured in Grand Rapids, however, and the company occasionally referred to the car as a Marquette, which tended to confuse. The only model offered, whatever its name, was a small tiller-steered electric runabout stylishly finished with black body and red running gear. It was available with Willard battery at $750, with an Edison at $1000. The Willard promised forty-five miles on a single charge, the Edison sixty. In addition to administrative difficulties, the Berwick's problem may have been its performance. Fifteen miles an hour was the car's top speed, modest even for an electric by this time.

BERWICK — Mahony City, Pennsylvania — (1917) — The Berwick Car Works was a company hastily organized for a quick profit courtesy of the United States Government. In July of 1917 it produced an armored car for the war effort in Europe. Army evaluation followed, but a government contract did not. Probably only the one car was ever built.

BESSEMER — A car called the Bessemer is indicated on some lists to have been built in Chicago in 1904 by the Robert M. Cutting Company. This has not been substantiated. There was no company by that name in the Windy City in 1904, though there was a Robert M. Cutting, who listed his occupation as "student" and his residence as 132 South Waller Avenue.

BESSERDICH & ZACHOW — William Besserdich and his brother-in-law Otto Zachow were the partners behind the four-wheel-drive vehicle built in Clintonville, Wisconsin which became known as the F.W.D. Refer to F.W.D.

BEST — The Best Automobile Company was organized with a capital stock of $20,000 in Indianapolis, Indiana during the fall of 1908. Edgar Updyke, William N. Gates and Edward E. Gates were among the incorporators. In 1909 and 1910 the firm was advertising in the trade press for the necessary capital to proceed into manufacture of a Best car, but there is not indication manufacture ever happened.

BEST — San Leandro, California — (1898-1899) — The Best Manufacturing Company was one of the most prominently known traction-engine building firms on the West Coast. It was a family business, with Otto, Leo and Daniel Best in charge. In 1898 the company completed an experimental gasoline carriage which was formidably large, with huge wagon wheels, and a two-cylinder 7 hp engine the gasoline for which was sprayed into the cylinders. Transmission was via belt, and a speed of up to 20 mph

1899 Best Gasoline Carriage, auto-buggy, NAHC

was claimed, though this reduced to 18 when the full complement of eight passengers was aboard. Left-hand drive was a most unusual feature for this early period. This first Best was the work of Daniel, and he demonstrated it for the first time during early September of 1898. A story about the car appeared in the February 18th, 1899 issue of *Mining & Scientific Press*, and it indicated that the Best company was contemplating manufacture: "This vehicle is especially designed for family carriages, stage coaches for carrying mail and passengers . . ." Production never did follow, however, though in 1899 Daniel Best did run up a two-passenger gasoline runabout. It was the last car from the Best company. When the Reverend Joseph Parker of Mendocino subsequently requested a mammoth carriage for use in his touring evangelical work, the Bests turned him down. The Best factory was taken over by the Holt Manufacturing Company in 1908. In 1914 the Sequoia Motor Car Company moved in to build the Sequoia.

BETHLEHEM — The car produced by the Bethlehem Automobile Company of Bethlehem, Pennsylvania from 1907-1908 was known as the Ideal. Refer to Ideal.

In April of 1920 the Bethlehem Motor Truck Corporation of Allentown, Pennsylvania announced its forthcoming manufacture of an export automobile which subsequently was also named the Ideal. Refer to Ideal.

1933 Betteridge, MVMA

BETTERIDGE — Los Angeles, California — (1933) — This racy little midget was built by young Billy Betteridge of Los Angeles in 1933. Its engine, which he sometimes used to power his outboard motorboat, developed 25 mph. The car's length was seven feet, its wheelbase sixty-five inches, its tread forty inches. The body was almost completely aluminum, and Betteridge claimed having hit 100 mph on the road.

BETZ — Chicago, Illinois — (1902) — Frank S. Betz & Company, which operated in suburban Chicago, began experimentation with gasoline carriages in late 1901, completing and testing its first single-cylinder car by February of 1902. A two-cylinder car followed, and Frank Betz indicated that if it proved satisfactory, his factory would immediately take up manufacture on an extensive scale. "The company will, however, not mingle with the automobile trade in the customary way," reported *The Motor Review*, "as its present line of manufacture being surgical instruments and apparatus, the new vehicle will for a time be pushed exclusively among the 'medics,' with whom the company has an intimate acquaintance." It does not appear the Betz car was pushed upon more than a few doctors before the company returned to manufacture of the products it knew best.

BEUTEL — Manitowoc, Wisconsin — (1911) — The Beutel Brothers were wagonmakers in Manitowoc who purchased the lot on St. Clair Avenue adjacent to their factory for the purpose of erecting a four-story building. "It will be utilized in the manufacture of automobiles," *The Motor World* reported in April 1911, "and also for garage purposes." The extent of Beutel automobile manufacture is not known.

1904 Beverly, tonneau, NAHC

BEVERLY — Beverly, Massachusetts — (1904) — The Beverly was successor to the Upton, a change made necessary when Colton Upton left the Upton Machine Company in Beverly, Massachusetts and took his name with him. There were further changes to the car as well: Its four-cylinder engine was pepped up to 22 hp from 16, and a honeycomb radiator replaced the previous coiled pipe. And there was another unusual feature, as described in the catalog: "Acetylene brass head-lights, fitted to swing with the forward wheels, thereby throwing the light directly ahead at all times. Two brass oil side lights and tail lamp, throwing white on step and red astern." The price was now $4000, as opposed to the previous $3500. And the Beverly survived but a year. In September of 1905 the Upton Machine Company was reorganized as the Beverly Manufacturing Company, and produced transmissions only until January 1908 when the factory was sold to the Cameron Car Company. Meanwhile, Colton Upton had moved to Lebanon, Pennsylvania where he built another car bearing his name in 1906-1907.

1904 BEVERLY
Four — 22 hp, 90" wb

	FP	5	4	3	2	1
Tour.-5P	4000	2900	3700	5600	9100	20,000

BEWIS — The Bewis of 1915 which has appeared on car rosters was simply the Lewis of Racine misspelled. Refer to Lewis.

BEYER — Leavenworth, Kansas — (1900) — The Beyer Brothers of Leavenworth had been building buggies and wagons since 1857. In 1900 they built a three-wheeled motor buggy which is believed to be the entire extent of their automotive production.

BEYSTER-DETROIT — Detroit, Michigan — (1910-1911) — The Beyster-Detroit Motor Car Company was organized in December of 1909 with a capital stock of $50,000 and manufacturing facilities secured at the factory of Beyster, Thorpe & Company at 1329 Woodward Avenue in Detroit. Although light delivery trucks were the principal focus of the Beyster-Detroit production efforts, a few runabouts — utilizing the Hupmobile 20 engine — were built as well. In April 1911 the company announced that it was "winding up its affairs" after having found "the field too crowded and the competition too strenuous."

B.G.S. — The appearance of the B.G.S. as a car built in America in 1900 is in error. The B.G.S. was produced in Neuilly, France from 1899 to 1906, and may have been imported but was never built in this country.

B & H — This was an alternative designation for the Brew-Hatcher built in Cleveland from 1904-1905. Refer to Brew-Hatcher.

BIANCHI — The Bianchi was an Italian car built in Milan from 1898 and imported into this country for a few years after the turn of the century by Percy Owen of New York City. The car was never built here, however. In 1907 there was incorporation of a Bianchi Automobile Company in New York City with $10,000 capital stock and the announced plan of manufacture but, again, only importation followed. Stephen Kjelsden, Francis Camwright and William Conners were the principals involved in that venture.

BI-AUTOGO — The Bi-Autogo, completed in 1912, was the first automobile built by James Scripps-Booth. Part motorcar, part motorcycle, it was powered by a 45 hp L-head V-8 engine, the first ever built in Detroit. Refer to Scripps-Booth.

BIBBS — The Bibbs which seemingly was built in New York City in 1904 was simply a misspelling of the venture promoted by the Gibbs Engineering Company of New York City. Refer to Gibbs.

BI CAR — No automobile was ever officially marketed under this name. Bi-Car was the sometime designation for two cyclecars produced in 1914; refer to Fauber (Elgin, Illinois) and Henderson (Indianapolis, Indiana). A Bi-Car was also offered as a chassis only by the Engineering Equipment Company of Indianapolis in 1915.

BI-CAR — Detroit, Michigan — (1911-1912) — The Bi-Car was the invention of John J. Chapin and was described as a motorcycle embodying some of the features of an automobile. Its engine was a four-cylinder four-stroke started by a crank at the side; shaft drive and a two-speed transmission were featured. The Detroit Bi-Car Company was organized in November of 1911 with a capital stock of $100,000. Joining Chapin in this venture was Alfred Roseroot as vice-president, John J. Berkery as secretary and Frank J. Gorman as treasurer. A temporary factory was secured at Greenwood and Baltimore avenues in Detroit, though the company had plans to build its own factory later. Those plans were never realized. The Bi-Car did not proceed beyond the prototype stage.

BIDDLE — Knoxville, Tennessee — (1902) — The Biddle Manufacturing Company announced in August that it would soon be in production with its line of high-powered gasoline automobiles. One John Biddle was behind this venture. He was not related to the Biddle family of Main Line Philadelphia, and his car did not enjoy the success of the Biddle from Pennsylvania. Probably only the prototype was built.

1917 Biddle, model D, touring, HAC

BIDDLE — Philadelphia, Pennsylvania — (1915-1922) — The Biddle was built in Philadelphia, and there was a member of the socially prominent Biddle family involved, one R. Ralston Biddle, although it would appear he lent little more to the venture than the credence to call it the Biddle Motor Car Company. The firm's president was A. Mc. I. Maris, and its designer was Charles Fry. The car was built for the carriage trade, a segment of the market more interested in aesthetics than mechanics. The Biddle company served that market admirably. Technically, the Biddle was a prosaic vehicle, assembled from components arriving at its factory from a variety of sources (i.e., rear axle from Salisbury, worm and gear steering from Warner, wire wheels from Rudge-Whitworth, electrics from Westinghouse). Engines were a 226.4 cubic inch 48 hp Buda four, and the 350.5 cubic inch walking-beam four from Duesenberg (later Rochester-Duesenberg) which delivered about 100 bhp in race tune, though it was sedated somewhat for the Biddle clientele. What the Biddle did best was to look good. Its coachwork was exquisite. A wide range of standard factory bodies sold in the $2000-$4000 range, and the chassis was priced at $1650 ($2095 in 1918) with Biddle willing to mount any coachwork to customer specifications. A small luxury car (wheelbase was 120 inches, raised to 121 in 1917) distinguished by the deep vee of its very Mercedes-like radiator (built for the company by English and Mersick), the Biddle had undeniable stylish panache, contributed in large measure by one of its earliest customer prospects: Miriam Warren Hubbard. It was Ms. Hubbard who suggested the car's vee radiator and who happily kibitzed on other aspects of the Biddle design. If she be given credit as America's first female automobile stylist, her relative success is given testimony by the number of component manufacturers picturing the car in their own advertising, Duesenberg Motors among them. But Biddle's low-key approach to production (100 cars each in 1915 and 1916, no more than 500 each in the three years following) came face to face with the postwar recession, and the company initially thought a move to new headquarters at Fifth Avenue and 142nd Street in New York City might help. When it didn't the firm was sold in 1920 to a syndicate whose members included H.C. Maihbohm of Maihbohm Motors Company. This group received forty orders immediately and soon had forty cars assembled save for two necessary parts which would be delivered by the supplier when the company paid its bills which alas it could not do. Consequently, the firm was sold again, early in 1921 to another consortium headed by F.L. Crane, who renamed it the Biddle-Crane Motor Car Company. Biddle-Crane paid the bills to the parts companies, and the forty half-finished cars were completed and delivered. A new line was prepared, with bodies to come from Rauch and Lang in Cleveland. No more than a handful were produced before Biddle-Crane went out of business toward the end of 1922. In all, approximately 1750 Biddles were built by the three different companies that tried. A particularly rakish Biddle roadster with Rochester-Duesenberg engine is on display at Harrah's Automobile Collection.

1915-1916 BIDDLE
Model D — 4-cyl., 23 hp, 120"wb

	FP	5	4	3	2	1
Rdstr.-2P	1700	3000	4000	6000	9500	21,000
Tour.-4P	1700	2900	3700	5600	9100	20,000
Tour.-5P	1800	2900	3700	5600	9100	20,000
Town Car-5P	3000	2700	3600	5300	8800	19,000

1917 Biddle, model D, semi-collapsible town car, HAC

1917 BIDDLE
Model D — 4-cyl., 23 hp, 121" wb

Collapsible Town Car	3900	2900	3700	5600	9100	20,000
Tour.-4P	2350	3000	4000	6000	9500	21,000
Rdstr.-2P	2200	3100	4200	6300	10,500	22,000
Town Car-5P	3800	2700	3600	5300	8800	19,000
Semi-Collapsible Town Car	2850	2800	3650	5500	9000	19,500
Brougham-6P	3800	2700	3600	5300	8800	19,000
Raceabout-2P	2100	2900	3700	5600	9100	20,000

1918 Biddle, Rosemont, touring, WLB

1918 Biddle, Ormond Speedway Special, roadster, WLB

1918 Biddle, Town Car, HAC

1918 BIDDLE
4-cyl., 23 hp, 121" wb

	FP	5	4	3	2	1
Rdstr.-4P	2600	3000	4000	6000	9500	21,000
Tour.-4P	2650	2900	3700	5600	9100	20,000
Rdstr.-3P	2650	2950	3900	5800	9300	20,500
Sed.-5P	4100	2500	3500	5000	8500	18,000
Town Car-5P	4000	2700	3600	5300	8800	19,000
Brougham-6P	3900	2800	3650	5500	9000	19,500

1919 Biddle, roadster, HAC

1920 Biddle, touring, JAC

1919 BIDDLE
4-cyl., 23 hp, 121" wb

Salon Sed.-5P	4400	2700	3600	5300	8800	19,000
Tour.-4P	2750	3100	4200	6300	10,500	22,000

1920-1921 BIDDLE
Model B-1 — 4-cyl., 33 hp, 121" wb

Rdstr.-2P	2900	3100	4200	6300	10,500	22,000
Rosemont-2P	3250	3200	4300	6500	11,000	23,000
Tour.-6P	3300	3000	4000	6000	9500	21,000
King Rdstr.-2P	3150	3200	4300	6500	11,000	23,000
Tour.-4P	3250	3000	4000	6000	9500	21,000
Sed.-5P	4600	2500	3500	5000	8500	18,000
Ormond-2P	3750	2400	3400	4800	8000	17,000

1922 BIDDLE
Model B-1 — 4-cyl., 33 hp, 121" wb

Rdstr.-3P	3475	3100	4200	6300	10,500	22,000
Tour.-4P	3475	3000	4000	6000	9500	21,000
Speedway-4P	4000	3500	4500	7000	13,000	25,000
Cpe.-4P	4350	2500	3500	5000	8500	18,000
Limo.-6P (126" wb)	5650	2700	3600	5300	8800	19,000
Brgm.-6P (125" wb)	6000	2900	3700	5600	9100	20,000

BIDDLE-MURRAY — Oak Park, Illinois — (1905-1907) — The Biddle-Murray Manufacturing Company was initially organized in Chicago in late 1905 by Ralph McShaw, John D. Black and Edward C. Maher. Capital stock was a modest $10,000. A year later the firm was incorporated again, under the lenient laws of Maine, its capitalization now a lofty $300,000. Apparently there was some production of the Biddle-Murray in a factory in Oak Park, Illinois. When stockholder Alfred E. Case petitioned the company into receivership in March 1907, the trade press noted that the firm had "made automobiles in a small way," though its factory doors had been closed since February 20th. Several other creditors — including McCord & Company, Kenilworth Machinery Company and Christ Hafner — followed Case in pressing legal action, and Biddle-Murray was no more.

BIG BROWN LUVERNE — The Big Brown Luverne was the most famous of the models produced by the Luverne Automobile Company of Luverne, Minnesota. Refer to Luverne.

BIG FOUR FLYER — Dayton, Ohio — (1908) — Harry Arnstein of Dayton built several cars which he called the Big Four Flyer. In its June 18th, 1908 issue, *The Motor World* reported that Arnstein was "preparing to engage in the business on a large scale. The organization of a stock company and the construction of a factory in Dayton are included in his plans." His plans went awry, however: there is no evidence that his Big Four Flyer ever flew.

BIGELOW — The Bigelow-Willey Motor Company was organized during the summer of 1913 in Philadelphia "to manufacture, buy, sell and deal in and with electric machines of all kinds." Jay Bigelow and G.A. Willey were the partners in this venture. Their capital stock was $50,000. Manufacture of an automobile has not been established.

BIGGELMAN — In 1910, in Troy, New York a man by the name of August Biggelman purportedly built an automobile. Documentation of this is lacking.

BILBRO — The Bilbro Auto Company was organized in New York City early in 1909 with a capital stock of $20,000 and the plan to manufacture and operate a garage. James E. Troy, William L. Brown and Ernest Mayer backed this venture. Manufacture of a car is doubted.

1914 Billiken, 2-pass. roadster, WLB

BILLIKEN — Milwaukee, Wisconsin — (1914) — Charles J. Eigel, his brother Stanley and Samuel P. Carroll were the men behind the Milwaukee Cyclecar Company at 511 First Avenue. The name they chose for their product was Billiken. During this period, the Billiken mascot (a small Buddha-like statuette that purportedly brought good luck) was a popular radiator ornament among car owners — and doubtless this was the derivation of this cyclecar's name. Though its planetary transmission, choice of 48-inch or standard 56-inch tread and shaft drive were unusual, the Billiken was otherwise typical of the cyclecar genre. And, like all other cyclecar builders, the company was in trouble almost immediately. In May a move to DePere, Wisconsin was considered, but by June the company decided going west might help and were in the process of negotiating with the town of West Sacramento, California for a factory site. The company was still negotiating when its money ran out.

1914 BILLIKEN
Cyclecar — 4-cyl., 12 hp, 96" wb

	FP	5	4	3	2	1
Rdstr.-2P	395	1600	2700	3800	5800	12,000
Light Delivery	410	1500	2500	3600	5500	11,000

BILLINGS — Hartford, Connecticut — (1900, 1905) — The steam car designed by Frederick Billings of the drop forging firm of Billings & Spencer in Hartford was introduced to the public on the American Bicycle Company stand in New York City's Madison Square Garden in November 1900. "It can go at a thirty-five-mile-an-hour clip without turning a hair," exhibit manager Mudge declared. Six and a quarter horsepower was claimed for its engine, and an attraction claimed for the tubular boiler was that "the dread corrosion is practically impossible in it." A novelty of the car's construction was the auxiliary hand water pump operated by the steering lever. A very handsome car finished in black with side panels of cast aluminum, the Billings had been built in the American Bicycle factory in Toledo, Ohio. Subsequently, Frederick Billings sold all rights to the machine to American Bicycle, and it was produced as the Toledo. In 1905 Frederick Billings built a gasoline automobile which quickly led to rumors in the trade press that a new Billings car was forthcoming. Frederick Billings immediately denied it. "He harbors no intentions of the sort," *The Motor World* reported that November. "He did build a gasoline car for his own use, and its behavior has been such as to attract the attention of some men of means. They have coquetted with Mr. Billings, and he has not proven averse to the flirtation. If they desire to buy he is not disinclined to sell — and that is all there is to the story." Attempts to organize the Town and Country Automobile Company in Hartford for manufacture of the Billings car came to naught, however.

BILLY FOUR — Atlanta, Georgia — (1910) — A.W. Keating was president and M.W. Lord treasurer of the McNabb Iron Works of Atlanta. The car they produced was perfectly named. It was a cute, rambunctious little $500 roadster which might have better fared had the McNabb company been properly set up for manufacture. Model 1 of the Billy Four had a four-cylinder 20 hp engine, thermo-syphon cooling, two-speed planetary transmission, 88-inch wheelbase, and a total weight of 1100 pounds. There was no Model 2.

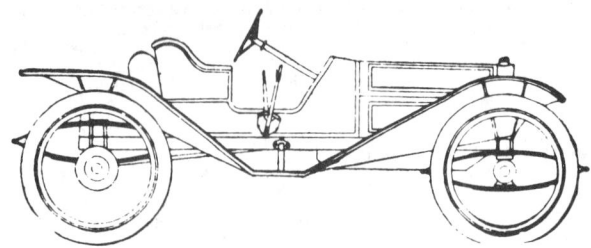

1910 Billy Four, roadster, NAHC

1910 BILLY FOUR
Four — 20 hp, 88" wb

	FP	5	4	3	2	1
Model 1 Rds.	500	1600	2700	3800	5800	12,000

BIMEL — Sidney, Ohio — (1916-1917) — The Bimel appears to have been simply a badge-engineered Elco. Rights to the car had been secured by the Bimel Buggy Company in August of 1915 when the Elwood Iron Works, producers of the Elco, went bankrupt. Initially the cars continued to be marketed under the Elco name, but an advertisement in the *Sidney Daily News* from August 25th, 1916 touted the four-cylinder roadster and touring models as Bimels and invited the public to stop by for a ride. Trade press references from the same period, however, continued to refer to the car as an Elco. Conceivably the name change may have been simply for home town use. A six-cylinder model utilizing a Caille engine was envisioned to carry the Bimel name solely, but that car does not appear to have been produced at all.

BIMOBILE — The Bimobile Company was organized in the summer of 1911 in New York City to manufacture "automobiles, motors, engines, balloons, aeroplanes and other airships." Capital stock was $60,000; backing this venture were Kimber A. George, Franklin A. Rhoades and Edwin P. Oakes. For a while it appears they gave thoughts to calling their products by the unlikely name of Bipmonobile. Whatever called and whatever eventually may have arrived, it was not an automobile.

BINATE — The Binate was the name of the engine which powered the Coffee car of 1902 produced in Richmond, Virginia. The engine itself was also sold under contract by Charles E. Miller, the successful automotive supply man and jobber operating out of New York City during this period. No automobile was ever called a Binate, however.

BINGHAM — The Bingham Manufacturing Company was organized in Cleveland, Ohio early in 1911 with a capital stock of $25,000 and the plan to manufacture "automobiles and other vehicles." Herbert Bingham, William H. Gillie, C.B. Dickey, C.F. Schied and W.C. Rhoades were the people involved. Early in 1912 they reorganized as the Bingham Motor Car Company to manufacture automobiles and trucks. Subsequently, in 1914, a Bingham truck did evolve of this venture. An automobile was never manufactured, however.

BINGHAMTON — The Binghamton Gas Engine Company was located at 1 Carroll Street in Binghamton, New York. In addition to engines, its product line at the turn of the century also included metal novelties, but there is no evidence, despite Binghamton's inclusion as a manufacturer in the Hiscox book, that any of these novelties was an automobile. J.G. Clonney was the Binghamton president in 1900. In 1901 his vice-president, E.C. Inderlied, took over and reorganized as the Rumsey Gas Engine Company. Rumsey did not build an automobile either.

Purportedly a two-passenger coupe was built in 1920 by the Binghamton Electric Truck Company of Binghamton, New York. No doubt this was a prototype for a projected production which never followed. The Binghamton company, which was located at 250 Main Street, apparently produced a modest number of trucks in 1920 and 1921, however.

BINGMAN — Detroit, Michigan — (1912) — In 1912 in Detroit a machinist by the name of Fred Bingman, together with his son Philip, built an automobile at the small shop they operated at 725 Fourteenth Avenue. Manufacture did not follow. The partners' first car had been a single-cylinder tricycle at the turn of the century.

1903 Binney & Burnham Steamer, runabout, NAHC

BINNEY & BURNHAM STEAM — Boston, Massachusetts — (1902) — In January of 1902, following the building of a steamer for George McQuesten, the Messrs. Binney and Burnham announced in Boston that they were ready for business and prepared to produce to order "any style of steam carriage" desired. James L. Binney and John Appleton Burnham believed in building heavy; 1100 pounds for a two-seater was a weighty proposition in those days, and capacities of forty gallons for the water tank and eight for the gasoline tank were exceptionally large. For this reason, the Binney & Burnham was described, even by its makers, as being only "moderately fast" though of "great efficiency in actual use." A Model B Runabout and a Model C Touring Car with accommodation for eight passengers, or six passengers and a lot of luggage, were the standard production choices. In December of 1902 one of the touring cars was delivered to Elliot C. Lee, the vice-president of the Massachusetts Automobile Club. This sale might logically have led to others among Boston's automobile crowd, but James Binney and John Burnham quarreled and by January 1903 dissolved their partnership. Burnham found a new partner named Lyman, and proceeded to build the Lyman & Burnham. Binney's further adventures are not known, but he may have returned to his previous trade as a carriage painter.

BIRCH — Burlington, New Jersey — (1899) — James H. Birch had been in the carriage business on Library Street in Burlington since 1862, and in 1899 he added a motor vehicle department. "Mr. Birch started in without capital, but by vigilance and strict attention to business he has built up a large institution and his productions are used in all quarters of the globe," *The Motor Vehicle Review* noted admiringly that year, adding that success in his automobile business seemed assured. The indications are that James H. Birch did produce a few automobiles, but never embarked substantially in the field.

1919 Birch, touring, NAHC

BIRCH — Chicago, Illinois — (1916-1923) — Birch Motor Cars, Inc. of Chicago sold its cars by direct mail only, predominantly through magazine advertisements. These were assembled cars with Lycoming, Herschell-Spillman, Beaver, Supreme or Le Roi engines and standard components, throughout. Unlike most automotive mail order businesses which had their cars built for them entirely by other factories, it would appear that Birch did some of its own assembly. The company was an adjunct of Birch Motor College, a technical school, and its labor force was entirely composed of students. More Birch cars, however, were probably put together by the professionals of Crow-Elkhart in Indiana and Seneca in Ohio.

1916 BIRCH
Four — 19.6 hp, 114" wb

	FP	5	4	3	2	1
Model 32 Tour.	695	2450	3450	4900	8300	17,500

1917 BIRCH
Four — 19.6 hp, 114" wb

Model 28 Rdstr.	695	2500	3500	5000	8500	18,000
Model 32 Tour.	765	2400	3400	4800	8000	17,000

1918 BIRCH
Four — 19.6 hp, 114" wb

Model 35 Tour.	845	2400	3400	4800	8000	17,000
Model 35 Rdstr.	925	2500	3500	5000	8500	18,000

Six — 21.6 hp, 116" wb

Model 45 Tour.	955	2450	3450	4900	8300	17,500

1919 BIRCH
Model 30 — 4-cyl., 14.4 hp, 108" wb

Tour.	895	2500	3500	5000	8500	18,500

Model 36 — 4-cyl., 19.6 hp, 115" wb

Chummy Rdstr.	1145	2600	3550	5200	8700	18,500
Tour.	1145	2500	3500	5000	8500	18,000

Model 45 — 6-cyl., 21.6 hp, 115" wb

Tour.	1395	2700	3600	5300	8800	19,000

1920 BIRCH
Model 30 — 4-cyl., 30 hp, 108" wb

Tour.	1295	2700	3600	5300	8800	19,000

Model 40 — 4-cyl., 40 hp, 117" wb

Tour.	1495	2800	3650	5500	9000	19,500

Model 6-45 — 6-cyl., 45 hp, 115" wb

Tour.	1795	3100	4200	6300	10,500	22,000

1921-1922 BIRCH
Model 44 — 4-cyl., 37 hp, 117" wb

Tour.-5P	1495	3100	4200	6300	10,500	22,000
Rdstr.-3P	1495	3200	4300	6500	11,000	23,000
Spt.-4P	1545	3250	4400	6600	11,500	23,500
Sed.-7P	2295	2300	3300	4600	7500	16,000

1922 Birch, 4-pass. Sport, touring, WLB

Model 66 — 6-cyl., 57 hp, 117" wb

	FP	5	4	3	2	1
Tour.-5P	1695	3200	4300	6500	11,000	23,000
Rdstr.-3P	1695	3300	4400	6700	12,000	24,000
Spt.-4P	1745	3400	4500	6900	12,500	24,500
Sed.-7P	2495	2400	3400	4800	8000	17,000

1923 BIRCH
Model 23-45 — 4-cyl., 28 hp, 114" wb

Tour.-5P	895	2800	3650	5500	9000	19,500
Rdstr.-3P	895	2900	3700	5600	9100	20,000
Spt.-4P	995	2950	3900	5800	9300	20,500
Sed.-5P	1195	2200	3200	4400	7000	20,500

Model 305 — 4-cyl., 39 hp, 108" wb

Tour.-5P	695	2900	3700	5600	9100	20,000
Rdstr.-2P	865	3000	4000	6000	9500	21,000

BIRD — A Bird from New York City in 1911 has been indicated on various car rosters. There was no Bird Automobile Company in town at the time, however.

1896 Bird Motor Trap, auto-buggy, NAHC

BIRD — Buffalo, New York — (1895-1898) — Henry R. Bird entered a friction-drive, kerosene-fueled car in the Chicago Times-Herald Contest of 1895. Returning to New York after his Thanksgiving weekend in the Windy City, he finished his second car, which was a wagonette with dos-a-dos seats, weighed 750 pounds and was claimed to have a speed of 30 mph, which would have been flying. Early in 1896 Henry Bird was at work on his third vehicle, which he said would be lighter and faster yet. It was in 1896, too, that announcement was made of the impending formation of a corporation for manufacture. Since references indicate only four vehicles ever being built, it would appear the Bird company never got off the ground.

BIRDSALL — "The Birdsall Automobile Company has been organized in New York by E.T. Birdsall, formerly connected with the Decauville Automobile Company," *Motor Way* announced during the early summer of 1906. "The new concern is to place on the market a six-cylinder touring car." Manufacture did not follow.

BIRMINGHAM — Three Birmingham ventures in Alabama announced the intention to manufacture automobiles but appear not to have followed through with production.
In August of 1903 the Birmingham Electric & Manufacturing Company declared itself "preparing to place an electric automobile on the market" and was not heard from again.
In 1910 the Birmingham Motor Company was organized with a capital stock of $5000 by Leo Loeb, Mrs. Joseph H. Loveman and Maurice Link.
In 1911 the Birmingham Automobile Company was organized with a capital stock of $10,000 by John B. Ransom, George Bennie and B.J. Banks, Jr.

1922 Birmingham, touring, WLB

BIRMINGHAM — **Jamestown, New York** — **(1921-1923)** — The Birmingham was a 55 hp Continental-engined six on a 124-inch wheelbase with standard components used throughout but a most unusual flexible suspension system. Three transverse springs and an independent rear axle were combined with two transverse springs in front which made for a four-wheel independent suspension and the "easiest riding car ever put on the market," as advertising said. Alas, getting the Birmingham on the market was the hard part. Because the suspension system was similar to that which had appeared on the Cornelian built by the Blood Brothers in Kalamazoo, Cyrus E. Weaver, the designer of the Birmingham, purchased all relevant patents held by the Blood Brothers. This was perhaps the only aspect of the Birmingham venture which went right. The first Birmingham prototype sedan was completed and tested in Detroit in May of 1921, but already Jamestown, New York had been selected as the factory site. The mayor of Jamestown, Samuel A. Carlson, agreed to serve as president of Birmingham Motors Corporation, accepting no salary for the position. Because he believed Birmingham would do for Jamestown what Franklin had done for Syracuse (and even, grandiosely, what Ford had done for Detroit), Carlson asked only for out-of-pocket expenses for promoting this new industry for his community. Demonstrations of the new Birmingham were set up in numerous towns in Upstate New York and elsewhere, with an office opened in each for the sale of stock. Five cars were assembled in nearby Falconer by early 1922, these joined the two further cars previously put together in Detroit, and this fleet of demonstrators had soon hit as many as fifty cities. One of them was New York City for the National Automobile Show in January 1922. In March James B. Mansfield (a noted automotive engineer and president of Mansfield Steel Corporation, Mansfield Truck Company and Detroit Trailer Company) had been hired as consulting engineer, and Charles A. Towne (who had served in both houses of the U.S. Congress and who had run for the vice-presidency of the United States with Williams Jennings Bryan) came aboard as counsel. Stock was selling like hotcakes. But Mayor Carlson soon fell victim to his political enemies. Already a defamatory article about the company had appeared in the stock market publication, *U.S. Investor*. Initially it was thought this malicious piece of journalism could be turned to Birmingham's advantage. But in August 1922 the AP wire service buzzed with the news that a Federal grand jury in Washington had filed a presentment following a ten-month investigation by the U.S. Post Office. The charge was fraudulent use of the mails to sell more than $300,000 of worthless stock, and among the eighteen Birmingham men named was Mayor Samuel Carlson. Newspapers not friendly to Carlson had a heyday. During the next two months Birmingham assembled 26 cars and chassis to prove its viability. But a stockholders meeting in October ended in bedlam, with one local stock salesman stabbed to death. A Birmingham official smashed his way through a plateglass window to escape. In June of 1923, the indictment against Birmingham officials was dismissed in court. But the exoneration came far too late for Birmingham Motors. A valiant attempt was made to generate favorable publicity with a Duesenberg-engined special-built Birmingham race car to compete in the 1923 Indianapolis 500, but the money ran out before it could be completed. In December mortgage foreclosure arrived. In 1924 there was an attempt to revive the Birmingham as a new car to be called the Wright for the Canadian market. This plan fell apart quickly. As many as 50 Birminghams may have been built during the contentious short life of the company. None of the cars are believed to exist today.

BISHOP — Late in 1906 the firm of Bishop, McCormick and Bishop was organized with a capital stock of $51,000 to manufacture and deal in automobiles and motors in Poughkeepsie, New York. The partners were Eli H. Bishop, John McCormick and Bartol T. Bishop. Manufacture has not been documented.

BISHOP — **Fargo, North Dakota** — **(1910)** — Alfred L. Bishop of Fargo built a four-passenger touring car for himself in 1910. Its engine was 18-20 hp, and all parts of the vehicle were apparently of his own devising. He reported the car as his "#1," but that another followed is not known.

BISON — **Buffalo, New York** — **(1904)** — A Bison from Buffalo was kind of a cute idea, but there is no evidence that more than a prototype was ever built. The Bison Motor Company was organized early in 1904 by Frank I. Alliger, the mayor of Tonawanda, and Frederick Wende and William A. Lutz of Buffalo. The firm's capital stock was only $25,000, which seemed hardly sufficient for the grand plans of manufacturing steam, electric and gasoline motors, automobiles and auto boats. The Bison was extinct by year's end.

BISSELL — **Toledo, Ohio** — **(1909)** — F.E. Bissell was the president of a Toledo jobbing company which dealt in electrical equipment generally, and Bissell hoped, in 1909, an automobile specifically. He had acquired patterns for a light electric earlier in the year, and a single prototype was built. The car was not put on the market, however, and by 1910 the Bissell Electric Company had returned to its usual endeavors.

BISSING — An automobile was purportedly built by Justus Bissing in Hays, Kansas in 1908. Documentation is lacking.

BJELLA — **McIntosh, Minnesota** — **(1906)** — The Bjella was completed in the spring of 1906 in the shops of the McIntosh Iron and Wood Works, a firm specializing in the manufacture of wooden harrows and horse-drawn sleighs. It had a flat opposed two-cylinder engine and high wagon wheels, and a comely appearance which belied its backyard origins. Probably its designer, Ole A. Bjella, never harbored other than the most wishful notions of manufacture, but he was luckier than most pioneer builders whose total output was but one vehicle. His Bjella survives and has been restored by a collector in the Southwest.

1897 Black, runabout, GR

1899 Black, physician's phaeton, JAC

BLACK — **Indianapolis, Indiana** — **(1893; 1897-1900)** — Charles H. Black was the proprietor of a wagon works and blacksmith shop in Indianapolis, and he got the urge to construct a horseless carriage after driving a neighbor's imported Benz in 1891. The two-seater gasoline car he completed in 1893 was, not surprisingly, designed along Benz-like lines. Its coachwork was a buggy. Final drive was via two different-sized belts, providing for a high and low gear. Motive force was a small single-cylinder internal combustion engine which was cranked by a turn of the flywheel. Ignition was by kerosene torch, which must have been risky. Nonetheless, the 1893 Black car survives to this day, on display at the Indianapolis Children's Museum. From 1897 to 1900 Black built a somewhat refined version of his gasoline buggy for sale. None are believed to exist. His operation was a small one, and there is no indication that his cars were sold other than locally. Most carried his name; a few he called Indianapolis in 1899 when he named his enterprise the Indianapolis Automobile and Vehicle Company. In 1900 Black sold his patents to a group of unidentified local capitalists for $20,000. They organized as the Indiana Motor & Vehicle Company and produced the Black car as the Indiana in 1901.

BLACK STEAM — West Chester, Pennsylvania — (1902) — The carpentry shop of Seth C. Black was located in the alley to the rear of Woodward's livery stables, on Church Street, in West Chester. Although he spent most of his life as a carpenter, Black had thoughts of becoming an automobile manufacturer in 1902. "S.C. Black has completed his new automobile, and expects to give it a trial this afternoon," reported the *Daily Local News* of West Chester on March 11th, 1902. "Mr. Black will construct several more, having on hand about one dozen boilers for that purpose." He may indeed have built several more cars, but that proved to be the extent of his automobile manufacturing activity.

1906 Black, runabout, HAC

BLACK — Fort Wayne, Indiana — (1906) — The Black Manufacturing Company shared the same 216 West Berry Street address as the Randall Motor Car Company. The latter, Fort Wayne's first dealership for automobiles, had been established in 1901 by Alfred L. Randall. A prominent and wealthy citizen in town, Randall had offered John Brisben Walker's Mobile Steamer early on, and is credited with bringing the first Cadillacs and Fords to Fort Wayne. Prior to automobiles, he had been a bicycle dealer through which activity he came to know Marion Black, a local bicycle racer of some renown. By 1906, dissatisfied with merely being a dealer of cars, Randall was fired with enthusiasm at the idea of becoming an automobile manufacturer. Marion Black's name being well known in the area, he latched onto it and Marion Black himself, whom he installed as president of the Black Manufacturing Company. Whether Black had the engineering skill to design the two-cylinder 12 hp runabout that was to be sold under his name is not known. It is known that the car weighed 900 pounds and was to be sold for $750. "Something for the Dealer This Time" was the gambit under which the Black Manufacturing Company offered its product in the trade press. How many Blacks were built a mystery, but total production may have been the one prototype that was pictured in the ads soliciting dealers. Obviously dealers didn't buy Randall's Black automobile idea because by 1909 Fort Wayne directories indicated the Black Manufacturing Company as marketing only automobile parts, which conceivably may have been bought for the Black car that never was. Thereafter the Black Manufacturing Company quietly disappeared. As for Randall, he sold his dealership in 1916 and turned to the automobile financing business.

1910 Black, model 15, stanhope, WLB

BLACK — Chicago, Illinois — (1908-1910)/BLACK CROW — (1909-1910) — When the Black Manufacturing Company took its product to the Iowa State Fair during the summer of 1908, the result was $50,000 in orders — and high hopes for this typical builder of highwheelers that had just been launched into business. The Black was a two-cylinder air-cooled buggy with chain drive and solid rubber tires, which was a simple enough specification, although Black also chose initially to offer another highwheeler even more primeval which it marketed under the name of Chicago Motor Buggy. In 1909 Black bought out the defunct Aurora Motor Works thirty miles to the west for the production of parts for its cars — and,

desiring to offer its customers an even broader choice, joined forces with the newly-formed Crow Motor Car Company of Elkhart, Indiana to produce the four-cylinder Black Crow. This larger car was built entirely in the Indiana factory, and was also marketed through the Crow organization. That this might not have been the wisest arrangement for president W.H. Black to have made was apparent the year following when Crow summarily cancelled the contract with Black and said it would henceforth produce and sell the vehicle itself as the Crow-Elkhart. That spelled the end for the Black, the Black Crow and the Black Manufacturing Company.

1908 BLACK
Chicago Motor Buggy — 2-cyl., 14 hp, 69 1/2" wb

	FP	5	4	3	2	1
Type 12 Rbt.-2P	375	2400	3400	4800	8000	17,000
Type 112 Rbt.-2P	450	2450	3450	4900	8300	17,500
Type 212 Rbt. Limo.-2P	475	2500	3500	5000	8500	18,000

Black — 2-cyl., 18 hp, 75" wb

Type 18 Surrey-4P	575	2500	3500	5000	8500	18,000
Type 118 Surrey-4P	650	2500	3500	5000	8500	18,000
Type 20 Surrey	575	2500	3500	5000	8500	18,000
Type 30 Dly. Wagon	900	2300	3300	4600	7500	16,000

1909 Black Crow, roadster, WLB

1909 BLACK/BLACK CROW
Chicago Motor Buggy — 2-cyl., 14 hp, 69 1/2" wb

Type 12 Rbt.-2P	450	2400	3400	4800	8000	17,000
Type 112 Rbt.-2P	475	2400	3400	4800	8000	17,000
Type 212 Rbt. Limo.-2P	525	2500	3500	5000	8500	18,000

Black — 2-cyl., 18 hp, 75" wb

Type 18 Surrey-4P	575	2450	3450	4900	8300	17,500
Type 118 Surrey-4P	650	2450	3450	4900	8300	17,500
Type 20 Surrey	575	2450	3450	4900	8300	17,500
Type 30 Dly. Wagon	900	2300	3300	4600	7500	16,000

Black Crow — 4-cyl., 35/40 hp, 112" wb

Rbt.-2P	1000	2600	3550	5200	8700	18,500
Rds.-3P	1050	2700	3600	5300	8800	19,000
Combination Car	1250	2500	3500	5000	8500	18,000

1910 BLACK/BLACK CROW
Black — 2-cyl., 12 hp, 69 1/2" wb

Model 12 Stanhope	450	2400	3400	4800	8000	17,000

Black — 2-cyl., 12 hp, 82 1/2" wb

Model 15 Stanhope	500	2400	3400	4800	8000	17,000
Model 215 Rds.-2P	550	2700	3600	5300	8800	19,000

Black — 2-cyl., 12 hp, 75" wb

Model 18 High Wheel-4P	575	2500	3500	5000	8500	18,000

Black Crow — 4-cyl., 25 hp, 107" wb

Model C Tour.-3P	1000	2700	3600	5300	8800	19,000
Model D Rds.-2P	1050	2800	3650	5500	9000	19,500
Model E Surrey-4P	1100	2500	3500	5000	8500	18,000
Model F Pony Tonneau-4P	1200	2600	3550	5200	8700	18,500

Black Crow — 4-cyl., 35 hp, 120" wb

Model M Tour.-7P	1750	3000	4000	6000	9500	21,000
Model L Tour.-5P	1500	3000	4000	6000	9500	21,000

BLACKBURN — Houston, Texas — (1920-1921) — Like the later Mayfair, the Blackburn was an attempt to make a better Model T Ford. Its engine and chassis were Tin Lizzie, though the former was beefed up to 23 hp and the latter was provided a sliding gear transmission. A five-passenger touring was the only body style offered, and the price was $400. The car was produced for two years only by the Blackburn Automotive Company of Houston. Reportedly, as many as 500 may have been sold.

1920-1920 BLACKBURN
Four — 23 hp, 100" wb

Tour.-5P	400	2500	3500	5000	8500	18,000

BLACK DIAMOND — Geneva, New York — (1903) — The Black Diamond Automobile Company was organized by a group of New York businessmen in the fall of 1903. Among them were Dewett Hallenbeck of Geneva, who served as president; George P. Rogers of Seneca Falls; Edward J. Cook of Geneva; and three men from Brooklyn, George W. Spencer, John F. Hylan and William Dieter. The last named was a mechanical engineer and the inventor of the Dieter motor, which was a combination steam-gasoline unit and slated to power the new Black Diamond car. A half-million-dollar factory was proposed to be built in Geneva, but the Black Diamond venture there does not seem to have proceeded further than the building of a single prototype with the Dieter combination engine. Black Diamond did move into automobile manufacture in 1904, however, following merger with the Buckmobile Company of Utica. The Buckmobile was produced into 1905. Though Black Diamond had plans to manufacture a rather more refined car in 1905 under its own name, those plans were abruptly halted when the sheriff showed up to close the Buckmobile doors in Utica later that year.

1903 Blackhawk, runabout, NAHC

BLACKHAWK — Moline, Illinois — (1903) — In 1897 W.E. Clark of Moline built his first automobile, a single-cylinder air-cooled car with fan mounted on the flywheel. He tinkered with it into the turn of the century. In 1901 his Clark Manufacturing Company announced completion of a single-cylinder 4 hp air-cooled runabout for which production was planned forthwith. In 1902 the decision was made to call it a Blackhawk, and in 1903 Clark was finally ready for the market. By now he had come up with a two-cylinder model as well, and both were placed on the same chassis, with the engine mounted in the rear above the frame and its flywheel fitted underneath in a horizontal position. Steering was by tiller, and the transmission was planetary. Prices were $750 for the single-cylinder runabout, $850 for the double-cylinder phaeton. The Blackhawk survived less than a year. But W.E. Clark was back again in 1906 with a new car called the Deere-Clarke.

1903 BLACKHAWK

	FP	5	4	3	2	1
Rbt. (1-cyl.)	750	2400	3400	4800	8000	17,000
Phae. (2-cyl.)	850	2500	3500	5000	8500	18,000

1929 Blackhawk, four-door speedster, HAC

BLACKHAWK — Indianapolis, Indiana — (1929-1930) — The Blackhawk was a less powerful, less expensive and less noteworthy car manufactured by the Stutz Motor Car Company of America — and doubtless it was for these reasons that Stutz chose to make it a separate marque rather than a model of the Stutz. The choice of its name was calculated to evoke Stutz association, however, although it tended to confuse rather than enhance. The Blackhawk (one word) had little in common with the fabled Stutz Black Hawk (two words) speedsters which had preceded the cheaper car into the marketplace. The new Blackhawk was introduced for 1929 and was enthusiastically promoted. At the end of 1929, company figures indicated 2320 Stutzes and 1310 Blackhawks sold. In 1930 Blackhawk production dropped to 280 and the marque was quietly discontinued at the end of the year.

1929 BLACKHAWK
Model L-6 — 6-cyl., 85 hp, 127 1/2" wb

Spdstr.-2P	2535	5400	7300	11,800	25,000	38,000
Spdstr.-4P	2635	5500	7500	12,000	26,000	39,000
Spdstr.-4P (Tonneau Cowl)	2835	5700	7800	12,300	27,000	39,500
Cpe.-5P	2395	3500	4500	7000	13,000	25,000
Cpe.-2P	2595	3200	4300	6500	11,000	23,000
Cabr. Cpe.-4P	2595	3700	4700	7300	13,700	26,000
Sed.-5P	2695	2700	3600	5300	8800	19,000
Weymann Chantilly-5P	2895	3000	4000	6000	9500	21,000
Weymann Monaco-4P	2955	3000	4000	6000	9500	21,000
Weymann Deauville-4P	2955	3000	4000	6000	9500	21,000

1929 Blackhawk, sedan, JAC

Model L-8 — 8-cyl., 90 hp, 127 1/2" wb

	FP	5	4	3	2	1
Spdstr.-2P	2485	5900	8300	12,800	29,000	41,000
Spdstr.-4P	2585	6000	8500	13,000	30,000	42,000
Spdstr.-4P (Tonneau Cowl)	2835	6100	8700	13,300	30,500	42,500
Cpe.-5P	2345	3900	4800	7700	14,300	27,000
Cpe.-2P	2545	3500	4500	7000	13,000	25,000
Cabr. Cpe.-4P	2545	4000	5000	8000	15,000	28,000
Sed.-5P	2645	2900	3700	5600	9100	20,000
Weymann Chantilly-5P	2895	3200	4300	6500	11,000	23,000
Weymann Monaco-4P	2955	3200	4300	6500	11,000	23,000
Weyman Deauville-5P	2955	3200	4300	6500	11,000	23,000

1930 Blackhawk, touring, JAC

1930 BLACKHAWK
Model L6 — 6-cyl., 85 hp, 127 1/2" wb

Sed.-5P	2395	3100	4200	6300	10,500	22,000
Cpe.-5P	1995	3500	4500	7000	13,000	25,000
Cpe.-2P	2495	3300	4400	6700	12,000	24,000
Spdstr.-2P	2535	6000	8500	13,000	30,000	42,000
Spdstr.-4P	2533	5900	8300	12,800	29,000	41,000
Spdstr.-4P (Tonneau Cowl)	2735	6200	8800	13,500	31,000	43,000
Cabr. Cpe.	2595	5800	8000	12,500	28,000	40,000
Weymann Chantilly-5P	2595	4000	5000	8000	15,000	28,000
Weymann Monaco-4P	2655	4000	5000	8000	15,000	28,000
Weymann Deauville-4P	2655	4000	5000	8000	15,000	28,000

Model L8 — 8-cyl., 90 hp, 127 1/2" wb

Sed.-5P	2395	3300	4400	6700	12,000	24,000
Cpe.-5P	1995	3700	4700	7300	13,700	26,000
Cpe.-2P	2495	3500	4500	7000	13,000	25,000
Spdstr.-2P	2535	6200	8800	13,500	31,000	43,000
Spdstr.-4P (Tonneau Cowl)	2735	6300	9000	14,000	32,000	44,000
Cabr. Cpe.	2595	5900	8300	12,800	29,000	41,000
Weymann Chantilly-5P	2595	4200	5200	8400	15,700	29,000
Weymann Monaco-4P	2655	4200	5200	8400	15,700	29,000
Weymann Deauville-4P	2655	4200	5200	8400	15,700	29,000

1912 Blackiston, runabout, LC

BLACKISTON — Canton, Ohio — (1912) — Though unquestionably it was a car, the vehicle built by G.P. Blackiston of Canton appeared as big as a locomotive. Its chassis was that of a former (and unidentified) racing car to which Blackiston fitted two radiators, one a honeycomb, the other a tubular. The hood was seven-and-a-half feet long and five-and-a-half feet high. "As the hood towers above the driver's head, the only direct view to the front is at one side of the car," *The Automobile Journal* reported, "but the ingenious placing of mirrors is expected to overcome this difficulty." The engine of the Blackiston developed 90 hp, and the car's top speed was expected to be about 137 mph. G.P. Blackiston insisted that he had not built the car for racing, however, but instead "to find enjoyment in making long distance tours therein."

BLACKSTONE — Momence, Illinois — (1916) — Other than the fact that it was an assembled car with a $845 price tag, little is known about the Blackstone. Executive offices were in Chicago, the factory in Momence, and the Blackstone Motor Company was a $100,000 incorporation. In November of 1916, Blackstone revealed its selection of A.E. Patchin, formerly general sales manager of the Double Service Tire & Rubber Company of Akron, to serve in the same capacity for the Blackstone. By the end of the year, however, Patchin had no car to sell, as the Blackstone company quickly went under. M.L. Rogers, L.L. Irwin and Harry W. Davis had been the entrepreneurs of the Blackstone venture.

BLAIR — A number of ventures called Blair were promoted, but the evidence suggests that none of the following ever produced a Blair car.
  The Blair-Forth Manufacturing Company was organized in Boston, Massachusetts with a capital stock of $100,000 during the early spring of 1908. Clarence Forth and William Blair were the partners involved. Forth subsequently built a car under his own name in Mansfield, Ohio in 1910.
  The Blair Manufacturing Company was organized in Newark, Ohio with a capital stock of $300,000 during the fall of 1911 by Frank M. Blair, John R. McCune, Willis A. Robbins, Edwin C. Wright and Harry H. Baird. The company was reorganized three years later as the Blair Motor Truck Company. Commercial vehicles only seem to have been produced.
  The Blair Manufacturing Company of Boston, Massachusetts was a million-dollar incorporation from early 1914 promoted by M.A. Daniher, E.T. Roche and J.B. Lazenby.
  The Blair Motor Company of Cincinnati, Ohio was incorporated early in 1911 with a capital stock of $25,000. Incorporators were John A. Deasy, P.F. Habercorn, John H. Monahan, J.W. Creaman and E.H. Bourk.
  Blair, Scofield & Company was a $100,000 Delaware incorporation organized during the fall of 1910.

BLAIR STEAMER — Northboro, Massachusetts — (1906) — The Blair Light Company of Northboro tested the steamer it built during the summer of 1906. The vehicle purportedly was entirely automatic in operation, requiring the use of neither fuel nor air pumps. Because the company did not proceed into manufacture, one must assume the tests did not turn out as expected.

1903 Blaisdell Steamer, NAHC

BLAISDELL — Brooklyn, New York — (1903) — J.F. Blaisdell of Brooklyn built a large steam delivery vehicle in 1903 which showed very well in the commercial vehicle tests held in New York City that June. That year he also built a steam stanhope for the use of Dr. S.C. Blaisdell, also of Brooklyn. "The doctor to date has owned a number of light steam vehicles," *The Horseless Age* reported, ". . . however, in time, many structural weaknesses were discovered and the machines were disposed of." The stanhope built for him by Blaisdell & Company appeared considerably more substantial. Although no family relationship between J.F. Blaisdell and Dr. S.C. Blaisdell was indicated, it would appear likely that they were related.

BLAKE — The Blake Automobile Company was organized with a capital stock of $100,000 during the summer of 1912 for the purpose of building automobiles in Cambridge, Massachusetts. E.C. Blake and L.E. Gibson were among the promoters involved. That fall the venture was reincorporated as the Cambridge Automobile Company. There was no manufacture.

BLAKE — Attleboro, Massachusetts — (1901) — That James E. Blake of Attleboro built one gasoline automobile in 1901 is documented. That many others followed is doubtful. Rights to the vehicle were acquired in July of 1901 by the United States Automobile Company in Attleboro, this firm having previously built the electric car designed by Frank Mossberg, who owned a big bicycle bell factory in town and who left the United States Automobile Company that year. Mossberg returned in 1903, however, and a few more of the Blake-designed gasoline cars were built that year — together with his electric — in the bicycle bell factory. All cars built carried the tradename of United States.

BLAKESLEE — The Blakeslee was one of four names under which the same electric victoria was marketed between 1905 and 1910 in Cleveland, Ohio. Refer to DeMars.
  The Blakeslee-Britten Company was organized early in 1910 with a capital stock of $50,000 for the manufacture of automobiles in Jersey City, New Jersey. G.E. Blakeslee, E.F. Britten, Jr. and E.E. Downs were the principals involved. Manufacture is doubted.

BLANCHARD — F.W. Blanchard was one member of the committee which came up with the Faulkner-Blanchard produced in Detroit in 1910. Refer to Faulkner-Blanchard.
  A.W. Blanchard, Inc. was organized in Brooklyn, New York during the fall of 1908 for the manufacture of motor cars and motor boats. Capital stock was $25,000. Manufacture is doubted.

BLANCHARD — Springfield, Massachusetts — (1826) — Among the twenty-five inventions patented by Thomas Blanchard during his lifetime was a steam carriage. It was completed by the inventor in 1826, and was demonstrated by him in November and December of that year. Springfield newspapers from that period indicate that the vehicle was successfully operated; it "could run forward and backwards, steer properly and climb hills, aided by a set of interchangeable gears which would transmit the driving force to the rear wheels in two speeds." The Blanchard steam carriage accommodated eight passengers. Its engine had a piston stroke of eleven inches; pine wood was used for fuel. Although the Massachusetts State Legislature supported his steam car development, Thomas Blanchard did not proceed further than the building of one machine. He turned his attention thereafter to other inventions, including a lathe for turning gunstocks, a device for making tacks, a steam process for bending hardwood for chairs and wheels, a machine for cutting and folding envelopes in one operation. He also devised a number of steamboats, and applied his ingenuity to locomotive construction as well. He died in 1864.

BLANCHE — The inclusion of the Blanche among automobiles built in 1906 in the United States is amusing, because it is incorrect on two counts. First, the name is a misspelling of Bianchi; and second, the Bianchi was an Italian car imported but never built in this country.

BLANK & SCHREIBER — Walcott, Iowa — (1914) — The cyclecar produced by the partnership of R.H. Blank and G. Schreiber weighed 400 pounds, had a wheelbase of 100 inches, a tread of 36 inches, was fitted with a 12 hp Deluxe motor and a friction transmission. There was a single seat in front for the driver, a rumble seat in the rear for the passenger — and undoubtedly only one example of this car ever was built. Blank and Schreiber had planned to manufacture the vehicle in Walcott, Iowa.

BLAUROCK — New York, New York — (1900) — Manufacture of a Blaurock automobile was considered at the turn of the century, and at least a single prototype was built, but it seems evident that the Blaurock Carriage Company of New York City never proceeded into serious automobile marketing. That the Blaurock organization was a financially healthy one during this period is equally evident, however, from press reports of the sumptuous banquet John A. Blaurock threw for newspaper men upon the occasion of the first New York Automobile Show that year.

BLEECK — Early in 1915 in St. Louis, Missouri the Bleeck Automobile Company was organized with a capital stock of $10,000 in order to "buy, sell and manufacture automobiles." John N. Bleeck, A.M. Bleeck and Eugene Herr were the principals involved. Manufacture is doubted.

BLEVINS — The Blevins-Garrity Motor Company was organized in Knoxville, Tennessee during the fall of 1910 with $50,000 capital stock and a plan to manufacture and deal in automobiles. R.C. Blevins, J.A. Dickey, S.S. McCormick, C.G. Avin and George W. Robertson were the people involved. Manufacture is doubted.

BLEVNEY STEAMER — Newark, New Jersey — (1901) — John C. Blevney of Newark built a vehicle in 1901 with two steam engines flanking a perpendicular boiler placed in the rear of the chassis. He experimented with this road wagon for two years, and then followed it in 1903 with a steam truck. He also invented a rear-wheel device for converting a horsedrawn wagon to a power vehicle. It does not appear that any of his inventions saw manufacture. In 1895 he had been superintendent of the De la Vergne Refrigerating Machine Company which had completed its first car the following year.

1899 Blimline Gasoline Carriage, auto-buggy, NAHC

BLIMLINE — Sinking Spring, Pennsylvania — (1898-1899) — Sebastian Blimline was a carriage builder in Sinking Spring, and in 1898 he built the first automobile in his area. It was a two-passenger runabout powered by a 1-1/2 hp gasoline engine. Two speeds — three and ten miles an hour — were obtained by means of a clutch on a countershaft and two pulleys. Almost immediately, Blimline began building another more powerful — 4 hp — carriage, and by February of 1899 he announced that he expected to being marketing his cars in the spring. His venture did not survive the turn of the century, however.

1906 Bliss, touring, WLB

BLISS — Brooklyn, New York — (1906) — Audacity was perhaps the most noteworthy attribute of the E.W. Bliss Company. "The Bliss Car, as the name implies, is the very best that can be produced," the company said. It had a four-cylinder T-head engine, integral flywheel and fan, double chain drive, and was available with a five-seater tonneau body for $5000 and with any custom body a purchaser desired for a lot more. Advertised as "The Car with a Reputation Behind It," the reputation was that of E.W. Bliss, who was claimed to be one of the ablest engineers in the business and renowned in both Europe and America. That may have been true, but Bliss' business prior to 1906 had been as builder of heavy presses. The Bliss car was purportedly designed by Harold E. Porter, but it was probably Bliss' expertise in metallurgy which had resulted in the extensive use of chrome-nickel steel throughout. "Too busy to go to Chicago," Bliss advertised early in 1906 with reference to the automobile show in the Windy City. A touring car and a chassis had been on display at the New York Show that January. Precisely one year later — in January 1907 — E.W. Bliss declared that he had "had enough of the automobile business." A total of ten cars had been built representing an investment of $250,000. The E.W. Bliss Company returned exclusively to its machinery and drop forging efforts.

1906 BLISS
Four — 30 hp, 114" wb

	FP	5	4	3	2	1
Tour.-5P	5000	3000	4000	6000	9500	21,000

124

1902 Bliss, touring, MVMA

BLISS — Attleboro, Massachusetts — (1901-1902) — Whether the vehicle's motive power was steam or gasoline mattered less to the Bliss Chainless Automobile Company than the method of driving that power. The father-son team of A.H. and F.H. Bliss disliked chains. In the experimental steam car they built in 1901 the drive to the rear axle was by spur gearing. In 1902 they put together a touring car with a 12 hp gasoline engine built by Edward F. Scholze and shaft drive of their own invention. Apparently only a single example of each car was produced. In early 1903 it was reported that one Napoleon P. Bliss of Attleboro was promoting a new company to manufacture motor vehicles. His relationship to A.H. and F.H. Bliss is a matter of question, but this venture failed before the production of a single car. Of the Bliss automobiles that were built, the ultimate destiny of the gasoline touring car is unknown: the Bliss steamer was consumed in a fire at the local commercial garage to which it had been sent for repairs. After their automotive venture had ended, A.H. and F.H. Bliss returned completely to their usual work as jewelry manufacturers.

1906 B.L.M., race car, runabout, WLB

B.L.M. — Brooklyn, New York — (1906-1907) — The initials stood for Sidney S. Breese, Charles l.. Lawrence and Andrew Moulton, three young men barely out of their teens who joined together to form the Breese, Lawrence, Moulton Motor Car and Equipment Company of Brooklyn for the production of quite extraordinary motorcars. Their initial idea, announced in August 1906, was a race car that was based on an experimental model Breese and Lawrence had put together in 1905. It had 85 hp and a price tag of $12,000 — and the young men quickly concluded there wasn't a sufficient market for such cars to build a viable business. Consequently, early in 1907, came the Pirate Runabout, powered by a 24 hp engine made by Mutel et Cie and imported from France, and placed in a 1400-pound shaft-drive chassis. Fifty-five miles an hour was guaranteed with the standard gear, and optional gears could be furnished for speeds from 35 to 70 mph. What B.L.M. was building would later become known as a sports car, though this had not been the B.L.M. idea at all, but instead "to fill the requirements of a private conveyance for the suburban motorist who prefers to use the automobile instead of the railway in going to and from his business." The ordinary runabout was too slow for this purpose, the average touring car was fast enough but too heavy and expensive to run. In the Pirate, the young men said, "we have solved the problem of a practical business man's conveyance by adopting the lines of a miniature racer." Then, for more elegant motoring, they came up with a lower-powered and lovely landaulet. It is a pity their enterprise did not succeed. Plans for the production of 250 cars were announced in September 1907, by December the company was in receivership. Conceivably, the B.L.M. marketing approach had been wrong. The sportiness of the Pirate should have been emphasized rather than its practicality. A few years later the T-head Mercer Raceabout, which bore a resemblance to the B.L.M., became something of a sensation. By that time, two of the B.L.M. partners were in Paris building a special sporting car just for themselves. Just two examples of the L.M. ensued, one for Lawrence, one for Moulton. Purportedly, they cost $30,000 apiece and were on the road in Paris in 1912.

1907 B.L.M., Pirate, runabout, HAC

1907 B.L.M.

	FP	5	4	3	2	1
Pirate Runabout	3500	3500	4500	7000	13,000	25,000
Four — 16 hp, 98" wb						
Land'et.	4500	3200	4300	6500	11,000	23,000

BLOCK BROTHERS — The inclusion of this car on automotive lists for 1905 is a typographical error. The Blood brothers were building their car in Kalamazoo, Michigan during this period. Refer to Blood.

1921 Blodgett, touring, SKY

BLODGETT — Detroit, Michigan — (1921) — The Blodgett was a five-passenger touring car with a six-cylinder Continental engine that was built as a prototype only by the Blodgett Engineering & Tool Company, a long-time family-operated business in Detroit, the Blodgetts at the helm being Frederick F., Alvah S. and Alexander H. The firm had prospered for years as designers and builders of dies, tools, jigs, fixtures, special machinery and metal stampings. Its plans to enter the automobile manufacturing field — with a sedan and a coupe addition to the touring car — were genuine, and thwarted probably by the depressed postwar economy.

1907 Blomstrom, model 30, runabout, WLB

BLOMSTROM — Detroit, Michigan — (1902-1903; 1907-1908) — C.H. Blomstrom was responsible for no fewer than five different cars: the Queen, the Gyroscope, the Rex cyclecar, the Frontmobile — and the Blomstrom. Actually there were two Blomstroms. After building an experimental car in 1897, and another in 1899, C.H. became a manufacturer in 1902 of a small single-cylinder runabout he named for himself. By the end of 1903 he had built twenty-five of these cars, and in 1904 established the C.H. Blomstrom Motor Company. He renamed his car the Queen at that time and built 1500 of them from 1904 to 1906, when legal difficulties forced him to move across town in Detroit. There, in August 1906, he

established the Blomstrom Manufacturing Company. His new Blomstrom 30 — a bigger car than his former Queen — was ready for the start of the 1907 season. It was little changed for 1908 when Blomstrom announced that production that year was being planned at 200 units: 125 touring cars and 75 runabouts. The Blomstrom was described in the press as "the last thing in motor car design throughout," but by now C.H. was fascinated by his next new thing, the Gyroscope car which was nearing production status in another section of the same factory. The Blomstrom probably died through neglect.

1907 BLOMSTROM
Model 30 — 4-cyl., 30 hp, 110" wb

	FP	5	4	3	2	1
Tour.-5P	2250	2700	3600	5300	8800	19,000
Rbt.-3P	2250	2800	3650	5500	9000	19,500

1908 BLOMSTROM
Model 30 — 4-cyl., 35 hp, 110" wb

	FP	5	4	3	2	1
Tour.-5P	2250	2900	3700	5600	9100	20,000
Rbt.-3P	2250	2950	3900	5800	9300	20,500

BLOOD — A Blood from Minneapolis, Minnesota has frequently appeared on rosters as a car built in 1900. This would appear not to be so. City directory listings from Minneapolis for the years from 1900 through 1902 include a Blood-Milli Motor Vehicle Company at 244 First Avenue North. J.D. Anderson was president, H.W. Benton vice-president, B. Tuchman secretary-treasurer. The listings do not indicate that any automobile was being manufactured. More than likely, the firm operated as an automobile dealership.

1903 Blood, model A, NAHC

BLOOD — Kalamazoo, Michigan — (1903, 1905-1906) — Maurice E. and Charles C. Blood were remarkably skilled mechanics and the proprietors of the Kalamazoo Cycle Company. Charles D. and Frank D. Fuller were good businessmen and the proprietors of a wood product manufacturing company in Kalamazoo. In December 1902, when the Fullers decided to become automobile producers, they got in touch with the Bloods — and the Michigan Automobile Company, Ltd. was formed. The Bloods' first prototype car was on the road in the spring of 1903, a tiny little vehicle with a 48-inch wheelbase that weighed all of 360 pounds. Although it was tested for over 3000 miles, the Blood brothers were aware that they had adhered too closely to bicycle practice in its construction. Their next prototype stretched out to a 54-inch wheelbase, and it was this car which was put into production as the Michigan. It was followed by a twin on a 78-inch wheelbase for 1904. And the brothers designed two models for 1905. All

1905 Blood Brothers, touring, NAHC

125

these cars would be called Michigans. But in 1905 they became Bloods too. Late in the previous year, the Bloods and the Fullers had quarreled, with the result that M.E. and C.C. left the Michigan organization to establish the Blood Brothers Automobile & Machinery Company which proceeded to manufacture the same cars under the Blood name. Earlier the Bloods had set themselves up as agents for the Pope and Cadillac motorcars, and they continued this business as well. The Blood was not built after 1906. In November that year the brothers issued a statement announcing cessation of automobile manufacture, the removal of the word "automobile" from their company name, and the forthcoming manufacture of universal joints exclusively. Less than a decade later, however, the brothers were back in the automobile business building a new car called the Cornelian. The Michigan, incidentally, survived one year longer than did the Blood.

1905-1906 BLOOD
Model C — 2-cyl., 12 hp, 78" wb

	FP	5	4	3	2	1
Light Touring	900	2700	3600	5300	8800	19,000
Model D — 2-cyl., 12 hp, 80" wb						
Demi-Tonneau	1100	2800	3650	5500	9000	19,500
Model E — 2-cyl., 16 hp, 90" wb						
Side Entrance Tonneau	1250	2900	3700	5600	9100	20,000

BLOOD CYCLECAR — The cyclecar built by the Blood Brothers Machine Company of Kalamazoo, Michigan from 1914-1915 was called the Cornelian. Refer to Cornelian.

BLOOM — A.J. Bloom was the brother-in-law of R.C. Hupp, founder of the Hupp Motor Company and the R.C.H. Corporation. His plan was to produce a cyclecar, but he was not nearly so lucky in this as his sister's husband had been in his automotive ventures. The Bloom never passed the prototype stage, nor was a company ever organized for its manufacture.

BLUE — Although initially indicated as simply the Blue, this 1910 Detroit automobile venture quickly became True Blue. Refer to True Blue.
In early 1912, in Brooklyn, New York, the Blue Taxi Company was organized for the manufacture of taxicabs. S.H. Miskind, H.M. Bemberger and M. May were the principals involved. Manufacture has not been substantiated.

BLUEBIRD — There were two cars called Bluebird, but they are more properly regarded as models. The first was built by Gilbert Loomis in Westfield, Connecticut in 1903-1904. Refer to Loomis. The second was merely a nickname for a race car built by the Chalmers company of Detroit in 1910.
In 1910 in New Rochelle, New York, the Bluebird Motor Cab Company was organized with a capital stock of $40,000 to "manufacture, rent and deal in motor cars, motor cycles, etc." Behind this venture were John K. Robinson, Jr., Theodore I. Bridgeman and E.W. Wilson. Whether any cars were produced has not been established, but the company remained in New Rochelle as a taxi operator for a number of years. In 1917 the firm's name was changed to Blue Bird Taxi and Garage.

BLUE & GOLD — Sacramento, California — (1910-1913) — "Will Sacramento be the center of the automobile manufacturing business with a $200,000 plant putting out upwards of 5000 machines a year for the coast trade, and with branch manufactories and distributing points at Los Angeles and Portland?" That was the question asked in a page one story appearing in the September 26th, 1910 issue of the Sacramento *Union*. The answer, as it turned out, was no. But for a while this venture promised to be something big. San Francisco businessmen were backing it, and the curious name they gave to their venture was A Automobile Company. E.C. Collins was president, J.H. Graham vice-president, C.E. Gibbs secretary, and T.F. Cooke treasurer. They spent the next several months looking over sites in the area, and exciting the Sacramento city fathers with the prospects of their idea. "We are figuring on our first production now," T.F. Cooke revealed in November. "It will be a torpedo body runabout machine, and the price will be within the reach of any one of moderate means. As we expand our business, larger cars will be placed on the market at considerably lower prices than those manufactured in the East." A lavish architectural drawing of the seven-building A Automobile Company complex appeared later that month. A site had been donated by the North Sacramento Land Company "under terms that call for the erection of the plant within a specified length of time." In January 1911 A Automobile Company established offices in Sacramento. In late May a company representative said that construction would begin "in the very near future." The A Automobile Company people did proceed far enough to select the name of Blue & Gold (the California state colors) for their car, and to build a few examples of both four and six cylinders (with electric lights, self starters and left hand drive) which were displayed in a local dealership in 1913, according to an article that May in the *San Francisco Examiner*. Advertisements for the Blue & Gold indicated a $2100 six-cylinder model for which no specifications were given and a $1150 four on a 108-inch wheelbase chassis featuring a three-speed selective sliding gear transmission, central control and multiple disc clutch. The San Francisco dealer had announced that output for "the present model season" would be 500 cars. But nowhere near that number resulted. One Blue & Gold registered in California during 1916-1917 carried serial number 10028, so a total production in two digits seems likely. Interestingly, after failing in Sacramento, the A Automobile Company considered making Richmond, California its home and naming one of its models after the town, but that idea fell through by the end of 1914 when the city fathers of Richmond failed to provide adequate financial inducements to bring the bereft A Automobile Company to town.

BLUE LIGHT — Hagerstown, Maryland — (1927-c. 1931) — Like the Aristocrat, the Astor, the Five-Boro, the Luxor, the Paramount, the Super Paramount and the Twentieth Century, the Blue Light was a taxicab produced by the Moller organization in Hagerstown. Its engine was a Buda, and its specifications a virtual carbon copy of the others. The only difference in the Blue Light was that it was built exclusively for use in the city of Baltimore, Maryland.

BLUE STREAK — Blue Streak was the model designation for a semi-racer runabout produced by the Logan Construction Company of Chillicothe, Ohio from 1907-1908. Refer to Logan.

BLUFF CLIMBER — St. Louis, Missouri — (1901-1902) — The Bluff Climber was a steam car sold in kit form by the Neustadt-Perry Company of St. Louis. "While it is a small machine in size," commented *The Automobile Review* in 1901, "it has excellent steaming capacity, making regular trips across the Mississippi bottoms and climbing the heavy grades known as the Bluff Hills, from which it obtained the name of 'The Bluff Climber'." The Neustadt company produced a variety of other kit cars in addition to and following the Bluff Climber, sometimes with catchy designations, other times under the Neustadt name.

BLUMBERG — San Antonio & Orange, Texas — (1920-1921) — The Blumberg represents one of the longer-lived frauds in the history of the American automobile. Some references indicate that it was in production from 1915 to 1922, but the fact was that it was never really in proper production at all. There was a lot of stock sold, however. Although there were a number of previous incorporations along the way, the Blumberg Motor Manufacturing Company as a two-million-dollar venture arrived in 1920. The incorporation took place in Delaware, with all principals indicated to be from Wilmington. Both tractors and passenger cars were slated to be built, and photos extant indicate that at least some of the former were. As for automobiles, Blumberg announcements proclaimed the building to custom order of either four-cylinder or V-8 cars, a seven-passenger touring of the latter to sell for $3000. A number of years ago George K. Holland of the Orange County Historical Society interviewed one of the former shareholders in the company, who remembered the "Blumberg" well. No dividends nor any correspondence having followed his purchase of shares, this disgruntled stockholder traveled to San Antonio to check out the company personally. He found that the Blumberg offices were a suite in the best hotel in town, and the address of the Blumberg factory turned out to be a deserted shed with no sign of any automotive activity ever having happened there. Blumberg company president, H.G. Blumberg was not in the hotel at the time of the stockholder's first visit there, and did not show up the second time when the stockholder made an appointment to see him. Conceivably he was already wearing his new hat — as president of the Lone Star Motor Truck and Tractor Association.

B & O — The B. & O. Auto Line was organized in Lansing, Michigan during the summer of 1906 to "buy, sell, repair, build and operate automobiles." Behind this $5000 venture were L.E. Bussey, W.H. Olmstead, W.S. Anderson and F.G. Withrow. Manufacture of any cars is doubted.
The B & O Engineering Company of 270 Watson Street in Buffalo was included in the "List of American Cyclecar Makers" in *Automobile Trade Journal's* January 1914 issue. Details regarding the company's car are lacking.

BOBCAT — Bobcat was the name given to a three-cylinder two-seater steam roadster planned to be built in Garfield, Ohio during the early Twenties. Refer to MacDonald.

BODE — Chicago, Illinois — (1903) — "The Bode Automobile Company, of Chicago, Ill., are putting through 200 gasoline runabouts," *The Horseless Age* announced brightly in July of 1903. The firm had been incorporated the month before with a capital stock of $50,000 by Leon S. Alschuler, James G. Condon and Charles W. Stiefel. Bode was not heard from again in 1904.

1902 Bohnet, steam runabout, LPL

BOHNET — Lansing, Michigan — (1901-1902) — George J. Bohnet of Lansing worked variously as a druggist and a machinist, in the bicycle business and in the music business — and in 1901 he completed building the first steam car in the city of Lansing. The task had required a year-and-a-half; the car's first test run was on the evening of June 6th. Almost immediately he sold the vehicle to a doctor from DeWitt for less than a thousand dollars, and he was at work building his second car for an executive from the Capital Electric Company. That one was completed and delivered in ten months. The Bohnet steamer was an attractive little runabout with wire wheels and tiller steering. Having sold his first two cars so easily, George Bohnet was encouraged to think bigger, and he persuaded J.W. Post of Lansing to think bigger with him. Together they established the Lansing Automobile Works in 1902, with Bohnet to do the designing and Post to handle, as the Twentieth Century Edition of *The Lansing Journal* put it that year, "the business end of the company." Alas, there was no business, and the partnership soon ended. Bohnet then joined W.K. Prudden as an automobile dealer, handling Oldsmobiles through 1906, Reos through 1917 and Dodges thereafter.

1901-1902 BOHNET

	FP	5	4	3	2	1
Bohnet Steam Car	—	2500	3500	5000	8500	18,000

BOISSELOT — Jersey City, New Jersey — (1901) — The Boisselot Automobile and Special Gasoline Motor Company of Jersey City had two ideas: the automobile itself and an introduction to it so "that the most modest purse may partake of its pleasure." This latter was a 1/4 hp motor and the necessary attachments that would transform an ordinary bicycle into a motorcycle in a few hours. It was the Boisselot hope that, thus introduced, the Boisselot motor purchaser would step up next to the Boisselot motor carriage. Boisselot automobiles were provided in two models: "The Pearl" two-seater with a 3-3/4 hp water-cooled engine, priced at $600; and the 6 hp "La Boisselot" voiturette for three or four passengers at $1200. Both vehicles featured the company's exclusive "carburated Thermo Auto Regulator which will secure a complete pulverization." Boisselot set up a sister company to produce auto parts and in 1902 was succeeded by the Holland Automobile Company which built a steam car.

1901 BOISSELOT

"The Pearl"	600	1600	2700	3800	5800	12,000
"La Boisselot"	1200	1700	2750	3900	6000	12,500

BOLENDER — Dayton, Ohio — (1914) — As a backyard creation, the cyclecar built by F.P. Bolender of Dayton was undoubtedly better than many. This was conclusively proved, so a Dayton newspaper stated in 1914, when Bolender was arrested for speeding through town at 32 mph. "The owner and manufacturer said it was the second time he had driven the contraption," it reported, "and he was not certain that he was making such good speed yet he was willing to accept as true the officer's statement, so he pleaded guilty." Bolender was fined $10 and costs.

BOLLEE — By the turn of the century Leon Bollee was famous as the builder of a fine car in France. In 1904 C.C. Worthington of New York City acquired the license to build the Leon Bollee in America. Refer to Worthington-Bollee.

BOLLSTROM — Battle Creek, Michigan — (1915, 1921) — Whether Maurice Bollstrom ever did manage to market a car under his own name is very much to be doubted, but that was not for lack of trying. An engineer who had bounced around in the industry for a good many years, Bollstrom was heading his own Bollstrom Products Sales Company in Battle Creek in 1915. His product then was a four-wheel-drive chassis of one-half ton capacity which was to be used as the basis for roadster, touring car and delivery bodies. Bollstrom himself had built only prototypes, but announced in June that he had closed a contract with a Michigan manufacturer to produce the vehicles for him, with deliveries slated to begin that November. They never did. Six years later Maurice Bollstrom was again back in the news, but his car this time was a front-drive. Again, he had built a prototype, which he demonstrated to potential investors in various Midwest cities. The car was described by a St. Louis reporter who saw it as resembling "an ordinary automobile except that the motor is somewhat higher atop the front axle, and tonneau is slung lower and the rear wheels extend somewhat further back behind the body." That Bollstrom never made it into production either.

1900 Bolte, runabout, NAHC

BOLTE — Kearney, Nebraska — (1900) — Thomas H. Bolte was the owner of a bicycle shop in Kearney who built a gasoline runabout in 1900. It was powered by a single cylinder 2 hp engine with belt drive to the countershaft and double chain drive to the rear wheels. The car was announced to the national automotive press, and Bolte indicated his plans to form a company for its manufacture with the factory to be located in Denver, Colorado. Apparently, he never got that far west, however. References from 1920 indicate that the Bolte Manufacturing Company in Kearney was engaged in the manufacture of cement mixers.

BOND — The Bond Brothers Company was organized with a capital stock of $10,000 to manufacture automobiles in Portland, Maine. This early 1907 venture was promoted by G.A. Hutchins and C.H. Tolman, both of Portland. No car seems to have been produced.

BONEBRAKE-ROBERTS — El Reno, Oklahoma — (1907) — "Another implement company contemplates 'going into automobiles,'" *The Motor World* announced in June of 1907. In El Reno, Oklahoma, the Bonebrake-Roberts company had completed a model of its automobile which it declared "appears to be practical, substantial and serviceable." Appearances deceived, however, because the Bonebrake-Roberts was not put into formal production. The Bonebrake half of the partnership tried again the following year, however. According to *The Motor World* in February 1908, "Mr Bonebrake entered into negotiations with the Chamber of Commerce of Wichita, Kansas, with a view of obtaining a factory site in that city." Those negotiations ultimately fell through, and Mr. Bonebrake returned to Oklahoma and the string of hardware stores that he had been operating profitably for some time around the state.

BONNER — The Bonner Automobile Company was organized in Brooklyn, New York early in 1910 by C.L. Bonner, J.G. Gastelger and J.W. Gastelger. The plan was manufacture of "horseless vehicles, motors, engines, etc.," and the capital stock was $2500. Manufacture did not follow.

In the fall of 1912, in Cambridge, Massachusetts, the D. Henry Bonner Company was organized with a capital stock of $20,000 to manufacture and deal in automobiles. In addition to Bonner, Edward S. Howland and William E. Furniss were involved. Manufacture has not been established.

BONNER — Chrisman, Illinois — (1910-1911) — Very little is known about this automobile save for the fact that two were built shortly after the establishment of the Bonner Manufacturing Company in Chrisman. Apparently, the cars, which used Rutenber engines, were experimental vehicles to test the viability of production, and the company soon decided to forgo the idea. Bonner was a machine-tool manufacturing concern which probably enjoyed its most significant success as the supplier of pipe wrenches for the building of the Panama Canal. Purportedly, the Bonner people also supplied the wrenches for the Rayfield cars built in Chrisman.

BOOTH-CROUCH — This pioneer vehicle of 1896 was built for Dr. Carlos C. Booth by W. Lee Crouch in his machine shop in New Brighton, Pennsylvania. Refer to Crouch.

1900 Borbein, electric runabout, HAC

BORBEIN — St. Louis, Missouri — (1900, 1904-1909) — In 1899 H.F. Borbein & Company began manufacturing solid steel axles and artillery wood wheels at the corner of Ninth and Clark in St. Louis. In 1900, when his quarters became cramped there, Henry Borbein moved to Cass Avenue — and within a year was crowded again, but without sufficient capital to make another move. During 1900 he had built an electric runabout and caught the "automotive bug." Consequently, early in 1901, he joined forces with the Brecht Butchers' Supply Company, which had decided to establish an automotive sideline. Borbein served as manager of the Brecht Automobile Company from 1901 until October 1903 when he had the wherewithal to buy out Brecht, immediately changing the name of the product from Brecht to Borbein and announcing that he stood ready "to fill all outstanding orders." Like the latterday Brechts, Borbeins were sold in diverse states of undress. Motors, tanks and connections were never supplied, but the rest varied according to model. Borbein's No. 26, for example, was a large 130-inch steel-framed touring car chassis "furnished ready for power with one coat of lead paint, with or without upholstering." No doubt Borbein's product was bought by both the backyard do-it-your-selfer and unimaginative entrepreneurs who wanted to get into manufacture the easy way. Precisely how long Borbein remained in business selling these quasi-kit cars is not known. Although he was pressed for receivership in August 1907, H.F. Borbein was still advertising late in 1909. Thereafter he continued in the automobile parts manufacturing field, selling out to his son Alfred Borbein in 1919.

1904 Borbein, 4-pass. runabout, NAHC

BORDENTOWN — The Bordentown Mobile & Transportation Company at Bordentown, New Jersey was organized with a capital stock of $50,000 and the object of manufacturing electric automobiles early in 1902. There was a veritable regiment of incorporators: Lewis C. Vandergrift, Jesse Smith, Edward K. Munnick, James A. Masterson, James W. Cain, Robert A. Holloway, Edward D. Preston, Frank P. Gray, W.F. Dewsnap, William C. Steele, James S. Gilbert, George W. Shreeve and Peter J. Magee, all of Bordentown, plus David O. Berrian of Beverley. Manufacture does not appear to have followed.

1912 Borland Electric, coupe, MVMA

BORLAND ELECTRIC — Chicago, Illinois — (1910-1914)/Saginaw, Michigan — (1914-1916) — The Borland Electric began its life in 1910 as the Ideal Electric, product of the Ideal Electric Vehicle Company of Chicago. The Borland name arrived at the Chicago Automobile Show in January 1912, the same time the firm's name was changed to Borland-Grannis Company. In November that year a Borland made a test run from Chicago to Milwaukee, a distance of 104 miles, on one battery charge. According to *The Horseless Age*, this was "one of the most extraordinary instances" indicating the great technical strides made by electric vehicles. The following year the company advertised its product as a 100-mile-per-charge car. Although initially introduced in chain-and-shaft-drive models, the Borland went shaft-drive exclusively soon after. Its speed range was 3 to 25 mph. In 1914 Borland combined with the Argo and Broc electrics to form the American Electric Vehicle Company, although the individual marque names were continued for the duration of each car's life. Bruce Borland and U.B. Grannis served as vice-presidents of the merged company; a Broc man was president, an Argo man secretary and treasurer. Soon after amalgamation, Borland manufacturing operations moved to Saginaw, Michigan.

1910 BORLAND ELECTRIC

	FP	5	4	3	2	1
Ideal (CD) Brgm. (92" wb)	1875	2000	3000	4200	6500	14,000

1911 BORLAND ELECTRIC

	FP	5	4	3	2	1
Ideal (CD) Brgm. (92" wb)	2200	2000	3000	4200	6500	14,000

1912 BORLAND ELECTRIC

	FP	5	4	3	2	1
Borland (CD) Brgm. (92" wb)	2200	2000	3000	4200	6500	14,000
Borland (SD) Brgm. (92" wb)	2000	2000	3000	4200	6500	14,000

Note: (CD) = Chain-Drive; (SD) = Shaft-Drive.

1913 BORLAND ELECTRIC

	FP	5	4	3	2	1
Model 45 Col. Cpe.-4P (92" wb)	2700	1800	2800	4000	6200	13,000
Model 50 Cpe.-4P (93" wb)	2900	1900	2900	4100	6400	13,500
Model 52 Rdstr.-2P (93" wb)	2550	2100	3100	4300	6800	14,500
Model 41 Cpe.-4P (93" wb)	2500	1600	2700	3800	5800	12,000
Model 60 Land'et. (123" wb)	5500	2000	3000	4200	6500	14,000

1914 Borland Electric, limousine, NAHC

1914 BORLAND ELECTRIC

	FP	5	4	3	2	1
Model 50 Cpe. (92" wb)	2900	1800	2800	4000	6200	13,000
Model 52 Rdstr. (92" wb)	2550	2100	3100	4300	6800	14,500
Model 60 Limo. (123" wb)	5500	2000	3000	4200	6500	14,000

1915-1916 BORLAND ELECTRIC

	FP	5	4	3	2	1
Model 50 Cpe. (96" wb)	2550	1800	2800	4000	6200	13,000
Model 56 Rdstr. (96" wb)	2250	2100	3100	4300	6800	14,500
Model 60 Limo. (96" wb)	5500	2000	3000	4200	6500	14,000

BORLAND — Dunseith, North Dakota — (1913) — Possibly H.W. Borland of Dunseith may have completed the building of his 12 hp highwheeler earlier than 1913. It is known that he licensed the vehicle that year in North Dakota, and he is not known to have built another.

1933 Borntraeger, MVMA

BORNTRAEGER — Chicago, Illinois — (1933) — The Borntraeger was a miniature race car built in one example only, and noteworthy because it featured front wheel drive. Its designer was Edward A. Borntraeger, who was described by *MoToR* as a "Chicago battery man." The Borntraeger was a trim little machine which had a four-cylinder air-cooled motorcycle engine and four-wheel brakes. It had a wheelbase of 66 inches and weighed 500 pounds. The car cost Borntraeger $2000 to build, and it took him two years to build it. Seventy miles an hour was its top speed.

BOROUGH & BLOOD — Marshall, Michigan — (1908) — During the fall of 1908, the Borough & Blood Buggy Company of Marshall announced that it had commenced the manufacture of motor vehicles. The company's product was a high-wheeled motor buggy, and it was produced for a short period only.

1908 BOROUGH & BLOOD

Borough & Blood	—	1600	2700	3800	5800	12,000

BOSS — Massillon, Ohio — (1904-1905) — The Boss was the idea of J.E. Long and John Crawford. It was powered by a four-cylinder 24 hp air cooled engine and offered in side-entrance tonneau touring form. In the late fall of 1904, the partners launched the Long-Crawford Automobile Company for its manufacture. The Boss faded from the automotive scene sometime during 1905.

1911 B.O.S.S., touring, WLB

B.O.S.S. — Detroit, Michigan — (1911) — This B.O.S.S. was so written because the initials represented the organizers' names: Frank A. Bowen, John A. Olson, Frank A. Smith and Franklin Stratton. The last named was the designer of the car which was a 35 hp four produced as a convertible passenger/delivery vehicle. The B.O.S.S. Company was organized in Detroit in early 1911 with a capital stock of $250,000 of which $135,000 had been paid in. Some production seems to have followed, but this B.O.S.S. venture was only shortly on the road.

1904 Boss Steam Car, runabout, NAHC

BOSS STEAM CAR — Reading, Pennsylvania — (1897-1909) — In 1892 James L. Eck established the Boss Knitting Machine Works. Five years later he built his first steam car, operated it successfully, and was ready for business. An unsprung subframe carried the running gear, the body was "so constructed as to hide all machinery, which is a very chief objection to most carriages," and initially the two models were available at $850 and $1200. The Boss running gear could be bought separately, at $140. James Eck was an ardent champion of steam power, contending that "anybody that runs a car and uses gasoline dislikes it" because of the danger of fire breaking out in the barn while refueling. He also noted the relative ease of obtaining kerosene anyplace, "where gasoline is always very scarce to be had." Prior to his retirement from both his knitting machine works and his sideline auto business, James Eck built 22 steam cars. When he died in 1924, his inventoried estate included "two junk automobiles, value $5." Today, the Historical Society of Berks County owns what is probably one of those two "junk" vehicles. It is on display at the Boyertown Museum of Historic Vehicles and is the only Boss Steam Car known to exist.

1897-1904 BOSS STEAM CAR
2-cyl., 7 hp, 70" wb

	FP	5	4	3	2	1
Rbt.-2P	1200	2400	3400	4800	8000	17,000
Dos-a-Dos-4P	850	2350	3350	4700	7800	16,500

1905-1906 BOSS STEAM CAR
2-cyl., 8 hp, 75" wb

Model D Rbt.	1000	2400	3400	4800	8000	17,000
Model B Dos-a-Dos	850	2350	3350	4700	7800	16,500

1907-1909 BOSS STEAM CAR
2-cyl., 10 hp, 75" wb

Model F Rbt.	1000	2450	3450	4900	8300	17,500

BOSTON — San Francisco, California — 1900) — Why William J. Woosley chose to call his Pacific Coast venture the Boston Automobile Company is a mystery, though perhaps he assumed an implied East Coast affiliation might better sell cars in the wild and wooly West. "Manufacturers of automobiles of every description" was Woosley's entry in the 1900 San Francisco city directory. How many he built is not known. By 1901 he had decided that "Boston Automobile Company" was not the sales-getter he had hoped, however. Woosley continued to indicate himself as an "automobile manufacturer," but amusingly his firm this time was the Universal Automobile Company.

1903 Boston & Amesbury Gas Carriage, runabout, NAHC

BOSTON-AMESBURY — Amesbury, Massachusetts — (1902-1903) — In 1900 H.A. Spiller left the Pringst-Spiller Power & Auto Company in Trenton, New Jersey and took his automotive ambitions to New England. Settling in Dorchester, Massachusetts, he had built a small gasoline runabout by October that year, but he tried without success to get his Spiller Motor Carriage Company going. Better luck arrived two years later in Amesbury. For a while it appeared that he would enter both the automobile and the engine-building field, but after he sold one of his engines to the carriage-building Miller brothers for their first car, they elected not to go into manufacture. By that time, the summer of '02, H.A. Spiller had organized his Boston & Amesbury Manufacturing Company, however, The Boston-Amesbury was introduced at the Mechanics Fair in Boston that November. The exhibition car had been driven 2000 miles already, its maker said proudly, "but shows no evidence of hard use." The Boston-Amesbury may have been the first automobile sold to someone handicapped. A one-armed visitor to the Mechanics Fair "was much taken with it," according to Spiller, "because it was the first motor vehicle he had seen that could be driven safely by a man deprived of the use of one hand." By the time the Fair had ended, Spiller had orders for fifteen cars, and was preparing for a production of 200 units for 1903. The Boston-Amesbury was distinguished by its front-mounted coil radiator, its early use of left-hand steering, and a very neat body design. It was available in a pair of two-cylinder models, an 8 hp 1800-pound two-seater and a 16 hp 2400-pound four-seater. Undercapitalization of his venture was probably the reason the Boston & Amesbury Manufacturing Company of H.A. Spiller failed.

1902-1903 BOSTON-AMESBURY

	FP	5	4	3	2	1
Boston-Amesbury Two-Seater	—	2300	3300	4600	7500	16,000
Boston-Amesbury Four-Seater	—	2350	3350	4700	7800	16,500

BOSTON ELECTRIC — Boston, Massachusetts — (1899) — Most probably the Boston Automobile Manufacturing Company never made it into production, but this was not for lack of ambition. Its directors were Francis A. Osborn, Joseph B. Moors, D. Webster King, Cyrus G. Beebe and George D. Burrage. The company was incorporated in the state of Maine with a capitalization of $750,000, two-thirds of that in preferred stock, one-third in common, both with a par value of $100 per share. According to the May 24th, 1899 issue of *The Horseless Age*, Boston Automobile Manufacturing would produce "package delivery wagons, pleasure carriages and cabs, to be run by electric power." The prototype stage seems to be as far as this venture proceeded.

BOSTON ELECTRIC — Concord, Massachusetts — (1907) — The Concord Motor Car Company apparently put its cart before the horse. Early in 1907 the firm announced that its new electric car would be exhibited at the Boston Automobile Show. But the Boston Electric didn't make it on time. Possibly the prototype was the only car built, and it may not have been successful. Certainly manufacture was never begun. The men behind this venture had been John S.P. Alcott, F. Alcott Pratt and John Edward Lavell, who had incorporated the Concord company with a capital stock of $10,000 during the summer of 1906.

BOSTON HAYNES-APPERSON — This car was a customized version of the Haynes-Apperson of Kokomo, Indiana — and was built in 1898 by O.H. Perry of Boston, Massachusetts who had earlier built a car of his own. Refer to Perry.

BOSTON HIGH WHEEL — Boston, Massachusetts — (1907) — Why anyone would choose to build a highwheeler in Boston is curious but the Boston High Wheel Manufacturing Company did. Its cylinders were two, horsepower twelve. Front tires were 44 inches in diameter, rear tires 48 inches, a size amenable to rutted country roads, but rather incongruous for city streets. Bostonians didn't buy, neither did any rural folk in the countryside outlying, and Boston High Wheel was out of business within the year.

129

BOSTON STEAMER — Curiously, the Boston Automobile Company which was in business from 1900 to 1901 located both its offices and its factory in Bar Harbor, Maine. In 1900 the car was referred to for a time as the Boston, but the name had been changed by early 1901. Refer to Bar Harbor.

BOSTONIA — The Bostonia Motor Manufacturing Company was a summer of 1914 incorporation with a capital stock of $200,000. Manufacture of cars in Boston was planned, but never realized.

1903 Bosworth, steamer, surrey, WLB

BOSWORTH — Saugus, Massachusetts — (1903-1904) — The Bosworth was a two-passenger steam surrey which developed 7-1/2 hp and was built by Frank C. Bosworth in the stable of his home at 19 Main Street in Saugus. It was begun in 1903, completed in 1904, and received Massachusetts Automobile Register No. 8634 on September 27th that year. Family members recall that the Bosworth Steamer was successfully tested and was driven on the roads around Saugus frequently.

BOULDING STEAM — Wells, Nevada — (1905) — "A freak of a looker, and so far only a promise of success" was the assessment of *Motor Field* in 1905 regarding the goliath of a steamer built by George R. Boulding which the inventor was then testing in the arid environs of Salt Lake City to Wells. "The object of the high wheels is to run over sagebrush, of the solid tires to avoid punctures by the cactus, of the steam power to get over the difficulty of the lack of gasoline depots, and the front wheel drive system to utilize three wheels in pulling one out of a chuck hole," *Motor Field* explained. And the magazine added laconically, "The inventor apparently knows more of the desert than he does of automobiling." This undoubtedly was the reason that Boulding's plan to proceed into manufacture of automobiles for the desert trade never went further than his first test drive.

BOULEVARD — The Boulevard Auto Company was organized in New York City early in 1910 with a capital stock of $20,000 and the plan to manufacture engines and cars. E.N. Dorgenfrei, W. Peters and A. Korsmeier were the incorporators. Manufacture is doubted.

The Boulevard Garage Company was organized in Albany, New York during the spring of 1912 with a capital stock of $50,000 by M.L. Ryder, S.W. Whitney and H.A. Rayno. Manufacture was planned but not realized.

1920 Bour-Davis, touring, WLB

BOUR-DAVIS — Detroit, Michigan — (1916-1917)/Frankfort, Indiana — (1918)/Cedar Grove, Louisiana — (1919-1922) — The idea for the Bour-Davis was conceived in Chicago by Robert C. Davis, an engineer for the Chicago, Duluth & Lake Superior Steam Ship Company; Charles J. Bour, a Chicago advertising man; and E.C. Noe, the general manager of the Chi-

cago Elevated Railroad. They moved to Detroit to produce a car designed by A.A. Gloetzner that was introduced in mid-1916 and was enthusiastically received by the press. "A novel effect is produced by having the front of the V-shaped radiator slant at about the same angle as the windshield," said *MoToR*, "and this together with the sloping of the steering post and the rear of the body gives a look of distinction." The Bour-Davis spent the rest of its life moving south. By 1918 it had been absorbed into the company owned by the Shadburne brothers and was produced in their Frankfort, Indiana plant. The following year the Bour-Davis entered Dixie and was reorganized as the Louisiana Motor Car Company of Shreveport, with factory in nearby Cedar Grove. It was this last incarnation of the Bour-Davis which was the most successful. The Southern aspect was particularly played upon in lavish, full-color brochures noting that the car was built in the South by men, "who know the wide extremes of service conditions which must be met in the South." Actually, it was quite the same car that had been built in the North — an assembled vehicle using a six-cylinder Continental Red Seal engine. Among the distinguishing features of the latterday Bour-Davis was the placement of its radiator slightly ahead of the front axle, a quite high hood — and, on touring cars, the sweeping of the front-seat leather pleats over the back seat and into a sort of ornamental dashboard. Bour-Davis went into receivership in June of 1921, but struggled on in manufacture for a while longer. In 1923 the firm was succeeded by the Ponder Motor Manufacturing Company but the Ponder automobile (a six with Continental engine and the same 126-inch wheelbase) never proceeded beyond the building of a prototype.

1916 Bour-Davis, touring sedan, NAHC

1916-1917 BOUR-DAVIS
Model 17 — 6-cyl., 26 hp, 118" wb

	FP	5	4	3	2	1
Tour.-5P	1250	2700	3600	5300	8800	19,000
Tour. Sed.-5P	1500	2450	3450	4900	8300	17,500

1918-1919 BOUR-DAVIS
Model 18B — 6-cyl., 29.4 hp, 118" wb

Tour.-5P	1650	2700	3600	5300	8800	19,000

1920 BOUR-DAVIS
Model 20 — 6-cyl., 42 hp, 118" wb

Tour.-5P	1700	2700	3600	5300	8800	19,000

Model 21 — 6-cyl., 55 hp, 118" wb

Tour.-5P	1850	2800	3650	5500	9000	19,500

1921 BOUR-DAVIS
Model 21S — 6-cyl., 50 hp, 126" wb

Tour.-5P	2535	3200	4300	6500	11,000	23,000
Tour.-7P	2585	3100	4200	6300	10,500	22,000
Rdstr.-2P	2585	3300	4400	6700	12,000	24,000

1922 Bour-Davis, roadster, HAC

1922 BOUR-DAVIS
Model 21S — 6-cyl., 50 hp, 126" wb

Tour.-7P	2385	3100	4200	6300	10,500	22,000
Tour.-5P	2300	3200	4300	6500	11,000	23,000
Rdstr.-3P	2300	3300	4400	6700	12,000	24,000

BOURNONVILLE — Bournonville Motors Company of Hoboken is frequently cited as the manufacturer of an automobile in 1914. The firm built motors only then, and had a devil of a time interesting any automobile manufacturers in them. By the early Twenties Bournonville had metamorphosed into the Bournonville Rotary Valve Company and during this period did enter the industry with a new car called the Rotary.

BOUTJES — The Boutjes-Hayes Automobile Company was organized in Peoria, Illinois in late 1908 for the manufacture of automobiles, parts and accessories. The capital stock was $2500, and manufacture is doubted.

BOUTON — Rumford Falls, Maine — (1902-1903) — Samuel Bouton said that he was a cousin of Georges Bouton of the famed French automobile company, De Dion-Bouton et Cie. Whether it was this fact, or the automobile he designed, which prompted businessmen of Rumford Falls to organize a half-million dollar company for manufacture of his car is not known. Dr. J.A. Nile was president of the new Bouton Automobile Company which was established in 1902 and began operations in a woolen mill in Rumford Falls the year following. The Bouton was a simple motorized buggy available as a two or four-seater. During the spring of 1903 the Bouton workforce was reported to be about a dozen men, and orders were on hand for fifty cars. One car a week was the production schedule. The company does not seem to have survived 1903.

BOUTON & BATEMAN — "Bouton & Bateman, Vineland, New Jersey, are establishing a motor vehicle manufactory," announced *The Motor Vehicle Review* in September 1899. Further details regarding this venture are lacking.

1901 Bowen Gasoline Carriage, auto-buggy, NAHC

BOWEN — Buffalo, New York — (1901) — In two summer issues of 1901, *The Horseless Age* described and pictured the experimental vehicle built in Buffalo by George B. Bowen. The picture perhaps was worth a thousand words; the little gasoline runabout looked rather like an overgrown baby buggy. Bowen said he had driven the vehicle about 2000 miles, and provided the magazine sufficient descriptive material for a lengthy two articles. But at the end of the final one, the editors noted cryptically, "nothing is said about speed changing devices; without any variable gear we should think the carriage would not be able to go far."

BOWKER — The Bowker Automobile & Machine Company, incorporated in Portland, Maine in 1900, was the successor to the automotive venture begun earlier that year as Belger & Bowker. Refer to Belger & Bowker.

BOWLING GREEN — That the Bowling Green Motor Car Company built automobiles in Bowling Green, Ohio from 1911 to 1915 has been indicated erroneously on numerous automobile rosters. The firm's name was deceptive, because its products were commercial vehicles only, which were marketed under the tradename of Modern. In November 1914 Bowling Green changed its name to "Truck Company" and continued in the manufacture of commercial vehicles into 1919.

BOWMAN — E. Wirt Bowman of Evanston, Illinois was certainly ambitious. In 1895 he announced his intention to enter "four types of vehicles" in the Chicago Times-Herald Contest. He did not, however, make it to the starting line with even one, and whether he ever successfully completed and tested any of his cars has not been documented.

BOWMAN — Bellefontaine, Ohio, (1900) — In 1900, John and Paul Bowman, who were machinists in Bellefontaine, received an order to build two motor vehicles. Flushed with this heady success, the brothers announced that following the completion of the cars, they planned to relocate in Chicago and begin the manufacture of automobiles in the Windy City. The evidence suggests, however, that the Bowmans remained in Bellefontaine and largely confined themselves to their machinist trade following their production of the two cars.

BOWMAN — New York, New York — (1902) — Sydney B. Bowman produced and sold bicycles as the Sydney B. Bowman Cycle Company in New York City from 1899 to 1904. By 1902 he had also organized the Bowman Automobile Company, which operated principally as a dealership and imported the French Clement-Bayard into this country until 1910. In addition, in 1902, however, Bowman did market a few small 6 hp $800 gasoline runabouts under his own name, and built an additional car, a 70 hp racer that was designed by N.W. Schlater and paid for by H.R. Morse who ordered it.

1922 Bowman, roadster, NAHC

BOWMAN — Covington, Kentucky — (1921-1922) — The Bowman Motor Car Company, Inc. of Covington was an interesting venture because, unlike so many other small independent firms coming into the field during this period, it appears that Bowman manufactured its own four-cylinder engine. Most other components of the automobile arrived from suppliers in the industry. The Bowman was a quite conventional vehicle offered as a roadster and touring on a 108-inch wheelbase. Interestingly, although the car did make the pages of the automotive press, it was never pictured in the local Covington newspaper. Bowman raised its price of $1045 in 1921 to $1185 in 1922 — and then departed the automobile industry as quietly as it had entered.

1921 BOWMAN
Model L — 4-cyl., 27 hp, 108" wb

	FP	5	4	3	2	1
Tour.-5P	1045	1600	2700	3800	5800	12,000
Rds.-3P	1045	1700	2750	3900	6000	12,500

1922 BOWMAN
Model L — 4-cyl., 27 hp, 108" wb

Tour.-5P	1185	1600	2700	3800	5800	12,000
Rds.-3P	1185	1700	2750	3900	6000	12,500

BOYD — The Boyd Steel Spring Company of Brooklyn, New York was listed in automobile trade directories of 1910 as an automobile manufacturer. This was in error. The company had earlier been incorporated by H.B. Boyd, C.A. Cook and A.R. Boyd, who announced their plans to manufacture "steel springs, motor car and machine parts" only.

Three four-wheel-drive cars were built in 1915 by the Neustadt Automobile & Supply Company of St. Louis, Missouri to the special order of H.M. Boyd. Refer to Neustadt.

BOYDEN — Grand Haven, Michigan — (1908) — Charles Boyden of Grand Haven invented a "new type of gasoline engine," *The Horseless Age* revealed in August of 1908. It was a four developing 30 hp, and apparently a prototype of a car was built around it. Plans to manufacture the car in Holland, Michigan followed, but plans were as far as the venture proceeded.

BOYER — San Francisco, California — (1906-1907) — The Boyer Motor Car Company was incorporated with a capital stock of $50,000 in 1906 in San Francisco. G.A. Boyer, F.M. Boyer and Lawrence T. Wagner were the men involved, and their stated purpose was the manufacture, repair and selling of all kinds of automobiles. A few cars may have been built by this firm, but the mainstay of company efforts was as a dealership for Franklin and Royal. Dogged by bad luck, Boyer suffered two fires in 1907, in addition to confronting the nationwide financial panic that year. In April of 1908 the business affairs of the company were described as being "wound up."

BOYERSDORFER — The Boyersdorfer appearing on several car lists was simply the Bayersdorfer misspelled. Refer to Bayersdorfer.

BOYNTON — During the early Twenties the Arthur-Boynton Corporation of Albany, New York built an export car called the A.B.C. Refer to A.B.C.

B. & P. — The B. & P. Company of Milwaukee, Wisconsin produced an automobile from 1902-1903 which was marketed under the name of Ideal. Refer to Ideal.

In late 1909 in Buffalo, New York, the B. & P. Motor Car Company was organized to manufacture and deal in automobiles. Initial capital stock was $1000, and the incorporators were Fred J. and J.A. Brodie and Mary G. Parkhurst. Manufacture is doubted.

BRACKETT — The Brackett Automobile Company was organized in Portland, Maine early in 1905 for the manufacture of motorcars. President of the venture was John W. Anderson, treasurer was James R. Parsons. Manufacture is doubted.

BRADDON — Downers Grove, Illinois — (1919) — Chicago capital saw to the formation of the Braddon Motors Company in early April 1919. The man behind the Braddon idea was George J. Fogle, formerly of the Locomobile and Maibohm companies, who would serve as vice-president and general sales manager. Braddon's president was F.J. Clark, the secretary-treasurer was John Voiral. If there was a Braddon in the company, he was a very silent partner — and perhaps wisely so, since this enterprise never did get off the ground. At least a prototype of the four-cylinder Braddon was built. It was an assembled car of completely standard components. A two-story brick factory building was secured in the Chicago suburb of Downers Grove, but whether an assembly line was ever set up is unknown. Production at the rate of four cars a day had been slated to begin in May of 1919. But with just $50,000 to start the company, Braddon Motors was severely undercapitalized and never really had a chance. So quickly did Braddon Motors arrive and depart the automotive scene, in fact, its presence went unnoticed in the news columns of the *Downers Grove Reporter*.

1929 Bradfield, taxi, HAC

BRADFIELD — Chicago, Illinois — (1929-1930) — Bradfield Motors, Inc. was organized in the late summer of 1928 by H.C. Bradfield for the manufacture of taxis, buses and trucks. Only the taxis appear to have reached the market, however. Bradfield was the former general sales manager for the Yellow Cab Manufacturing Company, and he brought with him George Daubner, Yellow Cab's chief engineer. There were two models of the Bradford taxi, both with six-cylinder engines, which was somewhat unusual since most taxis were fours, the larger $1850 car on a 125-inch wheelbase, the smaller $1495 model on a 117-inch. Both taxis were shown at the New York Automobile Show in January 1929. Manufacture of these cars was contracted to the Kissel company in Hartford, Wisconsin, that firm having dabbled in the taxicab business itself in recent years. Unfortunately, Kissel was by now in financial trouble, and in September of 1930, George and Will Kissel requested receivership. In November 1931, Bradfield leased two floors of the Kissel factory to complete an order from two taxi companies in Milwaukee for sixty of the Bradfield-type cabs, but the venture appears to have ended thereafter.

1929-1930 BRADFIELD
Model 57-B — 6-cyl., 117" wb

	FP	5	4	3	2	1
Sed. Taxi	1495	2400	3400	4800	8000	17,000
Model 67-B — 6-cyl., 125"						
Sed. Taxi	1850	2500	3500	5000	8500	18,000
1931 BRADFIELD						
Model 57-C — 6-cyl., 117" wb						
Sed. Taxi	—	2400	3400	4800	8000	17,000

BRADFORD — The Bradford Motor Works of Bradford, Pennsylvania built a kit car called the Bradford from 1904-1905. It was nothing more than leftover parts of the Holley. Refer to Holley.

"The Bradford Company, Wilmington, Delaware, are preparing to turn out assembled cars and would like catalogues of makers of engines, transmissions, differentials, pressed steel frames, etc.," reported *Cycle and Automobile Trade Journal* in August 1910. Bradford in Wilmington was not heard from again.

The Bradford Automobile Exchange was organized with a capital stock of $30,000 in Bradford, Pennsylvania late in 1911. Incorporators were F.H. Head, L.I. Holmes and F.H. Logan (all of Bradford), P.L. Gallup (of Smithport) and S.L. Libbits (of Custer City). Manufacture does not appear to have followed, though the firm operated as a dealership.

For a short period during 1914 the product of the Cycle Car Company of Wilmington, Delaware was known by the name of its designer, T.C. Bradford. The car ultimately was marketed as the Diamond. Refer to Diamond.

The Bradford-Sterne Auto Company was organized in Detroit during the spring of 1907 for the purpose of making automobiles and accessories. Incorporators were W.T. Bradford, Beecher Sterne, J.N. Bradford and F.I. Sterne. Manufacture does not appear to have followed.

That a Bradford was built in 1920 by the Consolidated Motor Car Company of Bradford, Connecticut has been a common error. There is no such city in Connecticut, the closest approximation being Branford. The Consolidated Motor Car Company did produce automobiles in Connecticut, however, under two marque names. Refer to Sterling and B.E.L.

BRADFORD — Lenox, Massachusetts — (1901) — Early in 1901, William H. Bradford, who was described as a "wealthy resident of Lenox," was reported to be building two automobiles at his "country residence." More than likely, the cars were being built for him, or with a healthy assist from his chauffeur. The Bradford automobile was specially designed for motoring in the Berkshire hills.

BRADLEY — In 1895 the firm of Bradley, Wheeler & Company of Kansas City, Missouri announced its entry in the Chicago Times-Herald Contest with a vehicle of its own design. Bradley, Wheeler did not make it to the starting line, and whether the car was subsequently finished and tested has not been documented.

Initially, in 1900, the car was known simply by the name of its designer, Hiram T. Bradley. By September, however, the Pacific Motor Company had been organized for its manufacture. Refer to Pacific.

1920 Bradley, Four, touring, WLB

BRADLEY — Cicero, Illinois — (1920-1921) — The Bradley Motor Car Company offered a Lycoming-engined assembled car that was available with either four or six cylinders and just one style of body, a five-passenger touring on a 116-inch wheelbase. Scarcely was the company in business when it was summarily out of it. The Bradley was introduced in late spring of 1920 as a four, with the Bradley six following that fall as a 1921 model. In November of 1920 Bradley underwent involuntary receivership. Among the petitioners were the Maremont Manufacturing Company of Chicago which claimed a Bradley debt of $872, the B.F. Goodrich Company which claimed $1100, and the Chicago Steel Foundry Company which noted petulantly that Bradley hadn't paid its bill of $43. The receivership petition indicated that the Bradley company had several finished automobiles on hand in addition to a number in process and a large inventory. Though the company's liabilities of $100,000 were said to be offset by assets somewhat larger, Bradley went under during receivership.

1920 BRADLEY

	FP	5	4	3	2	1
Model H Four Tour.	1265	3000	4000	6000	9500	21,000
1921 BRADLEY						
Model H Four Tour.	1265	3000	4000	6000	9500	21,000
Model F Six Tour.	1500	3050	4100	6200	10,000	21,500

BRAGER — Aneta, North Dakota — (1902) — That Albert Brager of Aneta built an automobile in 1902 has been established, but further details regarding it are lacking.

1899 Bramwell-Robinson Sociable, auto-buggy, NAHC

BRAMWELL-ROBINSON — Hyde Park, Massachusetts — (1899-1902) — The Bramwell-Robinson was the result of an alliance between John T. Robinson who manufactured paper box machinery and the father-son team of W.C. and C.C. Bramwell who were inventors and mechanics. Robinson put up the money, and the Bramwells came up with the cars. The first was a piquant little air-cooled single-cylinder three-wheeler called the Bramwell-Robinson Sociable, three of which were built and tested at the turn of the century, with preparations then being made for a lot of twenty-five more. By the time that run was completed, the Bramwells had come up with two more models, these with four wheels and more horsepower. The cars were favorably received in the press and presumably by the public. The Bramwell-Robinson alliance had fallen apart by 1900, however. No reason was given, but it may have been a case of Robinson's ego being wounded. Although the car was the product of the Bramwell-Robinson Company, it was occasionally referred to only as the Bramwell, with the Robinson name left off the company designation as well. Thereafter John T. Robinson proceeded to build a new four-cylinder car in Hyde Park called the Robinson, later to become the Pope-Robinson. And the Bramwells finished up the cars on hand in Hyde Park and then took off for Springfield, Ohio to carry on with their own car there.

132

	FP	5	4	3	2	1
Sociable (1-cyl., 3 hp three-wheeler)						

1900-1902 BRAMWELL-ROBINSON

	FP	5	4	3	2	1
Model A Rbt. (1-cyl., 5 hp)	750	1600	2700	3800	5800	12,000
Model B Rbt. (1-cyl., 8 hp)	850	1650	2750	3900	5900	12,200

1904 Bramwell, runabout, GR

BRAMWELL — Springfield, Ohio — (1904-1905) — In 1903, following the dissolution of their partnership with John T. Robinson, W.C. Bramwell and his son C.C. headed west to discover a place to continue the building of their car. In Ohio they found the Springfield Automobile & Industrial Company which had tried to build its own automobile in 1899 and failed. This firm was easily persuaded to change its name to Springfield Automobile Company, and to produce the Bramwells' effort as the Springfield. A refinement of the former Bramwell-Robinson, the car featured a single-cylinder two-stroke 8 hp water cooled engine fitted into a 72-inch wheelbase chassis. It had a laminated wood frame reinforced with steel sheathing, planetary transmission and a left-hand steering wheel with outside lever control. Though the Bramwells joined the Springfield Automobile Company as managers in 1903, by year's end they had bought out the venture. They didn't bother to change the firm's designation, but in 1904 changed the product name to Bramwell. The Bramwell sold for $800 and was quite substantially built, weighing 1125 pounds, hefty for a runabout. Not so substantial, however, was the Bramwell's treasury and their venture failed early in 1905. The Springfield Automobile Company was absorbed by the Columbus Buggy Company in December 1905, C.C. Bramwell remaining on to design the Firestone-Columbus highwheeler for the Columbus organization.

1904-1905 BRAMWELL
Single Cylinder — 8 hp, 72" wb

Rbt.	800	1800	2800	4000	6200	13,000

BRANDLE — The Brandle Motors Company was organized during the summer of 1917 in St. Louis, Missouri to manufacture, sell and deal in automobiles and automobile accessories. Capital stock was $50,000, and the incorporators were T.C. Brandle, Guy Wilson, C.P. Brandle and E.L. Frueh. Manufacture of a Brandle automobile does not appear to have followed.

BRANDON — Houston, Texas — (1911-1912) — In September of 1911 the Commercial Motor Car Company of Houston announced that manufacture was forthcoming of four-wheel-drive automobiles and trucks to be built under the Twyford patents and to be marketed under the tradename of Brandon. The Brandons were Z.Z. and L.J.; the Twyford was Robert E., who had earlier produced a four-wheel-drive car under his own name in Pennsylvania. Possibly a prototype or two of the new Brandon was built, but the company proceeded into receivership in June of 1912 before any manufacture was begun.

1916 Brasie, Packet, 2-pass. roadster, WLB

BRASIE — Minneapolis, Minnesota — (1914-1916) — In late July of 1914 the Brasie Motor Car Company succeeded the Brasie Motor Truck Company which had been marketing the Twin City truck since 1913. The reason for the new $100,000 incorporation was that Frank R. Brasie had a new idea. To help him he brought into his company as secretary one J.M.

Michaelson who had previously been a motorcycle manufacturer and the designer of the Michaelson cyclecar whose short life was just ending in Minneapolis. Brasie wanted to build a cyclecar too, and he hired Michaelson to take charge of its sales and promotion. The new vehicle would be marketed under the name of Brasie and would consist of two pleasure cars and a light delivery on the same chassis carrying the model names of Messenger and Packet respectively. Specifications were the usual for the cyclecar genre: 12 hp engine, 100-inch wheelbase, friction transmission, belt drive. An unusual feature was the use of two jacks mounted under the seats which saw to the tightening of the drive belts by the ingenuous expediency of forcing the rear axle backward. When the firm name was changed to Packet Motor Car Manufacturing Company in 1916, Packet became the name for both the pleasure and delivery cyclecars, although it would appear that production by then was principally the commercial vehicle.

1914-1916 BRASIE
Cyclecar — 4-cyl., 12 hp, 100" wb

	FP	5	4	3	2	1
Messenger Rdstr.-2P	400	1600	2700	3800	5800	12,000
Messenger Rdstr.-4P	400	1600	2700	3800	5800	12,000
Packet Delivery	400	1550	2600	3700	5700	11,500

Packet — 4-cyl., 12 hp, 100" wb

Rdstr.-2P	450	1600	2700	3800	5800	12,000
Rdstr.-4P	450	1600	2700	3800	5800	12,000
Delivery	450	1550	2600	3700	5700	11,500

1927 Brauks, touring, WLB

BRAUKS — St. Louis, Missouri — (1898-1927) — George S. Brauks was a cabinetmaker from St. Louis who built a total of seven cars between the years 1898 and 1927. His first effort was a small single-cylinder stanhope the materials for the building of which cost him $250. His most ambitious effort was his final one, every part of which he made himself, including the wheels. The car was a beautifully detailed diminutive of a full-size automobile. Its wheelbase was 86 inches, its tread 46, and the car was powered by a four-cylinder which provided a 60 mph performance and 35 mpg economy. And it had only cost George Brauks $185 to build. Of his previous efforts, one had collided with a streetcar and been demolished, another he traded in on a two-story house, and the remainder he sold. His last car he drove for a number of years following its completion in 1927.

BRAY — Waverly, New York — (1897) — James B. Bray, whose name has frequently been cited as "Bary" in various rosters, built an automobile for his own use in Waverly, New York in 1897. It was powered by two small single-cylinder gasoline motors and provided tandem seating for two passengers. What makes this automobile particularly interesting is that it is an early example of a vehicle designed for use by someone handicapped. Mr. Bray wrote *The Horseless Age* that he had been unable to walk for the past eighteen years.

1902 Brazier, touring, NAHC

BRAZIER — Philadelphia, Pennsylvania — (1902-1903) — H. Bartol Brazier was a Frenchman who built a heavy (2650 pounds), high (36-inch wheels) touring car in Philadelphia. It was powered by a two-cylinder 18 hp engine and featured a right-hand steering wheel which was straight upright in 1902, and tilted for 1903. Brazier did not build many of these vehicles, and never incorporated. A six-passenger touring was his regular production model at $2700, though he was willing to fit a variety of phaeton, surrey or wagonette bodies on the same chassis for prices ranging from $2550 to $3400. After 1903 he went into general machine work in Philadelphia.

BRAZIL — The Brazil Motors Company was organized with a capital stock of $125,000 early in 1917 in Brazil, Indiana. Incorporators were William M. Zellner, John F. Brown and Lewis McNutt. Documentation that this firm produced any cars is lacking. Another venture in Brazil in 1921 produced a car called the Vanderbilt, but none of the Brazil Motors Company people seem to have been involved.

1901 Brecht Steamer, "Rushmobile" runabout, HAC

1903 Brecht Electric, runabout, WLB

BRECHT — St. Louis, Missouri — (1901-1903) — The Brecht was the product of the Brecht Automobile Company, which was established in 1901 as an adjunct enterprise to the Brecht Butcher's Supply Company of St. Louis for the manufacture of automobiles, automobile running gear and automobile parts. The terms for purchase of any of these was the same: "strictly cash." Although the company was firm on this aspect of its business, it wavered on just about everything else. During its first two years, it offered an electric runabout for $1000 (1-1/2-inch solid rubber tires) and $1040 (3-inch pneumatics), as well as a two-cylinder steam car called the Rushmobile for which no price was quoted. In 1903 the purchaser had an even wider choice as Brecht cars were sold without engines, or as the company cutely phrased it, "ready for power." That was up to the owner, but Brecht was happy to make engine suggestions from its inventory stock. Interestingly, the last page of the company brochure that year advised that "we shall expect you to call on us" during the World's Fair in St. Louis in 1904. By the time the Fair opened, however, H.F. Borbein, manager of the automobile division from the beginning, had bought out the Brecht interests — and the new billboard over the plant entrance read Borbein. The Borbein was produced in kit form for several years thereafter. The Brecht brothers — Gus, Frank and Charles — went back to butcher supply business exclusively.

BREED — Detroit, Michigan — (1914) — A machinist by the name of George Breed was indicated to be building a cyclecar in the March 1914 issue of *Motor Print*. Further details are lacking.

1899 Breer, runabout, GR

BREER — Los Angeles, California — (1900) — In 1900, at the age of seventeen, Carl Breer built himself a steam car in his father's blacksmith shop at 215 San Pedro Street in Los Angeles. Its two-cylinder 5 hp engine was of his own devising, young Breer following a description he found of a Stanley steam engine in a technical magazine; its burner was cast iron, with 3000 holes drilled to produce a Bunsen effect. The car's fuel was gasoline. Various components of the drivetrain were purchased, and the body was built by a local carriagemaker. When at last the car was completed, it became the first Carl Breer ever drove, or rode in. And he drove it a lot, once all the way to Pasadena in reverse because of a problem in the forward valve linkage. Subsequently studying for a mechanical engineering degree at the University of Stanford, Carl Breer spent summers working on the Tourists that were built by the Auto Vehicle Company of Los Angeles. Two decades later, he became famous as one of Walter P. Chrysler's "Three Musketeers" (the other two Fred Zeder and Owen R. Skelton). It was this engineering triumvirate which was responsible for the first Chrysler in the mid-Twenties. In the mid-Thirties, it was largely Carl Breer's idea which resulted in the Chrysler Airflow. The steam car he built in 1900 remained in his possession for over seven decades. Following his death it was donated by the Breer family to the Los Angeles County Museum where it is on display today.

1921 Breese

BREESE — Airplane parts provided most of the components for the little speedster built by Lieutenant Robert P. Breese of the U.S. Aviation Service, but whether he put his car together over here or Over There is not certain. Weighing a total of 400 pounds, the Breese was powered by a two-cylinder 20 hp Harley-Davidson motorcycle engine and was fitted with a three-speed transmission. Its wheels and tires were standard airplane parts and the windshield was from a De Haviland. The car was completed shortly after the Armistice. A reference from *Motor Age* in 1921 indicates the Breese as an "American production" and calls it the "smallest car in the world." It was purchased that year by a French duke with a penchant for midget motoring.

BREESE & LAWRENCE — This car, built in 1905 in Brooklyn by Sidney S. Breese and Charles L. Lawrence, was the forerunner of the B.L.M. of 1906-1907. Refer to B.L.M.

1910 Breeze, auto-buggy, GR

BREEZE — Carthage, Ohio — (1910) — The Breeze was a high-wheeled buggy with a two-cylinder air-cooled engine, side crank and chain drive that was built for one short season by the Jewel Carriage Company of Carthage. It didn't have the ungainly appearance of most highwheelers, though perhaps mechanically it was found wanting. No other explanation offers itself for why the Breeze was on the market for such a brief period.

BREIDING — Sterling, Illinois — (1900) — In 1900, in Sterling, A.H. Breiding built himself a car. It was a highwheeler powered by a gasoline engine. In 1901, in partnership with a man named Korn, he built a prototype for hoped-for production. How many Korn & Breiding cars followed is not known.

BRELSFORD — Villisca, Iowa — (1900) — Late in 1900 C.W. Brelsford of Villisca reported his building of a gasoline-powered runabout which was fitted with a two-cylinder 4 hp engine, weighed about 350 pounds complete, and was tested at a speed as high as 25 mph. Evidence suggests he did not proceed into manufacture, however.

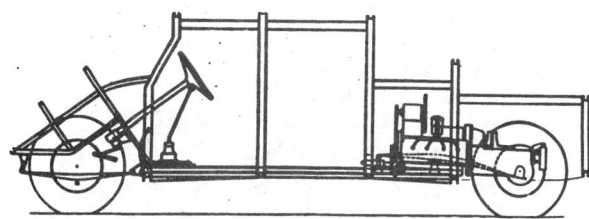

1932 Bremac, MVMA

BREMAC — Sidney, Ohio — (1932) — The name Bremac was coined from the first syllable of the names of Procter Brevard and William R. McCulla. McCulla, a noted designer of engines; Brevard, though not so well known, was the former sales engineer for Zenith-Detroit Corporation and had been assistant to Colonel Jesse G. Vincent when the latter was chief engineer for Hudson prior to joining the Packard Motor Car Company. Hudson also boasted McCulla as an alumnus, the engineer having served there as well as Belden and Thomas. Also involved in the new Bremac Motor Car Corporation were Amos Northup, chief designer of Murray Corporation, and Fred D. Clark of Sidney, who was backing the project financially. The project was a radical new idea in automobile construction. The Bremac had no chassis frame, no propeller shaft, no universal joint. As described by the company, it most closely resembled "an airplane monocoque fuselage, to which have been flexibly attached at the front end a front axle and steering unit, and at the rear a powerplant, transmission, clutch and axle unit." The powerplant was an 80 hp eight designed by Brevard, the prototype's wheelbase was 146 inches, and the coachwork was courtesy of Amos Northup who evolved "a new form of streamlining" for the Bremac that was designated the Teardrop. (Seating in the five-passen-

ger sedan was the reverse of the usual, three passengers in front, two in the rear.) Production on a strictly custom basis was planned, with wheelbase varying "in proportion to body design for streamlining." In mid-October of 1932, Bremac announced that its first prototype was under construction in Sidney — and that the company expected to complete three cars of different body model design for exhibition at the New York Automobile Show the following month. The Bremac never made it to the show.

BREMER — The Bremer Wilson Manufacturing Company was a $100,000 incorporation in Niles, Michigan organized during the summer of 1913 for the production of automobiles. No manufacture seems to have followed.

BRENENSTUL & CARPENTER — Wakeman, Ohio — (1900) — During the early spring of 1900, Brenenstul & Carpenter of Wakeman announced completion of their first gasoline automobile. A runabout weighing 500 pounds, the partners claimed several special features for their car. "The starter is operated by a lever which normally lies along the sill of the body on the floor," reported *Cycle and Automobile Trade Journal*. "To start the engine it is only necessary to lift this lever. To shut off the engine, the lever is depressed." Brenenstul & Carpenter planned to market their car for $800, with its motor to be offered as a separate package at $200. The evidence suggests they were not in business long.

BRENKEL-ANGER — Early in 1908 the Brenkel-Anger Company of Milwaukee, Wisconsin was organized with a capital stock of $10,000 and the plan to "engage in the manufacture of automobiles." The partners involved were A.C. Brenkel and W.A. Anger. No automobiles appear to have resulted of this venture, but Walter Anger later went to build the A.E.C. in Milwaukee in 1913.

1904 Brennan, runabout, WLB

BRENNAN — Syracuse, New York — (1902-1908) — The Brennan Manufacturing Company was an engine-building concern which supplied its High Powered Motor (14 hp at 700 rpm, 18 hp at 1000 rpm) and other lesser or higher powered units to a number of automobile manufacturers including George B. Selden during this the height of the famous Selden patent litigation. The date the company began producing its own car has been variously given as 1905 or 1907, but it would appear that Brennan was willing to put together automobiles at customer request as early as 1902. No concerted effort was ever made into manufacture although the Panic of '07 left Brennan with an overstock of engines and motivated the company to put together a few more cars. In 1913 Brennan tried the commercial vehicle field, but this again was a short-term venture.

BRENNAN — Mt. Vernon, New York — (1908-1910) — Arthur J. Brennan operated a machine shop on North Third and East Sidney Avenue in Mt. Vernon, and indicated himself as an automobile builder from 1908 through 1910. Further details are lacking.

BRENNING — Springfield, Ohio — (1900-1901) — In December of 1900, Brenning Brothers of Salem, Massachusetts announced the relocation of their electrical business to Grape Alley in Springfield, Ohio where a shop was being erected to carry on general electrical manufacturing as well as to build electric vehicles to the design of a car patented by Dr. C.W. Russell of Springfield. In February of 1901 L.F. Brenning advised the automotive trade press that production had begun. It ended soon thereafter, though the Brennings apparently remained in the general electrical business in Springfield. Dr. Russell did too, and in late 1902 tried again, with a gasoline car, under the name Russell-Springfield.

BREWER — Berlin, Wisconsin — (1908) — Dan Brewer of Berlin built a gasoline automobile for himself in 1908. In June that year, the *Berlin Evening Journal* reported that he had been out motoring again and "making much better speed and less noise." Most likely, he built the car because he couldn't afford to buy one. As the newspaper reported, most prophetically, "The auto so far is high priced, built for speed, a luxury of the wealthy or well-to-do, but the everyday, practical, self-propelled rig . . . is bound to come." Henry Ford introduced his Model T later that year.

1904 Brew-Hatcher, touring, NAHC

BREW-HATCHER — Cleveland, Ohio — (1904-1905) — The Brew-Hatcher, or B & H as it was also called, was an amalgam of the components that Francis O. Brew and William A. Hatcher had already been building for about a year as suppliers to the industry. "Practically all of the parts are of the firm's own design." the press said of the new car, "and will also be marketed separately . . . Some of its parts have no equivalent on the American market, as, for instance, the multiple feed, hand operated grease cup." The Brew-Hatcher was introduced at the Chicago Automobile Show in January 1904. It was discontinued in the fall of 1905 when Brew retired (later he became a tax authority in the Cleveland office of the Internal Revenue Service) and Hatcher elected to continue production of parts only (later he switched to tool manufacturing). Prior to the Brew-Hatcher, incidentally, William Hatcher had been chief engineer for Winton in Cleveland and subsequently had joined the engineering department of the Ohio Automobile Company in Warren where he had been instrumental in the design of the Model F Packard.

1904 BREW-HATCHER
Two — 16 hp, 79" wb

	FP	5	4	3	2	1
Tour.-5P	1750	2700	3600	5300	8800	19,000

1905 BREW-HATCHER
Two — 16 hp, 92" wb

	FP	5	4	3	2	1
Side Entrance Tonneau	1500	2700	3600	5300	8800	19,000

Four — 18/24 hp, 96" wb

	FP	5	4	3	2	1
Model C Tour.	2000	3000	4000	6000	9500	21,000

BREWSTER — Birmingham, Alabama — (1915) — The Brewster Motor Car Company was organized in Birmingham early in 1915. E.B. Van Keuren, who was described as a "consulting engineer for a number of southern companies for some time," was president and chief engineer. Simon Levy was vice-president and general manager; R.S. Levy secretary and treasurer. The Brewster was to be an assembled light car with a standard tread and a wheelbase of 104 inches for roadster, 108 inches for tourer. The price tag was stated as under $750. "The models will be out within a month," Carette reported, "while production will start early in the spring." Production never started. The Brewster ended with the prototypes.

1915 Brewster, town landau, OCW

BREWSTER — Long Island City, New York — (1915-1925)/Springfield, Massachusetts — (1934-1935) — The venerable house of Brewster & Company had been "Carriage Builders to American Gentlemen" since 1810, and began supplying gentlemen with coachwork for horseless carriages at the turn of the century. For a decade the company manufactured an automobile as well in its Long Island City plant. The prototype was completed in 1915, and the car was introduced a 1916 model. It had a four-cylinder Knight-type engine set in a 125-inch wheelbase chassis, with a variety of elegant body styles available, including a Glass-Quarter Brougham at $8300, a Town Landaulet at $8450 and a Falling Front Landaulet at $8500. The radiator of this first-generation Brewster was oval, the position of the steering wheel optional. Obviously, these cars were aimed at a mon-eyed clientele, although their practicality was stressed: The Brewster, the company said, "will cost less in general overhauling in a number of years

use, also cause less petty annoyance to the caretaker, than any car made to date." When Rolls-Royce of England decided to manufacture its car in Springfield, Massachusetts, Brewster initially was one of the coachbuilders supplying coachwork for the cars. The Brewster car was discontinued in 1925 shortly before the Brewster company was absorbed into Rolls-Royce of America in early 1926. It was back in 1934, however, following the demise of Rolls-Royce manufacture in this country, and the reorganization of the American Rolls-Royce company into the Springfield Manufacturing Corporation. The new Brewster's *raison d'etre* was quite the same as the original Brewster's had been — an elegant custom-built car but without the ostentation of the usual massive-wheelbase luxury types — and that was an even more important consideration now. The Great Depression had made flamboyant displays of wealth rather vulgar, and there simply wasn't as much wealth around in any case. Thus, these latterday Brewsters were built on the Ford V-8 chassis principally (though Buick, Lincoln, Cadillac and even Rolls-Royce among others could be requested) and were available in a variety of open and closed body styles distinguished by a captivating heart-shaped radiator grille. All body styles on the Ford chassis were sold at the single and very attractive price of $3500. (It should be noted, incidentally, that a few cars retained the Ford V-8 radiator and nomenclature which makes them Brewster-bodied Fords. Only the heart-shape-grille, flare-fendered, split-bumpered cars are proper Brewsters.) The Brewster idea was a fine one, but the company had been so hard hit financially by the hard times that it didn't have a chance to succeed. Although 300 has been the widely cited figure for second-generation Brewster production, in reality probably only about 113 were built. On June 24th, 1936, liquidation of the Springfield Manufacturing Corporation was ordered by the courts. And Brewster became a memory. Cole Porter saw to it that the memory would live on. In the musical *Anything Goes*, he included the company in his metaphoric list — "You're the top, You're a Brewster body" — of things that epitomize the absolutely first-rate.

1916 Brewster, coupe, HAC

1916 BREWSTER
Knight — 4-cyl., 26 hp, 125" wb

	FP	5	4	3	2	1
Twn. Car	6500	5000	6500	11,000	22,000	35,000
Tour.	5850	4300	5400	8700	16,500	30,000
Rbt.	5250	4500	5800	9500	18,000	32,000
Limo.	6650	4700	6100	9900	19,000	33,000
Limo.	6500	4700	6100	9900	19,000	33,000
Cpe.	6500	4200	5200	8400	15,700	29,000
Sed.	6500	3900	4800	7700	14,300	27,000

1917 Brewster, town landaulet, HAC

1917 BREWSTER
Knight — 4-cyl., 26 hp, 125" wb

Twn. Brgm.	7600	6000	8500	13,000	30,000	42,000
Converted Brgm.	7500	5900	8300	12,800	29,000	41,000
Glass-Quarter Brgm.	7500	6200	8800	13,500	31,000	43,000
Twn. Land'et.	7600	6000	8500	13,000	30,000	42,000
Falling Front Land'et.	7700	6400	9300	14,500	33,000	45,000
Tour.-Land'et.	7900	6700	9900	15,500	34,800	47,000
Limo.	7500	6200	8800	13,500	31,000	43,000
Enclosed-Drive Limo.	7500	6000	8500	13,000	30,000	42,000
Open Phae.	7000	6400	9300	14,500	33,000	45,000
Club Rbt.	6500	6000	8500	13,000	30,000	42,000
Rbt.	6700	5900	8300	12,800	29,000	41,000
Land'et. Rbt.	7500	6000	8500	13,000	30,000	42,000

1918 BREWSTER
Knight — 4-cyl., 25.6 hp, 125" wb

Country Brgm.	8300	6400	9300	14,500	33,000	45,000
Open Phae.	7700	6200	8800	13,500	31,000	43,000
Twn. Brgm.	8450	6000	8500	13,000	30,000	42,000

	FP	5	4	3	2	1
Twn. Land'et.	8400	6200	8800	13,500	31,000	43,000
Enclosed Drive	8400	5900	8300	12,800	29,000	41,000
Limo.	7700	6000	8500	13,000	30,000	42,000
Rbt.	7200	5900	8300	12,800	29,000	41,000

1919 Brewster, town brougham, HAC

1919 BREWSTER
Knight — 4-cyl., 25.6 hp, 125″ wb

	FP	5	4	3	2	1
Country Brgm.	8300	6400	9300	14,500	33,000	45,000
Open Phae.	7700	6200	8800	13,500	31,000	43,000
Twn. Brgm.	8300	6000	8500	13,000	30,000	42,000
Twn. Land'et.	8450	6200	8800	13,500	31,000	43,000
Tour. Land'et.	8800	5900	8300	12,800	29,000	41,000
Enclosed Drive	8400	5900	8300	12,800	29,000	41,000
Limo.	8500	6000	8500	13,000	30,000	42,000
Rbt.	7200	5900	8300	12,800	29,000	41,000

1920 BREWSTER
Knight — 4-cyl., 60 hp, 125″ wb

	FP	5	4	3	2	1
Club Rbt.	7900	6000	8500	13,000	30,000	42,000
Limo.	9600	6200	8800	13,500	31,000	43,000
Twn. Brgm.	9400	6300	9000	14,000	32,000	44,000
Country Brgm.	9400	6400	9300	14,500	33,000	45,000
Enclosed Drive	9400	6200	8800	13,500	31,000	43,000
Round Corner Land'et.	9500	6300	9000	14,000	32,000	44,000
Twn. Land'et.	9500	6200	8800	13,500	31,000	43,000

1920 Brewster, country brougham, HAC

1921 Brewster, club runabout, HAC

1921 BREWSTER
Knight, Model 91 — 4-cyl., 53 hp, 125″ wb

	FP	5	4	3	2	1
Club Rbt.	7900	6200	8800	13,500	31,000	43,000
Open Phae.	9000	6400	9300	14,500	33,000	45,000
Double Enclosed Drive	10,500	6700	9900	15,500	38,000	47,000
Twn. Brgm.	10,700	6500	9500	15,000	34,000	46,000
Glass Quarter Brgm.	10,500	6700	9900	15,500	38,000	47,000
Land'et.	10,700	6400	9300	14,500	33,000	45,000

1922-24 Brewster, enclosed drive limousine, HAC

1922 BREWSTER
Knight, Model 91 — 4-cyl., 53 hp, 125″ wb

	FP	5	4	3	2	1
Tour.	7000	6400	9300	14,500	33,000	45,000
Double Enclosed Drive	10,500	6700	9900	15,500	38,000	47,000
Limo.	10,600	6300	9000	14,000	32,000	44,000
Twn. Brgm.	10,700	6300	9000	14,000	32,000	44,000
Club Rbt.	7000	6200	8800	13,500	31,000	43,000
Glass Quarter Brgm.	10,500	6400	9300	14,500	33,000	45,000
Twn. Land'et.	10,700	6300	9000	14,000	32,000	44,000
Cabr.	10,800	6500	9500	15,000	34,000	46,000

1923 BREWSTER
Knight, Model 91 — 4-cyl., 58 hp, 125″ wb

	FP	5	4	3	2	1
Tour.	5000	6000	8500	13,000	30,000	42,000
Club Rbt.	5000	5900	8300	12,800	29,000	41,000
Twn. Land'et.	7000	6300	9000	14,000	32,000	44,000
Limo.	7000	6200	8800	13,500	31,000	43,000
Double Enclosed Drive	7000	6200	8800	13,500	31,000	43,000
Glass Quarter Brgm.	7000	6300	9000	14,000	32,000	44,000
Twn. Brgm.	7000	6400	9300	14,500	33,000	45,000
Cabr.	7000	6300	9000	14,000	32,000	44,000

1924 BREWSTER
Knight, Model 02 — 4-cyl., 54 hp, 125″ wb

	FP	5	4	3	2	1
Rbt.	4500	6200	8800	13,500	31,000	43,000
Tour.	5000	6300	9000	14,000	32,000	44,000
Double Enclosed Drive	7500	6400	9300	14,500	33,000	45,000
Twn. Land'et.	7500	6300	9000	14,000	32,000	44,000
Limo.-7P	7500	6200	8800	13,500	31,000	43,000
Glass Quarter Brgm.	7500	6300	9000	14,500	32,000	44,000
Twn. Brgm.	7500	6300	9000	14,000	32,000	44,000

1925 BREWSTER
Knight, Model 02 — 4-cyl., 54 hp, 125″ wb

	FP	5	4	3	2	1
Double Enclosed Drive	7500	6400	9300	14,500	33,000	45,000
Glass Quarter Brgm.	7500	6300	9000	14,000	32,000	44,000
Twn. Brgm.	8900	6200	8800	13,500	31,000	43,000
Limo.	7500	6200	8800	13,500	31,000	43,000
Twn. Land'et.	7500	6300	9000	14,000	32,000	44,000

1934 Brewster, roadster, OCW

1935 Brewster, town car, HAC

	FP	5	4	3	2	1
Brewster Ford (127" wb)	3500	8700	9900	15,500	34,800	47,000

BRICE — The Brice Motor Car Company was organized in Warrensville, Ohio late in 1911 with a capital stock of $200,000 for the purpose of manufacturing and selling automobiles. W.P. Kehres, Thomas J. Atkinson, John G. Schultz, E.B. Hecker and J.A. Hecker were the principals involved. This venture seems to have stalled soon after incorporation.

BRICK CHURCH — The Brick Church Automobile & Supply Company was organized with a capital stock of $100,000 for the manufacture of car accessories in South Orange, New Jersey during the early fall of 1907. John B. Todd and Melvin O.C. Hull were the principals behind this venture which moved to East Orange in late 1908 and was reincorporated for the manufacture of automobiles as the Brick Church Automobile Company. L. Burr Manning now joined the venture. That any cars were produced seems doubtful. The company did act as Buick dealers. In 1916 the firm was reincorporated as the Brick Church Auto & Taxi Company, but by that time automobile manufacture had long since disappeared from any of the firm's plans.

BRIDGEPORT — The Bridgeport Auto Company of Wheeling, West Virginia was organized with a capital stock of $5000 in January 1913 for the manufacture of automobiles. J.B. Handlan, W.G. Hamiton, G.T. Knote, E. Morrell and H. Miller were the incorporators. Manufacture did not follow.

The Bridgeport Auto Company of Bridgeport, Ohio announced in December 1913 its plans to erect a huge factory in town for the manufacture of automobiles. "It is said that an eastern concern will be merged with the Bridgeport company in the near future," reported *The Automobile*. Whether it was the Wheeling firm is not known, but again manufacture did not follow.

BRIDGEPORT — **Bridgeport, Connecticut** — **(1901)** — That the Bridgeport Boiler Works in Connecticut had a steam automobile under construction in 1901 was reported in both *The Motor Age* and *The Horseless Age*, the latter magazine noting that the vehicle was "substantial" and that the firm planned to market it. But marketing did not follow. Conceivably, the boiler of the Bridgeport car may have been the invention of Louis Morris and Charles S. Cole, two Bridgeport mechanics who had applied for a patent on a steam car boiler that year.

BRIDGES — The Bridges Motor Car & Rubber Company of Fort Worth, Texas has been indicated on various car rosters as producing an automobile in 1918. Probably this did not happen. During the spring of that year the firm, whose president and general manager was Clarence W. Bridges, announced plans for the construction of a factory on a commodious 289 acres of land outside Fort Worth. There is no evidence that plant was ever completed. Manufacture of "automobiles, automobile tires, trucks and tractors" had been the ambitious plan.

BRIDGES — **Carlisle, Pennsylvania** — **(1900-1901)** — John Miller Bridges of Carlisle completed his first single-cylinder gasoline runabout in early 1900 and announced his manufacturing intention thereafter. Runabouts only were to be his product, fitted with tubular running gear, and the purchaser's choice of either a 4-1/2 or 6 hp motor and either wood or wire wheels. He may have built a few cars for local sale, but not for long. By 1902 the Carlisle city directory was listing his occupation as clerk.

1936 Bridges, MVMA

BRIDGES — **Pasadena, California** — **(1936)** — This Bridges was another of the Dymaxion-inspired streamlined cars (like the Arrowhead, also from the West Coast) that was built to predict the future course of automobile design. This example had a single seat in the front which carried four passengers abreast. A four-cylinder engine developing 30 hp was at the rear. The monocoque frame/body was devised of airplane tubing. The Bridges was designed by California Institute of Technology professor Calvin B. Bridges. He claimed a 65 mph top speed and a 35 mph fuel economy for the car.

BRIETZKE — **Racine, Wisconsin** — **(1900)** — Charles F. Brietzke, chief engineer of the Fish Brothers Wagon Company of Racine, built the first gasoline automobile in town in 1900. The car was fitted with a Fish body, but Brietzke put the vehicle together in the basement of his home at 808 Union Street. Its two-stroke 10 hp engine was of his own invention; the wire wheels and tires he bought off a racing sulky in Milwaukee. The car sat two people and was tiller steered. Brietzke never envisioned going into manufacturing; in fact, he built the car only because his wife was afraid of horses and her doctor had said she should get out of the house more often. After using the vehicle for a couple of years, Brietzke acquired a White steamer and raffled his own car off. The year following he became a salesman for the new Mitchell car which had just gone into production in town, and in 1906 he opened Racine's first garage.

1934 Briggs Experimental Prototye, MVMA

BRIGGS — **Detroit, Michigan** — **(1933-1936)** — There never was a production automobile called Briggs, although the Briggs Manufacturing Company of Detroit produced bodies by the thousands for Ford and Chrysler, and several fascinating prototypes by the mid-Thirties. The man responsible for the prototypes was Dutch-born John Tjaarda, whose American design credentials included stints at Locke and Company, Duesenberg and GM's Art and Colour Section before he joined Briggs in 1932. Shortly thereafter he showed Edsel Ford preliminary sketches and models for an integral-construction car he had designed which could be fitted with either a rear or front-mounted engine. Build some prototypes, Ford said — which Tjaarda did, the rear-engined first, Tjaarda having been a rear-engine enthusiast since the mid-Twenties when he attempted in vain to obtain financing to proceed to production prototype on his rear-engine "Sterkenburg" designs. The wood-framed Tjaarda/Briggs mockup was displayed in New York at a "Ford Exhibition of Progress" in December 1933, and at Chicago's "Century of Progress" World's Fair in June 1934. An operational version followed in 1935, by which time Briggs had already built two front-engined versions. In October the rear-engined Briggs was introduced to the public. Built on a 125-inch wheelbase and powered by an 84 hp V-8, the car was so aerodynamically well designed that a speed of 110 mph was possible. The complete "propulsive mechanism," including engine, radiator, clutch, transmission, differential, driveshaft, transverse rear spring and rear wheels, was combined into a compact unit upon which the rear of the steel body rested, the two being connected by nine nuts and bolts. Although the car created something of a sensation, production did not follow. (Historians since have contended that this car influenced Ferdinand Porsche in his subsequent design of the German Volkswagen). What did see production, however, was a refinement of the front-engined prototype — with solid axles front and rear — which was introduced in November as the new Lincoln Zephyr. In 1936 Tjaarda worked up a four-cylinder rear-engined prototype for Briggs in which Germany's Auto Union was interested although, again, production did not follow. All of the Tjaarda-designed Briggs prototypes were later destroyed.

BRIGGS-DETROITER — Although occasionally referred to as the Briggs-Detroiter, this car built in Detroit from 1912 to 1917 was usually called simply the Detroiter. Refer to Detroiter.

1920 Briggs & Stratton, Flyer

BRIGGS & STRATTON — **Milwaukee, Wisconsin** — **(1919-1923)** — In 1918 the Briggs & Stratton Company of Milwaukee, manufacturers of automotive accessories, invested nearly a half-million dollars in new buildings and equipment — and in 1919 diversified. Manufacturing rights to the Smith Motor Wheel and the Smith Flyer were purchased that year from A.O. Smith (also of Milwaukee) and the little buckboard that had formerly been known as the Smith now became known as the Briggs & Stratton Flyer. Among other refinements, Briggs & Stratton beefed up the Smith Motor Wheel from 1 to 2 hp and added a flywheel magneto. In 1921, by which time, the company had added a Motor-Wheel-powered scooter to its line, the buckboard began to be referred to as the Red Bug. Prices that year were $100 for motor wheel, $150 for motor scooter and $200 for motor buckboard, though they were reduced the year following in the wake of the postwar recession. In 1924 Briggs & Stratton sold its manufacturing rights to a New Jersey company which continued the buckboard in production in North Bergen as the Red Bug. At the same time the buckboard rights were sold, Briggs & Stratton bought Toledo Automotive Products Company. Previously the Wisconsin company had manufactured the Ohio firm's window regulators under license, a venture which proved so financially lucrative that the entire Toledo firm was taken over.

1919-1920 BRIGGS & STRATTON
Flyer — 1-cyl., 62" wb

	FP	5	4	3	2	1
Model D Buckboard	—	1500	2500	3600	5500	11,000

1921-1923 BRIGGS & STRATTON
Red Bug — 1-cyl., 62" wb

	FP	5	4	3	2	1
Model D Buckboard	—	1500	2500	3600	5500	11,000

BRIGHT — Early in 1914 the Bright Auto & Repair Company was organized in Elmhurst, Illinois to manufacture and deal in motor vehicles. Incorporators were George Bright, Ralph H. Mears and Harvey J. Bright. Subsequent manufacture is doubtful.

BRIGHTON — Brighton was the name given by W. Lee Crouch to one of the cars he built in 1896 in New Brighton, Pennsylvania. Refer to Crouch. Brighton Six was the model name in 1913-1914 for a line of six-cylinder cars produced by Palmer-Singer following the company's fine performance in the twenty-four-hour race at Brighton Beach in 1911. Refer to Palmer-Singer.

BRILL — Appleton, Wisconsin — (1909) — Edward Brill of Appleton was a manufacturer of motors for automobiles and boats who, during the summer of 1909, built several automobiles on special order from Fox River Valley clients. This was strictly a sideline activity to his usual work, and he did not proceed into formal automobile manufacture.

BRINER — St. Louis, Missouri — (1902) — At his shop on Second Street and Franklin Avenue in St. Louis, Fred E. Briner built himself a steam car in 1902. Its boiler had as many half-inch copper tubes as there were days in a year, with a Bunsen burner underneath. Its body provided for four-passengers sitting dos-a-dos. A fire during a motoring trip was doused, with the help of onlookers and a healthy amount of water, but the incident seems to have extinguished Fred Briner's steam car enthusiasm too. He never built another automobile.

1915 Briscoe, model B, Cloverleaf, roadster, RM

BRISCOE — Jackson, Michigan — (1914-1921) — Benjamin Briscoe had a very good idea when he decided to ally himself with Jonathan D. Maxwell to produce the Maxwell car, and a very bad one when he decided to use the Maxwell-Briscoe company as the base around which to build a rival conglomerate to William C. Durant's General Motors. His United States Motor Company was a disaster. In 1913 he left the wreckage of it to Walter Flanders, took off for France to form Briscoe Freres with his brother Frank and to build a cyclecar that he would bring back to the U.S. to market as the Argo. And he had another idea, a car to be named for himself. Since the U.S. Motor fiasco had rendered him persona non grata in New York banking circles, he secured the financing for his new Briscoe Motor Corporation from the meat-packing Swifts of Chicago. The Briscoe, which would be built in Jackson, Michigan, made its debut at the New York Automobile Show in January 1914. Powered by a four-cylinder L-head engine of 33 hp, it was a typical medium-priced American light car except for the cyclops headlight that stared out of the radiator grille. This might have proved a marvelous identifying feature save for the fact that a car with only one headlight was against the law in many states. The Cloverleaf Roadster model also had a compressed papier-mache body, which was certainly unusual and perhaps not such a good idea either. Consequently,

for 1916, the Briscoe outwardly resembled any other American tourer, though Ben Briscoe came up with another exploitable gimmick: a choice of two engines, the four or the Ferro V-8. "Buy the Four. Use it a month," the brochures said. "If then you decide you want the Eight, simply pay the difference and a small charge for installation work." Later in 1916 he introduced a smaller 24 hp air-cooled four which, he said, he "and fourteen of the world's greatest engineers created in France." Following the First World War, Briscoe returned to France to talk to Bellanger Freres and from this came a plan to offer to any small community the chance to become an automobile maufacturer through the simple expedient of buying from Briscoe his easy-to-assemble plans for a four-cylinder automobile (Briscoe engine, Bellanger chassis). How many small towns bought this idea is unknown. Then, in 1920, he had yet another idea for his Briscoe car: production simplification. His chief engineer Jules Haltenberger devised a reversible propeller shaft, a single design for all spring shackles and bolts, identical clutch and brake pedal forgings and one drill size for most of the holes required in the chassis. This simplified production but proved calamitous for the car. Late in 1921 Briscoe decided he had had enough of all this and handed his company's presidency over to Clarence A. Earl. Earl continued building Briscoes for which parts remained on hand, selling them off as late as the spring of 1922, but in the meantime he renamed the company and its new car for himself. Briscoe betimes embarked upon other fields of endeavor, oil in California, gold mining in Colorado among them. Production figures for the Briscoe were 5000 units in 1914-1915, 7100 in 1916, 8100 in 1917-1918, 11,000 in 1919; 6000 in 1920. These are approximations, though reasonably accurate — and about four times less each year than Benjamin Briscoe had hoped to build.

1914-1915 BRISCOE
Model B — 4-cyl., 33 hp, 107" wb

	FP	5	4	3	2	1
Cloverleaf Rds.-3P	785	2700	3600	5300	8800	19,000
Deluxe Tour.-5P	785	2500	3500	5000	8500	18,000

The Latest Briscoe Beauty

1916 Briscoe, model 4-38, touring, HAC

1916 BRISCOE
Model 4-38 — 4-cyl., 33 hp, 114" wb

	FP	5	4	3	2	1
Tour.-5P	750	2700	3600	5300	8800	19,000
Cloverleaf Rds.-3P	750	2900	3700	5600	9100	20,000

Model 8-38 — 8-cyl., 35 hp, 114" wb

	FP	5	4	3	2	1
Tour.-5P	950	2900	3700	5600	9100	20,000
Cloverleaf Rds.-3P	950	3000	4000	6000	9500	21,000

1917-19 Briscoe, model B-4-24, touring, HAC

1917 BRISCOE
Model B 4-24 — 4-cyl., 24 hp, 105" wb

	FP	5	4	3	2	1
Tour.-5P	685	2900	3700	5600	9100	20,000
Club Rds.-4P	685	3000	4000	6000	9500	21,000
Rbt.-2P	685	2700	3600	5300	8800	19,000
Dly. Car	725	2500	3500	5000	8500	18,000
Coachaire	810	2800	3700	5500	9000	19,500

1918 BRISCOE
Model B 4-24 — 4-cyl., 24 hp, 104" wb

	FP	5	4	3	2	1
Tour.-5P	725	2900	3700	5600	9100	20,000
Rbt.-2P	725	3000	4000	6000	9500	21,000
Dly. Car	725	2500	3500	5000	8500	18,000
Rds.-4P	725	3000	4000	6000	9500	21,000
Coachaire	850	2900	3700	5600	9100	20,000

1919 BRISCOE
Model B 4-24 — 4-cyl., 24 hp, 104" wb

	FP	5	4	3	2	1
Tour.-5P	885	3000	4000	6000	9500	21,000
Rds.-2P	885	3100	4200	6300	10,500	22,000
Dly. Car	885	2500	3500	5000	8500	18,000

1920 Briscoe, model B-4-24, touring, HAC

1920 BRISCOE
Model B 4-24 — 4-cyl., 24 hp, 103'' wb

	FP	5	4	3	2	1
Tour.-5P	985	3100	4200	6300	10,500	22,000
Rbt.-2P	985	3200	4300	6500	11,000	23,000
Sed.-5P	1885	2400	3400	4800	8000	17,000
Cpe.-2P	1885	2500	3500	5000	8500	18,000

1921 Briscoe, model 4-34, sedan, HAC

1921 BRISCOE
Model 4-34 — 4-cyl., 35 hp, 109'' wb

Tour.-5P	1285	3100	4200	6300	10,500	22,000
Rds.-2P	1285	3200	4300	6500	11,000	23,000
Cpe.-3P	1885	2500	3500	5000	8500	18,000
Sed.-5P	1885	2400	3400	4800	8000	17,000

BRISCOE FRERES — Briscoe Freres had been the name selected by Benjamin Briscoe for his overseas venture in France. There he developed a cyclecar which he returned to America to build as the Argo in 1914. Refer to Argo.

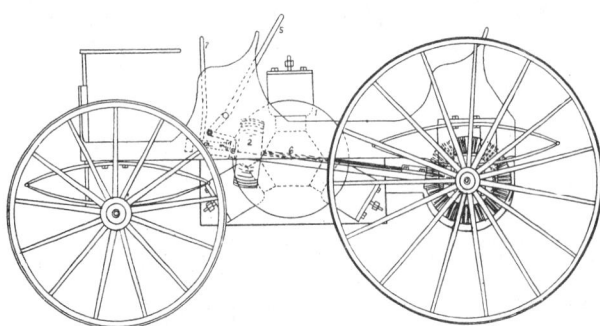

1896 Bristol

BRISTOL — Chicago, Illinois — (1896) — Harvey S. Bristol of Chicago patented both his automobile and its engine in 1896. Whether he ever completed and successfully tested the vehicle has not been documented. Interestingly, the engine was a six. The chassis featured the flywheel and friction wheel combined on the motor shaft.

BRISTOL — The Bristol Automobile Company was organized in December of 1906 in Waterbury, Connecticut with a capital stock of $10,000. The firm's plan was to ''manufacture, buy, sell, repair, lease and hire autos, auto parts and accessories.'' Edgar H. Bristol, Bennett B. Bristol and Watson E. Goodyear, all of Naugatuck, were the people involved. Manufacture is not believed to have followed.

Although occasionally referred to in the trade press as a Bristol, the landaulet taxicab designed by the Bristol Engineering Company and produced from 1909-1911 by the New Departure Manufacturing Company of Bristol, Connecticut was marketed under the tradename of Rockwell. Refer to Rockwell.

1903 Bristol, runabout, NAHC

BRISTOL — Bristol, Connecticut — (1903-1904) — The Bristol Motor Car Company was the second automotive venture of Frederick Newton Manross, a man whose many interests ranged from clockmaking to photography. In 1902 he had backed Frederick A. Law of Hartford in the design and building of an automobile, the rights to which were sold to the Electric Vehicle Company and many ideas of which subsequently found their way into various of the Pope motorcars. The rights to the 1903 Bristol — an air cooled 8 hp single-cylinder runabout with planetary transmission and thirty-inch wheels which Manross and a few friends designed — were also quickly sold. On May 21st that year the *Bristol Press* reported that a contract had been signed by Bristol Motor Car Company whereby it merged into the Russell & Erwin Company of Bristol and the American Hardware Corporation of New Britain. Ostensibly, manufacture was to center in the Bristol factory where production had begun in March. Very soon the Bristol was no more, however, as American Hardware decided to center operations in its own factory in New Britain, where it would proceed to build the famous Corbin car. In the meantime, in Bristol, sometime during 1904, F.N. Manross had again allied himself with Frederick Law in the establishment of the Law Auto Manufacturing Company, of which Manross was the principal owner. Although a few cars carrying the Law name were subsequently built and sold, this new company was organized not for the manufacture of cars but component parts. In 1907 the Corbin interests absorbed this firm as well. The following year F.N. Manross and his son Robert built another touring runabout, but this one was for their own use. In a photo caption appearing in the *Bristol Press* of March 29th, 1908, reference is made to the fact that this was the fifth machine built by Manross. This may have represented the total Bristol/Law/Manross production.

1903-1904 BRISTOL

	FP	5	4	3	2	1
Bristol Rbt.	—	2500	3500	5000	8500	18,000

1911 Broc Electric, model 19, roadster, WLB

BROC ELECTRIC — Cleveland, Ohio — (1909-1914)/Saginaw, Michigan — (1914-1916) — The Broc Carriage & Wagon Company began building automobile bodies as early as 1904, but did not build and market a complete car until 1909. Fresh from its maiden year's experience in the field, Broc announced that its product for 1910 was the perfect car. "That is a pretty broad statement," *Cycle and Automobile Trade Journal* allowed, "and . . . it might be pertinent to enumerate some of the points on which the company bases its claims, and which go far toward putting it in the perfect class. These include theft proof safety appliances, continuous torque control, efficiency and durability, interchangeable bodies, simple and effective controller, ample brakes, interchangeability of parts, imported German ball bearings throughout, and the highest quality of material and workmanship possible." Obviously Broc had a terrific press agent, and it may have been company president F.A. Brand. The Broc Electric was typical for its genre, with either chain or shaft-drive depending on model, and some models with tiller steering which was rather retrograde by now. In succeeding years, Broc went through organizational changes which resulted in its renaming to Broc Carriage Company first, and Broc Electric Vehicle Company second. Then in 1914 Broc emerged with Argo and Borland to become the American Electric Car Company. Though the marque name was continued for the product, its manufacture was soon moved to Saginaw, F.A. Brand served as president of the merged companies.

1912 Broc Electric, model 26, coupe, HAC

1912 BROC ELECTRIC

	FP	5	4	3	2	1
Model 19						
Rdstr. (85'' wb)	2100	3000	4000	6000	9500	21,000
Model 20						
Stanhope (85'' wb)	2000	2900	3700	5600	9100	20,000
Model 21						
Victoria (85'' wb)	2050	2700	3600	5300	8800	19,000
Model 22						
Cpe. (85'' wb)	2300	2500	3500	5000	8500	18,000
Model 30						
Brgm. (100'' wb)	3500	2700	3600	5300	8800	19,000
Model 26						
Cpe. (84'' wb)	2700	2500	3500	5000	8500	18,000
Model 28						
Brgm. (95'' wb)	3000	2600	3550	5200	8700	18,500

1910 Broc Electric, model D, stanhope, HAC

1909-1910 BROC ELECTRIC

	FP	5	4	3	2	1
Model D						
Straight Front Cpe. (80''wb)	1950	3000	4000	6000	9500	21,000
Model D						
Ext. Front Cpe. (80'' wb)	2700	3100	4200	6300	10,500	22,000
Model D						
Stanhope (80'' wb)	2000	2700	3600	5300	8800	19,000
Model D						
Victoria (80'' wb)	2000	2900	3700	5600	9100	20,000

1913 Broc Electric, model 20, brougham, HAC

1913 BROC ELECTRIC

Model 20						
Brgm.-2P (84'' wb)	2100	2700	3600	5300	8800	19,000
Model 28						
Brougham-5P (96'' wb)	3000	2800	3600	5500	9000	19,500
Model 29						
Brgm.-5P (96'' wb)	3100	2800	3600	5500	9000	19,500
Model 31						
Brgm.-5P (96'' wb)	3500	2800	3600	5500	9000	19,500

1911 Broc Electric, model 21, victoria, WLB

1911 BROC ELECTRIC

Model 25						
Cpe.-4P (83'' wb)	2700	2500	3500	5000	8500	18,000
Model 19						
Rdstr.-2P (83'' wb)	2100	3000	4000	6000	9500	21,000
Model 20						
Stanhope-2P (80'' wb)	2000	2900	3700	5600	9100	20,000
Model 21						
Victoria-2P (80'' wb)	2050	2700	3600	5300	8800	19,000
Model 22						
Cpe.-3P (80'' wb)	2300	2500	3500	5000	8500	18,000
Model 24						
Cpe.-4P (80'' wb)	2500	2500	3500	5000	8500	18,000

1914 Broc Electric, model 32, brougham, HAC

1914 BROC ELECTRIC

Model 30

	FP	5	4	3	2	1
Cpe. (96" wb)	3000	2700	3600	5300	8800	19,000
Model 32						
Rear Drive Brgm. (96" wb)	2900	2500	3500	5000	8500	18,000
Model 34						
Front Drive Brgm. (98" wb)	3100	2500	3500	5000	8500	18,000
Model 33						
Rear Drive Brgm. (98" wb)	3100	2700	3600	5300	8800	19,000
Model 36						
Double Drive Brgm. (98" wb)	3200	2600	3550	5200	8700	18,500

1915-16 Broc Electric, model 36, double drive brougham, HAC

1915-1916 BROC ELECTRIC

Model 36

Double Drive Brgm. (96" wb)	3200	2600	3550	5200	8700	18,500
Model 34						
Rear Drive Brgm. (96" wb)	3100	2700	3600	5300	8800	19,000
Model 33						
Front Drive Brgm. (96" wb)	3150	2700	3600	5300	8800	19,000

BROCK — Brock's Garage, Inc. was organized with a capital stock of $100,000 in March 1913 to manufacture and deal in automobiles in Trenton, New Jersey. Three Brocks — John L., Howard P. and Harry K. — were involved. Manufacture has not been documented.

BROCKSHIRE & ROBINSON — The Brockshire & Robinson Company was organized with a capital stock of $20,000 in Saint Paris, Ohio late in 1911. F.M. Brockshire, W.T. Robinson, John Schooler, H.L. Pentz and H.C. Brockshire were the people involved, and automobile manufacture was their plan. It does not appear to have been realized.

BRODHEAD — The Brodhead Car Company was organized early in 1910 in the Wisconsin city of that name by local businessmen intent upon producing an automobile. A four-cylinder 40 hp car for the 1910 market was planned, together with erection of a big factory in town. These plans seems to have been dashed early.

BROKAW — The C.B. Brokaw Auto Company was organized with a capital stock of $20,000 during the fall of 1909 for the manufacture of automobiles in Plainfield, New Jersey. Involved in this venture were C.B. and A.F. Brokaw of Plainfield and W.B. Hopping of New York City. Manufacture does not seem to have followed.

BRONX — Most likely there was never a Bronx manufactured but there were two companies organized in that New York City borough to do so.

The Bronx Automobile Company was a $25,000 incorporation by Herbert E. Van Hofne, George L. Whitney and Donald C. Roberts from early 1905.

The Bronx Taxicab Company was a 1910 $500 incorporation of H.L. and G.H. Hill and M. Monfied.

BROOK — Brook, Indiana — (1909) — "Brook Coming to the Front with Prospects for Another Factory in the Near Future" was the headline in *The Brook Reporter* of June 25th, 1909. One Lee Lowe and his brother had come to town and persuaded local businessmen to support them in the construction of a factory for automobile manufacture. Very little was recorded about what the car would be, but reportedly there were plans to call it the Ade, after George Ade, the famous author and humorist whose estate was two miles east of Brook. The car was never called that, however; neither was it called a Brook, as it has appeared on various rosters. No car was ever produced, and perhaps the prototype was not even completed. The factory was, however, and it remains extant today as the home of the Brook Plumbing and Heating Company. Lee Lowe moved to Royal Center, Indiana following the failure of his automotive venture.

1920 Brook, cyclecar, NAHC

BROOK — Indianapolis, Indiana — (1920-1921) — This Brook was a cyclecar, and the Spacke renamed. It was produced in Indianapolis by the Spacke Machine & Tool Company which had been bought out by Daniel S. Brooks of Peru Auto Parts in 1917. The new regime had entered automobile manufacturing ranks with the Spacke cyclecar two years later, but after one season as the Spacke, the car was redesignated the Brook (without the "s" of its namesake's surname nor the ending "e" that history has so frequently given it). The only significant design change from Spacke to Brook was the removal of the fuel tank from the rear deck to the front of the car where a radiator was usually positioned, certainly an engineering revision of dubious merit. In September of 1920 Daniel S. Brooks announced that his company was unable to meet due obligations. By November the Spacke Machine & Tool Company was operating under receivership. A few Brook cars were produced into 1921, but most of the units leaving the factory now were destined to be called Peters, that East Coast Company having negotiated the rights to sell the car under its own banner.

BROOKES — The Brookes Motor Car Company was a $5 million Delaware incorporation from 1913 to "manufacture, sell and deal in automobiles." The incorporators were Charles B. Bishop, Clarence J. Jacobs and Harry W. Davis. No manufacture is indicated.

BROOKLYN — Mention in the trade press during the fall of 1900 of the establishment of the Brooklyn Automobile and Machine Company was a misprint. The firm in question was Bowker. Refer to Belger & Bowker.

The Brooklyn & Long Island Auto Association was organized with a $20,000 capital stock in the fall of 1914 to manufacture motorcars, supplies and equipment. Involved in the venture were C.F. Batt, R.P. Lumely and J.G. Snyder. Manufacture is doubted.

BROOKS — During the summer of 1912, the Brooks Motor Car Company was incorporated in Buffalo, New York with a capital stock of $100,000 for the manufacture of gasoline automobiles of all kinds, including taxicabs. "It will operate a factory in Buffalo," the press reported, "and plans to turn out a large number of cars annually, increasing the capital stock as required by the business." It does not appear this venture proceeded any further than the grand plans of its incorporators, Herman G. Rechsteiner, George B. North and B.O. Kerr.

BROOKS — Detroit, Michigan — (1905-1907) — At some point during its brief two-year existence the Brooks Automobile Company of Detroit changed its name to the Brooks Motor Company. At another point it completed one car. That was the total Brooks production. The car was named for C.H. Brooks, the company's vice-president and chief designer who previously had been with Maxwell-Briscoe in Tarrytown (New York). E.C. Murray was Brooks president; also involved were Joseph and Peter Schulte and F.D. Van Normund. In October of 1905 the Brooks Automobile Company was organized with a capitalization of $100,000. A factory on Scotten Avenue and Lake Shore Railroad in Detroit was secured. In September of 1907 — when Dr. F.J. McHugh was indicated to be president — the Brooks Motor Company died. The Brooks demise was concisely summed up in *The Horseless Age* that month: ". . . in the production of one car its money has been expended, and the entire output was recently put up at auction to satisfy a claim of $718.78."

1912 Brooks, motor wagon, OCW

BROOKS — Saginaw, Michigan — (1911-1912) — The Brooks Manufacturing Company of Saginaw produced a light delivery wagon which could do double-duty in taking the family to church on Sunday, though Brooks never built an automobile per se. "Cheaper than a horse and wagon," the company advertised, "three times the mileage at one-third the upkeep." The Brooks delivery wagon business was acquired in 1913 by Charles Duryea, and the year following its factory was taken over by A.R. Thomas for production of the cyclecar which had begun its life as the Detroit Speedster.

BROOKS — Buffalo, New York — (1927) — Oland J. Brooks was an American who trekked to Stratford, Ontario for his automotive venture. There, in 1923, he established Brooks Steam Motors Ltd. and began production of Canada's most popular steam car. The Brooks also sold well in the United States during this period, and indeed was outsold only by the venerable Stanley. As the Twenties waned, however, Oland Brooks found himself in financial difficulty and his company was in receivership by 1927. Brooks did return to Buffalo at that time to try again, but whether any of his steam cars were produced there remains in question. Inconclusive references indicate that a few were. In 1929 the last Brooks cars were auctioned off at prices as low as $150. In 1931 the Ontario factory was put up for sale following what the press called a "maze of legal entanglement" for four years.

BROOKS-LATTA — St. Louis, Missouri — (1910-1911) — During the fall of 1910, Charles E. Brooks and the Latta brothers — Charles and Allan T. — organized the Brooks-Latta Automobile Manufacturing Company in St. Louis with a capital stock of $150,000. Temporary quarters were taken at 4255 Fairfax Avenue, where experimental models were begun. In the late summer of 1911, the Brooks-Latta company announced that it had secured an option on a parcel of land at Sullivan and Lambdin avenues at which site a factory for the manufacture of automobiles and commerical vehicles would be built. There is no evidence it ever was. The Brooks-Latta never proceeded beyond the prototype stage.

BROOMELL — The car was a six-wheeled behemoth built in York, Pennsylvania in 1903. The name refers to its designer, Albert P. Broomell. Broomell himself called the car a Pullman. Refer to Pullman Six-Wheeler.

BROTHERTON — Detroit, Michigan — (1910) — The Brotherton was a six-cylinder car that was the idea of N.T. Brotherton, although he did not design it. Performing that task for him was Charles Balough, who had formerly been a draftsman for the Reliance Motor Truck Company of Detroit and assistant chief engineer for the Rapid Motor Vehicle Company of Pontiac. A prototype was built, but a company for manufacture was not organized. Balough soon found greener pastures in Springfield (Ohio) and left the project in the fall of 1910 to become chief engineer of the Kelly Motor Truck Company. Although *Cycle and Automobile Trade Journal* reported in September that Balough was "still connected with the Brotherton Six in a consulting way," it would appear that little further consulting was necessary. The car never proceeded into manufacture.

1904 Brotz, auto-buggy, OCW

BROTZ SPECIAL — Kohler, Wisconsin — (1904) — The first automobile in Kohler was built by Anton F. Brotz, and he called it Special. Its two-cylinder horizontally-opposed motor, its chassis, steering gear, transmission and rear axle were all made by Brotz at his small machine shop, a foot-power lathe doubling as a drill press. Anton Brotz completed the car in 1904 and drove it until 1911. He never built another one, his interests turning to aviation. He was director of research for the Kohler Company for many years prior to his death in 1945.

1904 Brough, motor buggy, TP

BROUGH — Randall, Kansas — (1904) — George Brough was a mail carrier from Randall who decided to go horseless. A blacksmith in town helped him do it. The Brough automobile was a motorized buggy, and its motor was a 6 hp one-lunger which the smithy had used the year previous to operate machinery in his shop. Chain drive was featured. Most of the vehicle was made up of bits and pieces of old farm machinery, and its construction was very primitive — but it served George Brough well for several years of letter carrying. This car remains extant, and is on display today at Tommy Protsman's museum in Stone Mountain, Georgia.

1902 Brower, runabout, MVMA

BROWER — Syracuse, New York — (1884, 1902) — Fred G. Brower was a machinist from Syracuse who built a small electric car in 1884. In 1902 he designed a gasoline runabout for his twelve-year-old daughter Carrie. Its 3 1/2 hp engine was purchased, but all other parts of the vehicle were made by Brower. Initially the car was designed as a three-wheeler but was revised into a four-wheeler soon after. Brower may have built additional cars, but aside from supplying transportation for his family, it would appear he had no further automotive ambition.

BROWN — The Brown Auto Company was a $4500 incorporation from Marysville, Kentucky during the summer of 1913. Mike Brown, W.B. Tulley and S.M. King backed this venture to manufacture automobiles, though it appears none were.

The Brown-Barbier Company of New York City was organized with a capital stock of $500,000 during the summer of 1906 for the manufacture of automobiles, automobile supplies and appliances. Wilbur F. Wund, Theodore Broderick and Anton Barbier were the principals involved. Manufacture of a Brown-Barbier car did not follow.

The Brown Car Corporation was incorporated by W.P. Fargo, H.W. Torney and E.E. Beyer in early 1913 with a capital stock of $30,000 for the manufacture of automobiles in New York City. Manufacture was not forthcoming.

The Brown Cotton Gin Company of New London, Connecticut produced a car in 1910, but it was a single vehicle more appropriately designated by the name of its designer. Refer to Gardner.

The Brown-Darnell Company of Richmond, Indiana was organized with a capital stock of $2000 for the manufacture of automobiles and bicycles in 1902. Directors were Wesley Brown, John C. Darnell, John A. Spekenhier, John A. Walls, Fred M. Taft and Edward Valentine. Manufacture is doubted.

The Brown Development Company was frequently mentioned during the mid-Twenties as the name of the Syracuse, New York venture which actually was the Julian Brown Development Company. Refer to Julian Brown.

The Brown-Dryer Motor Company was organized in Tucson, Arizona during late 1916 for the manufacture and sale of automobiles and accessories. Bert O. Brown and Roland C. Dryer were the partners behind this $50,000 venture. Manufacture of a Brown-Dryer automobile is doubted.

The H. Oscar Brown Motor Car Company was organized to manufacture automobiles in Camden, New Jersey late in 1906. Capital stock was $100,000. Manufacture is questionable. By 1908 H. Oscar Brown was in Philadelphia trading in his local agency for the American Locomotive Motor Car Company for a job with the new Bergdoll company.

Howard H. Brown produced the Winner car in Elgin, Illinois from 1899-1901. Refer to Winner.

The James W. Brown Company of Pawtucket, Rhode Island was the sponsoring organization for the air-cooled Cameron from 1903-1906. Refer to Cameron.

The Brown Motor Company of Washington, Indiana has been indicated to have produced a car in 1910. Documentation is lacking.

The Brown Motor Vehicle Company was organized in New York City during the summer of 1903 with a capital stock of $2000 and the plan to manufacture automobiles. C.H.S. Brown, F.F. Goodman and F.D. Homan were behind this venture. Manufacture is doubted.

The P.J. Brown Carriage Company of West Brighton, New York was noted in *Motor Age* in February 1907 as the manufacturer of "carriages and motor cars." The company moved its factory that month to State and High streets near Broadway. Further details are lacking.

The Ralph E. Brown Motor Car Company of Buffalo, New York announced in January 1914 its plans to manufacture cyclecars. This does not appear to have happened.

The Brown & Robb Company was organized with a capital stock of $100,00 for the manufacture of automobiles in Gloucester City, New Jersey early in 1914. E.L. Brown and T.H. Robb were the partners involved. Manufacture does not appear to have followed.

The firm of Brown & Talbot is believed to have built automobiles to order in Salem, Massachusetts from 1900-1907. Trade directory listings indicate this, but documentation of the extent of this activity is lacking.

William H. Brown of Cleveland has been cited as the builder of an automobile in 1895. This has not been documented. Possibly this was the same William H. Brown who subsequently launched himself into the automobile accessory field in Chicago, exhibiting a dust shield of his design at the automobile show there in 1900.

A car called the Brown has appeared on various car rosters as being built by the Great Western Automobile Company in Kalamazoo, Michigan in 1914. City directories indicate no Great Western company in town until 1919 when Great Western Auto Parts set itself up in business in Kalamazoo.

BROWN — Fargo, North Dakota — (1899) — George D. Brown was a wholesale bicycle dealer from Fargo who decided to become an automobile producer late in 1899. According to the December 15th issue of *The Autobain* that year, Brown had "laid in a supply of machinery for the manufacture of the popular machines." He had completed his single-cylinder gasoline car and described the result as "gratifying." Gratifying it may have been, satisfying it was not. Purportedly, the belt drive on his car "always kept coming off." He tried to build an electric next, then gave up manufacturing plans and became the first automobile dealer (Locomobile) in the state of North Dakota.

BROWN STEAM — Stonington, Rhode Island — (1902) — In 1902 Dudley Brown of Stonington built an automobile of which, he proudly proclaimed, virtually every piece had been used for something else before. Motive power was a steam engine which had previously operated a thresher, the wheels were from an old mowing machine, and the body was rough timber. It couldn't have been very pretty, but Brown claimed his machine capable "of rolling off 25 miles an hour."

BROWN STEAM — Hutchinson, Kansas — (1905) — The Brown brothers of Hutchinson — H.H., J.D. and W.J. — built a steam automobile in 1905 which generated five horsepower, used coal oil for fuel, and was good for about eight miles an hour. In May that year, *The Motor World* declared the brothers "ready to undertake to supply the general public, if the public will but step up and take notice." Apparently the public didn't.

BROWN — Richmond, California — (1914) — "The success of experiments with a new low-priced car which have been in progress in Richmond, California for the past six months insure that enterprising city an automobile factory," *Motor Field* reported in April 1914. Herbert F. Brown, a local Richmond businessman, was behind the Brown Auto Company venture. Experimentation had been supervised by Charles Smith, formerly of the Ford and Chalmers factories in the Midwest. A roadster, the Brown featured solid steel wheels, an underslung body, cantilever springs, electric lights, a 25 hp engine good for speeds up to 60 mph on the road.Its first public showing and demonstration had been January 25th. A site for the Brown factory had been selected in the northern part of the city, but it appears not to have been built. The Brown, which was to have sold for $410, was stopped in its tracks soon after, for reasons unknown.

144

BROWN — Asbury Park, New Jersey — (1914) — The Brown cyclecar was a wire-wheeled, Spacke-engined, side-by-side two-seater whose specification could have been used as the prototype for the entire cyclecar genre. A friction countershaft drove to a jackshaft, thence a vee-belt took power to the rear wheels. The wheelbase was 96 inches, the tread 44, the price $375. The Brown Cyclecar Company did veer from the norm, however, in offering a companion model, the Monmouth Raceabout, which boasted twice the cylinders and twice the horsepower at twice the price. A standard selective transmission and shaft drive were also features of this model which had a 100-inch wheelbase and 52-inch tread. The diversity didn't help. The announcement of the formation of the Brown company in Asbury Park was quickly followed by a brief mention of its demise.

1914 BROWN
Cyclecar — 2-cyl., 10 hp, 96" wb

	FP	5	4	3	2	1
Rds.-2P	375	1200	2300	3300	5100	9500

Cyclecar — 4-cyl., 20 hp, 100" wb

	FP	5	4	3	2	1
Monmouth Raceabout-2P	650	1400	2400	3500	5300	10,000

1916 Brown, touring, NAHC

BROWN — Cincinnati, Ohio — (1916) — The Brown Carriage Company of Cincinnati, longtime builders of horsedrawn vehicles, entered the automotive ranks late, and with two ideas. The first was a 105-inch-wheelbase five-passenger touring car with a four-cylinder Le Roi engine, standard components throughout, and the appearance of at least a dozen other vehicles on the road. It was priced at $735. The second was a $675 commercial vehicle, also with Le Roi engine, which looked rather like the "business car" then being successfully produced by the Dodge Brothers. Neither of these ideas survived into 1917.

BROWN-BURTT — So far as has been determined, none of the vehicles built by the Burtt Manufacturing Company of Kalamazoo, Michigan from 1903-1906 were ever referred to as the Brown-Burtt. The car was the idea of Frank Burtt and Warren B. Cannon, and it was marketed under the latter's name. Refer to Cannon.

1898 Brown Touring Cart, auto-buggy, NAHC

BROWN TOURING CART — Chicago, Illinois — (1887, 1898) — Edwin F. Brown was a Chicago bicycle manufacturer who resided in Evanston and who had a penchant for bending the truth. In 1899 he claimed to have been Chicago's oldest cyclist and to have built three steam vehicles between the years 1884 and 1891. Both these claims are dubious, though he is known to have completed a single steamer in 1887. In 1898 Brown designed, after a fashion, a gasoline vehicle. Its engine was a 5 hp single-cylinder unit of the "Lewis type." The Lewis was George W., who built the engine for Brown and who had been experimenting with horseless vehicles for some time, winning a prize in the Chicago Times-Herald Contest of 1895 for a friction-drive device he had invented. Lewis apparently did not design the chassis of the Lewis-engined Brown Touring Cart, however.

That was the work of another mechanic named A.W. King, who devised an endless-belt drivetrain which he said he intended to patent. The design contributions made by Edwin F. Brown to the Brown Touring Cart would seem to have been minimal, though perhaps the body styling was one — and it was a handsome vehicle, a cross between trap, mail phaeton and victoria, with body a rich Brewster green, wheels in vermilion and all trimmings burnished brass. A "booking agency" for the Brown Touring Cart was said to have been opened at the corner of Jackson and Clinton in Chicago, but how many orders resulted is not known. In 1899 Brown took Chief Kack-Kack of the Pottawatomies for a ride in one of his cars; the Indian was impressed but did not buy.

1903 Browne, touring, OCW

BROWNE — Denver, Colorado — (1903) — In late 1903, F.O. Browne, an automobile dealer in Denver, sent a letter to various magazines in the automotive trade press announcing that he had built a touring car with a special purpose in mind. "It was built with the object in view of covering long runs over the deserted and unimproved roads that lead to the big game country in the Colorado wilds," *The Automobile* reported, "and should, therefore, be well adapted to the requirements of the cross-country tourist." Its engine, which was placed under the seat, developed fourteen horsepower. A short chain drive and two-speed transmission were fitted, as well as a sixteen-gallon gasoline tank good for about 300 driving miles between fill-ups. Though manufacture was Browne's intention, it does not appear to have resulted.

BROWNELL — Rochester, New York — (1907) — Three cars bearing the Brownell name were built, but the man who built them quickly decided that he should stick instead to what he knew best: building engines. There is some confusion as to the sequence of events, but apparently the first organization of F.A. Brownell's company was in association with another Rochester engine builder named Henry L. Trebert. This was during the summer of 1906, when the Brownell-Trebert Company was announced, its purpose ostensibly being the manufacture of automobiles as well as engines. (Ironically, the Trebert Gas Engine Company that Henry Trebert left to join Brownell went on to produce a car in 1907 as well, and it was called the Trebert.) References from 1907 also indicate that another company was being organized, the F.A. Brownell Motor Company. Whether Trebert was connected with it is problematical: his name was not among the roster of officers. One thing is certain: The Brownell motorcar building venture was halted soon after it began. And wisely so, as it turned out. The Brownell and Trebert engine-building forays proved to be the linear antecedent of Rochester Motors Company, producer of the famous Rochester-Duesenberg engine of the post-World War I era. Conceivably, the three Brownells built were simply for the private use of company executives. One of them was registered in Michigan in 1916 and remains extant.

1909 Brownie, touring, OCW

BROWNIE — Elmira, New York — (1909) — Brownie was the name given to the prototype car built by A. Ward LaFrance and Edgar Wemple in Elmira in 1909. It was a handsomely formidable machine. "The body, fenders, radiator, etc. were our own design and I believe its appearance was somewhat ahead of its time," Ward LaFrance reminisced in the *Chemung County Historical Journal* in 1957. "This car attracted considerable interest in Buffalo but efforts to manufacture it did not mature. It was later purchased by Herbert Brand." Ward LaFrance was the son of Asa LaFrance of fire-engine fame. He became rather famous himself as a truck and fire engine producer, organizing the Ward LaFrance Truck Company in 1918 which survived in Elmira into the 1980's.

BROWNIE — Hannibal, Missouri — (1916) — Aside from chopping $250 off the price, there was very little difference between the car that J.O. Carter marketed in 1915 in Hannibal as the Cartermobile and the car he hawked in 1916 as the Brownie. Both were four-cylinder touring cars, the Brownie at 23 hp and on an inch shorter 114-inch chassis. The price now was $735. The new car was introduced late in 1915 as a 1916 model; late in 1916 there was a press mention that the Brownie was being built by the Carter Manufacturing Company in Detroit. Conceivably, J.O. Carter may have been in negotiation for a site in Michigan to be closer to where most of the automotive action was, but his Brownie failed before ever leaving Missouri.

1910 Browniekar, roadster (Buster Keaton at wheel), JAC

BROWNIEKAR — Newark, New York — (1908-1911) — The Browniekar was a two-seater roadster on a 66-inch wheelbase, with a four-stroke 3 hp single-cylinder engine, belt drive, a price tag of $150, and a maximum speed of 10 mph. It was described as "a toy designed for harmless sport and amusement of the young folks . . . but nevertheless a real motor car." It was designed by a real motor car engineer, William H. Birdsall who was chief engineer of the Mora Motor Car Company. Although initially its producing organization was called the Child's Automobile Company, this was soon changed to the Omar Motor Car Company, a clever touch, Omar being an anagram of Mora.

1908-1911 BROWNIEKAR
Single Cylinder — 3 1/2 hp, 66" wb

	FP	5	4	3	2	1
Rds.	150	1200	2300	3300	5100	9500

BRUENING — Ackley, Iowa — (1901) — By the spring of 1901, Bruening Brothers of Ackley had completed their gasoline automobile. Details regarding it are lacking, but it is known the brothers forwarded the car to L. Rummel & Sons of Marshalltown for painting and trimming. This was the only Bruening known to have been built.

1906 Brunn, coupe, WLB

145

BRUNN — Buffalo, New York — (1906 et seq.) — The Brunn Carriage Manufacturing Company had been founded in the middle of the Nineteenth Century by Henry Brunn. In 1906 the firm entered automotive ranks with an electric, which was marketed for the company by James MacNaughton, also of Buffalo. Brunn catalogued the car in 1906 only, but continued to build vehicles on custom order until as late as 1911. A 1910 car is known to have been built as the Clark Electric. The firm's automotive activity was modest, however. Henry Brunn was an ardent carriage man, and his company largely devoted its efforts to the horsedrawn trade. The famous coachbuilding house of Brunn & Company in Buffalo was established in 1908 by Henry's nephew Hermann A. Brunn, who had apprenticed in his uncle's factory.

1906 BRUNN

	FP	5	4	3	2	1
Phae. Stanhope	2500	—	—	—	—	—
Inside Drive Cpe.	2500	—	—	—	—	—
Brunn Station Wagon	3500					

BRUNNER — Buffalo, New York — (1910) — The Brunner Motor Car Company marketed a two-cylinder 16 hp vehicle with shaft drive, planetary transmission, and solid tires on 36- and 38-inch wheels front and rear. Although a light delivery was most often advertised, a touring car was also available on the same 90-inch chassis. A distinguishing characteristic of the Brunner was the fitting of a muffler for each cylinder. B.S. Morden, A.L. Dixon and C.P. Miller were the principals behind the Brunner company which had been incorporated in November 1909 with a capital stock of $14,000. The Brunner venture was short-lived.

BRUNS — The Bruns Automobile Company was organized in Brooklyn, New York during the summer of 1906 with a capital stock of $5000 and the plan to manufacture automobiles and bicycles. Three Bruns — A.E., S. and F. — were behind this venture. Manufacture of a car is doubted.

1917 Brunswick, touring, WLB

BRUNSWICK — Newark, New Jersey — (1917) — The Brunswick Motor Car Company was organized in November of 1916 by Russell Smith, Everett Cadmus, J.T. Bunt and A.V. Weeks. Capitalization was $500,000, and the company's purpose was manufacture of an assembled car on a 120-inch wheelbase with a four-cylinder Wisconsin engine and amenities rather grand for a vehicle projected to be sold at $1950. Two Waltham clocks were to be provided, one each in the front and back compartments. In the rear section, too, would be five cabinets, each with a Yale lock, containing thermos bottles, sandwich trays and other niceties. Early in 1917 the company was operating out of temporary headquarters in Newark, though a permanent factory was slated to be built near the Pennsylvania Railroad tracks outside of town where an annual output of 500 to 1000 cars was planned. A prototype appears to be as far as this venture proceeded, however. Most likely the money ran out, but perhaps too the Brunswick backers ultimately realized they could not afford to build the car for its price tag, and raising its price would have lifted it out of the market for which its specifications intended it.

BRUSH — Cleveland, Ohio — (1886) — In 1886 the magazine *Electrical World* announced the completion of an electric tricycle built by the Brush Electric Company of Cleveland to the design of company superintendent H.S. Possons. This vehicle was reputed at the time to be the first practical three-wheeled electric vehicle in the United States. Shortly thereafter, in Des Moines, William Morrison built this nation's first practical four-wheeler electric.

BRUSH — Detroit, Michigan — (1907-1911) — In claiming the hill-negotiating superiority of its 6 hp product vis-a-vis automobiles of 20 or more horsepower, the Brush Runabout Company suggested that potential purchasers reflect upon the reason a squirrel can climb a tree better than an elephant. This proved an effective argument, and the little two-seater Brush was one of the most popular American cars of its genre. It was little changed during its career because its designer Alanson P. Brush, who had assisted in the engineering of the first single-cylinder Cadillac in 1902, believed he had reached "perfection of an original idea in motor car construction" early on. Horsepower and wheelbase were increased a bit in later models, and pneumatics replaced the original solid tires, but otherwise the Brush remained the same, with axles and frames fashioned from oak, hickory and maple woods, and coil springs at all four corners. Speeds of 35 mph were promised, and prices were in the $500 range. A Brush Runabout finished the 2636-mile Glidden Tour of 1909 "in good shape — a lot more than can be said of some of the big cars," as the company noted in a brochure — climbed Pikes Peak in eight hours, and crossed the

1910 Brush, model D, runabout, WLB

American continent handily. In addition to his own car, Alanson P. Brush designed the early Oaklands and served as consulting engineer to General Motors, particularly during the years William C. Durant — who regarded him as something of a protege — was in control. Unfortunately, to start his own company, Brush had been backed by Frank Briscoe, whose older brother Benjamin had empire building plans along GM lines. The Brush Runabout Company was absorbed into Briscoe's United States Motor Company in 1910 and died with the collapse of that unfortunate conglomerate. The last Brushes were built in 1911 though they continued to be sold into 1912. For the 1912 model year a new car was introduced called the Liberty Brush, though it was simply the old Brush reduced to its essentials and offered for the low price of $350.

1907 BRUSH
Model A — 1-cyl., 6 hp, 74" wb

	FP	5	4	3	2	1
Rbt.	500	2800	3700	5500	9000	19,500

1908 BRUSH
Model A — 1-cyl., 7 hp, 74" wb

Rbt.	500	2800	3700	5500	9000	19,000
Two-Cylinder — 88" wb						
Tour.	—	2900	3700	5600	9100	20,000

Note: A twin was offered only in 1908.

1909 Brush, model B, runabout, HAC

1909 BRUSH
Model B — 1-cyl., 7 hp, 74" wb

Rbt.	500	2900	3700	5600	9100	20,000

1910 BRUSH
Model D — 1-cyl., 10 hp, 80" wb

Rbt.-2P	485	2900	3700	5600	9100	20,000
Rbt.-3P	505	2900	3700	5600	9100	20,000
Rbt.-4P	510	2900	3700	5600	9100	20,000
Racy Type	600	3000	4000	6000	9500	21,000
Cpe.	850	2700	3600	5300	8800	19,000

1911 BRUSH
Model E — 1-cyl., 10 hp, 80" wb

Rbt.-2P	450	3000	4000	6000	9500	21,000
E22 Rbt.	465	2900	3700	5600	9100	20,000
E24 Rbt.	465	2900	3700	5600	9100	20,000
E28 Rbt.	470	2900	3700	5600	9100	20,000
Rds.	485	3100	4200	6300	10,500	22,000
Cpe.	850	2700	3600	5300	8800	19,000

1911 Brush, model E, runabout, WLB

1922 Bryan Steam Car, touring, NAHC

1921 Bryan Steam Car, brougham, KM

BRYAN — Peru, Indiana — (1918-1923) — The precise inclusive dates for this steam car are difficult to ascertain, but it is known that in approximately a half decade a half-dozen cars were produced. George A. Bryan was born in Albuquerque (New Mexico) and began his career as an engine wiper for the Santa Fe Railroad, rising through the ranks to fireman, engineer and locomotive inspector. His last railroad job was as chief inspector, and it was while in this position that Bryan conceived the idea of adapting the super-heated system for steam locomotives into light powerplants to operate automobiles and tractors. His first experimental steam car, built in 1913, was driven through the mountains and deserts of New Mexico. In 1916, with his father Oscar Bryan, he organized the Bryan Harvester Company, thereafter secured a manufacturing site in Peru, Indiana and built a factory there. The boiler of a Bryan steam car featured forty-four seven-foot-long tubes, with a burner of the Bunsen type. Maximum steam pressure was 600 pounds. The Bryan was a good-looking car, produced in touring style only, despite a handsome brougham model shown in the 1921 prospectus. George Bryan also built at least one steam truck. The Bryan steam tractor, which was developed at the same time, was quite successful in tests as well. During his tractor experimentation, George Bryan happened upon the idea of a home heating plant. It was to this venture that he turned in 1925, the first Bryan steam boilers being produced then, and the company name being changed to Bryan Steam Corporation. Subsequently, he expanded his work to include specially designed gas and oil heating burners. By 1930 these were being marketed in forty-three states and overseas.

BRYANT — The Bryant Sales Company was organized in New York City early in 1912 with a capital stock of $15,000 "to manufacture automobiles and engage in the automobile business." W.B. Haggerty, F.B. Mansfield and M.E. Wilson were behind this venture. Manufacture is doubted.

BUCKBOARD — Cleveland, Ohio — (1904) — "Out on Crawford Road is made the cheapest machine on the market," *The Automobile Review* reported in April 1904. "H.S. Moore is its maker and with the light and inexpensive buckboard he scored one of the successes of the auto show in Detroit." This success was short-lived however, because the Buckboard remained in production but a single year. The other car of Moore's manufacture, the Star, also eclipsed in 1904. Harry S. Moore thereafter became an automobile dealer.

BUCKEYE — The Buckeye Auto Sales and Renting Company was organized in New York City during the fall of 1908 to "engage in the manufacture of motor cars and locomotives." Capital stock was $10,000. Manufacture did not follow.

The Buckeye Engine Company of Salem, Ohio was included in the "List of American Cyclecar Makers" published in *Automobile Trade Journal's* January 1914 issue. Further documentation is lacking. A Buckeye Cyclecar Company in Columbus was also reported that year, and probably was affiliated as the selling organization for the Salem car.

In 1909 Buckeye was the company name of the firm producing the Frayer-Miller car of Columbus, Ohio. Refer to Frayer-Miller.

BUCKEYE — Anderson, Indiana — (1895) — Buckeye was the name given to the gasoline-powered three-wheeler built in 1891 by John W. Lambert four years later, in 1895, when he contemplated going into manufacture with it. He did not, however, follow through on this, confining his efforts thereafter to experimentation in automobiles and production only in the gasoline engine field. In 1902 manufacture of a Lambert-designed car did begin. This was the Union which was built in Union City, Indiana into 1905 when production was moved to Anderson, and the car was renamed the Lambert. The Lambert was manufactured from 1906 to 1917.

BUCKEYE — Cleveland, Ohio — (1901-1902) — The Buckeye was a single-cylinder 2-3/4 hp, center-tiller-steered, wire-wheeled, two-passenger runabout produced by the People's Automobile Company of Cleveland and offered in two guises. For $447.50 all the parts necessary for assembly were provided except for the body and tires. People's would add the body and tires itself, and build the car for $1000. The price differential between kit car and complete car seems to indicate that the company preferred to market the Buckeye for the do-it-yourselfer. Occasional references note the sponsoring firm to be the Buckeye Automobile Company, but this was merely an adjunct of the People's organization which also manufactured another car under its own name.

BUCKEYE — Chillicothe, Ohio — (1903) — The Buckeye from Chillicothe was produced by the Motor Storage and Manufacturing Company. It was a four-cylinder 12 hp 90-inch-wheelbase vehicle with a choice of either wire or artillery wheels. There was a cross seat in front, and two bench seats in the rear facing each other, for a total passenger capacity of eight. A canopy top with fringe was standard equipment. After one year in production, the Buckeye was discontinued, and Motor Storage and Maufacturing began building a new car called the Logan.

1903 BUCKEYE

	FP	5	4	3	2	1
Buckeye Surrey (4-cyl., 12 hp, 90" wb)	2000	2400	3400	4800	8000	17,000

BUCKEYE — Dayton, Ohio — (1911) — The Buckeye Wagon Company of Dayton was headed by Charles Anderson, Jr. as president/general manager and W.L. Wirsching as secretary. In 1911 they added "& Motor Car" to their firm's name and for that year only produced a high-wheeled motor buggy. By 1912 Buckeye factory at 34 North Canal Street had been returned to the manufacture of horsedrawn vehicles only.

BUCKLES — Manchester, Oklahoma — (1914) — This cyclecar, built by T.E. Buckles of Manchester, was powered by a two-cylinder Spacke engine and featured a friction transmission and vee-belt drive. Its wheelbase was 96 inches, its tread 36 inches, which was quite narrow even for a cyclecar. "At present the Buckles is in the experimental stage," *The Automobile* reported in January 1914, "the owner not yet having had an opportunity of testing the car thoroughly." No company was ever formed for manufacture; one can assume the Buckles cyclecar never strayed far from Buckles' backyard.

1914 BUCKLES

Rds. (2-cyl., 10 hp, 96" wb)	350	—	—	—	—	—

1904 Buckmobile, runabout, JAC

1905 Buckmobile, runabout, NAHC

BUCKMOBILE — Utica, New York — (1903-1905) — Given its name, "Ease of Riding Without a Peer" was a curious slogan for this little two-cylinder, two-seater roadster, but its makers insisted that their vehicle's "peculiar buckboard design" was responsible for the wonderful ride. The car was the idea of Albert J. Seaton; A. Vedder Brower provided the financing. Seaton was the president of the new Buckmobile Company, Brown the secretary-treasurer. The Buckmobile's designer was William H. Birdsall, who also served as company general manager. Buckmobile engines (which were available with both water and air cooling, both units having been designed by Seaton) were cast by Munson Brothers; the wheels came from Weston Mott; and Charles H. Childs, a local carriage builder, supplied the bodies. The Buckmobile was introduced at the New York Automobile Show at Madison Square Garden in January 1903, and the New York *Sun* said it was a sensation. The company factory at 547 Sunset Avenue in Utica had a capacity of two cars weekly, but the reception the car received at the New York show indicated that expansion was called for. By September plant additions raised capacity to a car a day; the Buckmobile people had overextended themselves, and never recovered. In October 1904 the firm was merged with the Black Diamond Automobile Company which continued Buckmobile manufacture in the Remington plant that Black Diamond had also purchased in Utica. There had been an automobile called the Remington. Although Black Diamond built an experimental steam vehicle in 1903, it never marketed a car under its own name. And Black Diamond didn't build the Buckmobile long. Total production has been estimated at forty cars. In August 1905 it was announced that the business would be sold at a sheriff's sale. The previous summer William Birdsall had left Buckmobile to design the new Regas for D.D. Dunn in Rochester. By the time of the Sheriff's sale in Utica, Birdsall was in Newark, New York where his new car was the Mora.

1903 BUCKMOBILE

	FP	5	4	3	2	1
Rbt. (2-cyl., 10 hp, 80'' wb)	850	2500	3500	5000	8500	18,000
1904 BUCKMOBILE						
Rbt. (2-cyl., 15 hp, 82'' wb)	1200	2600	3600	5200	8700	18,500
1905 BUCKMOBILE						
Rbt. (2-cyl., 15 hp, 83'' wb)	900	2700	3600	5300	8800	19,000
Detachable Tonneau (2-cyl., 15 hp, 83'' wb)	1050	2800	3600	5400	8900	19,200

BUEL STEAMER — Woburn, Massachusetts — (1897-1903) — Following the War between the States and his apprenticeship, James Frederick Buel took over management of the machine shop in Woburn which had been established by his father in 1857. Manufacture of drill presses and freight elevators followed, and in 1878 Buel and his friend James M. Kimball strung wires between their homes on Main and Fowle streets, establishing the first private telephone line in Woburn. That his inventive imagination

1903 Buel Steamer, touring, WNBC

would be fired by the horseless carriage was to be expected. Beginning in 1897 Buel began building steam cars which he sold for $500-$600 each to residents of the community. Their boilers and tires were purchased, but the remainder of a Buel Steamer was entirely Buel built. Engines were two-cylinder and horizontally fitted. Production was about a car a year. Buel's steamer building was strictly a sideline activity.

BUENING — Westport, Kansas — (1905) — In 1905 in the Kansas City suburb of Westport, seventeen-year-old Joe Buening and his fifteen-year-old brother Leo built their first gasoline car. "Crudely put together with wooden planks, odds and ends, the vehicle did function on the streets of Westport," the Buening family history reads. "The boys delighted in driving it through the area, much to the consternation of their more refined neighbors." Two years later, neither boy yet having turned twenty, the Buenings established an Apperson dealership in town and thereafter remained longtime Kansas City automobile retailers.

BUFFALO — A veritable herd of Buffaloes were planned in Upstate New York in addition to those which ultimately did ride the roads.

The Buffalo Co-Operative Motor Car Company has been indicated on various car rosters as having produced a car in 1913-1914. City directories indicate the presence of no such firm in town at that time; its name suggests in any case that it was organized as a dealership, a number of similar "co-operatives" being organized throughout the country during this period.

The Buffalo Garage Company was organized early in 1904 with a capital stock of $30,000 to "manufacture, sell, rent and store motor vehicles." Incorporators were George H. Smith, Benjamin F. Milsom and Byron D. Schultz. Manufacture is doubted.

The Buffalo General Manufacturing Company was organized in early 1909 by J.R. Kean and D.B. Doan with a capital stock of $6000 for manufacture of motorcars, a plan unrealized.

The Buffalo Maintenance Company was organized by Harold Kaiser, J.H. Preston, Jr. and Charles Hoxie during the fall of 1909 to "manufacture motor cars, power wagons and motor boats." Capital stock was $5000, and manufacture did not follow.

The Buffalo Motor Car Company was organized early in 1904 by Frank I. Alliger, Frederick Wende and William A. Lutz, who apparently looked around and saw all the other Buffaloes in town and almost immediately decided to change the name of their venture to Bison Motor Company.

The Buffalo Motor Vehicle Company was organized in late 1911 with a capital stock of $100,000 and the plan to "manufacture, sell and repair automobiles." W.R. Hunteley, J.H. Vailm and C.R. Hunteley were the incorporators. Manufacture has not been documented.

The Buffalo Specialty Company was organized with a capital stock of $500,000 during the early summer of 1905 by Oliver Cabana, Jr., Egbert T. Brown and M.T. Cabana. Manufacture of automobiles were planned, but has not been substantiated.

The Buffalo Spring and Gear Company at 1520 Niagara Street was listed as an automobile manufacturer in the Hiscox book *Horseless Vehicles, Automobiles, Motor Cycles* published in 1900. Further documentation is lacking.

The Buffalo Taxicab Company was organized in the spring of 1909 with a capital stock of $200,000 "to manufacture, sell and rent motor cars, as well as operate a livery and garage." This company was the taxicab-producing arm of the E.R. Thomas Motor Company which had been producing the Thomas cars in Buffalo since 1903.

The Buffalo Truck & Tractor Corporation was organized during the fall of 1917 with a capital stock of $150,000 "to manufacture various kinds of motors, cars, wagons, boats, vehicles, automobiles and airplanes." E.H. Oversmith, G.B. Burd and S.B. Simpkins were the incorporators. World War I delayed the onset of production, but following the Armistice this Buffalo venture did move into manufacture, although commercial vehicles only were its products.

BUFFALO — Buffalo, New York — (1899) — During the summer of 1899 the Buffalo Cycle Supply Company burned to the ground but by early fall had relocated into new premises at 895 Washington Street. And by September too, the firm had completed the prototype of its new automobile which Buffalo manager John W. Frey made available for a trial spin by an obviously enthusiastic reporter from *The Motor Vehicle Review*. "The vehicle is very springy and adaptable for easy riding," the reporter wrote. "There is very little vibration, no smoke, no odor, it is positively noiseless, is of hydro-carbon motive power, and it will run 20 hours without recharging at a cost of 1 1/2¢ per hour." Obviously this fellow needed a little counseling in proper automobile terminology. The Buffalo's engine was a one-lunger of just two horsepower, but in light runabout trim (its weight was 700 pounds, the same figure being its projected price tag) the car was good for up to 30 mph. The Buffalo Cycle Supply Company also held numerous patents on automobile components, this factor also contributing to the reporter's conclusion that "without delay" the Buffalo firm would become among the "most important factors in the industry." This did not happen, of course, nor does it seem the Buffalo saw any meaningful production.

1902 Buffalo Sr., model 7, NAHC

BUFFALO — Buffalo, New York — (1900-1902) — The Buffalo Automobile & Auto-Bi Company was the idea of a peripatetic bicycle manufacturer and gasoline engine builder by the name of Erwin Ross Thomas. The firm was established at the turn of the century. Auto-Bi referred to Thomas' motorized bicycles; when he began experimenting with motorized vehicles somewhat more sophisticated, he initially termed the results by such varying model designations as Auto-Two, Auto-Tri and Auto-Quad. These vehicles, basically bicycle based, were produced in very small numbers for the local citizenry. E.R. Thomas did not proceed into proper manufacture until 1902, and at that time he elected to call his new improved product a Buffalo. His company produced the Buffalo Junior at $650, the Buffalo Senior at $800 and the larger Buffalo Tonneau — "the only automobile suitable for family use" and sometimes referred to as the Buffalomobile — at $1000. These cars were distinguished by their use of three-speed sliding gear transmissions and roller bearing axles, at a time when two-speed planetary drive and plain-bearing axles were the norm. The cars became more distinguished yet after Erwin Thomas decided to rename the marque after himself in 1903. Among the vehicles to follow was the famous Thomas Flyer which won the epic New York to Paris race of 1908. Conceivably, E.R. Thomas had delayed putting his own name on his cars until he was sure of their merit.

1902 BUFFALO
Buffalo Junior — 1-cyl., 3-1/2 hp, 68" wb

	FP	5	4	3	2	1
Model No. 6 Rbt.-2P	650	2600	3600	5200	8700	18,500

Buffalo Senior — 1-cyl., 6 hp, 72" wb

	FP	5	4	3	2	1
Model No. 7 Rbt.-2P	800	2600	3600	5200	8700	18,500
Model No. 16 Tonneau-4P	1000	2700	3600	5300	8800	19,000

BUFFALO — Buffalo, New York — (1901-1902) — The Buffalo Gasoline Motor Company was incorporated in 1899 with $25,000 capital stock by Louis Langen, L. Belle Conrad and Louis A. Fisher. Gasoline engines, logically, were the firm's products. In 1901 the company fitted a few of its four-cylinder 7 hp units to chassis designed in-house and put the result on the market, leaving bodies, gasoline and water tanks to be added by the purchasers. Inconclusive references indicate a further foray by this company, into manufacture of complete vehicles this time, during 1902, but it ended equally as dismally as the bodyless Buffalo did in 1901. Among the reasons was the lawsuit brought by the Electric Vehicle Company early in 1903 for infringement of the Selden patent, litigation which resulted in the Buffalo company acquiring the requisite license from the Association of Licensed Automobile Manufacturers but ultimately deciding it wiser simply to forgo car building instead. The Buffalo Gasoline Motor Company did prosper awhile in the engine-building business. When the firm relocated into larger quarters in 1903, *The Motor World* enthused that "this move is eloquent of the prosperity the company have (sic) enjoyed and a lasting testimonial to the worth of their product, the famous Buffalo gasoline motors." Ironically, the Buffalo Gasoline Motor Company did ultimately move into a sustained automobile manufacture late in 1906 when, following negotiations with none other than George B. Selden himself, the firm's name was changed to Selden Motor Vehicle Company. That the company had become "Seldenized" was the way The *Motor World* put it. All of the subsequent cars would, of course, be called Seldens.

BUFFALO ELECTRIC — Buffalo, New York — (1901-1906)/(1912-1915) — There is certain confusion to the automobiles emanating from this upstate New York factory. Initially, the Buffalo Electric Carriage Company

1903 Buffalo Electric, touring, NAHC

was housed there, and produced a variety of stanhopes, golf brakes and touring cars. Although initial price was high, the company stressed that maintenance was low: "The battery can be fully recharged in forty-five minutes from any 110-volt circuit at a cost not to exceed twenty-five cents." Apparently, such practical advantages of the Buffalo Electric did not sell many cars, because in 1906 F.A. Babcock took over the factory to produce his own electric under his own name. He fared no better, and no longer. Consequently, in 1912, a Buffalo Electric was back, built this time by the Buffalo Electric Vehicle Company which incorporated Babcock's ill-fated enterprise. Prices of these Buffalo Electrics were even higher and, recognizing the industry trend, the cars were frankly announced to be "designed along lines of the latest type gasoline cars." The company did secure a lucrative contract with John Wanamaker for the sale of its cars in Philadelphia and New York City, but this was not enough to offset the growing public preference for gasoline-powered vehicles. The last Buffalo Electric became extinct faster than the two previous electrics built in the same factory.

1901 BUFFALO ELECTRIC

	FP	5	4	3	2	1
Electric Stanhope	1500	2500	3500	5000	8500	18,000

1902 Buffalo Electric, stanhope, HAC

1902 BUFFALO ELECTRIC

Electric Stanhope	1500	2500	3500	5000	8500	18,000
Electric Golf Brake	2000	2700	3600	5300	8800	19,000

1903 BUFFALO ELECTRIC

Electric Vic. Stanhope	1650	2600	3600	5200	8700	18,500
Electric Tour. Car	5000	2800	3700	5500	9000	19,500

1904 BUFFALO ELECTRIC

Electric Stanhope	1650	2600	3600	5200	8700	18,500
Electric Golf Brake	2200	2800	3700	5500	9000	19,500

1905-1906 BUFFALO ELECTRIC

Model 1 Stanhope-2/4P	1650	2700	3600	5300	8800	19,000
Model 3 Golf Brake	1800	2800	3700	5500	9000	19,500
Model 4 Stanhope-4P	2250	2900	3700	5600	9100	20,000

1904 Buffalo Electric, golf brake, WLB

1912 Buffalo Electric, model 20, runabout, HAC

1914 Buffalo Electric, model 30, coupe, HAC

1912-1914 BUFFALO ELECTRIC

	FP	5	4	3	2	1
Model 20 Rdstr.	2600	2700	3600	5300	8800	19,000
Model 30 Cpe.	2900	2400	3400	4800	8000	17,000
Model 30B Brgm.	3000	5000	3500	5000	8500	18,000

1915 BUFFALO ELECTRIC

	FP	5	4	3	2	1
Model 36 Cpe.	2900	2400	3400	4800	8000	17,000

BUFFALOMOBILE — Occasionally the car produced in 1902 by the Buffalo Automobile & Auto-Bi Company was called the Buffalomobile. More frequently, it was simply the Buffalo. Refer to Buffalo.

BUFFALO-ROCHESTER ELECTRIC — Buffalo, New York — (1899-1900) — Although the Buffalo-Rochester Electric Power and Auto Company is frequently cited as having manufactured an automobile at the turn of the century, this does not appear to have been so. The company was organized late in 1899 with a formidable capital stock of $5,000,000, its headquarters to be in Rochester and a factory in Buffalo, New York. Manufacture of automobiles was never envisioned, the purpose of the organization being, according to *The Autobain,* "to get possession of all the valuable patents along this line possible, develop the claims to public recognition and then sell them to others." The company was not at all successful in this, but conceivably a prototype or two might have been built before the venture failed.

1904 Buffum, model H, touring, WLB

BUFFUM — Abington, Massachusetts — (1901-1907) — The H.H. Buffum Company built both touring cars and motor boats, and made it a practice to depart from the traditional whenever possible. Probably this was the company's undoing. Initially its cars used horizontal motors and a composite chain and gear transmission, but in 1904 a switch was made to vertical engines, cone clutch and sliding gear transmission. This was trendy, but not untoward. However, the company also offered that year, as a catalog model, its Model G (Greyhound) race car with a horizontal eight-cylinder engine developing a claimed 80 hp; this was the first eight-cylinder car offered for regular sale in America. Subsequently, Buffum offered a V-8 in models designed for touring, but whether the Buffum or the Hewitt V-8 was the earlier to hit the marketplace is open to conjecture. One of the two, however, was America's first V-8. In addition to being a fine engineer, H.H. Buffum was also an admirable coachbuilder. The hand-hammered aluminum bodies of his Buffums weighed but 120 pounds. It is not known what occupied his talents immediately following the demise of the Buffum, but he had returned to the automotive manufacturing field by 1914 when he produced the Laconia cyclecar. Meanwhile Bicknell Hall of Taunton had purchased the defunct Buffum factory in October 1907 and marketed a few of the final eight-cylinder Buffum cars under his own name.

1901-1903 BUFFUM
Four — 20 hp, 94-1/2" wb

	FP	5	4	3	2	1
King of Belgium Tonneau	2500	2800	3700	5500	9000	19,500

1904 BUFFUM
Four — 28 hp, 94-1/2" wb

	FP	5	4	3	2	1
Model H Tonneau	2500	2800	3700	5500	9000	19,500

Eight — 80 hp, 120" wb

	FP	5	4	3	2	1
Model G Greyhound	—	3100	4200	6300	10,500	22,000

1905 Buffum
Four — 28 hp, 105" wb

	FP	5	4	3	2	1
Model K Touring	4000	2900	3700	5600	9100	20,000

Four — 12 hp, 86" wb

	FP	5	4	3	2	1
Model F Rdstr.	1200	2700	3600	5300	8800	19,000

1906-1907 BUFFUM
Eight — 40 hp, 100" wb

	FP	5	4	3	2	1
Rbt.	2500	3100	4200	6300	10,500	22,000

BUGGYABOUT — Buggyabout was the model designation of the highwheeler built by the Hatfield Motor Vehicle Company of Miamisburg, Ohio from 1907-1908. Refer to Hatfield.

BUGGY-AUT The Buggy-Aut was a model of the Duryea built from 1908 into 1914 in Reading, Pennsylvania and Saginaw, Michigan. Refer to Duryea.

BUGGY CAR — Cincinnati, Ohio — (1908-1909) — The Buggy Car Company brightly advertised its highwheeler as the result of four years experience. This was true, but the experience was that of the Postal Auto & Engine Company of New Bedford, Indiana, the complete assets of which the Ohio company purchased in September 1908. The highwheeler was offered in two twin-cylinder models providing either friction drive or a planetary transmission and priced in the $475-$750 range. The lack of ingenuity of the Buggy-Car Company was typified by its name, which honestly described the product.

1908 Buggy Car, model 1, piano box runabout, WLB

1909 Buggy Car, model A, runabout, JAC

1908-1909 BUGGY CAR
Friction drive — 2-cyl., 16/18 hp, 76" wb

	FP	5	4	3	2	1
Model A Rbt./Delivery	750	2400	3400	4800	8000	17,000
Model B Rbt./Delivery	650	2400	3400	4800	8000	17,000
Model C Surrey	775	2500	3500	5000	8500	18,000

Planetary — 2-cyl., 12-1/2 hp, 76" wb

	FP	5	4	3	2	1
No. 1 Rbt.-2P	475	2400	3400	4800	8000	17,000
No. 4 Rbt.-3P	625	2400	3400	4800	8000	17,000

BUGGYMOBILE — Buggymobile was an alternate designation for the high-wheeler produced by the Columbus Buggy Company from 1907 to 1908. Refer to Columbus.

BUGMOBILE — Chicago, Illinois — (1908-1909) — Few cars in the history of the American industry may be said to have been more unfortunately named than the product of the Bugmobile Company of America. The firm was incorporated in Chicago in July of 1907, with manufacture begun late that year at 208 Wabash Avenue. "Despite the title of this latest comer to the small car class . . .," *The Automobile* commented at the time, "the Bugmobile embodies many features of construction patterned after far higher-priced standards." Included among these features were an angle steel frame from which the entire engine/transmission was suspended. The transmission was selective with final drive to the rear wheels from a countershaft via steel cables. The price range was $500-$750. The company was out of business soon.

1908 BUGMOBILE
Model A — 2-cyl., 12 hp, 68" wb

Rbt.	500	2300	3300	4600	7500	16,000

Model B — 2-cyl., 12 hp, 76" wb

Rbt.	750	2350	3350	4700	7800	16,500

1909 BUGMOBILE
Model C — 2-cyl., 15 hp, 76" wb

Rbt.	750	2350	3350	4700	7800	16,500

1908 Bugmobile, runabout, NAHC

BUICK

BUICK — Detroit, Michigan — (1903)/Flint, Michigan — (1904-1942 et. seq.) — That the man behind the first Buick was also the man who developed a method of affixing porcelain to cast iron and thus gave the world the white bathtub is a piece of historical trivia that has become part of the popular saga of the automobile. Beyond that, however, little is known about David Dunbar Buick. An inveterate tinkerer, he was a consummately poor businessman. In 1899, finding the mechanical age more challenging than bathtubs, Buick sold off his plumbing business to the Standard Sanitary Manufacturing Company and organized the Buick Auto-Vim and Power Company to produce gasoline engines for farm and marine use, this venture reorganized in 1902 to Buick Manufacturing Company. Joining Buick's venture were Walter Marr (beginning an on-again, off-again relationship with Buick) and Eugene Richard (who worked for Olds prior to its historic fire). Among these three men, the famous Buick valve-in-head engine was developed, and the first Buick car was built and tested in 1903. Putting up the money was Detroit sheet-metal manufacturer Benjamin Briscoe, who soon tired of doing only that. Despite Briscoe's yet-again reorganization of the Buick venture into the Buick Motor Company in the spring of 1903, all he had to show thus far for his continuing infusions of cash was a factory facility, one Buick car and no sign that production was about to commence. Meanwhile, he had met another Olds veteran named Jonathan D. Maxwell who did not seem quite so tentative about the production side of the automobile industry. Divesting himself of David Dunbar Buick was next on Briscoe's agenda, and he did this neatly by unloading the whole Buick business to James H. Whiting of Flint Wagon Works during the late summer of 1903. In Flint the Buick pace did not pick up appreciably, the production prototype arriving only during the summer of 1904, the first sale of a Buick following in August. Within two months sixteen Buicks had been ordered, but Whiting's capital investment had been entirely expended, and David Buick's procrastination at the factory did not hold promise that the business would ever be a particularly profitable one. Thus the Buick business was again unloaded, Whiting turning over the company and its future on November 1st, 1904 to a fellow Flint resident, the co-owner of the Durant-Dort Carriage Company, one William Crapo Durant. Durant was a dynamo. Within a year he increased the capital stock of the Buick Motor Company from $75,000 to $1,500,000, reportedly selling a half million dollars of it in a single day to neighbors in Flint. Joining the company engineering staff in 1905 was Enos DeWaters, who had previously worked at Thomas and Cadillac and who would take over as chief engineer upon Walter Marr's retirement during World War I. Being lost in the shuffle somehow was David Dunbar Buick. By the end of 1908 he would leave the company, his series of financial misadventures thereafter to include carburetor manufacture and two automobiles (the Lorraine and the Dunbar); in 1928 he would be found working at the information desk at the Detroit School of Trades; in 1929 he would die impoverished at age seventy-four. That responsibility for David Buick's tragic career largely lay with David Buick himself is unassailable; unassailable too is the astonishing success Billy Durant made of Buick's company. Aside from their overhead-valve design, the early two-cylinder Buicks were conventional, with two-speed planetary transmissions and single chain final drive. But with Durant as super salesman, Buick production rose to 750 cars in 1905, 1400 in 1906, 4641 in 1907. For the 1907 model year, a four had joined the twin, this a T-head design featuring shaft drive and, depending upon model, either three-speed sliding gear or two-speed planetary transmission. In 1908, as production was practically doubling (to 8820 units), Billy Durant used Buick as his base for founding another company: General Motors, in mid-September. The most popular Buick that year was the four-cylinder Model 10 which was priced in the $1000 range and which was a close competitor of Henry Ford's new Model T. Ford's monolithic vision of the auto industry was not Durant's, however, and though the latter's multi-dimensional approach to setting up his new corporation would ultimately bear incredible fruit, Durant's idea of a bargain in companies to buy up for General Motors during these first years very frequently brought real lemons. Nineteen ten found Durant desperately in need of money, which the banks agreed to provide only if he gave up effective control of General Motors. He had no choice but to accept, and left GM to join forces with Louis Chevrolet in the establishment of another automobile company with which he ultimately planned to get GM back. Meanwhile, among his last suggestions before relinquishing control of GM was for his Durant-Dort superintendent to take over Buick. To this the banking interests agreed, and Charles W. Nash moved into Buick's presidential chair until November 1912, when he was promoted to the same one for General Motors itself. Taking over from Nash as Buick president at that time was Walter P. Chrysler. That both Nash and Chrysler were superb managers for Buick is undeniable, but the car Durant had left them was already a success: in the marketplace and in competition. Though Durant's interest in the latter was not overwhelming, he was aware that racing could sell cars. This was of paramount importance. It was Durant who recruited Bob Burman and Louis Chevrolet as the stars of the Buick racing team, and it was Burman and Chevrolet who made the Buick stock automobile a racing star. Though the factory seldom contested the major international events of the day, its record in middle-echelon contests was unsurpassed. In 1909 alone, Buick won 166 events, over ninety percent of those entered, and by 1913, when Buick racing ended, the company held a flurry of AAA speed records, thirty of which would still stand in the record books a decade later. In 1914 Buick's first six arrived. Like the first Buicks, the new 48 hp unit was an overhead valve, with the cylinders cast in pairs. Unlike earlier Buicks, it was a big car, set in a 130-inch wheelbase chassis more than a foot longer than most models which had preceded. Production for 1915 of 43,946 cars practically sextupled to 124,834 in 1916. Part of the reason for this astounding increase was the salesmanship of Richard H. Collins, who earned the nickname "Trainload" (which was how he sold Buicks) before moving over to the presidency of Cadillac in 1917 following the Lelands' departure. The Lelands' departure from Cadillac had followed Durant's triumphant return to the helm of General Motors which soon resulted in the departure from GM and Buick of Charles Nash and Walter Chrysler. Most people liked Billy Durant; few found it possible to work for him for long. Of brief duration, too, was Durant's second incumbency at GM. Getting himself into financial trouble again, he was forced out of the company for the last time in November 1920. As Alfred Sloan began to pick up the pieces of Durant's GM empire, he recognized Buick as its vital link. "It is far better that the rest of General Motors be scrapped than any chances taken with Buick's earning power," he wrote Pierre du Pont. But no chances would be taken at Buick. In charge since Chrysler's departure was Harry H. Bassett, the likeable, careful former Weston-Mott executive who would remain with Buick until his sudden death in 1926. Unlike sister GM companies, Buick had neither a long love affair nor even a brief flirtation with a V-8. Fours and sixes satisfied Buick just fine, with detachable cylinder heads and four-wheel brakes being the biggest engineering news from the company for '24, though the new styling caused some additional comment because it looked rather like a Packard. Packard, exercising noblesse oblige, did not take legal steps, but did rather cleverly plagiarize the famous Buick slogan in a few ads that year — "When prettier cars are built, Packard will build them" — with the result that Buick redefined its radiator configuration somewhat away from the Packard's for '25. In 1925, too, after vacillating for years as to whether fours or sixes were preferred, Buick opted for sixes across the board. Thereafter, Buick did very little, except gloat. The company was riding high, with one of America's most popular cars, routinely placing in the top five of the industry and, except for the 1921 recession year, with annual production in six figures (and usually over 200,000) throughout the Twenties. Buick's Silver Anniversary was in 1929, and the company chose to celebrate it with bigger and better Buicks featuring sloping non-glare windshields (which was fine) and new styling with side panels that bulged perceptibly (which was not). The infamous pregnant Buick had arrived. Compared to the good years of the Twenties, not many of these cars were delivered. Buick also conceived a cheaper companion car that year called the Marquette, which didn't deliver well either. The early Depression years were awful at Buick. In mid-1932, Edward T. Strong, the former Buick sales manager who had been elevated to Buick's presidency after Bassett's death, retired — and former Olds man Irving Reuter took over briefly. Still heading engineering was the conservative Ferdinand A. ("Dutch") Bower, who had taken over from DeWaters who had retired in ill health in '29. For 1931 the company had remained overhead valve, but went straight-eight across the board. Synchromesh came for '32, together with Wizard Control, a combined freewheeling and automatic clutch. But Buick's real wizard entered late in '33, when Harlow H. ("Red") Curtice, the former spark of the AC plug division, came onboard as Buick's president. Recognizing that the cars had become literally heavy with the success of the Twenties and that complacency had resulted in a Buick look that was by now old-fashioned, Curtice first attacked the remedial, making Buicks overall lighter in both weight and price tag, and introducing the Series 40, a smaller, less expensive car that could be counted upon for volume sales while Curtice geared up for the all-new Buick line for '36. These were the cars for which names joined designations: the Special (Series 40), Century (Series 60), Roadmaster (Series 80) and Limited (Series 90). Harley Earl at GM Art and Colour had contributed in great measure to their styling; Buick engineering had introduced aluminum pistons and, following the earlier lead of other GM cars, hydraulic brakes and turret tops. (Independent front suspension had been a feature since '34.) It was in a 1936 Roadmaster that Wallis Warfield Simpson made her celebrated escape to the Continent — and to worldwide headlines — during the British Abdication crisis which followed her romance with the Prince of Wales, briefly Edward VIII. Roadmasters, too, were driven for fine exposure by Joan Crawford and Bette Davis in vintage films of this period. The Curtice-era Buicks found considerable favor among movie folk; indeed the Estate Wagon of 1940 was conceived in Hollywood. But a *cause celebre* or cinema celebrity wasn't necessary to sell Buicks now. In 1937, for the first time since 1928, Buick surpassed the 200,000 mark. And in 1938, the Buick company, having been relegated to the bottom half of the top ten for a half-decade, returned to a solid number four spot it would enjoy until the war brought a halt to all automobile production. By now Charles A. Chayne was Buick's chief engineer and Chayne's handiwork for the '38 Buicks included all-around coil springs. Also new for '38 were domed high-compression pistons for the Buick engine which was now designated

"Dynaflash"; a Century model was clocked by Buick at 103 mph, which was admittedly a flashy performance. Dynaflow would follow postwar, but Buick did have a tentative go with a semi-automatic Self-Shifting Transmission in '39. A genuine industry first were the Buick's turn signals as standard equipment in '39, and though Harlow Curtice's attempts to go custom with Brunn and the Limited — to the consternation of Cadillac — produced only a few cars at decade's turn, he had to be pleased with what the Buick had become since he took over. Once again, it was one of America's most popular cars. Buick's record year production of 310,955 cars in 1940 was followed in 1941 by another new record: 316,251. Soon there were Hellcats on the Buick assembly line, but with the arrival of peace in '45, Curtice and Buick would be ready to take up where they had left off.

Buick Data Compilation
by Robert C. Ackerson

1904

1904 Buick, model B, touring, JAC

BUICK — MODEL B — TWO: The Model B Buick was a four-passenger touring car with an indigo blue body and bright yellow wheels. Typical of most early designs, right hand drive was installed and simple curved fenders were used. Doors were provided for the rear seat compartment but none were provided for the front passengers. Weather protection was nonexistent since neither a windshield or top were provided as standard equipment.

I.D. DATA: Serial numbers on plate on left side of frame.

Model No.	Body Type & Seating	Price	Weight	Prod. Total
B	Tr.-4P	950	1850	37

ENGINE: Inline. Valve in head. Two. Cast iron block. B & S: 4.5 x 5. Disp.: 159 cu. in. Brake H.P.: 21 @ 1230 R.P.M./N.A.C.C. H.P.: 16.2. Valve lifters: mechanical. Carb.: float feed.

CHASSIS: [Model B] W.B.: 87 in. Frt/Rear Tread: 56 in. Tires: 30 x 3.5.

TECHNICAL: Planetary transmission. Speeds: 2F/1R. Floor shift controls. Cone clutch. Chain drive. Mechanical brakes on two wheels. Wood spoke wheels.

OPTIONS: Top (100.00). Windshield (20.00). Acetylene headlamps and oil side lights (75.00).

HISTORICAL: Introduced August 13, 1904 (date of first Buick sold). Calendar year production: 37. Model year production: 37. The president of Buick was James Whiting to November 1, succeeded by Charles L. Begole. A Model B won its class in hill climb held at Eagle Rock, NJ on Thanksgiving Day 1904. Another Model B sans body and non-essential features won its class in the first "Race to the Clouds" up Mt. Washington, New Hampshire.

1904 Model B, 2-cyl.			5	4	3	2	1
Tr	FP	950		value not estimable			

1905

1905 Buick, model C, touring, HAC

BUICK — MODEL C — TWO: The Model C was virtually identical to the Model B, however, a new royal blue body, ivory wheels color combination was used. In addition room was provided for 5 passengers and the service brake was now foot-operated.

I.D. DATA: Serial numbers on plate on left side of frame. Body and engine were made in Flint and final assembly took place in Jackson.

Model No.	Body Type & Seating	Price	Weight	Prod. Total
C	Tr.-5P	1200	1850	750

ENGINE: Inline. Two. Cast iron block. B & S: 4.5 x 5 in. Disp.: 159 cu. in. Brake H.P.: 22 @ 1200 R.P.M./N.A.C.C. H.P.: 16.2. Valve lifters: mechanical. Carb.: float feed, Kingston adjustable.

CHASSIS: [Model C] W.B.: 87 in. Frt/Rear Tread: 56 in. Tires: 30 x 3.5.

TECHNICAL: Planetary transmission. Speeds: 2F/1R. Floor and steering column controls. Cone clutch. Chain drive. Mechanical brakes on two wheels. Wood spoke wheels.

OPTIONS: Cape Cart Top.

HISTORICAL: Buick claimed 3 major performance records in 1905. In Boston at the Readville track a world's record for two cylinder cars for the five mile distance was established. The Buick's time was 6 minutes, 19-3/5 seconds. At a one mile Newark, NJ track a Buick set a new track record of 62 seconds. In a six mile event held at the same location a Buick also was the overall winner. Calendar year production: 750. Model year production: 750. The president of Buick was Charles L. Begole.

1905
Model C, 2-cyl.

	FP	5	4	3	2	1
	1200	3900	7800	13,000	18,200	26,000

1906

1906 Buick, model G, runabout, HAC

BUICK — MODEL G — TWO: The Model G was a 2-seat roadster version of the Model F. Its running gear was identical to the Model F. All Buicks had as standard equipment acetylene headlight and oil side and tail lamps. Also included in the base price was a storage battery and vibrator horn.

BUICK — MODEL F — TWO: The Model F was a revised version of the Model C. A new radiator design ran the full height of the hood and provided easy identification. The paint scheme for 1906 consisted of a purple lake body with ivory wheels and running gear.

I.D. DATA: Serial numbers on plate on left side of frame. Starting: 1 to 1207 Model F.

Model No.	Body Type & Seating	Price	Weight	Prod. Total
F	Tr.-5P	1250	1850	1207
G	Rds.-2P	1150	—	193

Note 1: Model G Price reduced to $1000.

ENGINE: Inline. Two. Cast iron block. B & S: 4.5 x 5. Disp. 159 cu. in. Brake H.P.: 22 @ 1200 R.P.M./N.A.C.C. H.P.: 16.2. Valve lifters: mechanical. Carb.: float feed, Kingston adjustable.

CHASSIS: [Model G] W.B.: 87 in. Frt/Rear Tread: 56 in. Tires: 30 x 3.5. [Model F] W.B.: 87 in. Frt/Rear Tread: 56 in. Tires: 30 x 3.5

TECHNICAL: Planetary transmission. Speeds: 2F/1R. Floor and steering column controls. Cone clutch. Chain drive. Mechanical brakes on two wheels. Wood spoke wheels.

OPTIONS: Cape Cart top (100.00).

HISTORICAL: Introduced January, 1906. Calendar year production: 1,400. Model year production: 1,400. The president of Buick was Charles L. Begole. Buicks set new overall records at the Eagle Rock, NJ and Mt. Washington, NH hill climbs. Race victories were attained at Yonkers, NY and the New York City Empire City track in events of 100 mile duration. In addition a Model F Buick was the only car to complete a 1,000 mile, New York to Chicago Relay run.

1906
Model F & G, 2-cyl.

	FP	5	4	3	2	1
Tr	1250	3300	6600	11,000	15,400	22,000
Rds	1150	3150	6300	10,500	14,700	21,000

1907

BUICK — MODELS F TR & G RDS — TWO: These two Buick models were given a longer, 89'' wheelbase and a belly pan which enclosed the engine and transmission. A smaller 15 instead of 16 gallon fuel tank was installed.

BUICK — MODELS D TR & S RDS — FOUR: These two new Buick models were powered by Buick's first 4-cylinder engine linked to a 3-speed, sliding gear transmission. The Model D was introduced in May 1906 as a 1907 model and featured a royal blue body with ivory wheels. The sporty Model S had a French gray body accentuated by green striping.

BUICK — MODELS H TR & K RDS — FOUR: These two Buicks had the same finishes as the Model D and Model S models and were identical in all other areas except they used the 2-speed planetary transmission.

I.D. DATA: Serial numbers on plate on left side of frame. Starting: 101 (Models D and S). Ending: 523. During 1906 construction of a new Buick plant began in Flint and thus Buicks were constructed both in Jackson and Flint, Michigan. Engine No. Starting: 101 (Models D and S). Ending: 523.

Model No.	Body Type & Seating	Price	Weight	Prod. Total
F	Tr.-5P	1250	1850	3365
G	Rds.-2P	1150	1800	535
D	Tr.-5P	2000	2250	523
S	Rds.-2P	2500	2000	69
H	Tr.-5P	1750	2250	36
K	Rds.-2P	2500	NA	13

1907 Buick, model G, roadster, OCW

ENGINE: [Models F and G] Inline. Two. Cast iron block. B & S: 4.5 x 5. Disp.: 159 cu. in. Brake H.P.: 22 @ 1200 R.P.M./N.A.C.C. H.P.: 16.2. Valve lifters: mechanical. Carb.: float feed. [Models D, S, H and K] Inline. T-head. Four. Cast iron block. B & S: 4.25 x 4.5. Disp.: 255 cu. in. Brake H.P.: 30. Main bearings: 5. Valve lifters: mechanical.

CHASSIS: [Model F] W.B.: 89 in. Frt/Rear Tread: 59 in. Tires: 30 x 3.5. [Model G] W.B.: 89 in. Frt/Rear Tread: 59 in. Tires: 30 x 3.5. [Model D] W.B.: 102.5 in. Tires: 32 x 4. [Model S] W.B.: 106.5 in. Tires: 32 x 4. [Model H] W.B.: 102.5 in. Tires: 32 x 4. [Model K] W.B.: 106.5 in. Tires: 32 x 4.

TECHNICAL: Models F and G Planetary transmission. Speeds: 2F/1R. Floor and steering column controls. Cone clutch. Chain drive. Mechanical brakes on two wheels. Wooden spoke wheels. Models D and S Sliding gear transmission. Speeds: 3F/1R. Floor shift. Multiple disc in oil bath. Shaft drive. Mechanical brakes on two wheels. Wooden spoke wheels. Models K and H Planetary transmission. Speeds: 2F/1R. Floor and steering column controls. Cone clutch. Chain drive. Mechanical brakes on two wheels. Wooden spoke wheels.

OPTIONS: Top - Model G (70.00).

HISTORICAL: Introduced May 1906 Model D. The Model D was Buick's first 4-cylinder engine. Calendar year production: 4,641. Model year production: 4,641. The president of Buick was Charles L. Begole. The only automobile company to out produce the Buick in 1907 was Ford. Buick introduced torque tube drive on the Model D and Model S in 1907 and continued its use until 1962.

1907

Model F & G, 2-cyl.	FP	5	4	3	2	1
Tr	1250	3300	6600	11,000	15,400	22,000
Rds	1150	3150	6300	10,500	14,700	21,000
Model D, S, K & H, 4-cyl.						
Tr	1850	3400	6900	11,500	16,100	23,000
Rds	2500	3300	6600	11,000	15,400	22,000
Tr	1750	3300	6600	11,000	15,400	22,000

1908

1908 Buick, model 5, touring, HAC

BUICK — MODELS F & G — TWO: The Model F and Model G Buicks were extensively restyled with a longer wheelbase plus reshaped hoods, fenders and grille form. Both cars had wine-colored bodies with red wheels.

BUICK — MODELS D & S — FOUR: Body styles for the Model S were extended to include a rumble seat version and a 4-place tourabout as well as the original roadster. The Model D was virtually unchanged but a $100 price drop helped maintain its popularity. Even more dramatic was the Model S price reduction of $750.

1908 Buick, model 10, touring, JAC

BUICK — MODEL 10 — FOUR: This new Buick was its most popular model in 1908 and for good reason. With brass trim, an off-white Buick Gray finish and an attractive $900 price (which included acetylene headlights, oil-fired side and taillights and a bulb horn) it was bound to be a success.

BUICK — MODEL 5 — FOUR: Replacing the Model K was this big touring car available in either red or blue bodies with ivory wheels and appointments. Its engine was a new 4-cylinder with its cylinders cast in pairs and fitted with an aluminum crank case.

I.D. DATA: Serial numbers on plate on left side of frame. Starting: Models D & S 524, Model 10 1, Model 5 101. Ending: Models D & S 1692, Model 10 4002, Model 5 501. Starting: Models F & G 6301, Models D & S 524, Model 10 1, Model 5 1. Ending: Models F & G 15,010, Models D & S 1699, Model 10 4002, Model 5 405.

Model No.	Body Type & Seating	Price	Weight	Prod. Total
F	Tr.-5P	1250	1850	3281
G	Rds.-2P	1150	1800	219
D	Tr.-5P	1750	2250	543
S	Rds.-2P	1750	2000	373
10	Tr.-3P	900	NA	4002
5	Tr.-5P	2500	3700	402

Note 1: Model S, 4P Tourabout body available for 1800.

ENGINE: [Models F and G] Inline. Two. Cast iron block. B & S: 4.5 x 5. Disp.: 159 cu. in. Brake H.P. 22 @ 1200 R.P.M. SAE H.P.: 16.2 Valve lifters: mechanical. Carb.: float feed Schebler. [Models D and S] Inline. T-head. Four. Cast iron block. B & S: 4.25 x 4.5. Disp.: 255 cu. in. Brake H.P.: 30. Main bearings: 5. Valve lifters: mechanical. Carb.: Schebler. [Model 10] Inline. Valve in head. Four. Cast iron block. B & S: 3-3/4 x 3-3/4. Disp.: 165 cu. in. Brake H.P.: 22.5. Valve lifters: mechanical. Carb.: Schebler. Model 5 Inline. T-head, cast in pairs. Four. Cast iron block. B & S: 4-5/8 x 5. Disp.: 336 cu. in. Brake H.P.: 40. SAE H.P.: 34.2.

CHASSIS: [Model F] W.B.: 92 in. Frt/Rear Tread: 59 in. Tires: 30 x 3.5. [Model G] W.B.: 92 in. Frt/Rear Tread: 59 in. Tires: 30 x 3.5. [Model D] W.B.: 102.5 in. Tires: 32 x 4. [Model S] W.B.: 106.5 in. Tires: 32 x 4. [Model 10] W.B.: 88 in. Tires: 30 x 3. [Model 5] W.B.: 108 in. Tires: 34 x 4.

TECHNICAL: Models F & G Planetary transmission. Speeds: 2F/1R. Floor and steering column controls. Cone clutch. Chain drive. Mechanical brakes on two wheels. Wooden spoke wheels. Models D & S Sliding gear transmission. Speeds: 3F/1R. Floor shift. Multiple disc in oil. Shaft drive. Mechanical brakes on two wheels. Wooden spoke wheels. Model 10 Planetary transmission. Speeds: 2F/1R. Floor and steering column controls. Cone clutch. Shaft drive. Divided rear axle. Mechanical brakes on two wheels. Wooden spoke wheels. Model 5 Sliding gear transmission. Speeds: 3F/1R. Floor shift. Cone clutch. Shaft drive. Mechanical brakes on two wheels. Wooden spoke wheels.

OPTIONS: Model F — gas headlights, horn, tool kit (90.00). Model 10 — top (50.00).

HISTORICAL: Introduced November, 1907. Calendar year production: 8,820. Model year production: 8,820. The president of Buick was Charles L. Begole. Both the Model D and Model 5 Buicks served as the basis for racing ventures during 1908 that included victories in the light car class at the Vanderbilt Cup Races. Buicks also participated in the Savannah, GA races as well as in a Montreal 2-day affair where they won 11 of 14 races.

1908

Model F & G, 2-cyl.	FP	5	4	3	2	1
Tr	1250	4200	8400	14,000	19,600	28,000
Rds	1150	3600	7200	12,000	16,800	24,000
Model D & S, 4-cyl.						
Tr	1750	3600	7200	12,000	16,800	24,000
Rds	1750	3750	7500	12,500	17,500	25,000
Model 10, 4-cyl.						
Tr	900	3400	6900	11,500	16,100	23,000
Model 5, 4-cyl.						
Tr	2500	4200	8400	14,000	19,600	28,000

1909

1909 Buick, model 10, roadster, OCW

BUICK MODELS 10 & 15: Buick remained the nation's number two auto producer with a model lineup that retained its most popular models and replaced the poor sellers with improved offerings. No longer produced were the Model D, Model S and Model 5 styles. The Model 10 was offered in 4 body types all of which had a longer, 92 inch wheelbase and the new and racy Model 16 Buicks took on a modern appearance by virtue of their rounded front and rear fenders.

BUICK MODEL 6 — FOUR: Replacing the Model 5 was the Model 6A Rds with a 113'' wheelbase.

BUICK MODELS F & G — TWO: The 2-cylinder Model F and G Buick continued unchanged but remained strong sellers. Their exterior color schemes retained the same wine body finish with red wheels and running gear.

Overshadowing Buick's tremendous sales success which enabled it to hold onto second place in the industry were the machinations of William Durant which brought Buick into the fold of his newly created General Motors.

I.D. DATA: Serial numbers on plate on left side of frame. Starting: Models F and S 9950, Model 10 4003, Models 16 and 17 1, Model 6A 1. Ending: Models F and S 13900, Model 10 12152, Models 16 and 17 2500, Model 6A 6. Engine No. Starting: Models F and S 15011, Model 10 4003, Models 16 and 17 1, Model 6A 1. Ending: Models F and S 19050, Model 10 12111, Models 16 and 17 2517, Model 6A 6.

1909 Buick, model 17, touring, HAC

Model No.	Body Type & Seating	Price	Weight	Prod. Total
F	Tr.-5P	1250	1850	3856
G	Rbt.-2P	1150	1800	144
6A	Rds.-2P	2750	3700	6
10	Rds.-3P	1000	—	Note 2
10	Tourabout-4P	1050	—	Note 2
10	Toy Tonneau-4P	—	—	Note 2
16	Rds.-2P	1750	2620	Note 3
16	Tourabout-4P	1750	2620	Note 3
17	Tr.-5P	1750	2790	2003

Note 1: There was a mid-year price reduction on the Model F touring to $1000.
Note 2: Total production of all Model 10 styles were 8100.
Note 3: Total production of all Model 16 styles was 497.

ENGINE: [Models F and G] Inline. Two. Cast iron block. B & S: 4.5 x 5. Disp.: 159 cu. in. Brake H.P.: 22 @ 1200 R.P.M. SAE H.P.: 16.2. Valve lifters: mechanical. Carb.: float feed Schebler. [Model 6A] Inline, T-head, cast in pairs. Four. Cast iron block. B & S: 4-5/8 x 5. Disp.: 336 cu. in. Brake H.P.: 40. N.A.C.C. H.P.: 34.2. Valve lifters: mechanical. [Model 10] Inline, valve in head. Four. Cast iron block. B & S: 3-3/4 x 3-3/4. Disp.: 165 cu. in. Brake H.P.: 22.5. Valve lifters: mechanical. Carb.: Schebler. [Models 16 and 17] Inline. Four. Cast iron block. B & S: 4.5 x 5. Disp.: 318 cu. in. SAE H.P.: 32.4. Carb.: Schebler.

CHASSIS: [Model F] W.B.: 92 in. Frt/Rear Tread: 59 in. Tires: 30 x3.5. [Model G] W.B.: 92 in. Frt/Rear Tread: 59 in. Tires: 30 x 3.5. [Model 6A] W.B.: 113 in. [Model 10] W.B.: 92 in. Frt/Rear Tread: 56 in. Tires: 30 x 3. [Model 16] W.B.: 112 in. Tires: 34 x 4. [Model 17] W.B.: 112.5 in. Tires: 34 x 4.

TECHNICAL: Models 16 and 17 Sliding gear transmission. Speeds: 3F/1R. Floor shift controls. Shaft drive. Bevel gear, torque tube. Mechanical brakes on two wheels. Wooden spoke wheels. Models F and G Planetary transmission. Speeds: 2F/1R. Floor and steering column controls. Cone clutch. Chain drive. Mechanical brakes on two wheels. Wooden spoke wheels. Model 6A Sliding gear transmission. Speeds: 3F/1R. Floor shift controls. Cone clutch. Shaft drive. Mechanical brakes on two wheels. Wooden spoke wheels. Model 10 Planetary transmission. Speeds: 2F/1R. Floor and steering column controls. Cone clutch. Shaft drive. Divided rear axle. Mechanical brakes on two wheels. Wooden spoke wheels.

OPTIONS: Rumble Seat (Model 10) (100). Hood straps. Windshield. Side mounted spare.

HISTORICAL: Calendar year production: 14,606. Model year production: 14,606. The president of Buick was Charles L. Begole. Buick was an active, enthusiastic competitor in racing events during 1909. Modified Model 17's competed at the old Indianapolis raceway and at the Atlanta, GA race. At both locations the Buicks set track records with ease. Louis Chevrolet drove a Model 16 to a victory in the 200 race in Atlanta and a win in a 393 mile race, the Cobe Trophy Stock Car Road Race at Coren Point, IN. Other Buick successes took place at Daytona Beach and Giant's Despair hill climb at Wilkes-Barre, PA.

1909
Model G, (only 6 built in 1909).

	FP	5	4	3	2	1
Rds	2750	4350	8700	14,500	20,300	29,000
Model F & G						
Tr	1250	4050	8100	13,500	18,900	27,000
Rds	1150	4200	8400	14,000	19,600	28,000
Model 10, 4-cyl.						
Tr	1050	3900	7800	13,000	18,200	26,000
Rds	1000	4050	8100	13,500	18,900	27,000
Model 16 & 17, 4-cyl.						
Rds	1250	4200	8400	14,000	19,600	28,000
Tr	1150	4050	8100	13,500	18,900	27,000

1910

1910 Buick, touring, OCW

BUICK — MODEL 10 — FOUR: The Model 10 was essentially unchanged for 1910 but its basic appeal and 13 different body styles boosted output to nearly 11,000 cars.

BUICK — MODEL F — TWO: No changes for 1910 except for a new vertical tube radiator.

BUICK — MODELS 16 & 17: No changes for 1910 except for a new vertical tube radiator.

BUICK — MODEL 7 — FOUR: This new model with a big 392.6cid engine was Buick's prestige open vehicle for 1910.

BUICK — MODEL 19 — FOUR: The Model 19 touring car was a new model with a Buick green body and ivory wheels. Its engine was based on the Model D unit from 1907. However its wheelbase was increased from 102 to 105 inches.

BUICK — MODEL 41 — FOUR: With this limousine model Buick made its first venture into the closed car market. Among its prestige features was imported goatskin upholstery and a rear compartment speaking tube.

1910 Buick, model 41, limousine, JAC

I.D. DATA: Serial numbers on plate on left side of frame. Starting: Model 10 12152, Model F 13951, Models 16 & 17 2501, Model 7 1, Model 19 1, Model 41 1. Ending: Model 10 23150, Model F 17901, Models 16 & 17 10754, Model 7 85, Model 19 4012, Model 41 41. Engine No. Starting: Model 10 12251, Model F 19051, Models 16 & 17 2518, Model 7 1, Model 19 1, Model 41 1. Ending: Model 10 23267, Model F 25203, Models 16 & 17 10878, Model 7 96, Model 19 4023, Model 41 40.

Model No.	Body Type & Seating	Price	Weight	Prod. Total
10	Rbt.-3P	1000	NA	Note 1
10	Tourabout-4P	1050	NA	Note 1
10	Toy Tonneau-4P	1150	1730	Note 1
F	Tr.-5P	1000	2300	4000
16	Rds.-2P	1750	2620	Note 2
16	Surrey-4P	1750	2620	Note 2
16	Toy Tonneau-4P	1750	2620	Note 2
7	Tr.-7P	2750	3700	85
17	Tr.-5P	1750	2790	6002
19	Tr.-5P	1400	2500	4000
41	Limo.-5P	2750	3400	40

Note 1: Total production of all Model 10 styles was 10,998.
Note 2: Total production of all Model 16 styles was 2252.

ENGINE: [Model 19] Inline. T-head. Four. Cast iron block. B & S: 4.25 x 4.5. Disp.: 255 cu. in. Brake H.P.: 28.9. Main bearings: 5. Valve lifters: mechanical. Carb.: Schebler. Model 7 Inline. T-head, cast in pairs. Four. Cast iron block. B & S: 4-5/8 x 5. Disp.: 336 cu. in. Brake H.P.: 40. SAE H.P.: 34.2. Valve lifters: mechanical. [Model 10] Inline. Valve in head. Four. Cast iron block. B & S: 3-3/4 x 3-3/4. Disp.: 165 cu. in. Brake H.P.: 22.5. Valve lifters: mechanical. Carb.: Marvel 10-501. [Model F] Inline. Two. Cast iron block. B & S: 4.5 x 5. Disp.: 159 cu. in. Brake H.P.: 22. SAE H.P.: 16.2. Valve lifters: mechanical. Carb.: float feed Schebler. [Models 16, 17 and 41] Inline. Four. Cast iron block. B & S: 4.5 x 5. Disp.: 318 cu. in. SAE H.P.: 32.4. Valve lifters: mechanical. Carb.: Marvel 10-508.

CHASSIS: [Model 10] W.B.: 92 in. Frt/Rear Tread: 56 in. Tires: 30 x 3. [Model 16] W.B.: 112 in. Tires: 34 x 4. [Model 17] W.B.: 112.5 in. Tires: 34 x 4. [Model 7] W.B.: 122 in. Tires: 36 x 4. [Model 19] W.B.: 105 in. Tires: 32 x 4. [Model 41] Tires: 34 x 4.

TECHNICAL: Model 10 Planetary transmission. Speeds: 2F/1R. Floor and steering column controls. Cone clutch. Shaft drive. Divided rear axle. Mechanical brakes on two wheels. Wooden spoke wheels. Model F Planetary transmission. Speeds: 2F/1R. Floor and steering column controls. Cone clutch. Chain drive. Mechanical brakes on two wheels. Wooden spoke wheels. Models 16 & 17 Sliding gear transmission. Speeds: 3F/1R. Floor shift controls. Shaft clutch. Bevel gear, torque tube. Mechanical brakes on two wheels. Wooden spoke wheels. Model 7 Sliding gear transmission. Speeds: 3F/1R. Floor shift controls. Leather faced cone clutch. Shaft drive. Mechanical brakes on two wheels. Wooden spoke wheels. Model 19 Sliding gear transmission. Speeds: 3F/1R. Floor shift controls. Cone clutch. Shaft drive. Mechanical brakes on two wheels. Wooden spoke wheels. Model 41 Sliding gear transmission. Speeds: 3F/1R. Floor shift controls. Cone clutch. Shaft drive. Mechanical brakes on two wheels. Wooden spoke wheels.

OPTIONS: Model 7 — top, side curtains. Model 17 — spare tire. Model 10 — windshield, wicker picnic basket.

HISTORICAL: Calendar year sales: 29,425 (includes 2048 Model 14 Buicks generally regarded as 1911 models). Model year production: 27,377. The president of Buick was Thomas Neal. The famous Buick Bugs appeared in 1910 and in July 1910 they were driven by Bob Burman and Louis Chevrolet to an impressive array of records at the Grand Circuit Speedway Meet in Indianapolis. A total of 5 firsts, and 3 second place marks were set including a time trial record of 105.87 mph. Other victories were achieved in races ranging from 10 to 100 miles held at Indianapolis. At a 3 day meet held at Lowell, MA Buick won 7 of 10 races in the stock chassis division as well as the Vesper Trophy for cars in the 301 - 450 cid engine class. Marquette Buicks competed in the Vanderbilt Cup Race and one such racer driven by Burman finished 3rd in the 1910 Savannah, GA Grand Prize race behind two Benz racers.

1910

	FP	5	4	3	2	1
Model 6, 2-cyl.						
Tr	2750	4350	8700	14,500	20,300	29,000
Model F, 2-cyl.						
Tr	1000	3900	7800	13,000	18,200	26,000
Model 14, 2-cyl.						
Rds	550	3750	7500	12,500	17,500	25,000
Model 10, 4-cyl.						
Tr	1150	3400	6900	11,500	16,100	23,000
Rds	1000	3400	6900	11,500	16,100	23,000
Model 19, 4-cyl.						
Tr	1400	4350	8700	14,500	20,300	29,000
Model 16 & 17, 4-cyl.						
Rds	1750	4200	8400	14,000	19,600	28,000
Tr	1750	4050	8100	13,500	18,900	27,000
Model 7, 4-cyl.						
Tr	2750	4800	9600	16,000	22,400	32,000
Model 41, 4-cyl.						
Limo	2750	4050	8100	13,500	18,900	27,000

1911

1911 Buick, model 38, roadster, JAC

BUICK — MODELS 14 & 14B — TWO: The Model 14 or Buggyabout (also available as the 14B with the fuel tank moved from under the seat to the rear) was a tiny, 79 inch wheelbase 2-seater. It was the last Buick to be equipped with a 2 cylinder engine and chain drive. It's possible that if it had been produced in 1908 when it was first developed that the Model 14 could have provided the base for a Buick challenge to Ford's supremacy in the low priced field.

BUICK — MODELS 32 & 33 — FOUR: These two new Buicks used the 165cid engine of the discontinued Model 10 and were respectively a roadster and tourer. Both cars were equipped with an automatic high speed clutch release.

BUICK — MODEL 21 — FOUR: This touring model was one of the most attractive Buicks with its angular body particularly pleasing in its Buick green finish and available cream-colored wheels.

BUICK — MODELS 26 & 27 — FOUR: Both of these Buicks in roadster and touring bodies were powered by a new 210cid 4-cylinder engine. The standard color for the Model 26 was battleship gray. The Model 27 was given a dark blue body with white wheels.

BUICK — MODELS 38 & 39 — FOUR: In effect these two Buicks were larger versions of the Model 26 and Model 27 Buicks. The Model 38 roadster with its large, 27 gallon, rear mounted fuel tank was finished in a dark blue body and gray wheels. The Model 39 tourer attracted attention with its four door body. However the driver's door was inoperative. The standard color for the Model 39 was dark blue. Its wooden wheels were painted gray.

BUICK — MODEL 41 — FOUR: The Model 41 limousine was powered by a 4-cylinder engine of 318 cubic inch displacement.

I.D. DATA: Serial numbers on plate on left side of frame. Starting: Model 21 1, Model 26 & 27 1, Model 32 & 33 1, Model 38 & 39 1, Model 41 41. Ending: Model 21 300, Model 26 & 27 400, Model 32 & 33 3150, Model 38 & 39 1050, Model 41 67. Engine Nos. Starting: Model 21 1, Model 26 & 27 1, Model 32 & 33 1, Model 38 & 39 1, Model 41 41. Ending: Model 21 300, Model 26 & 27 405, Model 32 & 33 3153, Model 38 & 39 1059, Model 41 67.

Model No.	Body Type & Seating	Price	Weight	Prod. Total
14	Rds.-2P	550	1500	Note 1
21	Tr.-5P	1500	2610	Note 2
21	Tr. CIC.-5P	1500	2610	Note 2
21	Rds. R./S.-3P	1550	2610	Note 2
26	Rds.-2P	1050	2100	1000
27	Tr.-5P	1150	2280	3000
32	Rds.-2P	800	1695	1150
33	Tr.-5P	950	1855	2000
38	Rds.-2P	1850	2650	153
39	Tr.-5P	1850	3225	905
41	Limo.-5P	2750	3400	27

Note 1: Total production of 3300, includes 2048 built in late 1910.
Note 2: Total production of all Model 21 styles was 3000.

ENGINE: [Model 14] Inline. Two. Cast iron block. B & S: 4.5 x 40. Disp. 127 cu. in. SAE H.P.: 14.2. Valve lifters: mechanical. [Model 21] Inline. Four. Cast iron block. B & S: 4.25 x 4.5. Disp.: 255 cu. in. Brake H.P.: 40. SAE H.P.: 28.9. Main bearings: 5. Valve lifters: mechanical. Carb. Schebler. [Models 32 & 33] Inline. Valve in head. Four. Cast iron block. B & S: 3-3/4 x 3-3/4. Disp.: 165 cu. in. SAE H.P.: 22.5. Valve lifters: mechanical. Carb.: Schebler. [Models 26 & 27] Inline. Four. Cast iron block. B & S: 4 x 4. Disp. 201 cu. in. SAE H.P.: 25.6. Valve lifters: mechanical. Carb.: Marvel E 10-501. [Models 38 and 39] Inline. Four. Cast iron block. B & S: 4.5 x 5. Disp. 318 cu. in. Brake H.P.: 48. SAE H.P. 32.4. Valve lifters: mechanical. Carb.: Marvel E 10-502. [Model 41] Inline. Four. Cast iron block. B & S: 4.5 x 5. Disp.: 318 cu. in. (some sources credit Model 41 with a 338cid engine). SAE H.P.: 32.4. Valve lifters: mechanical.

CHASSIS: [Model 14] W.B.: 79 in. Tires: 30 x 3. [Model 21] W.B.: 110 in. Tires: 34 x 4. [Model 26] W.B.: 100 in. Tires: 32 x 3.5. [Model 27] W.B.: 106 in. Tires: 32 x 3.5. [Model 32] W.B.: 89 in. Tires: 30 x 3.5. [Model 33] W.B.: 100 in. Tires: 30 x 3.5. [Models 38 & 39] W.B.: 116 in. Tires: 36 x 4. [Model 41] W.B.: 112.5 in. Tires: 36 x 4.5.

TECHNICAL: Model 14 Selective sliding gear transmission. Speeds: 2F/1R. Floor & steering column controls. Disc clutch. Chain drive. Mechanical brakes on two wheels. Wooden wheels. Model 21 Sliding gear transmission. Speeds: 3F/1R. Floor shift controls. Cone clutch. Shaft drive. Mechanical brakes on two wheels. Models 26 & 27 Sliding gear transmission. Speeds: 3F/1R. Floor shift controls. Multiple disc clutch. Shaft drive. Mechanical brakes on two wheels. Wooden wheels. Models 32 & 33 Planetary transmission. Speeds: 2F/1R. Floor and steering column controls. Cone clutch. Shaft drive. Mechanical brakes on two wheels. Wooden rim wheels. Models 38 & 39 & 41 Sliding gear transmission. Speeds: 3F/1R. Floor shift controls. Multiple disc clutch. Shaft drive. Mechanical brakes on two wheels. Wooden rim wheels.

OPTIONS: Windshield. Top.

HISTORICAL: Calendar year production: 13,389. Model year production: 13,389. The president of Buick was Thomas Neal. Two Marquette-Buicks were entered in the first Indianapolis 500. However they retired after 30 and 46 laps respectively. Similarly two Marquette-Buicks competed in the Savannah, GA Grand Prize race but neither car finished.

1911
Model 14, 2-cyl.

	FP	5	4	3	2	1
Rds	550	2000	5100	8500	11,900	17,000
Model 21, 4-cyl.						
Tr	1500	2300	5400	9000	12,600	18,000
Model 26 & 27, 4-cyl.						
Rds	1050	2800	5700	9500	13,300	19,000
Tr	1150	2000	5100	8500	11,900	17,000
Model 32 & 33						
Rds	800	2300	5400	9000	12,600	18,000
Tr	2000	2000	5100	8500	11,900	17,000
Model 38 & 39, 4-cyl.						
Rds	1850	3900	7800	13,000	18,200	26,000
Tr	1850	3300	6600	11,000	15,400	22,000
Limo	2750	3600	7200	12,000	16,800	24,000

1912

1912 Buick, touring, OCW

1912 BUICK — OVERVIEW: Improvements common to all 1912 Buicks included improved lubrication arrangements for the pushrods and the addition of grease cups to the spring shackles, steering knuckles and clutch. All models were fitted with three-speed sliding-gear transmission.
Buick eliminated a number of Models for 1912 including Model 14, Model 21, Model 38 and Model 41.

BUICK — MODEL 28 — FOUR: This roadster as all Buicks for 1912 was fitted with true doors, thus acquiring a more modern appearance. A number of color combinations were available including a two-tone wine and black body and blue-black fenders as well as a body finish of Buick gray and black body with blue-black fenders, hood and tank.

BUICK — MODEL 29 — FOUR: Customers could also order this touring model in either of two color combinations. Its hood, fenders and wheels were finished in blue-black while body color could be gray or wine.

BUICK — MODEL 34: This roadster was fitted on a trim, 90.7'' wheelbase and was delivered with a gray body, matching wheels and blue hood and fenders.

BUICK — MODEL 35 — FOUR: This most popular Buick for 1912 was updated with a three-speed selective sliding gear transmission replacing the planetary transmission used previously. Also sharing in this change over was the Model 34. The driver's door on the Model 35 was inoperative. Standard body color was dark blue with the wheels finished in gray.

BUICK — MODEL 36 — FOUR: This model was one of three roadsters offered by Buick in 1912. It shared its 201cid engine with both the Model 28 and Model 29 Buicks and was available in two color schemes. A blue and gray body with blue-black hood, fenders and fuel tank was standard. A second choice was a Buick-brown body with blue-black fenders.

BUICK — MODEL 43 — FOUR: This was the largest Buick offered in 1912. The Model 43 318cid engine like all 1912 Buick engines had its spark plugs positioned in the cylinder head at a 45° angle instead of the older, horizontal location.

I.D. DATA: Serial numbers on plate on left side of frame. Starting: Model 29 1, Models 34, 35, 36 1, Model 43 1. Ending: Model 29 8,500, Models 34, 35, 36 9051, Model 43 1501. Engine No. Starting: Model 29 1, Models 34, 35, 36 1, Model 43, 1. Ending: Model 29 8500, Models 34, 35, 36 9059, Model 43 1506.

Model No.	Body Type & Seating	Price	Weight	Prod. Total
28	2-dr. Rds.-2/4P	1025	2375	2500
29	3-dr. Tr.-5P	1180	2600	6000
34	2-dr. Rds.-2P	900	1875	1400
35	3-dr. Tr.-5P	1000	2100	6050
36	2-dr. Rds.-2P	900	1950	1600
43	3-dr. Tr.-5P	1725	3360	1501

ENGINE: [Models 28 and 29] Inline. Four. Cast iron block. B & S: 4 x 4. Disp.: 201 cu. in. SAE H.P.: 25.5. Valve lifters: mechanical. Carb.: Marvel E 10-543. [Models 34, 35 and 36] Inline. Four. Cast iron block. B & S: 3.75 x 3.75. Disp.: 165 cu. in. SAE H.P.: 22.5. Valve lifters: mechanical. Carb.: Schebler. [Model 43] Inline. Four. Cast iron block. B & S: 4.5 x 5. Disp.: 318 cu. in. Brake H.P.: 48. SAE H.P.: 32.4. Valve lifters: mechanical. Carb.: Schebler.

CHASSIS: [Model 28] W.B.: 108 in. Tires: 34 x 3.5. [Model 29] W.B.: 108 in. Tires: 34 x 3.5. [Model 34] W.B.: 90.75 in. Tires: 30 x 3.5. [Model 35] W.B.: 101.75 in. Tires: 32 x 3.5. [Model 36] W.B.: 101.75 in. Tires: 32 x 3.5. [Model 43] W.B.: 116 in. Tires: 36 x 4.

TECHNICAL: All models Sliding gear transmission. Speeds: 3F/1R. Floor shift controls. Leather faced, aluminum cone clutch. Shaft drive. Mechanical brakes on two wheels. Wooden wheels.

OPTIONS: Top. Windshield.

HISTORICAL: Innovations: Buick enclosed the selective type shift lever and emerging brake in a panel attached to the non-operating front right hand door on all models. Calendar year production: 19,051. Model year production: 19,051. The president of Buick was Walter P. Chrysler. A Marquette-Buick was entered in the 1912 Indianapolis 500 but retired after 72 laps.

1912
Model 34, 35 & 36, 4-cyl.

	FP	5	4	3	2	1
Rds	900	3150	6300	10,500	14,700	21,000
Tr	1000	3300	6600	11,000	15,400	22,000
Model 28 & 29, 4-cyl.						
Rds	1025	2300	5400	9000	12,600	18,000
Tr	1180	2800	5700	9500	13,300	19,000
Model 43, 4-cyl.						
Tr	1725	3400	6900	11,500	16,100	23,000

1913

BUICK — MODEL 24 & 25 — FOUR: These two Buicks with roadster and touring bodies replaced the Models 34, 35 and 36 of 1912. Both were offered in maroon or Buick gray bodies with blue-black fenders and wheels.

BUICK — MODEL 30 & 31 — FOUR: These roadsters and touring Buicks were offered in blue-black or gray finished bodies.

BUICK — MODEL 40 — FOUR: The prestige Buick for 1913 was this touring model. An interesting design feature was the extension of its leather upholstery over the upper door surfaces.

I.D. DATA: Serial numbers on plate on left side of frame. Starting: Model 24 & 25 1, Model 30 6250 and 12751, Model 31 1 and 8000, Model 40 1. Ending: Models 24 & 25 11000, Model 30 7999 and 13501, Model 31 6250 and 12749, Model 40 1508. Engine No. Starting: Models 24 & 25 1, Models 30 & 31 1, Model 40 1. Ending: Models 24 & 25 11005, Models 30 & 31 13504, Model 40 1510.

1913 Buick, touring, OCW

1914 Buick, model B-25, touring, HAC

1914 BUICK: Highlighting the 1914 Buicks was a new 6-cylinder engine, the use of a Delco electric starter and lighting system and a switch to left hand drive with center mounted gear shift and emergency brake.

1913 Buick, touring (Louis Chevrolet at wheel), JAC

Model No.	Body Type & Seating	Price	Weight	Prod. Total
24	2-dr. Rds.-2P	950	2130	2850
25	3-dr. Tr.-5P	1050	2335	8150
30	2-dr. Rds.-2P	1125	2480	3500
31	3-dr. Tr.-5P	1285	2750	10,000
40	3-dr. Tr.-5P	1650	—	1506

ENGINE: [Models 24 and 25] Inline. Ohv. Four. Cast iron block. B & S: 3.75 x 3.75. Disp.: 165 cu. in. N.A.C.C. H.P.: 22.5. Valve lifters: mechanical. Carb.: Marvel E 10-501. [Models 30 and 31] Inline. Ohv. Four. Cast iron block. B & S: 4 x 4. Disp. 201 cu. in. N.A.C.C. H.P.: 25.6. Valve lifters: mechanical. Carb.: Schebler. [Model 40] Inline. Ohv. Four. Cast iron block. B & S: 4.25 x 4.5. Disp.: 255 cu. in. Brake H.P.: 40. N.A.C.C. H.P.: 28.9. Main bearings: 5. Valve lifters: mechanical. Carb.: Schebler.

CHASSIS: [Model 24] W.B.: 105 in. Frt/Rear Tread: 56 or 60 in. Tires: 32 x 3.5. [Model 25] W.B.: 105 in. Frt/Rear Tread: 56 or 60 in. Tires: 32 x 3.5. [Model 30] W.B.: 108 in. Tires: 34 x 3.5. [Model 31] W.B.: 108 in. Tires: 34 x 3.5. [Model 40] W.B.: 115 in. Tires: 36 x 4.

TECHNICAL: Sliding gear transmission. Speeds: 3F/1R. Floor shift control. Cone clutch. Shaft drive. Mechanical brakes on two wheels. Wooden wheels.

OPTIONS: Electric head, tail and side lights.

HISTORICAL: Calendar year production: 26,006. Model year production: 26,006. The president of Buick was Walter P. Chrysler. A Buick won a 102 mile "Corona Race" on the West coast in 1913. In addition, on July 17, 1913 a Model 10 Buick of 1910 vintage became the first car to climb Pike's Peak unassisted. 1913 was the last year for right hand drive in a Buick. Nickel plating instead of brass was also introduced.

1914 BUICK

1914 Buick, model B-24, roadster, JAC

BUICK — SERIES B — MODELS B-24 & B-25 — FOUR: These roadster and touring models retained Buick's familiar front end design with angular forms for the hood and radiator. Adding to their sales appeal were a standard top and windshield.

BUICK — SERIES B — MODELS B-36 & B-37 — FOUR: With their rounded hoods and grille outlines, these roadster and touring Buicks took on a more modern appearance which was accompanied by running boards free from supporting the battery boxes.

BUICK — SERIES B — MODEL B-38 — FOUR: In a year of major styling and engineering changes the B-38 was a benchmark Buick since it was the first production Buick with a fully enclosed coupe body.

BUICK — SERIES B — MODEL B-55 — SIX: This touring model was the first Buick available with a 6-cylinder, overhead valve engine. With the rounded hood and nose of the B-24 and B-25 models plus fenders set lower then previously, the B-55 represented a break from the styling confines of Buick's early years.

I.D. DATA: Serial numbers on plate on left side of frame. Starting: B-24 101, B-25 101, B-55 101. Ending: B-24 3226, B-25 13521, B-55 2137. Engine No. Starting: B-24 101, B-25 101, B-55 104. Ending: B-24 16674, B-25 16774, B-55 2103.

Model No.	Body Type & Seating	Price	Weight	Prod. Total
B-24	2-dr. Rds.-2P	950	2200	3126 (A)
B-25	4-dr. Tr.-5P	1050	2400	13446 (B)
B-36	2-dr. Rds.-2P	1375	2726	2550
B-37	4-dr. Trer.-5P	1485	2930	9050
B-38	2-dr. Cpe.-2P	1800	2930	50
B-55	4-dr. Tr.-5P	1985	3664	2045

Note 1: (A) — 239 built for export (chassis only).
Note 2: (B) — 1544 were built for export (chassis only).

1913

Model 30 & 31, 4-cyl.	FP	5	4	3	2	1
Rds	1125	2800	5700	9500	13,300	19,000
Tr	1285	3000	6000	10,000	14,000	20,000
Model 40, 4-cyl.						
Tr	1850	3600	7200	12,000	16,800	24,000
Model 24 & 25, 4-cyl.						
Rds	950	3400	6900	11,500	16,100	23,000
Tr	1050	3600	7200	12,000	16,800	24,000

ENGINE: [Models B-24 and B-25] Inline Ohv. Four. Cast iron block. B & S: 3.75 x 3.75. Disp.: 165 cu. in. SAE H.P.: 22. Main bearings: 3. Valve lifters: mechanical. Carb.: Marvel E 10-501. [Models B-36, B-37 and B-38] Inline Ohv. Four. Cast iron block. B & S: 3.75 x 5. Disp.: 221 cu. in. Brake H.P.: 35. Main bearings: 3. Valve lifters: mechanical. Carb.: Marvel E 10-502. [Model B-55] Inline Ohv. Six-cast in pairs. Cast iron block. B & S: 3.75 x 5. Disp.: 331 cu. in. Brake H.P.: 48. SAE H.P.: 33.75. Main bearings: 4. Valve lifters: mechanical. Carb.: Marvel.

CHASSIS: [Series B-24] W.B.: 105 in. Frt/Rear Tread: 56 in. or 60 in. Tires: 32 x 3.5. [Series B-25] W.B.: 105 in. Frt/Rear Tread: 56 in. or 60 in. Tires: 32 x 3.5. [Series B-36] W.B.: 112 in. Frt/Rear Tread: 56 in. or 60 in. Tires: 34 x 4. [Series B-37] W.B.: 112 in. Frt/Rear Tread: 56 in. or 60 in. Tires: 34 x 4. [Series B-38] W.B.: 112 in. Frt/Rear Tread: 56 in. or 60 in. Tires: 34 x 4. [Series B-55] W.B.: 130 in. Frt/Rear Tread: 56 in. Tires: 36 x 4.5.

TECHNICAL: Sliding gear transmission. Speeds: 3F/1R. Floor shift controls. Cone clutch. Shaft drive. 3/4 floating rear axle. Mechanical brakes on two wheels. Wooden wheels.

OPTIONS: Front bumper. Rear bumper. Spotlight.

HISTORICAL: Calendar year production: 21,217. Model year production: 21,217. The president of Buick was Walter P. Chrysler.

1914
Model B-24 & B-25, 4-cyl.

	FP	5	4	3	2	1
Rds	900	3400	6900	11,500	16,100	23,000
Tr	1050	3600	7200	12,000	16,800	24,000
Model B-36, B-37 & B-38, 4-cyl.						
Rds	1235	3600	7200	12,000	16,800	24,000
Tr	1335	3750	7500	12,500	17,500	25,000
Cpe	1800	3150	6300	10,500	14,700	21,000
Model B-55, 6-cyl.						
7P Tr	1985	3900	7800	13,000	18,200	26,000

1915

1915 Buick, model C-55, touring, HAC

1915 Buick, model C-36, roadster, HAC

1915 BUICK: This was a record production year for Buick. Lower prices and improvements such as cantilevered rear springs on 6-cylinder models, an improved electric starter on 4-cylinder Buicks and the use of concealed door hinges on all models were the most important revisions.

BUICK — SERIES C — MODELS C-24 & C-25 — FOUR: The roadster body of the C-24 with its exposed gas tank was definitely dated. However the rounded front end of this Buick and the C-25 tourer helped maintain their popularity with Buick customers.

BUICK — SERIES C — MODELS C-36 & C-37 — FOUR: These Buicks were visually nearly identical to their 1914 counterparts. Both models were offered with an all-black finish or a combination of blue-black hood and body with black fenders and wheels.

BUICK — SERIES C — MODELS C-54 & C-55 — SIX: Joining the C-55 Buick which now had a 7-passenger capacity was the C-54 roadster model.

I.D. DATA: Serial numbers on plate on left side of frame. Starting: C-24 and C-25 100000, C-36 and C-37 106000, C-54 and C-55 105000. Ending: C-24 and C-25 144713, C-36 and C-37 143913, C-54 and C-55 144715. Engine No. Starting: C-24 and C-25 100000, C-36 and C-37 100000, C-54 and C-55 100000. Ending: C-24 and C-25 144723, C-36 and C-37 144723, C-54 and C-55 144723.

Model No.	Body Type & Seating	Price	Weight	Prod. Total
C-24	2-dr. Rds.-2P	900	2200	3256 (A)
C-25	4-dr. Trer.-5P	950	2334	19080 (B)
C-36	2-dr. Rds.-2P	1185	2795	2849
C-37	4-dr. Trer.-5P	1235	2980	12450
C-54	2-dr. Rds.-2P	1635	3400	352
C-55	4-dr. Trer.-7P	1650	3680	3449

Note 1: (A) — 186 CX-24 export models were also produced.
Note 2: (B) — 931 CX-25 export models were also produced.

ENGINE: [Models C-24 and C-25] Inline. Ohv. Four. Cast iron block. B & S: 3.75 x 3.75. Disp.: 165 cu. in. N.A.C.C. H.P.: 22.5. Main bearings: 3. Valve lifters: mechanical. Carb.: Marvel E 10-501. [Models C-36 and C-37] Inline Ohv. Four. Cast iron block. B & S: 3.75 x 5. Disp.: 221 cu. in. Brake H.P.: 37. N.A.C.C. H.P.: 22.5. Main bearings: 3. Valve lifters: mechanical. Carb.: Marvel 10-502. [Models C-54 and C-55] Inline Ohv. Six. Cast iron block. B & S: 3.75 x 5. Disp.: 331 cu. in. Brake H.P.: 55. N.A.C.C. H.P.: 33.75. Main bearings: 4. Valve lifters: mechanical. Carb.: Marvel.

CHASSIS: [Model C-24] W.B.: 106 in. Frt/Rear Tread: 56 or 60 in. Tires: 32 x 3.5. [Model C-25] W.B.: 106 in. Frt/Rear Tread: 56 or 60 in. Tires. 32 x 3.5. [Model C-36] W.B.: 112 in. Frt/Rear Tread: 56 or 60 in. Tires: 34 x 4. [Model C-37] W.B.: 112 in. Frt/Rear Tread: 56 or 60 in. Tires: 34 x 4. [Model C-54] W.B.: 130 in. Frt/Rear Tread: 56 in. Tires: 36 x 4.5. [Model C-55] W.B.: 130 in. Frt/Rear Tread: 56 in. Tires: 36 x 4.5.

TECHNICAL: All models sliding gear transmission. Speeds: 3F/1R. Floor shift controls. Cone clutch. Shaft drive. 3/4 floating rear axle. Mechanical brakes on two wheels. Wooden wheels.

OPTIONS: Speedometer (C-24, C-25). Bumpers. Spot lighter.

HISTORICAL: The C-36 was the first Buick to carry its spare tire enclosed in the body. Calendar year production: 42,553. Model year production: 42,553. The president of Buick was Walter P. Chrysler.

1915
Model C-24 & C-25, 4-cyl.

	FP	5	4	3	2	1
Rds	900	3400	6900	11,500	16,100	23,000
Tr	950	3600	7200	12,000	16,800	24,000
Model C-36 & C-37, 4-cyl.						
Rds	1185	3600	7200	12,000	16,800	24,000
Tr	1235	3750	7500	12,500	17,500	25,000
Model C-54 & C-55, 6-cyl.						
Rds	1635	3750	7500	12,500	17,500	25,000
Tr	1600	3900	7800	13,000	18,200	26,000

1916

1916 Buick, funeral car, JAC

159

BUICK — SERIES D — MODELS D44 & D45 — SIX: These Buicks were powered by a new 6-cylinder engine with a single block casting and a displacement of 224 cubic inches. The D-44 roadster had trim new lines including a squared off rear deck while the D-45 was to become the most popular Buick of 1916.

BUICK — SERIES D — MODELS D46 & D47 — SIX: The D-46 Coupe was the first true Buick convertible and was equipped with plate glass windows. The D-47 was the first Buick with a sedan body style.

BUICK — SERIES D — MODELS D-54 & D-55: Both of these Buicks, unchanged from 1915, were discontinued at the end of the 1916 model year.

This was Buick's greatest production year to date with an output of 124,834 cars.

I.D. DATA: Serial numbers on plate on left side of frame. Starting: D-44 & D-45 144717, D-54 59217, D-55 156717. Ending: D-44 & D-45 254501, D-54 213022, D-55 214822. Engine No. Starting: All models — 144729 & up.

Model No.	Body Type & Seating	Price	Weight	Prod. Total
D-44	2-dr. Rds.-2P	985	2660	12,978 (A)
D-45	4-dr. Trer.-5P	1020	2760	73,827 (B)
D-46	2-dr. Cpe.-2P	1425	2900	1443
D-47	2-dr. Sed.-5P	1800	3130	881
D-54	2-dr. Rds.-2P	1450	3400	1194
D-55	4-dr. Trer.-5P	1485	3670	9866

Note 1: (A) — 541 were produced for export.
Note 2: (B) — 4741 were produced for export.

ENGINE: [Models D-44, D-45, D-46 and D-47] Inline. Ohv. Six. Cast iron block. B & S: 3.25 x 4.5. Disp.: 225 cu. in. Brake H.P.: 45. N.A.C.C. H.P.: 25.35. Main bearings: 4. Valve lifters: mechanical. Carb.: Marvel E 10-543. [Models D-54 and D-55] Inline. Ohv. Six. Cast iron block. B & S: 3.75 x 5. Disp.: 331 cu. in. Bearings: 4. Valve lifters: mechanical. Carb.: Marvel.

CHASSIS: [Model D-44] W.B.: 115 in. Frt/Rear Tread: 56 in. Tires: 34 x 4. [Model D-45] W.B.: 115 in. Frt/Rear Tread: 56 in. Tires: 34 x 4. [Model D-46] W.B.: 115 in. Frt/Rear Tread: 56. Tires: 34 x 4. [Model D-47] W.B.: 115 in. Frt/Rear Tread: 56. Tires: 34 x 4. [Model D-54] W.B.: 130 in. Frt/Rear Tread: 56 in. Tires: 36 x 4-1/2. [Model D-55] W.B.: 130 in. Frt/Rear Tread: 56 in. Tires: 36 x 4-1/2.

TECHNICAL: Sliding gear transmission. Speeds: 3F/1R. Floor shift controls. Cone clutch. Shaft drive. Full floating rear axle. Mechanical brakes on two wheels. Wooden spoke wheels.

OPTIONS: Front bumper. Cowl spot lights.

HISTORICAL: Introduced August, 1916. Calendar year production: 122,315. Model year production: 105,471. The president of Buick was Walter P. Chrysler. Calendar year production included Model D-34 and D-35 4-cylinder models which, while most Buick histories regard as 1916 models, Buick tended to almost totally ignore. Because of this inconsistency they will be examined in the 1917 model year section.

1916
Model D-54 & D-55, 6-cyl.

	FP	5	4	3	2	1
Rds	1450	3600	7200	12,000	16,800	24,000
Tr	1485	3750	7500	12,500	17,500	25,000

1917

1917 Buick, roadster, OCW

BUICK — SERIES D — D-34 & D-35 — FOUR: Buick production, due to limited supplies of strategic materials, fell to 115,267 in 1917. The large Model D-54 and D-55 Buicks were dropped while the D-34 and D-35 models were given considerable publicity. Their 4-cylinder engine developed an impressive 35hp and displaced 170 cubic inches. A detachable cylinder head was incorporated and the chassis used semi-elliptic springs rather than cantilever units.

The remaining cars in the Buick lineup remained unchanged.

I.D. DATA: Serial numbers on plate on left side of frame. Starting: Model D-34, D-35 — 215,823, D-44 154717. Ending: Model D-34, D-35 — 331774, D-44 289851.* Engine No. Starting: all models 144729 & up.
Note 1: Includes some D-54, D-55 models built in 1916.

Model No.	Body Type & Seating	Price	Weight	Prod. Total
D-34	2-dr. Rds.-2P	660	1900	2292 (A)
D-35	4-dr. Tr.-5P	675	2100	20,126 (B)
D-44	2-dr. Rds.-2P	1040	2660	4366 (C)
D-45	4-dr. Tr.-5P	1070	—	25,371 (D)
D-46	2-dr. Cpe.-3P	1440	2900	485
D-47	2-dr. Sed.-5P	1835	3130	132

Note 1: (A) — 238 more were built for export.
Note 2: (B) — 1097 more were built for export.
Note 3: (C) — 100 more were built for export.
Note 4: (D) — 1371 more were built for export.

ENGINE: [Model D-34 and D-35] Inline. Ohv. Four. Cast iron block. B & S: 3-3/8 x 4-3/4. Disp.: 170 cu. in. Brake H.P.: 35. N.A.C.C. H.P.: 18.2. Main bearings: 3. Valve lifters: mechanical. Carb.: Marvel E 10-502. [Model D-44, D-45, D-46, D-47] Inline. Ohv. Six. Cast iron block. B & S: 3-1/4 x 4-1/2. Disp.: 225 cu. in. Brake H.P.: 45. N.A.C.C. H.P.: 25.3. Main bearings: 4. Valve lifters: mechanical. Carb.: Marvel.

CHASSIS: [Model D-34] W.B.: 106 in. Frt/Rear Tread: 56 in. Tires: 31 x 4. [Model D-35] W.B.: 106 in. Frt/Rear Tread: 56 in. Tires: 31 x 4. [Model D-44] W.B.: 115 in. Frt/Rear Tread: 56 in. Tires: 34 x 4. [Model D-45] W.B.: 115 in. Frt/Rear Tread: 56 in. Tires: 34 x 4. [Model D-46] W.B.: 115 in. Frt/Rear Tread: 56 in. Tires: 34 x 4. [Model D-47] W.B.: 115 in. Frt/Rear Tread: 56 in. Tires: 35 x 4-1/2.

TECHNICAL: Sliding gear transmission. Speeds: 3F/1R. Floor shift controls. Cone clutch. Shaft drive. Full floating rear axle. Mechanical brakes on two wheels. Wooden spoke wheels.

OPTIONS: Front bumper. Rear bumper. Solid top — D-34.

HISTORICAL: Introduced Aug. 1916. Calendar year production: 115,267. Model year production: 55,578. The president of Buick was Walter P. Chrysler.

1916-1917
Model D-34 & D-35, 4-cyl.

	FP	5	4	3	2	1
Rds	660	3300	6600	11,000	15,400	22,000
Tr	675	3400	6900	11,500	16,100	23,000
Model D-44 & D-45, 6-cyl.						
Rds	985	3400	6900	12,000	16,100	24,000
Tr	1020	3600	7200	12,000	16,800	24,000
Model D-46 & D-47, 6-cyl.						
Conv Cpe	1425	2800	5700	9500	13,300	19,000
Sed	1800	1550	4500	7500	10,500	15,000

1918

1918 Buick, roadster, JAC

1918 Buick E-6-49, touring, HAC

BUICK — SERIES E — FOUR & SIX: Buick dropped the 225 cid six in favor of a larger 242 cid version. The 4-cylinder models continued with a new gear-driven oil pump and new oil and ammeter gauges were installed on the dash. Other changes included a trimmer instrument panel, revised seats with higher backs and the substitution of linoleum in place of rubber for the floor covering.

With windshields given a slight rearward slant the open Buick models took on a racier appearance. An interesting feature of the Model E-50 sedan was its removable rear door post. This early example of "hard top styling" was featured only in 1918.

I.D. DATA: Serial numbers on plate on left side of frame. Starting: 343,783. Ending: 480,995.

Model No.	Body Type & Seating	Price	Weight	Prod. Total
E-34	2-dr. Rds.-2P	795	1900	3800 (A)
E-35	4-dr. Tr.-5P	795	2100	27,125 (B)
E-37	2-dr. Sed.-5P	1185	2420	700
E-44	2-dr. Rds.-2P	1265	2750	10,391 (C)
E-45	4-dr. Tr.-5P	1265	2850	58,971 (D)
E-46	2-dr. Cpe.-2P	1695	2965	2965
E-47	4-dr. Sed.-5P	1845	3230	463
E-49	4-dr. Tr.-7P	1385	3075	16,148
E-50	4-dr. Sed.-7P	2175	3620	987

Note 1: (A) — 172 were built for export.
Note 2: (B) — 1190 were built for export.
Note 3: (C) — 275 were built for export.
Note 4: (D) — 3035 were built for export.

ENGINE: [Models E-34, E-35, E-37] Inline Ohv. Four. Cast iron block. B & S: 3-3/8 x 4-3/4. Disp.: 170 cu. in. Brake H.P.: 35. N.A.C.C. H.P.: 18.2. Valve lifters: mechanical. Carb.: Marvel E 10-517. [Models E-44, E-45, E-46, E-47, E-49, E-50] Inline Ohv. Six. Cast iron block. B & S: 3-3/8 x 4-1/2. Disp.: 242 cu. in. Brake H.P.: 60. N.A.C.C. H.P.: 27.3. Valve lifters: mechanical. Carb.: Marvel 10-520.

CHASSIS: [Models E-34, E-35, E-37] W.B.: 106 in. Tires: 31 x 4 (E-37 — 23 x 3.5). [Models E-44, E-45, E-46, E-47] W.B.: 118 in. Tires: 34 x 4. [Models E-49, E-50] W.B.: 124 in. Tires: 34 x 4.5.

TECHNICAL: Sliding gear transmission. Speeds: 3F/1R. Floor shift controls. Multiple disc clutch. Shaft drive. Full floating rear axle. Mechanical brakes on two wheels. Wooden rim wheels.

OPTIONS: Front bumper. Spotlight. Dual spare tire carrier.

HISTORICAL: Introduced Aug. 1917. Calendar year production: 77,691. Model year production: 126,222. The president of Buick was Walter P. Chrysler.

1918

Model E-34 & E-35, 4-cyl.	FP	5	4	3	2	1
Rds	660	3150	6300	10,500	14,700	21,000
Tr	675	3300	6600	11,000	15,400	22,000
Model E-37, 4-cyl.						
Sed	1185	2000	5100	8500	11,900	17,000
Model E-44, E-45 & E-49, 6-cyl.						
Rds	985	3400	6900	11,500	16,100	23,000
Tr	1020	3600	7200	12,000	16,800	24,000
7P Tr	1385	3750	7500	12,500	17,500	25,000
Model E-46, E-47 & E-50, 6-cyl.						
Conv Cpe	1425	2800	5700	9500	13,300	19,000
Sed	1800	1550	4500	7500	10,500	15,000
7P Sed	2175	1650	4650	7750	10,850	15,500

1919

BUICK — SERIES H — SIX: Only cosmetic changes were made in the appearance of the 1919 Buick. Thinner and more numerous hood louvers were used and the six cylinder engine which was common to all Buicks had new valve, push rod and spark plug covers.

The instrument panel was not illuminated and the pull-type switches for the ignition and lights gave way to a lever-action Delco combined ignition and light switch.

I.D. DATA: Serial numbers on left side of frame by gas tank and again behind left front wheel. Starting: 480996. Ending: 547523.

Model No.	Body Type & Seating	Price	Weight	Prod. Total
H-44	2-dr. Rds.-2P	1595	2813	7839 (A)
H-45	4-dr. Tr.-5P	1595	2950	44,589 (B)
H-46	2-dr. Cpe.-4P	2085	3100	3971
H-47	4-dr. Sed.-5P	2195	3296	501
H-49	4-dr. Tr.-7P	1985	3175	6795
H-50	4-dr. Sed.-7P	2585	3736	531

Note 1: (A) — 176 were also exported.
Note 2: (B) — 2595 were also exported.

ENGINE: Inline. Ohv. Six. Cast iron block. B & S: 3-3/8 x 4-1/2. Disp.: 242 cu. in. Brake H.P.: 60. N.A.C.C. H.P.: 27.3. Valve lifters: mechanical. Carb.: Marvel E 10-526.

CHASSIS: [Models H-44, H-45, H-46, H-47] W.B.: 118 in. Frt/Rear Tread: 56 in. Tires: 33 x 4. [Models H-49, H-50] W.B.: 124 in. Frt/Rear Tread: 56 in. Tires: 34 x 4.5.

TECHNICAL: Sliding gear transmission. Speeds: 3F/1R. Floor shift controls. Multiple disc clutch. Shaft drive. Full floating rear axle. Mechanical brakes on two wheels. Wooden spoke wheels.

1919 Buick H-6-46, coupe, HAC

OPTIONS: Front bumper. Spot light.

HISTORICAL: Calendar year production: 119,310. Model year production: 65,997. The president of Buick was Walter P. Chrysler.

1919

Model H-44, H-45 & H-49, 6-cyl.	FP	5	4	3	2	1
Rds	1595	3400	6900	11,500	16,100	23,000
Tr	1595	3600	7200	12,000	16,800	24,000
7P Tr	—	3750	7500	12,500	17,500	25,000
Model H-46, H-47 & H-50, 6-cyl.						
Cpe	1985	1650	4650	7750	10,850	15,500
Sed	2195	1025	2600	5250	7300	10,500
7P Sed	2585	1150	3600	6000	8400	12,000

1920

1920 Buick K-6-44, roadster, HAC

BUICK — SERIES K — SIX: The Series K Buicks were unchanged from the 1919 Series H versions.

I.D. DATA: Serial numbers on left side of frame by gas tank and repeated behind left front wheel. Starting: 547524. Ending: 687794. Engine numbers on crankcase on left side near front of oil filler tube.

Model No.	Body Type & Seating	Price	Weight	Prod. Total
K-44	2-dr. Rds.-3P	1495	2813	19,000 (A)
K-45	2-dr. Tr.-5P	1495	2950	85,245 (B)
K-46	2-dr. Cpe.-4P	2085	3100	6503
K-47	4-dr. Sed.-5P	2255	3296	2252
K-49	4-dr. Tr.-7P	1785	3175	16,801 (C)
K-50	4-dr. Sed.-7P	2695	3736	1499

Note 1: (A) — 200 built for export.
Note 2: (B) — 7400 built for export.
Note 3: (C) — 1100 built for export.

ENGINE: Inline Ohv. Six. Cast iron block. B & S: 3-3/8 x 4-1/2. Disp.: 242 cu. in. Brake H.P.: 60. N.A.C.C. H.P.: 27.3. Main bearings: 4. Valve lifters: mechanical. Carb.: Marvel E 10-526.

CHASSIS: [Models K-44, 45, 46] W.B.: 118 in. Frt/Rear Tread: 56 in. Tires: 33 x 4. [Model K-47] W.B.: 118 in. Frt/Rear Tread: 56 in. Tires: 34 x 4.5. [Models K-49, 50] W.B.: 124 in. Frt/Rear Tread: 56 in. Tires: 34 x 4.5.

TECHNICAL: Sliding gear transmission. Speeds: 3F/1R. Floor shift controls. Multiple disc clutch. Shaft drive. Full floating rear axle. Mechanical brakes on two wheels. Wooden spoke wheels with detachable rims.

OPTIONS: Front bumper. Spotlight.

HISTORICAL: Calendar year production: 115,176. Model year production: 140,000. The president of Buick was Harry H. Bassett.

1920
Model K, 6-cyl.

	FP	5	4	3	2	1
Cpe K-46	2085	1075	3000	5500	7700	11,000
Sed K-47	2255	950	2100	4750	6650	9500
Rds K-44	1495	3150	6300	10,500	14,700	21,000
Tr K-45	1495	3300	6600	11,000	15,400	22,000
7P Sed K-50	2695	1025	2600	5250	7300	10,500

1921

1921 Buick, model 48, coupe, HAC

1921 Buick, model 50, sedan, JAC

BUICK — SERIES 21 — SIX: Buick's styling was moderately changed for 1921 with its higher hood and radiator now forming a straight horizontal line to the windshield base. Technical improvements included cord tires on all models produced after Jan. 1, 1921.

I.D. DATA: Serial numbers on brass plate left side of frame by gas tank and repeated behind left front wheel. Starting: 687795. Ending: 760555. Engine numbers on brassplate next to timing gear inspection hole. Starting: 687795. Ending: 760555.

Model No.	Body Type & Seating	Price	Weight	Prod. Total
44	2-dr. Rds.-3P	1795	2845	7236 (A)
45	2-dr. Tr.-5P	1795	2972	31,877 (B)
46	2-dr. Cpe.-4P	2585	3137	4063
47	4-dr. Sed.-5P	2895	3397	2252
48	2-dr. Cpe.-4P	2985	3397	2606
49	4-dr. Tr.-7P	2060	3272	6424 (C)
50	4-dr. Sed.-7P	3295	3612	1460

Note 1: (A) — 56 produced for export
Note 2: (B) — 1192 produced for export
Note 3: (C) — 366 produced for export
Note 4: All models carry a 21 prefix i.e. 21-44.

ENGINE: Inline. Ohv. Six. Cast iron block. B & S: 3-3/8 x 4-1/2. Disp.: 242 cu. in. Brake H.P.: 60. N.A.C.C. H.P.: 27.3. Main bearings: 4. Valve lifters: mechanical. Carb.: Marvel E 10-526.

CHASSIS: [Models 44, 45, 46 and 47] W.B.: 118 in. Frt/Rear Tread: 56 in. Tires: 34 x 4.5. [Models 48, 49 and 50] W.B.: 124 in. Frt/Rear Tread: 56 in. Tires: 34 x 4.5.

TECHNICAL: Sliding gear transmission. Speeds: 3F/1R. Floor shift controls. Multiple disc clutch. Shaft drive. Full floating rear axle. Mechanical brakes on two wheels. Wooden spoke wheels with detachable rims.

OPTIONS: Tool box. Bumper. Spotlight. Step plates. 2 tops (Tr. Car)

HISTORICAL: A Buick Model 46 completed the 750 mile route between San Francisco and Portland in 29 hours which was 44 minutes less than the Southern Pacific's crack Shasta Limited train. Calendar year production: 82,930. Model year production: 55,337. The president of Buick was Harry H. Bassett.

1921 BUICK
Series 40, 6-cyl.

	FP	5	4	3	2	1
Rds	1795	3300	6600	11,000	15,400	22,000
Tr	1795	3400	6900	11,500	16,100	23,000
7P Tr	2060	3600	7200	12,000	16,800	24,000
Cpe	2585	950	2100	4750	6650	9500
Sed	2895	875	1700	4250	5900	8500
Ewb Cpe	2985	1000	2400	5000	7000	10,000
7P Sed	3295	1150	3600	6000	8400	12,000

1922

1922 Buick, model 22-44, roadster, OCW

BUICK — SERIES 22-FOUR — FOUR: Buick's big news for 1922 was the reintroduction of a 4-cylinder model in August 1921. Retained from 1921 were the smoother and higher radiators and hoods.

1922 Buick, model 22-36, coupe, JAC

BUICK — SERIES 22-SIX — SIX: Highlighting the 6-cylinder Buick line were new Sport Roadster and Sport Touring models with standard Houk wire wheels, red interior and dash-installed clock and speedometer manufactured by Van Sicklen.

I.D. DATA: Serial numbers on left side of frame by gas tank and repeated behind left front wheel. Starting: Models 34, 35, 36, 37 — 688795 & up. Models 44, 45, 46, 47, 48, 49, 50 — 753000 & up. Model 55 — 852537. Ending: Model 55 — 857599. Engine numbers on crank case.

Model No.	Body Type & Seating	Price	Weight	Prod. Total
34	2-dr. Rds.-2P	935	2310	5583 (A)
35	4-dr. Tr.-5P	975	2380	22,521 (B)
36	2-dr. Cpe.-3P	1475	2560	2225
37	4-dr. Sed.-5P	1650	2780	3118
44	2-dr. Rds.-3P	1495	2285	7666 (C)
45	4-dr. Tr.-5P	1525	3005	34,433 (D)
46	2-dr. Cpe.-4P	2135	3235	2293
47	4-dr. Sed.-5P	2435	3425	4878
48	2-dr. Cpe.-4P	2325	3430	8903
49	4-dr. Tr.-7P	1735	3280	6714 (E)
50	4-dr. Sed.-7P	2635	3615	4201
50L	4-dr. Limo.7P	2735	—	178
54	2-dr. Spt. Rds.-3P	1785	3180	2562
55	2-dr. Spt. Tr.-4P	1785	3270	900

Note 1: (A) — 5 built for export.
Note 2: (B) — 29 built for export.
Note 3: (C) — 9 built for export.
Note 4: (D) — 499 built for export.
Note 5: (E) — 71 built for export.
Note 6: All models carry a 22 prefix i.e. 22-34.

ENGINE: [Models 34, 35, 36, 37 Series 22-4] Inline. Ohv. Four. Cast iron block. B & S: 3-3/8 x 4-3/4. Disp.: 170 cu. in. Brake H.P.: 35-40. N.A.C.C. H.P.: 18.23. Main bearings: 3. Valve lifters: mechanical. Carb.: Marvel H 10-502. [Models 44, 45, 46, 47, 48, 49, 50, 50L, 54, 55 Series 22-Six] Inline. Ohv. Six. Cast iron block. B & S: 3-3/8 x 4-1/2. Disp.: 242 cu. in. Brake H.P.: 60. N.A.C.C. H.P.: 27.3. Main bearings: 4. Valve lifters: mechanical. Carb.: Marvel H 10-54.

CHASSIS: [Models 34, 35, 36, 37] W.B.: 109 in. Tires: 31 x 4. [Models 44, 45, 46, 47] W.B.: 118 in. Frt/Rear Tread: 56 in. Tires: 33 x 4. [Models 48, 49, 50, 50L] W.B.: 124 in. Frt/Rear Tread: 56 in. Tires: 34 x 4.5. [Models 54, 55] W.B.: 124 in. Frt/Rear Tread: 56 in. Tires: 32 x 4.5.

TECHNICAL: Sliding gear transmission. Speeds: 3F/1R. Floor shift controls. Multiple disc clutch. Shaft drive. Full floating rear axle. Mechanical brakes on two wheels. Wooden spoke wheels with detachable rims. (Models 54, 55 have Houk wire wheels).

OPTIONS: Dual Sidemount (124'' wheelbase cars only). Cowl lamps (open models).

HISTORICAL: Introduced Aug. 1921. Calendar year production: 123,152 (including truck models). Model year production: 106,788. The president of Buick was Harry H. Bassett.

1921-1922
Series 30, 4-cyl.

	FP	5	4	3	2	1
Rds	895	3000	6000	10,000	14,000	20,000
Tr	935	3150	6300	10,500	14,700	21,000
Cpe OS	1295	875	1700	4250	5900	8500
Sed	1395	825	1600	4000	5600	8000
Series 40, 6-cyl.						
Rds	1495	3400	6900	11,500	16,100	23,000
Tr	1525	3600	7200	12,000	16,800	24,000
7P Tr	1735	3750	7500	12,500	17,500	25,000
Cpe	2135	1000	2400	5000	7000	10,000
Sed	2435	775	1500	3750	5250	7500
Cpe	2325	1075	3000	5500	7700	11,000
7P Sed	2635	1075	3000	5500	7700	11,000
50 7P Limo	2735	1150	3600	6000	8400	12,000

1923

BUICK — SERIES 23-FOUR — FOUR: Buick styling was substantially improved with crowned fenders, cowl lights, new drum-shaped headlights and rounded window edges. Also providing the Buick with a fresh appearance was its new grille form which would remain virtually unchanged through 1927. Technical improvements included repositioned rear spring hangers, a lower suspension system and a transmission lock. Increased engine life was achieved through a harder cylinder casting, a larger crankshaft and stronger connecting rods, pistons and main bearings.

BUICK — SERIES 23-SIX — SIX: The 6-cylinder Buicks although sharing the styling of the Series 23-Four were identified by their longer 188 and 124'' wheelbases. In addition open bodied 6-cylinder Buicks had rectangular rear windows while those of the 4-cylinder models were oval-shaped.

I.D. DATA: Serial numbers on left side of frame by gas tank and repeated behind left front wheel. Starting: 4-cylinder models 34, 35, 36, 37, 38, 39 — 832673, 6-cylinder models 44, 45, 47, 48, 49, 50, 54, 55 — 871321. Ending: 4-cylinder models — 1051558, 6-cylinder models — 1060176. Engine numbers on left side of crankcase near front of oil filler tube.

1923 Buick, coupe, OCW

Model No.	Body Type & Seating	Price	Weight	Prod. Total
34	2-dr. Rds.-2P	865	2415	5768 (A)
35	4-dr. Tr.-5P	885	2520	36,935 (B)
36	2-dr. Cpe.-3P	1175	2745	7004
37	4-dr. Sed.-5P	1395	2875	8885 (C)
38	2-dr. Tr. Sed.-5P	1325	2750	6025
39	2-dr. Spt. Rds.-2P	1025	2445	1971
41	2-dr. Tr. Sed.-5P	1935	3380	8719
44	2-dr. Rds.-3P	1175	2940	6488 (D)
45	4-dr. Tr.-5P	1195	3085	45,227 (E)
47	4-dr. Sed.-5P	1985	3475	7358
48	2-dr. Cpe.-4P	1895	3440	10,847
49	4-dr. Tr.-7P	1435	3290	5906 (F)
50	4-dr. Sed.-7P	2195	3670	10,279 (G)
54	2-dr. Spt. Rds.-3P	1625	—	4501
55	2-dr. Spt. Tr.-4P	1675	3330	12,857

Note 1: (A) — 8 built for export.
Note 2: (B) — 7004 built for export.
Note 3: (C) — 1 built for export.
Note 4: (D) — 3 built for export.
Note 5: (E) — 47 built for export.
Note 6: (F) — 25 built for export.
Note 7: (G) — 1 built for export.
Note 8: All models carry a 23 prefix i.e. 23-34.

ENGINE: [Series 23-Four] Inline. Ohv. Four. Cast iron block. B & S: 3-3/8 x 4-3/4. Disp.: 170 cu. in. Brake H.P.: 35. N.A.C.C. H.P.: 18.23. Main bearings: 3. Valve lifters: mechanical. Carb.: Marvel K 10-514. [Series 23-Six] Inline Ohv. Six. Cast iron block. B & S: 3-3/8 x 4-1/2. Disp.: 242 cu. in. Brake H.P.: 60. N.A.C.C. H.P.: 27.3. Main bearings: 4. Valve lifters: mechanical. Carb.: Marvel K 10-511.

CHASSIS: [Models 34-39] W.B.: 109 in. Tires: 31 x 4. [Models 44, 45] W.B.: 118 in. Frt/Rear Tread: 56 in. Tires: 32 x 4. [Models 48, 49, 50] W.B.: 124 in. Tires: 33 x 4.5. [Models 54, 55] W.B.: 124 in. Tires: 32 x 4.5.

TECHNICAL: Sliding gear transmission. Speeds: 3F/1R. Floor shift controls. Multiple disc clutch. Shaft drive. Full floating rear axle. Mechanical brakes on two wheels. Wooden spoke wheels with detachable rims.

Note 1: Models 39 & 50 Spt. Rds. and Model 55 Spt. Tr. were offered with either Houk wire or Tuare steel disc wheels as well as wooden.

OPTIONS: Disc wheels. Front bumper. Spotlight. Wind wings. White sidewall tires. Taillights (diamond-shaped). Spare tire cover. Heater (Perfection types AB, GB).

HISTORICAL: Introduced Jan. 1923. Calendar year production: 210,572. Model year production: 181,657. The president of Buick was Harry H. Bassett. A modified Model 54 Series 23-Six was timed at 108.24mph in a run at the Muroc dry lake in California. Buick built its one-millionth car on March 21, 1923.

1923
Series 30, 4-cyl.

	FP	5	4	3	2	1
Rds	865	2800	5700	9500	13,300	19,000
Spt Rds	1025	3000	6000	10,000	14,000	20,000
Tr	885	3000	6000	10,000	14,000	20,000
Cpe	1175	875	1700	4250	5900	8500
Sed	1395	825	1600	4000	5600	8000
Tr Sed	1325	775	1500	3750	5250	7500
Series 40, 6-cyl.						
Rds	1175	3150	6300	10,500	14,700	21,000
Tr	1195	3300	6600	11,000	15,400	22,000
7P Tr	1435	3400	6900	11,500	16,100	23,000
Cpe	1895	875	1700	4350	6050	8700
Sed	1985	850	1650	4100	5700	8200
Master Series 50, 6-cyl.						
Spt Rds	—	3300	6600	11,000	15,400	22,000
Spt Tr	1675	3400	6900	11,500	16,100	23,000
7P Sed	2195	875	1700	4250	5900	8500

1924

1924 Buick 24-Six-55, sport touring, HAC

1924 Buick, model 24-Four-33, 4-pass. coupe, HAC

BUICK — SERIES 24-FOUR — FOUR: The Buicks for 1924 were with the exception of the engine in its 4-cylinder line, new automobiles. With a gently sloping hood and smoothly molded fenders the Buick attracted plenty of attention. With a radiator shell that was extremely close to Packard's familiar pattern it also became the center of controversy that Packard responded to with its "When prettier automobiles are built, Packard will build them."

BUICK — SERIES 24-SIX — SIX: Giving the 6-cylinder models added distinction was their nickel-plated trim and longer 128" wheelbase for some models.

Mechanically, Buick's 1924 models were noted for their 4-wheel mechanical brakes, stronger frames and axles. The 6 cylinder engine had a larger displacement and was equipped with a removable cylinder head and aluminum crankcase. 1924 was the last year for Buick's closed cars to have horizontally divided windshields.

I.D. DATA: Serial numbers on left side of frame by gas tank and repeated behind left front wheel. Starting: Series 24-Four 1060178 & up, Series 24-Six 1064324. Ending: Series 24-Six 1239258. Engine numbers on left side of crank case near front of oil filler tube.

Model No.	Body Type & Seating	Price	Weight	Prod. Total
33	2-dr. Cpe.-4P	1395	2845	5479 (A)
34	2-dr. Rds.-2P	935	2576	4296
35	4-dr. Tr.-5P	965	2680	21,857
37	4-dr. Sed.-5P	1495	2955	6563
41	4-dr. Dbl. Service Sed.-5P	1695	3675	14,094
44	2-dr. Rds.-2P	1275	3300	9700
45	4-dr. Tr.-5P	1295	3455	48,912
47	4-dr. Sed.-5P	2095	3845	10,377
48	2-dr. Cpe.-4P	1995	3770	13,009
49	4-dr. Tr.-7P	1565	3645	7224
50	4-dr. Sed.-7P	2285	4020	9561
50L	4-dr. Limo. Sed.-7P	2385	—	713
51	4-dr. Brgm. Tr. Sed.-5P	2235	3940	4991
54	2-dr. Spt. Rds.-3P	1675	3470	1938
54C	2-dr. Ctry. Clb. Cpe.-3P	1945	3765	1107
55	4-dr. Spt. Tr.-4P	1725	3605	4111
57	4-dr. Twn. Car-7P	2795	3860	25

Note 1: (A) A total of 6087 Buicks of various models and body styles were built for export.
Note 2: All models carry a 24 prefix i.e.: 24-33.

ENGINE: [Models 24-Four] Inline. Ohv. Four. Cast iron block. B & S: 3-3/8 x 4-3/4. Disp.: 170 cu. in. Brake H.P.: 35. N.A.C.C. H.P.: 18.23. Main bearings: 3. Valve lifters: mechanical. Carb.: Marvel K 10-514. [Models 24-Six] Inline. Ohv. Four. Cast iron block. B & S: 3-3/8 x 4-3/4. Disp.: 255 cu. in. Brake H.P.: 70. N.A.C.C. H.P.: 27.3. Main bearings: 4. Valve lifters: mechanical. Carb.: Marvel R 10-578.

CHASSIS: [24-Four] W.B.: 109 in. Tires: 31 x 4. [24-Six Models 41, 44, 45, 46, 47] W.B.: 120 in. Tires: 32 x4. [24-Six Models 48, 49, 50, 51, 54, 55] W.B.: 128 in. Tires: 32 x 4-1/2.

TECHNICAL: Series 24-Four. Sliding gear transmission. Speeds: 3F/1R. Floor shift controls. Multiple disc clutch. Shaft drive. 3/4 floating rear axle. Mechanical brakes on four wheels. Wooden spoke wheels with detachable rim. Series 24-Six. Sliding gear transmission. Speeds: 3F/1R. Floor shift controls. Multiple disc clutch. Shaft drive. Full floating rear axle. Mechanical brakes on four wheels. Wooden spoke wheels with detachable rims.

OPTIONS: Front bumper. Rear bumper. Wind wings. Motometer.

HISTORICAL: Introduced Aug. 1, 1923. Four wheel mechanical brakes. Calendar year production: 160,411. Model year production: 171,561. The president of Buick was Harry H. Bassett.

1924
Standard Series 30, 4-cyl.

	FP	5	4	3	2	1
Rds	935	3150	6300	10,500	14,700	21,000
Tr	965	3300	6600	11,000	15,400	22,000
Cpe	1395	875	1700	4250	5900	8500
Sed	1495	825	1600	4000	5600	8000
Master Series 40, 6-cyl.						
Rds	1275	3150	6300	10,500	14,700	21,000
Tr	1295	3300	6600	11,000	15,400	22,000
7P Tr	1565	3400	6900	11,500	16,100	23,000
Cpe	1995	950	2100	4750	6650	9500
Sed	2095	875	1700	4250	5900	8500
Demi Sed	1695	875	1700	4350	6050	8700
Master Series 50, 6-cyl.						
Spt Rds	1675	3400	6900	11,500	16,100	23,000
Spt Tr	1725	3600	7200	12,000	16,800	24,000
Cabr Cpe	1945	3000	6000	10,000	14,000	20,000
TwnC	2795	1750	4800	8000	11,200	16,000
7P Sed	2285	950	2100	4750	6650	9500
Brgm Sed	2235	1000	2400	5000	7000	10,000
Limo	2385	1075	3000	5500	7700	11,000

1925

1925 Buick, roadster, OCW

1925 Buick, model 25-Six-51, brougham sedan, HAC

BUICK — STANDARD SIX — SIX: Buick adopted a new series designation for 1925 and Standard Six models replaced the 24-Four's as the lower priced Buicks. A new six cylinder engine powered the 9 models of this series all of which were higher priced than their predecessors. A longer, 114.3" wheelbase was used.

BUICK — MASTER SIX — SIX: The Master Six was powered by the same engine used in 1924 by the 24-Six of 1924. Styling changes were extremely modest but several new body styles kept public interest in Buick high. The age of the open tourer as the dominant product of any manufacturer was passing and for the first time Buick's best selling body styles were closed models. An interesting response to the tourer's decline was Buick's introduction of "Enclosed Touring" models in both the Standard and Master series. These cars used normal Touring bodies fitted with permanently fixed tops.

I.D. DATA: Serial numbers on left side of frame by gas tank and repeated behind left front wheel. Starting: Std.-1239259 & up, Master — 1211720 & up. Engine numbers on crankcase on left side near front of oil filler tube.

Standard Six Series

Model No.	Body Type & Seating	Price	Weight	Prod. Total
20	4-dr. C'ch.-5P	1295	3050	21,900
21	4-dr. Dbl. Serivce Sed.-5P	1475	3185	9252
24	2-dr. Rds.-2P	1150	2750	3315
24A	2-dr. Encl. Rds.-2P	1190	2800	1725
24S	2-dr. Spt. Rds.-5P	1250	—	501
25	4-dr. Tr.-5P	1175	2920	16,040
25A	4-dr. Encl. Tr.-5P	1250	2970	4450
25S	4-dr. Spt. Tr.-5P	—	—	651
26	2-dr. Cpe.-2P	1375	2960	4398
26S	2-dr. Spt. Cpe.-4P	—	—	550
27	4-dr. Sed.-5P	1665	3245	10,772
28	2-dr. Cpe.-4P	1565	3075	7743

Master Six Series

Model No.	Body Type & Seating	Price	Weight	Prod. Total
40	2-dr. C'ch.-5P	1495	3560	30,600
44	2-dr. Rds.-2P	1365	3285	2975
44A	2-dr. Encl. Rds.-2P	1400	3335	850
45	4-dr. Tr.-5P	1395	3465	5203
45A	4-dr. Encl. Tr.-5P	1475	3540	1900
47	4-dr. Sed.-5P	2225	3850	4200
47A	4-dr. Encl. Tr.-7P	1475	3540	500
50	4-dr. Sed.-7P	2425	3995	4606
50L	4-dr. Limo.-7P	2525	4030	768
51	4-dr. Brgm. Sed.-5P	2350	3905	6850
54	2-dr. Spt. Rds.-3P	1750	3485	1917
54C	2-dr. Ctry. Clb. Cpe.-3P	2075	3745	2751
55S	2-dr. Spt. Tr.-4P	1800	3550	2774
57	4-dr. Twn. Car-7P	2925	3850	92

Note 1: All models had a 25 prefix i.e.: 25-20.
In addition a total of 9412 Buicks of all models were exported.

ENGINE: [Standard Six] Inline. Ohv. Six. Cast iron block. B & S: 3 x 4-1/2. Disp.: 191 cu. in. Brake H.P.: 50 at 2800 R.P.M. N.A.C.C. H.P.: 21.6. Main bearings: 4. Valve lifters: mechanical. Carb.: Marvel T38. Torque: 120 lbs.-ft. at 1600 R.P.M. [Master Six] Inline. Ohv. Four. Cast iron block. B & S: 3-3/8 x 4-3/4. Disp.: 255 cu. in. Brake H.P.: 70. N.A.C.C. H.P.: 27.3. Main bearings: 4. Valve lifters: mechanical. Carb.: Marvel T4S.

CHASSIS: [Standard Six] W.B.: 114.3 in. Tires: 5.00 x 22. [Master Six] W.B.: 120/128 in. Tires: 32 x 5.77 (6.00 x 22 opt.)

TECHNICAL: Sliding gear transmission. Speeds: 3F/1R. Floor shift controls. Multiple disc clutch. Shaft drive. 3/4 floating-Std. Six, full floating-Master Six. Mechanical brakes on four wheels. Wooden spoke wheels with detachable rims.

OPTIONS: White sidewall tires. Bumpers. Spotlight. Wind wings. Motometer.

HISTORICAL: Introduced Aug. 1924. Vacuum operated windshield wipers replaced hand-powered versions. 1925 was the first model year Buick equipped its car with balloon tires. Calendar year production: 192,100. Model year production: 157,071 plus 9412 for export. The president of Buick was Harry H. Bassett. Buick sent a touring model around the world via a dealer-to-dealer route. Each dealer was responsible for driving the car to the next and having its log book signed. 1925 was the first year Buick used a nitrocellulose lacquer in place of a varnish-color finish process.

1925
Standard Series 20, 6-cyl.

	FP	5	4	3	2	1
Rds	1150	3000	6000	10,000	14,000	20,000
Spt Rds	1250	3150	6300	10,500	14,700	21,000
Encl Rds	1190	3300	6600	11,000	15,400	22,000
Tr	1175	3000	6000	10,000	14,000	20,000
Encl Tr	1250	3150	6300	10,500	14,700	21,000
Bus Cpe	1375	950	2100	4750	6650	9500
Cpe	1475	975	2200	4850	6800	9700
Sed	1665	900	1900	4500	6300	9000
Demi Sed	1695	925	2000	4600	6400	9200

Master Series 40, 6-cyl.

	FP	5	4	3	2	1
Rds	1365	3150	6300	10,500	14,700	21,000
Encl Rds	1460	3300	6600	11,000	15,400	22,000
Tr	1395	3300	6600	11,000	15,400	22,000
Encl Tr	1475	3400	6900	11,500	16,100	23,000
Cpe	2125	1075	3000	5500	7700	11,000
2 dr Sed	1495	950	2100	4750	6650	9500
Sed	2225	975	2200	4850	6800	9700

Master Series 50, 6-cyl.

	FP	5	4	3	2	1
Spt Rds	1750	3400	6900	11,500	16,100	23,000
Spt Tr	1800	3600	7200	12,000	16,800	24,000
Cabr Cpe	2075	3000	6000	10,000	14,000	20,000
7P Sed	2425	1000	2400	5050	7050	10,100
Limo	2525	1025	2600	5200	7200	10,400
Brgm Sed	2350	1025	2600	5200	7200	10,400
TwnC	2925	1650	4650	7750	10,850	15,500

1926 Buick, Standard Six, 2-dr. coupe, HAC

BUICK STANDARD SIX, MASTER SIX — SIX: Both Buick series were restyled for 1926 with smoother radiator edges and on those cars with Fisher bodies, double belt moldings. Hubcaps and the gas filler caps were now constructed of aluminum and a straight tie rod running vertically across the grille supported the headlights.

Technical improvements included new air, oil and gas filters, a stronger clutch and one-piece brake linings. The Buick's new dual-beam headlights were mounted in interchangeable shells. The dimming switch for these lights was mounted in the steering wheel center. Components such as the chassis, drive shaft and rear axle were now of a heavier construction. In addition the Buick chassis had Zerk lubrication fittings.

1926 Buick, Master Six, sedan, JAC

BUICK MASTER SIX — SIX: Engine displacement and power was increased in both series. In addition to their longer wheelbase the Master series models were distinguished from their Standard running mates by such features as a Motometer, scuff plates, clock, cigarette lighter and heater that were included in their base price.

I.D. DATA: Serial numbers on right side of frame behind front wheel position. Starting: Std — 1398244, Master — 1426599. Ending: Std — 1638576, Master — 1638773. Engine numbers on left side of crankcase near front of oil filler tube.

Model No	Body Type & Seating	Price	Weight	Prod. Total
Standard Six Series				
20	2-dr. Sed.-5P	1195	3140	40,113
24	2-dr. Rds.-2P	1125	2865	1891
25	4-dr. Tr.-5P	1150	2920	4859
26	2-dr. Cpe.-2P	1195	3030	10,531
27	2-dr. Sed.-5P	1295	3210	43,375
28	2-dr. Cpe.-4P	1275	3110	8271
Master Six Series				
40	2-dr. Sed.-5P	1395	3655	21,861
44	2-dr. Rds.-2P	1250	3380	2654
45	4-dr. Tr.-5P	1295	3535	2630
47	2-dr. Sed.-5P	1495	3790	53,490
48	2-dr. Cpe.-4P	1795	3845	10,028
49	4-dr. Sed.-5P	1995	—	1
50	4-dr. Sed.-7P	1995	4040	12,690
50T	4-dr. Taxi Cab-7P	—	4040	220
51	4-dr. Brgm. Tr. Sed.-5P	1925	3945	10,873
54	2-dr. Spt. Rds.-3P	1495	3580	2501
54C	2-dr. C.C. Spt. Cpe.-3P	1765	3820	4436
55	4-dr. Spt. Tr.-4P	1525	3650	2051
58	2-dr. Cpe.-4P	1275	—	1

Note 1: All models carry a 26 prefix i.e. 26-20.

ENGINE: [Standard Six] Inline. Ohv. Six. Cast iron block. B & S: 3-1/8 x 4-1/2. Disp.: 207 cu. in. Brake H.P.: 60. N.A.C.C. H.P.: 23.4. Main bearings: 4. Valve lifters: mechanical. Carb.: Marvel T3. Torque: 140. [Master Six] Inline. Ohv. Six. Cast iron block. B & S: 3-1/2 x 4-3/4. Disp.: 274 cu. in. Brake H.P.: 75. N.A.C.C. H.P.: 29.4. Main bearings: 4. Valve lifters: mechanical. Carb.: Marvel T-4. Torque: 178.

CHASSIS: [Standard Six] W.B.: 114.5 in. Tires: 6.00 x 21. [Master Six] W.B.: 120/128 in. Tires: 6.00 x 21.

TECHNICAL: Sliding gear transmission. Speeds: 3F/1R. Floor shift controls. Multiple disc clutch. Shaft drive. 3/4 floating-Std Six, full floating-Master Six. Mechanical brakes on four wheels. Wooden spoke wheels with detachable rims.

OPTIONS: Bumpers. Fog lights. Motometer (Std Six). Running board step plates (Std Six). Instrument panel light. Cadmium rims. White side wall tires.

HISTORICAL: Introduced Aug. 1, 1925. The old combination starter-generator was replaced by separate Delco starter and generator units. Calendar year production: 266,753. Model year production: 240,533 (including 7480 for export and 1 experimental model). On Oct. 17, 1926 Harry Bassett (president of Buick) died of pneumonia. His successor was Edward Thomas Strong.

1926
Standard Series, 6-cyl.

	FP	5	4	3	2	1
Rds	1125	3000	6000	10,000	14,000	20,000
Tr	1150	3150	6300	10,500	14,700	21,000
2P Cpe	1195	1075	3000	5500	7700	11,000
4P Cpe	1275	1000	2400	5000	7000	10,000
2 dr Sed	1195	975	2200	4850	6800	9700
Sed	1295	975	2300	4950	6900	9900
Master Series, 6-cyl.						
Rds	1250	3300	6600	11,000	15,400	22,000
Tr	1295	3400	6900	11,500	16,100	23,000
Spt Rds	1495	3400	6900	11,500	16,100	23,000
Spt Tr	1525	3600	7200	12,000	16,800	24,000
4P Cpe	1275	1075	3000	5500	7700	11,000
Spt Cpe	1295	1150	3600	6000	8400	12,000
2 dr Sed	1295	1000	2400	5000	7000	10,000
4 dr Sed	1395	1025	2600	5250	7300	10,500
Brgm	1925	1050	2700	5350	7450	10,700
7P Sed	1995	1125	3450	5750	8050	11,500

1927

1927 Buick, 4-dr. sedan, OCW

1927 Buick, Standard Six, sport roadster, HAC

BUICK — STANDARD SIX — SIX: The appearance of both Buick lines was left almost unaltered for 1927. All open models in both series had one piece windshields and a reorganized dash which placed the speedometer directly before the driver and provided dashboard lighting on all models.

Technical advancements were headlined by new motor mounts, a counter balanced crankshaft, a "vacuum ventilation" for the crankcase, and a torsional balancer which enabled Buick to describe its engines as "Vibrationless Beyond Belief". The Standard Six models continued to have gas tank mounted fuel gauges.

BUICK MASTER SIX — SIX: Master Six Models on the 128'' wheelbase chassis had a Gothic Goddess radiator cap replete with wings. This ornament was also fitted to Models 24 and 25 of the Standard Six series. Master Six closed car interiors were finished in walnut, satin and broadcloth. With the exception of the 3 lowest priced Models 40, 47 and 48, the Master Six Buicks featured new dash-mounted fuel gauges.

I.D. DATA: Serial numbers on right side of frame behind front wheel position. Starting: Std. Six Ser.-1638800, Master Six Ser.-1661435. Engine numbers on crankcase on left side near front of oil filler tube.

Model No.	Body Type & Seating	Price	Weight	Prod. Total
Standard Six Series				
20	2-dr. Sed.-5P	1195	3215	33,190
24	2-dr. Spt. Rds.-4P	1195	2990	4985
25	4-dr. DeL. Spt. Tr.-5P	1225	3040	3272
26	2-dr. Cpe.-2P	1195	3110	10,512
26S	2-dr. Ctry. Clb. Cpe.-4P	1275	3190	11,688
26CC	2-dr. Clp. Top. Cpe.-4P	—	3200	1
27	4-dr. Sed.-5P	1295	3300	40,272
28	2-dr. Cpe.-4P	1275	3190	7178
29	4-dr. Twn. Brgm. Sed.-5P	1375	3305	11,032
Master Six Series				
40	4-dr. Sed.-5P	1395	3750	12,130
47	4-dr. Sed.-5P	1495	3870	49,105
48	2-dr. Cpe.-4P	1465	3800	9350
50	4-dr. Sed.-7P	1995	4115	11,259
50T	4-dr. Taxi Cab.-7P	—	—	60
51	4-dr. Brgm. Sed.-5P	1925	4050	13,862
54	2-dr. DeL. Spt. Rds.-4P	1495	3655	4310
54C	2-dr. Ctry. Clb. Cpe.-4P	1765	3905	7095
54CC	2-dr. Conv. Cpe.-4P	1925	3915	2354
55	4-dr. DeL. Spt. Tr.-4P	1525	3735	2092
58	2-dr. Cpe.-5P	1850	3940	7655

ENGINE: [Standard Six] Inline. Ohv. Six. Cast iron block. B & S: 3-1/8 x 4-1/2. Disp.: 207 cu. in. Brake H.P.: 63 @ 2800 R.P.M. N.A.C.C. H.P.: 23.4. Main bearings: 4. Valve lifters: mechanical. Carb.: Marvel T3. Torque: 140. [Master Six] Inline. Ohv. Six. Cast iron block. B & S: 3-1/2 x 4-3/4. Disp.: 274 cu. in. Brake H.P.: 75. N.A.C.C. H.P.: 29.4. Main bearings: 4. Valve lifters: mechanical. Carb.: Marvel T4. Torque: 178.

CHASSIS: [Standard Six] W.B.: 114.5 in. Tires: 33 x 6. [Master Six] W.B.: 120/128 in. Tires: 33 x 6.

TECHNICAL: Sliding gear transmission. Speeds: 3F/1R. Floor shift controls. Multiple disc clutch. Shaft drive. 3/4 floating rear axle - Std Six, full floating rear axle - Master Six. Mechanical brakes on four wheels. Wooden spoke wheels with detachable rims.

OPTIONS: Bumpers. Trunk.

HISTORICAL: Introduced August 1926. Calendar year production: 255,160. Model year production: 250,116 (includes 8109 for export). The president of Buick was Edward Thomas Strong. The two-millionth Buick was produced on November 1, 1927.

1927
Series 115, 6-cyl.

	FP	5	4	3	2	1
Rds	1195	3150	6300	10,500	14,700	21,000
Tr	1225	3300	6600	11,000	15,400	22,000
2P Cpe	1195	1075	3000	5500	7700	11,000
4P RS Cpe	1275	1150	3600	6000	8400	12,000
Spt Cpe	1275	1125	3450	5750	8050	11,500
2 dr Sed	1195	950	2100	4750	6650	9500
4 dr Sed	1295	975	2200	4850	6800	9700
Brgm	1375	1000	2400	5000	7000	10,000
Series 120, 6-cyl.						
4P Cpe	1465	1200	3750	6250	8750	12,500
2 dr Sed	1395	975	2200	4850	6800	9700
4 dr Sed	1495	1000	2400	5000	7000	10,000
Series 128, 6-cyl.						
Spt Rds	1495	3600	7200	12,000	16,800	24,000
Spt Tr	1525	3750	7500	12,500	17,500	25,000
Conv	1925	3150	6300	10,500	14,700	21,000
5P Cpe	1850	1150	3600	6000	8400	12,000
Spt Cpe RS	1765	1250	3900	6500	9100	13,000
7P Sed	1995	1025	2600	5250	7300	10,500
Brgm	1925	1075	3000	5500	7700	11,000

1928

1928 Buick, opera coupe, DM

BUICK STANDARD SIX — SERIES 115 — SIX: Buick's styling for 1928 featured thinner windshield and corner posts (on closed models) standard hood emblems and smooth-surfaced fenders. The older, barrel-shaped headlight cases gave way to bullet-shaped versions which along with the radiator, windshield molding and hood fasteners, were nickel-plated. Giving the Buick a new face was a smoother radiator shell which shed almost all that had remained of its Packard-look.

A new stronger, double-drop frame with deeper side channels allowed body height to be reduced by 3 inches. A noteworthy improvement in handling and roadability was attained by the use of 4-wheel Lovejoy hydraulic shock absorbers on all models. Engine changes for 1928 were highlighted by reshaped hemispherical combustion chambers.

Interior improvements were lead by Buick's adoption of the standard H-shift pattern, an adjustable steering column and dash-mounted engine temperature and fuel level gauges. Plush mohair was used for the upholstery.

Also added to the Buick's standard equipment list for 1928 were Wolverine bumpers. All Standard Six models had dash-mounted gas gauges and painted headlight shells. The exceptions to the latter were Models 24 and 25 which had chromed shells.

BUICK MASTER SIX — SERIES 120 — SIX: A new DeLuxe 4-door Sedan was added to the Master Six line while Models 54CC (Convertible Coupe) and 40 (2 door Sedan) were eliminated. The 4-door Sport Touring Master Six was the only Buick offered with standard side mounts. All Master Six models had chromed headlight shells. A new model on the 120'' wheelbase chassis was the 47S, 5-passenger DeLuxe Sedan. Its back was leather trimmed and was fitted with side landau hinges. Interiors were finished in Taupe and Green figured-design mohair plush. All closed models in both series had wide doors, new outside door handles and rear compartment carpets. The Master Six Buicks on the 128'' wheelbase has a 128 Series designation.

I.D. DATA: Serial numbers on right side of frame behind front wheel opening. Starting: Std. Six — 1901476, Master Six — 1911026. Ending: Std. Six — 2137872, Master Six — 2169650. Engine numbers on crankcase.

Model No.	Body Type & Seating	Price	Weight	Prod. Total
Std Six Series				
20	2-dr. Sed.-5P	1195	3310	32,481
24	2-dr. Spt. Rds.-4P	1195	3090	4513
25	4-dr. Spt. Tr.-5P	1225	3140	3134
26	2-dr. Cpe.-2P	1195	3215	12,417
26S	2-dr. Ctry. Clb. Cpe.-4P	1275	3300	13,211
27	4-dr. Sed.-5P	1295	3370	50,224
29	4-dr. Twn. Brgm.-5P	1375	3400	10,840
Master Six Series				
47	4-dr. Sed.-5P	1495	3920	34,197
47S	4-dr. DeL. Sed.-5P	1575	3930	16,398
48	2-dr. Cpe.-4P	1465	3835	9002
49	4-dr. Tr.-7P	NA	NA	2
50	4-dr. Sed.-7P	1995	4085	10,827
51	4-dr. Brgm. Sed.-5P	1925	3980	10,258
54	2-dr. Spt. Rds.-4P	1495	3655	3853
54C	2-dr. Ctry. Clb. Cpe.-4P	1765	3890	6555
55	4-dr. Spt. Tr.-5P	1525	3735	1333
58	2-dr. Cpe.-5P	1850	3925	9984

Note 1: All models carry a 28 prefix, i.e. 28-20.

ENGINE: [Standard Six] Inline. Ohv. Six. Cast iron block. B & S: 3-1/8 x 4-1/2. Disp.: 207 cu. in. Brake H.P.: 63 @ 2800 R.P.M. N.A.C.C. H.P.: 23.44. Main bearings: 4. Valve lifters: mechanical. Carb.: Marvel T3. Torque: 140. [Master Six] Inline. Ohv. Six. Cast iron block. B & S: 3-1/2 x 4-3/4. Disp.: 274 cu. in. Brake H.P.: 77 @ 2800 R.P.M. N.A.C.C. H.P.: 29.4. Main bearings: 4. Valve lifters: mechanical. Carb.: Marvel T4. Torque: 178.

CHASSIS: [Standard Six] W.B.: 114.5 in. Tires: 31 x 5.25. [Master Six] W.B.: 120 in. (Models 47 and 47S only). Tires: 33 x 6.00. (Models 50, 51, 54, 54C, 55 and 58): W.B.: 128 in. Tires: 33 x 6.

TECHNICAL: Sliding gear transmission. Speeds: 3F/1R. Floor shift controls. Multiple disc clutch. Shaft drive. 3/4 floating rear axle — (Std Six) full floating rear axle — (Master Six). Overall Drive Ratio: Models 20, 27, 29 — 5.1:1. Models 48, 54, 54C, 55, 58 — 4.72:1. Models 24, 25, 26, 26S, 47, 47S, 50, 51 — 4.9:1. Mechanical brakes on four wheels. Wooden spoke wheels with detachable rims.

OPTIONS: Buffalo wire wheels (Std Six Models 24 & 25 and 128'' wheelbase Master Six models only). Dual tire carrier. Motometer.

HISTORICAL: Introduced July 28, 1927. Calendar year production: 221,758. Model year production: 235,009 (including 5194 for export). The president of Buick was Edward Thomas Strong. A 1928 model coupe produced in November 1927 was the two-millionth Buick built.

1928 Buick, roadster, OCW

1928

Series 115, 6-cyl.	FP	5	4	3	2	1
Rds	1195	3150	6300	10,500	14,700	21,000
Tr	1225	3300	6600	11,000	15,400	22,000
2P Cpe	1195	1075	3000	5500	7700	11,000
Spt Cpe	1275	1125	3450	5750	8050	11,500
2 dr Sed	1195	950	2100	4750	6650	9500
4 dr Sed	1295	975	2200	4850	6800	9700
Brgm	1375	1000	2400	5000	7000	10,000
Series 120, 6-cyl.						
Cpe	1465	1200	3750	6250	8750	12,500
4 dr Sed	1495	1000	2400	5000	7000	10,000
Brgm	1575	1025	2600	5250	7300	10,500
Series 128, 6-cyl.						
Spt Rds	1495	3750	7500	12,500	17,500	25,000
Spt Tr	1525	3900	7800	13,000	18,200	26,000
5P Cpe	1765	1150	3600	6000	8400	12,000
Spt Cpe	1850	1250	3900	6500	9100	13,000
7P Sed	1995	1075	3000	5500	7700	11,000
Brgm	1925	1125	3450	5750	8050	11,500

1929

1929 Buick, series 129, model 58, coupe, JAC

1929 Buick, series 129, model 57, sedan, JAC

BUICK — SERIES 116 — SIX: The 1929 Buicks were the first cars styled in their entirety by General Motors Art and Colour department. Three new series the 116, 121 and 129 (which represented wheelbase measurements) replaced the older Standard and Master Six designations and all were fitted with the body form that earned them the label of Pregnant Buicks. This non-complimentary label was due to the 1-1/2'' body bulge below the beltline.

Aside from this feature which lasted only for one year the 1929 Buicks had slightly slanted windshields on closed body models and a radiator bearing the Buick nameplate in its center rather than on the shell. Major technical improvements included (on closed models) dual electric windshield wipers and side cowl ventilators.

Buick was also celebrating its silver anniversary with a total of 43 exterior color options. Standard in all models was a mechanical fuel pump in place of the vacuum tank.

The chassis' design of all three series was, with the exception of the external mechanical brakes, virtually all new. The frame was constructed of thicker steel with deeper cross sections and key suspension components were strengthened. Lovejoy shock absorbers were also installed. All engines were increased both in terms of displacement and power and steel-backed main bearings were also used by Buick for the first time.

The 116'' wheelbase chassis Buick now featured interiors with ashtrays and cigarette lighters as standard equipment.

1929 Buick, series 121, model 44, sport roadster, JAC

BUICK — SERIES 121 — SIX: Offered in 6 styles, the 121 Series Buick shared its walnut interior trim with all 1929 Buicks. Also common to all Buicks was a new molded rubber steering wheel.

1929 Buick, series 129, model 51, sport sedan, JAC

BUICK — SERIES 129 — SIX: Eight body styles all on the 129'' wheelbase were available in this series. The optional bumpers now consisted of 3 rather than 2 horizontal bars.

I.D. DATA: Serial numbers on right side of frame behind front fender opening. Starting: 2123926. Ending: 2313805. Engine numbers on crankcase. Starting: Ser. 116-22225361, Ser. 121,129-2340300.

Model No.	Body Type & Seating	Price	Weight	Prod. Total
Series 116				
20	2-dr. Sed.-5P	1220	3525	17,783
25	4-dr. Tr.-5P	1225	3330	2938
26	2-dr. Bus. Cpe.-2P	1195	3465	8745
26S	2-dr. Spt. Cpe. R/S-4P	1250	3520	10,308
27	4-dr. Sed.-5P	1320	3630	44,345
Series 121				
41	4-dr. Cl. C. Sed.-5P	1450	4180	10,110
44	2-dr. Spt. Rds.-4P	1325	3795	6195
46	2-dr. Bus. Cpe.-2P	1395	3990	4339
46S	2-dr. Spt. Cpe. R./S.-4P	1450	4055	6638
47	4-dr. Sed.-5P	1520	4175	30,356
48	2-dr. Cpe.-4P	1445	4010	4255

Model No.	Body Type & Seating	Price	Weight	Prod. Total
Series 129				
49	4-dr. Tr.-7P	1550	3990	1530
50	4-dr. Sed.-7P	2045	4360	8058
50L	4-dr. Imp. Sed. Limo.-7P	2145	4405	736
51	4-dr. Spt. Sed.	1875	4230	7014
54CC	2-dr. DeL. Conv. Cpe.-4P	1875	4085	2021
55	4-dr. Spt. Tr.-5P	1525	3905	1122
57	4-dr. Sed.-5P	1935	4260	5175
58	2-dr. Cpe.-5P	1865	4145	734

Note 1: All models carry a 29 prefix, i.e.: 29-20

ENGINE: [Series 116] Inline. Ohv. Six. Cast iron block. B & S: 3-5/16 x 4-5/8. Disp.: 239.1 cu. in. C.R.: 4.3:1. Brake H.P.: 94 at 2800 R.P.M. Taxable H.P.: 26.3. Main bearings: 4. Valve lifters: mechanical. Carb.: Marvel 3-jet, updraft T3-10-704. Torque: 172 lbs.-ft. at 1200 R.P.M. [Series 121, 129] Inline. Ohv. Six. Cast iron block. B & S: 3-5/8 x 5. Disp.: 309.6 cu. in. C.R.: 4.3:1. Brake H.P.: 91. N.A.C.C. H.P.: 31.5. Main bearings: 4. Valve lifters: mechanical. Carb.: Marvel 3-jet updraft T4-10-706.

CHASSIS: [Series 116] W.B.: 116 in. O.L.: 167-3/4 in. Height: 74-7/8 in. Frt/Rear Tread: 56-7/16 in./58 in. Tires: 30 x 5.50. [Series 121] W.B.: 121 in. Frt/Rear Tread: 56-7/16 in./58 in. Tires: 30 x 6.5. [Series 129] W.B.: 129 in. Frt/Rear Tread: 56-7/16 in./58 in. Tires: 32 x 6.50.

TECHNICAL: Sliding gear transmission. Speeds: 3F/1R. Floor shift controls. Multiple disc clutch. Shaft drive. Ser. 116-3/4 floating rear axle — all others — full floating rear axle. Overall Drive Ratio: 4.9:1. Mechanical external contracting brakes on four wheels. Wooden spoke wheels with detachable rims. Rim size: 20 in.

OPTIONS: Front bumper. Rear bumper. Clock. Welled fenders, side mounts. Wide-spoke artillery. Wire wheels. Step plates. Spare tire, tube. Spare tire cover. Spare tire lock. Disc wheels.

HISTORICAL: Introduced July 29, 1928. Calendar year production: 196,104. Model year production: 187,861 (includes 8932 cars built for export). The president of Buick was Edward Thomas Strong.

1929
Series 116, 6-cyl.

	FP	5	4	3	2	1
Spt Tr	1225	4350	8700	14,500	20,300	29,000
Bus Cpe	1195	1200	3750	6250	8750	12,500
RS Cpe	1250	1400	4200	7000	9800	14,000
2 dr Sed	1220	975	2200	4850	6800	9700
4 dr Sed	1320	1000	2400	5000	7000	10,000
Series 121, 6-cyl.						
Spt Rds	1325	4950	9900	16,500	23,100	33,000
Bus Cpe	1395	1400	4200	7000	9800	14,000
RS Cpe	1450	1550	4500	7500	10,500	15,000
4P Cpe	1445	1400	4200	7000	9800	14,000
4 dr Sed	1520	1025	2600	5250	7300	10,500
CC Sed	1450	1050	2700	5350	7450	10,700
Series 129, 6-cyl.						
Conv	1875	4200	8400	14,000	19,600	28,000
Spt Tr	1525	4650	9300	15,500	21,700	31,000
7P Tr	1550	4500	9000	15,000	21,000	30,000
5P Cpe	1865	1150	3600	6000	8400	12,000
CC Sed	1875	1150	3600	6000	8400	12,000
7P Sed	2045	1075	3000	5500	7700	11,000
Limo	2145	1250	3900	6500	9100	13,000

1930

1930 Buick, series 40, model 46S, sport coupe, JAC

BUICK — SERIES 40 — SIX: The Buicks for 1930 appeared as handsome and graceful as the 1929 models had been bulbous. As one observer noted, ''the cars retain the Buick individuality without . . . the bulge.'' A new vertically mounted, thermostatically controlled shutter system gave the Buick's radiator a long racy appearance. More importantly a height reduction of 2'' and a new around the body belt line worked visual wonders in the Buick's appearance. Also contributing to the Buick's more modern styling were flatter hubcaps for the increasingly popular wire wheel option.

The Series 40 Buicks replaced the Series 116 and were mounted on a longer 118'' wheelbase. Interiors carried rubber floor mats.

1930 Buick, series 50, model 57, sedan, JAC

BUICK — SERIES 50 — SIX: Series 50 models which replaced the Series 121 all had wheelbases of 124'' plus fully carpeted interiors as did the Series 60 Buicks.

1930 Buick, series 60, model 64, sport roadster, JAC

BUICK — SERIES 60 — SIX: Both the 132'' wheelbase Series 60 and the Series 50 shared a 331.5cid engine for 1931. All Buicks had a new dash panel with the instruments both directly and indirectly lighted. Beginning on Jan 1, 1930 a new sport roadster with rumble seat, model 30-64 was added to Series 60.

I.D. DATA: Serial numbers on right side of frame behind front fender opening. Starting: Series 40 — 2313806, Series 50, 60 — 2334956. Ending: Series 40 — 2459715, Series 50, 60 — 2460543. Engine numbers on crankcase. Starting: Series 40 — 2439593, Series 50, 60 — 2489593. Ending: Series 40 — 2568138, Series 50, 60 — 2613337.

Model No. Series 40	Body Type & Seating	Price	Weight	Prod. Total
40	2-dr. Sed.-5P	1270	3600	6101
44	2-dr. Spt. Rds.-4P	1310	3420	3476
45	4-dr. Phae.-5P	1310	3410	972
46	2-dr. Bus. Cpe.-2P	1260	3540	5695
46S	2-dr. Sp. Cpe.-4P	1300	3600	10,719
47	4-dr. Sed.-5P	1330	3700	47,294
Series 50				
57	4-dr. Sed.-5P	1540	4235	22,929
58	2-dr. Cpe.-4P	1510	4120	5275
Series 60				
60	4-dr. Sed.-7P	1910	4415	6583
60L	4-dr. Limo.-7P	2070	4475	690
61	4-dr. Sp. Sed.-5P	1760	4330	12,508
64	2-dr. Spt. Rds.-4P	1585	4015	2006
64C	2-dr. DeL. Cpe.-4P	1695	4225	5370
68	2-dr. Cpe.-4P	1740	4200	10,216
69	4-dr. Phae.-7P	1595	4100	807

Note 1: All models carry a 30 prefix, i.e. 30-40.

ENGINE: [Series 40] Inline. Ohv. Six. Cast iron block. B & S: 3-7/16 x 4-5/8. Disp.: 257.5 cu. in. Brake H.P.: 80.5 @ 2800 R.P.M. N.A.C.C. H.P.: 28.39. Main bearings: 4. Valve lifters: mechanical. Carb.: Marvel T3S-10-758. [Series 50, 60] Inline. Ohv. Six. Cast iron block. B & S: 3-3/4 x 5. Disp.: 331.4 cu. in. Brake H.P.: 99 @ 2800 R.P.M. N.A.C.C. H.P.: 33.75. Main bearings: 4. Valve lifters: mechanical. Carb.: Marvel T4-10-754.

CHASSIS: [Series 40] W.B.: 118 in. Tires: 29 x 5.50. [Series 50] W.B.: 124 in. Frt/Rear Tread: 56-7/8 in. / 58 in. Tires: 31 x 6.50. [Series 60] W.B.: 132 in. Frt/Rear Tread: 56-7/8 in. / 58 in. Tires: 19 x 6.50.

TECHNICAL: Sliding gear transmission. Speeds: 3F/1R. Floor shift controls. Multiple disc clutch. Shaft drive. 3/4 floating rear axle. Mechanical, internal expanding brakes on four wheels. Wooden spoke wheels with detachable rims.

OPTIONS: Wire wheels. Chrome grille guard. Side mounts. White sidewall tires. Luggage rack. Fog lights. Wind wings.

HISTORICAL: Introduced July 28, 1929. Calendar year production: 119,265. Model year production: 181,743 (including 6098 stripped chassis and cars for export.) The president of Buick was Edward Thomas Strong. Entered at Indianapolis was a Buick 6 powered car, The Butchers Brothers Special, which was credited with a 14th place finish.

1930
Series 40, 6-cyl.

	FP	5	4	3	2	1
Rds	1310	4500	9000	15,000	21,000	30,000
Phae	1310	4650	9300	15,500	21,700	31,000
Bus Cpe	1260	1150	3600	6000	8400	12,000
RS Cpe	1300	1550	4500	7500	10,500	15,000
2 dr Sed	1270	1075	3000	5500	7700	11,000
4 dr Sed	1330	1125	3450	5750	8050	11,500
Series 50, 6-cyl.						
4P Cpe	1510	1400	4200	7000	9800	14,000
4 dr Sed	1540	1150	3600	6000	8400	12,000
Series 60, 6-cyl.						
RS Rds	1585	4650	9300	15,500	21,700	31,000
7P Tr	1595	4700	9450	15,750	22,050	31,500
RS Spt Cpe	1695	2000	5100	8500	11,900	17,000
5P Cpe	1740	1650	4650	7750	10,850	15,500
4 dr Sed	1540	1150	3600	6000	8400	12,000
7P Sed	1910	1200	3750	6250	8750	12,500
Limo	2070	1250	3900	6500	9100	13,000

1930 Marquette, touring, OCW

1930 MARQUETTE — SIX: The Marquette, which was offered only for the 1930 model year represented a combination of Oldsmobile styling and engineering with a number of traditional Buick features. For several years Buick production had been declining. With the impact of the depression becoming more severe Buick decided to produce an economy car to shore up its position.

The Marquette's appearance was contemporary with thin vertical hood louvers and a radiator shell similar to Buick's but with angled ''Herring Bone'' bars. However its L-head six cylinder engine was definitely out of step with Buick design philosophy. Nonetheless the Marquette could make a good account of itself in acceleration, having the ability to travel from 5 to 25 mph in 8.8 seconds and from 10 to 60 mph in 31 seconds.

However with Buick planning an all-eight cylinder line for 1931 the Marquette really didn't have a future as a Buick product and thus it was manufactured only as a 1930 model.

I.D. DATA: Serial numbers on frame beneath left front fender. Starting: 10000. Ending: 52998. Engine numbers on crankcase. Starting: 10000. Ending: 48450.

Model No.	Body Type & Seating	Price	Weight	Prod. Total
30	2-dr. Sed.-5P	1000	2850	4630
34	2-dr. Spt. Rds.-4P	1020	2640	2397
35	4-dr. Phae.-5P	1020	2670	889
36	2-dr. Bus. Cpe.-2P	990	2760	2475
36S	2-dr. Sp. Cpe.-4P	1020	2760	4384
37	4-dr. Sed.-5P	1060	2925	15,795

Note 1: All models carried a 30 prefix i.e.: 30-30

ENGINE: Inline. L-head. Six. Cast iron block. B & S: 3-1/8 x 4-5/8. Disp.: 212.8 cu. in. Brake H.P.: 67.5 at 3000 R.P.M. N.A.C.C. H.P.: 23.4. Main bearings: 4. Valve lifters: mechanical. Carb.: Marvel.

CHASSIS: W.B. 114 in. Tires: 28 x 5.25.

TECHNICAL: Sliding gear transmission. Speeds: 3F/1R. Floor shift controls. Single plate clutch. Shaft drive. Semi-floating rear axle. Overall Ratio: 4.5:1. Mechanical brakes on four wheels. Wooden spoke wheels.

OPTIONS: Wire wheels. Side mounts. Demountable wood wheels. Trunk rack.

HISTORICAL: Calendar year production: 35,007. Model year production: 35,007 (including 4,437 stripped chassis and cars for export). The president of Buick was Edward Thomas Strong. The Marquette took part in a number of performance trials including a 778 mile run from Death Valley to Pikes Peak in 40 hours, 45 minutes.

1930 MARQUETTE
Marquette - Series 30, 6-cyl.

	FP	5	4	3	2	1
Spt Rds	1020	3750	7500	12,500	17,500	25,000
Phae	1029	3900	7800	13,000	18,200	26,000
Bus Cpe	990	1025	2600	5250	7300	10,500
RS Cpe	1020	1075	3000	5500	7700	11,000
2 dr Sed	1000	950	2100	4750	6650	9500
4 dr Sed	1060	975	2200	4850	6800	9700

1931

1931 Buick, series 90, model 96, coupe, OCW

BUICK — SERIES 50 — EIGHT: Buick's styling was all but unchanged (the only observable difference was a radiator cap bearing a figure 8) but that hardly mattered since three new straight-eight engines were introduced for 1931. None of these engines shared any interchangeable parts and the smallest, displacing 220 cubic inches was used for the Series 40 which had the same 114'' wheelbase of the discontinued Marquette.

The Series 50 interior was equipped with either mohair or cloth upholstery, carpeting for the rear seat floor area, dome lights and arm rests. A rear foot rail was provided as was an adjustable driver's seat. Midway through the model year the Series 50 received the synchromesh transmission previously available only on the more costly Buicks. Also appearing as a mid-season offering was a new convertible coupe model.

BUICK — SERIES 60 — EIGHT: In Buick's new lineup the Series 60 corresponded to the old Series 40 models with a 118'' wheelbase and a 272cid engine. Their interior of either mohair plush or cloth was of higher quality than that of the Series 50. Open models were finished in a leather interior. All Series 60, 80 and 90 Buicks closed cars had a std equipment passenger-side windshield wiper.

BUICK — SERIES 80 — EIGHT: Only 2 models were offered in this series with a 124'' wheelbase and 344cid engine. As were all 1930 Buicks, the Series 80's had a revamped instrument panel, lower front seats with deeper cushions and a new cooling system with thermostatically controlled shutters.

1931 Buick, series 90, model 94, sport roadster, JAC

BUICK — SERIES 90 — EIGHT: The Series 90 Buick was powered by the 344cid engine and had a wheelbase of 132''. Closed car interiors had mohair plush interiors with silk roller shades for the rear side and back windows; full floor carpeting was provided. The convertible coupe which had a mid-season introduction had a leather interior as did the other open-model Series 90 Buicks.

I.D. DATA: Serial numbers on right side of frame behind front fender opening. Starting: 2460544. Ending: 2602731. Engine numbers on crank case. Starting: 2624638. Ending: 2751921.

Model No.	Body Type & Seating	Price	Weight	Prod. Total
Series 50				
50	2-dr. Sed.-5P	1035	3145	3616
54	2-dr. Spt. Rds.-4P	1055	2935	907
55	4-dr. Phae.-5P	1055	2970	358
56	2-dr. Bus. Cpe.	1025	3055	2782
56C	2-dr. Conv. Cpe.-4P	1095	3095	1531
56S	2-dr. Sp. Cpe.-4P	1055	3155	5733
57	4-dr. Sed.-5P	1095	3265	33,184
Series 60				
64	2-dr. Spt. Rds.-4P	1335	3465	1050
65	4-dr. Phae.-5P	1335	3525	463
66	2-dr. Bus. Cpe.-2P	1285	3615	2732

Model No.	Body Type & Seating	Price	Weight	Prod. Total
66S	2-dr. Sp. Cpe.-4P	1325	3695	6489
67	4-dr. Sed.-5P	1355	3795	30,665
Series 80				
86	2-dr. Cpe.-4P	1535	4120	3579
87	4-dr. Sed.-5P	1565	4255	14,731
Series 90				
90	4-dr. Sed.-7P	1935	4435	4159
90L	4-dr. Limo.-7P	2035	4505	514
91	4-dr. Sed.-5P	1785	4340	7853
94	2-dr. Spt. Rds.-4P	1610	4010	824
95	4-dr. Phae.-7P	1620	4125	392
96	2-dr. Cpe.-5P	1765	4260	7705
96C	2-dr. Conv. Cpe.-4P	1785	4195	1066
96S	2-dr. Ctry. Club. Cpe.-4P	1720	4250	2990

ENGINE: [Series 50] Inline. Ohv. Eight. Cast iron block. B & S: 2-7/8 x 4-1/4. Disp.: 220.7 cu. in. C.R.: 4.75:1. Brake H.P.: 77 at 3200 R.P.M. N.A.C.C. H.P.: 26.45. Main bearings: 5. Valve lifters: mechanical. Carb.: 2 barrel Marvel updraft T-3-10-894. Torque (Compression): 156 lbs.-ft. at 1600 R.P.M. [Series 60] Inline. Ohv. Eight. Cast iron block. B & S: 3-1/16 x 5. Disp.: 272.6 cu. in. C.R.: 4.63:1. Brake H.P.: 90 at 3000 R.P.M. N.A.C.C. H.P.: 30.02. Main bearings: 5. Valve lifters: mechanical. Carb.: Marvel TD25-10-795, late 1931 TD-25-10-983. Torque: 200 lbs.-ft. 43.5 @ 1600 R.P.M. [Series 80, 90] Inline. Ohv. Eight. Cast iron block. B & S: 3-5/16 x 5. Disp.: 344.8 cu. in. C.R.: 4.5:1. Brake H.P.: 104 at 2800 R.P.M. N.A.C.C. H.P.: 35.12. Main bearings: 5. Valve lifters: mechanical. Carb.: Marvel TD-3 10-796, late 1931 TD-3 10-984. Torque: 250 lbs.-ft. at 1400 R.P.M.

CHASSIS: [Series 50] W.B.: 114 in. Frt/Rear Tread: 56-1/2 in./57 in. Tires: 18 x 5.25. [Series 60] W.B.: 118 in. Length: 175. Height: 72. Frt/Rear Tread: 56-3/4 in./58 in. Tires: 19 x 6.50. [Series 80] W.B.: 124 in. Frt/Rear Tread: 56-7/8 in./58 in. Tires: 19 x 6.50. [Series 90] W.B.: 132 in. Frt/Rear Tread: 56-7/8 in./58 in. Tires: 19 x 6.50.

TECHNICAL: Sliding gear, synchromesh transmission (Series 60, 80, 90). Speeds: 3F/1R. Floor shift controls. Ser. 50, 60 — single dry plate, Ser. 80, 90 — double dry plate clutch. Shaft drive. 3/4 floating rear axle, Ser. 50 — semi-floating rear axle. Overall Drive Ratio: Ser. 60-4.5:1, Ser. 80, 90 — 4.5:1, 4.18:1. Mechanical brakes on four wheels. Wooden spoke wheels on demountable rims. Ser. 50 — 18 x 4, Ser. 60, 19 x 4, Ser. 80, 90 — 19 x 4-1/2.

OPTIONS: Front bumper. Rear Bumper. Dual sidemount. Heater (two types, hot water and exhaust pipe types). Clock. Side mounts. Side mount covers (metal and wood). Trunk cover. Demountable wire wheels. Grille guard. Luggage rack. White side walls. Wind wings. Gravel deflectors.

HISTORICAL: Introduced July 26, 1930. The Buick 8-cylinder engines were equipped with an oil temperature regulator that cooled the oil at high speeds and warmed it in cold weather. Calendar year production: 88,417. Model year production: 138,965 (including 5642 stripped chassis and cars for export). The president of Buick was Edward Thomas Strong. The Butcher Brothers Special with a Buick 8 crashed at Indianapolis after 6 laps of racing. The Shafer 8 powered by a 272cid Buick engine qualified for the 500 at a speed of 105.103mph and finished in 12th place.

1931 Buick, series 50, model 56S, special coupe, OCW

1931

Series 50, 8-cyl.	FP	5	4	3	2	1
Spt Rds	1055	4650	9300	15,500	21,700	31,000
Phae	1055	4700	9450	15,750	22,050	31,500
Bus Cpe	1025	1750	4800	8000	11,200	16,000
RS Cpe	1055	2000	5100	8500	11,900	17,000
2 dr Sed	1035	1150	3600	6000	8400	12,000
4 dr Sed	1095	1200	3750	6250	8750	12,500
Conv	1095	4200	8400	14,000	19,600	28,000
Series 60, 8-cyl.						
Spt Rds	1335	4950	9900	16,500	23,100	33,000
Phae	1335	5000	10,050	16,750	23,450	33,500
Bus Cpe	1285	1750	4800	8000	11,200	16,000
RS Cpe	1325	2000	5100	8500	11,900	17,000
4 dr Sed	1355	1250	3900	6500	9100	13,000
Series 80, 8-cyl.						
Cpe	1535	2900	5850	9750	13,650	19,500
4 dr Sed	1565	1750	4800	8000	11,200	16,000
7P Sed	—	1400	4200	7000	9800	14,000
Series 90, 8-cyl.						
Spt Rds	1610	7650	15,300	25,500	35,700	51,000
7P Tr	1620	7800	15,600	26,000	36,400	52,000
5P Cpe	1765	3600	7200	12,000	16,800	24,000
RS Cpe	1720	3900	7800	13,000	18,200	26,000
Conv	1785	5700	11,400	19,000	26,600	38,000
5P Sed	1785	2200	5250	8750	12,250	17,500
7P Sed	1935	2300	5400	9000	12,600	18,000
Limo	2035	3150	6300	10,500	14,700	21,000

1932

1932 Buick, series 90, model 96, victoria coupe, JAC

1932 Buick, club sedan & convertible coupe, JAC

BUICK — SERIES 50 — EIGHT: The 1932 Buicks were easily identified by their new hood doors which replaced the long-used louvers, the elimination of external sun visors and a more pronounced 10° rearward windshield slope. The radiator grille was given a new tapered shape with a narrower base. All Buicks also were equipped with dual taillights and longer and more streamlined fenders. The Series 60 and 80 models were available with a thinner head gasket and different spark plugs at no extra cost which raised their compression ratio and boosted top speed by 3mph.

The Series 50 Buick which continued to use the 114'' wheelbase chassis was available, along with the rest of the Buick line, with Wizard Control which provided owners with both free wheeling and no clutch shifting between second and third gears. New styles for the Series 50 consisted of a 2-door 5-passenger Victoria Coupe, and an attractive 5-passenger Convertible Phaeton with a choice of either leather or whipcord upholstery. Setting the Series 50 from other Buicks was their lack of chrome beaded radiator shutters and chrome plated hood handles. Their headlight shells were painted rather than chromed. Only a single taillight was fitted.

BUICK — SERIES 60 — EIGHT: The larger 118'' wheelbase Series 60 line also added the Victoria Coupe and Convertible Phaeton models to its offerings. The interior of the latter model featured leather upholstery and dual rear ashtrays.

BUICK — SERIES 80 — EIGHT: Only 2 models were offered in this series on a new 126'' wheelbase. The Victoria Coupe version had a unit-type rear trunk.

BUICK — SERIES 90 — EIGHT: The top of the line Series 90 Buick used a new 134'' wheelbase chassis and among its various models were two new body styles, the 4-door Club Sedan and 2-door Victoria Coupe. Standard on all Series 90 Buicks were wire wheels and dual side mounts.

I.D. DATA: Serial numbers right side of frame behind front fender opening. Starting: 2602732. Ending: 2659522. Engine numbers on crankcase. Starting: 2751922.

Model No.	Body Type & Seating	Price	Weight	Prod. Total
Series 50				
55	4-dr. Spt. Phae.-5P	1155	3270	69
56	2-dr. Bus. Cpe.-2P	935	3275	1726
56C	2-dr. Conv. Cpe.-4P	1080	3335	630
56S	2-dr. Spe. Cpe.-4P	1040	3395	1905
57	4-dr. Sed.-5P	995	3450	10,803
57S	4-dr. Spe. Sed.-5P	1080	3510	9766
58	2-dr. Vic. Cpe.	1060	3420	2194
58C	2-dr. Conv. Phae.-5P	1080	3425	380
Series 60				
65	4-dr. Spt. Phae.-5P	1390	3795	79
66	2-dr. Bus. Cpe.-2P	1250	3796	636
66C	2-dr. Conv. Cpe.-4P	1310	3795	450
66S	2-dr. Spe. Cpe.-4P	1270	3860	1678
67	4-dr. Sed.-5P	1310	3980	9013
68	2-dr. Vic. Cpe.-5P	1290	3875	1514
68C	2-dr. Conv. Phae.-5P	1310	3880	366

Model No.	Body Type & Seating	Price	Weight	Prod. Total
Series 80				
86	2-dr. Vic. Trav. Cpe.-5P	1540	4335	1800
87	4-dr. Sed.-5P	1570	4450	4089
Series 90				
90	4-dr. Sed.-7P	1955	4695	1368
90L	4-dr. Limo.-7P	2055	4810	164
91	2-dr. Clb. Sed.-5P	1820	4620	2237
95	4-dr. Spt. Phae.-7P	1675	4470	131
96	2-dr. Vic. Cpe.-5P	1785	4460	1460
96C	2-dr. Conv. Cpe.-4P	1805	4460	289
96S	2-dr. Ctry. Clb. Cpe.-4P	1740	4470	586
97	4-dr. Sed.-5P	1805	4565	1485
98	2-dr. Conv. Phae.-5P	1830	4550	268

ENGINE: [Series 50] Inline. Ohv. Eight. Cast iron block. B & S: 2-15/16 x 4-1/4. Disp.: 230.4 cu. in. C.R.: 4.75. Brake H.P.: 82.5 @ 3200 R.P.M. N.A.C.C. H.P.: 27.61. Main bearings: 5. Valve lifters: mechanical. Carb.: 2 barrel Marvel updraft TD-15 10 982. Torque: 200 lbs.-ft. @ 1600 R.P.M. [Series 60] Inline. Ohv. Eight. Cast iron block. B & S: 3-1/16 x 5. Disp.: 272.6 cu. in. C.R.: 4.63:1. Brake H.P.: 90 (high compression 96) @ 3000 R.P.M. N.A.C.C. H.P.: 30.02. Main bearings: 5. Valve lifters: mechanical. Carb.: 2 barrel Marvel updraft TD-25 10-1501. Torque: 200 lbs.-ft. @ 1600 R.P.M. [Series 80, 90] Inline. Ohv. Eight. Cast iron block. B & S: 3-5/16 x 5. Disp.: 344.8 cu. in. C.R.: 4.5. Brake H.P.: High compression 113, 104 @ 2800 R.P.M. N.A.C.C. H.P.: 35.12. Main bearings: 5. Valve lifters: mechanical. Carb.: 2 barrel Marvel updraft TD-3 10-1503. Torque: 250 lbs.-ft. @ 1400 R.P.M.

CHASSIS: [Series 50] W.B.: 114 in. Frt/Rear Tread: 56-1/2 in. / 57 in. Tires: 18 x 5.50. [Series 60] W.B.: 118 in. Frt/Rear Tread: 56-3/4 in. / 58 in. Tires: 18 x 6.00. [Series 80] W.B.: 126 in. Tires: 18 x 7.00. [Series 90] W.B.: 134 in. Tires: 18 x 7.00.

TECHNICAL: Sliding gear, synchromesh transmission. Speeds: 3F/1R. Floor shift controls. Ser. 50, 60 — single dry plate, Ser. 80, 90 — double dry plate. Shaft drive. 3/4 floating rear axle. Ser. 50 — 4.6:1, Ser. 60 — 4.27, 4.545:1, Ser. 80 — 4.27:1, Ser. 90 — 4.18, 4.27:1. Mechanical brakes on four wheels. Painted wire wheels or 12 wooden spoke wheels with demountable rims. Wizard Control. Automatic clutch (series 80, 90).

OPTIONS: Heater. Clock. Chrome grille guard. Dual side mounts. Single bar bumpers. Tire locks. Tire covers. Cigarette lighter. Wheel trim rings. Trunk. Trunk rack. Vacuum windshield pump (Ser. 50 only, std on all others). 12 spoke wood wheel (Ser. 50, DeLuxe models).

HISTORICAL: Introduced Nov. 14, 1931. A Buick powered racer entered and driven by Phil Shafer finished 11th in the Indy. Shafer also won an Elgin, Ill. race with the same car. Innovations: Adjustable shock absorbers, Wizard Control free wheeling and automatic clutch. Calendar year production: 41,522. Model year production: 55,086 (another 1,704 stripped chassis and cars for export were produced). The president of Buick was Irving J. Reuter. Buick discontinued the use of wooden spoke wheels at the end of the 1932 model year.

1932
Series 50, 8-cyl.

	FP	5	4	3	2	1
Spt Phae	1155	5250	10,500	17,500	24,500	35,000
Conv	1080	4950	9900	16,500	23,100	33,000
2 dr Phae	1080	5400	10,800	18,000	25,200	36,000
Bus Cpe	935	1750	4800	8000	11,200	16,000
RS Cpe	1040	2000	5100	8500	11,900	17,000
Vic Cpe	1060	1400	4200	7000	9800	14,000
4 dr Sed	995	1075	3000	5500	7700	11,000
Spt Sed	1080	1075	3000	5500	7700	11,000
Series 60, 8-cyl.						
Spt Phae	1390	5700	11,400	19,000	26,600	38,000
Conv	1310	5400	10,800	18,000	25,200	36,000
2 dr Phae	1310	5550	11,100	18,500	25,900	37,000
Bus Cpe	1250	2000	5100	8500	11,900	17,000
RS Cpe	1270	2300	5400	9000	12,600	18,000
Vic Cpe	1290	2200	5250	8750	12,250	17,500
4 dr Sed	1310	1150	3600	6000	8400	12,000
Series 80, 8-cyl.						
Vic Cpe	1540	2300	5400	9000	12,600	18,000
4 dr Sed	1570	1350	4100	6800	9500	13,600
Series 90, 8-cyl.						
7P Sed	1955	2800	5700	9500	13,300	19,000
Limo	2055	3400	6900	11,500	16,100	23,000
Clb Sed	1820	3300	6600	11,000	15,400	22,000
Spt Phae	1675	6300	12,600	21,000	29,400	42,000
2 dr Phae	1830	6150	12,300	20,500	28,700	41,000
Conv Cpe	1805	6000	12,000	20,000	28,000	40,000
RS Cpe	1740	4050	8100	13,500	18,900	27,000
Vic Cpe	1785	3300	6600	11,000	15,400	22,000
5P Sed	1805	2000	5100	8500	11,900	17,000

1933

BUICK — SERIES 50 — EIGHT: This was a year of major styling changes for Buick. New front and rear fenders with deeper valances and more sweeping curves plus a 2¼'' height reduction, gave all models a fresh appearance. Adding to this sense of newness was the Buick's new V-shaped grille and the discontinuation of wooden spoke wheels throughout all series. Customers could now select either wire or steel spoke artillery wheels.

Technical improvements were headlined by a new x-crossmember frame and the Fisher No-Draft ventilation. In addition the free-wheeling unit now allowed the driver to switch back and forth from direct drive to free wheeling as desired. The adjustable shock absorber system wasn't offered in 1933. A new type of headlight whose passing beam brightly illuminated the pavement edge while shedding a far dimmer light on the traffic side was common to all Buicks.

The Series 50 Buicks continued to use a 114'' wheelbase chassis. Body styles were trimmed to 5 from the 1932 level of 8 as the Sport Phaeton, Special Sedan and Convertible Phaeton were dropped. Twin taillights were fitted to all models.

1933 Buick, series 50, model 57, sedan, JAC

1933 Buick, series 60, model 66C, convertible coupe, OCW

BUICK — SERIES 60 — EIGHT: A 127'' wheelbase was used for the Series 60 which also consisted of 5 models for 1933. Eliminated for the 1933 model year were the Sport Phaeton and Business Coupe models.

BUICK — SERIES 80 — EIGHT: The Series 80 wheelbase for 1933 was an impressive 130''. Whereas only 2 models were offered in this series in 1932, 3 new models, the Convertible Coupe, Sport Coupe and Convertible Phaeton were added for the new model year.

BUICK — SERIES 90 — EIGHT: 1933 was the poorest sales year for Buick since 1915 but in terms of prestige the Series 90 models with an ultra-long 138'' wheelbase took Buick to a new status level. However only 5 body styles were offered as Buick eliminated the Sport Phaeton, Country Club Coupe, 5-passenger Sedan, Convertible Coupe Roadster and Convertible Phaeton from the Series 90 line. Closed car interiors were available in mohair plush, whipcord or cloth.

I.D. DATA: Serial numbers on right side of frame behind front fender opening, on plate on firewall. Starting: 2659523. Ending: 2706452. Engine numbers on right side of crankcase. Starting: 2751922.

Model No.	Body Type & Seating	Price	Weight	Prod. Total
Series 50				
56	2-dr. Bus. Cpe.-2P	995	3520	1321
56C	2-dr. Conv. Cpe.-2P	1115	3525	346
56S	2-dr. Spt. Cpe.-2P	1030	3585	1643
57	4-dr. Sed.-5P	1045	3705	19,109
58	2-dr. Vic. Cpe.-5P	1065	3605	4118
Series 60				
66C	2-dr. Conv. Cpe.-2P	1365	3940	152
66S	2-dr. Spt. Cpe.	1270	3975	1000
67	4-dr. Sed.-5P	1310	4115	7450
68	2-dr. Vic. Cpe.-5P	1310	4005	2887
68C	4-dr. Conv. Phae.-5P	1585	4110	183
Series 80				
86	2-dr. Vic. Cpe.-5P	1540	4420	758
86C	2-dr. Conv. Cpe.-2P	1575	4325	90
86S	2-dr. Spt. Cpe.-2P	1495	4355	401
87	4-dr. Sed.-5P	1570	4505	1545
88C	4-dr. Conv. Phae.-5P	1845	4525	124

172

Model No.	Body Type & Seating	Price	Weight	Prod. Total
Series 90				
90	4-dr. Sed.-7P	1955	4705	890
90L	4-dr. Limo.-7P	2055	4780	299
91	2-dr. Clb. Sed.-5P	1820	4520	1637
96	2-dr. Vic. Cpe.-5P	1785	4520	556
97	4-dr. Sed.-5P	1805	4595	641

ENGINE: [Series 50] Inline. Ohv. Eight. Cast iron block. B & S: 2-15/16 x 4-1/4. Disp.: 230.4 cu. in. C.R.: 4.63. Brake H.P.: 86 @ 3200 R.P.M. N.A.C.C. H.P.: 27.61. Main bearings: 5. Valve lifters: mechanical. Carb.: 2 barrel Marvel updraft ED-18 10-1515. [Series 60] Inline. Ohv. Eight. Cast iron block. B & S: 3-1/16 x 5. Disp.: 272.6 cu in C.R.: 4.63:1. Brake H.P.: 97 @ 3200 R.P.M. N.A.C.C. H.P.: 30.02. Main bearings: 5. Valve lifters: mechanical. Carb.: 2 barrel Marvel updraft ED-28 10-1518. [Series 80, 90] Inline. Ohv. Eight. Cast iron block. B & S: 3-5/16 x 5. Disp.: 344.8 cu. in. C.R.: 4.63:1. Brake H.P.: 104 @ 2800 R.P.M. Main bearings: 5. Valve lifters: mechanical. Carb.: 2 barrel Marvel updraft ED-3 10-1514.

CHASSIS: [Series 50] W.B.: 119 in. Frt/Rear Tread: 59/60-1/2 in. Tires: 17 x 6. [Series 60] W.B.: 127 in. Frt/Rear Tread: 59/60-1/2 in. Tires: 17 x 6.50. [Series 80] W.B.: 130 in. Frt/Rear Tread: 58-1/2 in. / 60-1/2 in. Tires: 17 x 7. [Series 90] W.B.: 138 in. Frt/Rear Tread: 58-1/2 in. / 60-1/2 in. Tires: 17 x 7.

TECHNICAL: Sliding gear, synchromesh transmission. Speeds: 3F/1R. Floor shift controls. Single dry plate clutch — Ser. 50, 60. Double dry plate clutch — Ser. 80, 90. Shaft drive. 3/4 floating rear axle. Overall ratio: Ser. 50 - 4.7:1, Ser. 60 - 4.6:1, Ser. 80 - 4.273:1, Ser. 90 - 4.27, 4.36:1. Mechanical brakes on four wheels. Wire on steel spoke artillery wheels. Wizard control.

OPTIONS: Side mounts. Luggage rack. Trunk. Fog lights. Wire wheels. Artillery-type all steel wheels.

HISTORICAL: Introduced Dec. 3, 1932. The Shafer 8 Special powered by a 284cid Buick engine was driven by H. W. ''Stubby'' Stubblefield to a 5th place finish at an average speed of 100.762 mph. The top 4 cars were powered by Miller racing engines. Dash mounted starter button. Calendar year production: 40,620. Model year sales: 43,247. Model year production: 45,150 (1774 stripped chassis and cars for export were also produced). Harlow Herbert Curtice became Buick President on Oct. 23, 1933.

1933
Series 50, 8-cyl.

	FP	5	4	3	2	1
Conv	1115	4050	8100	13,500	18,900	27,000
Bus Cpe	995	1250	3900	6500	9100	13,000
RS Spt Cpe	1030	1550	4500	7500	10,500	15,000
Vic Cpe	1065	1400	4200	7000	9800	14,000
4 dr Sed	1065	1150	3600	6000	8400	12,000
Series 60, 8-cyl.						
Conv Cpe	1365	4350	8700	14,500	20,300	29,000
Phae	1585	4500	9000	15,000	21,000	30,000
Spt Cpe	1270	1750	4800	8000	11,200	16,000
Vic Cpe	1310	1550	4500	7500	10,500	15,000
4 dr Sed	1310	1250	3900	6500	9100	13,000
Series 80, 8-cyl.						
Conv	1575	4800	9600	16,000	22,400	32,000
Phae	1845	4950	9900	16,500	23,100	33,000
Spt Cpe	1495	1800	4950	8250	11,550	16,500
Vic	1540	1750	4800	8000	11,200	16,000
4 dr Sed	1570	1400	4200	7000	9800	14,000
Series 90, 8-cyl.						
Vic	1785	3150	6300	10,500	14,700	21,000
5P Sed	1805	1750	4800	8000	11,200	16,000
7P Sed	1955	2800	5700	9500	13,300	19,000
Clb Sed	1820	3000	6000	10,000	14,000	20,000
Limo	2055	3150	6300	10,500	14,700	21,000

1934

1934 Buick, series 40, model 41, sedan, AA

1934 BUICK: Buick's year old synchromesh transmission was improved by the adoption of helical gears. The actual gear shifting procedure was made more convenient by the shift lever's shorter movement. Also noteworthy was the mid-year revision made in the automatic starting mechanism that prevented the starter from being used to move the car when the ignition was locked.

An interesting feature of the Buick instrument panel was its octane selector handle which altered the spark timing to allow the use of either standard or premium fuel.

The headlights used on the 1934 models produced 20% more illumination and provided four different light patterns: city and country driving beams, a passing beam and a parking light. Series 40 Buicks had 3 horizontal hood louvers while models in the remaining series had 4. Also not included as standard equipment on the Series 40 were the dual chrome horns of the Series 50 through 90.

BUICK — SERIES 40 — EIGHT: In terms of Buick's recent past the introduction of this low priced series on May 12, 1934 was nothing short of revolutionary. But it came at a time when business as usual patterns could spell disaster. Although its wheelbase of 117'' was longer than the 1933 Series 50 Buick it was both considerably lighter in weight and less expensive. Series 40 models were the only Buicks not equipped with dual exterior mounted horns. Closed models in the Series 40 had either whipcord or mohair velvet upholstery with leather used for open models. All models in all series had their radiator filler cap placed under the hood.

1934 Buick, series 50, model 56S, sport coupe, JAC

BUICK — SERIES 50 — EIGHT: Body choices in this Buick line remained unchanged but a longer 119'' wheelbase was used. As was the case with all Buicks, the new Series 50 had narrow horizontal hood louvers and safety glass in their windshields and vent windows. Interiors featured (on closed models) wide walnut grained metal window trim.

BUICK — SERIES 60 — EIGHT: Series 60 Buicks had a longer, by one inch, wheelbase for 1934. A new Club Sedan model was added to its lineup. A more powerful 100hp, 278cid engine was also introduced. Common to all Buicks for 1934 was General Motors "Knee Action" independent front suspension and a "Ride Stabilizer" rear anti-roll bar.

1934 Buick, series 90, model 91, club sedan, JAC

BUICK — SERIES 90 — EIGHT: With the Series 80 dropped for 1934, the Series 90 received new Convertible Coupe, Sport Coupe and Convertible Phaeton models. The Series 90 was equipped both with safety glass in all windows and a Bendix vacuum power brake booster. The Series 90 models shared their combination accelerator-starter with the rest of the 1934 Buicks. Interiors of closed models featured mohair velvet plush upholstery.

I.D. DATA: Serial numbers on right side of frame, behind front fender opening. Starting: 2706453. Ending: 2777649. Engine numbers on crankcase. Starting. Ser. 40 — 2984900, Ser. 50, 60, 90 — 2861223.

Model No.	Body Type & Seating	Price	Weight	Prod. Total
Series 40				
41	4-dr. Sed. Built-in trunk-5P	925	3175	10,953
46	2-dr. Bus. Cpe.-2P	795	2995	1806
46S	2-dr. Spt. Cpe. R/S-4P	855	3085	1232
47	4-dr. Sed.-5P	895	3155	7425
48	4-dr. Tr. Sed. Built-in Trunk-5P	865	3120	4779
Series 50				
56	2-dr. Bus. Cpe.-2P	1110	3682	1078
56C	2-dr. Conv. Cpe.-2P	1230	3692	506
56S	2-dr. Sp. Cpe. R/S-4P	1145	3712	1150
57	4-dr. Sed.-5P	1190	3852	12,094

Model No.	Body Type & Seating	Price	Weight	Prod. Total
58	2-dr. Vic. Cpe. Built-in Trunk-5P	1160	4316	4405
Series 60				
61	2-dr. Clb. Sed. Built-in Trunk-5P	1465	4318	5395
66C	2-dr. Conv. Cpe. R/S-4P	1495	NA	253
66S	2-dr. Sp. Cpe.-2P	1375	4193	816
67	4-dr. Sed.-5P	1425	4303	5171
68	2-dr. Vic. Cpe. Built-in Trunk-5P	1395	4213	1935
68C	4-dr. Conv. Phae. Built-in Trunk-5P	1675	4353	444
Series 90				
90	4-dr. Sed.-7P	2055	4906	1151
90L	4-dr. Limo.-7P	2175	4876	262
91	2-dr. Clb. Sed. Built-in trunk-5P	1965	4696	1477
96C	2-dr. Conv. Cpe. R/S-4P	1945	4511	68
96S	2-dr. Spt. Cpe. R/S-4P	1875	4546	137
97	4-dr. Sed.-4P	1945	4691	635
98	2-dr. Vic. Cpe.-5P	1895	4571	347
98C	4-dr. Conv. Phae. Built-in trunk-5P	2145	4691	119

ENGINE: [Series 40] Inline. Ohv. Eight. Cast iron block. B & S: 3-3/32 x 3-7/8. Disp.: 233 cu. in. Brake H.P.: 93 @ 3200 R.P.M. N.A.C.C. H.P.: 30.63. Main bearings: 5. Valve lifters: mechanical. Carb.: 2 barrel Marvel downdraft BB-1, 10-1633. [Series 50] Inline. Ohv. Eight. Cast iron block. B & S: 2-31/32 x 4-1/4. Disp.: 235 cu. in. Brake H.P.: 88 @ 3200 R.P.M. N.A.C.C. H.P.: 28.2. Main bearings: 5. Valve lifters: mechanical. Carb.: 2 barrel Marvel updraft ED-1S, 10-1577. [Series 60] Inline. Ohv. Eight. Cast iron block. B & S: 3-3/32 x 4-5/8. Disp.: 278:1 cu. in. Brake H.P.: 100 @ 3200 R.P.M. N.A.C.C. H.P.: 30.63. Main bearings: 5. Valve lifters: mechanical. Carb.: 2 barrel Marvel ED-2S, 10-1579. [Series 90] Inline. Ohv. Eight. Cast iron block. B & S: 3-5/16 x 5. Disp.: 344.8 cu. in. Brake H.P.: 116 @ 3200 R.P.M. N.A.C.C. H.P.: 35.12. Main bearings: 5. Valve lifters: mechanical. Carb.: Marvel ED3S 10-1581.

CHASSIS: [Series 40] W.B.: 117 in. Tires: 16 x 6.25. [Series 50] W.B.: 119 in. Frt/Rear Tread: 59/60-1/2 in. Tires: 16 x 7.00. [Series 60] W.B.: 128 in. Tires: 16 x 7.50. [Series 90] W.B.: 136 in. Tires: 16 x 7.50.

TECHNICAL: Sliding gear, synchromesh transmission. Speeds: 3F/1R. Floor shift controls. Single dry plate clutch. Shaft drive. 3/4 floating rear axle. Overall Ratio: Ser. 40 — 4.33:1, Ser. 50 — 4.89:1, Ser. 60 — 4.7:1, Ser. 90 — 4.36:1. Mechanical brakes on four wheels. Steel spoke artillery wheels.

OPTIONS: White side walls. Two-tone paint. Safety glass (Ser 50 & 60) ($9.75 — $20.00). Radio (dealer installed). Metal spare tire cover. Luggage rack. Side mounts. Passenger side windshield wipers — Series 40.

HISTORICAL: Introduced Dec. 27, 1933. Calendar year production: 78,757. Model year production: 63,647 (plus 7362 stripped chassis and cars for export). The president of Buick was Harlow Curtice. Two Buick-powered Rigling cars were qualified in 6th and 8th places starting position in the Indy. One car retired with a broken cam drive after 130 laps. The second entry, the "Shafer Special" with a 286 cid Buick 8 finished in 6th position with an average speed of 98.26mph. The cars in front at the race's end were powered by either Duesenberg or Miller engines.

1934
Special Series 40, 8-cyl.

	FP	5	4	3	2	1
Bus Cpe	795	1075	3000	5500	7700	11,000
RS Cpe	855	1150	3600	6000	8400	12,000
2 dr Tr Sed	865	1000	2400	5000	7000	10,000
Tr Sed	925	1050	2800	5400	7500	10,800
4 dr Sed	895	1050	2700	5300	7400	10,600
Series 50, 8-cyl.						
Conv	1230	3900	7800	13,000	18,200	26,000
Bus Cpe	1110	1100	3300	5650	7900	11,300
Spt Cpe	1145	1200	3800	6300	8800	12,600
Vic Cpe	1160	1200	3800	6300	8800	12,600
4 dr Sed	1190	1000	2400	5050	7050	10,100
Series 60, 8-cyl.						
Conv	1495	4200	8400	14,000	19,600	28,000
Phae	1675	3900	7800	13,000	18,200	26,000
Spt Cpe	1375	1500	4350	7300	10,200	14,600
Vic	1395	1500	4350	7300	10,200	14,600
4 dr Sed	1425	1050	2700	5300	7400	10,600
Clb Sed	1465	1050	2800	5400	7500	10,800

1934 Buick, series 90, model 96C, convertible coupe, OCW

Series 90, 8-cyl.

	FP	5	4	3	2	1
Conv	1945	5700	11,400	19,000	26,600	38,000
Phae	2145	5850	11,700	19,500	27,300	39,000
Spt Cpe	1875	2400	5400	9050	12,700	18,100
5P Sed	1895	2200	5300	8800	12,300	17,600
7P Sed	2055	2100	5200	8650	12,100	17,300
Clb Sed	1965	2400	5400	9050	12,700	18,100
Limo	2175	3300	6600	11,000	15,400	22,000
Vic	1895	3150	6300	10,500	14,700	21,000

1935

1935 Buick, convertible coupe, OCW

BUICK — SERIES 40 — EIGHT: Visual changes in the Buick's appearance for 1935 were extremely modest consisting mainly of new colors and exterior trim revisions. The Series 40 models received a glove box lock and dual windshield wipers along with numerous design improvements intended to remedy complaints of poor clutch and timing chain durability. A Convertible Coupe was also added to the Series 40 model line. Whereas the more costly Buicks were fitted with chrome headlight shells, those on the Series 40 were painted. All models received automatic chokes and a girder-type frame was used on all Buick convertibles.

BUICK — SERIES 50 — EIGHT: Changes to the Series 50 were limited to the installation of center rear arm rests on closed models.

1935 Buick, series 60, model 61, club sedan, JAC

BUICK — SERIES 60 — EIGHT: All body styles were continued unchanged for 1935. Series 60 sedans shared the folding center rear seat arm rest with Series 90 models.

BUICK — SERIES 90 — EIGHT: Series 90 models were equipped with shatter proof glass in all windows.

I.D. DATA: Serial numbers on right side of frame, behind front fender opening. Starting: 2777650. Ending: 2830898. Engine numbers on crankcase. Starting: Ser. 40-42937408, Ser. 50, 60, 90 — 2922072. Ending: Ser. 40-42995237, Ser. 50, 60, 90 — 2984413.

Model No.	Body Type & Seating	Price	Weight	Prod. Total
Series 40				
41	4-dr. Sed.-5P	925	3210	18,638
46	2-dr. Bus. Cpe.-2P	795	3020	2850
46C	2-dr. Conv. Cpe.-4P	925	3140	933
46S	2-dr. Spt. Cpe.-4P	855	NA	1136
47	4-dr. Sed.-5P	895	3180	6250
48	2-dr. Tr. Sed.-5P	865	3160	4957

174

Model No.	Body Type & Seating	Price	Weight	Prod. Total
Series 50				
56	2-dr. Bus. Cpe.-2P	1110	3652	257
56C	2-dr. Conv. Cpe.-2P	1230	3662	170
56S	2-dr. Sp. Cpe.-4P	1145	3682	268
57	4-dr. Sed.-5P	1190	3822	3778
58	2-dr. Vic. Cpe.	1160	3737	1589
Series 60				
61	2-dr. Clb. Sed.-5P	1462	4288	2762
66C	2-dr. Conv. Cpe.-4P	1375	4163	111
66S	2-dr. Sp. Cpe.-4P	NA	NA	257
67	4-dr. Sed.-5P	1425	4273	1716
68	2-dr. Vic. Cpe.-5P	1395	4183	597
68C	4-dr. Conv. Phae.-5P	1675	4323	256
Series 90				
90	4-dr. Sed.-7P	2055	4766	609
90L	4-dr. Limo.-7P	2175	4846	191
91	4-dr. Clb. Sed.-5P	1965	4606	573
96C	2-dr. Conv. Cpe.-4P	1945	4481	10
96S	2-dr. Spt. Cpe.-4P	1875	4516	41
97	4-dr. Sed.-5P	1945	4661	117
98	2-dr. Vic. Cpe.-5P	1895	4541	32
98C	4-dr. Conv. Phae.-5P	2145	4661	38

1935 Buick series 90, model 98C, convertible phaeton, JAC

ENGINE: [Series 40] Inline. Ohv. Eight. Cast iron block. B & S: 3-3/12 x 3-7/8. Disp.: 233 cu. in. Brake H.P.: 93 @ 3200 R.P.M. N.A.C.C. H.P.: 30.63. Main bearings: 5. Valve lifters: mechanical. Carb.: 2 barrel, Stromberg downdraft EE-1 or Marvel ED-15. [Series 50] Inline. Ohv. Eight. Cast iron block. B & S: 2-31/32 x 4-1/4. Disp.: 235 cu. in. Brake H.P.: 88 @ 3200 R.P.M. N.A.C.C. H.P.: 28.2. Main bearings: 5. Valve lifters: mechanical. Carb.: Marvel ED-15, 10-157. [Series 60] Inline. Ohv. Eight. Cast iron block. B & S: 3-3/32 x 4-5/8. Disp.: 278.1 cu. in. Brake H.P.: 100 @ 3200 R.P.M. N.A.C.C. H.P.: 30.63. Main bearings: 5. Valve lifters: mechanical. Carb.: Marvel ED-25, 10-1579. [Series 90] Inline. Ohv. Eight. Cast iron block. B & S: 3-5/16 x 5. Disp.: 344.8. C.R.: 4.63. Brake H.P.: 116 @ 3200 R.P.M. N.A.C.C. H.P.: 35.12. Main bearings: 5. Valve lifters: mechanical. Carb. Marvel ED-3, 10-1581.

CHASSIS: [Series 40] W.B.: 117 in. Tires: 16 x 6.25. [Series 50] W.B.: 119 in. Frt/Rear Tread: 59/60-1/2 in. Tires: 16 x 7.00. [Series 60] W.B.: 128 in. Tires: 16 x 7.50. [Series 90] W.B.: 136 in. Tires: 16 x 7.50.

TECHNICAL: Sliding gear, synchromesh transmission. Speeds: 3F/1R. Floor shift controls. Single dry plate clutch. Shaft drive. 3/4 floating rear axle. Overall Ratio: Ser. 40-4.33:1, Ser. 50 4.88:1, Ser. 60 4.7:1, Ser. 90 4.36:1. Mechanical brakes on four wheels. Steel spoke artillery wheels.

OPTIONS: Sidemount (standard on Model 98C). Wire wheels. Luggage rack. Steel side mount tire covers. 2-tone paint.

HISTORICAL: Introduced Oct. 18, 1934. Calendar year production: 107,611. Model year production: 48,256 (4993 stripped chassis and cars for export were also produced). The president of Buick was Harlow Curtice. A Shafer Special with a Buick 8 cylinder engine was qualified by Cliff Bergers at 114.1 mph at Indy. After starting in 16th position it ran out of gas just 4 laps from the finish.

1935 Buick, series 50, model 57, 4-dr. sedan, OCW

1935

Special Series 40, 8-cyl.

	FP	5	4	3	2	1
Conv.	925	3600	7200	12,000	16,800	24,000
Bus Cpe	795	1050	2700	5300	7400	10,600
RS Spt Cpe	855	1125	3450	5800	8100	11,600
2 dr Sed	865	1000	2400	5000	7000	10,000
2 dr Tr Sed	865	1000	2500	5100	7100	10,200
4 dr Sed	895	1000	2400	5050	7050	10,100
4 dr Tr Sed	925	1025	2500	5150	7150	10,300
Series 50, 8-cyl.						
Conv	1230	3900	7800	13,000	18,200	26,000
Bus Cpe	1110	1000	2500	5100	7100	10,200
Spt Cpe	1145	1125	3450	5800	8100	11,600
Vic	1160	1125	3450	5800	8100	11,600
4 dr Sed	1190	1000	2400	5050	7050	10,100
Series 60, 8-cyl.						
Conv	1495	4200	8400	14,000	19,600	28,000
Phae	1675	3750	7500	12,500	17,500	25,000
Vic	1395	1350	4100	6800	9500	13,600
4 dr Sed	1425	1125	3450	5800	8100	11,600
Clb Sed	1465	1125	3450	5800	8100	11,600
Spt Cpe	1375	1350	4100	6800	9500	13,600
Series 90, 8-cyl.						
Conv	1945	4950	9900	16,500	23,100	33,000
Phae	2145	5250	10,500	17,500	24,500	35,000
Spt Cpe	1875	2950	5900	9800	13,700	19,600
Vic	1895	2950	5900	9800	13,700	19,600
5P Sed	1965	2200	5300	8800	12,300	17,600
7P Sed	2055	1900	5000	8300	11,600	16,600
Limo	2175	3150	6300	10,500	14,700	21,000
Clb Sed	1965	2600	5550	9300	13,000	18,600

1936

1936 Buick, Special, model 46C, convertible coupe, JAC

BUICK SPECIAL — SERIES 40 — EIGHT: Buick historians are unanimous in regarding the 1936 models as the cars that marked the start of the Buick renaissance. Across the board were Turret-Top bodies, hydraulic brakes and dramatic new styling with sharply slanted V-type windshields, high, wedged-shaped radiators, twin taillamps and bullet-shaped headlights. Technical advancements included an improved independent front suspension, new alloy pistons and an improved water temperature control. To celebrate the occasion Buick also assigned names to its traditional Series designations. Buick wasn't the least bit bashful about touting the top speed ability of these new cars. The Special was capable of 85 mph, the Limited, 87 mph and the Roadmaster, 90 mph. The hot new Century could achieve a sizzling 95 mph.

The Series 40 Special retained the 233 cid engine, which now featured Anolite aluminum pistons, as did the 320 cid Buick engine.

BUICK CENTURY — SERIES 60 — EIGHT: The first of the great Century Buicks shared a new 320.2 cid straight eight with the Series 80 (Roadmaster) and Series 90 (Limited) models that was destined to remain in production through 1952. On a relatively short, 118 inch wheelbase the Century's styling with its rearward sweeping lines and rounded grille with vertical bars was particularly appealing.

1936 Buick, Roadmaster, model 80C, convertible phaeton, AA

BUICK ROADMASTER — SERIES 80 — EIGHT: Only 2 body styles, a 4-door Trunk Sedan, and an elegant Convertible Phaeton were offered in this Roadmaster Series. Standard on the latter was a single side mount.

1936 Buick, Limited, model 91, sedan, JAC

BUICK LIMITED — SERIES 90 — EIGHT: The 4 Limited models all used the same 4-door body style with glass partitions provided for the Limousine and Formal Sedan versions. Standard on all Buick Limited models was a left side external tire mount.

I.D. DATA: Serial numbers on right side of frame, behind front fender opening. Starting: 2830899. Ending: 2999496. Engine numbers on crankcase. Starting: Ser. 40-42995239, Ser. 60, 80, 90 — 63001000. Ending: Ser. 40 — 43166224, Ser. 60, 80, 90 — 93166224.

Model No.	Body Type & Seating	Price	Weight	Prod. Total
Series 40 (Special)				
41	4-dr. Sed.-5P	885	3360	77,007
46	2-dr. Bus. Cpe.-2P	765	3150	10,912
46C	2-dr. Conv. Cpe.-4P	820	3190	1488
46S	2-dr. Spt. Cpe.-4P	820	3190	1086
46Sr	2-dr. Spt. Cpe.-4P	820	3190	1390
48	2-dr. Vic. Cpe.-5P	835	3305	21,214
Series 60 (Century)				
61	4-dr. Sed.-5P	1090	—	17,806
66C	2-dr. Conv. Cpe.-4P	1135	3775	717
66So	2-dr. Spt. Cpe.-4P	1035	3625	1078
66Sr	2-dr. Spt. Cpe.-4P	1035	3635	1001
68	2-dr. Vic. Cpe.-5P	1055	3730	3762
Series 80 (Roadmaster)				
80C	4-dr. Conv. Phae.-6P	1565	4228	1064
81	4-dr. Sed.-6P	1255	4098	14,985
Series 90 (Limited)				
90	4-dr. Sed.-8P	1845	4517	1590
90	4-dr. Limo.-8P	1945	4577	709
91	4-dr. Sed.-6P	1695	4477	1713
91F	4-dr. Formal Sed.-6P	1795	4487	74

ENGINE: [Series 40] Inline. Ohv. Eight. Cast iron block. B & S: 3-3/32 x 3-7/8. Disp.: 233 cu. in. Brake H.P.: 93 @ 3200 R.P.M. N.A.C.C. H.P.: 30.63. Main bearings: 5. Valve lifters: mechanical. Carb.: 2 barrel Stromberg downdraft EE1. [Series 60, 80, 90] Inline. Ohv. Eight. Cast iron block. B & S: 3-7/16 x 4-5/16. Disp.: 320.2 cu. in. C.R.: Brake H.P.: 120 @ 3200 R.P.M. N.A.C.C. H.P.: 37.81. Main bearings: 5. Valve lifters: mechanical. Carb.: 2 barrel Stromberg downdraft EE22. Torque: 238 lbs.-ft. @ 1600 R.P.M.

CHASSIS: [Series 40] W.B.: 118 in. Tires: 16 x 6.50. [Series 60] W.B. 122 in. O.L.: 197 in. Height: 68 in. Frt/Rear Tread: 58.1 in. / 57.5 in. Tires: 15 x 7.00. [Series 80] W.B.: 131 in. Tires: 16 x 7.00. [Series 90] W.B.: 138 in. Tires: 16 x 7.50.

TECHNICAL: Sliding gear transmission. Speeds: 3F/1R. Floor shift control. Single dry plate clutch. Shaft drive. Semi-floating rear axle. Overall Ratio: Ser. 40-4.44:1, Ser. 60-3.90:1, Ser. 80-4.22:1, Ser. 90-4.55:1. Hydraulic brakes on four wheels. Pressed steel wheels. 16 in. (Series 60-15'').

OPTIONS: Heater Master and DeLuxe. Dual side mounts. Fog lights. White side walls. Grille guard. Electric watch. Buick Master 5-tube radio. Buick Ranger 6-tube radio. Trim rings.

1936 Buick, Special, model 46, coupe, OCW

HISTORICAL: Introduced Sept. 28, 1935. Hydraulic brake, Turret top. Calendar year sales: 164,861. Calendar year production: 179,533. Model year production: 157,623 (in addition 10,973 stripped chassis and cars for export were produced). The president of Buick was Harlow Curtice. The 3 millionth Buick, a Series 40 Special 4-door sedan was built on May 28, 1936.

1936
Special Series 40, 8-cyl.

	FP	5	4	3	2	1
Conv	905	3600	7200	12,000	16,800	24,000
Bus Cpe	765	1125	3450	5800	8100	11,600
RS Cpe	820	1200	3800	6300	8800	12,600
2 dr Sed	835	1050	2700	5300	7400	10,600
4 dr Sed	885	1050	2700	5300	7400	10,600

Century Series 60, 8-cyl.

Conv	1135	4050	8100	13,500	18,900	27,000
RS Cpe	1035	1500	4350	7300	10,200	14,600
2 dr Sed	1085	1100	3400	5700	8000	11,400
4 dr Sed	1090	1125	3450	5800	8100	11,600

Roadmaster Series 80, 8-cyl.

Phae	1565	4050	8100	13,500	18,900	27,000
4 dr Sed	1255	1900	5000	8300	11,600	16,600

Limited Series 90, 8-cyl.

4 dr Sed	1695	2200	5300	8800	12,300	17,600
7P Cpe	1845	2600	5550	9300	13,000	18,600
Fml Sed	1795	2950	5900	9800	13,700	19,600
7P Limo	1945	3150	6300	10,500	14,700	21,000

1937

1937 Buick, Special, model 46C, convertible coupe, AA

BUICK SPECIAL — SERIES 40 — EIGHT: Buick's art deco styling of 1937 was substantially revised with a divided grille with horizontal bars, fenders with squared-off ends and extremely graceful streamlined head light shells. The center section of the die cast grille was painted to match the body color. While overall height was reduced by 1½ inches the floors were lowered 2½" to maintain interior head room.

Among Buick's technical improvements for 1937 was a quieter overhead valve mechanism, "streamlined" intake valves, a new oil pump and a cooling system with 7% greater capacity.

The Buick Special received both a longer 122" wheelbase chassis and a new 248 cid engine. Particularly attractive was the 4-door Model 47 with its swept-back rear deck. Another addition to the Special line was the 5 passenger Convertible Phaeton. Buick claimed the Series 40 Sedan could accelerate from 10 to 60 mph in 19.2 seconds.

1937 Buick, Century, model 66C, convertible coupe, JAC

BUICK CENTURY — SERIES 60 — EIGHT: The Century series with a 126" wheelbase was highlighted by 2 swept-back body styles, the Model 64 2-door Sedan and Model 67 4-door Sedan. With an official top speed of 101 mph the Century was one of the most impressive automobiles of 1937. The coupe bodies in both the Series 40 and Series 60 Buicks were lengthened to provide space for two passengers behind the front seat. These "opera" seats could also be folded flush into the body when not in use.

BUICK ROADMASTER — SERIES 80 — EIGHT: The Roadmaster, on the same 131" wheelbase of 1936 were available in 3 body styles, including a new 6 passenger Formal Sedan.

BUICK LIMITED — SERIES 90 — EIGHT: The 7 Limited models along with all other Buicks were available with a windshield defroster and a radio antenna installed in the running board. Unlike the Special and Century models which used all-steel body construction, the Limited and Roadmaster Buick retained composite wood and steel bodies.

I.D. DATA: Serial numbers on right side of frame, behind front fender opening. Starting: 2999497. Ending: 3219847. Engine numbers on crankcase. Starting: Ser. 40 - 43166225, all others - 63176225. Ending: Ser. 40 - 43396936, all others - 43388399.

Series 40 (Special)

Model No.	Body Type & Seating	Price	Weight	Prod. Total
40C	4-dr. Conv. Phae.-5P	1302	3630	1689
41	4-dr. Trunk Back Sed.-5P	1021	3490	82,440
44	2-dr. Tr. Sed.-5P	959	3490	9330
46	2-dr. Bus. Cpe.-2P	913	3380	13,742
46C	2-dr. Conv. Cpe.-4P	1056	3480	2265
46S	2-dr. Spt. Cpe.-4P	975	3445	5059
47	4-dr. Tr. Sed.	995	3510	22,312
48	2-dr. Trunk Back Sed.-5P	895	3480	15,936

Series 60 (Century)

60C	4-dr. Conv. Phae.-5P	1524	3840	410
61	4-dr. Trunk Back Sed.-5P	1233	3720	20,679
64	2-dr. Tr. Sed.-5P	1172	3720	1117
66C	2-dr. Conv. Cpe.-4P	1269	3715	787
66S	2-dr. Spt. Cpe.-4P	1187	3660	2840
67	4-dr. Tr. Sed.-5P	1207	3750	4750
68	2-dr. Trunk Back Sed.-5P	1197	3750	2874

Series 80 (Roadmaster)

80C	4-dr. Phae.-6P	1856	4214	1040
81	4-dr. Trunk Back Sed.-6P	1518	4159	14,637
81C	4-dr. Formal Sed.-6P	1641	4299	452

Series 90 (Limited)

90	4-dr. Trunk Back Sed.-8P	2240	4549	1592
90L	4-dr. Limo.-8P	2342	4599	720
91	4-dr. Trunk Back Sed.-6P	2066	4469	1229
91F	4-dr. Formal Sed.-6P	2240	4409	156

ENGINE: [Series 40] Inline. Ohv. Eight. Cast iron block. B & S: 3-3/32 x 11-1/8. Disp.: 248 cu. in. C.R.: 5.7:1. Brake H.P. 100 @ 3200 R.P.M. N.A.C.C. H.P.: 30.6. Main bearings: 5. Valve lifters: mechanical. Carb.: Stromberg AA1. [Series 60, 80, 90] Inline. Ohv. Eight. Cast iron block. B & S: 3-7/16 x 4-5/16. Disp.: 320.2 cu. in. C.R.: 5.9:1. Brake H.P.: 130 @ 3400 R.P.M. N.A.C.C. H.P.: 37.81. Main bearings: 5. Valve lifters: mechanical. Carb.: Stromberg AA2.

CHASSIS: [Series 40] W.B.: 122 in. O.L.: 200-1/16 in. Frt/Rear Tread: 58-7/16 in. / 59-5/32 in. Tires: 16 x 6.50. [Series 60] W.B.: 126 in. O.L.: 203-9/16 in. Frt/Rear Tread: 58-5/16 in. / 59-1/4 in. Tires: 15 x 7.00. [Series 80] W.B.: 131 in. O.L.: 210-1/4 in. Frt/Rear Tread: 59-19/32 in. / 62-1/2 in. Tires: 16 x 7.00. [Series 90] W.B.: 138 in. O.L.: 216-1/2 in. Frt/Rear Tread: 59-7/16 in. / 62-1/2 in. Tires: 16 x 7.50.

TECHNICAL: Sliding gear transmission. Speeds: 3F/1R. Floor shift controls. Single dry plate clutch. Shaft drive. Semi-floating rear axle (Ser. 40 & 60 - hypoid gears. Ser. 80 & 90 continues to use spiral bevel gears). Overall ratio: Ser. 40 - 4.44:1, Ser. 60 - 3.90:1, Ser. 80 - 4.22:1, Ser. 90 - 4.55:1. Hydraulic brakes on four wheels. Pressed steel wheels. Rim: 16 in. (Ser. 60 - 15 in.)

OPTIONS: Heater. Dual side mounts. Fog lights. White side wall tires. Grille Guard. Defroster in combination with heater. Heater. Dash installed radio with built-in speaker grille.

HISTORICAL: Introduced Oct. 18, 1936. Cowl-mounted windshield wipers on all models. Calendar year sales: 203,739. Calendar year production: 227,038. Model year production: 220,346 (including 14,290 stripped chassis and cars for export). The president of Buick was Harlow Curtice. The 3,000,000th Buick, a 1937 Model 81 Roadmaster 6 passenger sedan was presented to Arthur L. Newton on Oct. 25, 1936. Mr. Newton was president of Glidden Buick Corporation of New York City which had been Buick's largest dealer for 20 years.

1937
Special Series 40, 8-cyl.

	FP	5	4	3	2	1
Conv	1056	4650	9300	15,500	21,700	31,000
Phae	1302	4800	9600	16,000	22,400	32,000
Bus Cpe	913	1200	3800	6300	8800	12,600
Spt Cpe	975	1350	4100	6800	9500	13,600
2 dr FsBk	959	1250	3900	6550	9150	13,100
2 dr Sed	985	1225	3850	6400	8900	12,800
FsBk Sed	1021	1250	3900	6550	9150	13,100
4 dr Sed	995	1250	3900	6500	9100	13,000

Century Series 60, 8-cyl.

Conv	1302	5400	10,800	18,000	25,200	36,000
Phae	1524	5550	11,100	18,500	25,900	37,000
Spt Cpe	1187	1650	4650	7800	10,900	15,600
2 dr FsBk	1172	1400	4200	7050	9850	14,100
2 dr Sed	1197	1350	4150	6900	9700	13,800
FsBk Sed	1207	1450	4250	7100	9900	14,200
4 dr Sed	1233	1400	4150	6950	9750	13,900

Roadmaster Series 80, 8-cyl.

4 dr Sed	1518	1500	4350	7300	10,200	14,600
Fml Sed	1641	1650	4650	7800	10,900	15,600
Phae	1856	5700	11,400	19,000	26,600	38,000

Limited Series 90, 8-cyl.

4 dr Sed	2066	2200	5300	8800	12,300	17,600
7P Sed	2240	2600	5550	9300	13,000	18,600
Fml Sed	2240	2800	5700	9500	13,300	19,000
Limo	2342	3750	7500	12,500	17,500	25,000

1938

1938 BUICK: The major changes in the Buick line for 1938 consisted of the adoption of coil springs for its rear suspension and the availability of a semi-automatic transmission for the Series 40 models.

Styling changes were minor. The front line of the grille was now nearly vertical which enabled a longer hood to be used. The graceful form of the headlights was mirrored in the shape of the front fender-mounted parking lights and the front bumper guards were taller than previously.

Other engineering changes included a redesigned frame X-member of channel section rather than I-beam construction. Although it wasn't the first to move its battery to a location under the hood, this Buick feature for 1938 was a welcomed development.

BUICK SPECIAL — SERIES 40 — EIGHT: The Automatic Safety Transmission semi-automatic transmission option (which Oldsmobile had introduced in June 1937) required use of the clutch only when the car was started or stopped. A steering column-mounted lever with reverse, neutral, low-range and high range Forward position controlled the operation of the transmission. Low range provided first and second gears with an automatic upshift. High range encompassed first, third and fourth gears. Above 20mph in High range the car was in fourth gear with a downshift to third possible by fully depressing the accelerator. The use of crowned head pistons raised the Series 40 engine's compression ratio to 6.15:1 and increased maximum horsepower to 107 at 3400rpm.

BUICK CENTURY — SERIES 60 — EIGHT: The wheelbase of the Buick Century remained unchanged at 126''. The two-door Touring Sedan was dropped for 1938. Its engine, identical to that used in the Series 80 and 90 developed 141hp.

1938 Buick, Roadmaster, model 81, 4-dr. sedan, JAC

BUICK ROADMASTER & LIMITED — SERIES 80 & 90 — EIGHT: Wheelbases of the 80 and 90 Buick were increased 2'' to 133 and 140 inches respectively. The use of the crowned ''turbulator'' pistons raised their engine's compression ratio to 6.5:1. Horsepower was boosted to 141 at 3600rpm. The Series 90 Formal Sedan was not offered while the Four-door Sedan was added to the Series 80 line.

I.D. DATA: Serial numbers on riveted plate on right side cowling under hood, right frame rail at cowl. Starting: 13219848 (Flint), 23238767 (South Gate), 33245765 (Linden). Ending: 13388546 (Flint), 23386843 (South Gate), 33376283 (Linden). Identification of different numbers used at other factories: Prefix 1 — Flint Michigan assembly. Prefix 2 — South Gate, California assembly. Prefix 3 — Linden, New Jersey assembly. Engine numbers on low right rear side of crankcase adjacent to dipstick. Starting: 43396937 — Ser. 40, 63396937 — Ser. 60, 83396937 — Ser. 80, 93396937 — Ser. 90. Ending: 93544292 — Ser. 90.

Model No.	Body Type & Seating	Price	Weight	Prod. Total
Series 40 (Special)				
40C	2-dr. Conv. Phae.-5P	1406	3705	776
41	4-dr. Tr. Sed.-5P	1047	3560	79,510
44	2-dr. Spt. Sed.-5P	981	3515	5943
46	2-dr. Bus. Cpe.-2P	945	3385	11,337
46C	2-dr. Conv. Cpe.-4P	1103	3575	2473
46S	2-dr. Spt. Cpe.-4P	1001	3425	5381
47	4-dr. Spt. Sed.-5P	1022	3535	11,265
48	2-dr. Tr. Sed.	1006	3520	14,153
Series 60 (Century)				
60C	4-dr. Conv. Phae.-5P	1713	3950	208
61	4-dr. Tr. Sed.-5P	1297	3780	12,364
66C	2-dr. Conv. Cpe.-4P	1359	3815	642
66S	2-dr. Spt. Cpe.-4P	1226	3690	1991
67	4-dr. Spt. Sed.-5P	1272	3785	1515
68	2-dr. Tr. Sed.-5P	1256	3760	1380
Series 80 (Roadmaster)				
80C	4-dr. Spt. Phae.-6P	1983	4325	350
81F	4-dr. Tr. Sed.-6P	1645	4245	4505
81F	4-dr. Fml. Sed.-6P	1759	4305	247
87	4-dr. Spt. Sed.-6P	1645	4245	466
Series 90 (Limited)				
90	4-dr. Tr. Sed.-8P	2350	4608	644
90L	4-dr. Limo.-8P	2453	4653	410
91	4-dr. Tr. Sed.-6P	2077	4568	437

ENGINE: [Series 40] Inline. Ohv. Eight. Cast iron block. B & S: 3-3/32 x 4-1/8. Disp.: 248 cu. in. C.R.: 6.15:1. Brake H.P.: 107 @ 3400 R.P.M. Taxable H.P.: 30.63. Main bearings: 5. Valve lifters: mechanical. Carb.: Marvel CD1 or Stromberg AAV-1 dual downdraft. Torque: 203 lbs.-ft. @ 2000 R.P.M. [Series 60, 80, 90] Inline. Ohv. Eight. Cast iron block. B & S: 3-7/16 x 4-5/16. Disp.: 320.2 cu. in. C.R.: 6.35:1. Brake H.P.: 141 @ 3600 R.P.M. Taxable H.P.: 37.81. Main bearings: 5. Valve lifters: mechanical. Carb.: Marvel CD-2 or Stromberg AAV-2 dual downdraft (1-1/4 inch). Torque: 269 lbs.-ft. @ 2000 R.P.M.

CHASSIS: [Series 40] W.B.: 122 in. O.L.: 200-1/16 in. Frt/Rear Tread: 58-7/16 in. / 59-5/32 in. Tires: 15 x 6.50. [Series 60] W.B.: 126 in. O.L.: 203-9/16 in. Frt/Rear Tread: 58-5/16 in. / 59-1/4 in. Tires: 15 x 7.00. [Series 80] W.B.: 133 in. O.L.: 213-1/4 in. Frt/Rear Tread: 59-19/32 in. / 62-1/2 in. Tires: 16 x 7.00. [Series 90] W.B.: 140 in. O.L.: 219-1/2 in. Frt/Rear Tread: 59-7/16 in. / 62-1/2 in. Tires: 16 x 7.50.

TECHNICAL: Sliding gear transmission. Speeds: 3F/1R. Floor shift controls. Single dry plate clutch. Shaft drive. Semi-floating rear axle. Overall Ratio: 4.40:1 — Ser. 40, 3.90:1 — Ser. 60, 4.18:1 — Ser. 80, 4.56:1 — Ser. 90. Hydraulic brakes on four wheels. Pressed steel wheels. Automatic Safety transmission ($80.00). No Rol Hill-Holder (Series 60, 80, 90).

OPTIONS: Single sidemount. Dual sidemount. Electric clock (Special only). DeLuxe modern seat covers (6.55 — 9.35). Master heater ($13.95). DeLuxe heater (18.95). Grille guard (1.85). Ivory plastic steering wheel with full horn ring (Special Model 48 only). Fog lamps (5.50). Grille covers (1.35). Centerline radio (59.75). Centerline dual radio (67.50). Electric windshield defroster (3.00). Dual heater defroster (8.85).

HISTORICAL: Introduced Oct. 1937. A Shafer Special powered by a Buick engine was bumped from the starting line up after initially qualifying at 112.7 mph at Indy. The 1938 Series 80 and 90 models were the last Buicks using wood in the construction of their bodies. Innovations: Although Buick offered the Automatic Safety Transmission only for the 1938 model year it still represented an important step in the development of the modern automatic transmission. The use of coil springs at the rear was also an industry first. Calendar year production: 173,905. Model year production: 168,689 (including 12,692 stripped chassis and cars for export). The president of Buick was Harlow Curtice.

1938 Buick, Special, model 41, trunkback sedan, OCW

1938
Special Series 40, 8-cyl.

	FP	5	4	3	2	1
Conv	1103	4800	9600	16,000	22,400	32,000
Phae	1406	4950	9900	16,500	23,100	33,000
Bus Cpe	945	1350	4100	6800	9500	13,600
Spt Cpe	1101	1400	4200	7050	9850	14,100
2 dr FsBk	981	1350	4100	6800	9500	13,600
2 dr Sed	1006	1300	4050	6700	9400	13,400
FsBk Sed	1022	1350	4150	6900	9700	13,800
4 dr Sed	1047	1300	4050	6750	9450	13,500

1938 Buick, Century, model 68, 2-dr. sedan, OCW

Century Series 60, 8-cyl.	FP	5	4	3	2	1
Conv	1359	5550	11,100	18,500	25,900	37,000
Phae	1713	5700	11,400	19,000	26,600	38,000
Spt Cpe	1226	1650	4650	7800	10,900	15,600
2 dr Sed	1256	1400	4200	7050	9850	14,100
FsBk Sed	1272	1450	4250	7100	9900	14,200
4 dr Sed	1297	1350	4150	6900	9700	13,800
Roadmaster Series 80, 8-cyl.						
Phae	1983	5850	11,700	19,500	27,300	39,000
FsBk Sed	1645	1900	5000	8300	11,600	16,600
4 dr Sed	1645	1650	4650	7800	10,900	15,600
Fml Sed	1758	2200	5300	8800	12,300	17,600

1938 Buick, Limited, model 91, 4-dr. sedan, AA

Limited Series 90, 8-cyl.						
4 dr Sed	2176	3000	6000	10,000	14,000	20,000
7P Sed	2350	3150	6300	10,500	14,700	21,000
Limo	2453	3900	7800	13,000	18,200	26,000

1939

1939 BUICK: Buick's styling for 1939 was highlighted by a new two-piece "waterfall" grille with thin vertical bars and a substantial increase in window area. On the Series 40 and 60 bodies the windshield area was 26% larger, their front door windows were 16% larger and a 21% increase in area was claimed for their rear windows, which were on all models of a one-piece design. Other key design changes included a narrower hood, thinner front door pillars and larger hubcaps.

A new dash arrangement and "Handi-shift" column-mounted gearshifts were key interior changes. All major gauges except for the clock which was mounted on the passenger's side were positioned directly in front of the driver.

1939 Buick, Special, model 41, 4-dr. sedan, OCW

BUICK SPECIAL — SERIES 40 — EIGHT: The Series 40 wheelbase was reduced 2" to 120". Both a new clutch with only 9 parts as compared to 41 in 1938 and a new lighter and stronger transmission were introduced. In place of the normal running boards, optional narrow trim strips could be installed. The Series 40 interior was finished in walnut finish garnish moldings.

The Sport Sedan, Model 47 was dropped from the Special and Century lines and the Convertible Coupe now was fitted with rear opera seats rather than the rumble seat which was no longer offered for any Buick. The Convertible Phaeton model was also dropped for 1939. Its successor was the Convertible Sport Phaeton with a trunk-back body style in both the Special and Century lines.

BUICK CENTURY — SERIES 60 — EIGHT: The Series 60 shared the new clutch assembly with the Series 40 and was also available with the optional rocker panel trim strip. Its interior garnish molding was mahogany.

BUICK ROADMASTER — SERIES 80 — EIGHT: The Roadmaster shared stainless steel windshield and rear window trim plus mahogany interior trim panels with the Limited models. The Series 80 Sport Phaeton could be ordered with either the fastback or rear trunk style.

BUICK LIMITED — SERIES 90 — EIGHT: The 3 Series 90 Buicks continued to use a 140" wheelbase and the Limousine model featured a movable glass partition in back of the chauffeur's compartment. Standard equipment for Models 90 and 90L included rear compartment cigarette lighter and vanity case.

I.D. DATA: Serial numbers on riveted plate on right side cowling under hood. Starting: 13388547 (Flint), 23395088 (South Gate), 33405088 (Linden). Ending: 13596806 (Flint), 23592131 (South Gate), 33593652 (Linden). Same factory build identification as 1938. Engine numbers on low right rear side of crankcase adjacent to dipstick. Starting: 43572652 (Ser. 40), 63576652 (Ser. 60, 80, 90). Ending: 43786213 (Ser. 40), 93755912 (Ser. 60, 80, 90).

Note 1: Some cars were fitted with 0.010" overside pistons. These engines are identified by a dash (-) following the engine number.

Model No.	Body Type & Seating	Price	Weight	Prod. Total
Series 40				
41	4-dr. Tr. Sed.-5P	996	3547	109,213
41C	4-dr. Spt. Phae.-5P	1406	3707	724
46	2-dr. Bus. Cpe.-2P	849	3387	14,582
46C	2-dr. Conv. Cpe.-4P	1077	3517	4569
46S	2-dr. Spt. Cpe.-4P	950	3437	10,043
48	2-dr. Tr. Sed.-5P	955	3482	27,218
Series 60				
61	4-dr. Tr. Sed.-5P	1246	3832	18,462
61C	4-dr. Spt. Phae.-5P	1713	3967	249
66C	2-dr. Conv. Cpe.-4P	1343	3762	790
66S	2-dr. Spt. Cpe.-4P	1175	3687	3408
68	2-dr. Tr. Sed.-5P	1205	3557	521
Series 80				
80C	4-dr. Spt. Phae.-6P	1938	4932	3
81	4-dr. Tr. Sed.-6P	1543	4247	5460
81C	4-dr. Phae.-6P	1983	4362	311
81F	4-dr. Fml. Sed.-6P	1758	4312	303
87	4-dr. Spt. Sed.-6P	1543	4247	20
Series 90				
90	4-dr. Tr. Sed.-8P	2350	4608	650
90L	4-dr. Limo.-8P	2453	4653	423
91	4-dr. Tr. Sed.-6P	2074	4568	378

ENGINE: [Series 40] Inline. Ohv. Eight. Cast iron block. B & S: 3-3/32 x 4-1/8. Disp.: 248 cu. in. C.R.: 6.15:1. Brake H.P.: 107 @ 3400 R.P.M. Taxable H.P.: 30.63. Main bearings: 5. Valve lifters: mechanical. Carb.: Carter 4195. Torque: 126 lbs.-ft. @ 1000 R.P.M. [Series 60, 80, 90] Inline. Ohv. Eight. Cast iron block. B & S: 3-7/16 x 4-5/16. Disp.: 320.2 cu. in. C.R.: 635:1. Brake H.P. 141 @ 3600 R.P.M. Taxable H.P.: 37.81. Main bearings: 5. Valve lifters: mechanical. Carb.: Stromberg AAV26. Torque: 130 lbs.-ft. @ 1000 R.P.M.

CHASSIS: [Series 40] W.B.: 120 in. O.L.: 198-1/16 in. Frt/Rear Tread: 58-1/4- in. / 59-3/32 in. Tires: 15 x 6.50 4 ply. [Series 60] W.B.: 126 in. O.L.: 203-9/16 in. Frt/Rear Tread: 58-23/32 in. / 59-21/32 in. Tires: 15 x 7.00 4 ply. [Series 80] W.B.: 133 in. O.L.: 213-1/4 in. Frt/Rear Tread: 59-19/32 in. / 62-1/2 in. Tires: 16 x 7.00 4 ply. [Series 90] W.B.: 140 in. O.L.: 219-1/2 in. Frt/Rear Tread: 59-7/16 in. / 62-1/2 in. Tires: 16 x 7.50 6 ply.

TECHNICAL: Sliding gear transmission. Speeds: 3F/1R. Column controls. Single dry plate clutch. Shaft drive. Semi-floating rear axle. Overall Ratio: 4.40, 3.9, 3.6-Ser. 40, 3.9, 3.6, 3.4 — Ser. 60 4.18-Ser. 80 4.56 — Ser. 90. Hydraulic brakes on four wheels. Pressed steel wheels. No Rol Hill-Holder (Series 60, 80, 90).

OPTIONS: Dual sidemounts. Fender skirts. Push button radio. Leather interior. Sonomatic push button radio. White side walls. Sunshine turret roof. Fender-mounted parking lights.

HISTORICAL: Introduced Oct. 9, 1938. Standard equipment directional signals (rear only), push-button "Sonomatic" radio, "Sunshine Turret-Roof" (sun roof) optional for Series 40 and 60 2-door and 4-door. Calendar year production: 231,219. Model year production: 208,256 (including 10,932 stripped chassis and cars for export). The president of Buick was Harlow Curtice.

1939
Special Series 40, 8-cyl.

	FP	5	4	3	2	1
Conv	1077	5250	10,500	17,500	24,500	35,000
Phae	1406	5400	10,800	18,000	25,200	36,000
Bus Cpe	894	1300	4050	6750	9450	13,500
Spt Cpe	950	1400	4200	7000	9800	14,000
2 dr Sed	955	1200	3750	6250	8750	12,500
4 dr Sed	996	1250	3900	6500	9100	13,000

1939 Buick, Century, model 61, 4-dr. sedan, AA

Century Series 60, 8-cyl.

	FP	5	4	3	2	1
Conv	1343	5700	11,400	19,000	26,600	38,000
Phae	1713	5850	11,700	19,500	27,300	39,000
Spt Cpe	1175	1750	4800	8000	11,200	16,000
2 dr Sed	1205	1400	4200	7000	9800	14,000
4 dr Sed	1246	1400	4200	7050	9850	14,100

Roadmaster Series 80, 8-cyl.

	FP	5	4	3	2	1
Phae FsBk	1983	6900	13,800	23,000	32,200	46,000
Phae	1988	6750	13,500	22,500	31,500	45,000
FsBk Sed	1543	2800	5700	9500	13,300	19,000
4 dr Sed	1543	2300	5400	9000	12,600	18,000
Fml Sed	1758	3000	6000	10,000	14,000	20,000

Limited Series 90, 8-cyl.

	FP	5	4	3	2	1
8P Sed	2350	3000	6000	10,000	14,000	20,000
4 dr Sed	2074	2800	5700	9500	13,300	19,000
Limo	2453	3300	6600	11,000	15,400	22,000

1940

1940 Buick, Special, model 41, 4-dr. sedan, OCW

1940 Buick, Century, model 46S, sport coupe, JAC

BUICK SPECIAL — SERIES 40 — EIGHT: A 1 inch wheelbase increase to 121'' enabled the side mount option and front doors that fully opened to coexist. A full-width rear seat was installed in the Sport Coupe model and a dual diaphragm fuel pump was used to improve windshield wiper operation. Interior features included white trim panels and combination Bedford cloth and mohair upholstery.

BUICK SUPER — SERIES 50 — EIGHT: The new Series 50 Buick shared the 121'' wheelbase chassis with the Specials. Five body styles were offered, all of which were devoid of running boards. Bedford cord upholstery in a two-tone tan was standard. A midyear Estate wagon model was exclusive to the Super Series.

BUICK CENTURY — SERIES 60 — EIGHT: Five body styles were offered in the Century line.

BUICK ROADMASTER — SERIES 70 — EIGHT: To make room for the new Series 80 Limited models the Roadmaster was given a new Series 70 designation. It shared its body shell with the new Super line and was available in 4 body styles. Interiors of either gray or tan Bedford cord were offered.

BUICK LIMITED — SERIES 80 — EIGHT: These Limited models, mounted on 133 inch wheelbase chassis previously used for the Roadmasters had std equipment heaters and defrosters. All body styles were of a 6 passenger capacity. Interior appointments included a choice of Bedford cloth (either tan or grey), broadcloth or cloth (tan or grey) or leather.

BUICK LIMITED — SERIES 90 — EIGHT: Although all Buicks had the same front end design and 8 passenger capacity the 140'' wheelbase set the Series 90 models apart. Three body styles were offered.

I.D. DATA: Serial numbers on riveted plate on right side cowling under hood, right side of frame top near cowling. Starting: 13596807 (Flint), 23601856 (South Gate), 33611856 (Linden). Ending: 13880011 (Flint), 23871217 (South Gate), 33874783 (Linden). Same factory built identification as 1939. Engine numbers on right side of crankcase below pushrod cover toward front (Ser 40-50) same location except near rear of engine (Ser 60, 70, 80). Starting: 43786214 (Ser 40), 53786214 (50, 60, 70, 80, 90). Ending: 44074857 (Ser 40), 94074858 (Ser 50, 60 70, 80, 90).

Model No. Series 40	Body Type & Seating	Price	Weight	Prod. Total
41	4-dr. Tr. Sed.-5P	996	3660	67,308
41C	4-dr. Conv. Phae.	1355	3755	552
41T	4-dr. Taxi-5P	NA	NA	48
46	2-dr. Bus. Cpe.-2P	895	3505	12,372
46C	2-dr. Conv. Cpe.-4P	1077	3665	3664
46S	2-dr. Spt. Cpe.-4P	950	3540	8291
48	2-dr. Tr. Sed.-5P	955	3605	20,739

1940 Buick, Super, model 59, estate wagon, JAC

Series 50				
51	4-dr. Tr. Sed.-6P	1109	3790	95,875
51C	4-dr. Conv. Phae.-6P	1549	3895	1351
56C	2-dr. Conv. Cpe.-6P	1211	3785	4764
56S	2-dr. Spt. Cpe.-6P	1058	3735	26,251
59	4-dr. Est. Wag.-6P	1242	3870	495
Series 60				
61	4-dr. Tr. Sed.-5P	1211	3935	8597
61C	4-dr. Conv. Phae.-5P	1620	4050	194
66	2-dr. Bus. Cpe.-2P	1128	3800	44
66C	2-dr. Conv. Cpe.-4P	1343	3915	542
66S	2-dr. Spt. Cpe.-5P	1175	3765	96
Series 70				
71	4-dr. Tr. Sed.-6P	1359	4045	13,583
71C	4-dr. Conv. Phae.-6P	1768	4195	235
76C	4-dr. Conv. Cpe.6P	1431	4055	606
76S	2-dr. Spt. Cpe.-5P	1277	3990	3921
Series 80				
80C	4-dr. Conv. Phae.-6P	1952	4550	7
81	4-dr. Tr. Sed.-6P	1553	4400	3810
81C	4-dr. Fsbk. Conv. Phae.-6P	1952	4540	230
81F	4-dr. Fml. Sed.-6P	1727	4455	248
87	4-dr. Spt. Sed.-6P	1553	4380	14
87F	4-dr. Fml. Spt. Sed.-6P	1727	4435	7
Series 90				
90	4-dr. Tr. Sed.-8P	2096	4645	796
90L	4-dr. Limo.-8P	2199	4705	526
91	4-dr. Tr. Sed.-6P	1942	4590	417

ENGINE: [Series 40, 50] Inline. Ohv. Eight. Cast iron block. B & S: 3-3/32 x 4-1/8. Disp.: 248 cu. in. C.R.: 6.15:1. Brake H.P.: 107 @ 3400 R.P.M. Taxable H.P.: 30.63. Main bearings: 5. Valve lifters: mechanical. Carb.: Carter Model 440S, 474S or Stromberg AAV-16, A-19181. Torque: 126 lbs.-ft. @ 1000 R.P.M. [Series 60, 70, 80, 90] Inline. Ohv. Eight. Cast iron block. B & S: 3-7/16 x 4-5/16. Disp.: 320.2 cu. in. C.R.: 6.35:1. Brake H.P.: 141 @ 3600 R.P.M. Taxable H.P.: 37.81. Main bearings: 5. Valve lifters: mechanical. Carb.: Carter No 4485 or Stromberg AAV-25 A-19182. Torque: 130 lbs.-ft. @ 1000 R.P.M.

CHASSIS: [Series 40] W.B.: 121 in. O.L.: 204 in. Frt/Rear Tread: 58-7/16 in. / 59-5/32 in. Tires: 16 x 6.50. [Series 50] W.B.: 121 in. O.L.: 204 in. Frt/Rear Tread: 58-7/16 in. / 59-5/32 in. Tires: 16 x 6.50. [Series 60] W.B.: 126 in. O.L.: 209 in. Frt/Rear Tread: 58-5/16 in. / 59-1/4 in. Tires: 15 x 7.00. [Series 70] W.B.: 126 in. O.L.: 214 in. Frt/Rear Tread: 58-5/16 in. / 59-1/4 in. Tires: 15 x 7.00. [Series 80] W.B.: 133 in. O.L.: 213-1/4 in. Frt/Rear Tread: 59-19/32 in. / 62-1/2 in. Tires: 16 x 7.50. [Series 90] W.B.: 140 in. O.L.: 219-1/2 in. Frt/Rear Tread: 59-7/16 in. / 62-1/2 in. Tires: 16 x 7.50.

TECHNICAL: Sliding gear transmission. Speeds: 3F/1R. Column controls. Single dry plate clutch. Shaft drive. Semi-floating rear axle. Overall Ratio: 3.9 (Ser. 40). Hydraulic brakes on four wheels. Pressed steel wheels. No Rol Hill-Holder.

OPTIONS: Seat covers. Front bumper guard. Fog lights. Roof mounted radio antenna (closed cars). Telescoping vacuum-powered mounted on left front fender (open cars). Sonomatic radio (63.00). Fender skirts. Dual white sidewall tires. Fresh Aire underseat heater/defroster. DeLuxe steering wheel (12.50). Rear seat radio (Model 90-L). Outside mirrors. Grille guard. Electric clock (Std Series 60, 70, 80, 90). Folding rear center guard. Winter grille cover. Radiator insect screen. Twin comfort cushions. Front door scuff pads. Visor vanity mirrors.

HISTORICAL: Introduced Sept. 22, 1939. Innovations: All Buick engines were equipped with oil filters and sealed beam headlights were used on all models. A new feature was Fore-N-Aft Flash-Way directionals. Calendar year production: 310,995. Model year production: 283,404 (including 8288 stripped chassis and cars for export). The president of Buick was Harlow Curtice. Buick had its best production year in history in 1940. On Nov. 18, 1940 the 4 millionth Buick was produced. 1940 was the last year Buicks were available with side mounts.

1940
Special Series 40, 8-cyl.

	FP	5	4	3	2	1
Conv	1077	5400	10,800	18,000	25,200	36,000
Phae	1355	5550	11,100	18,500	25,900	37,000
Bus Cpe	895	1400	4200	7000	9800	14,000
Spt Cpe	950	1500	4350	7250	10,150	14,500
2 dr Sed	955	1250	3900	6500	9100	13,000
4 dr Sed	996	1300	4050	6750	9450	13,500

1940 Buick, Super, model 56C, convertible coupe, OCW

Super Series 50, 8-cyl.

	FP	5	4	3	2	1
Conv	1077	5400	10,800	18,000	25,200	36,000
Phae	1355	5550	11,100	18,500	25,900	37,000
Cpe	1058	1450	4250	7100	9900	14,200
4 dr Sed	1109	1300	4050	6750	9450	13,500
Sta Wag	1242	4800	9600	16,000	22,400	32,000

1940 Buick, Century, model 61C, convertible phaeton, OCW

1940 Buick, Roadmaster, model 76S, sport coupe, OCW

180

Century Series 60, 8-cyl.

	FP	5	4	3	2	1
Conv	1343	5850	11,700	19,500	27,300	39,000
Phae	1620	6000	12,000	20,000	28,000	40,000
Bus Cpe	1128	1750	4800	8000	11,200	16,000
Spt Cpe	1175	1800	4950	8250	11,550	16,500
4 dr Sed	1211	1550	4500	7500	10,500	15,000

Roadmaster Series 70, 8-cyl.

	FP	5	4	3	2	1
Conv	1431	6000	12,000	20,000	28,000	40,000
Phae	1768	6150	12,300	20,500	28,700	41,000
Cpe	1277	2000	5100	8500	11,900	17,000
4 dr Sed	1359	1750	4800	8000	11,200	16,000

Limited Series 80, 8-cyl.

	FP	5	4	3	2	1
FsBk Phae	1952	6900	13,800	23,000	32,200	46,000
Phae	1952	6750	13,500	22,500	31,500	45,000
FsBk Sed	1553	3300	6600	11,000	15,400	22,000
4 dr Sed	1553	3400	6900	11,500	16,100	23,000
Fml Sed	1727	3750	7500	12,500	17,500	25,000
Fml FsBk	1727	3900	7800	13,000	18,200	26,000

Limited Series 90, 8-cyl.

	FP	5	4	3	2	1
7P Sed	1942	3750	7500	12,500	17,500	25,000
Fml Sed	2096	3900	7800	13,000	18,200	26,000
Limo	2199	4050	8100	13,500	18,900	27,000

1941

1941 BUICK: For the 1941 model year which was destined to set new records Buick introduced twin carburetion, new bodies and on a very limited (5 cars in all) basis custom body work by Brunn on Roadmaster and Limited Series chassis. Buick's "Fireball" engine for 1941 was fitted with dome-shaped pistons and combustion chambers. All series were available with a choice of rear axle ratios at no extra cost. All cars were offered in two-tone color combinations with 19 selections at no extra charge.

1941 Buick, Special, model 44C, convertible coupe, OCW

BUICK SPECIAL — SERIES 40 — EIGHT: Both the Special and Century lines received new bodies for 1941. As with all 1941 Buicks they featured front fenders that extended nearly to the front door, headlights that were almost totally integrated into the front fender line and a broader front grille. The Estate model moved into the Series 40 line for 1941. On Feb. 3, 1941 four new Special series 40A models were introduced with a 118" wheelbase. These carried a 40-A designation which brought a new 40-B identification for the original Series 40.

BUICK SUPER — SERIES 50 — EIGHT: The Super Buicks as all other Buicks above Series 40 were equipped with standard compound carburetion. Bodies were carried over from 1940 but all Buicks had overall heights lowered from 9/10 to 2-3/4".

BUICK CENTURY — SERIES 60 — EIGHT: With its new body and 165 hp the Century Buick ranked both as America's most powerful automobile and one of its most attractive. It shared thin chrome strips on the front fenders with all production Buicks except the 40-B Specials. Introduced into both the Century and Special lines was the new Sedanet body style.

BUICK ROADMASTER — SERIES 70 — EIGHT: Four Roadmaster body styles were available, all with the 165hp carburetion engine.

BUICK LIMITED — SERIES 90 — EIGHT: The 133" wheelbase Limited Series was not offered in 1941. Standard equipment on the 139" Limited included rear fender skirts.

I.D. DATA: Serial numbers underhood, on right side of firewall. Starting: Ser. 40A-14034052 (Flint), 23994170 (South Gate), 34007924 (Linden). All others — 13880012 (Flint), 23892008 (South Gate), 33897008 (Linden). Ending: Ser. 40A — 14257441 (Flint). Engine numbers on crankcase as in 1940. Starting: Ser. 40 — 44074859, Ser. 40-A - A4074859, Ser. 50, 60, 70, 90 — 54074859. Ending: Ser. 40-A — A4457940, Ser. 50, 60, 70, 80, 90 — 94453893.

Model No. Series 40-A	Body Type & Seating	Price	Weight	Prod. Total
44	2-dr. Bus. Cpe.-3P	915	3530	3258
44C	2-dr. Conv. Cpe.-6P	1138	3780	4282
44S	2-dr. Spt. Cpe.-6P	980	3590	5269
47	4-dr. Tr. Sed.-6P	1021	3670	13,992
Series 40-B				
41	4-dr. Tr. Sed.-6P	1052	3730	91,138
44SE	4-dr. Sed. Sup. Equipment	NA	NA	13,378
46	2-dr. Bus. Cpe.-3P	735	3630	9185
46S	2-dr. S'net.	1006	3700	87,687
46SSE	2-dr. S'net. Sup. Equip.-6P	1063	NA	9591
49	4-dr. Est. Wag.-6P	1463	3980	838
Series 50				
51	4-dr. Tr. Sed.-6P	1185	3770	57,367
51C	2-dr. Conv. Phae.-6P	1555	4015	467
56	2-dr. Bus. Cpe.-3P	1031	3620	2449
56C	2-dr. Conv. Cpe.-6P	1267	3810	12,181
56S	2-dr. Spt. Cpe.-6P	1113	3670	19,603
Series 60				
61	4-dr. Tr. Sed.-6P	1288	4239	15,027
66	2-dr. Bus. Cpe.-3P	1195	4093	220
66S	2-dr. S'net.-6P	1241	4157	5521
Series 70				
71	4-dr. Tr. Sed.-6P	1364	4204	10,431
71C	4-dr. Conv. Phae.-6P	1457	4285	312
76C	2-dr. Conv. Cpe.-6P	1775	4451	1845
76S	2-dr. Spt. Cpe.-6P	1282	4109	2784
Series 90				
90	4-dr. Tr. Sed.-8P	2360	4680	885
90L	4-dr. Limo.-8P	2465	4760	605
91	4-dr. Tr. Sed.-6P	2155	4575	1223
90F	Fml. Sed.-6P	2310	4665	293

ENGINE: [Series 40A, 40B] Inline. Ohv. Eight. Cast iron block. B & S: 3-3/32 x 4-1/8. Disp.: 248 cu. in. C.R.: 6.15:1. Brake H.P.: 115 @ 3500 R.P.M. opt compound carburetion for Series 40A & 40B boosts H.P. to 125 at 3800 R.P.M. Main bearings: 5. Valve lifters: mechanical. Carb.: Carter 487-S or Stromberg AAV-16. Torque: 210 lbs.-ft. @ 2000 R.P.M. [Series 50] Inline. Ohv. Eight. Cast iron block. B & S: 3-3/32 x 4-1/8. Disp.: 248 cu. in. C.R.: 7:0. Brake H.P. 125 @ 3800 R.P.M. Main bearings: 5. Valve lifters: mechanical. Carb.: Carter 509S, 510S or Stromberg AAV-16, AA-1. Torque: 278 lbs.-ft. @ 2200 R.P.M. [Series 60, 70, 90] Inline. Ohv. Eight. Cast iron block. B & S: 3-7/16 x 4-5/16. Disp.: 320.2 cu. in. C.R.: 7.0:1. Brake H.P.: 165 @ 3800 R.P.M. Main bearings: 5. Valve lifters: mechanical. Carb.: Carter 509S, 510S or Stromberg AAV-16, AA1. Torque: 278 lbs.-ft. @ 2200 R.P.M.

CHASSIS: [Series 40-A] W.B.: 118 in. O.L.: 202-17/32 W-75-15/16 in. Height: 67-13/32 in. Frt/Rear Tread: 59-1/8 in. / 62-3/16 in. Tires: 15 x 6.50. [Series 40B] W.B.: 121 in. O.L.: 208-3/4 in. Height 66-11/16 in. Frt/Rear Tread: 58-7/16 in. / 59-5/32 in. Tires: 16 x 6.50. [Series 50] W.B.: 121 in. O.L.: 210-3/8 in. Height: 66 in. Frt/Rear Tread: 58-7/16 in. / 59-5/32 in. Tires: 16 x 6.50. [Series 60] W.B.: 126 in. O.L.: 213-1/2 in. Height: 66-13/16 in. Frt/Rear Tread: 58-5/16 in. / 59-1/4 in. Tires: 15 x 7.00. [Series 70] W.B.: 126 in. O.L.: 215 in. Height: 66-1/8 in. Frt/Rear Tread: 59-1/8 in. / 62-1/4 in. Tires: 15 x 7.00. [Series 90] W.B.: 139 in. O.L.: 228-5/8 in. Height: 68-7/8 in. Frt/Rear Tread: 58-11/32 in. / 62-1/2 in. Tires: 16 x 7.50.

TECHNICAL: Sliding gear transmission. Speeds: 3F/1R. Column controls. Single dry plate clutch. Shaft drive. Semi floating rear axle. Overall Ratio: Ser. 40 — single carburetor, 4.4:1, compound carburetor 4.1:1. Ser. 50, 4.4:1, Ser. 60, 70 — 3.9:1. Ser. 90 4.2:1. Hydraulic brakes on four wheels. Pressed steel wheels. Drivetrain Options: Hill-Holder No Rol (9.00). Compound carburetion (Ser. 40 except Models 41SE & 46SSE (15.39).

OPTIONS: Clock electric (special only). Super Sonomatic (shortwave & regular band). Underseat heater & defroster (standard on models 51C, 71C, & Ser. 90) (33.00). Rear stainless steel footrest molding (Sed.). Vacuum pump windshield washer (std. Ser. 90) (3.85). EZI, no glare mirrors. Fender skirts (std. on Ser. 90) (10.00). Fog lights (10.75). Sonomatic pushbutton radio & antenna (65.00). Special paint (41.05). DeLuxe Dash Heater (15.50). Dual Defroster (7.50).

HISTORICAL: Introduced Oct. 13, 1940. Buick introduced its 2-way hood which could be opened from either side for 1941. Calendar year sales: 297,381. Calendar year production: 316,251. Model year production: 377,428 (including 7597 stripped chassis & cars for export.) The president of Buick was Harlow Curtis.

1941 Buick, Super, model 51C, convertible phaeton, OCW

1941
Special Series 40-A, 8-cyl.

	FP	5	4	3	2	1
Conv	1138	4500	9000	15,000	21,000	30,000
Bus Cpe	915	1175	3600	6050	8450	12,100
Spt Cpe	980	1200	3800	6300	8800	12,600
4 dr Sed	1021	1175	3600	6050	8450	12,100
Special Series 40-B, 8-cyl.						
Bus Cpe	935	1200	3800	6300	8800	12,600
2 dr S'net	1006	1350	4100	6800	9500	13,600
Torp Sed	1134	1250	3900	6550	9150	13,100
Sta Wag	1463	4050	8100	13,500	18,900	27,000

NOTE: Add 5 percent for SSE.

	FP	5	4	3	2	1
Super Series 50, 8-cyl.						
Conv	1267	5100	10,200	17,000	23,800	34,000
Phae	1555	5400	10,800	18,000	25,200	36,000
Cpe	1031	1400	4200	7050	9850	14,100
4 dr Sed	1185	1350	4100	6800	9500	13,600
Century Series 60, 8-cyl.						
Bus Cpe	1195	1400	4200	7000	9800	14,000
2 dr S'net	1241	1800	4950	8250	11,550	16,500
4 dr Sed	1288	1650	4650	7750	10,850	15,500
Roadmaster Series 70, 8-cyl.						
Conv	1457	6750	13,500	22,500	31,500	45,000
Phae	1775	6900	13,800	23,000	32,200	46,000
Cpe	1282	1900	5000	8300	11,600	16,600
4 dr Sed	1364	1650	4650	7800	10,900	15,600
Limited Series 90, 8-cyl.						
7P Sed	2155	2900	5850	9750	13,650	19,500
4 dr Sed	2360	3000	6000	10,000	14,000	20,000
Fml Sed	2310	3300	6600	11,000	15,400	22,000
Limo	2465	4050	8100	13,500	18,900	27,000

1942

1942 BUICK: The 1942 Buicks offered the very appealing Sedanet fastback style which had been the sensation of 1941 in all series except the Limited line. New wider and lower bodies were offered for the Series 50 and Series 70 and "Airfoil" front fenders that flowed into the lines of the rear fenders were introduced on Convertibles and Sedanet models in Series 50 and Series 70. All models had new front fender trim featuring parallel chrome strips. Also featured for 1942 was a handsome new grille with a lower outline and thin vertical bars.

After the government prohibited the use of chrome trim on Jan. 1, 1942 Buick began production of the H models. A number of body styles were dropped and most trim was now painted. Cast iron pistons were used in the 248cid engine and the Series 90 cars were dropped. The last of the 1942 Buicks was completed on Feb. 4, 1942.

1942 Buick, Special model 41, 4-dr. sedan, AA

BUICK SPECIAL — SERIES 40-A, 40-B — EIGHT: All Series 40 Buicks had new front fenders that extended well into the front door region. Models 41SE and 46SSE were fitted with Century interiors.

BUICK SUPER — SERIES 50 — EIGHT: The swept-back fenders of the Convertible and Sedanet Supers made them styling leaders. A feature the Supers shared with other Buicks was a new interior air intake positioned near the front grille which eliminated the old cowl-level ventilator.

BUICK CENTURY — SERIES 60 — EIGHT: The Century 4-door models along with those in the Special and Limited series had 6 side windows. All Century models had, prior to Jan. 1942, added side trim in their rear fenders. This feature was also common to all Buicks except the Series 40A and the Series 50 and Series 70 models with "Airfoil" front fenders. Those cars had twin side bars that ran unbroken the full length of the body.

BUICK ROADMASTER — SERIES 70 — EIGHT: The new Roadmaster bodies were lower and wider than in 1941 and along with the Series 50 models featured small reflector lenses on their rear fenders.

1942 Buick, Roadmaster, model 71, 4-dr. sedan, JAC

BUICK LIMITED — SERIES 90 — EIGHT: The 3 Series 90 models combined the older notch back styling with the extended length front fender format of the Series 40, 50 and 60 Buicks. With standard rear fender skirts the Limited also carried twin chrome trim strips on their front and rear fenders.

I.D. DATA: Serial numbers under hood, on right side of firewall. Starting: 14257442 - Flint, 24273684 - South Gate, 3426384 - Linden. The same factory-built identification of 1941 was continued. Engine numbers on crankcase as in 1941. Starting: Series 40A 4457941A, Ser 40B 4457971-4, Ser 50 4457941-5, Ser 60 4457941-6, Ser 70 4457941-7, Ser 90 4457941-9. Ending: Series 40A 4556599A, Ser 40B 4556599-4.

Model No.	Body Type & Seating	Price	Weight	Prod. Total
Series 40A				
44	2-dr. Util. Cpe.-3P	990	3510	461
44C	2-dr. Conv. Cpe.-6P	1260	3790	1776
47	4-dr. Tr. Sed.	1080	3650	1611
48	2-dr. Bus. S'dnt.-3P	1010	3555	559
48S	2-dr. Family S'dnt.-6P	1045	3610	5981
Special 40-B				
41	4-dr. Tr. Sed.-6P	1203	NA	17,187
41SE	Sed. Sup. Equipment-4P	1287	NA	2286
46	2-dr. Bus. S'dnt.-3P	1020	3650	1406
46S	2-dr. Family S'dnt.-6P	1075	3705	11,856
46SSE	8-dr. S'dnt. Sup. Equipment	NA	NA	1809
49	4-dr. Est. Wag.	1450	3925	326
Series 50				
51	4-dr. Tr. Sed.-6P	1280	3890	16,001
56C	2-dr. Conv. Cpe.-6P	1450	4025	2454
56S	4-dr. S'dnt.-6P	1230	3800	14,579
Series 60				
61	4-dr. Sed.-6P	1350	4065	3342
66S	2-dr. S'dnt.-6P	1300	3985	1229
Series 70				
71	4-dr. Tr. Sed.-6P	1465	4150	5418
76C	2-dr. Conv. Cpe.-6P	1675	4300	509
76S	2-dr. S'dnt.-6P	1365	4075	2471
Series 90				
90	4-dr. Tr. Sed.-8P	2455	4710	144
90L	4-dr. Limo.-8P	2716	NA	192
91	4-dr. Tr. Sed.-6P	2245	4665	215
90F	Formal Sed.-6P	2395	4695	85

ENGINE: [Series 40A, 40B] Inline. Ohv. Eight. Cast iron block. B & S: 3-3/32 x 4-1/8. Disp.: 248 cu. in. Brake H.P.: 110* @ 3400 R.P.M. * 118hp @ 3600 with compound combustion. Main bearings: 5. Valve lifters: mechanical. Carb.: Carter 487-S or Stromberg AAV-16. [Series 50] Inline. Ohv. Eight. Cast iron block. B & S: 3-3/32 x 4-1/8. Disp.: 2118 cu. in. Brake H.P.: 118 @ 3600 R.P.M. Main bearings: 5. Valve lifters: mechanical. Carb.: Carter 509S, 510S or Stromberg AAV-16, AA1. [Series 60, 70, 90] Inline. Ohv. Eight. Cast iron block. B & S: 3-7/16 x 4-5/16. Disp.: 320.2 cu. in. C.R.: 6.7:1. Brake H.P.: 165 @ 3800 R.P.M. Main bearings: 5. Valve lifters: mechanical. Carb.: Carter 509S, 510S or Stromberg AAV-16, AA-1. Torque: 278 lbs.-ft. @ 2200 R.P.M.

CHASSIS: [Series 40A; 40B] W.B.: 118 in. O.L.: 202-17/32 in. Height: 67-13/32 in. Frt/Rear Tread: 59-1/8 in. / 62-3/16 in. Tires: 15 x 6.50. [Series 50] W.B.: 124 in. O.L.: 210 in. Height: 66-11/16 in. Frt/Rear Tread: 58-7/16 in. / 59-5/32 in. Tires: 16 x 6.5. [Series 60] W.B.: 126 in. O.L.: 213-1/2 in. Height: 66-13/16 in. [Series 70] W.B.: 129 in. O.L.: 217 in. Height: 66-1/16 in. Frt/Rear Tread: 59-1/8 in. / 62-1/4 in. Tires: 15 x 7.00. [Series 90] W.B.: 139 in. O.L.: 228-5/8 in. Height: 68-7/8 in. Tires: 15 x7.00. [Series 40B] W.B.: 121 in. O.L.: 208-3/4 in.

TECHNICAL: Sliding gear transmission. Speeds: 3F/1R. Column controls. Single dry plate clutch. Shaft drive. Semi-floating rear axle. Overall ratio: 3.90 - Ser 70, 3.6 or 3.9 - Ser 60. Hydraulic brakes on four wheels. Pressed steel wheels. Hill-holder: No Rol.

OPTIONS: Fender skirts on Series 40 & 50. Electric clock (special only). Super sonomatic radio. Under seat heater & defroster. Windshield washer. EZI mirrors. Fender skirts. Fog lamps. Sonomatic radio.

HISTORICAL: Introduced Oct. 3, 1941. Calendar year production: 16,601. Model year production: 94,442 (including 2575 stripped chassis and cars for export). The president of Buick was Harlow Curtice.
Production of 1942 model Buicks ended on Feb. 2, 1942.

1942

Special Series 40-A, 8-cyl.	FP	5	4	3	2	1
Bus Cpe	1067	1025	2600	5250	7300	10,500
2 dr S'net	1125	1075	3000	5500	7700	11,000
3P S'net	1088	1025	2600	5250	7300	10,500
Conv	1352	3350	6750	11,250	15,750	22,500
4 dr Sed	1162	1000	2400	5000	7000	10,000
Special Series 40-B, 8-cyl.						
3P S'net	1098	1025	2600	5250	7300	10,500
2 dr S'net	1156	1075	3000	5500	7700	11,000
4 dr Sed	1203	1125	3450	5750	8050	11,500
Sta Wag	1551	3900	7800	13,000	18,200	26,000
Super Series 50, 8-cyl.						
Conv	1560	3600	7200	12,000	16,800	24,000
2 dr S'net	1329	1175	3650	6100	8500	12,200
4 dr Sed	1381	1200	3750	6250	8750	12,500
Century Series 60, 8-cyl.						
2 dr S'net	1402	1200	3750	6250	8750	12,500
4 dr Sed	1454	1250	3900	6500	9100	13,000
Roadmaster Series 70, 8-cyl.						
Conv	1811	4200	8400	14,000	19,600	28,000
2 dr S'net	1517	1300	4050	6750	9450	13,500
4 dr Sed	1590	1350	4150	6900	9700	13,800
Limited Series 90, 8-cyl.						
8P Sed	2610	1500	4350	7250	10,150	14,500
4 dr Sed	2400	1300	4050	6750	9450	13,500
Fml Sed	2558	1650	4650	7750	10,850	15,500
Limo	2716	2600	5500	9250	12,950	18,500

BULKLEY-RIDER — That the Bulkley-Rider Tractor Company of Los Angeles (usually misspelled Buckley-Rider) built an automobile circa 1915 in Los Angeles has been indicated on numerous lists. This is in error. The firm built heavy-duty tractors and farm tractors designed by Jim Fouch and William A. Rider. Marcius Bulkley was a dealer/distributor for Autocar, Knox and Bulkley-Rider trucks, later Perfex commercial vehicles.

BULLARD STEAM — Springfield, Massachusetts — (1885-1886) — James H. Bullard began work on his steam car in 1885. It had a two-cylinder engine and a cylindrical boiler with fire tubes placed lengthwise. The latter was the most significant feature of the Bullard because it represented the first instance in steam car development in which essential functions of the vehicle were automatically controlled. Bullard's flash boiler used liquid rather than the more usual solid fuel, and it was made automatic by the simple expedient of a pilot fire which always remained lit. The car was ready for the road by the summer of 1886. In subsequent experiments Bullard switched from kerosene fuel to alcohol but found that it provided insufficient heat and also occasionally caused his vehicle to catch fire. Bullard was among the first to atomize fuel oil with a device similar to today's perfume atomizers. Most of his ideas were patented, and the majority dealt with automating a steam car's controls. He continued experimentation on his own until 1899 when he convinced A.H. Overman to build a steam car called the Victor.

BULLARD — Marshall, Michigan — (1904) — George A. Bullard began his foundry and machine shop business at the corner of Kalamazoo and Spruce in 1872, and within a decade it was one of the largest industries in Marshall. Furnaces and stoves were his principal products, though he developed a sideline enterprise in school and church furniture early on. In 1888 Bullard disposed of his furnace business, and spent the remainder of his career building school desks and church pews. In 1904 he also built an automobile, but it was for his own pleasure and use; manufacture was not contemplated. Upon his retirement in 1909, he sold his furniture factory.

BULL MOOSE — St. Paul, Minnesota — (1914) — Bull Moose was the name given to the axles, bodies and other automotive components that were manufactured by L.C. Erbes in St. Paul. During 1913 Erbes had bought the remains of the defunct Cutting car of Jackson, Michigan and consolidated both ventures as the Bull Moose-Cutting Automobile Company. In early 1914 he bought up the defunct Milwaukee Motor Company, including its stock of finished and unfinished engines, which nicely prepared him — he thought — for entry into the automobile manufacturing field. During the summer he announced plans to build a standard roadster based on the Cutting and to be called a Bull Moose, and a cyclecar designed by John E. Pfeffer of Minneapolis and to be called a Baby Moose. The Baby Moose was put into production in St. Paul, but almost immediately L.C. Erbes had second thoughts about the wisdom of calling the roadster the Bull Moose. Instead he renamed the car the L.C.E., with the pilot models built in the old Cutting factory in Michigan, though operations had moved to Waterloo, Iowa by the time production began later in 1914.

BULLOCK — Cincinnati, Ohio — (1900) — The Bullock Electric Manufacturing Company was located on East Norwood in Cincinnati. George Bullock was president and treasurer, J.S. Neave was vice-president, J.W. Bullock secretary and William Cooper superintendent. This company was indicated to be manufacturing an automobile in the Hiscox book *Horseless Vehicles, Automobiles, Motor Cycles* published in 1900. Details regarding the car being built are lacking.

BUNDY — Binghamton, New York — (1895) — W.L. Bundy was the superintendent of the Bundy Company of Binghamton and in 1895 he built a steam wagon for his own use. "Motion is communicated to the machine through the rear wheels, which are fastened to the revolving axle and connected with the engine by cogs, sprockets and chain" was the rather nice way he described it. The engine and boiler were placed just ahead of the rear wheels. Two sets of sprocket wheels provided for a two-speed transmission: fast and slow. "The fast speed is used on levels," Bundy explained, "and when a hill is reached the fast gear is thrown off and the other used. This decreases the speed one-half but gives double power for hill climbing." Ten miles an hour was possible on country roads, and the Bundy steam wagon could haul a load of two tons.

BURCH AUTO-SLEIGH — This automotive sleigh of 1905-1906 is more appropriately referred to by the name of its designer. Refer to Cook Auto-Sledge.

BURDETTE — New Athens, Ohio — (1870) — It must have been something to see. The vehicle was the idea of Oliver Burdette of New Athens, but he had the help (financial and otherwise) of area residents James Sharp and Robert Webb in seeing it through. The vehicle that resulted was a leviathan, fully eighteen feet in length, with a trailing fuel tender the length of a wagon and a water tank equally as long. This big steamer did move under its own power, its owners motoring one time as far as Smyrna (a distance of twenty miles) and reportedly causing a water famine in the area by pumping every well dry along the road, this undoubtedly an exaggeration. County fairs offered $50 to $100 for the trio to exhibit the car, which Burdette, Sharp and Webb did at every opportunity. "I had my first glimpse of that wonderful steam wagon at the Cadiz Fair," reported an eyewitness. ". . . a sharp whistle, a cloud of black smoke and the great fluffy puffs of white steam, a commotion and stir among the frightened horses and then a monster thing rolled, walked, crawled, into the course and wound its huge length around the quarter-mile track. Mr. Webb standing erect at the helm, on his face a look of pride, his long white beard floating down over his vest, was emblematic of Father Time or Noah steering the ark." Unfortunately, there were design flaws in the Burdette, among them an engine which was not reversible, resulting in the bolide once motoring gently through a roundhouse when it could not be halted. The Burdette also caused one fatality, which probably was the reason for its being taken off the road forever.

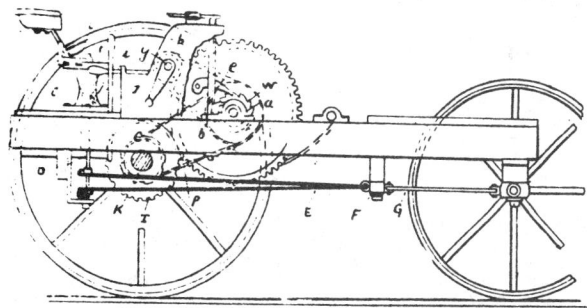

1895 Burdick

BURDICK — Hubbell, Nebraska — (1895) — Whether A. Burdick of Hubbell enjoyed success with a vehicle using his motor is not known, but he insisted it would work nicely. It was a spring motor which could be applied to any ordinary wagon or carriage. "The springs can be wound in three ways," Burdick explained, "namely: by the momentum of the vehicle in going down hill, by hand, or by a small electric battery of about one man power."

1909 Burdick, model C, touring, NAHC

BURDICK — Eau Claire, Wisconsin — (1909) — Ralph Burdick's American Motor Company of Eau Claire manufactured small two-cycle marine engines. But when Burdick decided to get into the automobile business, he did it big. Organizing as the Burdick Motor Car Company in 1909, he announced a 590-cubic-inch (Continental engine) that would deliver 60 hp in the standard touring car which was priced at $7000 and a special Greyhound model delivering 85 hp for which no price was announced. Both cars were to be placed on a huge 142-inch wheelbase chassis. The Greyhound was never built, the touring car was. "There was no research to it at all," mechanic Al Johnson remembered years later to an Eau Claire *Leader Telegram* reporter. "Assembling it was just a matter of buying a front end and putting it here, buying a transmission and putting it there, getting a rear axle and putting it there. Sometimes the parts fit and sometimes they didn't. It was fun as long as it lasted." It didn't last very long. Johnson recalled also that the Burdick rode like a lumber wagon.

BURG — Burlington, Iowa — (1902) — In early 1900 the Burg Wagon Company of Burlington wrote a letter to the editors of *The Motor Vehicle Review* indicating its intention to enter automobile-building ranks and its desire to correspond with engine builders whose products were "first class, reliable . . . and of four, six and eight horse power." Probably Burg was inundated with replies, but the firm ultimately decided against automobile manufacture. Ed Burg did build a car for himself in 1902, no doubt using a purchased engine. Its top speed was 15 mph, and it is believed to have been the only car produced in the Burg Wagon Company factory.

1910 Burg, touring, NAHC

BURG — Dallas City, Illinois — (1910-1913) — The L. Burg Carriage Company began with the building of four-cylinder cars. The firm soon mounted the six-cylinder bandwagon, however, and during its final year tried to pretend it had never built fours at all. The Burg Six was a big car with an L-head six developing 60 hp at 1500 rpm. Among the reasons perhaps for the demise of this old firm — it had begun in the carriage-building field during the Civil War — was the ill-disguised belligerence which was introduced to its advertising. Being told that "hundreds of thousands of dollars have been wasted by [those] indiscreet and inexperienced automobile buyers" choosing not to buy a Burg was a less-than-flattering approach to potential customers who had heretofore been thusly indiscreet and inexperienced. Heading Burg's automobile department had been Charles Zimmerman, who previously designed the Eureka in St. Louis. Some decades later, the Burg factory was turned into a dance hall.

1910-1911 BURG
4-cyl., 30 hp, 112" wb

	FP	5	4	3	2	1
Model K Tour.-5P	1750	2800	3700	5500	9000	19,500
Model L Rds.-5P	1750	2900	3700	5600	9100	20,000
Model M Rbt.-3P	1750	2900	3700	5600	9100	20,000

1912 BURG
Model K — **4-cyl., 26 hp, 114" wb**

Tour.-5P	1750	3000	4000	6000	9500	21,000

Model M — **4-cyl., 32 hp, 114" wb**

Tour.-7P	1750	3100	4200	6300	10,500	22,000

Model R — **6-cyl., 50 hp, 132" wb**

Tour.-7P	2400	3900	4800	7700	14,300	27,000

1913 Burg, six, touring, NAHC

1913 BURG
Six — **60 hp, 132" wb**

Tour.-7P	2400	5700	11,400	19,000	26,600	38,000

183

1899 Burgett & West Steamer, KM

BURGETT & WEST STEAM — Middleburgh, New York — (1899) —
Whether C. Edward Burgett or William S. West was the man responsible for the building of this steam vehicle remains a source of contention among descendants of both families. An article appearing in the *Cobleskill Times* in June 1926 credits Burgett with its design and building; retrospective articles from the 1950's tend to toss most of the laurels William West's way. One would suspect the car was a collaboration, and credit should be shared, though the evidence suggests the lion's share belongs to Burgett. The vehicle was built in Middleburgh in 1899 and was exhibited and driven at the Schoharie County Fairgrounds in September 1901. C. Edward Burgett, formerly a pattern-maker and machinist for General Electric in Schenectady, had opened a small machine shop in Middleburgh in the late 1890's; William West operated a laundry in town and was described as "an all-round-mechanic." The steamer was powered by an engine of two cylinders insulated with asbestos and shrouded in a polished jacket. The boiler was fifteen inches in diameter and eighteen inches high, mounted behind the front seat, and with 365 half-inch copper tubes inside. Final drive was by single chain to the rear axle. Gasoline was used for fuel. The car was used for several years thereafter, but was ultimately traded to Harry Cameron of Central Bridge for an Orient Buckboard and $100. Some time during the 1930's, it appears, it was scrapped. Though West is not known to have built another car, Burgett did or at the very least attempted to. "C.E. Burgett is building an automobile," a local newspaper reported in January 1902, "and he'll make it work if any live man can."

BURKS & GEMMILL — Los Angeles, California — (1907) — Dana Burks was the president, Jesse Gemmill the general manager and Mark Gemmill the superintendent of the Burks-Gemmill Engineering Company of 2418-2430 Sante Fe Avenue in Los Angeles. The firm manufactured marine and gasoline engines, and in 1907 announced that it was also "making ready to produce a runabout." Further documentation of the Burks & Gemmill automotive venture is lacking. The firm is known to have built farm tractors and a few truck-tractor units.

BURLINGAME — Worcester, Massachusetts — (1896) — Abraham Burlingame was a native of New England who arrived in Worcester in 1870 to establish a small machine shop on School Street. Shortly thereafter he invented a machine pulley from which, as his obituary noted, he "reaped a fortune." And he opened a big new factory at 22 Cypress Street. There he turned his inventive attention to the steam engine. In 1896 he built an experimental automobile to demonstrate the efficacy of his new powerplant, and it worked fine. He did not build another car, but turned his factory over to the production of steam engines, in which activity he prospered as well. On February 8th, 1900, as he was driving home from work for lunch, he was stricken and died of apoplexy the following morning. He was fifty-eight years old.

BURMAN — Jackson, Michigan — (1914) — Bob Burman was among America's most famous racing drivers of the pre-World War I era. His financial backer was L.C. Erbes, with whom he allied himself in late 1913 in a business venture which ultimately resulted in the L.C.E. car of 1915-1916. In 1914 Erbes also produced a limited run of race cars built to Burman's design and produced in the factory of the former Cutting in Jackson, Michigan. In April 1916, Bob Burman was killed in a race car accident in Corona, California.

BURNS — The Burns-Ramsden Motor Car Company was organized in St. Louis, Missouri during the summer of 1912 with a capital stock of $10,000 to manufacture and deal in automobiles. Incorporators were J.H. Ramsden, L. Burns, O.E. Carter and C.K. Rowland. Manufacture is doubted.

The Burns-Thomas Company was organized early in 1914 with a capital stock of $2500 to manufacture motorcars in New Haven, Connecticut. E.J. Burns, William H. Thomas, Jr., E.F. Shuster and J. Kegelmeyer were the incorporators. Manufacture is doubted.

BURNS — Buffalo, New York — (1903) — The Burns Typewriter Company of Buffalo was one of countless firms doing business in another field at the turn of the century which believed that an automobile might be a profitable sideline. Early in 1903 the Burns people built and tested a gasoline automobile, then changed their minds, announcing that fall that they "have decided not to manufacture for the present." Nor the future either, as it turned out.

1909 Burns, transformable coupe, NAHC

BURNS — Havre de Grace, Maryland — (1908-1912) — The Burns brothers — W.A., R.H. and A.G. — were among the few Eastern manufacturers of a highwheeler, which they realized by simply adding a two-cylinder air-cooled engine, friction transmission and double-chain drive to the carriages which their Burns Brothers company had been producing for decades before. Burns motor carriages sold dismally, and the brothers tried getting their vehicles closer to the ground with standard wheels but the result still resembled the buggy it was, and the car was discontinued.

1908-1909 BURNS
2-cyl., 16 hp, 90" wb

	FP	5	4	3	2	1
High Wheeled Buggy	750	2400	3400	4800	8000	17,000
Transformable Cpe.-2P	800	2300	3300	4600	7500	16,000

1910 BURNS
2-cyl., 14 hp, 96" wb

High Wheeled Buggy	800	2400	3400	4800	8000	17,000

4-cyl., 18/20 hp, 96" wb

Transformable Cpe.	800	2300	3300	4600	7500	16,000

1911 BURNS
2-cyl., 12 hp, 96" wb

Transformable Cpe.	800	2300	3300	4600	7500	16,000

1912 BURNS
2-cyl., 15 hp, 100" wb

Transformable Cpe.	800	2300	3300	4600	7500	16,000

BURR — The firm of Burr & Company in New York City has been indicated on various car rosters as building an automobile in 1897. Burr did provide the body for the Struss car produced that year, but this seems to have been the extent of its automotive activity. The company, which was at 1709 Broadway, was listed as a manufacturer of automobiles in the Hiscox book *Horseless Vehicles, Automobiles, Motor Cycles* published in 1900. Turn of the century references to the Burr company in New York City directories, however, mention carriages only as the firm's products. And it was as a coachbuilder that Burr & Company continued in business into the World War I era, specializing in bodies for foreign cars which arrived in New York as chassis only.

1906 Burr, touring, NAHC

BURR — Champaign, Illinois — (1906) — Ellis M. Burr graduated with a degree in mechanical engineering from the University of Illinois and remained in town to establish E.M. Burr & Company, a foundry and machine shop, and also to be president of the Chamber of Commerce of Champaign in 1906 when he built his automobile. A touring car on a 100-inch wheelbase and powered by a two-cylinder Cushman engine, the Burr was built for just one reason: to demonstrate the effectiveness of the three-speed transmission which Ellis Burr had invented and patented. It was a single gear engagement device with reverse drive. Hugh Dolnar, writing in *Cycle and Automobile Trade Journal*, regarded it as a break-through: ". . . only one pair of gears of any kind is in action at the same time, and hence never drives the car through more than one gear engagement between the crankshaft and the divided rear axle or the side-chain sprocket-shafts."

1902 Burrington, runabout, LC

BURRINGTON — Holyoke, Massachusetts — (1902) — B.G. Burrington of 144 Beech Street in Holyoke built a one-cylinder 6 hp car on a tubular frame stretching 60 inches between the wheels and featuring chain drive and right-hand tiller steering. Its top speed was about 20 mph, and its running range between fill-ups was about a hundred miles. Though Burrington never incorporated a company for manufacture, he sold a few examples in the neighborhood as registration lists of the period document.

BURROW — The Burrow Metal Works was a $150,000 incorporation from Albany, New York early in 1915 for the manufacture of motorcars and engines. This venture appears never to have left the paper stage.

1904 Burrowes, runabout, OCW

BURROWES — Portland, Maine — (1904-1908) — The E.T. Burrowes Company of Portland manufactured house screens. For a short while the firm also dabbled in the manufacture of automobiles, these being simple single-cylinder, chain-drive runabouts or tourers which were quite neat and tidy. The Burrowes car was strictly a sideline activity to the main business of the Burrowes company. No more than eight automobiles were ever built, and purportedly the first two met with accidents soon after delivery to their new owners. Interestingly, for a car with such a small production, the survival rate is phenomenal. One car in existence today has been documented to be a Burrowes, and another car extant is believed to be as well. When Edward Thomas Burrowes retired from his company in 1912, it was the largest screen manufacturer in the world, and also had branched into the billiard, pool table and folding card table fields.

1908 Burrowes, touring, GR

1904-1908 BURROWES

	FP	5	4	3	2	1
Burrowes	—	3300	4400	6700	12,000	24,000

1914 Burrows, 2-pass. tandem cyclecar, WLB

BURROWS — Ripley, New York — (1914-1915) — The Burrows Cyclecar Company was organized in July 1914 in Ripley with a capital stock of $30,000. Its product was typical in being a tandem two-seater with friction transmission, belt drive and a two-cylinder air-cooled 9 hp Mack engine. Not so typical was its wheelbase which was 106 inches, lengthy for a cyclecar, though a number of East Coast products stretched similarly. "Burrows Another New Yorker with Long Belt," headlined *The American Cyclecar*. The Burrows' headlamps were mounted above the level of the body, which looked rather peculiar. A tandem two-seater at $375 was the only Burrows offering for 1914; for 1915 the company featured side-by-side seating and a lower price tag, neither of which helped to make the marque survive longer. The Burrows involved in this venture were Watson and Robert P., both of Ripley.

1914 BURROWS

Tandem Cyclecar	375	2600	3600	5200	8700	18,500

1915 BURROWS

Model M Roadster	295	2450	3450	4900	8300	17,500

BURTT — The Burtt Manufacturing Company of Kalamazoo, Michigan produced an automobile from 1903 to 1906 that was marketed under the name of Cannon. Refer to Cannon.

BURWELL — Toledo, Ohio — (1899) — In April of 1899 *The Horseless Age* reported that the three-wheeled gasoline carriage built by George Burwell of Toledo "was first seen on the street the other day." Burwell was the superintendent of the Lozier bicycle factory in Toldeo, and he had designed the car in collaboration with John G. Perrin. Initially, Henry Lozier contemplated manufacture of this vehicle, but ultimately he sold out his business to the American Bicycle Company, with the tricycle design as part of the package. Subsequently, Burwell and Perrin persuaded Lozier to build a four-wheeled automobile, and the famous Lozier was the result.

BURY — New York, New York — (1927) — The Bury was an attempt to introduce an automobile patterned after the Austin Seven which had enjoyed phenomenal success in England since its introduction in 1922. The prototype was designed and built by Charles W. Bury of New York City. A roadster on a 73-inch wheelbase, it was powered by a 20 hp four-cylinder Continental Red Seal engine. Bury was intent upon manufacture, and traveled to Michigan to scout possible factory locations. Financing had already been secured, he announced. The car did attract a good deal of attention when driven to the plant of Continental Motors Corporation — and Continental was all set to supply engines. Whoever was set to supply the money, however, must have backed out quickly, because the Bury was never heard of again. Several years later the American Austin was produced in Pennsylvania, but Charles Bury was not a part of that organization. According to *The American Cyclecar* in 1914, Bury at that time had been associated with the Ritz Cyclecar Company as purchasing agent.

1927 Bury, roadster, KM

1918 Bush, touring, JAC

BUSH — The Bush Engine Company was organized in Newark, New Jersey early in 1902 by Edward T. Magoffin, Frank R. Serles and Alfred G. Brown. Capital stock was a cool $5 million. "The objects of the company are practically unlimited," *The Motor Review* reported, "and include the manufacture of boilers, engines, car-wheels, trucks, carriages, automobiles, etc." Whether Bush manufactured anything is questionable but an automobile definitely was not among its products.

Although early announcements of this 1902 automotive venture from Fond du Lac, Wisconsin gave priority to W.J. Bush, later references put his partner W.E. Hibbard in first place. Refer to Hibbard & Bush.

The Bush Manufacturing Company was organized during the spring of 1908 in Hartford, Connecticut with a capital stock of $2500 and the plan "to manufacture, buy, sell and deal in automobiles and automobile parts." Incorporators were Philip M. Bush, Edward J. Jetter and Bernard Garner. Manufacture is doubted.

1917 Bush, touring, NAHC

BUSH — **Chicago, Illinois** — **(1916-1925)** — In June 1915 John H. Bush decided to try the direct mail approach with the automobile business. He sent out brochures advertising the Bush motorcar and requesting payment in advance. When an order was received, it was forwarded together with his check to whatever company was willing to build cars for him wholesale. A Bush nameplate was fitted to the next whatever-the-car on the assembly line, and it was shipped directly to the customer. Bush never did sell many cars this way, but since his out-of-pocket expenses were few, he managed to stay in business quite a while. "Write any of these men," John Bush suggested in a 1918 flyer listing some 90 names (with addresses) of presumably satisfied Bush owners. "They will be glad to tell you honestly of their experience with Bush cars. We have not asked them if it was all right to use their names, but you can take a chance. Send postage for reply." For the most part, the addresses were places like Upper Frenchville, Maine; Sabetha, Kansas; Stady, North Dakota; Bokoshe, Oklahoma; Direct, Texas; Olga, North Dakota; Tyronza, Arkansas. Bush also claimed to have sold cars in Mexico, Ireland and the island of Mauritius in the Indian Ocean. Among the companies building his Bush car for him were Sphinx in York (Pennsylvania), Piedmont in Lynchburg (Virginia), Norwalk in Martinsburg (West Virginia), Huffman and Crow-Elkhart in Elkhart (Indiana). By the early Twenties all of these firms were irrevocably wending their way out of business, and John Bush's failure to find another factory interested in the same arrangement was doubtless the reason the Bush faded into oblivion. Like Birch Motor Cars, Inc., another Chicago direct mail house, the Bush Motor Company was affiliated with a trade school (the Bush Motor College, Inc.), but it does not appear any manufacturing was done there.

1916-1919 BUSH
Model 4-18 — 4-cyl., 19.6 hp, 116" wb

	FP	5	4	3	2	1
Tour.-5P	875	3100	4200	6300	10,500	22,000

1920 Bush, touring, KM

1920 BUSH
Model A — 4-cyl., 25 hp, 116" wb

	FP	5	4	3	2	1
Tour.-5P	1595	3100	4200	6300	10,500	22,000

Model 6 — 6-cyl., 45 hp, 121" wb

	FP	5	4	3	2	1
Tour.-5P	2010	3200	4300	6500	11,000	23,000

1921 BUSH
Model A — 4-cyl., 25 hp, 116" wb

	FP	5	4	3	2	1
Tour.-5P	1245	3100	4200	6300	10,500	22,000

Model 6 — 6-cyl., 45 hp, 121" wb

	FP	5	4	3	2	1
Tour.-5P	1575	3200	4300	6500	11,000	23,000

1922-1923 BUSH
Model EC-4 — 4-cyl., 35 hp, 116" wb

	FP	5	4	3	2	1
Tour.-5P	1125	3200	4300	6500	11,000	23,000

Model EC-6 — 6-cyl., 45 hp, 121" wb

	FP	5	4	3	2	1
Tour.-5P	1350	3300	4400	6700	12,000	24,000

1924-1925 BUSH
Model 4-24 — 4-cyl., 35 hp, 116" wb

	FP	5	4	3	2	1
Tour.-5P	1125	3200	4300	6500	11,000	23,000

Model 6-24 — 6-cyl., 45 hp, 116" wb

	FP	5	4	3	2	1
Tour.-5P	1350	3300	4400	6700	12,000	24,000

BUSHNELL — In September of 1911 *MoToR* magazine reported that the G.H. Bushnell Press Company of Thompsonville, Connecticut had sold all of its cottonseed oil machinery to the American Machine & Manufacturing Company of Greenville, South Carolina and planned to "shortly turn their attention to the manufacture of automobiles." The automobile that resulted was marketed under the name of Maxim Tri-Car.

BUSSE — **St. Louis, Missouri** — **(1903)** — H.F. Busse built a car for himself in St. Louis in 1903. Its specifications included a single-cylinder engine, planetary transmission, single chain drive, and solid rubber tires on wooden wheels. The body was a five-passenger touring with rear entrance tonneau. Busse drove the car regularly, his most memorable trip probably the jaunt he took to Belleville, Illinois. Because a rainstorm had preceded his arrival, he and his car were invited into a Belleville saloon for the evening. The car at least stayed dry thereafter. Probably H.F. Busse did not. The saloon keeper was reportedly pleased by the "unusually large business" he enjoyed that evening courtesy of Mr. Busse's car.

BUTCHER & GAGE — Two cars purportedly were produced by the partnership of Butcher & Gage in Jackson, Michigan in 1903. Documentation of this has not been discovered.

BUTLER — The Butler Automobile Supply Company was organized in Boston, Massachusetts during the fall of 1907 for the manufacture of motor cars and motor boats. Capital stock was $25,000; A.C. Hayes was the president of the company, H.M. Butler the treasurer. Manufacture of an automobile is doubted.

BUTLER — Butler, Pennsylvania — (1901) — In April of 1901 *The Horseless Age* reported the continuing experimentation with gasoline automobiles of the Butler Company of Butler. The engines used arrived from the Motor Vehicle Power Company of Philadelphia, and the Butler automobiles remained ever in the experimental stage. A truck called the Butler was subsequently marketed by the Huselton Automobile Company in Butler from 1913 to 1914. The town of Butler made considerably more automobile news during the 1930's when the American Austin and American Bantam were built there.

BUTLER HIGH WHEEL — Butler, Indiana — (1908) — That the Butler Company of Butler, Indiana did make it into production seems evident. Photographs of its product indicate it to be a simple two-passenger motor buggy with very high wheels. The company's motto, as noted on the company stationery, was "Always Ahead." The firm's automotive efforts were behind it by 1909, however.

BUURRASSA — Attleboro, Massachusetts — (1902) — The Buurrassa was a single automobile built for T.I. Smith & Company of North Attleboro by J.H.E. Buurrassa. Its engine was an 8 hp twin which was mounted at the front of a 73-inch chassis. Two speeds forward were provided, and the body was a tonneau.

BUYERS — The Buyers and Manufacturers Automobile Company was organized with a capital stock of $300,000 in Buffalo, New York during the spring of 1904. Directors Carl Thorden, W.H. Van Deusen and C.V. Roty indicated their intention to manufacture automobiles. This does not appear to have happened.

BYERS — The John F. Byers Machine Company of Ravenna, Ohio was listed as an automobile manufacturer in the Hiscox book *Horseless Vehicles, Automobiles, Motor Cycles* published in 1900. Further documentation is lacking.

BYRIDER ELECTRIC — The Byrider was one of four names under which the same electric victoria was marketed between 1905 and 1910 in Cleveland, Ohio. Refer to DeMars Electric.

1915 B-Z-T, Light Car, roadster, WLB

B-Z-T — Owego, New York — (1915) — C.K. Ball, W.H. Zeh and D.N. Thompson were the upstate New York men responsible for the B-Z-T. They put eight months into its development, completed their first prototype in April 1914, and tested it in May. Unsatisfied, they continued testing and refining. By the time their B-Z-T Car Company finally entered the cyclecar market, most other manufacturers were leaving it. Guilt by association not being desired, Ball, Zeh and Thompson elected to refer to their vehicle as a "light car." Most of the B-Z-T's specification was pure cyclecar, however: air cooled, two-cylinder 12/15 hp engine, friction transmission, 94-inch wheelbase, 36-inch tread, two-seater model only. But shaft drive was not the cyclecar norm, and supplying the car with a full set of fenders was unusual too. The price was right at $385. Still, the B-Z-T suffered the fate of all cyclecars, and just as quickly.

1915 B-Z-T

	FP	5	4	3	2	1
B-Z-T Rds.-2P	385	—	—	—	—	—

C-A-C — Chicago, Illinois — (1914-1915) — The C-A-C was a cyclecar produced by C.A. Coey of Chicago and initially introduced as the Coey Junior. "Nothing has been left undone and no expense spared to make the C-A-C a machine with low initial cost and minimum upkeep expense," Coey said. For $425 the purchaser received a side-by-side two-seat roadster on a 96-inch wheelbase with 42-inch tread, though the standard 56-inch was available for more portly types. The engine was a water-cooled four of 12 hp; shaft drive and a planetary transmission were featured. For $650 Coey also offered the C-A-C in an enclosed body style which was described as "the first limousine in the cyclecar class." That was rather overdoing it. The C-A-C was discontinued in 1915, though other Coey models were built for another two years.

1914-1915 C-A-C
Cyclecar — 4-cyl., 12 hp, 96" wb

	FP	5	4	3	2	1
Rds.	425	1100	2200	3200	4900	9000
Limo.	650	1000	2100	3100	4800	8500

1914 C-A-C, cyclecar, LC

CADET — Flint, Michigan — (1925) — The Cadet was General Motors' try at a new car for the export market, and it proceeded no further than myriad other export cars promoted by companies with considerably less petty cash at their disposal. The Cadet had a four-cylinder Chevrolet engine and a 90-inch wheelbase — and after building two prototypes, GM abandoned the project. The car had been designed by Fabio Segardi, the European-born engineer who was already well known in the United States via his work with Hudson, Olds and Willys, and who was about to become even more famous. In September 1925, shortly after finishing the design of the Cadet at General Motors Research, Segardi left GM and joined Reo, where he designed the popular Flying Cloud series introduced in 1927.

CADILLAC

CADILLAC — Detroit, Michigan — (1903-1942 et. seq.) — Henry Martyn Leland was born to Quaker parents in Vermont in 1843 and learned precision with Samuel Colt in Connecticut and with Brown and Sharpe, makers of tools and machinery in Rhode Island, for whom he developed a hair clipper that made a barber's work considerably easier for years thereafter. In 1890 he took his family and his talents to Detroit, where fine machining was virtually unknown and where he allied himself with wealthy lumberman Robert C. Faulconer and tool designer Charles H. Norton in the formation of Leland, Faulconer and Norton, the firm reduced by one in 1894 when Norton struck out on his own, later to become a successful manufacturer of crankshaft grinders. Precision gear making was the Leland and Faulconer specialty initially, though by 1896 the firm was into manufacture of steam engines for Detroit streetcars and gasoline units for marine use. In June 1901, contracted by Olds Motor Works to produce engines for the curved dash Oldsmobile, Leland came up with a refined version that developed 23 percent more horsepower but which was rejected by the Olds people because retooling for it would further delay production already delayed by the factory fire in March. But a year later Henry Leland was in the automobile business . . . courtesy of Henry Ford. In August 1902 William Murphy and Lemuel W. Bowen, who were among the financial backers behind Ford's automotive venture which to their dismay seemed to produce little more than racing cars, called in Leland as a consultant to appraise the automobile plant and equipment so they could sell it and get out. Leland showed them the engine rejected by Olds and

suggested they stay in. Thus was born the Cadillac Automobile Company, named for Le Sieur Antoine de la Mothe Cadillac, the French explorer who had discovered Detroit in the early Eighteenth Century. The first Cadillac was completed on October 17th, 1902 and was given its maiden test drive by Alanson P. Brush, the twenty-four-year-old Leland and Faulconer engineer who had contributed substantially to the car's design and who would later build the Brush Runabout. In January the Cadillac was taken to the New York Automobile Show where company sales manager William E. Metzger (formerly of Olds Motor Works, later the "M" of E-M-F) took orders for an astounding 2286 cars before declaring mid-week that the Cadillac was "sold out." What made the Model A Cadillac such a best-seller, in addition to Metzger's super-salesman technique, was its refinement. Though the 10 hp developed by its single-cylinder copper-jacketed engine was exemplary, its two-speed planetary transmission and center chain drive via Brown-Lipe differential was conventional. Still, in a day when many automobile productions had a machine shop look to them, the Cadillac, comparatively, looked like a jewel from Tiffany's. And the price was just $750. The deal made with the former Ford backers called for Leland and Faulconer merely to supply engines, transmissions and steering gears for the Cadillac, and that part of the operation moved with Leland-like precision. But at the Cadillac factory on Cass Avenue, chassis

1903 Cadillac, runabout with tonneau, OCW

and body assembly lagged woefully behind. In October 1905, the Cadillac and Leland and Faulconer operations were merged into a new Cadillac Motor Car Company, with Henry Leland — now in his sixties — as general manager, his son Wilfred as assistant treasurer under Murphy. The single-cylinder Cadillac would be built for a half-dozen years in America, but its most significant historical achievement happened in England in 1908. It was the idea of F.S. Bennett, the London importer for Cadillac who had contested the car successfully in hill climbs and endurance trials since 1903. At Brooklands in 1908, under Royal Automobile Club supervision, he directed the dismantling of three single-cylinder Cadillacs, the scrambling of their parts, and the reassembly thereafter of three cars, which were then run on Brooklands Track. The concept of precision manufacturing of interchangeable parts was a new one for the automobile industry. The Cadillac achievement in demonstrating it won the company the Dewar Trophy — the first ever for an American car — in 1908. The first four-cylinder Cadillac — with 28/30 hp vertical in-line engine mounted up front under a hood, planetary transmission (revised to selective in 1907) and shaft drive — had arrived for the 1905 model year, followed for 1909 by the Model Thirty, a refinement of the four which would advertise "1/1000th of an inch is the standard of measurement." Shortly after the announcement of the Model Thirty, there was another announcement that Cadillac had been bought by General Motors for over $5.5 million. This was undoubtedly the most substantial, and probably the wisest, purchase William C. Durant made for his new empire, and Durant was smart enough to keep the Lelands on board and in complete charge. In 1910, when Durant's free-spending had plunged GM into financial disaster, it was the persuasion of the Lelands and the strength of Cadillac which saved the corporation from possible dissolution. Closed coachwork — which had been introduced with the Osceola coupe model in 1906 — became prominent in Cadillac catalogues from 1910 which, while not pacesetting, did represent an early focus on closed cars as standard productions. In 1912 the Cadillac became "The Car That Has No Crank" with the introduction of the Delco self-starter and electric lights developed by Charles F. Kettering. Cadillac tried hard for the Dewar Trophy that year but didn't succeed, the Dewar Committee electing to award no prize at all in 1912. Interestingly, in October Cadillac inaugurated the slogan "Standard of the World," which may indicate the company had fully expected to receive the Dewar.

1903 Cadillac, runabout with tonneau, OCW

Amusingly, the Dewar Trophy was awarded to Cadillac in 1913 both for its "improved" starting-lighting-ignition system and its new two-speed rear axle. Unfortunately regarding the latter, the Austin Automobile Company of Grand Rapids, which had earlier that year introduced its own version, sued for patent infringement in late 1914 and won in January 1915. Needless to say, Cadillac dropped mention of the two-speed axle as concomitant to its second winning of the Dewar — and indeed was so embarrassed that the 1913 Dewar was hardly mentioned at all. Later the company chose to fudge by noting that "the 1912 electrics led to the second Dewar" — which was not entirely untrue. Wholly meritorious during this period was the new Cadillac V-8. Introduced in September 1914, three months later *The Automobile* would comment that it had "ushered in an epoch." Neither the world's first V-8 (Clement Ader's Paris-Madrid race car of 1903 was a V-8, and De Dion's V-8 of 1910 was first in series production) nor America's (Hewitt and Buffum preceding) the Cadillac version nonetheless was epochal. Inspired by the De Dion unit, Cadillac refined the V-8 concept into an engine of supreme sophistication and one that would become the hallmark of Cadillac for generations thereafter, far outliving its many competitors. Introduced in four open and four closed body styles ranging in price from $1975 to $3600, the cars were most attractively priced — and more than 20,000 were sold in 1915. In January that year "The Penalty of Leadership," written by Theodore MacManus for Cadillac and one of the most celebrated advertisements in automobile history, was published in *The Saturday Evening Post*. During World War I, more than 2000 Cadillac V-8's were sent overseas as staff cars, and it was during World War I, too, that the Lelands left Cadillac. According to William C. Durant, they were fired, principally because their personal egos now foreshadowed their interest in General Motors. According to the Lelands, they resigned because Durant refused to build the Liberty aero engine. Following their leavetaking, Cadillac did proceed into Liberty manufacture, as did the Lelands who organized the Lincoln Motor Company for that purpose. For a number of years after the Lelands' departure, Cadillac management was in some turmoil. Immediately succeeding as general manager was former Buick man Richard H. Collins, who left in 1921 for Peerless, taking with him chief engineer Benjamin H. Anibal who had succeeded D. McCall White who, incidentally, was now building a V-8 called the Lafayette in Indiana for Charles Nash. But by 1923, Ernest Seaholm, who had been on Anibal's design staff, was officially made chief engineer and would remain so until World War II, and in 1925, following the unremarkable tenure of Herbert H. Rice who had replaced Collins, Lawrence P. Fisher assumed the Cadillac presidency for a decade-long run. (As legend has it, all seven of the Fisher brothers had filed into Rice's office to complain one after the other about his management, and he resigned soon after.) By the mid-Twenties things had settled down nicely at Cadillac. Continuing refinements of the V-8 had brought detachable cylinder heads for 1918, an inherently balanced crankshaft in the V-63 of 1924 (which also introduced four-wheel brakes), and detail changes in the interim 85.5 hp Series 314 V-8 which endured until 1936 when Cadillac's new 165 hp V-8 introduced unit block construction and featured downdraft carburetion in a design that would survive until 1949. By the Twenties, Cadillac's price range was up to the $3000-$5000 league, but the cars were selling well, generally in the 20,000's annually, a figure that would nearly double in 1928. The Series 341 cars for '28 were the first Cadillacs designed by Harley J. Earl, and they bore a distinct resemblance to the smashing LaSalle, Cadillac's companion car introduced the year before. Cadillacs for 1929 pioneered synchromesh transmission and introduced safety glass. In January 1930 the V-16 Cadillac made its debut, followed in September by the V-12. Both engines (their design credited to Owen Nacker) were overhead valve units, developing 165 hp and 135 hp respectively at introduction, though the V-12 was up to 150 hp and the V-16 to 185 hp for 1934, by which model year the V-16's wheelbase was stretched to a mammoth 154 inches making the Cadillac America's lengthiest production car. The Harley Earl-designed and Fleetwood-built bodies, on the V-16 particularly, were elegant, and included the very striking and provocatively named Madame X. The lavish and luxurious excess of multi-cylinders made sense when the engines were developed by various manufacturers during the Roaring Twenties. Ultimately arriving on the market as they did after the stock market crash and as the Depression took hold, there was no real rationale for these cars. But, alone among manufacturers offering twelves or sixteens, Cadillac did surprisingly well, selling 15,207 of them in a decade, far more than anyone else. Meanwhile, Cadillac's engineering department, justifiably renowned in the industry, came up with ride control for '32, no-draft ventilation for '33 and independent front suspension for '34. By 1935 the Fisher all-steel turret top had arrived, and by now Nicholas Dreystadt was occupying Cadillac's general managership chair, having moved into it in June 1934 when Lawrence

Fisher moved on to another GM assignment. Though Cadillac had not suffered as horrendously as many other manufacturers during the depths of the Depression, the company was nonetheless hurting. Dreystadt's formula for easing the pain was to streamline operations and to cut costs. This resulted for 1938 in the discontinuation of the ohv V-16 and V-12, which were replaced by a new flat-head V-16 generating the same 185 hp of its predecessor, but a less troublesome engine and more economical to build. Nineteen thirty-eight also saw the Cadillac go to a steering-column-mounted gearshift a year before other GM cars — and the new V-8 Sixty Special with notched back, no running boards and a spunky new look courtesy of a young designer on Harley Earl's staff named Bill Mitchell. Nineteen forty-one saw the final rationalization of the Dreystadt streamlining program with the Cadillac V-16 and the LaSalle dropped, and production concentrated on seven V-8 models mounted on three wheelbases and offering as options air-conditioning (following Packard's lead of 1940) and Hydra-Matic (introduced by Oldsmobile in '40). Cadillac sales for 1941 approached 60,000 cars, the best in the company's history. In 1942 Cadillac turned to military production. Postwar, GM's premiere division would enjoy its best production year ever, amid some further pacesetting Cadillac cars.

Cadillac Data Compilation
by Philip S. Dumka

1903

1903 Cadillac, runabout with tonneau, OCW

CADILLAC — ONE: Note; Cadillac did not use the "A" designation in 1903. However, later Cadillac publications combined references to 1903 "Cadillac" and "1904 Model A" and used "Model A" in reference to all single cylinder cars.

Chassis: Angle steel frame. Two half-elliptic springs front and rear. Straight, tubular front axle. Right-hand, wheel steering. Controls to right. Adjustable rack and pinion steering gear. Single tube tires, wood wheels.

Engine: Leland & Faulconer "Little Hercules". Horizontal single cylinder mounted to the left under front seat. Water cooled, impeller pump circulation thru finned tube front-mounted sloping radiator. Detachable, special alloy, cast iron cylinder with copper water jacket. Detachable combustion/valve chamber. Valves vertical, in-line and perpendicular to the cylinder bore. Exhaust, at bottom, is operated by rocker and push rod from cam on gear driven half speed shaft in crankcase. Inlet, at top, is operated by rocker which is operated by a sliding cam driven by an eccentric on the half speed shaft. The fulcrum for the sliding cam is adjustable by movement of a lever on the steering column, giving variable lift to the inlet valve and, thus, throttle adjustment for the engine. Fuel is gravity fed from a tank under the driver's seat to an updraft mixer which automatically delivers the amount of fuel demanded by the inlet valve opening. Internal lubrication by splash from single-pipe, gravity feed oiler. External points, including mains, lubricated by grease and oil cups. Cranking from right or left side of vehicle thru jackshaft and chain to crankshaft.

Driveline: Two speed planetary transmission. Low speed on left foot pedal. High and reverse on controller lever at right. Single chain to spur gear differential.

Brakes: Foot pedal operated mechanical on inboard ends of rear half-axles. Engine can be used for additional braking by easing controller lever into reverse.

Body: Two passenger runabout convertible to four passenger by bolting on rear entrance tonneau. Sloping, curved dash. Body can be lifted from chassis without disconnecting any wiring, plumbing or controls.

Note. Alanson P. Brush, of Leland & Faulconer, held patents on copper water jacket, variable lift inlet valve, mixer, planetary transmission, and adjustable rack and pinion steering. By 1906, the impact of Brush patents would start a drastic change in Cadillac design.

I.D. DATA: Serial numbers were not used. Engine numbers were stamped two places on crankcase: 1. Top, right edge of cylinder flange, near water outlet. 2. Right, front face, just below top cover. (Blank spaces on patent plate are for additional patent dates, not engine number.) Engine No.: 1-2500 (Includes three prototypes built in 1902.)

Model No.	Body Type & Seating	Price	Weight	Prod. Total
NA	Runabout-2P	750	1370	Note 1
NA	W/Tonneau-4P	850	1450	Note 1

Note 1: Cadillac model year total was 2,497.

ENGINE: Horizontal, with cylinder to rear. One cyl. Cast iron cylinder, with copper water jacket. B & S: 5 x 5 in. Disp.: 98.2 cu. in. Brake H.P.: "Higher than advertised or calculated H.P." Advertised H.P.: 6-1/2. (ALAM, NACC, SAE H.P. calculated by identical formulae) (ALAM first used formula in 1908.) Main bearings: Two. Valve lifters: Mechanical (See "Description") Carb.: Updraft mixer, manufactured by Cadillac.

CHASSIS: W.B.: 72 in. O.L.: 9 ft. 3 in. Height: 5 ft. Frt/Rear Tread: 54-1/2 in. Tires: 28 x 3 single tube.

TECHNICAL: Planetary transmission. Speeds: 2F/1R. (3:1 low, rev. — direct high). Controls: low — foot pedal. Rev., high — lever to right. Low, rev. — bands. High — disc clutch. Chain drive. Spur gear differential. Overall ratio: 3.1:1 to 5:1 (see drivetrain options). Mechanical brakes on two wheels — contracting on inboard drums. Wood wheels — 12 spoke (14 spoke on prototype). Wheel size: 22 in.
Drivetrain Options: Different combinations of 9 or 10 tooth driving sprocket with 31, 34, 38, 41, or 45 tooth driven sprocket gave ten possible ratios from 3.1:1 to 5:1. Lower ratios for runabout to be run on smooth, level roads to higher ratios for loaded delivery to be run on rough, hilly roads. Instructions for changing sprockets were furnished to owners, but the change involved disassembly of the transmission and rear axle — definitely not a "quick-change" set-up.

OPTIONS: Tonneau (100.00). Leather top w/side curtains & storm apron (50.00). Rubber top w/side curtains & storm apron (30.00). Lights.

HISTORICAL: Advertised November, 1902, but was not at Auto Shows until January, 1903. Innovations: Interchangeable parts. Calendar year sales and production: 2,497. Model year sales and production: 2,497. The President of Cadillac was C.A. Black.

Although period photos exist of stripped single cylinder Cadillacs in speed contests, the as-delivered cars were only fast enough to travel at reasonable speeds on the roads of the time.

However, the cars soon gained a reputation for reliability, ease and economy of maintenance, and remarkable pulling and climbing capability. Publicity shots show Cadillacs pulling heavily loaded wagons up slopes and climbing the steps of public buildings.

The first Cadillac exported to England was entered by its promoter, F.S. Bennett, in the July, 1903 Sunrising Hill Climb — "The worst hill in England." The entry finished 7th in a field of 17, being the only one cylinder in a field otherwise made up of 2 & 4 cylinder cars with up to four times the displacement of the Cadillac. The same car was entered in the September, 1903 One Thousand Mile Reliability Trial in England and finished 4th in its price class on total points but 1st in its price class on reliability scoring.

1903
Model A, 1-cyl.

	FP	5	4	3	2	1
Rbt	800	4200	8400	14,000	19,600	28,000
Ton Rbt	900	4350	8700	14,500	20,300	29,000

1904

CADILLAC — MODEL A — ONE: Continuation of 1903, delivery body with detachable top added. Horsepower rating upped to 8-1/4. Clincher tires now standard equipment. Optional 60 in. tread available. Pressure fed multiple oiler introduced.

1904 Cadillac, model B, touring, OCW

CADILLAC — MODEL B — ONE: Same as Model A except:
Chassis: Pressed steel frame and axles. Front axle girder style (not available in wide tread). Single transverse half-elliptic front spring. Cranking (counterclockwise) at left side only. Compression relief provided for cranking. Safety device to prevent crank from being inserted when spark control lever is in advanced position. Horsepower rating upped to 8-1/4 — more a question of confidence than any engine design changes.
Body: Inverted box replaces sloping, curved dash. Radiator vertical and below frame. Joint in body at dash allows body to be slid off with no lifting. Surrey body style added — side entrance detachable tonneau. Delivery top no longer detachable. Weight of all body styles reduced by as much as 70 pounds. Prices increased $50.

I.D. DATA: Serial numbers were not used for model A or B. Engine numbers were stamped two places on crankcase: 1. Top, right edge of cylinder flange, near water outlet. 2. Right, front face, just below top cover. (Blank spaces on patent plate are for additional patent dates, not engine number.) Model A engine nos.: 3500 — 4018 with B. 8200 — 8350 with CEF (1905). 13501 — 13706 with CEF (1905-special). Model B engine nos.: 2500 — 3500. 3500 — 4018 with A. 4200 — 5000 with EF.

Model No.	Body Type & Seating	Price	Weight	Prod. Total
Model A				
NA	Rbt.-2P	750	1370	—
NA	W/Tonneau-4P	850	1450	—
NA	Del.-2P	850	1525	—
Model B				
NA	Rbt.-2P	800	1300	—
NA	Tr.-4P	900	1420	—
NA	Surrey-4P	900	1400	—
NA	Del.-2P	900	1525	—

ENGINE: Horizontal, with cylinder to rear. One. Cast iron cylinder, with copper water jacket. B & S: 5 x 5 in. Disp.: 98.2 cu. in. Brake H.P.: "Higher than advertised or calculated H.P." Advertised H.P.: 8-1/4. (ALAM, NACC, SAE H.P. calculated by identical formulae) (ALAM first used formula in 1908.) Main bearings: Two. Valve lifters: Mechanical (see "Description"). Carb.: Updraft mixer, manufactured by Cadillac.

CHASSIS: [Model A, except Delivery] W.B.: 72 in. O.L.: 9 ft., 3 in. Height: 5 ft. Frt/Rear Tread: 54-1/2 in. (60 optional). Tires: 28 x 3 Clincher. [Model A Delivery] W.B.: 72 in. O.L.: 9 ft., 3 in. Height: 7 ft., 1 in. Frt/Rear Tread: 54-1/2 in. Tires: 28 x 3 Clincher. [Model B, except Delivery] W.B.: 76 in. O.L.: 9 ft., 4 in. Height: 5 ft. Frt/Rear Tread: 54-1/2 in. Tires: 30 x 3 Clincher. [Model B Delivery] W.B.: 76 in. O.L.: 9 ft., 4 in. Height: Approx. 7 ft. Frt/Rear Tread: 54-1/2 in. Tires: 30 x 3-1/2 Clincher.

TECHNICAL: Planetary transmission. Speeds: 2F/1R (3:1 low, rev. — direct high). Low-foot pedal, rev., high — lever to right. Low, rev. — bands, High — disc clutch. Chain drive. Spur gear differential. Overall ratio: 3.1:1 to 5:1 (see drivetrain options). Mechanical brakes on two wheels — contracting on inboard drums. Wood wheels — 12 spoke (14 spoke on prototype). Wheel size: [Model A] 22 in. [Model B] 24 in., [Delivery] 23 in. **Drivetrain Options:** Different combinations of 9 or 10 tooth driving sprocket with 31, 34, 38, 41, or 45 tooth driven sprocket gave ten possible ratios from 3.1:1 to 5:1. Lower ratios for runabout to be run on smooth, level roads to higher ratios for loaded Delivery to be run on rough, hilly roads. Instructions for changing sprockets were furnished to owners, but the change involved disassembly of the transmission and rear axle — definitely not a "quick-change" set-up.

OPTIONS: Model A: same as 1903. Model B: Bulb Horn. Lights. Leather top w/sides and storm apron (50.00). Rubber top w/sides and storm apron (30.00). Deck to replace tonneau on Touring or Surrey (10.00).

1904 Cadillac, model B, runabout, JAC

HISTORICAL: Model A introduced 1903. Model B introduced January, 1904. Calendar year sales and production, Model A&B: 2,319. Model year sales and production: same. The President of Cadillac was C.A. Black.

Note: Factory burned in the Spring of 1904, reducing capacity to almost nothing for 45 days. Deposits on 1500 orders were returned. Volume of sales still exceeded those of any other make in the country.

When the street was muddy, cars with rear entrance tonneau were backed in perpendicular to the sidewalk so passengers needn't walk in the mud. The side entrance Surrey ended this inconvenience.

1904
Model A, 1-cyl.

	FP	5	4	3	2	1
Rbt	800-850	4050	8100	13,500	18,900	27,000
Ton Rbt	900	4200	8400	14,000	19,600	28,000

Model B, 1-cyl.

1905

1905 Cadillac, rear entrance tonneau, OCW

CADILLAC — MODEL B — ONE: Unchanged from 1904. Horsepower now rated at 9. Optional wide tread, not available on Model B in 1904, is now made available by use of tubular axle with 61 inch tread to replace pressed steel axle with standard tread.

CADILLAC — MODEL C — ONE: Mid-year offering, at reduced prices, of Model B with Model F "hood" and radiator. Cadillac called the Model C "an accommodation to customers who want a detachable tonneau." The Model F being non-detachable. This may be interpreted as "a program to move out the remaining Model B chassis."

CADILLAC — MODEL D — FOUR: Body: Five passenger touring with side entrance tonneau doors. Wood body. Aluminum skin available at extra cost. Running boards. Aluminum dash, carrying lubricator and running fuel tank with gravity feed to mixer. Storage fuel tank at rear of chassis — fuel transfer to running tank by exhaust pressure.
Chassis: Emphasis on strength and durability. Pressed steel frame. Two half-elliptic springs in front, platform spring in rear. Right hand steering, controls to right. Brake lever operates service brakes on rear drums. Foot pedal operates emergency brake on drive shaft. Application of either brake system disengages flywheel clutch thru an interlock. Engine and transmission mounted in tubular subframe. Patented double syphon muffling system.
Drive Line: Three speed planetary transmission (3:1, 2:1, direct). Progressive shift — all speeds on single lever. Twin disc clutch in flywheel, disc clutch and three bands on transmission, emergency brake drum behind transmission. Shaft drive (two U-joints) to bevel gear. Live rear axle with spur gear differential.
Engine: Four cylinder vertical in-line L-head, counterclockwise cranking. Individual cylinders with copper water jackets, heads detachable with factory equipment. Two piece crankcase — lower section carrying mains and patented sloping-trough splash lube system which insures lubrication to each cylinder regardless of grade. Horizontal commutator shaft projects forward into cavity in radiator — commutator is serviced from front of vehicle. With number one cylinder over the front axle and a stretched out accessory section on the front of the engine, the radiator extends forward of the front tires. The hood is one quarter the length of the car.
Engine throttle control is a complicated variation of the one cylinder throttling arrangement. The L-head valves are operated by in line push rods and roller tappets riding on extra wide cams on a spring-loaded, sliding camshaft. Exhaust cams are of constant cross section but inlet cams are cone shaped to effect a varying lift and timing as the camshaft is moved along its axis. Axial motion of the camshaft against its return spring is by hydraulic piston which receives pressure from an engine driven pump. The throttle control on the steering column operates a bypass valve in the hydraulic loop. Position of this valve regulates the percentage of system pressure acting on the camshaft piston, thus the nominal axial position of the camshaft. Governor action is automatic due to interaction between engine driven pump speed, hydraulic pressure, and cam position (overspeed increases pressure and drives cam back to a lower speed position). As on the one cylinder, inlet valve opening automatically determines the amount of fuel supplied by the mixer — identical to the one cylinder mixer except for the addition of an auxiliary air intake valve.

Note: In addition to patents pertaining to one cylinder cars, Alanson Brush also held patents on the splash lubrication system and the muffler system used on Model D. Although not patented, counterclockwise cranking was a Brush "trademark".

1905 Cadillac, model E, runabout, HAC

CADILLAC — MODEL E— ONE: Same as 1904 except: More normal looking "hood" with sharp corners and side louvers. Radiator raised to fit shape of "hood". Detachable tonneau not available. Front axle now tubular, arched, with truss. Rocker shaft between front axle and spring introduced mid-year. Balanced linkage on transmission bands.

Note: E, F, K, M, S, T are not six distinct models. E, K, S are runabouts; F, M, T all other body styles.

CADILLAC — MODEL F — ONE: Same chassis as Model E except 2 in. longer wheelbase. Body styles: First Cadillac one cylinder touring car with non-detachable tonneau and two side doors for tonneau entrance. Delivery.

I.D. DATA: Serial numbers were not used on any of these models. Engine numbers were stamped two places on crankcase. 1. Top, right edge of cylinder flange, near water outlet. 2. Right, front face, just below top cover. (Blank spaces on patent plate are for additional patent dates, not engine number.) Model B engine no.: 4200-5000 with EF (1904). Model C engine no.: 6600-8200 with EF, 8200-8350 with AEF, 13501-13706 with AEF-special. Model D engine numbers were stamped on top of crankcase — in front of and to the left of number one (front) cylinder. Starting: 10,001. Ending: 10,156. Model E engine no.: 4200-5000 with EF (1904), 5000-6600 with F, 6600-8200 with CF, 8200-8350 with ACF, 13501-13706 with ACF-special. Model F engine no.: 4200-5000 with BE (1904), 5000-6600 with E, 6600-8200 with CE, 8200-8350 with ACE, 13501-13706 with ACE-special, 13728-14200.

Model No.	Body Type & Seating	Price	Weight	Prod. Total
Model B				
NA	Tr.-4P	900	1450	
NA	Sur.-4P	900	1450	
Model C				
NA	Rbt.-2P	750	1330	—
NA	Tr.-4P	850	1450	
Model D				
NA	2-dr. Tr.-5P	2800	2600	156
Model E				
NA	Rbt.-2P	750	1100	—
Model F				
NA	2-dr. Tr.-4P	950	1350	—
NA	Del.-2P	950	1400	

ENGINE: Models B, C, E, F: Horizontal, with cylinder to rear. One cyl. Cast iron cylinder, with copper water jacket. B & S: 5 x 5 in. Disp.: 98.2 cu. in. Brake H.P.: "Higher than advertised or calculated H.P." Advertised H.P.: 9. (ALAM, NACC, SAE H.P. calculated by identical formulae) (ALAM first used formula in 1908). Main bearings: Two. Valve lifters: mechanical (See "Description"). Carb.: Updraft mixer, manufactured by Cadillac. Model D: Vertical, in-line, L-head. Four cyl. Cast iron cylinders, cast singly, copper water jacket. B & S: 4-3/8 x 5 in. Disp.: 300.7 cu. in. Advertised H.P.: 30. Main bearings: Five. Valve lifters: Mechanical, roller tappets, variable lift inlet. Carb.: Cadillac updraft mixer with auxiliary air valve.

CHASSIS: [Model B] W.B.: 76 in. O.L.: 9 ft., 4 in. Height: 5 ft. Frt/Rear Tread: 56-1/2 (61 opt.). Tires: 30 x 3 Clincher. [Model C] W.B.: 76 in. O.L.: 9 ft., 4 in. Height: 5 ft. Frt/Rear Tread: 56-1/2 (61 opt.). Tires: 30 x 3 Clincher. [Model E] W.B.: 74 in. O.L.: 9 ft. Height: 4 ft., 8 in. Frt/Rear Tread: 56-1/2 (61 opt.). Tires: 28 x 3 Clincher. [Model F Touring] W.B.: 76 in. O.L.: 9 ft., 4 in. Height: 5 ft., 4 in. Frt/Rear Tread: 56-1/2 (61 opt.). Tires: 30 x 3-1/2 Clincher. [Model F Delivery] W.B.: 76 in. O.L.: 9 ft., 4 in. Height: approx. 7 ft. Frt/Rear Tread: 56-1/2 in. Tires: 30 x 3-1/2 Clincher. [Model D] W.B.: 100 in. O.L.: approx. 12 ft., 10 in. Height: approx. 5 ft., 9 in. Frt/Rear Tread: 56-1/2 in. Tires: 34 x 4-1/2 Dunlop's.

TECHNICAL: Models B & C: Planetary transmission. Speeds: 2F/1R (3:1 low, rev. — direct high). Controls: low — foot pedal, rev., high — lever to right. Low, rev. — bands, high — disc clutch. Chain drive. Spur gear differential. Overall ratio: 3.1:1 to 5:1 (see drivetrain options). Mechanical brakes on two wheels — contracting on inboard drums. Wood wheels — 12 spoke. Wheel size: 24 in.

Drivetrain Options: Different combinations of 9 or 10 tooth driving sprocket with 31, 34, 38, 41, or 45 tooth driven sprocket gave ten possible ratios from 3.1:1 to 5:1. Lower ratios for runabout to be run on smooth, level roads to higher ratios for loaded Delivery to be run on rough, hilly roads.

Instructions for changing sprockets were furnished to owners, but the change involved disassembly of the transmission and rear axle — definitely not a "quick-change" set-up.

Model D: Planetary transmission. Speeds: 3F/1R. Right hand drive, controls to right. Clutch: twin disc in flywheel, disc and 3 bands on transmission. Shaft drive. Live axle, bevel drive, spur gear differential. Mech. brakes on two wheels — service-lever-rear drums — emerg.-pedal-drive shaft. Wood artillery wheels, 12 spoke. Wheel size: 25 in. Model E: Planetary transmission. Speeds: 2F/1R (3:1 low, rev. — direct high). Controls: low — foot pedal, rev., high — lever to right. Low, rev. — bands, High — disc clutch. Chain drive. Spur gear differential. Overall ratio: 3.1:1 to 5:1 (see drivetrain options). Mechanical brakes on two wheels — contracting on inboard drums. Wood wheels — 12 spoke. Wheel size: 22 in.

Drivetrain Options: Model E: Same as Models B & C.

Model F: Planetary transmission. Speeds: 2F/1R, (3:1 low, rev. — direct high). Controls: low — foot pedal, rev., high — lever to right. Low, rev. — bands, High — disc clutch. Chain drive. Spur gear differential. Overall ratio: 3.1:1 to 5:1 (see drivetrain options). Mechanical brakes on two wheels — contracting on inboard drums. Wood wheels — 12 spoke (14 spoke on prototype). Wheel size: 23 in.

Drivetrain Options: Same as Models B & C.

OPTIONS: [Model B] Bulb Horn. Lights. Rear deck to replace tonneau (10.00). [Models C & F] Bulb Horn. Lights. [Model E] Bulb Horn. Lights. Leather top w/sides & storm apron (50.00). Rubber top w/sides & storm apron (30.00)

HISTORICAL: Model B: Introduced 1904. Calendar year sales and production: 4029 with C, E, F. Model year sales and production: same. Model C: Introduced Summer, 1905. Calendar year sales and production a limited % of 4,029 with B, E, F. Model year sales and production: same. Model D: Introduced Jan., 1905. Innovations: Three speed planetary tranmission. Governed throttle. Variable lift inlet valve gear on multi-cylinder engine. Calendar year sales and production: 156. Model year sales and production: same. The President of Cadillac was C.A. Black.

Note: After designing the one cylinder and Model D Cadillacs, Alanson Brush left L&F/Cadillac and extracted lump sum and royalty payments for use of his patents. This action triggered a plan to purge Cadillac design of Brush influence.

Model E: Introduced January, 1905. Calendar year sales and production: 4,029 Model year sales and production: same.

Note: Cadillac Automobile Co. and Leland & Faulconer merged in Oct., 1905 to form Cadillac Motor Car Co., Henry Leland became General Manger of the new company. Maximum production capability one car every ten minutes of each ten hour working day.

Model F: Introduced January, 1905. Calendar year sales and production: 4,029 with B, C, E. Model year sales and production: same.

Note: The new front end styling was recognized as a desirable improvement. Not only did Cadillac update Model B's with the Model F "hood" and radiator (Model C), but owners of A's and B's had the new nose grafted to their cars. There was even an aftermarket supplier of update kits.

1905
Models B-E

	FP	5	4	3	2	1
Rbt	750-800	4000	7950	13,250	18,550	26,500
Ton Rbt	900	4050	8100	13,500	18,900	27,000
Model D, 4-cyl.						
Rbt	2800	4350	8700	14,500	20,300	29,000
Ton Rbt	3150	4500	9000	15,000	21,000	30,000

1906

CADILLAC — MODEL K — ONE: Chassis same as 1905 except spark control now on steering column and oiler has mechanical feed from a cam on the hub of the flywheel. Straight-side Dunlop tires are now standard equipment. Bodies restyled. All 1906 one cylinder passenger car bodies now Victoria style. Dash now pressed steel and corners of "hood" rounded. This "hood" and dash treatment was used thru 1908. 1906 cars can be identified by long muffler and severe cant to the nose of the front fenders. Tops were not shown in catalogs but undoubtedly were available. Cadillac was setting up its own top department and would be offering Cadillac-made tops for 1907.

CADILLAC — MODEL M — ONE: Same as 1906 Model K except for body styles and two inch longer wheelbase.

CADILLAC — MODEL L — FOUR: Based on 1905 Model D.
Bodies: Cadillac's first offering of a limousine body. Cadillac's first use of auxiliary (rear facing) seats in Touring tonneau to give seven passenger seating capacity.

1906 Cadillac, model M, touring, OCW

Engine: Bore increased from 4-3/8 to 5 in.; mixer replaced by throttled, float feed, jet type carburetor; hydraulic governor replaced by centrifugal ring-type governor linked to carburetor throttle butterfly; variable lift inlet valve feature dropped; commutator shaft changed from horizontal to vertical.
Chassis: Change in commutator drive allowed for shorter hood; dash now pressed steel; wheelbase lengthened to 110 in.; service and emergency brakes both act on rear drums.

1906 Cadillac, model H, coupe, HAC

CADILLAC — MODEL H — FOUR: Same as Model L except; No limousine offered; Touring is five passenger; Runabout and first production Cadillac Coupe offered. Wheelbase 102 in.; tires 32 x 4; rear springs 3/4 elliptic.

Note: Early ads, advance catalogs, and the 1906 ALAM Handbook listed the wheelbase of the Model H as 100 in. rather than the actual 102 in.

I.D. DATA: Model K & M serial numbers on plate on rear of body (with engine number). Engine numbers were stamped two placed on crankcase: 1. Top, right edge of cylinder flange, near water outlet. 2. Top surface of left, front mounting leg. Also on plate on rear of body (with serial number). (Blank spaces on patent plate are for additional patent dates, not engine or serial number.) Engine No.: 8350-10000 with M, 20001-21850 with M, 21851-22150 with M (1906-1907). Model L serial numbers on plate on rear of body or on dash (with engine no.). Engine numbers were stamped on top surface of crankcase — in front of and to the left of number one (front) cylinder. Model H serial numbers on plate on rear of body or on dash (with engine no.) Engine numbers were stamped on top surface of crankcase — in front of and to the left of number one (front) cylinder. Engine No.: 10201-10709 (1906-1908).

Model No.	Body Type & Seating	Price	Weight	Prod. Total
Model K				
NA	Vic. Rbt.-2P	750	1100	—
Model M				
NA	2-dr. Vic. Tr.-4P	950	—	—
NA	Delivery-2P	950	—	—
Model L				
NA	2-dr. Tr.-5/7P	3750	2850	—
NA	2-dr. Limo.-7P	5000	3600	—
Model H				
NA	2-dr. Tr.-5P	2500	2400	—
NA	Rbt.-2P	2400	—	—
NA	2-dr. Cpe.-2P	3000	2500	—

Note: The weight of the model K victoria runabout is approximate.

ENGINE: Models K&M: Horizontal, with cylinder to rear. One. Cast iron cylinder, with copper water jacket. B & S: 5 x 5 in. Disp.: 98.2 cu. in. Brake H.P.: "Higher than advertised or calculated H.P." Advertised H.P.: 10. (ALAM, NACC, SAE H.P. calculated by identical formulae) (ALAM first used formula in 1908). Main bearings: Two. Valve lifters: Mechanical (see "Description") P.1. Carb.: Updraft mixer, manufactured by Cadillac. Model L: Vertical, inline, L-head. Four. Individual cast iron cyl., copper water jacket. B & S: 5 x 5 in. Disp.: 392.7 cu. in. Advertised H.P.: 40. Five main bearings. Valve lifters: mechanical. Carb.: throttled, float feed, jet type made by Cadillac. Model H: Vertical, inline, L-head. Four. Individual cast iron cyl., copper water jacket. B & S: 4-3/8 x 5. Disp.: 300.7 cu. in. Advertised H.P.: 30. Five main bearings. Valve lifters: Mechanical. Carb.: throttled, float feed, jet type made by Cadillac.

CHASSIS: [Model K] W.B.: 74 in. O.L.: 9 ft., 2 in. Height: 4 ft., 6 in. Frt/Rear Tread: 56 in. (61 opt). Tires: 28 x 3. [Model M Touring] W.B.: 76 in. O.L.: 9 ft., 7 in. Height: 5 ft., 6 in. Frt/Rear Tread: 56 in. (61 opt). Tires: 30 x 3-1/2. [Model M Delivery] W.B.: 76 in. Frt/Rear Tread: 56 in. Tires: 30 x 3-1/2. [Model L Touring] W.B.: 110 in. O.L.: approx. 13 ft., 3 in. Height: approx. 6 ft., 3 in. Frt/Rear Tread: 56-1/2 in. Tires: 36 x 4 front, 36 x 4-1/2 rear. [Model L Limo] W.B.: 110 in. O.L.: approx. 13 ft., 6 in. Height: approx. 7 ft., 5 in. Frt/Rear Tread: 56-1/2 in. Tires: 36 x 4 front, 36 x 5 rear. [Model H] W.B.: 102 in. Frt/Rear Tread: 56-1/2 in. Tires: 32 x 4.

TECHNICAL: Model K&M: Planetary transmission. Speeds: 2F/1R (3:1 low, rev. — direct high). Controls: low — foot pedal, rev., high — lever to right. Low, rev. — bands, High — disc clutch. Chain drive. Spur gear differential. Overall ratio: 3.1:1 to 5:1 (see drivetrain options). Mechanical brakes on two wheels — contracting on inboard drums. Wood wheels — 12 spoke. Model K Wheel size: 22 in, Model M: 23 in.
Drivetrain Options: Different combinations of 9 or 10 tooth driving sprocket with 31, 34, 38, 41, or 45 tooth driven sprocket gave ten possible ratios from 3.1:1 to 5:1. Lower ratios for runabout to be run on smooth, level roads to higher ratios for loaded Delivery to be run on rough, hilly roads.
Instructions for changing sprockets were furnished to owners, but the change involved disassembly of the transmission and rear axle — definately not a "quick-change" set-up.

Model L&H: Planetary transmission. Speeds: 3F/1R. Right hand drive, controls to right. Clutch: Twin disc in flywheel, disc and 3 bands on transmission. Shaft drive. Live axle, bevel drive, bevel differential. Mechanical brakes on two wheels — service and emergency on rear drums. Wood artillery wheels, 12 spoke. Wheel size (Model L): 28 front, Touring rear 27, Limo rear 26 in. (Model H) 24 in.

OPTIONS: Model K: Bulb horn. Lights. Rubber top with sides & storm apron (30.00). Leather top with sides & storm apron (50.00). Model M: Bulb horn. Lights. Cape cart top for Touring (75.00). Model L: Bulb horn. Lights. Touring top (150.00). Model H: Bulb horn. Lights. Touring top (125.00). Runabout top (50.00).

HISTORICAL: Models K&M: Introduced January, 1906. Calendar year sales and production: 3,650 K&M. Model year sales and production: same. Model L: Introduced January, 1906. Calendar year sales and production: Unknown — probably very limited. Model year sales and production: same. The president of Cadillac was C.A. Black.

Note: Except for the V-16's, the Model L engine displacement was not equalled in a production Cadillac engine until 1964. Wm. K. Vanderbilt, Jr. owned a Model L Cadillac, but this type of customer was rare. Cadillac needed high production to make the concept of interchangeable parts pay off.

Model H: Introduced January, 1906. Calendar year sales and production: 509 (1906-1908). Model year sales and production: same.

Note: Purge of Alanson Brush design features started. Mixer and variable inlet valve opening no longer used on four cylinder Cadillacs. The real start of the purge was the design of the Model G for 1907.

1906
Model K-M, 1-cyl.

	FP	5	4	3	2	1
Rbt	800	3750	7500	12,500	17,500	25,000
Tr	1025	3900	7800	13,000	18,200	26,000
Model H, 4-cyl.						
Rbt	2450	3900	7800	13,000	18,200	26,000
Tr	2625	4050	8100	13,500	18,900	27,000
Model L, 4-cyl.						
7P Tr	3900	4350	8700	14,500	20,300	29,000
Limo	5000	4050	8100	13,500	18,900	27,000

1907

CADILLAC — MODEL G — FOUR: Although the Model L Cadillac Limousine had a planetary transmission and 5 x 5 bore and stroke like the single cylinder Cadillac Runabout, the two models were entirely opposite in concept. The single cylinder was a horseless carriage for the masses, the Model L a Nabob's throne-on-wheels. Whether due to the Alanson Brush patent squabble, acute marketing perception, or both; Cadillac came up with a four cylinder design which met the expectations of customers who wanted just a bit more than the best one cylinder car could offer — an inexpensive, easily maintained, long lasting, precision built car — a "single cylinder Cadillac with four cylinders" — the Model G.

1907 Cadillac, model M, victoria touring, OCW

Engine: Four cylinder, 4 x 4-1/2 in., L-head, 20 H.P.; cylinders cast singly, copper water jackets, detachable combustion valve chamber; main bearings replaceable without removing crankshaft; interchangeable inlet and exhaust valves operated by push rod & roller cam follower on single gear driven camshaft; belt driven fan, water pump, and oiler; splash lubrication; three point engine suspension; float feed carburetor controlled by foot throttle or automatic ring-type governor; clockwise cranking.
Chassis: Pressed steel frame; two half elliptic front, two full elliptic rear springs; foot brake internal, hand brake external on rear drums; worm and sector steering mechanism.
Driveline: Leather faced cone clutch; selective sliding gear transmission, independently attached to frame; single universal in drive shaft to bevel drive line rear axle with spur gear differential.
Bodies: Two door, five passenger Touring and three passenger (single rumble) Runabout, both with wooden dash. Cadillac-built tops available at extra cost.

CADILLAC — MODEL H — FOUR: Same as 1906 Model H except body lines of Touring simplified and five passenger Limousine offered.

1907 Cadillac, model K, light runabout, HAC

CADILLAC — MODEL K — ONE: Chassis same as 1906 except muffler much shorter with outlet at front rather than side, oiler drive changed from cam to pulley and belt, and engine/transmission drip pan added. Runabout bodies remained the same as 1906 but front fenders were changed — nose of fender was now flattened and an inside skirt was added (early 1907 catalogs still showed the canted fender). For the first time, a factory-installed-only Victoria style top was offered, as well as a buggy top.

Note: Prices on Cadillacs varied somewhat in different catalogs and ads, possibly due to severe economic crisis in 1907. Most-quoted (highest) prices shown herein.

CADILLAC — MODEL M — ONE: Chassis same as Model K except for two inch longer wheelbase. Additional body styles offered. Straight line Touring again available. Folding Tonneau new. Tonneau folds to look like runabout but this body not available on shorter Model K chassis. First production one cylinder Coupe offered.

I.D. DATA: Model G&H serial numbers on plate on rear of body or on dash (with engine no.) Engine numbers were stamped on top surface of crankcase — in front of and to the left of number one (front) cylinder. Model G engine no.: 30003-30425 (1907), 30426-30500 (1907-1908). Model H engine no.: 10201-10709 (1906-1908). Model K&M serial numbers on plate on rear of body (with engine number). Engine numbers were stamped two placs on crankcase. 1. Top, right edge of cylinder flange, near water outlet. 2. Top surface of left, front mounting leg. Also on plate on rear of body (with serial number). (Blank spaces on patent plate are for additional patent dates, not engine or serial number.) Engine No. 21851-22150 with M (1906-1907), 22151-24075 with M, 24075-24350 with M, S, T.

Model No.	Body Type & Seating	Price	Weight	Prod. Total
Model G				
NA	2-dr. Tr.-5P	2000	—	—
NA	Rbt.-2P	2000	—	—
NA	Rbt.-3P	2000	—	—
Model H				
NA	2-dr. Tr.-5P	2500	—	—
NA	2-dr. Limo.-6P	3600	—	—
NA	Rbt.-2P	2400	—	—
NA	2-dr. Cpe.-2P	3000	—	—
Model K				
NA	Vic. Rbt.-2P	800	1100	—
NA	W/Vic. top	925	—	—
Model M				
NA	2-dr. Straight line Tr.-4P	950	1350	—
NA	2-dr. Vic. Tr.-4P	950	—	—
NA	Folding Tonneau-4P	1000	—	—
NA	2-dr. Cpe.-2P	1350	—	—
NA	Del.-2P	950	—	—

Note: Weights are approximate.

ENGINE: Model G & H: Vertical, in-line, L-head. Four. Individual cast iron cyl., copper water jacket. B & S: 4 x 4-1/2 in. (Model H) B & S: 4-3/8 x 5 in. Model G Disp.: 226.2 c.i. Model H Disp.: 300.7 c.i. Model G Advertised H.P.: 20. Model H Advertised H.P.: 30. Main bearings: Five. Valve lifters: Mechanical. Carb.: throttled, float feed, jet type made by Cadillac. Models K & M: Horizontal, with cylinder to rear. One cyl. Cast iron cylinder, with copper water jacket. B & S: 5 x 5 in. Disp.: 98.2 cu. in. Brake H.P.: "Higher than advertised or calculated H.P." Advertised H.P.: 10. (ALAM, NACC, SAE H.P. calculated by identical formulae) (ALAM first used formula in 1908.) Main bearings: Two. Valve lifters: Mechanical. Carb.: Updraft mixer, manufactured by Cadillac.

CHASSIS: [Model K] W.B.: 74 in. O.L.: 9 ft., 2 in. H.: 5 ft., 6 in. Frt/Rear Tread: 56 in. (61 opt) Tires: 30 x 3. [Model M Touring] W.B.: 76 in. O.L.: 9 ft., 7 in. H.: 5 ft., 2 in. Frt/Rear Tread: 56 in. (61 opt) Tires: 30 x 3-1/2. [Model M — other bodies] W.B.: 76 in. Frt/Rear Tread: 56 in. (61 opt) Tires: 30 x 3-1/2. [Model G] W.B.: 100 in. Frt/Rear Tread: 56 in. Tires: 32 x 3-1/2. [Model H] W.B.: 102 in. Frt/Rear Tread: 56-1/2 in. Tires: 32 x 4.

TECHNICAL: Model G: Selective sliding gear transmission. Speeds: 3F/1R. Right hand drive, controls to right. Leather faced cone clutch. Shaft drive. Live axle, bevel drive, spur gear differential. Mechanical brakes on two wheels — Service and emergency on rear drums. Wood artillery wheels, 10 spoke front, 12 spoke rear. Wheel size: 25 in. Model H: Planetary transmission. Speeds: 3F/1R. Right hand drive, controls to right. Twin disc in flywheel, disc and three bands on transmission. Shaft drive. Live axle, bevel drive, bevel differential. Mechanical brakes on two wheels — service and emergency on rear drums. Wood artillery wheels, 12 spoke. Wheel size: 24 in. Models K & M: Planetary transmission. Speeds: 2F/1R (3:1 low, rev. — direct high) Low — foot pedal, rev., high — lever to right. Low, rev. — bands, High — disc clutch. Chain drive. Spur gear differential. Overall ratio: 3.1:1 to 5:1 (see drivetrain options). Mechanical brakes on two wheels — contracting on inboard drums. Wood wheels — 12 spoke. Model K Wheel size: 24 in., Model M: 23 in.
Drivetrain Options: [Model K&M] Different combinations of 9 or 10 tooth driving sprocket with 31, 34, 38, 41, or 45 tooth driven sprocket gave ten possible ratios from 3.1:1 to 5:1. Lower ratios for runabout to be run on smooth, level roads to higher ratios for loaded Delivery to be run on rough, hilly roads.
Instructions for changing sprockets were furnished to owners, but the change involved disassembly of the transmission and rear axle — definitely not a "quick-change" set-up.

OPTIONS: Model G: Bulb horn. Lights. Cape Cart top for Touring (120.00).

Note: Tops now being manufactured by Cadillac.

Model H: Bulb horn. Lights. Touring top (150.00). Model K: Bulb horn. Lights. Rubber top w/side curtains & storm apron (40.00). Leather top w/side curtains & storm apron (70.00). Model M: Bulb horn. Lights. Rubber cloth Cape Cart top for Touring (100.00)

HISTORICAL: Model G: Introduced January, 1907. Calendar year sales and production: 1030 (1907-1908). Model year sales and production: same. President of Cadillac was C.A. Black. Model G was first Cadillac without major Alanson Brush design influence. Model H: Introduced 1906. Calendar year sales and production: 509 (1906-1908). Model year sales and production: same. Models K & M: Introduced 1906. Calendar year sales and production: 2350 with M, K, S, T. Model year sales and production: same. In Feb.-Mar. 1908, four 1907 Model K's successfully completed the Royal Automobile Club's Standardisation Test. As a result of these test results, the Cadillac Automobile Company was awarded the Dewar Trophy for 1908 (actual award date was Feb., 1909). The Dewar Trophy was an annual award for the most important advancement of the year in the automobile industry.

1907
Model G, 4-cyl. 20 hp.

	FP	5	4	3	2	1
Rbt	2000	3600	7200	12,000	16,800	24,000
Tr	2000	3750	7500	12,500	17,500	25,000
Limo	3600	3400	6900	11,500	16,100	23,000
Model H, 4-cyl. 30 hp.						
Tr	2500	4050	8100	13,500	18,900	27,000
Limo	3600	3300	6600	11,000	15,400	22,000
Model K-M, 1-cyl.						
Rbt	800	3400	6900	11,500	16,100	23,000
Tr	1025	3600	7200	12,000	16,800	24,000

1908 Cadillac, model G, limousine, HAC

CADILLAC — MODEL G — FOUR: Same as 1907 Model G except: Limousine added to the line; One or two passenger rumble seats available, of different pattern than the single rumble of 1907.

Note: There were no changes in the Model G engine for 1908, but the advertised horsepower rating was increased from 20 to 25. This was due to the newly instituted ALAM horsepower formula, which gave the Model G a horsepower rating of 25.6. Cadillac had always been conservative in horsepower ratings. The ALAM rating was also conservative, and gave the same rating to every engine with the same bore and number of cylinders. There was no allowance for design, accuracy or precision of manufacture, superior practice in fits and tolerances, etc.. Cadillac, although having had a voice in establishing the ALAM formula, soon took exception to being rated the same as the least sophisticated manufacturer. Although engines were tested for actual developed horsepower, it was to be many years before horsepower curves were publicized.

CADILLAC — MODEL H — FOUR: Same as 1907 Model H except: Coupe body dropped from the line; Touring body now similar to Model G, with continuous molding across center of doors. Engine speed governor and interlock between brakes and clutch no longer supplied. Tire size increased to 34 x 4.

CADILLAC — MODEL M — ONE: Offered as Delivery only. Same as 1907 Delivery except that prices now include two oil side lamps, an oil tail lamp, and a bulb horn. Headlamps would not be included as standard equipment on Cadillacs until 1910. Does not have longer wheelbase or running boards of Models S & T.

1908 Cadillac, model S, runabout with rumble, HAC

CADILLAC — MODEL S — ONE: Chassis same as 1907 except wheelbase on all body styles increased to 82 in. and full running boards replaced step plates. Single and double rumble seat options on straight line or Victoria styles were available on runabouts. If rumble seat passengers were to be carried regularly, tire size increase from 30 x 3 to 30 x 3-1/2 was recommended.

CADILLAC — MODEL T — ONE: Chassis same as Model S except Coupe did not have running boards. Bodies were same as 1907 Model M except Folding Tonneau was dropped. Victoria style top now available for tonneau of Victoria Touring.

I.D. DATA: Model G & H serial numbers on plate on rear of body or on dash (with engine no.). Engine numbers were stamped on top surface of crankcase — in front of and to the left of number one (front) cylinder. Model G engine no.: 30426-30500 (1907-1908), 30501-31032 (1908). Model H engine no.: 10201-10709 (1906-1908). Model M, S & T serial numbers on plate on rear of body (with engine number). Engine numbers were stamped two placed on crankcase: 1. Top, right edge of cylinder flange, near water outlet. 2. Top surface of left, front mounting leg. Also on plate on rear of body (with serial number). (Blank spaces on patent plate are for additional patent dates, not engine or serial number.) Model M engine no.: 24075-24350 with K, S, T (1907). Model S engine no.: 24075-24350 with K, M, T (1907), 24351-25832 with T. Model T engine no.: 24075-24350 with K, M, S (1907), 24351-25832 with S.

Model No.	Body Type & Seating	Price	Weight	Prod. Total
Model G				
NA	2-dr. Tr.-5P	2000	—	—
NA	2-dr. Limo.-5P	3000	—	—
NA	Rbt.-3P	2000	—	—
NA	Rbt.-4P	2025	—	—
Model H				
NA	2-dr. Tr.-5P	2500	—	—
NA	2-dr. Limo.-6P	3600	—	—
NA	Rbt.-2P	2400	—	—
Model M				
NA	Delivery-2P	950	—	—
Model S				
NA	Straight Line Rbt.-2P	850	—	—
NA	Vic. Rbt.-2P	850	—	—
NA	Vic. Rbt. w/single rumble	875	—	—
NA	St. Line Rbt. w/double rumble	885	—	—
Model T				
NA	2-dr. St. Line Tr.-4P	1000	—	—
NA	2-dr. Vic. Tr.-4P	1000	—	—
NA	2-dr. Cpe.-2P	1350	—	—

ENGINE: Model H: Vertical, in-line, L-head. Four. Individual cast iron cyl., copper water jacket. (Model G) B & S: 4 x 4-1/2 in. (Model H) B & S: 4-3/8 x 5 in. Model G Disp.: 226.2 c.i. Model H Disp.: 300.7 c.i. (Model G) A.L.A.M. H.P.: 25.6 Advertised H.P.: 25. (Model H) A.L.A.M. H.P.: 30.625 Advertised H.P. 30. Main bearings: Five. Valve lifters: Mechanical. Carb.: throttled, float feed, jet type made by Cadillac. Models M, S, & T: Horizontal, with cylinder to rear. One. Cast iron cylinder, with copper water jacket. B & S: 5 x 5 in. Disp.: 98.2 cu. in. Brake H.P.: "Higher than advertised or calculated H.P." Advertised/A.L.A.M. H.P.: 10. (ALAM, NACC, SAE horsepower calculated by identical formulae) (ALAM first used formula in 1908.) Main bearings: Two. Valve lifters: Mechanical. Carb.: Updraft mixer, manufactured by Cadillac.

CHASSIS: [Model M Delivery] W.B.: 76 in. Frt/Rear Tread: 56. Tires: 30 x 3-1/2. [Model S] W.B.: 82 in. O.L.: 10 ft., 1 in. Height: 5 ft., 4 in. Frt/Rear Tread: 56 in. (61 opt) Tires: 30 x 3. [Model T Touring] W.B.: 82 in. O.L.: 10 ft., 2 in. Height: 5 ft., 4 in. Frt/Rear Tread: 56 in. (61 opt) Tires: 30 x 3-1/2. [Model T Coupe] W.B.: 82 in. Frt/Rear Tread: 56 in. (61 opt) Tires: 30 x 3-1/2. [Model G] W.B.: 100 in. Frt/Rear Tread: 56 in. Tires: 32 x 3-1/2 (34 x 4 Limo). [Model H] W.B.: 102 in. Frt/Rear Tread: 56-1/2 in. Tires: 34 x 4.

TECHNICAL: Model G: Selective sliding gear transmission. Speeds: 3F/1R. Right hand drive, controls to right. Leather faced cone clutch. Shaft drive. Live axle, bevel drive, spur gear differential. Mechanical brakes on two wheels — service and emergency on rear drums. Wood artillery wheels, 10 spoke front, 12 spoke rear. Wheel size: Tr. & Rdstr. 25 in., Limo. 26 in. Model H: Planetary transmission. Speeds: 3F/1R. Right hand drive, controls to right. Twin disc in flywheel, disc and three bands on transmission. Shaft drive. Live axle, bevel drive, bevel differential. Mechanical brakes on two wheels — service and emergency on rear drums. Wood artillery wheels, 12 spoke. Wheel size: 26 in. Models M, S&T: Planetary transmission. Speeds: 2F/1R (3:1 low). Low — foot pedal, rev., high — lever to right. Low, rev. — bands, High — disc clutch. Chain drive. Spur gear differential. Overall ratio: 3.1:1 to 5:1 (see drivetrain options). Mechanical brakes on two wheels — contracting on inboard drums. Wood wheels — 12 spoke. Models M & T Wheel size: 23 in., Model S: 24 in.
Drivetrain Options: [Models M, S & T] Different combinations of 9 or 10 tooth driving sprocket with 31, 34, 38, 41, or 45 tooth driven sprocket gave ten possible ratios from 3.1:1 to 5:1. Lower ratios for runabout to be run on smooth, level roads to higher ratios for loaded Delivery to be run on rough, hilly roads.
Instructions for changing sprockets were furnished by owners, but the change involved disassembly of the transmission and rear axle — definitely not a "quick-change" set-up.

OPTIONS: Model G: Headlights. Rubber, leather, and mohair tops in three-bow, cape cart, and victoria styles (90.00 to 200.00). Model H: Headlights. Lined Cape Cart top for Touring (150.00). Model M: Headlights. Model S: Headlights. 30 x 3-1/2 tires on Runabouts with rumble (50.00). Rubber top with side curtains & storm apron (60.00). Leather top with side curtains & storm apron (80.00). Victoria style top (factory installed only) (175.00). Storm front w/windows to replace storm apron (15.00). Model T: Headlights. Cape Cart top (115.00). Victoria style top (factory installed only) (175.00).

HISTORICAL: Model G: Introduced November, 1907. Calendar year sales and production: 1030 (1907-1908). Model year sales and production: same. The President of Cadillac was C.A. Black.

Note: The bulky, complicated, planetary transmission, luxury fours were too great a first leap from the single cylinder, which had become passe. The compromise Model G design formed a solid basis for the "Thirty", which was to be the single line for Cadillac thru 1914. Had Brush design concepts been perpetuated, the company might well have failed. Its move into a firm position in the luxury car field was to wait another seven years.

Model H: Introduced June, 1907. Calendar year sales and production: 509 (1906-1908). Model year sales and production: same.

Note: The last of the planetary transmission fours and the last of counter-clockwise cranking for Cadillac. The only remaining Brush features were to be the copper water jacket and the splash lube system; both of these were in use by Cadillac thru 1914.

Model M: Introduced 1906. Model year production: Included with 1907. Models S&T: Introduced Nov. 1907. Calendar year sales and production: 1482 with S&T. Model year sales and production: same.

Note: Several hundred of the approximately 16,000 single cylinder Cadillacs produced still exist in the hands of collectors all over the world. A prominent Australian collector visiting Hershey remarked, "Anyone wanting to restore, drive, and enjoy a one cylinder car best find a Cadillac" — no argument, mate.

1908
Model G, 4-cyl. 25 hp.

	FP	5	4	3	2	1
Rbt	2000	3000	6000	10,000	14,000	20,000
Tr	2000	3150	6300	10,500	14,700	21,000
Model H, 4-cyl. 30 hp.						
Rbt	2500	3300	6600	11,000	15,400	22,000
Tr	2500	3150	6300	10,500	14,700	21,000
Cpe	2950	3000	6000	10,000	14,000	20,000
Limo	3000	2800	5700	9500	13,300	19,000
Model S-T, 1-cyl.						
Rbt	850	2800	5700	9500	13,300	19,000
Tr	1000	3000	6000	10,000	14,000	20,000
Cpe	1350	2000	5100	8500	11,900	17,000

1909

1909 Cadillac, Thirty, touring, OCW

CADILLAC — MODEL "THIRTY" — FOUR: After an inauspicious trial in the luxury car field, and recognizing the disappearing market for the single cylinder cars which made their reputation, Cadillac settled down with a design which had originated in 1906 (the 1907-1908 Model G). With in-house mass production of a single line, Cadillac was able to offer a high quality automobile at a moderate price; $1400 for the Model "Thirty" as compared to $2000 for the Model G.

The "Thirty" differed from the Model G as follows:
Bodies: No closed bodies offered. Detachable tonneau once again available. Steel doors and cowl on Roadster and Demi-tonneau. Flaring, twisted front fenders replaced by flat fenders with filler between fender and frame. Full running boards and running board dust shields on all bodies. No louvers in hood. Bodies finished (painted) by Cadillac.
Chassis: 3/4 platform rear spring system. Single dropped frame. Wheelbase lengthened to 106 in. In mid-year, brake drum diameter was increased to 12 in.
Drive line: Transmission refined and mounted at three points to frame cross members rather than at four points to frame side rails. Universal joint housed in ball joint at rear of transmission. Rear axle with bevel gear differential made by American Ball Bearing.
Engine: Drive for water pump (gear type) and oiler changed from external belt to internal gears. Gear driven accessory shaft allows for optional magneto. Speed governor no longer used.

I.D. DATA: Serial numbers on plate on rear of body or on dash (with engine no.) Engine numbers were stamped on top surface of crankcase — in front of and to the left of number one (front) cylinder. Starting: 32002. Ending: 37904.

Model No.	Body Type & Seating	Price	Weight	Prod. Total
NA	2-dr. Touring-5P	1400	—	—
NA	2-dr. Demi-Tonneau-4P	1400	—	—
NA	Roadster-3P	1400	—	—

ENGINE: Vertical, in-line, L-head. Four. Individual cast iron cyl., copper water jacket. B & S: 4 x 4-1/2 in. Disp.: 226.2 cu. in. Brake H.P.: 30. A.L.A.M. H.P.: 25.6. Main bearings: Five. Valve lifters: Mechanical-push rod-roller cam followers. Carb.: Float feed; made by Cadillac.

CHASSIS: W.B.: 106 in. Frt/Rear Tread: 56 in. (61 opt.) Tires: 32 x 3-1/2.

TECHNICAL: Selective, sliding gear transmission. Speeds: 3F/1R. Right hand drive, controls to right. Leather faced cone clutch. Shaft drive. Plain live rear axle; bevel drive; bevel gear differential. Overall ratio: Tour., Demi-Tonn. 3.5:1, roadster 3:1. Mech. brakes on two wheels — Service/foot/contracting — emerg./lever/expanding. Wood artillery wheels, 10 & 12 spoke, quick detachable rims. Wheel rim size: 25 in. Optional: Final drive ratio: 3:1, 3.5:1, 4:1.

OPTIONS: Seat covers (45.00-75.00). ''Rubber'', mohair, or leather tops (55.00-125.00). Bosch, Dow, Eisemann, or Splitdorf magnetos (100.00-126.00) Rushmore style B headlamps with Rushmore No. 1 generator (46.50). With Prest-o-lite style B tank (59.50). Mezger windshield (50.00). Gabriel horns, style 1, 2, 3, 4 (15.00-35.00). Stewart & Clark speedometer (15.00-40.00).

HISTORICAL: Introduced December, 1908. Calendar year sales and production: 5903. Model year sales and production: same. The president/general manager of Cadillac was Henry Leland. On July 29, 1909, Cadillac Motor Car Co. became a wholly owned subsidiary of General Motors Co., and Henry Leland became President and General Manager of Cadillac Motor Car Co.

1909
Model 30, 4-cyl.

	FP	5	4	3	2	1
Rds	1400	3000	6000	10,000	14,000	20,000
demi T.C.	3000	2800	5700	9500	13,300	19,000
Tr	1400	3150	6300	10,500	14,700	21,000
Model T, 1-cyl.						
Tr	1000	1200	3750	6250	8750	12,500

emerg./lever/expanding. Wood artillery wheels, 10 & 12 spoke, quick detachable rims. Wheel size: 26 in. (Limo 25 in.) Optional Final drive ratios: 3:1, 4:1.

OPTIONS: Seat covers (40.00-60.00). ''Rubber'' or mohair tops (55.00-95.00). Prest-o-lite style B tank (25.00). Windshield (30.00). Jones speedometer No. 29, 33, 34 (25.00-35.00). Foot rail (3.50)

HISTORICAL: Introduced November, 1909. Innovations: Delco ignition system. Model year sales. Model year production: 8008. President & General Manager of Cadillac was Henry Leland.

Note: In the early days of automobiling in America, open cars and poor travel conditions precluded Winter motoring. Manufacturers displayed samples at the Winter auto shows and took orders for Spring and Summer delivery. Cadillac's model year coincided with the calendar year and the year's production was presold.

In 1910, Cadillac got more heavily into closed cars and had a solid reputation for quality and value. With a ready demand for their full factory capacity, they introduced the 1911 models in late Summer of 1910 and had delivered a significant percentage of the 1911 model production by the start of the calendar year. Cadillac was now producing below demand and customers were willing to accept delivery at any time or wait as long as necessary for delivery.

1910
Model 30, 4-cyl.

	FP	5	4	3	2	1
Rds	1600	4200	8400	14,000	19,600	28,000
demi-T.C.	2250	3600	7200	12,000	16,800	24,000
Tr	1600	4800	9600	16,000	22,400	32,000
Limo	3000	3150	6300	10,500	14,700	21,000

1910

1910 Cadillac, Thirty, limousine, HAC

CADILLAC — MODEL ''THIRTY'' — FOUR: Same as 1909 except: Basic price increased to $1600.
Bodies: Only open cars advertised before April, 1910. Limousine in early catalog, Coupe added in later catalog. Closed bodies by Fisher. Touring body of wood, large (rear) panel of Demi-tonneau and all doors of steel.
Chassis: Gas headlamps now standard. Wheelbase lengthened to 110 in. (120 in. on Limo).
Drive line: In mid-year, rear axle was changed to Timken semi-floating.
Engine: Bore increased to 4-1/4 in. Dual ignition consisting of new Delco four coil system and low tension magneto. Mid-year change to centrifugal water pump.

I.D. DATA: Serial numbers on plate on rear of body or on dash (with engine no.) Engine numbers were stamped on top surface of crankcase — in front of and to the left of number one (front) cylinder. Starting: 40001. Ending: 48008.

Model No.	Body Type & Seating	Price	Weight	Prod. Total
NA	2-dr. Touring-5P	1600	—	—
NA	2-dr. Demi-Tonneau-4P	1600	—	—
NA	Roadster-2P	1600	—	—
NA	Roadster-3P	1600	—	—
NA	2-dr. Limo.-7P	3000	—	—
NA	2-dr. Coupe-3P	2200	—	—

ENGINE: Vertical, in-line, L-head. Four. Individual cast iron cyl., copper water jacket. B & S: 4-1/4 x 4-1/2 in. Disp.: 255.4 cu. in. Brake H.P.: 33. A.L.A.M. H.P.: 28.9. Main bearings: Five. Valve lifters: Mechanical-push rod-roller cam followers. Carb.: Float feed — made by Cadillac.

CHASSIS: All except Limo. W.B.: 110 in. Frt/Rear Tread: 56 in. (61 opt) Tires: 34 x 4. Limo. W.B.: 120 in. Tires: 34 x 4-1/2.

TECHNICAL: Selective, sliding gear transmission. 3F/1R. Right hand drive, controls to right. Leather faced cone clutch. Shaft drive. Live; bevel drive; bevel gear diff.; ABB plain/Timken semi-floating. Overall ratio: 3.5:1 (Limo 4:1). Mech. brakes on two wheels. Service/foot/contracting —

196

1911

1911 Cadillac, Thirty, touring, OCW

CADILLAC — MODEL ''THIRTY'' — FOUR: Same as 1910 except: Basic price increased to $1700.
Bodies: First front (fore) door on an open Cadillac body — left side only on Foredoor Touring and Torpedo. Torpedo body all steel on wood frame. Limo body interchangeable with Touring and Coupe body interchangeable with Demi-tonneau (an inducement to year round motoring).
Chassis: Wheelbase lengthened to 116 in. Brake drum diameter increased to 14 in. Double dropped frame.
Drive line: Rear axle changed to Timken full floating, with torsion arm and two universal joints in the drive shaft.
Engine: Bore increased to 4½ in. Schebler Model L carburetor used. Bosch high tension magneto and Delco single coil system used for dual ignition.

I.D. DATA: Serial numbers on plate on dash (with engine no.) Engine numbers were stamped on top surface of crankcase — in front of and to the left of number one (front) cylinder. Starting: 50000. Ending: 60018.

Model No.	Body Type & Seating	Price	Weight	Prod. Total
NA	2-dr. Touring-5P	1700	—	—
NA	2-dr. Demi-Tonneau-4P	1700	—	—
NA	3-dr. Foredoor Tr.-5P	1800	—	—
NA	3-dr. Torpedo-4P	1850	—	—
NA	Roadster-2P	1700	—	—
NA	Roadster-3P	1700	—	—
NA	2-dr. Limo.-7P	3000	—	—
NA	2-dr. Coupe-3P	2250	—	—

ENGINE: Vertical, in-line, L-head. Four. Individual cast iron cyl., copper water jacket. B & S: 4-1/2 x 4-1/2 in. Disp.: 286.3. A.L.A.M. H.P.: 32.4. Main bearings: Five. Valve lifters: Mechanical — push rod — roller cam followers. Carb.: Float feed; Schebler Model L.

CHASSIS: All except Limo. W.B.: 116 in. Frt/Rear Tread: 56 in. (61 opt). Tires: 34 x 4. Limo. Tires: 36 x 4-1/2.

TECHNICAL: Selective, sliding gear transmission. Speeds: 3F/1R. Right hand drive, controls to right. Leather faced cone clutch. Shaft drive. Full floating rear axle, bevel drive, bevel gear differential. Overall ratio: 3.43:1 (roadster 3.05:1, limo. 3.66:1). Mech. brakes on two wheels — Service/foot/contracting — emerg./lever/expanding. Wood artillery wheels, 10 & 12 spoke, quick detachable rims. Wheel size: 26 in. (Limo. 27 in.). Optional Final drive ratios: 3.43:1, 3.66:1.

OPTIONS: Seat covers (40.00-60.00). Mohair tops (65.00-90.00). Prest-o-lite style B tank (25.00). Windshield (40.00). Jones electric horn, with storage battery (40.00).

HISTORICAL: Introduced August, 1910. Model year sales: 10019. Model year production: 10019. The President & General Manager of Cadillac was Henry Leland.

1911
Model 30, 4-cyl.

	FP	5	4	3	2	1
Rds	1750	2000	5100	8500	11,900	17,000
demi-T.C.	1850	3600	7200	12,000	16,800	24,000
Tr	1750	3750	7500	12,500	17,500	25,000
Cpe	2250	2300	5400	9000	12,600	18,000
Limo	3000	3150	6300	10,500	14,700	21,000

1912

1912 Cadillac, Four, roadster, HAC

1912 CADILLAC — FOUR: Same as 1911 except: Basic price increased to $1800.
Bodies: Demi-tonneau and Foredoor Touring replaced by Phaeton. Coupe accommodates extra passenger on folding seat. The only fully enclosed standard four cylinder Limo. Open bodies of steel, closed bodies of aluminum. Full set of doors on all body styles. Hoods once again louvered. Running board dust shields cover frame and running board brackets. Exterior trim Nickel plated. Electric side lights have external wiring. All controls inside except brake lever on open bodies.
Chassis: Brake drum diameter increased to 17 in.
Drive line: No significant change.
Engine: New carburetor, made by Cadillac to C.F. Johnson patents. Delco 6/24 volt starting - lighting - twin ignition system.

I.D. DATA: If serial numbers were used they were on the plate on dash (with engine no.) Engine numbers were stamped on top surface of crankcase — in front of and to the left of number one (front) cylinder. Starting: 61001. Ending: 75000.

Model No.	Body Type & Seating	Price	Weight	Prod. Total
NA	4-dr. Touring-5P	1800	—	—
NA	4-dr. Phaeton-4P	1800	—	—
NA	4-dr. Torpedo-4P	1900	—	—
NA	2-dr. Roadster-2P	1800	—	—
NA	4-dr. Limo.-7P	3250	—	—
NA	2-dr. Coupe-4P	2250	—	—

ENGINE: Vertical, in-line, L-head. Four. Individual cast iron cyl., copper water jacket. B & S: 4-1/2 x 4-1/2 in. Disp.: 286.3 cu. in. Brake H.P.: 40 plus. A.L.A.M. H.P.: 32.4. Main bearings: Five. Valve lifters: Mechanical - push rod - roller cam followers. Carb.: float feed; Made by Cadillac to C.F. Johnson patents.

CHASSIS: W.B.: 116 in. Frt/Rear Tread: 56 in. (61 opt). Tires: 36 x 4.

TECHNICAL: Selective, sliding gear transmission. Speeds: 3F/1R. Right hand drive, controls to right. Leather faced cone clutch. Shaft drive. Full floating rear axle, bevel drive, bevel gear differential. Overall ratio: 3.92:1 (Phaeton & Torpedo 3.66:1, Roadster 3.43:1). Mech. brakes on two wheels — service/foot/contracting — emerg./lever/expanding. Wood artillery wheels, 10 & 12 spoke, quick detachable rims. Wheel size: 28 in. Optional Final drive ratios: 3.05:1, 3.43:1, 3.66:1.

OPTIONS: Front bumper (18.00). Clock (15.00). Seat covers (32.00-50.00). Mohair tops (60.00-90.00). Windshields (35.00-40.00). Trunk rack (10.00). Kamlee No. 1000 trunk (30.00). Demountable rims (25.00). Electric horn (25.00). Power tire pump (35.00). Handy lamp (2.00).

HISTORICAL: Introduced September, 1911. Innovations: Electric starting-ignition-lighting system. Model year sales: 13995. Model year production: 13995. The President & general manager was Henry Leland.

1912 Cadillac, Four, touring, JAC

1912
Model 30, 4-cyl.

	FP	5	4	3	2	1
Rds	1850	3400	6900	11,500	16,100	23,000
4P Phae	1950	3400	6900	11,500	16,100	23,000
5P Tr	1900	4350	8700	14,500	20,300	29,000
Cpe	2250	2000	5100	8500	11,900	17,000
Limo	3250	2800	5700	9500	13,300	19,000

1913

1913 Cadillac, Four, touring

1913 CADILLAC — FOUR: Same as 1912 except: Basic price increased to $1975.
Bodies: Smoother, more integrated appearance. All controls inside. Cowls on all bodies except Coupe. Reverse curve in front fenders. Top and windshield standard equipment. Sidelight wiring concealed.
Chassis: Wheelbase lengthened to 120 in.
Drive line: No significant change.
Engine: Major changes in lower end. Stroke increased to 5-3/4 in. Main bearings now in upper half of crankcase — lower half becomes an oil pan. Camshaft and accessory shaft chain driven. Engine mounting points moved to top of crankcase. Engine suspended from arched cross members. Valve stems enclosed. Starter/generator simplified (six volt only) and more compact. Ring governor used once more; but for spark control, not speed control. Engine driven tire pump optional.

I.D. DATA: If serial numbers were used, they could be found on plate on the dash (with engine no.) Engine numbers were stamped on top surface of crankcase — in front of and to the left of number one (front) cylinder. Starting: 75001. Ending: 90018.

Model No.	Body Type & Seating	Price	Weight	Prod. Total
NA	4-dr. Touring-5P	1975	—	—
NA	4-dr. Torpedo-4P	1975	—	—
NA	4-dr. Touring-6P	2075	—	—
NA	4-dr. Phaeton-4P	1975	—	—
NA	2-dr. Roadster-2P	1975	—	—
NA	4-dr. Limo.-7P	3250	—	—
NA	2-dr. Coupe-4P	2500	—	—

ENGINE: Vertical, in-line, L-head. Four. Individual cast iron cyl., copper water jacket. B & S: 4-1/2 x 5-3/4 in. Disp.: 365.8 cu. in. Brake H.P.: 40-50. A.L.A.M. H.P.: 32.4. Main bearings: Five. Valve lifters: Mechanical — push rod — roller cam followers. Carb.: float feed; Made by Cadillac to C.F. Johnson patents.

CHASSIS: W.B.: 120 in. Frt/Rear Tread: 56 in. (61 opt.). Tires: 36 x 4-1/2.

TECHNICAL: Selective, sliding gear transmission. Speeds: 3F/1R. Right hand drive, controls to right. Leather faced cone clutch. Shaft drive. Full floating rear axle, bevel drive, bevel differential. Overall ratio: 3.43:1 (Roadster 3.05:1, Limo. 3.66:1). Mech. brakes on two wheels — Service/foot/contracting — emerg./lever/expanding. Wood artillery wheels, 10 & 12 spoke, Demountable rims. Wheel size: 27 in. Optional Final drive ratios: 3.43:1, 3.66:1, 3.92:1.

OPTIONS: Front bumper (15.00). Clock (35.00). Seat covers (32.50-65.00). Running board trunk (33.00). Tire trunk (16.50). Electric horn (25.00). Power tire pump (25.00). Handy lamp (2.00). Weed chains (8.00).

HISTORICAL: Introduced August, 1912. Model year sales: 15018. Model year production: 15018. The President & General Manager was Henry Leland.

Note: "Standard of the World" first used in the fall of 1912, in ads for the 1913 cars.

1913
Model 30, 4-cyl.

	FP	5	4	3	2	1
Rds	1975	3150	6300	10,500	14,700	21,000
Phae	1975	3400	6900	11,500	16,100	23,000
Torp	1975	3150	6300	10,500	14,700	21,000
5P Tr	1975	3750	7500	12,500	17,500	25,000
6P Tr	2075	4050	8100	13,500	18,900	27,000
Cpe	2500	1750	4800	8000	11,200	16,000
Limo	3250	2300	5400	9000	12,600	18,000

1914

1914 Cadillac, Four, landaulet coupe, HAC

1914 CADILLAC — FOUR: Same as 1913 except:
Bodies: Torpedo body no longer available. Landaulet treatment on Coupe. Five passenger "Inside drive Limousine" (actually a center door sedan) is a new style. Hinged steering wheel and hinged driver's seat cushion facilitate entrance and exit for front seat passengers at right side of car. With smaller side lamps, bodies now have the appearance of enclosing the occupants and all the machinery.
Chassis: Hinged steering wheel. Speedometer drive located in left steering knuckle.
Drive line: Rear axle changed to Timken two-speed.
Engine: Second ignition system for auxiliary use only. One distributor, one set of spark plugs. Fuel tank moved to rear of chassis. Hand pump on dash to pressurize tank for starting, camshaft driven pump for running. Power tire pump standard equipment.

I.D. DATA: There were no serial numbers for the 1914 Cadillac. Engine numbers were stamped on top surface of crankcase — in front of and to the left of number one (front) cylinder. Engine No.: 91005-99999; A-1 — A-5008.

Model No.	Body Type & Seating	Price	Weight	Prod. Total
NA	4-dr. Touring-7P	2075	—	—
NA	4-dr. Touring-5P	1975	—	—
NA	4-dr. Phaeton-4P	1975	—	—
NA	2-dr. Roadster-2P	1975	—	—
NA	2-dr. Landaulet Coupe-3P	2500	—	—

Model No.	Body Type & Seating	Price	Weight	Prod. Total
NA	4-dr. Standard Limo.-7P	3250	—	—
NA	2-dr. Inside Drive Limo.-5P	2800	—	—

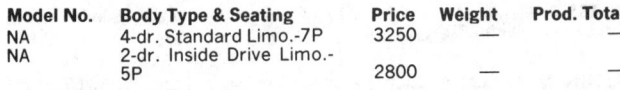

1914 Cadillac, Four, 7-pass. touring, JAC

ENGINE: Vertical, in-line, L-head. Four. Individual cast iron cyl., copper water jacket. B & S: 4-1/2 x 5-3/4 in. Disp.: 365.8 cu. in. Brake H.P.: 40-50. N.A.C.C. H.P.: 32.4. Main bearings: Five. Valve lifters: Mechanical-push-rod-roller cam followers. Carb.: float feed; made by Cadillac to C.F. Johnson patents.

CHASSIS: W.B.: 120 in. Frt/Rear Tread: 56 in. (61 opt). Tires: 36 x 4-1/2. Special chassis. W.B.: 134 in.

TECHNICAL: Selective, sliding gear transmission. Speeds: 3F/1R. Right hand drive, controls to right. Leather faced cone clutch. Shaft drive. Full floating rear axle, two speed, bevel drive, bevel gear differential. Overall ratio: 3.67:1/2.5:1. Mech. brakes on two wheels — Service/foot/contracting — emerg./lever/expanding. Wood artillery wheels, 10 & 12 spoke, demountable rims. Wheel size: 27 in. Optional Final drive dual ratio 4.07:1/2.5:1.

OPTIONS: Seat covers (32.50-65.00). Handy lamp (2.00).

HISTORICAL: Introduced July, 1913. Innovations: Production two-speed rear axle. Model year sales: 14,003. Model year production: 14,003. The President & general manager was Henry Leland.

Note: The last four cylinder Cadillac for 67 years; and the final use by Cadillac of Alanson Brush design features.

Note: A 1914 Cadillac Touring (engine number 92,524) was awarded the 1913 Dewar Trophy as a result of electrical and two-speed-axle performance during a 1000-mile test conducted in September/October 1913.

1914
Model 30, 4-cyl.

	FP	5	4	3	2	1
Rds	1975	3600	7200	12,000	16,800	24,000
Phae	1975	3650	7350	12,250	17,150	24,500
5P Tr	1975	3600	7200	12,000	16,800	24,000
7P Tr	2075	3650	7350	12,250	17,150	24,500
Lan Cpe	2500	1800	4950	8250	11,550	16,500
Encl dr Limo	2800	2300	5400	9000	12,600	18,000
Limo	3250	2800	5700	9500	13,300	19,000

1915

1915 Cadillac, Type 51, landaulet coupe, OCW

CADILLAC — TYPE 51 — EIGHT: Bodies: Similar to 1914 bodies except: Side lights smaller. Hood top panels blend smoothly into hood side panels. Shape of doors changed. Three piece "Rain Vision" windshield used on closed cars. Roof line of closed cars raised at front. Cadillac "One-man" top with inside operating curtains which open with the doors is standard equipment. Top fastened to windshield, eliminating straps. Four passenger Phaeton replaced by two door Salon with passageway between individual front seats (right front seat revolves). "Inside drive Limousine" of 1914 now designated "Five Passenger Sedan". Berline enclosed drive limousine added. The designation "Imperial" used with "Sedan" (or "Brougham", "Suburban", etc.) denotes a regular Sedan with a glass partition added between front and rear compartments.

Chassis: First left drive Cadillac (right drive available as an option). Tread 56 inches (61 inch optional wide tread still available). Wheelbase 122 inches (145 inch chassis available without body). Wood wheels with ten spokes in front, twelve spokes in rear. Speedometer drive changed to right steering spindle. Rear springs three-quarter platform, front springs half-elliptic, six inches longer than in 1914. Ladder type frame changed to six inch deep "H" frame with three cross members.

Drive Line: Multiple disc, dry plate clutch with 15 steel plates, 7-3/4 in. dia. Alternate plates faced with wire mesh asbestos. Selective sliding gear transmission. Aluminum case in unit with engine. Tubular drive shaft with two universal joints. Torque arm. Spiral bevel drive in full floating rear axle.

Engine: Ninety degree L-Head V-8, 3-1/8 x 5-1/8, 314 cu. in. Cast iron cylinders in two blocks of four located exactly opposite on Aluminum-Copper alloy crankcase. Water jackets and combustion chambers integral. Water circulation and temperature control is by an impeller type pump with thermostat for each block of cylinders. Three 1-7/8 diameter bearings on crankshaft with four throws all in one plane. Fork and blade connecting rods. Rod bearings available standard, .005 under, and .020 under. Three rings, solid wall pistons and cylinder blocks available standard, first, and second oversize. Single camshaft with eight cams. Camshaft and generator shaft driven by silent chain. Motor/generator/distributor at rear, two cylinder power tire pump at front, inside engine Vee. Updraft carburetor, water-heated intake manifold, and log-type exhaust manifolds located inside Vee. Dual exhaust system with no balance pipe. Valves 1-9/16 diameter, 5/16 lift. Exhaust valves flat, intake valves tulip shape. Valves actuated by adjustable tappets which are activated by rocker arms with roller riding on cams. Firing order is: 1L-2R-3L-1R-4L-3R-2L-4R, where R(right) and L(left) are as viewed from the rear, and each bank is numbered one thru four from the front. Valve chamber caps are stamped H, L, or LL for high or low compression ratios. Engine has three-point suspension. Ball and socket at front and solid at rear, forming an additional frame cross member. Before Engine No. A-7710, oil relief valve is cast integral with starter gear housing. Starting with Engine No. A-7710, oil relief valve is a separate unit mounted on angular face of crankcase. The lubrication system is recirculating, pressure fed from a gear type oil pump. The pump draws oil from the crankcase and forces it thru a header pipe running inside the crankcase. Leads run from this pipe to the main bearings and thence thru drilled holes in the crankshaft to the connecting rod bearings. Pistons, cylinders, etc. are lubricated by oil thrown from the lower ends of the connecting rods. Oil from the rear end of the header pipe runs to the pressure relief valve. Overflow from this valve is gravity fed to the camshaft and chains, then drains back to the crankcase.

I.D. DATA: Serial numbers were not used. Engine numbers stamped on the crankcase just back of the right hand bank of cylinders, and on a plate on the dash. Starting: A-6000. Ending: A-19001.

Style No.	Body Type & Seating	Price	Weight	Prod. Total
NA	4-dr. Touring-7P	1975	—	—
NA	4-dr. Touring-5P	1975	—	—
NA	2-dr. Salon-5P	1975	—	—
NA	2-dr. Roadster-2/4P	1975	—	—
602	2-dr. Landaulet Coupe-3P	2500	—	—
601	2-dr. Sedan-5P	2800	—	—
583	4-dr. Limo.-7P	3450	—	—
NA	4-dr. Berline Limo.-7P	3600	—	—
715	4-dr. Imperial Sedan-5P	—	—	—

Note: Thru 1919, Cadillac sometimes referred to Touring Cars and Roadsters as "Seven Passenger Car", "Five Passenger Car" or "Two Passenger Car". The designations "Touring" and "Roadster" are used herein for clarity.

ENGINE: Ninety degree V-8 L-head. Heads not detachable. Cast iron blocks of four on Aluminum crankcase. B & S: 3-1/8 x 5-1/8 in. Disp.: 314.5 cu. in. C.R.: 4.25:1. Brake H.P.: 70 @ 2400 R.P.M. 60 + advertised. S.A.E./N.A.C.C. H.P.: 31.25. Main bearings: Three. Valve lifters: Rockers with roller cam follower acting on mech. lifters. Carb.: float feed, aux air control; mfg by Cad under C.F. Johnson patents. Torque (Compression) 180 lbs.-ft. @ 2000 R.P.M.

1915 Cadillac, Type 51, 7-pass. touring, HAC

CHASSIS: [Type 51] W.B.: 122 in. Frt/Rear Tread: 56 in. (61 opt). Tires: 36 x 4-1/2. [Special Chassis] W.B.: 145 in.

TECHNICAL: Selective sliding gear transmission. Case in unit with engine. Speeds: 3F/1R. Left drive, center control (rhd opt). Multiple disc, dry plate, 15 discs. Shaft drive. Spiral bevel, full floating rear axle. Overall ratio: 4.44:1. Mech. brakes on two wheels, one external, one internal. Wood artillery wheels, demountable rims (wire wheels opt). Wheel size: 27 in. Optional Drive ratio 3.94:1, 5.07:1.

OPTIONS: Seat covers (35.00-65.00). Handy lamp (2.00).

HISTORICAL: Introduced September, 1914. Innovations: High production V-8 engine. Model year sales: 13002. Model year production: 13002. The President & General Manager was Henry Leland.

1915
Model 51, V-8

	FP	5	4	3	2	1
Rds	1975	3900	7800	13,000	18,200	26,000
Sal Tr	1975	4050	8100	13,500	18,900	27,000
7P Tr	1975	3900	7800	13,000	18,200	26,000
3P Cpe	2500	1750	4800	8000	11,200	16,000
Sed Brgm	2800	1750	4800	8000	11,200	16,000
7P Limo	3450	3000	6000	10,000	14,000	20,000
Berl Limo	3600	3300	6600	11,000	15,400	22,000

1916

1916 Cadillac, Type 53, victoria, HAC

CADILLAC — TYPE 53 — EIGHT: Bodies: Similar to Type 51 except: Hood line raised so that transition in cowl is less abrupt. Roof line of closed bodies raised again at front so that entire roof line is one gentle curve. Door shape changed. Five passenger Touring dropped. Salon now has four doors. Victoria body replaces Landaulet Coupe. Four passenger Coupe built by Cadillac added in mid-year. Five/seven (5/7p) Brougham replaces two door Sedan. (The seating arrangement 7p denotes two folding auxiliary seats facing forward in the rear compartment. The seating arrangement 5/7p denotes two emergency "seats" in ther rear compartment. These "seats" are rear-facing upholstered shelves hinged down out of the back of the front seat.) Touring body on special 132 inch chassis offered. Police Patrol, Ambulance, and Hearse bodies on special 145 inch chassis offered.

Chassis: Same as Type 51 plus 132 inch chassis also available.
Drive Line: Power tire pump moved from engine to transmission.
Engine: Power tire pump moved from engine to transmission. Distributor moved from rear to front of engine. Fan blades curved. Exhaust manifolds redesigned with curved connector pipes feeding into collector.

I.D. DATA: Serial numbers were not used. Engine numbers were stamped on the crankcase just back of the right hand bank of cylinders, and on a plate on the dash. Starting: A-20000. Ending: A-38003.

Style No.	Body Type & Seating	Price	Weight	Prod. Total
NA	4-dr. Touring-7P	2080	—	—
NA	4-dr. Salon-5P	2080	—	—
NA	2-dr. Roadster-2/4P	2080	—	—
1517	2-dr. Victoria-3P	2400	—	—
NA	2-dr. Coupe-4P	2800	—	—
1518	4-dr. Brougham-5/7P	2950	—	—
1744	4-dr. Limo.-7P	3450	—	—
1519	4-dr. Berline-7P	3600	—	—
NA	4-dr. 132 inch Touring	—	—	—
NA	Ambulance	3455	—	—
NA	Police Patrol	2955	—	—
NA	Hearse	3880	—	—

ENGINE: Ninety degree V-8 L-head. Heads not detachable. Cast iron block of four on Aluminum crankcase. B & S: 3-1/8 x 5-1/8 in. Disp.: 314.5 cu. in. Brake H.P.: 77 @ 2600 R.P.M. 60 plus advertised. S.A.E./N.A.C.C. H.P.: 31.25. Main bearings: Three. Valve lifters: Rockers with roller cam follower acting on mech. lifters. Carb.: float feed, aux air control; mfg by Cad under C.F. Johnson patents.

CHASSIS: [Type 53] W.B.: 122 in. Frt/Rear Tread: 56 in. (61 opt). Tires: 36 x 4-1/2. [Special Chassis] W.B.: 145 in. 132 in.

199

TECHNICAL: Selective sliding gear transmission. Case in unit with engine. 3F/1R. Left drive, center control (rhd opt). Multiple disc, dry plate clutch, 15 discs. Shaft drive. Spiral bevel, full floating rear axle. Overall ratio: 4.44:1. Mech. brakes on two wheels, one external, one internal. Wood artillery wheels, demountable rims (R-W wire wheels opt). Wheel size: 27 in. Optional Drive ratio: 3.94:1, 5.07:1.

OPTIONS: Seat covers (35.00-65.00).

HISTORICAL: Introduced July, 1915. Model year sales: 18004. Model year production: 18004. The president & general manager was Henry Leland. In May, 1916, Erwin G. "Cannonball" Baker and Wm. F. Sturm drove a V-8 Cadillac Roadster from Los Angeles to New York City in 7 days, 11 hours, 52 minutes. They bettered their previous time, driven in another make of car, by 3 days, 19 hours, 23 minutes.

1916
Model 53 V-8

	FP	5	4	3	2	1
Rds	2080	3900	7800	13,000	18,200	26,000
5P Tr	2080	4050	8100	13,500	18,900	27,000
7P Tr	2080	4200	8400	14,000	19,600	28,000
3P Cpe	2400	1750	4800	8000	11,200	16,000
Sed Brgm	2950	1750	4800	8000	11,200	16,000
7P Limo	3450	2900	5850	9750	13,650	19,500
Berl Limo	3600	3150	6300	10,500	14,700	21,000

1917

1917 Cadillac, Type 55, touring, OCW

CADILLAC — TYPE 55 — EIGHT: Bodies: Similar to Type 53 except: New crown fenders and elimination of molding on hood panels and around doors give smoother appearance overall. Phaeton and Roadster have six degree slope to windshield. Salon replaced by Phaeton with bench seat in front. Club Roadster added. Convertible Touring (a four door hardtop) manufactured by Cadillac and having a Vee windshield is introduced. Coupe with cast Aluminum body is also manufactured by Cadillac. Victoria is now five window with fixed top and removable pillars. Berlin/Berline is now called Imperial (undoubtedly due to nasty connotation of "Berlin" at the time). Landaulet body style added. One listing of closed body styles by Fisher mentions "Touring Couplet", with no description. Previous round, plain door (rim) of headlights now embellished with stylized outline of shield and crown.
Chassis: Frame depth increased to eight inches, and two tubular cross members added. Wide tread no longer available.
Drive Line: Number of clutch plates increased to 17.
Engine: Lighter pistons of "belted" design with large oil return holes in the piston walls. Exhaust manifolds have shorter connector pipes. Split, tapered collars used to retain valve spring feet.

I.D. DATA: Serial numbers were not used. Engine numbers were stamped on the crankcase just back of the right hand bank of cylinders, and on a plate on the dash. Engine No.: 55-A - 1 thru 55 - A-1000; 55-B - 1 thru 55-B-1000; etc., thru 55-S-2.

Style No.	Body Type & Seating	Price	Weight	Prod. Total
NA	4-dr. Touring-7P	2240	—	—
NA	4-dr. Phaeton-4P	2240	—	—
NA	2-dr. Roadster-2/4P	2240	—	—
NA	2-dr. Club Roadster-4P	2240	—	—
NA	2-dr. Conv. Victoria-4P	2710	—	—
NA	2-dr. Coupe-4P	2960	—	—
NA	4-dr. Conv. Touring-7P	2835	—	—
2460	4-dr. Brougham-5/7P	3110	—	—
2450	4-dr. Limo.-7P	3760	—	—
2440	4-dr. Imperial-7P	3910	—	—
2620	4-dr. Landaulet-7P	3910	—	—
2470	Touring Couplet	—	—	—
NA	Ambulance	3760	—	—
NA	Police Patrol	3160	—	—
NA	Hearse	4040	—	—

Note: Prices $160 less previous to 14 December 1916.
Note: Touring Couplet may be same as Conv. Victoria.

ENGINE: Ninety degree V-8 L-head. Heads not detachable. Cast iron blocks of four on Aluminum crankcase. B & S: 3-1/8 x 5-1/8 in. Disp.: 314.5 cu. in. S.A.E./N.A.C.C. H.P.: 31.25. Main bearings: Three. Valve lifters: Rockers with roller cam follower acting on mech. lifters. Carb.: Float feed, aux air control; mfg. by Cad under C.F. Johnson patents.

CHASSIS: [Type 55] W.B.: 125 in. Frt/Rear Tread: 56 in. Tires: 36 x 4-1/2. [Type 55 Limo, Land, Imp.] W.B.: 132 in. Frt/Rear Tread: 56 in. Tires: 37 x 5. [Special Chassis] W.B.: 145 in.

TECHNICAL: Selective sliding gear transmission. Case in unit with engine. Speeds: 3F/1R. Left drive, center control (rhd opt). Multiple disc, dry plate clutch, 17 discs. Shaft drive. Spiral bevel, full floating rear axle. Overall ratio: 4.44:1. Mech. brakes on two wheels, one external, one internal. Wood artillery wheels, demountable rims (R-W or Houk wire wheels opt). Wheel size: 27 in. Optional Drive ratio 3.94:1, 5.07:1.

HISTORICAL: Introduced August, 1916. Model year sales: 18,002. Model year production: 18,002.

Note: General Motors Corp. was incorporated 13 Oct. 1916 in Delaware. General Motors Co. was taken over by General Motors Corp. 1 Aug. 1917. General Motors Corp. was then an "operating" company and Cadillac Motor Car Co. became a Division of General Motors.
   Henry Leland left Cadillac in June, 1917 and Richard H. Collins became President & General Manager.

1917
Model 55, V-8

	FP	5	4	3	2	1
Rds	2240	3750	7500	12,500	17,500	25,000
Clb Rds	2240	3900	7800	13,000	18,200	26,000
Conv	2240	3600	7200	12,000	16,800	24,000
Cpe	2240	1650	4650	7750	10,850	15,500
Vic	2710	1750	4800	8000	11,200	16,000
Brgm	3110	1650	4650	7750	10,850	15,500
Limo	3760	2800	5700	9500	13,300	19,000
Imp Limo	3910	3000	6000	10,000	14,000	20,000
7P Lan'let	3910	3150	6300	10,500	14,700	21,000

1918

1918 Cadillac, Type 57, touring, OCW

CADILLAC — TYPE 57 — EIGHT: Bodies: Similar to Type 55 except: Top line of hood and cowl now a continuous straight line to the windshield on most body styles. Headlight reflectors tilted by mechanical linkage to lever on steering post. Nine hood louvers tilted six degrees. Windshield on all open cars tilted six degrees. Club Roadster, Coupe, Convertible Touring, and Touring Couplet dropped from the line. Town Limousine and Town Landaulet added. The main compartment of these two bodies was approximately four inches narrower than on the standard Limousine. Suburban added in mid-year.
Chassis: No significant change from Type 55.
Drive Line: Transmission redesigned and is not interchangeable with Types 51, 53, 55.
Engine: Detachable cylinder heads. "Belted" pistons replaced by ultra light weight pistons.

I.D. DATA: Serial numbers were not used. Engine numbers were stamped on the crankcase just back of the right hand bank of cylinders, and on a plate on the dash. Also stamped on the fan shaft housing. Engine No.: 57-A-1 thru 57-Z-1000 with 1919.

Style No.	Body Type & Seating	Price	Weight	Prod. Total
NA	4-dr. Touring-7P	2590	4035	—
NA	4-dr. Phaeton-4P	2590	3925	—
NA	2-dr. Roadster-2/4P	2590	3865	—
2750	2-dr. Conv. Victoria-4P	3075	3970	—
2730	4-dr. Brougham-5/7P	3535	4290	—
NA	4-dr. Brougham-7P	4145		—
2740	4-dr. Limo.-7P	4085	4425	—
2820	Limo.			—
2680	4-dr. Town Limo.-6P	4100	4295	—
3110	U.S. Govt. Limo.			—
2760	4-dr. Imperial-7P	4285		—
2770	4-dr. Landaulet-7P	4235	4510	—
2840	4-dr. Twn. Land.-6P	4250	4350	—
2910	4-dr. Suburban-7P	4090	4350	—

Style No.	Body Type & Seating	Price	Weight	Prod. Total
NA	Police Patrol	3850	—	—
NA	Ambulance	4350	—	—
NA	Hearse	4685	—	—

Note: Prices increased several times during the war years, partly due to war taxes. The lowest prices for the body style are given.

ENGINE: Ninety degree V-8 L-head. Heads detachable. Cast iron blocks of four on Aluminum crankcase. B & S: 3-1/8 x 5-1/8 in. Disp.: 314.5 cu. in. S.A.E./N.A.C.C. H.P.: 31.25. Main bearings: Three. Valve lifters: Rockers with roller cam follower acting on mech. lifters. Carb.: float feed, aux air control; mfg by Cad under C.F. Johnson patents.

CHASSIS: [Type 57] W.B.: 125 in. Frt/Rear Tread: 56 in. Tires: 35 x 5. [Type 57 Roadster] W.B.: 125 in. Frt/Rear Tread: 56 in. Tires: 34 x 4-1/2. [Type 57 Limo., Imp., Land., Tn. Limo., Tn. Land.] W.B.: 132 in. Frt/Rear Tread: 56 in. Tires: 35 x 5. [Special Chassis] W.B.: 145 in.

TECHNICAL: Selective sliding gear transmission. Case in unit with engine. Speeds: 3F/1R. Left drive, center control (rhd opt). Multiple, dry plate clutch, 17 discs. Shaft drive. Spiral bevel, full floating rear axle. Overall ratio: 4.44:1. Mech. brakes on two wheels, one external, one internal. Wood artillery wheels, demountable rims (R-W wire wheels opt). Wheel size: 25 in. Optional Drive ratio: 3.94:1, 5.07:1.

HISTORICAL: Introduced August, 1917. Model year sales: 45146 with 1919. Model year production: 45146 with 1919. The President & General Manager was Richard H. Collins.

1918-19
Type 57, V-8

	FP	5	4	3	2	1
Rds	2970	3750	7500	12,500	17,500	25,000
Phae	2970	3900	7800	13,000	18,200	26,000
Tr	2970	3600	7200	12,000	16,800	24,000
Conv Vic	3365	3400	6900	11,500	16,100	23,000
Brgm	3840	1650	4650	7750	10,850	15,500
Limo	4145	1250	3900	6500	9100	13,000
Twn Limo	4160	1250	3900	6500	9100	13,000
Lan'let	4295	1400	4200	7000	9800	14,000
Twn Lan'let	4310	2300	5400	9000	12,600	18,000
Imp Limo	4345	2000	5100	8500	11,900	17,000

1919

1919 Cadillac, Type 57, touring, OCW

CADILLAC — TYPE 57 — EIGHT: Bodies: Similar to 1918 Type 57 except: Twenty five vertical hood louvers. Phaeton 1-1/2" lower. Victoria no longer "convertible" and has aluminum rather than leather roof and rear quarter. Brougham replaced by sedan with full width front seat and no emergency seats. Town Limousine renamed Town Brougham. Landaulet, Town Landaulet, and Hearse dropped. As Fisher made minor changes in details on the Victoria, Suburban, and Sedan, the bodies were identified as 57-A and 57-B. This was a body designation only, not a Type designation. There was no Type 57-B Cadillac. The 57-B bodies had a square effect at body, door and window corners; and the lower edge of the windshields followed the curve of the cowl.
Chassis: No significant change.
Drive Line: No significant changes from 1918.
Engine: No significant changes from 1918.

I.D. DATA: Serial numbers were not used. Engine numbers were stamped on the crankcase just back of the right hand bank of cylinders, and on a plate on the dash. Also stamped on the fan shaft housing. Engine No.: 57-A - 1 thru 57 - Z-1000 with 1918, and 57-AA-1 thru 57- TT-146.

Style No.	Body Type & Seating	Price	Weight	Prod. Total
NA	4-dr. Touring-7P	3220	4035	—
NA	4-dr. Phaeton-4P	3220	3925	—
NA	2-dr. Roadster-2/4P	3220	3865	—
3040	2-dr. Victoria-4P	3990	3970	—
3050	4-dr. Sedan-5P	4215	—	—
3260	Imperial Sedan	—	—	—
3210	4-dr. Limo.-7P	4520	4425	—

Style No.	Body Type & Seating	Price	Weight	Prod. Total
NA	4-dr. Imperial-7P	4620	—	—
NA	4-dr. Twn. Brougham-6P	4520	4295	—
2830	Limo.-8P			—
3140	4-dr. Suburban-7P	4465	4350	—
3140-P1200	Imp. Suburban			—
NA	Police Patrol	4050	—	—
NA	Ambulance	4550	—	—

Note: Some overlap existed on new or deleted body styles for 1918 and 1919.

ENGINE: Ninety degree V-8 L-head. Heads detachable. Cast iron blocks of four on Aluminum crankcase. B & S: 3-1/8 x 5-1/8 in. Disp.: 314.5 cu. in. S.A.E./N.A.C.C. H.P.: 31.25. Main bearings: Three. Valve lifters: Rockers with roller cam follower acting on mech. lifters. Carb.: float feed, aux air control; mfg by Cad under C.F. Johnson patents.

CHASSIS: [Type 57] W.B.: 125 in. Frt/Rear Tread: 56 in. Tires: 35 x 5. [Type 57 Roadster] W.B.: 125 in. Frt/Rear Tread: 56 in. Tires: 34 x 4-1/2. [Type 57 Limo, Suburban] W.B.: 132 in. Frt/Rear Tread: 56 in. Tires: 35 x 5. [Special Chassis] W.B.: 145 in.

TECHNICAL: Selective sliding gear transmission. Case in unit with engine. Speeds: 3F/1R. Left drive, center control (rhd opt). Multiple disc, dry plate clutch, 17 discs. Shaft drive. Spiral bevel, full floating rear axle. Overall ratio: 4.44:1. Mech. brakes on two wheels, one external, one internal. Wood artillery wheels, demountable rims (R-W wire wheels opt). Wheel size: 25 in. Optional Drive ratio 3.94:1, 5.07:1.

OPTIONS: Front bumper (12.50). Rear bumper (12.50). Cigar lighter (5.00). Seat covers (13.50-125.00). Spotlight (7.50). Set of five Rudge-Whitworth wire wheels (150.00). Tire chains (9.00). Rear view mirror (3.75).

HISTORICAL: The 1919 Type 57 was a continuation of 1918 Type 57. Model year sales: 45,146 with 1918. Model year production: 45,146 with 1918. The President & General Manager was Richard H. Collins.

1920-1921

1920 Cadillac, Type 59, town car, HAC

CADILLAC — TYPE 59 — EIGHT: Similar to Type 57, with following exceptions:
Bodies: General lines slightly straighter and fuller. Cowl lengthened on Phaeton and Roadster. Windshield on Limousine and Town Brougham tilted slightly. Lower section of windshield fixed; ventilation to lower part of front compartment provided by vent in top of cowl. Hood hinge concealed. Narrow beading added on cowl at joint with hood. Smaller sidelights, closer to windshield. Shield shaped pattern on headlight doors changed to narrow bead with curved sides; detachable emblem at top. Headlights and sidelights optionally available in full nickel. Touring on 132 in. wheelbase. Two passenger Coupe new — this and Town Brougham dropped in mid run but picked up again for Type 61.
Chassis: Front wheels changed from ten to twelve spoke. Frame stiffened by lengthening the deep section. Radiator water condenser moved to outside of frame. Extra length chassis not available.
Drive line: Speedometer drive moved from front axle to transmission.
Engine: Intake manifold heated by exhaust gasses. Timing chains adjustable, from outside crankcase. Crankshaft diameter increased to 2 in.. New-style 4-pole motor-generator used.

I.D. DATA: Serial numbers were not used. Engine numbers were stamped on the crankcase just back of the right hand bank of cylinders, and on a plate on the dash. Engine No.: 59-A-1 thru 59-Z-1000 and 59-AA-1 thru 59-BB-12.

Style No. 1st Design	Body Type & Seating	Price	Weight	Prod. Total
	4-dr. Tr.-7P	3740	—	—
	4-dr. Phae.-4P	3590	—	—
	2-dr. Rds.-2/4P	3590	—	—
4000	2-dr. Vict.-4P	4340	—	—
	2-dr. Cpe.-2P	4290	—	—
4010	4-dr. Sed.-5P	4750	—	—
4020	4-dr. Sub.-7P	4990	—	—

201

Style No.	Body Type & Seating	Price	Weight	Prod. Total
4030	4-dr. Limo.-7P	5090	—	—
4050	4-dr. Imp. Limo.-7P	5190	—	—
4040	4-dr. Twn. Brgm.-7P	5090	—	—
2nd Design				
	4-dr. Tr.-7P	3940	—	—
	4-dr. Phae.-4P	3790	—	—
	2-dr. Rds.-2/4P	3790	—	—
4130	2-dr. Vict.-4P	4540	—	—
	2-dr. Cpe.-2P	—	—	—
4140	4-dr. Sed.-5P	4950	—	—
4120	4-dr. Sub.-7P	5190	—	—
4150	4-dr. Limo.-7P	5290	—	—
4170	4-dr. Imp. Limo.-7P	5390	—	—
4160	4-dr. Twn. Brgm.-7P	5290	—	—
3rd Design				
	4-dr. Tr.-7P	3940	—	—
	4-dr. Phae.-4P	3790	—	—
	2-dr. Rds.-2/4P	3790	—	—
4290	2-dr. Vict.-4P	4540	—	—
	2-dr. Cpe.-2P	—	—	—
4270	4-dr. Sed.-5P	4950	—	—
4300	4-dr. Sub.-7P	5190	—	—
4360	4-dr. Limo.-7P	5290	—	—
4350	4-dr. Imp. Limo.-7P	5390	—	—
	4-dr. Twn. Brgm.-7P	5690	—	—

Note 1: Some Fisher references designate 1st, 2nd, 3rd designs as 59-A, 59-B, 59-C. These designs differ only in detail and are not significant styling changes. The -A, -B, -C's refer only to bodies, not "Type" — there was no Type 59-A, Type 59-B, or Type 59-C Cadillac.

Note 2: The two passenger Coupe appeared only in early Type 59 catalogs. If produced at all as a Type 59 body style, this Coupe was dropped by April, 1920 but was picked up as a Type 61 style.

Note 3: The April 1, 1920 price list advanced all prices by $200 (2p Coupe not listed). The only price change on May 1, 1920 was an advance to $5690 for the Town Brougham. This body style was not shown in the later (1921) catalogs, but was picked up as a Type 61 style.

Note 4: Job (Body) number is stamped on right front door sill.

ENGINE: Ninety degree V-8. L-Head. Cast iron blocks of four on Aluminum crankcase. B & S: 3-1/8 x 5-1/8 in. Disp.: 314.5 cu. in. S.A.E./N.A.C.C. H.P.: 31.25. Main bearings: Three. Valve lifters: Rockers with roller cam follower acting on mech. lifters. Carb.: float feed, aux air control; mfg by Cad under C.F. Johnson patents.

CHASSIS: [Type 59 Phae., Rds., Vict., Cpe., Sed.] W.B.: 125 in. Frt/Rear Tread: 56 in. Tires: 34 x 4-1/2. [Others] W.B.: 132 in. Frt/Rear Tread: 56 in. Tires: 35 x 5.

TECHNICAL: Selective sliding gear transmission. Case in unit with engine. Speeds: 3F/1R. Left drive, center control (rhd opt.). Multiple disc, dry plate clutch. Shaft drive. Spiral bevel, full floating rear axle. Overall ratio: 4.44:1, 5.07:1. Mech. brakes on two wheels, one external, one internal. Wood artillery wheels, demountable rims, 12 spoke. Wheel size: 25 in. Optional Drive ratio: 3.94:1.

OPTIONS: All nickel headlamps, sidelamps, and hubcaps. R-W wire wheels.

HISTORICAL: Introduced January, 1920. Model year sales: 24878. Model year production: 24878. The president & general manager was Richard H. Collins (H.H. Rice as of May, 1921).

Note: The general state of the post war economy, shortages of materials, railway strikes, and the completion and occupation of a new factory resulted in a production slump at Cadillac during 1920-1921. With the outstanding war record of the Type 57; with long waiting lists of eager customers; and with reconstruction pressures in the nation and in the company — Cadillac built the new Type 59 for two years without significant styling or mechanical changes.

1921 Cadillac, Type 59, limousine, JAC

202

	FP	5	4	3	2	1
Rds	3590	3600	7200	12,000	16,800	24,000
Phae	3590	3750	7500	12,500	17,500	25,000
Tr	3740	3400	6900	11,500	16,100	23,000
Vic	4340	1650	4650	7750	10,850	15,500
Sed	4750	1150	3600	6000	8400	12,000
Cpe	5090	1200	3750	6250	8750	12,500
Sub	4990	1250	3900	6500	9100	13,000
Limo	5090	1650	4650	7750	10,850	15,500
Twn Brgm	5090	2200	5250	8750	12,250	17,500
Imp Limo	5190	1800	4950	8250	11,550	16,500

NOTE: Coupe and Town Brougham dropped for 1921.

1922-1923

1922 Cadillac, Type 61, touring, HAC

CADILLAC — TYPE 61 — EIGHT: Similar to Type 59, with the following exceptions:

Bodies: Higher radiator. Shoulders of hood raised. Lower center of gravity with same ground clearance. Hood made of Aluminum. Exterior door handles on all but front doors of Limousine. Soft-type roof construction on closed cars. Leather covered, fixed visor on closed cars. Trunk rack, vertical bars on rear of body, and running board kick plates on five passenger Sedan and Phaeton. Headlights mounted by single post rather than fork. Shield shaped bead on headlight door has straight rather than curved sides. Optional nickel plated lights and radiator shell offered. Horn moved under hood. New steering wheel, without hinge. Windshield cleaner and rearview mirror standard equipment. Two passenger Coupe and Town Brougham revived. Five passenger Coupe new. Landau Sedan new for 1923. Victoria for 1923 had roomier interior and doors hinged at front.

Chassis: Smaller wheels, giving lower center of gravity. All bodies on 132 in. wheelbase. Self lubricating bushings at many points in brake and clutch linkage. New, piston-type grease cups at other lube points.

Drive Line: Rear axle housing redesigned to maintain road clearance with smaller wheels. Final drive ratios now 4.50:1, 4.91:1, and 4.15:1 (special). Transmission lock provided.

Engine: Camshaft drilled to provide internal oil passage and replace oil tube. Two-pole generator replaced four-pole.

I.D. DATA: Serial numbers were not used. Engine numbers were stamped on the crankcase just back of the right hand bank of cylinders, and on a plate on the dash. Engine No.: 61-A-1 thru 61-Z-18006.

Style No.	Body Type & Seating	Price	Weight	Prod. Total
1st Design				
	4-dr. Tr.-7P	3940	4025	—
	4-dr. Phae.-4P	3790	3955	—
	2-dr. Rds.-2/4P	3790	3920	—
4420	2-dr. Vict.-4P	4540	4115	—
4470	2-dr. Cpe.-2P	4540	3980	—
4440	2-dr. Cpe.-5P	4690	4130	—
4430	4-dr. Sed.-5P	4950	4220	—
4400	4-dr. Sub.-7P	5190	4420	—
4450	4-dr. Limo.-7P	5290	4400	—
4460	4-dr. Imp. Limo.-7P	5390	4450	—
4480	4-dr. Town Brgm.-7P	—	—	—
5160	4-dr. Land. Sed.-5P	—	—	—
2nd Design				
	4-dr. Tr.-7P	3150	4025	—
	4-dr. Phae.-4P	3150	3955	—
	2-dr. Rds.-2/4P	3100	3920	—
4430	2-dr. Vict.-4P	3875	4115	—
5080	2-dr. Cpe.-2P	3875	3980	—
5050	2-dr. Cpe.-5P	3925	4130	—
5040	4-dr. Sed.-5P	4100	4220	—
4410	4-dr. Sub.-7P	4250	4420	—
5060	4-dr. Limo.-7P	4550	4400	—
5070	4-dr. Imp. Limo.-7P	4600	4450	—
	4-dr. Town Brgm.-7P	—	—	—
	4-dr. Land. Sed.-5P	—	—	—
3rd Design				
	4-dr. Tr.-7P	2885	4025	—
	4-dr. Phae.-4P	2885	3955	—
	2-dr. Rds.-2/4P	2885	3920	—
5090	2-dr. Vict.-4P	3675	4115	—
	2-dr. Cpe.-2P	—	3980	—
	2-dr. Cpe.-5P	3750	4130	—

Style No.	Body Type & Seating	Price	Weight	Prod. Total
	4-dr. Sed.-5P	3950	4220	—
5030	4-dr. Sub.-7P	3990	4420	—
	4-dr. Limo.-7P	4300	4400	—
	4-dr. Imp. Limo.-7P	4400	4450	—
	4-dr. Town Brgm.-7P	—	—	—
	4-dr. Land. Sed.-5P	3950	—	—

Note: Introductory prices were much the same as for Type 59. In January, 1922 came a drastic price reduction, followed by a smaller reduction in December, 1922. These were the first price reductions for Cadillac and followed an industry trend. Increased production schedules, higher efficiency in the new manufacturing facilities, and economic pressures combined to make the reductions possible as well as necessary.

1923 Cadillac, Type 61, touring, OCW

ENGINE: Ninety degree V-8. L-head. Cast iron blocks of four on Aluminum crankcase. B & S: 3-1/8 x 5-1/8 in. Disp.: 314.5 cu. in. Brake H.P.: 60 plus advertised. S.A.E./N.A.C.C. H.P.: 31.25. Valve lifters: Rockers with roller cam follower acting on mech. lifters. Carb.: float feed, aux air control; mfg by Cad under C.F. Johnson patents.

CHASSIS: [Type 61] W.B.: 132 in. Frt/Rear Tread: 56 in. Tires: 33 x 5.

TECHNICAL: Selective sliding gear transmission. Case in unit with engine. Speeds: 3F/1R. Left drive, center control (rhd opt.). Multiple disc, dry plate clutch. Shaft drive. Spiral bevel, full floating rear axle. Overall ratio: 4.50:1, 4.91:1. Mech. brakes on two wheels, one external, one internal. Wood artillery wheels, demountable rims, 12 spoke. Wheel size: 23 in. Optional Drive ratio: 4.15:1.

OPTIONS: All nickel headlamps, sidelamps, hubcaps, and radiator shell. R-W wire wheels.

HISTORICAL: Introduced September, 1921. Model two year sales: 41001. Model two year production: 41001. The President & General Manager was Herbert H. Rice.

1922-1923
Type 61, V-8

	FP	5	4	3	2	1
Rds	3790	3400	6900	11,500	16,100	23,000
Phae	3790	3600	7200	12,000	16,800	24,000
Tr	3940	3400	6900	11,500	16,100	23,000
Cpe	3975	1750	4800	8000	11,200	16,000
Vic	3875	1800	4950	8250	11,550	16,500
5P Cpe	4350	1400	4200	7000	9800	14,000
Sed	4550	1300	4050	6750	9450	13,500
Sub	4650	2300	5400	9000	12,600	18,000
7P Limo	4550	2600	5500	9250	12,950	18,500
Imp Limo	4950	2800	5700	9500	13,300	19,000
Lan'let Sed	5290	2900	5850	9750	13,650	19,500

1924

CADILLAC — V-63 — EIGHT: Similar to Type 61, with the following exceptions:
Bodies: Longer hood. One inch higher radiator. Roof and rear quarter lines of closed cars softened. Liberal use of non-functional landau bars (buggy bows). Two passenger Coupe has blind quarters. More interior room. Lower seating position in closed cars. Ventilator door set flush in cowl. 1-1/2 in. narrower windshield posts. Full width, curved division windows. Automatic, vacuum operated windshield cleaner. Bowl shape replaced bell shape of headlight bodies. Five passenger Sedan with Imperial division offered. New seven passenger Sedan offered mid-year.
Chassis: Front wheel brakes added. Service brake pedal acts on rear external and front internal bands. Emergency brake lever acts on rear internal bands. Front axle/steering knuckle design changed to reversed Elliott type. New tie rod with adjustable ball and socket ends moved from front to rear of axle. Two cross members added to frame. 145 in. wheelbase special chassis once more made available.
Drive line: No significant changes.
Engine: The engine is much the same as in the Type 61 cars except for the

1924 Cadillac, V-63, Suburban, HAC

new harmonized and inherently balanced two-plane crankshaft and the revisions dictated by this system. Firing order changed to: 1L-4R-4L-2L-3R-3L-2R-1R. Flywheel weight reduced as a result of increased flywheel effect of compensators and larger (2-3/8 in. dia.) crankshaft. Sixteen cams on camshaft. Rocker arms and plate redesigned. Chain adjustment no longer needed — a result of 1/4 in. wider chains and greater smoothness of engine.

I.D. DATA: There were no serial numbers used on the Cadillac V-63. Engine numbers were stamped on the crankcase just back of the right hand bank of cylinders, and on a plate on the dash. Starting: 63-A-1. Ending: 63-H-1550.

Style No.	Body Type & Seating	Price	Weight	Prod. Total
NA	4-dr. Touring-7P	3085	4280	—
NA	4-dr. Phaeton-4P	3085	4200	—
NA	2-dr. Roadster-2/4P	3085	4190	—
5490	2-dr. Victoria-4P	3275	4380	—
5380	2-dr. Coupe-2P	3875	4270	—
5280	2-dr. Coupe-5P	3950	4370	—
5270	4-dr. Sedan-5P	4150	4480	—
5290	4-dr. Landau Sedan-5P	4150	4480	—
5460	4-dr. Imperial Sedan-5P	4400	4600	—
5260	4-dr. Suburban-7P	4250	4560	—
5310	4-dr. Imp. Suburban-7P	4500	4640	—
5470	4-dr. Sedan-7P	3585	4610	—
5300	4-dr. Limousine-7P	4600	4640	—
5370	4-dr. Twn. Brougham-7P	4600	4530	—

Note: All Cadillac V-8's up to this time had been designated Type 51, Type 53, etc., thru Type 61; with no -A, -B, etc. to designate the first or second year of a two year production run (57, 59, 61). For 1924-1925, the designation became V-63; not Type V-63, not Series V-63, just V-63. However, some Cadillac master parts books covering V-63 plus Type 59 and Type 61 do refer to Type 63. Further, these parts books refer to 63-A and 63-B in reference to early **vs** late or 1924 **vs** 1925 V-63 chassis as well as body differences.

ENGINE: Ninety degree V-8. L-head. Cast iron blocks of four on Aluminum crankcase. B & S: 3-1/8 x 5-1/8 in. Disp.: 314.5 cu. in. Brake H.P.: 80 plus advertised. S.A.E./N.A.C.C. H.P.: 31.25. Main bearings: Three. Valve lifters: Rockers with roller cam follower acting on mech. lifters. Carb.: float feed, aux air control; mfg by Cad under C.F. Johnson patents.

CHASSIS: [V-63] W.B.: 132 in. Frt/Rear Tread: 56 in. Tires: 33 x 5. [Special Chassis] W.B.: 145 in. Frt/Rear Tread: 56 in. Tires: 33 x 5.

TECHNICAL: Selective sliding gear transmission. Case in unit with engine. Speeds: 3F/1R. Left drive, center control (rhd. opt.). Multiple disc, dry plate clutch. Shaft drive. Spiral bevel, full floating rear axle. Overall ratio: 4.50:1, 4.91:1. Mechanical brakes on four wheels. Wood artillery wheels, demountable rims, 12 spoke. Wheel size: 23 in. Optional Drive ratio 4.15:1.

OPTIONS: All nickel headlamps, radiator shell, and hubcaps. Wire wheels. Disc wheels. Five balloon tires on disc wheels (140.00). Six balloon tires on disc wheels, plus double carrier for spares (215.00). Five balloon tires on wire wheels (225.00). Six balloon tires on wire wheels, plus double carrier for spares (315.00).

HISTORICAL: Introduced September, 1923. Innovations: Compensated, inherently balanced, two-plane crankshaft. Four wheel brakes. Model year sales: 35,500 with 1925 Model V-63. Model year production 35,500 with 1925 Model V-63. The President & General Manager was Herbert H. Rice.

1925

1925 Cadillac, V-63, 2-dr. coach, OCW

CADILLAC — V-63 — EIGHT: A continuation of the 1924 line, expanded to include the "Custom" line introduced in October, 1924. Five "Custom" bodies were shown in the catalog, but a total of eight were listed by job number. The new line was custom to the extent that the customer could choose from 24 color harmonies and 10 upholstery patterns. The introduction of Duco finishes signaled this start to a color explosion which hit Cadillac in the next few years. Nickel plated radiator shell and lights became standard. The scrolled radiator shell, first exclusive to the "Custom" line, was adapted to the standard line. The "Custom" line was distinguished by sloping windshields and double belt molding. A two door, five passenger Coach body was added to the Standard line.

I.D. DATA: Serial numbers were not used. Engine numbers were stamped on the crankcase just back of the right hand bank of cylinders, and on a plate on the dash. Starting: 63-H-1551. Ending: 63-M-2572.

Style No.	Body Type & Seating	Price	Weight	Prod. Total
	Standard Body Styles			
1149	4-dr. Touring-7P	3185	—	—
1150	4-dr. Phaeton-4P	3185	—	—
1151	2-dr. Roadster-2/4P	3185	—	—
5690	2-dr. Victoria-4P	3485	—	—
6150	4-dr. Sedan-5P	3835	—	—
5700	4-dr. Landau Sedan-5P	3835	—	—
5680	4-dr. Sedan-7P	3885	—	—
6030	4-dr. Imp. Sedan-7P	4010	—	—
6010	2-dr. Coach-5P	3185	—	—
	"Custom" Body Styles			
5750	4-dr. Sedan-5P	4550	—	—
5720	4-dr. Suburban-5P	4650	—	—
NA	4-dr. Imp. Sedan-5P		—	—
5760	4-dr. Limousine-7P		—	—
5730	4-dr. Imp. Suburban-7P	4950	—	—
5770	4-dr. Twn. Brougham-7P		—	—
5740	2-dr. Coupe-5P	4350	—	—
5710	2-dr. Coupe-2P	3975	—	—

ENGINE: Ninety degree V-8. L-head. Cast iron blocks of four on Aluminum crankcase. B & S: 3-1/8 x 5-1/8 in. Disp.: 314.5 cu. in. Brake H.P.: 80 plus advertised. S.A.E./N.A.C.C. H.P.: 31.25. Main bearings: Three. Valve lifters: Rockers with roller cam follower acting on mech. lifters. Carb.: float feed, aux air control; mfg by Cad under C.F. Johnson patents.

CHASSIS: [All Standard body styles & Custom 2-P Coupe] W.B.: 132 in. Frt/Rear Tread: 56 in. Tires: 33 x 5. Special Chassis. W.B.: 145 in. Frt/Rear Tread: 56 in. Tires: 33 x 5. [All Custom body styles except 2-P Coupe] W.B.: 138 in. Frt/Rear Tread: 56 in. Tires: 33 x 5.

1925 Cadillac, V-63, Imperial sedan, JAC

TECHNICAL: Selective sliding gear transmission. Case in unit with engine. Speeds: 3F/1R. Left drive, center control (rhd. opt). Multiple disc, dry plate clutch. Shaft drive. Spiral bevel, full floating rear axle. Overall ratio: 4.50:1, 4.91:1. Mechanical brakes on four wheels. Wood artillery wheels, demountable rims, 12 spoke. Wheel size: 23 in. Optional Drive ratio 4.15:1, 5.55:1.

OPTIONS: Black radiator shell. Wire wheels. Disc wheels. Five balloon tires on disc wheels (140.00). Six balloon tires on disc wheels, plus double carrier for spares (215.00). Five balloon tires on wire wheels (225.00). Six balloon tires on wire wheels, plus double carrier for spares (315.00).

HISTORICAL: The 1925 Cadillac V-63 was a continuation of 1924 ("Custom" line introduced Oct., 1924). Innovations: Duco finish. Model year sales: 35,500 with 1924 model V-63. Model year production: 35,500 with 1924 model V-63. The president & general manager was Herbert H. Rice (L.P. Fisher as of May, 1925).

1924-1925
V-63, V-8

	FP	5	4	3	2	1
Rds	3085	4800	9600	16,000	22,400	32,000
Phae	3085	5250	10,500	17,500	24,500	35,000
Tr	3085	4650	9300	15,500	21,700	31,000
Vic	3275	3150	6300	10,500	14,700	21,000
Cpe	3950	3000	6000	10,000	14,000	20,000
Limo	4600	2600	5500	9250	12,950	18,500
Twn Brgm	4600	2800	5700	9500	13,300	19,000
Imp Sed	4400	2300	5400	9000	12,600	18,000
Custom models, (V-8 introduced Oct., 1924)						
Cpe	3875	2800	5700	9500	13,300	19,000
5P Cpe	3950	3000	6000	10,000	14,000	20,000
5P Sed	4150	2900	5850	9750	13,650	19,500
Sub	4250	2800	5700	9500	13,300	19,000
Imp Sub	4500	2900	5850	9750	13,650	19,500
Other models, V-8						
7P Sed	3585	2800	5700	9500	13,300	19,000
Vic	3275	2900	5850	9750	13,650	19,500
Lan Sed	4100	2950	5950	9900	13,800	19,800
2 dr Sed	4150	1750	4800	8000	11,200	16,000
8P Imp Sed	4400	2000	5100	8500	11,900	17,000

(All Custom and post-Dec. 1924 models have scrolled radiators).

1926

1926 Cadillac, Series 314, touring, OCW

"THE NEW NINETY DEGREE CADILLAC" — SERIES 314 — EIGHT:
Bodies: Open cars transferred to "Custom" line with 138 in. w.b., except Roadster, which retained 132 in. w.b. Two passenger "Custom" Coupe transferred to Standard line, keeping 132 in. w.b. Window added in rear quarter. Coach renamed Brougham. Landau Sedan, Limousine, and Town Brougham dropped. Semi-commercial chassis now 150 in. w.b. Cadillac offered funeral coaches and ambulance (bodies by Superior) plus armored car.

Narrower, higher radiator with thermostatically controlled shutters. Moto-meter on "Custom" cars. Greater distance radiator to windshield. Long sweeping front fenders containing battery and tool boxes. One piece windshield on all cars. Windshield swinging from pivot at top on open cars. Vertical "V-V" windshield on closed cars. Fourteen louvers to rear of hood. New nickel plated radiator shell with emblem set on badge shaped background. All front doors now hinged at windshield post. No side lights. New drum shaped headlights contain parking bulb plus double filament bulb for tilting beam. Small (9 in.) drum on Standard line, large (10 in.) drum on "Custom" line. Rear lamp on left fender instead of on tire carrier. Bumpers on "Custom" line. Motor driven horn attached to left hand headlight bracket instead of on intake manifold.

As of end of 1925: "Custom" closed bodies once more had sloping (V-V) windshield (More angle than on V-63). Triangular side glasses added forward of windshield posts.

In Spring of 1926: At Chassis Unit Number 1-25000, battery and tool boxes moved from front fenders back to location behind running board dust shields.

Mid-year 1926: Cabriolet (leather backed) version of "Custom" closed cars added to line.

By June, 1926: "Custom" Touring available on order with fender wells, six wire wheels and trunk rack at $360 extra.

Chassis: Rear springs now semi-elliptic with ball and socket rear shackles. Spring seats no longer oscillate on rear axle housing. Spring covers on "Custom" line. Torque arm relocated from right to left side and connected to frame thru fabric hanger. Radiator now cellular instead of tube and plate, and second radiator to cowl brace added. Balloon tires on split

rims with no side rings. Brake drums bell shaped to give clearance for balloon tires. Watson stabilators replace Gabriel snubbers. "American" ("National") threads replace special (Cadillac) threads. Chassis weight reduced by 263 lb. (130 lb. of this in engine weight reduction). In Spring of 1926, at Steering Gear Unit Number 1-23500, steering changed from worm and sector type to split nut type.
Drive Line: Axle shafts have 14 drive teeth instead of 6 lugs.
Engine: Crankcase ventilation system to eliminate dilution and condensation (this feature was used on the last 2000 V-63's). Oil filter added. Oil level indicator on right side of crankcase instead of inside Vee. Oil filler cap screw type instead of hinged. Camshaft bearings fed full oil pressure, not overflow from regulator. Rocker arms eliminated. Valves and tappets placed at an angle to the cylinder bores to line up directly with cams. One water pump, at left. Detachable water elbow on cylinder heads. Oil pump at right front corner of crankcase, in place of second water pump. Oil and water pumps driven directly from crossshaft. Starter and generator separate units for first time on Cadillacs. Starter vertical at top of flywheel housing, driving thru teeth on rear face of flywheel. Generator at front, in Vee. Generator/fan driven by belt, eliminating one chain. Tension on single chain maintained by idler sprocket. Front cover of engine made of steel instead of Aluminum. Intake manifold now a separate piece.

I.D. DATA: Serial numbers were not used. Engine numbers were stamped on crankcase immediately above the base of the oil filler spout and on plate on dash. Starting: (1925) 100001. (1926) 114250. Ending: (1925) 114249. (1926) 142020.

Up to the Series 314, Cadillac had used the engine number as the key identifying number for the vehicle, and all changes made during a model production run were recorded by engine number. Parts orders listing the part and the engine number insured receipt of the correct version of the part, including correct paint color, if applicable.

Starting with the Series 314, a "Unit and Car Number" scheme was put into effect. Each car was assigned an engine number, which was stamped on the engine and on a plate on the firewall just before the car was shipped. This engine number, as before, was the identifying number of the vehicle — to be used for registration, etc..

However, changes were recorded, for the most part, by Unit Number, which was the number stamped on each main assembly of the vehicle as that assembly was completed. Engine number and engine unit number bore no relation to each other. A change made at engine unit number 1-38009 might or might not have been included on the car carrying engine number 138009.

Various Cadillac manuals and parts books detail the various changes by unit number or, in rare cases, by engine/car number; but no cross reference exists. If the factory kept any cross reference of unit numbers against engine/car numbers, they did not pass it along with the car. Dealers were urged to make a unit number record for each of their customer's cars, so as to be able to service and supply parts for the car according to the exact requirements of the particular configuration of that vehicle.

Engine numbers for Series 314 cars consist of six digits, starting with the figure 1. Unit numbers for Series 314 cars consist of the figure 1, followed by a dash, followed by one to five digits. The generator and starter carried Delco serial numbers.

The various numbers are located as follows:
Engine/car Number — On the crankcase at the base of the oil filler and on the patent plate on the front face of the dash.
Engine Unit Number — On top of left hand crankcase support arm (rear).
Chassis/frame Unit Number — On the upper surface of the left hand side bar, opposite the steering gear.
Body Unit Number and Job/Style Number — On right front sill or on metal plate on the front face of the dash.
Steering Gear Unit Number — On housing, near lubrication fitting.
Transmission Unit Number — On top of flange holding brake and clutch pedal bracket.
Clutch Unit Number — On front and rear retaining plates.
Front Axle Unit Number — On upper surface of axle I-beam.
Rear Axle Unit Number — On rear surface of the housing, just to right of cover plate.
Carburetor Unit Number — On left hand rear face of flange by which carburetor is attached to intake header.
Generator Unit Number — On side of generator.
Starter Unit Number — On side of starter.

1926 Cadillac, Series 314, 4-dr. sedan, AA

Style No.	Body Type & Seating	Price	Weight	Prod. Total
	Standard Body Styles			
6400	2-dr. Brougham-5P	2995	4075	—
6430	2-dr. Coupe-2P	3045	4040	—
6490	2-dr. Victoria-4P	3095	4115	—
6420	4-dr. Sedan-5P	3195	4155	—
6410	4-dr. Sedan-7P	3295	4240	—
6440	4-dr. Imperial-7P	3435	4360	—
	"Custom" Body Styles (August, 1925)			
1154	4-dr. Touring-7P	3250	4300	—
1155	4-dr. Phaeton-4P	3250	3960	—
1156	2-dr. Roadster-2/4P	3250	3920	—
6460	2-dr. Coupe-5P	4000	4190	—
6470	4-dr. Sedan-5P	4150	4190	—
6450	4-dr. Suburban-7P	4285	4250	—
6480	4-dr. Imp. Suburban-7P	4485	4355	—
	"Custom" closed body styles (Jan '26), replacing closed bodies of Aug '25. (sloping windshield).			
6680	2-dr. Coupe-5P	4000	4465	—
6690	4-dr. Sedan-5P	4150	4465	—
6670	4-dr. Suburban-7P	4285	4580	—
6700	4-dr. Imp. Suburban-7P	4485	4615	—
	Mid-year additions to "Custom"			
6680-L	2-dr. Cab. Coupe-5P	—	—	—
6690-L	4-dr. Cab. Sedan-5P	—	—	—
6670-L	4-dr. Cab. Sub.-7P	—	—	—
6700-L	4-dr. Imp. Cab. Sub.-7P	—	—	—
	Semi-commercial line			
NA	5-dr Cus. Limo. Funeral Coach	—	—	—
NA	5-dr Imp. Limo. Ambulance	—	—	—
NA	5-dr Imp. Limo. Funeral Coach	—	—	—
NA	3-dr Armored Car	—	6500	—

Note: The weight of the 3-dr. Armored car is approximate.

ENGINE: Ninety degree V-8. L-head. Cast iron blocks of four on Aluminum crankcase. B & S: 3-1/8 x 5-1/8 in. Disp.: 314.5 cu. in. Brake H.P.: 80 plus advertised. S.A.E./Taxable/N.A.C.C. H.P.: 31.25. Main bearings: Three. Valve lifters: Mechanical lifters with roller acting directly on cams. Carb.: float feed, aux air control; mfd by Cad under C.F. Johnson patents.

CHASSIS: [All Standard Cars plus Custom Roadster] W.B.: 132 in. Frt/Rear Tread: 56 in. Tires: 33 x 6.75 low pressure. [All Custom Cars except Roadster] W.B.: 138 in. Frt/Rear Tread: 56 in. Tires: 33 x 6.75 low pressure. [Semi-commercial] W.B.: 150 in. Frt/Rear Tread: 56 in. Tires: 33 x 6.75 low pressure.

TECHNICAL: Selective sliding gear transmission. Case in unit with engine. Speeds: 3F/1R. Left drive, center control (rhd opt). Multiple disc clutch. Shaft drive. Spiral bevel, full floating rear axle. Overall ratio: 4.91:1, 4.5:1, 4.15:1. Mechanical brakes on four wheels. Wood artillery wheels, split rim, 12 spoke (Wire and Disc opt.). Wheel size: 21 in. Optional Drive ratio: 5.33:1 (Standard on armored car).

OPTIONS: Front bumper for Standard Cars (24.00). Rear bumper for Standard Cars (24.00). Heater (32.00). Spring covers for Standard Cars (20.00). 33 x 5 Tires on wooden wheels (NC) Tonneau windshields (90.00-120.00). Trunks (56.00-72.50).

Note: Cadillac still took the stand that their cars were complete and ready for entirely acceptable service as-built. However, accessories were recognized and dealers were encouraged to handle this business. Accessory catalogs were published by factory branches and the factory put out bulletins to dealers. It would be a few more years before the factory put out an accessory catalog directly to the public.

HISTORICAL: Introduced August, 1925. Innovations: Crankcase ventilation. Calendar year sales: (1925) 14249, (1926) 27771. Calendar year production: (1925) 14249, (1926) 27771. Model two year sales: 50619 (Aug. '25 thru Sep. '27). Model two year production: 50619 (Aug. '25 thru Sep. '27). The President & General Manager was Lawrence P. Fisher.
Other notes: With increasing consistency, Cadillac promotional material had mentioned the model designation alongside the name "Cadillac". For 1924/1925, practically every ad, catalog, manual, etc., carried the designation "V-63". Suddenly, in August, 1925, all mention of a model designation was withheld from promotional material. The public would learn to think "Cadillac", not "Model", and would be presented "The New Cadillac" periodically for many years to come. However, for practical considerations in the area of Parts and Service, a system of model designation was still required. The "New Cadillac" for 1926/1927 was known to insiders as Series 314, based on engine displacement.

1926-1927
Series 314, V-8

	FP	5	4	3	2	1
Cpe	3045	4350	8700	14,500	20,300	29,000
Vic	3095	4500	9000	15,000	21,000	30,000
5P Brgm	—	4350	8700	14,500	20,300	29,000
5P Sed	—	3150	6300	10,500	14,700	21,000
7P Sed	3295	3300	6600	11,000	15,400	22,000
Imp Sed	3435	3150	6300	10,500	14,700	21,000
Custom Line, V-8						
Rds	3295	12,000	24,000	40,000	60,000	80,000
Tr	3250	12,000	24,000	40,000	60,000	80,000
Phae	3250	12,300	24,600	41,000	62,000	82,000
Cpe	4000	6150	12,300	20,500	28,700	41,000
Sed	4150	4800	9600	16,000	22,400	32,000
Sub	4285	4950	9900	16,500	23,100	33,000
Imp Sed	4485	5850	11,700	19,500	27,300	39,000

205

1927

1927 Cadillac, Series 314, Fleetwood Imperial 7-pass. sedan, OCW

"THE NEW NINETY DEGREE CADILLAC" — SERIES 314 — EIGHT:
August, 1926 (Chassis Unit Number 1-29675. Steering Unit Number 1-30501):
Body: Sport Coupe and Sport Sedan added to Standard line. Convertible Coupe and Double Cowl (Sport) Phaeton added to "Custom" line. Custom bodies by Fleetwood, Brunn, Willoughby, and others available. Wheelbase on Standard seven passenger Sedan and Imperial now 138 in. Standard Victoria made five passenger by removing parcel compartment. New radiator shell with sharp corner between top and front surfaces and with round emblem on black background. Roadster and Phaetons have forward folding windshields. Monogram panel on Touring and Phaetons extended to cowl, and vertical molding in front of rear door moved back of door. Light controls moved from instrument panel to steering wheel. New instrument panel of walnut with silver inlay effect. "Custom" cars and Standard Sport models have Nickel cowl band and side lights. All cars have large (10 in.) headlights; black body on Standard, all Nickel on "Custom". Horn of vibrator type, with bent trumpet. Fender wells standard on Sport Coupe and Sedan, and on Sport Phaeton. Bumpers and motometer standard on "Custom" line and Standard Sport Models.
Chassis: At Steering Gear Unit Number 1-44906, steering gear was changed back to worm and sector type.
Drive Line: 4.9:1 is only final drive ratio offered.
Engine: Early 1927, at Engine Unit Number 1-41001 (Chassis Unit Number 1-40994): Practically everything on the outside of the engine, except the carburetor, was relocated. The overall appearance, except for the location of the starter, now resembled the soon to be introduced 303 LaSalle engine. Generator and water pump were moved to lower right front corner of engine and were driven by a common chain. The fan was once more on a separate bracket, still belt driven. The distributor went from the rear to the front of the engine and onto a common shaft with the oil pump, now inside the engine. The fuel pressure pump was now at the rear of the engine, driven by a connecting rod. The starter was moved forward and now drives thru gear teeth cut on the front face of the flywheel.

1927 Cadillac, Series 314, sport sedan, JAC

I.D. DATA: Serial numbers were not used on the 1927 Cadillac. Engine numbers stamped on crankcase immediately above the base of the oil filler spout and on plate on dash. Starting: 142021. Ending: 150619.

Style No.	Body Type & Seating	Price	Weight	Prod. Total
	Standard Body Styles			
6970	2-dr. Brgm.-5P	2995	4170	—
6980	2-dr. Cpe.-2P	3100	4105	—
7000	2-dr. Sport Cpe.-2P	3500	4460	—
7030	2-dr. Vic.-5P	3195	4190	—
6990	4-dr. Sed.-5P	3250	4270	—
7040	4-dr. Spt. Sed.-5P	3650	4590	—
7050	4-dr. Sed.-7P	3400	4370	—
7010	4-dr. Imp.-7P	3535	4480	—
	"Custom" Body Styles			
7020	2-dr. Conv. Cpe.-2/4P	3450	4300	—
6680	2-dr. Cpe.-5P	3855	4465	—

Style No.	Body Type & Seating	Price	Weight	Prod. Total
	"Custom" Body Styles			
6690	4-dr. Sed.-5P	3995	4465	—
6670	4-dr. Sub.-7P	4125	4580	—
6700	4-dr. Imp.-7P	4350	4615	—
6680-L	2-dr. Cab. Cpe.-5P	3955	—	—
6690-L	4-dr. Cab. Sed.-5P	4095	—	—
6670-L	4-dr. Cab. Suburban-7P	4225	—	—
6700-L	4-dr. Cab. Imp.-7P	4450	—	—
1165	2-dr. Rds.-2/4P	3350	4220	—
1164	4-dr. Phae.-4P	3450	4275	—
1164-B	4-dr. D.C. Phae.-4P	3975	4465	—
1163	4-dr. Tr.-7P	3450	4285	—
	Fleetwood Body Styles			
2891	Limo. Brgm.	5525	—	—
2925	Twn. Cab. (seats forward)-7P	5750	—	—
3200	Twn. Cab. (opera seats)-7P	5500	—	—
3202	Coupe with rumble-2P	4775	—	—
3260	Imp.-5P	4975	—	—
3260-S	Sed.-5P	4875	—	—
3261	Imp. Cab.-5	5125	—	—
3261-S	Sed. Cab.-5P	4975	—	—
3275	Imp.-7P	5150	—	—
3275-S	Sed.-7P	4975	—	—
3276	Imp. Cab.-7P	5375	—	—
3291	Limo. Brgm.	5525	—	—
3078	Cabr.-7P	—	—	—
3012	Trans. Cab.-7P	—	—	—
2950	Conv. Cab.-7P	—	—	—
	Brunn Body Styles			
1810	Collapsible Cab.-4P	—	—	—
1836	Sed.-4P	—	—	—
1915	Sed. Lan.-6P	—	—	—
NA	Twn. Cabr.	4800	—	—
	Willoughby Body Styles			
NA	Twn. Cabr.	4800	—	—

Semi-commercial line: Continuation of 1926.

1927 Cadillac, Series 314, 4-dr. phaeton, JAC

ENGINE: Ninety degree V-8. L-head. Cast iron blocks of four on Aluminum crankcase. B & S: 3-1/8 x 5-1/8 in. Disp.: 314.5 cu. in. S.A.E./Taxable/N.A.C.C. H.P.: 31.25. Main bearings: Three. Valve lifters: Mechanical lifters with roller acting directly on cams. Carb.: float feed, aux air control; mfd by Cad under C.F. Johnson patents.

CHASSIS: All Standard Cars except 7P Sedan and Imperial. Custom Roadster and Conv. Coupe. W.B.: 132 in. Frt/Rear Tread: 56 in. Tires: 33 x 6.75 low pressure. Semi-commercial. W.B.: 150 in. Frt/Rear Tread: 56 in. Tires: 33 x 6.75 low pressure. All Custom Cars except Roadster and Conv. Coupe. Standard 7P Sedan and Imperial. W.B.: 138 in. Frt/Rear Tread: 56 in. Tires: 33 x 6.75 low pressure.

TECHNICAL: Selective sliding gear transmission, case in unit with engine. Speeds: 3F/1R. Left drive, center control (rhd. opt.). Multiple dry disc clutch. Shaft drive. Spiral bevel, full floating rear axle. Overall ratio: 4.91:1. Mechanical brakes on four wheels. Wood artillery wheels, split rim, 12 spoke. (See Note). Wheel size: 21 in.

1927 Cadillac, Series 314, convertible coupe, JAC

1927 Cadillac, Series 314, Fleetwood limousine brougham, JAC

Note: Disc wheels standard on Standard Sport Coupe and Sedan. Wire wheels standard on Custom Sport Phaeton.

OPTIONS: Front bumper for Standard cars (25.00). Rear bumper for Standard cars (25.00). Tire cover(s) (6.25-17.50). Black radiator shell (NC). Heater (40.00). Trunk rack (55.00-91.00). Trunks (55.00-91.00). Arm rest on Std line (25.00). Motometer on Std line (10.00). Cowl lamps on Standard line (75.00). Nickel headlights on Standard line (10.00). 33 x 5 high pressure tires (NC). Disc wheels set of 5 (NC). Disc wheels set of 6, w/dual carrier (25.00). Wire wheels set of 5 (140.00). Wire wheels set of 6, w/dual carrier (175.00). 6 Wire wheels, fender wells (350.00). 6 Disc wheels, fender wells (240.00). 6 Wood wheels, fender wells (200.00).

HISTORICAL: The 1927 Cadillac Series 314 was a continuation of 1926 models. Some new body styles introduced August, 1926. Calendar year sales: (1927) 8599. Calendar year production: (1927) 8599. Model two year sales: 50619 (Aug. '25 thru Sep. '27). Model two year production: 50619 (Aug. '25 thru Sep. '27). The President & General Manager was Lawrence P. Fisher.
Note: "Fifty body styles and types — Five hundred color and upholstery combinations" was Cadillac's catch phrase for their new program to individualize the motor car. Change was constant; everything was tried; and pilot models were sold but not cataloged. The catalog was but a starting point — the customer could pick almost any combination of bits and pieces and have a unique motor car without the expense of a full custom. Authenticity of surviving cars may be in question because of the multitude of possible variations. In the final analysis; if it has a vertical starter motor, it's most likely a 314.

1927
Series 314 Std., V-8, 132" wb

	FP	5	4	3	2	1
Spt Cpe	3500	7200	14,400	24,000	33,600	48,000
Cpe	3100	6750	13,500	22,500	31,500	45,000
Sed	3250	5550	11,100	18,500	25,900	37,000
Spt Sed	3650	5700	11,400	19,000	26,600	38,000
Brgm	2995	5400	10,800	18,000	25,200	36,000
Imp	3535	5700	11,400	19,000	26,600	38,000
Std. Series, V-8, 132" wb						
7P Sed	3400	5400	10,800	18,000	25,200	36,000
Custom, 132" wb						
RS Rds	3350	12,900	25,800	48,200	66,000	86,000
RS Conv	3450	10,500	21,000	35,000	49,000	70,000
Phae	3450	13,800	27,600	46,000	73,500	92,000
Spt Phae	3975	14,400	28,800	48,000	76,000	96,000
Tr	3450	13,500	27,000	45,000	70,000	90,000
Conv	3450	10,200	20,400	34,000	47,600	68,000
Cpe	3855	7500	15,000	25,000	35,000	50,000
5P Sed	3995	5850	11,700	19,500	27,300	39,000
Sub	4125	6000	12,000	20,000	28,000	40,000
Imp Sed	4350	6150	12,300	20,500	28,700	41,000
Brn Twn Cabr	4450	6150	12,300	20,500	28,700	41,000
Wilby Twn Cabr	4225	6750	13,500	22,500	31,500	45,000
Fleetwood Bodies						
Limo Brgm	4875	7200	14,400	24,000	33,600	48,000
Twn Cabr	4975	7500	15,000	25,000	35,000	50,000
Trans Twn Cabr	5500	7800	15,600	26,000	36,400	52,000
Coll Twn Cabr	5750	7950	15,900	26,500	37,100	53,000
Vic	4775	6900	13,800	23,000	32,200	46,000

1928

CADILLAC — SERIES 341-A — EIGHT: General Motors now owned 100% of Fisher and had purchased Fleetwood and made it a division of Fisher. Practically all of Fleetwood's output was now on Cadillac/LaSalle chassis, and most Cadillac/LaSalle catalog or full customs were by Fleetwood. By using several variations and combinations of treatment above the belt line on a few basic body shells, Fleetwood was able to satisfy most customers' special desires and still offer short delivery (3-7 weeks). For the few who wanted something truly unique, Fleetwood produced full customs to order (4 months delivery).
The Fisher and Fisher "Custom" lines were merged. The Victoria was dropped. The two door Brougham was replaced by the four door Town Sedan. Funeral Coaches, Ambulances, and a combination of the two were offered on the new 152 in. wheelbase chassis; bodies by Superior. All passenger car bodies were on a 140 in. chassis.

1928 Cadillac, Series 341-A, Imperial Cabriolet

The longer wheelbase and underslung rear springs allowed for long, low-slung body lines. The deep, narrow, cellular radiator slung low in the frame and the slatted metal cover sweeping down over the fuel tank contributed to this effect, but the kick panels under the doors detracted somewhat.
Massive 12 in. bullet type headlights were mounted on a crossbar between the fenders. A monogram rod was attached between the headlights and nickeled wire-conduit stanchions were placed between headlights and frame. Matching sidelights were mounted on the cowl. Dual ball-shaped rear lights were fender mounted. The top of the hood and radiator shell were flattened and thirty narrow louvers were set toward the rear of the side panels. Dual ventilator doors were in the top of the cowl on open cars and in the sides on closed cars.
The wind split on the lights was also featured in panels and moldings on the hood and cowl. An extra wide single belt molding blended into the cowl and hood, as well as the pillars. The monogram panel on four door open bodies was back to rear-doors-only. Fleetwood bodies featured a molding sweeping down and forward on the sides of the cowl, except on the transformables, which had a bold molding sweeping up the cowl and forward across the top of the hood.
Other body details included 3½ inch wider rear compartment (rear tread had been increased by 2 inches), adjustable front seats on all but Imperials, and bumpers as standard equipment on all cars.
Chassis: Front brake drums increased from 16 to 17 in. in midyear. Rear springs under-slung. Fuel tank filler neck extended outside frame side rail. Hydraulic shock absorbers. Rear tread only increased to 58 in..
Drive line: New twin disc clutch, cast iron transmission housing, torque tube drive.
Engine: New dimensions of 3-5/16 x 4-15/16 were the first change for the Cadillac V-8 since the Type 51. The transition which had started with the final version of the Series 314 engine was now complete; the 341 Cadillac engine and the 303 LaSalle engine were practically identical in configuration. The 341 now had offset blocks, side by side connecting rods, single exhaust system, horizontal starter along right side of transmission, oil filter mounted on engine, oil level indicator behind right hand block, manifold vacuum plus vacuum pump operating fuel feed system and windshield wipers. Aside from differences due to displacement and power, the only noticeable difference was the enameled heat deflector over the Cadillac carburetor.

I.D. DATA: There were no serial numbers used. Engine numbers were stamped on plate on front of dash and on crankcase just below the water inlet on the right side. Starting: 300001. Ending: 320001.

1928 Cadillac, Series 341-A, 4-dr. sedan, JAC

Style No.	Body Type & Seating	Price	Weight	Prod. Total
Fisher — 140 in. wheelbase.				
1173	2-dr. Roadster-2/4P	3350	4590	—
1171	4-dr. Touring-7P	3450	4630	—
1172	4-dr. Phaeton-4P	3450	4640	—
1172-B	4-dr. Sport Phaeton-4P	3950	5145	—
7920	2-dr. Coupe-2/4P	3295	4820	—
7980	2-dr. Conv. Coupe-2/4P	3495	4665	—
7970	2-dr. Coupe-5P	3495	4760	—
7950	4-dr. Sedan-5P	3595	4880	—
7960	4-dr. Town Sedan-5P	3395	4875	—

Style No.	Body Type & Seating	Price	Weight	Prod. Total
7960-L	4-dr. Town Sedan-5P	3395	4875	—
7930	4-dr. Sedan-7P	3695	4965	—
7990	4-dr. Imp. Sedan-5P	3745	4925	—
7990-L	4-dr. Imp. Cabriolet-5P	3745	4925	—
7940	4-dr. Imp. Sedan-7P	3895	5025	—
7940-L	4-dr. Imp. Cabriolet-7P	3895	5025	—

Semi Commercial — 152 in. wheelbase:

Style No.	Body Type & Seating	Price	Weight	Prod. Total
NA	Limo. Funrl. Coach	—	—	—
NA	Limo. Amb.	—	—	—

Fleetwood — 140 in. wheelbase

Style No.	Body Type & Seating	Price	Weight	Prod. Total
8020	4-dr. Sedan-5P	4095	5120	—
8020-L	4-dr. Sed. (lea back)-5P	—	—	—
8030	4-dr. Imp. Sedan-5/7P	4245	5085	—
8030-L	4-dr. Imp. Seda. (l.b.)-5/7P	—	—	—
8025	4-dr. Sedan Cabriolet-5P	4095	5120	—
8035	4-dr. Imp. Sed. Cab.-5/7P	4245	5085	—
8045	4-dr. Sedan Cabriolet-5P	4095	5120	—
8045-C	4-dr. Coll. Landau-5P	4795	—	—
8055	4-dr. Imp. Sed. Cab.-5/7P	4245	5085	—
8055-C	4-dr. Coll. Landau-5/7P	4945	—	—
8000	4-dr. Sedan-7P	4195	5040	—
8000-L	4-dr. Sedan (l.b.)-7P	—	—	—
8010	4-dr. Imperial-7P	4445	5180	—
8010-L	4-dr. Imp. (leather back)-7P	—	—	—
8005	4-dr. Sedan Cabriolet-7P	4195	5040	—
8015	4-dr. Imp. Cab.-7P	4445	5180	—
3525	4-dr. Trans. Twn. Cab.-7P	5500	5180	—
3525-C	4-dr. Tr. Twn. Coll. Land.-7P	6200	—	—
3512	4-dr. Trans. Twn. Cab.-5/7P	5000	5180	—
3512-C	4-dr. Tr. Twn. Coll. Land.	5700	—	—
3520	4-dr. Trans. Twn. Cab.-7P	5500	5180	—
3520-C	4-dr. Tr. Twn. Coll. Cab.-7P	6200	—	—
3591	4-dr. Tr. Limo. Brougham-7P	5500	5180	—
3591-C	4-dr. Tr. Coll. Limo. Brgm.-7P	—	—	—
3550	Full Coll. Cab. (on order)	—	—	—
3550-C	(Twn. Car w/full coll top-7P)	—	—	—

Note: The following body styles are listed as Fleetwood 341, 341-A, 341-B, but are unconfirmed. All are on 140'' wheelbase except as noted. Included must be full customs and one-off variations of catalog customs.

1928/1929 CADILLAC SERIES 341-A, 341-B

Style No.	Body Type			
3015	Limo.-7P 138'' wb	—	—	—
3097	Limo.-5P	—	—	—
3133	All Weather Touring-5P	—	—	—
3135	Special Town Cabriolet	—	—	—
3144	Sedan-4P 132'' wb	—	—	—
3174	Sport Cabriolet-5P	—	—	—
3185	Sedan-7P	—	—	—
3199	Coupe-2P	—	—	—
3208	Imperial Cabriolet-5P 152'' wb	—	—	—
3238	Club Cabriolet-5P	—	—	—
3274	Sport Cabriolet Sedan-5P	—	—	—
3300	Convertible Cabriolet-7P	—	—	—
3360	Sedan-5P	—	—	—
3360-S	Imperial-5P	—	—	—
3361	Sedan-5P	—	—	—
3361-S	Imperial-5P	—	—	—
3375	Sedan-7P	—	—	—
3375-S	Imperial-7P	—	—	—
3376	Sedan-7P	—	—	—
3412	Town Car-7P 152'' wb	—	—	—
3435	Town Car-7P 152'' wb	—	—	—
3475	Limo.-7P	—	—	—
3512-P	Town Car-5P	—	—	—
3512-C-P	Town Car-5P	—	—	—
3515	Limo.-7P	—	—	—
3520-P	Town Car-5P	—	—	—
3520-C-P	Town Car-7P	—	—	—
3525-P	Town Car-7P	—	—	—
3525-C-P	Town Car-7P	—	—	—
3591-P	Town Car-7P	—	—	—
3591-C-P	Town Car-7P	—	—	—
3885	Convertible Sedan	—	—	—
3891	Imperial Sedan-7P	—	—	—

ENGINE: Ninety degree V-8, L-head. Eight. Cast Iron block on Copper/Aluminum crankcase. B & S: 3-5/16 x 4-15/16 in. Disp. 341 cu. in. C. R.: 4.8:1 std, 5.3:1 opt. SAE/Taxable/N.A.C.C. H.P.: 35.1. Main bearings: Three. Valve lifters: Mechanical, with rollers riding on cams. Carb.: Mfg by Cad under C.F. Johnson patents. (Compression) 90-92 PSI @ 1000 R.P.M., 105-107 PSI @ 1000 RPM with hi-comp. heads.

1928 Cadillac, Series 341-A, Fleetwood transformable town cabriolet, JAC

CHASSIS: [Series 341-A] W.B.: 140 in. O.L.: 213-1/4 in. Frt/Rear Tread: 56/58 in. Tires: 32 x 6.75 (7.00-20). [Series 341-A Comm Chassis] W.B.: 152 in. Frt/Rear Tread: 56/58 in. Tires: 32 x 6.75 (7.00-20).

TECHNICAL: Selective transmission. Speeds: 3F/1R. Left hand drive, center control (rhd opt). Twin disc clutch. Shaft drive (torque tube). Full floating rear axle, Spiral bevel drive. Overall ratio: 4.75:1 std; 5.08:1 opt. Mechanical brakes on four wheels. 16'' rear drums. 16'' front drums (17'' front mid-year). Artillery wheels. (wire and disc opt). Wheel size: 20 in.

OPTIONS: Folding trunk rack (25.00). Step plate (3.25 ea.). Tire mirrors (30.00). Wind wings (15.00-30.00). Trunks (65.00-100.00). Herald ornament (12.00). Seat covers. Spotlight (35.00). Tire covers (10.00). Tonneau windshield (120.00). Natural wood wheels (10.00 extra). 5 disc wheels (20.00). 6 disc wheels, fender wells, 2 spares (175.00). 5 wire wheels (95.00). 6 wire wheels, fender wells, 2 spares (250). Fender wells for wood wheels, 2 spares (140.00).

HISTORICAL: Introduced: September, 1927. Model year sales: 20001. Model year production: 20001. President & general manager of Cadillac: Lawrence P. Fisher.

1928
Fisher Custom Line, V-8, 140" wb

	FP	5	4	3	2	1
Rds	3350	13,500	27,000	45,000	70,000	90,000
Tr	3450	13,200	26,400	44,000	68,000	88,000
Phae	3450	13,500	27,000	45,000	70,000	90,000
Spt Phae	4000	13,800	27,600	46,000	73,500	92,000
Conv RS	3500	12,000	24,000	40,000	60,000	80,000
2P Cpe	3400	6900	13,800	23,000	32,200	46,000
5P Cpe	3500	6600	13,200	22,000	30,800	44,000
Twn Sed	3400	6150	12,300	20,500	28,700	41,000
Sed	3600	6000	12,000	20,000	28,000	40,000
7P Sed	3700	6150	12,300	20,500	28,700	41,000
5P Imp Sed	3800	6300	12,600	21,000	29,400	42,000
Imp Cabr	3745	8850	17,700	29,500	41,300	59,000
7P Imp Sed	3895	9600	19,200	32,000	44,800	64,000
7P Imp Cabr	3895	9900	19,800	33,000	46,200	66,000

Fisher Fleetwood Line, V-8, 140" wb

	FP	5	4	3	2	1
Sed	4095	6300	12,600	21,000	29,400	42,000
5P Cabr	4095	10,500	21,000	35,000	49,000	70,000
5P Imp Cabr	4245	10,800	21,600	36,000	50,500	72,000
7P Sed	4195	6600	13,200	22,000	30,800	44,000
7P Cabr	4445	10,500	21,000	35,000	49,000	70,000
7P Imp Cabr	4445	10,800	21,600	36,000	50,500	72,000
Trans Twn Cabr	5000	11,100	22,200	37,000	52,000	74,000
Trans Limo Brgm	5500	11,400	22,800	38,000	56,000	76,000

1929

1929 Cadillac, Series 341-B, roadster, OCW

1929 Cadillac, Series 341-B, roadster, JAC

CADILLAC — SERIES 341-B — EIGHT:
Similar to 1928 Cadillac Series 341-A except:
Bodies: Side lights moved to fenders. Security-Plate safety glass used in all windows and windshields. All brightwork chrome plated. Electric windshield wipers used. Fleetwood introduced the All Weather Phaeton. Fleetwood showed the sweep panel across cowl and hood on all body styles.
Chassis: Duplex-Mechanical brakes with all shoes internal used.
Drive line: Synchro-mesh transmission introduced.
Engine: Connecting rods drilled to give pressure lubrication to small ends. Metric spark plugs introduced midyear.

I.D. DATA: There were no serial numbers used. Engine numbers were stamped on plate on front of dash and on crankcase just below the water inlet on the right side. Starting: 320002. Ending: 338104.

1929 Cadillac, Series 341-B, town sedan, JAC

Style No.	Body Type & Seating	Price	Weight	Prod. Total
Fisher — 140 in. wheelbase				
1182	4-dr. Touring-7P	3450	4774	—
1183	4-dr. Phaeton-7P	3450	4635	—
1183-B	4-dr. Sport Phaeton-4P	3950	5110	—
1184	2-dr. Roadster-2/4P	3350	4678	—
8620	4-dr. Sedan-7P	3795	5145	—
8630	4-dr. Imp. Sedan-7P	3995	—	—
8640	4-dr. Sedan-5P	3695	5027	—
8650	4-dr. Imp. Sedan-5P	—	—	—
8660	4-dr. Town Sedan-5P	3495	5028	—
8670	2-dr. Coupe-5P	3595	4887	—
8680	2-dr. Conv. Coupe-2/4P	3595	4796	—
8690	2-dr. Coupe-2/4P	3295	4909	—
Semi-Commercial — 152 in. wheelbase				
NA	Limo. Funrl. Coach	—	—	—
NA	Limo. Ambulance	—	—	—
Fleetwood — 140 in. wheelbase				
3830	4-dr. Imperial-5P	4345	5130	—
3830-S	4-dr. Sedan-5P	4195	5120	—
3830-C	4-dr. Coll. Imp.-5P	5045	—	—
3830-SC	4-dr. Coll. Sedan-5P	4895	—	—
3830-L	4-dr. Imp. (leather back)-5P	4445	—	—
3830-SL	4-dr. Sedan (l.b.)-5P	4295	—	—
3861	4-dr. Imp. Twn.(club) Sed.-5P	—	—	—
3861-S	4-dr. Club Cabriolet-5P	4395	5120	—
3861-C	4-dr. Coll. Imp. Club. Cab.-5P	—	—	—
3861-SC	4-dr. Coll. Club Cab.-5P	5095	—	—
3855	4-dr. Imp. Cabriolet-5P	4345	5130	—
3855-S	4-dr. Sedan Cab.-5P	4195	5120	—

Style No.	Body Type & Seating	Price	Weight	Prod. Total
3855-C	4-dr. Coll. Imp. Cab.-5P	5045	—	—
3855-SC	4-dr. Coll. Sedan Cab.-5P	4895	—	—
3875	4-dr. Imperial-7P	4545	5210	—
3875-S	4-dr. Sedan-7P	4295	5200	—
3875-C	4-dr. Coll. Imp.-7P	5245	—	—
3875-L	4-dr. Imp. (leather back)-7P	4645	—	—
3875-SL	4-dr. Sedan (leather back)-7P	4395	—	—
3875-SC	4-dr. Coll. Sedan-7P	4995	—	—
3875-X	4-dr. Imp. (full lea. qrtr)-7P	4795	—	—
3875-SX	4-dr. Sed. (full lea. qrtr)-7P	4545	—	—
3180	All Weath. Phaeton-5P	5750	5130	—
3880	4-dr. Imp. A-W Phaeton-5P	5995	5140	—
3512	4-dr. Trans. Twn. Cab.-5/7P	5250	5180	—
3512-C	4-dr. Coll. Tr. Twn. Cab.-5/7P	5950	5180	—
3520	4-dr. Trans. Twn. Cab.-7P	5500	5180	—
3520-C	4-dr. Coll. Tr. Twn. Cab.-7P	6200	5180	—
3525	4-dr. Trans. Twn. Cab.-7P	5500	5180	—
3525-C	4-dr. Coll. Tr. Twn. Cab.-7P	5500	5180	—
3591	4-dr. Tr. Limo. Brougham-7P	5500	5180	—
3591-C	4-dr. Coll. Tr. Land. Brhn.-7P	6200	5180	—
3550	4-dr. Full. Coll. Tr. Cab.-7P	6700	—	—

ENGINE: Ninety degree V-8, L-head. Eight. Cast iron block on Copper/Aluminum crankcase. B & S: 3-5/16 x 4-15/16 in. Disp.: 341 cu. in. C.R.: 5.3:1 std, 4.8:1 opt. Brake H.P.: 90 plus advertised. SAE/Taxable/N.A.C.C. H.P.: 35.1. Main bearings: Three. Valve lifters: Mechanical, with rollers riding on cams. Carb.: Mfg. by Cad under C.F. Johnson patents. Compression: 90-92 PSI @ 1000 R.P.M., 105-107 PSI @ 1000 RPM with hi-comp heads.

CHASSIS: [Series 341-B] W.B.: 140 in. O.L.: 213-1/4 in. Frt/Rear Tread: 56/58 in. Tires: 7.00-20 (32 x 6.75). [Series 341-B Comm. Chassis] W.B.: 152 in. Frt/Rear Tread: 56/58 in. Tires: 7.00-20 (32 x 6.75).

TECHNICAL: Selective synchro-mesh transmission. 3F/1R. Left drive, center control (rhd opt). Twin disc clutch. Shaft drive (torque tube). Full floating rear axle, spiral bevel drive. Overall ratio: 5.08:1 std; 4.75:1, 4.39:1 opt. Duplex-mechanical brakes on four wheels. All shoes inside drums. 16-1/2 in. drums. Wood artillery wheels (wire and disc opt). Wheel size: 20 in.

OPTIONS: Folding trunk rack (25.00). Step plate (3.25 ea.). Tire mirrors (30.00). Wind wings (15.00-30.00). Heater (32.00). Trunks (65.00-100.00). Herald ornament (12.00). Seat covers (10.00). Spotlight (35.00). Tire covers (10.00). Tonneau windshield (120.00). Natural wood wheels (10.00 extra). 5 disc wheels (20.00). 6 disc wheels, fender wells, 2 spares (175.00). 5 wire wheels (95.00). 6 wire wheels, fender wells, 2 spares (250.00). Fender wells for wood wheels, 2 spares (140.00).

HISTORICAL: Introduced August, 1928. Innovations: Synchro-mesh transmission. Safety glass. Model year sales: 18103. Model year production: 18103. President & General Manager of Cadillac was Lawrence P. Fisher.

1929 Cadillac, Series 341-B, sport phaeton, JAC

1929
Series 341-B, V-8, 140" wb

	FP	5	4	3	2	1
Rds	3350	13,800	27,600	46,000	73,500	92,000
Phae	3450	13,500	27,000	45,000	70,000	90,000
Spt Phae	3950	13,800	27,600	46,000	73,500	92,000
Tr	3450	13,200	26,400	44,000	68,000	88,000
Conv	3595	12,900	25,800	48,200	66,000	86,000
2P Cpe	3295	9000	18,000	30,000	42,000	60,000
5P Cpe	3595	9300	18,600	31,000	43,400	62,000
5P Sed	3695	7500	15,000	25,000	35,000	50,000
7P Sed	3795	7350	14,700	24,500	34,300	49,000
Twn Sed	3495	7650	15,300	25,500	35,700	51,000
7P Imp Sed	3995	7800	15,600	26,000	36,400	52,000

Fleetwood Custom Line, V-8, 140" wb

	FP	5	4	3	2	1
Sed	4195	7650	15,300	25,500	35,700	51,000
Sed Cabr	4195	12,600	25,200	42,000	64,000	84,000
5P Imp Sed	4345	8100	16,200	27,000	37,800	54,000
7P Imp Sed	4545	8250	16,500	27,500	38,500	55,000
Trans Twn Cabr	5250	12,000	24,000	40,000	60,000	80,000
Trans Limo Brgm	5500	12,000	24,000	40,000	60,000	80,000
Clb Cabr	5500	12,000	24,000	40,000	60,000	80,000
A/W Phae	5750	24,100	42,000	68,000	98,000	126,000
A/W State Imp	5995	25,500	45,000	73,000	100,000	130,000

1930

1930 Cadillac, Series 353, 7-pass. sedan, OCW

CADILLAC — SERIES 353 — EIGHT: An extension of the Series 341-B, with the following changes:

Bodies: Fisher ("Fisher Custom") line reduced to seven closed bodies, including Convertible Coupe. Fleetwood ("Fleetwood Special Custom") line consolidated into eleven basic bodies, with many variations.

Louvers carried well to the front of the hood. Fleetwood Roadster had louvers in the sides of the cowl. Wider radiator. Larger headlights (12" lens, 13" overall). Windshield slopes a few degrees. Short, cadet-type visor. Valance across rear of car covers fuel tank and frame, and joins rear fenders. With wider rear tread, rear cushions made 4" wider. All but a few bodies were prewired for radio, with an aerial built into the top.

Chassis: Ball and socket spring shackles no longer used. Front tread increased from 56" to 59". Rear tread increased from 58" to 59-1/2". Third rear shoe for emergency brake dropped; lever now operates rear service brake shoes. Fan shaped end on exhaust tail pipe. Demountable wood wheels offered as an extra cost option.

Drive line: All cars have 3/4 floating rear axle.

Engine: Bore increased 1/16 inch. Reduction type starter used. Fan lubricated by engine oil return pressure. Cover used over spark plugs. New distributor has wires out rear, into single conduit.

I.D. DATA: There were no serial numbers on the 1930 Cadillac Series 353. Engine numbers were stamped on crankcase just below the water inlet on the right hand side. Starting: 500001. Ending: 511005.

1930 Cadillac, Series 353, Fleetwood sport cabriolet, JAC

Style No. Fisher	Body Type & Seating	Price	Weight	Prod. Total
30152	4-dr. Twn. Sed.-5P	3495	5040	—
30158	2-dr. Cpe.-2/4P	3295	4955	—
30159	4-dr. Sed.-5P	3695	5070	—

210

Style No.	Body Type & Seating	Price	Weight	Prod. Total
30162	4-dr. Sed.-7P	3795	5170	—
30163	4-dr. Imp.-7P	3995	5210	—
30168	2-dr. Conv. Cpe.-2/4P	3595	4860	—
30172	2-dr. Coupe-5P	3595	4945	—
Fleetwood Built-to-order				
4150	4-dr. Full Coll. Trans. Twn. Cab.	—	—	—
4157	4-dr. Tour.-7P	—	—	—
4160	4-dr. Spt. Phae.-5P	—	—	—
4160-A	4-dr. Spt. Phae.-5P	—	—	—
4160-B	4-dr. Spt. Phae.-5P	—	—	—
4161	4-dr. Sed. or Imp. Spt. Cab.-5P	—	—	—
4164	4-dr. Trans. Brougham-5P	—	—	—
4164-B	4-dr. Trans. Brougham w/cane work-5P	—	—	—
4176	2-dr. Spt. Sta. or Conv. Cpe.-2P	—	—	—
4185	2-dr. All Weather Cpe.-4P	—	—	—
3350	Trans. All Weather Phae., 152 in. wheelbase-7P	—	—	—
3950	Twn. Car w/Full Collapsible Top-7P	—	—	—
3902	2-dr. Rds.-2/4P	3450	4625	—
3930	4-dr. Imp.-5P	4395	5220	—
3930-S	4-dr. Sedan-5P	4195	5150	—
3930-C	4-dr. Collapsible Imp.-5P	5195	—	—
3930-SC	4-dr. Collapsible Sed.-5P	4995	—	—
3955	4-dr. Imp. Cabr.-5P	4445	5240	—
3955-S	4-dr. Sed. Cabr.-5P	4245	5200	—
3955-C	4-dr. Collapsible Imp. Cabr.-5P	5195	—	—
3955-SC	4-dr. Collapsible Sed. Cabr.-5P	4995	—	—
3975	4-dr. Imp.-7P	4595	5320	—
3975-S	4-dr. Sed.-7P	4295	5280	—
3975-C	4-dr. Collapsible Imp.-7P	5395	—	—
3975-SC	4-dr. Collapsible Sed.-7P	5095	—	—
3975-P	4-dr. Imp. (plain hood)-7P	4845	—	—
3981	4-dr. Sedanette Cabr.-5P	4500	5070	—
3982	4-dr. Sedanette Cabr.-5P	4595	5070	—
3980	4-dr. All Weather Phae.-5P	4700	4990	—
3912	4-dr. Transformable Twn. Cabr.-5/7P	4995	5230	—
3912-C	4-dr. Coll. Trans. Twn. Cabr.-5/7P	5745	—	—
3920	4-dr. Twn. Cab. (quarter window)-7P	5145	5150	—
3920-C	4-dr. Coll. Twn. Cab. (1/4 window)-7P	5945	—	—
3925	4-dr. Trans. Twn. Cab. (no 1/4 window)-7P	5145	5150	—
3925-C	4-dr. Coll. Tr. Twn. Cab. (no 1/4 window)-7P	5895	—	—
3991	4-dr. Trans. Limo. Brougham-7P	5145	5320	—
3991-C	4-dr. Coll. Tr. Limo. Brougham-7P	5945	—	—

1930 Cadillac, Series 353, Fleetwood transformable limousine brougham, JAC

ENGINE: Ninety degree V-8. L-head. Cast iron on silicon/aluminum crankcase. B & S: 3-3/8 x 4-15/16 in. Disp.: 353 cu. in. C.R.: 5.05:1 std, 4.92:1 opt. Brake H.P.: 96 @ 3000 R.P.M.. SAE/Taxable H.P.: 36.45. Main bearings: Three. Valve lifters: Mechanical, with rollers riding on cams. Carb.: mfg. by Cad under C.F. Johnson patents.

CHASSIS: [Series 353] W.B.: 140 in. Length: app. 210-5/8 in. Frt/Rear Tread: 59/59-1/2 in. Tires: 7.00-19. [Comm. Chassis] W.B.: 152 in.

TECHNICAL: Selective, synchro-mesh transmission. Speeds: 3F/1R. Left drive, center controls (rhd. opt). Twin disc clutch. Shaft drive (torque tube). 3/4 floating rear axle spiral bevel gears. Overall ratio: 5.08:1 std.;

4.39:1, 4.75:1 opt. (4.75:1 made std. in midyear). Safety-mechanical brakes on four wheels. (16-1/2 in. drums). Wood artillery wheels (disc, wire, wood demountable opt). Wheel size: 19 in.

1930 Cadillac, Series 353, Fleetwood Imperial phaeton, JAC

OPTIONS: Tire cover(s) (6.50-30.00). Wind Wings (25.00-55.00). Tonneau Shield (185.00). Radio (175.00). Heater (42.50). Radiator ornament (25.00). Trunks (80-115.00). Seat covers (26.75-230.25). Spotlight/driving lights (15.50-80.00). Tire mirrors (32.00/pair). 5 Wire wheels (70.00). 6 Wire wheels w/fender wells, trunk rack (210.00). 5 Demountable wood wheels (50.00). 6 dem. wood wheels w/fender wells, trunk rack (190.00). 5 Disc wheels (50.00). 6 disc wheels w/fender wells, trunk rack (190.00).

HISTORICAL: Introduced September, 1929. Innovations: Radio available. Most bodies prewired for radio, with aerial built into top. Model year sales: 14,995. Model year production: 14,995. The president & general manager was Lawrence P. Fisher.

1930-1931 (V-16)

1930 Cadillac, V-16, roadster, OCW

CADILLAC — SERIES 452/452-A — SIXTEEN: Bodies: Although full-custom bodies were built by Fleetwood, Murphy, Waterhouse, Saoutchik, VandenPlas, Pinin Farina, and others; most were "catalog customs" by Fleetwood. A few cars had Fisher bodies. Only about one fifth were open or convertible, two thirds were five or seven passenger sedans or Imperials, the rest Coupes or Town Cars.

More than 50 body styles were offered, but the list consists of only a few basic shells with several variations each: metal or leather quarters, with or without quarter windows, fixed or collapsible (Landau) quarters, with or without Imperial division, straight or coach sill, plain or recessed hood/cowl, etc..

With few exceptions, the "41" styles had plain hood and straight sill, the "42" styles had plain hood and coach sill, and the "43" styles had recessed hood/cowl and straight sill.

Windshield treatment varied from vertical Vee to 22 degree sloping, as follows:

Vertical Vee swing-out (Penna.) 4130, 4155
7 degree flat swing-out 4212, 4220, 4225, 4264, 4291
7 degree V-type swing-out 4312, 4320, 4325, 4335, 4376, 4380, 4391
7 degree flat crank-up (V-V) 4330, 4355, 4361, 4375, 4381
16 degree flat swing-out, folding 4302
18 degree flat crank-up (V-V) "Madame X" 4130, 4155, 4161, 4175, 4276, 4476
21 degree flat swing-out 4235
22 degree flat, divided 4260

The sobriquet "Madame X" (with an "e") is not prominent, if it appears at all, in Cadillac promotional literature. Perhaps the only place Cadillac printed it is in body style listings found in various parts lists, as early as March, 1930. The term is associated with job/style numbers 4130, 4155, 4161, 4175, in plain, -S, -C, and -SC variations. In later parts lists, job number 4476 is listed as having a "Madame X" windshield.

"Madame X" has a Hollywood flavor, but is no more inappropriate than the style designations "Fleetbourne", "Fleetdowns", etc.. The term must have arisen from a distinctive styling feature common to the four basic

body styles. Further, the term more likely came from Detroit than from Pennsylvania Dutch country. The most distinctive styling feature of the "41" series bodies built in Detroit is the 18 degree flat, crank-up (V-V) windshield. It is unlikely that the Penna. versions with vertical Vee swing-out windshields were thought of as "Madame X" bodies. Job/style number 4276, being style 4476 with coach sill, also has a "Madame X" windshield.

Chrome plated window reveals were used on "41" bodies but were not unique to those styles. Although early body specs listed chrome plated reveals, July 1930 body specs listed painted reveals on "41" bodies. Painted window reveals on "Madame X" bodies are probably as rare as the "standard" rear-mounted spare tire.

In simplest terms, 1930-31 Fleetwood four door bodies with 18 degree windshield, mounted on Cadillac V-16 chassis are "Madame X"; and two Coupe body styles have the "Madame X" windshield.

Body details unique to the V-16 or introduced with the V-16 and seen on the full 1931 line include: Single bar bumpers, dual horns, concave monogram bar, radiator screen, 13 inch Guide "Tiltray" headlights, dual rear lights matching the headlights, triple molding on dust shield panels of straight sill styles, five doors in the hood, single matching door in the side of the cowl, and none, one, or two rectangular vent doors in the top of the cowl. Most bodies with recessed hood/cowl had one triangular door in the top of the cowl.

1930 Cadillac, V-16, 4-dr. phaeton, JAC

Chassis: Frame similar to 353 except for five-point engine mount on V-16. Brake system had vacuum assist operated on manifold vacuum, not vacuum pump. Brake drums 16½ inch diameter. Specially balanced white wall tires used.
Drive Line: Rear engine support at tail of transmission. Heavier clutch linings (chassis unit 7-2991 and later used thinner lining of V-8). Rear axle shafts same as on 353 except made of special steel. Optional 3.47:1 final drive ratio dropped mid-model.
Engine: Extra effort and expense went into a polished, plated, enameled, uncluttered engine compartment. Wiring was concealed and covers were used on engine and dash to hide plumbing and controls.

Twin coils were mounted in recesses in the radiator top tank. Spark plug wires came out the rear of the double deck distributor cap and disappeared under the cover inside the Vee. The narrow (45 degree) Vee allowed for outboard mounting of manifolds and dual carburetors. Intake pipes from higher in the engine compartment were added at engine number 702502 to eliminate the problem of road splash entering the carburetors. Fuel feed was by dual vacuum tanks operated by vacuum pump. By May, 1930, the chrome plated vacuum tanks were superceded by painted units. The dual exhaust system ended in fan shaped tail pipe tips.

To silence the overhead valve system, hydraulically rotated eccentric bushings were used in the rocker arms. The early use of a different head thickness for various compression ratios was replaced by the use of a single head with gaskets of different thickness. Right and left heads and blocks were interchangeable. One row of head studs went thru the block to the crankcase, the second row seated in the block.

Engine lubrication was full pressure from oil pump on rear main bearing cap. At engine unit number 7-1038, the oil level indicator was moved from rear of right hand cylinder block to left side of crankcase. The belt driven fan was mounted on ball bearings, lubricated by grease fitting, not engine

1931 Cadillac, V-16, 7-pass. limousine, JAC

oil pressure. Crankshaft thrust was taken by center main. A harmonic balancer was mounted on front end of crankshaft. A single chain to drive camshaft and generator was provided with automatic adjuster incorporated in an idler acting on the outside of the chain. A thermostat was used to close the crankcase ventilation intake at higher engine temperatures.

The double outlet water pump on the right side of the engine was driven by an extension shaft from the rear of the generator. A cooling system condenser tank was used once again.

The engine, transmission assembly was mounted at the four corners of the engine plus a dual mount at the rear of the transmission. The front mounts were supported by diagonal members in the frame.

I.D. DATA: Serial numbers were not used on the 452/452-A series. Engine numbers were stamped on crankcase right hand side, on the generator drive chain housing. Starting: 700001. Ending: 703251.

Style No.	Body Type & Seating	Price	Weight	Prod. Total
4108-C	4-dr. Imp. Lan. Cabr.-5/7P	—	—	—
4130	4-dr. Imp.-5/7P	7300	5920	—
4130-S	4-dr. Sed.-5P	6950	5850	—
4155	4-dr. Imp. Cabr.-5/7P	7350	5940	—
4155-C	4-dr. Imp. Lan. Cabr.-5/7P	—	—	—
4155-S	4-d.r Sed. Cabr.-5P	7125	5900	—
4155-SC	4-dr. Lan. Sed. Cabr.-5P	—	—	—
4161	4-dr. Imp. Clb. Sed.-5P	—	—	—
4161-C	4-dr. Imp. Lan. Clb. Sed.-5P	—	—	—
4161-S	4-dr. Clb. Sed.-5P	6950	5740	—
4175	4-dr. Imp.-7P	7525	6020	—
4175-C	4-dr. Imp. Lan.-7P	—	—	—
4175-S	4-dr. Sed.-7P	7225	5980	—
4200	4-dr. Sed. Cabr.-7P	—	—	—
4206	2-dr. Cpe.-2/4P	—	—	—
4207	2-dr. Cpe.-2/4P	—	—	—
4208	4-dr. Imp. Cabr.-5/7P	—	—	—
4212	4-dr. Trans. Twn. Cabr.-5/7P	8750	5915	—
4212-C	4-dr. Coll. Trans. Twn. Cabr.-5/7P	—	—	—
4220	4-dr. Trans. Twn. Cabr.-7P	8750	5850	—
4220-B	4-dr. Trans. Twn. Cabr.-7P	—	—	—
4225	4-dr. Trans. Twn. Cabr.-7P	8750	5850	—
4225-C	4-dr. Coll. Trans. Twn. Cabr.-7P	—	—	—
4235	2-dr. Conv. Cpe.-2/4P	6900	5670	—
4243	4-dr. Phae.	—	—	—
4244	4-dr. Phae.	—	—	—
4246	4-dr. Phae.	—	—	—
4257-A	4-dr. Tr.-7P	—	—	—
4257-H	4-dr. Tr.-5P	—	—	—
4260	4-dr. Spt. Phae.-5P	6500	—	—
4260-A	4-dr. Spt. Phae.-5P	—	—	—
4260-B	4-dr. Spt. Phae.-5P	—	—	—
4262	4-dr. Imp. Cabr.-7P	—	—	—
4264	4-dr. Twn. Brgm.-5/7P	9200	5765	—
4264-B	4-dr. Town Brgm.-5/7P	9700	5675	—
4275	4-dr. Imp. Sed.-7P	—	—	—
4275-C	4-dr. Imp. Landau Sed.-7P	—	—	—
4276	2-dr. Cpe.-2/4P	6850	5765	—
4280	4-dr. All Weather Phae.-4P	7350	5675	—
4285	4-dr. All Weather Spt. Cabr.-5P	—	—	—
4291	4-dr. Transformable Limo. Brgm.-7P	8750	6020	—
4302	2-dr. Rds.-2/4P	5350	5325	—
4312	4-dr. Transformable Twn. Cabr.-5/7P	7000	5930	—
4312-C	4-dr. Collapsible Transformable Twn. Cabr.-5/7P	—	—	—
4320	4-dr. Transformable Twn. Cabr.-7P	7150	5850	—
4320-C	4-dr. Collapsible Transformable Twn. Cabr.-7P	—	—	—
4325	4-dr. Transformable Twn. Cabr.-7P	7150	5850	—
4325-C	4-dr. Collapsible Transformable Twn. Cabr.-7P	—	—	—
4330	4-dr. Imp.-5/7P	6300	5920	—
4330-S	4-dr. Sed.-5P	5950	5850	—
4335	2-dr. Conv. Cpe.-2/4P	5900	5655	—
4355	4-dr. Imp. Cabr.-5/7P	6350	5940	—
4355-C	4-dr. Collapsible Imp. Cabr.-5/7P	—	—	—
4355-S	4-dr. Sed. Cabr.-5P	6125	5885	—
4361	4-dr. Imp. Club Sed.-5P	—	—	—
4361-S	4-dr. Club Sed.-5P	5950	5740	—
4375	4-dr. Imp.-7P	6525	6020	—
4375-C	4-dr. Collapsible Imp.-7P	—	—	—
4375-S	4-dr. Sed.-7P	6225	5980	—
4376	2-dr. Cpe.-2/4P	5800	5750	—
4380	4-dr. All Weather Phae.-5P	6650	5690	—
4381	2-dr. Cpe.-5P	5950	—	—
4391	4-dr. Transformable			

Style No.	Body Type & Seating	Price	Weight	Prod. Total
	Limo. Brgm.-7P	7150	6020	—
4391-C	4-dr. Collapsible Transformable Limo. Brgm.-7P	—	—	—
4412	4-dr. Transformable Twn. Cabr.-5/7P	—	—	—
4476	2-dr. Cpe.-2/4P	5800	5765	—
3289-A	4-dr. Trans. Twn. Cabr.-7P	—	—	—
3981	4-dr. Sed. Cabr.-5P	—	—	—
3991	4-dr. Trans. Limo. Brgm.-7P	—	—	—
2950-X	4-dr. Sed.-7P	—	—	—
2901-LX	4-dr. Sed.-7P	—	—	—
2951-LX	4-dr. Sed.-7P	—	—	—
30-X	4-dr. Sed.-7P	—	—	—
LX-2905	4-dr. Twn. Sed.-5P	—	—	—
LX-2913	2-dr. Cpe.-5P	—	—	—
30-152	4-dr. Twn. Sed., Fisher-5P	—	—	—
30-158	2-dr. Cpe., Fisher-2/4P	—	—	—
30-159	4-dr. Sed., Fisher-5P	—	—	—
30-168	2-dr. Conv. Cpe., Fisher-2/4P	—	—	—
30-172	2-dr. Cpe., Fisher-5P	—	—	—

1931 Cadillac, V-16, 2-dr. coupe, JAC

ENGINE: 45 degree, overhead valve V-16. Cast Nickel Iron blocks on Silicon/Aluminum crankcase. B & S: 3 x 4 in. Disp.: 452 cu. in. C.R.: 5.35:1 early std., 5.11:1 std., 4.98:1 opt. Brake H.P.: 175-185 @ 3400 R.P.M. SAE/Taxable H.P.: 57.5. Main bearings: Five. Valve lifters: Push rod/rocker arm with hydraulic rotary eccentric silencer in rocker arm. Carb.: Cadillac/Johnson.

CHASSIS: [Series: 452/452-A] W.B.: 148 in. O.L.: approx. 222-1/2 in. Frt/Rear Tread: 59/59-1/2 in. Tires: 7.00-19 early, 7.50-19 mid-model.

TECHNICAL: Selective, synchro-mesh transmission. Speeds: 3F/1R. Left drive, center control, (rhd. opt.). Twin disc clutch. Shaft drive, torque tube. 3/4 floating rear axle, spiral bevel drive. Overall ratio: 4.39:1 std.; (3.47:1), 4.07:1, 4.75:1 opt. Vacuum assisted mechanical brakes on four wheels. Wood artillery wheels (wire, disc, demountable wood opt.). Wheel size: 19 in.

OPTIONS: Mirrors (10.00-32.00). Sidemount cover(s) (5.00-40.00). Tonneau windshield (185.00). Wind wings (47.50). Radio (200.00). Heater (41.00-55.00). Heron or Goddess ornament (20.00). Auxiliary lights (37.50-75.00). Seat covers (26.75-73.50). Trunks (100.00-119.00). 5 wire wheels (70.00). 6 wire wheels, fender wells, trunk rack (210.00). 5 demountable wood wheels (50.00). 6 demountable wood wheels, fender wells, trunk rack (190.00). 5 disc wheels (50.00). 6 disc wheels, fender wells, trunk rack (190.00). Fenders other than black (100.00).

HISTORICAL: Introduced January, 1930. Model year sales: 3251. Model year production: 3251. The President & General Manager was Lawrence P. Fisher.

Note: Although a token number (approximately one percent) of the V-16 chassis were sold to domestic and foreign coachbuilders, all body styles advertised by Cadillac were "Catalog Customs" by Fleetwood. The customer was able to order limited variations in the "Catalog Customs", or order a full-custom creation.

It is remarkable that Fleetwood was able to turn out four to five hundred bodies per month at a time when activities at the Pennsylvania shop were being phased out and "production" at a new location in Detroit was being set up.

Thru the Fall of 1930, dealers were required to furnish the factory with weekly and monthly owner reaction and service reports on each V-16 delivered.

1930
Series 353, V-8, 140" wb
Fisher Custom Line

	FP	5	4	3	2	1
Conv	3595	13,500	27,000	45,000	70,000	90,000
2P Cpe	3295	12,000	24,000	40,000	60,000	80,000
Twn Sed	3495	7500	15,000	25,000	35,000	50,000
Sed	3695	7800	15,600	26,000	36,400	52,000
7P Sed	3795	7950	15,900	26,500	37,100	53,000
7P Imp Sed	3995	8100	16,200	27,000	37,800	54,000
5P Cpe	3595	7500	15,000	25,000	35,000	50,000

Fleetwood Line, V-8

Rds	3450	31,100	58,000	88,000	114,000	150,000
5P Sed	4195	8250	16,500	27,500	38,500	55,000
Sed Cabr	4245	14,400	28,800	48,000	76,000	96,000
5P Imp	4395	8400	16,800	28,000	39,200	56,000
7P Sed	4295	8250	16,500	27,500	38,500	55,000
7P Imp	4595	8550	17,100	28,500	39,900	57,000
Trans Cabr	4995	14,700	29,400	49,000	78,000	98,000
Trans Limo Brgm	5145	14,400	28,800	48,000	76,000	96,000
Clb Cabr	4500	15,000	30,000	50,000	80,000	100,000
A/W Phae	4700	22,000	55,000	84,000	110,000	140,000
A/W State Imp	5145	30,300	57,000	86,000	112,000	145,000

Fleetwood Custom Line, V-16, 148" wb

Rds	5350	55,000	97,000	152,000	193,000	275,000
Phae	6150	54,000	95,000	149,000	189,000	270,000

"Flat Windshield" Models

A/W Phae	6650	53,000	93,000	146,000	186,000	265,000
Conv	6900	45,000	79,000	124,000	158,000	225,000
Cpe	6850	15,000	30,000	50,000	80,000	100,000
Clb Sed	6950	14,400	28,800	48,000	76,000	96,000
5P OS Sed	7300	14,400	28,800	48,000	76,000	96,000
5P Sed Cabr	7125	18,500	33,000	55,000	88,000	110,000
Imp Cabr	7350	18,500	33,000	55,000	88,000	110,000
7P Sed	7225	14,400	28,800	48,000	76,000	96,000
7P Imp Sed	7525	15,000	30,000	50,000	80,000	100,000
Twn Cabr 4212	8750	20,600	34,800	58,000	91,000	116,000
Twn Cabr 4220	8750	20,600	34,800	58,000	91,000	116,000
Twn Cabr 4225	8750	20,600	34,800	58,000	91,000	116,000
Limo Brgm	8750	15,000	30,000	50,000	80,000	100,000
Twn Brgm 05	9200	15,000	30,000	50,000	80,000	100,000

"Cane-bodied" Model

Twn Brgm	9700	18,500	33,000	55,000	88,000	110,000

Madam X Models

A/W Phae	6650	54,000	95,000	149,000	189,000	270,000
Conv	5900	46,000	81,000	127,000	161,000	230,000
Cpe	5800	15,000	30,000	50,000	80,000	100,000
5P OS Imp	6300	15,000	30,000	50,000	80,000	100,000
5P Imp	6300	13,500	27,000	45,000	70,000	90,000
Twn Cabr 4312	7000	18,500	33,000	55,000	88,000	110,000
Twn Cabr 4320	7150	18,500	33,000	55,000	88,000	110,000
Twn Cabr 4325	7150	18,500	33,000	55,000	88,000	110,000
Limo Brgm	7000	15,000	30,000	50,000	80,000	100,000

1931

1931 Cadillac, Series 355-A, town sedan, JAC

CADILLAC — SERIES 355-A — EIGHT: Similar to Series 353 except as follows:

Bodies: New body, longer and lower. Longer hood with five hood ports (doors). Matching doors in cowl. Modified coach sill, no compartments in splash pan. Battery and tool compartments under front seat. Metal floor boards. Oval instrument panel, with same grouping as Series 353. Radiator screen, single bar bumper, dual horns. Headlight diameter reduced one inch.

Chassis and drive line: New frame with divergent side rails. Rear springs mounted directly under frame rails. Metal covers on springs. Radiator mounted lower in frame. Condenser tank for cooling system.

Engine: Displacement same as Series 353. Series designation on V-8's no longer matches displacement. Five point engine suspension, similar to V-16. Intake muffler added. Distributor 1-1/2 inches higher than on 345. Fan lower to match lower radiator.

I.D. DATA: Serial numbers were not used. Engine numbers were stamped on crankcase just below the water inlet on the right hand side. Starting: 800001. Ending: 810717.

Style No. Fisher	Body Type & Seating	Price	Weight	Prod. Total
31252	4-dr. Twn. Sed.-5P	2845	4675	—
31258	2-dr. Cpe.-2/4P	2695	4480	—
31259	4-dr. Sed.-5P	2795	4660	—
31262	4-dr. Sed.-7P	2945	4760	—
31263	4-dr. Imp. Sed.-7P	3095	4835	—
31272	2-dr. Cpe.-5P	2795	4500	—

Style No. Fleetwood	Body Type & Seating	Price	Weight	Prod. Total
4502	2-dr. Rds.-2/4P	2845	4450	—
4503	4-dr. Sed.-7P	—	—	—
4535	2-dr. Conv. Cpe.-2/4P	2945	4450	—
4550	4-dr. Trans. Twn. Cab.-7P	—	—	—
4557	4-dr. Tr.-7P	3195	—	—
4560	4-dr. Phae.-4/5P	2945	4395	—
4580	4-dr. All Wthr. Phae.-5P	3795	4685	—

1931 Cadillac, Series 370-A, V-12, phaeton, OCW

ENGINE: 90 degree L-head. Eight. Cast Iron on Aluminum crankcase. B & S: 3-3/8 x 4-15/16 in. Disp.: 353 cu. in. C.R.: 5.35:1 std, 5.26:1 opt. Brake H.P.: 95 plus @ 3000 R.P.M. SAE/Taxable H.P.: 36.45. Main bearings: Three. Valve lifters: Mechanical. Carb.: Cad/Johnson, with intake silencer.

CHASSIS: [Series 355-A] W.B.: 134 in. O.L.: approx. 203 in. Height: 72-1/2 in. Frt/Rear Tread: 57-1/4 / 59-1/2 in. Tires: 6.50 x 19. (7.00 x 18 on opt wheels). [Series 355-A Comm. Chassis.]W.B.: 152 in.

1931 Cadillac, Series 370-A, V-12, coupe, JAC

TECHNICAL: Selective, synchro transmission. Speeds: 3F/1R. Lhd., center controls, rhd. opt. Twin disc clutch. Shaft drive, torque tube. 3/4 floating rear axle, spiral bevel drive. Overall ratio: 4.75:1 std.; 4.07:1, 4.54:1 opt. Mechanical brakes on four wheels. Wood artillery wheels std. (Wire, disc, demountable wood opt.). Wheel size: 19 in. std.; 18 in. w/opt. wheels.

1931 Cadillac, Series 370-A, V-12, roadster, JAC

OPTIONS: Trunks (100.00-119.00). Tonneau Windshield (185.00). Wind wings (25.00-47.50). Tire cover(s) (5.00-40.00). Mirrors (10.00-32.00/pair). Radio (price on application). Heater (41.00-55.00). Auxiliary lights (37.50-75.00). Seat covers (26.75-73.50). Heron or Goddess (20.00). 5 wire wheels (70.00). 6 wire wheels w/fender wells, trunk rack (240.00). 5 demountable wood wheels (50.00). 6 demountable wood wheels w/wells and rack (230.00). 4 Natural wood wheels (10.00).

HISTORICAL: Introduced August, 1930. Model year sales: 10717. Model year production: 10717. The President & General Manager was Lawrence P. Fisher.

1931
Series 355, V-8, 134" wb
Fisher Bodies

	FP	5	4	3	2	1
Rds	2845	31,900	59,000	90,000	116,000	155,000
Phae	2945	31,100	58,000	88,000	114,000	150,000
2P Cpe	2695	12,000	24,000	40,000	60,000	80,000
5P Cpe	2795	12,300	24,600	41,000	62,000	82,000
Sed	2795	8250	16,500	27,500	38,500	55,000
Twn Sed	2845	8550	17,100	28,500	39,900	57,000
7P Sed	2945	8700	17,400	29,000	40,600	58,000
Imp Limo	3095	9000	18,000	30,000	42,000	60,000
Fleetwood Bodies V-8						
Rds	3095	30,300	57,000	86,000	112,000	145,000
Conv	2945	22,000	36,000	60,000	93,000	120,000
Phae	3495	30,300	57,000	86,000	112,000	145,000
A/W Phae	3795	30,300	57,000	86,000	112,000	145,000
Series 370, V-12, 140" wb						
Rds	3945	35,100	63,000	98,000	124,000	175,000
Phae	4045	34,300	62,000	96,000	122,000	170,000
Conv	4045	32,700	60,000	92,000	118,000	160,000
A/W Phae	4895	35,100	63,000	98,000	124,000	175,000
2P Cpe	3795	11,400	22,800	38,000	56,000	76,000
5P Cpe	3895	11,700	23,400	39,000	58,000	78,000
Sed	3895	9000	18,000	30,000	42,000	60,000
Twn Sed	3945	9300	18,600	31,000	43,400	62,000
Series 370, V-12, 143" wb						
7P Sed	4195	9900	19,800	33,000	46,200	66,000
Imp Limo	4345	10,800	21,600	36,000	50,500	72,000
Series V-16, 148" wb						
2P Rds	5350	60,000	105,000	165,000	210,000	300,000
Phae	6500	62,000	109,000	171,000	217,000	310,000
A/W Phae	5750	61,000	107,000	168,000	214,000	305,000
4476 Cpe	5800	14,100	28,200	57,000	74,000	94,000
4276 Cpe	6850	14,400	28,800	48,000	76,000	96,000
5P Cpe	5950	14,100	28,200	57,000	74,000	94,000
Conv	6900	45,000	79,000	124,000	158,000	225,000
4361 Clb Sed	5950	14,100	28,200	57,000	74,000	94,000
4161 Clb Sed	6950	14,100	28,200	57,000	74,000	94,000
4330 Imp	6500	14,100	28,200	57,000	74,000	94,000
4330 Sed	6125	12,000	24,000	40,000	60,000	80,000
4130 Sed	7125	12,300	24,600	41,000	62,000	82,000
4130 Imp	7300	12,300	24,600	41,000	62,000	82,000
4335 Sed Cabr	6125	17,100	31,800	53,000	85,000	106,000
4355 Imp Cabr	6350	18,500	33,000	55,000	88,000	110,000
4155 Sed Cabr	7125	18,500	33,000	55,000	88,000	110,000
4155 Imp Cabr	7350	20,600	34,800	58,000	91,000	116,000
4375 Sed	6225	12,000	24,000	40,000	60,000	80,000
4175 Sed	7225	12,300	24,600	41,000	62,000	82,000
4375 Imp	6525	12,300	24,600	41,000	62,000	82,000
4175 Imp	7525	12,600	25,200	42,000	64,000	84,000
4312 Twn Cabr	6525	18,500	33,000	55,000	88,000	110,000
4320 Twn Cabr	6525	18,500	33,000	55,000	88,000	110,000
4220 Twn Cabr	8750	24,100	42,000	68,000	98,000	126,000
4325 Twn Cabr	6525	18,500	33,000	55,000	88,000	110,000
4225 Twn Cabr	8750	24,100	42,000	68,000	98,000	126,000
4391 Limo Brgm	6525	18,500	33,000	55,000	88,000	110,000
4291 Limo Brgm	8750	24,100	42,000	68,000	98,000	126,000
4264 Twn Brgm	9200	25,500	45,000	73,000	100,000	130,000
4264B Twn Brgm C/N	—	29,500	55,000	84,000	110,000	140,000

1932

1932 Cadillac, Series 355-B, town sedan, JAC

CADILLAC — SERIES 355-B — EIGHT: Series 355-B is representative of changes for 1932. Differences in other 1932 models are noted separately.
Bodies: Longer and lower, with an entirely restyled front assembly. Roof line lowered one to three inches. Longer hood has six ports. New front styling includes a flat grill built into the radiator shell, head and side lights

of streamlined bullet shape, and elimination of fender tie-bar and monogram bar. Trumpets of dual horns project thru headlight stanchions. Headlight lenses 9-1/2 inch diameter. Dual taillights match headlights. Super-safe lighting features three-filament bulbs and four control positions for degree and angle of illumination. Front license plate mounted on bumper.

Running boards curved to match sweep of front fenders and blend into rear fenders. The tail of the rear fenders is blended into the fuel tank valance. The trunk on the Town Coupe, Town Sedan, and five passenger Convertible Coupe is integral with the body.

Driver's vision is increased by 30%, as a result of elimination of the outside visor and construction of the 12 degree sloping windshield and corner posts. Large ventilator in top of cowl, none in sides of cowl. All separate body moldings eliminated. Three spoke steering wheel affords easy view of instrument cluster in front of driver. The right side of the panel is occupied by a "locker".
Chassis: Frame redesigned, using more box construction and no front or rear tubular cross member. Brake drums cast Molybdenum. "Cardan" shaft replaced by cable control for front brakes. "Full Range Ride Control" by driver adjustment of shock absorber valves. V-threaded spring shackle pins to control side play. Wire wheels standard, with optional full chrome covers to simulate disc wheels. Optional demountable wood wheels fit same hubs as wire wheels.
Drive Line: "Triple-Silent Synchro-Mesh" transmission, by use of constant-mesh helical gears with ground and lapped tooth profile for all forward gears. Rear axle redesigned to be lighter and stronger, thru use of improved heat treatments. Final drive ratios changed, but smaller tires give same net effect. "Controlled Free Wheeling" used — vacuum assist on clutch, controlled by foot button. Depressing button releases clutch; releasing button or depressing accelerator re-engages clutch.
Engine: Twenty one percent increase in power achieved mostly from new manifold design plus carburetor revisions. Intake manifold redesigned to give equal length path to each cylinder. Location of inlet and exhaust valves interchanged on middle cylinders of each block, placing inlet valves side by side at the center so that one leg of the inlet manifold can service both middle cylinders. Exhaust manifold placed atop the intake manifold, with single exhaust pipe to the rear. Air filter added to intake muffler. External tuning chamber on tail pipe. Mechanical fuel pump replaces vacuum tank fuel feed. Separate vacuum pump for wipers. Oil filter mounted along left side of crankcase. Increased capacity from battery and air cooled generator. Manual advance on distributor eliminated. Six point engine suspension (four corners of engine plus dual mount at rear of transmission).

Fan mounted closer to radiator. Close fitting fan shroud adjustable and must be moved up or down on radiator as fan assembly is moved for adjustment of belt tension. Radiator of full-bonded-fin construction. Thermostat controlled shutters retained.

I.D. DATA: There were no serial numbers used for the Series 355-B Cadillac. Engine numbers were stamped on crankcase near the water inlet on the right hand side. Starting: 1200001. Ending: 1202700.

Job No.	Body Type & Seating	Price	Weight	Prod. Total
Fisher 134" W.B.				
32-8-155	2-dr. Rds.-2/4P	2895	4635	—
32-8-178	2-dr. Cpe.-2/4P	2795	4705	—
32-8-168	2-dr. Conv. Cpe.-2/4P	2945	4675	—
32-8-159	4-dr. Std. Sed.-5P	2895	4885	—
Fisher 140" W.B.				
32-8-256	4-dr. Std. Phaeton-5P	2995	4700	—
32-8-280	4-dr. Spec. Phaeton-5P	3095	4750	—
32-8-273	4-dr. All Wthr. Phae.-5P	3495	5070	—
32-8-279	4-dr. Spt. Phae.-5P	3245	4800	—
32-8-272	2-dr. Cpe.-5P	2995	4715	—
32-8-259	4-dr. Spec. Sed.-5P	3045	4965	—
32-8-252	4-dr. Town Sed.-5P	3095	4980	—
32-8-262	4-dr. Sed.-7P	3145	5110	—
32-8-263	4-dr. Imp. Sed.-7P	3295	5150	—

Style No.	Body Type & Seating	Price	Weight	Prod. Total
Fleetwood 140" W.B.				
4930-S	4-dr. Sed.-5P	3395	4965	—
4975-S	4-dr. Sed.-7P	3545	5110	—
4975	4-dr. Limo-7P	3745	5150	—
4981	2-dr. Twn. Cpe.-5P	3395	4915	—
4912	4-dr. Twn. Cab.-5/7P	4095	4990	—
4991	4-dr. Limo. Brgm.-7P	4245	5100	—
4925	4-dr. Twn. Cab.-7P	4245	5100	—
4975-H4	4-dr. Limo.-7P	—	—	—
4985	2-dr. Conv. Cpe.-5P	—	—	—

1932 Cadillac, Series 355-B, phaeton, JAC

ENGINE: [Series 355-B] Ninety degree L-head. Eight. Cast Iron on Aluminum crankcase. B & S: 3-3/8 x 4-15/16 in. Disp.: 353 cu. in. C.R.: 5.38:1 std.; 5.70:1, 5.20 opt. Brake H.P.: 115 @ 3000 R.P.M. SAE Taxable/H.P.: 36.45. Main bearings: Three. Valve lifters: Mechanical. Carb.: Cad/Johnson.

CHASSIS: [Series: 355-B] W.B.: 134, 140 in. O.L.: 207, 213 in. Frt/Rear Tread: 59-7/8 // 61 in. Tires: 7.00 x 17. Series: 355-B Comm. Chassis. W.B.: 156 in.

TECHNICAL: Selective, synchro transmission. Speeds: 3F/1R. LHD., center controls, RHD opt. Twin disc clutch — selective vacuum-activation. Shaft drive, torque tube. 3/4 floating rear axle, spiral bevel drive. Overall ratio: 4.36:1, 4.60:1. Mechanical brakes on four wheels, (15" drums). Wire wheels std. Demountable wood opt. Wheel size: 17 in. drop center.

OPTIONS: Tire cover(s) ($5-$20 each). Trunks ($100-$180). Heron or Goddess ($20). Radio (Price on application). Heater ($37.50-$47.50). Auxiliary lights ($37.50-$57.50). Wind Wings ($25-$47.50). Tonneau Shield ($185). Seat covers ($26.50-$73.50). Mirrors ($8-$16 each). Full covers for wire wheels ($10 each). 6 Wire wheels w/fender wells and trunk rack ($130). 5 Demountable wood wheels ($30). 6 Demount. wood wheels w/wells and rack ($166). Colored fender set. ($50).

HISTORICAL: Introduced January, 1932. Model year sales: 2700. Model year production: 2700. The president & general manager was Lawrence P. Fisher.

1932 Cadillac, Series 370-B, V-12, touring, OCW

CADILLAC — SERIES 370-B — TWELVE: Overall styling and appearance identical to V-8, except for emblems.

Mechanical features same as V-8, except for minor differences dictated by increased power and weight (gear ratios, tire size, vacuum assist on brakes, battery/generator capacity). Dual exhaust system has tuning chambers in mufflers rather than attached to tail pipes. Dual ignition coils are mounted in top tank of radiator.

The engine is basically the same as the 370-A. Fuel feed changed from vacuum tank to mechanical pump. New Cuno disc type self-cleaning oil filter mounted at right hand side of clutch housing; connected to starter pedal to rotate discs each time pedal is depressed. New Detroit Lubricator dual carburetors are first departure by Cadillac in twenty years from a Cad/Johnson carburetor.

I.D. DATA: Serial numbers were not used. Engine numbers were stamped on the right hand side of the crankcase on the generator drive chain housing. Starting: 1300001. Ending: 1301740.

Job No.	Body Type & Seating	Price	Weight	Prod. Total
Fisher 134" W.B.				
32-12-155	2-dr. Rds.-2/4P	3595	4870	—
32-12-178	2-dr. Cpe.-2/4P	3495	4085	—
32-12-168	2-dr. Conv. Cpe.-2/4P	3645	5060	—
32-12-159	4-dr. Std. Sed.-5P	3595	5175	—

1932 Cadillac, Series 370-B, V-12, convertible coupe, JAC

Job No.	Body Type & Seating	Price	Weight	Prod. Total
Fisher 140" W.B.				
32-12-236	4-dr. Std. Phae.-5P	3695	5240	—
32-12-280	4-dr. Spec. Phae.-5P	3795	5290	—
32-12-273	4-dr. All Wthr. Phae.-5P	4195	5385	—
32-12-279	4-dr. Spt. Phae.-5P	3945	5340	—
32-12-272	2-dr. Cpe.-5P	3695	5220	—
32-12-259	4-dr. Spec. Sed.-5P	3745	5345	—
32-12-252	4-dr. Twn. Sed.-5P	3795	5370	—
32-12-262	4-dr. Sed.-7P	3845	5460	—
32-12-263	4-dr. Imp. Sed.-7P	3995	5500	—

Style No.	Body Type & Seating	Price	Weight	Prod. Total
Fleetwood 140" W.B.				
5030-S	4-dr. Sed.-5P	4095	5345	—
5075-S	4-dr. Sed.-7P	4245	5460	—
5075	4-dr. Limo.-7P	4445	5500	—
5081	2-dr. Twn. Cpe.-5P	4095	5225	—
5012	4-dr. Twn. Cab.-5/7P	4795	5380	—
5091	4-dr. Limo. Brgm.-7P	4945	5580	—
5025	4-dr. Twn. Cab.-7P	4945	5580	—
Fleetwood 140" W.B. Special				
5029	Imp.-5P	—	—	—
5030	4-dr. Imp. Sed.-5P	—	—	—
5030-FL	4-dr. Imp. Cab.-5P	—	—	—
5030-SFL	4-dr. Imp. Cab.-5P	—	—	—
5031	Imp. Sed.-5P	—	—	—
5031-S	Sed.-5P	—	—	—
5055	Imp. Sed.-5P	—	—	—
5055-C	Coll. Imp. Sed.-5P	—	—	—
5056	Imp. Cab.-5P	—	—	—
5057	Tr.-7P	4895	5295	—
5065	Imp. Sed.-7P	—	—	—
5075-FL	4-dr. Limo. Cab.-7P	—	—	—
5075-H4	Imp. Sed.-7P	—	—	—
5082	Sed.-5P	—	—	—
5085	2-dr. Conv. Cpe.-5P	4995	5200	—

1932 Cadillac, Series 370-B, V-12, town sedan, JAC

ENGINE: 45 degree overhead vlave. Twelve. Cast Iron on Aluminum crankcase. B & S: 3-1/8 x 4 in. Disp.: 368 cu. in. C.R.: 5.30:1 std.; 5.08:1, 4.90:1 opt. Brake H.P.: 135 @ 3400 R.P.M. SAE/Taxable H.P.: 46.9. Main bearings: Four. Valve lifters: Mechanical w/hydraulic silencer on rocker bushing. Carb.: Detroit Lubricator Type L-13, R-13/Model 51.

CHASSIS: [Series 370-B] W.B.: 134, 140 in. O.L.: 207, 213 in. Frt/Rear Tread: 59-7/8 / 61 in. Tires: 7.50 x 17. [Series 370-B Comm. Chassis] W.B.: 156 in.

TECHNICAL: Selective, synchro transmission. Speeds: 3F/1R. LHD, Center control, RHD opt. Twin disc clutch — selective vacuum-activation. Shaft drive, torque tube. 3/4 floating rear axle, spiral bevel drive. Overall Ratio: 4.60:1, 4.80:1. Mechanical brakes on four wheels, with vacuum assist (15" drums). Wire wheels std. Demountable wood opt. Wheel size: 17 in. Drop center.

OPTIONS: Tire cover(s) (5.00-20.00 each). Trunks (100.00-180.00). Heron or Goddess (20.00). Radio (price on application). Heater (37.50-47.50). Auxiliary lights (37.50-57.50). Wind wings (25.00-47.50). Tonneau Shield (185.00). Seat Covers (26.50-73.50). Mirrors (8.00-16.00 each). Full covers for wire wheels (10.00 each). 6 wire wheels w/fender wells and trunk rack (150.00). 5 demountable wood wheels (30.00). 6 demountable wd. whls. w/wells and rack (186.00). Colored fender set (50.00).

HISTORICAL: Introduced January, 1932. Model year sales: 1740. Model year production: 1740. The president & general manager was Lawrence P. Fisher.

CADILLAC — SERIES 452-B — SIXTEEN: Styling and appearance same as V-8 and V-12, except for emblems and longer hood with seven ports. A few Fleetwood body styles had an 18 degree rather than the typical 12 degree windshield. Some body styles achieved the ultimate proportions — radiator over front axle, windshield midway between the axles, and all seating between the axles.

With the longer wheelbase and more power and weight, some mechanical details were beefed up versions of the V-8, V-12 designs (10" deep frame, heavier axles, 18" rims, 11" clutch, 16" brake drums, different gear ratios, greater battery/generator capacity).

The engine remained basically the same as in 30-31. As on the V-12, carburetors were changed to Detroit Lubricator, and oil filter was changed to Cuno. Fuel feed was by mechanical pump. Intake silencers with filter took place of the vacuum tanks on the dash. In a departure from the smooth, uncluttered look of the earlier V-16, the spark plug wires sprouted from the top of the distributor cap. A more efficient and dependable design, but a real compromise in appearance.

I.D. DATA: Serial numbers were not used. Engine numbers were stamped on the right hand side of the crankcase on the generator drive chain housing. Starting: 1400001. Ending: 1400300.

Job No. Fisher 143" w.b.	Body Type & Seating	Price	Weight	Prod. Total
32-16-155	2-dr. Rds.-2/4P	4595	5065	—
32-16-178	2-dr. Cpe.-2/4P	4495	5530	—
32-16-168	2-dr. Conv. Cpe.-2/4P	4645	5505	—
32-16-159	4-dr. Std. Sed.-5P	4595	5625	—
Fisher 149" w.b.				
32-16-256	4-dr. Std. Phae.-5P	4695	5400	—
32-16-280	4-dr. Spec. Phae.-5P	4795	5450	—
32-16-273	4-dr. All Wthr. Phae.-5P	5195	5525	—
32-16-279	4-dr. Spt. Phae.-5P	4945	5500	—
32-16-252	4-dr. Twn. Sed.-5P	—	—	—
32-16-259	4-dr. Spec. Sed.-5P	—	—	—
32-16-262	4-dr. Sed.-7P	—	—	—
32-16-263	4-dr. Imp. Sed.-7P	—	—	—
32-16-272	2-dr. Cpe.-5P	—	—	—

Style No. Fleetwood 149" w.b.	Body Type & Seating	Price	Weight	Prod. Total
5130-S	4-dr. Sed.-5P	5095	5735	—
5175-S	4-dr. Sed.-7P	5245	5865	—
5175	4-dr. Limo.-7P	5445	5905	—
5181	2-dr. Twn. Cpe.-5P	5095	5605	—
5112	4-dr. Twn. Cab.-5/7P	5795	5775	—
5191	4-dr. Limo. Brgm.-7P	5945	5935	—
5125	4-dr. Twn. Cab.-7P	5945	5935	—
Fleetwood 149" w.b. Special				
5112-C	4-dr. Coll. Twn. Cab.-5/7P	—	—	—
5120	4-dr. Trans. Twn. Cab.-7P	—	—	—
5125	4-dr. Trans. Twn. Cab.-7P	—	—	—
5125-C	4-dr. Coll. Tr. Twn. Cab.-7P	—	—	—
5125-Q	4-dr. Trans. Cab.-7P	—	—	—
5129	4-dr. Imp.-5P	—	—	—
5130-FL	4-dr. Imp. Cab.-5P	—	—	—
5130-SFL	4-dr. Sed. Cab.-5P	—	—	—
5131	4-dr. Imp. Sed.-5P	—	—	—
5131-S	4-dr. Imp. Sed.-5P	—	—	—
5140-B	Spec. Sed.-5P	—	—	—
5155	4-dr. Imp. Sed.-5P	—	—	—
5155-C	4-dr. Coll. Imp. Sed.-5P	—	—	—
5156-C	4-dr. Coll. Imp. Sed.-5P	—	—	—
5164	4-dr. Trans. Twn. Brgm.-7P	—	—	—
5165	4-dr. Imp. Limo.-7P	—	—	—
5175-C	4-dr. Coll. Limo.-7P	—	—	—
5175-FL	4-dr. Limo. Cab.-7P	—	—	—
5175-H4	4-dr. Imp. Sed.-7P	—	—	—
5185	2-dr. Conv. Cpe.-5P	—	—	—
Fleetwood 165" w.b. Special				
5177	4-dr. Imp.-8P	—	—	—

1932 Cadillac, Series 452-B, V-16, town sedan, JAC

ENGINE: [Series 452-B] 45 degree overhead valve. Sixteen cylinders. Cast iron on aluminum crankcase. B & S: 3 x 4 in. Disp.: 452 cu. in. C.R.: 5.36 1 std.; 5.00:1, 4.90:1 opt. Brake H.P.: 165 @ 3400 R.P.M. Taxable H.P.: 57.5. Main bearings: Five. Valve Lifters: Mechanical w/hydraulic silencer on rocker bushing. Carb.: Detroit lubricator type L-14, R-14/Model 51.

216

CHASSIS: [Series 452-B] W.B.: 143, 149 in. O.L.: 216, 222 in. Frt/Rear Tread 59-7/8 / 61 in. Tires: 7.50 x 18.

TECHNICAL: Selective synchro transmission. Speeds: 3F/1R. LHD, Center control, RHD opt. Twin disc-clutch — Selective vacuum-activation. Shaft drive torque tube. 3/4 floating rear axle, spiral bevel drive. Overall ratio: 4.31:1, 4.64:1. Mechanical brakes on four wheels with vacuum assist (16" drums.) Wire wheels std. Demountable wood opt. Wheel size: 18 in. drop center.

OPTIONS: Tire covers (5-20 each). Trunks (100-180). Heron or Goddess (20). Radio (Price on application). Heater (37.50-47.50). (37.50-57.50). Wind Wings (25-47.50). Tonneau Shield (185). Seat Covers (26.50-73.50). Mirrors (8-16 each). Full covers for wire wheels (10 each). 6 Wire wheels w/fender wells and trunk racks (150). 5 demountable wood wheels (30). 6 demount. wd. whls. w/wells and rack (186). Colored fender set (50).

1932 Cadillac, Series 452-B, V-16, all-weather phaeton, JAC

HISTORICAL: Introduced January, 1932. Model year sales: 300. Model year production: 300. The president & general manager was Lawrence P. Fisher.

1932

Series 355B, V-8, 134" wb	FP	5	4	3	2	1
Rds	2895	14,400	28,800	48,000	76,000	96,000
Conv	2945	14,100	28,200	57,000	74,000	94,000
2P Cpe	2795	9000	18,000	30,000	42,000	60,000
Sed	2895	7500	15,000	25,000	35,000	50,000
Fisher Line, 140" wb						
Std Phae	2995	14,400	28,800	48,000	76,000	96,000
D W Phae	3095	17,100	31,800	53,000	85,000	106,000
D C Spt Phae	3245	18,500	33,000	55,000	88,000	110,000
A/W Phae	3495	17,100	31,800	53,000	85,000	106,000
Cpe	2995	9900	19,800	33,000	46,200	66,000
Spec Sed	3045	7800	15,600	26,000	36,400	52,000
Twn Sed	3095	7950	15,900	26,500	37,100	53,000
Imp Sed	3295	8250	16,500	27,500	38,500	55,000
Fleetwood Bodies, 140" wb						
Sed	3395	8250	16,500	27,500	38,500	55,000
Twn Cpe	3395	9900	19,800	33,000	46,200	66,000
7P Sed	3545	9000	18,000	30,000	42,000	60,000
7P Limo	3745	9900	19,800	33,000	46,200	66,000
5P Twn Car	4095	10,800	21,600	36,000	50,500	72,000
Twn Cabr	4245	10,800	21,600	36,000	50,500	72,000
Limo Brgm	4245	10,500	21,000	35,000	49,000	70,000
Series 370-B, V-12, 134" wb						
Rds	3595	33,500	61,000	94,000	120,000	165,000
Conv	3645	24,100	42,000	68,000	98,000	126,000
2P Cpe	3495	9900	19,800	33,000	46,200	66,000
Std Sed	3595	7650	15,300	25,500	35,700	51,000
Series 370-B, V-12, 140" wb						
Fisher Bodies						
Std Phae	3695	31,900	59,000	90,000	116,000	155,000
Spec Phae	3795	32,700	60,000	92,000	118,000	160,000
Spt Phae	3945	33,500	61,000	94,000	120,000	165,000
A/W Phae	4195	32,700	60,000	92,000	118,000	160,000
5P Cpe	3695	11,100	22,200	37,000	52,000	74,000
Spec Sed	3745	10,800	21,600	36,000	50,500	72,000
Twn Sed	3795	9300	18,600	31,000	43,400	62,000
7P Sed	3845	9600	19,200	32,000	44,800	64,000
7P Imp	3995	9900	19,800	33,000	46,200	66,000
Series 370-B, V-12, 140" wb						
Fleetwood Bodies						
Tr	4295	33,500	61,000	94,000	120,000	165,000
Conv	4045	34,300	62,000	96,000	122,000	170,000
Sed	4995	9900	19,800	33,000	46,200	66,000
Twn Cpe	5700	11,100	22,200	37,000	52,000	74,000
7P Sed	5075	9600	19,200	32,000	44,800	64,000
Limo	5275	9600	19,200	32,000	44,800	64,000
5P Twn Cabr	5700	22,000	36,000	60,000	93,000	120,000
7P Twn Cabr	5850	20,600	34,800	58,000	91,000	116,000
Limo Brgm	5850	15,000	30,000	50,000	80,000	100,000
Series 452-B, V-16, 143" wb						
Fisher Bodies						
Rds	4595	40,000	70,000	110,000	140,000	200,000
Conv	4645	39,000	69,000	108,000	137,000	195,000
Cpe	4495	15,000	30,000	50,000	80,000	100,000
Std Sed	4595	9900	19,800	33,000	46,200	66,000
Series 452-B, V-16, 149" wb						
Fisher Bodies						
Std Phae	4695	41,000	72,000	113,000	144,000	205,000
Spec Phae	4795	43,000	76,000	119,000	151,000	215,000
Spt Phae	4945	45,000	79,000	124,000	158,000	225,000
A/W Phae	5195	43,000	76,000	119,000	151,000	215,000
Fleetwood Bodies, V-16						
5P Sed	5095	10,800	21,600	36,000	50,500	72,000
Imp Limo	5945	11,400	22,800	38,000	56,000	76,000
Twn Cpe	5095	11,700	23,400	39,000	60,000	78,000
7P Sed	5245	11,100	22,200	37,000	52,000	74,000
7P Twn Cabr	5945	17,100	31,800	53,000	85,000	106,000
5P Twn Cabr	5795	18,500	33,000	55,000	88,000	110,000
Limo Brgm	5945	18,500	33,000	55,000	88,000	110,000

1933

1933 Cadillac, Series 355-C, Fleetwood sedan, OCW

CADILLAC — SERIES 355-C — EIGHT: In the mid twenties, Cadillac broke with functional body design and began a period of "stylish functional". The 1933 "C" cars ushered in the period of styling/streamlining for its own sake. A face lift, simple in execution but startling in effect, transformed the "B" cars and started the concept of selling cars on the basis of styling features and selling replacement cars on the basis of changes in style.

Bumpers were sectioned, with plain ends and a three-bar center. The grill was made Vee-shaped and blended into the painted (chrome optional) radiator shell. The radiator filler cap disappeared under the hood on the right side (same side as the oil level gauge). The fender tie-bar, after a year's absence, was sectioned and the center section hidden behind the grill. Six horizontal doors replaced the vertical hood doors. Skirts (valances) were added to front and rear fenders. The most significant change in body detail was the introduction of no-draft Individually Controlled Ventilation (I.C.V.) or pivoting vent windows in the front doors and rear quarter or rear door windows. In early production, the front door window had to be lowered to disengage the channel at its front edge from the vent window to allow the vent window to pivot. In later production, the sealing channel was attached to the door frame rather than the window glass so that the vent window could be operated independently of the window glass. Windshield and rear quarter windows were made stationary. Absence of windshield operating mechanism on closed cars allowed room to conceal wiper motor behind the headboard. The cowl ventilator was baffled and drained in such a way as to be rainproof. Chassis changes were few and of minor nature. Controlled free wheeling was discontinued. Vacuum assist was added to the V-8 brake system. Changes in shock absorber valves extended the range of the ride control system. At engine unit number 30-3607; the dual point, four lobe distributer was replaced by a single point, eight lobe unit.

I.D. DATA: Serial numbers were not used. Engine numbers were stamped on crankcase near the water inlet on the right hand side. Starting: 3000001. Ending: 3002100.

Job No.	Body Type & Seating	Price	Weight	Prod. Total
Fisher 134" wb				
33-8-155	2-dr. Rds.-2/4P	2795	—	—
33-8-168	2-dr. Conv. Cpe.-2/4P	2845	4825	—
33-8-178	2-dr. Cpe.-2/4P	2695	4855	—
Fisher 140" wb				
33-8-252	4-dr. Sed.-5P	2995	5060	—
33-8-256	4-dr. Phae.-5P	2895	4865	—
33-8-259	4-dr. Sed.-5P	2895	5000	—
33-8-262	4-dr. Sed.-7P	3045	5105	—
33-8-263	4-dr. Imp. Sed.-7P	3195	5140	—
33-8-272	2-dr. Cpe.-5P	2895	4850	—
33-8-273	4-dr. All Wthr. Phae.-5P	3395	5110	—
Style No.	**Body Type & Seating**	**Price**	**Weight**	**Prod. Total**
Fleetwood 140" wb				
5330-S	4-dr. Sed.-5P	3295	5000	—
5375-S	4-dr. Sed.-7P	3445	5140	—
5375	4-dr. Limo.-7P	3645	—	—
NA	2-dr. Cpe.-5P	—	—	—
5312	4-dr. Trans. Twn. Cab.-5/7P	3995	—	—
5391	4-dr. Trans. Limo. Brgm.-7P	4145	—	—
5325	4-dr. Trans. Twn. Cab.-7P	4145	—	—
5357	4-dr. Tr.-7P	—	—	—
5381	2-dr. Twn. Cpe.-5P	—	—	—
5312-C	4-dr. Coll. Trans. Twn. Cab.-5/7P	—	—	—
5325-C	4-dr. Coll. Trans. Twn. Cab.-7P	—	—	—
5375-C	4-dr. Coll. Limo.-7P	—	—	—
5375-H4	Limo. w/4" extra headroom-7P	—	—	—
5330-FL	4-dr. Imp. Cabr.-5P	—	—	—
5375-FL	4-dr. Imp. Cabr.-7P	—	—	—
5364	4-dr. Trans. Twn. Brgm.-5P	—	—	—
5320	4-dr. Trans. Twn. Cabr.-7P	—	—	—

ENGINE: [Series 355-C] Ninety degree L-Head. Eight. Cast Iron on Aluminum crankcase. B & S: 3-5/8 x 4-15/16 in. Disp.: 353 cu. in. C.R.: 5.4:1 std., 5.7:1 opt. Brake H.P.: 115 @ 3000 R.P.M. H.P.: 36.45. Main bearings: Three. Valve lifters: Mechanical. Carb.: Cad/Johnson.

CHASSIS: [Series 355-C] W.B.: 134, 140 in. O.L.: approx. 207-213 in. Frt/Rear Tread: 59-7/8 / 61 in. Tires: 7.00 x 17. [Series Semi-Comm. Chassis] W.B.: 156 in.

TECHNICAL: Selective, synchro transmission. Speeds: 3F/1R. LHD, Center control, RHD optional. Twin disc clutch. Shaft drive, torque tube. 3/4 floating rear axle, spiral bevel drive. Overall ratio: 4.36:1, 4.60:1. Mechanical brakes on four wheels with vacuum assist. (15" drums.) Wire wheels std. Demountable wood opt. Wheel size: 17 in. Drop center.

OPTIONS: Sidemount cover(s). Wheel discs (chrome 10.00 each/ Body color 12.50 ea.) Radio (Standard 64.50, Imperial 74.50). Heater Hot air or hot water. Draft deflector for Conv. Cpe. (35/pair). Luggage sets (37.00-110.00). Trunks w/luggage (104.00-180.00). Seat Covers (10.00/seat). Mirrors. Spotlight Lorraine (24.50). Dual Pilot Ray Lights (44.50). Heron radiator ornament (20.00). Six wire wheels with fender wells. Five demountable wood wheels. Six demountable wood wheels with fender wells.

HISTORICAL: Introduced January, 1933. Innovations: Fisher no-draft individually controlled ventilation (I.C.V.) (Vent windows). Model year sales: 2100. Model year production: 2100. The President & General Manager was Lawrence P. Fisher.

CADILLAC — SERIES 370-C — TWELVE: The only way to tell the difference between the V-8 and V-12 Cadillac for 1933 is to check the emblems or look under the hood. (Lift the left side to check water level in the radiator — the filler cap and oil level gauge are on the left side on V-12 and V-16, on the right side on V-8's.)

I.D. DATA: Serial numbers were not used. Engine numbers were stamped on the right hand side of the crankcase on the generator drive chain housing. Starting: 4000001. Ending: 4000953.

Job No.	Body Type & Seating	Price	Weight	Prod. Total
Fisher 134" w.b.				
33-12-155	Rds.-2/4P	3495	—	—
33-12-168	Conv. Cpe.-2/4P	3545	5125	—
33-12-178	Cpe.-2/4P	3395	5165	—
Fisher 140" w.b.				
33-12-252	Twn. Sed.-5P	3695	5385	—
33-12-256	Phae.-5P	3595	—	—
33-12-259	Sed.-5P	3595	5335	—
33-12-262	Sed.-7P	3745	5440	—
33-12-263	Imp. Sed.-7P	3895	5500	—
33-12-272	Cpe.-5P	3595	—	—
33-12-273	All Wthr. Phae.-5P	4095	5405	—
Style No.	**Body Type & Seating**	**Price**	**Weight**	**Prod. Total**
Fleetwood 140" w.b.				
5430-S	4-dr. Sed.-5P	3995	5335	—
5475-S	4-dr. Sed.-7P	4145	5440	—
5475	4-dr. Limo.-7P	4345	5500	—
NA	2-dr. Cpe.-5P	—	—	—
5412	4-dr. Trans. Twn. Cab.-5/7P	4695	—	—
5425	4-dr. Trans. Twn. Cab.-7P	4845	—	—
5491	4-dr. Trans. Limo. Brgm.-7P	4845	—	—
5420	4-dr/ Trans. Twn. Cab.-7P	—	—	—
5425-C	4-dr. Coll. Trans. Twn. Cab.-7P	—	—	—
5430-FL	4-dr. Imp. Cabr.-5P	—	—	—
5455	4-dr. Imp. Cab. (Madame X)-5/7P	—	—	—
5457-A	4-dr. Tr.-7P	—	—	—
5464	4-dr. Trans. Twn. Brgm.-7P	—	—	—
5475-H4	4-dr. Limo. w/4" extra headroom-7P	—	—	—
5475-FL	Limo. Cabr.-7P	—	—	—
5481	2-dr. Twn. Cpe.-5P	—	—	—
5482	4-dr. Sedanette-5P	—	—	—
5485	2-dr. Conv. Coupe-5P	—	—	—

ENGINE: 45 degree overhead value. Twelve cyl. Cast iron on aluminum crankcase. B & S: 3-1/8 x 4. Disp.: 368 cu. in. C.R.: 5.4:1 std.; 5.4:1, 5.1:1 opt. Brake H.P.: 135 @ 3400 R.P.M. H.P.: 46.9. Main bearings: Four. Valve lifters: mech. w/hydraulic silencer on rocker bushing. Carb.: Detroit Lubricator Type L-13, R-13/Model 51.

CHASSIS: [Series: 370-C] W.B.: 134, 140 in. Length: approx. 207-213 in. Frt/Rear Tread: 59-7/8 / 61 in. Tires: 7.50 x 17. Semi-comm. chassis. W.B.: 156 in.

TECHNICAL: Selective, synchro transmission. 3F/1R. LHD, Center control, RHD optional. Twin disc clutch. Shaft drive, torque tube. 3/4 Floating rear axle, spiral bevel drive. Overall Ratio: 4.60:1, 4.80:1. Mechanical brakes on four wheels with vacuum assist. (15" drums.) Wire wheels std. Demountable wood opt. Wheel size: 17 in. drop center.

OPTIONS: Sidemount cover (s). Wheel discs (chrome 10.00 each/body color 12.50 ea.). Radio (Standard 64.50, Imperial 74.50). Heater hot air or hot water. Draft deflector for conv. cpe. (35.00/pair). Luggage sets (37.00-110.00). Trunks w/luggage (104.00-180.00). Seat Covers (10.00/seat). Mirrors. Lorraine (24.50). Dual Pilot Ray Lights (44.50). Dual Pilot Ray Lights (44.50). Heron radiator ornament (20.00). Six wire wheels with fender wells. Five demountable wood wheels. Six demountable wood wheels with fender wells.

HISTORICAL: Introduced January, 1933. Innovations: Fisher no-draft individually controlled ventilation (I.C.V.) (Vent windows). Model year sales: 953. Model year production: 953. The General Manager was Lawrence P. Fisher.

1933 Cadillac, Series 452-C, V-16, coupe, OCW

CADILLAC — SERIES 452-C — SIXTEEN: For 1933, Cadillac announced that V-16 production would be limited to 400 cars. These were to be serially numbered — the number and the owner's name to be displayed on a plate inside the car. Nearly seventy body styles were suggested. Half this number of styles were actually built, but one half the total production of 126 cars was in the five most conservative five or seven passenger sedan styles.

V-16's had the Vee-shaped grill/radiator shell, skirted fenders, and no-draft ventilation common to the full line. Detail distinction was achieved with a new, winged goddess mascot; large, spinner hub caps; absence of crankhole cover in the grill; and an awkward, four-bar bumper. Hood side panels carried two vertical doors plus three stylized horizontal louvers. Vertical louvers on front fender skirts, shown in promotional literature and used on mockups, were replaced in "production" by three horizontal louvers matching the hood louvers.

Some new styling details were shown on various bodies. Instead of ending at the front of the cowl, some hoods were extended back over the cowl to the windshield. Many four door bodies sported a rear body panel which swept back over the fuel tank, with a door opening for carrying parcels. At least one open and one closed four door design offered a built-in trunk. A few styles even retained the "Madame X" look seen on some of the first V-16's.

Mechanical changes were few. A higher compression ratio was available to utilize improved gasolines. Except on early production, wheel size was reduced from 18" to 17". Beginning with engine unit number 50-24, the starter ring gear was moved from the clutch center-plate to the flywheel — same as on the V-8 and V-12.

I.D. DATA: Serial numbers were not used. Engine numbers were stamped on the right hand side of the crankcase on the generator drive chain housing. Starting: 5000001. Ending: 5000126.

Job No.	Body Type & Seating	Price	Weight	Prod. Total
Fisher 143" w.b.				
33-16-168	2-dr. Conv. Cpe.-2/4P	—	—	—
33-16-272	2-dr. Cpe.-5P	—	—	—
Style No.	**Body Type & Seating**	**Price**	**Weight**	**Prod. Total**
Fleetwood 143" w.b.				
5508	2-dr. Conv. Cpe.-2/4P	—	—	—
5509	2-dr. Cpe.-2/4P	—	—	—
Fleetwood 149" w.b.				
5502	2-dr. Rds.-2/4P	—	—	—
5512	4-dr. Twn. Cab.-5/7P	6850	6110	—
5513	4-dr. Twn. Cab.-5/7P	—	—	—
5514	4-dr. Twn. Cab.-5/7P	—	—	—
5520	4-dr. Twn. Cab.-7P	—	—	—
5521	4-dr. Twn. Cab.-7P	—	—	—
5524	4-dr. Twn. Cab.-7P	—	—	—
5525	4-dr. Twn. Cab.-7P	6850	6270	—
5526	4-dr. Twn. Cab.-7P	—	—	—
5530	4-dr. Imp. Sed.-5P	—	—	—
5530-S	4-dr. Sed.-5P	6250	6070	—
5530-FL	4-dr. Imp. Sed. Cab.-5/7P	—	—	—
5530-SFL	4-dr. Sed. Cab.-5/7P	—	—	—
5530-H4	4-dr. Imp. Sed.-5P	—	—	—
5531	4-dr. Imp. Sed.-5/7P	—	—	—
5531-S	4-dr. Sed.-5/7P	—	—	—
5532	4-dr. Imp. Sed.-5/7P	—	—	—
5532-S	4-dr. Sed.-5/7P	—	—	—
5533	4-dr. Twn. Imp.-5P	—	—	—
5533-S	4-dr. Twn. Sed.-5P	—	—	—
5535	2-dr. Conv. Cpe.-2/4P	—	—	—
5536	2-dr. Spt. Conv. Cpe.-2/4P	—	—	—
5540	4-dr. Imp. Cab.-5/7P	—	—	—
5540-S	4-dr. Sed. Cab.-5/7P	—	—	—
5545	4-dr. Imp. Cab.-5/7P	—	—	—
5545-S	4-dr. Sed. Cab.-5/7P	—	—	—
5550	4-dr. Full Coll. Twn. Cab.-7P	—	—	—
5555	4-dr. Imp. Cab.-5/7P	—	—	—
5555-C	4-dr. Coll. Imp. Cab.-5/7P	—	—	—
5557	4-dr. Tr.-7P	—	—	—
5558	4-dr. Phae.-5P	—	—	—
5559	4-dr. Spt. Phae.-5P	—	—	—

Job No.	Body Type & Seating	Price	Weight	Prod. Total
5560	4-dr. Spt. Phae.-5P	—	—	—
5561	4-dr. Close Cpld. Imp.-5P	—	—	—
5561-S	4-dr. Close Cpld. Sed.-5P	—	—	—
5563	4-dr. Spt. Imp.-5/7P	—	—	—
5563-S	4-dr. Spt. Sed.-5/7P	—	—	—
5564	4-dr. Twn. Brgm.-5/7P	—	—	—
5564-B	4-dr. Twn. Brgm. w/cane-5/7P	—	—	—
5565	4-dr. Limo.-7P	—	—	—
5565	4-dr. Sed.-7P	—	—	—
5566	4-dr. Limo.-7P	—	—	—
5566-S	4-dr. Sed.-7P	—	—	—
5573	4-dr. Limo.-7P	—	—	—
5573-S	4-dr. Sed.-7P	—	—	—
5574	4-dr. Imp. Cab.-7P	—	—	—
5574-S	4-dr. Sed.-7P	—	—	—
5575	4-dr. Limo.-7P	6600	6270	—
5575-S	4-dr. Sed.-7P	6400	6200	—
5575-FL	4-dr. Imp. Cab.-7P	—	—	—
5575-SFL	4-dr. Sed. Cab.-7P	—	—	—
5576	2-dr. Cpe.-2/4P	—	—	—
5577	2-dr. Spt. Cpe.-2/4P	—	—	—
5578	4-dr. All Wthr. Spt. Phae.-5P	—	—	—
5579	4-dr. All Wthr. Phae.-5P	8000	6110	—
5579-A	4-dr. All Wthr. Phae.-5P	—	—	—
5580	4-dr. Conv. Phae.-5P	—	—	—
5581	2-dr. Twn. Cpe.-5P	6250	6000	—
5583	2-dr. Cpe.-2P	—	—	—
5585	2-dr. Conv. Cpe.-5P	7500	5910	—
5586	2-dr. Conv. Cpe.-4P	—	—	—
5590	4-dr. Limo. Brgm.-7P	—	—	—
5591	4-dr. Limo. Brgm.-7P	6850	6300	—
5592	4-dr. Limo. Brgm.-7P	—	—	—
5599	2-dr. Aero Dyn. Cpe.-5P	—	—	—

1933 Cadillac, Series 452-C, V-16, 7-pass. sedan, JAC

ENGINE: [Series 452-C] 45 degree overhead valve. Sixteen. Cast iron on aluminum crankcase. B & S: 3 x 4 in. Disp.: 452 cu. in. C.R.: 5.7:1 std.; 5.4:1, 5.1:1 opt. Brake H.P.: 165 @ 3400 R.P.M. Taxable H.P.: 57.5. Main bearings: Five. Valve lifters: Mechanical w/hydraulic silencer on rocker bushing. Carb.: Detroit Lubricator Type L-14, R-14/Model 51.

CHASSIS: [Series 452-C] W.B.: 143, 149 in. O.L.: approx. 216-222 in. Frt/Rear Tread 59-7/8 / 61 in. Tires: 7.50 x 17.

TECHNICAL: Selective, synchro transmission. Speeds: 3F/1R. LHD, Center control, RHD optional. Twin disc clutch. Shaft drive, torque tube. 3/4 Floating rear axle, spiral bevel drive. Overall ratio: 4.31:1, 4.64:1. Mechanical brakes on four wheels with vacuum assist. (15" drums.) Wire wheels std. Demountable wood opt. Wheel size: 17 in. drop center.

1933 Cadillac, Series 452-C, V-16, 7-pass. limousine, JAC

218

OPTIONS: Wheel discs. Radio (Standard 64.50, Imperial 74.50). Heater hot air or hot water. Luggage sets (37.00-110.00). Trunks w/luggage (104.00-180.00). Mirrors. Spotlight Lorraine (24.50). Dual pilot ray lights (44.50). Goddess radiator ornament (Plated — gold 50.00, silver 40.00). Six wire wheels with fender wells. Five demountable wood wheels. Six demountable wood wheels with fender wells.

HISTORICAL: Introduced January, 1933. Innovations: Fisher no-draft individually controlled ventilation (I.C.V.) (Vent windows). The President & General Manager was Lawrence P. Fisher.

1933
Series 355C, V-8, 134" wb
Fisher Bodies

	FP	5	4	3	2	1
Rds	2795	18,500	33,000	55,000	88,000	110,000
Conv	2695	14,400	28,800	48,000	76,000	96,000
Cpe	2845	8550	17,100	28,500	39,900	57,000

Series 355C, V-8, 140" wb
Fisher Bodies

	FP	5	4	3	2	1
Phae	2895	17,100	31,800	53,000	85,000	106,000
A/W Phae	3395	15,000	30,000	50,000	80,000	100,000
5P Cpe	2895	8700	17,400	29,000	40,600	58,000
Sed	2895	8250	16,500	27,500	38,500	55,000
Twn Sed	2995	8400	16,800	28,000	39,200	56,000
7P Sed	3045	8550	17,100	28,500	39,900	57,000
Imp Sed	3195	9000	18,000	30,000	42,000	60,000

Series 355C, V-8, 140" wb
Fleetwood Line

	FP	5	4	3	2	1
5P Sed	2895	8550	17,100	28,500	39,900	57,000
7P Sed	3045	8700	17,400	29,000	40,600	58,000
Limo	2995	9000	18,000	30,000	42,000	60,000
5P Twn Cabr	2995	13,500	27,000	45,000	70,000	90,000
7P Twn Cabr	3045	13,800	27,600	46,000	73,500	92,000
Limo Brgm	3195	10,500	21,000	35,000	49,000	70,000

Series 370C, V-12, 134" wb
Fisher Bodies

	FP	5	4	3	2	1
Rds	3495	25,500	45,000	73,000	100,000	130,000
Conv	3545	17,100	31,800	53,000	85,000	106,000
Cpe	3395	11,400	22,800	38,000	56,000	76,000

Series, 370C, V-12, 140" wb
Fisher Bodies

	FP	5	4	3	2	1
Phae	3595	20,600	34,800	58,000	91,000	116,000
A/W Phae	4095	18,500	33,000	55,000	88,000	110,000
5P Cpe	3595	12,000	24,000	40,000	60,000	80,000
Sed	3595	10,200	20,400	34,000	47,600	68,000
Twn Sed	3695	10,500	21,000	35,000	49,000	70,000
7P Sed	3745	10,200	20,400	34,000	47,600	68,000
Imp Sed	3895	10,800	21,600	36,000	50,500	72,000

Series 370C, V-12, 140" wb
Fleetwood Line

	FP	5	4	3	2	1
Sed	3995	10,800	21,600	36,000	50,500	72,000
7P Sed	4145	10,800	21,600	36,000	50,500	72,000
Limo	4345	11,100	22,200	37,000	52,000	74,000
5P Twn Cabr	4695	15,000	30,000	50,000	80,000	100,000
7P Twn Cabr	4845	15,000	30,000	50,000	80,000	100,000
7P Limo Brgm	4845	12,000	24,000	40,000	60,000	80,000

Series 452-C V-16, 154" wb

	FP	5	4	3	2	1
Dual Cowl Spt Phae	—	40,000	70,000	110,000	140,000	200,000

Fleetwood Bodies, 149" wb

	FP	5	4	3	2	1
Conv	7500	35,100	63,000	98,000	124,000	175,000
A/W Phae	8000	35,900	64,000	100,000	126,000	180,000
Sed	6250	12,300	24,600	41,000	62,000	82,000
7P Sed	6400	12,300	24,600	41,000	62,000	82,000
Twn Cab	6850	31,100	58,000	88,000	114,000	150,000
7P Twn Cab	6850	31,100	58,000	88,000	114,000	150,000
7P Limo	6600	14,400	28,800	48,000	76,000	96,000
Limo Brgm	6850	15,000	30,000	50,000	80,000	100,000
5P Twn Cpe	6850	12,900	25,800	48,200	66,000	86,000
Imp Cab	5540	20,600	34,800	58,000	91,000	116,000

1934

1934 Cadillac, Model 355-D, convertible sedan, OCW

CADILLAC — MODEL 355-D — SERIES 10, 20, FLEETWOOD (30) — EIGHT: 1934 Cadillacs were completely restyled and mounted on an entirely new chassis, but used the same basic engines as in 1933.
Bodies: Bodies on the Series 10 and 20 cars were built by Fisher. Bodies on the V-8 Fleetwood Series were shared with the twelves and sixteens. Styling emphasized streamlining, including concealment of all chassis features except the wheels. Body construction was improved for better insulation against engine heat and reduction of engine, road, and wind noise. Bumpers were a stylish but ineffective biplane design, mounted against telescoping springs. The grill was Vee shaped and sloping, set into a painted shell. Although restricted use of chrome was a feature of the overall ornamentation, a chrome plated radiator shell was available as an option. Horns and radiator filler cap were concealed under the hood. Teardrop Guide Multibeam headlights were mounted on streamlined supports attached to the fenders. Parking lamps were mounted in the headlight supports. Airfoil shaped front fenders were brought low over the chassis. The hood sills were high, with the entire fender shape molded into the radiator shell. A curious horizontal crease broke the nose contour of the fenders. Hoods extending nearly to the windshield carried shutter type louvers in the side panel. Windshields were fixed and steeply sloping; 18 degrees flat on Fisher bodies, 25 degrees flat or 29-1/2 degrees Vee on Fleetwood bodies. Cowl vents opened toward the windshield; one vent on flat windshield bodies, two vents projecting through openings in the hood on Vee windshield bodies. Bodies were two inches lower than on previous models. Added passenger space in the front compartment was achieved by moving the hand brake lever to the left of the driver, under the instrument panel. On twelves and sixteens, the gearshift lever was moved forward to the clutch housing. Rear fenders were airfoil shaped and carried rear lights which matched the headlights. The gas tank filler on Fisher bodies was on the left side at the rear of the body; on Fleetwood bodies in the left rear fender. All bodies featured a beaver tail rear deck which completely covered the chassis. On Fleetwood bodies, the spare was concealed inside the rear deck, unless optional fender mounts were specified.
Chassis: Significant changes in chassis design resulted in improved riding and handling plus decreased driver fatigue. The new independent "knee action" front suspension with coil springs and center point steering resulted in greatly reduced unsprung weight. Front shocks were now an integral part of the suspension; the shock arm being the upper suspension arm. An inverted steering box, mounted on the outside of the frame, was used on Fleetwood bodied cars. Hotchkiss drive replaced the torque tube drive. Rear brakes were operated by pull rods and cables. A new frame of X design added to chassis strength and allowed for the reduction in overall vehicle height. A stabilizer bar to control body roll in turns was added at the rear of the chassis. The brake and clutch pedal assembly was relocated from transmission to frame. Mufflers on Fleetwood bodied cars were relocated to the outside of the frame. In Fisher bodies, the battery was under the front seat, on the right side. In the Fleetwood bodies, the battery was under the right front fender and was removed from underneath.
Engine: Engine changes were few, but horsepower was increased. All engines used Lynite Aluminum pistons. Compression ratios were increased. Intake ducting to the carburetor air cleaner was extended to the radiator casing, providing cold, dense air rather than the hot air in the engine compartment. The combination of Aluminum pistons, cold intake air, and higher compression with improved fuels resulted in increased horsepower and engine speeds. Detail changes in the V-8 engine included a change to Detroit Lubricator carburetor, use of dual valve springs, discontinuation of the oil filter, and solenoid starter control with starter button on instrument panel. One V-8 engine change to be appreciated by anyone removing a cylinder head was the change from head studs to cap screws. The change was actually made so that the heads could be turned before lifting, so as to clear the hood shelf. Another change, not necessarily appreciated was the elimination of provision for hand cranking.

I.D. DATA: Serial numbers were on top surface of frame side bar, right side, just ahead of dash. Same as engine number. Starting no.: 3100001. Ending: 3108318 (with 1935). Engine numbers were stamped on crankcase near the water inlet on the right hand side. Starting engine no.: 3100001. Ending: 3108318 (with 1935).

Style No.	Body Type & Seating	Price	Weight	Prod. Total
Series 10 Fisher 128 in. w.b.				
34728	2-dr. Spt. Cpe.-2/3P	2395	4550	—
34718	2-dr. Conv. Cpe.-2/4P	2495	4515	—
34721	4-dr. Conv. Sed.-5P	2695	4750	—
34722	2-dr. Twn. Cpe.-5P	2545	4630	—
34709	4-dr. Sed.-5P	2495	4715	—
34702	4-dr. Twn. Sed.-5P	2545	4735	—
Series 20 Fisher 136 in. w.b.				
34678	2-dr. Spt. Cpe.-2/3P	2595	4660	—
34668	2-dr. Conv. Cpe.-2/4P	2695	4625	—
34671	4-dr. Conv. Sed.-5P	2895	4860	—
34659	4-dr. Sed.-5P	2695	4825	—
34652	4-dr. Twn. Sed.-5P	2745	4815	—
34662	4-dr. Sed.-7P	2845	4945	—
34663	4-dr. Imp. Sed.-7P	2995	4970	—
Series Fleetwood (30) 146 in. w.b. Vee windshield				
Some listings show these as 56___ styles.				
5702	Rdst.-2P	—	—	—
5712-C	Coll. Twn. Cab.-5P	—	—	—
5712-LB	Twn. Cab.-5P	5495	5540	—
5712-MB	Twn. Cab.-5P	—	—	—
5720	Twn. Cab.-7P	—	—	—
5720-C	Coll. Twn. Cab.-7P	—	—	—
5725-B	Twn. Cab.-7P	—	—	—
5725-LB	Twn. Cab.-7P	5595	5650	—
5725-MB	Twn. Cab.-7P	—	—	—
5730	Imp. Sed.-5P	—	—	—
5730-FL	Imp. Cab.-5P	4145	5500	—
5730-FM	Imp. Brgm.-5P	—	—	—
5730-S	Sed.-5P	3745	5465	—
5733	Imp. Twn. Sed.-5P	—	—	—
5733-S	Twn. Sed.-5P	3795	5415	—
5735	Conv. Cpe.-2P	4045	5115	—
5757	Tr.-7P	—	—	—
5759	Spt. Phae.-5P	—	—	—
5775	Imp. Sed. (Limo.)-7P	4095	5580	—
5775-B	Limo.-7P	—	—	—
5775-E	Imp. Sed.-7P	—	—	—
5775-FL	Imp. Cab.-7P	4295	5580	—
5775-FM	Imp. Brgm.-7P	—	—	—
5775-H4	Imp. Sed.-7P	—	—	—
5775-S	Sed.-7P	3895	5545	—
5775-W	Limo.-7P	—	—	—
5776	Cpe.-2P	3895	5150	—

Style No.	Body Type & Seating	Price	Weight	Prod. Total
5780	Conv. Sed. w/div.-5P	4295	5465	—
5780-B	Conv. Sed.-5P	—	—	—
5780-S	Conv. Sed.-5P	5430	—	—
5785	Coll. Cpe.-5P	4295	5415	—
5788	Stat. Cpe.-5P	—	—	—
5789-A	Vict. Cpe.-4P	—	—	—
5791	Limo. Brgm.-7P	5495	5580	—
5791-B	Limo. Brgm.-7P	—	—	—
5799	Aero. Cpe.-5P	4295	5430	—

Series Fleetwood (30) 146 in. w.b. flat windshield

Style No.	Body Type & Seating	Price	Weight	Prod. Total
6030-B	Imp. Sed.-5P	—	—	—
6030-FL	Imp. Cab.-5P	3695	5500	—
6030-FM	Imp. Brgm.-5P	—	—	—
6030-S	Sed.-5P	3295	5465	—
6033-S	Twn. Sed.-5P	3345	5415	—
6035	Conv. Cpe.-2P	—	—	—
6075	Imp. Sed.-7P	3645	5580	—
6075-B	Limo. (spec. back)-7P	—	—	—
6075-D	Limo.-7P	—	—	—
6075-E	Limo.-7P	—	—	—
6075-FL	Imp. Cab.-7P	3845	5580	—
6075-FM	Imp. Brgm.-7P	—	—	—
6075-H3	Limo.-7P	—	—	—
6075-H4	Limo.-7P	—	—	—
6075-O	Imp. Sed.-7P	—	—	—
6075-S	Sed.-7P	3445	5545	—

Some confusion exists as regards style numbers on 1934-35 Fleetwood bodies. Following the previous Fleetwood system, V-8's would be 56____ or 60____ styles, V-12's would be 57____ or 61____ styles, and V-16's would be 58____ or 62____ styles. This system was followed in promotional literature, in the 1934 Master Parts List, and in early factory records. However, since the bodies were identical for all these series, Fleetwood stamped all body plates 57____ or 60____. Master Parts Lists after 1934 used only 57____ and 60____ style numbers for 1934-35 Fleetwood bodies. Starting in 1936, V-8 and V-12 style numbers reflected the new 1936 series designations, but V-16's retained the 57____ system. 60____ styles were no longer offered.

1934 Cadillac, Model 355-D, town sedan, JAC

ENGINE: Ninety degree L-head. Eight. Cast iron block on aluminum crankcase. B & S: 3-3/8 x 4-15/16 in. Disp.: 353 cu. in. C.R.: 6.25:1 std. 5.75:1 opt. Brake H.P.: 120 @ 3000 R.P.M. SAE/Taxable H.P.: 36.45. Main bearings: Three. Valve lifters: Mechanical. Carb.: Detroit Lubricator, Model 51.

CHASSIS: [Series 10] W.B.: 128 in. O.L.: 205-3/4 - 207-1/2 in. Frt/Rear Tread: 59-3/8 / 62 in. Tires: 7.00 x 17. [Series 20] W.B.: 136 in. O.L.: 213-3/4 - 215-1/2 in. Frt/Rear Tread: 59-3/8 / 62 in. Tires: 7.00 x 17. [Series Fleetwood (30)] W.B.: 146 in. O.L.: 227-9/16 in. Frt/Rear Tread: 59-3/8 / 62 in. Tires: 7.00 x 17.

TECHNICAL: Selective synchro transmission. Speeds: 3F/1R. LHD, center control, emerg brake at left-under panel (RHD opt). Twin disc clutch. Shaft drive, Hotchkiss. 3/4 floating rear axle, spiral bevel drive. Overall ratio: [Series 10, 20] 4.60:1 std, 4.36, 4.8:1 opt. [Series 30] 4.80:1 std, 4.60:1 opt. Mechanical brakes with vacuum assist on four wheels. Wire wheels. Wheel size: 17 in. drop center.

OPTIONS: Sidemount cover(s) (20.00 ea.). Radio (standard/master 64.50/74.50). Heater (44.50). Seat covers. Spotlight (24.50). Flexible steering wheel.

HISTORICAL: Introduced: January, 1934. Model year sales: 8318 (with 1935). Model year production: 8318 (with 1935). The president & general manager was Lawrence P. Fisher to May 31, 1934. Nicholas Dreystadt General Manager after June 1, 1934.

1934
Series 355D, V-8, 128" wb
Fisher Bodies

	FP	5	4	3	2	1
Conv	2645	11,400	22,800	38,000	56,000	76,000
Conv Sed	2845	12,000	24,000	40,000	60,000	80,000
2P Cpe	2545	7500	15,000	25,000	35,000	50,000
Twn Cpe	2695	7200	14,400	24,000	33,600	48,000
Sed	2645	6300	12,600	21,000	29,400	42,000
Twn Sed	2695	6300	12,600	21,000	29,400	42,000

Series 355D, V-8, 136" wb
Fisher Bodies

	FP	5	4	3	2	1
Conv	2845	12,000	24,000	40,000	60,000	80,000
Conv Sed	3045	12,900	25,800	48,200	66,000	86,000
Cpe	2745	7800	15,600	26,000	36,400	52,000
Sed	2845	6450	12,900	21,500	30,100	43,000
Twn Sed	2895	6450	12,900	21,500	30,100	43,000
7P Sed	2995	6600	13,200	22,000	30,800	44,000
Imp Sed	3145	6750	13,500	22,500	31,500	45,000

1934
Series 355D, V-8, 146" wb
Fleetwood bodies with straight windshield

	FP	5	4	3	2	1
Sed	3495	6750	13,500	22,500	31,500	45,000
Twn Sed	3545	6750	13,500	22,500	31,500	45,000
7P Sed	3645	6900	13,800	23,000	32,200	46,000
7P Limo	3845	8250	16,500	27,500	38,500	55,000
Imp Cab	3895	13,500	27,000	45,000	70,000	90,000
7P Imp Cab	4045	13,800	27,600	46,000	73,500	92,000

Series 355D, V-8, 146" wb
Fleetwood bodies with modified "V" windshield

	FP	5	4	3	2	1
Conv	4095	12,300	24,600	41,000	62,000	82,000
Aero Cpe	4495	11,400	22,800	38,000	56,000	76,000
Cpe	4495	9900	19,800	33,000	46,200	66,000
Spl Sed	3945	6750	13,500	22,500	31,500	45,000
Spl Twn Sed	5695	6750	13,500	22,500	31,500	45,000
Conv Sed Div	4495	13,500	27,000	45,000	70,000	90,000
7P Spl Sed	5795	6750	13,500	22,500	31,500	45,000
Spl Limo	5695	7050	14,100	23,500	32,900	47,000
Sp Twn Cab	3975	13,200	26,400	44,000	68,000	88,000
7P Twn Cab	4095	12,900	25,800	48,200	66,000	86,000
5P Spl Imp Cab	4345	13,500	27,000	45,000	70,000	90,000
7P Spl Imp Cab	4495	13,500	27,000	45,000	70,000	90,000
Limo Brgm	4295	9000	18,000	30,000	42,000	60,000

1934 Cadillac, Model 370-D, V-12, town sedan (with Jean Harlow), JAC

CADILLAC — MODEL 370-D — TWELVE: Except for the engine and various emblems, the V-12 was much the same car as the 146 inch wheelbase V-8.

I.D. DATA: Serial numbers were located on top surface of frame side bar, right side, just ahead of dash. Same as engine number. Starting no.: 4100001. Ending: 4101098 (with 1935). Engine numbers stamped on the right hand side of the crankcase, on the generator drive chain housing. Starting engine no.: 4100001. Ending: 4101098 (with 1935).

Style No.	Body Type & Seating	Price	Weight	Prod. Total
Fleetwood 146 in w.b. Vee Windshield				
5702	Rds.-2P	—	—	—
5712-C	Coll. Twn. Cab.-5P	—	—	—
5712-LB	Twn. Cab.-5P	6195	5990	—
5712-MB	Twn. Cab.-5P	—	—	—
5720	Twn. Cab.-7P	—	—	—
5720-C	Coll. Twn. Cab.-7P	—	—	—
5725-B	Twn. Cab.-7P	—	—	—
5725-LB	Twn. Cab.-7P	6295	6040	—
5725-MB	Twn. Cab.-7P	—	—	—
5730	Imp. Sed.-5P	—	—	—
5730-FL	Imp. Cab.-5P	4845	5765	—
5730-FM	Imp. Brgm.-5P	—	—	—
5730-S	Sed.-5P	4445	5735	—
5733	Imp. Twn. Sed.-5P	—	—	—
5733-S	Twn. Sed.-5P	4995	5700	—
5735	Conv. Cpe.-2P	4745	5485	—
5757	Tr.-7P	—	—	—
5759	Spt. Phae.-5P	—	—	—
5775	Imp. Sed. (Limo.)-7P	4795	5790	—
5775-B	Limo.-7P	—	—	—
5775-E	Imp. Sed.-7P	—	—	—
5775-FL	Imp. Cab.-7P	4995	5790	—
5775-FM	Imp. Brgm.-7P	—	—	—

Style No.	Body Type & Seating	Price	Weight	Prod. Total
5775-H4	Imp. Sed.-7P	—	—	—
5775-S	Sedan-7P	4595	5760	—
5775-W	Limo.-7P	—	—	—
5776	Cpe.-2P	4595	5520	—
5780	Conv. Sed. w/div.-5P	4995	5800	—
5780-B	Conv. Sed.-5P	—	—	—
5780-S	Conv. Sed.-5P	—	5770	—
5785	Coll. Cpe.-5P	4995	5685	—
5788	Stat. Cpe.-5P	—	5720	—
5789-A	Vict. Cpe.-4P	—	—	—
5791	Limo. Brgm.-7P	6195	6030	—
5791-B	Limo. Brgm.-7P	—	—	—
5799	Aerodynamic Cpe.-5P	4995	5720	—

Fleetwood 146 in. w.b. Flat Windshield
Some listings show these as 61____ styles.

Style No.	Body Type & Seating	Price	Weight	Prod. Total
6030-B	Imp. Sed.-5P	—	—	—
6030-FL	Imp. Cab.-5P	4395	5765	—
6030-FM	Imp. Brgm.-5P	—	—	—
6030-S	Sed.-5P	3995	5735	—
6033-S	Twn. Sed.-5P	4045	5700	—
6035	Conv. Cpe.-2P	—	—	—
6075	Imp. Sed.-7P	4345	5790	—
6075-B	Limo. (spec. back)-7P	—	—	—
6075-D	Limo.-7P	—	—	—
6075-E	Limo.-7P	—	—	—
6075-FL	Imp. Cab.-7P	4545	5790	—
6075-FM	Imp. Brgm.-7P	—	—	—
6075-H3	Limo.-7P	—	—	—
6075-H4	Limo.-7P	—	—	—
6075-O	Imp. Sed.-7P	—	—	—
6075-S	Sed.-7P	4145	5760	—

Some confusion exists as regards style numbers on 1934-35 Fleetwood bodies. Following the previous Fleetwood system, V-8's would be 56____ or 60____ styles, V-12's would be 57____ or 61____ styles, and V-16's would be 58____ or 62____ styles. This system was followed in promotional literature, in the 1934 Master Parts List, and in early factory records. However, since the bodies were identical for all these series, Fleetwood stamped all body plates 57____ or 60____. Master Parts Lists after 1934 used only 57____ and 60____ style numbers for 1934-35 Fleetwood bodies. Starting in 1936, V-8 and V-12 style numbers reflected the new 1936 series designations, but V-16's retained the 57____ system. 60____ styles were no longer offered.

ENGINE: 45 degree, overhead valve. Twelve. Cast iron block on aluminum crankcase. B & S: 3-1/8 in. x 4 in. Disp.: 368 cu. in. C.R.: 6.0:1 std.; 5.65:1 opt. Brake H.P.: 133 @ 3400 R.P.M. SAE/Taxable H.P.: 46.9. Main bearings: Four. Valve lifters: Mechanical w/hydraulic silencer on rocker bushing. Carb.: Dual Detroit Lubricator, Type R-13, L-13, Model 51.

CHASSIS: W.B.: 146 in. O.L.: 227-9/16 in. Frt/Rear Tread: 59-3/8 in./62 in. Tires: 7.50 x 17.

TECHNICAL: Selective, synchro transmission. Speeds: 3R/1R. LHD, center control; emerg at left under panel (RHD opt). Twin disc clutch. Shaft drive, Hotchkiss. 3/4 floating rear axle, spiral bevel drive. Overall ratio: 4.80:1 std., 4.60:1 opt., 5.11:1 opt. Mechanical brakes with vacuum assist on four wheels. Wire wheels. Wheel size: 17 in. drop center.

OPTIONS: Sidemount cover(s) (20.00 each). Radio (Standard/Master) (64.50/74.50). Heater (44.50). Seat covers. Spotlight (24.50). Flexible steering wheel.

HISTORICAL: Introduced January, 1934. Model year sales: 1098 (with 1935). Model year production: 1098 (with 1935). The president & general manager was Lawrence P. Fisher to May 31, 1934. Nicholas Dreystadt was general manager after June 1, 1934.

1934
Series 370D, V-12, 146" wb
Fleetwood bodies with straight windshield

	FP	5	4	3	2	1
Sed	4195	7200	14,400	24,000	33,600	48,000
Twn Sed	4245	7350	14,700	24,500	34,300	49,000
7P	4345	7500	15,000	25,000	35,000	50,000
7P Limo	4545	7650	15,300	25,500	35,700	51,000
5P Imp Cab	4595	14,400	28,800	48,000	76,000	96,000
7P Imp Cab	4745	14,100	28,200	57,000	74,000	94,000

Series 370D, V-12, 146" wb
Fleetwood bodies with modified "V" windshield

	FP	5	4	3	2	1
Conv	4945	13,500	27,000	45,000	70,000	90,000
Aero Cpe		30,300	57,000	86,000	112,000	145,000
RS Cpe	5195	10,500	21,000	35,000	49,000	70,000
Spl Sed	4645	7200	14,400	24,000	33,600	48,000
Spl Twn Sed	4695	7350	14,700	24,500	34,300	49,000
Conv Sed	5195	15,000	30,000	50,000	80,000	100,000
7P Spl Sed	4795	7500	15,000	25,000	35,000	50,000
Spec Limo	4995	7650	15,300	25,500	35,700	51,000
5P Twn Cab	6395	15,000	30,000	50,000	80,000	100,000
7P Twn Cab	6495	14,700	29,400	49,000	78,000	98,000
5P Spl Imp Cab	5045	17,100	31,800	53,000	85,000	106,000
7P Spl Imp Cab	5195	15,000	30,000	50,000	80,000	100,000

CADILLAC — MODEL 452-D — SIXTEEN: V-16's shared the Fleetwood bodies with the eights and twelves, but were given a few distinctive styling details. The grill was of eggcrate design. Headlights were mounted on the radiator shell rather than the fenders, and the parking lights were on the fenders rather than in the headlight supports. Three spears were placed on the hood side panels and front fender skirts. There was no crease across the nose of the front fenders.

Chassis changes were the same as on the eights and twelves, with minor differences to accomodate the added weight, power, and tremendous 154 inch wheelbase.

1934 Cadillac, Model 454-D, V-16, town sedan, JAC

I.D. DATA: Serial numbers were on top surface of frame side bar, right side, just ahead of dash. Same as engine number. Starting no.: 5100001. Ending: 5100150 (with 1935). Engine numbers were stamped on the right hand side of the crankcase, on the generator drive chain housing. Starting engine no.: 5100001. Ending: 5100150 (with 1935).

Style No.	Body Type & Seating	Price	Weight	Prod. Total

Fleetwood 154 in. w.b. Vee Windshield
Some listings show these as 58____ styles.

Style No.	Body Type & Seating	Price	Weight	Prod. Total
5702-C	Rds.-2P	—	—	—
5712-C	Coll. Twn. Cab.-5P	—	—	—
5712-LB	Twn. Cab.-5P	8850	—	—
5712-MB	Twn. Cab.-5P	—	—	—
5720	Twn. Cab.-7P	—	—	—
5720-C	Coll. Twn. Cab.-7P	—	—	—
5725-B	Twn. Cab.-7P	—	—	—
5725-LB	Twn. Cab.-7P	8950	6390	—
5725-MB	Twn. Cab.-7P	—	—	—
5730	Imp. Sed.-5P	—	—	—
5730-FL	Imp. Cab.-5P	7700	—	—
5730-FM	Imp. Brgm.-5P	—	—	—
5730-S	Sed.-5P	7300	6100	—
5733	Imp. Twn. Sed.-5P	—	—	—
5733-S	Twn. Sed.-5P	7350	6085	—
5735	Conv. Cpe.-2P	7600	5900	—
5757	Tr.-7P	—	—	—
5759	Spt. Phae.-5P	—	—	—
5775	Imp. Sed. (Limo.)-7P	7650	6210	—
5775-B	Limo.-7P	—	—	—
5775-E	Imp. Sed.-7P	—	—	—
5775-FL	Imp. Cab.-7P	7850	—	—
5775-FM	Imp. Brougham-7P	—	—	—
5775-H4	Imp. Sed.-7P	—	—	—
5775-S	Sed.-7P	7450	6190	—
5775-W	Limo.-7P	—	—	—
5776	Cpe.-2P	7450	5840	—
5780	Conv. Sed. w/div.-5P	7850	6100	—
5780-B	Conv. Sed.-5P	—	—	—
5780-S	Conv. Sed.-5P	—	—	—
5785	Coll. Cpe.5P	7885	—	—
5788	Stat. Cpe.-5P	—	—	—
5789-A	Vict. Cpe.-4P	—	—	—
5791	Limo. Brgm.-7P	8850	—	—
5791-B	Limo. Brgm.-7P	—	—	—
5799	Aerodynamic Cpe.-5P	7850	—	—

Fleetwood 154 in. w.b. Flat Windshield
Some listings show these as 62____ styles.

Style No.	Body Type & Seating	Price	Weight	Prod. Total
6030-B	Imp. Sed.-5P	—	—	—
6030-FL	Imp. Cab.-5P	7050	—	—
6030-FM	Imp. Brgm.-5P	—	—	—
6030-S	Sed.-5P	6650	—	—
6033-S	Twn. Sed.-5P	6700	6085	—
6035	Conv. Cpe.-2P	—	—	—
6075	Imp. Sed.-7P	7000	6210	—
6075-B	Limo. (spec. back)-7P	—	—	—
6075-D	Limo.-7P	—	—	—
6075-E	Limo.-7P	—	—	—
6075-FL	Imp. Cab.-7P	7200	—	—
6075-FM	Imp. Brgm.-7P	—	—	—
6075-H3	Limo.-7P	—	—	—
6075-H4	Limo.-7P	—	—	—
6075-O	Imp. Sed.-7P	—	—	—
6075-S	Sed.-7P	6800	6190	—

Some confusion exists as regards style numbers on 1934-35 Fleetwood bodies. Following the previous Fleetwood system, V-8's would be 56____ or 60____ styles, V-12's would be 57____ or 61____ styles, and V-16's would be 58____ or 62____ styles. This system was followed in promotional literature, in the 1934 Master Parts List, and in early factory records. However, since the bodies were identical for all these series, Fleetwood stamped all body plates 57____ or 60____. Master Parts Lists after 1934 used only 57____ and 60____ style numbers for 1934-35 Fleetwood bodies. Starting in 1936, V-8 and V-12 style numbers reflected the new 1936 series designations, but V-16's retained the 57____ system. 60____ styles were no longer offered.

ENGINE: 45 degree, overhead valve. Sixteen. Cast iron block on aluminum crankcase. B & S: 3 x 4 in. Disp.: 452 cu. in. C.R.: 6.0:1 std. 5.57:1 opt. Brake H.P.: 169.2 @ 3400 R.P.M. SAE/Taxable H.P.: 57.5. Main bearings: Five. Valve lifters: Mechanical w/hydraulic silencer on rocker bushing. Carb.: Dual Detroit lubricator, type R-14, L-14, Model 51.

221

CHASSIS: [Series 452-D] W.B.: 154 in. O.L.: 240 in. Frt/Rear Tread: 59-3/8 / 62 in. Tires: 7.50 x 17.

TECHNICAL: Selective synchro transmission. Speeds: 3F/1R. LHD, center control, emerg at left under panel (RHD opt). Twin disc clutch. Shaft drive, Hotchkiss. 3/4 floating rear axle, spiral bevel drive. Overall ratio: 4.64:1 std. 4.31:1 opt, 4.07:1 opt. Mechanical brakes with vacuum assist on four wheels. Wire wheels. Wheel size: 17 in. drop center.

OPTIONS: Sidemount cover(s) (20.00 ea.). Radio (standard/master 64.50/74.50). Heater (44.50). Seat covers. Spotlight (24.50). Flexible steering wheel.

HISTORICAL: Introduced: January, 1934. Model year sales: 150 (with 1935). Model year production: 150 (with 1935). The president & general manager was Lawrence P. Fisher to May 31, 1934. Nicholas Dreystadt was general manager after June 1, 1934.

1934
Series 452D, V-16, 154" wb
Fleetwood bodies with straight windshield

	FP	5	4	3	2	1
Sed	6950	9900	19,800	33,000	46,200	66,000
Twn Sed	7000	10,200	20,400	34,000	47,600	68,000
7P Sed	7100	10,500	21,000	35,000	49,000	70,000
Limo	7300	10,500	21,000	35,000	49,000	70,000
5P Imp Cab	7350	15,000	30,000	50,000	80,000	100,000

Series 452D, V-16, 154" wb
Fleetwood bodies with modified "V" windshield

	FP	5	4	3	2	1
4P Conv	7900	31,100	58,000	88,000	114,000	150,000
Aero Cpe	8150	25,500	45,000	73,000	100,000	130,000
RS Cpe	7750	12,000	24,000	40,000	60,000	80,000
Spl Sed	7600	11,400	22,800	38,000	56,000	76,000
Spl Twn Sed	7650	11,400	22,800	38,000	56,000	76,000
Conv Sed	8150	31,900	59,000	90,000	116,000	155,000
7P Spl Sed	7750	11,400	22,800	38,000	56,000	76,000
Spl Limo	7950	11,700	23,400	39,000	58,000	78,000
5P Twn Cab	9150	22,000	36,000	60,000	93,000	120,000
7P Twn Cab	9250	20,600	34,800	58,000	91,000	116,000
5P Spl Imp Cab	8000	24,100	42,000	68,000	98,000	126,000
7P Spl Imp Cab	8150	22,000	36,000	60,000	93,000	120,000
Limo Brgm	9150	12,000	24,000	40,000	60,000	80,000

1935

1935 Cadillac, Series 10, V-8, town coupe, HAC

CADILLAC — MODEL 355-D — SERIES 10, 20, 30 — EIGHT: V-8 Cadillac for 1935 remained virtually unchanged from 1934. The biplane bumpers of 1934 were replaced by more conventional units. One major change was introduced on Fisher bodies - the all steel Turret Top. Fleetwood bodies did not have the steel top until 1936. For 1934, Fleetwood bodied V-8's on 146 in. wheelbase were designated Series 30. Fisher bodied cars continued under the designations Series 10 and Series 20.

Having been associated with funeral and ambulance equipment for many years, Cadillac embarked on an extra effort in 1935 to consolidate this business. Three Fleetwood bodied seven passenger livery sedans were offered on the V-8 Series 30 chassis. Additionally, a 160 in. wheelbase commercial V-8 chassis was offered for hearse and ambulance adaptation.

I.D. DATA: Serial numbers were on top surface of frame side bar, right side, just ahead of dash. Same as engine number. Starting no.: 3100001 (with 1934). Ending: 3108318. Engine numbers were stamped on crankcase near the water inlet on the right hand side. Starting engine no.: 3100001 (with 1934). Ending: 3108318.

Style No.	Body Type & Seating	Price	Weight	Prod. Total
Series 10 Fisher 128 in. w.b.				
35728	2-dr. Spt. Cpe.-2/3P	2345	4550	—
35718	2-dr. Conv. Cpe.-2/4P	2445	4515	—
35721	4-dr. Conv. Sed.-5P	2755	4750	—
35722	2-dr. Twn. Cpe.-5P	2495	4630	—
35709	4-dr. Sed.-5P	2445	4715	—
35702	4-dr. Twn. Sed.-5P	2495	4735	—
Series 20 Fisher 136 in. w.b.				
35678	2-dr. Spt. Cpe.-2/3P	2545	4660	—
35668	2-dr. Conv. Cpe.-2/4P	2645	4625	—
35671	4-dr. Conv. Sed.-5P	2955	4860	—
35659	4-dr. Sed.-5P	2645	4825	—

Style No.	Body Type & Seating	Price	Weight	Prod. Total
35652	4-dr. Twn. Sed.-5P	2695	4815	—
35662	4-dr. Sed.-7P	2795	4945	—
35663	4-dr. Imp. Sed.-7P	2945	4970	—
Series 30 Fleetwood Livery 146 in. w.b.				
6075-L	4-dr. Livery Limo.-7P	—	—	—
6075-LL	4-dr. Livery Limo.-7P	—	—	—
6075-SL	4-dr. Livery Sed.-7P	—	—	—
Series 30 Fleetwood 146 in. w.b. Vee Windshield				
Some listings show these as 56____ styles.				
5702	Rds.-2P	—	—	—
5712-C	Coll. Twn. Cab.-5P	—	—	—
5712-LB	Twn. Cab.-5P	5495	5540	—
5712-MB	Twn. Cab.-5P	—	—	—
5720	Twn. Cab.-7P	—	—	—
5720-C	Coll. Twn. Cab.-7P	—	—	—
5725-B	Twn. Cab.-7P	—	—	—
5725-LB	Twn. Cab.-7P	5595	5650	—
5725-MB	Twn. Cab.-7P	—	—	—
5730	Imp. Sed.-5P	—	—	—
5730-FL	Imp. Cab.-5P	4145	5500	—
5730-FM	Imp. Brgm.-5P	—	—	—
5730-S	Sed.-5P	3745	5465	—
5733	Imp. Twn. Sed.-5P	—	—	—
5733-S	Twn. Sed.-5P	3795	5415	—
5735	Conv. Cpe.-2P	4045	5115	—
5757	Tr.-7P	—	—	—
5759	Spt. Phae.-5P	—	—	—
5775	Imp. Sed. (Limo.)-7P	4095	5580	—
5775-B	Limo.-7P	—	—	—
5775-E	Imp. Sed.-7P	—	—	—
5775-FL	Imp. Cab.-7P	4295	5580	—
5775-FM	Imp. Brgm.-7P	—	—	—
5775-H4	Imp. Sed.-7P	—	—	—
5775-S	Sed.-7P	3895	5545	—
5775-W	Limo.-7P	—	—	—
5776	Cpe.-2P	3895	5150	—
5780	Conv. Sed. w/div.-5P	4295	5465	—
5780-B	Conv. Sed.-5P	—	—	—
5780-S	Conv. Sed.-5P	—	5430	—
5785	Coll. Cpe.-5P	4295	5415	—
5788	Stat. Cpe.-5P	—	—	—
5789-A	Vict. Cpe.-4P	—	—	—
5791	Limo. Brgm.-7P	5495	5580	—
5791-B	Limo. Brgm.-7P	—	—	—
5799	Aero. Cpe.-5P	4295	5430	—
Series 30 Fleetwood 146 in. w.b. Flat Windshield				
6030-B	Imp. Sed.-5P	—	—	—
6030-FL	Imp. Cab.-5P	3695	5500	—
6030-FM	Imp. Brgm.-5P	—	—	—
6030-S	Sed.-5P	3295	5465	—
6033-S	Twn. Sed.-5P	3345	5415	—
6035	Conv. Cpe.-2P	—	—	—
6075	Imp. Sed.-7P	3645	5580	—
6075-B	Limo. (spec. back)-7P	—	—	—
6075-D	Limo.-7P	—	—	—
6075-E	Limo.-7P	—	—	—
6075-FL	Imp. Cab.-7P	3845	5580	—
6075-FM	Imp. Brgm.-7P	—	—	—
6075-H3	Limo.-7P	—	—	—
6075-H4	Limo.-7P	—	—	—
6075-O	Imp. Sed.-7P	—	—	—
6075-S	Sed.-7P	3445	5545	—

Some confusion exists as regards style numbers on 1934-35 Fleetwood bodies. Following the previous Fleetwood system, V-8's would be 56____ or 60____ styles, V-12's would be 57____ or 61____ styles, and V-16's would be 58____ or 62____ styles. This system was followed in promotional literature, in the 1934 Master Parts List, and in early factory records. However, since the bodies were identical for all these series, Fleetwood stamped all body plates 57____ or 60____. Master Parts Lists after 1934 used only 57____ or 60____ style numbers for 1934-35 Fleetwood bodies. Starting in 1936, V-8 and V-12 style numbers reflected the new 1936 series designations, but V-16's retained the 57____ system. 60____ styles were no longer offered.

ENGINE: Ninety degree L-head. Eight. Cast iron block on aluminum crankcase. B & S: 3-3/8 x 4-15/16 in. Disp.: 353 cu. in. C.R.: 6.25:1 std. 5.75:1 opt. Brake H.P.: 130 @ 3400 R.P.M. SAE /Taxable H.P.: 36.45. Main bearings: Three. Valve lifters: Mechanical. Carb.: Detroit lubricator, model 51.

CHASSIS: [Series 10] W.B.: 128 in. O.L.: 207-1/2 in. Frt/Rear Tread: 59-3/8 / 62 in. Tires: 7.00 x 17. [Series 20] W.B.: 136 in. O.L.: 215-1/2 in. Frt/Rear Tread: 59-3/8 x 62 in. Tires: 7.00 x 17. [Series 30] W.B.: 146 in. O.L.: 227-9/16 in. Frt/Rear Tread: 59-3/8 / 62 in. Tires: 7.00 x 17. [Commercial Chassis] W.B.: 160 in.

TECHNICAL: Selective, synchro transmission. Speeds: 3F/1R. LHD, Center control, emerg brake at left-under panel (RHD opt). Twin disc clutch. Shaft drive, Hotchkiss. 3/4 floating rear axle, spiral bevel drive. Overall ratio: [Series 10, 20] 4.60:1 std., 4.36, 4.8:1 opt. [Series 30] 4.80:1 std., 4.60:1 opt. Mechanical brakes with vacuum assist on four wheels. Wire wheels. Wheel size: 17 in. drop center.

OPTIONS: Sidemount cover(s) (20.00 ea.). Radio (standard/master 64.50/74.50). Heater (44.50). Seat covers. Spotlight (24.50). Flexible steering wheel.

HISTORICAL: Introduced: January, 1935 (continuation of 1934 line). Innovations: All steel Turret Top — Fisher bodies only. Model year sales: 8318 (with 1934). Model year production: 8318 (with 1934). The general manager was Nicholas Dreystadt.

1935 Cadillac, Series 40, V-12, town cabriolet, OCW

CADILLAC — MODEL 370-D — SERIES 40 — TWELVE: Virtually the same as 1934, except for new bumper. Designation changed to Series 40.

I.D. DATA: Serial numbers were on top surface of frame side bar, right side, just ahead of dash. Same as engine number. Starting no.: 4100001 (with 1934). Ending: 4101098. Engine numbers were stamped on the right hand side of the crankcase, on the generator drive chain housing. Starting engine no.: 4100001 (with 1934). Ending: 4101098.

Style No.	Body Type & Seating	Price	Weight	Prod. Total
Series 40 Fleetwood 146 in. w.b. Vee Windshield				
5702	Rds.-2P	—	—	—
5712-C	Coll. Twn. Cab.-5P	—	—	—
5712-LB	Twn. Cab.-5P	6195	5990	—
5712-MB	Twn. Cab.-5P	—	—	—
5720	Twn. Cab.-7P	—	—	—
5720-C	Coll. Twn. Cab.-7P	—	—	—
5725-B	Twn. Cab.-7P	—	—	—
5725-LB	Twn. Cab.-7P	6295	6040	—
5725-MB	Twn. Cab.-7P	—	—	—
5730	Imp. Sed.-5P	—	—	—
5730-FL	Imp. Cab.-5P	4845	5765	—
5730-FM	Imp. Brgm.-5P	—	—	—
5730-S	Sed.-5P	4445	5735	—
5733	Imp. Twn. Sed.-5P	—	—	—
5733-S	Twn. Sed.-5P	4995	5700	—
5735	Conv. Cpe.-2P	4745	5485	—
5757	Tr.-7P	—	—	—
5759	Spt. Phae.-5P	—	—	—
5775	Imp. Sed. (Limo.)-7P	4795	5790	—
5775-B	Limo.-7P	—	—	—
5775-E	Imp. Sed.-7P	—	—	—
5775-FL	Imp. Cab.-7P	4995	5790	—
5775-FM	Imp. Brgm.-7P	—	—	—
5775-H4	Imp. Sed.-7P	—	—	—
5775-S	Sed.-7P	4595	5760	—
5775-W	Limo.-7P	—	—	—
5776	Cpe.-2P	4595	5520	—
5780	Conv. Sed. w/div.-5P	4995	5800	—
5780-B	Conv. Sed.-5P	—	—	—
5780-S	Conv. Sed.-5P	—	5770	—
5785	Coll. Cpe.-5P	4995	5685	—
5788	Stat. Cpe.-5P	—	5720	—
5789-A	Vict. Cpe.-4P	—	—	—
5791	Limo. Brgm.-7P	6195	6030	—
5791-B	Limo. Brgm.-7P	—	—	—
5799	Aero. Cpe.-5P	4995	5720	—
Series 40 Fleetwood 146 in. w.b. Flat Windshield				
Some listings show these as 61_____ styles.				
6030-B	Imp. Sed.-5P	—	—	—
6030-FL	Imp. Cab.-5P	4395	5765	—
6030-FM	Imp. Brgm.-5P	—	—	—
6030-S	Sed.-5P	3995	5735	—
6033-S	Twn. Sed.-5P	4045	5700	—
6035	Conv. Cpe.-2P	—	—	—
6075	Imp. Sed.-7P	4345	5790	—
6075-B	Limo. (spec. back)-7P	—	—	—
6075-D	Limo.-7P	—	—	—
6075-E	Limo.-7P	—	—	—
6075-FL	Imp. Cab.-7P	4545	5790	—
6075-FM	Imp. Brgm.-7P	—	—	—
6075-H3	Limo.-7P	—	—	—
6075-H4	Limo.-7P	—	—	—
6075-O	Imp. Sed.-7P	—	—	—
6075-S	Sed.-7P	4145	5760	—

Some confusion exists as regards style numbers on 1934-35 Fleetwood bodies. Following the previous Fleetwood system, V-8's would be 56_____ or 60_____ styles, V-12's would be 57_____ or 61_____ styles, and V-16's would be 58_____ or 62_____ styles. This system was followed in promotional literature, in the 1934 Master Parts List, and in early factory records. However, since the bodies were identical for all these series, Fleetwood stamped all body plates 57_____ or 60_____. Master Parts Lists after 1934 used only 57_____ and 60_____ style numbers for 1934-35 Fleetwood bodies. Starting in 1936, V-8 and V-12 style numbers reflected the new 1936 series designations, but V-16's retained the 57_____ system. 60_____ styles were no longer offered.

ENGINE: 45 degree, overhead valve. Twelve. Cast iron block on aluminum crankcase. B & S: 3-1/8 in. x 4 in. Disp.: 368 cu. in. C.R.: 6.0:1 std., 5.65:1

opt. Brake H.P.: 150 @ 3600 R.P.M. SAE/Taxable H.P.: 46.9. Main bearings: Four. Valve lifters: Mechanical w/hydraulic silencer on rocker bushing. Carb.: Dual Detroit Libricator, Type R-13, L-13, Model 51.

CHASSIS: W.B.: 146 in. Frt/Rear Tread: 59-3/8 in./62 in. Tires: 7.50 x 17.

TECHNICAL: Selective, synchro transmission. Speeds: 3F/1R. LHD, center control; emerg at left under panel (RHD opt). Twin disc clutch. Shaft drive, Hotchkiss. 3/4 floating rear axle, spiral bevel drive. Overall ratio: 4.80:1 std., 4.60:1 opt., 5.11:1 opt. Mechanical brakes with vacuum assist on four wheels. Wire wheels. Wheel size: 17 in. drop center.

OPTIONS: Sidemount cover(s) (20.00 each). Radio (standard/master) (64.50/74.50). Heater (44.50). Seat covers. Spotlight (24.50). Flexible steering wheel.

HISTORICAL: Introduced January, 1935 (continuation of 1934 line). Model year sales: 1098 (with 1934). Model year production: 1098 (with 1934). The general manager was Nicholas Dreystadt.

CADILLAC — MODEL 452-D — SERIES 60 — SIXTEEN: Virtually the same as 1934, except for new bumper. Designation changed to Series 60.

I.D. DATA: Serial numbers were on top surface of frame side bar, right side, just ahead of dash. Same as engine number. Starting: 5100001 (with 1934). Ending: 5100150. Engine numbers were stamped on the right hand side of the crankcase, on the generator drive chain housing. Starting engine no.: 5100001 (with 1934). Ending: 5100150.

Style No.	Body Type & Seating	Price	Weight	Prod. Total
Series 60 Fleetwood 154 in. w.b. Vee Windshield				
Some listings show these as 58_____ styles.				
5702	Rds.-2P	—	—	—
5712-C	Coll. Twn. Cab.-5P	—	—	—
5712-LB	Twn. Cab.-5P	8950	6100	—
5712-MB	Twn. Cab.-5P	—	—	—
5720	Twn. Cab.-7P	—	—	—
5720-C	Coll. Twn. Cab.-7P	—	—	—
5725-B	Twn. Cab.-7P	—	—	—
5725-LB	Twn. Cab.-7P	9050	6390	—
5725-MB	Twn. Cab.-7P	—	—	—
5730	Imp. Sed.-5P	—	—	—
5730-FL	Imp. Cab.-5P	7800	6150	—
5730-FM	Imp. Brgm.-5P	—	—	—
5730-S	Sed.-5P	7400	6085	—
5733	Imp. Twn. Sed.-5P	—	6140	—
5733-S	Twn. Sed.-5P	7450	6050	—
5735	Conv. Cpe.-2P	7700	5800	—
5757	Tr.-7P	7700	5800	—
5759	Spt. Phae.-5P	—	—	—
5775	Imp. Sed. (Limo.)-7P	7750	6210	—
5775-B	Limo.-7P	—	—	—
5775-E	Imp. Sed.-7P	—	—	—
5775-FL	Imp. Cab.-7P	7950	—	—
5775-FM	Imp. Brgm.-7P	—	—	—
5775-H4	Imp. Sed.-7P	—	—	—
5775-S	Sed.-7P	7550	6190	—
5775-W	Limo.-7P	—	—	—
5776	Cpe.-2P	7550	5840	—
5780	Conv. Sed. w/div.-5P	7950	6100	—
5780-B	Conv. Sed.-5P	—	—	—
5780-S	Conv. Sed.-5P	—	6080	—
5785	Coll. Cpe.-5P	—	6000	—
5788	Stat. Cpe.-5P	—	—	—
5789-A	Vict. Cpe.-4P	—	—	—
5791	Limo. Brgm.-7P	8950	6225	—
5791-B	Limo. Brgm.-7P	—	—	—
5799	Aerodynamic Cpe.-5P	8150	6050	—
Series 60 Fleetwood 154 in. w.b. Flat Windshield				
Some listings show these as 62_____ styles.				
6030-B	Imp. Sed.-5P	—	—	—
6030-FL	Imp. Cab.-5P	7150	—	—
6030-FM	Imp. Brgm.-5P	—	—	—
6030-S	Sed.-5P	6750	6050	—
6033-S	Twn. Sed.-5P	6800	6085	—
6035	Conv. Cpe.-2P	—	—	—
6075	Imp. Sed.-7P	7100	6210	—
6075-B	Limo. (spec. back)-7P	—	—	—
6075-D	Limo.-7P	—	—	—
6075-E	Limo.-7P	—	—	—
6075-FL	Imp. Cab.-7P	7300	—	—
6075-FM	Imp. Brgm.-7P	—	—	—
6075-H3	Limo.-7P	—	—	—
6075-H4	Limo.-7P	—	—	—
6075-O	Imp. Sed.-7P	—	—	—
6075-S	Sed.-7P	6900	6190	—

Some confusion exists as regards style numbers on 1934-35 Fleetwood bodies. Following the previous Fleetwood system, V-8's would be 56_____ or 60_____ styles, V-12's would be 57_____ or 61_____ styles, and V-16's would be 58_____ or 62_____ styles. This system was followed in promotional literature, in the 1934 Master Parts List, and in early factory records. However, since the bodies were identical for all these series, Fleetwood stamped all body plates 57_____ or 60_____. Master Parts Lists after 1934 used only 57_____ and 60_____ style numbers for 1934-35 Fleetwood bodies. Starting in 1936, V-8 and V-12 style numbers reflected the new 1936 series designations, but V-16's retained the 57_____ system. 60_____ styles were no longer offered.

ENGINE: 45 degree, overhead valve. Sixteen. Cast iron block on aluminum crankcase. B & S: 3 in. x 4 in. Disp.: 452 cu. in. C.R.: 6.0:1 std. Brake H.P.: 185 @ 3800 R.P.M. SAE/Taxable H.P.: 57.5. Main bearings: Five. Valve lifters: Mechanical w/hydraulic silencer on rocker bushing. Carb.: Dual Detroit Lubricator, Type R-14, L-14, Model 51.

CHASSIS: W.B.: 154 in. O.L.: 240 in. Frt/Rear Tread: 59-3/8 in./62 in. Tires: 7.50 x 17.

TECHNICAL: Selective, synchro transmission. Speeds: 3F/1R. LHD, center control, emerg at left under panel (RHD opt.). Twin disc clutch. Shaft drive, Hotchkiss. 3/4 floating rear axle, spiral bevel drive. Overall ratio: 4.64:1 std., 4.31:1 opt., 4.07:1 opt. Mechanical brakes with vacuum assist on four wheels. Wire wheels. Wheel size: 17 in. drop center.

OPTIONS: Sidemount cover(s) (20.00 each). Radio (standard/master) (64.50/74.50). Heater (44.50). Seat covers. Spotlight (24.50). Flexible steering wheel.

HISTORICAL: Introduced January, 1935 (continuation of 1934 line). Model year sales: 150 (with 1934). Model year production: 150 (with 1934). The general manager was Nicholas Dreystadt.

1935
Series 355E, V-8, 128" wb
Fisher Bodies

	FP	5	4	3	2	1
RS Conv	2445	10,800	21,600	36,000	50,500	72,000
Conv Sed	2755	10,500	21,000	35,000	49,000	70,000
RS Cpe	2345	9000	18,000	30,000	42,000	60,000
5P Twn Cpe	2495	8250	16,500	27,500	38,500	55,000
Sed	2445	6900	13,800	23,000	32,200	46,000
Twn Sed	2495	7050	14,100	23,500	32,900	47,000

Series 355E, V-8, 136" wb
Fisher Bodies

RS Conv	2645	11,400	22,800	38,000	56,000	76,000
Conv Sed	2955	11,100	22,200	37,000	52,000	74,000
RS Cpe	2545	8550	17,100	28,500	39,900	57,000
Sed	2645	7050	14,100	23,500	32,900	47,000
Twn Sed	2695	7200	14,400	24,000	33,600	48,000
7P Sed	2795	8250	16,500	27,500	38,500	55,000
Imp Sed	2945	9000	18,000	30,000	42,000	60,000

Series 355E, V-8, 146" wb
Fleetwood bodies with straight windshield

Sed	3295	7350	14,700	24,500	34,300	49,000
Twn Sed	3345	7500	15,000	25,000	35,000	50,000
7P Sed	3445	7650	15,300	25,500	35,700	51,000
Limo	3645	7800	15,600	26,000	36,400	52,000
5P Imp Cabr	3695	12,900	25,800	48,200	66,000	86,000
7P Imp Cabr	3845	12,600	25,200	42,000	64,000	84,000

Series 355E, V-8, 146" wb
Fleetwood bodies with modified "V" windshield

4P Conv	4045	12,000	24,000	40,000	60,000	80,000
4P Cpe	3895	9000	18,000	30,000	42,000	60,000
Spec Sed	3745	7500	15,000	25,000	35,000	50,000
Spec Twn Sed	3795	7650	15,300	25,500	35,700	51,000
Conv Sed	4295	12,300	24,600	41,000	62,000	82,000
7P Spec Sed	3895	7650	15,300	25,500	35,700	51,000
Spec Limo	4095	8250	16,500	27,500	38,500	55,000
5P Twn Cabr	5495	11,400	22,800	38,000	56,000	76,000
7P Twn Cabr	5595	11,100	22,200	37,000	52,000	74,000
5P Imp Cabr	4145	11,700	23,400	39,000	58,000	78,000
7P Imp Cabr	4295	11,400	22,800	38,000	56,000	76,000
Limo Brgm	5495	9000	18,000	30,000	42,000	60,000

Series 370E, V-12, 146" wb
Fleetwood bodies with straight windshield

Sed	3295	8550	17,100	28,500	39,900	57,000
Twn Sed	3345	8700	17,400	29,000	40,600	58,000
7P Sed	3445	8850	17,700	29,500	41,300	59,000
Limo	3645	9300	18,600	31,000	43,400	62,000
5P Imp Cabr	3695	12,900	25,800	48,200	66,000	86,000
7P Imp Cabr	4295	12,600	25,200	42,000	64,000	84,000

Series 370E, V-12, 146" wb
Fleetwood bodies with modified "V" windshield

Conv	4045	13,500	27,000	45,000	70,000	90,000
4P Cpe	3895	10,500	21,000	35,000	49,000	70,000
Spec Sed	3745	9000	18,000	30,000	42,000	60,000
Spec Twn Sed	3795	9300	18,600	31,000	43,400	62,000
Conv Sed	4295	13,200	26,400	44,000	68,000	88,000
7P Spec Sed	3895	9300	18,600	31,000	43,400	62,000
Spec Limo	4095	9900	19,800	33,000	46,200	66,000
7P Twn Cabr	5495	13,500	27,000	45,000	70,000	90,000
5P Twn Cabr	5595	13,500	27,000	45,000	70,000	90,000
5P Spec Imp Cabr	4145	14,400	28,800	48,000	76,000	96,000
7P Spec Imp Cabr	4295	14,100	28,200	57,000	74,000	94,000
Limo Brgm	5495	12,000	24,000	40,000	60,000	80,000

Series 452E, V-16, 154" wb
Fleetwood bodies with straight windshield

Sed	6750	11,700	23,400	39,000	58,000	78,000
Twn Sed	6800	11,700	23,400	39,000	58,000	78,000
7P Sed	6900	12,000	24,000	40,000	60,000	80,000
7P Limo	7100	12,300	24,600	41,000	62,000	82,000
5P Imp Cabr	7150	14,400	28,800	48,000	76,000	96,000
7P Imp Cabr	7300	14,100	28,200	57,000	74,000	94,000

Series 452D, V-16, 154" wb
Fleetwood bodies with modified "V" windshield

2-4P Cpe	7700	27,900	51,000	79,000	106,000	136,000
4P Cpe	7550	24,100	42,000	68,000	98,000	126,000
Spec Sed	7400	12,000	24,000	40,000	60,000	80,000
Spec Twn Sed	7450	12,300	24,600	41,000	62,000	82,000
7P Spec Sed	7550	12,600	25,200	42,000	64,000	84,000
Spec Limo	7750	12,900	25,800	48,200	66,000	86,000
5P Twn Cabr	8950	35,100	63,000	98,000	124,000	175,000
7P Twn Cab	9050	34,300	62,000	96,000	122,000	170,000
5P Spec Imp Cabr	7800	37,000	65,000	102,000	130,000	185,000
7P Spec Imp Cabr	7950	35,900	64,000	100,000	126,000	180,000
Limo Brgm	8950	18,500	33,000	55,000	88,000	110,000
5P Conv	8150	38,000	67,000	105,000	133,000	190,000
Conv Sed	8150	37,000	65,000	102,000	130,000	185,000

1936 Cadillac, Series 36-70, coupe, OCW

CADILLAC — SERIES 36-60 — EIGHT: A new model for 1936 — more than a LaSalle, less than a full size Cadillac — the same concept as the LaSalle, but with that name — Cadillac. Smaller, shorter, lighter, less powerful, less expensive, but with full Cadillac quality. Limited to three body styles, by Fisher. The Convertible Coupe had a rumble seat, but the closed Coupe had only a small folding seat inside for an extra passenger. Both these body styles had a single fenderwell on the side opposite the driver. Vee windshield, grill and fender treatment were the same as on the larger V-8's. The engine was the same new engine as in the Fleetwood bodies V-8's, but with a 3/8 in. smaller bore. The transmission was the smaller unit, similar to that in the LaSalle. Many dimensions were less than on the larger V-8's, to fit the concept of a lower priced, less pretentious, but equally high-quality product.

I.D. DATA: Engine numbers were on top of the crankcase, just behind the fan support. Starting: 6010001. Ending: 6016712.

Model No.	Body Type & Seating	Price	Weight	Prod. Total
36-6077	Cpe.-2P	1645	3830	—
36-6067	Conv. Cpe.-2P	1725	3940	—
36-6019	Tr. Sed.-5P	1695	4010	—

ENGINE: Ninety degree, L-head. Eight. Cast iron block (blocks cast enbloc with crankcase). B & S: 3-3/8 x 4-1/2 in. Disp.: 322 cu. in. C.R.: 6.25:1. Brake H.P.: 125 @ 3400 R.P.M. SAE/Taxable H.P.: 36.45. Main bearings: Three. Valve lifters: Hydraulic. Carb.: Stromberg EE-25.

CHASSIS: W.B.: 121 in. O.L.: 196 in. H.: 65-3/4 - 67-1/2 in. Frt/Rear Tread: 58/59 in. Tires: 7.00 x 16.

TECHNICAL: Selective, synchro transmission. Speeds: 3F/1R. LHD, center control, emerg at left under panel (RHD opt.). Single disc clutch. Shaft drive, Hotchkiss. Semi-floating rear axle, spiral bevel drive. Hydraulic brakes on four wheels. Disc wheels. Wheel size: 16 in.

OPTIONS: Sidemount cover(s) (20.00). Radio (master/standard 89.50/54.50). Heater (18.50). Seat covers. Flexible steering wheel (16.00). Trim rings (1.50 each). Wheel discs (4.00 each).

HISTORICAL: Introduced: October, 1935. Model year sales: 6712. Model year production: 6712. The general manager was Nicholas Dreystadt.

1936 Cadillac, Series 36-70, 4-dr. sedan, JAC

CADILLAC — SERIES 36-70, 36-75 — EIGHT: Though not the best seller in 1936, the Series 36-70 and 36-75 were the basic Cadillacs. Lower priced LaSalles and Series 60's were better sellers; V-12's and V-16's were better cars; but the 346 cu. in. V-8's were the ones which survived to form the main source of Cadillac business for years to come.
Bodies: Bodies were all Vee windshield styles by Fleetwood. A narrower radiator shell supported the new louver-style ''Convex Vee'' grill. Headlights were mounted on the radiator shell; parking lights were inside the headlights. Front fenders were new, with a crease along the center line.

Cowl vent was changed back to opening forward. Built in trunks on "Touring" styles, Town Sedans, and Convertibles Sedans. Stationary and Convertible Coupes had rumble seats plus a separate door for the spare tire at the extreme rear of the deck. All bodies now used the all steel Turret Top. Engine: The Cadillac V-8 for 1915 got detachable cylinder heads for 1918, compensated crankshaft for 1924, side by side rods for 1928, and a complete replacement design for 1936. The new engine, produced in two displacements, featured: Blocks and crankcase cast enbloc. Water jacket full length of the cylinder bore, more rigid crankshaft with six counterweights. New connecting rods with large ends split at an angle to allow for removal from top of engine. Hydraulic valve silencers. New manifolding and downdraft carburetor. Suction type crankcase ventilation (fumes taken out thru exhaust system). Simplified lubrication system (only piping was to hydraulic lifters). Combination fuel and vacuum pump on front engine cover. Starter on right hand side, in front of bell housing. Generator serviced by removing panel under left front fender. Pressure cap on radiator. Chassis: New chassis features: Two mufflers in series. Battery under left side of front seat. Double universal joint in steering shaft. Single plate clutch. Ride control discontinued, but ride stabilizer added at front. First hydraulic brakes on a Cadillac (used on LaSalle two years earlier).

I.D. DATA: Engine numbers were on top of the crankcase, just behind the fan support. Starting: 3110001. Ending: 3115248.

Style No.	Body Type & Seating	Price	Weight	Prod. Total
Series 36-70 Fleetwood 131 in. w.b.				
36-7057	Cpe.-2P	2595	4620	—
36-7067	Conv. Cpe.-2P	2695	4690	—
36-7019	Tr. Sed.-5P	2445	4670	—
36-7029	Conv. Sed.-5P	2745	4710	—
Fleetwood Series 36-75 138 in. wb.				
36-7509	Sed.-5P	2645	4805	—
36-7519	Tr. Sed.-5P	2645	4805	—
36-7509F	Formal Sed.-5P	3395	4805	—
36-7529	Conv. Sed.-5P	3395	5040	—
36-7539	Twn. Sed.-5P	3145	4840	—
36-7503	Sed.-7P	2795	4885	—
36-7513	Imp. Sed.-7P	2995	5045	—
36-7523	Tr. Sed.-7P	2795	4885	—
36-7533	Imp. Tr. Sed.-7P	2995	5045	—
36-7543	Twn. Car-7P	4445	5115	—
Fleetwood Commercial Cars				
36-7503L	Comm. Sed.-7P	2695	—	—
36-7513L	Comm. Imp. Sed.-7P	2865	—	—
36-7523L	Comm. Tr. Sed.-7P	2695	—	—
36-7533L	Comm. Imp. Tr. Sed.-7P	2865	—	—

ENGINE: Ninety degree, L-head. Eight. Cast iron block (blocks cast enbloc with crankcase). B & S: 3-1/2 x 4-1/2 in. Disp.: 346 cu. in. C.R.: 6.25:1. Brake H.P.: 135 @ 3400 R.P.M. SAE/Taxable H.P.: 39.20. Main bearings: Three. Valve lifters: Hydraulic. Carb.: Stromberg EE-25.

CHASSIS: [Series 36-70] W.B.: 131 in. O.L.: 206-1/4 in. H.: 66 - 69-1/2 in. Frt/Rear Tread: 60-3/16 / 60-1/2 in. Tires: 7.50 x 16. [Series 36-75] W.B.: 138 in. O.L.: 213-1/2 in. H.: 68-13/16 in. Frt/Rear Tread: 60-3/16 / 62-1/2 in. Tires: 7.50 x 16. [Series 36-75 Commercial Chassis] W.B.: 156 in.

TECHNICAL: Selective, synchro transmission. Speeds: 3F/1R. LHD, center control, emerg at left under panel (RHD opt). Single disc clutch. Shaft drive, Hotchkiss. Semi-floating rear axle, spiral bevel drive. Overall ratio: [36-70] 4.55:1 std.; 4.3:1 opt. [36-75] 4.6:1 std.; 4.3:1 opt. Hydraulic brakes on four wheels. Wheel size: 16 in.

OPTIONS: Sidemount cover(s) (20.00). Radio (master/standard 89.50/54.50). Heater (18.50). Seat covers. Flexible steering wheel (16.00). Trim rings (1.50 each). Wheel discs (4.00 each).

HISTORICAL: Introduced: October, 1935. Model year sales: 5248. Model year production: 5248. The general manager was Nicholas Dreystadt.

For the first time since 1914, Cadillacs were designated as a year model — "The 1936 Cadillacs". Annual model changes and introduction in the Fall of the year would now become regular practice.

1936 Cadillac, Series 36-85, touring sedan, OCW

CADILLAC — SERIES 36-80, 36-85 — TWELVE: The 1936 V-12 was essentially a 1936 V-8 with a twelve cylinder engine. Performance was greatly improved over previous V-12's. Identification with the hood closed was only possible by reading emblems. Even dual exhaust pipes would no longer identify the V-12. A crossover pipe from left to right manifold resulted in a single exhaust system (with two mufflers in series). Commercial Cars and Chassis also shared the V-8 and the V-12 engines.

I.D. DATA: Engine numbers were on the upper left surface of the generator drive chain housing. Starting: 4110001. Ending: 4110901.

Style No.	Body Type & Seating	Price	Weight	Prod. Total
Fleetwood Series 36-80 131 in. wb.				
36-7057	Cpe.-2P	3295	4690	—
36-7067	Conv. Cpe.-2P	3395	4800	—
36-7019	Tr. Sed.-5P	3145	4945	—
36-7029	Conv. Sed.-5P	3445	4990	—
Fleetwood Series 36-85 138 in. wb.				
36-7509	Sed.-5P	3345	5115	—
36-7509F	Formal Sed.-5P	4095	5115	—
36-7519	Tr. Sed.-5P	3345	5115	—
36-7529	Conv. Sed.-5P	4095	5230	—
36-7539	Twn. Sed.-5P	3845	5065	—
36-7503	Sed.-7P	3495	5195	—
36-7513	Imp. Sed.-7P	3695	5230	—
36-7523	Tr. Sed.-7P	3495	5195	—
36-7533	Imp. Tr. Sed.-7P	3695	5230	—
36-7543	Twn. Car-7P	5145	5300	—
Fleetwood Commercial Cars				
36-7503L	Comm. Sed.-7P	—	—	—
36-7513L	Comm. Imp. Sed.-7P	—	—	—
36-7523L	Comm. Tr. Sed.-7P	—	—	—
36-7533L	Comm. Imp. Tr. Sed.-7P	—	—	—

Note that V-12's used same style numbers as V-8's.

ENGINE: 45 degree, overhead valve. Twelve. Cast iron block on aluminum crankcase. B & S: 3-1/8 x 4 in. Disp.: 368 cu. in. C.R.: 6.0:1 std. 5.65:1 opt. Brake H.P.: 150 @ 3600 R.P.M. Main bearings: Four. Valve lifters: Mechanical with hydraulic silencer on rocker bushing. Carb.: Dual Detroit lubricator, type R-13, L-13, Model 51.

CHASSIS: [Series 36-80] W.B. 131 in. O.L.: 206-1/4 in. H.: 66 - 69-1/2 in. Frt/Rear Tread: 60-3/16 / 60-1/2 in. Tires: 7.50 x 16. [Series 36-85] W.B.: 138 in. O.L.: 213-1/2 in. Frt/Rear Tread: 60-3/16 / 62-1/2 in. Tires: 7.50 x 16. [Series 36-85 Commericial Chassis] W.B.: 156 in.

TECHNICAL: Selective, synchro transmission. Speeds: 3F/1R. LHD, center control, emerg at left under panel (RHD opt). Single disc clutch. Shaft drive, Hotchkiss. Semi-floating rear axle, spiral bevel drive. Overall Ratio: 4.6:1 std. 4.3:1 opt. Hydraulic brakes on four wheels. Disc wheels. Wheel size: 16 in.

OPTIONS: Sidemount cover(s) (20.00). Radio (master/standard 89.50/54.50). Heater (18.50). Seat covers. Flexible steering wheel (16.00). Trim rings (1.50 each). Wheel discs (4.00 each).

HISTORICAL: Introduced: October, 1935. Model year sales: 901. Model year production: 901. The general manager was Nicholas Dreystadt.

CADILLAC — SERIES 36-90 — SIXTEEN: The 1936 V-16 was a continuation of the 1935 cars. Built to order only, nearly half of the fifty two units were seven passenger limousines. As with V-8 and V-12 lines, Fleetwood bodies for the V-16 now used the all steel Turret Top. All body styles had Vee windshields. A minor mechanical change involved the use of the "Peak-load" generator.

I.D. DATA: Engine numbers were on the upper surface of the generator drive chain housing. Starting: 5110201. Ending: 5110252.

Style No.	Body Type & Seating	Price	Weight	Prod. Total
Fleetwood Series 36-90, 154 in. wb.				
Some listings show these as 58___ styles.				
36-5725LB	Twn. Cab.-7P	8850	6390	—
36-5725C	Twn. Cab.-7P	—	—	—
36-5730FL	Imp. Cab.-5P	—	—	—
36-5730S	Sed.-5P	—	—	—
36-5733S	Twn. Sed.-5P	7250	6085	—
36-5735	Conv. Cpe.-2P	—	—	—
36-5775	Imp. Sed. (Limo.)-7P	7750	6190	—
36-5775FL	Imp. Cab.-7P	7850	6210	—
36-5775S	Sed.-7P	7555	6190	—
36-5776	Cpe.-2P	—	—	—
36-5780	Conv. Sed. w/Div.-5P	7850	6100	—
36-5791	Limo. Brgm.-7P	—	—	—
36-5799	Aero. Cpe.-5P	—	—	—

Some confusion exists as regards style numbers on 1934-35 Fleetwood bodies. Following the previous Fleetwood system, V-8's would be 56___ or 60___ styles, V-12's would be 57___ or 61___ styles, and V-16's would be 58___ or 62___ styles. This system was followed in promotional literature, in the 1934 Master Parts List, and in early factory records. However, since the bodies were identical for all these series, Fleetwood stamped all body plates 57___ or 60___. Master Parts Lists after 1934 used only 57___ and 60___ style numbers for 1934-35 Fleetwood bodies. Starting in 1936, V-8 and V-12 style numbers reflected the new 1936 series designations, but V-16's retained the 57___ system. 60___ styles were no longer offered.

ENGINE: 45 degree, overhead drive. Sixteen. Cast iron block on aluminum crankcase. B & S: 3 x 4 in. Disp.: 452 cu. in. C.R.: 6.0:1 std. 5.65:1 opt. Brake H.P.: 185 @ 3800 R.P.M. SAE/Taxable H.P.: 57.5. Main bearings: Five. Valve lifters: Mechanical with hydraulic silencer on rocker bushing. Carb.: Dual Detroit lubricator, type R-14, L-14, Model 51.

CHASSIS: W.B.: 154 in. O.L.: 238 in. Frt/Rear Tread: 59-3/8 / 62 in. Tires: 7.50 x 17.

TECHNICAL: Selective, synchro transmission. Speeds: 3F/1R. LHD, center control, emerg at left under panel (RHD opt.). Twin disc clutch. Shaft drive Hotchkiss. 3/4 floating rear axle, spiral bevel drive. Overall Ratio: 4.64:1 std. 4.31:1 opt. 4.07:1 opt. Mechanical brakes with vacuum assist on four wheels. Wire wheels. Wheel size: 17 in. drop center.

OPTIONS: Sidemount covers (20.00). Radio (master/standard 89.50/54.50). Heater (18.50). Seat covers. Flexible steering wheel (16.00). Trim rings (1.50 each).

HISTORICAL: Introduced: October, 1935 (continuation of 1935 series). Model year sales: 52. Model year production: 52. The general manager was Nicholas Dreystadt.

1936

Series 60, V-8, 121" wb

	FP	5	4	3	2	1
Conv	1725	9900	19,800	33,000	46,200	66,000
2P Cpe	1645	4800	9600	16,000	22,400	32,000
Tr Sed	1695	3900	7800	13,000	18,200	26,000

Series 70, V-8, 131" wb, Fleetwood bodies

Conv	2695	10,500	21,000	35,000	49,000	70,000
2P Cpe	2595	4950	9900	16,500	23,100	33,000
Conv Sed	2745	10,800	21,600	36,000	50,500	72,000
Tr Sed	2445	4500	9000	15,000	21,000	30,000

Series 75, V-8, 138" wb, Fleetwood bodies

Sed	2645	6000	12,000	20,000	28,000	40,000
Tr Sed	2645	6150	12,300	20,500	28,700	41,000
Conv Sed	3395	11,400	22,800	38,000	56,000	76,000
Fml Sed	3395	6000	12,000	20,000	28,000	40,000
Twn Sed	3145	6150	12,300	20,500	28,700	41,000
7P Sed	2795	6300	12,600	21,000	29,400	42,000
7P Tr Sed	2795	6750	13,500	22,500	31,500	45,000
Imp Sed	2995	6900	13,800	23,000	32,200	46,000
Imp Tr Sed	2995	7050	14,100	23,500	32,900	47,000
Twn Car	4445	7500	15,000	25,000	35,000	50,000

Series 80, V-12, 131" wb, Fleetwood bodies

Conv	3395	11,400	22,800	38,000	56,000	76,000
Conv Sed	3445	11,100	22,200	37,000	52,000	74,000
Cpe	3295	6000	12,000	20,000	28,000	40,000
Tr Sed	3145	6300	12,600	21,000	29,400	42,000

Series 85, V-12, 138" wb, Fleetwood bodies

Sed	3345	6750	13,500	22,500	31,500	45,000
Tr Sed	3845	6750	13,500	22,500	31,500	45,000
Conv Sed	4095	11,700	23,400	39,000	58,000	78,000
Fml Sed	4095	7050	14,100	23,500	32,900	47,000
Twn Sed	3845	7200	14,400	24,000	33,600	48,000
7P Sed	3495	7350	14,700	24,500	34,300	49,000
7P Tr Sed	3495	7500	15,000	25,000	35,000	50,000
Imp Sed	3695	7800	15,600	26,000	36,400	52,000
Imp Tr Sed	3695	7950	15,900	26,500	37,100	53,000
Twn Car	5145	8250	16,500	27,500	38,500	55,000

Series 90, V-16, 154" wb, Fleetwood bodies

2P Conv	7850	26,300	47,000	75,000	102,000	132,000
Conv Sed	7850	27,900	51,000	79,000	106,000	136,000
2P Cpe	7350	15,000	30,000	50,000	80,000	100,000
Aero Cpe	7450	17,100	31,800	53,000	85,000	106,000
Sed	7850	12,000	24,000	40,000	60,000	80,000
Twn Sed	7250	12,300	24,600	41,000	62,000	82,000
7P Sed	7350	12,600	25,200	42,000	64,000	84,000
5P Imp Cabr	7850	25,500	45,000	73,000	100,000	130,000
7P Imp Cabr	7850	26,300	47,000	75,000	102,000	132,000
Imp Sed	7850	27,900	51,000	79,000	106,000	136,000
Twn Cabr	7850	28,700	53,000	81,000	108,000	138,000
Twn Lan	8850	17,800	32,400	54,000	86,000	108,000
5P Conv	7850	25,500	45,000	73,000	100,000	130,000

1937

1937 Cadillac, town cabriolet, OCW

CADILLAC — SERIES 37-60, 37-65, 37-70, 37-75 — EIGHT: A new body style for the Series 60 line was the Convertible Sedan. Body changes included: Eggcrate grill and hood louvers; Higher fenders with lengthwise crease along the top; Set of three horizontal bars each side of grill; Bumpers carrying the Cadillac emblem; Swinging rear quarter windows; All steel body construction. Series 60 shared many features with the LaSalle, but used the 346 cu. in. V-8 engine. A Series 60 Commercial Chassis with 160-3/8 in. wheelbase was offered.

Series 37-65
A new Series, offered in only one body style — a five passenger Touring Sedan built by Fisher on the 131 in. wheelbase used on Series 70 cars. This car offered a longer, heavier car than the Series 60 at a price below that of the Fleetwood bodies cars.

1937 Cadillac, Series 37-65, touring sedan, JAC

Series 37-70, 75
Bodies same as 1936 except for: Drip molding running from the bottom of the front pillar up and over the doors and rear quarter window; New fenders and bumpers; Headlights rigidly attached (adjusted by moving reflector); Wheel discs incorporated a hub cap; Built-in trunk used on most bodies. A diecast eggcrate grill was used, but the hood louver treatment differed from that used on Fisher bodied cars. Chrome diecast strips were used at the rear of the hood side panels. A seven passenger Fisher bodied Special Touring Sedan, with or without division, was offered on the 138 in. wheelbase. These two body styles had the eggcrate hood louvers typical of all Fisher bodied Cadillacs for 1937. The Business Car line included eight passenger versions of these Special Sedans plus eight passenger versions of four Fleetwood body styles. The eighth passenger was seated with two others on the auxiliary seats. A Commercial Chassis on a 156 in. wheelbase was offered. Engine changes included: Lighter flywheel; Generator relocated in the Vee; oil filter installed; New carburetor with full-automatic electric choke; oil bath air cleaner; relocated distributor. A new transmission design featured: Pin-type synchronizers; shifter rails relocated to side of case; Cover on bottom of case; extension integral with transmission mainshaft.

I.D. DATA: Engine numbers were on the crankcase, just behind the left cylinder group, parallel to the dash. Starting: [Series 37-60] 6030001; [Series 37-65] 703001; [Series 37-70, 75] 3130001. Ending: [Series 37-60] 6037003; [Series 37-65] 7032401; [Series 37-70, 75] 3134232.

Style No.	Body Type & Seating	Price	Weight	Prod. Total
Series 37-60 Fisher 124 In. w.b.				
37-6019	Tr. Sed.-5P	1545	3845	—
37-6049	Conv. Sed.-5P	1885	3885	—
37-6067	Conv. Cpe.-2P	1575	3745	—
37-6027	Spt. Cpe.-2P	1445	3710	—
Series 37-65 Fisher 131 In. wb.				
37-6519	Tr. Sed.-5P	1945	4835	—
Series 37-75 Fisher 138 In. wb.				
37-7523S	Spec. Tr. Sed.-7P	2445	4825	—
37-7533S	Spec. Imp. Tr. Sed.-7P	2645	4985	—
Series 37-70 Fleetwood 131 In. wb.				
37-7019	Tr. Sed.-5P	2445	4420	—
37-7029	Conv. Sed.-5P	2795	4460	—
37-7057	Spt. Cpe.-2P	2645	4285	—
37-7067	Conv. Cpe.-2P	2745	4325	—
Series 37-75 Fleetwood 138 In. wb.				
37-7503	Sed.-7P	—	—	—
37-7509-F	Fml. Sed.-5P	3495	4745	—
37-7513	Imp. Sed.-7P	—	—	—
37-7519	Tr. Sed.-5P	2645	4745	—
37-7523	Tr. Sed.-7P	2795	4825	—
37-7529	Conv. Sed.-5P	3445	4980	—
37-7533	Imp. Tr. Sed.-7P	2995	4985	—
37-7539	Twn. Sed.-5P	3145	4780	—
37-7543	Twn. Car-7P	4545	5055	—
37-7589-A	Cpe.-5P	—	—	—
37-7592	Limo. Brgm.-7P	—	—	—
Series 37-75 Fisher 138 In. w.b. Business Cars				
37-7523-SL	Spec. Bus. Tr. Sed.-8P	2575	4825	—
37-7533-SL	Spec. Bus. Imp. Tr. Sed.-8P	2775	4985	—
Series 37-75 Fleetwood 138 In. w.b. Business Cars				
37-7503-L	Bus. Sed.-8P	—	—	—
37-7513-L	Bus. Imp. Sed.-8P	—	—	—
37-7523-L	Bus. Tr. Sed.-8P	—	—	—
37-7533-L	Bus. Imp. Sed.-8P	—	—	—

ENGINE: Ninety degree, L-head. Eight. Cast iron block (blocks cast enbloc with crankcase). B & S: 3-1/2 x 4-1/2 in. Disp.: 346 cu. in. C.R.: 6.25:1 std. 5.75:1 opt. Brake H.P.: 135 @ 3400 R.P.M. SAE/Taxable H.P.: 39.20. Main bearings: Three. Valve lifters: Hydraulic. Carb.: Stromberg AA-25.

CHASSIS: [Series 37-60] W.B.: 124 in. O.L.: 201-1/4 in. Frt/Rear Tread: 58/59 in. Tires: 7.50 x 16. [Series 37-65] W.B.: 131 in. O.L.: 208-3/16 in. Frt/Rear Tread: 60-3/16 / 60-1/2 in. Tires: 7.50 x 16. [Series 37-70] W.B.: 131 in. O.L.: 208-3/16 in. Frt/Rear Tread: 60-3/16 / 60-1/2 in. Tires: 7.50 x 16. [Series 37-75] W.B.: 138 in. O.L.: 215-7/8 in. Frt/Rear Tread: 60-3/16 / 62-1/2 in. Tires: 7.50 x 16. [Series 37-60 Commercial Chassis] W.B.: 160-3/8 in. O.L.: 237-7/8 in. Tires: 7.00 x 16. [Series 37-75 Commercial Chassis] W.B.: 156 in. O.L.: 231-1/4 in. Tires: 7.50 x 16.

TECHNICAL: Selective, synchro transmission. Speeds: 3F/1R. LHD, center control, emerg at left under panel (RHD opt.). Single disc clutch. Shaft drive, Hotchkiss. Semi-floating rear axle, spiral bevel drive. (Series 37-60 Hypoid). Overall ratio: 4.3:1 (Series 37-60 3.69:1). Hydraulic brakes on four wheels. Disc wheels. Wheel size: 16 in.

OPTIONS: Sidemount cover(s) (15.00 - 17.50). Radio (master/standard 79.50/59.50). Heater (19.50 - 60.00). Seat covers (7.50 per seat). Wheel disc (4.00 each). Trim rings (1.50 each). Flexible steering wheel (15.00).

HISTORICAL: Introduced: November, 1936. Model year sales: [Series 60] 7003; [Series 65] 2401; [Series 70, 75] 4232. Model year production: [Series 60] 7003; [Series 65] 2401; [Series 70, 75] 4232. The general manager was Nicholas Dreystadt.

CADILLAC — SERIES 37-85 — TWELVE: Series 37-85 was, once more, a Series 37-75 with a V-12 engine. 1937 was the final model year for this engine. The Series 80, with 131 in. wheelbase was dropped from the line. Oil bath air cleaner and pressure radiator cap were new to the 1937 V-12.

I.D. DATA: Engine numbers were on the upper surface of the generator drive chain housing. Starting: 4130001. Ending: 4130478.

Style No.	Body Type & Seating	Price	Weight	Prod. Total
Series 37-85 Fleetwood 138 in. w.b.				
37-7509F	Formal Sed.-5P	4195	5050	—
37-7513	Imp. Sed.-7P	3695	5165	—
37-7519	Tr. Sed.-5P	3345	5050	—
37-7523	Tr. Sed.-7P	3495	5130	—
37-7529	Conv. Sed.-5P	4145	5165	—
37-7533	Imp. Tr. Sed.-7P	3695	5165	—
37-7539	Twn. Sed.-5P	3845	5000	—
37-7543	Twn. Car-7P	5245	5230	—
37-7511	Tr. Cpe.-5P	—	—	—
37-7518	Sed.-5P	—	—	—
37-7589A	Cpe.-5P	—	—	—
37-7591	Limo. Brgm.-7P	—	—	—
Series 37-85 Fisher 138 in. wb. Business Cars				
37-7523SL	Spec. Buss Tr. Sed.-8P	2575	4825	—
37-7533SL	Spec. Buss Imp. Tr. Sed.-8P	2775	4985	—
Series 37-85 Fleetwood 138 in. wb. Business Cars				
37-7503L	Buss Sed.-8P	—	—	—
37-7513L	Buss Imp. Sed.-8P	—	—	—
37-7523L	Buss Tr. Sed.-8P	—	—	—
37-7533L	Buss Imp. Tr. Sed.-8P	—	—	—

ENGINE: 45 degree, overhead valve. Twelve. Cast iron block on aluminum crankcase. B & S: 3-1/8 x 4 in. Disp.: 368 cu. in. C.R.: 6.0:1 std. 5.65:1 opt. Brake H.P.: 150 @ 3600 R.P.M. SAE/Taxable H.P.: 46.9. Main bearings: Four. Valve lifters: Mechanical with hydraulic silencer on rocker bushing. Carb.: Dual Detroit lubricator, type R-13, L-13, Model 51.

CHASSIS: [Series 37-85] W.B.: 138 in. O.L.: 215-7/8 in. Frt/Rear Tread: 60-3/16 / 61-1/2 in. Tires: 7.50 x 16.

TECHNICAL: Selective, synchro transmission. Speeds: 3F/1R. LHD, center control, emerg at left under panel (RHD opt.). Single disc clutch. Shaft drive, Hotchkiss. Semi-floating rear axle, spiral bevel drive. Overall ratio: 4.6:1. Hydraulic brakes on four wheels. disc wheels. Wheel size: 16 in.

OPTIONS: Sidemount cover(s) (15.00 - 17.50). Radio (master/standard 79.50/59.50). Heater (19.50 - 60.00). Seat covers (7.50 per seat). Wheel discs (4.00 each). Trim rings (1.50 each). Flexible steering wheel (15.00).

HISTORICAL: Introduced: November, 1936. Model year sales: 478. Model year production: 478. The general manager was Nicholas Dreystadt.

CADILLAC — SERIES 37-90 — SIXTEEN: The 1937 Series 90 remained essentially the same as the 1934-36 cars. 1937 was the final model year for the overhead valve V-16 engine. For the first time, hydraulic brakes (with a vacuum booster on the pedal) were used on these cars. A stabilizer bar was added to the front suspension. A Handy oil filter replaced the Cuno self-cleaning unit. A pressure cap was used on the radiator.

I.D. DATA: Engine numbers were on the upper surface of the generator drive chain housing. Starting: 5130301. Ending: 5130350.

Style No.	Body Type & Seating	Price	Weight	Prod. Total
Series 37-90 Fleetwood 154 in. w.b.				
37-5725LB	Imp. Twn. Cab.-7P	—	—	—
37-5730S	Sed.-5P	—	—	—
37-5730FL	Imp. Cab.-5P	—	—	—
37-5733S	Twn. Sed.-5P	7350	6085	—
37-5735	Conv. Cpe.-2P	—	—	—
37-5775	Imp. Sed.-7P	7550	6190	—
37-5775S	Sed.-7P	7350	6190	—
37-5775SF	Sed.-7P	—	—	—
37-5775FL	Imp. Cab.-7P	7950	6210	—
37-5775H4	Limo.-7P	—	—	—
37-5776	Cpe.-2P	—	—	—
37-5780	Conv. Sed.-5P	7950	6100	—
37-5785	Coll. Cpe.-5P	—	—	—
37-5791	Limo. Brgm.-7P	—	—	—
37-5799	Aero. Cpe.-5P	7500	—	—

ENGINE: 45 degree, overhead valve. Sixteen. Cast iron block on aluminum crankcase. B & S: 3 x 4 in. Disp.: 452 cu. in. C.R.: 6.0:1 std. 5.65:1 opt. Brake H.P.: 185 @ 3800 R.P.M. SAE/Taxable H.P.: 57.5. Main bearings: Five. Valve lifters: Mechanical with hydraulic silencer on rocker bushing. Carb.: Dual Detroit lubricator, type R-14, L-14, Model 51.

CHASSIS: W.B.: 154 in. O.L.: 238 in. Frt/Rear Tread: 59-3/8 / 62 in. Tires: 7.50 x 17.

TECHNICAL: Selective, synchro transmission. Speeds: 3F/1R. LHD, center control, emerg at left under panel (RHD opt.). Twin disc clutch. Shaft drive Hotchkiss. 3/4 floating rear axle, spiral bevel drive. Overall ratio: 4.64:1 std. 4.31:1 opt., 4.07:1 opt. Hydraulic brakes with vacuum booster on four wheels. Wire wheels with disc cover. Wheel size: 17 in. drop center.

OPTIONS: Sidemount cover(s) (15.00 - 17.50). Radio (master/standard 79.50/59.50). Heater (19.50 - 60.00). Seat covers (7.50 per seat). Wheel discs (4.00 each). Trim rings (1.50 each). Flexible steering wheel (15.00).

HISTORICAL: Introduced: November, 1936. Model year sales: 50. Model year production: 50. The general manager was Nicholas Dreystadt.

1937

	FP	5	4	3	2	1
Series 60, V-8, 124" wb						
Conv	1790	8250	16,500	27,500	38,500	55,000
Conv Sed	2120	8550	17,100	28,500	39,900	57,000
2P Cpe	1655	5250	10,500	17,500	24,500	35,000
Tr Sed	1760	4500	9000	15,000	21,000	30,000
Series 65, V-8, 131" wb						
Tr Sed	2190	4800	9600	16,000	22,400	32,000
Series 70, V-8, 131" wb, Fleetwood bodies						
Conv	3005	8550	17,100	28,500	39,900	57,000
Conv Sed	3060	9000	18,000	30,000	42,000	60,000
Spt Cpe	2905	5700	11,400	19,000	26,600	38,000
Tr Sed	2695	5100	10,200	17,000	23,800	34,000
Series 75, V-8, 138" wb, Fleetwood bodies						
Tr Sed	2915	5550	11,100	18,500	25,900	37,000
Twn Sed	3425	5700	11,400	19,000	26,600	38,000
Conv Sed	3730	9900	19,800	33,000	46,200	66,000
Fml Sed	3785	6000	12,000	20,000	28,000	40,000
Spec Tr Sed	2710	6150	12,300	20,500	28,700	41,000
Spec Imp Tr Sed	2910	6300	12,600	21,000	29,400	42,000
7P Tr Sed	3070	6450	12,900	21,500	30,100	43,000
7P Imp	3270	6300	12,600	21,000	29,400	42,000
Bus Tr Sed	2845	6150	12,300	20,500	28,700	41,000
Bus Imp	3050	7500	15,000	25,000	35,000	50,000
Twn Carb	4855	10,500	21,000	35,000	49,000	70,000
Series 85, V-12, 138" wb, Fleetwood bodies						
Tr Sed	3635	6300	12,600	21,000	29,400	42,000
Twn Sed	4135	6450	12,900	21,500	30,100	43,000
Conv Sed	4450	10,500	21,000	35,000	49,000	70,000
7P Tr Sed	3790	6750	13,500	22,500	31,500	45,000
Imp Tr Sed	3990	7500	15,000	25,000	35,000	50,000
Twn Car	5575	10,800	21,600	36,000	50,500	72,000
Series 90, V-16, 154" wb, Fleetwood bodies						
2P Conv	7900	30,300	57,000	86,000	112,000	145,000
5P Conv	8205	29,500	55,000	84,000	110,000	140,000
Conv Sed	8205	30,300	57,000	86,000	112,000	145,000
Cpe	7745	18,500	33,000	55,000	88,000	110,000
Twn Sed	7595	12,900	25,800	48,200	66,000	86,000
7P Sed	7645	13,200	26,400	44,000	68,000	88,000
Limo	7900	13,500	27,000	45,000	70,000	90,000
5P Imp Cabr	8155	29,500	55,000	84,000	110,000	140,000
5P Twn Cabr	9125	30,300	57,000	86,000	112,000	145,000
7P Imp Cabr	8205	30,300	57,000	86,000	112,000	145,000
7P Twn Cabr	9230	31,100	58,000	88,000	114,000	150,000
Aero Cpe	9200	18,500	33,000	55,000	88,000	110,000
Limo Brgm	9125	15,000	30,000	50,000	80,000	100,000
Fml Sed	9230	17,100	31,800	53,000	85,000	106,000

1938

1938 Cadillac, Sixty Special, sedan

CADILLAC — SERIES 38-60, 38-60S, 38-65, 38-75 — EIGHT: For 1938, the Series 70 and Fisher bodied Series 75 Specials were dropped, but a Convertible Sedan was added to the Series 65 line. The styling bonanza for 1938 was the sensational new Sixty Special Sedan.

Series 60 was restyled with a squared off grille made up of horizontal bars extending around front and sides of the nose. Three sets of four chrome bars decorated the side panel louvers. Hood was front opening alligator style and headlights were fixed to the sheet metal between fenders and grille.

Sixty Special had much the same nose as the Sixty, with one less bar in the grille assembly. The body was entirely new and unique, on a double dropped frame three inches lower than the Sixty. There were no runningboards, the floor being at normal runningboard height. Large side windows in chrome frames were flush with the sides of the body. The convertible-shaped top featured a thin roof section and a notched back.

Series 65 (Custom V-8) and Series 75 (Fleetwood) shared a new front end style featuring a massive vertical cellular grille, three sets of horizontal bars on the hood sides, alligator hood, and headlights on the filler piece between fenders and hood. Optional sidemount covers were hinged to the fenders. Quarter windows were of sliding rather than hinged construction. Rear of bodies had rounder corners and more smoothly blended lines; trunks had more appearance of being an integral part of the body. Bodies were all steel except for wooden main sills.

New chassis details included: Column gear shift; horns just behind grille; battery under right hand side of hood; transverse muffler just behind fuel tank; wheels by different manufacturer (not interchangeable with 1937); "Synchro-Flex" flywheel; hypoid rear axle on all series; deletion of oil filter. Compression ratio on Series 75 was raised to 6.70:1, necessitating use of high octane fuel.

I.D. DATA: Serial numbers were on left frame side bar, at the rear of the left front motor support. Starting: Same as engine number. Ending: Same as engine number. Engine numbers were on crankcase, just behind left cylinder block. Starting Engine No.: [Series 38-60] 8270001; [Series 38-60S] 6270001; [Series 38-65] 7270001; [Series 38-75] 3270001. Ending: [Series 38-60] 8272052; [Series 38-60S] 6273704; [Series 38-65] 7271476; [Series 38-75] 3271911.

Style No.	Body Type & Seating	Price	Weight	Prod. Total
Fisher Series 38-60, 124" wb				
38-6127	Cpe.-2P	1695	3855	—
38-6167	Conv. Cpe.-2P	1810	3845	—
38-6149	Conv. Sed.-5P	2215	3980	—
38-6119	Sed.-5P	1775	3940	—
Fisher Series 38-60S, 127" wb				
38-6019S	Spec. Sed.-5P	2085	4170	—
Fisher Series 38-65 132" wb				
38-6519	Sed.-5P	2285	4540	—
38-6519-F	Imp. Sed.-5P	2360	4580	—
38-6549	Conv. Sed.-5P	2600	4580	—
Fleetwood Series 38-75, 141" wb, Business Cars				
38-7523-L	Bus. Tr. Sed.-7P	3105	4945	—
38-7533-L	Bus. Tr. Imp.-7P	3255	5105	—
Fleetwood Series 38-75 141 in. wb				
38-7557	Cpe.-2P	3275	4675	—
38-7557-B	Cpe.-5P	3380	4775	—
38-7567	Conv. Cpe.-2P	3380	4665	—
38-7519	Sed.-5P	3075	4865	—
38-7519-F	Imp. Sed.-5P	3155	4925	—
38-7559	Formal Sed.-5P	3990	4865	—
38-7539	Town Sed.-5P	3635	4900	—
38-7529	Conv. Sed.-5P	3940	5110	—
38-7523	Sed.-7P	3205	4945	—
38-7533	Imp. Sed.-7P	3360	5105	—
38-7533-F	Formal Sed.-7P	3990	5105	—
38-7553	Town Car-7P	5115	5175	—

1938 Cadillac, Series 65, sedan, OCW

ENGINE: Ninety degree. L-head. Eight. Cast iron block (blocks cast enbloc with crankcase). B & S: 3-1/2 in. x 4-1/2 in. Disp.: 346 cu. in. C.R.: [Series 60, 60S, 65] 6.25:1; [Series 75] 6.7:1. Brake H.P.: 135 (140 on 75) @ 3400 R.P.M. SAE/Taxable H.P.: 39.20. Main bearings: Three. Valve lifters: Hydraulic. Carb.: Stromberg AAV-25.

CHASSIS: [Series 38-60] W.B.: 124 in. O.L.: 207-5/8 in. Frt/Rear Tread: 58/61 in. Tires: 7.00 x 16. [Series 38-60S] W.B.: 127 in. O.L.: 207-5/8 in. Frt/Rear Tread: 58/61 in. Tires: 7.00 x 16. [Series 38-65] W.B.: 132 in. O.L.: 211-3/8 in. Frt/Rear Tread: 60-1/2/62-3/8 in. Tires: 7.00 x 16. [Series 38-75] W.B.: 141 in. O.L.: 220-5/8 in. Frt/Rear Tread: 60-1/2/62-1/2 in. Tires: 7.50 x 16. [Series 38-60 Commercial Chassis] W.B.: 160 in. [Series 38-65 Commercial Chassis] W.B.: 160 in. [Series 38-75 Commercial Chassis] W.B.: 161 in.

TECHNICAL: Selective synchro manual transmission. Speeds: 3F/1R. LHD; gearshift on column; handbrake at left (RHD opt.). Single disc clutch. Shaft drive Hotchkiss. Semifloating rear axle. Hypoid gears. O.R.: [60, 60S, 65] 3.92:1; [75] 4.58:1. Hydraulic brakes on four wheels. Disc wheels. Wheel size: 16 in.

OPTIONS: Radio for Fleetwood Bodies (95.00). Radio Master/Standard (79.50/65.00). Heater (26.50-42.50). Seat covers (7.50 per seat). Spotlight (18.50). Automatic battery filler (7.50). Flexible steering wheel (15.00). fog lights (17.50 pair). Wheel discs (4.00 each). Trim rings (1.50 each).

HISTORICAL: Introduced: October, 1937. Model year sales and production: [Series 60] 2052; [Series 60S] 3704; [Series 65] 1476; [Series 75] 1911. The general manager was Nicholas Dreystadt.

CADILLAC — SERIES 38-90 — SIXTEEN: The Series 90 for 1938 became essentially a Series 75 with a V-16 engine. Even though the wheelbase was thirteen inches shorter, the bodies were equal or larger in all dimensions than previous Cadillac V-16's. This was accomplished by fitting the nearly flat engine low in the frame and partially behind the line of the firewall. V-16's were distinguished from the counterpart V-8's by a coarser pitch eggcrate grille, fender lamps, and streamlined louvers on the hood side panels and all fender skirts.

The new V-16 engine was of L-head, short stroke square design, cast-enbloc, with 135 degree Vee. With each block in running balance, the engine was basically a twin-eight. Dual accessories included carburetors, oil bath air cleaners, manifolds, distributors, coils, fuel pumps, and water pumps. The fuel pumps were interconnected so that either one could supply both carburetors if needed. Only the left hand distributor contained breaker arms; the two arms being electrically independent but operated by a single eight-lobe cam. The right hand unit acted only to distribute the high tension voltage to the spark plugs in the right bank. A cross pipe connected both exhaust manifolds and fed into a single down-pipe at the left. The generator was placed low in the Vee and was driven by an internal rubber ring in the fan hub acting on a driven wheel on the generator shaft. This arrangement allowed for fan speeds less than engine speed and generator speeds nearly twice engine speed — it lasted only one year.

I.D. DATA: Serial numbers were on frame side bar, just ahead of the steering gear. Starting: Same as engine number. Ending: Same as engine number. Engine numbers were on upper rear left hand corner of left cylinder block, parallel with cylinder head. Starting Engine No.: 5270001. Ending: 5270315.

Style No.	Body Type & Seating	Price	Weight	Prod. Total
Fleetwood Series 38-90 141 in. w.b.				
38-9057	Cpe.-2P	5335	4915	—
38-9057-B	Cpe.-5P	5440	5015	—
38-9067	Conv. Cpe.-2P	5440	4905	—
38-9019	Sed.-5P	5135	5105	—
38-9019-F	Imp. Sed.-5P	5215	5165	—
38-9059	Formal Sed.-5P	6050	5105	—
38-9039	Twn. Sed.-5P	5695	5140	—
38-9029	Conv. Sed.-5P	6000	5350	—
38-9023	Sed.-7P	5265	5185	—
38-9033	Imp. Sed.-7P	5420	5345	—
38-9033-F	Formal Sed.-7P	6050	5345	—
38-9053	Twn. Car-7P	7170	5415	—

ENGINE: 135 degree Vee. L-Head. Sixteen. Cast iron block. B & S: 3-1/4 in. x 3-1/4 in. Disp.: 431 cu. in. C.R.: 7:1. Brake H.P.: 185 @ 3600 R.P.M. SAE/Taxable H.P.: 67.6. Main bearings: Nine. Valve lifters: Hydraulic. Carb.: Carter WDO 407s(L) — 408s(R).

CHASSIS: [Series 38-90] W.B.: 141 in. O.L.: 200-5/8 in. Frt/Rear Tread: 60-1/2 in./62-1/2 in. Tires: 7.50 x 16.

TECHNICAL: Selective synchro manual transmission. Speeds: 3F/1R. LHD; gearshift on column; handbrake at left. Single disc clutch. Shaft drive, Hotchkiss. Semifloating rear axle. Hypoid gears. O.R.: 4.31:1. Hydraulic brakes on four wheels. Disc wheels. Wheel size: 16 in.

OPTIONS: Radio (95.00). Heater (26.50-42.50). Seat covers (7.50 per seat). Spotlight (18.50). Automatic battery filler (7.50). Flexible steering wheel (15.00). Fog lights (17.50 pair).

HISTORICAL: Introduced October, 1937. Model year sales and production: 315. The general manager of Cadillac was Nicholas Dreystadt.

1938						
Series 60, V-8, 124" wb	FP	5	4	3	2	1
Conv	1815	8250	16,500	27,500	38,500	55,000
Conv Sed	2215	8550	17,100	28,500	39,900	57,000
2P Cpe	1695	5550	11,100	25,900	37,000	—
Tr Sed	1780	5400	10,800	18,000	25,200	36,000
Series 60 Special, V-8, 127" wb						
Tr Sed	2090	6000	12,000	20,000	28,000	40,000
Series 65, V-8, 132" wb						
Tr Sed	2290	5550	11,100	18,500	25,900	37,000
Div Tr Sed	2360	6300	12,600	21,000	29,400	42,000
Conv Sed	2605	9900	19,800	33,000	46,200	66,000
Series 75, V-8, 141" wb, Fleetwood bodies						
Conv	3380	9900	19,800	33,000	46,200	66,000
Conv Sed	3945	10,200	20,400	34,000	47,600	68,000
2P Cpe	3280	7050	14,100	23,500	32,900	47,000
5P Cpe	3380	6750	13,500	22,500	31,500	45,000
Tr Sed	3080	6300	12,600	21,000	29,400	42,000
Div Tr Sed	3155	6750	13,500	22,500	31,500	45,000
Twn Sed	3635	6600	13,200	22,000	30,800	44,000
Fml Sed	3995	6750	13,500	22,500	31,500	45,000
7P Fml Sed	3995	7050	14,100	23,500	32,900	47,000
7P Tr Sed	3210	6750	13,500	22,500	31,500	45,000
Imp Tr Sed	3360	6900	13,800	23,000	32,200	46,000
8P Tr Sed	3105	6750	13,500	22,500	31,500	45,000
8P Imp Tr Sed	3260	6900	13,800	23,000	32,200	46,000
Twn C	5115	9000	18,000	30,000	42,000	60,000
Series 90, V-16, 141" wb, Fleetwood bodies						
Conv	5440	12,900	25,800	48,200	66,000	86,000
Conv Sed Trk	6000	12,900	25,800	48,200	66,000	86,000
2P Cpe	5340	9000	18,000	30,000	42,000	60,000

	FP	5	4	3	2	1
5P Cpe	5440	9600	19,200	32,000	44,800	64,000
Tr Sed	5140	9300	18,600	31,000	43,400	62,000
Twn Sed	5695	9600	19,200	32,000	44,800	64,000
Div Tr Sed	5215	10,500	21,000	35,000	49,000	70,000
7P Tr Sed	5270	10,500	21,000	35,000	49,000	70,000
Imp Tr Sed	5420	10,500	21,000	35,000	49,000	70,000
Fml Sed	6055	10,500	21,000	35,000	49,000	70,000
Fml Sed Trk	6055	10,500	21,000	35,000	49,000	70,000
TwnC	7175	12,000	24,000	40,000	60,000	80,000

1939

1939 Cadillac, Sixty Special, touring sedan, JAC

CADILLAC — SERIES 39-60S, 39-61, 39-75 — EIGHT: For 1939, Series 61 replaced Series 60 and 65 of 1938. All V-8's had new grille styling; similar in appearance but different in detail dimensions on each series. The pointed center grille and the functional side grilles were diecast, with fine-pitch bars. A single diecast louver was positioned to the rear of each hood side panel. Headlights were once again attached to the radiator casing.

Sixty Special, now bodied by Fleetwood, was offered with optional Sunshine Turret Top or center division. These options were also available on the Series 61 Sedan. Series 61 was available with or without running boards; had concealed door hinges except for the lower front hinge; and had chrome reveals on all windows.

Chassis changes included: Tube and fin radiator core; Sea shell horns under the hood; 10 mm spark plugs; Cross-link steering on Series 61; Slotted disc wheels on Series 60S and 61.

I.D. DATA: Serial numbers were located on the left frame side bar, opposite the steering gear. Starting: Same as engine number. Ending: Same as engine number. Engine numbers were on the crankcase, just behind the left cylinder block, parallel to the dash. Starting Engine No.: [Series 39-60S] 6290001; [Series 39-61] 8290001; [Series 39-75] 3290001. Ending: [Series 39-60S] 6295513; [Series 39-61] 8295913; [Series 39-75] 3292069.

Style No.	Body Type & Seating	Price	Weight	Prod. Total
Fleetwood Series 39-60S, 127 in. w.b.				
39-6019S	Spec. Sed.-5P	2195	4110	—
39-6019S-A	Spec. Sed. (STT)-5P	2245	—	—
39-6019S-F	Spec. Sed. (Div)-5P	—	—	—
Fisher Series 39-61, 126 in. w.b.				
39-6127	Cpe.-2P	1695	3685	—
39-6167	Conv. Cpe.-2P	1855	3765	—
39-6129	Conv. Sed.-5P	2265	3810	—
39-6119	Tr. Sed.-5P	1765	3770	—
39-6119-A	Tr. Sed. (STT)-5P	1805	—	—
39-6119-F	Tr. Sed. (Div)-5P	—	—	—
Fleetwood Series 39-75, 141 in. w.b. Business Cars				
39-7523-L	Buss. Tr. Sed.-8P	3215	4865	—
39-7533-L	Buss. Tr. Imp.-8P	3370	5025	—
Fleetwood Series 39-75, 141 in. w.b.				
39-7557	Cpe.-2P	3395	4595	—
39-7557-B	Cpe.-5P	3495	4695	—
39-7567	Conv. Cpe.-2P	3495	4675	—
39-7519	Sed.-5P	3100	4785	—
39-7519-F	Imp. Sed.-5P	3265	4845	—
39-7559	Formal Sed.-5P	4115	4785	—
39-7539	Twn. Sed.-5P	3750	4820	—
39-7529	Conv. Sed.-5P	4065	5030	—
39-7523	Sed.-7P	3325	4865	—
39-7533	Imp. Sed.-7P	3475	5025	—
39-7533-F	Formal Sed.-7P	4115	5025	—
39-7553	Twn. Car-7P	5245	5095	—

ENGINE: Ninety degree. L-Head. Eight. Cast iron block (blocks cast enbloc with crankcase). B & S: 3-1/2 in. x 4-1/2 in. Disp.: 346 cu. in. C.R.: [60S, 61] 6.25:1, [75] 6.7:1. Brake H.P.: 135 (140 on 75) @ 3400 R.P.M. SAE/Taxable H.P.: 39.20. Main bearings: Three. Valve lifters: Hydraulic. Carb.: Stromberg AAV-26.

CHASSIS: [Series 39-60S] W.B.: 127 in. O.L.: 214-1/4 in. Frt/Rear Tread: 58/61 in. Tires: 7.00 x 16. [Series 39-61] W.B.: 126 in. O.L.: 207-1/4 in. Frt/Rear Tread: 58/59 in. Tires: 7.00 x 16. [Series 39-75] W.B.: 141 in. O.L.: 225-1/8 in. Frt/Rear Tread: 60-1/2 in./62-1/2 in. Tires: 7.50 x 16. [Series 39-61 Commercial Chassis] W.B.: 162-1/4 in. O.L.: 243-1/2 in. Tires: 7.00 x 16. [Series 39-75 Commercial Chassis] W.B.: 161-3/8 in. O.L.: 245-3/8 in. Tires: 7.50 x 16.

1939 Cadillac, Sixty Special, touring sedan, OCW

TECHNICAL: Selective synchro manual transmission. Speeds: 3F/1R. LHD; gearshift on column; handbrake at left (RHD opt.). Single disc clutch. Shaft drive, Hotchkiss. Semifloating rear axle. Hypoid gears. O.R.: [60S, 61] 3.92:1, [75] 4.58:1. Hydraulic brakes on four wheels. Slotted disc wheels. Wheel size: 16 in.

OPTIONS: Radio (69.50). Heater (31.50). Seat covers (8.25 per seat). Spotlight (18.50). Windshield washer (5.75). Automatic battery filler (7.50). Fog lights (14.50 pair).

HISTORICAL: Introduced October, 1938. Model year sales and production: [Series 60S] 5513, [Series 61] 5913, [Series 75] 2069. The general manager of Cadillac was Nicholas Dreystadt.

1939 Cadillac, Series 39-90, V-16, 7-pass. sedan, JAC

CADILLAC — SERIES 39-90 — SIXTEEN: Same as 1938 except for a few detail changes. Chrome strips used along runningboard edges. Spears on hood and fender skirts fully chromed. New instrument panel and minor differences in bumpers and tail lights. Generator relocated high in the Vee and belt driven.

I.D. DATA: Serial numbers were located on the left frame side bar, opposite the steering gear. Starting: Same as engine number. Ending: Same as engine number. Engine numbers were on the left rear corner on the flat top of the crankcase, parallel to the dash. Starting Engine No.: 5290001. Ending: 5290138.

Style No.	Body Type & Seating	Price	Weight	Prod. Total
Fleetwood Series 39-90, 141 in. wb				
39-9057	Cpe.-2P	5440	4915	—
39-9057-B	Cpe.-5P	5545	5015	—
39-9067	Conv. Cpe.-2P	5545	4995	—
39-9019	Sed.-5P	5240	5105	—
39-9019-F	Imp. Sed.-5P	5315	5165	—
39-9059	Formal Sed.-5P	6165	5105	—
39-9039	Town Sed.-5P	5800	5140	—
39-9029	Conv. Sed.-5P	6110	5350	—
39-9023	Sed.-7P	5375	5185	—
39-9033	Imp. Sed.-7P	5525	5345	—
39-9033-F	Formal Sed.-7P	6165	5345	—
39-9053	Town Car-7P	7295	5415	—

ENGINE: 135 degree Vee. L-head. Sixteen. Cast iron block. B & S: 3-1/4 in. x 3-1/4 in. Disp.: 431 cu. in. C.R.: 6.75:1. Brake H.P.: 185 @ 3600 R.P.M. SAE/Taxable H.P.: 67.6. Main bearings: Nine. Valve lifters: Hydraulic. Carb.: Carter WDO-407s (L) — 408s (R).

CHASSIS: W.B.: 141 in. O.L.: 222 in. Frt/Rear Tread: 60-1/2/62-1/2 in. Tires: 7.50 x 16.

TECHNICAL: Selective synchro manual transmission. Speeds: 3F/1R. LHD; gearshift on column; handbrake at left. Single disc clutch. Shaft drive Hotchkiss. Semifloating rear axle. Hypoid gears. O.R.: 4.31:1. Hydraulic brakes on four wheels. Disc wheels. Wheel size: 16 in.

OPTIONS: Radio (69.50). Heater (31.50). Seat covers (8.25 per seat). Spotlight (18.50). Windshield washer (5.75). Automatic battery filler (7.50). Fog lights (14.50 pair).

HISTORICAL: Introduced: October, 1938. Model year sales and production: 138. The general manager of Cadillac was Nicholas Dreystadt.

1939
Series 61, V-8, 126" wb

	FP	5	4	3	2	1
Conv	1770	8100	16,200	27,000	37,800	54,000
Conv Sed	2170	8400	16,800	28,000	39,200	56,000
Cpe	1610	4500	9000	15,000	21,000	30,000
Tr Sed	1680	4050	8100	13,500	18,900	27,000

Series 60 Special, V-8, 127" wb, Fleetwood

	FP	5	4	3	2	1
Sed	2090	4350	8700	14,500	20,300	29,000
SR Sed	—	4500	9000	15,000	21,000	30,000
SR Imp Sed	—	4800	9600	16,000	22,400	32,000

Series 75, V-8, 141" wb, Fleetwood bodies

	FP	5	4	3	2	1
Conv	3380	8250	16,500	27,500	38,500	55,000
Conv Sed Trk	3945	8550	17,100	28,500	39,900	57,000
4P Cpe	3280	5250	10,500	17,500	24,500	35,000
5P Cpe	3380	5400	10,800	18,000	25,200	36,000
Tr Sed	2995	4950	9900	16,500	23,100	33,000
Div Tr Sed	3155	5100	10,200	17,000	23,800	34,000
Twn Sed Trk	3635	5250	10,500	17,500	24,500	35,000
Fml Sed Trk	3995	5400	10,800	18,000	25,200	36,000
7P Fml Sed Trk	3995	5400	10,800	18,000	25,200	36,000
7P Tr Sed	3210	5250	10,500	17,500	24,500	35,000
7P Tr Imp Sed	3360	5400	10,800	18,000	25,200	36,000
Bus Tr Sed	3105	5250	10,500	17,500	24,500	35,000
8P Tr Imp Sed	3260	5400	10,800	18,000	25,200	36,000
Twn Car Trk	5115	5550	11,100	18,500	25,900	37,000

Series 90, V-16, 141" wb, Fleetwood bodies

	FP	5	4	3	2	1
Conv	5440	15,000	30,000	50,000	80,000	100,000
Conv Sed	6000	17,100	31,800	53,000	85,000	106,000
4P Cpe	5340	10,500	21,000	35,000	49,000	70,000
5P Cpe	5440	9900	19,800	33,000	46,200	66,000
5P Tr Sed	5140	8550	17,100	28,500	39,900	57,000
Twn Sed Trk	5695	8700	17,400	29,000	40,600	58,000
Div Tr Sed	5215	9000	18,000	30,000	42,000	60,000
7P Tr Sed	5270	9300	18,600	31,000	43,400	62,000
7P Imp Tr Sed	5395	9600	19,200	32,000	44,800	64,000
Fml Sed Trk	6055	9900	19,800	33,000	46,200	66,000
7P Fml Sed Trk	6055	9900	19,800	33,000	46,200	66,000
Twn Car Trk	7175	10,500	21,000	35,000	49,000	70,000

1940

1940 Cadillac, Sixty Special, sedan, OCW

CADILLAC — SERIES 40-60S, 40-62, 40-72, 40-75 — EIGHT: For 1940, Series 61 was replaced by Series 62, featuring the "Projectile" or "Torpedo" bodies. The one-year-only Series 72 was introduced as a less expensive companion to the Series 75. 1940 was the final year for optional sidemounts.

The identifying feature for all V-8 Cadillacs was once again the grille. Although the grilles were the same pointed shaped as in 1939, the grille bars were heavier and fewer in number. Two sets of louver bars appeared on each hood side panel.

Sixty Special was available as a Town Car as well as a Sedan.

Series 62 featured a low, sleek body with chrome window reveals, more slant to the windshield, and a curved rear window. Runningboards were no-cost options. Convertible Coupes and Sedans were introduced in mid-year.

Series 72 had the general appearance of the Series 75, but was three inches shorter and was set apart by rectangular tail lights set high on the sides of the trunk. Re-circulating ball steering was tried on Series 72 in 1940, to be adopted on all series in 1941.

Sealed beam headlights and turn indicators were standard equipment. The engine manifold was set at five degrees to the engine to cancel the rearward tilt of the engine and give balanced fuel distribution.

I.D. DATA: Serial numbers were located on the left frame side bar, opposite the steering gear. Starting: Same as engine number. Ending: Same as engine number. Engine no. location: On the crankcase, just behind the left cylinder block, parallel to the dash. Starting Engine No.: [Series 40-60S] 632001; [Series 40-62] 832001; [Series 40-72] 7320001; [Series 40-75] 3320001. Ending: [Series 40-60S] 6324600; [Series 40-62] 8325903; [Series 40-72] 7321525; [Series 40-75] 3320956.

1940 Cadillac, Series 62, 4-dr. sedan, OCW

Style No.	Body Type & Seating	Price	Weight	Prod. Total
Fleetwood Series 40-60S, 127" wb				
40-6019S	Spec. Sed.-5P	2090	4070	—
40-6019S-A	Spec. Sed. (STT)-5P	—	—	—
40-6019S-F	Spec. Sed. (Div)-5P	2230	4110	—
40-6053S	Town Car-5P	—	—	—
40-6053-LB	Town Car-5P	3820	4365	—
40-6053-MB	Town Car-5P	3465	4365	—
Fisher Series 40-62, 129" wb				
40-6219	Tr. Sed.-5P	1745	4030	—
40-6227C	Cpe.-2P	1685	3940	—
40-6229	Conv. Sed.-5P	2195	4230	—
40-6267	Conv. Cpe.-2P	1795	4045	—
Fleetwood Series 40-72, 138" wb				
40-7219	Tr. Sed.-5P	2670	4670	—
40-7219-F	Tr. Sed. (Div)-5P	2790	4710	—
40-7223	Tr. Sed.-7P	2785	4700	—
40-7233	Imp. Sed.-7P	2915	4740	—
40-7259	Formal Sed.-5P	3695	4670	—
40-7233-F	Formal Sed.-7P	3695	4780	—
Fleetwood Series 40-72, 138" wb, Business Cars				
40-7223-L	Bus. Tr. Sed.-9P	2690	4700	—
40-7233-L	Bus. Tr. Imp.-9P	2824	4740	—
Fleetwood Series 40-75, 141" wb				
40-7557	Cpe.-2P	3280	4785	—
40-7557-B	Cpe.-5P	3380	4810	—
40-7567	Conv. Cpe.-2P	3380	4915	—
40-7519	Sed.-5P	2995	4900	—
40-7519-F	Imp. Sed.-5P	3155	4940	—
40-7559	Formal Sed.-5P	3995	4900	—
40-7539	Town Sed.-5P	3635	4935	—
40-7529	Conv. Sed.-5P	3945	5110	—
40-7523	Sed.-7P	3210	4930	—
40-7533	Imp. Sed.-7P	3360	4970	—
40-7533-F	Formal Sed.-7P	3995	4970	—
40-7553	Town Car-7P	5115	5195	—
Fleetwood Series 40-75, 141" wb, Business Cars				
40-7523-L	Bus. Tr. Sed.-8P	—	—	—
40-7533-L	Bus. Tr. Imp.-8P	—	—	—

ENGINE: Ninety degree. L-head. Eight. Cast iron block (blocks cast enbloc with crankcase). B & S: 3-1/2 in. x 4-1/2 in. Disp.: 346 cu. in. C.R.: [Series 60S, 62] 6.25:1; [Series 72, 75] 6.7:1. Brake H.P.: 135 (140 on 72, 75) @ 3400 R.P.M. SAE/Taxable H.P.: 39.20. Main bearings: Three. Valve lifters: Hydraulic. Carb.: Stromberg AAV-26.

1940 Cadillac, Series 62, convertible coupe, OCW

CHASSIS: [Series 40-60S] W.B.: 127 in. O.L.: 216-7/8 in. Frt/Rear Tread: 58/61 in. Tires: 7.00 x 16. [Series 40-62S] W.B.: 129 in. O.L.: 216-1/16 in. Frt/Rear Tread: 58/59 in. Tires: 7.00 x 16. [Series 40-72S] W.B.: 138 in. O.L.: 226-11/16 in. Frt/Rear Tread: 58/62-1/2 in. Tires: 7.50 x 16. [Series 40-75] W.B.: 141 in. O.L.: 228-3/16 in. Frt/Rear Tread: 60-1/2/62-1/2 in. Tires: 7.50 x 16. [Series 40-72 Commercial Chassis] W.B.: 165-1/4 in. O.L.: 253-13/16 in. Tires: 7.50 x 16. [Series 40-75 Commercial Chassis] W.B.: 161-3/8 in. O.L.: 248-11/16 in. Tires: 7.50 x 16.

TECHNICAL: Selective synchro manual transmission. Speeds: 3F/1R. LHD; gearshift on column; handbrake at left (RHD opt.). Single disc clutch. Shaft drive Hotchkiss. Semifloating rear axle. Hypoid gears. O.R.: [60S, 62] 3.92:1; [72] 4.31:1; [75] 4.58:1. Hydraulic brakes on four wheels. Slotted disc wheels. Wheel size: 16 in. Drivetrain Options: Hill-Holder (Norol) (13.50).

1940 Cadillac, Series 62, convertible sedan, OCW

OPTIONS: Radio (69.50). Heater (26.50-52.50). Seat covers (8.25 per seat). Spotlight (18.50). Automatic battery filler (7.50). Flexible steering wheel (15.00) Fog lights (14.50 pair). Windshield washer (6.50). Grille guard. Wheel discs (4.00 each). Trim rings (1.50 each).

HISTORICAL: Introduced: October, 1939. Model year sales and production: [Series 60S] 4600; [Series 62] 5903; [Series 72] 1525; [Series 75] 956. The general manager of Cadillac was Nicholas Dreystadt.

CADILLAC — SERIES 40-90 — SIXTEEN: The last Cadillac with other than a V-8 engine for more than forty years to come. Only such detail changes as new instrument panel, tail lights, and bumpers; plus the introduction of sealed beam headlights and directional signals distinguished the 1940 from the 1939 V-16.

I.D. DATA: Serial numbers were located on the left frame side bar, opposite the steering gear. Starting: Same as engine number. Ending: Same as engine number. Engine numbers were on the upper rear corner of the left cylinder block, parallel to the cylinder head. Starting Engine No.: 5320001. Ending: 5320061.

Style No.	Body Type & Seating	Price	Weight	Prod. Total
Fleetwood Series 40-90, 141 in. wb				
40-9057	Cpe.-2P	5340	4915	—
40-9057-B	Cpe.-5P	5440	5015	—
40-9067	Conv. Cpe.-2P	5440	4995	—
40-9019	Sed.-5P	5140	5190	—
40-9019-F	Imp. Sed.-5P	5215	5230	—
40-9059	Fml. Sed.-5P	6055	5190	—
40-9039	Twn. Sed.-5P	5695	5140	—
40-9029	Conv. Sed.-5P	6000	5265	—
40-9023	Sed.-7P	5270	5215	—
40-9033	Imp. Sed.-7P	5420	5260	—
40-9033-F	Fml. Sed.-7P	6055	5260	—
40-9053	Twn. Car-7P	7175	5415	—

ENGINE: 135 degree Vee. L-Head. Sixteen. Cast iron block. B & S: 3-1/4 in. x 3-1/4 in. Disp.: 431 cu. in. C.R.: 6.75:1. Brake H.P.: 185 @ 3600 R.P.M. SAE/Taxable H.P.: 67.6. Main bearings: Nine. Valve lifters: Hydraulic. Carb.: Carter WDO- 407s(L) — 408s (R).

CHASSIS: W.B.: 141 in. O.L.: 255-11/16 in. Frt/Rear Tread: 60-1/2 in./62-1/2 in. Tires: 7.50 x 16.

TECHNICAL: Selective synchro manual transmission. Speeds: 3F/1R. LHD; gearshift on column; handbrake at left. Single disc clutch. Shaft drive, Hotchkiss. Semifloating rear axle. Hypoid gears. O.R.: 4.31:1. Hydraulic brakes on four wheels. Disc wheels. Wheel size: 16 in.

OPTIONS: Radio (69.50). Heater (26.50-52.50). Seat covers (8.25 per seat). Spotlight (18.50). Automatic battery filler (7.50). Flexible steering wheel (15.00). Fog lights (14.50 pair). Windshield washer (6.50).

HISTORICAL: Introduced October, 1939. Model year sales and production: 61. The general manager of Cadillac was Nicholas Dreystadt.

1940

Series 62, V-8, 129" wb	FP	5	4	3	2	1
Conv	1795	7500	15,000	25,000	35,000	50,000
Conv Sed	2195	7800	15,600	26,000	36,400	52,000
Cpe	1685	4650	9300	15,500	21,700	31,000
Sed	1745	4050	8100	13,500	18,900	27,000
Series 60 Special, V-8, 127" wb, Fleetwood						
Sed	2090	5550	11,100	18,500	25,900	37,000
SR Sed	2190	5850	11,700	19,500	27,300	39,000
Imp Sed	2230	5850	11,700	19,500	27,300	39,000
SR Imp Sed	2330	6000	12,000	20,000	28,000	40,000
MB Twn Car	4365	6150	12,300	20,500	28,700	41,000
LB Twn Car	4365	6150	12,300	20,500	28,700	41,000
Series 72, V-8, 138" wb, Fleetwood						
Sed	2675	5250	10,500	17,500	24,500	35,000
4P Imp Sed	2915	5400	10,800	18,000	25,200	36,000
7P Sed	2785	5550	11,100	18,500	25,900	37,000
7P Bus Sed	2690	5250	10,500	17,500	24,500	35,000
7P Imp Sed	2825	5550	11,100	18,500	25,900	37,000
7P Fml Sed	2915	5700	11,400	19,000	26,600	38,000
7P Bus Imp	2915	5400	10,800	18,000	25,200	36,000
5P Fml Sed	3695	5850	11,700	19,500	27,300	39,000
Series 75, V-8, 141" wb, Fleetwood						
Conv	3380	9300	18,600	31,000	43,400	62,000
Conv Sed	3945	9600	19,200	32,000	44,800	64,000

	FP	5	4	3	2	1
2P Cpe	3280	6750	13,500	22,500	31,500	45,000
5P Cpe	3380	6600	13,200	22,000	30,800	44,000
Sed	2995	6300	12,600	21,000	29,400	42,000
5P Imp Sed	2995	6600	13,200	22,000	30,800	44,000
7P Sed	3155	6450	12,900	21,500	30,100	43,000
7P Imp Sed	3360	6750	13,500	22,500	31,500	45,000
5P Fml Sed	3995	6750	13,500	22,500	31,500	45,000
7P Fml Sed	3995	6900	13,800	23,000	32,200	46,000
Twn Sed	5115	7200	14,400	24,000	33,600	48,000
Twn Car	5115	7500	15,000	25,000	35,000	50,000
Series 90, V-16, 141" wb, Fleetwood						
Conv	5440	14,400	28,800	48,000	76,000	96,000
Conv Sed	6000	14,400	28,800	48,000	76,000	96,000
2P Cpe	5340	8400	16,800	28,000	39,200	56,000
5P Cpe	5440	8100	16,200	27,000	37,800	54,000
Sed	5140	7800	15,600	26,000	36,400	52,000
7P Sed	5270	7950	15,900	26,500	37,100	53,000
7P Imp Sed	5420	8100	16,200	27,000	37,800	54,000
5P Fml Sed	6055	8550	17,100	28,500	39,900	57,000
7P Fml Sed	6055	8700	17,400	29,000	40,600	58,000
5P Twn Sed	5695	8700	17,400	29,000	40,600	58,000
7P Twn Car	7175	9000	18,000	30,000	42,000	60,000

1941

1941 Cadillac, Series 62, coupe, OCW

CADILLAC — SERIES 41-60S, 41-61, 41-62, 41-63, 41-67, 41-75 — EIGHT: For 1941, the Series 61 designation was brought back, replacing LaSalle in the Cadillac price structure. A new Series 63 was offered in one body style. A new Series 67, with Fisher sedan bodies and the longest wheelbase (139 in.), replaced the 1940 Series 72. For the first time since 1926, all Cadillac products used the same engine.

Front end stylists adopted a theme which was to be repeated for years to come. The one piece hood came down lower in front, included the side panels, and extended sideways to the fenders. A single, rectangular panel of louver trim was used on each side of the hood. Access to the engine compartment was improved, to say the least. The rectangular grill was wide, vertical, and bulged forward in the middle. Rectangular parking lights were built into the top outer corners of the grille. Headlights were built into the nose of the fenders, and provision for built in accessory fog lights was provided under the headlights. Three chrome spears were on the rear section of all four fenders, except on the Sixty Special. Rear wheel shields (fender skirts) were standard on most bodies.

Sixty Special front fenders extended into the front doors.

Series 61 Coupe and Sedan were fastback styles reminiscent of the Aerodynamic Coupes of the Thirties.

Series 62 came in the standard body style lineup, including the only Convertible Sedan for 1941 and the last such body style offered by Cadillac.

Running boards were concealed or no-cost options on all but the 60S and 75; the Sixty Special had none and the 75's had nothing but. Power tops, electric divisions, factory installed air conditioning, and Hydra-Matic transmissions were available.

1941 Cadillac, Series 60 Special, 4-dr. sedan, OCW

I.D. DATA: Serial numbers were located on the left frame side bar, opposite the steering gear. Starting: Same as engine number. Ending: Same as engine number. Engine numbers were on the crankcase, just behind the left cylinder block, parallel to the dash. Starting Engine No.: [Series 41-60S] 6340001; [41-61] 5340001; [41-62] 8340001; [41-67] 9340001; [41-75] 3340001. Ending: [Series 41-60S] 6344101; [41-61] 5369258; [41-62] 8364734; [41-63] 7345050; [41-67] 9340922; [41-75] 3342104.

Style No.	Body Type & Seating	Price	Weight	Prod. Total
Fleetwood Series 41-60S, 126 in. wb				
41-6019S	Sed.-5P	2195	4230	—
41-6019S-A	Sed. (STT)-5P	—	—	—
41-6019S-F	Sed. (Div)-5P	2345	4290	—
Fisher Series 41-61, 126 in. wb				
41-6127	Cpe.-5P	1345	3985	—
41-6127D	Cpe. Del.-5P	1435	4005	—
41-6109	Tr. Sed.-5P	1445	4065	—
41-6109D	Tr. Sed. Del.-5P	1535	4085	—
Fisher Series 41-62, 126 in. wb				
41-6227	Cpe.-2/4P	1420	3950	—
41-6227D	Cpe. Del.-2/4P	1510	3970	—
41-6219	Tr. Sed.-5P	1495	4030	—
41-6219D	Tr. Sed. Deluxe-5P	1535	4050	—
41-6267D	Con. Cpe. Del.-2/4P	1645	4055	—
41-6229D	Con. Sed. Del.-5P	1965	4230	—
Fisher Series 41-63, 126 in. wb				
41-6319	Tr. Sed.-5P	1696	4140	—
Fisher Series 41-67, 139 in. wb				
41-6719	Tr. Sed.-5P	2595	4555	—
41-6719-F	Tr. Sed. (Div)-5P	2745	4615	—
41-6723	Tr. Sed.-7P	2735	4630	—
41-6733	Imp. Tr. Sed.-7P	2890	4705	—
Fleetwood Series 41-75, 136 in. wb				
41-7519	Tr. Sed.-5P	2995	4750	—
41-7519-F	Tr. Sed. (Div)-5P	3150	4810	—
41-7523	Tr. Sed.-7P	3140	4800	—
41-7533	Tr. Imp.-7P	3295	4860	—
41-7559	Fml. Sed.-5P	3920	4900	—
41-7533-F	Fml. Sed.-7P	4045	4915	—
Business Cars Series 41-75; 136 in. wb				
41-7523-L	Buss Tr. Sed.-9P	2895	4750	—
41-7533-L	Buss Tr. Imp.-9P	3050	4810	—

ENGINE: Ninety degree. L-Head. Eight. Cast iron block (blocks cast enbloc with crankcase). B & S: 3-1/2 in. x 4-1/2 in. Disp.: 346 cu. in. C.R.: 7.25:1. Brake H.P.: 150 @ 3400 R.P.M. SAE/Taxable H.P.: 39.20. Main bearings: Three. Valve lifters: Hydraulic. Carb.: Stromberg AAV-26, Carter WDO 506s.

1941 Cadillac, Series 62, 4-dr. sedan, JAC

CHASSIS: [Series 41-60S] W.B.: 126 in. O.L.: 217-3/16 in. Frt/Rear Tread: 59/63 in. Tires: 7.00 x 15. [Series 41-61] W.B.: 126 in. O.L.: 215 in. Frt/Rear Tread: 59/63 in. Tires: 7.00 x 15. [Series 41-62] W.B.: 126 in. O.L.: 216 in. Frt/Rear Tread: 59/63 in. Tires: 7.00 x 15. [Series 41-63] W.B.: 126 in. O.L.: 215 in. Frt/Rear Tread: 59/63 in. Tires: 7.00 x 15. [Series 41-67] W.B.: 139 in. O.L.: 228 in. Frt/Rear Tread: 58-1/2 in./62-1/2 in. Tires: 7.50 x 16. [Series 41-75] W.B.: 136 in. O.L.: 226-1/8 in. Frt/Rear Tread: 58-1/2 in./62-1/2 in. Tires: 7.50 x 16. [Series 41-62 Commercial Chassis] W.B.: 163 in. O.L.: 252-7/8 in. Tires: 7.00 x 16. [Series 41-75 Commercial Chassis] W.B.: 163 in. O.L.: 252-7/8 in. Tires: 7.50 x 16.

1941 Cadillac, Series 63, 4-dr. sedan, OCW

232

TECHNICAL: Selective synchro manual transmission. Speeds: 3F/1R. LHD; gearshift on column; handbrake at left (RHD opt. except 60S and 67). Single disc clutch. Shaft drive, Hotchkiss. Semifloating rear axle. Hypoid gears. O.R.: [60S, 61, 62, 63] 3.77:1 (3.36:1 opt.); [67, 75] 4.27:1 (3.77:1 opt.). Hydraulic brakes on four wheels. Slotted disc wheels. Wheel size: 15 in. (16 in. on 67 and 75). Drivetrain Options: Automatic transmission (125.00), Hill-holder (Norol) (11.50).

OPTIONS: Fender skirts (17.50 pair). Radio (69.50). Heater (59.50-65.00). Seat covers (8.75/seat). Spotlight (18.50). Fog lights (14.50). Backup light (7.50). Windshield washer (7.50). Wheel discs (4.00 each). Trim rings (1.50 each).

HISTORICAL: Introduced September, 1940. Model year sales and production: [Series 60S] 4101; [Series 61] 29258; [Series 62] 24734; [Series 63] 5050; [Series 67] 922; [Series 75] 2104. The general manager of Cadillac was Nicholas Dreystadt.

1941 Cadillac, Series 75, Fleetwood limousine, OCW

1941

Series 61, V-8, 126" wb	FP	5	4	3	2	1
Cpe	1345	3300	6600	11,000	15,400	22,000
DeL Cpe	1435	3400	6900	11,500	16,100	23,000
Sed	1445	2300	5400	9000	12,600	18,000
DeL Sed	1535	2800	5700	9500	13,300	19,000
Series 62, V-8, 126" wb						
Conv	1645	7500	15,000	25,000	35,000	50,000
Conv Sed	1965	7650	15,300	25,500	35,700	51,000
Cpe	1420	3600	7200	12,000	16,800	24,000
DeL Cpe	1510	3750	7500	12,500	17,500	25,000
Sed	1495	3000	6000	10,000	14,000	20,000
DeL Sed	1585	3150	6300	10,500	14,700	21,000
Series 63, V-8, 126" wb						
Sed	1695	3300	6600	11,000	15,400	22,000
Series 60 Special, V-8, 126" wb, Fleetwood						
Sed	2195	4350	8700	14,500	20,300	29,000
SR Sed	2345	4500	9000	15,000	21,000	30,000
Series 67, V-8, 138" wb						
5P Sed	2595	3000	6000	10,000	14,000	20,000
Imp Sed	2745	3150	6300	10,500	14,700	21,000
7P Sed	2735	3000	6000	10,000	14,000	20,000
7P Imp Sed	2890	3300	6600	11,000	15,400	22,000
Series 75, V-8, 136-1/2" wb, Fleetwood						
5P Sed	2995	3150	6300	10,500	14,700	21,000
5P Imp Sed	3150	3350	6750	11,250	15,750	22,500
7P Sed	3140	3350	6750	11,250	15,750	22,500
9P Bus Sed	3050	3300	6600	11,000	15,400	22,000
7P Imp Sed	3295	3400	6900	11,500	16,100	23,000
Bus Imp Sed	3050	3150	6300	10,500	14,700	21,000
5P Fml Sed	3920	3400	6900	11,500	16,100	23,000
7P Fml Sed	4045	3400	6900	11,500	16,100	23,000

1942

1942 Cadillac, Series 61, 4-dr. sedan, OCW

CADILLAC — SERIES 42-60S, 42-61, 42-62, 42-63, 42-67, 42-75 — EIGHT: For 1942, the Series lineup remained the same as in 1941. The grille became more massive, with fewer bars. Parking lights became round and fog light sockets became rectangular and were included within the grille area. A bullet shape appeared on the tops of the bumper guards. Fenders were rounded and longer. Front fenders on all but Series 75 extended into the front doors. Series 62 and 60S rear fenders extended forward into rear doors. The new fenders had heavy moldings along the sides.

Series 75 had the new grille but retained the 1941 fender treatment. A detail trim change on the 75's was a rounded nose on the hood louvers.

The first general styling change on the Sixty Special destroyed the character of the car. Bulbous lines plus superfluous trim in the form of louver bars on the quarters and numerous short vertical bars low on the fenders spoiled its appeal. The only convertible was the Series 62, showing quarter windows for the first time.

A new fresh air ventilating system with air ducts leading from the grille, replaced cowl ventilators. Handbrake control was changed from lever to tee shaped pull handle. Radiator shutter control of engine temperature was replaced by a blocking-type thermostat in the water return fitting on the radiator.

I.D. DATA: Serial numbers were on the right frame side bar, just behind the engine support bracket. Starting: Same as engine number. Ending: Same as engine number. Engine numbers were on the right hand side of the crankcase, just above the water pump. Chrome or polished stainless steel brightwork. Starting Engine No.: [Series 42A-60S] 6380001; [Series 42A-61] 5380001; [Series 42A-62] 8380001; [Series 42A-67] 9380001; [Series 42A-75] 3380001. Ending: [Series 42A-60S] 6381500; [Series 42A-61] 5385237; [Series 42A-62] 8384401; [Series 42A-63] 7381500; [Series 42A-75] 3381200. Painted "brightwork": [Series 42B-60S] 6386001; 6386375; [Series 42B-61] 5386001; 5386463; [Series 42B-62] 8386001; 8386560; [Series 42B-63] 7386001; 7386250; [Series 42B-67] 9386001; 9386180; [Series 42B-75] 3386001; 3386327.

Style No.	Body Type & Seating	Price	Weight	Prod. Total
Fleetwood Series 42-60S, 133" wb				
42-6069	4-dr. Sed.	2435	4310	—
42-6069-F	4-dr. Sed. (Div)	2589	4365	—
Fisher Series 42-61, 126" wb				
42-6107	Club Cpe.-5P	1560	4035	—
42-6109	4-dr. Sed.	1647	4115	—
Fisher Series 42-62, 129" wb				
42-6207	Club Cpe.-5P	1667	4105	—
42-6207D	Opt. Club Cpe.-5P	1754	4125	—
42-6269	4-dr. Sed.	1754	4185	—
42-6269D	4-dr. Opt. Sed.	1836	4205	—
42-6267D	Opt. Con. Clb. Cpe.-5P	2020	4365	—
Fisher Series 42-63, 126" wb				
42-6319	4-dr. Sed.	1882	4115	—
Fisher Series 42-67, 139" wb				
42-6719	Sed.-5P	2896	4605	—
42-6719-F	Sed. (Div)-5P	3045	4665	—
42-6723	Sed.-7P	3045	4680	—
42-6733	Imp.-7P	3204	4775	—
Fleetwood Series 42-75, 136" wb				
42-7519	Sed.-5P	3306	4750	—
42-7519-F	Sed. (Div)-5P	3459	4810	—
42-7523	Sed.-7P	3459	4800	—
42-7533	Imp.-7P	3613	4860	—
42-7559	Formal Sed.-5P	4330	4900	—
42-7533-F	Formal Sed.-7P	4484	4915	—
Businss Cars Series 42-75, 136" wb				
42-7523-L	Bus. Sed.-9P	3152	4750	—
42-7533-L	Bus. Imp.-9P	3306	4810	—

ENGINE: Ninety degree. L-head. Eight. Cast iron block (blocks cast enbloc with crankcase). B & S: 3-1/2 in. x 4-1/2 in. Disp.: 346 cu. in. C.R.: 7.25:1. Brake H.P.: 150 @ 3400 R.P.M. SAE/Taxable H.P.: 39.20. Main bearings: Three. Valve lifters: Hydraulic. Carb.: Stromberg AAV-26; Carter WDO 486S.

CHASSIS: [Series 42-60S] W.B.: 133 in. O.L.: 224 in. Frt/Rear Tread: 59/63 in. Tires: 7.00 x 15. [Series 42-61] W.B.: 126 in. O.L.: 215 in. Frt/Rear Tread: 59/63 in. Tires: 7.00 x 15. [Series 42-62] W.B.: 129 in. O.L.: 220 in. Frt/Rear Tread: 59/63 in. Tires: 7.00 x 15. [Series 42-63] W.B.: 126 in. O.L.: 215 in. Frt/Rear Tread: 59/63 in. Tires: 7.00 x 15. [Series 42-67] W.B.: 139 in. O.L.: 228 in. Frt/Rear Tread: 58-1/2/62-1/2 in. Tires: 7.50 x 16. [Series 42-75] W.B.: 136 in. O.L.: 227 in. Frt/Rear Tread: 58-1/2/62-1/2 in. Tires: 7.50 x 16. [Series 42-75 Commercial Chassis] W.B.: 163 in. O.L.: 253-1/32 in. Tires: 7.50 x 16.

TECHNICAL: Selective synchro manual transmission. Speeds: 3F/1R. LHD; gearshift on column; handbrake at left (RHD opt except 60S, 62, 67, 75). Single disc clutch. Shaft drive Hotchkiss. Semifloating rear axle. Hypoid gears. O.R.: [60S, 61, 62, 63] 3.77:1. (3.36:1 opt); [67, 75] 4.27:1 (3.77:1 opt). Hydraulic brakes on four wheels. Slotted disc wheels. Wheel size: 15 in (16 in. on 67 and 75). Drivetrain Options: Automatic transmission (135.00). Hill-holder (Norol) (12.50).

1942 Cadillac, Series 62, 4-dr. sedan, JAC

OPTIONS: Radio (65.00). Heater (59.50-65.00). Seat covers (9.75/seat). Spotlight (19.50). Fog lights (24.50). Backup light (12.50). Windshield washer (8.25) Wheel discs (4.00 each). Trim rings (1.50 each)

HISTORICAL: Introduced: September, 1941. Model year sales and production: [Series 60S] 1875; [Series 61] 5700; [Series 62] 4961; [Series 63] 1750; [Series 67] 700; [Series 75] 1527. The general manager of Cadillac was Nicholas Dreystadt.

1942
Series 61, V-8, 126" wb

	FP	5	4	3	2	1
Cpe	1560	1250	3900	6500	9100	13,000
Sed	1647	1225	3850	6450	9000	12,900
Series 62, V-8, 129" wb						
DeL Clb Cpe	1754	1650	4650	7750	10,850	15,500
Clb Cpe	1667	1550	4500	7500	10,500	15,000
DeL Conv Cpe	2020	4950	9900	16,500	23,100	33,000
Sed	1754	1225	3850	6450	9000	12,900
DeL Sed	1836	1250	3900	6550	9150	13,100
Series 63, V-8, 126" wb						
Sed	1882	1250	3950	6600	9200	13,200
Series 60 Special, V-8, 133" wb, Fleetwood						
Sed	2435	2300	5400	9000	12,600	18,000
Imp Sed	2589	2800	5700	9500	13,300	19,000
Series 67, V-8, 139" wb						
5P 4 dr Sed	2896	1400	4200	7000	9800	14,000
5P 4 dr Sed Div	3045	2000	5100	8500	11,900	17,000
7P 4 dr Sed	3045	1550	4500	7500	10,500	15,000
7P 4 dr Sed Imp	3204	2000	5100	8500	11,900	17,000
Series 75, V-8, 136" wb, Fleetwood						
5P Imp	3080	1750	4800	8000	11,200	16,000
5P Imp Sed	3230	2000	5100	8500	11,900	17,000
7P Sed	3230	1750	4800	8000	11,200	16,000
9P Bus Sed	3080	1750	4800	8000	11,200	16,000
7P Imp Sed	3375	2300	5400	9000	12,600	18,000
9P Bus Imp	3080	2000	5100	8500	11,900	17,000
5P Fml Sed	4060	2800	5700	9500	13,300	19,000
7P Fml Sed	4205	2900	5850	9750	13,650	19,500

CADY — Auburn, New York — (1899) — Frank E. Cady built an automobile in Auburn in 1899 for his own use. A lawyer, real estate investor, the president of the Cady Manufacturing Company (which produced carpet stretchers) and the Cady Filter and Cooler Company, Cady never envisioned embarking upon automobile manufacture.

CAESAR — Anderson, Indiana — (1914) — In July of 1914, after leaving the Painesville (Ohio) company which built his Vulcan, Alonzo R. Marsh announced that next he would produce a light car in Anderson (Indiana) to be known as the Caesar. So far as is known, only a single prototype of this car was built. No company was ever incorporated for its manufacture. By 1915 Alonzo Marsh had returned to his home Brockton, Massachusetts to rejoin his brothers in the building of another car called the Eastern.

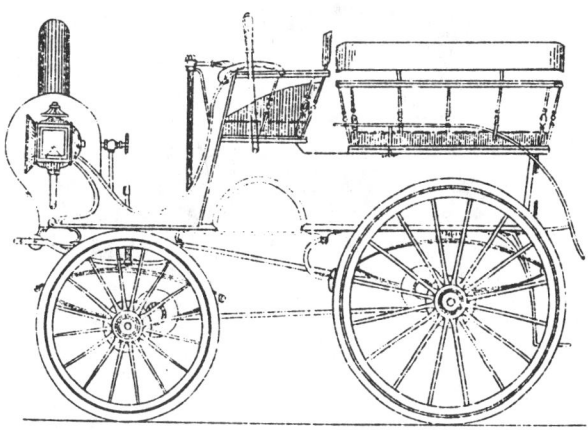

1895 Caffrey Steam Carriage, NAHC

CAFFREY STEAM — Camden, New Jersey — (1895) — In 1895 the Charles F. Caffrey Company of Camden built a steam carriage for a Philadelphia physician named F.L. Sweany. Petroleum was used as fuel, and a small motor was attached to each of the vehicle's four wheels. These motors could be run independently of one another, for a minimum of 3 and a maximum of 12 hp. The complete carriage weighed in at only 1350 pounds, and was comely in appearance. Oil and water tanks were hidden from view under the seats. Across the front of the body, the boiler was placed, presenting "a very neat appearance," *The Horseless Age* reported, "as it is covered with patent leather." A maximum speed of 16 to 20 mph was claimed. A foot pedal shut off the steam and simultaneously applied braking to the wheels. This was the only complete car built by the Charles F. Caffrey Company. The firm remained in the automobile field, however, building bodies for the Morris & Salom cars during this period and for the Biddle in 1917.

233

1897 Caffrey Electric, NAHC

CAFFREY ELECTRIC — Reno, Nevada — (1897) — W.G. Caffrey of Reno had an interesting idea in 1897. It was a four-wheeled electric carriage, but one to be operated like a trolley car with power provided by overhead electrified wires. He constructed one carriage in his Reno foundry and set up a line of poles outside with a dynamo placed thereon. According to contemporary reports, the vehicle performed successfully and Caffrey envisioned its application "in outlying districts where water power is available for the generation of electricity." Given the character of the Nevada terrain, that would have meant a good many poles and a lot of wire. Caffrey's trolley passenger car never proceeded beyond the prototype stage.

CAILLE — Although the Caille Brothers of Detroit were half of the partnership, this 1904 car bore the name of its designer too. Refer to Du Brie-Caille.

CAIRO — The Cairo Auto Sales Company was organized in Cairo, Illinois late in 1913 to "manufacture, sell, rent and repair motor cars." John P. Glynn, Joseph J. Glynn and Albert D. Teer were the incorporators. Capital stock was $2500. Manufacture is doubted.

1908 Caldwell

CALDWELL — Waterloo, Iowa — (1908) — "Cylinderless, boltless, noiseless, cussedless" were the attributes of the Caldwell, according to its inventor. This automotive fore-carriage — or "iron horse," as its inventor preferred — was propelled by a hollow moving piston which slid back and forth along a stationary head. Attached to the front of any horsedrawn buggy, it immediately transformed the vehicle into an automobile, if peculiarly so. Caldwell published a formidable catalog espousing the virtues of his "iron horse." Reported *The Motor World* laconically, "A company to manufacture the thing is in existence in Waterloo, Iowa." But not for long.

CALIFORNIA — The California Cycle Company was organized in San Francisco in the fall of 1899 to manufacture and deal in bicycles and motor vehicles. Capital stock was $5000, and the firm was backed by S. Green, W. Levy, G.M. Gunzberger, J.O. Malley and M. Lichenstein. That a California automobile resulted is doubted.

During the summer of 1914 the California Manufacturing Company of San Diego announced that production of a cyclecar would soon begin in its factory on Second Street between A and Ash. "The first models turned out will be commercial cars equipped with six-horsepower single-cylinder

motors," *Cyclecar Age* reported. Further details are lacking.

California Midget was the nickname given to the 1908 Los Angeles car which is more properly designed by the name of its designer. Refer to Cowan.

The California Motor Car Company was organized in Los Angeles with a capital stock of $100,000 early in 1904. Manufacturing automobiles was the firm's plan, with its total stock subscribed by Charles A. Anthony, Earle C. Anthony, H.K. Anthony, Roy P. Hillman and G.L. Hillman. That any manufacture resulted has not been documented. Earle C. Anthony had earlier built an electric car of his own and later, of course, would become very famous in the area as a Packard dealer.

California Tourist was the designation in 1910 for the car which had been produced in Los Angeles since 1902 as the Tourist. Refer to Tourist.

CALIFORNIA — San Diego, California — (1899) — Dr. George M. Calmus resided at 2845 K Street in San Diego and was the inventor of a rotary engine weighing but fifteen pounds which he claimed would develop 5 hp. In 1899 he announced that, following an investigation of the "motor vehicle industry in the East," he was preparing to organize the California Automobile Company in San Diego for the manufacture of automobiles. This he never did do, nor is it certain that a vehicle with his engine was ever successfully tested,

1902 California, runabout, GR

CALIFORNIA — San Francisco, California — (1900-1902) — The California Automobile Company had its offices and plant at 346 McAllister Street in San Francisco. "Our factory, where the machine is made, is at your disposal for any repairs or breakage," the company said. "These can be attended to without the troublesome delays necessarily encountered when dealing with Eastern firms." Moreover, California promised prices cheaper by $100 to $300 than the East Coast competition. The price range from California was $500 to $3000, "according to style, power and speed," and the vehicles offered included gasoline, electric and steam. The "stylish little runabout" was tiller steered, with air-cooled motor under the seat, side chain drive, a high bench seat and very low dash — and a look that was the spitting image of the French Henriod. Pictures were identical as a matter of fact. Possibly California was building the Henriod under license from the French company — or possibly a lookalike without benefit of license. In any case, the California Automobile Company was organized in October of 1900 by Henry C. Whittemore, Michael J. Kirwin, Charles E. Hancock, Sherwood Bird and Norton C. Hulse, all of California. In early December of 1901 *The Motor Age* reported that California planned to have its first "six machines ready for customers" by the 10th. Other early California gasoline vehicles were referred to by the name of their designer (and the company manager), Bainridge L. Ryder. After 1902, following a managerial shakeup, the firm elected to confine production to a steam car only which was marketed under the tradename of Calimobile. B.L. Ryder remained in charge at the factory.

CALIFORNIA — San Francisco, California — (1901-1905) — This California was product of the California Motor Company which was established by Louis H. Bill in 1901. Its San Francisco address was 2212 Folsom Street through 1904, at which time the operation moved to 304 McAllister Street, not far from the erstwhile California Automobile Company. Bicycles and motorcycles appear to have been California Motor's chief activity, but trade directory listings from the era indicate the firm as an automobile manufacturer too. Most likely any cars built were to specific customer order. After 1905 Louis Bill became the Bay Area distributor for the Rambler and appointed the Fageol brothers (Frank and William) as Rambler agents for Oakland. In 1913 Bill answered the Thomas B. Jeffery Company call to come to Kenosha as assistant general manager at the Rambler factory. He remained with the Wisconsin company until Charles W. Nash acquired Jeffery in 1916, then returned to California to join the Fageol brothers in their automotive venture.

CALIFORNIA — Los Angeles, California — (1910) — In November of 1909 the newly-formed California Automobile Company bought out the Auto Vehicle Company of Los Angeles, makers of the Tourist car. Former Auto Vehicle general sales manager Volney S. Beardsley was the new firm's president, with Fred Hooker Jones secretary and treasurer. Sitting on the board were John D. Hooker, Dr. George W. Tape and Russell J. Waters. For the 1910 model year the firm continued production of the two- and four-cylinder Tourist models and added a line of fours carrying the California name, which had occasionally been used as a Tourist model designation in years past. The California Automobile Company exhibited at the Southern California Automobile Show in February 1910, and in April announced a 1910 model year production of 150 Tourist and California cars. Parts shortages, which had plagued the non-Selden-licensed Auto Vehicle Company, continued to hamper California Automobile Company efforts. By year's end the firm elected to continue in business only as a dealership, with the Firestone-Columbus, Warren-Detroit and Columbus Electric among the cars offered. In June 1913 (two years after the Selden patent was effectively disposed of by court decision), the California Automobile Company began making plans to return to the manufacturing field. An electrical engineer named John T. Shannon designed the new car, which would carry the name of company president Volney Beardsley. The Beardsley electric was produced from 1914 to 1917.

1910 CALIFORNIA
Four — 40 hp, 118" wb

	FP	5	4	3	2	1
Tour.	2250	2300	3300	4600	7500	16,000
Four — 50 hp, 118" wb						
Tour.	3000	2300	3300	4600	7500	16,000
Four — 30 hp, 106" wb						
Torpedo	1300	2200	3200	4400	7000	15,000

CALIFORNIA — Oakland, California — (1911) — The California Motor Car Company was organized early in 1911 in Oakland by a contingent of local businessmen headed by Walter C. Sachs. A "disused cotton mill" was secured as preliminary headquarters in May. That month, according to *The Horseless Age*, the California people "asked the local Chamber of Commerce to investigate their bona fide intentions and aid them so far as possible to secure capital for the enterprise." Thus far $100,000 of the venture's stock had been subscribed; $75,000 more was needed. Subsequently the firm acquired a factory in nearby Fruitvale. But the first California was also the last. Made aware that a Los Angeles firm had preempted the name, the Oakland people decided to call their production car the Pacific Special!

CALIFORNIA — Los Angeles, California — (1913) — L.E. French was a former writer for *The Horseless Age* who designed himself a cyclecar in 1913 which he said could travel at speeds of 60 mph. Conceivably, with a good tailwind. Its engine was a 10 hp air-cooled twin; friction transmission and double vee belt drive were fitted. The wheelbase was 102 inches, the tread 44; French planned to sell the car for $395. He called it a California, and the California Cycle Car Company was organized in Los Angeles for its manufacture. This venture went precisely nowhere. Later in 1913 French found new backers for the organization of a new company, and the Los Angeles cyclecar followed.

CALIFORNIA — Los Angeles, California — (1923-1925) — This California was a companion car to the Leach, the expensive six-cylinder automobile produced by the Leach Biltwell Motor Company of Los Angeles. Its four-cylinder ohv overhead cam 50 hp engine was designed by Harry A. Miller, who had also designed the six-cylinder 100 hp unit used in the Leach. The car was exhibited in January 1923 in Oakland at the Ulrey-Noteware Company, the Leach Biltwell dealer for Alameda County. "An oiling system has been built that keeps the oil cool at all times under the most trying conditions," *The Oakland Tribune* reported. "The oil runs through a portion of the radiator which has been built for same, where it is cooled, and this arrangement saves the base of the oil, and more mileage per gallon should be received." Indeed, the dealership's H.D. Noteware claimed a fuel economy of 35 mpg. By this time the Leach Biltwell Motor Company was in financial trouble, and had retreated from its original Sante Fe Avenue factory in Los Angeles to more modest premises at 112 West 9th Street where it shared space with the newly formed California Motors, Incorporated. Martin Andrew Leach was the president of this venture (as well as Leach Biltwell), allied in the California enterprise with Samuel G. Miles. The Leach motor car was discontinued later in 1923. The California may have been built in very small numbers into 1925.

CALIFORNIAN — The Californian Motor Car Company has been indicated on various rosters as producing an automobile in San Francisco in 1912. There is no evidence this ever happened. Possibly this car-that-wasn't has been confused with the California Motor Car Company across the bay in Oakland during this period.

Californian was the name given to the specially-disguised Mercers designed by George Bentel of Los Angeles which, circa 1915-1916, were campaigned under that name, as a fourth car when race regulations limited a team's entry to three. Refer to Bentel.

CALIFORNIAN SIX — Los Angeles, California — (1920) — "The Car of the King's Highway" was a "product of the Golden West" which offered "unsurpassed beauty of design combined with a mechanical perfection representing the utmost in construction." If advertising hyperbole had sold cars in 1920, the California Motor Car Corporation of Los Angeles couldn't have built its Californian Six fast enough to meet the demand. It was an assembled car (Beaver six engine), but an extremely handsome one defiled only by the outlandishly vainglorious tenor of its advertising prose. A seven-passenger touring and a four-passenger sport "club express" stretched rakishly over a long 134-inch wheelbase. Alas, the California Motor Car Corporation did not stretch into 1921. Purportedly, the

1920 Californian Six, touring, KM

company failed after the building of just one complete car and a couple of unfinished chassis. The men behind the Californian Six were all from the Midwest, production manager Edward Lawrence and sales manager Allison L. Tull being veterans of Elgin in Illinois, and chief engineer Robert J. Schefferly having worked previously for Studebaker and Wichita Falls.

CALIMOBILE — San Francisco, California — (1902) — After selling its California as a steam, electric or gasoline car in 1900-1901, and after a managerial shakeup which brought William Corbin, Dr. J.G. Crawford and E.R. Harper to the board of directors, the California Automobile Company of San Francisco chose to confine production for 1902 to a single steam car called the Calimobile. B.L. Ryder remained in charge at the factory and, according to company secretary A.E. Ruddell in March 1902, was "turning out machines that are giving such satisfaction that buyers are coming our way as fast as we can attend to them." Four automobiles a month was the factory capacity. Models included a $900 runabout and a $1600 four-passenger touring, two of the latter being sold to San Francisco's Palace Hotel. The largest Calimobiles were nine-passenger steam stage coaches, at least three of which were built. The company does not seem to have survived 1902, however.

CALL — New York, New York — (1911) — Little is known about the Call Motor Car Company of New York and its product. The few cars built by the firm were produced in 1911. According to a tax assessor's book, the model range included a 25 hp Model H, and 28 hp models designated O, R and S.

CALLIHAN — Woonsocket, South Dakota — (1883-1905) — Just three years earlier, with his young wife, E. Scott Callihan had arrived in the Dakota territory by covered wagon. There, on the edge of Indian country, about twenty miles from Woonsocket, the closest trading post, they selected a parcel of land to homestead. By 1883 Callihan had built a fine log house — and a three-wheeled steam car, undoubtedly the first in the still largely unsettled western territory. Its two-cylinder engine used hay for fuel, the water boiler was two feet high and produced a pressure of 175 pounds. The bearings were brass, the frame steel, the crank disc cast iron. Except for the hard rubber of the wheels, every piece of the Callihan was made by E. Scott. The car's top speed was 15 mph. For the forty-mile round trip to Woonsocket, it required ten gallons of water, five of kerosene and replenishments of hay, which was easily gathered along the prairie trail. To the rugged individualism which was a integral part of the pioneer spirit, E. Scott Callihan added an inventive genius all the more remarkable for the primitiveness of the territory in which he exercised it. As his son later remembered, "Over a period of years, up to 1905, he built several automobiles, very successful they were. He also made a threshing machine model, and many interesting things. I can remember our home was lighted with electric lights; the electric plant made by my father."

1903 Caloric, runabout, NAHC

CALORIC — Chicago, Illinois — (1903-1904) — The Chicago Motocycle Company was organized late in 1898 at 107 Madison Street in Chicago by Charles Dickinson, L.F. Douglass and Henry B. Babson. Although an ambi-

1904 Caloric, runabout, WLB

tious program for the manufacture of gasoline, electric and steam vehicles was announced, it does not appear the firm got around to manufacturing much of anything until after the turn of the century. In the meantime, a repair station was operated. References from 1902 indicate that a car carrying the Chicago name and a two-cylinder motor was produced by the company that year. By 1903, however, the company had settled on Caloric for its product's name, and its product line now included a three-cylinder model. The Chicago-cum-Caloric was interesting in that it could be run on hot air in addition to the more usual gasoline or kerosene fuels. To start the engine required the heating of the cylinder head by a torch until it was red hot. One cannot imagine this working well. The Caloric must have been one of the more unusual exhibits at the Chicago Automobile Show in 1903: It was a closed coupe as high as it was long. By August 1904 Chicago Motocycle had merged with the Auto Motor Cycle Company and announced that henceforth it would concentrate on automobile repair and the manufacture of marine engines, and would build further automobiles only to order. At the Chicago Automobile Show in January 1905, the firm did exhibit a gasoline runabout called the Fostler, and may have built a few of these that season.

1903-1904 CALORIC
Two Cylinder — 4 1/2 hp, 66" wb

	FP	5	4	3	2	1
Rbt.	800	1600	2700	3800	5800	12,000
Two Cylinder — 6 1/2 hp, 66" wb						
Rbt.	1000	1600	2700	3800	5800	12,000
Three Cylinder — 9 hp						
Cpe.	—	1400	2400	3500	5300	10,000

CALUMET — Chicago, Illinois — (1916-1917) — G.A. Holcombe was the president, Albert R. Hulbert the secretary and H.A. Zimmerman the treasurer of the Calumet Motors Corporation which had its headquarters at 9154 Commercial Avenue in Chicago. In November of 1916 the firm announced its forthcoming manufacture of a six-cylinder car to be offered as a four-passenger clubster and five- and seven-passenger touring. Production was slated to begin March 1st, 1917 in a new factory then under construction in Lamont. Possibly prototypes were built, but the new Lamont factory was never occupied by Calumet.

CALVERT — Early in 1912 F.G. Kitchi founded the Calvert Motor Company in Baltimore, Maryland. He does not appear to have proceeded further than a $25,000 incorporation of the company. Probably not even a prototype was built.

CALVERT — Baltimore, Maryland — (1927) — How many of the Cavalier Motor Associates of Mt. Vernon, New York were among the Calvert Motor Associates of Baltimore is not known, but these two companies followed closely upon one another. The designer of both cars was Norton L. Dods, whose usual work was for the Baltimore publishing company which produced the used car value guides called the Blue Book and the Red Book. The Cavalier had been a four, the new Calvert a six (Continental engine) carrying the model designation Duplex Three. The wheelbase was 105 inches. Projected price tags were $550 for chassis, $795 for roadster with rumble seat and disc wheels. But Calvert Motor Associates never did get an assembly line going. A prototype roadster was built, and a few more open cars one of which is believed to remain extant.

CAMBRIDGE — The Cambridge Automobile Company was incorporated with a capital stock of $100,000 for the manufacture of automobiles in Cambridge, Massachusetts during the fall of 1910. E.C. Blake and L.E. Gibson were the partners behind this venture. This was simply a reincorporation of the venture organized that summer as the Blake Automobile Company. Manufacture still did not result.

CAMDEN — The Camden Motor Company was organized early in 1904 for the manufacture of automobiles in Camden, New Jersey. Josiah G. Reeves, John T. Bottomley, C.M. Reeves and E.G. Reeves were the promoters of this venture which was headquartered at 1068 North Seventh Street. Capital stock was $2000. Manufacture did not result, though the firm may subsequently have operated as a dealership in automobiles and accessories.

The Camden & Atlantic Automobile Company was organized with a capital stock of $25,000 early in 1906 for the manufacture of automobiles in Camden, New Jersey. L. Dare Ginhart, Jr., Charles Summer Wesley and M. Leon Berry were the incorporators. Manufacture is doubted.

CAMERON — A car called the Cameron was listed in *MoToR* magazine in 1911 as the product of the Indiana Motor & Manufacturing Company in Franklin, Indiana. This was an editorial error. The car was actually the Continental.

1903 Cameron, runabout, HAC

CAMERON — Rhode Island, Massachusetts, Connecticut/Michigan & Ohio — (1903-1920) — The Cameron couldn't stay put. Few automobiles in the history of the U.S. industry ever moved around quite as much as the car that Everett S. Cameron in association with his brother Forrest F. Although water-cooled models would be manufactured later, the Cameron is best remembered today for its air-cooled cars. The first automobiles built by Everett S. Cameron were not gasoline cars at all, however, but steamers, the Eclipse and the Taunton produced in Easton and Taunton, Massachusetts at the turn of the century. But as early as 1900, the Camerons believed the future limited for steam cars and built their first experimental single-cylinder gasoline vehicle. Some three years later they talked an established manufacturer of textile machinery, the James W. Brown Company of Pawtucket, Rhode Island into producing it for them. For the first two years, the Cameron was marketed by a separate corporation (United Motors Company), but when sales reached almost 500 in 1904 the Brown company decided to become identified with the car and thus took over sales and advertising under its own name. Wheel steering and torque tube drive were among the advanced features of the first Camerons. Two- and three-cylinder cars were added to the line in 1904, the Cameron appearance improved, and so did its performance. Camerons won numerous hill climbs and dirt track events, including a half-mile world record in Cincinnati, Ohio. A Cameron was the first air-cooled car to climb to the top of Mount Washington without a stop. For a while air cooling appeared to be the one constant in the life of the Cameron, but even that was to change. Meanwhile, early in 1906, the Brown company was sold to outsiders not interested in automobile manufacture, so the Camerons moved back to Brockton, Massachusetts where they had built racing bicycles less than a decade before. With the help of local investors, they organized the Cameron Car Company and developed a rear-mounted gearbox which became a much publicized feature of the Cameron for the rest of its days, no matter where it was built. Four- and six-cylinder versions of the same basic air-cooled engine were developed. In 1908, the need for more capital and manufacturing space moved the Cameron forty miles away, to Beverly, Massachusetts, where the former Upton factory became the main plant and headquarters. In 1909 branch plants were established in New London, Connecticut (where the six-cylinder cars were produced), in Attica, Ohio (where local financing beckoned), and in Alma, Michigan (where Cameron trucks were built in 1912). Production for 1911 was 600 units, and Camerons continued winning races in the United States, and abroad at Brooklands Track in England and in Pretoria, South Africa. Additional financing and larger facilities elsewhere soon resulted in the Beverly, New London, Attica and Alma plants being phased out. In 1913, amidst a hoopla of publicity, twenty freight car loads of Cameron machinery were moved to the old Methusek Piano plant in West Haven, Connecticut, and the new million-dollar Cameron Manufacturing Company was incorporated in nearby Orange. And the Cameron became water cooled. Still utilizing the patented rear-mounted transmission (now up to four speeds forward), a new line of water-cooled, pointed-radiator Cameron cars was introduced, including a racy roadster marketed as the Yale Featherweight Flyer. One thousand cars was the projected output for the 1914 model year, but the war in Europe and the failure of local investors to come through with expected financing forced the company into bankruptcy instead. Part of the plant was leased to the Avis Gun Company, the balance to the Euclid Motor Car Company for the building of a cyclecar of that name. (Everett Cameron was involved in that venture, as was his sales manager Frank S. Corlew.) It appeared that the Cameron was dead, but the appearance deceived. Instead a new company showed up in 1916 in nearby Norwalk, Connecticut. The plan now was to develop a water-cooled six to sell for $1000, a few prototypes were built — and that was the end of that. The news for 1919 was yet another factory relocation — to Stamford this time — and another new Cameron, this one to feature a return to air cooling. A new engine was developed, and although it may

236

have been put in a few cars for sale, its principal application would be for a front-wheel-drive farm tractor also called the Cameron. The Cameron car was gone forever during 1920. Forrest F. Cameron moved to Cleveland where he tried again with an altogether new Cameron. Everett S. Cameron decided to confine his talents thereafter to the design and manufacture of aviation and marine engines.

1903-1904 CAMERON
Single — 6 hp, 76" wb

	FP	5	4	3	2	1
Rbt.	650	4400	5500	9000	16,000	30,500
Rbt. w/Tonneau	750	4500	5700	9400	17,700	31,500
Canopy Top Rbt. w/Tonneau	800	4700	6100	9900	19,000	33,000

1905 Cameron, model L, side entrance tonneau, HAC

1905 CAMERON
Twin — 8 hp, 76" wb

Rbt.	650	4400	5500	9000	16,900	30,500
Rbt. w/Tonneau	775	4500	5700	9400	17,700	31,500

Three — 12/15 hp, 90" wb

Rbt.	950	4700	6100	9900	19,000	33,000
Side Entrance Tonneau	1050	4800	6200	10,100	20,000	33,500
Surrey	1050	4900	6300	10,300	21,000	34,000

1906 CAMERON
No new cars manufactured in 1906 although some leftover cars from the James Brown era, which ended in December 1905, may have been sold. The Camerons announced in November-December 1906 were 1907 models.

1907 Cameron, model 6, light touring car, HAC

1907 CAMERON
Four — 16 hp, 86" wb

Tourist Three-Seater	1050	4000	4900	7900	14,700	27,500

Four — 16 hp, 86" wb

Light Tour.	850	3900	4800	7700	14,300	27,000

Four — 16 hp, 96" wb

Tour.	1200	4000	5000	8000	15,000	28,000
Rbt.	750	3900	4800	7700	14,300	27,000

Four — 16 hp, 98" wb

Side Entrance Tonneau	1200	4000	4900	7900	14,700	27,500

Four — 24 hp, 112" wb

Tour.	1800	4100	5100	8200	15,400	28,500

1908 Cameron, model 8, special fire dept. car, HAC

1908 CAMERON
Four — 20 hp, 86" wb

	FP	5	4	3	2	1
Model 6 Rbt.	850	3800	4800	7500	14,000	26,500

Four — 16/20 hp, 96" wb

Model 9 Open Tour.	1100	4000	4900	7900	14,700	27,500

Four — 20 hp, 98" wb

Model 8 Tour.-3P	1050	3900	4800	7700	14,300	27,000

1909 Cameron, model 14, runabout, HAC

1909 CAMERON
Four — 20/24 hp, 96" wb

Model 14 Rbt.-2P	900	4000	5000	8000	15,000	28,000
Model 14 Rbt.-3P	950	4000	5000	8000	15,000	28,000
Model 15 Featherweight Flyer-2P	1000	4200	5200	8400	15,700	29,000
Model 16 Rds.-4P	1050	4200	5200	8400	15,700	29,000
Model 16 Tour.-5P	1100	4100	5100	8200	15,400	28,500

Six — 30/36 hp, 114" wb

Model 11 Tour.	1500	4200	5200	8400	15,700	29,000
Model 11 Rds.	1500	4300	5400	8700	16,500	30,000
Model 11 Rbt.	1500	4300	5300	8600	16,100	29,500

1910 CAMERON
Four — 24 hp, 102" wb

Model 14 Rbt.-2P	950	4200	5200	8400	15,700	29,000
Model 14 Rbt.-3P	985	4200	5200	8400	15,700	29,000

Four — 24 hp, 96" wb

Model 15-4 Featherweight Flyer (optional 86" or 92" wb)	1000	4400	5600	9200	17,300	31,000

Four — 24 hp, 104" wb

Model 16 Tour.-5P	1100	4300	5400	8700	16,500	30,000
Model 16 Rds.-4P	1100	4400	5600	9200	17,300	31,000

Six — 36 hp, 110" wb

Model 11-Six Flyer	1500	4500	5800	9500	18,000	32,000

Six — 30/36 hp, 114" wb

Model 11 Tour.-5P	1500	4300	5400	8700	16,500	30,000
Model 11 Tour.-4P	1500	4300	5400	8700	16,500	30,000
Model 11 Rds.-2P	1500	4400	5600	9200	17,300	31,000
Model 11 Rds.-3P	1500	4500	5700	9400	17,700	31,500

1911 Cameron, model 30, roadster, WTC

1911 CAMERON
Four — 24 hp, 104" wb

Model 24 Open-Back Rbt.-2P	800	4000	5000	8000	15,000	28,000
Model 25 Closed-Back Rbt.-2P	825	4100	5100	8200	15,400	28,500
Model 25A Rds.-3P	850	4200	5200	8400	15,700	29,000
Model 25B Surrey-4P	875	4400	5600	9200	17,300	31,000
Model 27 Tour.-5P	1050	4300	5400	8700	16,500	30,000
Model 26 Flyer-2P	885	4400	5600	9200	17,300	31,000
Model 28 Fore-Door Rbt.	1000	4300	5400	8700	16,500	30,000
Model 29 Fore-Door Tour.	1250	4400	5600	9200	17,300	31,000

Six — 36 hp

Model 30 Fore-Door Rbt. (114" wb)	1250	4500	5800	9500	18,000	32,000
Model 31 Fore-Door Tour. (120" wb)	1550	4700	6100	9900	19,000	33,000

1912 CAMERON
Four — 24 hp, 104" wb

Model 28 Fore-Door Flyer-4P	800	4300	5400	8700	16,500	30,000

Four — 24 hp, 110" wb

Model 29 Baby Tonneau	950	4000	5000	8000	15,000	28,000
Model 29A Fore-Door Tour.-5P	950	4200	5200	8400	15,700	29,000

237

1912 Cameron, model 29A, touring, WTC

Six — 36 hp, 114" wb
Model 30 Fore-Doore Flyer-

	FP	5	4	3	2	1
2P	1200	4300	5400	8700	16,500	30,000
Six — 36 hp, 120" wb						
Model 31 Baby Tonneau	1400	4200	5200	8400	15,700	29,000
Model 32 Fore-Door Tour.-						
5P	1400	4300	5400	8700	16,500	30,000

1913 CAMERON
The only Cameron cars sold in 1913 were leftover air-cooled models from 1912. The new cars announced late in 1913 were water-cooled models for the 1914 model year.

1914 Cameron Yale Featherweight Flyer, WTC

1914 CAMERON
Four — 21 hp, 115" wb

	FP	5	4	3	2	1
Model 30 Tour.-5P	1200	4400	5600	9200	17,300	31,000
Yale Featherweight Flyer-						
2P	1200	4500	5800	9500	18,000	32,000

1915-1918 CAMERON
Although Cameron cars were projected and advertised for these model years, none were produced or sold. Cars sold in 1919 and in early 1920 were doubtless minimal, but the following were advertised and pictured during those years.

1919 CAMERON

	FP	5	4	3	2	1
Model 45 Standard Water-Cooled	1700	4300	5300	8600	16,100	29,500
Model 55 Cameron Air-Cooled	1400	4200	5200	8400	15,700	29,000

1920 CAMERON
Model 55 Air Cooled Six

	FP	5	4	3	2	1
Spt. Rds. (108" wb)	2000	4300	5400	8700	16,500	30,000
Tour.-5P (118" wb)	2000	4200	5200	8400	15,700	29,000

CAMERON — Cleveland, Ohio — (1922) — Following the demise of the Cameron on the East Coast, Forrest F. Cameron journeyed west to try again in Cleveland. There a prototype of his air-cooled four-cylinder small tourer was built in the machine shop of F.H. Bultman Company. The vehicle had a 104-inch wheelbase, weighed a thousand pounds, and sported disc wheels and a unique cantilever spring suspension system. A price tag of $600 was contemplated, and fuel consumption of 30 mpg was claimed. Road test results were encouraging, but financing for the manufacture of the car, which was to come from the East Coast, never arrived. While in Cleveland, incidentally, Forrest Cameron also collaborated on the design and engineering of the Marsh and Pomeroy cars.

CAMPBELL ELECTRIC — Providence, Rhode Island — (1897) — An electric automobile was built at the Campbell Machine Company in Providence in 1897. It was designed by Harry E. Dey, a pioneer in the electric car field, and it was produced for a local doctor named J.A. Chase. "The carriage is a novel affair and attracted much attention," the *Providence Telegram* noted that year following the vehicle's first appearance on the streets."

[It] is fitted with three storage batteries capable of driving the carriage fifteen miles an hour; if necessary, however, the speed can be increased about five miles per hour." So far as is known, this was the only automobile built in the Campbell shops.

CAMPBELL — Kingston, New York — (1918-1919) — The Campbell was the Emerson renamed and, it was hoped, cleansed of the taint of the stock manipulation and fraud charges that had quickly killed the Emerson Motors Company in 1917. Theodore A. Campbell and his brother George N., who had been principals in the Emerson organization, though not involved in the skull-duggery, reorganized as the Campbell Motor Car Company and continued production in the same Kingston factory. The Emerson, with a price tag of $395, had been enthusiastically touted as the "lowest-priced five-passenger car in the world." The Campbells quickly found they could not produce profitably at that figure and more than doubled it. At $835, the Campbell was grossly overpriced for the market in which its specifications indicated it belonged. The Campbell Motor Car Company was in the hands of receivers by May 1919.

1918-1919 CAMPBELL
Four — 4-cyl., 22 hp, 110" wb

	FP	5	4	3	2	1
Tour.-5P	835	—	—	—	—	—

CAMPBELL-CORWIN — Brooklyn, New York — (1907) — During the spring of 1907 the bicycle-manufacturing Campbell-Corwin Company of Brooklyn increased its capital stock by $5000 for the purpose of manufacturing automobiles. Gilbert M. Stratton was president of the company, Ambrose D. Corwin and Edward R. Strong were directors. The firm temporarily headquartered its new venture at 522 Vanderbilt Avenue until its new facility at 902-908 Union Street was completed. Manufacture of a Campbell-Corwin car has not been documented, but it is certainly possible that a few automobiles may have been built. Late in 1908 G.M. Stratton announced that his firm's name had been changed to Montauk Garage Company. Automobile repair probably was the firm's principal activity thereafter.

CAMPUS — The Campus Auto Garage was organized in Rochester, New York with a capital stock of $10,000 during the early summer of 1910. Rochester businessmen E.A. Stein, James Barry and H.B. Shield were behind this venture and they indicated their plans to "manufacture and deal in automobiles, bicycles and supplies." A Campus automobile is not believed to have followed.

1900 Canda, Auto Quadricycle, HAC

CANDA — Carteret, New Jersey — (1900-1902) — In 1896 the Canda Manufacturing Company, producers of railroad hand cars, acquired manufacturing rights to the gasoline engine invented by the Duryea brothers and announced a forthcoming production of omnibuses, express and delivery wagons with Charles E. Duryea to superintend the factory. This alliance was of short duration, and Duryea (who already was quarreling with his brother J. Frank) soon took off to pursue his own ventures. In 1900 Canda decided to get into the automobile business on its own. The Auto-Quadricycle, powered by a 1-3/4 hp gasoline engine "of the Otto type" and carrying two passengers in tandem, was put on the market that year. Its price was $485 exclusive of lamps and signal bell. By 1901 a Quadricycle Van and an Auto-Tricycle had been added with the same engine, though "greater power" was available for an additional ten dollars. The line was also broadened with a Stanhope and a Spider Runabout, these vehicles powered "by a pair of gasoline engines of about 2 1/2 horsepower each" and featuring a variable speed mechanism permitting the carriage "to move at any desired speed from a moderate walk, say 2 1/2 miles up to 15 miles per hour (and) to be run backwards as well." When the Canda company folded during the summer of 1902, its remaining inventory was acquired by George W. Condon of Newark who sold the cars for $195 with only twenty-five percent down. That had to be one of the better new-car buys in America at the time.

1900 CANDA
One Cylinder — 1-3/4 hp, 46" wb

	FP	5	4	3	2	1
Auto-Quadricycle	485	1200	2300	3300	5100	9500

1901 Canda, Spider Runabout, HAC

1901-1902 CANDA
One Cylinder — 1-3/4 hp, 46" wb

Auto-Quadricycle	485	1100	2200	3200	4900	9000
Auto-Quadricycle Van	485	1000	2100	3100	4800	8500
Auto-Tricycle	400	1000	2100	3100	4800	8500

Two Cylinder — 5 hp, 50" wb

Spider Rbt.	625	1100	2200	3200	4900	9000

Two Cylinder — 5 hp, 54" wb

Stanhope	700	1100	2200	3200	4900	9000

CANFIELD — "William Canfield of Canaan, Connecticut is about to erect a factory which will be used for the manufacture of automobiles," *The Horseless Age* reported in May 1905. There is no evidence that Canfield ever did this.

1904 Cannon, runabout, WLB

CANNON — **Kalamazoo, Michigan** — **(1903-1906)** — Frank Burtt and Warren B. Cannon were machinists from Kalamazoo. In 1901 Burtt was working as superintendent of the Municipal Lighting Plant, and Cannon was serving in the same capacity for the Williams Manufacturing Company, producers of windmills and silos. In 1902 they quit their respective jobs to establish the Burtt Manufacturing Company for the production of an automobile called the Cannon. Earlier that year, in addition to designing the Cannon car, Warren Cannon had begun the Automatic Machine Company for the manufacture of gasoline engines, and it was into that factory that the car-building venture moved. The plant had an annual capacity of forty units. The Cannons built there featured single-, twin- and four-cylinder engines, spur gear or planetary transmissions, and were available as lever-steered runabouts and wheel-steered touring cars. In 1906 the company began building larger quarters, but by the time construction had been completed, automobile manufacture had been discontinued. Subsequent production was confined to friction clutches and the Kalamazoo gasoline engine. An advertisement from 1914 indicated that more than 4000 of the latter were in use throughout the world.

1903-1905 CANNON

	FP	5	4	3	2	1
Rbt. (1-cyl., 7 hp, 72" wb)	650	2400	3400	4800	8000	17,000
Tonneau (2-cyl., 15 hp, 84 1/2" wb)	1350	2500	3500	—	8500	18,000

1906 CANNON
Model 3 — 2-cyl., 24 hp, 104" wb

Side Entrance Tonneau	1650	2500	3500	5000	8500	18,000

Model 2 — 4-cyl., 50 hp, 120" wb

Side Entrance Tonneau	3500	2700	3600	5300	8800	19,000

CANNON — **Des Moines, Iowa** — **(1912)** — The Cannon Motor Car Company was organized in Des Moines in late 1912 with offices in the Utica Building downtown and no factory site yet decided upon. The firm's products were slated to be a roadster "fully equipped with top" to sell between four and five hundred dollars, and a 500-pound light delivery to sell "a shade lower." J.F. Cannon was the man behind all this, and he was reported in the press to have been "connected with nearly all the leading automobile factories in Detroit." One might get the impression that he couldn't hold a job. He proved no better as his own boss. One reference indicates that he planned to name his vehicles after the town of their manufacture. But whether anything more than a prototype of the Des Moines or the Cannon was ever built is open to question.

1921 Cannon Ball, 6-60, touring, WLB

CANNON BALL — **Texico, New Mexico** — **(1918-1921)** — "6-60, Star of the Highway" was the slogan, $10 million was the capital stock, and "Quick Prosperity" was promised investors. W.L. Mansfield, C.A. Roberson, J.B. Hanlin, D.A. Randall and J.C. Milne were the men behind the Cannon Ball Motor Company which was organized in Texico, New Mexico in January 1918. A surviving brochure of the company indicates the Cannon Ball as a 1921 model. What happened in the three intervening years from incorporation is not known. Conceivably, a prototype of the car was never completed. Most certainly, stock in the company was sold.

1901 Cannon Steam Racer, WLB

CANNON STEAM RACER — **Cambridge, Massachusetts** — **(1901-1902)** — George C. Cannon was a student at Harvard with a yen for speed. In 1901 he had a steam car built with a Peter Forg burner from Somerville and the chassis devised by Charles E. Miller, the big auto accessory man from New York City. On August 23rd, 1902, at Brighton Beach track in Brooklyn, he drove this vehicle a mile in 1 minute 7-3/5 seconds. He may have had a touring version built as well. He did not go into manufacture, however. When he graduated from Harvard, he took a job with Grout Brothers in 1905 to race and test their steam cars.

CANTON — **Canton, Ohio** — **(1909-1910)** — In December of 1909, D.L. Tschantz, president of the Canton Buggy Company, announced that he had set aside a portion of his buggy plant for the production of automobiles. Cars both for passenger and delivery use were to be built, with the emphasis on the latter. "The idea is to take advantage of the present state of the art," Tschantz said, "produce a wagon of the greatest possible utility from the point of view of radius of action, low cost per ton mile of the goods transported, with a particular eye to the future, considering depreciation." The extent of production which followed is not known, but the Canton Buggy Company did apparently build a few motorized buggies in the year which followed.

1906 Cantono Electric, brougham, WLB

CANTONO ELECTRIC — Marion, New Jersey — (1904-1907) — The idea was that of Capt. Eugene Cantono of the Italian Army. It was produced under license in New Jersey by the Cantono Electric Tractor Company. The idea was an electric fore-carriage, a two-wheel attachment to make a horsedrawn buggy horseless, with batteries mounted over the axle, and electric motors with independent gear drive to each wheel. Cantono also built complete models using this device. The company was bankrupt by September 1907. In commenting on the Cantono demise, *The Motor World* referred to the captain's invention as "a ponderous creation" which had "failed to cut a figure in the electric field."

1904-1905 CANTONO ELECTRIC

	FP	5	4	3	2	1
Electric Fore-Carriage	1750	1200	2300	3300	5100	9500
Electric Brgm.	3500	1500	2500	3600	5500	11,000

1905 Cantono Electric, brougham, RBB

1906 CANTONO ELECTRIC

Electric Fore-Carriage	1750	1200	2300	3300	5100	9500
Electric Victoria	2900	1400	2400	3500	5300	10,000
Electric Extension Brgm.	3100	1500	2500	3600	5500	11,000

1907 CANTONO ELECTRIC

Electric Fore-Carriage	1750	1200	2300	3300	5100	9500
Electric Extension Brgm.	3500	1500	2500	3600	5500	11,000

CANZOL — Cleveland, Ohio — (1931) — This promotional midget was built to be the official messenger car for the National Air Races held at Cleveland in 1931. Instead of the usual motive force, it featured a propeller driven by a small air-cooled engine. Speeds of up to 90 mph were claimed, but probably never realized.

1931 Canzol

CAPITAL — The Capital Auto Company was organized in Indianapolis, Indiana during the fall of 1906 with a capital stock of $25,000 for the purpose of building "motor cars, parts and appurtenances." Russell R. Irwin, Fred W. Eisle and Harry Seibert backed this venture. Manufacture is doubted.

The Capital Engine Company of 1913 was a million-dollar incorporation to manufacture and sell automobiles which most likely was organized to sell stock to the gullible.

c.1889 Capitol Steam Chariot, NAHC

CAPITOL STEAM — Washington, D.C. — (c.1889) — Only one of these two-cylinder 6 hp light steam cars was ever built. Extravagantly styled, its body a web of undulating lines and provocative curves, the vehicle was called a "Steam Chariot" by its inventor who decided in 1902 to attach a $1200 price tag to it and to market it through the Capitol Automobile Company which he established. According to a descendant of the inventor, he was unable to interest potential investors because the styling of the vehicle — which had purportedly been built in 1889 — was by then outdated. Indubitably. The car looked like it had leapt from the pages of *Ben Hur*. It remains extant.

CAPITOL ELECTRIC — Washington, D.C. — (1911-1912) — The Washington Motor Vehicle Company commenced business in the District of Columbia in 1909. Its product was an electric commercial vehicle manufactured in four models ranging from a 750-pound light delivery to a two-ton truck. In 1911 the tradename of the vehicles was changed from Washington to Capitol (or Capitol Car). Apparently a handful of passenger cars was produced under the Capitol name but trade press articles about the company focus on the commercial vehicles only. Some rosters indicate the Washington Motor Vehicle Company as remaining in business into 1914, which seems highly doubtful. In February of 1912, W.H. Cowant, who had been appointed receiver for the company, indicated that "its assets and liabilities are small."

CAPITOL CITY — The Capitol City Automobile Company was organized during the early fall of 1900 with a capital stock of $100,000 to manufacture and sell automobiles in Washington, D.C. Behind this venture were C.F. Norment, E.B. Evans, E. Reynolds, E. Wilson and M.A. Ballinger. Manufacture is doubted.

CAPS — Kansas City, Missouri — (1905) — The Caps brothers were printing machine manufacturers in Kansas City who built a two-cylinder 14 hp two-seater gasoline runabout in 1902, ran up a tonneau for a couple of extra passengers, and then spent three years trying to find someone to finance manufacture. By 1905, after the Caps had sold a few cars to neighbors, a local bank decided to help, and the Farmer's Auto-Motor Car Company was formed. It was a $250,000 incorporation, with the bankers taking charge, F. Burleigh Johnson as president, J.K. Hudson as chairman of the board. A factory in Sheffield was contemplated, but a site in Kansas City was ultimately selected. Production of the Caps had barely begun, however, when the bankers found another group of entrepreneurs in whom they had more faith. The Caps were booted out of their factory, and the Kansas City Motor Car Company moved in to produce the Kansas City.

CAR — Car Motors Corporation of New York City was organized in early 1923 presumably for the manufacture of automobiles but obviously for the selling of stock. That fall the firm, and its promoter Arthur H. Kliesrath, were enjoined in the State Supreme Court from selling any more. The Attorney General reported that Car Motors had issued $5 million in stock, had sold a total of $70,000 in the few months past, and had not completed a single car.

1907 Car De Luxe, 7-pass. touring, WLB

CAR DE LUXE — Toledo, Ohio — (1906-1907)/Detroit, Michigan — (1908-1909) — Costliness of manufacture was the keynote of the De Luxe Motor Car Company, and there was a decided pretentiousness in its marketing. De Luxe, for example, chose to refer to the Hess-Bright ball bearings it used as "genuine imported Deutsche Waffen Fabrik." There were a lot of them in the Car De Luxe, thirty-three in all, including three on the crankshaft, four in the steering post, five in the transmission, six in the gearbox, eight in the wheels, six in the axles, and one in the clutch. The De Luxe company was originally housed in the old Yale factory in Toledo. In October of 1906 De Luxe president Nathan M. Kaufman and De Luxe general manager Daniel W. Kaufman orchestrated a merger with C.H. Blomstrom, builder of the Blomstrom and Queen cars in Detroit. Subsequently the De Luxe company moved to Detroit, into a new factory all its own which some years later was purchased by Walter Flanders for the car bearing his name. Although the Car De Luxe was discontinued by the end of 1909, the memory of the company lingered on a while longer. In 1912 a disgruntled former stockholder named Roswell R. Robinson took De Luxe to court charging that he had been "induced to purchase stock by fraudulent representation." He won his case.

1907 CAR DE LUXE
Model A — 4-cyl., 50 hp, 121" wb

	FP	5	4	3	2	1
Tour. Car-7P	4750	5000	6500	11,000	22,000	35,000

1908 Car De Luxe, touring, JAC

1908 CAR DE LUXE
Model B — 4-cyl., 50 hp, 121" wb

	FP	5	4	3	2	1
Tour.-7P	5000	5000	6500	11,000	22,000	35,000
Rbt.-4P	5000	4900	6300	10,300	21,000	34,000
Limo.-Land'et.-7P	5000	4700	6100	9900	19,000	33,000

1909 CAR DE LUXE
Model B — 4-cyl., 50/60 hp, 121" wb

	FP	5	4	3	2	1
Tour.-7P	5000	5000	6500	11,000	22,000	35,000
Close-Coupled Tour.-4/5P	5000	5200	6800	11,300	23,000	36,000
Limo.-7P	6250	4700	6100	9900	19,000	33,000

1930 Cardon, steam touring, MVMA

CARDON — Chicago, Illinois — (1929-1930) — The Cardon was simply the conversion of a 1930 Nash into a steam car. Its name was derived from the two men responsible for its building: Jeffery Carqueville and Duncan MacDonald. Carqueville was the grandson of Thomas B. Jeffery; Mac-Donald was an engineer whose checkered career in the industry had included the Gearless and the MacDonald steam cars of the early Twenties. The engine in the Cardon was a four, with the cylinders operating independently of each other, and with a pilot light which reportedly was perpetually burning. The car was tested in Chicago in 1930 and was driven by Carqueville to New York in search of potential investors. When they were not found, Carqueville sold the car in the East and went home.

1923 Cardway, touring, KM

CARDWAY — New York, New York — (1923-1924) — While sitting in his office at 342 Madison Avenue in New York City, one Colonel Frederick Cardway decided to produce an automobile. He never did incorporate a company to do it, but he did get further than many firms that were capitalized with high hopes and glowing prospectuses during that era. Cardway actually built at least five, and possibly six, cars. They were paragons of the unrelievedly ordinary, with six-cylinder Continental engines, varied components from companies supplying accessory car manufacturers of the day, and the appearance of having been designed by a committee of former employees who had worked for Hupmobile and Crawford, among others. There is no evidence that the coachwork was designed by anyone other than Colonel Cardway, however; he simply borrowed liberally from the look of other cars on the road. Two models, with little discernible difference between them, were offered. Possibly all Cardways had right-hand drive, because export seems to have been the aim from the beginning, which was not illogical since Colonel Cardway had previously handled export overseas sales for both Packard and Pierce-Arrow. One of the Cardway cars remains extant, in a collection in Canada. In 1925, after his automotive venture failed, Colonel Cardway took on a Rollin dealership. In 1929 he became a vice-president of Sanford Motor Truck Company in Syracuse, where he was placed in charge of European sales and distribution.

1923-1924 CARDWAY
Six — 40 hp, 118" wb

	FP	5	4	3	2	1
Std. Spt. Tour.	1295	—	—	—	—	—
Super Spt. Tour.	1495	—	—	—	—	—

CARETTE — The Carette Manufacturing Company of Chicago has been indicated on various car rosters as building an automobile in 1913. Doubtless this was not so. Chicago city directories for the period indicate no such company in town.

CAREY — Fairmount, Indiana — (1905) — In a 1905 *Cycle and Automobile Trade Journal* "Buyer's Guide," the Carey Motor Car Company of Fairmount was listed as a manufacturer of both steam and gasoline automobiles. The total lifetime production of the company was just one gasoline car, however, the Carey factory having a workforce of one man: William Carey. In 1905 he spent approximately three months building the car which purportedly had been "the only order received by the factory." Problems arose when the Westerfield Motor Company of Anderson demanded payment for the gasoline engine which had been purchased for it, and further creditors became rather testy regarding payment for machinery and equipment bought but not paid for. William Carey ultimately solved these problems by leaving town; his wife shut up the shop and followed him. "The automobile, which had reached a state of partial completion and could be run at a low rate of speed by one who understood its character and peculiarities, was left at the shop," *The Motor World* reported that December. "It will probably be partitioned among the creditors."

1906 Carey, rotary-engine runabout, NAHC

CAREY — New York, New York — (1906) — Two addresses were given at the time for the Carey Motor Company. One was West 125th Street, in the heart of Harlem and was probably the administrative office or showroom. The other was Girard Avenue in the Bronx, which was probably the factory since Stephen M. Balzer was also located on that street and the Carey was powered by one of Balzer's rotary engines. Unlike the automobiles built under the Balzer name before the turn of the century which carried three-cylinder engines, the Balzer in the Carey was a five. The Carey also differed from the rotary-engined Adams-Farwell then being built in Dubuque (Iowa) in that its vertical-crankshaft engine was front mounted, while the Adams-Farwell's horizontal-crankshaft powerplant was positioned in the rear. Although the Carey was exhibited at the Automobile Club of America show in New York in 1906, it is not known how many orders were taken there, nor how many cars were subsequently produced. By 1907, however, the Carey had faded from sight entirely.

1871 Carhart Steam Vehicle, "The Spark", WLB

CARHART STEAM — Racine, Wisconsin — (1871) — J.W. Carhart was a doctor of medicine, his brother H.S. Carhart was a professor of physics (Northwestern University and Michigan State University). The idea for this pioneer steam carriage was the doctor's, the working drawings were the professor's, and a wealthy citizen of Racine named George Slauson put up the money to have it built. The boiler was made by Button Fire Engine Works of Waterford, New York (Dr. Carhart had moved to Racine from Saratoga County, New York), and much of the machine work was done by the J.I. Case company in Racine. The vehicle ran, and so successfully that it persuaded the legislature of the State of Wisconsin to offer a prize of $10,000 to any citizen of the state who could produce "a cheap and practical substitute for use of horses and other animals on the highway and farm." J.W. Carhart was not persuaded to enter, though he did ride on the Oshkosh during its contest trial for the $10,000 prize. After the turn of the century, in letters to the editors of *MoToR* and *The Horseless Age*, J.W. Carhart, who by now had relocated his medical practice to Texas, declared his continuing belief in the efficacy of steam as the automobile's prime motive force, and mentioned that he was building another steam automobile for his own pleasure. Early in 1914 he reminisced about the Spark, the nickname for his 1871 car. "Since then I frequently have heard the cannonading of racing motors lined up for the start (of a race), but, frankly, even Disbrow's Jay-Eye-See (a popular race car of the period) could not compare with it for genuine peace-disturbing qualities," he said. "Of course, the steam whistle with which it was equipped did not tend to make matters any better. In fact, it was not long before we had the street entirely to ourselves, for, when they had seen it, the citizens were unanimous in predicting that the Spark would blow up. I think it was due to this fact that there were only a few runaways and no casualties connected with our premier appearance." On December 21st, 1914, Dr. J.W. Carhart died. His 1871 vehicle remained extant as long as 1942. Its whereabouts since that date are unknown; sadly, it may have been sacrificed to the scrap drive for World War II.

1911 Carhartt, model A, Gunboat Special, roadster, WLB

CARHARTT — Detroit, Michigan — (1911-1912) — "Twenty-eight years' progressive manufacturing success culminates in Carhartt Cars" read the advertisements in 1911. That the success was as a manufacturer of overalls was a matter that Hamilton Carhartt did not believe necessary to mention. In March of 1910 he incorporated his Carhartt Automobile Corporation and was in production by August on a flurry of 1911 models offered as 25 hp and 35 hp fours on a single chassis. For 1912 he trimmed his model line considerably, but increased horsepower and added another chassis. How many 1912 models Hamilton Carhartt produced is not known, but there could not have been many. In March that year, with $4000 cash on hand and liabilities of $20,000, he decided to return to the manufacture of wearing apparel exclusively. The new Monarch moved into the old Carhartt plant.

1911 CARHARTT
Junior — 4-cyl., 25 hp, 118" wb

	FP	5	4	3	2	1
Model J Rds.	1100	—	—	—	—	19,000
Model J Tour.	1250	—	—	—	—	20,000

Four — 4-cyl., 35 hp, 118" wb

	FP	5	4	3	2	1
Model A Gunboat Spec.	2250	3100	4200	6300	10,500	22,000
Model B Phae.	2250	3200	4300	6500	11,000	23,000
Model C Rbt.	2250	3200	4300	6500	11,000	23,000
Model D Cpe.	2250	2700	3600	5300	8800	22,000
Model G Land'et.	2250	2900	3700	5600	9100	20,000
Model H Limo.	2250	2700	3600	5300	8800	19,000

1912 CARHARTT
Junior Model J — 4-cyl., 30 hp, 108" wb

	FP	5	4	3	2	1
Fore-Door Tour. Rbt.	1350	—	—	—	—	—
Limo.	2200	—	—	—	—	—
Cpe.	1750	—	—	—	—	—

Model B — 4-cyl., 50 hp, 118" wb

	FP	5	4	3	2	1
Fore-Door Tour. Rbt.	2500	—	—	—	—	—
Limo.	3500	—	—	—	—	—
Cpe.	3200	—	—	—	—	—

CARL ELECTRIC — Toledo, Ohio — (1913) — The Carl Electric Vehicle Company was organized in November of 1913 by Arnold Goss, A.O. Garford, H. Sulzberger and former Willys-Overland chief engineer C.A. Neracher. The firm was capitalized at $300,000, and purchased much of the machinery of the Chicago Electric Motor Car Company in the Windy City. This was moved to a new factory in Toledo, where the production of electric delivery vehicles was scheduled to begin in early 1914. A few prototypes were assembled, but the venture fell apart before manufacture began.

CARLEY — Colfax, Washington — (1900-1902) — The Carley brothers operated an ironmongery in Colfax where in 1900 they built their first experimental car. Apparently, they were dissatisfied with the results because when the brothers announced their forthcoming entrance into the automobile field late the following year they indicated their intention to "buy parts and assemble them." Perhaps a few cars followed, but by the end of 1902 the Carley Iron Works had returned wholeheartedly to the business it knew best.

CARLISLE — The Carlisle Body and Gear Company of Carlisle, Pennsylvania was organized with a capital stock of $30,000 late in 1904 to manufacture "automobiles, carriages, wagons and sleighs." A large passel of Carlisle businessmen backed this venture: David S. Wagner, John W. Plank, Arthur R. Rupley, John C. Eckels, L.S. Eisenhour, William H. Crossley, John A. Heffelfinger, George B. Brandon, Abram Null, J.C. Hoover, F.D. Clymer, E.J. Gardner, R.E. Cabish, John A. Means, John W. Wetzel. That a Carlisle automobile resulted has not been documented.

CARLISLE — Chicago, Illinois — (1899-1900) — In October of 1899 when the Carlisle Manufacturing Company of 69-75 Jackson Street in Chicago announced its entry into the automobile field, the firm proudly stated that it planned to be the "first motor vehicle assembler, purchasing parts and motors elsewhere." Carlisle was not the first to do this, though the company was typical in not doing it long. The engine the company purchased was a small gasoline unit. "This motor has been given a thorough test and has not been found wanting," president Carlisle said. "E.F. Brown, of the Brown Manufacturing Company, our next door neighbor, has one and has been using it for months." A few months turned out to be the extent of the Carlisle life in the automobile industry. References from early 1900 indicate an increase in the firm's capital stock for expansion purposes, but the company was out of the assembling business by year's end.

CARLSON — Brooklyn, New York — (1904) — Charles A. Carlson had formerly been in charge of the New York City repair department for the Winton Motor Carriage Company of Cleveland, and during the summer of 1903 he struck out on his own, opening a garage at 623 Bergen Street in Brooklyn and announcing his forthcoming manufacture of pleasure and commercial vehicles. Not until January 1904, however, was the Carlson Motor Vehicle Company organized. The investors were Leopold Sandhelm and his brother Eugene, and the capital stock was $100,000. In addition to powering the Carlson vehicles, the four-cylinder four-stroke 40 hp engine Charles Carlson had designed was sold as a separate package to the trade. In 1904 only was a Carlson passenger car offered, a 20 hp runabout on the same 90-inch chassis as the firm's delivery truck. Thereafter the Carlson company built trucks exclusively, production continuing into 1910.

CARLSON-WENSTROM — Philadelphia, Pennsylvania — (1914) — The Carlson-Wenstrom Mfg. Company, Inc. was a machinery producer located at Richmond and Erie Avenue in Philadelphia. J.L. Carlson was president, W.R. Wenstrom was secretary-treasurer, and in 1914, in the midst of the cyclecar craze, they directed their engineer, Jacob Lundgren, to construct a cyclecar for potential manufacture. Whether the cyclecar built was unworthy or whether the cyclecar fad had died before Carlson-Wenstrom could get into production is not known. The first cyclecar from this company, however, was also the last.

CARMM — During the early Twenties, the Carmm Convertible Body Company of New York City, New York was engaged in the business of what its name suggests. No evidence has been found to indicate the firm built a complete car.

1913 Car-Nation, tandem cyclecar, WLB

CAR-NATION — Detroit, Michigan — (1912-1915) — "The Car for the American Public" was more than a cyclecar, the American Voiturette Company said, and in part that was true. The four-passenger touring car model was large for the genre, but the two-passenger roadster and tandem were typical. Prices for all three cars were in the $500 range, and each had the same four-cylinder air-cooled engine, 104-inch wheelbase and three-speed transmission. That American Voiturette was not entirely sure of its own convictions is indicated by the fact that late in 1913 company president Charles S. Shaffer bought out the Keeton Motor Car Company of Detroit and continued manufacture of the full-size Keeton along-side the Car-Nation. By September 1914 American Voiturette was in receivership. Six hundred Car-Nations and 100 Keetons were slated to be assembled under receivership control. Although a new firm, the Car-Nation-Motor Car Company, was formed in 1915 to continue manufacture, nothing ever came of it. What remained of the Car-Nation was ultimately purchased by Sam Winternitz for $100,000. In announcing the car in 1913, incidentally, *Automobile Topics* magazine called it a Coronation. This was an error perpetrated either at the reporter's typewriter or in the magazine's composing room. There never was a car in America called the Coronation.

1914 Car-Nation, roadster, WLB

1912-1915 CAR-NATION
Cyclecar — 4-cyl., 18 hp, 104" wb

	FP	5	4	3	2	1
Tandem-2P	510	—	—	—	—	—
Rds.-2P	495	—	—	—	—	—
Tour.-4P	520	—	—	—	—	—

CARNEGIE — New York, New York — (1915) — "The only sign of an automobile of any sort was a wash drawing in the New York office, on which a car designer worked patiently for several weeks before the exposure of the scheme, trying to reconcile the proportions of wheels, tires, hood, body and steering wheel as shown in the drawing, with the possibilities of motor car construction and the specifications given in the Carnegie circulars." Thus reported *Automobile Topics* late in 1915. The Carnegie circulars were handsome pieces of literature, provided by a New York printer in exchange for a percentage of the profits. The literature deftly implied a relationship with Andrew Carnegie's steel empire in Pittsburgh. A five-passenger touring car to be priced at $595 and sold for export exclusively was to be the product of the Carnegie Engineering Corporation. William J.A. Bailey was the mastermind behind this scheme, and he engineered it well, taking offices in the prestigious Whitehall Building in lower Manhattan (which he furnished, as said in the press, "with ancient-looking files in the endeavor to obtain the appearance of an established firm") and boasting of a huge factory in Kalamazoo, Michigan. Promotional material was circulated by mail advertising the availability of both dealerships (for a deposit of $510, eight prospective dealers purportedly sent in the money) and the car ($50 deposit, and some orders did come in from Europe). Associated with Bailey in this endeavor were Robert F. Norwalk and Chauncey Holt, Jr. They were all quickly found out. The company's factory in Kalamazoo was discovered to be an abandoned saw mill. In addition to the wash drawing, the firm's other tangible assets included a box of rusty tools. Those "ancient-looking files" had been rented. In November 1915 Bailey pleaded guilty to a charge of using the mails to defraud and was sentenced to thirty days in jail. The lightness of the sentence was due to the fact that Bailey had paid back $5400 of the $7000 he had received in deposits, and gave his notes for the remainder.

CARPENTER — The Carpenter Motor Vehicle Company of Brooklyn, New York was indicated in trade directories as a manufacturer in 1910. That a car was actually produced has not been documented. There was such a company in Brooklyn at the time, at 1239 Fulton Street, but the evidence suggests it operated as a dealership.

1895 Carpenter Electric, auto-buggy, NAHC

CARPENTER — Denver, Colorado — (1895) — H.H. Carpenter of Denver built a very light electric runabout featuring a storage battery of his own invention which was placed under the seat. The vehicle was tiller steered, with two bicycle wheels in front, two high carriage wheels in the rear. Though Carpenter never marketed his car, it was among the earliest built in the state of Colorado.

CARQUEVILLE — The steam car built in 1929-1930 by Jeffery Carqueville in association with Duncan MacDonald is more properly referred to as the Cardon. Refer to Cardon.

CARR — "W.E. Carr of Tacoma, Washington reports his car still in the experimental stage." *The American Cyclecar* reported in February 1914. Possibly it remained ever thus; certainly it was never put into manufacture.
The Carr Road Tour Automobile Company was an early 1917 Delaware incorporation capitalized at $500,000 for the manufacture of automobiles. None were.

CARRIAGE — The Carriage Machine Company of 87 Elm Street in Amesbury, Massachusetts was indicated as an automobile manufacturer in the Hiscox book *Horseless Vehicles, Automobiles, Motor Cycles* published in 1900. Further documentation is lacking.
Although occasionally referred to as the Carriage-Mobile, the car built in Waterloo, Iowa from 1907-1909 by the Summit Carriage-Mobile Company is more properly designated as a Summit. Refer to Summit.

CARRICO — Cincinnati, Ohio — (1896, 1909) — In 1896, while working for the Speed Changing Pulley Company of Indianapolis, F.D. Carrico assisted in the building of an experimental gasoline carriage called the Carrico-De Tamble. That car was never produced, though the Speed Changing Pulley Company subsequently built the De Tamble automobile beginning in 1908. By that time, Carrico had departed for Cincinnati to build two-cylinder air-cooled engines, some of which were used in the De Tamble, some of which he fitted into a buggy-type chassis of his own. He did not sell many of his bodyless Carricos, however, nor sell them long. In October 1909 the Carrico Motor Company's affairs were described as "being wound up."

CARROLL — A car called the Carroll or Carrol was reported to have been built by the Compressed Air Power Company of East Boston, Massachusetts in 1901. Refer to Compressed Air.
The George L. Carroll Company was a $25,000 Delaware incorporation from 1917 for the manufacture of automobiles and motor trucks. Neither followed.
The William A. Carroll Corporation was organized with a capital stock of $50,000 during the late spring of 1912 for the manufacture of motor vehicles in Merrimac, Massachusetts. Involved in this venture were William A., William E. and Annie E. Carroll, Charlotte B. Case and Walter R. Mitchell. Manufacture does not appear to have followed.

1908 Carroll, carbonic acid prototype, NAHC

CARROLL — Philadelphia, Pennsylvania — (1908) — John Carroll, a mechanic in Philadelphia, spent years perfecting his invention, but finally during the summer of 1908, he was ready. His idea was an engine run by carbonic acid, which he had already bench-tested, and which he had now installed in an old curved-dash Oldsmobile chassis that he was ready to take for a test ride, with a reporter for *The Motor Age* tagging along. "The street test was really quite convincing," the reporter wrote, "and what-

ever the merits of his system, Carroll made good on this occasion." The car was driven up Broad Street, out to Fairmount Park, and up the steep City Line hill from the Schuylkill River, being stopped and started several times on the incline to demonstrate the engine's flexibility and power. Whatever its merits, and undoubtedly it didn't develop the 100 hp its inventor claimed for it, the Carroll engine was a compact and nice piece of work. Just 13 1/2 by 10 1/2 by 4 1/2 inches, it was machined from a solid piece of steel, with three cylinders and six pistons, the latter moving longitudinally. "After returning from its trip from City Line hill the motor was cool," the reporter remarked, "indeed, the operation of the engine produced little, if any, heat. Carroll says his motor cannot burn out or freeze. To prevent corrosion or oxidization in the tanks, a mixture composed mostly of kerosene is used." An engine requiring neither radiator nor fan nor carburetor nor any of the various accoutrements of the gasoline engine seemed almost too good to be true. Had John Carroll's engine been practical as well, the industry doubtless would have beat a path to his door.

1912 Carroll-40, touring, NAHC

CARROLL — Strasburg, Pennsylvania — (1911-1912) — The Carroll from Strasburg is probably the only automobile in American history with tobacco and bologna figuring in its origins. The car was created by two brothers, Carroll and Chester Aument; their father was a Strasburg tobacconist who purchased the former Sharpe bologna factory in town so the young men could pursue their dream. Carroll, a Drexel Institute graduate, was chief engineer; Chester was salesman and general manager; and the Carroll Motor Car Company was organized in January 1911. To fill the company coffers while the prototype was being built, the brothers sold tires, repaired cars and became the local dealers for the Marion, Cutting and Jackson cars. Meantime, a four-cylinder 40 hp Continental engine was purchased, and Carroll Aument proceeded to run up a chassis for it, which was ready in time for the Lancaster Fair in September. Thereafter he put himself to work on the body, and on February 23rd, 1912 the completed car had its first test run. By now the brothers had decided to call it the Carroll-40. Obviously the Aument had grand dreams because for 1913 they informed the trade press that roadster, tourabout and touring models of three different Carroll cars (a 32 hp four in the $2400 price range, a 40 hp four in the $3250 range, a 40 hp six in the $3500 range) would be forthcoming. They never arrived. Rosters listing the Carroll as produced until 1926 have been grossly in error. The only Carroll built in Strasburg was the first prototype, though the Carroll Motor Car Company continued as a dealership for some time. Until it was sold for scrap in the late 1930's, the Carroll prototype was used as a tow car.

1921 Carroll Six, touring, WES

CARROLL SIX — Lorain, Ohio — (1921-1922) — The West Coast dealer for the Carroll Six claimed it to be the first car "to come out from a factory fully equipped." For $3985, a purchaser received a permanent California top, six disc or wire wheels, cord tires, tire covers, trunk rack, bumper, and a host of other accessories which put the usual automobile buyer back at least a thousand dollars over purchase price. The car was offered in two body styles only, on a 128-inch wheelbase. Initial plans called for the fitting of a Rochester (Trego) engine, but when the car was introduced it carried a 66 hp Beaver six. Because the radiator of the Carroll Six was recessed seven-and-a-half inches behind the front axle, it was one of the more distinctive-looking cars on the road. None of the distinctive buying inducements offered by the Carroll Automobile Company caused it to stay in business long in Lorain, however. Carelessness at the factory probably also helped to see to the car's quick demise. As legend has it, a trainload of Carrolls was shipped west in the wintertime, without anti-freeze. The cars arrived on the Pacific Coast with all their blocks cracked. One Carroll Six is known to survive today.

1921-1922 CARROLL SIX
Six — 66 hp, 128" wb

	FP	5	4	3	2	1
Rds.-2P	3985	3200	4300	6500	11,000	23,000
Tour.-5P	3985	3100	4200	6300	10,500	22,000

CARSON — In 1920 a venture in Detroit styling itself as the Carson Motor Company indicated its intention to build an automobile. No documentation remains regarding the vehicle intended to be built, but manufacture certainly did not follow. The entrance and exit of Carson on the Detroit scene was so abbreviated that the firm never made the city directory.

1901 Carter Steamer, runabout, MVMA

CARTER STEAM — Grand Rapids, Michigan — (1901) — In his native Jackson, Michigan, Byron J. Carter had been experimenting with horseless carriages since before the turn of the century, building a gasoline car as early as 1899. None of his designs were produced, however, until 1901 when the Michigan Automobile Company was organized in Grand Rapids to manufacture Carter's steam stanhope. Its boiler featured an automatic burner, a victoria top was provided as standard equipment, and the vehicle was lever steered from the right side. The price was $1000. The evidence suggests this car was built for one year only. In 1902 Carter improved his design and persuaded some businessmen in his hometown to organize the Jackson Automobile Company for its manufacture. Carter did not remain with that organization long, however. Subsequently, he went on to design and build the famous Cartercar.

1901 CARTER STEAM

Carter Steam Stanhope	1000	2700	3600	5300	8800	19,000

1920 Carter Steam Car, touring, WLB

CARTER STEAM — Gulfport, Mississippi — (1920-1921) — Having patented various elements of a new steam car he designed, Dr. A. Richard Carter of Hammond, Louisiana trekked to Gulfport to build a factory for his Richard Carter Automobile Company. Kerosene sprayed on a coil boiler furnished the steam in Dr. Carter's car. "There are two cylinders to each engine, with two pistons to each cylinder," he advised, "and the entire motor is similar in appearance to a gasoline engine." Carter claimed a fuel efficiency of twenty miles to a gallon of kerosene. The last press release he issued to the trade publications was late in 1920 and indicated

that the Gulfport factory was nearly complete and that production would begin December 1st. Some production did follow, at least three and maybe as many as twenty-five cars. These were all five-passenger touring cars priced at $2350. Possibly he may also have produced a few steam tractors as well. A surviving catalog indicates the name "Arc" (representing Carter's initials) at the bottom of the chassis drawing of the car, but whether the cars were officially marketed under the Arc name is not known.

1920-1921 CARTER STEAM

	FP	5	4	3	2	1
Carter Steam	2350	3100	4200	6300	10,500	22,000

1907 Carter Two-Engine Car, HAC

CARTER TWO-ENGINE — Hyattsville, Maryland — (1907-1908) — In 1905, after the car he was driving stalled in the midst of a downpour and would not start again, Howard O. Carter decided it was time for the automobile to have a fail-safe system. The result was a vehicle with two four-cylinder engines — and separate radiators, ignitions and exhausts — which could be operated either singly or together. The engines were put in a shaft-drive five-seater touring car, and promotion was begun. Locating the executive offices of the Carter Motor Car Corporation in the District of Columbia provided the pleasant rationale for comparing the Fourth of July 1776 which commemorated "our absolution from the thraldom of monarchy" to the 19th of May 1905 which would be remembered as "the birth of an epoch of transportation unparalleled in the history of the world." Initially, manufacture was considered for Detroit. There the Carter International Motor Car Corporation was announced, "international" being added to the firm's name because now the two-engined Carter was to be exported, too, under the name of Carter Duplex. Ultimately, a factory nearer the Carter main office was deemed preferable, however, and a site was found in Hyattsville, Maryland where construction was begun in 1907 and completed just about the time Howard O. Carter discovered that the American public preferred taking its chances to playing it safe with two engines. The Hyattsville plant was thereafter turned over to manufacture of a new car called the Washington which had only one.

1908 Carter Two-Engine Car, HAC

1907-1908 CARTER TWO-ENGINE
Model 3A — 8-cyl., 40 hp, 129"

Semi-Rds.	4000	5400	7300	11,800	25,000	38,000

Model 3B — 8-cyl, 60 hp, 129" wb

Tour.-7P	5000	5300	7000	11,500	24,000	37,000

Model 3C — 8-cyl., 75 hp, 129" wb

Limo.-7P	6000	5300	7000	11,500	24,000	37,000

1905 Cartercar, model C, runabout, HAC

CARTERCAR — Jackson, Michigan — (1905)/Detroit, Michigan — (1906)/Pontiac, Michigan — (1907-1915) — Unable to convince his partners of the Jackson Automobile Company that the number of drive speeds should be left up to the driver not his car's transmission, Byron J. Carter left his job as manufacturing superintendent for the Jackson car in 1905. He casually organized the Motorcar Company in Jackson later that year, but soon relocated to Detroit after securing financial backing there. Two years later the firm's name was changed to the Cartercar Company, and was relocated again, to the factory of the Pontiac Spring & Wagon Works in Pontiac. The Cartercar was extremely well received by the press and aggressively promoted as the car of "A Thousand Speeds . . . no clutch to slip . . . no gears to strip . . . no universal joints to break . . . no shaft drive to twist . . . no bevel gears to wear and howl . . . no noise to annoy." After 4000 miles the paper fiber rims could be replaced for about three to five dollars, "at least one-half the amount expended on grease packing in a geared transmission." Cartercar sales rose nicely from 101 in 1906 to 264 in 1907 and 325 in 1908. On April 6th, 1908 Byron Carter died suddenly of pneumonia at age forty-four. On October 26th, 1909 the Cartercar Company became one of almost thirty firms bought up by William Crapo Durant in the two years following his incorporation of General Motors. Initially Cartercars were all two-cylinder machines, in 1909 a couple of fours were added, and by 1910 all Cartercars had four cylinders. There were few other changes; as a 1910 ad declared, "It's Hard to Improve a Cartercar." By 1910, however, Billy Durant had been tossed out of GM; by the time he regained control in September 1915 it was too late for Cartercar. Because sales figures had never approximated the 1000-2000 units a year Durant had envisioned, GM board directors had earlier decided to use the Cartercar facilities for the production of a Northway-powered six to sell under the name of Oakland, another of the companies Durant acquired for GM. The Cartercar plant was ordered closed on May 22nd, 1915. Durant had bought Cartercar for its friction drive: "How was anyone to know that the Cartercar wasn't the thing," he later lamented. There were similar cars on the market, Lambert, Metz, Petrel, Sears, Simplicity and others, many probably infringing on Byron Carter's patent. But of all friction-drive automobiles built in America, the Cartercar was the most famous, the most successful and the longest lived. At least two dozen Cartercars are known to survive. Byron J. Carter, incidentally, had also built a steam car called the Carter at the turn of the century but it was neither famous nor long-lived.

1905 CARTERCAR
Model A — 1-cyl., 6-1/2 hp, 75" wb

	FP	5	4	3	2	1
Rbt.	650	2500	3500	5000	8500	18,000

Model B — 1-cyl., 7 1/2 hp, 75" wb

	FP	5	4	3	2	1
Rbt.	700	2600	3600	5200	8700	18,500

Model C — 2-cyl., 10 hp, 78" wb

	FP	5	4	3	2	1
Rbt.	850	2700	3600	5300	8800	19,000

1906 Cartercar, model A, touring, HAC

1906 CARTERCAR
Twin — 20 hp, 94" wb

Model A Tour.	1350	2900	3700	5600	9100	20,000
Model B Vict.	1350	2700	3600	5300	8800	19,000

1907 Cartercar, model D, runabout, HAC

1907 Cartercar, model E, folding tonneau roadster, OCW

1907 CARTERCAR
Twin — 22/24 hp, 94" wb

	FP	5	4	3	2	1
Model A Tour.	1350	2900	3700	5600	9100	20,000
Model D Rbt.	1250	3000	3900	5800	9300	20,500
Model C Tonneau	1400	3000	4000	6000	9500	21,000
Model E Folding Tonneau	1350	3100	4200	6300	10,500	22,000

1908 Cartercar, model A, touring, HAC

1908 CARTERCAR
Twin — 25 hp, 96" wb

Model A Tour.	1350	2900	3700	5600	9100	20,000
Model D Rbt.	1250	3000	3900	5800	9300	20,500
Model E Folding Tonneau	1350	3000	4000	6000	9500	21,000
Model F Detachable Tonneau	1400	3100	4200	6300	10,500	22,000

1909 CARTERCAR
Twin — 20 hp, 100" wb

Model H Gentleman's Rds.	1000	2900	3700	5600	9100	20,000

Twin — 22/24 hp, 103" wb

Model K Tour.	1350	3000	4000	6000	9500	21,000
Model G Gentleman's Rds.	1350	3100	4200	6300	10,500	22,000

1909 Cartercar, model K, touring, HAC

1910 Cartercar, model H, gentleman's roadster, HAC

1910 CARTERCAR
Four — 25 hp, 100" wb

	FP	5	4	3	2	1
Model H Tour.	1150	3700	4700	7300	13,700	26,000
Model H Rds.	1100	3900	4800	7700	14,300	27,000
Model H Double-Rumble	1150	4000	4900	7900	14,700	27,500
Four — 35 hp, 10" wb						
Model L Tour.	1600	3900	4800	7700	14,300	27,000
Model L Land'et. Taxi	2000	3100	4200	6300	10,500	22,000

1911 Cartercar, model L, touring, HAC

1911 Cartercar, model H, roadster, OCW

1911 CARTERCAR
Four — 30 hp, 102" wb

	FP	5	4	3	2	1
Model H Baby Tonneau	1150	3900	4800	7700	14,300	27,000
Model H Rds.	1150	4100	5100	8200	15,400	28,500
Four — 35 hp, 110" wb						
Model L Tour.	1600	3700	4700	7300	13,700	26,000
Four — 40 hp, 120" wb						
Model M Tour.	1875	5100	10,200	17,000	23,800	34,000

1912 Cartercar, model R, roadster, HAC

1912 CARTERCAR
Four — 30 hp, 102" wb

	FP	5	4	3	2	1
Model H Tour.	1200	5250	10,350	17,500	24,500	35,000
Four — 40 hp, 112" wb						
Model R Tour.	1600	3900	4800	7700	14,300	27,000
Model R Cpe.	1700	3500	4500	7000	13,000	25,000
Model R Rds.	1500	5500	10,750	18,250	25,000	36,000
Four — 45 hp, 122" wb						
Model S Tour.	2100	5700	11,400	19,000	26,600	38,000

1913 Cartercar, model 5, coupe, HAC

1913 CARTERCAR
Model 5 — 4-cyl., 40 hp, 116" wb

	FP	5	4	3	2	1
Tour.	1700	5250	10,350	17,500	24,500	35,000
Rds.	1600	5500	10,950	18,250	25,000	36,000
Cpe.	1900	3300	4400	6700	12,000	24,000
Sed.	2000	3100	4200	6300	10,500	22,000

1914 Cartercar, model 5, coupe, HAC

1914 CARTERCAR
Model 5 — 4-cyl., 40 hp, 116" wb

	FP	5	4	3	2	1
Tour.	1700	5250	10,350	17,500	24,800	35,000
Rds.	1600	5500	10,950	18,250	25,000	36,000
Cpe.	1900	3300	4400	6700	12,000	24,000
Sed.	2000		4200	6300	10,500	22,000

Model 7 — 4-cyl., 31 hp, 106" wb

	FP	5	4	3	2	1
Tour.	1250	3700	4700	7300	13,700	26,000
Rds.	1250	3900	4800	7700	14,300	27,000

1915 Cartercar, model 9, roadster, HAC

1915 CARTERCAR
Model 9 — 4-cyl., 31 hp, 106" wb

	FP	5	4	3	2	1
Rds.	1250	3700	4700	7300	13,700	26,000
Tour.	1250	3900	4800	7700	14,300	27,000

CARTERMOBILE — Hannibal, Missouri — (1915) — "This long looked for mechanical masterpiece is known by practically every mechanic in the United States," advertised the Carter Motor & Manufacturing Company in an outrageous bending of the truth that could only have been accepted by the irrevocably gullible. The Cartermobile was a quite ordinary four-cylinder 115-inch wheelbase touring car priced at $985 which, J.O. Carter said, bending the truth a little more, was half what it was worth. When the motoring public did not immediately rally to his Cartermobile cause, J.O. Carter simply rethought his car and reintroduced it late in 1915 as the $735 Brownie.

CARTERMOBILE — Hyattsville, Maryland — (1921-1922) — In October of 1921, L.L. Stephens, Frank L. Carter and A. Gary Carter incorporated the Carter Motor Car Company with a capital stock of $2,000,000. Company offices were in Washington, D.C., with the former plant of the Washington Motor Car Company in Hyattsville to serve as the factory. The Carter brothers owned that plant, because they had formerly been the producers of the Washington car (which had been discontinued in 1912), and the C.B. (which survived from 1917-1918). The Cartermobile was slated to be a low-priced ($895) four to compete with the Model T Ford. References have indicated the use of Herschell-Spillman engines and a variety of open and closed body styles, but if any of these cars were built, it was very quietly and obviously unsuccessfully. Possibly the Cartermobile did not proceed beyond the prototype stage.

CARTHAGE — Carthage, Ohio — (1914-1915) — The Carthage Motor Car Company at 7540 Carthage Pike was in business one year, and apparently produced some cars, though details regarding making them are lacking. George R. Babbs was the man in charge. In May 1915 the Puritan Machine Company of Detroit announced its purchase of the bankrupt Carthage company (Puritan's 63rd such purchase), and thereafter advertised and supplied parts for the car to Carthage owners.

1901 Carver, three-wheeler, NAHC

CARVER — New York, New York — (1901) — At the turn of the century, A.F. Carver of New York City designed himself a small three-wheeled 3 hp gasoline carriage that was sweetly quaint. It weighed all of 255 pounds, and was fitted with a one-gallon gasoline tank with an extra reserve tank of seven quarts placed under the footboard. This presumably would provide for a touring range of 100 miles at a 15 mph speed. The car was built for Carver across the Hudson (in South Orange, New Jersey) by W.L. Mead. Carver was so delighted with his little vehicle that he immediately told *The Motor World* all about it. "This little carriage has made seventeen miles on its trial day's run," the magazine reported enthusiastically in May, "and completed forty more miles the day following without a single mishap of any kind." There is no evidence that A.F. Carver had any plans for production.

CASADAY — The W.S. Casaday Manufacturing Company of South Bend, Indiana produced commercial vehicles under the Casaday name as well as a passenger car called the Williams in 1905. Refer to Williams.

CASE — The Case Motor Car Company was organized during the summer of 1910 to "manufacture and deal in motor cars and to operate a repair shop" in New Bremen, Ohio. Capital stock was $50,000, and the backers of this venture were J.H. Grothaus, Edmund Grothaus, J.F. Laufersieck, Louis Huenke and Otto J. Bossel. The steel-plow-producing Grothaus-Lautersieck factory was subsequently outfitted for vehicle production, but it appears the only vehicles to follow were trucks.

1911 Case, touring, OCW

CASE — Racine, Wisconsin — (1911-1927) — In 1871 one Dr. J.M. Carhart built a steam buggy in Racine, much of the work on which was completed in the nearby J.I. Case Threshing Machine Company. Promotional advantage was taken of this many years later when Case suggested that perhaps it deserved some credit for having built America's first automobile. Though the Carhart connection was tenuous, the Case claim to pioneering was not. In 1842 Jerome Increase Case had left his father's hard scrabble farm in Williamstown, New York to venture to Wisconsin where he set up an agricultural machinery business which by 1848 was the largest in Racine and which by 1886 was the largest in the world in steam engine manufacture. J.I. Case died in 1891 at the age of seventy-three, but his company thereafter proceeded from strength to strength. In 1895 Case planned to enter a car in the Chicago Times-Herald Contest but could not complete it on time. That year the first Case gasoline tractor was produced, and the firm continued to focus efforts in the agricultural field, its automotive involvement largely confined to the presence of many Case officers and stockholders in the executive ranks of the Pierce Motor Company, producers of the Pierce-Racine. In 1910 Case took over the Pierce company, and the first Case car arrived for the 1911 model year. It represented a modification of the former four-cylinder Pierce-Racine 30. By 1913 a 40 hp model was added, and Case continued with its medium-priced fours through World War I. Racing was aggressively promoted during the early years, the company hiring sports impresario J. Alex Sloan to oversee things. Although the three-car team entered for the inaugural running of the Indianapolis 500 in 1911 retired, Case scored impressive wins that year in Algonquin and Hawthorne in Illinois, though the death that fall of Case driver Lewis Strang near Blue River, Wisconsin cast a pall over the season. Though the Case record in major races was composed largely of crashes and retirements, the cars were a smash, figuratively, at small county fairs where the Case name in agriculture was known to virtually everyone in the crowd. By the end of 1915 Case retired from motor sport selling much of its equipment to Alex Sloan, who proceeded to become the dominant promoter in dirt track racing for the next two decades. And Case went on building the Case car. In 1918 a 50 hp six (Continental engine) was added to the line. By now, and probably because the company believed its agricultural origins should be downplayed, the automotive business had been renamed the Case Motor Car Division of J.I. Case T.M. Company, though testimonial letters from satisfied owners indicated that a Case was as sturdily built as a tractor, and would last just as long. The company reputation for robust quality ranged beyond American borders; during the summer of 1915, Case shipped 101 cars to Czarist Russia. Whether they survived the Revolution is not known. By the 1920's all Case cars were sixes, with engines built by Continental in a variety of sizes. Later models were designated by the parent company's initials phonetically as the Jay-Eye-See cars. In the face of increasing competition by the major manufacturers, the automotive department was closed down during 1927. The eagle-on-a-globe emblem of the Case was modeled after "Old Abe," the Civil War era mascot of the 8th Wisconsin regiment and was used for decades thereafter on the farm vehicles for which the company remains renowned.

1911 Case, torpedo, HAC

1911 CASE
Four — 30 hp, 115" wb

	FP	5	4	3	2	1
Fore-Door Tour.-5P	1850	4000	5000	8000	15,000	28,000
Torpedo-4P	1950	4200	5200	8400	15,700	29,000
Limo.-7P	2850	3700	4700	7300	13,700	26,000
Rds.-2P	1750	4200	5200	8400	15,700	29,000
Suburban-4P	1850	3900	4800	7700	14,300	27,000

1912 Case, Forty, touring, HAC

1912 CASE
Model L — 4-cyl., 30 hp, 116" wb

Fore-Door Tour.-5P	1850	4200	5200	8400	15,700	29,000

Model M — 4-cyl., 40 hp, 120" wb

Fore-Door Tour.-5P	2050	4400	5600	9200	17,300	31,000
Torpedo-4P	2050	4500	5700	9400	17,700	31,500
Rds.-2P	2050	4500	5800	9500	18,000	32,000

1913 Case, Forty, touring, HAC

1913 CASE
Model U — 4-cyl., 30 hp, 115" wb

Tour.-5P	1500	4200	5200	8400	15.700	29,000
Rds.-2P	1500	4300	5400	8700	16,500	30,000

Model O — 4-cyl., 40 hp, 124" wb

Tour.-5P	2200	4500	5800	9500	18,000	32,000
Tour.-7P	2400	4600	6000	9700	18,500	32,500
Limo.-7P	3200	4200	5200	8400	15,700	29,000

1914 CASE
Model 25 — 4-cyl., 25 hp, 110" wb

Tour.-5P	1250	4200	5200	8400	15,700	29,000

Model 35 — 4-cyl., 35 hp, 120" wb

Tour.-5P	1850	4300	5400	8700	16,500	30,000

Model 40 — 4-cyl., 40 hp, 124" wb

Tour.-5P	2300	4400	5600	9200	17,300	31,000
Tour.-7P	2500	4500	5800	9500	18,000	32,000

1914 Case, limousine, JAC

1915 Case, model 25, touring, HAC

1915 CASE
Model 25 — 4-cyl., 25 hp, 115 1/2" wb

	FP	5	4	3	2	1
Tour.-5P	1350	4200	5200	8400	15,700	29,000

Model 35 — 4-cyl., 35 hp, 120" wb

Tour.-5P	1600	4300	5400	8700	16,500	30,000

Model 40 — 4-cyl., 40 hp, 124" wb

Tour.-5P	1800	4300	5400	8700	16,500	30,000
Tour.-7P	2000	4400	5600	9200	17,300	31,000

1916 Case, model T, touring, HAC

1916 CASE
Model T — 4-cyl., 40 hp, 120" wb

Tour.-7P	1090	4500	5800	9500	18,000	32,000
Rds.-3P	1090	4700	6100	9900	19,000	33,000

1917 Case, model T, "New York Special", touring, HAC

1917 CASE
Model T — 4-cyl., 40 hp, 120" wb

Tour.-7P	1190	4500	5800	9500	18,000	32,000
Rds.-4P	1190	4700	6100	9900	19,000	33,000

1918 Case Six, All-Seasons, touring, HAC

1918 CASE
Model U — 6-cyl., 50 hp, 125" wb

	FP	5	4	3	2	1
Family Tour.-7P	1875	4400	5600	9200	17,300	31,000
Spt.-4P	1875	4500	5800	9500	18,000	32,000
All-Seasons Tour.-7P	2375	4600	6000	9700	18,500	32,500

1919 CASE
Model U — 6-cyl., 50 hp, 125" wb

Tour.-7P	2100	4700	6100	9900	19,000	33,000
Rds.-4P	2100	4900	6300	10,300	21,000	34,000

1920 Case, model V, coupe, HAC

1920 CASE
Model V — 6-cyl., 50 hp, 126" wb

Tour.-7P	2400	4500	5800	9500	18,000	32,000
Spt.-4P	2400	4700	6100	9900	19,000	33,000
Sed.-7P	3300	3900	4800	7700	14,300	27,000
Cpe.-4P	3100	4000	5000	8000	15,000	28,000

1921 Case, model V, sport, HAC

1921 CASE
Model V — 6-cyl., 50 hp, 126" wb

Tour.-7P	2650	4500	5800	9500	18,000	32,000
Rds.-4P	2650	4700	6100	9900	19,000	33,000
Cpe.-4P	3400	4000	5000	8000	15,000	28,000
Sed.-7P	3750	3900	4800	7700	14,300	27,000

1922 CASE
Model V-22 — 6-cyl., 50 hp, 126" wb

Tour.-7P	1935	4400	5600	9200	17,300	31,000
Spt.-4P	1935	4500	5800	9500	18,000	32,000
Cpe.-4P	2585	3700	4700	7300	13,700	26,000
Sed.-7P	3375	3500	4500	7000	13,000	25,000

Model X — 6-cyl., 55 1/2 hp, 122" wb

Tour.-5P	1890	4300	5400	8700	16,500	30,000

Model W — 6-cyl., 70 hp, 129" wb

Tour.-7P	2380	4700	6100	9900	19,000	33,000
Sed.-7P	3375	3700	4700	7300	13,700	26,000

1922 Case, model V, touring, HAC

1923 Case, model W, touring, HAC

1923 CASE
Model X — 6-cyl., 55 1/2 hp, 122" wb

	FP	5	4	3	2	1
Tour.-5P	1790	4200	5200	8400	15,700	29,000
Rds.-3P	1750	4300	5400	8700	16,500	30,000
Sed.-5P	2575	3300	4400	6700	12,000	24,000
Suburban Cpe.-4P	2480	3500	4500	7000	13,000	25,000
Jay-Eye-See Tour.-5P	2230	4300	5400	8700	16,500	30,000

Model W — 6-cyl., 70 hp, 129" wb

Tour.-7P	1990	4300	5400	8700	16,500	30,000
Spt.-4P	1950	4400	5600	9200	17,300	31,000
Cpe.-4P	2480	3700	4700	7300	13,700	26,000
Sed.-7P	2975	3500	4500	7000	13,000	25,000

1924 Case, model Y, sedan, HAC

1924 CASE
Model X — 6-cyl., 55 1/2 hp, 122" wb

Tour.-5P	1790	4200	5200	8400	15,700	29,000
Rds.-3P	1750	4300	5400	8700	16,500	30,000
Surburban Cpe.-4P	2480	3500	4500	7000	13,000	25,000
Sed.-5P	2575	3300	4400	6700	12,000	24,000
Jay-Eye-See Spt. Phae.-5P	2230	4300	5400	8700	16,500	30,000

Model Y — 6-cyl., 70 hp, 132" wb

Tour.-7P	2475	4400	5600	9200	17,300	31,000
Sed.-7P	3325	3700	4700	7300	13,700	26,000

1925 CASE
Jay-Eye-See — 6-cyl., 52 hp, 122" wb

Rds.-3P	1840	4200	5200	8400	15,700	29,000
Tour.-5P	1885	3900	4800	7700	14,300	27,000
Spec. Tour.-5P	2160	4200	5200	8400	15,700	29,000
Brgm.-5P	2590	3200	4300	6500	11,000	23,000
Sed.-5P	2590	3100	4200	6300	10,500	22,000

Model X — 6-cyl., 52 hp, 122" wb

Rds.-3P	1670	4000	5000	8000	15,000	28,000
Tour.-5P	1695	3700	4700	7300	13,700	26,000
Suburban Cpe.-5P	2390	3200	4300	6500	11,000	23,000
Vict.-5P	2390	3250	4400	6600	11,500	23,500
Sed.-5P	2485	3000	4000	6000	9500	21,000

1925 Case Jay-Eye-See, sedan, HAC

Model Y — 6-cyl., 66 hp, 132" wb

	FP	5	4	3	2	1
Tour.-7P	2475	4400	5600	9200	17,300	31,000
Sed.-7P	2325	3500	4500	7000	13,000	25,000

1926 Case, model Y, sedan, HAC

1926 CASE
Jay-Eye-See — 6-cyl., 52 hp, 122" wb

Tour.-5P	1885	4200	5200	8400	15,700	29,000
Sed.-5P	2950	3100	4200	6300	10,500	22,000
Brgm.-5P	2590	3200	4300	6500	11,000	23,000

Model Y — 6-cyl., 66 hp, 132" wb

Tour.-7P	2225	4500	5800	9500	18,000	32,000
Sed.-7P	2975	3700	4700	7300	13,700	26,000

1927 Case Jay-Eye-See, sedan, HAC

1927 CASE
Jay-Eye-See — 6-cyl., 52 hp, 122" wb

Tour.-5P	1885	4200	5200	8400	15,700	29,000
Sed.-5P	2590	3100	4200	6300	10,500	22,000
Brgm.-5P	2590	3200	4300	6500	11,000	23,000

Model Y — 6-cyl., 66 hp, 132" wb

Tour.-7P	2225	4500	5800	9500	18,000	32,000
Sed.-7P	2975	3700	4700	7300	13,700	26,000

CASEY — Billerica, Massachusetts — (1901, 1914) — F.A. Casey operated a garage, motor repair and machine shop in Billerica. He was the son of a railroad engineer, and he built his first automobile after the turn of the century, using a marine motor and bicycle wheels. The vehicle he built in 1914, however, was considerably more sophisticated. Although believed for decades to have been an automobile, it was instead a 2 1/2 ton truck, fitted with a four-cylinder (Wisconsin or Continental) engine, axles purchased from Columbia Axle Company, and most other parts fabricated in the Casey machine shop. The frame was channel iron, the body a flatbed; there was a seat for two people, and no windshield. The vehicle was used for a considerable period by Trull Brothers Farm in

Tewksbury to carry produce to Boston Market once a week. According to F.A. Casey's son, Frederick A. Casey, only the one vehicle was built. Although manufacture was contemplated, the cost of doing so was prohibitive. The Casey garage and machine shop remains extant in Billerica, occupied today by the Knights of Columbus.

CASH — Hiawatha, Kansas — (1904) — William Cash built the first automobile in Hiawatha. It had a single-cylinder engine, rubber buggy wheels, a black body with a red leather seat, and was capable of 12 mph. Cash constructed the car in the foundry he owned. It is not known if he ever built another.

1901 Casler, electric runabout, MVMA

CASLER — Chicago, Illinois — (1901) — "The Wagon That Runs," B.G. Casler of 1025 Monadnock Block in Chicago advertised. "No danger, smoke, noise or heat. Always ready, Always reliable." The Casler was an electric, with a claimed 60 miles per battery charge, and available in passenger and delivery models priced from $500 to $2500. B.G. Casler advertised his cars extensively in 1901, although almost certainly he did not build them himself. Possibly the cars were produced for him by the Wood company in Chicago.

CASWELL — Sandusky, Ohio — (1901, 1905) — Myron J. Caswell operated a machine shop out of the back of his home at 901 Central Avenue in Sandusky. In 1901 George J. Schade, who was the first automobilist in town, asked Caswell to build him a steam engine, using gasoline for fuel, in order to motorize a horsedrawn stanhope he had. Caswell did this, and the resulting automobile was said to develop 10 hp and to run noiselessly. This appears to have been the sole automotive effort of Myron J. Caswell, though his twelve-year-old son Harold built a gasoline runabout for himself in 1905 which was described as "odd-looking," though it did run.

CATARACT — Niagara Falls, New York — (1904) — The new Cataract Machine and Automobile Company of Niagara Falls announced the election of its officers during early fall of 1904: S.P. Franchot as president, Fred V. Simpson as vice-president, H.W. Kellogg as secretary, and Max Amberg as treasurer. According to an official company announcement, Cataract was prepared to "begin the manufacture of automobiles and (to) do other work in the machine line." Cataract stuck to the other work. No car of that name ever appeared on the market, though a single example may have been built as a prototype. A decade later a Cataract Motor Company appeared in Paterson, New Jersey, although it seems unrelated to this Niagara Falls venture and was devoted to engine manufacture exclusively.

CATO — San Francisco, California — (1910, 1912) — Most probably all of the vehicles built by J.L. Cato of San Francisco were experimental, with no production realized. Although there may have been others, two cars are indicated in a source contemporary to the period. G.D. Angle's *Engineering Encyclopedia* of 1910 notes a car with six-cylinder air-cooled opposed engine, the 1912 edition a car with four-cylinder water-cooled vertical engine.

CATROW — Miamisburg, Ohio — (1899) — "Herbert Catrow of Miamisburg . . . threatens to start an automobile factory at that place," reported *The Motor Age* in December 1899. Whether Catrow ever followed through on his threat has not been documented, but it is known that the cars he planned to build would have been gasoline powered.

CAUSEWAY — Causeway Auto Mart, Inc. was organized in Dover, Delaware late in 1919 with a capital stock of $10,000 and the plan to "manufacture, sell and repair automobiles." Incorporators were Harry B. Grandeffo, W.G. Singer and L.A. Irwin. Manufacture is doubted.

1911 Cavac, roadster, WLB

CAVAC — Detroit, Michigan — (1910-1911) — The Small Motor Car Company of Detroit had one automobile idea. It was a 24 hp L-head four-cylinder engine cast en bloc and offset from the center of the crankshaft, which was carried in two ball bearings with all moving parts enclosed. All this was placed in a pressed steel underslung chassis of 100-inch wheelbase and offered as a racy roadster only at $1050. The Cavac made its first and last public appearance at the automobile shows in early 1911. The Small Automobile Company, which was headquartered in Room 605 in the Whitney Building in Detroit, had planned manufacture in both Detroit and Winnipeg, Canada. The few prototypes built were put together in a local machine shop. During the fall of 1911 the trade press announced the $500,000 incorporation of a Cavac Motor Car Company in Philadelphia. But this venture fared no better there than it had in Detroit.

1926 Cavalier, roadster, WLB

CAVALIER — Mt. Vernon, New York — (1926) — "The first of the 'Pony' cars has arrived," *Automobile Topics* announced in April of 1926, "or at least is in the offing." And this pony was a frolicsome little roadster on a 98-inch wheelbase, powered by a 32 hp four-cylinder overhead valve engine and running on smart-looking disc wheels. A two-passenger vehicle with a rumble-seat option, the Cavalier was designed by Norton L. Dods — and a prototype was built. Manufacturing the Cavalier was the idea of Cavalier Motor Associates of Mt. Vernon, and this group presented an interesting variation on the usual production theme. The Cavalier was an assembled car, which was common of course, but it was designed to be assembled by the dealer, which was an untoward idea — "unique, if not radical," *Automobile Topics* said. "No trouble is expected through having the dealers virtually build the car. As the Associates say, 'If a dealer's mechanics can't put the parts together, how could he expect to service the car'?" There was a certain logic to that. The Cavalier was to sell for $595 "a.g.d.," which translated to "at garage door." Unfortunately, Cavalier Motor Associates couldn't find enough dealers to go along with their Cavalier idea, and the venture that was "in the offing" never made it on. The following year Norton Dods tried again with another new car called the Calvert. It was his third effort, incidentally, his first having been the Vernon (also in Mt. Vernon) a half decade prior to the Cavalier.

CAWLEY — Salt Lake City, Utah — (1917) — Early in 1917, fresh from the demise of the Waco car in Seattle, C.A. Cawley turned up in Salt Lake City where he completed a prototype car and announced that a company would be organized for its manufacture. Designed specifically "to meet all western requirements," the Cawley production car was to be a 41 hp four with five-passenger touring body and a thousand-dollar price tag. A search through the local history archives of the University of Utah has revealed no evidence of manufacture. An earlier inquiry in the local Salt Lake City newspaper brought the same. No doubt C.A. Cawley's dream of manufacture remained just that.

CAYE-JONES — The Caye-Jones Motor Company was a $10,000 incorporation from August 1911 for the manufacture of cars in Hopkinsville, Kentucky. This venture appears not to have left the paper stage.

C.B. — Hyattsville, Maryland — (1917-1918) — In late 1916 the Carter Brothers of Hyattsville began phasing out their involvement with the Washington automobile they had been producing since 1909 and phasing in their newest automotive venture. In November *Automobile Topics* announced that the Carters had acquired all rights to the Monarch car designed by Robert C. Hupp. (The Monarch company had gone into bankruptcy in Detroit the previous April.) Both the Monarch eight- and twelve-cylinder models would be produced, and a small car to sell for under $600 and to be known as the Monarch Midget would be added. "To conserve the value of the name" was the reason given for the Carters' decision to stay with the designation Monarch. They quickly changed their minds, however. When the product of the new Carter Brothers Motor Company arrived, it was called a C.B. It survived just two seasons, and production may not have passed the pilot model stage. The Carters were back again in 1921 with another new car called the Cartermobile, but it was even shorter-lived.

1917-1918 C.B.

	FP	5	4	3	2	1
C.B. Four-28	575	—	—	—	—	—
C.B. Eight-35	1100	—	—	—	—	—
C.B. Twelve-65	2500	—	—	—	—	—

C.B. & H. — The C.B. & H. Company was incorporated in Albany, New York during the fall of 1914 for the manufacture of automobiles. Capital stock was $50,000; incorporators were F.T. Harback, J.H. Pease and F.W. Ritter. Manufacture did not follow.

C. de L. — Nutley, New Jersey — (1913) — The C. de L. Engineering Works of Nutley was in the automobile manufacturing business for one year only. It offered two four-cylinder passenger cars, as well as two truck models, and furnished both in chassis form only. Aside from the feature of pistons that were either single- or double-acting "at the pleasure of the operator," there was nothing further to distinguish the C. de L. chassis from hundreds like it on the road — which was probably the reason C. de L. was out of the automobile manufacturing business in 1914.

1913 C. de L.

Four (20/40 hp, 118" wb) chassis	1500	—	—	—	—	—
Four (30/60 hp, 140" wb) chassis	2800	—	—	—	—	—

CECIL — Lincoln, Nebraska — (1901) — R.E. Cecil built an automobile in Lincoln in 1901. He made wooden forms for his one-cylinder, gasoline engine from which an Omaha foundry molded parts. A buggy body and racing wheels were featured. Though he never built another, R.E. Cecil's car was probably the first ever produced in Lincoln.

CECO — Minneapolis, Minnesota — (1914)/Chicago, Illinois — (1914-1915) — This cyclecar began its life as the Continental in Minneapolis and was designed by John E. Pfeffer of that city. It became the Ceco, a slightly larger car, following the substantial financial investment of W.C. Shrobisher of Sturgis, Michigan and Emory Nonnast of Chicago, both of whom were described as millionaires. The result was the reorganization of the original Continental Engine Manufacturing Company into the million-dollar incorporation of the Continental Engineering Company. The Minnesota operation was soon moved entirely to Chicago, with headquarters at 1305 South Michigan Avenue. Though John Pfeffer was among the officers of this new venture, it seems his title was more honorary than operative since he elected to remain behind in Minnesota and market a cyclecar himself called the Baby Moose. Thomas H. Mars was the production manager of the Chicago operation. The new Ceco was introduced in the fall of 1914, having been preceded in the marketplace by numerous other cyclecars, most of which had already earned a dreadful reputation. Continental decided to capitalize on this by advertising the Ceco as "Latest Announced — First Perfected." The car's specifications included four-cylinder 12 hp air cooled engine, friction transmission and 103-inch wheelbase, quite long for a cyclecar. A roadster, tandem two-seater and two delivery models were offered in a price range of $350 to $395. Like most cyclecars, the Ceco did not long survive, though production does seem to have continued into 1915.

1914-1915 CECO
Cyclecar — 4-cyl., 12 hp, 103" wb

Tandem-2P	375	—	—	—	—	—
Rds.-2P	350	—	—	—	—	—
Parcel Post Dly.	395	—	—	—	—	—
Light Dly.	350	—	—	—	—	—

CENTAUR — Buffalo, New York — (1902-1903) — The Centaur Motor Vehicle Company at 642 Linwood Avenue in Buffalo was incorporated for $100,000 in the spring of 1902 for the manufacture of both gasoline and electric vehicles. The former cars were offered as 5 and 6 hp $700 runabouts and $800 light tourers, while the $850 electrics were said to be capable of 15 mph and 60 miles on a single charge. There was little doubt as to the Centaur preference among its products: "The Shrewdest Dealers are pushing electrics," one company trade press ad read, "and will be established when the Boom comes for the pleasure vehicle." Despite what seemed to be a healthy advertising budget, the company failed to make a marketable proposition of its cars. Press reports from early 1904 that

1903 Centaur, Electric, runabout, WLB

Centaur had sold out totally to Towanda Motor Vehicle Company were in error. Instead, following the discontinuation of its own car, Centaur continued in business as an agency for Cadillacs and Yales, and as a general garage. Behind the Centaur venture was J.C. Eccleston (formerly of the William Hengerer Company in Buffalo), H.C. Wilcox (of the American Wood Rim Company) and Fisher Atherton (formerly of the Buffalo Cycle Manufacturing Company).

CENTRAL — A goodly number of ventures titled Central seem to have entered the automobile field with the intention of automobile manufacture but then left it before the onset of any production, or continued in business only as a dealership.

The Central Automobile Company of Chicago, organized in early 1905 with a capital stock of $2500 by Alfred D. Plamondon, James E. Higgins and Benjamin F. Nicholson. A venture of the same name and capital stock organized about the same time and also in Chicago by John Vennema, H.I. Westphal and C. Stephens.

The Central Automobile Company of Pittsfield, Massachusetts, organized with a capital stock of $15,000 during the summer of 1905 by Franklin Weston, L.A. Merchant and E.H. Kennedy, all of Pittsfield.

The Central Automobile Company of New Haven, Connecticut, organized in late 1905 with a $20,000 capital stock by James F. English of New Haven, Harry B. Tuttle of Cheshire and Samuel F. Taylor of New York City.

The Central Automobile Corporation of Morgantown, West Virginia organized in the spring of 1918 with a capital stock of $100,000 by O.O. Donley, Charles G. Baker, Rufus F. Lazzelle, M.J. Malamphry, Jr. and Walter M. Johnston.

The Central City Automobile Company of Syracuse, New York, organized in the spring of 1903 with a $10,000 capital stock by Myron C. Blacksmith, Charles L. Kennedy and Frank L. Wightman, all of Syracuse.

The Central Garage and Machine Works of New York City, organized during the fall of 1908 with a capital stock of $5000.

The Central Motor Company of Brooklyn, New York, organized late in 1911 with a capital stock of $10,000 by W.B. Burradell, R. Dubecq and A.M. Beres.

The Central Motor Car Company of Bloomfield, New Jersey, organized late in 1906 with a capital stock of $25,000 by C.W. Smith, E.H. Cadmus and C.R. Underwood.

The Central New York Automobile Company of Oneonta, New York, organized during the fall of 1909 with a $50,000 capitalization of G.A. Flint, C.M. Bates and J.C. Cameron.

CENTRAL — Cleveland, Ohio — (1903) — A two-cylinder horizontal opposed engine with mechanical valves, a planetary transmission, center chain drive, fuel and water tanks under a hood up front, and a tilting steering wheel were among the specifications of the product of the Central Automobile Company of Cleveland. That its car was exhibited at the booth of the Ralph Temple & Austrian Company during the 1903 Chicago Automobile Show is known. The extent of production is not.

CENTRAL — Indianapolis, Indiana — (1903) — In the early spring of 1903 the Central Motor Car Company was organized in Indianapolis by Harry C. Stutz and two gentlemen named Hardin and Spratt. The firm proposed to manufacture automobiles and the Stutz gasoline engine. Interestingly, Stutz had only recently moved from Ohio to Indiana, following sale of the rights to manufacture his engine to the Lindsay Automobile Parts Company of Indianapolis. Obviously, a falling-out with the Lindsay people had been quick in coming. His new partners Hardin and Spratt left Lindsay to join him. But Stutz's tenure with the Central venture was brief as well. In the fall of 1903, Central announced its building of a prototype gasoline automobile "which possesses some features which are original." Apparently among these was a carburetor of the firm's own design. Whether it was Stutz's work is problematical. By 1904 he had hired on at the G & J Tire Company in Indianapolis, and by that time Central's production output was carburetors only. Its automobile production had been scant, and indeed may have ended with the one prototype.

CENTRAL — Detroit, Michigan — (1904) — Trade directory references from 1904 indicate the Central Machine & Engineering Company of Detroit as the manufacturer of an automobile that year. No doubt the car was built as a prototype only and probably for a local entrepreneur anxious to get into the automobile business. According to the 1904 Detroit city directory, the Central company, which was located at 62 Second Street, was headed by William F. Koeller, Sr., with his son serving as manager — and they advertised themselves as "machinists, tool makers and engineers; installation of complete heating apparatus."

CENTRAL — Connersville, Indiana — (1905) — In October of 1905 a prototype automobile which had been built by the Central Manufacturing Company of Connersville was destroyed in a fire at the firm's 127 West Seventh Street plant. Central decided to forgo any plans for automobile manufacture thereafter. Eleven blocks to the north, in a new factory, the company went on to become one of the most prominent automobile body makers in the field, providing coachwork to as many as seventeen Indiana car manufacturers. In 1913 the Central Car Company was organized as an offshoot to produce the Howard for a Chicago distributor. The company's greatest celebrity followed Errett Lobban Cord's purchase of Central during the Twenties and his attaching of the more chic designation LaGrande for the custom bodies it built.

CENTRAL STEAM — Providence, Rhode Island — (1905-1906) — In November of 1905, the plans of the Central Automobile Company of Providence were reported as "not fully developed," in which state probably they ever remained. Central's better-mousetrap idea was a rotary steam engine, several units of which had been imported from Europe for the building of pilot models. Runabouts of 10 hp and $850 price tags, together with 20 hp touring cars to sell in the $1200-$1500 range, were to compose Central's model line-up. The expectation was for the marketing of 100 cars during the 1906 season, but most probably many fewer than that were built before this venture went under.

CENTRAL GREYHOUND — This 1905 eight-cylinder race car was built by the H.H. Buffum Company of Abington, Massachusetts for the Central Automobile Company of New York City. This same car had been offered as a catalogued Buffum model in 1904. Refer to Buffum.

CENTURY — In the January 1906 "Buyer's Guide" section of the *Cycle and Automobile Trade Journal*, the Century Cash Register Company, Ltd. of 656-672 Humboldt Avenue in Detroit was listed as manufacturing a gasoline automobile. Further documentation is lacking.

The Century Motors Corporation was organized in Phoenix, Arizona late in 1916 to "manufacture, buy, sell and deal in motor cars and trucks." Capital stock was $250,000; the incorporators were Ben C. Lindsay and George H. Black. Manufacture is doubted.

CENTURY — St. Louis, Missouri — (1901) — Details regarding the car built by the Century Manufacturing Company of 2113 South Second Street in St. Louis are lacking, but it is known that the firm commenced production during the late spring of 1901 and suffered a fire two months later resulting in $7500 in damages, which apparently was sufficient to render the venture asunder.

1902 Century, steam runabout, NAHC

CENTURY — Syracuse, New York — (1900-1903) — The Century Motor Vehicle Company aimed to please. It offered automobiles with a choice of electric, steam and gasoline engines. The founders of the company were Charles F. Saul, Charles Listman, Charles A. Bridgman, Hiram W. Plumb and William Van Wagoner, this venture evolving out of the earlier partnership of Saul and Van Wagoner which had produced the Van Wagoner prototypes in 1899. Prototypes of the new Century cars were finished in 1900, and early in 1901 production began with an electric and steam runabout, the latter's shaft drive being most unusual for the period. By November the company reported the building of sixty-odd vehicles to date. Some of the steamers were exported to England where they were sold under the tradename of Ophir. A gasoline automobile followed for 1902. Powered by a single-cylinder 7 hp engine placed in a 72-inch wheelbase chassis, it carried the name Century Tourist and was priced at $750. Prices never were quoted for the Century electric or steam cars, though in late December of 1902 the firm announced that it had sold all of its steam cars on hand and would build no more. Few Century cars of any kind were built thereafter. By early 1903 production had been halted for lack of funds, and in August that year Century asked for an extension of credit. Bankruptcy was declared in January 1904. The Century plant was sold in June to the Dunn Salmon Shoe Company. Century creditors received eight percent on their claims.

1901 CENTURY

	FP	5	4	3	2	1
No. 1 Electric Rbt.	—	2400	3400	4800	8000	17,000
No. 1 Steam Rbt.	—	3100	4200	6300	10,500	22,000

1903 Century, Tourist, gasoline dos-a-dos, WLB

1902-1903 CENTURY

		5	4	3	2	1
No. 1 Electric Rbt.-2P	—	2400	3400	4800	8000	17,000
No. 2 Electric Carriage-4P	—	2400	3400	4800	8000	17,000
No. 3 Electric Dly.	—	2200	3200	4400	7000	15,000
No. 1 Steam Rbt.-2P	—	3100	4200	6300	10,500	22,000
No. 2 Steam Carriage-4P	—	3100	4200	6300	10,500	22,000
Century Tourist Gasoline Car	—	2900	3700	5600	9100	20,000

CENTURY — Detroit, Michigan — (1908) — A two-cylinder runabout to sell for $600 was the proposed product of the Century Motor Car Company which was organized early in 1908 by F.A. Hamilton and C.A. Linke. Their offices were at 32 John R Street in Detroit, but their venture never moved into a factory. This Century died at the prototype stage.

1912 Century Electric, roadster, WLB

CENTURY ELECTRIC — Detroit, Michigan — (1912-1915) — The Century Electric Motor Car Company was organized by John Gillespie, Inc. in May of 1912 with a total capitalization of $100,000 of which $80,000 was paid in. An underslung frame distinguished the Century from most other electrics in the field, but this was not enough to make this latecomer to the ranks a going concern. In May of 1914, Edwin Denby (a member of the law firm of Chamberlin, Denby & Webster, and a stockholder of the Hupp Motor Car Company) bought control and reorganized as the Century Manufacturing Company. One year later, with listed assets of $23,226 and liabilities of $48,295, the company was bankrupt.

1912 CENTURY ELECTRIC

Model E Rds. (97" wb)	1750	4400	5600	9200	17,300	31,000
Model E Brgm. (97" wb)	1950	4200	5200	8400	15,700	29,000

1913 CENTURY ELECTRIC

Model B Brgm. (98" wb)	2550	4200	5200	8400	15,700	29,000

1914 CENTURY ELECTRIC

Model LB Brgm. (104" wb)	3250	4200	5200	8400	15,700	29,000

1915 CENTURY ELECTRIC

	FP	5	4	3	2	1
Model SB Brgm.-4P (104" wb)	2650	4300	5400	8700	16,500	30,000
Model LB Brgm.-5P (104" wb)	3250	4300	5400	8700	16,500	30,000

CENTURY STEAMER — East Orange, New Jersey — (1906) — The Century Auto Power Company was organized with a capital stock of $125,000 early in 1906 by East Orange businessmen Henry R. Waite, C.A. Waite and H.L. Cadmus. A New York office was established at 102 Fulton Street, with a small factory built in East Orange "so designed that it can be easily enlarged," as was said. There a kerosene burner and flash steam generator invented by Robert J. Minor would be produced, with steam automobiles, auto-boats and launches built to order. The orders were few, and the company was out of business by year's end.

1901 Century Tourist, runabout, NAHC

CENTURY TOURIST — Bronxville, New York — (1901) — The Century Tourist was built by H. Ward Leonard, who by the turn of the century was one of America's most prominent inventors in the electrical field. Ironically, with regard to automobiles, Ward Leonard was convinced that gasoline was the way to go, the first car that he marketed being powered by a 3 1/2 hp De Dion engine. A small three-passenger $1000 runabout introduced in February of 1901, the Century Tourist was joined within months by a larger 5 hp $1400 car called the Knickerbocker. By July of 1901, Ward Leonard decided to call the smaller version a Knickerbocker too. Knickerbocker cars were produced through 1903.

CEYTON — The Ceyton Filles Company was organized early in 1912 in Camden, New Jersey with a capital stock of $3000 for the manufacture of automobiles. The people behind this venture were Howard L. Merrick, John A. Kinney, William Williams and Thomas W. Shora, all of Collingswood. Manufacture is doubted.

1907 C-F, runabout, WLB

C-F — Chicago, Illinois — (1907-1909) — The Cornish-Friedberg Motor Car Company had its first C-F cars off the production line in late spring of 1907, but did not formally introduce the marque until the Chicago Automobile Show that December. One reporter at the show noted that the new car was built "to meet the requirements of that large class of buyers usually included under the generic title of 'average automobilist'." The C-F was a thoroughly standard water-cooled four with shaft drive and a $2000-range price tag. Unfortunately, there was nothing unusual either in the company entering the marketplace quite undercapitalized, and the venture didn't last two years. Interestingly, its founders — F.W. Cornish, Charles and Louis W. Friedberg — had hedged their bets by becoming the Chicago dealers for the Aerocar as well, but that firm failed even before theirs did. Louis Friedberg tried again, briefly, in 1909 with the Chicago Forty.

1907-1909 C-F
Four — 35 hp, 114" wb

	FP	5	4	3	2	1
Tour.-5P	2250	3100	4200	6300	10,500	22,000
Rds.-3P	2250	3200	4300	6500	11,000	23,000
Rds.-4P	2265	3250	4400	6600	11,500	23,500

C & G — Automobile trade directory references from 1910 indicate the C & G Auto Company of 62 West 43rd Street in New York City as an automobile manufacturer. The firm did operate as a dealership, but manufacture has not been substantiated.

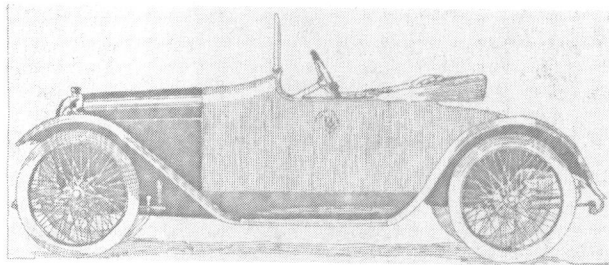

1914 C.G.P. Light Car

C.G.P. — **New York, New York** — **(1915)** — The C.G.P. was a single car that was designed and built by Dr. Charles G. Percival who was the president of the Light Car Association of America. Considerable traveling was required by Percival in the dispatch of his presidential duties, and he preferred doing it in a car that was, literally, custom built. It was quite ordinary, nonetheless: a Farmer engine (four-cylinder, water cooled, L-head, 12.1 hp), thermo-syphon cooling, cone clutch, low tension magneto, Allis-Chalmers single starting and lighting, 104-inch wheelbase, and 48-inch tread. The body lines of the two-seater runabout were attractive, however, and Charles G. Percival affixed his initials to the side of the car.

C.G.V. — The C.G.V. was a French car imported into the United States by Smith & Mabley of New York City. During 1902-1903 a few cars were built in this country as well. Refer to American C.G.V.

1905 Chadwick, type 9, touring, HAC

CHADWICK — **Philadelphia & Pottstown, Pennsylvania** — **(1904-1916)** — While working for the Searchmont company in Philadelphia, Lee Sherman Chadwick was able to study and drive the Mors racer in which Henri Fournier (who was also associated with Searchmont) had put up the fastest straightaway mile yet recorded in the Western Hemisphere (51.8 seconds along New York's Coney Island Boulevard in 1901). When Searchmont went under, Chadwick bought some of the parts for the proposed four-cylinder car he had designed, incorporated what he had learned from the Mors and a lot of ideas of his own and the result was the first Chadwick. Operating initially as the Fairmount Engineering Works in Philadelphia, the company became the Chadwick Engineering Works in March of 1907 with the move to larger quarters in Pottstown. Chadwick's first six had been built in 1906, and it was put on the market in 1907 as the Great Chadwick Six, which was not an overstatement. It displaced 706.86 cubic inches, developed 75 hp at 1100 rpm, and was good for at least 80 mph in standard runabout trim. Its cylindrical copper water jackets, carburetor, direct-drive double bevel gear transmission, cone clutch and aluminum dust-proof cases for the double chain drive were all patented Chadwick designs. Chain drive might appear retrograde for so progressive a car as the Chadwick, but there was a reason for it. As Lee Chadwick pointed out, though European manufacturers employed shaft drive in their production cars, they invariably used double chain "when they enter the world's great racing contests . . . in which they have always been supreme." Lee Chadwick meant to go racing; his Chadwick was America's first great high performance production car. It was also the first car in the world to have a supercharger, which would become available as a $375 option on the production runabout. The Chadwick, with Willie Haupt driving, was virtually unbeatable in hill climbs. With Len Zengle driving, it took the world's one-mile straightaway record away from the 120 hp Fiat at 88 mph, beat Barney Oldfield and his big Benz at the 1909 inaugural races at the Indianapolis Motor Speedway, and was victorious in the 1910 Fairmount Park epic after a breathtaking duel with Ralph Mulford's Lozier. Then Chadwick quit racing. There were problems in the front office. The Chadwicks were huge and expensive cars which Lee Chadwick was continually refining. The Great Chadwick Six evolved into the Perfected Great Chadwick Six, a slight exaggeration because Lee Chadwick believed it should be refined further yet. His backers didn't agree, and in 1911 Chadwick left for other pursuits, including manufacture of the Chadwick Road Guide which he had designed. Lee Chadwick's cars continued to be built without him, until the company went bankrupt late in 1915 and its factory was taken over by an armaments manufacturer. The number of Chadwicks built have been reported as 235 or 264; only two are known to exist, and they are both in the collection of Pollock's Auto Showcase.

1904-1905 CHADWICK
Type 9 — 4-cyl., 32 hp, 107 1/2" wb

	FP	5	4	3	2	1
Tour.-7P	4000	7800	13,000	20,000	43,500	58,000

1906 Chadwick, type II, touring, HAC

1906 CHADWICK
Type 11 — 4-cyl., 40/45 hp, 108" wb

	FP	5	4	3	2	1
Tour.-5P	5000	7800	13,200	20,200	43,800	59,000

Type 12 — 4-cyl., 24/30 hp, 102" wb

	FP	5	4	3	2	1
Tour.-5P	4000	7800	12,900	19,900	43,300	57,000

1907 Great Chadwick Six, touring, HAC

1907 CHADWICK
Model 12 — 4-cyl., 40/45 hp, 108" wb

	FP	5	4	3	2	1
Tour.-7P	5000	7800	13,000	20,000	43,500	58,000

Great Chadwick Six — 75 hp, 124" wb

	FP	5	4	3	2	1
Tour.-7P	5000	10,000	20,000	30,000	60,000	80,000

1908 Great Chadwick Six, runabout, HAC

1908 CHADWICK
Great Chadwick Six — 75 hp, 124" wb

	FP	5	4	3	2	1
Tourabout-5P	5500	10,500	20,500	31,000	62,000	82,000
Rbt.-3P	5500	10,300	20,300	30,500	61,000	81,000
Tour.-7P	5500	10,000	20,000	30,000	60,000	80,000

255

1909 Great Chadwick Six, semi-racer, JAC

1909 CHADWICK
Great Chadwick Six — 80 hp

	FP	5	4	3	2	1
Tour.-7P (130" wb)	5500	10,000	20,000	30,000	60,000	80,000
Tourabout-5P (130" wb)	5500	10,300	20,300	30,500	61,000	81,000
Semi-Racer-2P (112" wb)	6500	10,800	20,800	31,500	63,000	83,000

1910 Great Chadwick Six, runabout, HAC

1910 CHADWICK
Great Chadwick Six — 80 hp, 130" wb

	FP	5	4	3	2	1
Tour.-7P	5500	10,000	20,000	30,000	60,000	80,000
Std. Tourabout-5P	5500	9800	19,500	28,500	57,500	78,000
Guy Vaughan Tourabout-4P	5500	9900	19,800	29,300	58,800	79,000
Limo.-7P	6500	8200	14,500	21,500	45,800	65,000
Rbt.-2P (112" wb)	6500	10,300	20,300	30,500	61,000	81,000

1911 Great Chadwick Six, runabout, WLB

1911 CHADWICK
Great Chadwick Six — 80 hp, 133" wb

	FP	5	4	3	2	1
Tour.-7P	5500	10,500	20,500	31,000	62,000	82,000
Std. Tourabout-5P	5500	10,000	20,000	30,000	60,000	80,000
Miniature Tonneau-4P	5500	9900	19,800	29,300	58,800	79,000
Limo.-7P	6500	8200	14,500	21,500	45,800	65,000
Land'et.-7P	6500	8400	15,500	22,500	47,300	67,000
Rbt.-2P (112" wb)	5500	10,800	20,800	31,500	63,000	83,000

1912-1913 CHADWICK
Great Chadwick Six — 60 hp, 133" wb

	FP	5	4	3	2	1
Tour.-7P	5500	10,500	20,500	31,000	62,000	82,000
Tourabout-5P	5500	10,000	20,000	30,000	60,000	80,000
Limo.-7P	6500	8200	14,500	21,500	45,800	65,000
Rbt.-2P (112" wb)	5500	10,800	20,800	31,500	63,000	83,000

1914 CHADWICK
Model R-19 — 6-cyl., 60 hp, 112" wb

	FP	5	4	3	2	1
Tour.-7P	5500	10,000	20,000	30,000	60,000	80,000
Rds.-2P	5500	10,300	20,300	30,500	61,000	81,000
Limo.	6500	8000	14,000	21,000	45,000	64,000

Model T-19 — 6-cyl., 60 hp, 133" wb

	FP	5	4	3	2	1
Tour.-5/7P	5500	11,000	21,000	32,000	64,000	84,000

1912 Great Chadwick Six, runabout, HAC

1913 Great Chadwick Six, touring, HAC

1914 Chadwick, model 19, touring, HAC

1915 Chadwick, model 19, touring, HAC

1915 CHADWICK
Model 19 — 6-cyl., 60 hp, 133" wb

	FP	5	4	3	2	1
Rds.-2P	5500	9900	19,800	29,300	58,800	79,000
Limo.-7P	6500	7800	13,300	20,300	44,000	60,000
Tour.-5P	5500	9800	19,500	28,500	57,500	78,000
Tour.-7P	5500	9700	19,300	27,800	56,300	77,000

1916 CHADWICK
Model 19 — 6-cyl., 60 hp, 133" wb

	FP	5	4	3	2	1
Tour.-7P	5500	9700	19,300	27,800	56,300	77,000
Rds.-2P	5500	9900	19,800	29,300	58,800	79,000
Limo.-7P	6500	7800	13,300	20,300	44,000	60,000

1916 Chadwick, model 19, roadster, HAC

1907 Chalfant, touring, NAHC

CHALFANT — Lenover, Pennsylvania — (1907) — The Chalfant Gasoline Motor Car Company of Lenover produced a conventional touring car with a two-cylinder water-cooled engine, planetary transmission and double chain drive. The company entered the market in December 1906 with a price tag of $1250 for the touring car, and made known the availability of a runabout with the same motor and chassis and a price "of which they will quote on application." References from March of 1907 indicate that Chalfant raised its touring car price to $1300, and there was no mention of a runabout. Interestingly, latterday references often note the Chalfant as having been built until 1912. But documentation from the period indicates the car did not survive beyond 1907. A total of 50 Chalfants had been built. This venture was very much a family affair, with Millard F. Chalfant, Harry Chalfant and W. Howard Chalfant in charge, Horace S. Boyd and William Michener assisting.

1907 CHALFANT
Model C — 2-cyl., 22 hp, 90" wb

	FP	5	4	3	2	1
Tour.-5P	1300	—	—	—	—	—

1910 Chalmers-Detroit, Thirty, touring, HAC

CHALMERS-DETROIT/CHALMERS — Detroit, Michigan — (1908-1910)/**CHALMERS** — (1922-1924) — In the beginning, the Chalmers-Detroit was simply the Thomas-Detroit under another name. When Howard Coffin and Roy Chapin, whose idea the Thomas-Detroit had been, decided they preferred running their own show to being controlled cross-continent by Erwin Ross Thomas in Buffalo, they talked Hugh Chalmers of

Detroit into buying out their New York State sponsor. Chalmers could afford it because, as vice-president of the National Cash Register Company, he was earning $72,000 a year, which was a considerable sum in those days. So, late in 1907, Chalmers resigned his NCR vice-presidency and got out of cash registers and into cars. In July of 1908 the Chalmers-Detroit Motor Car Company was born to produce vehicles in the $1500-$2800 range. The first cars arrived that month and were marketed as 1909 models. Meantime, Chapin and Coffin were thinking about marketing a car in the under-thousand-dollar field, and Coffin designed a 20 hp four for that purpose. Hugh Chalmers was only mildly enthusiastic, so the duo persuaded Detroit department store magnate J.L. Hudson into taking a financial interest in exchange for having the car named after him. By the end of 1909 the first 1000 Hudsons had been sold. A quick swap of money and stock saw the new Hudson group buy out Hugh Chalmers and in turn sell out Chalmers-Detroit to him — and so Chapin and Coffin went off with their Hudson, and Chalmers had the Chalmers-Detroit all to himself. Already the Chalmers-Detroit had distinguished itself in racing, taking five firsts, a second and a third in six premier light car contests of 1908-1909. And already Chalmers-Detroits were in the garages of Vanderbilts and Rockefellers; John Herreshoff of America's Cup fame also had one, as did the superintendent of inventions for the Burroughs Adding Machine Company, one Jesse G. Vincent, who was soon to join Packard and become one of its greatest chief engineers. Late in 1910 Chalmers-Detroit was reorganized into the Chalmers Motor Car Company — and all cars thereafter were known simply as Chalmers. For more than a decade they were among the most popular automobiles in America. A Chalmers won the Glidden Trophy in 1910, in 1912 a six-cylinder model was introduced, and from 1915 on production was concentrated on sixes. By now sales were in the 20,000 range annually. "The Ram's horn with a hot spot" colorfully described the Chalmers' famous exhaust-heated curved manifold. Chalmers sixes carried on their predecessors' sporting prowess, winning in class at Pikes Peak and overall in a twenty-four-hour marathon at Sheepshead Bay. Soon, however, business as usual at Chalmers met with the recession following World War I, sales dropped drastically, and receivership loomed. Hugh Chalmers noticed that the Maxwell company across town was suffering similarly, but not as drastically. He leased part of the Chalmers property to Maxwell, but differences arose over an accounting under the terms of the lease and it was cancelled in mid-1921. The Maxwell-Chalmers marriage was consummated the following year, however, when Chalmers was hit with both a mortgage foreclosure and a general creditors suit. Maxwell agreed to buy the Chalmers property — for $1,987,000 — and to assume the Chalmers' debts. It looked good on paper; in practice the marriage was foundering already. An outsider was summoned. Fresh from his similar salvage job at Willys-Overland, Walter Percy Chrysler strode into the affairs of Maxwell-Chalmers. The last Chalmers were 1924 models built in late 1923. The Maxwell survived one year longer. In January 1924 the new Chrysler was introduced.

1908 Chalmers-Detroit, Thirty, roadster, OCW

1908 CHALMERS-DETROIT
Model F — 4-cyl., 24 hp, 110" wb

	FP	5	4	3	2	1
Tour.-5P	1500	4000	5000	8000	15,000	28,000
Rds.-2P/3P/4P	1500	4200	5200	8400	15,700	29,000
Limo.-5P	2500	3100	4200	6300	10,500	22,000

Model E — 4-cyl., 40 hp, 112" wb

	FP	5	4	3	2	1
Tour.-5P	2750	5800	11,550	19,250	26,950	38,500
Rds.-2P/3P/4P	2750	5700	11,400	19,000	26,600	38,000
Speed Rds.-2P	2800	5850	11,700	19,500	27,300	39,000

1909 Chalmers-Detroit Forty, runabout, HAC

1909 CHALMERS-DETROIT
Thirty — 4-cyl., 30 hp, 110" wb

	FP	5	4	3	2	1
Tour.	1500	4000	5000	8000	15,000	28,000
Tourabout	1500	4200	5200	8400	15,700	29,000
Rbt.	1500	4300	5400	8700	16,500	30,000

Forty — 4-cyl., 40 hp, 112" wb

	FP	5	4	3	2	1
Tour.	2750	5800	11,550	19,250	26,950	38,500
Rbt.	2750	5700	11,400	19,000	26,600	38,000

1910 CHALMERS-DETROIT
Thirty — 4-cyl., 30 hp, 115" wb

	FP	5	4	3	2	1
Tour.	1500	4200	5200	8400	15,700	29,000
Rds.	1500	4400	5600	9200	17,300	31,000
Pony Tonneau	1600	4300	5400	8700	16,500	30,000
Limo.	3000	3100	4200	6300	10,500	22,000
Inside Drive Cpe.	2400	3200	4300	6500	11,000	23,000
Land'et.	3000	3300	4400	6700	12,000	24,000

Forty — 4-cyl., 40 hp, 122" wb

Tour.	2750	5800	11,550	19,250	26,950	38,500
Rds.	2750	5700	11,400	19,000	26,600	38,000
Pony Tonneau	3000	5850	11,700	19,500	27,300	39,000

1911 Chalmers, touring, OCW

1911 CHALMERS
Thirty — 4-cyl., 30 hp, 115" wb

Tour.	1500	4300	5400	8700	16,500	30,000
Rds.	1500	4500	5800	9500	18,000	32,000
Pony Tonneau	1600	4400	5600	9200	17,300	31,000
Limo.	3000	3100	4200	6300	10,500	22,000
Inside Drive Cpe.	2400	3200	4300	6500	11,000	23,000
Land'et.	3000	3300	4400	6700	12,000	24,000

Forty — 4-cyl., 40 hp, 122" wb

Tour.	2800	4400	5600	9200	17,300	31,000
Torpedo	3000	4500	5800	9500	18,000	32,000
Rds.	2750	4700	6100	9900	19,000	33,000

1912 Chalmers Thirty-Six, torpedo roadster, HAC

1912 CHALMERS
Thirty, Models 9 & 11 — 4-cyl., 30 hp, 115" wb

Tour.	1500	4300	5400	8700	16,500	30,000
Torpedo Rds. (104" wb)	1500	4500	5800	9500	18,000	32,000
Fore-Door Pony Tonneau	1500	4400	5600	9200	17,300	31,000
Cpe. (104" wb)	2000	3300	4400	6700	12,000	24,000

Thirty-Six, Model 10 — 4-cyl., 36 hp, 115" wb

Tour.	1800	4400	5600	9200	17,300	31,000
Fore-Door Tour.	1800	4700	6100	9900	19,000	33,000
Pony Tonneau	1800	4500	5800	9500	18,000	32,000
Rds.	1900	4700	6100	9900	19,000	33,000
Cab-Side Limo.	3000	4000	5000	8000	15,000	28,000
Berlin Limo.	3250	4200	5200	8400	15,700	29,000

Six, Model 12 — 6-cyl., 54 hp, 130" wb

Tour.	3250	5000	6500	11,000	22,000	35,000
Fore-Door Pony Tonneau	3250	5200	6800	11,300	23,000	36,000

258

1913 Chalmers Six, coupe, HAC

1913 CHALMERS
Thirty, Model 16 — 4-cyl., 30 hp, 115" wb

	FP	5	4	3	2	1
Tour.-5P	1600	4300	5400	8700	16,500	30,000
Torpedo-4P	1600	4200	5200	8400	15,700	29,000

Thirty-Six, Model 17 — 4-cyl., 36 hp, 118" wb

Tour.-5P	1950	4400	5600	9200	17,300	31,000
Tour.-7P	2150	4300	5400	8700	16,500	30,000
Torpedo-4P	1950	4200	5200	8400	15,700	29,000
Rds.	1950	4500	5800	9500	18,000	32,000
Cpe.	2250	3500	4500	7000	13,000	25,000
Limo.-7P	3250	3300	4400	6700	12,000	24,000

Six, Model 18 — 6-cyl., 54 hp, 130" wb

Torpedo-4P	2400	5000	6500	11,000	22,000	35,000
Tour.-5P	2400	4900	6300	10,300	21,000	34,000
Tour.-7P	2600	4700	6100	9900	19,000	33,000
Rds.	2400	5200	6800	11,300	23,000	36,000
Cpe.	2700	3900	4800	7700	14,300	27,000
Limo.-7P	3700	3500	4500	7000	13,000	25,000

1914 Chalmers Six, coupelet, HAC

1914 CHALMERS
Model 19 — 4-cyl., 36 hp, 118" wb

Tour.-5P	1775	4300	5800	9500	18,000	32,000
Torpedo-4P	1775	4700	6100	9900	19,000	33,000

Model 24 — 6-cyl., 60 hp, 132" wb

Tour.-5P	2175	5000	6500	11,000	22,000	35,000
Torpedo-4P	2175	5200	6800	11,300	23,000	36,000
Rds.-3P	2175	5300	7000	11,500	24,000	37,000
Tour.-6P	2275	4900	6300	10,300	21,000	34,000
Cpe.-3P	2850	3300	4400	6700	12,000	24,000
Limo.-7P	3600	3700	4700	7300	13,700	26,000

1915 CHALMERS
Light Six — 48 hp, 126" wb

Tour.-5P	1650	4300	5400	8700	16,500	30,000
Tour.-6P	1725	4200	5200	8400	15,700	29,000
Cpl.-2P/3P	1900	3100	4200	6300	10,500	22,000
Sed.-5P	2750	2900	3700	5600	9100	24,000
limo.-7P	3200	3500	4500	7000	13,000	25,000

Master Six — 60 hp, 132" wb

Tour.-5P	2400	4500	5800	9500	18,000	32,000
Tour.-7P	2400	4400	5600	9200	17,300	31,000

1916 Chalmers Six-48, touring, HAC

1916 CHALMERS

Model 6-30 — 6-cyl., 30 hp, 115" wb

	FP	5	4	3	2	1
Tour.-5P	1050	3300	4400	6700	12,000	24,000

Model 6-40 — 6-cyl., 40 hp, 124" wb

Tour.-7P	1350	4300	5400	8700	16,500	30,000
Rds.-3P	1350	4400	5600	9200	17,300	31,000
Vict.-Cabr.	1450	4200	5200	8400	15,700	29,000
Planquin Sed.	1700	3700	4700	7300	13,700	26,000

Model 6-48 — 6-cyl., 48 hp, 126" wb

| Tour.-7P | 1550 | 4400 | 5600 | 9200 | 17,300 | 31,000 |

Model 6-54 — 6-cyl., 54 hp, 132" wb

Master Six Tour.-7P	2175	4500	5800	9500	18,000	32,000
Master Six Limo.-7P	3350	4000	5000	8000	15,000	28,000
Master Six Phae.-5P	2175	4700	6100	9900	19,000	33,000

1917 Chalmers Six-30, touring sedan, HAC

1917 CHALMERS

Model Six-30 — 6-cyl., 30 hp, 115" wb

Tour.-5P	1090	4200	5200	8400	15,700	29,000
Rds.	1070	4300	5400	8700	16,500	30,000
Cabr.	1440	4000	5000	8000	15,000	28,000

Model Six-30 — 6-cyl., 30 hp, 122" wb

Tour. Sed.-7P	1850	3300	4400	6700	12,000	24,000
Twn. Car	2550	3700	4700	7300	13,700	26,000
Limo.	2550	4000	5000	8000	15,000	28,000
Tour.-7P	1350	4300	5400	8700	16,500	30,000

1918-19 Chalmers Six-30, touring, HAC

1918 CHALMERS

Model Six-30 — 6-cyl., 30 hp, 117" wb

Tour.-5P	1485	4200	5200	8400	15,700	29,000
Duplex-4P	1485	3500	4500	7000	13,000	25,000
Cabr.-3P	1775	3900	4800	7700	14,300	27,000
Rds.-3P	1485	4300	5400	8700	16,500	30,000
Tour.-7P	1535	4000	5000	8000	15,000	28,000
Tour. Sed.-7P	1950	3200	4300	6500	11,000	23,000
Limo.-7P	3025	3500	4500	7000	13,000	25,000

1919 CHALMERS

Model Six-30 — 6-cyl., 30 hp, 117" wb

Tour.-5P	1565	4200	5200	8400	15,700	29,000
Tour.-7P	1615	4000	5000	8000	15,000	28,000
Limo. Land'et.-7P	3025	3700	4700	7300	13,700	26,000
Rds.-3P	1565	4300	5400	8700	16,500	30,000
Cabr.-3P	1985	3900	4800	7700	14,300	27,000
Limo.-3P	2985	3500	4500	7000	13,000	25,000
Sed.-7P	2250	3100	4200	6300	10,500	22,000
Twn. Land'et.-7P	3025	3900	4800	7700	14,300	27,000
Twn. Car-7P	2925	3700	4700	7300	13,700	26,000

1920 CHALMERS

Model 35-C — 6-cyl., 45 hp, 117" wb

Rds.-2P	1685	4200	5200	8400	15,700	29,000
Sed.-5P	2370	2700	3600	5300	8800	19,000
Cpe.-3P	2105	3000	4000	6000	9500	21,000
Tour.-5P	1685	3900	4800	7700	14,300	27,000
Spt.-4P	1845	4000	5000	8000	15,000	28,000

Model 35-B — 6-cyl., 45 hp, 122" wb

Tour.-7P	1765	4000	5000	8000	15,000	28,000
Limo.-7P	3075	2900	3700	5600	9100	20,000
Twn. Car-7P	3175	3100	4200	6300	10,500	22,000
Land'et.-7P	3175	3200	4300	6500	11,000	23,000

1920 Chalmers, model 35-C, sport model, JAC

1921 Chalmers, model 35-C, touring, HAC

1921 Chalmers, model 35-C, coupe, HAC

1921 CHALMERS

Model 35-C — 6-cyl., 45 hp, 117" wb

	FP	5	4	3	2	1
Tour.-5P	1795	3900	4800	7700	14,300	27,000
Rds.-2P	1795	4200	5200	8400	15,700	29,000
Spt.-5P	1995	4200	5200	8400	15,700	29,000
Cpe.-4P	2595	3000	4000	6000	9500	21,000
Sed.-5P	2745	2500	3500	5000	8500	18,000

Model 35-B — 6-cyl., 45 hp, 122" wb

| Tour.-7P | 1795 | 4200 | 5200 | 8400 | 15,700 | 29,000 |

1922 Chalmers Six, touring, HAC

259

1922 CHALMERS
Six — 45 hp, 117" wb

	FP	5	4	3	2	1
Rds.-3P	1245	4000	5000	8000	15,000	28,000
Tour.-5P	1295	3900	4800	7700	14,300	27,000
Tour.-7P	1395	3700	4700	7300	13,700	26,000
Coach	1585	—	—	—	—	—
Cpe.-4P	1995	3100	4200	6300	10,500	22,000
Sed.-5P	2295	2900	3700	5600	9100	20,000

1923 Chalmers, model Y, touring, HAC

1923 CHALMERS
Model Y — 45 hp, 117" wb

	FP	5	4	3	2	1
Rds.-3P	1185	3900	4800	7700	14,300	27,000
Tour.-5P	1185	3700	4700	7300	13,700	26,000
Tour.-7P	1345	3500	4500	7000	13,000	25,000
Sed. C'ch.-5P	1585	2500	3500	5000	8500	18,000
Spt. Tour.-5P	—	—	—	—	—	—
Sed.-5P	2295	—	—	—	—	—
Tour.-7P	1395	—	—	—	—	—

CHAMPION — From 1908-1909 the Famous Manufacturing Company of Chicago produced a highwheeler alternately called the Famous or the Champion. Refer to Famous.

The Champion Motor Car Company of South Milwaukee, Wisconsin was organized during the early summer of 1906 for the manufacture of motor vehicles. Capital stock was $10,000; the incorporators were C.B. Kubach, C. Megow and A.W. Walter. That any Champion car followed has not been documented.

The Champion Motor Car Company of Indianapolis, Indiana was a venture from the summer of 1913 to manufacture touring cars (a 50 hp six and a 36 hp four) in a plant owned by J.T. Elwell at Arthur Avenue and the Northern Pacific tracks. Actual manufacture of any cars has not been substantiated.

The Champion Motor Car Company of St. Louis, Missouri proceeded to the point of publishing a brochure in the fall of 1914 to announce the forthcoming manufacture of a Champion "small four" and "little six" in the former plant of the St. Louis Car Company at 5200 North Second Street. Two months later the venture was in bankruptcy court.

The Champion which was announced as forthcoming from Fort Madison, Iowa in late 1915 ultimately arrived as the Champion of Wabash, Indiana in 1916.

The Champion Wagon Company, Inc. was a $25,000 incorporation from Oswego, New York during the fall of 1913. Promoters F.C. Hill, J.S. Truman and F.S. Truman announced manufacture of automobiles as their agenda, but this Champion never arrived at all.

CHAMPION — Minneapolis, Minnesota — (1913) — "Shrouded in mystery, and yet with a flare of trumpets, comes the announcement that Minneapolis is to have a real full-grown automobile plant before winter's snows render its streets slippery." Thus did *Automobile Topics* herald the arrival of the new Champion Motor Car Company in July 1913. The spokesman for the company was described as the "industrial commissioner of the Minneapolis Civic & Commerce Association," and he declined to mention any of the people involved. The Champion was to be built as a $2750 50 hp six and a $1800 36 hp four. A factory was being outfitted at 14th Avenue NE and the Northern Pacific Railroad tracks. Nothing further was heard of this Champion before Minneapolis streets became slippery that winter. Nothing was heard after, either. The Champion Motor Car Company departed the automotive vale shrouded in the same mystery as its entrance. Whether prototypes were successfully tested has not been documented.

CHAMPION — Wabash, Indiana — (1916) — This product of the Champion Auto Equipment Company had a 188-cubic-inch 36 hp L-head four-cylinder engine mounted in a 110-inch wheelbase chassis and priced at $750 for either roadster or touring car. All this was quite conventional, what was not was the Automatic Tire Inflator which was standard equipment and which allowed the tires to be inflated while the car was in motion. Apparently, Champion had begun production of this better mousetrap a few months previously, together with what the company referred to as its "stupendously successful" Champion Duplex Diaphragm Pump. Initially the company planned to locate its new factory in Fort Madison, Iowa, but plans fell through there and when the Champion arrived, it was in Wabash, Indiana. The car, with Automatic Tire Inflator fitted, was dis-

1916 Champion, roadster, WLB

played at the Chicago Automobile Show in 1916. Reporters were intrigued, but Champion did not disclose any details of the device. The car did not appear at the Chicago Automobile Show in 1917.

1919 Champion, touring, WLB

CHAMPION — Pottstown, Pennsylvania — (1919-1924) — Henry G. Crowther was the president and L.V. Goebbels the chief engineer of the Direct Drive Motor Car Company that was organized in Philadelphia in January of 1919 to build cars at Pottstown in the old Chadwick factory. Direct drive referred to the grooved rings on the rear wheels which meshed with grooved pulleys on each end of a jackshaft, a drive system reminiscent of the Duryea patents. The Champion might have been a linear successor to the Crowther-Duryea, though it does not appear that Charles Duryea was involved with the company. The Duryea system was abandoned in any case by mid-1920, a conventional rear axle was fitted, and the company was renamed Champion Motors Corporation. Although a Falls-engined six was announced, it never saw the assembly line. The Champion remained a four throughout its life, a Lycoming in the Tourist, a Herschell-Spillman in the Special. On the outside, Champions varied only in their radiator configuration, the Tourist looking rather like a Packard, the Special more Rolls-Royce-ish. Interestingly, when the plagiarism was on the other foot, Champion reacted immediately. In 1923, when Overland announced its new Champion model, the Pottstown company cried "foul" — and Overland quietly ceased use of the name. Although 1924 models were announced by Champion, they were built for a short time only. Some references indicate factory sites in Gloucester (New Jersey) and Primos (Pennsylvania). These might have been planned, but were never moved into.

1919-1920 CHAMPION
Model KO — 4-cyl., 40 hp, 116" wb

	FP	5	4	3	2	1
Tour.-5P	1495	3100	4200	6300	10,500	22,000
Tourist-5P	1150	3000	4000	6000	9500	21,000

1921 CHAMPION
Tourist — 4-cyl., 35 hp, 118" wb

	FP	5	4	3	2	1
Tour.-5P	1350	3000	4000	6000	9500	21,000

Special — 4-cyl., 40 hp, 118" wb

	FP	5	4	3	2	1
Tour.-5P	1595	3100	4200	6300	10,500	22,000

1922 CHAMPION
Tourist — 4-cyl., 35 hp, 116" wb

	FP	5	4	3	2	1
Tour.-5P	1095	2900	3700	5600	9100	20,000

Special — 4-cyl., 40 hp, 118" wb

	FP	5	4	3	2	1
Tour.-5P	1395	3100	4200	6300	10,500	22,000

1923 CHAMPION
Special/Tourist — 4-cyl., 40 hp, 116" wb

	FP	5	4	3	2	1
Tourist Tour.-5P	895	2500	3500	5000	8500	18,000
Spc. Tour.-5P	1050	2700	3600	5300	8800	19,000

1924 CHAMPION
Special/Tourist — 4-cyl., 40 hp, 112" wb

	FP	5	4	3	2	1
Tourist Tour.-5P	975	2500	3500	5000	8500	18,000
Spc. Tour.-5P	1295	2700	3600	5300	8800	19,000

1923 Champion Tourist, touring, KM

CHAMPION ELECTRIC — New York, New York — (1912-1913) — Although the Champion Electric Vehicle Company of 100 William Street in New York City has been indicated as a manufacturer of a passenger car from 1912-1913, documentation of this is lacking. The only vehicles exhibited by the firm at the New York Automobile Show in October 1912 were a light delivery wagon and a one-ton truck, although other models reportedly were to be "developed later." The company appears to have failed before this was done, although prototype work may have begun.

CHAMPION — Cleveland, Ohio — (1920) — The Champion Motor Car Company was organized in Cleveland early in 1920 with a capital stock of $525,000. Manufacture of a four-cylinder touring car on a 108-inch wheelbase to be sold for $950 was the company's plan, and a prototype was shown at a local industrial meeting that April. That was the last of this Champion. The company failed soon thereafter.

CHANDLER STEAM — Akron, Ohio — (1902) — The first Chandler in America was a steamer built in Akron by a mechanic named P.J. Chandler. As *The Motor Review* noted in April of 1902, Chandler was building "several trial steam vehicles" and expected to enter the field "on a somewhat extensive basis." There is no evidence he ever did, however.

1914 Chandler, model 14, touring, HAC

CHANDLER — Cleveland, Ohio — (1914-1929) — In February of 1913 a group of former officers of the Lozier Motor Company of Detroit moved to Cleveland to form their own company to build a six-cylinder car similar to the Lozier Light Six. Among the men involved were F.C. Chandler, W.S. Mead, T.V. Whitbeck, Sam Regar, and C.A. Emise who had been so successful as the sales manager of Lozier. Interestingly, the new firm was initially called Emise Motor Car Company, but the name was changed within weeks to Chandler. The new Chandler Motor Car Company was successful immediately, and the Chandler motorcar became among the most highly regarded medium-priced automobiles in America. Not surprisingly, the radiators of the first cars looked very Lozier-like. Although not a competition car by any means, a Chandler's performance on the road was meritorious. In 1915 a Chandler Six was driven the nearly 2000 miles from Tiajuana, Mexico to Vancouver, Canada without a motor or wheel stop: in 1926 Ralph Mulford drove a Chandler 1000 miles in 689 minutes. Victory at Pikes Peak in 1925 had been followed by heavy promotion of the company's "Pikes Peak engine." Chandler roared into the Twenties. Its operating profit for 1922 was close to $4 million. Production had doubled that year from 5000 to 10,000 cars, and the latter figure remained the norm thereafter. Nineteen twenty-seven was the marque's peak year, when units built approached 20,000. Chandler's constant-mesh Traffic Transmission was introduced in 1924, and its Bowen "One-Shot" chassis lubrication followed in 1926, the same year the distinctive four-paneled radiator design made its debut. In 1919 the subsidiary Cleveland Automobile Company had been organized by Chandler for the building of a smaller and cheaper car called the Cleveland. In December of 1926 the parent company absorbed its subsidiary and discontinued its car. Now the official company name was Chandler-Cleveland Corporation. Among the surprises Chandler offered for 1927 was a new eight, which like its six was Chandler-built. By now, however, things had begun to sour for Chandler. The company's public relations office put up a marvelously brave front, with releases to the trade press that president F.C. Chandler had been able to take "a breathing spell in Bermuda" because Chandler cars were "going great guns at the factory." For the year ending December 31st, 1927, Chandler lost $473,109. In early December the following year, the announcement was made that Chandler-Cleveland Motors Corporation had been absorbed by Hupp Motor Car Corporation. Hupp president DuBois Young was now Chandler's president. Among his first official acts was to discontinue the Chandler motorcar. Interestingly, Chandlers remained available until 1931 in Switzerland, where they were famous for losing all oil pressure in left-hand bends.

1927 Chandler, Royal Eight, touring, OCW

1914 CHANDLER
Model 14 — 6-cyl., 27 hp, 120" wb

	FP	5	4	3	2	1
Light Six Tour.-5P	1785	2500	3500	5000	8500	18,000
Limo.	3600	2300	3300	4600	7500	16,000
Cpe.	2850	2200	3200	4400	7000	15,000

1915 Chandler Six, runabout, HAC

1915 CHANDLER
Six — 6-cyl., 27 hp, 120" wb

Tour.-5P	1595	2500	3500	5000	8500	18,000
Limo.	2750	2300	3300	4600	7500	16,000
Sed.	2750	2200	3200	4400	7000	15,000
Rbt.-2P	1595	2700	3600	5300	8800	19,000
Cpe.	2200	2300	3300	4600	7500	16,000
Cpl.	1950	2200	3200	4400	7000	15,000

1916 Chandler Six, sedan, HAC

1916 CHANDLER
Six — 6-cyl., 27 hp, 122" wb

Tour.-5P	1295	2700	3600	5300	8800	19,000
Rds.	1295	2900	3700	5600	9100	20,000
Limo.	2450	2300	3300	4600	7500	16,000
Sed.	2250	1800	2800	4000	6200	13,000

	FP	5	4	3	2	1
Conv. Sed.	1795	2500	3500	5000	8500	18,000
Cpe.	1950	2300	3300	4600	7500	16,000
Cabr.	1650	2400	3400	4800	8000	17,000

1917 Chandler, type 17, roadster, HAC

1917 CHANDLER
Type 17 — 6-cyl., 27 hp, 123" wb

Rds.-4P	1395	2900	3700	5600	9100	20,000
Tour.-7P	1395	2700	3600	5300	8800	19,000
Conv. Cpe.-4P	1995	2500	3500	5000	8500	18,000
Conv. Sed.-7P	2095	2700	3600	5300	8800	19,000
Limo.-7P	2695	2300	3300	4600	7500	16,000

1917 CHANDLER
Type 17 — 6-cyl., 27 hp, 123" wb

Rds.-4P	1395	3100	4200	6300	10,500	22,000
Tour.-7P	1395	3000	4000	6000	9500	21,000
Conv. Cpe.-4P	1995	2700	3600	5300	8800	19,000
Conv. Sed.-7P	2095	2900	3700	5600	9100	20,000
Limo.-7P	2695	2300	3300	4600	7500	16,000

1918 Chandler Six, touring, HAC

1918 CHANDLER
Six — 6-cyl., 30 hp, 123" wb

Rds.-2P	1595	3200	4300	6500	11,000	23,000
Tour.-7P	1595	3100	4200	6300	10,500	22,000
Spt.	1675	3200	4300	6500	11,000	23,000
Cpe.	2195	2200	3200	4400	7000	15,000
Sed.	2295	1800	2800	4000	6200	13,000
Limo.	2895	2300	3300	4600	7500	16,000

1919 Chandler Six, touring, JAC

1919 CHANDLER
Six — 6-cyl., 30 hp, 123" wb

Rds.-4P	1795	3200	4300	6500	11,000	23,000
Tour.-7P	1795	3100	4200	6300	10,500	22,000
Disp. Car	1875	2500	3500	5000	8500	18,000
Cpe.	2395	2000	3000	4200	6500	14,000
Sed.	2495	2300	3300	4600	7500	16,000
Limo.	3095	2700	3600	5300	8800	19,000
Spt.-4P	2175	3000	4000	6000	9500	21,000
Conv. Cpe.	2695	2900	3700	5600	9100	20,000

1920 Chandler Six, coupe, HAC

1920 CHANDLER
Six — 6-cyl., 30 hp, 123" wb

	FP	5	4	3	2	1
Rds.-4P	1895	3200	4300	6500	11,000	23,000
Disp.-4P	1975	2500	3500	5000	8500	18,000
Tour.-7P	1895	3100	4200	6300	10,500	22,000
Sed.-7P	2795	2300	3300	4600	7500	16,000
Cpe.-4P	2695	2500	3500	5000	8500	18,000
Limo.-7P	3295	2900	3700	5600	9100	20,000

1921 Chandler Six, sedan, HAC

1922 Chandler Six, Chummy Sedan, JAC

1921-1922 CHANDLER
Six — 45 hp, 123" wb

Tour.-7P	1930	3200	4300	6500	11,000	23,000
Rds.-2P	1930	3500	4500	7000	13,000	25,000
Rds.-2P	1930	3700	4700	7300	13,700	26,000
Disp.-4P	2010	2500	3500	5000	8500	18,000
Cpe.-4P	2930	2300	3300	4600	7500	16,000
Sed.-7P	3030	2000	3000	4200	6500	14,000
Limo.-7P	3530	2500	3500	5000	8500	18,000

1923 CHANDLER
Six — 45 hp, 123" wb

Rds.-4P	—	3200	4300	6500	11,000	23,000
Tour.-5P	—	3100	4200	6300	10,500	22,000
Tour.-7P	—	3000	4000	6000	9500	21,000
Ryl. Disp.	—	2900	3700	5600	9100	20,000
Chy. Sed.	—	2300	3300	4600	7500	16,000
Metropolitan Sed.	—	2400	3400	4800	8000	17,000
Sed.-7P	—	2500	3500	5000	8500	18,000
Limo.	—	2900	3700	5600	9100	20,000

1923 Chandler Six, Metropolitan Sedan, HAC

1924 Chandler Royal Dispatch Sport Model, HAC

1924 CHANDLER
Model 32-A — 6-cyl., 123" wb

	FP	5	4	3	2	1
Tour.-5P	1485	3200	4300	6500	11,000	23,000
Tour.-7P	1635	3100	4200	6300	10,500	22,000
Rds.-4P	1685	3500	4500	7000	13,000	25,000
Rds.-2P	1695	3300	4400	6700	12,000	24,000
Ryl. Disp.-4P	1785	2900	3700	5600	9100	20,000
Chy. Sed.-5P	1785	2300	3300	4600	7500	16,000
Metropolitan Sed.-5P	2270	2400	3400	4800	8000	17,000
Sed.-7P	2385	2500	3500	5000	8500	18,000
Limo.-7P	2995	2900	3700	5600	9100	20,000

1925 Chandler Comrade Roadster, HAC

1925 CHANDLER
Model 33 — 6-cyl., 55 hp, 123" wb

Tour.-5P	1585	3500	4500	7000	13,000	25,000
Tour.-7P	1735	3300	4400	6700	12,000	24,000
Spc. Rds.-3P	1795	3700	4700	7300	13,700	26,000
Comrade Rds.-4P	1785	3900	4800	7700	14,300	27,000
Ryl. Disp.-4P	1885	3100	4200	6300	10,500	22,000
Chy. Sed.-5P	2045	2500	3500	5000	8500	18,000
Four-Door Sed.-5P	1995	2300	3300	4600	7500	16,000
Metropolitan Sed.-5P	2195	2400	3400	4800	8000	17,000
Sed.-7P	2195	2300	3300	4600	7500	16,000
Limo.-7P	3095	2900	3700	5600	9100	20,000

1926 CHANDLER
Model 35 — 6-cyl., 55 hp, 124" wb

20th Century Sed.-5P	1590	2200	3200	4400	7000	15,000
Spt. Tour.-5P	1495	3100	4200	6300	10,500	22,000
Tour.-7P	1595	3000	4000	6000	9500	21,000
Comrade Rds.-4P	1695	3300	4400	6700	12,000	24,000
Ryl. Disp.-4P	1735	3100	4200	6300	10,500	22,000
Metropolitan Sed.-5P	1895	2300	3300	4600	7500	16,000
Sed. DeL.-7P	1995	2400	3400	4800	8000	17,000
Brgm.-5P	1695	2500	3500	5000	8500	18,000
Limo.-7P	3095	2900	3700	5600	9100	20,000

1927 CHANDLER
Standard Six

Sed.-5P	995	2000	3000	4200	6500	14,000
DeL. Sed.-5P	1135	2200	3200	4400	7000	15,000
Cpe.-3P	1035	2400	3400	4800	8000	17,000
DeL. Cpe.-3P	1125	2500	3500	5000	8500	18,000
Tour.-5P	945	3000	4000	6000	9500	21,000
DeL. Tour.-5P	1005	3100	4200	6300	10,500	22,000
Rds.-3P	1135	3300	4400	6700	12,000	24,000

1926 Chandler, model 35, sedan, AA

Special Six

	FP	5	4	3	2	1
Sed.-5P	1295	2200	3200	4400	7000	15,000
Cpe.-3P	1195	2500	3500	5000	8500	18,000
DeL. Cpe.-3P	1285	2700	3600	5300	8800	19,000
Tour.-5P	1145	3200	4300	6500	11,000	23,000
Spt. Tour.-5P	1295	3500	4500	7000	13,000	25,000
Big Six						
Metropolitan Sed.-5P	1595	2300	3300	4600	7500	16,000
Metropolitan Sed. DeL.-5P	1695	2400	3400	4800	8000	17,000
DeL. Sed.-7P	1895	2500	3500	5000	8500	18,000
20th Century Sed.-5P	1495	2200	3200	4400	7000	15,000
Cpe.-4P	1675	2500	3500	5000	8500	18,000
Tour.-5P	1545	3100	4200	6300	10,500	22,000
Tour.-7P	1695	3000	4000	6000	9500	21,000
Comrade Rds.-3P	1695	3500	4500	7000	13,000	25,000
Royal Eight						
Sed.-5P	2195	2400	3400	4800	8000	17,000
Sed. DeL.-7P	2295	2500	3500	5000	8500	18,000
Cpe.-4P	2195	2900	3700	5600	9100	20,000
Rds.-3P	2195	5000	6500	11,000	22,000	35,000
Tour.-5P	2050	4500	5800	9500	18,000	32,000
Tour.-7P	2195	4400	5600	9200	17,300	31,000

1928 Chandler Special Six Sportster, HAC

1928 CHANDLER
Special Six

Tour.-5P	995	3900	4800	7700	14,300	27,000
Rds.-4P	1135	4300	5400	8700	16,500	30,000
Sptstr.-5P	1145	4500	5800	9500	18,000	32,000
Sed.-5P	995	2300	3300	4600	7500	16,000
Cpe.-2P	1035	2700	3600	5300	8800	19,000
Cpe. DeL.-2P	1125	2900	3700	5600	9100	20,000
Sed. DeL.-5P	1135	2400	3400	4800	8000	17,000
Cpe.-4P	1135	2900	3700	5600	9100	20,000
Cpe. DeL.-4P	1235	3000	4000	6000	9500	21,000
Big Six						
Tour.-7P	1695	4200	5200	8400	15,700	29,000
Metropolitan Sed.-5P	1495	2900	3700	5600	9100	20,000
DeL. Sed.-5P	1595	3000	4000	6000	9500	21,000
Cpe.-4P	1675	3500	4500	7000	13,000	25,000
Cpe.-3P	1675	3300	4400	6700	12,000	24,000
Sed.-7P	1795	3100	4200	6300	10,500	22,000
Ryl. Six Sed.-5P	1795	3200	4300	6500	11,000	23,000
Royal Eight						
Tour.-7P	1995	4700	6100	9900	19,000	33,000
Cpe.-4P	1995	3900	4800	7700	14,300	27,000
Cpe.-3P	1995	3700	4700	7300	13,700	26,000
Sed.-5P	1995	3300	4400	6700	12,000	24,000
Sed.-7P	2095	3500	4500	7000	13,000	25,000
Sed. DeL.-5P	2195	3700	4700	7300	13,700	26,000

1929 CHANDLER
Model 65 — 6-cyl., 55 hp, 109" wb

Tour.-5P	895	4400	5600	9200	17,300	31,000
Sptstr.-5P	995	4900	6300	10,300	21,000	34,000
Cpe.-3P	875	3700	4700	7300	13,700	26,000
Sed.-5P	895	3300	4400	6700	12,000	24,000
Cpe.-4P	955	3900	4800	7700	14,300	27,000
DeL. Sed.-5P	995	3500	4500	7000	13,000	25,000
Cabr.-3P	1075	4000	5000	8000	15,000	28,000

1929 Chandler Eight, sedan, HAC

Royal 75 — 8-cyl., 80 hp, 118" wb

	FP	5	4	3	2	1
Brgm.-5P	1295	4200	5200	8400	15,700	29,000
Cpe.-3P	1295	4000	5000	8000	15,000	28,000
Cpe.-4P	1295	4200	5200	8400	15,700	29,000
Sed.-5P	1395	3700	4700	7300	13,700	26,000
DeL. Sed.-5P	1495	3900	4800	7700	14,300	27,000
Big Six — 83 hp, 124" wb						
Tour.-7P	1725	4500	5800	9500	18,000	32,000
Metropolitan Sed.-5P	1525	3700	4700	7300	13,700	26,000
Cpe.-4P	1725	3900	4800	7700	14,300	27,000
Ctry. Clb. Cpe.-4P	1725	4000	5000	8000	15,000	28,000
Cabr.-4P	1825	4400	5600	9200	17,300	31,000
Sed.-7P	1925	3500	4500	7000	13,000	25,000
Ber.-7P	2025	3700	4700	7300	13,700	26,000
Royal 85 — 8-cyl., 95 hp, 124" wb						
Tour.-7P	1995	4500	5800	9500	18,000	32,000
Sed.-5P	1795	4200	5200	8400	15,700	29,000
Ctry. Clb. Cpe.-3P	1925	4300	5400	8700	16,500	20,000
Cpe.-4P	1925	4200	5200	8400	15,700	29,000
DeL. Sed.-5P	1995	4500	5800	9500	18,000	32,000
Cabr.-4P	2095	4000	5000	8000	15,000	28,000
Sed.-7P	2195	4200	5200	8400	15,700	29,000
Ber.-7P	2295	4300	5400	8700	16,500	30,000

CHAPARRAL — The Chaparral was the first car built by Harry Eugene Luck of Cleburne, Texas. It was completed in 1910 and its successful testing resulted in Luck obtaining the venture capital necessary to produce the Luck Utility in 1911. Refer to Luck Utility.

CHAPIN — The Chapin Automobile Company was organized in Chicago during the late summer of 1910 to manufacture and deal in automobiles and supplies. Capital stock was $50,000; D.C. Dell and M.N. Davis were the partners involved. Manufacture is doubted.

CHAPLIN — The Chaplin-Dille Motor Car Company was organized in Morgantown, West Virginia late in 1912 with a capital stock of $25,000 to manufacture and deal in motorcars. Behind this venture were B.M. Chaplin, J.E. Dille and M.C. Wildman. Manufacture is doubted.

CHAPMAN — Chapman & Sons Manufacturing Company of Stoughton, Massachusetts was indicated as an automobile producer in the Hiscox book *Horseless Vehicles, Automobiles, Motor Cycles* published in 1900. A man named Edward D. Chapman has been noted as one of the Chapmans involved. Further documentation is lacking. The town records of Stoughton include no information on an Edward Chapman nor a Chapman company. In some car rosters this automobile venture is indicated to have survived from 1895 through 1905, this doubtless in error and resulting from confusion with the other Chapmans in the field during this period.

1899 Chapman Electric, auto-buggy, NAHC

CHAPMAN ELECTRIC — Portland, Maine — (1899-1901) — In 1899 *Motor Age* said it was probably the lightest four-wheel electric carriage in the world. It weighed only 360 pounds, half of that being the battery. Although occasionally being called the Electromobile, the car was more often given the name of its inventor, W.H. Chapman, who was an electrician employed by the Belknap Motor Company of Portland. Chapman intended his vehicle to carry one person "normally and two on smooth roads." Mileage between charges was about twenty with two people riding; with only one, an extra battery could be carried, which raised the figure to forty or fifty. The chassis rested on four 32-inch bicycle wheels shod with four-inch tires. Two half-horsepower motors were fitted, each geared to the rear wheels. Several different designs of body were offered, and although prices were not quoted, it appears the Chapman was produced into 1901.

1905 Chapman Steamer, auto-buggy, NAHC

CHAPMAN — Stonington, Connecticut — (1905) — There were only two cars in Stonington in 1905. One was a single-cylinder Cadillac, the other was the steam car built by Odell M. Chapman. Its engine was a two-cylinder double-acting 6/8 hp Mason, its boiler was from the Oswego Boiler Works. Both engine and boiler were under the driver's seat, with an eight-gallon copper water tank and a ten-gallon gasoline tank mounted to the rear. "As this car was of the non-condensing type, a brook or watering trough was much in demand," Odell Chapman remembered in the late Forties. "The water gauge was of considerable concern, often breaking, losing steam and water before the gauge cocks could be closed. This would result in a scorched boiler and melted fuse plug and a tow home behind old 'Nell,' as my parents maintained a horse and buggy for their own use." Odell Chapman built just the one car.

CHAPMAN — Napa, California — (1908 et seq.) — Lyman A. Chapman of Napa seems to have built several cars for himself. The first was in 1908 and was not very successful. "Although belt-drive seems to be making great strides with the majority of manufacturers in this country," he penned to *The American Cyclecar* in 1914, "the writer is anxious to know if these manufacturers have tried out their machines on dusty and rutty roads." His 1908 car had been belt drive, he advised, and bad roads had resulted in the belts becoming clogged and buried in dust. On subsequent cars, he had tried a belt only to the countershaft with chain to the rear wheels, and ultimately chain drive completely, which he found eminently more satisfactory. Since a healthy percentage of cyclecars on the market in 1914 sported belt drive, *The American Cyclecar*, which had a vested interest in the cyclecar genre, printed the Chapman letter but penned a postscript of its own: "In all probability Mr. Chapman used flat belts, as vee belts were not used at the time he mentioned. Experience disspells any doubt as to the success of vee belts."

CHAPPAQUA — The Chappaqua Garage, Inc. was organized during the summer of 1917 with a capital stock of $5000 to manufacture and deal in automobiles in Chappaqua, New York. P. Jensen, S. Jensen and D. Connelly, all of Chappaqua, were indicated as the incorporators. Manufacture is doubted.

CHARLES GATE — The Charles Gate Engineering Company was organized in East Orange, New Jersey early in 1906 for the manufacture of automobiles. Five thousand dollars was the capital stock. Behind this venture were A.R. Bangs, H.A. Bangs, H.B. Hollings, G.H. Bauman and H.H. Puking, all of East Orange. Manufacture is doubted.

CHARRON, GIRARDOT & VOIGHT — This French car was more popularly known by its initials, C.G.V. In addition to importing these cars into this country, the firm of Smith & Mabley in New York City produced a few of them as well during 1902-1903. Refer to American C.G.V.

CHARTER — The Charter Automobile Company was organized in Baltimore, Maryland with a capital stock of $750,000 early in 1912. Automobile manufacture was the announced plan of Charter backers Clinton R. Voutz, William Edgar Byrd and George H. Reinert. That any cars were built has not been established.

1903 Charter, tonneau, GR

CHARTER — Chicago, Illinois — (1903-1904) — Late in 1903, James A. Charter, a mechanic for Fairbanks-Morse whom *Motor Age* described as having been "directly interested in gas engine design and manufacture for a score of years," completed his new idea in automobile design. It was a car which used a half-gasoline/half-water mixture for fuel. Gasoline vapor and atomized water entered the cylinder at the same time, heat from the explosion formed super-heated steam, and its expansion assisted in the downstroke of the piston. Otherwise, Charter's car was a conventional four of 50 hp, with a conventional, if cumbersome, rear-entrance tonneau body. It was probably the unconventional aspect of the Charter which resulted in the car not being manufactured. In 1908 the Fairbanks-Morse Company did enter the automobile industry, but with a vehicle not designed by James A. Charter.

CHARTER OAK — New Britain, Connecticut — (1917) — In November of 1916 Eastern Motors Syndicate established itself in Hartford, Connecticut and prepared to market a six-cylinder car with a Herschell-Spillman engine. The company's technical man had been selected, but Eastern Motors admitted that it had not yet found a factory site. Fred A. Law was the firm's new chief engineer, and he was a good one, with a long resume including designs for both Pope and the Electric Vehicle Company, and association with Frederick Newton Manross for a car of his own. In February of 1917 Eastern Motors announced its new factory, a one-story plant in New Britain which it had leased for manufacture. That August, after spending $30,000 and producing only one automobile, which at the time was still in the paintshop, Eastern Motors Syndicate went into bankruptcy because, as *Automobile Topics* said, its promoters found "the present not time to offer a high-priced machine." The Charter Oak was slated to sell for $5000. The marque name, incidentally, referred to the tree in which the royal colonial charter of Connecticut had been hidden in 1662.

CHASE — In August 1900 one Charles H. Chase of Danbury, Connecticut completed a working model of an electric automobile, according to *The Motor Vehicle Review*, and "will soon begin work on a full-size machine." Whether he ever completed it is not known.

CHASE STEAM — Worcester, Massachusetts — (1902) — A former engineer for the New York, New Haven & Hartford Railroad, F.W. Chase of Worcester completed his first steam automobile in April 1902. In May it was demolished when the gasoline tank exploded while the inventor was preparing for a trial run. Five people were injured. Though history does not record, the likelihood is that Chase did not try again.

CHASE — Syracuse, New York — (1907-1912) — The Chase Motor Truck Company was founded in 1906 by Aurin Chase, the former vice-president of the Syracuse Chilled Plow Company which was his father's business. Because the focus of young Chase's new company was truck production, the $900 highwheeler it produced was larger than the norm for that genre. Indeed, although it was called a Surrey (and occasionally Businessman's Runabout), the vehicle was easily convertible from car to light truck. The

1909 Chase, model F, 5-pass. surrey, NAHC

wheelbase was 100 inches. Chain drive and solid rubber tires were featured, and though other powerplants were used, a 20 hp three-cylinder air-cooled two-stroke was the Chase mainstay. The company continued in commercial vehicle manufacture after discontinuing its automobile department in 1912.

CHASE — Minneapolis, Minnesota — (1909) — In 1907 A.F. Chase was in Chicago managing the local agency for Maxwell-Briscoe and announcing that he planned to return to his native Minneapolis and begin an automobile factory. Return to Minneapolis later that year he did, but initially his efforts were concentrated on establishing a dealership there for the Mitchell. In 1909, however, he returned again to the manufacturing idea he had originally had in Chicago. The Chase proposition was a simple one: a high-wheeled solid-tired buggy powered by a two-cylinder air-cooled motor and carrying a $550 price tag. By March of 1909 the prototype had been built. How many further buggies were produced and sold is not known, but the logistics of their manufacture had already been seen to, the motors contracted to be built by a local steam engine plant, the bodies in a local carriage works, with Chase assembling the cars in the shop adjoining his Mitchell dealership.

CHATTANOOGA — During the fall of 1905 the Chattanooga Automobile Company was organized for the purpose of building automobiles and motorcycles in Chattanooga, Tennessee. The capital stock was $10,000, and the incorporators were Charles Forstner, Joseph C. Forstner, W.S. White, J.L. Foust and A.S. Dickey. Manufacture is doubted.

1914 Chautauqua Cyclecar, runabout, WLB

CHAUTAUQUA — Jamestown, New York — (1914) — The Chautauqua was a cyclecar produced by the Chautauqua Cyclecar Company which was in all ways save two similar to virtually every other cyclecar on the market. The first difference was its standard 56-inch tread, the second was its steering-column-mounted gearshift. This novelty was not sufficient to cause the Chautauqua to survive longer than any other cyclecar. Indeed, it may not have proceeded much beyond the prototype stage. In June of 1914 Chautauqua president and designer H.J. Newman — a veteran of Stoddard-Dayton — announced plans to locate his factory in New Castle, Pennsylvania, this because the vehicle's frame and axles were to be manufactured in nearby Sharon (home of the Driggs company which produced components for numerous cyclecar builders) and the tubing was to come from Elwood City, Pennsylvania. This strategic location, he said, would eliminate considerable overhead expense for freighting. Newman estimated that he would require about $50,000 working capital to get his business started on a basis of 1000 cars the first year. Probably he never got the money, and he certainly never produced a thousand cars. Newman is known to have driven the prototype of his cyclecar (powered by a two-cylinder 12 hp Spacke engine) over 1000 miles in the mountains of New York and Pennsylvania. His price tag for the car was $400. Later in 1914 he announced plans to upgrade the vehicle with a four-cylinder engine and shaft drive, though undoubtedly he was out of business before this could be done.

1914 CHAUTAUQUA
Cyclecar — 2-cyl., 12 hp, 102" wb

	FP	5	4	3	2	1
Model C Rds.	400	—	—	—	—	—

CHAUTAUQUA ELECTRIC — Jamestown & Falconer, New York — (1919)
— Two companies were organized in Upstate New York in 1919 for manufacture of a $600 electric car, and the likelihood is that there was a link between the two. The first announced was the Chautauqua Electric Car Company, Inc. in Jamestown, preliminary announcements indicating that the adjacent plants of the Supreme Furniture Company and Lynndon Mirror Company were being purchased with an additional building to be erected to connect them — and there some 250 workers would produce 600 Chautauqua Electrics during the coming year. Soon after, announcement came from Falconer of the creation there of the Chautauqua Electric Manufacturing Company. That even prototypes resulted in either Jamestown or Falconer has not been confirmed. Interesting, the Falconer plant that had been destined for the Chautauqua was later turned into a furniture factory. A number of area residents recall their fathers having lost a lot of money in the Chautauqua Electric venture.

CHAUTAUQUA STEAMER — Dunkirk, New York — (1911) — Only prototypes were built by the Chautauqua Motor Company of Dunkirk, though the firm had certainly intended to become a factor in the motor industry. That Chautauqua built at least one automobile was indicated in a Timken bearing ad in *MoToR* in January 1911. That a truck was produced as well was documented by the appearance of same at the Chicago Automobile Show that February where the vehicle was demonstrated. Chautauqua faded from the scene soon after. This venture, incidentally, seems to have evolved out of the Webb Jay Motor Company which produced a steamer in Chicago in 1908 and continued thereafter as a steam car dealership until the brothers Jay found more lucrative courses to pursue. A reference from March of 1910 indicates that the Webb Jay organization had that month changed its name to Chautauqua Motor Company.

1922 Checker, model C, HAC

CHECKER — Kalamazoo, Michigan — (1922-1942 et. seq.) — The Checker was born of the merger between Commonwealth Motors of Joliet, Illinois (producers of the Commonwealth) and the Markin Body Corporation of Chicago. The merger took place in October 1921, the famous taxi followed one year later. Initially there had been the plan for Checker to continue the manufacture as well of the Handley car formerly made by Handley Motors, Inc., but nothing came of this. All Checker fortunes were placed on the taxi. A Buda-engined four in the beginning, the Checker was provided a Continental six-cylinder engine by the turn of the decade. Although it has been commonly believed that Checker Motors Corporation did not begin marketing passenger cars until after the Second World War, the company did offer a model called the Checker Utility (Continental six) from late summer of 1931 into 1932 and possibly later. The Utility was a $1795 all-purpose vehicle which could convert easily from passenger car to light delivery. During the early Thirties, too, Checker produced a few one-off custom cars for individual customers, the most notable being a bullet-proof sedan for Sam Insull. The corporation's most significant venture into passenger car production, of course, followed in 1959 and continued until the firm's demise in the early Eighties. Morris Markin, whose idea Checker had been, remained in charge at the company until his death at the age of seventy-seven in 1970.

1920 CHECKER CAB
Model C, 4-cyl. (Lycoming engine)

	FP	5	4	3	2	1
4-dr. Taxicab-5P	1595	2000	3000	4200	6500	14,000

Note: Taxi version of Commonwealth car; about two per day being built by winter of 1920 in Joliet, Ill.

1921 CHECKER CAB
Model C, 4-cyl. (Herschell-Spillman engine)

4-dr. Taxicab-5P	1595	2000	3000	4200	6500	14,000

Note: Markin Auto Body Co. took over Commonwealth operations Oct. 1921; moved headquarters to Chicago.

1922 CHECKER CAB
Model C-44, 4-cyl., 40 hp

4-dr. Limo. Taxi-5/7P	2680	2300	3300	4500	7200	15,500
4-dr. Lan. Taxi-5/7P	2785	2300	3300	4600	7500	16,000
Chassis	1800	—	—	—	—	—

Note: Morris Markin ordered 1800 Checker Cab engines from National Mas-Gore Corp., of Kalamazoo, Mich., in Jan. 1922. In May 1922, Commonwealth entered receivership and Checker Cab Mfg. Co. was formed.

1923 Checker, model H, HAC

1923 CHECKER CAB
Model H-2, 4-cyl., 22.5 hp, 117" wb

	FP	5	4	3	2	1
4-dr. Lan. Taxi-5P	2440	2300	3300	4600	7500	16,000
4-dr. Limo. Taxi-5P	2340	2300	3300	4500	7200	15,500

Note: Serial nos. 1 to 4501. In Jan. 1923, production was running at 112 units per month. Model year production based on serial number range: approximately 4500. Buda 4-cyl. engine. New factory in Kalamazoo opened June 23, 1923.

1924 Checker, model E, HAC

1924 CHECKER CAB
Model E, 4-cyl., 22.5 hp, 117" wb

4-dr. Lan. Taxi-5P	2440	2300	3300	4600	7500	16,000
4-dr. Limo. Taxi-5P	2340	2300	3300	4500	7200	15,500

Note: Serial nos. 4501 to 5089; approximately 600 built.

1925 CHECKER CAB
Model E, 4-cyl., 22.5 hp, 117" wb

4-dr. Limo. Taxi-5P	2690	2100	3100	4300	6700	14,500
4-dr. Limo. Cab.-5P	2500	2000	3000	4200	6500	14,000
4-dr. Limo. Cab.-5P	2600	2000	3000	4200	6500	14,000
4-dr. Limo. Cab.-5P	2700	2000	3000	4200	6500	14,000

Note: Serial nos. 5090 to 6019; approximately 930 built. Production was an average of 75 per week. Fleet discount prices were "available upon application."

1926 Checker, model F, OCW

1926 CHECKER CAB
Model E, 4-cyl., 22.5 hp, 117" wb

4-dr. Limo. Taxi-5P	2500	2000	3000	4200	6500	14,000

Model F, 4-cyl., 22.5 hp, 117" wb

4-dr. Limo. Taxi-5P	2500	2000	3000	4200	6500	14,000

Note: Serial nos. 6020 to 8018; approximately 2000 built. A 1937 McQuay-Norris parts catalog lists 1926 Models K, KX6 and BX using a Buda HS6A engine, but no additional information about such models is available.

1927 Checker, model G-4, HAC

1927 CHECKER CAB
Model F, 4-cyl., 22.5 hp, 117" wb

	FP	5	4	3	2	1
4-dr. Limo. Taxi-5P	2500	2000	3000	4200	6500	14,000

Model G-4, 4-cyl., 22.5 hp, 117" wb

	FP	5	4	3	2	1
4-dr. Lan. Taxi-5P	2592	2100	3100	4300	6700	14,500
4-dr. Limo. Taxi-5P	2600	2000	3000	4200	6500	14,000

Model G-6, 6-cyl., 27.30 hp, 124-3/4" wb

	FP	5	4	3	2	1
4-dr. Lan. Taxi-5P	2692	2200	3200	4500	7200	15,500
4-dr. Limo. Taxi-5P	2700	2300	3300	4600	7500	16,000

Note: Serial nos. 8019 and up. No production estimate available.

1928 Checker, model G, HAC

1928 CHECKER CAB
Model G-4, 4-cyl., 22.5 hp, 117" wb

	FP	5	4	3	2	1
4-dr. Lan. Taxi-5P	2592	2100	3100	4300	6700	14,500
4-dr. Limo. Taxi-5P	2600	2200	3200	4400	7000	15,000

Model G-6, 6-cyl., 27.34 hp, 124-3/4" wb

	FP	5	4	3	2	1
4-dr. Lan. Taxi-5P	2692	2200	3200	4500	7200	15,500
4-dr. Limo. Taxi-5P	2700	2300	3300	4600	7500	16,000

Note: Serial nos. and production estimates not available. Prices listed as "subject to change."

1929 Checker, model K-6, HAC

1929 CHECKER CAB
Model K-6, 6-cyl., 27.30 hp, 127" wb

	FP	5	4	3	2	1
4-dr. Twn. Car Taxi-6P	2492	2300	3300	4600	7500	16,000

Note: Serial nos. and production not available. Buda CS engine.

1930 Checker, model K-6, HAC

1930 CHECKER CAB
Model K-6, 6-cyl., 27.30 hp, 127" wb

	FP	5	4	3	2	1
4-dr. Twn. Car Taxi-6P	2492	2300	3300	4600	7500	16,000

Note: Serial numbers and production not available. Buda CS engine. Models M and MU-6 may have appeared in late 1930.

1931 Checker, model M, HAC

1931 CHECKER CAB
Model K-6, 6-cyl., 27.3 hp, 127" wb

	FP	5	4	3	2	1
4-dr. Twn. Car Taxi-6P	2500	2400	3400	4800	8000	17,000

Model M, 6-cyl., 61.5 bhp, 122" wb

	FP	5	4	3	2	1
M6 4-dr. Lan. Taxi-6P	NA	2500	3500	5000	8500	18,000
MU6 4-dr. Sub. Utility	1795	2300	3300	4700	7800	16,500

Note: The MU6 Suburban Utility was a combination Landau Limousine and Station Wagon with folding center seats, a rear liftgate and tailgate. It used a Buda J-214 engine. The Model K used a Buda CS6 engine. Serial numbers and production unavailable.

1932 CHECKER CAB
Model K-6, 6-cyl., 27.3 hp, 127" wb

	FP	5	4	3	2	1
4-dr. Twn. Car Taxi-6P	2500	2400	3400	4600	8000	17,000

Model M, 6-cyl., 61.5 bhp, 122" wb

	FP	5	4	3	2	1
M6 4-dr. Lan. Taxi-6P	NA	2500	3500	5000	8500	18,000
MU6 4-dr. Sub. Utility	1795	2300	3300	4700	7800	16,500

Note: The Series M models used a Buda JC-214 engine in 1932. About 1,000 Suburban Utility models were built in 1931-1932.

1933 CHECKER CAB
Model T, 8-cyl. (Lycoming), 98 bhp

	FP	5	4	3	2	1
4-dr. Lan. Taxi-6P	NA	2400	3400	4800	8000	17,000
4-dr. Sub. Utility-8P	1795	2300	3300	4600	7500	16,000

Note: The Lycoming GU or GUC straight eight engine was used in 1933-1934 models. About 500 Model T trucks were also built. In June, 1933, E.L. Cord gained control of Checker Motors and produced the Saf-T-Cab for his Auburn Motor Co. The Saf-T-Cabs were used in Cleveland, Ohio.

1934 CHECKER CAB
Model T-8, 8-cyl. (Lycoming), 98 bhp

	FP	5	4	3	2	1
4-dr. Lan. Taxi-6P	NA	2200	3200	4400	7000	15,000
4-dr. Sub. Utility-8P	NA	2000	3000	4200	6500	14,000

Note: Lycoming GU engine. Production was about 1000 vehicles.

1936 Checker, model Y, HAC

1935-1936
Model Y-6, 6-cyl. (Continental), 80 hp

	FP	5	4	3	2	1
4-dr. Taxi-5P	NA	2200	3200	4400	7000	15,000
6-dr. LWB Suburban-9P	NA	2000	3000	4200	6500	14,000

Model Y-8, 8-cyl. (Lycoming), 148 bhp

	FP	5	4	3	2	1
4-dr. Taxi-5P	NA	2300	3300	4600	7500	16,000
6-dr. LWB Suburban-9P	NA	2200	3200	4400	7000	15,000

Note: Krause Publications' *Encyclopedia of Commercial Vehicles* describes the Series Y Checker as "a cheaper vehicle than the T, with a 6-cylinder Continental engine and the sloping lines typical of cars of the era." However, both AEA and McQuay-Norris parts catalogs of 1936, 1937 and 1942 list only an 8-cylinder Model Y using a Lycoming GFD straight eight engine. The GFD motor was the same engine used in the Auburn 850. It had a 3.06 x 4-3/4 in. bore and stroke and developed 30.01 SAE hp and 148 bhp @ 4000 rpm. Morris Markin regained control of the company from E.L. Cord in 1936.

1937-1939 CHECKER CAB
Model Y-8, 8-cyl. (Lycoming). 148 bhp

	FP	5	4	3	2	1
4-dr. Chicago Taxi-5P	NA	2300	3300	4600	7500	16,000
4-dr. N.Y. Taxi-5P	NA	2300	3300	4600	7500	16,000

Note: Lycoming GFD engine used.

1940 Checker, model A, HAC

1940-1941 CHECKER CAB
Model A, 6-cyl. (Continental), 80 bhp

	FP	5	4	3	2	1
4-dr. Lan. Taxi-5P	NA	2400	3400	4800	8000	17,000

Note: The Model A had unusual streamlined styling with radically cut front fenders, a roof vent over the driver's compartment and an open rear body section that could be covered with a removable, padded rear roof panel.

CHELSEA — The car produced by the Chelsea Manufacturing Company of Chelsea, Michigan from 1903-1904 was marketed as the Welch Tourist. Refer to Welch.

1914 Chelsea Cyclecar, roadster, NAHC

CHELSEA — **Newark, New Jersey** — (1914) — Despite specifications which indicated otherwise, the Chelsea Manufacturing Company of Newark insisted upon referring to its product as a cyclecar. This most assuredly was a mistake. The Chelsea's 56-inch tread, shaft drive and selective transmission represented standard-car features rarely present in a cyclecar. Its wheelbase at 102 inches was longer than most, and its four-cylinder 12 hp engine somewhat more powerful. A side-by-side roadster of torpedo pattern was the only body style offered, and its price was $390. In the early spring of 1914 Chelsea indicated its scheduled output that year to be about 500 cars. In September there was reference to a Chelsea being entered in a reliability run, though no further indication as to how it fared. Possibly not well. And probably the year's output of 500 cars was not reached before the Chelsea Manufacturing Company went under.

CHENEY — **Milwaukee, Wisconsin** — (1914) — Herbert W. Cheney was an electrical engineer living at 121 31st Street in Milwaukee who built a cyclecar in 1914. That he may have considered manufacture was indicated by the inclusion of his name among cyclecar builders in the March 1914 issue of *Motor Print*. Manufacture did not follow, however.

CHERRY — The Cherry Autocab Company was organized in New York City during the fall of 1908 to "make, sell and rent automobiles." The capital stock was $25,000, and the incorporators included L.L. Doblin of 583 Broadway and A.S. Gilbert of 310 West 93rd Street. Manufacture has not been documented.

CHESTER — The Chester Auto Company was organized in Buffalo, New York early in 1908 with a capital stock of $7500 for the manufacture of motor vehicles. A.J. Chester, E.E. Williams and Fred D. Russell backed this venture. Manufacture is doubted.

The Chester Gas Engine Company of Sterling, Illinois was listed as an automobile manufacturer in the Hiscox book *Horseless Vehicles, Automobiles, Motor Cycles* published in 1900. Further documentation is lacking.

The Chester Rubber Tire & Tool Company was a $250,000 incorporation arriving from East Liverpool, Ohio during the early fall of 1913. Manufacture of both tires and motor cars was announced. Behind this venture were John E. Newell, James C. Freshwater, George A. Hasson and George Arner. Manufacture of a car is doubted.

CHESTERTOWN — The Chestertown Automobile and Garage Company was organized with a capital stock of $25,000 during the fall of 1911 to "manufacture, keep for hire, lease, repair and deal in motorcars and supplies" in Chestertown, Maryland. The people behind this venture were H. Berge Simmons, A. Parks Rasin and L. Bates Russell, all of Chestertown. Manufacture of an automobile is doubted.

CHEVROLET

CHEVROLET — **Detroit and Flint, Michigan** — (1912-1942 et. seq.) — The Chevrolet was a car built for a purpose. It was the vehicle by which William C. Durant intended to regain control of General Motors, the corporation he had founded in 1908 and which he lost to the bankers in 1910. A businessman/entrepreneur of the swashbuckling adventurer sort, Billy Durant was not always wise, but he was ever resourceful. Initially his Chevrolet — which he envisioned as a light car of "French type" to be sold at popular prices — didn't work out exactly as planned, but that was Louis' fault. To put his plan into operation, Durant had contacted Louis Chevrolet, one of the stalwarts on the successful racing team Durant had established while heading Buick. Durant was aware that Chevrolet had ambitions to build a car of his own, and since the Chevrolet name was already well known in motor sport, and since Chevrolet had been born in Europe and knew what "French type" meant, Durant was sure he was the man for the job. Chevrolet hired a Frenchman to help him, Etienne Planche, whom he had known from his days with the Walter in Brooklyn and who had designed the Roebling-Planche (antecedent to the Mercer) — and this Billy thought boded well too. In May of 1911 a Detroit newspaper leaked the news of the forthcoming Chevrolet car from Durant. Meanwhile Durant began organizing a whole bunch of companies: the Chevrolet Motor Company in Detroit (initially Chevrolet Motor Car but the "Car" was soon dropped), the Little Motor Car Company in Flint (to build a less expensive car called the Little to bring some quick cash into the coffers), the Mason Motor Company in Flint (to build engines for these cars, with former Buick engineer Arthur Mason at its head), the Republic Motor Company (for which he bought an entire block in New York City to be used as an auxiliary assembly plant), among others. And meanwhile, too, Louis was taking his time coming up with the new Chevrolet. The Little arrived first, during the summer of 1912, as a $650 four. Some months later a $1285 Little Six was added, this a last-minute decision because the car Louis Chevrolet was building was turning out to be not a light French type at all, but a big car that Durant knew he couldn't sell for less than $2150. Still, when Louis Chevrolet finally had the car ready, Durant felt he had no other choice but to get it on the market right away, since a year-and-a-half had passed since that first press mention it was coming. And thus it was, late in 1912, that the Chevrolet Six Type C Classic arrived, with an overhead valve T-head engine of 299 cubic inches (the largest displacement of any Chevrolet engine until introduction of the 348-cubic-inch V-8 in 1958) and a wheelbase of 120 inches (as long as any Chevy ever). The car was well built — three point motor suspension, a three-speed selective transmission on a full-floating rear axle — but it was also ponderous, and it didn't sell. Billy Durant definitely had a problem. With cheaper prices, the Little was selling, but it had been a shoestring operation and Durant was aware that the cars were not very durable. His solution was to combine the good points of the Chevrolet and the Little into one new car to be sold as a Chevrolet. And to gather all the various companies he had organized under the Chevrolet banner too, and to move the whole operation to Flint, where he had enjoyed boy-wonder status since his carriage-making days. This irritated Louis Chevrolet, who took off on his own to build the Frontenac; therefter Etienne Planche received an offer he couldn't refuse from Durant's old partner J. Dallas Dort and took off to build the Dort. Subsequently Durant finished up the run of Chevrolet Classic Sixes for which parts remained, and introduced the Chevrolet Light Six or Model L for the 1914 model year (this the former Little Six, and the only L-head in Chevrolet history). More important in 1914 was the arrival of the H Series, powered by a 170.9-cubic-inch four-cylinder engine designed by Arthur Mason which would remain in production until 1928. These were the first Chevrolets not to include a self-starter as standard equipment (it was available optionally), but they were also the first Chevrolets to be sold for under a thousand dollars. Baby Grand for the $875 touring and Royal Mail for the $750 roadster were the delightful names for these automobiles and there was a sporty Amesbury Special available at $985 too. All these cars carried a new emblem, the famous Chevrolet bowtie, which was Durant's idea and one which he'd carried around with him for a long time, having been inspired to it by either the wallpaper in a Paris hotel room (as he liked to say) or something he saw in the rotogravure section of a Hot Springs, Virginia newspaper (which is the way his wife remembered it). Durant's plan to assemble Chevrolets in the heart of New York City, however, ran into an indisputable snag, the factory being located in one of the worst sections in town with the result that he had to buy protection from both Tammany Hall and street toughs. Thus when the former Maxwell-Briscoe plant became available in Tarrytown, he bought it up right away. A few months later, on December 16th, 1914, he introduced the Chevrolet

Four-Ninety, that figure being its price tag and just happening to be also the price tag at which Henry Ford was selling his Model T. The car — designed by Alfred Sturt, another former Buick man — was essentially a Series H stripped to essentials and offered in any color so long as it was black. This copycat approach from Chevrolet brought an immediate rejoinder from Ford; he lowered the Model T's price to $440. Durant began selling Four-Nineties by the tens of thousands anyway, though by 1917 their price tags were $550, this including a self-starter which of course the Model T did not have. Because of Henry Ford's headstart with mass production of the T, however, he could consistently lower his car's price tag with the result that the differential between the cars widened through the years — and the Model T swamped the Chevrolet in sales. But as this was happening, Billy Durant was otherwise occupied. Mysteriously, large chunks of General Motors stock were being bought up, and proxies procured, and on September 16th, 1915 — the seventh anniversary of Billy Durant's founding of General Motors — he had the corporation back again. "Chevrolet Buys General Motors" was the headline — and though that was a simplification of the Durant maneuvers, it pretty much told the story. Unfortunately, with GM again his, Billy Durant began to neglect Chevrolet. The $1400 Model D ohv 90° V-8 on a 120-inch wheelbase — designed by Mason and Sturt, and an admirable car — was really a step backwards insofar as the Chevrolet marketing philosophy was concerned; introduced late in 1917, it was ushered out at the end of 1918. The Series F had replaced the H for 1917, and was a bigger car, and bigger yet with the FB for 1919. Bigger, too, were the Chevrolet's price tags. Bigger yet was the trouble Billy Durant was getting himself into at the helm of General Motors. Just as the first time around, Durant was on a buying spree, and many of his purchases (especially Samson tractor which he hoped to be a competitor to the Fordson) proved disastrous. When the postwar recession hit in 1920, Billy Durant lost everything: Chevrolet, General Motors, the whole works. Undaunted, he would come back, of course, with Durant Motors, but the question now was what would happen to Chevrolet. Heading GM was Pierre du Pont who initially favored scuttling the car, but Alfred Sloan, Jr., the man du Pont brought in to make sense of the wreckage of Durant's empire, talked him out of it. Instead of eliminating Chevrolet, Sloan eliminated most of the Durant men in the organization and replaced them with his own people: K.W. Zimmerscheid as Chevrolet general manager and president, O.E. Hunt (formerly of Packard and Mercer) as chief engineer. And recognizing that tackling Henry Ford head-on was ludicrous ("suicidal," Sloan said), the decision was made to create a price class of its own for the Chevrolet, low but not the lowest, a step up in dollars but a step up also in refinement and creature comforts which those dollars bought and which the Model T didn't have. Billy Durant himself had moved the Chevrolet toward this concept, but hadn't followed through. Sloan would — and it worked beautifully, though not immediately. First there was the misstep of the copper-cooled Chevrolet. It was an interesting idea; its engine, at 135 cubic inches, was the smallest in Chevrolet history but it promised fewer parts, less weight, lower cost and higher performance than a water-cooled unit; air cooling was certainly something the Model T didn't have, and the promotional potential for the car looked terrific. Unfortunately, the copper-cooled Chevrolet was terrible. Some 759 of the cars were built, 239 of which were scrapped before ever leaving the factory. Of the cars dispatched to dealers, in June 1923 the company asked for every one of them back, in the first massive recall in Chevrolet history. Fortunately, there had been another Chevrolet to sell that year called Superior, successor to the Four-Ninety, the Model FB being dropped because it encroached on Olds and Oakland territory which was a market area in which Sloan didn't want the Chevrolet anyway. Meanwhile, Zimmerscheid, who had suffered a nervous breakdown during the copper-cooled fiasco, elected to retire — and on January 15th, 1924, Danish-born William S. Knudsen, Henry Ford's former production manager, became Chevrolet's president and general manager. "I vant vun for vun," he said at a dealer meeting in Chicago. That would take a while, but unquestionably the Chevrolet was making inroads into Model T territory. In 1924 Ford outsold Chevrolet by more than eight to one, in 1925 four to one, in 1926 less than three to one. Among the reasons for this was the, literally, superior Superior beginning in 1925 when the "infamous rear end," as Sloan called it — or the "Chevrolet hum" as had been the nickname for the noise made by the car's bevel gear rear axle since the first Four-Ninety days — was at last eliminated. Chevy's new rear axle was a one-piece banjo type with the entire differential mounted in a carrier which included the torque tube. Also new for '25 was variety of colors: Chevrolet was the first low-priced car to go Duco. And the car's standard transmission, sported since the beginning, was by now an even greater plus in the marketplace, since the jokes about the Model T's planetary were no longer as funny as they used to be. In 1927 Knudsen went all out: "The Most Beautiful Chevrolet in Chevrolet History" read the ads. The bodies of the new Capitol series had a double belt, full crown fenders, bullet-shaped headlamps, and the $715 sport cabriolet was America's first low-priced car with a rumble seat. In 1927 Chevrolet built over 1.7 million cars. For the first time since 1906 a car other than a Ford was number one in the industry. But Ford had virtually given away the number one spot in 1927 by shutting down his factory for six months, and ensuing production delays with the new Model A Ford would give Chevrolet easy victory in 1928 too. Thereafter the top spot would have to be earned. Like the new Model A, the new National series Chevrolet for '28 had four-wheel brakes. But the all-new Chevrolet for '29 had something the Ford didn't have: two more cylinders. The Cast Iron Wonder had arrived, Chevy now had a six for the price of a four, and a sturdy overhead valve engine that would endure into the early Fifties. The new cars were called International, appropriately since their body styling had the Continental flair that Harley Earl of GM's Art and Colour Department was trying to introduce to all corporation cars. Nonetheless, Ford, having sorted out the Model A production problems was now in full swing and delivering cars to the tens of thousands of people who had never driven anything else but a Ford and who had been desperately waiting for a new one since the T assembly line shutdown. Ford won the sales race in 1929 and in 1930, when the Chevrolet was called the Universal. In 1931 Chevy had it back with the Independence series, and retained the top spot in 1932 when Ford went to a V-8, which Chevy countered with the Confederate series offering synchromesh, free-wheeling, four-point rubber engine mounts, downdraft carburetion and further engine tweaks to get 60 hp out of the Cast Iron Wonder, only five less than Ford's V-8. With the Great Depression in full cry, Chevrolet

ushered in a cheaper six called the Standard in '33, which made a Master of the old six — and first place again in the industry. In 1933 the cast of characters in the Chevrolet management team changed, as the corporation moved top men around to troublespots within the GM family. William Knudsen was appointed executive vice-president for General Motors, his place at Chevrolet taken by his understudy of many years, Marvin Coyle. Harry Klingler, the super sales manager of Chevrolet since 1929, moved over to help troubled Pontiac, his place taken by the aptly named William Holler, who was a super salesman too. Only chief engineer Jim Crawford (who had replaced O.E. Hunt in 1929) remained at Chevy, and he begged Knudsen to do what he could to get Knee Action for Chevrolet for '34, initial thought having been that it should be reserved for the top-of-the-line GM cars. Knudsen won the argument, a good thing too, since Plymouth also went i.f.s. in '34. Ford stuck to transverse springs — and Chevy won the sales race again. Chevy lost in '35, partly because of a labor strike, partly because the new Ford V-8 had pizzazz and was advertising 90 hp, as opposed to the 80 of Chevy's Blue Flame six (it had been called the Blue Streak in '34 and there was no explicable reason for the name change to Blue Flame, though probably both designations were coined by Chevrolet P.R. in hopes that people would start using them instead of Stovebolt Six, which Chevrolet's venerable engine was nicknamed). Henry Ford helped Chevrolet regain the top spot in '36 by offering nothing new, which made Chevy's introduction of hydraulic brakes (Ford wouldn't have them until '39) something to shout about. But the 1937 Chevrolet gave William Holler even more crowing opportunity, because the car was all-new, with a more compact and powerful (85 hp) version of the Cast Iron Wonder, a stiffer box-girder frame and hypoid rear axle. The 15,000,000th Chevrolet was built in 1939; in 1940 a General Motors dealer from Argentina, Juan Manuel Fangio, began his remarkable racing career behind the wheel of a Chevrolet Master 85 which he drove to victory in the 5900-mile Buenos Aires-Lima-Buenos Aires race at an average of 53.6 mph. From 1937 Chevrolet had remained solidly in first place in the industry, a position it would not relinquish for the remainder of the years before America's entrance into World War II brought a halt to automobile production. Postwar, Chevrolet's status as number one — indeed as the best-selling car in the world — would become a virtual tradition.

Chevrolet Data Compilation by M.C. "Pinky" Randall

1912

CHEVROLET — CLASSIC SIX — SERIES C — SIX: The first Chevrolet bore a resemblance to the Republic Four, but was primarily an all-new automobile. Only one model — the Classic Six touring car — was available. It was built on a 120 inch wheelbase chassis. Features included ignition by dual system and dry cells, an English Air starter, dro-forged "I" front axle, full-floating rear axle and cone clutch. The springs were semi-elliptic up front and three-quarter platform in the rear. The steering gear was of the worm and gear type. The body, frame and wheels were finished in Chevrolet Blue-Black. The fenders, splash aprons and hood were black. A light gray stripe decorated the body and wheels. A German silver radiator bore the Chevrolet name in script. Standard equipment included a top, top boat, windshield, speedometer, electric speedometer light, self starter, demountable rims, extra tire holders, electric lights, gas gauge, two gallon auxiliary oil tank, 20 gallon gas tank and running board mounted tool kit.

1912 Chevrolet, Classic Six, touring, OCW

I.D. DATA: Serial numbers were not used.

Model No.	Body Type & Seating	Price	Weight	Prod. Total
C	4-dr. Tr.-5P	2250	NA	2999

ENGINE: T-head. Twin cam. Six (Cast in three banks of two). Cast iron block. B & S: 3-9/16 x 5 in. Disp.: 299 cu. in. Brake H.P.: 40. Net H.P.: 30 NACC. Main bearings: Three. Valve lifters: Solid.

CHASSIS: W.B.: 120 in. Frt/Rear Tread: 56/56 in. Tires: 35 x 4.5.

TECHNICAL: Rear axle mounted selective sliding transmission. Speeds: 3F/1R. Floor-mounted gearshift controls. Cone type clutch. Full-floating rear axle. Internal expanding rear brakes. Wood spoke artillery wheels.

OPTIONS: Front bumper, Motometer. Spare tire(s). 60 in. Southern tread. OSRV mirror. Running board luggage gate. Whitewall tires.

HISTORICAL: Introduced Nov., 1911. Calendar year production: 2,999. Innovations: First car to bear Chevrolet nameplate. Chevrolet Motor Company was incorporated Nov. 3, 1911.

1912 Classic Series, 6-cyl.	FP	5	4	3	2	1
Tr	2150	4650	9300	15,500	21,700	31,000

1913

1913 Chevrolet, Classic Six, touring, OCW

CHEVROLET — CLASSIC SIX — SERIES C — SIX: The 1913 Classic Six was virtually unchanged from the original, except for the design of the windshield. The method of mounting the windshield was now to bolt it to a swept back cowl, instead of directly to the dashboard. Also, the braces ran from the dash to the center hinges of the windshield frame. There is no record of exactly when the change took place — it may have been phased into production in late 1912. Thus, the later design cannot be used to date a car, but all 1913 models have swept back cowls. Colors and equipment were as in 1912.

I.D. DATA: Serial numbers were not used. Engine numbers identified the cars. Numbers are not available.

Model No.	Body Type & Seating	Price	Weight	Prod. Total
C	4-dr. Tr.-5P	2500	NA	5987

ENGINE: T-head. Twin cam. Six (Cast in three banks of two). Cast iron block. B & S: 3-9/16 x 5 in. Disp.: 299 cu. in. Brake H.P.: 40. Net H.P.: 30 NACC. Main bearings: Three. Valve lifters: Solid. Carb.: Stromberg (exhaust heated type).

CHASSIS: W.B.: 120 in.

TECHNICAL: Rear axle mounted selective sliding transmission. Speeds: 3F/1R. Floor-mounted gearshift controls. Cone type clutch. Full-floating rear axle. Internal expanding rear wheel brakes.

OPTIONS: Front bumper. Motormeter. Spare tire(s). 60 in. Southern tread. Rearview mirror. Running board luggage gate. Whitewall tires.

HISTORICAL: Introduced: Late 1912. Calendar year production: 5,987. Innovations: New windshield mounting and bracing system. W.C. Durant merged the Little Motor Car Company with Chevrolet in 1913. He gave the Chevrolet name to the Little car and moved the Detroit plant to his Flint Wagon Works. A second assembly plant was leased in New York City. The Chevrolet "Bow-Tie" trademark was used for the first time this year, on all Light Six models.

1913 Classic Series, 6-cyl.						
Tr	2500	4300	8550	14,250	19,950	28,500

1914

CHEVROLET — SERIES H — FOUR: The all-new 1914 H Series came in two body styles called the "Royal Mail" roadster and "Baby Grand" touring. (These names would be used on Chevrolet F, FA and FB models built through 1922.) Early versions had a flat wooden dash. This was replaced in mid-year with a streamlined, all-metal dash and cowl. The folding windshield was braced to the cowl. The touring had a two-man top and came in Chevrolet gray or Plum color finish with black chassis and gray wheels. The roadster was finished only in Chevrolet gray with black chassis and gray wheels. The Royal Mail had a flat rear deck. "Standard" equipment included top, curtains, windshield, speedometer, horn, spare tire and complete tool kit. Early Royal Mails had 30 x 3-1/2 clincher type tires.

1914 Chevrolet, roadster, OCW

CHEVROLET — LIGHT SIX — SERIES L — SIX: Available only as a touring car, the new Light Six came in Chevrolet blue or Gun metal gray. The chassis and wheels were blue. Standard equipment included Mohair top, top boot, side curtains, ventilating windshield, foot rail, robe rail, speedometer, electric horn, demountable rims, spare tire carrier on rear, (with extra rim), two double bulb electric headlamps, electric taillamp, Auto-Lite starter, LBA battery and complete tool kit.

CHEVROLET — CLASSIC SIX — SERIES C — SIX: This large touring car was in the last season. The Chevrolet name appeared in script on the front. The radiator shell and Chevrolet nameplate were silver. The finish color was a dark (almost black) color called Chevrolet blue. It was used on the body, frame and wheels. The fenders and splash aprons and hood black. Light gray striping was seen onthe body and wheels. Standard equipment included a top, boot, windshield, speedometer, electric lights, self-starter, demountable rims, extra tire holders, electric lights and gas gauge. A two gallon auxiliary oil tank was under the car. Side curtains stored in a compartment under the rear seat. Tools were stored in a box located under the runningboard, which was integral with it. There was a console-like storage fixture betwee the front seats.

I.D. DATA: [Series H] Serial numbers were not used. Engine numbers identified the cars. Starting: 1. Ending: 6243. [Series L] Serial numbers were not used. Engine numbers identified the cars. Starting: 1. Ending: 6243. [Series C] Serial numbers were not used. Engine numbers identified the cars. Engine numbers are not available.

Model No.	Body Type & Seating	Price	Weight	Prod. Total
H-2	2-dr. Rds.-2P	750	1975	Note 3
H-4	4-dr. Tr.-5P	875	2500	Note 3
L	4-dr. Tr.-5P	1475	3050	Note 3
C	4-dr Tr.-5P	2500	3750	Note 3

Note 1: Above price is for cars with Presto-Lite lights and magneto. With an Auto-Lite system the roadster was $875 and the touring was $1000.
Note 2: With Presto-Light lighting and magneto the price was $125 higher.
Note 3: Total production was 5,005 Chevrolets of all models.

ENGINE: [Model H] Engine OHV. Inline. (Casten block). Four cylinder. Cast iron block. B & S: 3-11/16 x 4 in. Disp.: 171 cu. in. Brake H.P.: 24. Net H.P.: 21.75 NACC. Main bearings: Three. Valve lifters: Solid. Carb.: Zenith two-jet. [Model L] Engine: L-head. Inline. (Cast in blocks of three). Six. ast iron block. B & S: 3-5/16 x 5-1/4 in. Disp.: 271 cu. in. Brake H.P.: 35. Net H.P. 26 NACC. Main bearings: Three. Valve lifters: Solid. Carb.: Zenith two-jet. [Model C] Engine T-head. Twin cam. Inline. Six (cast in three banks of two). Cast iron block. B & S: 3-9/16 x 5 in. Disp.: 299 cu. in. Brake H.P.: 40. Net H.P.: 30 NACC. Main bearings: Three. Valve lifters: Solid. Carb.: Stromberg (exhaust heated type).

CHASSIS: [Series H] W.B.: 104 in. Frt/Rear Tread: 56/56 in. Tires: 32 x 3.5. [Series L] W.B.: 112 in. Frt/Rear Tread: 56/56 in. Tires: 34 x 4. [Series C] W.B.: 120 in. Frt/Rear Tread: 56/56 in. Tires: 35 x 4.5. A special 60 in. thread for use on roads in the South was available.

TECHNICAL: Selective sliding (mounted on rear axle on Light/Classic sixes). Speeds: 3F/1R. Floor-mounted gearshift controls. Cone type clutch. [Model C] full-floating. Rear axle: [Model L] three-quarter floating. [Model H] semi-floating. [Classic Six] Internal expanding rear wheel brakes. [Others] External contracting rear wheel brakes. Wood spoke artillery wheels. Drivetrain options: Free-wheeling. Vacuum clutch. Hill-holder. Automatic transmission. Overdrive.

OPTIONS: Bumper front. Motometer. Auto-Lite electrical system. Spare tire(s). 60-in. Southern tread. Rearview mirror. Runningboard luggage gate. Houk wire wheels on "H" series.

HISTORICAL: Introduced: Late 1913. Calendar year production: (All) 5,005. Innovations: (H) First Chevrolet ohv four-cylinder engine. (L) only L-head Chevrolet ever built. Large 112 inch wheelbase. (also used on 1917-19 V-8). Gray & Davis electric starter. Sims ignition. Longest wheel base in Chevrolet history (also used on 1917-19 V-8). Louis Chevrolet leaves company over dispute with W.C. Durant. In June 1914 the Maxwell Motor Company's Tarrytown, N.Y. plant was purchased by Chevrolet. A new sales office was set up in Oakland, Calif.

1914 Chevrolet, touring, OCW

1914
Series H2 & H4, 4-cyl.

	FP	5	4	3	2	1
Rds	750	2300	5400	9000	12,600	18,000
Tr	875	2600	5500	9250	12,950	18,500
Series C, 6-cyl.						
Tr	2500	3300	6600	11,000	15,400	22,000
Series L, 6-cyl.						
Tr	1475	3150	6300	10,500	14,700	21,000

1915

1915 Chevrolet, roadster, HAC

CHEVROLET — SERIES H — FOUR: The 1915 Chevrolet fours had the same general appearance as 1914 editions, but the wheelbase grew to 106 in. Another change was the use of concealed door hinges. Larger tires with demountable rims were a new feature. The windshield cowl braces were removed. A starter became standard equipment. The diameter of the steering wheel went up to 17 inches. A new "Amesbury Special" roadster was introduced. It had the racy lines of an imported car and an exposed wooden dash board. A lockable rear deck was featured. The one piece windshield fitted behind the seat. Standard on all models were the top, top hood, windshield, speedometer and demountable rims.

CHEVROLET — SERIES L — SIX: The Light Six, Model L, was the only Chevrolet ever to use an L-head engine. It came only as a touring car available in Chevrolet blue or Gun metal gray. The chassis and wheels were blue. Standard equipment included Mohair top, cover, side curtains, ventilating windshield, foot rail, robe rail, speedometer, electric horn, demountable rims, spare tire carrier on rear, extra rim, two double-bulb electric headlamps, electric taillamp, Auto-Lite starter, LBA battery and complete tool equipment.

I.D. DATA: [Series H] Serial numbers were not used. Engine numbers located on flywheel and on the left front engine mount. Starting: 6244. Ending: 13000. [Series L] Serial numbers ran from 501 to 1000.

Model No.	Body Type & Seating	Price	Weight	Prod. Total
H-2	2-dr. Rds.-2P	750	2000	Note 1
H-4	4-dr. Tr.-5P	850	2500	Note 1
H-3	2-dr. Spl. Rds.-2P	985	2100	Note 1

Note 1: Total production for calendar 1915 was 13,605 Chevrolets including 313 cars built in Canada.
Note 2: Model H-2 also called "Royal Mail"; Model H-4 also called "Baby Grand"; Model H-3 also called "Amesbury Special".

L	4-dr. Tr.-5P	1475	3050	1000

ENGINE: [Series H] OHV. Inline. Four. Cast iron block. B & S: 3-11/16 x 4 in. Disp.: 171 cu. in. Brake H.P.: 24. Net H.P.: 21.75 N.A.C.C.: Main bearings: Three. Valve lifters: Solid. Carb.: Zenith two-jet. [Series L] L-head. Inline (Three banks of two each). Six. Cast iron block. B & S: 3-5/16 x 5-1/4 in. Disp.: 271 cu. in. Brake H.P.: 30. Net H.P.: 26.3. Main bearings: Three. Valve lifters: Solid. Carb.: Zenith double-jet.

CHASSIS: [Series H] W.B.: 106 in. Frt/Rear Tread: 56/56 in. Tires: 32 x 3.5. [Series L] W.B.: 112 in. Frt/Rear Tread: 56/56 in. Tires: 34 x 4.

TECHNICAL: Selective Sliding Gear transmission. Speeds: 3F/1R. Floor-mounted gearshift controls. Cone type clutch. Rear axles: (H) semi-floating; (L) three-quarter floating. Contracting and expanding rear wheel brakes. Wood artillery spoke wheels. Transaxle on Series L six.

OPTIONS: Front bumper. Spare tire. OSRV mirror. Houk quick-detachable wire wheels ($125). Auto lite electric system, on H ($60); on L ($125). Motometer. "Fat Man" steering wheel. Southern gauge (60 in. track).

HISTORICAL: Introduced: 1915 (490 introduced in Jan. 1915 and placed on sale June 1, 1915). Innovations: (H) Larger wheelbase. Starter option mounted on flywheel at rear of engine. New "Amesbury Special" roadster. Electric lights became standard equipment. Calendar year production: 13,605. Model year production: (H) 13,600; (L) 1000; (Total) 14,600.
    Chevrolet sales offices opened in Kansas City, Mo. and Atlanta, Ga. New factories established in St. Louis, Mo. and Oshawa, Canada. Chevrolet also licensed Gardner Buggy Co. to assemble cars in St. Louis. Within 17 days of putting the new 490 on the market, Chevrolet Motor Co. had accepted 46,611 orders for the car valued at $23,329,390.

1915
Series H2 & H4, 4-cyl.

	FP	5	4	3	2	1
Rds	750	1750	4800	8000	11,200	16,000
Tr	875	2300	5400	9000	12,600	18,000
Series H3, 4-cyl.						
2P Rds	985	2800	5700	9500	13,300	19,000
Series L, 6-cyl.						
Tr	1425	3000	6000	10,000	14,000	20,000

1916

1916 Chevrolet, Series Four-Ninety, touring, HAC

CHEVROLET — SERIES 490 — FOUR: Named after the price of the two basic models, the Chevrolet 490 series was new for 1916. Neither the touring or the roadster had a left front door. A vertical windshield was one styling trait. Front fenders followed a straight line from behind the center of the front wheels to the front of the running boards and no splash guards were used. Standard equipment included a top, top hood and the windshield. The rear curtain in the top hood had a single celluloid window. With an electric lighting and starting system the price was $550. Cars so equipped had a Connecticut automatic ignition system instead of a magneto.

CHEVROLET — SERIES H — FOUR: The Model H Chevrolet was about the same as in 1915. Both the flat deck "Royal Mail" and the "Baby Grand" touring car were carried over. The Model H-2-1/2 Special Roadster replaced the "Amesbury Special." It had a conventional rear deck and Brewster Green finish. The other cars were finished in French gray with green patent leather upholstery. Standard equipment included a top, top hood, windshield, speedometer, ammeter and demountable rims on all models.

I.D. DATA: Serial numbers were not used on 1916 models in the 490 series. Series H Serial numbers were not used. Engine numbers located on the flywheel. Engine numbers for 1916 were 13001 to 29390.

Model No.	Body Type & Seating	Price	Weight	Prod. Total
490	1-dr. Rds.-2P	490	1820	Note 1
490	3-dr. Tr.-5P	490	1910	Note 1
H-2	2-dr. Rds.-2P	720	2000	Note 1
H-4	4-dr. Rds.-5P	720	2500	Note 1
H-2-1/2	2-dr. Spl. Rds.-2P	750	2100	Note 1

Note 1: Total production was 70,701 Chevrolets including 7,721 cars made in Canada.
Note 2: Model H-2 also called "Royal Mail"; Model H-4 also called "Baby Grand"; Model H-2-1/2 also called "Royal Mail" Turtledeck Roadster.

ENGINE: OHV. Inline. Four. Cast iron block. B & S: 3-11/16 x 4 in. Disp.: 171 cu. in. Brake H.P.: 24. 21.74 N.A.C.C. Main bearings: Three. Valve lifters: Solid. Carb.: Zenith one-inch double-jet.

CHASSIS: [Series 490] W.B.: 102 in. Frt/Rear Tread: 56/56 in. Tires: (frt.) 30 x 3; (rear) 30 x 3.5. [Series H] W.B.: 106 in. Frt/Rear Tread: 56/56 in. Tires: 32 x 3.5.

TECHNICAL: Selective sliding transmission. Speeds: 3F/1R. Floor-mounted gearshift controls. Cone type clutch. Rear axles: (490) three-quarter floating; (H) semi-floating. External contracting rear wheel brakes. Wood spoke artillery wheels.

OPTIONS: Front bumper. Spare tire. OSRV mirror. Motometer. Southern gauge (60 in track). (H) A Simms high tension magneto was standard equipment. For $125 extra buyers could order the Auto-Lite starting, generating and lighting system with battery. Cars so equipped had a Connecticut coil and distributor in place of magneto. (490) similar electrical equipment was $60 extra. "Fat Man" steering wheel.

HISTORICAL: Introduced during late 1915. Calendar year production: 62,898. Model year production: (490) 18,000 approximate; (H) 52,000 approximate. Innovations: (490) New 490 Series designed as low cost auto to compete with Model T Ford. (H) Open Hotchkiss drive used on cars built at Tarrytown. Radius rods for improved rear axle alignment.
Chevrolet was now operating plants in Ft. Worth, Tex. and Bay Cities, Mich. The Warner Gear factory in Toledo, Ohio was purchased as a Chevrolet manufacturing plant. Chevrolet also opened the auto industry's first West Coast plant in Oakland, Calif. First closed car bodies built by Chevrolet this year. Production hits 70,701 unit mark.

1916
Series 490, 4-cyl.

	FP	5	4	3	2	1
Tr	490	2000	5100	8500	11,900	17,000
Series H2, 4-cyl.						
Rds	720	1800	4950	8250	11,550	16,500
Torp Rds	750	2300	5400	9000	12,600	18,000
Series H4, 4-cyl.						
Tr	750	2800	5700	9500	13,300	19,000

1917

1917 Chevrolet, touring, HAC

CHEVROLET — SERIES 490 — EIGHT: For 1917 the 490 was changed little in appearance. A left front door was added. Electric lamps became standard equipment. A new model called the All-Season touring car had a permanent hardtop replacing the folding top. Flexible sliding windows disappeared into the roof and removable side sections were used. The top even had a dome lamp. The interior was trimmed in cloth upholstery. All models were finished in black. A self-starter was now standard equipment. New touring car body improvements included foot and robe rails, a tilted windshield, a one-man top with curtains of the improved type, protection flaps on the door tops, door storage pockets, a kickpad at the rear of the front seat and demountable rims.

CHEVROLET — SERIES F — FOUR: A new Series F replaced the Series H for the 1917 season. It had a longer wheelbase. Two models were offered. The "Royal Mail" was the roadster and the "Baby Grand" was the touring car. On both models the front fenders followed a straight line from just behind the center of the front wheels to the running board. A vertical, non-folding windshield was standard equipment. An Auto-Lite generator, starter and lighting system with Remy ignition was standard.

I.D. DATA: [Series 490] Serial number system same as on Model F except 490s were also built in St. Louis (code 3), Oakland (code 6) and Ft. Worth (code 7) plants. Serial numbers not used prior to July 1. Starting: 1-8972. Ending: 1-37468. Also: 2-22507 to 2-36488; 3-8512 to 3-15000; 6-5977 to

6-10089; 7-3001 to 7-5842 and 9-151 to 9-1935. Engine numbers located on flywheel. Engine numbers not available. [Series F] Serial number located on dashboard nameplate. Factory codes: 1 is Flint; 2 is Tarrytown and 9 is Oshawa (Canada). Starting: 1-1222. Ending: 1-3430. Also: 2-2894 to 2-4113 and 9-466 to 9-532. Engine numbers located on flywheel. Engine numbers not availble.

Model No.	Body Type & Seating	Price	Weight	Prod. Total
490	2-dr. Rds.-2P	535	1820	Note 1
490	4-dr. Tr.-5P	550	1890	Note 1
490	4-dr. A-Str.-5P	625	NA	Note 1
F-2	2-dr. Rds.-2P	800	2640	Note 1
F-5	4-dr. Tr.-5P	800	2745	Note 1

Note 1: Total production was 125,882 Chevrolets including 14,005 cars built in Canada.
Note 2: Price of both models increased to $875 during the year.

ENGINE: [Series 490] OHV. Inline. Four. Cast iron block. B & S: 3-11/16 x 4 in. Disp.: 171 cu. in. Brake H.P.: 24. Net H.P.: 21.75 N.A.C.C. Main bearings: Three. Valve lifters: Solid.. Carb.: Zenith double-jet. [Series F] OHV. Inline. Four. Cast iron block. B & S: 3-11/16 x 4 in. Disp.: 171 cu. in. Brake H.P.: 24. Net H.P.: 21.75 N.A.C.C. Main bearings: Three. Valve lifters: Solid. Carb.: Zenith double-jet.

CHASSIS: [Series 490] W.B.: 108 in. Frt/Rear Tread: 56/56 in. Tires: 32 x 3-1/2. [Series F] W.B.: 102 in. Frt/Rear Tread: 56/56 in. Tires: (frt.) 30 x 3; (rear) 30 x 3.5.

TECHNICAL: Selective sliding. Speeds: 3F/1R. Floor-mounted gearshift controls. Cone type clutch. Three-quarter floating rear axle. Overall ratio: 3.5:1. External contracting rear wheel brakes. Artillery spoke wood wheels.

OPTIONS: Self-starter and electric lights ($60). Motometer. OSRV mirror. Spare tire. Demountable rims (on roadster). Southern gauge (60 in. track). "Fat Man" steering wheel. Front bumper.

HISTORICAL: Introduced 1917. Innovations: (490) Plunger type oil pump. Open valve train. Cone type clutch. Ball bearing front wheels. Quarter elliptic springs. Duplex type front spring deleted. New All-Season car. (F) Larger wheelbase. Calendar year production: 110,839. Model year production: (490) 57,692; (F) 3,493; (Total) 61,185. Company President: William C. Durant.
Early in 1917 the Monroe Motor Co. was sold to William Small of Flint, Mich. Thereafter, this brand was no longer sold by Chevrolet dealers. Also on the business front, the Mason Motor Co., of Flint, merged with Chevrolet to build engines. Chevrolet was not yet part of General Motors. Chevrolet introduced its V-8 Model D in 1917. Specifications for this model are given in the 1918 Chapter.

1917
Series F2 & F5, 4-cyl.

	FP	5	4	3	2	1
Rds	875	2000	5100	8500	11,900	17,000
Tr	875	2300	5400	9000	12,600	18,000
Series 490, 4-cyl.						
Rds	535	1750	4800	8000	11,200	16,000
Tr	550	1750	4800	8000	11,200	16,000
HdTp Tr	625	2000	5100	8500	11,900	17,000
Series D2 & D5, V-8						
Rds	1385	3000	6000	10,000	14,000	20,000
Tr	1385	3150	6300	10,500	14,700	21,000

1918

1918 Chevrolet, center-door sedan, OCW

CHEVROLET — SERIES 490 — FOUR: New models this year were All-Season coupes and sedans with removable center posts. Open cars had a windshield with a 15° backwards slant. Wheel felloes were square and demountable rims were standardized. Closed cars featured a rear mounted gas tank. Standard equipment included a top, top hood, windshield, speedometer, ammeter, tire pump, electric horn and demountable rims. The bodies were built by Ionia Body Co. and finished by Chevrolet.

CHEVROLET — SERIES FA — FOUR: The FA series replaced the F. It was much the same as far as appearance. Open cars had a windshield with a 15° slant. The sedan had removable roof center posts. Standard equipment included top, top hood, windshield, speedometer, ammeter, tire pump, electric horn and demountable rims.

CHEVROLET — SERIES D — V-8: The Chevrolet V-8 Series D came in two models. The D-4 was a four-passenger roadster, the D-5 a five-passenger touring. Both were finished in Chevrolet green and had French-pleated leather upholstery. A 20-gallon gas tank was mounted at the rear of the frame. The touring was a four-door model. The roadster was actually more of a two-door "dual-cowl" touring car. Rear slanting hood louvers were used. The body was described as "a delight to the eye" and "a series of curves that blend harmoniously." All visible woodwork was of genuine mahogany and metal parts were nickle. The body foundation was of pressed steel. Standard equipment included a one-man waterproof top with side curtains and Bair brackets; windshield; sixteen candle power headlights; speedometer; demountable rims with extra rim; tire carrier; license holder and tools. Experts believe that production started late in 1917, and that the car was discontinued late in 1918. This was most likely the only full year for the model. To conserve space we are listing specifications in this book under 1918 only, although the Master Price Lists from Chevrolet include the model in 1917, 1918 and 1919. Production breakdown for those three years are indicated below..

I.D. DATA: [Series 490] Serial number located on dash nameplate. Factory codes were: 1 is Flint; 2 is Tarrytown; 3 is St. Louis; 6 is Oakland; 7 is Ft. Worth and 9 is Oshawa (Canada). Starting: 1-37469. Ending: 1-59674. Also: 2-36489 to 2-59958; 3-15001 to 3-24000; 6-10090 to 6-20097; 7-5843 to 7-15110 and 9-1936 to 9-1935. Engine numbers located on flywheel. Engine numbers not available. [Series FA] Serial number system same as on 490. Starting: 1-3431. Ending: 1-10241. Also: 2-4114 to 2-7432 and 9-772 to 9-2047. Engine numbers located on flywheel. Engine numbers not available. [Series D] Serial number system same as on 490 and FB. Starting: (1917) 1-8; (1918) 1-242. Ending: (1917) 1-241; (1918) 1-1557. Also: (1917) 2-2894 to 2-4112; (1918) 2-4113 to 2-7437 and (1917) 9-466 to 9-532; (1918) 9-533 to 9-727.

Model No.	Body Type & Seating	Price	Weight	Prod. Total
490	4-dr. Tr.-5P	685	1890	Note 1
490	2-dr. Rds.-2P	660	1820	Note 1
490	2-dr. A/W Cpe.-3P	1060	2040	Note 1
490	3-dr. A/W Sed.-4P	1060	2160	Note 1
FA-2	2-dr. Rds.-2P	935	2640	Note 1
FA-5	3-dr. Tr.-5P	935	2680	Note 1
FA-4	2-dr. A/W Sed.-4P	1475	2950	Note 1
D-4	2-dr. Rds.-4P	1550	3150	Note 1
D-5	4-dr. Tr.-5P	1550	3200	Note 1

Note 1: Total production of the Chevrolet 490 was 95,660 cars including 13,840 made in Canada. Total production of the Series D (V-8) was 511 in 1917; 2,199 in 1918 and 71 in 1919.
Note 2: Prices in 1917 were $1385 for both models.

1918 Chevrolet, Series 490, touring, JAC

ENGINE: [Series 490] OHV. Inline. Four. Cast iron block. B & S: 3-11/16 x 4 in. Disp.: 171 cu. in. Brake H.P.: 26 @ 1800 R.P.M. Net H.P.: 21.75 N.A.C.C. Main bearings: Three. Valve lifters: Solid. Carb.: 1V. [Series FA] OHV. Inline. Four. Cast iron block. B & S: 3-11/16 x 5-1/4 in. Disp.: 224. Brake H.P.: 37 @ 2000 R.P.M. Net H.P.: 21.75 N.A.C.C. Three main bearings. Solid valve lifters. Carb.: 1V. [Series D] 90# V-Block. OHV. Eight. Cast iron block. B & S: 3-3/8 x 4 in. Disp.: 288 cu. in. Net H.P.: 36 N.A.C.C. Main bearings: Three. Valve lifters: Solid. Carb.: Zenith double-jet.

CHASSIS: [Series 490] W.B.: 102 in. Frt/Rear Tread: 56/56 in. Tires: 30 x 3.5. [Series FA] W.B.: 108 in. Frt/Rear Tread: 56/56 in. Tires: 33 x 4. [Series D] W.B.: 120 in. Tires: 34 x 4 (non-skid on rear).

TECHNICAL: Selective sliding transmission. Speeds: 3F/1R. Floor-mounted gear shift controls. Cone type clutch. Three-quarter rear axle. Overall ratio: (490) 3.63:1; (FB) 4.62:1; (D) 4.25:1. External contracting rear wheel brakes. Wood spoke wheels.

OPTIONS: Spare tire. Motometer. OSRV mirror (fender mount). "Fat Man" steering wheel. Sixty inch Southern gauge.

HISTORICAL: Introduced late 1917. Calendar year production: 80,434. Model year production: (490) 86,200; (FA) 11,403; (D) 4833. Innovations: (490) New water pump. New gear oil pump. Spur and gear steering with one piece main shaft. New oil pressure gauge. (FA) larger displacement engine. New water pumps. (D) All new V-8 (introduced in late 1917 as 1917 model).

Chevrolet joined GM in 1918. St. Louis assembly plant opens. Truck production started, Chevrolet headquarters still at 57th St. and Broadway in N.Y.C. Royal Mail and Baby Grand names dropped. Same style continue as roadster and touring in FA series.

1918
Series 490, 4-cyl.

	FP	5	4	3	2	1
Tr	685	2000	5100	8500	11,900	17,000
Rds	660	1750	4800	8000	11,200	16,000
Cpe	1060	750	1450	3300	4900	7000
Sed	1060	650	1250	2400	4200	6000
Series FA, 4-cyl.						
Rds	935	2000	5100	8500	11,900	17,000
Tr	935	2300	5400	9000	12,600	18,000
Sed	1475	750	1450	3300	4900	7000
Series D, V-8						
4P Rds	1550	3600	7200	12,000	16,800	24,000
Tr	1550	3750	7500	12,500	17,500	25,000

1919

1919 Chevrolet, touring, HAC

CHEVROLET — SERIES 490 — FOUR: Only a few minor changes were made in 1919 models. On open cars a Bair top saddle replaced the old-fashioned, bolt-on type. The spare tire carrier was now of three-quarter circle design with a lever. Fixed center posts and a full frame door were now used on the 490 coupe. Prices included top, top hood, windshield, speedometer, ammeter, tire pump, electric horn and demountable rims.

CHEVROLET — SERIES FB — FOUR: The first 1,514 Chevrolet sedans built used the body and all chassis sheet metal from the FA. Later sedans and all other body types were completely new for 1919. New front fender featured a stylish reverse curve. A new 110 inch wheelbase was used. The later sedans were 4-door models. The new FB coupe had fixed center posts and a full frame door. Prices included top, top hood, windshield, speedometer, ammeter, tire pump, electric horn and demountable rims.

I.D. DATA: [Series 490] Serial number located on dash nameplate. Factory codes: 1 is Flint; 2 is Tarrytown; 3 is St. Louis; 6 is Oakland; 7 is Ft. Worth and 9 is Oshawa (Canada). Starting: 1-59675. Ending: 1-92474. Also: 2-59959 to 2-90421; 3-24001 to 3-47100; 6-20098 to 6-36684; 7-15111 to 7-25429 and 9-14187 to 9-28153. Engine numbers located on flywheel. Engine numbers not available. [Series FB] Serial number system was same as on 490. Starting: 1-100. Ending: 1-9384. Also: 2-100 to 2-4738; 6-1001 to 6-1289 and 9-104 to 9-1335. Engine numbers located on flywheel. Engine numbers unknown.

Model No.	Body Type & Seating	Price	Weight	Prod. Total
490	2-dr. Rds.-2P	715	1820	Note 1
490	4-dr. Tr.-5P	735	1890	Note 1
490	4-dr. Sed.-4P	1185	2160	Note 1
490	2-dr. Cpe.-3P	1100	2040	Note 1
FB-20	2-dr. Rds.-2P	1110	2640	Note 1
FB-30	4-dr. Tr.-5P	1235	2880	Note 1
FB-50	2-dr. Cpe.-3P	1635	2820	Note 1
FB-40	4-dr. Sed.-4P	1685	2950	Note 1
FB-40	2-dr. Sed.-4P*	1685	2950	Note 1

Note 1: Total production of Chevrolets was 149,904 including 17,431 cars made in Canada.
Note 2: * This was the FB sedan using the old FA body with a center opening door on passenger side.

ENGINE: [Series 490] OHV. Inline. Four. Cast iron block. B & S: 3-11/16 x 4 in. Disp.: 171 cu. in. Brake H.P.: 26 @ 1800 R.P.M. Net H.P.: 21.75 N.A.C.C. Main bearings: Three. Valve lifters: Solid. Carb.: 1V. [Series FB] OHV. Inline. Four. Cast iron. B & S: 3-11/16 x 5-1/4 in. Disp.: 224 cu. in. Brake H.P.: 37 @ 2000 R.P.M. Net H.P.: 21.75. Main bearings: Three. Carb.: 1V.

CHASSIS: [Series 490] W.B.: 102 in. Frt/Rear Tread: 56/56 in. Tires: 30 x 3.5. [Series FB] W.B.: 110 in. Frt/Rear Tread: 56/56 in. Tires: 33 x 4.

TECHNICAL: Selective sliding. Speeds: 3F/1R. Floor-mounted gearshift controls. Cone type clutch. Three-quarter floating rear axle. Overall ratio: (490) 3.63:1; (FB) 4.62:1. External contracting two-wheel brakes. Artillery spoke wheels.

OPTIONS: OSRV mirror (fender mounted). Spare tire. Motometer. "Fat Man" steering wheel. Sixty inch Southern gauge.

HISTORICAL: Introduced late 1918. Calendar year production: 123,371. Model year production: [Series 490] 127,231; [Series FB] 14,516. Innovations: (490) Speedometer drive taken from universal joint. Four-button switch changed to lever type. Fixed center post coupe. (FB) completely new line introduced this year.
This was Chevrolet's first full year as part of General Motors Corp. Some sources show the Series D V-8 as a 1919 model, but there are no 1919 serial numbers for V-8s. Some 1918 models may have been sold as 1919s.

1919
Series 490, 4-cyl.

	FP	5	4	3	2	1
Rds	715	1400	4200	7000	9800	14,000
Tr	735	1550	4500	7500	10,500	15,000
Sed	1185	650	1250	2400	4200	6000
Cpe	1100	700	1350	2800	4550	6500
Series FB, 4-cyl.						
Rds	—	1750	4800	8000	11,200	16,000
Tr	1235	2000	5100	8500	11,900	17,000
Cpe	1635	825	1600	4000	5600	8000
2 dr Sed	1685	775	1500	3750	5250	7500
4 dr Sed	1685	750	1450	3300	4900	7000

1920

1920 Chevrolet, coupe, HAC

CHEVROLET — SERIES 490 — FOUR: Although automotive styling wasn't around in 1920, Chevrolet did make a change in the 490's appearance. It was done by replacing the old straight fenders with a reverse curve type. They also mounted the headlights on steel brackets and eliminated the tie-bar. New for open models was a top with two round windows in the rear.

CHEVROLET — SERIES FB — FOUR: Reverse curve front fenders were also used on the FB Series Chevrolets for 1920. Otherwise there was little change from first FB models of 1919.

I.D. DATA: [Series 490] Serial number located on nameplate on dash. Prefix indicates plant. 1 is Flint; 2 is Tarrytown; 3 is St. Louis; 6 is Oakland; 7 is Ft. worth and 9 is Oshawa (Canada). Starting: 1-92475. Ending: 1A-20160. Also: 2-90422 to 2A-23673; 3-47101 to 3A-70100; 6-36685 to 6A-51094; 7-25430 to 7A-34121; 9-28154 to 9-A40225. Engine numbers located on flywheel. Engine numbers not available. [Series FB] Serial number system same as on 490 Series. Starting: 1-9385. Ending: 1-20516. Also: 2-4739 to 2-10634; 3-54 to 3-1600; 6-1290 to 6-4990 and 9-1336 to 9-4604. Engine numbers located on flywheel. Engine numbers not available.

Series 490

Model No.	Body Type & Seating	Price	Weight	Prod. Total
490	2-dr. Rds.-2P	795	1820	Note 2
490	4-dr. Tr.-5P	810	1895	Note 2
490	4-dr. Sed.-5P	1285	2160	Note 2
490	2-dr. Cpe.-3P	1210	2040	Note 2

Note 1: Prices dropped about $100 during 1920 model year.

Model No. Series FB	Body Type & Seating	Price	Weight	Prod. Total
FB	2-dr. Rds.-2P	1270	2160	Note 2
FB	4-dr. Tr.-5P	1355	2800	Note 2
FB	4-dr. Sed.-5P	1885	2950	Note 2
FB	2-dr. Cpe.-3P	1855	2820	Note 2

Note 2: Total production was 150,226 Chevrolets including 18,847 cars made in Canada.
Note 3: Prices dropped $60-100 during 1921.

ENGINE: [Series 490] OHV. Inline. Four. Cast iron block. B & S: 3-11/16 x 4 in. Disp.: 171 cu. in. Brake H.P.: 26 @ 1800 R.P.M. Net H.P.: 21.75 N.A.C.C. Main bearings: Three. Valve lifters: Solid. Carb.: 1V. [Series FB] OHV. Inline. Four. Cast iron block. B & S: 3-11/16 x 5-1/4 in. Disp.: 224 cu. in. Brake H.P.: 37 @ 2000 R.P.M. Net H.P.: 21.75. Main bearings: Three. Valve lifters: Solid. Carb.: 1V.

CHASSIS: [Series 490] W.B.: 102. Tires: 30 x 3-1/2. [Series FB] W.B.: 110. Tires: 33 x 4.

TECHNICAL: Selective sliding. Speeds: 3F/1R. Floor-mounted gearshift controls. Cone type clutch. (490) two-piece rear axle. (FB) 3/4 floating rear axle. Overall ratio: (490) 3.63:1; (FB) 4.62:1. External contracting rear brakes. Wood spoke wheels.

OPTIONS: Front bumper. Rear bumper. Spare tire. Spare tire cover. Step plates. "Fat Man" steering wheel. Motometer. Cowl lights. Wind wings. OSRV mirror. Special paint.

HISTORICAL: Introduced: Jan. 1920. Model year production: (490) 129,106; (FB) 17,137; Total 146,243 approximate. Calendar year production: 121,908. Innovations: Gravity fuel feed on 490. Vacuum fuel feed on FB.
W.C. Durant leaves General Motors for second time. Karl W. Zimmerschield becomes president of Chevrolet.

1920
Series 490, 4-cyl.

	FP	5	4	3	2	1
Rds	795	1400	4200	7000	9800	14,000
Tr	810	1550	4500	7500	10,500	15,000
Sed	1285	775	1500	3750	5250	7500
Cpe	1210	825	1600	4000	5600	8000
Series FB, 4-cyl.						
Rds	1270	1750	4800	8000	11,200	16,000
Tr	1355	2000	5100	8500	11,900	17,000
Sed	1885	875	1700	4250	5900	8500
Cpe	1885	900	1900	4500	6300	9000

*NOTE: Factory prices reduced during the year due to economic depression.

	FP	5	4	3	2	1
Cpe	—	150	450	1000	1750	2500

1921

1921 Chevrolet, Series 490, sedan, HAC

CHEVROLET — SERIES 490 — FOUR: The 1921 Chevrolet 490 was virtually unchanged in appearance from last year. The passenger side door on the sedan was moved to a position in the center of the car. Larger size 31 x 4 tires were used on closed models only.

CHEVROLET — SERIES FB — FOUR: There were no basic changes in Series FB Chevrolets from 1920. The same four body styles remained in production.

I.D. DATA: [Series 490] Serial number located on nameplate on dash. Prefix indicates plant. 1A is Flint; 2A is Tarrytown; 3 is St. Louis; 6 is Oakland and 9 is Oshawa (Canada). Starting: 1A-20161. Ending: 1A-59938. Also: 2A-23674 to 2A-55239; 3-70101 to 3A-53241; 6-51095 to 6A-54958; 9-40226 to 9A-47848. Engine numbers on flywheel. Engine numbers not available. [Series FB] The serial number system was the same as on the 490 series. Starting: 1-20517. Ending: 1-24853. Also: 2-10635 to 2-15651; 3-1601 to 3-2316; 6-4991 to 6-6121; 9-4605 to 9-6436. Engine numbers located on flywheel. Engine numbers not available.

Series 490

Model No.	Body Type & Seating	Price	Weight	Prod. Total
490	Chassis	NA	NA	Note 2
490	2-dr. Rds.-2P	795	1820	Note 2
490	4-dr. Tr.-5P	820	1890	Note 2
490	2-dr. Cpe.-3P	1325	2040	Note 2
490	2-dr. Sed.-5P	1375	2160	Note 2

Note 1: During the year prices dropped to the 1922 factory prices.

Series FB

FB	2-dr. Rds.-2P	1320	2640	Note 2
FB	4-dr. Trs.-5P	1345	2780	Note 2
FB	2-dr. Cpe.-3P	2075	2820	Note 2
FB	2-dr. Sed.-5P	2075	2950	Note 2

Note 2: Total production was 76,370 Chevrolets including 8,187 cars made in Canada.

Note 3: Prices dropped about $500 in late 1921 due to recession.

ENGINE: [Series 490] OHV. Inline. Four. Cast iron block. B & S: 3-11/16 x4 in. Disp.: 171 cu. in. Brake H.P.: 26 @ 1800 R.P.M. N.A.C.C. H.P.: 21.75. Main bearings: Three. Valve lifters: Solid. Carb.: 1V. [Series FB] OHV. Inline. Four. Cast iron block. B & S: 3-11/16 x 5-1/4 in. Disp.: 224 cu. in. Brake H.P.: 37 @ 2000 R.P.M. N.A.C.C. H.P.: 21.75. Main bearings: Three. Valve lifters: Solid. Carb.: 1V.

CHASSIS: [Series 490] W.B.: 102 in. Tires: 30 x 3-1/2 (open); 31 x 4 (closed). [Series FB] W.B.: 110 in. Tires: 33 x 4.

TECHNICAL: Selective sliding transmission. Speeds: 3F/1R. Floor mounted gear shift controls. Cone clutch. Shaft drive (torque tube). Rear axle: (FB) 3/4-Floating; (490) 2-piece. Overall Ratio: (FB) 4.62:1; (490) 3.63:1. External contracting rear brakes. 12-spoke wood artillery wheels.

OPTIONS: Spare tire. Spare tire cover. Step plates. "Fat Man" steering wheel. Motometer. Cowl lights. Wind wings. OSRV mirror. Special paint.

HISTORICAL: Introduced Jan. 1921. Innovations: New center door sedan. Larger tires on 490 closed models. Calendar year production: 61,717. Model year production: (490) 117,827 approximate; (FB) 13,028 approximate.

A management survey recommended the discontinuance of Chevrolet production.

1921
Series 490, 4-cyl.

	FP	5	4	3	2	1
Rds	795	2300	5400	9000	12,600	18,000
Tr	820	2300	5400	9000	12,600	18,000
Cpe	1325	825	1600	4000	5600	8000
C-D Sed	1375	875	1700	4250	5900	8500

Series FB, 4-cyl.

	FP	5	4	3	2	1
Rds	1320	2300	5400	9000	12,600	18,000
Tr	1345	2800	5700	9500	13,300	19,000
Cpe	2075	875	1700	4250	5900	8500
4 dr Sed	2075	875	1700	4250	5900	8500

1922

1922 Chevrolet, sedan, OCW

CHEVROLET — SERIES 490 — FOUR: The appearance of 490 models stayed about the same. Steel wheel felloes were new. The sedan became a 4-door model. Gypsy style rear curtains were now seen on open cars. Also, the windshield was lower and a hand-operated emergency brake was used for the first time. A Utility Coupe was added to the line in March, 1922.

CHEVROLET — SERIES FB — FOUR: This was the final season for the FB Chevrolet. There were no basic styling changes. New features included steel felloe wheels, a 10 gallon gas tank, a shorter steering column and a 4-1/2 in. lower seat cushion. New 32 x 4 size tires were introduced during the year.

I.D. DATA: [Series 490] Serial number located on name plate on dash. Prefixes indicated plant. 1 is Flint; 2 is Tarrytown; 3 is St. Louis; 6 is Oakland and 9 is Oshawa (Canada). Starting: 1A-59939. Ending: 1A-92881. Also: 2A-55240 to 2A-88765. 3A-33242 to 3A-66294. 6A-54959 to 6A-72319. 9A-47849 to 9A-70543. Engine numbers on flywheel. Engine numbers not available. [Series FB] Serial number system same as on 490 Series. Starting: 1-24854. Ending: 1A-39542. Also: 2-15652 to 2A-30267; 3-2317 to 3A-30599; 6-6122 to 6A-30704; 9-6436 to 9A-7593. Engine numbers located on flywheel. Engine numbers not available.

Model No.	Body Type & Seating	Price	Weight	Prod. Total
490	Chassis	NA	1435	Note 1
490	2-dr. Rds.-2P	510	1725	Note 1
490	4-dr. Tr.-5P	525	1770	Note 1
490	2-dr. Utl. Cpe.-2P	850	1945	Note 1
490	2-dr. Cpe.-4P	680	2015	Note 1
490	4-dr. Sed.-5P	875	2150	Note 1
FB	2-dr. Rds.-2P	865	2310	Note 1
FB	4-dr. Tr.-5P	885	2595	Note 1
FB	2-dr. Cpe.-4P	1325	2735	Note 1
FB	2-dr. Sed.-4P	1395	2890	Note 1

Note 1: Total production was 243,479 Chevrolets including 19,895 cars made in Canada.

ENGINE: [Series 490] OHV. Inline. Four. Cast iron block. B & S: 3-11/16 x 4 in. Disp.: 171 cu. in. Brake H.P.: 26 @ 1800 R.P.M. Main bearings: Three. Valve lifters: Solid. Carb.: 1V. [Series FB] OHV. Inline. Four. C.I. Block. B & S: 3-11/16 x 5-1/4 in. Disp.: 224 cu. in. Brake H.P.: 37 @ 2000 R.P.M. N.A.C.C. Horsepower 21.75. Main bearings: Three. Valve lifters: Solid. Carb.: 1V.

1922 Chevrolet, touring, JAC

CHASSIS: [Series 490] W.B.: 102 in. Tires: 30 x 3-1/2 or 31 x 4. [Series FB] W.B.: 110 in. Tires: 32 x 4.

TECHNICAL: Selective sliding transmission. Speeds: 3F/1R. Floor mounted gear shift controls. Cone clutch. Shaft drive. (torque tube). Rear axle: (FB) 3/4-floating; (490) 2-piece. Overall Ratio: (FB) 4.62:1; (490) 3.63:1. External contracting rear brakes. Steel felloe wheels.

OPTIONS: Spare tire. Spare tire cover. Step plates. "Fat Man" steering wheel. Motometer. Cowl lights. Wind wings. OSRV mirror. Special paint.

HISTORICAL: Introduced: Jan. 1922. Innovations: (Series FB) New poured con rods. New crank w/two-inch longer throws. Improved cylinder head w/three exhaust ports. Reverse Elliot front axle. (Series 490) Valve adjustment on rocker arms. Larger diam. King pins. Single pedal brakes. Spiral cut ring and pinion. Calendar year production: 208,848. Model year production: (490) 109,473 approximate; (FB) 29,459 aproximate. W.S. Knudsen became the new president of Chevrolet.

1922
Series 490, 4-cyl.

	FP	5	4	3	2	1
Rds	510	2300	5400	9000	12,600	18,000
Tr	525	2800	5700	9500	13,300	19,000
Cpe	850	825	1600	4000	5600	8000
Utl Cpe	680	600	1200	2200	3850	5500
Sed	875	875	1700	4250	5900	8500

Series FB, 4-cyl.

	FP	5	4	3	2	1
Rds	865	2300	5400	9000	12,600	18,000
Tr	885	2800	5700	9500	13,300	19,000
Sed	1395	875	1700	4250	5900	8500
Cpe	1325	900	1900	4500	6300	9000

1923

1923 Chevrolet, Copper Cooled, coupe, HAC

CHEVROLET - COPPER-COOLED — SERIES C — FOUR: The Copper Cooled Chevrolet looked like a conventional 1923 Series B Superior model, except that the radiator was replaced by louvers and the "bow tie" emblem had a copper colored background. The word "Copper" appeared above the Chevrolet logo and the word "Cooled" was below it. There was a functional nickle plated hood ornament.

The unusual air-cooled engine in these Chevrolets was designed by Charles F. Kettering. The model evolved from two years of experimentation with the air-cooled concept, but the car was still unperfected when released for sale at the New York Automobile Show in Jan. 1923. Production was suspended five months later and a complete recall was issued.

Only 759 of the cars were built, of which 239 were scrapped before leaving the factory. Of the 500 cars shipped, 150 were used by Chevrolet representatives and about 300 were sent to dealerships. About 100 were sold before the recall. Two are known to survive today. One is part of the Harrah's Automobile Collection. The other is in the Henry Ford Museum. In addition, several engines still survive. Well-known Chevrolet collector "Pinky" Randall says, "I have one of them. They were used as stationary engines in Chevrolet factories."

1923 Chevrolet, Superior, roadster, JAC

CHEVROLET - SUPERIOR — MODEL B — FOUR: The 1923 Chevrolet Superior had much smoother lines for open models. The hood line was raised and the cowl section was narrowed. Drum type headlights were featured. The radiator was higher and had a flatter curvature at its top. Late in the year, deluxe versions of the touring, coupe and sedan were introduced. They featured disc wheels, bumpers, nickel plated radiator shells, deluxe radiator caps, motometers, running board kick plates and locking steering wheels. The Deluxe touring had outside door handles and deluxe upholstery.

I.D. DATA: [Series C] Serial numbers were located on a plate on the left side of the front seat frame. They took the form 1-C-1001 and up. Ending number is not recorded. The car in Mich. is 1-C-1109; the car in Nevada is 1-C-1268. The location of engine numbers is not recorded. [Series B] Serial number located on nameplate on the left side of front seat frame. Prefixes indicated the plant. 1 is Flint; 2 is New York; 3 is St. Louis; 6 is Oakland. Up to the later part of 1923 a 9 is Oshawa; later 9 is Norwood; 12 is Buffalo and 21 is Janesville. Starting: 1-B20391. Ending: 1-B98854. Also: 2-B19269 to 2-B111787; 3-B24459 to 3-B132178; 6-B8087 to 6-B51547; 9-B1928 to 9-B9077; 12-B1190 to 12-B7340 and 21-B1000 to 21-B38352. Engine numbers located on flywheel. Engine numbers not available.

Model No.	Body Type & Seating	Price	Weight	Prod. Total
M	2-dr. Rds.-2P	710	NA	Note 3
M	4-dr. Tr.-5P	695	NA	Note 3
M	4-dr. Sed.-5P	1060	NA	Note 3
M	2-dr. Coach-5P	1050	NA	Note 3
M	2-dr. Vtl. Cpe.-2P	880	1700*	Note 3
M	4-dr. Del. Tr.-5P	725	NA	Note 3

Note 1: Based on *Special Interest Autos* "Drive Report" Sept.-Oct. 1975. Indicated that copper-cooled was 215 lbs. lighter than conventional Chevrolet.
Note 2: Total production: 500; Total Sales: 100.

B	Chassis	NA	1390	Note 3
B	2-dr. Rds.-2P	510	1715	Note 3
B	4-dr. Tr.-5P	495	1795	Note 3
B	2-dr. UH. Cpe.-2P	680	1915	Note 3
B	2-dr. S'net-4P	850	2055	Note 3
B	4-dr. Sed.-5P	860	2095	Note 3

Note 3: Total production was 480,737 Chevrolets including 25,751 cars made in Canada.
Note 4: Prices for Deluxe models slightly lower than prices for 1924 Deluxe models.

ENGINE: [Copper-Cooled] OHV. Inline. Four. Cast iron block w/borded copper fins. B & S: 3.5 x 3.5 in. Disp.: 135 cu. in. C.R.: 4.0:1. Brake H.P.: 22 @ 1750 R.P.M. Main bearings: Three. Valve lifters: Solid. Carb.: Carter 1V (updraft). Torque: 50 lbs.-ft. @ 1300 R.P.M. [Superior] OHV. Inline. Four. Cast iron block. B & S: 3-11/16 x 4 in. Disp.: 171 cu. in. Brake H.P.: 26 @ 2000 R.P.M. N.A.C.C. H.P.: 21.75. Main bearings: Three. Valve lifters: Solid. Carb.: Carter 1V.

CHASSIS: [Both Series] W.B.: 103 in. O.L.: 142 in. O.H.: 74.25 in. Frt/Rear Tread: 58/58 in. Tires: 30 x 3.5.

TECHNICAL: Selective sliding transmission. Speeds: 3F/1R. Floor-mounted gearshift controls. Cone clutch. Shaft drive. Semi-floating rear axle. Overall ratio: [Model M] 4.44:1; [Model B] 3.77:1. External contracting rear wheel brakes. Wood spoke 3.0 x 24.75 wheels.

OPTIONS: Front bumper. Rear bumper. Disc wheels. Plated radiator. Wind wings. Spare tire. Tire cover. Motor meter. Kick plates. Deluxe upholstery. Deluxe radiator cap. Locking steering wheel. OSRV mirror. Sun visor (open cars). Special paint. Cowl lamps.

HISTORICAL: Superior B introduced Jan. 1923. Innovations: Increased wheelbase. Copper Cooled Series. New serial number system used letter or number to identify model year. Calendar year registrations: 291,761. Calendar year production: 415,814. Model year production: 323,182 (approx.)

New plants opened in Norwood, Ohio; Buffalo, N.Y. and Janesville, Wis. Some Model B engines had Holley carburetors.

1923 Chevrolet, Superior, 4-dr. sedan, OCW

1923
Superior B, 4-cyl.

	FP	5	4	3	2	1
Rds	510	2300	5400	9000	12,600	18,000
Tr	495	2800	5700	9500	13,300	19,000
Sed	860	750	1450	3300	4900	7000
2 dr Sed	850	750	1450	3300	4900	7000
Utl Cpe	680	775	1500	3750	5250	7500
DeL Tr	525	1075	3000	5500	7700	11,000

1924

CHEVROLET - SUPERIOR — SERIES F — FOUR: The Superior Series F was virtually unchanged in appearance from 1923 models. New body styles included a 2-door coach and four-passenger coupe. The sedanette was dropped. Standard equipment on open cars included tools; jack; speedometer; ammeter; oil pressure gauge; dashlight; choke pull; electric horn; ignition theft lock; demountable rims with extra rim; spare tire carrier; legal headlights; headlight dimmer; license bracket and double adjustable windshield. Closed models also had a windshield cleaner; plate glass windows; window regulator; sun visor and door locks. Deluxe equipment available for some mid-year models included disc wheels; bumpers; nickel radiator shells; runningboard kick plates and (on the touring) outside door handles.

1924 Chevrolet, Superior, touring, OCW

I.D. DATA: Serial numbers were located on the right or left side of dash under cowl and seat frame. Starting: 1B72774. Ending: 1F38881. Also: 2B92892 to 2F51140; 3B98371 to 3F56585; 6B41756 to 6F29296; 9B1166 to 9F27125; 12B1064 to 12F35270 and 21B22374 to 21F33581. Note: Cars built late in the run were sold as 1925 models. They had the following serial numbers: 1F38882 to 1K-1; 2F51141 to 2K-1; 3F56586 to 3K-1; 6F297 to 6K-1; 9K27126 to 9K-1; 12F35271 to 12K-1 and 21F33582 to 21K-1.

Model No.	Body Type & Seating	Price	Weight	Prod. Total
F	2-dr. Rds.-2P	490	1690	Note 1
F	4-dr. Tr.-5P	495	1875	Note 1
F	4-dr. Sed.-5P	795	2070	Note 1
F	2-dr. Cpe.-2P	640	1880	Note 1
F	2-dr. Cpe.-4P	725	2005	Note 1
F	2-dr. Coach-5P	695	2030	Note 1
Deluxe Equipped				
F	4-dr. Del. Tr.-5P	640	1955	Note 1
F	4-dr. Del. Sed.-5P	940	2240	Note 1
F	2-dr. Del. Cpe.-4P	775	2050	Note 1

Note 1: Total production was 307,775 Chevrolets including 20,587 cars made in Canada.

ENGINE: OHV. En Bloc. Four. Cast iron block. B & S: 3-11/16 x 4 in. Disp.: 171 cu. in. Brake H.P.: 26 @ 2000 R.P.M. N.A.C.C. H.P.: 21.7. Main bearings: Three. Valve lifters: Solid. Carb.: 1V.

CHASSIS: W.B.: 103 in. Tires: 30 x 3-1/2 non-skid.

TECHNICAL: Selective sliding transmission. Speeds: 3F/1R. Floor mounted gear shift controls. Semi-floating rear axle. 3.82: 1. External contracting rear brakes. Steel felloe, woodspoke.

OPTIONS: Step plates. OSRV mirrors. Tire cover. Motometer. Special paint. Spare tire. Disc wheels. Deluxe equipment.

HISTORICAL: Introduced: Aug. 1, 1923. Innovations: New coach and four-passenger coupe. New Deluxe models. Improved front axle. Improved brakes. Calendar year registrations: 289,962. Calendar year production: 262,100. Model year production: 264,868 (Aug. 1, 1923 to Aug. 1, 1924).
Curved front axles and cable operated brakes characterized early models in this series. Straight front axles and brake rods were used on later Series F Superior Chevrolets. New plant in Norwood, Ohio opened this year. Cars built before Aug. 1, 1923 were series B Superior Chevrolets.

1924
Superior, 4-cyl.

	FP	5	4	3	2	1
Rds	490	2300	5400	9000	12,600	18,000
Tr	495	2800	5700	9500	13,300	19,000
DeL Tr	640	2900	5850	9750	13,650	19,500
Sed	795	650	1250	2400	4200	6000
DeL Sed	940	675	1300	2600	4400	6300
2P Cpe	640	700	1350	2800	4550	6500
4P Cpe	725	650	1250	2400	4200	6000
DeL Cpe	775	725	1400	3000	4700	6700
2 dr Sed	695	650	1250	2400	4200	6000

1925

CHEVROLET - SUPERIOR — SERIES K — FOUR: The 1925 Chevrolet had a new radiator design. The upper part of the nickle plated shell curved down at the center. Fisher Body vertical ventilating (v.v.) windshields were used on closed cars. A Cadet style visor was another new feature. Wood spoke wheels were standard on open cars; sedans and coupes in late pro-

duction had steel disc wheels. New Klaxon horns and a new steering wheel with walnut-like rim were other features of Superior K Chevrolets built after Aug. 1, 1925.

I.D. DATA: Serial numbers were located on the right or left side of dash under cowl and seat frame. Starting: 1K1000. Ending: 1K33571. Also: 2K1000 to 2K45727; 3K1000 to 3K48220; 6K1000 to 6K27866; 9K1000 to 9K27519; 12K1000 to 12K36081 and 21K1000 to 21K32544.

1925 Chevrolet, Superior, Series K, coupe, JAC

Note: Cars built late in the run were sold as 1926 models. They had the following serial numbers: 1K33752 to 1V-1; 2K45728 to 2V-1; 3K48221 to 3V-1; 6K27867 to 6V-1; 9K27520 to 9V-1; 12K36082 to 12V-1 and 21K32545 to 21V-1.

Model No.	Body Type & Seating	Price	Weight	Prod. Total
K	2-dr. Rds.-2P	525	1690	Note 1
K	4-dr. Tr.-5P	525	1855	Note 1
K	2-dr. Cpe.-2P	715	1880	Note 1
K	4-dr. Sed.-5P	825	2070	Note 1
K	2-dr. Coach-5P	735	2030	Note 1

Note 1: Total production was 519,229 Chevrolets including 30,968 cars made in Canada.

1925 Chevrolet, Superior, Series K, coach, OCW

ENGINE: OHV. Inline. Four. Cast iron block. B & S: 3-11/16 x 4 in. Disp.: 171 cu. in. Brake H.P.: 26 @ 2000 R.P.M. N.A.C.C. H.P.: 21.7. Main bearings: Three. Valve lifters: Solid. Carb.: 1V Model RXO.

CHASSIS: W.B.: 103 in. Tires: 30 x 3-1/2 (open cars); 29 x 4.40 (closed cars).

TECHNICAL: Selective sliding transmission. Speeds: 3F/1R. Floor-mounted gearshift controls. Cluth: sinale plate dry disc. Semi-floating rear axle. Overall Ratio: 3.82:1. External contracting rear wheel brakes. Spoke wheels (open); Disc wheels (closed).

OPTIONS: Front bumper. Rear bumper. Step plates. OSRV mirrors. Tire cover. Motometer. Special paint. Spare tire. Heater. Clock. Wood spoke wheels (closed cars). Steel disc wheels (open cars).

HISTORICAL: Introduced: Jan. 1925. Innovations: Redesigned engine with new block, rods and crank. New disc clutch. Semi-elliptic springs. Calendar year registrations: 341,281. Calendar year production: 444,671. Model year production: 306,479 (Jan. 1925 — Aug. 1925).
Cars built after August 1, 1925 had the new Klaxon horns and walnut steering wheel. They also had spark/throttle controls on the dash above the steering wheel and a headlight brace bar. They were sold as 1926 models. Bloomfield, N.J. factory purchased. First year of production over 500,000 units (incl. early 1926 models).

1925
Superior K, 4-cyl.

	FP	5	4	3	2	1
Rds	525	3600	7200	12,000	16,800	24,000
Tr	525	3750	7500	12,500	17,500	25,000
Cpe	715	750	1450	3300	4900	7000
Sed	825	700	1350	2800	4550	6500
2 dr Sed	735	700	1350	2700	4500	6400

1926

1926 Chevrolet, Superior, Series V, 4-dr. sedan, OCW

CHEVROLET - SUPERIOR — SERIES V — FOUR: The Super Series V was introduced in mid-1926 and was marketed into the first part of the 1927 sales year. It was similar to the previous Series K except that a tie-bar connected the drum-shaped headlights.

I.D. DATA: Serial Number located on right or left side of dash under cowl and seat frame. Starting: 1V1000. Ending: 1V48499. Also: 2V1000 to 2V49550; 3V1000 to 3V83277; 6V1000 to 6V27138; 9V1000 to 9V52906; 12V1000 to 12V38701 and 21V1000 to 21V54755.

Model No.	Body Type & Seating	Price	Weight	Prod. Total
V	2-dr. Rds.-2P	510	1790	Note 1
V	4-dr. Tr.-5P	510	1950	Note 1
V	2-dr. Cpe.-2P	645	2035	Note 1
V	4-dr. Sed.-5P	735	2225	Note 1
V	2-dr. Coach-5P	645	2150	Note 1
V	4-dr. Lan. Sed.-5P	765	2220	NA

Note 1: Total production was 732,147 Chevrolets including 39.967 cars made in Canada.

ENGINE: OHV. Inline. Four cyl. Cast iron block. B & S: 3-11/16 x 4 in. Disp.: 171 cu. in. Brake H.P.: 26 @ 2000 R.P.M. Net H.P.: 21.7 N.A.C.C. Main bearings: Three. Valve lifters: Solid. Carb.: 1V.

CHASSIS: W.B. 103 in. Tires: 29 x 4.40.

TECHNICAL: Selective sliding transmission. Speeds: 3F/1R. Floor-mounted gearshift controls. Clutch: Single plate dry disc. Semi-floating rear axle. Overall ratio: 3.82:1. External Contracting rear wheel brakes. Wood spoke wheels.

OPTIONS: Step plates. OSRV mirror. Tire covers. Whitewall tires. Motormeter. Special paint. Spare tire. Wood spoke wheels. Commercial pickup equipment.

HISTORICAL: Introduced: Mid-1926. Calendar year registrations: 486,366. Calendar year production: 588,962. Model year production: 547,724. Innovations: Belt driven generator. Cam operated oil pump. Improved brakes. New Landau sedan.
Spark/throttle control moved above steering wheel on late models. Combination stop/taillamp (instead of round taillight) on late models. New Detroit axle factory. Eight million dollars appropriated to make Chevrolet more competitive with Ford.

1926
Superior V, 4-cyl.

Rds	510	3600	7200	12,000	16,800	24,000
Tr	510	3750	7500	12,500	17,500	25,000
Cpe	645	750	1450	3300	4900	7000
Sed	735	700	1350	2800	4550	6500
2 dr Sed	645	700	1350	2700	4500	6400
Lan Sed	765	825	1600	4000	5600	8000

1927

CHEVROLET - CAPITOL — SERIES AA — FOUR: The 1927 Chevrolets had a new radiator shell on which the top portion no longer bowed downwards. There was a downward pointing "peak" in the center of the upper shell. New bullet shaped headlight buckets were finished in black enamel with bright metal trim rings. Fuller crown fenders were seen. Rectangular brake

1927 Chevrolet, Capitol, landau sedan, AA

and clutch pedals were used. There was a new parking brake release and a coincidental ignition/steering wheel lock. A new body style was the Sports Cabriolet. An Imperial Landau sedan was introduced in May 1927. Equipment on open cars included tools; jack; speedometer; ammeter; oil pressure gauge, dash light; choke pull, electric horn, extra rim; spare tire carrier; bullet type cowl lamps; headlight dimmer; license brackets; double-adjustable windshield; foot accelerator; air cleaner; oil filter; pedal enclosure; rear-vision mirror; gas gauge and automatic stop light. Closed cars also had V.V. windshields; wipers; plate glass windows; window regulators; sunvisor; door locks; dome lights; rear window roller shade; door pockets and remote control door handles.

I.D. DATA: Serial Number located on right or left side of dash under cowl and seat frame. Starting: AA1 & up. Engine numbers located on base ahead of oil filter.

1927 Chevrolet, Capitol, coach (with Alfred Sloan), JAC

Model No.	Body Type & Seating	Price	Weight	Prod. Total
AA	2-dr. Rds.-2P	525	1960	41,313
AA	4-dr. Tr.-5P	525	1895	53,187
AA	2-dr. Cpe.-2P	625	2090	124,101
AA	2-dr. Spt. Cabr.-2/4P	715	2135	41,137
AA	2-dr. Coach-5P	695	2190	239,566
AA	4-dr. Sed.-5P	695	2275	99,400
AA	4-dr. Imp. Lan.-5P	NA	NA	37,426
AA	4-dr. Lan. Sed.-5P	745	2270	42,410

Note 1: The Sports Cabriolet was a closed car not a convertible.

ENGINE: OHV. Inline. Four. Cast iron block. B & S: 3-11/16 x 4 in. Disp.: 171 cu. in. Brake H.P.: 26 @ 2000 R.P.M. Net H.P.: 21.7. Main bearings: Three. Valve lifters: Solid. Carb.: 1V; Model: Carter.

CHASSIS: W.B.: 103 in. Tires: 29 x 4.40 (balloon).

TECHNICAL: Selective sliding transmission. Speeds: 3F/1R. Floor-mounted gearshit controls. Single plate dry disc. Semi-floating rear axle. Overall ratio: 3.82:1. External Contracting rear-wheel brakes. Steel disc wheels.

OPTIONS: Window awnings. Step plates. Whitewall tires. Woodspoke wheels. Motometer. Special paint. OSRV mirror. Spare tire. Tire cover.

HISTORICAL: Introduced: Jan. 1927. Total production: 1,001,820 Chevrolets including 61,740 cars made in Canada. Innovations: First Chevrolet rumble seat on Capitol AA Sports Cabriolet. First year for natural wood spoke wheel option. New Remy distributor and Carter carburetor. Air and oil filters standard for first time.
In 1927, Chevrolet outsold Ford for the first time. Saginaw gray iron foundry was opened. First million car sales year for Chevrolet. General Manager: William S. Knudsen.

1927
Model AA, 4-cyl.

	FP	5	4	3	2	1
Rds	525	3750	7500	12,500	17,500	25,000
Tr	525	3900	7800	13,000	18,200	26,000
Utl Cpe	625	725	1400	3000	4700	6700
2 dr Sed	595	725	1400	3100	4800	6800
Sed	695	750	1450	3300	4900	7000
Lan Sed	745	775	1500	3600	5100	7300
Cabr	715	2300	5400	9000	12,600	18,000
Imp Lan	745	1750	4800	8000	11,200	16,000

1928

1928 Chevrolet, National, Imperial landau, HAC

CHEVROLET — NATIONAL — MODEL AB — FOUR: The 1928 Chevrolets were larger cars. New, full crown fenders were used. There were larger, bullet type headlamps and a higher cowl line. Standard equipment included. Fisher V.V. windshield, vacuum wiper, inside rear view mirror, stop light, parking lights, door pockets and gas gauge. Smoking set and robe rails on sedans.

I.D. DATA: Serial numbers on front seat heel board at left or right side. Starting: AB 1000 and up. A numerical prefix indicated assembly plant as follows: ''1'' = Flint, Mich.; ''2'' = Tarrytown, N.J.; ''3'' = St. Louis; ''5'' = Kansas City, Mo.; ''6'' = Oakland, Calif.; ''8'' = Atlanta, Ga.; ''9'' = Norwood, Ohio; ''12'' = Buffalo, N.Y. and ''21'' = Janesville, Wis. Engine number on base ahead of oil filter. Codes not available.

Model No.	Body Type & Seating	Price	Weight	Prod. Total
AB	2-dr. Rds.-2P	495	2030	NA
AB	4-dr. Tr.-5P	495	2090	26,973
AB	2-dr. Cpe.-2P	595	2235	150,356
AB	2-dr. Cabr.-2/4P	665	2270	NA
AB	2-dr. Cpe. Spt. Conv.-2P	695	2265	38,268
AB	2-dr. Coach-5P	585	2360	346,976
AB	4-dr. Sed-5P	675	2435	127,819
AB	4-dr. Imp. Lan.-5P	715	2405	54,998

ENGINE: OHV. Inline. Four. Cast iron block. B & S: 3-11/16 x 4 in. Disp.: 171 cu. in. Brake H.P.: 35 @ 2200 R.P.M. NACC H.P.: 21.7. Valve lifters: Solid. Carb. Carter 1V.

CHASSIS: W.B.: 107 in. Length: 156 in. (less bumpers). Tread: 56 in. Tires: 30 x 4.50 in.

TECHNICAL: Manual transmission. Straight cut gears. Speeds: 3F/1R. Floor shift controls. Overall Ratio: 3.82:1. Mechanical brakes on four wheels. Disc wheels.

OPTIONS: Front bumper. Rear bumper. Heater. Wood spoke wheels. Outside rear view mirror. Leatherette spare tire cover. Spare tire (rim std.). Fluid canisters. Runningboard step plates. Wind wings (open cars).

HISTORICAL: Introduced Jan. 1928. Indirect lighted instrument panel. Four-wheel brakes. Thermostat. Alemite chassis lubrication. Total production: 1,193,212 Chevrolets including 69,217 cars made in Canada. Hibbard & Darrin constructed at least one custom-bodied National series AB sedan. General manager: W.S. Knudsen.

1928
Model AB, 4-cyl.

	FP	5	4	3	2	1
Rds	495	3750	7500	12,500	17,500	25,000
Tr	495	3900	7800	13,000	18,200	26,000
Utl Cpe	595	775	1500	3600	5100	7300
Sed	675	775	1500	3750	5250	7500
2 dr Sed	585	750	1450	3300	4900	7000
Cabr	665	2300	5400	9000	12,600	18,000
Imp Lan	715	1750	4800	8000	11,200	16,000
Conv Cabr	695	3150	6300	10,500	14,700	21,000

1929

1929 Chevrolet, International, 4-dr. sedan, HFM

CHEVROLET — INTERNATIONAL — MODEL AC — SIX: The 1929 Chevrolets had a more rectangular radiator with the company ''bow-tie'' logo in an upright oval at the top of the chrome plated radiator shell. Fewer vertical louvers were seen towards the rear of the hood side panels. Wider, single belt moldings decorated the body. New, one-piece full crown fenders and new bullet type lamps were used. A rumble seat Sport Roadster was a mid-year addition to the line.

I.D. DATA: Serial number on right body sill under floor mat, except roadster and phaeton (right side of seat frame on these models). Starting: AC1000 and up. Numerical prefixes used for each factory; same as 1928. Each factory built only one body style. Engine numbers on right side of block behind fuel pump. Codes not available.

Model No.	Body Type & Seating	Price	Weight	Prod. Total
1AC	2-dr. Rds.-2P	525	2175	27,988
2AC	4-dr. Phae.-5P	525	2240	8,632
3AC	2-dr. Cpe.-2P	595	2425	Note 1
5AC	2-dr. Spt. Cpe.-2/4P	645	2470	Note 1
6AC	2-dr. Cabr.-2/4P	695	2440	45,956
8AC	2-dr. Coach-5P	595	2500	367,360
9AC	4-dr. Sed.-5P	675	2585	196,084
21AC	4-dr. Imp. Sed.-5P	695	2555	41,983
12AC	4-dr. Lan. Conv.-5P	725	2560	300
1AC	2-dr. Spt. Rds.-2/4P	545	2230	1,210

Note 1: Combined production total for coupe and Sport Coupe was 157,230 cars.
Note 2: Model number prefix shown above indicates assembly point. Refer to factory codes in 1928 Chevrolet serial number data.

ENGINE: OHV. Inline. Six. Cast iron block. B & S: 3-5/16 x 3-3/4 in. Disp.: 194 cu. in. Brake H.P.: 46 @ 2600 R.P.M. NACC H.P.: 26.3 Main bearings: Three. Valve lifters: Solid. Carb. Carter 1V.

CHASSIS: W.B.: 107 in. Length: 156 in. (less bumpers). Tread: 56 in. Tires: 20 x 4.50.

TECHNICAL: Manual transmisson. Straight cut gears. Speeds: 3F/1R. Floor shift controls. Banjo rear axle. Single plate dry disc clutch. Overall ratio: 3.82:1. Four wheel mechanical brake. Rod activated. Internal front/external rear. Disc wheels.

OPTIONS: Front bumper. Rear bumper. Single sidemount. Dual sidemount. Sidemount cover(s). Rear spare cover. Trunk rack. Steamer type trunk. Heater. Outside rear view mirror. Cigar lighter. Runingboard step plates. Wire spoke wheels. Wind wings (open cars). Accessory hood mascot.

HISTORICAL: Introduced: December 1928. Banjo type rear axle. Electro lock. Rubber covered 17-in. steering wheel. New six-cylinder engine. Total production: 1,328,605 Chevrolets including 73,918 cars made in Canada. Advertised as ''A Six for the Price of a Four.'' Fuel consumption: App. 19 m.p.g. General manager: W.S. Knudsen.

1929
Model AC, 6-cyl.

	FP	5	4	3	2	1
Rds	525	4200	8400	14,000	19,600	28,000
Tr	525	4350	8700	14,500	20,300	29,000
Cpe	595	1750	4800	8000	11,200	16,000
Spt Cpe	645	2000	5100	8500	11,900	17,000
Sed	675	1500	4350	7250	10,150	14,500
Imp Sed	695	1550	4500	7500	10,500	15,000
Conv Lan	725	3300	6600	11,000	15,400	22,000
2 dr Sed	595	1400	4200	7000	9800	14,000
Conv Cabr	695	3400	6900	11,500	16,100	23,000

1930

1930 Chevrolet, Universal, coach, OCW

CHEVROLET — UNIVERSAL — SERIES AD — SIX: The major change in 1930 Chevrolets was the addition of a slanting, non-glare windshield. The gas gauge was moved to the dashboard. Other instruments had a new, circular shape with dark colored faces. Smaller tires were used. The Special Sedan replaced the Imperial Sedan. Its standard equipment included six wire wheels with fender wells, front and rear bumpers, robe rail, dome light and silk assist cords.

I.D. DATA: Serial numbers in same locations as 1929. AD 1000 and up. Numerical prefixes used for each factory; same as 1929. Each factory built one body style. Engine numbers same location; codes not available.

Model No.	Body Type & Seating	Price	Weight	Prod. Total
1AD	2-dr. Rds.-2P	495	2195	5,684
2AD	2-dr. Spt. Rds.-2/4P	515	2250	27,651
3AD	4-dr. Phae.-5P	495	2265	1,713
5AD	2-dr. Cpe.-2P	565	2415	100,373
6AD	2-dr. Spt. Cpe-2/4P	615	2525	45,311
8AD	2-dr. Coach-5P	565	2515	255,027
9AD	4-dr. Club Sed.-5P	625	2575	24,888
12AD	4-dr. Sed.-5P	675	2615	135,193
21AD	4-dr. Spec. Sed.-5P	685	2665	35,929
5AD	2-dr. R/S Cpe.-2/4P	—	—	9,211

Note 1: Model number prefix shown above indicates assembly point. Refer to factory codes in 1928 Chevrolet serial number data.

1930 Chevrolet, Universal, coupe, JAC

ENGINE: OHV. Inline. Six. Cast iron block. B & S: 3-5/16 x 3-3/4 in. Disp.: 194 cu. in. C.R.: 5.02:1. Brake H.P.: 50 @ 2600 R.P.M. NACC H.P.: 26.3. Main bearings: Three. Valve lifters: Solid. Carb.: Carter 1V.

CHASSIS: W.B.: 107 in. Tires: 19 x 4.75.

TECHNICAL: Manual transmission. Speeds: 3F/1R. Floor shift controls. Single plate clutch. Semi-floating rear axle. Overall ratio: 4.1:1. Four wheel internal (mechanical) brakes. Disc wheels.

OPTIONS: Front bumper. Rear bumper. Single sidemount. Dual sidemount. Sidemount cover(s). Trunk rack. Steamer trunk. Wood spoke wheels. Heater. Wire spoke wheels (std. on Sports models). Cigar lighter. Rear spare cover. Outside rear view mirror.

HISTORICAL: Introduced: Jan. 1930. New type manifold. Three-spoke steering wheel. Hydraulic shock absorbers added. Total production: 864,243 Chevrolets, including 39,773 cars made in Canada. The 7-millionth Chevrolet since 1912 was built on May 28, 1930 at Flint, Mich. General manager: W.S. Knudsen.

1930 Chevrolet, Universal, sport roadster, JAC

1930
Model AD, 6-cyl.

	FP	5	4	3	2	1
Rds	495	4350	8700	14,500	20,300	29,000
Spt Rds	525	4500	9000	15,000	21,000	30,000
Phae	495	4500	9000	15,000	21,000	30,000
2 dr Sed	565	1400	4200	7000	9800	14,000
Cpe	565	1750	4800	8000	11,200	16,000
Spt Cpe	625	2000	5100	8500	11,900	17,000
Clb Sed	625	1650	4650	7750	10,850	15,500
Spec Sed	685	1550	4500	7500	10,500	15,000
Sed	675	1500	4350	7250	10,150	14,500
Con Lan	725	3300	6600	11,000	15,400	22,000

1931

1931 Chevrolet, Independence, roadster, OCW

CHEVROLET — INDEPENDENCE — SERIES AE — SIX: The 1931 Chevrolet had a higher, larger radiator. The headlights were mounted on a bowed tie-bar. The hood sides featured multiple vertical louvers within a raised panel. There were new type panel and body moldings. Wire spoke wheels became standard equipment.

I.D. DATA: Serial numbers in same location as 1930. Starting: AE 1000 and up. Numerical prefixes used for each factory; same as 1929. Each factory built one body style. Engine numbers same location. Starting: 2100285. Ending: 2951552.

Model No.	Body Type & Seating	Price	Weight	Prod. Total
1AE	2-dr. Rds.-2P	475	2295	2,939
2AE	2-dr. Spt. Rds.-2/4P	495	2340	24,050
3AE	4-dr. Phae.-5P	510	2370	852
5AE	2-dr. Cpe.-2P	535	2490	57,741
6AE	2-dr. Spt. Cpe.-2/4P	575	2565	66,029
8AE	2-dr. 5-W Cpe.-2P	545	2490	28,379
21AE	2-dr. Cpe.-5P	595	2610	20,297
21AE	2-dr. Conv. Cabr.-2/4P	615	2520	23,077
9AE	2-dr. Coach-5P	545	2610	228,316
12AE	4-dr. Sed.-5P	635	2685	52,465
21AE	4-dr. Spec. Sed.-5P	650	2725	109,775
21AE	2-dr. Lan. Phae.-5P	650	2610	5,634

Note 1: Model number prefixes shown above indicate assembly point. Refer to factory codes in 1928 Chevrolet serial number data.

ENGINE: OHV. Inline. Six. Cast iron block. B & S: 3-5/16 x 3-3/4 in. Disp.: 194 cu. in. C.R.: 5.02:1. Brake H.P.: 50 @ 2600 R.P.M. NACC H.P.: 26.3. Main bearings: Three. Valve lifters: Solid. Carb.: Carter 1V.

1931 Chevrolet, Independence, coupe, JAC

CHASSIS: W.B.: 109 in. Tires: 19 x 4.75.

TECHNICAL: Manual transmission. Speeds: 3F/1R. Floor shift controls. Disc clutch. Semi-floating rear axle. Overall ratio: 4.1:1. Internal mechanical brakes on four wheels. Wire wheels standard.

OPTIONS: Front bumper. Rear bumper. Single sidemount. Dual sidemount. Sidemount cover(s). Rear spare cover. Pedestal mirrors. Dual taillamps. Heater. Dual chrome sidemount trim rings. Cigar lighter. Luggage rack. Touring trunk. Spotlight. Wind wings. Quail radiator mascot. Guide lamps.

HISTORICAL: Introduced: Nov. 1930. Lovejoy shock absorbers. Semi-elliptic springs. Engine vibration dampener added. Heavier frame. More rigid crankshaft. Improved flywheel. New ribbed block and crankcase castings. Calendar year registrations: 583,429. Calendar year production: 627,104. Model year production: 623,901. General managers: W.S. Knudsen and M.E. Coyle. Chevrolet produced its 8-millionth car on Aug. 25, 1931.

1931 Chevrolet, Independence, sedan, JAC

1931
Model AE, 6-cyl.

	FP	5	4	3	2	1
Rds	475	4500	9000	15,000	21,000	30,000
Spt Rds	495	4800	9600	16,000	22,400	32,000
Cabr	615	4350	8700	14,500	20,300	29,000
Phae	510	4500	9000	15,000	21,000	30,000
2 dr Sed	545	1550	4500	7500	10,500	15,000
5P Cpe	595	2000	5100	8500	11,900	17,000
5W Cpe	545	2300	5400	9000	12,600	18,000
Spt Cpe	575	3000	6000	10,000	14,000	20,000
Cpe	535	2800	5700	9500	13,300	19,000
DeL 2 dr Sed	545	1750	4800	8000	11,200	16,000
Sed	635	1650	4650	7750	10,850	15,500
Spec Sed	650	1800	4950	8250	11,550	16,500

1932

CHEVROLET - CONFEDERATE — SERIES BA — SIX: Styling changes for 1932 Chevrolets included a longer hood and new deep crown front fenders. Door type louvers were used in the hood. They were chrome plated on Deluxe models. A built in radiator grille was part of the new design. New 18-inch wire wheels were adopted. Standard equipment included a built in sun visor, tilting windshield and adjustable seat. New technical features included a downdraft carburetor, counter-balanced crank shaft and added frame cross member.

I.D. DATA: Serial numbers on closed cars were on the right body sill under floor mat. Serial numbers on open cars were on the right side of the seat frame. Starting: BA 1000 and up. Numerical prefixes used for each factory; same as 1931. Each factory built one body style. Engine numbers in same location; codes not available.

1932 Chevrolet, Confederate, landau phaeton, OCW

Model No.	Body Type & Seating	Price	Weight	Prod. Total
1BA	4-dr. Phae.-5P	495	2495	419
1BA	2-dr. Rds.-2P	445	2410	1,118
2BA	2-dr. Spt. Rds.-2/4P	485	2480	8,552
5BA	2-dr. Cpe.-2P	490	2580	8,874
6BA	2-dr. Spt. Cpe.-2/4P	535	2645	2,226
8BA	2-dr. 5W Cpe.-2P	490	2580	34,796
21BA	2-dr. Cpe.-5P	575	2700	7,566
21BA	2-dr. Del. 5W Cpe.-2P	510	2580	26,623
21BA	2-dr. Conv.-2/4P	595	2590	Note 2
9BA	2-dr. Coach-5P	495	2665	132,109
12BA	2-dr. Del. Coach-5P	515	2665	9,346
12BA	4-dr. Sed.-5P	590	2750	27,718
21BA	4-dr. Spec. Sed.-5P	615	2800	52,446
21BA	2-dr. Lan. Phae.-5P	625	2700	1,602

NOTE 1: Model number prefix shown above indicated assembly point. Refer to factory codes in 1928 Chevrolet serial number data.
NOTE 2: No production total available.

1932 Chevrolet, Confederate, coupe, JAC

ENGINE: OHV. Inline. Six. Cast iron block. B & S: 3-5/16 x 3-3/4 in. Disp.: 194 cu. in. C.R.: 5.2:1. Brake H.P.: 60 @ 3000 R.P.M. N.A.C.C. H.P.: 26.3. Main bearings: Three. Valve lifters: Solid. Carb.: Carter 1V Model 150S.

CHASSIS: W.B.: 109 in. Tires: 18 x 5.24.

TECHNICAL: Manual Synchromesh transmission. Speeds: 3F/1R. Floor shift controls. Single plate clutch. Semi-floating rear axle. Overall Ratio: 4.1:1. Four wheel internal (mechanical) brakes. Wire wheels standard. Drivetrain Options: Free-Wheeling.

OPTIONS: Front bumper. Rear bumper. Single sidemount. Dual sidemount. Trunk rack. Standard tire cover ($1). Deluxe tire cover ($2.50). Heater. Outside mirror. Pedastal mirrors. Dual wipers. Cowl lights. Dual horns. Metal tire covers ($6). Fender well tire lock ($5). Rear tire lock ($2.50). DeLuxe equipment included chrome hood louvers; two ash trays; assist cords; arm rests; curtains for rear and rear quarter windows and vanity case.

HISTORICAL: Introduced: Dec. 5, 1931. Innovations: Synchromesh transmission. Selective free wheeling. Counter-balanced crank shaft. Added frame cross member. Calendar registrations: 332,860. Calendar year production: 306,716. Model year production: 323,100. General Manager: M.E. Coyle.
The 1932 Chevrolet Sports Roadster could go from 0-35 mph in 6.7 seconds. Some station wagon bodies were constructed on Chevrolet chassis by Mifflinburg Body Co. of Mifflinburg, PA.

1932 Chevrolet, Confederate, special sedan, JAC

1932
Model BA Standard, 6-cyl.

	FP	5	4	3	2	1
Rds	445	4950	9900	16,500	23,100	33,000
Phae	495	4950	9900	16,500	23,100	33,000
Lan Phae	625	4800	9600	16,000	22,400	32,000
3W Cpe	490	3000	6000	10,000	14,000	20,000
5W Cpe	490	3150	6300	10,500	14,700	21,000
Spt Cpe	520	3300	6600	11,000	15,400	22,000
2 dr Sed	495	1750	4800	8000	11,200	16,000
Sed	615	2000	5100	8500	11,900	17,000
5P Cpe	575	3150	6300	10,500	14,700	21,000

Model BA DeLuxe, 6-cyl.

Spt Rds	485	5100	10,200	17,000	23,800	34,000
Lan Phae	640	4950	9900	16,500	23,100	33,000
Cabr	610	4800	9600	16,000	22,400	32,000
3W Bus Cpe	510	3150	6300	10,500	14,700	21,000
5W Cpe	505	3300	6600	11,000	15,400	22,000
Spt Cpe	535	3400	6900	11,500	16,100	23,000
2 dr Sed	515	2000	5100	8500	11,900	17,000
Sed	590	2300	5400	9000	12,600	18,000
Spec Sed	630	2800	5700	9500	13,300	19,000
5P Cpe	590	3300	6600	11,000	15,400	22,000

1933

1933 Chevrolet, Master Eagle, sedan, OCW

CHEVROLET - MASTER EAGLE — SERIES CA — SIX: A slightly larger, more streamlined car was Chevrolet's Master Eagle series for 1933. New styling features included a V-shaped radiator, rear slanting hood door louvers, skirted fenders and a beaver tail back panel. This was called "Airstream" design. It also brought in a fixed position windshield and Fisher Body No-Draft ventilation system. Door lock buttons were on the window sills. Chrome headlight buckets were used. An eagle radiator mascot was available to identify cars in this series.

CHEVROLET — STANDARD MERCURY — SERIES-CC — SIX: Chevrolet introduced an all-new series in the middle of the year. These cars had slanting v-type radiators and skirted fenders. The headlight buckets were painted black and had chrome plated rims. Conventional hood louvers were featured. Overall dimensions were scaled down from those of the Master Eagle Series. Otherwise the two lines looked similar.

I.D. DATA: [Series CA] Serial numbers locations were as on 1932 models. Starting: CA 1000 & up. Engine numbers in same location; codes not available. [Series CC] Serial number locations were the same as on Master Eagle models. Starting: CC 1000 & up. Engine numbers in same location as on Master Eagle Motors; codes not available.

1933 Chevrolet, Master Eagle, phaeton, JAC

Model No.	Body Type & Seating	Price	Weight	Prod. Total
CA	2-dr. Spt. Rds.-2/4P	485	2555	2,876
CA	4-dr. Phae.-5P	515	2600	543
CA	2-dr. Cpe.-2P	495	2665	60,402
CA	2-dr. Spt. Cpe.-2/4P	535	2730	26,691
CA	2-dr. Conv.-2/4P	565	2820	4276
CA	2-dr. Coach-5P	515	2770	162,629
CA	4-dr. Sed.-5P	565	2830	162,361
CA	4-dr. Twn. Sed.-5P	545	2795	30,657
CC	2-dr. Cpe.-2P	445	2425	8909
CC	2-dr. Spt. Cpe.-2/4P	475	2485	1903
CC	2-dr. Sed.-5P	455	2515	25,033

ENGINE: [Series CA] OHV. Inline. Six. Cast iron block. B & S: 3-5/16 x 4 in. 194 cu. in. C.R.: 5.2:1. Brake H.P.: 65 @ 2800 R.P.M. N.A.C.C. H.P.: 26.3 Three main bearings. Valve lifters: solid. Carb.: Carter 1V Model W1. [Series CC] OHV. Inline. Six. Cast iron block. B & S: 3-5/16 x 3-1/2 in. Disp.): 181 cu. in. C.R.: 5.2:1. Brake H.P.: 60 @ 3000 R.P.M. N.A.C.C. H.P.: 26.3. Main bearings: Three. Valve lifters: Solid. Carb.: Carter 1V Model W1.

CHASSIS: [Master Eagle Series] W.B.: 110 in. Tires: 18 x 5.25. [Mercury Series] W.B.: 107 in. Tires: 17 x 5.25.

TECHNICAL: Manual transmission (Synchromesh on Master Eagle). Speeds: 3F/1R. Floor shift controls. Single plate clutch. Semi-floating rear axle. Overall Ratio: (Master Eagle) 4.11:1; (Standard) 4.4:1. Four wheel internal mechanical brakes. Wire wheels standard. Selective standard on Master Eagle; not available on Standard Mercury.
Note: Synchromesh transmission with Master Eagles. Selective constant mesh transmission on Mercury standard models.

OPTIONS: Oval wipers. Foglights. Trunk rock. Twin horns. Step plates. Outside mirrors. Sidemount pedestal mirrors.
Note: Deluxe equipment for Chevrolets included dual horns, dual taillights, vanity set and other special interior furnishings.

HISTORICAL: (Master Eagle) Dec. 1932; (Mercury) Mar. 1933. Innovations: An airplane type dashboard was employed on Master Eagle models. Both Chevrolet engines featured an octane selector. Safety plate glass used in Mercury series windshield. Model year production: (Eagle Series) 450,530; (Mercury Series) 35,848; (Total) 486,378. General Manager: M.E. Coyle.
Chevrolet dealers sponsored the first Soap Box Derby in Dayton, Ohio this year. It was created by M.E. Scott, who later joined the company's public relations dept.

1933 Chevrolet, Master Eagle, town sedan, JAC

1933

Mercury, 6-cyl.

	FP	5	4	3	2	1
2P Cpe	445	1025	2600	5250	7300	10,500
RS Cpe	475	1125	3450	5750	8050	11,500
2 dr Sed	455	825	1600	4000	5600	8000

Master Eagle, 6-cyl.

	FP	5	4	3	2	1
Spt Rds	485	4400	8850	14,750	20,650	29,500
Phae	515	4600	9150	15,250	21,350	30,500
2P Cpe	495	1075	3000	5500	7700	11,000
Spt Cpe	535	1150	3600	6000	8400	12,000
2 dr Sed	515	850	1650	4150	5800	8300
2 dr Trk Sed	545	875	1700	4250	5900	8500
Sed	565	875	1700	4250	5900	8500
Conv	565	3200	6450	10,750	15,050	21,500

1934

1934 Chevrolet, roadster, OCW

1934 Chevrolet, coach, JAC

OPTIONS: Front bumper. Rear bumper. Dual taillights. Dual sidemount ($30). Sidemount cover(s). Fender skirts ($8). Bumper Guards. Radio. Heater. Clock. Cigar lighter. Radio antenna. Seat covers. Rear view mirror. Spotlight.

HISTORICAL: Introduced: (Master) Jan. 1934; (Standard) Jan. 1934. Innovations: Knee Action coil spring front suspension on Master Chevrolet. External horns not available. New X-Y frame on Master. New type valve and rocker arm arrange for Master "Blue Flame" six. Calendar year registrations: 534,906. Calendar year production: 620,726. Model year production: (Master) 457,167; (Standard) 99,499; (Total) 556,666. General Manager: M.E. Coyle.
   The phaeton, offered only in the Standard Series, is very rare today. Fender skirts were a new Chevrolet accessory in 1934. In an unusual promotion to prove the power of the improved Chevrolet engine, a 1934 Chevy six was used to tow a train called the Burlington Zephyr into a Chicago railroad station.

CHEVROLET — MASTER — SERIES DA — SIX: Cars in Chevrolet's top priced series grew slightly larger in 1934, but the basic features of "Airstream" styling were unchanged. A new V-type radiator and grille appeared. The hood was even longer and wider, too. Deeper crown fenders were seen. There were three horizontal hood louvers which decreased in length from top to bottom. A new, winged hood ornament graced the radiator shell. Prices increased significantly this year.

CHEVROLET — STANDARD — SERIES DC — SIX: The Standard models for 1934 were much the same as last year. A new longer hood with horizontal streamlined louvers was used. The No-Draft ventilation system was also improved. A fancier, winged hood ornament made the cheaper Chevrolets look more like the expensive ones. The standard models had painted headlight buckets and less bright metal trim. The vertical grille bars were spaced wider apart than on the Master Series models.

I.D. DATA: [Series DA] Serial number locations were the same as on 1933 models. Starting: DA-1001 & up. Engine numbers were in the same location. Master series engine numbers were M-3964078 to M-4708994. [Series DC] Serial number locations were the same as on Master Series models. Starting: DC-1001 & up. Engine numbers were in same location as on Master Series motors. Starting: M-40549. Ending: M-166168.

Model No.	Body Type & Seating	Price	Weight	Prod. Total
DA	2-dr. Rds.-2/4P	540	2830	1,974
DA	2-dr. Bus. Cpe.-2P	560	2895	53,018
DA	2-dr. Spt. Cpe.-2/4P	600	2995	18,365
DA	2-dr. Cabr.-2/4P	695	2990	3,276
DA	2-dr. Coach-5P	580	2995	163,948
DA	4-dr. Sed.-5P	640	3080	124,754
DA	2-dr. Twn. Sed.-5P	615	3020	49,431
DA	4-dr. Spt. Sed.-5P	675	3155	37,646

Note 1: The Sport Sedan was a touring sedan style with integral rear trunk.

Model No.	Body Type & Seating	Price	Weight	Prod. Total
DC	2-dr. Spt. Rds.-2/4P	465	2380	1,038
DC	4-dr. Phae.-5P	520	2400	234
DC	2-dr. Cpe.-2P	485	2470	16,765
DC	2-dr. Coach-5P	495	2565	69,082
DC	4-dr. Sed.-5P	540	2655	11,840

Note 2: The 4-dr Sedan was added to the Standard Series as a mid-year model in Oct. 1934.

ENGINE: [Series DA] OHV. Inline. Six. Cast iron block. B & S: 3-5/16 x 4 in. Disp.: 206.8 cu. in. C.R.: 5.45:1. Brake H.P.: 80 @ 3300 R.P.M. N.A.C.C. H.P.: 26.3. Main bearings: Three. Valve lifters: Solid. Carb.: Carter 1V Model W1. [Series DC] OHV. Inline. Six. Cast iron block. B & S: 3-5/16 x 3-1/2 in. Disp.: 181 cu. in. C.R.: 5.2:1. Brake H.P.: 60 @ 3000 R.P.M. N.A.C.C. H.P.: 26.3. Main bearings: Three. Valve lifters: Solid. Carb.: Carter 1V Model W1.

CHASSIS: [Master Series] W.B.: 112 in. Tires: 5.50 x 17. Note: The Master Chevrolet featured "Knee Action" front suspension with coil springs. [Standard Series] W.B.: 107 in. Tires: 5.25 x 17.

TECHNICAL: Manual transmission. Speeds: 3F/1R. Floor shift controls. Single-plate clutch. Semi-floating rear axle. Overall ratio: 4.11:1. Four wheel mechanical brakes. Wire wheels. Selective free-wheeling optional on Master.

1934 Chevrolet, 4-dr. sedan, JAC

1934

Standard, 6-cyl.

	FP	5	4	3	2	1
Sed	540	825	1600	4000	5600	8000
Spt Rds	465	4000	7950	13,250	18,550	26,500
Phae	520	4100	8250	13,750	19,250	27,500
Cpe	485	1025	2600	5250	7300	10,500
2 dr Sed	495	800	1550	3900	5450	7800

Master, 6-cyl.

	FP	5	4	3	2	1
Spt Rds	540	4100	8250	13,750	19,250	27,500
Bus Cpe	560	1075	3000	5500	7700	11,000
Spt Cpe	600	1125	3450	5750	8050	11,500
2 dr Sed	580	875	1700	4300	6000	8600
Twn Sed	615	875	1700	4350	6050	8700
Sed	640	900	1800	4450	6250	8900
Conv	695	3650	7350	12,250	17,150	24,500

1935

CHEVROLET — STANDARD — SERIES EC — SIX: Standard series 1935 Chevrolets had styling that was very similar to 1934 models. Two changes were painted headlight shells and the repositioning of gauges in the center of the dashboard. Semi-elliptic front springs were carried over on these models. An 11-gallon fuel tank was used on standard Chevrolets.

CHEVROLET — MASTER DELUXE — SERIES ED/EA — SIX: The Master DeLuxe series 1935 Chevrolets had completely new styling. They featured Fisher Abody Division's latest innovation — all-steel "Turret Top" body construction. It allowed smoother, rounder, more streamlined designs.

1935 Chevrolet, Standard, coupe, OCW

Cars in the EA series featured "Knee-Action" front suspension with coil springs. (Dubonnet suspension). An option was semi-elliptic front springs and a straight front axle. Cars so equipped were designated ED series models and cost $20 less. A split type front windshield was part of the all-new body styling. The doors opened from the front in "suicide door" style. There were no open cars in the Master DeLuxe series. A 14-gallon fuel tank was used on Master DeLuxe models.

I.D. DATA: [Series EC] Serial numbers were on the body sill under the floor mat at right front door, near front seat; also on seat frame on right side. Starting: EC-1001. Ending: EC-39050. Engine numbers were on right side of block near fuel pump. Starting: M4709885. Ending: M5500178. [Series ED/EA] Serial numbers were in the same location as on Standard models. Starting: ED-1001/EA-1001. Ending: ED-3043/EA-54937. Engine numbers were in the same location as on Standard models. Starting: 4708995. Ending: 5500178.

Model No.	Body Type & Seating	Price	Weight	Prod. Total
EC	2-dr. Spt. Rds.-2/4P	465	2410	1,176
EC	4-dr. Phae.-5P	485	2465	217
EC	2-dr. Cpe.-2P	475	2520	32,193
EC	2-dr. Coach-5P	485	2625	126,138
EC	4-dr. Sed.-5P	550	2675	42,049
Series ED (Without Knee-Action)				
ED	2-dr. Cpe.-2P	560	2910	40,201
ED	2-dr.Spt. Cpe.-2/4P	600	2940	11,901
ED	2-dr. Coach-5P	580	3010	102,996
ED	4-dr. Sed.-5P	640	3055	57,771
ED	2-dr. Twn. Sed.-5P	615	3050	66,231
ED	4-dr. Spt. Sed.-5P	675	3120	67,339

Note 1: Cars with "Knee Action" were designated EA models. They cost $20 more and weighed 30 pounds more. Production of ED and EA models was lumped together as a single total.

ENGINE: [Series EC] OHV. Inline. Cast iron block. B & S: 3-5/16 x 4 in. Disp.: 206.8 cu. in. C.R.: 5.45:1. Brake H.P.: 74 @ 3200 R.P.M. N.A.C.C. H.P.: 26.3. Main bearings: Three. Valve lifters: Solid. Carb.: Carter 1V Model 284S. [Series ED/EA] OHV. Inline. Six. Cast iron block. B & S: 3-5/16 x 4 in. Disp.: 206.8 cu. in. C.R.: 5.45:1. Brake H.P.: 80 @ 3300 R.P.M. N.A.C.C. H.P.: 26.3. Main bearings: Three. Valve lifters: Solid. Carb.: Carter 1V Model 284S.

CHASSIS: [Standard Series] W.B.: 107 in. Tires: 17 x 5.25. [Master DeLuxe ED Series] W.B.: 113 in. Tires: 17 x 5.50 without knee-action. Master DeLuxe EA Series W.B.: 113 in. Tires: 17 x 5.50 with knee action.

1935 Chevrolet, Master Deluxe, sport sedan, JAC

284

TECHNICAL: Manual transmission. Speeds: 3F/1R. Floor shift controls. Single plate clutch. Semi-floating rear axle. Overall ratio: 4.11:1. Four wheel mechanical brakes. Wire wheels. Selective free-wheeling (optional on Master DeLuxe).

OPTIONS: Bumper guards. Radio. Heater. Clock. Cigar lighter. Radio antenna. Seat covers. Spotlight. Cowl lamps. Fender skirts. License plate frame. Wire wheels. Rearview mirror. Dual sidemounts (rare).

HISTORICAL: Introduced: Dec. 15, 1934. Introduced Fisher Body with "Turret Top." The 1935 "Blue Flame" 6-cylinder engine had an improved head design, better lubrication and redesigned combustion chambers. Calendar year registrations: 656,698. Calendar year production: 793,437. Model year production: (standard) 207,976; (Master DeLuxe) 346,481; (Total) 554,457. General Manager: M.E. Coyle.

The 10 millionth Chevrolet ever produced was built on Nov. 13, 1934. The car — a 1935 model — was donated to the City of Flint (Mich.) for police safety patrol duties. The Standard Sports Roadster and Phaeton were discontinued in the early part of the 1935 production run. A new assembly plant (Code 14) opened in Baltimore. New manufacturing plants were added in Saginaw, Mich. and Muncie, Ind.

1935
Standard, 6-cyl.

	FP	5	4	3	2	1
Rds	465	3500	7050	11,750	16,450	23,500
Phae	485	3800	7650	12,750	17,850	25,500
Cpe	475	1025	2600	5250	7300	10,500
2 dr Sed	485	825	1600	4000	5600	8000
Sed	550	850	1650	4150	5800	8300
Master, 6-cyl.						
5W Cpe	560	1075	3000	5500	7700	11,000
Spt Cpe	600	1125	3450	5750	8050	11,500
2 dr Sed	580	850	1650	4100	5700	8200
Sed	640	875	1700	4250	5900	8500
Spt Sed	675	875	1700	4350	6050	8700
Twn Sed	615	850	1650	4150	5800	8300

NOTE: (Knee-action models: add $20 to factory prices and 25 percent to current values).

1936

1936 Chevrolet, convertible coupe, OCW

CHEVROLET — STANDARD — SERIES FC — SIX: The Standard series Chevrolets adopted the all-steel Fisher Body with "Turret Top" styling. They had more rounded front fenders and radiator grilles and shells. A split front windshield (as used on 1935 Master DeLuxes) was new. The number of horizontal hood louvers was reduced to two, with the top ones being longer. Rear fenders were skirted and more streamlined. Steel disc wheels were used this year. A 14-gallon fuel tank was now used on all Chevrolets.

MASTER DELUXE — SERIES FD/FA — SIX: A thicker, rounder radiator shell characterized cars in the Master DeLuxe lines. The grille was also larger and more rounded at the top; more pointed at the bottom. A lower hood ornament had its wings pointing back horizontally. The doors were now hinged toward the rear; no more "suicide" style front doors. The FD designation was for cars without coil spring front suspension; the FA designation was for cars with this feature. There were still no open cars in the Master DeLuxe series. In mid-year, steel spoke wheels were adopted for all models.

Model No.	Body Type & Seating	Price	Weight	Prod. Total
FC	2-dr. Cpe.-2P	495	2645	59,356
FC	2-dr. Cabr.-2/4P	595	2745	3629
FC	2-dr. Coach-5P	510	2750	76,646
FC	4-dr. Sed.-5P	575	2775	1,142
FC	2-dr. Twn. Sed.-5P	535	2775	220,884
FC	4-dr. Spt. Sed.-5P	600	2805	46,760
SERIES FD (WITHOUT KNEE-ACTION)				
FD	2-dr. Cpe.-2P	560	2895	49,319
FD	2-dr. Spt. Cpe.-2/4P	590	2940	10,985
FD	2-dr. Coach-5P	580	2985	40,814
FD	4-dr. Sed.-5P	640	3060	14,536
FD	2-dr. Twn. Sed.-5P	605	3030	244,134
FD	4-dr. Spt. Sed.-5P	665	3080	140,073

Note 1: Cars with "Knee Action" were designated FA models. They cost $20 more and weighed 30 pounds more. Production of FD and FA models was lumped together as a single total.

ENGINE: OHV. Inline. Six. Cast iron block. B & S: 3-5/16 x 4 in. Disp.: 206.8 cu. in. C.R.: 6.0:1. Brake H.P.: 79 @ 3200 R.P.M. N.A.C.C. H.P.: 26.3. Main bearings: Three. Valve lifters: Solid. Carb.: Carter 1V Model 319S.
Note 2: The same engine was used in both series in 1936.

CHASSIS: [Standard Series] W.B.: 109 in. Tires: 17 x 5.25. [Master DeLuxe FD Series] W.B.: 113 in. Tires: 17 x 5.50 without knee-action. [Master DeLuxe FA Series] W.B.: 113 in. Tires: 17 x 5.50 with knee-action.

TECHNICAL: Manual transmission. Speeds: 3F/1R. Floor shift controls. Single-plate clutch. Semi-floatin rear axle. Overall ratio: 4.11:1. Four-wheel hydraulic brakes. Steel spoke wheels (slotted).

OPTIONS: Fender skirts. Bumper guards. Radio. Heater. Clock. Cigar lighter. Radio antenna. Seat covers. External sun shade. Spotlight. Cowl lamps. Fog lamps. License plate frame. Wire wheels. Rear view mirror. Dual sidemounts. (Rare).

HISTORICAL: Introduced: Nov. 2, 1935. Innovations: Hydraulic brakes introduced for Chevrolets. Cabriolet reintroduced in Standard series. Box-girder frame on standard models. Early standards had composite wood/steel doors. Later cars were all-steel. Calendar year registrations: 930,250. Calendar year production: 975,238. Model year production: (Standard) 431,016; (Deluxe) 499,996; (Total) 975,238. General Manager: M.E. Coyle.
  Chevrolet reclaimed the Number 1 position in U.S. automobile sales this season. A new transcontinental speed record was set by Bob McKenzie driving a 1936 Standard Chevrolet.

1936 Chevrolet, Master Deluxe, sedan, HAC

1936
Standard, 6-cyl.

	FP	5	4	3	2	1
Cpe	495	1025	2600	5250	7300	10,500
Sed	575	825	1600	4000	5600	8000
Spt Sed	600	850	1650	4150	5800	8300
2 dr Sed	510	825	1600	3950	5500	7900
Cpe P.U.	—	950	2100	4750	6650	9500
Conv	595	1650	4650	7750	10,850	15,500

Master, 6-cyl.

	FP	5	4	3	2	1
5W Cpe	560	1075	3000	5500	7700	11,000
Spt Cpe	590	1125	3450	5750	8050	11,500
2 dr Sed	580	850	1650	4100	5700	8200
Twn Sed	605	850	1650	4150	5800	8300
Sed	640	850	1650	4200	5850	8400
Spt Sed	665	875	1700	4250	5900	8500

NOTE: (Knee-action models: add $20 to factory prices and $200 to current values).

1937

1937 Chevrolet, 2-dr. sedan, AA

CHEVROLET — MASTER — SERIES GB — SIX: Chevrolets had completely new "Diamond Crown" styling with safety glass in all windows and straight side fenders. A streamline groove ran from the fenders onto the doors, where it blended into the sheet metal. The grille was swept in on each side. Headlamp buckets on all models were painted body color. Master models had less trim, single taillamps, single wipers and no front fender parking lamps. Inside there was no front seat armrest or dashboard head indicator gauge. The sides of the hood were decorated with a tapering, spear-shaped panel incorporating cooling louvers. Semi-elliptic springs and a straight axle suspension were at the front of these cars. The standard Cabriolet featured Master Deluxe style bumper guards. Safety-Plate glass was used in all Chevrolets. Trunks, on most models, were now larger, with enclosed spare tires.

MASTER DELUXE — SERIES GA — SIX: The Master Deluxe models had the same size and styling features as Masters. Knee-Action front suspension was standard. Other standard equipment included dashboard heat indicator; front passenger armrest; dual taillamps; double wipers; twin sunvisors, fancy bumpers with guards.

I.D. DATA: Starting: GB-1001. Ending: GB-60674. Engine numbers were on the right side of block near fuel pump. Starting: 1. Ending: 1187821. Series GA Serial numbers were in the same location as Master Models. Starting: GA-1001. Ending: GA-82134. Engine numbers were the same as on Master models.

1937 Chevrolet, Master, sport sedan, HAC

Model No.	Body Type & Seating	Price	Weight	Prod. Total
GB	2-dr. Cpe.-2P	619	2770	54,683
GB	2-dr. Cabr.-2/4P	725	2790	1724
GB	2-dr. Coach-5P	637	2800	15,349
GB	2-dr. Twn. Sed.-5P	655	2830	178,845
GB	4-dr. Sed.-5P	698	2845	2755
GB	4-dr. Spt. Tr. Sed.-5P	716	2885	43,240
GA	2-dr. Cpe.-2P	685	2840	56,166
GA	2-dr. Spt. Cpe.-2/4P	724	2870	8935
GA	2-dr. Coach-5P	703	2910	7260
GA	2-dr. Twn. Sed.-5P	721	2935	300,332
GA	4-dr. Sed.-5P	770	2935	2221
GA	4-dr. Spt. Sed.-5P	788	2960	144,110

ENGINE: [Series GA] OHV. Inline. Six. Cast iron block. B & S: 3-1/2 x 3-3/4 in. Disp.: 216.5 cu. in. C.R.: 6.25:1. Brake H.P.: 85 @ 3200 R.P.M. N.A.C.C. H.P.: 29.4 Main bearings: Four. Valve lifters: Solid. Carb.: Carter 1V Model W1.

CHASSIS: [Master Series] W.B.: 112-1/4 in. Tires: 16 x 6.00. [Master Deluxe Series] W.B.: 112-1/4 in. Tires: 16 x 6.00.

TECHNICAL: Manual transmission. Speeds: 3F/1R. Floor shift controls. Single-plate clutch. Semi-floating rear axle. Overall Ratio: (Master) 3.73:1; (Master Deluxe) 4.22:1. Four wheel hydraulic brakes. Steel spoke wheels.

OPTIONS: Fender skirts. Bumper guards. Radio. Heater. Clock. Cigar lighter. Radio antenna. Seat covers. External sun shade. Spotlight. Fog lamps. License frames. Whitewall tires. Front fender marker lamps. Rear tire cover. Slide in express box. Wheel trim rings.
Note 1: Sidemounts were no longer a standard accessory.

HISTORICAL: Introduced: Nov. 1936. Innovations: Completely new all-steel Unisteel Body by Fisher with updated styling. Completely re-engineered 6-cylinder engine with larger bore; shorter stroke. Four main bearings. Boxgirder type frame now used on all models. Calendar year registrations: 768,040. Calendar year production: 868,250. Model year production: (Master) 306,024; (Master Deluxe) 519,196; (Total) 825,220. General Manager: M.E. Coyle.
  Chevrolet was again America's best selling automotibile.

1937
Master, 6-cyl.

	FP	5	4	3	2	1
Conv	725	4000	7950	13,250	18,550	26,500
Cpe	619	925	2000	4600	6400	9200
Cpe P.U.	—	975	2200	4850	6800	9700
2 dr Sed	637	850	1650	4100	5700	8200
2 dr Twn Sed	655	850	1650	4150	5800	8300
4 dr Trk Sed	698	850	1650	4200	5850	8400
4 dr Spt Sed	716	875	1700	4250	5900	8500

Master DeLuxe, 6-cyl.

	FP	5	4	3	2	1
Cpe	685	975	2200	4850	6800	9700
Spt Cpe	724	1000	2500	5100	7100	10,200
2 dr Sed	703	850	1650	4200	5850	8400
2 dr Twn Sed	721	875	1700	4250	5900	8500
4 dr Trk Sed	770	875	1700	4250	5900	8500
4 dr Spt Sed	788	875	1700	4300	6000	8600

1938

1938 Chevrolet, Master Deluxe, 4-dr. sedan, AA

CHEVROLET — MASTER — SERIES HB — SIX: Chevrolet advertised that its 1938 models had new modern body styling. In reality, the body shell, fenders and running boards were the same as in 1937. A new grille was composed of horizontally arranged chromium bars, alternating one wide and four narrow. It was in two pieces, right and left. A center molding divided them. New bumper had a full width indentation, about one half inch wide, that was painted black. Headlights and taillamps were of a carryover design. The hood had ventilators highlighted by three chrome horizontal moldings. The bullet shaped headlights were mounted closely to the radiator grille. Inside the seats were two inches wider. Improved worm and roller sector steering was used. The front suspension was of semi-elliptic springs and a straight axle on all Master Series models, plus the Master Deluxe cabriolet. Master Chevrolets had single taillamps as standard equipment.

CHEVROLET — MASTER DELUXE — SERIES HA — SIX: The Master DeLuxe featured styling changes identical to Master models. The main difference was that bumper guards were standard equipment on the Master DeLuxe. These guards were now braced to the frame. The Master DeLuxe designation appeared on the center chrome molding running across the oblong shaped hood ventilators. Dual taillamps were standard equipment.

1938 Chevrolet, Master Deluxe, sport coupe, HAC

I.D. DATA: [Series HB] Serial numbers were on a plate under hood on right side of cowl. Starting: HB-1001. Ending: HB-30097. Engine numbers were on the right side of block near fuel pump. National 1938 and later series on milled pad on crankcase to rear of distributor on right side of engine. Engines with a "B" prefix were built at Buffalo, N.Y. Starting: 1187822. Ending: 11915446; also B-1 to B-10502. [Series HA] Serial numbers were in the same location as on Master models. Starting: HA-1001. Ending: HA-46134. Engine numbers were the same as on Master models.

Model No.	Body Type & Seating	Price	Weight	Prod. Total
HB	2-dr. Cpe.-2P	648	2770	39,793
HB	2-dr. Cabr.-4P	755	2790	2,787
HB	2-dr. Coach-5P	668	2795	3,326
HB	2-dr. Twn. Sed.-5P	689	2825	95,050
HB	4-dr. Sed.-5P	730	2840	522
HB	4-dr. Spt. Sed.-5P	750	2845	20,952
HA	2-dr. Cpe.-2P	714	2840	36,106
HA	2-dr. Spt. Cpe.-4P	750	2855	2,790
HA	2-dr. Coach-5P	730	2900	1,038
HA	2-dr. Twn. Sed.-5P	750	2915	186,233
HA	4-dr. Sed.-5P	796	2915	236
HA	4-dr. Spt. Sed.-5P	817	2940	76,323

Note 1: The slant-back 4-door sedan is an unusually rare Chevrolet. Other sedans were trunk-back models.

ENGINE: OHV. Inline. Six. Cast iron block. B & S: 3-1/2 x 3-3/4 in. Disp.: 216.5 cu. in. C.R.: 6.25:1. Brake H.P.: 85 @ 3200 R.P.M. N.A.C.C. H.P.: 29.4. Main bearings: Four. Valve lifters: Solid. Carb.: Carter 1V Model W1.

CHASSIS: [Master Series] W.B.: 112-1/4 in. Tires: 16 x 6.00. [Master DeLuxe Series] W.B.: 112-1/4 in. Tires: 16 x 6.00.

TECHNICAL: Manual transmission. Speeds: 3F/1R. Floor shift. Single-plate clutch. Semi-floating rear axle. Overall ratio: (Master) 3.73:1; (Master DeLuxe) 4.22:1. Four wheel hydraulic brakes. Steel spoke wheels.

OPTIONS: White sidewall tires. Fender marker lamps. Rear tire cover. Dual sidemount (rare). Sidemount cover (rare). Fender skirts ($8). Bumper Guards (std. on Master DeLuxe). Radio. Heater. Clock. Cigar lighter. Radio antenna. Seat covers. External sun shade. Spotlight. Fog lamps. wheel trim rings. License plate holder.
Note 2: At least one U.S. built 1938 Chevrolet had factory equipment dual sidemounts. This car is owned by a Dutch collector who lives in Holland.

HISTORICAL: Introduced: Oct. 23, 1937. Innovations: Heavier valve springs. Cutoff exhaust valve guides. Langer water pump shaft. New ball bearing water pump (mid-year). Improved generator and starter systems. New diaphram spring type clutch. New Departure throw-out bearing. Lighter flywheel. Longer rear axle housing and shaft. Calendar year registrations: 464,337. Calendar year production: 490,447. Model year production: (Master) 167,926; (Master DeLuxe) 302,840; (Total) 470,766. General Manager: M.E. Coyle.

1938

Master, 6-cyl.	FP	5	4	3	2	1
Conv	755	4100	8250	13,750	19,250	27,500
Cpe	648	925	2000	4600	6400	9200
Cpe P.U.	—	975	2200	4850	6800	9700
2 dr Sed	668	850	1650	4200	5850	8400
2 dr Twn Sed	689	875	1700	4250	5900	8500
4 dr Sed	730	875	1700	4250	5900	8500
4 dr Spt Sed	750	450	1050	1700	3200	4600
Master DeLuxe, 6-cyl.						
Cpe	714	975	2300	4950	6900	9900
Spt Cpe	750	1025	2600	5200	7200	10,400
2 dr Sed	730	875	1700	4250	5900	8500
2 dr Twn Sed	750	875	1700	4300	6000	8600
4 dr Sed	797	875	1700	4300	6000	8600
4 dr Spt Sed	817	875	1700	4350	6050	8700

1939

1939 Chevrolet, Master Deluxe, 4-dr. sedan, AA

CHEVROLET MASTER 85 — SERIES JB — SIX: The 1939 Chevrolets had longer hoods. Their redesigned hoods, fenders, wheels and runningboards made for a lower, longer appearance. The body shell was basically the same as 1938, but looked more modern. The grille extended back along the fender line at the top and narrowed to around four inches at the bottom. It had a well rounded grille mouldings and a horizontal bar effect on the splash aprons. The radiator was more upright. Headlights were mounted atop the front fenders. The door panel creases were eliminated and all four fenders were raised at the rear. Mounted at the center of the decklid, except on sedans and coaches, was the license plate lamp. Combination taillamps were of smaller size and incorporated stop lamps. The front bumpers had a more rounded face bar and were otherwise unchanged. Four spoke steel wheels replaced the old eight spoke type. Inside, the hand brake lever was moved to the cowl. A vacuum gearshift mounted on the steering column was a $10 option.

MASTER DELUXE — SERIES JA — SIX: The Master Deluxe was a fancy version of the Master. It had bumperguards as standard equipment. Twin taillights were regular equipment. An all-new body style was the 4-passenger coupe with folding opera seats replacing the rumble seat. The "Knee Action" coil spring front suspension was utilized.

I.D. DATA: [Series JB] Serial numbers were on a plate underhood on right side of cowl. Starting: JB-1001. Ending: JB-33221. Engine numbers were on the right side of engine on milled pad on crankcase near rear of distributor. Starting: 1915447. Ending: 2697267; also B-10503 to B-105461. [Series JA] Serial numbers were in the same location as on Master 85 models. Starting: JA-1001. Ending: JA-58510. Engine numbers were the same as on Master models.

Model No.	Body Type & Seating	Price	Weight	Prod. Total
JB	2-dr. Cpe.-2P	628	2780	41,770
JB	2-dr. Coach-5P	648	2795	1404
JB	2-dr. Twn. Sed.-5P	669	2820	124,059
JB	4-dr. Sed.-5P	689	2805	336
JB	4-dr. Spt. Sed.-5P	710	2845	22,623
JB	4-dr. Sta. Wag.-8P	848	3010	430

Note 1: The 4-door slant-back sedan continued to sell poorly. The new station wagon came in two variations. Production total given above includes 229 station wagons with folding end gates and 201 with rear door.

JA	2-dr. Bus. Cpe.-2P	684	2845	33,809
JA	2-dr. Spt. Cpe.-4P	715	2845	20,908
JA	2-dr. Coach-5P	699	2865	180
JA	2-dr. Twn. Sed.-5P	720	2875	220,181
JA	4-dr. Sed.-5P	745	2875	68
JA	4-dr. Spt. Sed.-5P	766	2910	110,521
JA	4-dr. Sta. Wag.-8P	883	3060	989

Note 2: Rare models included the Master Deluxe coach and 4-dr slant-back sedan.

ENGINE: OHV. Inline. Six. Cast iron block. B & S: 3-1/2 x 3-3/4 in. Disp.: 216.5 cu. in. C.R.: 6.25:1. Brake H.P.: 85 @ 3200 R.P.M. N.A.C.C. H.P.: 29.4. Main bearings: Four. Valve lifters: Solid. Carb.: Carter IV Model W1-4205.

CHASSIS: [Master Series] W.B.: 112-1/4 in. Tires: 16 x 6.00. [Master Deluxe Series] W.B.: 112-1/4 in. Tires: 16 x 6.00.

TECHNICAL: Manual transmission. Speeds: 3F/1R. Floor shift controls. Single-plate. Semi-floating rear axle. Overall Ratio: (Master) 3.23:1; (Master Deluxe) 4.22:1. Four wheel hydralic brakes. Four spoke steel wheels. Vacuum clutch (10.00).
Note 3: Column gear shift used with vacuum clutch option.

OPTIONS: White sidewall tires. Rearview mirror. Single sidemount (standard on sta. wag.). License plate frame. Sidemount cover (on sta. wag.). Fender skirts (8.90). Bumper guards. Radio. Heater. Clock. Cigar lighter. Radio antenna. Seat covers. External sun shade. Spotlight. Fog lamps. Wheel trim rings. Slip-in coupe pickup box. Fender marker lamps.

HISTORICAL: Introduced: Oct. 1938. Innovations: Double-acting (airplane type) shock absorbers on Master 85. Rubber bushed front suspension on Master. Diaphram clutch spring riveted to clutch cover. New open spring front suspension on Master Deluxe. Double-acting rear shock absorbers. New folding trunk guard braced to frame. Town and Country deluxe horn package. Calendar year registrations: 598,341. Calendar year production: 648,471. Model year production: (Master) 200,058; (Master Deluxe) 387,119, (Total) 587,177. General Manager: M.E. Coyle.

The new station wagon bodies were built by Mid-States Body Corp. The Master Deluxe was said to be the fastest accelerating American passenger car of 1939. It went from 10 to 60 m.p.h. in high gear. A new manufacturing plant in Tonawanda, N.Y. was opened this year. The 15 millionth Chevrolet was built in 1939. No convertible cabriolets were built this year.

1939 Chevrolet, Master Deluxe, coach, HAC

1939
Master 85, 6-cyl.

	FP	5	4	3	2	1
Cpe	628	975	2300	4900	6850	9800
2 dr Sed	648	925	2000	4600	6400	9200
2 dr Twn Sed	669	925	2000	4650	6500	9300
4 dr Sed	689	925	2000	4650	6500	9300
4 dr Spt Sed	710	950	2100	4700	6600	9400
Sta Wag	848	1125	3450	5750	8050	11,500

Master DeLuxe, 6-cyl.

	FP	5	4	3	2	1
Cpe	684	1025	2500	5150	7150	10,300
Spt Cpe	715	1025	2600	5250	7300	10,500
2 dr Sed	699	1000	2500	5100	7100	10,200
2 dr Twn Sed	720	1025	2500	5150	7150	10,300
4 dr Sed	745	1025	2500	5150	7150	10,300
4 dr Spt Sed	766	1025	2600	5200	7200	10,400
Sta Wag	610	1550	4450	7450	10,400	14,900

1940

CHEVROLET — MASTER 85 — SERIES KB — SIX: A longer wheelbase and completely new body and sheet metal were changes for 1940. The New "Royal Clipper" styling started with an "alligator" type front opening hood. The side panels were removable to get at the engine. The grille had a narrow vertical center bar, topped in name by a horizontal bar. It was of one piece design. The headlights were on top of the fenders and featured sealed beam bulbs. Parking lights were mounted on top of the front fenders. The trunk had more flowing lines with flush taillamps. The license plate lamp was again in the center of the trunk lid. The bumpers featured two

1940 Chevrolet, Special Deluxe, convertible coupe, OCW

black-finished in dentations running the length of the face bar. The Master 85 models did not have stainless steel belt hood or running board moldings. They had plainer upholstery and slightly less standard equipment. Front suspension was still of the leaf-spring, I-beam axle design.

CHEVROLET — MASTER DELUXE — SERIES KH — SIX: Master DeLuxe was now Chevrolet's mid-priced line. These cars had the same styling as Master 85s, with more trim. Master DeLuxe identification appeared at the rear of the hood side ventilators. Stainless steel body and hood moldings were omitted. Knee-Action front suspension was standard equipment.

CHEVROLET — SPECIAL DELUXE — SERIES KA — SIX: The Special DeLuxe, Chevrolet's new top-priced line, was a fancier edition of the Master DeLuxe. Stainless steel moldings trimmed the hood and body belt line. Standard equipment included a 30 hour clock, front door arm rests, right-hand windshield wiper, twin air horns and a deluxe steering wheel with horn ring. A convertible with a full width rear seat and power-operated top was new. The opera seat coupe was replaced with a 5-passenger coupe having a full rear seat. A choice of different colors of upholstery and convertible tops was offered for the first time by Chevrolet.

I.D. DATA: [Series KB] Serial numbers were on a plate on right side of Floor pan in front of front seat. Starting: KB-1001. Ending: KB-20946. Engine numbers were on the right side of engine on milled pad on crankcase near rear of distributor. Starting: 2697268. Ending: 3665902; also B-105462 to B-221935. "B" prefix on engine number indicates Buffalo N.Y. factory. [Series KH] Serial numbers were in the same location as on Master 85 models. Starting: KH-1001. Ending: KH-37644. Engine numbers were the same as on Master 85 models. [Series KA] Serial numbers were in the same location as on other models. Starting: KA-1001. Ending: KA-72089. Engine numbers were the same as on other models.

1940 Chevrolet, Special Deluxe, coupe, JAC

Model No.	Body Type & Seating	Price	Weight	Prod. Total
KB	2-dr. Bus. Cpe.-2P	659	2865	25,734
KB	2-dr. Twn. Sed.-5P	699	2915	66,431
KB	4-dr. Spt. Sed.-5P	740	2930	11,468
KB	4-dr. Sta. Wag.-8P	903	3106	411
Note 1: Station wagon was low production model.				
KH	2-dr. Bus. Cpe.-2P	684	2920	28,090
KH	2-dr. Spt. Cpe.-2/4P	715	2925	17,234
KH	2-dr. Twn. Sed.-5P	725	2965	143,125
KH	4-dr. Spt. Sed.-5P	766	2990	40,924
KA	2-dr. Bus. Cpe.-2P	720	2930	25,537
KA	2-dr. Spt. Cpe.-4P	750	2945	46,628
KA	2-dr. Conv.-4P	898	3160	11,820
KA	2-dr. Twn. Sed.-5P	761	2980	205,910
KA	4-dr. Spt. Sed.-5P	802	3010	138,811
KA	4-dr. Sta. Wag.-8P	934	3158	2,493

Note 2: A total of 367 station wagons had double rear doors.

ENGINE: OHV. Inline. Six. Cast iron block. B & S: 3-1/2 x 3-3/4 in. Disp.: 216.5 cu. in. Compression Ratio: 6.25:1. Brake H.P.: 85 @ 3400 R.P.M. N.A.C.C. H.P.: 29.4. Main bearings: Four. Valve lifters: Solid. Carb.: Carter 1V Model W1-420S.

CHASSIS: [Master 85 Series] W.B.: 113 in. Tires: 16 x 6.00. [Master DeLuxe Series] W.B.: 113 in. Tires: 16 x 6.00. [Special DeLuxe Series] W.B.: 113 in. Tires: 16 x 6.00.

TECHNICAL: Manual Synchromesh transmission. Speeds: 3F/1R. Column gearshift (vacuum type) controls. Single-plate clutch. Semi-floating rear axle. Overall ratio: (Master) 3.73:1; (Others) 4.11:1. Four wheel hydraulic brakes. Steel spoke wheels.

OPTIONS: Whitewall tires. Wheel trim rings. Rearview mirror. Master grille guard. Full wheel discs. Fender skirts. Bumper guards. Radio. Heater. Clock. Cigar lighter. Radio antenna. Seat covers. External sun shade. Spotlight. Fog lamps. Accessory (plastic) hood ornament.

HISTORICAL: Introduced Sept. 1939. Innovations: First use of plastic parts. First stainless steel trim. New shape oil pan. Redesigned valve lifters. Higher charging rate. Helical gear transmission. Cross trunion type u-joint. Redesigned front cross member. Calendar year registrations: 853,529. Calendar year production: 895,734. Model year production: (Master) 116,618; (Master DeLuxe) 232,510; (Special DeLuxe) 430,945; (Total) 775,073. General Manager: M.E. Coyle.
   A Model 85 business coupe driven by Juan Manuel Fangio won the 6,000 mile Gran Primo Internacional Del Norte race in Argentina. Fangio averaged 55 mph. He came in over an hour ahead of the second place car. Three Chevys were among the top ten finishers in this contest. Chevrolet also signed its first contract for U.S. Government weapons production in April, 1940.

1940 Chevrolet, Master Deluxe, 4-dr. sedan, OCW

1940
Master 85, 6-cyl.

	FP	5	4	3	2	1
Cpe	659	1000	2400	5000	7000	10,000
Twn Sed	699	900	1900	4500	6300	9000
Spt Sed	740	950	2100	4750	6650	9500
Sta Wag	903	1550	4500	7500	10,500	15,000
Master DeLuxe, 6-cyl.						
Cpe	684	1025	2600	5250	7300	10,500
Spt Cpe	715	1075	3000	5500	7700	11,000
2 dr Sed	725	1000	2400	5000	7000	10,000
Spt Sed	766	975	2200	4850	6800	9700
Special DeLuxe, 6-cyl.						
Cpe	720	1075	3000	5500	7700	11,000
Spt Cpe	750	1125	3450	5750	8050	11,500
2 dr Sed	761	1025	2600	5250	7300	10,500
Spt Sed	802	1000	2500	5100	7100	10,200
Conv	898	3400	6900	11,500	16,100	23,000
Sta Wag	934	3150	6300	10,500	14,700	21,000

1941

CHEVROLET — MASTER DELUXE — SERIES AG — SIX: Longer, lower, wider bodies were mounted on a Chevrolet chassis with a three inch longer wheelbase. The grille resembled last years, but was new. It had six chromeplated die cast moldings. The hood was a front opening type with side panels eliminated. The headlights were now blended into the fenders. Chrome moldings decorated the front fender tops. There were parking lamps below each headlight. The new body featured concealed safety steps instead of runningboards. The slope of the windshield, rear window and upper bodysides was increased. Concealed hinges were used on the doors and hood. The Master DeLuxe had body belt moldings and model identification plates at the rear of the hood sides. Standard upholstery and trimmings were plain. There were no arm rests on the front doors.

1941 Chevrolet, Special Deluxe, convertible coupe, OCW

SPECIAL DELUXE — SERIES AH — SIX: The Special Deluxe had the same new body and basic styling as the Master Deluxe. The series name appeared in chrome block letters on the rear sides of the hood. Additional standard equipment included a deluxe steering wheel with horn ring, stainless steel hood moldings, stainless steel window reveal moldings, a chrome plated license pate lamp and arm rests on the front doors. Richer upholstery material was used. In the spring, the Fleetline sedan was introduced. It was a close-coupled 4-door model without ventipanes.

I.D. DATA: [Series AG] Serial numbers were on a plate on right side of floor pan in front of front seat. Starting: AG-1001. Ending: AG-62708. Engine numbers were on the right side of engine on milled pad on crankcase near rear of distributor. Starting: AA-1001. Ending: AA-1163729. Engines built in Tonawanda factory were numbered AC-1001 to AC-195459. [Series AH] Serial numbers were in the same location as on Master Deluxe. Starting: AH-1001. Ending: AH-02375. Engine number were the same as Master Deluxe.

Model No.	Body Type & Seating	Price	Weight	Prod. Total
AG	2-dr. Bus. Cpe.-2P	712	3020	48,763
AG	2-dr. Cpe.-5P	743	3025	79,124
AG	2-dr. Twn. Sed.-5P	754	3050	219,438
AG	4-dr. Spt. Sed.-5P	795	3090	59,538
AH	2-dr. Bus. Cpe.-2P	769	3040	17,602
AH	2-dr. Cpe.-5P	800	3050	155,889
AH	2-dr. Cabr.-5P	949	3285	15,296
AH	2-dr. Twn. Sed.-5P	810	3095	228,458
AH	4-dr. Spt. Sed.-5P	851	3125	148,661
AH	4-dr. Sta. Wag.-8P	995	3410	2045
FLEETLINE SERIES				
AH	4-dr. Sed.-5P	877	3130	34,162

ENGINE: OHV. Inline. Six. Cast iron block. B & S: 3-1/2 x 3-3/4 in. Disp.: 216.5 cu. in. C.R.: 6.5:1. 90 @ 3300 R.P.M. N.A.C.C. H.P.: 29.4. Main bearings: Four. Valve lifters: Solid. Carter 1V Model W1483S.

CHASSIS: [Master Deluxe] W.B.: 116. in. Tires: 16 x 6.00. [Special Deluxe Series] W.B.: 116 in. Tires: 16 x 6.00.

TECHNICAL: Manual Synchromest transmission. Speeds: 3F/1R. Column gear shift controls. Single-plate clutch. Semi-floating rear axle. Overall Ratio: 4.11:1. Four wheel hydraulic brakes. Steel spoke wheels.

1941 Chevrolet, Special Deluxe, station wagon, JAC

OPTIONS: Whitewall tires. Stainless steel fender trim. Short wave radio. Exhaust deflector. Fender skirts. Bumper guards. Radio. Heater. Clock. Cigar lighter. Radio antenna. Seat covers. External sun shade. Spotlight. Fog lamps. Wheel trim rings. Full wheel discs. License plate frame. Accessory hood ornament. Bumper wing guards. Rearview mirror.

HISTORICAL: Introduced Sept. 1940. Innovations: Increased compression ratio. Flat top pistons. Smaller combustion chamber. New 10 mm. spark plugs. New design rocker arms. Redesigned water pump. Improved ignition points. Knee-Action front coil spring suspension standard on all Chevrolets. Calendar year registrations: 880,346. Calendar year production: 930,293. Model year production: (Master Deluxe) 419,044; (Special Deluxe) 602,327; (total) 1,021,371. General Manager: M.E. Coyle.

Last full production year prior to WWII. Chevrolet conducted a promotional contest in which Spencer Tracy was picked as America's top movie star. He was given a new Chevrolet station wagon.

1941
Master DeLuxe, 6-cyl.

	FP	5	4	3	2	1
2P Cpe	712	1000	2400	5000	7000	10,000
4P Cpe	743	1025	2600	5250	7300	10,500
Twn Sed	754	900	1900	4500	6300	9000
Spt Sed	795	925	2000	4650	6500	9300

Special DeLuxe, 6-cyl.

	FP	5	4	3	2	1
2P Cpe	769	1025	2500	5150	7150	10,300
4P Cpe	800	1050	2700	5350	7450	10,700
Twn Sed	810	925	2000	4650	6500	9300
Spt Sed	851	950	2100	4750	6650	9500
Flt Sed	877	1000	2400	5000	7000	10,000
Conv	949	3900	7800	13,000	18,200	26,000
Sta Wag	995	3600	7200	12,000	16,800	24,000
Cpe P.U.	—	1150	3600	6000	8400	12,000

1942

1942 Chevrolet, Special Deluxe Fleetline, aerosedan, AA

CHEVROLET — MASTER DELUXE — SERIES BG — SIX: A heavier "American Eagle" grille with lower and wider horizontal bars characterized the 1942 Chevrolet. A front bumper gravel shield was added. Parking lights were in the grille side moldings. A new hood extended back to the edge of the door. The cowl panel was eliminated. Headlights were flush-mounted in the front fenders. Bolt-on caps extended the fenders onto the doors. At the rear the fenders and taillights were unchanged, but the license lamp and gravel shields were of new designs. There was no nameplate on the sides of the Master DeLuxe hood. Seats, steering wheel and interior trim were plain. On Jan. 1, 1942 all bright metal trim — with the exception of bumpers and guards — was eliminated as part of the war effort. These "black out" models had trim parts painted in body color.

CHEVROLET — SPECIAL DELUXE — SERIES BH — SIX: Better upholstery, more trim and a longer list of standard equipment were seen on Special DeLuxe Chevrolets. Extras included a deluxe steering wheel with horn ring, chrome hood nameplates, and front door arm rests. The Cabriolet now had rear quarter windows. A new model was a fastback 2-door Fleetline Aero sedan. Like the Fleetline Sportmaster sedan it had three stainless steel trim strips on the sides of the fenders and fender caps. After Jan. 1, Special DeLuxes were also sold with painted, rather than plated, trim.

I.D. DATA: [Series BG] Serial numbers were on a plate on right side of floor pan in front of front seat. Starting: BG-1001. Ending: BG-13310. Engine numbers were on the right side of engine on milled pad on crankcase near rear of distributor. Starting: 2AA-1001 & up; BA-1001 & up; 2AC-1001 & up. [Series BH] Serial numbers were in the same locations as on Master DeLuxe. Starting: BH-1001. Ending: BH-27530. Engine numbers were the same as on Master DeLuxe.

Model No.	Body Type & Seating	Price	Weight	Prod. Total
BG	2-dr. Cpe.-2P	760	3055	8,089
BG	2-dr. Cpe.-5P	790	3060	17,442
BG	2-dr. Twn. Sed.-6P	800	3090	41,872
BG	4-dr. Spt. Sed.-6P	840	3110	14,093
Fleetmaster Series				
BH	2-dr. Cpe.-2P	815	3070	1,716
BH	2-dr. Cpe.-5P	845	3085	22,187
BH	2-dr. Cabr.-5P	1080	3385	1,182
BH	2-dr. Twn. Sed.-6P	855	3120	39,421
BH	4-dr. Spt. Sed.-6P	895	3145	31,441
BH	4-dr. Sta. Wag.-8P	1095	3425	1,057

Model No.	Body Type & Seating	Price	Weight	Prod. Total
Fleetline Series				
BH	2-dr. Aerosedan-6P	880	3105	61,855
BH	4-dr. Spt. Master-6P	920	3165	14,530

Note 1: The new Aerosedan was a fastback model.

ENGINE: OHV. Inline. Six. Cast iron block. B & S: 3-1/2 x 3-3/4 in. Disp.: 216.5 cu. in. C.R.: 6.5:1. Brake H.P.: 90 @ 3300 R.P.M. N.A.C.C. H.P.: 29.4. Main bearings: Four. Valve lifters: Solid. Carb.: Carter 1X Model 483S.

CHASSIS: [Master DeLuxe Series] W.B.: 116 in. Tires: 16 x 6.00. [Special DeLuxe Series] W.B.: 116 in. Tires: 16 x 6.00.

TECHNICAL: Manual Synchromesh transmission. Speeds: 3F/1R. Column gear shift controls. Single-plate clutch. Semi-floating rear axle. Overall ratio: 4.11:1. Four wheel hydraulic brakes. Steel spoke wheels.

OPTIONS: Whitewall tires. Short wave radio. Signal-seeking radio. Exhaust deflector. Fender skirts. Bumper Guards. Radio. Heater. clock. Cigar lighter. Radio antenna. Seat covers. External sun shade. Spotlight. Fog lamps. Wheel trim rings. License plate lamp. Bumper wing guards. OSRV mirror.

HISTORICAL: Introduced: Sept. 1941. Innovations: Signal-seeking radio with station tuner introduced as an option. Aerosedan introduced. Calendar year production: 45,472. Model year production: (Master DeLuxe) 84,806; (Special DeLuxe) 173,989; (Total) 258,795. General Manager: M.E. Coyle.

All automobile production halted Feb. 1, 1942. Last pre-war Chevrolet built Jan. 30. All factories except Saginaw Service Mfg. plant converted for war production.

1942 Chevrolet, Special Deluxe, Fleetmaster cabriolet, HAC

1942
Master DeLuxe, 6-cyl.

	FP	5	4	3	2	1
2P Cpe	760	825	1600	4000	5600	8000
4P Cpe	790	850	1650	4100	5700	8200
Cpe P.U.	—	825	1600	4050	5650	8100
Twn Sed	800	700	1350	2800	4550	6500
Spt Sed	840	725	1400	3000	4700	6700

Special DeLuxe, 6-cyl.

	FP	5	4	3	2	1
2P Cpe	815	850	1650	4150	5800	8300
5P Cpe	845	875	1700	4250	5900	8500
Twn Sed	855	725	1400	3000	4700	6700
Spt Sed	895	750	1450	3300	4900	7000
Conv	1080	3600	7200	12,000	16,800	24,000
Sta Wag	1095	3150	6300	10,500	14,700	21,000

Fleetline, 6-cyl.

	FP	5	4	3	2	1
2 dr Aero	880	825	1600	4000	5600	8000
4 dr Spt Mstr	920	800	1550	3850	5400	7700

CHICAGO — The Chicago Auto Car Company was a $2 million Maine incorporation from early 1907 for the making of automobiles and appliances. J.E. Manter and C.D. Fullerton were the indicated incorporators. Manufacture did not follow.

The Chicago Auto Service Company was organized early in 1905 with a capital stock of $10,000 to manufacture and deal in automobiles. The incorporators were Lewis W. Parker, Henry M. Hagan and Charles W. Kefer. Manufacture is doubted.

The Chicago Automobile Company was organized with a capital stock of $50,000 during the fall of 1904 for the manufacture of automobiles and motor boats. M.F. Mogg, M.E. Mogg and W.A. Whirlwall were the incorporators. Manufacture is doubted.

The Chicago Automobile Self-Starting Appliance Company was organized with a capital stock of $70,000 during the fall of 1909 for the manufacture of automobiles and appliances. Edward J. Kelly was backing this venture. Manufacture of a car is doubted.

The Chicago Car Company was organized late in 1914 with a capital stock of $125,000 for the manufacture of automobiles and engines. E.M. Roehrborn, J.J. Gorman and M. O'Leary were the incorporators. Manufacture is doubted.

The Chicago Carriage Motor Company was the shop in which C.O. Hansen built his car in 1895. Refer to Hansen.

Chicago Flyer was the name given in 1907 to a car produced by the Automobile Parts & Equipment Company of Chicago, this firm using a flurry of designations for the cars it marketed through 1914. Refer to Auto Parts.

Chicago Light Six was the designation used in 1917 only for the car produced by the Pan-American Motors Corporation of Decatur, Illinois. Refer to Pan-American.

Chicago Motor Buggy was the designation of one model produced by the Black Manufacturing Company of Chicago from 1908-1909. The other cars built by the firm carried only the Black name, later Black Crow. Refer to Black.

The Chicago Pneumatic Tool Company built fifty highwheelers in 1906 for use by its traveling salesmen. Refer to C.P.T.

The Chicago Recording Scale Company of Waukegan, Illinois produced an automobile from 1906-1907 which was marketed under the tradename of Apollo. Refer to Apollo.

Chicago Runabout was an occasional designation for the car produced from 1907-1910 by the Chicago Coach and Carriage Company. More often the car carried the name of the man who had designed it and superintended its building. Refer to Duer.

The Chicago Vehicle Company was organized in Trenton, New Jersey in 1899 with a capital stock of $400,000. David Harvey of Asbury Park was the New Jersey incorporator, all remaining principals — Orson O. Fox, Smith C. Shadrick, John Trier, Gustave Lukas, M.M. Chestown, J.W. Creekmur — being from Chicago. "The company is formed to manufacture, sell and operate all kinds of vehicles," reported *The Hub* in August 1899.

1899 Chicago hydro-carbon carriage, HAC

CHICAGO — Harvey, Illinois — (1895-1899) — The Chicago Motor Vehicle Company, Ltd. had its offices at 341 Wabash Avenue and its factory in nearby Harvey where, the company said, the capacity was a hundred vehicles weekly. Most of the firm's production prior to the turn of the century was probably horsedrawn vehicles, though Chicago offered to outfit any of its numerous carriage styles available with a "double-cylinder hydro-carbon motor" using "ordinary stove gasoline." The company was especially proud of its "No. 4 Gear, No. 20 Body" an example of which it had built for the famous Chicago Times-Herald Contest of 1895: "She has out-run everything on wheels in Chicago, steam cars alone excepted, and is still running." By the turn of the century, the focus of the Chicago Motor Vehicle Company changed as president W.R. Donaldson decided to enter another field. Although an occasional automobile might have been built to customer order thereafter, production was concentrated on commercial vehicles. These included omnibuses and delivery cars, all of them using the Worth friction drive system developed by William O. Worth, who was a member of the Chicago company's directorate and who would later build the Worth car. According to *The Harvey Tribune-Citizen* in its 1902-1903 manufacturing supplement, the Chicago Motor Vehicle Company was the first in the world to manufacture hydro-carbon street railway cars. The company went bankrupt in late 1904.

1902 Chicago, motocycle carriage, RD

290

CHICAGO — Chicago, Illinois — (1902) — The Chicago Motocycle Company was organized in 1898 at 107 Madison Street by Charles Dickenson, L.F. Douglas and Henry B. Babson. Repair work occupied the firm for its first few years, but in 1902 the manufacture of automobiles was embarked upon. The motive force for the Chicago was a two-cylinder engine which could be run on hot air in addition to the more usual gasoline or kerosene fuels. "No water is used for cooling purposes," *The Motor World* reported, "the heat being all utilized and converted into power, an asbestos jacket to retain the heat being used instead of a water jacket for getting rid of it." To start the engine required the use of a torch on the cylinder head until it was red-hot. One cannot imagine this to be a feature of appeal to many customers. Beginning in 1903, the Chicago car was marketed under the tradename of Caloric, though manufacture had been discontinued by the end of 1904. At the Chicago Automobile Show in January 1905, the company exhibited a standard gasoline runabout called the Fostler, a few examples of which may have been built that year.

CHICAGO — Chicago, Illinois — (1914) — The Chicago Cyclecar Company declared that its aim was to provide side-by-side seating in a vehicle which still retained "the advantages of a 36-inch tread." What those advantages were, the company did not enunciate; but it did manage to produce at least a prototype of a roadster model seating two people none too comfortably. The car's friction transmission and chain drive were the usual, though the latter was enclosed which was rare in a cyclecar. The engine was a Mack. Whether the Chicago cyclecar ever proceeded into quantity manufacture is not known, but extremely doubtful.

CHICAGO ELECTRIC — Chicago, Illinois — (1899-1901) — Both the Chicago Electric Vehicle & Transportation Company and the Chicago Electric Vehicle Company were organized during the spring of 1899, but only the latter venture proceeded beyond the incorporation notice. The men behind it were Edward L. Brewster, William G. Beale and Samuel Insull, and they bought out the business of the Fischer Equipment Company at 118 East Twentieth Street. The Chicago Electric Vehicle Company was capitalized at two million dollars. Runabouts, phaetons, broughams, dogcarts and electric cabs were the announced products, although it would appear only the last-named vehicles were built in any numbers in a plant in Faribault, Minnesota. Until approximately 1901, the Chicago Electric Vehicle Company operated a fleet of cabs in the Windy City. The firm faded out thereafter. The subsequent ventures of Messrs. Brewster and Beale are not known, but Sam Insull, of course, went on to a rather colorful career.

1914 Chicago Electric, brougham, WLB

CHICAGO ELECTRIC — Chicago, Illinois — (1913-1916) — The Chicago Electric Motor Car Company was organized by a group of alumni of the Woods Electric Company, among them Frederick J. Newman who would serve as president of the new firm, C.J. Blakeslee as chief engineer, and Penrose Reed as general sales manager. The Chicago Electric featured a low-slung, shaft-drive chassis and a high arched door, and was available initially in two brougham body styles. Two horizontal levers operated the car, one for steering, the other for regulating the speed from 5 mph to the maximum of 25 mph. Although the background and experience of its founders provided "virtual surety," as *Automobile Topics* said, that the new company would take hold immediately, apparently it did not. In November of 1913, the announcement came that the Carl Electric Vehicle Company had purchased much of the Chicago Electric machinery and was moving same to Toledo (Ohio) to begin building electric commercial vehicles. The design of the Chicago Electric pleasure car was bought by the Walker Vehicle Company of Chicago in late 1914 and the car was continued in production into 1916. Among the more notable purchasers of the latter-day Chicago Electric was the Vatican in Rome, for the use of Pope Pius X. And among the more novel marketing gimmicks for the car was the selling of its 1916 models in the Chicago area without battery if the purchaser desired to rent same instead. In an arrangment with the Rental Battery Company of Chicago, Walker leased batteries (with service included) to Chicago Electric owners for twenty dollars a month for the first year, sixteen dollars for the second. The Rental Battery Company was out of business by the end of 1916, however, and the Walker Vehicle Company was taken over by the Detroit Electric people soon after.

1913 CHICAGO ELECTRIC

	FP	5	4	3	2	1
No. 131 Front-Drive Brgm. (96" wb)	2800	3200	4300	6500	11,000	23,000
No. 132 Rear-Drive Brgm. (104" wb)	3100	3300	4400	6700	12,000	24,000

1914 CHICAGO ELECTRIC

	FP	5	4	3	2	1
No. 141 Front-Drive Brgm. (96" wb)	3000	3200	4300	6500	11,000	23,000
No. 142 Rear-Drive Brgm. (104" wb)	3300	3300	4400	6700	12,000	24,000

1915-1916 CHICAGO ELECTRIC

	FP	5	4	3	2	1
Rear-Drive Brgm. (96" wb)	2600	3300	4400	6700	12,000	24,000
Cabr. Rds. (96" wb)	2600	3700	4700	7300	13,700	26,000
Front-Drive Limo. (104" wb)	2800	3500	4500	7000	13,000	25,000

(Note: for 1916 prices were lowered to $1985 and $2150 respectively)

CHICAGO FORTY — Chicago, Illinois — (1909) — The evidence suggests that the Chicago Forty was nothing more than the C-F renamed. It was a 35 hp shaft-drive four selling for $2250, precisely what the C-F had been prior to the demise earlier in 1909 of the Cornish-Friedberg Motor Car Company. Louis Friedberg was the only member of the C-F team involved, and probably what *Motor World* called his "automobile manufacturing enterprise on a modest scale" was simply the using up of parts on hand and the marketing of the result under a new name.

CHICAGO MOTOR BUGGY — Chicago, Illinois — (1908) — Although the designation was entirely appropriate for the vehicle it bought, the Chicago Motor Buggy Company might have been better advised to have chosen another name for its product. It was a two-cylinder, air-cooled solid-tire highwheeler priced in the $550 to $750 range. Unfortunately, across town in Chicago, the Black Manufacturing Company was producing a model of its highwheeler that it also called the Chicago Motor Buggy and the price range for its variation was $375 to $475. The Chicago Motor Buggy Company was out of business by the end of the year.

1908 CHICAGO MOTOR BUGGY
2-cyl., 15 hp, 72" wb

Rbt.	550	2400	3400	4800	8000	17,000
Surrey	750	2500	3500	5000	8500	18,000

1906 Chicago Steamer, touring, NAHC

CHICAGO STEAM CAR — Chicago, Illinois — (1905-1907) — Just two minutes to start steam from cold water was the claim of the Chicago Automobile Manufacturing Company and, if true, the Chicago Steam Car would have been one of the quickest of any steamer on the market to get away. It probably was not true. The Chicago did, however, have a V-4 engine which was certainly unusual, and tanks for water/gasoline sufficient for 150 and 125 miles. The vehicle was shaft drive, and offered in one five-passenger body style only. In August of 1906 the company announced that it was considering a move to Connersville, Indiana if that town provided enough inducement. The inducement was the purchase of $17,000 of the $50,000 capital stock to be subscribed. Connersville didn't buy.

1905-1907 CHICAGO STEAM CAR
Model C — 4-cyl., 25/30 hp, 114" wb

Detachable Tonneau-5P	2500	2500	3500	5000	8500	18,000

CHICOPEE — The Chicopee Motor Car Company was organized in St. Louis, Missouri to manufacture and deal in motor cars in late 1910. Capital stock was $3000. The incorporators were H.C. Carr, F.V. Carr and J.J. Blincoe. Manufacture is doubted.

CHIEF — Buffalo, New York — (1908) — The Chief from Buffalo was a small two-stroke, water-cooled runabout with friction transmission, center chain drive and right-hand wheel steer. It was totally akin to dozens of other runabouts being manufactured during this period in the East, and the Chief Manufacturing Company was akin as well in not long surviving in the industry.

1908 Chief, runabout, NAHC

1908 CHIEF
Model A — 2-cyl., 10/12 hp, 84" wb

	FP	5	4	3	2	1
Rbt.-2P	600	2300	3300	4600	7500	16,000

CHIEF — Detroit, Michigan — (1911) — The Chief from Detroit was a touring car with a rear tonneau easily convertible to a light delivery body (which was not unusual) and fitted with a V-8 engine (which was). The Chief Motor Car Company had been organized in December 1910 by Francis A. Mueller, Thomas J. Atkinson and Jere F. Oundy. In February 1911 they announced their plans for manufacture. Nothing further was heard of the car or the company. Probably only a prototype was built.

CHILDERS & LOWE — "Childers & Lowe and Charles Stone, San Luis Obispo, California, are building an auto," reported *The Horseless Age* in March 1902. Further documentation is lacking.

CHIPPEWA — Chippewa Falls, Wisconsin — (1912) — So far as is known, the Chippewa Valley Auto Company built only one car and strictly for its own use. Most of the work involved was farmed out to the Phoenix Manufacturing Company of Eau Claire. A unique feature of the Chippewa automobile was its removable unit powerplant "which may be hoisted out of the car and transferred to a motorboat hull constructed especially for the purpose." Why was not addressed.

CHIVILLE — Chicago, Illinois — (1914) — Of the cyclecar he was building in Chicago in 1914, Gerald D. Chiville said that it would be "different from anything on the market . . . simple as a motorcycle and yet have all the necessary features of most successful automobiles." Chiville's cyclecar may have been different, but certainly it never did reach the market.

CHOATE — Portland, Maine — (1896) — Parker C. Choate, a metallurgical engineer from Portland, designed a gasoline motor vehicle with no flywheel, no crankshaft, no drive chain and no sprocket wheels in its transmission. The entire unit powerplant attached directly to the rear axle. Speed control was electrical, although without the use of storage batteries. "The power is claimed to be most elastic," *The Horseless Age* said, "the explosions occurring with a frequency of from five to the minute up to the full capacity of the cylinders, which is said to be 200 to 300 per minute." A great economy of power was the result, Choate advised, and he hoped to complete his carriage in time for the Cosmopolitan Race in Providence. He didn't make it to the starting line.

CHRISTIE — New York & New Jersey — (1904-1910) — Christie Iron Works of New York evolved into the Christie Direct Action Motor Car Company in 1906 and the Walter Christie Automobile Company in 1908. J. Walter Christie was America's first serious exponent of front wheel drive. His system was patented in the United States, Europe, Russia and Australia, and he sought to prove the soundness of his ideas through racing. The car Christie took to Ormond-Daytona Beach in January 1904 had a four-cylinder 30 hp engine mounted transversely, the crankshaft supplanting the front axle, with front wheels driven directly by flywheels coupled via leather-faced clutches to the crank ends and telescoping universal joints heavily packed with grease. A half-dozen racers were built in all, one of which had two 60 hp engines mounted at either end of the car, and another of which had two distinctions — it was the first American entrant in a French Grand Prix (1907) and it was powered by the largest engine (a 19,881 cc V-4) ever to compete in any Grand Prix. Though he had completed a 50 hp, 100-inch wheelbase, 2300-pound touring car with body by Healey to sell for $6500 by the summer of 1906, Christie was too busy racing to market it. When his Direct Action company went into receivership, an undaunted Christie simply formed a new company and designed a

291

1907 Christie, touring, WLB

tidy little ohv 18 hp four that he planned to produce as a $2600 taxicab for New York City. Only three were built, however; Christie was sidetracked into racing once more. "It's no shame to be poor," he once told a friend, "but it's damn inconvenient." Motorcar production interested him probably only as a means to finance further experimentation. In 1908 he had patented a tractor device to convert fire department rigs from horse-drawn to automotive, and in 1912 he formed the Front Drive Motor Company in Hoboken (New Jersey) for its marketing. Six hundred such tractors were built. Walter Christie spent the rest of his life designing airplane engines, tanks and other military machines which were ingenious but brought him neither fame nor fortune. He died in 1944 at age eighty, in obscurity. But if modern front wheel drive can be said to have a single inventor, it was J. Walter Christie.

1908 Christie Taxi landaulet, HAC

CHRISTENSEN — Milwaukee, Wisconsin — (1908) — N.A. Christensen was the inventor of an air brake and an automatic air compressor which he had been selling profitably to garages and automobile manufacturers since 1905. In 1908 he sold out that business to join the gasoline-engine-producing C.P. & L. Lauson Company of Milwaukee which later that year increased its capital stock from $75,000 to $150,000, changed its name to Christensen Engineering Company, and announced that "the manufacture of motor cars will hereafter be the principal line of activity." A.H. Lauson remained onboard as the new Christensen company's secretary-treasurer, with Christensen taking the presidency. The evidence suggests that gasoline-engine manufacture remained the mainstay of the Christensen Engineering Company, though the firm perhaps built a few automobiles to special order of specific clients. The Christensen plant was at 841-847 Thirtieth Street.

CHRISTMAN — San Jose, California — (1901-1902)/Los Angeles, California — (1907) — Charles G. Christman first launched himself into the automobile business with his Christman Motor Carriage Company in 1901. Located at 86-88 East San Fernando Street in San Jose, the Christman firm produced a few small gasoline-powered runabouts beginning in 1901, but by July of 1902 Charles Christman had sold out to the Golden State Automobile Company which proceeded to build the Golden State car, while in another portion of the factory Christman stayed on to manufacture a muffler he had invented. In 1907 Christman had another automotive idea and incorporated the Christman Motor Car Company in Los Angeles to build it. The latterday Christman was termed a Desert Car, and

featured large wheels, a wide tread, low gear ratio and other accoutrements to lend itself well for use in mining districts. Christman's Desert Car adventure was even shorter than his runabout's, though his 1907 vehicle is known to have been exhibited at local automobile shows.

CHRISTOPHER — For a time the Christopher Brothers of Chicago were the selling agents for the Triumph car built in the Windy City from 1907-1912. Refer to Triumph.

CHRYSLER

CHRYSLER — Detroit, Michigan — (1924-1942 et. seq.) — The evolution of the Chrysler represents one of the more stirring sagas in the history of the American automobile. First, there is the fact that no other individual since has managed to do what Walter Percy Chrysler was the last to accomplish in the mid-Twenties — and that is, simply to start a new automobile company and to make it survive. But second, there is the marvelous tale about how he managed to do it. From an early career as a farm hand, grocery boy, silverware salesman, and round-house sweeper for the Union Pacific. Walter Chrysler had moved up to Pittsburgh plant manager of the American Locomotive Company when his talents first came to the attention of the automobile industry and he was brought to Flint, Michigan as the works manager for Buick in 1910. In 1919, when he slammed the door on his way out of General Motors, he was Buick's president. Though he had liked the job, he found working with William C. Durant taxed his patience beyond the endurable. He left Buick a very wealthy man, Durant later commenting that he had paid Chrysler $10 million for his stock, enough to provide a comfortable kitty with which to start his own automobile company. One suspects Walter Chrysler had that in mind all along. But first another job from Chase National Bank beckoned which promised to be both challenging (taking over management of the faltering automotive business of John North Willys) and lucrative (Chrysler's fee was a cool million dollars a year). At this point, mid-1919, the Willys car lineup was focused on three cars: an Overland to compete with the Model T Ford, a line of Willys-Knight fours, and a Willys Six then under development and under wraps in the former Duesenberg plant in Elizabeth, New Jersey. Working on the last-named car for Willys Corporation (the holding company for all John North Willys' interests, and separate from Willys-Overland) were three former Studebaker engineers named Fred Zeder, Owen Skelton and Carl Breer. Neither the low-priced field nor sleeve-valve engines piqued Chrysler's interest much, which meant he didn't care particularly about the Overland or the Willys-Knight. But that Willys Six prototype in the Elizabeth plant intrigued him. Indeed, during 1920, rumors floated that the car would be introduced as the Chrysler Six, and at least one published ad alluded to that effect as late as January 1921, which provides an idea of the power Chrysler was exerting at the time over Willys affairs. But Chrysler remained with Willys for only two years, and then left ostensibly because his job of streamlining the organization was finished, or conceivably because he thought Willys was. From banker friends he immediately launched himself into a similar salvage operation with another faltering automobile company, the Maxwell Motor Corporation which had recently been merged, none too happily, with Chalmers. Meanwhile, the Willys Six prototype had not yet been marketed because John North Willys remained in a fight to wrest control of Willys from the banks, which he deftly accomplished by maneuvering Willys-Overland stock and moving his Willys Corporation holding company into receivership. This resulted in the Elizabeth plant and the prototype inside being sent to the auction block. And there, ironically, Walter Chrysler (now Maxwell's president) was outbid by his old boss William C. Durant, who had meanwhile been kicked out of General Motors and was beginning his second empire. Fortunately for Chrysler, Durant wanted a car that was bigger and more expensive than the Willys Six that he had bought with the Elizabeth factory, and consequently that prototype was extensively revamped to become the new Flint. This left Zeder, Skelton and Breer free to develop their original design further, which they did at the enthusiastic urging of Walter Chrysler. By mid-1923 they were installed in the Chalmers plant in Detroit, where the Chalmers car was by now being phased out of production. In January 1924, at the Commodore Hotel in New York City, the new Chrysler was introduced. By the end of December, 32,000 had been sold, a new first-year sales record in the industry. What the Chrysler represented was something new in America. Its six-cylinder L-head engine displaced only 201.5 cubic inches, but with a 4.7:1 compression ratio (the industry norm was 4.0:1) developed 68 bhp at 3200 rpm. And the Chrysler could be had for $1395. It was America's first medium-priced car with a high compression engine. Nor was that all; the specification also included four-wheel hydraulic brakes, aluminum pistons, full-pressure lubrication, and tubular front axle amongst other features never before combined on a volume-produced car. Seventy miles an hour was the Chrysler's comfortable top speed. As *Fortune* magazine noted a few years later, here was a car perfectly suited to the Twenties, "a period when desires had supplanted needs . . . an era when a car which could give for $1500 the 'thrills' of a car of $5000 was precisely what the people who could buy it would most wish to buy." In competition the Chrysler fared nicely. On July 16th, 1924 Ralph De Palma drove one of the cars to the top of Mt. Wilson, not only winning the event and bettering the previous stock car record by over two minutes, but faster by more than a minute than the previous race car record too. At the Culver City Board Speedway in 1925, De Palma and the Chrysler won a 1000-mile stock car race at a 76.3 mph average. The Chrysler was the first American car to contest Le Mans, competing there four times, finishing third and fourth in 1928. But the contest of most interest to Walter P. Chrysler was within the industry itself. In mid-1925, he took his first step, with the organization of Chrysler Corporation, succeeding Maxwell. By year's end, "in response to a public demand for another car bearing the Chrysler name," as the press release put it, a four-cylinder Chrysler was introduced. It was really just an updated Maxwell, a fact which went unmentioned, of course. Also introduced for 1926 were two more Chrysler sixes, one a price echelon below the original, the other the Imperial, a 92 hp car designed to compete with Lincolns and the like. By 1927, in three short years, Walter Chrysler had moved up from the bottom rung (32nd place) in the industry to fourth. In 1928 he purchased Dodge, introduced the Plymouth and the De Soto, and slipped neatly into third, In 1929 Chryslers were styled longer, lower and with a thin-profile radiator that would be widely copied in Europe — and on the now lengthened Imperial chassis. Chrysler entered the custom field with limited production series of designs by LeBaron, Locke and Dietrich. By 1931 most Chrysler models were straight-eights. In 1934 the Airflow arrived. It was perhaps Chrysler's first mistake. A revolutionary car, and a most interesting one, the Airflow had begun in a miniature wind tunnel with Chrysler's engineering triumvirate — or the Three Musketeers as Zeder, Breer and Skelton were now known — determining that a zeppelin-like oval tapering to the rear was the automobile's optimum shape. From this followed an engine placed over the axle, not behind it, and a welded chassis/body construction with the passenger compartment cradled between the axles. Body styling was the province of Oliver Clark (who had designed the first Chrysler), though aerodynamic considerations really styled the Airflow. Its hood cascaded into a grille that looked like a waterfall with flush-mounted headlamps (designed by Breer and consulting engineer C. Harold Wills) on each side. A curved one-piece windshield was an innovation on the Custom Imperial model. ''The beauty of nature itself'' was the way Chrysler described the Airflow's appearance; ''breathlessly different-looking'' was the assessment of a *Harper's Bazaar* fashion editor. Unfortunately, the vast majority of the public found it bizarre, or just plain ugly. Combined with these were production delays occasioned by the necessity for retooling, which resulted in rumors spreading that the cars were faulty. The Airflow was a disaster in the marketplace. In 1934 only 11,292 of them were sold in three model lines, two-and-a-half times less than the single conventional Chrysler in the model lineup that year. Attempts to make the Airflow more palatable in appearance followed, plus the addition of more comely Airstream models, though it was 1937 before all Chryslers became conventionally styled again. By now Ray Dietrich had been brought in as chief body designer, with Oliver Clark moving up to executive rank. In 1940-1941 Ralph Roberts of LeBaron designed two gorgeous idea cars — the Thunderbolt (a retractable hardtop coupe) and the Newport (a dual cowl phaeton) — of which six examples each were built and displayed 'round the country. On August 18th, 1940, Walter P. Chrysler died. Five years earlier he had relinquished the presidency of his corporation to right-hand-man Kaufman Thuma Keller. It would be K.T. Keller who would lead Chrysler into the postwar era.

Chrysler Data Compilation
by John A. Gunnell

1924

1924 Chrysler, Six, model B-70, touring, OCW

CHRYSLER — MODEL B-70 — SIX: The Chrysler was introduced at the New York Auto Show in the city's Hotel Commodore. There was a full range of nine different body styles. Styling features included steppe type fenders, drum headlights, vertical hood louvers and a prominent double belt line molding on closed cars. The distinctive Chrysler radiator had a thick, rounded shell and a double winged radiator cap with the Chrysler Viking helmet logo located at the upper center. Split windshields were used on early production open cars.

I.D. DATA: Serial numbers stamped on a plate attached to front of dash and on left frame side member at rear spring horn. Starting: 1001. Ending: 32813. Engine numbers were stamped on a boss on top of chain case. Engine number info. not available.

Model No.	Body Type & Seating	Price	Weight	Prod. Total
B-70	2-dr. Rds.-4P	1525	2805	Note 1
B-70	4-dr. Tr.-5P	1335	2730	Note 1
B-70	4-dr. Phae.-5P	1395	2785	Note 1
B-70	4-dr. Sed.-5P	1625	3060	Note 1
B-70	4-dr. Imp. Sed.-5P	1895	3085	Note 1
B-70	2-dr. Brgm.-5P	1795	2995	Note 1
B-70	4-dr. Crw. Imp. Sed.-5P	2195	3090	Note 1
B-70	2-dr. Cpe.-4P	1195	2935	Note 1
B-70	4-dr. Twn. Car-5P	3725	3225	Note 1

Note 1: Total calendar year production of Chryslers and Maxwells combined was 79,144.

ENGINE: Inline. L-head. Six. Cast iron block. B & S: 3 in. x 4-3/4 in. Disp.: 201 cu. in. C.R.: 4.7:1. Brake H.P.: 68 @ 3000 R.P.M. N.A.C.C. H.P.: 21.60. Main bearings: Seven. Valve lifters: Solid. Carb.: Ball & Ball.

CHASSIS: W.B.: 112-3/4 in. O.L.: 160 in. Tires: 30 x 5.75 or 29 x 4.5 on demountable, six-lug rims.

TECHNICAL: Manual transmission. Speeds: 3F/1R. Floor shift controls. Conventional clutch. Shaft drive. Four-wheel hydraulic brakes. Steel disc wheels on touring. Wood-spoke wheels on other models.

OPTIONS: Double bar front bumpers. Double bar rear fender guards. Wind wings. Step plates. Trunk rack. Spare tire. Sidemounted spare tires. Accessory radiator cap. Whitewall tires. Sidemount covers (leather). Side curtains. OSRV mirror. Touring trunk.

HISTORICAL: Introduced in January, 1924. High compression engine used Ricardo type cylinder head. The new Chryslers were only five mph slower than the Packard eight; they had a top speed of 70-75 mph. The Chrysler replaced the Maxwell and calendar year production figures include both marques. More than 32,000 of these cars were Chryslers. A total of 19,960 Chryslers were registered during the calendar year. Ralph DePalma used a Chrysler to win the famous Mt. Wilson hill climb. He then drove the same car 1,000 miles in 1,007 hours at the Fresno, Calif. board racing track setting numerous stock car racing records.

1924
Model B, 6-cyl., 112.75" wb

	FP	5	4	3	2	1
Rds	1625	2300	5400	9000	12,600	18,000
Phae	1495	2800	5700	9500	13,300	19,000
Tr	1395	2000	5100	8500	11,900	17,000
RS Cpe	1795	1000	2400	5000	7000	10,000
4 dr Sed	1725	975	2300	4900	6850	9800
Brgm	1895	975	2300	4950	6900	9900
Imp Sed	1995	1000	2400	5000	7000	10,000
Crw Imp	2095	1025	2500	5150	7150	10,300
TwnC	3725	1400	4200	7000	9800	14,000

1925

1925 Chrysler, model B-70, 4-dr. sedan, OCW

CHRYSLER — MODEL B-70 — SIX: There were relatively few changes in the 1925 Chryslers. Open cars now used a one-piece windshield which was hinged at the top instead of a horizontally split two piece type. After Nov. 1924, Chrysler bodies were built by Fisher Body Co. At the middle of the year, Chrysler purchased the Kercheval Body factory, in Detroit, and started producing its own bodies. A longer gearshift lever was used for 1925 models and there were a number of technical refinements including the addition of a vibration damper and the use of rubber engine mounts.

I.D. DATA: Serial numbers were in the same locations. Starting: B-32813. Ending: B-81000. Engine numbers were in the same location. Engine numbers not available.

Model No.	Body Type & Seating	Price	Weight	Prod. Total
B-70	2-dr. Rds.-4P	1625	2805	Note 1
B-70	4-dr. Tr.-5P	1395	2730	Note 1
B-70	4-dr. Phae.-5P	1495	2785	Note 1
B-70	4-dr. Sed.-5P	1825	3060	Note 1
B-70	4-dr. Imp. Sed.-5P	2065	3085	Note 1
B-70	2-dr. Brgm.-5P	1965	2995	Note 1
B-70	2-dr. Coach-5P	1545	2895	Note 1
B-70	2-dr. Roy. Cpe.-4P	1895	2935	Note 1
B-70	4-dr. Crw. Imp. Sed.-5P	2195	3090	Note 1
B-70	4-dr. Twn. Car-5P	3725	3225	Note 1

Note 1: Total 1925 calendar year production of Chryslers and Maxwells combined was 132,343.

ENGINE: Inline. L-head. Six. Cast iron block. B & S: 3 in. x 4-3/4 in. Disp.: 201 cu. in. C.R.: 4.7:1. Brake H.P.: 68 @ 3000 R.P.M. N.A.C.C. H.P.: 21.60. Main bearings: Seven. Valve lifters: Solid. Carb.: Ball & Ball.

CHASSIS: W.B.: 112-3/4 in. O.L.: 160 in. Tires: 30 x 5.75 on demountable, six-lug rims.

TECHNICAL: Manual transmission. Speeds: 3F/1R. Floor shift controls. Conventional clutch. Shaft drive. Four-wheel hydraulic brakes. Wood-spoke wheels.

OPTIONS: Double bar front bumper. Double bar rear guards. Wind wings. Step plates. Trunk rack. Spare tire. Sidemount spares. Accessory radiator cap. White sidewall tires. Sidemount covers (leather). Side curtains. OSRV mirror. Special Duco paint colors. Wire spoke wheels.

HISTORICAL: Introduced January, 1925. Chrysler calendar year production was approximately 76,600. New car registrations for Chrysler were 68,793. On June 26, 1925 Maxwell was reorganized and incorporated in the state of Delaware as Chrysler Corporation. Lawyer Nicholas Kelley was president of the new company for two weeks, after which Walter P. Chrysler became president. Chrysler of Canada, Ltd. was also formed this year. Ralph DePalma set more new stock car records at Culvar City, Calif. by driving a stripped down touring car 1,000 miles in 786 minutes on Jan. 5, 1925. In England, Sir Malcom Campbell drove a streamlined Chrysler to a new lap record of 100 mph at Brooklands race track. Another Chrysler was raced at the French Grand Prix at LeMans.

1925 Chrysler, model B-70, roadster, JAC

1925
Model B-70, 6-cyl., 112.75" wb

	FP	5	4	3	2	1
Rds	1625	2300	5400	9000	12,600	18,000
Phae	1495	2800	5700	9500	13,300	19,000
Tr	1395	2000	5100	8500	11,900	17,000
Roy Cpe	1795	1075	3000	5500	7700	11,000
4 dr Sed	1695	975	2300	4900	6850	9800
Brgm	1865	975	2300	4950	6900	9900
Imp Sed	1995	1000	2400	5000	7000	10,000
Crw Imp	2095	1025	2500	5150	7150	10,300
TwnC	3725	1400	4200	7000	9800	14,000

1926

1926 Chrysler, model G70, roadster, OCW

CHRYSLER — MODEL F-58 — FOUR: The four-cylinder Chrysler was a continuance of the Maxwell with a new, rounded radiator sheel. The design was thinner than that used on Chrysler sixes, but had a family resemblance. Also, belt line moldings of the Chrysler type were used along with new "cadet" type visors on closed cars. These bodies were designed and

built by Budd Mfg. Co. of Philadelphia. Closed cars had one piece wind-shields; open cars had two piece types of the swing out style. The winged Viking hood ornament identified the cars.

1926 Chrysler Imperial, Series E80, touring, OCW

CHRYSLER — MODEL G70 — SIX: The Chrysler G-70 was a refinement of the previous B-70 and had basically the same styling except that the door openings were raised a bit higher off the body sills. Minor variations in headlamp design were seen as running changes between early and late production units. The early cars of 1925-26 manufacture had drum head-lamps with hooded rings. The early 1926 series had plain drum headlights. The later 1926 models had bullet shaped headlamps.

CHRYSLER — SERIES E80 — SIX: The Chrysler Imperial E80 was a luxury series with distinctive styling, longer wheelbases and a larger and more powerful engine. A styling innovation was a scalloped hood and radiator design. The Imperials also used bullet shaped headlamps. Standard equipment was on the rich end of the scale including many fancy trim features not offered in other Chryslers.

I.D. DATA: [Model F-58] Serial numbers were in the same locations. Numbers for the 1925-1/2 F series were WW100P to WY560W; those for the 1926 F-58 series were YC200P to YRO56S. Engine numbers were F-25000 to F-110000. [Model G-70] Serial numbers were in the same locations. G-70 numbers for the 1925-26 series were WY580W to WD999D; G-70 numbers for the first 1926 series were PP580P to PP454R and G-70 numbers for the late 1926 series were PP930S to PS287D. Engine numbers were G-81001 to G-142300. [Series E-80] Serial numbers were in the same locations. Serial numbers were ED000W to EW655S. Engine numbers were also in the same locations. Engine numbers unavailable.

Model No.	Body Type & Seating	Price	Weight	Prod. Total
F-58	2-dr. Rds.-2P	890	2375	Note 1
F-58	4-dr. Tr.-5P	895	2390	Note 1
F-58	2-dr. Cpe.-2P	995	2495	Note 1
F-58	2-dr. Coach-5P	1045	2590	Note 1
F-58	4-dr. Sedan-5P	1095	2680	Note 1

Note 1: Approximately 81,089 Series F-58 Chryslers were built to the 1926 specifications.

Model No.	Body Type & Seating	Price	Weight	Prod. Total
G-70	2-dr. Rds.-2/4P	1625	2805	Note 2
G-70	2-dr. Roy. cpe.-2/4P	1795	2935	Note 2
G-70	4-dr. Tr.-5P	1395	2785	Note 2
G-70	2-dr. Coach-5P	1445	2895	Note 2
G-70	2-dr. Brgm.-5P	1865	2995	Note 2
G-70	4-dr. Sed.-5P	1695	3060	Note 2
G-70	4-dr. Crw. Sed.-5P	2095	3090	Note 2

Note 2: Total G-70 production was 72,039 cars.
Note 3: The Brougham is also called a "leather trimmed touring sedan" and the Crown sedan is also called a "Landau sedan."

Model No.	Body Type & Seating	Price	Weight	Prod. Total
E-80	2-dr. Rds.-2/4P	2885	3730	Note 4
E-80	4-dr. Phae.-5P	2645	3775	Note 4
E-80	2-dr. Cpe.-4P	3195	4015	Note 4
E-80	4-dr. Sed.-5P	3395	4104	Note 4
E-80	4-dr. Imp. Sed.-7P	3595	4225	Note 4
E-80	4-dr. Ber. Limo.-7P	3695	4260	Note 4
Custom Bodies				
E-80	4-dr. L'let.-7P	NA	NA	Note 4
E-80	4-dr. Twn. Car-7P	NA	NA	Note 4

Note 4: Total E-80 production was 9,114 cars.
Note 5: The custom body models were designed for the 127 inch extended wheelbase. It's possible other custom body Imperials were built on a special 133 inch wheelbase available for special order coachwork.

ENGINE: [Model F-58] L-head. Inline. Four. Cast iron block. B & S: 3-5/8 in. x 4-1/2 in. Disp.: 185.8 cu. in. Brake H.P.: 38 @ 2200 R.P.M. N.A.C.C. H.P.: 21.03. Valve lifters: Solid. Carb.: Stewart. [Model G-70] Inline. L-head. Six. Cast iron block. B & S: 3-1/8 in. x 4-3/4 in. Disp.: 218.6 cu. in. C.R.: 4.7:1. Brake H.P.: 68 @ 3000 R.P.M. N.A.C.C. H.P.: 21.60. Main bearings: Seven. Valve lifters: Solid. Carb.: Ball & Ball. [Series E-80] Inline. L-head. Six. Cast iron disp. B & S: 3-1/2 in. x 5 in. Disp.: 288 cu. in. C.R.: 4.7:1. Brake H.P.: 92 @ 3000 R.P.M. N.A.C.C. H.P.: 29.4. Main bearings: Seven. Valve lifters: Solid. Carb.: Ball & Ball.

CHASSIS: [Model F-58] W.B.: 109 in. Tires: 30 x 5.25. [Model G-70] W.B.: 112-3/4 in. O.L.: 160 in. Tires: 30 x 5.77. [Series E-80] Standard W.B.: 120 in.; Seven-passenger wheelbase: 127 inches; Special order wheelbase: 133 in. Tires: 32 x 6.25.

1926 Chrysler, model G70, Crown sedan, JAC

TECHNICAL: Manual transmission. Speeds: 3F/1R. Conventional clutch. Shaft drive. Mechanical rear wheel brakes on early F-58s. Hydraulic rear wheel brakes on late F-58s. Four-wheel hydraulic brakes on other models. Wood-spoke wheels on all models.

OPTIONS: Double bar front bumpers. Double bar rear guards. Wind wings. Step plates. Trunk rack. Spare tire. Sidemount spares. Accessory radiator cap. Touring trunks. White sidewall tires. Side curtains. OSRV mirrors. Pedestal mirrors for sidemounts. Special paint. Wire spoke wheels.

HISTORICAL: Introduced at various points throughout the year. Calendar year production: 162,242. Calendar year registrations: 129,565. An Imperial roadster was the Indy 500 Pace Car. The Fleetwood Body Corp. cataloged several custom body designs for the 127 inch wheelbase Chrysler Imperial chassis. Chrysler was America's 7th ranked automaker this year. Walter P. Chrysler remained as president of the company bearing his name. The Fedco serial numbering system was adapted for the 1926 season and was used through 1930 by Chrysler.

1926
Series 58, 4-cyl., 109" wb

	FP	5	4	3	2	1
Rds	890	2000	5100	8500	11,900	17,000
Tr	845	1750	4800	8000	11,200	16,000
Clb Cpe	895	825	1600	4000	5600	8000
2 dr Sed	935	750	1450	3500	5050	7200
4 dr Sed	995	700	1350	2900	4600	6600

Series 60, 6-cyl., 109" wb
Introduced: May, 1926.

	FP	5	4	3	2	1
Rds	1145	2000	5100	8500	11,900	17,000
Tr	1075	1750	4800	8000	11,200	16,000
Cpe	1165	875	1700	4250	5900	8500
2 dr Sed	1195	800	1550	3900	5450	7800
Lthr Tr Sed	1225	825	1600	4000	5600	8000
4 dr Sed	1295	800	1550	3800	5300	7600
Lan Sed	1330	800	1550	3900	5450	7800

Series G-70, 6-cyl., 112.75" wb

	FP	5	4	3	2	1
Rds	1525	2300	5400	9000	12,600	18,000
Phae	1395	2800	5700	9500	13,300	19,000
Roy Cpe	1695	950	2100	4750	6650	9500
2 dr Sed	1395	825	1600	4000	5600	8000
Lthr Trm Sed	1415	875	1700	4250	5900	8500
Brgm	1745	950	2100	4750	6650	9500
4 dr Sed	1545	875	1700	4250	5900	8500
Roy Sed	1795	975	2200	4850	6800	9700
Crw Sed	1895	975	2300	4950	6900	9900

Series E-80 Imperial, 6-cyl., 120" wb

	FP	5	4	3	2	1
RS Rds	2595	3750	7500	12,500	17,500	25,000
Phae	2495	3900	7800	13,000	18,200	26,000
Cpe	2895	1150	3600	6000	8400	12,000
5P Sed	3095	1075	3000	5500	7700	11,000
7P Sed	3195	1150	3600	6000	8400	12,000
Berl	3595	1200	3750	6250	8750	12,500

1927

1927 Chrysler, Series 50, sedan, JAC

CHRYSLER — SERIES 50 — FOUR: The wheelbase on the four cylinder Chryslers was reduced by three inches, although the basic styling was carried over from the previous year. The number of models was expanded to eight with the addition of a rumbleseat roadster, a leather trimmed sedan and a landau sedan which had the rear quarters upholstered with rubberized fabric and decorated with dummy landau irons.

1927 Chrysler, Series 60, roadster, JAC

CHRYSLER — SERIES 60 — SIX: The Chrysler 60 was an all new car which was introduced as a mid-1926 model. It was carried over, with minor changes, through the 1927 model year. These cars had typical Chrysler styling with bullet shaped headlights. The wheelbase was 109 inches, the same formerly used on the 4-cylinder models, but the engine was an improved type six. Early 60 series cars had 30 x 5.25 tires and five lug wheels. Later versions had smaller tires, four lug wheels and an illuminated instrument panel that was finished in white.

1927 Chrysler, Series 70, roadster, JAC

CHRYSLER —- SERIES 70 — SIX: This was a carryover of the 1926 G-70 series with several new models including "sport" and "Custom Sport" versions of the phaeton, a rumbleseat cabriolet, rumbleseat coupe and a Landau Brougham. New bullet shaped headlights were used on the open bodied models only, while the closed cars continued to feature drum type headlights. Standard equipment included Delco Remy ignition, hydraulic brakes and one piece windshields. A new equipment feature was a coincidental transmission lock. Early 1927 Series 70 models had five lug wheels and 30 x 5.75 tires, while later versions had four lug wheels with 30 x 6 tires. These cars were known as Chrysler's "Finer 70s."

1927 Chrysler Imperial, Series 80, roadster, OCW

IMPERIAL — SERIES 80 — SIX: This was Chrysler's prestige car line. It was marketed as a 1927-28 series. Features included lower, longer bodies, hydraulic brakes, Delco Remy ignition and Chrysler's high-compression "Red Head" engine. Standard equipment on open styles included wind wings and leather exterior door trim panels. Bullet shaped headlights were featured. The scalloped hood and radiator shell design was used for Imperials and many of the cars had two-tone finish. Chrysler's first true convertible, with functional landau irons, was offered in this line. A richly appointed Town car was available on special order. Custom body builders offered coachcraft designs for the long wheelbase Imperials.

I.D. DATA: [Series 50] Serial numbers were in the same locations. Starting: FWOOOP. Ending: HWOOOW. Engine numbers were in the same locations. Engine numbers are not available. [Series 60] Serial numbers were in the same locations. (1926-1/2) Starting: YR500W. Ending: YYD242D. (1927) Starting: YD243W. Ending: LWOOOW. Engine numbers were in the same locations. Starting: H-21001. Ending: H-72800. [Series 70] Serial numbers were in the same locations. (1926-1/2) Starting: PP930S. Ending: PS287D. (1927) Starting: PP454Y. Ending: CWOOOW. Engine numbers were in the same locations. Starting: G-142301. Ending: G-151600. [Series 80] Serial numbers were in the same locations. Starting: EW655L. Ending: EPOOOR. Engine numbers were also in the same locations. Engine numbers are not available.

Model No.	Body Type & Seating	Price	Weight	Prod. Total
50	2-dr. Rds.-2P	750	2025	Note 1
50	R.S. Rds.-2/4P	795	2130	Note 1
50	4-dr. Tr.-5P	750	2125	Note 1
50	2-dr. Cpe.-2P	750	2230	Note 1
50	2-dr. Coach-5P	780	2335	Note 1
50	2-dr. Lthr. Trim Sed.-5P	795	2410	Note 1
50	4-dr. Sed.-5P	830	2410	Note 1
50	4-dr. Lan. Sed.-5P	855	2410	Note 1

Note 1: Total series production was 82,412.

60	2-dr. Rds.-2P	1145	2545	Note 1
60	RS Rds.-2/4P	1175	2615	Note 1
60	4-dr. Tr.-5P	1075	2575	Note 1
60	2-dr. Cpe.-2P	1125	2585	Note 1
60	2-dr. RS Cpe.-2/4P	1245	2685	Note 1
60	2-dr. Coach-5P	1195	2780	Note 1
60	2-dr. Lthr. Trim Sed.-5P	1225	2780	Note 1
60	4-dr. Sed.-5P	1295	2840	Note 1

Note 1: Total series production is not available.

70	2-dr. RS Rds.-2/4P	1495	2845	Note 1
70	4-dr. Phae.-5P	1395	2905	Note 1
70	4-dr. Spt. Phae.-5P	1495	2905	Note 1
70	4-dr. Cus. Spt. Phae.-5P	1650	2950	Note 1
70	2-dr. RS Cabr.-2/4P	1745	2935	Note 1
70	2-dr. Cpe.-2P	1545	2850	Note 1
70	2-dr. RS Cpe.-2/4P	1595	2950	Note 1
70	2-dr. Clb. Cpe.-4P	1565	2905	Note 1
70	2-dr. Brgm.-5P	1525	3090	Note 1
70	2-dr. Lan. Brgm.-5P	1550	3090	Note 1
70	4-dr. Roy. Sed.-5P	1595	3150	Note 1
70	4-dr. Crw. Sed.-5P	1795	3160	Note 1

Note 1: Total series production was 48,254.

80	2-dr. RS Rds.-2/4P	2595	3805	Note 1
80	2-dr. Spt. Rds.-2/4P	2795	3850	Note 1
80	4-dr. Phae.-5P	2495	3925	Note 1
80	4-dr. Spt. Phae.-5P	2895	4240	Note 1
80	4-dr. Phae.-7P	2645	4115	Note 1
80	2-dr. Bus. Cpe.-2P	2895	4220	Note 1
80	2-dr. Clb. Cpe.-4P	2895	4090	Note 1
80	2-dr. Clb. Cpe.-5P	3095	4220	Note 1
80	4-dr. Std. Sed.-5P	2695	4055	Note 1
80	4-dr. Sed.-5P	3195	4260	Note 1
80	4-dr. Lan Sed.-5P	3295	4215	Note 1
80	4-dr. LWB Sed.-5P	3295	4450	Note 1
80	4-dr. Limo.-7P	3595	4370	Note 1
80	4-dr. Twn. Car.-7P	5495	4265	Note 1

Note 1: Total series production is not available.

1927 Chrysler, Series 80, Imperial phaeton, JAC

ENGINE: [Series 50] Inline. L-head. Four. Cast iron block. B & S: 3-5/8 in. x 4-1/8 in. Disp.: 170.3 cu. in. Brake H.P.: 38 @ 2200 R.P.M. N.A.C.C. H.P.: 21.03. Main bearings: Three. Valve lifters: Solid. Carb.: Ball & Ball. [Series 60] Inline. L-head. Six. Cast iron block. B & S: 3 in. x 4-1/4 in. Disp.: 180.2 cu. in. Brake H.P.: 54 @ 3000 R.P.M. N.A.C.C. H.P.: 21.6. Valve lifters: Solid. Carb.: Stromberg. [Series 70] Inline. L-head. Six. Cast iron block. B & S: 3 in. x 4-3/4 in. Disp.: 218.6 cu. in. Brake H.P.: 68 @ 3000 R.P.M. N.A.C.C. H.P.: 23.44. Valve lifters: Solid. Carb.: Stromberg. [Series 80] Inline. L-head. Six. Cast iron block. B & S: 3-1/2 in. x 5 in. Disp.: 288.6 cu. in. Brake H.P.: 92 @ 3200 R.P.M. N.A.C.C. H.P.: 29.40. Main bearings: Seven. Valve lifters: Solid. Carb.: Stromberg.

CHASSIS: [Series 50] W.B.: 106 in. Tires: 29 x 4.75. [Series 60] W.B.: 109 in. Tires: (early) 30 x 5.25; (late) 28 x 5.25. [Series 70] W.B.: 112-3/4 in. Tires: (early) 30 x 5.75; (late) 30 x 6. [Series 80] W.B.: (standard) 120 in.; (custom) 127 in.; (special order) 133 in. Tires: 30 x 6.75.

DRIVETRAIN: Manual transmission. Speeds: 3F/1R. Floor shift controls. Conventional clutch. Shaft drive. Overall gear ratios: [Series 50] 4.7:1; [Series 60] 4.6:1; [Series 70] 4.3:1; [Series 80] 4.82:1. Mechanical rear wheel brakes standard on Series 50. Hydraulic rear wheel brakes available at extra cost on Series 50. Four wheel hydraulic brakes available on other series. Wood spoke wheels standard. Starting in Aug. 1926, Budd-Michelin steel disc wheels were available on all 1927 series Chryslers.

OPTIONS: Double bar front bumper. Double bar rear fender guards. Side-mount spare tires. Leather sidemount covers. Heater. Clock. Cigar lighter. Wind wings. Step plates. Rear mount spare. Rumbleseat windshield. Rumbleseat wind winds. OSRV mirror. Trunk rack. Touring trunk. Dual wipers. Dual taillights. Steel disc wheels. Wire spoke wheels on Sport models. Side curtains. Custom coachwork bodies.

HISTORICAL: Early series introduced August, 1926. Late series introduced Jan. 1927. Calendar year production: 182,195. Calendar year new car registrations: 154,234. An Imperial made a high-speed, non-stop run of 6,726 miles from San Francisco to New York to Los Angeles. The car's average speed was 40.2 mph. Walter P. Chrysler was again president of the company. Chrysler ranked 7th in U.S. auto sales.

1927
Series I-50, 4-cyl., 106" wb

	FP	5	4	3	2	1
2P Rds	750	2800	5700	9500	13,300	19,000
RS Rds	795	3000	6000	10,000	14,000	20,000
Tr	845	2800	5700	9500	13,300	19,000
Cpe	750	875	1700	4250	5900	8500
2 dr Sed	780	775	1500	3750	5250	7500
Lthr Trm Sed	795	825	1600	4000	5600	8000
4 dr Sed	830	775	1500	3600	5100	7300
Lan Sed	855	775	1500	3750	5250	7500

Series H-60, 6-cyl., 109" wb

2P Rds	1145	3300	6600	11,000	15,400	22,000
RS Rds	1175	3400	6900	11,500	16,100	23,000
Tr	1075	3300	6600	11,000	15,400	22,000
2P Cpe	1125	900	1900	4500	6300	9000
RS Cpe	1245	950	2100	4750	6650	9500
2 dr Sed	1145	825	1600	4050	5650	8100
Lthr Trm Sed	1165	875	1700	4250	5900	8500
4 dr Sed	1245	750	1450	3400	5000	7100

Series 'Finer' 70, 6-cyl., 112.75" wb

RS Rds	1495	3300	6600	11,000	15,400	22,000
Phae	1395	3400	6900	11,500	16,100	23,000
Spt Phae	1495	3600	7200	12,000	16,800	24,000
Cus Spt Phae	1595	3750	7500	12,500	17,500	25,000
RS Cabr	1745	3150	6300	10,500	14,700	21,000
2P Cpe	1595	900	1900	4500	6300	9000
RS Cpe	1545	950	2100	4750	6650	9500
4P Cpe	1565	900	1800	4450	6250	8900
Brgm	1525	875	1700	4300	6000	8600
Lan Brgm	1550	875	1700	4350	6050	8700
Roy Sed	1595	900	1800	4400	6150	8800
Crw Sed	1795	900	1800	4450	6250	8900

1927-Early 1928
Series E-80 Imperial, 6-cyl., 120" & 127" wb

RS Rds	2595	4200	8400	14,000	19,600	28,000
Spt Rds	2795	4350	8700	14,500	20,300	29,000
5P Phae	2495	4350	8700	14,500	20,300	29,000
Spt Phae	3995	4500	9000	15,000	21,000	30,000
7P Phae	2645	4200	8400	14,000	19,600	28,000
RS Cabr	3495	4050	8100	13,500	18,900	27,000
Bus Cpe	2895	1400	4200	7000	9800	14,000
4P Cpe	3095	1400	4200	7000	9800	14,000
5P Cpe	3095	1150	3600	6000	8400	12,000
Std Sed	2695	1000	2400	5050	7050	10,100
4 dr Sed	3195	1000	2400	5000	7000	10,000
Lan Sed	3295	1075	3000	5500	7700	11,000
7P Sed	2895	1100	3200	5600	7800	11,200
Limo	3595	1250	3900	6500	9100	13,000
TwnC	5495	1800	4950	8250	11,550	16,500

1928

CHRYSLER — SERIES 52 — FOUR: The Series 52 was basically a continuation of the Chrysler 50. Styling differences included bullet shaped headlights and a new kind of visor on closed cars. The visor was narrower and had a greater slope; it did not jut out quite as far when viewed in profile. A new instrument panel featured indirect illumination and had the gauges and controls housed in a rectangular panel, instead of an oval one. Standard equipment included an adjustable steering wheel and I-beam front axle. Hydraulic brakes were available at extra cost. This series became the Plymouth in 1929.

CHRYSLER — SERIES 62 — SIX: Chrysler's "small" six had a higher radiator. These cars returned to the use of drum type headlights and cowl lights were eliminated. Standard equipment included an electric gas gauge, hydraulic brakes, rubber engine mounts, ignition lock on dash, ventilating type windshield and light control on steering wheel. The design of the instrument board was changed from an oval to rectangular panel, as on the Chrysler 50. The new cadet sun visor design was used on the 62 also.

1928 Chrysler, Series 72, 4-dr. sedan, JAC

CHRYSLER — SERIES 72 — SIX: A higher radiator and cowl were used on the Chrysler 72. Headlight posts were now firmly attached to the frame of the cars. Standard equipment included hydraulic brakes, tubular front axle, rubber shock insulators on springs and a new, oblong instrument panel. Throttle and headlight controls were repositioned on a thinner new steering wheel.

IMPERIAL — SERIES 80 —SIX: Early 1928 Chrysler Imperials were a carryover of the 1927 Series 80. These cars had Fedco serial numbers EW853S through EW911R and engine numbers E9709 through E10248. There were no important changes in styling or specifications. Refer to 1927 specifications for these cars.

IMPERIAL — SERIES 80L — SIX: The "new" 1928 Imperials were on a 136 inch wheelbase. They retained the scalloped type radiator and hood design. There was a line of factory bodied models, a second line of semi-custom LeBaron bodied models, a third line of Dietrich bodied semi-custom models and one design from Locke. These were all richly appointed cars intended for prestige class buyers. Styling traits included the removal of the monogram from the radiator and the use of large, plated, bullet shaped headlights.

I.D. DATA: [Series 52] Fedco numbering system used 1926-1929. Serial number symbol plate built into instrument panel above and to left of the instruments or in center of panel over instrument board. Starting: HW000P. Ending: HL685L. Engine numbers were on upper left side of block, between first and second cylinders, just below head. Starting: I-83074. Ending: I-166185. [Series 62] Fedco serial numbers were in the same location. Starting: LW000P. Ending: LS101C. Engine numbers were in the same location. Starting: M-72641. Ending: M-135784. [Series 72] Fedco serial numbers were in the same location. Starting: CW000P. Ending: CR838L. Engine numbers were in the same location. Starting: J192950. Ending: J242900. [Series 80 & 80L] Fedco serial numbers were in the same location. Starting: EP000P. Ending: EP315C. Engine numbers were stamped on top of the timing gear chain case. Starting: L1201. Ending: L4069.

Model No.	Body Type & Seating	Price	Weight	Prod. Total
52	2-dr. Rds.-2/4P	670	2075	Note 1
52	4-dr. Tr.-5P	695	2130	Note 1
52	2-dr. Cpe.-2P	670	2180	Note 1
52	2-dr. Del. Cpe.-2/4P	720	2240	Note 1
52	2-dr. Coach-5P	670	2300	Note 1
52	4-dr. Sed.-5P	720	2375	Note 1
52	4-dr. Del. Sed.-5P	790	2375	Note 1

Note 1: Total series production was 76,857.

62	2-dr. Rds.-2/4P	1075	2705	Note 1
62	4-dr. Tr.-5P	1095	2740	Note 1
62	2-dr. Bus. Cpe.-2P	1065	2780	Note 1
62	2-dr. Cpe.-2/4P	1145	2855	Note 1
62	2-dr. Coach-5P	1095	2855	Note 1
62	4-dr. Sed.-5P	1175	2905	Note 1
62	4-dr. Lan. Sed.-5P	1235	2940	Note 1

Note 1: Total series production was 64,136.

72	2-dr. Rds.-2/4P	1495	3005	6416
72	2-dr. Spt. Rds.-2/4P	1595	3005	Note 1
72	2-dr. Cpe.-4P	1595	3160	6869
72	2-dr. RS Cpe.-2/4P	1545	3130	Note 2
72	2-dr. Conv. Cpe.-2/4P	1745	3100	1729
72	4-dr. Twn. Sed.-5P	1695	3270	4977
72	4-dr. Roy. Sed.-5P	1595	3235	3266
72	4-dr. Crw. Sed.-5P	1795	3235	Note 3
72	4-dr. C.C. Sed.-5P	1595	3240	Note 4
72	4-dr. Imp. Twn. Cabr.-5P	3595	3485	36

Note 1: Production of the standard roadster and Sport roadster was a single total with no breakouts available.
Note 2: Production of the standard coupe and Rumbleseat coupe was a single total with no breakouts available.
Note 3: Production of the Crown sedan and Royal sedan was a single total with no breakouts available.
Note 4: Production of the closed-coupled sedan and the Town sedan was a single total with no breakouts available.

80L	2-dr. Rds.-2/4P	2795	3870	281
80L	4-dr. Sed.-5P	2945	4125	790
80L	4-dr. Twn. Sed.-5P	2995	4140	431
80L	4-dr. Sed.-7P	3075	4250	374
80L	4-dr. Limo.-7P	3495	4285	86
(LeBaron Bodies)				
80L	4-dr. Trav. D.C. Phae.-4P	4185	4200	31
80L	2-dr. Clb. Cpe.-2/4P	3995	4150	25
80L	2-dr. Twn. Cpe.-4P	3995	4150	21
80L	2-dr. Conv. Cpe.-2/4P	3995	4150	39
80L	4-dr. C.C. Conv. Sed.-4P	6485	4250	4
80L	4-dr. Twn. Cab.-7P	3595	NA	1
(Dietrich Bodies)				
80L	4-dr. D.C. Phae.-7P	6795	4300	5
80L	4-dr. Imp. Conv. Sed.-5P	6795	4300	10
80L	4-dr. Sed.-4P	5795	4300	4
(Locke Bodies)				
80L	2-dr. Imp. Trav'let-4P	4485	4165	21

Note 1: Total 80L series production included 1,962 factory bodied cars and 161 custom bodied cars. Grand total: 2,123.

1928 Chrysler Imperial, Locke, dual cowl phaeton, OCW

ENGINE: [Series 52] Inline. L-head. Four. Cast iron block. B & S: 3-5/8 in. x 4-1/8 in. Disp.: 170.3 cu. in. C.R.: 4.7:1. Brake H.P.: 38-45 @ 2600 R.P.M. N.A.C.C. H.P.: 21.03. Valve lifters: Solid. Carb.: Carter. [Series 62] Inline. L-head. Six. Cast iron block. B & S: 3 in. x 4-1/2 in. Disp.: 180.2 cu. in. C.R.: 5.2:1. Brake H.P.: 54 @ 3000 R.P.M. N.A.C.C. H.P.: 21.60. Main bearings: Seven. Valve lifters: Solid. Carb.: Stromberg (Note: Above specifications for engine with standard "Silver Dome" head. The high-compression "Red Head" with 6.2:1 compression and 60 Brake H.P. was optional). [Series 72] Inline. L-head. Six. Cast iron block. B & S: 3-1/4 in. x 5 in. Disp.: 248.9 cu. in. C.R.: (Std.) 5.1:1; (Opt.) 6.2:1. Brake H.P.: (Std.) 75 @ 3200 R.P.M.; (Opt.) 85 @ 3200 R.P.M. N.A.C.C. H.P.: 25.36. Main bearings: Seven. Valve lifters: Solid. Carb.: Ball & Ball. [Series 80 & 80L] Inline. L-head. Six. Cast iron block. B & S: 3-5/8 in. x 5 in. Disp.: 309.3 cu. in. C.R.: (Std.) 4.75:1; (Opt.) 6.0:1. Brake H.P.: 100 @ 3200 (Std. head); 112 @ 3300 ("Red Head"). Invarstrut pistons. Valve lifters: Solid. Carb.: Stromberg.

CHASSIS: [Series 52] W.B.: 106 in. Tires: 29 x 4.75. [Series 62] W.B.: 108-3/4 in. Tires: 28 x 5.25. [Series 72] W.B.: 118-3/4 in. Tires: 30 x 6. [Series 80] W.B.: (Std.) 120 in.; (Custom) 127 in.; (Special) 133 in. Tires: 30 x 6.75. [Series 80L] W.B.: 136 in. O.L.: 203 in. Tires: 30 x 6.75.

TECHNICAL: Manual transmission. Speeds: 3F/1R. Floor shift controls. Conventional clutch. Shaft drive. Overall gear ratio: [Series 52] 4.7:1; [Series 62] 4.6:1; [Series 72] 4.3:1; [Series 80] 4.83:1 and [Series 80L] 4.08:1. Two-wheel mechanical brakes standard on Series 52. Four-wheel hydraulic brakes standard on other series. Wood spoke wheels were standard equipment on factory bodied cars.

OPTIONS: Front bumper. Rear bumper. Sidemount tire(s). Leather sidemount covers. Trunk rack. Touring trunk. Wind wings. Rear mount spare tire. Rear fender guards. Rear covered spare. OSRV mirror. Accessory radiator cap. Pedastal mirrors for sidemounts. Trippe lights. Radiator guard. Spotlight(s). Disc wheels. Wire wheels. Rear windshield on dual cowl phaetons. Special paint. Special order custom coachwork.

HISTORICAL: All series, except for the 80L, were introduced in July, 1927. The 80L series was introduced in Nov., 1927. Calendar year production: 160,670. Calendar year registrations: 142,024. This was Chrysler's all-time highest production year for the prewar era and also the highest until 1950. Chrysler entered four Imperial roadsters in the Twenty-Four Hours of LeMans. The Chrysler team placed 3rd and 4th in class. The winning car averaged 64.5 mph for the race. Another Imperial placed 2nd in the Belgian 24-hour Grand Prix and two Series 72 Chryslers took 3rd and 4th in the same race. Chrysler purchased Dodge Brothers this year.

1928

Series 52, 4-cyl., 106" wb

	FP	5	4	3	2	1
RS Rds	670	3750	7500	12,500	17,500	25,000
Tr	695	3600	7200	12,000	16,800	24,000
Clb Cpe	670	875	1700	4250	5900	8500
DeL Cpe	720	900	1900	4500	6300	9000
2 dr Sed	670	825	1600	4000	5600	8000
4 dr Sed	720	825	1600	4000	5600	8000
DeL Sed	790	800	1550	3850	5400	7700

Series 62, 6-cyl., 109" wb

	FP	5	4	3	2	1
RS Rds	1075	3900	7800	13,000	18,200	26,000
Tr	1095	3750	7500	12,500	17,500	25,000
Bus Cpe	1065	875	1700	4250	5900	8500
RS Cpe	1145	950	2100	4750	6650	9500
2 dr Sed	1095	825	1600	4000	5600	8000
4 dr Sed	1175	800	1550	3900	5450	7800
Lan Sed	1235	825	1600	4050	5650	8100

Series 72, 6-cyl., 120.5" wb

	FP	5	4	3	2	1
RS Rds	1495	3900	7800	13,000	18,200	26,000
Spt Rds	1595	4200	8400	14,000	19,600	28,000
Conv	1745	3600	7200	12,000	16,800	24,000
RS Cpe	1545	1075	3000	5500	7700	11,000
4P Cpe	1595	1000	2400	5000	7000	10,000
CC Sed	1595	1000	2400	5000	7000	10,000
Roy Sed	1595	875	1700	4250	5900	8500
Crw Sed	1795	900	1900	4500	6300	9000
Twn Sed	1695	975	2300	4900	6850	9800
LeB Imp Twn Cabr	3595	1750	4800	8000	11,200	16,000

Series 80 L Imperial, 6-cyl., 136" wb

	FP	5	4	3	2	1
RS Rds	2795	4350	8700	14,500	20,300	29,000
Sed	2495	1000	2400	5000	7000	10,000
Twn Sed	2995	1000	2400	5050	7050	10,100
7P Sed	3075	1000	2400	5000	7000	10,000
Limo	3495	1150	3600	6000	8400	12,000

Series 80 L Imperial, 6-cyl., 136" wb, Custom Bodies

	FP	5	4	3	2	1
LeB DC Phae	—	9300	18,600	31,000	43,400	62,000
LeB CC Conv Sed	4185	8250	16,500	27,500	38,500	55,000
LeB RS Conv	3995	7800	15,600	26,000	36,400	52,000
LeB Clb Cpe	3995	3900	7800	13,000	18,200	26,000
LeB Twn Cpe	3995	3750	7500	12,500	17,500	25,000
LeB Lan Limo	3995	175	525	1050	2100	3000
Der Conv Sed	—	175	525	1050	2100	3000
Dtrch Conv. Sed	6795	9000	18,000	30,000	42,000	60,000
Dtrch 4P Phae	—	9300	18,600	31,000	43,400	62,000
Dtrch 7P Phae	—	9300	18,600	31,000	43,400	62,000
Dtrch Sed	5795	3300	6600	11,000	15,400	22,000
Lke Phae	4485	7500	15,000	25,000	35,000	50,000

1929

1929 Chrysler, Series 75, roadster, OCW

CHRYSLER — SERIES 65 — SIX: The four-cylinder Chryslers were renamed Plymouths this year. The company's basic line was now a six called the Series 65. These cars featured narrow profile radiators and higher cowls. A longer wheelbase was used. An ignition keyhole replaced the old switch type. Other styling features included bowl shaped headlights, full crown ''Air Wing'' fenders and a new silver and black finished instrument panel. Arched windows were another advance in design for closed cars. Standard equipment included Lockheed internal hydraulic brakes and hydraulic shock absorbers.

CHRYSLER — SERIES 75 — SIX: The 75 series Chryslers had about the same appearance changes as the Chrysler 65. They included narrow profile radiators, full crown fenders, arched windows on closed cars (a more rounded sun visor was also used), bowl shaped headlights, dual cowl ventilators, vertical hood louvers and a lengthened wheelbase. Standard equipment included Lockheed hydraulic brakes and Lovejoy shock absorbers. The Chrysler 75 instrument panel was done in black and gold. These were the first Chryslers to feature built in radiator shutters.

IMPERIAL ''L'' — SERIES IMP L — SIX: A narrow profile radiator, automatic radiator shutter, slender front body pillars, shatterproof glass, arched windows, dual cowl ventilators, fuel gauge on dash and arched vertical hood louvers were features of 1929 Imperials. Eight factory body styles were listed by the National Automobile Dealers Association and a few custom bodies were available, too. Standard equipment included hydraulic brakes and Houdaille shock absorbers. The factory semi-custom bodies were by Locke.

1929 Chrysler, Series 75, 4-pass. coupe, JAC

I.D. DATA: [Series 65] Fedco serial numbers were in the same locations. Starting: LS400P and DWOOOW. Ending: LD999D and DC507D. Engine numbers were on the upper left side of block in same location. Starting: P175001. Ending: P241336. [Series 75] Fedco serial numbers were in the same locations. Starting: CY050P and ZWOOOP. Ending: CD999D and ZW672L. Motor numbers were in the same location as on 65s. Starting: R250001. Ending: R309150. [Series IMP L] Fedco serial numbers were in the same locations. Starting: EP320P. Ending: EP542P. Engine numbers were located on the top of timing gear chain case. Starting: L4070. Ending: L6358.

Model No.	Body Type & Seating	Price	Weight	Prod. Total
65	2-dr. Rds.-2/4P	1065	2730	4953
65	4-dr. Tr.-5P	1075	2770	65472
65	2-dr. Bus. Cpe.-2P	1040	2780	4655
65	2-dr. 5W Cpe.-2/4P	1145	2875	7603
65	2-dr. Sed.-5P	1065	2905	8846
65	4-dr. Sed.-5P	1145	2960	24958

Note 1: Total series production was 116,487.

75	2-dr. Rds.-2/4P	1550	3190	6414
75	4-dr. Phae.-5P	1795	3110	248
75	4-dr. Phae.-7P	1865	3235	11
75	4-dr. Ton. Phae.-4P	1835	3290	227
75	2-dr. 3W Cpe.-2P	1535	3235	9488
75	2-dr. Conv. Cpe.-2/4P	1795	3320	1430
75	2-dr. 5W Cpe.-2/4P	1655	3335	1016
75	4-dr. Roy. Sed.-5P	1535	3280	22456
75	4-dr. Twn. Sed.-5P	1655	3360	3408
75	4-dr. Crw. Sed.-5P	1655	3365	3814
75	4-dr. Conv. Sed.-5P	2345	3430	337
75	2-dr. Jan. Tr. Cabr.-2P	NA	NA	1

Note 1: Total series production was 48,850 (approximate).
Note 2: The custom bodied touring cabriolet was built by French coachmaker Carrosserie Janssen of Paris. Other custom bodies may have been sold on the Series 75 chassis.

L	2-dr. Rds.-2/4P	2675	3955	41
L	4-dr. Phae.-7P	3095	3925	15
L	2-dr. Cpe.-2P	2895	4020	149
L	2-dr. Conv. Cpe.-2/4P	2995	4035	142
L	4-dr. Sed.-5P	2975	4335	838
L	4-dr. Twn. Sed.-5P	2975	4310	379
L	4-dr. Sed.-7P	3095	4460	442
L	4-dr. Limo. Sed.-7P	3475	4510	99
L	2-dr. Locke Cus. Rds.-2/4P	NA	NA	NA
L	2-dr. Imp. Rds.-2/4P	2895	NA	401
L	4-dr. Locke Conv. Sed.-5P	NA	NA	NA
L	2-dr. Dtrch Cpe.-2/4P	NA	NA	NA

Note 1: Total series production for 1929-1930 was 2,506 cars, excluding an unknown amount of custom body jobs.
Note 2: This series was carried over as a 1930 series. The 1930 Imperials were those with serial numbers EP542C to EP608R and engine numbers L6359 to L6998. The 1930 prices increased $100-200, but other specifications were basically the same except that a 4-speed ''Multi-Range'' transmission was used in 1930 production units along with smooth, non-corrugated bumpers.

1929 Chrysler, Imperial 7-pass. sedan, JAC

ENGINE: [Series 65] Inline. L-head. Six. Cast iron block. B & S: 3-1/8 in. x 4-1/4 in. C.R.: (Std.) 5.2:1; (Opt.) 6.0:1. Brake H.P.: (Std.) 65 @ 3000 R.P.M.; (Opt.) 70 @ 3200 R.P.M. N.A.C.C. H.P.: 23.44. Valve lifters: Solid. Carb.: Stromberg. [Series 75] Inline. L-head. Six. Cast iron block. B & S: 3-1/4 in. x 5 in. Disp.: 248.9 cu. in. C.R.: (Std.) 5.2:1; (Opt.) 6.0:1. Brake H.P.: (Std.) 75 @ 3200 R.P.M.: (Opt.) 84 @ 3400 R.P.M. N.A.C.C. H.P.: 25.35. Main bearings: Seven. Valve lifters: Solid. Carb.: Ball & Ball. [Series IMP L] Inline. L-head. Six. Cast iron block. B & S: 3-5/8 in. x 5 in.. Disp.: 309.3 cu. in. C.R.: (Std.) 5.2:1; (Opt.) 6.0:1. Brake H.P.: (Std.) 110 @ 3200 R.P.M.; (Opt.) 112 @ 3300 R.P.M. N.A.C.C. H.P.: 31.54. Valve lifters: Solid. Carb.: Stromberg

CHASSIS: [Series 65] W.B.: 112-3/4 in. Tires: 5.50 x 18. [Series 75] W.B.: 121 in. Tires: 6.00 x 18. [Series 80L] W.B.: 136 in. O.L.: 203 in. Tires: 17 x 7.00.

TECHNICAL: Manual transmission. Speeds: 3F/1R. Floor shift controls. Conventional clutch. Shaft drive. Overall ratio: [Series 65] 4.9:1; [Series 75] 4.3:1; [Series 80L] 3.77:1 to 4.45:1. Four wheel hydraulic brakes on all models. Wood spoke wheels or wire wheels as standard equipment.

OPTIONS: See 1928 options.

HISTORICAL: The 65 and 75 series were introduced June, 1928. The Imperial 80L series was introduced in Oct. 1928. Calendar year production: 92,034. Calendar year new car registrations: 84,520. A team of two stripped down Imperial roadsters and two Series 75 roadsters competed at LeMans in 1928, placing 6th and 7th in their class. The same cars took part in other European Grands Prix, but did not do well. A Series 65 Chrysler ran 53,170 non-stop miles to set a World Class endurance record in Germany.

1929 Chrysler, Imperial roadster, Locke, JAC

1929
Series 65, 6-cyl.), 112.75" wb

	FP	5	4	3	2	1
RS Rds	1065	4350	8700	14,500	20,300	29,000
Tr	1075	4500	9000	15,000	21,000	30,000
Bus Cpe	1040	1000	2400	5000	7000	10,000
RS Cpe	1145	1250	3900	6500	9100	13,000
2 dr Sed	1065	950	2100	4750	6650	9500
4 dr Sed	1145	950	2100	4750	6650	9500
Series 75, 6-cyl.						
RS Rds	1550	4950	9900	16,500	23,100	33,000
5P Phae	1795	5100	10,200	17,000	23,800	34,000
DC Phae	—	5400	10,800	18,000	25,200	36,000
7P Phae	1865	4950	9900	16,500	23,100	33,000
RS Conv	1795	4800	9600	16,000	22,400	32,000
Conv Sed	2345	4650	9300	15,500	21,700	31,000
RS Cpe	1535	1075	3000	5500	7700	11,000
Cpe	1655	1000	2400	5000	7000	10,000
Roy Sed	1535	975	2300	4950	6900	9900
Crw Sed	1655	975	2300	4950	6900	9900
Twn Sed	1655	1075	3000	5500	7700	11,000
1929-30						
Series 80 L Imperial, 6-cyl., 136" wb						
RS Rds	2895	9000	18,000	30,000	42,000	60,000
Lke DC Spt Phae	—	10,500	21,000	35,000	49,000	70,000
Lke 7P Phae	3095	10,200	20,400	34,000	47,600	68,000
Lke Conv Sed	—	9900	19,800	33,000	46,200	66,000
Lke RS Conv	—	8250	16,500	27,500	38,500	55,000
2P Cpe	2675	2800	5700	9500	13,300	19,000
RS Cpe	2895	3600	7200	12,000	16,800	24,000
4 dr Sed	2975	1400	4200	7000	9800	14,000
Twn Sed	2975	1750	4800	8000	11,200	16,000
7P Sed	3095	1150	3600	6000	8400	12,000
Limo	3475	1550	4500	7500	10,500	15,000

1930

CHRYSLER — SERIES 66 — SIX: A number of styling changes on the 1930 Chrysler 66 included heavier fenders, bowl shaped headlights, slender profile radiators and pennon type hood louvers. Standard equipment consisted of Delco Remy ignition, hydraulic brakes, rubber spring shackles and a new 3-spoke steering wheel. Cars with serial numbers above H143EY and engine numbers above C16440 had larger more powerful engines and vertical hood louvers. On some cars split vertical louvers, located inside an arch shaped panel, were used.

1930 Chrysler, Series 70, coupe, AA

CHRYSLER — SERIES 70 — SIX: Styling features of the Chrysler 70 included narrow profile radiator, bowl shaped headlights and pennon type hood louvers on early year cars. Standard equipment included Delco Remy ignition, hydraulic brakes, 4-speed transmission, mechanical fuel pump, downdraft carburetor and new "paraflex" springs. Late year cars with serial numbers above P-116SS and engine numbers above V-13595 had a larger engine, vertical hood louvers, new type instrument panel and thermostatic radiator shutters.

1930 Chrysler, Series 77, roadster, AA

CHRYSLER — SERIES 77 — SIX: The Chrysler 77 featured hydraulic internal brakes, 4-speed transmission, double-drop frame, parking lamps on the front upper corner pillars and distinctive concave moldings on the open cars. Pennon type hood louvers were used on early production units, while later cars switched to a vertical louver design.

1930 Chrysler, Imperial 7-pass. sedan, JAC

IMPERIAL — SERIES IMP — SIX: The 1930 Imperial was a carryover of the 1929 Imperial 80L. New features were automatic radiator shutters, vertical hood louvers and 4-speed transmission. The only specifications changes from 1930 were the prices. The roadster was $2,995; the phaeton was $3,195; the coupe was $3,095; the sedan was $3,075; the Town Sedan was $3,075; the 7-passenger sedan was $3,195 and the limousine was $3,575. Consult 1930 specifications chart for additional information.

CHRYSLER — SERIES CJ — SIX: The Series CJ was a line of all-new, downsized models bearing the Chrysler name. This series was actually a 1930-1/2 series and was introduced in Feb. 1930. Features included a new, low-slung chassis, hydraulic internal brakes, fuel pump, rubber spring shackles, hydraulic shock absorbers and rubber engine mounting system. Like other Chryslers, they had bowl shaped headlights, narrow profile radiators and standard wood spoke wheels. Three groupings of vertical hood louvers were carried in an arched shaped panel on the sides of the hood. This was the first Chrysler built since 1925 that did not carry a model designation indicating the top speed of the car.

I.D. DATA: [Series 66] Serial numbers were in the same locations. Starting: H001WP. Ending: H252SY. Engine numbers on upper left side of block, between cylinders one and two, just below cylinder head. Starting: C1001 to C28055. [Series 70] Serial numbers were in the same locations. Starting: P001WP. Ending: P180YE. Engine numbers were in the same locations. Starting: V1001. Ending: V27181. [Series 77] Serial numbers were in the same locations. Starting: C001WP. Ending: C187DH. Engine numbers were in the same locations. Starting: W1001. Ending: W26976. [Series CJ] Fedco serial numbers were in the same locations. Starting: H400WP. Ending: H471CS. Engine numbers were in the same locations. Starting: CJ1001. Ending: CJ24494. (Note: When the Fedco numbering system was dropped in late 1930, some CJ-6s carried conventional type serial numbers. Starting: 6500001. Ending: 6514919).

Model No.	Body Type & Seating	Price	Weight	Prod. Total
66	2-dr. Rds.-2/4P	1025	2625	1213
66	4-dr. Phae.-5P	1025	2695	26
66	2-dr. Bus. Cpe.-2P	995	2750	2014
66	2-dr. Roy. Cpe.-2/4P	1075	2850	3257
66	2-dr. Brgm. Sed.-5P	1000	2850	2343
66	4-dr. Roy. Sed.-5P	1095	2930	13753
Note 1: Total series production was 22,606.
70	2-dr. Rds.-2/4P	1345	3205	1431
70	4-dr. Phae.-5P	1295	3315	279
70	2-dr. Bus. Cpe.-2P	1345	3410	766
70	2-dr. Roy. Cpe.-2/4P	1395	3490	3135
70	2-dr. Conv. Cpe.-2/4P	1545	3450	705
70	2-dr. Brgm. Sed.-5P	1345	3490	1204
70	4-dr. Roy. Sed.-5P	1445	3590	11213
Note 1: Total series production was 18,733.
77	2-dr. Rds.-2/4P	1665	3370	1729
77	4-dr. Phae.-5P	1795	3495	173
77	2-dr. Bus. Cpe.-2P	1625	3560	230
77	2-dr. Roy. Cpe.-2/4P	1725	3615	2954
77	2-dr. Crw. Cpe.-4P	1795	3580	883
77	2-dr. Conv. Cpe.-2/4P	1825	3580	418
77	4-dr. Roy. Sed.-5P	1725	3750	436
77	4-dr. Crw. Sed.-5P	1795	3760	2654
77	4-dr. Twn. Sed.-5P	1795	3720	436
Note 1: Total series production was 9,913.
CJ	2-dr. Rds.-2/4P	835	2390	1616
CJ	4-dr. Tr.-5P	835	2455	22
CJ	2-dr. Bus. Cpe.-2P	795	2560	2267
CJ	2-dr. Roy. Cpe.-2/4P	835	2590	3593
CJ	2-dr. Conv. Cpe.-2/4P	925	2540	579
CJ	4-dr. Roy. Sed.-5P	845	2695	20748
Note 1: Total series production was 10,915.

1930 Chrysler, Series 66, 4-dr. sedan, JAC

ENGINE: [Series 66] (Early): Inline. L-head. Six. Cast iron block. B & S: 3-1/8 in. x 4-1/2 in. Disp.: 195.6 cu. in. Brake H.P.: 65 @ 3200 R.P.M. N.A.C.C. H.P.: 23.44. Carb.: Stromberg. (Late): Inline. L-head. Six. Cast iron block. B & S: 3-1/8 in. x 4-3/4 in. Disp.: 218.6 cu. in. Brake H.P.: 68 @ 3000 R.P.M. N.A.C.C. H.P.: 23.44. Carb.: Stromberg. [Series 70] (Early): Inline. L-head. Six. Cast iron block. B & S: 3-1/8 in. x 4-3/4 in. Disp.: 218.6. Brake H.P.: 75 @ 3200 R.P.M. N.A.C.C. H.P.: 23.44. Carb.: Stromberg. (Late): Inline. L-head. Six. Cast iron block. B & S: 3-3/8 in. x 5 in. Disp.: 268.4. Brake H.P.: 93 @ 3200 R.P.M. N.A.C.C. H.P.: 27.34. Carb.: Stromberg. [Series 77] Inline. L-head. Six. Cast iron block. B & S: 3-3/8 in. x 5 in. Disp.: 268.4 cu. in. Brake H.P.: 93 @ 3200 R.P.M. N.A.C.C. H.P.: 27.34. Carb.: Stromberg. [Series CJ] Inline. L-head. Six. Cast iron block. B & S: 3-1/8 in. x 4-1/4 in. Disp.: 195.6 cu. in. Brake H.P.: 62 @ 3200 R.P.M. N.A.C.C. H.P.: 23.44. Carb.: Carter.

CHASSIS: [Series CJ-6] W.B.: 109 in. Tires: 19 x 5.00. [Series 66] W.B.: 112-3/4 in. Tires: 18 x 5.50. [Series 70] W.B.: 116-1/2 in. Tires: 18 x 5.50. [Series 77] W.B.: 124 in. Tires: 18 x 6.00. [Imp Series] W.B.: 136 in. Tires: 18 x 7.00.

TECHNICAL: Three-speed manual transmission on Series CJ-6 and Series 66 models. Four-speed "multi-range" manual transmission on other series. Speeds: 3F/1R and 4R/1R. Floor shift controls. Conventional clutch. Shaft drive. Overall ratio: [Series CJ-6] 4.7:1; [Series 66] 4.7:1; [Series 70] 4.1:1; [Series 77] 3.58:1 on open cars and 3.82:1 on closed cars. [Imperial Series] 3.77:1 to 4.45:1. Wood spoke wheels standard on all models. Hydraulic brakes standard on all models.

OPTIONS: Front bumper. Rear bumper. Rear fender guards. Spare tire. Sidemounted spare tire(s). Wire spoke wheels. OSRV mirror. Pedestal sidemount mirror(s). Cowl lights. Cigar lighter. Trunk rack. Touring trunk. Special solid paint. Two-tone sweep panel finish on Series 77 roadsters and phaetons. Leather side mount covers. Metal sidemount covers. Metal sidemount cover trim moldings. Spotlight(s). Trippe lights. Wind wings. Imperial custom bodies.

HISTORICAL: The CJ Series six was introduced in February, 1930. All other series introduced in July 1929. Calendar year production: 60,199. Calendar year new car registrations: 60,908. Innovations: Four-speed transmission. Fuel pump. "Futura" design instrument panels on 70/77. CJ six-cylinder engine was first Chrysler six to have four main bearings instead of seven. A Chrysler powered racing car owned by Julius Slade qualified for the Indianapolis 500 mile race. Driver Roland Free drove it for 69 laps until the clutch burned out. The Chrysler Building, in New York City, was completed this year.

1930 Chrysler, Series 77, 4-dr. sedan, JAC

1930-1931 (through December)
Series Six, 6-cyl, 109" wb
(Continued through Dec. 1930).

	FP	5	4	3	2	1
RS Rds	785	3900	7800	13,000	18,200	26,000
Tr	785	3750	7500	12,500	17,500	25,000
RS Conv	785	3600	7200	12,000	16,800	24,000
Bus Cpe	745	950	2100	4750	6650	9500
Roy Cpe	785	950	2100	4750	6650	9500
Roy Sed	795	875	1700	4250	5900	8500

1930-1931
Series 66, 6-cyl, 112 3/4" wb
(Continued through May 1931).

	FP	5	4	3	2	1
RS Rds	1025	4350	8700	14,500	20,300	29,000
Phae	1025	4500	9000	15,000	21,000	30,000
Bus Cpe	995	950	2100	4750	6650	9500
Roy Cpe	1075	1000	2400	5000	7000	10,000
Brgm	995	900	1900	4500	6300	9000
Roy Sed	1095	950	2100	4750	6650	9500

Series 70, 6 cyl, 116 1/2" wb
(Continued through Feb. 1931).

	FP	5	4	3	2	1
RS Rds	1345	4950	9900	16,500	23,100	33,000
RS Conv	1545	4500	9000	15,000	21,000	30,000
Phae	1295	5100	10,200	17,000	23,800	34,000
Bus Cpe	1245	1000	2400	5000	7000	10,000
Roy Cpe	1295	1075	3000	5500	7700	11,000
Brgm	1245	1000	2400	5000	7000	10,000
Roy Sed	1295	1025	2600	5250	7300	10,500

Series 77, 6-cyl., 124.5" wb

	FP	5	4	3	2	1
RS Rds	885	6750	13,500	22,500	31,500	45,000
DC Phae	970	6000	12,000	20,000	28,000	40,000
RS Conv	970	5250	10,500	17,500	24,500	35,000
Bus Cpe	865	1075	3000	5500	7700	11,000
Roy RS Cpe	1295	1150	3600	6000	8400	12,000
Crw Cpe	—	1075	3000	5500	7700	11,000
Roy Sed	1295	1000	2400	5000	7000	10,000
Crw Sed	—	1025	2600	5250	7300	10,500

1931

1931 Chrysler, Series CG, Imperial town car, LeBaron, AA

CHRYSLER — SERIES CJ — SIX: The Series Six Chrysler was carried over as a 1931 model with very little change, except that cowl lamps were now mounted on the surcingle and new special type spring shackles were introduced.

CHRYSLER — SERIES 66 — SIX: This was another carryover series. A new feature was a curved headlamp tie-bar with "66" in center. Serial numbers for the 1931 series were H252SS to H262ER. Engine numbers for the 1931 series were C28056 to C28968. Specifications were the same as for late 1930 Series 66 models. Prices were unchanged. Weights increased by five pounds. Consult 1930 listings for further information.

CHRYSLER — SERIES 70 — SIX: This was another carryover series. A styling change was seen in the use of a new, low, flat, V-type radiator. Serial numbers for the 1931 series were P180YD to P188DW for early year cars with Fedco type numbers and 79970001 to 7998712 for later in the year cars. Engine numbers for the 1931 series were V27182 to V29413. Specifications were the same, except that prices and weights on closed cars changed as follows: Business coupe was $1,245 and 3425 pounds; Royal coupe was $1,295 and 3520 pounds; Brougham was $1,245 and 3530 pounds and Royal Sedan was $1295 and 3590 pounds. Consult 1930 listing for additional information.

1931 Chrysler, Series CD, convertible coupe, OCW

CHRYSLER — SERIES CD — EIGHT: Chrysler's first eight had a wide profile V-type radiator that somewhat resembled the radiator of the L-29 front wheel drive Cord. Other styling features included two cowl ventilators, vertical louver hoods, sloping windshields and cowl lamps. The first series CD (80 HP) was built from July 1930 to about Jan. 1931. It was succeeded by a second series CD (88 HP) built from approximately Jan. 1931 to April 1931. Body styling for these two lines was virtually identical.

1931 Chrysler, Series CG, Imperial dual-cowl phaeton, LeBaron, JAC

IMPERIAL — SERIES CG — EIGHT: A totally new Imperial was seen for 1931. With its V-type radiator, long hood, broad sweeping fenders and slanting split windshield, it took Chrysler's new "L-29 look" one step further than the smaller cars. Features included interior sun visors, adjustable front seats and steering columns, hydraulic brakes, 4-speed transmission, hydraulic shocks, rubber spring shackles and a new instrument panel. Standard factory bodies were by Briggs. Semi-custom bodies were by LeBaron. Waterhouse, Locke, Derham and Murphy also produced individual custom bodies on the Imperial chassis.

CHRYSLER — SERIES CM — SIX: This so-called "New Series Six" for 1931 was introduced in Jan. 1931 as a mid-year model, probably at the New York salon. It featured a new, wide profile, V-type radiator, vertical hood louvers, cowl lamps and two cowl ventilators. A new double-drop frame design gave extremely low-slung, sporty lines which followed Chrysler's "L-29 look" theme. Early closed cars were even built without external sun visors. Most likely, this change proved unpopular as later editions had very small, rounded visors. Sport models were highlighted by including several accessories — like sidemounts and wire wheels — as regular equipment.

1931 Chrysler, Series CD, roadster, JAC

CHRYSLER — DELUXE CD SERIES — EIGHT: The Deluxe CD series replaced the second series CD line in May 1931. It was a fancier more powerful version of this sporty looking 1931 Chrysler eight. Identification features included dual (split) windshields, screened V-type radiators and winged radiator caps. Standard equipment included hydraulic brakes, 4-speed transmission, four-point engine mounting and rubber spring shackles.

I.D. DATA: [Series CJ] Serial numbers were now on the right front door hinge pillar. Starting: 6514920. Ending: 6520171. Engine numbers remained in the previous location. Starting: CJ24495. Ending: CJ30292. [Series CD] Serial numbers were in the same location. (First Series) Starting: 7500001. Ending: 7510538. (Second Series) Starting: 7510539. Ending: 7514222. Engine numbers were in the same location. (First Series) Starting: CD-1001. Ending: CD-11531. (Second Series) Starting: CD-11532. Ending: CD-15671. Note: The use of the first and second series designations is believed to be relatively modern and both were probably considered a single line when new. Production figures for both seem to be lumped together. The CD series should not be confused with the CD Deluxe Eight line introduced in May 1931, which had a more powerful 100 HP engine. [Series CG] Serial numbers were in the same locations. Starting: 7800001. Ending: 7802915. Engine numbers were stamped on top of the timing gear chain cover. Starting: CG1001. Ending: CG3924. [Series CM] Serial numbers were in the same location. Starting: 6520501. Ending: 6548433. Engine numbers were in the same location as on other Chrysler engines (but not Imperial engines). Starting: CM1001. Ending: CM30828. [Series CD] Serial numbers were in the same locations. Starting: 7514601. Ending: 7519758. Engine numbers were in the same locations. Starting: CD16001. Ending: CD21140.

Model No.	Body Type & Seating	Price	Weight	Prod. Total
CJ	2-dr. Rds.-2/4P	785	2390	1616
CJ	4-dr. Tr.-5P	785	2455	279
CJ	2-dr. Cpe.-2P	745	2560	2267
CJ	2-dr. Roy. Cpe.-2/4P	785	2590	3593
CJ	2-dr. Conv. Cpe.-2/4P	875	2550	705
CJ	4-dr. Roy. Sed.-5P	795	2695	20748

Note 1: Total production was 29,239.
Note 2: Bold face indicates 1930-31 combined total.

CD	2-dr. RS Rds.-2/4P	1495	3100	1462
CD	2-dr. Spt. Rds.-2/4P	1595	3270	Note 2
CD	4-dr. D.W. Phae.-5P	1970	3490	85
CD	2-dr. Std. Roy. Cpe.-2/4P	1495	3290	3000
CD	2-dr. Spl. Roy. Cpe.-2/4P	1535	3290	Note 3
CD	2-dr. Spl. Conv. Cpe.-2/4P	1665	3195	700
CD	4-dr. Std. Roy. Sed.-5P	1525	3405	9000
CD	4-dr. Spl. Roy. Sed.-5P	1565	3405	Note 4

Note 1: Total Series CD production was 14,355. This includes all first and second series cars including 108 chassis only supplied to custom coach builders.
Note 2: Production totals of the roadster and Sports roadster is combined.
Note 3: Production of the standard and special Royal coupes is combined.
Note 4: Production of the standard and special Royal sedans is combined.

Model No.	Body Type & Seating	Price	Weight	Prod. Total
(Semi-Custom)				
CG	2-dr. LeB. Rds.-2/4P	3220	4530	100
CG	4-dr. LeB. D.C. Phae.-5P	3575	4645	85
CG	2-dr. LeB. Cpe.-2/4P	3150	4605	135
CG	2-dr. LeB. Conv. Cpe.-2/4P	3320	4570	10
(Standard Factory)				
CG	4-dr. Sed.-5P	2745	4705	909
CG	4-dr. C.C. Sed.-5P	2845	4685	1195
CG	4-dr. Sed.-7P	2945	4825	403
CG	4-dr. Limo. Sed.-7/8P	3145	4915	271
(Individual Custom)				
CG	2-dr. Waterhouse Conv. Vic.-5P			6
CG	2-dr. LeBaron Spdstr. Conv.-2P			1
CG	2-dr. Drauz (German) Conv. Sed-5P			1
CG	2-dr. LeBaron Conv. Sed.-5P			1
CG	4-dr. LeBaron Twn. Car-7P			unknown

Note: Total Imperial Series CG production was 3,228 cars of all types. This includes 99 chassis supplied to custom coach builders on which individual custom models were constructed. The above list of individual customs illustrates some models known to have been made. It does not represent a complete list and the production totals provided are strictly estimates.

CM	2-dr. RS Rds.-2/4P	885	2565	2281
CM	2-dr. Bus. Cpe.-2P	865	2730	802
CM	2-dr. RS Cpe.-2/4P	885	2775	5327
CM	2-dr. Conv. Cpe.-2/4P	970	2870	1492
CM	4-dr. Sed.-5P	895	2850	28620
CM	4-dr. DW Phae.-5P	915	2740	196
CM	Chassis	NA	NA	99

Note 1: Total Series CM production was 38,817.

Del CD	2-dr. RS Rds.-2/4P	1545	3330	511
Del CD	4-dr. Phae.-5P	1970	3545	113
Del CD	2-dr. RS Cpe.-2/4P	1525	3525	1506
Del CD	2-dr. Bus. Cpe.-2/4P	1565	3575	500
Del CD	2-dr. Conv. Cpe.-2/4P	1585	3445	501
Del CD	4-dr. Sed.-5P	1565	3640	5843
Del CD	Chassis Only	NA	NA	126

Note 1: Total DeLuxe CD series production was 9,106.

ENGINE: [Series CJ] Inline. L-head. Six. Cast iron block. B & S: 3-1/8 in. x 4-1/2 in. Disp.: 195.6 cu. in. C.R.: 5.2:1. Main bearings: Four. Valve lifters: Solid. Carb.: Carter 1V. [Series CD] (First Series): Inline. L-head. Eight. Cast iron block. B & S: 3 in. x 4-1/4 in. Disp.: 240.33 cu. in. C.R.: 5.2:1. Brake H.P.: 80 @ 3400 R.P.M. N.A.C.C. H.P.: 28.8. Valve lifters: Solid. Carb.: Stromberg Model BXV-2. (Second Series): Inline. L-head. Eight. Cast iron block. B & S: 3-1/8 in. x 4-1/4 in. Disp.: 217.8 cu. in. C.R.: 5.2:1. Brake H.P.: 88 @ 3400 R.P.M. N.A.C.C. H.P.: 31.25. Valve lifters: Solid. Carb.: Stromberg. [Series CG] Inline. L-head. Eight. Cast iron block. B & S: 3-1/2 in. x 5 in. Disp.: 384.84 cu. in. C.R.: 5.2:1. Brake H.P.: 125 @ 3200 R.P.M. N.A.C.C. H.P.: 39.2. Main bearings: Nine. Valve lifters: Solid. Carb.: Stromberg Model DD-3. [Series CM] Inline. L-head. Six. Cast iron block. B & S: 3-1/8 in. x 4-3/8 in. Disp.: 217.8 cu. in. C.R.: 5.35:1. Brake H.P.: 78 @ 3400 R.P.M. N.A.C.C. H.P.: 25.35. Main bearings: Seven. Valve lifters: Solid. Carb.: Stromberg UR-2. [Deluxe CD Series] Inline. L-head. Eight. Cast iron block. B & S: 3-1/4 in. x 4-1/4 in. Disp.: 282.1 cu. in. C.R.: 5.2:1. Brake H.P.: 100 @ 3400 R.P.M. N.A.C.C. H.P.: 33.8. Valve lifters: Solid. Carb.: Stromberg Model DXC-3.

CHASSIS: [Series CJ] W.B.: 109 in. Gas tank: 15.5 gal. Tires: 19 x 5.00. [Series 66] W.B.: 112-3/4 in. Gas tank: 11 gal. Tires: 18 x 5.50. [Series 70] W.B.: 116-1/2 in. Gas tank: 19.5 gal. Tires: 18 x 5.50. [Series CD] W.B.: 124 in. O.L.: 186 in. Gas tank: 19.5 gal. Tires: 18 x 5.50. [Series CG/Imperial] W.B.: 145 in. Gas tank: 21.5 gal. Tires: 18 x 7.00 or 18 x 7.50. [Series CM] W.B.: 116 in. Gas tank: 15.5 gal. Tires: 19 x 5.00 or 19 x 5.25. [Series DeL. CD] W.B.: 124 in. Gast tank: 19.5 gal. Tires: 17 x 6.50.

TECHNICAL: Three-speed manual transmission in CJ and CM sixes. Speeds: 3F/1R. Four-speed manual "multi-range" transmission in other series. Speeds: 4F/1R. Floor shift controls. Conventional clutch. Shaft drive. Overall gear ratio: [Series CJ] 4.7:1. [Series 66] 4.7:1. [Series 70] 3.82:1. [Series CD] 4.10:1. [Series CG] 4.1:1. [Series CM] 4.66:1 and [Series DeL. CD] 4.3:1. Hydraulic brakes standard on all Chryslers and Imperials. Wire wheels standard on CD/CG; wood spoke wheels standard on other series.

1931 Chrysler, Series CD, 4-dr. sedan, JAC

OPTIONS: Front bumper. Rear bumper. Rear fender guards. Spare tire. Sidemounted spare tire(s). Wire spoke wheels. OSRV mirror. Pedestal sidemount mirror(s). Cowl lights. Cigar lighter. Trunk rack. Touring trunk. Special solid paint. Two-tone sweep panel finish on Series 77 roadsters and phaetons. Leather side mount covers. Metal sidemount covers. Metal sidemount cover trim moldings. Spotlight(s). Trippe lights. Wind wings. Imperial custom bodies.

HISTORICAL: The CM series was introduced in January, 1931. The DeLuxe CD series was introduced in May 1931. All other series introduced in July 1930. Calendar year production: 52,819. Calendar year new car registrations: 52,650. The 1931 Imperial CG is often considered the most beautiful Imperial ever built. Chrysler appeared in the Indy 500 and European Grand Prix racing again this year. Stock car driver Harry Hartz set numerous speed records with an Imperial sedan at Daytona Beach, Fla. Mayor Al Smith, of New York City, drove an Imperial LeBaron Phaeton.

1931-1932

New Series Six, CM, 6-cyl., 116 wb
(Produced Jan. – Dec. 1931).

	FP	5	4	3	2	1
RS Rds	885	5100	10,200	17,000	23,800	34,000
Tr	915	4950	9900	16,500	23,100	33,000
RS Conv	970	4800	9600	16,000	22,400	32,000
Bus Cpe	865	950	2100	4750	6650	9500
Roy Cpe	885	1000	2400	5000	7000	10,000
Roy Sed	895	950	2100	4750	6650	9500

Series 70, 6-cyl., 116 1/2" wb

Bus Cpe	1245	1075	3000	5500	7700	11,000
Roy Cpe	1295	1125	3450	5750	8050	11,500
Brgm	1245	1000	2400	5000	7000	10,000
Roy Sed	1295	1000	2400	5000	7000	10,000

First Series, CD, 8--cyl., 80 hp, 124" wb
(Built 7/17/30 – 1/31).

RS Rds	1545	5550	11,100	18,500	25,900	37,000
Spt Rds	1650	6000	12,000	20,000	28,000	40,000
Conv	1585	5400	10,800	18,000	25,200	36,000
Cpe	1525	1400	4200	7000	9800	14,000
Spec Cpe	1565	1500	4350	7250	10,150	14,500
Roy Sed	1565	1025	2600	5200	7200	10,400
Spec Roy Sed	1565	1025	2600	5250	7300	10,500

Second Series, CD, 8-cyl., 88 hp, 124" wb
(Built 2/3/31 – 5/18/31).

RS Spt Rds	3220	6000	12,000	20,000	28,000	40,000
Lke DC Phae	3575	6150	12,300	20,500	28,700	41,000
RS Conv	3320	5850	11,700	19,500	27,300	39,000
Roy Cpe	2000	1200	3750	6250	8750	12,500
Spec Roy Cpe	3150	1250	3900	6500	9100	13,000
Roy Sed	2745	1025	2600	5250	7300	10,500

2nd Series CD

Spec Roy Sed	2845	1075	3000	5500	7700	11,000

DeLuxe Series, CD, 8-cyl., 100 hp, 124" wb
(Built 5/19/31 – 11/31).

RS Rds	1545	6150	12,300	20,500	28,700	41,000
Lke DC Phae	1970	6300	12,600	21,000	29,400	42,000
RS Conv	1585	6000	12,000	20,000	28,000	40,000
RS Cpe	1525	1400	4200	7000	9800	14,000
Roy Cpe	1565	1300	4050	6750	9450	13,500
4 dr Sed	1565	1200	3750	6250	8750	12,500

Imperial, CG, 8-cyl., 125 hp, 145" wb
(Built July 17, 1930 thru Dec. 1931)

Standard Line

CC Sed	2845	6750	13,500	22,500	31,500	45,000
5P Sed	2745	4500	9000	15,000	21,000	30,000
7P Sed	2945	4500	9000	15,000	21,000	30,000
Limo	3145	5000	10,050	16,750	23,450	33,500

Custom Line

LeB RS Rds	3295	25,500	45,000	73,000	100,000	130,000
LeB DC Phae	3395	27,900	51,000	79,000	106,000	136,000
LeB Conv Sed	3595	18,500	33,000	55,000	88,000	110,000
Conv Sed (LeBaron)	—	12,900	25,800	48,200	66,000	86,000
LeB RS Cpe	3295	6750	13,500	22,500	31,500	45,000
Wths Conv Vic	—	14,700	29,400	49,000	78,000	98,000
LeB Conv Spds	—	17,100	31,800	53,000	85,000	106,000

1931-32

CHRYSLER — CM SERIES — SIX: After July 1931 the Chrysler CM Six was sold as a first series 1932 model. This was basically a carryover series with only small changes in the cars. The changes included a narrow profile radiator, cowl lights mounted on the body surcingle and the introduction of freewheeling as an option. Horsepower ratings increased slightly.

CHRYSLER — 70 SERIES — SIX: This series was also sold as a carryover line during the first part of the 1932 model year, which began in July 1931. Styling features included a new narrow profile radiator with the pennon type hood design. Standard equipment included 4-speed transmission, downdraft carburetor, rubber spring shackles and fuel pump.

CHRYSLER — CD SERIES — EIGHT: The Deluxe Eight series was also carried over into the early part of the 1932 model year. Features were unchanged.

IMPERIAL — CG SERIES — EIGHT: In July 1931, the Chrysler Imperial CG series was also carried over into the first part of the 1932 model year. Features included dual sloping windshields, interior sun visors, vertical hood louvers and a streamlined V-type radiator. Standard equipment included 4-speed transmission, hydraulic brakes and four point engine mounting.

I.D. DATA: [CM Series] Serial numbers were in the same location. Starting: 6548434. Ending: 6557326. Engine numbers were also in the same location. Starting: CM30829. Ending: CM39467. [70 Series] Serial numbers were in the same location. Starting: 7998713. Ending: 7999974. Engine numbers were also in the same location. Starting: V29414. Ending: V30378. [CD Series] Serial numbers were in the same locations. Starting: 7519759. Ending: 7523531. Engine numbers were also in the same locations. Starting: CD21141. Ending: CD25182. [CG Series] Serial numbers were in the same location. Starting: 7802916. Ending: 7803273. Engine numbers were in the same location. Starting: CG3925. Ending: CG4268.

Model No.	Body Type & Seating	Price	Weight	Prod. Total
CM	2-dr. Rds.-2/4P	885	2615	Note 1
CM	4-dr. Phae.-5P	915	2740	Note 1
CM	2-dr. Bus. Cpe.-2P	865	2765	Note 1
CM	2-dr. RS Cpe.-2/4P	885	2830	Note 1
CM	2-dr. Conv. Cpe.-2/4P	935	2785	Note 1
CM	4-dr. Sed.-5P	895	2935	Note 1

Note 1: See 1931 Chrysler CM Series production totals.

SPECIFICATIONS: [70 Series] Only four body styles in the Chrysler 70 series were carried over as 1932 model year offerings. They were the Business coupe, Royal coupe, Brougham and Royal sedan. Prices and weights for the four models were unchanged. Refer to the 1931 specifications for details. [CD Series] There were no changes in available body styles, prices or weights. Refer to the 1931 specifications for details. [CG Series] There was now a total of nine models. Eight were the same ones offered in 1931. The descriptions, prices, weights and production totals were unchanged except that the former Custom Phaeton was now called a Custom Sport Phaeton. There was also one new model:

Model No.	Body Type & Seating	Price	Weight	Prod. Total
CG	4-dr. Cus. Conv. Sed.-5P	3995	4825	25

ENGINE: [CM Series] Inline. L-head. Six. Cast iron block. B & S: 3-1/4 in. x 4-3/8 in. Disp.: 217.8 cu. in. C.R.: 5.35:1. Brake H.P.: 78 @ 3400 R.P.M. N.A.C.C. H.P.: 25.35. Carb.: Schebler model UR-2. [70 Series] The Chrysler 70 series engine was unchanged. Refer to the 1931 engine specifications for details. [CD Series] The Chrysler CD Deluxe Eight engine was unchanged. Refer to the 1931 engine specifications for details. [CG Series] The Imperial CG engine was unchanged. Refer to the 1931 engine specifications for details.

CHASSIS: Chassis specifications for all models were the same as 1931 specifications except: 1932 CM sixes used 19 x 5.25 tires and 1932 Imperial CGs used 17 x 7.50 tires.

TECHNICAL: Same as 1931 models.

OPTIONS: Same as 1931 models.

HISTORICAL: Same as 1931 models. While these cars were sold as 1932 models, their production was included in 1931 Chrysler production records.

Pricing: Consult 1931 price listings.

1932

1932 Chrysler, Series CI, roadster, OCW

CHRYSLER — SERIES CI — SIX: The second series 1932 Chrysler sixes were extensively updated. Styling changes included a new oval instrument board, new dual (split) V-type windshields on closed cars (one-piece on open cars), dual cowl ventilators and larger hub caps that covered the wheel lugs. Standard equipment included Delco Remy ignition, hydraulic brakes, flexible "Floating Power" type engine suspension system, double drop frame, dash controlled freewheeling and hydraulic shock absorbers. New optional features included an automatic vacuum controlled clutch and silent gear selector. Six wire wheels were standard equipment on the Convertible sedan. For the English market, these cars were sold as the Richmond and Kingston; a third six-cylinder car was called the Mortlake but it was based on the DeSoto SC.

CHRYSLER — SERIES CP — EIGHT: This new second series 1932 series featured all steel bodies, a new double drop "girder truss" frame, narrow V-type radiator, split V-type windshields on closed cars, interior sun visors, cowl lamps and twin trumpet type horns. Standard equipment included Delco Remy ignition, hydraulic brakes, Floating Power, 4-speed transmis-

1932 Chrysler, Series CP, roadster, JAC

sion, dash button controlled freewheeling, rubber spring shackles and six wire wheels on the Convertible sedan and limited edition LeBaron Town Car. Automatic vacuum controlled clutch was optional. Following the practice of naming models after suburbs of London, this model was sold in England as the Hurlingham.

IMPERIAL — SERIES CH — EIGHT: This new second series 1932 line featured dual V-type windshields, cowl lamps, twin inside sun visors, twin trumpet horns, an indirectly lighted oval instrument panel and luxury appointments. Standard equipment included Delco Remy ignition, hydraulic brakes, Floating Power, double drop frame, freewheeling, 4-speed transmission, downdraft carburetor, rubber spring shackles, wire wheels, and rear mounted spare (on most body types). Six wire wheel equipment was standard on the Convertible sedan. The optional automatic vacuum operated clutch feature was available.

1932 Chrysler, Series CL, Imperial, convertible sedan, LeBaron, AA

CUSTOM IMPERIAL — SERIES CL — EIGHT: The 1932 Custom Imperial CL models had a special lengthened hood with door type hood ventilators instead of vertical louvers. Differences from the Imperial CH models included a longer wheelbase, larger overall size, bigger tires, a walnut dashboard with machine tooled instrument cluster and twin glove boxes and custom bodies. Most of the cars had LeBaron semi-custom coachwork, but five chassis were supplied for individual custom bodies, of which two were done for the Walter P. Chrysler family.

I.D. DATA: [Series CI] Serial numbers were again found on a plate located on the right front door hinge pillar post. Starting: 6557401. Ending: 6575639. Engine numbers were again located on the upper left side of the cylinder block between one and two cylinders, just below the cylinder head. Engine Nos. Starting: CI1001. Ending: CI19425. [Series CP] Serial numbers were in the same location. Starting: 7523601. Ending: 7528546. Engine numbers were in the same location. Engine Nos. Starting: CP10001. Ending: CP6171. [Series CH] Serial numbers were in the same location. Starting: 7900001. Ending: 7901362. Engine numbers were in the same location. Engine Nos. Starting: CH1001. Ending: CH2416. [CL Series] Serial numbers were in the same location. Starting: 7803301. Ending: 7803527. Engine numbers were in the same location. Engine Nos. Starting: CL1001. Ending: CL1247.

Model No.	Body Type & Seating	Price	Weight	Prod. Total
CI	2-dr. Rds.-2/4P	885	2830	474
CI	4-dr. Phae.-5P	915	2905	59
CI	2-dr. Bus. Cpe.-2P	865	2915	345
CI	2-dr. R/S Cpe.-2/4P	885	3040	2913
CI	2-dr. Conv. Cpe.-2/4P	935	2970	1000
CI	4-dr. Sed.-5P	895	3135	13,772
CI	2-dr. Conv. Sed.-5P	1125	3160	322
CI	Chassis only	NA	NA	70

Note 1: Total series production was 18,964.
Note 2: A limited amount of custom bodied cars were built on the Chrysler CI six chassis. They are eligible for full Classis status upon individual application.

Model No.	Body Type & Seating	Price	Weight	Prod. Total
CP	2-dr. R/S Cpe.-2/4P	1435	3735	718
CP	2-dr. Cpe.-5P	1475	3810	396
CP	2-dr. Conv. Cpe.-2/4P	1495	3705	502
CP	4-dr. Sed.-5P	1475	3885	3198
CP	4-dr. Conv. Sed.-5P	1695	4090	251
CP	Chassis only	NA	NA	48
CP	4-dr. LeB. Twn. Car-5P	3975	4320	(-12)

Note 1: Total series production was 5,113.
Note 2: A limited amount of custom bodies were built on the Chrysler CP eight chassis. Of the 48 chassis supplied to custom coachbuilders, it is believed that less than one dozen had the semi-factory LeBaron Town Car body for which the price and weight are listed above. Specifications for other individual customs are not available.

CH	2-dr. R/S Cpe.-2/4P	1925	4480	239
CH	4-dr. Sed.-5P	1945	4645	1002
CH	4-dr. Conv. Sed.-5P	2195	4890	152
CH	Chassis only	NA	NA	9

Note 1: Total series production was 1,402.
Note 2: Nine custom bodies were built on the 1932 Imperial CH chassis.
Note 3: All Imperial CH models are considered full Classics.

CL	4-dr. LeB. D.C. Phae.-5P	3395	5065	14
CL	2-dr. LeB. Conv. Rds.-2/4P	3295	4930	28
CL	4-dr. LeB. C.C. Sed.-5P	2895	5150	57
CL	4-dr. LeB. Conv. Sed.-5P	3595	5125	49
CL	4-dr. LeB. Sed.-7P	2995	5295	35
CL	4-dr. LeB. Sed. Limo.-7/8P	3295	5330	32

Individual Customs

CL	2-dr. LeB. Rds./Spds.-2P	NA	NA	1
CL	4-dr. LeB. Land. Limo.-7P	NA	NA	1
CL	Others	NA	NA	3

Note 1: Total series production was 220.
Note 2: Five chassis were supplied to coachbuilders for individual custom bodies. The LeBaron Landau Limousine was built for Walter P. Chrysler. It was fitted with early bowl type headlights and a special fabric covered hard top. The LeBaron roadster-speedster was built for one of Walter P. Chrysler's sons.

1932 Chrysler, Series CI, convertible coupe, OCW

ENGINE: [Series CI] Inline. L-head. Six. Cast iron block. B & S: 3-1/4 in. x 4-1/2 in. Disp.: 223.98 cu. in. C.R.: 5.35:1. Brake H.P.: 82 @ 3400 R.P.M. N.A.C.C. H.P.: 25.35. Valve lifters: Solid. Carb.: Ball & Ball model 6A1. [Series CP] Inline. L-head. Eight. Cast iron block. B & S: 3-1/4 in. x 4-1/2 in. Disp.: 298.6 cu. in. C.R.: 5.2:1. Brake H.P.: 100 @ 3400 R.P.M. N.A.C.C. H.P.: 33.80. Valve lifters: Solid. Carb.: Stromberg model DXR-3. [Series CH] Inline. L-head. Eight. Cast iron block. B & S: 3-1/2 in. x 5 in. Disp.: 384.84 cu. in. C.R.: 5.2:1. Brake H.P.: 125 @ 3200 R.P.M. N.A.C.C. H.P.: 39.20. Valve lifters: Solid. Carb.: Stromberg model DD-3. [Series CL] See 1932 Imperial CH series engine specifications.

CHASSIS: [Series CI] W.B.: 116 in. Tires: 18 x 5.50. Gas tank: 15.5 gal. [Series CP] W.B.: 125 in. Tires: 17 x 6.50. Gas tank: 19.5 gal. [Series CH] W.B.: 135 in. Tires: 17 x 7.00. Gas tank: 21.5 gal. [Series CL] W.B.: 146 in. Tires: 17 x 7.50. Gasl tank: 21.5 gal.

TECHNICAL: Three-speed manual transmission in Series CI Chrysler Six. Speeds: 3F/1R. Four-speed manual transmission in all other series. Speeds: 4F/1R. Floor shift controls. Conventional clutch. Shaft drive. Overall gear ratios: [CI] 4.6:1; [CP] 4.3:1. [CH/CL] 4.1:1. Four wheel hydraulic brakes on all series. Wood spoke wheels standard on Chryslers; wire spoke wheels standard on Imperials.

OPTIONS: Front bumper. Rear bumper. Rear fender guards. Rare spare (on Chryslers). Sidemounted spares. Leather sidemount covers. Metal sidemount covers. Chrome plated side mount covers. OSRV mirror. Pedestal type OSRV mirrors with sidemounts). Jumbo type Goodyear "Air Wheel" tires. Steel spoke wheels on Chrysler sixes and eights. Trunk rack. Touring trunk. Leather rear tire cover. Wire wheels (on Chrysler sixes and eights). Cigar lighter. Radio. Radio antenna. Wind wings. Heater. Clock. Spotlight(s). Trippe lights. Rear windshield (Phaeton). Automatic vacuum operated clutch. Silent gear transmission.

1932 Chrysler, Series CL, Imperial coupe, JAC

HISTORICAL: The second series 1932 models were introduced in January, 1932. Calendar year production: 25,291. Calendar year registrations: 26,016. Model year production: 25,699. Innovations: Freewheeling. Automatic vacuum clutch. Silent gear transmission. "Floating Power" flexible engine mounts. Chrysler was 10th in U.S. model year sales and 11th in calendar year output. The Chrysler powered George Howie Special qualified for the Indy 500, but was bumped from the field before the race started. The Chrysler powered Golden Seal Special started 36th in the Indy 500 and went out with a burned clutch on lap no. 17. Two "Trifon Special" prototypes for the Chrysler Airflow were built.

1932
Second Series, CI, 6-cyl., 116-1/2" wb, 82 hp
(Begun 1/1/32).

	FP	5	4	3	2	1
RS Rds	885	4500	9000	15,000	21,000	30,000
Phae	915	4350	8700	14,500	20,300	29,000
RS Conv	885	4200	8400	14,000	19,600	28,000
Conv Sed	1125	4350	8700	14,500	20,300	29,000
Bus Cpe	865	1075	3000	5500	7700	11,000
RS Cpe	885	1150	3600	6000	8400	12,000
4 dr Sed	895	925	2000	4650	6500	9300

Series CP, 8-cyl., 125" wb, 100 hp
(Began 1/1/32).

	FP	5	4	3	2	1
RS Conv	1495	4950	9900	16,500	23,100	33,000
Conv Sed	1695	5100	10,200	17,000	23,800	34,000
RS Cpe	1435	1550	4500	7500	10,500	15,000
Cpe	1475	1400	4200	7000	9800	14,000
4 dr Sed	1475	1300	4050	6750	9450	13,500
LeB TwnC	3975	3300	6600	11,000	15,400	22,000

Imperial Series, CH, 8-cyl., 135" wb, 125 hp
(Began 1/1/32).
Standard Line

	FP	5	4	3	2	1
Conv Sed	2195	25,500	45,000	73,000	100,000	130,000
RS Cpe	1925	6750	13,500	22,500	31,500	45,000
4 dr Sed	1945	5250	10,500	17,500	24,500	35,000

Imperial Series, CL, 8-cyl., 146" wb, 125 hp
(Began 1/1/32).
Custom Line -- LeBaron bodies

	FP	5	4	3	2	1
RS Conv	3295	29,500	55,000	84,000	110,000	140,000
DC Phae	3395	31,100	58,000	88,000	114,000	150,000
Conv Sed	3595	27,900	51,000	79,000	106,000	136,000

1933

1933 Chrysler, convertible coupe, OCW

CHRYSLER — CO SERIES — SIX: The Chrysler sixes were the company's best selling cars for 1933. They had more massive streamlined fenders that swept lower in the front. Other styling changes included a long, cowl-less hood with door type ventilators, single bar bumpers, "suicide" rear hinged doors, sloping V-type radiators, slanting V-type windshields and more rakish, slanted door openings. Standard equipment included Delco Remy ignition, hydraulic brakes, ''Floating Power'', automatic vacuum clutch, freewheeling, silent helical gear transmission, Oilite springs and a new coincidental starter/accelerator pedal. The sixes came with single windshield wipers and without external trumpet horns. Six wire wheel equipment was standard on convertible sedans.

1933 Chrysler, Series CT, Royal convertible coupe, JAC

CHRYSLER ROYAL — CT SERIES — EIGHT: The Royal eights for 1933 also had the new sweeping fenders, single bar bumpers, ''suicide'' doors, sloping V-type radiator, slanting V-type windshield, door type hood vents and more streamlined looks. Distinctive features of the Royal eights included all steel body construction, dual windshield wipers, dual taillights and dual chrome trumpet horns. Standard equipment included Delco Remy ignition, Lockheed hydraulic brakes, ''Floating Power'', coincidental starter, automatic vacuum clutch, adjustable front seats, automatic-control shock absorbers and six wire wheel equipment on the convertible sedan. A high horsepower engine option was available.

IMPERIAL — SERIES CQ — EIGHT: The Imperial CQ was an all new, smaller car which was downsized about nine inches from comparable 1932 models. It shared the annual styling theme of sweeping fenders, sloping V-type radiators, a cowl-less hood with door type ventilators, single bumpers and slanting V-type windshields. Rear hinged ''suicide'' doors were, however, found only on the Imperial CQ convertible sedan. Standard equipment included dual wipers, taillights and external chrome trumpet horns, a covered rear spare, Delco Remy ignition, Lockheed hydraulic brakes, ''Floating Power'', automatic vacuum clutch and freewheeling. Six wire wheel equipment, landau irons and a touring trunk were standard on convertible sedans. In a new twist, Imperial buyers were offered a *lower* horsepower engine option.

CUSTOM IMPERIAL — CL SERIES — EIGHT: This richest of all Chrysler series also had sweeping fenders, sloping V-radiators, sloping dual windshields, a cowl-less hood with door type ventilators, single bar bumper and chrome external trumpet horns. Rear hinged ''suicide'' doors were used on all Custom Imperials, except the Limousine. As usual, the factory cataloged semi-custom bodies were by LeBaron. Only six chassis and cowls were supplied to custom coachbuilders and at least two of them were bodied in Switzerland by the shops of Lagenthawl and Jean Oygaz. Standard Custom Imperial features included Delco Remy ignition, Lockheed hydraulic brakes, ''Floating Power'', automatic vacuum clutch, coincidental starter and freewheeling. The Custom Imperials also had rust proofed fenders, automatic heat control, downdraft carburetion and safety glass throughout. Wire wheels were standard on all models, but could be deleted upon owner request. Six wire wheels and a trunk were standard on phaetons and convertible sedans.

CHRYSLER — WIMBLEDON — SIX: Following its practice of selling a smaller or less expensive car in overseas markets, Chrysler marketed what was in reality the model SD DeSoto in Great Britain. Although fitted with a small-bore export engine, the Chrysler Wimbledon was generally equipped with deluxe appointments such as dual fender-mounted spare tires.

CHRYSLER — KEW — SIX: The smallest and least expensive Chrysler sold in the United Kingdom was in reality a rebadged Plymouth Six. The Chrysler Kew appears to have made its English debut in 1931 and would survive until England's entry into World War II in 1939.

I.D. DATA: [CO Series] Serial numbers were again found on a plate located on the right front door hinge pillar post. Starting: 6576001. Ending: 6592816. Engine numbers were again located on the upper left side of the cylinder block between the one and two cylinders, just below the cylinder head. Starting: C01001. Ending: C018608. [CT Series] Serial numbers were in the same location. Starting: 7000001. Ending: 7010035. Engine numbers were in the same location. Starting: CT10001. Ending: CT11396. [Series CQ] Serial numbers were in the same location. Starting: 7529001. Ending: 7532779. Engine numbers were in the same location. Starting: CQ1001. Ending: CQ4864. [CL Series] Serial numbers were in the same location. Starting: 7803551. Ending: 7803705. Engine numbers were in the same location. Starting: CL1251. Ending: CL1408.

1933 Chrysler, Series CO, business coupe, JAC

Model No.	Body Type & Seating	Price	Weight	Prod. Total
CO	2-dr. Bus. Cpe.-2P	745	2968	587
CO	2-dr. RS Cpe.-2/4P	775	3018	1454
CO	2-dr. Conv. Cpe.-2/4P	795	3013	677
CO	2-dr. Brgm.-5P	745	3078	1207
CO	4-dr. Sed.-5P	785	3143	13264
CO	4-dr. Spl. Int. Sed.-7P	825	3160	51
CO	2-dr. Conv. Sed.-7P	945	3212	207
CO	4-dr. Sed.-7P	NA	NA	151
CO	Chassis & Cowl	NA	NA	267

Note 1: Total series production was 17,814.
(120 in. wheelbase)

CT	2-dr. Bus. Cpe.-2P	895	3303	226
CT	2-dr. RS Cpe.-2/4P	915	3343	1033
CT	2-dr. Conv. Cpe.-2/4P	945	3363	539
CT	4-dr. Sed.-5P	925	3483	7993
CT	2-dr. Conv. Sed.-5P	1085	3617	257

(128 in. wheelbase)

CT	4-dr. Sed.-7/8P	1125	3658	246
CT	Chassis & Cowl	NA	NA	95

Note 1: Total series production was 10,389.
Note 2: Custom bodied cars built on the 128 in. wheelbase CT Series chassis may be accepted by the Classic Car Club of America on an individual application basis.

CQ	2-dr. RS Cpe.-2/4P	1275	3734	364
CQ	2-dr. Vic. Cpe.-5P	1295	3754	267
CQ	2-dr. Conv. Cpe.-2/4P	1325	3754	243
CQ	4-dr. Sed.-5P	1295	3864	2584
CQ	4-dr. Conv. Sed.-5P	1495	4144	364
CQ	Chassis & Cowl	NA	NA	16

Note 1: Total series production was 3,838.
(LeBaron semi-custom)

CL	4-dr. Phae.-5P	3395	4890	36
CL	2-dr. Rds. Conv.-2/4P	3295	4910	9
CL	4-dr. C.C. Sed.-5P	2895	5045	43
CL	4-dr. Sed.-8P	2995	5240	21
CL	4-dr. Limo.-8P	3295	5245	22
CL	4-dr. Conv. Sed.-5P	3395	5135	11

(Individual Customs)

CL	2-dr. Stationary Cpe.	NA	NA	3
CL	Chassis & Cowl	NA	NA	6

Note 1: Total series production was 151.

ENGINE: [CO Series] Inline. L-head. Six. Cast iron block. B & S: 3-1/4 in. x 4-1/2 in. Disp.: 223.98 cu. in. C.R.: 5.35:1. Brake H.P.: 83 @ 3400 R.P.M. N.A.C.C. H.P.: 25.35. Main bearings: Four. Valve lifters: Solid. Carb.: Stromberg IV. (Note: Optional engine with 6.2:1 high compression ''Red Head'' and 89 BHP @ 3400 R.P.M. available). [CT Series] Inline. L-head. Eight. Cast iron block. B & S: 3-1/4 in. x 3-1/8 in. Disp.: 273.7 cu. in. C.R.: (Std.) 5.4:1; (Opt.) 6.2:1. Brake H.P.: (Std.) 90 @ 3400 R.P.M.; (Opt.) 98 @ 3400 R.P.M. N.A.C.C. H.P.: 25.35. Main bearings: Five. Valve lifters: Solid. Carb.: Stromberg 1V model EX-32. [Series CQ] Inline. L-head. Eight. Cast iron block. B & S: 3-1/4 in. x 4-1/2 in. Disp.: 298.65 cu. in. C.R.: (Std.) 6.2:1; (Opt.) 5.2:1. Brake H.P.: (Std.) 108 @ 3400 R.P.M.; (Opt.) 100 @ 3400 R.P.M. N.A.C.C. H.P.: 33.80. Main bearings: Nine. Valve lifters: Solid. Carb.: Stromberg 1V model EX-32. [CL Series] Inline. L-head. Eight. Cast iron block. B & S: 3-1/2 in. x 5 in. Disp.: 384.84 cu. in. C.R.: (Std.) 5.8:1; (Opt.) 5.2:1. Brake H.P.: (Std.) 135 @ 3200 R.P.M.; (Opt.) 125 @ 3200 R.P.M. N.A.C.C. H.P.: 39.20. Main bearings: Nine. Valve lifters: Solid. Carb.: Stromberg 2V model EE-3.

CHASSIS: [Series CO] W.B.: 117 in. Tires: 17 x 5.50. Gas tank: 15.5 gal. [Series CT] W.B.: 120/128.5 in. Tires: 17 x 6.00. Gas tank: 16 gal. [Series CQ] W.B.: 126 in. Tires: 17 x 6.50. Gas tank: 19.5 gal. [Series CL] W.B.: 146 in. Tires: 17 x 7.50. Gas tank: 21.5 gal.

TECHNICAL: Manual transmission. Speeds: 3F/1R. (Note: The four-speed transmission with four speeds forward and one reverse was still used on Imperials.) Floor shift controls. Conventional clutch. Overall ratios: (CO) 4.37:1; (CT/CQ) 4.3:1; (CL) 4.10:1. Wire wheels were standard equipment on all Chryslers. Lockheed four-wheel brakes used on all series.

OPTIONS: Front bumper. Rear bumper. Rear spare (Chryslers). Side-mounted spares. Leather sidemount covers. Metal sidemount covers. Chrome sidemount covers. OSRV mirror. Pedestal OSRV sidemount mirrors. Special Goodrich spoke wheels with General Jumbo tires. Trunk rack.

Touring trunk. Leather rear tire cover. Wire wheels (chrome plated). Cigar lighter. Radio. Antenna. Wind wings. Heater. Clock. Spotlight(s). Trippe lights. Rear windshield (Phaeton). Demountable wood spoke wheels. Chrome steel spoked wheels. Chrome plated hood ventilator doors. Retractable tonneau windshield (Custom Imperial Phaeton).

HISTORICAL: Introduced: The CL series was introduced at mid-model year in Feb. 1933. Other series introduced in December, 1932. Calendar year production: 30,220. Model year production: 32,241. Calendar year new car registrations: 28,677. Chrysler was America's 9th largest auto manufacturer on a model year basis and 10th ranked auto maker on a calendar year sales basis. Innovations: new 3-speed silent helical gear transmission on Chryslers. Improved steel alloy exhaust valve seats. New type oil filter. Automatic choke. Finishing 14th at the Indy 500, the Golden Seal special was the last Chrysler powered car to compete at Indianapolis in the pre-war years. Development work on the Airflow design continued in 1933. This was also the last year that Chrysler produced a roadster.

1933 Chrysler, Imperial dual cowl phaeton, LeBaron, AA

1933
Series CO, 6-cyl., 116.5" wb

	FP	5	4	3	2	1
RS Conv	795	2600	5500	9250	12,950	18,500
Conv Sed	945	2800	5700	9500	13,300	19,000
Bus Cpe	745	1125	3450	5750	8050	11,500
RS Cpe	775	1150	3600	6000	8400	12,000
Brgm	745	1075	3000	5500	7700	11,000
4 dr Sed	785	950	2100	4750	6650	9500

Royal Series CT, 8-cyl., 119.5 wb

RS Conv	945	4000	7950	13,250	18,550	26,500
Conv Sed	1085	4050	8100	13,500	18,900	27,000
Bus Cpe	895	1250	3900	6500	9100	13,000
RS Cpe	915	1400	4200	7000	9800	14,000
4 dr Sed	925	1000	2400	5000	7000	10,000
7P Sed	1175	1125	3450	5750	8050	11,500

Imperial Series CQ, 8-cyl., 126" wb

RS Conv	1325	5250	10,500	17,500	24,500	35,000
Conv Sed	1495	5550	11,100	18,500	25,900	37,000
RS Cpe	1275	3750	7500	12,500	17,500	25,000
5P Cpe	1295	3500	7050	11,750	16,450	23,500
4 dr Sed	1295	3400	6900	11,500	16,100	23,000

Imperial Custom, Series CL, 8-cyl., 146" wb

RS Conv	3295	15,000	30,000	50,000	80,000	100,000
WS Phae	3395	31,100	58,000	88,000	114,000	150,000
CC Sed	2895	7950	15,900	26,500	37,100	53,000

1934

1934 Chrysler, Series CA, sedan, JAC

CHRYSLER — SERIES CA/CB — SIX: The Chrysler sixes for 1934 were the company's only conventional cars, as Chrysler and Imperial Eights took the new Airflow styling. New features included valanced front and rear fenders, horizontal hood louvers, body color radiator shells and one-piece windshields. "Suicide" doors were used on all models in the short wheelbase CA line and on all models, except the Convertible sedan, in the long wheelbase CB line. Standard equipment included Delco Remy ignition, independent front suspension, "Floating Power", front vent windows, dual windshield wipers and steel spoke wheels.

CHRYSLER AIRFLOW — SERIES CY — SIX: Following a confusing corporate policy of building special models for the export or Canadian markets, the CY Airflow fits neatly into this category. The CY was actually a DeSoto Airflow fitted with Chrysler trim. The CY sold for about $60 more than the SE DeSoto upon which it was based. Based on serial number sequence, only 444 were built.

1934 Chrysler, Series CU Airflow, 4-dr. sedan, OCW

CHRYSLER AIRFLOW — SERIES CU — EIGHT: The Chrysler eight used the new, ultra streamlined Airflow design with unit body construction. Features included an alligator hood, recessed headlights mounted in teardrop shaped housings that incorporated the parking lights, triple bar bumpers, valanced fenders with full shroud rear fender skirts, a waterfall grille with multiple vertical blades, sloping V-type windshield, front and rear vent windows (most models) and six vertical hood louvers arranged in groups of two with each pair of descending size. Standard equipment included Delco Remy ignition, Lockheed hydraulic brakes, cross flow radiator, automatic vacuum operated clutch and "Floating Power". The Town sedan had a blind rear quarter styling treatment.

IMPERIAL AIRFLOW — SERIES CV — EIGHT: This was a larger version of the new Airflow with more luxurious equipment and appointments. Features included a split windshield and triple bar bumpers. Standard equipment was the same as on the Chrysler CU Airflow eights, plus downdraft carburetor and vacuum assisted "power" brakes.

CUSTOM IMPERIAL AIRFLOW — SERIES CX — EIGHT: This was a new intermediate sized series in the Airflow line. It was actually a long wheelbase version of the Imperial Airflow CV and used the same styling and equipment features. Even the engine had the same specifications. Although four body styles were cataloged, it appears that only two Town Limousines and one prototype version of the Town Sedan were built.

CUSTOM IMPERIAL AIRFLOW — SERIES CW — EIGHT: These were very special models built in limited production quantities. They included the largest and heaviest models ever made by Chrysler Corporation. Special features included the first ever curved one-piece windshield, dual "step plate" running boards with chrome trim moldings, an extended length cowl with longer trim moldings and four bar bumpers. They had rounded radiator grilles and headlamps and parking lights that were integral with the hood. Full chrome wheel disks were available only on this series. Standard equipment included everything found on lower priced Airflows, plus automatic overdrive and ride stabilizer bars.

1934 Chrysler, Kew, 2-dr. sedan, JB

CHRYSLER — KEW — SIX: Again the smallest and least expensive Chrysler model sold in Great Britain, the Kew was in reality a rebadged Plymouth, fitted with the small-bore export engine of 170 cubic inches.

CHRYSLER — WIMBLEDON — SIX: Based on the Plymouth this year, the Wimbledon differed in appointments and had the regular bore Plymouth engine. Among the items special to England was a sliding roof panel. The Plymouth was shipped as a CKD (completely knocked down) unit to Chrysler Kew assembly plant for final trim and finish.

CHRYSLER — CROYDON — SIX: This Chrysler model was in reality a DeSoto Airflow SE sold in the English market.

I.D. DATA: [Series CA/CB] Serial numbers were again found on a plate on the right front door hinge pillar post. Starting: 6650001. Ending: 6672665. Engine numbers were again located on the upper left side of the cylinder block between the one and two cylinders, just below the cylinder head. Starting: CA1001 and CB1001. [Series CU] Serial numbers were in the same location. Starting: 6593001. Ending: 6601154. Engine numbers were located in the same location. Starting: CU1001 (& up). [Series CV] Serial numbers were in the same location. Starting: 7010101. Ending: 7012191. Engine numbers were in the same location. Starting: CV1001 (& up). [Series CX] Serial numbers were in the same location. Starting: 7901401. Ending: 7901528. Engine numbers: See CV series engine codes. [Series CW] Serial numbers were located in the same location. Starting: 7803751. Ending: 7803798. Engine numbers were in the same location. Starting: CW1001. Ending: CW1071. CY serial numbers (Canada): starting: 9820676. Ending: 9821120.

1934 Chrysler, Series CA, coupe, OCW

Model No. (CA Series)	Body Type & Seating	Price	Weight	Prod. Total
CA	2-dr. Bus. Cpe.-2p	775	2879	1650
CA	2-dr. Del. Cpe.-2/4P	830	2903	1875
CA	2-dr. Conv. Cpe.-2/4P	865	2889	700
CA	2-dr. Brgm.-5P	795	3019	1575
CA	4-dr. Sed.-5P	845	3123	17,617
CA	Chassis & Cowl	NA	NA	385
(CB Series)				
CB	4-dr. C.C. Sed.-5P	935	3094	980
CB	4-dr. Conv. Sed.-5P	985	3069	450
CB	Chassis & Cowl	NA	NA	20

Note 1: Total CA series production was 23,802.
Note 2: Total CB series production was 1,450.

CU	2-dr. Cpe.-5P	1345	3736	732
CU	2-dr. Brgm.-6P	1345	3741	306
CU	4-dr. Twn. Sed.-6P	1345	3716	125
CU	4-dr. Sed.-6P	1345	3760	7226

Note 1: Total series production was 8,389.

CV	2-dr. Cpe.-5P	1625	3929	212
CV	4-dr. Sed.-6P	1625	3974	1997
CV	4-dr. Twn. Sed.-6P	1625	3969	67
CV	Chassis & Cowl	NA	NA	1

Note 1: Total series production was 2,277.

CX	4-dr. Sed.-6P	2245	4154	25
CX	4-dr. Twn. Sed.-6P	2245	4160	1
CX	4-dr. Limo.-8P	2345	4299	78
CX	4-dr. Twn. Limo.-8P	2345	4304	2

Note 1: Total series production was 106.

CW	4-dr. Sed.-8P	5000	5780	17
CW	4-dr. Twn. Sed.-8P	5000	5815	28
CW	4-dr. Cus. Limo.-8P	5145	5900	20
CW	4-dr. Twn. Limo.-8P	5145	5935	2

Note 1: Total series production was 67.

1934 Chrysler Imperial, Airflow, limousine, OCW

ENGINE: [Series CA/CB] Inline. L-head. Six. Cast iron block. B & S: 3-3/8 in. x 4-1/2 in. Disp.: 241.6 cu. in. C.R.: (Std.) 5.4:1; (Opt.) 6.2:1. Brake H.P.: (Std.) 93 @ 3400 R.P.M.; (Opt.) 100 @ 3400 R.P.M. N.A.C.C. H.P.: 27.34. Main bearings: Four. Valve lifters: Solid. Carb.: Ball & Ball 1V. [Series CU] Inline. L-head. Eight. Cast iron block. B & S: 3-1/4 in. x 4-1/2 in. Disp.: 299 cu. in. C.R.: 6.5:1. Brake H.P.: 122 @ 3400 R.P.M. N.A.C.C. H.P.: 33.80. Valve lifters: Solid. Carb.: Stromberg model EX-32. [Series CV]

Inline. L-head. Eight. Cast iron block. B & S: 3-1/4 in. x 4-7/8 in. Disp.: 323.5 cu. in. C.R.: 6.5:1. Brake H.P.: 130 @ 3400 R.P.M. N.A.C.C. H.P.: 33.80. Valve lifters: Solid. Carb.: Stromberg 1V model EE-22. [Series CX] See Imperial Airflow CV engine data. [Series CW] Inline. L-head. Eight. Cast iron block. B & S: 3-1/2 in. x 5 in. Disp.: 384.84 cu. in. C.R.: 6.5:1. Brake H.P.: 145 @ 3200 R.P.M. N.A.C.C. H.P.: 39.20. Valve lifters: Solid. Carb.: Stromberg 2V model EE-3.

CHASSIS: [Series CA] W.B.: 117 in. Tires: 16 x 6.50. Gas tank: 15 gal. [Series CB] W.B.: 121 in. Tires: 16 x 6.50. Gas tank: 15 gal. [Series CU] W.B.: 122.8 in. Tires: 16 x 7.00. Gas tank: 21 gal. [Series CV] W.B.: 128 in. Tires: 16 x 7.50. Gas tank: 21 gal. [Series CX] W.B.: 137.5 in. Tires: 16 x 7.50. Gas tank: 21 gal. [Series CW] W.B.: 146 in. Tires: 17 x 7.50. Gas tank: 30 gal.

TECHNICAL: [Custom Imperial Airflow CW] Manual transmission. Speeds: 4F/1R. [Other Series] Manual transmission. Speeds: 3F/1R. Floor shift. Conventional clutch. Shaft drive. Overall gear ratios: (CA/CB) 4.11:1; (CU/CV/CX) 4.10:1; (CW) 4.14:1. Steel spoke wheels standard on all series. Lockheed hydraulic four wheel brake standard on all series (vacuum assisted on CW).

OPTIONS: Front bumper. Rear bumper. Sidemount(s) on series CA/CB Six. Leather sidemount cover. Steel sidemount cover. Chrome sidemount cover. Spotlight(s). Trippe lights. Rear spare (Chrysler sixes). Rear spare cover. Pedestal mirrors (with sidemounts). OSRV mirror(s). Clock. Cigar lighter. Radio. Antenna. Electric horns. Trunk rack. Touring trunk. Chrome wheel trim rings. Fender skirts (Airflow). Full wheel disks (Custom Imperial CW).

HISTORICAL: Introduced January, 1934. Calendar year production: 36,929. Model year production: 36,091. Calendar year new car registrations: 28,052. Chrysler was America's 10th ranked automaker on a model year production basis and 11th ranked automaker on a calendar year sales basis. Innovations: five-degree tip to Airflow engine. Airflow steering gear in front of axle. Power brakes on Imperial CW Airflows. First curved one-piece windshield. Softer Airflow springs. Ten inch wider seats in Airflows. Driver Harry Hartz established 72 stock car speed and endurance records, at Daytona Beach, Fla., with a 1934 Airflow CU Coupe. Hartz also averaged 18.1 miles per gallon while driving a similar car coast-to-coast from Los Angeles to New York City.

1934
Series CA, 6-cyl., 117" wb

	FP	5	4	3	2	1
RS Conv	865	5300	10,650	17,750	24,850	35,500
Bus Cpe	775	1075	3000	5500	7700	11,000
RS Cpe	865	1175	3700	6150	8600	12,300
Brgm	795	1050	2800	5400	7500	10,800
4 dr Sed	845	1025	2600	5250	7300	10,500
Series CB, 6-cyl., 121" wb						
Conv Sed	970	5500	10,950	18,250	25,550	36,500
CC Sed	900	1300	4000	6650	9300	13,300
Airflow, Series CU, 8-cyl., 123" wb						
Cpe	1345	3600	7200	12,000	16,800	24,000
Brgm	1345	3650	7350	12,250	17,150	24,500
4 dr Sed	1345	3350	6750	11,250	15,750	22,500
Twn Sed	1345	3500	7050	11,750	16,450	23,500
Imperial Airflow, Series CV, 8-cyl., 128" wb						
Cpe	1625	4000	7950	13,250	18,550	26,500
4 dr Sed	1625	3500	7050	11,750	16,450	23,500
Twn Sed	1625	3800	7650	12,750	17,850	25,500
Imperial Custom Airflow, Series CX, 8-cyl., 137.5" wb						
4 dr Sed	2245	4600	9150	15,250	21,350	30,500
Twn Sed	2245	4600	9150	15,250	21,350	30,500
Limo	2345	5300	10,650	17,750	24,850	35,500
Twn Limo	2345	6450	12,900	21,500	30,100	43,000
Imperial Custom Airflow, Series CW, 8-cyl., 146.5" wb						
4 dr Sed	5000	8400	16,800	28,000	39,200	56,000
Twn Sed	5000	9300	18,600	31,000	43,400	62,000
Limo	5000	9600	19,200	32,000	44,800	64,000

1935

1935 Chrysler, Series CZ, Airstream Deluxe, 4-dr. sedan, AA

CHRYSLER AIRSTREAM — SERIES C-6 — SIX: Chrysler's conventional cars were now called Airstream models. They had new, all-steel uni[t] bodies, slightly convex grilles, horizontal hood louvers and sloping rea[r] panels with built-in luggage compartments. Standard equipment include[d]

Autolite ignition, hydraulic brakes, "Floating Power", Synchromesh transmission and a ventilated clutch. Sixes had single windshield wipers and taillights, as standard equipment. There was also only one interior sun visor.

CHRYSLER AIRSTREAM — SERIES CZ — EIGHT: Chrysler's CZ Airstream Eight had a three inch longer wheelbase than the Airstream Six. The cars in both lines looked basically the same otherwise, but the Eights had dual sun visors, wipers and taillights added to the standard equipment list. They also had slightly larger tires.

CHRYSLER DELUXE AIRSTREAM — CZ (DEL.) — EIGHT: Deluxe Airstream Eights could be readily identified by their dual chrome trumpet horns, fender mounted parking lights, twin bullet-shaped taillights and winged "8" emblem on the front sides of the hood. Runningboards on the Deluxe models had chrome trim moldings. These cars were actually a CZ sub-series, but had specific serial numbers. Two body styles were offered with a longer than normal wheelbase and it's likely that most — if not all — of the bare chassis sold were also long wheelbase units.

1935 Chrysler, Airflow, 4-dr. sedan, OCW

CHRYSLER AIRFLOW — SERIES C-1 — EIGHT: The 1935 Airflow had a new hood that extended forward in a V-shape. Single broad bumpers were used and the louvers on the hood were decorative, rather than functional. The new grille had a greater slope from top to bottom and ended squarely at the top of the radiator instead of tapering over the center. Standard equipment included Autolite ignition, hydraulic brakes, "Floating Power," automatic choke and a stabilizer in back of the front axle.

IMPERIAL AIRFLOW — SERIES C-2 — EIGHT: The front fender valances, cowl sides and decorative hood louvers on Imperial Airflows were longer than on the Chrysler Airflows. Tire sizes were larger, too. Interior appointments were correspondingly richer. An aluminum cylinder head and over-drive transmission were standard equipment for Imperials. Another feature was a Stromberg two-barrel carburetor. The Imperial Airflows also had vacuum assisted power brakes.

IMPERIAL CUSTOM AIRFLOW — SERIES C-3 — EIGHT: The C-3 Imperial Custom Airflow was a big car with a wheelbase nearly 10 inches longer than the regular Imperial Airflow. Most of this extra room was evident in the car's longer front doors and side windows. There were four body styles in this series but two were built in extremely limited quantities and had a mixture of 1934 and 1935 features. For example, one Town Sedan Limousine had triple bar bumpers and 1934 type hood doors combined with the new 1935 style grille and hood.

CUSTOM IMPERIAL AIRFLOW — SERIES CW* — EIGHT: In 1935, the CW Custom Imperial was replaced with the CW* with one-piece front and rear bumpers and decorative louvers instead of hood doors. These cars again had a distinctive, one-piece curved windshield. The interior featured rich upholstery and trim. A disappearing partition window was used in the limousines. Available records show 32 production units sold in 1935. However, it seems likely that additional cars were assembled this year and, later, updated for sale in subsequent years.

I.D. DATA: [Series C-6] Serial numbers were on a plate on the front door hinge pillar post. Starting: 6800001. Ending: 6823250. Engine numbers were on the left side of cylinder block, between one and two cylinders, just below cylinder head. Starting: C6-1001. Ending: C6-25519. [Series CZ] Serial numbers were in the same locations. Starting: 6701501. Ending: ̄707676. Engine numbers were in the same locations. Starting: CZ-1001. ̄nding: CZ-10341. [Series CZ (Del.)] Serial numbers were in the same ̄ation. Starting: 6707677. Ending: 6710401. Engine numbers were in the same location. Starting: CZ-1001. Ending: CZ-10341. [Series C-1] ̄ numbers were in the same location. Starting: 6601201. Ending: ̄ ̄00. Engine numbers were in the same location. Starting: C1-1001. ̄ C1-6037. [Series C-2] Serial numbers were in the same location. ̄: 7012301. Ending: 7014900. Engine numbers were in the same ̄Starting: C2-1001. Ending: C2-3632. [Series C-3] Serial numbers ̄ e same locations. Starting: 7528551. Ending: 7528675. Engine ̄ere in the same locations. Starting: C3-1001. Ending: C3-1135. ̄ Serial numbers were in the same location. Starting: 7803799. ̄ ̄835. Engine numbers were in the same locations. Starting: ̄ing: CW-1080.

1

Model No.	Body Type & Seating	Price	Weight	Prod. Total
C6	2-dr. Bus. Cpe.-2P	745	2863	1975
C6	2-dr. RS Cpe.-2/4P	810	2953	861
C6	2-dr. Conv. Cpe.-2/4P	870	3053	Note 2
C6	2-dr. Tr. Brgm.-5P	820	2988	1901
C6	4-dr. Sed.-5P	830	3013	6055
C6	4-dr. Tr. Sed.-5P	860	3048	12,790
C6	Chassis	NA	NA	476
C6	2-dr. Fs. Bk. Sed.-5P	820	2990	400

Note 1: Total series production was 24,458.
Note 2: There is no available record of production of the C6 convertible coupe.

CZ	2-dr. Bus. Cpe.-2P	910	3103	Note 1
CZ	2-dr. RS Cpe.-2/4P	935	3138	Note 1
CZ	2-dr. Tr. Brgm.-5P	960	3203	Note 1
CZ	4-dr. Sed.-5P	975	3213	Note 1
CZ	4-dr. Tr. Sed.-5P	995	3263	Note 1

Note 1: Production of the Airstream Eights and DeLuxe Airstream Eights was recorded as a single, combined total. See figures listed below for DeLuxe Airstream Eight.

CZ	2-dr. Bus. Cpe.-2P	930	3138	100
CZ	2-dr. RS Cpe.-2/4P	955	3233	550
CZ	2-dr. Conv. Cpe.-2/4P	1015	3298	101
CZ	2-dr. Tr. Brgm.-5P	980	3293	500
CZ	4-dr. Sed.-5P	985	3333	2958
CZ	4-dr. Tr. Sed.-5P	1015	3338	4394
CZ	4-dr. LWB Trav. Sed.-5P	1235	3513	245
CZ	4-dr. LWB Sed.-7P	1235	3538	212
CZ	Chassis	—	—	237

Note 1: Total production of CZ Airstream Eights and CZ Deluxe Airstream Eights together was 9,297.
Note 2: The designation LWB means long wheelbase.

C-1	2-dr. Bus. Cpe.-2P	1245	3823	72
C-1	2-dr. Cpe.-6P	1245	3883	307
C-1	4-dr. Sed.-6P	1245	3828	4617

Note: Total series production was 4,996.

C-2	2-dr. Cpe.-6P	1475	4003	200
C-2	4-dr. Sed.-6P	1475	3998	2398

Note 1: Total series production was 2,598.

C-3	4-dr. Sed.-6P	2245	4208	69
C-3	4-dr. Twn. Sed.-6P	2245	4308	1
C-3	4-dr. Sed. Limo.-8P	2345	4378	53
C-3	4-dr. Twn. Sed. Limo.-8P	2345	4478	2

Note 1: Total series production was 125.

CW*	4-dr. Sed.-8P	5000	5785	15
CW*	4-dr. Twn. Sed.-8P	5000	5885	0
CW*	4-dr. Sed. Limo.-8P	5145	5990	15
CW*	4-dr. Twn. Sed. Limo.-8P	5145	6090	2

Note 1: Total series production (per available records) was 32.
Note 2: Some sources show production of non-Custom Imperial CW Airflows as follows: 4-dr. Sedan (17); 4-dr. Limousine (28) and 4-dr. Town Sedan (2). These figures cannot be substantiated by contemporary historical sources which show no listings for a non-custom series. It's likely that the figures could apply to cars sold in later years with updated sheet metal.

ENGINE: [Series C-6] Inline. L-head. Six. Cast iron block. B & S: 3-3/8 in. x 4-1/2 in. Disp.: 241.5 cu. in. C.R.: (Std.) 6.0:1; (Opt.) 6.5:1. Brake H.P.: (Std.) 93 @ 3400 R.P.M.; (Opt.) 100 @ 3400 R.P.M. N.A.C.C. H.P.: 27.34. Main bearings: Four. Valve lifters: Solid. Carb.: Carter 1V model E6F2. Torque: (Std.) 180 lbs.-ft. @ 1200 R.P.M.; (Opt.) 185 lbs.-ft. @ 1200 R.P.M. [Series CZ] Inline. L-head. Eight. Cast iron block. B & S: 3-1/4 in. x 4-1/8 in. Disp.: 273.8 cu. in. C.R.: (Std.) 6.2:1; (Opt.) 7.0:1. Brake H.P.: (Std.) 105 @ 3400 R.P.M.; (Opt.) 110 @ 3400 R.P.M. N.A.C.C. H.P.: 33.8. Main bearings: Five. Valve lifters: Solid. Carb.: Stromberg 1V model EX-32. Torque: (Std.) 200 lbs.-ft. @ 1200 R.P.M.; (Opt.) 206 lbs.-ft. @ 1200 R.P.M. [Series CZ (Del.)] The Deluxe Airstream Eights used the same engines as the standard Airstream Eights. See specifications above. [Series C-1] Inline. L-head. Eight. Cast iron block. B & S: 3-1/4 in. x 4-7/8 in. Disp.: 323.5 cu. in. C.R.: (Std.) 6.2:1; (Opt.) 6.5:1. Brake H.P.: (Std.) 115 @ 3400 R.P.M.; (Opt.) 120 @ 3400 R.P.M. N.A.C.C. H.P.: 33.8. Main bearings: Five. Valve lifters: Solid. Carb.: Stromberg 1V model EX-32. Torque: (Std.) 240 lbs.-ft. @ 1200 R.P.M.; (Opt.) 250 lbs.-ft. @ 1200 R.P.M. [Series C-2] Inline. L-head. Eight. Cast iron block. B & S: 3-1/4 in. x 4-7/8 in. Disp.: 323.5 cu. in. C.R.: (Std.) 6.5:1; (Opt.) 7.45:1. Brake H.P.: (Std.) 130 @ 3400 R.P.M.; (Opt.) 138 @ 3400 R.P.M. N.A.C.C. H.P.: 33.8. Main bearings: Five. Valve lifters: Solid. Carb.: Stromberg 2V model EE-22. Torque: (Std.) 250 lbs.-ft. @ 1600 R.P.M.; (Opt.) 265 lbs.-ft. @ 1600 R.P.M. [Series C-3] The Custom Imperial Eights (C-3) used the same engines as the Imperial Eights (C-2). See specifications above. [Series CW*] Inline. L-head. Eight. Cast iron block. B & S: 3-1/2 in. x 5 in. Disp.: 384.8 cu. in. C.R.: 6.5:1. Brake H.P.: 150 @ 3200 R.P.M. N.A.C.C. H.P.: 39.2. Main bearings: Five. Valve lifters: Solid. Carb.: Stromberg 2V model EE-3.

CHASSIS: [Series C6] W.B.: 118 in. Tires: 16 x 6.25. [Series CZ] W.B.: 121 in. Tires: 16 x 6.50. [Series CZ (DeL.)] W.B.: 121 in. Tires: 16 x 6.50. [Series CZ (DeL./LWB)] W.B.: 133 in. Tires: 16 x 6.50. [Series C-1] W.B.: 123 in. Tires: 16 x 7.00. [Series C-2] W.B.: 128 in. Tires: 16 x 7.50. [Series C-3] W.B.: 130 in. Tires: 16 x 7.50. [Series CW*] W.B.: 146-1/2 in. Tires: 17 x 7.50.

TECHNICAL: Manual transmission (with automatic overdrive in Imperial Airflows). Speeds: 3F/1R (Imperials have overdrive fourth). Floor shift controls. Conventional clutch. Shaft drive. Overall ratios: (C6) 4.11:1; (C2) 3.95:1; (C1) 4.1:1; (C2/C3 & CW) 4.3:1, & CW. Lockheed four wheel brakes. Steel spoke wheels.

OPTIONS: Front bumper. Rear bumper. Trumpet horns. Dual sidemounts. Sidemount cover(s). Fender skirts (Std. on Airflows). Bumper guards. Radio. Heater. Clock. Cigar lighter. Radio antenna. Seat covers. Spotlight(s). OSRV mirror. Full wheel disks. Chrome wheel trim rings. Trunk rack (Airstream). Touring trunk (Airstream). Division window. Overdrive (C1 Series). Power brakes (C1 Series).

HISTORICAL: Date of Introduction: (DeLuxe Airstream) May 1, 1935; (others) Jan. 2, 1935. Innovations: (Airstream) All-steel body. Balanced weight distribution. New Autolite ignition. New 8-cylinder engine. Engine repositioned six inches forward. More sloping windshield. Synchromesh transmission. Independent front suspension. (Airflow) New grille. Automatic Overdrive and aluminum head on Imperials. Calendar year production: 50,010. Model year production: 38,533. In 1935, Chrysler was America's 10th ranked auto maker in both model year and calendar year production. Walter P. Chrysler was elected chairman of the corporation bearing his name. K.T. Keller took his place as Chrysler's new president. Chrysler experimented the concept of a compact car during 1935. The Custom Imperial CW models are full Classics.

1935 Chrysler, Wimbledon, 4-dr. sedan, JB

1935

Airstream Series C-6, 6-cyl., 118" wb

	FP	5	4	3	2	1
RS Conv	870	3800	7650	12,750	17,850	25,500
Bus Cpe	745	1025	2500	5150	7150	10,300
RS Cpe	810	1025	2500	5150	7150	10,300
Tr Brgm	820	925	2000	4650	6500	9300
4 dr Sed	830	850	1650	4150	5800	8300
Tr Sed	830	850	1650	4150	5800	8300

Airstream Series C-Z, 8-cyl., 121" wb

Bus Cpe	910	1075	2900	5450	7600	10,900
RS Cpe	935	1125	3450	5800	8100	11,600
Tr Brgm	960	975	2300	4900	6850	9800
4 dr Sed	975	975	2300	4900	6850	9800
Tr Sed	995	975	2300	4900	6850	9800

Airstream DeLuxe Series C-1, 121" wb

RS Conv	1015	4000	7950	13,250	18,550	26,500
Bus Cpe	930	1100	3300	5650	7900	11,300
RS Cpe	955	1175	3700	6150	8600	12,300
Tr Brgm	980	975	2300	4900	6850	9800
4 dr Sed	985	925	2000	4650	6500	9300
Tr Sed	1015	925	2000	4650	6500	9300

Airstream DeLuxe, Series C-1, 8-cyl., 133" wb

Trav Sed	1235	975	2300	4900	6850	9800
7P Sed	1235	975	2300	4900	6850	9800

Airflow Series C-1, 8-cyl., 123" wb

Bus Cpe	1245	3650	7350	12,250	17,150	24,500
Cpe	1245	3800	7650	12,750	17,850	25,500
4 dr Sed	1245	3650	7350	12,250	17,150	24,500

Imperial Airflow Series C-2, 8-cyl., 128" wb

Cpe	1475	4000	7950	13,250	18,550	26,500
4 dr Sed	1475	3800	7650	12,750	17,850	25,500

Imperial Custom Airflow Series C-3, 8-cyl., 137" wb

4 dr Sed	2245	4400	8850	14,750	20,650	29,500
Twn Sed	2245	4600	9150	15,250	21,350	30,500
Sed Limo	2345	6100	12,150	20,250	28,350	40,500
Twn Limo	2345	6450	12,900	21,500	30,100	43,000

Imperial Custom Airflow Series C-W, 8-cyl., 146.5" wb

4 dr Sed	5000	9300	18,600	31,000	43,400	62,000
Sed Limo	5145	10,200	20,400	34,000	47,600	68,000
Twn Limo	5145	10,500	21,000	35,000	49,000	70,000

1936

CHRYSLER AIRSTREAM — SERIES C-7 — SIX: Changes to Chrysler's 1936 Airstream models were minor ones. The new die-cast grille was oval shaped when viewed head on. It consisted of multiple vertical blades which swept over the nose of the car in waterfall style. The center vertical molding was thicker. A molding on the sides of the hood continued, horizontally, across the nose. The headlights were again torpedo-shaped and torpedo-shaped parking lamps were mounted on the front-fender catwalks. Open cars had flat one-piece windshields. Closed cars had split two-piece windshields. Standard equipment included Autolite ignition, Lockheed hydraulic brakes, dual sun visors, wipers and taillights, no draft ventilation and safety glass all around. The convertible sedan made its return this season.

1936 Chrysler, Series C-8, Airstream 4-dr. sedan, AA

CHRYSLER DELUXE AIRSTREAM — SERIES C-8 — EIGHT: DeLuxe Airstream styling changes were similar to those on 1936 Airstream Sixes. The Eights featured special trim like bright metal running board moldings and a winged ''8'' badge on the hoodside louvers. Both regular 121 inch and extended 133 inch chassis were available. Standard equipment included Autolite ignition, hydraulic brakes and the small Chrysler Straight-Eight with a downdraft Stromberg carburetor.

CHRYSLER AIRFLOW — SERIES C-9 — EIGHT: Slight modifications to the basic Airflow design included a hump-back style built-in luggage compartment, all-steel top construction, new grille similar in design to the Airstream type and egg-crate style hood ventilators. ''Life Guard'' tire tubes and vertically adjustable front seats were new innovations. Only one coupe was available.

1936 Chrysler Imperial, Airflow Custom, 7-pass. 4-dr. sedan, AA

IMPERIAL AIRFLOW — SERIES C-10 — EIGHT: The front fender valance panels, cowl side panels and hood ventilators were longer on Imperial Airflows. An aluminum cylinder head and automatic overdrive transmission were standard, as was a two-barrel carburetor. Imperials continued to offer power brakes at regular price.

CUSTOM IMPERIAL AIRFLOW — C-11 — EIGHT: The C-11 Custom Imperial Airflow used the new grille, egg-crate hood trim, all-steel top construction and hump-back luggage compartment introduced on 1936 Airflows. The longer chassis length was consumed with lengthened front doors having larger door windows. Single bar bumpers with guards, split V-type windshields and larger tires were other features of these rare cars.

CUSTOM IMPERIAL AIRFLOW — SERIES CW — EIGHT:** Ten long wheelbase CW type Custom Imperial Airflows were sold this year. These cars may have been 1934 chassis with updated sheet metal and trim parts. They were not regular production models and exact specifications are not available. Prices and weights were about the same as in 1935. Engine specifications were unchanged. These cars featured one piece curved windshields. Body style breakouts of the ten cars are not available.

I.D. DATA: [Series C-7] Serial numbers were on a plate on the front door hinge pillar post. Starting: 6823301. Ending: 6865003. Engine numbers were on the left side of cylinder block, between one and two cylinders, just below cylinder head. Starting: C7-1001. Ending: C7-44530. [Series C-8] Serial numbers were in the same location. Starting: 6710501. Ending: 6719499. Engine numbers were in the same location. Starting: C8-1001. Ending: C8-10554. [Series C-9] Serial numbers were in the same locations. Starting: 6606201. Ending: 6607879. Engine numbers were in the same locations. Starting: C9-1001. Ending: C9-2852. [Series C-10] Serial numbers were in the same location. Starting: 7014901. Ending: 7019398. Engine numbers were in the same location. Starting: C10-1001. Ending: C10-5536. [Series C-11] Serial numbers were in the same locations. Starting: 7803851. Ending: 7803925. Engine numbers were in the same locations. Starting: C11-1001. Ending: C11-1075.

Model No.	Body Type & Seating	Price	Weight	Prod. Total
C-7	2-dr. Bus. Cpe.-2P	760	2962	3703
C-7	2-dr. Conv. Cpe.-2/4P	925	3053	650
C-7	2-dr. R/S Cpe.-2/4P	825	3037	759
C-7	2-dr. Tr. Brgm.-5P	825	3082	3177
C-7	4-dr. Conv. Sed.-5P	1125	3282	497
C-7	4-dr. Tr. Sed.-5P	875	3137	34099
C-7	Chassis	NA	NA	586

Note 1: Total production was 43,471.

(121 in. wheelbase)

C-8	2-dr. Bus. Cpe.-2P	925	3155	520
C-8	2-dr. R/S Cpe.-2/4P	995	3220	325
C-8	2-dr. Conv. Cpe.-2/4P	1075	3350	240
C-8	2-dr. Tr. Brgm.-5P	995	3330	268
C-8	4-dr. Conv. Sed.-5P	1265	3495	362
C-8	4-dr. Tr. Sed.-5P	1045	3345	6547

(133 in. wheelbase)

C-8	4-dr. Trav. Sed.-5P	1245	3500	350
C-8	4-dr. Sed.-7P	1245	3550	619
C-8	4-dr. Sed. Limo.-7P	1865	NA	67
C-8	4-dr. Leb. Twn. Car-7P	4995	NA	8
C-8	Chassis	NA	NA	196

Note 1: Total series production was 9,502.
Note 2: The long wheelbase LeBaron Town Sedan, a true Town Car, was built only on special order.

C-9	2-dr. Cpe.-6P	1345	3997	110
C-9	4-dr. Sed.-6P	1345	4102	1590

Note 1: Total series production was 1,700.

C-10	2-dr. Cpe.-6P	1475	4105	240
C-10	4-dr. Sed.-6P	1475	4175	4259
C-10	Chassis	NA	NA	1

Note 1 Total series production was 4,500.

C-11	4-dr. Sed.-5P	2475	NA	38
C-11	4-dr. Sed. Limo.-7P	2575	NA	37

Note 1: Total series production was 75 cars.

1936 Chrysler, Series C-8, Airstream convertible sedan, JAC

1936 Chrysler, Kew "Airglide," Carlton, JB

1936
Airstream Series C-7, 6-cyl., 118" wb

	FP	5	4	3	2	1
RS Conv	925	4100	8250	13,750	19,250	27,500
Conv Sed	1125	4300	8550	14,250	19,950	28,500
Bus Cpe	760	1025	2500	5150	7150	10,300
RS Cpe	825	1050	2800	5400	7500	10,800
Tr Brgm	825	975	2300	4900	6850	9800
Tr Sed	875	900	1800	4400	6150	8800

Airstream DeLuxe Series C-8, 8-cyl., 121" wb

	FP	5	4	3	2	1
RS Conv	1075	4300	8550	14,250	19,950	28,500
Conv Sed	1265	4400	8850	14,750	20,650	29,500
Bus Cpe	925	1025	2500	5150	7150	10,300
RS Cpe	995	1175	3600	6050	8450	12,100
Tr Brgm	995	975	2300	4900	6850	9800
Tr Sed	1045	925	2000	4650	6500	9300

Airstream DeLuxe, 8-cyl., 133" wb

	FP	5	4	3	2	1
Trav Sed	1245	925	2000	4650	6500	9300
4 dr Sed	1245	925	2000	4650	6500	9300
Sed Limo	1865	975	2300	4900	6850	9800
LeB Twn Sed	4995	1225	3850	6400	8900	12,800

Airflow, 8-cyl., 123" wb

	FP	5	4	3	2	1
Cpe	1345	3500	7050	11,750	16,450	23,500
4 dr Sed	1345	3350	6750	11,250	15,750	22,500

Imperial Airflow, 8-cyl., 128" wb

	FP	5	4	3	2	1
Cpe	1475	3650	7350	12,250	17,150	24,500
4 dr Sed	1475	3500	7050	11,750	16,450	23,500

Imperial Custom Airflow, 8-cyl., 137" wb

	FP	5	4	3	2	1
4 dr Sed	2475	3800	7650	12,750	17,850	25,500
Sed Limo	2475	4100	8250	13,750	19,250	27,500

Imperial Custom Airflow, 8-cyl., 146.5" wb

	FP	5	4	3	2	1
8P Sed	5145	7650	15,300	25,500	35,700	51,000
Sed Limo	5145	7950	15,900	26,500	37,100	53,000

ENGINE: [Series C-7] Inline. L-head. Six. Cast iron block. B & S: 3-3/8 in. x 4-1/2 in. Disp.: 241.5 cu. in. C.R.: (Std.) 6.0:1; (Opt.) 6.5:1. Brake H.P.: (Std.) 93 @ 3400 R.P.M.; (Opt.) 100 @ 3400 R.P.M. N.A.C.C. H.P.: 27.34. Main bearings: Four. Valve lifters: Solid. Carb.: Carter 1V model EGG1 (BB). Torque: (Std.) 180 lbs.-ft. @ 1200 R.P.M.; (Opt.) 185 lbs.-ft. @ 1200 R.P.M. [Series C-8] Inline. L-head. Eight. Cast iron block. B & S: 3-1/4 in. x 4-1/8 in. Disp.: 273.8 cu. in. C.R.: (Std.) 6.2:1; (Opt.) 7.0:1. Brake H.P.: (Std.) 105 @ 3400 R.P.M.; (Opt.) 110 @ 3400 R.P.M. N.A.C.C. H.P.: 33.8. Main bearings: Five. Valve lifters: Solid. Carb.: Stromberg 1V model EXV-3. Torque: (Std.) 200 lbs.-ft. @ 1200 R.P.M.; (Opt.) 206 lbs.-ft. @ 1200 R.P.M. [Series C-9] Inline. L-head. Eight. Cast iron block. B & S: 3-1/4 in. x 4-7/8 in. Disp.: 323.5 cu. in. C.R.: (Std.) 6.2:1; (Opt.) 6.5:1. Brake H.P.: (Std.) 115 @ 3400 R.P.M.; (Opt.) 120 @ 3400 R.P.M. N.A.C.C. H.P.: 33.8. Main bearings: Five. Valve lifters: Solid. Carb.: Stromberg 1V model EXV-3. Torque: (Std.) 240 lbs.-ft. @ 1200 R.P.M.; (Opt.) 250 lbs.-ft. @ 1200 R.P.M. [Series C-10] Inline. L-head. Eight. Cast iron block. B & S: 3-1/4 x 4-7/8. Disp.: 323.5 cu. in. C.R.: (Std.) 6.5:1; (Opt.) 7.45:1. Brake H.P.: (Std.) 130 @ 3400 R.P.M.; (Opt.) 138 @ 3400 R.P.M. N.A.C.C. H.P.: 33.8. Main bearings: Five. Valve lifters: Solid. Carb.: Stromberg 2V model EE-22. Torque: (Std.) 250 lbs.-ft. @ 1600 R.P.M.; (Opt.) 265 lbs.-ft. @ 1600 R.P.M. [Series C-11] The Custom Imperial C-11 engines were the same as those used on Imperial C-10. See specifications above.

CHASSIS: [Series C-7] W.B.: 118 in. Tires: 16 x 6.25. [Series C-8] W.B.: 121 or 133 in. Tires: 16 x 6.50. [Series C-9] W.B.: 123 in. Tires: 16 x 7.00. [Series C-10] W.B.: 128 in. Tires: 16 x 7.50. [Series C-11] W.B.: 137 in. Tires: 16 x 7.50. [Series CW**] W.B.: 146.5 in. Tires: 17 x 7.50.

TECHNICAL: Same as 1935.

OPTIONS: Same as 1935.

HISTORICAL: Date of Introduction: (C-11) Feburary 5, 1936; (others) November 2, 1935. Innovations: (Airstream): New rear axle with silent hypoid gears. New automatic overdrive option ($37.00). Redesigned rear fenders. (Airflow) "Life Guard" tire tubes. Vertically adjustable front seat. All-steel top. Calendar year registrations: 58,698. Calendar year production: 71,295. Model year production: 59,248. The President was K.T. Keller.

The 1936 season was Chrysler's best year since 1929. The company fell to 11th position on the U.S. sales charts. A prototype small car with front wheel drive and a five cylinder radial engine was the company's experimental project this year. The CW Imperial Custom Airflows are genuine CCCA Classic cars.

1937

1937 Chrysler, Series C-16, Royal 4-dr. sedan, AA

CHRYSLER ROYAL — SERIES C-16 — SIX: Chrysler's six-cylinder line was named Royal this season. These cars had all-new styling combined with a shorter chassis. The grille consisted of multiple horizontal bars which were longer at the top and shorter towards the bottom. Horizontal moldings decorated the sides of the hood and swept around the nose, but did not quite touch at the center. Bullet shaped headlights were mounted high on the front fenders. New features included built-in windshield defroster vents, fully insulated body mountings and safety padding on back of the front seats. A long-wheelbase Royal sub-series featured two body styles.

IMPERIAL — SERIES C-14 — EIGHT: The true 1937 Imperial was no longer an Airflow. These cars had the same basic styling as the new Royal six with a longer hood and cowl. The Imperial name appeared on the nose between the grille and the wraparound hood louvers. Imperials had a longer wheelbase, larger tires and more luxurious interior appointments than the sixes. They also had the new, built-in defroster vents, insulated body mountings, and seat safety padding. The Imperial engine continued to use an aluminum cylinder head in both its low and optional high-compression forms.

1937 Chrysler, Series C-17, Imperial sedan, JAC

CHRYSLER AIRFLOW — SERIES C-17 — EIGHT: The only true 1937 Airflows were a Chrysler Series. They had new, safety instrument panels with no protruding knobs. There was a concealed crank for raising the windshield. The hood was hinged at the cowl and opened from the front; side hood panels were released by catches on the inside. Other features included built-in defroster vents, padded front seat backs, safety type controls and hardware, soft arm rests, and a flat floorboard. Standard equipment included hydraulic brakes, double acting hydraulic telescoping shock absorbers, fully insulated engine mountings and a hypoid rear axle. The 1937 models had horizontal hood louvers and chrome plated beads. headlamps mounted on the front hood sides and license plate lamps and brackets mounted in the center of the body. The grille was similar to that used on conventional models. The name ''Chrysler Airflow'' appeared, in chrome scripts, on the body color panel between the grille and the wrap-around hood louvers.

1937 Chrysler, Series C-15, Imperial, touring sedan, AA

IMPERIAL CUSTOM — SERIES C-15 — EIGHT: The Custom Imperial had basically the same styling and equipment features as the Imperial C-14s. A longer wheelbase was used and body and door panels were stretched accordingly. The Custom Imperial Town Sedan Limousine, with blind rear quarter panels, was available on special order. Custom coach built bodies ranging from a fastback Town Car to a beautiful Derham Convertible Victoria were produced on the 16 Custom Imperial chassis supplied by Chrysler. The Custom Imperials, whether factory built or custom bodied, had extra-rich upholstery and trim.

CUSTOM IMPERIAL — SERIES CW — EIGHT: Although no Custom Imperial CW models were actually built in 1937, three such cars were updated with 1937 style bumpers, grilles and trim and sold as 1937 automobiles. One was built for the Hershey family of candy bar and antique car fame. A second one was built for Manuel L. Querzon, President of the Philippines. A third car was delivered to radio personality Major Edward Bowes. The Querzon and Major Bowes cars survive today. One is owned by the Government of the Philippines; the other by collector Frank Kleptz of Terre Haute, Ind. All of the cars seem to have been specially equipped, by Chrysler and LeBaron, with numerous features not found in other CWs. A 1940 *Life* magazine article put the value of the Major Bowes car at $25,000.

CHRYSLER — KEW — SIX: For the English motorist who wanted a small Chrysler, this badge-converted Plymouth was just the ticket. Fitted with the small-bore 170-cubic-inch engine, the Kew was rated at a tax-beating 19.8 horsepower.

CHRYSLER — WIMBLEDON — SIX: A slightly more upscale version of the Kew Six, the Wimbledon utilized Plymouth's 201-cubic-inch six-cylinder engine and featured such amenities as a sliding roof panel and overdrive transmission. The Wimbledon was rated at 23.4 horsepower for Great Britain's taxation purposes. Shipped as CKD units from Detroit to the Chrysler works at Kew, Surrey, even chassis and engines were shipped in knocked-down form for 1937.

CHRYSLER — RICHMOND — SIX: For the wise English motorist who preferred something more than a disguised Plymouth but who couldn't afford a ''real'' Chrysler, there was always the Richmond which was based on the U.S. S-3 DeSoto Airstream.

I.D. DATA: [Series C-16] Serial numbers were on a plate on the front door hinge pillar. Starting: 6865101. Ending: 6948225. Engine numbers were on the left side of the block, between cylinders no. 1 and no. 2, just below the cylinder head. Starting: C16-1001. Ending: C16-88640. [Series C-14] Serial numbers were in the same location. Starting: 6719601. Ending: 6733606. Engine numbers were in the same location. Starting: C14-1001. Ending: C14-15572. [Series C-17] Serial numbers were in the same location. Starting: 7019401. Ending: 7024000. Engine numbers were in the same location. Starting: C17-1001. Ending: C17-5618. [Series C-15] Serial numbers were located in the same positions. Starting: 7804001. Ending: 7805201. Engine numbers were in the same positions. Starting: C15-1001. Ending: C15-2237. [Series CW] Serial numbers were in the same location. These cars were numbered in the years they were built and do not have 1937 serial numbers. Serial and engine numbers are not available.

Model No.	Body Type & Seating	Price	Weight	Prod. Total
(116 in. wheelbase)				
C-16	2-dr. Bus. Cpe.-2P	810	3049	9830
C-16	2-dr. Conv. Cpe.-2/4P	1020	3274	767
C-16	2-dr. R/S Cpe.-2/4P	860	3099	1050
C-16	2-dr. Brgm.-5P	870	3114	750
C-16	2-dr. Tr. Brgm.-5P	880	3094	7835
C-16	4-dr. Sed.-5P	910	3124	1200
C-16	4-dr. Tr. Sed.-5P	920	3134	62,408
C-16	4-dr. Conv. Sed.-5P	1355	3484	642
(133 in. wheelbase)				
C-16	4-dr. Tr. Sed.-7P	1145	3544	856
C-16	4-dr. Sed. Limo.-7P	1245	3550	138
C-16	Chassis	NA	NA	524

Note 1: Total series production was 86,000.

C-14	2-dr. Bus. Cpe.-2P	1030	3374	1075
C-14	2-dr. R/S Cpe.-2/4P	1070	3449	225
C-14	2-dr. Conv. Cpe.-2/4P	1170	3609	351
C-14	2-dr. Tr. Brgm.-5P	1070	3544	430
C-14	4-dr. Tr. Sed.-5P	1100	3564	11,976
C-14	4-dr. Conv. Sed.-5P	1500	3824	325
C-14	Chassis	NA	NA	118

Note 1: Total series production was 14,500.

C-17	2-dr. Cpe.-6P	1610	4225	230
C-17	2-dr. Tr. Sed.-6P	1610	4300	4370

Note 1: Total series production was 4,600.

(Factory Semi-Customs)				
C-15	4-dr. Tr. Sed.-5P	2060	4500	187
C-15	4-dr. Tr. Sed.-7P	2060	4522	721
C-15	4-dr. Sed. Limo.-7P	2160	4644	276

(Individual Customs)				
C-15	4-dr. LeB. FsBk. Twn. Car-7P	NA	NA	1
C-15	2-dr. Der. Conv. Vic.-5P	NA	NA	1
C-15	4-dr. Der. Conv. Sed.-7P	NA	NA	1
C-15	4-dr. Der. Conv. Twn. Car-5P	NA	NA	1
C-15	2-dr. Der. Vic. Twn. Car-5P	NA	NA	?
C-15	4-dr. LeB. Twn. Sed. Limo.-7P	NA	NA	?

Note 1: Total series production was 1,200 including 16 chassis supplied to custom coach builders. The individual customs listed above represent some body styles known to have been produced on the 16 chassis. The production totals given are estimates.

CW	4-dr. Sed. Limo.-7P	NA	NA	3

Note 1: The figure of three cars built with 1937 trim and appointments is a rough estimate based on known facts. It's possible that others of these cars were made.

1937 Chrysler, Series C-16, Royal coupe, JAC

ENGINE: [Series C-16] Inline. L-head. Six. Cast iron block. B & S: 3-3/8 in. x 4-1/4 in. Disp.: 228.1 cu. in. C.R.: (std.) 6.5:1; (opt.) 7.0:1. Brake H.P.: (std.) 93 @ 3600 R.P.M.; (opt.) 100 @ 3600 R.P.M. N.A.C.C. H.P.: 27.34. Main bearings: Four. Valve lifters: Solid. Carb.: Carter 1V model E6K1-4 (BB). Torque: (std.) 168 lbs.-ft. @ 1200 R.P.M.; (opt.) 176 lbs.-ft. @ 1200 R.P.M. [Series C-14] Inline. L-head. Eight. Cast iron block. B & S: 3-1/4 in. x 4-1/8 in. Disp.: 273.8 cu. in. C.R.: (std.) 6.7:1; (opt.) 7.4:1. Brake H.P.: (std.) 110 @ 3600 R.P.M.; (opt.) 115 @ 3600 R.P.M. N.A.C.C. H.P.: 33.80.

Main bearings: Five. Valve lifters: Solid. Carb.: Stromberg 2V model EE-22. Torque: (std.) 212 lbs.-ft. @ 1600 R.P.M.; (opt.) 220 lbs.-ft. @ 1600 R.P.M. [Series C-15] Inline. L-head. Eight. Cast iron block. B & S: 3-1/4 in. x 4-7/8 in. Disp.: 323.5 cu. in. C.R.: (std.) 6.2:1. (opt.) 6.5:1. Brake H.P.: (std.) 130 @ 3400 R.P.M.; (opt.) 138 @ 3400 R.P.M. N.A.C.C. H.P.: 33.80. Main bearings: Five. Valve lifters: Solid. Carb.: Stromberg 2V model AAOV-1. Torque: (std.) 250 lbs.-ft. @ 1600 R.P.M.; (opt.) 265 lbs.-ft. @ 1600 R.P.M. [Series C-15] The Custom Imperial engine was the same as the Airflow engine. See specifications in chart above. [Series CW] Inline. L-head. Eight. Cast iron block. B & S: 3-1/2 in. x 5 in. Disp.: 384.4 cu. in. C.R.: (std.) 5.8:1. (opt.) 5.2:1. Brake H.P.: 150 @ 3200 R.P.M. N.A.C.C. H.P.: 39.2. Main bearings: Five. Valve lifters: Solid. Carb.: Stromberg 2V model EE-3. Torque: 260 lbs.-ft. @ 1200 R.P.M.

CHASSIS: [Series C-16] W.B.: 116 in. Tires: 16 x 6.25. [Series C-16 (LWB)] W.B.: 133 in. Tires: 16 x 6.25. [Series C-14] W.B.: 121 in. Tires: 16 x 6.50. [Series C-17] W.B.: 128 in. Tires: 16 x 7.50. [Series C-15] W.B.: 140 in. Tires: 16 x 7.50. [Series CW] W.B.: 146.5 in. Tires: 17 x 7.50.

TECHNICAL: Manual synchromesh transmission. Speeds: 3F/1R. Floor shift controls. Conventional clutch. Shaft drive. Hypoid rear axle. Overall ratios: (C16/C14) 4.10:1; (C17) 4.30:1; (C15) 4.27:1, (CW) 4.30:1. Four wheel hydraulic brakes. Steel spoke-wheels.

OPTIONS: Front bumper. Rear bumper. Single sidemount (Airstream). Dual sidemount (Airstream). Sidemount cover(s). Fender skirts. Bumper guards. Radio. Heater. Clock. Cigar lighter. Radio antenna. Seat covers. OSRV mirror. Spotlight(s). Trippe lights. Whitewall tires. Special paint. Special upholstery.

HISTORICAL: Introduced October, 1936. Innovations: Built-in defroster vents. Safety type interior hardware and seat back padding. Fully insulated engine mountings. Improved six-cylinder engine. Increased horsepower on eight. Calendar year registrations: 91,622. Calendar year production: 107,872. Model year production: 106,120.
Chrysler was America's 9th largest auto-maker on a model year basis and the 10th largest automaker on a calendar year basis. A Custom Imperial convertible sedan was used on an AAA Official Car at the Indy 500. The car was painted silver and black to commemorate the speedways 25th anniversary. K.T. Keller was president of Chrysler Motors.

1937
Royal, 6-cyl., 116" wb

	FP	5	4	3	2	1
RS Conv	1020	4000	7950	13,250	18,550	26,500
Conv Sed	1355	4100	8250	13,750	19,250	27,500
Bus Cpe	810	975	2300	4900	6850	9800
RS Cpe	860	1025	2500	5150	7150	10,300
Brgm	870	800	1550	3900	5450	7800
Tr Brgm	880	800	1550	3900	5450	7800
4 dr Sed	910	800	1550	3900	5450	7800
Tr Sed	920	850	1650	4150	5800	8300
Royal, 6-cyl., 133" wb						
4 dr Sed	1145	900	1800	4400	6150	8800
Sed Limo	1245	925	2000	4650	6500	9300
Der TwnC	—	1100	3300	5650	7900	11,300
Airflow, 8-cyl., 128" wb						
Cpe	1610	3650	7350	12,250	17,150	24,500
4 dr Sed	1610	3500	7050	11,750	16,450	23,500
Imperial, 8-cyl., 121" wb						
RS Conv	1170	4100	8250	13,750	19,250	27,500
Conv Sed	1500	4300	8550	14,250	19,950	28,500
Bus Cpe	1030	1550	4400	7400	10,400	14,800
RS Cpe	1070	1600	4600	7650	10,700	15,300
Tr Brgm	1070	1450	4250	7150	10,000	14,300
Tr Sed	1100	1550	4400	7400	10,400	14,800
Imperial Custom, 8-cyl., 140" wb						
5P Sed	2060	4600	9150	15,250	21,350	30,500
7P Sed	2060	4900	9750	16,250	22,750	32,500
Sed Limo	2160	6750	13,500	22,500	31,500	45,000
Twn Limo	2160	6750	13,500	22,500	31,500	45,000
Custom Built Models						
Der Fml Conv Twn Car	—	9300	18,600	31,000	43,400	62,000
Der Conv Vic	—	8400	16,800	28,000	39,200	56,000

1938

1938 Chrysler, Series C-18, Royal 4-dr. sedan, OCW

CHRYSLER ROYAL — SERIES C-18 — SIX: The Airflow disappeared in 1938, but the Chrysler Royal was back for its second year. There were obvious styling changes to the grille, headlights and hood trim. The new grille consisted of horizontal bars filling a shield-shaped opening that tapered towards the bottom. There was a vertical center molding and chrome chevron trim below the grille. Scripts on the nose of the car read "Chrysler Royal." The torpedo shaped headlights now sat on top of the fenders, instead of alongside the grille. The hood was of the side-opening type with removable side panels. The hood louvers were a long, narrow casting with three openings at the rear. All Chryslers used a deluxe steering wheel on which a narrow inner rim acted as the horn button. The emergency brakelever was mounted under the cowl, at its center. Standard equipment included hydraulic brakes, Autolite ignition and a larger, more powerful engine. The standard wheelbase was increased by three inches and the two long wheelbase models were stretched accordingly. At least one Derham Custom Town Car was constructed on the Chrysler Royal Six chassis, although most of the units built were probably ambulances and funeral cars.

1938 Chrysler, Series C-19, New York Special sedan, JAC

IMPERIAL AND N.Y. SPECIAL — SERIES C19 — EIGHT: Imperials had the same basic styling changes as Royals for 1938. They could be identified by the addition of chrome chevrons on the front of each front fender and the model scripts on the hubcaps and above the grille. Naturally, the Imperials had richer interior upholstery and trim. A longer hood was used, too. A brand new Imperial sub-series was the New York Special line. Interestingly, the New York Specials were considered Chryslers, although they were built on the Imperial Chassis and used the Custom Imperial engine. As listed in contemporary reference sources, the New York Special line consisted of a Business coupe and Touring sedan. However, no coupes are known to have been built. The New York Special used a distinctive grille with wider horizontal openings. Special broadcloth upholstery was available only in this model. It came in two single color and four two-tone combinations. The New York Special model later grew into the Chrysler New Yorker series. Instrument panels in the Imperials had highly polished woodgrain finish; New York Special instrument panels were finished to harmonize with the upholstery colors.

CUSTOM IMPERIAL — SERIES C-20 — EIGHT: The Custom Imperials were larger, fancier versions of the Imperials on a longer wheelbase chassis. Their longer length required larger front doors and rear doors with correspondingly longer window openings. The seven passenger sedan had two auxiliary folding seats in the front seat back. The five passenger sedan had storage compartments in the same space. The limousine had folding seats and a division window between the front and rear compartments. Eleven individual customs were built on chassis supplied to coach makers. Most, if not all, of these units carried special Derham bodies. Instrument panels on Custom Imperials were finished to harmonize with the upholstery colors.

1938 Chrysler, Wimbledon, 7-pass. limousine, JB

CHRYSLER — KEW/WIMBLEDON — SIX: Buyers in Great Britain had their choice of two Chrysler models this year, both based on the Plymouth body shell and drivetrain. There is some confusion as to whether the 201-cubic-inch-engine-equipped car was sold as a Wimbledon as had been practice in previous years, some references noting only "two models" of the Kew, a standard and a deluxe. Previously all Kew models were fitted with the 170-cubic-inch export Plymouth engine. Deluxe Kew models featured 12-volt electrics (which U.S. Plymouths would not see until 1956), leather upholstery, sunshine roof, twin wipers and a rear-seat center armrest.

1938 Chrysler, Series C-18, Royal convertible sedan, JAC

I.D. DATA: [Series C-18] Serial numbers were located on the right front door hinge pillar post. Starting: 7532801. Ending: 7573257. Engine numbers were located on the left side of block, between cylinders one and two, just below the cylinder head. Starting Engine No.: C18-1001. Ending: C18-43001. [Series C-19] Serial numbers were in the same location. Starting: 6734001. Ending: 6742105. Serial numbers for the New York Special were 6607901 to 6609802. Engine numbers were in the same location. Starting Engine No.: C19-1001. Ending: C19-9172. Engine numbers for the New York Special were C20-1001 to C20-3525. [Series C-20] Serial numbers were in the same location. Starting: 7805501. Ending: 7806033. Engine numbers were in the same location. Numbers were the same as those given above for New York Specials.

Model No.	Body Type & Seating	Price	Weight	Prod. Total
(Standard wheelbase)				
C-18	2-dr. Bus. Cpe.-2P	918	3090	4840
C-18	2-dr. R/S Cpe.-2/4P	963	3135	363
C-18	2-dr. Conv. Cpe.-2/4P	1085	3250	480
C-18	2-dr. FsBk. Brgm.-5P	963	3160	88
C-18	2-dr. Tr. Brgm.-5P	975	3165	3802
C-18	4-dr. Tr. Sed.-5P	1010	3180	31,991
C-18	4-dr. FsBk. Sed.-5P	998	3170	112
C-18	4-dr. Conv. Sed.-5P	1425	3450	177
(Long wheelbase)				
C-18	4-dr. Tr. Sed.-7P	1235	3450	722
C-18	4-dr. Sed. Limo.-7P	1325	3545	161
C-18	Chassis	NA	NA	564

Note 1: Total series production was 43,300.

(Imperial Eight)				
C-19	2-dr. Bus. Cpe.-2P	1123	3450	766
C-19	2-dr. R/S Cpe.-2/4P	1160	3515	80
C-19	2-dr. Conv. Cpe.-2/4P	1275	3630	189
C-19	2-dr. Tr. Brgm.-5P	1165	3560	245
C-19	4-dr. Tr. Sed.-5P	1198	3565	8554
C-19	4-dr. Conv. Sed.-5P	1595	3835	113
C-19	Chassis	NA	NA	55
(New York Special)				
C-19	2-dr. Bus. Cpe.-2P	1255	3475	Note 2
C-19	4-dr. Tr. Sed.-5P	1370	3600	Note 3

Note 1: Total series production was 10,002.
Note 2: Records indicate that no New York Special Business coupes were built.
Note 3: Production of the New York Special Touring Sedan included in Imperial Eight touring sedan total.

(Factory Models)				
C-20	4-dr. Tr. Sed.-5P	2295	4495	252
C-20	4-dr. Tr. Sed.-7P	2295	4510	122
C-20	4-dr. Sed. Limo.-7P	2395	NA	145
(Individual Customs)				
C-20	2-dr. Der. Conv. Vic.-5P	NA	NA	Note 2
C-20	4-dr. Der. Twn. Sed.-5P	NA	NA	Note 2
C-20	4-dr. Der. Conv. Sed.-5P	NA	NA	Note 2
C-20	4-dr. Der. Twn. Limo.-7P	NA	NA	Note 2
C-20	Chassis	NA	NA	Note 2

Note 1: Total production of factory models was 519.
Note 2: A total of 11 Custom Imperial chassis were built. The four cars listed are among those known to have been made on these chassis.

ENGINE: [Series C-18] Inline. L-head. Six. Cast iron block. B & S: 3-3/8 in. x 4-1/2 in. Disp.: 241.5 cu. in. C.R.: (std.) 6.2:1. (opt.) 7.0:1. Brake H.P.: (std.) 95 @ 3600 R.P.M. (opt.) 102 @ 3600 R.P.M. N.A.C.C. H.P.: 27.34. Main bearings: Four. Valve lifters: Solid. Carb.: Carter 1V model E6M1. Torque: (std.) 180 lbs.-ft. @ 1200 R.P.M. (opt.) 190 lbs.-ft. @ 1200 R.P.M. [Series C-19] Imperial Engine: Inline. L-head. Eight. Cast iron block. B & S: 3-1/4 in. x 4-1/2 in. Disp.: 298.7 cu. in. C.R.: (std.) 6.2:1. (opt.) 7.4:1. Brake H.P.: (std.) 110 @ 3400 R.P.M. (opt.) 122 @ 3400 R.P.M. N.A.C.C. H.P.: 33.80. Main bearings: Six. Valve lifters: Solid. Torque: (std.) 214 lbs.-ft. @ 1600 R.P.M. (opt.) 238 lbs.-ft. @ 1600 R.P.M.; New York Special Engine: Inline. L-head. Eight. Cast iron block. B & S: 3-1/4 in. x 4-1/2 in. Disp.: 298.7 cu. in. C.R.: (std.) 6.5:1. (opt.) 7.4:1. Brake H.P.: (std.) 115 @

3400 R.P.M.; (opt.) 122 @ 3400 R.P.M. N.A.C.C. H.P.: 33.80. Main bearings: Six. Valve lifters: Solid. Torque: (std.) 225 lbs.-ft. @ 1600 R.P.M. (opt.) 238 lbs.-ft. @ 1600 R.P.M. [Series C-20] Engine specifications were the same as those given above for New York Specials.

CHASSIS: [Series Royal (std.)] W.B.: 119 in. Tires: 16 x 6.25 [Series Royal (LWB)] W.B.: 136 in. Tires: 16 x 6.25. [Series Imperial] W.B.: 125 in. Tires: 16 x 6.50. [Series N.Y. Spl.] W.B.: 125 in. Tires: 16 x 6.50. [Series Custom Imp.] W.B.: 130 in. Tires: 16 x 7.50.

TECHNICAL: Three-speed manual Synchromesh transmission. Speeds: 3F/1R. Floor shift controls. Conventional clutch. Shaft drive. Hypoid rear axle. Overall Ratios: (C18) 4.1:1; (C19) 3.91:1; (C20) 4.55:1. Four wheel hydralic brakes. Steel spoke wheels.

OPTIONS: Whitewall tires. Wheel trim rings. Full wheel disks. Dual sidemounts. Sidemount cover(s). Fender skirts. Bumper guards. Radio. Heater. Clock. Cigar lighter. Radio antenna. Seat covers. Trippe lights. Spotlight(s). Fog lamps. OSRV mirror. Special paint. Special upholstery. Custom coach built bodies. License plate frame.

HISTORICAL: Introduced: October, 1937. Innovations: New side opening hood. Repositioned emergency brake. New steering wheel with chrome horn ring. Introduced rubber insulated steering gear; an industry first. Front and rear sway bars in all Imperials. Calendar year registrations: 46,184. Calendar year production: 41,496. Model year production: 52,949. Chrysler was America's 9th largest automaker in terms of model year production and 11th largest in terms of calendar year output. Major Bowes "Original Amateur Hour" radio show was sponsored by Chrysler and the Major continued to drive his $25,000 Airflow CW limousine. George Dammann's book 70 Years of Chrysler suggests that some Custom Imperials built late in 1938 may have had Fluid Drive semi-automatic transmissions.

1938 Chrysler, Series C-19, Imperial touring sedan, AA

1938
Royal (6-cyl.) 119" wb

	FP	5	4	3	2	1
RS Conv	1085	4100	8250	13,750	19,250	27,500
Conv Sed	1425	4300	8550	14,250	19,950	28,500
Bus Cpe	918	925	2000	4650	6500	9300
RS Cpe	963	975	2300	4900	6850	9800
Brgm	963	725	1400	3100	4800	6800
Tr Brgm	975	775	1500	3600	5100	7300
4 dr Sed	998	775	1500	3500	5100	7300
Tr Sed	1010	800	1550	3900	5450	7800
Royal, 6-cyl., 136" wb						
7P Sed	3450	850	1650	4150	5800	8300
7P Limo Sed	3545	900	1800	4400	6150	8800
Imperial, 8-cyl., 125" wb						
Rs Conv	1275	4300	8550	14,250	19,950	28,500
Conv Sed	1595	4400	8850	14,750	20,650	29,500
Bus Cpe	1123	1025	2500	5150	7150	10,300
RS Cpe	1160	1050	2800	5400	7500	10,800
Tr Brgm	1165	925	2000	4650	6500	9300
Tr Sed	1198	925	2000	4650	6500	9300
New York Special, 8-cyl., 125" wb						
Tr Sed	1370	900	1800	4400	6150	8800
Imperial Custom, 8-cyl., 144" wb						
5P Sed	2295	925	2000	4650	6500	9300
4 dr Sed	2295	975	2300	4900	6850	9800
Limo Sed	2395	1025	2500	5150	7150	10,300
Derham customs on C-20 chassis						
Twn Sed	—	1600	4600	7650	10,700	15,300
Twn Limo	—	1800	4900	8150	11,400	16,300
Conv Vic	—	4100	8250	13,750	19,250	27,500
Conv Sed	—	4600	9150	15,250	21,350	30,500

1939

CHRYSLER ROYAL — SERIES C-22 — SIX: For 1939, Chrysler brought out new body styling with narrower runningboards and the headlamps recessed into the fenders. The grilles on the various series were similar, but differed in details. A chrome strip ran vertically up the prow-shaped nose of the cars, with horizontal moldings on either side running a short distance back. Multiple vertical moldings ran down the fender aprons and

1939 Chrysler, Series C-22, Royal sedan, JAC

front panel in "waterfall" style. Royal sixes had five of the horizontal moldings on either side and 19 bars in the waterfall. A long molding traveled along the side of the hoods and was underscored by three horizontal slashes near the cowl. An upper belt molding began at the cowl and continued to the rear of the body. The word Chrysler appeared, in script, on either side of the nose. Other new styling features included a v-shaped windshield, concealed rear luggage compartment and an attractive front bumper with a dip in its center and a twin bar guard arrangement. Cars in the Windsor sub-series had this model name spelled out with a small chrome signature behind three vertical bars on the front hoodsides. Standard equipment included Solar Spark ignition, hydraulic brakes, steering wheel mounted gear selector and an illuminated speedometer. Royal Windsors had fancier interior appointments. Two long wheelbase models were found in the Standard Royal line only.

1939 Chrysler, Series C-23, New Yorker, 4-dr. sedan, OCW

IMPERIAL/NEW YORKER/SARATOGA — SERIES C-23 — EIGHT: Imperials, New Yorkers and Saratogas were all built on the same chassis and shared the same powerplants. These cars were styled similarly to other Chryslers but had fewer horizontal and vertical grille bars on the two new sub-series. There were three horizontal bars on either side of the nose and only 11 bars in the lower "waterfall" grille on New Yorkers and Saratogas. Imperials had five horizontal bars (like Royals) but had 23 bars in their wider waterfall lower grilles. Each series also had small chrome signatures bearing the model name incorporated into the decorative trim on the front of the hoodsides. New Yorkers were the "luxury" line and had two-tone upholstery and rich appointments. Saratogas were "sports luxury" cars with their leather and Bedford cord upholstery selections. Both lines included a special Victoria coupe built in limited production by the Hayes Body Co. of Grand Rapids, Mich. They had a rounded top, fastback rear deck and split rear window treatment. A sun roof was optional on New Yorker and Saratoga sedans. Solar Spark ignition, hydraulic brakes, a new eight-cylinder engine and larger tires were standard equipment on cars in each of the three lines. The optional high-compression engine available in these cars had the aluminum cylinder head.

CUSTOM IMPERIAL — SERIES C-24 — EIGHT: Custom Imperials had basically the same trim features as C-23 Imperials combined with a longer wheelbase, correspondingly longer body panels, richer interior appointments and standard full wheel discs. A new "Cruise and Climb" overdrive transmission was standard in cars of this line and optional in other 1939 models. The Custom Imperials also had larger tires and the standard engine, while having the same compression ratio as the C-23 engine, was slightly more powerful because the aluminum "Silver Dome" cylinder head was standard. The optional Custom Imperial engine was, however, the same as the optional C-23 engine. Several individual customs were built on C-24 running gear.

CHRYSLER — PLYMOUTH — SIX: For the first time since the early 1930's Chrysler of Great Britain used the word Plymouth in selling its smaller line of Chryslers. This car was a badge-engineered Plymouth P-7 Roadking replete down to its standard floor shift transmission. The Chrysler Plymouth was available only in a five-passenger "touring saloon" body style. The only engine offered was the 170-cubic-inch Plymouth export unit.

CHRYSLER — KEW — SIX: Now the middle series, the Kew was badge-engineered from the U.S. P-8 Deluxe Plymouth, which included column-mounted transmission controls and the choice of either the small-bore export engine or the regular Plymouth 201-cubic-inch engine, as well as the choice of cloth or leather upholstery. Standard equipment included a single fog lamp. The Kew could be had as either a five-passenger sedan or a two-passenger convertible coupe.

CHRYSLER — WIMBLEDON — SIX: The '39 Wimbledon would prove to be the last badge-engineered Plymouth sold overseas as a Chrysler. The only engine offered in the Wimbledon was the Plymouth 201-cubic-inch. Buyers could specify cloth or "English trim" (leather) upholstery. Body styles included a five-passenger saloon, a long wheelbase eight-passenger sedan or eight-passenger limousine, a convertible coupe and a Carlton-bodied four-place convertible victoria. Standard equipment included a single fog lamp and "dual power" overdrive transmission; all eight-passenger models were fitted with fender skirts. "Real" Chryslers could also be had in Royal, Imperial or Custom Imperial models.

I.D. DATA: [Series C-22] Serial numbers were located on the right front door hinge pillar post. Starting: (Royal) 7574001; (Royal Windsor) 6948301. Ending: (Royal) 7624876; (Royal Windsor) 6954947. Engine numbers were located on the left side of the block, between cylinders one and two, just below the cylinder head. Starting Engine No.: (All) C22-1001. Ending: (All) C22-58748. [Series C-23] Serial numbers were in the same location. Starting: (Imp.) 6742201; (N.Y.) 6609901; (Sar.) 6672701. Ending: (Imp.) 6750055; (N.Y.) 6613333; (Sar.) 6673414. Engine numbers were in the same locations. Starting Engine No.: C23-1001. Ending: C23-13107. [Series C-24] Serial numbers were in the same location. Starting: 7806201. Ending: 7806507. Engine numbers were in the same location. Starting Engine No.: C24-1001. Ending: C24-1322.

1939 Chrysler, Series C-24, Imperial sedan, OCW

Model No.	Body Type & Seating	Price	Weight	Prod. Total
(Royal)				
C-22	2-dr. Cpe.-2P	918	3120	(4780)
C-22	2-dr. Vic. Cpe.-4P	970	3160	(239)
C-22	2-dr. Brgm.-5P	975	3200	4838
C-22	4-dr. Sed.-5P	1010	3265	(45,955)
(LWB Royal)				
C-22	4-dr. Sed.-7P	1235	3520	621
C-22	4-dr. Limo.-7P	1325	3625	191
(Royal Windsor)				
C-22	2-dr. Cpe.-2P	983	3130	(4780)
C-22	2-dr. Vic. Cpe.-4P	1035	3165	(239)
C-22	2-dr. Clb. Cpe.-5P	1185	3245	2983
C-22	4-dr. Sed.-5P	1075	3275	(45,955)
C-22	Chassis	NA	NA	394

Note 1: Total series production was 60,001.
Note 2: The figures in brackets indicate where the production of Royal and Royal Windsor models is a combined total. No breakouts for either sub-series are available.

Model No.	Body Type & Seating	Price	Weight	Prod. Total
(Imperial)				
C-23	2-dr. Cpe.-2P	1123	3520	492
C-23	2-dr. Vic. Cpe.-4P	1160	3555	35
C-23	2-dr. Brgm.-5P	1165	3610	185
C-23	4-dr. Sed.-5P	1198	3640	(10,536)
(New Yorker)				
C-23	2-dr. Cpe.-2P	1223	3540	(606)
C-23	2-dr. Vic. Cpe.-4P	1260	3580	99
C-23	2-dr. Clb. Cpe.-5P	1395	3665	(606)
C-23	4-dr. Sed.-5P	1298	3695	(10,536)
(Saratoga)				
C-23	2-dr. Clb. Cpe.-5P	1495	3665	134
C-23	4-dr. Sed.-5P	1443	3720	(10,536)
C-23	Chassis	NA	NA	48

Note 1: Total series production was 12,001.
Note 2: Combined production of Imperial, New Yorker and Saratoga sedans was 10,536 (as shown in parenthesis). No further series breakouts are available.
Note 3: Combined production of the New Yorker business coupe and club coupe was 606 (as shown in parenthesis).

Model No.	Body Type & Seating	Price	Weight	Prod. Total
C-24	4-dr. Sed.-5P	2595	4590	88
C-24	4-dr. Sed.-7P	2595	4620	95
C-24	4-dr. Limo. Sed.-7P	2695	4665	117
C-24	4-dr. Der. Conv. Twn. Car	NA	NA	1
C-24	4-dr. Der. Conv. Sed.	NA	NA	1
C-24	4-dr. Der. Tr. Phae.-7P	NA	NA	1
C-24	Chassis	NA	NA	(7)

Note 1: Total series production was 307.

Note 2: The three individual customs listed above were among special models built on the seven (total shown in parenthesis) Custom Imperial Chassis delivered to coach builders this year. The Convertible Town Car, by Derham, was built for the visit of England's King George VI and Queen Elizabeth to the U.S. This car was later donated to a Detroit American Legion post.

ENGINE: [Series C-22] Inline. L-head. Six. Cast iron block. B & S: 3-3/8 in. x 4-1/2 in. Disp.: 241.5 cu. in. C.R.: (std.) 6.5:1; (opt.) 7.0:1. Brake H.P.: (std.) 100 @ 3600 R.P.M.; (opt.) 107 @ 3600 R.P.M. N.A.C.C. H.P.: 27.34. Main bearings: Four. Valve lifters: Solid. Carb.: Carter 1V model E6N1. Torque: (std.) 184 lbs.-ft. @ 1200 R.P.M.; (opt.) 190 lbs.-ft. @ 1200 R.P.M. [Series C-23] Inline. L-head. Six. Cast iron block. B & S: 3-1/4 in. x 4-7/8 in. Disp.: 323.5 cu. in. C.R.: (std.) 6.8:1; (opt.) 7.45:1. Brake H.P. (std.) 130 @ 3400 R.P.M.; (opt.) 138 @ 3400 R.P.M. N.A.C.C. H.P.: 33.80. Main bearings: Five. Valve lifters: Solid. Carb.: Stromberg 2V model AAV-Z. Torque: (std.) 250 lbs.-ft. @ 1600 R.P.M.; (opt.) 265 lbs.-ft. @ 1600 R.P.M. [Series C-24] Inline. L-head. Eight. Cast iron block. B & S: 3-1/4 in. x 4-7/8 in. Disp.: 323.5 cu. in. C.R.: (std.) 6.8:1; (opt.) 7.45:1. Brake H.P.: (std.) 132 @ 3400 R.P.M.; (opt.) 138 @ 3400 R.P.M. N.A.C.C. H.P.: 33.80. Main bearings: Five. Valve lifters: Solid. Carb.: Stromberg 2V model AAV-Z. Torque: (std.) 254 lbs.-ft. @ 1600 R.P.M.; (opt.) 265 lbs.-ft. @ 1600 R.P.M.

1939 Chrysler, 2-dr. brougham, OCW

CHASSIS: [Series C-22 (SWB)] W.B.: 119 in. Tires: 16 x 6.25. [Series C-22 (LWB)] W.B.: 136 in. Tires: 16 x 6.50. [Series C-23] W.B.: 125 in. Tires: 16 x 7.00. [Series C-24] W.B.: 144 in. Tires: 16 x 7.50.

TECHNICAL: (Chrysler): Synchromesh transmission (Imp.) Fluid Drive. Speeds: 3F/1R (overdrive std. on Cus. Imp.). Steering column gear selector. Conventional clutch. Shaft drive. Hypoid rear axle. Overall Ratios: (C-22) 4.1:1 or 4.3:1; (C-23) 3.91:1; (C-24) 4.9:1. Lockheed four-wheel hydraulic brakes. Steel spoke wheels.

OPTIONS: Whitewall tires. Wheel trim rings. Full wheel discs (std. Saratoga and Cus. Imp.). Dual sidemounts (Imperials-last year). Metal sidemount cover(s). Fender skirts. Bumper guards. Radio. Heater. Clock. Cigar lighter. Radio antenna. Seat covers. External sun shade. Spotlight(s). Trippe lights. Ski rack. Rooftop "Tour Rack". Sun roof (used on 239 N.Y. and Saratoga sedans). Runningboard courtesy lamps. Fog light(s). Exhaust pipe extension. License plate frames. Individual custom bodies (special order). Signal lights. Padded roof (Customs). Oversized tires. Special paint. Special upholstery. Fluid Drive transmission (std. in Cus. Imp./opt. in all other eights).

HISTORICAL: Introduced: October, 1938. Innovations: Fluid Drive on Custom Imperials. Improved eight-cylinder engine. "Super finish" paint jobs. Column mounted gearshift. New sun roof option. Calendar year registrations: 63,956. Calendar year production: 67,749. Model year production: 72,443.

In terms of model year output, Chrysler was America's 11th largest auto-maker this season. The company slipped to 12th place in calendar year sales. Radio personality Major Bowes drove a new 1939 Custom Imperial limousine. Derham also created a number of individual customs on the smaller chassis and produced a one-off Saratoga sedan with a padded leather roof treatment.

1939

Royal, 6-cyl., 119" wb

	FP	5	4	3	2	1
Cpe	918	900	1800	4400	6150	8800
Vic Cpe	970	900	1800	4400	6150	8800
Brgm	975	850	1650	4150	5800	8300
4 dr Sed	1010	800	1550	3900	5450	7800

Royal, 6-cyl., 136" wb

7P Sed	1235	850	1650	4150	5800	8300
Limo	1325	900	1800	4400	6150	8800

Royal Windsor, 6-cyl., 119" wb

Cpe	983	900	1800	4400	6150	8800
Vic Cpe	1035	925	2000	4650	6500	9300
Clb Cpe	1185	925	2000	4650	6500	9300
4 dr Sed	1075	850	1650	4150	5800	8300

Imperial, 8-cyl., 125" wb

Cpe	1123	925	2000	4650	6500	9300
Vic Cpe	1160	975	2300	4900	6850	9800
Brgm	1165	800	1550	3900	5450	7800
4 dr Sed	1198	900	1800	4400	6150	8800

New Yorker, 8-cyl., 125" wb

Cpe	1223	925	2000	4650	6500	9300
Vic Cpe	1260	975	2300	4900	6850	9800
Clb Cpe	1395	975	2300	4900	6850	9800
4 dr Sed	1298	850	1650	4150	5800	8300

Saratoga, 8-cyl., 125" wb

	FP	5	4	3	2	1
Clb Cpe	1495	1025	2500	5150	7150	10,300
4 dr Sed	1443	900	1800	4400	6150	8800

Imperial Custom, 8-cyl., 144" wb

5P Sed	2595	975	2300	4900	6850	9800
7P Sed	2595	1025	2500	5150	7150	10,300
Limo	2695	1300	4000	6650	9300	13,300

Special Derham customs on C-24 chassis

7P Tr	—	3800	7650	12,750	17,850	25,500
Conv Sed	—	4100	8250	13,750	19,250	27,500
Conv TwnC	—	4600	9150	15,250	21,350	30,500

1940

1940 Chrysler, Series C-25, Royal coupe, JAC

CHRYSLER — SERIES 25 — SIX: The Chrysler Six came in five sub-series this year; Royal; long wheelbase Royal; Windsor; long wheelbase Windsor and Windsor Highlander. All were basically similar in appearance. New styling features included more massive fenders with recessed headlamps, sealed beam headlights, longer wheelbases, wider front and rear seats, longer hoods and "Airfoam" seat cushions. Horizontal grille bars extended across the lower half of the radiator and fender aprons. The model name appeared spelled out on each side of the hood at the forward end. Highlanders had authentic Scotch plaid and moleskin leather upholstery. Convertibles were re-introduced and two-tone paint jobs were made available again. Standard equipment included Solar Spark ignition, hydraulic brakes, dual sun visors, dual taillights and dual windshield wipers. Buyers had the option of ordering their cars with conventional running boards or more streamlined chrome trimmed rocker panels. The Chrysler Six was available with an optional high-compression engine utilizing the "Silver Dome" aluminum head.

1940 Chrysler, Series C-26, New Yorker convertible coupe, JAC

CHRYSLER — SERIES 26 — EIGHT: The Chrysler Eight came in four subseries; Traveler; New Yorker; New Yorker Highlander and Saratoga. All were on the same 128-1/2 inch wheelbase. Styling features were like those on Chrysler Sixes except for the slightly longer sheet metal and the addition of front fender parking lights. Model names appeared on each side of the hood near the front end. The Traveler was the economy eight with the plainest interior and standard transmission. The New Yorker had upgraded interior appointments and Fluid Drive was optional. The Saratoga was available only as a 4-door sedan in two interior configurations; sport or formal. The Sport sedan had leatherette trimmed seats and door panels. The Formal sedan had a lowerable division window. Standard equipment included Solar Spark ignition, hydraulic brakes, dual sun visors, dual taillights, dual wipers, an improved six main bearing engine and two-barrel carburetor. The Chrysler Eight was available with an optional high-compression engine utilizing the "Silver Dome" aluminum head.

1940 Chrysler, Series C-27, Crown Imperial, limousine, AA

CROWN IMPERIAL — C-27 — EIGHT: There were only three Imperials in 1940 and all were Crown models on a stretched wheelbase. Basic styling was similar to that of other Chryslers with larger doors and sheet metal. The Crown Imperials featured front fender parking lights and came only with conventional running boards. In six passenger cars the front seat-back incorporated storage compartments and there were foot rests on the rear floor. Eight passenger models had jump seats in place of storage compartments and no foot rest. The limousine had a division window and could be ordered with leather upholstery in the driver's compartment. Fluid drive, automatic overdrive and vacuum operated power brakes continued to be standard equipment on this line. Both low and high-compression versions of the Crown Imperial engine used the aluminum cylinder head. The engine was the updated 323.5 cu. in. job with six main bearings. Only one individual custom — a parade phaeton by Derham — was made on the Crown Imperial chassis.

I.D. DATA: [Series 25] Serial numbers were located on the right front door hinge pillar post. Starting: (Roy.) 7625001; (Wind.) 6955201. Ending: (Roy.) 7657487; (Wind.) 6993727. Engine numbers were on the left side of block, between one and two cylinders, just below cylinder head. Starting: (Roy.) C25-1001; (Wind.) C25-70147. Ending: (Roy.) C25-1001; (Wind.) C25-72067. [Series 26] Serial numbers were in the same location. Starting: (Trav.) 6750101; (N.Y.) 6613401; (Sara.) 6673501. Ending: (Trav.) 6756417; (N.Y.) 6624087; (Sara.) 6674100. Engine numbers were in the same location. Starting: (Trav.) C26-1001; (N.Y.) C26-1001; (Sara.) C26-1001. Ending: (Trav.) C26-18753; (N.Y.) C26-18761; (Sara.) C26-18700. [Series C-27] Serial numbers were in the same location. Starting: 7806551. Ending: 7807401. Engine numbers were in the same location. Starting: C27-1001. Ending: C27-1875.

Model No. (Royal)	Body Type & Seating	Price	Weight	Prod. Total
C25	2-dr. Cpe.-3P	895	3075	Note 2
C25	2-dr. Cpe.-6P	960	3110	Note 3
C25	2-dr. Vic. Sed.-6P	960	3150	Note 4
C25	4-dr. Sed.-6P	995	3175	23,274
(LWB Royal)				
C25	4-dr. Sed.-8P	1235	3550	Note 5
C25	4-dr. Limo.-8P	1310	3640	Note 6
C25	Chassis	NA	NA	152
(Windsor)				
C25	2-dr. Cpe.-3P	935	3095	Note 2
C25	2-dr. Cpe.-6P	995	3135	Note 3
C25	2-dr. Vic. Sed.-6P	995	3175	Note 4
C25	2-dr. Conv. Cpe.-6P	1160	3360	Note 7
C25	4-dr. Sed.-6P	1025	3210	Note 8
(LWB Windsor)				
C25	4-dr. Sed.-8P	1275	3575	Note 5
C25	4-dr. Limo.-8P	1350	3660	Note 6
(Highlander)				
C25	2-dr. Cpe.-6P	1020	3135	Note 3
C25	2-dr. Conv. Cpe.-6P	1185	3360	Note 7
C25	4-dr. Sed.-6P	1050	3210	Note 8

Note 1: Total series production was 73,998.
Note 2: Combined production was 5,117.
Note 3: Combined production was 4,315.
Note 4: Combined production was 9,851.
Note 5: Combined production was 439.
Note 6: Combined production was 98.
Note 7: Combined production was 2,275.
Note 8: Combined production was 28,477.

(Traveler)	Body Type & Seating	Price	Weight	Prod. Total
C26	2-dr. Cpe.-3P	1095	3475	Note 2
C26	2-dr. Cpe.-6P	1150	3525	Note 3
C26	2-dr. Vic. Sed.-6P	1150	3555	Note 4
C26	4-dr. Sed.-6P	1180	3590	Note 5
(New Yorker)				
C26	2-dr. Cpe.-3P	1175	3490	Note 2
C26	2-dr. Cpe.-6P	1230	3570	Note 3
C26	2-dr. Conv. Cpe.-6P	1375	3775	Note 6
C26	2-dr. Vic. Sed.-6P	1230	3610	Note 4
C26	4-dr. Sed.-6P	1260	3635	Note 5
C26	4-dr. Fml. Sed.-6P	1335	NA	Note 5
(Highlander)				
C26	2-dr. Cpe.-6P	1255	3570	Note 3
C26	2-dr. Conv. Cpe.-6P	1400	3775	Note 6
C26	4-dr. Sed.-6P	1285	3635	Note 5

Model No. (Saratoga)	Body Type & Seating	Price	Weight	Prod. Total
C26	4-dr. Sed.-6P	1375	3790	Note 5
C26	4-dr. Fml. Sed.-6P	1450	NA	Note 5
C26	Chassis	NA	NA	29

Note 1: Total series production was 17,600.
Note 2: Combined production was 711.
Note 3: Combined production was 1,117.
Note 4: Combined production was 275.
Note 5: Combined production was 14,603.

C27	4-dr. Sed.-6P	2245	4340	355
C27	4-dr. Sed.-8P	2345	4330	284
C27	4-dr. Limo.-8P	2445	4365	210
C27	4-dr. Par. Phae.-6P	NA	NA	1

Note 1: Total series production was 850.

ENGINE: [Series 25] Inline. L-head. Six. Cast iron block. B & S: 3-3/8 in. x 4-1/2 in. Disp.: 241.5 cu. in. C.R.: (Std.) 6.5:1. (Opt.) 7.0:1. Brake H.P.: (Std.) 108 @ 3600 R.P.M.; (Opt.) 112 @ 3600 R.P.M. N.A.C.C. H.P.: 27.34. Main bearings: Four. Valve lifters: Solid. Carb.: Carter 1V model BB-E6S1. Torque: (Std.) 188 lbs.-ft. @ 1200 R.P.M.; (Opt.) 194 lbs.-ft. @ 1200 R.P.M. [Series 26] Inline. L-head. Eight. Cast iron block. B & S: 3-1/4 in. x 4-7/8 in. Disp.: 323.5 cu. in. C.R.: (Std.) 6.8:1. (Opt.) 7.45:1. Brake H.P.: (Std.) 135 @ 3400 R.P.M.; (Opt.) 143 @ 3400 R.P.M. N.A.C.C. H.P.: 33.80. Main bearings: Six. Valve lifters: Solid. Carb.: Stromberg 2V model AAV-2. Torque: (Std.) 255 lbs.-ft. @ 1600 R.P.M.; (Opt.) 270 lbs.-ft. @ 1600 R.P.M. [Series C-27] Inline. L-head. Eight. Cast iron block. B & S: 3-1/4 in. x 4-7/8 in. Disp.: 323.5 cu. in. C.R.: (Std.) 6.8:1. (Opt.) 7.45:1. Brake H.P.: (Std.) 132 @ 3400 R.P.M.; (Opt.) 143 @ 3400 R.P.M. N.A.C.C. H.P.: 33.80. Main bearings: Six. Valve lifters: Solid. Carb.: Stromberg 2V model AAV-2. Torque: (Std.) 260 lbs.-ft. @ 1600 R.P.M.; (Opt.) 270 lbs.-ft. @ 1600 R.P.M.

CHASSIS: [Series C-25] W.B.: 122.5 in. Tires: 16 x 6.25. [Series C-25 (LWB)] W.B.: 139.5 in. Tires: 16 x 6.50. [Series C-26] W.B.: 128.5 in. Tires: 16 x 6.50 or 16 x 7.00. [Series C-27] W.B.: 143 in. Tires: 15 x 7.50.

TECHNICAL: Trans: (C-27) Fluid Drive; (Others) Synchromesh manual. Speeds: 3F/1R (overdrive std. on C-27). Column mount gearshift. Multiple dry disc clutch. Shaft drive. Hypoid rear axle. Overall ratio: (C-25) 4.1:1; (C-26) 3.9:1; (C-27) 4.55:1. Lockheed 4-wheel hydraulic brakes. Steel spoke wheels.

OPTIONS: Whitewalls. Full wheel discs. Wheel trim rings. Two-tone paint. OSRV mirror. Fender skirts. Bumper guards. Radio. Heater. Clock. Cigar lighter. Radio antenna. Seat covers. External sun shade. Spotlight(s). Fog light(s). Front fender parking lights (six). Rear fender gravel guards. Chrome trimmed rocker panels. Leather driver's seat (limo.). Bumper crash bars. Wind wings (conv.).

HISTORICAL: Introduced Sept. 1939. Innovations: Sealed beam headlights. Six main bearing eight. "Airfoam" seat cushions. Calendar year registrations: 100,117. Calendar year production: 115,824. Model year production: 92,419. Chrysler held 10th place in U.S. model year production. The company was 9th in calendar year output. The Derham Crown Imperial parade phaeton survives in the Henry Ford Museum. Derham also produced a special order Crown Imperial Town Limousine, a Royal Six Town Car, a Saratoga Town Car, six Newport prototype parade phaetons and six Thunderbolt prototype sport roadster-hardtops. One of the Newports was the Indianapolis 500 Pace Car in 1940. Walter P. Chrysler died on Aug. 18, 1940.

1940 Chrysler, Series C-26, Travelers sedan, JAC

1940

Royal, 6-cyl., 122.5" wb	FP	5	4	3	2	1
3P Cpe	895	800	1550	3900	5450	7800
6P Cpe	960	850	1650	4150	5800	8300
Vic Sed	960	775	1500	3600	5100	7300
4 dr Sed	995	725	1400	3100	4800	6800
Royal, 6-cyl., 139.5" wb						
8P Sed	1235	800	1550	3900	5450	7800
8P Limo	1310	850	1650	4150	5800	8300
Royal Windsor, 6-cyl., 122.5 wb						
Conv Cpe	1160	3350	6750	11,250	15,750	22,500
3P Cpe	935	800	1550	3900	5450	7800
6P Cpe	995	850	1650	4150	5800	8300
2 dr Vic Sed	995	775	1500	3600	5100	7300
4 dr Sed	1025	725	1400	3100	4800	6800
Royal Windsor, 6-cyl., 139.5 wb						
8P Sed	1275	800	1550	3900	5450	7800
8P Limo	1350	850	1650	4150	5800	8300

Traveler, 8-cyl., 128" wb	FP	5	4	3	2	1
3P Cpe	1095	850	1650	4150	5800	8300
6P Cpe	1150	900	1800	4400	6150	8800
2 dr Vic Sed	1150	800	1550	3900	5450	7800
4 dr Sed	1180	800	1550	3900	5450	7800
New Yorker, 8-cyl., 128.5" wb						
Conv Cpe	1375	3650	7350	12,250	17,150	24,500
3P Cpe	1175	900	1800	4400	6150	8800
6P Cpe	1230	925	2000	4650	6500	9300
2 dr Vic Sed	1230	800	1550	3900	5450	7800
4 dr Sed	1260	850	1650	4150	5800	8300
Fml Sed Div	1335	900	1800	4400	6150	8800
Saratoga, 8-cyl., 128.5" wb						
4 dr Sed	1375	900	1800	4400	6150	8800
Fml Sed Div	1450	925	2000	4650	6500	9300
TwnC Der	—	1025	2500	5150	7150	10,300
Crown Imperial, 8-cyl., 145.5" wb						
6P Sed	2245	925	2000	4650	6500	9300
6P Twn Limo	—	1025	2500	5150	7150	10,300
8P Twn Limo	2445	1025	2500	5150	7150	10,300
8P Sed	2345	1025	2500	5150	7150	10,300
8P Sed Limo	—	1025	2500	5150	7150	10,300
8P Limo	2445	1025	2500	5150	7150	10,300
Parade Phae	—	6100	12,150	20,250	28,350	40,500
Nwpt Parade	—	19,200	33,600	56,000	89,000	112,000
Thunderbolt	—	31,900	59,000	90,000	116,000	155,000

1941

1941 Chrysler, Town & Country, station wagon, OCW

CHRYSLER — SERIES 28 — SIX: The 1941 Chrysler Six came in the same five sub-series. Styling was basically the same as in 1940, except the bodies were slightly wider and lower and had increased glass area in the front and rear. The number of horizontal grille bars was reduced from nine to six, with wider spaces between them. The Chrysler script nameplate appeared directly on the nose and trim louvers were not used on the hood sides. Decorations on the trunk were redesigned as were the bumper guards, which had three horizontal ribs. All models came with or without runningboards. Fluid Drive was standard and a new "Vacamatic" semi-automatic transmission was available at extra-cost. Innovations included a new "Spitfire" engine, Automatic Safety control gearshift, inside hood lock and a steering wheel with no spokes in the upper half. An important new model was the Windsor Six Town & Country Wagon, a "barrel-back" suburban type vehicle designed by Chrysler president David A. Wallace. It had a steel top, but the body was covered with White Ash wood framing and genuine mahogany veneer panels.

1941 Chrysler, New Yorker, convertible coupe, OCW

CHRYSLER — SERIES 30 — EIGHT: The Traveler economy series was deleted. Remaining were the Saratoga, New Yorker and New Yorker Highlander sub-series. General styling features were like those on Chrysler Sixes except for slightly longer sheet metal. Small signature scripts placed on the trailing edge of the hood supplied model identification. In the middle of the year, the New Yorker line was made Chryslers top sub-series. Standard equipment included Solar Spark ignition, hydraulic brakes, dual sun visors, dual taillights, dual wipers, a "Spitfire" eight-cylinder engine

with a two-barrel carburetor and Fluid Drive. One Town & Country Wagon was constructed, upon special order, on the Saratoga chassis.

1941 Chrysler, Crown Imperial, landau limousine, TVB

CROWN IMPERIAL — SERIES C-33 — EIGHT: There was one new hybrid in the 1940 Imperial line. Called the Special Town sedan, it used the New Yorker chassis, but had a Crown Imperial nameplate. New Crown Imperial features included Laidlaw interior fabrics, safety rim wheels, Double Eagle tires and optional, hydro-electric power windows. The master control unit for the power windows was mounted on top of the instrument panel. Crown Imperials had the general styling of other models, with body panels "stretched" to fit the longer wheelbase. Custom Imperial chrome signatures appeared on the rear of the hood sides, below the beltline trim. Fluid Drive was among the Crown Imperial's standard equipment.

I.D. DATA: [Series 28] Serial numbers were located on the right front door hinge pillar post. Starting: (Roy.) 7657501; (Wind.) 7901601. Ending: (Roy.) 7736429; (Wind.) 7957099. Engine numbers were located on the upper left side of the block, between cylinders one and two, just below the cylinder head. Starting: (All) C28-1001. Ending: (All) C28-135725. [Series 30] Serial numbers were in the same location. Starting: (Sar.) 6756501; (N.Y.) 6624101. Ending: (Sar.) 6762251; (N.Y.) 6642655. Engine numbers were in the same location. Starting: (All) C30-1001. Ending: (All) C30-25734. [Series C-33] Serial numbers were in the same location. Starting: 7807501. Ending: 7808214. Note: The Special Town sedans had New Yorker serial numbers. Engine numbers were in the same location. Starting: C33-1001. Ending: C33-1735. Note: The Special Town sedans had New Yorker engine numbers.

1941 Chrysler LeBaron Custom Town Limousine

Model No. (Royal)	Body Type & Seating	Price	Weight	Prod. Total
C-28	2-dr. Cpe.-3P	995	3170	6846
C-28	2-dr. Clb. Cpe.-6P	1085	3260	10,830
C-28	2-dr. Lux. Brgm.-6P	1066	3270	8006
C-28	4-dr. Sed.-6P	1091	3300	51,378
C-28	4-dr. Twn. Sed.-6P	1136	3320	1277
(LWB Royal)				
C-28	4-dr. Sed.-8P	1345	3650	297
C-28	4-dr. Limo.-8P	1415	3740	31
C-28	Chassis	NA	NA	3
(Windsor)				
C-28	2-dr. Cpe.-3P	1045	3170	1921
C-28	2-dr. Clb. Cpe.-6P	1142	3260	8513
C-28	2-dr. Conv. Cpe.-6P	1315	3470	4432
C-28	2-dr. Lux. Brgm.-6P	1128	3270	2898
C-28	4-dr. Sed.-6P	1165	3300	36,396
C-28	4-dr. Twn. Sed.-6P	1198	3315	2704
(LWB Windsor)				
C-28	5-dr. T&C Sta. Wag.-6P	1412	3540	200
C-28	5-dr. T&C Sta. Wag.-9P	1492	3595	797
C-28	4-dr. Sed.-8P	1410	3650	116
C-28	4-dr. Limo.-8P	1487	3740	54
(Highlander)				
C-28	2-dr. Cpe.-3P	1065	3170	Note 2
C-28	2-dr. Clb. Cpe.-6P	1162	3260	Note 2
C-28	2-dr. Conv. Cpe.-6P	1335	3470	Note 2
C-28	2-dr. Lux. Brgm.-6P	1148	3270	Note 2

Model No.	Body Type & Seating	Price	Weight	Prod. Total
C-28	4-dr. Sed.-6P	1185	3300	Note 2
C-28	4-dr. Twn. Sed.-6P	1218	3315	Note 2
(LWB Highlander)				
C-28	4-dr. Sed.-8P	1430	3650	Note 2
C-28	4-dr. Limo.-8P	1507	3740	Note 2

Note 1: Total series production was 136,701.
Note 2: Production of cars with the plaid "Highlander" interior was lumped together with Windsor production. No breakout is available.

Model No.	Body Type & Seating	Price	Weight	Prod. Total
(Saratoga)				
C-30	2-dr. Cpe.-3P	1245	3600	Note 2
C-30	2-dr. Clb. Cpe.-6P	1299	3685	Note 3
C-30	2-dr. Lux. Brgm.-6P	1293	3715	Note 4
C-30	4-dr. Sed.-6P	1320	3755	Note 6
C-30	4-dr. Twn. Sed.-6P	1350	3750	Note 7
C-30	5-dr. T&C Sta. Wag.-9P	NA	NA	1
C-30	Chassis	NA	NA	9
(New Yorker)				
C-30	2-dr. Cpe.-3P	1325	3635	Note 2
C-30	2-dr. Clb. Cpe.-6P	1369	3690	Note 3
C-30	2-dr. Conv. Cpe.-6P	1548	3945	Note 5
C-30	2-dr. Lux. Brgm.-6P	1369	3745	Note 4
C-30	4-dr. Sed.-6P	1389	3775	Note 6
C-30	4-dr. Twn. Sed.-6P	1399	3785	Note 7
(N.Y. Highlander)				
C-30	2-dr. Cpe.-3P	1345	3635	Note 2
C-30	2-dr. Clb. Cpe.-6P	1389	3690	Note 3
C-30	2-dr. Conv. Cpe.-6P	1568	3945	Note 5
C-30	2-dr. Lux. Brgm.-6P	1389	3745	Note 4
C-30	4-dr. Sed.-6P	1409	3775	Note 6
C-30	4-dr. Twn. Sed.-6P	1419	3785	Note 7

Note 1: Total series production was 24,301.
Note 2: Combined production was 771.
Note 3: Combined production was 2845.
Note 4: Combined production was 293.
Note 5: Combined production was 1295.
Note 6: Combined production was 15,868.
Note 7: Combined production was 2326.

Model No.	Body Type & Seating	Price	Weight	Prod. Total
(C-30 Crown Imperial Line)				
C-30	4-dr. Spl. Twn. Sed.-6P	1760	3900	894
(C-33 Crown Imperial Line)				
C-33	4-dr. Sed.-6P	2595	4435	179
C-33	4-dr. Sed.-8P	2695	4495	205
C-33	4-dr. Limo.-8P	2795	4560	316
C-33	Chassis	NA	NA	1

Note 1: Total C-33 series production was 701. (This does not include the Special Town sedan which is totaled as part of the New Yorker Series above).
Note 2: The limousine production total includes an undetermined number of LeBaron Custom Town Limousines, a limited edition model built only on special order.
Note 3: The single Crown Imperial chassis was used for a Custom Landaulet Limousine built for Chrysler president Walter O. Briggs.

1941 Chrysler, Windsor, sedan, JAC

1941 Chrysler, Thunderbolt, convertible show car, FR

1941 Chrysler, Newport, dual cowl phaeton show car, FR

1941 Chrysler, Royal, coupe, JAC

ENGINE: [Series 28] Inline. L-head. Six. Cast iron block. B & S: 3-3/8 in. x 4-1/2 in. Disp.: 241.5 cu. in. C.R.: (std.) 6.5:1 or 6.8:1; (opt.) 7.2:1. Brake H.P.: (std.) 108 @ 3600 R.P.M. or 112 @ 3600 R.P.M.; (opt.) 115 @ 3600 R.P.M. N.A.C.C. H.P.: 27.34. Main bearings: Four. Valve lifters: Solid. Carb.: Carter 1V model BB-E6W1. Torque: (std.) 188/190 lbs.-ft. @ 1200 R.P.M.; (opt.) 196 lbs.-ft. @ 1200 R.P.M. (Note: Cars built early in the year had the 6.5:1 low-compression engine. Cars built later in the year had the 68:1 low-compression engine.) [Series 30] Inline. L-head. Eight. Cast iron block. B & S: 3-1/4 in. x 4-7/8 in. Disp.: 323.5 cu. in. C.R.: (std.) 6.8:1; (opt.) 6.8:1 w/alum. head. Brake H.P.: (std.) 137 @ 3400 R.P.M.; (opt.) 140 @ 3400 R.P.M. N.A.C.C. H.P.: 33.80. Main bearings: Six. Valve lifters: Solid. Carb.: Stromberg 2V model AAV-2. Torque: (std.) 225 lbs.-ft. @ 1600 R.P.M.; (opt.) 260 lbs.-ft. @ 1600 R.P.M. [Series C-33] Inline. L-head. Eight. Cast iron block. B & S: 3-1/4 in. x 4-7/8 in. Disp.: 323.5 cu. in. C.R.: 6.8:1 (with aluminum head). Brake H.P.: 140 @ 3400 R.P.M. N.A.C.C. H.P.: 33.80. Main bearings: Six. Valve lifters: Solid. Carb.: Stromberg 2V model AAV-2. Torque: 260 lbs.-ft. @ 1600 R.P.M.

CHASSIS: [Series C-28] W.B.: 121.5 in. Tires: 16 x 6.25. [Series C-28 (LWB)] W.B.: 139.5 in. Tires: 16 x 6.50. [Series C-30] W.B.: 127.5 in. Tires: 15 x 7.00. [Series C-33] W.B.: 145.5 in. Tires: 15 x 7.50.

TECHNICAL: Fluid Drive transmission. Speeds: 3F/1R. Column mounted gearshift. Conventional clutch. Shaft drive. Hypoid rear axle. Overall Ratio: (C-28) 3.9:1; (C-30) 3.91:1; (C-33) 4.55:1. Four wheel hydraulic brakes. Steel disc wheels.

OPTIONS: Whitewalls. Full wheel discs. Wheel trim beauty rings. Two-tone paint. OSRV mirror(s). Fender skirts. Bumper guards. Radio. Heater. Clock. Cigar lighter. Radio antenna. Seat covers. External sun shade. Spotlight(s). Fog lamps. Vacamatic transmission. Conventional runningboards (on C-30s). Leather driver's seat. (limo). Bumper crash bars. Master grille guard. Chrome exhaust extension. Hydro-electric power windows (Imp.). Highlander plaid upholstery (Windsor & New Yorker). Navajo style interior. Saran trim package. Rear fender gravel guards.

HISTORICAL: Production started: August, 1940. Production ended: July, 1941. Introduced: September, 1940. Innovations: New "Spitfire" engines. Automatic safety control. Power windows optional on Crown Imperial. Town & Country introduced. Vacamatic four-speed transmission. Convertible has rear quarter windows. Calendar year registrations: 143,025. Calendar year production: 141,522. Model year production: 161,704. Company president: Walter O. Briggs. Chrysler was America's 10th ranked auto-maker in model year 1941. On a calendar year basis, the company was the 8th largest car-maker. Chrysler buyers had a choice of 13 color combinations and 27 interior trim combinations. Chrysler showrooms enjoyed increased traffic as crowds thronged to view the exciting Newport and Thunderbolt "dream" cars. Six of each were built and exhibited until the U.S. entry in World War II. Walter Chrysler, Jr. kept one of the Newports; the other eleven cars were sold.

1941 Chrysler, Crown Imperial, town sedan, TVB

1941
Royal, 6-cyl., 121.5" wb

	FP	5	4	3	2	1
3P Cpe	995	800	1550	3900	5450	7800
6P Clb Cpe	1085	850	1650	4150	5800	8300
2 dr Brgm	1066	725	1400	3100	4800	6800
4 dr Sed	1091	775	1500	3600	5100	7300
Twn Sed	1136	800	1550	3900	5450	7800
Royal, 6-cyl., 121.5" wb						
Twn & Ctry Wag	1492	3650	7350	12,250	17,150	24,500
Royal, 6-cyl., 139.5" wb						
8P Sed	1345	800	1550	3900	5450	7800
8P Limo Sed	1415	850	1650	4150	5800	8300
Windsor, 6-cyl., 121.5" wb						
Conv Cpe	—	3650	7350	12,250	17,150	24,500
3P Cpe	1045	850	1650	4150	5800	8300
6P Clb Cpe	1142	900	1800	4400	6150	8800
2 dr Brgm	1128	775	1500	3600	5100	7300
4 dr Sed	1165	800	1550	3900	5450	7800
Twn Sed	1198	850	1650	4150	5800	8300
Windsor, 6-cyl., 139.5" wb						
8P Sed	1410	850	1650	4150	5800	8300
8P Sed Limo	1487	800	1550	3900	5450	7800
Saratoga, 8-cyl., 127.5" wb						
3P Cpe	1245	900	1800	4400	6150	8800
6P Clb Cpe	1299	925	2000	4650	6500	9300
2 dr Brgm	1293	775	1500	3600	5100	7300
4 dr Sed	1320	800	1550	3900	5450	7800
Twn Sed	1350	850	1650	4150	5800	8300
New Yorker, 8-cyl., 127.5" wb						
Conv Cpe	1548	3800	7650	12,750	17,850	25,500
3P Cpe	1325	975	2300	4900	6850	9800
6P Cpe	1369	1025	2500	5150	7150	10,300
2 dr Brgm	1369	900	1800	4400	6150	8800
4 dr Sed	1389	900	1800	4400	6150	8800
Twn Sed	1399	925	2000	4650	6500	9300
6P Sed	2595	975	2300	4900	6850	9800
8P Sed	2695	975	2300	4900	6850	9800
Sedan Limo 8P	—	975	2300	4900	6850	9800
8P Limo	2795	1025	2500	5150	7150	10,300
Laudalet Limo	—	1025	2500	5150	7150	10,300
LeB Twn Limo	—	1050	2800	5400	7500	10,800
New Yorker Special/Crown Imperial, 8-cyl., 127.5" wb						
Twn Sed	—	1050	2800	5400	7500	10,800

C-33 series.

1942

1942 Chrysler, Windsor, convertible, TVB

CHRYSLER — SERIES C-34 — SIX: The 1942 Chrysler grille consisted of five chrome, horizontal bars that ran across the front end and part of the fenders. Horizontal parking lamps were recessed into the grille. The one-

piece alligator hood was unlocked by a knob in the drivers compartment. The were also five chrome bars on the rear fenders. Runningboards were concealed for a streamlined appearance. Standard equipment for all sixes included Solar Spark ignition, hydraulic brakes, full circle horn rings and dual visors, wipers and horns. Windsor models also had "Air Foam" seat cushions, broadcloth upholstery, electric clock, white wall wheel rims, mirror hub caps and front carpets. The Windsor sedan and brougham had folding arm rests in the rear seat. Cars built late in the year had painted "blackout" trim instead of chrome parts. The available car-lines included the Royal and Windsor and each had a long wheelbase sub-series. Consisting of two models. Highlander plaid interiors were optional on Windsors at $20 extra.

CHRYSLER — SERIES C-36 — EIGHT: The Chrysler Eights had the same general styling as sixes, with slightly longer front end sheet metal. Small chrome signatures on the rear sides of the hood, under the beltline trim, identifed the cars as Saratogas or New Yorkers. New Yorkers had upscale interiors with front carpets, clocks and folding rear seat arm rests. Highlander plaid or Indian style "Thunderbird" upholstery was optional in New Yorkers at $20 extra. Derham converted at least one New Yorker convertible into a sports model with cut-down doors, sweep spear side moldings and fender skirts. Its production is included with that of the regular convertible.

1942 Chrysler, Crown Imperial, limousine, OCW

CROWN IMPERIAL — SERIES C-37 — EIGHT: The Crown Imperial was on Chrysler's longest wheelbase and had larger hoods, fenders and doors to eat up the extra space. Interiors were richly upholstered and appointed with folding auxiliary seats in eight passenger cars. The limousine had a leather front seat and division window. Chrysler built two C-37 Chassis, but Derham made at least three special Crown Imperials. The first was a semi-custom Blind Rear Quarter Open Town Car; actually a converted limousine. The two real customs were a 4-door Convertible Sedan and a distinctive-looking Formal Open Town Car.

I.D. DATA: [Series C-34] Serial numbers were located on the right front door hinge pillar. Starting: (Roy.) 70001001; (Wind.) 70010179. Ending (Roy.) 70010179; (Wind.) 70514481. Engine numbers were located on the left side of the block just below the cylinder head. Starting: (All) C34-1001. Ending: (Roy.) C34-2392; (Wind.) C34-23922. [Series C36] Serial numbers were in the same location. Starting: (Sar.) 6762501; (N.Y.) 6674201. Ending: (Sar.) 6764094; (N.Y.) 6684754. Engine numbers were in the same location. Starting: (Sar.) C36-1001; (N.Y.) C36-1001. Ending: (Sar.) C36-13516; (N.Y.) C36-13526.

1942 Chrysler, Royal, 2-dr. brougham, TVB

Model No. (Royal)	Body Type & Seating	Price	Weight	Prod. Total
C-34	2-dr. Cpe.-3P	1075	3331	479
C-34	2-dr. Clb. Cpe.-6P	1168	3406	779
C-34	2-dr. Brgm.-6P	1154	3431	709
C-34	4-dr. Sed.-6P	1177	3476	7424
C-34	4-dr. Twn. Sed.-6P	1222	3481	73
(LWB Royal)				
C-34	4-dr. Sed.-8P	1535	3854	79
C-34	4-dr. Limo.-8P	1605	3944	21
(Windsor)				
C-34	2-dr. Cpe.-3P	1140	3351	250
C-34	2-dr. Clb. Cpe.-6P	1228	3426	1713
C-34	2-dr. Conv. Cpe.-6P	1420	3661	574
C-34	2-dr. Brgm.-6P	1220	3441	317
C-34	4-dr. Sed.-6P	1255	3496	10,054
C-34	4-dr. Twn. Sed.-6P	1295	3506	479
C-34	4-dr. T&C Wag.-6P	1595	3614	150
C-34	4-dr. T&C Wag.-9P	1685	3699	849

Model No.	Body Type & Seating	Price	Weight	Prod. Total
(LWB Windsor)				
C-34	4-dr. Sed.-8P	1605	3879	29
C-34	4-dr. Limo.-8P	1685	3954	12

Note 1: Total series production was 23,991.

Model No.	Body Type & Seating	Price	Weight	Prod. Total
(Saratoga)				
C-36	2-dr. Cpe.-3P	1325	3703	80
C-36	2-dr. Clb. Cpe.-6P	1380	3788	193
C-36	2-dr. Brgm.-6P	1365	3798	36
C-36	4-dr. Sed.-6P	1405	3833	1239
C-36	4-dr. Twn. Sed.-6P	1450	3843	46
C-36	Chassis	NA	NA	2
(New Yorker)				
C-36	2-dr. Cpe.-3P	1385	3728	158
C-36	2-dr. Clb. Cpe.-6P	1450	3783	1234
C-36	2-dr. Conv. Cpe.-6P	1640	4033	401
C-36	2-dr. Brgm.-6P	1440	3798	62
C-36	4-dr. Sed.-6P	1475	3873	7045
C-36	4-dr. Twn. Sed.-6P	1520	3893	1648
C-36	4-dr. T&C Wag.-9P	NA	NA	1

Note 1: Total series production was 12,145.

Model No.	Body Type & Seating	Price	Weight	Prod. Total
C-37	4-dr. Sed.-6P	2815	4565	—
C-37	4-dr. Sed.-8P	2915	4620	—
C-37	4-dr. Limo.-8P	3065	4685	—
(Derham Semi-Custom)				
C-37	4-dr. Twn. Car-8P	NA	NA	NA
(Derham Custom)				
C-37	4-dr. Conv. Sed.-6P	NA	NA	1
C-37	4-dr. Fml. Twn. Car-6P	NA	NA	1

Note 1: Total series production was 450.

1942 Chrysler, Town & Country, station wagon

ENGINE: [Series C-34] Inline L-head. Six. Cast iron block. B & S: 3-7/16 in. x 4-1/2 in. Disp.: 250.6 cu. in. C.R.: 6.6.:1. Brake H.P.: 120 @ 3800 R.P.M. N.A.C.C. H.P.: 27.34. Main bearings: Four. Valve lifters: Solid. Carb.: Carter 1V model EE-1. Torque: 200 lbs.-ft. @ 1600 R.P.M. [Series C-36] Inline L-head. Eight. Cast iron block. B & S: 3-1/4 in. x 4-7/8 in. Disp.: 323.5 cu. in. C.R.: 6.8:1. Brake H.P.: 140 @ 3600 R.P.M. N.A.C.C. H.P.: 33.80. Main bearings: Six. Valve lifters: Solid. Carb.: Stromberg 2V model AAV-2. Torque: 260 lbs.-ft. @ 1800 R.P.M. [Series C-37] The Crown Imperial used the Saratoga/New York engine.

CHASSIS: [Series C-34] W.B.: 121-1/2 in. Tires: 16 x 6.25. [Series C-34 (LWB)] W.B.: 139-1/2 in. Tires: 16 x 6.50. [Series C-36] W.B.: 127-1/2 in. Tires: 15 x 7.00.

TECHNICAL: Transmission: (six) manual; (eight) Fluid Drive. Speeds: 3F/1R. Column shift controls. Multiple disc clutch. Shaft drive. Hypoid rear axle. Overall Ratio: (C-34) 3.9:1; (C-36) 3.9:1; (C-37) 3.58:1. Four wheel hydraulic brakes. Steel disc wheels.

OPTIONS: Whitewall wheel discs. Mirror hub caps. OSRV mirror(s). License plate frame. Chrome exhaust extension. Fender skirts. Bumper guards. Radio. Heater. Clock. Cigar lighter. Radio antenna. Seat covers. External sun shade. Spotlight(s). Fog lamps. Highlander plaid upholstery (20.00). Thunderbird American Indian upholstery (20.00). Two-tone paint. Special paint colors. Fluid drive (std. on T&C wagon and eights). Vacamatic transmission. Fender skirt medallions.

HISTORICAL: Production started: August, 1941. Production ended: January, 1942. Introduced September, 1941. Innovations: Dash controlled alligator hood. Larger more powerful six-cylinder engine. Blackout trim on cars built after Dec. 1941. Concealed runningboards on all models. Thunderbird interior. Calendar year registrations: None. Calendar year production: 5,292. Model year production: 36,586. Chrysler was 12th in calendar year sales for 1942. The company's model year ranking was 10th. A unique semi-custom built this season was the "Laura A.," a Town & Country Wagon converted into an open, 4-door touring car. It appeared in Hollywood films and is believed to have been built by the shop of Bohman & Schwartz in Pasadena, Calif.

1942 Chrysler, New Yorker convertible coupe, JAC

1942
Royal, 6-cyl., 121.5" wb

	FP	5	4	3	2	1
3P Cpe	1075	800	1550	3900	5450	7800
6P Clb Cpe	1168	850	1650	4150	5800	8300
2 dr Brgm	1154	675	1300	2600	4400	6300
4 dr Sed	1177	675	1300	2600	4400	6300
Twn Sed	1222	800	1550	3900	5450	7800
Royal, 6-cyl., 139.5" wb						
8P Sed	1535	775	1500	3600	5100	7300
8P Limo	1605	800	1550	3900	5450	7800
Windsor, 6-cyl., 121.5" wb						
Conv Cpe	1420	3350	6750	11,250	15,750	22,500
3P Cpe	1140	850	1650	4150	5800	8300
6P Cpe	1228	900	1800	4400	6150	8800
2 dr Brgm	1220	725	1400	3100	4800	6800
4 dr Sed	1255	725	1400	3100	4800	6800
Twn Sed	1295	775	1500	3600	5100	7300
6P T&C Wag	1595	3100	6150	10,250	14,350	20,500
9P T&C Wag	1685	3200	6450	10,750	15,050	21,500
Windsor, 6-cyl., 139.5" wb						
8P Sed	1605	800	1550	3900	5450	7800
8P Limo	1685	850	1650	4150	5800	8300
Saratoga, 8-cyl., 127.5" wb						
3P Cpe	1325	925	2000	4650	6500	9300
6P Cpe	1380	975	2300	4900	6850	9800
2 dr Brgm	1365	775	1500	3600	5100	7300
4 dr Sed	1405	775	1500	3600	5100	7300
Twn Sed	1450	900	1800	4400	6150	8800
New Yorker, 8-cyl., 127.5" wb						
Conv Cpe	1640	3650	7350	12,250	17,150	24,500
3P Cpe	1385	975	2300	4900	6850	9800
6P Cpe	1450	1025	2500	5150	7150	10,300
2 dr Brgm	1440	800	1550	3900	5450	7800
4 dr Sed	1475	800	1550	3900	5450	7800
Twn Sed	1520	925	2000	4650	6500	9300
Der Conv Cpe	—	4000	7950	13,250	18,550	26,500
Crown Imperial, 8-cyl., 145.5" wb						
6P Sed	2815	850	1650	4150	5800	8300
8P Sed	2915	850	1650	4150	5800	8300
8P Sed Limo	3065	925	2000	4650	6500	9300
Derham Customs						
Conv Sed	—	3800	7650	12,750	17,850	25,500
TwnC	—	1600	4600	7650	10,700	15,300
Fml TwnC	—	1700	4700	7900	11,100	15,800

CHURCH — "Messrs. Church & Jones, representing the Church Automobile Company of Pittsburgh, are said to be looking for a location for an automobile factory and to have given Youngstown, Ohio, and Duquesne, Pennsylvania their favorable consideration," reported *The Horseless Age* in May 1901. Obviously neither Youngstown nor Duquesne reciprocated. Church never proceeded into manufacture.

The Church Balanced Import Steam Turbine Company was organized in Portland, Maine early in 1904 to "build and sell boats, automobiles, engines, etc." George F. Gould of Portland was president and treasurer of this venture; directors included J.T. Fagan and B.M. Welch of Portland; B.S. Church of Plainfield, New Jersey; T.C. Hillhouse of Yonkers, New York; S.M. Hitchcock of New York City. Capital stock in this venture was $750,000 of which $300 was paid in at incorporation. Probably lots more was hoped to be sold. Manufacture did not follow.

The Church Motor Car Company from early 1913 was a million-dollar Delaware incorporation for the manufacture of motor cars. Herbert E. Latter was the indicated incorporator. Manufacture did not follow.

CHURCH — Cincinnati, Ohio — (1920) — In April of 1920, F.S. Church, the longtime manager of the Chevrolet dealership in Cincinnati, resigned his job to devote all energies to the car he had invented. "The main feature of the new design is the absence of metal springs," *Motor Age* reported that month. "Other innovations are four wheel driving, braking and steering, one reduction gear for starting and an estimated speed of 60 mph." The entire car weighed less than 500 pounds and that figure was also the price at which Church expected to retail it. The venture failed almost immediately. Whether F.S. Church went back to his old job is not known.

1920 CHURCH

	FP	5	4	3	2	1
Church						

1913 Church-Field Electric, roadster, WLB

CHURCH-FIELD ELECTRIC — Sibley, Michigan — (1912-1913) — Austin Church and H. George Field claimed their electric car to be the first ever with a two-speed planetary transmission which combined with ten electrical selector positions to provide for a total of twenty speed ranges, and a potential hill climbing prowess most unusual for an electric. An underslung frame and aluminum body with Renault-type hood were featured. The Church-Field was available in two models, a roadster capable of 30 mph, and a coupe capable of 25 mph. The Church-Field Motor Company introduced the new car at the Detroit Automobile Show in January 1912. By September 1913 the firm was in financial trouble, and the plant was closed. Conceivably, some cars may have been put together from parts on hand thereafter. What remained of the Church-Field assets was sold for $600 in May 1915.

1912-1913 CHURCH-FIELD ELECTRIC

	FP	5	4	3	2	1
Rds.-2P (100" wb)	2300	2700	3600	5300	8800	19,000
Cpe.-5P (100" wb)	2800	2400	3400	4800	8000	17,000

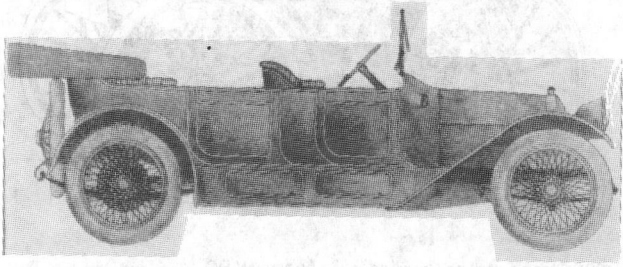

1914 Church, Mackenzie model, touring, WLB

CHURCH PNEUMATIC — Chicago, Illinois — (1913-1914) — "The Car with the Bother Left Out" left out almost everything else too. It had no transmission, no clutch, no carburetor, no shift levers, no timing gears, no sleeves, no intake or exhaust poppet valves and springs. What it did have was the Church Pneumatic System the engineering charts and data for which were available from the company: "They're the most interesting automobile engineering papers of the decade. They are yours free on request." These papers, alas, are not known to have survived, neither did the Church Motor Car Company for long. Advertising proclaimed the Church Pneumatic System as the sensation of the 1913 Chicago Automobile Show. Chicago newspapers reported that the company had been incorporated for a million dollars. The Church Pneumatic was gone before the end of 1914.

1913-1914 CHURCH PNEUMATIC
4-cyl., 90 hp, 132" wb

Mackenzie Model	2500	—	—	—	—	—

CHURCHILL — Spokane, Washington — (1913) — In 1913 D.D. Churchill of Spokane claimed that the vehicle he had just finished building was "the smallest motor car capable of service on the roads." Built at a cost of $250 and powered by a 20 hp engine, it was less than six-and-a-half feet long, with the highest part of the body just three feet from the ground. Churchill also claimed that, with four people aboard, his car had attained a speed of 25 mph and had "proved effective in city and country travel."

CIESMONT — The Ciesmont Automobile Company was organized during the summer of 1907 to manufacture motorcars in Camden, New Jersey. The capital stock was $50,000. J.F. Stevens, W.F. Dill and H.R. Miller backed this venture. Manufacture is not indicated.

CINCINNATI — The Cincinnati Motor Car Company was organized during the summer of 1912 with a capital stock of $10,000 for the manufacture of "automobiles for pleasure and commercial purposes." Incorporators were C.D. Wilson, H.C. Heisey, C.W. Shepler, J.C. Miller and R.M. Comer. Manufacture is doubted.

The Cincinnati Motors Company was organized during early 1912 with a capital stock of $10,000 for the manufacture of automobiles and motor trucks. Incorporators were Franklin Alter, J.B. Doan and Harry T. Alter. This venture did move into production, but of commercial vehicles only which were marketed under the tradename of Alter from 1914-1916.

1903 Cincinnati Steamer, runabout, NAHC

CINCINNATI STEAM — Cincinnati, Ohio — (1903-1904) — The Cincinnati Automobile Company of 807-809 Race Street produced a steam runabout which was more rakishly low in stature than the norm, but was otherwise typical of small-steam-car practice, with its 10 hp single-acting steam engine fitted under the seat, final drive by chain, and steering by tiller. The car was relatively high priced for the specifications it afforded, and was not produced long. President of the company had been Emmet P. Gray, who had also designed the Cincinnati.

1903-1904 CINCINNATI STEAM

	FP	5	4	3	2	1
Steam Rbt.	1000	2700	3600	5300	8800	19,000
Steam Rbt./Tonneau	1500	2900	3700	5600	9100	20,000

CINCINNATI — Cincinnati, Ohio — (1923) — The Cincinnati Automotive Trades Association built an automobile in 1923, this the result of a nifty promotion idea of the organizations general manager, John J. Behle. The car was put together at the Automotive Accessory and Radio Exposition held in Cincinnati from November 22nd to 29th, an eighth of the car being completed each day. The purpose of all this, according to Behle, was to "demonstrate that the exhibitors will have on display everything needed for an automobile." The finished car was donated to a local charity.

1910 Cino, touring, HAC

CINO — Cincinnati, Ohio — (1910-1913) — Prior to 1910, the Queen City of Cincinnati had been noted as a carriage-making center and for its many manufacturers of machine tools. In 1910, however, an even half-dozen automobile manufacturers began in Cincinnati and, according to *The Automobile*, one of the most important was the carriage-producing Haberer & Company, builders of the new Cino. It was a conventional car throughout, but very well crafted; entered into dirt-track competition by the factory, the Cino did very well, winning 32 prizes in 44 starts. The decision of Haberer to discontinue the Cino in May of 1913 came as something of a surprise to the industry. Al Haberer subsequently explained that the Ohio River floods that spring had inundated the factory and made continuation of production impossible.

1910 CINO
4-cyl., 40 hp, 112" wb

Model A Pony Tonneau						
Tour.	2250	3000	4000	6000	9500	21,000
Model A Rds.	2250	3100	4200	6300	10,500	22,000

1911 Cino, semi-racer, WLB

1911 CINO
4-cyl., 40 hp, 113" wb

	FP	5	4	3	2	1
Fore-Door Tour.	2350	3000	4000	6000	9500	21,000
Tour.	2250	2900	3700	5600	9100	20,000
Semi-Racer Rbt.	2250	3100	4200	6300	10,500	22,000
Toy Tonneau	2250	3100	4200	6300	10,500	22,000

1912 CINO
6-cyl., 60 hp, 130" wb

	FP	5	4	3	2	1
Tour.-7P	2750	5900	11,850	19,750	27,650	39,500

4-cyl., 50 hp, 117" wb

	FP	5	4	3	2	1
Tour.-5P	1850	5250	10,500	17,500	24,500	35,000

1913 CINO
Model 450-A — 4-cyl., 50 hp, 120" wb

	FP	5	4	3	2	1
Silent Cino Tour.-5P	1850	5000	10,500	16,750	23,450	33,500
Silent Cino Rds.-2P	1850	5100	10,200	17,000	23,800	34,000

Model 660-A — 6-cyl., 60 hp, 132" wb

	FP	5	4	3	2	1
Tour.-7P	2700	6000	12,000	20,000	28,000	40,000
Rds.-2P	2700	5900	11,850	19,750	27,650	39,500

CIRCLE — The Circle Motor Car Company was organized in New York City during the spring of 1911 with a capital stock of $25,000 for the manufacture of automobiles. Involved in the venture were three people named Boyle — J.M., J.W. and E.M. — all of New York City. Manufacture is doubted.

CIRCLEVILLE — Circleville, Ohio — (1914) — The Circleville Automobile Company was a dealership which planned to enter the manufacturing arena in 1914 via a cyclecar powered by an engine invented by W. Lee Crouch. With self-starter and electric lights, the car was planned to be sold at $425. Whether a prototype of the Circleville was ever completed has not been determined; given W. Lee Crouch's procrastination in his own automobile adventures at the turn of the century, possibly it was not. Certainly the car did not proceed into manufacture.

1938 Cissel

CISSEL — Rockville, Maryland — (1938) — The Cissel was a little midget single-seater built by Humphrey Cissel of Rockville in 1938. It was undoubtedly the cheapest car built in America that year. Its cost was three dollars. Cissel used an old washing machine motor for power and claimed a tidy fuel efficiency of eighty miles a gallon.

CITIZENS — The Citizens' Automobile Company was organized in Birmingham, Alabama during the fall of 1909 with a capital stock of $25,000. Incorporators were J.C. Turner, M.F. Hinckman, H.G. Robinson and G.W. Yancey. Their plan was to "engage in the manufacture, selling and leasing of motorcars, taxicabs and accessories." Manufacture is not believed to have followed.

CITY — The City Auto Company was organized with a capital stock of $10,000 in late 1917 to manufacture and deal in automobiles in Bridgeport, Connecticut. Incorporators were Francis C. Eisenman, Leo C. Eisenman and John J. Grills. Manufacture is doubted.

The City Automobile Company was organized with a capital stock of $4800 in the fall of 1912 for the manufacture of automobiles in Morgantown, West Virginia. Incorporators were J. Leonard Yates, B.S. Deering, N.B. Yost, Margaret Smith and Cora B. Deering. Manufacture is doubted.

The City Machine Company was organized in Detroit during the fall of 1905 to manufacture and sell automobiles and supplies. Involved in this venture were Myron E. Benjamin, Lewis W. Raulet, George S. Benjamin, Frederick J. Nicholson, Alonzo L. Johnson, Franklin O. Prussia, Andrew W. Smith, M.E. Benjamin. Manufacture of an automobile is doubted.

The City Motor Service was a $50,000 New York City incorporation from the summer of 1908 "to manufacture and deal in motorcars and operate the same." Manufacture is doubted.

CLA-HOLME — Denver, Colorado — (1922) — The Cla-Holme was America's second four-wheel-drive car of the Twenties. The first, the McGill from Fort Worth, arrived in 1921. It began and ended its life as a prototype. The Cla-Holme from Denver arrived in 1922. It was a six (either Continental or Falls engine, references differ), and a two-seater roadster slated to sell for $1665. A transmission with eight forward speeds was a provocative feature. Like McGill, the Cla-Holme Motor Car Company managed a total production of just one prototype.

1898 Clapp Gasoline Carriage, auto-buggy, NAHC

CLAPP — Connecticut & New Jersey — (1898-1900) — Henry W. Clapp had worked with the Duryea brothers on their early vehicles in Massachusetts, and moved to New Haven, Connecticut to try a car of his own. His first was the Eastern of 1896, which failed quickly. In 1898 he came up with a two-cylinder 6 hp water-cooled engine which he mounted in a buggy chassis with 48-inch wheels shod with three-inch pneumatic tires. Completing the car in August that year, Clapp began laying grand plans for its manufacture and found the New Haven Chair Company which had recently abandoned bicycle manufacture and "was anxious to devote (its factory) to some more promising industry." Production of three vehicles a day was envisioned "as soon as the shop can be got in running order." Apparently the shop could not be so got, because in 1900 Henry Clapp showed up in Jersey City, New Jersey and attempted to establish the Clapp Motor Vehicle Company with an envisioned capitalization of $300,000 and/or the Clapp Motor Carriage Company capitalized at $600,000 — sources differ. Clapp never did go into manufacture. But the Clapp he built might have been the first example of what would decades later be called a "fuel efficient" car. It used only six gallons of gasoline for a 100-mile run.

CLARK — The Clark built in Lansing, Michigan from 1910-1911 was the linear descendant of the Clarkmobile. Refer to Clarkmobile.

The Clark Special from Tell City, Indiana was the rechristened and revised Herrmann of 1905. Refer to Herrmann.

In 1910 the A.C. Clark Carriage Company of Chicago announced its intention to move into the automotive field. When Albert C. Clark reincorporated that year, however, it was as the Clark Delivery Car Company for the manufacture of commercial vehicles only.

Clark & Company of Cleveland, Ohio has been indicated on various rosters as producing a steam car in 1900-1901. This has not been substantiated.

The Clark Motor Company of Buffalo, New York was one of the firms consolidated into the Buffalo Electric Vehicle Company which produced the Buffalo Electric from 1912-1915. No cars were sold under the Clark name.

The Clark Motor Car Company of Louisville, Kentucky announced an increase in its capital stock from $30,000 to $60,000 and declared itself a manufacturer of automobiles in 1911. Further documentation is lacking.

The James A. Clark Company in Upstate New York produced an automobile following the turn of the century which was marketed as the Herkimer. Refer to Herkimer.

322

CLARK STEAM — Cambridge, Massachusetts — (1899-1905) — William G. Clark of 33 Chester Street in North Cambridge produced steam engines developing horsepower ranging from two to twenty. Although he offered to fit these engines into any vehicle of the purchaser's choosing, he envisioned commercial application predominantly, his steam traction unit being designed particularly well for road-building work or for harvesting cane and beet-root sugar in Cuba. Whether any Clark-designed vehicles made it to the Caribbean is not known. No doubt, precious few Clark vehicles of any kind ever saw production, though William G. Clark continued to indicate himself as a manufacturer through 1905.

CLARK — Moline, Illinois — (1897, 1901) — A single-cylinder air-cooled car with its fan mounted on the flywheel was the singular feature of the experimental car produced by W.E. Clark in Moline in 1897. In 1901 his Clark Manufacturing Company announced completion of another gasoline car, this one with a 4 hp engine designed by W.E. Clark. "The vehicle is now being tested and has been sold to Doctor Ludwig of Rock Island," the trade press reported in July that year. "If it behaves well in every-day use, the company will proceed with the manufacture of others." Apparently it did not behave well. In 1903 Clark did briefly market a subsequent automobile called the Blackhawk. In 1906 he was convinced he had hit the big time when he interested the famous John Deere company in town to finance his next effort. The Deere-Clark was the result.

CLARK STEAM — Vicksburg, Michigan — (1901) — Two cars were built by the Clark Brothers Company of Vicksburg in 1901. They were steam runabouts and quite standard for the period, with the exception of one feature which was the reason for the cars being built. This was the Clark Regular Alarm Column, which was described as a device to maintain a predetermined water level in the boiler "without attention from the operator, making it impossible to burn or scorch the boiler even though the water tank should become empty without the knowledge of the operator." Homer Clark was its inventor; the cars were built to demonstrate his invention and promote its sale to other manufacturers. The Clark Brothers Company had been producing feed water regulating devices for the three years past.

1904 Clark, runabout, NAHC

CLARK — Detroit, Michigan — (1904) — In January of 1904 the E.C. Clark Machine Company of 59 Woodbridge Street in Detroit announced the ongoing road-testing of its first experimental car. Its engine was a four-cylinder air-cooled vertical unit with a cooling device described as "simple and unique, doing away with the possibility of overheating." Although the firm announced its plans to market the vehicle, this does not appear to have been done. Instead the Clark company focused attention on the manufacture of motors only. The company may have moved to Lansing in 1905.

CLARK — Bozeman, Montana — (1908) — This Clark was a motor sleigh built by a letter carrier from Bozeman named Lee R. Clark. "However crude the machine may be, and whatever its practical value in Arctic exploration," commented *Motor Field* in January 1908, "certain it is that it will run over snow in Montana without sinking into it." Lee Clark had already proven that. This vehicle was built as an ordinary automobile, with the addition of a fifth wheel for gripping the snow or ice and raised or lowered by electric motor depending on road conditions, and with runners that were adjustable as well. Clark claimed speeds of up to 20 mph, and planned to build more of his sleigh cars, but whether he did is not known.

CLARK ELECTRIC — Buffalo, New York — (1910) — The Model A Clark of 1910 used a 3 1/2 hp Westinghouse motor and a 28-cell Niagara battery. It was a three-passenger electric runabout on a 106-inch wheelbase and featured shaft drive, semi-elliptic springs in front and full elliptics in the rear. The car was built by Brunn's Carriage Manufacturing Company in Buffalo, most likely to the custom order of a client named Clark. Brunn built a number of such cars beginning in 1906. So far as is known, there was no Model B of this electric.

1910 Clark, runabout, NAHC

CLARK — Shelbyville, Indiana — (1910-1912) — In 1912, in an effort perhaps to suggest a longer experience in the automobile industry, the Clark Motor Car Company advertised its three-body-style range of cars as the Models X, Y and Z. These did not differ much from the cars produced for the two previous seasons as Models A and B, with four-cylinder Rutenber engines, Remy magnetos, Schebler carburetors, Fisk tires and bodies which were said to be "aluminoid." The people behind the company were John D. Clark, J.H. Akers, A.J. Thurston, Arthur Woodward and, as general manager, Maurice Wolfe, lately of the Wolfe car from Minnesota. Following an involuntary bankruptcy in June 1912, the Clark was resumed in production under fresh management. By the following June, however, John Clark announced defeat — and the sale of his factory to Maurice Wolfe whose new car would be called the Meteor.

1912 Clark, model Y, torpedo roadster, WLB

1910-1911 CLARK
4-cyl., 30 hp, 114" wb

	FP	5	4	3	2	1
Model A Tour.	1175	3000	4000	6000	9500	21,000
Model B Rds.	1175	3100	4200	6300	10,500	22,000
4-cyl., 40 hp, 124" wb						
Model A Tour.	1600	3300	4400	6700	12,000	24,000
Model B Rds.	1800	3500	4500	7000	13,000	25,000
1912 CLARK						
4-cyl., 30/40 hp, 114" wb						
Model X Tour.	1000	—	—	—	—	22,000
Model Y Torpedo Rds.	1000	—	—	—	—	23,000
Model Z Fore-Door Tour.	1050	—	—	—	—	23,000

1903 Clark Electric, NAHC

CLARK ELECTRIC — Philadelphia, Pennsylvania — (1903-1905) — A.F. Clark & Company was vigorously launched in 1903 for the manufacture of electric delivery trucks and pleasure vehicles, as well as batteries, motors and controllers for the industry. In addition to all of this, the company made a combination vehicle equipped with a 7 hp gasoline engine and a dynamo that charged the batteries at 35 amperes "and 45 or 48 amperes when speeding at 30 miles per hour." The gasoline engine was said to be started via the dynamo "by simply turning a knob." The standard Clark Electrics had a maximum of 18 mph and 40 miles between charges. The man behind this venture was Albert F. Clark. Whether his product was found wanting in some particular, or it was simply a case of too much too soon, Clark's company was in trouble from the beginning. He struggled for a couple of years in Philadelphia, then gave up and moved to Toledo where he tried to help the Cooney Carriage Company move into the automotive age. When that didn't pan out, he remained in Toledo and tried again with another Clark Electric in 1909.

1903 Clark Gasoline-Electric, NAHC

1903-1905 CLARK ELECTRIC.

	FP	5	4	3	2	1
Electric Stanhope	1250	2700	3600	5300	8800	19,000
Electric Combination Brgm.	3500	2900	3700	5600	9100	20,000

CLARK ELECTRIC — Toledo, Ohio — (1909-1910) — This 1909 effort was Albert F. Clark's third automobile, preceded by the Clark Electric of Philadelphia from 1903-1905 and the Cooney Electric of Toledo from 1906. Experimentation began in 1908, and early in 1909 Clark attempted to interest New Orleans capital in organization of the Toledo Electric Motor Works. This didn't work. Then he happened upon the Allen Manufacturing Company, a successful purveyor of plumbing supplies in Toledo. The Allen & Clark Company resulted, with Clark continuing his experiments at the Allen premises at 2014 Adams Street. This new Clark Electric runabout, he said, was capable of 30 mph and with the new battery he had invented would "at low current, carry an electric car further than any other battery known." Unfortunately, this venture did not travel far. In September of 1908 the Toledo Electric Vehicle Company was organized with a capital stock of $50,000 for manufacture of the Clark Electric. An old riding academy on Collingwood Avenue was leased for factory use, and machinery was installed there. Production was begun, but the Clark Electric survived less than a year, whereupon the Allen people went on to plumbing, and Albert Clark to pursuits which history has not recorded with certainly, though probably the Clark from Buffalo in 1911 was among them.

CLARK ELECTRIC — Buffalo, New York — (1910-1911) — During the spring of 1910 the Clark Motor Company was organized with a capital stock of $50,000 in Buffalo. The incorporators included Stanley B. DeLong, John W. Van Allen and Henry J. Rente. The firm was said to have been "financed entirely by Buffalonians," but the Clark for whom it was named was probably Albert F., whose most recent automotive adventure had been in Toledo. In addition to the Clark patents for electric cars, this new enterprise had also secured rights to patents of William Van Wagoner, whose experience in the automobile field dated back to the turn of the century in Syracuse. That the Clark Motor Company ever moved into viable production of electric cars and trucks is to be doubted, but it is known that pilot models of both had been assembled by June 1911 in a rented factory at 1738 Elmwood Avenue in Buffalo before this venture went under.

CLARK-HATFIELD — Oshkosh, Wisconsin — (1908-1909) — Like many other horsedrawn vehicle builders, J.L. Clark believed that changing the name of his Clark Carriage Company to the Clark-Hatfield Automobile Company, and providing horsepower to his traditional product was sufficient to make it in the automobile industry. In July of 1908 he announced his plans, having secured either the necessary capital or engineering expertise from a Mr. Hatfield in exchange for the hyphenated marque name. Possibly the Mr. Hatfield was Charles B., either Jr. or Sr., who had produced a Hatfield motorized buggy in Ohio the year previous. The Clark-Hatfield was a typical highwheeler with two-cylinder 14 hp engine, $650 price tag and but one unusual feature; its friction transmission was

1908 Clark Hatfield, runabout, WLB

mounted ahead of, rather than behind, the car's two-cylinder engine. This did not work at all well, nor long. Subsequently, as the J.L. Clark Manufacturing Company, the firm produced truck bodies.

1908-1909 CLARK-HATFIELD
Model No. 23 — 2-cyl., 14 hp

	FP	5	4	3	2	1
Motor Buggy	650	2200	3200	4400	7000	15,000

CLARK-NORWALK — Cleveland, Ohio — 1910 — This Clark refers to the sales agency in Cleveland that sold the Norwalk that was built in the Ohio city of that name. Badge engineering literally — the name in brass script on the radiator core — was the sole difference between this car and the Norwalk sold elsewhere. Likewise, the Rock Hill that year was another Norwalk with new brass script. The Clark-Norwalk was shown at the Cleveland Armory Automobile Show in late 1910. It did not reappear in 1911, most likely because of the resulting confusion — which should have been predicted in any case — with the Clark being built in Shelbyville, Indiana.

CLARK SPECIAL — Anderson, Indiana — (1908) — The J.D. Clark Auto Company of Anderson operated chiefly as a dealership and garage, but in 1908 built one 50 hp custom car for Dr. W.C. Rousch of that city. Rousch drove the car, which he christened the Clark Special, on a trip of 1692 miles that year from Anderson into New York State.

1901 Clark Steam Car, experimental, NAHC

CLARK STEAM CAR — Boston, Massachusetts — (1900-1909) — Edward S. Clark began his steam boiler factory in Boston in 1895 and his experiments with steam cars soon thereafter. By the turn of the century he was ready to market a quite advanced steamer powered by a 20 hp four-cylinder horizontally opposed engine with flash boiler placed under the hood. A double-side-entrance tonneau was the only body style, and a novel feature was the steering wheel which tilted forward for ease of entrance and egress and which also locked the throttle valve in its vertical position, "removing the danger of starting of the car by unauthorized persons." The initial asking price for a Clark Steam Car was $5000, and although this was halved in 1909, it was still a thousand dollars more than the Stanley and other steamers on the market. Apparently Clark never envisioned quantity production, indeed he never even bothered to incorporate a company. There was a wide variation among body styles and specifications through the years. The Clark Steam Car sold in very small numbers and, with the cessation of its manufacture, its inventor simply went back to the reboring of cylinders, the fitting of pistons and valves, the furnishing of parts, and the repairing, remodeling and painting of automobiles of all kinds which had been his principal source of income all along. After his steam car adventure, he got into the commercial vehicle field awhile, though most of the few trucks he produced were gasoline powered. It would appear that Edward S. Clark epitomized the compleat tinkerer.

1900-1902 CLARK STEAM CAR

	FP	5	4	3	2	1
Double Side-Entrance Tonneau	5000	3500	4500	7000	13,000	25,000

1903 CLARK STEAM CAR

	FP	5	4	3	2	1
Model B Tour.	3500	3100	4200	6300	10,500	22,000
Model K Dly.	2000	3000	4000	6000	9500	21,000
Model D Tour.	3500	3200	4300	6500	11,000	23,000
Model E Tour.	3500	3200	4300	6500	11,000	23,000
Model A Tour.	5000	3500	4500	7000	13,000	25,000

1904 Clark Steam Car, HAC

1904 CLARK STEAM CAR

Style H Dos-a-Dos (84" wb)	4000	4000	5000	8000	15,000	28,000
Style D Surrey (99" wb)	2500	3300	4400	6700	12,000	24,000
Style K Dly. (69" wb)	2000	2900	3700	5600	9100	20,000
Suburban Car (72" wb)	1000	3100	4200	6300	10,500	22,000

1905 Clark Steam Car, HAC

1905 CLARK STEAM CAR

Side Entrance Tonneau (108" wb)	5000	3300	4400	6700	12,000	24,000

1907 Clark Steam Car, HAC

1906-1907 CLARK STEAM CAR

Tour.-7P (110" wb)	5000	3300	4400	6700	12,000	24,000

1909 Clark Steam Car, model LXX, HAC

1908-1909 CLARK STEAM CAR

	FP	5	4	3	2	1
Model LXX Rds.-4P (110" wb)	2750	3500	4500	7000	13,000	25,000

CLARKE — In 1907 the Clarke Automobile & Launch Company of Jacksonville, Florida was bought out by M.C. Hutto and Claude Nolan. Included in the sale were fourteen second-hand automobiles, machinery, tires, tools, and two new touring cars. It seems unlikely that Clarke had built any of the cars itself, serving instead as an agency. A few cars called the Hutto had been produced, though Hutto and Nolan's buying out of the Clarke facilities was simply to combine them with their own for "one of the most extensive repair shops and supply stores in the South."

CLARKE-CARTER — From 1909 to 1913 the Clarke-Carter Automobile Company of Jackson, Michigan produced a car called the Cutting. Refer to Cutting.

1903 Clarkmobile, runabout, WLB

CLARKMOBILE — Lansing, Michigan — (1903-1904)/CLARK — (1910-1911) — Clark & Company of Lansing had been in the buggy business since 1865. The "Clark" was Albert Clark, the "& Company" was his son Frank G., one of the earliest automobile enthusiasts in town. Indeed, it was Frank Clark who built the body for the first experimental gasoline vehicle of a Detroit horseless carriage enthusiast by the name of Ransom Olds. This was in 1896. But Albert Clark cautioned his son about the riskiness of the nascent automobile industry, and so the son stayed away — that is, until Albert Clark died in 1901. Then Frank Clark jumped in with both feet. He spent eighteen months designing a quite wonderful little single-cylinder 7 hp runabout. In April 1902 he organized the Clarkmobile Company. In early 1903 he introduced his car to the public. The Clarkmobile featured wheel steering, a long body slung low on a reachless running gear, and a bonnet-like box in front. "They Go and Go Right" was the company slogan, but by January 1905 it was Frank Clark who left, selling out his business to the New Way Motor Company. Precisely why he left the automobile field at that time is something of a mystery, because he ultimately returned to it. Having disposed of his automobile plant to New Way, he found himself in need of another and allied with Claude E. Furgason of Lansing who ran a machine shop in town. Together they established the Furgason Motor Company for the manufacture of the second-generation automobile designed by Frank Clark. This one would be called simply the Clark, and it had twice the cylinders and twice the horsepower of the Clarkmobile. With a 92-inch wheelbase, it was twenty inches longer than its predecessor; at $650, it was a hundred dollars cheaper. But like the Clarkmobile, the Clark was marketed for a little less than two years. By 1911 Frank Clark decided his future lay in the commercial vehicle field. His Clark Power Wagon Company moved into the Furgason Motor Company factory. Two years thereafter, in 1913, Frank Clark moved to Pontiac (Michigan) where he founded the Columbia Motor Truck and Trailer Company, an organization he headed until his retirement in 1929. He died in 1957, at age eighty-five.

1903-1904 CLARKMOBILE
Clarkmobile — 1-cyl., 7 hp, 72" wb

Rbt.-3P	750	2500	3500	5000	8500	18,000

1910-1911 CLARK
Clark — 2-cyl., 14 hp, 92" wb

Rbt.-3P	650	2700	3600	5300	8800	19,000

CLAROTTA — The Clarotta Manufacturing Company was the name of a new one-million-dollar corporation organized in Milwaukee, Wisconsin in March 1920. The principals involved were Walter A. Kuebler, Otto G. Pfeifer and Thomas C. Hanson. The manufacture of motors, motorvehicles, automotive equipment and machinery was their plan. Said *Automotive Industries:* "The project has not matured sufficiently to make possible a detailed explanation of its purposes at this time." Maturity was never reached.

1917 Classic, model 4-40, touring, WLB

CLASSIC — Chicago, Illinois — (1916-1917)/Lake Geneva, Wisconsin — (1920) — The name Classic was rather a misnomer for this low-priced four-cylinder car, though it did possess one factor of distinction: a slanting windshield introduced somewhat earlier than the rest of the industry. A Lycoming engine was used, and initial sales were modest but reassuring. Components shortages due to the First World War put an end to production of the first Classic, however. Following the war, the Classic Motor Car Company was reincorporated in Lake Geneva, with plans to produce a Classic Four and a Classic Six using Classic-built engines on a common wheelbase of 118 inches. The Lake Geneva *News* reported the Classic's coming to town in its December 16th, 1920 issue. The company was so quickly out of business this time, however, the production of the second Classic was minuscule at best.

1916-1917 CLASSIC
Model 4-40 — 4-cyl., 20 hp, 114" wb

	FP	5	4	3	2	1
Tour.-5P	885	—	—	—	—	—
Cloverleaf Rds.-3P	885	—	—	—	—	—

CLAWSEN — Lansing, Michigan — (1903) — A runabout powered by a horizontal opposed four-cylinder engine was the product of Smith Clawsen who operated a machine shop at 324 Washington Avenue in Lansing. No doubt, his tenure as a manufacturer, which he announced in the early spring of 1903, was short-lived, and his production small.

CLEAR & DUNHAM — According to some rosters, the partnership of Clear & Dunham produced an automobile in Cleveland, Ohio in 1900. This appears to be in error. Cleveland city directories for the turn of the century reveal that there was no one in town named Clear, and the only Dunhams were not likely to have had a mechanical bent.

CLEAVER — Fond du Lac, Wisconsin — (1903) — Early in 1903 F.C. Cleaver, formerly superintendent of motive power and cars for the Wisconsin Central Railroad, decided to enter the automotive industry. He formed the Cleaver Motor Vehicle Company of Fond du Lac and had his first car on the road around the Fourth of July. According to a news release dated July 6th, 1903, the company planned to manufacture two gasoline vehicles: a 12 hp four-passenger car weighing 1000 pounds and a truck with the engine under the front seat. Sources extant indicate these plans were probably never realized.

CLEBURNE — The company was called the Cleburne Auto Car Manufacturing Company, but the car it produced in Cleburne, Texas from 1911 to 1914 was the Luck Utility. Refer to Luck Utility.

CLEGGMOBILE — Memphis, Michigan — (1884-1886) — John Clegg was a mechanic who had been trained in his native England, and who operated a machine shop in Memphis, where he built a steam tractor in the early 1880's. His son Thomas nagged him continually thereafter to build an automobile next, and the father finally relented in 1884. During that winter they worked on, and in the spring of '85 completed, a steam car with a single-cylinder engine and seating capacity for driver, stoker and two pas-

sengers. The tubular boiler was carried in the rear; the fuel used was coal. Rear wheels were a gigantic five feet eight inches in diameter. Final drive was via leather belts which featured spring adjustments in order to provide enough play for the turning of corners. The Cleggmobile — or "The Thing," as the Cleggs called it — turned corners throughout the area. It was tested on nearby roads for more than 500 miles, in short trips of not more than fourteen miles each. A second car was built in 1886, three years before John Clegg's death in 1899. It was also the last Clegg car built. In 1975 the town of Memphis celebrated the 95th anniversary of the Cleggmobile, erecting a plaque to Thomas J. Clegg as the "inventor of the first self-propelled vehicle in Michigan." Although a $100 reward was offered by the local newspaper for anyone possessing a photograph of the Cleggmobile, no one in town, alas, could provide one.

CLEMENT — Hartford, Connecticut — (1903) — The Clement works in Hartford had been manufacturing gasoline engines since the turn of the century. In April of 1903 the firm's name was changed to A. Clement Cycle Motor & Light Carriage Company and the announcement was made that the Hartford factory would be enlarged for the manufacture of automobiles. Whether a prototype followed of the Clement automobile is not known; almost assuredly production never did begin. This never-was American marque is interesting, however, because the man behind it was the son of the celebrated French automotive pioneer, Adolphe Clement.

CLERMONT STEAMER — Although this designation appeared in a brochure, the steam car venture of George A. Coats during the early Twenties in Columbus, Ohio is more properly designated by his name. Refer to Coats Steam.

CLETRAC — The pilot models may have borne the same emblems as the famous tractor being built in the same plant, but the production car which resulted was called the Rollin. Rollin cars were built in Cleveland from 1923-1925. Refer to Rollin.

CLEVELAND — Cleveland and Hansen were the names used alternatively by the Hansen Automobile Company of Cleveland to designate the firm's car in 1902. Refer to Hansen.

The Cleveland Auto Company was indicated to be an automobile manufacturer in the Hiscox book *Horseless Vehicles, Automobiles, Motor Cycles* published in 1900. This appears to have been an error. The only automobile company in town with the Cleveland name at the turn of the century was the Cleveland Automobile, Storage and Repair Company, which was headed by the peripatetic Owen brothers. Refer to Owen.

The Cleveland Auto Cab Company of Geneva, Ohio produced a taxi from 1908-1911 which was marketed under the name of Ewing. Refer to Ewing.

The Cleveland Auto Sales & Manufacturing Company was organized in early 1911 with a capital stock of $25,000 to manufacture and deal in automobiles. The incorporators were Charles A. Aaron, J.A. Burke, Jr., Thomas P. Corey and William M. Byrnes. Manufacture is doubted.

The Cleveland, Beck and Lyman Motor Corporation was organized with a capital stock of $8600 during the spring of 1909 to "manufacture motors, motor boats and vehicles." C. Cleveland, A.L. Beck and H.B. Lyman were behind this venture. Manufacture is doubted.

The Cleveland Cycle and Auto Company was organized late in 1905 with a capital stock of $2500 by James MacNaughton and F. Louis DuBroy. Why they chose to call their venture that is a mystery, since the partners were in Buffalo, New York. A quick change of mind saw the venture renamed the MacNaughton & DuBroy Company. Refer to MacNaughton.

CLEVELAND — Cleveland, Ohio — (1901) — Thomas Shehan designed the prototypes of this Cleveland, and prototypes proved to be as far as this venture proceeded. F.D. Dorman, Charles Drabek, George W. Dunham, C.O. Ahn and John T. Morris were the men behind the Cleveland Motor Carriage Company which was incorporated during the summer of 1901. Steam, gasoline and electric vehicles were planned to be built in the company's factory at 66 Chestnut Street, but the firm's capital stock was a mere $10,000 which didn't take the company far. The venture was finished by year's end.

CLEVELAND — Cleveland, Ohio — (1902-1904) — Following the sale to American Bicycle Company of the Sperry Electric he had been producing for several years past, A.L. Moore, the president of the Cleveland Machine Screw Company, decided to build a gasoline car. In June of 1902 he established the Cleveland Automobile Company, and made himself president of that firm too. Also involved in this new venture were M.B. Johnson, H.H. Johnson, H.N. Ensworth and J.B. Russell. The pilot car was ready that summer, and production was begun that fall, with parts for 100 units ordered immediately. The Cleveland company would build its own engines, a single and two-cylinder initially, a four to follow for '04, and all cars would have chain drive and right-hand steering. A.L. Moore's Cleveland was on the market an even shorter time than his Sperry Electric.

1903 Cleveland, tonneau, WLB

1902-1903 CLEVELAND

	FP	5	4	3	2	1
Rds. (1-cyl., 72" wb)	750	2700	3600	5300	8800	19,000
Tour. (2-cyl., 15 hp, 78" wb)	1750	3000	4000	6000	9500	21,000

1904 CLEVELAND

Tour. (4-cyl., 20 hp, 97" wb)	2500	3100	4200	6300	10,500	22,000
Rbt. (1-cyl., 72" wb)	750	2700	3600	5300	8800	19,000
Tonneau (1-cyl., 72" wb)	850	2700	3600	5300	8800	19,000

1905 Cleveland, touring, WLB

CLEVELAND — Cleveland, Ohio — (1905-1909) — "The Car Without a Weak Spot" had one rather droll feature. By removing the hubcaps, the driving shafts of the rear axle could be slid out easily. This better-mouse-trap idea, however, did not result in a path being beaten to the door of the Cleveland Motor Car Company. That this Cleveland was a durable car, though, was demonstrated in 1906 when a Model D Runabout owned by a Mr. and Mrs. Walter Hale toured 3251 miles through Spain and France, and received a rave notice in the Paris edition of the *New York Herald*. The cars performed well in competition events in this country too. Louis Chevrolet heading the team which finished fifth in the Twenty-Four-Hour Race at Brighton Beach in 1908. The Cleveland was successor to the Meteor, a car produced for Worthington in New York by the Federal Manufacturing Company of Cleveland. Federal's sales manager, William L. Colt, resigned his position to organize the Cleveland Motor Car Company, which absorbed the Meteor venture in December 1904, though the Cleveland firm was not formally incorporated (with a capital stock of $100,000) until September 1906. Early Clevelands were small fours carrying a price tag of $2800. Subsequently, both horsepower and prices were raised, and the car without a weak spot had now acquired a bad one. It was too expensive for the market at which it was aimed. Company headquarters moved to New York City in 1907, but the announced plan to relocate the factory in Milwaukee never came to pass. Instead the company went under in Cleveland in 1909 after a production of approximately a thousand cars in four years. William L. Colt immediately took himself back to New York City where, later that year, he allied himself with Harry L. Stratton and became a very prosperous automobile dealer.

1905 CLEVELAND
4-cyl., 18 hp, 91" wb

Model C Rbt./Tour.	2800	2900	3700	5600	9100	20,000

1906 CLEVELAND
4-cyl., 20 hp, 91" wb

Model D Rbt.	2800	2900	3700	5600	9100	20,000

4-cyl., 30/35 hp, 104" wb

Model F Tour.	3500	3000	4000	6000	9500	21,000
Model F Dbl. Phae.	3500	3050	4100	6200	10,000	21,500

1906 Cleveland, model F, phaeton, WLB

1907 Cleveland, model H, limousine, HAC

1907 Cleveland, Speed Car, runabout, WLB

1907 CLEVELAND
4-cyl., 30/35 hp, 104" wb

	FP	5	4	3	2	1
Model F-H Speed Car	3750	3100	4200	6300	10,500	22,000
Model H Tour.	4000	3200	4300	6500	11,000	23,000
Model H Limo.	5000	2900	3700	5600	9100	20,000

1908 CLEVELAND
4-cyl., 40/45 hp, 122" wb

Tour.	3500	4000	5000	8000	15,000	28,000
Rbt.	3500	3700	4700	7300	13,700	26,000
Limo.	5000	3000	4000	6000	9500	21,000

1909 CLEVELAND
4-cyl., 40/45 hp

Tour. (122" wb)	3500	4000	5000	8000	15,000	28,000
Rbt. (112 1/2" wb)	3500	3700	4700	7300	13,700	26,000

CLEVELAND — Cleveland, Ohio — (1914) — The Cleveland Cyclecar Company was incorporated with a capital stock of $200,000 in March of 1914. Promoting the venture were W.E. Burnes (a veteran of the Garford and F.B. Stearns companies) and W.H. Hoyes (a Stearns graduate as well, and a former executive with the Royal Motor Car Company). The Cleveland's designer was Robert Clark, who reputedly had worked for Daimler and Humber in his native England before arriving on these shores to serve as machine-shop superintendent for Columbia in Hartford (Connecticut) and chief inspector at F.B. Stearns before resigning his position there to enter the cyclecar field. He probably should have stayed put. "The Aristocrat of Cyclecars" and "The Peer of Cyclecars," as the Cleveland was variously called, had a four-cylinder 16 hp water-cooled engine, friction transmission, final drive by vee belt, and a $395 price tag. And it was discontinued before the end of 1914.

1914 Cleveland Cyclecar, roadster, WLB

1914 CLEVELAND
Cyclecar — 4-cyl., 16 hp, 96" wb

	FP	5	4	3	2	1
Rds.-2P	395	—	—	—	—	—

1922 Cleveland, model 41, touring, HAC

CLEVELAND — Cleveland, Ohio — (1919-1926) — This Cleveland was really just a small Chandler that was given its own name and its own factory. It featured the Chandler's overhead valve six in a shorter-wheelbase chassis and with cheaper price tags. All this notwithstanding, there was a concerted effort on the part of Chandler to emphasize the independence of the Cleveland Automobile Company. Indeed, in 1923, when merger rumors appeared in the trade press, Chandler vice-president George M. Graham vigorously denied them, adding that he was unaware of the source of the stories but hoped "that the (Chandler) company was given a generous cut of the proceeds of such a transaction." Thereafter, Cleveland president Sid Black increased his company's issuance of press releases, none of which even mentioned the Chandler name. In December of 1924, veteran race driver Ralph Mulford climbed Mount Wilson in a stock Cleveland Six for a new speed record there, and in January 1925 Mulford drove another stock Cleveland Six on the Culver City (California) Speedway for a thousand miles without an engine stop and to another record. (His fourteen-hour elapsed time broke the old mark by more than two-and-a-half hours.) This was a final blaze of independent Cleveland glory. In December that year the Cleveland Automobile Company was succeeded by Chandler-Cleveland Corporation, and a lower-priced Chandler replaced the Clevelands. A readily identifiable feature of both Clevelands and Chandlers was the radiator-badge shape of the rear windows on all open models.

1919 Cleveland, model 40, 4-pass. coupe, WLB

1920 Cleveland, model 40, touring, HAC

1919-1920 CLEVELAND
Model 40 — 6-cyl., 45 hp, 112" wb

	FP	5	4	3	2	1
Tour.-5P	1385	3100	4200	6300	10,500	22,000
Rds.-2P	1385	3200	4300	6500	11,000	23,000
Cpe.-4P	2195	2700	3600	5300	8800	19,000
Sed.-5P	2195	2300	3300	4600	7500	16,000

1921 Cleveland, model 41, touring, HAC

1921 CLEVELAND
Model 41 — 6-cyl., 45 hp, 112" wb

	FP	5	4	3	2	1
Tour.-5P	1435	3100	4200	6300	10,500	22,000
Rds.-3P	1435	3200	4300	6500	11,000	23,000
Cpe.-4P	2345	2700	3600	5300	8800	19,000
Sed.-5P	2445	2300	3300	4600	7500	16,000

1922 Cleveland, model 41, roadster, WLB

1922 Cleveland, model 41, sedan, WLB

1922 CLEVELAND
Model 41 — 6-cyl., 45 hp, 112" wb

	FP	5	4	3	2	1
Sed.-5P	2195	2300	3300	4600	7500	16,000
Cpe.-4P	2295	2700	3600	5300	8800	19,000
Tour.-5P	1295	3100	4200	6300	10,500	22,000
Rds.-3P	1295	3200	4300	6500	11,000	23,000

1923 Cleveland, model 42, sport touring, WLB

1923 CLEVELAND
Model 42 — 6-cyl., 45 hp, 112 1/2" wb

	FP	5	4	3	2	1
Tour.	995	3300	4400	6700	12,000	24,000
Rds.	1085	3500	4500	7000	13,000	25,000
Spt.	1260	3700	4700	7300	13,700	26,000
Two-Door Sed.	1295	2200	3200	4400	7000	15,000
Spc. Two-Door Sed.	1395	2300	3300	4600	7500	16,000
Four-Door Sed.	1485	2300	3300	4600	7500	16,000
Spc. Four-Door Sed.	1685	2400	3400	4800	8000	17,000

1924 Cleveland, model 42, touring deluxe, HAC

1924 CLEVELAND
Model 42 — 6-cyl., 45 hp, 112 1/2" wb

	FP	5	4	3	2	1
Tour.-5P	1045	3300	4400	6700	12,000	24,000
Rds.-3P	1085	3500	4500	7000	13,000	25,000
DeL. Tour.-5P	1145	3700	4700	7300	13,700	26,000
Cpe.-3P	1245	2900	3700	5600	9100	20,000
Spt. Tour.-5P	1295	3900	4800	7700	14,300	27,000
Spc. Cpe.-3P	1345	3000	4000	6000	9500	21,000
Two-Door Sed.-5P	1365	2300	3300	4600	7500	16,000
Spc. Two-Door Sed.-5P	1445	2400	3400	4800	8000	17,000
Four-Door Sed.-5P	1545	2400	3400	4800	8000	17,000
Spc. Four-Door Sed.-5P	1645	2500	3500	5000	8500	18,000

1925 Cleveland, model 42, sport model, HAC

1925 CLEVELAND
Model 42 — 6-cyl., 45 hp, 115" wb

	FP	5	4	3	2	1
Tour.-5P	1095	3300	4400	6700	12,000	24,000
Tour. DeL.-5P	1195	3500	4500	7000	13,000	25,000
Cpe.-3P	1295	2700	3600	5300	8800	19,000
Spc. Cpe.-3P	1395	2900	3700	5600	9100	20,000
Four-Door Sed.-5P	1495	2300	3300	4600	7500	16,000
Sed. DeL.-5P	1695	2400	3400	4800	8000	17,000
Brgm.-5P	1545	2500	3500	5000	8500	18,000
Spt. Tour.-5P	1295	3900	4800	7700	14,300	27,000

1926 Cleveland, model 43, special sedan, HAC

1926 CLEVELAND
Model 31 — 6-cyl., 45 hp, 108 1/2" wb

	FP	5	4	3	2	1
Tour.-5P	895	3500	4500	7000	13,000	25,000
Tour. DeL.-5P	1025	3700	4700	7300	13,700	26,000
Cpe.-3P	1035	2700	3600	5300	8800	19,000
Sed.-5P	1090	2300	3300	4600	7500	16,000

Model 43 — 6-cyl., 60 hp, 115" wb

	FP	5	4	3	2	1
Tour.-5P	1095	3900	4800	7700	14,300	27,000
Spt. Tour.-5P	1245	4300	5400	8700	16,500	30,000
Cpe.-4P	1225	2900	3700	5600	9100	20,000
C'ch.-5P	1295	2500	3500	5000	8500	18,000
Four-Door Sed.-5P	1395	2700	3600	5300	8800	19,000
DeL. Sed.-5P	1595	2900	3700	5600	9100	20,000
Spt. Sed.-5P	1625	3000	4000	6000	9500	21,000

CLEVELAND ELECTRIC — The Cleveland Electric Company was indicated as an automobile manufacturer in the Hiscox book *Horseless Vehicles, Automobiles, Motor Cycles* published in 1900. This venture probably had remained ever a hopeful. Turn of the century Cleveland city directories do not include such a company.

Although the first electric cars produced by the Cleveland Machine Screw Company were designated by the title Cleveland, Sperry System, the later cars were called simply Sperry. These turn of the century electrics had been designed by Elmer A. Sperry. Refer to Sperry.

CLEVELAND ELECTRIC — Cleveland, Ohio — (1909-1910) — This electric from Cleveland had a schizophrenic existence. Initially, it was planned as the product of the Cuyahoga Motor Car Company which operated a dealership and garage on Euclid Avenue. Announcement of the forthcoming manufacture of the Cuyahoga Electric was made in October 1908, but only a prototype followed, and it was called the Cleveland Electric. In May of 1909 the firm was reorganized into the Cleveland Electric Vehicle Company, but the intention now was for manufacture of taxicabs. Minds were changed once again by year's end, however, and the Cleveland Electric finally emerged in 1910 as a production car designed by Raymond B. Doty and available on a 100-inch wheelbase as a $2250 runabout, $2500 victoria and $2800 coupe. The final change of mind came in 1911 when the Cleveland Electric Vehicle Company decided to forget the automobile manufacturing field altogether and get into the battery-producing business instead. Apparently it had been the bipolar battery invented by J.L. and M.O. Smith which had been the impetus behind the entire venture from the beginning.

CLEVELAND THREE-WHEELER — Cleveland, Ohio — (1900-1901) — This motor tricycle was introduced by Harry A. Lozier at the annual bicycle show at New York City's Madison Square Garden in January 1900. Lozier at the time manufactured the Cleveland bicycle in Ohio, and he planned to add this vehicle to his line. His plans quickly changed, however, and he sold out his Ohio interests to the American Bicycle Company, retiring to Plattsburgh (New York) where his engineers would design the famous Lozier automobile. The American Bicycle Company meantime proceeded into manufacture of the Lozier-company-designed Cleveland Three-Wheeler. Its price was $350. Purportedly, a hundred of the trikes were built by A.B.C., and marketed through that company's extensive bicycle branches on the East Coast.

CLIMAX — New Salem, Massachusetts — (1906-1911) — Humble origins are part of the lore of automobile history. The Climax Electric Works of New Salem exemplifies this nicely. Its business was begun in a henhouse in 1906. The henhouse belonged to Levi W. Flagg, who allied himself that year with William E. Taft (erstwhile promoter of a steamer bearing his name), and together they decided to build an inexpensive electric car. Finding it too expensive, they immediately switched to gasoline. The Climax which followed was powered by a two-cylinder 18 hp engine set in a 90-inch wheelbase and offered as a runabout for $500, or in kit form for $290. A friction transmission was featured, as well as a center-mounted steering wheel so the car could be either left- or right-hand drive. Precisely when the first Climax was sold is not known, but about 1908 the venture had proven successful enough for Climax Electric Works to move out of the henhouse on the Flagg homestead and into a cement block building on Main Street in town. Shortly thereafter Taft left the enterprise; Flagg con-

1908 Climax, roadster, WLB

tinued building Climax cars until forestalled by bankruptcy in late 1911. The business had been augmented early on with the manufacture of air-cooled gasoline engines for the trade, which a 1907 advertisement indicated were in use in "thirty-nine states of the Union and two provinces of Canada, giving universal satisfaction." At some point the name of the firm changed to T & F Cycle Car Company although no complete vehicles were marketed under that name. T & F supplied components for the building of automobiles (a friction transmission with Hyatt roller bearings and aluminum disc for $21.00, with plain bronze bearings and cast iron disc for $14.00) and advertised itself as the first in the United States to build parts expressly for cyclecars. This side of the business continued beyond Climax car manufacturing, since T & F supplied components for the Westfield light car of 1915. Among Levi W. Flagg's other ventures was the construction of a telephone system in the area and extensive work with the Tri-County Electric Company to secure electric power for outlying farms and homes. Levi W. Flagg died in New Salem in 1939. The building in which his Climax was assembled remains standing and is today part of the campus of New Salem Academy. It is listed on the National Register of Historic Places, as part of the New Salem Common Historic District.

5-PASS. TOURING CAR $2750

1921 Climber, touring, HAC

CLIMBER — Little Rock, Arkansas — (1919-1924) — Early in 1919 three men of Little Rock — William Drake, Clarence Roth and David Hopson — organized the Climber Motor Corporation and purchased a 20 1/2-acre site on the east side of town. There was built a one-story plant measuring 100 by 300 feet for the production of an assembled car (Herschell-Spillman four or six) designed by chief engineer George Schoeneck, who had been imported from Detroit. Production began later that year, and by December the marque was represented by no fewer than ten dealerships, most of them in Arkansas. The problems arrived early. First, there was internal dissension; Drake and Hopson left the company in October of 1919. Second, ordered parts were slow to be delivered. Though 3000 cars had been optimistically planned for the first year, George Schoeneck found he could not complete even fifty. To maintain any production schedule, he tried to devise and "manufacture" his own parts — which did not work well. There was a chronic shortage of funds. Climber was broke by mid-1923. In June 1924 the company was sold at the receiver's sale to a Dr. R.L. Saxon and John W. Dickerson who resumed manufacture as the New Climber Company, which was something of a misnomer because all they were doing was assembling cars from material already on hand. When that project was finished, so was the Climber. An estimated total of 100 Climber Fours and 100 Climber Sixes had been built. The last news from the company was in mid-December 1924, to the effect that stockholders would receive 88.4% on their claims, which was considerably better than the percentage enjoyed by stockholders of other automobile companies so quickly defunct.

1919-1922 CLIMBER
Model K — 4-cyl., 35 hp, 116" wb

	FP	5	4	3	2	1
Tour.-5P	1385	4000	5000	8000	15,000	28,000
Rds.-2P	1495	4300	5400	8700	16,500	30,000
Sed.-5P	2400	2700	3600	5300	8800	19,000

Model S — 6-cyl., 57 hp, 126" wb

	FP	5	4	3	2	1
Tour.-5P	2250	4300	5400	8700	16,500	30,000
Rds.-2P	2250	4500	5800	9500	18,000	32,000
Sed.-5P	3250	2900	3700	5600	9100	20,000

Factory prices quoted are for the 1919 model year. Prices increased yearly thereafter.

1920 Climber, touring, FR

1922 Climber, Simplex Six, touring, WLB

1923 Climber, roadster, JAC

1923 Climber, phaeton, NAHC

1923-1924 CLIMBER
Six — 72 hp, 125 1/2" wb

	FP	5	4	3	2	1
Tour.-5P	2250	4300	5400	8700	16,500	30,000
Rds.-2P	2250	4500	5800	9500	18,000	32,000
Tr.-7P	2385	4200	5200	8400	15,700	29,000
Cpe.-3P	2490	2700	3600	5300	8800	19,000
Sed.-5P	2750	2300	3300	4600	7500	16,000

CLINTON — The Clinton Automobile Company was organized in Hoboken, New Jersey with a capital stock of $10,000 during the fall of 1912 to manufacture and deal in automobiles. B.F. Krom and W.A. Schuette were the partners behind this venture, which was headquartered at 132 Third Street in Union Hill. Manufacture is doubted.

The Clinton Machine & Dusting Works of Clinton, Massachusetts has been indicated on various car rosters as manufacturing a car in 1902. The listing was apparently the result of the company's classified advertisement in the December issue of *Cycle and Automobile Trade Journal* that year. The ad read: "Steam Automobile, Fair Condition, First check of $75 gets it." Perhaps Clinton had built the car, perhaps not. One thing is certain, if the car was any good at all, it was a steal at the price.

Walter R. Clinton operated a machine and engine-building shop at 36 Elm Street in West Haven, Connecticut. In the 1907-1908 West Haven city directory he also included himself under automobile manufacturers. Further documentation is lacking.

1901 Clinton E. Woods, NAHC

CLINTON E. WOODS — Chicago, Illinois — (1897-1901) — Clinton E. Woods was the son of a carriage manufacturer and one of the most enthusiastic early proponents of electric cars in America. His tragic flaw was an inability to latch onto — or get along with — suitable backers. Following a sojourn with the American Electric Vehicle Company in 1896 in Chicago, he designed his own car which was promoted by the Aluminum Motor Vehicle Company the year following, and went nowhere. In 1898 the Fisher Equipment Company of Chicago backed him in the production of what *The Horseless Age* referred to as "fine artistic carriages," mostly in the hansom cab configuration, but output was modest, sixty cars at most. In 1899 Clinton E. Woods believed he had it made when prominent Chicago and New York capitalists organized the Woods Motor Vehicle Company in the former city, bought Clinton Woods' patents and installed him as superintendent of a vast new factory for production of his cars. Manufacture began, but Woods was soon eased out of the company. By early 1901 he was in business again for himself, building a variety of electrics which *The Automobile* said were distinguished by their departure from horse vehicle forms. "I build automobiles," Clinton E. Woods said, "not horseless carriages." But, alas, he did not do so for long. The Woods-Waring Company of 21 Van Buren Street in Chicago failed by the end of 1901. In early 1902, Clinton E. Woods was in Erie, Pennsylvania where he became an automobile tire salesman for the Penn Rubber Company; in 1903 he was manager of an automobile dealership on East 57th Street in New York City. His further activities are not known. Meanwhile, back in Chicago, the Woods Motor Vehicle Company, which had been organized under his patents, was reorganized and went on to become one of America's longest-lived electric car manufacturers.

1898-1899 CLINTON E. WOODS

	FP	5	4	3	2	1
Hansom Cab	—	—	—	—	—	—
Road Buggy	—	—	—	—	—	—

1901 CLINTON E. WOODS

	FP	5	4	3	2	1
Light Stanhope	850	2500	3500	5000	8500	18,000
Brgm. Cab	2250	2700	3600	5300	8800	19,000
Dly.	3100	2700	3600	5300	8800	19,000
Vict. Stanhope	1850	2900	3700	5600	9100	20,000

CLIPPER — Grand Rapids, Michigan — (1902) — The Clipper was a continuation of the Michigan, the steam car designed by Byron J. Carter and produced by the Michigan Automobile Company in 1901. Elmer Pratt took over the Michigan business in 1902, which he renamed the Clipper Autocar Company. According to Pratt, the plan was to occupy the old Clipper bicycle plant in Grand Rapids and to build "Clipper automobiles of Clipper quality by Clipper mechanics, and advertised and sold by Clipper salesmen." The company was capitalized at $400,000. Apparently, Pratt's ambition ran away with him, because his Clipper venture never got off the ground. Only a few of the former Michigan steam cars were marketed under the Clipper name. Meanwhile, Byron Carter had returned to his native Jackson, Michigan to build the Jaxon steamer car and the Jackson gasoline car. Later he was responsible for the famous friction-drive Cartercar.

CLOSE — Olean, New York — (1902-1907) — The Close brothers of Olean — Fred and Frank — operated a bicycle manufactory in Olean called the Close Cycle Company. Frank Close was the mechanic of the duo, and in 1902 he built his first automobile. In 1904 the firm was renamed the Close Cycle and Automobile Company, but the year following its name changed to Olean Garage Company, and it was in the field of automobile repair that the brothers decided to concentrate. Total production of Close automobiles is not known, but according to a special industrial edition of the *Olean Evening Herald* published in 1908, five cars had been built to special order in the two years previous. The brothers also served as the local agent for the Cartercar. "The garage is open at all hours of the day or night," the newspaper reported. Apparently, it was one of the best known and most popular in town.

1869 Clough, runabout, WLB

CLOUGH — Lakeport, New Hampshire — (1869) — In 1869, in his native Springfield, Enos Merrill Clough built a steam carriage, the first in the state of New Hampshire, and one of the earliest in New England. It was a surprisingly attractive-looking vehicle, with two small engines placed on each side of a boiler in the rear. Wood was used as fuel. The steamer cost Clough $1300 to build. It had a three-speed-forward, three-speed-backward transmission, a wheel for steering, and a purported 3463 parts, which must have been an exaggeration. Enos Clough introduced his vehicle to the public at the Fourth of July celebration in Newport in 1869 — and was promptly ordered off the scene for disturbing the equine population of the town. Soon thereafter Clough moved to Lakeport to work in the Boston & Maine Railway roundhouse, and his vehicle was more favorably received there. It was driven through town at speeds of up to 10 mph. Ultimately, Clough sold the car to a jeweler in Laconia named Richard Gove. The purchase price was a magnificent gold watch and chain. Soon after its new owner took possession of the car, he smashed it. The vehicle was repaired, and upon Gove's death in 1883 was sold for $50 at auction. The new owner, A.S. Gordon, dismantled the vehicle, storing the carriage and the engine/drivetrain in separate places; the former was later burned in a fire, the latter survives to this day. Enos Clough had nicknamed his vehicle "The Faerie Queen," after the Edmund Spenser epic poem. On August 2nd, 1916, The Faerie Queen's inventor died, killed by an automobile while returning home from his job as a flagman at the Black Brook railroad crossing in Laconia.

1903 Cloughley, surrey, NAHC

CLOUGHLEY — Cherryvale & Parsons, Kansas — (1896-1903) — Robert H. Cloughley took out his first patents on automotive vehicles in 1891, and tested his first steamer near Cherryvale in 1896. This was doubtless the first steam car built west of the Mississippi. That Cloughley worked on the railroad was evident in its design; there was a stovepipe-like stack on the back of the car to get rid of the smoke. Cloughley used the car as a taxi and offered to take passengers anywhere in town for a quarter. He found few takers, however, since the boiler was under the rear seat, which made for a rather toasty ride on a warm day. He continued tinkering and improved the design. In April 1901 he organized the Cloughley Automobile Manufacturing Company. The first car produced was sold to the owner of the Tannehill Manufacturing Company who said he would buy if the car could climb Serber Hill just west of Cherryvale. The car climbed the hill, but the company went nowhere. Cloughley reorganized as the Cloughley Motor Vehicle Company in Parsons early in 1903. All Cloughleys were in the surrey body style, and by 1903 these included gasoline cars as well. Among the distinctive features of the production Cloughley chassis were: a ball-bearing compensating gear; solid axles with hollow axles turning on the outside; spring blocks forming a case for driving boxes on roller bearings. But like many ventures with a perpetual tinkerer at their head, the second Cloughley company was no better organized than the first, and failed just as quickly.

	FP	5	4	3	2	1
1896-1901 CLOUGHLEY						
Steam Surrey Taxicab						
1902 CLOUGHLEY						
Steam Surrey (2-cyl., 8 hp)	1200	3100	4200	6300	10,500	22,000
1903 CLOUGHLEy						
Steam Surrey (2-cyl., 8 hp)	1200	3100	4200	6300	10,500	22,000
Gasoline Surrey (2-cyl., 9 hp)	1500	3000	4000	6000	9500	21,000
Gasoline Surrey (2-cyl., 12 hp)	1500	3100	4200	6300	10,500	22,000

CLOVER — H.K. Clover of Salt Lake City announced his invention of a steam car early in 1901. Subsequently he promoted it as the Royalmobile. Refer to Royalmobile.

1911 Cloyd, touring, RLB

CLOYD — Nashville, Tennessee — (1911) — Percival C. Cloyd ran an auto repair shop at 1110 Third Avenue South in Nashville, and in 1911 decided if he could repair cars, he could also build them. Restyling his business the Cloyd Auto Company, he offered a touring car (123-inch wheelbase), runabout and roadster (110-inch wheelbase) powered by a four-cylinder 40 hp gasoline engine with three-speed transmission by selective sliding gear. His price for the Cloyd "40" was $1400 f.o.b. Nashville. His production was modest.

1911 Club Car, 7-pass. touring, WLB

CLUB CAR — New York, New York — (1910-1911) — The Club Car Company of America was an interesting, and almost whimsically unique, idea. One had to join the club to buy one of its cars. "The origin of this selling method is due to a party of New York Bank officials, who realizing the relatively small portion of the actual investment in the car itself which the final buyer receives, owing to the agent's commissions, advertising, racing, etc., decided to combine and build a limited number of cars for themselves and others entering a club," explained *Cycle and Automobile Trade Journal*. No more than five shares in the company were allowed any single individual, and only one share of preferred stock was necessary for membership and to secure the benefit of the company. The one share served as the lifetime initiation fee, and the benefit was the purchase of one car

annually by company members. Club Cars were built by Merchant & Evans of Philadelphia, with engines supplied by American & British Manufacturing of Bridgeport, Connecticut, and coachwork from Biddle & Smart of Amesbury, Massachusetts. This was an interesting albeit somewhat snobbish new idea in automobile manufacture. Unfortunately, after a single year, the lifetime membership in the Club Car Company of America bought nothing. Merchant & Evans sold off the cars remaining in stock as Devons.

1910-1911 CLUB CAR
Club Car — 4-cyl., 40 hp, 125" wb

	FP	5	4	3	2	1
Model A-A Tour.	3000	4500	5800	9500	18,000	32,000
Model B-B Torpedo	2900	4700	6100	9900	19,000	33,000
Model B-C Rbt.	2800	4400	5600	9200	17,300	31,000
Model A-D Land'et.	3750	4000	5000	8000	15,000	28,000
Model A-E Limo.	3750	3900	4800	7700	14,300	27,000

CLUTS — Illinois — (1903) — There were two Cluts vehicles built in Illinois in 1903, and possibly one of them never did run. It was built by Dr. A.C. Cluts, who was a coroner and who put together a two-cylinder 12 hp gasoline machine, though he lamented in March of 1903 that "I have been at it for three days, but have so far been unable to get more than two explosions at a time." The other was built by Oliver Cluts, whose relationship to the coroner is not known, and it was an experimental vehicle assembled to test the automobile hub that Cluts had patented. During the fall of 1903 this Cluts organized the Cluts Manufacturing Company with a capital stock of $25,000, a venture which seems to have gone nowhere. References differ as to whether the Illinois city in which the Cluts was sited was Cuba or Canton.

CLYDE SPECIAL — Whether Clyde Special was simply a typographical error, or whether the Pacific Motor and Automobile Company really meant to call its car that in 1908, is not known, but this California car from Redondo was never marketed as other than the Coyote Special. Refer to Coyote Special.

1908 Clymer, roadster, GR

CLYMER — St. Louis, Missouri — (1908) — The Clymer was a 12 hp highwheeler with solid rubber tires and a claimed top speed of 30 mph. It was available in four body styles at prices ranging upwards from $675 and was produced by the Durable Motor Car Company of St. Louis. "Guaranteed For One Year," advertising headlines ballyhooed. "That means something. Most manufacturers will not guarantee for any specified time." Amusingly, the time specified for the Clymer was longer than the company was in business.

1909 Coates-Goshen, roadster, NAHC

COATES-GOSHEN — Goshen, New York — (1909-1910) — In his youth Joseph Saunders Coates had been an enthusiast of harness racing, and in 1884 he bought Historic Track in Goshen, the birthplace of sulky racing. Thereafter, as the proprietor of the Miller Cart Company, he manufactured high quality sulkies — and it was in his sulky factory that he built his first experimental four-cylinder car in 1905. Three years later he came up with the financing necessary to go into manufacture. The Coates-Goshen was one of the classiest new automotive entries at the 1909 Automobile Show in New York City's Crystal Palace. Among its progressive features was the lowering of its pressed steel frame between the dash and the rear seat, anticipating the modern dropped frame by decades. Among Coates-Goshen owners were opera star Fritzi Scheff and actor Monty Woolley. A total of thirty-two cars had been built when the Coates-Goshen Automobile Company plant burned to the ground in a dreadful fire which also destroyed a church, a lumberyard, an eight-story tenement and many private homes in Goshen. Joseph Coates could not continue. His automobile company declared bankruptcy in October 1911. In 1912 Coates tried something else, a two-cylinder $450 three-wheeler commercial van, which he marketed as the Coates Tricar, but this venture lasted only two years. The remainder of his career Joseph Coates devoted predominantly to the design of horse racing tracks, an activity in which he persisted into his late eighties.

1909 COATES-GOSHEN
Model 25 — 4-cyl., 25 hp, 112" wb

	FP	5	4	3	2	1
Twn. Car-6P	3250	2000	3000	4200	6500	14,000
Rbt.-4P	2450	2700	3600	5300	8800	19,000
Baby Tonneau-4P	2600	2700	3600	5300	8800	19,000

Model 32 — 4-cyl., 32 hp, 116" wb

Rbt.-4P	2850	2700	3600	5300	8800	19,000
Baby Tonneau-4P	3000	2700	3600	5300	8800	19,000
Tour.-5P	3000	2500	3500	5000	8500	18,000

1910 COATES-GOSHEN
Thirty-Two — 4-cyl., 32 hp, 116" wb

Baby Tonneau-4P	2925	2900	3700	5600	9100	20,000
Tour.-5P	3000	2900	3700	5600	9100	20,000

Forty-Five — 4-cyl., 45 hp, 123" wb

Rbt.-4P	3250	3100	4200	6300	10,500	22,000
Tour.-5P	3500	3000	4000	6000	9500	21,000
Tour.-7P	3500	2900	3700	5600	9100	20,000

Sixty — 4-cyl., 60 hp, 140" wb

Tour.-7P	4200	4200	5200	8400	15,700	29,000

COATS — Chicago, Illinois — (1914) — The first Coats in America was a cyclecar built by Paul Coats of Chicago. Manufacture was intended, but never realized. The prototype was completed, however, and was under test by January of 1914, according to *The American Cyclecar*.

1921 Coats Steamer, touring, WLB

1922 Coats Steamer, touring, WLB

COATS STEAM — Columbus, Ohio — (1921-1923) — George A. Coats was a former automobile distributor who made a small fortune when he acquired some coal mines in Indiana and who decided to sink part of his windfall into a steam car venture. An unnamed Norwegian engineer whom he had met abroad prior to the outset of the First World War was the designer of the Coats, which was said at the time to be the most progressive new steam car introduced in this country. It was powered by a three-cylinder single-expansion engine, with water tube boiler. No flywheel was fitted; the two-speed gearshift was floor-mounted (unusual for a steamer), and another floor pedal, when depressed, allowed steam to

enter the cylinders for the full length of the stroke. The Coats was initially announced in March 1921, but it was not until September that a company — Coats Steamers, Inc. — was organized in Columbus for its manufacture. The initial selling price of $1000 was revised to "a shade under $1100" in October in "order to add little refinements that will give the car a greater sales value." The final announced price was $1085 which was to buy a touring, roadster and sedan, all on a common 115-inch wheelbase. George Coats revealed that pilot models of the car were at that time being assembled at the leased plant in Indianapolis "to try out dies and the like." By the spring of 1922 the Coats Steam Car Company (as the venture was now renamed) seemed to have found a permanent home in Bowling Green, Ohio when George Coats contracted with the (Y.F.) Stewart Motor Car Company for manufacture. A partnership resulted, and the car thereafter was occasionally referred to as the Stewart-Coats, this most likely by the Stewart people, George Coats preferring only his own name. Curiously, the name Clermont Steamer was also used in one sales brochure. But whatever it was called, where was it? By November 1922 a trade press headline read "Coats Steamer Promised Soon." It finally did officially arrive on the market early in 1923 but by then the money was gone. The number of pilot models produced in Indianapolis is not known; a single prototype is documented to have been built in Bowling Green. Mortgage foreclosure proceedings began in Columbus in late July 1923, and it was all over soon. Interestingly, the advance payments of about $20,000 which had been made by prospective Coats dealers were said to have been recovered "in a rather large amount," which was most unusual in those days.

CO-AUTO — The Co-Auto Motor Company was organized in Indianapolis, Indiana early in 1910 with a capital stock of $25,000 to manufacture and deal in automobiles. Incorporators were M.G. Beckner, J. Harrison and F.W. Wiese. Manufacture is doubted.

COBB — The Cobb Motor Car Company was organized in White Plains, New York early in 1910 with a capital stock of $5000 to manufacture and deal in automobiles and accessories. Incorporators were Frederick W. Cobb, J.O. Hobby, Jr. and Arthur I. Strang. Manufacture is doubted.

COBE — The Cobe Automobile Company was organized in New York City during the summer of 1906 with a capital stock of $5000 to manufacture automobiles. Incorporators were A.J. Cobe, H.H. Cobe and H. Kosch. Manufacture is doubted.

COBURN — That there was to be a Coburn from Norfolk, Virginia in 1911 was reported, but whether it arrived even as a prototype has not been documented. Certainly manufacture did not follow. Formal dissolution of the Coburn Bunting Motor Corporation arrived December 31st, 1920 according to the *Marvyn Scudder Manual of Extinct or Obsolete Companies*.

CODY — Cody Motors Company was organized with a capital stock of $100,000 in early 1911 for the manufacture of automobiles in New York City. Arthur McMullen, Jr., R.L. Kelly and John C. Mullin were the incorporators. Manufacture is doubted.

COE — Lima, Ohio — (1883) — In 1883, in his native Lima, Ohio, Adelbert Brown Coe built a steam automobile powered by a three-cylinder engine and capable of 12 mph. Apparently he didn't mind at the time that the vehicle didn't attract much attention. Forty years later, however, he did. Now nearing retirement age and employed in the automotive department of the Williams Manufacturing Company in Macon, Georgia, Coe secured documentation in 1922 from several Lima businessmen who recalled seeing his automobile successfully tested in the fall of 1883. His claim, however, that it was "the first automobile that was ever built" was patently false.

COEY — Chicago, Illinois — (1901-1902, 1913-1917) — Charles A. Coey was something of a character. In 1901, from his company headquarters at 177 LaSalle Street in Chicago, he announced that he was building several styles of motor vehicles "From the ground up." C.A. Coey & Company would offer both electric and gasoline cars. The electric motors he bought, the gasoline engine was Coey's own — a two-stroke one-lunger complete with water jacket that weighed 225 pounds and developed five horsepower. Said C.A.: "Any person of ordinary intelligence and ability to handle tools can take it apart and put it together again." This seemed to imply that something might go wrong with the engine; still, Coey guaranteed the unit for five years "against imperfect workmanship and poor material." In 1902 Coey had yet another idea. Moving into a building at 5311-13 Cottage Grove Avenue, he proclaimed it the first "automobile livery and repository" in the United States. Reposing there were ten Coey electrics which were for rent "the same as a person would rent a horse and buggy." Coey would also teach people to drive for a fee of ten dollars, a hefty

1901 Coey, electric runabout, RD

1913 Coey Flyer, 5-pass. touring, WLB

sum in those days, though apparently he enjoyed some success because he grandly incorporated the C.A. Coey School of Motoring. Subsequently he became the Chicago agent for the Thomas Flyer, which was a prosperous venture though Coey seems to have spent a good deal of time being sued or being duped. "Chicago dealer Victimized by Peculiar Systems of Bookkeeping," one trade press headline read, "His Forgiving Spirit Imposed Upon." When finally Coey decided to become an automobile manufacturer in 1913, it was with a bunch of ideas for gasoline cars, the boast that "the faults of others have been our engineers," and a claim "to beat the world." The world-beater that the Coey Motor Company (initially organized as Coey-Mitchell) produced was sold direct to the customer, eliminating the middleman's profit and enabling the company "to put $350 more cash value in the Coey Flyer than we could otherwise do" — and it was sold with a ten-year guarantee "under ordinary care . . . estimating a mileage of 5000 miles to a year." The Flyer was offered as both a four and a six. A smaller four, the Model A, was raced by Coey himself in Detroit and in various East Coast events, winning an impressive number of contests, though not so many to justify Coey's claim for it as "The Worlds' (sic) Champion Light Car." In 1914 he introduced the Coey Bear and the Coey Junior, both cyclecars which, like most vehicles of that genre, survived just one winter. The Junior was soon upgraded and renamed the C-A-C. Coey drove a Bear to second place in the International Cyclecar Race in Detroit in July 1914, and subsequently it was beefed up to Coey Flyer specifications. In 1916 Coey's company was absorbed by Wonder Motor Truck which produced a smaller flyer for a while into 1917.

1914 Coey Junior, roadster, WLB

334

1913 COEY
Model A — 4-cyl., 18 hp, 96" wb

	FP	5	4	3	2	1
Rdstr.	425	5400	7300	11,800	25,000	38,000

Coey Flyer — 4-cyl., 24 hp, 104" wb

Tour.	650	7000	10,800	16,900	37,100	49,000

Coey Flyer — 6-cyl., 60 hp, 128" wb

Tour.	2000	7800	13,000	20,000	43,500	58,000

1914 Coey Flyer, HAC

1915 Coey Bear, roadster, HAC

1914-1915 COEY
Coey Bear — 4-cyl., 12 hp, 96" wb

	FP	5	4	3	2	1
Rdstr.	425	5400	7300	11,800	25,000	38,000

Coey Junior — 2-cyl., 9 hp, 96" wb

Rdstr.	425	5300	7000	11,500	24,000	37,000
Cpe.	650	5200	6800	11,300	23,000	36,000

Coey Flyer — 6-cyl., 48 hp, 128" wb

Tour.	995	7800	13,000	20,000	43,500	58,000

Coey Flyer — 4-cyl., 24 hp, 104" wb

Tour.	650	7000	10,800	16,900	37,100	49,000

1916 Coey Flyer, roadster, HAC

1916-1917 COEY
Coey Flyer — 4-cyl., 16 hp, 96" wb

	FP	5	4	3	2	1
Tour.	650	5400	7300	11,800	25,000	38,000
Rdstr.	425	5500	7500	12,000	26,000	39,000

COFFEE — Richmond, Virginia — (1902) — R.W. Coffee & Sons, Inc. of 908 East Cary Street in Richmond was a well established general machinery manufacturing firm which added stationary and marine gasoline engines to its product line before the turn of the century and contemplated automobile manufacture shortly thereafter. A prototype single-cylinder twelve-horsepower touring car was completed late in 1902. Its engine was called a "Binate," and was described thusly: "Two pistons, with the rod of one placed inside the other, travel in opposite directions. The charge is introduced between the two piston heads, and is compressed as they are brought together. The explosion forces them apart, causing the crank of one to pull on the shaft while the other pushes it in the opposite direction, thus neutralizing the shock and causing the car to run with a very noticeable smoothness." That it might have succeeded in doing just that was indicated by a journalist from *The Motor World* who

1902 Coffee, Binate, touring, surrey, NAHC

traveled to Virginia to check out the car and reported enthusiastically on the demonstration that was given him: "a smooth running car, simple in its control and operation, and with ample power for any contingencies that might arise." The reporter seemed somehow more impressed with R.W. Coffee than his machine, however: "His flowing white beard gives him a patriarchial appearance, and his unhurried speech, which to the initiated stamps him unmistakably as a Southerner, has a 'before-the-war' flavor that is as attractive as it is unusual in this busy city." Richmond was not to see production of the Coffee for long, however. By 1903 R.W. Coffee & Sons had returned exclusively to its previous manufacturing endeavors.

1901 Coffin Steamer, runabout, WLB

COFFIN STEAMER — Ann Arbor, Michigan — (1901) — While he was an engineering student at the University of Michigan, Howard E. Coffin built a steam car the working parts of which were said to be a "model of economy." The car was completed in 1901. In 1902 there was a brief press mention from West Bay city that a $30,000 stock company was in the process of formation for the manufacture of a new Coffin car. This did not ensue, however, and young Coffin went back to his engineering studies. Subsequently he did enter the automobile industry, and fortunately with no plans to name a car for himself. Instead, Coffin became most famous as the chief engineer of a new company whose product was called a Hudson. The Coffin Steamer remains extant, and is in the collection of the Henry Ford Museum.

COFFMAN & CHERRY — "Coffman & Cherry, Lincoln, Illinois are planning to organize a company for the manufacture of a new automobile recently, designed by them," reported *The Horseless Age* in March of 1906. Further details regarding this short-lived venture are lacking.

COGGSWELL — Grand Rapids, Michigan — (1910-1911) — Seldom has local pride been more fulsomely extolled. "A Grand Rapids car, designed by a Grand Rapids man, assembled by Grand Rapids workmen and carrying a Grand Rapids name will be manufactured by a company composed exclusively of Grand Rapids men," the announcement read. One H. Coggswell was the designer of the car, and the Coggswell Motor Car Company was formed to build it. "The identity of those interested is being withheld at the present time for business reasons," H. Coggswell said provocatively in November of 1910. History has not since learned who the Coggswell

backers were because the company did not survive long enough for a grand introduction of the product. A workforce of about seventy-five Grand Rapids men did, however, manage to produce some cars before Coggswell failed.

1910-1911 COGGSWELL
Model 35 — 4-cyl., 35 hp, 112" wb

	FP	5	4	3	2	1
Tour.	1600	—	4	3	2	1

1907 Colburn, touring, NAHC

COLBURN — Denver, Colorado — (1906-1911) — "It was not so very long since that Colorado was not considered a particularly good place for automobiles, much less for manufacturing them," the East Coast-based magazine *The Automobile* sniffed in 1907. But the new Colburn Automobile Company of Denver promised to change all that. Firstly, the four-cylinder engine of its car was especially designed to perform in a high altitude, and the company envisioned Rocky Mountain area marketing only. Secondly, Colburn did not plunge recklessly into manufacture, beginning late in 1906 and scheduling fifty cars only for production in 1907. The workforce was approximately thirty-five men. Interesting model names were another distinction of the Colburn: Rex Alta in 1906 (which Colburn translated from the Latin as "King of the Heights") and Skyscraper in 1907 (which was a very trendy new coinage then in vogue). In 1909 a Colburn won a race in Denver amidst a field of Chalmers, Moons, Oldsmobiles and Marmons. Nineteen ten was Colburn's best year ever, but by 1911 the company realized that it could not continue profitably as a manufacturer. In February of 1912 Colburn announced the cessation of production and the transformation of the company into a dealership for National cars. While producing the Colburn, the company had also served as an agency for Rauch & Lang electrics and White steam cars.

1906 COLBURN
Rex Alta — 4-cyl., 25 hp, 107" wb

Model C Tour.	3250	4000	5000	8000	15,000	28,000
Model D Rdstr.	3250	4200	5200	8400	15,700	29,000

1907 COLBURN
Skyscraper — 4-cyl., 25 hp, 107" wb

Model C Tour.	3250	4000	5000	8000	15,000	28,000
Model D Rdstr.	3250	4200	5200	8400	15,700	29,000

1908 COLBURN
4-cyl., 30 hp, 108" wb

Model C Tour.	3250	4200	5200	8400	15,700	29,000
Model D Rdstr.	3250	4300	5400	8700	16,500	30,000

1909 COLBURN
4-cyl., 30 hp, 108" wb

Model C Tour.	2750	4200	5200	8400	15,700	29,000
Model D Rdstr.	2750	4300	5400	8700	16,500	30,000

4-cyl., 40/45 hp, 116" wb

Model H Tour.	4500	5800	8000	12,500	28,000	40,000

1910 Colburn, touring

1910 COLBURN
Model M — 4-cyl., 30 hp, 112" wb

Tour.-5P	2750	4500	5800	9500	18,000	32,000
Rdstr.-4P	2500	5000	6500	11,000	22,000	35,000

Model E — 4-cyl., 35 hp, 108" wb

Tour.-5P	2750	5000	6500	11,000	22,000	35,000
Rdstr.-3P	2750	5300	7000	11,500	24,000	37,000

Model H — 4-cyl., 45 hp, 114" wb	FP	5	4	3	2	1
Tour.-7P	4500	7000	10,800	16,900	37,100	49,000
1911 COLBURN						
Model N — 4-cyl., 38 hp, 122" wb						
Tour.-7P	3500	6800	10,300	16,000	35,500	48,000

1911 Colby, model G, roadster, WLB

COLBY — Mason City, Iowa — (1911-1914) — There seemed to be every reason that the company should succeed. By the fall of 1910, when William Colby decided to become an automobile manufacturer, there lay behind him an impressive roster of companies he had promoted or been instrumental in organizing, including the People's State Bank in Mason City. Everything went extraordinarily well in the beginning. To design his car and superintend its manufacture, Colby hired David W. Henry, who had a decade of experience in the field and whose Henry car had been introduced in Muskegon, Michigan the year previous. A factory site was quickly found where construction of the five-story plant of the Colby Motor Company would be begun. But since the Chicago Automobile Show in February 1911 was targeted for the car's introduction, a temporary assembly line was set up in another plant in town. Machinery was installed there on November 1st; two days later the first Colby rolled off the line. By January 4th, 1911 three automobiles were ready for the Chicago show, and one hundred more awaited final assembly. The first Colbys were 40 hp fours, but these were quickly followed by smaller 30 hp variations — and by Colby race cars. Three Colbys were entered in the Kane County Cup at the famed Elgin road races in August 1911, and the car driven by Indianapolis Speedway veteran Billy Pearce placed third, an excellent showing for a brand-new automobile. Pearce thereafter became the factory's number one driver, winning a series of events including the Silver Trophy of the Omaha Speedway Association. His Colby "Red Devil" appeared all-conquering in its class, but ultimately the "Red Devil" conquered Billy Pearce. He was killed late in the year in a contest in Sioux City. Though the car was repaired, it was never again raced. The new underslung production Colby for 1912 became all the rage, however. Meanwhile, problems aplenty were revealed in the front office. In early December 1911 Colby merged with the National Cooperative Farm Machinery Company of Davenport. Though its name remained the same, little else did. William Colby stayed on as president, but David Henry was booted out, and showed up soon after in Nebraska with a new car idea called the Omaha. H.O. Ogren (who would later build a car under his own name) was now Colby chief engineer — and H.S. Murphy arrived as the new general manager. Frugality was Murphy's forte, and he found many areas of the Colby operation where it had not previously been practiced. Apparently his automobile company had been the one William Colby venture in which he had flown too high, wide and handsome. The company's finances were in total disarray. Murphy laid down the law, but his attempts to reduce inventory, streamline production and control ordering procedures proved to be remedial measures only. In late October of 1913, following a failure the year previous to merge with the Western Implement & Motor Company (National Cooperative's parent organization in Davenport), the Colby company was acquired by the Standard Motor Company, a new incorporation composed chiefly of Iowa bankers, which planned to acquire the Minneapolis Motor Company in Minnesota as well. C.H. MacNider (a Mason City citizen representing Standard interests) was in. Lavish plans were made for the building of "the largest automobile manufacturing plant in the west" in Minneapolis. They died aborning. Meanwhile, production of the Colby limped along in Mason City. And soon as the Standard Motor Company, which had been largely a gigantic promotion scheme, found itself in deep trouble. Purportedly the Colby company had been kept alive through the generosity of a seventy-four-year-old Iowa widow who had been left a fortune estimated between $200,000 and $500,000.

1912 Colby Forty, touring, HAC

According to press reports, "whenever money was needed to operate the Colby plant, she was visited and prevailed upon to give accommodation notes which were cashed by bankers and others throughout the northern half of Iowa. It is said that the old lady's paper is widely scattered and that should any of its holders attempt to enforce collection the attempt will be legally resisted, as it is claimed that she was not of sound mind when she signed the notes." The widow's son was immediately appointed as her guardian. Colby was bankrupt. Its liabilities were more than a half million dollars, and it was estimated that during the three years of its existence the company lost a thousand dollars a day. Probably not many more than a thousand Colbys had been built. Just one is believed to exist today, and it is on display at the Kinney Pioneer Museum in Mason City.

1911 COLBY						
Forty — 4-cyl., 40 hp, 121" wb	FP	5	4	3	2	1
Tour.	1750	4200	5200	8400	15,700	29,000
Rdstr.	1750	4300	5400	8700	16,500	30,000
1912 COLBY						
Thirty — 4-cyl., 30 hp, 116" wb						
Model L Underslung Tour.	1250	4500	5800	9500	18,000	32,000
Model N Underslung Cpe.	2250	2700	3600	5300	8800	19,000
Model M Underslung Rdstr.	1250	5000	6000	11,000	22,000	35,000
Forty — 4-cyl., 40 hp, 121" wb						
Model H Tour.	1750	4400	5600	9200	17,300	31,000
Model D Racer	1750	5000	6500	11,000	22,000	35,000
Model G Rdstr.	1750	4700	6100	9900	19,000	33,000
Model A Limo.	3500	4200	5200	8400	15,700	29,000
Model R Cpe.	2500	3900	4800	7700	14,300	27,000
Model K Torpedo	2000	4000	5000	8000	15,000	28,000
1913 COLBY						
Model C-40 — 4-cyl., 40 hp, 118" wb						
Rdstr.-2P	1800	4200	5200	8400	15,700	29,000
Tour.-5P	1800	4000	5000	8000	15,000	28,000
Model E-50 — 5-cyl., 50 hp, 128" wb						
Tour.-7P	2100	4400	5600	9200	17,300	31,000
Tour.-5P	2060	4500	5800	9500	18,000	32,000
Six — 6-cyl., 60 hp, 135" wb						
Tour.-7P	2500	5400	7300	11,800	25,000	38,000

COLD AIR — Louisville, Kentucky — (1910) — The Cold Air Regenerative Motor Car Company was organized in Louisville, Kentucky during the spring of 1910. Behind this venture were John F. French, W.F. Dawson, J.H. Miller, S.B. Simmons, Charles Shepherd, O.M. Rayman, J.F. Miller, William Kinney, Leo French, Charles Dawson and H.S. Ferguson. Their plan was manufacture of a car which was said to be "run by leverage power produced by cold air pressure." This venture did not pass the prototype stage.

COLE — Rockford, Illinois — (1903) — According to an edition of the *Rockford Register-Gazette* published in late 1904, the firm of Cole & Son of Rockford was doing "a large business in wheels, motor cycles, automobiles, lawn mowers . . . and an immense amount of repair work." In late 1903 J.J. Cole and his son built a prototype of a gasoline touring car which was initially planned to be marketed under the tradename of Rockford. Plans changed, however, and the car ultimately was not manufactured at all. The Coles continued as repairers of automobiles, and secured the local dealership for the Rambler.

COLE — Charles City, Iowa — (1904) — In the early spring of 1904, W.H. Cole of Charles City announced completion of his first automobile which he said had proven "most satisfactory" in road testing — and that he was at the time endeavoring to organize a company for its manufacture. The evidence indicates his endeavors proved futile. The Cole was never manufactured in Charles City.

1909 Cole, 4-pass. runabout, NAHC

COLE — Indianapolis, Indiana — (1909-1925) — Until 1908, it seemed, Joseph J. Cole hadn't made any mistakes. Born in 1869 on a farm in Indiana, he left the rural life as soon as he finished high school, took a year in business school and then worked his way into top management jobs with two carriage-making concerns until in 1904 he had amassed enough capital to buy out the Gates-Osborne Carriage Company of Indianapolis and rename it the Cole Carriage Company. The business prospered with a 3000-unit per year production. His mistake arrived with the first car he built, the high-wheeled motor buggy he called the Cole Solid Tire Automobile. As legend has it, in October 1908, he took the prototype on a test drive around the Soldier's and Sailor's Monument in Indianapolis that lasted rather longer than he had anticipated because he had neglected the matter of installing brakes, a situation solved by continuing to circle the monument until he ran out of gas. The braking oversight was rectified on the production version (with the help of engineer Charles S. Crawford, who would later become famous with Stutz), but after selling 170 units, Cole concluded that manufacturing a highwheeler was a mistake too. In June 1909, therefore, he organized the Cole Motor Car Company and introduced a conventional four-cylinder Model 30 of which he had sold over 100 units by the end of the year. By year's end 1910, Cole output had reached 783 vehicles. A Model 30 Flyer captured the Massapequa Trophy in the Vanderbilt Cup Race of 1910, in addition to numerous other contests on both the East and West coasts, including a 24-hour marathon at Brighton Beach. Wild Bill Endicott was usually behind the Flyer's wheel. A Cole six followed and, in 1913, so did electric lighting and starting. Although initially eschewing the annual model change ("Cole motor cars do not bloom once a year, like Easter lilies"), the company soon began following the industry with yearly revisions. In 1915, one year after Cadillac, Cole introduced a V-8 and soon dropped fours and sixes altogether. Throughout its history the Cole was an assembled car (its V-8 came from General Motors' Northway division, which also built Cadillac's version). It was J.J. Cole's belief that specialists provided better examples of their specialty than automobile manufacturers could design themselves. Because this was not a view shared by companies producing their own parts (they routinely pooh-poohed "mere assemblers"), Cole conjured the phrase "Standardized Car" for his product, indicating the use in the Cole of components which were the standard for quality in the industry. Considering his car's natural competition to be the Cadillac, Cole never ventured into the lower-priced field, although in 1915 he did consider awhile a merger with several companies, including Inter-State of Muncie, for a proposed "General Motors of Indiana." He turned down all offers made by William C. Durant to become a GM subsidiary. The Aero-Eight introduced in 1918 put Cole in the forefront of the razor-edge school of styling, and the company pioneered the use of balloon tires. "Did you ever go ballooning in a Cole?" the ads said. "There's a touch of tomorrow in all Cole does today" was another appealing slogan. By now Cole promotion, previously a paragon of the common-sense approach, had taken a decidedly lofty tone, with "Cole Equipages" including such models as "Tuxedo Foursome," "Sportosine," "Tourosine" and "Ultra-Sportster." The 6225 Cole automobiles produced in 1919 was second only to Cadillac among America's high-priced automakers. After enjoying more than a decade of prosperity, Cole began losing money in the wake of the postwar depression. Just 1722 cars left the newly-expanded Cole factory in 1922, just 1522 in 1923. While his company was still solvent, J.J. Cole chose to liquidate rather than jeopardize his personal fortune. This process was begun early in 1925, and was not quite completed ten months later when Cole died suddenly of an infection at age fifty-six.

1909 COLE
Model 30 — 2-cyl., 14 hp, 90" wb

	FP	5	4	3	2	1
Rbt.-3/4P	750	2700	3600	5300	8800	19,000
Rbt.-2P	725	2600	3500	5200	8700	18,500
Rbt.-4P	775	2500	3500	5000	8500	18,000
Solid Tire Automobile	—	—	—	—	—	—

1910 Cole, Flyer, roadster, WLB

1911 Cole, model L, roadster, WLB

1910 COLE
Series 30 — 4-cyl., 30 hp, 108" wb

	FP	5	4	3	2	1
Model G Palace Tour.-5P	1500	3000	4000	6000	9500	21,000
Model G Light Tour.-5P	1500	2900	3700	5600	9100	20,000
Model E Flyer-2P	1500	4000	5000	8000	15,000	28,000
Model F Tourabout-4P	1400	3900	4800	7700	14,300	27,000

1911 COLE
Series 30 — 4-cyl., 30 hp, 118" wb

	FP	5	4	3	2	1
Model O Tour.-5P	1600	4000	5000	8000	15,000	28,000
Model Q Fore-Door Tour.-5P	1650	3900	4800	7700	14,300	27,000
Model M Toy Tonneau	1650	4000	5000	8000	15,000	28,000
Model L Rds.-2P	1600	4200	5200	8400	15,700	29,000

1912 Cole Forty, coupe, JAC

1912 COLE
Forty — 4-cyl., 40 hp, 122" wb

	FP	5	4	3	2	1
Model A Spdstr.	1885	4500	5800	9500	18,000	32,000
Model B Rds.	1885	4700	6100	9900	19,000	33,000
Model C Toy Tonneau	1885	4300	5400	8700	16,500	30,000
Model D Tour.	1885	4200	5200	8400	15,700	29,000
Model I Colonial Cpe.	2500	2700	3600	5300	8800	19,000
Model T Inside Drive Limo.	3250	3000	4000	6000	9500	21,000
Model U Limo.	3000	2900	3700	5600	9100	20,000

1913 Cole Sixty, roadster, HAC

1913 COLE
Forty — 4-cyl., 40 hp, 116" wb

	FP	5	4	3	2	1
Tour.-5P	1685	4500	5800	9500	18,000	32,000
Rds.-2P	1685	5000	6500	11,000	22,000	35,000

Fifty — 4-cyl., 50 hp, 122" wb

	FP	5	4	3	2	1
Rds.-2P	1985	5300	7000	11,500	24,000	37,000
Toy Tonneau-4/6P	1985	5400	7300	11,800	25,000	38,000
Tour.-5/7P	1985	5200	6800	11,300	23,000	36,000

Sixty — 6-cyl., 40 hp, 132" wb

	FP	5	4	3	2	1
Tour.-7P	2485	5400	7300	11,800	25,000	38,000
Toy Tonneau-4P	2485	5500	7500	12,000	26,000	39,000
Rds.-2P	2485	5800	8000	12,500	28,000	40,000
Cpe.-4P	3000	2900	3700	5600	9100	20,000
Ber. Limo.-7P	4250	3500	4500	7000	13,000	25,000

1914 Cole, 2-pass. roadster, WLB

1914 Cole, sedan, Willoughby, HAC

1914 Cole, 4-pass. coupe, WLB

1914 COLE
Four — 4-cyl., 28.9 hp, 120'' wb

	FP	5	4	3	2	1
Toy Tonneau	1925	4200	5200	8400	15,700	29,000
Tour.-5P	1925	4000	5000	8000	15,000	28,000
Rds.-2P	1925	4300	5400	8700	16,500	30,000
Cpe.-3P	2350	2700	3600	5300	8800	19,000

Six — 6-cyl., 43.8 hp, 136'' wb

Tour.-7P	2600	4500	5800	9500	18,000	32,000
Toy Tonneau-6P	2600	5000	6500	11,000	22,000	35,000
Rds.-2P	2600	5000	6500	11,000	22,000	35,000
Cpe.-4P	3000	2900	3700	5600	9100	20,000
Limo.-7P	4000	3500	4500	7000	13,000	25,000

1915 Cole Eight, prototype, HAC

1915 COLE
Standard 4-40 — 4-cyl., 40 hp, 120'' wb

Tour.-7P	1485	4200	5200	8400	15,700	29,000
Rds.-2P	1485	4400	5600	9200	17,300	31,000
Cpe.-3P	1885	2700	3600	5300	8800	19,000

Model 6-50 — 6-cyl., 29 hp, 126'' wb

Tour.-4P	1865	4300	5400	8700	16,500	30,000
Tour.-7P	1865	4500	5800	9500	18,000	32,000
Rds.-2P	2465	4900	6300	10,300	21,000	34,000
Cpe.-3P	2250	2800	3700	5500	9000	19,500

Big Six 6-60 — 6-cyl., 60 hp, 136'' wb

Tour.-7P	2465	4500	5800	9500	18,000	32,000
Rds.-2P	2465	5000	6500	11,000	22,000	35,000
Cpe.-4P	2750	2900	3700	5600	9100	20,000
Limo.-7P	3750	3500	4500	7000	13,000	25,000

1916 COLE
Model 8-50 — 8-cyl., 39.2 hp, 127'' wb

Tour.-7P	1785	5000	6500	11,000	22,000	35,000
Rds.-3P	1785	5300	7000	11,500	24,000	37,000
Ber.-Limo.-8P	3250	3900	4800	7700	14,300	27,000
Cpe.-4P	2185	3100	4200	6300	10,500	22,000
Demountable Sed.-7P	2285	2900	3700	5600	9100	20,000

1916 Cole Eight, touring, JAC

1917 Cole Eight, touring, HAC

1917 COLE
Series 860 — 8-cyl., 39.2 hp, 127'' wb

	FP	5	4	3	2	1
Tuxedo Rds.-4P	1695	5400	7300	11,800	25,000	38,000
Tour.-7P	1695	5000	6500	11,000	22,000	35,000
Trsedan.-7P	2295	3100	4200	6300	10,500	22,000
Tourcope-4P	2295	3500	4500	7000	13,000	25,000
Foredoor Trsedan-7P	2495	3200	4300	6500	11,000	23,000

1918 Cole Eight, roadster, HAC

1918 COLE
Series 870 — 8-cyl., 39.2 hp, 127'' wb

Rds.-2P	2395	5400	7300	11,800	25,000	38,000
Tour.-7P	2395	5000	6500	11,000	22,000	35,000
Sptstr.-4P	2395	5800	8000	12,500	28,000	40,000

1919 Cole Eight, touring sedan, HAC

1919 COLE
Series 870 — 8-cyl., 39.2 hp, 127'' wb

Tourstr.-7P	2595	4500	5800	9500	18,000	32,000
Trsedan.-7P	3695	3100	4200	6300	10,500	22,000
Rds.-2P	2595	5200	6800	11,300	23,000	36,000
Sptstr.-4P	2595	5400	7300	11,800	25,000	38,000
Tourcoupe-4P	3795	3300	4400	6700	12,000	24,000
Trsedan.-7P	3595	3100	4200	6300	10,500	22,000
Twn. Car-7P	3795	3900	4800	7700	14,300	27,000

1920 Cole, Aero Eight, sport coupe, WLB

1920 COLE
Aero Eight — 8-cyl., 80 hp, 127" wb

	FP	5	4	3	2	1
Rds.-2P	2750	5500	7500	12,000	26,000	39,000
Sptstr.-4P	2750	5800	8000	12,500	28,000	40,000
Sportsedan-6P	3895	3500	4500	7000	13,000	25,000
Sportosine-6P	3995	3900	4800	7700	14,300	27,000
Sportcoupe-4P	3795	4000	5000	8000	15,000	28,000
Tourosine-7P	3995	4200	5200	8400	15,700	29,000
Trsedan.-7P	3995	3700	4700	7300	13,700	26,000
Towncar-6P	3895	4000	5000	8000	15,000	28,000
Tourstr.	2850	4300	5400	8700	16,500	30,000

1921 Cole Aero Eight, brougham, Willoughby, HAC

1921 Cole, Aero Eight, sport sedan, JAC

1921 Cole, Aero Eight, Sportosine, WLB

1921 COLE
Aero Eight — 8-cyl., 80 hp, 127" wb

	FP	5	4	3	2	1
Tour.-7P	3250	5800	8000	12,500	28,000	40,000
Rds.-2P	3250	6000	8500	13,000	30,000	42,000
Spt.-4P	3250	5800	8000	12,500	28,000	40,000
Cpe.-4P	4250	4200	5200	8400	15,700	29,000
Sed.-4P	4350	3900	4800	7700	14,300	27,000
Tourosine-7P	4450	4000	5000	8000	15,700	28,000
Sportosine-4P	4450	4200	5200	8400	15,700	29,000
Trsedan.-7P	4450	3900	4800	7700	14,300	27,000

1922 Cole, Aero Eight, Tourosine, HAC

1922 COLE
Aero Eight 890 — 8-cyl., 80 hp, 127 1/4" wb

	FP	5	4	3	2	1
Tour.-7P	2485	6000	8500	13,000	30,000	42,000
Rds.-2P	2485	6400	9300	14,500	33,000	45,000
Spt.-4P	2485	6000	8500	13,000	30,000	42,000
California Spt.-4P	2835	6700	9900	15,500	34,800	47,000
California Tour.-7P	2835	6900	10,800	16,900	36,100	49,000
Cpe.-3P	3385	4300	5400	8700	16,500	30,000
Sportosine-6P	3685	4400	5600	9200	17,300	31,000
Sportsedan-4P	3685	4200	5200	8400	15,700	29,000
Sub.-5P	3685	4300	5400	8700	16,500	30,000
Trsedan.-7P	3685	4400	5600	9200	17,300	31,000
Tourosine-7P	4185	4500	5800	9500	18,000	32,000

1923 Cole, touring, HAC

1923 COLE
Series 890 — 8-cyl., 80 hp, 127 1/4" wb

Tour.-7P	2685	6200	8800	13,500	31,000	43,000
Spt.-4P	2685	6300	9000	14,000	32,000	44,000
Rds.-2P	2685	6500	9500	15,000	34,000	46,000
Cpe.-4P	3285	4400	5600	9200	17,300	31,000
Sed.-7P	3280	4000	5000	8000	15,000	28,000
Trsedan.-7P	3685	4200	5200	8400	15,700	29,000
Sub.-5P	3685	4300	5400	8700	16,500	30,000
Ber.-7P	3885	4500	5800	9500	18,000	32,000

1924 Cole, Master Model Royal, sedan, WLB

1924 COLE
Series 890 — 8-cyl., 80 hp, 127 1/4" wb

Westchester Tour.-7P	2175	6200	8800	13,500	31,000	43,000
Spt.-4P	2175	6300	9000	14,000	32,000	44,000
Cpe.-4P	2750	4400	5600	9200	17,300	31,000
Imp. Cpe.-4P	3075	4500	5800	9500	18,000	32,000
Sed.-7P	3075	4200	5200	8400	15,700	29,000
Brouette-5P	3075	4300	5400	8700	16,500	30,000
Aero-Volante-4P	3075	6500	9500	15,000	34,000	46,000

1924 Cole, Master Model Volante, 4-pass. touring, WLB

1925 Cole Brouette, JAC

1925 COLE
Series 890 — 8-cyl., 80 hp, 127 1/4'' wb

	FP	5	4	3	2	1
Aero-Volante-4P	2325	6500	9500	15,000	34,000	46,000
Westchester Tour.-7P	2325	6400	9300	14,500	33,000	45,000
Cpe.-4P	2900	5200	6800	11,300	23,000	36,000
Brouette-5P	3225	4900	6300	10,300	21,000	34,000
Ryl. Sed.-7P	3225	5000	6500	11,000	22,000	35,000

COLE & LANG — Topeka, Kansas — (1900) — In 1900 two machinists from Kansas, James E. Cole of Alma and Andrew Lang of Topeka, completed their first automobile which, according to *The Motor Age*, was ''an oil-propelled machine which they believe they can make and sell, at a profit, at $250.'' Had they been able to do that, they would have become millionaires. But it appears this venture died before even a factory in Topeka, which had been the partners' plan, was realized.

COLE & WOOP — New York, New York — (1901-1902) — This juvenile car of 1901 was designed by J.O. McDonnell and built by Cole & Woop of 50 West 67th Street in New York City. It was four feet long, weighed 200 pounds, and featured wire wheels 20 inches in diameter in the rear, 16 inches in front, shod with 1 1/2-inch pneumatic tires. Its power was derived from a ten-cell storage battery providing one-quarter horsepower, speeds up to seven miles an hour, and a running range of twenty miles between battery charges. The little Cole & Woop electric was a Christmas present from his mother to Master George Jay Gould, Jr. In the spring of 1902, Cole & Woop built a second little electric car — this one a victoria — for young Master Gould, possibly as a birthday present or possibly because the lad was already bored with the first. Building juvenile cars was a diversion for Cole & Woop. The firm usually provided custom bodies for full-size versions. New York City had dozens of carriage builders so occupied during this era.

1934 Coleman, 2-dr. sedan, HAC

COLEMAN — Littleton, Colorado — (1930-1935) — The cars were designed by Harleigh Holmes; they were paid for by George L. Coleman. Having patented a steerable driving axle in 1919, Holmes had established

the Four Wheel Drive Company in Carbondale, Colorado in 1921, a firm he sold out the year following to lead-and-zinc mining magnate Coleman. Coleman Motors Corporation began producing four-wheel-drive trucks in Littleton about 1925. Holmes seems to have been kept on in the Coleman organization in an ex officio capacity, being given such assignments as the design of race cars, first for Coleman's son to take to Pikes Peak, then for the famous Unser family, even for the Indy 500 in 1930-1931. The idea behind the Coleman passenger car was probably Holmes', though Coleman was congenially willing to fund the project because some patentable engineering features might result which would provide tidy royalties. Although in 1933 the company announced plans for marketing of the Coleman, with a $995 price tag, this never in fact happened — and probably was only briefly considered. Total Coleman production was five cars; all of them utilizing Ford components but offering a good many interesting, if sometime bizarre, Holmes' ideas. The first two vehicles were front wheel drive, the last three rear-drive but with a front axle which arched formidably into a huge U over the engine, this to effect a very low center of gravity, though some problems in road-going must have been effected as well. Overall height and width were the same 58 inches, ground clearance was a mere eight. Front and rear fenders formed a continuous line with the deeply flanged running boards to allow sufficient reinforcement for the perimeter-type frame, which presaged somewhat the ''stepdown'' idea of the post-war Hudson. Unconventional, too, was the Coleman's body styling. Although perhaps it could not be called unrelievedly ugly, neither could it be called handsome.

COLEMAN ELECTRIC — Chicago, Illinois — (1892 et seq.) — Among the early pioneers in the electric field was Clyde J. Coleman of Chicago, who built a two-seated surrey in 1892 which he drove successfully and often in the Chicago area. Later that year, as the World's Columbian Exposition drew near, he joined with two other Chicagoans in a venture to produce Columbia Electric chair cars for use in transporting visitors at the fair. By the turn of the century, Coleman had traveled east to work for the Electric Vehicle Company, among others, though he continued developing and patenting his electric ideas (ultimately he had no fewer than 165 patents to his credit) and apparently dabbling on occasion in the building of electric cars for his own use and pleasure. The Coleman electric which news reports indicate made a successful run in the contests staged by the Massachusetts Automobile Club in 1901 was most likely a car built by Clyde J. Coleman.

COLISEUM — The Coliseum Machine & Garage Company was incorporated with a capital stock of $40,000 early in 1914 for the manufacture, repair and sale of motorcars in South Bend, Indiana. John Wlaz, William P. Furey and J. Elmer Peak were behind this venture. Manufacture is doubted.

COLLINGS — The Collings Carriage Company of Camden, New Jersey has been indicated to have manufactured an automobile from 1913-1915 on various car rosters. That this was the case has not been documented, and seems unlikely.

COLLINS — A steam car called Collins is indicated on various car rosters as having been built in 1902 by the Hartford Motor Machine Company in Hartford, Connecticut. That firm was located at 902 Main Street, but city directory references offer no indication of the firm's activity.

The Collins Gear and Motor Company was organized in Philadelphia, Pennsylvania during the summer of 1910 with a capital stock of $250,000. The incorporators were F.R. Hansell of Philadelphia, and E.T. Vennell and George H.B. Martin of Camden. Their plan was to ''manufacture and deal in motor cars, power boats, portable boats and engines.'' The firm subsequently purchased the factory of the defunct Simpson Stove and Manufacturing Company in Canonsburg. Manufacture of an automobile is not believed to have followed, however.

The Collins Motor Company was organized late in 1917 to manufacture automobiles, gasoline engines and tractors in Collins, Wisconsin. The incorporators were M.S. Valeskey, John A. Draheim, G.W. Valeskey and H.A. Allhiser. Manufacture of an automobile has not been documented.

COLLINS ELECTRIC — Scranton, Pennsylvania — (1900) — Patrick J. Collins was the manager of the Scranton Electric Works at 504 Lackawanna Avenue in Scranton. In 1900 he built his first car there, an electric delivery wagon which was completed that summer. He immediately organized himself as the Collins Electric Vehicle Company and in the autumn announced to the trade press that he planned to establish an electric car factory in Scranton. ''It is the purpose of the company to furnish light-weight and easy-running electric vehicles which will travel long distances without recharging of the batteries,'' reported *Electrical World and Engineer*. Alas, Collins' plans fell through. Subsequent city directory references indicate that he remained at his job as manager of Scranton Electric, which specialized in armature winding and general repairing, as well as x-ray supplies.

1921 Collinet, roadster, WLB

COLLINS — Huntington, New York — (1919-1921)/**COLLINET** — Garden City, New York — (1920-1921) — The Collins behind this Long Island venture was Albert H. Collins, whose Wolverine had just died in Kalamazoo. Joining him as his vice-president was Will B. Brewster of the renowned New York coachbuilding house. The idea of Collins Motors, Inc. was to build quite special motorcars to compete with the best Europe had to offer. A 120-inch wheelbase chassis (references differ as to whether the engine would be a four or a six) was slated to carry a roadster body "for the clubman and amateur sportsman," while a longer wheelbase would be utilized for touring, town and custom-built cars. Further plans were made for the testing of each car on the Long Island Speedway, with a certificate of performance to be issued with each vehicle sold. Then there was a halt to all these plans. Quite possibly, not even the prototype chassis was completed. A Collins four with a Herschell-Spillman engine and a $2500 price tag was announced for the 1920 model year, but it never even approached an assembly line. References to the Collins continued into 1921, though by now Albert H. had left Huntington for Garden City where he showed up with a new company and pretty much the same idea. His Collinet Motor Company did manage to have a car built and ready for the New York Automobile Salon in November 1920. It was powered by a four-cylinder 90 hp Wisconsin engine, fitted into a 132-inch wheelbase chassis, and featured a sporty two-seater body with a wedge-like shape. The price tag for this one was $5500. Future production, it was stated, would be on a custom basis. Despite further pronouncements from the company, including two models for the 1922 model year (a 65 hp four for $5000 and a 90 hp six for $6500), it would appear there was no production at all. The Collinet, like the Collins, never proceeded beyond the prototype stage.

COLLINS SIX — Detroit, Michigan — (1921) — In April of 1921, Richard H. Collins vigorously denied rumors that he planned to resign his position as president of the Cadillac Motor Car Company and join his former boss, William C. Durant, in the latter's recently incorporated Durant Motors. He was telling only half a lie. In May he did announce his impending retirement from Cadillac, but it was for the establishment of his own company for which he had already picked out a factory. It was the old Cass and Amsterdam avenue plant which for years had been the home of the Cadillac, and Collins proceeded in the next few months to continue borrowing liberally from his old employer. In June Cadillac chief engineer Ben Anibal joined him in his new venture, in July so did Cadillac research engineer Fenn Holden. Enormous excitement attended the announcement of the forthcoming Collins Six. Anibal and Holden were already working up the prototype. In December, however, the Collins Motor Car Company announced that production of the new car in Detroit had been "postponed indefinitely." The reason was that, in the meantime, Richard Collins had bought control of the Peerless company in Cleveland. Ironically, upon his departure from General Motors, there had been much buzzing in Detroit that the new Collins Six would probably be a cross between a Buick and a Cadillac. When it was finally introduced, it was a Peerless. The "Collins Six" name appeared only on the prototype. In December 1924, when Collins resigned from Peerless, he sold the company his car for a purported half-million dollars.

COLONIAL — Colonial was the name given to the passenger car produced by the Walden W. Shaw Livery Company of Chicago during 1920-1921, in order to differentiate it from the firm's taxicabs. Refer to Shaw.

The Colonial Automobile Company of Boston produced a steam car from 1899-1901 which was marketed under the tradename of Kent's Pacemaker. Refer to Kent's Pacemaker.

The Colonial Beach Motor Company was organized with a capital stock of $500 late in 1912 to manufacture automobiles in Richmond, Virginia. F.W. Alexander, George Staples and H.W.B. Williams were the incorporators. Manufacture is doubted.

The Colonial Car Company was organized in Jonesville, Michigan in 1916 for the manufacture of an electric car to be marketed under the tradename of American Beauty. Refer to American Beauty.

COLONIAL ELECTRIC — Circleville, Ohio — (1902) — In 1902 the Colonial Carriage Company of Circleville built a sample electric vehicle to the order of a client from New York. "The machine has proven very satisfactory," *The Automobile and Motor Review* reported that July, "and it is probable that the company will engage permanently in the business." Although Colonial may have built a few more electrics to specific customer order, manufacture was not embarked upon.

1912 Colonial Electric, coupe, WLB

COLONIAL ELECTRIC — Detroit, Michigan — (1912) — The Colonial Electric Car Company was organized in September of 1911 by Otto F. Bartlett A.D. Stansell, Fred C. Willis, Albert Webb, Jr., Dr. L.C. Moore, Mark W. Allen and William E. Storms. Manufacture was concentrated on a single model, a $2700 five-passenger brougham capable of 25 miles per hour and 75 miles per charge. A cut-glass flower vase and a vanity were included as standard equipment. A three-passenger coupe on the same 93-inch wheelbase chassis was announced, but was built only as a prototype. In June of 1912 *Motor Age* commented that the Colonial company had "scored a marked local success." Rumors were afloat that the firm was to be sold to General Motors, though these were denied. The Colonial Electric Car Company simply faded away after that. There is evidence that it might have been absorbed by the Anderson Electric Car Company, makers of the Detroit Electric. It is known that three years later one of the Colonial Electric people returned to the field with a rather unique idea: William E. Storms, who built an electric cyclecar under his own name.

1921 Colonial Six, four-passenger sportster, HAC

COLONIAL — Boston, Massachusetts — (1921-1922) — The executive board of Colonial Motors Corporation included General John H. Sherburne and Melvin F. Hill of Brookline, James W. Milner of Newton, Earl E. Beveridge of Springfield, James J. Donahue of Lynn, and Hugh H. Lally of Braintree. On its advisory board were V.A. Charles, Harry A. Eisner and Judge George H. Bruce. The tenor and marketing approach of this Colonial adventure might be indicated by the manner in which the company chose to write its address: "Nine Twenty Six Commonwealth Avenue." The company chose not to mention that the engine powering its car was a pedestrian six-cylinder from Beaver. If looks could have deceived, the Colonial might have managed it nicely. Built on a long 130-inch wheelbase, the car was available in four handsome body styles, each of them sporting disc wheels. "Production at the rate of five hundred cars a year is being established pending the construction of the Colonial factory," the brochure said. At the moment, the company had to make do with "ten thousand feet of show room and engineering space." How many Colonials were built, and at what prices they were sold remains a mystery. But the logical assumption would be that the production was very low, and the prices very high, probably the $5000 range.

1921-1922 COLONIAL

	FP	5	4	3	2	1
Colonial Six Sptstr.-4P	—	6400	9300	14,500	33,000	45,000
Colonial Six Tour.-6P	—	6000	8500	13,000	30,000	42,000
Colonial Six Rds.-2P	—	6700	9900	15,500	34,800	47,000
Colonial Six Cpe.-3P	—	4500	5800	9500	18,000	32,000

COLONIAL SIX — Detroit & Indianapolis — (1917) — In January of 1917 announcement came from Detroit that the Colonial Automobile Company had begun the manufacture of a $995 car. In July the announcement came that this $995 car was a 35 hp six on a 116-inch wheelbase, but now the company was in Indianapolis. Colonial's next move was into oblivion.

1917 Colonial, Six, touring, WLB

The men behind this venture were R.C. Fulcher, D.A. Alig, H.M. McDermid and a virtual battalion of kibitzing bystanders. "One of the outstanding features of the Colonial Six is the fact that the specifications were suggested by about one thousand automobile dealers at the request of the Colonial company," *Automobile Trade Journal* reported, "and its design is said to follow out these general suggestions as to a car which would nearly meet the average buyer's demands." Apparently not. Design by a committee of a thousand produced a car that many fewer than a thousand bought.

COLONIAL SIX — Warren, Ohio — (1922) — After declaring bankruptcy on May 1st, 1922 from his home in Racine, Wisconsin, Otis Friend turned up the month following in Warren, Ohio to organize Colonial Motors for manufacture of a new car. His late lamented Friend had been a four, the new Colonial was to be a six. The only Colonial produced undoubtedly was the prototype which had been planned to be manufactured by the Friend Motor Corporation before that venture went under. Only a new emblem was necessary. During the summer of 1922, there were reports that Colonial Motors Company and Supreme Motors Corporation (also of Warren) would consolidate with Apperson of Kokomo, Indiana. Instead, the Colonial venture died aborning.

1921 Colonial, Straight 8, 4-dr. sedan, WLB

COLONIAL STRAIGHT 8 — San Francisco, California — (1921) — This Colonial was built as a prototype only at a cost which may have been as high as $50,000. Backing the project was the Mechanical Development Corporation of San Francisco, which financed an engineer named W.A. Rider. "A car that promises to produce a sensation equal almost to that created by the first automobile" was the advertising cry. Slated to sell for $1800, the 60 hp Colonial Straight 8 was claimed to offer 28 mpg and 2000 miles to a gallon of oil. Considering the 125 1/2-inch wheelbase and the car's overall size, this seems unlikely. The Colonial was, however, probably the first straight-eight on the West Coast. It was also among the first cars in America to feature four-wheel hydraulic brakes, made by Binn's Machine & Tool Works of San Francisco. During this period both Duesenberg and Kenworthy announced their own straight-eight, four-wheel-brake cars. They saw production, which the Colonial did not. The Colonial Straight 8 remains extant.

COLORADO SPRINGS — The Colorado Springs Garage Company was organized with a capital stock of $25,000 during the spring of 1904 to "manufacture, purchase or otherwise acquire, operate, sell and dispose of and generally deal in automobiles and vehicles similar thereto." The directors of this Colorado venture were Paul Schwalbach, Theodore H. Braasch and A.M. Schwalbach. Manufacture of an automobile is doubted.

COLT — Yonkers, New York — (1907) — William Mason Turner had been an automobile salesman in Yonkers since 1898. In 1907 he turned to automobile manufacture, establishing the Colt Runabout Company. For his car's engine, he turned to his friend William S. Howard, who offered Turner space in his gas-engine works at 17 Nepperhan Avenue in exchange for a

1907 Colt, runabout, WLB

vice-presidency. The Howard-built engine used in the Colt was a 40 hp six fitted into a 105-inch wheelbase chassis. A two-seater was the only body style offered and was advertised as the "Mile-a-Minute" runabout. That was probably stretching the truth some. Turner was, however, engagingly honest in determining what to ask for his car: $1500, or "a price to the public which pays a fair percentage of profit to the company," as he put it. Unfortunately, no profit at all followed. By December of 1907 three creditors with total claims of $1874 petitioned the Colt Runabout Company into bankruptcy. Sources vary as to Turner's total production. One magazine of the period indicates "at least two," another less than a hundred. Probably the former is the more accurate. Though Turner apparently gave up the automobile manufacturing idea after this one attempt, an undaunted William S. Howard decided to try again under his own name.

COLT-STRATTON — The Colt-Stratton Company, Inc. was organized in New York City late in 1909 with a capital stock of $125,000 for the manufacture of "motors, engines, machines, cars, carriages, etc." Very quickly William L. Colt (the former president of the Cleveland Motor Car Company) and Harry L. Stratton (erstwhile president of the Amalgamated Copper Company) decided to do otherwise, and became dealers instead, initially of the Cole and the Paige-Detroit, later (and most famously) of the Dodge.

COLUMBIA — The Columbia-Knight was a model of the Columbia produced in Hartford, Connecticut. It was marketed for two seasons only, 1912-1913. Refer to Columbia.

The Columbia Magnetic was a gas-electric hybrid that was produced by the Electric Vehicle Company in Hartford Connecticut from 1907-1908. The designation was informal jargon, however. The car was marketed simply as the Columbia.

The Columbia Taxicab Company of St. Louis, Missouri produced and sold its own taxis from 1915-1917 under the designation of L.W.C. Refer to L.W.C.

The Columbia Vehicle Company was organized late in 1911 in Hamilton, Ohio to manufacture and deal in motor vehicles. Samuel Zielonski, M.M. Dermody, E.F. Alexter and George W. Platt were among the incorporators. Manufacture is doubted.

The Columbia Wagonette was a large eleven-passenger electric depot wagon produced in 1902-1903 by the Electric Vehicle Company of Hartford, Connecticut as a model of its Columbia. Refer to Columbia.

1897 Columbia, electric carriage, SR

1899 Columbia Mark VIII, gasoline runabout, HAC

COLUMBIA — Hartford, Connecticut — (1897-1913) — If things had gone as planned, there might not be a Big Three in the American automobile industry today, there might be a Big One — and the company that built the Columbia would be it. The story is rather confusing. Colonel marketed under the tradename of Columbia by his Pope Manufacturing Company of Hartford. On May 13th, 1896 — after several months of testing — the company was satisfied with its first experimental automobile, which was an electric; a gasoline car had been tried the year before apparently. In 1897 Hiram Percy Maxim was hired to head Pope's motor carriage department, and in the two years that followed 500 electric and 40 gasoline carriages were built, all carrying the name Columbia. In 1899, in New York City, financiers William Collins Whitney bought out the Electric Vehicle Company owned by Isaac Rice, with the idea of manufacturing 2,000 electric taxicabs for service in America's major cities. Whitney went to Pope to talk merger of his new company and the Pope automobile-manufacturing facilities, and the result in 1899 was the Columbia Automobile Company to manufacture the cars, with Electric Vehicle as a holding com-

1900 Columbia Mark XI, electric wagonette, HAC

discontinued. Interestingly, the Columbia brochure for 1911 describing the new Mark 48 and Mark 85 cars devoted a full page to extolling the validity of the Selden Patent, though just a few months after the brochure was published — in January 1911 — the final decision in the Selden case spelled finis to the monopoly over the gasoline vehicle industry which the holders of the patent had hoped to forever enjoy. And, ironically, Columbia by now had become part of another grand scheme destined to even quicker failure. In 1910 the company was absorbed by United States Motor, Benjamin Briscoe's try at emulating Billy Durant's General Motors Corporation. In 1911, ironically, Columbia was paying license royalties to Charles Yale Knight for the 38 hp sleeve-valve four-cylinder model which would be marketed as the Columbia Knight. By 1913, with the collapse of United States Motor, there were no more Columbias at all.

1899 Columbia Mark V, electric victoria, JAC

pany for the taxicab fleet subsidiaries to be set up in various cities. Electric Vehicle also acquired the Selden patent for gasoline automobiles. About 2000 Columbia electric cabs were built, but they were enormously expensive and not very profitable. Electric Vehicle therefore decided that the Selden Patent was a more financially lucrative proposition and sought to enforce it, demanding royalties frm every gasoline car manufacturer in the United States. Most complied, but some did not, including a maverick in Detroit named Henry Ford. A lawsuit followed; not until 1911 would it be settled, in favor of the gasoline car manufacturers. In the meantime, though royalties from other manufacturers were bringing the most cash into the company coffers, Columbia motorcars were being produced in both electric and gasoline versions. The gasoline car Hiram Maxim designed in 1899 was quite advanced, featuring full-elliptic springs, a front-mounted coil radiator and a left-hand steering wheel in 1900 Electric Vehicle bought the Riker Electric and began marketing it. In 1901 the Columbia Automobile Company name was dropped, Electric Vehicle thereafter becoming the sponsoring company for all Columbia automobiles, be they gasoline or electric. Hirma Maxim having departed, Frederick A. Law was the engineer responsible for the new Columbia gasoline car. In 1904 Columbians ranged from a small Mark LX electric runabout capable of 15 mph and priced at $850 to a very European-looking 30-36 hp four-cylinder Mark XLII gasoline touring car capable of 45 mph and priced at $5000. There were thirty-seven Columbia models in all. In 1906 the 45 hp Mark LXVI gasoline touring car was introduced with a seven-speed "Direct Electric Transmission." In 1907 Electric Vehicle Company went into receivership, from which it recovered, but it remained an invalid ever after. Gradually through the years the ratio of gasoline to electric Columbias produced had been moving in the gasoline car's favor. In 1907-1908 a hybrid gas-electric was referred to informally as the Magnetic. In 1909, when there were five gasoline models and just two electrics, the firm's name changed again, from Electric Vehicle to Columbia Motor Car Company — and the cumbersome practice of using roman numerals to designate models was

1901 Columbia Mark VIII, gasoline runabout, HAC

1901 Columbia Mark XXXI, electric victoria, OCW

1902 Columbia Mark XXXI, electric runabout, HAC

1897-1902 COLUMBIA
Electric Cars

	FP	5	4	3	2	1
Mark III Stanhope Phae.	—	—	—	—	—	—
Mark XXXI Elberon Vic.	—	—	—	—	—	—
Mark XXXI Seabright Rbt.	—	—	—	—	—	—
Mark XIX Tonneau	—	—	—	—	—	—
Mark XIX Cabriolet	—	—	—	—	—	—
Mark XI Omnibus	—	—	—	—	—	—
Mark XI Wagonette	—	—	—	—	—	—
Mark XI Delivery	—	—	—	—	—	—
Mark XVIII Hansom	—	—	—	—	—	—

Gasoline cars — 1-cyl., 4-1/2 hp, 67-1/2" wb

	FP	5	4	3	2	1
Mark VIII Rbt.	—	—	—	—	—	—

1903 Columbia Mark XLI, gasoline touring, HAC

1903 COLUMBIA
Electric cars

Mark XXI Rbt.	1000	2900	3700	5600	9100	20,000
Mark XXXVIIII Rbt.	900	2900	3700	5600	9100	20,000
Mark XXXI Seabright Rbt.	1000	2900	3700	5600	9100	20,000
Mark XXI Vic.	1500	2700	3600	5300	8800	19,000
Mark III Phae.	1500	3100	4200	6300	10,500	22,000
Mark XIX Surrey	1500	3200	4300	6500	11,000	23,000
Mark XIX Tonneau	1800	3000	4000	6000	9500	21,000
Mark XIX Cabriolet	2250	2900	3700	5600	9100	20,000
Mark XIX Spec. Ser. Wag.	2000	2700	3600	5300	8800	19,000
Mark XXXV Ext. Frt. Brgm.	3500	3500	4500	7000	13,000	25,000
Mark XXXV Hamsom	3500	3700	4700	7300	13,700	26,000
Mark XXXVI Rear Driven Cpe.	3000	4000	5000	8000	15,000	28,000
Mark XXXVI Cpe.*	2800	3900	4800	7700	14,300	27,000
* (Inside Operated)						
Mark XXXIX Vic. Phae.	3000	4000	5000	8000	15,000	28,000
Mark XI Opera Bus	2000	3900	4800	7700	14,300	27,000
Mark XI Wagonette	2500	3700	4700	7300	13,700	26,000
Mark XI Ambulance	3500	3100	4200	6300	10,500	22,000
Mark XI Police Patrol	3500	3000	4000	6000	9500	21,000
Mark XI Delivery Wag.	1800	2900	3700	5600	9100	20,000
Mark XXXII Delivery Wag.	2250	2700	3600	5300	8800	19,000

Gasoline cars — 2-cyl., 12/14 hp, 82" wb

Mark XLI Tour.	5000	3100	4200	6300	10,500	22,000

1904 COLUMBIA
Electric cars

Mark XXXI Rbt.	1000	—	—	—	—	22,000
Mark XXXVIII Rbt.	750	—	—	—	—	23,000
Mark LX Rbt.	850	—	—	—	—	24,000
Mark XXXI Vic.	1500	—	—	—	—	21,000
Mark XIX Surrey	1500	—	—	—	—	23,000
Mark XIX Tonneau	1800	—	—	—	—	24,000
Mark XIX Cabriolet	2250	—	—	—	—	22,000
Mark XIX Spec. Serv. Wag.	2000	—	—	—	—	20,000
Mark XXXV Ext. Frt. Brgm.	3500	—	—	—	—	27,000
Mark XXXV Brgm.*	3500	—	—	—	—	25,000
* (Straight Front)						
Mark XXXV Landau*	3500	—	—	—	—	26,000
* Leather Head						
Mark XXXV Glass Fnt. Landau	3500	—	—	—	—	25,000

1904 Columbia Mark XXXVI, inside operated electric coupe, HAC

	FP	5	4	3	2	1
Mark XXXV Land'et.	3500	—	—	—	—	24,000
Mark XXXV Hanson	3500	—	—	—	—	24,000
Mark XXXXI Rear Driven Cpe.	3000	—	—	—	—	25,000
Mark XXXVI Cpe.*	2800	—	—	—	—	24,000
(* Inside Operated)						
Mark XXXIX Vic. Phae.	3000	—	—	—	—	27,000
Mark XI Ambulance	3500	—	—	—	—	22,000
Mark XI Police Patrol	3500	—	—	—	—	21,000
Mark XI Delivery Wag.	1800	—	—	—	—	20,000
Mark XXXII Delivery Wag.	2250	—	—	—	—	20,000
Mark LII Delivery Wag.	2500	—	—	—	—	19,000

Gasoline cars — 2-cyl., 12/14 hp, 82" wb

Mark XLIII Tonneau-4P	1750	—	—	—	—	24,000

Gasoline cars — 4-cyl., 30/35 hp

Mark XLII Tonneau-6P*	4000	—	—	—	—	25,000
* (106" wb)						
Mark XLII Limo. (110" wb)	5000	—	—	—	—	27,000

1905 Columbia Mark XLV, gasoline tonneau, HAC

1905 COLUMBIA
Electric cars

Mark XXXV Hansom	3500	3300	4400	6700	12,000	24,000
Mark XXXV Brgm.	3500	3500	4500	7000	13,000	25,000
Mark XXXV Landau	3500	3500	4500	7000	13,000	25,000
Mark XXXV Land'et.	3500	3700	4700	7300	13,700	26,000
Mark LX Rbt.	900	3200	4300	6500	11,000	23,000
Mark LXI Vic. Phae.	1350	3300	4400	6700	12,000	24,000

Gasoline cars — 2-cyl., 12/14 hp, 81-1/2 wb

Mark XLIII Tonneau	1500	3700	4700	7300	13,700	26,000
Mark XLIV Tonneau (18 hp)	1750	3900	4800	7700	14,300	27,000

Gasoline cars — 4-cyl., 35/40 hp, 112" wb

Mark XLV Land'et.	5000	4000	5000	8000	15,000	28,000
Mark XLV Royal Vic.	5000	4200	5200	8400	15,700	29,000
Mark XLV Limo.	5500	4200	5200	8400	15,700	29,000
Mark XLV Tonneau (108" wb)	4000	3900	4800	7700	14,300	27,000

1906 COLUMBIA
Electric cars

Mark LXVIII* Brgm.	4000	3300	4400	6700	12,000	24,000
* (Extension Front)						
Mark LXVIII Land'et.	4000	3200	4300	6500	11,000	23,000
Mark LXVIII Hansom	4000	3200	4300	6500	11,000	23,000
Mark LXVIII Vic.	4000	3300	4400	6700	12,000	24,000
Mark LX Rbt.	900	3000	4000	6000	9500	21,000
Mark XIX Surrey	1900	3100	4200	6300	10,500	22,000

1906 Columbia Mark LXVIII, electric victoria, HAC

	FP	5	4	3	2	1
Mark XI Opera Bus	2500	3700	4700	7300	13,700	26,000
Mark XI Private Bus	6000	3300	4400	6700	12,000	24,000
Gasoline cars — 2-cyl., 18 hp, 90" wb						
Mark XLIV Tour.	1750	3900	4800	7700	14,300	27,000
Gasoline cars — 4-cyl., 24/28 hp, 98" wb						
Mark XLVI Tour.	3000	4000	5000	8000	15,000	28,000
Gasoline cars — 4-cyl., 40/45 hp, 112" wb						
Mark XLVII Tour.	4500	4200	5200	8400	15,700	29,000
Mark XLVII Double Vic.	5000	4300	5400	8700	16,500	30,000
Mark XLVII Land'et.	5500	4400	5600	9200	17,300	31,000
Mark XLVII Limo.	5500	4500	5800	9500	18,000	32,000

1907 Columbia Mark XIX, electric surrey, HAC

1907 COLUMBIA
Electric cars

Mark LXVIII Brgm.*	4000	3300	4400	6700	12,000	24,000
* (Extension Front)						
Mark LXVIII Land'et.	4000	3300	4400	6700	12,000	24,000
Mark LXVIII Hamsom	4000	3200	4300	6500	11,000	23,000
Mark LXVIII Vic.	4000	3300	4400	6700	12,000	24,000
Mark LX Rbt.	900	2700	3600	5300	8800	19,000
Mark XIX Surrey	1900	3000	4000	6000	9500	21,000
Mark XI Opera Bus	2500	3200	4300	6500	11,000	23,000
Mark XI Private Bus	6000	3100	4200	6300	10,500	22,000
Gasoline cars — 2-cyl., 18/19 hp, 91" wb						
Mark XLIV Tour.	1650	3900	4800	7700	14,300	27,000
Gasoline cars — 4-cyl., 24/28 hp, 109" wb						
Mark XLVIII Tour.	3000	4000	5000	8000	15,000	28,000
Mark XLVIII Limo.	4200	3500	4500	7000	13,000	25,000
Gasoline cars — 4-cyl., 40/45 hp, 112" wb						
Mark XLIX Tour.	4500	4200	5200	8400	15,700	29,000
Mark XLIX Limo.	5500	3700	4700	7300	13,700	26,000
Gasoline cars — 4-cyl., 40/45 hp, 119-1/2" wb						
Mark XLIX Land'et.	5500	3900	4800	7700	14,300	27,000
Mark XLIX Limo.	5500	4000	5000	8000	15,000	28,000

1908 COLUMBIA
Electric cars

Mark LX Rbt.	900	2700	3600	5300	8800	19,000
Mark XIX Surrey	1900	3100	4200	6300	10,500	22,000
Mark LXX Vic. Phae.	1600	3200	4300	6500	11,000	23,000
Mark LXVII Brgm.	3500	3900	4800	7700	14,300	27,000

1908 Columbia Mark LXVII, electric brougham, HAC

Gasoline cars — 4-cyl., 29 hp, 109" wb	FP	5	4	3	2	1
Mark XLVIII Tour.	3000	3100	4200	6300	10,500	22,000
Mark XLVIII Rbt.	3000	3000	4000	6000	9500	21,000
Mark LXVIII Limo.	4200	3500	4500	7000	13,000	25,000
Gasoline cars — 4-cyl., 48 hp, 124" wb						
Mark LXVI Tour.	6500	3300	4400	6700	12,000	24,000
Mark LXVI Limo.	8500	3700	4700	7300	13,700	26,000

1909 Columbia Mark 48, gasoline roadster, HAC

1909 COLUMBIA
Electric cars

Mark 70 Vic. Phae.	1600	3200	4300	6500	11,000	23,000
Mark 67 Brgm.	3500	3500	4500	7000	13,000	25,000
Gasoline cars — 4-cyl., 29 hp, 115" wb						
Mark 48 Tour.	2750	3300	4400	6700	12,000	24,000
Mark 48 Rbt.	2750	3100	4200	6300	10,500	22,000
Mark 48 Rdstr.	2750	3200	4300	6500	11,000	23,000
Mark 48 Limo.	3750	3500	4500	7000	13,000	25,000
Mark 48 Land'et.	3850	3700	4700	7300	13,700	26,000

1910 COLUMBIA
Electric cars

Mark 70 Vic. Phae.	1600	3100	4200	6300	10,500	22,000
Mark 67 Brgm.	3500	3200	4300	6500	11,000	23,000
Mark 68 Land'et.	3500	3500	4500	7000	13,000	25,000
Gasoline cars — 4-cyl., 32.4 hp, 115" wb						
Mark 48 Tour.	2750	3300	4400	6700	12,000	24,000
Mark 48 Rdstr.-4P	2750	3500	4500	7000	13,000	25,000
Mark 48 Limo.	3850	3700	4700	7300	13,700	26,000
Mark 48 Land'et.	3950	3900	4800	7700	14,300	27,000

1910 Columbia Mark 48, gasoline touring, HAC

1911 Columbia Mark 85, gasoline vestibuled roadster, HAC

1911 COLUMBIA
Electric cars

	FP	5	4	3	2	1
Mark 70 Vic. Phae.	1600	3100	4200	6300	10,500	22,000
Mark 67 Brgm.	3500	3500	4500	7000	13,000	25,000
Gasoline cars — 4-cyl., 38 hp, 120" wb						
Mark 85 Tour.-4/6P	3100	4200	5200	8400	15,700	29,000
Mark 85 Limo.	4800	4300	5400	8700	16,500	30,000
Mark 85 Rdstr.-2/4P	3300	4300	5400	8700	16,500	30,000
Mark 85 Vestibule Rdstr.-6P	2400	4400	5600	9200	17,300	31,000
Mark 85 Land'et.	4900	4500	5800	9500	18,000	32,000
Gasoline cars — 4-cyl., 32 hp, 115" wb						
Mark 48 Tour.-5P	2700	4200	5200	8400	15,700	29,000
Mark 48 Tour.-7P	3000	4000	5000	8000	15,000	28,000
Mark 48 Rdstr.	2750	4200	5200	8400	15,700	29,000
Mark 48 Land'et.-Limo.	3850	4400	5600	9200	17,300	31,000
Mark 48 Inside Operated Cpe.	3500	4200	5200	8400	15,700	29,000

1912 Columbia Cavalier, touring, HAC

1912 COLUMBIA
Cavalier — 4-cyl., 38 hp, 120" wb

	FP	5	4	3	2	1
Rdstr.-2P	3300	4000	5000	8000	15,000	28,000
Rdstr.-4P	3300	4200	5200	8400	15,700	29,000
Tour.-6P	3400	4000	5000	8000	15,000	28,000
Tour.-7P	3500	3900	4800	7700	14,300	27,000
Limo.	4800	4300	5400	8700	16,500	30,000
Knight — 4-cyl., 38 hp, 129" wb						
Rdstr.-2/4P	4500	4200	5200	8400	15,700	29,000
Tour.-4P	4500	4000	5000	8000	15,000	28,000
Limo.-6P	4500	4400	5600	9200	17,300	31,000
Land'et.-7P	4500	4500	5800	9500	18,000	32,000

1913 Columbia Knight, touring, HAC

1913 COLUMBIA
Cavalier — 4-cyl., 38 hp, 120" wb

	FP	5	4	3	2	1
Tour.-7P	3500	4000	5000	8000	15,000	28,000
Limo.-7P	4800	4300	5400	8700	16,500	30,000
Tour.-6P	3400	4000	5000	8000	15,000	28,000
Rdstr.-2/4P	3300	4200	5200	8400	15,700	29,000
Land'et.-7P	4900	4500	5800	9500	18,000	32,000
Knight — 4-cyl., 38 hp, 129" wb						
Tour.-5/7P	4500	4400	5600	9200	17,300	31,000
Rdstr.-2/4P	4500	4700	6100	9900	19,000	33,000
Limo.-7P	5800	4400	5600	9200	17,300	31,000
Land'et.-7P	6000	4500	5800	9500	18,000	32,000

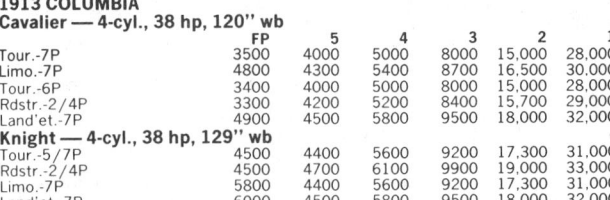

1900 Columbia Steamer

COLUMBIA STEAM — Baltimore, Maryland — 1899-1900 — The Columbia Motor & Manufacturing Company was organized during the summer of 1899 with a capital stock of five million dollars. Officers were Theodore J. King (president), A.O. Babendrerer (secretary and treasurer), and Thomas Downey, W.H. Schrom and W. Cator (directors). The plans for immediate manufacture of horseless carriages apparently didn't leave paper during 1899. In 1900, however, the Columbia people attempted to pick up the pieces of the Crouch Automobile Manufacturing & Transportation Company and make a go of the steam-car venture with which W. Lee Crouch had failed after five years of trying. Columbia failed even more quickly. Following the purchase of the Crouch assets, nothing further was heard of the Columbia venture. Probably the one steam car built was more Crouch than Columbia.

COLUMBIA — Fort Wayne, Indiana — (1902) — That the Columbia Machine Works in Fort Wayne built one automobile in 1902 has been documented. Its six horsepower engine was constructed at the plant as apparently were all other components of the vehicle. "The castings and all parts were received recently from the foundry," *The Motor Age* reported in May, "and are now being turned and trued up on the lathe." Whether Columbia intended the car as a prototype for production was not recorded, but manufacture does not seem to have followed in any case.

COLUMBIA STEAM — Brooklyn, New York — (1904-1905) — From 1901 to 1903 the Columbia Engineering Works at William and Inlay streets in Brooklyn built the steam vehicles designed by Arthur Herschmann and marketed under his own name. When Herschmann orders stopped arriving, Columbia decided to produce a steamer of its own, in both passenger and commercial version. Details regarding the vehicles are lacking, but Columbia did not build them long. "Out of the Game," *The Motor Age* headlined in August 1905 in announcing that Columbia had "discontinued the manufacture of cars for the present." Manufacture was not resumed.

COLUMBIA — Seattle, Washington — (1914) — This Columbia was built by the American Cyclecar Company of Seattle. A side-by-side two-seater, it had a two-cylinder ohv engine, friction transmission, belt drive, 96-inch wheelbase and 40-inch tread — and most probably only prototypes were built. In May of 1914, *The American Cyclecar* announced that the Columbia remained in the experimental stage. "Developments constantly leading to some modification or improvements that have been thought advisable have caused delays," the magazine said. Evidence is lacking that production ever began. Daniel Murray and George L. Grant had been the backers of this venture.

COLUMBIA ELECTRIC — The Columbia Electric Company of Indiana produced an automobile in McCordsville from 1905-1906 and in Knightstown into 1912 that was marketed under the tradename of Leader. Refer to Leader.

The Columbia Electric Vehicle Company was incorporated in New Jersey in May of 1899 to "manufacture and operate motor vehicles driven by electricity or other power." This venture was an offshoot of the Electric Vehicle Company, producers of the Columbia in Hartford, Connecticut.

The Columbia Electric Vehicle Company of Detroit produced the Columbia Electric only in 1914. Thereafter both the car and the company's name was changed to Columbian. Refer to Columbian Electric.

COLUMBIA MOTOR BUGGY — Hamilton, Ohio — (1909) — Thomas L. Curley was the president, J.E. Wright the vice-president and Robert Kennedy the secretary-treasurer of the Columbia Carriage Company of Hamilton. In October of 1908 they announced the completion of their company's first experimental motorized vehicle. In January of 1909 followed the announcement that production had begun. The Columbia Motor Buggy (also occasionally referred to as the Hamilton) was powered by a two-cylinder 16 hp engine mounted in an 86-inch wheelbase chassis. It was a completely conventional highwheeler with the simplest of specifications. But obviously it was too much for Columbia Carriage. That August, after building twenty-five motor buggies, the company informed the press that it intended to stick to horsedrawn vehicles from now on.

1893 Columbia Perambulator, electric dos-a-dos, NAHC

COLUMBIA PERAMBULATOR — Chicago, Illinois — (1892-1896) — In 1892, as the World's Columbian Exposition drew near in Chicago, three electric vehicle proponents (Clyde J. Coleman, Fred Dagenhardt and E.E. Keller) joined together to form the Columbia Perambulator Company with the expectation of obtaining a franchise from the fair promoters to produce motorized transport for visitors. Three pilot vehicles were built, two of them rolling three-wheel chairs with electric motors. The third was a four-wheeler with two seats placed dos-a-dos and steering by an upright wheel on the right side. Its top speed was 10 mph. Unfortunately no lucrative franchise was offered by the Columbia Exposition people, and consequently this venture was abandoned with the building of the pilot models. The four-wheeler as well as one of the motorized chairs were exhibited at the Electrical Building at the Exposition. The only motorized vehicle seen on the grounds was the electric car built by William Morrison which was then being promoted by Harold Sturges. Subsequently Columbia Perambulator produced at least two electric tricycles (with motor supplied by Frank Perret of New York City), but that the company entered sustained manufacture has not been documented.

1917 Columbia Six, touring, HAC

COLUMBIA SIX — Detroit, Michigan — (1916-1924) — In 1915 the executive suite of the King Motor Car Company in Detroit became a temporarily lonely place as the firm's president, sales manager and manufacturing superintendent took an abrupt leave to start their own company. Joining J.G. Bayerline, Walter L. Daly and T.A. Bollinger in the formation of the Columbia Motors Company of Detroit were William E. Metzger, one of the founders of the E-M-F Company, and A.T. O'Connor, formerly of Olds and Packard. With a roster like that, success seemed assured — and for a while it was. The Columbia Six was an assembled car, but a particularly fine one: Continental engines, Timken axles and roller bearings, Detroit Self-Lubricating springs, Warner transmission and steering gear, Borg & Beck clutch, Stromberg carburetor, Harrison radiator. But one feature which belonged exclusively to Columbia was its motor temperature control: a thermostat placed just above the fan which automatically opened the radiator shutters as temperature increased. The Columbia Six was probably the first car in its price class to feature such a device. Most Columbias sold for under $2000, and were very nicely finished. The $1475 Sport Model, for example, had a walnut instrument panel, French beveled plate window, and hassocks instead of the usual footrail. An even sportier model was rather cleverly called the Columbia Six Shooter. When sales reached 6000 units in 1923, however, the men who had so wisely guided Columbia's fortunes thus far became overenthusiastic. Anticipating a boom, they bought out the Liberty Motor Car Company across town in Detroit, and both Liberty and Columbia went bust the following year.

1917 COLUMBIA SIX
Model D — 6-cyl., 25.35 hp, 115" wb

	FP	5	4	3	2	1
Tour.-5P	1175	4200	5200	8400	15,700	29,000

1918 Columbia Six, touring sedan, HAC

1918 COLUMBIA SIX
Model C — 6-cyl., 25.35 hp, 115" wb

Tour.-5P	1350	4200	5200	8400	15,700	29,000
Spt.-4P	1495	4300	5400	8700	16,500	30,000
Sed.-5P	1995	2700	3600	5300	8800	19,000

1919 Columbia Six, sport touring, KM

1919 COLUMBIA SIX
Six — 6-cyl., 25.35 hp, 115" wb

Tour.-5P	1600	4200	5200	8400	15,700	29,000
Spt.-4P	1745	4300	5400	8700	16,500	30,000
Tour. Sed.-5P	2445	2700	3600	5300	8800	19,000

1920 Columbia Six, 20-E roadster, HAC

1920 COLUMBIA SIX
Six, Series 20 — 6-cyl., 38 hp, 115" wb

	FP	5	4	3	2	1
Tour.-5P	1695	4200	5200	8400	15,700	29,000
Spt.-4P	1845	4400	5600	9200	17,300	31,000
Rds.-2P	1845	4900	6300	10,300	21,000	34,000
Sed.-5P	2850	2700	3600	5300	8800	19,000
Cpe.-4P	2850	2900	3700	5600	9100	20,000

1921 Columbia Six, 20-D sport, HAC

1921 COLUMBIA SIX
Six, Series 20 — 6-cyl., 55 hp, 115" wb

	FP	5	4	3	2	1
Tour.-5P	1795	4300	5400	8700	16,500	30,000
Spts.-4P	1945	4400	5600	9200	17,300	31,000
Rds.-2P	1945	4900	6300	10,300	21,000	34,000
Sed.-5P	2895	2700	3600	5300	8800	19,000
Cpe.-4P	2895	2900	3700	5600	9100	20,000

1922 Columbia Six, deluxe touring, HAC

1922 COLUMBIA SIX
Six — 6-cyl., 55 hp, 115" wb

	FP	5	4	3	2	1
Model CC DeL. Tour.-5P	1475	4400	5600	9200	17,300	31,000
Model D Spt.-4P	1475	4500	5800	9500	18,000	32,000
Model E Rds.-2P	1475	4900	6300	10,300	21,000	34,000
Model H Cpe.-4P	2295	2900	3700	5600	9100	20,000
Model CS Sed.-5P	2350	2800	3700	5500	9000	19,500
Challenger Tour.-5P	1195	4200	5200	8400	15,700	29,000
Challenger Cpe.-4P	1995	2500	3500	5000	8500	18,000
Challenger Sed.-5P	1995	2300	3300	4600	7500	16,000
Six Shooter	—	2400	3400	4800	8000	17,000

1923 Columbia Light Six, touring, HAC

1923 COLUMBIA SIX
Light Six — 6-cyl., 50 hp, 115" wb

	FP	5	4	3	2	1
Tour.-5P	985	4500	5800	9500	18,000	32,000
Rds.-2P	995	5000	6500	11,000	22,000	35,000
Spc. Six Phae.	1095	4900	6300	10,300	21,000	34,000
Cpe.-2P	1235	2700	3600	5300	8800	19,000
Spc. Six Spt.-4P	1395	3000	4000	6000	9500	21,000

	FP	5	4	3	2	1
Sed.-5P	1395	2300	3300	4600	7500	16,000
Spc. Six Cpe.-4P	1685	2900	3700	5600	9100	20,000
Elite — 6-cyl., 55 hp, 115" wb						
Spt.-5P	1475	3900	4800	7700	14,300	27,000
Cpe.-4P	1925	3100	4200	6300	10,500	22,000
Sed.-5P	1995	2700	3600	5300	8800	19,000
Tour.-5P	1475	4000	5000	8000	15,000	28,000

1924 Columbia Six, sedan, HAC

1924 COLUMBIA SIX
Six — 6-cyl., 50 hp, 115" wb

	FP	5	4	3	2	1
Stnd. Phae.-5P	995	4200	5200	8400	15,700	29,000
Rds.-2P	995	4500	5800	9500	18,000	32,000
Hollywood Phae.-5P	1195	4500	5800	9500	18,000	32,000
Cpe.-2P	1295	2900	3700	5600	9100	20,000
Tiger Spt.-4P	1395	4700	6100	9900	19,000	33,000
Sed.-5P	1495	2500	3500	5000	8500	18,000
Hollywood Cpe.-4P	1585	3000	4000	6000	9500	21,000
Sed.-5P	1650	2700	3600	5300	8800	19,000
Hollywood Spc. Sed.-5P	1995	3000	4000	6000	9500	21,000

1914 Columbian Electric, 2-pass. runabout, WLB

COLUMBIAN ELECTRIC — Detroit, Michigan — (1914-1917) — During those years when lower prices seemed to be the salvation for the electric car industry, C.F. Krueger of Detroit came up with a particularly nice rendition of an inexpensive battery-powered car. In February of 1914 he announced the formation of his Columbia Electric Vehicle Company to produce the Columbia Electric. Subsequently, when several articles appeared in the trade press noting for the reader's interest that this new concern should not be confused with the electric-producing Columbia Motor Car Company which had just gone to the wall in Hartford (Connecticut), Krueger decided to further ameliorate any confusion and by 1915 had changed both his car and his company's name to Columbian. The Columbia(n) Electric was offered in two (later three) body styles on one chassis (88-inch wheelbase). These were perky little cars with wire wheels and curvaceous fenders and a bargain at under $1000, but alas the initial price tags were not sufficient to produce a profit. When Krueger raised his prices in order to make a profit, sales plummeted. By late 1917, he was convinced he was in a can't-win situation and simply closed up shop.

1914 Columbian Electric, 3-pass. coupelette, WLB

348

1914-1915 COLUMBIAN ELECTRIC

	FP	5	4	3	2	1
Columbia(n) Electric Rbt.-2P	785	3000	4000	6000	9500	21,000
Columbia(n) Electric Coupelette-3P	985	2900	3700	5600	9100	20,000

1914 Columbian Electric, 4-pass. brougham, WLB

1916 COLUMBIAN ELECTRIC

	FP	5	4	3	2	1
Columbian Electric Rbt.-2P	995	3000	4000	6000	9500	21,000
Columbian Electric Brgm.-4P	1495	2900	3700	5600	9100	20,000
Columbian Electric Coupelette-3P	1275	2900	3700	5600	9100	20,000

1917 COLUMBIAN ELECTRIC

	FP	5	4	3	2	1
Columbian Electric Rbt.-2P	1175	3000	4000	6000	9500	21,000
Columbian Electric Brgm.-4P	1575	2900	3700	5600	9100	20,000
Columbian Electric Coupelette-3P	1375	2900	3700	5600	9100	20,000

COLUMBUS — Columbus was the name used in a trade periodical for the cars produced in 1903-1904 by Rodgers & Company of Columbus, Ohio. The magazine had simply and erroneously referred to the car by its location rather than its name, however. Refer to Imperial.

The Columbus Auto Parts Company was organized during the fall of 1912 with a capital stock of $25,000 and the plan to manufacture automobiles. The incorporators of this Ohio venture were R.E. Klages, C.J. Krag, C.K. Klages, J.C. Stoddart and W.D. McKinney. Manufacture is doubted.

The Columbus Automobile Company built a car called the Benz Spirit in 1900. Refer to Benz Spirit.

The Columbus Motor Vehicle Company produced automobiles from 1902-1904 which were named for the famous French balloonist of the period. Refer to Santos-Dumont.

COLUMBUS — Columbus, Ohio — (1903) — Late in 1903 the Columbus Carriage & Harness Company announced the completion of its first prototype two-cylinder air-cooled shaft-drive motorcar. The company planned to build light runabout, doctor's closed phaeton and delivery wagon versions once production commenced. Production never commenced, however; the prototype was the only car built.

1907 Columbus, auto-buggy, NAHC

COLUMBUS — Columbus, Ohio — (1907-1908) — The Columbus Buggy Company, whose origins dated back to early post-Civil War days, was among the largest producers of horsedrawn vehicles in America. Atypically for a buggy producer, Columbus entered the automotive industry with an electric car which was marketed beginning in 1903 as the Columbus Electric. In December of 1905 the firm bought out the gasoline automobile company operated by the Bramwells in Springfield (Ohio), together with the services of C.C. Bramwell who came up with the first Columbus entry into gasoline car ranks. It was a highwheeler on a 72-inch wheelbase with rope drive, and powered by a two-cylinder 10 hp air-cooled engine. Alternately referred to as the Buggymobile or the Columbus, the car's price was $750 and its slogan "a Vehicle for the Masses, not a Toy for the Classes," which was a rather pointed put-down of more expensive and more powerful standard cars. Ironically, Columbus Buggy began producing one of these itself in 1909, called the Firestone-Columbus, after company president Clinton D. Firestone. The highwheeler was immediately forgotten. The Firestone-Columbus and the Columbus Electric were continued in production into 1915.

1907-1908 COLUMBUS
Buggymobile — 2-cyl., 10 hp, 72" wb

	FP	5	4	3	2	1
Highwheeler	750	2500	3500	5000	8500	18,000

COLUMBUS — Columbus, Ohio — (1913-1914) — In December of 1913 the Columbus Brass Company completed the building of its prototype cyclecar and began testing it on the streets in town. In January 1914 *The American Cyclecar* reported that "some changes in the car are being made, but these are of minor importance, as the model has been demonstrated a success." There is no evidence, however, that Columbus Brass ever introduced its cyclecar on the market.

1907 Columbus Electric, model 1100, surrey, WLB

COLUMBUS ELECTRIC — Columbus, Ohio — (1903-1915) — Unlike most Midwest wagon builders, the Columbus Buggy Company entered the automobile field not with a highwheeler but with an electric. Manufacture was begun in a small way as early as 1903, though it was not until 1906 that the model line grew from a single body style, and an aggressive promotion and marketing plan was set up. By 1909 business was booming, and the schedule for 1910 called for the production of 1000 Columbus Electrics, the best year thus far. By now, too, Columbus Buggy had finally entered the gasoline car field, typically with a highwheeler at first, which was marketed from 1907 to 1908 as the Columbus, and which then grew into a large standard car marketed beginning in 1909 as the Firestone-Columbus. Clinton D. Firestone was the president of Columbus Buggy. Obviously, he made a mistake somewhere because his flourishing company rather rapidly began to founder. In January 1913 bankruptcy was declared, and Columbus Buggy's creditors took over. In August 1913 Clinton Firestone, with his old treasurer O.H. Perry, organized the Columbus Electric Vehicle Company for the manufacture of pleasure and commercial cars, though rumor quickly spread that the real reason for this organization was to allow Firestone to bid on the assets of Columbus Buggy when the creditors' committee elected to sell. Ultimately, in May 1914, sell the creditors did, but not to Firestone. Instead, Columbus Buggy went to a group of Buffalo (New York) businessmen headed by Charles A. Finnegan of the E.R. Thomas Motor Car Company. Reorganization plans immediately followed for the continuing production of gasoline and electric cars, in addition to horsedrawn vehicles. There was a name change to New Columbus Buggy Company (capitalized at $500,000), and the possibility loomed that the Thomas Flyer might be built in Ohio as well. George Lattimer, a wholesale druggist who had been operating the firm in the interests of the creditors, was retained as president. He was soon out of a job, however, as were most of the workers who were laid off summarily, a skeleton crew being retained to finish vehicles on hand. In May of 1915 the factory of the New Columbus Buggy Company was sold at public auction. Included in the sale were thirty-five new Columbus Electrics, twelve new Firestone-Columbuses and eighteen used cars.

349

1903-1905 COLUMBUS ELECTRIC

	FP	5	4	3	2	1
Folding Top Rbt.	—	—	—	—	—	—

1906 COLUMBUS ELECTRIC

No. 100 Vict. Phae.	—	—	—	—	—	—
No. 1102 Sta. Wag.	—	—	—	—	—	—
No. 1100 Surrey	—	—	—	—	—	—
No. 1102 Inside Operated Cpe.	—	—	—	—	—	—

1907 Columbus Electric, model 1000, runabout, WLB

1907 COLUMBUS ELECTRIC

	FP	5	4	3	2	1
Model 1002 Cpe. (69" wb)	1900	2700	3600	5300	8800	19,000
Model 1000 Rbt. (69" wb)	1900	2900	3700	5600	9100	20,000
Model 1100 Surrey (89" wb)	2500	3000	4000	6000	9500	21,000
Model 1102 Sta. Wag. (89" wb)	3000	2900	3700	5600	9100	20,000

1908 COLUMBUS ELECTRIC

	FP	5	4	3	2	1
Model 1000 Phae. (69" wb)	—	2700	3600	5300	8800	19,000
Model 1002 Cpe. (69" wb)	—	2500	3500	5000	8500	18,000
Model 1100 Surrey (89" wb)	—	2900	3700	5600	9100	20,000

1909 Columbus Electric, model 1001, victoria stanhope, WLB

1909 Columbus Electric, model 1002, coupe, HAC

1909 COLUMBUS ELECTRIC

	FP	5	4	3	2	1
Model 1000 Stanhope (74" wb)	1700	2900	3700	5600	9100	20,000
Model 1202 Brgm. (76" wb)	2200	2500	3500	5000	8500	18,000
Model 1002 Cpe. (74" wb)	2000	2400	3400	4800	8000	17,000
Model 1001 Stanhope (74" wb)	1750	3000	4000	6000	9500	21,000
Model 1100 Surrey (86" wb)	2500	3100	4200	6300	10,500	22,000

1910 COLUMBUS ELECTRIC

	FP	5	4	3	2	1
Model 1010 Rbt. (83" wb)	—	2900	3700	5600	9100	20,000
Model 1001 Vict. (75" wb)	—	2500	3500	5000	8500	18,000
Model 1202 Cpe. (75" wb)	—	2400	3400	4800	8000	17,000
Model 1000 Phae. (75" wb)	—	2700	3600	5300	8800	19,000

1911 COLUMBUS ELECTRIC

	FP	5	4	3	2	1
Model 1000 Stanhope (75" wb)	—	2900	3700	5600	9100	20,000
Model 1002 Cpe. (75" wb)	—	2500	3500	5000	8500	18,000
Model 1220 Cpe. (88" wb)	—	2700	3600	5300	8800	19,000

1912 COLUMBUS ELECTRIC

	FP	5	4	3	2	1
Model 1220 Cpe. (88" wb)	—	2700	3600	5300	8800	19,000
Model 1202 Cpe. (77" wb)	—	2500	3500	5000	8500	18,000

1913 COLUMBUS ELECTRIC

	FP	5	4	3	2	1
Model 1230 Colonial Cpe. (86" wb)	2550	2500	3500	5000	8500	18,000
Model 1234 Colonial Cpe. (92" wb)	3000	2700	3600	5300	8800	19,000
Model 1250 Colonial Cpe. (92" wb)	3200	2700	3600	5300	8800	19,000

1914 COLUMBUS ELECTRIC

	FP	5	4	3	2	1
Model 1234 Colonial Cpe. (92" wb)	2800	2700	3600	5300	8800	19,000
Model 1230 Colonial Cpe. (86" wb)	2350	2500	3500	5000	8500	18,000
Model 1250 Colonial Cpe. (100" wb)	3000	2900	3700	5600	9100	20,000

1915 COLUMBUS ELECTRIC

	FP	5	4	3	2	1
New Columbus Model 1234 Cpe. (92" wb)	—	2900	3700	5600	9100	20,000
New Columbus Model 1230 Cpe. (86" wb)	—	2700	3600	5300	8800	19,000

1908 Comet, V-8, runabout, WLB

COMET — San Francisco, California — (1907-1909) — The Comet is perhaps the least known of Elbert John Hall's achievements. Together with Jesse G. Vincent, Hall is credited with the design of the renowned Liberty aircraft engine of World War I. His Hall-Scott engine powered the fabulous Fageol car of that period, and subsequently became famous for its dependability in truck and bus applications for a generation. The Comet preceded all this activity; it was his first automobile. Elbert Hall was a native Californian who began his career as a machinist and in 1902 was awarded half ownership in the I.L. Burton Machine Works for which he was then employed. He spent several years thereafter building heftier engines for cars shipped from the East Coast which could not manage the formidable San Francisco hills, and in 1905 he did some work for the Heine-Velox company as well. Both the Burton and Heine-Velox factories were destroyed in the San Francisco earthquake, and in 1907 Hall joined the newly organized Comet Automobile Company. When that firm died aborning, Hall kept the name and set himself up elsewhere in San Francisco as the Hall Auto Repair Company, and allied with Walter C. Morris (the San Francisco Autocar dealer) in the Hall Automobile Company. From the latter came the Comet, a 25 hp ohv four that was advertised lustily: "A guarantee of 75 miles an hour goes with every $1,500 Comet sold." Most of the cars that followed were two-seater roadsters with victoria tops on 102-inch wheelbase chassis. But not all of the engines were fours. A six was built on special order in 1909; the year previous had seen a roadster stuffed with a V-8. Comets were quite competitive in West Coast racing, highlighted in August of 1908 by overwhelming domination at the Santa Rosa races (Comets won seven of the eight races in which they were entered). On another occasion Elbert Hall managed zero to 45 mph in three blocks uphill in San Francisco. Total Comet production is believed to have been seven cars. Although not a commercial success, this venture, was a beginning. In 1910 Elbert Hall met Bert Scott and formed the partnership which resulted in the noteworthy continuation of his career.

COMET — Buffalo, New York — (1913-1914) — The Comet from Buffalo was a 25 hp four available as a $750 roadster and a $950 touring car — and was produced by the Continental Motors Corporation. This venture had been incorporated in Buffalo on September 7th, 1912 by Gordon L.

Matthews, Frank V. Whyland, Allen E. Choate, Walter F. Schmiding and Reverdy L. Hurd. Of this quintet, Frank Whyland is known to have had previous automobile experience, with the Whyland-Nelson and Whyland cars, both ventures which proved as quickly futile as the Comet would.

1914 Comet, model A, runabout, WLB

COMET — Indianapolis, Indiana — (1914) — "Have you seen the Comet?," the advertisement read. "Not a luminous celestial body, according to Webster's definition, but a speedy, snappy little cyclecar, virtually a four-wheeled motorcycle built on automobile lines." The Comet was a belt-drive tandem two-seater powered by an air-cooled two-cylinder Spacke engine. Its wheelbase was 100 inches, its tread 36. One interesting feature was the fitting of the front fenders to the wheel spindles as in motorcycle practice. "The cyclecar has a far different dust proposition than a big car," the company said, "and must have fenders to fit the new condition." The Comet was designed by Fred B. Mertz and financed by E.R. Parry and St. Clair Parry, whose brother David M. had earlier produced the Parry automobile which lasted a year longer than would the Comet. Twenty-five Comets had been assembled by early 1914 for test purposes before beginning large-scale manufacturing operations in the Comet Cyclecar Company plant in Indianapolis. Probably not many more than those first test cars were ever built. Interestingly, this firm had begun life as the Economy Cyclecar Company but this was quickly changed when it was discovered there was another cyclecar on the East Coast with the Economy name.

1914 COMET
Cyclecar — 2-cyl., 10 hp, 100" wb

	FP	5	4	3	2	1
Tandem Rds.	500	—	—	—	—	—

1920 Comet Six, model C-53, touring, HAC

COMET — Decatur, Illinois — (1917-1922) — George W. Jagers was a native of Racine (Wisconsin) and began his career as a costing clerk for the J.I. Case Threshing Machine Company. Subsequently acquiring control of the Racine Manufacturing Company, a novelty and toy producer which had fallen on hard times in Racine, Jagers used it as a base from which to launch himself into the automobile industry. During the fall of 1916 he opened an office in Chicago, rented loft space in nearby Rockford, and under the aegis of Racine Manufacturing had about a dozen prototypes of his new Comet assembled. The car was introduced at the Chicago Automobile Show in January of 1917, though production didn't begin until August when a factory was set up in downstate Decatur. The product of the new Comet Automobile Company was an assembled car with a six-cylinder engine and the straight-line body styling which was very much in vogue. Initially, the powerplant was a Lewis (the same six which had powered the Lewis from Racine), but soon a switch to Continental was made. Sales of the Comet in the Midwest were modest, but consistent, and the company seemed to be faring well. "This Comet Has Come to Stay," advertising enthused. In 1920 Comet received an order for forty cars from Antwerp, Belgium — and grand plans were immediately made in Decatur for going international. Construction was begun on a huge and expensive new factory with a 200-car-per-day capacity. But huge foreign orders never materialized and there were no Comets even in Decatur anymore. By December of 1920 the company was in deep trouble, following the failure of its bond issue sale. In voluntary receivership, and with a plan to refinance, production continued. A smaller four in the $1000 range was introduced as a companion to the Comet Six. Reportedly, George Jagers wanted to return to Racine and relocate his Comet factory

there, but this never materialized. Neither did a viable refinancing plan. The company's administrative affairs were in a tangle, and authorities were looking askance at its stock selling operations. There were no bidders when the company was offered for sale as a whole late in 1922. In the personal property sale that followed in 1923, one Comet Six touring car brought only $35, while stacks of wheels sold at eight cents each. In 1924 eight former officers of the company were indicated for using the mails to defraud. Most of them appear to have ultimately been cleared of the charges.

1918 Comet Six, model 6-50, touring, HAC

1917-1918 COMET
Six-50 — 6-cyl., 50 hp, 125" wb

	FP	5	4	3	2	1
Tour.-5P	1285	4000	5000	8000	15,000	28,000

1919 COMET
Six-50 — 6-cyl., 50 hp, 125" wb

Tour.-5P	1685	4000	5000	8000	15,000	28,000

1920 COMET
Model C-53 — 6-cyl., 55 hp, 125" wb

Tour.-5P	2150	4200	5200	8400	15,700	29,000

1921 Comet Six, model C-53-2, touring, WLB

1921 COMET
Model C-53-2 — 6-cyl., 55 hp, 125" wb

Sed.-5P	3650	4200	5200	8400	15,700	29,000

1922 Comet, Light Four, touring, WLB

1922 COMET
Light Four — 30/32 hp

Tour.-5P	985	3900	4800	7700	14,300	27,000

Model C-53-2 — 6-cyl., 55 hp, 125" wb

Tour.-5P	2350	4200	5200	8400	15,700	29,000
Sed.-5P	3650	2700	3600	5300	8800	19,000
Sed.-7P	3750	2500	3500	5000	8500	18,000

COMET RACER — In 1904 a special eight-cylinder racer called the Comet was built by the Marion Motor Car Company of Indianapolis, Indiana. Refer to Marion.

1922 Commander, Six, sedan, KM

COMMANDER — New York, New York — (1922) — The Commander existed in a nifty brochure that was headlined "The Automobile Without an Equal." That wasn't exactly true, since the Commander was an Ogren with a new radiator badge. In September of 1922 Hugo W. Ogren left the presidency of the car and company named for him in Milwaukee, Wisconsin and headed east. Most probably, he recognized the reality that his Ogren was about to fail (which it was) and he had in the meantime happened upon a group of New York financiers willing to back him in a new automotive venture. Commander Motors Corporation was organized later that month with a capital stock of $2,000,000 and headquarters at 49 Wall Street. A factory for manufacture was now under construction in Chicago and expected to be ready by November. A press note indicated that the Commander would be built in the Ogren plant in Wisconsin until the Chicago facility was ready, which seemed rather unlikely since one might have imagined Hugo Ogren to have been *persona non grata* in Milwaukee. None of the Ogren company people seem to have been involved in this Commander venture. President of the new company was Charles H. Wilcox, vice-president was Nicholas Schmidt, secretary-treasurer was Sidney R. Flett, sales director was K.W. Zoeller. Zoeller quickly found himself with nothing to sell, because the Commander venture died aborning. The only car produced was the single Ogren sporting new badge and hubcaps. Meanwhile, the real Ogren in Milwaukee struggled on for a while longer.

COMMERCE — Detroit, Michigan — (1907-1908) — In 1906 the American Machine Manufacturing Company of Detroit announced its intention to embark upon the manufacture of automobile engines and parts. David Blumenthal was the president of this firm, Charles C. Simons the vice-president, F.V. Nicol the secretary-treasurer and W.J. Grant the superintendent. That fall the capital stock in the company was increased by $60,000 to allow the firm to enter the automobile manufacturing field as well, with Paul Arthur hired to design the company's vehicles which would be sold under the tradename of Commerce. As the name suggests, the American Machine product line consisted chiefly of commercial vehicles, though convertible passenger/delivery cars were also built, as well as a few large touring cars for use by hotels. Production at the American Machine factory at Beaubien and Champlain streets in Detroit continued through 1908.

1922 Commerce, 10-pass. touring, JAC

COMMERCE — Detroit, Michigan — (1922) — The Commerce Motor Car Company had been building trucks in Detroit since 1911. In 1922 the company added a ten-passenger touring car to its line. It was powered by a six-cylinder 73 hp Continental 9A engine, placed in a 127-inch wheelbase. Its price tag was $2350, its comfortable touring speed was 40 mph, and its slogan was "the wonder of motordom." Commerce produced its wonder for 1922 only, however. By 1923 it had returned to the manufacture of trucks and large buses exclusively.

COMMERCIAL — The Commercial Automobile Company of Chicago produced an automobile in 1908 known as the Hennegin. Refer to Hennegin.

The Commercial Car Company of Keyport, New Jersey was organized with a capital stock of $125,000 during the fall of 1909. Manufacture of automobiles and motor boats was the plan of G.F. Smith, P. and W. Cherry and C. Russell. It does not seem to have been realized.

The Commercial Car Sales & Service Company was organized in Chicago late in 1911 to manufacture automobiles, engines and accessories. The capital stock was $10,000; incorporators were G.H. Taylor, B. McWilliams and F.A. Rinehart. Manufacture of an automobile is doubted.

The Commercial Motor Company of Jersey City, New Jersey took over the assets of the defunct Panam of Mamaroneck, New York in the late spring of 1903. Commercial proceeded to build a truck and only as a prototype before going out of business.

The Commercial Motor Car Company of San Antonio, Texas promoted a car called the San Antonio in 1910. Refer to San Antonio.

The Commercial Motor Car Company of Houston, Texas promoted a car called the Brandon in 1911. Refer to Brandon.

The Commercial Motor Car Company was organized in Cincinnati, Ohio during the summer of 1913 to manufacture and deal in automobiles. The capital stock was $50,000. Incorporators were Walter G. Vosler and a lot of people named Hoelscher — H.A., E.H., W.H. and George. These same people incorporated the Commercial Motor Transportation Company the month following with a capital stock of $250,000. Neither venture is believed to have proceeded anywhere.

The Commercial Motor Car Company of St. Louis, Missouri was incorporated in the spring of 1906 to manufacture and deal in automobiles. Capital stock was $10,000. Involved in this venture were Charles B. McKinney, Frank E. Stevens and Lou E. Stevens of St. Louis, and Eugenia E. McKinney of Irving, Illinois. Manufacture is doubted.

The Commercial Motor Car Company was organized with a capital stock of $25,000 in the summer of 1911 to "manufacture, buy and sell motor cars, appliances, etc., make repairs and maintain a garage" in Wilkes Barre, Pennsylvania. Behind this venture were Edward W. Davis, J. Wallace Davis and Thomas W. Haines. Manufacture of an automobile is doubted.

The Commercial Motors Company was organized in Louisville, Kentucky in the spring of 1912 with a capital stock of $10,000 to manufacture and sell automobiles. The incorporators were Harry B. Fitch, R.J. Hurt and R.E. Scharf. Manufacture is doubted.

The Commercial Truck & Automobile Company was organized in New Orleans, Louisiana late in 1911 to make automobiles and trucks. The incorporators were Richard Brook and John D. Edwards. An automobile did not follow.

COMMERCIAL ELECTRIC — Detroit, Michigan — (1903-1904) — The Commercial Motor Vehicle Company of 108 St. Antoine Street in Detroit desired so vigorously that it be recognized as a manufacturer of commercial vehicles only that it termed its sole passenger-car model as a "business man's carriage." It was a small 500-pound runabout with a top speed of 14 mph and was good for 40 miles on one charge of its ten-cell battery. The motor was three-quarter horsepower. Everything else the Commercial Motor Vehicle Company built was considerably bigger. The delivery wagon was equipped with two 2 1/2 hp motors and a 40-cell battery. A ten-ton truck, called the Quadray, had four 4 hp motors and an 80-cell battery. A forty-passenger bus was similarly powered. The Commercial Motor Vehicle Company was in production through 1904, and may have lingered for a short while into 1905, although this cannot be documented.

COMMODORE — New York, New York — (1921-1922) — In 1921 the Commodore was offered with a six-cylinder Continental engine in two body styles ranging in price from $4000-$5200; in 1922 the car was a four with Wisconsin engine offered in five models ranging from $2850-$3500. No doubt its name had been chosen to elicit association with the famed Hotel Commodore in New York City, the site often for the prestigious Automobile Salons of the period. But something went wrong somewhere, as the wide discrepancy between the car's offerings in the two years it was produced indicates. Production doubtless was minimal. Very little is known about the Commodore Motors Corporation which was located at 1552 Broadway in New York. Its charter was repealed in 1925, following a two-year delinquency in paying taxes.

1921 COMMODORE
Six — 60 hp, 132-1/2" wb

	FP	5	4	3	2	1
Spt. Sed.-5P	5200	3200	4300	6500	11,000	23,000
Spt. Rdstr.-4P	4000	4500	5800	9500	18,000	32,000

1922 COMMODORE
Four — 60 hp, 132-1/2" wb

Tour.-4P	2950	4300	5400	8700	16,500	30,000
Spt. Rdstr.-2P	2850	4500	5800	9500	18,000	32,000
Cabriolet-2P	3250	4200	5200	8400	15,700	29,000
Cpe.-4P	3250	2700	3600	5300	8800	19,000
Sed.-5P	3500	2300	3300	4600	7500	16,000

COMMONWEALTH — Boston, Massachusetts — (1903-1904) — In the *Motor Age* edition of September 17th, 1903, A.J. Coburn & Company of Boston announced the development of an automobile called the Commonwealth which was said to be "almost ready for introduction." It was never introduced. What happened is not known, but the Coburn company quickly returned the focus of its attention to the selling of Crestmobiles and Elmores, which had been its business prior to the Commonwealth idea. Only a prototype was built.

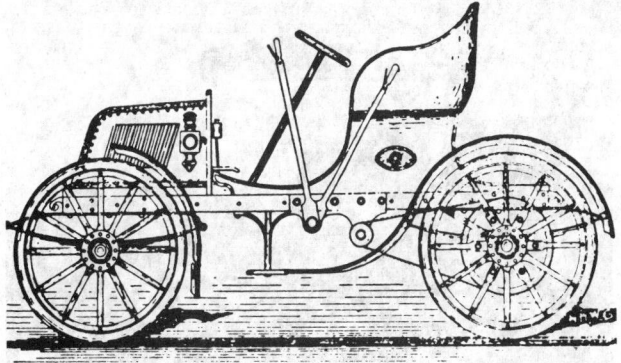
1904 Commonwealth, runabout, GR

1918 Commonwealth, Four, roadster, HAC

COMMONWEALTH — Joliet, Illinois — (1917-1922) — Commonwealth Motors Corporation was the name to which the company manufacturing the Partin-Palmer was changed in 1915 after it got into financial trouble in Chicago. In 1917 the car's name was changed to Commonwealth too, and the factory was relocated in Joliet. The Commonwealth slogan, "The Car with the Foundation," had nothing to do with the checkered existence of the Partin-Palmer, but instead referred to the overkill exercised in the construction of the Commonwealth frame: chrome nickel alloy steel from Parish & Bingham, with five-inch channel section, extra wide body flanges "super-reinforced" with heavily gussetted cross members, the top of the frame lined with thick felt to prevent body squeaks. On the exterior, the series of rivets along the seams of the hood were a distinguishing feature. Engines were generally fours from Lycoming or Herschell-Spillman, though two more cylinders were available for 1919 in a Victory Six model. The little roadster was available with the option of a tent — and was dubbed the American Traveler. A new car designed by Leland F. Goodspeed, and carrying his name, was tried in 1922. But more noteworthy certainly was the car from Commonwealth Motors which followed its merger with the Markin Body Corporation in October 1921. It was a taxicab called Checker which proceeded to make a good deal of history. The Commonwealth, and the Goodspeed, were promptly forgotten.

1917-1918 COMMONWEALTH
Four — 19.6 hp, 112" wb

	FP	5	4	3	2	1
Rdstr.-4P	895	3000	4000	6000	9500	21,000
Tour.-5P	895	2900	3700	5600	9100	20,000

1919 Commonwealth, Four, 5-pass. touring, WLB

1919 COMMONWEALTH
Four — 19.6 hp, 115" wb

Rdstr.-4P	1095	3000	4000	6000	9500	21,000
Tour.-5P	1095	2900	3700	5600	9100	20,000

Six — 25.3 hp, 115" wb

Vic. Six Tour.	1295	3100	4200	6300	10,500	22,000

1920 Commonwealth, model 4-40, touring, HAC

1920 COMMONWEALTH
Model 4-40 — 4-cyl., 35 hp, 117" wb

	FP	5	4	3	2	1
Tour.-5P	1395	3000	4000	6000	9500	21,000

1921 Commonwealth, model 4-35, sedan, HAC

1922 Commonwealth, taxi, HAC

1921-1922 COMMONWEALTH
Model 4-35 — 4-cyl., 37 hp, 117" wb

Tour.-5P	1595	3000	4000	6000	9500	21,000
Sport-4P	1785	3200	4300	6500	11,000	23,000
Sed.-5P	2465	2300	3300	4600	7500	16,000

COMPOUND — Middletown, Connecticut — (1904-1908) — Although engine builder John W. Eisenhuth designed an experimental automobile in San Francisco in 1896, the vehicle was not built there but instead at a machine shop in Newark, New Jersey — and at the turn of the century, Eisenhuth himself migrated east to the comparative hotbed of automotive activity in the Greater New York area. In continuing his experiments in Newark, he happened upon one D.F. Graham whose Graham-Fox compound engine intrigued him. Taking a cue from steam engine development, this three-cylinder gasoline powerplant represented, according to Eisenhuth and Graham, a "marked improvement over the single expansion 'and then into the muffler' concept." In the Graham-Fox, the pressure of exhaust gases from the two explosive cylinders operated the third center cylinder, this system both saving power and reducing muffler noise. The prototype show car displayed at Madison Square Garden in 1903 carried the Graham-Fox name. But production would be begun under a new name and with a brand-new company: the Compound car manufactured by the

353

1898 Compound, experimental auto-buggy, NAHC

Eisenhuth Horseless Vehicle Company of Middletown, Connecticut. Eisenhuth had taken over the Keating automobile company in Middletown during 1901, though not very quietly. Charges of blackmail and grand larceny were bandied about awhile, and John W. Eisenhuth was arrested on at least two occasions. Obviously an amicable settlement of some sort was arrived at, because the Compound automobile itself arrived for the 1904 model year. In 1905 it performed admirably in the New York Motor Club's National Economy Test, and the company asked professors at both M.I.T. and Stevens Institute to make independent studies of the Compound engine's horsepower and fuel efficiency which were published. But already the E.H.V. Company had made a serious mistake. During its inaugural year, when the vehicle received the most attention, the Compound was introduced only as a high-powered touring car that was grossly overpriced at $6000. A lesser-powered $2000 car followed later that year, and the $2000-and-under range remained the Compound's principal market for the rest of its life. Interestingly, the firm's name being seen as a liability, the Eisenhuth Horseless Vehicle Company became the Eagle Motor Car Company at some point during its history, and some of the cars may have been marketed under the Eagle marque name. This did not undo the earlier E.H.V. mistake, however, and most probably the lingering effects of the contretemps surrounding the company's formation co-mingled to cause the Compound never to establish a really solid footing in the industry. About a decade later, John Eisenhuth was back in the automotive press. His new car this time was the Poppy.

1904 COMPOUND

	FP	5	4	3	2	1
Three-cyliner — 20 hp, 100" wb						
Tour.-5P	2000	2500	3500	5000	8500	18,000
Three-cylinder — 60 hp, 112" wb						
Tour.-7P	6000	3100	4200	6300	10,500	22,000

1905 Compound, series 4, runabout, HAC

1905 COMPOUND
Model 3 — 3-cyl., 24/28 hp, 100" wb

Side Entrance Tonneau	2000	2400	3400	4800	8000	17,000
Series 4 — 3-cyl., 12/15 hp, 81" wb						
Side Entrance Tonneau	1400	2200	3200	4400	7000	15,000
Rbt.-2P	1200	2700	3600	5300	8800	19,000

1905 Compound, model 3, tonneau, HAC

1906 Compound, model 5, touring, HAC

1906 COMPOUND
3-cyl., 16 hp, 81-1/2" wb

	FP	5	4	3	2	1
Doctor's Stanhope-2P	1400	2400	3400	4800	8000	17,000
3-cyl., 16 hp, 96-1/2" wb						
Model 5 Tour.-5P	1400	2500	3500	5000	8500	18,000
Model 7-1/2 Tuxedo-5P	1300	2300	3300	4600	7500	16,000
Model 8 Royal Vic.-4P	1700	2700	3600	5300	8800	19,000

1907 Compound, Doctor's Stanhope, HAC

1907 COMPOUND
3-cyl., 16 hp, 82" wb

Doctor's Stanhope-2P	1400	2400	3400	4800	8000	17,000
2-cyl., 20 hp, 96-1/2" wb						
Model L Rbt.-2P	1600	2500	3500	5000	8500	18,000
Model I Vic.-4P	2250	2700	3600	5300	8800	19,000
Model K Tour.-5P	2000	2500	3500	5000	8500	18,000
2-cyl., 16 hp, 96-1/2" wb						
Model M Tour.-5P	1600	2300	3300	4600	7500	16,000
6-cyl., 40 hp, 115" wb						
Model H Tour.-7P	3750	3100	4200	6300	10,500	22,000

354

1908 Compound, model N, touring, HAC

1908 COMPOUND
2-cyl., 20 hp. 96-1/2" wb

	FP	5	4	3	2	1
Model N Tour. Rbt.	1550	2700	3600	5300	8800	19,000
Model O Tonneau-4P	1700	2900	3700	5600	9100	20,000
Model P Tonneau-5P	1900	3000	4000	6000	9500	21,000

COMPRESSED AIR — Boston, Massachusetts — (1909) — Cars driven by compressed air enjoyed a certain vogue in the automobile industry after the turn of the century, and among those promoting the idea was the Compressed Air Power Company of 35 Congress Street in Boston. William H. McMasters was the firm's president. One vehicle is known to have been built in 1909 to demonstrate the efficacy of the system. That it was called the Carrol has been indicated on some car rosters, which is a curiosity. The vehicle itself was given no name by the company and was registered with the Massachusetts motor vehicle bureau that year only as a "25 hp" from the Compressed Air Power Company. That any further vehicles may have been built is not known.

CONCORD — Early in 1907 the Concord Motor Car Company of Concord, Massachusetts announced its forthcoming introduction of a car to be marketed under the tradename of Boston Electric. Refer to Boston Electric.

The Concord of 1924-1925 was, like the Minute Man, a model of the Lexington built in Connersville, Indiana. Refer to Lexington.

1902 Conger, touring, NAHC

CONGER — Groton, New York — (1902-1903) — The Conger Manufacturing Company had been producing farm implements in Groton since 1849 and traction engines for agricultural and road use since about 1860. In 1902 Conger acquired the gasoline engine formerly manufactured by the Stoltz Automobile Company of Brooklyn and proceeded to refine it — in the process, as Conger said, "making it a very desirable, reliable, and efficient motor for automobile and similar use." Conger also built a touring car in which to demonstrate the engine. It was a peculiar looking machine with a very low hood and a very high tonneau. "It is perhaps enough to say that it has never failed to negotiate the hills around Groton or to satisfactorily perform its functions," *Cycle and Automobile Trade Journal* reported in August 1902. Conger announced its immediate intention to market a 14 hp four-cylinder engine, with deliveries of single, twin, three and four-cylinder units to follow in sixty days. It does not appear that the company built any automobile other than the first test car. The last heard from Conger was in September 1903, when it was announced that the firm had been succeeded by the American Road Roller Company.

CONKLIN ELECTRIC — Dayton, Ohio — (1895) — This electric built by Oliver F. Conklin of Dayton was a tricycle. It had a tubular steel frame, brown wire-bound wood rims, pneumatic tires and oak battery case. The battery case and motor were spring-mounted, the seat of leather, hammock style. The weight of the machine complete with motor and batteries was 160 pounds. It could carry a maximum load of 500 pounds, riders and

baggage. Conklin believed he had built his vehicle "on strictly scientific principles for durability, comfort and everyday business and pleasure use." There is no evidence that he built other than one car. Originally he had intended the vehicle for entry in the Chicago Times Herald Contest, but he did not make it to the starting line.

CONLEY — Chicago, Illinois — (1914) — The Conley was a tandem two-seater cyclecar on a 100-inch wheelbase with 38-inch tread, though other of its specifications were not quite so cyclecar-like. Its engine was a 123-cubic-inch water-cooled four, and the Conley featured a two-speed selective transmission, a differential and shaft drive, as well as the novelty of an adjustable steering column. The car was designed and built by G.F. Conley of Chicago, and he priced it at $375. He never incorporated a company for manufacture, however, and the cars he built must have been few.

CONNECTICUT — The Connecticut Auto Engineering Corporation was organized late in 1906 in Meriden with a capital stock of $24,000 to manufacture and deal in automobiles. E.C. Wilcox, L.E. Wilcox, B.C. Rogers, B.L. Lawton, Charles Cuno, J.H. White and Wilbur F. Rogers were the incorporators. Manufacture is doubted.

The Connecticut Automobile Company from New Haven in 1908 was a flim-flam venture presumably for the manufacture of a car called the Fulton. Refer to Fulton.

The Connecticut Cab Company was organized in Bristol in early 1910 to carry on the business of the Rockwell taxi. Refer to Rockwell.

The Connecticut Motor Vehicle Company was organized in New York City early in 1909 for the manufacture of engines and automobiles. Capital stock was $50,000, and the incorporators were C.M. Gilpin, H.A. Stuart and H.C. Murray. Manufacture of an automobile is doubted.

CONNERSVILLE — The Connersville Motor Vehicle Company was incorporated with a capital stock of $50,000 late in 1906 in Connersville, Indiana by John B. McFarlan, Sr., and his son and namesake, John, Jr. Apparently the incorporation was for development purposes prior to the McFarlans' entry into the automobile field. When this Connersville car arrived late in 1909, it carried the name McFarlan. Refer to McFarlan.

CONNERSVILLE — Connersville, Indiana — (1914) — In the midst of the cyclecar craze, the Connersville Buggy Company at Eastern and Charles streets built a prototype of the genre with plans for manufacture. Alas, the cyclecar craze ended before the Connersville ever saw any production. Subsequently, Howard Van Auken did build electric vans at the Connersville plant, but this venture was only of eight-months' duration.

CONNOLLY STEAM — Rochester, New York — (1901) — C.J. Connolly was a bicycle and automobile dealer located at 47 Exchange Street in Rochester. Early in 1901 he announced the completion of his first steam runabout, and that he was now at work on a surrey model. The Connolly was a sturdy vehicle, heavier built and with larger water and fuel tanks than was the norm for the period. A nicety was the gauge indicating water level in the boiler which was placed on the dashboard; a mirror and an outside water glass was the usual. *The Motor Vehicle Review* was quite impressed with the prospects of this venture: "Mr. Connolly has associated with him a number of skilled mechanics and, when completed, his wagons will doubtless meet with much favor. His popularity as a bicycle dealer is known throughout the county and if his motor vehicles come up to expectations, a considerable trade locally at least may be expected." For whatever reason, inadequate financing probably, the Connolly steam car was no longer in production in 1902.

1907 Conover, touring, WLB

CONOVER — Paterson, New Jersey — (1907-1912) — Although the Conover Motor Car Company, Paterson was the name and address used on the business stationery, the Conover was actually built by the Watson Machine Company, also of Paterson. Edwin K. Conover was the mechanical engineer who designed the car, with A.B. Watson and S.J. Watson producing it as an adjunct to their cordage machinery business. Powered by a four-cylinder 35/40 hp Rutenber engine fitted into a 104-inch wheelbase chassis, the shaft-drive Conover was a five-seater touring with removable tonneau and a detachable deck which transformed the vehicle into a "High Power Runabout" of Olympian proportion. The base price of $3000 included five lamps, one three-chime whistle, a 7 1/2-inch horn, and a muffler cutout. Further niceties brought the touring's price up to $3475 and the runabout's to $3375. Total production was about twenty-five cars. Watson lost money on every one of them; reputedly had Conovers been priced at what they cost the machine company to build, they would have been tagged at over $9,000. Obviously Watson was building the car for reasons other than profit, and it is interesting that although production was minimal, the company did not discontinue its automobile department until 1912. Fortunately, its Conover venture was not debilitating. The Watson Machine Company remains in existence to this day as manufacturers of wire rope machinery at the same address in Paterson.

1902 Conrad, runabout, HAC

CONRAD — Buffalo, New York — (1900-1903) — The Conrad Motor Carriage Company began business in Buffalo building light, tiller-steered and chain-driven steam cars. In 1902 it added a brace of two-cylinder gasoline models, a runabout at $750 and a $1250 touring car which was not pictured in the catalog "owing to the inability of the engraver to complete his work in time." Sadly, that catalog for the 1903 line illustrates the probable reason for the quick demise of the firm. In its list of officers, a heavy black line through one name was accompanied by an asterisk which footnoted: "The office of the President, made vacant by the death of Mr. Schuyler L. Fisher, will be filled at the next annual meeting of the Company." But at the next annual meeting of the company six months later, the main order of business was its dissolution. In 1904 there was a brief attempt to revive the car as the Lackawanna.

1901 CONRAD

	FP	5	4	3	2	1
Steam Rbt.	750	3000	4000	6000	9500	21,000

1902 CONRAD
Steam cars

	FP	5	4	3	2	1
Style 50 Rbt.	750	3000	4000	6000	9500	21,000
Style 70 Dos-a-Dos	850	3100	4200	6300	10,500	22,000
Style 77 1/2 Spc. Rbt.	1200	3200	4300	6500	11,000	23,000
Style 80 Surrey	1050	3200	4300	6500	11,000	23,000
Style 60 Buggy Top Stanhope	800	3250	4350	6600	11,500	23,500
Style 65 Vict. Top Stanhope	850	3300	4400	6700	12,000	24,000
Style 90 Surrey	1200	3500	4500	7000	13,000	25,000
Gasoline cars						
Rbt. (2-cyl., 8 hp, 78" wb)	750	3100	4200	6300	10,500	22,000
Tour. (2-cyl., 12 hp, 84" wb)	—	3300	4400	6700	12,000	24,000

1903 Conrad, touring, WLB

1903 Conrad, runabout, WLB

1903 CONRAD
Steam cars

	FP	5	4	3	2	1
Style 65 Spc. Rbt.	850	3200	4300	6500	11,000	23,000
Style 70 Dos-a-Dos	800	3300	4400	6700	12,000	24,000
Style 77 1/2 Panel-Seat Rbt.	1200	2900	3700	5600	9100	20,000
Gasoline cars						
Rbt. (2-cyl., 8 hp, 78" wb)	750	3300	4400	6700	12,000	24,000
Tour. (2-cyl., 12 hp, 84" wb)	1250	3200	4300	6500	11,000	23,000
Rbt. (2-cyl., 9 hp, 78" wb)	850	3400	4500	6900	12,500	24,500

CONSOLIDATION — The Consolidation Auto Supply Company was a $500,000 Delaware incorporation to "manufacture, sell, deal in and prepare for market all kinds of motor cars and boats" in New York City. The venture was organized during the summer of 1913 by H.O. Coughlan and F. Schmidt. Manufacture of an automobile is doubted.

CONSOLIDATED — The Consolidated Equipment Company was organized in Chicago early in 1906 with a capital stock of $5000 to manufacture automobiles and accessories. Incorporating the venture were Foree Bain, George T. May, Jr. and M.F. Allen. Manufacture of an automobile is doubted.

The Consolidated Motor Company was the name to which the Moyea Automobile Company of Ohio and New York was changed in January 1904. The car remained the Moyea. Refer to Moyea.

The Consolidated Motor Company of Lafayetteville, North Carolina was a $25,000 incorporation from the fall of 1911 to deal in automobiles. H. Lutterloh and I.U. McKethan were the incorporators. Manufacture of an automobile is doubted.

The Consolidated Motor Car Company of Columbus, Ohio was a $4 million incorporation from the fall of 1910 to "manufacture gasoline and electric motor cars, boats and other motor-propelled and electric-propelled vehicles." The incorporators were G.A. Howells, L.R. Canfield, Thomas D. Russell, J.L. Bradley and Ralph Blue. Manufacture of an automobile is doubted.

The Consolidated Motor Manufacturing Company of Philadelphia, Pennsylvania was a $250,000 incorporation from the fall of 1919 to manufacture automobiles and automobile parts. Incorporators were W.F. O'Keefe, George G. Steigler and J.H. Dowdell. Manufacture of an automobile is doubted.

The Consolidated Motors Company of America was a $10 million Delaware incorporation from late 1917 for the manufacture of motor cars and trucks. No doubt this was strictly a stock-selling venture.

Consolidated Motors, Inc. of Los Angeles, California has been indicated on various car rosters as the producer of an automobile in 1934. City directories of the early Thirties reveal no such company in town. According to the *Marvyn Scudder Manual of Extinct or Obsolete Companies*, Consolidated Motors, Inc. was a Delaware incorporation and was dissolved in 1935.

CONSOLIDATED — Toledo, Ohio — (1908) — The Consolidated Manufacturing Company was incorporated as a million-dollar venture during the summer of 1905 by William B. Duck, Frank W. Caughling, Harry E. Dumuid, James P. Hampton and Edgar C. Hampton. Apparently bicycles and motorcycles were the mainstay of production for this Toledo firm's first two years, but in 1908 the company also introduced a motor trike which could be fitted with either a basket or a cab-shaped box between its front wheels and was thus interchangeable for pleasure driving or commercial use.

CONSTANTINE — Following the demise of the Hawley in Mendon, Michigan, the organizers of that company moved back to where their adventure had begun: Constantine, Michigan. There in September of 1908 they established the new Constantine Motor Car Company and took over the business of the Crescent Motor Car Company of Detroit. The plan was to build a runabout designed by J.C. Forrester of the latter city. It was, however, never called a Constantine. Refer to Crescent.

CONTINENTAL — The Continental Automobile Company was incorporated in Trenton, New Jersey in October of 1899 with a whopping capital stock of $8 million. Incorporators were Julius M. Ferguson, Michael B. Caffey and Charles E. Pennoyer, all of New York City. "The company is empowered to manufacture motor vehicles," *The Motor Vehicle Review* reported. It does not appear the company ever did, however.

The Continental Motors Corporation of Buffalo, New York produced a car in 1914 that was marketed under the tradename of Comet. Refer to Comet.

The Continental Motor Car Company was organized in Springfield, Illinois during the summer of 1907 with a capital stock of $10,000 to manufacture automobiles and engines. Incorporators were John A. Beebe, B.C. Farmietzer and Charles C. Stillwell. Manufacture of an automobile is doubted.

The Continental Motor Vehicle Company of Camden, New Jersey was incorporated with a capital stock of $100,000 during the summer of 1903 to manufacture and sell "motor vehicles of all kinds." Daniel M. Pfautz, Henry S. Mansfield, L. Charles Bechtle, William F. Robinson and Robert C. Taylor were the incorporators. Manufacture of an automobile is doubted.

1907 Continental, touring, WLB

CONTINENTAL — **New Haven, Connecticut** — **(1907-1908)** — Because it was built in the same town as Yale, and perhaps because its makers thought an implied association with that revered seat of learning might work to their promotional advantage, this Continental was initially produced under the name of University Automobile Company. Whether Yale objected is not known, but the firm became the Continental Automobile Manufacturing Company the following year, though its catalog did still read rather like a dissertation. The four-cylinder Continental was available in three models: a 25 hp 100-inch wheelbase $2400 runabout, a 30 hp 112-inch wheelbase $2700 tonneau and a 35 hp 120-inch wheelbase $3000 touring. The company might have been well advised on the efficiency of a more standardized production. A Continental runabout did show well at the Yale University Automobile Club spring meet of 1907, its designer C.S. Johnston driving, and putting up a mile a minute on the straight. And it showed up in the Glidden Tour soon after, though less meritoriously, as *Motor Age* noted, "being eliminated owing to the driver's arrest at Richmond, Indiana, for speeding and the subsequent collision of the car with a trolley in Dayton, Ohio." In addition to Johnston, an engineer from Washington, D.C., the promoters of the Continental had included Constant A. Moeller, the president of Narragansett Breweries in Rhode Island and a substantial investor in New Haven real estate, and Frank J. Schollhorn, vice-president of the William Schollhorn Company, a large manufacturer of small tools in New Haven.

1908 Continental, runabout, NAHC

	FP	5	4	3	2	1
Model A Rbt.	2400	3000	4000	6000	9500	21,000
Model B Tonneau	2700	3100	4200	6300	10,500	22,000
Model C Tour.	3000	3000	4000	6000	9500	21,000

1910 Continental, 35, touring, NAHC

CONTINENTAL — **Franklin, Indiana** — **(1910-1914)** — This Continental was built by the Indiana Motor & Manufacturing Company of Franklin and marketed by the Indiana Motor Sales Company whose offices were in the Odd Fellows Building in Indianapolis. It was a fine medium-priced motorcar featuring such high-priced appointments as machine-buffed leather upholstery and a mahogany dashboard. The car was put on the market in December of 1909; the company was in receivership by spring of 1912. John C. Billheimer, the state Auditor of Indiana, had been its president. In June the Security Trust Company sold Indiana Motor & Manufacturing to Frank M. Millikan. The purchase price was $20,000. Millikan brought in fellow Franklinite, Frank N. Martindale, to assist, reorganized the company and continued the Continental in production. Among the marketing plans he tried was the sale of Continentals on a time payment plan providing for one-year financing. But this was not enough to make a going concern of an automobile venture which had been undercapitalized from the beginning. For the 1914 model year the Continental was offered as the Martindale & Millikan, but that was the end of it. Ultimately, the venture evolved into the Continental Auto Parts Company which moved to Knightstown (Indiana) in January 1916 and continued in business supplying parts, as the *Knightstown Banner* put it, "for any and all machines, and especially Orphan cars." In 1915 Frank Martindale tried again, with a horsedrawn vehicle conversion kit called the Ultimotor.

1910 CONTINENTAL
Thirty-Five — 4-cyl., 35 hp, 116" wb

Tour.-5P	1400	3000	4000	6000	9500	21,000

1911 CONTINENTAL
Thirty-Five — 4-cyl., 35 hp, 116" wb

Tour.-5P	1400	3000	4000	6000	9500	21,000
Torpedo-4P	1500	2900	3700	5600	9100	20,000
Rbt.-2P	1500	3100	4200	6300	10,500	22,000

1912 CONTINENTAL
Thirty-Five — 4-cyl., 35 hp, 116" wb

Fore-Door Tour.-5P	1500	3100	4200	6300	10,500	22,000
Fore-Door Rds.-2P	1500	3200	4300	6500	11,000	23,000

1913 CONTINENTAL
Thirty — 4-cyl., 30 hp, 116" wb

Tour.-5P	1000	3000	4000	6000	9500	21,000

Forty — 4-cyl., 40 hp, 117" wb

Fore-Door Tour.-5P	1725	3200	4300	6500	11,000	23,000
Fore-Door Rds.-2P	1725	3300	4400	6700	12,000	24,000

1914 CONTINENTAL
Martindale & Millikan — 4-cyl., 30 hp, 110" wb

Model XXX Tour.	1000	3200	4300	6500	11,000	23,000

Martindale & Millikan — 4-cyl., 32 hp, 118" wb

Model XXVII Tour.	1800	3300	4400	6700	12,000	24,000

CONTINENTAL — **Minneapolis, Minnesota** — **(1914)** — This Continental was a cyclecar which featured a four-cylinder air-cooled engine, friction transmission, 92-inch wheelbase, 32-inch tread, a choice of chain or belt drive, and a price tag of $360. The Continental Engine Manufacturing Company was a Chicago venture set up to produce the car in what the firm said was its own factory in Minneapolis. The Minneapolis address, however, was the same as that of the Dispatch Motor Company. Possibly a few Continentals were built in the Dispatch factory, but not for long because within months this venture had been renamed the Continental Engineering Company with all operations moved to Chicago and the product now made somewhat bigger and called a Ceco. Meanwhile, John E. Pfeffer, who had designed the Continental and the Ceco, stayed behind in Minnesota and tried again himself with a new Continental-like cyclecar he named the Baby Moose.

CONTINENTAL — **Grand Rapids, Michigan** — **(1933-1934)** — This Continental began life as the De Vaux. When De Vaux-Hall Motors failed in January 1932, Continental Motors Corporation stepped in and continued to build a revised version of the De Vaux as the De Vaux Continental (or Continental De Vaux) for the remainder of 1932. In November that year, however, the Continental-De Vaux Company became the Continental Automobile Company — Norman de Vaux was out, and three new models of a new car called the Continental were built for 1933. Previously a single six had been offered, now there were two sixes as well as a four that would be advertised as America's lowest priced, full-sized car. Respective model

357

1933 Continental, Ace Standard, 4-dr. sedan, WLB

designations were Flyer, Ace and Beacon. The Continental did not survive any longer than had the De Vaux. Sales in 1933 were a mere 3310 cars. In 1934 only the four-cylinder Beacon was offered, with sales further plummeting, to 953 cars. Despite its short life, the Continental did show well in demonstration runs, the Beacon especially, its 65 mph/32 mpg performance being declared a speed-economy record. By the end of 1934 Continental returned exclusively to its former business of supplying engines to those of its clients who were still managing to stay in the automobile business during the Great Depression. Norman de Vaux decided to pick up the pieces this time, initially planning to produce a Beacon-like De Vaux Four Forty-Four. When that failed, he tried again, Beaconizing the Four Forty-Four into the De Vo.

1933 Continental, Beacon, roadster, WLB

1933 Continental, sedan, JAC

1933 CONTINENTAL

Beacon — 4-cyl., 38 hp, 101 1/2" wb

	FP	5	4	3	2	1
Rds.-2P	355	3900	4800	7700	14,300	27,000
Commercial Cpe.	380	3300	4400	6700	12,000	24,000
Two-Door Sed.	380	3200	4300	6500	11,000	23,000
Four-Door Sed.	395	3300	4400	6700	12,000	24,000
DeL. Commercial Cpe.	425	3500	4500	7000	13,000	25,000
DeL. Two-Door Sed.	440	3300	4400	6700	12,000	24,000
DeL. Four-Door Sed.	460	3500	4500	7000	13,000	25,000

1933 Continental, Flyer, commercial coupe, WLB

Flyer — 6-cyl., 65 hp, 107" wb

Rds.-2P	450	4200	5200	8400	15,700	29,000
Commercial Cpe.	490	3700	4700	7300	13,700	26,000
Two-Door Sed.	510	3300	4400	6700	12,000	24,000
Four-Door Sed.	535	3500	4500	7000	13,000	25,000

Ace — 6-cyl., 85 hp, 114" wb

	FP	5	4	3	2	1
Rumble-Seat Cpe.	725	4000	5000	8000	15,000	28,000
Sed.-5P	745	3000	4000	6000	9500	21,000
DeL. Sed.-5P	816	3100	4200	6300	10,500	22,000

1934 CONTINENTAL

Beacon — 4-cyl., 38 hp, 101 1/2" wb

Cpe.	380	3700	4700	7300	13,700	26,000
Two-Door Sed.	380	3300	4400	6700	12,000	24,000
Four-Door Sed.	395	3500	4500	7000	13,000	25,000
DeL. Four-Door Sed.	460	3600	4600	7200	13,400	25,500

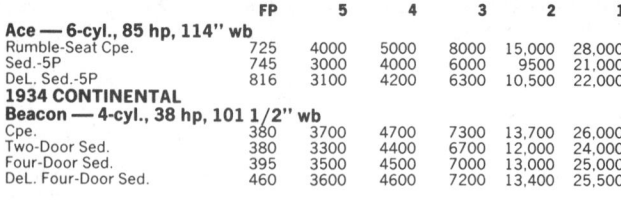
1907 Continental, Roadster, WLB

CONTINENTAL ROADSTER — Chicago, Illinois — (1907) — The Continental Motor Car Company of 209-217 Robey Street in Chicago manufactured one model only: a piquant little roadster with a sprightly radiator badge, a hood that was a perfect circle, and a meritorious fuel consumption guarantee of 26 mpg. Planetary transmission and shaft drive were featured, and its two-cylinder engine was offered with a choice of water- or air-cooling. The first advertisements for the car appeared late in 1907. They had disappeared by 1908. Inconclusive references indicate that Continental tried a commercial vehicle venture before going under.

1907 CONTINENTAL ROADSTER
2-cyl., 12 hp, 90" wb

	FP	5	4	3	2	1
Rds.	—	—	—	—	—	—

COOK — "The Cook Manufacturing Company, Albion, Michigan, will build an automobile for 1904," reported *The Horseless Age* in the spring of 1903. Apparently the Cook Manufacturing Company did not.

The Cook Motor Vehicle Company of St. Louis, Missouri produced a highwheeler called the Simplo from 1908-1909. Refer to Simplo.

The Cook & Wilkinson Company, Inc. of New York City was a $25,000 venture from early 1910 to "manufacture and deal in wagons, motor cars, bicycles, vehicles and all kinds and supplies for same." The incorporators were William M. Blain, George Cook and Lyman M. Wilkinson. Manufacture of an automobile is doubted.

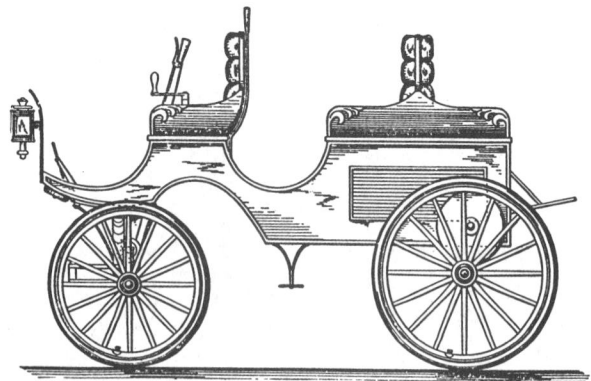
1896 Cook, gasoline carriage

COOK — Mt. Gilead, Ohio — (1896) — James M. Cook of Mt. Gilead was its inventor, but he graciously allowed that the motor carriage he designed was "put into practical working shape" by two mechanical engineers from Indianapolis named Thurman and Silvius. The vehicle was a six-seater with a gracefully styled body and power provided by a two cylinder gasoline engine developing four horsepower. At the time, its transmission — friction clutches actuating the gears — was considered quite novel. Fuel cost, Cook estimated, was "from one-fourth to three-eighths of a cent per mile." There is no indication that he ever contemplated manufacture.

COOK — Salem, Massachusetts — (1897) — In 1897 Frank P. Cook of Salem built an automobile in his workshop at the rear of his home at 31 Forrester Street. "The carriage would look just like a beach wagon if it were not for the absence of the shafts and the running gear which shows underneath," the *Salem Gazette* reported that year. "The power is derived from a five-horsepower kerosene water tubular boiler and a four horse upright engine. The heat is supplied by a blaze of a spray of kerosene which is forced into the firebox by a jet of steam." Frank Cook built all the parts of his steamer himself, equipping it with water and kerosene tanks good for a fifty-mile run. "The carriage will travel as fast as anybody cares to go," the *Gazette* went on. "Its exact speed is not known but it is safe to say that it will lose any ambitious officers who attempt to arrest the driver for going faster than the law allows."

COOK — Delaware, Ohio — (1900) — Perhaps the gasoline car C.E. Cook was testing on the streets of Delaware during the summer of 1900 was the only car he ever built. "Mr. Cook has embodied many good ideas in the construction of his vehicle," *The Motor Vehicle Review* reported, "but the motors he put in are too small and he does not get the speed that he otherwise would have." C.E. Cook continued his motor development, however, and later organized the Cook Motor Company for engine manufacture. Its capital stock was increased from $15,000 to $25,000 in 1906 with the enthusiastic support of local businessmen, which seems to indicate that C.E. Cook had his under-powered problems licked.

COOK — Elba, New York — (1901) — Louis Cook of Elba built an automobile in 1901 which used wood for fuel. He intended to make his first trial trip with the car to visit the Pan-American Exposition in Buffalo, but he never got that far, his vehicle coming to a stop in "Zeb Crosby's yard" after the discovery of "several weaknesses in the system."

COOK AUTO-SLEDGE — Calicoon, New York — (1905-1906) — Although most standard history references cite Admiral Robert E. Peary as the first man to reach the North Pole in 1909, numerous scholars believe that Dr. Frederick A. Cook got there first, in 1908. (The Dr. Frederick A. Cook Society was established in 1939 to support this claim, and it remains a vigorous organization to this day.) In the matter of automobile history, there can be no doubt, however, that Dr. Cook was the first explorer ever to consider such an expedition in an automobile, or more accurately an auto-sledge (or sled). Both Frederick Cook and his brother Theodore were avid automobilists. It was Theodore who was the wizard mechanic, however, and who was principally responsible for designing and building in Calicoon during 1905-1906 a sledge powered by an air-cooled gasoline engine that his brother contemplated using on his expedition. The auto-sledge was tested in the Catskills during 1906, but Dr. Cook decided to leave it behind in 1907 when he set off for the North Pole, believing that it would be too heavy for the icy crust of the Arctic. Following his return in 1908, and the controversy which erupted over his claim, Dr. Cook retired from polar exploration. His brother Theodore, however, continued to design and build sledges for other explorers, though most of these would be dog-drawn. An unconfirmed reference indicates that Theodore Cook built three 24 hp auto-sledges for C.E.H. and F.R. Burch in 1906, for their proposed trip to the South Pole. Whether these were used is not known; the Burch brothers didn't make it to their destination in any case. The South Pole was discovered in 1911 by Roald Amundsen, who used a sledge designed by Theodore Cook. Like the Frederick Cook vehicle which had set off for the North Pole four years earlier, the Amundsen sledge was dog-drawn. Amundsen's claim of discovery has, of course, not been challenged.

COOK & GOWDEY — Chicago, Illinois — (1895) — The Cook & Gowdey Company of 6324 Madison in Chicago entered the Chicago Times-Herald Contest with a vehicle of its own design. The car was not completed in time for the event, however, and that it was ever successfully tested has not been documented.

COOKE — The Cooke, Fitz & Dillingham Company was a $25,000 Maine incorporation from the summer of 1909 to manufacture, repair and deal in automobiles. Dr. J.W.K. Shaw, George W. Dallas, Preston King, G.J. Leblanc, Jr. and Henry Broussard were the incorporators. Manufacture is doubted.

COOLEY — Batavia, New York — (1900-1901) — On April 2nd, 1900, *The Daily News* of Batavia reported that Robert L. Cooley, who was the proprietor of a bicycle shop in town, was building an automobile which he would fit with a 4 hp gasoline engine and 28-inch bicycle wheels. On September 25th, the newspaper announced that "a trial run of about five miles was made about the village last night" and "although the machine is not entirely finished, it ran nicely and proved to be a success." The year following, in partnership with Daniel W. Tomlinson, Cooley built another automobile patterned after a steamer that Tomlinson had purchased that summer. This car may have been revised from the gasoline car of the previous

1900 Cooley, gasoline buggy, LC

year. Subsequently, Cooley and Tomlinson built another steam car for an ex-railroad engineer living in nearby Corfu. This represented the total extent of Cooley/Tomlinson automobile production. Thereafter Robert Cooley operated an automobile dealership and repair station, until 1917 when he joined the Colonial Radio Corporation of Buffalo as a research technician. It was while working there, in 1937, that he was killed when struck down by an automobile as he returned home from work on May 11th.

COOLEY STEAM — Boston, Massachusetts — (1903) — John F. Cooley of Boston was the inventor of a steam engine the principle of which he termed "cycloidal." Most trade press reporters seemed confused. "It would appear that the central member or 'piston' revolves in one direction, while the surrounding member or cylinder, with the three-lobed recess, revolves in the opposite direction about an axis eccentric to that of the piston," explained *The Automobile*. "Steam appears to be admitted through the ports in the casing on the right hand side, and exhausted through the corresponding ports on the other side, the casing of course being stationary." Cooley's engine was successfully tested in early March 1903 at the Massachusetts Institute of Technology, and three versions of horsepower varying from 10 to 70 were installed in the chassis of three different steam cars (a Stanley, a Mobile and a Grout). Road tests were reported to have proceeded smoothly. Later in March the Cooley Epicycloidal Engine Company was organized with a whopping $10 million stock to promote manufacture of this engine for steam car use. It vanished from view soon thereafter. Something must have gone wrong somewhere.

COONEY — Toledo, Ohio — (1906-1907) — Fresh from defeat with his Clark Electric in Philadelphia, Albert F. Clark traveled to Toledo where he talked the Cooney Carriage Company into going automotive. His idea was a good one: an electric car chassis in which the entire mechanism was free from attachment in any way to the body of the car; any style of body could thus be fitted with facility — and Cooney would be able not only to produce its own electric car but also to market the chassis to other carriage builders who didn't wish to bother with the mechanical end of things. Cooney & Company was organized in January of 1906 for this venture. Its officers included Charles R. Bowman as president, James J. Cooney as vice-president, George L. Shanks as general manager. A working prototype had been thoroughly tested by February of 1907, but the project seems to have ended soon after. No doubt undercapitalization was the principal reason. Only $10,000 had been invested in the Cooney electric. Cooney went back to carriages, and Albert Clark remained in Toledo to try again with the Clark electric.

COOPER — The Cooper Auto Exchange was a $25,000 incorporation in New York City during the summer of 1910 to manufacture, deal in and repair motor cars and accessories. Incorporators were C.C. Cooper, J.H. Lent, W.O. Lent and H.A. Miln. Manufacture of an automobile is doubted.

The Cooper Brothers Motor Company was organized in Safford, Arizona during the summer of 1917 to manufacture, repair and deal in automobiles and auto accessories. Capital stock was $10,000. Behind this venture were Arthur H. Cooper, Horace E. Cooper and Howard M. Hunt. Manufacture of an automobile is doubted.

COOPER — Kansas City, Missouri — (1921) — Among the many would-be challengers to the Model T Ford was the Cooper of Kansas City. A four on a 106-inch wheelbase, the car was slated to sell for $750 as a five-passenger sedan with wooden artillery wheels. Only prototypes were built, however, before the Cooper Motor Company motored into oblivion.

CO-OPERATIVE — The Co-Operative Automobile Company was organized in Pittsburgh, Pennsylvania late in 1908 to manufacture and deal in automobiles. This $25,000 venture was backed by L.E. Negley, J.P. Vance and A.C. Martin. Manufacture of an automobile is doubted.

The Co-Operative Engineering Works was organized in Chicago, Illinois with a capital stock of $10,000 early in 1908 for the manufacture of automobiles and supplies. F.W. Ritchie, J. Smalley and G.E. Schmidt were the incorporators. Manufacture of an automobile is doubted.

The Co-Operative Trading Syndicate was a $100,000 Delaware incorporation from the summer of 1910 "to manufacture, construct, maintain and operate automobiles." It went nowhere.

COOPER HEWITT — New York, New York — (1903-1904) — Peter Cooper Hewitt was the scion of two of the most prominent families in New York City at the turn of the century. In 1845 Peter Cooper had turned over the Trenton Iron Works which he had founded to his son Edward and Edward's close friend, Abram Stevens Hewitt. The revolutionary wrought-iron beams rolled at the Trenton Iron Works and used in the construction of the Cooper Union Foundation Building in Manhattan were forerunners of today's steel I-beams. (That 1859 building still stands.) Following the Civil War, the first mass-produced steel in America resulted from the Cooper/Hewitt partnership. By the turn of the century, a goodly fortune had been amassed, naturally. Undoubtedly Peter Cooper Hewitt's forays into the automobile field were largely a caprice. The number of cars that he designed and had built for himself at the Trenton Iron Works is not known, but at least one racing car and sporting car have been documented. Peter Cooper Hewitt was a member of the fashionable racing fraternity in New York during this period, but not as spectacularly so as Willie K. Vanderbilt. A tantalizing reference from March 1903 indicates that the young man was "about to enter the market with an 800-pound automobile with aluminum body." Conceivably the Trenton Iron Works produced a prototype of this effort, but manufacture never followed.

1930 Cootie, HAC

COOTIE — Dayton, Ohio — (1920-1942) — The Cootie was a juvenile car built by the Custer Specialty Company of Dayton. It was powered by a General Electric motor, had a top speed of 10 mph, and could travel that distance on one battery charge at a cost of 15¢. Although its price varied through the years, it made a grand Christmas present for a youngster in 1920 at just $95. Interestingly, the Cootie was occasionally used by adults; examples are known to have been licensed for the road in both the United States and England. The Custer Specialty Company produced a number of further automotive vehicles under its own name.

COPE — The Cope Company was organized in Newark, New Jersey late in 1908 for the manufacture of carriages and automobiles. Capital stock was $50,000. Behind this venture were M.M. Dodd, Grace G. Conley and Alonzo Church. Manufacture of an automobile is doubted.

COPELAND — Phoenix, Arizona & Camden, New Jersey — (1881-1890) — Lucius D. Copeland was among America's most persistent early automotive pioneers. His first attempt at motorizing a vehicle was in 1881 when he attached a small motor to a Columbia bicycle with results which he said were "very inefficient and dangerous." Subsequently, the Star bicycle (which unlike the Columbia carried its large wheel at the rear in a frame and was steered by the small front wheel) appeared on the market. Copeland immediately bought one. On the front frame tube, he attached a small boiler and then fitted a small engine just below the saddle with belt drive to a large pulley on the rear wheel. After testing the vehicle at 15 mph, he exhibited it for the first time at the Maricopa County Fair in Phoenix in the fall of 1884. Deciding that he had come up with something eminently worthy of manufacture, he took his steam bicycle first to the

1887 Copeland, runabout, GR

Mechanics' Pavilion in San Francisco, and then to skating rinks and exhibition halls in cities all along the California coast. When he couldn't find financial backing in the West, he traveled to the East Coast and found a financial angel in Philadelphia by the name of Sanford Northrup. The Northrup Manufacturing Company was the result, and in its shop in Camden (New Jersey) Copeland built a steam tricycle which he drove often in Fairmount Park (Philadelphia) and once to Atlantic City and back, sixty miles each way. His tricycle was patented and he assigned rights to the Moto-Cycle Manufacturing Company of Philadelphia. Other experimental vehicles followed, one of them anticipating the side-car design which was ten years in the future. In Phoenix, in 1881, he had even tried an electric. Unfortunately, no sales resulted from any of this. Even Lucius Copeland's persistence had its limits. Ultimately, he retired to California, believing that people "would not pay more than $500 for a motor vehicle and that there would be little or no profit in the business."

COPPOCK — Although Lembert W. Coppock was the man whose idea the venture was, the car which was ultimately produced in 1910 was called the Decatur. Refer to Decatur.

CORBALEY & THORPE — The Corbaley & Thorpe Auto Company was organized in Palo Alto, California during the fall of 1906 to manufacture and deal in automobiles. Capital stock was $25,000. Behind this venture were H.G. Corbaley, Ray P. Thorpe and T.C. Thorpe. Manufacture of an automobile is doubted.

1905 Corbin, model D, touring, HAC

CORBIN — New Britain, Connecticut — (1905-1912) — The Corbin Motor Vehicle Company was a wholly owned subsidiary of American Hardware Corporation. And it was begun principally because Philip Corbin, whose family had established the Corbin Screw Corporation and the Corbin Cabinet Lock Company (also divisions of American Hardware) was a horseless carriage enthusiast. Although production began in 1903 in Bristol (Connecticut) with commercial vehicles and small quantities of a runabout called the Bristol, Corbin did not enter the passenger car market in earnest until 1905, when production was moved to New Britain. Initially the Corbin model line was composed of two air-cooled models which featured metal brake shoes, apparently a first in an American production car though this feature was not continued. In 1908 Corbin added water-cooled models, and in 1910 the air-cooled version was discontinued. The car was known as "The Full Jeweled Corbin," a slogan to which one reporter of the day lent credence when he remarked that its half-century history of high quality hardware manufacture had made the name Corbin "synonymous with the sterling mark on silver." The Corbin enjoyed commercial success. Indeed, the word used to announce the company's discontinuation of motorcar manufacture in early 1912 was "retirement." Philip Corbin himself had retired a few years before. American Hardware is still in business.

1905 CORBIN
Model D — 4-cyl., 16//20 hp, 94" wb

	FP	5	4	3	2	1
Tour.	2000	2900	3700	5600	9100	20,000

Model C — 4-cyl., 24/30 hp, 106" wb

	FP	5	4	3	2	1
Tour.	4000	3100	4200	6300	10,500	22,000

1906 Corbin, model E, touring, WLB

1906 Corbin, model G, runabout, JAC

1906 CORBIN
Model G — 4-cyl., 24 hp, 93" wb

	FP	5	4	3	2	1
Rbt.-2P	1800	2700	3600	5300	8800	19,000

Model E — 4-cyl., 24 hp, 100" wb

	FP	5	4	3	2	1
Tour.-5P	2000	3000	4000	6000	9500	21,000

1907 Corbin, model I, runabout, WLB

1907 CORBIN
Model I — 4-cyl., 24 hp, 100" wb

	FP	5	4	3	2	1
Rbt.-2P	2250	3500	4500	7000	13,000	25,000

Model H — 4-cyl., 24 hp, 108" wb

	FP	5	4	3	2	1
Tour.-5P	2500	3700	4700	7300	13,700	26,000
Limo.-5P	3500	3200	4300	6500	11,000	23,000

1908 Corbin, model R, touring, HAC

1908 CORBIN
Air cooled — 4-cyl., 30 hp, 108" wb

	FP	5	4	3	2	1
Model R Tour.-5P	2650	4000	5000	8000	15,000	28,000
Model R Limo.-5P	3500	3500	4500	7000	13,000	25,000
Model S Rds.-2P/3P/4P	2650	4200	5200	8400	15,700	29,000

Water cooled — 4-cyl., 30 hp, 108" wb

	FP	5	4	3	2	1
Model K Tour.-5P	2500	4200	5200	8400	15,700	29,000
Model K Limo.-5P	3650	3700	4700	7300	13,700	26,000
Model O Rds.-2P/3P/4P	3650	4300	5400	8700	16,500	30,000

1909 Corbin, model O² small tonneau, WLB

1909 CORBIN
Air cooled — 4-cyl., 32 hp, 108" wb

	FP	5	4	3	2	1
Model R¹ Tour.-5P	2500	4000	5000	8000	15,000	28,000
Model S¹ Rds.-2P/3P/4P	2500	4200	5200	8400	15,700	29,000
Model S² Small Tonneau-4P	2650	3900	4800	7700	14,300	27,000

Water cooled — 4-cyl., 32 hp, 108" wb

	FP	5	4	3	2	1
Model K¹ Tour.-5P	2500	4200	5200	8400	15,700	29,000
Model O² Rds.-2P/3P/4P	2500	4300	5400	8700	16,500	30,000
Model O³ Small Tonneau-4P	2650	4000	5000	8000	15,000	28,000

Model 14 — 4-cyl., 32 hp, 114" wb

	FP	5	4	3	2	1
Limo.-5/7P (air of water cooled)	3500	4400	5600	9200	17,300	31,000
Land'et.-5/7P (air of water cooled)	3650	4500	5800	9500	18,000	32,000
Twn. Car-5/7P (air of water cooled)	3000	4400	5600	9200	17,300	31,000

1910 Corbin, model 18, limousine, WLB

1910 CORBIN
Model 18 — 4-cyl., 30 hp, 120" wb

	FP	5	4	3	2	1
Tour.-5P	2750	7200	14,400	24,000	33,600	48,000
Toy Tonneau-4P	2750	7350	14,700	24,500	34,300	49,000
Rds.-3P	2750	7100	14,200	23,400	32,000	46,000
Limo.-7P	3750	3500	4500	7000	13,000	25,000

1911 Corbin, model 30, roadster, HAC

1911 CORBIN
Model 30 — 4-cyl., 30 hp, 115" wb

	FP	5	4	3	2	1
Tour.	2000	4000	5000	8000	15,000	28,000
Rbt.	2000	4200	5200	8400	15,700	29,000

Model 18 — 4-cyl., 30 hp, 120" wb

Toy Tonneau	2750	7200	14,400	24,000	33,600	48,000
Tour.	2750	7100	14,200	23,400	32,000	46,000

Model 40 — 4-cyl., 40 hp, 120" wb

Tour.-5P	3000	7400	14,700	24,500	34,300	49,000
Tour.-7P	3050	7500	15,000	25,000	35,000	50,000
Toy Tonneau	3000	7400	14,700	24,500	34,300	49,000
Torpedo	3100	7500	15,000	25,000	35,000	50,000
Limo.	4000	3700	4700	7300	13,700	26,000

1912 Corbin, model 30, roadster, WLB

1912 CORBIN
Model 30 — 4-cyl., 32.4 hp, 115" wb

Tour.	2000	4200	5200	8400	15,700	29,000
Rds.	2000	4400	5600	9200	17,300	31,000

Model 40 — 4-cyl., 36.1 hp, 120" wb

Tour.-5P	3000	7200	14,400	24,000	33,600	48,000
Toy Tonneau-5P	3000	7300	14,700	24,500	34,500	49,000
Tour.-7P	3050	7300	15,000	25,000	35,000	50,000
Torpedo	3100	7300	14,700	24,500	34,500	49,000
Limo.	4000	3900	4800	7700	14,300	27,000

CORBITT — Henderson, North Carolina — (1907-1914) — Richard J. Corbitt was a native North Carolinian, who moved from Enfield to Henderson in the 1890's. Initially his idea was to make his fortune in the tobacco industry, but the coming of the "tobacco trusts" soon pushed the small buyers out of business — so he turned to wagon-building instead. His Corbitt Buggy Company was successful from the beginning and, having learned from his tobacco experience of the advantages of monopoly, he bought into or helped organize three other buggy enterprises in town. With the advent of the automobile, these other buggy companies turned to the manufacture of such varied products as hosiery, veneers and furniture, but Corbitt himself decided to give the automotive industry a whirl. The Corbitt Automobile Company followed, and the first Corbitt automobile appeared in 1907. It was a highwheeler with virtually no accoutrements; in 1908 Corbitt added fenders, in 1909 acetylene lights. All of these vehicles were sold locally. In 1910, however, Corbitt began to announce and advertise in the national press, and also to expand his model line and production. In 1910, too, he built his first truck, which sold measurably better than his automobile and which was the reason for his ultimate discontinuation of pleasure cars to concentrate on commercial vehicles exclusively. By 1916 Corbitt trucks were in use in twenty-three countries. Corbitts saw duty in both the World Wars, and the first school buses in North Carolina were Corbitts as well. The company continued successfully in the commercial vehicle field until the mid-Fifties when Richard Corbitt retired and sold out his business interests.

1907-1909 CORBITT

	FP	5	4	3	2	1
Two-Seater High-Wheel Buggy	—	—	—	—	—	—

1910-1911 CORBITT
2-cyl., 18/20 hp, 90" wb

Model A Tour.-4P	800	2400	3400	4800	8000	19,000
Model B Rbt.-2P	800	2900	3700	5600	9100	20,000

1912 CORBITT
4-cyl., 30 hp, 120" wb

	FP	5	4	3	2	1
Model A Rds.-2P	1750	4500	5800	9500	18,000	32,000
Model B Tour.-4P	2000	4300	5400	8700	16,500	30,000
Model C Tour.-5P	2000	4200	5200	8400	15,700	29,000

1913 CORBITT
4-cyl., 30/35 hp, 120" wb

Model D Rds.-2P	1800	5000	6500	11,000	22,000	35,000
Model E Tour.-4P	1975	4500	5800	9500	18,000	32,000
Model F Tour.-5P	1975	4700	6100	9400	19,000	33,000

1914 CORBITT
4-cyl., 26 hp, 120" wb

Model D Rds.-2P	1450	5000	6500	11,000	22,000	35,000
Model E Tour.-4P	1600	4500	5800	9500	18,000	32,000
Model F Tour.-5P	1650	4700	6100	9900	19,000	33,000

1929 Cord, L-29, cabriolet, AA

CORD L-29 — Auburn & Connersville, Indiana — (1929-1932)/**CORD 810-812** — (1936-1937) — There were two front-wheel-drive American motorcars announced in 1929, and they were produced by two of the most dynamic and colorful entrepreneurs in the American automobile industry at the time. Errett Lobban Cord managed to get his L-29 into the marketplace faster than Archie Andrews did his Ruxton, and initially this worked to Cord's advantage. The rationale for the car was certainly a viable one: Cord needed something to fill the price gap in his Cord Corporation between the popularly priced Auburn and the grand Model J Duesenberg he had just introduced — and, although the front-wheel-drive idea had languished in America since Walter Christie failed commercially before the First World War, it was now enjoying public attention because of its successful application in several race cars for the Indianapolis 500. Race car engineers Harry Miller and Cornelius Van Ranst, as well as Indy driver Leon Duray, would be advisers to the L-29 project. Auburn chief engineer Herb Snow would devise the industry's first X-frame bracing for the new Cord, this after E.L. Cord himself had driven the ladder-framed prototype over a plowed field behind his home in Auburn, and all the doors popped open. Fix it, he said. Powering the L-29 was a 298.6-cubic-inch 125 hp L-head eight supplied by Lycoming (a company Cord owned), and the car was priced at $3095 for sedan and brougham, $3295 for cabriolet and phaeton. These were uncommonly lovely cars; indeed, many connoisseurs today consider the L-29 the best-looking American car of the period. Front wheel drive made for a much lower and more rakish silhouette than the norm, and the L-29 proved particularly attractive to master coachbuilders on both sides of the Atlantic. A blue coupe designed by Alexis de Sakhnoffsky took the prestigious Concours d'Elegance in Monaco by storm in 1930, this but one of dozens of "beauty contest" victories the car won throughout Europe. Two months after the introduction of the L-29, however, the crash on Wall Street effectively killed its chances for commercial success. Prices were lowered to the $2395-$2595 range for '31, but it didn't help; for the 1932 model year the L-29 engine was bored out an eighth-inch for 322 cubic inches and 132 hp, which didn't help either. Interestingly, the total production run of the L-29 — 5010 units — was almost precisely what Cord had scheduled for the car from the beginning. Five thousand L-29's had been the plan, with the car thereafter to be followed by the improved L-30. When the Depression saw to it that the L-30 would never happen, many of the changes commited for it (i.e., the larger engine) were incorporated into the last L-29's built. Production ceased December 31st, 1931, the last 157 cars titled as 1932 models. And that, seemingly, was that. Four years later, however, the front-drive Cord was back, with startlingly modern "coffin nose" styling by Gordon Buehrig. Perhaps the single most instantly recognizable car in the history of the American automobile, the Cord 810 happened almost by accident. By this time E.L. Cord's automotive empire was faltering, and Cord himself was devoting considerably less time to it than to many of his other activities. But he recognized that the "specialty merchandise field" was where his automobile company belonged, and the 810 Cord was his last attempt to put it there. Originally designed as a "baby Duesenberg," the car became a Cord when front wheel drive was decided upon in order to make for a lower silhouette. And the decision was made quickly, with just fifteen weeks to build enough cars for presentation at the November automobile shows. There was a Keystone Kops semblance to the entire operation, but the cars made it to the shows, where they received a rousing reception — and then the problems moved to the production line, where haste made further waste, and though the kinks were worked out as the cars were being built, it was not before unflattering rumors spread. The 810 of 1936 was powered by Lycoming's 125 hp V-8, which did not change for the 812 models in '37, though a supercharger did become available, which boosted horsepower to 170. "Specialty merchandise" that it was, the $2000-$3000 price range for the cars was not the 810/812's undoing. Nor were the teething problems of the car, since most new cars had

1930 Cord, L-29, convertible sedan, AA

those. Errett Lobban Cord's exit from the automobile industry in 1937 was. On August 7th that year, after the production of not quite 3000 810/812's, the assembly line stopped. Auburn production had already ceased. So had Duesenberg. The last car to come from the Cord empire, fittingly, was a Cord.

1930 Cord L-29, de Sakhnoffsky coupe, JAC

1930 Cord L-29, town car, LeBaron, JAC

1930
Series L-29, 8-cyl., 137.5" wb

	FP	5	4	3	2	1
4P Cab	3295	17,100	31,800	53,000	85,000	106,000
5P Brgm	3095	9900	19,800	33,000	46,200	66,000
5P Sed	3095	9600	19,200	32,000	44,800	64,000
Sed Phae	3295	29,500	55,000	84,000	110,000	140,000

1931 Cord L-29, sedan, ACD

1931
Series L-29, 8-cyl., 137.5" wb

	FP	5	4	3	2	1
2-4P Cabr	2495	18,500	33,000	55,000	88,000	110,000
5P Brgm	2395	10,200	20,400	34,000	47,600	68,000
5P Sed	2395	9900	19,800	33,000	46,200	66,000
Sed Phae	2595	29,500	55,000	84,000	110,000	140,000

1932 Cord L-29, convertible sedan, ACD

1932
Series L-29, 8-cyl., 137.5" wb

2-4P Cabr	2495	18,500	33,000	55,000	88,000	110,000
5P Brgm	2395	10,200	20,400	34,000	47,600	68,000
5P Sed	2395	9900	19,800	33,000	46,200	66,000
Sed Phae	2595	29,500	55,000	84,000	110,000	140,000

1933-34-35
(Not Manufacturing)

1936 Cord, Sportsman, convertible, AA

1936 Cord, Beverly, sedan, OCW

1937 Cord, Westchester, sedan, OCW

363

1936
Model 810, 8-cyl., 125" wb

	FP	5	4	3	2	1
Phae	2195	14,400	28,800	48,000	76,000	96,000
Sportsman	2145	14,700	29,400	49,000	78,000	98,000
West Sed	1995	6750	13,500	22,500	31,500	45,000
Bev Sed	2095	7050	14,100	23,500	32,900	47,000

1937
Model 812, 8-cyl., 125" wb

	FP	5	4	3	2	1
Phae	2645	14,400	28,800	48,000	76,000	96,000
Sportsman	2585	14,700	29,400	49,000	78,000	98,000
West Sed	2445	6750	13,500	22,500	31,500	45,000
Bev Sed	2545	7050	14,100	23,500	32,900	47,000

Model 812, 8-cyl., 132" wb

	FP	5	4	3	2	1
Cus Bev	2960	7200	14,400	24,000	33,600	48,000
Cus Berline	3060	7350	14,700	24,500	34,300	49,000

NOTE: Add $2000 for supercharged models; factory prices for supercharged Cords.

CORDNER — The Cordner Motor Car Company was organized in New York City early in 1909 to "manufacture, lease and sell horseless vehicles." Behind this $25,000 venture were A.B. Cordner, Robert E. Graham and W.H. Flinn. No Cordner car is believed to have resulted, but it is known that the company served as a dealership for the Acme. Later that year the firm moved from its original quarters at 176th Street and Broadway into the former Studebaker salesrooms along Automobile Row.

1922 Corinthian, touring, NAHC

CORINTHIAN — Philadelphia, Pennsylvania — (1922-1923) — Corinthian Motors, Inc. was organized in late November of 1921 for the manufacture of a four-cylinder assembled car which was enormously expensive and which was offered in a "racer" version in addition to more sedate open and closed models. When initial sales in 1922 did not fulfill expectations, Corinthian came back for 1923 with a cheaper-line addition. The Junior was powered by a Herschell-Spillman four, the Senior by Wisconsin's T-head. The diversity did not boost sales sufficiently for the company to survive into 1924. Corinthian's president and engineer was Charles B. Lewis, who earlier had tried and failed in the manufacture of a truck in San Francisco. References indicate that the Lewis truck arrived in 1912 and disappeared in 1914.

1922 CORINTHIAN
Model M-1 — 4-cyl., 65 hp, 130" wb

Racer	4500	5000	6500	11,000	22,000	35,000
Cpe.-3P	6875	4200	5200	8400	15,700	29,000
Sed.-5P	7290	3900	4800	7700	14,300	27,000
Rdstr.-2P	5000	5400	7300	11,800	25,000	38,000

1923 CORINTHIAN
Junior — 4-cyl., 35 hp, 110" wb

Tour.-5P	985	4200	5200	8400	15,700	29,000
Rdstr.-2P	985	4400	5600	9200	17,300	31,000
Cpe.-3P	1385	3100	4200	6300	10,500	22,000
Sed.-5P	1385	3000	4000	6000	9500	21,000

Senior — 4-cyl., 65 hp, 132" wb

Tour.-5P	5000	4500	5800	9500	18,000	32,000
Rdstr.-2P	5000	5400	7300	11,800	25,000	38,000
Cpe.-3P	6875	4200	5200	8400	15,700	29,000
Sed.-5P	7290	3900	4800	7700	14,300	27,000
Racer	4500	5000	6500	11,000	22,000	35,000

CORL — The Corl Motor Car Company was a $300,000 Delaware incorporation from late 1915 for the manufacture of motor cars and trucks. J.E. Corl, P.W. Sullivan and Lee D. Mathias were the incorporators. Manufacture is doubted.

CORLISS — In the fall of 1909 the Corliss Motor Company was organized in Wisconsin by Ernest E. Smith, Albert K. Stebbins and John A. Wallis for the manufacture of a six-cylinder car designed by W. Owen Thomas. Although the production plans for the Owen Thomas were short-lived, the Corliss company did subsequently enter the commercial field. Refer to Owen Thomas.

1914 Cornelian, roadster, WLB

CORNELIAN — Kalamazoo & Allegan, Michigan — (1914-1915) — The Blood brothers — M.E. and C.C. — were pioneer machinists in Kalamazoo, the manufacturers of a car bearing their name from 1902 to 1906, and the successful producers of universal joints thereafter. Probably it was young Howard E. Blood — son of Maurice E. Blood — who was the motivation for the return of the Blood Brothers Machine Company into automotive manufacture. What young Howard designed was a cyclecar, one of the very best of its type. Unlike most cyclecars, the Cornelian's tread was the standard fifty-six inches, which provided comfortable side-by-side seating. Progressive features included unit body construction (no chassis, the body serving as same), independent rear suspension, and a full-floating rear axle. Proper fenders were fitted and were uniquely shaped ("ridge-board type" was what they were called then). The Cornelian was a neat job throughout, and it was introduced at the New York Automobile Show at Grand Central Palace in January 1914. Apparently, early prospects were sufficiently encouraging to prompt the company to move its plant from Kalamazoo to Allegan where larger facilities were available. The move was completed by March 1915. And the Bloods decided to enter a specially-designed Cornelian in that year's Indianapolis 500. Its 103 cubic inch engine was the smallest thus far ever entered in the 500, and its driver was one of the sport's biggest: Louis Chevrolet. Chevrolet's qualifying speed for the race was 81.2 mph, and he was in the money on the 77th lap when he broke a valve and was out of the contest. Soon thereafter hopes were dashed for the Cornelian cyclecar as well. In June, a month after the 500, the company reported a workforce of 248 men and a workday of 24 hours in order for the factory to gear up for production of 25 cars per week. By October the announcement came of the discontinuation of the Cornelian, after a total production of approximately 100 units. Doubtless the publicity attendant to Indy had spurred sales momentarily, the by-now dastardly reputation of the cyclecar genre squelched it permanently. The Cornelian that raced at Indianapolis survives and is in the collection of the Indianapolis Motor Speedway Museum.

1915 Cornelian, roadster, WLB

1914-1915 CORNELIAN
4-cyl., 13 hp, 96" wb

	FP	5	4	3	2	1
Cyclecar Rdstr.-2P	435	—	—	—	—	—

CORNING — The Corning Automobile Company was organized in early 1906 with a capital stock of $5000 for the manufacture of automobiles in Corning, New York. George T. Wolcott, Samuel K. Wolcott and William W. Cowan were behind this venture. Manufacture is doubted.

CORNISH-FRIEDBERG — The firm was called the Cornish-Friedberg Motor Car Company, but the car it produced in Chicago from 1907 to 1909 was more popularly known by its initials. Refer to C-F.

1922 Corona, buckboard, MVMA

CORONA — The Corona was a variation of the buckboard produced by Briggs & Stratton and was built by a manufacturer unknown during 1922. It even made the pages of chic *Vanity Fair* that year. "Here is a practical two-passenger buckboard for running about beaches and other resorts," the magazine said. "(It) does eighty miles to the gallon of gasoline and half pint of oil, and its top speed is from three to nearly thirty miles an hour." The vehicle used a standard Briggs & Stratton Motor Wheel, though its wheelbase at 72 inches was ten inches longer than the Briggs & Stratton version. The Corona might be viewed as a forerunner of the modern-day dune buggy. Conceivably, it may have been built by Briggs & Stratton, but documentation of this is lacking.

CORONATION — Possibly a dreadful handwriting or terrible typing on the part of the company itself resulted in the Coronation car of 1913 from Detroit, references to which were made by both *The Automobile* and *Automobile Topics* that year. The car actually was the Car-Nation.

1909 Correja, touring car, HAC

CORREJA — Iselin & Elizabeth, New Jersey — (1909-1914) — Precisely when F.C. and Edwin Vandewater began building their Correja car is not known. In December 1909 when Vandewater & Co., Inc. moved from Iselin to Elizabeth, the purpose was — according to a press release — to expand production of the vehicle which they had "been making in a small way for several years." However, the vehicle which had been built in a "small way" was the Eagle, which had failed in Rahway. The new Correja was a much better car, and though pilot models may have arrived earlier, a production version didn't until August of 1908 as a 1909 model. A heavy and well-built car, the Correja was remarkably dependable. "Takes Every Hill and Always Will" was the company's slogan. Interestingly, in 1911, the Vandewaters curtailed their unusual production of tourers and runabouts, and concentrated production on a single two-seater model called the "Speed Runabout." Nineteen eleven proved to be Correja's best year ever, with 120 cars sold. It is curious that for 1912 the Vandewaters decided to return to a flurry of models and obviously it was not a good idea. The new cars did not sell, and the company paid its bills for the next two years largely through parts and repair work. In February 1914 the Vandewaters declared bankruptcy, which infuriated the Thomas Howard Company of Brooklyn, the Correja distributor. Howard contended that the bankruptcy move by the Vandewaters was merely an attempt to evade completing the cars they had been contracted to build. But the Vandewaters proved they were indeed broke. That someone named Correja had been a financial angel in this venture seems likely, but who that was is not known. Interestingly, California registration lists for 1919 indicate an Emma A. Correja of Riverside as owner of a Correja touring car.

1909 CORREJA

	FP	5	4	3	2	1
Four — 40 hp, 110'' wb						
Tour.-5P	1900	2700	3600	5300	8800	19,000
Rbt.-2/3P	1900	2900	3700	5600	9100	20,000

1909 Correja, runabout, WLB

1910 CORREJA
Four — 30 hp, 116' wb
Model 30 (Close Coupled)

	FP	5	4	3	2	1
Torpedo-4P	1500	2900	3700	5600	9100	20,000
Four — 50 hp, 116'' wb						
Model 50						
Torpedo-5P	2200	3100	4200	6300	10,500	22,000
Four — 50 hp, 127'' wb						
Model 50						
Torpedo-7P	2300	3500	4500	7000	13,000	25,000

1911 Correja, runabout, HAC

1911 CORREJA
Four — 35 hp, 105'' wb

Speed Rbt.-2P	1450	4000	5000	8000	15,000	28,000

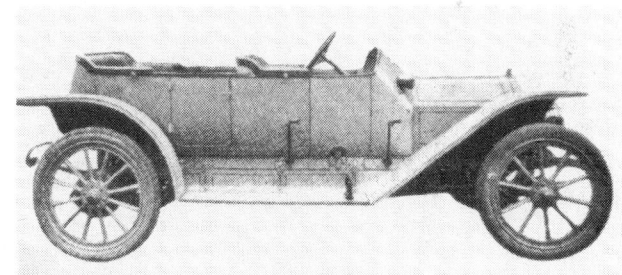

1912 Correja, model T, torpedo touring, HAC

1912 CORREJA
Four — 35 hp, 105'' wb
Model A

Torpedo Rbt.	1450	3500	4500	7000	13,000	25,000
Model B						
Torpedo	1450	3300	4400	6700	12,000	24,000
Model C						
Rdstr.	1450	3500	4500	7000	13,000	25,000
Model T						
Torpedo Tour. (125'' wb)	1650	3900	4800	7700	14,300	27,000
Six — 60 hp, 125'' wb						
Model R						
Torpedo Rdstr.	1950	4200	5200	8400	15,700	29,000
Model S						
Torpedo Tour.	2150	4000	5000	8000	15,000	28,000
1913 CORREJA						
Six — 45 hp, 125'' wb						
Model C						
Speed Rdstr.	1850	4300	5400	8700	16,500	30,000
Model J						
Torpedo Tour.	1850	4200	5200	8400	15,700	29,000
Six — 65 hp, 125'' wb						
Model R						
Speed Rdstr.	2250	4500	5800	9500	18,000	32,000
Model S						
Torpedo Tour.	2250	4300	5400	8700	16,500	30,000

1914 Correja Six, touring, HAC

1914 CORREJA
Six — 34 hp, 128" wb

	FP	5	4	3	2	1
Tour.-5P	1800	5000	6500	11,000	22,000	35,000
Knickerbocker Tour.-6P	2100	5200	6800	11,300	23,000	36,000

CORRICK — Detroit, Michigan — (1914) — In 1914 a machinist from Detroit named J.B. Corrick built himself a cyclecar. Details are lacking, but documentation of its building appeared in *Motor Print* that March.

CORTLAND — The Cortland Motor Wagon Company was organized to manufacture and deal in automobiles and accessories in Cortland, New York during the spring of 1910. The firm did move into manufacture, but of a truck only which was built from 1911-1912.
The Cortland Cart & Carriage Company produced the Hatfield automobile in Sidney, New York from 1916-1924. Refer to Hatfield.

CORWEG — That the Corweg Shuttle Valve Motor Company of Atlantic City, New Jersey was engaged in the automobile manufacturing business as early as 1905 and as late as 1921 has been indicated on numerous car rosters. Undoubtedly not. The city directory for Atlantic City does not reveal a company in town by that name for the years from 1900 through 1921.

CORWIN — In 1906 the Corwin Manufacturing Company of Peabody, Massachusetts produced an automobile called the Gas-au-lec. Refer to Gas-au-lec.

CORY — Albany, Indiana — (1907) — The Cory was a $300 runabout on a 63-inch wheelbase chassis that weighed 450 pounds and was only a foot longer than it was wide. It was powered by a single-cylinder two-stroke water-cooled engine of four horsepower, and used a friction transmission, and solid tires on very high wheels. The Cory Automobile Company announced its entrance onto the automotive scene in February of 1907. Its quick departure, which occurred late that year, was not announced.

COSHOCTON — The Coshocton Motor Car Company has appeared on various car rosters as an automobile producer in Coshocton, Ohio during 1913. No documentation of this has been found.

COSMOPOLITAN — The Cosmopolitan Power Company was incorporated in Jersey City, New Jersey in May of 1900 with a capital stock of a stupendous $40 million. "It is a Chicago enterprise, and its officers, it is stated, will include some of the leading capitalists of that city," reported *Electrical World and Engineer.* "The corporation has been established to operate and construct all sorts of carriages driven by compressed air, electricity and gasoline. Its market will be sought mainly in the West . . . its factories are to be scattered through the country." None of this ever happened.

COSMOPOLITAN — St. Louis, Missouri — (1907-1910) — The D.W. Haydock Motor Car Manufacturing Company of St. Louis built a highwheeler with a difference. At least in the prototype. It had an absolutely round radiator and was driven by a single chain to the front axle, this to obviate skidding in corners and facilitate hill climbing. An ingenuous imitation of the front-wheel-drive principle advocated with more sophistication by Walter Christie, the car was introduced as the Haydock Front Drive. D.W.

1907 Cosmopolitan, runabout, NAHC

quickly decided the vehicle deserved a name with more style, and all production cars would be called Cosmopolitan. They would also be rear-driven. Actually, front drive had been the answer to a question no other highwheeler manufacturer bothered to ask. Skidding in curves was not a problem for highwheelers since their speed was generally modest enough to forestall that possibility, and hill climbing proclivity was not particularly an advantage in the flat farm lands of the Midwest.

1907 Cosmopolitan, Haydock Front Drive, NAHC

1907 COSMOPOLITAN
Model B — 1-cyl., 5 hp, 60" wb

	FP	5	4	3	2	1
High Wheel Rbt.	350	2700	3600	5300	8800	19,000

1908 COSMOPOLITAN
2-cyl., 10/12 hp, 87" wb

	FP	5	4	3	2	1
Type 4 Rbt.-2P	625	2900	3700	5600	9100	20,000
Type 5 Rbt.-3P	675	3000	4000	6000	9500	21,000
Type 6 Rbt.-4P	725	3100	4200	6300	10,500	22,000

1909 COSMOPOLITAN
Model No. 4 — 2-cyl., 14 hp, 87" wb

	FP	5	4	3	2	1
High Wheel Rbt.	625	3000	4000	6000	9500	21,000

1910 COSMOPOLITAN
Model No. 5 — 2-cyl., 18 hp, 97" wb

	FP	5	4	3	2	1
Rbt.	800	3100	4200	6300	10,500	22,000

1921 Cotay, roadster, KM

COTAY — New York, New York — (1920-1921) — Cotay was an abbreviation of Coffyn and Taylor. Frank Coffyn was an aviation enthusiast who was described as one of the three surviving members of the "Wright team"; James B. Taylor, Jr. was a test pilot. The designer of the engine for the Cotay, however, had his feet firmly planted on the ground, though they moved around a lot. This was none other than Everett S. Cameron, who had spent the previous decade traveling to the numerous factories in the East and Middle West where his Cameron had been built. Like most Cameron designs, the Cotay's ohv 18 hp four-cylinder engine was air cooled. The car in which it was fitted was a perky two-seater roadster that might be described as an oversized and sophisticated cyclecar. It featured shaft drive, a three-speed sliding gear transmission built in unit with the engine, cantilever springs and electric lighting and starting. The wheelbase was 105 inches. The unit chassis/body was a plywood and aluminum composite; the disc wheels were wood. The result was a very light car weighing but 900 pounds and with a 45 mpg fuel economy. The price tag was $1200. Everett Cameron had a financial interest in the Coffyn-Taylor Motor Company, but reaped no financial reward. Neither did Coffyn or Taylor. Although the Cotay was offered on the domestic market, apparently it was the export trade which the company envisioned from the beginning as its road to fame and profit. The Cotay was introduced at the White City during the 1920 Motor Show in London, where it elicited some interest on the part of spectators and the British press, although it was not enough to make a going concern of Coffyn-Taylor Motors.

COTE — The Cote Automobile Company was organized in Castleton, New York during the fall of 1910 for the manufacture of motor sleighs and automobiles in Tupper Lake. The capital stock was $15,000; Michael Kennedy, Charles H. Marsha, Theodore Cote and Almson Snell were the incorporators. Manufacture of an automobile is doubted.

1901 Cotta, steam runabout, JAC

COTTA STEAM — **Lanark & Rockford, Illinois** — **(1901-1903)** — This steam car was also referred to as the Cottamobile, and it was unique in being the only steamer then on the market to boast four-wheel-drive and steering. Its two-cylinder engine was mounted precisely mid-ship, with individual chain drive to each wheel. "No slipping of wheels when you 'auto-go'" was the cute way the company put it. The Cotta was designed by Charles E. Cotta, who assembled the pilot model in 1901 in Lanark, where his father operated a thriving nursery. Four more pilot models followed in 1902, built by the Love Manufacturing Company of Rockford, as Cotta busied himself in trying to establish a company and find a factory site. Not until January of 1903 was the announcement made by the newly-established Cotta Automobile Company of Rockford that its first production machine had been completed, and that ten more cars were in the process of construction. Whether all of these cars were ever finished is not known. In November Cotta sold his patent rights to the Four Wheel Drive Wagon Company of Milwaukee which had recently been organized to enter the commercial field. Although it was mentioned that Charles Cotta would join that company as vice-president, if he did move to Milwaukee, he did not stay long. Instead he returned to Rockford to organize the Cotta Gear Company for the manufacture of transmissions which he had been building alongside his Cotta steamer from the beginning. In 1912 a brief reference noted the impending manufacture of motorcars by Cotta Gear, but this latterday Cotta never appeared.

COTTON — **Topeka, Kansas** — **(1901)** — Isaac F. Cotton was a gunsmith and machinist from Topeka who purportedly built an automobile in 1901. He very well might have, like many machinists of that period, but solid documentation appears lacking.

1904 Country Club, tonneau, HAC

COUNTRY CLUB — **Boston, Massachusetts** — **(1903-1904)** — If ever a car could be said to have built-in snob appeal before a single example was ever seen, it was the product of the Country Club Car Company of Boston. The name was the idea of H.M. Woodward, and he was also responsible for the "pneumatic speed change," a three-speed sliding gear transmission operated by compressed air from one of the car's two cylinders. The Country Club was otherwise restricted to the usual, and after only a few were built, H.M. Woodward sallied forth to build "auto boats" with the Country Club name.

1904 COUNTRY CLUB
2-cyl., 16 hp, 86-1/2" wb

	FP	5	4	3	2	1
Tonneau-4P	2500	—	—	—	—	—

COURIER — **Sandusky, Ohio** — **(1904-1905)** — The Courier was built by the Sandusky Automobile Company and was a slightly larger companion car to the Sandusky. The only significant engineering difference was its sliding gear transmission, which the company said was a first for a runabout. This was plainly not true, and few potential purchasers bought either the boast or the Courier. Petitioned into bankruptcy in October of 1904, the Sandusky Automobile Company was reorganized in April 1905 and continued production for a few more months. As many as 225 Couriers may have been built.

1904 COURIER
Style D — 1-cyl., 7 hp, 70" wb

	FP	5	4	3	2	1
Rbt.	700	3000	4000	6000	9500	21,000
Style F — 1-cyl., 7 hp, 70" wb						
French-Front Rbt.	800	3100	4200	6300	10,500	22,000
1905 COURIER						
Model F — 1-cyl., 7 hp, 70" wb						
Rbt.-2P	650	3000	4000	6000	9500	21,000
Model H — 1-cyl., 8 hp, 76" wb						
Tonneau-4P	700	3100	4200	6300	10,500	22,000

1904 Courier, runabout, WLB

COURIER — **Stoneham, Massachusetts** — **(1905)** — The Courier Motor Company was successor to the Phelps Motor Vehicle Company — and was very short-lived. In September of 1905, L.J. Phelps retired from business and moved to California, turning his company over to Elliott C. Lee (the president of the American Automobile Association) who reorganized in October as the Courier Motor Company with a capital stock of $150,000. Possibly a few of the Phelps cars in the process of construction were driven out the door with a Courier emblem, but Elliott Lee decided against this entire venture very soon. By December the Shawmut Motor Company moved into the Phelps factory to build its own car.

1910 Courier, roadster, WLB

COURIER — Dayton, Ohio — (1910-1912) — The Courier Car Company was organized by Charles G. Stoddard, John W. Stoddard and others of the Dayton Motor Car Company. In essence, this Courier was a smaller and cheaper Stoddard-Dayton, and the Courier company was merely a Stoddard-Dayton subsidiary, the only reason for its existence being the belief that the respected Stoddard-Dayton name should not be sullied by the production of an inexpensive car. The new company was announced during the summer of 1909, the first Couriers arrived in January 1910 as roadsters (with an oval gas tank or "mother-in-law" seat in the rear) and touring cars. In 1912 the cars were called Courier Clermonts, and they were the last. Earlier Stoddard-Dayton had been taken over by the United States Motor Company (Benjamin Briscoe's aborted attempt to emulate General Motors), and of course Courier had gone along. When Walter Flanders was hired to pick up the pieces of the U.S. Motor debacle, he decided the only company in the combine worth salvaging was Maxwell. In 1913 the Courier plant in Dayton was sold for $50,000, and the money promptly went into the Maxwell treasury.

1912 Courier, Clermont, roadster, WLB

1910 COURIER
4-cyl., 20 hp, 100" wb
Model 10-A-3

	FP	5	4	3	2	1
Tour.-5P	1200	3700	4700	7300	13,700	26,000
Model 10-A-1						
Rdstr.-2P	1050	4000	5000	8000	15,000	28,000
1911 COURIER						
4-cyl., 25 hp, 112" wb						
Model 11-M						
Tour.-5P	1350	3900	4800	7700	14,300	27,000
1912 COURIER						
4-cyl., 30 hp, 108" wb						
Clermont Fore-Door Tour.	1150	3700	4700	7300	13,700	26,000
Clermont Fore-Door Rdstr.	1150	3900	4800	7700	14,300	27,000

1923 Courier, sedan, JAC

COURIER — Sandusky, Ohio — (1923) — Courier was the name for the new car with a six-cylinder Falls engine which the previous year had been called the Maibohm. When Maibohm Motors collapsed in July of 1922, it was resuscitated by the newly incorporated Arrow Motors, headed by Albert C. Burch who had formerly been involved with the Signal and Clydesdale truck companies. In August of 1922, when initial plans went awry, Arrow Motors reorganized as Courier Motors, and A.C. Burch announced "big things" — the Courier, while retaining the basic Maibohm body lines, would have "practically new 'inners'" which included a central tank chassis oiling system operated by a plunger on the dash, and dry sump full-pressure engine lubrication. "The Most Completely and Conveniently Lubricated Car in America" crowded the ads. The Courier, which was introduced for the 1923 model year, just seemed to fade away after that. The trade press didn't ever bother with an obituary. Total production had probably been no more than fifty cars. A right-hand-drive Courier extant in Australia indicates that part of the output was exported.

1923 Courier, phaeton, WLB

1923 COURIER
Model D — 6-cyl., 46, hp, 116" wb

	FP	5	4	3	2	1
Tour.-5P	1395	4500	5800	9500	18,000	32,000
Rdstr.-3P	1295	5000	6500	11,000	22,000	35,000
Spt.-4P	1495	5200	6800	11,300	23,000	36,000
Cpe.-3P	1965	3700	4700	7300	13,700	26,000
Sed.-5P	1995	3500	4500	7000	13,000	25,000

COURTNEY — New Castle, Pennsylvania — (1896) — Philip T. Courtney was an engineer and draftsman at the Vulcan Foundry in New Castle who completed and began testing his first automobile in late 1896. Conceivably, the results were not congenially to his expectation because although he promised full particulars regarding his car to *The Horseless Age*, he did not deliver on them.

COVELL — The Covell & Crosby Motor Company was organized in Bay Shore, Long Island, New York early in 1906 with a capital stock of $20,000 and the plan to manufacture and deal in automobiles. The plan to manufacture was disbanded early, C.H. Covell and Arthur A. Crosby electing to become Ariel dealers instead.

1902 Covert, runabout, HAC

COVERT — Lockport, New York — (1902-1907) — Byron V. Covert & Company was founded early in 1902 ostensibly to produce the steam car Covert had designed in 1901, but in the meantime he had come up with a chain-drive gasoline runabout he preferred, and it was this car which he took to market later that summer. Then he had another idea, introduced at the New York Automobile Show in January 1903: the Covert Chainless, with sliding gear transmission, running gear "of the reachless pattern" and gearbox attached directly to the rear axle. By 1904, when the firm name changed to Covert Motor Vehicle Company, a four-cylinder touring car had been introduced. In the World's Fair Buffalo to St. Louis endurance run that same year, a Covert runabout was the only car in its class to successfully make it to Missouri. Unfortunately, the company was never able to capitalize on this performance on a national basis. The car appears to have been sold mainly to customers in New York State. By 1908 Byron Covert decided to concentrate his manufacture on running gear components solely, and axles particularly.

1902 COVERT
1-cyl., 3 hp, 62" wb

	FP	5	4	3	2	1
Rbt.	600	3100	4200	6300	10,500	22,000

1903 Covert Chainless, runabout, HAC

1903 COVERT
1-cyl., 3 hp, 62" wb

Rbt.	500	3100	4200	6300	10,500	22,000
1-cyl., 5 hp, 62" wb						
Chainless Rbt.	750	3200	4300	6500	11,000	23,000

1904 Covert Chainless, runabout, WLB

1904 COVERT
1-cyl., 6-1/2 hp, 72" wb

Chainless Rbt.	750	3200	4300	6500	11,000	23,000
4-cyl., 20/24 hp, 94" wb						
Tour.	2250	3300	4400	6700	12,000	24,000

1905 COVERT
1-cyl., 6-1/2 hp, 72" wb

Chainless Rbt.	650	3200	4300	6500	11,000	23,000
4-cyl., 24 hp, 94" wb						
Tour.	2250	3300	4400	6700	12,000	24,000
1906-1907 COVERT						
1-cyl., 6-1/2 hp, 72" wb						
Chainless Rbt.	650	3200	4300	6500	11,000	23,000

1905 Covert Chainless, runabout, HAC

1908 Cowan, runabout, WLB

COWAN — Los Angeles, California — (1908) — This car, which was nicknamed the California Midget, was built by Brice Cowan of Los Angeles. It was powered by an air-cooled 3 hp Aster engine which Cowan tweaked into providing the horses sufficient for a 25-30 mph performance. Friction transmission with nine speeds forward and two in reverse, and double chain drive, were featured. The two-seater was approximately six feet long with a three-foot tread. Only the one example was built, and although it was successful, the Cowan would not be noteworthy except for one fact. Brice Cowan was fifteen years old. He didn't need any help building it. Young Brice's father, W.K. Cowan, was one of the pioneer automobile dealers in Los Angeles.

COWLES — From 1914-1915 the Cowles-MacDowell Pneumobile Company of Chicago produced an automobile which it marketed as the Pneumobile, although it was occasionally called the Cowles Light Six as well. Refer to Pneumobile.

1906 Cox, roadster, HS

COX — The name Jas. I. Cox appears carved into the trunk lid of this beguiling little roadster built circa 1906, but whether Cox built the car himself or commissioned it to be built for him, and where, is not known. The engine is a small two-stroke, the transmission is friction, the drive by belts. One adult or a couple of pubescent children could be accommodated on the small seat. The car's wheelbase measures 52 inches, its tread 25 1/2 inches; its total weight is but 245 pounds. The Cox remains extant in an East Coast collection.

369

COX — Detroit, Michigan — (1914) — In 1909, following a dispute with John North Willys, the new owner of Overland in Indianapolis, Claude E. Cox left the company to set himself up in business in Detroit as the Commercial Engineering Laboratories at 88 Congress Street. Building prototypes for entrepreneurs anxious to get into the automobile industry was his principal focus of activity, but at least a few cars were built under his own name too. Among these was a cyclecar and a motor buggy in 1914. The former was built only as a prototype, the latter may have seen a small production.

COYOTE — Albany, Indiana — (1909) — Whether this venture produced anything more than the prototype is not known. The Coyote, a small gasoline-engined runabout, was the idea of the Union Automobile Company of Albany. A single example was completed early in 1909. That March the company revealed its plans to move to Seymour. "No bonus will be asked," reported *The Motor Age*, "but instead a commodius factory building is to be provided, and the company will remove here as soon as the plant is ready." For some reason, the Coyote died before ever leaving Albany, Indiana.

1909 Coyote Special, roadster, GR

COYOTE SPECIAL — Redondo, California — (1908-1909) — The Coyote Special was a rakish two-seater roadster powered by a 50 hp eight-cylinder engine and capable of a claimed, and probably exaggerated, 75 mph. The car was produced by the Pacific Motor and Automobile Company which announced its presence on the automotive scene during the summer of 1908, indicating that a factory site was being sought near Long Beach. By December, however, Redondo had been chosen after businessmen of that community subscribed to 10,000 shares in the company's stock. Undoubtedly no dividends were ever declared. The Pacific Motor and Automobile Company was out of business before 1909 ended. Just two Coyote Specials had been built, one of them being raced locally with no resounding success. For years it had been believed that the car's engine was simply two Franklin fours coupled together. This was not the case, but the Syracuse, New York company had unwittingly contributed substantially to the Coyote Special's design. In the engine, the crankcase and crankshaft were Coyote's own, but many of the other parts were courtesy of Franklin. Likewise, Franklin full-elliptic springs, axles, wheels and steering gear found their way into the Coyote Special as well. Obviously Pacific Motor and Automobile Company did most of its shopping in a junkyard.

C.P.T. — Chicago, Illinois — (1906) — The initials translated to Chicago Pneumatic Tool Company, a firm well known in Cook County as the manufacturers of air compressors and pneumatic and electric tools. The firm entered the automotive field as the builders of commercial vehicles, the Duntley Commercial and the Little Giant Truck being the best known of its efforts. Apparently C.P.T. was also a name used by the company for its trucks, and for the firm's single foray into passenger automobile manufacture. The C.P.T. was a solid-tired, two-cylinder, 22 hp runabout that was produced in 1906 only and was never marketed. The cars were solely for the use of the company's traveling salesmen. A total of fifty were built.

C. & R. — The C. & R. Garage was organized in Chicago, Illinois during the spring of 1913 to manufacture, sell and repair motor cars and to operate a general livery. Capital stock was $1000; Albert E. Cosey, K.R. Ballentine and S.J. Mathews were the incorporators. Manufacture of an automobile is doubted.

CRAGAR — Los Angeles, California — (1933-1934) — Cragar Corporation, Ltd. of 940 North Ocean Drive in Los Angeles was headed by Crane Gartz, who had made his wealth in plumbing and who took the first three letters of his first and last names to designate this new venture. Cragar specialized in the production of speed accessories and assorted go-fast equipment for the sporting set. Associated with Gartz in this activity was Harlan Fengler. In addition to ohv Ford conversions and race car equipment, Cragar did produce complete automobiles in 1933-1934, most of them for race competition and to custom order.

1920 Craig-Hunt, touring

CRAIG-HUNT — Indianapolis, Indiana — (1920) — For five years Craig-Hunt, Inc. had enjoyed prosperity by manufacturing speed specialties for the lucrative Ford Model T aftermarket industry. In 1920 the company decided that it could build a better Ford, and this decision was its undoing. In May the Craig-Hunt Motor Company was incorporated with a capital stock of $1,000,000 by John R. Craig, W.L. Hunt and C.L. Zechiel with the promise that a low-priced 103-inch wheelbase roadster and touring car of "wonder performance" would be forthcoming. Preliminary advertisements boasted about the sixteen-valve engine with overhead camshaft, and the special Craig-Hunt spring suspension. But this super Model T never arrived. Less than a month later Craig-Hunt was enjoined against building its new plant on Maple Road Boulevard by a recently enacted city ordinance prohibiting manufacturing plants within 500 feet of a boulevard. By October the company was in receivership, for an outstanding debt amounting to $125.50. Production had never begun, the only Craig-Hunt was the prototype.

1907 Craig-Toledo, roadster, WLB

CRAIG-TOLEDO — Toledo, Ohio — (1907) — Although it was the Craig shipbuilding family of Toledo that put up the money, the Craig-Toledo idea belonged to Frank M. Blair. An engineer whose resume included work with Woods, Jackson, Yale and Ford, Blair wanted to build the "best possible car to carry three passengers on our rough American roads as fast as the driver cares to go." And he convinced George L. and John F. Craig of the practical wisdom of his idea. The prototype car was built in Dundee (Michigan) and was called the Maumee. It was on the road March 1st, 1906, put up 65 mph with ease, and subsequently 18,000 miles of testing without stress. The reason for this extended test period was the three-point suspension which was the distinctive, and patented, feature of the design. In January of 1907 the new Craig-Toledo Motor Company and the new car were announced, followed by lavish advertising and plans to build one hundred $4000 roadsters for 1907. How many were built in the next six months is unknown, how many were on hand in June when the company went into involuntary receivership is. The following February Joseph W. Lane, trustee for the company, sued George L. Craig for $18,000, which was the difference between $2000 held to be a fair settlement to a creditor and $20,000 allowed Craig in the form of eight Craig-Toledo automobiles at the time the company went into bankruptcy.

1907 CRAIG-TOLEDO
4-cyl., 40 hp, 112" wb

	FP	5	4	3	2	1
Rds.-3P	4000	—	—	—	—	—

CRAMER — Garrett, Indiana — (1901) — In an August 1901 issue of *The Motor Age*, it was reported that Claude Cramer of Garrett had built an automobile. Details regarding the car are lacking.

CRANDALL — Groton, New York — (1902) — In March of 1902 the Crandall Machine Company announced to the trade press that the automobile it was building was just about completed. Crandall wasn't giving just due, because said vehicle was a collaborative effort. The car had been designed by W.G. Stolz, an automobile man from Brooklyn, and its body was being seen to by the Groton Carriage Works. By May the car was finished and given its first test run up Savercool Hill. "It seemed to work well in going up," reported *The Motor Age* thereafter, "but on returning the operator lost control of it and the occupants had a not altogether enjoyable ride. It was finally guided into a field and there stopped." So far as is known, this was the first and last automobile produced by the Crandall Machine Company.

1913 Crane, model 3, touring, Brewster, FR

CRANE — Bayonne, New Jersey — (1912-1914)/CRANE-SIMPLEX — Long Island City, New York — (1922) — Henry Middlebrook Crane was an M.I.T.-trained engineer who was responsible for some of the most rapid motorboats and most expensive motorcars in America during the pre-World War I period. The Harmsworth Trophy was won no fewer than four times by Dixie speedboats powered by Crane-designed engines, his most puissant being a V-8 of more than 200 hp. Interestingly, when Henry M. Crane turned his talents to the automobile, it was elegance not speed that was his principal design focus. The Crane & Whitman Company of Bayonne, after experimenting with several automobile designs, evolved into the Crane Motor Car Company about 1910, and the Model 3 Crane Six was ready for market in 1912. At $8000 for the chassis alone, the market was naturally a limited one. The Crane six-cylinder engine was a 563.7-cubic-inch L-head nominally rated at 46 hp but developing 110 hp. The chassis stretched 136 inches between the axles, and the coachwork was to custom order. The Crane Six was built in small numbers until the end of 1914, less than 40 cars total being produced, about half that number the improved Model 4. Crane also built three experimental automobiles for Alco. During the fall of 1914 the Crane operation was purchased by the Simplex Automobile Company of New Brunswick. Henry Crane moved his old company to New Brunswick, where the Model 4 Crane Six engine was refined, a new longer chassis of 144-inch wheelbase was designed to accept it, and the resulting car was put into production as the Simplex, Crane Model 5. Although frequently shortened to then, and alluded to since, as the Crane-Simplex, that designation was unofficial and, indeed, incorrect. The car was a Simplex and marketed as such until 1917 when the New Brunswick factory was turned over entirely to the manufacture of Hispano-Suiza aircraft engines. Although a few Crane-designed Simplex cars were produced during the war, the Simplex Automobile Company was destined for oblivion by February 1920 when it became part of Hare's Motors, an operating company established by Emlen S. Hare which now controlled Simplex, Locomobile and Mercer. In the late fall of 1922, with the collapse of Hare's Motors, Henry M. Crane purchased the Simplex property and equipment, organized the Crane-Simplex Company and secured a factory in Long Island City which had previously served as a Wright-Martin facility and the New York service station for Simplex automobiles. His plan was to revive the car he had designed for Simplex and to call it the Crane-Simplex, officially this time. Slated to sell in chassis form only at a price of $10,000, very few Crane-Simplexes were built before this venture went under.

1912-1914 CRANE/CRANE SIMPLEX
Crane Six — 36 hp, 136" wb

	FP	5	4	3	2	1
Chassis	8000	—	—	—	—	—

1922 CRANE/CRANE SIMPLEX
Crane-Simplex — 46 hp, 144" wb

Chassis	10,000	—	—	—	—	—

CRANE & BREED — Cincinnati, Ohio — (1912) — A carriage builder since 1850, the Crane & Breed Manufacturing Company of Cincinnati experimented with an electric runabout in 1902 but did not enter the automobile industry until 1909 and did so then with a gasoline-powered ambulance and hearse. Like Cunningham in New York, Crane & Breed was a pioneer exponent of providing elegant coachbuilt bodies for those vehicles which might or definitely would represent a person's last ride. Unlike Cunningham, however, Crane & Breed built a car for the definitely living only in 1912, and it was big, expensive and offered in eight body styles. The engine was the same as had powered the earlier ambulances and hearses. After 1912 Crane & Breed no longer built complete vehicles, concentrating exclusively on coachwork (predominantly professional cars) until the company's demise in 1924.

1912 CRANE & BREED
Crane & Breed — 6-cyl., 48 hp, 152" wb

	FP	5	4	3	2	1
Tour.	3000	6400	9300	14,500	33,000	45,000
Rds.	3000	6700	9900	15,500	34,800	47,000
Toy Tonneau	3000	6500	9500	15,000	34,000	46,000
Torpedo	3250	6800	10,300	16,000	35,500	48,000
Cpe.	4200	4200	5200	8400	15,700	29,000
Limo.	4250	4500	5800	9500	18,000	32,000
Twn. Car	4250	5000	6500	11,000	22,000	35,000
Land'et. Limo.	4500	5800	8000	12,500	28,000	40,000

CRANE & WHITMAN — Bayonne, New Jersey — (1907-1908) — The Crane & Whitman Automobile Works was located at Seventh Street near the Boulevard in Bayonne and built engines under contract. It was here that Henry Crane began his automotive experiments. His first car, a four-cylinder model, was tested in September 1907. The first car he sold was a six that was custom built for Harry Payne Whitney, who still owned it at the time of his death in 1924. Documentation regarding any other cars built by Henry Crane during this period is lacking. Crane went on to considerable renown, of course, following his association with Simplex.

1908 CRANE & WHITMAN

	FP	5	4	3	2	1
Crane & Whitman	—	—	—	—	—	—

CRAVEN — Late in 1905 the capital stock of the Craven Sectional Tire Company of Albany, Indiana was increased by $40,000 to finance the firm's entrance into the manufacture of automobiles. Apparently, H.O. Craven must have had a change of heart, however, because no Craven automobile ever appeared on the market.

CRAWFORD — Le Mars, Iowa — (1901) — Details regarding the car built by J.B. Crawford of Le Mars are lacking, but it is known the vehicle was nearing completion during the spring of 1901 and, according to *The Motor Age*, "a new company, formed to make it, expects to give it a trial in a few days." Perhaps the trial was unsuccessful; there is no evidence the car was put into production.

1905 Crawford, model A, runabout, HAC

CRAWFORD — Hagerstown, Maryland — (1904-1923) — The Crawford was the result of an alliance between a pipe organ manufacturer in Hagerstown and a bicycle builder from Philadelphia. The man who made the music was Mathias Peter Moller, a Danish immigrant; the two-wheelers were the product of Robert S. Crawford, a Scotsman who had developed a two-cylinder gasoline automobile around 1902. In 1904 they joined together with another Hagerstown businessman named Henry Holzapfel to form the Crawford Automobile Company. Two small runabouts were built in 1904, five in 1905. Their two-cylinder 10 hp water-cooled engines were mounted up front under a hood, with planetary transmission, chain drive and wheel steering featured. A four was added in 1906, when production was 41 cars, and fours only were produced through 1912. Early engines were Rutenbers, with Continentals later substituted. Crawford automobiles switched from chain drive to shaft and from planetary transmissions to sliding gear in 1908; the transmission was fitted on the rear axle beginning in 1911, this transaxle arrangement continuing through 1914. From 1916 onward all Crawfords were sixes, which were light and medium sized initially, but got heavier and bigger later on. A distinguishing feature was the curved-arc bracket attached to the filler cap for fitting of the rear license plate; the front tag was positioned with practicality in mind, not encumbering the radiator honeycomb from its supply of much needed cool air. There seemed to be a good deal of vacillation within the Crawford Automobile Company. Annual output had peaked way back in 1910 with 275 cars; thereafter it dwindled, with 104 cars produced in 1916, just 38 in 1917 when materials shortages became critical. The company had produced a few trucks through the years, and a twelve-cylinder Crawford was promised, but never arrived. Robert Crawford had left the firm early on, though his brother George stayed on awhile as office manager. In 1921 Moller became sole owner of the Crawford Automobile Company, and the vacillation ended soon after that. A new car called the Dagmar — named for Moller's daughter — was introduced during the summer of 1922. That fall the full Crawford line for 1923 was presented, and these were the biggest cars yet. Only 54 Crawfords had been built in 1922, in 1923 the last units were assembled, the final car for E.L. Schulenberger, the superintendent of Moller's pipe organ company. The official announcement followed in March of 1924. "Crawford Passes Out of Picture After Twenty Years; Makers Say Dagmar Is to Take Its Place," read the headline.

1904-1905 CRAWFORD
Model A — 2-cyl., 10 hp, 78" wb

	FP	5	4	3	2	1
Rbt.-2P	—	3000	4000	6000	9500	21,000

1906 Crawford, model C, touring, HAC

1906 CRAWFORD
Model A — 2-cyl., 10 hp, 78" wb

Rbt.-2P	850	3000	4000	6000	9500	21,000
Model C — 4-cyl., 24/28 hp, 100" wb						
Tour.-5P	2000	3100	4200	6300	10,500	22,000

1907 Crawford, model E, touring, WLB

1907 CRAWFORD
Model E — 4-cyl., 35 hp, 106" wb

Tour.-5P		2500	3100	4200	6300	10,500	22,000
Model F — 4-cyl., 50 hp, 118" wb						
Tour.-7P		3000	3200	4300	6500	11,000	23,000

1908 Crawford, model G, touring, HAC

1908 CRAWFORD
Model D — 4-cyl., 35 hp, 106" wb

Rbt.-3/4P		2500	3000	4000	6000	9500	21,000
Model E — 4-cyl., 35 hp, 106" wb						
Tour.-5P		2500	3000	4000	6000	9500	21,000
Model G — 4-cyl., 40 hp, 114" wb						
Tour.-5P		3000	3100	4200	6300	10,500	22,000
Model F — 4-cyl., 50 hp, 114" wb						
Tour.-7P		3500	7000	14,000	23,500	35,900	47,000

1909 Crawford, model H, touring, HAC

1909 CRAWFORD
Model H — 4-cyl., 25 hp, 106" wb

	FP	5	4	3	2	1
Tour.-5P	1300	3100	4200	6300	10,500	22,000
Rbt.-4P	1200	3000	4000	6000	9500	21,000
Model G — 4-cyl., 40 hp, 114" wb						
Tour.-5P	3000	3000	4000	6000	9500	21,000
Model D — 4-cyl., 40 hp, 114" wb						
Rds.-3/4P	3000	3200	4300	6500	11,000	23,000
Model F — 4-cyl., 50 hp, 114" wb						
Tour.-7P	3250	7000	14,000	23,500	32,900	47,000
Limo.-7P	4250	2900	3700	5600	9100	20,000

1910 Crawford, model 10, touring, HAC

1910 CRAWFORD
Model 10 — 4-cyl., 30 hp, 110" wb

Tour.-5P	1300	3100	4200	6300	10,500	22,000
Rds.-3P	1300	3300	4400	6700	12,000	24,000
Model F-G — 4-cyl., 50 hp, 130" wb						
Tour.	3500	3200	4300	6500	11,000	23,000

1911 Crawford, model 11-30, roadster special, HAC

1911 CRAWFORD
Model 11-30 — 4-cyl., 30 hp, 112" wb

Tour.-5P	1375	3100	4200	6300	10,500	22,000
Model 11-35 — 4-cyl., 35 hp, 120" wb						
Fore-Door Tour.-5P	1650	3200	4300	6500	11,000	23,000

1912 Crawford, model 12-30, roadster, HAC

1912 CRAWFORD
Model 12-30 — 4-cyl., 30 hp, 115" wb

	FP	5	4	3	2	1
Fore-Door Tour.-5P	1500	3200	4300	6500	11,000	23,000
Fore-Door Rds.-2P	1400	3500	4500	7000	13,000	25,000

Model 12-35 — 4-cyl., 35 hp, 129" wb

Fore-Door Tour.-5P	1650	3300	4400	6700	12,000	24,000

1913 Crawford, model 13-30, touring, HAC

1913 CRAWFORD
Model 13-30 — 4-cyl., 30 hp, 115" wb

Rds.-2P	1700	3500	4500	7000	13,000	25,000
Tour.-5P	1750	3200	4300	6500	11,000	23,000

Model 13-40 — 4-cyl., 40 hp, 125" wb

Rds.-2P	2050	3700	4700	7300	13,700	26,000
Tour.-5P	2100	3300	4400	6700	12,000	24,000

Model 13-6-45 — 6-cyl., 45 hp, 132" wb

Tour.-7P	3250	7000	14,000	23,500	32,900	47,000

1914 Crawford, model 4-40, touring, HAC

1914 CRAWFORD
Model 4-40 — 4-cyl., 40 hp, 125" wb

Rds.-2P	2100	3700	4700	7300	13,700	26,000
Tour.-5P	2100	3300	4400	6700	12,000	24,000

1915 Crawford, touring (with Moller family), KM

1915 CRAWFORD
Model 6-35 — 6-cyl., 35 hp, 120" wb

Tour.-5P	2100	3700	4700	7300	13,700	26,000

Model 4-40 — 4-cyl., 40 hp, 125" wb

Rds.-2P	2100	3500	4500	7000	13,000	25,000
Tour.-5P	2100	3200	4300	6500	11,000	23,000

1916 CRAWFORD
Model 6-40 — 6-cyl., 40 hp, 120" wb

Tour.-5P	1650	3700	4700	7300	13,700	26,000
Rds.-3P	1650	4000	5000	8000	15,000	28,000
Sed.-5P	2000	2900	3700	5600	9100	20,000

1916 Crawford, model 6-40, cloverleaf roadster, HAC

1917 Crawford, model 6-40, touring, HAC

1917 CRAWFORD
Model 6-40 — 6-cyl., 40 hp, 120" wb

	FP	5	4	3	2	1
Tour.-5P	1650	3700	4700	7300	13,700	26,000
Rds.-3P	1650	4000	5000	8000	15,000	28,000
Sed.-5P	2000	2900	3700	5600	9100	20,000

1918 Crawford, model 6-40, touring, HAC

1918-1919 CRAWFORD
Model 6-40 — 6-cyl., 40 hp, 122 1/2" wb

Tour.-5P	2250	3700	4700	7300	13,700	26,000
Rds.-2P	2250	3900	4800	7700	14,300	27,000
Toy Tonneau-4P	2250	3900	4800	7700	14,300	27,000
Sed.-5P	2750	3000	4000	6000	9500	21,000

1920 Crawford, model 6-40, sport touring, WLB

1920-1921 CRAWFORD
Model 6-40 — 6-cyl., 40 hp, 122 1/2" wb

Tour.-7P	3000	3700	4700	7300	13,700	26,000
Rds.-3P	3000	3900	4800	7700	14,300	27,000
Spt.-6P	3000	3900	4800	7700	14,300	27,000
Sed.-7P	3000	3000	4000	6000	9500	21,000

1921 Crawford, model 6-40, touring, HAC

1922 CRAWFORD
Model 6-40 — 6-cyl., 40 hp, 122 1/2" wb

	FP	5	4	3	2	1
Tour.-7P	2750	3700	4700	7300	13,700	26,000
Rds.-3P	2750	4000	5000	8000	15,000	28,000
Spt.-6P	2750	4000	5000	8000	15,000	28,000
Sed.-7P	2750	3000	4000	6000	9500	21,000

1923 CRAWFORD
Model 6-70 — 6-cyl., 70 hp, 138" wb

Tour.-7P	3100	4200	5200	8400	15,700	29,000
Cpe.-5P	4500	3200	4300	6500	11,000	23,000
Sed.-7P	4500	3100	4200	6300	10,500	22,000

CRAWFORD-HOUGH — The Crawford-Hough Garage Company was organized in Cleveland early in 1910 to manufacture, rent and repair motor cars. Richard H. Lee. G.R. Collar, G.H. Gallagher, George E. Bradbury and Henry R. Gall were the incorporators of this $10,000 venture. Subsequent manufacture is doubted.

CREDLEBAUGH — New Carlisle, Ohio — (1900) — H.S. Credlebaugh built himself a gasoline engine in 1900 that he thought was pretty good. As described in *The Motor Vehicle Review:* "The only moving parts when the motor is running are a 1-3/4-inch pipe check valve, a round piece of steel 1/4x5 inches that makes 1-25 of a revolution at each stroke of the piston, the piston and pitman, the crankshaft and flywheels. The speed of the motor is entirely under the control of the operator and there is not the pretense of either a carburetor or an atomizer." At this point, Credlebaugh was checking the trade publication ads for the simplest and most practical running gear so that he could build himself a car. "He does not claim the earth and all that it contains," remarked *MVR* admiringly, "but does claim simplicity and practibility and a motor that is as near fool proof as any that are made up to the present time." Credlebaugh did not plan manufacture.

CRELL — Ionia, Michigan — (1901) — "Ionia, Michigan is to have an automobile factory," *The Motor World* enthused in March 1901. "A motor carriage is being built there according to the ideas of A.C. Crell, and new machinery has arrived and is being placed in an old electric light plant building. A stock company will back the new motor carriage business." Alas, no manufacturing followed in Ionia.

CRESCENT — The Crescent Automobile Company was organized in 1908 in New York City for the manufacture of automobiles. The firm was incorporated with a capital stock of $1000 by James C. Stoopes of 267 West 22nd Street, and William V. and Triphena E. Stoopes of 345 West 35th Street. Manufacture is doubted.
   The Crescent City Automobile Company was incorporated in New Orleans, Louisiana during the fall of 1907 with $30,000 capital to manufacture, sell and repair automobiles. The incorporators were J.P. John, D.C. Johnson and W.P. Parkhouse. Manufacture is doubted.
   The Crescent Motor Car Company was organized with a capital stock of $100,000 during the summer of 1908 to "manufacture and deal in motor cars and auxiliary machinery" in Chicago. Incorporators were F.D. Moor, C.P. Hatter and W.J. Crumpton. Manufacture of an automobile has not been documented.
   The Crescent Parts Company was organized in New York City early in 1907 for the manufacture of motors, machinery, motor cars and accessories. Capital stock was $150,000. The incorporators were T.J. Press, J.E. Cheeseman, S.S. Slater and F. Frediger, all of New York City. Manufacture of an automobile is doubted.
   Crescent Tricycle was an occasional designation used in the automotive press for the turn-of-the-century three-wheeler built in Chicago by the American Bicycle Company and marketed as the Trimoto. Refer to Trimoto.

CRESCENT — New York, New York — (1900) — Although incorporated in Wilmington, Delaware, the Crescent Automobile Manufacturing Company was a New York City firm with headquarters and a small machine shop at 130 Broadway. Initially, Crescent's purpose was manufacture of the P.T. 1 hp bicycle motor, the rights to which were acquired. But Cres-

1900 Crescent, runabout

cent also developed a two-cylinder 4 hp engine of its own, which was installed in a runabout with bicycle wheels and tiller steering which *Cycle and Automobile Trade Journal* commended as a "handsome vehicle of substantial construction." Crescent planned to market this car at $550, though these plans went awry. As *CATJ* noted, "only experimental machines have been made as yet, pending the sale of sufficient stock to establish a factory of sufficient capacity to manufacture economically." Sufficient stock was not sold, and Crescent faded away. Interestingly, the year following, the P.T. Motor Company moved into manufacture of an automobile of its own.

CRESCENT — St. Louis, Missouri — (1905) — In early summer of 1905 the Crescent Automobile & Supply Company was organized in St. Louis by O.H. Van Kleck for the purpose of manufacturing gasoline automobiles, "making a specialty of racing cars designed by Mr. Van Kleck." How many examples of the firm's "specialty" arrived is not known, but very few production cars followed. The Crescent was a simple two-cylinder car offered as a touring (100-inch wheelbase, $950) and roadster (96-inch wheelbase, $885). This venture did not survive the winter. Interestingly, a decade later, a new organization called the Crescent Motor Car Company was established in St. Louis. Its product was called the Crescent too, but after the building of three cars there was a marque name change to Superior. Possibly the memory of the earlier short-lived Crescent was the reason.

CRESCENT — Detroit, Michigan — (1907-1908) — The Crescent Motor Car Company was organized in May of 1907 with a capital stock of $75,000 which may seem modest, but since the plan of the firm was to produce the Reliance touring car and the Marvel roadster (the two companies previously building those automobiles having elected not to any longer), there was not an overwhelming need for much start-up money. Still, Crescent didn't manage to make any money either. In September of 1908 when the Constantine Motor Car Company was formed in Constantine in order to take over the business of Crescent in Detroit, the latter's worth was valued at $50,000. The people behind the Constantine venture had formerly been associated with the Hawley Automobile Company which had recently removed itself from the town of Constantine to the town of Mendon, where it had quickly died. The new Crescent which would now be built by Constantine in Constantine was not to be a Reliance or Marvel however, but a new runabout designed by J.C. Forrester of Detroit. The Crescent plant at Meldrum and Champlain streets in Detroit was sold. But the Crescent never made it to Constantine. Two months later, in November, there was a report that the car would instead be built in a vacated soap factory in Goshen, Indiana. Amidst all the confusion, perhaps a few pilot model second-generation Crescents were built somewhere. But the car never did see a production line.

1914 Crescent, Royal Six, touring, WLB

CRESCENT — Carthage, Ohio — (1913-1914) — The Crescent was the linear descendant of the Ohio and was built in the same factory in Carthage. In December 1912 Ralph E. Northway, who had just sold his Northway engine factory in Detroit to General Motors for a nice profit, bought out the Ohio Motor Car Company and reorganized as the Crescent Motor Company. The former Ohio four was renamed the Crescent although Ohio remained as its model name. Northway added a Crescent six which carried the model name Royal and, not surprisingly, a Northway engine from Detroit. But what Northway had purchased was an invalid company, and it quickly succumbed. Reports that the Crescent Motor Company had moved to St. Louis in late 1914 were unfounded and probably based on another St. Louis company with a similar name. Meanwhile, Ralph Northway was liquidating what remained of his Crescent in Carthage in early 1915. When next heard from a few years later, Ralph Northway was in Natick, Massachusetts preparing to build cars and trucks under his own name.

1913-1914 CRESCENT
Four — 29 hp, 116" wb

	FP	5	4	3	2	1
Ohio Tour.-5P	1275	—	—	—	—	—
Six — 38 hp, 132" wb						
Royal Tour.-5P	1985	—	—	—	—	—

CRESSON-MORRIS — During 1914-1916, the Cresson-Morris Company of Philadelphia built two cyclecars. The first was for Charles Duryea, the second was for the Crowther Motor Company. Refer to Duryea and Crowther.

1901 Crest, model A, runabout, HAC

1901 Crestmobile, model C, runabout, HAC

CRESTMOBILE — Cambridge & Dorchester, Massachusetts — (1901-1905) — At the turn of the century the Crest Manufacturing Company produced gasoline engines and "all the parts to construct automobiles." After proving that this was so in 1900 by building a car out of Crest parts, the company proudly announced its entrance into automobile manufac-

turing ranks in early 1901. Its car would be called the Crestmobile. A three-wheeler was offered briefly, but most of the Cambridge company's initial output was a single-cylinder chain-drive two seater of varying horsepower. The engines were air cooled. By 1903 shaft drive had replaced the former chain. With the car's comfortable maximum a modest 20 mph, Crest noted rather cleverly in a brochure of testimonial letters that "our best speed record is our rapid rise to favor." Thus far, the company claimed, 1000 Crestmobiles had been produced, and the changes for 1904 were "in every case improvements and not corrections of previous fault." Among these was a new 8½ hp air-cooled engine, still a single, the company averring that any objection to one-lungers was not based on logic, because not only was a single cylinder "slightly more efficient than two," but it was obviously more simple. By 1904, however, that argument was wearing thin in the marketplace. At East Coast automobile shows in both 1904 and 1905 Crest did exhibit a two-cylinder 15 hp surrey but the company virtually ignored it in promotion and conceivably that car was not marketed at all. The firm was by now in big trouble. "The Crest Manufacturing Company have been on financial shoals during the year," *The Motor World* reported in December 1904, "and for some time its future has been problematical. A 'for sale' sign on the factory at Cambridge, however, seems to settle all doubts on that score." In 1905 Crest was absorbed into the Alden-Sampson Manufacturing Company of Pittsfield, producers of commercial vehicles. Alden-Sampson sold leftover Crestmobiles through 1906, and possibly into 1907. Meanwhile the Dorchester factory which Crest had established earlier as a branch plant was sold to the Hub Motor Car Exchange which proceeded to build a car called the Dorchester there.

1901 CRESTMOBILE
Crestmobile — 1-cyl., 57" wb

	FP	5	4	3	2	1
Model A Rbt. (2 hp)	550	2500	3500	5000	8500	18,000
Model B Rbt. (3-1/2 hp)	600	2700	3600	5300	8800	19,000
Model C Rbt. (5 hp)	650	2800	3700	5500	9000	19,500

1903 Crestmobile, model D, runabout, WLB

1903 Crestmobile, model F, touring, FR

1903 CRESTMOBILE
Crestmobile — 1-cyl., 3-1/2 hp, 57" wb

	FP	5	4	3	2	1
Model C Rbt.	500	2700	3600	5300	8800	19,000
Model F Tour.	600	2800	3700	5500	9000	19,500
Crestmobile — 1-cyl., 5 hp, 72" wb						
Model D Rbt.-2P	750	2700	3600	5300	8800	19,000
Model D Rbt.-4P	850	2800	3700	5500	9000	19,500

1904-1905 CRESTMOBILE
Crestmobile — 1-cyl., 8-1/2 hp, 76" wb

	FP	5	4	3	2	1
Model D Rbt.-2P	800	2700	3600	5300	8800	19,000
Model D Tonneau-4P	900	2800	3700	5500	9000	19,500

C.R.G. — Wilkes-Barre, Pennsylvania — (1908) — The initials represent Charles R. Greuter, and the car was one he tried unsuccessfully to market in 1908. The C.R.G. was Greuter's least successful automotive venture, and resulted in no more than a prototype. At the turn of the century, Greuter had produced the Holyoke car in Massachusetts, and was chief engineer to the Matheson Motor Car Company in Wilkes-Barre prior to his abortive try with the C.R.G. Subsequent to it, Greuter became an engineering consultant, setting up shop in Saugus, Massachusetts, where he developed carburetors of his own design and appears to have built a number of automobiles for others, including the prototype K-D. His most wonderful automotive efforts followed in the mid-Twenties when he joined Stutz, became that company's chief engineer and was the man most responsible for engine development of the famed DV-32.

C.R.G. SPECIAL — Dayton, Ohio — (1920) — The Green Engineering Company of Dayton manufactured aluminite pistons and connecting rods, piston rings and pins, and also engaged in cylinder regrinding and general job work in the automotive line. This business was begun in 1912, and by 1920 Green was well known in the field. Briefly, in 1920, the company also built to special order a car called the C.R.G. Special. It had a 120-inch wheelbase, was powered by a four-cylinder engine using the Green aluminite pistons, and was capable of an easy 60 mph. "The acceleration is wonderful," *American Automobile Digest* commented, "and the vibration common to a four-cylinder car entirely absent . . . The gasoline mileage is approximately 18 and the oil mileage about 1000. The company does not believe this can be equalled by any stock car on the market." Custom orders for the car may have continued into the early Twenties.

1914 Cricket Cyclecar, roadster, WLB

CRICKET — Detroit, Michigan — (1913-1914) — The product of the Cricket Cyclecar Company was perfectly named. It was a little bug of a car on an 84-inch wheelbase, weighing 500 pounds, and powered by a 9 hp vee-twin that was mounted beside the driver. An extension on the left side of a motorcycle-type frame allowed for four wheels and two-abreast seating. The original design was attributed to English engineer Anthony New who had put his first car on the road in London in August of 1912. The refined American version hit the streets of Detroit on November 15th, 1913. The idea did not travel well. Some production did follow by the spring of 1914 when a factory was secured at 80 Walker Street and a showroom on Woodward Avenue in Detroit. But by late 1914, Tracy Lyon and O.C. Hutchinson, the U.S. backers, had sold out to Motor Products Company of Detroit, the motorcycle-building firm that had produced the engine for the Cricket.

1914 CRICKET
Cyclecar — 2-cyl., 9 hp, 84" wb

	FP	5	4	3	2	1
Rdstr.-2P	325	—	4	3	2	1

1937 Cricket, rear-engined sedan, FR

CRICKET — Boston & Holliston, Massachusetts — (1930's) — Cricket was the name Samuel Eliot gave to the series of three cars that he built in the Thirties as showcases for his mechanical innovations. While the chronology of the first two is not precisely known, one of them had fluid drives in the rear hubs and the other had torsion bar suspension. Much more is known about Cricket No. 3, a rear-engined, all-stainless-steel sedan with sliding doors that was built in 1937. Driving controls were combined in one joystick which steered the car when moved left or right and applied the brakes when pushed forward. The tail fin incorporated a special exhaust. This Cricket was bathed in light inside from a fixture on the roof which also provided road lighting for the driver. In 1950 Sam Eliot had plans to install a pancake engine of his own design in this car, but more than likely that never happened. Sam is fondly remembered as among the stalwarts of the Veteran Motor Car Club of America during its borning years.

CRIMMELL & HAILMAN — Hartford, Indiana — (1903) — In 1903, in Hartford, two mechanics named Clyde Crimmell and Paul Hailman built a gasoline automobile. Details are lacking, but the partners are not believed to have built another.

1907 Crist, roadster, JHV

CRIST — Los Angeles, California — (1907) — Royal Crist, who had formerly been associated with the Western Iron Works in Los Angeles, began building an automobile ostensibly for himself in 1906 which proved so successful upon completion in late 1907 that almost immediately it was purchased by a local doctor. Its engine and transmission had been purchased, but all other parts of the car were made by Crist, with the help of a blacksmith. The frame was of forged steel, and all body and fender parts were hand formed. The vehicle was good for 55 mph. Despite this admirable first effort, evidence is lacking that Royal Crist ever built another car.

CRITERION — The Criterion Motor Company of Des Moines, Iowa and later Kent, Ohio was one of several ventures floated by W.H. Kitto between the years of 1905 and 1911. He sold quite a bit of stock, but did not build a Criterion car. Refer to Kitto.

CRITTY — The Jere C. Critty Company was organized in Chicago early in 1907 with a capital stock of $2500 and the plan "to engage in the manufacture and sale of motor cars and accessories." The incorporators were L.E. Hart, J.B. Montgomery and F.W. Kraft. Manufacture of an automobile is doubted.

CROCK — The Crock Motor Company was located at the corner of South Water and Broad streets in Cuyahoga Falls. Keith Crock was its president, W.T. Evans its secretary-treasurer. The firm operated as a dealership, but in 1920 a trade directory reference indicates the firm as a manufacturer. Further documentation is lacking. The company was gone from Cuyahoga Falls by 1925, leaving no impression whatsoever on local history.

CROCKETT — New York, New York — (1918) — The J.B. Crockett Company was located at 4244 Whitehall Street in New York's Financial District and in early 1918 indicated its intention to produce an automobile for export. Later that year, under the lenient laws of Delaware, the firm was formally incorporated with a capital stock of $3 million. C.L. Rimlinger, M.M. Clancy and P.B. Drew were the incorporators. There is no evidence an automobile ever resulted.

CROESUS — Kansas City, Missouri — (1906) — George W. Curtiss was a photographer and W.L. Bell sold school furniture, and in January of 1906 they formed the Croesus Motor Car Company in Kansas City and leased a shop at First and Main streets. The Croesus was to be built in two models, both of them designed by Curtiss who had become interested in automobiles after purchasing and putting together one of the small Holley kit cars. The Croesus was another matter entirely, however, and promised to live up to its name; all fittings that were normally brass on an automobile, for example, would be silver plated on the Croesus. But the venture came to a tawdry end in January 1907 when Curtiss filed suit against Bell alleging that he was to furnish the brains and skill and Bell the cash, that two cars had already been built but they were still on hand, and that Bell had made no effort to push their sale. Whether those two cars were subsequently sold is not known, but no more Croesuses were built.

1906 CROESUS
Junior — 4-cyl., 18/20 hp, 88" wb

	FP	5	4	3	2	1
Rbt.-2P	2000	—	—	—	—	—

Four — 4-cyl., 35/40 hp, 108" wb

	FP	5	4	3	2	1
Tour.-7P	4000	—	—	—	—	—

1922 Croft

CROFT — Zion City, Illinois — (1922) — This curiosity, built by William Edgar Croft of Zion City for reasons of his own, featured a two-cylinder motorcycle engine combined with a 48-inch airplane propeller. Croft claimed sixty miles per hour and fifty miles per gallon.

1903 Crompton, runabout, NAHC

CROMPTON — Worchester, Massachusetts — (1902-1905) — In 1901 the people who made the Crompton Loom decided to make an automobile, two versions as a matter of fact, a steamer and an electric. The Crompton Motor Carriage Company was incorporated for $5000 in March, with Charles H. Crompton taking its presidency. Early experimentation soon convinced the company that steam power was preferable, and the electric was abandoned. By April of 1902 the first Crompton steamer was undergoing tests. It was introduced to the public at the Boston Automobile Show in March 1903, where it attracted considerable attention. The Crompton represented a radical departure from standard steam car practice. It featured twenty-four separate fire-tube boilers, twelve on each side at the rear of the body, and all fed from a common water supply and delivering steam into a common pipe. Apparently, some examples were sold in the two years that followed, until May of 1905 when the factory in Worcester caught fire. That ended the Crompton.

CRON — The William Cron Sons Company was organized in Columbus, Ohio late in 1910 for the manufacture of motor cars. Capital stock was $35,000, and the Cron sons involved were John A., F.J. and A.W. That a Cron car followed is doubted.

CRONHOLM & STENWALL — Chicago, Illinois — (1895) — The Cronholm & Stenwall Company of 319 Le Moyne Street in Chicago was yet another entry into the Chicago Times-Herald Contest of 1895 which failed to make the starting line. Whether the Cronholm & Stenwall car was ever successfully completed is not known.

1939 Crosley, convertible coupe, JAC

CROSLEY — Cincinnati, Ohio — (1939-1942 et. seq.) — The Crosley was the third automobile built by Powel Crosley, Jr. His first was an inexpensive six-cylinder car prototype on a 114-inch wheelbase called the Marathon Six, which died aborning in 1909; his second was a cyclecar called the DeCross in 1913 which didn't survive much longer. When announcing his new car in 1939, Powel Crosley chose not to remember those two earlier efforts, though public relations releases did note his work during the pre-World War I period as assistant sales manager for the Parry, National and Inter-State automobile companies. In the period since, of course, Crosley had become a millionaire several times over. In 1922 he was the largest manufacturer of radios in the world; his subsequent Crosley "Shelvadoor" pioneered refrigerators with shelves mounted in the doors; by 1934 he owned the Cincinnati Redlegs baseball team. His new Crosley car represented both "wish-fulfillment," as his associates later termed it, and a personal crusade on Crosley's part to popularize the small-car idea in America. He was several decades ahead of his time. His Crosley was part latterday cyclecar, part progenitor of the sub-compact that necessity would finally make a dominant U.S. reality in the 1970's. Powel Crosley began sketching designs for his new car as early as 1934, assisted by engineers L.C. Oswald and S.F. Clifton. The car would be built in his Marion plant, near Cincinnati. The production Crosley was introduced to the press and dealers at the Indianapolis Speedway in April 1939; its public debut was at the New York World's Fair that June; by year's end, 2017 Crosleys had been sold. Powered by an air-cooled Waukesha-built 12 hp twin, the Crosley was mounted on an 80-inch wheelbase chassis and weighed all of 924 pounds total. At the Fair, the Crosley was called "The Car of Tomorrow"; subsequently, "The Forgotten Man's Car" became the more usual tagline. Crosley dealers included stores which handled other Crosley products; Macy's in New York and Bamberger's in New Jersey became Crosley agencies, the first Macy's customer to purchase a car was Mrs. Averell Harriman. Sales in 1940 plummeted to 422 cars. Numerous production problems had arisen, broken bellhousings the most serious, these caused by the lack of a universal joint in the driveshaft and poor design of the motor mounts. Paul Klotsch, chief engineer for Briggs, became Crosley's chief engineer in December 1940. A universal joint was installed in the car, and motor mount design was revised. Sales rose to 2289 in 1941; 1029 Crosleys for 1942 were sold prior to the cessation of manufacture follow-

1940 Crosley, convertible coupe, JAC

ing Pearl Harbor. The most famous of the Crosleys of the prewar period was the soft-top station-wagon model (Covered Wagon) that Cannon Ball Baker drove cross-country, averaging 50.4 mpg for 6517.3 miles. Postwar the Crosley gained even greater fame, uprated with an overhead cam four-cylinder engine, the Hotshot model enjoying considerable cachet and competition success in the sports car world.

1939
2-cyl., 80" wb

	FP	5	4	3	2	1
Conv	350	250	750	1150	2450	3500

1940
2-cyl., 80" wb

Conv	299	250	750	1150	2450	3500
Sed	349	200	600	1100	2250	3200
Sta Wag	450	250	750	1150	2500	3600

1941 Crosley, station wagon, OCW

1941
2-cyl., 80" wb

Conv	390	250	750	1150	2450	3500
Sed	400	200	600	1100	2250	3200
Sta Wag	496	250	750	1150	2500	3600

1942
4-cyl., 80" wb

Conv	412	250	750	1150	2400	3400
Sed	515	200	600	1100	2250	3200
Sta Wag	581	250	750	1150	2450	3500

CROSS — E.D. Cross was a physician living at 3149 Indiana Avenue in Chicago who entered the Chicago Times-Herald Contest of 1895 with a vehicle of his own design. His car was not completed in time for the event, however, and whether Dr. Cross ever did indeed finish the car has not been documented.

1897 Cross Steam Carriage, NAHC

CROSS STEAM — Providence, Rhode Island — (1897) — The Cross Writing Instrument Company of Providence (later A.T. Cross Company of Lincoln) was the principal pursuit of Alonzo T. Cross. But he also has the distinction of having built the first automobile in Rhode Island. It was a steamer begun late in 1896 and completed in 1897. Its chassis was put together in Cross' pencil factory; the body arrived from H.M. Howe Company, a carriage builder in town. Two engines were produced for the car, the first a four horsepower, the second a six. With the latter fitted, a top speed of six miles an hour was realized. Both engines were produced by L.F.N. Baldwin of the Cruickshank Engine Works in Providence. Subsequently, Baldwin would attempt to manufacture his own car, bearing his own name. Alonzo Cross meantime had returned to his pencil business.

1924 Cross, roadster, WSH

CROSS — Indianapolis, Indiana — (1924) — At least two different chassis were built and equipped with varying bodies in 1924 as Harry E. Cross of Indianapolis attempted to enter the automobile manufacturing field. His prospectus indicated a four-cylinder 12/14 hp L-head engine built in unit with a three-speed selective transmission. The 105-inch wheelbase chassis featured an I-beam front axle with semi-floating rear and bevel-type differential. Suspension was quarter elliptics in front, with a special three-point spring suspension ("pivoting frame at center permitting either rear wheel to be raised twelve inches or more without tilting frame") at the rear. Cross planned to provide either wire or demountable disc wheels in his production car. Unfortunately, his attempts to charter a manufacturing company in New York State proved futile. Indianapolis city directories of the early Twenties reveal that Cross was involved in machine work principally, but dabbled in real estate. He died in 1934.

1923 Crossland Steamer, KM

CROSSLAND STEAM — Chicago & Peoria, Illinois — (1923) — In 1921 Harry C. Pfaff, an engineer whose credits included stints with General Motors, Ford and Maxwell, disappeared from the automobile industry to a laboratory in Chicago. The only knowledge the trade had of what he was doing was a short press release stating that the Crossland Steam Motive Corporation had been formed to manufacture a Pfaff-designed steam car with a 131-inch wheelbase to sell for $3600. Pfaff had reportedly begun experimenting with the car in 1919. The car didn't show up, however, until late January of 1923 when it was exhibited at the Congress Hotel in Chicago during automobile show week. The wheelbase was 125 inches, and the price ws $1985. The five-passenger touring body was finished in aluminum. The car attracted crowds. "In the Crossland, we have a car that is absolutely automatic," Harry Pfaff said at a press conference. "The driver must fill the kerosene tank every 500 miles and the water tank every 800 miles. Beyond this he turns a button on the dash and his fires start." Apparently no burning desire on the part of the public followed, and if the Crossland saw any production at all, it was minimal and did not survive into 1924.

CROSSLEY — That Albert D. Crossley was an automobile manufacturer was indicated in Connecticut Motor Vehicle Registers of 1913 and 1914. Whether Crossley indeed produced an automobile under his own name has not been documented. During the summer of 1911, in partnership with George I. Whitehead, he had established the Auto Shop at 4 Crescent Street in Hartford indicating that "rebuilding and repairing" would be the specialty. Crossley had formerly worked for Pope in Hartford, Whitehead for Columbia.

In 1936, in East Haven, Connecticut, Richard Crossley built a three-wheeled speedster he called the Aerocoupe. Whether he was related to Albert D. Crossley is not known. Refer to Aerocoupe.

CROTON — The Croton Motor Car Company was organized with a special stock of $300,000 late in 1912 for the manufacture of automobiles in Washington, D.C. Incorporators included J.P. Stoltz, A.M. Linn, J.I. Brownson, J.H. Donnan, H.C. Warne, C.S. Caldwell and R.M. Paxton. Manufacture is doubted.

1896 Booth-Crouch, Gasoline Carriage

CROUCH — **Pennsylvania & Maryland** — **(1895-1900)** — Procrastination and inconstancy appear to have been human failings of W. Lee Crouch. His small machine shop of Pierce & Crouch of New Brighton, Pennsylvania had built an experimental and not wholly successful gasoline carriage in 1895. In 1896 the shop was given the assignment of designing and building another gasoline engine for Dr. Carlos C. Booth of Youngstown, Ohio. The physician sketched out the drivetrain and coachwork himself, and Crouch furnished the single-cylinder 3 hp engine. "This vehicle was entered in the Cosmopolitan race under rather discouraging circumstances, due to haste and imperfect experimental work," *The Horseless Age* stated in July 1896. Reportedly, a "rotten belt and gasoline of too high test" was the problem — and at some point after Yonkers the "sparking apparatus" acted up and the Cosmopolitan had to be abandoned. In September *The Horseless Age* reported that Crouch, who had entered a race in Providence himself with a new car called Brighton, would not be at the starting line because he could not complete his new gasoline carriage on time. Next Crouch mentioned his intention to manufacture light gasoline engines to sell to builders of motor vehicles. But he subsequently changed his mind about that. By 1899 he was into steam and built a new car so powered which he drove in January that year from Rochester to Beaver Falls, Pennsylvania "over frozen, hilly and muddy roads, 4 1/2 miles in fifteen minutes." He was associated in this enterprise with D.A. Clark, and Lewis R. and Fre-

1899 Crouch Steam Carriage, auto-buggy, NAHC

derick Davidson, of Beaver Falls. Next he turned up in Baltimore, Maryland where he established his Crouch Automobile Manufacturing & Transportation Company. Here he built at least one steam car before February of 1900 when this venture went into receivership and what was left of it was purchased by the Columbia Motor and Manufacturing Company. Apparently, W. Lee Crouch remained in the automobile business thereafter; in 1914 he was in Lancaster, Ohio and had a short fling with a proposed Circleville cyclecar.

CROUCH — **Stoneham, Massachusetts** — **(1905-1906)** — In 1914 *The Automobile* published a roster of "abandoned automobile manufacturing enterprises" in the United States. Included was a firm called Gray & Couch of Stoneham, Massachusetts. Who the "Gray" was cannot be determined, but "Couch" was no doubt A. Stillman Crouch, a pioneer bicycle manufacturer of Stoneham. In 1905-1906 Crouch extended his manufacture to motorcycles. Most likely he also produced three- and four-wheeled gasoline vehicles for anyone in town who asked. Upon retiring from business, Crouch accepted a permanent position in the Stoneham Fire Department in 1912, the year the department received its first motorized piece of apparatus. Doubtless with his background, he was a handy man to have around. He died in 1940.

1911 Crow, model 10, roadster, NAHC

CROW — **Elkhart, Indiana** — **(1911)/CROW-ELKHART** — **(1911-1923)** — According to Martin E. Crow, the Crow automobile was born because he and his father, Dr. E.C. Crow, had been interested in the Menges self-starter, built a prototype in order to demonstrate it, ultimately gave up on the starter, but stuck with the car. That isn't precisely how it happened. A prototype of the Menges car had indeed been built in the Elkhart factory of the Sterling-Hudson Whip Company, the Crows involved at that time with Willard W. Sterling and F.O. Hudson in an automotive venture begun during the spring of 1908 and resulting in the Sterling car for the 1909 model year. By the time the Sterling appeared, however, Albert Menges had long since departed for Tennessee to try to find financial backing there, and the Crows were on their own in Elkhart producing a car that was neither a Sterling nor a Menges. Their Crow Motor Car Company was incorporated in July of 1909, with production beginning the following month. For the first two years the Crows were not building their own cars, but rather the Black Crow distributed by the Black Manufacturing Company of Chicago. This deal had undoubtedly been made to bring ready cash into the Crow treasury because late in 1910 the Crows cancelled the contract with Black and began to build and distribute their own line of cars — called simply Crow for a few months, then Crow-Elkhart the name change most probably to accentuate its difference from the Black Crow which had been widely regarded as a Chicago product. The Crow-Elkhart was a conventional automobile offered in a plethora of body styles, all in the medium-price range. A six was added to the original four in 1913, and occasionally the line was referred to as "Elk-Hart Four" and "Elk-Hart Six." Engines were usually proprietary — Rutenber, Lycoming, Herschell-Spillman, Gray, Atlas — though an in-house ohv unit was produced at the end of the First World War. In 1917 the "9-Year Chassis," as advertising termed it, was offered in just two body styles — the usual touring, and a very attractive cloverleaf roadster — and now the proliferation was in colors available, a total of ten during an era when, as Crow-Elkhart pointed out, the automobile purchaser was usually "pinned down" to a few, or occasionally just one. "Made to make good" was a Crow-Elkhart slogan. And the Crow-Elkhart Motor Car Company — as the firm was renamed late in 1916 — was willing to make good cars for other companies as well, most particularly those which, like Birch and Bush, specialized in the mail order trade. It was perhaps the ordinariness of the Crow-Elkhart that resulted in its never becoming a best-selling car. The Elkhart factory had a thirty-car-per-day capacity, but never was worked to its full potential. Peak year was 1917 when output was 3800 cars. In mid-October 1918 the company was in trouble, and plant operations were put under a receiver. In early 1919 Crow-Elkhart was reorganized, the Crows were out, and J.A. Harps was in as president. Production in 1921 was a dismal 600 units. Early in 1922 receivership arrived again, and this time the press reported that another reorganization seemed unlikely. Instead, on June 22nd, 1923, the Crow-Elkhart assets were sold for $78,700 "subject to a mortgage" to Century Motors Company. Century was the Crow-Elkhart subsidiary which built the Morriss-London, an export car. The only Crow-Elkharts built after the sale were 1923 and earlier models for which parts remained at the factory. Ironically, the Crow-Elkharts of the early Twenties, with their vee noses, were the prettiest cars the company had ever produced. A few may have been sold as late as 1925.

1911 Crow-Elkhart, model 13, touring, NAHC

1913 Crow-Elkhart, model C-4, touring, HAC

1911 CROW

	FP	5	4	3	2	1
Four — 25/29 hp, 109" wb						
Model 10 Rds.	1000	3000	4000	6000	9500	21,000
Model 11 1/2 Encl. Rds.	1150	3100	4200	6300	10,500	22,000
Model 11 Surrey-4P	1100	3100	4200	6300	10,500	22,000
Model 12 Tourabout-4P	1150	3100	4200	6300	10,500	22,000
Four — 32 hp, 110" wb						
Model 13 Tour.-5P	1300	3200	4300	6500	11,000	23,000
Four — 35/38 hp, 112" wb						
Model 15 Fore-Dr. Tr.-5P	1500	3300	4400	6600	11,500	23,500
Four — 40 hp, 120" wb						
Model 16 Speedway Rds.	1650	3500	4500	7000	13,000	25,000
Model 17 Fore-Dr. Tr.-5P	1750	3300	4400	6700	12,000	24,000
Model 20 Fore-Dr. Tr.-7P	2000	3200	4300	6500	11,000	23,000

1914 Crow-Elkhart, model D-65, touring, HAC

1914 CROW-ELKHART

	FP	5	4	3	2	1
Four — 26 hp, 114" wb						
Model D-45 Tour.-5P	1185	3300	4400	6700	12,000	24,000
Model D-42 Rds.-2P	1150	3700	4700	7300	13,700	26,000
Four — 29 hp, 120" wb						
Model D-55 Tour.-5P	1600	3500	4500	7000	13,000	25,000
Model D-52 Rds.-2P	1575	3900	4800	7700	14,300	27,000
Model D-54 Tour.-4P	1625	3700	4700	7300	13,700	26,000
Model D-56 Tour.-6P	1650	3500	4500	7000	13,000	25,000
Six — 34 hp, 130" wb						
Model 62 Rds.-2P	2225	4000	5000	8000	15,000	28,000
Model D-65 Tour.-5P	2250	3700	4700	7300	13,700	26,000
Model D-64 Tour.-4P	2275	3700	4700	7300	13,700	26,000
Model D-66 Tour.-6P	2300	3500	4500	7000	13,000	25,000

1912 Crow-Elkhart, model 60, 3-pass. coupe, WLB

1915 Crow-Elkhart, model E-66, touring, HAC

1915 CROW-ELKHART

	FP	5	4	3	2	1
Four — 16 hp, 104" wb						
Model E-25 Tour.-5P	725	3100	4200	6300	10,500	22,000
Four — 26 hp, 114" wb						
Model E-42 Rds.-2P	1165	3500	4500	7000	13,000	25,000
Model E-45 Tour.-5P	1175	3200	4300	6500	11,000	23,000
Four — 29 hp, 120" wb						
Model E-52 Rds.-2P	1475	3700	4700	7300	13,700	26,000
Model E-54 Tour.-4P	1500	3300	4400	6700	12,000	24,000
Model E-55 Tour.-5P	1495	3200	4300	6500	11,000	23,000
Model E-56 Tour.-6P	1525	3200	4300	6400	10,800	22,500
Six — 34 hp, 130" wb						
Model E-62 Rds.-2P	1895	4000	5000	8000	15,000	28,000
Model E-64 Tour.-4P	1920	3700	4700	7300	13,700	26,000
Model E-65 Tour.-5P	1895	3500	4500	7000	13,000	25,000
Model E-66 Tour.-5P	1945	3400	4500	6900	12,500	24,500

1912 Crow-Elkhart, model 57, 2-pass. torpedo roadster, WLB

1912 CROW-ELKHART

Four — 20 hp, 110" wb					
Model 50 Rds.-3P	875	3000	4000	6000	9500	21,000
Four — 26 hp, 114" wb					
Model 51 Rds.-2P	1000	3100	4200	6300	10,500	22,000
Model 52 Tour.-5P	1100	3000	4000	6000	9500	21,000
Model 53 Rbt.-2P	1250	3000	4000	6000	9500	21,000
Model 54 Tour.-5P	1200	3100	4200	6300	10,500	22,000
Four — 27 hp, 116" wb					
Model 55 Tour.-5P	1450	3200	4300	6500	11,000	23,000
Four — 29 hp, 118" wb					
Model 56 Tour.-5P	1600	3300	4400	6600	11,500	23,500
Model 57 Rds.-2P	1650	3300	4400	6700	12,000	24,000
Four — 32 hp, 122" wb					
Model 58 Tour.-5P	1750	3300	4400	6700	12,000	24,000
Model 59 Tour.-7P	2000	3200	4300	6500	11,000	23,000
Model 60 Cpe.-3P	1475	3500	4500	7000	13,000	25,000

1913 CROW-ELKHART

Series C — 4-cyl., 33 hp, 114" wb					
C-1 Rds. (112" wb)	1200	3200	4300	6500	11,000	23,000
C-2 Tour.-5P	1400	3100	4200	6300	10,500	22,000
C-3 Rds.-2P	1400	3300	4400	6700	12,000	24,000
C-4 Tour.-5P	1500	3200	4300	6500	11,000	23,000
Model C-5 — 4-cyl., 38 hp, 116" wb					
Fore-Door Tour.-5P	1650	3300	4400	6700	12,000	24,000
Model C-6-A — 6-cyl., 50 hp, 122" wb					
Tour.-5P	2250	3500	4500	7000	13,000	25,000
Model C-6-B — 6-cyl., 60 hp, 137" wb					
Tour.-7P	2500	3900	4800	7700	14,300	27,000

1916 Crow-Elkhart, model 30, sedan deluxe, HAC

380

1916 CROW-ELKHART
Model 30 — 4-cyl., 20 hp, 112" wb

	FP	5	4	3	2	1
Tour.-5P	725	3100	4200	6300	10,500	22,000
Cpe.-3P	995	2500	3500	5000	8500	18,000
Sed.-5P	1095	2300	3300	4600	7500	16,000

1917 Crow-Elkhart, model 33, cloverleaf roadster, WLB

1917 CROW-ELKHART
Four — 20 hp, 114" wb

	FP	5	4	3	2	1
Model 35 Tour.-5P	795	3300	4400	6700	12,000	24,000
Model 33 Cloverleaf Rds.-4P	845	3500	4500	7000	13,000	25,000

1918 Crow-Elkhart, model C-E-36 Standard, touring, WLB

1918 CROW-ELKHART
Model C-E-36 — 20 hp, 114" wb

	FP	5	4	3	2	1
Cloverleaf Rds.-4P	995	3700	4700	7300	13,700	26,000
Tour.-5P	935	3300	4400	6700	12,000	24,000
DeL. Tour.-5P	995	3400	4500	6900	12,500	24,500
Conv. Sed.-5P	1275	3500	4500	7000	13,000	25,000
Conv. Cpe.-3P	1195	3300	4400	6700	12,000	24,000

1919 Crow-Elkhart, model C-E-36, touring, HAC

1919 CROW-ELKHART
Model C-E 36 — 4-cyl., 20 hp, 115" wb

	FP	5	4	3	2	1
Tour.-5P	1095	3300	4400	6700	12,000	24,000
Rds.-2P	1095	3700	4700	7300	13,700	26,000
DeL. Rds.-4P	1155	3900	4800	7700	14,300	27,000
DeL. Tour.-5P	1155	3500	4500	7000	13,000	25,000
Conv. Sed.-5P	1445	3000	4400	6700	12,000	24,000
Tour. (6-cyl.)	1295	3500	4500	7000	13,000	25,000

1920 Crow-Elkhart, model H-57, sedan, HAC

1920 CROW-ELKHART
Model L — 4-cyl., 34.9 hp, 117" wb

	FP	5	4	3	2	1
L-55 Tour.-5P	1295	3500	4500	7000	13,000	25,000
L-54 Rds.-4P	1445	3900	4800	7700	14,300	27,000
L-53 Rds.-3P	1295	3800	4800	7500	14,000	26,500
L-56 Cpe.	1945	2400	3400	4800	8000	17,000

Model H — 6-cyl., 57 hp, 117" wb

	FP	5	4	3	2	1
H-55 Tour.-5P	1545	3900	4800	7700	14,300	27,000
H-54 Rds.-4P	1695	4200	5200	8400	15,700	29,000
H-53 Rds.-3P	1545	4100	5100	8200	15,400	28,500
H-57 Sed.-7P	2395	2500	3500	5000	8500	18,000
H-56 Cpe.	2195	2700	3600	5300	8800	19,000

1921 Crow-Elkhart, Series S, roadster, WLB

1921 CROW-ELKHART
Series L — 4-cyl., 34.9 hp, 117" wb

	FP	5	4	3	2	1
L-65 Tour.-5P	1295	3500	4500	7000	13,000	25,000
L-63 Rds.-3P	1295	3900	4800	7700	14,300	27,000
L-64 Spt.-4P	1345	3700	4700	7300	13,700	26,000
L-67 Sed.-7P	2195	2500	3500	5000	8500	18,000

Series S — 6-cyl., 57 hp, 117" wb

	FP	5	4	3	2	1
S-65 Tour.-5P	1545	3900	4800	7700	14,300	27,000
S-64 Spt.-4P	1595	4000	5000	8000	15,000	28,000
S-63 Rds.-3P	1545	4200	5200	8400	15,700	29,000
S-67 Sed.-7P	2395	2700	3600	5300	8800	19,000

1922 Crow-Elkhart, Series L, roadster, HAC

1922-1923 CROW-ELKHART
Series L — 4-cyl., 34.9 hp, 117" wb

	FP	5	4	3	2	1
Model L-55 Tour.-5P	1295	3300	4400	6700	12,000	24,000
Model L-54 Spt.-4P	1345	3500	4500	7000	13,000	25,000
Model L-54-B Spc. Spt.-4P	1595	3700	4700	7300	13,700	26,000
Model L-55 Rds.-3P	1295	4200	5200	8400	15,700	29,000
Model C-65 (4-cyl.) Spc. Tour.-5P	1195	4000	5000	8000	15,000	28,000
Model CS-65 (6-cyl.) Spc. Tour.-5P	1445	4200	5200	8400	15,700	29,000

Series S — 6-cyl., 57 hp, 117" wb

	FP	5	4	3	2	1
Model S-65 Tour.-5P	1545	3700	4700	7300	13,700	26,000
Model S-64 Spt.-4P	1595	3900	4800	7700	14,300	27,000
Model S-64-B Spc. Spt.-4P	1845	4000	5000	8000	15,000	28,000
Model S-63 Rds.-3P	1545	4200	5200	8400	15,700	29,000
Model S-67 Sed.-7P	2395	2700	3600	5300	8800	19,000

CROWDUS ELECTRIC — Chicago, Illinois — (1899-1902) — The Crowdus was introduced on the marketplace around Christmas time in 1899. It was a quite conventional light electric with a tubular frame, wood wheels and the look of a horse-drawn buggy. A tiller was typical for vehicles of this kind, but the one on the Crowdus was unusual, being a multipurpose device controlling the steering, speed changing and braking. Not until 1901 was the Crowdus Automobile Company formally incorporated with a capital stock of $100,000. Most of the new money came from F.H. Cooper, who was described as "the well-known drygoods millionaire." An electric vehicle that would run 100 miles at an average speed of 10 mph was promised. This provided a longer between-charge range than the former Crowdus, but a penalty had been made in performance; turn of the century Crowduses would do about 23 mph. The Crowdus was produced into 1902 but did not survive the year.

1899 Crowdus Electric, stanhope, NAHC

CROWE THIRTY — Detroit, Michigan — (1911) — In the fall of 1911 W.A. Crowe of Detroit placed on the market a four-cylinder 30 hp touring car. It was designed by W.W. McIntyre. Later in September Crowe was reported to be negotiating with the Industrial Association of Grand Rapids for the purpose of establishing the Crowe Motor Car Company in that city. Apparently the negotiations went awry, because the Crowe Thirty never did move to Grand Rapids. It died later that year in Detroit. The car's designer, incidentally, should not be confused with W.H. McIntyre who enjoyed considerably more success in Auburn, Indiana building the McIntyre.

CROWN — Although early in 1915 the word from Kalamazoo, Michigan was that the Crown Automobile Manufacturing Company was the organization in charge, the cyclecar built that year was known only by the tradename Greyhound. Refer to Greyhound.

1905 Crown, touring, NAHC

CROWN — Detroit, Michigan — (1905-1907) — The Detroit Auto Vehicle Company was organized in the late later summer of 1904 with a capital stock of $150,000. F.H. Blackman was president, H.H. Lind was secretary, B. Wuryburger was treasurer — and the vice-president was Detroit department store magnate J.L. Hudson. Their car was called the Crown, the first prototype on the road early in 1905, with production commencing later that year. The Crown was available as a two-cylinder 12 hp runabout, a four-cylinder 24 hp touring car, and a two-cylinder 16 hp delivery car. The last named had chain drive, the passenger cars bevel gear. A planetary transmission was featured on the touring and delivery, but the runabout had friction drive which "does not slip, has no gears, and all wear can be taken up in five minutes, and at the end of a season's use $1.75 will replace all worn friction surfaces." Most probably this Crown was not much good. By 1906 Edward T. Ross, the former assistant superintendent for Cadillac, had been hired to design a new two-cylinder car. Given his Cadillac experience and the exemplary reputation of the Cadillac engine, Ross was regarded in the press as "perfectly competent to secure the first grand requisite of a successful car, a powerful, flexible and well-finished motor." His prototype was on the road in August of 1906, and into production thereafter for the 1907 season. The entire '07 output was presold to an Elmira automobile dealer by the name of John North Willys. Apparently,

Detroit Auto Vehicle sought to downplay Crown associations that year, frequently referring to the new car simply as a Detroit. But the company was in trouble anyway, the problems hearkening back to the initial organization. Detroit Auto Vehicle was successor to the Detroit Novelty Machine Works, some of whose stockholders objected vociferously to the automotive venture and instituted litigation. With such a shaky beginning, it is not surprising that the firm was bankrupt by October 1907. Both John North Willys and J.L. Hudson, of course, remained in the automobile field.

1905 Crown, runabout, WLB

1905-1906 CROWN
Two — 12 hp, 78" wb

	FP	5	4	3	2	1
Rbt.	750	2400	3400	4800	8000	17,000

Two — 16 hp, 78" wb

	FP	5	4	3	2	1
Light Delivery	1250	2500	3500	5000	8500	18,0000

Four — 24 hp, 99" wb

	FP	5	4	3	2	1
Tour.	2150	2700	3600	5300	8800	19,000

1907 (Crown) Detroit, touring, WLB

1907 CROWN/DETROIT
Two — 22/24 hp, 96" wb

	FP	5	4	3	2	1
Rbt.	1500	2700	3600	5300	8800	19,000
Tour.	1500	2500	3500	5000	8500	18,000

1908 Crown, auto-buggy, NAHC

CROWN — Amesbury, Massachusetts — (1908-1910) — The Crown Motor Vehicle Company was organized early in 1908 for the manufacture of a highwheeler. Its president was W.A. Shafer, who was the New England distributor for the Glide car. Its secretary was J.R. Graves, whose Graves & Congdon machine shop was the site for manufacture. Its treasurer was Frank Dodge, who was described as a "mechanical engineer and designer of automatic machinery." The Crown featured tiller steering, a "reach" frame, platform springs — and was powered by a two-cylinder horizontally opposed air-cooled engine of 12 hp mounted under the seat. The vehicle was well described in *Cycle and Automobile Trade Journal* as having "a neat, carriage-like appearance, there being nothing special to indicate the presence of machinery or mechanism of any kind, other than the side driving chains, which in future models will be entirely encased." Alas, there were not many future models. By 1910, W.A. Shafer had gone back to selling Glides exclusively, and J.R. Graves took over the Crown for the remainder of its short life, with his partner Arthur G. Congdon overseeing production. Occasionally, the car was referred to as the Graves & Congdon.

1908-1909 CROWN
Model A — 2-cyl., 12 hp, 74" wb

	FP	5	4	3	2	1
High Wheel Rbt.	775	2700	3600	5300	8800	19,000
Spec. Rbt. (80" wb)	850	2800	3700	5500	9000	19,500

1910 CROWN
Model A — 2-cyl., 12 hp, 74" wb

High Wheel Rbt.	750	2700	3600	5300	8800	19,000

1913 Crown, roadster, WLB

CROWN — Louisville, Kentucky — (1913-1914) — In March of 1913 the Crown Motor Car Company was organized in Louisville with B.F. Lambert as president, A.B. Lambert as vice-president, and C.H. Lambert as secretary-treasurer. Of that trio B.F. Lambert had just recently sold out his interest in the Buckeye Manufacturing Company, builders of the Lambert automobile in Anderson, Indiana. It cannot be verified that C.H. and A.B. Lambert, who were father and son, were also associated with the Buckeye company, but it would seem likely. Interestingly, the new car the Lamberts announced their intention to build in June was a 30 hp standard four, but when the Crown finally arrived later in 1913 it was a cyclecar, albeit with standard tread. Obviously the trio had spotted what they thought was a more financially lucrative business, but the cyclecar proved to be a fad and they quickly changed their minds after minimal production of the Crown cyclecar. In June of 1914 the Lamberts left Louisville for New Albany, Indiana where the factory of the Ohio Falls Company was newly vacant because of the failure of the Pilgrim car. Although they moved in as the Crown Motor Car Company, the Lamberts soon reorganized as the Hercules Motor Car Company, and Hercules was the name given to the car manufactured there.

1914 Crown, roadster, WLB

1913-1914 CROWN
Cyclecar — 4-cyl., 14 hp, 90" wb

Model A Rdstr.	385	2400	3400	4800	8000	17,000

CROWN MAGNETIC — The Crown Magnetic was an export version of the Owen Magnetic ordered in early 1920 by the English firm Crown Limited. Refer to Owen Magnetic.

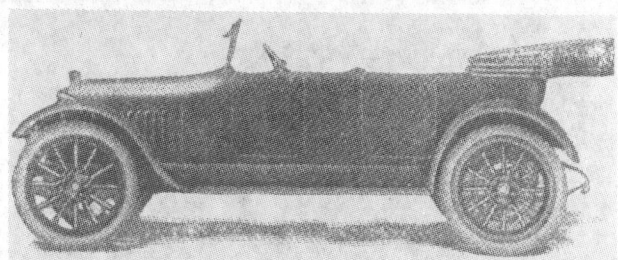

1916 Crowther, model 5-30, 5-pass. touring, WLB

CROWTHER/CROWTHER-DURYEA — Rochester, New York — (1915-1916)/(1917) — The Crowther Motor Company was established in October of 1915 by Henry Crowther to market a light car assembled for him by Cresson-Morris in Philadelphia and utilizing the transmission developed by Charles E. Duryea. As it happened, Cresson-Morris was also assembling a cyclecar for Charles E. Duryea which he was marketing under his own name. Late in 1916 Mr. Crowther found Mr. Duryea, and Cresson-Morris lost two clients. The Crowther-Duryea Motor Company established itself in Crowther's hometown of Rochester (New York), the enterprises of Charles E. Duryea having become something of a moveable feast in recent years. According to a report in early January 1917, one hundred of the new Crowther-Duryeas were being assembled, with plans to step up production once those were completed. Production was never stepped up. The company discontinued operations later during 1917, its factory being sold to a Buffalo tire concern in 1918. Charles Duryea meantime had returned to Reading (Pennsylvania) to build his Duryea Gem.

1917 Crowther-Duryea, model 5-35, roadster, WLB

1916 CROWTHER
Model 5-30 — 4-cyl., 23 hp, 110" wb

	FP	5	4	3	2	1
Tour.-5P	650	3000	4000	6000	9500	21000
Tour.-4P	650	3100	4200	6300	10,500	22,000

1917 CROWTHER-DURYEA
Model 5-35 — 4-cyl., 23 hp, 112" wb

Rbt.-2P	450	3100	4200	6300	10,500	22,000
Tour.-5P	650	3000	4000	6000	9500	21000

1909 Croxton-Keeton, French type, touring, WLB

CROXTON-KEETON/CROXTON — Massillon, Ohio/Cleveland, Ohio & Washington, Pennsylvania — (1909-1910)/(1911-1914) — Herbert A. Croxton was a Massillon iron and steel man who had previously built the Jewel motorcar, and Forrest M. Keeton was a Detroiter formerly associated with the Pope-Toledo and the De Luxe car companies. Together they formed the Croxton-Keeton Motor Car Company in late summer of 1909 for the production of two different types of motorcar, what they called their "German" (based on the Rutenber-engined Jewel) and their "French" (which cradled its passengers between the axles and sported a Renault-type hood with dashboard-mounted radiator). Neither of these cars was built for long. In August of 1910, H.A. Croxton announced that he had requested receivership "in order to protect creditors from ill-advised and hasty action." He alleged further that two members of the company

1910 Croxton-Keeton, German type, touring, WLB

had tried to undermine Croxton-Keeton and the receivership had been instituted to forestall this. Obviously, one of the two people involved was F.M. Keeton, because he promptly left for Detroit to build his own car called the Keeton. Meantime, H.A. Croxton reorganized as the Croxton Motor Company of Cleveland. Because production had not been completely halted during receivership, the old Croxton-Keeton was simply continued as the new Croxton, with a couple of new models added. In March of 1911, the Croxton company was merged with Royal Tourist to form a holding company called Consolidated Motor Car Company, with H.A. Croxton at its head, but this merger did not survive more than a few months and Croxton was on his own again. He reorganized once more as Croxton Motor Company and began taking bids for a new plant to be erected in Washington, Pennsylvania. The new factory was completed by early fall of 1912, and Croxton quickly moved in. He was in financial trouble almost immediately. The Croxton production line in Washington was stopped forever early in 1914. The Universal Motor Car Company immediately moved in to build its own car there.

1910 Croxton-Keeton, German type, roadster, WLB

1910 Croxton-Keeton, French type, touring, JAC

1909-1910 CROXTON-KEETON

Thirty — 4-cyl., 28.9 hp, 115-1/2" wb

	FP	5	4	3	2	1
French Suburban-4P	2850	4400	5600	9200	17,300	31,000
French Tour.-6P	3250	5000	6500	11,000	22,000	35,000
French Land'et.-6P	3300	4200	5200	8400	15,700	29,000
Forty-Five — 4-cyl., 48 hp, 130" wb						
German Tour.-7P	3500	5200	6800	11,300	23,000	36,000
German Rdstr.-3/4P	3500	5300	7000	11,500	24,000	37,000

1911 CROXTON

Thirty — 4-cyl., 30 hp, 115" wb

	FP	5	4	3	2	1
French Roadster	2250	5000	6500	11,000	22,000	35,000
French Suburban	2500	4500	5800	9500	18,000	32,000
French Tour.	2600	4900	6300	10,300	21,000	34,000
French Taxi	3300	4200	5200	8400	15,700	29,000
Thirty-Eight — 4-cyl., 38 hp, 120" wb						
French Fore-Door Tour.	2650	5000	6500	11,000	22,000	35,000
Forty — 4-cyl., 40 hp, 130" wb						
German Touring-4P*	3000	5200	6800	11.300	23.000	36.000

1911 Croxton, German type, touring, KM

	FP	5	4	3	2	1
* (Close-Coupled)						
German Tour.-7P	3000	5000	6500	11,000	22,000	35,000
Forty-Eight — 4-cyl., 48 hp, 130" wb						
German Fore-Door Tour.-7P	3250	5400	7300	11,800	25,000	38,000
1912 CROXTON						
Thirty — 4-cyl., 30 hp, 120" wb						
Model R Rdstr.-2P	2250	5000	6500	11,000	22,000	35,000
Model S Tour.-4P	2500	4700	6100	9900	19,000	33,000
Model T Land'et.-5P	3300	4500	5800	9500	18,000	32,000
Model U Tour.-4/5P	2650	4900	6300	10,300	21,000	34,000
Forty-Five — 4-cyl., 45 hp, 130" wb						
Model L Fore-Door Tour.-7P	3500	5200	6800	11,300	23,000	36,000
Model N Tour.-5P*	3500	5300	7000	11,500	24,000	37,000
* (Close-Coupled)						
Model O Rdstr.-2/4P	3500	5400	7300	11,800	25,000	38,000
French Six — 6-cyl., 44 hp, 130" wb						
Land'et.-5P	3000	4300	5400	8700	16,500	30,000
1913-1914 CROXTON						
Model A-4 — 4-cyl., 30 hp, 121" wb						
Rdstr.-2P	2250	5200	6800	11,300	23,000	36,000
Tour.-4/5P	2500	5000	6500	11,000	22,000	35,000
Model B — 6-cyl., 48 hp, 140" wb						
Tour.-6/7P	3000	5300	7000	11,500	24,000	37,000

CRUICKSHANK — In 1896 a steam-powered delivery van was built at the Cruickshank Steam Engine Works in Providence, Rhode Island. The vehicle was one of several designed by L.F.N. Baldwin. Refer to Baldwin.

1917 Cruiser, roadster, WLB

CRUISER — Madison, Wisconsin — (1917-1919) — The Cruiser was offered as a standard touring and roadster, but it was apparent from promotional literature that the company believed its fame and fortune would be made via its Special Camping Roadster, which might be regarded as a pioneer RV. The recreational aspects of the Cruiser were seen to by such fittings as a tent, sliding and folding bed, table, chairs, bed clothing, lavatory commode, and hot and cold "running" water provided in two large storage compartments located on each running board. With the war on, the Cruiser people thought their product a natural for service Over There. The Cruiser Motor Car Company initially had its main offices in Portland, Maine, but a Midwest factory location was envisioned from the beginning. Winthrop J. Burdick of Indianapolis was the company's first president; D.S. Bobb, a Chicago lawyer, its first secretary. Two prototypes of the camping Cruiser, with all accoutrements aboard, were built in Indianapolis for exhibition purposes. Subsequently, temporary facilities were set up in the former New Era factory in Joliet, Illinois where production was begun. (Burdick had been a New Era director.) The money ran out rather quickly, however, and by September of 1917 fresh capital from Chicago and Madison saw to the removal of offices and factory to Wisconsin, with W.D. Curtis of Madison as the firm's new president. Production began anew in temporary quarters in Madison while a new factory site was found and construction begun. Ironically, by the fall of 1919, when Cruiser was able to move into its new plant, the company was in sufficient financial difficulties again not to be able to remain there long.

1917-1919 CRUISER
Six — 21.6 hp, 117 1/2" wb

	FP	5	4	3	2	1
Tour.-5P	1075	3900	4800	7700	14,300	27,000
Rds.-3P	1075	4200	5200	8400	15,700	29,000
Spc. Camping Rds.	1195	4400	5600	9200	17,300	31,000

CRUSADER — Although Crusader Motors Corporation of York, Pennsylvania was listed in a 1923 trade directory as a manufacturer of automobiles, that seems to have been in error. There indeed was such a company in town at that time, but more than likely it operated only as a dealership.

CRUSADER — Joliet, Illinois — (1914-1915) — The Crusader Motor Car Company moved into the plant formerly occupied by the Dayton Cyclecar Company, confident in the belief that it would succeed where Dayton had failed. Refinements were made to the former Dayton to take it out of the cyclecar category. The four-cylinder engine remained the same, but the wheelbase was shortened to 101 inches, while the tread was widened to the standard 56 inches. Shaft drive and a three-speed sliding gear transmission were fitted. "The list price on these cars has not been decided yet," the company wrote *Carette* magazine in December of 1914, "but we think the roadster will sell under $500 and the touring car for something like $600." Whether prices ever were finalized is not known. Quite possibly, the only Crusaders built were the pilot models. Certainly, the company did not survive 1915. Crusader designer W.O. Dayton quickly moved across town to design another car called the New Era.

CRYDER — Cryder & Company was organized in New York City early in 1906 for the manufacture of automobiles. H.C. Cryder, T.A. Havemeyer and Townsend Morgan were the principals involved. Manufacture of a Cryder car did not follow, but the firm did move into automobile importation, becoming the agents for the French Mors and Leon-Bollee.

CRYSTAL CITY — Corning, New York — (1914) — Raymond Troll and Charles Manning were mechanics from Corning who, in 1914, produced a two-passenger cyclecar powered by a four-cylinder water-cooled 18 hp Farmer engine built in unit with a three-speed selective transmission and set into a quite lengthy chassis of 106-inch wheelbase. They called their vehicle the Crystal City, a reference of course to Corning's famous glass-making center, though the car's home was considerably more modest — the garage of Dr. C.A. Carr at 22 East First Street which was said to have been "leased for the purpose." About twenty-five cars were to be built in that garage in 1914, Troll and Manning announced. Whether production reached that figure is not known, but at least one car was built, an area resident having recalled seeing it in town. According to *The Carette and American Cyclecar*, by the summer of 1914, Troll and Manning had taken to grandiosely referring to themselves as the Corning Motor Car Company.

C.T.M. — The C.T.M. Manufacturing Company was organized in Newark, New Jersey during the spring of 1910 for the manufacture of automobiles and parts. Capital stock was $100,000, and the firm's initials translated to Allen C. Coats, A. Morris Thompson and William McKay, all of Newark. Manufacture of a C.T.M. car has not been documented.

1914 Cub Cyclecar, runabout, NAHC

CUB — Richmond, Virginia — (1914) — The Cub cyclecar was the product of two alumni of the University of Berlin in Germany: Otto E. Szekely and Charles J. Berthal, both of whom had earned engineering degrees there. This represents the only point of distinction for this automotive venture. The Cub's tubular frame, belt drive, vee-type air-cooled engine, $350 price and other specifications were typical of the cyclecar genre. The Szekely Cyclecar Company, as the firm was named, did not survive into 1915.

CUBE — The Cube Hub Company of Port Huron, Michigan was an early 1907 venture organized to manufacture automobiles. Capital stock was $10,000. The firm seems to have gone nowhere.

1901 Cull, gasoline touring, HAC

CULL — St. Louis, Missouri — (1899-1901) — In 1899 two St. Louis electricians by the names of A.B. Cull and A.A. King built their first car, apparently without a great deal of forethought. The running gear purchased for it had been designed for an electric, but the engine they used was a Fairbanks-Morse gasoline unit which they cooled via a few coils of pipe connected to a tank under the rear of the body. Despite its makeshift aspect, the vehicle ran well, and at about 10 mph. In 1901 A.B. Cull built himself another car which was considerably more sophisticated, powered by a single-cylinder engine mounted midship, with two-speed planetary transmission, chain drive, and wheel steering. This effort was put together at the Briner Electric Company on Second Street and Franklin Avenue, and the result was driven by A.B. Cull until 1904 when he sold it. Subsequently, Cull became prominent in St. Louis motoring circles through his employment with the South Side Automobile Company.

CULLMAN — Chicago, Illinois — (1902) — The only automobile built by the Cullman Wheel Company of Chicago was a steamer in 1902 for experimental purposes only. The firm, which specialized in the manufacture of sprockets and differentials, was located on Larrabee Street in the Windy City until 1904 when quarters were moved to 1027 Dunning Street.

1905 Culver, auto-buggy, NAHC

CULVER — Aurora, Illinois — (1905) — Dr. D.D. Culver believed he had discovered "the motor car's shortcomings from a physician's standpoint." He built a car that overcame them, and organized the Practical Automobile Company to manufacture it. Whether he would locate its factory in his hometown of Aurora or in Genoa, he had not yet decided. The specifications of the Culver indicate it to be a completely conventional two-cylinder two-seater highwheeler of the period, except for the tilting steering column which made getting in and out of the car easier, important naturally for house calling. This feature was not sufficient, however, to make a success of his automobile business, and Dr. Culver returned to his medical practice in 1906, although apparently not before he designed the Aurora for some businessmen in town who had decided to have to fling themselves in the automobile industry.

1905 CULVER
Highwheeler Buggy — 2-cyl., 6 hp, 72" wb

	FP	5	4	3	2	1
Highwheeler Buggy		—	—	—	—	—

1917 Culver, runabout, NAHC

CULVER — Culver City, California — (1917) — The Culver Manufacturing Company produced its own small single-cylinder 4 hp engine and put it into a small 66-inch wheelbase two-seater for youngsters. The selling price of $225 was attractive for a vehicle of this type. References do not indicate, however, that the Culver survived beyond 1917.

CUMMINGS — The Cummings Automobile Company at 257 Washington Street in Boston, with one A.M. Cummings in charge, was indicated as an automobile manufacturer in the Hiscox book *Horseless Vehicles, Automobiles, Motor Cycles* published in 1900. Further documentation is lacking. The 1900 Boston city directory reveals an Arthur M. Cummings with a business address of Room 95 at 1 Beacon, but no Cummings Automobile Company. By 1901 Arthur Cummings had left town. W.J. Cummings of 6th Street in Wellston, Ohio was indicated as an automobile manufacturer in the Ware yearbook for 1908. Further documentation has not been discovered.

1894 Cummings Electric, HAC

CUMMINGS ELECTRIC — Chicago, Illinois — (1894) — The electric car built by G.K. Cummings of Chicago in 1894 featured a wheel for steering and a foot pedal for speed control. A two-seated buggy with straight dash perched high over a box with batteries and the 2 hp motor. The front axle was aluminum bronze, and the band clutch of the brake was leather-lined steel. Dual chains drove to the rear wheels, and the differential was a steel roller. Although ungainly, the car reportedly was tested successfully. There is no documentation that G.K. Cummings built another.

CUMMINGS — Carrington, North Dakota — (1908) — In 1908 Clarence Cummings of Carrington built a two-stroke gasoline-engined automobile for himself. The vehicle is remembered as being crude, but Clarence was only sixteen years old.

1934 Cummins, Diesel, race car, NAHC

CUMMINS — Columbus, Indiana — (1929 et seq.) — The most famous Cummins automobiles of the late Twenties and Thirties were race cars built by Clessie L. Cummins to demonstrate the advantages of diesel power. In 1931 a Cummins set a world record for diesel-engined cars with a speed of 100.75 mph at Daytona, and that year at Indianapolis, Dave Evans drove a Cummins diesel the entire 500-mile distance without a stop, finishing thirteenth at 86.17 mph. But perhaps an even more impressive achievement had been realized the year before when Clessie Cummins himself drove a four-cylinder Cummins-engined passenger car from Indianapolis to New York City, a distance of 792 miles, with only $1.38 being expended for fuel. Interestingly, the car — which used a standard automobile chassis of unspecified make — had been equipped with a governor limiting speed to 55 mph. Five years later, another Cummins-engined passenger car was again seen in New York, at the automobile show this time and on an Auburn chassis. This Cummins diesel engine was a six developing 85 mph. Though the Cummins Engine Company subsequently provided diesel power for several Indy race cars, the last in 1952, the firm never manufactured a production car.

CUMMINS-MONITOR — Although the Columbus, Ohio firm was known briefly during 1915 and 1916 as the Cummins-Monitor Company, its product was referred to only as the Monitor. In December 1916 the firm's name was changed to Monitor Motor Car Company, and it remained in production into 1922. Refer to Monitor.

1917 Cunard electric juvenile car, NAHC

CUNARD — New York, New York — (1917) — Though the company was famous for its steam ships, the only automobile ever built at Cunard was an electric. A child's car capable of 15 mph, it was produced in 1917 by employees of the Cunard line for the son of Captain Roberts, superintendent of the Cunard docks in New York City.

CUNNINGHAM — Although the Massachusetts Steam Wagon Company was organized in Pittsfield, Massachusetts in December of 1900 for manufacture of the vehicles developed by the Cunningham Engineering Company of Boston, it would appear the resulting vehicles were of commercial type only. The Cunningham steam truck was a four-wheel-drive produced through 1901.

1908 Cunningham, Electric, stanhope, HAC

CUNNINGHAM — Rochester, New York — (1907-1936) — James Cunningham, Son & Company was incorporated in 1882. With the death of the founding father in 1886, son Joseph took over, and within a decade Cunningham was America's leading producer of high quality dogcarts, vis-a-vis, sleighs, cutters, berlins, tally-hos and victorias. Like many other carriage-building concerns, Cunningham successfully made the transition from horse drawn to horseless vehicles. The company had experimented with an electric car before the turn of the century, and casually marketed it after. Cunningham entered the market in earnest beginning in 1907, with gasoline cars powered by Buffalo or Continental engines, and custom coachwork to order. For the 1911 model year Cunningham began offering catalogued production models powered by a Cunningham-built 40 hp four-cylinder engine. By 1916 the company had its own 442-cubic-inch 45 hp V-8. In 1919 Ralph De Palma drove a V-8 Cunningham special roadster 98 mph in a six-mile trial at Sheepshead Bay. But it was neither the Cun-

1929 Cunningham, Series V-7, boattail speedster, HAC

ningham's specifications nor its performance — both of which were meritorious — that distinguished the marque. It was, not surprisingly, its coachwork. During the World War I era and into the Twenties, Cunninghams were among the most handsome cars in America and the most expensive as well, averaging $5000, and reaching as high as $9000. They were huge vehicles, on wheelbases of 132 and 142 inches. The Cunningham clientele included Mary Pickford, Harold Lloyd, William Randolph Hearst, Blanche Sweet, Marshall Field, Philip Wrigley, Fatty Arbuckle and Cecil B. De Mille. Following the Wall Street crash, Cunningham focused production on the hearse and ambulance business which had been its mainstay practically from the beginning. Interestingly, during Cunningham's production car days, undertakers who used Cunningham equipment frequently served as Cunningham dealers. The last production Cunninghams had been built in 1931, but may have been sold as new into 1933. In the mid-Thirties the company produced a handful of town car bodies on Ford V-8 chassis (as did Brewster), the last known example completed in 1937. At about $2600, these Cunninghams were considerably less expensive than the gigantic and grand cars of the glory years.

1911 CUNNINGHAM
Model J — 4-cyl., 40 hp, 124" wb

	FP	5	4	3	2	1
Touring-7P	3500	7600	12,500	19,400	42,400	55,000
Runabout	3250	7800	12,900	19,900	43,300	57,000
Limousine	4500	7000	10,800	16,900	37,100	49,000
Landaulet	4500	7200	11,300	17,700	38,700	50,000

1912 CUNNINGHAM
Model J — 4-cyl., 40 hp, 124" wb

Runabout	3250	7600	12,500	19,400	42,400	55,000
Phaeton-5P	3500	7500	12,300	19,100	41,700	54,000
Touring-7P	3500	7200	11,300	17,700	38,700	50,000
Torpedo-4P	3500	7300	11,800	18,400	40,400	52,000

	FP	5	4	3	2	1
Toy Tonneau-4P	3500	7400	12,100	18,800	41,100	53,000
Limousine-7P	4500	7200	11,300	17,700	38,700	50,000
Landaulet-7P	4500	7300	11,600	18,100	39,600	51,000

1912 Cunningham, model J, 7-pass. touring, WLB

1913 Cunningham, model M, touring, HAC

1913 CUNNINGHAM
Model M — 4-cyl., 36.1 hp, 124" wb

Touring-7P	3500	7200	11,300	17,700	38,700	50,000
Phaeton-5P	3500	7500	12,300	19,100	41,700	54,000
Torpedo-5P	3500	7300	11,800	18,400	40,400	52,000
Runabout	3250	7600	12,500	19,400	42,400	55,000
Limousine-7P	4600	7200	11,300	17,700	38,700	50,000
Landaulet-7P	4500	7300	11,600	18,100	39,600	51,000
Berlin Limousine-7P	4600	7300	11,600	18,100	39,600	51,000

1914 Cunningham, model R, limousine, HAC

1914 CUNNINGHAM
Model R — 4-cyl., 36.1 hp, 129" wb

Touring-7P	3750	7200	11,300	17,700	38,700	50,000
Runabout	3500	7400	12,100	18,800	41,100	53,000
Touring-4P	3750	7300	11,800	18,400	40,400	52,000
Touring-5P	3750	7300	11,700	18,300	40,000	51,500
Limousine	5000	7000	10,800	16,900	37,100	49,000
Landaulet	5000	7200	11,300	17,700	38,700	50,000

1915 CUNNINGHAM
Model S — 4-cyl., 36.1 hp, 129" wb

Touring-7P	3750	7200	11,300	17,700	38,700	50,000
Touring-5P	3750	7300	11,600	18,100	39,600	51,000
Touring-4P	3750	7300	11,700	18,300	40,000	51,500
Runabout	3500	7400	12,100	18,800	41,000	53,000
Limousine	5000	7000	10,800	16,900	37,100	49,000
Landaulet	5000	7200	11,300	17,700	38,700	50,000

1916 CUNNINGHAM
Model S — 4-cyl., 36.1 hp, 129" wb

Touring-7P	3750	7300	11,600	18,100	39,600	51,000
Touring-4P	3750	7400	12,000	18,600	40,800	52,500
Runabout	3500	7500	12,300	19,100	41,700	54,000
Limousine	5000	7200	11,300	17,700	38,700	50,000
Landaulet	5000	7300	11,600	18,100	39,600	51,000

387

1916 Cunningham, model S, landaulet, HAC

1919 Cunningham, Series V, touring victoria, JAC

1917 Cunningham, Series V, touring, HAC

1917 CUNNINGHAM
Series V — 8-cyl., 45 hp, 132" wb

	FP	5	4	3	2	1
Touring-5P	3750	7600	12,500	19,400	42,400	55,000
Touring-7P	3750	7500	12,300	19,100	41,700	54,000
Roadster-2P	3750	7800	12,900	19,900	43,300	57,000
Runabout-3P	3750	7700	12,700	19,700	43,000	56,000
Limousine-8P	5000	7300	11,800	18,400	40,400	52,000
Berline-8P	5000	7300	11,800	18,400	40,400	52,000
Toy Tonneau-4P	3750	7400	12,100	18,800	41,100	53,000
Coupe-4P	4500	7000	10,800	16,900	37,100	49,000
Sedan-5P	4500	6000	8500	13,000	30,000	42,000
Town Car-6P	5000	6400	9300	14,500	33,000	45,000
Touring Sedan-5P	5000	5900	8300	12,800	29,000	41,000
Roadster Coupe-4P	4500	7600	12,500	19,400	42,400	55,000

1919 Cunningham, Series V, boattail speedster, BC

1919 CUNNINGHAM
Series V — 8-cyl., 45 hp, 132" wb

	FP	5	4	3	2	1
Touring-7P	4250	7700	12,700	19,700	43,000	56,000
Touring-4P	4250	7800	12,900	19,900	43,300	57,000
Roadster-4P	4250	7800	13,300	20,300	44,000	60,000
Limousine	5500	7300	11,800	18,400	40,400	52,000
Landaulet	5750	7400	12,100	18,800	41,100	53,000

1918 Cunningham, Series V, touring, HAC

1918 CUNNINGHAM
Series V — 8-cyl., 45 hp, 132" wb

	FP	5	4	3	2	1
Touring-7P	4250	7600	12,500	19,400	42,400	55,000
Touring-4P	4250	7700	12,700	19,700	43,000	56,000
Roadster-4P	4250	7800	13,000	20,000	43,500	58,000
Landaulet	5750	7300	11,800	18,400	40,400	52,000
Limousine	5500	7300	11,600	18,100	39,600	51,000
Berline	5500	7300	11,600	18,100	39,600	51,000
Coupe	5500	7000	10,800	16,900	37,100	49,000
Town Card	5500	6000	8500	13,000	30,000	42,000

1920 Cunningham, Series V, touring victoria, JAC

1920 CUNNINGHAM
Series V — 8-cyl., 95 hp, 132" wb

Touring-4P	6200	7800	12,900	19,900	43,000	57,000
Roadster	6200	7800	13,300	20,300	44,000	60,000
Sedan	7600	7200	11,300	17,700	38,700	50,000

Series V — 8-cyl., 95 hp, 142" wb

Touring-6P	6700	7800	13,300	20,300	44,000	60,000
Inside Drive Limousine	8100	7300	11,800	18,400	40,400	52,000
Town Limousine	8100	7400	12,100	18,800	41,100	53,000
Landaulet	8100	7500	12,300	19,100	41,700	54,000

1919 Cunningham, Series V, brougham, HAC

1921 Cunningham, Series V, touring victoria, JAC

1921 CUNNINGHAM
Series V — 8-cyl., 95 hp, 132" wb

	FP	5	4	3	2	1
Touring-6P	6200	7800	12,900	19,900	43,300	57,000
Limousine	7600	7400	12,100	18,800	41,100	53,000
Town Car	6000	7500	12,300	19,100	41,700	54,000
Cabriolet	6000	7600	12,500	19,400	42,400	55,000
Series V — 8-cyl., 95 hp, 142" wb						
Touring-6P	6700	7800	13,300	20,300	44,000	60,000
Touring-7P	6800	7800	13,200	19,800	43,800	59,000
Town Car	8100	7600	12,500	19,400	42,400	55,000
Cabriolet	8100	7700	12,700	19,700	43,000	56,000

1922 Cunningham, Series V-4, touring victoria, HAC

1922 CUNNINGHAM
Series V-4 — 8-cyl., 95 hp, 132" wb

	FP	5	4	3	2	1
Special Speed Roadster	—	8200	14,500	21,500	46,800	65,000
Touring-4P	6000	7800	13,200	20,200	43,800	59,000
Special Speed Touring	—	7900	13,700	20,700	44,500	62,000
Touring-7P	6200	7800	13,300	20,300	44,000	60,000
Coupe	6300	7200	11,300	17,700	38,700	50,000
Sedan	6400	6800	10,300	16,000	35,500	48,000
Roadster	6000	7800	13,300	20,300	44,000	60,000
Series V-4 — 8-cyl., 95 hp, 142" wb						
Touring-7P	6800	7900	13,700	20,700	44,500	62,000
Sedan-6P	7200	7200	11,300	17,700	38,700	50,000
Inside Drive Limousine	8100	7800	13,200	20,200	43,800	59,000
Landaulet	8100	7800	13,300	20,300	44,000	60,000

1923 Cunningham, Series V-4, touring, HAC

1923 Cunningham, Series V-4, landaulet, HAC

1923 CUNNINGHAM
Series V-4 — 8-cyl., 95 hp, 132" wb

	FP	5	4	3	2	1
Touring-4P	5650	7800	13,300	20,300	44,000	60,000
Roadster-3P	5650	7400	12,100	18,800	41,100	63,000
Touring-6P	6150	7800	13,200	20,200	43,800	59,000
Coupe-4P	7150	7200	11,300	17,700	38,700	50,000
Series V-4 — 8-cyl., 95 hp, 142" wb						
Enclosed Drive Limousine-7P	7650	7300	11,800	18,400	40,400	52,000
Landaulet-6P	7650	7400	12,100	18,800	41,000	53,000
Town Car-6P	7650	7500	12,300	19,100	41,700	54,000
Limousine-6P	7650	7300	11,600	18,100	39,600	51,000

1924 Cunningham, Series V-5, dual cowl phaeton, HAC

1924 CUNNINGHAM
Series V-5 — 8-cyl., 90 hp, 132" wb

	FP	5	4	3	2	1
Touring-4P	5800	7800	13,300	20,300	44,000	60,000
Series V-5 — 8-cyl., 90 hp, 142" wb						
Touring-6P/7P	6300	7900	13,700	20,700	44,500	62,000
Limousine-4P	7700	7300	11,600	18,100	39,600	51,000
Limousine-6P	7700	7300	11,800	18,400	40,400	52,000

1925 Cunningham, Series V-5, 4-dr. sedan, OCW

1926 Cunningham, Series V-6, 5-pass. touring, HAC

1925-1926 CUNNINGHAM
Series V-6 — 8-cyl., 90 hp, 132" wb

	FP	5	4	3	2	1
Roadster	5800	8200	14,500	21,500	46,800	65,000
Sport Touring-4P	6300	7900	13,700	20,700	44,500	62,000
Touring-6P	6300	7800	13,300	20,300	44,000	60,000
Touring-7P	6300	7800	13,000	20,000	43,500	58,000
Series V-6 — 8-cyl., 90 hp, 142" wb						
Sedan-4P	7150	5800	8000	12,500	28,000	40,000
Inside Drive Limousine	7650	7200	11,300	17,700	38,700	50,000
Inside Drive Cabriolet	7650	7300	11,800	18,400	40,400	52,000
French Brougham	7650	7400	12,100	18,800	41,100	53,000
Cabriolet	7650	7600	12,500	19,400	42,400	55,000

1927 Cunningham, Series V-6, 7-pass. touring, HAC

1927 CUNNINGHAM
Series V-6 — 8-cyl., 90 hp, 132" wb

	FP	5	4	3	2	1
Roadster-4P	6150	8200	14,500	21,500	46,800	65,000
Touring-4P	6150	7900	13,700	20,700	44,500	62,000
Sedan-4P	7600	5000	6500	11,000	22,000	35,000
Limousine-6P	8100	7200	11,300	17,700	38,700	50,000
Town Car-6P	8100	7600	12,500	19,400	42,400	55,000

Series V-7 — 8-cyl., 106 hp, 142" wb

	FP	5	4	3	2	1
Touring-6P	7000	9400	18,800	26,500	53,800	75,000
Touring-7P	7000	9300	18,500	26,000	52,500	74,000
Special Speed Roadster	7750	11,300	21,300	32,500	65,000	85,000
Special Speed Four-Passenger	7750	11,800	21,800	33,500	67,000	87,000
Enclosed Drive Limousine	8500	9000	18,000	25,000	50,000	72,000
Town Sedan	9100	8200	14,000	21,000	45,000	65,000

1928 Cunningham, Series V-7, touring, OCW

1929 Cunningham, Series V-7, town car, OCW

1929 Cunningham, Series V-7, roadster, HAC

1930 Cunningham, Series V-7, landaulet, JAC

1928-1929 CUNNINGHAM
Series V-7 — 8-cyl., 106 hp, 132" wb

	FP	5	4	3	2	1
Roadster	7000	9000	18,000	25,000	50,000	72,000
Touring-4P	7000	8200	14,500	21,500	46,800	65,000
Cabriolet	8500	8500	16,000	23,000	48,000	68,000
Enclosed Drive-4P	8500	8700	16,500	23,500	48,500	69,000
Petit Cabriolet	8500	8700	16,500	23,500	48,500	69,000
Coupe-2P	8000	7800	13,300	20,300	44,000	60,000

CUNO — The Cuno Engineering Company was organized with a capital stock of $50,000 during the spring of 1913 to ''design and manufacture motor cars'' in Meriden, Connecticut. The Cunos involved were initialed C., C.H. and A. Manufacture of a Cuno did not follow, although conceivably the firm may have built prototypes for anxious automobile entrepreneurs.

CURRAN — New York, New York — (1923) — Purportedly, in addition to commercial vehicles, the Curran Steam Auto Company of America produced two touring cars powered by three-cylinder engines and set into 128-inch wheelbase chassis in 1923. Such was reported that year in any case. Possibly wishful thinking was the only thing produced. New York City directories of the early Twenties do not include any mention of a Curran. But, in San Francisco, there was a branch office of the Curran company at 681 Market Street, with Frank J. Curran indicated as president. Possibly any vehicles built were put together there.

CURTIN-HEBERT — ''Preparations are being made by the Curtin-Hebert Manufacturing Company of Gloversville, New York to begin the manufacture of automobiles in that city,'' reported *The Automobile* in March 1904. Preparation seems to have been as far as this venture proceeded.

CURTIN & SCHILLE — Columbus, Ohio — (1899 et seq.) — Thomas E. Curtin and Frank H. Schille were the proprietors of a carriage-making company in Columbus at the turn of the century. In 1899 the firm built an electric carriage for a local manufacturer of screws, the vehicle intended for inter-factory use in conveying company stock from one department to another. Probably other vehicles followed for local Columbus customers. In 1905 Thomas Curtin organized the Curtin-Williams Automobile Company for the manufacture of automobiles. Apparently this venture died aborning, however, for the year following found Curtin among the initial investors in another Columbus automotive venture which would result in the Harmer car.

CURTIS — The Curtis-Pembroke Company was organized early in 1904 to manufacture and deal in automobiles in Rochester, New York. Capital stock was $10,000, and the partners involved were H.A. Curtis and C.J. Pembroke. Manufacture is doubted.

The Harry Curtis Automobile Company was organized in New York City late in 1907 with a capital stock of $10,000 for the manufacture of automobiles. Amanda Curtis, H.S. Rogers and J.C. Brown were the incorporators. Whether the Harry Curtis was the H.A. Curtis from Rochester is not known, but manufacture of this Curtis car is doubted as well.

Although the Pittsburgh Machine and Tool Company of 201 Corey Avenue in Braddock, Pennsylvania produced trucks for in-house use from 1912-1915, the company never built an automobile. It is believed, however, that Pittsburgh company president Curtis had a White custom made for himself.

1867 Curtis Steamer, NAHC

CURTIS STEAM — Newburyport, Massachusetts — (1867) — Francis Curtis was the superintendent of the Gas Works in Newburyport and in 1866 he invented a steam engine which was attached to a piece of fire-fighting apparatus and which, the Newburyport *Daily Herald* reported, ran "as self-reliant and independent as though it were a living thing." Nehemiah S. Bean, designer of the Amoskeag fire engine, sat next to Curtis during its test run, and it may be that Curtis' engine idea ultimately found its way into the famous Amoskeag. Curtis, however, had difficulty convincing the Newburyport City Council of the wisdom of steam power, and thus he never was able to establish a steam fire-engine factory in town. But he did build another steamer the following year, and this was a passenger carriage built to specification for an unnamed client. Its vertical boiler, made for Curtis by the Whittier Machine Works, was placed in front of the seat, with a coal box at the rear. There was a twenty-gallon water tank; coal capacity was eighty pounds. Steam pressure generated was forty to forty-five pounds, horsepower generated was five, maximum speed was 25 mph. With a full load of coal, the car would run approximately thirty miles, provided about a half-dozen stops were made for water. The longest non-stop run recorded was nine miles in twenty-six minutes. Whether this run was made by the owner or the inventor is not known. Reportedly, the price agreed upon for the Curtis Steam Carriage was $1000, to be paid in installments. When the owner did not meet his payments, Francis Curtis took his steam carriage back. This has to have been the first automobile repossession in American history. Most probably, the Curtis steam car has another first to its credit as well. During the testing period before delivery to its client, the car aroused the wrath of Curtis' Newburyport neighbors, one of whom swore out a warrant for his arrest. When the sheriff arrived, Francis Curtis left, in his car, with the lawman in hot pursuit on foot — the first getaway by automobile in American history.

1920 Curtis, touring, NAHC

CURTIS — Little Rock, Arkansas — (1920-1921) — The Curtis Motor Car Company was the idea of Little Rock mayor Charles E. Taylor and, save for chief engineer F.H. Berger who was imported from General Motors up north, its officers were composed chiefly of Little Rock people. There was little "engineering" necessary for chief engineer F.H. Berger to do, however, because the Curtis engines would be a Herschell-Spillman four and a Continental six, and the Curtis would be an assembled car completely. It may be that Curtis didn't assemble the car either. "We expect to begin the building of a factory as soon as sufficient stock has been sold," the company's lone brochure of 1920 read. "Unless something very unusual should happen to prevent, we shall begin the manufacture of cars not later than the summer of 1920." Subsequent references in neither trade publications nor the local press mention a factory; the thirty units which were later said to have been built may have been assembled by another manufacturer. Although export of the Curtis to Europe had initially been envisioned, according to *Motor West* magazine, the car was never promoted except locally. In April of 1921 the Curtis Motor Car Company went into receivership, its assets at the time reported to be a grand $87. Interestingly, during receivership, it was revealed that the Curtis company had been not incorporated but had operated instead as a trust. There were rumors, too, that a judicial investigation would be opened into the company's affairs, but apparently Curtis was simply allowed to fade away instead.

1920-1921 CURTIS

	FP	5	4	3	2	1
Curtis Four (45 hp, 112" wb)	1045	—	—	—	—	—
Curtis Six (55 hp, 112" wb)	1565	—	—	—	—	—

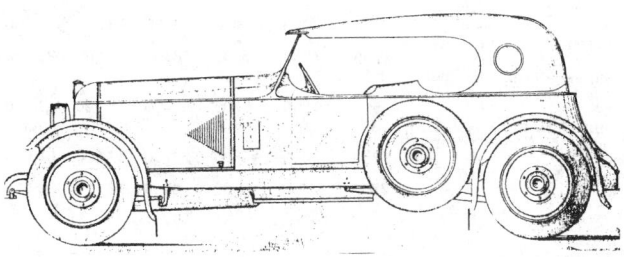

1920-21 Curtiss, touring, HAC

CURTISS AUTOPLANE — Garden City, New York — (1917)/**CURTISS** — Hammondsport, New York — (1920-1921) — Renowned aviator Glenn Curtiss had been an automobile enthusiast since his earliest motorcycle days in his hometown of Hammondsport. Indeed, he owned the first automobile in town, and later was a dealer for the Orient Buckboard, the Frayer-Miller and the Ford. As early as 1912 he tried to talk Henry Ford into fitting an aviation motor into the Model T, which intrigued Ford, but not enough to follow through on the project. In 1917 Curtiss combined his automotive and aviation interests, and the result was the first flying car perhaps to have been built. Standard aircraft wheels were used, with the Curtiss OXX engine mounted up front under the hood. The car section was peculiar looking. The wings and boom-mounted tail were secured to the vehicle in a complicated series of fasteners and guy wires; changing from one mode of transport to the other had to have been time consuming. The vehicle was unveiled in February 1917 at the New York Pan-American Aeronautic Exposition. It is known to have been driven, it is doubtful if it ever flew. Curtiss' next automotive venture was with a car for the road only. Following the First World War, he found himself with a surplus of his OX-5 aviation engines. Adapting them to automotive use seemed a good sporting idea, and indeed he would not be the only one to try it. Both the Prado and the Wharton during this period used the OX-5. Curtiss was lucky to have the services of Charlie Kirkham, chief engineer for the Curtiss Aeroplane Company, to revise the OX-5 (a 100 hp V-8) for him, and the talents of Miles Carpenter of Phianna, who designed and produced the car for Curtiss on the Phianna chassis. How many were built is questionable, probably only a few, and maybe just one. The Curtiss Motor Car Company was casually organized, and the car was just as casually promoted. No attempt at serious manufacture seems to have been undertaken. The several biographies of Glenn Curtiss ignore this automotive venture completely, giving considerably more attention to his Aerocar enterprise of 1929. This evolved out of a camp-car he had built for his own use and adapted into a streamlined design for utilization in vehicles ranging from touring car to school bus. The Aerocar Company of Detroit was incorporated in June of 1929 and included among its stockholders and directors such stalwarts of the industry as Barney Everett, Roy D. Chapin, Howard E. Coffin and Walter O. Briggs. Four months later, however, the stock market crashed — and all Aerocar plans crashed with it.

CUSHMAN — In late 1903 the Cushman Motor Company of Lincoln, Nebraska increased its capital stock to $300,000 in order to begin the manufacture of automobiles. Of the total stock increase, only $50,000 was paid in. It does not appear that a car from Cushman followed.

1907 Custead, runabout, JHV

CUSTEAD — Whittier, California — (1907) — The Custead was a home-built automobile which occupied H.H. Custead at home for two years. Begun in 1905 and completed in 1907, it was a small, light (just 440 pounds) roadster powered by a single-cylinder air-cooled engine, with two-speed planetary transmission. H.H. Custead realized 35 mph and 30 mpg with his car.

CUSTER — The Custer Manufacturing Company was organized in Marion, Indiana with a capital stock of $12,000 during the summer of 1909 for the purpose of building motorcars. Directors of the venture were L.A. Pickett and a quartet of Custers — Burr, George D., Robert J. and Angela G. Manufacture of an automobile is doubted.

1930 Custer Electric, coupe, HAC

1930 Custer Electric Chair, HAC

CUSTER ELECTRIC — Dayton, Ohio — (1920-1942) — L. Luzern Custer purportedly built an experimental electric car in 1898, but it was not until 1920 that he began his Custer Specialty Company in Dayton for the production of electric vehicles. The Custer was built as a Cootie (children's car), Cabbie (miniature railroad), Chair (automotive wheelchair), Carrier (factory truck) and Coupe (two-passenger city car). Of all varieties, the most significant in production was the automotive wheelchair, which was doubtless to Luzern Custer's personal satisfaction because he happened to be an invalid himself. The Cootie was perhaps the second most produced of the Custer vehicles and was catalogued by F.A.O. Schwartz of New York City. As for the Coupe, it weighed 550 pounds, was not much longer than it was high (78 inches versus 62), was rather cute, and might have been a marvelous proposition for crowded metropolitan areas except for one thing; its cruising speed was eight miles an hour. The Custer Specialty Company was in business a long time in Dayton (into the 1960's), but no more than a handful (and possibly only one) of the Coupes was ever built.

1910 Cutting, model A-40, touring, HAC

CUTTING — Jackson, Michigan — (1909-1913) — The Cutting was produced by the Clarke-Carter Automobile Company in the factory which had previously seen the production of the C.V.I. car. Clarke was Horatio E., a

Jackson investment broker, who served as president; Carter was Wedworth W., whose uncle was a leading Jackson banker and who served as secretary-treasurer. Former C.V.I. designer Charles Cutting was chief engineer, and he designed a wide variety of models powered by Wisconsin, Model and Milwaukee four-cylinder engines. Cuttings raced in the Indianapolis 500 in 1911 and 1912, placing among the top fifteen the first year, and being formidably in contention the year following until Wild Bob Burman lived up to his not-always-desired nickname and crashed. But it was on the road rather than the race track that a Cutting had its best performance. It was a well-thought-out and well-built automobile. In 1912 Cutting advertising stressed the fact that "no radical change has been made from the original design" — and the company claimed its product cost less per horsepower and per wheelbase inch than any other $1200-plus car in America, proceeding to prove it in a carefully detailed chart. The Cutting's only problem, it appeared, was Clarke-Carter's initial under-capitalization. In 1913, when the Jesco Starting Device was offered as an option, the firm was reorganized as Cutting Motor Car Company, but it was too late to undo the mistake that had been made in 1909. "Wealthy sponsors fail to come to the rescue and receivership results" was the trade press headline. Cutting liabilities exceeded $350,000. The company was sold in October 1913 for $30,000 and the assumption of two mortgages. The purchaser was L.C. Erbes, who subsequently built the L.C.E.

1910 CUTTING
Four — 40 hp, 116" wb

	FP	5	4	3	2	1
Model A-40 Tourabout	1650	4000	5000	8000	15,000	28,000
Model A-40 Touring	1650	3900	4800	7700	14,300	27,000

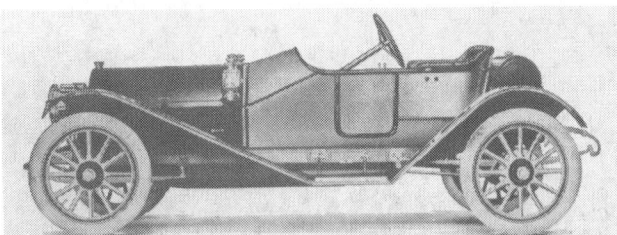

1911 Cutting, model A-30, roadster, WLB

1911 CUTTING

Four — 32 hp, 116" wb					
Model A-30 Roadster	1200	3900	4800	7700	14,300	27,000
Four — 35 hp, 116" wb					
Model B-40 Touring	1350	4000	5000	8000	15,000	28,000
Four — 40 hp, 116" wb					
Model C-50 Touring	1650	3900	4800	7700	14,300	27,000
Model D-50 Fore-Door Touring	1700	4000	4900	7900	14,700	27,500
Model E-50 Torpedo	1750	4000	5000	8000	15,000	28,000
Four — 60 hp, 122" wb					
Model F-60 Touring-7P	2250	4000	5000	8000	15,000	28,000
Model G-60 Torpedo Touring-7P	2350	4200	5200	8400	15,700	29,000

1912 Cutting, model A-30, torpedo roadster, HAC

1912 CUTTING

Four — 30 hp, 116" wb					
Model A-30 Torpedo Roadster	1200	4200	5200	8400	15,700	29,000
Model D-35 Fore-Door Touring	1250	4000	5000	8000	15,000	28,000
Model T-35 Torpedo Touring	1250	4000	5000	8000	15,000	28,000
Four — 40 hp, 116" wb					
Model D-40 Fore-Door Touring	1500	4200	5200	8400	15,700	29,000
Four — 50 hp, 124 & 126" wb					
Model T-55 Torpedo Touring-5P	1850	4400	5600	9200	17,300	31,000
Model F-60 Torpedo Touring-7P	2250	4300	5400	8700	16,500	30,000

1913 CUTTING

Four — 40 hp, 120" wb					
Model A-40 Torpedo Rbt.-2P	1475	4400	5600	9200	17,300	31,000
Model B-40 Touring-5P	1475	4300	5400	8700	16,500	30,000

1913 Cutting, model A-40, roadster, WLB

1913 Cutting, model B-40, touring, WLB

CUYAHOGA ELECTRIC — Although initially announced in 1909 from Cleveland as the product of the Cuyahoga Motor Car Company, by the time the prototype was built, the car's name was changed to Cleveland. Refer to Cleveland Electric.

1908 C.V.I., touring, NAHC

C.V.I. — Jackson, Michigan — (1908) — The C.V.I. Motor Car Company was organized in Jackson with a capital stock of $100,000 in order to manufacture a six-cylinder motorcar designed by Charles D. Cutting. The incorporators were W.S. Kessler, W.M. Thompson, H.S. Reynolds, P.H. Withington, Winthrop Withington and H.L. Smith, and the date of incorporation was October 1906. By February of 1907 the first prototype was successfully tested on the road, and the C.V.I. was first publicly exhibited in December at the Chicago Automobile Show. A factory in Jackson had meantime been equipped, and production began there in January 1908. The first year's output was planned at fifty cars. Whether this total was reached is not known, but by year's end the numerous incorporators of C.V.I. decided not to continue in business. That this decision had nothing to do with the merit of the C.V.I. automobile is evident from a test run reported by Hugh Dolnar in *Cycle and Automobile Trade Journal*. It was made in the midst of a snowstorm, with the C.V.I. side-curtained against the weather and, as Dolnar reported, "The return run was rapid and really delightful, though we were headed into the storm, and this C.V.I. blizzard excursion gave the writer an entirely new conception of the delights of mid-winter motoring made possible by a big car, well covered and driven by a motor which can give any desired pace, slow or fast, on high-gear." Further evidence of the worthiness of the C.V.I. is indicated by the fact that Charles Cutting had no difficulty securing other backers to try again in the automotive industry. His next car was a four called the Cutting, which was built in the C.V.I. factory until 1913. The name change was necessary because the previous initials had referred to Cutting Six (C.V.I.) in roman numerals.

1908 C.V.I.
Model A — 6-cyl., 40 hp, 117" wb

	FP	5	4	3	2	1
Touring-5P	4000	3700	4700	7300	13,700	26,000
Touring-7P	4000	3500	4500	7000	13,000	25,000
Runabout-3/4P	4000	3900	4800	7700	14,300	27,000

1928 C.W.B., sports car, FR

C.W.B. — New Haven, Connecticut — (1927-1929) — The initials translate to Charles Wakefield Bishop, and the company which built them was C.W.B. Sports Automobiles Ltd. of New Haven. The firm was a figment of the Bishop imagination, the cars were not. They were built by Charlie Bishop when he was a student at Yale, and each of the four was different, and a bit of the one preceding. The first, in 1927, combined Ford Model T engine, '23 small Buick suspension, custom-built radiator around a Poughkeepsie Fiat top tank, spheroid from an Itala speedster circa 1927. It was called S.F., for Semper Fidelis, which was a misnomer. Car No. 2, built in the spring of '28 and called Wendy, combined Continental six engine, box girder frame, cantilever suspension all-around, Jacox steering box, Pierce-Arrow gas tank and the aforementioned radiator of the S.F. Then, later in 1928, Car No. 3 — its inventor cannot recall its name — was cannibalized from S.F. and Wendy, with the box frame dropped for an overslung front and underslung rear of structural channel and with a full two feet (from 120 to 144 inches) added to the wheelbase. Car No. 4 was called Tigger, with a nod to A.A. Milne, and was essentially Car No. 3 with three feet lopped off its chassis. Improved chassis design, low weight and a low profile was ever the Bishop objective. There might have been a No. 5 save for the fact that Charlie Bishop graduated from Yale and, though while in London the year following he began planning a Tracta-style front-drive car with two rear axles for off-road work, the Great Depression connived to intervene. Charles Wakefield Bishop thereupon went on to a distinguished career as an engineer — and to becoming one of the earliest and foremost historians of the automobile.

CYCLECAR — Initially, in 1914, the product of the Cycle Car Company of Wilmington, Delaware was known simply by its generic name. Ultimately the vehicle was marketed as the Diamond. Refer to Diamond Cyclecar.

1914 Cycleplane, 2-pass. tandem, WLB

CYCLEPLANE — Westerly, Rhode Island — (1914) — The Cycleplane was a cyclecar whose mechanical specification was typical for vehicles of its type but whose look decidedly was not. Arthur W. Ball was its designer, and he claimed streamlining was the factor he kept most in mind in coming up with the Cycleplane body. Set on a "truss bridge" frame, the car sported shelf-like fenders which ran the length of the car and were purported to have a shock-absorbing effect, although most probably they were more useful as armrests for the vehicle's two passengers. Actually, the car looked less like a plane than a boat. In addition to the standard two-cylinder air-cooled Spacke-engined roadster with planetary transmission and belt drive, the Cyclecar Company of Westerly also planned to offer more sophisticated four-cylinder water-cooled models with three-speed sliding gear transmissions and shaft drive. But production apparently never began. It is believed that Arthur Ball's prototype was his first and last Cycleplane.

CYCLETTE — Nashville, Tennessee — (1914) — The Cyclette was the second idea of Henry E. Neal, Jr. His first was an unnamed cyclecar he built with W.L. McFarland in 1913 which was said to be the first car built in Nashville weighing less than 750 pounds, a distinction but scarcely a noteworthy one. The Cyclette was distinctive for other reasons. It was typically cyclecar in its two-cylinder 13 hp DeLuxe engine, friction transmission, vee-belt drive, and staggered two-seater body. But Henry Neal has to have been the first person to come up with the idea of fitting a Mercedes vee-type radiator to a cyclecar. It looked rather peculiar. An interesting idea, however, was the use of small doors fitted to the body which, when swung down, doubled as steps. The Cyclette prototype was completed and tested on the streets of Nashville in February of 1914. Although Neal announced his intention at that time to proceed into manufacture, apparently he never found the backing to do so.

CYCLOID — Minneapolis, Minnesota — (1910) — The Cycloid Manufacturing Company was incorporated in Minneapolis during the fall of 1910 with plans, as *Cycle and Automobile Trade Journal* reported, to "erect a factory in that city and commence the manufacture of trucks and automobiles." There is no evidence that either of these plans came to fruition. A.F. Pagel, Colonel W.P. Cockey and C.O. Furbush were the men behind the Cycloid venture. *Automobile Topics* reported that "a special transmission which will not strip is said to be the special feature of the new machines." Perhaps it didn't "strip" but probably it didn't work well either.

1920 Cyclomobile, 2-pass. runabout, WLB

CYCLOMOBILE — Toledo, Ohio — (1920) — Charles D. Hamel referred to his vehicle as a "light-weight car," but the marque name he chose for it left little doubt as to what it was — a cyclecar born a half-decade after the death of the cyclecar industry. Friction transmission, chain drive and air-cooled Spacke vee engine had been the specification for dozens of the cyclecars produced in 1914, and was again for the Cyclomobile produced in 1920. The dummy radiator up front was the gasoline tank. Initially, Hamel stated that his Cyclomobile Manufacturing Company of Toledo would produce a one-passenger vehicle only, although he soon decided this would severely limit his market. Consequently, he merely widened the 36-inch tread of his vehicle into 44 inches for two-passenger and light-delivery models. A longer wheelbase version with a rear deck was known as the Manexall. That designation lengthened out to Manufacturers' & Exporters' Alliance, Inc., a New York City concern which was to handle distribution of the Cyclomobile. Obviously, overseas sales were envisioned. Few sales from either side of the Atlantic resulted before both companies went under, however. A certain taint attaches itself here. Early in 1921 the Wizard Automobile Company of Charlotte, North Carolina was chastised for flagrantly offending truth by the national vigilance committee of the Associated Advertising Clubs of the World. Charles D. Hamel was noted as the sales manager for Wizard, and the Manufacturers' & Exporters' Alliance was indicated as the company which reportedly had ordered several trainloads of Wizard cars. No more Wizards had been produced than Cyclomobiles.

1920 CYCLOMOBILE
Cyclomobile — 2-cyl., 13 hp, 90" wb

	FP	5	4	3	2	1
Roadster-1P	395	2700	3600	5300	8800	19,000
Roadster-2P	425	2800	3700	5500	9000	19,500
Light Delivery	425	2400	3400	4800	8000	17,000
Manexall — 2-cyl., 23 hp, 102" wb						
Roadster-2P	475	2800	3700	5500	9000	19,500

CYCLONE — Greenville, South Carolina — (1921-1922) — Cyclone Motors Corporation of Greenville was organized late in 1920 for the manufacture of trucks principally. No automobile produced by the company was marketed under the Cyclone name, but the firm did build a taxi which it called the W.B.C. (for Well Built Cab). A fleet of these cars was sold to the Black and White Cab Company of New York City, whose president declared to Cyclone that "you have solved our problem." Cyclone had problems of its own, however, and in the fall of 1922 its president, C.G. Eidson, announced receivership. Liabilities were set at $200,000; assets at $500,000. The company had been incorporated with a million-dollar capitalization.

CYCLOP — Indianapolis, Indiana — (1910) — In association with his brothers, L. Porter Smith operated a garage at 2409 North Penn Street in Indianapolis. There, in 1910, a number of four-cylinder friction drive runabouts were built and sold under the name of Cyclop. A total production of fifty Cyclops has been estimated.

CYCLOPS — Indianapolis, Indiana — (1914) — During the summer of 1914, Joseph W. Ferrer, Charles A. Hargrave and James W. Smith announced that they were about to place their cyclecar with one headlight and an appropriate name on the market soon. Already dozens of cyclecar ventures had gone to the wall, and the new Cyclops Cyclecar Company quickly joined them. Probably no more than the prototype was built.

CYCO LECTRIC — The Cyco Lectric Car Company of New York City produced an electric light car from 1914-1916 which was marketed as the Volta-Car. Refer to Volta-Car.

CYGNET — The Cygnet Motor Company of Detroit, Michigan was organized early in 1912 for the manufacture of an $850 light car to be sold as runabout and delivery. "The promoters are not ready to disclose their whole hand yet," *The Automobile* commented in February, "but the new car, it is promised, will be quite a departure from the conventional design." Alas, we shall never know. This venture appears to have disappeared soon after.

CYRIACKS — The Cyriacks Motor Company was organized in Eaton, Ohio during the fall of 1910 for the purpose of manufacturing motor cars and accessories. F.R. Cyriacks, F.R. Christman and F.C.H. Kurzrock were the principals involved. Manufacture of an automobile is doubted.

1922 D.A.C., 5-pass. touring, WLB

D.A.C. — Detroit & Wayne, Michigan — (1922-1923) — Everything about the new venture seemed to assure its success. The Detroit Air Cooled Car Company was established in the spring of 1922 by W.J. Doughty, formerly of Hupp, and more recently the Franklin distributor for Detroit. Doughty surrounded himself with men prominent in industrial circles, among them engineer G.R. Tremolada, C.H. Bennett who was president of the Daisy Air Rifle Company, and August Gieseler, the superintendent of the National Tool Company. D.A.C.'s sales manager would be Frank Sanders of Chicago, formerly well known as a Franklin distributor. Its sheet aluminum coachwork would be seen to by veteran body builder John McArthur at Detroit. Also involved in the enterprise were officials of the Mansfield Steel Corporation and the King Trailer Company. The company was capitalized at a healthy $1.2 million, and plans called for the production of 10,000 D.A.C. motorcars the first year. In February of 1922 a touring car prototype was displayed at the Detroit Automobile Show, and in December a sedan was exhibited in New York and later in Chicago. Two patented fea-

1923 D.A.C., 5-pass. phaeton, WLB

tures of the D.A.C. powerplant were regarded by the press as "interesting developments in air-cooled engine design." The first was the concentrated application of air by specially devised and attached air-conducting chutes which brought the in-rushing fan-impelled air to the radiating surfaces. The second was the staggered vee arrangement of the six cylinders — or

twin three, as the company preferred — which was said to facilitate cooling by permitting air to be directed to each cylinder in equal volume and at the same temperature. But something went awry somewhere, either in the car's design or the company's organization. It was not until October of 1922 that the D.A.C. found a home, a small factory on Cass Avenue in Detroit where production was expected to begin not later than January 1st of 1923, although more than likely it never did. By April of 1923 the company had moved into a new factory in Wayne, the woefully inadequate Cass Avenue facility being sold to the Detroit distributor of Stephens cars. The D.A.C. did proceed into production in Wayne, but the assembly line was almost immediately shut down when the company quickly went under.

1922-1923 D.A.C.
Twin-Three — 6-cyl., 32 hp, 115" wb

	FP	5	4	3	2	1
Touring-5P	1250	—	—	—	—	—
Coupe-4P	1700	—	—	—	—	—
Sedan-5P	1750	—	—	—	—	—

1922 Dagmar, sport sedan, HAC

DAGMAR — Hagerstown, Maryland — (1922-1926) — The Dagmar was introduced in the summer of 1922 as a sporting companion car to the Crawford. It carried the same six-cylinder 70 hp Continental engine on the same 138-inch-wheelbase chassis, but it looked very little like a Crawford. Indeed, its straight-line military fenders and its use of brass trim all over set it apart from most round-fendered, nickel-trimmed American cars on the road. Mathias P. Moller, who owned the Crawford Automobile Company and whose daughter was named Dagmar, decided to cast his fortunes entirely with his new car in 1923. By early 1924, following his purchase of a new factory in Hagerstown, he had dropped the Crawford and renamed his firm the M.P. Moller Motor Car Company. Various open and closed models had been added by now to the original Dagmar sport victoria, and were joined in 1925 by a smaller version on a 120-inch wheelbase chassis, sporting nickel trim. This car was initially called "Petite," but soon earned the nickname Baby Dagmar. There were other changes too, some which M.P. Moller may have preferred not to make. Those straight-line military fenders were thought chic by some, freakish by others. Rounded fenders were offered optionally early on, and became standard by 1924. The first cars carried an emblem bearing the royal Danish coat of

1923 D.A.C., 5-pass. sedan, WLB

1923 Dagmar, model 6-70, coupe, WLB

arms, which was eliminated in 1924 when the Danish embassy objected — and a pipe organ (the other product M.P. Moller was manufacturing in Hagerstown) became the emblem motif. The original Dagmar hexagonal hubcaps were removed when Packard put up a fuss. Packard hadn't liked Dagmar's copying of its radiator either, but didn't press that matter legally, only the Packard hubcaps being a registered trademark. A total of 135 Dagmars were built in 1923, most probably the marque's peak year. In 1924 a Dagmar was presented to the Philadelphia lass who won the Miss America contest; it was the sport victoria which, with its ornately bowed folding top, was the perfect automobile for her year of glory. Though an assembled car of standard components, the Dagmar was virtually custom built. ''An Automobile Classic,'' the brochures said. Production ceased after 1926. Most likely it wouldn't have survived that long save for the fact that in 1924 the company received a very lucrative contract to build taxicabs. Moller had long been known as the pipe-organ king; he made a new empire in the cars-for-hire field, producing one taxi named for himself and a plethora of others like Blue Light, Aristocrat, Paramount, Super Paramount, Astor, Five-Boro, and Twentieth Century. This diversification allowed him the pleasure of continuing the Dagmar despite its unprofitability. The last Dagmar built was a huge seven-passenger sedan for Moller himself to take to Europe in 1927 for a visit to his native Denmark. The Moller company continued manufacturing taxicabs and custom bodies for trucks into the mid-Thirties.

1923 Dagmar, model 6-70, sport victoria, WLB

1922 DAGMAR
Model 6-70 — 6-cyl., 70 hp, 138'' wb

	FP	5	4	3	2	1
Sport Victoria-4P	3500	7500	15,000	25,000	35,000	50,000

1925 Dagmar, model 6-60, sport victoria, JAC

1923-1924 DAMGAR
Model 6-70 — 6-cyl., 70 hp, 138'' wb

Sport Victoria-4P	3500	7500	15,000	25,000	35,000	50,000
Brougham	—	5200	6800	11,300	23,000	36,000
Sedan-7P	4500	4900	6300	10,300	21,000	34,000
Roadster-2/3P	—	7500	15,000	25,000	35,000	50,000
Coupe	—	4400	5600	9200	17,300	31,000

1925 Dagmar, model 6-80, roadster, HAC

396

1926 Dagmar, model 6-60, roadster, KM

1925-1926 DAGMAR
Model 6-60 — 6-cyl., 60 hp, 120'' wb

	FP	5	4	3	2	1
Sport Victoria-4P	1775	7500	15,000	25,000	35,000	50,000
Sedan-5P	—	4400	5600	9200	17,300	31,000
Model 6-80 — 6-cyl., 80 hp, 138'' wb						
Sport-Victoria-4P	3500	7800	15,500	25,700	36,000	51,000
Sedan-5P	4500	5200	6800	11,300	23,000	36,000

DAIMLER — The Daimler Manufacturing Company which had its headquarters in Long Island City, New York manufactured motors, launches and a few commercial vehicles beginning before the turn of the century. This German company's automobiles were imported into this country as well, but it was not until 1905 that a car was manufactured here. Refer to American Mercedes.

DAISY — Flint, Michigan — (1902-1903) — Frank McPhillips of Flint allied himself with some former executives of the Ash-Harper Company of Lansing, and together they established the Daisy Automobile Company during the summer of 1902. ''It is the intention of the company to build a standard machine in all respects and not to waste time or money in experimental work,'' *The Motor Age* reported in August,'' . . . contracts have been let for all the material necessary to complete the first twenty-five machines and as soon as the first lot are under headway material sufficient for 100 machines will be ordered.'' For whatever reason, the Daisy venture seems never to have made much headway, and did not survive 1903.

1914 Daisy, cyclecar, JHV

DAISY — Los Angeles, California — (1914) — Given the appeal of the name, as well as its connotation, it's surprising that more cyclecar ventures were not named Daisy as this West Coast venture was. The name and the car were the idea of Eugene W. Jump and Harry H. Fouch, who incorporated the Daisy Cyclecar Company, with a $100,000 capital stock, for manufacture. The prototype of their Daisy was first shown in the Los Angeles area in January 1914. Powered by a 10 hp air-cooled four-cylinder engine built by the Pacific Mechanical Company, the Daisy featured friction transmission, double chain drive and full elliptic springs in a 95-inch wheelbase chassis. The little two-passenger roadster weighed but 600 pounds and was planned to be marketed in the $400 price range. Plans went awry, however, and production never followed. Within months Eugene Jump had left to superintend the Los Angeles factory producing the Eaglet. Harry H. Fouch's further adventures are not known. His brother James R. Fouch was also involved in automobile-building in Los Angeles and Harry may have joined him.

1910 Dakota, touring, JB

DAKOTA — Wimbledon, North Dakota — (1910) — The Dakota was a De Tamble with high wheels that was marketed by Alexander and John More, erstwhile schoolteachers from Fountain City, Wisconsin who had established a hardware business in Wimbledon in the mid-1890's, added farm implements soon after, then automobiles in 1904. The More brothers, both of whom would serve as mayor of Wimbledon, were dealers for National, White, Westcott, Continental, Richmond, Lambert and Demot. Whether they approached the De Tamble Motor Company of Anderson, Indiana with the Dakota idea, or vice versa, is not known. In any case, in 1909 a trainload of the Indiana cars was on its way to North Dakota where they were fitted with 36-inch solid rubber tires (replacing the De Tamble's 30-inch pneumatics) and given the name Dakota. "There are many people that want an automobile but do not want to be bothered with the constant troubles occasioned by the use of pneumatic tires," the Mores advertised. "...By the use of high wheels the car has high clearance...roads with high centers are no hindrance to the Dakota." The car was introduced at the first automobile show in the state of North Dakota — at Jack's Auditorium in Grand Forks in February 1910. At $675, the Dakota was $25 more expensive than the De Tamble. The More brothers sold the car in their Wimbledon showroom as well as at More branches in Fargo, Jamestown, Portal and elsewhere. Indeed, the brothers indicated their Dakota's territory as both North and South Dakota in addition to Montana. North Dakota vehicle records of the period include at least seven Dakotas, which doubtless was many fewer than the Mores sold since not everyone in the state licensed their cars at the time.

DALEY — In Barre, Vermont at the turn of the century, W.A. Lane and F.A. Daley collaborated on the building of a number of steam cars. Refer to Lane & Daley.

1895 Daley Motor Carriage, auto-buggy, NAHC

DALEY — Charles City, Iowa — (1895-1898) — M.H. Daley of Charles City manufactured disc and lever harrows for the farm and was an ardent proponent of motorized travel for the road. He built his first car in 1895, powered initially by a rotary gasoline engine of his own design, which proved ineffective, so he designed a two-cylinder gasoline engine to replace it. The advantage of two cylinders over a single, M.H. Daley averred, was that "one explodes while the other is compressing, giving an explosion every revolution, whether little or much power is used." He also devised an interesting front suspension allowing the forward wheels to rise

or fall as much as twelve inches in going over uneven ground, thus relieving the body of excessive strain. Daley believed his to be the lightest four-wheeled vehicle in the world and, at only 195 pounds, it perhaps was. Gasoline consumption was an extraordinary 100 miles to the gallon. In December Daley advised the press that he was organizing a company for manufacture, that his harrow factory could easily be revised for automobile building, and that he expected to be able to sell his vehicles for $500. He probably never sold many, but in 1898 he wrote *The Horseless Age* to let them know he was "still at it." Perhaps he tinkered out a few more vehicles thereafter, but his livelihood remained farm equipment.

DALTON — Flint, Michigan — (1911-1912) — In 1911, Hubert K. Dalton, the factory manager for the Whiting Motor Car Company, decided to labor no more building a car named for someone else and sallied forth to produce one named for himself. This venture had the complete support of his old boss, James H. Whiting, who happened to be Dalton's father-in-law. The August 5th, 1911 issue of *The Flint Journal* announced the imminent formation of the Dalton Motor Car Company and the forthcoming new Dalton automobile. The Dalton was a Whiting lookalike. It had a four-cylinder 175-cubic-inch 20 hp L-head engine, and a 106-inch wheelbase and was to be offered as a runabout only for $900. Rather quickly, Dalton learned that superintending a factory was one thing, starting an automobile company was another. Only three Daltons were built before Hubert K. Dalton gave up on the idea. In 1913 he moved to New York where he established Dalton Manufacturing Company, and he did very well there producing marine hardware for Allied ships during World War I.

DANIELS — The Daniels Motor Car Company has been indicated on various car rosters as producing an automobile in East St. Louis, Missouri in 1912. St. Louis city directories reveal a multitude of automobile businesses in the area during this period, but Daniels was not among them.

1916 Daniels, model A, 5-pass. victoria, WLB

DANIELS — Reading, Pennsylvania — (1916-1924) — The Daniels Motor Car Company of Reading had two very good things going for it. One was George E. Daniels, former president of Oakland and vice-president of General Motors, who knew how to manage a business. The other was Neff E. Parish, whose Parish Pressed Steel Company had built frames for numerous manufacturers, including Pierce-Arrow, and who knew metallurgy. The Daniels was advertised as "The Distinguished Car to the Discriminating," and the discriminating could have it exactly as desired, each car tailored to individual preference. Production began late in 1915 at a healthy 300 cars a year. Initially using Herschell-Spillman 331-cubic-inch V-8 engines, Daniels developed its own eight-cylinder for the Model C introduced in 1919, and apparently a little too hastily because bugs in the unit resulted in less than 200 of this model being built. All problems were corrected with the 404-cubic-inch 90 hp Model D which arrived before the first roar of the Twenties, and clear sailing appeared ahead. The Daniels was a formidable machine, weighing about three tons, with radiator shell and core of one-piece cast pewter, though the body was of lighter aluminum. Coachwork by Fleetwood was a distinguishing feature of the marque. Prices had risen to the luxury range by now, which probably would not have represented a problem except that George Daniels had decided to expand production to

1918 Daniels, model A, sedan, JAC

1500 vehicles annually. To do so, he reorganized as the Daniels Motor Company, issuing 10,000 shares of preferred stock at $95 with an 8.42 percent yield. This was, unfortunately, far too generous a dividend for a company the size of Daniels to support. A personality clash between George Daniels and Neff Parish was the company's coup-de-grace. When the latter withdrew his financial support, the marque was doomed. With massive layoffs in the workforce, office clerks were commandeered into the factory to complete cars on the assembly line. In January 1924 the Daniels company was sold to Levene Motors, a Philadelphia concern specializing in the sale of parts and service for moribund cars. Levene announced that it planned to continue production of the Daniels, but this was only to complete those cars for which parts remained on hand. There were only a few of those, and reportedly they were put together miserably and expensively ($10,000 each). Among the Daniels cars which remain extant are three on display at the Boyertown (Pennsylvania) Museum of Historic Vehicles.

1918 Daniels, model A, five passenger brougham, HAC

1916-1918 DANIELS
Model A — 8-cyl., 34 hp, 127" wb

	FP	5	4	3	2	1
Touring	2350	7600	12,500	19,400	42,400	55,000
Landaulet	3500	6800	10,300	16,000	35,500	48,000
Limousine	3400	6700	9900	15,500	34,800	47,000
Roadster	2350	7800	13,300	20,300	44,000	60,000
Sedan	3250	5800	8000	12,500	28,000	40,000

1919 DANIELS
Model C — 8-cyl., 45 hp, 127" wb

Touring	3750	7800	13,200	20,200	43,800	59,000
Roadster	3750	7900	13,700	20,700	44,500	62,000

1920 Daniels, model D, Sportster, dual windshield touring, WLB

1920 Daniels, model D, 7-pass. victoria, WLB

1920 DANIELS
Model D — 8-cyl., 90 hp, 132-1/4" wb

Touring-4P/6P/7P	4500	7900	13,700	20,700	44,500	62,000
Submarine Roadster-3P	4500	9400	18,800	26,500	53,800	75,000
Sedan-5P	6000	6000	8500	13,000	30,000	42,000
Brougham-5P	6000	6300	9000	14,000	32,000	44,000
Suburban-7P	6250	6400	9300	14,500	33,000	45,000
Limousine-7P	6250	6500	9500	15,000	34,000	46,000

1921 Daniels, model D, touring, HAC

1922 Daniels, model D, submarine speedster, HAC

1921 DANIELS
Model D — 8-cyl., 90 hp, 132-1/4" wb

Submarine Roadster-3P	5350	9400	18,800	26,500	53,800	75,000
Coupe-3P	6250	6800	10,300	16,000	35,500	48,000
Touring-4P	5689	7900	13,700	20,700	44,500	62,000
Submarine Speedster-2P	5350	9700	19,300	27,800	56,300	77,000
Touring-6P	5350	8200	14,500	21,500	45,800	65,000
Collapsible Winter Roadster	6500	7800	13,300	20,300	44,000	60,000
Sedan-4P	6950	6400	9300	14,500	33,000	45,000

1922 Daniels, 4-pass. sedan, JAC

1922 DANIELS
Model D — 8-cyl., 90 hp, 132-1/4" wb

Speedster-2P	5350	9800	19,500	28,500	57,500	78,000
Roadster-3P	5350	9400	18,800	26,500	53,800	75,000
Roadster-4P	5350	9500	19,000	27,000	55,000	76,000
Touring-7P	5350	8200	14,500	21,500	45,800	65,000
Coupe-4P	6250	6800	10,300	16,000	35,500	48,000
Cabriolet-4P	6500	7800	13,000	20,000	43,500	58,000
Sedan-4P	7000	5800	8000	12,500	28,000	40,000
Suburban-7P	7025	6000	8500	13,000	30,000	42,000
Brougham-5P	7250	6400	9300	14,500	33,000	45,000

1923 Daniels, model D, landau brougham, HAC

1923 DANIELS
Model D — 8-cyl., 90 hp, 132" & 138" wb

	FP	5	4	3	2	1
Touring-7P	4350	8200	14,500	21,500	45,800	65,000
Sport-4P	4350	8400	15,500	22,500	47,300	67,000
Roadster-2P	4350	9500	19,000	27,000	55,000	76,000
Coupe-4/5P	5350	6800	10,300	16,000	35,500	48,000
Sedan-4P	6000	5800	8000	12,500	28,000	40,000
Sedan-6/7P	6000	5900	8300	12,800	29,000	41,000
Town Limousine-7P	6900	6400	9300	14,500	33,000	45,000
Brougham-6/7P	7250	6700	9900	15,500	34,800	47,000

1924 DANIELS
Model D — 8-cyl., 90 hp, 132 & 138" wb

	FP	5	4	3	2	1
Touring Sedan-4P	6800	5900	8300	12,800	29,000	41,000
Touring-4P	5000	8200	14,500	21,500	45,800	65,000
Touring-7P	5150	8000	14,000	21,000	45,000	64,000
Sedan-7P	6800	5800	8000	12,500	28,000	40,000
Town Brougham-7P	6750	6300	9000	14,000	32,000	44,000
Suburban Limousine-7P	6800	6700	9900	15,500	34,800	47,000
Landau Brougham-7P	6950	6800	10,300	16,000	35,500	48,000

DANIELSON — Frank Danielson of Chicago made two attempts to enter the automobile manufacturing business. The first was in 1902 with his incorporation of the Danielson Machinery Company with a capital stock of $25,000; his second was in 1914 with his $50,000 incorporation of the Danielson Engine Works. In neither case does an automobile appear to have been built.

DANN-DODGE — Dann, Dodge & Company was organized in Chicago during the summer of 1911 by E.G. Dann, Henry H. Dodge and Donald D. Dodge. Capital stock was $5000, and the partners' plan was to manufacture and deal in motorcars and accessories. Manufacture of an automobile is doubted.

1911 Dan Patch, model 51, torpedo, HAC

DAN PATCH — Minneapolis, Minnesota — (1910-1911) — "A car with a horsey sounding name is to be placed on the market shortly by the M.W. Savage Factories Company," *The Horseless Age* noted brightly in April of 1910. The reason for the horsey sounding name was that the Savage family, prominent manufacturers of cattle feed in Minneapolis, also owned and promoted the famous harness racer named Dan Patch. In addition to an automobile, the Savages put the Dan Patch name on gasoline engines and such widely diverse products as stoves, stopwatches, sewing machines and cream separators. Obviously the clever and lucrative merchandising of a famous name is not a contemporary phenomenon that began with *Star Wars*. The Savages got into the automobile business the easy way, by purchasing the output of an unnamed Indiana automobile factory (which probably was W.H. McIntyre in Auburn) and transporting it to Minneapolis for distribution to the Minnesota trade. Fifteen hundred machines in eighteen different models were promised for 1911, but neither production output nor range of models approached those figures. Instead of a line which was to include commercial vehicles, cheap runabouts, highwheelers and light tourers, the Dan Patch name appeared only on a quartet of medium-priced fours. Apparently some of the cars were marketed under the Savage name as well, and they may have been sold into early 1912.

1910-1911 DAN PATCH
Thirty-Five — 4-cyl., 35 hp, 110" wb

	FP	5	4	3	2	1
Model 71 Roadster	1250	3900	4800	7700	14,300	27,000
Model 70 Touring	1350	3500	4500	7000	13,000	25,000

Forty — 4-cyl., 40 hp, 126" wb

	FP	5	4	3	2	1
Model 50 Touring-5P	1650	4000	5000	8000	15,000	28,000
Model 51 Torpedo-4P	1850	4200	5200	8400	15,700	29,000

DARBY — The Darby Motor Car Company was incorporated in Westfield, New Jersey during the summer of 1912 by Harry C. Darby, Aaron B. Darby and Levy Douglass. The manufacture and sale of motorcars, bicycles and auto machinery was the intention; capital stock was $25,000. Manufacture of an automobile is doubted.

1910 Darby, model 20, roadster, WLB

DARBY — St. Louis, Missouri — (1909-1910) — C.T. Darby of St. Louis designed the car, and two local automobile enthusiasts named Harvey D. Dunham and Allen Whittemore put up the money for its manufacture. The first two pilot models produced for the Darby Motor Car Company were on display at the Coliseum exhibition in St. Louis from February 15th to the 20th of 1909. Production began almost immediately thereafter, and in August was reported to be increased. "The Simplest Automobile on Earth" was perhaps overdoing it for the company slogan, but the Darby was indeed an ingenuous machine. Its engine was a two-stroke, its transmission a friction drive. It was a stylish little vehicle aimed "to sell at a price commensurate with the rapid advance of the low-priced automobile." Another low-priced automobile called the Model T Ford rapidly undersold it, however, Darby was out of business, and the Messrs. Dunham and Whittemore took their automobile enthusiasm to other established marques.

1909-1910 DARBY
Model 20 — 2-cyl., 16 hp, 100" wb

	FP	5	4	3	2	1
Roadster-3P	750	2500	3500	5000	8500	18,000
Surrey-4P	800	2700	3600	5300	8800	19,000

DARLING — In 1905 Edward S. Darling of Salt Lake City built a front-wheel-drive car which he hoped to manufacture. Refer to Autocrat.

In 1913 the Darling Automobile Manufacturing Company was organized in Britton, Oklahoma for the manufacture of automobiles and internal combustion engines. Capital stock was $25,000. Behind this venture were C.P. Stealey, A.W. Hedge, H.O. Crum, G.E. Crawford, S.L. Shintaffer, D.L. Sellers, W.C. Settle and H.S. Emmerson. Manufacture of an automobile is doubted.

DARLING STEAM — Franklin, Massachusetts — (1899) — During the summer of 1899 F.A. Darling of Franklin completed work on a steam carriage that weighed 1000 pounds and was fitted with pneumatic tires. The upright boiler was thirteen inches high, thirty inches in diameter, and contained twenty-six tubes and a water firebox. Some 250 pounds of steam could be generated. The water tank in back held ten gallons of water. Coke was used for fuel, with 100 pounds of it being carried. A storage battery provided illumination, a red light at the rear, a green one in front of the steam gauge. When the vehicle was completed, F.A. Darling said he had no plans to build another.

1902 Darling, model I, 4-pass. rig, WLB

DARLING — Mansfield & Shelby, Ohio — (1901-1902) — In November of 1900 *Motor Age* reported that R.R. Darling had closed a deal with the Beardsley & Hubbs Manufacturing Company whereby the latter would build the Darling car in its Mansfield factory. A flurry of varied gasoline cars followed in 1901, but only for a short while. By the end of the year Volmer Beardsley and Charles Hubbs had moved to Shelby, and R.R. Darling had moved on to Cleveland to form a new company for the building of another car which he said he had "perfected." Darling's new company never got off the ground in Cleveland. Meanwhile in Shelby, Beardsley & Hubbs continued the Darling tradename into 1902, then reorganized as the Shelby Motor Car Company to build another car called the Shelby.

1901 DARLING
Two-Cylinder — 10/12 hp

	FP	5	4	3	2	1
Model 1 Stanhope	850	2700	3600	5300	8800	19,000
Model 2 Stanhope with Top	950	2800	3700	5500	9000	19,500
Style 3 Combination Sthp.	1000	2900	3700	5600	9100	20,000
Style 4 Combination Sthp.	1000	2900	3700	5600	9100	20,000
Model 5 Physicians' Car	1200	3000	3900	5800	9300	20,500
Style 6 Combination Brake	1100	3000	3900	5800	9300	20,500
Style 7 Combination Brake	1200	3000	3900	5800	9300	20,500

1902 DARLING
Two-Cylinder — 10/12 hp

	FP	5	4	3	2	1
Model 1 Stanhope	850	2700	3600	5300	8800	19,000
Model 1 2/4 Passenger Rig	1000	2800	3700	5500	9000	19,500
Style 7 Combination Brake	1200	2900	3700	5600	9100	20,000
Style 6 Combination Brake	1100	2900	3700	5600	9100	20,000

1917 Darling, Six, touring, WLB

DARLING — Dayton, Ohio — (1917) — Late in 1916 it was announced that the Darling Motors Company had been organized by a group of men from the National Cash Register Company who were automobile enthusiasts. Among them were George W. Dillman, M.M. Dugan and J.D. Frock. The car about which they had enthusiasm was a six-cylinder tourer with Continental engine and 130-inch wheelbase that was designed by James Guthrie. Enthusiasm quickly waned. Soon after production of the $1600 Darling was begun in the spring of 1917 in the old Wright-Martin airplane plant in Dayton, it was summarily concluded.

1917 DARLING

Darling Six — 130" wb						
	1600	4000	5000	8000	15,000	28,000

1903 Darrow, runabout, NAHC

DARROW — Owego, New York — (1903) — Like Ward Decker, Stuart Darrow produced telephone switching devices in Owego and decided to build an automobile too. Unlike Decker who built at least several cars, Darrow's total production seems to have been but one. It was a small two-seater runabout with a 3-1/2 hp Thomas engine, chain drive and wood wheels. Although one reference indicates the forthcoming formation of the Darrow Motor Vehicle Company, it is doubtful that Stuart Darrow ever progressed that far. His plans for marketing the car appear to have ended soon after he decided on $550 for its price tag.

DART — Early in 1909 the Dart Engineering Company was organized in New York City for the manufacture of automobiles and motorcycles. Capital stock was $10,000; the incorporators were J.R. Del Rio of Manhattan, G.C. Autenrieth of Westchester County and P.S. Tice of Brooklyn. Manufacture of an automobile is doubted. Although indicated on some car rosters as surviving through 1911, the Dart Engineering Company does not appear in any New York City directories of the period.

Dart was the name selected by James V. Martin of Garden City, New York for a small coupe he hoped to sell both at home and abroad during the late Twenties. Refer to Martin.

DART — Anderson, Indiana — (1910) — The Dart Manufacturing Company of Anderson occupied itself principally in the production of gasoline engines. A catalog from 1910 indicates that the company made available during that year at least a chassis with its two-cylinder engine and a planetary transmission installed upon which the body of any carriagemaker could be mounted. One such Dart motor buggy is known to remain extant. There appears to be no relationship, incidentally, between this firm and the famous Dart truck-producing company which had begun manufacture in Anderson, but which had moved to Waterloo, Iowa by this time. That company's sole passenger car effort was the Dartmobile.

1914 Dart, 2-pass. roadster, WLB

DART — Jamestown, New York — (1914) — The Dart cyclecar had a two-cylinder air-cooled engine, spur gear transmission and chain drive to the left rear wheel only. Disc wheels were standard equipment because, as promotion, said, they are unbreakable, "will always run true and have a large radiating surface to prevent overheating of tires." If wire wheels were desired, they were a $15 extra. The officers of the company were William Shillaber (president), S.A. Van Derveer (secretary and treasurer), W.J. Lausterer (superintendent), H.A. Bubb (sales manager) and M.L. Badhorn (purchasing agent). These were the same men who guided the fortunes of the Automatic Registering Machine Corporation, the largest manufacturer of voting machines in the world. "The same workmen that have been building the voting machines are working on the construction of the cyclecar," the press reported in late summer of 1914. Deliveries of the Dart cyclecar began in September and ended soon after, when the men of Automatic Registering Machine returned wholeheartedly to the business they knew best.

1914 DART
Cyclecar — 2-cyl., 15 hp, 102" wb

	FP	5	4	3	2	1
Roadster-2P	300	—	—	—	—	—

DARTMOBILE — Waterloo, Iowa — (1922) — The Dartmobile was the sole passenger car effort of the Dart Truck and Tractor Corporation. The firm had begun in 1890 as a bicycle manufacturer which had branched into automobile engines at the turn of the century, and commercial vehicle manufacture in 1903. Dart took especial pride in its image of durability, emphasizing that its trucks "are not a delivery car built on a pleasure car basis, but are trucks built of truck design and materials." Whether the Dartmobile was built on one of the company's smaller truck chassis is not known, but the car was powered by a four-cylinder L-head engine. Apparently second thoughts regarding entry into passenger car ranks were rather quick in arriving, because the Dartmobile never proceeded beyond the prototype stage.

DARWIN — The Darwin Motor Car Company was organized in Eau Claire, Wisconsin during the fall of 1913 for the purpose of automobile manufacture. O.S. Darwin, M.D. Garrison and W.C. Tufts backed this $10,000 venture. Manufacture of a Darwin car is doubted.

DASHIELL — The Dashiell Motor Company was organized in Chicago during the summer of 1914 with a capital stock of $25,000 for the manufacture of automobiles. C.R. Dashiell, Emil C. Wetten and Charles H. Pegler were behind this venture. Manufacture of an automobile is doubted.

DAVENPORT — Although the Davenport Cycle Works of Davenport, Iowa reported itself in the automobile manufacturing business in 1902, if any cars were produced at all, they were few. The company's factory was closed that October when the Davenport landlord objected to not being paid his rent.

DAVENPORT STEAM — Minneapolis, Minnesota — (1902-1903) — Although it is conceivable that lesser-passengered vehicles may have been built by the Davenport Manufacturing Company in Minneapolis, apparently it was Birge W. Davenport's idea to corner the bus market. A twelve-passenger steam stage coach was the Davenport company's first, followed by vehicles for up to twenty-six passengers. In 1903 the firm was reported to be building two steam buses of twenty-passenger capacity each for Leopold E. Wagner of Binghamton (New York) to be operated from downtown to a park several miles outside the city. This was probably Davenport's last order because the company disappeared soon after.

DAVIDSON — Mayville, North Dakota — (1900) — At the turn of the century, in Mayville, Will T. Davidson built an automobile. Except that its engine had two cylinders delivering three horsepower, details of the vehicle are not known.

DA VINCI — The Da Vinci was the last automotive idea of James Scripps-Booth and was built in 1925 as a prototype, with a Pup cyclecar variation following in 1930. Refer to Scripps-Booth.

DAVIS — The A.R. Davis Motor Car Company was organized during the summer of 1911 in Cleveland, Ohio with a capital stock of $10,000 to "manufacture motorcars and motorcar accessories and parts and to carry on a garage business." Incorporators were Charles A. Rolfe, F.H. Grace, George V. Gunderman, C.A. Lemmon and J.K. Kirkpatrick. Manufacture of a car is doubted.

The Davis Car Company of Seattle, Washington produced an automobile from 1921-1922 which was marketed under the tradename of Totem. Refer to Totem.

In January 1900, D.L. Davis, who was described as the superintendent of the Salem (Ohio) electric railroad, was reported to be building an automobile. Further details are lacking.

The Davis Manufacturing Company of Milwaukee, Wisconsin produced the Vixen from 1914-1916. Refer to Vixen.

DAVIS — Waterloo, Iowa — (1895) — Although its entry in the Chicago Times-Herald Contest of 1895 was announced, the Davis Gasoline Engine Company of Waterloo didn't make it to the starting line. The vehicle was subsequently completed, but the Davis firm remained thereafter in the gasoline business exclusively.

DAVIS — Portland, Maine — (1901) — In 1901 G.H. Davis of Portland built what was described in *The Motor Age* as a "successful acetylene vehicle." Two years of study and experiment had preceded completion of the car, and Davis was assisted by W.M. Bardwell of New York in this endeavor. Said *The Motor Age:* "The machine carries 100 pounds of carbide, which is fed, automatically, no doubt, into a water tank."

1911 Davis, model 50, touring, HAC

DAVIS — Richmond, Indiana — (1908-1929) — George W. Davis had long been a wagon builder in Richmond when, in 1908, he announced his entry into the automotive field as the George W. Davis Motor Car Company. His first cars were simply motorized buggies, though by 1911 he was building proper touring cars, their four-cylinder engines from Continental, as was the six which was introduced in 1914. A twelve was promised the following year, but was never marketed. Instead, Davis ran with sixes only from 1916 until 1927 when an eight arrived. Production was in the several thousands annually during the good years, of which Davis had quite a few. Export trade was brisk; a Davis took first place in a hill climb near Madrid, Spain in 1917, the same year the company expanded into another factory building in Richmond recently vacated by Westcott. An assembled car, but quite well built, the Davis was distinguished by the wide variety of body styles available and by the use of imaginative two-tone paint schemes long before these became generally popular. Sporting versions carried pleasant model designations like Legionare, Man o' War and Fleetaway, though Mountaineer to designate the Series 80 of 1923 was a curious choice for a car built in Indiana. As with many assembled car producers, the Davis fortunes wavered as the Twenties wore on. In February of 1928 the company was purchased by the Automotive Corporation of America. The last days of the Davis are confusing. Villor P. Williams was the man behind the Davis now, and he wanted the company principally to have a car available on which to put his Parkmobile, a device which slid an automobile sideways into a parallel parking place. The smaller Davis he renamed the New York Six; the larger Davis was to remain the Davis Eight. Both cars were to get the Parkmobile. Only a handful did, however. Though a few Davises may have been built in 1929, they were the 1928 cars for which stock remained on hand. By 1930 all activity in Richmond was concentrated on the production of power lawn mowers and related products. Meanwhile, Villor Williams had returned to Baltimore, Maryland where his Automotive Corporation of America was headquartered. As late as January of 1931 he was still announcing the forthcoming manufacture of the Parkmobile-equipped New York Six and Davis Eight. But he gave up soon after that.

1908-1910 DAVIS	FP	5	4	3	2	1
Motor Buggy	—	—	—	—	—	—
1911 DAVIS						
Thirty-Five — 4-cyl., 35 hp, 112" wb						
Fore-Door Tour. Torpedo-5P	1750	3100	4200	6300	10,500	22,000
Fifty — 4-cyl., 50 hp, 120" wb						
Fore-Door Tour. Torpedo-5P	2250	3200	4300	6500	11,000	23,000
1912 DAVIS						
Series 40 — 4-cyl., 40 hp, 112" wb						
Touring-5P	1850	3100	4200	6300	10,500	22,000
Torpedo Touring-4P	1850	3200	4300	6500	11,000	23,000
Roadster-2P	1850	3300	4400	6700	12,000	24,000

1913 Davis, model 40-F, 2-pass. roadster, WLB

1913 Davis, model 40-D, 5-pass. touring, WLB

1913 DAVIS	FP	5	4	3	2	1
Series 40 — 4-cyl., 40 hp, 118" wb						
Touring-5P	1850	3100	4200	6300	10,500	22,000
Roadster-2P	1850	3300	4400	6700	12,000	24,000
Series 50 — 4-cyl., 50 hp, 118" wb						
Touring-5P	2100	6500	13,200	22,000	30,800	41,500
1914 DAVIS						
Model 35-K — 4-cyl., 20 hp, 112" wb						
Roadster-2P	1335	3300	4400	6700	12,000	24,000
Model 50-A — 4-cyl., 32 hp, 118" wb						
Touring-5P	1985	3000	4000	6000	9500	21,000
Six-50 — 6-cyl., 50 hp, 129" wb						
Touring-5P	2150	7000	14,000	23,500	32,900	47,000

1912 Davis, model 40-C, torpedo, HAC

1915 Davis, model 38-B, roadster, HAC

1915 DAVIS	FP	5	4	3	2	1
Model 38 — 4-cyl., 23 hp, 112" wb						
Touring-5P	1235	3100	4200	6300	10,500	22,000
Roadster-2P	1235	3500	4500	7000	13,000	25,000

401

Six-50 — 6-cyl., 50 hp, 128" wb

	FP	5	4	3	2	1
Touring-5P	2150	6500	13,200	22,000	30,800	42,000
Touring-6P	2150	7000	14,000	22,500	31,200	43,000

1916 DAVIS
Model C-38 — 4-cyl., 23 hp, 112" wb

Touring-5P	1165	3100	4200	6300	10,500	22,000
Roadster-2P	1165	3500	4500	7000	13,000	25,000

Model 6-F — 6-cyl., 30 hp, 120" wb
Roadster-4P	1250	3700	4700	7300	13,700	26,000

Model 6-G — 6-cyl., 30 hp, 120" wb
Touring-5P	1250	3300	4400	6700	12,000	24,000

Model 6-E — 6-cyl., 50 hp, 124" wb
Touring-7P	1495	3200	4300	6500	11,000	23,000

1917 Davis, model 6-H, 7-pass. Springfield sedan, WLB

1917 DAVIS
Model 6-H — 6-cyl., 30 hp, 119" wb

Touring-7P	1195	3200	4300	6500	11,000	23,000
Club Roadster-5P	1195	3700	4700	7300	13,700	26,000
Sedan-7P	1795	2900	3700	5600	9100	20,000

Model 6-H — 6-cyl., 50 hp, 124" wb
Touring-7P	1495	3500	4500	7000	13,000	25,000

1918 Davis, model 6-H, club roadster, HAC

1918 DAVIS
Model 6-H — 6-cyl., 30 hp, 119" wb

Touring-7P	1485	3200	4300	6500	11,000	23,000
Club Roadster-5P	1485	3500	4500	7000	13,000	25,000
Sedan-7P	1850	2900	3700	5600	9100	20,000
Touring-4P	1485	3300	4400	6700	12,000	24,000

Model 6-K — 6-cyl., 30 hp, 125" wb
Touring-7P	1485	3300	4400	6700	12,000	24,000
Club Roadster-5P	1485	3700	4700	7300	13,700	26,000
Sedan-7P	1850	3000	3900	5800	9000	20,500
Touring-4P	1485	3500	4500	7000	13,000	25,000

1919 Davis, model 6-H, touring, HAC

1919 DAVIS
Model 6-H — 6-cyl., 30 hp, 120" wb

Touring-7P	1685	3500	4500	7000	13,000	25,000
Chummy Roadster	1685	3900	4800	7700	14,300	27,000
Touring-4P	1685	3700	4700	7300	13,700	26,000
Sedan-7P	2300	2900	3700	5600	9100	20,000
Coupe-4P	2300	3100	4200	6300	10,500	22,000

1920 Davis, model 53, 4-pass. Special Sport Car, touring, WLB

1920 DAVIS
Series 50 — 6-cyl., 38 hp, 120" wb

Touring-5P	1985	3500	4500	7000	13,000	25,000
Sport-4P	2025	3700	4700	7300	13,700	26,000
Special Sport-4P	2150	3900	4800	7700	14,300	27,000
Sedan-5P	2985	2900	3700	5600	9100	20,000
Coupe-4P	2985	3100	4200	6300	10,500	22,000

1921 Davis, series 50, touring, HAC

1921 DAVIS
Series 50 — 6-cyl., 58 hp, 120" wb

Touring-5P	2085	3500	4500	7000	13,000	25,000
Sport-4P	2125	3700	4700	7300	13,700	26,000
Roadster-3P	2125	4000	5000	8000	15,000	28,000
Special Roadster-3P	2250	4200	5200	8400	15,700	29,000
Coupe-4P	3085	3300	4400	6700	12,000	24,000
Sedan-5P	3085	3100	4200	6300	10,500	22,000
Special Sport-4P	2250	3200	4300	6500	11,000	23,000

1923 Davis, series 70, touring, WLB

1923 Davis, series 60, Man O' War, HAC

1923 DAVIS
Series 60 — 6-cyl., 64 hp, 120" wb

Man o' War-3P	1595	2500	3500	5000	8500	18,000
Fleetaway-4/5P	1695	2500	3500	5000	8500	18,000

Series 70 — 6-cyl., 52 hp, 115" wb
Touring-5P	1195	3500	4500	7000	13,000	25,000
Phaeton-5P	1295	3700	4700	7300	13,700	26,000
Sport-4P	1495	3800	4800	7700	14,300	27,000
Roadster-3P	1495	4200	5200	8400	15,700	29,000
Sedan-5P	1795	2900	3700	5600	9100	20,000
Coupe-4P	1795	3100	4200	6300	10,500	20,000
California-5P	1445	2900	3700	5600	9100	20,000

Series 80 — 6-cyl., 68 hp, 118" wb
Sedan-5P	2195	3000	4000	6000	9500	21,000
Touring-5P	1695	3700	4700	7300	13,700	26,000
Roadster-3P	1695	4300	5400	8700	16,500	30,000
Berline Sedan-5P	2295	3500	4500	7000	13,000	25,000
Utility Brougham	1895	3100	4200	6300	10,500	22,000

1923 Davis, touring, WLB

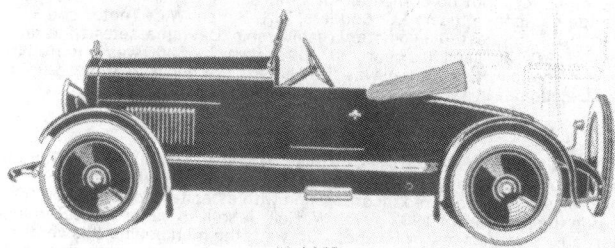

1923 Davis, series 60, Man O' War, HAC

1924 DAVIS
Series 70 — 6-cyl., 52 hp, 115" wb

		5	4	3	2	1
Phaeton-5P	1295	3900	4800	7700	14,300	27,000
Legionaire-4P	1495	3200	4300	6500	11,000	23,000
Man o' War-3P	1495	2900	3700	5600	9100	20,000
Utility Brougham-5P	1695	3100	4200	6300	10,500	22,000
Broudan-4P	1695	3200	4300	6500	11,000	23,000
Sedan-5P	1795	3000	4000	6000	9500	21,000
Berline-5P	1895	3100	4200	6300	10,500	22,000

1925 Davis, model 90, touring phaeton, WLB

1925 DAVIS
Model 90 — 6-cyl., 52 hp, 118" wb

Phaeton-5P	1395	3900	4800	7700	14,300	27,000
Man o' War-4P	1495	2900	3700	5600	9100	20,000
Legionaire-4P	1495	3200	4300	4300	6500	23,000
Utility Brougham-5P	1595	3300	4400	6700	12,000	24,000
Sedan-5P	1895	3000	4000	6000	9500	21,000
Berline Sedan-5P	1995	3100	4200	6300	10,500	22,000

Model 91 — 6-cyl., 68 hp, 116" wb

Phaeton-5P	1695	4000	5000	8000	15,000	28,000
Roadster-4P	1795	4200	5200	8400	15,700	29,000
Brougham-5P	1895	3300	4400	6700	12,000	24,000
Sedan-5P	2195	2900	3700	5600	9100	20,000
Berline-5P	2295	3100	4200	6300	10,500	22,000

1926 DAVIS
Model 93 — 6-cyl., 48 hp, 109" wb

Sedan-5P	1255	3000	4000	6000	9500	21,000

Model 92 — 6-cyl., 68 hp, 118" wb

Touring-5P	1395	3700	4700	7300	13,700	26,000
Man o' War-4P	1495	3000	4000	6000	9500	21,000
Sedan-5P	1595	3100	4200	6300	10,500	22,000
Imperial Sedan-5P	1795	3200	4300	6500	11,000	23,000
Berline Sedan-5P	1795	3500	4500	7000	13,000	25,000
Legionaire-5P	1495	3300	4400	6700	12,000	24,000

1927 DAVIS
Model 93 — 6-cyl., 48 hp, 109" wb

Sedan-5P	1255	3000	4000	6000	9500	21,000
Coupe-3P	1285	3300	4400	6700	12,000	24,000

Model 92 — 6-cyl., 68 hp, 118" wb

Touring-5P	1495	3900	4800	7700	14,300	27,000
Roadster-4P	1495	4300	5400	8700	16,500	30,000
Sedan-5P	1595	3100	4200	6300	10,500	22,000
Imperial Sedan-5P	1795	3200	4300	6500	11,000	23,000
Berline Sedan-5P	1795	3300	4400	6700	12,000	24,000
Legionaire-5P	1495	3000	4000	6000	9500	21,000

Model 98 — 8-cyl., 85 hp, 119" wb

	FP	5	4	3	2	1
Polo Roadster-4P	1795	4300	5400	8700	16,500	30,000
Princess Coupe-4P	1885	3300	4400	6700	12,000	24,000
Emperor Sedan-5P	1885	3100	4200	6300	10,500	22,000
Legionaire Touring-5P	1795	3500	4500	7000	13,000	25,000

1928 DAVIS
Model 99 — 8-cyl., 85 hp, 119" wb

Polo Roadster-4P	1885	4300	5400	8700	16,500	30,000
Princess Coupe-4P	1885	3300	4400	6700	12,000	24,000
Emperor Sedan-5P	1885	3100	4200	6300	10,500	22,000
Legionaire Touring-5P	1885	3500	4500	7000	13,000	25,000

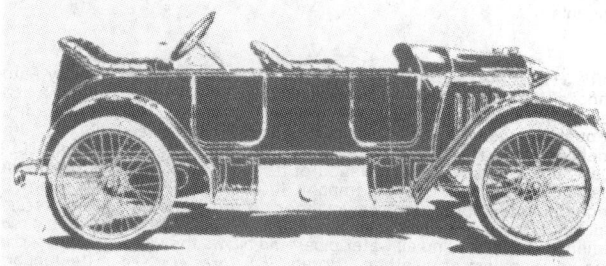

1914 Davis, 2-pass. tandem, WLB

DAVIS — Detroit, Michigan — (1914) — This tandem cyclecar from Detroit had a two-cylinder 10 hp air-cooled engine mounted in a 93-inch wheelbase chassis, and was slated to sell for $425. It was, its designer William Norris Davis frankly admitted, a line-for-line copy of the French Bedelia, the grand-daddy of all cyclecars which was still enjoying commercial success in Europe. The Davis, however, went nowhere. After trying in vain to secure capital to form the Davis Cyclecar Company for manufacture in Detroit, then attempting to do the same in Buffalo, Davis found a job out west and joined the staff of the Los Angeles Cyclecar Company. Whether he drove to the Pacific Coast in the prototype of his Davis is not known.

DAVIS STEAM — Detroit, Michigan — (1921) — Davis Steam Motors, Inc. was organized in Detroit in March 1921 with a capital stock of $100,000. The principals involved were Merrill Davis, E.M. Bliss, F.D. Sieberg and A.B. Eggert, and the purpose of the company was stated to be the marketing of a two-cylinder steam engine for use in both passenger cars and trucks. Later in August, Eggert announced that, in addition to the steam engine, a car also would be produced, and apparently a few were. The Davis seems to have been built as a touring car only, on a 120-inch wheelbase and with a $2300 price tag. The company ran out of steam rather quickly.

1904 Dawson, touring, NAHC

DAWSON — Chicago, Illinois — (1904) — The J.H. Dawson Machinery Company of Chicago produced a touring car for two or four passengers powered by a two-cylinder 16 hp engine that was claimed capable of 35 mph. Its slogan was "A Faultless Automobile," which had to be an exaggeration. The long single chain which drove to the rear axle was insubstantial, and the Dawson's two-speed ("one slow and one fast") transmission probably would have caused problems in use as well. All this was averted by a factory fire in March of 1904 which quickly spelled the end of the Dawson automotive enterprise.

1904 DAWSON

	FP	5	4	3	2	1
Rbt. (2-cyl., 16 hp, 72" wb)	1300	—	—	—	—	—
Tr. (2-cyl., 16 hp, 72" wb)	1500	—	—	—	—	—

DAWSON AUTO-MOBILE — Basic City, Virginia — (1899-1901) — The Dawson Auto-Mobile was a small two-cylinder tiller-steered chain-drive steam runabout with room for three on its front bench seat and a top speed of from 25 to 30 mph "on fair roads." The "fair roads" upon which the Dawson Auto-Mobile coursed were in the state of Virginia. It was there that an Ohio native named George Dawson had arrived, in 1899, at the railroad station in Basic City. He had spent a day and a night en route on the Chesapeake & Ohio from Cincinnati. In Basic City he set up a machine shop, built his first car, and began his second. He also called himself the Dawson Manufacturing Company and advertised his steam car for sale in an automotive trade journal. Some inquiries arrived from the ad, but no solid offers. Because he needed money to complete his second car, he ultimately sold the first at a loss to two area residents: Luther Gaw and John Clark of Waynesboro, across the river, that town's first auto mechanic and its only barber respectively. Unable to encourage local businessmen to invest in his steam car enterprise, and unable even to find a buyer for his second incomplete car, George Dawson closed up shop, returned to the railroad station and took the next C&O train bound for Cincinnati. Though his sojourn in Basic City was short, George Dawson does have the distinction of having built the first automobile in the state of Virginia.

DAY STEAM — Kansas City, Missouri — (1901-1902) — The Day Automobile Company of Kansas City was established in April of 1901 as a dealership for Locomobile steamers and Oldsmobile gasoline cars. The firm proudly boasted that prior to its coming to town there were only two automobiles in use in Kansas City, both of them electrics. Later during 1901 Day built a steam delivery wagon of its own design for the use of the George P. Peck Dry Goods Company. It featured a 10 hp engine, an 18-inch-diameter boiler, and was claimed to provide an 18 mph average speed. "The wagon also has an anti-freeze device which keeps up a circulation of steam around all water pipes and allows the wagon to be used in the very coldest of weather," noted *The Horseless Age* in its January 22nd, 1902 edition. The company was stated to be now arranging for facilities in St. Louis to be used as a distributing point for automobiles and an assembly plant for the Day steam wagons. It would appear, however, that the Day Automobile Company continued as an automobile dealership only.

1912 Day Utility, touring, WLB

DAY UTILITY — Detroit, Michigan — (1911-1913) — The Day Automobile Company of Detroit was organized by former Locomobile dealer Thomas W. Day, who brought in Hugh Jennings, the manager of a Detroit baseball club, as his vice-president. Day himself designed the car which would carry the model name of Utility and which was styled for maximum use by farmers. "All the room possible is provided for carrying produce," the company said. "The car has been designed to be neither a large touring car not a little dinky runabout." As a combination vehicle (the produce-carrying area was a substantial clear space under the two seats), the Day Utility was a particularly attractive success. But as a commercial venture it was not. Initial sales were sufficiently good to prompt the company to move from its initial Trumbull Avenue factory in Detroit to large quarters at 25 East Milwaukee in the spring of 1912. But soon after the money ran out, and Thomas Day could find no more in Detroit. In August of 1913 he reported that he had secured financial support in Spokane and would remove his factory to the state of Washington. But he never got there. There appears to be no connection between this Day and the one in Kansas City, save for the fact that both had handled the Locomobile.

1911 DAY UTILITY
Utility — 4-cyl., 21 hp, 100" wb

	FP	5	4	3	2	1
Model 1 Roadster	950	3000	4000	6000	9500	21,000
Model 2 Touring	1150	2900	3700	5600	9100	20,000

1912 DAY UTILITY
Utility — 4-cyl., 26 hp, 110" wb

	FP	5	4	3	2	1
Touring-5P	1150	2900	3700	5600	9100	20,000

1913 DAY UTILITY
Utility — 4-cyl., 33 hp, 115" wb

	FP	5	4	3	2	1
Model D Touring-7P	1500	3000	4000	6000	9500	21,000

DAYTON — The Dayton Automobile Company was organized in that Ohio city during the fall of 1906 with a capital stock of $25,000 and a motorcar manufacturing plan. Incorporators were A.M. Dodds, John L. Baker, E.E. Burkhart, N.A. Tressler and John N. Vandeman. No manufacture is believed to have resulted from this venture, but four years later John L. Baker returned with the Dayton Electric Car Company which did move into production.

Yet another Dayton Automobile Company was organized in Dayton, Ohio during the early spring of 1911 with a capital stock of $30,000 to "manufacture, sell and repair automobiles and deal in accessories and supplies." Incorporators were J.N. Agentroad, C.N. Hunter, A.S. Iddings, D.W. Iddings and J.E. Studebaker. Manufacture of an automobile is doubted.

In 1909 at the Dayton Automobile Supply Company in Dayton, Ohio an automobile was built by T.J. Kehoe. Refer to T.J.K. Special.

DAYTON STEAM — Dayton, Ohio — (1900-1902) — In November of 1900 the Warner Manufacturing Company, which had not succeeded in getting its steam car venture going, was succeeded by the Dayton Motor Vehicle Company. The new firm was capitalized at $40,000 and was said to be preparing "a complete line of patterns and designs for a steam wagon at a price not to exceed other manufacturers." Among the patented features of the new Dayton was its double-boiler arrangement providing "an absolute condensation of steam, none of which will be seen except in extreme heavy pulls." An article in *The Motor Vehicle Review* for December 27th, 1900 indicates that a steam runabout was being built, and that the company expected to add light and heavy delivery wagons to its line. However, it would appear that the Dayton Motor Vehicle Company thereafter concentrated not on motor vehicles but their component parts. Advertisements from 1902 offered running gears, burners, steam motors and regulators, but no complete automobiles. By December of that year Dayton company officers I.C. Souders, B.N. Bierce, W.C. Teeter and H.L. Warner had requested a voluntary receivership. Dayton assets at the time totaled $10,000, liabilities nearly $15,000 of which $6000 was indebted to banks. Possibly H.L. Warner was the Hugh L. Warner who showed up in Muncie, Indiana in 1903 as the designer of the new Warner car.

DAYTON ELECTRIC — Jersey City, New Jersey — (1902) — The Dayton Autoelectric Company, which noted its address as 230 Washington Street in Jersey City, announced incorporation with a capital stock of $600,000 during the summer of 1902. Alvah W. Hall, John Kirby, Eugene J. Barney, Harrie N. Reynolds and W.H. Spear, Jr. were the men behind this venture which was slated to manufacture electric vehicles, but which does not appear to have ever been charged up sufficiently to have produced more than a prototype.

DAYTON ELECTRIC — Dayton, Ohio — (1911-1914) — For several years the Dayton Electric Car Company (initially incorporated as the Dayton Electromobile Company) manufactured a very attractive electric with pneumatic tires and wheel steering in several closed body styles. Production was never very high, and the company could not have long survived in any case. But Dayton Electric went out of business with dignity. In November 1914 president John L. Baker announced he was surety on notes aggregating $20,000, of which $19,000 was past due, and since other creditors were demanding payment, he thought best to petition for a receiver. Because company assets were not sufficient to meet claims against the company should the business continue, and because the company had a large number of vehicles on hand, he suggested that all personal and real property be sold and the proceeds distributed. His suggestion was accepted. Following receivership, the J.L.B. Motor Car Company was set up to complete cars for which parts remained in stock and to handle the business of supplying parts for older models.

1911 Dayton Electric, coupe, NAHC

1911 DAYTON ELECTRIC

	FP	5	4	3	2	1
Mod. 101 Cpe.-3P (80" wb)	2500	3000	4000	6000	9500	21,000
Mod. 101 Cpe.-2P (80" wb)	2300	2900	3700	5600	9100	20,000
Model 101 Vic. (80" wb)	2000	3100	4200	6300	10,500	22,000
Model 101 Sthp. (80" wb)	1900	2700	3600	5300	8800	19,000
Model 101 Cpe.-4P (86" wb)	3000	3200	4300	6500	11,000	23,000

1912 DAYTON ELECTRIC
Model 104 — 80" wb

	FP	5	4	3	2	1
Double Chain Drive Victoria	2000	3300	4400	6700	12,000	24,000
Shaft Drive Victoria	2100	3400	4500	6900	12,500	24,500
Model 103 — 80" wb						
Dbl. Chain Drive Str. Ft. Cp.	2300	3500	4500	7000	13,000	25,000
Shaft Drive Str. Front Coupe	2400	3600	4600	7200	13,400	25,500
Model 102 — 86" wb						
Double Chain Drive Coupe	2600	3700	4700	7300	13,700	26,000
Shaft Drive Coupe	2700	3800	4800	7500	14,000	26,500

1913-1914 DAYTON ELECTRIC

	FP	5	4	3	2	1
Model 1021 Cpe. (86" wb)	2600	3700	4700	7300	13,700	26,000
Model 1022 Cpe. (92" wb)	2800	3800	4800	7500	14,000	26,500

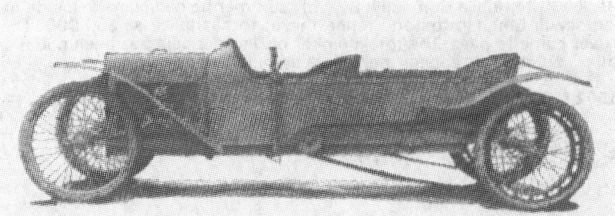

1914 Dayton, 2-pass. tandem, WLB

DAYTON — Joliet, Illinois — (1914) — During the final year of Reliable Dayton production in Chicago in 1909, William O. Dayton referred to one of the models by his last name only. But it would not be until 1914 that his name would grace another motorcar, and this time it was a cyclecar which he moved south of Chicago to build. In the beginning, the town of Joliet was enormously enthusiastic about the Dayton, as was the automotive press. "This car conforms to the absolute cyclecar idea of maximum of efficiency and minimum weight and cost," said *Motor Age*, "and obtains surprising results with surprisingly few mechanisms." Following a test trip made from Chicago to Joliet in 1 hour 35 minutes, *The Automobile* enthused in January 1914 that "the Dayton is one of the fastest cyclecars so far built in America, the speedometer needle having pointed to over 60 on several occasions." The Dayton's frame was hickory wood, the transmission was friction, the drive by belt, the power by Spacke. Both a tandem and a side-by-side two-seater were in production in the Dayton factory in Joliet by late spring of 1914. By July the plant was described as being so heavily taxed to meet the demand that Dayton had secured the premises formerly occupied by the defunct Economy Automobile Company in order to enlarge. By November, however, the Dayton Cyclecar Company was succeeded by the Crusader Motor Car Company. The Dayton cyclecar was finished. One is known to remain extant.

1914 DAYTON
Cyclecar — 4-cyl., 18 hp, 105" wb

Tandem Two-Seater	375	2500	3500	5000	8500	18,000
Side-by-Side Two-Seater	375	2600	3600	5200	8700	18,500

D-D — D-D was the nickname given to the cars of the Detroit-Dearborn Motor Car Company in 1910. The cars were, however, always marketed under their full name. Refer to Detroit-Dearborn.

1910 Deal, model S, 4-pass. runabout, NAHC

DEAL — Jonesville, Michigan — (1908-1911) — The Deal Buggy Company of Jonesville had been a successful manufacturer of horsedrawn carriages and sleighs since 1865, eight years after Jacob J. Deal had arrived in Jonesville to set up a blacksmith shop. In 1891 Jacob's son George Varnum Deal joined his father as a full partner and the business was renamed J.J. Deal & Son. In 1905 George Deal motorized his first buggy, and may have built a few more of these for local customers in the two years following. It was not until 1908 that the Deal automobile was introduced, however, and the Deal Motor Vehicle Company organized. The Deal was a 30 hp four, and a very pretty car with an abundance of brass. It had been designed entirely by George Deal, and undoubtedly it was his death late in 1908 which shortened the life also of the Deal automobile. Omar Dickerson, who was related to the Deal family by marriage, took over as manager of the factory. Automobile production was discontinued after 1911; Dickerson left the company at the end of 1913; the Deal company was out of business by 1915. The Deal plant was later turned into a toy factory. Among the Deals surviving today is one on display in the front window of the Jonesville Village Office.

1908-1910 DEAL
Model S — 4-cyl., 30 hp, 102" wb

	FP	5	4	3	2	1
Runabout-4P	950	3000	4000	6000	9500	21,000

1911 DEAL
Model C — 4-cyl., 30 hp, 102" wb

Surrey-4P	1000	3100	4200	6300	10,500	22,000

Model R — 4-cyl., 30 hp, 104" wb

Touring-5P	1250	3300	4400	6700	12,000	24,000

DEALERS — The Dealers Vehicle Company of Detroit was listed as an automobile manufacturer in the Hiscox book *Horseless Vehicles, Automobiles, Motor Cycles* published in 1900. Further documentation is lacking.

The Dealers' Automobile Exchange & Development Company was organized late in 1906 with a capital stock of $125,000 to "manufacture motor cars and wood machines and to repair machines" in Rahway, New Jersey. Incorporators included S.D. Mershon and C.W. Nichols of Rahway and H.H. Walker of New York City. Manufacture of an automobile is doubted.

DEARBORN — Dearborn was the model designation of the car built in 1911 by the J & M Motor Company of Lawrenceburg, Indiana. Refer to James.

The Dearborn Autmobile Company was a $10,000 incorporation from Chicago during the summer of 1912 to manufacture automobiles and accessories. Incorporators were Sidney Oppenheimer, Arthur Rosenthal and John C. Ahrensfield. Manufacture of a car is doubted.

DE BARRES — The De Barres Automobile Company was organized in New York City during the spring of 1906 to "manufacture, deal in and rent automobiles." Capital stock was $50,000, and the incorporators were W.H. Barnard, A.E. Solomon and R. De Barres. Manufacture of a car did not follow, although the company operated a garage at Park Avenue and 63rd Street and later became the agents for the French Delahaye and Pilain with showrooms at 1966 Broadway.

DeCAMP — Late in 1906 the E.L. DeCamp Motor Company was organized in Kansas City, Missouri, with a capital stock of $10,000, and the stated purpose of automobile manufacture, E.L. DeCamp himself had formerly been a salesman with the Hyde Park Automobile Company in Kansas City and more recently had been made general manager of the Kansas City Motor Car Company which was about to go to market with its Kansas City car. No doubt there was never a DeCamp car, the DeCamp company being set up to handle Kansas City distribution.

DECATUR — Decatur, Illinois — (1896) — During the summer of 1896, C.V. Walls, the manager of the Decatur Gasolene Engine Company, announced that he had refitted a horseless carriage with two of his Walls 4 hp gasoline engines and that now it was good for 15 mph on good roads and hill climbing at a speed of 3 mph. The vehicle had originally been produced the year previous in Jacksonville as the Hall Gasoline Trap. "The carriage was built too light," reported C.V. Walls, "but as the builder designed it for a 4 hp Kane-Pennington engine, which was guaranteed to weigh only 50 pounds (but didn't), his error in this direction is pardonable." The Walls engines set the vehicle right. But the Decatur Gasolene Engine Company did not subsequently enter the automobile field, contenting itself instead with gasoline engine manufacture exclusively.

1911 Decatur, 4-pass. utility, NAHC

DECATUR — Decatur, Indiana — (1910-1911) — The Decatur, in essence, was born in the Indiana town of Marion. The history is somewhat confusing. Lembert W. Coppock was an engineer who originally worked for the Apperson brothers in Kokomo, but moved to Marion to join the Murillo Manufacturing Company when he learned that firm planned to enter the automotive field. When Murillo did not do this, Coppock formed his own company in December 1906, and designed his first automotive vehicle, a light delivery truck, but the Coppock Motor Car Company was a shoestring operation, and by July of 1907 was in financial trouble. To the rescue came the Decatur Commercial Club with an offer of monetary support if Coppock would move his factory from Marion to Decatur. Coppock readily agreed. The new plant was in operation by New Year's Day of 1908. Delivery trucks remained the company's sole output. On October 8th, 1909 the Coppock Motor Car Company was reorganized as the Decatur Motor Car Company in order that operations could be enlarged. It would appear that Lembert Coppock left the firm at this time. The truck he designed remained in production, but added to the line now was a two-cylinder air-cooled four-passenger car that sold for $750. It was known as the "Deca-

405

tur Utility Car'' and was quickly convertible to carrying parcels in the rear quarter. The first of these cars was completed in April 1910; 200 more were produced before year's end. A factory representative was quoted in the *Decatur Democrat* as enthusing that ''they could sell one thousand cars if they could get them out.'' The Decatur Utility Car was discontinued in 1911, nevertheless. What killed it was a brand-new model truck called the Hoosier Limited. It sold for $2500, was a smash best-seller, and became the mainstay of the company. In 1912, when the Decatur factory proved woefully inadequate to meet the demand for its trucks, the company accepted an offer of $100,000 from the city of Grand Rapids (Michigan) to move its plant to that town. In the subsequent reorganization, the firm was renamed the Grand Rapids Motor Truck Company, later the United Motor Truck Company. It prospered in Grand Rapids until felled by the Depression.

1914-1915 DECATUR
Four — 12/14-hp, 102" wb

	FP	5	4	3	2	1
Delivery/Roadster	790	2400	3400	4800	8000	17,000

DECATUR — Grand Rapids, Michigan — (1914-1915) — The Parcel Post Equipment Company of Grand Rapids introduced its vehicle at the Boston Truck Show in 1914 in the guise that the firm's name suggests. Later that year the company got the notion that the parcel carrier mounted in front could be replaced with a long, long hood and the same vehicle could be sold as a roadster. The respective bodies were interchangeable; the Parcel Post Equipment Company now had a double-threat and it deserved a name more appealing to the general trade than Parcel Post. Thus was the name Decatur chosen. Powered by a four-cylinder 12/14 hp water-cooled engine, the Decatur was mounted on a 102-inch wheelbase chassis which featured a three-speed selective sliding gear transmission and chain drive. The price was $790. Production continued through 1915.

1914 Decatur, runabout, WLB

1915 Decatur, roadster parcel wagon, WLB

1914-1915 DECATUR
Four — 12/14-hp, 102" wb

Delivery/Roadster	790	2400	3400	4800	8000	17,000

1903 Decker, tonneau, NAHC

406

DECKER — Owego, New York — (1902-1903) — Ward Decker was the president of the Automatic Telephone Exchange Company of Owego. He was also the designer of a small and pretty runabout with a single-cylinder engine of initially 5-1/2 hp, which he soon upped to seven. Wheel steering and shaft drive were quite advanced features for the period. Sometime early in 1903 he decided to give his car a company, and organized the Decker Automobile Company. By early summer he had plans to locate his factory in Binghamton and, once there, to capitalize at $50,000. This never came to pass. The total number of Deckers built has been noted as three, but it would appear there were a few more than that.

1902 DECKER

	FP	5	4	3	2	1
Runabout (1-cyl., 5-1/2 hp)	1000	—	—	—	—	—

1903 DECKER

Runabout (1-cyl., 7 hp)	1200	—	—	—	—	—

1914 De Cross, 2-pass. cyclecar, WLB

DE CROSS CY-CAR — Cincinnati, Ohio — (1913-1914) — The De Cross was a cyclecar which its makers preferred to abbreviate somewhat. Its friction transmission, belt drive and air-cooled Spacke engine were typical, as was its tandem seating arrangement, but with a difference. In the Cy-Car the front seat was lower because the car was operated from the rear seat. In November of 1913 the prototype was driven from Cincinnati to Hamilton (Ohio) and back, a distance of 45 miles on one gallon of fuel. ''Fifteen miles of the return trip was (sic) covered in 45 minutes,'' the report read, ''when a stop was made to light the lamps. A number of other such trips, in all about 250 miles, have been run with the same success.'' Whether a company was ever properly organized for the De Cross Cy-Car's manufacture, or indeed whether the vehicle ever proceeded beyond the prototype stage, is problematical. What remains most interesting about the Cy-Car, in addition to its curious seating/driving arrangement, is the identity of one of its builders. The partnership behind the vehicle was composed of G.A. Doeller, whose further contributions to automobile history remain obscure, and Powel Crosley, Jr., who later made a considerable name for himself in Cincinnati building refrigerators, radios and cars.

DE DIETRICH — The De Dietrich was one of the most famous French cars in America during the pre-World War I era, but it was never manufactured here. It was imported certainly. And there was a bit of flim-flam involving the name too, this courtesy of a Detroit engineer, L.M. Dietrich, whose employers in 1906 thought an implied association with the renowned French car might boost sales of the Kansas City they were producing in Missouri. Refer to Kansas City.

DE DION-BOUTON — This French car was both imported and manufactured in this country at the turn of the century. Refer to American De Dion.

1923 Deemster, touring, NAHC

DEEMSTER — Hazleton, Pennsylvania — (1923) — The Deemster Corporation of America represents one of the rare examples of a foreign car manufacturer proceeding to the prototype stage in the post-World War I era. Most of these ventures never left paper. At least one example of a U.S. version of the English Deemster was produced, however. It carried the same four-cylinder 50 hp engine, but its wheelbase was fourteen inches longer (110 inches), and its tread two inches wider (50 inches). Initially the idea was to make the Deemster in America as a $375 export product, then later to introduce it in the United States with a $1100 price tag. Initially, too, the plan was for manufacture in Hazleton, but by the summer of 1923 there was word of a possible relocation to Detroit ''due to a change of plans.'' Ultimately, there was another change of plans, and that was not to produce the Deemster in the United States at all. George F. Summers, who was representing British Deemster interests in this country, promptly returned home. Julius Keller, the American most prominently involved in the venture, found another line of work. Most of the company's activity had emanated from its headquarters at 342 Madison Avenue in New York City.

1907 Deere, type A, roadster, WLB

DEERE-CLARK — Moline, Illinois — (1906)/DEERE — (1907) — In 1897 W.E. Clark of Moline built a single-cylinder air-cooled car with fan mounted on the flywheel. It was never marketed, nor was a 1901 effort, though in 1903 Clark did briefly manufacture a car called the Blackhawk. For the two years following its demise, he sought financing in order to try again. Finally, late in 1905, he persuaded the famous John Deere company in Moline to help him. Deere bought out the defunct Clarkmobile Company of Lansing (the automotive venture of E.G. Clark, presumably no relation to W.E.) and moved the relevant tools and machinery to Moline. The Deere-Clark Motor Company of Moline was formally established in January of 1906. In the decade since his first experiments Clark had made the decision for water-cooling, and the Deere-Clark of 1906 and the Deere which followed in 1907 were four-cylinder water-cooled models offered as tourers, limousines and runabouts. "A Car Designed to Satisfy," the brochure said, but the John Deere people weren't satisfied sufficiently to back the project long. By the end of 1907 they decided to stick to agriculture, took their name off the car and their money out of the company. The firm was reorganized to produce another car called the Midland, which survived a little longer. More successful in Moline were the automotive efforts of the Velie family, who were related to the Deeres by marriage.

1907 Deere, type B, touring, WLB

1906 DEERE-CLARK
Deere-Clark — 4-cyl., 30 hp, 100" wb

	FP	5	4	3	2	1
Side Entrance Touring-5P	2850	2700	3600	5300	8800	19,000
Limousine	3500	2500	3500	5000	8500	18,000

1907 DEERE
Deere — 4-cyl., 30 hp, 106" wb

	FP	5	4	3	2	1
Side Entrance Touring-5P	2500	2700	3600	5300	8800	19,000
Gentleman's Roadster	2500	2900	3700	5600	9100	20,000
Limousine	3500	2500	3500	5000	8500	18,000

DEERING — Chicago, Illinois — (1902) — In 1902 R.S. Deering of Chicago built himself an automobile. The Deering Works at Fullerton and Clybourn was an adjunct of the International Harvester Company. Manufacture of the Deering car was never contemplated, though possibly the "automobile mowing machine" designed by Deering in 1900 did see manufacture.

DEERING MAGNETIC — Chicago, Illinois — (1918-1919) — The Deering Magnetic represented a combining of Dorris ohv six-cylinder engine and Entz transmission. Rights to the latter were acquired from the Owen Magnetic people, and the car would be built in the Dorris plant in St. Louis, Missouri. Magnetic Motors Corporation of Chicago was the Deering Magnetic parent organization. The car was luxury throughout with straight-line styling on a long 132-inch wheelbase. Designer of the Deering Magnetic was Karl H. Martin, the remarkable engineer whose further credits included the Roamer, the Kenworthy and the Wasp. Why this fine car failed might be attributed to the bad timing of its entry into the marketplace and by the weak base its sponsoring Magnetic Motors Corporation afforded it.

1918 Deering Magnetic, 7-pass. touring, WLB

1918 DEERING MAGNETIC
Six — 38.4 hp, 132" wb

	FP	5	4	3	2	1
Touring Car-7P	3950	4500	5800	9500	18,000	32,000
Town Car-5P	5950	4300	5400	8700	16,500	30,000

1919 DEERING MAGNETIC
Six — 38.4 hp, 132" wb

	FP	5	4	3	2	1
Touring-7P	4700	4500	5800	9500	18,000	32,000
Touring-4P	4700	4700	6100	9900	19,000	33,000
Coupe-4P	5850	4000	5000	8000	15,000	28,000
Sedan-7P	5950	3500	4500	7000	13,000	25,000
Town Car-5P	6500	4200	5200	8400	15,700	29,000

DEFENDER — One trade press reference from January 1914 indicates the name Defender for the car designed by A.A. Gloetzner, the former Olds Motor Works engineer. If that name indeed was contemplated, it was swiftly discarded. The car which resulted was never marketed as other than the Flyer. Refer to Flyer.

DEFIANCE — Early in 1907 the Defiance Chain Company of Boston, Massachusetts was capitalized at $10,000 for the purpose of manufacturing automobiles. Behind this venture were G.H. Burg, D.W. Dunn and H.B. Lent. Manufacture did not follow.

DEFIANCE — Defiance, Ohio — (1909) — During the summer of 1909 the Miller Machine Company of Defiance announced its impending manufacture of a touring car to be called the Defiance "40" — with bodies to be made at the Defiance Carriage Company, machining and assembly to take place at the Defiance bicycle factory which had been dormant for some time. Previously the Miller Machine Company had conducted an automobile garage in town, but this foray into manufacture probably never left the prototype stage. An examination of the local newspapers — *The Defiance Herald* and the *Crescent News* — for the period 1909-1912 reveals that Miller operated as a dealership only. An ad in the *Herald*, a German-language paper, offered as "Gut fur Farmer und Stadter...dus Winton Automobil zu $3,000, das Cadillac Automobil zu $1600, Maxwell Autos zu $600, $900 and $1500." There was a Defiance manufactured in Defiance, but it was a motor truck, and there was no Miller connection. The Defiance Motor Truck Company was organized in 1916 and took over the plant of the Turnbull Wagon Company, one of the largest factories in town.

DE FREET — Thomas M. De Freet was an employee of the state Adjutant General's office in Indianapolis, Indiana and decided to build himself a car for entry in the Chicago Times-Herald Contest in 1895. He did not complete the vehicle in time for the event, however, nor is it certain that he ever did.

DeGALLIER — Cleveland, Ohio — (1902) — According to the *Automobile Motor Review* in February 1902, one E.P. DeGallier of 317 Electric Building in Cleveland was experimenting with an automobile. No doubt this was a one-off effort; De Gallier was not heard from thereafter as a motorcar builder.

1902 DeGroot Mail Wagon, HAC

DeGROOT — Morristown, New Jersey — (1901) — George F. DeGroot was a Morristown letter carrier who designed a small 20 hp gasoline vehicle which he enclosed for the full length of its body to ensure that neither mailman nor mail would be subjected to inclement weather during the conduct of appointed rounds. The Morris County *Chronicle* for February 22nd, 1901 published detailed drawings of the DeGroot vehicle and indicated that "a gentleman from Morristown and also one from New York" were avidly interested in the project and were planning to "place the wagons in the market as soon as possible." This did not happen. Indeed, only the building of a prototype can be documented with certainty. What can also be documented is that George DeGroot was employed by the Morristown Post Office for twenty-eight years, and that he walked a lot. In 1917, three years before he received his pension, an article in the *Morristown Jerseyman* revealed that DeGroot had walked 146,805 miles and had worn out about 100 pairs of shoes in a quarter-century of delivering the Morristown mail. He spent his final three years behind the general delivery window. He died a little less than two years following his retirement, on February 14th, 1922.

DeHART — The DeHart Motor Car Company was organized late in 1910 with a capital stock of $10,000 and the plan to manufacture automobiles in Jersey City, New Jersey, William F. Ely, Frank J. Higgins and Rachel G. Butler were behind this venture. Manufacture is doubted.

DE HAVEN — Chicago, Illinois — (1904) — The De Haven Brothers — Elmer and Howard — advertised themselves as automobile manufacturers at 87 South Center Avenue in Chicago in 1904. The De Havens seem to have operated principally as a dealership, though they may have built a few cars to custom order as well.

DEIBLER — "Deibler & Johnson, who are assembling cars (in Berlin, Wisconsin), making some of the parts on a small scale, are organizing a stock company to go into the manufacturing business on an extensive scale," reported *The Motor Age* during the summer of 1908, not quite getting the story straight. Ed Deibler did build a car that year, but it was in association with Frank Russell. Refer to Russell-Deibler.

DEKALB — The Dekalb Manufacturing Company was an enterprise of the Vesey Family — W.J., A.J. and W.J., Jr. — of Ft. Wayne, Indiana. During the fall of 1915 the Veseys announced a capitalization of $150,000 for the purpose of entering into automobile manufacture. A car does not appear to have followed.

DeKALB — St. Louis, Missouri — (1915) — During the summer of 1915 the DeKalb Motor Car Company of St. Louis announced that it had completed its first six-cylinder 45 hp Beaver-engined delivery car. Flexibility would be the mark of this new venture. The same 130-inch wheel-base chassis was to be used as well for a large touring car. Very few of either were produced before the DeKalb company succumbed later that year.

DE LAMATER — The De Lamater-Byrnes Automobile Company was organized in New York City early in 1912 with a capital stock of $30,000. J.W. De Lamater and M.B. Byrnes announced their intention to manufacture and deal in automobiles and motor vehicles. Only the latter did they subsequently do.

DELANOY — Alameda, California — (1897) — In 1897 in Alameda, Frederick W. Delanoy built himself an automobile at his home at 1122 Grand Street. It was described wonderfully that year by the Alameda *Daily Argus*: "The carriage runs at the rate of eight or ten miles an hour. It is supplied with a tank carrying three gallons of gasoline, sufficient to keep the engine going four hours. In five hours the fifty miles between Alameda and San Jose could be covered without refilling the tank. The engine is of one horse power and is the kind known as the 'Pacific.' It was originally a vertical engine. Young Delanoy bought it for $75, converted it into a horizontal engine and fitted it into his horseless carriage. It is quite a complicated piece of machinery, but every piece of metal is hidden under the seat of the vehicle. Back of it is a tank holding eight gallons of water which is used to cool the cylinders. When the water gets hot it is drained off and the nearest water trough suffices to fill the tank again." Two bicycle lanterns were fitted to the dash of Delanoy's car, and its four bicycle wheels were made expressly for him by Edward Mohaig of San Francisco. The body was ash, painted "black and Indian red." The vehicle had cost Frederick Delanoy about $200 to build.

1895 De La Vergne Motor Drag, auto-buggy, NAHC

DE LA VERGNE — New York, New York — (1895-1896) — The De La Vergne Refrigerating Machine Company was located at the foot of 138th Street in Manhattan. The company entered a German Benz in the Chicago Times-Herald Contest of Thanksgiving Week in 1895, and returned to New York to complete four horseless carriages of its own (two traps with single-cylinder engines and two drags with two-cylinder engines) in December. Apparently the firm had a number of other vehicles in the making because in December it was reported that De La Vergne had sold "motocycles" to a number of New York's wealthiest citizens, including William Rockefeller, John Jacob Astor, William Waldorf Astor, George Gould, Edwin Gould and William Havemeyer. Further sales went to beer barons Jacob Rupert of New York and Fred Pabst of Milwaukee. Why this company chose to leave the automotive industry is something of a mystery. De La Vergne cars were apparently built for the company by Hincks & Johnson Company (Bridgeport, Connecticut) and Valentine, Linn & Son (Brooklyn). De La Vergne superintendent John C. Blevney later built a car of his own.

DELAWARE — The Delaware Garage Company was a $100,000 Wilmington incorporation from late 1909 to manufacture and deal in automobiles and motor vehicles. C.B. Holt, P.C. Hanson and W.H. Hayes were the incorporators. Manufacture of a car is doubted.

The Delaware Motors Company was a $150,000 Delaware incorporation from early 1911 (sometimes misspelled Delavan) for the purpose of manufacturing automobiles and engines. G.G. Stiegler, R.G. Lupton and H.W. Nock were the incorporators. Manufacture of a car is doubted.

DE LEON — New York, New York, — (1905-1906) — Archer & Company of New York City imported the French Hotchkiss into the United States and from late 1905 through 1906 also assembled a car known as the De Leon which was an amalgam of components supplied by various French parts makers. A 35 hp four was the only model offered. By 1907 Archer & Company had returned to the importation of complete French cars exclusively.

1916 Delia Amphibian, HAC

DELIA AMPHIBIAN — San Francisco, California — (1916) — "A few weeks ago, bathers on a famous beach near San Francisco . . . were startled to see a rakish-looking motor car roll onto the beach and plunge into the surf," *Automobile Topics* reported in its March 4th, 1916 issue. "The car didn't disappear in the waves, but rode high over the swell, cutting the water with its blunt prow; it took a short cruise and returned to the beach, climbing it with ease, and disappeared as suddenly as it had arrived." The vehicle was called the Delia, or Motor Duck, by Michael de Cosmo, who claimed to be its inventor. On land, the Delia drove through shaft and conventional differential to the rear wheels, with worm-and-sector steering connected to the front axle. When the car hit the waves, a switch of a lever engaged a friction wheel which drove a propeller shaft, and the steering shifted from front axle to rear rudder. Although the Delia could be driven through inclement conditions on land, at sea it was a fair-weather friend only since its sides were not high enough to prevent swamping in rough water. Reportedly, ten miles an hour had been reached when the Delia went asea. Its speed ashore was not mentioned, although *Automobile Topics* noted that "it looks much like any other roadster, except that the propeller and rudder can be plainly seen." Michael de Cosmo said he planned to market a "much improved model," but he was not heard from again. Interestingly, de Cosmo's Delia was, in fact, the Hydromotor and the history of that venture reveals no Michael de Cosmo as being involved. Perhaps the name was being used pseudonymously for testing, or perhaps de Cosmo had taken himself for a splashy joyride.

DELLING — West Collingswood, New Jersey — (1923-1929) — The Delling was a steam car which was produced in small numbers as a $2500 touring and a $3200 sedan. The man behind it was Eric H. Delling, veteran of the Stanley and Mercer companies whose previous independent efforts had included the Deltal and the Delta built in his native Brooklyn. With his brothers as partners, Delling established Delling Motors Company in 1923. Although initially Philadelphia was planned as the factory site, operations soon moved to West Collingswood in New Jersey. Among the advantages noted for the Delling in a very handsome brochure were its ease of operation: "It can be throttled down to one mile per hour; it can be accelerated instantly, without the use of a clutch and without shifting gears, to a speed

1924 Delling Steamer, sedan, HAC

1926 Delling Steamer, phaeton, WLB

of sixty miles per hour." And touted too was the Delling's economy, the steamer averaging sixteen miles on one gallon of kerosene: "Kerosene costs about one-third less than gasoline, and no state tax is levied on it." The Delling Una-Flow was a three-cylinder double-acting engine with poppet valves, said to deliver the same amount of power impulses as a twelve-cylinder gasoline motor. The wheelbase for both touring and sedan was 126 inches. The company envisioned use of the Delling powerplant in taxicabs, passenger buses, trucks, unit railroad cars, tractors, marine applications and small stationary power units. How many of these applications were tried is not known. In 1930, by which time the Delling Motors Company had failed, it was reported that a Delling steam bus in regular operation between Philadelphia and Atlantic City since 1929 had just turned 40,000 miles on its odometer. Eric Delling was also the chief engineer for the Brooks steam car, and in 1938 was in Newton, Massachusetts as chief engineer of Alma Steam Motors.

DELMORE — New York, New York — (1923) — The Delmore was a three-wheeler produced by Delmore Motors Corporation of New York City. Production began in 1923 and probably ended that year. The corporation's Delaware charter was repealed in January 1926 following a two-year non-payment of taxes. Delmore had rather preciously referred to its car as a "passengermobile." It was powered by a two-cylinder Indian engine of 22 hp, fitted into a 68-inch wheelbase and offered only as a wire-wheeled roadster at $525.

1923 DELMORE
Two-Cylinder — 22 hp, 68" wb

	FP	5	4	3	2	1
Roadster	525	2500	3500	5000	8500	18,000

DE LONG — Phoenix, New York — (1902-1903) — In late 1901 George Erwin De Long left his job as superintendent of the Leggett Carriage Company in Syracuse and allied himself with the Industrial Machine Company of nearby Phoenix which was reorganized in January 1902 with a new capitalization of $25,000. Directors were William H. Haberle, Edward Oswald, F.P. Mermance, J.I. Van Dorn, and George and August Fink. The company was slated to build an automobile designed by De Long, who would serve as production manager. The car was a two-cylinder air-cooled 3½ hp runabout, with one forward and one reverse speed, and a gasoline tank capacity good for a 100-mile run. The vehicle weighed 500 pounds and was priced at 500 dollars. Production was scheduled to begin in February, but it didn't. What seems to have happened is that the directors of the Industrial Machine Company became disenchanted with De Long, or vice versa. By October George De Long had announced that he was endeavoring to organize a new company, and in April of 1903 he advised further that it would be called the Syracuse Automobile & Motor Company and its capitalization would be $100,000. Interestingly, just about this same time, De Long's old employer Leggett had gone into the automobile building business himself with the Iroquois. De Long never did get into manufacture, though he was still trying as late as 1908 to organize a company to do so.

DE LOURA — Ottumwa, Ft. Madison, et al., Iowa — (1902-1903) — H.E. De Loura was the general manager of the Rochester Gasoline Carriage & Motor Company in New York State at the turn of the century. In 1902 he decided to strike out on his own. "Gents —," he wrote to *Cycle and Automobile Trade Journal* that March, "I am desirous of finding some city that is willing to donate a site and building for me to move my factory into." His "factory" at the time consisted of some machinery, a couple of proto-

types, and his plan to build steam and gasoline automobiles ranging from light runabout to five-ton truck, and also including gasoline engines of up to 150 hp. He preferred a location west or south of Chicago, and apparently he did elicit some interest from several communities in Iowa. His first address in the state was Ottumwa, thereafter he was briefly in Ft. Madison, and in September 1902 he indicated that he was moving to Perry. During the summer of the following year, a further reference placed him in Fort Dodge. There is no indication that manufacture followed in any of these locations.

1913 Deltal, race car, GR

DELTAL — Brooklyn, New York — (1913-1914)/DELTA — (1923-1925) — These two motorcars built a decade apart have one thing in common: their designer. Eric H. Delling was a Brooklyn-born engineer who rose to prominence through his design work for the famous Stanley Steamer and the equally famous Mercer gasoline car. His first venture into designing a vehicle of his own came in 1914 with the Deltal, a four-cylinder 300-cubic-inch gasoline car which received considerable attention in the press because of its high-speed, high-efficiency engine. Just one of these cars was built, a racer which showed well at Elgin in August of 1913. Because Delling was hired shortly thereafter to design the new L-head Mercer, there has been speculation that the car he designed for the Trenton company was based upon his Deltal racer. Delling left Mercer in June of 1916, subsequently to toil for Stanley in Massachusetts, but he was soon back home in Brooklyn with ideas for further cars of his own. His first now was the Delta, a six-cylinder car (Continental engine) set in a 133-inch wheelbase chassis with an L-head Mercer-like radiator up front. Delling developed the car in association with Andrew Moulton (the "M" of the troika that had produced the B.L.M.). The Delta did not proceed beyond the prototype. At the same it was being developed, however, Delling began a steam car venture which carried his last name, and that automobile did see some production.

1923 Delta, touring, KM

DE LUXE — The car built by the De Luxe Motor Car Company in Toledo, Ohio from 1906-1907 and then in Detroit into 1909 was generally referred to in brochures and advertisements as the Car De Luxe. Refer to Car De Luxe.

The De Luxe Automobile Company was organized in Jersey City, New Jersey during the spring of 1906 with a capital stock of $125,000 for the manufacture of "automobiles and all kinds of mechanically propelled vehicles." Incorporators were Ralph R. Caldwell, H.O. Coughlan, John R. Turner, Henry T. Hung, W.C. Caldwell and Stanley H. Merrell. Manufacture is doubted.

DELUXE — Cleveland, Ohio — (1910) — The Deluxe Motor Car Company was organized in Cleveland in 1910 by W.G. Moore to manufacture a two-wheeled automobile. It featured thirty-inch artillery wheels and wheel steering with a small windshield clamped to the steering post. There was a small rear deck in back. Either one- or two-cylinder motors were to be fitted, with speeds up to 70 mph claimed for the twin. Small caster-type support wheels held the vehicle vertical when not in motion and could be folded up via a foot lever when the Deluxe Two-Wheeler was running. Prototypes were built, and apparently there was some production. A Deluxe is included in California registration lists during the World War I period, wherein it was identified as a "cyclecar."

DEMAR — The J.E. Demar Company was organized in New York City during the summer of 1907 with a capital stock of $15,000 to "engage in the manufacture of motors, engines, carriages, vehicles, boats, etc." Incorporators were J.E. Demar and R.E. and J.R. Beatty — and they seem to have done none of those things.

DEMAREST — Greenwich, Connecticut — (1908) — References from 1908 indicate that A.T. Demarest & Company of Greenwich, Connecticut was engaged in the manufacture of both carriages and automobiles. Details regarding the latter are lacking, but the venture apparently came to an end in August that year when Aaron T. Demarest was described as having ''died suddenly of ptomaine poisoning.''

1905 DeMars Electric, victoria, NAHC

DeMARS ELECTRIC — Cleveland, Ohio — (1905-1906)/BLAKESLEE ELECTRIC — (1906)/WILLIAMS ELECTRIC — (1906-1907)/BYRIDER ELECTRIC — (1907-1910) — This electric car from Cleveland had four very short lives. William O. DeMars started the first one. He had been experimenting with horseless carriages since 1902 but it was not until December of 1904 that his garage was grandly evolved into the DeMars Electrical Vehicle Company. Among the principals in this $25,000 incorporation was John R. Blakeslee, whose son C.J. was given a job at the plant. In February 1906 C.J. Blakeslee put together a group to buy out DeMars; the Blakeslee Electric Automobile Company was established, and the car's name was changed to Blakeslee. Meanwhile William DeMars went off to manage the Oliver Electric Vehicle Company, also in Cleveland, which had been newly formed to service, repair, charge and store electric automobiles. Although the press was informed that ''a few machines may be assembled to order,'' it does not seem that Oliver received any orders to do so. Meanwhile the Blakeslee Electric was in production. But only for a few months. After about twenty were built, during the summer of 1906, J.F. Townsend, H.A. Williams and several members of the Byrider family, who had been having no luck at all trying to build their Williams gasoline car in Akron, came to town and bought out Blakeslee. Now the company was called the Williams Motor Carriage Company, and the car the Williams Electric. This lasted less than a year. In May 1907 John and William A. Byrider bought out Williams, established the Byrider Electric Automobile Company and renamed the car the Byrider Electric. This one survived into early 1910. Through all these reincarnations, there were minimal changes in the product. It began life as a 71-inch wheelbase victoria, and thus did it end it. Even the price remained the same. The cyclops headlight which had been a distinguishing feature of the DeMars was continued through the Blakeslee and Williams and Byrider. The Williams and Byrider had painted wheel flanges instead of polished brass, the Williams covered the

driving chain, and Byrider, curiously, offered a second Victoria model at the same price on a 72-inch wheelbase. But that was about it. Following the takeover by Williams in 1906, incidentally, C.J. Blakeslee had left to work for the Woods Electric Vehicle Company in Chicago. In 1912 he allied with another Woods man, chief engineer F.J. Newman, to form another company to produce another Blakeslee, but that one was never built at all.

1905-1906 DEMARS ELECTRIC

	FP	5	4	3	2	1
DeMars Elec. Vic. (71'' wb)	1800	3000	4000	6000	9500	21,000

1906 BLAKESLEE ELECTRIC

	FP	5	4	3	2	1
Blakeslee Ele. Vic. (71'' wb)	1800	3000	4000	6000	9500	21,000

1906-1907 WILLIAMS ELECTRIC

	FP	5	4	3	2	1
Williams Elec. Vic. (71'' wb)	1800	3000	4000	6000	9500	21,000

1908-1910 BYRIDER ELECTRIC

	FP	5	4	3	2	1
Byrider Elec. Vict. (71'' wb)	1800	3000	4000	6000	9500	21,000

DEMARS — St. Thomas, North Dakota — 1907 — In 1907 R.A. Demars of St. Thomas built himself a four-passenger touring car powered by a 25/35 hp engine. Further details are lacking.

DE MOOY — Cleveland, Ohio — (1900-1904) — The De Mooy Brothers of Cleveland had been building marine gasoline engines at their small shop on Granger Street near Prospect since before the turn of the century. Although their output was both two- and four-cycle units, the De Mooys ardently favored the two-strokes. In 1900 the brothers installed one of these 3 hp units in a carriage, which was a fine success, as attested to by their friend C.M. Giddings, who was building a car of his own in Rockford, Illinois. De Mooy Brothers did not move into vehicle manufacture, however, explaining in a letter to *Cycle and Automobile Trade* Journal published in December 1902 that ''we had all we could do with marine engines.'' Any vehicles subsequently produced by the De Mooys were strictly for their own use. In April of 1904, C.W. De Mooy was among the organizers who took over the defunct American Motor Carriage Company of Cleveland (the builders of the former American Gas car), but the American Automobile Company which resulted from that takeover is believed to have died aborning.

DEMOT — Detroit, Michigan — (1910-1911)/DEMOTCAR — (1910-1911) — The curious name was a constriction of Detroit Motor Car, it was spelled DeMot in the first brochure, DeMotCar and Demotcar in the second. A final decision on nomenclature was never necessary because the Demotcar Company never printed a third brochure. The car, which was also occasionally referred to as a Little Detroit, was introduced as a two-cylinder 8/10 hp $550 runabout that weighed 1100 pounds including ''two people of average size,'' and its specifications were average as well, except perhaps for the use of asbestos and camel's hair for brake linings. The Demotcar venture had been spearheaded by C.H. Ritter, a wealthy, retired wholesale liquor dealer in Detroit who hired George T. Homeier as factory manager and Guy Hamilton as chief engineer, both these men having had prior experience in the automobile industry. The rest of the Demotcar management team was apparently composed of Ritter's friends, since none of them had any automotive background. The company was in trouble almost immediately. The Demot was introduced in September of 1909, and the Demotcar Company was bankrupt by August of 1910. Production continued under receivership for a while. Then in December of 1911, through a curious set of circumstances, C.H. Ritter again acquired possession of Demotcar. This time he brought with him R.A. Skinner, who previously had been in the printing business, and A.W. Voege, one of the trustees of his bankrupt company. They reorganized as the Ritter Automobile Company and moved to Madison, Wisconsin. There they added two cylinders to the engine and ten inches to the wheelbase — and renamed the product the Ritter. It failed as quickly as the Demotcar.

1910 Demotcar, runabout, WLB

1910-1911 DEMOT
Two-Cylinder — 8/10 hp, 80'' wb

Runabout	550	—	—	—	—

DE MOTTE — Valley Forge, Pennsylvania — (1904) — The De Motte Motor Car Company of Valley Forge was certainly ambitious. ''They have a very complete factory . . . and a system which has been thoroughly tried out,'' *Cycle and Automobile Trade Journal* enthused in February of 1904. ''Their line includes solid and detachable tonneaus, solid and detachable surreys, runabouts, light and heavy deliveries, trucks, passenger coaches, etc., but the same chassis does for nearly all models . . .'' While simplifica-

1908 Byrider Electric, victoria, WLB

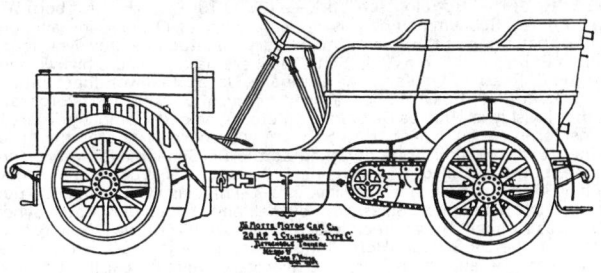

1904 De Motte

tion of production was a quality to be admired, it would seem that De Motte overdid it. There was a variety in horsepower, however, a 20 hp four being the norm, with a smaller engine for runabouts, a bigger one for trucks and coaches. Chain drive and wheel steering was featured throughout the line. An advertising slogan was "Quaker Staunchness and French Perfection." The company did not make it into 1905.

1904 DE MOTTE
Four — 20 hp, 90" wb

	FP	5	4	3	2	1
Touring-5P	2200	3000	4000	6000	9500	21,000
Surrey-4P	—	2900	3700	5600	9100	20,000
Two — 10 hp, 90" wb						
Runabout-2P	—	2900	3700	5600	9100	20,000

DENISON — New Haven, Connecticut — (1898-1902) — Julian F. Denison, an electrical engineer from New Haven, was involved with three different cars during the turn of the century period, and not one of them was an electric. Apparently, he developed a preference early on for gasoline power, and by 1898 had developed a water-jacketed two-stroke internal combustion engine. That year he also organized the Denison Motor Carriage Company with his long-time partner E.S. Walton, and Julian R. Tinkham of the Tinkham Cycle Company of New York City. The tricycle he built would be marketed as a Tinkham. Probably more of them were produced than the cars marketed under his own name, though among the latter were a few four-wheeled carriages and a nine-passenger omnibus for George D. Jones, a liveryman from Torrington. In 1901 Denison began using the name Yale for both his engines and his cars, and a few more units of each were built. The Yale Motor Company succeeded the Denison Motor Carriage Company that year, and remained separate from his Denison Electric Engineering Company. This was no doubt a good idea, since the Yale company, which was located at 424 State Street in New Haven, was sued for back rent of $150 early in 1902. This appears to have ended J.F. Denison's automobile manufacturing career, though his Denison Electric Engineering Company survived. Conceivably that firm may have built an electric car, but only experimentally, no Denison electric was ever marketed.

DENNIS — The Dennis Motor Company was organized in Toledo, Ohio during the late spring of 1912 with a capital stock of $25,000 to manufacture automobiles and engines. Incorporators were C.H. Dennis, C.W. Close, Allen L. Reid and R.S. Woodrow. Manufacture of a car is doubtful.

DENNISTON — Early in 1911, from Buffalo, New York, came word that the Denniston Company was taking over the business of the E.E. Denniston Company and recapitalizing at $150,000 for the purpose of motor car manufacture. During the late summer of the year following, however, when Denniston went into bankruptcy, it was revealed that the firm's product had been bodies for automobiles only. The Buffalo Electric Vehicle Company moved into the old Denniston plant.

DENVER — Early in 1900 the Denver Electric Vehicle Company was organized with a capital stock of $3000 to manufacture and sell automobiles in Colorado. W.H. Smith, C.S. Rogers and W.E. Humphrey were the Denver residents behind this venture which is not believed to have proceeded into production.

DE PALMA — New York, New York — (1905)/DE PALMA — Detroit, Michigan — (1916) — Ralph De Palma was one of the greatest drivers in the history of American motor sport. A hero to youngsters for two generations, he won approximately 2000 races during a twenty-five-year career. On occasion he assayed being an automobile producer too. In 1905 he built two cars in New York City, and in 1911 he announced plans to form a company there to "make a specialty of touring cars and roadsters." This did not happen, however, and De Palma returned to the track. Although an occasional custom-built special may have been sold under his name thereafter, it was not until 1916 that he made a concerted effort to enter the field. In early spring that year the De Palma Manufacturing Company was incorporated in Detroit with a capital stock of $100,000 for the purpose of producing aero engines and motorcars. Behind the venture was wealthy Detroit capitalist Frank P. Book, who served as president. De Palma was vice-president, and H.V. Book was secretary-treasurer. The automobiles to be built were principally racing cars, although The Automobile indicated in November that the company would build "special speedsters for those who want cars of that type." There is no indication that De Palma Manufacturing Company ever really got going. By 1917 De Palma had allied himself with the Packard Motor Car Company and spent the next several seasons campaigning the Liberty-engined Packard race cars in events throughout the country, including a one-mile standing start of 92.71 mph at Daytona Beach in February 1919 which was a record that stood into the early 1950's.

DEPPE — New York & Watertown, New York — (1919-1920) — Early in 1917 William P. Deppe organized the Deppe Motors Corporation, locating its offices at 149 Church Street in New York City. The purpose of the company was to exploit the Deppe superheater, a carburetor apparatus which was claimed to eliminate carbonization, double the power secured from gasoline, and permit the use of any low-grade engine fuel. In November 1919, in Watertown, the New York Air Brake Company announced that it was entering the truck-producing field, and in December New York Air Brake and Deppe joined forces for the production of an automobile to be called the Deppe, or possibly the Starbuck, after the president of New York Air Brake. According to the local Watertown paper, the car was to "be more or less of an aristocrat, as motors go, and will be something between a Stutz and the Rolls-Royce." A public relations release indicated that some 10,000 cars selling in the $3500 price range were expected to be built during 1920. Shortly thereafter the Wall Street Journal investigated and reported that "the passenger cars . . . will serve principally to demonstrate the value of the Deppe superheater, right to manufacture which will be sold to any other concern on a royalty basis." Whether Deppe found any takers for his superheater is not known. But only a single prototype Deppe was built. When last heard from in the press, in 1921, Deppe Motors Corporation and New York Air Brake Company were in court, saying very unpleasant things about each other.

1911 Derain, 7-pass. touring, NAHC

DERAIN — Cleveland, Ohio — (1908-1911) — Hugh Dolnar, veteran reporter for the Cycle and Automobile Trade Journal, said it all, said it best and also said it in one formidable sentence: "The Derain car driven by a two-cycle four-cylinder motor, same torque as an eight-cylinder motor running on the four-stroke cycle would give, and therefore very smoothly driven, was designed by Earl H. Sherbondy, who took up the small gas-engine at the age of sixteen, in 1904, and having means and shop facilities, pursued his quest of the best small internal combustion motor through his studies at the University School, Cleveland, whence he graduated in 1906, and reached such a degree of gas-engine success as to make a single-cylinder two-cycle motor, 4-1/2 by 4 inches, water cooled, 110 pounds compression, show 16-1/2 bhp at 1320 rpm, this being the high prony brake record for any piston and cylinder motor of equal dimensions within the writer's knowledge." In 1908, at the age of twenty, Earl Sherbondy organized the Simplex Manufacturing Company in Cleveland and exhibited a touring car at the local automobile show, although at that time he indicated he did not plan to manufacture anything other than motors and transmissions. By August of 1909, however, he had changed his mind and announced that he would assemble twenty-five cars to sell for $4000 each. He was still doing this late in 1910 when he met Hugh Dolnar who gave him the rave review noted above. His Derain Motor Company did not survive 1911 anyway.

1908 DERAIN
Show Car — 4-cyl., 38 hp, 112" wb

	FP	5	4	3	2	1
	—	—	—	—	—	—

1909-1911 DERAIN
Production car — 4-cyl., 30 hp, 125-1/2" wb

	FP	5	4	3	2	1
Touring-7P	4000	4000	5000	8000	15,000	28,000

DERIGHT — In the fall of 1905 the Deright Automobile Company was organized in Omaha, Nebraska with a capital stock of $50,000 "to buy, sell and make automobiles." J.J. Deright ultimately decided to do only buying and selling, however, and in the years prior to 1909 he held the local agencies for such divers cars as Stoddard-Dayton, Ford, Waverley, Rauch & Lang and Velie. That year he sold out the Deright Automobile Company and took on local dealerships for Locomobile and Matheson.

DERRICKSON — The Derrickson Manufacturing Company was organized in Muncie, Indiana early in 1903 with a capital stock of $125,000 to manufacture automobiles. Harry S. Osborn, H.L. Kitselman and R.C. White were the incorporators. Manufacture is doubted.

DERR STEAM — From 1926 to about 1939, Thomas S. Derr built steam automobiles in West Newton, Massachusetts. His venture's name was the American Steam Automobile Company, and the cars produced were generally referred to as American Steam Cars. Refer to American Steam Car.

DESBERON — New York City & New Rochelle, New York — (1901-1904) — The Desberon Motor Car Company was a New York City venture with plants at 51st Street and Twelfth Avenue in Manhattan and at 12 Rose Street in suburban New Rochelle. Although Desberon commercial vehicles were both steamers and gasoline-powered, the passenger cars were internal combustion from the beginning. These engines featured the Desberon "patented head wherein there are no water joints whatever," and the company pointed with pride to the "genuine scientific novelty" of its radiator, "the air going upward through its sections in the natural manner

411

1902 Desberon, runabout, HAC

whether the car be moving or standing still.'' Having deemed ball and roller bearings unsuited to American running, Desberon used a ''substantial bronze sleeve'' in its wheels. ''If you go out on a Desberon,'' the company said, ''you will come home on time and on the machine.'' Perhaps but probably not very quickly. The only known sporting contest entered by Desberon was a hill climb at Eagle Rock near Newark, New Jersey in November 1904. In two events, a Desberon finished sixth and eleventh; there were six cars entered in the first event, eleven in the second. The company faded away after 1904. Total production is not known, but late in 1901 the firm indicated having received ten passenger car orders for delivery the following spring, and subsequent production appears to have been on the basis of one runabout a week, two tonneaus and a single truck per month.

1904 Desberon, runabout, GR

1901-1904 DESBERON
Style C — 2-cyl., 7 hp, 78'' wb

	FP	5	4	3	2	1
Runabout	3000	3000	4000	6000	9500	21,000
Style D — 4-cyl., 12/15 hp, 78'' wb						
Tonneau	3000	2900	3700	5600	9100	20,000
Style E — 4-cyl., 30/36 hp, 90'' wb						
Tonneau	4000	3100	4200	6300	10,500	22,000

1908 De Schaum, highwheeler, WLB

DE SCHAUM — Buffalo, New York — (1908-1909) — He was born William Andrew Schaum and he was in the car-building business in Baltimore under that name at the turn of the century. Nineteen six, however, found him in Buffalo as William A. de Schaum where he designed a highwheeler for the C. Rossler Manufacturing Company. Unsatisfied with that venture, de Schaum left Rossler and secured financial backing to incorporate rather lavishly in 1908 as De Schaum Motor Syndicate Company. There is considerable evidence that de Schaum was more promoter than producer. Still, the vehicle he designed as the De Schaum was very handsome, but it was also a highwheeler — and buggy types were by now ebbing in the marketplace. Naming his 1909 models the Seven Little Buffalos didn't help either. Sales were dismal, and De Schaum Motor Syndicate was through. Undaunted, de Schaum moved to Hornell, New York to establish the De Schaum-Hornell Motor Company in 1910, which never built a car. Thereupon he traveled to Michigan, where his car this time was the Suburban, and where he got into a peck of trouble.

1908 DE SHAUM
Model W — 2-cyl., 10 hp, 74'' wb

	FP	5	4	3	2	1
Stanhope	600	2500	3500	5000	8500	18,000
Model S — 2-cyl., 10 hp, 84'' wb						
Surrey	700	2600	3600	5200	8700	18,500
1909 DE SCHAUM						
Model W — 2-cyl., 10 hp, 72'' wb						
Stanhope	500	2500	3500	5000	8500	18,000
Model A — 2-cyl., 10 hp, 76'' wb						
Stanhope	600	2600	3600	5200	8700	18,500
Model A — 2-cyl., 14 hp, 82'' wb						
Stanhope	600	2800	3700	5500	9000	19,500
Model S — 2-cyl., 14 hp, 82'' wb						
Runabout	750	2900	3700	5600	9100	20,000
Model S — 2-cyl., 20 hp, 87'' wb						
Touring	850	3000	3900	5800	9300	20,550

DESERT FLYER — Reno, Nevada & Council Bluffs, Iowa — (1908) — The first news of this venture appears to have come from Tonopah, Nevada. The April 1st, 1907 edition of the *Tonopah Sun* revealed that the Nevada Motor Car Company had been established a few days previous and that a factory would be built in Reno in the next six months. The idea was production of massive touring cars for stage coach service in the mining districts of Nevada. The men behind the idea were George Bertzchy of Reno, who was described as ''one of the pioneers'' of the gold and silver rush; A.J.P. Bertzchy, undoubtedly a relative, who had been working for various automobile companies in Chicago since the turn of the century; and George W. Tibbetts, a wealthy Colorado physician who had invested heavily in the Nevada mines. Tex Rickard was also involved in the project. A four-cylinder prototype car weighing five tons (and conjured mostly from Pope-Toledo parts) was built in Chicago that winter and headed west the following spring. According to the *Reno Gazette* of May 25th, 1908, it developed 80 hp, had forty-inch solid wooden disc wheels that were iron bound and fitted with solid rubber tires, and sported a double radiator and large fuel and oil capacities ''for passage through the long stretches of uninhabited country.'' Occasionally called the Nevada Flyer or the Reno Flyer, this behemoth was most often referred to as the Desert Flyer and never arrived in the desert. Meanwhile, in Omaha, Bertzchy tried to secure venture capital with the help of one William Clifford, who said he was from Rawhide, Nevada. The Nevada Motor Car Company, as this project was thus far styled, ended with the building of the single prototype which itself ended up in Council Bluffs, Iowa where it finished its career as the Nevada truck. Thereafter, A.J.P. Bertzchy sued the Nevada firm for back salary and adjourned to Council Bluffs, where in the early fall of 1908 he organized the Bertzchy Motor Company with the assistance of the Council Bluffs Commercial Club. His new automotive idea would be named for himself.

1909 De Shaw, touring, NAHC

DE SHAW — Brooklyn, New York — (1907-1909) — Charles De Shaw was a mechanic from Brooklyn who was an enthusiast of the two-stroke principle and the lightweight motorcar. Following extensive experimentation, he came up with a three-cylinder engine weighing just 119 pounds and put it in a runabout weighing less than 800. ''Arrangements have been made for installing a fan if necessary,'' said De Shaw, ''but so far . . . the engine works satisfactorily without any, and is capable of carrying two people up any of the hills around New York or Brooklyn on the high speed.'' The car was offered only as a runabout, although a rumble seat would be provided at extra cost. De Shaw sold these cars rather casually for over a year. Late in 1908 their marketing became more serious with the formation of the De Shaw Motor Company organized by P.H. Clark (president), W.E. Vogt (vice-president), S.W. Bates (treasurer) and E.W. Lester (secretary), with Charles De Shaw serving as mechanical engineer and superintendent in a new shop set up in Evergreen, Long Island, which was described as a suburb of Brooklyn. Although De Shaw continued to insist that his car really didn't need one, a fan had been added by now, probably at the insistence of his backers. And in addition to the three-cylinder runabout, there was a four-cylinder touring car and runabout added in 1909. Perhaps De Shaw might have fared better had his business not been expanded from its modest beginnings. The car and the company simply faded away in 1910.

1907-1908 DE SHAW

	FP	5	4	3	2	1
Rbt. (3-cyl., 12/14 hp)	—	—	—	—	—	—
1909 DE SHAW						
Rbt. (3-cyl., 12/14 hp)	—	—	—	—	—	—
Touring (4 cyl., 28 hp)	2250	—	—	—	—	—
Runaout (4 cyl., 4 hp)	2150	—	—	—	—	—

DESMARAIS — Holyoke, Massachusetts — (1904) — P. Desmarais & Sons Motor Company of Holyoke was launched into business in 1904 by Pierre, Arthur J.N. and Joseph H. Desmarais for the manufacture of motors and automobiles. Two years earlier, Joseph H. Desmarais (who was a medical doctor and then living in Bristol, Connecticut) had reported his successful completion of a gasoline motor. Now a prototype gasoline car was built around it, but promptly thereafter all concerned decided there was an easier way to get into the automobile industry. In 1905 the Desmarais family secured the Holyoke dealership for the Matheson.

DES MOINES — In 1912 J.G. Cannon organized the Cannon Motor Car Company in Des Moines, Iowa for the manufacture of an automobile which he only briefly considered calling the Des Moines. Refer to Cannon.

1902 Des Moines, motorette, NAHC

DES MOINES — Des Moines, Iowa — (1902) — The Des Moines Automobile Company was incorporated in January 1902 with a paid-up capital stock of $50,000. "Dr. C.B. Paul is president of the new company," *The Motor World* reported, "and it is understood that he has interested a large number of influential men who will furnish all the capital necessary to operate the plant." Obviously one of these influential men attached a string to his furnishing of capital, because within a month the new president of Des Moines was W.F. Pillsbury. Dr. Paul remained on the board, however, and his brother J.E. Paul was the company secretary. To run the factory, Des Moines recruited W.E. Stone who arrived from H.H. Franklin in Syracuse. Although both electric and gasoline vehicles were originally projected for manufacture, only the latter made it into production. The Des Moines car was built for less than a year. Following its demise, apparently the company continued in the automobile repair business. Its plant was on Ninth, between Locust and Grand Streets.

1902 DES MOINES

Des Moines Motorette	650	2400	3400	4800	8000	17,000
Des Moines Imperial	850	2450	3500	4900	8300	17,500
Des Moines Stanhope	1000	2500	3500	5000	8500	18,000
Des Moines Tonneau	1600	2700	3600	5300	8800	19,000

DES MOINES DAZZLER — Des Moines, Iowa — (1906) — Late in 1906 a new venture called the Motor Components Manufacturing Company announced from Des Moines the imminent manufacture of a 50 hp two-stroke car positively bristling with new features — among them the "Arctic Cooler," a device said to be so efficient that the car's engine would actually be cooler when running at top speed than when slowed down. Des Moines Dazzler was the name chosen for this wonderful new automobile. "A trial car of the runabout order is now reported to be undergoing the refinement of a series of road trials," *The Motor World* declared around Christmas. Whether that was the truth was anyone's guess, since the Motor Components Manufacturing Company was another of the enterprises of the talented con artist, William H. Kitto.

DESMOND — The Desmond Automobile company was an automobile venture organized in Chicago which announced in January 1906 its plans for the erection of a factory in Oklahoma City, Oklahoma. The Desmond was not heard from again.

DE SOTA — There never was a De Sota car, despite its presence on automotive rosters. This phantom was simply a misspelling of the de Soto which was produced in Auburn, Indiana from 1913-1914. Interestingly, in a reference from April 1913, not only did *Automobile Topics* get the name wrong, but the place as well, noting the "De Sota" as being built in Des Moines, Iowa.

1914 de Soto, 2-pass. tandem cyclecar, WLB

DE SOTO — Auburn, Indiana — (1913-1914) — The de Soto Motor Car Company was incorporated by L.M. Field (of Auburn), Hayes and Glenn Fry (of Iowa City) and V. H. Van Sickle and H.J. Clark (of Des Moines) during November of 1912. Capital stock was $20,000. Although it was not mentioned at that time, nor subsequently, the de Soto venture was actually a subsidiary to the Zimmerman Manufacturing Company of Auburn, and the de Soto six-cylinder car a counterpart to the six produced by Zimmerman. The de Soto (and the company preferred that spelling, though other variations appeared in the trade press) was a 55 hp automobile (somewhat more powerful than the Zimmerman) and pricier, at $2185. That figure bought electric lights and a compressed air starter, though if a purchaser didn't desire the latter, $100 was deducted from the list price. The de Soto six was continued in 1914 and was joined that year by a two-cylinder 10 hp cyclecar with tandem seats, wheel steering and body lines considerably more pleasing than the cyclecar norm. Plans for 1915 included moving de Soto production from Auburn to Fort Wayne and renaming the cyclecar the Motorette. Instead, the de Soto was discontinued that year. Deaths in the Zimmerman family had left John Zimmerman alone to manage the Zimmerman enterprises, and he simply decided to concentrate efforts under the family name alone.

1913 DE SOTO
Six — 55 hp, 130" wb

	FP	5	4	3	2	1
Touring-5P	2185	4500	5800	9500	18,000	32,000
1914 DE SOTO						
Cyclecar — 2-cyl., 10 hp, 100" wb						
Tandem Roadster	385	2700	3600	5300	8800	19,000
Six — 55 hp, 132" wb						
Touring-5/7P	2185	5000	6500	11,000	22,000	35,000
Roadster-2/4P	2185	4900	6300	10,300	21,000	34,000

DESOTO

DESOTO — Detroit, Michigan — (1929-1942 et. seq.) — The DeSoto was a phenomenon. In its first twelve months in the industry, a total of 81,065 cars were delivered, a first-year sales record which eclipsed the previous high marks made by Graham-Paige (1928), Pontiac (1926) and Chrysler (1924), and a record that would endure far longer, for nearly three decades in fact. If any car seemed destined to be a winner, it was the DeSoto. "Most emphatically, it is not just another model, to be dragged along by the tractive effort of Chrysler advertising, prestige and popularity," *Automobile Topics* enthused upon its introduction. "Nor is it to suffer the unkindly fate that so often befalls the proverbial stepchild." But that is precisely what happened, ultimately, though the unkindly fate of this companion car was more leisurely in coming than most. Actually, the DeSoto wasn't a necessary car when it arrived, for the market gap it was intended to fill between the Chrysler and the new Plymouth could very nicely be plugged by Dodge, which company Walter Chrysler had just managed to buy. Indeed, there is reason to believe that the DeSoto had been planned by Chrysler to intimidate the bankers controlling Dodge into selling the company to him. By the time that happened and the papers were signed, the DeSoto was on the assembly line, however. In the heady optimism of the Twenties, its sensational first year seemed to indicate that the car, though somewhat superfluous, could do very nicely on its own. It was a nice automobile, though not extraordinary in any way, its 174.9-cubic-inch L-head six-cylinder engine delivering 55 hp for a pleasantly snappy and vigorous performance, and Lockheed hydraulic brakes, Lovejoy shock absorbers, Hotchkiss drive, and the same thin-profile (or "ribbon") radiator of the more expensive Chrysler making for an admirable $845 DeSoto package. The car was named, of course, for the Spanish explorer Hernando DeSoto who, comparatively, probably encountered no more difficulties in discovering the Mississippi in 1541 than DeSoto would in surviving the 1930's. The car's fortunes plummeted during the Depression. In 1930 the DeSoto line of sixes was augmented by a straight-eight, its engine and chassis similar to the new Dodge eight also introduced that year. During 1930, 34,889 DeSotos and 68,159 Dodges were produced, the same vis-a-vis ratio of the two cars since 1928, which seemed to auger well. The eight was discontinued after '32, replaced by a fine new 75 hp six, the first DeSoto featuring a body design completely its own, though it shared the new Plymouth PB chassis with free wheeling and Floating Power engine mounts. In that depth-of-Depression year, DeSoto's sales of more than 25,000 cars practically equalled Dodge's. By 1933, however, two decisions were made for the car, one of which perhaps wasn't wise, the other an unmitigated disaster. First, the DeSoto's price range was modified; from a car priced somewhat less than the Dodge, it now became a car priced somewhat higher. Since this moved the DeSoto closer to the Chrysler than heretofore, it perhaps followed that the car would become more Chrysler-like. In 1934 that meant the Airflow. DeSoto sold just over 15,000 of them that year, which was better than Chrysler's 11,000 Airflows, but Chrysler also offered a conventionally-styled car (DeSoto didn't) which brought overall Chrysler sales up to a more respectable near-37,000. Meanwhile Dodge passed the 100,000 mark. In 1935 and 1936, only 11,797 DeSoto Airflows were built, though the more conventional Airstream introduced in '35 helped to boost respective production figures to 34,276 and 52,789 cars during those years. But Dodge was up past the 200,000 mark now. And so it would go. Still, DeSoto did enjoy some good fortune in the later 1930's. The beginnings of a lucrative taxicab business and an upswing in sales following introduction of the completely conventional Ray Dietrich-designed cars of '37 were positives in the DeSoto history. The superlative arrived for '42, the most expensive DeSotos ever, with scads of chrome and disappearing headlights. Just 24,771 of them were built before February 9th, 1942 when all production stopped. When it resumed after the war, the DeSoto continued its teeter-totter life within Chrysler Corporation for a decade and a half. Ironically, the car's last year, 1960, was also the year the new Ford Falcon took away the sales record that DeSoto had enjoyed holding since 1929.

DeSoto Data Compilation
by John A. Gunnell

1929

1929 DeSoto Six, Series K, roadster, OCW

DESOTO — SERIES K — SIX: The DeSoto was introduced in the middle of 1928 as a 1929 automobile. The new marque was named after the Spanish explorer and aimed at the low-priced six market. After its Aug. 4 introduction, the DeSoto sold at a record setting pace and hit an all-time high for any American car in its first year at this point in time. Appearance features included an arched headlamp tie-bar, triple groups of vertical hood louvers and cowl lamps integral with the surcingle molding. Deluxe equipment included fender wells, six wheel equipment, special paint, chrome headlamp tie-bar and richer upholstery. Standard equipment included Delco-Remy ignition, hydraulic brakes, Lovejoy shock absorbers and rubber mounted motor suspension.

I.D. DATA: Serial numbers followed the Fedco coding system. They were located on a plate built into the center of the instrument board. Starting No.: KW000P. Ending No.: KL300L. Engine numbers were located on the upper left side of cylinder block between no. 1 and no. 2 cylinders, just below cylinder head. Starting Engine No.: K1001. Ending: K83099.

Model No.	Body Type & Seating	Price	Weight	Prod. Total
K	2-dr. Rds.-2/4P	845	2350	Note 1
K	4-dr. Phae.-5P	845	2445	Note 1
K	2-dr. Bus. Cpe.-2P	845	2465	Note 1
K	2-dr. Del. Cpe.-2/4P	885	2525	Note 1
K	2-dr. Coach-5P	845	2580	Note 1
K	4-dr. Sed.-5P	885	2645	Note 1
K	4-dr. Del. Sed.-5P	955	2655	Note 1

Note 1: Total production was over 80,000 cars.

ENGINE: Inline. L-head. Six. Cast iron block. B & S: 3 x 4-1/8. Disp.: 174.9 cu. in. C.R.: 5.2:1. Brake H.P.: 55 @ 3000 R.P.M. N.A.C.C. H.P.: 21.6. Four main bearings. Solid valve lifters. Carb.: Stromberg 1V. Torque: 110 lbs.-ft. @ 1200 R.P.M.

CHASSIS: [Series K] W.B.: 109.75 in. O.L.: 169 in. Tires: 5.00 x 19.

TECHNICAL: Selective sliding gear transmission. Speeds: 3F/1R. Floor shift control. Conventional clutch. Shaft drive. Semi-floating rear axle. Overall drive ratio: 4.7:1. Lockheed hydraulic 4-wheel brakes. Wood spoke wheels.

OPTIONS: Front bumper. Rear bumper. Single sidemount. Dual sidemount. Sidemount cover(s). Rear spare. Wire spoke wheels. Special paint. Special upholstery. Cigar lighter. High compression cylinder head. Trippe lights. Spotlight(s). Cowl lamps.

HISTORICAL: Introduced: Aug. 6, 1928. All new light six-cylinder from Chrysler Corp. Calendar year registrations: (1928) 14,538; (1929) 59,614. Calendar year production: (1929) 64,911; (1928) 33,345. Model year production: (1929) 62,191. Corporate president Walter P. Chrysler. First announced in the *Detroit Free Press* on May 6, 1928. Over 500 dealers signed up immediately and by the end of 1928, over 34,000 cars were shipped to a dealer network of 1,500. J.E. Fields, a Chrysler vice president of sales was named president of DeSoto Division.

1929 DeSoto Six, Series K, 4-dr., sedan, OCW

1929
Model K, 6-cyl.

	FP	5	4	3	2	1
Rds	845	4050	8100	13,500	18,900	27,000
Phae	845	4200	8400	14,000	19,600	28,000
Bus Cpe	845	900	1900	4500	6300	9000
DeL Cpe	885	950	2100	4750	6650	9500
2 dr Sed	845	850	1650	4100	5700	8200
4 dr Sed	885	850	1650	4100	5700	8200
DeL Sed	955	875	1700	4250	5900	8500

1930

1930 DeSoto Six, Series K, roadster, OCW

DESOTO — SERIES K — SIX: The Series K DeSoto six continued to be marketed when the 1930 model year began in July, 1929. The cars were unchanged in terms of appearance features or equipment. The model year designation was simply changed to make the cars seem more up-to-date. Refer to the previous listing for models, prices, weights and technical specifications.

1930 DeSoto Eight, Series CF, coupe, JAC

DESOTO — SERIES CF — EIGHT: In January, 1930, DeSoto continued to market the Series K six as a 1930 model, but also introduced the new Series CF eight. This was a low-priced eight-cylinder car. It had undivided vertical hood louvers, instead of the three separate groupings used on sixes. The radiator had a deeper, chrome plated shell. A unit grouped instrument panel was featured. Standard equipment included NorthEast ignition, hydraulic brakes, mono-piece body construction, fuel pump, rubber spring shackles, downdraft carburetor, Lovejoy shock absorbers and a seven cross member frame.

1930 DeSoto Eight, Series CF, phaeton, JAC

FINER DESOTO — SERIES CK — SIX: The CK DeSoto six was introduced in May 1930. Its appearance features included a deeper radiator shell and cowl lamps mounted on top of the front fenders. Otherwise it looked much like the original DeSoto six. Standard equipment additions included Delco-Remy ignition and a larger bore engine.

I.D. DATA: [Series K] Serial numbers were in the same location. Starting: KL300E. Ending: KK142W. Engine numbers were in the same location. Starting: K83100. Ending: K113744. [Series CF] Serial numbers were in the same location. Both Fedco and conventional type numbers were used. Starting: L001WP. Ending: L172PH. (Conventional) 6000001 to 6000212. Engine numbers were in the same location. Starting: CF1001. Ending: CF19388. [Series CK] DeSoto switched completely to the use of conventional serial numbers. They were in the same location. Starting: 5000001. Ending: 5006932. Engine numbers were in the same location. Starting: CK-1001. Ending: Ck-8443.

1930 DeSoto Six, Series CK, roadster, JAC

Model No.	Body Type & Seating	Price	Weight	Prod. Total
K	2-dr. Rds.-2/4P	845	2350	Note 1
K	4-dr. Phae.-5P	845	2445	Note 1
K	2-dr. Bus. Cpe.-2P	845	2465	Note 1
K	2-dr. Del. Cpe.-2/4P	885	2525	Note 1
K	2-dr. Sed.-5P	845	2580	Note 1
K	4-dr. Sed.-5P	885	2645	Note 1
K	4-dr. Del. Sed.-5P	955	2655	Note 1

Note 1: See 1929 Series K production totals.

CF	2-dr. Rds.-2/4P	985	2720	1457
CF	4-dr. Phae.-5P	1035	2800	179
CF	2-dr. Bus. Cpe.-2P	965	2835	1015
CF	2-dr. Del. Cpe.-2/4P	1025	2875	2735
CF	2-dr. Conv. Cpe.-2/4P	1075	2845	524
CF	4-dr. Sed.-5P	995	2965	9653
CF	4-dr. Del. Sed.-5P	1065	2975	4139
CF	Chassis	NA	NA	373

Note 2: Total series production was 20,075.

CK	2-dr. Rds.-2/4P	810	2385	1086
CK	4-dr. Phae.-5P	830	2475	209
CK	2-dr. Bus. Cpe.-2P	830	2515	858
CK	2-dr. R/S Cpe.-2/4P	860	2585	1521
CK	2-dr. Conv. Cpe.-2/4P	945	2540	184
CK	4-dr. Sed.-5P	875	2705	8248
CK	Chassis	NA	NA	94

Note 3: Total series production was 12,200.

ENGINE: [Series K] Inline. L-head. Six. Cast iron block. B & S: 3 x 4-1/8 in. Disp.: 174.9 cu. in. C.R.: 5.2:1. Brake H.P.: 55 @ 3000 R.P.M. N.A.C.C. H.P.: 21.6. Four main bearings. Solid valve lifters. Carb.: Stromberg 1V. Torque: 110 lbs.-ft. @ 1200 R.P.M. [Series CF] Inline. L-head. Eight. Cast iron block. B & S: 2-7/8 x 4 in. Disp.: 207.7 cu. in. C.R.: 5.2:1. Brake H.P.: 70 @ 3400 R.P.M. N.A.C.C. H.P.: 26.45. Five main bearings. Solid valve lifters. Carb.: Carter model 188 SR. Torque: 132 lbs.-ft. @ 1200 R.P.M. [Series CK] Inline. L-head. Six. Cast iron block. B & S: 3-1/8 x 4-1/8 in. Disp.: 189.8 cu. in. C.R.: 5.2:1. Brake H.P.: 60 @ 3400 R.P.M. Four main bearings. Solid valve lifters. Carb.: Stromberg 1V model DX3. Torque: 120 lbs.-ft. @ 1200 R.P.M.

CHASSIS: [Series K] W.B.: 109 in. O.L.: 169 in. Tires: 19 x 5.00. [Series CF] W.B.: 114 in. O.L.: 177 in. Tires: 19 x 5.25. [Series CK] W.B.: 109 in. O.L.: 169 in. Tires: 19 x 5.00.

TECHNICAL: Selective sliding gear transmission. Speeds: 3F/1R. Floor shift controls. Single-plate dry disc clutch. Shaft drive. Semi-floating rear axle. Overall ratios: (K) 4.7:1; (CF) 4.9:1; (CK) 4.7:1. Four wheel hydraulic brakes. Wood spoke wheels.

OPTIONS: Front bumper. Rear bumper. Single sidemount. Dual sidemount. Sidemount cover(s). Wire wheels. Bumper guards. OSRV mirror. Heater. Clock. Cigar lighter. Special paint. Special upholstery. Wind wings. Spotlight(s). Cowl lamps. Trumpet horn. Pedestal sidemount mirrors. Fender wells.

HISTORICAL: Date of Introduction: (K) July 1929; (CF) Jan. 1930; (CK) May 1930. Innovations: First DeSoto Eight. Larger more powerful "CK" six. Delco Remy ignition. Calendar year registrations: 35,267. Calendar year production: 34,889. Model year production: 32,091. DeSoto was America's 15th largest auto-maker in model year 1930. The 100,000 DeSoto was built this year.

1930
Model CK, 6-cyl.

	FP	5	4	3	2	1
Rds	845	3900	7800	13,000	18,200	26,000
Tr	845	4050	8100	13,500	18,900	27,000
Bus Cpe	845	875	1700	4250	5900	8500
DeL Cpe	885	900	1900	4500	6300	9000
2 dr Sed	845	775	1500	3750	5250	7500
Sed	885	825	1600	4000	5600	8000

Model CF, 8-cyl.

Rds	985	4050	8100	13,500	18,900	27,000
Phae	1035	4200	8400	14,000	19,600	28,000
Bus Cpe	965	900	1900	4500	6300	9000
DeL Cpe	1025	950	2100	4750	6650	9500
Sed	995	900	1900	4500	6300	9000
DeL Sed	1065	950	2100	4750	6650	9500
Conv	1075	3900	7800	13,000	18,200	26,000

1930-31

DESOTO (FINER) — SERIES CK — SIX: The Finer Six was carried over as an early 1931 series. There were no obvious styling or equipment changes. The rear axle ratio was numerically lowered and new serial number ranges were used. July 1, 1930 was the date after which CKs were considered first series 1931 DeSotos.

DESOTO — SERIES CF — EIGHT: The DeSoto Eight was carried over as an early 1931 model. There were no obvious styling or equipment changes. The rear axle ratio was numerically lowered and a new range of serial numbers was used. July 1, 1930 was the date after which CFs were considered first series 1931 models.

I.D. DATA: [Series CK] Serial numbers were in the same locations. Starting: 5006933. Ending: 5011672. Engine numbers were in the same location. Starting: CK8444. Ending: CK13217. [Series CF] Serial numbers were in the same location. Starting: L172PR. Ending: L185PC. Engine numbers were in the same location. Starting: CF19389. Ending: CF21448.

NOTE: Body styles, prices, weights and production totals for the 1930-31 DeSoto CK models are given in the 1930 section. Body styles, prices, weights and production totals for the 1930-31 CF models are also given in the 1930 section.

ENGINE: Specifications for the DeSoto six-and eight-cylinder engines were unchanged. See 1930 charts above.

CHASSIS: Chassis specifications were the same as 1930 model specifications.

TECHNICAL: Drivetrain specifications were the same as 1930 model specifications except cars now had a 4.6:1 rear axle ratio.

OPTIONS: Options available for the 1930-31 series were the same as offered for the 1930 models.

HISTORICAL: See 1930 DeSoto historical notes. Calculations based on serial and engine numbers suggest that approximately 4800 sixes (CK) and 2100 eights (CF) were sold as 1931 first series cars.

1931

DESOTO — SERIES SA — SIX: The 1931 DeSoto Six SA was introduced in January, 1931 at the New York Automobile Show. The restyled body appearance emphasized a longer hood. Other styling features included a narrow profile radiator, vertical radiator shutters and hood louvers, twin cowl ventilators, new type swinging windshield and an oval instrument board. Standard equipment included Delco-Remy ignition, hydraulic brakes, double drop frame and hydraulic shock absorbers.

DESOTO — SERIES CF* — EIGHT: The 1931 DeSoto CF* Eight used a new headlamp cross-bar with the DeSoto crest in the center of it to distinguish it from the six. The eight had two-bar bumpers, a stripe on the sun visor and matching body and fender finish. Other features included a new, narrow profile radiator shell, vertical radiator shutters and hood louvers, twin cowl ventilators, an oval instrument panel and new French type sun visor and top. Standard equipment included Delco-Remy ignition, hydraulic brakes, new counter balanced crankshaft, a non-glare slanting windshield, adjustable front seats and hydraulic shock absorbers.

1931 DeSoto Six, Series SA, roadster, OCW

I.D. DATA: [Series SA] Serial numbers were in the same location. Starting No.: 5011801. Ending: 5030806. Engine numbers were in the same location. Starting Engine No.: SA1001. Ending: SA20305. [Series CF*] Serial numbers were in the same locations. Both Fedco and conventional numbers were used on the eights. Starting: L-185PH. Ending: L-192LD. Conventional serial numbers 6000801 to 6001888 were also used. Engine numbers were in the same locations. Starting Engine No.: CF*22001. Ending: CF*24308.

Model No.	Body Type & Seating	Price	Weight	Prod. Total
SA	2-dr. Rds.-2/4P	795	2520	1949
SA	4-dr. Phae.-5P	795	2645	100
SA	2-dr. Std. Cpe.-2P	740	2630	1309
SA	2-dr. Del. Cpe.-2/4P	775	2685	2663
SA	2-dr. Conv. Cpe.-2/4P	825	2630	638
SA	2-dr. Sed.-5P	695	2715	2349
SA	4-dr. Sed.-5P	775	2745	17,866
SA	4-dr. Del. Sed.-5P	825	2835	1450
SA	Chassis	—	—	32

Note 1: Total series production was 28,356.

CF*	2-dr. Rds.-2/4P	995	2825	73
CF*	2-dr. Bus. Cpe.-2P	965	2935	102
CF*	2-dr. Del. Cpe.-2/4P	995	2970	486
CF*	2-dr. Conv. Cpe.-2/4P	1110	2970	48
CF*	4-dr. Sed.-5P	995	3065	3490
CF*	4-dr. Del. Sed.-5P	1065	3115	Note 3
CF*	Chassis	NA	NA	3

Note 2: Total series production was 4,224.
Note 3: Production of the Deluxe sedan is included in the total for the regular 4-door sedan.

ENGINE: [Series SA] Inline. L-head. Six. Cast iron block. B & S: 3-1/4 x 4-1/8 in. Disp.: 205.3 cu. in. C.R.: 5.4:1. Brake H.P.: 72 @ 3400 R.P.M. N.A.C.C. H.P.: 25.35. Four main bearings. Solid valve lifters. Carb.: Carter 1V model 188SR. Torque: 139 lbs.-ft. @ 1200 R.P.M. [Series CF*] Inline. L-head. Eight. Cast iron block. B & S: 2-7/8 x 4-1/4 in. Disp.: 220.7 cu. in. C.R.: 5.4:1. Brake H.P.: 77 @ 3400 R.P.M. N.A.C.C. H.P.: 26.45. Five main bearings. Solid valve lifters. Carb.: Stromberg 1V model DX3. Torque: 140 lbs.-ft. @ 1200 R.P.M.

CHASSIS: [Series SA] W.B.: 109 in. Tires: 19 x 5.00. [Series CF*] W.B.: 114 in. Tires: 19 x 5.25.

TECHNICAL: Selective sliding gear transmission. Speeds: 3F/1R. Floor shift controls. Single plate dry disc clutch. Shaft drive. Semi-floating rear axle. Overall gear ratios: (SA) 4.33:1; (CF*) 4.60:1. Hydraulic four wheel brakes. Wood spoke wheels (except convertibles).

OPTIONS: Front bumper. Rear bumper. Single sidemount. Dual sidemounts. (standard on CF convertible). Metal sidemount cover(s). Leather sidemount covers. OSRV mirrors. Wire spoke wheels (std. on convertibles). Heater. Clock. Cigar lighter. Wind wings. Trunk rack. Touring trunk. Spotlight(s). Cowl lamps. Trumpet horn. Spare tire(s). Chrome headlights.

1931 DeSoto Six, Series SA, deluxe coupe, JAC

HISTORICAL: Introduced: Jan. 1, 1931. Innovations: (Six) Double drop frame. Hydraulic shock absorbers. Visor-less styling on closed cars. (Eight) Unisteel enclosed bodies. Increased stroke. Heavier crankshaft. New rubber center clutch hub. Calendar year registrations: 28,430. Calendar year production: 32,091. DeSoto was America's 15th ranked producer in terms of model year production. Some depot hack bodies for the DeSoto chassis were custom built by J.T. Cantrell & Co. Peter Paolo drove a DeSoto Eight across the country as a promotional stunt. Production figures above cover 1931 models (built Jan. to June 1931) and 1931-32 models (built July to Dec. 1931). About 75 percent of the sixes and 50 percent of the eights were sold as "true" 1931 models.

1931
Model SA, 6-cyl.

	FP	5	4	3	2	1
Rds	795	4050	8100	13,500	18,900	27,000
Phae	795	4200	8400	14,000	19,600	28,000
Cpe	740	775	1500	3750	5250	7500
DeL Cpe	775	900	1900	4500	6300	9000
2 dr Sed	695	775	1500	3700	5200	7400
Sed	775	775	1500	3700	5200	7400
DeL Sed	825	825	1600	4000	5600	8000
Conv	825	3900	7800	13,000	18,200	26,000

Model CF, 8-cyl.

	FP	5	4	3	2	1
Rds	995	4200	8400	14,000	19,600	28,000
Bus Cpe	965	950	2100	4750	6650	9500
DeL Cpe	695	975	2300	4950	6900	9900
Sed	995	925	2000	4650	6500	9300
DeL Sed	1065	950	2100	4750	6650	9500
Conv	1110	4050	8100	13,500	18,900	27,000

1931-32

DESOTO — SERIES SA — SIX: The Series SA DeSoto Six was carried over as an early 1932 series. There were no obvious styling changes. New technical features included "Easy-Shift" transmission with silent second gear and the optional availability of freewheeling at $20 extra. July 1, 1931 was the date after which SAs were considered 1932 models.

DESOTO — CF* — EIGHT: The Series CF* DeSoto Eight was carried over as an early 1932 series. There was no obvious styling changes. New technical features included "Easy-Shift" transmission with silent second gear and the optional availability of freewheeling at $20 extra. July 1, 1931 was the date after which CF* models were considered 1932 automobiles.

I.D. DATA: [Series SA] Serial numbers were in the same location. Starting: 5030807. Ending: 5040056. Engine numbers were in the same location. Starting: SA20306. Ending: SA29328. [Series CF*] Serial numbers were in the same location. Both Fedco and conventional numbers were used on the eights. Starting: L192EW. Ending: L192DS. Conventional serial numbers 6001889 to 6004021 were also used. Engine numbers were in the same location. Starting: CF* 24309. Ending: CF* 26621.

Note 1: Body styles, prices, weights and production totals for the 1931-32 DeSoto SA models are given in the 1931 section. About 25 percent of the sixes were sold as 1932 models.

Model No.	Body Type & Seating	Price	Weight	Prod. Total
CF*	4-dr. Phae.-5P	1035	2750	22

Note 1: The 4-door phaeton was an all new model produced only in the early 1932 series. Body styles, prices, weights and production totals for other 1931-32 DeSoto CF* models are given in the 1931 section. About 50 percent of the eights were sold as 1932 models.

ENGINE: [Series SA] DeSoto Six engine specifications were unchanged from 1931 specifications. See data in charts above. [Series CF*] DeSoto Eight engine specifications were unchanged from 1931 specifications. See data in charts above.

CHASSIS: Chassis specifications were the same as 1931 model specifications.

TECHNICAL: Drivetrain specifications were the same as 1931 model specifications except the transmission now had a silent second gear and freewheeling was an available option.

OPTIONS: Options available for the 1931-32 series were the same as offered for the 1931 models.

HISTORICAL: See 1931 DeSoto historical notes. Calculations based on serial numbers suggest that approximately 9,022 sixes (CA) and 2,312 eights (CF*) were sold as 1932 first series cars.

1932

DESOTO — SERIES SC — SIX: Introduced in Jan., 1932, the SC series was characterized by a rounded grille that resembled that of a Miller racing car. It had horizontal bars divided by three vertical bars. New styling features included one-piece fenders, twin cowl ventilators, wider body belt moldings, interior (instead of exterior) sun visors and wire wheels. Standard equipment included Delco-Remy ignition, hydraulic brakes, "Floating Power," free wheeling, fuel pump, double drop X-type frame, safety all-steel body, silent gear selector, Synchromesh transmission, and a rear spare wheel. Buyers could have their car with a painted grille shell or a chrome plated one (at extra cost). There was also a custom SC sub-series in which all models featured external trumpet horns, dual taillamps, dual windshield wipers, safety glass, cigar lighters, adjustable seats, and fenders painted to match the body color. Both standard and custom models could also be ordered with "deluxe" equipment including bumpers and six wire wheels. Chrome headlights were standard on all SCs. The Custom roadster and coupe were models with a rumbleseat and six wheel equipment was standard on the custom SC convertible sedan.

1932 DeSoto Six, Series SC, convertible coupe, OCW

I.D. DATA: Serial numbers were in the same location. Starting: (std.) 5040201; (cus.) 6005001. Ending: (std.) 5055921; (cus.) 6012580. Engine numbers were in the same location. Starting Engine No.: (std.) SC1001; (cus.) SC1001. Ending: (std.) SC23584; (cus.) SC24800.

Model No. (Standard SC)	Body Type & Seating	Price	Weight	Prod. Total
SSC	2-dr. Rds.-2P	675	2720	(894)
SSC	2-dr. Cpe.-2P	695	2843	1691
SSC	2-dr. R/S Cpe.-2/4P	735	2888	(2897)
SSC	2-dr. Brgm.-5P	695	2903	3730
SSC	4-dr. Sed.-5P	775	2993	8924
SSC	4-dr. Sed.-7P	925	3148	221
SSC	Chassis	NA	NA	83
(Custom SC)				
CSC	2-dr. Rds.-2/4P	775	2738	(894)
CSC	2-dr. Cpe.-2/4P	790	2913	(2897)
CSC	2-dr. Conv. Cpe.-2/4P	845	2858	960
CSC	4-dr. Sed.-5P	835	3028	4791
CSC	4-dr. Conv. Sed.-5P	975	3043	275
CSC	4-dr. Phae.-5P	775	NA	30

Note 1: Total series production was 24,496.
Note 2: Figures in brackets are combined totals for standard and custom models and are shown in both places.

ENGINE: Inline. L-head. Six. Cast iron block. B & S: 3-1/4 x 4-3/8 in. Disp.: 217.8 cu. in. C.R.: 5.4:1. Brake H.P.: 75 @ 3400 R.P.M. N.A.C.C. H.P.: 25.35. Four main bearings. Solid valve lifters. Carb.: Ball & Ball 1V model 6B2. Torque: 140 lbs.-ft. @ 1400 R.P.M.

CHASSIS: [Series SC (std.)] W.B.: 112-3/8 in. Tires: 18 x 5.25. [Series SC (cus.)] W.B.: 112-3/8 in. Tires: 17 x 5.50. [Series SC (Sed.-7P)] W.B.: 121 in. Tires: 18 x 5.25.

TECHNICAL: Transmission: Selective sliding w/constant mesh. and freewheeling. Speeds: 3F/1R. Floor shift controls. Single disc dry plate clutch. Shaft drive. Semi-floating rear axle. Overall Ratio: 4.62:1. Four wheel hydraulic brakes. Wire wheels.
Note: A vacuum operated automatic clutch was available at extra cost.

1932 DeSoto Six, Series SC, sedan, JAC

OPTIONS: Front bumper. Rear bumper. Single sidemount. Dual sidemount(s). Sidemount cover(s). Wood spoke wheels. Spare tire. Radio. Heater. Clock. Cigar lighter. Radio antenna. Special upholstery. Wind wings. Spotlight(s). Cowl lamps. Trumpet horns (std. models). Trunk rack. touring trunk. Safety glass (std. models). Dual taillights (std. models). Chrome radiator shell. Dual sun visors (std. models). Chrome sidemount trim bands. Special paint.

HISTORICAL: Introduced: Jan., 1932. Innovations: Fuel pump. Automatic clutch option. Constant mesh transmission. New double drop X frame. Freewheeling standard. Longer wheelbase. "Floating Power" engine

mounting system. Calendar year registrations: 25,311. Calendar year production: 27,441. Model year production: 24,496. For the calendar year, DeSoto was the 9th ranked U.S. auto-maker. The company placed 12th in model year production. At least two SC Custom Town Cars were constructed on the 121 inch wheelbase chassis. The 1932 DeSoto was advertised as "America's Smartest Low-Priced Car." Race driver Peter DePaolo made a 10-day cross-country promotional run in a new DeSoto SC. It culminated with a 300-mile race track trial at speeds up to 80 mph. Production and sales of the SC DeSoto continued into 1933 in Great Britain, where a badge-engineered version was marketed as the Chrysler Mortlake Six.

1932

SA, 6-cyl., 109" wb						
Phae	—	4350	8700	14,500	20,300	29,000
Rds	—	4200	8400	14,000	19,600	28,000
Cpe	—	1000	2400	5000	7000	10,000
DeL Cpe	—	1000	2400	5000	7000	10,000
Conv	—	4050	8100	13,500	18,900	27,000
2 dr Sed	—	775	1500	3750	5250	7500
Sed	—	800	1550	3850	5400	7700
DeL Sed	—	825	1600	4000	5600	8000
SC, 6-cyl., 112" wb						
2 dr Conv Sed	975	4050	8100	13,500	18,900	27,000
Rds	775	4200	8400	14,000	19,600	28,000
Phae	775	4350	8700	14,500	20,300	29,000
Conv	845	3900	7800	13,000	18,200	26,000
Bus Cpe	735	1000	2400	5000	7000	10,000
RS Cpe	790	1075	3000	5500	7700	11,000
Sed	775	775	1500	3750	5250	7500
DeL Sed	835	825	1600	4050	5650	8100
CF, 8-cyl., 114" wb						
Rds	—	4350	8700	14,500	20,300	29,000
Bus Cpe	—	1025	2600	5250	7300	10,500
DeL Cpe	—	1125	3450	5750	8050	11,500
Brgm	—	775	1500	3750	5250	7500
Sed	—	825	1600	4000	5600	8000
DeL Sed	—	850	1650	4100	5700	8200

1933

1933 DeSoto Six, Series SD, convertible coupe, OCW

DESOTO — SERIES SD — SIX: The 1933 DeSotos had a horizontal radiator grille and front fenders that came to the center of the radiator. One way to tell standard models was that they did not have a vertical trim divider on the headlight lenses. Twin sun visors, taillights and trumpet horns were standard on only the Customs early in the year, but later became standard equipment on the low-priced cars, as well. Other 1933 DeSoto features included Delco-Remy ignition, hydraulic brakes, "Floating Power," automatic vacuum clutch, coincidental starter, automatic choke, double drop X-type frames and safety plate glass. Six wire wheel equipment was standard on the Custom Convertible sedan.

I.D. DATA: Serial numbers were in the same location. Starting: (Std.) 5056001; (Cus.) 6013001. Ending: (Std.) 5068056; (Cus.) 60234023. Engine numbers were in the same location. Starting: SD-1001. Ending: SD-23800.

Model No. (Standard SD)	Body Type & Seating	Price	Weight	Prod. Total
SD	2-dr. Cpe.-2P	665	2905	800
SD	2-dr. R/S Cpe.-2/4P	705	2975	(2705)
SD	2-dr. Brgm.-5P	665	2995	2436
SD	2-dr. Spl. Brgm.-5P	725	3015	8133
SD	4-dr. Sed.-5P	735	3070	(7890)
(Custom SD)				
SD	2-dr. R/S Cpe.-2/4P	750	2995	(2705)
SD	2-dr. Conv. Cpe.-2/4P	775	2990	412
SD	4-dr. Sed.-5P	795	3150	(7890)
SD	2-dr. Conv. Sed.-5P	875	NA	132
SD	Chassis	NA	NA	124
SD	4-dr. Exp. Sed.-7P	NA	NA	104

Note 1: Total series production was 22,736.
Note 2: Figures in parenthesis indicate combined production totals for standard and custom models. No additional breakouts are available.

ENGINE: Inline. L-head. Six. Cast iron block. B & S: 3-1/4 x 4-3/8. Disp.: 217.8 cu. in. C.R.: 6.2:1. Brake H.P.: 100 @ 3400 R.P.M. N.A.C.C. H.P.: 25.35. Five main bearings. Solid valve lifters. Carb.: Ball & Ball 1V model E6A3. Torque: 160 lbs.-ft. @ 1200 R.P.M.

CHASSIS: [Series SD] W.B.: 114-3/8 in. Tires: (std.) 17 x 5.50; (cus.) 15 x 7.00.

1933 DeSoto Six, Series SD, standard brougham, JAC

TECHNICAL: All-silent helical gear transmission. Speeds: 3F/1R. Floor shift controls. Single plate dry disc clutch. Shaft drive. Semi-floating rear axle. Overall Ratio: 4.375:1. Four wheel hydraulic brake. Wire wheels supplied on standard models. Goodyear "Airwheels" standard on Custom models.

OPTIONS: Front bumper. Rear bumper. Single sidemount. Dual sidemount(s). Sidemount cover(s). Trumpet horns. Bumper guards. Radio (all cars wired for radios). Heater. Clock. Cigar lighter. Radio antenna. Seat covers. OSRV mirror(s). Spotlight(s). Cowl lamps. Rear spare tire. Wind wings. Special paint. Special upholstery. Trunk rack. Touring trunk.

HISTORICAL: Introduced: Dec., 1932. Automatic choke. Automatic manifold heat control. All helical-gear transmission. Coincidental starter operated by accelerator pedal. Calendar year registrations: 21,260. Calendar year production: 20,186. Model year production: 22,736. Race driver Harry Hartz drove a specially modified DeSoto backwards across the U.S. this year. The stunt was designed to herald the 1934 DeSoto Airflows. The SD was sold in Great Britain as the Chrysler Wimbledon this year only.

1933 DeSoto Six, Series SD, custom coupe, JAC

1933
SD, 6-cyl.

	FP	5	4	3	2	1
Conv	795	3750	7500	12,500	17,500	25,000
2 dr Conv Sed	975	4050	8100	13,500	18,900	27,000
2P Cpe	695	850	1650	4150	5800	8300
RS Cpe	790	1000	2400	5000	7000	10,000
DeL Cpe	735	1000	2400	5000	7000	10,000
2 dr Std Brgm	725	850	1650	4100	5700	8200
Cus Brgm	755	875	1700	4250	5900	8500
Sed	765	825	1600	4000	5600	8000
Cus Sed	795	850	1650	4150	5800	8300

1934

DESOTO — SERIES SE — SIX: All 1934 DeSotos featured Chrysler Corp.'s new, streamlined, Airflow design. They had built-in headlamps. Wider front seats accommodated three passengers. The hood extended beyond the front axle. The rear fenders were shrouded with full fender skirts. Other design features included horizontal hood louvers, a rounded radiator grille and a modified, V-shaped windshield. Standard equipment included Delco-Remy ignition, 4-wheel hydraulic brakes, unit body construction, "Floating Power," and Goodyear "Airwheels."

I.D. DATA: Serial numbers were in the same location. Starting: 5068501 and up. Engine numbers were in the same location. Starting: SE1001 and up.

1934 DeSoto Airflow, Series SE, 4-dr. sedan, OCW

Model No.	Body Type & Seating	Price	Weight	Prod. Total
SE	2-dr. Cpe.-5P	995	3323	1584
SE	2-dr. Brgm.-6P	995	3323	522
SE	4-dr. Sed.-6P	995	3378	11,713
SE	4-dr. Twn. Sed.-6P	995	3343	119
SE	Chassis	NA	NA	2

Note 1: Total series production was 13,940.

ENGINE: Inline. L-head. Six. Cast iron block. B & S: 3-3/8 x 4-1/2 in. Disp.: 241.5 cu. in. C.R.: 6.2:1. Brake H.P.: 100 @ 3400 R.P.M. N.A.C.C. H.P.: 27.34. Four main bearings. Solid valve lifters. Carb.: Ball & Ball 1V model E6B1. Torque: 185 lbs.-ft. @ 1200 R.P.M.

CHASSIS: W.B.: 115-1/2 in. Tires: 16 x 6.50.

TECHNICAL: Manual transmission with freewheeling. Speeds: 3F/1R. Floor shift controls. Conventional clutch. Shaft drive. Semi-floating rear axle. Overall ratio: 4.11:1. Four wheel hydraulic brakes. Goodyear "Airwheels."

OPTIONS: Front bumper. Rear bumper. Fender skirt ornament. Fender skirts (std. models). Bumper guards. Radio. Heater. Clock. Cigar lighter. Radio antenna. Seat covers. Steel artillery spoke wheels (no extra cost). Spotlight. Steel disc wheels (no extra cost). License plate frames. Automatic vacuum clutch.

HISTORICAL: Introduced Jan. 1934. Innovations: Radically new Airflow design. Balanced weight distribution. Unit body construction. Extra long leaf springs. Low radiator core. Fresh air ventilation. Calendar year registrations: 11,447. Calendar year production: 15,825. Model year production: 13,940. DeSoto ranked 13th in terms of U.S. model year output. Byron C. Foy was president of DeSoto. He helped promote sales of the new model at Chrysler's exhibit at the "Century of Progress" exposition in Chicago. Airflows were capable of up to 22 mpg fuel economy. Race driver Harry Hartz set 32 stock car records driving a DeSoto Airflow at Muroc Dry Lake in California. Hartz also made a New York to San Francisco cross-country trip with a total fuel bill of just $33.06. The SE was sold in Great Britain as the Chrysler Croydon.

1934
Airflow SE, 6-cyl.

	FP	5	4	3	2	1
Cpe	995	1000	2400	5000	7000	10,000
Brgm	995	1025	2600	5250	7300	10,500
Sed	995	875	1700	4250	5900	8500
Twn Sed	995	1075	3000	5500	7700	11,000

1935

1935 DeSoto, Airstream, Series SF, 4-dr. sedan, OCW

1935 DeSoto Airstream, Series SF, convertible coupe, JAC

AIRSTREAM — SERIES SF — SIX: Because of the Airflow's lack of acceptance, DeSoto added the conventional Airstream series as a companion car this year. Styling features included a sloping V-type radiator grille, two rows of horizontal windstream hood louvers and bullet shaped headlights mounted on pedestals above the front fender catwalks. The bumper had a V-shaped dip in its center and three vertical chrome "hash marks" decorated the lower front fender aprons. The Airstreams were about $220 cheaper than comparable Airflows in the DeSoto line. Standard equipment included Autolite ignition, hydraulic brakes, independent front suspension, balanced weight distribution, "Floating Power" and new centrifuse brake drums. A Deluxe equipment package including two-tone paint, small front fender lamps, dual taillights, dual trumpet horns, two windshield wipers, wheel trim rings, chrome fender and runningboard moldings, a cigar lighter and front compartment carpeting was available for $35 extra after June 1935.

1935 DeSoto Airflow, Series SG, 4-dr. sedan, OCW

AIRFLOW — SERIES SG — SIX: In an attempt to make it look slightly less radical, the DeSoto Airflow was given a new front end with a slightly V-shaped radiator. The 1935 grille was more sloping than rounded, increasing the length of the hood. There were now only three horizontal hood louvers instead of 11. Standard equipment included Autolite ignition, Lockheed 4-wheel hydraulic brakes, balanced weight distribution, centrifuse brake drums, "Floating Power," and fender skirts. A hypoid rear axle was adopted this year and the anti-sway stabilizer bar was moved from the rear of the car to the front. Freewheeling was no longer used.

I.D. DATA: [Series SF] Serial numbers were in the same location. Starting: 6023501. Ending: 6043679. Engine numbers were in the same locations. Starting: SF-1001. Ending: SF-21874. [Series SG] Serial numbers were in the same location. Starting: 5082201. Ending: 5088967. Engine numbers were in the same location. Starting: SG-1001. Ending: SG-7843.

Model No.	Body Type & Seating	Price	Weight	Prod. Total
SF	2-dr. Bus. Cpe.-2P	695	2840	1760
SF	2-dr. R/S Cpe.-2/4P	760	2925	900
SF	2-dr. Conv. Cpe.-2/4P	835	3035	226
SF	2-dr. Sed.-5P	745	2915	1350
SF	2-dr. Tr. Sed.-5P	775	2960	2035
SF	4-dr. Sed.-5P	795	2990	5714
SF	4-dr. Tr. Sed.-5P	825	3035	8018

Note 1: Total series production was 20,784.

SG	2-dr. Bus. Cpe.-3P	1015	3390	70
SG	2-dr. Cpe.-5P	1015	3390	418
SG	4-dr. Sed.-6P	1015	3390	6269
SG	4-dr. Twn. Sed.-6P	1015	3400	40

Note 2: Total series production was 6,797.
Note 3: Above factory prices (for Airflows) in effect after Feb. 7, 1935. Earlier price was $1,195 for all models.

ENGINE: [Series SF] Inline. L-head. Six. Cast iron block. B & S: 3-3/8 x 4-1/2. Disp.: 241.5 cu. in. C.R.: 6.0:1. Brake H.P.: 93 @ 3400 R.P.M. N.A.C.C. H.P.: 27.34. Four main bearings. Solid valve lifters. Carb.: Ball & Ball 1V model E6F2. Torque: 180 lbs.-ft. @ 1200 R.P.M. [Series SG] Inline. L-head. Six. Cast iron block. B & S: 3-3/8 x 4-1/2. Disp.: 241.5 cu. in. C.R.: 6.5:1. Brake H.P.: 100 @ 3400 R.P.M. N.A.C.C. H.P.: 27.34. Four main bearings. Solid valve lifters. Carb.: Ball & Ball 1V E6F2. Torque: 185 lbs.-ft. @ 1200 R.P.M.

CHASSIS: [Series SF] W.B.: 116 in. Tires: 16 x 6.25. [Series SG] W.B.: 115-1/2 in. Tires: 16 x 6.50.

TECHNICAL: Manual transmission (Synchromesh). Speeds: 3F/1R. Floor shift controls. Conventional clutch. Shaft drive. Hypoid rear axle. Overall ratio: (SF) 3.89:1; (SG) 4.0:1. Lockheed 4-wheel centifuse hydraulic brakes. Steel spoke wheels with Goodyear "Airwheel" tires.

OPTIONS: Front bumper. Rear bumper. Whitewall tires. Dual sidemount (Airstream). Sidemount covers (Airstream). Fender skirts. Bumper guards. Radio. Heater. Clock. Cigar lighter. Radio antenna. Seat covers. Chrome wheel trim rings. Spotlight(s). Parking lamps. Trumpet horns. Fender skirt ornaments. Fender moldings. Runningboard moldings. Carpets. Twin wipers. Righthand taillight. Righthand interior sun visor. Spare tire metal cover. Overdrive transmission. Special paint colors.

HISTORICAL: Production began: Nov. 1934. Production ended: (SF) Aug. 1935; (SG) Sept. 1935. Introduced Jan. 2, 1935. Innovations: Both models have engine over axles and redistribution of weight. Improved hydraulic brakes on centrifuse drums. Freewheeling eliminated. Independent front suspension on Airstreams. Hypoid rear axle. Ventilated clutch in Airflow. Calendar year registrations: 26,952. Calendar year production: 34,276. Model year production: 27,581. Company president was Byron C. Foy. DeSoto was America's 13th largest producer on a model year basis. For the second year in a row, the DeSoto Airflow won the Grand Prix Award for aerodynamic styling at the Monte Carlo Concours d' Elegance. Taxicab specials were produced in some quantities this year. DeSoto provided dealers with a kit that could be used to update 1934 Airflows to give them generally the same appearance as 1935 models. DeSoto experimented with a streamlined compact car this year. The SG was sold in Great Britain as the Chrysler Croydon; leftover '34 models were slightly modified and sold into 1935.

1935
Airstream, 6-cyl.

	FP	5	4	3	2	1
Bus Cpe	695	725	1400	3100	4800	6800
Cpe	760	775	1500	3600	5100	7300
Conv	835	3650	7350	12,250	17,150	24,500
2 dr Sed	745	550	1150	2100	3800	5400
2 dr Tr Sed	775	600	1200	2200	3900	5600
Sed	795	650	1250	2400	4150	5900
Tr Sed	825	650	1250	2400	4200	6000

Airflow, 6-cyl.

Bus Cpe	1195	975	2300	4900	6850	9800
Cpe	1195	1025	2500	5150	7150	10,300
Sed	1195	850	1650	4150	5800	8300
Twn Sed	1195	1050	2800	5400	7500	10,800

1936

1936 DeSoto Airstream, Series S-1, coupe, OCW

AIRSTREAM — SERIES S-1 — SIX: The DeSoto Airstream came in Deluxe and Custom car-lines for 1936. Both carried conventional body work with a new horizontal bar radiator grille and "pennon" style hood louvers. DeLuxes had one-piece flat windshields. Customs (except the convertibles) had split v-type windshields, chrome moldings on top of headlamps, fender skirt and runningboard moldings and rear wheel shrouds (fender skirts). Standard equipment included Autolite ignition, hydraulic brakes, "Floating Power," extra-long springs, independent front suspension, ride stabilizer and Goodyear's "Airwheel Magic Carpet" ride. The Custom Traveler and limousine were built on a long-wheelbase chassis. Special seven passenger taxicabs had the long wheelbase Custom bodies, Deluxe type windshields and sliding sunroofs (in 2,200 cars).

AIRFLOW III — SERIES S-2 — SIX: The DeSoto Airflow had a new, flanged steel roof panel insert. It was bolted to the perimeter of the roof, acoustically treated and electrically insulated to serve as a radio antenna. New styling features included a die-cast grille with vertical moldings and curved diagonal trim, twin "pennon" style hood louvers, new bumpers, redesigned bodyside moldings, new taillights and an updated instrument panel. Standard equipment included Autolite ignition, 4-wheel hydraulic brakes, balanced weight distribution, "Floating Power," unitized body construction and Goodyear "Airwheels."

I.D. DATA: [Series S-1] Serial numbers were in the same location. Starting: (Del.) 6043701; (Cust.) 5500001. Ending: (Del.) 6061693; (Cust.) 5517216. Engine numbers were in the same location. Starting Engine No.: S1-1001. Ending: S1-39756. [Series S-2] Serial numbers were in the same location. Starting: 5089001. Ending: 5093971. Engine numbers were in the same location. Starting Engine No.: S2-1001. Ending: S2-6038.

1936 DeSoto Airflow, Series S-2, 4-dr. sedan, OCW

Model No.	Body Type & Seating	Price	Weight	Prod. Total
(Deluxe)				
S-1	2-dr. Bus. Cpe.-2P	695	2941	2592
S-1	2-dr. Tr. Brgm.-5P	770	3051	2207
S-1	4-dr. Tr. Sed.-5P	810	3111	13,093
S-1	Chassis	NA	NA	99
(Custom)				
S-1	2-dr. Bus. Cpe.-2P	745	3000	940
S-1	2-dr. R/S Cpe.-2/4P	795	3085	641
S-1	2-dr. Conv. Cpe.-2/4P	895	3031	350
S-1	2-dr. Tr. Brgm.-5P	825	3031	1120
S-1	4-dr. Tr. Sed.-5P	865	3126	13,801
S-1	4-dr. Conv. Sed.-5P	1095	3246	215
(LWB Custom)				
S-1	4-dr. Trav. Sed.-5P	1075	3256	23
S-1	4-dr. Sed.-7P	1075	3340	208
S-1	4-dr. N.Y. Taxi-7P	NA	NA	2500
S-1	Chassis	NA	NA	460
S-1	4-dr. Calif. Taxi-7P	NA	NA	451

Note 1: Total Deluxe series production was 17,991; Total Custom series production was 20,719; Grand total Series S-1 production was 38,710.

S-2	2-dr. Cpe.-5P	1095	3540	250
S-2	4-dr. Sed.-6P	1095	3540	4750

Note 2: Total series production was 5,000.

1936 DeSoto Airstream, Series S-1, 4-dr. sedan, JAC

ENGINE: [Series S-1] Inline. L-head. Six. Cast iron block. B & S: 3-3/8 x 4-1/2. Disp.: 241.5 cu. in. C.R.: 6.0:1. Brake H.P.: 93 @ 3400 R.P.M. N.A.C.C. H.P.: 27.34. Four main bearings. Solid valve lifters. Carb.: Ball & Ball 1V model E6G1. Torque: 180 lbs.-ft. @ 1200 R.P.M. [Series S-2] Inline. L-head. Six cyl. Cast iron block. B & S: 3-3/8 x 4-1/2. Disp.: 241.5 cu. in. C.R.: 6.5:1. Brake H.P.: 100 @ 3400 R.P.M. N.A.C.C. H.P.: 27.34. Four main bearings. Solid valve lifters. Carb.: Ball & Ball model E6G1. Torque: 185 lbs.-ft. @ 1200 R.P.M.

CHASSIS: [Series S-1] W.B.: 118 in. Tires: 16 x 6.25. [Series (LWB) S-1] W.B.: 130 in. Tires: 16 x 6.25. [Series S-2] W.B.: 115-1/2 in. Tires: 16 x 6.50.

TECHNICAL: Manual transmission (Synchromesh). Speeds: 3F/1R. Floor shift controls. Conventional clutch. Shaft drive. Spiral bevel gear axle (hypoid with overdrive). Overall Ratio: (S-1) 3.89:1; (S-1) 4.1:1. Lockheed 4-wheel centrifuse brakes. Steel spoke wheels with Goodyear "Airwheel" tires.

OPTIONS: Front bumper. Rear Bumper. Whitewalls. Dual sidemount(s). Fender skirts. Bumper guards. Radio. Heater. Clock. Cigar lighter. Radio antenna. Seat covers. Spotlight(s). Fog lamps. Trumpet horn (Airstreams). Overdrive (Deluxe Airstream). Wind wings (convertibles). Chrome wheel covers. Special paint. OSRV mirror. Righthand taillight (Deluxe). Righthand sun visor (Deluxe). Twin wipers (Deluxe).

HISTORICAL: Production began: Sept., 1935. Production ended: Aug., 1936. Introduced: Nov. 2, 1935. Steel top insert. One inch lower Airstream chassis is claimed to be "twice as rigid." Airstream wheelbase increased two inches. DeSoto officially enters the taxi building business with N.Y. City "Sunshine" Cabs. Calendar year registrations: 45,088. Calendar year production: 52,789. Model year production: 43,710. Company president: Byron C. Foy. DeSoto was America's 13th ranked auto-maker for model year 1936. The convertible sedan was reintroduced in the Airstream Custom series. This was the last year for the DeSoto Airflow. DeSoto production facilities were expanded this season and also separated from Chrysler production facilities. The DeSoto S-1 was sold as the Chrysler Richmond in Great Britain.

1936

DeLuxe Airstream S-1, 6-cyl.

	FP	5	4	3	2	1
Bus Cpe	695	700	1350	2700	4500	6400
Tr Brgm	770	675	1300	2600	4400	6300
Tr Sed	810	700	1350	2900	4600	6600

Custom Airstream S-1, 6-cyl.

	FP	5	4	3	2	1
Bus Cpe	745	700	1350	2800	4550	6500
Cpe	795	725	1400	3100	4800	6800
Conv	895	4000	7950	13,250	18,550	26,500
Tr Brgm	825	725	1400	3000	4700	6700
Tr Sed	865	725	1400	3200	4850	6900
Conv Sed	1095	4100	8250	13,750	19,250	27,500
Trv Sed	1075	750	1450	3500	5050	7200
7P Sed	1075	775	1500	3600	5100	7300

Airflow III S-2, 6-cyl.

	FP	5	4	3	2	1
Cpe	1095	925	2000	4650	6500	9300
Sed	1095	825	1600	4000	5600	8000

1937

1937 DeSoto, Series S-3, 4-dr. sedan, OCW

DESOTO — SERIES S-3 — SIX: There was just one DeSoto series in 1937. These cars had a new hood that was hinged at the cowl. The grille featured horizontal bars divided by a vertical center panel finished in body color. The six upper grille bars swept back along the sides of the hood. The DeSoto name was spelled out by vertically stacked chrome letters on the center panel. Bullet shaped headlamps were attached to the sides of the hood. A wide, ribbed bumper was used. Standard equipment included Autolite ignition, hydraulic brakes, all-steel body construction with 14 rubber float body mountings, hypoid rear axle and independent front suspension. A "safety-styled" interior was a 1937 innovation. The speedometer was mounted in front of the steering column, instrument panel knobs were recessed, gauges were flush-mounted and door handles curved inward to prevent snagging. The top of the front seat back was heavily padded and even the overhead windshield wiper knob was made of soft rubber. Several accessories including bumpers, bumper guards, spare tire and safety glass were standard equipment for the first time this year. Dual wipers, taillights, sun visors, horns and door arm rests were standard in convertibles.

I.D. DATA: Serial numbers were in the same location. Starting: 5517301. Ending: 5597700. Engine numbers were in the same location. Starting: S3-1001. Ending: S3-77210.

Model No.	Body Type & Seating	Price	Weight	Prod. Total
S-3	2-dr. Bus. Cpe.-3P	770	3038	11,050
S-3	2-dr. R/S Cpe.-3/5P	820	3088	1,030
S-3	2-dr. Conv. Cpe.-3/5P	975	3225	992
S-3	2-dr. FsBk. Brgm.-6P	830	3123	1200
S-3	2-dr. Tr. Brgm.-6P	840	3148	11,660
S-3	4-dr. FsBk. Sed.-6P	870	3123	2265
S-3	4-dr. Tr. Sed.-6P	880	3148	51,889
S-3	4-dr. Conv. Sed.-5P	1300	3441	426
(Long Wheelbase [LWB])				
S-3	4-dr. Tr. Sed.-7P	1120	3451	695
S-3	4-dr. Limo. Sed.-7P	1220	3536	71
S-3	4-dr. Calif. Taxi-7P	NA	NA	225
S-3	Chassis	NA	NA	497

Note 1: Total series production was 82,000.

ENGINE: Inline. L-head. Six. Cast iron block. B & S: 3-3/8 x 4-1/4. Disp.: 228.1 cu. in. C.R.: 6.5:1. Brake H.P.: 93 @ 3600 R.P.M. N.A.C.C. H.P.: 27.34. Four main bearings. Solid valve lifters. Carb.: Ball & Ball 1V model E6K4. Torque: 168 lbs.-ft. @ 1200 R.P.M.

CHASSIS: [Series S-3] W.B.: 116 in. Tires: 16 x 6.00. [Series (LWB) S-3] W.B.: 133 in. Tires: 16 x 6.50.

1937 DeSoto, Series S-3, coupe, JAC

TECHNICAL: Synchromesh manual transmission. Speeds: 3F/1R. Floor shift controls. Conventional clutch. Shaft drive. Hypoid rear axle. Overall ratio: (SWB) 4.11:1; (LWB) 4.33:1. Four-wheel hydraulic brakes. Steel disc wheels.

OPTIONS: Front bumper (standard). Rear bumper (standard). Whitewall tires. Dual sidemounts. Sidemount cover(s). Fender skirts. Bumper guards (standard). Transitone radio. Heater. Clock. Cigar lighter (std. in Convertibles). Radio antenna. Seat covers. External sun shade. Spotlight(s). Fog lamps. "Gas-Saver" overdrive transmission ($35). Wheel trim rings. Sliding sun roof. License plate frames. OSRV mirror. Vent wings (convertibles).

1937 DeSoto, Series S-3, convertible sedan, JAC

HISTORICAL: Production started: Sept. 1936. Production ended: Aug. 1937. Introduced Sept. 1936. Innovations: Shorter stroke engine. Safety styled interior. Alligator hood with removable side panels. Steel roof construction. One-piece flat windshield on all DeSotos. First DeSoto station wagons built by J.C. Cantrell on DeSoto S-3 chassis. Rubber body mounting. Calendar year registrations: 74,424. Calendar year production: 86,541. Model year production: 82,000. DeSoto was America's 12th ranked auto-maker for model year 1937. World's first three-way radios installed in Eastchester, N.Y. Police Department's 1937 DeSoto squad cars. A specially finished Silver DeSoto convertible sedan was used as an "Official Car" at the 1937 Indy 500. DeSoto claimed its "Gas Saver" transmission was so economical that it gave one free mile for every four miles the car was driven. The 1937 DeSotos were designed by former custom coachbuilder Ray Dietrich, Chrysler Corp.'s new chief designer. The S-3 DeSoto continued to be sold in Great Britain as a Chrysler Richmond.

**1937
S-3, 6-cyl.**

	FP	5	4	3	2	1
Conv	975	4100	8250	13,750	19,250	27,500
Conv Sed	1300	4300	8550	14,250	19,950	28,500
Bus Cpe	770	675	1300	2600	4400	6300
Cpe	820	725	1400	3100	4800	6800
Brgm	830	650	1250	2400	4150	5900
Tr Brgm	840	650	1250	2400	4200	6000
Sed	870	675	1300	2500	4300	6100
Tr Sed	880	675	1300	2500	4350	6200
7P Sed	1120	675	1300	2600	4400	6300
Limo	1220	875	1700	4300	6000	8600

1938

DESOTO — SERIES S-5 — SIX: The 1938 DeSotos had a new, die-cast grille. It was shorter than last year's grille and had a chrome Chevron effect at the bottom on the fender apron. The DeSoto had a three inch longer wheelbase. The bullet-shaped headlamps were recessed into the fenders. A cowl vent was used to draw fresh air into the car; eliminating the use of crank-open windshields. Wipers were moved from the windshield header, back to the cowl. Standard equipment included Autolite

1938 DeSoto, Series S-5, 4-dr. sedan, OCW

ignition, hydraulic brakes, independent front suspension, semi-elliptic rear leaf springs, ten percent larger brake drums, a new and stronger chassis frame, dash mounted emergency brake and rubber mounted steering system. Two 7-passenger body styles were again available on the long wheelbase chassis. Optional this year was a high-compression engine with an aluminum cylinder head.

I.D. DATA: Serial numbers were in the same location. Starting: 5598301. Ending: 5632912. Engine numbers were in the same location. Starting: S5-1001. Ending: S5-39664.

Model No.	Body Type & Seating	Price	Weight	Prod. Total
S-5	2-dr. Bus. Cpe.-3P	870	3039	5160
S-5	2-dr. R/S Cpe.-3/5P	920	3089	38
S-5	2-dr. Tr. Brgm.-6P	930	3119	5367
S-5	2-dr. FsBk Sed.-6P	920	3104	11
S-5	4-dr. Tr. Sed.-6P	970	3139	23,681
S-5	4-dr. FsBk Sed.-6P	958	3134	498
S-5	4-dr. Conv. Sed.-5P	1375	3394	431
(LWB)				
S-5	4-dr. Tr. Sed.-7P	1195	3439	513
S-5	4-dr. Sed. Limo.-7P	1285	3524	81
S-5	4-dr. Calif. Taxi-7P	NA	NA	372
(Chassis)				
S-5	Chassis	NA	NA	413
S-5	4-dr. Cantrell Sta. Wag.	NA	NA	NA
S-5	4-dr. Der. Twn. Car	NA	NA	(1)

Note 1: Total series production was 39,203.
Note 2: The Cantrell station wagons and Derham Town Car were among models built on the chassis which DeSoto supplied to coachbuilders for special bodies or professional conversions.

1938 DeSoto, Series S-5, coupe, JAC

ENGINE: Inline. L-head. Six. Cast iron block. B & S: 3-3/8 x 4-1/4. Disp.: 228.1 cu. in. C.R.: (Std.) 6.5:1; (Opt.) 7.0:1. Brake H.P.: (Std.) 93 @ 3600 R.P.M.; (Opt.) 100 @ 3600 R.P.M. N.A.C.C. H.P.: 27.34. Four main bearings. Solid valve lifters. Carb.: Carter 1V model E6M1 (Ball & Ball). Torque: (Std.) 172 lbs.-ft. @ 1200 R.P.M.; (Opt.) 176 lbs.-ft. @ 1200 R.P.M.

CHASSIS: [Series S-5] W.B.: 119 in. Tires: 16 x 6.00. [Series (LWB) S-5] W.B.: 136 in. Tires: 16 x 6.50.

TECHNICAL: Synchromesh manual transmission. Speeds: 3F/1R. Floor shift controls. Conventional clutch. Shaft drive. Hypoid rear axle. Overall ratio: 4:1:1. Four wheel hydraulic brakes. Steel disc wheels.

OPTIONS: Front bumper. Rear bumper. Whitewall tires. OSRV mirror. "Butterfly" ventipanes (Convertible). Fender skirts. Bumper guards. Radio. Heater. Clock. Cigar lighter. Radio Antenna. Seat covers. External sun shade. Spotlight(s). Fog lamps. Wheel trim rings. Righthand sun visor (std. on Convertible). Righthand taillight (std. on Convertible). Dual horns (std. on Convertible). Righthand windshield wiper (std. on Convertible). High-compression aluminum cylinder head. Leather driver's seat (Limousine). "Gas Saver" overdrive transmission.

HISTORICAL: Production started: Sept. 1937. Production ended: July 1938. Introduced Sept. 1, 1937. Innovations: New rubber mounted steering gear. Parking brake control positioned below instrument panel. Cowl mounted wipers. Non-opening one-piece windshields. High-compression engine with aluminum head (used on all long wheelbase models). Calendar year registrations: 35,259. Calendar year production: 32,688. Model year production: 39,203. DeSoto was America's 13th ranked auto-maker in model year 1938.

1938
S-5, 6-cyl.

	FP	5	4	3	2	1
Conv	1045	4100	8250	13,750	19,250	27,500
Conv Sed	1375	4300	8550	14,250	19,950	28,500
Bus Cpe	835	700	1350	2700	4500	6400
Cpe	870	725	1400	3200	4850	6900
Tr Brgm	930	675	1300	2600	4400	6300
Sed	958	700	1350	2800	4550	6500
Tr Sed	970	700	1350	2700	4500	6400
7P Sed	1195	800	1550	3900	5450	7800
Limo	1285	925	1900	4550	6350	9100

1939

1939 DeSoto, Seres, S-6, 4-dr. sedan, OCW

DESOTO — SERIES S-6 — SIX: The 1939 DeSoto had more streamlined styling with a newly designed hood. The nose of the car had horizontal chrome grille bars running rearward. There were also chrome horizontal bars running across the front splash aprons. The headlamps were entirely recessed in the fenders. The DeSoto name appeared on both sides of the nose and there were horizontal decorations with four square vents on the rear end of the hood side panels. Two-piece V-type windshields made their return this year. DeSoto again marketed two bodies on an extended wheelbase chassis and all models, except the Custom Club Coupe, were available in deluxe or custom trim. Custom models had all features of deluxe cars plus dual sun visors, dual horns, dual taillights and richer interiors with darker colored fabrics. Innovations for 1939 included column mounted gearshift levers, constant speed electric windshield wipers and "Superfinish," an exclusive Chrysler Corp. method of giving engine parts a smooth, mirror-like surface. Standard equipment included Solar Spark ignition, hydraulic brakes and coil spring independent front suspension. The Custom Club coupe name with "Airfoam" rubber cushion front seats. There was no convertible in the DeSoto line this year and an optional sliding sun roof was introduced as an alternative sports feature. All 1939 sedans, limousines and taxis were fastback models.

I.D. DATA: Serial numbers were in the same location. Starting: 5634001. Ending: 5687134. Engine numbers were in the same location. Starting: S6-1001. Ending: S6-55461.

Model No. (DeLuxe Line)	Body Type & Seating	Price	Weight	Prod. Total
S-6	2-dr. Bus. Cpe.-2P	870	3064	5176
S-6	2-dr. AS Cpe.-2/4P	925	3089	2124
S-6	2-dr. Tr. Sed.-5P	930	3129	7472
S-6	4-dr. Tr. Sed.-5P	970	3174	31,513
(LWB DeLuxe Line)				
S-6	4-dr. Calif. Taxi-7P	NA	NA	1250
S-6	4-dr. Tr. Sed.-7P	1195	3454	425
S-6	4-dr. Sed. Limo.-7P	1285	3549	84
S-6	Chassis	NA	NA	154
(Custom Line)				
S-6	2-dr. Bus. Cpe.-2P	923	3069	498
S-6	2-dr. Cus. AS Cpe.-2/4P	978	3094	287
S-6	2-dr. Cus. Clb. Cpe.-4P	1145	3164	264
S-6	2-dr. Tr. Sed.-5P	983	3134	424
S-6	4-dr. Tr. Sed.-5P	1023	3179	5993
(LWB Custom Line)				
S-6	4-dr. Tr. Sed.-7P	1248	3459	30
S-6	4-dr. Limo. Sed.-7P	1338	3554	5

Note 1: Total series production was 55,699.
Note 2: The AS Coupe had auxiliary (jump) seats.
Note 3: The Custom Club Coupe was built by Hayes Body Co.

ENGINE: Inline. L-head. Six. Cast iron block. B & S: 3-3/8 x 4-1/4. Disp.: 228.1 cu. in. C.R.: (Std.) 6.5:1. (Opt.) 7.0:1. Brake H.P.: (Std.) 93 @ 3600 R.P.M.; (Opt.) 100 @ 3600 R.P.M. N.A.C.C. H.P.: 27.34. Four main bearings. Solid valve lifters. Carb.: Ball & Ball 1V model E6N1. Torque: (Std.) 172 lbs.-ft. @ 1200 R.P.M.; (Opt.) 176 lbs.-ft. @ 1200 R.P.M.

CHASSIS: [Series S-6] W.B.: 119 in. Tires: 16 x 6.00. [Series (LWB) S-6] W.B.: 136 in. Tires: 16 x 6.50.

TECHNICAL: Manual Synchromesh transmission. Speeds: 3F/1R. Column mounted gearshift. Conventional multiple disc clutch. Shaft drive. Hypoid rear axle. Overall ratio: 4.1:1. Four wheel hydraulic brakes. Steel disc wheels.

1939 DeSoto, Series S-6, 4-dr. sedan, JAC

OPTIONS: Whitewall tires. Chrome beauty rings. OSRV mirror(s). Vent wings. Bumper wing guards. Fender skirts. Bumper guards. Radio. Heater. Clock. Cigar lighter. Radio antenna. Seat covers. External sun shade. Spotlamp(s). Fog lamps. Dual tone horns (std. on Custom). Righthand sun visor (deluxe). Righthand taillight (deluxe). Sliding sun roof. "Perfected Controlled" overdrive transmission. "Airfoam" seat cushions (except Custom Club Coupe). License plate frames. Special paint colors.

HISTORICAL: Started production: Aug. 1938. Ended production: July 1939. Introduced Oct. 1938. Innovations: New streamlined bodies including limited production. Custom Club Coupe made by Hayes Body Co. Remote control gearshift. Improved overdrive. "Superfinish" engine parts. Calendar year registration: 51,951. Calendar year production: 53,269. Model year production: 55,699. DeSoto was America's 13th ranked auto-maker for model year 1939. DeSoto claimed that its new step-down type overdrive gave the equivalent of five forward speeds. Spencer Tracy, Walt Disney and Myrna Loy were among personalities who participated in DeSoto's advertising and promotional campaign this year.

1939
S-6 DeLuxe, 6-cyl.

	FP	5	4	3	2	1
Bus Cpe	870	725	1400	3100	4800	6800
Cpe	925	750	1450	3300	4900	7000
Tr Sed	930	675	1300	2600	4400	6300
Tr Sed	970	700	1350	2700	4500	6400
Limo	1285	750	1450	3500	5050	7200
S-6 Custom, 6-cyl.						
Cpe	923	700	1350	2700	4500	6400
Custom Cpe	978	700	1350	2800	4550	6500
Custom Clb Cpe	1145	800	1550	3900	5450	7800
2 dr Tr Sed	983	750	1450	3300	4900	7000
Tr Sed	1023	750	1450	3400	5000	7100
7P Sed	1248	750	1450	3500	5050	7200
Limo	1338	925	1900	4550	6350	9100

1940

1940 DeSoto, Series S-7, 4-dr. sedan, OCW

DESOTO — SERIES S-7 — SIX: The 1940 DeSotos were even more streamlined. They had more massive fenders and concealed door hinges. The frontal design featured horizontal chrome grille bars in a special configuration having two separate grilles on either side of a V-shaped body color panel in the center. The V-pointed downward. DeSoto script nameplates were positioned on either side of the center panel on the nose of the car. Conventional running boards were available on all models, but optional on customs, which had chrome trimmed rocker panels as standard equipment. All of the cars had wider front and back seats and larger windows. Both the Deluxe and Custom lines included long wheelbase models. New innovations included sealed beam headlights and an "All-Weather" air control system with dual heater and blower units. Also available, as an option, was "Simplimatic" Fluid-Drive — a type of semi-automatic transmission. A chrome script applied to the rear of the hood sides, below beltline level, identified each car as a "Custom" or "Deluxe" trimmed car. Custom models also had chrome moldings around the windshield and windows and chrome trim above and below the taillights. Deluxe models did not have such brightwork.

1940 DeSoto, Series S-7, deluxe coupe, JAC

1941 DeSoto, Series S-8, custom brougham, OCW

I.D. DATA: Serial numbers were in the same locations. Starting: (Del.) 6064301; (Cus.) 5688001. Ending: (Del.) 6095928; (Cus.) 5720329. Engine numbers were in the same location. Starting: (All) S7-1001. Ending: (All) S7-67427.

Model No. (Deluxe)	Body Type & Seating	Price	Weight	Prod. Total
S-7	2-dr. Bus. Cpe.-2P	845	3001	3650
S-7	2-dr. AS Cpe.-2/4P	905	3026	2098
S-7	2-dr. Tr. Sed.-5P	905	3066	7072
S-7	4-dr. Tr. Sed.-5P	945	3086	18,666
(LWB Deluxe)				
S-7	4-dr. Tr. Sed.-7P	1175	3490	142
S-7	4-dr. Calif. Taxi-7P	/NA	NA	2323
(Custom)				
S-7	2-dr. Cus. Cpe.-2P	885	3024	1898
S-7	2-dr. AS Cus. Cpe.-2/4P	945	3044	2234
S-7	2-dr. Conv. Cpe.-4P	1095	3329	1085
S-7	2-dr. Tr. Sed.-5P	945	3084	3109
S-7	4-dr. Tr. Sed.-5P	985	3104	25,221
(LWB Custom)				
S-7	4-dr. Tr. Sed.-7P	1215	3490	206
S-7	4-dr. Limo.-7P	1290	3635	34
S-7	Chassis	NA	NA	52

Note 1: Total series production was 67,790.

ENGINE: Inline. L-head. Six. Cast iron block. B & S: 3-3/8 x 4-1/4. Disp.: 228.1 cu. in. C.R.: (Std.) 6.5:1; (Opt.) 6.8:1. Brake H.P.: (Std.) 100 @ 3600 R.P.M.; (Opt.) 105 @ 3600 R.P.M. N.A.C.C. H.P.: 27.34. Four main bearings. Solid valve lifters. Carb.: Ball & Ball 2V model E6N2. Torque: (Std.) 176 lbs.-ft. @ 1200 R.P.M.; (Opt.) 178 lbs.-ft. @ 1200 R.P.M.

CHASSIS: [Series S-7] W.B.: 122.5 in. Tires: 16 x 6.00. [Series (LWB) S-7] W.B.: 139.5 in. Tires: 16 x 6.50.

TECHNICAL: Manual synchromesh transmission. Speeds: 3F/1R. Column mounted gearshift. Conventional multiple disc clutch. Shaft drive. Hypoid rear axle. Overall ratio: 4.1:1. Four wheel hydraulic brakes. Steel disc wheels.

OPTIONS: Whitewall tires. Chrome beauty trim rings. OSRV mirror(s). Bumper wind guards. Master grille guard. Fender skirts. Bumper guards. Radio. Heater. Clock. Cigar lighter. Radio antenna. Seat covers. External sun shade. Spotlight(s). Fog lamps. Dual note horns. Conventional runningboards (on Customs). Two-tone "Sportsman" exterior finish (4-door sedan). Special paint colors. License plate frames.

HISTORICAL: Production started: Aug. 1939. Production ended: July 1940. Introduced Sept. 1939. Innovations: Sealed beam headlights. Fluid drive semi-automatic transmission. "All-Weather" fresh air circulation system. Autolite ignition. New "high-lift" camshaft. Stronger and lower chassis frame. Sportsman sedan introduced at mid-year. Calendar year registrations: 71,943. Calendar year production: 83,805. Model year production: 67,790. Walter P. Chrysler died on Aug. 18, 1940. DeSoto, a Chrysler Corp. company, was America's 13th ranked auto-maker for model year 1940. The company had a much higher 10th place ranking in terms of calendar year sales. Production of early 1940 models was delayed by a strike. DeSoto was advertised as "America's Family Car."

1940
S-7 DeLuxe, 6-cyl.

	FP	5	4	3	2	1
Bus Cpe	845	775	1500	3600	5100	7300
Cpe	905	800	1550	3900	5450	7800
2 dr Tr Sed	905	675	1300	2500	4350	6200
4 dr Tr Sed	945	700	1350	2700	4500	6400
7P Sed	1175	825	1600	3950	5500	7900

S-7 Custom, 6-cyl.

Conv	885	3800	7650	12,750	17,850	25,500
2P Cpe	945	700	1350	2800	4550	6500
Clb Cpe	1095	700	1350	2900	4600	6600
2 dr Sed	945	700	1350	2800	4550	6500
Sed	985	700	1350	2900	4600	6600
7P Sed	1215	850	1650	4150	5800	8300
Limo	1290	900	1800	4400	6150	8800

DESOTO — SERIES S-8 — SIX: DeSoto's 1941 styling changes started with longer, lower, wider "Rocket" bodies. They had flatter windshields and alligator hoods with the lock control inside the driver's compartment. The grille consisted of 14 curved, vertical bars on either side of a body color center panel. There were three, short, horizontal strips on either side of the nose. Headlamps were round with ornamental trim extensions top and bottom. Runningboards were fully concealed. Standard equipment included Autolite ignition, hydraulic brakes, Fluid Drive, Simplimatic transmission, flipper windows for rear seat ventilation, "Hold-open" front doors, Safety-Rim wheels, oil bath air cleaner, a new steering wheel with a single horizontal spoke and a speedometer with a needle that glowed red when driving over 50 mph. Custom models also had "Air Foam" seat cushions, chrome window moldings and dual electric wipers. Both lines — Custom and Deluxe — included long wheelbase models. Rear vision was greatly improved by enlarged rear windows.

I.D. DATA: Serial numbers were in the same location. Starting: (Del.) 6096001; (Cust.) 5720401. Ending: (Del.) 6141720; (Cust.) 5770881. Engine numbers were in the same location. Starting Engine No: (All) S8-1001. Ending: (All) S8-100247.

1941 DeSoto, Series S-8, custom coupe, HAC

Model No. (Deluxe)	Body Type & Seating	Price	Weight	Prod. Total
S-8	2-dr. Bus. Cpe.-2P	945	3134	4449
S-8	2-dr. Cpe.-5P	1025	3219	5603
S-8	2-dr. Sed.-5P	1008	3224	9228
S-8	4-dr. Sed.-5P	1035	3254	26,417
(Deluxe LWB)				
S-8	4-dr. Sed.-7P	1270	3629	101
S-8	4-dr. Calif. Taxi-7P	NA	NA	2502
(Custom)				
S-8	2-dr. Cus. Cpe.-2P	982	3144	2033
S-8	2-dr. Clb. Cpe.-5P	1080	3239	6726
S-8	2-dr. Conv. Cpe.-5P	1240	3494	2937
S-8	2-dr. Brgm.-5P	1060	3264	4609
S-8	4-dr. Sed.-5P	1085	3269	30,876
S-8	4-dr. Twn. Sed.-5P	1133	3329	4362
(Custom LWB)				
S-8	4-dr. Sed.-7P	1310	3649	120
S-8	4-dr. Limo.-7P	1390	3754	35
S-8	Chassis	NA	NA	1

Note 1: Total series production was 99,999.

ENGINE: Inline. L-head. Six. Cast iron block. B & S: 3-3/8 x 4 1/4. Disp.: 228.1 cu. in. C.R.: (Del.) 6.5:1; (Cust.) 6.8:1. Brake H.P.: (Del.) 100 @ 3600 R.P.M.; (Cust.) 105 @ 3600 R.P.M. N.A.C.C. H.P.: 28.36. Four main bearings. Solid valve lifters. Carb.: Carter 1V model EE-1. Torque: (Del.) 176 lbs.-ft. @ 1200 R.P.M.; (Cust.) 178 lbs.-ft. @ 1200 R.P.M.

CHASSIS: [Series S-8] W.B.: 121.5 in. O.L.: 208 in. Tires: 16 x 6.25. [Series S-8 (LWB)] W.B.: 139.5 in. Tires: 16 x 6.50.

TECHNICAL: Transmission: Synchromesh (manual). Speeds: 3F/1R. Column mounted gearshift. Multipledisc clutch. Shaftdrive. Hypoid rear axle. Overall ratio: 4.1:1. Four wheel hydraulic brakes. Safety-Rim wheels.

OPTIONS: Whitewall tires. Chrome beauty trim rings. OSRV mirror(s). Bright fender edge molding (std. at mid-year). Fender guardrails. Fender skirts. Bumper guards. Radio. Heater. Clock. Cigar lighter. Radio antenna. Seat covers. External sun shade. Spotlight(s). Fog lamps. Twin horns. Sportsman club coupe trim package. Two-tone paint. Special paint colors. Fluid drive. Simplimatic transmission. "Skyview" taxicab window. Front fender parking lamps. Conventional runningboards. Oversize tires.

HISTORICAL: Production started: Aug. 1940. Production ended: July 1941. Introduction: Oct. 8, 1940. Innovations: Simplimatic semi-automatic transmission. Higher second gear ratio. Battery located under left fender shield. Oil bath air cleaner. Single spoke steering wheel. Alligator type hood. Safety-rim wheels. Calendar year registrations: 91,004. Calendar year production: 85,980. Model year production: 99,999. Chrysler was America's tenth ranked auto-maker in calendar year 1941. Model year output was also 10th highest for a domestic manufacturer. DeSoto prices increased $42.50 in the middle of the year.

1941
S-8 DeLuxe, 6-cyl.

Bus Cpe	945	775	1500	3600	5100	7300
Cpe	1025	800	1550	3900	5450	7800
2 dr Sed	1008	700	1350	2700	4500	6400
Sed	1035	700	1350	2900	4600	6600
7P Sed	1270	850	1650	4100	5700	8200

S-8 Custom, 6-cyl.

Conv	1240	4000	7950	13,250	18,550	26,500
Cpe	982	800	1550	3900	5450	7800
Clb Cpe	1080	850	1650	4150	5800	8300
2 dr Brgm	1060	725	1400	3100	4800	6800
4 dr Sed	1085	725	1400	3100	4800	6800
Twn Sed	1133	750	1450	3300	4900	7000
Limo	1390	925	2000	4650	6500	9300
7P Sed	1310	800	1550	3900	5450	7800

1942

1942 DeSoto, Series S-10, sedan, OCW

DESOTO — SERIES S-10 — SIX: Styling characteristics for 1942 included headlights that were concealed behind retractable doors. The grille featured S-shaped vertical bars running fully across the front. More massive wraparound bumpers curved around the front and rear fenders. Rectangular parking lamps were mounted in the front fenders. The upper grille bar was trimmed with a center ornament, on the nose, and also wrapped around and down the front fenders. Standard equipment included Autolite ignition, hydraulic brakes, concealed runningboards, a larger-bore "Powermaster" six-cylinder engine, and key lock front doors. Custom line models also had bolster type upholstery, "Air Foam" seat cushions, dual electric wipers, front and rear door arm rests, and a folding rear seat arm rest on sedans, limousines and broughams. Both trim levels came on standard and long wheelbase chassis.

I.D. DATA: Serial number were in the same location. Starting: (Del.) 6142001; (Cust.) 5771001. Ending: (Del.) 6153101; (Cust.) 5783503. Engine numbers were in the same locations. Starting: (Both) S10-1001. Ending: (Both) S10-25551.

Model No. (Deluxe)	Body Type & Seating	Price	Weight	Prod. Total
S-10	2-dr. Bus. Cpe.-2P	1010	3190	469
S-10	2-dr. Cpe.-5P	1092	3270	1968
S-10	2-dr. Sed.-5P	1075	3270	1781
S-10	4-dr. Sed.-5P	1103	3315	6463
S-10	4-dr. Twn. Sed.-5P	1147	3335	291
S-10	2-dr. Del. Conv. Cpe.-5P	1250	3495	79
(Deluxe LWB)				
S-10	4-dr. Sed.-7P	1455	3705	49
S-10	4-dr. Calif. Taxi-7P	NA	NA	756
(Custom)				
S-10	2-dr. Cus. Cpe.-2P	1046	3205	120
S-10	2-dr. Clb. Cpe.-5P	1142	3270	2236
S-10	2-dr. Conv. Cpe.-5P	1317	3510	489
S-10	2-dr. Brgm.-5P	1142	3305	913
S-10	4-dr. Sed.-5P	1152	3330	7974
S-10	4-dr. Twn. Sed.-5P	1196	3365	1084
(Custom LWB)				
S-10	4-dr. Sed.-7P	1504	3725	79
S-10	4-dr. Limo.-7P	1580	3820	20

Note 1: Total series production is 24,771.

1942 DeSoto, Series S-10, custom convertible coupe, HAC

ENGINE: Inline. L-head. Six. Cast iron block. B & S: 3-7/16 x 4-1/4. Disp.: 236.7 cu. in. C.R.: 6.6.:1. Brake H.P.: 115 @ 3800 R.P.M. N.A.C.C. H.P.: 28.36. Four main bearings. Solid valve lifters. Carb.: Carter 1V model EE-1. Torque: 190 lbs.-ft. @ 1600 R.P.M.

CHASSIS: [Series S-10] W.B.: 121.5 in. Tires: 16 x 6.25. [Series S-10 (LWB)]. W.B.: 139.5 in. Tires: 16 x 6.50.

TECHNICAL: Transmission: Synchromesh (manual). Speeds 3F/1R. Column mounted gearshift. Multiple disc clutch. Shaft drive. Hypoid rear axle. Overall ratio: 3.9:1. Four wheel hydraulic brakes. Safety-rim wheels.

OPTIONS: Whitewall tires. Whitewall plastic wheel discs. OSRV mirror(s). Chrome rear fender edge shields. Chrome wheel trim rings. Fender skirts. Bumper Guards. Radio. Heater. Clock. Cigar Lighter. Radio Antenna. Seat Covers. External Sun Shade. Spotlight(s). Fog lamps. Dual horns. Fluid Drive. Simplimatic transmission. Directional signals. License plate frame. "Skyview" taxicab window. Sportsman interior trim package. Two-tone paint. Special paint colors. Oversize tires.

HISTORICAL: Production started: Aug. 1941. Production ended: Jan. 1942. Introduction: Sept. 1, 1941. Hidden "Airfoil" headlights. Higher horsepower engine. Larger valves. Numerically lower rear axle ratio. Key locks on both front doors. Calendar year registrations: none. Calendar year production: 4,186. Model year production: 24,771. DeSoto fell from 10th place to 14th in calendar year sales. Its model year output was 13th highest in the auto industry. A specially trimmed DeSoto was driven around the country promoting sales of U.S. War Bonds. DeSoto's prewar production ended Feb. 9, 1942.

1942
S-10 DeLuxe, 6-cyl.

	FP	5	4	3	2	1
Bus Cpe	1010	750	1450	3300	4900	7000
Cpe	1092	775	1500	3600	5100	7300
2 dr Sed	1075	700	1350	2900	4600	6600
Sed	1103	700	1350	2900	4600	6600
Twn Sed	1147	725	1400	3100	4800	6800
7P Sed	1455	925	1900	4550	6350	9100

S-10 Custom, 6-cyl.

Conv	1317	3800	7650	12,750	17,850	25,500
Cpe	1046	800	1550	3900	5450	7800
Clb Cpe	1142	850	1650	4150	5800	8300
Brgm	1142	775	1500	3700	5200	7400
4 dr Sed	1152	775	1500	3750	5250	7500
Twn Sed	1196	800	1550	3800	5300	7600
7P Sed	1504	950	2100	4750	6650	9500
Limo	1580	950	2200	4800	6700	9600

DE SOUCHET — The De Souchet Motor Appliance Company was organized in Springfield, Illinois late in 1907 with a $100,000 capital stock for the purpose of manufacturing automobiles. Z.L. De Souchet was the man behind this venture. Manufacture of a car is doubted.

1909 De Tamble, model B, roadster, JAC

DE TAMBLE — Indianapolis & Anderson, Indiana — 1908-1913 — The De Tamble never had a chance. It began life as a little two-cylinder runabout produced in small numbers by the Speed Changing Pulley Company of Indianapolis, which was headed by Edward S. De Tamble. In August of 1909 the car moved to Anderson to be built by a new organization called the De Tamble Motor Company. The De Tamble was shown at the St. Louis Automobile Show in March of 1910, but production remained minimal and in August that year a group of money men from the East took over. By now DeTamble had sold out most of the output of the two-cylinder runabout which continued life as the James (Lawrenceburg, Indiana) and the Dakota (Wimbledon, North Dakota). DeTamble production now centered on four-cyliner cars. Early in 1911 the company narrowly avoided receivership, and another new management team composed of creditors and dealers now had the reins, with J.J. Appel succeeding Edward S. De Tamble as president. Meanwhile, a De Tamble roadster dashed from Louisiana to Tennessee in the 1911 New Orleans-Memphis race and won first prize. Precisely when Charles H. Walters, previously vice-president of the Mansfield Rubber Company, entered the De Tamble's life cannot be determined, but in various managerial changes he served as secretary, general manager, general superintendent, vice-president and president. From 1908 through 1910 approximately 2000 De Tambles had been produced. Because of plant shutdowns at each financial crisis, 1911 was a spotty year. It was Walters who announced that although the factory had a 3000-per-year capacity, De Tamble would not build that many cars in 1912, preferring to "sacrifice quantity for quality." In February that year Walters was arrested and placed under $10,000 bail on charges of embezzling $16,654 from the company. De Tamble was bankrupt, or so it appeared. Walters must have been cleared of the charges, though, because his name popped up occasionally among the veritable regiment of people now struggling to save De Tamble. In late February 1912 James W. Sansberry, president of the National Exchange Bank of Anderson, was the new De Tamble general manager. Receivership proceedings followed in June, but precisely one year later De Tamble was in operation again. Then it was shut down once more, with the promise that production would be resumed by January 1st, 1914 at the latest. The last mention of De Tamble is from November 1915, a brief announcement that the company's equipment had been sold for taxes to Elmer Eckhouse of Indianapolis. He indicated he might resume De Tamble production. Of course, he did not, but somehow his statement was the perfect curtain call for the ill-fated De Tamble.

1910 De Tamble, model G, torpedo roadster, WLB

1908-1909 DE TAMBLE
2-cyl., 16 hp, 90" wb

	FP	5	4	3	2	1
Model B Roadster-3P	650	4500	5800	9500	18,000	32,000

1910 DE TAMBLE
2-cyl., 16 hp, 90" wb

Model B Roadster-3P	650	4500	5800	9500	18,000	32,000

4-cyl., 30 hp, 113" wb

Model C Touring-5P	1250	4400	5600	9200	17,300	31,000
Model G Torpedo-2P	1000	4300	5400	8700	16,500	30,000

1911 DE TAMBLE
2-cyl., 16 hp, 90" wb

Model B Roadster	750	4500	5800	9500	18,000	32,000

4-cyl., 36 hp, 115" wb

Model J Touring-5P	1200	4400	5600	9200	17,300	31,000
Model H Touring-5P	1150	4400	5600	9200	17,300	31,000
Model G Runabout-2P	1000	4300	5400	8700	16,500	30,000

4-cyl., 40 hp, 120" wb

Model K Touring-7P	1675	4700	6100	9900	19,000	33,000

1912 De Tamble, model M, roadster, HAC

1912 DE TAMBLE
4-cyl., 36 hp, 116" wb

	FP	5	4	3	2	1
Model K Touring-5P	1250	4300	5300	8600	16,100	29,500
Model L Torpedo-5P	1500	4300	5400	8700	16,500	30,000
Model M Roadster-2P	1075	4400	5600	9200	17,300	31,000

1913 DE TAMBLE
Model 4-24 — 4-cyl., 17 hp, 103" wb

Roadster-2P	795	4400	5600	9200	17,300	31,000
Touring-5P	845	4300	5400	8700	16,500	30,000

DETMAR — The Detmar Auto Sales Company was organized in New York City late in 1911 for the purpose of manufacturing and selling automobiles and engines. Behind this $20,000 venture were John J. McLaran, F.B. Knowlton and Edward C. Inderlied. Manufacture of an automobile is doubted.

DETRICK — The Detrick Company was organized in Oakland, California early in 1910 with a $5000 capital stock for the manufacture of automobiles. W.G. Gardiner of San Francisco, G.A. McDougald of Oakland and G.F. Detrick of Berkeley were the backers of this venture. Manufacture is doubted.

DETROIT — The Detroit Air Cooled Car Company produced an automobile from 1922-1923 which was marketed by its initials. Refer to D.A.C.

The Detroit Auto Vehicle Company produced an automobile from 1905-1907 that was marketed under the tradename of Crown. Refer to Crown.

The Detroit Automobile Manufacturing Company was organized by J.P. La Vigne to produce his La Petite car in 1905. Refer to La Petite.

The Detroit Automobile Syndicate was organized in early 1907 to build touring cars in Detroit. Ralph Dyar, John Dyar, B.S. Warren and W.T. McGraw were the incorporators. Manufacture is doubted.

The Detroit Horseless Carriage Company built a gasoline car in 1897-1899 which is more properly attributed to its inventor, Barton Lee Peck. Refer to Peck.

The Detroit Motor Car & Supply Company was organized in New York City late in 1906 with a capital stock of $30,000 to manufacture "motors, engines and machinery, cars, wagons, boats, etc." F.F. Weston of New York City, A.P. Morrow of Elmira and J.A. Van Wie of Cortland were the incorporators. Manufacture is doubted.

The Detroit Spring Wheel Company was organized in late 1906 with a capital stock of $100,000 for the manufacture of automobiles and supplies. Walter Parker, William T. McGraw, Frank G. Smith, Jr., Harry Bennett and Benjamin S. Warren were the incorporators, all of Detroit. Manufacture of a car is doubted.

The Detroit Steam Engine Company was organized early in 1905 with a capital stock of $50,000 to manufacture and deal in automobiles and engines. Incorporators were John D. MacLachlin, Ovid B. Law, William E. Higginbotham and William G. Malcomson, all of Detroit. Manufacture of a car is doubted.

1900 Detroit Surrey, auto-buggy, NAHC

DETROIT — Detroit, Michigan — (1899-1902) — Early in 1899, William H. Murphy, a wealthy businessman of Detroit, was given a ride in the second experimental automobile built by a local enthusiast named Henry Ford. Murphy was impressed with the vehicle, talked a group of his moneyed friends into joining him to back Ford and thus, on July 24th, 1899 was born the Detroit Automobile Company. Its purpose was the manufacture of motorcars, and company manager Frank R. Alderman was soon telling a representative of *Motor Age* to expect a full line of Detroit models, including trap, phaeton, touring cart, runabout, physican's stanhope and surrey. But Henry Ford was still experimenting. His next vehicle was a heavy delivery wagon. By late 1899 he commented to an acquaintance that he had "one and a half (cars) started"; soon after the turn of the century about seven were in planning stages, maybe a dozen more followed in all. As its first anniversary approached, the Detroit Automobile Company had spent $86,000 and had little to show for it save for a delivery wagon and a pitiful number of runabouts. In January 1901 the firm was officially dissolved, though several of the backers still had faith in Ford, moved him to smaller quarters and told him to keep working, convinced he would come up with something. He did, a racing car. After an impressive victory at the Grosse Pointe race in October 1901, Ford's backers were enthusiastic, though they decreed that any further race cars could not be built on company time. The directors were desperate to get into production. Ford was furious: "I expect to make $ (racing) where I can't make ¢ manufacturing," he fumed. He left the company soon after. In August 1902 William Murphy and an associate visited a Detroit engineer named Henry M. Leland to ask him to appraise their automobile plant and equipment persuant to its sale. Leland recommended that the company be reorganized instead. It was, and it was renamed. The new automobile from the former Detroit company would be called a Cadillac. Henry Ford went on to build a production car too.

DETROIT — Detroit, Michigan — (1900) — The Detroit Motor Works at 1383 Jefferson Avenue both manufactured and dealt in gasoline engines. In the late fall of 1900 the company reported its ongoing experimentation with an automobile but, as *The Motor Vehicle Review* advised, the firm "will not put vehicles on the market until it can do so with perfect confidence." Apparently the Detroit Motor Works never felt thusly confident.

1904 Detroit, tonneau, NAHC

DETROIT — Detroit, Michigan — (1904) — When its new car was announced early in 1904, the Wheeler Manufacturing Company of Detroit declared that it was the result of considerable work "for some time past" and was now perfected. The Detroit was also quite versatile, available with both a tonneau and delivery body which were easily exchangeable, and with neither fitted the car could do service as a quite large sporting runabout. Gasoline and water tanks were placed under a modified Renault hood, "which arrangement," the company said, "not only distributes the weight but allows for filling without difficulty." Seventeen coats of paint were used on the body; this Detroit was a bright vehicle, finished in red and green, with yellow trimmed running gear. Despite what appeared to be a fine automobile, the Wheeler Manufacturing Company did not continue the Detroit in production beyond 1904. Conceivably, it may have returned to the manufacture of auxiliary seats for cars which had been its principal product previously.

1904 DETROIT
2-cyl., 15 hp, 84" wb

	FP	5	4	3	2	1
Rbt./Tr./Dly.	1500	—	—	—	—	—

DETROIT — Detroit, Michigan — (1912) — The Detroit Motor Chassis Company was organized in the early fall of 1912 and moved soon thereafter into a factory at 960 Champlain Street. Company officers were A.J. Kinncan, M.D. Dewitt, L.J. Stringer and William P. Culver. Allowing carriage builders to go horseless the easy way was the firm's purpose, and the Detroit chassis offered a four-cylinder 37 hp engine, with three-speed Warner transmission and Weston-Mott axles. Conceivably, this venture evolved several years later into the Detroit Chassis Company.

DETROIT — Detroit, Michigan — (1915-1917) — The Detroit Chassis Company was organized in November of 1915 and leased the former plant of the Vitralite Company on West Grand Boulevard and Hubbard Avenue in Detroit. The building of complete cars was not the company's purpose but rather to "cater especially to carriage and buggy makers and offer them a chassis at a reasonable price." The Detroit standard chassis was of 110-inch wheelbase fitted with a four-cylinder gasoline engine, with all other components of the purchaser's choosing. How many buggy and carriage makers were supplied by the Detroit Chassis Company is not known, but among its clients during the three years the company was in business were Smith & Sons of London, England and Charles E. Duryea for whom Detroit built the chassis for the GEM.

DETROIT-DEARBORN — Dearborn, Michigan — (1910) — The Detroit-Dearborn Motor Car Company was organized by Edward Bland, Arthur E. Kiefer, Elmer W. Foster and Samuel D. Lapham in the summer of 1909, and they had their first pilot models on the road on November 15th. The D-D cars, as they were nicknamed, were 35 hp fours engineered by former Regal designer Paul Arthur and offered as a touring torpedo called the Minerva and a touring roadster called the Nike, both priced at $1650. Appointments in the Detroit-Dearborn were selected "with a view of putting the proper thing in each place." Front floorboards were covered in

1910 Detroit-Dearborn, touring, WLB

aluminum alloy, cocoa mat was fitted in the tonneau, and the running-boards had a cork covering. This, and the rather nice mythological reference in model names, represented the most distinctive aspects of the Detroit-Dearborn. It was simply a good, sturdy car. "The company is organized along conservative lines, the capitalization being $50,000, but the progressive methods and thoroughness manifested from the outset augur well," reported *Cycle and Automobile Trade Journal* in March 1910. The company was bankrupt that fall after a total production of 110 cars. The Detroit-Dearborn assets were bought by Vernon C. Fry.

1910 DETROIT-DEARBORN
4-cyl., 35 hp, 112" wb

	FP	5	4	3	2	1
Nike Touring Roadster	1650	4700	6100	9900	19,000	33,000
Minerva Touring Torpedo	1650	4500	5800	9500	18,000	32,000

1907 Detroit Electric, runabout, HAC

DETROIT ELECTRIC — Detroit, Michigan — (1907-c.1939) — The Anderson Carriage Company, which had been established in Port Huron (Michigan) in 1884, was moved to Detroit by its founder in 1895. And in 1907 William C. Anderson moved his company into the automotive age. The first Detroit Electric was designed by George M. Bacon and was ready by June of that year, with 125 more being built before Christmas. Production rose to 400 in 1908, 650 in 1909, 1500 in 1910. In 1909 Anderson had purchased the Elwell-Parker Company of Cleveland (the electric motor builders who had previously supplied the Baker Electric), and now Anderson was able to build all components for its cars save the tires and wheels. Business boomed. In 1911 the firm was renamed the Anderson Electric Car Company. That year too saw the introduction of the company's "Chainless" Direct Shaft Drive (with no chain or gear reductions from motor to driveshaft) which had been many years in development. The new Underslung Roadster model was one of the lowest electrics in the field. Despite the excellent performance of the Detroit Electric in a number of endurance runs, the company was always careful to insist that its product was not a touring car, though it would "take you anywhere that an automobile may go with a mileage radius farther than you will ever care to travel in a day." In a company-sponsored test, a Detroit Electric ran 211.3 miles on a single battery charge, though 80 miles between charges was the figure generally advertised. It was as an urban vehicle, one for women drivers especially, that the Detroit Electric enjoyed most of its commercial success. In 1913 Detroit Electrics were built awhile under license in Scotland by Arrol-Johnson, in 1916 Anderson bought out the Chicago Electric (which had been in business since the turn of the century). Production in 1914 was 4669 cars; war year 1916 dropped to 3000. In 1918 William Anderson retired, and was succeeded as president by M.S. Towsen, formerly of Elwell-Parker. In 1919 the company name was changed from Anderson to Detroit Electric Car Company. With the electric vehicle having rapidly fallen from public favor, the Detroit Electric remained one of the few in the field. By 1920, though averring that "the Electric was the pioneer enclosed car — and it is still the best," Detroit Electric closed cars began to take on the semblance of gasoline cars with the introduction of a false hood and a mock radiator that resembled the Italian Fiat. As the Twenties wore on, the company backed off on its passenger car production to concentrate more in the commercial field. William Anderson, who

426

had remained a dominant factor in his business even after his retirement, died in mid-November 1929. In the wake of the Great Depression, Detroit Electric production plummeted, and was ultimately curtailed to an individual-order basis. Though a standard factory body was available, coachwork more often arrived courtesy of Willys-Overland, which resulted in an electric car with hood louvers. The hood and grille from the Dodge were used on some of the last cars built. Since shortly after the stock market crash, the Detroit Electric fortunes had been guided by A.O. Dunk, who had gained fame in the pre-World War I years as the purchaser of defunct companies. Dunk kept the Detroit Electric alive for a number of years. That his death in 1936 would spell the end for the company was rumored widely in the press, but the firm remained on the scene for awhile thereafter, until at least as late as 1938. Then, sometime before World War II, America's most famous and longest-lived electric car quietly disappeared from the automotive scene.

1909 DETROIT ELECTRIC

	FP	5	4	3	2	1
Model L Runabout (87" wb)	1400	3100	4200	6300	10,500	22,000
Model A Victoria (74" wb)	1850	2900	3700	5600	9100	20,000
Model B Victoria (74" wb)	1900	2900	3700	5600	9100	20,000
Model C Coupe (74" wb)	2300	3000	4000	6000	9500	21,000
Model D Coupe (74" wb)	2400	3000	4000	6000	9500	21,000

1910 Detroit Electric, model H, roadster, JAC

1910 DETROIT ELECTRIC

Model D Coupe (80" wb)	2500	3100	4200	6300	10,500	22,000
Model L Runabout (87" wb)	1700	2900	3700	5600	9100	20,000
Model A Victoria (80" wb)	1900	3000	4000	6000	9500	21,000
Model B Victoria (80" wb)	1925	3000	4000	6000	9500	21,000
Model C Coupe (80" wb)	2500	3100	4200	6300	10,500	22,000
Model E Coupe (87" wb)	2100	3200	4300	6500	11,000	23,000
Model F Victoria (87" wb)	1800	3300	4400	6700	12,000	24,000
Model G Victoria (87" wb)	1825	3300	4400	6700	12,000	24,000
Model H Roadster (87" wb)	1650	3500	4500	7000	13,000	25,000

1908 Detroit Electric, inside-drive coupe, HAC

1911 Detroit Electric, model 17, gentlemen's underslung roadster, HAC

1911 DETROIT ELECTRIC

Model 10 Brgm. (85" wb)	2800	3500	4500	7000	13,000	25,000
Model 15 Victoria (80" wb)	2000	3100	4200	6300	10,500	22,000
Model 17 Rds. (96" wb)	2000	3200	4300	6500	11,000	23,000
Model 21 Brgm. (85" wb)	2700	3500	4500	7000	13,000	25,000
Model 22 Brgm. (80" wb)	2500	3500	4500	7000	13,000	25,000
Model 23 Victoria (85" wb)	1900	3300	4400	6700	12,000	24,000
Model 18 Rds. (87" wb)	1800	3700	4700	7300	13,700	26,000
Model 19 Vic. Rds. (87" wb)						
	1800	3800	4800	7500	14,000	26,500
Model 20 Rds. (87" wb)	1700	3300	4400	6700	12,000	24,000
Model 16 Victoria (80" wb)	2025	3200	4300	6500	11,000	23,000
Model 11 Brgm. (80" wb)	2600	3300	4400	6700	12,000	24,000
Model 14 Victoria (85" wb)	2200	3300	4400	6700	12,000	24,000

(Note: Models 10 through 16 were shaft drive; models 17 through 23 chain drive)

1909 Detroit Electric, model C, coupe, NAHC

1909 Detroit Electric, model L, runabout, WLB

1912 Detroit Electric, model 29, limousine, HAC

427

1912 DETROIT ELECTRIC

	FP	5	4	3	2	1
Model 14 Victoria (85" wb)	2200	3100	4200	6300	10,500	22,000
Model 27 Vic. Open Top (85" wb)	2000	3200	4300	6500	11,000	23,000
Model 32 Vic. Cl. Top (85" wb)	2025	3100	4200	6300	10,500	22,000
Model 33 Brgm. (85" wb)	2700	3300	4400	6700	12,000	24,000
Model 30 Fore-Dr. Rds. (96" wb)	2200	3500	4500	7000	13,000	25,000
Model 31 Coupe (96" wb)	2600	2900	3700	5600	9100	20,000
Model 25 Extension Brougham (90" wb)	2800	3700	4700	7300	13,700	26,000
Model 26 Extension Brougham (90" wb)	2800	3700	4700	7300	13,700	26,000
Model 28 Taxicab (112" wb)	3400	3200	4300	6500	11,000	23,000
Model 28 Landaulet (112" wb)	3400	3300	4400	6700	12,000	24,000
Model 28 Town Car (112" wb)	3400	3500	4500	7000	13,000	25,000
Model 29 Limousine (112" wb)	3750	3900	4800	7700	14,300	27,000

1913 Detroit Electric, model 36, brougham, HAC

1913 DETROIT ELECTRIC

Model 42 Brgm. (96" wb)	3000	3100	4200	6300	10,500	22,000
Model 35 Brgm. (90" wb)	2850	3000	4000	6000	9500	21,000
Model 36 Brgm. (85" wb)	2700	2900	3700	5600	9100	20,000
Model 37 Brgm. (104" wb)	3600	3300	4400	6700	12,000	24,000
Model 39 Rds. (96" wb)	2350	3500	4500	7000	13,000	25,000
Model 40 Victoria (85" wb)	2300	3200	4300	6500	11,000	23,000

1914 Detroit Electric, model 47, brougham, OCW

1914 DETROIT ELECTRIC

Model 48 Dupl. Drive Brgm. (100" wb)	3000	3500	4500	7000	13,000	25,000
Model 47 Brgm. (100" wb)	2850	3300	4400	6700	12,000	24,000
Model 46 Rds. (100" wb)	2500	3700	4700	7300	13,700	26,000
Model 45 Forward-Drive Brougham (100" wb)	2800	3200	4300	6500	11,000	23,000
Model 44 Vic. (100" wb)	2300	3100	4200	6300	10,500	22,000
Model 43 Brgm. (100" wb)	2550	3100	4200	6300	10,500	22,000

1915 DETROIT ELECTRIC

Model 54 Rear-Seat Brougham (100" wb)	2950	3200	4300	6500	11,000	23,000
Model 50 Cabr. (100" wb)	2650	3300	4400	6700	12,000	24,000
Model 51 Small Brgm. (100" wb)	2850	3000	4000	6000	9500	21,000
Model 52 Dupl.-Drive Brougham (100" wb)	3000	3100	4200	6300	10,500	22,000
Model 53 Front-Drive Brougham (100" wb)	2950	3000	4000	6000	9500	21,000
Model 55 Small Brgm. (100" wb)	2600	3000	4000	6000	9500	21,000

1915 Detroit Electric, model 54, brougham, HAC

1916 DETROIT ELECTRIC

Model 57 Brgm. (100" wb)	2175	3200	4300	6500	11,000	23,000
Model 56 Cabr. (100" wb)	2075	3300	4400	6700	12,000	24,000
Model 60 Dupl. Drive (100" wb)	2275	3100	4200	6300	10,500	22,000
Model 58 Front Drive (100" wb)	2250	3100	4200	6300	10,500	22,000
Model 59 Rear Drive (100" wb)	2225	3100	4200	6300	10,500	22,000
Model 61 Rear Drive (94" wb)	1975	3100	4200	6300	10,500	22,000

1917 DETROIT ELECTRIC

Model 63 Brougham-4P	2275	3200	4300	6500	11,000	23,000
Model 64 Brougham-5P	2350	3300	4400	6700	12,000	24,000
Model 62 Cabriolet-3P	2175	3100	4200	6300	10,500	22,000
Model 68 Touring-4P	1775	3200	4300	6500	11,000	23,000
Model 68 Roadster-5P	2375	3300	4400	6700	12,000	24,000
Model 68 Runabout-5P	2325	3200	4300	6500	11,000	23,000

(Note: All cars with 100-inch wheelbase)

1918 Detroit Electric, model 75, brougham, HAC

1918 DETROIT ELECTRIC

Model 71 Brougham-4P	2940	3200	4300	6500	11,000	23,000
Model 72 Brougham-5P	2015	3000	4000	6000	9500	21,000
Model 73 Brougham-5P	2990	3300	4400	6700	12,000	24,000
Model 74 Brougham-5P	3040	3500	4500	7000	13,000	25,000
Model 75 Brougham-4P	2125	3100	4200	6300	10,500	22,000
Model 76 Convertible Rds.	2375	3700	4700	7300	13,700	26,000

(Note: All cars with 100-inch wheelbase)

1920 Detroit Electric, model 75-A, brougham, HAC

1919 DETROIT ELECTRIC

	FP	5	4	3	2	1
Model 71-A Brougham-4P	2940	3100	4200	6300	10,500	22,000
Model 72-A Brougham-5P	3015	3200	4300	6500	11,000	23,000
Model 73-A Brougham-5P	3040	3300	4400	6600	11,500	23,500
Model 75-A Brougham-5P	3040	3300	4400	6600	11,500	23,500
Model 75-A Brougham-4P	2175	3000	4000	6000	9500	21,000
Model 76-A Convertible Rds.	2175	3300	4400	6700	12,000	24,000

1920 DETROIT ELECTRIC

	FP	5	4	3	2	1
Model 72-A Brougham-5P	3300	3100	4200	6300	10,500	22,000
Model 73-A Brougham-5P	4000	3200	4300	6500	11,000	23,000
Model 71-A Brougham-4P	3200	3100	4200	6300	10,500	22,000
Model 75-A Brougham-4P	3300	3100	4200	6300	10,500	22,000

1921 Detroit Electric, model 88, brougham, HAC

1921 DETROIT ELECTRIC

Model 88 Brougham-5P	4000	3300	4400	6700	12,000	24,000
Model 82 Brougham-4P	4000	3300	4400	6700	12,000	24,000

1922 Detroit Electric, model 90, town car, HAC

1922 DETROIT ELECTRIC

Model 90 Town Car	2985	3500	4500	7000	13,000	25,000
Model 85 Duplex Drive Sedan	3450	3700	4700	7300	13,700	26,000
Model 91 Rear Drive Brougham	3985	3300	4400	6700	12,000	24,000
Model 92 Forward Drive Brougham	3985	3500	4500	7000	13,000	25,000
Model 93 Dupl. Drive Brougham	3985	3500	4500	7000	13,000	25,000

1923 Detroit Electric, model 93, brougham, NAHC

1923 DETROIT ELECTRIC

Model 90, 4.29 hp (NACC), 100" wb

	FP	5	4	3	2	1
Cpe.-4P	2800	3300	4400	6700	12,000	24,000

Model 91, 5.58 hp (NACC), 100" wb

Brgm.-4P	3500	3500	4500	7000	13,000	25,000

Model 92, 5.58 hp (NACC), 100" wb

Brgm.-5P	3500	3600	4600	7500	13,500	25,500

Model 93, 5.58 hp (NACC), 100" wb

Dup. Brgm.-5P	3500	3700	4700	7300	13,700	26,000

Note: Advertised output for Model 90 was 25 bhp. Advertised output for Models 91-14 was 30 bhp. Models 90-91 had rear drive. Model 92 had forward drive. Model 93 had duplex drive. Serial nos. 13151 & up. Production: approximately 50.

1924 DETROIT ELECTRIC

Model 90, 4.29 hp (NACC), 100" wb

Brgm.-4P	2800	3200	4300	6500	11,000	23,000

Model 91, 5.58 hp (NACC), 100" wb

Brgm.-5P	3500	3300	4400	6700	12,000	24,000

Model 92, 5.58 hp (NACC), 100" wb

Dup. Brgm.-5P	3500	3300	4400	6700	12,000	24,000

Model 93, 5.58 hp (NACC), 100" wb

Dup. Brgm.-5P	3500	3500	4500	7000	13,000	25,000

Model 94, 5.58 hp (NACC), 100" wb

Dup. Brgm.-5P	3200	3500	4500	7000	13,000	25,000

Note: Model 90-93 similar to 1923. Model 94 had duplex drive. Serial nos.: [Model 90] 13200 & up; [Others] 13500 & up. Production: approximately 70.

1925 DETROIT ELECTRIC

Model 95, 4.00 hp (NACC), 100" wb

Brgm.-4P	2800	3200	4300	6500	11,000	23,000

Note: Serial nos. 13270 & up. Production unknown. *Branham Automobile Reference Book* (1928) says "discontinued after 1925." Other sources indicate Model 95 built 1925-28.

1926 Detroit Electric, model 95, brougham, NAHC

1926 DETROIT ELECTRIC

Model 95, 4.00 hp (NACC), 100" wb

Brgm.-4P	2800	3300	4400	6700	12,000	24,000

1927 DETROIT ELECTRIC

Model 95, 4.00 hp (NACC), 100" wb

Brgm.-4P	2800	3300	4400	6700	12,000	24,000

1928 DETROIT ELECTRIC

Model 95, 4.00 hp (NACC), 100" wb

Brgm.-4P	2800	3300	4400	6700	12,000	24,000

Note: Serial numbers indicate production of 136 cars 1925-1928.

1929 DETROIT ELECTRIC

Model 99S, 4.00 hp (NACC), 112" wb

Cpe.-5P	4250	3200	4300	6500	11,000	23,000

Note: Serial numbers 13406 to 13432. Production: 26 (app.)

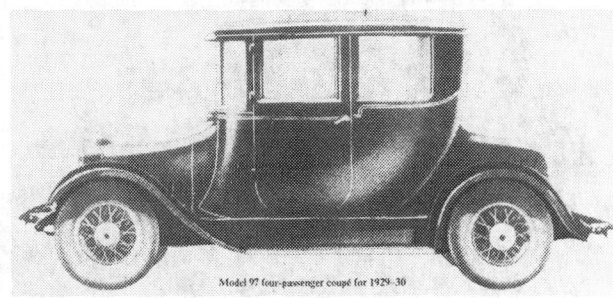

Model 97 four-passenger coupé for 1929-30

1929-1930 Detroit Electric, model 97, coupe, KM

1930 DETROIT ELECTRIC

Model 97, 4.00 hp (NACC), 100" wb

Cpe.-4P	2800	3100	4200	6300	10,500	22,000

Model 99, 4.00 hp (NACC), 112" wb

Cpe.-4P	4250	3200	4300	6500	11,000	23,000

Note: Serial nos. 13433 to 13611. Production: 178 (app.)

1931 Detroit Electric, model 99, coupe, OCW

1931 DETROIT ELECTRIC
Model 97, 4.00 hp (NACC), 100" wb

	FP	5	4	3	2	1
Cpe.-4P	2800	3100	4200	6300	10,500	22,000

Model 99, 4.00 hp (NACC), 112" wb

Cpe.-4P	4250	3200	4300	6500	11,000	23,000

Note: Serial nos. 13612 to 13743. Production: 131 (app.).

1932 Detroit Electric, model 99, coupe, OCW

1932 DETROIT ELECTRIC
Model 97, 4.00 hp (NACC), 100" wb

Brgm.-4P	2940	3100	4200	6300	10,500	22,000

Model 99, 4.00 hp (NACC), 112" wb

Cpe.-5P	4250	3200	4300	6500	11,000	23,000

Note: Serial nos. 13685 to 13744. Production: 59 (app.).

1933 DETROIT ELECTRIC
Model 97, 5.00 hp (NACC), 100" wb

Cpe.-4P	2800	3100	4200	6300	10,500	22,000

Model 99, 5.00 hp (NACC), 112" wb

Cpe.-4P	3750	3200	4300	6500	11,000	23,000

Note: Serial nos. 13745 to 19350. Production: inestimable.

1934 DETROIT ELECTRIC
Model 97, 5.00 hp (NACC), 100" wb

Cpe.-4P	2800	3100	4200	6300	10,500	22,000

Model 99, 5.00 hp (NACC), 112" wb

Cpe.-4P	3750	3200	4300	6500	11,000	23,000

Note: Serial nos. 19351 & up.

1935 DETROIT ELECTRIC
Model 97, 5.00 hp (NACC), 100" wb

Cpe.-4P	2345	3200	4300	6500	11,000	23,000

Model 99, 5.00 hp (NACC), 112" wb

Cpe.-4P	2960	3300	4400	6700	12,000	24,000

Note: Serial nos. not available.

1936 Detroit Electric, coupe, FR

1936-1939 DETROIT ELECTRIC
Note: After 1936, some Detroit Electrics of the previous style were apparently turned out. Others were built in modern models to simulate a gas car. Some, if not all of the latter used the exterior sheet metal of contemporary Dodges and were, in fact, identical to Dodges of this period.

1912 Detroiter, model No. 1., touring, HAC

DETROITER — Detroit, Michigan — (1912-1917) — In October of 1911 Claude S. Briggs resigned as sales manager of the Brush Runabout Company to join forces with John A. Boyle of Detroit. Together they incorporated the Briggs-Detroiter Company (capital stock $200,000) for the manufacture of a low-priced car that would be a bigger and better Brush Runabout. W.S. Lee was appointed chief engineer; Zach C. Barber, formerly a distributor for the E-M-F, would take charge of sales. The Detroiter was introduced at the Detroit Automobile Show in January 1912. It was an assembled car powered by a Continental four, then a Perkins V-8, then a Continental six. (Occasionally the car was referred to as a Briggs-Detroiter, but most often Detroiter was used as the marque name.) Despite high initial sales, the company did not fare well, requesting receivership during the summer of 1915 when its assets were computed to be $150,000, its liabilities $250,000. The company was bought outright later that summer by A.O. Dunk of the Puritan Machine Company. Thereupon Claude Briggs departed for the C.R. Wilson Body Company. Dunk reorganized as the Detroiter Motor Car Company and continued production until early in 1917 when he elected to kick himself upstairs to become chairman of the executive board and allow J.S. Kuhn, a New York banker who had been active in the reorganization, to take over as president. In March 1917 Kuhn reorganized yet again as the Detroiter Motors Company. By October Detroiter was again in receivership. In December its entire stock of finished cars, machinery, tools, parts and good will were bought by Sam Winternitz who immediately began planning his next auction.

1912 DETROITER
Model No. 1 — 4-cyl., 25 hp, 104" wb

	FP	5	4	3	2	1
Touring-5P	850	3300	4400	6700	12,000	24,000

1913 Detroiter, model A, touring, HAC

1913 DETROITER
Model A — 4-cyl., 25 hp, 104" wb

Touring-5P	900	3300	4400	6700	12,000	24,000
Roadster-2P	900	3500	4500	7000	13,000	25,000

1914 DETROITER
Series A — 4-cyl., 20 hp, 104" wb

Model A-1 Touring-5P	900	3300	4400	6700	12,000	24,000
Model A-2 Touring-5P	900	3300	4400	6700	12,000	24,000
Model A-3 Roadster-2P	900	3500	4500	7000	13,000	25,000
Model A-4 Roadster-2P	900	3500	4500	7000	13,000	25,000
Model A-5 Roadster-2P	1025	3700	4700	7300	13,700	26,000
Model A-6 Touring-5P	1025	3500	4500	7000	13,000	25,000
Kangaroo Speedster-2P	1025	4000	5000	8000	15,000	28,000

1914 Detroiter, Kangaroo, speedster, WLB

1915 DETROITER
Model C-5 — 4-cyl., 20 hp, 112" wb

	FP	5	4	3	2	1
Touring-5P	1050	3300	4400	6700	12,000	24,000

1916 Detroiter, model F, touring, HAC

1916 DETROIER
Model F — 4-cyl., 23 hp, 112" wb

	FP	5	4	3	2	1
Touring-5P	985	4000	5000	8000	15,000	28,000
Sedan-5P	1150	2700	3600	5300	8800	19,000

Model F-8 — 8-cyl., 31 hp, 112" wb

	FP	5	4	3	2	1
Touring-5P	1295	4500	5800	9500	18,000	32,000
Sedan-5P	1460	3200	4300	6500	11,000	23,000

1917 Detroiter, model 6-45, convertible coupe, HAC

1917 DETROITER
Model 6-45 — 6-cyl., 45 hp, 119" wb

	FP	5	4	3	2	1
Touring-5P	1250	4200	5200	8400	15,700	29,000
Roadster-3P	1250	4300	5400	8700	16,500	30,000
Luxemor Roadster-4P	1300	4500	5800	9500	18,000	32,000
Convertible Coupe	1525	2700	3600	5300	8800	29,000
Touring Sedan-5P	1550	2500	3500	5000	8500	18,000

DETROIT-OXFORD — Although the company building it was called the Detroit-Oxford Manufacturing Company, the car itself was more usually called the Oxford. It was built in Oxford, Michigan from 1905-1906. Refer to Oxford.

1914 Detroit Speedster, runabout, NAHC

DETROIT SPEEDSTER — Detroit, Michigan — (1913-1914)/SAGINAW SPEEDSTER — Saginaw, Michigan — (1914) — In August of 1913, A.R. Thomas announced that he was promoting the Detroit Cyclecar Company which would soon be in production with a side-by-side two-seater roadster. Designed by Ernest Weigold, former engineer for E.R. Thomas and chief engineer for Herreshoff, it featured a water-cooled four-cylinder engine, which was more cylinders than the average cyclecar, and the vehi-

cle weighed in at 850 pounds which represented more avoirdupois. Shaft drive was an unusual feature as well. Initially the vehicle was referred to as the Little Detroit, but promoter Thomas decided that might have a negative connotation. The vehicle did not succeed any better as simply the Detroit, however, nor as the Detroit Speedster, whereupon in May of 1914 A.R. Thomas showed up in Saginaw to promote another venture he had just organized called the Saginaw Motor Car Company. In July he announced his closing of a deal for the factory of the Brooks Manufacturing Company, producers of the erstwhile light delivery car which Charles Duryea had tried to make a go of during his short sojourn in Saginaw. The Brooks factory now was to see production of a car called the Saginaw Speedster. The new Saginaw Speedster was the old Detroit. It fared no better in its new location, and indeed may not have seen any production there. Apparently among the reasons for Thomas' moving to Saginaw was the legal tangle he got himself into in Detroit selling stock.

1913-1914 DETROIT SPDSTR./SAGINAW SPDSTR.
Cyclecar — 4-cyl., 95 c.i.d., 92" wb

	FP	5	4	3	2	1
Roadster	375	—	—	—	—	—

DETROIT STEAM CAR — This was the designation for 1923 for the car which had been produced in 1922 as the Trask or Trask-Detroit. Refer to Trask Steam.

1915 Detroit Taxicab, hansom, FR

DETROIT TAXICAB — Detroit, Michigan — (1914-1915) — The Detroit Taxicab & Transfer Company built its own cars simply because no one else in Detroit seemed anxious to. "They were all too busy to give us much thought," explained I.S. Scrimger, "and claimed they could do nothing for us unless we were willing to accept the chassis for the pleasure car they were building." The fact that the Detroit people, after eight years of using gasoline cars, had decided an electric was more viable for taxi service meant there were not many firms in the area capable of meeting their request, but those that could have missed out on a good deal. Instead Detroit Taxicab & Transfer developed its own electric, engineer W.J. Behn in charge. The car was designed, apparently, so that a gasoline unit could be installed should the electric version fail. It did not. Specifications regarding the Detroit Taxicab (other than its 121-inch wheelbase) are lacking, but relevant dates are not. The prototype was placed in service at the Hotel Pontchartrain at 2:00 p.m. on June 25th, 1914. After a successful test period, eleven more were built and placed in service by the following January. By the fall of 1915 another fifteen cars had been completed, and twenty more were underway and scheduled to be finished by year's end. That appears to have given Detroit Taxicab & Transfer the full fleet desired, because there is no evidence of production beyond these forty-seven cars. How long they remained in service is not known.

DEVAC — Newark, New Jersey — (1907) — The letters in the name represented "double explosion, valveless, air cooled" — and the Devac Automobile Company was organized in early 1907 with a capital stock of $500,000 to produce this two-stroke car. Company president was Elmer S. Smith, vice-president was William H. Wallace, and secretary-treasurer was C.W. Leonard. They seem to have proceeded little further than settling on a name for their product. The new Devac certainly never passed the prototype stage.

DEVAULT — Livingston, Montana — (1930's) — Re-manufactured Model T Fords were relatively numerous during the 1920's. The DeVault of the 1930's was a re-manufactured car with a difference. First-hand observers disagree as to whether it looked more like a Plymouth or a Model A Ford. Ironically, the chassis on which it was based was a Nash. The DeVault Motor Company was located at 109 South "B" Street in Livingston; downstairs was showroom and office for the Nash dealership, upstairs was the family residence of Feris J. DeVault. French-born, DeVault apparently retained his Continental flair. Though no one is certain how long he marketed his DeVault, word is unanimous that it was a very stylish car.

DE VAUX — Grand Rapids, Michigan & Oakland, California — (1931-1932) — Norman de Vaux was a native Californian who was a close friend of William C. Durant's. During Durant's General Motors days, de Vaux organized the Chevrolet Motor Company of California for him, and later the West Coast companies for Star and Durant when the irrepressible Billy was setting up his second empire. Colonel Elbert J. Hall was a native Californian who built high-powered race cars called Sunset and in 1908, with the backing of a wealthy Stanford University student named Bert Scott, established the Hall-Scott Motor Company. Hall designed aircraft, tractor

1931 De Vaux, custom coupe, WLB

and bus engines, worked with Packard's Colonel Jesse Vincent on development of the Liberty aircraft engine for World War I, and was associated with the Fageol brothers in their $12,000+ luxury motorcar of 1917. Late in 1930, de Vaux and Hall got together with an automotive idea on the precise opposite end of the automotive scale from the Fageol. In California they decided to build a new economy car, then traveled to Grand Rapids to get things started. They leased one of the plants of the Hayes Body Corporation, and contracted with Hayes for the building of bodies. Another plant was planned for Oakland, California. The new de Vaux was shown at the automobile shows in New York and Chicago in early 1931; it had an L-head six-cylinder engine designed by Hall and a range of four models selling from $595 to $795. It was a very well equipped car for its price class, but neither de Vaux nor Hall were equipped to handle the marketing of a new automobile in the wake of the Depression. The first car came off the line in Grand Rapids in early April, with production there up to sixty-five cars a day within the month, and the Oakland plant in operation by April 15th. But sales were dismal. Only 4808 cars were sold in all of 1931. By January of 1932 the partners gave up. In February Continental Motors Corporation stepped in, bought the De Vaux name and the Michigan assets of the company, refined the product, raised both horsepower and prices and tried to succeed where De Vaux-Hall Motors Corporation had failed, offering the car as the De Vaux Continental (or Continental De Vaux) for the remainder of 1932. In September one of these cars, a stock coupe, averaged 66 mph for 1000 miles at Muroc Lake, a new Class C record. But only 1358 cars were sold that year. Then Continental had another idea, a model line of two sixes and a new four and the marketing of the car as a Continental only. Both de Vaux and Hall were out of the Continental picture now. The new cars were introduced in 1933, but by the end of 1934 Continental decided to return to engine building exclusively. Norman de Vaux stepped back into the picture, with plans to produce the Beacon model of the 1934 Continental as the 1935 De Vaux Four Forty-Four. A brochure indicated that production was planned only for Oakland, California. But no production at all resulted. Instead Norman de Vaux would try again in 1936 with another idea, an export-only car called the De-Vo.

1931 De Vaux, sedan, JAC

1931 DE VAUX
6-cyl., 70 hp, 113" wb

	FP	5	4	3	2	1
Phaeton	545	4400	5600	9200	17,300	31,000
Standard Sedan	595	2300	3300	4600	7500	16,000
Standard Coupe	595	2500	3500	5000	8500	18,000
Custom Sedan	795	2400	3400	4800	8000	17,000
Custom Coupe	795	2700	3600	5300	8800	19,000

1932 DE VAUX
(Continental) — 6-cyl., 80 hp, 113" wb

Standard Sedan	775	2400	3400	4800	8000	17,000
Standard Coupe	725	2700	3600	5300	8800	19,000
Custom Sedan	845	2500	3500	5000	8500	18,000
Custom Coupe	845	2900	3700	5600	9100	20,000
Custom Convertible Coupe	895	4000	5000	8000	15,000	28,000
Standard R/S Cpe.	775	3000	4000	6000	9500	21,000

DEVENDORF — The Perl W. Devendorf Corporation was organized in Watertown, New York early in 1919 with a capital stock of $150,000 for the manufacture of automobiles. Joining P.W. Devendorf in this venture were G.F. Wallis and C.B. Winslow. Manufacture is doubted.

DE-VO — Dover, Delaware — (1936-1937) — De-Vo represented the phonetic spelling of the last name of the man whose idea it was. Following the failure of his De Vaux car, Norman de Vaux was trying again, this time in association with former Packard vice-president F.F. Beall, and with a car designed for export only. The De-Vo Motor Car Corporation was organized in Maryland late in 1936, but manufacture was slated for Dover, Delaware. The De-Vo was to be an economy car, as had been the De Vaux. It would rather resemble the Continental Beacon, which was the car de Vaux's De Vaux had become when bankruptcy forced him to give up on it. Norman de Vaux would have to give up on the De-Vo soon too. A four/five-passenger sedan on a 102-inch wheelbase, the car was powered by a four-cylinder Continental Red Seal engine. A single prototype — which remains extant — was put together at the M.P. Moller works in Hagerstown, Maryland. The project died soon thereafter. Subsequently Norman de Vaux joined Hupp and as general manager was responsible for producing the Hupmobile Skylark of 1939-1940.

DEVON — Philadelphia, Pennsylvania — (1911) — The Devon was simply the name under which Merchant & Evans marketed the last of the Club Cars it had produced for the New York-based Club Car Company of America. The idea of buying membership in a club in order to purchase one of its automobiles had quickly proven to to be the answer to a question no one had asked — and with dismal membership, the New York company quickly faded into oblivion. Convinced that the idea would fare no better in Philadelphia, Merchant & Evans ordered new script bearing the "Devon" name and offered the cars for sale without a membership application.

1901 Dewabout, runabout, WLB

DEWABOUT — Lexington, Kentucky — (1900-1901) — In 1900 Thomas B. Dewhurst, who ran a bicycle agency and repair shop in the basement of the Phoenix Hotel in Lexington, decided to build an automobile. Since his would be Kentucky's first, he designed the vehicle, as he later said, by using his own imagination and "by following to a certain extent the pictures of machines of various kinds published by newspapers and magazines." The result was a pneumatic-tired, wire-wheeled, tiller-steered two-seater powered by a two-cylinder 4 hp air-cooled engine. Begun in the fall of 1900, the machine was completed early the following year and successfully completed its maiden run from Lexington to nine miles past Georgetown and return in May. Dewhurst called the car the Dewabout and continued to tinker with it for the next several years. When he decided to enter the automobile business, however, it was as a dealer and not a manufacturer. His Buick agency was one of the pioneer dealerships in the industry. His Dewabout was retained as an attraction in the Dewhurst showroom. In 1918 Thomas Dewhurst wrote a lively account of the Dewabout ("The First Automobile in the Blue Grass") for *The Kentucky Magazine* noting that observers along the route of the first run concluded the car was a "new-fangled peanut roaster." The last contemporary reference to the Dewabout appeared in the January 1925 issue of *Automobile Trade Journal*. Under a picture of Thomas B. Dewhurst sitting in his Dewabout was the caption, "This car has recently found its way to the junk pile."

1909 DeWitt, auto-buggy, NAHC

DEWITT — **North Manchester, Indiana** — **(1909-1910)** — During the early years of this century, Virgil L. DeWitt emigrated from his native Switzerland to settle in Auburn (Indiana) and work for the W.H. Kiblinger Company, then a prosperous manufacturer of high-wheeled motor buggies. Believing that with a little backing he could produce an automobile equally as fine, he approached the Industrial Association of North Manchester with his idea, which was enthusiastically received. DeWitt was offered a parcel of land worth $600 in addition to $1500 in cash to bring his factory to town. As the North Manchester *News Journal* reported in July of 1908, the Association "is made up of practically everyone in town, so all are interested. It is a big family affair and will be best done by everybody doing his share, and doing it right now." The money DeWitt needed to begin construction of his factory was immediately put up by the townspeople, and a fine structure was built. The first DeWitt — "A Handsome Red Buzz Buggy" — rolled out of the factory on April 15th, 1909. It was very Kiblinger-like, with a two-cylinder 13.6 hp engine mounted under the seat, a piano-box two-seater body, a top speed of 30 mph and a price tag of $592.50. In May a sympathy strike following the firing of a clumsy workman halted production for a month, but by June the output of the DeWitt factory was up to four vehicles a day, and sales were high. Less than a year later, however, on May 5th, 1910, the DeWitt factory burned to the ground. Ironically, just a few days before, Virgil DeWitt had given three of his cars to an insurance agency in exchange for insurance coverage. Following the fire, the equipment that could be salvaged was sold to a Chicago machinery company. Virgil DeWitt sold his home in North Manchester in 1912 and reportedly moved to California. At least one DeWitt motor buggy is known to be extant.

1909-1910 DeWITT
2-cyl., 13.6 hp, 78" wb

	FP	5	4	3	2	1
Motor Buggy-2P	592.50	2700	3600	5300	8800	19,000

DEXTER — The Dexter Stocking Company was organized in Rochelle, Illinois during the fall of 1913 with a capital stock of $5000 to manufacture and deal in automobiles and accessories. Dexter Stocking, Thad M. Graves and Elmer E. Holmes were behind this venture. Manufacture of a car is doubted.

1895 Dey-Griswold Electric, phaeton, NAHC

DEY-GRISWOLD — **New York, New York** — **(1895-1898)/DEY** — **(1917-1919)** — Harry E. Dey had two electric car ideas. The first was a combination electric-fluid drive which forced oil through turbines attached to the rear wheels. Too much slippage in the turbines resulted, but the concept did allow the later, somewhat tenuous, claim that the Dey-Griswold featured the world's first torque converter. A few of these electrics were produced in Rhode Island by the Pawtucket Motor Carriage Company, but Dey-Griswold & Company was out of business before the turn of the century. For a while thereafter, Harry Dey was associated with Dr. Charles

1917 Dey Electric, roadster, WLB

Steinmetz in his electric experiments. And he was applying for a lot of patents on his own too as the Dey Electric Vehicle Syndicate, which was followed in mid-1915 by the Dey Electric Corporation, with the promise that new models of a Dey Electric would show up at the New York Automobile Show in January 1917. They did — and thus followed the second Dey electric car idea, this time an electric motor that was part of the rear axle, "the rotating armature driving the one, the rotating field the other car wheel." The motor was its own differential, and no transmission was required. It was an interesting idea, but it didn't work any better than Dey's Nineteenth Century electric notion. There were some Steinmetz ideas as well in this second-generation Dey — a $1000 runabout on a 100-inch wheelbase chassis — which originally was to be built in York, Pennsylvania under the aegis of J.W. Guthrie and H.W. Hayden. That venture was bankrupt by August 1917. Dey took over himself in 1919 and prepared for manufacture which never came in Jersey City, New Jersey. Very few of either the Dey-Griswold or the Dey were ever produced. Harry Dey died in 1927.

D.H.K. — **Detroit, Michigan** — **(1909)** — Light runabouts to sell for under $500 were to be the product of the D.H.K. Motor Car Company which was organized in Detroit during the spring of 1909. The firm was defunct by that fall, probably before viable manufacture had commenced.

DIAMOND — Although Diamond was indicated in a January 1907 press report as the name of the new car to be produced by the Barnes Manufacturing Company, the firm ultimately decided to market the vehicles under the Servitor name and its own. Refer to Barnes and Servitor.

Diamond was one of three names used by J.W. Ricketts of South Bend, Indiana to designate the cars he produced from 1909-1911. Refer to Ricketts.

The Diamond Motor Car Company was organized in Philadelphia during the spring of 1912 to manufacture and deal in automobiles in Pelham Manor, New York. Behind this $10,000 venture were Carl W. Runlett, Charles W. Jaycox and Frank Davis. Manufacture of a car is doubted.

The Diamond State Automobile Company was organized in Delaware early in 1914 to "manufacture and sell motor cars and other vehicles and deal in supplies for same." J.F. Chapple and N.B. Mancile of Wilmington, T.C. Marshall of Yorklyn, were behind this $25,000 venture. Manufacture of a car is doubted.

DIAMOND — **Wilmington, Delaware** — **(1902)** — The Diamond Automobile Company of Wilmington was organized to manufacture a gasoline runabout and a tricycle featuring a new compensating gear invented by John H. Parsons. The principals behind this venture were James Baily and C.B. Harris of Wilmington, Charles Burton of Philadelphia, W.F. Pierce of St. Paul, Minnesota and Martin Mainogue of Springfield, Ohio. Prototypes of the two vehicles appear to have been completed, but no more than that. In November it was reported that the Diamond Automobile Company "has been closed up under a landlord's warrant."

DIAMOND — **Meriden, Connecticut** — **(1905)** — The Diamond Motor Company was organized in New Haven in 1904 and soon found a suitable factory for manufacture at the corner of Center and Britannia streets in Meriden. Conceivably the selection of Meriden was made partly because of John T. Murphy who was Diamond's chief engineer and a resident of that city. In January of 1905, *The Horseless Age* reported that the Diamond Motor Company expected "to begin production of a lot of motor cars by the 1st of February." That first lot was also its last. Diamond disappeared from the Meriden City Directory in 1905, and John T. Murphy had found work as an engineer with another company in town.

DIAMOND — **Wilmington, Delaware** — **(1914-1915)** — The Cycle Car Company of Wilmington was incorporated by a local business firm trading under the wonderfully whimsical name of Marvel, Marvel and Wolcott — and by a local automobile enthusiast named T.C. Bradford. The company's shops were at 224 French Street. With a four-cylinder 16/20 hp engine, the firm's product was rather high-powered for a cyclecar, and the company would have been better advised to have called it just about anything else. Interestingly, the car was simply referred to as Cyclecar for several months, then Bradford for a few weeks, until finally Diamond was chosen as the name for the product. Fuel consumption of the Diamond Cyclecar was meritorious (30-40 mpg), and so was the maximum road speed of 55 mph. Houk wire wheels were featured, and complete electrics ("lights flashing both strong and dim") were fitted. T.C. Bradford stated that numerous orders, some even from abroad, had already been received, and the press indicated that the location of the firm in Wilmington, with its central East Coast advantage, bade well for the success of the venture. What did not bode well was the company's product; fewer than one percent of the cyclecars manufactured in the United States in 1914 survived 1915 — and the cyclecar from Wilmington was not one of them. The company beefed up its product into a light car with standard tread for 1915, but the public relations damage already done could not be undone, and the Cycle Car Company of Wilmington was out of business by year's end.

1914 DIAMOND
Cyclecar — **4-cyl., 16/20 hp, 100" wb**

	FP	5	4	3	2	1
Roadster-2P	350	2500	3500	5000	8500	18,000

1915 DIAMOND
Light Car — **4-cyl., 16/20 hp, 100" wb**

	FP	5	4	3	2	1
Roadster-2P	450	2500	3500	5000	8500	18,000
Touring-4P	475	2700	3600	5300	8800	19,000

DIAMOND — **Detroit, Michigan** — **(1922)** — This Diamond was a taxi promoted by Frank L. Klingensmith, president of the Gray Motor Corporation, and his associate Frank F. Beall, together with H.T. Hanover, who headed Apex Motor Corporation, and Nat Jacoby, who operated the Black and White Cab Company of New York. Klingensmith's new low-priced Gray car was already big news in Detroit, Hanover had money and would soon be nicely at liberty since the Ace car he had been building in Ypsilanti was on its way out, and Jacoby was known as a real go-getter in taxicab circles in New York City. This venture had success written all over it. The Diamond Taxicab Company, a $10 million New York State incorporation, was formally announced in the early spring of 1922. To build the taxi, Diamond turned to Elkhart, Indiana and Elcar. Elcar's chief engineer A.M. Graffis designed the Diamond taxi, with some kibitzing from Jacoby. A standard cab in most particulars, the Diamond was distinguished by its use of less glass than the norm, the windows it had being easily removed panels which could be replaced in case of accident. Doubtless this feature was Jacoby's idea, a practical one, and also quite "marketable" in the taxi sense, since the privacy of a landaulet was frequently desirable among taxi patrons. It is known that the original order to Elcar for Diamond taxis was for a run of a thousand, but how many more cars than that may have been built is something of a mystery. As is how long the Diamond was produced. After satisfying the market in New York City, plans called for a Diamond invasion of such other East Coast cities as Boston, Philadelphia, Washington and Baltimore. But by that time, Gray Motor Corporation was in trouble in Detroit and although Diamond was not officially associated with Klingensmith's passenger-car-producing venture, its fortunes necessarily had to have some ties to it. By January of 1925 Frank Klingensmith had left Gray, by then a virtual corpse, and no doubt the Diamond taxi was dead too.

1907 Diamond T, touring, NAHC

DIAMOND T — Chicago, Illinois — (1907-1911) — The Diamond T Motor Car Company of Chicago was organized in 1905 by C.A. Tilt, who had just completed the building of his first car. Tilt was obviously a careful man, because he did not plunge headlong into manufacture. Not until 1907 was the Diamond T placed on the market in three body styles. These were big cars, and very substantially built. Fifty units were produced that first year. Tilt continued to build his four-cylinder Diamond T passenger cars through 1911. The only reason he stopped then, reportedly, was that a client happened to ask him if he could build a truck as well. And, of course, he could. Thereafter production was focused on the commercial field, and Diamond T trucks became a conspicuous part of the American scene for more than a half century. Total Diamond T car production probably numbered in the hundreds. More than 250,000 Diamond T trucks were built through 1966.

1907 DIAMOND T
Four — 40 hp, 114" wb

	FP	5	4	3	2	1
Touring-5P	3500	4000	5000	8000	15,000	28,000
Limousine	4250	3900	4800	7700	14,300	27,000
Runabout	3250	3700	4700	7300	13,700	26,000

1908 DIAMOND T
Four — 50 hp, 114" wb

Roadster	3500	4200	5200	8400	15,700	29,000
Touring	4300	4000	5000	8000	15,000	28,000
Limousine	5200	3900	4800	7700	14,300	27,000

1909 DIAMOND T
Four — 50 hp, 114" wb

Touring-7P	3250	4000	5000	8000	15,000	28,000
Tourabout-4P	3000	4200	5200	8400	15,700	29,000
Roadster-3P	2750	4300	5400	8700	16,500	30,000

1910 DIAMOND T
Model D — 4-cyl., 30 hp, 108" wb

Speedster-2P	2250	5200	6800	11,300	23,000	36,000
Touring-4P	2300	4000	5000	8000	15,000	28,000
Roadster-3P	2250	4300	5400	8700	16,500	30,000

Model E — 4-cyl., 45 hp, 124" wb

Touring-7P	3200	4000	5200	8400	15,700	29,000
Roadster-3P	2850	4400	5600	9200	17,300	31,000
Touring-5P	3000	4300	5400	8700	16,500	30,000

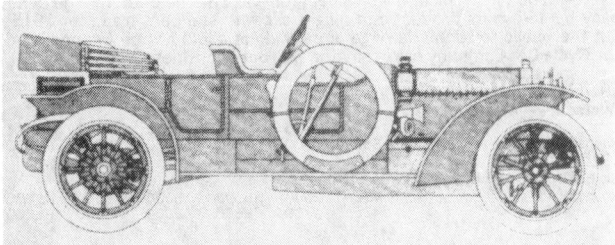

1911 Diamond T, touring, NAHC

1911 DIAMOND T
Four — 45 hp, 124" wb

Fore-Door Touring-5P	3500	4200	5200	8400	15,700	29,000
Limousine-7P	4200	3900	4800	7700	14,300	27,000

1925 Diana, roadster, JAC

DIANA — St. Louis, Missouri — (1925-1928) — Diana Motors Company of St. Louis was a wholly owned subsidiary of the Moon Motor Car Company. In Roman mythology Diana is goddess of the moon, which obviously was the reason for the name but, curiously, the company never dwelled on that fact much. It might be said that another goddess was involved as well, since the Diana's radiator shell was a virtual carbon copy of the Belgian Minerva. Diana/Moon did not dwell on that at all. The new company and the new car were announced by Stewart McDonald (president of Moon, who would hold the same position in Diana) in late May of 1925. The Diana itself arrived on June 25th, and was sensationally received. The company referred to it as "the easiest steering car in America," "the only car built entirely for balloon tires," and "a car for women drivers." In performance testing the Diana reported fuel consumption of 15 to 18 mpg, with maximum speeds up to 70 mph. The car's engine was a 72 hp Continental straight-eight. It was as an upmarket motorcar of high style that the Diana truly shown. Prices were generally in the $2000 range, though one had to pay extra for a fancy sports roadster with radiator and wire wheels in bronze. A town car at $5000 was another limited production model designed to generate showroom traffic. Diana Motors claimed its "Composite Steel Body" to be a first, which is moot, though narrow steel windshield posts effectively enhanced visability. Hydraulic four-wheel brakes were fitted, as well as the Lanchester Vibration Dampener, both progressive features, though the Diana is perhaps better remembered for sporting one of the loveliest radiator mascots ever to appear on an American car. Seven thousand cars had been the projected Diana production its first year, though it was not realized that first twelve months, nor in the two years that followed. In the midst of internal problems within the Moon organization — as well as some purported structural problems in the car itself — the Diana faded away. Models for 1928 were announced, but by early in the new year the Diana had simply become another Moon.

1926 Diana, roadster, HAC

1926 DIANA
Eight — 72 hp, 125½" wb

	FP	5	4	3	2	1
Touring-5P	1895	3700	4700	7300	13,700	26,000
Roadster-4P	1895	4000	5000	8000	15,000	28,000
Two-Door Sedan-5P	2095	2300	3300	4600	7500	16,000
Cabriolet Roadster-4P	2095	3300	4400	6700	12,000	24,000
Sedan-5P	1995	2200	3200	4400	7000	15,000
Deluxe Sedan-5P	2195	2250	3300	4500	7300	15,500

1927 Diana, 4-dr. sedan, WLB

1927 Diana "Palm Beach Special," roadster, HAC

1927 Diana, town car, HAC

1927 DIANA
Eight — 72 hp, 125½" wb

	FP	5	4	3	2	1
Touring-7P	1995	3700	4700	7300	13,700	26,000
Roadster-5P	1795	4000	5000	8000	15,000	28,000
Two-Door Sedan-5P	1995	2300	3300	4600	7500	16,000
Cabriolet Roadster-5P	2095	3300	4400	6700	12,000	24,000
Sedan-7P	2695	2100	3100	4300	6800	14,500
Deluxe Sedan-5P	2195	2250	3300	4500	7300	15,500

1928 DIANA
Eight — 72 hp, 125½" wb

	FP	5	4	3	2	1
Roadster Deluxe	1695	4200	5200	8400	15,700	29,000
Brougham Deluxe	2095	2500	3500	5000	8500	18,000
Sedan Deluxe	2295	2700	3600	5300	8800	19,000
Phaeton Deluxe	1895	4000	5000	8000	15,000	28,000

1901 Diebel, runabout, NAHC

DIEBEL — Philadelphia, Pennsylvania — (1901) — In 1899 William Diebel was the proprietor of the Fairmount Cycle Company at 832 Arch Street in Philadelphia. Deciding to get into the manufacture of running gear and engines for automobiles, Diebel moved to the factory of the Howard Manufacturing Company in Mt. Holly, New Jersey where he allied himself with a man named Eppler. By the fall of 1900, however, Diebler had moved back to Philadelphia into a new plant at Randolph and Fairmont avenues. Apparently, Eppler moved with him because the firm remained styled as the Diebel-Eppler Manufacturing Company, although not for long. By the fall of 1901 the Diebel-Cox Manufacturing Company ensued, and this firm now moved into a new plant at Fairmount and Fifth. From the new partner-

ship arrived a little gasoline runabout called the Diebel. William Diebel air cooled his little 7hp two-cylinder car in an unusual way. Rings with radiating arms were shrunk unto the cylinder casting which made for a shark-toothed look and perhaps did not work well. The car's price of $650 was attractive, however, and probably front office problems were more responsible for the Diebel's short life.

DIEBOLD — "Henry C. Diebold of Belleville, Illinois has completed an experimental automobile," reported *The Horseless Age* during the summer of 1901. Further details are lacking.
The Diebold Products Company was organized in Cleveland, Ohio early in 1913 "to manufacture machinery, motor trucks and motor pleasure cars." Behind this $25,000 venture were Charles R. Diebold, Max Friedman, Louis P. Diebold, Martin W. Sanders and Mabel M. Hummell. Manufacture of a car is doubted.

DIEHL — Portland, Oregon — (1935) — The Diehl looked rather like a dirigible. Yet another experimental car from the teardrop school, this one was designed by G.A. Diehl of Portland. Its rear-mounted engine was of Diehl's own construction, as was everything else about the car. The body was streamlined and fenderless, the frame was of duralumin — and the vehicle was a three-wheeler, "making parking and steering easier," as G.A. Diehl said. A single headlight was used in front, with side marker lamps similar to the running lights on a ship fitted. This was a safety feature. "With present cars, when passing a 'one-eyed' car at night," G.A. Diehl said, "it is difficult to determine which light is out, and collison may result, especially on narrow roads." So far as is known, this was the only car built by G.A. Diehl.

DIEHNART — Lafayette, Indiana — (1901) — In 1901 in Lafayette, and in association with Edgar F. Smith, one Frank Diehnart built an automobile. That the car was tested with success was reported in *The Motor Age* that June. That the partners never built another is probable.

DIFFERENTIAL — The Differential Steel Car Company has appeared on many rosters as a maker of automobiles or trucks, or both, in Findlay, Ohio during the 1930's. According to someone associated with the firm during that period, Differential produced neither. Railroad cars and parts were the company's sole products. An automobile was never tried, and the single truck which had been produced as a prototype was a complete failure.

1915 Dile, model A, roadster, WLB

DILE — Reading, Pennsylvania — (1914-1917) — In November of 1913, Fred K. Dick and Irvin D. Lengel of Reading put the first two letters of their last names and their automobile ideas together, and produced a piquant little four-cylinder, wire-wheeled sport roadster with a sliding gear transmission and a price tag less than $500. A custom version was ordered by Pearl White, with coachwork in dramatic stripes of black and white, to match the movie serial actress' favorite costume scheme. Apparently the shortage of parts occasioned by the First World War hastened the demise of the Dile Motor Car Company. In August 1916 backruptcy was declared. Winding up the firm's affairs took some time. In early fall of 1918 it was announced that all Dile cars in the process of construction, trademarks, patents, patterns, blueprints, et al. had been purchased by Belmont Motors Corporation, which had just been launched into business in Lewistown as a commercial vehicle maker.

1914-1917 DILE
Model A — 4-cyl., 11 hp, 96" wb

	FP	5	4	3	2	1
Sport Roadster-2P	485	2300	3300	4600	7500	16,000

DIMMER — The Dimmer Company of America was organized in Chicago during the fall of 1913 with a $21,000 capital stock for the manufacture and sale of automobiles. Behind the venture were A.A. Pantelis, O.O.H. Weldner, and J.H. Lally. Manufacture of a car is doubted.

DINGFELDER — Detroit, Michigan — (1903) — The Dingfelder was a 500-pound, 500-dollar motor buggy with a delightful name and little else to distinguish it from hundreds of other horsedrawn-vehicles-gone-horseless on the market in 1903. Its engine was a little 3½ hp one-lunger doubt-

435

less similar to the small marine gas engines the Dingfelder Motor Company, located at 958 Jefferson in Detroit, also manufactured. "The machine has been very well received by the local trade, and a nice business is anticipated," *Cycle and Automobile Trade Journal* reported in June 1903. "Mr. Dingfelder is held in high esteem for his honorable business methods and sterling integrity." Unfortunately, there were a good many scoundrels who would make more money in the automobile business than poor Mr. Dingfelder. His car did not survive into 1904.

DIRECT DRIVE — The car built in Pottstown, Pennsylvania from 1919 to 1924 by the Direct Drive Motor Car Company was marketed under the tradename Champion. Refer to Champion.

DIRECTOR — The Director Wagon Company of Hartford, Connecticut was noted as an automobile manufacturer in the Hiscox book *Horseless Vehicles, Automobiles, Motor Cycles* published in 1900. Further documentation is lacking.

1917 Disbrow, roadster, WLB

DISBROW — Cleveland, Ohio — (1916-1917) — Renowned race driver Louis Disbrow had a lot of help, but everything in the Disbrow was built to his detailed specifications. Wisconsin supplied the T-head fours of 90 and 110 hp; Warner Gear provided steering, transmission and clutch; Parish & Bingham the pressed steel frame, Perfex the radiator, Bosch the ignition, and Houk the wire wheels. The aluminum body design on the 114-inch wheelbase chassis was Disbrow's alone, however, and it was very racy with no runningboards but with bicycle-style fenders that turned with the front wheels to protect the driver from mud spray in a corner. Though demurring that the Disbrow "is not particularly a racing vehicle," the company nonetheless let it be known that, in its highest-powered version, 90 mph was guaranteed. This was the "Special Disbrow" roadster, a limited production car powered by an in-house engine with aluminum block and sixteen overhead valves. Prices were $2650-$3000. A four-seater version called the Quad Express was developed, but not marketed. Though initial sales of the Disbrow were salutary, the company was quickly hit by materials shortages occasioned by the First World War. Soon Louis Disbrow found competition in this arena fiercer than he had encountered in motor sport, and Disbrow Motors Corporation of Cleveland quietly faded from the scene during the summer of 1917. In January 1918 Louis Disbrow joined the Moore Motor Vehicle Company in Minneapolis as chief engineer, but he was not long there either. In later years he worked for a Milwaukee firm making spark plugs, continued to race occasionally (as late as 1929), and officiated at various race events. Shortly before his death in 1939, he was a clerk in the Philadelphia city morgue.

1916-1917 DISBROW

	FP	5	4	3	2	1
Model A 90 hp Roadster	2650	4700	6100	9900	19,000	33,000
Model B 110 hp Roadster	3500	5000	6500	11,000	22,000	35,000
Model C Spc. Disbrow Rds.	3000	4900	6300	10,300	21,000	34,000

1911 Dispatch, model E, runabout, WLB

DISPATCH — Minneapolis, Minnesota — (1910-1919) — Few automobiles ever survived so long without much being known about the company behind them as the Dispatch of Minneapolis. Prior to December of 1910 the Dispatch Motor Company was unknown in the trade press. In that month's issue of *Cycle and Automobile Trade Journal*, however, the firm's small two-cylinder roadster was fully described. And there was this note: "At first the demand for the car among the company's stockholders was so great that it was impossible to fill any other orders; but with the greatly increased factory facilities which the company now possesses, '1911 orders should be filled promptly." Larger four-cylinder models followed in 1912, and the trade press was thereafter kept informed of the complete lineup of Dispatch cars, but little ever was revealed about the company. R.E. Carswell and John Hoppins were the firm's principal officers. Dispatch cars used two-stroke engines until 1914 when the company substituted a four-stroke Wisconsin engine; more interestingly, Dispatches continued with chain drive until 1918, assuredly one of the last cars on the American road to do so. Although the Dispatch Motor Company was listed in Minneapolis city directories until 1923, the company had ceased manufacture by late January 1919 as revealed in *Motor Age* that month. Apparently, the firm survived a few years longer as an agency or garage.

1910-1911 DISPATCH
Model E — 2-cyl., 16 hp, 96" wb

	FP	5	4	3	2	1
Roadster-2P	675	4400	5600	9200	17,300	31,000

1912 DISPATCH
Model E — 2-cyl., 16 hp, 96" wb

	FP	5	4	3	2	1
Roadster-2P	700	4400	5600	9200	17,300	31,000

Four — 35 hp, 120" wb

Model D Torpedo Roadster	850	4500	5800	9500	18,000	32,000
Model G-2 Fore-Door Tour.	900	4600	6000	9700	18,500	32,500

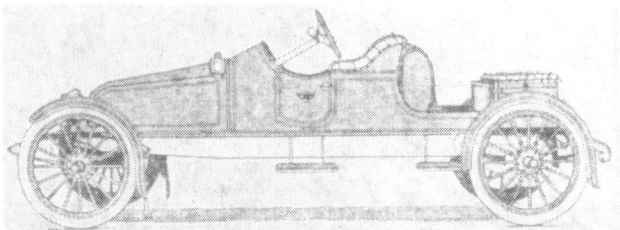

1913 Dispatch, model D, torpedo roadster

1913 DISPATCH
Four — 35 hp, 120" wb

Model D Torpedo Roadster	850	4500	5800	9500	18,000	32,000
Model G-2 Fore-Door Touring	900	4700	6100	9900	19,000	33,000
Model H Coupe-2P	1000	3000	4000	6000	9500	21,000

1914-1915 DISPATCH
Model G-3 — 4-cyl., 23 hp, 120" wb

Roadster-2P	850	4500	5800	9500	18,000	32,000
Touring-5P	900	4300	5400	8700	16,500	30,000
Tourist-5P	1210	4400	5600	9200	17,300	31,000
Coupe	1025	2900	3700	5600	9100	20,000

1916 DISPATCH
Model G — 4-cyl., 23 hp, 120" wb

Touring-5P	1210	4300	5400	8700	16,500	30,000
Roadster-2P	935	4500	5800	9500	18,000	32,000
Coupe-2P	1000	2900	3700	5600	9100	20,000

1917 DISPATCH
Model G — 4-cyl., 23 hp, 120" wb

Touring-5P	1210	4300	5400	8700	16,500	30,000
Roadster-2P	1135	4500	5800	9500	18,000	32,000
Coupe-2P	1400	2900	3700	5600	9100	20,000

1918-1919 DISPATCH
Model D — 4-cyl., 23 hp, 120" wb

Touring-5P	1250	4400	5600	9200	17,300	31,000
Coupe-2P	1400	3000	4000	6000	9500	21,000
Sedan-5P	1450	2700	3600	5300	8800	19,000
Cloverleaf Roadster-3P	1225	4500	5800	9500	18,000	32,000

1898 Dittlinger, auto buggy, GR

DITTLINGER — St. Louis, Missouri — (1898) — Emil V. Dittlinger was a practicing physican from St. Louis who during the late 1890's, in his own words, "saw the dawning of the physician's emancipation from the care and expense of the horse-drawn vehicle." In 1897 he visited automobile manufacturing plants in Detroit and in Decatur, Illinois (the latter Mueller) and returned home to build a car for himself. It was powered by a two-cylinder engine and was fitted with large wooden wheels and a surrey-topped five-passenger body. A planetary transmission was installed, but no brakes, throwing the car into reverse substituting, though not too well on one occasion when Dr. Dittlinger, in order to avoid a collison with a street-car, swerved toward a tree the low-hanging branches of which cut off his surrey top. Subsequently Dr. Dittlinger built a larger six-passenger vehicle, also with two-cylinder engine, but he never considered manufacture.

DITWILER — **Galion, Ohio** — **(1914)** — In early spring of 1914 the Ditwiler Manufacturing Company, producers of automobile steering gears in Galion, announced plans for manufacture of a shaft-drive cyclecar on a 100-inch wheelbase priced at under $400. A prototype was built, but although Ditwiler declared its expectation "to have a number of cars ready for the market within 90 days," it does not appear the firm ever moved into manufacture.

DIVINE — The Divine Motor Car Company was organized in Chicago during the summer of 1913 with a capital stock of $10,000 to manufacture motor vehicles. E.C. Divine, H.E. Campbell and W.R. Mitchell were the incorporators. Manufacture of a car is doubted.

DIXIE — Among Dixie ventures organized but which do not appear to have proceeded into manufacture of Dixie cars were the following.

The Dixie Motor and Boat Company in New Orleans in 1906, which also was organized as the New Orleans Autocar and Boat Company. Refer to New Orleans.

The Dixie Motor Company of High Point, North Carolina, organized early in 1907 with a capital stock of $125,000 by E.W. Van Brunt, C.S. Dutton and H.A. McGraw.

The Dixie Motor Car Company organized in 1910 in Frederick, Oklahoma with a capital stock of $250,000. Incorporators were R.C. Benner, C.M. Fuller, Jr., E.I. Holt, T.H. Lindley, J.A. Piliam, Oscar M. Abt and W.E. Taylor, all of Oklahoma City. The plan was manufacture of a $1050 gasoline car.

The Dixie Motor Car Company organized in November of 1909 with a capital stock of $100,000 in Oklahoma City, with Guthrie indicated as the probable factory site. Incorporators were R.C. Benner, T.H. Lindley and O.K. Sutton, and the plan was manufacture of motor buggies and high-wheeler trucks. One N.E. Lamphere (sic) of Carthage, Missouri was also reported to be involved in this venture. There was a Lanpher being built at that time in Carthage. The Dixie Flyer Automobile Manufacturing Company organized in early 1910 in Atlanta, Georgia by M.C. Morris, Stiles Hopkins, J.A. Chaney and W.K. Cleveland. Capital stock was $100,000. Although no car resulted from this venture, a four-wheel-drive-and-steer truck designed by Cleveland was announced the year following. The Dixie Motor Company organized in Asheville, North Carolina in 1913 with a capital stock of $10,000 and the plan to manufacture and deal in automobiles and to operate a garage and livery service. J.C. Arbogast, J.E. Craddock and J.B. Anderson were the people involved.

1908 Dixie Flier, runabout, NAHC

DIXIE — **Houston, Texas** — **(1908-1910)** — Early in 1908 E.M. Pavey reported that he was building a number of experimental cars in a shop at Capitol and Caroline streets in Houston, and that he was negotiating with the Business Men's League of Houston regarding the inducements that might be made to persuade him to locate his factory in that city. Obviously the inducements arrived, including financial backing from a local publisher named Marcellus Foster, because soon the Southern Motor Car Company was organized with a capital stock of $60,000, and Pavey's experimental cars became Dixies. They were offered in two basic variations: a high-wheeled buggy called the Junior and a low-wheeled runabout called the Flier, which with a tonneau became a standard touring. By the end of the year it was apparent to Pavey that his highwheeler was going nowhere and his Flier was overpriced. Consequently in 1909 he discontinued the former and revised the latter into the Tourist, which he made bigger and priced smaller. Unfortunately, the Houston bank in which he kept his money failed that year, so he never had the chance to find out if his new Dixie plan would be profitable. Pavey attempted reorganization in 1910 but failed. His total production in three years was seventeen cars. Among the interesting historical footnotes to this venture, incidentally, is that the Dixie was probably the only automobile in America produced in a factory with stained glass windows. The building into which the Southern Motor Car Company had moved in 1908 had formerly been a church.

1908 DIXIE
Two — 10/12 hp, 72" wb

	FP	5	4	3	2	1
Junior High Wheeled Rbt.	700	2700	3600	5300	8800	19,000
Four — 24 hp, 102" wb						
Flier Runabout	2000	3100	4200	6300	10,500	22,000
Touring-5P	2000	3000	4000	6000	9500	21,000

1909 Dixie Tourist, touring, HAC

1909-1910 DIXIE
Four — 30 hp, 110" wb

	FP	5	4	3	2	1
Tourist Runabout	1500	3100	4200	6300	10,500	22,000
Tourist Touring	1500	3000	4000	6000	9500	21,000

1916 Dixie, model 36, 2-pass. roadster, WLB

DIXIE — **Vincennes, Indiana** — **(1916)** — This Dixie was an attempt to produce a light car at cyclecar prices after the latter genre had disappeared from the American scene. It was offered in three models, two of them with standard tread, the speedster with a 36-inch tread. The use of coil springs was the one feature to which the Dixie Fiscal Company pointed with particular pride. Had the Dixie more to boast about, conceivably it might have survived longer than the one short year it did. At some point during its brief existence, the firm's name was changed to Dixie Manufacturing Company. Mac Price of Allendale, Illinois had spearheaded the Dixie venture, in collaboration with a number of prominent citizens of Vincennes.

1916 DIXIE
Model 36 — 4-cyl., 13 hp, 108" wb

	FP	5	4	3	2	1
Speedster-2P	385	2900	3700	5600	9100	20,000
Model 56 — 4-cyl., 13 hp, 108" wb						
Touring-4P	585	2500	3500	5000	8500	18,000
Roadster-2P	525	2700	3600	5300	8800	19,000

1917 Dixie Flyer, roadster, WLB

DIXIE FLYER — **Louisville, Kentucky** — **(1916-1923)** — The Kentucky Wagon Works (later Kentucky Wagon Manufacturing Company) had been in business in Louisville since 1878 and entered the automotive industry in 1912 following its purchase of the Electric Vehicle Company in town. Although some rosters indicate that a car called the Kentucky Electric was subsequently built, this was not the case. An electric pleasure car was planned but not produced; instead electric vehicle production of the firm was confined to trucks which were marketed as the Urban Electric from 1912 to 1916. A gasoline-powered truck was introduced in 1914 called Old Hickory and was continued until 1923. Kentucky Wagon's first experience in automobile building arrived in 1914 when the Hercules Motor Car Company of New Albany (Indiana) contracted for some outside coachwork and then conveniently went out of business the following year. Kentucky Wagon bought everything that was left of Hercules and moved it to Louisville. There is some confusion about what happened next. The Dixie Motor Car Company was established, as a subsidiary of Kentucky Wagon, and a surviving brochure indicates production plans for a Hercules touring car at $675. But that was the last heard of the Hercules, because in February 1916 a new car called the Dixie Flyer was introduced which Kentucky Wagon said had been under development as the Kentucky Kar for over a year. Conceivably a few Hercules parts found their way into the Dixie Flyer, but no more than that. Immediately noticeable on the Dixie Flyer was its windshield, which was bolt upright and built integral with the curved cowl dash. Less noticeable, but most unusual, was the Dixie radiator which was mounted on springs to ameliorate strain and vibration. Neither of these features survived for the Dixie's lifetime, but all subsequent cars were fours as was the company's first (Lycoming engines, followed by Herschell-Spillmans). Meantime, there were a couple of administrative changes. In late 1917 the Shadburne Brothers bought the Dixie company, but Kentucky Wagon bought it back almost immediately. There does not appear to have been any disruption in production of the car during this period. The sportiest Dixie arrived in 1921, a wire-wheeled speedster that was called the Firefly in 1922. It was also Kentucky Wagon's last Dixie, the company deciding not to fight the postwar depression any longer later that year. Truck manufacture was also phased out, though the company continued building wagons for nine more years. In 1923 Associated Motor Industries and Corporation took over the Dixie Flyer as well as the Jackson from Jackson, Michigan and the National from Indianapolis, announcing that all remaining Dixie Flyers and Jacksons would be "sold at sacrifice" and that only the National would be continued in production. The National was soon gone too. Total Dixie Flyer production in seven years had been approximately 10,000 cars. Many of the last Dixie Flyers of 1923 became "Nationals" by the simple expediency of replacing the radiator emblems and hubcaps.

1916 DIXIE FLYER
Flyer — 4-cyl., 17 hp, 112" wb

	FP	5	4	3	2	1
Touring-5P	775	3200	4300	6500	11,000	23,000

1917-1918 DIXIE FLYER
Flyer — 4-cyl., 17 hp, 112" wb

	FP	5	4	3	2	1
Patrician Touring-5P	845	3200	4300	6500	11,000	23,000
Thoroughbred Roadster-4P	845	3300	4400	6700	12,000	24,000
Delite Convertible Sedan	1275	3100	4200	6300	10,500	22,000

1919 Dixie Flyer, touring, HAC

1919 DIXIE FLYER
Model HS-50 — 4-cyl., 17 hp, 112" wb

	FP	5	4	3	2	1
Touring-5P	1095	3300	4400	6700	12,000	24,000
Roadster	1095	3500	4500	7000	13,000	25,000
Sedan	1450	2700	3600	5300	8800	19,000

1920 Dixie Flyer, sedan, HAC

1920 DIXIE FLYER
Model H — 4-cyl., 40 hp, 112" wb

Roadster-2P	1465	3500	4500	7000	13,000	25,000
Touring-5P	1465	3300	4400	6700	12,000	24,000
Sedan-5P	1965	2700	3600	5300	8800	19,000
Coupe-2P	1965	2900	3700	5600	9100	20,000

1921 DIXIE FLYER
Model H — 4-cyl., 40 hp, 112" wb

Touring-5P	1595	3300	4400	6700	12,000	24,000
Roadster-2P	1595	3500	4500	7000	13,000	25,000
Coupe-3P	2570	2900	3700	5600	9100	20,000
Sedan-5P	2570	2700	3600	5300	8800	19,000
Sport Roadster-4P	1845	3700	4700	7300	13,700	26,000

1921 Dixie Flyer, touring, HAC

1922 Dixie Flyer, touring, HAC

1922 DIXIE FLYER
Model H — 4-cyl., 40 hp, 112" wb

	FP	5	4	3	2	1
Touring-5P	1195	3500	4500	7000	13,000	25,000
Roadster-2P	1195	3900	4800	7700	14,300	27,000
Coupe-3P	1895	3000	4000	6000	9500	21,000
Sedan-5P	1895	2700	3600	5300	8800	19,000
Sport Touring-5P	1395	3700	4700	7300	13,700	26,000
Firefly Speedster	1395	4500	5800	9500	18,000	32,000

1923 Dixie Flyer, touring, JAC

1923 DIXIE FLYER
Model H — 4-cyl., 35 hp, 112" wb

	FP	5	4	3	2	1
Touring-5P	995	3500	4500	7000	13,000	25,000
Roadster-2P	995	3900	4800	7700	14,300	27,000
Speedster-2P	1095	4500	5800	9500	18,000	32,000
Sport-5P	1145	3700	4700	7300	13,700	26,000
Sedan-5P	1395	2700	3600	5300	8800	19,000
Coupe-3P	1395	3000	4000	6000	9500	21,000

DIXON — The Dixon Motor Company was organized in Pittsburgh, Pennsylvania during the summer of 1917 with a capital stock of $75,000 for the manufacture of automobiles and motor vehicles. M.L. Rogers, L.A. Irwin and Harry W. Davis were the incorporators. Manufacture of a car is doubted.

D.K. & K. — The D.K. & K. Company was organized in New York City during the summer of 1912 with a $5000 capital stock to manufacture automobiles and engines. Eckford DeKay, Sidney G. DeKay and Andrew C. Dam were the incorporators. Manufacture is doubted.

438

1907 D.L.G., runabout, NAHC

D.L.G. — St. Louis, Missouri — (1907) — The initials of the D.L.G. Motor Car Company represented Dyke, Liebert and Givens. Dyke was A.L., the automotive parts supply magnate who had earlier built a car bearing his own name. Liebert was B.L., a German-born engineer, and Givens was V.R., another engineer. Both Liebert and Givens had designed cars which Dyke considered producing. The only D.L.G. which ever arrived, however, was the overhead valve six with Mercedes-type radiator that was the work of Liebert. After production of very few cars, the D.L.G. venture was abandoned. Dyke returned to his prospering supply business. The further whereabouts of Liebert and Givens are unknown.

1907 D.L.G.
6-cyl., 35 hp chassis

	FP	5	4	3	2	1
Runabout (113" wb)	4000	—	—	—	—	—
Touring (130" wb)	4500	—	—	—	—	—

DOAN — Newtown, Pennsylvania — (1900) — George R. Doan was a physician from Newtown who built an automobile for himself in 1900. Details regarding the car are not known, but *The Horseless Age* documented its building that year.

1914 Doble, model A, roadster, NAHC

DOBLE — Waltham, Massachusetts — (1914-1915)/Detroit, Michigan — (1916-1918)/Emeryville, California — (1923-1931) — Born in San Francisco in 1895, Abner Doble was the eldest of four brothers and the namesake of his paternal grandfather who had put the family into the business of forging mining tools in 1850, an enterprise which naturally prospered during the California Gold Rush. Abner's father, W.A. Doble, and his uncle invented the Doble Water Wheel, and the family fortune was made. As a high school student in San Francisco, Abner Doble built his first steam car, and in 1910 he was sent to the Massachusetts Institute of Technology to study engineering. Steam power would remain the consuming passion of his life. While at M.I.T., he visited the factory of the Stanley brothers in Newton and came away wholly unimpressed. Shortly after the visit, he completed his first Model A which featured a twin-cylinder double-acting single-expansion engine with water tube boiler and a Harrison cellular radiator built to his specifications which condensed all exhaust steam. He paid a return visit to the Stanley twins whose cars still required an exhaust outlet, their tubular condensers being able to cope with only part of the steam used. Seeing the Doble drive up without a vestige of escaping steam brought the brothers immediately out of the factory screaming "Goddam. . . STOP!" Abner Doble had built the most sophisticated steam car in America up to that time. (Stanleys had condensers a few years later.) The Doble would remain the most technologically advanced steamer in the United States, and the world, for all of its days. But marketing it successfully was another matter. Its designer was part of the problem; he was more perfectionist than practical businessman. Five Model A's were built, four of them sold, the fifth retained for experimentation. In late October of 1914 the Abner Doble Motor Vehicle Company of Waltham (Massachusetts) was established to produce its successor, the refined Model B. Abner Doble was just nineteen years old. Underfinancing of his firm meant that the Model B never was produced, but Doble took the prototype to the Midwest and interested C.L. Lewis (erstwhile head of the Consolidated Car Company) of Detroit in the venture. The result was a new company, the General Engineering Company, formed in 1916 to build the Model C, or G.E.C. Doble, which was improved from the Model B. Doble's uniflow principle (steam flowed in one direction only with lower heat losses resulting) was introduced on this car. Starting a 1916 Doble required no more advance preparation than a gasoline car, and in less than three minutes there was enough generated to get underway. Elimination of the pilot light, the necessity of one fuel only for both starting and running, and the use of fuel atomization and electric ignition were further advanced features of the G.E.C. Doble. The car was introduced at the New York Automobile

Show and was a smash. Fifty thousand letters followed from people either wanting to become stockholders or dealers. In three months, 11,000 orders were received, but almost as soon as the assembly line was started up, wartime restrictions on steel allocation shut it down. Doble quickly reorganized as the Doble-Detroit Steam Motors Company later during 1917 to produce the Doble-Detroit, an improved G.E.C. Production estimates for this car range from three to two hundred, but a figure closer to the former is likely because in 1919 a disgruntled Doble sold manufacturing rights to the car to Amalgamated of Chicago and returned to California. His brother John returned with him, and his brother Warren joined the new enterprise as well. In 1920, in San Francisco, Doble Steam Motors of California was organized to produce the new Doble Model D, which featured a monotube boiler and a two-cylinder compound engine replacing the former uniflow. But this was merely prelude, as was a Doble-Simplex prototype assembled on a Jordan Big Six chassis in 1922. Doble wanted to build a car to rank with the most exemplary in the world, and the four cylinder Series E (with flash boiler, about 75 bhp, and a large efficient condenser providing a range of 1500 miles on 24 gallons of water) was it. In 1923 a new factory in Emeryville was established and production begun on Series E Dobles carrying eight body styles by Murphy and price tags from $8800 to $11,200. This put the Doble into the most rarefied segment of the marketplace. Its luxury and performance (a working head of steam in less than a minute and a half, an officially timed top speed for a 5000-pound tourer at over 93 mph) endeared it to a select clientele. An Indian maharajah ordered a special shooting brake (bodied by Hooper in England) for tiger hunts, and in Hollywood, Norma Talmadge, Joseph Schenk and Howard Hughes were Doble fanciers. Factory capacity was initially set at 300 Series E's per year, with an annual production of 1000 contemplated after factory additions. This did not come to pass. Stock manipulation, of which the Dobles were unaware, led to several lawsuits against the Doble company being filed in January of 1924. Abner Doble was held liable and sentenced to prison, though his appeal was successful and he was not jailed. But the company never recovered; further capital could not be raised. The Dobles carried on by themselves, introducing the Model F (with water-walled firebox) but the stock market crash finished them. Doble Steam Motors went into liquidation in April of 1931. In all, probably no more than forty-five Dobles were ever built.

1914 DOBLE
Model A — 2-cyl., 25 hp, 133" wb

	FP	5	4	3	2	1
Touring/Roadster	4000	3200	4300	6500	11,000	23,000

1915 Doble, model B, roadster, HAC

1915 DOBLE

Model B prototype	—	—	—	—	—	—

1916-1917 DOBLE
G.E.C./Model C — 2-cyl., 128" wb

Touring-7P	2500	3100	4200	6300	10,500	22,000
Roadster-2P	—	3300	4400	6700	12,000	24,000
Town Car-5P	—	2900	3700	5600	9100	20,000
Roadster-Coupe-4P	—	3200	4300	6500	11,000	23,000

1918 Doble-Detroit, touring, HAC

1918 DOBLE
Doble-Detroit — 2-cyl., 135" wb

Touring-7P	2700	3200	4300	6500	11,000	23,000

1920 DOBLE
Model D — 2-cyl.

Touring-7P	3750	3300	4400	6700	12,000	24,000

1922 Doble-Simplex, prototype, KM

1922 Doble, model D, touring, HAC

1923 Doble, Series E, phaeton, HAC

1923 Doble, Series E, dual windshield touring, OCW

c.1924 Doble E-11, all-weather touring, Murphy, FR

1925 Doble E-18, sedan, KM

1923-1931 DOBLE
Series E — 4-cyl., 75 hp, 142" wb

	FP	5	4	3	2	1
Phaeton-5P	—	7500	15,000	25,000	35,000	50,000
Phaeton-7P	—	7600	15,300	25,500	35,500	51,000
Phaeton DeLuxe-5P	—	7700	15,500	26,000	36,000	52,000
Sedan-5P	—	3300	4400	6700	12,000	24,000
Vestibule Sedan-5P	—	3500	4500	7000	13,000	25,000
Limousine-7P	—	3700	4700	7300	13,700	26,000
Runabout-3P	—	4000	5000	8000	15,000	28,000
Runabout Deluxe-3P	—	4200	5200	8400	15,700	29,000

DOCK — The Dock Gas Engine Company was organized in Jersey City, New Jersey late in 1906 with a $400,000 capital stock for the manufacture of engines, boats and vehicles of all kinds. John R. Turner, H.O. Coughlin and B. Stafford Mantz were the incorporators. Manufacture of a car is doubted.

DODGE — Detroit, Michigan — (1914) — It's a dreadful but appropriate pun. Early in 1914 an executive recognized the writing on the Wahl and decided to leave that Detroit automobile manufacturer before it went under. By February Alvan M. Dodge had allied himself with Edwin Herzog, E.O. Millay and J. Major Leman to form another enterprise, the Dodge Motor Car Company of Detroit. It was a shoestring venture, capitalized at only $1000 for the building of a light car that had initially been planned as a Wahl. Two models would be offered with four-cylinder 25 hp engines, friction transmission, double chain drive, 102-inch wheelbase chassis, and prices in the cyclecar range: $495 for roadster, $595 for touring. These Dodges had a standard tread, however, and were not properly cyclecars, although their entrance onto the scene in the midst of the cyclecar rage sometimes caused them to be mistaken as such in the trade press. During the summer of 1914 Alvan Dodge exhibited his new car at the Michigan State Fair, and happened to notice that another company in town named Dodge had also elected to get into automobile manufacturing. In August Alvan Dodge took John and Horace Dodge to court, suing them for infringement of the Dodge name. The case was finally settled in January 1916, and Alvan Dodge lost. Indeed it was he who was enjoined against further use of the name, the court deciding that although the Dodge Motor Car Company had been first on the market with a car called the Dodge, it had ceased production a few months after starting; meanwhile Dodge Brothers was faring very well. Incidentally, Alvan Dodge had been right about his former employer. The Wahl Motor Company had gone under, ironically just about the same time as Alvan's Dodge went to the wall too.

1914 DODGE
Four — 102" wb

	FP	5	4	3	2	1
Roadster	495	1500	2500	3600	5500	11,000
Touring	595	1400	2400	3500	5300	10,000

DODGE

DODGE BROTHERS — Detroit, Michigan — (1914-1930)/**DODGE** — (1930-1942 et. seq.) — In 1914 the announcement was likened in the trade press to "another Comstock lode or a second Klondike." The famous Dodge brothers were about to build a car. From the turn of the century when they established a small machine shop in Detroit, John and Horace Dodge had supplied engines and transmissions to Ransom Eli Olds, then engines, transmissions and axles to Henry Ford. As both manufacturers for and stockholders in the Ford venture, they made a fortune, but by 1913 had recognized the Ford company was moving toward self-sufficiency and, as John Dodge put it, "being carried around in Henry Ford's vest pocket" had become tiresome. And so now these respected engine builders would produce an automobile called, like their company itself, Dodge Brothers. Planning began in 1913, and the first Dodge Brothers left the factory on November 14th, 1914. The brothers were never ones to rush things, nor were they particularly loath to change once they felt they had things right. Probably there was no more sturdy a car built in America in 1915 than the Dodge Brothers. Its 35 hp L-head four-cylinder engine was strength personified, as was its welded all-steel body by Budd, though the brothers would add rivets here and there for a few years just for safety's sake. The Dodge Brothers was America's first mass-produced automobile with an all-steel body. Distinctive too was the car's twelve-volt electrical system and its three-speed selective transmission with enclosed heat-treated vanadium gears and "back-to-front" gear change. The wheelbase was 110 inches, and its dimension (raised to 114 for 1917 and 116 for 1924) would represent just about the only change made to the Dodge Brothers for the next decade. The car was immediately successful, with some 45,000 units built in 1915, the best first year for a new car thus far in American automobile history. In 1916 Dodge stood in fourth place in the industry. Certainly the brothers' renown in the industry was partly responsible for this splendid beginning, but responsible too was the reputation their car quickly earned for its straightforward honesty and dependability. In 1916 General Pershing used a Dodge Brothers to chase Pancho Villa over much of Mexico, and probably more of the brothers' cars saw overseas service during World War I than those of any other single manufacturer. Following the Armistice, John and Horace Dodge added an all-steel sedan for 1919 which, at $1900, was their most expensive car to date, and for 1920 they slightly raked the windshield on all models, which for the conservative Dodge Brothers was a styling move that almost bordered on the risque. Nineteen-twenty was the year that Dodge moved into second place in the industry; it was also the year that both brothers died, John of pneumonia in January, Horace of cirrhosis in December. That the Dodge brothers were raucous and roistering big drinkers had been widely known; John had wrecked at least one saloon and though his drinking habits may have hastened his death, it was his death which hastened Horace's. The brothers had been incredibly close. Dodge Brothers company now fell to their widows, with Frederick Haynes, a longtime company man, installed in the presidency in January 1921. Unfortunately, also in 1921, the company fell to third place in the industry, which didn't make Haynes' position very tenable, though he endured in it into 1925, during which year Dodge Brothers dropped to fifth and the Dodge widows decided to sell out to the New York banking house of Dillon, Read & Company for $146 million, the largest cash transaction thus far in the history of industrial finance. (A facsimile of the check was widely published in the press.) A financial man with no automobile experience, one E.G. Wilmer, was installed as Dodge Brothers' president that year. The company's position continued downward. Continued too were the traditional cars, though the wood-framed Fisher-bodied coach offered in '25 would have been abhorred by the brothers. In 1927 a new Fast Four (40 hp, 108-inch wheelbase) and for 1928 an L-head 60 hp six (designed by Dodge but built by Continental) were added to the line. In 1928 Dillon, Read sold the company (for $170 million, a stock transaction not cash) to Walter P. Chrysler, who had first tried to buy Dodge two years earlier. Though a relative newcomer in the industry, Walter Chrysler's Chrysler was an immensely popular medium-priced car, but he needed the formidable Dodge facilities and distributorship network in order to crack the lower-priced field. That he wished to lose no time is indicated by Clarence Dillon's phone call to him the morning following the sale to say everything was in order at the Dodge Brothers factory and it could run itself sight unseen for three months. "Hell, Clarence, our boys moved in yesterday" was Walter Chrysler's response. And so they had; E.G. Wilmer and crew were immediately informed their services were no longer needed. From an unlucky thirteenth place in the industry in 1928, the Dodge Brothers moved into the lucky seven spot within a year under Chrysler Corporation aegis. Most cars were sixes by 1928, with the hydraulic front-wheel brakes and standard gearshift adopted the year before being retained; retained too for the next few years was the car's individual identity. The transition of its name from Dodge Brothers to simply Dodge took place around 1930. A radio as standard equipment was offered on the top-of-the-line six that year. Gradually, the Dodge moved into a specific niche within the multi-division corporate framework: Chrysler as the top-market car, Plymouth the mass-volume car, and the Dodge and De Soto inbetween, the Dodge initially the more expensive, later the less, of the two. A straight-eight was offered from 1930 to 1933; sixes only were produced from 1934 to the war. In 1933 the Dodge became the industry's fourth best-seller (behind Plymouth), a position it would hold through 1937, the result no doubt of the car being spared the calamitous Airflow styling of the Chrysler and the De Soto. Though Dodge did not weather the "depression within the depression" of the later Thirties as well as other makers, the division did bounce back to an above 200,000-unit-per-year mark in 1940. When production ceased in early 1942, and Chrysler Corporation turned its efforts to war work, the position of Dodge on the American automotive scene was as solid as it had been during John's and Horace's Dodge Brothers days.

Dodge Data Compilation
by John A. Gunnell

1914

1914 Dodge Brothers, touring, OCW

DODGE — MODEL 30-35 — FOUR: Horace and John Dodge took delivery of the first Dodge car on Nov. 14, 1914. Cars built during 1914 carried serial numbers 1-370. Most historians consider all of these cars to be 1915 models, although many collectors prefer to call them 1914 models. Standard equipment included leather seats, a folding top, electric lighting, an electric self-starter, windshield, speedometer and demountable rims. The only model available was a touring car with "four" doors, one of which (driver's) was non-opening. Styling characteristics of early Dodge cars included headlights positioned high on the fenders and set back from the radiator, splash aprons which angled back and down and no splash aprons below the radiator.

I.D. DATA: Serial numbers were located on a plate on the toe board. Also prior to car number 761408 the serial number is stamped on the center cross member of the frame on the right side under the rear floorboard. Starting: 1. Ending: 370. Engine numbers were located on the front flange of cylinder block just ahead of the starter generator. Engine numbers are not available.

Model No.	Body Type & Seating	Price	Weight	Prod. Total
30-35	4-dr. Tr.-5P	785	2200	Note 1

Note 1: Total series production has been established as 370 cars in calendar year 1914.

ENGINE: Inline, L-head. Four. Cast iron block. B. x S.: 3-7/8 in. x 4-1/2 in. Disp.: 212.3 cu. in. C.R.: 4.0:1. Brake H.P.: 35 @ 2000 R.P.M. N.A.C.C. H.P.: 24. Main bearings: Four. Valve lifters: Solid.

CHASSIS: W.B.: 110 in. Tires: 33 x 4.

TECHNICAL: Selective sliding transmission. Speeds: 3F/1R. Floor shift controls. Cone type clutch. Shaft drive. Two wheel mechanical brakes. Demountable wood spoke wheels.

OPTIONS: Spare tire. Side curtains. Tool kit. Runningboard luggage rack. Horn. Wind wings. Motometer. Windshield wiper. Spotlight. Wire wheels.

HISTORICAL: Introduced: Nov. 14, 1914. First Dodge car. Unique manual transmission gearshift pattern. Calendar year production: 370 (built in calendar 1914). Dodge Brothers was organized on July 17, 1914. John and Horace Dodge capitalized the company with $5 million in common stock. The Dodge factory was located in Hamtramck, Mich. The first car to leave the factory was photographed extensively. It had hood louvers, but production models had plain side hoods.

1914
4-cyl., 110" wb

	FP	5	4	3	2	1
(Serial #1-249)						
Tr	785	1000	2400	5000	7000	10,000

1915

1915 Dodge Brothers, touring, HAC

DODGE — MODEL 30-35 — FOUR: There were no styling changes on 1915 Dodge touring cars. A new roadster was introduced. It had a slanting deck with an integral storage compartment and a spare tire carrier. Standard equipment for both models was leather seats, folding tops, electric lights, electric self-starters, windshields, speedometers and demountable wheel rims.

I.D. DATA: Serial numbers were in the same locations. Starting: 371. Ending: 45,000. Engine numbers were in the same location. Engine numbers are not available.

Model No.	Body Type & Seating	Price	Weight	Prod. Total
30-35	4-dr. Tr.-5P	785	2200	Note 1
30-35	2-dr. Rds.-2P	785	2155	Note 1

Note 1: Total 1914-1915 series production was 45,000.

ENGINE: Same as 1914 engine. See previous specifications.

CHASSIS: W.B.: 110 in. Tires: 33 x 4.

TECHNICAL: Selective sliding transmission. Speeds: 3F/1R. Floor shift controls. Leather-faced cone clutch. Shaft drive. Two wheel mechanical brakes. Demountable wood spoke wheels.

OPTIONS: Spare tire. Side curtains. Tool kit. Runningboard luggage rack. Horn. Wind wings. Motometer. Windshield wiper. Spotlight. Wire wheels.

HISTORICAL: Introduced Jan. 1, 1915. Calendar year production: 45,000 (includes 1914 models). Due to start-up costs, John and Horace Dodge lost money on the production of their earliest Dodge cars. Dodge was ranked America's number 3 auto-maker in 1915.

1915
4-cyl., 110" wb

	FP	5	4	3	2	1
Rds	785	875	1700	4250	5900	8500
Tr	785	825	1600	4000	5600	8000

1916

1916 Dodge Brothers, touring, OCW

DODGE — MODEL 30-35 — FOUR: History books are in dispute over the specific models and features offered in Dodge Brothers' 1916 line. *The Manual of Automobile Liability Insurance*, which was published Jan. 1, 1916 by The Fidelity and Casualty Co. of New York, indicates that the 1916 line had no basic changes from the 1915 offerings. According to this book, these cars were still rated 30-35 horsepower and still came in only two body styles — roadster and touring. The book describes them as 1915-1916 models, indicating the 1916 (model year) Dodges were a direct carryover from 1915. This information also agrees with a similar insurance guide published in 1918. It can thus be assumed that other sources showing several minor changes in "1916" Dodges have confused the true 1916 models with cars built in that calendar year, but marketed as 1917 models. We are going to consider the 1916 models a continuation of the 1915 series, using these contemporary sources for documentation. These cars had no styling changes. Standard equipment included leather seats, folding tops, electric lights, electric self-starter, windshield, speedometer and demountable wheel rims.

I.D. DATA: Serial numbers were in the same locations. Starting 45001. Ending: 110000. Engine numbers were in the same location. Engine numbers are not available.

1916 Dodge Brothers, California top touring, OCW

Model No.	Body Type & Seating	Price	Weight	Prod. Total
30-35	2-dr. Rds.-2P	785	2155	Note 1
30-35	2-dr. Tr.-5P	785	2200	Note 1

Note 1: Total series production was 71,400.

ENGINE: Same as 1914-15 engine. See previous specifications.

CHASSIS: W.B.: 110 in. Tires: 33 x 4 in.

TECHNICAL: Selective sliding transmission. Speeds: 3F/1R. Floor shift controls. Leather-faced cone clutch. Shaft drive. Two wheel mechanical brakes. Demountable wood spike wheels.

OPTIONS: Spare tire. Side curtains. Tool kit. Runningboard. Luggage rack. Horn. Wind wings. Motometer. Windshield wiper. Spotlight. Wire wheels.

HISTORICAL: Introduced: July, 1915. The true 1916 models seem to be a continuation of the 1915 models and had no more than very minor running production changes. Calendar year production: 71,400.

Dodge coined the slogan "It speaks for itself" in 1916 and started stressing the dependability of its products. U.S. Army general John Pershing placed an order for 150 Dodge Bros. touring cars for delivery July 15, 1916. The cars were used in the Campaign against Mexican bandit Pancho Villa. Lt. George Patton, Jr. led the first mechanized cavalry charge with three of these cars and 15 soldiers.

1916
4-cyl., 110" wb

	FP	5	4	3	2	1
Rds	785	900	1900	4500	6300	9000
W.T. Rds	950	950	2100	4750	6650	9500
Tr	785	875	1700	4250	5900	8500
W.T. Tr	950	900	1900	4500	6300	9000

1917

1917 Dodge Brothers, limousine (custom), OCW

DODGE — MODEL 30 — FOUR: According to the contemporary sources used for our research, the 1917 Dodge was referred to as the Dodge Model 30. It was rated at 35 advertised horsepower. These cars had a longer 114 inch wheelbase. There were four new models, in addition to the roadster and touring. Two of these were simply "Rex" top models. This term referred to a type of removable hardtop fitted with snap-on glass windows and detachable side panels. Built by the Rex Manufacturing Co. of Connersville, Ind., these tops allowed the owner to "convert" his roadster or touring car into a variety of configurations: open car, open-side hardtop or fully enclosed. The other models were a permanently enclosed center door sedan coupe with lowerable windows. Mechanically, a multiple disc clutch was used in place of the leather-faced cone type. Cars built after approximately Oct. 1, 1916 (for model year 1917) also had higher radiators, headlights mounted ahead of the radiator, splash aprons on the inner sides of the fenders and a rear cross bar (inside the spare tire carrier) supporting the rear license plate bracket and an electric taillamp.

I.D. DATA: Serial numbers were in the same location. Starting: 116,339. Ending: 210,000. Engine numbers were in the same location. Engine numbers are not available.

Model No.	Body Type & Seating	Price	Weight	Prod. Total
30	2-dr. Rds.-2P	835	2200	Note 1
30	4-dr. Tr.-5P	835	2200	Note 1
30	2-dr. Rex Rds.-2P	1000	2500	Note 1
30	4-dr. Rex Tr.-5P	1000	2700	Note 1
30	2-dr. C/D Sed.-5P	1265	2795	Note 1
30	2-dr. Cpe.-2P	1265	2520	Note1

Note 1: Total series production was 90,000.

ENGINE: Same as 1914-16 engines. See previous specifications.

CHASSIS: W.B.: 114 in. Tires: 33 x 4.

TECHNICAL: Selective sliding transmission. Speeds: 3F/1R. Floor shift controls. Multiple dry disc clutch. Shaft drive. Two-wheel mechanical brakes. Wood spoke wheels.

OPTIONS: Spare tire. Side curtains. Tool kit. Running board luggage rack. Horn. Wind wings. Motometer. Windshield wiper. Spotlight. Wire wheels.

HISTORICAL: Introduced July, 1916. Innovations: Longer wheelbase. Multiple dry disc clutch. Four new body styles. New hood styling. Repositioned headlights and taillights. New splash aprons. Calendar year production: 90,000. Dodge entered the commercial vehicle field in 1917, building both civilian and military trucks. Dodge dropped to fifth sales rank in the American auto industry.

1917
4-cyl., 114" wb

	FP	5	4	3	2	1
Rds	835	900	1900	4500	6300	9000
W.T. Rds	1000	950	2100	4750	6650	9500
Tr	835	900	1900	4500	6300	9000
W.T. Tr	1000	900	1900	4500	6300	9000
Cpe	1265	650	1250	2400	4200	6000
C.D. Sed	1265	700	1350	2800	4550	6500

1918

DODGE — MODEL 30 — FOUR: There were no significant changes in the 1918 Dodges. Styling was of the later 1917 type with high radiators, headlights ahead of radiator, inner side fender aprons and rear accessories mounted on a cross bar inside the spare tire carrier. Standard equipment included leather seats, windshield, self-starter, electric lights, speedometer, demountable rims and side curtains. Prices were up and civilian production was down due to the outbreak of World War I in Europe. Wire wheels seem to have received heavy promotion in ads this year.

I.D. DATA: Serial numbers were in the same locations. Starting: 217926. Ending: 300000. Engine numbers were stamped above the carburetor on the left side of the cylinder block. Engine numbers were also stamped on the left side of the engine rear support. In 1918, the right side of a few engine rear supports were also stamped with engine numbers. The engine numbers are not available.

Model No.	Body Type & Seating	Price	Weight	Prod. Total
30	2-dr. Rds.-2P	985	2200	Note 1
30	4-dr. Tr.-5P	985	2200	Note 1
30	2-dr. Rex Rds.-2P	1150	2500	Note 1
30	4-dr. Rex Tr.-5P	1150	2700	Note 1
30	2-dr. C/D Sed.-5P	1425	2795	Note 1
30	2-dr. Cpe.-2P	1425	2520	Note 1

Note 1: Total series production was 62,000.

ENGINE: Same as 1914-17 engine. See previous specifications.

CHASSIS: W.B.: 114 in. Tires: 33 x 4.

TECHNICAL: Selective sliding transmission. Speeds: 3F/1R. Floor shift controls. Multiple dry disc clutch. Shaft drive. Two-wheel mechanical brakes. Wood spoke wheels.

OPTIONS: Spare tire(s). Side curtains. Tool kit. Runningboard luggage rack. Horn. Wind wings. Motometer. Windshield wiper. Spotlight. Wire wheels. Sidemounts (on commercial vehicles).

HISTORICAL: Introduced: July 1, 1917. Calendar year production: 62,000. Dodge continued as the 5th largest auto-maker in the U.S. Commercial vehicles ranged from a panel delivery truck called the "Business Car" to a chemical fire truck ordered by the Clear Lake, Minn. Fire Department.

1918
4-cyl., 114" wb

	FP	5	4	3	2	1
Rds	985	950	2100	4750	6650	9500
W.T. Rds	1150	1000	2400	5000	7000	10,000
Tr	985	875	1700	4250	5900	8500
WT Tr	1150	875	1700	4350	6050	8700
Cpe	1425	600	1200	2200	3850	5500
Sed	1425	700	1350	2800	4550	6500

1919

1919 Dodge Brothers, 4-dr. sedan, JAC

DODGE — MODEL 30 — FOUR: Originating as a carryover series, the 1919 Dodge Brothers' line underwent a number of running production changes during the model year. One was the adoption of narrower windshields for all open cars. A four-door sedan with standard wire wheels was introduced in February 1919. In April, the Rex "convertible" roadster/coupe was replaced with a conventional five window coupe. General styling characteristics and equipment features were the same as seen on 1918 models.

I.D. DATA: Serial numbers were in the same locations. Starting: 303,107. Ending: 420,000. Engine numbers were in the same locations. Engine numbers are not available.

Model No.	Body Type & Seating	Price	Weight	Prod. Total
30	2-dr. Rds.-2P	1085	NA	Note 1
30	4-dr. Tr.-5P	1085	NA	Note 1
30	2-dr. Rex Rds.-2P	1250	NA	Note 1
30	4-dr. Rex Tr.-5P	1250	NA	Note 1
30	2-dr. C/D Sed.-5P	1425	NA	Note 1
30	4-dr. Sed.-5P	1900	2815	Note 1
30	2-dr. 5W Cpe.-3P	1750	NA	Note 1
30	4-dr. Cus. Limo.-6P	NA	NA	Note 1
30	4-dr. Taxi-3/6P	1650	NA	Note 1

Note 1: Total series production was 106,000.

ENGINE: Same as 1914-18 engine. See previous specifications.

CHASSIS: W.B.: 114 in. Tires: 33 x 4.

TECHNICAL: Selective sliding transmission. Speeds: 3F/1R. Multiple dry disc clutch. Shaft drive. Two-wheel mechanical brakes. Wood spoke wheels.

OPTIONS: Spare tire(s). Side curtains. Tool kit. Runningboard luggage rack. Horn. Wind wings. Motometer. Windshield wiper. Spotlight. Wire wheels (std. 4-door sedan). Sidemounts (commercial vehicles). Kerosene coach lamps (on limousine). Front bumper. Rear fender guards.

HISTORICAL: Announced: July 1, 1918. New models including 4-door sedan, five window coupe, town car taxicab and custom-built limousine. Thinner windshield on open cars as a running production change. Calendar year production: 106,000. Dodge capacity was up to 500 cars per day this year. The company put its 400,000th car together. The number of commercial vehicle offerings enjoyed a large increase.

1919
4-cyl., 114" wb

	FP	5	4	3	2	1
Rds	935	900	1900	4500	6300	9000
Tr	935	900	1900	4500	6300	9000
Cpe	1650	600	1200	2200	3850	5500
Rex Cpe	1350	650	1250	2400	4200	6000
Rex Sed	1350	700	1350	2700	4500	6400
4 dr Sed	1650	700	1350	2800	4550	6500
Dep Hk	882	650	1250	2400	4200	6000
Sed Dely	885	750	1450	3300	4900	7000

1920

1920 Dodge Brothers, touring, OCW

DODGE — MODEL 30 — FOUR: Dodge continued to follow its policy of phasing in minor alterations as running production changes and avoiding annual styling updates. When introduced on July 1, 1919, the 1920 Dodges looked very much like the company's original designs. During the model run, a slanted windshield was adopted on both open models and the touring car was fitted with new, longer rear fenders. There was also a new convertible top, with wraparound rear curtains. And longer, 45 inch rear springs provided a smoother ride. General styling and equipment features were the same as on previous models. The Rex Top models were no longer offered.

I.D. DATA: Serial numbers were in the same locations. Starting: 424146. Ending: 569548. Engine numbers were in the same location. Engine numbers are not available.

Model No.	Body Type & Seating	Price	Weight	Prod. Total
30	2-dr. Rds.-2P	1085	2240	Note 1
30	4-dr. Tr.-5P	1085	2425	Note 1
30	2-dr. Cpe.-3P	1750	2520	Note 1
30	4-dr. Sed.-5P	1900	2795	Note 1
30	4-dr. Taxi.-5P	1650	2710	Note 1

Note 1: Total series production was 141,000.

ENGINE: The 1920 engine was the same as the 1914-19 engine. See previous specifications.

CHASSIS: W.B.: 114 in. Tires: 33 x 4.

TECHNICAL: Selective sliding transmission. Speeds: 3F/1R. Floor shift controls. Multiple disc clutch. Shaft drive. Two-wheel mechanical brakes. Wood spoke wheels (wire wheels on sedan).

OPTIONS: Front bumper. Rear bumper. Single sidemount (commercial). Wire wheels (except sedan). Spare tire cover. Runningboard luggage rack. Motometer. OSRV mirror. Wind wings (open cars). Spare tire. "Fat Man" steering wheel. Side curtains. Spotlight(s).

HISTORICAL: Introduced: July 1, 1919. Longer rear springs. Slant windshields on open cars. New style top. Longer rear fenders on touring car. Calendar year production: 141,000.
Dodge was America's second best selling car in 1920. John Dodge died on Jan. 14, 1920 after a bout with pneumonia. Horace Dodge died Dec. 20, 1920 after contracting the flu. Soon there after, Frederick J. Hayes became president of Dodge Brothers, Inc. Commercial vehicles offered this year include a panel truck and screen side delivery van.

1920
4-cyl., 114" wb

	FP	5	4	3	2	1
Rds	1085	900	1900	4500	6300	9000
Tr	1085	775	1500	3750	5250	7500
Cpe	1750	650	1250	2400	4200	6000
Sed	1900	600	1200	2200	3850	5500

1921

1921 Dodge Brothers, touring, OCW

DODGE — MODEL 30 — FOUR: There were additional minor changes in Dodge Brothers' cars this season. On the touring car the "cathedral" style windows used since 1914 were replaced with a horizontal, rectangular glass window. Closed cars got a new, full-width front seat. The diameter of the wood spoke wheels was reduced by one inch to 24 inches, with a corresponding reduction in tire size. A brand new feature was a heater. Wire wheels were now standard on the coupe and sedan and were used on roadsters built late in the model year. Some 1921 Dodges still came with cathedral style tops and some had a new headlamp tie-bar.

I.D. DATA: Serial numbers were in the same locations. Starting: 569549. Ending: 663096. Engine numbers were in the same location. Engine numbers were not available.

Model No.	Body Type & Seating	Price	Weight	Prod. Total
30	2-dr. Rds.-2P	1235	2305	Note 1
30	4-dr. Tr.-5P	1285	2500	Note 1
30	2-dr. Cpe.-3P	1900	2590	Note 1
30	4-dr. Sed.-5P	2150	2890	Note 1

Note 1: Total calendar year production was 81,000.

ENGINE: The 1921 engine was the same as the 1914-20 engine. See previous specifications.

CHASSIS: W.B.: 114 in. Tires: 33 x 4.

TECHNICAL: Selective sliding transmission. Speeds: 3F/1R. Floor shift controls. Multiple dry disc clutch. Shaft drive. Two-wheel mechanical brakes. Wood spoke or wire wheels.

OPTIONS: Front bumper. Rear bumper. Single sidemount (commercial). Spare tire. Spare tire cover. Runningboard luggage rack. Wire wheels (open cars except late roadsters). Motometer. Heater. OSRV mirror. Wind wings (open cars). "Fat Man" steering wheel. Side curtains. Window shades (coupe/sedan). Spotlight(s).

HISTORICAL: Introduced July, 1920. Smaller diameter wheels and tires. Rectangular rear window design adopted as a running change. Full-width front seat for closed cars. Calendar year production: 81,000. Dodge placed third in the U.S. sales race for calendar 1921. Frederick J. Haynes was the new president of Dodge Bros., Inc. A custom-bodied Landau Touring with disc wheels was built on a 1921 Dodge chassis by Stratton-Bliss. Graham Bros., of Evansville, Ind., made an agreement to market its trucks through the Dodge dealer network in mid-1921. Graham became an independent affiliate of Dodge Bros., Inc.

1921
4-cyl., 114" wb

	FP	5	4	3	2	1
Rds	1235	950	2100	4750	6650	9500
Tr	1285	900	1900	4500	6300	9000
Cpe	1900	500	1100	1900	3500	5000
Sed	2150	400	1000	1650	3150	4500

1922

DODGE — FIRST SERIES — FOUR: There were two series of 1922 Dodges. The first series models had "low" hoods of the 1921 style. There were, however, changes in some bodystyles. On the sedan, the roof was four inches lower, the beltline was straighter and the rear side window opening was now square-cornered. Budd-Michelin steel discs replaced the former wire wheels. This model had the sparetire mounted at the rear. A small taillight and license plate holder were mounted on the left rear fender and a new semi-floating rear axle was used. Similar changes were used in the three-passenger coupe. Open models were nearly a direct carryover from 1921. Due to the economic effects of a postwar (WWI) recession, Dodge prices were lowered considerably.

1922 Dodge Brothers, touring, OCW

SECOND SERIES — FOUR: Second series models had an altered radiator, hood, cowl line that was raised 3-1/2 inches. Other changes included outside door handles, fluted head lamp lenses, a slanted instrument panel, windshield visors and buttonless upholstery. Prices were again lowered, although major specifications were unchanged. A new bodystyle was a two-passenger Business Coupe with fabric covered blind rear roof quarters. The cowl on the second series models had a more curved appearance and the windshield on open cars was bowed slightly outward.

I.D. DATA: [First Series] Serial numbers were in the same locations. Starting: 663097. Ending: 761407. Engine numbers were in the same location. Engine numbers are not available. [Second Series] Serial numbers were located on a plate on the toe board and were now also stamped on the right side frame member just to the rear of the front spring rear hanger. Starting: 761408. Ending: 826401. Engine numbers were in the same location. Engine numbers are not available.

Model No.	Body Type & Seating	Price	Weight	Prod. Total
S/1	2-dr. Rds.-2P	935	2305	Note 1
S/1	4-dr. Tr.-5P	985	2450	Note 1
S/1	2-dr. Cpe.-3P	1585	2650	Note 1
S/1	4-dr. Sed.-5P	1785	2940	Note 1

Note 1: There is no separate breakout available for first series production. Serial numbers indicate that approximately 98,310 cars were built in this series.
Note 2: The S/1 designation indicates "Series One" and is not a factory designation.

Model No.	Body Type & Seating	Price	Weight	Prod. Total
S/2	2-dr. Rds.-2P	850	2300	Note 1
S/2	4-dr. Tr.-5P	880	2500	Note 1
S/2	2-dr. Bus. Cpe.-2P	980	2600	Note 1
S/2	4-dr. Bus. Sed.-5P	1195	2965	Note 1
S/2	4-dr. Sed.-5P	1440	2940	Note 1

Note 1: There is no separate breakout available for first series production. Serial numbers indicate that approximately 65,000 cars were built in this series.
Note 2: The S/2 designation indicates "Series Two" and is not a factory designation.

ENGINE: [First Series] Inline. L-head. Four. Cast iron block. B & S: 3-7/8 in. x 4-1/2 in. Disp.: 212.3 cu. in. C.R.: 4.0:1. Brake H.P.: 35 @ 2000 R.P.M. N.A.C.C. H.P.: 24.03. Main bearings: Four. Valve lifters: Solid. [Second Series] Selective sliding transmission. Speeds: 3F/1R. Floor shift controls. Multiple dry disc clutch. Shaft drive. Semi-floating rear axle. Two-wheel mechanical brakes. Wood spoke wheels.

CHASSIS: (All Series) W.B.: 114 in. Tires: 32 x 4.

OPTIONS: Front bumper. Rear bumper. Single sidemount (commercial). Spare tire. Spare tire cover. Wire spoke wheels. Budd-Michelin steel disc wheels. "Fat Man" steering wheel. Heater. Motometer. Wind wings (open cars). OSRV mirror. Spotlights. Side curtains. Runningboard luggage rack.

HISTORICAL: First series introduced July 1921. Square window sedan introduced Aug. 1921. Square window coupe introduced Sept. 1921. Second series introduced June 1922. Higher radiator and hood. Higher, rounder cowl styling. Disc wheels. Windshield visor. Buttonless upholstery. Semi-floating rear axle. Lower rooflines. Calendar year production: 142,000. Model year production: 152,673. Dodge set record breaking sales figures this season and regained third rank in the U.S. industry. The company expanded its production facilities, achieving the 600 vehicle per day level. The Babcock Body Co. built a luxurious Town Car Brougham on the Dodge chassis this year. The commercial vehicle lineup of Dodge and Graham Bros. models included over six models and numerous funeral vehicles were built on Dodge running gear by various specialty manufacturers.

1922
1st series, 4-cyl., 114" wb, (low hood models)

	FP	5	4	3	2	1
Rds	935	900	1900	4500	6300	9000
Tr	985	875	1700	4250	5900	8500
Cpe	1585	550	1150	2000	3600	5200
Sed	1785	500	1100	1900	3500	5000

2nd series, 4-cyl., 114" wb, (high hood models)

	FP	5	4	3	2	1
Rds	850	875	1700	4350	6050	8700
Tr	880	850	1650	4200	5850	8400
Bus Cpe	980	600	1200	2200	3850	5500
Bus Sed	1195	500	1100	1950	3600	5100
Sed	1440	500	1100	1900	3500	5000

1923

1923 Dodge Brothers, 4-dr. sedan, OCW

DODGE — SERIES 116 — FOUR: A 1923 Dodge Bros. innovation was the introduction of the automotive industry's first all-steel bodies. A business coupe, introduced in June 1922 (as a 1923 model) was the first car to ever feature this type of construction. The Type B four door sedan, also featuring an all-steel body, made its debut in Sept. Other 1923 models were carried over from the previous season with only minor changes in specifications. A number of special, custom-bodied Dodges were also built during the year. Around Oct. 1, the design of the new coupe was updated to include a sun visor and a larger rear window. The Type B Business Sedan also had a sun visor. The front seat was hinged to fold forward and the rear seat completely removable. With the seat removed, the rear compartment became a cargo carrying area. The Type A sedan had mohair velvet upholstery. The all-steel Type B Business Sedan had genuine Spanish leather upholstery.

I.D. DATA: Serial numbers were in the same locations. Starting: 826402. Ending: 1000000. Engine numbers were in the same locations. Engine numbers are not available.

Model No. (Standards)	Body Type & Seating	Price	Weight	Prod. Total
Std. A	2-dr. Rds.-2P	850	2375	Note 1
Std. A	4-dr. Tr.-5P	880	2545	Note 1
Std. A	4-dr. Sed.-5P	1440	2990	Note 1
Std. B	2-dr. Bus. Cpe.-2P	980	2590	Note 1
Std. B	4-dr. Bus. Sed.-5P	1195	2965	Note 1
(Customs)				
Cus.	4-dr. Sed.-7P	NA	NA	Note 1
Cus.	2-dr. Lang. Cpe.-4P	NA	NA	Note 1
Cus.	2-dr. C.C. Cpe.-4P	NA	NA	Note 1
Cus.	3-dr. Depot Wag.-7P	NA	NA	Note 1

Note 1: Total calendar year production was 151,000.

ENGINE: Inline. L-head. Four. Cast iron block. B & S: 3-7/8 in. x 4-1/2 in. Disp.: 212.3 cu. in. C.R.: 4.0:1. Brake H.P.: 35 @ 2000 R.P.M. N.A.C.C. H.P.: 24.03. Main bearings: Three. Valve lifters: Solid.

CHASSIS: W.B.: 114 in. Tires: 32 x 4.

TECHNICAL: Selective sliding transmission. Speeds: 3F/1R. Floor shift controls. Multiple dry disc clutch. Shaft drive. Semi-floating rear axle. Two wheel mechanical brakes. Wood spoke wheels.

OPTIONS: Front bumper. Rear bumper. Single sidemount (commercial). Steel disc wheels. Motometer. Spare tire. Custom bodies. "Fat Man" steering wheel. Heater. OSRV mirror. Runningboard luggage rack. Spotlight(s).

HISTORICAL: Introduced: June, 1922. Industry's first all-steel bodies. Baker enamel finish replaces varnish type paint on all-steel models. Last year for the 114 inch wheelbase. Calendar year registrations: 114,076. Calendar year production: 151,000. Model year production: 171,421.

Dodge was America's sixth best selling car in 1923. A total of 6,971 Dodge/Graham Bros. trucks were made this year. J.T. Cantrell & Co. built a limited number of depot hack bodies for the Dodge chassis. A wide range of Dodge funeral vehicles were also produced.

1923
4-cyl., 114" wb

	FP	5	4	3	2	1
Rds	850	875	1700	4350	6050	8700
Tr	880	850	1650	4200	5850	8400
Bus Cpe	980	550	1150	2100	3700	5300
Bus Sed	1195	550	1150	2000	3600	5200
Sed	1440	500	1100	1900	3500	5000

1924

1924 Dodge Brothers, touring, OCW

DODGE — SERIES 116 — FOUR: This was a year of big changes in Dodge Brothers products. Appearance updates included a taller radiator and a higher hood line. The side hood panels now had vertical louvers. Drumhead lights were another new styling feature. The cars had a longer wheelbase and lower overall height. The former three-quarter elliptic springs were replaced with those of semi-elliptic configuration. Inside, the seats were lowered. Gear and brake levers were moved forward, providing more useable leg room. Budd-Michelin steel disc wheels were now available for the roadster, as well as the closed body styles. All closed cars had a flat, slanted sun visor supported by curved corner brackets. A rear brake light was now made standard equipment for all models. Introduced at the New York Automobile Show, in January 1924, was a line of "special" models with deluxe equipment features like nickel-plated radiators, bumpers, automobile windshield wipers, motometer type radiator caps and bright metal runningboard step plates. Custom bodies appearing on the 1924 Dodge chassis included an Open-Drive Taxi, Enclosed-Drive Taxi and Landau Sedan.

I.D. DATA: Serial numbers were in the same locations. Starting: A-1. Ending: A-132,706. Engine numbers were in the same location. Engine numbers not available.

Model No.	Body Type & Seating	Price	Weight	Prod. Total
Std.	2-dr. Rds.-2P	865	2513	Note 1
Std.	4-dr. Tr.-5P	880	2610	Note 1
Std.	2-dr. Bus. Cpe.-2P	1035	2755	Note 1
Std.	2-dr. Cpe.-4P	1375	2809	Note 1
Std.	4-dr. Bus. Sed.-5P	1250	3050	Note 1
Std.	4-dr. Std. Sed.-5P	1385	3098	Note 1
(Special)				
Spec.	2-dr. Rds.-2P	1025	2653	Note 1
Spec.	4-dr. Tr.-5P	1055	2755	Note 1
Spec.	2-dr. Bus. Cpe.-2P	1035	2865	Note 1
Spec.	2-dr. Cpe.-4P	1535	2929	Note 1
Spec.	4-dr. Bus. Sed.-5P	1545	3050	Note 1
Spec.	4-dr. Sed.-5P	1385	3195	Note 1
(Custom Bodies)				
Cus.	4-dr. O.D. Taxi-6P	NA	NA	Note 1
Cus.	4-dr. E.D. Taxi-6P	NA	NA	Note 1
Cus.	4-dr. Lan. Sed.-6P	NA	NA	Note 1

Note 1: Total calendar year production was 193,861.
Note 2: Taxi prices were usually determined by the quantity ordered. Taxi weights depended upon final equipment specifications.

ENGINE: Inline. L-head. Four. Cast iron block. B & S: 3-7/8 in. x 4-1/2 in. Disp.: 212.3 cu. in. C.R.: 4.0:1. Brake H.P.: 35 @ 2000 R.P.M. Net H.P.: 24.03. Main bearings: Three. Valve lifters: Solid.

CHASSIS: [Standard Series] W.B.: 116 in. Tires: 32 x 4. [Special Series] W.B.: 116 in. Tires: 30 x 5.77.

TECHNICAL: Selective sliding transmission. Speeds: 3F/1R. Floor shift controls. Multiple dry disc clutch. Semi-floating rear axle. Two-wheel mechanical brakes. Wood-spoke wheels.

OPTIONS: Front bumper (std. on Spec.). Rear bumper (std. on Spec.) Spare tire. Budd-Michelin steel disc wheels (std. on Spec.). Rear taillight (std. on all). Motometer (std. on Spec.). Goodyear balloon tires (std. on Spec.). Runningboard step plates (std. on Spec.). Heater. OSRV mirror. Wind wings (open models). Nickel plated radiator (std. on Spec.). Sidemount spare tire (commercial vehicles). "Fat Man" steering wheel. Spotlight(s). Cowl lamps (std. on Spec.). Automatic windshield wiper (std. on Spec.). Custom-built bodies. Deluxe equipment packages.

HISTORICAL: Introduced: July, 1923. Calendar year registrations: 157,982. Calendar year production: 193,861. Model year production: 207,687. Innovations: New styling. Optional balloon tires. Semi-elliptic rear springs. Increased wheelbase. Increased front seat legroom. Lower center of gravity. Drum headlights. Increased cooling system with 2-1/2 quart capacity.

Dodge regained its former position as third ranked U.S. auto producer. Additional plant expansion was accomplished this year. New Canadian assembly plant starts operation in Walkerville, Ontario. Roy Chapman Andrew took three Dodges on a 10,000 mile fossil-hunting expedition into China and inner Mongolia.

1924
4-cyl., 116" wb

	FP	5	4	3	2	1
Rds	865	975	2300	4900	6850	9800
Tr	880	925	2000	4600	6400	9200
Bus Cpe	1035	650	1250	2400	4200	6000
4P Cpe	1375	675	1300	2500	4350	6200
Bus Sed	1250	650	1250	2400	4200	6000
Sed	1385	650	1250	2400	4150	5900
Special Series (deluxe equip.-introduced Jan. 1924)						
Rds	1025	1000	2400	5000	7000	10,000
Tr	1055	950	2100	4750	6650	9500
Bus Cpe	1035	650	1250	2400	4200	6000
4P Cpe	1535	700	1350	2800	4550	6500
Bus Sed	1545	650	1250	2400	4200	6000
Sed	1385	675	1300	2500	4300	6100

1925

1925 Dodge Brothers, 4-dr. sedan, OCW

DODGE — SERIES 116 — FOUR: The 1925 Dodges looked nearly identical to the previous year's models. New features included automatic windshield wipers, lift-open rear windows, cowl vents and a one-piece windshield. All cars had 20 inch wheels and balloon type tires. Technical improvements included sil-chrome exhaust valves, rubber motor mountings and new oil-drain piston rings. Introduced at the New York Automobile Show, in Jan., 1925, was a coach (2-door sedan) with a Fisher body. A new "cadet" style sun visor was used on this model. All Dodge Bros. body styles were available with special equipment features at modestly higher prices. The Special equipment again included double bar bumpers and rear fender guards, nickel plated radiator shell, Budd-Michelin steel disc wheels, a motometer type radiator cap, runningboard step plates, rear taillamp, Goodyear balloon tires and cowl lamps on closed body cars. Among custom creations turned out on the 1925 Dodge Bros. chassis were a depot hack type station wagon built by J.T. Cantrell, Inc. and a Custom Town Car built for Thomas J. Doyle, a Dodge distributor in the Detroit area.

I.D. DATA: Serial numbers were located on toeboard on either right or left side; also on cross member under floor board. Starting: A132707. Ending: A372474. Engine numbers located above carburetor on left side of cylinder block. Engine numbers not available.

Model No. (Standard Line)	Body Type & Seating	Price	Weight	Prod. Total
Std.	2-dr. Rds.-2P	855	2494	Note 1
Std.	4-dr. Tr.-5P	885	2591	Note 1
Std.	2-dr. Bus. Cpe.-2P	995	2725	Note 1
Std.	2-dr. Cpe.-4P	1375	2793	Note 1
Std.	4-dr. Bus. Sed.-5P	1095	3011	Note 1
Std.	4-dr. Sed.-5P	1245	3063	Note 1
Std.	2-dr. Coach-5P	1095	2783	Note 1
(Special Line)				
Spec.	2-dr. Rds.-2P	955	2650	Note 1
Spec.	4-dr. Tr.-5P	985	2750	Note 1
Spec.	2-dr. Bus. Cpe.-2P	1095	2865	Note 1
Spec.	2-dr. Cpe.-4P	1475	2932	Note 1
Spec.	4-dr. Bus. Sed.-5P	1195	3150	Note 1
Spec.	4-dr. Sed.-5P	1330	3195	Note 1
Spec.	2-dr. Coach-5P	1110	2823	Note 1
(Customs)				
Cus.	4-dr. Cant. Sta. Wag.-8P	NA	NA	Note 1
Cus.	4-dr. Twn. Car-6P	NA	NA	Note 1

Note 1: Total calendar year production was 201,000.

ENGINE: Inline. L-head. Four. Cast iron block. B & S: 3-7/8 in. x 4-1/2 in. Disp.: 212.3 cu. in. C.R.: 4.0:1. Brake H.P.: 35 @ 2000 R.P.M. Net H.P.: 24.03. Main bearings: Three. Valve lifters: Solid.

CHASSIS: [Standard Series] W.B.: 116 in. Tires: 30 x 5.77. [Special Series] W.B.: 116 in. Tires: 30 x 5.77.

TECHNICAL: Selective sliding gear transmission. Speeds: 3F/1R. Floor shift controls. Multiple dry disc clutch. Semi-floating rear axle. Two-wheel mechanical brakes. Wood-spoke wheels.

OPTIONS: Front bumper (std. on Spec.). Rear bumper (std. on Spec.) Spare tire. Budd-Michelin steel disc wheels (std. on Spec.). Rear taillight (std. on Spec.). Motometer (std. on Spec.). Goodyear balloon tires (std. on Spec.). Runningboard step plates (std. on Spec.). Heater. OSRV mirror. Wind wings (open models). Nickel plated radiator (std. on Spec.). Side-mount spare tires (commercial vehicles). "Fat Man" steering wheel. Spotlight(s). Cowl lamps (std. on Spec. closed cars). Automatic windshield wiper (std. on Spec.). Deluxe equipment packages. Whitewall tires.

Dodge was the fifth best-selling American nameplate this year. A consortium of New York bankers purchased the Dodge Bros. properties for $146,000,000. E.J. Wilmer was appointed chief executive officer of the company by the new owners.

1925
4-cyl., 116" wb

	FP	5	4	3	2	1
Rds	885	950	2100	4750	6650	9500
Spec Rds	955	1000	2400	5000	7000	10,000
Tr	885	950	2100	4750	6650	9500
Spec Tr	985	950	2100	4700	6600	9400
Bus Cpe	995	675	1300	2500	4300	6100
Spec Bus Cpe	1095	675	1300	2500	4350	6200
4P Cpe	1375	700	1350	2700	4500	6400
Sp Cpe	1475	700	1350	2800	4550	6500
Bus Sed	1095	650	1250	2400	4200	6000
Spec Bus Sed	1195	675	1300	2500	4300	6100
Sed	1245	675	1300	2500	4350	6200
Spec Sed	1330	675	1300	2600	4400	6300
2 dr Sed	1095	650	1250	2400	4200	6000
Spec 2 dr Sed	1110	675	1300	2500	4300	6100

1926

1926 Dodge Brothers, touring, OCW

DODGE — SERIES 116 — FOUR: The 1925 Dodges looked nearly identical to the previous year's models. New features included automatic windshield wipers, lift-open rear windows, cowl vents and a one-piece windshield. All cars had 20 inch wheels and balloon type tires. Technical improvements included sil-chrome exhaust valves, rubber motor mountings and new oil-drain piston rings. Introduced at the New York Automobile Show, in Jan., 1925, was a coach (2-door sedan) with a Fisher body. A new "cadet" style sun visor was used on this model. All Dodge Bros. body styles were available with special equipment features at modestly higher prices. The Special equipment again included double bar bumpers and rear fender guards, nickel plated radiator shell, Budd-Michelin steel disc wheels, a motometer type radiator cap, runningboard step plates, rear taillamp, Goodyear balloon tires and cowl lamps on closed body cars. Among custom creations turned out on the 1925 Dodge Bros. chassis were a depot hack type station wagon built by J.T. Cantrell, Inc. and a Custom Town Car built for Thomas J. Doyle, a Dodge distributor in the Detroit area.

I.D. DATA: Serial numbers were located on toeboard on either right or left side; also on cross member under floor board. Starting: A132707. Ending: A372474. Engine numbers located above carburetor on left side of cylinder block. Engine numbers not available.

Model No. (Standard Line)	Body Type & Seating	Price	Weight	Prod. Total
Std.	2-dr. Rds.-2P	855	2494	Note 1
Std.	4-dr. Tr.-5P	885	2591	Note 1
Std.	2-dr. Bus. Cpe.-2P	995	2725	Note 1
Std.	2-dr. Cpe.-4P	1375	2793	Note 1
Std.	4-dr. Bus. Sed.-5P	1095	3011	Note 1
Std.	4-dr. Sed.-5P	1245	3063	Note 1
Std.	2-dr. Coach-5P	1095	2783	Note 1
(Special Line)				
Spec.	2-dr. Rds.-2P	955	2650	Note 1
Spec.	4-dr. Tr.-5P	985	2750	Note 1
Spec.	2-dr. Bus. Cpe.-2P	1095	2865	Note 1
Spec.	2-dr. Cpe.-4P	1475	2932	Note 1
Spec.	4-dr. Bus. Sed.-5P	1195	3150	Note 1
Spec.	4-dr. Sed.-5P	1330	3195	Note 1
Spec.	2-dr. Coach-5P	1110	2823	Note 1
(Customs)				
Cus.	4-dr. Cant. Sta. Wag.-8P	NA	NA	Note 1
Cus.	4-dr. Twn. Car-6P	NA	NA	Note 1

Note 1: Total calendar year production was 201,000.

ENGINE: Inline. L-head. Four. Cast iron block. B & S: 3-7/8 in. x 4-1/2 in. Disp.: 212.3 cu. in. C.R.: 4.0:1. Brake H.P.: 35 @ 2000 R.P.M. Net H.P.: 24.03. Main bearings: Three. Valve lifters: Solid.

Model No. (Special Line)	Body Type & Seating	Price	Weight	Prod. Total
Spec.	2-dr. Rds.-2P	955	2595	Note 1
Spec.	4-dr. Tr.-5P	975	2695	Note 1
Spec.	2-dr. Cpe.-2P	1060	2718	Note 1
Spec. A	4-dr. Sed.-5P	1295	3107	Note 1
Spec. B	4-dr. Bus. Sed.-5P	1145	3077	Note 1
Spec.	2-dr. Coach-5P	1135	2823	Note 1
(Deluxe/Sport Models)				
Del.	2-dr. Spt. Rds.-2P	880	2497	Note 1
Del.	4-dr. Spt. Sed.-5P	1075	2930	Note 1
Del.	4-dr. Spt. Tr.-5P	880	2617	Note 1
(Customs)				
Cus.	4-dr. Lan. Sed.-6P	NA	NA	Note 1
Cus.	4-dr. Est. Car.-8P	NA	NA	Note 1

Note 1: Total calendar year production was 265,000.
Note 2: The prices shown for Standard and Special Line models are early year prices. These were reduced by an average of $135 later in the year when the Deluxe and Sport models were introduced.

ENGINE: Inline. L-head. Four. Cast iron block. B & S: 3-7/8 in. x 4-1/2 in. Disp.: 212.3 cu. in. C.R.: 4.0:1. Brake H.P.: 35 @ 2000 R.P.M. Net H.P.: 24.03. Main bearings: Three. Valve lifters: Solid. Carb.: 1V.

CHASSIS: [Series 126] W.B.: 116 in. Tires: (Early) 30 x 5.77; (Late) 31 x 5.25.

TECHNICAL: Selective sliding transmission. Speeds: 3F/1R. Floor shift controls. Multiple dry disc clutch. Semi-floating rear axle. Two-wheel mechanical brakes. Wood-spoke wheels.
Note 3: In Jan., 1926, all Dodges switched to 21 inch wheels and larger balloon tires.

OPTIONS: Front bumper. Rear fender guards. Spare tire. Steel disc wheels. Taillight. Motometer. Step plates. OSRV mirror. Heater. Wind wings (open cars). Nickel plated radiator. Automatic windshield wiper. Whitewall tires. Special paint. Spotlight(s). Cowl lamps. Nickel plated headlight rims.
Note 4: Special, Deluxe and Sport models had a front bumper, rear fender guards, disc wheels, taillight, motometer, step plates, nickel plated radiator and automatic windshield wiper as standard equipment. Special models and early Deluxe Sedans had nickel plated headlight rims. Sport models and late Deluxe Sedans had new bullet-shaped headlights with nickel-plated rims.

HISTORICAL: Introduced: July, 1925. Calendar year registrations: 219,446. Calendar year production: 265,000. Model year production: 249,869. Innovations: Two-unit 6-volt electrical system introduced. SAE standard "H" gearshift pattern introduced. Bullet-shaped headlights on Sport and late Deluxe models. Triple door hinges on all Dodge Bros. cars.
Dodge came in fourth in the U.S. auto sales race this season. Custom models included a padded top, oval rear quarter window Landau Sedan built by E.J. Thompson Co. of Pittsburgh, Pa. and a wood-bodied estate car, with cane accent panels, built by H.H. Babcock Co., of Watertown, N.Y. The Graham Bros. resigned from Dodge Bros. to begin a new firm known as Graham-Paige.

1926
4-cyl., 116" wb

	FP	5	4	3	2	1
Rds	795	950	2100	4750	6650	9500
Spec Rds	845	1000	2400	5000	7000	10,000
Spt Rds	975	1000	2400	5000	7000	10,000
Tr	795	950	2100	4750	6650	9500
Spec Tr	845	1000	2400	5000	7000	10,000
Spt Tr	895	1000	2400	5000	7000	10,000
Cpe	845	650	1250	2400	4200	6000
Spec Cpe	895	700	1350	2800	4550	6500
2 dr Sed	1095	650	1200	2300	4100	5800
2 dr Spec Sed	1100	650	1250	2400	4200	6000
Bus Sed	895	600	1200	2300	4000	5700
Spec Bus Sed	975	675	1300	2500	4300	6100
Sed	895	650	1200	2300	4100	5800
Spec Sed	995	650	1250	2400	4200	6000
Del Sed	1075	675	1300	2500	4300	6100

1927

1927 Dodge Brothers, 4-dr. sedan, OCW

DODGE — SERIES 126/124 — FOUR: In the appearance department, 1927 Dodges were much the same as in the past. Standard models had painted radiators and no cowl lamps. Special models had nickel plated radiators, cowl lamps, motometers, runningboard step plates, bumpers, and drum headlights with nickel plated rims. Deluxe and Sport models had special equipment plus bullet-shaped headlamps. New body styles included a Convertible Cabriolet introduced in April and an All-Purpose Sedan. The latter model was built by Millspaugh & Irish Corp. of Indianapolis. It had a curb-side opening rear door similar to the type used on sedan deliveries and panel trucks. Standard equipment on 1927 Dodges included a speedometer, ammeter, electric horn, coincidental lock, bumpers (extra cost on Std.), rear tire carrier, headlamp dimmer, inside rearview mirror, tool kit and jack. Special models also had an exhaust body heater. The Special Coupe was now of the three-window type. The new Convertible Cabriolet was built for only 2-1/2 months. It had genuine Spanish leather upholstery, landau irons, door glass window regulators, a rumble seat and Armory green finish.

I.D. DATA: Serial numbers were located on toeboard on either side and also on the cross member under the floorboard. First series (126) serial numbers were A702243 to A875379. Second series (124) serial numbers were A875380 to A934104. Engine numbers were located above carburetor on left side of cylinder block. Engine numbers are not available.

1927 Dodge Brothers, Special, coupe, HAC

Model No. (Std.)	Body Type & Seating	Price	Weight	Prod. Total
Std.	2-dr. Rds.-2P	795	2448	Note 1
Std.	4-dr. Tr.-5P	795	2584	Note 1
Std.	2-dr. Cpe.-2P	845	2568	Note 1
Std.	4-dr. Sed.-5P	895	2816	Note 1
(Spec.)				
Spec.	2-dr. Rds.-2P	845	2541	Note 1
Spec.	4-dr. Tr.-5P	845	2669	Note 1
Spec.	2-dr. Cpe.-2P	895	2672	Note 1
Spec.	4-dr. Sed.-5P	975	2893	Note 1
Spec.	4-dr. AP Sed.-5P	1245	NA	Note 1
(Del./Spt.)				
Del.	4-dr. Sed.-5P	1075	2609	Note 1
Spt.	2-dr. Rds.-2/4P	975	2604	Note 1
Spt.	4-dr. Tr.-5P	895	2633	Note 1
Del.	2-dr. Cabr.-2/4P	995	2727	Note 1
(Custom)				
Cus.	2-dr. Clb. Cpe.-4P	[495]	NA	Note 1

Note 1: Total calendar year production was 146,000.
Note 2: The Custom Club Coupe was built by Pioner Body Co. of Sidney, Ohio and the price shown in brackets is the price of the body only. There was also a $30 destination change.

ENGINE: Inline. L-head. Four. Cast iron block. B & S: 3-7/8 in. x 4-1/2 in. Disp.: 212.3 cu. in. C.R.: [Series 126] 4.0:1; [Series 124] 4.1:1. Brake H.P.: 35 @ 2000 R.P.M. Net H.P.: 24.03. Main bearings: Five. Valve lifters: Solid.

CHASSIS: W.B.: 116 in. Tires: 31 x 5.25.

TECHNICAL: Selective sliding transmission. Speeds: 3F/1R. Floor shift controls. Multiple dry disc clutch. Semi-floating rear axle. Two-wheel mechanical brakes. Wood-spoke wheels.
Note 3: Wire wheels were standard equipment on the Convertible Cabriolet.

OPTIONS: Front bumper. Rear bumper. Spare tire. Spare tire cover. Steel disc wheels. Wire wheels (std. on Cabriolet). Taillight. OSRV mirror. Heater. Automatic windshield wipers. Motometer. Wind wings. Nickel plated radiator. Nickel plated headlight rims. Spotlight(s). Cowl lamps. Step plates. Special colors. Trunk rack. Touring trunk.
Note 4: Special equipment features were again standard on some Special, Deluxe and Sport models.

HISTORICAL: Introduced: [Series 126] July 1926-Jan. 1927; [Series 124] Jan. 1927-July 1927. Calendar year registrations: 123,918. Calendar year production: 146,000. Model year production: 146,001. Innovations: [Series 126] Five main bearing crankshaft. New instrument panel with white faced gauges having black figures. [Series 124] Four-point engine mounting. Nickel plated drum headlights. Higher compression ratio. New Convertible Cabriolet produced between April 25, 1927 and Aug. 7, 1927, then discontinued.
Dodge slipped to seventh position on the U.S. auto sales charts this season. The Graham Bros. truck factory built all 1927 Dodge commercial vehicles. This was to be the last full season that the New York based banking firm Dillon, Reed and Co. would retain ownership of the Dodge Bros. name and facilities.

447

1927-28

DODGE SENIOR — SERIES 2249 — SIX: The Dodge Senior Six Series was the first of three new lines that the company introduced in late 1927 for the 1928 model year. Appearance features included a narrow, nickel plated radiator shell, new horizontal hood louvers, double body bead moldings and swinging type windshields. The Senior Six was aimed at the high-priced market and had a 116 inch wheelbase. Standard equipment included a Stromberg carburetor, NorthEast ignition, four-wheel hydraulic brakes, worm and sector steering and an I-beam front axle. The Senior Six entered production in May, 1927.

DODGE FAST FOUR — SERIES 128 — FOUR: The Dodge Fast Four (or Fastest Four) Model 128 was the second of three new lines that were introduced in late 1927 for the 1928 model year. Appearance features on these cars included "cadet" type sun visors, new lower bodies, a shorter wheelbase, new type body molding and vertical hood louvers. These cars looked similar to earlier four-cylinder Dodges but had more rounded rear roof corners and window openings, "cadet" type visors, lower body sills and a slightly concave type of A-pillar that blended more smoothly into the cowl area. Standard, Special and Deluxe trim models were available. Standard equipment included a Stewart carburetor, NorthEast ignition, mechanical two-wheel brakes, speedometer, ammeter, horn, coincidental lock, rear tire carrier, headlamp dimmer, inside rearview mirror, tool kit and jack. This series entered production in July, 1927.

DODGE FAST FOUR — SERIES 129 — FOUR: The Dodge Fast Four Model 129 was the last of three new lines that were introduced in late 1927 for the 1928 model year. These cars were the same as those in the Fast Four Model 128 series except they now had four wheel steeldraulic brakes. This increased the shipping weights of some models although prices did not change. This series entered production in Aug. 1927.

I.D. DATA: [Series 2249] Serial numbers were located on a plate on the toeboard near the steering column; also stamped on right front frame, below fender. Starting: IS10001. Ending: IS29156. Engine numbers were located on the left rear side of cylinder block, right side of cylinder block and right side (either front or rear) below exhaust manifold. Starting: S10001. Ending: S25109. [Series 128] Serial numbers were in the same locations. Starting: A934105. Ending: A961722. Engine numbers were in the same locations. Starting: A1005968. Ending: A1037113. [Series 129] Serial numbers were in the same locations. Starting: A961723. Ending: A1019544. Engine numbers were in the same locations. Starting: A1037114. Ending: A1104269.

Model No.	Body Type & Seating	Price	Weight	Prod. Total
2249	2-dr. Cpe.-2P	1495	3236	NA
2249	2-dr. Cpe.-4P	1570	3315	NA
2249	2-dr. Cabr.-2/4P	1595	3353	NA
2249	4-dr. Sed.-5P	1595	3421	NA
128	2-dr. Cpe.-2P	855	2428	NA
128	2-dr. Spl. Cpe.-2P	895	2725	NA
128	2-dr. Cabr.-2/4P	955	2463	NA
128	4-dr. Sed.-5P	875	2600	NA
128	4-dr. Spl. Sed.-5P	945	2924	NA
128	4-dr. Del. Sed.-5P	950	2609	NA
129	2-dr. Cpe.-2P	855	2486	NA
129	2-dr. Spl. Cpe.-2P	895	2725	NA
129	2-dr. Cabr.-2/4P	955	2521	NA
129	4-dr. Sed.-5P	875	2694	NA
129	4-dr. Spl. Sed.-5P	945	2924	NA
129	4-dr. Del. Sed.-5P	950	2695	NA

ENGINE: [Series 2249] Inline. L-head. Six. Cast iron block. B & S: 3-1/4 in. x 4-1/2 in. Disp.: 224.3 cu. in. C.R.: 5.3:1. Brake H.P.: 60 @ 2800 R.P.M. Net H.P.: 25.34. Valve lifters: Solid. Carb.: Stromberg 1V. [Series 128] Inline. L-head. Four. Cast iron block. B & S: 3-7/8 in. x 4-1/2 in. Disp.: 212.3 cu. in. C.R.: 4.1:1. Brake H.P.: 44 @ 2700 R.P.M. Net H.P.: 24.03. Main bearings: Five. Valve lifters: Solid. Carb.: Stewart 1V. [Series 129] See Series 128 engine specifications.

CHASSIS: [Series 2249] W.B.: 116 in. Tires: 31 x 6. [Series 128] W.B.: 108 in. Tires: 29 x 5. [Series 129] W.B.: 108 in. Tires: 29 x 5.

TECHNICAL: Selective sliding gear transmission. Speeds: 3F/1R. Floor shift controls. Single plate dry disc clutch. Hotchkiss drive. O.R.: [128/129] 3.76:1. [2249] 4.45:1. [128] Two-wheel mechanical brakes; [129] Four-wheel steeldraulic brakes; [2249] Four-wheel hydraulic brakes. Wood-spoke or wire wheels.

OPTIONS: Front bumper. Rear bumper. Spare tire. Dual sidemounts (Senior Six Sport models). Sidemount cover(s). Motometer. Wood-spoke wheels. Wire wheels. Heater. Nickel plated radiator. Nickel headlight rims. Nickel-plated headlight buckets. Taillight(s). OSRV mirror. Spotlight(s). Cowl lamps. Steel disc wheels. Trunk rack. Touring trunk. Automatic windshield wiper. Special paint colors. Wind wings (open models).

HISTORICAL: Introduced: [2249] May 1927; [128] July 1927; [129] Aug. 1927.
Note: For calendar year production information see 1927 section. No separate breakout is available for the early 1928 (1927-1928) series. All of the cars in this series were built during the 1927 calendar year. Innovations: New Dodge Six. Steel body framework eliminated; new construction features welded inner reinforcement panels. Four wheel hydraulic brakes on Senior Six. Hotchkiss drive. Four-point motor suspension.

1927-28
4-cyl., 116" wb

	FP	5	4	3	2	1
Rds	795	1125	3450	5750	8050	11,500
Spec Rds	845	1150	3600	6000	8400	12,000
Spt Rds	975	1200	3750	6250	8750	12,500
Cabr	995	1075	3000	5500	7700	11,000
Tr	795	1075	3000	5500	7700	11,000
Spec Tr	845	1125	3450	5750	8050	11,500
Spt Tr	895	1150	3600	6000	8400	12,000
Cpe	845	675	1300	2500	4300	6100
Spec Cpe	895	700	1350	2800	4550	6500
Sed	895	650	1250	2400	4200	6000
Spec Sed	975	675	1300	2500	4300	6100
DeL Sed	1075	675	1300	2500	4350	6200
A-P Sed	1245	700	1350	2800	4550	6500

1928

1928 Dodge Brothers, Senior Six, 4-dr. sedan, OCW

VICTORY — SERIES 130/131 — SIX: The Victory Six entered production in Nov. 1927 and was introduced on Jan. 7, 1928 at the New York Automobile Show. These all-new cars were recognized as the fastest and smartest vehicles in their price class available from an American auto-maker. They had a 112 inch wheelbase. Victory Six bodies were built by the Budd Manufacturing Co. and featured a prominent beltline molding which ran entirely around the back of the cars, small sun visors and round cornered windows. The hood had four separate groups of vertical louvers inside a raised rectangular panel. There were three louvers in each of the first three groups and two louvers in the rearmost group. Other features included nickel-plated drum type headlights, nickel-plated radiators and one-piece crown fenders. The difference between the 130 and 131 series was that the latter had larger wheels for added road clearance. Standard equipment on all Victory Sixes included NorthEast ignition, internal hydraulic brakes, a large frame, Zerk chassis lubrication and aluminum alloy pistons. Deluxe/Sport equipment included bumpers, sidemount spares and wire wheels.

SENIOR — SERIES 2251/2252 — SIX: In January 1928, the Senior Six received a few changes and became a "true" 1928 series designated with the number 2251. One change was the addition of Sport models with welled fenders, sidemount spares, wire spoke wheels, larger headlamps with a nickel-plated tie bar and vertical stanchions, cowl lamps, a nickel-plated cowl molding and folding trunk rack. The Sport Sedan was the first to appear. It debuted in January. Sport equipment became available for other body styles later in the year. There was also a change in the engine, which increased its horsepower to 68. When equipped with standard size tires, the Senior Six was designated Series 2251; with oversize tires, Series 2252.

STANDARD — SERIES 140/141 — SIX: The Standard Six was the third new line from Dodge and was offered in two Series 140 and 141, the latter using larger wheels for improved road clearance. These cars had 22 multiple vertical hood louvers, cadet type sun visors and drum type headlights. Standard equipment included a NorthEast ignition system, steeldraulic brakes and a starting system with the starter control mounted on the instrument board. The rumbleseat Cabriolet came with "sport" type equipment including nickel-plated drum headlights and wire spoke wheels. The sedan also came in "deluxe" type trim with contrasting body color and nickel-plated drum headlights. These cars entered production in March, 1928 and were introduced on April 27, 1928 with additional body styles added later in the year.

1928 Dodge Brothers, Victory Six, sedan, JAC

I.D. DATA: [Series 130/131] Serial numbers were in the same location. Starting: M1. Ending: M51929. Engine numbers were in the same location. Starting: M10001. Ending: M69396. [Series 2251/2252] Serial numbers and engine numbers were continued from 1927-28. See number listed in the previous section. [Series 140/141] Serial numbers were in the same locations. Starting: J1. Ending: J42686. Engine numbers were in the same locations. Starting: J10001. Ending: J55556.

Model No.	Body Type & Seating	Price	Weight	Prod. Total
130-1	4-dr. Tr.-5P	1030	2785	NA
130-1	2-dr. Cpe.-2P	1045	2660	NA
130-1	2-dr. Cpe.-4P	1170	2860	NA
130-1	2-dr. Brgm.-5P	1170	2849	NA
130-1	4-dr. Sed.-5P	1095	2767	NA
130-1	4-dr. Del. Sed.-5P	1170	2867	NA
2251-2	2-dr. Cpe.-2P	1495	3236	NA
2251-2	2-dr. Spt. Cpe.-2/4P	1725	3410	NA
2251-2	2-dr. Clb. Cpe.-4P	1570	3315	NA
2251-2	2-dr. Spt. Clb. Cpe.-4P	1800	3495	NA
2251-2	2-dr. Cabr.-2/4P	1595	3353	NA
2251-2	2-dr. Spt. Cabr.-2/4P	1720	3533	NA
2251-2	4-dr. Sed.-5P	1595	3421	NA
2251-2	4-dr. Spt. Sed.-5P	1770	3643	NA
140-1	2-dr. Cpe.-2P	875	2502	NA
140-1	2-dr. Spt. Cabr.-2/4P	945	2585	NA
140-1	4-dr. Sed.-5P	895	2721	NA
140-1	4-dr. Del. Sed.-5P	970	2790	NA

ENGINE: [Series 130/131] Inline. L-head. Six. Cast iron block. B & S: 3-3/8 in. x 3-7/8 in. Disp.: 208 cu. in. C.R.: 5.2:1. Brake H.P.: 58 @ 3000 R.P.M. Net H.P.: 27.34. Valve lifters: Solid. Carb.: Stromberg 1V. [Series 2251/2252] Inline. L-head. Six. Cast iron block. B & S: 3-1/4 x 4-1/2 in. Disp.: 224 cu. in. Brake H.P.: 68 @ 2800 R.P.M. Net H.P.: 25.34. Valve lifters: Solid. Carb.: Stromberg 1V. [Series 140/141] Inline. L-head. Six. Cast iron block. B & S: 3-3/8 in. x 3-7/8 in. Disp.: 208 cu. in. Brake H.P.: 58 @ 3000 R.P.M. Net H.P.: 27.3. Valve lifters: Solid. Carb.: Stromberg 1V.

CHASSIS: [Victory Six] W.B.: 112 in. Tires: 29 x 5. [Senior Six] W.B.: 116 in. Tires: 31 x 6. [Standard Six] W.B.: 110 in. Tires: 29 x 5.00.

TECHNICAL: Selective sliding transmission. Speeds: 3F/1R. Column shift controls. Single plate dry disc clutch. Semi-floating rear axle. Overall Ratio: [Victory] 4.45:1; [Senior] 4.45:1; [Standard] 4.45:1. [Standard] Steeldraulic brakes; (others) hydraulic brakes. Wood-spoke or wire-spoke wheels. Hotchkiss drive.

OPTIONS: Front bumper. Rear bumper. Spare tire. Dual sidemount. Sidemount cover(s). Nickel-plated headlights. Wire-spoke wheels. Steel disc wheels. Heater. Motometer. OSRV mirror. Special paint colors. Oversize tires and wheels. Spotlight(s). Cowl lamps. Wind wings. Trunk rack. Touring trunk.

HISTORICAL: Introduced: Jan. 1928; (Standard Six) March 1928. Calendar year registrations: 149,004. Calendar year sales: 67,327.
Note: The above calendar year totals also include 1929 (model year) cars built during calendar year 1928. Innovations: Senior Six Sport Models introduced. All-new Victory Six series introduced. All-new Standard Six series introduced. Horsepower of Senior Series six-cylinder engine increased. New aluminum alloy pistons in Victory engine.
History: Walter P. Chrysler purchased Dodge from Dillon, Reed & Co. (a New York banking firm) for a $170 million stock exchange merger on July 30, 1928. This led to a major reorganization of the company and caused Dodge to drop to 13th sales rank in the U.S. auto industry.

1928

'Fast Four', 4-cyl., 108" wb

	FP	5	4	3	2	1
Cabr	955	1000	2400	5000	7000	10,000
Cpe	855	675	1300	2500	4350	6200
Sed	875	650	1250	2400	4200	6000
DeL Sed	950	675	1300	2500	4300	6100

Standard Series, 6-cyl., 110" wb

	FP	5	4	3	2	1
Cabr	945	1125	3450	5750	8050	11,500
Cpe	875	750	1450	3300	4900	7000
Sed	895	700	1350	2800	4550	6500
DeL Sed	970	725	1400	3200	4850	6900

Victory Series, 6-cyl., 112" wb

	FP	5	4	3	2	1
Tr	1030	2000	5100	8500	11,900	17,000
Cpe	1045	775	1500	3750	5250	7500
RS Cpe	1170	825	1600	4000	5600	8000
Brgm	1170	775	1500	3750	5250	7500
Sed	1095	750	1450	3300	4900	7000
DeL Sed	970	775	1500	3750	5250	7500

Series 2249, Standard 6-cyl., 116" wb

	FP	5	4	3	2	1
Cabr	875	2000	5100	8500	11,900	17,000
RS Cpe	945	775	1500	3700	5200	7400
Sed	895	700	1350	2800	4550	6500
DeL Sed	970	750	1450	3300	4900	7000

Series 2251, Senior 6-cyl., 116" wb

	FP	5	4	3	2	1
Cabr	1595	2800	5700	9500	13,300	19,000
Spt Cabr	1725	3000	6000	10,000	14,000	20,000
RS Cpe	1495	775	1500	3750	5250	7500
Spt Cpe	1570	825	1600	4000	5600	8000
Sed	1595	750	1450	3300	4900	7000
Spt Sed	1770	775	1500	3750	5250	7500

1928-29

STANDARD — SERIES J — SIX: Beginning in July 1928, the Dodge Standard Six line was carried over as a "new" series for the first part of the 1929 model year. There were no major changes in specifications from the 1928 Standard Six, except that the shipping weights of two models increased slightly for an undetermined reason. A new molding, running from the radiator to the windshield pillar, was added on these cars and fender beading was slightly changed. Beginning in September, bullet headlights were used on Cabriolets and sedans.

VICTORY — SERIES M — SIX: Beginning in July 1928, the Dodge Victory Six line was also carried over as a "new" series for the first part of the 1929 model year. There were no major changes in specifications from the 1928 Victory Six, except that prices were lowered and several new body styles were added. These cars had lower, longer bodies with three inch wider doors and smaller rear quarter windows on sedans.

SENIOR — SERIES S — SIX: New styling was used on Senior Sixes marketed after July 1928 as "new" first series 1929 models. Appearance features included a new, higher radiator shell, vertical hood louvers, automatic radiator shutters, cadet type sun visors and a new type instrument panel with silver finish. Standard equipment included a larger, more powerful six-cylinder engine, NorthEast ignition, hydraulic brakes, Lovejoy shock absorbers and a new type emergency brake handle. These cars also had automatic windshield wipers, complete gauges, front and rear bumpers, a cigar lighter, two smoking cases and interior courtesy lamps. Rich interior appointments included plush velvet mohair upholstery, a mahogany finish steering wheel, rear door assist straps and the frosted silver dash treatment. The Senior Six wheelbase also increased four inches, bringing a corresponding increase in overall body proportions.

I.D. DATA: [Series J] Serial numbers were in the same locations. Starting: J42687. Ending: J75519. Engine numbers were in the same locations. Starting: J55557. Ending: J91561. [Series M] Serial numbers were in the same locations. Starting: M51930. Ending: M87759. Engine numbers were in the same locations. Starting: M69397. Ending: M128387. [Series S] Serial numbers were in the same locations. Starting: S50001. Ending: S60487. Engine numbers were in the same locations. Starting: S60001. Ending: S70595.

Model No.	Body Type & Seating	Price	Weight	Prod. Total
J	2-dr. Cpe.-2P	875	2515	NA
J	2-dr. Cabr.-2/4P	945	2585	NA
J	4-dr. Sed.-5P	895	2721	NA
J	4-dr. Del. Sed.-5P	970	2827	NA
M	2-dr. Rds.-2/4P	995	2673	NA
M	4-dr. Tr.-5P	995	2703	NA
M	2-dr. Cpe.-2P	1045	2629	NA
M	2-dr. Del. Cpe.-4P	1170	2860	NA
M	4-dr. Sed.-5P	1095	2870	NA
M	4-dr. Del. Sed.-5P	1170	2943	NA
M	4-dr. Spt. Sed.-5P	1295	3100	NA
S	2-dr. Rds.-2/4P	1615	3303	NA
S	2-dr. Cpe.-2P	1545	3389	NA
S	2-dr. Spt. Cpe.-2/4P	1627	3438	NA
S	2-dr. Brgm. Vic.-5P	1575	3468	NA
S	2-dr. Sed.-5P	1495	3403	NA
S	4-dr. Sed.-5P	1545	3507	NA
S	4-dr. Lan. Sed-5P	1595	3470	NA
S	4-dr. Spt. Sed-5P	1795	3719	NA

ENGINE: [Series J] See 1928 Standard Six engine specifications. [Series M] See 1928 Victory Six engine specifications. [Series S] Inline. L-head. Six. Cast iron block. B & S: 3-3/8 in. x 4-1/2 in. Disp.: 241.6 cu. in. C.R.: 5.2:1. Brake H.P.: 78 @ 3000 R.P.M. Net H.P.: 27.34. Valve lifters: Solid. Carb.: Stromberg 1V.

CHASSIS: [Standard Six] W.B.: 110 in. Tires: 29 x 5.00. [Victory Six] W.B.: 112 in. Tires: 29 x 5.00. [Senior Six] W.B.: 120 in. Tires: 31 x 6.00.

TECHNICAL: Light-weight selective sliding gear transmission. Speeds: 3F/1R. Floor shift controls. Single plate dry disc clutch. Semi-floating rear axle. Overall Ratio: (all) 4.45:1. (Std.) Steeldraulic brakes; (others) hydraulic brakes. Wood-spoke or wire-spoke wheels. Hotchkiss drive.

OPTIONS: Front bumper. Rear bumper. Spare tire. Dual sidemounts. Gordon sidemount cover(s). Nickle-plated headlamps. Wire-spoke wheels. Steel disc wheels. Heater. Motometer. Cigar lighter. OSRV mirror. Special paint colors. Oversize tires and wheels. Spotlight(s). Cowl lamps. Wind wings. Dual taillights. Trunk rack. Touring trunk. Clock. Dual chrome trumpet horns. Trippe lights. Trunk cover.

HISTORICAL: Introduced: July 1928.
Note: The cars in these series were built during calendar year 1928. For production information, see the 1928 section.
Innovations: Corrosion resistant fenders introduced. Styling refinements on Standard Six. Larger, lower bodies on Victory Six. Senior Six has longer wheelbase, Lovejoy shock absorbers, automatic radiator shutters and larger bore engine with increased horsepower. The Standard Six and Victory Six were discontinued in Dec. 1928, while the Senior Six was carried over, until June 1929, as a First Series 1929 line.

1929

DODGE — SERIES DA — SIX: The DA Six was an off-shoot of the Victory Six. New styling characteristics reflective of the Chrysler design influence were headlamps mounted on a bowed tie-bar and a narrow, bright metal molding attached to the rear edge of the hood. The hood was longer, the fenders were of one-piece full crown design and the bodies were of monopiece construction. Chromium plating was used on exterior hardware, in place of nickle plating. Standard equipment included NorthEast ignition, a gasoline filter, Lovejoy shock absorbers and a new exhaust manifold that ran to the front of the motor instead of the rear. The DAs had new bowl shaped headlights which were painted on standard models and chrome-plated on sporty or Deluxe cars.

1929 Dodge Brothers, Standard Six, 4-dr. sedan, OCW

SENIOR — SERIES S — SIX: Beginning in Jan. 1929, the Dodge Senior Six line was carried over as a "second series" 1929 offering. There were no basic alterations in styling or engineering features. Serial numbers, models, prices, weights and engine specifications were identical to those listed for 1928-29 models. Refer to the previous section for information.

I.D. DATA: Serial numbers were in the same locations. Starting: DA1. Ending: DA83714. Engine numbers were in the same locations. Starting Engine No.: H1001. Ending: H99485.

1929 Dodge Brothers, Victory Six, brougham, HAC

Model No.	Body Type & Seating	Price	Weight	Prod. Total
DA	2-dr. Rds.-2/4P	995	2695	NA
DA	4-dr. Phae.-5P	1025	2730	NA
DA	2-dr. Bus. Cpe.-2P	945	2770	NA
DA	2-dr. Del. Cpe.-2/4P	1025	2812	NA
DA	2-dr. Vic. Cpe.-4P	1025	2831	NA
DA	2-dr. Brgm.-5P	995	2830	NA
DA	4-dr. Sed.-5P	995	2900	NA
DA	4-dr. Del. Sed.-5P	1065	2920	NA

ENGINE: Inline. L-head. Six. Cast iron block. B & S: 3-3/8 in. x 3-7/8 in. Disp.: 208 cu. in. C.R.: 5.2:1. Brake H.P.: 63 @ 3000 R.P.M. Net H.P.: 27.34. Valve lifters: Solid. Carb.: Stromberg 1V.

CHASSIS: [DA Six] W.B.: 112 in. Tires: 29 x 5.00. [Senior Six] W.B.: 120 in. Tires: 31 x 6.00.

TECHNICAL: Selective sliding gear transmission. Speeds: 3F/1R. Floor shift controls. Single plate dry disc clutch. Semi-floating rear axle. Overall Ratio: [DA Six] 4.45:1 to 4.72:1; [Senior Six] 4.45:1. Hydraulic brakes. Wood-spoke or wire-spoke wheels. Hotchkiss drive.

OPTIONS: Front bumper. Rear bumper. Spare tire. Dual sidemounts. Gordon sidemount cover(s). Plated headlamps. Wire wheels. Motometer. Heater. Clock. Cigar lighter. OSRV mirror. Special paint colors. Wind wings. Spotlight(s). Cowl lamps. Dual taillights. Trunk rack. Touring trunk. Dual chrome trumpet horns. Trippe lights. Trunk cover. Whitewall tires. Chrome hood molding. Rear windscreen (Phaeton).

1929 Dodge Brothers, Senior Six, 2-dr. sedan, HAC

HISTORICAL: Introduced: Jan. 1929. Calendar year registrations: 115,774. Calendar year production: 124,557.
Note: The above calendar year totals also include 1930 (model year) cars built during calendar year 1929.
Model year production: 121,457.
Note: The preceeding model year production figure includes cars built in calendar year 1929 as 1930 models. Innovations: Chrysler influence reflected in design of new DA Six. Horsepower on small six increased. Shock absorbers on smaller Dodge DA series. New pastel colors available. Dodge first in U.S. industry to adopt downdraft carburetors. Dodge sales improved considerably. The company was America's seventh ranked automaker of 1929 on both calendar and model year basis. Production of the DA Six continued into March 1930, while the S Series Senior Six was replaced by a new DB Series Senior Six in June of 1929. The DB is considered a 1930 model.

1929

Standard Series, 6-cyl., 110" wb

	FP	5	4	3	2	1
Bus Cpe	945	900	1900	4500	6300	9000
Cpe	875	950	2100	4750	6650	9500
Sed	895	825	1600	4000	5600	8000
DeL Sed	970	875	1700	4250	5900	8500
Spt DeL Sed	1075	900	1900	4500	6300	9000
A-P Sed	1245	925	2000	4600	6400	9200
Victory Series, 6-cyl., 112" wb						
Rds	995	3750	7500	12,500	17,500	25,000
Spt Rds	1025	3900	7800	13,000	18,200	26,000
Tr	995	3900	7800	13,000	18,200	26,000
Spt Tr	1025	4050	8100	13,500	18,900	27,000
Cpe	1045	900	1900	4500	6300	9000
DeL Cpe	1170	950	2100	4750	6650	9500
Sed	1095	775	1500	3750	5250	7500
Spt Sed	1295	825	1600	4000	5600	8000
Standard Series DA, 6-cyl., 63 hp, 112" wb						
(Introduced Jan. 1, 1929).						
Rds	995	3900	7800	13,000	18,900	26,000
Spt Rds	1025	4050	8100	13,500	18,900	27,000
Phae	1025	4200	8400	14,000	19,600	28,000
Spt Phae	1065	4350	8700	14,500	20,300	29,000
Bus Cpe	945	950	2100	4750	6650	9500
DeL RS Cpe	1025	1000	2400	5000	7000	10,000
Vic	1025	900	1900	4500	6300	9000
Brgm	995	775	1500	3750	5250	7500
Sed	995	750	1450	3300	4900	7000
DeL Sed	1065	775	1500	3600	5100	7300
DeL Spt Sed	1170	775	1500	3750	5250	7500
Senior Series, 6-cyl., 120" wb						
Rds	1615	4050	8100	13,500	18,900	27,000
2P Cpe	1545	1000	2400	5000	7000	10,000
RS Spt Cpe	1627	1075	3000	5500	7700	11,000
Vic Brgm	1575	1000	2400	5000	7000	10,000
Sed	1495	900	1900	4500	6300	9000
Spt Sed	1795	950	2100	4750	6650	9500
Lan Sed	1595	1000	2400	5000	7000	10,000
Spt Lan Sed	1625	1025	2600	5200	7200	10,400

1929-30

DODGE — SERIES DA — SIX: Starting July 1, 1929 the DA Six was redesignated a "first series" 1930 Dodge. One new model was added to the line and the shipping weights changed slightly for several other body styles. Gemmer worm and sector type steering gear was now listed as a feature of these cars. General specifications were, however, the same as 1929 models.

DODGE SENIOR — SERIES DB — SIX: A new Series in Dodge's "first series" 1930 model line-up was the DB Senior Six. It was introduced in July 1929. Specifications and appearance features were basically the same as those for the 1929 Senior Six. New technical features included a 4-speed transmission and rubber mounted engine suspension system. In the styling department, chrome plated vertical supports were added below the headlights. Standard equipment included NorthEast ignition, hydraulic brakes, Lovejoy shock absorbers and automatic radiator shutters.

I.D. DATA: [Series DA] Serial numbers were in the same locations. Starting: DA83715. Ending: DA123481. Engine numbers were in the same locations. Starting Engine No.: H99486. Ending: H149821. [Series DB] Serial numbers were in the same locations. Starting: DB1. Ending: DB2999. Engine numbers were in the same locations. Starting Engine No.: O-1. Ending: O-3019.

Model No.	Body Type & Seating	Price	Weight	Prod. Total
DA	2-dr. Rds.-2/4P	995	2687	NA
DA	4-dr. Phae.-5P	1025	2730	NA
DA	2-dr. Bus. Cpe.-2P	945	2750	NA
DA	2-dr. Del. Cpe.-2/4P	1025	2812	NA
DA	2-dr. Cpe. Vic.-4P	1025	2846	NA
DA	2-dr. Sed.-5P	925	2876	NA
DA	2-dr. Brgm.-5P	995	2834	NA
DA	4-dr. Sed.-5P	995	2867	NA
DA	4-dr. Del. Sed.-5P	1065	2898	NA
DB	2-dr. Rds.-2/4P	1615	3303	NA
DB	2-dr. Cpe.-2/4P	1595	3426	NA
DB	2-dr. Brgm. Vic.-5P	1545	3419	NA
DB	4-dr. Sed.-5P	1595	3513	NA

ENGINE: [Series DA] See 1929 DA Series engine specifications. [Series DB] See 1929 Senior Six Series engine specifications.

CHASSIS: [DA Series] W.B.: 112 in. Tires: 19 x 5.50. [DB Series] W.B.: 120 in. Tires: 19 x 6.00.

TECHNICAL: Selective sliding gear transmission. Speeds: [DA] 3F/1R, [DB] 4F/1R. Floor shift controls. Single plate dry disc clutch. Semi-floating rear axle. Overall Ratio: (Both) 4.72:1. Hydraulic brakes. Wood-spokes or wire-spoke wheels.

OPTIONS: Front bumper. Rear bumper. Spare tire. Dual sidemounts. Sidemount cover(s). Wire spoke wheels. Trunk rack. Touring trunk. Heater. Clock. Cigar lighter. Spotlight(s). Cowl lamps. Trunk cover. Dual windshield wipers. OSRV mirror. Chrome plated headlamps. Twin wipers. Twin taillights. Twin trumpet horns. Special paint colors. Wind wings.
Note: Some of these accessories were standard equipment on DeLuxe models.

HISTORICAL: Introduced: July 1, 1929. See 1929 section for calendar year production figures. Model year production figures same as 1930. Innovations: Four-speed transmission on Series DB Senior Six. Also, four-point engine mounting system. Both the DA and DB Series were continued into calendar year 1930. The Dodge DA Six was produced until March 1930. The Dodge DB Six was produced until June 1930.

1930

1930 Dodge Six, Series DD, convertible coupe, JAC

DODGE — SERIES DD — SIX: Introduced in Jan. 1930, the DD Six was an all-new, "second series" 1930 Dodge car-line. Appearance characteristics included a smaller 109 inch wheelbase, monopiece body construction, wider radiator and a V.V. (vision and ventilating) type windshield. Very early DD models had uniform size vertical hood louvers and no cowl lamps. Later DD models also had vertical hood louvers, but the louvers grew smaller in size towards the front and the rear. This gave them an arch-like pattern. The later cars also had cowl lamps. Headlamps were of the bowl type with the buckets finished in black enamel and trimmed with chrome plated rims. They were mounted on a bow-shaped, chrome plated tie-bar. Standard equipment included NorthEast ignition, hydraulic brakes, AC fuel pump, new type instrument panel and a 3-spoke steering wheel.

DODGE — SERIES DA — SIX: After Jan. 1, the Dodge DA Six continued to be produced and sold as part of the "second series" 1930 line. There are no separate serial number breakouts for the cars built between January and the end of production in March. Appearance and equipment features, models, prices, weights and engine specifications are believed to be the same as listed in the 1929 section for this series.

1930 Dodge Eight, Series DC, 4-dr. sedan, JAC

DODGE — SERIES DC — EIGHT: The new Dodge DC Eight was said to be "more attractive, more powerful, longer and roomier." It was brought out in Jan. 1930, despite the worsening depression in America. Appearance characteristics included all-steel monopiece body construction, a wide shell radiator, chrome-plated bowl shape headlights, a chrome-plated bow-shaped headlight tie-bar and cowl lamps. The hood had vertical louvers that were fatter than those used on sixes. They formed an arch pattern, top and bottom, as they grew progressively smaller towards the front and rear. The eights measured a sizeable 163 inches overall and were mounted on a 114 inch wheelbase. Standard equipment included Delco-Remy ignition, hydraulic brakes, a new type slanting windshield, new instrument panel, AC fuel pump, hydraulic shock absorbers, 3-spoke steering wheel, rubber shackled springs, wood-spoke wheels and a rumb-

leseat in the roadster and convertible. A badge at the upper center of the radiator read "DODGE 8." Six wheel equipment (with wire wheels) was standard with Phaetons.

DODGE SENIOR — SERIES DB — SIX: After Jan. 1, the Dodge DB Senior Six continued to be produced and sold as part of the 1930 "second series" line. There are no separate serial number breakouts for the cars built between January and the end of production in June. Appearance and equipment features, models, prices, weights and engine specifications are believed to be the same as listed in the 1929 section covering this series.

ENGINE: [Series DD] For the new 1930 models, Dodge adopted the Fedco serial numbering system. Fedco plates were mounted on the center of the instrument panel, above the instruments. Conventional numbers were also used. Conventional numbers were in the same locations on a plate on the toeboard, also on a plate on the right front door hinge pillar post and also on the frame below the right front fender. For DD models the Fedco numbers were D001WP to D255PO and the conventional numbers were 3500001 to 3504188. Engine numbers were on the right rear side of cylinder block below exhaust manifold. Starting Engine No.: DD1001. Ending: DD32787. [Series DC] Serial numbers were in the same location as on the DD Sixes. Starting: (Fedco) E001WC; (conventional) 4500001. Ending: (Fedco) E191HY; (conventional) 4501083. Engine numbers were in the same location as on the DD Sixes. Starting Engine No.: DC1001. Ending: DC22400.

Model No.	Body Type & Seating	Price	Weight	Prod. Total
DD	2-dr. Rds.-2/4P	855	2462	772
DD	2-dr. Bus. Cpe.-2P	835	2534	3877
DD	2-dr. Cpe.-2/4P	855	2603	3363
DD	2-dr. Conv. Cpe.-2/4P	935	2605	620
DD	4-dr. Sed.-5P	865	2668	33,432
DD	Chassis	NA	NA	899

Note 1: Total series production was 42,963. (This includes DD Sixes sold as 1931 models).

DC	2-dr. Rds.-2/4P	1095	2802	598
DC	4-dr. Phae.-5P	1225	2960	234
DC	2-dr. Cpe.-2/4P	1125	2981	2999
DC	2-dr. Conv. Cpe.-2/4P	1195	2938	728
DC	4-dr. Sed.-5P	1145	3043	20,315
DC	Chassis	NA	NA	253

Note 1: Total series production was 25,127. (This includes DC Eights sold as 1931 models).

ENGINE: [Series DD] Inline. L-head. Six. Cast iron block. B & S: 3-1/8 in. x 4-1/8 in. Disp.: 189.8 cu. in. C.R.: 5.2:1. Brake H.P.: 60 @ 3400 R.P.M. Net H.P.: 23.44. Main bearings: Four. Valve lifters: Solid. Carb.: Carter 1V. Torque: 120 lbs.-ft. @ 1200 R.P.M. [Series DC] Inline. L-head. Eight. Cast iron block. B & S: 2-7/8 in. x 4-1/2 in. Disp.: 220.7 cu. in. C.R.: 5.4:1. Brake H.P.: 75 @ 3400 R.P.M. Net H.P.: 26.45. Main bearings: Five. Valve lifters: Solid. Carb.: Stromberg. Torque: 145 lbs.-ft. @ 1400 R.P.M.

CHASSIS: [Series DD Six] W.B.: 109 in. O.L.: 155-7/8 in. Tires: 19 x 5.00 [Series DA Six] W.B.: 112 in. Tires: 19 x 5.50. [Series DC Eight] W.B.: 114 in. O.L.: 163 in. Tires: 18 x 5.50. [Series DB Senior Six] W.B.: 120 in. Tires: 19 x 6.00.

TECHNICAL: Selective sliding transmission. Speeds: [DB] 4F/1R; [others] 3F/1R. Floor shift controls. Single plate dry disc clutch. Semi-floating rear axle. Overall Ratio: [DA/DB] 4.72:1; [DC] 4.6:1 and [DD] 4.9:1. Hydraulic brakes. Wood-spoke wheels.

OPTIONS: Front bumper. Rear bumper. Single sidemount. Dual sidemounts. Sidemount cover(s). Spare tire. Wire-spoke wheels. Silvertone radio. Heater. Clock. Cigar lighter. Radio antenna. Trunk rack. Touring trunk. Spotlight(s). Cowl lamps. Trumpet horns. Twin taillights. Twin horns. Folding bed option. Wind wings (open cars). Trunk cover. OSRV mirror. Special paint. Dual windshield wipers.
Note: Some accessories standard equipment on higher-priced models.

HISTORICAL: Introduced: Jan. 1, 1930. Calendar year registrations: 64,105. Calendar year production: 68,158. Model year production: 90,755. Innovations: First Dodge Eight introduced. Fuel pumps used on all-new 1930 models (vacuum tanks on carryover models). New instrument panels. Vision and ventilating windshields on all-new models. Hydraulic shock absorbers. For the model year, Dodge was fifth in U.S. sales. The company also ranked seventh in calendar year output. About 80 percent of DC Series production was sold as 1930 models. About 70 percent of DD Series production sold as 1930 models. These series were produced into the 1931 calendar year ending May 1931 and Sept. 1931 respectively.

1930
Series DA. 6-cyl., 112" wb

	FP	5	4	3	2	1
Rds	995	4350	8700	14,500	20,300	29,000
Phae	1025	4500	9000	15,000	21,000	30,000
Bus Cpe	945	875	1700	4250	5900	8500
DeL Cpe	1025	900	1900	4500	6300	9000
Vic	1025	925	2000	4600	6400	9200
Brgm	995	775	1500	3750	5250	7500
2 dr Sed	925	750	1450	3500	5050	7200
Sed	995	775	1500	3600	5100	7300
DeL Sed	1065	775	1500	3750	5250	7500
RS Rds	1025	4500	9000	15,000	21,000	30,000
RS Cpe	1065	1000	2400	5000	7000	10,000
Lan Sed	1065	825	1600	4000	5600	8000

Series DD, 6-cyl., 109" wb
(Introduced Jan. 1, 1930).

RS Rds	855	4200	8400	14,000	19,600	28,000
Phae	875	4350	8700	14,500	20,300	29,000
RS Conv	935	4050	8100	13,500	18,900	27,000
Bus Cpe	835	900	1900	4500	6300	9000
RS Cpe	855	950	2100	4750	6650	9500
Sed	865	750	1450	3300	4900	7000

Series DC, 8-cyl., 114" wb
(Introduced Jan. 1, 1930).

	FP	5	4	3	2	1
Rds	1095	4350	8700	14,500	20,300	29,000
RS Conv	1195	4200	8400	14,000	19,600	28,000
Phae	1225	4500	9000	15,000	21,000	30,000
Bus Cpe	1125	950	2100	4750	6650	9500
RS Cpe	1165	1000	2400	5000	7000	10,000
Sed	1145	775	1500	3750	5250	7500

1930-31

STANDARD DODGE — SERIES DD — SIX: After July, 1930, the Dodge DD Six was slightly updated and carried over as part of the 1931 "first series." Changes included a new Delco-Remy ignition system, the relocation of the starter control to the instrument panel and the addition of a new five-passenger phaeton. Prices were lowered $100 and shipping weights did not change. A new radiator featured a slanting "DODGE 6" emblem.

STANDARD DODGE — SERIES DC — EIGHT: After July, 1930, the Dodge DC Eight was slightly updated and carried over as part of the 1931 "first series." Changes included a lower overall body height, the addition of twin cowl vents, a sloping windshield, oblong type windows, and a new radiator emblem with a figure "8". Prices were cut $100-145.

I.D. DATA: [Series DD] Serial numbers were in the same locations. Starting: (Fedco) D255CW; (conventional) 3504189. Ending: (Fedco) D257PH; (conventional) 3516105. Engine numbers were in the same location. Starting Ending No.: DD32788. Ending: DD44576. [Series DC] Serial numbers were in the same locations. Starting: (Fedco) E191HS; (conventional) 4501084. Ending: (Fedco) E192EL; (conventional) 4504533. Engine numbers were in the same location. Starting Engine No.: DC22401. Ending: DC26018.

Model No.	Body Type & Seating	Price	Weight	Prod. Total
DD	2-dr. Rds.-2/4P	755	2462	Note 1
DD	4-dr. Phae.-5P	775	2521	542
DD	2-dr. Bus. Cpe.-2P	735	2534	Note 1
DD	2-dr. Cpe.-2/4P	755	2603	Note 1
DD	2-dr. Conv. Cpe.-2/4P	835	2605	Note 1
DD	4-dr. Sed.-5P	765	2668	Note 1
DD	Chassis	NA	NA	Note 1

Note 1: For carryover models see 1930 production totals.
Note 2: Total production of this series for the 1931 model year was approximately 12,900. The DD Six remained in actual production until May 1931.

DC	2-dr. Rds.-2/4P	995	2802	Note 1
DC	4-dr. Phae.-5P	1080	2960	Note 1
DC	2-dr. Bus. Cpe.-2P	1025	2910	123
DC	2-dr. Cpe.-2/4P	1065	2981	Note 1
DC	2-dr. Conv. Cpe.-2/4P	1095	2938	Note 1
DC	4-dr. Sed.-5P	1045	3043	Note 1
DC	Chassis	NA	NA	Note 1

Note 1: For carryover models see 1930 production totals.
Note 2: Total production of this series for the 1931 model year was approximately 4,300. The DC Eight remained in actual production until Sept., 1931.

ENGINE: [Series DD] See 1930 DD Series engine specifications. [Series DC] See 1930 DD Series.

CHASSIS: [Series DD] W.B.: 109 in. O.L.: 155-7/8 in. Tires: 19 x 5.00 [Series DC] W.B.: 114 in. O.L.: 163 in. Tires: 18 x 5.50.

TECHNICAL: Selective sliding transmission. Speeds: 3F/1R. Floor shift controls. Single plate dry disc clutch. Semi-floating rear axle. Overall Ratio: [DD] 4.9:1; [DC] 4.6:1. Hydraulic brakes. Wood-spoke wheels.

OPTIONS: Front bumper. Rear bumper. Single sidemount. Dual sidemounts. Sidemount cover(s). Spare tire. Wire-spoke wheels. Radio. Heater. Clock. Cigar lighter. Radio antenna. Trunk rack. Touring trunk. Spotlight(s). Cowl lamps. Trumpet horn(s). Twin taillights. Twin horns. Folding bed option. Wind wings. Trunk cover. OSRV mirror. Special paint. Dual windshield wipers.
Note: Some accessories standard on some models.

HISTORICAL: Introduced: July, 1930. See 1929 section for calendar year production figures. Model year production figures same as 1931. Innovations: Lower DC Eight bodies. Starting control on dashboard. New DD Phaeton. Twincowl vents on Eight.
The Model DC was nicknamed the "Marathon Eight" after one car was driven over 102,000 miles during the year. Many Dodge chassis were supplied to taxicab companies. They had special features like steel disc wheels, leather front seats and special lighting. Some station wagons were also turned out by J.. Cantrell & Co. of Huntington, N.Y.

1931

DODGE — SERIES DD — SIX: Starting in Jan., 1931, the Dodge DD Six was carried over as a part of the true 1931 series. There were no changes in the appearance features, standard equipment, availability of models, factory prices, shipping weights or engine specifications. Refer to the 1930-31 section for specifications and production information. The DD Six line remained in production through May, 1931.

DODGE — SERIES DH — SIX: The new DH models entered production in November 1930, as a "true" 1931 series. The line was made up of six medium priced six-cylinder cars on a five inch longer wheelbase. Appearance features included a wider and deeper radiator grille, lever type radia-

tor, shutters, twin cowl ventilators, fuller crown front fenders, a longer hood, a new front bumper with a V-shaped upper bar, a beaded sun visor and an ebony finished instrument panel. Standard equipment included a double drop frame, Delco Remy ignition, hydraulic brakes, a new vibration dampener, adjustable seats and wire spoke wheels.

DODGE — SERIES DC — EIGHT: Starting in Jan., 1931, the Dodge DC Eight was carried over as part of the true 1931 series. There were no changes in the appearance features, standard equipment, model availability, factory prices, shipping weights or engine specifications. Refer to the 1930-31 section for specifications and production information.

1931 Dodge Six, Series DH, 4-dr. sedan, JAC

DODGE — SERIES DG — EIGHT: The new DG models entered production in Jan., 1931, as a "true" 1931 series. The line was initially made up of four eight-cylinder cars. Appearance characteristics included a wider radiator, lever operated radiator shutters, twin cowl ventilators, new instrument panel and a swinging windshield. These cars were the first to use the Rocky Mountain ram as a hood ornament. Equipment features included Delco-Remy ignition, hydraulic brakes, double drop frame, downdraft Stromberg carburetor, rubber mounted motor suspension, three spoke steering wheel, adjustable seats and five wire spoke wheels. The wheelbase was over four inches longer than that of the DC Eight.

I.D. DATA: [Series DH] Serial numbers were located on a plate on the toeboard, also on the front right door hinge pillar post and also on frame below right front fender. Starting: 3518001. Ending: 3548559. Engine numbers were in the same location. Starting Engine No.: DH1001. Ending: DH33442. [Series DG] Serial numbers were in the same locations. Starting: 4508001. Ending: 4517521. Engine numbers were in the same location. Starting Engine No.: DG1003. Ending: DG11086.

Model No.	Body Type & Seating	Price	Weight	Prod. Total
DH	4-dr. Phae.-5P	865	2655	164
DH	2-dr. Bus. Cpe.-2P	815	2661	3178
DH	2-dr. R/S Cpe.-2/4P	853	2745	4187
DH	4-dr. Sed.-5P	845	2820	33,090
DH	2-dr. Rds.-2/4P	825	2638	160
DH	2-dr. Conv. Cpe.-2/4P	895	NA	NA
DH	Chassis	NA	NA	47

Note 1: Total production in the 1931 series was approximately 20,558 based on the range of serial numbers.
Note 2: The individual totals given in the righthand column above include DH Sixes carried over into the 1932 "first series".
Note 3: Dodge records do not show any production figures for the DH convertible coupe, although this model does appear in sales literature.

DG	2-dr. Rds.-2/4P	1095	NA	64
DG	2-dr. Cpe.-2/4P	1095	3094	2181
DG	2-dr. Conv. Cpe.-2/4P	1170	NA	NA
DG	4-dr. Sed.-5P	1135	3175	8937
DG	Chassis	NA	NA	20

Note 1: Total production in the 1931 series was approximately 9,500 based on the range of serial numbers.
Note 2: The individual totals given in the righthand column above include DG Eights carried over into the 1932 "first series."
Note 3: Dodge records do not show any production figures for the DG convertible coupe, although this model does appear in sales literature.

ENGINE: [Series DH] Inline. L-head. Six. Cast iron block. B & S: 3-1/4 in. x 4-1/4 in. Disp.: 211.5 cu. in. C.R.: 5.2:1. Brake H.P.: 68 @ 3200 R.P.M. Net H.P.: 25.35. Main bearings: Four. Valve lifters: Solid. Carb.: Carter 1V model 197S. Torque: 140 lbs.-ft. @ 1400 R.P.M. [Series DG] Inline. L-head. Eight. Cast iron block. B & S: 3 in. x 4-1/4 in. Disp.: 240.3 cu. in. C.R.: 5.2:1. Brake H.P.: 84 @ 3400 R.P.M. Net H.P.: 28.8. Main bearings: Five. Valve lifters: Solid. Carb.: Stromberg 1V model DXC-3. Torque: 158 lbs.-ft. @ 1400 R.P.M.

CHASSIS: [Series DD] W.B.: 109 in. O.L.: 155-7/8 in. Tires: 19 x 5.00 [Series DH] W.B.: 114 in. Tires: 19 x 5.00. [Series DC] W.B.: 114 in. O.L.: 163 in. Tires: 18 x 5.50. [Series DG] W.B.: 118-1/4 in. Tires: 18 x 5.50.

TECHNICAL: Selective sliding transmission. Speeds: 3F/1R. Floor shift controls. Conventional clutch. Semi-floating rear axle. Overall Ratio: [DD] 4.9:1; [DH] 4.66:1 to 4.3:1; [DC] 4.6:1; [DG] 4.6:1 to 4.3:1. Hydraulic brakes. Wood-spoke or wire-spoke wheels.

OPTIONS: Front bumper. Rear bumper. Spare tire. Dual sidemounts. Leather sidemount cover(s). Metal sidemount covers. Wire wheels. Disc wheels (taxi). Radio. Heater. Clock. Cigar lighter. Radio antenna. Trunk rack. Touring trunk. Spotlights. Cowl lamps. Trumpet horns. Wind wings. Trunk cover. Trippe lights. OSRV mirror. Special paint.

HISTORICAL: Introduced: Jan. 1931. Calendar year registrations: 53,090. Calendar year production: 56,003. Model year production: 52,364. Innovations: Fully rust proof bodies. Valve seat inserts. Fully automatic spark control. Dodge was America's 9th ranked auto-maker for the model year. This was the last time a Dodge roadster would be offered until 1949.

1931
Series DH, 6-cyl., 114" wb
(Introduced Dec. 1, 1930).

	FP	5	4	3	2	1
Rds	835	4050	8100	13,500	18,900	27,000
RS Conv	865	3900	7800	13,000	18,200	26,000
Bus Cpe	815	950	2100	4750	6650	9500
RS Cpe	853	1000	2400	5000	7000	10,000
Sed	845	750	1450	3300	4900	7000

Series DG, 8-cyl., 118.3" wb
(Introduced Jan. 1, 1931).

	FP	5	4	3	2	1
RS Rds	995	4200	8400	14,000	19,600	28,000
RS Conv	1095	3400	6900	11,500	16,100	23,000
Phae	1080	4350	8700	14,500	20,300	29,000
RS Cpe	1095	1000	2400	5000	7000	10,000
Sed	1135	825	1600	4000	5600	8000
5P Cpe	1145	1000	2400	5000	7000	10,000

1931-32

DODGE — SERIES DD — SIX: Chrysler Corp. records indicate that production of the Series DD Dodge Six ended in May of 1931. However, *Red Book National Used Car Market Report* (1935 edition) contains a listing for this series as an "early" 1932 line. This would suggest that the depression kept sales so low that Dodge continued to sell these cars even after production had ended. The cars marketed after July 1, 1931 were sold as part of the "first series" for 1932 and had serial numbers 3516106 and up; engine numbers DD44501 and up. Appearance features, standard equipment, model listings, factory prices, shipping weights and engine specifications did not change. Refer to the 1930-31 section for specifications and production information. Serial numbers indicate that only nine of these cars were sold as 1932 models.

DODGE — SERIES DH — SIX: Beginning in July, 1931, the Series DH Dodge Six was carried over as part of the company's "first series" for 1932. Appearance features were slightly changed in that swinging type windshields and lever operated radiator shutters were adopted. Standard equipment included a new type gearshifter and freewheeling. Brake horsepower was slightly increased due to a higher compression ratio being used. Other features were the same as on 1931 Dodge DH Sixes.

DODGE — SERIES DC — EIGHT: Starting in July, 1931, the Series DC Dodge Eight was carried over as part of the company's "first series" for 1932. These cars can be identified by a new instrument panel with three control buttons. Other appearance features, standard equipment, models, factory prices, shipping weights and engine specifications were unchanged. Cars sold as 1932 models had Fedco serial numbers E192EE to E193PS and conventional serial numbers 4504534 to 4505165. Engine numbers were DC26019 to DC26774. The DC Eight remained in production until Sept., 1931 and was then discontinued.

DODGE — SERIES DG — EIGHT: Starting in July, 1931, the Series DG Dodge Eight was carried over as part of the company's "first series" for 1932. These cars can be identified by a new type mahogany instrument panel, new type gearshift and new rubber-bushed spring shackles. There were a number of changes in the body style offerings with the Convertible Coupe being deleted and a Phaeton and two new coupes being added.

I.D. DATA: [Series DH] Serial numbers were in the same locations. Starting: 3548560. Ending: 3557371. Engine numbers were in the same location. Starting Engine No.: DH33443. Ending: DH41772. [Series DG] Serial numbers were in the same locations. Starting: 4517522. Ending: 4519534. Engine numbers were in the same locations. Starting Engine No.: DG11807. Ending: DG13028.

Model No.	Body Type & Seating	Price	Weight	Prod. Total
DH	4-dr. Phae.-5P	865	2655	Note 1
DH	2-dr. Bus. Cpe.-2P	815	2661	Note 1
DH	2-dr. R/S Cpe.-2/4P	835	2745	Note 1
DH	4-dr. Sed.-5P	845	2840	Note 1
DH	2-dr. Rds.-2/4P	850	2638	Note 1

Note 1: See 1931 Dodge DH Six section for production totals. About 8,800 cars were built in the 1931-32 Series.

DG	2-dr. Rds.-2/4P	1095	2976	Note 1
DG	4-dr. Phae.-5P	1155	2985	43
DG	2-dr. Bus. Cpe.-2P	1095	3003	119
DG	2-dr. R/S Cpe.-2/4P	1095	3094	Note 1
DG	2-dr. Clb. Cpe.-5P	1145	3240	500
DG	4-dr. Sed.-5P	1135	3175	Note 1
DG	Chassis	NA	NA	Note 1

Note 1: Production totals for the Roadster, R/S Coupe, Sedan and Chassis — only are listed in the 1931 Series DG eight section.
Note 2: About 2,000 cars were built and sold as 1932 models, according to the range of serial numbers.

ENGINE: [Series DH] Inline. L-head. Six. Cast iron block. B & S: 3-1/4 in. x 4-1/4 in. Disp.: 211.5 cu. in. C.R.: 5.4:1. Brake H.P.: 74 @ 3400 R.P.M. Net H.P.: 25.35. Main bearings: Solid. Valve lifters: Solid. Carb.: Carter 1V. Torque: 140 lbs.-ft. @ 1400 R.P.M. [Series DG] See 1931 Series DG Eight engine specifications.

CHASSIS: [Series DD] W.B.: 109 in. O.L.: 155-7/8 in. Tires: 19 x 5.00. [Series DH] W.B.: 114-1/4 in. Tires: 19 x 5.00. [Series DC] W.B.: 114 in. O.L.: 163 in. Tires: 18 x 5.50. [Series DG] W.B.: 118-1/4 in. Tires: 18 x 5.50.

TECHNICAL: Selective sliding transmission. Speeds: 3F/1R. Floor shift controls. Conventional clutch. Semi-floating rear axle. Overall Ratio: [DD] 4.9:1, [DH] 4.66:1, [DC] 4.6:1, [DG] 4.6:1. Hydraulic brakes. Wood-spoke or wire-spoke wheels. Free-wheeling.

OPTIONS: Front bumper. Rear bumper. Spare tire. Dual sidemounts. Leather sidemount cover(s). Metal sidemount covers. Wire wheels. Disc wheels (taxi). Radio. Heater. Clock. Cigar lighter. Radio antenna. Trunk rack. Touring trunk. Spotlights. Cowl lamps. Trumpet horns. Wind wings. Trunk cover. Trippe lights. OSRV mirror. Special paint.

HISTORICAL: Introduced: July 1931. See 1931 section for calendar year production. See 1932 section for model year production. Innovations: DH Six has new type gear shifter and free-wheeling feature; engine compression and horsepower rating increased. DG Eight has new dash, new gear shifter and rubber shackled springs. DC Eight has new instrumentation controls. The depression had a negative effect on Dodge sales and led to all of the late 1931 models being carried over into the early part of the 1932 selling season.

1932

1932 Dodge Six, Series DL, 4-dr. sedan, OCW

DODGE — SERIES DL — SIX: A new DL Series Dodge Six entered production in Nov. 1931 and was introduced in Jan. 1932. Appearance characteristics included a rakishly sloped windshield with no external sun visor, a new Dodge ram hood ornament, a curved-V double bar bumper, a higher and more rounded cowl line, chrome plated bowl type headlamps, longer, lower body feature lines and cowl lamps mounted further back on the surcingle molding. Standard equipment included Delco-Remy ignition, hydraulic brakes, double drop bridge type frame and a silent second gear transmission with an optional automatic vacuum-operated clutch and free-wheeling device operated by a button on the instrument panel. A single control on the new satin-finished instrument panel locked both the automatic clutch and the free-wheeling unit in or out. Mono-piece all-steel body construction was featured again and there were two, hand-operated ventilators on the top of the cowl.

DODGE — SERIES DK — EIGHT: Known as the "New Eight", the DK Series Dodge lineup entered production in Nov. 1931 for Jan. 1932 auto show introduction. Cars in this series were mounted on a larger double drop bridge frame and had a 122 in. wheelbase. Appearance features included a sloping windshield, interior (only) sun visors, longer and lower body feature lines and wire-spoke wheels. On these cars, only the top bar of the bumper was curved and "veed" downward at its center. The bottom bar was straight. Standard equipment included Delco-Remy ignition, hydraulic brakes, "Floating Power" type engine suspension, silent second gear transmission, hydraulic shocks and an adjustable windshield. Free-wheeling and an automatic clutch were standard on the New Eight. Cars built after mid-year had a high-compression cylinder head and ten additional horsepower.

1932 Dodge Four, Series DM, 2-dr. sedan, JB

DODGE — SERIES DM — FOUR: Beginning in 1932 and continuing until Pearl Harbor, Chrysler Corporation built a series of "junior" Dodges, based on the Plymouth body shell and drivetrain, for sale in the Canadian and export markets. This move came as a result of the corporate structural organization outside the U.S. Dodge dealers in these markets were not dualed with Plymouth, which eliminated the dealer from pursuing sales in the low-priced end of the market. The DM was an answer to these problems. Engine and chassis for the DM was supplied by the PB model Plymouth, with Dodge supplying the body and trim. In succeeding years Plymouth would supply even the body with Dodge lookalike grilles and trim applied. A total of 1,173 Dodge DM's was built in the United States for foreign export, with an additional 16 cars built in Windsor, Ontario.

I.D. DATA: [Series DL] Serial numbers were in the same locations. Starting: 3558101. Ending: 3578392. Engine numbers were in the same location. Starting Engine No.: DL1001. Ending: DL21030. [Series DK] Serial numbers were in the same locations. Starting: 4520101. Ending: 4526087. [Series DM] Serial numbers on a tag on the right front door post. Starting: 9905001. Ending: 9906173. Engine numbers on flat spot on left side of block, beginning number DM-1001.
Note: Starting with serial number 4524540 the higher compression cylinder head is used. Engine numbers were in the same location. Starting Engine No.: DK1001. Ending: DK7123.
Note: Engines above number DK5667 had the high compression cylinder head.

1932 Dodge Eight, Series DK, coupe, JAC

Model No.	Body Type & Seating	Price	Weight	Prod. Total
DL	2-dr. Bus. Cpe.-2P	795	2928	1963
DL	2-dr. R/S Cpe.-2/4P	835	2995	1815
DL	2-dr. Conv. Cpe.-2/4P	895	2988	224
DL	2-dr. Conv. Sed.-5P	915	3068	12
DL	2-dr. Vic. Cpe.-5P	865	3085	1
DL	4-dr. Sed.-5P	845	3094	16,901
DL	Chassis	NA	NA	126

Note 1: Total series production was 21,042.

DK	2-dr. R/S Cpe.-2/4P	1115	3417	821
DK	2-dr. Bus. Cpe.-2P	1095	3350	57
DK	2-dr. Conv. Cpe.-2/4P	1220	3438	88
DK	4-dr. Sed.-5P	1145	3527	4422
DK	4-dr. Conv. Sed.-5P	1395	3706	88
DK	2-dr. Vic. Cpe.-5P	1145	3504	651
DK	Chassis	NA	NA	22

Note 1: Total series production was 6,187.

DM	Phaeton	NA	NA	92
DM	Roadster	NA	NA	54
DM	4-dr. Sed.	NA	NA	760
DM	Conv. Sed.	NA	NA	48
DM	Sta. Wag.	NA	NA	1
DM	Chassis	NA	NA	235

ENGINE: [Series DL] Inline. L-head. Six. Cast iron block. B & S: 3-1/4 in. x 4-3/8 in. Disp.: 217.8 cu. in. C.R.: (std.) 5.35:1; (opt.) 6.35:1. Brake H.P.: 79 @ 3400 R.P.M. Net H.P.: 25.35. Main bearings: Four. Valve lifters: Solid. Carb.: Carter 1V. Torque: 150 lbs.-ft. @ 1200 R.P.M. [Series DK] Inline. L-head. Eight. Cast iron block. B & S: 3-1/4 in. x 4-1/4 in. Disp.: 282.1 cu. in. C.R.: (std.) 5.2:1; (opt.) 6.2:1 with "Red Head" engine. Brake H.P.: (std.) 90 @ 3400 R.P.M.; (opt.) 100 @ 3400 R.P.M. Net H.P.: 33.8. Main bearings: Five. Valve lifters: Solid. Carb.: Stromberg 1V model DXR-3. Torque: (std.) 185 lbs.-ft. @ 1200 R.P.M.; (opt.) 195 lbs.-ft. @ 1200 R.P.M. [Series DM] Inline. L-head. Four. Cast iron block. B&S 3⅜ in. x 4¾ in. Disp.: 196.1 cu. in. Brake H.P.: 65 @ 3400 R.P.M.

CHASSIS: [Series DL] W.B.: 114-1/2 in. Tires: 18 x 5.50. [Series DK] W.B.: 122 in. Tires: 18 x 6.00. [Series DM] W.B.: 112 in.

TECHNICAL: Selective sliding transmission. Speeds: 3F/1R. Floor shift controls. Single plate dry disc clutch. Semi-floating rear axle. Overall Ratio: [DL] 4.6:1-4.3:1; [DK] 4.1:1. Hydraulic brakes. Wood-spoke or wire-spoke wheels. Drivetrain Options: Free-wheeling (std. on DK). Vacuum clutch (std. on DK).

OPTIONS: Front bumper. Rear bumper. Spare tire. Dual sidemounts. Metal sidemount covers. Chrome sidemount trim ring. Wire wheels (on DL Six). Radio. Heater. Clock. Cigar lighter. Radio antenna. Trunk rack. Touring trunk. Spotlight(s). Cowl lamps. Dual trumpet horns. Whitewall tires. OSRV mirror. Special paint. Dual windshield wipers. Right-hand taillight. Right-hand sun visor. Wheel trim rings.

HISTORICAL: Introduced: Jan. 1932. Calendar year registrations: 28,111. Calendar year production: 30,216. Model year production: 27,555. Innovations: Lower center of gravity. Free-wheeling. Vacuum operated automatic clutch. Double drop bridge frame. Silent gear transmission. "Floating Power" engine suspension. "Red Head" high compression engine. Dodge was America's seventh largest auto-maker in model year 1932. The company held eighth rank in sales for the calendar year. Shipments of Dodge DM's began in April and ended in December of 1932.

1932
Series DL, 6-cyl., 114.3" wb
(Introduced Jan. 1, 1932).

	FP	5	4	3	2	1
RS Conv	895	3900	7800	13,000	18,200	26,000
Bus Cpe	795	900	1900	4500	6300	9000
RS Cpe	835	1000	2400	5000	7000	10,000
Sed	845	825	1600	4000	5600	8000

Series DK, 8-cyl., 122" wb
(Introduced Jan. 1, 1932).

	FP	5	4	3	2	1
Conv	1220	4050	8100	13,500	18,900	27,000
Conv Sed	1395	4200	8400	14,000	19,600	28,000
RS Cpe	1115	1000	2400	5000	7000	10,000
5P Cpe	1145	950	2100	4750	6650	9500
Sed	1145	875	1700	4250	5900	8500

1933

1933 Dodge Six, Series DP, coupe, JAC

DODGE — SERIES DP — SIX: The all-new Series DP Dodge Six was introduced on Nov. 23, 1932 as a 1933 model. At this time, Series DK Dodge Eights were still being made and sold in Dodge showrooms, but they were considered 1932 models since the company had changed to an annual model year policy. The DP Six had front-opening doors which were popular at this time and were often called "suicide" doors. Other appearance characteristics included a V-type radiator which was slanted and slightly curved at the bottom, double interior sun visors, single bar front bumper (and rear bumper), fuller crowned fenders, chrome plated bowl type headlights, no cowl lamps and a generally more streamlined look. Standard equipment included Delco-Remy ignition, hydraulic brakes, "Floating Power" engine suspension, double drop "x" frame construction, free-wheeling, automatic vacuum clutch, tubular front axle, downdraft carburetor, air cleaner, safety glass windshield and Zerk chassis lubrication. Dodge DP Sixes built from Nov. 1932 to April 1933 had a 111-1/4 in. wheelbase. Those made after April 1933 had a 115 in. wheelbase. The two types of DP Sixes are considered separate series, although factory records combine the body style production totals of both.

DODGE — SERIES DO — EIGHT: The DO Series Dodge Eight entered production in Dec. 1932 for introduction Jan. 1, 1933. It was the last eight-cylinder Dodge product marketed before the outbreak of World War II. These luxurious cars rode a 122 in. wheelbase. Appearance characteristics included a sloping V-type radiator that curved forward at the bottom, "beaver-tail" rear body styling, single bar bumpers, vertical hood louvers, chrome plated bullet-shaped headlamps, a visor-less slanting windshield, dual chrome plated horns and front-hinged, rear opening door. Standard equipment included Delco-Remy ignition, hydraulic brakes, Tri-beam headlights, coincidental transmission lock, I-beam front axle, downdraft carburetor, "Floating Power" engine suspension, free-wheeling and a safety glass windshield.

1933 Dodge Six, Series DP, convertible coupe, JAC

DODGE — SERIES DP — SIX: The long wheelbase version of the Series DP Dodge Six was introduced on April 5, 1933. Other specifications were identical to the 1933 DP first series. The extra length of these cars was apparent in the design of the front sheet metal, particularly the forward edge of the hood where the space between the radiator and the louvers was increased. The runningboards and sill plates were also obviously longer. Otherwise the styling of the short and long wheelbase cars was identical. Prices were also unchanged. Factory records do not breakout the body style production figures for the two lines separately.

DODGE — SERIES DQ — SIX: Once again, Plymouth provided the base for Dodge to build this model. Differing from the DM of 1932, Plymouth now also supplied the body as well as the engine and chassis for this conversion for the Canadian and overseas markets. Each car was fitted with a Dodge-appearing grille and other various trim pieces to differentiate it from its Plymouth heritage.

1933 Dodge Six, Series DP, 4-dr. sedan, JAC

I.D. DATA: [Series DP] Serial numbers were located on a plate on the right front door hinge pillar post. Starting: 3579001. Ending: 3594421. Engine numbers located on left side of engine block just below cylinder head. Starting Engine No.: DP1001. Ending: DP17793. [Series DO] Serial numbers were in the same location. Starting: 4527001. Ending: 4528601. Engine numbers were in the same location. Starting Engine No.: DO1001. Ending: DO2649. [Series DP] Serial numbers were in the same locations. Starting: 3594422. Ending: 3680000. Engine numbers were in the same location. Starting Engine No.: DP17794. Ending: DP105429. Canadian built cars located serial number on right front door post. Starting: 9452951. Ending: 9455705. Engine numbers located on flat spot on left corner of block.

Model No.	Body Type & Seating	Price	Weight	Prod. Total
DP	2-dr. Bus. Cpe.-2P	595	2452	11,236
DP	2-dr. R/S Cpe.-2/4P	640	2506	8879
DP	2-dr. Conv. Cpe.-2/4P	695	2511	1563
DP	2-dr. Sed.-5P	630	2591	8523
DP	2-dr. Salon Brgm.-5P	660	2620	(4200)
DP	4-dr. Sed.-5P	675	2632	69,074
DP	2-dr. Del. Salon Brgm.-5P	775	2825	(4200)
DP	Chassis	NA	NA	980

Note 1: Production totals above are for both short and long wheelbase versions of the DP Six. Serial numbers indicate that approximately 15,420 short wheelbase cars were built.
Note 2: The production total in parenthesis represents the combined total (4200) for the Standard and Deluxe 2-dr. Salon Brougham. No further breakout is available.

DO	2-dr. R/S Cpe.-2/4P	1115	3451	212
DO	2-dr. Vic. Cpe.-5P	1145	3540	159
DO	2-dr. Conv. Cpe.-2/4P	1185	3465	56
DO	4-dr. Sed.-5P	1145	3580	1173
DO	4-dr. Conv. Sed.-5P	1395	3961	39
DO	Chassis	NA	NA	13

Note 1: Total series production was 1,652.

DP	2-dr. Bus. Cpe.-2P	595	2501	Note 1
DP	2-dr. R/S Cpe.-2/4P	640	2551	Note 1
DP	2-dr. Conv. Cpe.-2/4P	695	2556	Note 1
DP	2-dr. Sed.-5P	630	2591	Note 1
DP	4-dr. Sed.-5P	675	2661	Note 1
DP	2-dr. Salon Brgm.-5P	660	2651	Note 1
DP	Chassis	NA	NA	Note 1

Note 1: See production totals listed above for the 1933 DP first series. Serial numbers indicate that approximately 87,635 long wheelbase cars were built.

ENGINE: [Series DP] Inline. L-head. Six. Cast iron block. B & S: 3-1/8 in. x 4-3/8 in. Disp.: 201.3 cu. in. C.R.: (std.) 5.5:1; (opt.) 6.2:1. Brake H.P.: 75 @ 3600 R.P.M.; (opt.) 81 @ 3600 R.P.M. Net H.P.: 23.44. Main bearings: Four. Valve lifters: Solid. Carb.: Stromberg 1V model EX-22. Torque: (std.) 136 lbs.-ft. @ 1200 R.P.M.; (opt.) 144 lbs.-ft. @ 1200 R.P.M. [Series DO] Inline. L-head. Eight. Cast iron block. B & S: 3-1/4 in. x 4-1/4 in. Disp.: 282.1 cu. in. C.R.: (std.) 6.5:1; (opt.) 5.2:1. Brake H.P.: (std.) 100 @ 3400 R.P.M; (opt.) 94 @ 3400 R.P.M. Net H.P.: 33.8. Main bearings: Five. Valve lifters: Solid. Carb.: Ball & Ball 2V model E8A. Torque: (std.) 200 lbs.-ft. @ 1200 R.P.M.; (opt.) 184 lbs.-ft. @ 1200 R.P.M. [Series DP] Inline. L-head. Six. Cast iron block. B & S: 3-1/8 in. x 4-3/8 in. Disp.: 201.3 cu. in. C.R.: (std.) 5.5:1; (opt.) 6.2:1. Brake H.P.: (std.) 75 @ 3600 R.P.M.; (opt.) 81 @ 3600 R.P.M. Net H.P.: 23.44. Main bearings: Four. Valve lifters: Solid. Carb.: Stromberg 1V model EX-22. Torque: (std.) 136 lbs.-ft. @ 1200 R.P.M.; (opt.) 144 lbs.-ft. @ 1200 R.P.M. [Series DQ] Inline. L-head. Six. Cast iron block. B&S: 3-⅛ in. x 4-⅛ in. Disp.: 189.8 cu. in. Brake H.P.: 70 @ 3600 R.P.M.

CHASSIS: [Series DP] W.B.: 111-1/4 in. Tires: 16 x 6.00. [Series DO] W.B.: 122 in. Tires: 17 x 6.50. [Series DP] W.B.: 115 in. Tires: 16 x 6.00.

TECHNICAL: Selective sliding transmission. Speeds: 3F/1R. Floor shift controls. Single plate dry disc clutch. Semi-floating rear axle. Overall Ratio: 4.375:1. Hydraulic brakes. Artillery or wire-spoke wheels. Drivetrain options: Free-wheeling. Vacuum clutch.

OPTIONS: Front bumper. Rear bumper. Dual sidemounts. Metal sidemount cover(s). Chrome sidemount trim bands. Rear spare metal cover. Radio. Heater. Clock. Cigar lighter. Radio antenna. Trunk rack. Touring trunk. Spotlights. OSRV mirror. Dual chrome trumpet horns (std. on "DO" Eight). Built-in trunk. Dual taillights. Dual windshield wipers. Wind wings. License plate frames. Goodyear "Airwheel" tires. White stripe tires.

HISTORICAL: Introduced: [DP/SWB] 11/23/32; [DO] 1/1/33; [DP/LWB] 4/5/33. Calendar year registrations: 86,062. Calendar year production: 91,403. Model year production: 106,103. Innovations: Silent helicalgear transmissions. First 100 horsepower Dodge; most powerful model up to 1933. New long wheelbase Six. New pressed steel artillery spoke wheels. New six-cylinder engine. Dodge was America's fourth ranked auto-maker for model year 1933. A Dodge DP convertible competed in the 1933 Elgin Road Races. Numerous Dodge promotions including a "Hell Driver's" demonstration highlighted the Chrysler display at the 1933 "Century of Progress Exposition" in Chicago.

1933
Series DP, 6-cyl., 111.3" wb

	FP	5	4	3	2	1
RS Conv	695	3900	7800	13,000	18,200	26,000
Bus Cpe	595	825	1600	4000	5600	8000
RS Cpe	640	900	1900	4500	6300	9000
Sed	630	650	1250	2400	4200	6000
Brgm	660	675	1300	2500	4350	6200
DeL Brgm	775	700	1350	2800	4550	6500

NOTE: Second Series DP introduced April 5, 1933 increasing WB from 111" to 115" included in above.

Series DO, 8-cyl., 122" wb

RS Conv	1220	3750	7500	12,500	17,500	25,000
Conv Sed	1395	4050	8100	13,500	18,900	27,000
RS Cpe	1115	1000	2400	5000	7000	10,000
Cpe	1145	950	2100	4750	6650	9500
Sed	1395	900	1900	4500	6300	9000

1934

1934 Dodge Six, Series DR, 4-dr. sedan, OCW

DELUXE — SERIES DR — SIX: The 1934 Dodge was completely restyled to reflect a much more streamlined look. Appearance characteristics included a new V-type radiator, skirted front and rear fenders, multiple horizontal hood louvers of descending length, larger bullet-shaped chrome plated headlamps and a single-bar bumper with a flat dip in its center. Standard equipment included Delco-Remy ignition, hydraulic brakes, new independent front suspension, "Floating Power," X-type frame, new type ventilating system, steel spoke wheels, dual horns and a new "leaping ram" type hood ornament. Pinstriping highlighted the body feature lines of the DR Series Dodge Six. An optional high-compression engine featured an aluminum "Silver Dome" cylinder head. Also standard was "Duplate" safety glass windshields and the automatic vacuum clutch. These models were retroactively designated "DeLuxe Sixes" after the Standard Six was introduced in June. At this point, the design of the hood side panels was changed replacing the multiple louvers with four plainer louvers, as used on the Standard Six.

SPECIAL — SERIES DS — SIX: The DS sub-series was basically a long wheelbase version of the DR containing only two distinctive body styles. They were an aerodynamically-styled 4-door "slantback" sedan and a 4-door convertible sedan, also with a "slantback" body. These cars were known as Specials and had a 121 inch stance. Appearance features included the V-shaped radiator, skirted fenders, horizontal hood louvers, large chrome bullet-shaped headlights, dual trumpet horns and body pinstriping. As standard equipment, these cars had Delco-Remy ignition, hydraulic brakes, independent front suspension, X-type frame, the new seven point "Finger Touch" ventilation system with control on dash, "Floating Power" engine suspension and "Floating Cushion" wheels with Goodyear "Airwheel" tires. An automatic vacuum clutch and "Ouplate" safety glass were also featured. The 4-door Special Aerodynamic Brougham was also known as a close-coupled sedan.

STANDARD — SERIES DRXX — SIX: The 1934 Dodge DRXX series was introduced on June 2, 1934 to sell alongside the DR and DS models. These cars were part of a mid-season economy line designed to offer buyers cars with the same general appearance as Deluxe Sixes, but slightly less fea-

1934 Dodge Six, Series DRXX, 4-dr. sedan, JAC

tures. They did not have safety-type "Duplate" glass, or an automatic vacuum clutch or the ventilating body. Other characteristics of the two lines were practically the same, except most standard models had body colored radiator shells and no pinstriping (although both of these trim features were optional at slight extra cost). As mentioned earlier, the Standard Six introduced the plainer hood design with only four horizontal louvers.

DODGE — SERIES DT — SIX: Continuing the practice of providing Canadian and overseas Dodge dealers with a smaller, less expensive car to sell, Plymouth again supplied body, chassis and running gear for a junior series Dodge. Again, only minor trim differences were made to the basic Plymouth to make it look like a smaller Dodge.

I.D. DATA: [Series DR] Serial numbers were in the same location. Starting: 3680001. Ending: 3756367. Engine numbers were in the same location. Starting Engine No.: DR-1001. Ending: DR-95158. [Series DS] Serial numbers were in the same location. Starting: 4528651. Ending: 4530400. Engine numbers were in the same location. Starting Engine No.: DR1009 and up. [Series DRXX] Serial numbers were in the same location. Starting: 4000001. Ending: 4015004. Engine numbers were in the same location. Starting: DRXX-59585. Ending: DRXX-95861. Canadian-built cars located serial numbers on right front door post. Starting: 9455721. Ending: 9460020. Engine numbers were located on that spot on left front corner of block.

Model No.	Body Type & Seating	Price	Weight	Prod. Total
DR	2-dr. Bus. Cpe.-2P	665	2695	8723
DR	2-dr. R/S Cpe.-2/4P	715	2745	5323
DR	2-dr. Conv. Cpe.-2/4P	765	2725	1239
DR	2-dr. Sed.-5P	715	2855	7308
DR	4-dr. Sed.-5P	765	2940	53,479
DR	4-dr. Sed.-7P	NA	NA	710
DR	Chassis	NA	NA	1475

Note 1: Total series production was 78,257.

DS	4-dr. Spl. Aero. Brgm.-5P	845	2905	1397
DS	4-dr. Spl. Aero. Conv. Sed.-5P	875	2915	350
DS	Chassis	NA	NA	3

Note: Total series production was 1750.

DRXX	2-dr. Bus. Cpe.-2P	645	2695	2284
DRXX	2-dr. R/S Cpe.-2/4P	690	2745	105
DRXX	2-dr. Conv. Cpe.-2/4P	745	2845	NA
DRXX	2-dr. Sed.-5P	695	2855	3133
DRXX	4-dr. Sed.-5P	745	2940	9481
DRXX	Chassis	NA	NA	1

Note 1: Total series production (excluding Convertible Coupe) was 15,004.
Note 2: Convertible Coupe production is not included in available factory records; possibly none were built.

ENGINE: [Series DR] Inline. L-head. Six. Cast iron block. B & S: 3-1/4 in. x 4-3/8 in. Disp.: 217.8 cu. in. C.R.: (Std.) 5.6:1; (Opt.) 6.5:1. Brake H.P.: (Std.) 82 @ 3600 R.P.M.: (Opt.) 87 @ 3600 R.P.M. Net H.P.: 25.35. Main bearings: Four. Valve lifters: Solid. Carb.: Stromberg 1V model EX-22. Torque: (Std.) 150 lbs.-ft. @ 1200 R.P.M.; (Opt.) 160 lbs.-ft. @ 1200 R.P.M. [Series DS] Inline. L-head. Six. Cast iron block. B & S: 3-1/4 in. x 4-3/8 in. Disp.: 217.8 cu. in. C.R.: 6.5:1. Brake H.P.: 87 @ 3600 R.P.M. Net H.P.: 25.35. Main bearings: Four. Valve lifters: Solid. Carb.: Stromberg 1V model EX-22. Torque: 160 lbs.-ft. @ 1200 R.P.M. [Series DRXX] Inline. L-head. Six. Cast iron block. B & S: 3-1/4 in. x 4-3/8 in. Disp.: 217.8 cu. in. C.R.: 5.6:1. Brake H.P.: 82 @ 3600 R.P.M. Net H.P.: 25.35. Main bearings: Four. Valve lifters: Solid. Carb.: Stromberg 1V model EX-22. Torque: 150 lbs.-ft. @ 1200 R.P.M. [Series DT] Inline. L-head. Six. Cast iron block, B&S: 3-1/8 in. x 4-3/8 in. Disp.: 201 cu. in. Brake H.P.: 77 @ 3600 R.P.M.

CHASSIS: [Deluxe Six] W.B.: 117 in. Tires: 16 x 6.25. [Special Six] W.B.: 121 in. Tires: 16 x 6.25. [Std. Six] W.B.: 117 in. Tires: 16 x 6.25.

TECHNICAL: Selective sliding transmission. Speeds: 3F/1R. Floor shift controls. Single plate dry disc clutch. Semi-floating rear axle. Overall Ratio: [DR] 3.8:1 or 5.1:1; [DS] 3.4:1 or 5.1:1; [DRXX] 3.8:1 or 5.1:1. Hydraulic brakes. "Floating Cushion" steel spoke wheels. Drivetrain Options: Vacuum clutch (Std. on Deluxe and Special). Overdrive.

1934 Dodge Six, Series DS, aero brougham, JAC

OPTIONS: Front bumper. Rear bumper. Dual sidemount(s). Metal sidemount cover(s). Wire spoke wheels. Bumper guards. Radio. Heater. Clock. Cigar lighter. Radio antenna. Seat covers. OSRV mirror(s). Spotlight(s). Chrome plated radiator shell (on Standard). Metal spare tire cover. Body pinstriping (on Std. Six). Wind wings (open models). License plate frame. Special paint.

HISTORICAL: Introduced: [DR/DS] Jan. 2, 1934; [DRXX] June 2, 1934. Calendar year registrations: 90,139. Calendar year production: 108,687. Model year production: 95,011. Innovations: Synchronized front and rear springs. Larger, improved brake drums. "Draft Free" body ventilation. First automatic overdrive. Independent front suspension.
Dodge was America's 4th ranked auto-maker in model year 1934. This was the year that Dodge began promoting "showdowns." These comparison tests with contemporary cars were highlighted in many film strips produced by Chrysler's advertising agency Ross Roy. This technique is still used to sell Dodge products today. Production of the DR/DS Series started in Jan. 1934 and ended the following November.

1934
DeLuxe Series DR, 6-cyl., 117" wb

	FP	5	4	3	2	1
RS Conv	765	3600	7200	12,000	16,800	24,000
Bus Cpe	665	825	1600	4000	5600	8000
RS Cpe	715	875	1700	4250	5900	8500
2 dr Sed	715	650	1250	2400	4150	5900
Sed	765	600	1200	2300	4000	5700

Series DS, 6-cyl., 121" wb

Conv Sed	875	3750	7500	12,500	17,500	25,000
Brgm	845	750	1450	3300	4900	7000

DeLuxe Series DRXX, 6-cyl., 117" wb
(Introduced June 2, 1934).

Conv	745	3600	7200	12,000	16,800	24,000
Bus Cpe	645	825	1600	4000	5600	8000
Cpe	690	875	1700	4250	5900	8500
2 dr Sed	695	600	1200	2200	3850	5500
Sed	745	600	1200	2200	3850	5500

1935

1935 Dodge Six, Series DU, convertible coupe, JAC

NEW VALUE — SERIES DU — SIX: Dodge's "New Value" line for 1935 was totally restyled. Appearance characteristics included a narrower, more sloping radiator grille, horizontal "Wind Stream" hood louvers, all-steel bodies that extended down to the runningboards, lower rooflines, a 3-3/4 inch lower floor, a more fastback rear body treatment and parking lamps mounted on the front fender aprons. The new "humpback" touring sedans were advertised as "Century" sedans. Standard equipment included Autolite ignition, hydraulic brakes, ventilated clutch, "Floating Power," automatic choke, leaf spring front suspension, concealed radiator cap, "Finger Tip" steering, "Air-Glide" ride and a crank-open windshield. The engine was moved eight inches forward in the chassis this season and the seats were also moved forward for better weight distribution. Two models, the Caravan sedan and 7-passenger sedan, had a foot longer wheelbase and correspondingly longer bodies

1935 Dodge Six, Series DU, touring sedan, OCW

DODGE — SERIES DV & DV-6 — SIX: This was once again a Plymouth-based small Dodge for the Canadian and overseas export markets. While full production figures are unknown, 1170 right-hand-drive DV's were built in Detroit for export. In Canada the DV was sold in two trim levels, the DV or standard, and the DV-6 or Deluxe. Again, only minor trim differences were made to the Plymouth to make it look like a Dodge.

I.D. DATA: Serial numbers were in the same location. Starting: 3756501. Ending: 3913106. Engine numbers were in the same location. Starting Engine No.: DU-1011. Ending: DU-159821. Canadian-built cars located serial numbers on right front door post. DV starting: 9460021. DV ending: 9464305. DV-6 starting: 9316226. DV-6 ending: 9316895. Engine numbers were located on left from corner of block.

Model No.	Body Type & Seating	Price	Weight	Prod. Total
DU	2-dr. Bus. Cpe.-2P	645	2731	17,800
DU	2-dr. R/S Cpe.-2/4P	710	2801	4499
DU	2-dr. Conv. Cpe.-2/4P	770	2883	950
DU	2-dr. Sed.-5P	690	2821	7891
DU	2-dr. Tr. Sed.-5P	715	2868	18,069
DU	4-dr. Sed.-5P	735	2861	33,118
DU	4-dr. Tr. Sed.-5P	760	2903	74,203
(Long Wheelbase)				
DU	4-dr. Caravan Sed.-5P	995	3118	193
DU	4-dr. Sed.-7P	995	3221	1018
DU	Chassis	NA	NA	1258

Note 1: Total series production was 158,999.

DV	Bus. Cpe.2-P	755	2745	
DV	2-dr. Sed.-5P	810	2795	
DV-6	Bus. Cpe.-2P	770	NA	
DV-6	R/S Cpe.-4P	840	2840	
DV-6	2-dr. Sed.-5P	835	NA	
DV-6	2-dr. Tr. Sed.-5P	880	2865	
DV-6	4-dr. Sed.-5P	880	2875	
DV-6	4-dr. Tr. Sed.-5P	910	2910	

Note: Prices shown in 1935 Canadian dollars.

ENGINE: Inline. L-head. Six. Cast iron block. B & S: 3-1/4 in. x 4-3/8 in. in. Disp.: 217.8 cu. in. C.R.: 6.5:1. Brake H.P.: 87 @ 3600 R.P.M. Net H.P.: 25.35. Main bearings: Four. Valve lifters: Solid. Carb.: Stromberg 1V model EX-22. Torque: 155 lbs.-ft. @ 1200 R.P.M. [Series DV & DV-6] Inline. L-head. Six. Cast iron block. B&S: 3-⅛ in. x 4-⅜ in. Disp.: 201 cu. in. Brake H.P.: 82 @ 3600 R.P.M.

CHASSIS: [Standard DU] W.B.: 116 in. Tires: 16 x 6.00. [Long Wheelbase DU] W.B.: 128 in. Tires: 16 x 6.00. [Series DV & DV-6] W.B.: 113 in. Tires: 5.25 x 17 standard, 6.00 x 16 deluxe.

TECHNICAL: Selective sliding transmission. Speeds: 3F/1R. Floor shift controls. Single plate dry disc clutch. Semi-floating rear axle. Overall Ratio: 4.7:1. Hydraulic brakes. Steelspoke wheels. Drivetrain Options: Vacuum clutch. Overdrive.

OPTIONS: Front bumper. Rear bumper. Dual sidemounts. Metal sidemount cover(s). Wheel trim rings. Bumper guards. Radio. Heater. Clock. Cigar lighter. Radio antenna. Dual windshield wipers. Spotlight(s). OSRV mirror. Trunk rack. Touring trunk. Police equipment package. Licence plate frames. Special paint.

HISTORICAL: Introduced: Jan. 2, 1935. Calendar year registrations: 178,770. Calendar year production: 211,752. Model year production: 158,999. Innovations: Synchromatic gear shift control. Easier front steering. Leaf springs replace coil springs in front suspension. Sliding window replace pivot type vent windows. High strength carbon molybdenum steel used for chassis parts. Dodge slipped on place to 5th position in U.S. model year production for 1935. The three millionth Dodge in history was built this year. Abram VanderZee was general sales manager of Dodge Division of Chrysler Corp. A number of wood-bodied Westchester Suburban station wagons were constructed on Dodge chassis by U.S. Body & Forging Co. of Tell City, Ind. Production of 1935 Dodges started in Nov., 1934 and ended in Sept., 1935.

1935
Series DU, 6-cyl., 116" wb - 128" wb, (*)

	FP	5	4	3	2	1
RS Conv	770	3800	7650	12,750	17,850	25,500
Cpe	645	850	1650	4150	5800	8300
RS Cpe	710	900	1800	4400	6150	8800
2 dr Sed	690	675	1300	2500	4300	6100
2 dr Tr Sed	715	675	1300	2500	4350	6200
Sed	735	675	1300	2600	4400	6300
Tr Sed	760	700	1350	2700	4500	6400
Car Sed (*)	995	800	1550	3900	5450	7800
7P Sed (*)	995	850	1650	4150	5800	8300

1936

1936 Dodge Six, Series D-2, touring sedan, JAC

BEAUTY WINNER — SERIES D-2 — SIX: Dodge's new "Beauty Winner' Six line entered production in Sept., 1935. Styling characteristics included a more rounded, but slightly convex radiator grille with four horizontal bars on each side, twin rows of transverse hood louvers with five chrome horizontal stripes, built-in horn housings below the torpedo-shaped headlamps and an all steel top that blended smoothly into the roof surface and also was wired for a radio antenna. Only one long wheelbase car, the seven-passenger sedan, remained in the D-2 series. Standard equipment included Autolite ignition, hydraulic brakes, a built-in foot rest in the rear compartment, "Silent" front spring shackles and a new instrument panel design with a large, airplane type speedometer in the center and horizontal chrome moldings. Dodge headlight buckets were now finished in body color with chrome trim rings. Chair height seats were used inside the cars, which also featured more interior space. A 4-door convertible sedan reappeared in the Dodge line this year and the U.S. Body & Forging Co. continued to build Westchester Suburban station wagons on Dodge chassis. These wood-bodied wagons had fabric roof inserts and snap-on canvas side curtains at the rear of the body. Also available from the factory was a new "Commercial" sedan which represented a cross between a passenger car and a sedan delivery truck.

DODGE — SERIES D-3 & D-4 — SIX: Advertised as "The Money Saving Dodge," the D-3 standard and D-4 deluxe Dodges were once again based on the 1936 Plymouth P-1 and P-2 series cars. Built for export and the Canadian market, these "junior" Dodges put Dodge in the low-priced field in their respective selling markets. These cars varied only in grille and trim differences from the Plymouths upon which they were based, with Plymouth again supplying the engine, drivetrain and body for the conversion. These models were built in the United States for export and in the Windsor, Ontario plant for Canadian consumption. Almost 3,100 D-3's were built in Detroit for export, with 36 cars being shipped with a small bore (2-⅞ in.) export engine and right-hand drive.

I.D. DATA: Serial numbers were in the same locations. Starting: 4015051. Ending: 4276687. Engine numbers were in the same locations. Starting Engine No.: D2-1001. Ending: D2-266089. Canadian-built cars: [D-3] Starting: 9316901. Ending: 9318219. [D-4] Starting 9464311. Ending: 9469955.

1936 Dodge Six, Series D-2, touring sedan, OCW

457

Model No.	Body Type & Seating	Price	Weight	Prod. Total
D2	2-dr. Bus. Cpe.-2P	640	2773	32,952
D2	2-dr. R/S Cpe.-2/4P	695	2823	4317
D2	2-dr. Conv. Cpe.-2/4P	795	2887	1525
D2	2-dr. Sed.-5P	695	2903	2453
D2	2-dr. Tr. Sed.-5P	720	2893	37,468
D2	4-dr. Sed.-5P	735	2923	5996
D2	4-dr. Tr. Sed.-5P	760	2958	174,334
D2	4-dr. Conv. Sed.-5P	995	3018	750
D2	4-dr. Sed.-7P	975	3238	1942
D2	Chassis	NA	NA	1910
D2	4-dr. Comm. Sed.	665	1935	1358

Note 1: Total series production was 265,005.

Model No.	Body Type & Seating	Price	Weight
D3	Bus. Cpe.-2P	730	2770
D3	2-dr. Sed.-5P	785	2840
D3	4-dr. Sed.-5P	825	2890
D3	2-dr. Tr. Sed.-5P	815	2850
D3	4-dr. Tr. Sed.-5P	855	2920
D3	Sed. Del.	800	2890
D4	Bus. Cpe.-2P	775	2805
D4	R/S Cpe.-4P	830	2890
D4	R/S Conv.-4P	965	2960
D4	2-dr. Tr. Sed.-5P	860	2920
D4	4-dr. Tr. Sed.-5P	900	2980

Note: Prices shown in 1936 Canadian dollars.

ENGINE: Inline. L-head. Six. Cast iron block. B & S: 3-1/4 in. x 4-3/8 in. Disp.: 217.8 cu. in. C.R.: 6.5:1. Brake H.P.: 87 @ 3600 R.P.M. Net H.P.: 25.35. Main bearings: Four. Valve lifters: Solid. Carb.: Stromberg 1V model EXV-2. Torque: 155 lbs.-ft. @ 1200 R.P.M. [Series D-3 & D-4] Inline. L-head. Six. Cast iron block. B&S: 3-⅛ in. x 4-⅜ in. Disp.: 201 cu.in. Brake H.P.: 82 @ 3600 R.P.M.

CHASSIS: [Regular Chassis] W.B.: 116 in. Tires: 16 x 6.00. [Extended Chassis] W.B.: 128 in. Tires: 16 x 6.00. [Series D-3 & D-4] W.B.: 113 in. Tires: D-3 5.50 x 17, D-4 6.00 x 16.

TECHNICAL: Selective sliding transmission. Speeds: 3F/1R. Floor shift controls. Single plate dry disc clutch. Semi-floating rear axle. Overall Ratio: 4.125:1 or 3.88:1. Hydraulic brakes. Steel artillery spoke wheels. Drivetrain Options: Vacuum clutch. Overdrive.

OPTIONS: Front bumper. Rear bumper. Single sidemount (comm. Sed.). Dual sidemounts. Metal sidemount cover(s). Fender skirts. Bumper guards. Radio. Heater. Clock. Cigar lighter. Radio antenna. Seat covers. Dual windshield wipers. Spotlights. Chrome wheel beauty trim rings. OSRV mirror. Chrome license plate frames. Whitewall tires. Metal spare tire cover. Special paint.

HISTORICAL: Introduced: Nov. 2, 1935. Calendar year registrations: 248,518. Calendar year production: 274,904. Model year production: 263,647. Innovations: All-steel top construction wired for radio antenna. New Commercial Sedan introduced. Silent front spring shackles.
  Dodge battled its way back into 4th place in U.S. model year production for 1936. Although Dodge did not produce Airflow passenger cars, the company manufactured 112 distinctive Airflow trucks between Jan., 1935 and Dec., 1936. For more information on Dodge trucks consult Krause Publication's *Encyclopedia of Commercial Vehicles*. Production of 1936 models ended in Aug. of that year.

1936
Series D2, 6-cyl., 116" wb - 128" wb, (*)

	FP	5	4	3	2	1
RS Conv	795	3800	7650	12,750	17,850	25,500
Conv Sed	995	4000	7950	13,250	18,550	26,500
2P Cpe	640	800	1550	3900	5450	7800
RS Cpe	695	900	1800	4400	6150	8800
2 dr Sed	695	725	1400	3100	4800	6800
2 dr Tr Sed	720	750	1450	3300	4900	7000
Sed	735	725	1400	3200	4850	6900
Tr Sed	760	750	1450	3400	5000	7100
7P Sed (*)	975	775	1500	3600	5100	7300

1937

1937 Dodge Six, Series D-5, touring sedan, OCW

DODGE — SERIES D5 — SIX: For 1937, the Dodge styling theme was patterned after that of other Chrysler products. A new split grille featured several vertical chrome moldings running down the center which were paralleled by wider body colored panels. The grilles, on either side, had multiple, chrome plated, horizontal strips. Larger, more deeply crowned, bullet-shaped headlamps were mounted on either side of the grille. There were no longer any horn parts in the fender aprons, the horns being moved into a new behind-the-grille location. A chrome drip molding now extended the full length of the all-steel body on all models and door handles were curved inward for safety. Hood louvers were again of a transverse design, but had slightly fewer vents and chrome moldings. Standard equipment included Autolite ignition, hydraulic brakes, all-steel disc wheels, "No-Draft" ventilation, reading lamps over rear windows (in lieu of dome lamps), ventipane type windows, new 16-gallon fuel tanks, dual taillamps, divided rear windows on all sedans and single windshield wipers. A new hypoid rear axle allowed a flat floor in the rear compartment as well as a lower driveshaft tunnel. Interior safety was emphasized this year with the introduction of non-snag door handles, recessed dash knobs and flush-mounted gauges. Built-in defroster vents were another new Dodge feature.

DODGE — SERIES D6 & D7 — SIX: The junior Dodge was once again Plymouth based, the D6 corresponding to the P3 business line with the D7 in deluxe trim like the P4 Plymouth. Plymouth once again supplied the engine, chassis and body, with Dodge supplying the grille and other corporate identity items. Detroit-built conversions were shipped overseas to the tune of better than 7,000 cars, including 39 fitted with a small-bore (2-⅞ in.) export engine. These cars were shipped both completed and knocked-down for overseas final assembly. Total Canadian production is uncertain.

I.D. DATA: Serial numbers were in the same location. (Detroit factory) Starting: 4530451. Ending: 4789907. (Evansville, Ind. factory) Starting: 9118501. Ending: 9149361. Engine numbers were in the same location. Starting Engine No.: D5-1001. Ending: D5-295935. (Canadian-built cars) D6 Starting 9318226 and 9387361. D6 Ending 9319000 and 9388420. D7 Starting: 9469961. D7 Ending 9478110.

Model No.	Body Type & Seating	Price	Weight	Prod. Total
D5	2-dr. Bus. Cpe.-2P	715	2902	41,702
D5	2-dr. R/S Cpe.-2/4P	770	2967	3500
D5	2-dr. Conv. Cpe.-2/4P	910	3057	1345
D5	2-dr. FsBk. Sed.-5P	780	2992	5302
D5	2-dr. Tr. Sed.-5P	790	2997	44,750
D5	4-dr. FsBk. Sed.-5P	820	2982	7555
D5	4-dr. Tr. Sed.-5P	830	2997	185,483
D5	4-dr. Conv. Sed.-5P	1230	3262	473
(Long Wheelbase)				
D5	4-dr. Sed.-7P	1075	3367	2207
D5	4-dr. Limo.-5P	1175	NA	216
D5	Chassis	NA	NA	2514
D5	2-dr. Murray Conv. Vic.-5P	NA	NA	(Chassis)
D6	Bus. Cpe.-2P	720	2850	
D6	2-dr. Sed.-5P	775	2880	
D6	4-dr. Sed.-5P	820	2930	
D6	2-dr. Tr. Sed.-5P	795	2895	
D6	4-dr. Tr. Sed.-5P	840	2950	
D7	Bus. Cpe.-2P	760	2895	
D7	R/S Cpe.-4P	820	2995	
D7	2-dr. Tr. Sed.-5P	850	2970	
D7	4-dr. Tr. Sed.-5P	890	2975	

Note: Prices shown in 1937 Canadian dollars.

Note 1: Total series production was 295,047.
Note 2: The custom-built Murray Convertible Victoria was constructed on the Dodge chassis by Murray Body Corp. This car was first used by engineering executive Fred Zeder and later used by Dean Clark, a Chrysler designer who worked in the Art & Colour Studio.

ENGINE: Inline. L-head. Six. Cast iron block. B & S: 3-1/4 in. x 4-3/8 in. Disp.: 217.8 cu. in. C.R.: 6.5:1. Brake H.P.: 87 @ 3600 R.P.M. Net H.P.: 25.35. Main bearings: Four. Valve lifters: Solid. Carb.: Stromberg 1V model EXV-2. Torque: 155 lbs.-ft. @ 1200 R.P.M. [Series D6 & D7] Inline. L-head. Six. Cast iron block. B&S: 3-⅛ in. x 4-⅜ in. Disp.: 201 cu.in. Brake H.P.: 82 @ 3600 R.P.M.

CHASSIS: [Series D5; regular chassis] W.B.: 115 in. Tires: 6.00 x 16. [Series DS, extended chassis] W.B.: 132 in. Tires: 6.50 x 16. [Series D6 & D7] W.B. 112 in. Tires: D6 5.50 x 16; D7 6.00 x 16.

TECHNICAL: Selective sliding transmission. Speeds: 3F/1R. Floor shift controls. Single plate dry disc clutch. Hypoid rear axle. Overall Ratio: 4.1:1; (Coupes) 3.9:1. Hydraulic brakes. Steel disc wheels. Drivetrain Options: Vacuum clutch. Overdrive.

OPTIONS: Front bumper. Rear bumper. Chrome wheel beauty trim rings. Dual sidemounts (Westchester Suburban). Metal sidemount covers. Fender skirts. Bumper guards. Radio. Heater. Clock. Cigar lighter. Radio antenna. Seat covers. OSRV mirror. Spotlights. Whitewall tires. Chrome license plate frames. Dual windshield wipers. Special paint.

HISTORICAL: Introduced: Oct. 1936. Calendar year registrations: 255,258. Calendar year production: 288,841. Model year production: 295,047. Innovations: First in auto industry to feature fully-insulated rubber body mountings. Safety padding on front seatbacks. Steel disc wheels made standard equipment. Safety recessed door handles and gauges. Hypoid rear axles. Longer wheelbase on extended chassis models.
  Dodge remained America's fourth largest auto-maker in model year 1937. The wood-bodied Westchester Suburban was again available for the Dodge chassis this season. Actor Clark Gable owned a 1937 Dodge Westchester Suburban fitted with dual sidemounted spares and twin spotlights. Production of 1937 models started in Sept. 1936 and ended in Aug. 1937.

1937
Series D5, 6-cyl., 115" wb - 132" wb, (*)

	FP	5	4	3	2	1
RS Conv	910	3350	6750	11,250	15,750	22,500
Conv Sed	1230	3500	7050	11,750	16,450	23,500
Bus Cpe	715	850	1650	4150	5800	8300
RS Cpe	770	900	1800	4400	6150	8800
2 dr Sed	780	650	1200	2300	4100	5800
2 dr Tr Sed	790	650	1250	2400	4200	6000
Sed	820	675	1300	2500	4300	6100
Tr Sed	830	675	1300	2600	4400	6300
7P Sed (*)	1075	775	1500	3600	5100	7300
Limo (*)	1175	775	1500	3750	5250	7500

1938

1938 Dodge Six, Series D8, touring sedan, AA

1938 Dodge Six, Series D8, 2-dr. sedan, JAC

DODGE — SERIES D8 — SIX: The 1938 Dodge was mildly facelifted from 1937. The new radiator grille had narrower stripes down the center, with narrower horizontal bars on either side. These bars harmonized with the new, horizontal hood louvers. The headlamps were moved on top of the fenders. A Dodge Bros. type emblem was again used on the grille, but this would be the last time for such identification. A leaping ram hood ornament was on top of the nose of the cars. The factory offered ten body styles, with the seven-passenger sedan and division window limousine on a lengthened wheelbase. New 1938 features were all-steel, "silent-safety" body construction with insulated roofs, rear quarters, body, cowl and door panels and adjustable seats with a lever at the driver's left hand. Standard equipment included Autolite ignition, hydraulic brakes, single windshield wipers, dual taillights, improved engine mountings, self-lubricating clutch and 16-gallon fuel tank. The limousine again had a leather front seat, velvet mohair rear seat and division window between the driver's and passengers' compartment. The 7-passenger sedan had a pair of folding jump seats in the passengers' compartment.

DODGE — SERIES D9 & D10 DELUXE — SIX: Dodge juniors this year were based on the Plymouth P5 and P6 models. Again, Plymouth supplied body, chassis and drivetrain while Dodge supplied the grille and other identity items. Conversions were built in both the U.S. (for export) and in Windsor (for the Canadian market). Only the D9 was built in the U.S., with nearly 7,500 units shipped, 81 with the small-bore (2-7/8 in.) engine; 4,285 of these had right-hand drive as well. Canadian production came to over 10,000 units.
I.D. DATA: Serial numbers were in the same location. (Detroit) Starting: 3001001. Ending: 30097065. (Evansville) Starting: 4001001. Ending: 4001625. Engine numbers were in the same location. Starting Engine No.: D8-1001. Ending: D8-114530. (Canada) D9 Starting: 9388426. Ending: 9390904. D10 Starting: 9478116. Ending: 9486415.

Model No.	Body Type & Seating	Price	Weight	Prod. Total
D8	2-dr. Bus. Cpe.-2P	808	2877	15,552
D8	2-dr. R/S Cpe.-2/4P	858	2952	950
D8	2-dr. Conv. Cpe.-2/4P	960	3122	701
D8	2-dr. FsBk. Sed.-5P	858	2977	999
D8	2-dr. Tr. Sed.-5P	870	2957	17,282
D8	4-dr. FsBk. Sed.-5P	898	2977	714
D8	4-dr. Tr. Sed.-5P	910	2967	73,417
D8	4-dr. Conv. Sed.-5P	1275	3308	132
(Long Wheelbase)				
D8	4-dr. Tr. Sed.-7P	1095	3332	1953
D8	4-dr. Limo.-5P	1185	3380	153
D8	Chassis	NA	NA	2301
(Semi-Custom)				
D8	4-dr. W'chest. Sub.-7P	1028	3200	375
Note 1: Total series production was 114,529				
D9	Bus. Cpe.-2P	850	2875	
D9	2-dr. Sed.-5P	913	2915	
D9	2-dr. Tr. Sed.-5P	928	2925	
D9	4-dr. Sed.-5P	960	2950	
D9	4-dr. Tr. Sed.-5P	975	2955	
D10	Bus. Cpe.-2P	915	2925	
D10	R/S Cpe.-4P	964	3005	
D10	2-dr. Sed.-5P	966	3005	
D10	2-dr. Tr. Sed.-5P	981	3020	
D10	4-dr. Sed.-5P	1003	3000	
D10	4-dr. Tr. Sed.-5P	1018	3035	

Note: Prices given in 1938 Canadian dollars.

ENGINE: Inline. L-head. Six. Cast iron block. B & S: 3-1/4 in. x 4-3/8 in. Disp.: 217.8 cu. in. C.R.: 6.5:1. Brake H.P.: 87 @ 3600 R.P.M. Net H.P.: 25.35. Main bearings: Four. Valve lifters: Solid. Carb.: Stromberg 1V model EXV-2. Torque: 155 lbs.-ft. @ 1200 R.P.M. [Series D9 & D10] Inline. L-head. Six. Cast iron block. B&S: 3-1/8 in. x 4-3/4 in. Disp.: 201 cu. in. Brake H.P.: 82 @ 3600 R.P.M.

CHASSIS: [D8; reg. chassis] W.B.: 115 in. Tires: 6.00 x 16. [Series D8; extended chassis] W.B.: 132 in. Tires: 6.50 x 16. [Series D9 & D10] W.B.: 112 in.

TECHNICAL: Selective sliding transmission. Speeds: 3F/1R. Floor shift controls. Single plate dry disc clutch. Hypoid rear axle. Overall Ratio: [Sed.] 4.1:1; [Cpe.] 3.9:1; [opt.] 4.3:1. Hydraulic brakes. Steel disc wheels. Drivetrain Options: Vacuum clutch. Overdrive.

OPTIONS: Front bumper. Rear bumper. Single sidemount (sta. wag.). Metal sidemount cover (sta. wag.). Fender skirts. Bumper guards. Radio. Heater. Clock. Cigar lighter. Radio antenna. Seat covers. Dual windshield wipers. Spotlight(s). Whitewall tires. Chrome wheel beauty trim rings. Master grille guard. Chrome license plate frames. Special paint. OSRV mirror.

1938 Dodge Six, Series D9, 4-dr. sedan, JB

HISTORICAL: Introduced: Oct., 1937. Calendar year registrations: 104,881. Calendar year production: 106,370. Model year production: 114,529. Innovations: Improved body insulation. Parking brake mounted on cowl to right of driver. Longer life engine mountings. Larger, self-lubricating clutch bearing. Rubber windshield mountings without metal frames. Dodge placed fifth in model year production during this recession year. The company continued to build Airflow type heavy trucks this season and introduced a new Route Van type truck. A new Dodge truck factory was opened in Detroit, Mich. Production of 1938 models began in Sept., 1937 and ended in July, 1938.

1938
Series D8, 6-cyl., 115" wb - 132" wb, (*)

	FP	5	4	3	2	1
Conv Cpe	960	3350	6750	11,250	15,750	22,500
Conv Sed	1275	3500	7050	11,750	16,450	23,500
Bus Cpe	808	775	1500	3600	5100	7300
Cpe 2-4	858	800	1550	3900	5450	7800
2 dr Sed	858	650	1250	2400	4200	6000
2 dr Tr Sed	870	675	1300	2500	4350	6200
Sed	898	700	1350	2700	4500	6400
Tr Sed	910	700	1350	2900	4600	6600
Sta Wag	—	900	1800	4400	6150	8800
7P Sed (*)	1095	775	1500	3700	5200	7400
Limo	1185	800	1550	3900	5450	7800

459

1939

1939 Dodge, Deluxe Six, Series D11, 4-dr. sedan, OCW

LUXURY LINER — SERIES D11 — SIX: Heralding the 25th anniversary of the Dodge nameplate were ten cars featuring all-new styling. There were three cars in the low-priced Special sub-series and seven in the Deluxe line. Two of the Deluxe models were on the extended length chassis, which now had a 134 inch wheelbase. The regular chassis also grew about two inches. Appearance characteristics of these "Luxury Liners" included a rounded hood with narrow, horizontal grille bars in the nose, near the top center. Below this were larger grilles (with horizontal bars) in the fender splash aprons, divided by a "V" extending up to the sides of the hood. The all-new bodies were longer and wider, with the door bottoms flared outward. Headlamps were fully recessed into the front fenders. Each side of the hood had two groupings of short, horizontal louvers with one group at the front and the other at the rear. New features included a "Remote Control" gearshift mounted on the steering column and independent front suspension with coil springs. Two-piece split windshields were used and a new "Safety Light" speedometer had a lighted bead that glowed different colors depending on car speed. Standard equipment included Autolite ignition, hydraulic brakes, dual taillights, door safety buttons on garnish moldings, 18-gallon fuel tank, steel disc wheels and No-Draft ventilation. A special turret-top coupe with a rear "split window" look was built by the Hayes Body Corp. and known as the Town Coupe.

1939 Dodge Six, Series D12, coupe, JB

DODGE — SERIES D12 & D13 DELUXE — SIX: Continuing the practice of offering a junior series Dodge in the Canadian and export markets, Plymouth again supplied body, chassis and running gear to Dodge. A Dodge grille and trim gave the cars separate identity. Export junior Dodges were again built in the U.S. while Windsor built conversions mainly for the Canadian marketplace. Nearly 6,800 D12 Sixes of U.S. origin were sold, 3,438 were right-hand drive, 38 fitted with the small-bore (2-⅞ in.) export engine; 2,924 were shipped as built-up units, the remaining 3,885 as CKD (completely knocked down) units for final overseas assembly. Windsor accounted for an additional 10,328 units for the Canadian trade.

I.D. DATA: Serial numbers were in the same location. Starting: (Spl.) 4276701; (Del.) 30100001. Ending: (Spl.) 4347700; (Del.) 30214458. Engine numbers were in the same location. Starting Engine No.: (Spl.) D11-1001; (Del.) D11-1001. Ending: (Spl.) D11-186148; (Del.) D11-186527. (Canada) D12 Starting: 9390906. Ending: 9393277. D13 Starting: 9486416. Ending: 9494715.

Model No.	Body Type & Seating	Price	Weight	Prod. Total
Special				
D11	2-dr. Bus. Cpe.-2P	756	2905	12,300
D11	2-dr. Sed.-5P	815	2955	26,700
D11	4-dr. Sed.-5P	855	2995	32,000
Deluxe				
D11	2-dr. Bus. Cpe.-2P	803	2940	Note 2
D11	2-dr. A/S Cpe.-2/4P	860	2985	Note 2
D11	2-dr. Twn. Cpe.-5P	1055	3075	602
D11	2-dr. Sed.-5P	865	3010	Note 2
D11	4-dr. Sed.-5P	905	3045	Note 2
Deluxe Long Wheelbase				
D11	4-dr. Sed.-7P	1095	3440	Note 2
D11	4-dr. Limo.-7P	1185	3545	Note 2

Note 1: The range of serial numbers suggests that approximately 70,999 Special and 114,457 Deluxe Dodge "Luxury Liners" were built.
Note 2: Several books show production totals for the D13 Series built in Canada and apply these figures to the Deluxe D11 Series. We believe this to be an error and feel that production totals for U.S.-built Specials are not available at this time.
Note 3: Hayes Body Corp. supplied 1,000 Town Coupe bodies to Chrysler. Since 264 DeSoto Town Coupes and 134 Chrysler Town Coupes were made, it can be assumed that the remaining 602 cars were Dodge Town Coupes.

D12	Bus. Cpe.-2P	860	2850
D12	2-dr. Sed.-5P	927	2900
D12	2-dr. Tr. Sed.-5P	944	2895
D12	4-dr. Sed.-5P	979	2935
D12	4-dr. Tr. Sed.-5P	995	2935
D13	Bus. Cpe.-2P	948	2900
D13	2-dr. Sed.-5P	1004	2985
D13	2-dr. Tr. Sed.-5P	1020	2990
D13	4-dr. Tr. Sed.-5P	1061	2995
D13	4-dr. Sed.-5P	1044	3000

Note: Prices given in 1939 Canadian dollars.

ENGINE: Inline. L-head. Six. Cast iron block. B & S: 3-1/4 in. x 4-3/8 in. Disp.: 217.8 cu. in. C.R.: 6.5:1. Brake H.P.: 87 @ 3600 R.P.M. Net H.P.: 25.35. Main bearings: Four. Valve lifters: Solid. Carb.: Stromberg 1V model BXV-3. Torque: 158 lbs.-ft. @ 1200 R.P.M. [Series D12 & D13] Inline. L-head. Six. Cast iron block. B&S: 3-⅛ in. x 4-⅜ in. Disp.: 201 cu. in. Brake H.P.: 82 @ 3600 R.P.M.

CHASSIS: [Special Series] W.B.: 117 in. Tires: 16 x 6.00. [Deluxe SWB Series] W.B.: 117 in. Tires: 16 x 6.00. [Deluxe LWB Series] W.B.: 134 in. Tires: 16 x 6.50. [Series D12 & D13] W.B.: 114 in.

TECHNICAL: Selective sliding transmission. Speeds: 3F/1R. Column shift controls. Single plate dry disc clutch. Hypoid rear axle. Overall Ratio: [Reg. W.B.] 4.1:1; [Extended W.B.] 4.3:1. Hydraulic brakes. Steel disc wheels.

OPTIONS: Front bumper. Rear bumper. Whitewall tires. Chrome beauty rings. OSRV mirror. Fender skirts. Bumper guards. Radio. Heater. Clock. Cigar lighter. Radio antenna. Seat covers. Dual taillight (on Bus. Cpe.). Spotlights. Front bumper guard extension rails. Fender mounted parking lamps. Directional signals. Chrome license plate frames. Special paint.

HISTORICAL: Introduced: Oct., 1938. Calendar year registrations: 176,585. Calendar year production: 186,474. Model year production: 179,300. Innovations: Column gearshift controls. Cowl mounted windshield wipers. Independent front suspension with coil springs. "Safety Light" speedometer. Roomier interiors with wider seats. Improved carburetion. Increased torque. Dodge was America's fifth largest auto-maker in model year 1939, which was also the company's 25th anniversary year. Production of 1939 models started in August, 1938 and ended in July, 1939.

1939 Dodge, Deluxe Six, Series D11, Town Coupe, Hayes, OCW

1939
Special Series D11S, 6-cyl., 117" wb

	FP	5	4	3	2	1
Cpe	756	850	1650	4150	5800	8300
2 dr Sed	915	675	1300	2600	4400	6300
Sed	855	700	1350	2800	4550	6500

DeLuxe Series D11, 6-cyl., 117" wb - 134" wb, (*)

	FP	5	4	3	2	1
Cpe	803	875	1700	4250	5900	8500
A/S Cpe	860	900	1800	4400	6150	8800
Twn Cpe	1055	925	2000	4650	6500	9300
2 dr Sed	865	700	1350	2800	4550	6500
Sed	905	725	1400	3000	4700	6700
Ewb Sed (*)	1095	900	1800	4400	6150	8800
Limo (*)	1185	900	1900	4500	6300	9000

1940

LUXURY LINER SPECIAL — SERIES D17 — SIX: A longer wheelbase and larger body highlighted the restyled 1940 Dodge "Luxury Liner." The year's new frontal treatment sported a two-piece grille with horizontal chrome bars extending across the radiator and fender aprons. The upper and lower grilles were separated by a horizontal, body color panel. The upper grille tapered to a sharp point on the nose of the car, which had a ram hood ornament on top and the Dodge name on either side. A horizontal chrome molding trimmed the hoodside. It had short, slanting chrome hash marks at the front, center and rear. A wide chrome molding ran, from the grille, down the center of the hood. Sealed beam headlights were fully recessed into the front fenders, with parking lights incorporated into the chrome bezels. The front fenders were decorated with three, long "wind stream" bead moldings along their sides. Base trim features were found on the D17 Specials which had no lower bodyside moldings. The beltline was decorated with a paint stripe instead of chrome molding. Standard equipment included Autolite ignition, hydraulic brakes, single vacuum windshield wiper, standard steering wheel, regular seat cushions, instrument panel safety signals, wider front and rear seats, full-floating suspension system and concealed door hinges. Conventional runningboards were now optional equipment.

Model No.	Body Type & Seating	Price	Weight	Prod. Total
D17	2-dr. Bus. Cpe.-2P	755	2867	12,001
D17	2-dr. Sed.-5P	815	2942	27,700
D17	4-dr. Sed.-5P	855	2997	26,803

Note 1: Total series production was 66,504.
Note 2: Add 25 pounds for cars with conventional runningboards.

Model No.	Body Type & Seating	Price	Weight	Prod. Total
D14	2-dr. Bus. Cpe.-2P	803	2905	12,750
D14	2-dr. A/S Cpe.-2/4P	855	2973	8028
D14	2-dr. Conv. Cpe.-5P	1030	3190	2100
D14	2-dr. Sed.-5P	860	2990	19,838
D14	4-dr. Sed.-5P	905	3028	84,976
(Extended Chassis)				
D14	4-dr. Sed.-7P	1095	3460	932
D14	4-dr. Limo.-7P	1170	3550	79
D14	Chassis	NA	NA	298

Note 1: Total series production was 129,001.
Note 2: Add 25 pounds for cars with conventional runningboards.

Model No.	Body Type & Seating	Price	Weight	Prod. Total
D14	4-dr. Sed.-6P	995	2980	
D14	2-dr. Sed.-6P	944	2965	
D14	Bus. Cpe.-3P	860	2890	
D15	Deluxe 4-dr. Sed.-6P	1061	3060	
D15	Deluxe 2-dr. Sed.-6P	1020	3010	
D15	Deluxe Bus. Cpe.-3P	948	2930	
D15	Del. Spec. 4-dr. Sed.-6P	1088	3060	
D15	Del. Spec. 2-dr. Sed.-6P	1048	3020	
D15	Del. Spec. Bus. Cpe.-3P	975	2950	
D15	Del. Spec. Clb. Cpe.-4P	1037	3000	

Note: Prices shown in 1940 Canadian dollars.

1940 Dodge, Deluxe Six, Series D14, 4-dr. sedan, OCW

LUXURY LINER DELUXE — SERIES D14 — SIX: The Deluxe Series for 1940 was again separated into standard and extended chassis car-lines, both of which had D14 model designations. The smaller cars had a 2-1/2 inch longer wheelbase than 1939 Dodges, while the big, seven-passenger wheelbase grew 5-1/2 inches. Deluxe models had the same basic appearance as the Specials, but carried slightly more trim and equipment. Interior appointments were also plusher. Some of the distinctive Deluxe features included "Air Foam" seat cushions, dual electric windshield wipers, chrome beltline trim moldings, deluxe steering wheel with horn ring, chrome moldings on the lower bodysides (or runningboards) and richer upholstery. As in 1939, the fancier version of the Deluxe coupe carried folding auxiliary seats inside the body, rather than a rumbleseat. The larger, seven-passenger models had wider doors, door windows and front sheet metal. The long wheelbase sedan featured folding jump seats and the limousine also had a leather front seat and glass partition window. Optional two-tone finish was available for the Deluxe 4-door sedan and included a harmonizing interior with special dress-up trim and a chrome exterior molding between the upper and lower sections of the grille.

DODGE — SERIES D14 KINGSWAY, D15 DELUXE & D15 DELUXE SPECIAL — SIX: This year's junior Dodge series expanded into three distinct groups, at least in the Canadian market, although the Deluxe Special differed from the Deluxe only in being equipped with dual sun visors and horns, horn rings, cigar lighter and front door armrests. Whether three models were offered in the foreign export cars is unknown. Again, these cars were based on the Plymouth body shell and chassis with a Canadian sourced engine; a Dodge grille and trim differentiated from the Plymouth. Only the D15 version was built in the U.S. for export, production totaling 4,317 units, nearly two-thirds of which were right-hand drive vehicles; none had the small bore export engine fitted, however.

1940 Dodge, Series D17, 2-dr. sedan, OCW

I.D. DATA: [D17] Serial numbers in same location. Starting: 4349001. Ending: 4415505. Engine numbers in same location. Starting Engine No.: D14-1001. Ending: D14-19385.
Note: Since both series used the same engine, all engines are coded "D-14." [D14] Serial numbers in same location. Starting: 30216001. Ending: 30342333. Engine numbers in same location. Starting Engine No.: D14-1001. Ending: D14-193835.
(Canadian) D14 Starting: 9420231. Ending: 9422897. D15 Starting: 9669926. Ending: 9673662.

1940 Dodge, sedan (Australian), JB

ENGINE: Inline. L-head. Six. Cast iron block. B & S: 3-1/4 in. x 4-3/8 in. Disp.: 217.8 cu. in. C.R.: 6.5:1. Brake H.P.: 87 @ 3600 R.P.M. Net H.P.: 25.35. Main bearings: Four. Valve lifters: Solid. Carb.: Stromberg 1V model BXV-3. Torque: 166 lbs.-ft. @ 1200 R.P.M. [Canada/Export] Inline. L-head. Six. Cast iron block. B&S: 3-1/4 in. x 4-3/8 in. Disp.: 218 cu. in. Brake H.P.: 84 @ 3600 R.P.M.

CHASSIS: [Special Series] W.B.: 119-1/2 in. Tires: 16 x 6.00. [Deluxe Std. W.B. Series] W.B.: 119-1/2 in. Tires: 16 x 6.00. [Deluxe LWB Series] W.B.: 139-1/2 in. Tires: 16 x 6.50. [Canada/Export] W.B.: 117 in. Tires: D14 5.50 x 16, D15 6.00 x 16.

TECHNICAL: Selective sliding transmission. Speeds: 3F/1R. Column shift controls. Single plate dry disc clutch. Hypoid rear axle. Overall Ratio: [Sed.] 4.1:1; [Cpe.] 3.9:1. Hydraulic brakes. Steel disc wheels.

OPTIONS: Front bumper. Rear bumper. Whitewall tires. Wheel trim rings. Oversize tires. Fender skirts. Bumper guards. Radio. Heater. Clock. Cigar lighter. Radio antenna. Seat covers. External sun shade. Spotlights. Master grille guard. Two-tone paint (Deluxe 4-door sed.). Special paint. Chrome license plate frames. Deluxe trim package (Spl. models). Conventional runningboards. Rear fender rubber scuff pads. OSRV mirror.

HISTORICAL: Introduced: Sept., 1939. Calendar year registrations: 197,252. Calendar year production: 225,595. Model year production: 195,505. Innovations: Sealed beam headlights. Longer wheelbase. Increased torque rating. Two leading shoe front wheel brakes. Safety wheel rims introduced. Dodge fell to seventh position in the model year production charts. Dodge accounted for 26 percent of Chrysler Corp.'s sales volume this year. Production of 1940 models began in Aug., 1939 and ended in July, 1940.

1940
Special Series D17, 6-cyl., 119.5" wb

	FP	5	4	3	2	1
Cpe	755	800	1550	3900	5450	7800
2 dr Sed	815	650	1250	2400	4200	6000
Sed	855	675	1300	2500	4350	6200

DeLuxe Series D14, 6-cyl., 119.5" wb - 139.5" wb, (*)

	FP	5	4	3	2	1
Conv	1030	3500	7050	11,750	16,450	23,500
Cpe	803	825	1600	4000	5600	8000
4P Cpe	855	800	1550	3900	5450	7800
2 dr Sed	860	700	1350	2800	4550	6500
Sed	905	725	1400	3100	4800	6800
Ewb Sed (*)	1095	725	1400	3100	4800	6800
Limo (*)	1170	775	1500	3700	5200	7400

1941

1941 Dodge, Custom, Series D19, 6-pass. town sedan, OCW

DODGE — SERIES D19 — SIX: The 1941 Dodge models featured larger, v-shaped windshields. The size of rear windows was also increased. Two large, horizontal-bar grilles were separated by a v-shaped panel done in body color. The grilles stretched completely over the fender aprons to the headlamps. A chrome molding ran over the nose and down the center of the hood. Decorative elements included a winged crest bearing the Dodge family coat-of-arms mounted at the front of the nose and a streamlined ram ornament mounted on top. All models had a chrome beltline molding running from the front of the hood to the rear of the body. Although all 1941 Dodges had the same D19 series designation, there were still three types of cars. The base trim level now used "Deluxe" nomenclature, while the fancier models were called "Customs." The Custom Six featured certain extras like "Air Foam" seat cushions, dual electric windshield wipers, a righthand inside arm rest, Deluxe steering wheel and chrome beading around the outside windows. The third type of Dodge was the extended chassis models which accommodated seven passengers with the addition of jump seats in the rear. Standard equipment included Autolite ignition, hydraulic brakes, hump-rim safety wheels, vertical uplift door handles, oil bath air cleaner and more powerful engine. Fluid drive was optional on all Dodge products.

DODGE — SERIES D20 KINGSWAY, D21 DELUXE & D21 DELUXE SPECIAL — SIX: Once again, at least for the Canadian market, the junior Dodges were broken down into three categories although differences among them were minimal — the Deluxe Special being noted only as having a cigar lighter and front door armrests to differentiate it from the Kingsway and Deluxe versions. Based on the P11 and P12 Plymouth series, the junior Dodges were built in the U.S. for export and in Windsor for the Canadian markets. Leaving the Detroit assembly line were 1,180 D20's and 2,094 D20 Deluxes, while nearly 14,000 units came off the Windsor line. Again Plymouth supplied the body and chassis with a Dodge 218-cubic-inch engine (which Plymouth would begin using in its 1942 U.S. production).

I.D. DATA: Serial numbers in same location. Starting: 30342401. Ending: 30576861. Engine numbers in same location. Starting Engine No.: D19-1001. Ending: D19-235536. [Canadian] D20 Starting: 9673666. Ending: 9681156. D21 Starting: 9503606. Ending: 9510870.

Model No.	Body Type & Seating	Price	Weight	Prod. Total
Deluxe Series				
D19	2-dr. Bus. Cpe.-2P	862	3034	22,318
D19	2-dr. Sed.-5P	915	3109	34,566
D19	4-dr. Sed.-5P	954	3149	49,579
Custom Series, 119.5 in. wb				
D19	2-dr. Clb. Cpe.-6P	995	3154	18,024
D19	2-dr. Conv. Cpe.-5P	1162	3384	3554
D19	2-dr. Brgm.-6P	962	3169	20,146
D19	4-dr. Sed.-6P	999	3194	72,067
D19	4-dr. Twn. Sed.-6P	1062	3234	16,074
Custom Series, 137.5 in. wb				
D19	4-dr. Sed.-7P	1195	3579	601
D19	4-dr. Limo.-7P	1262	3669	50
D19	Chassis	NA	NA	20

Note 1: Total series production was 236,999.
Note 2: The Custom Club Coupe was a five-window coupe; the Convertible Coupe now had rear quarter windows; the Custom Brougham was a 2-door sedan with vent panes in the rear side window; the 4-door Sedan had separate rear quarter windows; the Town Sedan had large rear door windows with vent panes at the rear.

Kingsway Series			
D20	Cpe.-3P	1079	2945
D20	Clb. Cpe.-5P	1167	3010
D20	2-dr. Sed.-6P	1178	3015
D20	4-dr. Sed.-6P	1241	3030
Kingsway Special Series			
D20	Cpe.-3P	1105	2960
D20	Clb. Cpe.-5P	1192	3025
D20	2-dr. Sed.-6P	1203	3030
D20	4-dr. Sed.-6P	1266	3045
Deluxe Series			
D21	Cpe.-3P	1191	2990
D21	2-dr. Sed.-6P	1277	3060
D21	4-dr. Sed.-6P	1327	3100
Deluxe Special Series			
D21	Cpe.-3P	1222	3015
D21	Clb. Cpe.-5P	1297	3085
D21	2-dr. Sed.-6P	1309	3080
D21	4-dr. Sed.-6P	1359	3135
D21	4-dr. Sed.-7P	1676	3565

Note: Prices given in 1941 Canadian dollars.

ENGINE: Inline. L-head. Six. Cast iron block. B & S: 3-1/4 in. x 4-3/8 in. Disp.: 217.8 cu. in. C.R.: 6.5:1. Brake H.P.: 91 @ 3800 R.P.M. Net H.P.: 25.35. Main bearings: Four. Valve lifters: Solid. Carb.: Stromberg 1V model BXV-3. Torque: 170 lbs.-ft. @ 1200 R.P.M. [Canada/Export] Inline. L-head. Six. B&S: 3-3/8 in. x 4-1/6 in. Disp.: 218 cu. in. Brake H.P.: 88 @ 3800 R.P.M.

CHASSIS: [Deluxe Series] W.B.: 119.5 in. Tires: 16 x 6.00. [Custom SWB Series] W.B.: 119.5 in. Tires: 16 x 6.00. [Custom LWB Series] W.B.: 137.5 in. Tires: 16 x 6.50. [Canada/Export] W.B.: 117-1/2 in.

TECHNICAL: Selective sliding transmission. Speeds: 3F/1R. Column shift controls. Single plate dry disc clutch. Hypoid rear axle. Overall Ratio: 4.3:1. Hydraulic brakes. Safety steel disc wheels. Drivetrain Options: Fluid drive.

1941 Dodge, Custom, Series D19, 4-dr. sedan, OCW

OPTIONS: Front bumper. Rear bumper. Whitewall tires. Wheel trim beauty rings. Oversize tires. Fender skirts. Bumper guards. Radio. Heater. Clock. Cigar lighter. Radio antenna. Seat covers. External sun shade. Spotlights. Fender mounted turn signals. OSRV mirror. Conventional runningboards. Master grille guards. Full wheel discs. Chrome fender speed line moldings. Special paint. Chrome license plate frames. Custom trim package.

HISTORICAL: Introduced: Sept., 1940. Calendar year registrations: 215,563. Calendar year production: 215,575. Model year production: 236,999. Innovations: Fluid Drive. Safety rim wheels. Shorter wheelbase on seven-passenger models. Taillights mounted in chrome, fin-like housings on top of rear fenders. Higher horsepower six-cylinder engine. Torque rating increased again. Dodge came in as the seventh most active U.S. auto-maker for the 1941 model year. Production of the D19 Series began in Aug., 1940 and ended in Sept., 1941.

1941
DeLuxe Series D19, 6-cyl., 119.5" wb

	FP	5	4	3	2	1
Cpe	862	775	1500	3600	5100	7300
2 dr Sed	915	675	1300	2600	4400	6300
Sed	954	700	1350	2800	4550	6500
Custom Series D19, 6-cyl., 119.5" wb - 137.5" wb, (*)						
Conv	1162	3650	7350	12,250	17,150	24,500
Clb Cpe	995	800	1550	3900	5450	7800
Brgm	962	725	1400	3000	4700	6700
Sed	999	700	1350	2900	4600	6600
Twn Sed	1062	725	1400	3100	4800	6800
7P Sed (*)	1195	800	1550	3900	5450	7800
Limo (*)	1262	850	1650	4150	5800	8300

1942

1942 Dodge, Deluxe, Series D22, 2-dr. sedan, OCW

DODGE — SERIES D22 — SIX: The 1942 Dodge had a more massive front end appearance. The front grille design had a square effect with heavy horizontal bars extending to the head lamps. The hood was hinged at the rear and opened with a pull control button mounted below the instrument panel. The fenders were of a more sweeping, streamlined design. Dual "Air-Line" moldings were placed low on the front and rear fenders. Other features included concealed runningboards and an airplane type speedometer. At the rear, rectangular taillamps were moved back onto the body and mounted flush in small chrome housings. Deluxe models represented the base trim car-line. Custom models included "Air-Foam" seat cushions, dual electric windshield wipers and chrome beading around the outside windows as standard equipment. All models had Autolite ignition, hydraulic brakes, a new "Power Flow" six-cylinder engine and a heavier crankshaft. New, "All-Fluid" drive was optional at extra cost. Dodge sales ceased on Feb. 21, 1942, after the outbreak of World War II. Cars built between mid-December and January had "blackout" style trim with most bright metal parts painted.

DODGE — SERIES D23S DELUXE & D23C SPECIAL DELUXE — SIX: The Plymouth-based junior series Dodge enjoyed brisk sales in Canada, while U.S. production for export dropped dramatically as a result of World War II: 1,113 units compared to Canada's 6,461. Again two distinct series were offered corresponding to the similar P14S and P14C models from Plymouth on which the cars were based. Canadian-built cars utilized the 25-inch "long-block" engine from the Canadian foundry while U.S. sourced vehicles continued to use the shorter 23-inch block.

I.D. DATA: Serial numbers in same location. Starting: 30577001. Ending: 30644378. Engine numbers in same location. Starting Engine No.: D22-1001. Ending: D22-68416. [Canada] D23 Starting: 9681161. Ending: 9687621.

1942 Dodge, Custom, Series D22, convertible coupe, OCW

Model No. Series	Body Type & Seating	Price	Weight	Prod. Total
Deluxe Series				
D22	2-dr. Cpe.-3P	895	3056	5257
D22	2-dr. Clb. Cpe.-6P	995	3131	3314
D22	2-dr. Sed.-6P	958	3131	9767
D22	4-dr. Sed.-6P	998	3171	13,343
Custom Series, 119.5 in. wb				
D22	2-dr. Clb. Cpe.-6P	1045	3171	4659
D22	2-dr. Conv. Cpe.-5P	1245	3476	1185
D22	2-dr. Brgm.-6P	1008	3171	4685
D22	4-dr. Sed.-6P	1048	3206	22,055
D22	4-dr. Twn. Sed.-6P	1105	3256	4047
Custom Series, 137.5 in. wb				
D22	4-dr. Sed.-7P	1395	3693	201
D22	4-dr. Limo.-7P	1475	3768	9

Note 1: Total series production was 68,522.

ENGINE: Inline. L-head. Six. Cast iron block. B & S: 3-1/4 in. x 4-5/8 in. Disp.: 230.2 cu. in. C.R.: 6.7:1. Brake H.P.: 105 @ 3600 R.P.M. Net H.P.: 25.35. Main bearings: Four. Valve lifters: Solid. Carb.: Stromberg 1V model BXV-3. Torque: 185 lbs.-ft. @ 1600 R.P.M.

CHASSIS: [Deluxe Series] W.B.: 119.5 in. Tires: 16 x 6.00. [Custom SWB Series] W.B.: 119.5 in. Tires: 16 x 6.00. [Custom LWB Series] W.B.: 137.5 in. Tires: 16 x 6.50.

TECHNICAL: Selective sliding transmission. Speeds: 3F/1R. Column shift controls. Single plate dry disc clutch. Hypoid rear axle. Overall Ratio: (std.) 3.9:1; (opt.) 3.73:1 or 4.1:1. Hydraulic brakes. Safety rim steel disc wheels. Drivetrain Options: All-Fluid Drive.

OPTIONS: Front bumper. Rear bumper. Whitewall tires. Wheel trim rings. Full wheel discs. Fender skirts. Bumper guards. Radio. Heater. Clock. Cigar lighter. Radio antenna. Seat covers. External sun shade. Spotlights. OSRV mirror. Turn signals. Parking brake "on" buzzer. Master grille guard. Chrome license plate frames. Oversize tires. Special paint. Custom trim package.

1942 Dodge, Custom, Series D22, town sedan, OCW

HISTORICAL: Introduced: Sept., 1941. Calendar year production: 11,675. Model year production: 68,522. Innovations: Longer stroke "Power Flow" six has higher compression with more horsepower and torque. Improved Fluid Drive feature optional. Heavier crankshaft. Stoplight mounted in center of trunk lid. For the war-shortened 1942 model run, Dodge wound-up as America's sixth largest auto-maker. Production of 1942 models began in Aug., 1941 and ended in Jan., 1942.

1942
DeLuxe Series D22, 6-cyl., 119.5" wb

	FP	5	4	3	2	1
Cpe	895	775	1500	3600	5100	7300
Clb Cpe	995	800	1550	3900	5450	7800
2 dr Sed	958	650	1250	2400	4200	6000
Sed	998	675	1300	2600	4400	6300

Custom Series D22, 6-cyl., 119.5" wb - 137.5" wb, (*)

	FP	5	4	3	2	1
Conv	1245	3200	6450	10,750	15,050	21,500
Clb Cpe	1045	800	1550	3900	5450	7800
Brgm	1008	775	1550	3750	5250	7500
Sed	1048	775	1500	3600	5100	7300
Twn Sed	1105	775	1500	3700	5200	7400
7P Sed (*)	1395	800	1550	3900	5450	7800
Limo (*)	1475	925	1900	4550	6350	9100

DODGESON — Detroit, Michigan — (1926) — This car was precisely named. "Designed and engineered by Mr. John Duval Dodge, son of John F. Dodge, President and Builder of the Famous Dodge Bros. Motor Car," the brochure announced. That was really allowing undue credit. Dodge's son was responsible for putting together the standard components of an assembled car, but the distinctive feature of the Dodgeson was designed by C.E. Wyrick. This was its straight-eight 196-cubic-inch rotary valve engine which was claimed to develop 72 bhp at 3000 rpm. Although a company called Dodgeson Motors was organized for manufacture, the car never proceeded beyond the building of a few prototypes. It was announced in January 1926, and it died soon thereafter.

1926 DODGESON

	FP	5	4	3	2	1
Dodgeson prototype (8-cyl., 72 hp, 116" wb)	—	—	—	—	—	—

1912 DODO, cyclecar, NAHC

DODO — Detroit, Michigan — (1912) — The DODO is an interesting vehicle historically for two reasons. First, it was the progenitor of an automotive idea which took America by storm in 1914 and was virtually dead the following year. The DODO was a cyclecar; its name was certainly prophetic. A tandem two-seater on a 100-inch wheelbase, the DODO was powered by an air-cooled two-cylinder 9hp engine and featured front wheel drive. Second, the car was designed by a brilliant young engineer named Karl Probst. It was built for him by his employer, the Auto Parts Manufacturing Company of Detroit. Although the prototype had a standard 56-inch tread, Probst planned to slim the production version down to 38 inches. But a production version was never built. When Auto Parts eschewed manufacture, Probst resigned and moved to Toledo to work for the electric-car-producing Milburn Wagon Company. Later, while working for American Bantam, he would be one of the principal engineers responsible for the development of the Jeep.

DOE-WAH-JACK — The Doe-Wah-Jack was planned as the successor to the Lindsley which was produced in Dowagiac, Michigan from 1908-1909. Refer to Lindsley.

DOHERTY — The H.B. Doherty Company was organized in Binghamton, New York with a capital stock of $5000 early in 1908 for the manufacture of engines, cars and boats. Manufacture is doubted.

DOLAN — Philadelphia, Pennsylvania — (1900) — Clarence W. Dolan of Philadelphia had an electric carriage built for himself in 1900 which, according to *The Motor World*, was expected to provide a "touring radius of 125 miles at an average speed of 25 miles per hour." Had the vehicle indeed had that fine between-charge capability at this early period doubtless it would have been put into production.

DOLFINI — Brooklyn, New York — (1900) — A.W. Dolfini & Company of 332 Classon Avenue in Brooklyn manufactured automobile running gear and fittings for fire engines — and in the fall of 1900 announced completion of the firm's first gasoline carriage. Although manufacture was contemplated, Dolfini is believed to have decided against it and remained thereafter in the components field.

DOLLITA — Washington, D.C. — (1903) — The Dollita was a midget car built for a midget vaudeville performer of that same name. Even its performance was downsized: 10 miles an hour, 15 miles between battery charges. A victoria in body style, upholstered in leather, the Dollita was dark green with bright red running gear, and nickel plated wheels shod with pneumatic tires. "It is an exact miniature of a full grown victoria," reported *The Motor World*, "with everything complete down to the tiny gong."

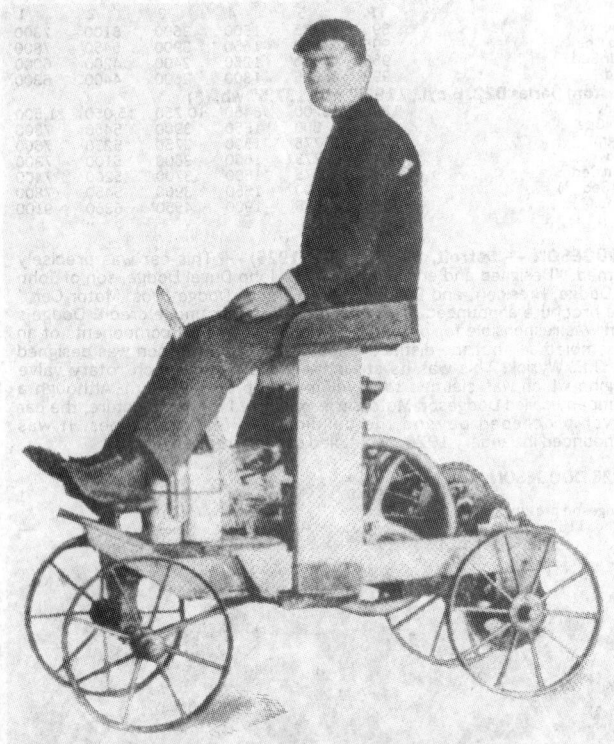

1903 Dollwet, runabout, NAHC

DOLLWET — San Francisco, California — (1903) — "With a soapbox as material and the label 'It floats' for inspiration, John Dollwet of San Francisco has built an automobile that will go from 8 to 10 miles an hour." Thus reported *The Motor Age* rather wittily in 1903, though young John Dollwet (he was sixteen years old) needed more than a soapbox (it served as the seat) to complete his car. Its frame was oak, attached to a solid axle in the rear, the front axle turning buggy-like on a kingbolt. A small vertical gasoline engine was mounted under the seat, with the gasoline tank serving as a surface carburetor. Because the car's seat was so high, the bicycle handlebars which served to steer had to be operated by foot. Dollwet's ingenuity was appealing, but whether he entered the automobile industry when he grew up is not known.

DOLLY MADISON — Dolly Madison was the name used in 1915 for the cars produced by the Madison Motor Company of Anderson, Indiana. The historical reference was perhaps flatteringly meant, but egregiously wrong; President James Madison's First Lady spelled her name Dolley. From 1916 through 1919 the company's cars were called simply Madison. Refer to Madison.

1904 Dolson, model A, touring, NAHC

DOLSON — Charlotte, Michigan — (1904-1907) — The member of the Dolson family who was most anxious to go automotive was D. Elmore. His father (John L.) and his brother (W. Elton) were apparently quite content manufacturing horsedrawn vehicles in Charlotte, the annual output of John L. Dolson & Sons being about 5000 units. Young D. Elmore was persistent, however, and after beginning experimentation in 1902, the com-

pany entered the automotive market with a two-cylinder touring car in 1904. This was followed by bigger and considerably more powerful fours, including a Cannon Ball Roadster that was guaranteed to do 75 mph. Late in 1906 the firm was renamed the Dolson Automobile Company, and its stock was increased from $100,000 to $300,000. The Dolsons built well, with bodies fashioned of wood, galvanized sheet steel and sheet copper which were widely reputed to be more durable than the most costly all-wood constructions. "Not one single Dolson composite car body has ever shown a panel crack or required repairs of any sort," *Cycle and Automobile Trade Journal* reported in 1906, "save in case of overturn or collision, and in these extreme instances the body was always capable of repair by removing the upholstering and bending the panels back to original form, instead of having to be replaced by a wholly new structure, as is the usual case with all wood or with aluminum casting bodies." Unfortunately, the Dolsons' automobile venture was not so solidly based. Although in the spring of 1907 they had purchased the equipment of the St. Anne Kerosine Motor Company in order to expand, they found themselves in financial trouble very soon after that. Involuntary bankruptcy followed late in 1907. Early in 1908 the Dolson trustee stated that the directors of the company were liable for three times the amount of stock subscribed for and held by them "because a sufficient amount of stock was not bona fidely subscribed for at the time the company commenced to do business." This was doubtless less wrong-doing on the part of the Dolsons than the fact that running an automobile business was a bit beyond their ken. Early in 1909 the Charlotte factory was sold to the truck-producing Duplex Power Car Company. The last twenty-five Dolson cars, which had been in the process of construction when the company went under, were completed in the spring of 1908 by court order. Remaining stock was sold to the Times Square Automotive Company of New York City. John Dolson turned to agriculture next, and began peppermint farming. His sons remained in the automotive business, but as salesmen and parts dealers. Total Dolson production was approximately 700 cars. Half of them remained on the road three years after production had ceased — a striking percentage for that era and testament that the company did not exaggerate when it termed its car the "Durable Dolson."

1904 DOLSON
Model A — 2-cyl., 15 hp, 82" wb

	FP	5	4	3	2	1
Touring-5P	1450	3100	4200	6300	10,500	22,000

1905 Dolson, model C, touring, HAC

1905 DOLSON
Model C — 2-cyl., 20 hp, 90" wb

Side Entrance Tonneau	1500	3100	4200	6300	10,500	22,000

Model B — 4-cyl., 28/32 hp, 103" wb

Side Entrance Tonneau	2500	3200	4300	6500	11,000	23,000

1906 Dolson, model F, touring

1906 DOLSON
Model C — 2-cyl., 2/24 hp, 100" wb

Touring-5P	1250	3100	4200	6300	10,500	22,000

Model D — 2-cyl., 22/24 hp, 101" wb

Touring-5P	1500	3200	4300	6400	10,800	22,500

Model E — 4-cyl., 28/32 hp, 106" wb

Touring-5P	2000	4500	9000	15,000	21,000	30,000

Model F — 4-cyl., 45/50 hp, 112" wb

Touring-5P	3000	5500	10,950	18,250	25,500	36,500

1907 Dolson, model F, "Cannon Ball", roadster, HAC

1907 DOLSON
Model H — 4-cyl., 35/40 hp, 111" wb

	FP	5	4	3	2	1
Touring-5P	2500	3000	4000	6000	9500	21,000

Model F — 4-cyl., 55/60 hp, 125" wb

	FP	5	4	3	2	1
Touring-7P	3250	3100	4200	6300	10,500	22,000
Cannon Ball Roadster	3250	3300	4400	6700	12,000	24,000

DOMAN — **Oshkosh, Wisconsin** — **(1899)** — H.C. Doman was the proprietor of the Union Iron Works at 118 Marion Street in Oshkosh and in October of 1899 he reported to *The Horseless Age* that he had completed a gasoline motor carriage weighing 700 pounds and that he expected to manufacture others like it. That expectation does not appear to have been realized, but Doman did proceed into the manufacture of engines, mostly marine and stationary type, and he is believed to have entered the automobile field as a dealer and mechanic about a decade later.

DOMAN-MARKS — There was no Doman-Marks automobile in 1937, despite its frequent roster reference. But Carl Doman and Ed Marks, formerly engineers for the H.H. Franklin Company, did contribute formidably to the building of the Airomobile produced that year. Refer to Airomobile.

DONALDSONVILLE — During the fall of 1911 the Donaldsonville Auto Company, Ltd. was organized in Donaldsonville, Louisiana with a $10,000 capital stock to manufacture and deal in automobiles. Behind this venture were K.A. Aucoin, Dr. S. Moore, Dr. V. Painchaud, Dr. Henry Le Blanc, P.H. Gilbert, A.L. Shaw, A.A. Sarrdet, A. Schroeder, Adolphe Netter, Charles H. Landry, Dr. E.K. Sims and A. Bloomensteil. Manufacture is doubted.

1906 Dorchester, runabout, NAHC

DORCHESTER — **Dorchester, Massachusetts** — **(1906)** — In the spring of 1906 the Hub Motor Car Exchange purchased the plant of the Crest Manufacturing Company which had just discontinued manufacture of the Crestmobile and proceeded to build a car very much like the Crestmobile there. The Crest people might have cautioned about the wisdom of doing that, since it was diminishing sales of their simple little runabout which had prompted them to forgo their business and merge themselves instead into the Alden-Sampson group. The new Dorchester, indeed, was a step backward from the Crestmobile in progressive runabout design. It featured chain drive, right hand tiller steering, and its tiny one-cylinder 4 hp engine was naked to the world, mounted ahead of the front axle and immediately in front of the dashboard. The Dorchester weighed 400 pounds and was priced at 400 dollars, and didn't survive 1906. The company tried again in 1907 with a slightly more powerful, slightly more sophisticated car called the Hub.

DORMAN — The Dorman Motor Company was organized early in 1907 in Geneva, New York for the manufacture of motor cars "and other self-propelling carriages and trucks." The incorporators of this $10,000 venture were D.M. Dorman, S.F. Dey and J.C. Rose. Manufacture of a car is doubted.

DORMANDY — **Troy, New York** — **(1903-1905)** — Although unassailable uniqueness is not a factor to be applied without trepidation for many vehicles in American automobile history, it can be safely asserted that the Dormandy was the only automobile in the United States ever to be pro-

duced in a shirt collar factory. The factory was that of the United Shirt & Collar Company of Troy whose president James Knox Polk Pine ordered the Dormandy to be built. It was named for its inventor, Gary Dormandy, who was a machinist and an employee of Pine's company. Although a few of the parts for the air-cooled engine were purchased from Frayer-Miller, most of its components were put together by blacksmiths of the collar company. The chassis was assembled alongside the shirt collars as well. The coachwork was contracted for outside, however, from the Troy Carriage Works. So pleased was president Pine with the first Dormandy built, a limousine, that he immediately ordered two more, both touring cars, for his sons. Then he allowed Gary Dormandy to build a fourth, another touring car, for himself. Each of these cars carried a floor-mounted brass plate the script for which included "Dormandy," the date 1903, and either the company's name or its president's. The four-cylinder air-cooled Dormandy was an absolutely successful motorcar. The first Dormandy was completed in 1903, the next two in 1904, and the fourth in 1905. In 1906 the United Shirt & Collar Company returned to soft goods exclusively.

DORN — There was no Dorn Motor Car Company in St. Louis, Missouri in 1910. This seems to have been an error perpetrated in a trade magazine that year, when a typesetter mis-set the word Dorris.

1897 Dorris, gasoline buggy, HAC

DORRIS — **St. Louis, Missouri** — **(1906-1926)** — George Preston Dorris had built an experimental gasoline car in 1896-1897 in his native Nashville (Tennessee) and in 1898 headed west to Missouri where he joined his old friend John L. French in organizing the St. Louis Motor Carriage Company, and in serving as its chief engineer. In 1905, when French elected to move to Peoria (Illinois), Dorris decided to stay behind in St. Louis and start his own business, a wise choice as it turned out because his old firm quickly failed in Peoria, while Dorris went on to become a respected and successful manufacturer in St. Louis. The Dorris Motor Car Company took over the former St. Louis company's plant and the first ohv 30 hp four-cylinder Dorris touring car on a 101-inch wheelbase was introduced at the New York Automobile Show in January 1906. Always an advanced vehicle, the Dorris became more powerful (an 80 hp six), bigger (132-inch wheelbase) and more expensive (as high as $7000 for closed cars) through the years. Truck production began prior to the First World War; in 1917 capital stock in the company was increased from $300,000 to $1,000,000 for the purpose of expansion. That year, too, Dorris president H.B. Krenning stepped aside "because of needed rest" and W.R. Colcord took over the helm. Though George Preston Dorris was the real force in the Dorris venture, he preferred not exercising his power from a presidential chair. In 1920 the Dorris company maneuvered the buying of Astra, another automobile-building company in town — and reorganized as Dorris Motors

1906 Dorris, model A, touring, HAC

Corporation. In 1923 the industry was abuzz with rumors of a proposed merger among the Dorris, Haynes and Winton companies, but that plan fell through. Nineteen twenty-three was Dorris' last full year as an automobile manufacturer. Production virtually ceased, and the car which the company had advertised as being "practically hand-built" was actually hand-built to special order for a few years following, as Dorris died a slow death in the courtroom. A newspaper headline of December 1926 sadly said it all: "Competition was too keen, Dorris company head tells referee." Total Dorris production had been 3100 cars and 900 trucks.

1906 DORRIS
Model A — 4-cyl., 30 hp, 101" wb

	FP	5	4	3	2	1
Touring-5P	2500	3000	4000	6000	9500	21,000

1910 Dorris, model E, touring, HAC

1910 DORRIS
Model E — 4-cyl., 30 hp, 110" wb

	FP	5	4	3	2	1
Touring-5P	2500	3100	4200	6300	10,500	22,000
Roadster-2/3P	2500	3200	4300	6500	11,000	23,000
Close-Coupled-4P	2500	2900	3700	5600	9100	20,000
Limousine-6P	3600	3300	4400	6700	12,000	24,000

1907 Dorris, model B, touring, WLB

1907 DORRIS
Model B — 4-cyl., 30 hp, 102" wb

Touring-5P	2500	3000	4000	6000	9500	21,000

1911 Dorris, model F, limousine, HAC

1911 DORRIS
Model F — 4-cyl., 30-hp, 115" wb

Touring-5P	2500	3200	4300	6500	11,000	23,000
Roadster-2/3P	2500	3300	4400	6700	12,000	24,000
Limousine-6P	3600	3300	4400	6700	12,000	24,000

1908 Dorris, model C, touring, JAC

1908 DORRIS
Model C — 4-cyl., 30 hp, 106" wb

Touring-5P	2500	3000	4000	6000	9500	21,000

1912 Dorris, model G, touring, HAC

1912 DORRIS
Model G — 4-cyl., 30 hp, 115" wb

Touring-5P	2500	3200	4300	6500	11,000	23,000
Roadster-2P	2500	3300	4400	6700	12,000	24,000
Torpedo-4P	2500	3100	4200	6300	10,500	22,000
Coupe	2700	2500	3500	5000	8500	18,000
Limousine-5P	3500	2900	3700	5600	9100	20,000
Limousine-7P	3600	3000	3900	5800	9300	20,500

1909 Dorris, model D, touring, HAC

1909 DORRIS
Model D — 4-cyl., 30 hp, 108" wb

Touring-5P	2500	3000	4000	6000	9500	21,000
Limousine-4P	3600	3200	4300	6500	11,000	23,000
Roadster-2/3/4P	2500	3100	4200	6300	10,500	22,000
Convertible Car-4P	2500	3000	4000	6000	9500	21,000

1913 Dorris, model H, touring, HAC

1913 DORRIS
Model H — 4-cyl., 30 hp, 121" wb

	FP	5	4	3	2	1
Touring-4/5P	2500	3200	4300	6500	11,000	23,000
Touring-6/7P	2550	3200	4300	6400	10,800	22,500
Limousine-7P	3600	3100	4200	6300	10,500	22,000

1914 Dorris, model I, limousine, OCW

1914 DORRIS
Model I — 4-cyl., 30 hp, 121" wb

	FP	5	4	3	2	1
Touring-7P	2550	3200	4300	6500	11,000	23,000

1915 Dorris, model A-1-4, touring, HAC

1915 DORRIS
Model A-1-4 — 4-cyl., 31 hp, 121" wb

	FP	5	4	3	2	1
Touring-5P	2200	3200	4300	6500	11,000	23,000
Roadster-2P	2200	3300	4400	6700	12,000	24,000
Limousine	3400	3100	4200	6300	10,500	22,000
Coupe-4P	2600	2500	3500	5000	8500	18,000
Sedan-4P	2800	2300	3300	4600	7500	16,000
Touring-7P	2250	3100	4200	6300	10,500	22,000

1916 Dorris, model A-1-6, touring, HAC

1916 DORRIS
Model A-1-4 — 4-cyl., 31 hp, 121" wb

	FP	5	4	3	2	1
Touring-7P	2250	3000	4000	6000	9500	21,000
Touring-5P	2200	3100	4200	6300	10,500	22,000
Roadster-2P	2200	3200	4300	6500	11,000	23,000
Limousine-7P	3475	3000	4000	6000	9500	21,000
Coupe-4P	3000	2400	3400	4800	8000	17,000

Model A-1-6 — 6-cyl., 38 hp, 128" wb

	FP	5	4	3	2	1
Coupe-4P	3250	2500	3500	5000	8500	18,000
Touring-7P	2475	3100	4200	6300	10,500	22,000
Roadster-2P	2475	3300	4400	6700	12,000	24,000
Limousine-7P	3675	3100	4200	6300	10,500	22,000

1917 DORRIS
Model 1-B-6 — 6-cyl., 38.4 hp, 128" wb

	FP	5	4	3	2	1
Touring-7P	2475	3100	4200	6300	10,500	22,000
Limousine-7P	3675	2900	3700	5600	9100	20,000
Coupe-4P	3250	2500	3500	5000	8500	18,000
Sedan-5P	3350	2300	3300	4600	7500	16,000

1918 DORRIS
Model 1-C-6 — 6-cyl., 80 hp, 130" wb

	FP	5	4	3	2	1
Touring-4P	—	3100	4200	6300	10,500	22,000
Touring-7P	—	3000	4000	6000	9500	21,000
Coupe	—	2400	3400	4800	8000	17,000
Sedan	—	2200	3200	4400	7000	15,000
Limousine	—	2900	3700	5600	9100	20,000

1917 Dorris, model 1-B-6, limousine, HAC

1918 Dorris, model 1-C-6, touring, HAC

1919 Dorris, model 6-80, touring, HAC

1919 DORRIS
Model 6-80 — 6-cyl., 80 hp, 132" wb

	FP	5	4	3	2	1
Touring-7P	3500	3300	4400	6700	12,000	24,000
Touring-4P	3500	3500	4500	7000	13,000	25,000
Limousine	4850	3000	4000	6000	9500	21,000

1920 Dorris, model 6-80, touring, HAC

1920 DORRIS
Model 6-80 — 6-cyl., 80 hp, 132" wb

	FP	5	4	3	2	1
Touring-7P	4350	3500	4500	7000	13,000	25,000
Roadster-4P	4350	3900	4800	7700	14,300	27,000
Sedan-7P	5720	2400	3400	4800	8000	17,000
Coupe-5P	5280	2700	3600	5300	8800	19,000
Limousine	5800	3100	4200	6300	10,500	22,000

1921 Dorris, model 6-80, touring, HAC

1921 DORRIS
Model 6-80 — 6-cyl., 80 hp, 132" wb

	FP	5	4	3	2	1
Touring-7P	4785	3500	4500	7000	13,000	25,000
Touring-4P	4785	3700	4700	7300	13,700	26,000
Sedan-7P	6690	2400	3400	4800	8000	17,000
Coupe-4P	5800	2700	3600	5300	8800	19,000

1922 Dorris, model 6-80, sedan, HAC

1922 DORRIS
Model 6-80 — 6-cyl., 80 hp, 132" wb

Touring-7P	4785	3700	4700	7300	13,700	26,000
Tourist-4P	4785	3900	4800	7700	14,300	27,000
Coupe-4P	5800	2900	3700	5600	9100	20,000
Sedan-7P	7190	2500	3500	5000	8500	18,000

1923 Dorris, model 6-80, 4-pass. coupe, JAC

1923 DORRIS
Model 6-80 — 6-cyl., 73 hp, 132" wb

Touring-7P	3950	3700	4700	7300	13,700	26,000
Touring-4P	3950	3900	4800	7700	14,300	27,000
Pasadena Touring	4150	4000	5000	8000	15,000	28,000
Coupe-4P	4985	2900	3700	5600	9100	20,000
Sedan-7P	5750	2500	3500	5000	8500	18,000

1924 DORRIS
Model 6-80 — 6-cyl., 70 hp, 132" wb

Touring-7P	3950	3700	4700	7300	13,700	26,000
Pasadena Phaeton-4P	4150	4000	5000	8000	15,000	28,000
Coupe-4P	4985	2900	3700	5600	9100	20,000
Sedan-7P	5800	2500	3500	5000	8500	18,000
Sedan-5P	5500	2700	3600	5300	8800	19,000

1924-25 Dorris, model 6-80, Pasadena phaeton, HAC

1925-1926 DORRIS
Model 6-80 — 6-cyl., 70 hp, 132" wb

	FP	5	4	3	2	1
Touring-7P	4150	3900	4800	7700	14,300	27,000
Pasadena Phaeton-4P	4150	4200	5200	8400	15,700	29,000
Coupe-4P	4985	3000	4000	6000	9500	21,000
Sedan-5P	5550	2700	3600	5300	8800	19,000
Sedan-7P	5800	2500	3500	5000	8500	18,000

DORSETT — Alton, Illinois — (1914) — This miniature mono-car was built by William Dorsett of Alton in 1914 for his five-year-old son. Its 3 hp air-cooled engine and friction transmission were purchased, but all other parts of the car were built by Dorsett. The wheelbase was 61 inches, the tread 27 inches — and the young boy apparently enjoyed the vehicle immensely . . . until he grew out of it.

1916 Dort, touring, HAC

DORT — Flint, Michigan — (1915-1924) — Together they had formed the Flint Road Cart Company in 1886, which evolved into the Durant-Dort Carriage Company — and, for the whole of their lives, Josiah Dallas Dort and William Crapo Durant remained the closest of friends. When Durant went off to his adventures with Buick and General Motors and Chevrolet, Dort stayed behind with the carriage business, but always lent his support, both moral and financial. In 1915 the Dort Motor Car Company was born, and J. Dallas Dort became an automobile manufacturer too, perhaps reluctantly because he had been a confirmed carriage man for years. The Dort he produced was a fine little car. Chief engineer for the company from beginning to end was Etienne Planche, who had helped Louis Chevrolet build the first Chevrolet. From the beginning the Dort was assembled in Canada as well by William Gray, under the name Gray Dort. The only real contretemps the firm suffered during the early years was the attempt by the Dart Motor Truck Company of Waterloo, Iowa to force Dort not to use that name because of conflict with its own. Dort's 1914 priority of registration was established, but the case was thrown out of court in 1917 — and the Dort sanguinely sailed on. A four-cylinder car only was offered through 1916, but the year following saw a cloverleaf roadster and two closed cars added to the line. Prices hovered gently around the $1000 mark. Nineteen twenty was the Dort's peak year, with 30,000 cars sold. Nineteen twenty-one brought a radiator restyling which flattered Rolls-Royce by imitation; the year following an interesting nine-window sedan was introduced. Harvard and Yale were designations given closed cars in 1923, and sporting open models were given disc wheels. Lycoming fours had powered Dorts since 1915; a Falls six was added in 1923, and was the only car offered in '24, the last year of Dort production. Total production over the decade had been more than 107,000 cars. Dort began the liquidation of his company's assets in the fall of 1924. He sold his factory to A.C. Spark Plug early in 1925. In May that year, on a local golf course, J. Dallas Dort died following a heart attack at age sixty-four.

1915-1916 DORT
Four — 17 hp, 105" wb

Touring-5P	650	2400	3400	4800	8000	17,000

1917 DORT
Four — 16.9 hp, 105" wb

Touring-5P	695	2500	3500	5000	8500	18,000
Sedan-5P	1065	2200	3200	4400	7000	15,000
Sedanet	815	2000	3000	4200	6500	14,000
Cloverleaf Roadster	695	2700	3600	5300	8800	19,000

1917 Dort, Cloverleaf, roadster, HAC

1918 DORT
Four — 19.6 hp, 105" wb

	FP	5	4	3	2	1
Touring-5P	—	2700	3600	5300	8800	19,000
Roadster-3P	—	3000	4000	6000	9500	21,000
Sedan-5P	—	2000	3000	4200	6500	14,000
Coupe-3P	—	2300	3300	4600	7500	16,000
Sedanet-5P	—	1800	2800	4000	6200	13,000

1918-19 Dort, touring, HAC

1919 DORT
Four — 19.6 hp, 105-1/2" wb

Touring-5P	925	2700	3600	5300	8800	19,000
Sedan-5P	1355	2000	3000	4200	6500	14,000
Sedanet	1090	1800	2800	4000	6200	13,000
Coupe	1355	2300	3300	4600	7500	16,000
Roadster	925	3000	4000	6000	9500	21,000

1920 Dort, four season coupe, HAC

1920 DORT
Four — 30 hp, 105-1/2" wb

Touring-5P	985	2900	3700	5600	9100	20,000
Roadster-3P	985	3100	4200	6300	10,500	22,000
Sedan-5P	1535	2000	3000	4200	6500	14,000
Coupe-3P	1535	2400	3400	4800	8000	17,000

1921 DORT
Four — 30 hp, 108" wb

Touring-5P	1215	2900	3700	5600	9100	20,000
Roadster-2P	1215	3100	4200	6300	10,500	22,000
Coupe-4P	1865	2400	3400	4800	8000	17,000
Sedan-5P	1995	2000	3000	4200	6500	14,000

1921 Dort, touring, JAC

1922 Dort, coupe, JAC

1922 DORT
Four — 30 hp, 108" wb

	FP	5	4	3	2	1
Touring-5P	985	3000	4000	6000	9500	21,000
Roadster-2P	985	3200	4300	6500	11,000	23,000
Coupe-3P	1165	2500	3500	5000	8500	18,000
Sedan-5P	1195	2200	3200	4400	7000	15,000
Coupe-4P	1495	2600	3600	5200	8700	18,500
Sedan-5P	1645	2250	3300	4500	7300	15,500

1923 Dort, touring, JAC

1924 Dort, 3-dr. coupe, JAC

469

1923 DORT
Four — 32 hp, 108" wb

	FP	5	4	3	2	1
Touring-5P	865	3000	4000	6000	9500	21,000
Roadster-2P	865	3200	4300	6500	11,000	23,000
Sport Touring-5P	995	3100	4200	6300	10,500	22,000
Sport Roadster-2P	995	3300	4400	6700	12,000	24,000
Yale Coupe-2P	1020	2900	3700	5600	9100	20,000
Yale Sedan-5P	1070	2700	3600	5300	8800	19,000
Harvard Coupe-3P	1240	3000	4000	6000	9500	21,000
Harvard Sedan-3P	1370	2900	3700	5600	9100	20,000

Six — 45 hp, 115" wb

Touring-5P	990	3100	4200	6300	10,500	22,000
Roadster-2P	990	3300	4400	6700	12,000	24,000
Sport Touring-5P	1120	3200	4300	6500	11,000	23,000
Sport Roadster-2P	1120	3500	4500	7000	13,000	25,000
Yale Coupe-2P	1145	3000	4000	6000	9500	21,000
Yale Sedan-5P	1195	2900	3700	5600	9100	20,000
Harvard Coupe-3P	1365	3100	4200	6300	10,500	22,000
Harvard Sedan-3P	1495	3000	4000	6000	9500	21,000

1924 Dort, touring, WLB

1924 Dort, brougham, WLB

1924 DORT
Six — 45 hp, 115" wb

Touring-5P	1095	3100	4200	6300	10,500	22,000
Sport Touring-5P	1245	3200	4300	6500	11,000	23,000
Brougham-5P	1535	2700	3600	5300	8800	19,000
Coupe-5P	1535	3100	4200	6300	10,500	22,000
Sedan-5P	1595	2500	3500	5000	8500	18,000

DOUGLAS — During the summer of 1909 the Douglas County Automobile Company was organized in Tuscola, Illinois with a capital stock of $5000 for the manufacture of motorcars and accessories. Guy R. Jones was the man behind this venture. Manufacture of a car is doubted.

1905 Douglas Electric

470

DOUGLAS ELECTRIC — Belleville, New Jersey — (1905) — This electric coupe from 1905 was invented by W.H. Douglas of Belleville and was built for him by Healey & Company of New York. The Douglas was elegant in the carriage trade sense and quite unusual in being front wheel drive, the motors suspended from the front axle and driven through universal joints. Only one example of this car was apparently produced.

1918 Douglas, 8, model G, touring, WLB

DOUGLAS — Omaha, Nebraska — (1918-1919) — In the early spring of 1918, the Douglas Motor Corporation succeeded the Drummond Motor Company in Omaha. Douglas revised the former Drummond V-8 into the new Douglas V-8, increasing its horsepower, lengthening its wheelbase, and raising its prices. The Douglas powerplant was a Herschell-Spillman, and "supplying the Middlewest with a high-powered car at a reasonable price" was the stated purpose of the company. A racy Speedster Special was thrown in for good measure. None of this resulted in the Douglas surviving any longer than had the Drummond. Douglas Motor Corporation was, however, also engaged in the manufacture of commercial vehicles in Omaha, and truck production continued into the mid-Thirties, though a temporary receivership was suffered in 1923.

1918-1919 DOUGLAS
Eight — 75 hp, 122" wb

	FP	5	4	3	2	1
Touring-5P	2000	3000	4000	6000	9500	21,000
Touring-7P	2100	2900	3700	5600	9100	20,000
Roadster-3P	2000	3300	4400	6700	12,000	24,000
Spds. Spc. (126" wb)	2250	4000	5000	8000	15,000	28,000

DOUGLASS — "Dr. J.P. Douglass, Harrisonville, Missouri is building an automobile for his own use," reported *The Horseless Age* in 1903. Details are lacking.

DOVER — The Dover Garage Company was organized with a capital stock of $10,000 in December of 1904 to "manufacture, deal in and repair motor vehicles" in Dover, New Jersey. The incorporators were Robert A. Bennett, Charles E. Clark and Hiram P. Hall. No manufacturing seems to have come of this venture, although the year previous Hiram Hall had had a brief fling as the manufacturer of an automobile named for himself.

DOVETAIL — Crawfordsville, Indiana — (1900) — In 1900 the Dovetail Carriage Company of Crawfordsville designed and built a gasoline motor carriage to the general specification of Mills Gregg, a mechanical engineering student at Purdue University. All parts of the car, including the engine, were the product of the Dovetail shops and, according to *The Autobain*, the company was so pleased with the results that it planned "to go into the building of horseless carriages as a sideline." How long the firm might have continued in this activity is not known.

DOW — Longmont, California — (1900) — Details regarding its construction are lacking, but *The Horseless Age* in January 1900 documented that A.L. Dow of Longmont was building a gasoline automobile.

DOWAGIAC — The Dowagiac was planned as the successor to the Lindsley which was produced in Dowagiac, Michigan from 1908-1909. Refer to Lindsley.

DOWNING — That a car called the Downing was built in New York City in 1901 has been indicated on various car rosters. This does not appear to be the case. In late November of 1900 a C.J. Downing & Company had been organized in New York, but only to "deal in bicycles and automobiles." That was the only automotive-related venture named Downing in town at the turn of the century.

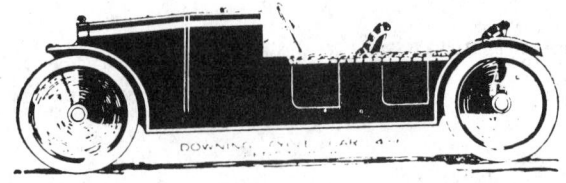

1914 Downing Cyclecar, 2-pass. tandem, NAHC

DOWNING — Detroit & Cleveland — (1913-1915)/DOWNING-DETROIT — (1914-1915) — The Downing Cyclecar Car Company of Detroit made a very serious mistake. It chose to call its vehicle a cyclecar. True, one of its two-passenger models featured tandem seating, but the other provided comfortable side-by-side, and there was a four-passenger model as well. The wheelbase for all 18 hp four-cylinder models was 105 inches, the tread a standard 56 inches, the wheels optional wire or wood, the frame pressed steel, the transmission a three-speed selective. The 10 hp two-cylinder models shared similar specs but the wheelbase was 103 inches. Just about the most cyclecar aspect of the Downing was its price range of under five hundred dollars. Had it been advertised as a light car at cyclecar prices, it might have survived longer. There is some confusion regarding the Downing company. Brochures indicate its designation as the Downing Cyclecar Company, as do most trade press references, with the Detroit address listed. During the summer of 1913 the firm announced its intention to build a cyclecar in Cleveland, as well, the specifications of this Downing differing chiefly in wheelbase and price. References following this indicate a change of firm name to Downing Motor Car Company, with the Detroit-produced cars being called the Downing-Detroits thereafter. This probably was to avoid confusion with the Cleveland car.

1915 Downing, model B, touring, WLB

1913-1915 DOWNING/DOWNING-DETROIT
Model A — 2-cyl., 10 hp, 103" wb

	FP	5	4	3	2	1
Tandem Runabout-2P	450	3100	4200	6300	10,500	22,000
Side-by-Side Roadster-2P	450	3300	4400	6700	12,000	24,000

Model B — 4-cyl., 18 hp, 105" wb

	FP	5	4	3	2	1
Tandem Runabout-2P	450	3100	4200	6300	10,500	22,000
Side-by-Side Roadster-2P	480	3300	4400	6700	12,000	24,000
Touring-4P	530	3700	4700	7300	13,700	26,000
Light Delivery	450	2900	3700	5600	9100	20,000

Cleveland-built Downing
Two — 12 hp, 98" wb

	FP	5	4	3	2	1
Side-by-Side Roadster	400	3300	4400	6700	12,000	24,000

Four — 18 hp, 98" wb

	FP	5	4	3	2	1
Side-by-Side Roadster	400	3400	4500	6900	12,500	24,500

DOWNTOWN — The Downtown Garage and Automobile Repair Company was organized early in 1906 in New York City to "manufacture automobiles and parts." Capital stock was $5000; the incorporators were Eugene R. Geddes and Frank M. Raynor of Brooklyn, and Alva Collins of New York City. Manufacture is doubted.

DOYLE — West Homestead, Pennsylvania — (1900) — The Borough of West Homestead, Pennsylvania was established in 1900, and the first man to set himself up in business in town was Al Leuschner. Leuschner operated a wagon shop, which proved to be a flourishing business, and later that year he was called upon to provide the coachwork for a horseless carriage devised by a mechanically minded Homestead physician named Joseph Doyle. Dr. Doyle's was the first automobile in the area, and created a great stir. Although the physician was momentarily carried away with the idea of going into manufacture as the Homestead Motor Vehicle Company, he quickly decided to confine his talents to the medical profession. Doyle Avenue in West Homestead is named after him.

1907 Dragon, Golden Dragon, runabout, WLB

DRAGON — Detroit & Philadelphia — (1906-1908) — The Dragon Automobile Company hired an excellent engineer to design its automobile: Leo Melanowski, who had apprenticed with the Otto Gas Engine Company in Vienna, worked for Panhard-Levassor and Clement-Bayard in France and Waltham in the United States and who was part of the engineering team responsible for the racing Winton Bullets of 1901-1903 in America. Dragon also enlisted the services of famed racing driver Joe Tracy as an engineering consultant and test driver. The result was a very fine four-cylinder motorcar which featured sliding gear transmission and shaft drive, and price tags in the $2000 range which were quite reasonable considering the specification. The matter Dragon skimped upon, it would appear, was quality control in production. Melanowski left early on to design the Aerocar from Detroit, and Joe Tracy didn't hang around long either. The company had been organized in the summer of 1906. Production began in Detroit in late fall, and the first models were ready for the New York Automobile Show at Grand Central Palace that December. Meanwhile the plant of the J.G. Brill Company in Philadelphia had been secured, and operations were moved there. Soon thereafter two attachments were served by the Sheriff of New York County on the cars and property of the Dragon Automobile Company. These resulted from two complaints. The first was from C.W. Ward, the Dragon agent for Newark (New Jersey), who stated that three cars had been delivered to him which "were not up to the standard guaranteed, and it was found impossible to get the company to put them in proper repair." Ward wanted his advance deposit back. The other complainant was W.S. Daniels of Boston, a former Dragon employee, who demanded back salary and commissions amounting to $1700. Nor was this all. It was further reported that the Dragon Automobile Company had borrowed $136,000 from a Philadelphia bank, using as security 200 Dragon touring cars that had been placed in storage in Philadelphia, to be removed therefrom only under the bank's direction and with a percentage of their sale price to be applied as part payment for the loan. By this time screaming creditors included the Herschell-Spillman engine manufacturers and the coil-and-spark-plug-producing C.F. Splitdorf company. By December of 1907 the Dragon Automobile Company had given up, its president John Kane Mills declaring personal bankruptcy three months later. By that time the firm had been succeeded by the Dragon Motor Company organized by J.E. Calhoun with a grand capitalization of a million dollars and the idea of entering the taxicab market. In March of 1908 Calhoun, already in trouble, agreed to receivership although he denied insolvency. Among his problems was the five months back rent that had been owed the J.B. Brill Company by Dragon Automobile Company, the payment for which Brill was now demanding of Dragon Motor Company. By late March Calhoun decided to give up too. Seventy touring car chassis remained to be completed when the Dragon plant and its assets were sold at public auction in early April 1908. Gorson Auto Exchange of Philadelphia bought everything, and presumably finished building the last fifty Dragons.

1906-1907 DRAGON
4-cyl., 24/26 hp, 104" wb

	FP	5	4	3	2	1
Touring-5P	2000	4000	5000	8000	15,000	28,000
Runabout-2P	2000	3900	4800	7700	14,300	27,000

1908 Dragon, roadster, HAC

1908 DRAGON
4-cyl., 35 hp, 96 wb

	FP	5	4	3	2	1
Roadster-2P	1850	3900	4800	7700	14,300	27,000

4-cyl., 24/26 hp, 104" wb

	FP	5	4	3	2	1
Touring-5P	2100	4000	5000	8000	15,000	28,000
Town Car-5P	2100	4200	5200	8400	15,700	29,000

1920 Dragon, victoria, WLB

471

DRAGON — Chicago, Illinois — (1920-1921) — In 1908, in Chicago, a company called the Dragon Automobile Works was organized with offices on State Street and plans to enter automobile manufacture. Production was never begun, and the company faded quietly out of sight later that year. The second Dragon from the Windy City arrived over a decade later, and did not fade quietly. In late July of 1920 the Dragon Motors Corporation announced that it had been capitalized at a million dollars and had just purchased the W.N. Selig motion picture plant for $360,000. The former movie studio was to be turned into an automobile factory for production of a taxicab as well as "America's Most Elegant Car." Herman Neidick, Joseph Stein and Hyman Edelman were the men behind this new Dragon. They immediately began an extensive advertising campaign to sell stock, mailing out photographs of the Selig studio and claiming that production was already ongoing there at the rate of one "America's Most Elegant Car" per day. Brochure photographs indicated the model line to include a touring car that looked a lot like a ReVere, a victoria, and a roadster called a Pup. The Dragon Company was also predicting a rosy future for itself as a taxicab producer. By late January of 1921 the further sale of Dragon stock was banned in the state of Illinois. By that summer the officers of the Dragon Motors Corporation were indicted for fraud. Approximately 300 people had been swindled out of sums ranging from $100 to $5000. Bankruptcy proceedings followed that September, and it was determined at that time that a grand total of thirteen Dragons had been built in the company's studio-factory. Subsequently, the Dragon organizers went on trial on charges of misuse of the mails and violations of the blue sky laws, and thereafter they went to jail.

1920-1921 DRAGON
Four — 58 hp, 120" wb

	FP	5	4	3	2	1
Touring-5P	3230	4500	5800	9500	18,000	32,000
Victoria-4P	3230	4400	5600	9200	17,300	31,000
Pip Roadster-2P	3230	4400	5600	9200	17,300	31,000

DRAKE — The Drake Electric Company was organized in Chicago late in 1904 with a $10,000 capital stock to "manufacture automobiles and electric appliances." The incorporators were James M. Wilson, William Herrick and Frank E. Drake. Manufacture of a car is doubted.

1921 Drake Six, touring, KM

DRAKE — Knoxville, Tennessee — (1921-1922) — The Drake Motor & Tire Manufacturing Company was incorporated in 1921 with an authorized capitalization of three million dollars. W.F. Drake was the organizer, and he proposed to manufacture automobiles, trucks, tires, tractors, rubber by-products, bodies and sheet metal parts. This was an ambitious effort that was backed, as Drake said, by "substantial citizens and men of acknowledged business sagacity." With the exception of A.J. Sisk, a "retired farmer and capitalist" from Byington, all of the officers of the Drake company were Knoxville men, retired contractors, real estate dealers and merchants among them. The Drake automobile was offered as a four and six (Herschell-Spillman). The former was pretty much a standard artillery-wheeled touring car of the day, but the latter was quite comely, with rakishly pleasing lines and smart disc wheels. The Drake chassis was said to be "built like the Rock of Gibraltar," but its solid foundation was apparently not shared by the Drake Motor & Tire Manufacturing Company. In June of 1921 the company offered a "special rebate agreement" to stockholders holding ten or more shares, offering them a ten-percent discount on the purchase of any Drake automobile, truck or farm tractor. The Drake company soon succumbed to the reality of the postwar recession, although not before producing a modest number of standard cars and one spectacularly special version of its six for silent film actress Mildred Reardon. It was a huge seven-passenger touring car with a hood of polished aluminum.

1921-1922 DRAKE
Drake Four — 100" wb

Touring-5P	795	4200	5200	8400	15,700	29,000

Drake Six — 57 hp, 127" wb

Touring-5P	2500	5400	7300	11,800	25,000	38,000
Sport Model-5P	2695	5800	8000	12,500	28,000	40,000

DRAPER — The Draper Corporation of Hopedale, Massachusetts has been cited as having built an automobile in 1904. Residents of Hopedale in the employ of the company during that period indicate that no automobile ever was built, that the Draper production was devoted exclusively to

weaving looms. George Otis Draper, who was a cousin of Massachusetts Governor Eben Draper, did own the first automobile in town, but it was a Stanley steam car. *The Horseless Age* in 1903 reported that George Draper was "building a new automobile" but no one in Hopedale apparently knew about it.

DREADNOUGHT — This was a model of the Moline built in East Moline, Illinois from 1904-1913. The designation was used beginning in 1912, to call promotional attention to the car's fine performance in numerous endurance contests of that period. Refer to Moline.

1917 Drexel, model 4-60, 4-pass. club roadster, WLB

DREXEL — Chicago, Illinois — (1916-1917) — In essence, the Drexel Motor Car Corporation of Chicago was the Farmack Motor Car Company with a fresh infusion of capital. Albert J. Farmer required extra cash to bring out a more advanced version of his Farmack, and if calling it a Drexel was necessary, he didn't mind that at all. His 41 hp overhead camshaft Farmer four-cylinder engine was continued in a $985 Drexel five-seat touring car. But now he could hopefully also introduce a seven-passenger touring with a new Farmer four-cylinder engine developing 63 hp at 3600 rpm (an unusually high-revving powerplant for that era) and featuring a double overhead camshaft with four valves per cylinder (which was equally unusual). At $1650 this Drexel would have been a remarkable buy and, with the optional four-passenger club roadster body, was probably the fastest car produced in Chicago. A brilliant engineer, Albert Farmer was not nearly so astute as a businessman. In the spring of 1917 he was asked to resign from the Drexel company for reasons of mismanagement, although the internal dissension abated somewhat when the Drexel backers realized that their most valuable asset was the sixteen-valve engine to which Farmer held the patents. Unfortunately, two Chicago banks which had invested heavily in the company subsequently failed, and by mid-summer of 1917 Drexel was bankrupt, with Harry B. Staver (who had earlier produced the Staver car in Chicago) appointed as receiver. Initially, there was a plan to reorganize the firm to produce a new automobile powered by the Ferro V-8 engine (A.J. Farmer had by now irrevocably left the company), but this never materialized. Instead the property of the Drexel Motor Corporation — valued at $122,410 — went to the auction block in late October 1917. Probably no more than pilot models of the new Drexel had ever been built.

1916 DREXEL
Model 5-40 — 4-cyl., 41 hp, 112" wb

	FP	5	4	3	2	1
Touring	985	3900	4800	7700	14,300	27,000

Model 7-60 — 4-cyl., 63 hp, 118" wb

Touring	1650	4200	5200	8400	15,700	29,000

Model 4-60 — 4-cyl., 63 hp, 118" wb

Club Roadster	1650	4400	5600	9200	17,300	31,000

1917 DREXEL
Model R-30/35 — 4-cyl., 35 hp, 112" wb

Touring-5P	855	3900	4800	7700	14,300	27,000
Roadster-2P	855	4000	5000	8000	15,000	28,000

1921 Driggs, roadster, WLB

DRIGGS-SEABURY — Sharon, Pennsylvania, (1915)/DRIGGS — New Haven, Connecticut — (1921-1923) — The Driggs Seabury Ordnance Corporation was one of several U.S. armaments producers to go into automobile manufacture, the most famous being J. Stevens Arms and Tool Company with its Stevens-Duryea. Actually, Driggs attempted the automotive field twice. The first time around the company tried the shotgun rather than the rifle approach. Prior to the First World War, the firm, embarked upon commercial vehicle production (1912) and followed this in 1915 with a cyclecar offered in two models sporting a four-cylinder engine and an underslung frame. The roadster featured a cone clutch and two-speed progressive transmission, the tandem sported a friction transmission and chain drive. The Driggs-Seabury was not, however, the only cyclecar being produced in the company's Sharon factory. Driggs also manufactured cyclecars for the Twombly and Ritz companies of New York City, as well as the somewhat larger Vulcan light car for an Ohio firm. Late in 1915 the Driggs-Seabury cyclecar was renamed the Sharon cyclecar, and its production was discontinued shortly thereafter. In its second time around in the automobile field six years later, the Driggs Ordnance & Manufacturing Corporation (as it was now renamed) decided to try the rifle method: a single model offered in varying body styles on a uniform chassis. During the summer of 1921 president L.L. Driggs announced that he had set up executive offices in New York City and a factory in New Haven, Connecticut (the same plant in which Driggs had manufactured war material for the U.S. Government during World War I) and that 100 units of the new Driggs were already in the works. They remained there quite some time, because it was not until October that the first lot of twenty-five was shipped out to dealers. Production remained minimal through the following year. In early October 1922 Driggs decided that better fortune might be had in the taxicab business, and most of the cars which followed were designed with meters for the taxi market. In a reorganization which followed receivership in November of 1923, the decision was made to concentrate on taxis exclusively. Thought "Built with the Precision of Ordnance" had been an appealing slogan for the Driggs production car, it had suffered one fatal flaw. For a small vehicle, it carried big prices. Driggs taxis were built into 1925.

1915 DRIGGS-SEABURY

	FP	5	4	3	2	1
Model A Tandem (4-cyl., 100" wb)	395	2500	3500	5000	8500	18,000
Model C Roadster (4-cyl., 100" wb)	395	2700	3600	5300	8800	19,000

1921-1922 DRIGGS
Model D — 4-cyl., 22 hp, 104" wb

	FP	5	4	3	2	1
Touring-4P	1275	3000	4000	6000	9500	21,000
Roadster-2P	1275	3100	4200	6300	10,500	22,000
Sedan-4P	1975	2500	3500	5000	8500	18,000

1922 Driggs, sedan, JAC

1923 DRIGGS
Model D — 4-cyl., 22 hp, 104" wb

Touring-4P	1275	3000	4000	6000	9500	21,000
Roadster-2P	1275	3100	4200	6300	10,500	22,000
Coupe-2P	1675	2700	3600	5300	8800	19,000
Sedan-4P	1975	2500	3500	5000	8500	18,000

1916 Drummond, Four, touring, WLB

DRUMMOND — Omaha, Nebraska — (1915-1918) — In the fall of 1909 the Drummond Carriage Company of Omaha — which had been founded by James Drummond in 1906 — decided to sell out its line of horsedrawn vehicles and to engage itself henceforth in the auto repair business. Six years later Drummond decided that if it could repair cars it could build them as well — and the Drummond Motor Car Company was the result.

J.W. Griffith was its president, F.W. Bacon vice-president and general manager, W.L. Griffith secretary and treasurer, R.W. Craig general sales manager. Initially the Drummond was offered as a four and a six, and its model range included a town car with a detachable top. For the 1917 model year all Drummonds were V-8's (Herschell-Spillman engine), and precious few of them were built. By early spring of 1918, the Drummond Motor Company of Omaha was succeeded by the Douglas Motor Corporation of Omaha. The new Douglas survived for an even shorter period than the old Drummond.

1916 DRUMMOND
Six — 22 hp, 120" wb

	FP	5	4	3	2	1
Touring-5P	1275	3900	4800	7700	14,300	27,000
Roadster-2P	1275	4200	5200	8400	15,700	29,000
Town Car Sedan-5P	1625	4000	5000	8000	15,000	28,000

Four — 36 hp, 115" wb

Touring-5P	1095	3700	4700	7300	13,700	26,000
Roadster-2P	1095	4000	5000	8000	15,000	28,000
Town Car Sedan-5P	1445	3900	4800	7700	14,300	27,000

1917 DRUMMOND
Model 17 — 8-cyl., 28 hp, 120" wb

Touring-5P	1600	4300	5400	8700	16,500	30,000
Roadster-2P	1600	4400	5600	9200	17,300	31,000
Cloverleaf Roadster-3P	1600	4500	5700	9400	17,700	31,500

DRURY-WELLS — Early in 1912 the Drury-Wells Motor Company was organized in Youngstown, Ohio with a capital stock of $10,000 for the manufacture of automobiles and parts. F.E. Drury was the only announced partner. Manufacture is doubted.

D-S — New York, New York — (1902) — "The D-S electro-gasoline automobile of New York is another claimant for the honor of revolutionizing the automobile industry," *The Motor Age* said somewhat skeptically during the fall of 1902, adding, "This machine uses a 6 horsepower gasoline motor, in which the flywheel is the armature of a dynamo or generator of electricity, to furnish electric energy to drive electric motors which form the hubs of the four wheels of the vehicle." The Hub Motor Vehicle Company and the Fischer Equipment Company had earlier introduced the same idea; this johnny-come-lately was even less successful, and not heard from again.

DUAL — Los Angeles & Midway City, California — (1922-1923)/Pomona, California — (1924) — Among the cars Los Angeles automobile dealer Theodore E. Felt represented were the Standard Electric, the Vulcan and the Woods. He was most impressed with the last named, especially the Woods Dual Power model. Early in 1922 the *Los Angeles Times* revealed that Felt had "secured the exclusive rights for California to build and sell this car." This was interesting since the Woods Dual Power had failed in Chicago about the time of the Armistice. Its resurrection would now be seen by the T.E. Felt Motor Car Company. Initially, a factory in Los Angeles was planned but early 1923 brought the news that the new Dual would be produced in a one-story cement factory in Midway City which was already under construction. Felt mentioned that he had built twenty Duals six years previously which he had put into taxi service in Los Angeles and they were still running "good as new." (More than likely, he had simply purchased and possibly refurbished Wood Dual Powers.) So convinced was Felt of the Dual's durability that he planned to offer a three-year guarantee. "He is preparing now to start quantity production," one trade press reporter wrote. "He also is selling stock." Doubtless that reporter had a good deal of fun writing that story. T.E. Felt vanished into the western sunset soon after. But the Dual automobile idea remained around awhile longer. It just moved to Pomona. The people behind it now were also the people promoting the Balboa in Fullerton. The Pomona connection was, specifically, the Pomona Pump Company which was interested in using the Balboa-Kessler engine in a new tractor and the Kessler four in tree-spraying wagons. That project fizzled, though for awhile the Balboa people did occupy a disused shed on the pump company's property. And perhaps it was in that shed that the Dual idea was reborn. Again, reference to the Woods Dual Power was made, but the engine for the Dual now was to be reworked from the Kessler four. Old-timers in the area recall that five automobiles (three touring cars and two roadsters) with "odd four-cylinder engines" were secretly built in a factory about twenty miles away. Probably the secrecy was necessary because the Balboa venture was mired in stock promotion fraud charges at the time. The Dual ended its career in the same shroud of bad feeling that the Balboa did.

DUBLIN — The Dublin Buggy Company announced during the summer of 1909 its plan to bring automobile manufacturing to Dublin, Georgia. The firm increased its capital stock by $50,000 for the purpose of erecting a one-story brick building in which to produce low-priced vehicles. Whether any cars were built is not known.

DuBOIS — The DuBois Automobile Agency was organized during the fall of 1900 in Jersey City, New Jersey for the manufacture of motor vehicles. Behind this $100,000 incorporation were J.I. Billings, K. McLarne and T. Barker. Manufacture is doubted.

DU BRIE-CAILLE — Detroit, Michigan — (1904) — Stanley R. Du Brie was a mechanical engineering graduate of the University of Ohio, and the Caille Brothers were Detroit manufacturers who claimed to have invented the slot machine. Their partnership was a long time coming. Following his graduation in 1896, Du Brie had built his first experimental car and had established the Du Brie Motor Works in Fremont (Ohio) for the manufacture of two-stroke marine engines. He sold this business to the Clauss Shear Works in 1900 and went north to Canada where he built his second car for the Charles Beck Manufacturing Company of Penetang, Ontario. Then he designed a line of two-stroke marine engines for Peter Payette & Company, also of Penetang and the largest gasoline marine engine makers

1904 DuBrie-Caille, touring, GB

in the Dominion. Shortly thereafter, Du Brie returned to the United States convinced that the two-cycle principle was the answer for the automobile industry, and in Detroit he found the Caille Brothers who were happily building their slot machines and who were willing to take a gamble on his proposition. With the Cailles' financial backing, Du Brie produced a prototype touring car with a two-cylinder, two-stroke engine and began testing it in July 1904 in the countryside surrounding Detroit. It put up 30 mph on high speed, and from 12-15 mpg on rough rural roads. This was probably the only example built. Although Hugh Dolnar gave the car a rave review in *Cycle and Automobile Trade Journal*, there is no evidence that production ever followed. The Caille Brothers returned to their one-armed bandits, and Du Brie returned to the marine engine field. A decade later Caille began producing engines too. And in 1910 Stanley Du Brie tried again with the Templeton-Du Brie.

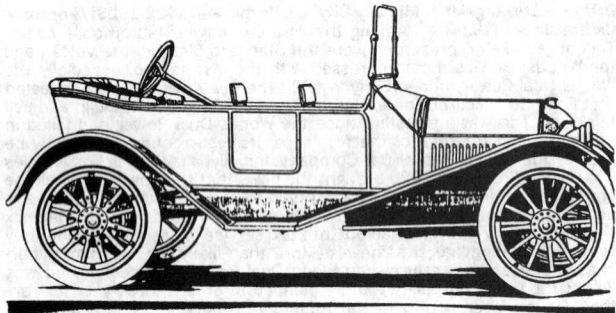

1913 Duck, KM

DUCK — The Duck was a model of the Jackson produced in Jackson, Michigan from 1903 to 1923. It was available only in 1913, and was also known as the Jackson Back Seat Steer, which literally described its difference from the rest of the Jackson line. Two passengers sat in front; the driver and another passenger in the back.

1866 Dudgeon Steam Wagon, NAHC

DUDGEON STEAM — New York, New York — (1857, 1866) — In 1857 Richard Dudgeon of New York City completed his work on America's first practical steam carriage. A prolific inventor, Dudgeon enjoyed financial

success principally through the hydraulic jack he had designed in the early 1850's. With shipbuilding and the railroad business booming, his jacks found ready acceptance and his machine shop in lower Manhattan boomed. Dudgeon's first steam carriage was a success as well. "Considerable attention has been excited during the last year by the occasional appearance on Broadway of a steam locomotive built by Mr. Richard Dudgeon," reported the *Annual of Scientific Discovery* in 1858. "Its speed was about equal with the average speed of horses in stages and it was apparently controlled with much ease, and with more certainty." Unfortunately, the vehicle was also destroyed that year when fire raged through the Crystal Palace where it was on exhibit as part of the annual fair of the American Institute. Business matters prevented Dudgeon from building another one until after the Civil War. His 1866 vehicle differed from the first only in particulars. Steam cylinders were located on each side of a horizontal boiler connected with the rear wheels. The front axle was on a kingpin, as was traditional wagon practice. Although Dudgeon stood ready to produce examples of the vehicle for anyone asking for same, apparently no one asked. Dudgeon used his car to carry himself to and from business, and to convey his family to church. Reportedly, it was noisy and consumed two bushels of coal and "a hogshead of water" on each trip. Reportedly, too, after he had driven it for about ten years, New York City authorities outlawed him from the road. Dudgeon died in Manhattan in 1895. Following the New York World's Fair in 1940, where it was on exhibition, the Dudgeon steam carriage was purchased for $500 by early car collectors George H. Waterman, Jr. and Kirkland H. Gibson. About thirty years ago historian Phil Dumka joined Joe Knowles, who maintained many of the Waterman cars, on a test drive of the vehicle. It was memorable. Said Phil: "The steering wheel at the stand-up operator's station at the rear rotated a screw the length of the vehicle. The screw acted directly on one end of the axle to push or pull the axle around the king pin for a turn — with what seemed fifty turns lock-to-lock — slower steering than an oil tanker. The iron shod wheels tended to drift away from the crown of the blacktop road surface. Joe wore himself out correcting for the drift, then correcting for the correction. I sat alongside the boiler. The total trip was less than one mile, but the blessed beast did run." The Dudgeon remains extant today as one of America's earliest pioneers of the automotive age.

1913 Dudly Bug, cyclecar, OCW

DUDLY BUG — **Menominee, Michigan** — **(1913-1915)** — The Dudly Bug was designed by H.F. Tideman, president of the Dudly Tool Company of Menominee, with the assistance of his younger brother William J. The pilot model was completed in early November of 1913. Production began before year's end. The Dudly Bug featured a two-speed planetary transmission, double belt drive, side-by-side staggered seating, and front fenders that turned with the wheels. Viewed head-on, with the fender latticework and two headlights precariously bulging out, it looked decidedly insectean. "Everybody is 'Bugs,'" advertisements said. The Dudly survived longer than many American cyclecars, probably because the Dudly Tool Company was an already well established firm. When the four-cylinder version for 1915 fared no better than the two-cylinder of 1914, the car was discontinued. H.F. Tideman immediately tried again, this time with an electric called the Menominee.

1914 Dudly Bug, cyclecar, WLB

1913-1914 DUDLEY BUG
Model A-1 — 2-cyl., 10 hp, 96" wb

	FP	5	4	3	2	1
Cyclecar Roadster-2P	375	2200	3200	4400	7000	15,000

1915 DUDLEY BUG
Model B-1 — 4-cyl., 12 hp, 100" wb

	FP	5	4	3	2	1
Cyclecar Roadster-2P	385	2300	3300	4600	7500	16,000

1908 Duer, model A, auto-buggy, WLB

DUER — Chicago, Illinois — (1907-1910) — The Chicago Coach and Carriage Company had been incorporated in 1898, but it was not until 1905 that superintendent Charles Duer was able to persuade company officials to allow him to build an experimental automobile, which he did that year. Yet another two years were required before Duer was allowed to go into production with it, although in the meantime the company began manufacturing automobile components and accessories. The Duer was claimed to be "neither a made-over buggy nor an assemblage of miscellaneous parts." But it was a highwheeler. Like the Holsman, it used rope drive, though in 1908 there was an attempt at modernity with the relocation of the air-cooled engine from beneath the set to underneath a hood, and the fitting of a mock radiator up front. Later Duer even opted for bucket seats instead of the usual bench. When its new contemporary look failed to ignite sales, the Duer was just quietly allowed to die. Occasionally, this car was also referred to as the Chicago Runabout. A few years later the company served as the Chicago agency for the Owen-Magnetic.

1907 DUER
Model A — 2-cyl., 12 hp, 72" wb

	FP	5	4	3	2	1
Runabout-2P	750	2400	3400	4800	8000	17,000

1908 DUER
Model A — 2-cyl., 12 hp, 76" wb

Runabout-2P	750	2500	3500	5000	8500	18,000

1909 DUER
Model A — 2-cyl., 12 hp, 78" wb

Runabout-2P	750	2700	3600	5300	8800	19,000

1910 DUER
Model A — 2-cyl., 16 hp, 74" wb

Runabout-2P	750	2500	3500	5000	8500	18,000
Coupe-2P	900	2300	3300	4600	7500	16,000

1920 Duesenberg, model A, prototype, HAC

DUESENBERG — Indianapolis, Indiana — (1920-1937) — In the March 1903 issue of *Cycle and Automobile Trade Journal*, in the column entitled "Injunctions, Lawsuits, Fires, Judgments, Failures, Etc.," it was revealed that one F.S. Duesenberg, a bicycle builder from Iowa, had filed a petition in bankruptcy, reporting assets of $1075.50 and liabilities of $2115.95. This little-known historic fact is insignificant, perhaps, but mentioned for a reason. If but one of all the automobiles ever built in America had to be singled out as the most glorious achievement in this country's automotive history, that car would have to be the Duesenberg. It transcended the ordinary in full measure, created legends in its wake which will live forever, and became a literal metaphor — "It's a Duesy" — for anything unrelentingly superlative. And yet, just as the man who built it might fail insignificantly in his career, the Duesenberg had its insignificant failings too. But they scarcely mattered in the overall scheme of what the Duesenberg was. Following the bankruptcy of his bicycle business, Fred Duesenberg remained in Iowa where the first car he designed and raced was the Mason. By 1913, in partnership with his brother Augie, he relocated in St. Paul, Minnesota where the Duesenberg Motor Company was organized

1921 Duesenberg, model A, town car, Fleetwood, FR

and where manufacture of auto and marine engines was commenced. The horizontal-valve rocker-arm (or "walking-beam") engine he had designed for the Mason race cars was continued in competition cars which bore the Duesenberg name from 1914. Their success was wonderful; Ralph Mulford and Eddie Rickenbacker drove Duesenbergs to commanding victories on Midwest board tracks. Eddie O'Donnell largely saw to the car's triumphs on the West Coast. The Duesenberg name became famous, and investment capital in the brothers' activities came easier. It is significant that the Duesenbergs never owned but instead were merely employees in their various enterprises. Duesenberg Motors Corporation, a $1.5 million venture, was organized in 1916 by New York capitalists, with construction of a huge factory in Elizabeth, New Jersey following. The war on, and racing largely over for the duration, the Duesenbergs undertook production there of aero engines (and some artillery tractor units) under government contract. The war over, the brothers found themselves with a big factory and nothing commercially significant to manufacture, except their four-cylinder auto engine for a number of new budding automotive manufacturers who had asked for it. This prospect didn't tantalize, since the Duesenbergs by now believed the four passe and were anxious to move into eight-cylinder development. The New York capitalists behind the Duesenbergs seemed unenthused. Consequently, the rights to the Duesenberg four were sold to Rochester Motors Company, Inc. (which ultimately marketed developed versions to Biddle, Roamer, ReVere, Richelieu, Meteor, Kenworthy and Argonne). Duesenberg Motors Corporation and the Elizabeth plant were acquired by Willys. This left the brothers free to continue development in nearby Newark on the single-overhead-camshaft, in-line eight-cylinder racing engine the development of which they had begun about the time of the Armistice. Interestingly, the prototype of the Duesenberg Model A passenger car which was introduced at the Hotel Commodore in November 1920 was fitted with a horizontal-valve, rocker-arm straight eight, though even by the time it appeared, Fred Duesenberg had decided that production cars would use the overhead camshaft design. Hydraulic four-wheel brakes — a first for America — had been fitted to the prototype, however. By now the Duesenbergs were part of a new $1.5 million company in Indianapolis: the Duesenberg Automobile and Motors Corporation. The new Model A created a sensation at its debut. Unfortunately, two problems ensued: first, Fred Duesenberg's decision to switch to the ohc design for production meant initially delayed deliveries (indeed, it would be the 1922 model year before the car was available): second, the people who were backing the venture, though businessmen of standing, had scant experience in managing an automobile company. (The Duesenbergs themselves had always been pretty much lackluster in administrative matters.) The Indiana venture was reorganized as Duesenberg Motors Company in 1925, but fared little better. More than 600 Model A's were built in five years, but not profitably, and the car has since been practically forgotten, or consigned to bridesmaid's status to the later Model J. The Model A Duesenberg is that rarity: a great car that still remains overlooked. Impossible to overlook during the period it was produced, however, was the phenomenal success the brothers enjoyed in competition.

1922 Duesenberg, model A, roadster, FR

There were two great names in American racing during the Twenties: one was Duesenberg, the other was Miller. Meanwhile, one day in 1926, Auburn president Errett Lobban Cord strode into Duesenberg history, acquired the company (subsequently renamed Duesenberg, Inc.) and instructed Fred Duesenberg to build a super car that could stand alongside — hopefully surpass — the world's most magnificent automobiles. That took time, of course, and in the interim the Model X — which had been a shoestring attempt by Fred Duesenberg to revamp the Model A — was produced during 1927. Only about a dozen cars were built, the number for which parts had been on hand at the time Cord bought the Duesenberg company. On December 1st, 1928, at the New York Automobile Salon, the mighty Model J moved center stage in Duesenberg history. It was big, it was fast, it was gorgeous, it was expensive. How big and how fast has since

475

become a subject of conjecture. Its race-inspired engine (twin overhead camshafts operating four valves per cylinder) was said to develop 265 hp which it probably did on the dynamometer though doubtless not in the heroically-sized (142½ and 153½ wheelbase inches) car itself. Still, whatever the figure, it was perhaps twice that of any other American car on the road. Likewise, the speed of 116 mph in high which was achieved in tests at Indianapolis Motor Speedway was probably not approached by those production cars which tipped the scales at 5000 pounds. But what did it matter; the Duesenberg was still king of the American road, "He drives a Duesenberg" was the only copy in many company advertisements. Owning a Duesenberg was an expensive proposition, of course. The chassis price was $8500 (about $2000 more than the price tag of a Model A with open car coachwork), and although the epic length and low stance of the Duesenberg chassis made it a favorite among coachbuilders on both sides of the Atlantic for special one-off efforts, the Duesenberg company itself preferred selling its own car complete, either with the superb in-house bodies designed by Gordon Buehrig or the limited series productions of approved coachbuilders. Tragically, in July 1932, Fred Duesenberg died following an automobile accident. Already he had designed the centrifugal supercharger which boosted horsepower of the J to 320 and with the later ram's horn — developed by brother Augie who took over as chief engineer — to perhaps almost 400. A supercharged J convertible coupe was purportedly tested at the Indy Speedway at 129 mph, and in 1935 Ab Jenkins sped 152.1 mph in an hour and averaged 135.5 for twenty-four at Bonneville in the supercharged Duesenberg Special. But by now the end was near for the Duesenberg. About 500 cars for the first production run had been the figure agreed upon by E.L. Cord and Fred Duesenberg at the outset, with no parameters regarding the time span in which they would be built. Certainly neither of them foresaw the stock market crash at that time, and obviously its aftermath affected the Duesenberg's fortunes as it did everything else. By the end of 1931, approximately 360 cars had been produced. From May of 1932 through October of 1935, about 36 supercharged J's were built. There were ten JN's (by Rollston, distinguished by wider, dropped bodies and deeper doors than the Duesenberg norm), and two SSJ's (not an official designation, but an apt one to describe the pair of supercharged J's built on a shortened 125-inch wheelbase chassis, one for Clark Gable, the other for Gary Cooper). The approximate total Duesenberg J production was 480 cars. Of these, probably more were delivered to people with famous (sometimes infamous) names than a likewise percentage of any other American manufacturer's production. The Duesenberg was more than a status symbol; it was status pure and simple, whether the owner was a maharajah, movie star, politician, robber baron, gangster or evangelist. In 1937 the Duesenberg was no more, discontinued with the Auburn and Cord following E.L. Cord's sale of his corporation. Probably few would cavil that the Duesenberg is the single most sought after car in America today.

1922 DUESENBERG
Model A — 8-cyl., 88 hp, 134" wb

	FP	5	4	3	2	1
Touring-4P	6500	10,000	20,000	30,000	60,000	80,000

1923 Duesenberg, model A, town car, FR

1923 DUESENBERG
Model A — 8-cyl., 88 hp, 134" wb

Touring-5P	6500	10,000	20,000	30,000	60,000	80,000
Roadster-2P	6500	10,500	20,500	31,000	62,000	82,000
Touring-7P	6750	9900	19,800	29,300	58,800	79,000
Sedan-7P	7800	6400	9300	14,500	33,000	45,000
Four-Window Sedan-4P	7800	6500	9400	14,800	33,500	45,500
Town Car-5P	8800	6500	9500	15,000	34,000	46,000

1924 Duesenberg, model A, roadster, JAC

1924 DUESENBERG
Model A — 8-cyl., 88 hp, 134" & 141" wb

	FP	5	4	3	2	1
Phaeton-4/5P	6250	23,800	41,000	67,000	97,500	125,000
Roadster-3P	6500	25,500	45,000	73,000	100,000	130,000
Sport-4P	6500	26,300	47,000	75,000	102,500	132,000
Phaeton-7P	6750	22,000	37,000	62,000	93,000	120,000
Four-Door Cabriolet-4P	7500	7600	12,500	19,400	42,400	55,000
Brougham-4P	7800	7800	12,900	19,900	43,300	57,000
Sedan Limousine-7P	7800	7800	13,300	20,300	44,000	60,000

1925 Duesenberg, model A, touring, JAC

1925 Duesenberg, model A, touring, IMS

1925 DUESENBERG
Model A — 8-cyl., 88 hp, 134" & 141" wb

Phaeton-5P	6250	25,500	45,000	73,000	100,000	130,000
Roadster-2P	6500	27,500	50,000	78,000	105,000	135,000
Sport-4P	6500	28,300	52,000	80,000	107,000	137,000
Phaeton-7P	6750	23,800	41,000	67,000	97,500	125,000
Four-Door Cabriolet-4P	7500	7800	13,300	20,300	44,000	60,000
Limousine-7P	7800	8000	13,900	20,900	44,800	63,000
Brougham-7P	7800	7900	13,700	20,700	44,500	62,000

1926 Duesenberg, model A, Schutte, roadster, IMS

1926 DUESENBERG
Model A — 8-cyl., 88 hp, 134" wb

Roadster-2P	6850	25,500	45,000	73,000	100,000	130,000
Roadster-4P	6850	27,500	50,000	78,000	105,000	135,000
Touring-5P	6650	25,500	45,000	73,000	100,000	130,000
Touring-7P	6850	25,200	44,500	71,500	99,500	129,000
Sport Touring-4P	6850	29,500	55,000	84,000	110,000	140,000
Sedan-5P	7700	10,000	20,000	30,000	60,000	80,000
Sedan-7P	8300	9400	18,800	26,500	53,800	75,000

1927 DUESENBERG
Model A — 8-cyl., 88 hp, 134" wb

Roadster-2P	5750	27,500	50,000	78,000	105,000	135,000
Phaeton-4/5P	5500	29,500	55,000	84,000	110,000	140,000
Sport-4P	5750	31,100	58,000	88,000	114,000	150,000
Phaeton-7P	5900	34,700	68,500	104,000	140,000	185,000
Deluxe Sedan	7500	13,800	23,800	37,500	75,000	95,000
Fleetwood Deluxe Sedan	7500	14,300	24,300	38,500	77,000	97,000
Town Brougham	7800	15,000	25,000	40,000	80,000	100,000

1927 Duesenberg, model X, Locke dual cowl phaeton, AA

1929 Duesenberg, model J, Fernandez & Darren s.w.b. convertible roadster, AA

1929 Duesenberg, model J, dual cowl phaeton, OCW

1927 DUESENBERG
Model X — 8-cyl., 100 hp, 135'' & 141'' wb
1929-1937 DUESENBERG
Model J — 8-cyl., 265 hp, 142½'' & 153½'' wb
All of the following automobiles were custom built and have values in excess of $250,000.
Phaeton
All-Weather Cabriolet
Enclosed Drive Sedan
Sedan-5P
Convertible Sedan
Convertible Roadster
Tourster
Convertible Berline
Convertible Victoria
Convertible Roadster
Beverly
Limousine
Prince of Wales Sedan
Coupe
Town Limousine
Town Car
Town Sedan
Coupe-4P
Convertible Phaeton
Town Limousine
Arlington
All-Weather Landau
Formal Town Car
Note: Chassis price at introduction was $8500, later increased to $9500.

1930 Duesenberg, model J, convertible coupe, OCW

1930 Duesenberg, model J, Derham cabriolet, OCW

1931 Duesenberg, model J, Rollston convertible victoria, AA

1932 Duesenberg, model J, Derham convertible sedan, AA

477

1932 Duesenberg, model SJ, torpedo phaeton, Brunn, HAC

1933 Duesenberg, model J, torpedo sedan, Rollston, JAC

1934 Duesenberg, model SJ, town car, Murphy, JAC

1935 Duesenberg, model J, convertible coupe, Bohman & Schwartz, FR

1936 Duesenberg, model JN, convertible sedan, Rollston, FR

1937 Duesenberg, model J, convertible berline, Rollston, FR

BODY STYLES BY COACHBUILDER
LeBaron Double Cowl Phaeton (sweep panel) — 1929-1930
LaGrande Double Cowl Phaeton (sweep panel) — 1930-1934
Murphy Convertible Coupe — 1929-1932
Murphy Convertible Sedan — 1929-1932
Murphy Clear Vision Sedan — 1929-1932
Murphy Beverly Sedan — 1930-1932
Murphy Double Cowl Phaeton — 1930-1931
Murphy Boattail (Torpedo) Convertible Coupe — 1930-1932
Derham Five-Passenger Sedan (Arlington) — 1929-1932
Holbrook Five-Passenger Sedan — 1929-1930
Weymann Five-Passenger Sedan — 1930-1931
Holbrook Town Car — 1929-1930
Murphy Town Car — 1930-1932
Rollston Town Car — 1930-1934
Willoughby Limousine — 1930-1934
Willoughby Berline — 1930-1934
Judkins Limousine — 1930-1934
Derham Tourster — 1930-1934
Rollston Convertible Coupe (JN) — 1933-1936
Rollston Convertible Sedan (JN) — 1933-1936
Rollston Sport Sedan (JN) — 1933-1936
LaGrande Torpedo Phaeton — 1934-1936
LaGrande Convertible Coupe — 1934-1936
LeBaron Convertible Berline — 1930-1933
Rollston Convertible Victoria — 1930-1933

DUKE — Early in 1919 the Duke Motor Company was organized in Pittsburgh, Pennsylvania for the manufacture of motor vehicles. Behind this $500,000 venture were A.M. Holloran, S.A. Williams and Ferris Giles. Manufacture of a car is doubted.

DULUTH — In April of 1909 the Duluth Motor Vehicle Company was organized in that Minnesota city with a capital stock of $50,000 to "manufacture, buy, sell, import and export automobiles, motors, engines, machines, etc., sell gasoline, do a general garage business, etc." A.G. Fitzgerald and C.W. Fitzgerald were the partners involved. Manufacture of a car is doubted.

DUM — Lancaster, Ohio — (1902) — Ed and Harley Dum worked for the Hocking Valley Bridge Works in Lancaster and in 1902 built an automobile for themselves. Details regarding it are lacking, but its building was documented in *The Motor Age* that year.

DUMONT — Occasionally during 1904 the Santos Dumont from Columbus, Ohio was advertised simply as the Dumont. Refer to Santos Dumont.

DUMORE — The Dumore was the light delivery version of the American Junior that was built by the American Motor Vehicle Company of Lafayette, Indiana during the World War I era. Piquant it may have been, but the vehicle is properly a truck and not a car. Refer to American Junior.

DUNBAR — **Chicago, Illinois** — **(1904)** — Dunbar & Company, located at 10 North Des Plaines Street in Chicago, was well known at the turn of the century for its manufacture of horse-and-man-drawn peanut and popcorn roasters. In 1904 the firm entered the automotive field. Although its work was largely in repairing and rebuilding cars, Dunbar is known to have produced a few automobiles as well on custom order.

1923 Dunbar, roadster, KM

DUNBAR — **Walden, New York** — **(1922-1923)** — "The project has been hatching for some little time," reported *Automobile Topics* in August 1922 when the magazine announced that David Dunbar Buick was returning to automotive ranks. In 1908 Buick had left the company bearing his name and embarked upon a variety of ventures all of which turned out badly. With his son Tom, he tried manufacturing carburetors, and lost money. In 1921 he was the president of Lorraine Motors in Grand Rapids, Michigan, but the company failed and he was out of a job. Thereafter some promoters in New York beckoned, and Buick headed east. Initially, the Dunbar venture held promise. The David Dunbar Buick Corporation was to be capitalized at five million dollars. Production was slated to be begun by early 1923. By early 1923, however, a site for manufacture had not yet been found, though one was in mid-April, a plant in Walden about seventy miles from New York City. One Dunbar chassis was ready, and work on three more was said to be in progress. Production of four models to range in price from $1100 to $1400 was slated now to begin in mid-May. The Dunbar never did proceed into manufacture. Only one prototype was ever built, a roadster with a Continental six-cylinder (52 hp) engine mounted on a 112-inch wheelbase chassis. Buick was out of another job. Thereafter, David Dunbar Buick launched himself into a variety of further ill-fated ventures, including oil in California and real estate in Florida. Finally, broke and beaten, he took a job at the Detroit School of Trades. The writer Bruce Catton discovered him there in 1928. So feeble was he now that he had been transferred to the school's information desk. The man who had created the first Buick ended his career as a receptionist. He died in 1929, at age seventy-four.

DUNHAM — During the summer of 1904 the firm of D.R. Dunham & Son was organized in Rahway, New Jersey with a capital stock of $100,000 to "manufacture and deal in automobiles, coaches, cars, bicycles and boats." Emma F. Dunham, Frederic W. Dunham and T.B. Lindsay were the incorporators. Manufacture of an automobile is doubted.

DUNKLE — **Pana, Illinois** — **(1908)** — In 1908, W.R. Dunkle of Pana built an automobile of his own invention which featured four wheel drive and a "special safety lever." Further details regarding the Dunkle car are lacking, but he is believed to have built one example only.

1910 Dunkle, runabout, NAHC

DUNKLE — **Greenville, Ohio** — **(1910)** — "The man with mechanical tastes can get much more instruction and pleasure through building a car himself than from using one already made," *The Automobile* commented in 1910 in depicting Ralph W. Dunkle's "maiden effort as an automobile manufacturer." The magazine was impressed with Dunkle's ingenuity, "the whole construction . . . being somewhat different from any type of automobile on the market." That was certainly true. Dunkle indicated that his engine was only a 2hp unit, and yet was good for "quite a little speed."

DUNLOP-TAYLOR — The Dunlop-Taylor Motor Company was organized during the summer of 1910 in New York City with a capital stock of $5000 to manufacture and deal in automobiles and accessories. Charles M. Dunlop and Ben C. Taylor were the partners involved. Manufacture of a car is doubted.

1916 Dunn, runabout, WLB

DUNN — **Ogdensburg, New York** — **(1916-1918)** — Just about the time everyone else in America had given up on the cyclecar idea, Walter Dunn, whose Dunn Motor Works built marine engines in Ogdensburg, decided to give it a go. The Dunn variation on the theme featured a four-cylinder vee-type air-cooled engine of Walter Dunn's own design, which he manufactured and also sold separately. The Dunn cyclecar featured a two-speed transmission, shaft drive, wire wheels — and a $295 price tag that was phenomenally low. Despite this, sales were minimal, and after limping through several unprofitable seasons, the Dunn was done in Ogdensburg.

1916-1918 DUNN
Cyclecar — 4-cyl., 15 hp, 84" wb

	FP	5	4	3	2	1
Roadster-2P	295	1600	2700	3800	5800	12,000

1896 Dunton electric tricycle, NAHC

DUNTON — **Jamaica, New York** — **(1896)** — Frederick W. Dunton was a mechanic from Jamaica, Long Island who built a small three-wheeled electric carriage in 1896. The motor and the batteries were suspended on either side of the axle of the front wheel, which Dunton called his "horse." A long handlebar extended therefrom to the front seat and included the controlling device for regulating speed. Three speeds of 4, 8 and 12 mph were available forward, with 4 mph provided in reverse. The total weight of the carriage was less than 500 pounds. Its capacity was 40 miles on a single charge, with recharging costs about thirty cents. The Dunton carriage was never put into manufacture.

DUO — During the spring of 1906 the Duo Motor Company was organized in Boston, Massachusetts with a capital stock of $250,000 for the manufacture and sale of automobiles. Behind this venture were Christopher T. Whitney, Daniel L. Culton, Nathan H. Harriman and Philip O. Jack. Manufacture is doubted.

1908 Duplex, model No. 1, stanhope, NAHC

479

DUPLEX — Chicago, Illinois — (1908-1909)— The Duplex Motor Car Company was organized in Chicago during the summer of 1907 with a capitalization of $30,000. It was owned and operated by the Bendix Company, which also marketed cars under its own name. Unlike the Bendix which was built in Logansport (Indiana), the Duplex appears to have been produced entirely in Chicago, though in September of 1908 there were negotiations ongoing for a factory in nearby Ottawa. The Duplex an unusual automobile featuring a double friction transmission and double driveshaft. Each of the transmissions had its own driveshaft and its own differential on the rear axle. Among the benefits realized from this system, Duplex said, was the better engine balance possible by the use of two flywheels and "because of the even pressure against the flywheels, at both sides, the engine runs freely on its bearings and no end thrust is created." A saving of power and a lessening of wear for the Duplex two-cylinder air-cooled engine was the expected result, but the car did not survive long enough for the company to advertise this advantage. The Duplex was discontinued early in 1909, shortly before the Bendix also met its demise.

1908 DUPLEX
No. 1 — 2-cyl., 10 hp, 88" wb

	FP	5	4	3	2	1
Stanhope	650	3100	4200	6300	10,500	22,000
No. 2 — 2-cyl., 15 hp, 88" wb						
Stanhope	—	3200	4300	6500	11,000	23,000
No. 3 — 2-cyl., 15 hp, 88" wb						
Surrey	—	3300	4400	6700	12,000	24,000

1909 Duplex, model A, touring, NAHC

1909 DUPLEX
Type B — 2-cyl., 20 hp, 90" wb

Touring Roadster-4P	1500	3300	4400	6700	12,000	24,000

DuPONT — In July 1915 announcement was made that the Sphinx Motor Car Company of York, Pennsylvania was being reorganized as the DuPont Motor Car Company. Whether any subsequent cars were marketed under the DuPont name is problematical. Refer to Sphinx.

1919 Du Pont, prototype, HAC

DU PONT — Wilmington, Delaware — (1919-1931) — In the beginning, when announcement of the new car was made, particular emphasis was placed on the fact that no association existed with General Motors. The Du Pont behind the new car was not Pierre S., president of E.I. Du Pont de Nemours & Company of Wilmington, who was majority stockholder, about to become president, and obviously heavily involved in picking up the pieces of the empire left in tatters by William C. Durant. Instead, the Du Pont behind the new car was E. Paul Du Pont, who was associated with the Ball Grain Explosive Company of Wilmington, headed by Alfred I. Du Pont. Du Pont Motors, Inc. had been organized just before America went to war for the building of marine engines. With the Armistice, the decision was made to produce an automobile. That the Du Pont would be quite un-GM-like in its approach to the automobile business was indicated by the coterie of talent Paul Du Pont gathered to produce it. General manager Arthur M. Maris came from Biddle; chief engineer John A. Pierson was from Wright-Martin Aircraft; sales manager William A. Smith was former general manager for Mercer. Moreover, the Du Pont was introduced not at an automobile show, but at the 1919 International Salon in New York City's Commodore Hotel. Obviously, the Du Pont was to be a class act. At first the Du Pont was powered by a four-cylinder engine produced in-house in Wilmington, with bodies built in Springfield (Massachusetts). In 1922

final assembly moved to a new plant in Moore (Pennsylvania), but moved back to Wilmington in October 1925. A total of 188 first-generation (Models A and B) Du Ponts were produced prior to July of 1923 when the Model C, with a six-cylinder engine from Herschell-Spillman, arrived. Forty-eight of these cars were built, followed by twenty-eight of the Wisconsin-engined Model D's and eighty-three of the ensuing Model E. Only one of the latter was fitted with the supercharger that created a good deal of attention for the company but was otherwise a lamentable failure. The Model E on a stretched 136-inch wheelbase was offered as the Model F, two of these cars being built. Before the stock market crashed, the most famous Du Pont of all was introduced: the Model G, powered by a Continental straight-eight developing 125 bhp, set into a chassis with wheelbases ranging from 125 to 150 inches and offered in a dazzling array of twelve body styles. Elegant and graceful coachwork had been the mark of the Du Pont since its introduction. The Model G carried these attributes to their zenith — except for one body style that was neither elegant nor graceful, but was assuredly the most singular, and best known, Du Pont ever built. This was the Model G Speedster, the show car of which was purchased by Mary Pickford for her husband Douglas Fairbanks, a four-seater version of which outran both Stutz and Chrysler at Le Mans in 1929, although alas for only three of the twenty-four hours. In May of 1930, Paul Du Pont bought the Indian Motorcycle Company of Springfield (Massachusetts) and moved his engineering department there to be closer to Merrimac, producer of many of the Model G bodies. Coachwork by Waterhouse and Derham also graced Du Pont chassis; celebrity clients included Will Rogers, Huntington Hartford and Jack Dempsey. The Depression killed the Du Pont. A total of 273 Model G's were produced in three-and-a-half years; three Model H's (the G mounted on a 146-inch Stearns-Knight frame) were built for the 1931 New York Automobile Show. One was a limousine, one a sedan, the third was a "Sport Phaeton with Tonneau Cowl." Production of all Du Ponts ceased in January 1932. A receiver was appointed in February 1933.

1919-1920 DU PONT
Model A — 4-cyl., 55 hp, 124" wb

	FP	5	4	3	2	1
Touring-5P	4000	4500	5800	9500	18,000	32,000
Roadster-2P	4000	5000	6500	11,000	22,000	35,000
Suburban Sedan-5P	5600	4000	5000	8000	15,000	28,000
Sedan-5P	5500	3700	4700	7300	13,700	26,000

1921 Du Pont, model A, roadster, HAC

1922 Du Pont, model A, roadster, JAC

1921-1923 DU PONT
Model B — 4-cyl., 55 hp, 124" wb

Touring-5P	3200	4700	6000	10,000	14,000	34,000
Roadster-2P	3000	5000	6500	11,000	22,000	35,000
Suburban Sedan-5P	4000	4000	5000	8000	15,000	28,000
Sedan-5P	4000	3700	4700	7300	13,700	26,000

1924 DU PONT
Model C/D — 6-cyl., 57 hp, 124" wb

Roadster-2P	2090	5200	6800	11,300	23,000	36,000
Touring-5P	2090	4700	6100	9900	19,000	33,000
Suburban Sedan-5P	3085	4200	5200	8400	15,700	29,000
Touring-Sedan-5P	3085	4000	5000	8000	15,000	28,000

1923 Du Pont, model B, touring, HAC

1924 Du Pont, model D, roadster, JAC

1925 Du Pont, model D, touring, HAC

1925 DU PONT
Model D — 6-cyl., 75 hp, 124" wb

	FP	5	4	3	2	1
Sport Roadster-2P	2600	5400	7300	11,800	25,000	38,000
Sport Touring-5P	2600	5200	6800	11,300	23,000	36,000
Sedan-5P	3400	3900	4800	7700	14,300	27,000
Touring-7P	3400	5000	6500	11,000	22,000	35,000

1926 Du Pont, model E, rumbleseat, coupe, WLB

1926 Du Pont, model E, sport phaeton, HAC

1926 DU PONT
Model D — 6-cyl., 75 hp, 124" wb

	FP	5	4	3	2	1
Touring-5P	2600	5200	6800	11,300	23,000	36,000
Roadster-2P	2600	5400	7300	11,800	25,000	38,000
Sedan-5P	3400	3900	4800	7700	14,300	27,000

1927 Du Pont, model E, sport phaeton, WLB

1927-1928 DU PONT
Model E — 6-cyl., 70 hp, 125" wb

	FP	5	4	3	2	1
Sport Phaeton-4/5P	2800	15,000	30,000	50,000	80,000	100,000
Roadster-4P	2800	14,000	28,000	48,000	76,000	96,000
Coupe-4P	3200	4300	5400	8700	16,500	30,000
Convertible Coupe	—	13,500	27,000	45,000	70,000	90,000
Sedan-5P	3400	4000	5000	8000	15,000	28,000

Model F (136-inch wheelbase, introduced 1928, built into 1929)

1929 Du Pont, model G, two-passenger speedster, OCW

1930 Du Pont, model G, town car, OCW

1931 Du Pont, model H, sport phaeton, RER

1929-1932 DU PONT
Model G — 8-cyl., 125 hp, 125″ to 150″

	FP	5	4	3	2	1
Sport Phaeton	4560	16,400	31,200	52,000	83,000	104,000
Touring-7P	4560	15,000	30,000	50,000	80,000	100,000
Roadster	4360	15,700	30,600	51,000	81,000	102,000
Convertible Coupe	4360	14,000	28,000	48,000	76,000	96,000
Club Sedan	4360	4300	5400	8700	16,500	30,000
Sedan-5P	4410	4000	5000	8000	15,000	28,000
Victoria-5P	4410	4400	5600	9200	17,300	31,000
Limousine-5P	4675	4500	5800	9500	18,000	32,000
Sedan-7P	4675	4200	5200	8400	15,700	29,000
Limousine-7P	4875	4500	5800	9500	18,000	32,000
Convertible Sedan	5150	15,000	30,000	50,000	80,000	100,000
Town Cabriolet	5750	15,500	30,600	51,000	81,000	102,000
Speedster-2P	5335.	—	—	—	—	—
Speedster-4P	6125	—	—	—	—	—
Sport Sedan	—	—	—	—	—	—
Club Berline	—	—	—	—	—	—

Model H (146-inch wheelbase, introduced 1931 automobile show)

1906 Duquesne, touring, WLB

DUQUESNE — Jamestown, New York — (1904-1906) — The Duquesne was built by a consortium of upstate New York businessmen who got together first as the Duquesne Motor Car Company in Buffalo, and moved to Jamestown early in 1904 where they chose to call themselves, curiously, the Duquesne Construction Company. Why they chose to move to Jamestown, however, is no mystery, that city having offered the company a cash bonus of $5000 and a plot of ground adjoining the Straight Manufacturing Company plant which was purchased outright by Duquesne. From this factory came a five-seater touring car with shaft drive, a round radiator and a number of novel features. Headlights which turned with the steering wheel were unusual, but not a Duquesne exclusive, though the company insisted its self-starter was. The latter was a ratchet mechanism operating on the flywheel by the foot pedal: "Once having used it," the company said, "you would as leave return to the primitive key winding watch as a crank-started motor car." Other gasoline vehicle manufacturers of this period were experimenting with starting devices too, though contemporary driving impresions by industry reporters would seem to indicate this one worked better than most. One feature, however, was almost certainly a first and only for Duquesne, and that was the tilting front seat which when moved to its forward position automatically opened the rear tonneau door. The fully-equipped Duquesne was priced in the $2000 range, and it failed despite gimmicks as meritorious as any offered in the industry probably because of internal dissension. Among the dissenters in the Duquesne team was LeRoy Pelletier (variously the president or vice-president of the firm depending upon managerial shakeup) who was a former newspaper man who had covered the rush to the Klondike for *The New York Times* and who would follow his Duquesne adventure by moving to Detroit to serve first as Henry Ford's private secretary and later as the industry's first great advertising man, for the E-M-F and Rickenbacker companies most memorably. The demise of the Duquesne was swift. Although a six-cylinder car had been promised to join the Duquesne four, it never arrived. Early in 1906 the company sold out to R.J. Straight who held the mortgage on its plant. Total production has been estimated as six cars. Duquesne creditors ultimately received ten percent on debts outstanding.

1904-1906 DUQUESNE
Model C — 4-cyl., 16/21 hp, 90″ sb

	FP	5	4	3	2	1
Side Entrace Tonneau	2000				--	1

DUQUESNE — Pittsburgh, Pennsylvania — (1912-1913) — The Pittsburgh Cage & Supply Company was the progenitor of the Duquesne Motor Car Company which launched itself onto the market in July of 1912. The assembled car it produced was designed by Oscar J. Howick and used a four-cylinder Wisconsin engine, Frank H. Morse (who had been among the founders of the Wisconsin Motor Manufacturing Company) being imported to serve as chief engineer. A six-cylinder model followed for the 1913 model year. That was the last Duquesne, and the last announcement from the company. Production must have been minimal. Frank Morse remained in town to build a cyclecar under his own name. Oscar Howick moved on to Michigan to design the Fenton and the Elgin Light Car.

1912 DUQUESNE
Four — 50 hp, 124″ wb

Touring-5P	2500	4400	5600	9200	17,300	31,000

1913 DUQUESNE
Four — 50 hp, 124″ wb

Touring-5P	2750	4500	5800	9500	18,000	32,000

Six — 50 hp, 133″ wb

Touring-7P	3250	4300	5400	8700	16,500	30,000

DURABILE — Cleveland, Ohio — (1902) — The Amstutz-Osborn Company was a machine shop which since the turn of the century had built experimental vehicles for entrepreneurs in the Cleveland area who were considering automotive manufacture. During the summer of 1902 Amstutz-Osborn decided to build a car for itself. The Durabile, as it was called, was a gasoline runabout with a Renault-type hood. The firm announced that production would begin within sixty days. Doubtless it did not. The Durabile was not heard from again in the automotive press; Amstutz-Osborn probably returned to machine work exclusively.

1921 Durant, roadster, HAC

DURANT — New York, New Jersey, Indiana, Michigan & California — (1921-1932) — On January 12th, 1921 Durant Motors, Inc. was formally organized as a $5 million company in New York State. A few years later the firm purportedly had more stockholders — 146,000 of them — than any other company in America except for American Telephone and Telegraph. Such was the drawing power of William Crapo Durant, one of American automobile history's most spectacular and colorful entrepreneurs. And also, perhaps, one of its most tragic. Having founded General Motors and lost it — twice — Durant had now begun the creation of his second empire. Not surprisingly, Durant Motors was conceived along GM lines. His prestige car would be the Locomobile, following his purchase of that famed though nearly bankrupt company in 1922. His Model T competitor would be the Star, also introduced that year. Though the Princeton would be stillborn, the Eagle would provide the basis for what became the Flint 40, the Flint being Durant's car in the Buick range, which arrived in 1923. But the most long-lived of his new cars would carry his name: the Durant, planned as an upmarket automobile in the Oakland mode. Forty-seven days after the January incorporation of Durant Motors, the first Durant prototypes were on the road. They were also the first of his new-empire cars in production (at his Long Island City, New York plant) in 1921. Their engines were 35 hp ohv fours built by Continental and set into 109-inch wheelbase chassis, with price tags beginning at $890. In February 1922 a six (Ansted engine) on a 123½-inch wheelbase joined the line, offering twice the horsepower at about twice the price. It was built in the Muncie, Indiana plant which had previously been home to the Sheridan, one of Billy Durant's last new projects at General Motors prior to his final leavetaking of that company. GM had sold him the plant. In 1922 a total of 55,000 Durant cars were delivered to new owners, and on March 27th, 1923 the 100,000th car to be built in Durant's new empire left the assembly line. His manufacturing domain was far-flung during this period: the Durant Six in Muncie, the Durant Four in Oakland (California), the Star and Durant Four in Elizabeth (New Jersey) and Lansing (Michigan), the Flint Six in Long Island City, and of course the Locomobile in Bridgeport (Connecticut). Moreover, in July of 1922 Durant had purchased the Mason Motor Truck Company of Flint (Michigan) outright, and a new factory was planned there, as well as production in Leaside (Ontario, Canada). It all looked wonderful for a while. But affairs quickly turned sour. In truth, Billy Durant himself was responsible for many of the problems of Durant Motors. As during his GM days, he was overextending himself. Unlike the GM days, however, when its component companies were his sole concern, Billy was now dabbling in a good many other ventures — and in the stock market. He wasn't around Durant Motors much, and his associates were reluctant to make decisions in his absence. Some decisions were made, though. In September 1923 the Ansted-engined Durant Six was dropped; it had been costly to build, and had enjoyed only lackluster sales. Fours only were produced from 1924 through August 1926, with four-wheel brakes, disc wheels and balloon tires fitted as standard equipment beginning in April of '24. During the summer of 1926, desperately in need of working capital, Durant sold his Flint, Michigan factory to General Motors. On April 1st, 1927, he sold the Long Island City plant to Ford. There was no production at all of the Durant car that year, and Billy lost $3.6 million in the first eight months. Nineteen twenty-eight was the 25th anniversary of Durant's career in the automobile industry. "Back on the job," he reported enthusiastically, but he had to be tired. He had begun Durant Motors at the age of sixty, when most men start thinking of retirement, and now he was sixty-five, when most men do retire. But still, Billy soldiered on. There were entirely new Durants for the 1928 model year, three sixes (Continental engine) of 40, 47 and 70 hp, the lowest powered having been the Star six the year previous. Mid-model year there was a change in radiator configuration, the second series without the bars of the first, and with an oval replacing the former round radiator badge. In January 1929 the former Star four became the Durant 4-40; and the 6-66 and 6-70 with four-speed gearboxes were announced, though they wouldn't arrive until late spring because, Durant explained, more time was necessary to perfect the transaxle. More than likely, the research and development money had been hard to come by. In the meantime, the old models were sold as new 1929's, which wasn't good public relations. But the real problem with the Durant was that it lived up to its slogan, "Just a Real Good Car," during an

1922 Durant, touring, WLB

era when car buyers had begun to demand more than that. Even before the stock market crash, Durant was faltering, and when it arrived both he and his company were dealt a staggering blow. Durant's efforts to soften the blow with an infusion of approximately $90 million of his own money did indeed help the market, but sent Billy reeling. By now the only car he had left was the Durant, though one of his last-ditch efforts, in 1930-1931, was an attempt to produce an American version of the French Mathis in Lansing. The Durant empire had pretty much centralized in that Michigan factory in 1929, though some manufacture continued in Oakland, California as well as Leaside, Ontario. Certainly there was no need for a plethora of Durant factories now: Durant sales of 43,951 cars in 1928 had been halved by 1930. In 1931 only 7270 cars would be sold, some of them with the novelty of "Pullman equipment," a concealed lever converting the seats into a bed, and a first for an American production car. Only a handful of Durants — mostly show cars and all of them facelifted 1931 models — were built in 1932. By the end of January that year Durant Motors had called it quits. The company was liquidated in 1933. Billy Durant declared personal bankruptcy in February 1936, indicating his only assets to be his clothing. None of his further activity — a combination grocery store/lunchroom, a bowling alley (housed in the former Flint agency in Asbury Park, New Jersey), a drive-in restaurant — had anything to do with the automobile industry, though it's been said that one probably unlikable car dealer used to relish taking salesmen to the Durant restaurant so that he could be served a hamburger by the man who had founded General Motors. On March 18th, 1947, at the age of eighty-five, William Crapo Durant died in New York City.

1921
Model A, 4-cyl., 35 hp, 109" wb

	FP	5	4	3	2	1
5P Tr	890	3000	6000	10,000	14,000	20,000
4P Cpe	1365	1400	4200	7000	9800	14,000
5P Sed	1365	1250	3900	6500	9100	13,000

1923 Durant, touring sedan, HAC

1922
Model A-22, 4-cyl., 35 hp, 109" wb

	FP	5	4	3	2	1
5P Tr	890	3000	6000	10,000	14,000	20,000
4P Cpe	1365	1400	7000	9800	14,000	
5P Sed	1365	1250	3900	6500	9100	13,000

Model B-22, 6-cyl., 70 hp, 123-1/2" wb

5P Tr	1650	3600	7200	12,000	16,800	24,000
2P Rds	1600	3900	7800	13,000	18,200	26,000
4P Cpe	2250	1550	4500	7500	10,500	15,000
5P Sed	2400	1400	4200	7000	9800	14,000

1923
Model A-22, 4-cyl., 35 hp, 109" wb

5P Tr	890	3300	6600	11,000	15,400	22,000
2P Rds	890	3750	7500	12,500	17,500	25,000
5P Sed	1365	1400	4200	7000	9800	14,000
4P Cpe	1365	1550	4500	7500	10,500	15,000

Model B-22, 6-cyl., 70 hp, 123-1/2" wb

5P Tr	1650	3750	7500	12,500	17,500	25,000
2P Rds	1600	3900	7800	13,000	18,200	26,000
5P Sed	2250	1550	4500	7500	10,500	15,000
4P Cpe	2400	1750	4800	8000	11,200	16,000

1924 Durant, coupe, HAC

1924
Model A-22, 4-cyl., 35 hp, 109" wb

5P Tr	890	3300	6600	11,000	15,400	22,000
2P Bus Cpe	1035	2300	5400	9000	12,600	18,000
Spt Rds	1040	3750	7500	12,500	17,500	25,000
4P Spt Tr	1090	3600	7200	12,000	16,800	24,000
Coach	1185	1750	4800	8000	11,200	16,000
2P Cpe	1365	2800	5700	9500	13,300	19,000
5P Sed	1365	1550	4500	7500	10,500	15,000
Spt Sed	1465	1750	4800	8000	11,200	16,000

1925 Durant, coach, HAC

1925-1926
Model A-22, 4-cyl., 37 hp, 109" wb

5P Tr	830	3300	6600	11,000	15,400	22,000
2P Bus Cpe	935	1750	4800	8000	11,200	16,000
4P Cpe	1160	2000	5100	8500	11,900	17,000
5P Sed	1190	1550	4500	7500	10,500	15,000
4P Sed	1310	1750	4800	8000	11,200	16,000
4P Cpe	1340	2300	5400	9000	12,600	18,000

NOTE: No production in 1927.

1928
Model 55, 6-cyl., 40 hp, 107" wb

2P Cpe	795	2000	5100	8500	11,900	17,000
5P 2 dr Sed	795	1550	4500	7500	10,500	15,000
5P Twn Sed	895	1400	4200	7000	9800	14,000

NOTE: This model was the former Star M-2 and was redesignated the M-4 in August, 1928.

Model 65, 6-cyl., 47 hp, 110" wb

5P Tr	795	3300	6600	11,000	15,400	22,000
4P Spt Rds	1025	3900	7800	13,000	18,200	26,000
4P Cpe	975	2300	5400	9000	12,600	18,000
5P 2 dr Sed	975	1750	4800	8000	11,200	16,000
4P Cabr	1045	2800	5700	9500	13,300	19,000
5P Sed	1075	1550	4500	7500	10,500	15,000
5P Twn Sed	1175	1750	4800	8000	11,200	16,000

Model 75, 6-cyl., 70 hp, 119" wb

5P 4 dr Sed	1385	1800	4950	8250	11,550	16,500
5P Twn Sed	1550	2000	5100	8500	11,900	17,000

1929 Durant, deluxe roadster, HAC

1929
Model 4-40, 4-cyl., 36 hp, 107" wb

	FP	5	4	3	2	1
4P Rds	595	3600	7200	12,000	16,800	24,000
4P DeL Rds	675	3900	7800	13,000	18,200	26,000
2P Cpe	595	2300	5400	9000	12,600	18,000
5P 2 dr Sed	595	1750	4800	8000	11,200	16,000
5P Sed	695	1550	4500	7500	10,500	15,000
5P DeL Sed	775	1750	4800	8000	11,200	16,000

NOTE: This was the former Star four and replaced the M-4 in January.

1929
Model 6-60, 6-cyl., 43 hp, 109" wb

		5	4	3	2	1
Spt Rds	685	4050	8100	13,500	18,900	27,000
2P Cpe	685	2800	5700	9500	13,300	19,000
5P 2 dr Sed	695	2000	5100	8500	11,900	17,000
5P Sed	750	1750	4800	8000	11,200	16,000
4P Cabr	750	2300	5400	9000	12,600	18,000

Model 6-70, 6-cyl., 65 hp, 119" wb

		5	4	3	2	1
5P Sed	1285	2300	5400	9000	12,600	18,000
4P Cpe	1195	3000	6000	10,000	14,000	20,000

Model 6-66, 6-cyl., 47 hp, 112" wb

		5	4	3	2	1
5P Sed	975	2600	5500	9250	12,950	18,500
4P Cpe	895	3150	6300	10,500	14,700	21,000
Phae	—	4200	8400	14,000	19,600	28,000

1930 Durant, roadster, AA

1930
Model 6-14, 6-cyl., 58 hp, 112" wb

		5	4	3	2	1
Std Sed	—	2300	5400	9000	12,600	18,000
Bus Cpe	—	2800	5700	9500	13,300	19,000
Spt Phae	—	4200	8400	14,000	19,600	28,000
Spt Rds	—	4350	8700	14,500	20,300	29,000

Model 6-17, 6-cyl., 70 hp, 115" wb

		5	4	3	2	1
DeL Sed	—	2800	5700	9500	13,300	19,000
DeL Cpe	—	3150	6300	10,500	14,700	21,000

1931 Durant, model 614, sedan, JAC

484

1931
Model 6-10, 4-cyl., 50 hp, 112" wb

	FP	5	4	3	2	1
Cpe	675	2800	5700	9500	13,300	19,000
Sed	695	2000	5100	8500	11,900	17,000

Model 6-12, 6-cyl., 58 hp, 112" wb

		5	4	3	2	1
Cpe	705	2900	5850	9750	13,650	19,500
Sed	725	2200	5250	8750	12,250	17,500

Models 6-14/6-19, 6 cyl., 58 hp, 112" wb

		5	4	3	2	1
Cpe	—	2800	5700	9500	13,300	19,000
Sed	—	2000	5100	8500	11,900	17,000

1932 Durant, model 6-22, sedan, KM

1932
Models 6-21/6-22, 6-cyl., 71 hp, 109" wb

		5	4	3	2	1
Sed	695	2000	5100	8500	11,900	17,000

DURENSEN — Minneapolis, Minnesota — (1921) — Andrew Durensen of Minneapolis worked for the Quaker States Sales Company, a firm dealing in jewelry and specialties, which apparently did not provide him sufficient challenge. In 1921 he built the pilot model of a four-passenger touring car he hoped to manufacture. It was powered by a two-cylinder 12 hp Spacke engine, set in a 100-inch wheelbase chassis. His plans did not progress far enough for him to affix a price tag. After the building of the prototype did not produce the necessary financing to continue further, Andrew Durensen reluctantly returned to jewelry and specialties.

DURHAM — The Durham Automobile Company was organized early in 1909 with a capital stock of $50,000 for the manufacture of a two-cylinder $600 high-wheeled roadster in Durham, North Carolina. One hundred cars were expected to be built during Durham's first season in the field. That any production at all followed has not been documented.

The Durham Engineering Company was organized in Newark, New Jersey during the summer of 1907 with a capital stock of $10,000. A. Durham and F.A. Reeve were the partners behind this venture to "engage in the manufacture of motor cars and motor cycles as well as doing a general engineering work." Manufacture of a car is doubted.

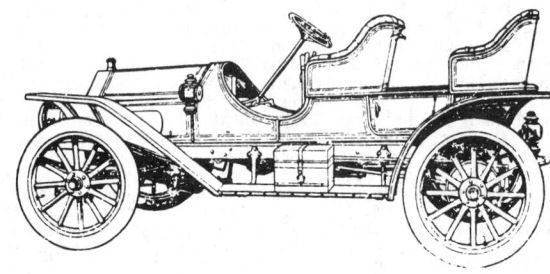

1909 Durocar, type N, surrey, NAHC

DUROCAR — Los Angeles, California — (1907-1911) — At the turn of the century, Alexander Winton sent one of his mechanics from Cleveland to the West Coast to see to the repairs of a Winton car in Southern California. This was not unusual in those days nor perhaps was it unusual that the mechanic didn't come back. Instead, Watt Moreland remained in the Los Angeles area where his first two automotive ventures were the Magnolia and the Tourist. The Long Beach dealer for the latter car was William M. Varney. In 1906 Varney and Moreland decided to begin their own automobile company, with Varney to serve as president, Moreland as secretary and superintendent, in addition to chief engineer. The Durocar he engineered featured a water-cooled two-cylinder engine, two-speed planetary transmission and shaft drive. It was formally introduced to the public at the Los Angeles Automobile Show in January 1907, in February the Durocar Manufacturing Company was in business, and shortly thereafter the first production Durocar was sold to A.P. Fleming, secretary of the Automobile Club of Southern California. Only seven cars were completed by September 1907, but soon after the factory logistics were finalized, output rose to five cars a day. Dealerships were established up and down the Pacific Coast and as far away as Montana and Honolulu. Matters appeared to be proceeding splendidly. But then, in November 1908, Watt Moreland resigned when the Durocar board of directors vetoed his suggestion to add a four-cylinder car to the line. "Two Cylinder Durocar Wins, Famous Eastern Make Four Cylinder Cars Also Ran," advertising headlines shouted thereafter, as Durocar raced extensively in local events to prove that a four was really two too many. Ultimately, however, Durocar produced a four anyway, for the 1910 season. But another change was now in the offing. Varney reorganized as the Amalgamated Motors Company, and although an announcement early in 1912 indicated that Amalgamated intended to resume manufacture of the Durocar following a move of the factory to Santa Ana, this did not transpire. Instead, Amalgamated moved to Alhambra. A few cars were put together there from parts on hand, but the only regular production Durocars which followed were trucks. Ironically, following his resignation from Durocar, Watt Moreland had moved to Burbank to produce the Moreland automobile, but he had changed his mind about that, and the only Morelands being built now were trucks too. That Durocars were durable cars is indicated by the presence of seventy-two of them on California registration lists of 1916-1917.

1907 DUROCAR
2-cyl., 26 hp, 102" wb

	FP	5	4	3	2	1
Runabout	—	2300	3300	4600	7500	16,000
Touring	—	2400	3400	4800	8000	17,000
Landalet	—	2300	3300	4600	7500	16,000

1908 DUROCAR
2-cyl., 26 hp, 102" wb

Model L Touring	1600	2400	3400	4800	8000	17,000
Model K Runabout	1550	2300	3300	4600	7500	16,000

1909 DUROCAR
2-cyl., 26 hp, 104" wb

Model L Touring	1600	2500	3500	5000	8500	18,000
Model K Runabout	1550	2500	3500	5000	8500	18,000
Model N Tourabout	1650	2400	3400	4800	8000	17,000

1910-1911 DUROCAR
2-cyl., 26 hp, 105" wb

Model 26 Touring	1500	2500	3500	5000	8500	18,000
Model 26 Tourabout	1500	2400	3400	4800	8000	17,000

4-cyl., 35 hp, 114" wb

Model 35 Touring	1750	2700	3600	5300	8800	19,000

4-cyl., 45 hp, 124" wb

Model 45 Touring	3500	3000	4000	6000	9500	21,000

1893 Duryea, OCW

DURYEA — Springfield, Massachusetts — (1893-1898)/Peoria, Illinois — (1898-1899)/Reading, Pennsylvania — (1900-1911)/Waterloo, Iowa — (1902-1903)/Saginaw, Michigan — (1911-1914)/Philadelphia, Pennsylvania — (1914-1915)/Reading, Pennsylvania — (1916-1917) — The Duryea was one of America's first gasoline cars. It was begun in Chicopee, Massachusetts by Charles E. and J. Frank Duryea, and was completed by J. Frank Duryea after his brother moved to Peoria, Illinois to pursue his bicycle enterprise. The vehicle's single-cylinder 4 hp engine was mounted underneath a carriage body and friction drive was featured. The first outdoor test run was in September 1893. The second Duryea was built entirely by J. Frank, and his brother joined him as a passenger in it for the epochal Chicago Times-Herald contest of 1895. The Duryea took winning honors in the event. It was Charles Duryea who was responsible for the organization in 1895 of America's first company for the manufacture of gasoline cars, the Duryea Motor Wagon Company of Springfield, Massachusetts. Thirteen vehicles, with belt drive, were produced, two of which were taken to England for the London to Brighton Emancipation Run of 1896. The car driven by J. Frank Duryea was the first to arrive in Brighton. Three-wheelers were produced during 1898, during which year the enterprise moved to Peoria, and the brothers began quarreling. When the partnership dissolved, J. Frank remained on the East Coast and soon decided that Massachusetts and the Stevens Arms and Tool Company was where he wanted to be, with the result being the Stevens-Duryea motorcar. And Charles E. decided he no longer wanted to be in Peoria. Scouting for a new location and fresh capital, he seems to have tried the West Coast first, references from September of 1899 announcing the intended establishment of the Henderson Horseless Carriage Company in Los Angeles for the manufacture of Charles E.'s three-wheeler. That venture went nowhere, but subsequently another Duryea (Otho) would try L.A. as well. Meanwhile Charles E. happened upon Reading (Pennsylvania) and Herbert M. Sternbergh ("son of the richest man in town, an iron-master of highest character and ability," according to Duryea). On April 6th, 1900 the Duryea Power Company of Reading was incorporated. For the next seven years Duryea produced three-cylinder, three-wheel (and an occasional four-wheel) vehicles that were capable of 20 mph. He was frequently seen on the streets of Reading, demonstrating the ease with which his single driving lever could handle gear selection and acceleration in addition to steering. Duryea was an ardent devote of the tiller, and detested the coming vogue of the steering wheel. Duryeas of this period sold in the $1500

1896 Duryea, HAC

range, with one larger 25 hp three-cylinder tourer at $2000 and up. Duryea vehicles were also being built in Coventry, England under license, and for a short period by the Waterloo Motor Works in Waterloo, Iowa. In 1903 New York City capitalists — Francis D. Carley and Henry Van Arsdale among them — organized the United States Rapid Vehicle Company in Manhattan with plans to acquire the Duryea patents together with the Reading and Waterloo plants, and to produce a new $1200 Duryea car on a massive scale. Charles Duryea was vice-president of this venture, which went nowhere. Meanwhile, in Peoria, squabbles with his associates were ongoing for Charles Duryea, and the Duryea Power Company plant there was taken over by receivers in 1907 after the production of 300 vehicles. Duryea learned of the takeover by telegram while attending the Chicago Automobile Show, returned to Reading and set up shop again in a garage, his new company name being simply his own. From this venture came the Buggyaut in 1908, a highwheeler powered by a two-stroke, two-cylinder, rear-mounted engine with drive by grooved rollers on the crankshaft engaging driving rims on the rear wheels. Again, this Duryea was tiller steered, the lever centrally mounted so that either the left or the right could be the driver's seat. The $750 Buggyaut was aptly named because, save for its hood in the front and turtle deck in the rear, it was simply a buggy. As an example of the highwheeler genre, the Buggyaut was longer lived than most, although Charles Duryea took a sabbatical from it in 1911 to hop over to Saginaw (Michigan) to form the Duryea Automobile Company. There he built his new Duryea Electa and some Buggyauts as well, took over the delivery wagon business of the Brooks Manufacturing Company — and went broke in January 1914. He returned to Reading to find himself in financial hot water there too, and left town again late in 1914. Next he tried a cyclecar, this being the very short era for its vogue, which was built for him by Cresson-Morris in Philadelphia. The Duryea cyclecar was powered by a four-stroke two-cylinder engine and featured the same roller drive as the Buggyaut. Unlike many cyclecars, seating was side-by-side rather than tandem. Within a year, however, the Duryea cyclecar became the Crowther-Duryea. The Crowther Motor Car Company, its cyclecar having been built by Cresson-Morris also, was in Rochester (New York), and Charles Duryea soon moved there to make it the Crowther-Duryea Motor Company, which discontinued operations by mid-1917. By that time Charles Duryea was back in Reading with a new idea and another financial angel to help, one Keyser Fry. The Duryea GEM was the "Biggest Idea in the History of the Motor-Car and the Last Word in Automobile Construction." Less a cyclecar than a motorcycle/automobile hybrid, the GEM had a 100-inch wheelbase, two wheels and the running gear in the rear, one wheel in front, and featured the Duryea Roller Drive. The chassis

1896 Duryea, HFM

was built in Detroit by the Detroit Chassis Company. The GEM weighed 500 pounds and cost $250; 50 mph was possible, Charles Duryea said, and 65 miles to a gallon of gasoline. A "Light Car" variation with four wheels and a $400 price tag was planned, although probably only the prototype was built. Of the GEM, production was no more than a half-dozen. It was the last car produced by Charles E. Duryea. Automobile history, however, remained important to him for the remainder of his life, and he continued his writings on the subject. On September 28th, 1939, at age seventy-six, he died in Philadelphia.

1903 Duryea, surrey, WLB

1895-1898 DURYEA

	FP	5	4	3	2	1
1900-1901 DURYEA **3-cyl., 6 hp, 66" wb**						
Dos-a-Dos Trap/Surrey	1500	2400	3400	4800	8000	17,000
Phaeton	1250	2500	3500	5000	8500	18,000
1902 DURYEA **3-cyl., 6/10 hp, 66" wb**						
Dos-a-Dos Trap/Surrey	1600	2400	3400	4800	8000	17,000
Phaeton	1250	2500	3500	5000	8500	18,000
1903 DURYEA **3-cyl., 10 hp, 66" wb**						
Four-Wheeled Phaeton	1350	2500	3500	5000	8500	18,000
Three-Wheeled Phaeton	1250	2300	3300	4600	7500	16,000
Rumble Phaeton	1500	2400	3400	4800	8000	17,000
Folding Front Phaeton	1500	2700	3600	5300	8800	19,000
Enclosed Phaeton	1600	2500	3500	5000	8500	18,000
Tonneau-7P (96" wb)	2000	2400	3400	4800	8000	17,000
Surrey (96" wb)	1750	2400	3400	4800	8000	17,000

1904 Duryea, folding rear phaeton, HAC

1904 DURYEA
3-cyl., 15 hp, 72" wb

	FP	5	4	3	2	1
Three-Wheeled Phaeton-2P	1250	2300	3300	4600	7500	16,000
Folding Rear Phaeton-4P	1500	2500	3500	5000	8500	18,000
Enclosed Doctor's Phaeton	1600	2400	3400	4800	8000	17,000
Surrey-5P	1750	2500	3500	5000	8500	18,000
Folding Front Phaeton-4P	1500	2300	3300	4600	7500	16,000
Straight-Line Phaeton-4P	1350	2200	3200	4400	7000	15,000
Park Wagon	1250	2000	3000	4200	6500	14,000
Tonneau-4P	2000	2300	3300	4600	7500	16,000
Delivery Wagon, Small	1000	2000	3000	4200	6500	14,000
Delivery Wagon, Large	1500	2200	3200	4400	7000	15,000

1905 DURYEA
3-cyl., 12/15 hp, 75" wb

	FP	5	4	3	2	1
Three-Wheeled Phaeton-2P	1200	2300	3300	4600	7500	16,000
Four-Wheeled Phaeton-2P	1300	2400	3400	4800	8000	17,000
Folding Seat Phae. (78" wb)	1500	2500	3500	5000	8500	18,000

1904 Duryea, enclosed phaeton, HAC

1905 Duryea, folding seat phaeton, HAC

1906 DURYEA
3-cyl., 12/15 hp chassis

	FP	5	4	3	2	1
Folding Rear Phae. (78" wb)	1500	2500	3500	5000	8500	18,000
Doctor's Phaeton (78" wb)	1300	2300	3300	4600	7500	16,000
Light Stage Coach (78" wb)	1200	2200	3200	4400	7000	15,000
Three-Wheel Phae. (81" wb)	1250	2000	3000	4200	6500	14,000
Delivery Wagon (96" wb)	1250	2200	3200	4400	7000	15,000
Touring-5P (96" wb)	1750	2300	3300	4600	7500	16,000
3-cyl., 25/30 hp, 106" wb						
Double Victoria-5P	2000	2400	3400	4800	8000	17,000

1908 Duryea, Buggyaut, HAC

1907 DURYEA
3-cyl., 15/18 hp chassis

	FP	5	4	3	2	1
Folding Rear Seat Phaeton (80" wb)	1500	2500	3500	5000	8500	18,000
Doctor's Phaeton (75" wb)	1250	2300	3300	4600	7500	16,000

3-cyl., 25/30 hp, 102" wb

Touring-4P	2500	2700	3600	5300	8800	19,000

1908 DURYEA
3-cyl., 15 hp, 80" wb

Folding Rear Phaeton	1500	2500	3500	5000	8500	18,000
Doctor's Phaeton	1250	2300	3300	4600	7500	16,000

2-cyl., 10/12 hp, 84" wb

Buggyaut	750	1800	2800	4000	6200	13,000

1909 DURYEA
2-cyl., 15 hp, 84" wb

Buggyaut, Single Seat	700	1800	2800	4000	6200	13,000
Buggyaut, Folding Rear Seat	750	1900	2900	4100	6400	13,500

1912 Duryea, Electa, HAC

1910 Duryea, Buggyaut, HAC

1910 DURYEA
2-cyl., 12/15 hp, 84" wb

Buggyaut, Single Seat	650	2000	3000	4200	6500	14,000
Buggyaut, Folding Rear Seat	750	2200	3200	4400	7000	15,000
Electa Victoria	900	1800	2800	4000	6200	13,000

1913 Duryea, Buggyaut, surrey, HAC

1911 Duryea, Electa, HAC

1911 DURYEA
2-cyl., 12/15 hp, 84" wb

Buggyaut, Single Seat	600	2000	3000	4200	6500	14,000
Electa Victoria	850	1800	2800	4000	6200	13,000
Buggyaut Surrey	700	2200	3200	4400	7000	15,000
Buggyaut Rbt. (100" wb)	850	2300	3300	4600	7500	16,000

1912 DURYEA
2-cyl., 12/15 hp chassis

Buggyaut, Single Seat (84" wb)	600	2000	3000	4200	6500	14,000
Buggyaut Surrey (84" wb)	650	2200	3200	4400	7000	15,000
Buggyaut Rbt. (100" wb)	700	2200	3200	4400	7000	15,000
Electa Victoria (80" wb)	750	2300	3300	4600	7500	16,000

1913 DURYEA
2-cyl., 12/15 hp chassis

Buggyaut, Single Seat (92" wb)	487	2000	3000	4200	6500	14,000
Buggyaut Surrey (92" wb)	537	2200	3200	4400	7000	15,000
Buggyaut Runabout (100" wb)	625	2200	3200	4400	7000	15,000
Electa Victoria (80" wb)	625	2300	3300	4600	7500	16,000

1914 Duryea, Cyclecar, roadster, WLB

1914 DURYEA
2-cyl., 19 hp chassis

	FP	5	4	3	2	1
Buggyaut, Single Seat (86" wb)	450	2000	3000	4200	6500	14,000
Buggyaut Surrey (96" wb)	500	2200	3200	4400	7000	15,000
Cyclecar Rds. (100" wb)	400	2000	3000	4200	6500	14,000

1917 Duryea GEM, roadster, HAC

1915 DURYEA
2-cyl., 19 hp, 100" wb

Cyclecar Roadster-2P	400	2000	3000	4200	6500	14,000

1917 DURYEA
2-cyl., 15 hp, 100" wb

GEM Roadster-2P	250	2000	3000	4200	6500	14,000

DURYEA — Los Angeles, California — (1900-1901) — Depending upon the reporter to whom he was speaking at the time, Otho C. Duryea either claimed no relationship, said he was the third of the Duryea brothers, or that he was the son of Charles E. In any case, at the turn of the century this Duryea was trying to get himself into the automobile business. After experimentation in New York City, O.C. Duryea headed west and settled in Los Angeles in 1901. There the Western Duryea Manufacturing Company was organized that summer as a half-million-dollar company. The manufacture of automobile carriages, tallyhos, delivery wagons and motor wagons "of every description," as well as high speed-motor boats and launches, was planned. A $75,000 factory, reputed to be "the most complete of its kind west of the Rocky Mountains," was already under construction. What the *Los Angeles Press* called "the largest order for automobile vehicles ever chronicled on the Pacific Coast" had already been received: ten auto-delivery wagons for J.R. Newberry's delivery company. Just how much production ever resulted from all this is not known. But the likelihood is not much. A single prototype motor carriage to O.C. Duryea's designs is documented to have been completed, however, and it was put together at the Maine Machine Shop near Alameda. If O.C. Duryea had been sent to Los Angeles by brother Charles E. to promote the Duryea car there, he seems not to have managed it well. A few years later he turned his talents to the invention of various kinds of rock-drilling equipment.

DUSSEAU — Toledo, Ohio — (1910-1911) — The Dusseau Fore and Rear Drive Automobile Company completed its first experimental touring model in late November of 1910 and displayed the car in its newly leased showroom on Erie Street in Toledo in December. The following January the company took the Dusseau to the Detroit Automobile Show. "The car is of the five-passenger type," reported *Automobile Topics*, "and, aside from the fore drive, is little different in appearance from the ordinary style of machine." That fact, and inadequate financing, may have been among the reasons this car never reached the assembly line. The Dusseau company had originally been organized with a capital stock of $30,000 in May of 1910 to operate a sales agency and garage. There were a good many Dusseaus involved — S.V., M.G., F.X. and R. — and which of them was the "Dr. Dusseau" who had patented the company's four-wheel drive system is not known. A subsequent brochure indicated the plan "to sell the right on a royalty basis to reliable concerns to make and use axles fitted with this device, for old or new cars." The Dusseaus do not appear to have been any more successful in this than they had been in getting a Dusseau automobile on the market. In 1913 they tried to launch a Dusseau truck with the same results. The Dusseaus seemed to be most successful at patenting stuff. After relocating to the West Coast, Maurice G. Dusseau patented two different universal joints amongst other devices, one of which he assigned 95% to the Positive Traction Motors Corporation.

D & V — Paterson, New Jersey — (1903) — In 1903 two machinists from Paterson named Jules Devigne and Levi E. Van Sickle were assembling automobiles of the "simplified French type" at their shop at 442 Broadway, equipping them with a 226-cubic-inch 12 hp three-cylinder engine of their own design. They were no longer doing so in 1904. No company had ever been incorporated for manufacture; the number of D & V's built could not have been more than a handful.

1900 Dyke, gasoline runabout, WLB

DYKE/ST. LOUIS — St. Louis, Missouri — (1899-1901)/**DYKE-BRITTON** — (1904) — Andrew Lee Dyke was born in Dykesville (Louisiana) in 1875 and made his fortune in St. Louis at the turn of the century as a pioneer in several aspects of the nascent automobile industry. In 1899 he established the first automobile supply business in America and issued the first automobile supply catalogue. Since there were just a few automobile factories in the whole of the United States at the time, there was really no overwhelming need for automobile supplies, so while he waited for an industry to catch up, he became a pioneer in the kit car business too. He designed and produced all the varying parts which might necessarily make up an automobile, from float-feed carburetor (in association with George Dorris) to reachless running gear. He offered a wide repertoire of engines ranging from a 5 hp one-lunger to a 12 hp twin, bodies for two, four or five passengers, and either solid or pneumatic tires. All components, plus blueprints and working drawings, were made available for about six hundred to a thousand dollars total. "Any ordinary mechanic," he said, could put them together. In order to test his components, Dyke put together many of his own cars too, as demonstrators and experimental models. He claimed to have built the first car with a canopy top and glass front. Some of his kit cars were made available as complete chassis, needing only bodies. He advertised widely in all of the early automobile magazines. His St. Louis Automobile Supply & Parts Company was a smashing success. On three occasions, A.L. Dyke offered complete cars on the market. In

1904 Dyke-Britton, touring, HAC

1899 he organized the St. Louis Electric Automobile Company and produced a stanhope and a runabout variously called a Dyke or St. Louis, the first electric vehicles in production west of the Mississippi. He sold this business to the Scott Automotive Company in 1901. In 1904 he built a 20 hp four-cylinder gasoline touring car that sold for $2500 and was marketed under the name of Dyke-Britton (Robert Britton was then serving as president of his supply house). In 1907 a big six called the D.L.G. Earlier A.L. Dyke had turned author. His first book was *Diseases of a Gasoline Auto, and How to Cure Them*, followed in 1903 by *Dr. Dyke's Anatomy of the Automobile* which explained the workings and maintenance of such cars as the curved dash Oldsmobile, the one-lunger Cadillac and the first Model A Ford. In 1909 he compiled *Dyke's Automobile and Gasoline Engine Encyclopedia*, and offered a mail-order course of instruction (twenty-four lessons each in pamphlet form) for "auto owners, chauffeurs and the 'uninitiated' generally." He died a very rich man.

DYLANDE — A.E. Dylande is known to have planned to produce a cyclecar in 1914, but whether he ever built a prototype is not. That he had formed a company for manufacture in Woonsocket, Rhode Island was revealed by *The American Cyclecar* in April that year. Dylande was not heard from again.

1934 Dymaxion, 4-dr. sedan, GR

DYMAXION — Bridgeport, Connecticut — (1933-1934) — A Renaissance man living always in the future, R. Buckminster Fuller was considered a crackpot for much of his life. He is regarded as a genius today. Prior to the Second World War, he used the name Dymaxion for his futuristic designs of houses, a boat, a bathroom and a car. The last named, which he designed in collaboration with well-known naval architect W. Starling Burgess, he hoped also to manufacture, but circumstances prevented that; just three Dymaxion cars were built. A three-wheeler on a 125-inch wheelbase chassis, the Dymaxion was powered by a Ford V-8 engine, had a top speed of 120 mph (almost double the prevailing American car norm) and fuel economy of 40 mpg (almost triple). An ultra-streamlined car, it was designed with practicality in mind; the Dymaxion had a turning radius of its own length, and could be parked in a spot only a foot longer. The first car was completed during the summer of 1933 in the old Locomobile plant in Bridgeport. Subsequently, officials of the New York Automobile Show invited Fuller to exhibit his car at that show but, at the eleventh hour, reneged — rumor had it because Chrysler Corporation complained, wishing no attention grabber from its new streamlined Airflow. Fuller took the car to the show anyway and parked it outside Grand Central Palace, where it attracted a good deal of attention. The Dymaxion was sent on tour thereafter, and tragedy struck. Outside of Chicago, the Dymaxion collided with another car and its occupants were killed, sensationalist headlines implied that the "freak"car's instability was a factor; the second car, which belonged to a Chicago politician, went unmentioned as even being at the scene of the accident. Doubtless, it was this adverse publicity which killed the Dymaxion's chances of marketability. The group of British automobile enthusiasts who had contracted to buy the second Dymaxion, by now completed, backed out. Fuller, short of funds, sold it to mechanics in the Bridgeport plant. The third car, then under construction, was exhibited at the Century of Progress in Chicago; it had been sold to a buyer who didn't back out — Leopold Stokowski, leader of the Philadelphia Symphony Orchestra. Of the three Dymaxions produced, each had visual differences, and only one (the second built and now in Harrah's Automobile Collection) is known to remain extant. After the war, Buckminster Fuller became recognized for the man of genius he was, largely through his invention of the geodesic dome, an architectural concept which has seen worldwide applications, including, interestingly, an automobile showroom/museum in Holland. On July 1st, 1983 Buckminster Fuller died in Los Angeles at the age of eighty-seven.

EADIE — The Eadie Vehicle & Gear Company was organized in Buffalo, New York early in 1912 with a capital stock of $200,000 for the manufacture of motorcars and parts. John M. Eadie, George P. Keating and Seward H. Millener, all of Buffalo, were the people involved. Incorporation was in New Jersey. Previous and subsequent to this venture Eadie was involved designing devices for use on farm wagons. Possibly the "motorcar" being planned here was a commercial vehicle. Manufacture is doubted.

EAGLE — At some point between 1904 and 1908, the name of the Eisenhuth Horseless Vehicle Company of Middletown, Connecticut was changed to the Eagle Motor Company. While a few subsequent cars may have been called Eagle too, the automobile generally continued to be marketed under its traditional name of Compound. Refer to Compound.

Scarcely had the Eagle Motor Car Company of Columbus, Ohio been established in late 1911 for the manufacture of the Eagle Roadster than the firm elected to change its name to the Union Sales Company and its product to the Union 25. This move was made to avoid confusion with all the other Eagles that had preceded this one into the marketplace. Refer to Union 25.

The Eagle Sales Company was incorporated in Bridgeport, Connecticut during the summer of 1917 with a capital stock of $50,000 to manufacture and market automobiles. George N. Kickey of Detroit, Michigan; George H. Day of Bridgeport, Connecticut and N.R. Goodman of Boston, Massachusetts were the incorporators. Manufacture of an automobile is doubted.

The Eagle & Vincent Automobile Company was incorporated with a capital stock of $15,000 during the summer of 1912 to manufacture automobiles in Mansfield, Ohio. C.H. Engle was behind this venture. Manufacture is doubted.

1905 Eagle, touring, (Buffalo), NAHC

EAGLE — Buffalo, New York — (1905) — The Eagle Automobile Company of Buffalo entered and exited the automobile industry so quickly that probably few people outside of town were ever aware of its existence. The company produced two models, both featuring an air-cooled engine and chain drive, the Model A a 12 hp two, the Model B a 24 hp four. Neither of them, nor the company, survived into 1906.

1905 EAGLE
Model A — 2-cyl., 12 hp

	FP	5	4	3	2	1
Touring-5P	950	2200	3200	4400	7000	15,000

Model B — 4-cyl., 24 hp

	FP	5	4	3	2	1
Touring-5P	2250	2300	3300	4600	7500	16,000

EAGLE — Rahway, New Jersey — (1905-1907) — The Eagle Automobile Company of Rahway put its cart before the horse. In mid-1905 the company announced that it was placing on the market a low-priced car with a four-cylinder air-cooled engine designed by H.J. Muntz of Poughkeepsie. If any cars were produced that year, one might wonder where and how. It was not until March of 1906 that the Eagle Automobile Company was incorporated for $60,000 capital; a week following that came the announcement, as *The Motor World* put it, that the Eagle was to "alight in Rahway." The Thorp property on Georges Avenue had just been purchased and "a factory will be erected at once." Apparently the factory was built, and Eagle cars were produced there. But not for long. The men behind the Eagle were Frank C. Vandewater, Edwin Vandewater, A. Gibbey Spencer, George W. Loft and Henry S. Griffin, all of Rahway. The Vandewaters moved from Rahway to Iselin soon thereafter. When next they were heard from, they had moved again, to Elizabeth — and they were producing another car called the Correja which was a considerably more admirable and successful venture than their short-lived Eagle.

1906 EAGLE
Four-cyl., 20/24 hp, 110" wb

Touring-5P	1400	2500	3500	5000	8500	18,000

1907 EAGLE
Four-cyl., 30 hp, 108" wb

Model E Touring-5P	1750	2400	3400	4800	8000	17,000

EAGLE — Milwaukee, Wisconsin — (1906) — During the summer of 1906 the Eagle Automobile Company of Milwaukee announced that it had completed its first car. This Eagle was powered by a two-cylinder 13/15 hp engine, featured friction drive, and sported a long hood "as on high power roadsters." Wheelbase was 98 inches. A price tag of $800 was put on the first car. And it may have been the last. The Eagle from Milwaukee was not heard from again.

1908 Eagle, auto-buggy, (Elmira), NAHC

EAGLE — Elmira, New York — (1908) — The Eagle Motor Carriage Company of Elmira declared that the "lightness and still-running qualities" of its product, "together with its easy riding long spring . . . place this car in a class by itself." Actually, the Eagle was a member of a very large class. It was a highwheeler, featuring a two-cylinder air-cooled engine (possibly a Brennan), planetary gear, rope/steel cable drive, wheel steering, and 48-inch rear wheels (32-inch front.) Long 74-inch single cantilever springs stretched between the axles on each side. "This car has no transmission, no jack shaft, no differential, no friction clutches, no universal joints, and yet, it is claimed, the car runs perfectly, going around sharp curves with perfect ease, as the cables on the inside wheel will slip a little when rounding a curve." Thus reported *Cycle and Automobile Trade Journal*, somewhat skeptically. Reportedly, too, the men behind this Eagle had tested their car every day for over two weeks "without turning a nut or using a tool of any kind." Nonetheless, the Eagle Motor Carriage Company did not survive the year. Production of this very primitive highwheeler — even at its bargain $350 price — was minimal.

1909 Eagle, roadster, (St. Louis), NAHC

EAGLE — St. Louis, Missouri — (1909) — The Eagle Automobile Company of St. Louis began and ended business with a $650 Model N two-passenger roadster featuring a two-cylinder 14 hp air-cooled engine, friction transmission and shaft drive on a 94-inch wheelbase. The company also referred to this car on occasion as the American Eagle. Under neither name did it sell well, and manufacture was discontinued in St. Louis by the end of 1909. Inconclusive references indicate that the company may thereafter have tried the commercial vehicle field, but with equally mediocre results.

EAGLE — Appleton, Wisconsin — (1910) — In 1910 the Eagle Manufacturing Company of Appleton, which had previously tiptoed into the automobile industry with the making of accessories, now decided to plunge stalwartly into automobile manufacture. In the reorganization, capital stock was increased from $6000 to $200,000, and the firm's name was changed to Eagle Automobile Manufacturing Company. Appleton residents were expected to provide the needed new capital, and W.D. Legge, an engineer with the Tuttle Press Company in town, took charge of engineering the new Eagle product, which was to be offered in two models: a 30 hp four at $2000 and a 40 hp four at $3000. A prototype is known to have been built, but then this venture was stopped abruptly in its tracks. Doubtless Appleton residents had not come through with the necessary capital.

EAGLE — Detroit, Michigan — (1911) — Martin Brazinski was the man behind this Eagle and, so far as is known, he built just one. The firm he headed was the Eagle Motor Car Company, at 427 Gratoit Avenue in Detroit, but it operated principally as a dealership. The reason for the building of an Eagle automobile was to demonstrate Brazinski's patented aluminum tires. Most component parts of the vehicle were purchased from suppliers. Its engine was a 60 hp Wisconsin six; surviving letters indicate that Brazinski bought his bearings, hubs and axles from Timken in Canton, Ohio; universal joints from Blood Brothres' Machine Company in Kalamazoo, Michigan; and wheels to order from Turnbull Wagon Company of Defiance, Ohio. The wheels were the rub — literally. Brazinski's patent described permanently affixed cast aluminum sidewall tires onto them, with spring-loaded canvas and rubber tread sections surrounding the perimeter of the sidewalls and held slightly apart by a strange rectangular cross-section inner tube. The idea was a blowout-free tire, but the result was that whenever the car hit a hard bump it would bottom on the aluminum sides of the wheel. This made for a horrible ride, needless to say, and was probably among the reasons Brazinski drove his Eagle only 224 miles before getting on to more profitable pursuits. The car — a seven-passenger touring on a 132-inch-wheelbase chassis — remains extant but runs on standard wheels and tires today.

1915 Eagle, model 1-A, roadster, WLB

EAGLE — Los Angeles & Chicago — (1914-1915), EAGLE-MACOMBER — Sandusky, Ohio — (1916-1918) — This Eagle had two lives with the same engine. Like the Balzer and the Adams-Farwell, it was a rotary, a five-cylinder air-cooled unit developed by Walter G. Macomber in Los Angeles, and placed like a merry-go-round in the front of a conventional staggered seat cyclecar with a 104-inch wheelbase. The Eagle Cyclecar Company, established in 1914, was succeeded by the Eagle-Macomber Motor Car Company that December. That deal swapped 20% of $1.5 million stock for the firm, its good will and bills. The reorganized firm remained in Chicago until a larger plant in Ohio was found, where operations moved in November 1915. By now the Model 1 Eagle with 36-inch tread had been joined by the Model 1-A with standard 56-inch track. From 800 pounds, the Eagle had doubled to 1600. And it would become even bigger as the Eagle-Macomber which, although commonly thought to be a cyclecar, was a light car instead. It retained the standard 56-inch tread and weighed in complete at 2350 pounds. The Macomber rotary engine fitted was more than twice the horsepower of the cyclecar original. But it shared the same fate as its predecessor. Interestingly, the company tried redesigning the chassis and coachwork for more passengers and a pricier asking fee the second year but to no commercial success.

1915 Eagle, model 1, roadster, HAC

1914-1915 EAGLE
Cyclecar — 5-cyl., 12/14 hp, 104" wb

	FP	5	4	3	2	1
Model 1 Stagger Seat Roadster	395	—				

1915-1916 EAGLE
Cyclecar — 5-cyl., 18 hp, 110" wb

Model 1-A Roadster-2P	700	—				

1917 Eagle-Macomber, touring, KM

1917 EAGLE MACOMBER
Light Car — 5-cyl., 28 hp, 108" wb

	FP	5	4	3	2	1
Cloverleaf Roadster-3P	700	—	—	—	—	—
Roadster-2P	700	—	—	—	—	—

1918 EAGLE MACOMBER
Light Car — 5-cyl., 28 hp, 118" wb

Model D Touring-5P	1500	—	—	—	—	—
Model D Touring Sedan-5P	1850	—	—	—	—	—

1924 Eagle, Six, touring, WLB

EAGLE — Flint, Michigan — (1923-1924) — This Eagle was Billy Durant's idea. In June of 1923, Durant Motors, Inc. announced the car as a "complete line of four and six-cylinder automobiles" to be built in the Star plant in Flint. The four was to sell for $525 and compete with the Chevrolet; Durant withheld details of the six because he wanted it to be a "complete surprise." Only the surprise arrived. The Eagle which appeared at the New York Automobile Show in January 1924 was a 50 hp six on a 115-inch wheelbase chassis with a price tag of $820, the lowest-priced six in America save for the Oldsmobile. The Eagle four was ignored completely, and it might be that Durant had mentioned it merely as a ruse to throw the industry off guard. The Eagle Six sported four-wheel brakes, and an announcement immediately followed that these would be available on the Durant, Flint and Star cars as well. The Eagle was ceremoniously treated to a grand display at the Flint Motor Company at 57th and Broadway in New York City, and showed up at the Chicago and San Francisco automobile shows too. After the hoopla died, however, so did the Eagle. In March Durant announced that the Eagle had been dropped, and that the Flint "40" would take its place. The only Eagles built were the pilot and show models.

EAGLE ELECTRIC — Detroit, Michigan — (1915, 1916) — The Eagle Electric Automobile Company of Detroit was organized in the spring of 1915 to build an electric motorcar designed by Herman A. Schmidt. In addition to Schmidt, the other promoters of this venture were Cass C. Smith and Henry Clay Judson. By early June the company had been officially incorporated with a capital stock of $100,000, and at its temporary headquarters at 169 Howard Street, the first models had been completed. Whether the company ever moved into permanent headquarters is not known. But the Eagle Electric Automobile Company did not survive the 1916 model year. Just one Eagle Electric was registered in Michigan in 1916.

1915-1916 EAGLE ELECTRIC

Cpl.-3P (without battery)	1100	2200	3200	4400	7000	15,000
Limo.-5P (without battery)	1325	2300	3300	4600	7500	16,000
Cpl.-3P (with battery)	1250	2200	3200	4400	7000	15,000
Limo.-5P (with battery)	1475	2300	3300	4600	7500	16,000

EAGLET — Los Angeles, California — (1914-1915) — Aside from being very well named for a cyclecar, the Eaglet had little further to recommend it. Shaft drive and planetary transmission were rather progressive features, but the remaining Eaglet specs were pedestrian. A two-cylinder runabout and a light delivery on a 95-inch wheelbase with 48-inch tread were planned, with a $425 price tag for each. The organization of the Eagle Motors Company was announced by Percy O. Gordon in July of 1914. In September the construction of a factory at 1875 West Jefferson in LA was the next news. Since very little was heard from the company thereafter, it may be assumed the Eaglet never left the nest. Prototypes were built, however, and perhaps a few production cars, before the hopes of the company were clipped. A couple of Eaglets might have been built on West Pico Boulevard in 1916. By 1917 Percy Gordon had changed his mind about automobiles and entered the real estate business.

1908 Earl, roadster, NAHC

EARL — Milwaukee & Kenosha, Wisconsin — (1907-1908) — Retrospectively, the makers of the Earl claimed that they began development of their first car in 1904 and had it on the road in 1905. They declined to mention, but the place was Milwaukee. It was not until the summer of 1907, however, that Earl Motor Car Company was incorporated, with a capital stock of $25,000 and at that time the firm transferred operations from Milwaukee to the former plant of the Visible Typewriter Company in Kenosha. If there had been any production in Milwaukee, it was minimal. An assembly line was set up in a new factory in Kenosha, and the Earl was definitely put into production there, offered in both two-and four-cylinder models. Apparently initial sales were sufficiently encouraging for the company to increase its capital stock to $350,000 early in 1908. But equally apparent the company should not have been so encouraged. By mid-summer all visible assets of the Earl Motor Car Company were seized by the Kenosha sheriff. Reportedly, fifteen cents on the dollar was offered in settlement of claims. When this was done, the remainder of the personal effects of the Earl company were sold for a grand total of $70. By the end of the year the Earl plant was taken over by the Petrel Motor Car Company which would enjoy considerably more commercial success than had the Earl.

1907 EARL
2-cyl., 15 hp, 100" wb

	FP	5	4	3	2	1
Roadster-2P	950	2500	3500	5000	8500	18,000

1908 EARL
2-cyl., 18 hp, 100" wb

Tiger Roadster-2P	950	2500	3500	5000	8500	18,000

4-cyl., 22 hp, 106" wb

Rumble-Seat Roadster	985	2600	3600	5200	8700	18,500
Touring-4P	1200	2700	3600	5300	8800	19,000

1922 Earl, model 40, roadster, WLB

EARL — Jackson, Michigan — (1922-1923) — In March of 1921, Benjamin Briscoe appointed Clarence A. Earl (the recently fired vice-president of Willys-Overland) as president of Briscoe Motor Corporation. By October, having wearied of the calamities that had greeted him at every turn in his automobile career, Briscoe departed abruptly to try his hand in new fields, and left his car, his company and his Jackson factory to Earl. Clarence Earl immediately called in the press to announce the formation of Earl Motors, Inc. and its forthcoming "new" four-cylinder motorcar. Actually the new Earl would be the old Briscoe with some of its problems worked out and made a little bit bigger and a little bit more powerful. Nonetheless, the rejuvenated car was greeted elaborately in trade publications, and there was much talk of the "spread of enthusiasm through the organization." From the beginning, there were problems. The financial burden that Earl assumed with the Briscoe takeover was reported to be nearly $1.5 million, and although he was greeted amiably in banking circles and found little difficulty in raising new capital, his was an uphill battle. It was complicated in the summer of 1922 by the appearance on the scene of a bewhiskered "Mr. Branigan" who, posing as a representative of Earl Motors, visited scores of Detroit companies placing gargantuan orders for various products and services. One week 10,000 menu cards for a company banquet were delivered to Earl Motors, another week an expensive set of new awnings for the factory. The identity of the hoaxster

was never discovered. In setting up his new organization, Earl found himself faced with a board of directors composed of bankers (Chicago Trust Company, Chemical National Bank of New York, Jackson City Bank of Jackson) and vice-presidents of various supplier companies. George C. Scobie, formerly of Price-Waterhouse and the Hayes Wheel Company, was appointed vice-president and comptroller. Clarence Earl quickly found that he did not agree with any of these people regarding the future course of Earl Motors, and he resigned as president in November of 1922. (He subsequently became the president of National.) The bankers and vice-presidents took over, with George Scobie as president, and reorganized as the Earl Motor Manufacturing Company in early 1923. Capitalization was set at a million dollars. Clarence Earl had envisioned his company as a high-volume producer. His opponents preferred a more conservative lower-quantity manufacturing policy. They fared dismally in pursuing it. Early in 1924 the service rights to the defunct Earl car were sold to Standard Motor Parts Company of Detroit. Approximately 2000 Earls had been produced.

1922 EARL
Model 40 — 4-cyl., 37.5 hp, 112" wb

	FP	5	4	3	2	1
Touring-5P	1285	2500	3500	5000	8500	18,000
Roadster-2P	1375	2700	3600	5300	8800	19,000
Brougham-4P	1995	2400	3400	4800	8000	17,000
Sedan-5P	1995	1800	2800	4000	6200	13,000
Screen Delivery	1085	1600	2700	3800	5800	12,000
Panel Delivery	1160	1500	2500	3600	5500	11,000

1923 Earl, model 40, coupe, HAC

1923 EARL
Model 40 — 4-cyl., 37.5 hp, 112" wb

Touring-5P	1095	2500	3500	5000	8500	18,000
Cabriolet-4P	1395	2450	3500	4900	8300	17,500
Roadster-2P	1485	2700	3600	5300	8800	19,000
Sedan-5P	1795	1800	2800	4000	6200	13,000
Coupe-4P	1795	2200	3200	4400	7000	15,000
Sport Phaeton-5P	1275	2700	3600	5300	8800	19,000

EARLY — The Early Motor Car Company of Columbus, Ohio has frequently been cited in rosters as a manufacturer of automobiles in 1911. It was not. In mid-January of 1912, when Early went into receivership, it was indicated that the company had been a sales agency for several lines of automobiles — Rambler, Halladay, Herreshoff and Paige-Detroit among them — and had dealt in parts and accessories. Of the 159 people to whom Early owed money, the largest creditor was Dr. L.M. Early, president of the company, who was said to be "in very bad health owing to experimentation with x-rays early in the history of that branch of science."

EAST — The East Jersey Motor & Transportation Company was organized during the spring of 1906 with a capital stock of $100,000 for the manufacture of "cars, cabs, carriages and ship chandlery" in Elizabeth, New Jersey. Among the incorporators were R.T. Potts and E.M. Wood. Manufacture of a car is doubted.

The East Liberty Sales Company was organized in Pittsburgh, Pennsylvania with a capital stock of $5000 early in 1915 to manufacture and deal in automobiles and supplies. Incorporators were W.H. Verner, L. Atwell and N.M. Harrower. Manufacture of an automobile is doubted.

The East Orange Automobile & Machine Company was organized in Newark, New Jersey during the summer of 1912 to "manufacture, deal in and store automobiles." Capital stock was $10,000. L.C. Stringham, F.L. Barr and Henry Seib were the incorporators. Manufacture is doubted.

The East Tennessee Motor Car Company was organized during the summer of 1910 in Knoxville with a capital stock of $10,000 to "manufacture and sell automobiles, gasoline engines, motorcycles, trucks, accessories and iron fences, and to do a general garage business." Incorporators were A.P. Rutherford, D.H. Jenkins, W.H. Bowman, A.A. Schmid and E.P. Rutherford. Manufacture of an automobile is doubted.

EASTABROOK — Grand Rapids, Michigan — (1916) — The Eastabrook was yet another of the "world's smallest" cars, as these lilliputian one-off automobiles built for either midgets or children during this era were often claimed to be. This one was built by a mechanic from Grand Rapids, P.H. Eastabrook, for his four-year-old son. And it was a darling. Unlike most, which were electric powered, the Eastabrook moved courtesy of a small single-cylinder gasoline engine. The car's wheelbase was 50 inches, its tread 22½ inches. And it was fully equipped: electric lights, electric horn, duplex steering gear, external contracting brakes, speedometer, clock and

1916 Eastabrook, NAHC

1899 Eastman, runabout, NAHC

gas pump. "Eastabrook's son drives the machine at will about the neighborhood and occasionally goes out for a spin of a mile or more," *Motor Age* reported. "The gears are low and it is impossible for him to make more than 8 or 10 miles an hour."

EASTERN — The Eastern Auto Distributing Company was organized in New York City during the summer of 1910 with a capital stock of $1200 to "manufacture and deal in automobiles, carriages, etc." Incorporators were Leonard K. Clark, Albert C. Baldwin and Stephen C. Piero. Manufacture of an automobile is doubted.

The Eastern Auto Service Company was organized in New York City late in 1907 with a capital stock of $100,000 for the manufacture of automobiles. F.D. Hollister, J. Seitz and M. Kram were the incorporators. Manufacture is doubted.

The Eastern Automobile Company was organized in Columbus, Ohio during the summer of 1911 with a capital stock of $10,000 to manufacture and deal in automobiles. Incorporators were Jacob Goldstein, J.E. Lacey, E.F. Cain, W.C. Adams and Charles Sylvester. Manufacture is doubted.

The Eastern Electric Vehicle Company established itself at 179 West First Street in South Boston, Massachusetts in 1921. Intended manufacture was probably commercial vehicles, but the firm never made it into production.

The Eastern Indiana Motor Car Company produced a car called the E.I.M. in Richmond, Indiana in 1915. Refer to E.I.M.

The Eastern Motor Company was organized in Atlantic City, New Jersey early in 1911 with a capital stock of $50,000 to "manufacture automobiles, motor cars, motorcycles, etc." Incorporators were E.G. Harris, W.E. Riley and P.G. Clerk. Manufacture of an automobile is doubted.

The Eastern Motor Company was organized in Camden, New Jersey during the fall of 1910 with a capital stock of $100,000 to construct motor vehicles and engines. Frank R. Hansell, William F. Eidell and John A. MacPeak were the incorporators. Manufacture of an automobile is doubted.

In 1916 the Eastern Motors Syndicate of New Britain, Connecticut announced its entry into the automotive field. The car it was to produce was the Charter Oak. Refer to Charter Oak.

The Eastern Parts Manufacturing Company was incorporated with a capital stock of $6000 during the summer of 1914 for the manufacture of motor vehicles in Albany, New York. Incorporators were J. Greenthal, G.C. Young and R. Frankel. Manufacture of an automobile is doubted.

The Eastern Transit Company was organized in Hartford, Connecticut with a capital stock of $50,000 during the summer of 1908 to "manufacture, lease, sell, buy, equip, license and operate airships of all kinds, also stages, cars, boats, motorcars, taxicabs, taxivans, etc." Behind this ambitious venture were J.L. Loomis, J.W. Knox and Mary E. Kellogg. Manufacture of an automobile is doubted.

EASTERN — **New Haven, Connecticut** — **(1896-1897)** — "Well pleased with its performance" was the assessment of the Eastern Motor Carriage Company of New Haven after trying out its first experimental car in 1896. It was powered by a seven-horsepower gasoline engine and provided accommodations for four passengers. The vehicle was so high that two steps were required for ascension to the seats. According to the December 1896 issue of *The Horseless Age*, "after making a few minor changes," the company expected to begin manufacturing. Conceivably some production may have resulted, the cars were probably put together in the shops of the Hoggson & Pettis Manufacturing Company which had assembled the prototype. Eastern Motor Carriage was out of business by 1898, however, and its promoter, Henry W. Clapp, immediately tried again with a new car he named for himself.

EASTERN — **Brockton, Massachusetts** — **(1910-1911)** — The Eastern Motor Company was organized by Alonzo R. Marsh, who seems to have been the one of four Marsh brothers least daunted by failure. Five years earlier, the Marshes of Brockton had assayed the automotive industry with production of the two-cylinder Marsh runabout but had quickly changed their minds and sold out to C.H. Metz. The Eastern was the second Marsh automobile, but only Alonzo was intimately involved with it. The car was a four-cylinder 24 hp touring on a 105-inch wheelbase that sold for $1250. Trade press references from January 1910 indicate that Marsh had "his entire raw material for 2,500 machines on the ground." Whether he managed to get that many cars put together before this venture went under is not known. Still undaunted, Alonzo Marsh next headed west, settling first in Painesville, Ohio to build the Vulcan, later in Cleveland where his brothers joined him to build another car under the Marsh name.

1900 Eastman Steamer, runabout, WLB

EASTMAN — **Cleveland, Ohio** — **(1898-1900)** — Henry F. Eastman was a bicycle man who had worked awhile with Alexander Winton in putting together Winton two-wheelers and who spent three years thereafter experimenting with both electric and steam vehicles. Ultimately he decided to forgo further development of his electric — a three-wheeler he called an Electro Cycle — and to go to market with his steam car. Early in 1900 he allied himself with a few local businessmen, and with H. Jay Hayes who had designed the all-steel body for his first electric, and together they established the Eastman Automobile Company of Cleveland. The steam runabout Eastman had designed was an attractive two-seater with wickerwork decoration on its side panels. Its tubular frame and bicycle wheels betrayed Eastman's earlier cycle experience, but its all-steel body was probably a first for an American production car. As explained rather ponderously in *The Motor Age*, it was "made of sheet metal backed by an asbestos covering, which retains the heat and muffles any possible noise, making a practically indestructible body which will not crack or warp and which admits of a high finish that can be baked on the same as in finishing bicycles, making it also possible to re-enamel in new colors in a few hours, while in ordinary carriage painting a number of days are necessary to secure a good finish." Another certainly unique feature, though not so commendable, was the steering tiller which was devised so "an operator . . . can ride for miles literally 'hands off,' it being necessary to use the steering lever only when it is desired to part from a straight line." Despite what was assuredly a fine horseless carriage, Henry Eastman produced it for only a short while, deciding in late November of 1900 to concentrate on the carriage part only. In May 1901 he sold his automobile department to A.M. Benson, who organized the Benson Automobile Company in Cleveland. Eastman reorganized as the Eastman Metallic Body Company, with H. Jay Hayes remaining with him awhile before taking off for Detroit to get into the body business himself.

EASTON — From 1910 to 1916 the Easton Machine Company produced automobiles in South Easton, Massachusetts under the tradename Morse. Refer to Morse.

EASTSIDE — The Eastside Auto Repair Company was organized in Paterson, New Jersey during the summer of 1911 with a capital stock of $20,000 to "construct and repair motor vehicles and engines." Incorporators were Vernon Ettinger, Matthew Weinstein and Chester C. Boggs, all of Paterson. Manufacture of an automobile is doubted.

492

EATON — South Hampton, New Hampshire — (1896) — In April of 1896 W.S. Eaton of South Hampton announced that he was building an automobile to enter in the Cosmopolitan Race on Decoration Day. He was one of twenty-six entries in the event, and also one of twenty not to make it to the starting line. (Four of the six cars that did make it were Duryeas.) How successful Eaton's vehicle subsequently was has not been documented.

1898 Eaton Electric Carriage, runabout, NAHC

EATON ELECTRIC — Boston, Massachusetts — (1898-1900) — At the Mechanics Fair in Boston in 1898, a small electric carriage called the Eaton was exhibited. Reportedly, it had been designed and built in a short six weeks by Howard F. Eaton, "a well-known electrical engineer of Boston." Following the fair, Eaton opened an office at 383 Washington Street and went into business as the Eaton Electric Motor Carriage Company. This business was very quickly superseded, in February of 1899, by the Eaton Motor Carriage Company with new offices at 8 Waltham Street and a grand capitalization of $500,000, though a mere $40 was paid in. To say that the Eaton Electric venture was underfinanced is an exercise in understatement. Very few Eaton Electrics were built; Royal Sheldon, owner of the Palace Theatre, bought one of them; several more were exported to London. By late fall of 1900, the bankruptcy of the Eaton Motor Carriage Company was revealed.

EBY — In York, Nebraska, following the turn of the century, the Eby Company manufactured the De Jarnette automobile wheel. In the late fall of 1907 the company reported the enlarging of its factory and plans for starting "the manufacture of complete automobiles." Subsequent manufacture is doubted, however.

ECK — From 1897 to 1909, in Reading, Pennsylvania, James L. Eck built steam cars which he sold under the name Boss. Refer to Boss Steam Car.

ECKENROTH — Early in 1912 the Eckenroth Automobile Livery Company was organized in Cleveland, Ohio with a capital stock of $5000 to build and repair automobiles. Rudolph H., Harry S. and Peter L. Eckenroth were behind this venture, in association with Carlton F. Schultz. Manufacture of an automobile is doubted.

ECKERSON — During the spring of 1911 the Eckerson Motor and Carriage Works was organized in New York City with a capital stock of $25,000 for the manufacture of motorcars and carriages. G.D. Eckerson, D.G. Moore, H.M. Bertody and C.R. Neidlinger were the principals involved. Manufacture of an automobile is doubted.

ECKERT — Charles Eckert of Cincinnati, Ohio is listed as an automobile manufacturer in the Hiscox book *Horseless Vehicles, Automobiles, Motor Cycles* published in 1900. Further documentation is lacking. Turn of the century city directory listings for the Charles Eckert Manufacturing Company, which was at 1518 Race Street, indicate its activity as bicycle manufacture only.

ECKHARDT & SOUTER — Buffalo, New York — (1903) — The Eckhardt & Souter was introduced at the Buffalo Automobile Show at City Convention Hall on March 9th, 1903. Designed by John Eckhardt, it was a four-cylinder two-stroke 25 hp touring car with a three-speed sliding gear transmission and wooden wheels with sixteen spokes. Said to be "very substantially built," it weighed 2400 pounds. A price was not quoted. The car was intended to be manufactured by the new Eckhardt & Souter Automobile Company at premises leased at 288 Triangle Street in Buffalo. Available sources do not indicate that production ever resulted.

ECKHART — In 1900 the Eckhart brothers of Auburn, Indiana organized the Auburn Automobile Company. Refer to Auburn.

ECKHOFF — The Eckhoff Automobile Company was organized in New York City late in 1910 with a capital stock of $5000 to manufacture and deal in motor cars and accessories. Behind this venture were John H. Eckhoff, Jr., John H. Eckhoff, Sr. and Edward J. Flanagan. Manufacture of an automobile is doubted.

ECLIPSE STEAM — Easton, Massachusetts — (1900-1903) — The Eclipse Automobile Company had its offices in Boston and its factory in nearby Easton. It produced a thousand-dollar steam runabout on a 62-inch wheelbase with tiller steering, wire wheels and coachwork quite typical for the period. The use of shaft drive was unusual, however. In January 1901 three Eclipse steamers were exhibited at the automobile show in Mechanic's Hall in Boston, where reportedly seven orders were received, the most important from the Boston Headquarters of the U.S. Postal Service. The local Back Bay Station postmaster announced his belief that use of the Eclipse cars would cut mail delivery time by twenty minutes. Whether it did or not is not known, but this sale to the post office resulted in one of the earliest uses of a motorized road vehicle for mail collection and delivery. Unfortunately, the post office didn't follow through with orders for a full fleet, and the Eclipse Automobile Company — undercapitalized as so many of these early ventures — faded away a couple of years later. The designer of the Eclipse's three-cylinder engine and steam boiler had been Everett S. Cameron. It was his first car. By 1901 Cameron had left Eclipse to build the Taunton in nearby Taunton, Massachusetts; in 1903 he went on to build his own car, the well-known air-cooled Cameron.

1903 Eclipse, steam runabout, NAHC

ECLIPSE — Fort Wayne, Indiana — (1902) — The Eclipse Buggy Company of Fort Wayne entered the automotive industry in the easiest possible way. It simply revised its carriage design sufficiently to be rendered horseless, but left up to the purchaser the means to make it so. This Eclipse was offered without an engine. "You supply the Power, we do the rest," the company advertised . . . but only in 1902.

ECLIPSE — Columbus, Ohio — (1904) — The Eclipse Machine Company was a small machine shop in Columbus whose proprietors liked to dabble with engines and cars. During the summer of 1904, they announced their invention of a new air-cooled motor which they would fit to some carriages "shortly." It would seem that a handful of Eclipse cars followed that year, though a viable production was never embarked upon. Building to customer order was as far as this Eclipse Machine Company venture proceeded.

ECLIPSE — Elmira, New York — (1904) — The Eclipse from Elmira was a four-cylinder 20 hp air-cooled touring car on a 94-inch wheelbase. The Eclipse Bicycle Company had first experimented with a horseless carriage in 1896, but had cold feet about proceeding into manufacture at that time. To produce the Eclipse in 1904, the firm changed its name to Eclipse Manufacturing Company. The name was quickly changed back when Eclipse discovered it had been right the first time around; the company's financial fortunes were better served by sticking to two-wheelers.

1905 Eclipse, touring

ECLIPSE — Milwaukee, Wisconsin — (1905-1906) — Eclipse was the name given to the automobiles produced by the Krueger Manufacturing Company in 1905. Harry F. Krueger and William F. Krueger were the men behind the Eclipse, and they had a background of twenty years of machine-shop training in the Milwaukee area, the last six of which had been focused on the rebuilding and repairing of automobiles. When finally they decided to build a car themselves, they incorporated a number of progressive ideas. Among them was a one-cylinder air-cooled engine produced by a single casting which the brothers tested on hot summer days in runs of from 100 to 175 miles without its ever overheating; indeed, an article in *Automobile Review* stated the brothers' claim that after a continual running of more than an hour "a person can always place the hand on the flange edges without any danger of as much as a blister." Shaft drive and planetary transmission were featured. More significantly, perhaps, Harry Krueger (who was the guiding spirit of the partnership) decided to place the steering wheel on the left-hand side of the car. In 1927 when he died, his obituary in *Motor Age* included the note that the Eclipse "is believed to have been" the first automobile in America to feature left-hand drive. (Actually, a turn-of-the century Columbia had preceded it.) In 1906, which was the last year the Kruegers manufactured their car, it was marketed as a Krueger rather than an Eclipse.

1905 ECLIPSE
Eclipse Model A - 1-cyl., 86" wb

	FP	5	4	3	2	1
Light Tour.-5P	1250	1600	2800	4000	6200	13,000
Light Delivery	1250	1600	2700	3800	5800	12,000

Eclipse Model B - 2-cyl., 22 hp

Tour.-5P	1800	2000	3000	4200	6500	14,000

1906 KRUEGER
Krueger - 2-cyl., 20 hp, 100" wb

Model C Tour.-5P	1800	2300	3300	4600	7500	16,000

ECLIPSE — Detroit, Michigan — (1907) — In December of 1906 the Eclipse Machine Company of Detroit announced that it would shortly place a "light, high grade" four-cylinder car on the market. Such production as followed was minimal, and strictly a sideline activity to the firm's general manufacturing of components for the automobile field. The Eclipse Machine Company's greatest coup in this regard probably occurred in November 1913 at the motorcycle show in Chicago when Vincent Bendix visited the Eclipse booth and showed president E.J. Dunn the starter drive he had invented. Within minutes Dunn had closed with Bendix for exclusive rights to the device.

1916 Eclipse, model 28, roadster, WLB

ECLIPSE — Detroit, Michigan — (1916) — The Eclipse Motor Car Company of Detroit was organized with a capital stock of $30,000 by A.S. Keller, A.P. Schulte and P.J. Murphy — and offered a lineup of four models: one roadster and three touring cars. The roadster was a 28 hp four on a 96-inch wheelbase at $595. The tourers included a five-passenger version on a 110-inch wheelbase powered by a 34 hp four-cylinder engine and priced at $745, and two seven-passenger cars on 115-inch wheelbases at $995 with 40 hp four-cylinder engine or $1295 with a V-8. Company literature also boasted of truck, motorcycle and motorboat manufacture. In advertising for dealers, Eclipse offered a free car to any go-getter anxious to "get out of the 'shirt sleeve class'," though with a few strings naturally, among them that the potential agent take a special Eclipse course of instruction from the Detroit Correspondence Institute of Motoring. "Our board of directors has made this a requirement," Eclipse said, "and our president has no authority to appoint any person as an agent of this company who does not agree to study this course." The odds are that the board of directors and president of Eclipse and the Institute were one and the same. Both ventures appear to have been short-lived.

1916 ECLIPSE
Model 34 — 4-cyl., 34 hp, 110" wb

	FP	5	4	3	2	1
Touring-5P	745	2700	3600	5300	8800	19,000

Model 28 — 4-cyl., 28 hp, 96" wb

Roadster-2P	595	2900	3700	5600	9100	20,000

Model 40 — 4-cyl., 40 hp, 115" wb

Touring-7P	995	2800	3700	5500	9000	19,500

Model 45 — 8-cyl., 45 hp, 115" wb

Touring-7P	1295	2900	3700	5600	9100	20,000

ECO — Detroit, Michigan — (1921) — The Eco was yet another of the numerous automobiles of the early post-World War I period which was planned for export only. This one was destined for Australia. It was designed by a Detroit engineer with the marvelous name of G. Hamilton-Grapes whose goal it was for a motorcar that would not overheat in the "tropical climate" Down Under and which would be fuel efficient because of the high gasoline prices there. Hamilton-Grapes intended the car to be built of American-made parts entirely, but envisioned assembly of the vehicle in Australia. The pilot model sported a Turmo engine and Zenith carburetor; two engineers from Zenith ran a chassis on test which resulted in fuel economy of 34.9 mpg. In September of 1921 *Automotive Industries* reported that G. Hamilton-Grapes was in the midst of a cross-country trip in the Eco prototype. It was a 108-inch wheelbase car, but its builder was

contemplating an increase to 110 inches for the production version. The Eco prototype made it back to Detroit, but the Eco production car never made it to Australia.

ECONOMIC STEAM — East Orange, New Jersey — (1902) — The Economic Manufacturing Company, with address given as 118-120 Main Street in East Orange, was listed as a producer of steam cars by *Cycle and Automobile Trade Journal* in January 1902. Undoubtedly, this was more expectation than fulfillment. The area was prominent as a hat manufacturing center at the turn of the century, and Thomas Edison's laboratories brought prosperity to the Oranges, but nowhere in the city's considerable historical record is there any indication a steam car was manufactured there.

ECONOMY — A number of ventures were organized under the Economy name indicating manufacture of an automobile as part of the forthcoming activity, though this seems not to have been realized. The companies were the following.

The Economy Auto and Garage Company, organized early in 1908 in Buffalo, New York with a capital stock of $15,000. Incorporators were J.L. McGrane, C.A. Stredbing and A.L. Dixon.

The Economy Automobile Company, organized in Grand Rapids, Michigan during the summer of 1911 with a capital stock of $7500. Incorporators were F.P. Oswald, H.J. Hagen and H.A. Brink.

The Economy Distributing Company, organized during the summer of 1909 in Albany, New York with a capital stock of $15,000. Incorporators were A.W. Rosen, Isaac Cohen and Aaron Benjamin.

The Economy Manufacturing Company, organized during the summer of 1908 in Chicago, Illinois with a capital stock of $2500. Incorporators were F.W. Detray, W. Demms and A.M. Searles.

1908 Economy, model B, high wheel buggy, WLB

ECONOMY — Indiana & Illinois — (1908-1911) — The Economy Motor Buggy Company of Fort Wayne, Indiana was a typical producer of highwheelers which could not seem to find a solution to its special problem. Its product infringed upon patents of the Success highwheeler from St. Louis, and when the Success Company took Economy to court for royalty nonpayment, the only solution the Economy people could come up with was to get out of town. The officers moved quietly to Illinois, trying Kankakee first but finding no available home there, and finally settling down in Joliet and returning to manufacture — until the Success Company found them again. Bankruptcy soon followed. Changing the Economy gasoline buggy design sufficiently to avoid royalties apparently was never considered, though the firm's president, William R. Everett, had earlier developed an experimental electric roadster and light delivery. In late 1909 the firm's name had been changed to Economy Motor Car Company, and most of its production in 1910 and 1911 was focused on commercial vehicles. Early in 1912 the assets of the now defunct Economy company were purchased by William E. Pratt of the Pratt Manufacturing Company in Joliet, who immediately announced that he would put Everett's electric roadster and delivery car into production under his own name.

1909 Economy, high wheel runabout, JAC

1908-1911 ECONOMY
Model B — 1-cyl., 10 hp, 86" wb

	FP	5	4	3	2	1
High Wheel Buggy	450	1800	2800	4000	6200	13,000

1909-1911 ECONOMY
Models E & G — 2-cyl., 22/24 hp, 86" wb

	FP	5	4	3	2	1
High Wheel Buggy		1800	2800	4000	6200	13,000

1916 Economy, Three-Dor roadster, HAC

ECONOMY — Tiffin & Bellefontaine, Ohio — (1916-1919), ECONOMY-VOGUE — Tiffin, Ohio — (1920), VOGUE — Tiffin, Ohio — (1921-1922) — The Economy Motor Company of Tiffin manufactured a line of conventional medium-priced assembled cars with the exception of one body style. It was the Three-Dor (sic) Roadster providing accommodation for five passengers. The rear seat, the company averred, was not the usual skimpy variety — "in this car all five passengers are 'in' the party and no one is slighted" — and the seat was reached by a third door which Economy claimed as an original feature. The people behind the Economy Motor Company were six Tiffin businessmen: John A. Manecke, Stanton J. Lewis, H.E. Cook, C.J. Larger, Raymond W. Miller, and George Wiseman. (Wiseman was the car's designer.) Late in 1916 they leased the old woolen mill at the corner of Washington and Riverside Drive in Tiffin, and they were in production by year's end. Almost immediately, Economy caught the eye of the Bellefontaine Automobile Company nearby — the Three-Dor was probably the reason — and consolidation plans were being made by January 1917. Initially, Economy "repudiated" the merger, but finally it was accomplished in April of 1917 — and a move was made to Bellefontaine where the Three-Dor was renamed a Chummy, and a Ferro V-8 was added to the usual Economy fours. Production apparently continued in Tiffin as

1917 Economy, model G4-36, touring, WLB

well. By the end of 1919, Economy was broke in Bellefontaine, but in Tiffin the marque was resurrected as a six called the Economy-Vogue to be built by the newly-restyled Vogue Motor Car Company. The marque name became simply Vogue for 1921 with the introduction of a larger and more expensive line of sixes. Production of these cars continued the following year. In January 1923 a trustee was named for the Vogue Motor Car Company, and its plant was ordered sold. Among the company's problems was its failure to pay taxes due. The Internal Revenue Service in Washington claimed $5000; the state of Ohio $2000.

1921 Vogue, model 6-55, touring, WLB

1916-1917 ECONOMY
Economy — 4-cyl., 115" wb

	FP	5	4	3	2	1
Touring	1695	2400	3400	4800	8000	17,000
Touring-Sedan	2295	2000	3000	4200	6500	14,000
Thre-Dor Roadster	1695	2300	3300	4600	7500	16,000

1918-1919 ECONOMY
Economy G4-36 — 4-cyl., 22.5 hp, 115" wb

	FP	5	4	3	2	1
Touring-5P	985	2300	3300	4600	7500	16,000
Chummy Roadster-5P	1040	2400	3400	4800	8000	17,000

Economy C8-48 — 8-cyl., 28.8 hp, 115" wb

	FP	5	4	3	2	1
Touring-5P	1395	2350	3400	4700	7800	16,500
Chummy Roadster-5P	1395	2450	3500	4900	8300	17,500

1920 ECONOMY-VOGUE
Economy-Vogue 6-46 — 6-cyl., 45.8 hp, 115" wb

	FP	5	4	3	2	1
Touring-5P	1795	2400	3400	4800	8000	17,000
Roadster-4P	1795	2500	3500	5000	8500	18,000
Sedan-5P	2475	1600	2700	3800	5800	12,000
Coupe-3P	2475	2000	3000	4200	6500	14,000

1921-1922 VOGUE
Vogue 6-55 — 6-cyl., 55 hp, 124" wb

	FP	5	4	3	2	1
Touring-5P	2285	3000	4000	6000	9500	21,000
Coupe-5P	3250	2300	3300	4600	7500	16,000
Sedan-7P	3250	2000	3000	4200	6500	14,000

1914 Economycar, cyclecar 2-pass. tandem, WLB

ECONOMYCAR — Providence, Rhode Island — (1914) — The Economycar people preferred use of the term "new motoring" to mention of the word "cyclecar," which is what their 400-pound $385 two-passenger tandem runabout was. The transmission was planetary, the final drive by vee belt, the engine a 9 hp air-cooled two-cylinder guaranteeing 40 mpg. The car was designed by Charles A. Trask, who formerly had been chief engineer for Cartercar and more recently had been affiliated with Nordyke & Marmon. Spearheading the Economycar venture was Fred K. Parke, whose previous credits included vice-presidential chairs at E-M-F, Studebaker and Universal Motor Truck. A factory with 100,000 square feet of floor space was secured in Providence, Rhode Island. Headquarters of the new International Cyclecar Company were at 1790 Broadway in New York City. Six thousand Economycars were planned to be built in 1914. Actual production was probably many thousand fewer than that. The Economycar was, however, comparatively one of the more successful American cyclecars. Indeed, so strong had been its initial impact on the market that a company in Indianapolis which had begun with the same name very quickly decided to call its cyclecar a Comet.

1914 ECONOMYCAR
Cyclecar — 2-cyl., 9 hp, 104" wb

	FP	5	4	3	2	1
Tandem Runabout	385	1800	2800	4000	6200	13,000
Parcel Car	400	1500	2500	3600	5500	11,000

EDDY ELECTRIC — Windsor, Connecticut — (1900-1901) — The Eddy Manufacturing Company of Windsor produced a small electric motor that was used by several electric vehicle manufacturers as early as 1898 and which earned a sterling reputation in the turn of the century trade press. In 1900 the company began building a few small carriages itself using the Eddy motor, although this activity did not continue past 1901. In 1902 the Eddy company was taken over by General Electric.

EDGAR — The Edgar Motor Livery Company was organized with a capital stock of $10,000 late in 1912 to manufacture and deal in automobiles in Chicago, Illinois. Behind this venture were James Edgar, E.A. Zimmerman and Abram L. Myers. Manufacture of an automobile is doubted.

EDIE MAC — Reading, Pennsylvania — (1900) — The Edie Mac Automobile Company was an ambitious venture capitalized at $250,000 for the building of a steam automobile said to feature "automatic igniters for the burners and automatic boiler feeders." Undoubtedly, no more than a prototype or two were ever built. It is known that the company had acquired a Reading bicycle plant formerly used by Irwin D. Lengel for its experimental work. Lengel later was the "I" of the four partners who got together to build the Dile.

EDISON ELECTRIC — West Orange, New Jersey — (1903-1904), Detroit & New York — (1914, 1927) — The daily press was abuzz with rumors early in 1903 that Thomas Alva Edison was planning to become an automobile manufacturer. He was not. In a marvelous interview published in the August 15th, 1903 issue of The Automobile, Edison said he was building four large electric touring cars for three reasons: the pleasurable use of himself and his friends, to demonstrate the advantage of his nickel-iron battery, and to put into effect some notions he had about how an automobile should be built in the first place. Before embarking upon this venture, Thomas Edison bought a Pan-American gasoline car, for which he was

1914 Edison Electric, brougham, WLB

1913 Edwards-Knight, 5-pass. touring, WLB

widely criticized in electric circles. "I wanted to build an electric touring car for my own use and I wanted to get a chassis that would not give me any trouble," he explained to the reporter for *The Automobile*. "I had the Mors racer used by Fournier out here last year, and we ripped it all apart and had a good look at it. I thought the running-gear was the best I had seen, but I wasn't able to test it. The Pan-American chassis is a copy of the Mors, only they made the steering knuckles larger, which was a most excellent thing. We drove to Atlantic City purposely to test the running-gear of that car, and I believe there is not a better chassis made, for we really tried to smash it by driving at high speed over the roughest roads we found. We tore the gears up badly though — come out and I'll show you." One only wishes one could. The advantages of an electric car have perhaps never been better explained than in these words from Thomas Edison in 1903: "Electricity is the thing," he said. "There is no reciprocating motion about an electric car; all is rotary, beautifully perfect and wonderfully efficient, and best of all it is so very simple. There are no whirring and grinding gears with their numerous levers to confuse. There is not that almost terrifying uncertain throb and whirr of the powerful combustion engine. There is no water circulating system to get out of order - no dangerous and evil-smelling gasoline and no noise. Perfect freedom from vibration assures both comfort and peace of mind." Thomas Alva Edison built his touring cars, and then moved on to other things. On two subsequent occasions the Edison name was again attached to an experimental electric car: in 1914, a project in Detroit in association with Edison's good friend Henry Ford, and a miniature 200-pound roadster produced in New York City in 1927.

1900 Edmond, tricycle, NAHC

EDMOND — Matteawan, New York — (1899-1901) — The Edmond tricycle was recommended especially for use by physicians, but pictures indicate that no provision was made for the carrying of a doctor's bag. It was a cute little trike, however, powered by a 1½ hp Otto-type one-lunger engine, with electric ignition. The gasoline tank was good for a fifty-mile run, top speed was 25 mph, and E.J. Edmond insisted that his vehicle was capable of taking any hill that a bicycle could, which was a curious claim contingent on the comparative foot-power of a cyclist. The pedals were necessary only to start the machine, serving thereafter as footrests. But Edmond provided a fail-safe system: "In case of accident to the motor it can be disengaged by removing a small pin, and the rider can then propel the machine by foot power." The complete machine weighed but 135 pounds and its price was $350. Evidence suggests that the E.J. Edmond Cycle Manufacturing Company may have produced the trike well into 1901. A two-wheeled motorcycle was produced too.

EDWARDS — In 1912 the Edwards Motor Car Company succeeded the company begun in Louisville, Kentucky by the Longest brothers in 1906. Refer to Longest.

EDWARDS-KNIGHT — Long Island City, New York — (1912-1913) — H.J. Edwards had been the man responsible for the engineering of the cars which C.G. Stoddard's Dayton Motor Car Company marketed as Stoddard-Daytons. Among these was a Knight-engined model. When the Stoddard factory was bought by United States Motor Company, which Benjamin Briscoe was attempting to organize in emulation of Billy Durant's General Motors, Stoddard joined Briscoe's empire as a vice-president,

Edwards as chief engineer. But they got out a few months later when the getting was still good, in February 1912, before the collapse of Briscoe's New York City based conglomerate. Immediately the new partners formed the Edwards Motor Car Company with offices in downtown Manhattan and a plant across the East River in Long Island City. Meantime they secured what was referred to in the press as the "last American license" to build cars in the United States with the Knight sleeve-valve engine. The Edwards-Knight was a handsome car on a 120-inch wheelbase, featuring electric self-starter, four-speed transmission (with third direct, overdrive in fourth), Lanchester patent springs and a double-dropped frame. It was introduced in December 1912, and production began in the Long Island City plant that month. In July of 1913, Stoddard and Edwards contemplated a move of their company to Louisville, Kentucky. A move was made in October, but it was not to Louisville. Instead, late that month, John North Willys purchased the Edwards Motor Car Company outright, including Knight license, all patents, drawings and factory equipment, and the services of H.J. Edwards. Kit and koboodle were shipped to the former Garford plant in Elyria (Ohio) which was now one of the Willys-Overland factories. Although initially there were plans to rename the car the Garford-Knight, John North Willys ultimately decided against that. All subsequent cars were called Willys-Knights.

1912-1913 EDWARDS-KNIGHT
Model 25 — 4-cyl., 40/50 hp, 120" wb

	FP	5	4	3	2	1
Touring-4/5P	3500	2700	3600	5300	8800	19,000
Speedster-2P	3500	3500	4500	7000	13,000	25,000
Roadster-2P	3500	3000	4000	6000	9500	21,000
Limousine-7P	4600	2500	3500	5000	8500	18,000
Landaulet-7P	4700	2700	3600	5300	8800	19,000

EHRENTRAUT — One Carl P. Ehrentraut has been indicated on various automobile rosters as building cars to custom order in Pittsburgh, Pennsylvania during 1911. This cannot be documented. The only Ehrentraut listed in the Pittsburgh city directory for this period was P.B., and he noted his occupation as "massage."

EHRLICH ELECTRIC — Chicago, Illinois — (1918) — The Ehrlich Electric was an experimental car built in the shops of the components-producing Lammert & Mann Company at 217 North Wood Street in Chicago. The car had been designed by company engineer L.B. Ehrlich. Manufacture was never considered. By the early Twenties, Ehrlich was on the engineering staff of Gray & Davis, Inc.

E.H.V. — The initials were that of the Eisenhuth Horseless Vehicle Company, which produced cars in Middletown, Connecticut from 1904 to 1908. E.H.V. was simply a nickname. The car was marketed as the Compound. Refer to Compound.

1898 Eichstaedt, MCHS

EICHSTAEDT — Michigan City, Indiana — (1898-1902) — Roman Eichstaedt was a native of Germany, arriving in Michigan City just before the turn of the century, after sojourns in New Orleans, St. Louis and Chicago as a machinist and patternmaker. Initially he hired himself out to the Michigan Central Railway Company where he worked in the machine shops, but soon he left to establish his own factory. He completed his first automobile there in 1898, a single-cylinder two-seater gasoline car that reached a speed of 20 mph. Thereafter the principal focus of his shop was the manufacture of the "Roman" bicycle, though he apparently was willing to build an occasional automobile for Michigan City residents who had been impressed with his first effort. Both his factory and his home were the same address: 121 West Market. His entry in the 1902 Michigan City Directory indicates that Roman Eichstaedt believed diversification was the key to success. He is listed as dealing in "bicycles, automobiles, sewing machines, repair shop, guns, ammunition, etc."

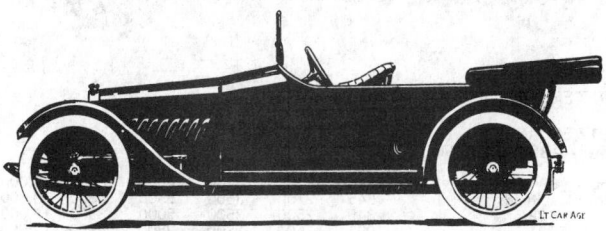

1915 E.I.M., touring, WLB

E.I.M. — **Richmond, Indiana** — **(1915)** — Just about the time every other cyclecar manufacturer in America had given up on the minimal-transport idea for the U.S. market, the Eastern Indiana Motor Car Company in Richmond decided to give it a try. The $450 E.I.M. used a four-cylinder 18 hp engine, which was considerably heftier than the powerplants of most cyclecars. Its 104-inch underslung chassis featured three-point suspension of the entire rear quarter, and the motor and transmission were mounted upon the frame rather than being cradled between the sills. As *Light Car Age* explained, "The lowest part of the chassis is, therefore, the plain side frame members, and as these are parallel to and in the very immediate proximity of the wheels there is no possibility for 'bedding' the car as is the case with most underslung designs." This seemed to make sense. Nonetheless, the E.I.M. did not survive the year.

1896 Einig Steam Carriage, NAHC

EINIG STEAM — **Jacksonville, Florida** — **(1896)** — In 1896 John Einig, a marine engineer from Jacksonville, built a steam carriage which used gasoline as fuel, consumption being about a quart-and-a-half per hour. "The sound of the escaping steam is said to be successfully muffled," reported *The Horseless Age*, "and the vapor itself rendered invisible, so that horses pay no attention to the carriage." That must have been over-statement, since Einig had difficulty obtaining a permit to operate the vehicle from the Jacksonville city fathers. Locally, it was known as the Chug Chug Wagon. The Einig became nationally known as well, through *The Horseless Age* article and a long descriptive account of it in *The Scientific American*, which drew a number of inquiries regarding possible purchase. Ultimately, Einig did sell the vehicle for $1000 to a *Scientific American* subscriber from England, this being one of the very early export sales of an American car. Subsequently, Einig built another vehicle which he sold to a party in New York but when problems were encountered with it, the vehicle was returned to Einig who revised it and then sold it to two local plumbers named Koons and Golder who converted it to a truck, the first one in operation in Jacksonville. Although Einig never built another car, he remained famous in Jacksonville long after his death in 1912 as the inventor of "Big Jim," the mammoth whistle atop the city's waterworks plant.

EISENHUTH — **Newark, New Jersey** — **(1896-1900)** — John W. Eisenhuth designed his first automobile in San Francisco in 1896 but it was built for him by a machine shop in Newark, New Jersey. His experimentation continued into the turn of the century, resulting in more Eisenhuth vehicles but whether they were developed on the East or West Coast is unclear. When he became a manufacturer in 1904, however, he was permanently settled in the Greater New York areas — or so he thought. His Eisenhuth Horseless Vehicle Company produced the Compound car from

1898 Eisenhuth Motor Carriage, NAHC

1904 to 1908 in Middletown, Connecticut. What occupied his time immediately after that is unknown, but 1913 found him back in San Francisco attempting to promote a new idea — "a noiseless engine." According to the *Oakland Tribune* that September, his plans included an automobile factory on 1000 acres of land near Palo Alto, with a model city for workers being built around it. How noiseless his engine was is anyone's guess, but in 1914 an unhappy investor in this project hollered long and loud that Eisenhuth had taken his money under false pretenses. He was arrested. And by 1915 he had left town. Interestingly, he had been arrested at least twice during his Compound days too. In 1917 Eisenhuth showed up in Los Angeles. His San Francisco venture of four years previous had gone unreported in the automotive press. But this time he wrote extensively to trade publications about his new automobile which would carry the name Poppy. The Poppy car died with him on May 14th, 1918. Eisenhuth was fifty-seven years old. His obituary in the *Berkeley Gazette* indicated that he was the holder of forty-eight patents.

ELEANOR — The Eleanor Automobile Company was organized in Washington, D.C. during the summer of 1904 with a capital stock of $300,000 for the manufacture of automobiles. Behind this venture were A. Von McCallister, B.A. Horst, Robert McElroy, L.T. Everett, M. Ochsenreiter, among others. Manufacture of an automobile is doubted.

ELBERON — The Elberon was the victoria model of the Columbia produced by the Electric Vehicle Company. Introduced in 1902, it proved to be one of the most popular of all Columbias and was frequently referred to simply as the Elberon in the trade press. It was a model, however, and not a specific make.

1915 Elbert, 2-pass. tandem roadster, WLB

ELBERT — **Seattle, Washington** — **(1914-1915), Sunnyvale, California** — **(1915)** — F.W. Topkin, formerly mechanical engineer for the Chicago Pneumatic Tube Company, was the designer of the Elbert. Doubtless a man named Elbert put up the money for this venture, but he appears to have been a silent partner. In late summer of 1914, the Elbert Motor Car Company was incorporated, and a factory was found at 2012 Fifteenth Avenue West in Seattle. Apparently this facility proved wanting, however, because the following March the company announced that it had completed negotiations for a "completely equipped" plant in Sunnyvale, California, thirty-eight miles south of San Francisco. Elbert moved there just a few months prior to its demise. As an example of a cyclecar, the Elbert was a particularly admirable one, with graceful big-car-like coachwork on a 102-inch wheelbase, shaft drive, a "gearless" differential and a four-cylinder water-cooled engine. Both underslung and overslung models were offered. At $295, the Elbert was also very low priced, even for a cyclecar.

The fortunes of the Elbert company had been guided by L.H. Beamish of Vancouver, N.F. Wilson of San Francisco and L.W. O'Connell of Chicago. Nicholas Wilson was the firm's president. As admirable as the Elbert cyclecar was, it does not appear that same nobility manifested itself in other aspects of this venture. The widely-touted Sunnyvale plant, for example, was the Goudy Machine Company, all six large buildings of which the Elbert company had purchased. Or that was what the Elbert people had said in Seattle anyway, and it was sufficient to lure a number of prospective employees to Sunnyvale. What they found there was something else. Nine Seattle families, who had also invested in the company, arrived to their chagrin to discover, in the words of the *San Francisco Bulletin*, that "the plant of the company consists of one wayside blacksmith shop" on the Goudy property. They swore out a complaint against Wilson. The Elbert venture was finished. Interestingly, among the company's grandiose plans had been publication of a monthly magazine called *Motor Car Thrift*. It might better have been called *Motor Car Fraud*.

1914-1915 ELBERT
Cyclecar — 4-cyl., 10 hp, 102" wb

	FP	5	4	3	2	1
Tandem Roadster-2P	295	1800	2800	4000	6200	13,000
Delivery Wagon	305	1500	2500	3600	5500	11,000

ELBRIDGE — The Elbridge Engine Company was organized in Rochester, New York during the fall of 1908 for the manufacture of engines and automobiles. Capital stock was $25,000. Backing this venture were L.J. Seeley of Rochester, G.E. De Long of Syracuse, and W.H. Salmon of Buffalo. Manufacture of an automobile is doubted. George De Long had been trying since 1902 to become an automobile manufacturer, incidentally. Refer to De Long.

1916 Elcar, model A, touring, HAC

ELCAR — Elkhart, Indiana — (1916-1931) — Shortly before Halloween in 1915, the Pratt brothers — William B. and George B. — who had changed their minds frequently before regarding the Pratt car they were building, changed their minds once again. Now, they decided, they would no longer build it, but a new car called the Elcar instead. Unlike the Pratt, which had been provided as a four and a six in the $2000 range, the Elcar was introduced as a four (Lycoming engine) only at $795. "The Car for the Many" would be a company slogan, and the Pratts reorganized the firm producing it to Elkhart Carriage & Motor Car Company. If the curious inclusion of "carriage" in the organization's title seemed a step backward at this late date, it was in fact, but the Pratts soon changed their minds about continuing in the horsedrawn vehicle building business anyway. In order to make way for the building of ambulance bodies for World War I, the brothers destroyed the equipment they had been using since before the turn of the century to build carriages — and even some partially finished carriages as well — and never built another. Meanwhile, a six (Continental engine) was added to the Elcar line for model year 1918. Two days before the Fourth of July in 1921, the Pratts had their last change of mind about their company. They sold out to a group of former Auburn executives — F.B. Sears, A.M. Graffis, G.W. Bundy, W.H. Denison — and retired shortly thereafter. Though the firm's name was subsequently changed to Elcar Motor Company, it was business as usual for the Elcar for the next few years, with the car being continued in a line of fours and sixes, though their prices edged upward increasingly. F.B. Sears would sit in the Elcar's presidential chair, and Mike Graffis would be chief engineer for the remainder of the marque's life. Beginning in late 1922, Elcar entered the taxicab field, after beating out Driggs for the contract to manufacture 1000 cabs for the Diamond Taxicab Company of New York City. Taxicab production continued to the end as well — with Elcar producing its own taxis (both fours and sixes) as well as variations (the Elfay, Martel, Royal Martel) for other taxi entrepreneurs. The biggest news from Elcar during the mid-Twenties was the introduction of a Lycoming-engined straight-eight for 1925, and the dropping of the Elcar four after 1926. Lockheed hydraulic brakes were introduced on the eight, which began as a 65 hp car offered in one series and which was expanded to several model lines of increasing horsepower thereafter, culminating in a top-of-the-line 140 hp eight which was among the most puissant engines in America of the period, outpowered only by the Duesenberg and Cadillac V-16. Late in 1926, Elcar president Sears was quoted as saying that "as long as the small producer of automobiles realizes his limitations and makes the most of his opportunities, he is assured a 'place in the sun'." But there wasn't one any longer for the Elcar after the stock market crash. Although receivership was temporarily averted in 1930, it arrived irrevocably in 1931. In final desperate attempts to save the company, the Elcar people collaborated with Alvah Powell, designer of the Lever engine, and with Harry Wahl who was attempting to revive the Mercer. Prototypes of both the Lever and the new Mercer were built on the Elcar chassis in the Elkhart factory. But then it was all over, though some of the Elcar people stayed on awhile producing taxicabs called El-Fay and Allied.

1916 ELCAR
Four — 35 hp, 114" wb

Touring-5P		795	2400	3400	4800	8000	17,000
Runabout-2P		795	2500	3500	5000	8500	18,000

1917 Elcar, model E, cloverleaf roadster, HAC

1917 ELCAR
Four — 35 hp, 115" wb

	FP	5	4	3	2	1
Touring-5P	845	2400	3400	4800	8000	17,000
Cloverleaf Roadster-4P	845	2700	3600	5300	8800	19,000
Roadster-2P	845	2500	3500	5000	8500	18,000
Sedan-5P	995	1600	2700	3800	5800	12,000

1918 Elcar, model E-Four, touring, HAC

1918 ELCAR
Model E-Four — 37.5 hp, 116" wb

Touring-5P	1095	2400	3400	4800	8000	17,000
Roadster-4P	1095	2500	3500	5000	8500	18,000
Sedan-5P	1625	1600	2700	3800	5800	12,000

Model D-Six — 40 hp, 116" wb

Touring-5P	1295	2500	3500	5000	8500	18,000
Sedan-5P	1795	1800	2800	4000	6200	13,000
Roadster-4P	1295	2700	3600	5300	8800	19,000

1919 Elcar, model D-Six, touring, HAC

1920 Elcar, model H-Four, sportster, HAC

1919 ELCAR
Model H-Four — 37.5 hp, 116" wb

	FP	5	4	3	2	1
Touring-4P	1175	2400	3400	4800	8000	17,000
Touring-5P	1175	2300	3300	4600	7500	16,000
Sedan-5P	1625	1600	2700	3800	5800	12,000

Model D-Six — 40 hp, 116" wb

	FP	5	4	3	2	1
Touring-5P	1375	2500	3500	5000	8500	18,000
Touring Roadster-4P	1375	2700	3600	5300	8800	19,000
Sedan-5P	1795	1800	2800	4000	6200	13,000
Sportster-4P	1375	2700	3600	5300	8800	19,000

1920 ELCAR
Four — 37.5 hp, 116" wb

Touring-5P	1395	2500	3500	5000	8500	18,000
Sportster-4P	1395	2900	3700	5600	9100	20,000
Sedan-5P	1595	1600	2700	3800	5800	12,000
Coupe-3P	1595	2000	3000	4200	6500	14,000

Six — 55 hp, 116" wb

Touring-5P	1595	2700	3600	5300	8800	19,000
Sportster-4P	1595	3000	4000	6000	9500	21,000
Sedan-5P	1295	1800	2800	4000	6200	13,000
Coupe-3P	2195	2200	3200	4400	7000	15,000

1921 Elcar, model G-4, sedan, HAC

1921 ELCAR
Four — 37.5 hp, 117" wb

Roadster-3P	1495	2900	3700	5600	9100	20,000
Touring-5P	1495	2500	3500	5000	8500	18,000
Sportster-4P	1495	3000	4000	6000	9500	21,000
Coupe-3P	2095	2000	3000	4200	6500	14,000
Sedan-5P	2195	1600	2700	3800	5800	20,000

Six — 55 hp, 117" wb

Touring-5P	1795	2700	3600	5300	8800	19,000
Roadster-3P	1795	3000	4000	6000	9500	21,000
Sportster-4P	1795	3100	4200	6300	10,500	22,000
Coupe-3P	2395	2200	3200	4400	7000	15,000

1922 Elcar, model 22-7-R, sedan, HAC

1923 Elcar, model 4-40H, speedway sport, HAC

1922 ELCAR
Model 22-K-4 — 37.5 hp, 118" wb

	FP	5	4	3	2	1
Touring-5P	1145	2900	3700	5600	9100	20,000
Sport-4P	1145	3100	4200	6300	10,500	22,000
Roadster-3P	1145	3200	4300	6500	11,000	23,000
Coupe-4P	1545	2300	3300	4600	7500	16,000
Sedan-5P	1645	1800	2800	4000	6200	13,000

Model 22-7-R — 55 hp, 118" wb

Touring-5P	1595	3000	4000	6000	9500	21,000
Sport-4P	1595	3200	4300	6500	11,000	23,000
Roadster-3P	1595	3300	4400	6700	12,000	24,000
Coupe-4P	2395	2400	3400	4800	8000	17,000
Sedan-5P	2495	2000	3000	4200	6500	14,000
Suburban-5P	2495	2000	3000	4200	6500	14,000

1923 Elcar, taxicab, NAHC

1923 ELCAR
Model 4-40 — 40 hp, 118" wb

Touring-5P	1095	2700	3600	5300	8800	19,000
Sport-4P	1095	2900	3700	5600	9100	20,000
Roadster-3P	1095	3000	4000	6000	9500	21,000

Model 6-60 — 55 hp, 118" wb

Touring-5P	1395	2900	3700	5600	9100	20,000
Sport-4P	1395	3100	4200	6300	10,500	22,000
Roadster-3P	1395	3200	4300	6500	11,000	23,000
Coupe-4P	2015	2400	3400	4800	8000	17,000
Brougham-5P	2065	2200	3200	4400	7000	15,000
Sedan-5P	2065	2000	3000	4200	6500	14,000

1924 Elcar, model 6-60, 3-dr. sedan, JAC

1924 ELCAR
Model 4-40 — 42 hp, 112" wb

Phaeton-5P	995	2900	3700	5600	9100	20,000
Demi-Sport-5P	1095	3000	4000	6000	9500	21,000
Speedway Sport	1195	3200	4300	6500	11,000	23,000
Standard Brougham-5P	1265	2200	3200	4400	7000	15,000
Sport Brougham	1395	2250	3300	4500	7300	15,500
Sedan-5P	1425	1800	2800	4000	6200	13,000
Sport Sedan	1125	1900	2900	4100	6400	13,500

Model 6-50 — 50 hp, 112" wb
Note: this smaller six carried basically the same body styles as the 4-40.

Model 6-60 — 55 hp, 118" wb

Phaeton-5P	1395	3000	4000	6000	9500	21,000
Sport-5P	1595	3200	4300	6500	11,000	23,000
Brougham-4P	1995	2300	3300	4600	7500	16,000
Brougham Sedan-5P	1995	2300	3300	4600	7500	16,000

1925 Elcar, model 8-80, sedan, HAC

499

1925 ELCAR
Model 4-40 — 4-cyl., 42 hp, 112" wb

	FP	5	4	3	2	1
Touring-5P	995	2900	3700	5600	9100	20,000
Demi Sport-5P	1095	3000	4000	6000	9500	21,000
Sport-5P	1195	3100	4200	6300	10,500	22,000
Brougham-5P	1265	2200	3200	4400	7000	15,000
Sport Brougham-5P	1395	2250	3300	4500	7300	15,500
Sedan-5P	1495	2000	3000	4200	6500	14,000
Sport Sedan-5P	1695	2100	3100	4300	6800	14,500

Model 6-50 — 6-cyl., 50 hp, 116" wb

Demi Sport-5P	1220	3100	4200	6300	10,500	22,000
Sport-5P	1420	3200	4300	6500	11,000	23,000
Brougham-5P	1490	2300	3300	4600	7500	16,000
Sport Brougham-5P	1620	2350	3400	4700	7800	16,500
Standard Sedan-5P	1720	2200	3200	4400	7000	15,000
Sport Sedan-5P	1920	2250	3300	4500	7300	15,500

Note: A model 6-60 (55 hp, 118" wb) was offered as well, both it and the 6-50 being replaced in July by the new 6-65.

Model 8-80 — 8-cyl., 65 hp, 127" wb

Touring-5P	2165	3200	4300	6500	11,000	23,000
Touring-7P	2265	3100	4200	6300	10,500	22,000
Roadster-3P	2765	3500	4500	7000	13,000	25,000
Brougham-5P	2865	2400	3400	4800	8000	17,000

1926 Elcar, model 8-81, roadster, HAC

1926 ELCAR
Model 4-55 — 4-cyl., 46 hp, 116" wb

Phaeton-5P	1095	3100	4200	6300	10,500	22,000
Coach-5P	1195	2000	3000	4200	6500	14,000
Sedan-5P	1395	2200	3200	4400	7000	15,000

Model 6-65 — 6-cyl., 55 hp, 116" wb

Phaeton-5P	1295	3200	4300	6500	11,000	23,000
Coach-5P	1395	2100	3100	4300	6800	14,500
Sedan-5P	1595	2250	3300	4500	7300	15,500

Model 8-81 — 8-cyl., 82 hp, 132" wb

Phaeton-5P	2165	3500	4500	7000	13,000	25,000
Phaeton-7P	2265	3300	4400	6700	12,000	24,000
Roadster-4P	2315	3700	4700	7300	13,700	26,000
Coupe-3P	2315	2500	3500	5000	8500	18,000
Sedan-5P	2265	2300	3300	4600	7500	16,000
Sedan-7P	2765	2250	3300	4500	7300	15,500
Brougham-5P	2865	2350	3400	4700	7800	16,500

1927 Elcar, model 8-90, sedan, HAC

1927 ELCAR
Model 6-70 — 6-cyl., 60 hp, 117" wb

Brougham-5P	1295	2300	3300	4600	7500	16,000
Sedan-5P	1395	2200	3200	4400	7000	15,000
Landaulet Roadster-4P	1475	3900	4800	7700	14,300	27,000

Model 8-82 — 8-cyl., 62 hp, 123" wb

Brougham-5P	1595	2400	3400	4800	8000	17,000
Sedan-5P	1790	2250	3300	4500	7300	15,500
Landaulet Roadster-4P	1870	4000	5000	8000	15,000	28,000

Model 8-90 — 8-cyl., 82 hp, 132" wb

Brougham-5P	2195	2450	3500	4900	8300	17,500
Landaulet Roadster-4P	2295	4200	5200	8400	15,700	29,000
Sedan-5P	2465	2300	3300	4600	7500	16,000
Sedan-7P (134" wb)	2765	2350	3400	4700	7800	16,500

1928 ELCAR
Model 6-70 — 6-cyl., 60 hp, 117" wb

Brougham-5P	1295	2300	3300	4600	7500	16,000
Sedan-5P	1295	2200	3200	4400	7000	15,000

Model 8-78 — 8-cyl., 62 hp, 123" wb

Standard Roadster-4P	1395	3900	4800	7700	14,300	27,000
Royal Roadster-4P	1495	4000	5000	8000	15,000	28,000
Standard Sedan-5P	1395	2250	3300	4500	7300	15,500
Standard Coupe-4P	1395	2450	3500	4900	8300	17,500
Royal Sedan-5P	1495	2300	3300	4600	7500	16,000
Royal Coupe-4P	1495	2500	3500	5000	8500	18,000

1928 Elcar, model 8-78, sedan, HAC

Model 8-82 — 8-cyl., 70 hp, 123" wb

	FP	5	4	3	2	1
Roadster-4P	1695	4200	5200	8400	15,700	29,000
Coupe-4P	1695	2600	3600	5200	8700	18,500
Sedan-5P	1695	2350	3400	4700	7800	16,500
Princess Sedan-5P	1895	2400	3400	4800	8000	17,000

Model 8-91 — 8-cyl., 84 hp, 127" wb

Roadster-4P	1995	4300	5300	8600	16,100	29,500
Prince Sedan-5P	2295	2450	3500	4900	8300	17,500
Prince Brougham-5P	2295	2500	3500	5000	8500	18,000
Coupe-4P	2295	2700	3600	5300	8800	19,000
Sedan-5P	2465	2500	3500	5000	8500	18,000
Sedan-7P	2565	2600	3600	5200	8700	18,500

Note: also offered were models 8-92 and 8-120 with the same 84 hp engine but on longer 132" wb chassis.

1929 Elcar, model 95, coupe, HAC

1929 ELCAR
Model 75 — 6-cyl., 61 hp, 117" wb

Roadster-2P	995	3900	4800	7700	14,300	27,000
Touring-5P	1075	3700	4700	7300	13,700	26,000
Roadster-4P	1145	4000	5000	8000	15,000	28,000
Club Sedan-5P	1095	2200	3200	4400	7000	15,000
Convertible Coupe-4P	1165	3300	4400	6700	12,000	24,000
Coupe-4P	1165	2500	3500	5000	8500	18,000
Sedan-5P	1195	2300	3300	4600	7500	16,000

Model 95 — 8-cyl., 90 hp, 123" wb

Roadster-2P	1295	4000	5000	8000	15,000	28,000
Roadster-4P	1435	4200	5200	8400	15,700	29,000
Touring-5P	1495	3900	4800	7700	14,300	27,000
Club Sedan-5P	1395	2300	3300	4600	7500	16,000
Convertible Sedan-4P	1465	3500	4500	7000	13,000	25,000
Coupe-4P	1465	2700	3600	5300	8800	19,000
Sedan-5P	1495	2400	3400	4800	8000	17,000

Model 96 — 8-cyl., 90 hp, 123" wb

Roadster-4P	1635	4200	5200	8400	15,700	29,000
Convertible Coupe-4P	2295	3500	4500	7000	13,000	25,000
Coupe-4P	2295	2800	3700	5500	9000	19,500
Sedan-5P	1695	2450	3500	4900	8300	17,500
Sedan-5P	1895	2500	3500	5000	8500	18,000

Model 120 — 8-cyl., 115 hp, 134" wb

Roadster-4P	2265	4300	5400	8700	16,500	30,000
Touring-5P	2465	4000	5000	8000	15,000	28,000
Convertible Coupe-4P	2295	3700	4700	7300	13,700	26,000
Coupe-4P	2295	2900	3700	5600	910	20,000
Sedan-5P	2295	2500	3500	5000	8500	18,000
Sedan-5P	2465	2600	3600	5200	8700	18,500
Sedan-7P	2645	2700	3600	5300	8800	19,000

1930 Elcar, model 140, convertible sedan, KM

1930 Elcar, 4-dr. sedan, JB

1930 ELCAR
Model 75A — 6-cyl., 61 hp, 117" wb

	FP	5	4	3	2	1
Sedan-5P	1195	2200	3200	4400	7000	15,000
Club Sedan-5P	1095	2300	3300	4600	7500	16,000
Touring-5/7P	1075	3700	4700	7300	13,700	26,000
Convertible Coupe-4P	1165	3500	4500	7000	13,000	25,000
Coupe-4P	1165	2500	3500	5000	8500	18,000
Roadster-4P	1145	4000	5000	8000	15,000	28,000
Roadster-2P	995	3900	4800	7700	14,300	27,000

Model 95 — 8-cyl., 90 hp, 123" wb
Sedan-5/7P	—	2250	3300	4500	7300	15,500
Club Sedan	—	2350	3400	4700	7800	16,500
Convertible Landau	—	3700	4700	7300	13,700	26,000
Coupe-4P	—	2600	3600	5200	8700	18,500
Touring-5/7P	—	3900	4800	7700	14,300	27,000
Roadster-2P	—	4000	4900	7900	14,800	27,500
Roadster-4P	—	4100	5100	8200	15,400	28,500

Model 96 — 8-cyl., 90 hp, 123" wb
Fleetwing Sedan-5/7P	1695	2300	3300	4600	7500	16,000
Princess Sedan-5P	1895	2400	3400	4800	8000	17,000
Coupe-4P	1665	2700	3600	5300	8800	19,000
Roadster-4P	1635	4200	5200	8400	15,700	29,000
Convertible Coupe-4P	1665	3700	4700	7300	13,700	26,000

Model 130 — 8-cyl., 140 hp, 130" wb
Coupe-4P	—	2900	3700	5600	9100	20,000
Sedan-5/7P	—	2300	3300	4600	7500	16,000
Business Coupe	—	2800	3700	5500	9000	19,500
Club Sedan	—	2350	3400	4700	7800	16,500
Convertible Landau	—	3700	4700	7300	13,700	26,000
Touring-5/7P	—	3900	4800	7700	14,300	27,000
Roadster-4P	—	4300	5400	8700	16,500	30,000

Note: Also offered was a model 120 with 8-cyl. 115 hp engine on a 134" wb chassis. Produced this year as well as the experimental lever-engined car, and three model 140 cars (two sedans and one convertible sedan) on 135" wb chassis which are believed to have formed the basis for the 1931 Mercer.

1931 ELCAR
Model 86 — 6-cyl., 61 hp, 117" wb
Roadster-2P	995	3900	4800	7700	14,300	27,000
Roadster-4P	1245	4000	5000	8000	15,000	28,000
Coupe-2P	1245	2500	3500	5000	8500	18,000
Coupe-4P	1265	2700	3600	5300	8800	19,000
Club Sedan	1295	2300	3300	4600	7500	16,000
Convertible Landaulet	1265	3500	4500	7000	13,000	25,000
Sedan	1295	2200	3200	4400	7000	15,000

Model 100 — 8-cyl., 90 hp, 123" wb
Roadster-4P	1635	4100	5100	8200	15,400	28,500
Coupe-2P	1645	2600	3600	5200	8700	18,500
Coupe-4P	1665	2800	3700	5500	9000	19,500
Convertible Landaulet	1665	3700	4700	7300	13,700	26,000
Club Sedan	1695	2350	3400	4700	7800	16,500
Fleet Sedan	1695	2300	3300	4600	7500	16,000
Princess Sedan	1695	2300	3300	4600	7500	16,000

Model 130 — 8-cyl., 140 hp, 130" wb
Roadster-4P	1995	4200	5200	8400	15,700	29,000
Coupe-2P	1945	2700	3600	5300	8800	19,000
Coupe-4P	1995	2800	3700	5500	9000	19,500
Convertible Landaulet	1995	3900	4800	7700	14,300	27,000
Club Sedan	1995	2400	3400	4800	8000	17,000
Sedan-5P	1995	2350	3400	4700	7800	16,500
Sedan-7P	2120	2400	3400	4800	8000	17,000

1916 Elco, model 30, roadster, OCW

ELCO — Sidney, Ohio — (1915-1917) — Originally the Elco four was to have been built in Elwood (Indiana) by the Elwood Iron Works which also planned production of a V-8 to be known as the Bailey-Klapp. Elwood Iron Works went bankrupt before getting to market, however, and consequently the rights to the Elco were assumed by the Bimel people of Sidney, Ohio in August of 1915. The Bimel Buggy Company had a checkered history. Established in Sidney in 1844, the firm moved subsequently to St. Mary's, but was later moved back to Sidney by William Bimel, son of the original founder. In Sidney the business failed in 1904, and Bimel was out, though his name remained. The factory was revised for manufacture of auto parts as the Bimel Spoke and Auto Wheel Works, with A.C. Noble as president and T.M. Miller as manager and treasurer. It was these two gentlemen who decided on automobile manufacture when the Elco became available. The Elco was an absolutely ordinary four-cylinder 30 hp gasoline car, though with a very attractive $585 price tag. A six to carry the Bimel name was projected and advertised though it does not seem to have been produced. In April 1916 the Bimel Automobile Company was incorporated with a capital stock of $500,000. It survived a year. In May 1917 the firm's stock, machinery and parts were purchased for $15,715 by the American Motor Parts Company of Indianapolis. A few finished cars remained on hand, and these were sold individually. Apparently some of the four-cylinder Elcos produced by Bimel were also sold under the Bimel name, but this seems to have been simply a case of badge engineering.

1915-1917 ELCO
Model 30 — 4-cyl., 30 hp, 102" wb

	FP	5	4	3	2	1
Roadster-2P	585	2500	3500	5000	8500	18,000
Touring-5P	585	2400	3400	4800	8000	17,000

ELDREDGE — The Eldredge Company was organized in Camden, New Jersey during the summer of 1912 for the manufacture of motor vehicles. Capital stock was $75,000. Behind this venture were W.E. Eldredge, C.P. Sharpless and H.L. Adams. Manufacture of an automobile is doubted.

1904 Eldredge, runabout, NAHC

ELDREDGE — Belvidere, Illinois — (1903-1906) — The National Sewing Machine Company, seeing similarity in principles of operation, saw no reason why it should not produce bicycles and automobiles alongside its main product and consequently embarked upon same. Bicycles were first, in 1894, and they were named Belvidere after the town in which the sewing machines were built. Automobiles followed in 1903, and they were named after the company president, B. Eldredge. The two-wheelers had presented no significant production problems, but already the company recognized the large difference between sewing machines and automobiles. In 1901 National Sewing Machine had contracted with Oscar Friedman in Chicago to build his automobile for him, and Friedman had sued in early 1903 charging that the goods had not been delivered. Undaunted, National Sewing Machine launched into manufacture of its own car later that year. A light two-cylinder two-seater that was occasionally referred to as the National Road Car, the first Eldredges had tiller steering on the left side, followed by left-hand wheel steering in 1905, which the Eclipse from Wisconsin also featured that year. The Eldredge's sliding-gear transmission was rather avant-garde for the period too. Conceivably, given the company's name and principal product, "Just What It Ought to Be" as a slogan for the Eldredge confused more than it enticed. Automobile manufacture was discontinued in 1906 after the production of approximately 300 Eldredges.

1903 ELDREDGE
Two-Cylinder — 8 hp, 68" wb
Runabout-2P	1000	1800	2800	4000	6200	13,000

1904-1905 ELDREDGE
Two-Cylinder — 8 hp, 68" wb
Runabout-2P	750	1800	2800	4000	6200	13,000

1906 ELDREDGE
Two-Cylinder — 10 hp, 68" wb
Runabout-2P	750	2000	3000	4200	6500	14,000

ELECTA — The Electa was a model of the Duryea built from 1910 to 1913 in Reading, Pennsylvania and Saginaw, Michigan. Refer to Duryea.

ELECTRA — Chicago, Illinois — (1913) — For a single short season the Storage Battery Power Company of Chicago produced a whole car around the batteries and other components which the firm had been supplying for some time to various manufacturers in the electric vehicle industry. The car was called the Electra and it was offered only as a roadster on an 85-inch wheelbase chassis at $750. In 1914 the Storage Battery Power Company elected to return to the supplying of components.

1914 Electra, model C, 2-pass. roadster, CATJ

ELECTRA — Los Angeles, California — **(1913-1915)** — How far one could travel in this Electra depended upon how much one was willing to spend. The $750 Model C provided 40 miles between charges; the $1250 Model D was good for 75. Both cars were two-passenger roadsters of similar body style, the C on a 90-inch wheelbase *sans* doors, the D a fore-door on a 96-inch wheelbase. William Piddington was president of the Electra Manufacturing Company, Inc. which was located at 1333 South Main Street in Los Angeles. After a small production run of the roadsters, and a change of management, the company focused production on storage batteries only.

1913-1915 ELECTRA
Model C — 90" wb

	FP	5	4	3	2	1
Roadster-2P	750	1900	2900	4100	6400	13,500
Model D — 96" wb						
Roadster-2P	1250	2000	3000	4200	6500	14,000

ELECTRETTE — The Electrette was a model of the Lansden Electric produced in Newark, New Jersey from 1906 to 1908. Refer to Lansden Electric.

ELECTRIC — The Electric Carriage Works of Los Angeles, California produced a car called the Hafer from 1903-1904. Refer to Hafer.

The Electric Maintenance Company was organized in Chicago, Illinois during the summer of 1913 with a capital stock of $50,000 for the manufacture of automobiles and supplies. W.P. Christie, C.E. Winters and W.A. Baehr were behind this venture. Manufacture of a car is doubted.

The Electric Motocycle was the designation occasionally given to the pioneer car built by William Morrison of Des Moines, Iowa and entered by Harold Sturges in the Chicago Times-Herald Contest of 1895. Refer to Morrison Electric.

The Electric Road Carriage Company of Boston, Massachusetts produced two electrics designed by Dr. Orazio Lugo in 1891. Refer to Lugo.

The Electric Service Company was organized in New York City during the summer of 1909 for the manufacture of automobiles and accessories. Incorporators were W.L. Ernst, M.E. Harby and A.A. Ernst. Manufacture of a car is doubted.

The Electric Storage Battery Company at 19th and Allegheny Avenue in Philadelphia, Pennsylvania was listed as an automobile manufacturer in the Hiscox book *Horseless Vehicles, Automobiles, Motor Cycles* published in 1900. If an automobile was built, it was for experimental purposes only. The firm was the manufacturer of exide and chloride batteries in Cleveland into the mid-1930's.

The Electric Undertakings Company at 52 Broadway in New York City was indicated in the Hiscox book *Horseless Vehicles, Automobiles, Motor Cycles* published in 1900 as the manufacturer of an automobile. City directory references of the period indicate no such company in town.

The Electric Vehicle Company was organized in Minneapolis, Minnesota early in 1910 with a capital stock of $20,000 to "manufacture, repair, purchase, sell and deal in motor cars and parts." Behind this venture were W.S. Hathaway, B.E. Stimson and E.B. Stimson. Manufacture of an automobile is doubted.

The Electric Vehicle Company was organized in Louisville, Kentucky late in 1910 for manufacture of a car to be called the Louisville Electric. Refer to Louisville.

The Electric Vehicle Service Company was organized in Chicago during the spring of 1913 with a capital stock of $20,000 to "manufacture, repair and rent motor cars." Incorporators were George C. Tripp, Francis E. Ingalls and H.J. Murphy. Manufacture of a car is doubted.

ELECTRIC CARRIAGE — New York, New York — **(1896-1897)** — The Electric Carriage & Wagon Company was organized in New York City in 1896. The firm planned initially to build open or covered carriages, delivery wagons, omnibuses and coaches, but the decision was almost immediately made to concentrate on electric hansoms and coupes which would be offered in just two cities: New York and Philadelphia. The company directors reason for thus confining its market was explained in *The Horseless Age:* "An indiscriminate putting forth of such vehicles they regard as unwise, because it would be impossible for them to send a skilled engineer out with every carriage they sold, and the average layman knows nothing about the electric business." The partners behind the Electric Carriage & Wagon Company were Henry G. Morris and Pedro G. Salom, who also produced electrics under their own names. The Electric Vehicle Company took over Electric Carriage & Wagon during the fall of 1897.

1896 Electric Carriage & Wagon Co., auto-buggy, NAHC

ELECTRIC VEHICLE — New York, New York — **(1897-1899)** — The Electric Vehicle Company was founded by Isaac L. Rice for the purpose of manufacturing hansom cabs. Rice was also the founder of the Electric Storage Battery Company and the Electric Boat Company, and he was the inventer of the Rice gambit in chess. There is no indication that he gave a name to the electric vehicles he built, though there were several dozen of them on the streets of Manhattan by the time the blizzard of '99 hit. One February evening in the midst of the storm, from the window of his Fifth Avenue mansion, financier William Collins Whitney happened to notice that the only vehicles able to negotiate the snowbound street were electric hansoms. Before the snows melted, he found out who was responsible for them, bought the Electric Vehicle Company, and Isaac Rice's cars were given a name: Columbia.

1897-1899 ELECTRIC VEHICLE

	FP	5	4	3	2	1
Electric Vehicle	—	2000	3900	8000	17,000	21,000

ELECTRICAL — Los Angeles, California — **(1906)** — The Electrical Construction Company of 1126 South Main Street in Los Angeles advertised itself as the manufacturer of an automobile in 1906 only. Leslie R. Saunders was president, Morris K. Benagh vice-president and Edmund Locke secretary of the firm. How many cars were built is not known, though the firm did serve as a dealership for the Baker Electric that year. By 1907 the company was advertising itself only as an electrical supply house and contractor with retail sales of automobiles as a sideline.

1914-15 Electriquette, JHV

ELECTRIQUETTE — Los Angeles, California — **(1914-1915)** — Clyde H. Osborn was a lawyer from San Diego who had invested in and was secretary of the dealership in that city which handled the Fritchle electric. When plans began being made for the 1915 San Diego Exposition, Osborn recognized a fine opportunity for a potentially profitable little business. He organized himself as the Electriquette Manufacturing Company of Los Angeles with headquarters at 1234 South Main Street, and commenced to have built 200 Electriquettes for comfortable sightseeing use by Exposition visitors. A small two-passenger vehicle distinguished by its all-wicker body, the Electriquette was good for eight hours between charges and rented at a pricey one dollar per hour. Whether this venture proved a handsomely profitable one for Osborn is not known, but he did not continue in manufacture following the Exposition. Apparently he sold off the Exposition cars for $325 each.

ELECTRO — The Electro Lighting Company of Indianapolis, Indiana was organized early in 1911 with a capital stock of $100,000 for the manufacture of electric automobiles in Indianapolis, Indiana. S.C. Renick, Charles C. Wedding and Joseph E. Bell were the president, vice-president and secretary-treasurer of the company respectively. Manufacture of a car is doubted.

ELECTROBAT — Electrobat was the name given to many of the electric cars built between 1894 and 1897 by Henry G. Morris and Pedro G. Salom of Philadelphia, Pennsylvania. Refer to Morris & Salom.

ELECTROBILE — Electrobile was the designation occasionally given to the electric cars more usually referred to as National Electric, which were built in Indianapolis, Indiana from 1901 to 1906. Refer to National Electric.

1922 Electrocar, taxicab, WLB

ELECTROCAR — **New Brunswick, New Jersey** — **(1922)** — The Electrocar was a taxicab designed by Joseph Anglada whose previous credits included a cyclecar named Liberty. Because electric cars by the early Twenties had lost their appeal in the marketplace, Anglada did his utmost to make this one resemble a gasoline car. Externally it did certainly, with a proper hood and an oval radiator grille. Inside Anglada did his best too, with two driver's pedals which were described as having the "appearance of the clutch and brake pedals on a gasoline car." The brake pedal indeed was that, the other pedal was the controller, which raised the car's speed as it was depressed further. The Electrocar's motor was by General Electric and was up front under the hood; the battery was from Exide, with the battery tray fitted with a jack arrangement and operated by a crank from outside the car. The wheelbase was 112 inches, and the price $2975. Following two years of experimentation the Electrocar Corporation of New Brunswick announced its new taxi from its chic New York City offices at 501 Fifth Avenue in late March 1922. The Electrocar was introduced on the exhibition floor of the New York Edison Company at Irving Place and 15th Street during the Annual Electric Automobile Show that April. Despite what seemed to be an altogether fine vehicle, it does not appear the Electrocar survived 1922.

ELECTROMOBILE — Although occasionally called Electromobile, the electric car built from 1899-1901 in Portland, Maine was more often designated by the name of the man who had designed it. Refer to Chapman Electric.
The Electromobile Company was organized with a capital stock of $100,000 in Wilmington, Delaware during the spring of 1913 for the manufacture of an electric automobile. Incorporators were H.E. Latter, W.J. Maloney and O.J. Reichard. Manufacture of a car is doubted.

ELECTROMOBILE — **Detroit, Michigan** — **(1906-1907)** — The American Electromobile Company of Detroit announced early in 1906 its forthcoming production of a two-passenger roadster and a truck. Initial experimentation was in a small machine shop in Detroit, though operations were transferred to the Massnick Manufacturing Company toward year's end. Frank Rae and Charles W. Beaumont were the men behind the Electromobile, and in February 1907 they announced that a new factory for manufacture would be constructed at 1567 River Street. The factory was completed, but they never moved in. Instead the partners quarreled, and Beaumont sued Rae early in 1908 charging conspiracy to reorganize the company with the object of freezing him out. Only one Electromobile had been thus far built, and it also appears to have been the last.

ELECTRONOMIC — Electronomic Steamer was one of three names used by Ralph Otho Hood for the steam cars he produced in Danvers, Massachusetts from 1899 to 1901. Refer to Hood Steamer.

EL-FAY — **Elkhart, Indiana** — **(1931-1935)** — The El-Fay was a taxi produced by the Elcar Motor Company for a taxi entrepreneur named Larry Fay, the name of the vehicle indicating the collaboration this venture was. Details regarding the car itself are difficult to determine since Elcar was building taxis under its own and other names as well. It is believed, however, that the El-Fay used Elcar 70, 75 75A and 86 chassis. Production continued until early 1935.

ELGIN — The Elgin Automobile Company of Chicago, Illinois produced an automobile from 1899-1901 that was marketed under the tradename of Winner. Refer to Winner.
The Elgin Motor Company was organized in Elgin, Illinois late in 1912 with a capital stock of $20,000 for the manufacture of automobiles. Incorporators were Edward J. O'Beirne, E.J. Adamek and Charles D. Adamek. Manufacture of a car is doubted.

1917 Elgin Six, roadster, HAC

ELGIN — **Argo, Illinois** — **(1916-1923), Indianapolis, Indiana** — **(1923-1924)** — "The Car of the Hour" and "Built like a Watch" were scarcely subtle reminders that several executives of the famed Illinois company producing clocks and timepieces had decided to enter the automotive arena. They did this by taking over the defunct New Era Motor Car Company of Joliet and moving it part and parcel to Argo. The Elgin was a conventional car that performed exceedingly well in Midwest endurance contests which demonstrated that "Illinois roads are not roads." The most interesting model was a six arriving in 1922 which featured the Cutler-Hammer pre-selective gearbox, double transverse rear suspension, and a built-in trunk. Apparently the Elgin Motor Car Corporation was an immensely popular proposition for small investors. Attendance at annual stockholders meetings was so large they had to be held in a tent. A stock dividend of ten percent had been paid in July 1916 and a cash dividend of five percent in July 1920. Nineteen-twenty was Elgin's best year ever — with sales totalling over $7 million. Then Elgin hit the postwar recession hard, and sold a bond issue of $500,000 to pay bank loans and "provide additional working capital." In June of 1923 Elgin stockholders formed a new corporation — Elgin Motors, Inc. — with J.H. McDuffee, formerly an officer with the Willys-Overland and Cole companies, as president and general manager. Indianapolis was selected as the new home of the Elgin car, and the buildings of the old Federal Motor Works in that city were purchased. Manufacture began in Indianapolis, but in late June of 1924 the new Elgin company was placed in receivership, following a suit brought by plant manager M.S. Black on a salary claim.

1916 ELGIN
Six - 21 hp, 114" wb

	FP	5	4	3	2	1
Tour.	845	2500	3500	5000	8500	18,000
Rds.	845	2700	3600	5300	8800	19,000

1917 ELGIN
Six - 21 hp, 116" wb

Tour.-6P	985	2500	3500	5000	8500	18,000
Rds.-4P	985	2700	3600	5300	8800	19,000

1918 Elgin Six, series F, touring, HAC

1918 ELGIN
Series F - 6-cyl., 21.6 hp, 117" wb

Tour.-5P	1095	2500	3500	5000	8500	18,000
Rds.-4P	1095	2700	3600	5300	8800	19,000
Sed.-5P	1645	1600	2700	3800	5800	12,000

1919 ELGIN
Series H - 6-cyl., 23.44 hp, 118" wb

Tour.-5P	1395	2500	3500	5000	8500	18,000
Military Scout-4P	1495	2200	3200	4400	7000	15,000
Conv. Sed.	1950	2800	3700	5500	9000	19,500

1919 Elgin Six, series H, touring, HAC

1920-21 Elgin Six, series K, touring, HAC

1920 ELGIN
Series K — 6-cyl., 37 hp, 118" wb

	FP	5	4	3	2	1
Tour.-5P	1485	2600	3600	5200	8700	18,500
Vict. Scout-4P	1585	2200	3200	4400	7000	15,000
Sed.-5P	2450	1600	2700	3800	5800	12,000

1921 ELGIN
Series K - 6-cyl., 37 hp, 118" wb

		5	4	3	2	1
Tour.-5P	1775	2600	3600	5200	8700	18,500
Vict. Scout-4P	1895	2200	3200	4400	7000	15,000
Cpe.-4P	2685	2000	3000	4200	6500	14,000
Sed.-5P	2685	1600	2700	3800	5800	12,000

1922 Elgin, Series K-1, touring, WLB

1922 ELGIN
Series K-1 - 6-cyl., 27 hp, 118" wb

Scout-4P	1595	2200	3200	4400	7000	15,000
Rds.-2P	1595	2700	3600	5300	8800	19,000
Cpe.-4P	2395	2300	3300	4600	7500	16,000
Sed.-5P	2395	2000	3000	4200	6500	14,000
Tour.-5P	1495	2500	3500	5000	8500	18,000

1923 Elgin Six, touring, NAHC

1923 ELGIN
Six - 6-cyl., 37 hp, 118" wb

	FP	5	4	3	2	1
Tour.-5P		2500	3500	5000	8500	18,000
Scout-4P	1125	2200	3200	4400	7000	15,000
Rds.-2P	1125	2700	3600	5300	8800	19,000
Sed.-5P	1695	1600	2700	3800	5800	12,000
Cpe.-4P	1695	2000	3000	4200	6500	14,000

1924 Elgin Six, coupe, JAC

1924 ELGIN
Six - 6-cyl., 46 hp, 118" wb

Sportsman-4P	1895	2500	3500	5000	8500	18,000
Coupe-3P	2145	2100	3100	4300	6800	14,500
Sed.-5P	2345	1800	2800	4000	6200	13,000

ELGIN ELECTRIC — Elgin, Illinois — (1899) — The first automobile built in this Wright Avenue factory was a $1200 electric produced by the Elgin Sewing Machine and Bicycle Company for American Electric Vehicle in Chicago. Called the "acme of perfection," it was guaranteed to do 75 miles at an average speed of 8 mph on a single charge. Five of these cars were built (two of them sold to Montgomery Ward) before Elgin Sewing Machine and Bicycle went out of business during the fall of 1899. Another group moved in immediately to build a gasoline car called the Winner. Prior to burning to the ground in 1904, this same factory saw two further attempts at manufacture by other automotive hopefuls.

ELGIN LIGHT CAR — Fenton, Michigan - (1914) — The Elgin Light Car was the second automobile designed in Fenton by Oscar J. Howick. It had two more cylinders and accommodations for one more passenger than his first, the Fenton cyclecar. The wheelbase was the same 96 inches. Howick's new car was powered by a water-cooled ohv 24 hp four-cylinder engine built in unit with a three-speed transmission. The frame was pressed steel, as was the streamlined body which seated two in front, one in the rear. The price tag was $455. The Elgin Light Car Company was organized in Fenton for its manufacture, but whether this car ever saw an assembly line is open to question. The company was said to be "seeking a factory location." Later in 1914 the press reported that Elgin had been taken over by a Detroit concern and would be manufactured there in 1915. It never was.

ELIJAH WARE — In about 1861 in Bayonne, New Jersey, one Elijah Ware built the first of at least several steam cars, one of which may have been America's first exported car. Refer to Ware.

ELITE — The Elite was a model of the Johnson produced from 1908 through 1910. The Johnson Service Company of Milwaukee, Wisconsin manufactured automobiles from 1905 through 1912. Refer to Johnson.

1901 Elite Steam, runabout, GR

ELITE STEAM — Utica, New York — (1901-1902) — D.B. Smith & Company of Utica produced a typical light steam runabout that was designed "only for the finest trade." The Elite gilded the lily with a vengeance. Its body was a mass of conjoining and contrasting and confusing curves, and there was brass all over, including an ornament atop the dash which looked very much like a tiara. "It must be seen to be appreciated," the company said. Presumably, this same ornate coachwork was also provided a 12 hp gasoline car the firm also offered under the name of Saratoga Tourist. Neither car was produced for long.

1907 Elite Junior, runabout, NAHC

ELITE JUNIOR — Newark, New Jersey — (1907) — The Elite Junior was a miniature automobile intended for children, as the company said, "ranging in age from four to eight years, and whose weight does not exceed sixty pounds." Its powerplant was a coil spring good for a one-eighth-mile running per windup. Two foot pedals were provided, one for acceleration, the other for braking — and the vehicle was "intended for level sidewalks or asphalt roads" only. The Elite Junior was produced by the Hughson & Burchett Motor Company of Newark, and it was an absolutely delectable little car. Why it was produced for just one season is unknown. Conceivably its price — which was never alluded to — was the reason.

ELIZABETH — The Elizabeth Taxicab Company was organized during the fall of 1909 in Elizabeth, New Jersey with a capital stock of $100,000 for the purpose of manufacturing automobiles. Incorporators were W.H. Cole and F.V. Price, Jr. Manufacture is doubted.

ELKHART — On sporadic occasions during its dozen years in the automobile field, the Crow-Elkhart Company of Elkhart, Indiana referred to various of its models as the Elk-hart. Crow-Elkhart remained the dominant name of the car from 1911-1923, however. Refer to Crow-Elkhart.

In 1909 the Elkhart Carriage & Harness Manufacturing Company of Elkhart, Indiana entered the automobile field. The cars it produced through 1915 were marketed under the name of Pratt-Elkhart, later Pratt. Refer to Pratt-Elkhart.

The Elkhart Motor Car Company of Elkhart, Indiana produced cars from 1909 through 1911 under the tradenames of Sterling and Komet. Refer to Sterling and Komet.

ELLICOTT — The Ellicott Steam Vehicle Company was organized during the fall of 1906 as a $1.5 million Maine incorporation for the manufacture of automobiles in Buffalo, New York. Thomas G. Shaw and Andrew Borst were among the people involved. Whether any cars at all resulted has not been documented. During the fall of 1907 the Standard Oil Company petitioned Ellicott (then styled the Ellicott Motor Car Company) into involuntary bankruptcy with indicated debts of $889.89. The firm was discharged in bankruptcy during the summer of 1908, and returned to the automobile business as the Ellicott Garage at 988 Ellicott Street where it repaired and remodeled cars, and that fall branched into body building.

ELLINGEN & PARKS — W. Ellingen and W.J. Parks have been indicated as the builders of an automobile in LaSalle, Illinois in 1896. Documentation of this is lacking.

1897 Elliott Gasoline Carriage, NAHC

ELLIOTT — Oakland, California — (1897-1899) — The Elliott was one of the first gasoline automobiles to be built on the Pacific Coast. It was named for its inventor, Willaim L. Elliott, who was the manager of the Oakland branch of the California Cycle Company of San Francisco. The Elliott was powered by a single-cylinder 2 hp Otto-type engine, which the inventor built following drawings in a French technical journal, with transmission by belt to a countershaft on the rear axle. It was a neat two-seater weighing 600 pounds. In the spring of 1897, Elliott wrote the editors of *The Horseless Age* that he intended to place his vehicle on the market at once. Although he did not do this, he tested the car extensively, including a run of fifty-six miles up Mt. Hamilton on September 13th, 1898. The Elliott made it to the top of the 4400-foot summit handsomely, but in coming down the brakes of the vehicle were worn out completely. Continuing experimentation ensued, and in April of 1899 Elliott reported that he was in progress on two new gasoline cars, one for himself, the other for a patron. The car he sold carried a $1200 price tag but Elliott declared his intention to "make them for $800 for anyone who wants one." In June he announced that, finally, he had been able to secure capital to back the serious manufacture of his automobile. Precisely what happened next is not known, but obviously Elliott's financial backing was not secure. By March 1900 he was advertising "a good gas engine for sale cheap." Interviewed seven years later by the *Oakland Tribune*, Elliott said his total production was the aforementioned three cars.

ELLIOTT — Dayton, Ohio — (1925) — This Elliott was a new car with an air-cooled engine designed by H.E. Elliott in collaboration with C.W. Lang. In the June 25th, 1925 issue of *Automotive Industries*, the partners announced that the prototype of the Elliott had been completed and manufacture was planned in Dayton. Apparently the venture failed soon after that.

ELLIS — Ellis was an alternative name for the electric car built in Chicago from 1900-1901 and usually marketed as a Triumph. Refer to Triumph.

ELLIS & TURNER — Peoria, Illinois — (1901) — The Ellis & Turner Company had been among the firms with which Charles E. Duryea was associated during his Peoria period. When Duryea left for Reading, Pennsylvania, Ellis and Turner decided to build their own car, returning from their first test trip in it on August 14th, 1901. After 600 miles of driving over dirt roads, they itemized their expenses: 25¢ for repairs, 40 gallons of gasoline at 13¢ a gallon or $5.20, two gallons of oil at 50¢ a gallon. They were sure they were on to something, and announced immediately their plans for manufacture. Ultimately, they decided to become automobile dealers instead.

ELLS — Vicksburg, Michigan — (1902) — In August of 1902, *The Horseless Age* reported that one T.A. Ells of Vicksburg had "completed a gasoline carriage after designs of his own." Further details of the vehicle are lacking.

ELLSWORTH — New York, New York — (1907) — In October of 1906 Thomas J. Fay resigned from Smith & Mabley of New York to join with John Mager Ellsworth to market a touring car. Fay had invented a clutch that was novel, Ellsworth had the money — and thus the incorporation papers read Ellsworth & Fay, and the car carried the name of the man who put up the money. The special clutch design, which in production was called the Fay-Ellsworth, was described as follows: "It consists essentially of a hardened cone shaped drum attached to the driven shaft and a spiral band attached to the driving member. The whip end of the Ellsworth tapered spiral band is pinched between the drum and the housing, due to a difference in the angle. The result is, the band constricts, when its tail is pinched, and the motor winds it up." The Ellsworth was powered by a 40 hp four-single overhead cam T-head engine. Special pride was taken by Fay and Ellsworth in the special grades of chrome, nickel, and vanadium steel which were used in the Ellsworth motor. Very few examples of the $5000 Ellsworth car were built. By the fall of 1907 the partners decided to concentrate production at their 518 West 22nd Street factory in New York upon the manufacture of chrome nickel steel parts exclusively.

E.L.M. — The E.L.M. Auto Company was organized for the manufacture of automobiles in Springfield, Massachusetts early in 1906. Capital stock was $15,000. Harry S. Elkins and Harry C. Medcraft were the "E" and "M" of this venture, the "L" apparently was a silent partner. Silence, too, followed on this venture, with undoubtedly not a single automobile produced. Harry C. Medcraft was back the following year with a new partner, however — one George B. Bowersox. The result of their collaboration was the Med-Bow Automobile Company and the Springfield car, produced in the Massachusetts city of that name in 1907-1908 and subsequently in Illinois from 1909-1910. Refer to Springfield.

ELMER — Kalkaska, Michigan — (1898-c.1906) — Elmer F. Johnson established his bicycle shop on Cedar Street in Kalkaska in 1863. Thirty-five years later he built his first automobile there, which he called the Elmer. It was a gasoline buggy using a two-speed transmission, wire-spoke wheels and a frame composed of tubular bicycle parts. The car was obviously much used, because it was rebuilt twice, first in 1901 and then again in 1905 when its original engine had worn out and was replaced by a Cushman. In 1905, too, Elmer Johnson built his second car, this one steam powered. A total of five more automobiles emanated from the Elmer F. Johnson Cycle Works in the months that followed. Undoubtedly these were built at the request of local people who were aware of Johnson's fine reputation as a quality bicycle builder — and who had probably seen his Elmer in action in the neighborhood. Only Johnson's first car was called the Elmer, incidentally, its inventor deciding on the more formal Johnson designation for the other six cars. The final destiny of the Johnsons is unknown, but the Elmer remains extant and is on permanent exhibit at the Kalkaska County Historical Society Museum.

1904 Elmer, KCHSM

1911 Elmer Six, touring, RBB

ELMER SIX — Elkhart, Indiana — (1911) —
Harry H. Elmer was the former general manager of the Haynes Automobile Company of Kokomo. Together with four other members of the Haynes executive echelon, he organized the Elmer Auto Corporation in Elkhart during the spring of 1911. A six-cylinder car had been designed already. To get into production quickly and, it was thought at the time, efficiently, the Elmer group bought out the Elkhart Motor Car Company, unknowingly buying a passel of problems with it. A lawyer by the name of John R. O'Shaughnessy, acting on behalf of the Elkhart company, negotiated the deal. He became secretary of the new Elmer company. Prototypes of the new Elmer six were built and tested before year's end. Then in February 1912 the roof fell in. The transfer of real estate from the Elkhart to the Elmer company was claimed to be fraudulent. Several creditors of the old Elkhart company had charged that although Elkhart had received more than $12,000 for the factory, they had not received any of the money due them. Meanwhile the Elmer Six prototypes languished, and now the factory in which manufacture was to begin was the subject of a court case. Desperately, Harry Elmer searched for a solution, and within a month he had found it. The Grant-Lees Machine Company of Cleveland liked the Elmer Six well enough to help sponsor its production. Within two months, the entire Elmer operation, moved to Cleveland, with the exception of lawyer O'Shaughnessy who was left behind. The Elmer Six, which had briefly been referred to as the Lohr during its days in Elkhart, became the Grant Six in Cleveland.

ELMERE —
The Elmere Motor Car Company was organized late in 1909 in New York City with a capital stock of $20,000 for the manufacture of "motors, machines, motor cars, carriages, boats, etc." G.W. Post, Jr., C.J. Post and J.N. Blair were the incorporators. Manufacture of an automobile is doubted.

1903 Elmore, model 7, runabout, HAC

ELMORE — Clyde, Ohio — (1899-1912) —
Elmore was the name of the small parcel of land near Clyde, Ohio where H.V. Becker operated a stave mill. His two sons, James and Burton, expanded the small company into bicycle production — and thereafter they inched into automobile manufacture. A total of ten cars were built by the Beckers before they incorporated their Elmore Manufacturing Company in 1902. Early Elmores had a single-cylinder engine mounted under the seat, another cylinder was added in 1903 which Elmore claimed to be "the only double cylinder motor in the world that can be started without cranking." Elmore was almost belligerent in its championing of the two-stroke idea; "The Car That Has No Valves" remained the company slogan for all its life. In 1903 the Beckers wrote *The Horseless Age* that certain comparisons between two-stroke and four-stroke engines appearing in the magazine's columns had been damaging to their interests and strongly suggested that a rebuttal treatise written by Elmore chief engineer E.W. Roberts be published. *The Horseless Age* duly printed Roberts' two-stroke argument, but the editors appended a note saying that whether a two-stroke or four-stroke engine was to be preferred remained to be proven. Although a dummy hood was provided a 1904 Elmore, it was not until 1906 that the cars had front-mounted engines, these now including a four-cylinder model. A three-cylinder Elmore became popular as a taxicab. In 1907 Elmore built 400 cars, its best year ever. Like the Cartercar with its friction drive, the Elmore with its two-stroke engine appealed to William C. Durant when he was creating General Motors, and he bought both companies specifically for their novelty, Elmore in November of 1909 for a reported half-million dollars. Neither the Cartercar nor the Elmore survived Durant's first ouster from GM. Elmore production was discontinued in the fall of 1912.

1900-1902 ELMORE

	FP	5	4	3	2	1
Trap (1-cyl., 6 hp, 62" wb)	1200	1600	2700	3800	5800	12,000
Rbt. (1-cyl., 3½ hp, 62" wb)	750	1500	2500	3600	5500	11,000

1903 ELMORE
Model 6 - 1-cyl., 5 hp, 62" wb

	FP	5	4	3	2	1
Rbt.	750	1600	2700	3800	5800	12,000
Model 7 Rbt. - 2-cyl., 6 hp	800	1500	2500	3600	5500	11,000
Model 8 Tour. - 2-cyl., 10 hp	1400	1600	2700	3800	5800	12,000

1904 Elmore, model 9, touring, HAC

1904 ELMORE
Model 9 - 1-cyl., 10 hp, 78" wb

	FP	5	4	3	2	1
Tonneau-4P	850	1600	2700	3800	5800	12,000
Rbt.-2P	750	1500	2500	3600	5500	11,000
Dly. Wagon	850	1100	2200	3200	4900	9000

1905 Elmore, model 11, touring, WLB

1905 ELMORE
Model 10 - 1-cyl., 10 hp, 78" wb

	FP	5	4	3	2	1
Tonneau-4P	950	1600	2700	3800	5800	12,000

Model 11 - 2-cyl., 16 hp, 83" wb

Pathfinder Tonneau	1250	1600	2700	3800	5800	12,000
Canopy Top Tonneau	1350	1700	2800	3900	6000	12,500

1906 Elmore, model 14, touring, HAC

1906 ELMORE
Model 14 - 3-cyl., 24 hp, 92" wb

Tour.-5P	1500	1800	2800	4000	6200	13,000

Model 15 - 4-cyl., 35 hp, 104" wb

Tour.-5P	2500	1900	2900	4100	6400	13,500

1907 Elmore, model 18, touring, HAC

1907 ELMORE
Models 16/17 - 3-cyl., 24 hp, 104" wb

Model 16 Tour.-5P	1750	1800	2800	4000	6200	13,000
Model 17 Rbt.-2P	1750	1900	2900	4100	6400	13,500

Model 18 - 4-cyl., 35 hp, 110" wb

Tour.-5P	2500	2000	3000	4200	6500	14,000

1908 Elmore, model 40, touring, HAC

1908 ELMORE
Model 30 - 3-cyl., 24 hp, 102" wb

Tour.	1750	1900	2900	4100	6400	13,500
Rdst.	1750	2000	3000	4200	6500	14,000

Model 40 - 4-cyl., 35 hp, 109" wb

Tour.	2500	2000	3000	4200	6500	14,000

1909 ELMORE
Model 33 - 3-cyl., 24 hp, 104" wb

Tour.-5P	1750	2100	3100	4300	6800	14,500
Cape Top Tour.-5P	1850	2200	3200	4400	7000	15,000
Land.-5P	2250	1800	2800	4000	6200	13,000
Rdst.-4P	1750	2200	3200	4300	6800	15,000

Model 44 - 4-cyl., 35 hp, 110" wb

Tour.-5P	2500	2200	3200	4400	7000	15,000
Cape Top Tour.-5P	2625	2250	3300	4500	7300	15,500

1909 Elmore, model 33, landaulet, HAC

1910 Elmore, model 46, touring, HAC

1910 ELMORE
Model 36 - 4-cyl., 36 hp, 110" wb

Tour.	1750	2200	3200	4400	7000	15,000
Demi-Tonneau	1750	2200	3200	4400	7000	15,000

Model 46 - 4-cyl., 46 hp, 120" wb

Tour.-7P	2500	5500	11,100	18,500	25,900	37,000

1911 Elmore, model 25, torpedo roadster, HAC

1911 ELMORE
Model 25 - 4-cyl., 25 hp, 108½" wb

Tour.	1250	2300	3300	4600	7500	16,000
Rdst.	1200	2400	3400	4800	8000	17,000

Model 36-B - 4-cyl., 50 hp, 114" wb

Tour.-7P	1750	2350	3400	4700	7800	16,500

Model 46-B - 4-cyl., 70 hp, 127½" wb

Tour.	—	2500	3500	5000	8500	18,000

1912 Elmore, model 26, torpedo roadster, JAC

1912 ELMORE

Four - 25.6 hp, 108½″ wb

	FP	5	4	3	2	1
Model 26 Rdst.	1150	2400	3400	4800	8000	17,000
Model 26 Tour.	1200	2300	3300	4600	7500	16,000
Model 27 Tour.	1250	2350	3400	4700	7800	16,500

Four - 32.4 hp, 114″ wb

	FP	5	4	3	2	1
Model 37 Fore-Door Tour.	1600	2500	3500	5000	8500	18,000
Model 27 Demi-Tonneau	1600	2500	3500	5000	8500	18,000
Model 38 Fore-Door Tour.	1750	2700	3600	5300	8800	19,000

ELRICK — Joliet, Illinois — (1896) — Apparently this car was completed and tested, but it would surely appear that its inventor had a very tenuous hold on truth in describing it. The car was invented by George Elrick of Joliet. It was a four-wheeler for two passengers, but with the simple removal of four pins it could be converted to a motorcycle to carry one person. Its single-cylinder gasoline engine weighed twenty pounds, and the whole vehicle as a four-seater only one hundred. The cost of running was approximately ten cents per hundred miles, Elrick said, and its maximum speed was 25 mph. Elrick had grand visions for production, believing his vehicle "admirably adapted" to delivery, express, postal and military service. These visions were clouded early on.

1895 Elston Gasoline Vehicle, NAHC

ELSTON — Charlevoix, Michigan — (1895) — In 1895 R.W. Elston of Charlevoix began building a four-passenger carriage powered by a 4 hp Kane-Pennington gasoline motor with the intention of entering the Chicago Times-Herald Contest to be held in November. Although the car was not finished on time, Elston did subsequently complete it, but never could make it travel further than around the block before experiencing problems. Elston never did build another car, but turned his talents instead to devising a new type of differential about which history seems to have recorded nothing.

ELWELL-PARKER ELECTRIC — Cleveland, Ohio — (1905-1908) — Motors produced by the Elwell-Parker Electric Company of 4224 St. Clair Avenue in Cleveland were used by a variety of electric car manufacturers during the early years of the industry, and Elwell-Parker also manufactured controllers, front and rear axles, complete power packages and chassis ready for body, tires and batteries. The company did build and market commerical vehicles under its own name, though never a passenger car. A few passenger cars, however, were built to demonstrate the various Elwell-Parker components. In 1909 the Elwell-Parker components business was acquired by the Anderson Carriage Company, makers of the Detroit Electric. Elwell-Parker remained in business building industrial electric fork-lift trucks.

ELWOOD — In 1915 the Elwood Iron Works announced its entry into the automotive field and its plans for production of a four-cylinder car to be known as the Elco. Although Elwood went bankrupt before getting the car onto the market, Elco manufacture was subsequently taken on by the Bimel Buggy Company. Elcos were produced in Sidney, Ohio from 1915 through 1917. Refer to Elco.

ELYRIA — The Elyria Auto Sales Company was organized in Elyria, Ohio late in 1912 with a capital stock of $10,000 to manufacture and deal in automobiles. Behind this venture were W.G. Bennett, I.W. Lyon, F.S. Bates, Carrell H. Smith and J.J. Dillon. Manufacture of a car is doubted.

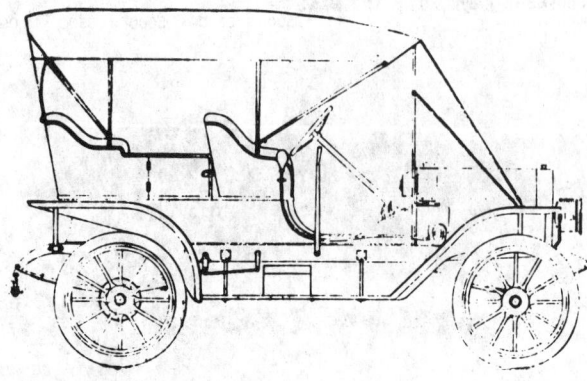

1909 Emancipator, touring, NAHC

508

EMANCIPATOR — Aurora, Illinois — (1909) — The Emancipator — the "Free From Trouble" car — was a four-cylinder 20 hp touring on a 100-inch wheelbase chassis which was built by the same people who produced the two-cylinder Aurora runabout. Shaft drive and a two-speed planetary transmission were featured, and the price tag was $1100. Unlike the Aurora which was built from 1907 to 1909, the Emancipator was produced only in 1909, following its introduction at the Chicago Automobile Show that January. The Emancipator Automobile Company, as the Aurora Motor Works had been renamed, was out of business by year's end.

EMBLEM — Despite car roster references to the contrary, there was no automobile built in America prior to the First World War which carried the name Emblem. The name was used for two motorcycles, however.

EMBREE-McLEAN — St. Louis, Missouri — (1909-1910) — The Embree-McLean Carriage Company had been producing carriages and bodies for twenty years in St. Louis when, in September of 1909, the firm elected to enter the automobile field. The vote to do so was one the board of directors possibly should never have taken, at least insofar as production plans were concerned. The schedule called for the building of 500 four-cylinder cars for the season following: a 30 hp roadster on a 105-inch wheelbase chassis, a 35 hp light touring on a 116-inch wheelbase, and a 40 hp seven-passenger touring on a 120-inch wheelbase. The first cars were off the line in November. By July of 1910 the company was forced into bankruptcy. The cost of preparing for production of three models with three different engines on three different chassis saw to the firm's undoing before any profit could be made.

EMENDORFER — Saginaw, Michigan — (1902-1909) — Although the total automobile production of F.A. Emendorfer & Company of 213 North Harrison Street in Saginaw was no doubt small, the firm advertised itself as a manufacturer of automobiles, gas engines and bicycles between the years 1902 and 1909. Michigan vehicle registrations indicate at least a few Emendorfers on the road, though repairing automobiles was the company's specialty.

EMER — The Emer Motor Livery Company was organized early in 1909 with a capital stock of $50,000 to manufacture cars and operate a garage in Chicago, Illinois. W.W. Dixon and W.S. Jamieson were behind this venture. Manufacture of an automobile is doubted.

EMERSON — The Emerson Company was organized in Fort Worth, Texas with a capital stock of $50,000 early in 1917 to assemble and deal in automobiles and automobile supplies. Included among the incorporators were J.H. Price, O.B. McCoy and S.O. Lovejoy. Manufacture is doubted.

1896 Emerson & Fischer Motor Wagon, NAHC

EMERSON — Cincinnati, Ohio — (1885)/EMERSON-FISCHER — (1896) — "I think it was about 1885 that I built my first vehicle operated by an engine which used gas derived from vaporizing coal oil of 150° test," Victor L. Emerson wrote The Horseless Age in 1903. "This machine at the time created quite a sensation among my neighbors and I think it would put to shame some of the present automobiles." A becoming modesty was not among Victor Emerson's virtues, and whether his three-wheeled carriage was, as he stated, "the first one in this country operated with an explosive engine" cannot be documented. Emerson drove the car on a number of test runs, the longest being about thirty miles, but riding on dirt roads in those days before pneumatic tires was "a very rough sort of sport," he said, and he abandoned the machine "after the novelty had worn off" and used it thereafter in his barn "as an elevator to lift grain by." In 1896, when he was associated with the Emerson & Fischer Company in Cincinnati, Emerson built another vehicle using a Duryea-King motor which when completed was delivered to a circus. Though reportedly further vehicles were under construction at that time, manufacture was not seriously embarked upon. At the turn of the century, Victor Emerson did attempt to organize a going company in Cincinatti, but he did not succeed. His subsequent automotive adventures included the Military and the S.S.E.

1917 Emerson, touring, WLB

EMERSON — Kingston, New York — (1917) — The Emerson was the result of a collaboration among Robert C. Hupp, founder of the Detroit company that produced the Hupmobile, and the brothers Theodore A. and George N. Campbell, who had founded the Imperial Automobile Company in Jackson, Michigan. It was their idea to produce a low-priced four-cylinder world-beater, and they talked New York financier Willis George Emerson into backing the project. A factory for the new Emerson Motors Company was secured in November 1916 in Kingston, New York and, in the grandiose publicity which announced the new Emerson, pointed mention was made of the sterling automotive credentials of Hupp and the Campbells and the success currently being enjoyed in the marketplace by one Henry Ford with his Model T. That the Emerson was meant to challenge the Ford head-on was unmistakable; it had a four-cylinder 22 hp engine, a wheelbase ten inches longer than the T, a selective sliding-gear transmission at a time when jokes already were rampant about the Tin Lizzie's planetary, and a very low $395 price tag. Advertisements carefully noted that the Emerson was the lowest-priced 110-inch wheelbase car in the world. Seemingly, success was assured. But from January to March of 1917, only sixty-nine cars were built, and although production was then stepped up to five cars per day, Robert C. Hupp now abruptly resigned. The official reason given was that he had ''completed his design assignment,'' but more than likely he discovered what was going on. By June of 1917 Emerson Motors Company was in receivership, and a whole passel of company officials were indicted for using the mails to defraud. Neither Hupp nor Emerson nor the Campbells were involved, but fourteen other people associated with the company were, most specifically the four brokers who had sold $1.5 million worth of Emerson stock. Production, now up to eighteen cars a day, continued awhile under receivership, but by September the Campbells had disassociated themselves from Emerson and reorganized as the Campbell Motor Car Company to produce the former Emerson as the new Campbell. The old Emerson company remained in the news for several years thereafter, however, as the fraud case wound its way through various appeals courts. In July of 1921, by unanimous decision of the judges of the United States Circuit Court of Appeals, the sentences of three Emerson officials were upheld. Two of them went to jail immediately, the third jumped bail and was a fugitive for more than a year until in November of 1922 he was arrested near Buffalo and sent to the Atlanta penitentiary to begin serving a seven-year sentence.

1908 E.M.F., model 30, touring, OCW

E-M-F — Detroit, Michigan — (1908-1912) — Although its initials had the unhappy effect of being lampooned into ''Every Morning Fix-it,'' ''Every Mechanical Fault'' and ''Eternally Missing Fire,'' among others, the E-M-F was a fine little car for the period. Its name had been logically chosen to designate its founders: E was Barney Everitt, who had made a fortune in Detroit as a body builder; M was William Metzger, the salesman par excellence who had played such a leading role during the early years of the Cadillac; F was Walter Flanders, who had learned how to build cars efficiently as Henry Ford's production manager. The E-M-F was planned as a mass quantity car at the same time Ford was getting his assembly line in order, with the difference that the E-M-F people opted for a ''well-finished'' vehicle in the medium-price range and didn't succeed nearly so well as Ford did with his low-priced Model T. The formation of the Everitt-Metzger-Flanders Company of Detroit was formally announced June 2nd, 1908, following acquisition of the Northern and Wayne companies and their plants and equipment. Chief engineer for the E-M-F was William E. Kelly, who had designed the Wayne. The car was a 30 hp four set into a sturdy pressed steel U-section frame featuring a three-speed sliding gear transmission incorporated into the rear axle. On the first cars, cooling was

by thermo-syphon but overheating problems arose, and William Kelly personally recalled the vehicles and installed water pumps. Production through 1909 totaled 8,132 units, and for 1910 would rise to 15,300. But, in addition to the unfair jibes its name occasioned (''oh, they were awfully peevish,'' wrote E-M-F advertising man LeRoy Pelletier), the E-M-F was plagued also by quarreling among its partners (Everitt and Metzger left in a huff in 1909 to build their own car called the Everitt, taking William Kelly with them, and Flanders would spread himself thin building his Flanders 20 extracurricularly) and by a distribution agreement with the wagon-building Studebaker Brothers which gave South Bend virtually a co-starring role in the E-M-F act. After a bitter court fight, Studebaker took E-M-F over completely by 1912, and all subsequent cars were marketed as Studebakers. Final E-M-F production was 25,967 cars for 1911-1912. Late in 1912 Flanders rejoined his old partners who were still building the Everitt. Following the First World War, Everitt, Metzger and Flanders got together again to build the Rickenbacker.

1909 E.M.F., model 30, touring, WLB

1908-1909 E.M.F.
Model 30 — 4-cyl., 30 hp, 106'' wb

	FP	5	4	3	2	1
Touring-5P	1250	2700	3600	5300	8800	19,000
Tourabout-4P	1250	2500	3500	5000	8500	18,000
Demi-Tonneau-4P	1250	2700	3600	5300	8800	19,000
Roadster-3P	1250	2900	3700	5600	9100	20,000

1910 E.M.F., model 30, touring, OCW

1910 E.M.F.
Model 30 — 4-cyl., 30 hp, 108'' wb

Touring-5P	1250	2700	3600	5300	8800	19,000

1911 E.M.F., model 30, touring, HAC

1911 E.M.F.
Model 30 — 4-cyl., 30 hp, 108'' w

Touring-5P	1000	2700	3600	5300	8800	19,000
Coupe	1400	2200	3200	4400	7000	15,000
Roadster-2P	1000	2900	3700	5600	9100	20,000

1912 E-M-F, model 30, roadster, HAC

1912 E.M.F.
Model 30 — 4-cyl., 30 hp, 112" wb

	FP	5	4	3	2	1
Fore-Door Touring-5P	1100	2700	3600	5300	8800	19,000
Demi-Tonneau-4P	1100	2900	3700	5600	9100	20,000
Roadster-2P	1100	3000	4000	6000	9500	21,000
Coupe	1450	2300	3300	4600	7500	16,000

EMISE — Early in 1913 announcement was made that the new Emise Motor Car Company of Cleveland, Ohio was about to enter the automotive field. It did, but within weeks its name had been changed to the Chandler Motor Car Company, which remained in production until 1929. Refer to Chandler.

EMPIRE — The Empire Garage Company of 185 Maine Avenue in Passaic, New Jersey was incorporated with a capital stock of $20,000 for the manufacture of automobiles and motor vehicles during the summer of 1906. Incorporators were A. Bretthauer, H.C. Fairchild and Alfreda Fairchild. Manufacture of a car is doubted.

The Empire Motor Carriage Company was organized in New York City during the fall of 1901 with a capital stock of $250,000 for the manufacture of automobiles. Behind this venture were Bradley S. Teale of Oneida; and George B. Burley, Henry T. Clinton, Thomas P. Payne and William A. Fitzpatrick, all of New York City. Manufacture of a car is doubted.

The Empire Motors Company was organized early in 1914 as a $100,000 Delaware corporation for the manufacture of "engines, automobile and airships." Incorporators of this venture were E.V. Webster of Baltimore, Maryland; G.G. Schroeder of Washington, D.C., and G.G. Guyer of Wilmington, Delaware. Manufacture of a car is doubted.

EMPIRE — Pittsburgh, Pennsylvania — (1896) — In January of 1896 the Empire Motor Company of Pittsburgh was organized with a capital stock of $150,000, and by February had begun testing its first 1½ hp motor buggy. Its power was transmitted by power and chain, with the speed regulated by a friction wheel on the driveshaft. The public test of the vehicle was seen to by William Morgan (manager of the Empire Motor Company) and E.W. Walker (a machinist for the Pennsylvania Railway Supply Company). Although they reported themselves pleased with the results, Morgan said that he was already at work on a new two-cylinder gasoline engine which he hoped would "give as steady power as a steam engine." Although occasional references indicate the company's sporadic appearance on the scene as late as 1899, it would seem that Empire Motor Company never did proceed into manufacture.

1909 Empire Twenty, model A, roadster, WLB

EMPIRE — Indianapolis, Indiana — (1909-1919)/Greenville, Pennsylvania — (1912-1914) — In 1909 four of the biggest names in Indianapolis — Arthur Newby, president of the company producing the popular National car; Carl Fisher, founder of Prest-O-Lite; James Allison, of subsequent Allison aircraft fame; engineer Robert Hassler from National — decided to build a sprightly, altogether admirable 20 hp four-cylinder $800 car that would be nicknamed "The Little Aristocrat." Unfortunately, three of them — Newby, Fisher, and Allison, together with Frank H. Wheeler of Wheeler-Schebler — also decided to build an oval race track in town, and the problems they had there diverted concentration from their Empire. When a disastrous inaugural race meet on the dirt of the new Indianapolis Motor Speedway brought threats by the A.A.A. that no further races would be sanctioned there, the track promoters concluded that bricks might be

better. In late December 1909, when the last brick (a gold-plated one) was ceremonially laid on the new Indy Speedway, the first car to try out the track was the new Empire, the first one off the line. This was probably the most attention its builders ever paid their car. Thereafter, they went back to worrying about how to make their race track a paying proposition, ultimately deciding that one big race of 500 miles every Memorial Day just might do it. Early in 1911 Harry C. Stutz was hired as a consulting engineer for the Empire, changed its specifications from chain to shaft drive, then left to build his own car which he introduced at the inaugural Indianapolis 500 that May. The new shaft-drive Empire was introduced the month following, but the men behind it remained basking in the success of their Memorial Day race. Convinced they were on to a good thing, they promptly forgot about their car altogether. Late in 1911 the Empire Motor Car Company was sold to another group of Indianapolis businessmen who reorganized as the Empire Automobile Company and began looking for someplace to build the Empire since its original factory had already been turned over to the manufacture of Prest-O-Lite starters. The Greenville Metal Products Company in Pennsylvania was happy to help, though for 1912 insisted that the cars assembled from Empire parts remaining to be marketed under the name of the Greenville president, Frank Fay. Consequently, the old Empire Twenty became the new Fay, though there was a new Empire too, the bigger Model 25. Meanwhile, the Empire people looked further for a factory to call their own, and acquired the Connersville Wheel Company in the city of that name. At last they were back home in Indiana, though obviously the Empire people weren't completely satisfied because in July 1915 they acquired the former Federal Motors factory in Indianapolis, right in their own neighborhood. Empires by now, however, were no longer Little Aristocrats, but quite ordinary four- (Teetor engine) and six-cylinder (Continental engine) cars sold in a welter of models which brochures indicate, even the people building them were confused about. The Empire was in chaos, and not surprisingly it quickly fell. Interestingly, among the Empires surviving today is a Model 31 for which the Greenville Steel Car Company (successor to Greenville Metal Products) assiduously searched as a tangible reminder of the firm's short sojourn as an automobile producer. When the car was found, it was given a homecoming, a museum all its own at the Greenville factory, and probably more attention than ever the Empire had during its lifetime.

1910 Empire Twenty, model A, roadster, HAC

1909-1910 EMPIRE
Twenty — 4-cyl., 20 hp, 96" wb

	FP	5	4	3	2	1
Model A Rdstr.	800	2500	3500	5000	8500	18,000
Model B Sptsr.	850	2700	3600	5300	8800	19,000

1911 Empire Twenty, model C, roadster, HAC

1911 EMPIRE
Twenty — 4-cyl., 20 hp, 96" wb

	FP	5	4	3	2	1
Model C Rdstr.	950	2500	3500	5000	8500	18,000

1912 EMPIRE
Model 25 — 4-cyl., 25 hp, 104" wb

	FP	5	4	3	2	1
Semi-Torpedo Rdstr.-2P	850	2600	3600	5200	8700	18,500
Touring-5P	950	—	—	—	—	—

1912 Empire, model 25, touring, RM

1913 Empire, model 25, touring, HAC

1913 EMPIRE
Model 25 — 4-cyl., 25 hp, 104" wb

	FP	5	4	3	2	1
Touring-5P	950	2600	3600	5200	8700	18,500

Model 31 — 4-cyl., 23 hp, 108" wb

Touring-5P	950	2700	3600	5300	8800	19,000

1914 Empire, model 31, touring, HAC

1914 EMPIRE
Model 31 — 4-cyl., 23 hp, 109" wb

Touring-5P	900	2700	3600	5300	8800	19,000

1915 Empire, model 31-40, touring, HAC

1915 EMPIRE
Model 31 — 4-cyl., 23 hp, 110" wb

Touring-5P	850	2700	3600	5300	8800	19,000
Roadster-2P	875	2900	3700	5600	9100	20,000

Model 31-40 — 4-cyl., 23 hp, 110" wb

Touring-5P	975	2800	3700	5500	9000	19,500
Roadster-2P	975	3000	3900	5800	9300	20,500

1916 Empire, model 60, touring, JAC

1916 EMPIRE
Model 33 — 4-cyl., 24 hp, 112" wb

	FP	5	4	3	2	1
Touring-5P	895	2700	3600	5300	8800	19,000
Tour. Sedan-5P	1095	2700	3400	4800	8000	17,000

Model 45 — 4-cyl., 24 hp, 116" wb

Touring-5P	1095	2800	3700	5500	9000	19,500
Tour. Sedan-5P	1295	2450	3500	4900	8300	17,500

Model 60 — 6-cyl., 25 hp, 120" wb

Touring-7P	1095	5500	10,950	18,250	25,500	36,500

1917-18 Empire, model 70-A, touring, JAC

1917 EMPIRE
Model 70 — 6-cyl., 25 hp, 120" wb

Touring-7P	1235	2900	3700	5600	9100	20,000
Sedan-7P	1625	2400	3400	4800	8000	17,000

1918 EMPIRE
Model 50 — 4-cyl., 20 hp, 116" wb

Touring-5P	1125	2900	3700	5600	9100	20,000
Roadster-2P	1165	3100	4200	6300	10,500	22,000

Model 70A — 6-cyl., 25 hp, 120" wb

Touring-5P	1345	3000	4000	6000	9500	21,000
Touring-7P	1375	2900	3700	5600	9100	20,000
Sedan-5P	1685	2300	3300	4600	7500	16,000

1919 Empire, model 72, touring, HAC

1919 EMPIRE
Model 72 — 6-cyl., 25 hp, 120" wb

Touring-7P	1445	3000	4000	6000	9500	21,000

EMPIRE STEAM — New York, New York — (c.1927) — The Cruban Machine & Steel Corporation of New York City was operated by the Banzhaf brothers — Albert H.T. and E.J. — and located in downtown Manhattan near the Financial District. Around 1927 a steam car carrying the name of Empire was designed for the firm by Carl Ubelmesser and was built probably for experimental or prototype purposes. Part of the car and its chassis remain in existence. It was the only automobile believed ever built at Cruban.

c.1927 Empire Steam Car, touring, KM

EMPIRE STATE — The Empire State General Vehicle Company was organized in Rochester, New York during the summer of 1910 with a capital stock of $100,000 for the manufacture of "vehicles and appliances." Incorporators were G.A. Hallister, R.M. Searle and J.T. Hutchings. Manufacture of an automobile is doubted.

The Empire State Motor Car Company was incorporated late in 1906 with a capital stock of $25,000 for the manufacture of engines and automobiles in New York City. Behind this venture were Herman Raub of Brooklyn and John J. McCutchan of the Empire State Automobile Garage at 2150 Broadway. Manufacture of an automobile is doubted.

Although the Empire State Motor Wagon Company of Catskill, New York did not build an automobile in 1898, as has occasionally been said, it does have another distinction. The company operated what was probably one of the first used car lots in the United States. The firm was organized during the early spring of 1898 for the sale, rental and exchange of motor vehicles of all kinds, with "second-hand motors and motor carriages" being offered at "reasonable rates." Leasing vehicles for county fairs and other exhibitions was another specialty. The man behind the Empire State Motor Wagon Company was P.C. Lewis, who had been a pump manufacturer in Catskill before entering the borning automobile industry.

1900 Empire State, runabout, NAHC

EMPIRE STATE — Rochester, New York — (1900-1901) — The Empire State Automobile Company of 26 Courtland Street in Rochester was organized in May of 1900 with a capital stock of $20,000. The specifications of the company's product read like a prototype for the generic turn-of-the-century gasoline runabout: small 4-1/2 hp engine mounted under the seat, chain drive, tiller steering and flimsy bicycle-type wire wheels. The price was $750. The Empire State survived less than two seasons.

In 1901 the Empire Manufacturing Company, Sterling, Illinois, built this unusual steam car. Note the "V" engine.

1901 Empire Steamer, runabout, GR

EMPIRE STEAMER — Sterling, Illinois — (1899-1900)/Sterling, Illinois — (1901-1902) — The Empire and the Sterling were essentially the same car built by two different sponsoring companies. Powered by a two-cylinder vee-type engine geared directly to the rear axle, this steamer was unusual in its transverse placement of a rectangular boiler with horizontal tubes across the frame and under the seat of the car. Outwardly, it was a typical wire-wheeled steam buggy of the day. The price tag was $750. Each attempt to manufacture the car survived a little over a year. Initially, the Empire Manufacturing Company evolved into the Empire Automobile Company for its production. This venture was superseded sometime during 1901 by the Sterling Automobile & Engine Company. During the fall of 1902 the Sterling property was sold at a sheriff's sale for $1300 to satisfy payments due on the factory mortgage.

1904 Empire Steamer, MVMA

EMPIRE STEAMER — Amsterdam, New York — (1904) — The Terwilliger brothers of Amsterdam built their first experimental steam car in 1897. In 1902 they announced the forthcoming formation of a "stock company" to manufacture steam automobiles of their own design. Although no cars immediately followed, a formal organization did: William T. Terwilliger & Company. When finally in 1904 the Terwilligers got their car to market, they decided against using their own name for it, and chose Empire Steamer instead. Available in one model only, the Empire Steamer had its two-cylinder 15 hp motor with Stephenson valve gear "hung pivotally from the rear axle" with "the cylinder end suspended from the midships boiler." The steering was right hand, the wheelbase eighty-seven inches, and the price $2000. The car did not survive into 1905.

EMPRESS — The Empress was a model of the Johnson produced in 1910. The Johnson Service Company of Milwaukee, Wisconsin manufactured automobiles from 1905 through 1912. Refer to Johnson.

EMRICK — Oakland, California — (1903) — William Emrick's machine shop was located at 1265 Seventh Street in Oakland and that he built an automobile there in 1903 is lent credence by his inclusion among participants in a motor tour of the Alameda County Automobile Club that May. Emrick also indicated himself as an "automobile manufacturer" in the Oakland city directory that year, which doubtless meant that he would be happy to put together a car for anyone who asked.

ENDURANCE — The Endurance Motor Car Company was organized in New York City early in 1906 with a capital stock of $35,000 and a plan to manufacture automobiles. Behind this venture were Harold Mable of Hackensack, Henry W. Johns of Bronxville and A. Parker Smith of New York City. Manufacture of a car is doubted.

1924 Endurance Steam Car, 4-dr. sedan, WLB

ENDURANCE STEAM — Long Beach, California — (1924) — The "possibility of fuel shortage — some day" was among the reasons *Motor West* provided for the enthusiastic interest generated among Los Angeles area reporters when the Endurance Steam Car Company demonstrated its new product to the press in late October of 1924. The Endurance was an entirely conventional steamer, and its description in *Motor West* as a "somewhat rough-and-ready model" indicates that the prototype had not been detailed throughout. With six passengers aboard, however, it did wend its way smartly through city traffic and up the steepest hill in Long Beach. The fact that the company had no stock for sale was taken as evidence of the sincerity of its organizers, who were Graydon P. Hickle as president, A.R. Waterman as chief engineer, C.A. French as consulting engineer and C.R. Newby as production engineer. Though sincere, alas, they were not successful. Five open and closed body styles on 124-inch wheelbase chassis were planned, but possibly only the $1985 touring car was produced before the company went under. The Pacific Steam Car Company was indicated as the manufacturing organization, incidentally, with the Endurance Steam Car Company handling the vehicle's marketing. Both firms shared the same Long Beach address. Production may have extended into 1925, but by spring of that year the W.Y. Jackman Company, which had been appointed national distributor, found itself with no more cars to sell. The administrative affairs of the company were wound up in Dayton, Ohio to which city the firm had moved in early 1925. No cars were produced there.

1909 Enger, model B, runabout, HAC

ENGER — Cincinnati, Ohio — (1909-1917) — Frank J. Enger of Cincinnati had a lot of ideas about automobiles, and he formed the Enger Motor Car Company in 1909 to bring them into reality. The first Engers were two-cylinder highwheelers, but within a year Enger had proceeded to standard cars which used the four-cylinder overhead valve engine he had designed. After trying a conventional six for the 1915 model year, Enger turned unconventional late that year with his introduction of a twelve-cylinder car, among the first in America, which he called the Enger Twin Six and which he offered for sale at only $1095. As he explained it, "the camshaft, which is located in the 'V' of the motor, has 24 cams, each valve being operated by an individual cam." In late 1916, he added a new wrinkle; his twelve could be run as a six by manipulating a lever that sent the flow of fuel to one cylinder bank only. (George Schebler also built a similar engine.) An Enger four developed 36 hp, an Enger twelve 55; what half of the twelve developed was not indicated. In August of 1916 Enger's company was reorganized to bring in new capital. In March of 1917 the company was in receivership. There was but one overwhelming reason for that. On January 4th, 1917, at age fifty-eight, Frank Enger shot and killed himself in his office. He was reported to have been in ill health for only a short time. Although he left a note for his vice-president Daniel McLaren giving full instructions for the continuing of the business, Enger's widow subsequently petitioned for receivership to protect her investment in the company which she stated had total assets of $330,000.

1909 ENGER
Highwheeler — 2-cyl., 14 hp chassis

	FP	5	4	3	2	1
Model B Rbt. (90" wb)	—	1600	2700	3800	5800	12,000
Model C Vict.	—	1700	2800	3900	6000	12,500
Model D Vict. Sthp. (88"wb)	1800	2800	4000	6200	13,000	

1910 Enger, model 40, touring, GR

1910 ENGER
Forty — 4-cyl., 35/40 hp, 116" wb

Touring-5P	2000	1700	2800	3900	6000	12,500

1911 Enger, model IV, close-coupled torpedo, HAC

1911 ENGER
Forty — 4-cyl., 40 hp, 119" wb

	FP	5	4	3	2	1
Model II Tour.-5P	2000	1700	2800	3900	6000	12,500
Model III Torpedo-5P	2150	1800	2800	4000	6200	13,000
Model IV Torpedo-4P	1875	1800	2800	4000	6200	13,000
Model V Tour.-4P	1800	1900	2900	4100	6400	13,500
Model VI Torpedo-3P	1775	1800	2800	4000	6200	13,000
Model VII Rbt.-2P	1700	1700	2800	3900	6000	12,500

1913 Enger, model F, touring, HAC

1912-1913 ENGER
Forty — 4-cyl., 40 hp, 120" wb

	FP	5	4	3	2	1
Model F Tour.-5P	1475	2500	3500	5000	8500	18,000
Model J Tourabout-4P	1475	2400	3400	4800	8000	17,000
Model E Rds.-2P	1475	2700	3600	5300	8800	19,000
Model P Tour.-5P	1750	2600	3600	5200	8700	18,500

1914 Enger, model A, touring, HAC

1914 ENGER
Forty — 4-cyl., 40 hp, 120" wb

	FP	5	4	3	2	1
Model A Tour.-5P	1285	2400	3400	4800	8000	17,000
Model B Tour.-5P	1435	2450	3500	4900	8300	17,500
Model C Rds.-2P	1285	2500	3500	5000	8500	18,000
Model G Tour.-5P	1585	2450	3500	4900	8300	17,500

1915 ENGER
Model 6-50 — 6-cyl., 30 hp, 125" wb

	FP	5	4	3	2	1
Tour.-7P	1495	2500	3500	5000	8500	18,000
Rds.-2P	1495	2600	3600	5200	8700	18,500

1916 ENGER
Four — 4-cyl., 36 hp, 106" wb

	FP	5	4	3	2	1
Tour.-5P	695	2700	3600	5300	8800	19,000

Twin Six — 12-cyl., 55 hp, 115" wb

	FP	5	4	3	2	1
Tour.-5P	1095	4300	5300	8600	16,100	29,500
Rds.-3P	1095	4300	5400	8700	16,500	30,000

1915 Enger, model 6-50, touring, HAC

1916 Enger, Twin-Six, touring, HAC

1917 ENGER
Four — 4-cyl., 36 hp, 106" wb

	FP	5	4	3	2	1
Tour.-5P	695	2700	3600	5300	8800	19,000

Twin Unit 12 — 12-cyl., 55 hp, 116" wb

	FP	5	4	3	2	1
Tour.-5P	1295	4200	5200	8400	15,700	29,000

ENGLAND — In late 1912, in Kansas City, Missouri, the England Brothers Motor Car Company was organized with a capital stock of $2000 for the manufacture of automobiles. The brothers involved were Edward and E.W. Manufacture of a car is doubted.

1901 Englehart Gasoline Carriage, NAHC

ENGLAND — Amesbury, Massachusetts — (1901) — In 1901 Arthur England built the first automobile in Amesbury. All components, including its engine, were hand built, and the car was displayed for public view that August in the machine shop of George W. England.

ENGLEHART — Northampton, Massachusetts — (1901) — A.J. Englehart operated a bicycle repair shop in Northampton which he said was the most complete in the country. In 1901 he built a gasoline car. Whether he ever envisioned manufacture is not known, but his car was tested and driven for a considerable period. Its bicycle wheels were insubstantial, but the rest of his dos-a-dos four-seater appeared quite sturdy. The Englehart sported a tubular frame of truss pattern, and was powered by a two-cylinder water-cooled engine. A water tank was placed in front of the dashboard, with the gasoline tank just inside the dash. The change gear provided two forward speeds and reverse, and was enclosed in a dustproof case. The total weight of the Englehart was 800 pounds.

ENGLER — Pontiac & Detroit, Michigan — (1913-1914) — The first Engler cyclecar was a tandem two-seater of 110-inch wheelbase and 36-inch tread, with power provided by a two-cylinder air-cooled 10 hp De Luxe motor, rear spring suspension by cantilever, transmission by friction disc and final drive by vee belt to the rear wheels. It was designed and built by William B. Engler, a former General Motors engineer. The car was first tested near Engler's home in Pontiac, but thereafter Engler moved to Detroit where he set up shop at 69 Alfred Street. Though he named his cyclecar for himself, his venture never proceeded far enough for him to organize a company for manufacture. In the spring of 1914 he built a new version of his cyclecar with 92-inch wheelbase and 44-inch tread which he took on a 900-mile run in Ohio, Indiana and Michigan. Apparently, he did build a few examples of this car for sale at $385.

ENGLISH — The English Automobile & Motor Company was a $5 million incorporation from Chicago, Illinois during the fall of 1899 for the manufacture and sale of rotary engines and automobiles. Behind this venture were Chicagoans F. English, T.M. Moe, A.F. Ross, F.A. Loomis, in association with one P. English of Benton Harbor, Michigan. Benton Harbor was selected as the location for manufacture. That this firm was an automobile manufacturer was indicated in the Hiscox book *Horseless Vehicles, Automobiles, Motor Cycles* published in 1900. Further documentation is lacking.

The English Motor and Automobile Works of Oakfield, New York was noted as an automobile manufacturer in the Hiscox book *Horseless Vehicles, Automobiles, Motor Cycles* published in 1900. Further documentation is lacking.

ENLIND — The Enlind Manufacturing Company was a million-dollar incorporation from the fall of 1900 to manufacture and deal in automobiles in Trenton, New Jersey. Behind this venture were K. Arvid Enlind, George Coughleton and P.C.B. Thornton. Enlind is known to have been the inventor of a "non-slipping pneumatic tire." Manufacture of an automobile is doubted.

ENSLEN — During the summer of 1909, Eugene F. Enslen, in collaboration with his son E.F. Enslen, Jr., announced the forthcoming incorporation of a $200,000 company in Birmingham, Alabama for the manufacture of an automobile they had designed. This venture almost immediately disappeared from newsprint.

ENSLOW — One Frank Enslow has been indicated as the builder of an automobile in Huntington, West Virginia in 1910. Documentation is lacking.

ENTERPRISE — The Enterprise Auto Machine Works of Pontiac, Michigan was described during the summer of 1912 as "composed of a number of experts from foreign automobile factories" who had just completed "a new factory building with up-to-date equipment, and will soon have a new car on the market." There is no evidence the car ever appeared.

The Enterprise Automobile Company was a $100,000 incorporation from the summer of 1908 to manufacture automobiles and engines in Hasbrouck Heights, New Jersey. Behind this venture were J.F. Coleman, J.L. Lotsch, E.S. and H.B. Schultz. Manufacture of a car is doubted.

ENTERPRISE — Chicago, Illinois — (1913) — Late in 1913, at the dawn of the cyclecar's short day in the American industry, the Enterprise Machinery Company of Chicago announced its development of a friction transmission that was cheap and promised to solve the problem of a long belt drive. "The power is transmitted from the engine friction disc through a double friction wheel, either half of which drives a rear wheel by a short chain," *The American Cyclecar* explained. "There are only eight working parts, no gears and it furnishes its own differential." A car was built by Enterprise to test and demonstrate the transmission, though the company had no plans for manufacture.

ENTYRE — The Entyre which has appeared on numerous car rosters was simply the Etnyre misspelled.

1914 Entz Six, touring, HAC

ENTZ — New York, New York — (1914) — Justus B. Entz was a Philadelphia electrical engineer who first began experimenting with an automatic electric transmission in the 1890's. His initial application of the device to a motor vehicle, in 1898, ended dismally however, when an electric arc melted a hole in the gas tank and the machine caught fire. Entz transmissions were fitted to some Columbia Electrics prior to the turn of the century, and a variation found its way into the U.S. battleship *New Mexico*. In late June of 1914, the Society of Automobile Engineers met at the seaside resort of Cape May (New Jersey) to, among other diversions, listen to a paper read by Justus Entz regarding the most recent developments to the electric transmission he had invented. An "animated discussion" was said to have followed Entz's reading of his paper, and even further stir was caused by the appearance of the Entz six-cylinder motorcar which its inventor had just happened to bring along. All routine operations of the car were seen to by a single controller lever swinging over a sector on the steering wheel. In average driving, the accelerator pedal was the only one on the floor necessary to use. As Entz explained his transmission, "the system consists of a dynamo-electric machine, one member of which replaces the ordinary engine flywheel, while the other occupies the general mechanical relation of the driven or male member of the ordinary cone clutch. In addition an electric motor is mounted on the driving-shaft behind the so-called clutch-generator, which serves the general purpose of a torque multiplier, or, in other words, serves to boost the turning effort developed by the engine under certain circumstances." The Entz had been introduced at the New York Automobile Show in January of 1914, shortly following the incorporation in New York of the Entz Motor Car Corporation. At the time of the Cape May meeting, Entz indicated that production would be forthcoming. It would, but not by Justus Entz. Instead the Entz patents were acquired by people with more experience in the automobile industry who introduced the Owen Magnetic at the New York Automobile Show in January of 1915.

EPHM Σ — This was the Hermes rendered into Greek letters. The car was built in New York in 1920 by Demos Tsaconas, for potential export sale to his native Greece. Refer to Hermes.

EPPS — Chicago, Illinois — (1902) — The Epps of 1902 was sold by the Mead Company of Chicago which during the years 1902 to 1905 specialized in the reconditioning of vehicles that were then resold under whatever name a prospective purchaser might wish. Presumably this car was bought by a Mr. Epps.

EQUIPOISE — Baltimore, Maryland — (1911) — Equipoise was the name given by E.L. Tunis of Windsor Mills in the suburbs of Baltimore to the gasoline vehicle he built in 1911. A two-wheeler with side balancing wheels, Tunis claimed his car capable of 100 mph, which probably provides all-new meaning to the dictionary definition of the word hyperbole. Tunis is known to have built only the one Equipoise.

EQUITABLE — The Equitable Automobile & Truck Company was indicated in the Hiscox book *Horseless Vehicles, Automobiles, Motor Cycles* published in 1900 as an automobile manufacturer in Boston, Massachusetts. Boston city directories of the period reveal the firm's correct designation to be Equitable Auto Truck and Power Company. The firm's principal activity was manufacture of brake and power equipment. In August of 1899 Equitable indicated its plans to build a steam carriage but whether it was completed has not been documented.

ERIE — The Erie Cycle and Motor Carriage Company of St. Louis, Missouri was indicated as the manufacturer of an automobile in the Hiscox book *Horseless Vehicles, Automobiles, Motor Cycles* published in 1900. No such company existed in St. Louis at that time. Undoubtedly the firm in question was the Erie venture in Anderson, Indiana.

The Erie Supply Company was organized in Toledo, Ohio early in 1912 with a capital stock of $10,000 to manufacture automobiles and supplies. Incorporators were W.J. Fritsche, F.H. Kruse, F.A. Brown, J. Samson and M. Winchester. Manufacture of a car is doubted.

ERIE — Anderson, Indiana — (1899-1902) — The Erie Cycle & Motor Carriage Company was incorporated during the late fall of 1898 to succeed the Erie Cycle & Manufacturing Company which had been producing two-wheelers for the two years past. "J.B. Lott is the president, inventor and mechanical head," *The Horseless Age* reported. The balance of company's business was looked after by Robert F. Schenk and Charles F. Lott. Small gasoline cars were built in small numbers during the turn-of-the-century period. Their price range was $350-$600, and they were all fitted with single-cylinder engines of J.B. Lott's design. Most of the cars were called Erie, but a few were marketed under the trade name of Werts, and Lott had considered calling the car a Herald for a while. Apparently the company experimented with a steam car as well early in 1902. By late fall that year, however, the Erie organization — by now renamed Erie Motor Carriage and Maufacturing Company — was taken over by L.P. Halladay and moved to Streator, Illinois. The well-known Halladay automobile followed.

1917 Erie, model 34, 2-pass. roadster, WLB

ERIE — Painesville, Ohio — (1916-1919) — The Erie Motor Car Company was financed, as *The Telegraph-Republican* of Painesville put it, on April 20th, 1916, by "Cleveland, Ashtabula and Painesville parties [who asked]

no assistance whatever from the city and [offered] no stock for sale." Frank Meket was the company president, W.E. Brown general manager, H. Percy secretary and treasurer. Percy had previously been purchasing agent for the Vulcan Manufacturing Company, which was helpful since Erie had launched itself into business by buying out Vulcan and made a little money on the side by continuing to service Vulcan automobiles. There is no evidence that the Erie Motor Car Company made much money marketing the Erie motorcar. It was powered by a four-cylinder water-cooled engine, and offered as touring car and roadster on a common 118-inch wheelbase and with a common price tag of $795, raised to $850 in 1918. By the latter year, it would appear that the Erie Motor Car Company's principal output was devoted to E.M.C. trucks for the war effort. The company did not long survive the Armistice. Though a considerably more expensive, four-cylinder Erie was announced for the 1920 model year, it does not seem this $1975 touring car was ever built.

1916-1917 ERIE
Erie — 4-cyl., 33 hp, 118" wb

	FP	5	4	3	2	1
Model 33 Tour.-5P	795	2700	3600	5300	8800	19,000
Model 34 Rdstr.-2P	795	2900	3700	5600	9100	20,000

1918-1919 ERIE
Erie — 4-cyl., 33 hp, 118" wb

Model 33 Tour.-5P	850	2700	3600	5300	8800	19,000
Model 34 Rdstr.-2P	850	2900	3700	5600	9100	20,000

1897 Erie & Sturgis Carriage, NAHC

ERIE & STURGIS — Los Angeles, California — (1897) — James Philip Erie was a New York engineer who migrated west in 1895 for reasons of his health. He settled in Los Angeles, near the S.D. Sturgis & Brother Machine Works, and it was at that shop that he spent most of the next two years. The automobile that resulted was his conception, and was translated into reality with the help of Samuel D. Sturgis. It featured a four-cylinder engine, one pair of cylinders located with the flywheel behind the rear axle, the other pair at the forward end of the steel frame. Drive was taken by direct gear from the main shaft to parallel countershafts where friction rollers provided for changes of speed. The vehicle was given its first test on May 30th, 1897 and was described in the following day's edition of the *Los Angeles Times:* "In appearance the motor-wagon is not unlike a massive tally-ho. The body of the carriage is high above all the machinery, which is enclosed below in a black box. This box is lined with asbestos, giving perfect ventilation to the engines and preventing any heat from reaching the body of the carriage. The fumes of the gasoline are barely noticeable, being all below and behind the carriage, and nearly all noise is prevented by the device of making all gears alternately of wood, fiber and steel." Only one of the four cylinders was used in the test, and there were problems with the vehicle. The asbestos reportedly "burned out like brown paper," and some of the Los-Angeles-bought steel was found to be defective. Subsequent news stories indicated that the faulty parts would be replaced with "honest material" imported from the East. Despite what seemed to be a splendid beginning — its first trial was described as succeeding "beyond any previous hopes" — and a purported expenditure of $30,000 in development work, it does not appear that the Erie & Sturgis gasoline car ever proceeded beyond this one example. Subsequently, James Philip Erie organized the Erie Pneumatic Hub Company in Los Angeles, but he had returned to New York by the turn of the century to continue a general engineering career there. Most of his patents were in the electrical field. Samuel D. Sturgis remained in Los Angeles in the general machining field with his brother William W. for a number of years. They manufactured gasoline engines and put together an occasional automobile or truck. A photograph of a Sturgis truck from 1905 is extant, and the brothers briefly built the Rocket gasoline car in 1903-1904, and possibly a single example of a Sturgis electric.

ERNST STEAM — New York, New York — (1895-1896) — The Ernst Power Vehicle Company was the formidable name given to the venture which resulted from the collaboration of two New Yorkers named Victor H. Ernst and Vincent F. Lake. Ernst was an inventor of various steam engine components and designs, and Lake reportedly had been "working on a type-setting machine." Together they announced their plans to build a steamer, a gasoline car and another vehicle with a secret type of engine. Only the steamer was built, and in one example only. What their secret had been was never divulged. The Ernst Power Vehicle Company was located at 245 Broadway in lower Manhattan. About five years later Ernst showed up as the front-half of the Ernst-Merkel Company, whose back-half may have been the motorcycle-building Merkel. The last heard of Victor H. Ernst was another firm, the Ernst Flying Machine Company, the New Jersey charter for which was voided in 1916.

1929 Erskine, model 52 Royal, 2-dr. sedan, AA

ERSKINE — South Bend, Indiana — (1927-1930) — The Erskine was named for Albert Russel Erskine, president of the Studebaker Corporation. It resulted from its namesake's fondness for things European and his desire to move his company smartly into a lower-priced field. "The Little Aristocrat" had a six-cylinder 146-cubic-inch Continental-built engine with a low European taxable rating of 16.54 hp, but developed 40 bhp at 3200 rpm and guaranteed 60 mph with 25-30 mpg. The Erskine was placed on a 108-inch wheelbase, with classy styling courtesy of Ray Dietrich. Introduced at the Grand Palais in Paris (where it was proclaimed the "clou du salon," the hit of the show), it appeared next at Olympia in London (where 2000 orders were taken at the stand, press headlines noting "Greatest auto value in British History — How can they do it?") and arrived in New York with Studebaker promotion burbling that the Erskine "comes to Broadway via Champs-Elysees and Piccadilly Circus." The European cachet was further played upon in advertisements touting "Studebaker's New 2-1/3 Litre Car." The Erskine sold well in Europe, but failed to catch on in the United States. Partly the reason was its price. The car was introduced at $995; a year later Henry Ford had his four-cylinder Model A on the market for $525, and Chevy was waiting in the wings with its Cast Iron Wonder six. What happened to the Erskine was typical of the trend in the American industry of the period. It got bigger and sold better. By 1930 the Erskine had 3.4 liters and a 114-inch wheelbase. In May that year the Erskine name was dropped, and the car was unceremoniously absorbed into the Studebaker line. Total production of the Erskine for its four model seasons was: 1927, 24,893 units; 1928, 22,275 units; 1929, 25,565 units; 1930, 22,371 units.

1927 Erskine, model 50, coupe, AA

1927 ERSKINE
Model 50 — 6-cyl., 40 hp, 108" wb

	FP	5	4	3	2	1
Tourer-5P	945	2400	3400	4800	8000	17,000
Sedan-5P	975	900	1300	2300	3300	5500
Custom Cpe.-4P	—	950	1400	2500	3700	6000
Bus. Cpe.-2P	—	900	1350	2400	3400	5700

1928 Erskine, model 51, convertible coupe, AA

1928 ERSKINE
Model 51 — 6-cyl., 43 hp, 108" wb

	FP	5	4	3	2	1
Clb. Sed.- 5P	795	1000	1600	2700	4000	6500
Sedan-5P	885	1000	1650	2700	4100	6700
Ryl. Sed.-5P	985	1000	1700	2800	4100	6800
Conv. Cpe.-2P	—	1200	3800	6300	8800	12,600

1929 Erskine, model 53 Regal, cabriolet, AA

1929 ERSKINE
Model 52 — 6-cyl., 43 hp, 109" wb

	FP	5	4	3	2	1
Clb. Sed.-5P	—	1000	1600	2700	4000	6500
Cabriolet-2P	—	2100	5200	8750	12,250	17,500
Cabriolet-4P	—	2300	5300	8900	12,400	17,800
Sedan-5P	—	1000	1700	2800	4100	6800

1930 Erskine, model 53, landau sedan, AA

1930 ERSKINE
Model 53 — 6-cyl., hp, 114" wb

	FP	5	4	3	2	1
Roadster	1285	4000	5000	8000	15,000	28,000
Touring	1385	3700	4700	7300	13,700	26,000
Bus. Cpe.	1255	950	1400	2400	3500	5800
Coupe	1315	950	1400	2500	3700	6000
Sedan	1295	900	1300	2300	3300	5500
Reglr. Sed.	1415	900	1350	2400	3400	5700
Clb. Sed.	1195	900	1300	2200	3200	5400

ERWIN — Philadelphia, Pennsylvania — (1913-1914) — Whether the output of the Erwin Motor & Machine Company was sold under the Erwin or Bergdoll name is not known. The company, which was located at the southeast corner of 31st and Dauphin in Philadelphia, was headed by Erwin R. Bergdoll, with his brothers Grover Cleveland and Charles A. assisting. As the firm's name indicates, engines and machinery were the principal products, though it does appear that the last few Bergdoll automobiles were built there after the Louis J. Bergdoll Motor Company went to the wall elsewhere in Philadelphia early in 1913. Louis J. Bergdoll meanwhile was attempting to reorganize and relocate in Trenton, New Jersey. This never happened, and after the assembling of the last few Bergdoll cars in the Erwin plant, that factory returned entirely to its usual efforts.

ESPLANADE —— The Esplanade Garage & Supply Company was organized during the summer of 1914 in Chicago, Illinois with a capital stock of $12,000 to manufacture and deal in automobiles. Incorporators were Erwin W. Roemer, Ambrose Ryan and James L. Bottourns. Manufacture of an automobile is doubted.

ESS EFF — Buffalo, New York — (1912) — The Ess Eff was a step backwards. It had a wonderfully low price tag of $350, but it bought the most primeval of specifications, chain drive particularly being quite outmoded by 1912 for a car of its type. The firm's name was the Ess Eff Silent Motor Company, though the car's air-cooled two-cylinder 17 hp engine probably was not. Friction transmission was featured. Offered as a runabout only on an 88-inch wheelbase, the Ess Eff was pictured and described in the 1912 roster of American makes published in the *Automobile Trade Journal*. It did not make the 1913 edition.

1912 Ess Eff, runabout, HAC

ESSENKAY — The Essenkay Empire Company was organized with a capital stock of $10,000 in Albany, New York during the fall of 1912 for the manufacture and sale of automobiles. Herman C. Cowen, John G. Cummings and Howard Wilbur were the principals involved. Manufacture of a car is doubted.

ESSEX — The Essex Automobile Company was organized in Newark, New Jersey during the fall of 1906 with a $5000 capital stock for the manufacture of automobiles. Incorporators were A. Somerville, C.E. Wyckoff and J.M. Somerville. Manufacture is doubted.

1901 Essex, auto buggy, NAHC

ESSEX — **Haverhill & Lynn, Massachusetts** — **(1901-1902)** — In 1901 the Essex Automobile & Supply Company was in Haverhill producing a four-cylinder 5 hp runabout, on a 60-inch wheelbase chassis with Upton direct tranmission gear and final drive by chain and sprocket. The car's weight was 600 pounds and its price was $700. In 1902 the Essex Automobile Company was in Lynn producing the same car. It did not survive the year there.

ESSEX STEAM — **Boston, Massachusetts** — **(1906)** — The Essex Motor Car Company of Boston was incorporated during the spring of 1905 by Arthur Hovering, Lawrence W. Cushman and Frank D. Branan for the purpose of building a steamer with a four-cylinder single-acting 15/20 hp engine featuring poppet valves. Only one model would be offered, at $3000, a side-entrance tonneau on a 107-inch wheelbase which resembled the famous Serpollet from France. Early in 1906 it was revealed that Essex had contracted with the Bailey Carriage Company of Amesbury, one of the largest carriage manufacturing plants in New England, for the building of the Essex. Most probably, all the Essexes to follow were produced in Amesbury. Most probably, too, there were not many made before the company went under.

ESSEX

ESSEX — **Detroit, Michigan** — **(1919-1932)** — The Hudson was named for the Detroit department store magnate who had put up much of the money for the company; the Essex was named a decade later after Hudson officials let their fingers walk over a map of England in pursuit of a name with snob appeal. Initially, the car had its own sponsoring organization, the Essex Motor Company, which in October of 1917 leased the old No. 5 Studebaker plant on Franklin Avenue in Detroit for the manufacture of a lower-priced companion car to the Hudson. Ninety-two cars were built in 1918, but were designated as 1919 models. The first-generation Essex was a four-cylinder 55 hp four on a 108 1/2-inch wheelbase, with quite angular body lines and a robust performance. Tests conducted under AAA supervision at the Cincinnati Speedway in December 1919 resulted in 3037.4 miles in 50 hours for a 60.75 mph average. Even more impressive was the transcontinental trek in August 1920 of four Essexes (two starting from each coast) which resulted in a 4 day 21 hour 32 minute average for

1922 Essex, coach, WRG

the quartet — and scads of publicity because a pouch of mail was carried in each car, with relief drivers sworn in as official letter carriers, and local newspaper headlines all across the country. But the most spectacular of the Essex achievements was in another area altogether: closed coachwork. The four-passenger coach introduced for 1922 at $1495 was the lowest-priced closed car in America. "Only $300 More Than Touring Model," headlined an incredulous *Motor Age*. By 1925 the Essex coach was priced five dollars *less* than the touring model. This was unheard of in the industry. A "packing crate" the competition might deride, but the car sold like hotcakes. In 1922 the facade of a separate company for the Essex was dropped, and both Essex and Hudson were now produced by the Hudson Motor Car Company. For the 1924 model year the Essex became a 28 hp L-head six, which though smoother than the four was not as robust. A perky boattail speedster was offered from 1927, four-wheel brakes became standard for 1928. In 1929 Essex sales contributed handsomely to the over 300,000 Hudson total, and the company was third in the industry. In 1932 the Essex had free wheeling, a vee radiator, a six-cylinder engine by now beefed up to 70 bhp — and a new model designation called Terraplane. In 1933 the Essex name was dropped, and the car became known simply as the Terraplane thereafter.

***

Essex Data Compilation
by Robert C. Ackerson

1919

1919 Essex, roadster, HAC

ESSEX — **SERIES A** — **FOUR:** "Everyone says nice things about the Essex" said one early ad for the Essex and few critics chose to dispute this assertion. The Essex was a conventional car in appearance but its angular body shape gave it a pleasing and easily identifiable style. But the real source of the Essex's appeal was its engine. Of F-head design it turned out an impressive 55hp and that was more than sufficient to make Essex synonomous with Performance. Dealers nationwide capitalized on this big selling point by staging demonstrations of Essex performance to initially skeptical customers who soon became enthusiastic Essex owners. In December 1919 an Essex successfully completed a fifty-hour endurance test in Cincinnati at an average speed of 60.75 mph. Initially the Essex was available only in Touring Car form but before the model year's end, Roadster and Sedan models were available.

I.D. DATA: Serial numbers on dash and right rear frame cross member. Starting: 5000. Ending: 75999. Engine numbers on left front motor mount.

Model No.	Body Type & Seating	Price	Weight	Prod. Total
NA	4-dr. Tr. Car-5P	1395	2450	NA
NA	4-dr. Sed.-5P	2250	2955	NA
NA	2-dr. Rds.-2P	1595	2625	NA

517

1919 Essex, phaeton, WRG

ENGINE: Inline Four. Cast iron block. B & S: 3-3/8 x 5 in. Disp.: 180 cu. in. Brake H.P.: 55 @ 2800 R.P.M. N.A.C.C. H.P.: 18.2. Main bearings: 3. Valve lifters: mechanical. Carb.: Essex bronze piston type.

CHASSIS: [Series A] W.B.: 108.5 in. Frt/Rear Tread: 56/56 in. Tires: 32 x 4.

TECHNICAL: Sliding gear transmission. Speeds: 3F/1R. Floor shift controls. Cork insert, wet clutch. Shaft drive. Hotchkiss rear axle. Overall ratio: 4.67:1. Mechanical brakes on rear wheels. Wooden spoke wheels. Rim size: 32 in.

OPTIONS: Houk wire wheels.

TECHNICAL: Introduced January 1919. Essex made 21,879 shipments to dealers during the 1919 calendar year. The President of Essex was William S. McAneeny.

Essex Motors was formed in 1917 and while technically independent of Hudson, was Hudson financed and staffed. For example, McAneeny was Hudson's factory manager, and such Hudson executives as Roscoe B. Jackson, and A. E. Barit held administrative positions at Essex. In addition, Hudson president Roy D. Chapin and other Hudson leaders served on the board of directors at Essex.

1919
Model A (4-cyl.)

	FP	5	4	3	2	1
Rds	1395	1150	3600	6000	8400	12,000
Tr	1395	1125	3450	5750	8050	11,500
Sed	1495	950	2100	4750	6650	9500

1920

1920 Essex, sedan

ESSEX — SERIES 5-A, 6-A & 7-A — FOUR: No changes, except for a higher headlight position on later models, either in appearance or design were made in the Essex for 1920. However there were plenty of activities in which Essex cars were involved to keep the Essex name in the public's view. The most sensational was the trans-continental mail run of four stock Essex Touring cars. Divided into two teams, leaving from San Francisco and New York, all four cars broke the old records for their respective directions, which had been set by the Hudson Super-Six in 1916. The fastest of the four Essex cars, traveling from San Francisco to New York City completed its run in 4 days, 14 hours, and 43 minutes.

I.D. DATA: Serial numbers on dash and right rear frame cross member. Starting: 5000. Ending: 89999. Engine numbers on left front motor mount.

Model No.	Body Type & Seating	Price	Weight	Prod. Total
NA	2-dr. Rds.-2P	1795	2545	NA
NA	4-dr. Tr. Car-5P	1795	2560	NA
NA	4-dr. Sed.-5P	2650	2900	NA
NA	2-dr. Cabr.-2P	2100	2675	NA

During 1920 Essex prices were reduced.

ENGINE: F-head. Inline Four. Cast iron block. B & S: 3-3/8 x 5 in. Disp.: 180 cu. in. Brake H.P.: 55 @ 2800 R.P.M. N.A.C.C. H.P.: 18.2. Main bearings: 3. Valve lifters: mechanical. Carb.: Essex bronze piston type.

CHASSIS: [Series 5A] W.B.: 108.5 in. Frt/Rear Tread: 56/56 in. Tires: 32 x 4. [Series 67] W.B.: 108.5 in. Frt/Rear Tread: 56/56 in. Tires: 32 x 4. [Series 7A] W.B.: 108.5 in. Frt/Rear Tread: 56/56 in. Tires: 32 x 4.

1920 Essex, sedan, WRG

TECHNICAL: Sliding gear transmission. Speeds: 3F/1R. Floor shift controls. Multiple disc clutch, cork inserts, running in oil. Shaft drive. Semi floating, Hotchkiss rear axle. Overall Ratio: 4.67:1. Mechanical brakes on two wheels. Wooden spoke wheels with detachable rims.

OPTIONS: Bumpers. Houk wire wheels. Spare tire.

HISTORICAL: Introduced Dec. 1919. Essex made 23,669 shipments to dealers during the 1920 calendar year. The president of Essex was William S. McAneeny.

1920
4-cyl.

	FP	5	4	3	2	1
Rds	1795	1150	3600	6000	8400	12,000
Tr	—	1125	3450	5750	8050	11,500
Sed	2650	950	2100	4750	6650	9500

1921

1921 Essex, touring, OCW

ESSEX — NO SERIES I.D. — FOUR: Essex adopted Hudson's strategy of abandoning both series and serial number codes from 1921 through 1923. At the same time it also offered a second line of 1921 models identified as the "New, Improved Essex," in October 1921. In the main, these cars were changed only in minor mechanical and styling details. The 4-door sedans received an ivory white panel on their rear door surfaces with the 2-door Cabriolet having the same feature on its doors. The open touring cars received new tops with improved weather protection.

I.D. DATA: Serial numbers on dash and right rear frame cross member. Starting: 500000. Ending: 630411 (Serial number range for 1921-23 models). Engine number on left front motor mount.

1921 Essex, cabriolet, WRG

Model No.	Body Type & Seating	Price	Weight	Prod. Total
NA	2-dr. Rds.-2P	1595	2545	NA
NA	4-dr. Tr. Car.-5P	1595	2560	NA
NA	4-dr. Sed.-5P	2450	2900	NA
NA	2-dr. Cabr.-2P	2100	2675	NA

Essex prices were reduced during the 1921 model year.

ENGINE: F-head. Inline Four. Cast iron block. B & S: 3-3/8 x 5 in. Disp. 180 cu. in. Brake H.P.: 55 @ 2800 R.P.M. N.A.C.C. H.P.: 18.2. Main bearings: 3. Valve lifters: mechanical. Carb.: Essex bronze piston type.

CHASSIS: No series identification 1921-23. W.B.: 108.5 in. Frt/Rear Tread: 56/56 in. Tires: 32 x 4.

TECHNICAL: Sliding gear transmission. Speeds: 3F/1R. Floor shift controls. Multiple disc clutch, cork inserts, running in oil. Shaft drive. Semi-floating rear axle. Overall ratio: 4.67:1. Mechanical brakes on two wheels. Wooden spoke wheels with detachable rims.

OPTIONS: Bumpers. Houk wire wheels. Spare tires.

HISTORICAL: Introduced Dec. 1920 - 1st line, Oct. 1921 2nd version. Essex made 13,422 shipments to dealers during the 1921 calendar year. The president of Essex was William S. McAneeny.

**1921
4-cyl.**

	FP	5	4	3	2	1
Rdst	1375	1200	3750	6250	8750	12,500
Tr	1595	1075	3000	5500	7700	11,000
Cabr	2100	1150	3600	6000	8400	12,000
2 dr Sed	2330	725	1400	3000	4700	6700
Sed	2450	725	1400	3100	4800	6800

1922

1922 Essex, touring, WRG

ESSEX — NO SERIES I.D. — FOUR: Hudson and Essex were merged into a single company in 1922 and shares in the new company were listed on the New York Stock Exchange. Essex, like Hudson offered two versions of 1922 models with the first type phasing in the new drum-shaped fuel tank. A new wider body was adopted for the Touring car with wider doors with front hinges. The Essex engine, in conjunction with the Super Six engine adopted a Morse timing chain. Other engine refinements included a new cylinder head with a more efficient fuel intake and repositioned spark plugs now on the right side of the engine. New pistons with aluminum skirts were also used. However the Essex line for 1922 was best remembered for its new coach model which proved to be a key catalyst speeding up the demise of the open cars as the predominant body style among American automobiles. Alfred P. Sloan later wrote that the introduction of

the Essex coach was "an event which was to profoundly influence the fortunes of Pontiac, Chevrolet, and the Model T." Although its styling was less than sensational the low price of the coach which after being reduced from $1492 to $1245 was only $100 above a comparable closed car assured its success.

I.D. DATA: Serial numbers on dash and right rear frame cross member. Starting: 500000. Ending: 630411 (Serial number range for 1921-1923 models). Engine numbers on left front motor mount.

Model No.	Body Type & Seating	Price	Weight	Prod. Total
NA	4-dr. Tr. Car-5P	1045	2600	NA
NA	4-dr. Sed.-5P	1895	2900	NA
NA	2-dr. Cabr.-2P	1145	2575	NA
NA	2-dr. C'ch.-5P	1245	2685	NA

The Rds. model was initially listed as available for 1922. However, it appears none were produced during the model year. The Cabr. was produced in the second portion of the model year.

1922 Essex, coupe, HAC

ENGINE: F-head. Inline Four. Cast iron block. B & S: 3-3/8 x 5 in. Disp.: 180 cu. in. Brake H.P.: 55 @ 2800 R.P.M. N.A.C.C. H.P.: 18.2. Main bearings: 3. Valve lifters: mechanical. Carb.: Essex bronze piston type.

CHASSIS: No series identification used 1921-23. W.B.: 108.5 in. Frt/Rear Tread: 56/56 in. Tires: 32 x 4.

TECHNICAL: Sliding gear transmission. Speeds: 3F/1R. Floor shift. Multiple disc clutch, cork inserts, running in oil. Shaft drive. Semi-floating rear axle. Overall Ratio: 4.67:1. Mechanical brakes on two wheels. Wooden spoke wheels with detachable rims.

OPTIONS: Bumpers. Houk wire wheels. Spare tire.

HISTORICAL: Introduced Dec. 1921, 2nd versions — Apr. 1922. Speed records: An Essex won the 183cid and under engine size class at Pikes Peak with a run of 20 munutes, 41 seconds. Essex made 36,222 shipments to dealers during the 1922 calendar year. The president of Essex was Roy D. Chapin.

**1922
4-cyl.**

	FP	5	4	3	2	1
Tr	1095	1075	3000	5500	7700	11,000
Cabr	1145	1150	3600	6000	8400	12,000
2 dr Sed	1345	725	1400	3000	4700	6700
Sed	1895	725	1400	3100	4800	6800

1923

1923 Essex, phaeton, OCW

ESSEX — NO SERIES — FOUR: Changes in Essex were very minor. During the model year the open Touring Car body adopted slightly narrower front doors and beginning in April a longer 28-inch gearshift was installed on all models.

I.D. DATA: Serial numbers on dash and right rear frame cross member. Starting: 500000. Ending: 630411 (Serial number range for 1921-23 models). Engine numbers on left front motor mount.

Model No.	Body Type & Seating	Price	Weight	Prod. Total
NA	4-dr. Tr. Car-5P	1045	2630	NA
NA	2-dr. Cabr.-2P*	1145	2575	NA
NA	2-dr. C'ch.-5P	1145	2685	NA

Note: * This model was dropped from the Essex line in Aug. 1923.

ENGINE: F-head. Inline Four. Cast iron block. B & S: 3-3/8 x 5 in. Disp. 180 cu. in. Brake H.P.: 55 @ 2800 R.P.M. N.A.C.C. H.P.: 18.2. Main bearings: 3. Valve lifters: mechanical. Carb.: Essex bronze piston type.

CHASSIS: No Series identification for 1923. W.B.: 108.5 in. Frt/Rear Tread: 56/56 in. Tires: 32 x 4.

TECHNICAL: Sliding gear transmission. Speeds: 3F/1R. Floor shift controls. Multiple disc clutch, cork inserts, running in oil. Shaft drive. Semi-floating rear axle. Overall ratio: 4.67:1. Mechanical brakes on two wheels. Wooden spoke wheels with detachable rims.

OPTIONS: Spare tire. Bumpers. Houk wire wheels.

HISTORICAL: Introduced Dec. 1922. Essex made 42,577 shipments to dealers during the 1923 calendar year. The president of Essex was Roscoe B. Jackson. Essex not only won its class at the Pikes Peak Hill Climb but came away the overall victor of the Penrose trophy with a time of 18 minutes, 47 3/4 seconds.

1923
4-cyl.

	FP	5	4	3	2	1
Cabr	1145	1150	3600	6000	8400	12,000
Phae	1045	1075	3000	5500	7700	11,000
2 dr Sed	1245	725	1400	3000	4700	6700

1924

1924 Essex, touring

ESSEX — NO SERIES — SIX: Beyond any doubt the most controversial feature of the 1924 Essex was its engine. Replacing the almost legendary F-head 4 was a 6-cylinder of conventional L-head design. Its physical dimensions were decidedly on the small size; 2-5/8 inch bore and a 4 inch stroke which yielded 130 cubic inches. Hudson did not (and would not until 1929) report this engine's horsepower but a prominent Hudson-Essex-Terraplane historian once estimated it as 34. Later in the model year Hudson increased the bore and stroke of this engine to 2-11/16 inches and 4-1/4 inches respectively which provided a displacement of 144.5 cubic inches and an estimated 40 horsepower. At the same time deeper oil troughs were installed which helped alleviate the tendency of its splash-type lubrication to inadequately supply the rear bearings with oil on down grades. As expected of a Hudson-built engine, the new Essex Six was fitted with a fully balanced, 3-bearing crankshaft, aluminum pistons, roller valve lifters, a Morse timing chain, automatic spark advance and a cast enbloc intake manifold. The 1924 Essex's styling was less controversial although it was all new. The industry was moving towards a longer and lower look and new frame brackets allowing for a lower body mounting level plus a smooth hoodline and peaked fenders put the Essex in line with the times. Hudson offered two versions of the 1924 Essex and the latter featured 31 x 5.25 balloon tires in place of the older 31 x 3.3-4 tires.

I.D. DATA: Serial numbers on dash and right rear frame cross member. Starting: 100001. Ending: 177750. Engine numbers on left side of cylinder block near water inlet elbow.

Model No.	Body Type & Seating	Price	Weight	Prod. Total
NA	2-dr. C'ch.-5P	975	2305	NA
NA	4-dr. Tr. Car.-5P	900	2185	NA
NA	2-dr. C'ch.-5P (A)	945	2370	NA
NA	4-dr. Tr. Car.-5P (B)	850	2130	NA

Note 1: (A & B) These models replaced the initial Essex offerings in June 1924.

ENGINE: L-head. Inline Six. Cast iron block. B & S: 2-11/16 x 4-1/4 in. Disp.: 144.6 cu. in. Taxable H.P.: 17.32. Main bearings: 3. Valve lifters: mechanical. Carb.: Stewart.

1924 Essex, coach, WRG

CHASSIS: No series identification for 1924. W.B.: 110.5 in. O.L.: 156.5 in. Frt/Rear Tread: 56/56 in. Tires: 31 x 5.25.

TECHNICAL: Sliding gear transmission. Speeds: 3F/1R. Floor shift controls. Multiple disc clutch, cork inserts, running in oil. Shaft drive. Semi-floating rear axle. Mechanical (14-1/2 x 1-1/2") brakes on rear wheels. Wooden spoke wheels with detachable rims.

OPTIONS: Front bumper. Rear bumper. Steel disc wheels.

HISTORICAL: Introduced Dec. 1923, superseded by models introduced in June 1924. Essex made 74,523 shipments to dealers during the 1924 calendar year. The president of Essex was Roscoe B. Jackson. The Essex Six set a new record time for a climb up Mt. Wilson in California of 31 minutes, 29 seconds.

1924
Six, 6-cyl.

	FP	5	4	3	2	1
Tr	850	1150	3600	6000	8400	12,000
2 dr Sed	975	750	1450	3300	4900	7000

1925

1925 Essex, coach, OCW

ESSEX — NO SERIES — FOUR: There were no changes of any consequence in the design of the Essex when the 1925 model year began. However during the year the size of the balloon tires fitted to the Essex were changed from 31 x 5.25 to 30 x 4.95 and minor engine modifications were made. Often criticized for its somewhat somber styling, the Essex coach was given a new, fresh appearance in March. The new body featured a curved windshield base, much thinner windshield and door posts and a reshaped windshield visor. As a step towards the adoption of a new Hudson-built body with a steel framework the Essex Coach used more steel in its construction than had the older model. As was the case with Hudson, prices of Essex models were reduced significantly during the model year.

I.D. DATA: Serial numbers on dash and right rear frame cross member. Starting: 177751. Ending: 337949. Engine numbers on left side of cylinder block near water inlet elbow.

Model No.	Body Type & Seating	Price	Weight	Prod. Total
NA	4-dr. Tr. Car.-4P	765 (B)	2185	NA
NA	2-dr. C'ch.-4P	895	2370	NA
NA	2-dr. C'ch.-4P (A)	765 (B)	2370	NA

Note 1: (A) This model replaced the older version in March 1925.
Note 2: (B) Initial price of the Tr. Car and C'ch were respectively $900 and $895.

ENGINE: L-head. Inline Six. Cast iron block. B & S: 2-11/16 x 4-1/4 in. Disp.: 144.6. N.A.C.C. H.P.: 17.32. Main bearings: 3. Valve lifters: mechanical. Carb.: Stewart.

CHASSIS: No series designations for 1925. W.B.: 110.5 in. O.L.: 156.5 in. Frt/Rear Tread: 56/56 in. Tires: 31 x 5.25 replaced by 30 x 4.95 in Jan. 1925.

TECHNICAL: Sliding gear transmission. Speeds: 3F/1R. Floor shift controls. Multiple disc clutch, cork inserts, running in oil. Shaft drive. Semi-floating rear axle. Overall ratio: 5.6:1. Mechanical (14-1/2 x 1-1/2 in.) brakes on two (rear) wheels. Wooden spoke wheels with detachable rims.

OPTIONS: Front bumper. Rear bumper. Steel disc wheels.

HISTORICAL: Introduced Dec. 1925. Essex made 159,634 shipments to dealers during the 1925 calendar year. The president of Essex was Roscoe B. Jackson. Profits of the Hudson Motor Car Company reached an all time high of $21,378,504 in 1925.

1925
Six, 6-cyl.

	FP	5	4	3	2	1
Tr	900	1150	3600	6000	8400	12,000
2 dr Sed	895	725	1400	3100	4800	6800

1926

1926 Essex, phaeton

ESSEX — NO SERIES — SIX: As was the case with Hudson, there were no changes in the appearance of the Essex until the Hudson-bodied versions of the Sedan and Coach appeared. The Coach was two inches lower than its predecessor. Those cars built after July 24 featured a nickel-plated radiator shell. An addition to the Essex line was a four-door sedan.

I.D. DATA: Serial numbers on dash and right rear frame cross member. Starting: 337845. Ending: 499999. Engine numbers on left side of cylinder block near water inlet elbow.

Model No.	Body Type & Seating	Price	Weight	Prod. Total
NA	2-dr. C'ch.-4P	735	2455	NA
NA	4-dr. Tr. Car	795	2260	NA
NA	2-dr. C'ch.-4P (*)	695	2500	NA
NA	4-dr. Sed.-5P	795	2540	NA

Note 1: (*) Hudson-built body introduced in July 1926.

ENGINE: L-head. Inline Six. Cast iron block. B & S: 2-11/16 x 4-1/4 in. Disp.: 144.6 cu. in. N.A.C.C. H.P.: 17.32. Main bearings: 3. Valve lifters: mechanical. Carb.: Stewart.

1926 Essex, sedan, OCW

CHASSIS: No series designations. W.B.: 110.5 in. O.L.: 156.5 in. Frt/Rear Tread: 56/56 in. Tires: 31 x 4.95.

TECHNICAL: Sliding gear transmission. Speeds: 3F/1R. Floor shift controls. Multiple disc clutch, cork inserts, running in oil. Shaft drive. Semi-floating rear axle. Overall Ratio: 5.6:1. Mechanical (14-1/2 x 1-1/2 in.) brakes on two (rear) wheels. Wooden spoke wheels with detachable rims.

OPTIONS: Front bumpers. Rear bumpers.

HISTORICAL: Introduced Dec. 1926. Essex made 157,247 shipments to dealers during the 1926 calendar year. The president of Essex was Roscoe B. Jackson. The new Hudson-built bodies for the Essex Coach and Sedan represented important steps towards the adoption of all-steel body construction.

1926
Six, 6-cyl.

	FP	5	4	3	2	1
Tr	765	1150	3600	6000	8400	12,000
2 dr Sed	765	700	1350	2800	4550	6500
4 dr Sed	795	700	1350	2900	4600	6600

1927

1927 Essex, sedan, OCW

ESSEX SUPER SIX — NO SERIES — SIX: Essex moved much closer to Hudson in terms of both style and name in 1927. It was now labeled as the Essex Super Six and its appearance, highlighted by a very Hudson-like hoodline, radiator plus a sensational boattailed Speedabout model made it a standout among American automobiles for 1927.

During the model year the Essex engine received a longer, 4.5 inch stroke which increased its displacement to 153.2 cubic inches. Although no horsepower rating was released its output was significantly increased.

In mid-summer, Hudson revised Essex styling by adding a full body length beltline molding, curving the rear body line and adopting smaller wheels and 30 x 5.00 tires.

I.D. DATA: Serial numbers on dash and right rear frame cross member. Starting: 500,001. Ending: 706,270. Engine numbers on left side of cylinder block near water inlet elbow.

Model No.	Body Type & Seating	Price	Weight	Prod. Total
NA	2-dr. Spdbt.-2P	700	2150	NA
NA	4-dr. Spds.-4P	785	2230	NA
NA	2-dr. Cpe.-2P	735	2340	NA
NA	2-dr. C'ch.-4P	735	2450	NA
NA	4-dr. Sed.-5P	785	2510	NA
NA	4-dr. Sed. DeL.-5P	895	2490	NA

1927 Essex, speedabout (late model year), WRG

ENGINE: L-head. Inline Six. Cast iron block. B & S: 2-11/16 x 4-1/4 in.(stroke later lengthened to 4-1/2 in. on June 25, 1927). Disp.: 144.7 - later model 153.2 cu. in. Brake H.P.: @ 4000 R.P.M. N.A.C.C. H.P.: 17.32. Main bearings: 3. Valve lifters: mechanical. Carb.: Stewart downdraft.

CHASSIS: No series designation. W.B.: 110.5 in. O.L.: 156.5 in. Frt/Rear Tread: 56/56 in. Tires: 31 x 5.00, later changed to 30 x 5.00 on June 25, 1927.

521

1927 Essex, coupe, HAC

TECHNICAL: Sliding gear transmission. Speeds: 3F/1R. Floor shift controls. Single plate clutch, cork inserts, running in oil. Shaft drive. Semi-floating rear axle. Overall ratio: 5.6:1, later 5.4:1 installed except for Spdbt. Mechanical brakes on two rear wheels. Wooden wheels. Rim size: 21 x 4 in.

OPTIONS: Front bumper. Rear bumper. Wire wheels. Spot lights. Leather upholstery (15.00).

HISTORICAL: Introduced Jan. 1927. Essex made 210,380 shipments to dealers during the 1927 calendar year. The president of Essex was Roscoe B. Jackson.

1927
Six, 6-cyl.

	FP	5	4	3	2	1
Tr	735	1400	4200	7000	9800	14,000
2 dr Sed	735	500	1100	1900	3500	5000
Sed	735	550	1150	2000	3600	5200
Super Six, 6-cyl.						
BT Spds	700	3600	7200	12,000	16,800	24,000
Tr	735	1400	4200	7000	9800	14,000
4P Spds	785	3000	6000	10,000	14,000	20,000
Cpe	735	700	1350	2800	4550	6500
2 dr Sed	735	600	1200	2200	3850	5500
Sed	795	600	1200	2200	3900	5600
DeL. Sed	895	650	1250	2400	4200	6000

1928

1928 Essex, coupe, OCW

ESSEX SUPER SIX — NO SERIES — SIX: The Essex for 1928 had an appearance which the *New York Times* described as "low hung." Its styling closely approximated, on a smaller scale, that of the Hudson. Thus it featured a trim, narrow radiator with vertical lines, and a winged man mascot in place of the old motometer. Other styling details included a bead line running from the radiator to the front windshield post, a shorter windshield visor, cowl mounted "saddle lights", and wider fenders. Although the boat-tailed Speedabout Essex wasn't offered in 1928 the Coupe models were given a more curved rear deck which in conjunction with other styling changes gave them a contemporary appearance. The Essex was also fitted with Hudson's new black rubber steering wheel. A major technical advance for Essex was the adoption of four-wheel Bendix, three-shoe mechanical brakes.

I.D. DATA: Serial numbers on dash and right rear frame cross member. Starting: 70627. Ending: 928657. Engine numbers on left side of cylinder block near water inlet elbow.

Model No.	Body Type & Seating	Price	Weight	Prod. Total
NA	2-dr. Rds.-3P	850	2365	NA
NA	4-dr. Tr. Car-5P	750	2305	NA
NA	2-dr. Cpe.-2P	745	2475	NA
NA	2-dr. Cpe. R/S-3P	775	2535	NA
NA	2-dr. C'ch.-5P	735	2560	NA
NA	4-dr. Sed.-5P	795	2660	NA

522

1928 Essex, sedan, WRG

ENGINE: Inline Six. Cast iron block. B & S: 2-11/16 x 4-1/2 in. Disp.: 153.2 cu. in. N.A.C.C. H.P.: 17.32. Main bearings: 3. Valve lifters: mechanical. Carb.: Stewart down draft.

CHASSIS: No series designation. W.B.: 110-1/2. O.L.: 156.5 in. Frt/Rear Tread: 56/56. Tires: 30 x 5.00.

TECHNICAL: Sliding gear transmission. Speeds: 3F/1R. Floor shift controls. Single plate clutch, cork inserts, running in oil. Shaft drive. Semi-floating rear axle. Overall ratio: 5.4:1. Mechanical brakes on four wheels. Wooden spoke wheels. Rim size: 20 x 4 in.

OPTIONS: Front bumper. Rear bumper. Leather upholstery.

HISTORICAL: Introduced Jan. 1928. Essex made 229,887 shipments to dealers during the 1928 calendar year. The president of Essex was Roscoe B. Jackson. This was the greatest sales year for the Essex.

1928
First Series, 6-cyl.

	FP	5	4	3	2	1
BT Spds	835	3200	6450	10,750	15,050	21,500
4P Spds	700	3100	6150	10,250	14,350	20,500
Cpe	735	700	1350	2700	4500	6400
2 dr Sed	735	600	1200	2200	3900	5600
Sed	835	650	1200	2300	4100	5800
Second Series, 6-cyl.						
Spt Rds	880	3350	6750	11,250	15,750	22,500
Phae	750	3200	6450	10,750	15,050	21,500
2P Cpe	775	725	1400	3200	4850	6900
RS Cpe	805	750	1450	3500	5050	7200
2 dr Sed	735	600	1200	2200	3900	5600
Sed	795	650	1200	2300	4100	5800

1929

1929 Essex, boattail speedabout, OCW

ESSEX THE CHALLENGER — NO SERIES — SIX: Essex styling for 1929 continued the basic form introduced in 1928 but there were a number of minor revisions. The beltline now fully encircled the body and a slightly larger radiator shell was adopted. Hudson officially labeled the Essex for 1929, "Essex the Challenger" and not too surprisingly revived the old "National Challenge Week" promotion in early March. During that time Essex distributors and dealers staged various acceleration, braking, fuel consumption and general performance events. In one such demonstration an Essex sedan climbed Fort George Hill, then regarded as one of New York's steepest grades from a standing start in high gear. In another run an Essex completed 30.5 miles through New York City on 1.5 gallons of gas. For the first time since the Essex F-head Six had been introduced Hudson officially released its horsepower rating, which turned out to equal the 55hp of the old Essex four.

1929 Essex, town car, WRG

I.D. DATA: Serial numbers on dash and right rear frame cross member. Starting: 928658. Ending: 1165673. Engine numbers on left side of cylinder block near water inlet elbow.

Model No.	Body Type & Seating	Price	Weight	Prod. Total
NA	2-dr. Spdbt.-4P	965	2500	NA
NA	4-dr. Phae.-5P	695	2490	NA
NA	2-dr. Rds.-4P	850	2460	NA
NA	2-dr. Cpe.-2P	695	2540	NA
NA	2-dr. cpe. w/R/S-2P	725	2600	NA
NA	2-dr. Conv. Cpe.-4P	895	2570	NA
NA	2-dr. C'ch.-5P	695	2635	NA
NA	4-dr. Std. Sed.-5P	795	2745	NA
NA	4-dr. Twn. Sed.-5P	850	2795	NA

1929 Essex, phaeton, WRG

ENGINE: L-head. Inline Six. Cast iron block. B & S: 2-3/4 x 4-1/2 in. Disp.: 161.4 cu. in. C.R.: 5.8:1. Brake H.P.: 55 @ 3600 R.P.M. N.A.C.C. H.P.: 19.4. Main bearings: three. Valve lifters: mechanical. Carb.: Marvel 5 downdraft 1-1/8 in.

CHASSIS: No series designation. W.B.: 110.5 in. O.L.: 156.5 in. Frt/Rear tread: 56/56 in. Tires: 30 x 5.00.

TECHNICAL: Sliding gear transmission. Speeds: 3F/1R (Spdbt. had 3 speed plus overdrive). Floor shift controls. Single plate clutch, cork inserts, running in oil. Shaft drive. Semi-floating rear axle. Overall Ratio: 5.6:1, Spdbt — 5.09. Bendix mechanical brakes on four wheels. 10 wooden spokes on wheels with detachable rims.

1929 Essex, coupe, HAC

OPTIONS: Front bumper. Rear bumper. Single sidemount. Dual sidemount. Steel sidemount cover(s). Eight Day Automatic radio. Cigar lighter. Wire wheels. Rumble roof for rumble seat. Utility trunk. Special trunk. Ball-jointed tire mount mirrors. Protectahood. Lap robes. Spring covers. Window awnings. Spare tire locks.

HISTORICAL: Introduced Jan. 1929. Essex made 227,653 shipments to dealers during the 1929 calendar year. The president of Essex was William J. McAneeny. Last year of phaeton until 1932. The 1929 Essex chassis was used for Hudson's first commercial offering, the Dover, which continued into 1931.

1929
Challenger Series, 6-cyl.

	FP	5	4	3	2	1
Rds	880	3300	6600	11,000	15,400	22,000
Phae	750	3150	6300	10,500	14,700	21,000
2P Cpe	745	725	1400	3000	4700	6700
4P Cpe	775	725	1400	3200	4850	6900
2 dr Sed	735	650	1250	2400	4150	5900
Sed	795	700	1350	2700	4500	6400
RS Rds	850	3400	6900	11,500	16,100	23,000
Phae	735	3300	6600	11,000	15,400	22,000
Conv	895	3000	6000	10,000	14,000	20,000
RS Cpe	725	900	1800	4450	6250	8900
Twn Sed	850	750	1450	3400	5000	7100
DeL Sed	895	775	1500	3600	5100	7300

1930

1930 Essex, Sun sedan, OCW

ESSEX CHALLENGER — NO SERIES — SIX: Essex was a significantly changed automobile for 1930. It had a longer, 113'' wheelbase, bodies that were on the average five inches wider than the 1929 versions along with a wider, by one inch, rear tread. Hudson said that "All Essex bodies are designed along modernistic lines" and this meant the Essex featured chrome plated hood hinges, a beaded body belt line and beaded running board aprons. The front doors now hinged at the windshield instead of the side pillars which, in conjunction with wider doors provided easier entrance and exit. Both Essex and Hudson featured rear fenders that were lengthened to cover the rear springs. The 1930 Essex was also equipped with a 3-spoke rubber steering wheel. In response to critics who believed the older 4-spoke, wood rimmed wheels were superior, Hudson retorted that "the new wheel has such a strength factor that repeated blows of a sledge hammer are necessary to demolish it." Additional interior features for 1930 included a new toggle handle windshield control and (on closed models) mohair and velour upholstery. Throttle and light controls were moved from the steering wheel to the dash. The Essex chassis was constructed of deeper, 7-1/16'' (4-1/2'' was used in 1925) side members and five cross-members were fitted. Due to the double-drop design of the side members the center of gravity was lowered by 1-1/2'' without any loss of road clearance. The Essex brake system was basically unchanged from 1929 but the shoes were redesigned to provide more uniform pressure over the drum contact area. The front suspension now was fitted forged cross ribs between the spring and king pin for additional axle

1930 Essex, Sun sedan, WRG

strength. At the rear a new axle design provided both greater rigidity and improved gear contact. All four wheels double-acting hydraulic shock absorbers replaced the single-action strap types used previously. The Essex Challenger was also equipped with worm and sector steering which Hudson reported was a boon particularly to women drivers "who find little physical exertion necessary to operate the new Essex Challenger many miles a day."

Hudson also redesigned the Essex engine for 1930. A larger, heavier crankshaft was adopted with a Lanchester torsional dampener, as well as a dual flow automatic lubrication system. This feature pumped oil alternately to the front and rear of the engine. The return to the crankcase was in the engine's center not the rear as previously.

I.D. DATA: Serial numbers on dash and right rear frame cross member. Starting: 1070300. Ending: 1234266. Engine numbers on left side of cylinder block near water inlet elbow.

Model No.	Body Type & Seating	Price	Weight	Prod. Total
NA	2-dr. Rds. R/S-4P*	695	2550	NA
NA	2-dr. Cpe.-2P	650	2660	NA
NA	2-dr. C'ch.-5P	650	2730	NA
NA	2-dr. Cpe. R/S-4P	685	2700	NA
NA	4-dr. Std. Sed.-5P	715	2805	NA
NA	4-dr. Tr. Sed.-5P*	775	2850	NA
NA	4-dr. Brgm.-5P	795	2850	NA
NA	2-dr. Sun. Sed.-5P*	695	2760	NA

* Composite steel and wood bodies built by Biddle & Smart, Amesbury, MA. Remaining model bodies of all steel construction by Hudson in Detroit.

ENGINE: L-head. Inline Six. Cast iron block. B & S: 2-3/4 x 4-1/2 in. Disp.: 161.4 cu. in. C.R.: 5.8:1. Brake H.P.: 58 @ 3300 R.P.M. N.A.C.C. H.P.: 19.8. Main bearings: 3. Valve lifters: mechanical. Carb.: Marvel 1-1/4 in.

1930 Essex, coupe, WRG

CHASSIS: No series designation. W.B.: 113 in. O.L.: 159 in. Frt/Rear Tread: 56/57 in. Tires: 18 x 5.00.

TECHNICAL: Sliding gear transmission. Speeds: 3F/1R. Floor shift controls. Single plate clutch, cork inserts, running in oil. Shaft drive. Semi-floating rear axle. Overall Ratio: 5.6:1. Bendix mechanical brakes on four wheels. 10 spoke wooden wheels with detachable rims. Rim size: 18 in.

OPTIONS: Front bumper. Rear bumper. Single sidemount. Dual sidemount. Steel sidemount cover(s). Radio. Cigar lighter. Wire wheels. Rumble roof for rumble seat. Utility trunk. Special trunk. Tire mount mirrors. Protectahood. Lap robes. Spring covers. Window awnings. Spare tire locks.

HISTORICAL: Introduced Jan. 1930. Innovations: new automatic choke, adjustable heat riser, Marvel carburetor had a new accelerator pump, three spoke rubber wheel, Lanchester torsional dampers, Dual flow lubrication system. Essex made 76,158 shipments to dealers during the 1930 calendar year. The president of Essex was William J. McAneeny.

1930
First Series, Standard, 6-cyl.

	FP	5	4	3	2	1
Rds	695	3900	7800	13,000	18,200	26,000
Conv	695	3300	6600	11,000	15,400	22,000
Phae	695	3350	6750	11,250	15,750	22,500
2P Cpe	650	700	1350	2700	4500	6400
RS Cpe	685	725	1400	3200	4850	6900
2 dr Sed	650	675	1300	2500	4350	6200
Std Sed	775	675	1300	2600	4400	6300
Twn Sed	700	850	1350	2700	4500	6400

Second Series, Standard, 6-cyl.

RS Rds	695	4200	8400	14,000	19,600	28,000
Phae	695	4050	8100	13,500	18,900	27,000
Sun Sed	695	1200	3700	6200	8700	12,400
Tr	695	1650	4600	7700	10,800	15,400
2P Cpe	650	700	1350	2700	4500	6400
RS Cpe	685	775	1500	3700	5200	7400
2 dr Sed	650	500	1100	1850	3350	4900
Sed	715	500	1100	1950	3600	5100
Twn Sed	850	650	1250	2400	4150	5900
DeL Sed	775	700	1350	2700	4500	6400
4 dr Brgm	850	725	1400	3200	4850	6900

1931 Essex, sport roadster, OCW

ESSEX SUPER SIX — MODEL E — SIX: Essex styling changes for 1931 were highlighted by a bronze chromium plated grid for the radiator shell, a straight, instead of curved tie bar for the headlights and fenders with a deeper flange that were designed to coincide symetrically with the general flow of the body lines. The double row of hood louvers found on the 1930 models were replaced by a single set that were considerably larger. All models had new bumpers, hubcaps, running boards and exterior hardware. The belt line moldings now extended the full length of the hood to the radiator shell. At the rear the body molding above the dust shield was higher and a larger rectangular rear window was featured. Essex interiors were available in Bedford cord, flat fabrics or velours and a new method of trimming significantly increased head room in all closed models. As much as five more inches of leg room was available in the Essex sedan models. A small but welcomed innovation was a new door lock mechanism which Hudson said maintained the outside handles in a rigid horizontal position, thus preventing the door rattle common to conventional designs. As was the case with all Hudson-built bodies those offered for the Essex had steel instead of wood roof rails. The Essex engine had the same 4½" stroke as in 1930 but its bore was increased by 1/8" to 2-7/8". Total displacement was 175.28 cubic inches. After many years of being extremely coy about the Essex engine's power Hudson became quite bold about its rating. In comparison to the 1930 Essex engine the new version developed 3 more horsepower at 20 mph and 5 more horsepower at 30 mph. Shared with Hudson was the Essex dual-flow oil system and new duralumin clutch disc.

I.D. DATA: Serial numbers on dash and right rear frame cross member. Starting: 1234267. Ending: 1281684. Engine numbers on left side of cylinder block near water inlet elbow.

1931 Essex, brougham, WRG

Model No.	Body Type & Seating	Price	Weight	Prod. Total
NA	2-dr. Spt. Rds.-2P	725	2400	NA
NA	2-dr. Cpe.-2P	595	2595	NA
NA	2-dr. Cpe. R/S-4P	645	2645	NA
NA	2-dr. Sp. Cpe. R/S-4P	725	2800	NA
NA	2-dr. C'ch.-5P	595	2690	NA
NA	4-dr. Std. Sed.-5P	695	2750	NA
NA	4-dr. Tr. Sed.-5P	775	2815	NA
NA	4-dr. Twn. Sed.-5P	735	2815	NA
NA	4-dr. Sp. Sed.-5P	855	2950	NA
NA	4-dr. Sed.-7P	895	2945	NA
NA	Phaeton	725	—	NA

ENGINE: L-head. Inline Six. Cast iron block. B & S: 2-7/8 x 4-1/2 in. Disp.: 175.28. C.R.: 5.8:1. Brake H.P.: 60 @ 3300 R.P.M. N.A.C.C. H.P.: 19.8. Main bearings: 3. Valve lifters: mechanical. Carb.: 1-1/4 in. Marvel 10-948.

CHASSIS: [Series E] W.B.: 113 in. Frt/Rear Tread: 58/58 in. Tires: 19 x 5.00.

TECHNICAL: Sliding gear transmission. Speeds: 3F/1R. Floor shift controls. Single plate clutch, cork inserts, running in oil. Shaft drive. Semi-floating rear axle. Bendix mechanical brakes on four wheels. 10 spoke wooden wheels with detachable rims. Free-Wheeling (35.00).

OPTIONS: Single sidemount. Heater. Wire wheels. Chrome windshield frames. Dual windshield wipers. Twin taillights. White sidewall tires. Spare tire cover.

HISTORICAL: Introduced Dec. 1930. Essex made 40,338 shipments to dealers during the 1931 calendar year. The president of Essex was William J. McAneeny.

1931
Standard, 6-cyl.

	FP	5	4	3	2	1
BT Rds	725	7500	15,000	25,000	35,000	50,000
Phae	725	4350	8700	14,500	20,300	29,000
RS Cpe	725	1025	2600	5200	7200	10,400
2P Cpe	595	950	2100	4700	6600	9400
Sed	695	700	1350	2700	4500	6400
2 dr Sed	595	675	1300	2600	4400	6300
Tr Sed	775	700	1350	2800	4550	6500

1932

1932 Essex, town sedan, WRG

ESSEX — SERIES E — SIX: The Essex had both all-new styling and numerous mechanical improvements for 1932. With their V-shaped radiators single piece bumpers and molded rear panels, the Essex models bore a close resemblance to the larger Hudsons. Making the 1931 appear extremely dated were the new models' curved windshield pillar, rounded rear body contour and deeper crowned fenders. The Essex's list of standard equipment included a "Quick-vision" instrument panel with tell-tale oil and generator signals, startix, adjustable front and rear seats and twin "Neutraltone" muffler. During the year the name of the Series E Essex was altered from its original Greater Essex Super-Six to Essex Super-Six Pacemaker before ending up as just the Essex Pacemaker when the Essex Standard Series was introduced in May 1932.

ESSEX — SERIES EC — SIX: The four EC models lacked dual cowl lights and were available only in a Louise Blue finish. The radiator shell was not chrome plated but painted to match the body. The EC Essex also lacked the chromed hood hinges and running board trim found on the Pacemaker Series.

I.D. DATA: Serial numbers on dash, right rear frame cross member. Starting: 1281685. Ending: 1300384. Engine numbers on left side of cylinder block near water inlet elbow.

Model No.	Body Type & Seating	Price	Weight	Prod. Total
Series E	4-dr. Phae.-5P	765	NA	NA
Series E	2-dr. Bus. Cpe.-2P	695	2775	NA
Series E	2-dr. Cpe.-4P	745	2840	NA
Series E	2-dr. C'ch.-5P	705	2860	NA
Series E	2-dr. Sp. Cpe. R/S-4P	795	2895	NA
Series E	4-dr. Twn. Sed.-5P	745	2950	NA
Series E	4-dr. Sp. Sed.-5P	845	3010	NA
Series E	2-dr. Conv. Cpe.	845	2760	NA
Series E	4-dr. St. Sed.-5P	775	2980	NA
Series EC	2-dr. C'ch.-5P	665	2785	NA
Series EC	4-dr. 3 Window Sed.-5P	735	2870	NA
Series EC	2-dr. Cpe.-2P	660	2680	NA
Series EC	2-dr. Cpe. R/S-4P	710	2750	NA

ENGINE: Inline. Six. Cast iron block. B & S: 2-15/16 x 4-3/4 in. Disp. 193.1 cu. in. C.R.: 5.8:1. Brake H.P.: 70 @ 3200 R.P.M. Main bearings: 3. Valve lifters: mechanical. Carb.: Marvel 10-997.

CHASSIS: [Series E] W.B.: 113 in. Frt/Rear Tread: 58/58 in. Tires: 19 x 5.00. [Series EC] W.B.: 113 in. Frt/Rear Tread: 58/58 in. Tires: 19 x 5.00 in.

TECHNICAL: Sliding gear transmission. Speeds: 3F/1R. Floor shift controls. Single plate clutch, cork inserts, running in oil. Shaft drive. Semi-floating rear axle. Overall ratio: 4.64:1, 5.0:1. Bendix mechanical brakes on four wheels. Choice of wire or wooden spoke wheels. Selective-control automatic clutch.

OPTIONS: Single sidemount. Dual sidemount. Fabric/metal sidemount cover(s). Clock. Cigar lighter. Interior visors. Passenger-side windshield wiper. Folding rear trunk rack. Shatter proof glass (windshield only or all around). Leather upholstery. Radio antenna. Glove compartment lock.

HISTORICAL: Introduced: Jan. 1932. An Essex Pacemaker set a new cross country, from Los Angeles to New York City of 60 hours, 20 minutes. Essex made 17,425 shipments to dealers during the 1932 calendar year. The president of Essex was William J. McAneeny.

1932
Pacemaker, 6-cyl.

	FP	5	4	3	2	1
Conv	845	3150	6300	10,500	14,700	21,000
Phae	765	3400	6900	11,500	16,100	23,000
2P Cpe	745	900	1800	4450	6250	8900
RS Cpe	795	975	2300	4950	6900	9900
2 dr Sed	705	850	1650	4200	5850	8400
Sed	705	875	1700	4250	5900	8500

ESTELMANN — The A. Estelmann Company was organized during the summer of 1913 with a capital stock of $15,000 to manufacture and deal in automobiles in New York City. In addition to A. Estelmann, H.A. Bell and P.A. Warnocke were involved. Manufacture is doubted.

E & T — Charlotte, Michigan — (1914) — In the inaugural Indianapolis 500 of 1911, Jack Tower drove a Jackson and his riding mechanic was Bob Evans. They didn't finish in the money there, but they teamed up afterwards to drive such diverse cars as the E-M-F, Warren-Detroit and Mason and to earn a good reputation for themselves in sporting circles. In 1914 Evans and Tower sought to parlay this renown into profit as the builders of a cyclecar called the E & T. Early that year they announced the formation of their E & T Cyclecar Company, with preliminary work on their car to be done in a machine shop in Charlotte, Michigan. Probably only the prototype was built; no evidence has been found indicating the E & T moved into manufacture.

1910 Etnyre, model T, touring, NAHC

ETNYRE — Oregon, Illinois — (1910-1911) — E.D. Etnyre announced during the fall of 1908 that he had "perfected a car" and would manufacture it. Interestingly, he also said that it would be of modest price. It was not until 1910 that he got into production, however, and by that time the price tag of his Etnyre had risen to the scarcely modest $3500 range. Several body styles were offered on a common 128-inch wheelbase, with 50 hp provided by the Etnyre four-cylinder engine. The Etnyre Motor Car Company was underfinanced, it limped into the 1911 season and did not survive it. Presumably, E.D. Etnyre returned thereafter to his longtime profitable business of manufacturing road-building machinery.

1910 ETNYRE
Four — 50 hp, 128" wb

Model E Touring-7P	3500	3100	4200	6300	10,500	22,000
Model T Cl.C.-5P	3450	2900	3700	5600	9100	20,000
Model N Rds.-4P	3400	3200	4300	6500	11,000	23,000

1911 ETNYRE
Four — 50 hp, 128" wb

Model E Touring-7P	3500	3100	4200	6300	10,500	22,000
Model T Dbl. Rumble-4P	3250	3000	4000	6000	9500	21,000

EUCLID — The Euclid Avenue Automobile Company was organized during the spring of 1904 in Cleveland, Ohio for the manufacture and sale of automobiles. Incorporators were Wade McIlrath, E.V.K. Hopkins, Clyde Martin, Webster A. McIlrath, Harry W. Orndorf and Benson McIlrath. Manufacture is doubted.

The Euclid Motor Car Company has been listed on various car rosters as producing an automobile in Trenton, New Jersey in 1909-1910. Business directories of the period indicate the firm operated only as a dealership.

EUCLID — Cleveland, Ohio — (1903-1904) — The Euclid was the second car produced by Hart O. Berg, and it was built alongside the vehicle bearing his name by the Berg Automobile Company of Cleveland. While the Berg was an unabashed imitation of the Panhard, the Euclid, as the company said, "crystallized whatever is best in American and foreign automobile building practice." The car was designed by J.G. Heaslet. Production began in July of 1903. Later in 1904 Berg sold out his business to the Worthington Automobile Company and although the Berg was continued awhile the Euclid was immediately dropped. It had been a $2750 touring car on a 90-inch wheelbase chassis powered by a four-cylinder 18 hp engine.

EUCLID — Cleveland, Ohio — (1907-1908) — The second Euclid from Cleveland had a lifespan which almost paralleled the first. It was also the second car produced by Herbert R. Palmer, whose first, the Palmer, had just died in Astabula. The Euclid Motor Car Company was organized in 1907 to produce two models of varying horsepower featuring Palmer's air-cooled three-cylinder two-stroke engine. Friction transmission and double chain drive were fitted on a common 100-inch wheelbase chassis. Production began later in 1907, and ended about a year after that.

1908 Euclid, runabout, NAHC

1908 EUCLID
Euclid — 3-cyl., 100" wb

	FP	5	4	3	2	1
Roadster (20 hp)	850	—	—	—	—	—
Tourer (35 hp)	1000	—	—	—	—	—

1914 Euclid, cycle-light car, NAHC

EUCLID — West Haven, Connecticut — (1914) — The Euclid Motor Car Company of West Haven called its product a "cycle-light car." And the Euclid indeed was part typical cyclecar, part typical light car. It had an air-cooled 15 hp four-cylinder engine, shaft drive, two-speed transmission, 100-inch wheelbase, 40-inch tread, total weight of 775 pounds — and was priced at $445. The Euclid company was headed by Edward A. Scheu, who began his career in the automobile business as a stock boy for Packard in 1903 and most recently had served as general manager of the Invader Oil Company of New York. Joining him in this venture were Everett S. Cameron, builder of the Cameron car, and his sales manager Frank S. Corlew, both somewhat at liberty because the Cameron company was in the throes of bankruptcy. The Euclid would be built in a portion of the Cameron factory. Response to the introduction of the car in Boston was most favorable, and extensive advertising plans were made, including a decision to call the car the Euclid Baby Grand. The people from Chevrolet immediately fired off a letter stating they had copyrighted that name for one of their models and would take legal action if Euclid used it. Litigation being undesirable, Frank Corlew solved that problem by renaming the Euclid the Grand Baby. But it did not long survive. By July of 1914 Everett Cameron had divested himself of his Euclid interests to return to his Cameron and other endeavors, that fall Frank Corlew and Edward Scheu quarreled, and by December the Euclid was no more. Incidentally, a water-cooled engine had initially been developed for the Euclid but had been found too expensive to manufacture for a car in the cyclecar class. Patented by Everett Cameron and called the C.S.C. (for Cameron, Scheu and Corlew), this engine, in both air- and water-cooled variations, subsequently found its way into such diverse automobiles as the Cotay, Parenti, Liberty and Sun.

EUREKA — The Eureka Automobile Company was organized in Jersey City, New Jersey during the fall of 1902 with a capital stock of $400,000 and the plan to manufacture automobiles. The venture took offices at 1 Montgomery Street. Incorporators were Nathan Metzenbaum of 11 Woodland Court in Cleveland, Ohio; Eugene W. Schneider of 600 Leonard Street in Brooklyn, New York, and Clatonia J. Dorticos of 58 West 109th Street in New York City. Manufacture of a car is doubted.

The Eureka Supply Company was organized in Buffalo, New York early in 1907 with a $10,000 capital stock to manufacture automobiles and motor boats. Incorporators were John W. Henry, Albert J. Nabinger and Ella M. White, all of Buffalo. Manufacture of a car is doubted.

The Eureka Taximeter Cab Company was organized in New York City late in 1908 with a capital stock of $25,000 to "manufacture, deal in and rent automobiles." Incorporators were H.M. Browne, F.W. Mills and E.J. Forhan. Manufacture of a car is doubted.

EUREKA — San Francisco, California — (1899-1900) — This gasoline car was built to order for one Charles L. Fair of San Francisco. It boasted some rather progressive features for this early period, including a three-cylinder 10 hp engine and a speed-changing lever providing four forward speeds. The car was designed by two local engineers named J.M. Ough and George Waltenbaugh. Maximum horsepower was generated at 650 rpm, and the car put up 30 mph in test runs, though as its inventors commented, "this speed is admittedly too fast for ordinary roads in California." The produc-

1900 Eureka, gasoline carriage (San Francisco), NAHC

tion possibilities of the vehicle were recognized early on, and rights to the carriage itself as well as patents acquired by Ough & Waltenbaugh were purchased almost immediately by the newly formed Eureka Automobile & Transportation Company. The aforementioned Mr. Fair was among the incorporators of Eureka. Ongoing negotiations for the buying "of a very large factory" in San Francisco followed, and several varieties of carriage, delivery wagon and truck were promised to be on the market within twelve months. Meantime, Ough and Waltenbaugh took themselves to Chicago where they too announced the forthcoming manufacture of an automobile. For some reason, probably undercapitalization, neither of these ventures resulted in production. With regard to the San Francisco effort, probably the subsequent death in an automobile accident of Charles L. Fair was involved too. Fair, who was the son of silver King James Fair, was killed racing a Mercedes in Europe. Early in 1903 one Sanford Bennett brought litigation against the Fair estate to collect money due him for an automobile patent of his which had been purchased by Fair.

EUREKA — New York, New York — (1902) — Early in 1902 the Eureka Automobile Agency opened a storage and repair depot at 2285 Eighth Avenue (between 122nd and 123rd streets) in New York City. There the company served as a distributorship for automobile parts and supplies, as agents for the P.T. car, and for a short time as the producer of a small 4 1/2 hp gasoline carriage sold under the name of Eureka. The P.T. Motor Company was out of business by the end of 1902, at which time production of the Eureka (which used a P.T. engine) also ceased. The company continued as a storage and repair depot.

1905 Eureka, touring (Detroit), HAC

EUREKA — Detroit, Michigan — (1905) — In early February of 1905 the Eureka Manufacturing Company of Detroit announced its forthcoming production of a four-cylinder car on a 96-inch wheelbase featuring a sliding gear transmission, right-hand wheel steering and King of Belgium side-entrance tonneau coachwork. "We are a little late to get to the shows," the company advertised after the shows were all over. This venture didn't survive the year.

EUREKA — Seattle, Washington — (1906-1907) — The Eureka Motor Company was incorporated in Seattle in October of 1906 with a capital stock of $50,000 and the "trans-Mississippi" rights to the Duo four-cylinder 20/24 hp engine. Behind this enterprise were A.D. Campbell, James H. De Veauve and H.R. Harriman in the company's executive posts, and F.A. Mitchell as general manager. Mitchell had previously been division master mechanic for the Sante Fe and mechanical designer for several Seattle components-manufacturing firms — and was Eureka's resident automobile expert. "In a general way the new car will be constructed to conform with Puget Sound conditions, as the sale is expected to be confined largely to this section of the country," *The Motor Way* reported in October 1906. "The company will build the frame and engine and follow the usual course of construction by buying the parts from the parts makers and assembling them here." To do all this, Eureka purchased the shop, machinery and location of the Seattle Manufacturing & Supply Company at 1409-13 Broadway (where Mitchell had formerly worked) and began construction there of a two-story plant. Probably the building was not completed before the venture went under. Probably the venture went under because $1900 was an absurdly high price tag for a pedestrian two-passenger runabout.

1906-1907 EUREKA
Model 1 — 4-cyl., 20/24 hp, 104" wb

	FP	5	4	3	2	1
Runabout-2P	1900	—	—	—	—	—

1908 Eureka, model D, motor buggy, (Beavertown), NAHC

EUREKA — Beavertown, Pennsylvania — (1907-1909) — The Eureka Motor Buggy Company of Beavertown produced a typical highwheeler. It featured friction transmission, solid tires, right-hand lever or wheel steering, and an air-cooled two- or three-cylinder two-stroke Speedwell engine. The car did not sell. Searching for a solution to this problem, the Eureka people believed they had found it late in 1908 when they persuaded a local businessman named Maxwell Kearns to invest in their venture. Kearns had ideas of his own, including the renaming of the car after himself, and an altogether new organization. The Kearns Motor Car Company was the result. Some Kearns in 1909 were also sold as Eurekas.

1907-1909 EUREKA
Model D — 2-cyl., 12/14 hp

Motor Buggy	650	—	—	—	—	—

Model L — 3-cyl., 15/18 hp

Motor Buggy	—	—	—	—	—	—

1909 Eureka, model L, motor buggy (Beavertown), NAHC

EUREKA — St. Louis, Missouri — (1907-1909) — The Eureka Motor Buggy Company of St. Louis produced a highwheeler that differed from the norm in featuring shaft drive, a selective transmission, and engine (air cooled twin) and gearbox built in unit. The car sported a right-hand steering wheel, was rather more racy looking than the usual motor buggy, and was probably faster too: A Eureka won the climb up Solomon's Hill in 1908. Charles Zimmerman was the designer of the car and the moving force behind the company. In 1907-1908 he offered his buggy in a wide variety of wheelbase sizes, though all body styles were of the runabout type, one of them with a modish rumble seat. In 1909, when he moved to a new factory on Olive Street, he changed his firm's name to Eureka Motor Car Manufacturing Company and settled on one 90-inch wheelbase chassis for all his cars. Though Eureka proved to be a popular name for an automobile, Zimmerman was the only one using it who gave a nod to Archimedes with the translation "I have found it" appearing in many of his ads. Conceivably, he may have been dissuaded from using his own name for his car because another highwheeler manufacturer in Auburn (Indiana) had preempted him. Following his Eureka venture, Charles Zimmerman found further work in the field, heading the automotive department of the L. Burg Carriage Company in Dallas City, Illinois beginning in 1910.

1907-1908 EUREKA
Two-Cylinder — 10/12 hp, 64, 70, 73 & 80" wb

Runabout	650	1600	2700	3800	5800	12,000

1909 Eureka, runabout, (St. Louis), NAHC

1909 EUREKA
Two-Cylinder — 14/16 hp, 90" wb

	FP	5	4	3	2	1
Runabout-2P	450	1600	2700	3800	5800	12,000
Runabout-2P	700	1800	2800	4000	6200	13,000
Roadster-3P	750	1800	2800	4000	6200	13,000
Surrey-4P	850	1900	2900	4100	6400	13,500
Light Delivery	850	1600	2700	3800	5800	12,000

1908 Eureka, auto-buggy, (Rock Falls), NAHC

EUREKA — Rock Falls, Illinois — (1908-1909) — The Eureka Manufacturing Company of Rock Falls produced furniture and caskets, and for a short while beginning in 1908 a motor buggy too. It featured a two-cylinder 15 hp engine, planetary transmission and wheel steering. The car had been introduced that year at the Farmer's Fair across the river in Sterling, with a number of orders resulting there. Eureka filled them, and built a hasty addition to its factory. In 1909 the wheelbase of the Eureka Motor Buggy was increased from 75 to 92 inches. But the car was discontinued later that year, the Eureka people deciding to confine efforts to a field they already knew. The production of custom hearse bodies followed, with Eureka continuing in this activity into the early 1960's.

EVANS — Bob Evans was one-half of the partnership which promoted the E & T cyclecar in Charlotte, Michigan in 1914. Refer to E & T.

The Evans-Eich Manufacturing Company was organized in Cincinnati, Ohio early in 1911 with a capital stock of $5000 to manufacture and repair automobiles. Behind this venture were William C. Evans, Wendel Eich and Earle C. Blair. Manufacture is doubted.

The F.S. Evans Company of Detroit, Michigan has appeared on various car rosters as the manufacturer of an electric automobile in 1903-1905. There was no such company in town at that time. A Frederick S. Evans was listed as the manager of the Commercial Motor Vehicle Company in Detroit, this firm building the Quadray truck from 1904-1905.

The Evans Pneumatic Motor Company of 126 Market Street in Camden, New Jersey was listed as an automobile manufacturer in the Hiscox book *Horseless Vehicles, Automobiles, Motor Cycles* published in 1900. Further documentation is lacking.

EVANS — Detroit, Michigan — (1910-1911) — Most likely, the Evans car did not proceed beyond the prototype stage. The first word of this venture arrived in late December of 1910 when the Evans Motor Car & Parts Company of Detroit announced its forthcoming manufacture of an automobile incorporating the two-stroke engine produced by the English Valveless Engine Company. The next word of this venture arrived in mid-1911 and revealed that the firm was now the Automobile Manufacturing & Engine Company and its product would be limited to commercial vehicles powered by four-cylinder four-stoke engines. Evans Limited trucks were built into 1913, the company moving from the Detroit area that year to Nashville, Tennessee. Although advance announcements from the firm indicated that it would once again try the passenger car field with a 1914 model, the company failed before ever getting to it.

EVANS STEAM AMPHIBIAN — Philadelphia, Pennsylvania — (1805) — The "Orukter Amphibolos," or "Amphibious Digger," as its inventor called it, was America's first recorded automotive vehicle. It was built by Oliver Evans who had nurtured ideas of steam road transport since before the American Revolution and it was built in 1805, when Evans was fifty years old. The Orukter was a steam dredge produced under contract from the Board of Health of Philadelphia for the purpose of cleaning the city docks. When he completed it, Evans fitted the machine with wheels, which broke down under the ponderous weight. His workmen built and fitted a new set. During the second week of July 1805, the vehicle moved under its own

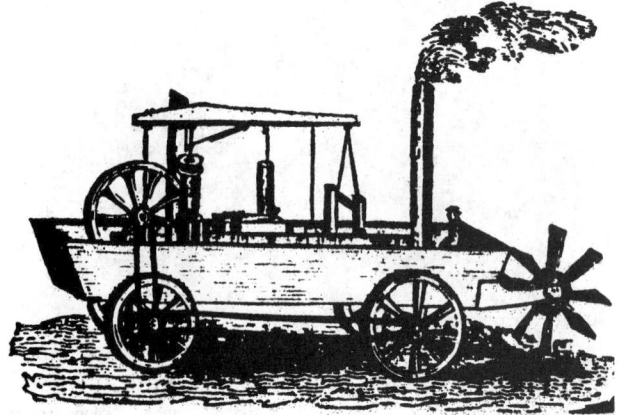

1805 Evans Steam Amphibian

1910 Everitt, model 30, touring, HAC

power. Further demonstrations followed at Centre Square (the site of Philadelphia City Hall today), and a short while later the Orukter was driven down to river's edge to do the job for which it had been built. Until his death in 1819, Oliver Evans manufactured and sold high-pressure steam engines, but never again was he able to secure financing to produce an automotive vehicle. Outside the town of Newport, Delaware — birthplace of Oliver Evans — a handsome sign bears testament to this "auto inventor."

EVANSVILLE — From 1907 to 1911, the Evansville Automobile Company of Evansville, Indiana produced a car called the Simplicity. Refer to Simplicity.

1900 Everett Steamer, carriage, WLB

EVERETT STEAM — Everett, Massachusetts, — (1898-1899) — The partnership of Milne & Killam began building light steam engines under Whitney patent at their shop at 10 Crescent Street in Everett in 1897. The year following they fitted one of their engines to a buggy and were sufficiently pleased with the results to organize themselves as the Everett Motor Carriage Company, and run up a few more examples that year for local sale. By 1899, however, Milne & Killam decided to abandon the manufacture of complete carriages and concentrate on just boilers and engines instead. In 1900 they sold their business to a group of Boston entrepreneurs who moved to town to establish the Oxford Automobile Company. In 1901 Frank Milne did build another steam car under his own name and offered to build others to custom order, but serious manufacture did not follow.

EVERETT — Joliet, Illinois — (1912) — During the waning days of the Economy Motor Buggy Company, producers of a highwheeler in Joliet, Illinois from 1908 through 1911, company president William R. Everett had designed an experimental electric-powered roadster and light delivery car which remained on hand when the firm's assets were sold to the Pratt Manufacturing Company early in 1912. William E. Pratt immediately announced his intention to produce the Everett electric under his own name, but the number of Pratts which followed had to be minimal or nonexistent. By September that year William Everett was in Valparaiso with his car and a proposition that the Commercial Club support him financially in setting up a factory there. Unfortunately, the Commercial Club proved loath to do this. No doubt, the only Everett ever in Valparaiso was the one William Everett had brought with him from Joliet.

EVERGLADE — In March 1907 *Automobile Topics* reported the formation in St. Petersburg, Florida of the Everglade Automobile Company. President was W.K. Cleveland, vice-president was F.E. Muller, and secretary-treasurer was A.T. Mullins. Said *Automobile Topics*: "This company owns a patent on a new appliance for the direct application of the power to each of the four wheels of a vehicle." Whether even a prototype of a four-wheel-drive automobile resulted is not known.

EVERITT — Detroit, Michigan — (1910-1912) — Essentially, the Everitt was the E-M-F without the F. After quarreling with their partner Walter Flanders, Barney Everitt and William Metzger left in mid-1909 to build their own car. It would be called the Everitt and it would be produced by the Metzger Motor Car Company, both partners thus being given equal billing in the new enterprise. The four-cylinder Everitt Four-30 was a specifications lookalike to the E-M-F Thirty built across town, which was not surprising since Everitt and Metzger had taken E-M-F chief engineer William Kelly with them. The planned output of 2500 units for 1910 was pre-sold before production began. Added in mid-1911 was a Four-36, and the year following a new Six-48. The slogan of "Self-Starting Everitt" for the latter referred to a compressed air device. Like Chalmers and Winton, among others, the Metzger Company was anxious to do away with the crank. Flanders, meantime, having tired of arguing with the Studebaker brothers about distribution of the E-M-F, decided to rejoin his old partners late in 1912. For reorganization purposes, the Metzger Company metamorphosed into the Everitt Motor Car Company which very soon was renamed the Flanders Motor Company. The new Flanders Six would be the old Everitt Six-48 with the addition of Gray & Davis electric lighting and starting. Latterday Everitt production figures are unknown, as are the number of Everitts produced in Canada by the Tudhope Company, to whom the rights had been sold in 1910.

1910 EVERITT
Four-30 — 4-cyl., 30 hp, 110" wb

	FP	5	4	3	2	1
Touring-5P	1350	2400	3400	4800	8000	17,000
Runabout 20	1350	2500	3500	5000	8500	18,000

1911 Everitt, model 30, inside drive coupe, HAC

1911 EVERITT
Four-30 — 4-cyl., 30 hp, 110" wb

Touring-5P	1350	2400	3400	4800	8000	17,000
Fore-Door Tour.-5P	1400	2500	3500	5000	8500	18,000
Roadster-2P	1500	2900	3700	5600	9100	20,000
Coupe-4P	1750	2200	3200	4400	7000	15,000

Four-36 — 4-cyl., 36 hp, 115" wb

Roadster-2P	1500	3000	4000	6000	9500	21,000
Touring-5P	1500	2700	3600	5300	8800	19,000

1912 Everitt, runabout, WLB

528

1912 Everitt, touring, WLB

1912 EVERITT
Four-30 — 4-cyl., 30 hp, 110" wb

	FP	5	4	3	2	1
Roadster-2P	1250	2900	3700	5600	9100	20,000
Touring-5P	1250	2500	3500	5000	8500	18,000

Four-36 — 4-cyl., 36 hp, 115" wb

Roadster-2P	1500	3000	4000	6000	9500	21,000
Touring-5P	1500	2700	3600	5300	8800	19,000

Six-48 — 6-cyl., 48 hp, 127" wb

Roadster-2P	1850	3100	4200	6300	10,500	22,000
Torpedo-4P	1850	3000	4000	6000	9500	21,000
Touring-5P	1850	2900	3700	5600	9100	20,000
Touring-6P	1900	2700	3600	5300	8800	19,000

1909 Everybody's, runabout, NAHC

EVERYBODY'S — St. Louis, Missouri — (1907-1909) — Everybody's Motor Car Manufacturing Company was organized in St. Louis in March of 1907. Its product was a two-cylinder runabout developing 10 hp at 650 rpm and featuring wheel steering, friction transmission and double chain drive. The Everybody's weighed 800 pounds and was priced at $450. Initially, production of the car was taken care of by the Success Auto-Buggy Manufacturing Company in St. Louis, but it would appear that Everybody's moved into its own plant shortly before going under in 1909, during which year the Everybody's price tag was raised to $500.

1907-1909 EVERYBODY'S
Everybody's — 2-cyl., 10 hp, 78" wb

Model C Rbt.-2P	500	—	—	—	—	—

EVINRUDE — Milwaukee, Wisconsin — (1914) — Although the detachable motor he had invented for rowboats would ever remain Ole Evinrude's chief claim to fame, he did dabble in the automobile business too, initially in 1910 by establishing the Evinrude Motor Company as a dealership in Milwaukee. In 1914 he announced his plans to manufacture a cyclecar but this venture seems to have proceeded no further than his working up of a prototype.

EWBANK — The Ewbank Power Transmission Company was organized in Portland, Oregon during the fall of 1911 with a capital stock of $250,000 for the manufacture and sale of motor vehicles. Herbert B. Ewbank and G.W. Stapleton were the people involved. Despite Ewbank's inclusion in various rosters, it does not appear an automobile was ever manufactured.

EWING — Geneva, Ohio — (1908-1911) — "The debutante of the season, the Ewing car, will make its bow to the Public on New Year's Eve, before the footlights of the American Motor Car Manufacturers' Association, at their Ninth International Automobile Show at Central Palace, New York." Although this advertising announcement from late December 1908 might seem rather fulsome for a taxicab, the Ewing was undoubtedly one of the prettiest on the market. It was designed by Louis P. Mooers, who had already earned a considerable reputation as engineer and race driver for the early Peerless cars. It was built by the Cleveland Auto Cab Company, and although the name Geneva had initially been considered, and some trade magazines called it such as well, the car was introduced as the Ewing, for Levi Edward Ewing who had formerly managed a match factory in Cleveland. Ewing was a substantial investor in the Cleveland Auto Cab

1909 Ewing, town car, MVMA

Company, and by February 1909 took over the firm completely and renamed it the Ewing Automobile Company. The Ewing was powered by a four-cylinder 24 hp engine and was made available as a taxi or town car on a 108-inch wheelbase chassis, both to sell at $3000. Approximately 30 cars were built in 1908, a total of 47 in 1909. Though this production was not estimable, it produced a small profit, though Levi Ewing found himself faced with another problem which had nothing to do with money. The town of Geneva was a small one, which offered no nightlife and scant diversion, and maintaining an adequate workforce of skilled mechanics was not easy. At first Ewing considered moving operations to Erie, Pennsylvania, but in October of 1909 he decided to sell out instead to William C. Durant who was in the midst of a buying spree of companies for his new venture called General Motors. Like so many of his purchases, the Ewing proved a financial liability and in June 1911 Durant dispatched the six taxicabs which remained unsold in Geneva to Buick and dissolved the Ewing Company. Levi Ewing, meanwhile, had moved to Findlay, Ohio to build a truck named for himself. And Louis Mooers, who had left Ewing in June 1909, was in Chicago building engines.

1914 Excel, 2-passenger roadster, LC

EXCEL — Detroit, Michigan — (1914) — The friction transmission and belt drive of the Excel were typical for a cyclecar, but its 1000 pounds dry was weighty and its appearance more substantial. The car's 91.5-cubic-inch four-cylinder water-cooled engine developed 12 hp. One model was offered, a two-passenger roadster on a 96-inch-wheelbase chassis at $450, marketed by the Excel Distributing Company of Detroit.

EXCELLENT SIX — Excellent Six was the slogan for the car designed by Ralph Lewis and financed by George D. Rider, which was produced in Muncie and Anderson, Indiana from 1908 to 1911. Refer to Rider-Lewis.

EXCELSIOR — The Excelsior Auto Garage Company was organized in Hoboken, New Jersey during the summer of 1913 with a capital stock of $25,000 for the manufacture of vehicles of all kinds. The incorporators were A.H. McMahon, C.B. Hermans and J.F. Marion, all of Jersey City. Manufacture of an automobile is doubted.

The Excelsior Compressor Company of New York City was organized with a capital stock of $25,000 during the spring of 1907 to manufacture "engines, cars and wagons" in Manhattan. W.J. Jeandron, H. Wallace and H.E. Taylor were the principals involved. Manufacture of a car is doubted.

The Excelsior Motor Manufacturing & Supply Company was organized in Chicago, Illinois early in 1912 with a capital stock of $500,000 for the manufacture of automobiles and parts. The incorporators were A.A Worseley, M. Lochwing and S.W. Jackson. Manufacture of a car is doubted.

The Excelsior Steam Car Company was a $500,000 Maine incorporation

529

from early 1905 for the manufacture of automobiles. J. Colby Bassett and P.C. Jack of Boston, and Norman L. Bassett and M.T. Leadbetter of Augusta, were the principals involved. Manufacture of a car is doubted.

The Excelsior Machine Company of Buffalo, New York has appeared on various car rosters as the manufacturer of an automobile in 1899. The firm does not appear in the Buffalo city directory for that year or the years surrounding. The Excelsior Machine Company is indicated, however, at Military Road near City Line in 1895. Documentation of any automobile built is lacking.

E.Z. GO-CART — Beloit & Monroe, Wisconsin — (1909) — Very little is known about the E.Z. Go-Kart Company except that its product was an early example of a genre that would only come into popular prominence many decades later. The company was organized in Beloit in November 1908 by Frederick Kaplan, Abraham Kaplan and A. Knells. Capital stock was $25,000. In the early fall of 1909 the firm moved to Monroe following the purchase of the Blue Label Cheese Company's factory in that town. The extent of production to follow is not known.

FACTOR • FWICK

FACTOR — A car called the Factor was cited in trade directories as having been built in 1915 in Bloomfield, New Jersey, with company headquarters across the Hudson in New York City. No company by that name appears in the directories of either city, nor do automotive trade publications of that era provide any further documentation. The Factor obviously wasn't one for long.

FADELEY-HILL — The Fadeley-Hill Company at 1336 New York Avenue in Washington, D.C. was listed in the Ware yearbook of the industry in 1910 as the manufacturer of an automobile. Further documentation is lacking.

1917 Fageol, touring, WLB

FAGEOL — Des Moines, Iowa — (1900)/Oakland, California — (1917) — The Fageol brothers — Frank R. and William B. — built an experimental gasoline car in their hometown of Des Moines in 1900. It was never marketed, the brothers becoming car dealers in Iowa instead. Not until their subsequent move to California did the Fageols contemplate automobile manufacture, and when they did, they thought big. In November of 1916, in association with Louis H. Bill (the man behind the turn-of-the-century California Motor Company of San Francisco), Fageol Motors Company was established for the manufacture of trucks, tractors and one of the largest and most expensive production cars ever to be made in the U.S.A. Wheelbases were to be 135 or 145 inches, with prices beginning at $9500 for chassis, $12,000 for production touring or speedster models, and soaring up to $17,000 complete with open or closed custom coachwork. Ivory

1917 Fageol, touring, HAC

door handles would be a special feature, as would be a sporting gearbox with five speeds forward and two reverse. Powering these cars would be the six-cylinder 125 hp aviation engine developed by the Hall-Scott Motor Company, also of California. Eighty miles an hour was guaranteed. How many Fageols automobiles were built perplexed historians for years. *Automobile Topics* in November 1916 indicated a planned output of 25 cars for 1917 but that was more hope than promise on Fageol's part. Two chassis were completed by early 1917 for use as exhibition models on the automobile show circuit. According to the Oakland Tribune, the coachwork for these two chassis was being seen to by C.P. Kimball of Chicago and Larkin of San Francisco. At the Chicago Automobile Show in February, Frank Fageol said, "There is no question regarding the sale of the first year's output." *Motor West* noted that 20 cars had been ordered at the Hotel Biltmore in New York City when the car was shown there. So selling the Fageol didn't seem to be the big problem, but producing it did. Not until August of 1917 did the company move into its new factory. And although

Fageol continued to promote its new car vigorously into early 1918, the idea of manufacture was given up soon after that. What had happened? The Fageol timing was bad. America's entrance into World War I brought shortages of materials, and Colonel Elbert J. Hall became preoccupied with government military contracts. The two Fageol cars thus far built were sold, one to a Dr. Antonio S. de Bustamante, Jr. of Havana, Cuba and the other purportedly to William Andrews Clark, Jr. (son of the one-time California senator). A third, and no doubt final, Fageol was built in 1921 for company president Louis Bill. A custom four-passenger speedster, it was fitted with an eight-cylinder Rutenber engine and Fageol's own seven-speed compound transmission. The Fageol company continued to build its farm tractors into the early 1920's, then turned full efforts to the truck, and later bus, production for which it would become well known. Interestingly, more than a decade later, Colonel Hall would become involved in another motorcar enterprise at the opposite end of the automotive scale from the Fageol — the economy DeVaux, powered by a 70 hp six of his design.

1917 FAGEOL
Six — 125 hp, 135 & 145" wb

	FP	5	4	3	2	1
Touring	12,000	3000	4000	6000	9500	21,000
Speedster	12,000	3500	4500	7000	13,000	25,000

FAIRBANKS-GRANT — Ithaca, New York — (1905) — In February of 1905 the Fairbanks-Grant Manufacturing Company of Ithaca, New York announced to the automotive trade press its intention to produce automobiles and motor boats. This announcement probably accounts for the appearance of the 1905 Fairbanks-Grant on automobile rosters. The company indeed was formed that year by Herbert C. Fairbanks, a machinist and model maker, but all references to the firm in the *Ithaca Weekly Journal* that year as well as the Fairbanks-Grant advertisement in the city directory indicate the production of motor boats, gasoline engines, power lawn mowers and experimental machinery only. Any car built, it was experimental only too.

FAIRBANKS-MORSE — Chicago, Illinois — (1908) — Prior to 1908 the only automobile built by the Fairbanks-Morse Company of Chicago was a single example of the Charter, a car designed by one of the firm's mechanics. In 1908 another car was built, and again most probably in a single example. The new Fairbanks-Morse was a touring car powered by a four-cylinder engine in a 108-inch wheelbase chassis featuring double chain drive. It was labeled "Model 1, Number 1" and was given a $3850 price tag. Undoubtedly this car was not put into production because Fairbanks-Morse concluded its fortunes would be better served in the commercial field. The company had built a railway inspection car in 1905, and would become quite well known for its tractors which would be produced into the early Twenties. Trucks of up to three ton capacity were built for a short time as well.

FAIRBURY — The Fairbury Motor Car Works was indicated in a trade directory from 1909 as the producer of a highwheeler in Fairbury, Illinois. Further details are lacking.

FAIRCHILD — The Fairchild Auto Company was incorporated with a capital stock of $100,000 in New Orleans, Louisiana in early 1910 to "manufacture, buy, sell, repair and rent motor cars and all kinds of vehicles." Incorporators were L.H. Fairchild, E.H. Fairchild, S.J. White and F.C. Bowlus, all of New Orleans. Manufacture of an automobile is doubted.

The Fairchild Electric Vehicle Company was organized in Brooklyn, New York with a capital stock of $50,000 early in 1912 for the manufacture and sale of automobiles. Incorporators were F.K. Fairchild, M.D. Fairchild and A.E. King. Manufacture is doubted.

FAIRFIELD — The Fairfield Motor Company was organized in late 1900 in Jersey City, New Jersey with a capital stock of $25,000 for the manufacture of automobiles. The venture was headquartered at 76 Montgomery Street. Incorporators were Joseph H. Sturgis, Bacon Wakeman and Frank K. Grain. Manufacture is doubted.

An automobile — or a truck — called the Fairfield has been indicated on car rosters as having been built in 1926 by the Automotive Development Corporation of Stamford, Connecticut. No documentation of this has been found. Stamford city directories for the period do not reveal such a company in town. A firm called Automotive Development Corporation was shown in the *Marvyn Scudder Manual of Extinct or Obsolete Companies* as having been chartered in the state of Delaware and officially dissolved in 1939.

FAIRFIELD — Portland, Maine — (1896) — "C.S. Fairfield . . . endeavored to apply a 10 hp kerosene motor to a buckboard, which he uses to convey summer excursion parties to resorts in the neighborhood of Portland," *The Horseless Age* reported in August of 1896. "He found, however, that the motor was unable to furnish the required power, either because of faulty transmission machinery or for some other reason." It does not appear that C.S. Fairfield ever motorized another buckboard.

1896 C.S. Fairfield, motor buckboard, NAHC

1909 F.A.L., touring, WLB

F.A.L. — Chicago, Illinois — (1909-1914) — The F.A.L. was built in the factory of the former Reliable-Dayton Automobile Company in Chicago. That this was planned as only a temporary measure is indicated by the fact that the Fal Motor Company spent much of its short life trying to find someplace else to go. In the spring of 1910, the company announced its forthcoming move to Champaign, that city having agreed to provide a site. Champaign reneged, however, and by early summer Fal was checking out Kenosha, Wisconsin. By late summer, the company was back in Illinois, prospecting in Waukegan. As it happened, the Fal people never did leave Chicago; instead they remained in the Windy City and moved from tribulation to tribulation. The F.A.L. or Falcar, as it was occasionally referred to, was a medium-sized four (Buda engine) offered in several body styles on a common 116-inch wheelbase. Originally introduced as A Car Without a Name, the men behind it quickly decided to use their own, that is their initials. The F.A.L.'s president was T.S. Fauntleroy, general sales manager was H.R. Averill and general manager was E.H. Lowe. This trio sold considerable stock in the Chicago area, much of it to farmers, but soon depleted all their available cash. N.H. Van Sicklen then stepped in and was made president, but quickly stepped out. Following him was E.H. Marhoefer, also of Chicago, and receivership in August of 1911. Petitioning creditors alleged that the assets of the company were being "neglected and dissipated" and that had certain unfulfilled contracts been carried through, substantial profits would have resulted. Early in 1912, C.J. Marhoefer, brother to E.H., announced that he had taken over and was reorganizing as the F-A-L Automobile Company. Late in 1913 he introduced a new model called the Grayhound, a two-passenger roadster with a cyclops headlight and sleeping provisions, the somewhat claustrophobic bed realized by pushing the seat cushion forward unto the floorboards for use as a pillow with the rear deck serving as legroom. "The entire length of the sleeping portion is eight feet," commented *Motor Age*, "and the height sufficient to permit of the sleeper turning." But the Grayhound didn't turn the F.A.L. fortunes around. In the spring of 1914 the company assets were sold at auction to A.O. Dunk of the Puritan Machine Company of Detroit. Total F.A.L. production, including the sleeper Grayhound, was claimed at the time to be 65,000 units. That was probably an exaggeration.

1909 F.A.L.
Four — 30 hp, 116" wb

	FP	5	4	3	2	1
Toy Tonneau	1650	2500	3500	5000	8500	18,000
Roadster	1650	2700	3600	5300	8800	19,000
Touring	1650	2600	3600	5200	8700	18,500

1910 F.A.L.
Four — 35/40 hp, 116" wb

Toy Tonneau	1750	2800	3700	5500	9000	19,500
Town Car	2250	2500	3500	5000	8500	18,000
Speed Car	2000	2600	3600	5200	8700	18,500
Touring	1650	2700	3600	5300	8800	19,000

1911 F.A.L.
Four — 35/40 hp, 116" wb

Fore-Door Touring	1850	2800	3700	5500	9000	19,500
Fore-Door Roadster	1850	2800	3700	5500	9000	19,500
Toy Tonneau	1850	2800	3700	5500	9000	19,500

1912 F.A.L.
Four — 35/40 hp, 116" wb

Fore-Door Touring	1850	2800	3700	5500	9000	19,500
Fore-Door Roadster	1850	2800	3700	5500	9000	19,500
Toy Tonneau	1850	2800	3700	5500	9000	19,500
Speed Car	1850	2800	3700	5500	9000	19,500

1913 F.A.L.
Four — 35/40 hp, 116" wb

Speedtype-2P	2500	2900	3700	5600	9100	20,000
Roadster-4P	2500	2900	3700	5600	9100	20,000
Toy Tonneau-4P	2800	2900	3700	5600	9100	20,000
Touring-7P	3000	3100	4200	6300	10,500	22,000

1914 F.A.L. Grayhound, NAHC

1914 F.A.L.
Grayhound — 4-cyl., 35/40 hp, 114" wb

	FP	5	4	3	2	1
Roadster-2P	2500	3000	4000	6000	9500	21,000

FALCON — The Falcon Motor Car Manufacturing Company was organized in Camden, New Jersey during the summer of 1910 with a capital stock of $125,000 for the manufacture and sale of motorcars. A factory site near Philadelphia was planned. Incorporators were Frank A. Kuntz, Joseph P. Murray and William S. Kell. Manufacture is doubted.

The Falcon Motor Vehicle Company of 1621 Fort Dearborn Building in Chicago, Illinois was organized during the spring of 1909 with a capital stock of $1000 for the manufacture of automobiles and accessories. Incorporators were Harry M. Fisher, Paulina Friedman and Leon Hornstein. Manufacturer is doubted.

FALCON — Youngstown, Ohio — (1905) — Walter F. Flynn was a young man with a lot of ambition and very little luck. In December of 1903 he bought a small piece of property in Youngstown near Court House hill from local rubber millionaire Henry B. Wick, who had just finished having an automobile built for himself. Flynn was anxious to get into the automobile business too, but satisfied himself initially by running a garage and a charging station for electric cars on his new premises. A factory would follow, he said, as soon as he could get the money. He did manage to build one gasoline car by early 1905, and he gave it a name: Falcon. Endeavoring mightily to interest local townspeople in manufacture — including Henry Wick, whose experience with his own car, alas, had sworn him off automobiles for the moment — Walter Flynn ultimately gave up on Youngstown and took his car to Michigan later that year. "Falcon Swoops Down on Bay City" was the headline in *The Motor World*. Having expended most of his funds already, Flynn couldn't afford to advertise, so he took local newsmen for a drive instead. That they were favorably impressed is indicated by an editorial appearing in the local Bay City newspaper which, commenting upon Flynn's desire to sell stock to form an automobile manufacturing company, noted: "Any one having money to invest in a legitimate industry which promises reasonably large returns from the outset will certainly find it to their advantage to confer with the secretary of the Board of Trade. Bay City should certainly leave no stone unturned to secure this industry." Apparently Bay City did. References from late 1905 indicate Flynn's intention to also establish a company to build a rolling mill in Bay City. Probably he had no better luck there either.

1909 Falcon, touring, NAHC

FALCON — Chicago, Illinois — (1907-1909) — John M. Larsen made ice machines in Chicago which provided him a comfortable living and a few motorcars called Falcon which probably never made him any money. Larsen's first effort was a gentleman's roadster with all brightwork silverplated and a price tag of $7500. A high-powered machine with a claimed 120 bhp, this Falcon purportedly was capable of two miles a minute. One would suspect that Larsen exaggerated his car's performance. In 1909 the Falcon Engineering Company was announced, and a new Falcon was introduced: a six-cylinder 90 hp nine-passenger touring car on a 136-inch wheelbase. It was priced at $12,500. Like the first Falcon, the second was built to order only — and one can safely assume the orders were few. By 1910 John Larsen returned full-time to the usual work of his Larsen Ice Machine Company. Although his car has on occasion been referred to as a Larsen, it was never marketed under any name other than Falcon.

1907-1908 FALCON

	FP	5	4	3	2	1
Falcon Gentleman's Rds.	7500	2500	4500	10,000	15,000	20,000

1909 FALCON

	FP	5	4	3	2	1
Falcon Touring Car-9P	12,500	3000	6000	12,000	24,000	30,000

1914 Falcon, 2-pass. roadster, WLB

FALCON — Staunton, Virginia — (1913-1914) — Although originally organized in Cleveland, Ohio, the Falcon Cyclecar Company moved its factory within months to Staunton, Virginia, and by early 1914 the sales and advertising departments had followed there too. As designed by Francis R. Hoyt, the Falcon was a racy-looking cyclecar with no doors. Belt drive was typical for the genre, as was friction transmission although the Falcon's was controlled by a wheel inset with the steering wheel rather than the usual lever. Hoyt was particularly proud of this feature, noting that it "obviates the necessity of the driver leaning forward and fussing with the gearshift lever, which is particularly aggravating under heavy traffic conditions." Pride was also taken in the automatic electric ignition system which permitted the car to be cranked from the seat. Not so meritorious was the Falcon's freakish suspension. It was wagon-like, with the front wheels turning from a kingpin in the center of the chassis. Transverse springs performed as the axle and turned with the wheels by cable control. The Falcon was probably pretty much shaken apart on the road after a few thousand miles. One of the roadsters did, however, successfully travel from Cleveland to Staunton on a factory test trip.

1913-1914 FALCON
Cyclecar — 2-cyl., 10 hp, 96" wb

	FP	5	4	3	2	1
Staggered-Seat Roadster	385	1000	2000	3000	5000	7000

FALCON — Memphis, Tennessee — (1916) — In December 1916 an announcement came from Memphis that a new four-wheel-drive automobile would be produced by the Falcon Motor Car Company which had recently been organized with a capital stock of $150,000 by a group of local businessmen. Heading this enterprise were J.G. Hamblett, E.E. Karlson, J.R. Manley, G.A. McGill and C.F. Kessler. Certainly manufacture did not follow, the prototype stage was as far as this venture proceeded. But the Falcon car idea was later resurrected by one of the promoters, George A. McGill, who showed up in Fort Worth, Texas in 1921 to promote a "new" four-wheel drive car named after himself.

FALCON — Newark, Ohio — (1922) — The Falcon from Newark was a 20 hp four-cylinder car on a 115-inch wheelbase featuring a streamlined body with silvered radiator and individual aluminum step-plates. It was the last-gasp effort of Halladay Motors Corporation to stay alive. Planned as a $1295 small-car companion to the Halladay six, it was announced to the press in December of 1921 and introduced to the public at New York City's Grand Central Palace in January of 1922. "A Car of Class Built for the Mass" was the optimistic slogan. By late March Halladay Motors Corporation was in receivership. Conceivably the Grand Central Palace show car may have been the only real Falcon built; the evidence suggests that all further Falcons were simply re-badged Halladays. Most probably, Halladay Motors had been entirely unaware of the other new Falcon from the Moller company of Pennsylvania which was introduced at the New York Automobile Salon shortly before.

1922 FALCON
Four — 20 hp, 115" wb

	FP	5	4	3	2	1
Touring	1295	2000	6000	12,000	18,000	23,000
Roadster	1395	2500	6500	13,000	19,000	24,000
Sedan	2085	1500	3000	6000	7500	8000
Coupe	1990	1600	3100	6200	7700	8400

Six — 46 hp, 115" wb

	FP	5	4	3	2	1
Touring	1595	3000	8000	16,000	24,000	30,000
Roadster	1595	3500	8500	17,000	25,000	31,000
Coupe	2295	2000	4000	8000	10,000	12,000
Sedan	2395	2200	4300	8400	10,500	12,600

FALCON — Lewistown, Pennsylvania — (1922) — The Falcon from Lewistown was introduced at the prestigious New York Automobile Salon held at the Hotel Commodore in late November of 1921. In essence, this Falcon was a light four-cylinder Moller with the added appeal of custom coachwork. Bodies were by Healey & Company, and three cars were on hand at the Salon. A center-door sedan was exhibited at the Healey stand, and a touring car and roadster were displayed under the aegis of H.P.M. Motors, Inc., this company being described as "Distributors of the Falcon, a High Class Light Car designed and built by the Moller Motor Company." In its *Automotive Reference Manual* published in November of 1922, the Automotive Service Bureau was careful to point out that the Falcon produced by Moller was not the same as the Falcon produced by Halladay, magazine editors having confused the two egregiously since the beginning of the year. All confusion had ended for the press by 1923, however, because both of the Falcons were dead by then. Historians have fre-

1922 Falcon, roadster, MVMA

quently been confused since. The Moller Falcon apparently did see a modicum production, the Halladay Falcon probably did not.

1922 FALCON
Four — 20 hp, 100" wb

	FP	5	4	3	2	1
Touring	—	—	—	—	—	—
Roadster	—	—	—	—	—	—
Sedan	4000	—	—	—	—	—
Coupe	3600	—	—	—	—	—
Speedster-2P	2800	—	—	—	—	—
Sportster-4P	3000	—	—	—	—	—

1927 Falcon-Knight, 4-dr. sedan, NAHC

FALCON-KNIGHT — Elyria, Ohio — (1927-1929) — Although former Dodge Brothers vice-president John A. Nichols, Jr. was the president of Falcon Motors Corporation, everyone in the trade press was aware that the man calling the shots in the company's affairs was John North Willys. The Falcon-Knight was planned as a companion car to bridge the marketing gap between the Whippet and the Willys-Knight. With prices in the $1000 range, the Falcon-Knight did this nicely. It featured a six-cylinder 45 hp Knight sleeve-valve engine and a full range of bodies on a 109-1/2 inch wheelbase. Eight demonstrators traveled a total of 400,000 miles in tests conducted by the Falcon company, and initially the Falcon-Knight was flying high. Production began at sixty cars a day, and on May 31st of 1927 the 3000th Falcon-Knight left the Elyria assembly line. Ten thousand cars were sold in the first nine months of production. "Just now is a wonderful time to keep sane," John Nichols commented in December of 1927, as the trade press enthused over the sensational performance of Falcon Motors Corporation during its first year. Possibly he was already aware of what was to follow. The last Falcon-Knight officially left the assembly line late in 1928, though a few remaining cars were assembled from parts on hand in January 1929. Then the Falcon company was quietly absorbed into the parent organization and its plant turned over to the production of Willys bodies. All Knight-engined cars from Ohio thereafter carried the Willys name.

1928 Falcon-Knight, coupe, HAC

533

1927-1929 FALCON-KNIGHT
Model 12 — 6-cyl., 45 hp, 109½ wb

	FP	5	4	3	2	1
Coupe-2P	995	2500	3500	5000	8500	18,000
Brougham-4P	995	2400	3400	4800	8000	17,000
Two-Door Sedan-5P	1025	2200	3200	4400	7000	15,000
Four-Door Sedan-5P	1195	2300	3300	4600	7500	16,000
Gray Ghost Roadster	1250	3300	4400	6700	12,000	24,000

Note: In June 1928 prices were changed to $1045 for coupe, $995 for two-door sedan, $1095 for four-door sedan, $1195 for Gray Ghost roadster.

FALLS — The Falls City Vulcanizing Company was organized early in 1904 in Louisville, Kentucky with a capital stock of $5000 for the manufacture of automobiles, bicycles and supplies. Incorporators were Albert H. Drake, Joseph C. Kirchdorfter and Herman Jansen. Manufacture of an automobile is doubted.

The Falls City Motor Company was organized in New Albany, Indiana during the spring of 1913 with a capital stock of $50,000 for the manufacture of automobiles. Ferdinand Kahler was the man behind this venture, which he soon reincorporated under the company name of Ohio Falls for the production of a car called the Pilgrim. Refer to Pilgrim.

The Falls Garage Company of Chagrin Falls, Ohio was organized late in 1912 with a capital stock of $10,000 to manufacture and deal in automobiles. O.S. Gore, T.O. Walts, H.D. Bishop, T.H. and A.E. Huggett were the people behind this venture. Despite occasional trade directory references from 1913 eluding to this firm as a manufacturer, it is believed never to have entered into formal production.

1921 Falls, roadster, JAC

FALLS — Sheboygan Falls, Wisconsin — (1921, 1924) — The Falls Machine Company was organized in 1901 in Sheboygan Falls for the manufacture of woodworking and milling machines. In 1908 single-cylinder gasoline engines for industrial or agricultural use were added, most of the production being sold to Montgomery Ward. A few years later gasoline engines for automotive use were introduced, and the firm was reorganized as Falls Motors Corporation. Its former woodworking business was sold to Jenkins Machinery Company. Falls engines were subsequently used in a number of assembled cars, the Grant, the Dort and the Elgin most prominently, though Courier, Maibohm, Ogren, Velie, Henney, Gardner, Apperson and Moon occasionally relied on the Falls as well. In 1921 Falls modified an Elgin roadster chassis into a smart boattailed roadster of which three examples were built for in-house use in the road testing of Falls engines. Until 1923 Falls engines had been principally fours and sixes, but in that year the company introduced a new straight-eight. Eight units were built, three of which went to the Elgin company just shortly before that firm went under. With the rapid dying off of so many assembled car manufacturers during this period, it was inevitable that Falls would fall too. By the end of 1924 the corporation had sold its equipment and service parts to varying firms in the field, and its buildings to Jenkins Machinery Company. A single Falls straight-eight remains extant, probably one of the three that had been destined for Elgin. Although the vehicle built around it in 1924 was most likely a tourer or sedan, it was revised into a race car prior to the Second World War.

F.A.M. — The initials represented French-American Motor, and a company by that name was organized in Cleveland in 1907 with automobile production slated to begin in 1908. Refer to French-American.

FAMILY — The Family Automobile Service Company was organized in Brooklyn, New York early in 1910 to "manufacture and deal in various kinds of motors, engines, vehicles, motor cars, motor boats, etc." Capital stock was $1000. The incorporators were John N. Williamson, Eliza De Mott and William G. Cooke. Manufacture of an automobile is doubted.

FAMOUS — East Chicago, Indiana — (1908-1909) — The Famous Manufacturing Company of East Chicago produced a completely conventional highwheeler with an air-cooled two-cylinder engine, two-speed planetary transmission, side lever steering, and rear wheels larger than those in front. (The friction transmission made available optionally in 1908 didn't survive into 1909.) When sales of the car under the company name didn't fare well, the decision was made to call the car a Champion. This allowed for promotional references to the "Famous Champion," but this did not help sales much either. Prior to automobiles, the Famous company had manufactured baling presses. After it failed with its Famous and Champion cars, the company went into the hardware business.

1909 Famous, model A, roadster, NAHC

1908-1909 FAMOUS
Famous/Champion — 2-cyl., 10/12 hp, 80" wb

	FP	5	4	3	2	1
Model A Rds.-2/3P	450	—	—	—	—	—
Model A Rds.-4P	600	—	—	—	—	—

1902 Fanning Electric, runabout, NAHC

FANNING — Chicago, Illinois — (1901-1903) — The business affairs of the Fanning Manufacturing Company were seen to by Frank Fanning, and the shop was run by his brother John. It would appear that Frank Fanning was responsible for the design of the Fanning cars. There were two varieties offered, the first a 2 hp $750 electric runabout with a sixty-mile range, the second a 9 hp two-cylinder air-cooled gasoline car available as a $1250 runabout or $1500 tonneau. The gasoline car had steel tubing in a wooden frame, a gear-driven fan which resembled a water wheel, chain drive and wheel steering. Frank Fanning was obviously a good merchandiser, because the cars were distributed by a number of motor companies on the East Coast. John Fanning was adept in production matters, because Fannings rolled out of the company in modest numbers but with commendable regularity. But on May 29th, 1903, there was a disastrous fire in the company's plant at Pratt and Morgan streets in Chicago, and the Fanning business did not survive it.

FANVIEN — The Fanvien Motor Company is indicated on various car rosters as being an automobile manufacturer in Detroit in 1910. There was no such company listed in the Detroit city directories from this period.

FARGO — The Fargo Motor Car Company was organized in Chicago, Illinois during the late summer of 1912 with a capital stock of $50,000 for the manufacture of automobiles and accessories. Three people named Kral — E.G., B.F. and J.J. — were the incorporators. Manufacture of an automobile is doubted.

FARGO — Detroit, Michigan — (1929) — The Fargo was introduced by Chrysler Corporation in the fall of 1928 as its entry into the commercial vehicle field. Both four-cylinder half-ton Packet and six-cylinder three-quarter-ton Clipper models were offered, and Chrysler sought to embue these vehicles with an "automobile" aura. "Passenger car lines of the most modern accepted standards are characteristic throughout the Fargo line," the company said. "Belt mouldings, passenger car type radiator shells, color scheme, general body steamlining, rounded rear body corners, fenders all contribute to that end." Also contributing in 1929 was the availability of an actual automobile on both the Packet and the Clipper chassis. The car was alternately called a sedan or station wagon by Chrysler, the latter more appropriately.

1929 Fargo, Clipper, station wagon, CHC

1929 FARGO
Packet — 4-cyl., 45 hp, 169" overall length

	FP	5	4	3	2	1
Sedan/Station Wagon	895	1500	2500	3600	5500	11,000

Clipper — 6-cyl., 65 hp, 175" overall length

	FP	5	4	3	2	1
Sedan/Station Wagon	1075	1600	2700	3800	5800	12,000

1916 Farmack, model B-30-35, roadster, WLB

FARMACK — Chicago, Illinois — (1915-1916) — Albert J. Farmer had an impressive automotive pedigree. On the East Coast he apprenticed at Pratt & Whitney and the Cole Firearms Company in New England and traveled to New York to become superintendent for Smith & Mabley, the European car importers who went on to build the famous Simplex automobile. He remained in New York to superintend the Rainier company and, when that firm was bought by General Motors, trekked west to Detroit to join GM's Northway engine building division and design motors for use in such cars as Cole, Oakland, Cartercar and Jackson. Thereafter he designed a four-cylinder engine with overhead camshaft which he built himself in Detroit and which ultimately interested some automobile people in Chicago. The result was the incorporation of the Farmack Motor Car Company in the Windy City in May of 1915. Among the incorporators of the firm was M.M. McIntyre who had previously been associated with the Coey company. Production of the Farmack began in the old Staver plant, and with prices in the thousand-dollar range, initial sales were good. Within the year, however, Albert Farmer happened upon some more Chicago businessmen who were anxious to invest and who liked everything about the Farmack except its name. In the reorganization that followed, the Farmack became the Drexel.

1915-1916 FARMACK
Four — 20 hp, 122" wb

	FP	5	4	3	2	1
Touring-5P	855	2200	3200	4400	7000	15,000
Roadster-2P	855	2400	3400	4800	8000	17,000
Cabriolet-2P	1155	2000	3000	4200	6500	14,000

FARMER-MOBILE — In 1907 the Summit Carriage-Mobile Company of Waterloo, Iowa advertised its highwheeler as the Farmer-Mobile. Beginning in 1908, only the Summit name was used. Refer to Summit.

FARMER'S AUTO — The Farmer's Auto-Motor Car Company was the designation given to the automobile venture of the Caps brothers of Kansas City, Missouri in 1905. The car was called a Caps, however. Refer to Caps.

Among the model designations of cars produced by the International Harvester Company from 1907 through 1911 was Farmer's Auto. Refer to International (I.H.C.).

The Farmers' Automobile Company was organized in Van Buren, Indiana early in 1909 with a capital stock of $10,000. Spearheading this venture was Zan Lozure who offered to transfer his carriage shop and half of the surrounding ground to the company for $800, or eight shares of stock. Plans called for the production of a highwheeler to sell for $425. The plans seem to have fallen through, however.

FARMOBILE — Despite its presence on automobile rosters, the Farmobile was not a car but instead was a gasoline-powered agricultural machine that was claimed to "plow 12 furrows at a time and . . . average 35 acres per day of 10 hours," among other farming uses. Its engine was an air-

cooled Frayer-Miller, and the Farmobile Manufacturing Company was an offshoot of the Oscar Lear Automobile Company, the producers of the Frayer-Miller car. The Farmobile was built in Columbus, Ohio from 1908-1909.

FARNER — Streator, Illinois — (1922-1923) — O.M. Farner of Streator put together an assembled car on a 115-inch wheelbase using a six-cylinder Falls engine and standard components throughout, and grandly incorporated the Farner Motor Car Company for its manufacture. Very few cars were built before Farner came to the stark realization that there was more to running an automobile company than putting a car together. In 1923 O.M. Farner reduced his 1922 price by a hundred dollars. By 1924 he had given up.

1922 FARNER
Model A — 6-cyl., 50 hp, 115" wb

	FP	5	4	3	2	1
Touring-5P	1195	2400	3400	4800	8000	17,000

1923 FARNER
Model A — 6-cyl., 50 hp, 115" wb

	FP	5	4	3	2	1
Touring-5P	1095	2400	3400	4800	8000	17,000

FARNSWORTH — The Farnsworth Motor Company was organized in Chehalis, Washington with a capital stock of $25,000 during the fall of 1911 to manufacture and deal in motors and motor vehicles. H.F. Farnsworth and Dick Balfour were the partners behind this venture. Manufacture of an automobile is doubted.

FARNUM — Baraboo, Wisconsin — (1901) — That C.H. Farnum of Baraboo had built an automobile to his own design was documented in *The Motor Age* in August 1901. Further details are lacking.

FARRAR — All that we know about this car is that an emblem exists which indicates Woodville, Massachusetts as the location of its manufacture. Historian William J. Lewis discovered it, and has a hypothesis. Years ago the very small town of Woodville had a general store called Farrar's Market. The only automobile known to have been built in Woodville was the Barnhard-Briggs in 1906. Conceivably, Farrar put up the money for A.H. Barnhard and J.L. Briggs to launch their venture and received top billing in exchange.

FARRINGTON — The Farrington Automobile Company was organized in Chicago, Illinois during the summer of 1910 with a $10,000 capital stock to manufacture and deal in automobiles and accessories. Incorporators were Joseph T. Delfosse, W.H. Farrington and Samuel F. Scott. Manufacture of an automobile is doubted.

1904 Fast, gasoline touring, NAHC

FAST — Milwaukee, Wisconsin — (1904) — H. Fast of Milwaukee manufactured motors, transmissions, running gears and accessories in a small shop the business title of which he changed to Fast Machine & Tool Works in 1903. In 1904 the George O. Francke Automobile Company of Milwaukee announced its forthcoming manufacture of a two-cylinder 12 hp gasoline car which was the result of "three years' experimenting." The experimenting was that of H. Fast, however, and the car was named after him. When sales did not immediately boom, the Francke company quickly lost interest, and Fast returned to his machine shop.

FAUBER — Indianapolis, Indiana — (1914) — In one year William Harrison Fauber failed with two different cars. The first he called a Bi-car, a two-wheeler with "spring stabilizers" for use upon entrance or when standing, a motorcycle-type frame and engine, tandem seating, a wheel for steering, and a wheelbase of 66 inches. It was priced at $295, but Fauber advised that "any man can save $100 by assembling the Bi-car himself." The second he called an Auto-Cyclecar which had the same engine but on an 80-inch wheelbase chassis, with a runabout offered in standard tread, a light delivery on a 44-inch tread. Although Fauber maintained his offices at 15 Murray Street in New York City, his cars were built for him by Cyclecar Engineering Company of Indianapolis. In announcing his entry into the automobile industry in late 1913, Fauber reported that he had produced 100 cars in 1902, neglecting to mention that he had not designed them but instead assembled them in Elgin, Illinois for Walter L.

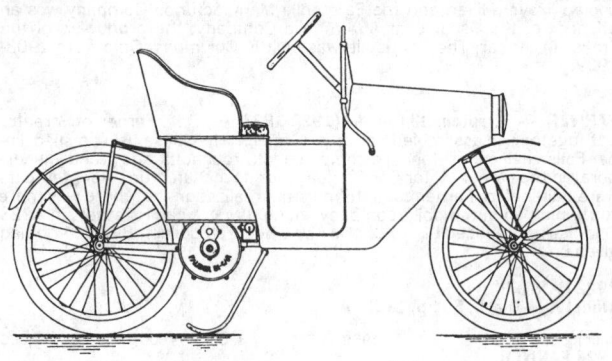

1914 Fauber, Bi-car, runabout, WLB

Marr, whose name they bore. (His previous business in Elgin had been the manufacture of a one-piece crank hanger for bicycles.) In announcing his exit from the automobile industry late in 1914, Fauber indicated that he would now pursue aeronautical interest, including the Fauber Hydroplane he had invented.

1914 FAUBER
Bi-car — 2-cyl., 8 hp, 66" wb

	FP	5	4	3	2	1
Tandem Two-Seater	295	1400	2400	3500	5300	10,000
Auto-Cyclecar — 2-cyl., 8 hp, 80" wb						
Standard Tread Runabout	285	1450	2450	3600	5400	10,500
Light Delivery	285	1100	2200	3200	4900	9000

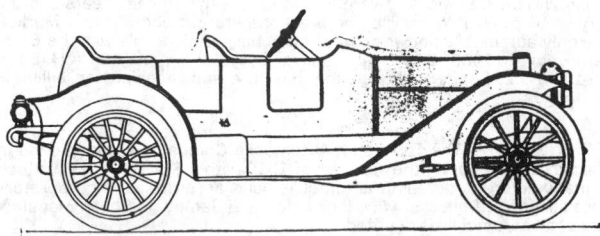

1910 Faulkner-Blanchard, Gunboat Six, MVMA

FAULKNER-BLANCHARD — Detroit, Michigan — (1910) — M.A. Faulkner was the major domo behind the Faulkner-Blanchard, and the car was designed by a committee composed of F.W. Blanchard, E.J. Cook and W.I. Dagg. The first prototype was on the road in mid-August of 1910. Production was to be centered on one $2500 model called the Gunboat Six, a 33 hp touring car on a 121-inch wheelbase. In early September the formation of the Faulkner-Blanchard Motor Car Company was announced, and the press was advised that a location for manufacture had not yet been found. Conceivably, it never was, since the Faulkner-Blanchard quietly slipped from sight shortly thereafter.

FAULTLESS — Although the cyclecar produced by the Valley Boat & Engine Company of Saginaw, Michigan was originally announced to the trade press under the name of Faultless, by the time the car arrived on the market, its name had been changed to Saginaw. Refer to Saginaw.

1909 Fawick Flyer, "Silent Sioux," OCW

FAWICK FLYER — Sioux Falls, South Dakota — (1908-1912) — Thomas L. Fawick was an ambitious young man. In 1906, while in his mid-teens, he left his job in his brother's Sioux Falls plumbing firm and spent the next year designing and building his first automobile which he finished soon after his eighteenth birthday. It had two cylinders, ran well, and elicited the interest of a number of Sioux Falls businessmen — John F.D. Mundt, R.J. Wells, Richard Brown and G.W. Burnside — in backing its manufacture. At this point, the car was called the Silent Sioux and the new firm for its building the Silent Sioux Auto Manufacturing Company — and the story becomes a bit confused. Although Fawick's first car was a twin, the next

one was a four, as were all subsequent. The engine was supplied by the Waukesha Motor Company in Wisconsin, and the hand-forged aluminum body was built to Fawick's specifications by the Charles Abresch Company of Milwaukee. Trade press references of the day indicate that the Silent Sioux Company itself had located in Milwaukee. Undoubtedly, this could have been considered because of the superior manufacturing facilities there, but the idea was quickly abandoned, and the project returned to Sioux Falls. The Silent Sioux Auto Manufacturing Company which had been organized in 1909 became the Fawick Motor Car Company in 1910. Of the original investors, only John F.D. Mundt remained, joined by Nevis O. Fawick, young Tom's plumber brother, and Harry N. Hanson, a machinist. The Fawick Flyer, like the Silent Sioux, remained a 40 hp four (Waukesha engine) on a 124-inch wheelbase. A five-passenger touring was the only body style built, and the price tag was $3000. A Flyer built late in 1910 sported four doors, which was claimed at the time to be a first in America, and it was in this car that former President Theodore Roosevelt rode when he visited Sioux Falls later that year. A total of five cars were produced. Although the profit on each of the Flyers sold was $600 — a fine figure for the day — Tom Fawick decided that manufacturing a car in Sioux Falls was not a viable proposition. Subsequently, he found a number of others that were. During the World War I years, he was in Wisconsin with his Twin-Disc Clutch Company. In the late Twenties, he designed an overdrive mechanism for automobile transmissions which he sold to Borg-Warner. In the Thirties Chrysler bought his engine rubber-mount design. Following the Second World War, he acquired the Federal Motor Truck Company. At the time of his death in the late Sixties, he was president of Fawick Corporation, a manufacturer of industrial clutches and brakes in Cleveland.

FAY — Thomas J. Fay was one-half of the partnership which produced the Ellsworth in New York City in 1907. Refer to Ellsworth.

The C.E. Fay Company was organized in Boston, Massachusetts during the summer of 1917 with a capital stock of $100,000 to manufacture automobiles and motor vehicles. Incorporators were C.E. Fay, E.H.M. Evans and A.M. Fay. Manufacture of an automobile is doubted. C.E. Fay had formerly been manager of the Ford assembly plant in Cambridge. Subsequently he became a Maxwell (later Chrysler) dealer.

FAY — Greenville, Pennsylvania — (1912) — The Fay was perhaps a bit of good-natured blackmail. When the Empire Automobile Company of Indianapolis was sold in December 1911, the new owners found themselves with a car but no place to build it since its factory had already been turned over to production of Prest-O-Lite starters. Their search for a new site took them to Greenville, Pennsylvania and the Greenville Metal Products Company, an automotive parts manufacturing concern organized in 1910 as a subsidiary of the Salisbury Axle Company of Jamestown, New York. Greenville president Frank Fay said he would be delighted to build the new Empire Model 25 that had been developed if the old Empire Model Twenty for which parts still remained would be marketed as the Fay. And so it was. The Fay survived as long as the remaining parts did. Production of the Empire was continued awhile in Pennsylvania, but by 1914 Greenville turned its attention to railroad car manufacture, in which business it remains today as the Greenville Steel Car Company. Frank Fay later became a Pennsylvania state senator.

1912 FAY
Model Twenty — 4-cyl., 20 hp, 96" wb

	FP	5	4	3	2	1
Fay Touring	—	—	—	—	—	—

FAY — New York, New York — (1921) — That Fay Motors Company of 203 West 54th Street in New York City was the manufacturer of an automobile for export only was indicated in the *Chilton Automobile Directory* of 1921. If there was indeed any manufacture at all, the trade press was not made aware of it. Conceivably, the people behind Fay may have had a quick change of mind and evolved into the Fay Taxicab Company, Inc. which turned up in New York the year following and sold out to Yellow Cab in 1923. The taxis in Fay's fleet numbered 400, but they had been purchased not manufactured.

FEAR NAUGHT — The Fear Naught Company was organized in New York City during the fall of 1911 with a capital stock of $100,000 for the manufacture of automobiles and other vehicles. Incorporators were J.M. Davis and F.C. Munson of New York City, and R.T. Hughes of Rutherford, New Jersey. Manufacture of an automobile is doubted.

FEDERAL — A number of automobile-manufacturing ventures carrying the Federal name seem to have entered and exited the field without producing any cars. They are the following:

The Federal Company of Cleveland, Ohio, organized during the late spring of 1905 with a capital stock of $10,000. Incorporators were T.G. Hogrett, George C. Whitcomb, B.F. Williams, C.G. Easty and W.G. McAleenan.

The Federal Automobile Company of America, organized in Sioux Falls, South Dakota early in 1902 with a capital stock of $2 million. Incorporators were William F. Buckley, Edward F. Wade and J.W. Boyce.

The Federal Motor Company of Buffalo, New York, organized with a capital stock of $10,000 early in 1910. Incorporators were Henry A. Dann, Troilus C. Koons, Ernest C. Anderson and Clyde R. Sikes.

The Federal Motor Car Company of Chicago, Illinois, organized late in 1911 with a capital stock of $10,000. Incorporators were C.W. Rhoades, D.F. Rosenthal and L.S. Kositchek.

The Federal Motor Manufacturing Company of Washington, D.C., organized with a $100,000 capital stock early in 1915. Incorporators were R.B. Owen, B. Buehner and W.F.A. Buehner.

The Federal Motor Supply Company of Cincinnati, Ohio, organized during the fall of 1912 with a capital stock of $250,000. Incorporators were G.W. Platt, E.C. Schmitt, R.L. Dollings, A.M. Braddy and M.F. Platt.

The Federal Taxicab Company of Jersey City, New Jersey, organized early in 1908 with a capital stock of $200,000. Incorporators were E. McMills, R.F. Tully and C.A. Cole.

1901 Federal Steam, runabout, NAHC

FEDERAL STEAM — Brooklyn, New York — (1901-1902) — Chief engineer of the Federal Motor Vehicle Company of Brooklyn was one Charles L. King, and he was completely responsible for the design of the Federal steam carriage. Its two-cylinder 10 hp compound engine and boiler were placed in the rear of the seat, its frame was rigid angle iron, and the entire body was made of metal. The solid construction throughout, "to withstand hard usage," its makers said, was admirable, and so was the price tag of $750. Nonetheless, it does not appear that the Federal Motor Vehicle Company survived into 1903.

1909 Federal, runabout, NAHC

FEDERAL — Chicago & Rockford, Illinois/Elkhart, Indiana — (1907-1909/1909) — The Federal was designed and promoted by John F. Waters of Chicago. A typical highwheeler, it was manufactured early in 1907 by the Federal Motor Car Company, later that year by the Federal Automobile Company, yet another reorganization ensuing early in 1908 with a move to nearby Rockford and reincorporation as the Rockford Automobile & Engine Company. The car was briefly renamed the Rockford in 1908. Waters remained with the organization throughout. An air-cooled two-cylinder two-stroke machine with its flywheel serving as the friction disc for the transmission, the Federal was offered only as a two-seater, fully fendered and with folding top by 1909, and fitted with solid tires as standard equipment, pneumatics available for $100 more. Factory superintendent Adam Ziska took journalist Hugh Dolnar on a test drive in April of 1909 during which the solid narrow tires "were often ten inches below the top surface of the mud, which obstructed the carburetor intake more than once." With pneumatic tires, Dolnar observed tellingly, the tires would have stayed on top of the frozen mud crust. In May of 1909 the Federal venture suffered its final reorganization when the Industrial Automobile Company of Elkhart, Indiana bought the Rockford Company lock, stock and barrel, though possibly without John F. Waters. A few cars may have been built in Indiana before Industrial failed later that year.

1907 FEDERAL
Model B — 2-cyl., 14 hp, 80" wb

	FP	5	4	3	2	1
Runabout-2P	475	2300	3300	4600	7500	16,000

1908 FEDERAL
Model C — 2-cyl., 14 hp, 80" wb

Runabout-2P	600	2300	3300	4600	7500	16,000

1909 FEDERAL
Model E — 2-cyl., 14 hp, 80" wb

Runabout-2P	800	2300	3300	4600	7500	16,000
Victoria-2P	800	2200	3300	4400	7000	15,000

FEE-AMERICAN — Detroit, Michigan — (1907-1908) — The Fee-Bock Automobile Company of Detroit was an authorized agency for the two-stroke Elmore that was produced in Clyde, Ohio. Robert L. Fee headed the company, and one member of his staff, Edward Zolle, convinced him that they could build a two-stroke car equally as meritorious as the Elmore. The Fee-American was the result, a shaft-drive 18-20 hp two-cylinder touring car with a $1500 price tag. Work on the prototype was done entirely in secret, and therefore reporters were surprised at its appearance at the Fee-Bock Automobile Company stand during the Detroit Automobile Show of February 1907. "The first car is rather pretty," one journalist noted, "with its dress of French gray and red running gear." Limited production did follow, but by 1909 Fee-Bock had come to the conclusion that selling cars was easier than manufacturing them, and the only vehicles shown at the company's stand during Detroit automobile show time thereafter were Elmores.

FEENY — Muncie, Indiana — (1914) — In 1910 Edmund J. Feeny of Muncie invented a new and effective type of vacuum cleaner and by 1914 his Feeny Manufacturing Company at the corner of Ohio and Washington was prospering in its manufacture as well as that of clothes reels. While a cyclecar might seem far removed from those products, Feeny was regarded in Muncie as the inventive sort, and he believed the machinery in his plant as "well suited" to automobile manufacture as household equipment. Though specifications regarding the Feeny are lacking, apparently a few cars were built and provided company salesmen to test in their travels. Whether Edmund Feeny found his cyclecar itself lacking in some particular, or whether he was a smart enough businessman to recognize the ultimate failure of the entire cyclecar genre, is not known. But the Feeny cyclecar never joined the Feeny vacuum cleaners and clothes reels in manufacture.

FEERRAR — Lock Haven, Pennsylvania — (1895) — In 1895 J.C.W. Feerrar of Lock Haven submitted his entry into the Chicago Times-Herald contest to be held that November. The car he was preparing for the event was not completed on time, however, and whether he ever did successfully test it has not been documented.

FEISTER — During the summer of 1901 the Feister Engineering Company was organized in the state of Delaware for the manufacture of automobiles. H.P. Feister was the promoter of this venture. Manufacture of an automobile is doubted.

FELL — Winchendon, Massachusetts — (1905) — Edward S. Fell of Winchendon was the inventor of a motor sleigh in 1905 which he described thusly: "It is steered by moving the front runners in the same manner as the front wheels of an automobile. The frame is supported on springs on the runners. The power is supplied by a high speed air cooled gasoline motor at the forward part of the sleigh. The propulsion is gained by two pushers operated by cranks and connecting rods at the rear of the sleigh." There was an American Motor Sleigh Company organized in Boston in 1905, but Edward Fell does not appear to have been involved in that venture.

FELLWOCK — Evansville, Indiana — (1907-1908) — The Fellwock Automobile Manufacturing Company was organized in Evansville in early 1907 with a capital stock of $20,000. Manufacturing automobiles was the stated intent, and the venture was a family affair, with P.B. Fellwock, W.E. Fellwock and J.F. Fellwock involved. Such manufacture as followed was strictly a sideline activity, and to specific customer order. The Fellwock mainstay was automobile repair, and in this the shops at 210 East Pennsylvania Street were kept busy. Fellwock also built tonneau bodies for the Maxwells, Mitchells and Fords that were sold in town.

FENKER — The H.W. Fenker Company of Cincinnati, Ohio was organized during the summer of 1916 with a capital stock of $50,000 for the manufacture of automobiles and accessories. Incorporators were H.W. Fenker, J.L. Clarke, J.D. Henry and James R. Steward. Manufacture of an automobile is doubted.

FENN — The Fenn-Sadler Machine Company of Hartford, Connecticut was indicated in a trade directory of 1904 as having produced an automobile that year. Further documentation is lacking. There was such a company at Hartford at the time, at 734 Main Street, though aside from general machine work, no references remain extant regarding its activity.

FENTON — In October of 1904 a venture styling itself the Fenton Automobile Company was noted in the trade press as building a 20 hp car in Fenton, Michigan. Further details are lacking.

FENTON — Fenton, Michigan — (1913-1914) — Oscar J. Howick, formerly of Lozier and Packard, and more recently Duquesne, was the designer of the product, but the moving spirit behind the Fenton Cyclecar Company was George Jenks, a former automobile salesman. The Fenton's two-cylinder air-cooled engine, belt drive and friction transmission were typically cyclecar, but its body styling with a deep vee front, full doors and fenders, and leather upholstery was more elegant than the norm. The wheelbase was 96 inches, the tread 36. Two passengers sat side-by-side in the Fenton, and the price was $375. Preliminary announcements of the new car, from September 1913, indicate that Signet was being considered for its name. By the time production began later that fall, however, the decision had been made for Fenton. On March 23rd, 1914, tragedy struck this automotive enterprise with the sudden death of George Jenks. The Fenton Cyclecar Company was reorganized within two months as the Koppin Motor Company by H.S. Koppin, who owned the former A.J. Phillips plant in Fenton which had been vacant for two years. Koppin planned to

537

1914 Fenton, 2-pass. roadster cyclecar, WLB

1920 Ferris, Six, touring, WLB

move manufacture into this plant, and he seems to have done so, but by the end of 1914 the Fenton-cum-Koppin cyclecar had died too. Meantime Oscar Howick was busying himself across town in Fenton designing the Elgin Light Car.

1913-1914 FENTON
Cyclecar — 2-cyl., 10 hp, 96" wb

	FP	5	4	3	2	1
Model A Rds.-2P	375	—	—	—	—	—

Note: as the Koppin, the car was raised in price to $385.

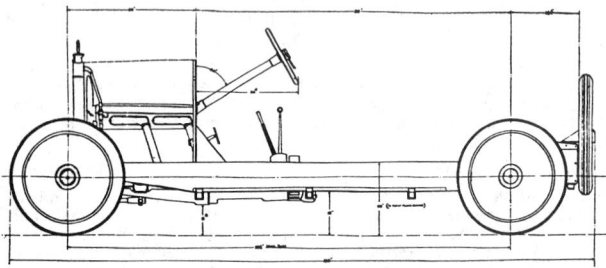

1920 Fergus, chassis, HAC

FERGUS — Newark, New Jersey — (1916-1922) — It was popularly called the Irish car, and although it appeared only in chassis form at the New York Automobile Show at Grand Central Palace in January 1916, it caused a sensation. In a rigid box girder frame with cantilever springs at all four corners, a four-cylinder single overhead camshaft engine was mounted on rubber, a first in the industry. The fuel tank contained a bypass from the exhaust to heat the gasoline to maintain pressure and a reserve gadget was built into the tank. The tire inflator was engine driven. Starting and lighting motors, spark plugs and all appendages were completely enclosed. But most innovative of all, perhaps, was the complete automatic chassis lubrication system. The Fergus was the idea of J.B. Ferguson, a body builder and machine shop owner from Belfast who had made his first trip to the United States in 1909 during which he met Walter Flanders and after which he began the importation of E.M.F. (later Studebaker) cars into Northern Ireland. In its design, he was assisted by aero engine designer Roland Chilton and motorcyle enthusiast Jack Maxwell. Initially the plan was to build the car in Ireland and import it into the United States. But the First World War quickly made that impossible. Thus it was that Fergus Motors of America was organized in 1916, with headquarters in New York City, and a factory site in nearby Newark, New Jersey. In the fall, it was announced that the company would require six months to get into production. Wartime curtailment of material halted this effort as well. The Fergus was not shown again until 1920, by which time it sported a six-cylinder 80 hp engine and front wheel brakes. The chassis price was listed at $7500 in 1920, $8500 in 1922. But in the midst of the postwar recession, no one bought. One of the two remaining chassis in Ireland was imported by an East Coast doctor and fitted with a Holbrook body. Following the doctor's death twenty-eight years later, the car was acquired by J.B. Ferguson, and later passed to his son who, following the Second World War, built a sports car himself also called the Fergus, which also never saw production. After the First World War, J.B. Ferguson had tried to revive the idea of building the car in Ireland under the new name O.D. (for owner/driver, to emphasize its ease of maintenance) but this venture failed almost immediately. Total Fergus production was three cars, all of the chassis having been built in Ireland. The official demise of the venture was announced in January 1923. The Fergus represents a pristine example of the unfortunate reality that a good idea is not all that is necessary to make it in the automobile industry.

FERGUSON — Ann Arbor, Michigan — (1902) — During the summer of 1902 the Ferguson Buggy Company which was located at 607-613 Detroit Street in Ann Arbor announced that it was "actively engaged in getting out the first models of an automobile." The only specification provided was that the vehicle was equipped with a two-cylinder engine. Its price tag was to be about $600. The Ferguson people announced further plans later that summer. As the *Cycle and Automobile Trade Journal* reported cheerily, "They expect to be on the market by September 15." There is no evidence that they ever made it.

FERRIS — Cleveland, Ohio — (1920-1922) — Late in 1919 the Ohio Trailer Company of Cleveland became the Ohio Motor Vehicle Company in order to produce "The Car of Character" called the Ferris which had been named after Ohio secretary-treasurer William E. Ferris. Despite the implication in promotion that the Ferris engine had been designed in-house, the six-cylinder unit was from Continental. The Ferris automobile was an assembled one, though very well built — and very expensive. Where it differed most significantly from other assembled cars was in its coachwork. The Ferris was dedicated "to the man who would not live on a street where all houses are alike." Its aluminum bodies had the custom-built look, its very high radiator was distinctive, and disc wheels as standard equipment was a departure from the norm. Most publicity photos of the car were taken in front of the posh Union Club in Cleveland. Probably less than a thousand Ferrises were produced. The postwar recession was largely responsible for the car's failure. In June of 1921 Ohio Motor Vehicle president Charles Riegler asked that his company's receiver be given authority to continue production. The last Ferris motorcars were new models completed under receivership.

1920-1921 FERRIS
Model C-20 & C-21 — 6-cyl., 50 hp, 130" wb

	FP	5	4	3	2	1
Touring-6P	3350	2700	3600	5300	8800	19,000
Sport-6P	3350	2900	3700	5600	9100	20,000
Sedan-4P	4875	2000	3000	4200	6500	14,000

1922 FERRIS
Model 60 — 6-cyl., 60 hp, 130" wb

	FP	5	4	3	2	1
Touring-6P	2595	2700	3600	5300	8800	19,000
Roadster-2P	2695	3000	4000	6000	9500	21,000
Sport Touring-6P	2795	2900	3700	5600	9100	20,000
Sport Roadster-2P	2845	3100	4200	6300	10,500	22,000
Sedan-4P	3695	2000	3000	4200	6500	14,000
Sport Sedan-4P	3895	2100	3100	4300	6800	14,500

Model 70 — 6-cyl., 70 hp, 130" wb

	FP	5	4	3	2	1
Touring-6P	2795	2900	3700	5600	9100	20,000
Roadster-2P	2895	3100	4200	6300	10,500	22,000
Sport Touring-6P	2995	3000	4000	6000	9500	21,000
Sport Roadster-2P	2995	3200	4300	6500	11,000	22,000
Sedan-4P	3895	2200	3200	4400	7000	15,000
Sport Sedan-4P	4100	2250	3300	4500	7300	15,500

FETZGER — The Fetzger Automobile Manufacturing Company has been indicated as the producer of an automobile in Galion, Ohio in 1910. Documentation is lacking.

1914 Fewmal, motorette, MVMA

FEWMAL — New York, New York — (1914) — The Fewmal was a good-looking sporting two-seater powered by a water-cooled four-cylinder overhead cam 18 hp engine that was fitted into a 100-inch wheelbase chassis with standard 56-inch tread. Shaft drive, sliding gear transmission, electric lights, wire wheels and left-hand steering were featured. Although *The American Cyclecar* reported the venture as emanating from California, it would appear that Fewmal Motors Company was entirely an East Coast operation. The firm had its offices at 27 West 60th Street in New York City.

"The company is capitalized for $200,000," noted *Cyclecar and Motorette*, "the full amount of which has been subscribed by prominent New England capitalists." Fewmal officers were M. Laogaire, president; H. G. Woodbury, Jr., treasurer; R. Remick, secretary, R.A. Loomis, general manager. The prototype Fewmal had been tested for over 12,000 miles, including a New York City-Providence-Boston demonstration trek. In late spring of 1914 Fewmal pronounced itself almost set, though the lines of its car, which the company called a motorette, "are to be smoothed out somewhat, more luggage space being provided in the rear, and the whole body is to be of pure stream-line design." Two more cars were already under construction, and they perhaps were the last Fewmals. There is no mention that a factory site was ever occupied. Fewmal's problem was that, although it was by no means a cyclecar, it was often referred to as such, which was a pity. At $500, it had to be one of the best small sporting car buys in America.

1901 Fey, touring, WLB

FEY — Northfield, Minnesota — (1897-1904) — A case of asthma was the motivating force behind the building of this pioneer car from Northfield. Lincoln H. Fey was allergic to horses, and as an habitue of the Fox and Ferris Machine Shop in town, he learned to work metal and got the idea of building an automobile. Steam power attracted him first; he built a steam engine in 1896, but quickly decided that an internal combustion unit made more sense, so he sold the steam engine for $25 and built a gasoline carriage in 1897. It was a tricycle with the single wheel at the rear. By now his brother Frank E. Fey had joined him in his automotive pursuit. The first Fey car was sold to Alfred J. Smith in New Prague for $65. This provided the brothers the money to build a second car, with four wheels, which was completed in 1898 and sold locally for $170. Two further automobiles were produced by Lincoln and Frank Fey, the last one in 1904 powered by a four-cylinder air-cooled engine of the brothers' own design. Aside from allowing a means to get from point A to point B with less wheezing, providing an occasional sale to finance building their next car, and having a good time tinkering, it does not appear likely that the Fey brothers ever contemplated a further expansion of their automobile adventure.

FIAT — From 1910 to 1918 the Fiat automobile of Italy was manufactured in the United States under license. The factory was in Poughkeepsie, New York. Refer to American Fiat.

FICHTER — Sutter, California — (1910) — Though his was strictly a shoestring operation, it appears that R.M. Fichter produced a few gasoline automobiles to customer order at his machine shop on Acadia and Clousia streets in Sutter around 1910. He was indicated in the Ware yearbook of the industry that year as an automobile builder.

FICKLING — The Fickling brothers — W. Irving and W. Webb — began their automotive venture in New York City during the early fall of 1906 with a capital stock of $15,000 and the plan to manufacture and deal in motor vehicles. Early on, automobile production was decided against, the Ficklings instead buying out the Automobile Cover & Top Company and continuing in business at 154 East 57th Street as limousine and tonneau body builders only.

1914 Fidelia, 2-pass. tandem cyclecar, WLB

FIDELIA — Cleveland, Ohio — (1914) — "Local engineers" were purportedly responsible for the design of the Fidelia, but they were obviously of the backyard sort. This cyclecar from Cleveland featured a two-cylinder

air-cooled De Luxe motor, friction transmission, spidery wire wheels, and a long vee belt drive that probably ripped apart after a few hundred miles of rough road motoring. "The seating is tandem," *Cyclecar Age* reported, "with special hammock seats, spring-hung at very lowest center of gravity, and seated only seventeen inches from the ground." The body design was rather snappy, though the cyclops headlight provided minimal illumination. John H. Sizelan introduced the Fidelia at the Cleveland Automobile Show in January 1914. He said at that time that the 61 Penrose Street address of the J.H. Sizelan Company was "of a temporary nature." Apparently, it was right next to his home. There is no evidence that the Fidelia ever found permanent headquarters.

1914 FIDELIA
Cyclecar — 2-cyl., 10 hp, 96" wb

	FP	5	4	3	2	1
Tandem Roadster-2P	395	—	—	—	—	—

FIDELITY — The Fidelity Motor Car Works of Chicago, Illinois has been indicated on various car rosters as the manufacturer of an automobile in 1909. This is not the case. The firm was organized that year in Sycamore by F.C. Brinkley, B.J. Snow and J.F. Waters for the manufacture of automobiles and accessories. The company's first vehicle arrived shortly thereafter, and it was a one-ton delivery wagon. Fidelity announced its plan to build "five different types of commercial vehicles," but seems to have failed before getting into formal manufacture.

FIEDLER — The Allen Fiedler Company was organized in Chicago, Illinois with a $5000 capital stock during the spring of 1909 to manufacture and deal in motor vehicles and accessories, as well as to conduct a garage. C.R. Browne, Charles Martin and H. Ryall were the incorporators. Manufacture of an automobile is doubted.

FIELD STEAM — Lewiston, Maine — (1886/1905) — In 1886 Edwin F. Field of the Field & Cranshaw Machine Shop of Lewiston finished work on the steam car he had designed in association with Frank Cranshaw. In later years Field claimed it was his steamer which gave the Stanley brothers their idea, although that was only partly true. The Stanleys were in Lewiston at the time, did see the Field car demonstrated and made an attempt to build a steamer of their own the year following. The project was aborted, however, and the brothers did not consider trying again until a decade later, after seeing George Whitney's steamer in Boston. In Lewiston, betimes, Field and Cranshaw continued their experimentation, though growing public resentment of their car's noise meant that most testing on the roads had to be conducted in the dead of night. It was not until late in 1903 that the Field Motor Carriage Company was organized for the manufacture of steam vehicles. Whether Cranshaw remained involved is not known. In the spring of 1905 announcement was made that the production prototype of the Field steam car had been completed and was being tested. But manufacture did not follow. Meantime the Stanley brothers were faring very well with their steamer in Massachusetts.

1910 Field, touring, NSHS

FIELD — Lincoln, Nebraska — (1910-1911) — Among the officers of the Field Automobile Manufacturing Company, it is known that vice-president Charles E. Gibbs was a barber, treasurer Peter F. Zimmer was an insurance man, and secretary Frank Farrell was in real estate, as were Gibbs and Zimmer as well. Precisely what had occupied William T. Field prior to his automotive venture is not known, but most assuredly he did design the Field car, in addition to being the company's president and general manager. The Field was a substantial automobile, a 30/35 hp four (Continental engine) on a 115-inch wheelbase offered as a five-passenger touring. "The reputation of the automobile industry on the manufacturers demands that at whatever price we may build a car," the Field company announced in the December 31st, 1910 edition of the *Lincoln Trade Review*, "it must be able to compare side by side with automobiles of whatever price." A masterpiece of obfuscation. A 1911 advertisement for the Field Automobile Manufacturing Company revealed the Field's price as $1500, and indicated that Field was an agent for the Velie and was into "repairing, storage and auto livery" as well. All this apparently ended very quickly. Field was not subsequently mentioned in an April 1911 *Lincoln Trade Review* article summarizing the automobile activity in town, nor did the company make the 1912 city directories. Most probably, the Messrs. Gibbs, Zimmer and Farrell had returned to their barbering, insurance and real estate by then. The name William T. Field appeared in Lincoln city directories for several decades thereafter as a machinist predominantly, working at a variety of local shops.

FIELD — Rice Lake, Wisconsin — (1922-1923) — On the face of it, the venture promised to be a success. One of the earliest Ford dealers in America, Arthur Field had been around automobiles for the whole of his life and had spent five years quietly working on his own perfecting a new design for a light car to be powered by a "twin-two" air-cooled engine and to feature a novel spring suspension system. The suspension was described by its inventor as occupying a "triangular cantilever position" and two cylinders of his engine were located on each side of a centrally-mounted flywheel. Rice Lake, Wisconsin was chosen as the site for manufacture, although the prototype was built in Minnesota, with many of its component parts farmed out to the O.E. Szekely Company of Moline, Illinois. The car was finished in August of 1922. Up to this point, financing of the venture had been entirely seen to by Field's own money and "voluntary advances" from Rice Lake citizens who were to become stockholders in the new Field Motor Company. Arthur Field and his car arrived in Rice Lake soon after. Following a careful investigation of the project, the Wisconsin State Railroad Commission granted Field a permit to sell stock. As reported in *Automotive Industries* during 1923, "practically all of the capital of the new corporation has been subscribed for and will suffice to finance the operations planned for the present." Capitalization was set at $50,000. Officers of the company included Field as president, J.H. Wallis as vice-president, R.C. Peck as secretary and T.W. Quinn as treasurer. Assembly of Field automobiles in Rice Lake was scheduled to begin in either March or April of 1924. The Field car project died well before that. Only the prototype was ever built.

FIELD & FEYDT — R.C. Field and H.G. Feydt, both of Waterbury, Connecticut, went into partnership with A.H. Dayton of Naugatuck during early 1915 for the purpose of manufacturing automobiles. Capital stock was $50,000. Manufacture does not seem to have been realized.

FIFTY-FIFTY — A cyclecar carrying the curious name of Fifty-Fifty has been indicated on various car rosters as having been built in 1914 by the Sheppard Manufacturing Company of Chicago. This cannot be documented. The firms in Chicago at the time with the Sheppard name were two, one of which manufactured loose-leaf binders and stationery supplies, the other dealt in wholesale groceries.

FILBY — A car called the Filby has been indicated on various car rosters to have been built in Columbus, Kansas. According to someone who had worked for the company, this was not so. The Filby Carriage Company, which had originated at Chetopa and later moved to Columbus, produced carriages and wagons, and subsequently engaged itself in the rebuilding of automobiles. At no time, however, was a car called the Filby manufactured.

FILLOW — Danbury, Connecticut — (1901) — A. Homer Fillow was an engineer from Danbury who created quite a sensation in town in 1901 when he built an automobile equipped with solid rubber tires instead of the usual steel variety most often seen on neighborhood streets. In partnership with him on this endeavor was John R. Hill of the Danbury Hardware Company on 242 Main Street. Fillow and Hill later got together as the Fillow Auto Company on 87 West Street. But this was not an automobile manufacturing firm. Instead it was a dealership for the E-M-F, and specialized in automobile repairing.

FINCH LIMITED — W.A. Pungs and his son-in-law E.B. Finch formed a partnership in 1904 which resulted in the production of the Pungs-Finch in Detroit. Among the most memorable Pungs-Finch models was the Finch Limited of 1906, which Henry Ford commented was the finest car he had ever seen. Refer to Pungs-Finch.

FINDEISEN & KROPF — The Findeisen & Kropf Manufacturing Company was organized in New York City during the summer of 1913 with a capital stock of $5000 and the plan to manufacture automobiles and aeroplanes. Incorporators were F. Findeisen of Berwin, Illinois; O.F. Kropf of Statford Place in Chicago; and Charles A. Riegelman of Woodmere, New York. Manufacture of an automobile is doubted.

FINDLAY — The Findlay Motor Car Company has frequently appeared on rosters as an automobile manufacturer in Findlay, Ohio from 1910 to 1912. This is not the case. The venture was the idea of Levi Edward Ewing, who previously had built the Ewing taxi in Geneva, Ohio. In 1910 he merged his newly-formed Findlay Motor Car Company with the American Motor Truck Company of Lockport, New York, and a steel stamping firm, and the whole combine was named Findlay Motor Company and moved into a factory in Findlay, Ohio which had originally manufactured nails. Manufactured there now were the Ewing truck and the American truck, but no passenger cars. Truck production came to an abrupt end when Findlay was plunged into bankruptcy early in 1913. Later that year its factory was taken over by the new Grant Motor Company — and the Grant car was produced there beginning in 1914.

FINDLAY — Findlay, Ohio — (1910) — "The first automobile ever made in Findlay, Ohio will be ready for inspection about March 1st," *The Automobile* announced in its January 27th, 1910 edition. For years the Findlay Carriage Company had been noted for its building of high-quality horse-drawn vehicles, and it was ready to go horseless. John N. Doty was president of the company, J. Calvin Moyer was secretary, Allen H. Moyer treasurer and manager. The car they built had a four-cylinder 40 hp engine mounted in a 124-inch wheelbase chassis and a maximum speed of 60 mph with five-passenger touring body. "The company has laid plans for making ten cars at once," *Motor Age* reported, "and they will be completed as soon as possible, after which work in real earnest will be begun

on an order of 150." Findlay did not pursue its automotive-building venture in earnest for long, however. $2500 was more for a car than most Findlay residents cared to spend — and the car was not advertised nationally. The Findlays returned to their carriage business, although it is known they produced a motor ambulance for funeral director Frank Barnhart in 1913, and thereafter the other two undertakers in town had to have one too. Financial difficulties had been plaguing the company since 1911. A fire destroyed the Findlay plant in 1916. The company never reopened.

1910 Firestone-Columbus, model 70-A, runabout, HAC

FIRESTONE-COLUMBUS — Columbus, Ohio — (1909-1915) — The Firestone-Columbus was the third car produced by the Columbus Buggy Company, preceded by the Columbus Electric introduced in 1903 and the Columbus highwheeler introduced in 1907. Though the electric was retained in production, the highwheeler was discontinued upon the arrival of the Firestone-Columbus, which was named for Columbus Buggy president Clinton DeWitt Firestone. "A Vehicle for the Masses, not a Toy for the Classes" had been the slogan for the simple two-cylinder $750 highwheeler, "The Car Complete" became the slogan for the four-cylinder $1800 Firestone-Columbus. Five hundred of these cars were produced in 1909. The Columbus Buggy people were opposed to the annual model change, noting with derision in 1910 that most manufacturers "have been chasing up and down the country making a great ado about their 'next year's styles'." That was not the way things were done in Columbus; instead all department heads met every morning at nine o'clock to suggest improvements and, whenever same were approved, they were incorporated into the Firestone-Columbus immediately. That this policy may not have proven successful is indicated by the fact that Columbus Buggy went broke in 1913. On February 22nd, 1914, Clinton Firestone was found dead at his apartment in the Vendome Hotel in Columbus, a victim of apoplexy. In June of 1914 his firm was sold to Charles A. Finnegan and Eugene D. Hofeller of the E.R. Thomas company in Buffalo, New York. They reorganized as the New Columbus Buggy Company, and a small further production followed. But it was all over early in 1915. On May 12th that year the final auction sale was begun. Sold that first day were sixty-five automobiles: thirty-five new electrics, twelve new gasoline cars, and eighteen used cars. The horsedrawn end of the business was sold on day two to one A. Webber of Louisville, Kentucky who planned to move it to that city.

1909 FIRESTONE-COLUMBUS
Model 5001 — 4-cyl., 35 hp, 110" wb

	FP	5	4	3	2	1
Baby Tonneau	1800	3200	4300	6500	11,000	23,000

1910 FIRESTONE-COLUMBUS
Series 6 — 4-cyl., 36 hp, 117" wb

	FP	5	4	3	2	1
Model 6-B Family Car	—	3100	4200	6300	10,500	22,000
Model 62-A Limousine	—	3300	4400	6600	11,500	23,500
Model 65-A Landaulet	—	3300	4400	6700	12,000	24,000

Series 7 — 4-cyl., 24/25 hp, 100" wb

	FP	5	4	3	2	1
Model 7-A Rbt.	—	3200	4300	6500	11,000	23,000
Model 70-A	—	—	—	—	—	—
Model 75-A Rbt.	—	3300	4400	6600	11,500	23,500
Model 72-A Coupe	—	3100	4200	6300	10,500	22,000
Model 73-A Light Tour. (103" wb)	—	3300	4400	6700	12,000	24,000

1911 Firestone-Columbus, model 74D, torpedo, WLB

1911 FIRESTONE-COLUMBUS
Series 74 — 4-cyl., 26/30 hp, 108" wb

	FP	5	4	3	2	1
Model A Fore-Door Tour.-4P	—	3200	4300	6500	11,000	23,000
Model B Tour.-4P	—	3200	4300	6500	11,000	23,000
Model C Surrey-4P	—	3100	4200	6300	10,500	22,000
Model D Torpedo-4P	—	3000	4000	6000	9500	21,000

Series 86 — 4-cyl., 32 hp, 113" wb

	FP	5	4	3	2	1
Model C Fore-Door Tour.	—	3300	4400	6700	12,000	24,000

Series 6 — 4-cyl., 42 hp, 120" wb

	FP	5	4	3	2	1
Model 6-C Tour.-5P	—	3400	4500	6900	12,500	24,500
Model 6-C Limo.-7P	—	3300	4400	6700	12,000	24,000

1912 Firestone-Columbus, model 68-D, touring, HAC

1912 FIRESTONE-COLUMBUS
Model 60-D — 4-cyl., 33 hp, 120" wb

		5	4	3	2	1
Fore-Door Tour.-5P		3300	4400	6700	12,000	24,000

Model 86-D — 4-cyl., 27 hp, 116" wb

		5	4	3	2	1
Fore-Door Tour.-5P		3200	4300	6500	11,000	23,000

Model 68-D — 4-cyl., 32 hp, 122" wb

		5	4	3	2	1
Fore-Door Tour.-7P		3400	4500	6900	12,500	24,500

Model 78-D — 4-cyl., 26 hp, 108" wb

		5	4	3	2	1
Vis-a-Vis Torpedo-3P		3200	4300	6500	11,000	23,000

1913 Firestone-Columbus, model 60-E, touring, HAC

1913 FIRESTONE-COLUMBUS
Model 86-E — 4-cyl., 35 hp, 116" wb

		5	4	3	2	1
Roadster-3P		3200	4300	6500	11,000	23,000
Touring-7P		3200	4300	6400	10,800	22,500

Model 60-E — 4-cyl., 45 hp, 122" wb

		5	4	3	2	1
Touring 5/7P		3200	4300	6500	11,000	23,000
Limousine-7P		3100	4200	6300	10,500	22,000

Model 90-E — 6-cyl., 60 hp, 130" wb

		5	4	3	2	1
Touring 5/7P		3300	4400	6700	12,000	24,000
Limousine-7P		3200	4300	6500	11,000	23,000

1914 Firestone-Columbus, model 82-E, raceabout, HAC

1914-1915 FIRESTONE-COLUMBUS
Model 86-E — 4-cyl., 27 hp, 116" wb

		5	4	3	2	1
Touring-5P	1850	3300	4400	6700	12,000	24,000

Model 60E — 4-cyl., 32 hp, 122" wb

		5	4	3	2	1
Touring-5P	2125	3500	4500	7000	13,000	25,000

Model 69D — 4-cyl., 32 hp, 122" wb

		5	4	3	2	1
Roadster-3P	1850	3900	4800	7700	14,300	27,000

Model 82E — 4-cyl., 32 hp, 122" wb

	5	4	3	2	1
Raceabout-2P	1050	4000	5000	8000	15,000	28,000

Model 90E — 6-cyl., 41 hp, 130" wb

	5	4	3	2	1
Touring-7P	2650	3700	4700	7300	13,700	26,000

Model 98E — 6-cyl., 41 hp, 130" wb

	5	4	3	2	1
Touring-5P	2500	3900	4800	7700	14,300	27,000

FIRTH — The Firth automobile appearing on many automotive rosters was merely a misspelling of the Forth. The car was produced in Mansfield, Ohio in 1910. Refer to Forth.

FISCHER — The Fischer Courant Company was organized in New York City early in 1919 for the manufacture of automobiles and bicycles. Capital stock was $25,000. The incorporators were L. Fischer, A. Fischer and E. Courant. Manufacture of an automobile is doubted.

J. George Fischer of Saginaw, Michigan indicated himself as an automobile manufacturer in 1902 in addition to his usual work as a bicycle builder, general machinist and dealer in electric supplies at his shop at 214-216 North Franklin. Only during this single year was an automobile a part of Fischer's advertised activity.

The Fischer Motor Vehicle Promotion Syndicate was organized in Jersey City, New Jersey early in 1902 with a capital stock of $100,000 and the plan to manufacture motor vehicles. I.B. Newcomb, George V. Sims and H.S.C. Thorton were the backers of this venture. Manufacture of an automobile is doubted.

In 1914-1915 an American version of the Swiss Fischer was produced in New York City. Refer to Mondex Magre.

FISCHER — Hoboken, New Jersey — (1901-1905) — The Fischer Motor Vehicle Company was located at 1311 Hudson Street in Hoboken and was in the business of manufacturing trucks which used a combined electric/gasoline power system. The presence of the Fischer name on various automobile rosters is probably because Fischer produced vehicles for the transporting of people as well as goods. But these were sightseeing and city transit buses and not passenger cars. Probably the smallest Fischer ever built was a twelve-passenger car for touring.

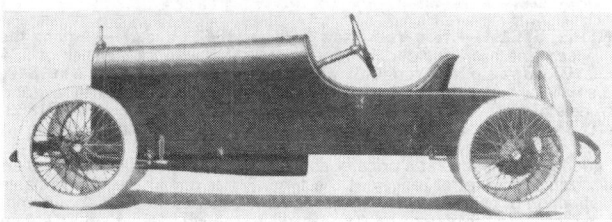

1914 Fischer-Detroit, model A, 2-pass. speedster, WLB

FISCHER-DETROIT — Detroit, Michigan — (1914) — The Fischer-Detroit was a light car with a four-cylinder water-cooled Perkins engine, selective transmission, shaft drive and a vee radiator. It was produced by the C.J. Fischer Company of Detroit and had its formal debut at the Grand Central Palace automobile show in New York City in late December of 1913. The Fischer-Detroit's price range was $595 to $845, and the latter bought a sedan, a remarkably good buy for a closed car of that period. Nonetheless, the Fischer-Detroit did not survive into 1915. In November of 1914, C.J. Fischer attempted to relocate in York, Pennsylvania. Purportedly local citizens had provided $50,000 to launch the new Fischer Motor Vehicle Company there, with operations to begin immediately at the plant of the Glen Rock Stamping Company. Samples of the Fischers built in Detroit were already in York. Probably no further Fischers followed, however. Soon thereafter the assets of the Fischer Motor Vehicle Company were sold by the receiver for $8000.

1914 FISCHER-DETROIT
Four — 104" wb

	5	4	3	2	1	
Speedster-2P	595	2700	3600	5300	8800	19,000
Tourist-2P	645	2400	3400	4800	8000	17,000
Cabriolet-2P	645	2300	3300	4600	7500	16,000
Sedan-4P	845	1800	2800	4000	6200	13,000

FISH — Bloomington, Illinois — (1906-1907) — In late December of 1906, *Motor World* reported that George L. Fish of Bloomington had organized the Fish Automobile Company for the manufacture of engines capable of burning any kind of fuel and automobiles to sell for $250 and up. Certainly no meaningful manufacture followed, but it would appear that at least one prototype of a Fish gasoline automobile did.

FISHBACK — Waterloo, Iowa — (1912) — "Fishback Angling for a Factory Site" was the droll headline in the February 1912 issue of *The Motor World* announcing the recent incorporation with a capital stock of $3,000,000, of the Fishback Motor Company in Newark, New Jersey. R. Wilton Fishback, previously the general manager of a Detroit marine and stationary engine building company, was the moving spirit behind this venture — and he allied himself with a New York real estate man named Julius J. Wittenberg and a banker named Peter R. Gilligan. Gilligan revealed that a factory location was being sought and that the company was "flirting with Youngstown, Ohio, among other places" and that Fishback was prepared to deposit $300,000 "in any local bank as a guarantee of good faith." By June the promoters announced their discovery of a "very desirable tract of land" in Waterloo, Iowa. And they issued a glowing prospectus of the profits to be made. By this time *The Motor World* had caught on to the scam, editorializing that month: "The Fishback promoters have improved on the ways of others by presenting in black and white a statement which is of uncommon interest as showing how it is possible to figure handsome profits before even a factory has been built or a wheel turned, the profits being of a nature that will cause not a few of those who actually are operating automobile factories to bite their lips for chagrin and disappointment and hide their diminished heads." The Fishback venture disappeared soon after. But R. Wilton Fishback did not. He revised his name a bit, to Robert W. Fishback and tried again in 1914 with the Savage Motor Car Company. That one ended in indictments.

FISHER — The Fisher Automobile Company was organized in Mooresville, Morgan County, Indiana in September of 1903 with a capital stock of $25,000 for the manufacture of automobiles. J.S. Comer, H.C. Scearce and D.F. Swain, Jr. were the directors of this new firm, and their earliest major endeavor seems to have been instigating legal proceedings against the newly incorporated Fisher Automobile Company of Bridgeport, Indiana regarding use of that name. Automobile manufacture does not appear to have followed, in either Mooresville or Bridgeport.

The Fisher Electric Manufacturing Company of Detroit, Michigan was indicated as an automobile manufacturer in the Hiscox book *Horseless Vehicles, Automobiles, Motor Cycles* published in 1900. Further documentation is lacking.

The Fisher Equipment Company of Chicago, Illinois was the sponsoring firm for production of the Clinton E. Woods in 1898. Refer to Clinton E. Woods.

The Fisher-Gibson Company was organized in Indianapolis, Indiana during the fall of 1911 with a capital stock of $50,000 for the manufacture of automobiles and accessories. The partners involved were Carl G. Fisher and Cecil E. Gibson, who were already involved with the Empire car in Indianapolis. No manufacture resulted from the Fisher-Gibson venture, though the company did serve as Indiana distributors for the Stearns, Overland, Stoddard-Dayton and Alco.

A Fisher was indicated as among the cyclecars on hand in July 1914 at the light car exhibit at the Michigan State Fairgrounds. Possibly the Fisher was a racing cyclecar, or a prototype for possible production, though manufacture did not follow.

The Fisher Motor Corporation has been indicated on various car rosters as an automobile manufacturer in New York City from 1914-1920. There is no indication that such a company existed in New York City during that entire period.

FISHER STEAM — New York, New York — (1840 et seq.) — Among the pioneer steam car builders of America was John Kenrick Fisher of 234 East Broadway in New York City, who constructed his first vehicle in 1840, a small carriage with a two-cylinder engine, a boiler of steel tubes, and wheels of full five feet in diameter. His next vehicle, completed in 1853, was a hackney and was produced by his newly-organized American Steam Carriage Company which offered to build steamers good for 15 mph on "good gravel roads" at a price of about $2000 each. Though that was an enormous amount of money at the time, Fisher does have the probable distinction of being the first entrepreneur in America to offer an automobile for sale to the general public. Alas, no one bought. Fisher's third steam carriage followed in 1859, a ten-passenger vehicle which was claimed to have been driven a mile in 2 minutes 40 seconds. In addition to designing the chassis for three fire engines built by Lee & Larned shortly before the Civil War, Fisher is believed to have built at least one more steam carriage himself, in 1869.

1917 Fisher

FISHER — Baltimore, Maryland — (1917) — This Fisher from 1917 was a sporting three-wheeler powered by a four-cylinder engine and capable of a reported, but probably none too stable, 75 mph. It was the invention of F.E. Fisher of Baltimore, and presumably was the only car he built.

FITCH — The Fitch of 1909 was successor to the Rome, New York car which was earlier promoted as the Maxwell-Fitch. Refer to Maxwell-Fitch.

FITT — Rochester, New York — (1903-1904) — In the Rochester city directory for 1903-1904, James Fitt indicated his occupation as "auto repairer and builder." Details regarding the cars he may have built are lacking.

FITZGIBBON — Fitzgibbon & Crisp was a $100,000 venture for the manufacture of automobiles emanating from Trenton, New Jersey early in 1913. The identity of Fitzgibbon and Crisp was not revealed; L.L. Woodward was the indicated incorporator of this idea to build automobiles which seems to have gone nowhere. The firm did go places, however, as the builders of automotive bodies for Mercer & Crane-Simplex — and as a truck body builder. Mid-1930's trade publications featured photographs of Fitzgibbon & Crisp streamlined integrated semi-trailer designs.

FIVE-BORO — Hagerstown, Maryland — (1924-1927) — The Five-Boro was a Buda-engined taxicab on a 118-inch wheelbase produced by the Moller works in Hagerstown. Its name derived from the location in which these cabs were used — New York City, where they served the five boroughs of Manhattan, Queens, Brooklyn, Staten Island and the Bronx. Moller was also responsible for the Aristocrat, Astor, Blue Light, Luxor, Paramount, Super Paramount and Twentieth Century taxis.

FLAGLER — The Flagler Company of Brooklyn, New York was granted a charter to manufacture and sell automobiles and to operate a garage early in 1907. Directors of the company were F.W. Flagler, A.R. Pardington and C.F. Hart. Capital stock for the venture was $25,000. A Flagler automobile does not appear to have resulted.

1914 Flagler, cyclecar, NAHC

FLAGLER — Cheyboygan, Michigan — (1914) — The Flagler was a smartly styled cyclecar with side-by-side seating and wheel steering. It was initially fitted with a two-cylinder 10/12 hp engine, friction transmission and vee-belt final drive. The wheelbase was 90 inches, the tread 42. Fuel economy was sensational: "54 Miles at 40 Miles Speed on One Gallon of Gasoline," the advertisements said. The price for all this was $375. The Flagler Cyclecar Company was organized in Chicago by Elias S. Flagler, but he chose Cheyboygan as his manufacturing site when the local chamber of commerce offered the pea canning plant on the south side of town. Cheyboygan townspeople also put up cash, and got in on the action. The new Flagler vice-president A.M. Gerow was president of the local First National Bank, and Flagler secretary-treasurer W.L. Hagadorn was described as a "local capitalist." Manufacturing had begun in temporary headquarters at 1324 Michigan Avenue in Chicago, but operations moved immediately to the pea canning plant in Cheyboygan. By this time the Flagler specifications had been uprated to a four-cylinder Perkins engine, standard sliding gear transmission and shaft drive. This raised the price to $450. Total Flagler production was probably about 100 cars.

1914 FLAGLER
Cyclecar — 2-cyl., 10/12 hp, 90" wb

	FP	5	4	3	2	1
Roadster-2P	375	1500	2500	3600	5500	11,000
Cyclecar — 4-cyl., 18 hp, 94" wb						
Roadster-2P	450	1600	2700	3800	5800	12,000

FLAIR — St. Louis, Missouri — (1902-1903) — In 1901, during the time he was not occupied working for the Meyer Brothers Drug Company, Henry Flair of St. Louis began building himself a car, which he completed in 1902. He used a steam engine to power it the first time around but was unsatisfied with the results, so he tore the car apart and substituted a two-cylinder gasoline engine which was mounted up front, and fitted with a planetary transmission, and chain drive to the rear axle. A four-passenger side-entrance tonneau body was fashioned, and the steering was by wheel. The conversion was completed by 1903, and Flair enjoyed the car for some time thereafter. He remained in the drug business, however.

FLANDERMOBILE — Anderson, Indiana — (1901) — Just what the Flandermobile Company of Anderson might have been building has not been documented for certain. All *The Horseless Age* reported of the firm's efforts was that it was "exploiting 'the primordial power of the world' for motor vehicle purposes," which would mean the Flandermobile was a steamer.

FLANDERS ELECTRIC — Chelsea & Pontiac, Michigan — (1912-1914) — In January 1911 the Flanders Manufacturing Company was founded, capitalized at $2.25 million, most of the money coming from former E-M-F backers, including Clement Studebaker, Jr. By now, Walter Flanders was the only original partner still with E-M-F, and Studebaker was sole distributor for its cars. Flanders Manufacturing was initially set up to produce, in a huge plant in Chelsea, a two-wheeled vehicle introduced as the Flanders Bi-Mobile, which everyone recognized for what it was, and thus it was soon called a motorcycle, with about 2500 built. The electric car introduced for 1912 was the idea of LeRoy Pelletier, advertising manager for E-M-F. It featured worm drive, cradle spring suspension and a coupe body about a foot lower than the electric car norm. The price was $1775. Although orders for 3000 cars were taken, production totaled less than a hundred before Flanders Manufacturing, badly overextended, found itself in receivership after moving to Pontiac. In October 1913, Pelletier bought the Flanders business, renamed the product the Tiffany, relocated in Flint and fared very poorly. In March 1914, with his former employer's blessing, he moved the business back to Chelsea and renamed it Flanders Electric Company, but fared no better. By this time the E-M-F had become the Studebaker, Walter Flanders was looking after the fortunes of Maxwell,

1912 Flanders Electric, coupe, WLB

and in November 1914 LeRoy Pelletier decided to give up and open an advertising agency in Detroit. Probably only a handful of the second-generation Flanders Electrics had been built.

1912 FLANDERS ELECTRIC

	FP	5	4	3	2	1
Colonial Coupe (100" wb)	1775	1800	2800	4000	6200	13,000
Victoria(100" wb)	1775	1800	2800	4000	6200	13,000

1913 FLANDERS ELECTRIC

Colonial Cpe. (100" wb)	2500	1800	2800	4000	6200	13,000

1914 FLANDERS ELECTRIC

Colonial Cpe. (100" wb)	1750	1800	2800	4000	6200	13,000

FLANDERS SIX — Detroit, Michigan — (1913) — Named for Walter Flanders, this car was essentially the Everitt which had been produced by the Metzger Motor Car Company and which now would be produced under the aegis of the new Flanders Motor Company. Earlier, Barney Everitt and William Metzger had been partners with Flanders in the E-M-F company which by now had been taken over by Studebaker. The Flanders Six brought the original E-M-F partners together again. The car was introduced at the New York Automobile Show in January 1913. The production that followed could not have been more than a handful of vehicles, however, because a month after the show, Benjamin Briscoe asked Flanders to help out with the fiasco he had created called United States Motor Company (an attempt to emulate General Motors) and in exchange for his services Flanders insisted Briscoe buy the Flanders Motor Company. Thereafter Flanders scrapped every weak company in Briscoe's corporate monstrosity, including his own, and found himself left with one good organization and one good car. It was the Maxwell.

1913 FLANDERS SIX
Model 50-Six — 38.4 hp, 130" wb

Touring-7P	2250	3000	4000	6000	9500	21,000
Roadster-3P	2200	3100	4200	6300	10,500	22,000

1911 Flanders 20, touring, OCW

FLANDERS 20 — Detroit, Michigan — (1910-1912) — Nettled because his partners Everitt and Metzger had left him in mid-1909, and also because the E-M-F was being drastically undersold and outproduced by the Model T Ford the production procedures for which he had largely set up when he worked for Henry Ford, Walter Flanders decided to build a new low-priced car. In July 1909 he talked the Studebaker brothers, the distributors of the E-M-F, into buying the factory of the defunct DeLuxe Motor Company of Detroit in order to compete with Ford head-on. The Flanders 20 was a four-cylinder car on a 100-inch wheelbase selling in the $750 price range, which at the time of its planning was less than the Model T. Unfortunately, Ford kept lowering the price of the Model T, and the Flanders 20 never could undersell it. Although production was far under the Model T's as well, the Flanders 20 total figure for three seasons of 31,514 units was a healthy one and, with E-M-F sales, was good for the number two spot in the industry in 1911. After 1912, by which time Studebaker had taken over completely, all E-M-F and Flanders cars became Studebakers.

1910 FLANDERS 20
Model 20 — 4-cyl., 20 hp, 100" wb

	FP	5	4	3	2	1
Runabout-2P	750	2500	3500	5000	8500	18,000
Touring-4P	790	2700	3600	5300	8800	19,000

1911 FLANDERS 20
Model 20 — 4-cyl., 20 hp, 100" wb

Runabout-2P	700	2700	3600	5300	8800	19,000
Roadster-3P	725	2800	3700	5500	9000	19,500
Suburban-4P	725	2500	3500	5000	8500	18,000
Coupe-3P	975	2400	3400	4800	8000	17,000

1912 Flanders 20, roadster, OCW

1912 FLANDERS 20
Model 20 — 4-cyl., 20 hp, 102" wb

Touring	800	2400	3400	4800	8000	17,000
Suburban	800	2300	3300	4600	7500	16,000
Runabout	775	2500	3500	5000	8500	18,000
Roadster	750	2700	3600	5300	8800	19,000
Coupe	1000	2400	3400	4800	8000	17,000

1922 Flapper, camping car, MVMA

FLAPPER — New York, New York — (1922) — The Flapper was not a car but a conversion, built by an unidentified company in New York City during the early 1920's. Available in sizes to fit the low-priced Ford, Gray and Star chassis, the medium-range chassis of such cars as Chevrolet, Essex, Maxwell and Dort, and all general chassis up to 116 inches, the Flapper was officially said to be a "camping" vehicle, its seats forming a bed for two people, with luggage space in the rear and an icebox below it. The name chosen for this conversion suggests, however, that its makers might have considered the car useful for purposes other than camping.

FLATBUSH — The Flatbush Automobile Company was organized early in 1906 with a capital stock of $5000 to make automobiles in Brooklyn, New York. Behind this venture was E.G. Applegate, Annie E. Applegate and S.E. Maires, all of Brooklyn. Manufacture is doubted.

FLEISCHMANN — The Fleischmann Vehicle Company was organized early in 1910 in New York City with a capital stock of $25,000 to "engage in the manufacture of carriages, motor cars and vehicles of all kinds." Incorporators were O.F. Fleischmann, R.H. Fleischmann and P. Damm. Manufacture of an automobile is doubted.

FLEMING — White Plains, New York — (1901) — In February of 1901, Peter G. Fleming of Elizabeth, New Jersey; Angel Afanador of Brooklyn, New York; and William J. Brewster of East Orange, New Jersey incorporated the Fleming Motor Vehicle Company in White Plains, New York with a capital stock of $10,000 for the stated purpose of manufacturing "motors, marine and automobile, and complete motor vehicles." The business was headquartered in Ossining, home of the penitentiary called Sing-Sing. So far as is known, this venture failed soon after incorporation. Possibly it was allied, however, with the Fleming Manufacturing Company which had a factory at 93-97 Elizabeth Street in New York City and which produced small gasoline engines of 1-1/4 to 3 hp for automotive use during this period. The new incorporation could have been an attempt to expand the Fleming horizon, but that more than a prototype automobile resulted from it is not known.

1895 Fletcher, runabout, WLB

FLETCHER STEAM — Hollis, Maine — (c.1895) — In 1909 *The Automobile* referred to this car built before the turn of the century as the first ever in the state of Maine, although this ignored the considerably previous effort of Richard D. Rice of Hallowell. Like the Rice car of 1858, Levi Fletcher's of c.1895 was a steamer. "It was not a sightly looking contrivance, but the principle was right, and it ran," reported *The Automobile.* "With much snorting, and grinding and hissing, the steam vehicle went slowly ahead. It made excellent progress down a grade, but when it struck a hill there was absolutely 'nothing doing.' Levi saw there must be improvements, so the contrivance was hauled back to the barn." There Fletcher continued tinkering with the machine, until he could realize a fair amount of speed on a level road, but the car still balked at hills. So it was back to the barn where Fletcher resumed tinkering until around 1908, when he was attracted by a noise outside and left the barn long enough to see an automobile go by. "He gazed in open-mouthed wonder, dropped his tools and went into the house," *The Automobile* said. "He never again touched his steam carriage and seemed to lose all interest in life. It is said he died of a broken heart."

FLEUR DE LIS — The Fleur de Lis Automobile Company was incorporated with a capital stock of $25,000 late in 1907 for the manufacture and sale of motor cars in New York City. Incorporators were F. Knowlton and E.A. Monfret. Manufacture is doubted.

FLEXIBLE — The Flexible Aeroplane Company was organized in Newark, New Jersey during the summer of 1909 with a capital stock of $100,000 for the manufacture of aeroplanes and automobiles. Incorporators were J. Formanns, J.K. Murgatroyd and H. Taylorson. Manufacture of an automobile is doubted.

FLINN STEAM — West Roxbury, Massachusetts — (1902-1903) — That Richard J. Flinn of West Roxbury was building an automobile for the market in 1902-1903 was indicated in December 1902 when *The Horseless Age* noted its receipt of a brochure from the inventor regarding "The Flinn Steam Trap." Flinn was further indicated in trade directory listings of steam automobile manufacturers in 1903. Richard J. Flinn, incidentally, is not to be confused with Thomas F. Flinn of Brooklyn, who was also involved in steam car development during this period. The compound steam engine invented and patented by Thomas Flinn was the powerplant used in the Volomobile produced by the New York Motor Vehicle Company.

FLINT — The Flint Motor Car Company was organized in Providence, Rhode Island early in 1905 with a capital stock of $30,000 to "manufacture, buy, sell and repair automobiles." Incorporators were Elliott Flint, Franklin M. Chenery and Thomas P. Allen. Manufacture is doubted.

FLINT — Long Island City, New York — (1923-1924) — Elizabeth, New Jersey & Flint, Michigan — (1924-1926)/Elizabeth, New Jersey — (1927) — When first announced, the press referred to this new car from the Durant empire as a "modified Chrysler," this because in acquiring the former plant of the Willys Corporation in Elizabeth, New Jersey, Durant had also acquired the prototype developed there by the engineering triumvirate of Zeder-Breer-Skelton in which Walter P. Chrysler had taken an especial interest. That trio continued developing their original concept, which ultimately was introduced as the Chrysler in 1924; the prototype they left behind in the Willys plant was revamped by the Durant people — headed by Alfred T. Sturt, designer of the Durant and Star — and became the Flint Six. Its seven-bearing crankshaft was carried over from the prototype, but the chassis was extensively reworked (at 120 inches, it was eight inches longer), and the body styling was all-new. Introduced at the Hotel Commodore in New York City during January 1923, the press now began referring to the new Flint as a "junior Locomobile," Durant having acquired that

1923 Flint, model E, touring, AA

company as well for his new empire. Indeed, the Flint did resemble the Locomobile somewhat, which no doubt was quite intentional. With price tags beginning as low as $1195, a mind's-eye association with the luxury Locomobile certainly was not at all a bad thing. And with 65 bhp generated from its six-cylinder engine, the Flint promised a performance uncommon for its price class. The first 500 Flint cars were produced in the Durant-owned factory in Long Island City, prior to the transfer of production in 1924 to Elizabeth and to a brand-new factory Durant built in Flint, Michigan, where he had enjoyed favorite-son status since his Buick days. In March 1924 the 65 hp Flint was joined by a smaller 49 hp companion car on a 115-inch wheelbase which Durant had originally planned to call the Eagle but was now the Flint 40. Lockheed hydraulic four-wheel brakes were adopted on both these Flint models; in 1926 another smaller companion — the 40 hp Junior on a 110-inch wheelbase — arrived with rear brakes only. Somewhat less than 15,000 Flints had been produced in both 1924 and 1925, but production dropped to almost half that in 1926. The car wasn't selling well, obviously, but the really insurmountable problem with the Flint was the instability of Billy Durant's second empire. During the summer of 1926, desperately in need of working capital, Durant sold his Flint, Michigan plant to General Motors. All production of the Flint car was then transferred to New Jersey. There, in 1927 less than 2000 units were built; then the Flint was discontinued, as Billy Durant struggled to save his business.

1924 Flint, model E, touring, OCW

1923-1924 FLINT
Model E — 6-cyl., 65 hp, 120" wb

	FP	5	4	3	2	1
Touring-5P	1195	3700	4700	7300	13,700	26,000
Special Touring-5P	1295	3900	4800	7700	14,300	27,000
Sport Roadster-3P	1630	4000	5000	8000	15,000	28,000
Sport Touring-4P	1695	4000	5000	8000	15,000	28,000
Coupe-4P	1895	2400	3400	4800	8000	17,000
Sedan-5P	1985	2000	3000	4200	6500	14,000
Special Coupe-4P	1995	2500	3500	5000	8500	18,000
Special Sedan-5P	2085	2200	3200	4400	7000	15,000

The Flint 40, which had been announced as the Eagle, was introduced in March 1924.

1925 Flint, model E-55, roadster, WLB

1925 FLINT
Model H-40 — 6-cyl., 49 hp, 115" wb

	FP	5	4	3	2	1
Touring-5P	1075	3500	4500	7000	13,000	25,000
Brougham-5P	1640	3100	4200	6300	10,500	22,000

Model E-55 — 6-cyl., 65 hp, 120" wb
Touring-5P	1595	3700	4700	7300	13,700	26,000
Roadster-4P	1950	4000	5000	8000	15,000	28,000
Sedan-5P	2285	2000	3000	4200	6500	14,000
Coupe-4P	2195	2400	3400	4800	8000	17,000
Sport Touring-4P	2050	4000	5000	8000	15,000	28,000

1926 Flint, model 60, roadster, HAC

1926 FLINT
Junior — 6-cyl., 40 hp, 110" wb
Coach	1085	2200	3200	4400	7000	15,000
Deluxe Coach	1185	2250	3300	4500	7300	15,500

Model 60 — 6-cyl., 49 hp, 115" wb
Touring-5P	1185	3900	4800	7700	14,300	27,000
Sedan-5P	1495	2200	3200	4400	7000	15,000
Brougham-5P	1575	2300	3300	4600	7500	16,000

Model 80 — 6-cyl., 65 hp, 120" wb
Touring-5P	1595	4000	5000	8000	15,000	28,000
Sport Touring-5P	2050	4200	5200	8400	15,700	29,000
Roadster-3P	1950	4300	5400	8700	16,500	30,000
Coupe-4P	1195	2400	3400	4800	8000	17,000
Sedan-5P	2285	2300	3300	4600	7500	16,000
Brougham-5P	2485	2400	3400	4800	8000	17,000
Sedan-7P	2750	2350	3400	4700	7800	16,500

1927 Flint, model 60, touring, HAC

1927 FLINT
Junior Model Z-18 — 6-cyl., 40 hp, 110" wb
Coach-5P	960	2200	3200	4400	7000	15,000
Deluxe Coach-5P	1075	2250	3300	4500	7300	15,500

Model B-60 — 6-cyl., 49 hp, 115" wb
Touring-5P	1260	3900	4800	7700	14,300	27,000
Sedan-5P	1495	2200	3200	4400	7000	15,000
Brougham-5P	1495	2300	3300	4600	7500	16,000
Sport Roadster-4P	1495	4200	5200	8400	15,700	29,000
Roadster-4P	1360	4000	5000	8000	15,000	28,000
Coupe Roadster-4P	1495	4200	5200	8400	15,700	29,000

Model E-80 — 6 cyl., 65 hp, 120" wb
Touring-5P	1450	4000	5000	8000	15,000	28,000
Sport Touring-5P	1645	4200	5200	8400	15,700	29,000
Coupe-4P	1850	2400	3400	4800	8000	17,000
Sedan-5P	1925	2300	3300	4600	7500	16,000
Sedan-7P	2125	2350	3400	4700	7800	16,500
Roadster-4P	1645	4200	5200	8400	15,700	29,000

FLINT ROADSTER — Flint, Michigan — (1902-1904) — In 1901, when he could not convince his associates in the Durant-Dort Carriage Company of Flint that getting into the automobile business was a good idea, A.B.C. (Alexander Brunnell Cullen) Hardy abruptly took leave to begin his own firm. The Flint Automobile Company which he organized in 1902 produced a one-cylinder 8 hp two-seater on a 72-inch wheelbase with wire wheels and left-hand tiller steering that was alternately called the Flint Roadster and the Hardy. "The Touring Car for Two" was the company slogan, and the price was $850. Fifty-two of these vehicles were built before A.B.C. Hardy voluntarily folded his company because he did not wish to pay royalties to the Association of Licensed Automobile Manufacturers, nor did he countenance a lawsuit for violation of the Selden Patent. Very soon thereafter he rejoined his old carriage partners who by this time had decided to get into the automobile business with a car called the Buick. Interestingly, in 1909, Hardy revived the Flint Automobile Company in order to sue the A.L.A.M. for restraint of trade, demanding $75,000 in

1903 Flint, roadster, NAHC

damages for his firm's failure. That litigation was still pending when the A.L.A.M. collapsed a few years later.

FLINTLO — Denver, Colorado — (1905-1908) — Its name had not been decided upon when this car was introduced at the Denver Automobile Show in April 1905; indeed so rushed had its makers, Flint & Lomax, been to get to the coliseum on time that the car appeared there in what was described as "an unfinished condition." The month following, *Motor Field* reported that the new car, now named Flintlo, was about to emerge from the paintshop for its first testing on the road. A five-passenger side-entrance tonneau, the Flintlo was powered by an ohv four-cylinder engine and featured a three-speed sliding-gear transmission and shaft drive. "If the car proves as successful as anticipated," *Motor Field* said, "the company will undertake the manufacturing of cars on a large scale." The Flintlo obviously did not prove successful; Flint & Lomax did not reappear at the Denver Coliseum in 1906.

FLORI — St. Louis, Missouri — (1900) — In 1900 George Flori built a single-cylinder gasoline automobile in his machine shop on Seventh Street near Elm in St. Louis, and he had numerous adventures with it subsequently. Indeed, its very first road test ended ignominiously because Flori had elected to devise his steering wheel so that a turn of it to the right turned the wheels to the left, a fact he forgot and thus motored gently into a trolley pole. On another occasion, Flori's car frightened a horse hitched to a sidewalk porch post with the result that when the horse took off, it took the porch along too. George Flori is not known to have built another car.

FLORIDA — Late in 1903 the Florida Automobile and Acetylene Gas Company was incorporated with a capital stock of $25,000 in Jacksonville, Florida for the manufacture, rental and repair of automobiles. The incorporators were Hugh Partridge, M.C. Hutto and Albert Jenkins. No automobile called the Florida was ever marketed, although two years later one of the incorporators, M.C. Hutto, did build a car in Jacksonville under his own name.

Early in 1916 the Florida Motors Corporation was organized with a capital stock of $6000 for the manufacture of motorcars, engines and accessories in Jacksonville, Florida. Behind this venture were R.H. Shackleford and C.E. Beloate. Manufacture of an automobile is doubted.

FLYER — The Flyer was one of three models produced by the Continental Automobile Company of Grand Rapids, Michigan in 1933-1934. Refer to Continental.

1914 Flyer, 2-pass. roadster, WLB

FLYER — New Jersey/Michigan — (1913-1914) — The Flyer Motor Company began its short life in Elizabeth, New Jersey and ended it in Mt. Clemens, Michigan. In addition to a disruptive change of address, the Flyer was also encumbered by journalistic references to it as a cyclecar. Its 100-inch wheelbase, standard 56-inch tread, sliding gear transmission, four-cylinder water-cooled 20 hp engine, torque tube drive, self-starter and full electric system were features enjoyed by no other cyclecar, in fact, its horsepower and wheelbase equaled the Model T Ford's. The Flyer Company described its product more aptly, if awkwardly, as a "reproduction of the larger modern automobile of today only of lesser size." Its price of

$495 was most attractive, though the Flyer Company couldn't hold to it long, raising early on to $600, which remained a bargain. The Flyer was designed by A.A Gloetzner, formerly of Olds Motor Works. On the East Coast it was produced under the aegis of the Thomas Howard Company of Brooklyn, selling agents for the Correja car. Though Minneapolis beckoned the Flyer awhile, the move to Mt. Clemens was ultimately made following the attractive offer the Flyer Company received from that city's Business Men's Association: exemption from city taxes and the use of free water for five years. Unfortunately, the Flyer wasn't around very long to take advantage. A.A. Gloetzner went on to design the Bour-Davis.

FLYING DUTCHMAN — Yakima, Washington — (1908) — Newton C. Gauntt was another of the pioneers who foresaw the emergence of the recreational vehicle market better than a half-century before it truly emerged. He was a native of the state of Washington and an architect whose design credits included the first Y.M.C.A. in Yakima. In 1908 he designed a six-cylinder 50 hp touring car complete with kitchenette and convertible to a sleeping room at night. This type of vehicle, he said, was unusually well adapted to the motoring conditions of the West. He called the car the Flying Dutchman, and planned to build four and seven-passenger models to sell for $4000 and $4500. Mid-year he made arrangements to buy out the defunct Perfection Automobile Company of South Bend (Indiana) with the intention of removing it part and parcel to the Pacific Northwest where he expected to recruit a workforce of 100 men to manufacture twenty cars a month in a new factory for which he had made provisional production arrangements in North Yakima. Unfortunately the Perfection deal fell through, and with it so did Gauntt's plans for the Flying Dutchman. Probably only the prototype was built.

FLYNN — The automobile Walter F. Flynn built in Youngstown, Ohio in 1905 and later tried to sell to the Board of Trade in Bay City, Michigan was called the Falcon. Refer to Falcon.

F. & M. — The F. & M. Specialty Company was organized in New York City late in 1910 to "manufacture and sell self-propelled vehicles and engines." Capital stock was $50,000 and the partners behind this venture were R.F. Fitzgerald of Newark, New Jersey and O.S. McFarland of New York City. Manufacture of an automobile is doubted.

FOLEY — The Foley Motor Car Company was organized in Newark, New Jersey during the summer of 1917 to manufacture and deal in automobiles. Capital stock was $25,000. Involved in this venture were E.J. Foley of Montclair and Peter A. Bannigan of Paterson. Manufacture is doubted.

FOOS — Springfield, Ohio — (1901-1906) — The Foos Gas Engine Company of Springfield was founded in 1887 and following the turn of the century claimed itself to be among the largest gasoline engine builders in the world. Scipio E. Baker was the firm's president, Charles E. Patric the vice president, Randolph Coleman the secretary and Harry E. Snyder the treasurer. The company assuredly was a prosperous one, routinely increasing its facilities during this period. Never, however, did Foos consider automobile manufacture. Any cars it assembled were strictly for experimental purposes, to test or demonstrate the company's products.

FORBES — Cromanton, Florida — (1896) — Joseph Forbes was a native of New York who served during the Civil War as a soldier in Company H, 1st New York Dragoons. He moved to Cromanton, Florida in 1886 where he continued his profession as a dentist, patenting several of his ideas, including a tooth extractor known as the Forbes forceps. Although he had been interested in the horseless carriage idea since apprenticing in a wagonmaker's shop in New York as a teenager, it was not until 1896 that he found the time and resources to build his automobile. It was a light gasoline-powered runabout that was a complete success, and which hundreds of Floridians traveled great distances to see in operation. It was the first gasoline automobile in the state of Florida. Joseph Forbes patented his invention, and dreamed of proceeding into manufacture. His later years were filled with pain, resulting from the atrocities visited upon him when he had been a prisoner at Andersonville and Libby Prison during the Civil War. Joseph Forbes was never able to secure the financing to produce his automobile. His dream died with him in January 1911. The town of Cromanton no longer exists, incidentally. In 1941 the United States Government took possession of all land in that area to build what is today Tyndall Air Force Base.

FORBES-CRUICKSHANK — The firm of Forbes Cruickshank, Inc. was organized in Passaic, New Jersey during the summer of 1917 with a capital stock of $25,000 to manufacture and deal in automobiles and accessories. Cyril P. Forbes of Paterson and Alexander G. Cruikshank of Hawthorne were the partners involved. Manufacture is doubted.

FORD — Two ventures named Ford, with no apparent connection to the Dearborn company, were organized for automobile manufacture and seem to have exited the field before any production was seen.

The Ford Automobile Company of Paterson, New Jersey, organized in early 1909 with a capital stock of $50,000 by R.W. Bates and G.M. Dorwart.

The Ford Taxicab Corporation, a $10,000 venture organized in Portland, Maine during April of 1913 by Newton R. Dexter, Joseph B. Reed and Emery G. Wilson.

FORD

1896 Ford, Quadricycle, runabout, HFM

FORD — Dearborn, Michigan — (1903-1942 et. seq.) — Henry Ford was born on a farm in rural Michigan on July 30th, 1863 and, as his father later said, grew up with "wheels in his head." At age sixteen he took himself to Detroit and a variety of machine shop and other jobs which brought him close to engines. In 1888 he married a lovely young farmer's daughter named Clara Jane Bryant, and in 1891 became an engineer for the Edison Illuminating Company. On November 6th that year the Fords' only child, Edsel, was born, and on Christmas Eve Henry, with Clara helping to dribble gasoline into the intake valve, tested his first gasoline engine in the kitchen sink of the Ford home. Although for awhile the practical matters of his employment and providing for his family took precedence, already Henry Ford envisioned building an automobile. An acquaintance of his beat him to it, however, Henry cycling behind Charles Brady King when King tested his first gasoline automobile on the streets of Detroit in March 1896. Henry completed his first car that summer in the shed behind the Ford home, half of the side of which had to be removed to get it out since its inventor had neglected to consider that the door was too small. Once out, the car — he called it a quadricycle — performed well, its drive by leather belt and chain, its two-cylinder four-stroke horizontal engine producing about 4 hp, which was good for about 20 mph on excursions into the country to the Ford or Bryant farms, with Henry driving, Clara sitting beside with Edsel on her lap. Henry Ford was on his way to becoming a legend. Although selling the vehicle was not his original intention, when Charles Ainsley offered $200 for it, Ford accepted, using the money to finance his second car, which was completed in late 1897 or early 1898. In mid-1899, his efforts by now having come to the attention of Detroit businessmen with money to invest — including Detroit's mayor William C. Maybury and William H. Murphy, one of the wealthiest men in town — the Detroit Automobile Company was organized, with Henry Ford as superintendent of a forthcoming automobile production which never came forth. Initially, Henry Ford couldn't make up his mind about what he wished to build, and when he did, his decision, much to the dismay of his backers, was for a race car — which beat a Winton at Grosse Pointe race track in October 1901. Though only about a dozen cars of any sort had thus far resulted, some of the Ford backers still retained a modicum of faith in their superintendent and a new organization called the Henry Ford Company resulted on November 30th, 1901. By March of 1902, however, disgruntled by a production that was ever forthcoming but never arriving, even the faithful Ford backers had lost faith. Moreover, they had brought in one Henry Martyn Leland as a consultant, which infuriated Ford. He left the company abruptly, taking as settlement $900 and William Murphy's promise not to use the Ford name henceforth. Murphy was good to his word; the car which Henry Leland would now build for the former Ford backers was called the Cadillac. Meanwhile, Henry Ford set himself up in a shop elsewhere in town and, with the help of Tom Cooper, built two race cars: the

1901 Ford, runabout, OCW

Arrow and the famous 999, a four-cylinder brute displacing an overwhelming 1155.3 cubic inches and in which, at Grosse Pointe in June 1903, Barney Oldfield became the first driver to circle a one-mile track in less than a minute: 59.6 seconds was his speed, 999 was the first car Oldfield had ever driven, and his performance made him a star. In January 1904, Henry Ford himself drove a revised version of 999 on the ice at Lake St. Clair to a world land speed record of 91.37 mph. Meanwhile, Ford had finally decided to become an automobile manufacturer too, with the help of money supplied by coal baron Alexander Young Malcolmson. On June 16th, 1903 the Ford Motor Company evolved from the previous short-lived incorporations of the Ford & Malcomson Company, Ltd. and the Fordmobile Company, Ltd., under neither of which had any cars been produced. But one month later, in July 1903, the first Ford Model A runabouts were loaded onto freight cars, and in the fifteen months to follow an impressive total of 1700 cars would be built and sold at $750 ($850 with tonneau) apiece. These and all subsequent cars from Ford were renegades, unrecognized by the Association of Licensed Automobile Manufacturers. Rebuffed in his initial attempt to obtain an A.L.A.M. license, Ford elected to fight instead. Though others joined him, it was Ford who protested the loudest and whose maverick stance in contesting the monopolistic Selden Patent group made him a folk hero by January 1911 when, finally, the patent was declared ineffective by court decision. By late 1904 the Model A had evolved into the C, which was different from the A mainly in the moving of its two-cylinder engine up front under a hood — Model C had a hood but engine still under seat as in Model A and there was a new Ford called the Model B which was a different car altogether save for the two-speed planetary transmission and gravity lubrication system it shared with predecessor Fords. The B was a vertical in-line 24 hp four with shaft drive and a $2000 price tag, and Henry Ford didn't like it at all. It was built mainly because Malcolmson wanted a piece of the upper-price-market action. As early as 1903, Henry Ford had said, "The way to make automobiles is to make one automobile like another, to make them all alike, to make them come through the factory just alike" — already he was thinking universal car. But the Model B was not that, neither was the two-cylinder 16 hp $1200 Model F of 1905, nor especially the 40 hp six-cylinder $2500 Model K introduced later in 1905, a car Henry Ford positively detested — though, with Frank Kulick driving, one did establish a world record for twenty-four hours of 47.2 mph and 1135 miles, which bettered the previous mark by 309 miles. By this time Ford had taken two steps toward the autonomy he desperately wanted; he made plans to extend his manufacturing to engines and running gear (previously this work had been farmed out, to Dodge Brothers especially), and he bought out Alexander Malcolmson (which meant he'd never be forced into building another expensive Ford). Henry Ford was in control now, and knew precisely where he was going. Introduced with the Model K had been the four-cylinder 15/18 hp Model N at $500, underselling the curved dash Oldsmobile (America's best-selling car of that period) and outselling the K by ten cars to one. By 1906 Ford production topped the 8000 mark, which was good for first place in the industry; in February the N was joined by the R and was followed by the S in the fall of 1907, good sellers too. In October of 1908 the Model T arrived; Henry Ford was through experimenting for almost two decades. This was exactly the car he had wanted to build since 1903. Helping him realize it were Charles Sorenson, Joseph Galamb, Jimmy Smith and especially Childe Harold Wills whose metallurgical experiments with vanadium steel would result in the lightness with durability that was one of the hallmarks of the Model T. Helping him to set the car up for production was Walter Flanders, who would leave the company, however, before the T's introduction to become the "F" of the E-M-F. The Model T Ford was a remarkable automobile, with 20 hp side-valve four-cylinder engine, two-speed planetary transmission, and a 100-inch wheelbase chassis of blessed simplicity and dogged reliability. (The countless jokes which grew up around the Model T were largely that, and affectionately told.) Considering its price class, the T was a powerful car with 45 mph possible, and it was an economical one too, needing only a gallon of gasoline every twenty-five miles or so. But more important than what the Model T was, was what the Model T did. American became a vastly different place in the wake of the Tin Lizzie, and indeed the Ford concept realized with the Model T revolutionized the world. The mass production of automobiles had its birth in August 1913 when the Ford final (or chassis) assembly line began to move. Although earlier, Ford and others (notably Ransom Eli Olds) had put together some elements (including sequential positioning of machines, men and material) necessary for mass production, it was only with the moving assembly line that a definitive mass production arrived. At Ford, chassis time was cut from 12 1/2 hours to 1 hour 33 minutes by January 1914, the month Henry Ford introduced the $5 day — and that year Ford produced more than 300,000 Model T's at the same time the entire rest of the American industry was producing approximately 100,000 less. It was in that year, too, that the Model T, previously available in black, red, green, pearl or French grey, became available in "any color so long as it's black." Mass production, of course, allowed the Model T to be profitably sold at ever-decreasing prices; introduced at $850, Ford's "Flivver" thereafter enjoyed yearly decreases to a low of $290 in December of 1924. The T's price tag was one of the few things to change during the car's lifetime. The radiator shell was revised from brass to black in 1916, electric lights had been introduced in 1915, and January, 1919 brought the option of an electric starter — but that was about all into the mid-Twenties. In 1922 the Model T passed the million mark in annual sales, and would continue to enjoy million-plus years thereafter, but no longer would the car enjoy its utter dominance in the marketplace. Everyone at Ford recognized what the emergence of popular competitors like the Chevrolet meant, except Henry Ford who through clever maneuvering shortly after the First World War — which include his resignation from the company and the placing of his son Edsel in the Ford presidency — had rid himself of all other Ford stockholders and thus now had no one to answer to but himself. Initally, Ford answered his associates' complaints regarding the Model T's old-fashionedness by introducing balloon tires in 1925, and providing the option of wire wheels and the availability of colors other than black in 1926. Ultimately, by the year following and after the building of 15,000,000 Model T's, even Henry Ford had to admit that the day of his beloved Tin Lizzie was over. The Ford assembly line was shut down at the end of May, 1927; when it was started up again six months later, the Model A was on it. Like the T, it was a side-valve four, but twice as powerful at 40 hp, and set in a 103.5-inch wheelbase chassis with three-speed sliding gear transmission and four-wheel brakes. The Tin Lizzie's planetary gearset and two-wheel brakes had by the mid-Twenties become two big marks against it, together with its ungainly appearance, this very nicely rectified in the Model A with sprightly body styling attributable mainly to Henry's son Edsel who had been guiding Lincoln fortunes since the Ford takeover of that company in 1922. No car in America had been so feverishly anticipated as the Model A Ford, and rumor ran rife during the half-year following the Ford shutdown until December 2nd, 1927 when the car made its official debut. Interestingly, among the rumors had been that the new car would be a hybrid of the Lincoln and Ford called the Linford. Though there was a pretty Lincoln look to the car, the Model A with introductory prices as low as $385 was indisputably a Ford. In the four years to follow, Ford and Chevrolet (which had become Number One with the Ford shutdown in '27) divided the production race, the Model A winning in 1929 and 1930, Chevy the victor in 1928 and 1931. Nearly five million Model A's had been built by March 31st, 1932 when its successor arrived, the Ford V-8, offering 65 hp for as little as $460. Never before had so many cylinders and so much power been offered for so little. Because Ford enjoyed coming up with the revolutionary and because experimentation with eight-cylinder engines had been ongoing at the company since the mid-Twenties, the V-8 was no doubt the car that Henry Ford would have wished to follow the Model T, though its development status had precluded that in 1927. A refined version of the Model A called Model B was introduced along with the V-8 but once the latter car got rolling, the four was forgotten altogether. In 1933 the V-8's wheelbase was increased to 112 inches from the rather short 106.5 with which it had been introduced. In 1934 when the Chevrolet went to independent front suspension, Ford was in the seemingly uncomfortable position of having to justify its continued use of all-round transverse leaf suspension (which had been introduced on the T), but a by-now increasingly stubborn Henry Ford explained it away by saying, "We use transverse springs for the same reason that we use round wheels — because we have found nothing better for the purpose." In 1935 Ford outsold Chevrolet, but for all other years in the Thirties, Chevy was on top. This is not to suggest that the V-8 Ford was an unpopular automobile. It most certainly was popular, its performance potential particularly providing an appeal to the go-faster crowd, whether its member be interested in an illegal fast getaway (as the bank-robbing Clyde Barrow who wrote Henry Ford a testimonial letter) or a legal one (Ford V-8's virtually ruled stock car racing for several years, and Ford racing specials were a mainstay of the Automobile Racing Club of America in the mid-to-late Thirties). But many average drivers preferred technical advances and more creature comforts than the V-8 had. In 1936 Chevrolet introduced hydraulic brakes; in 1937 Ford countered with a smaller 60 hp V-8 for a cheaper line of cars, but both it and the traditional V-8 (now at 85 hp) had mechanical brakes. The smaller V-8 was not a success, and Ford dealers began clamouring for a six to sell. But they were not to get it for awhile. Among numerous other problems the company had now, the labor situation at Ford during the later Thirties was ominous and life-threatening. As the Ford Motor Company moved toward the brink of disaster, an aging Henry Ford, always a mercurial man, grew increasingly recalcitrant. His son Edsel, together with long-time Ford associate Charles Sorenson, became convinced that the Ford Motor Company could only survive despite Henry Ford and not because of him. The Ford V-8 was finally given four-wheel hydraulic brakes for 1939, and the company had a new car that year, another V-8, called the Mercury. About the time it was introduced, Edsel Ford finally convinced his father to produce the car that he and Ford dealers had wanted for several years already. "A Ford Six, At Last" headlined *Business Week* when the new Special was introduced for 1941. It was the first six from Ford since the Model K that Henry had hated so much in 1905, and he had nothing to do with the engine. It was, however, introduced in any color so long as it was black, and the elder Ford may have had something to do with that. (Other colors were quickly added, however.) A pacifist since his peace ship days of the First World War, Henry Ford remained one as World War II approached and, with Charles Lindbergh, was a member of the America First Committee. His son Edsel was not. Prior to Pearl Harbor, the elder Ford had refused to aid the international war effort, believing in military production geared only for American defense purposes, but following the attack in Hawaii, he ordered a complete changeover to military production even before the War Production Board ordered it. But personal tragedy would strike Henry Ford soon. On May 26th, 1943, his son Edsel, weary and ill from the difficult years when he had become the conscience of the company and an adversary of his father, died of cancer, undulant fever and — as has been written — a broken heart. He was forty-nine years old. At the funeral Henry Ford stood tight-lipped in grief, and afterwards he appointed himself president of the Ford Motor Company. He was eighty years old. The Ford Motor Company lay in chaos now. On September 21st, 1945 — with the endorsement of his grandmother and his mother, including a threat by the latter to sell her stock — the eldest son of Edsel Ford became the president of the Ford Motor Company, over Henry Ford's objection. On April 7th, 1947 Henry Ford was gone; "The Father of the Automobile Dies," headlined *Life* magazine. It would be Henry Ford II who would guide Ford Motor Company fortunes in the postwar era.

Ford Data Compilation by Robert C. Ackerson

Model T Data Compilation by Bruce McCally

1903

FORD — MODEL A — TWO: The first production automobile produced by the Ford Motor Company, which was incorporated on June 16, 1903, the Model A, was a 2-seater runabout capable of a maximum speed of 30 mph.

With a weight of just 1250 pounds it was an early manifestation of Henry Ford's grasp of the automotive concept that would be fully exhibited in the Model T. As was common to most early automobiles the Model A had a horse buggy (without the horse of course!) appearance. The motor was positioned under the seat and a detachable tonneau provided seating for two additional passengers who gained access to their seats through a rear door.

1903 Ford, model A, runabout, OCW

I.D. DATA: Serial numbers were dash mounted, adjacent to steering column.

Model No.	Body Type & Seating	Price	Weight	Prod. Total
A	Rbt.-2P	850	1250	Note 1
A	Rbt. w/ton.-2P	950	—	Note 1

Note 1: Total production for Model A Series was 670 or 1708, depending upon the source referred to. Ford officially used the 670 figure.

ENGINE: Opposed. Two. Cast iron block. B & S: 4 in. x 4 in. Disp.: 100.4 cu. in. Brake H.P.: 8. Valve lifters: Mechanical. Carb.: Schebler (early), Holley.

CHASSIS: W.B.: 72 in.

TECHNICAL: Planetary transmission. Speeds: 2F/1R. Floor controls. Chain drive. Differential, band brakes. Wooden, spoke wheels.

HISTORICAL: Introduced July 1903. On June 19, 1903 Barney Oldfield drove the Ford 999 to a new one mile record time of 59.6 seconds. Calendar year production: 1708. Model year production: (1903-1904) 1700. The president of Ford was John S. Gray.

1904

1904 Ford, model C, runabout with tonneau, OCW

FORD — MODELS AC, C — TWO: These two Ford models replaced the Model A in late 1904. Both were powered by a larger engine developing 10hp. Ford claimed the top speed of both cars was 38mph. The Model AC was essentially a Model A with the new Model C engine. The Model C had its fuel tank positioned under the hood while that of the AC was located beneath the seat. Both cars had a longer, 78 inch wheelbase than that of the Model A.

FORD — MODEL B — FOUR: The Model B was a drastic shift in direction for Henry Ford. With its 4 passenger body, polished wood and brass trim, it was an elegant and expensive automobile. Powered by a 24hp, 318 cubic inch four it was capable of a top speed of 40mph. In place of the dry cells carried by earlier Fords, the Model B was equipped with storage batteries. A 15 gallon fuel tank was also fitted. Other features separating the $2000 Model B from other Fords was its shaft drive and rear hub drum brakes.

1904 Ford, model B, touring, JAC

I.D. DATA: Location of Serial No.: dash mounted, adjacent to steering column.

Model No.	Body Type & Seating	Price	Weight	Prod. Total
Model A	Rbt.-2P	850	1250	Note 1
Model A	Rbt. w/ton.-2P	950	1250	Note 1
Model AC	Rbt.-2P	850	1250	Note 1
Model AC	Rbt. w/ton.-2P	950	1250	Note 1
Model C	Rbt.-2P	850	1250	Note 1
Model C	Rbt. w/ton.-2P	950	1250	Note 1
Model B	2-dr. Tr.-4P	2000	1700	Note 1

Note 1: Total production in 1904 was 1,695 cars. Ford reported building a total of 670 model As and 1900 models A and AC altogether. Other sources show figures that vary.

ENGINE: [Model A] Cylinder layout: opposed. Two. Cast iron block. B & S: 4 in. x 4 in. Disp.: 100.4 cu. in. Brake H.P.: 8. Valve lifters: Mechanical. Carb.: Holley. [Model AC, C] Cylinder layout: opposed. Two. Cast iron block. B & S: 4-1/4 in. x 4-1/4 in. Disp.: 120.5 cu. in. Brake H.P.: 10. Valve lifters: Mechanical. Carb.: Holley. [Model B] Inline. Four. Cast iron block. B & S: 4-1/4 in. x 5 in. Disp.: 283.5 cu. in. Brake H.P.: 24. Valve lifters: Mechanical. Carb.: Holley.

CHASSIS: [Model A] W.B.: 72 in. [Model B] W.B.: 92 in. [Model C, Model AC] W.B.: 78 in. Tires: 28.

TECHNICAL: [Models A, AC, C] Planetary transmission. Speeds: 2F/1R. Floor shift controls. Cone clutch. Chain drive. Differential band brakes. Wooden spoke wheels. [Model B] Planetary transmission. Speeds: 2F/1R. Floor shift controls. Cone clutch. Shaft drive. Drum brakes. Two rear wheels. Wooden spoke wheels.

HISTORICAL: Date of Introduction: Sept. 1904 (Model C, AC). Calendar year production: 1695. Model year production: (1904-1905) 1745. Antique. The president of Ford was John S. Gray.

Model A
1903, 2-cyl., Ser. No. 1-670, 8 hp
1904, 2-cyl., Ser. No. 671-1708, 10 hp

	FP	5	4	3	2	1
Rbt	800	3750	7500	12,500	17,500	25,000
Rbt W/ton	850	4100	8250	13,750	19,250	27,500

Model B
10 hp, 4-cyl.

Tr	2000			Value inestimable		

Model C
10 hp, 2-cyl., Ser. No. 1709-2700

Rbt	800	3750	7500	12,500	17,500	25,000
Rbt W/ton	950	4100	8250	13,750	19,250	27,500
Dr's Mdl	850	3750	7500	12,500	17,500	25,000

Model F
16 hp, 2-cyl., (Produced 1904-05-06)

Tr	1100	3000	6000	10,000	14,000	20,000

Model K
40 hp, 6-cyl., (Produced 1905-06-07-08)

Tr	2800	10,500	21,000	35,000	49,000	70,000
Rds	2800	10,500	21,000	35,000	49,000	70,000

Model N
18 hp, 4-cyl., (Produced 1906-07-08)

Rbt	600	1400	4200	7000	9800	14,000

Model R
4-cyl., (Produced 1907-08)

Rbt	750	1400	4200	7000	9800	14,000

Model S
4-cyl.

Rbt	750	1400	4200	7000	9800	14,000

1905

FORD — MODEL F — TWO: The Ford Models C and B were carried into 1905. The Model C was given light yellow painted running gear in place of the former red finish along with wider 3 x 28 wheels.

In February 1905, these Fords were joined by the Model F powered by a 2 cylinder engine developing approximately 16hp. The Model F had a wheelbase of 84 inches and was fitted with a green body, cream colored wheels and running gear.

1905 Ford, model B, touring, OCW

I.D. DATA: Serial numbers were dash mounted, adjacent to steering column

Model No.	Body Type & Seating	Price	Weight	Prod. Total
C	Rbt.-2P	800	1250	Note 1
C	Rbt. w/ton.	950	1250	Note 1
B	2-dr. Tr.-4P	2000	1700	Note 1
F	2-dr. Tr. Car-4P	1000	1400	Note 1
F	2-dr. Dr. Cpe.-2P	1250	—	Note 1

Note 1: Total production for 1905 was 1,599 cars.

ENGINE: [Model C] Opposed. Two. Cast iron block. B & S: 4-1/4 in. x 4-1/2 in. Disp.: 120.5 cu. in. Brake H.P.: 10. Valve lifters: Mechanical. Carb.: Holley. [Model B] Inline. Four. Cast iron block. B & S: 4-1/4 in. x 4 in. Disp.: 283.5 cu. in. Brake H.P.: 24. Valve lifters: Mechanical. Carb.: Holley. [Model F] Opposed. Two. Cast iron block. B & S: 4-1/2 in. x 4 in. Disp.: 127 cu. in. Brake H.P.: 16+. Valve lifters: Mechanical. Carb.: Holley.

1905 Ford, model C, runabout with tonneau, OCW

CHASSIS: [Model C] W.B.: 78 in. Tires: 28. [Model F] W.B.: 84 in. Tires: 30. [Model B] W.B.: 92 in. Tires: 32.

TECHNICAL: [Model C] Planetary transmission. Speeds: 2F/1R. Floor controls. Cone clutch. Chain drive. Differential band brakes. Wooden spoke wheels. Wheel size: 28. [Model B] Planetary transmission. Speeds: 2F/1R. Floor controls. Cone clutch. Shaft drive. Drum brakes on two rear wheels. Wooden spoke wheels. Wheel size: 32. [Model F] Planetary transmission. Speeds: 2F/1R. Floor controls. Cone clutch. Chain drive. Differential band brakes. Wooden spoke wheels. Wheel size: 30.

OPTIONS: Top. Windshield. Lights.

HISTORICAL: Introduced February 1905 (Model F). Calendar year production: 1599. Model year production: (1905-1906) 1599. The President of Ford was John S. Gray.

1906

FORD — MODEL K — SIX: Late in 1905 the Model K Ford, priced at $2500 in touring form debuted. Since Henry Ford was moving close to the final design of his "car for the multitudes", it's not surprising that he cared little for this expensive automobile. Along with the touring model a roadster version was offered that was guaranteed to attain a 60 mph top speed.

FORD — MODEL N — FOUR: The $500 Model N with its front-mounted 4-cylinder engine developing over 15 hp was capable of 45 mph. Its styling, highlighted by such features as twin nickel-plated front lamps and a boat-tail rear deck, plus an 84 inch wheelbase, and a reputation for reliability represented a solid step forward by Henry Ford in his quest for a low-priced car for the mass market.

1906 Ford, model K, touring, JAC

FORD — MODEL F — TWO: The Model F was continued into 1906 unchanged. No longer available were Models B and C.

I.D. DATA: Dash mounted, adjacent to steering column.

Model No.	Body Type & Seating	Price	Weight	Prod. Total
Model F	2 dr. Tr. Cr.-4P	1100	1400	Note 1
Model K	2 dr. Tr. Cr.-4P	2500	2400	Note 1
Model K	Rbt.-4P	2500	2400	Note 1
Model N	Rbt.-2P	600	800	Note 1

Note 1: Total production was 2,798 or 8,729 depending upon the source referred to. Ford Motor Co. records show both figures.

1906 Ford, model N, roadster, OCW

ENGINE: [Model F] Opposed. 2. Cast iron block. B x S: 4-1/4 in. x 4-1/2 in. Disp: 128 cu. in. Brake H.P.: 10. Valve lifters: Mechanical. Carb.: Holley. [Model K] In line. Six. Cast iron block. B x S: 4-1/2 in. x 4-1/4 in. Disp.: 405 cu. in. Brake H.P. 40. Valve lifters: Mechanical. Carb.: Holley. [Model N] In line Four. Cast iron block. B x S: 3-3/4 in. x 3-3/8 in. Disp.: 149 cu. in. Brake H.P.: 15-18. Valve lifters: Mechanical. Carb.: Holley.

CHASSIS: [Series Model F] W.B.: 84. Tires: 30. [Series Model N] W.B.: 84. Tires: 2-1/2'' width. [Series Model K] W.B.: 114/120.

TECHNICAL: [Model F] Transmission: Planetary. Speeds: 2F/1R. Floor shift controls. Cone clutch. Chain drive. Differential band. Wooden spokes. Wheel size: 30. [Model K] Transmission: Planetary. Speeds 2F/1R. Floor shift controls. Disc clutch. Shaft drive. [Model N] Transmission: Planetary. Speeds: 2F/1R. Floor. Disc clutch. Chain drive.

OPTIONS: Cowl lamps. Bulb horn. 3'' wheels (Model N) (50.00).

HISTORICAL: Henry Ford became president of the Ford Motor Company, following the death of John S. Gray on July 6, 1906. A racing version of the Model K set a new world's 24 hr record of 1135 miles of 47.2 mph at Ormond Beach.

1907

FORD — MODEL K — SIX: The Model K was unchanged for 1907.

FORD — MODEL N — FOUR: The Model N was continued unchanged for 1907. As before it was a handsome automobile with nickel hardware and quarter-circle fenders. Volume production didn't begin until late 1907 when the price rose to $600.

1907 Ford, model K, touring, OCW

FORD — MODEL R — FOUR: The Model R was introduced in February 1907 as a more elaborate version of the Model N with foot boards in place of the Model N's carriage step. A mechanical lubrication ststyem also replaced the forced-feed oiler of the Model N.

FORD — MODEL S — FOUR: The Model S had the same mechanical and appearance features as that of the Model R, in addition to a single seat tonneau.

I.D. DATA: Serial numbers wer dash mounted, adjacent to steering column.

Model No.	Body Type & Seating	Price	Weight	Prod. Total
K	2-dr. Tr. Car-4P	2800	2000	—
K	Rbt.-4P	2800	2000	—
N	Rbt.-2P	600	1050	—
R	Rbt.-2P	750	1400	Note 1
S	Rbt. w/ton.-4P	700	1400	—
S	Rds.-2P	750	—	—

Note 1: Total production of the Model R was approximately 2,500 cars.

ENGINE: [Model K] Inline. Six. Cast iron block. B & S: 4-1/2 in. x 4-1/4 in. Disp.: 405 cu. in. Brake H.P.: 40. Valve lifters: Mechanical. Carb.: Holley. [Model N, R, S] Inline. Four. Cast iron block. B & S: 3-3/4 in. x 3-3/8 in. Disp.: 149 cu. in. Brake H.P.: 15-18. Valve lifters: Mechanical. Carb.: Holley.

1907 Ford, model S, roadster, OCW

CHASSIS: [Model K] W.B.: 120 in. [Model N, R, S] W.B.: 84 in. Tires: 3" width.

TECHNICAL: [Model K] Planetary transmission. Speeds: 2F/1R. Floor controls. Disc clutch. Shaft drive. [Model N, R, S] Planetary transmission. Speeds: 2F/1R. Floor controls. Disc clutch. Chain drive.

HISTORICAL: Calendar year production was 6,775 according to some sources and 14,887 according to others. The president of Ford was Henry Ford.

1908

FORD — MODELS K, N, R, S — FOUR: For the 1908 model year Ford continued to produce the K, N, R, and S models until production of the Model T began in October 1908.

I.D. DATA: Serial numbers were dash mounted, adjacent to steering column.

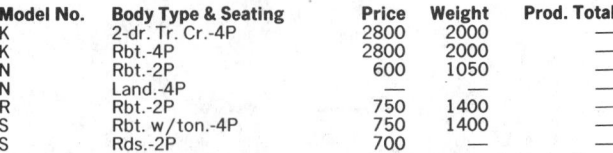

Model No.	Body Type & Seating	Price	Weight	Prod. Total
K	2-dr. Tr. Cr.-4P	2800	2000	—
K	Rbt.-4P	2800	2000	—
N	Rbt.-2P	600	1050	—
N	Land.-4P	—	—	—
R	Rbt.-2P	750	1400	—
S	Rbt. w/ton.-4P	750	1400	—
S	Rds.-2P	700	—	—

1908 Ford, model S, roadster, OCW

ENGINE: [Model K] Inline. Six. Cast iron block. B & S: 4-1/2 in. x 4-1/4 in. Disp.: 405. Brake H.P.: 40. Valve lifters: Mechanical. Carb.: Holley. [Model N, R, S] Inline. Four. Cast iron block. B & S: 3-3/4 in. x 3-3/8 in. Disp.: 149. Brake H.P.: 15-18. Valve lifters: Mechanical. Carb.: Holley.

CHASSIS: [Model K] W.B.: 120 in. [Model N, R, S] W.B.: 84 in. Tires: 3" width.

TECHNICAL: [Model K] Planetary transmission. Speeds: 2F/1R. Floor shift controls. Disc clutch. Shaft drive. [Model N, R, S] Planetary transmission. Speeds: 2F/1R. Floor shift controls. Disc clutch. Chain drive.

HISTORICAL: Calendar year production was 6,015 according to some sources and 10,202 according to others (including early Model T Fords). The president of Ford was Henry Ford.

1908
Model T, 4-cyl., 2 levers, 2 foot pedals (1,000 produced)

	FP	5	4	3	2	1
Tr	825	3000	6000	10,000	14,000	20,000

1909

1909 Ford, model T, touring, HFM

FORD — EARLY 1909 — MODEL T: The Model T Ford was introduced in October 1908, and was an entirely new car when compared to Ford's previous models. The engine had four cylinders, cast en-bloc; with a removable cylinder head, quite unusual for the time. The engine pan was a one-piece steel stamping and had no inspection plate.

The chassis featured transverse springs, front and rear; a rear axle housing which was drawn steel rather than a casting. Rear axles were non-tapered; the hubs being held with a key and a pin, with the pin being retained by the hub cap. The front axle was a forged "I" beam with spindles which had integral arms.

The use of Vanadium steel almost throughout made for a stronger yet lighter machine which gave the Ford impressive performance for its time.

Wheels were 30" with 30x3" tires on the front, and 30x3-1/2" on the rear. The wheel hub flanges were 5-1/2" diameter (compared with 6" from 1911 until the end of production in 1927).

Windshields and tops were optional equipment on the open cars, as were gas headlights, speedometers, robe rails, Prestolite tanks, foot rests, auto chimes, car covers and other accessories which Ford would install at the factory.

The radiator was brass, as were any lamps furnished (oil cowl and tail lamps were standard equipment). The hood had no louvres and was made of aluminum.

Body styles offered were the Touring, Runabout (roadster), Coupe, Town Car and Landaulet.

Bodies were generally made of wood panels over a wood frame, and were offered in red, gray and green; gray being primarily on the Runabouts, red on the Tourings, and green on the Town Cars and Landaulets.

These early cars (first 2500) were so unique that they are generaly considered a separate subject when discussing the Model T. Essentially, the engines had built-in water pumps; and the first 800 cars came with two foot pedals and two control levers (the second lever being for reverse) instead of the usual three pedals and one lever.

Front fenders were square tipped, with no bills.

FORD — LATE 1909 - MODEL T: Beginning about car number 2500, the Model T became more or less standardized. Through most of 1909 the windshields and tops on the open cars remained optional, but more and more were delivered with this equipment, as well as gas headlights, factory installed. By the end of the year, they were standard.

Body types and styling continued unchanged. Colors continued as in the early production except that green and red Tourings were both produced, along with a mixture of colors in the other models as well. Red was not offered after June 1909. Black was not listed as an available color and only one of the shipping invoices showed black, but early cars extant today seem to indicate that black was used. This could be due to oxidation of the top color coat, but black early Fords are an enigma to the Model T student. The one aluminum-paneled Touring body, built by Pontiac Body, was discontinued about September 1909.

Fenders were similar in design to the earlier 1909's but now had rounded fronts with small "bills."

The engine no longer had the water pump. It was now cooled by thermo-syphon action and set the pattern for all later Model T engines.

I.D. DATA: [Early 1909 (Oct. '08 to Apr. 09)] Serial number was between center exhaust ports on side of engine. Starting: 1 (October 1908). Ending: 2500 (approx.) (The first of the non-water pump engines was 2448, built on April 22, 1909 but there was some mixture of the old and the new in production for a short time.) Calendar year engine numbers: 1 to 309. (October to December 1908.) Car numbers were stamped on a plate on the front seat kick panel and these were the same as the engine numbers. Other numbers stamped on the body sills, etc. were manufacturer's numbers and not an identifying number. [1909] Serial number was behind the timing gear on the lower right side of the engine. Starting: 2501 (approx.) Ending: 11145 (approx.) (There is no "break" between the 1909 and 1910 cars. 11146 was the first number assembled in October 1909, the beginning of Ford's fiscal year 1910.). 1909 calendar year engine numbers: 310 to 14161 (approx.) Car numbers were stamped on a plate on the front seat kick panel and these were the same as the engine numbers. Other numbers stamped on the body sills, etc. were manufacturer's numbers and not an identifying number.

Model No.	Body Type & Seating	Price	Weight	Prod. Total
T	Tr.-5P	850 (A)	1200	7728 (B)
T	Rbt.-2P	825 (A)	NA	2351 (B)
T	Town Car-7P	1000 (A)	NA	236 (B)
T	Landaulet-7P	950 (A)	NA	298 (B)
T	Cpe.-2P	950 (A)	NA	47 (B)

Note: 1200 pounds was the figure given for the Touring car and "others in proportion." The bare chassis weighed about 900 pounds.

All body styles except the roadster had two doors; the front compartment being open and without doors on all but the Coupe.

(A) Prices effective October 1, 1908 (at introduction of the Model T).
(B) Fiscal year: October 1, 1908 to September 30, 1909.

1909 Ford, model T, coupe, HAC

ENGINE: [Early 1909 (first 2500)] L-head. Four. Cast iron block. B & S: 3-3/4 in. x 4 in. Disp.: 176.7 cu. in. C.R.: 4.5:1 (approx.) Brake H.P.: 22 @ 1600 R.P.M. N.A.C.C. H.P.: 22.5. Main bearings: Three. Valve lifters: Solid. Carb.: Kingston 5-ball, Buffalo. Torque: 83 lbs.-ft. @ 900 R.P.M.
Note: The first 2500 engines had an integral gear-driven water pump and a gear driven fan. There was no babbitt in the upper half of the main bearings. No inspection plate in the crankcase. Valve stems and lifters are exposed (no cover door).

[1909] L-head. Four. Cast iron block. B & S: 3-3/4 in. x 4 in. Disp.: 176.7 cu. in. C.R.: 4.5:1 (approx.) Brake H.P.: 22 @ 1600 R.P.M. N.A.C.C. H.P.: 22.5. Main bearings: Three. Valve lifters: Solid. Carb.: Kingston 5-ball, Holley, Buffalo. Torque: 83 lbs.-ft. @ 900 R.P.M.
Note: No water pump; now cooled by thermo-syphon action. There was no babbitt in the upper half of the main bearings. No inspection plate in the crankcase. Valve stems and lifters are exposed (no cover door).

CHASSIS: W.B.: 100 in. O.L.: 10 ft. 8 in. (Chassis) 11 ft. 2-1/2 in. (car). Frt/Rear Tread: 56 in. (60 in. optional until 1916). Tires: 30 x 3 front, 30 x 3-1/2 rear, standard equipment 1909-1925.
Note: Chassis essentially identical except those after mid-1913 have a longer rear crossmember.

TECHNICAL: [Early 1909 (First 800)] Planetary transmission. Speeds: 2F/1R. 2 pedal controls and two levers on floor. (See "General Comments") Multiple disk clutch (24 disks). Torque tube drive. Straight bevel rear axle. Overall ratio: 3.63:1. Brakes: contracting band in transmission. Hand-operated external expanding in rear wheels. Foot brake stops driveshaft. Parking brake on two rear wheels. Wheel size: 30 in.

OPTIONS: The basic equipment included three oil lamps only. (Two side and one tail.)
Options listed included: Windshield. Headlamps. Tops. Horns. Prestolite tanks (instead of the carbide tank). Robe rails. Tire chains. Top boots. Foot rests. Spare tire carriers. Speedometers. Bumpers. No prices were given.

1909 Ford, model T, touring, OCW

**1909
Model T, 4-cyl.**

	FP	5	4	3	2	1
Rbt	825	2300	5400	9000	12,600	18,000
Tr	850	2000	5100	8500	11,900	17,000
Trbt	950	2800	5700	9500	13,300	19,000
Cpe	950	2000	5100	8500	11,900	17,000
TwnC	1000	3300	6600	11,000	15,400	22,000
Lan'let	950	2800	5700	9500	13,300	19,000

GENERAL COMMENTS

Clutch & Brakes [thru car 800]: Clutch pedal gives low when pressed to floor, high when released, neutral in-between. Reverse lever puts clutch in neutral and applies reverse brake band. Second lever is the parking brake. [1909-1927] Planetary transmission. Speeds: 2F/1R. 3 pedal controls and 1 lever on floor. * Multiple disk clutch (26 disks 1909-1915). (25 disks 1915-1927). Torque tube drive. Straight bevel rear axle. Overall ratio: 3.63:1. Brakes: Contracting band in transmission. Hand-operated internal expanding in rear wheels. Foot brake stops driveshaft. Parking brake on two rear wheels. Wheel size: 30 in. (21 in. optional in 1925, standard in 1926-1927). Drivetrain options: 4 to 1 optional rear axle ratio beginning in 1919.

Clutch & Brakes [after car 800]: Clutch pedal gives low when pressed to floor, high when released, neutral in-between. Control lever puts clutch in neutral and applies parking brake. Center foot pedal applies reverse. Third (right hand) pedal is the service brake, applying transmission brake band.

Model T Wheels: Standard wheels are wooden spoke with demountable rims an option beginning in 1919. In 1925, 21" wood-spoke demountable rim wood wheels were an option; these became standard in 1926. Beginning January 1926 optional 21" wire wheels became available, and these became standard on some closed cars in calendar year 1927.

In mid-1925 (1926 models) the transmission brake was made about a half-inch wider, and the rear wheel brakes were enlarged to 11" with lined shoes. (1909-1925 were 7" with cast iron shoes (no lining).

Springs were transverse semi-elliptic, front and rear.

Model T Steering: 3 to 1 steering gear ratio by planetary gear at top of steering column until mid-1925 when ratio was changed to 5 to 1.

1910

1910 Ford, model T, runabout, OCW

FORD — MODEL T: The 1910 Fords were unchanged from 1909, except for a number of mechanical modifications in the rear axle, and the use of one standard color on all models, dark green. The Landaulet and Coupe were discontinued in 1910 and a new Tourabout (basically a touring car using two separate seat sections) was added. All 1910 Model Ts had windshields.

I.D. DATA: Serial number was behind the timing gear on the lower right side of the engine. Starting: 11146 (approx.) Ending: 31532 (approx.) (there is no "break" between the 1910 and 1911 cars. 31533 was the first number assembled in October 1910, the beginning of Ford's fiscal year 1911. The first "1911" car built was a Torpedo Runabout in which the chassis was assembled October 5, and the final assembly October 26. The first "blue" cars were built during October and are presumed to be "1911" models.) 1910 Calendar year engine numbers: 14162 (approx.) to 34901. Car numbers were stamped on a plate on the front seat kick panel and these were the same as the engine numbers. Other numbers stamped on the body sills, etc. were manufacturer's numbers and not an identifying number.

Model No.	Body Type & Seating	Price	Weight	Prod. Total
T	Tr.-5P	950 (A)	1200	16,890 (B)
T	Tourabout-4P	950 (A)	NA	** (C)
T	Rbt.-2P	900 (A)	NA	1486 (B)
T	Town Car-7P	1200 (A)	NA	377 (B)
T	Landaulet-7P	1100 (A)	NA	2 (B)
T	Cpe.-2P	1050 (A)	NA	187 (B)
T	Chassis	NA	900	108 (D)

Note: 1200 pounds was the figure given for the Touring car, and "others in proportion." The bare chassis weighed about 900 pounds.
All body styles except the Roadster and the Tourabout had two doors; the front compartment being open and without doors on all but the Coupe. The Tourabout was similar to the Touring but had two roadster-like seat sections and no doors.
(A) Prices effective October 1, 1909
(B) Fiscal year, October 1, 1909 to September 30, 1910
(C) Tourings and Tourabouts grouped. 16,890 is the total of the two.
(D) Chassis not shown in the catalog.

ENGINE: L-head. Four. Cast iron block. B & S: 3-3/4 in. x 4 in. Disp.: 176.7 in. C.R.: 4.5:1 (approx.) Brake H.P.: 22 @ 1600 R.P.M. N.A.C.C. H.P.: 22.5. Main bearings: Three. Valve lifters: Solid. Carb.: Kingston 5-ball, Holley, Buffalo (early 1910 only). Torque: 83 lbs.-ft. @ 900 R.P.M.
Note: No water pump; now cooled by thermo-syphon action. There was no babbitt in the upper half of the main bearings. No inspection plate in the crankcase. Valve stems and lifters are exposed (no cover door).

CHASSIS: [1909-1925] W.B.: 100 in. O.L.: 10 ft. 8 in. (Chassis) 11 ft. 2-1/2 in. (car). Frt/Rear Tread: 56 in. (60 in. optional until 1916). Tires: 30 x 3 front, 30 x 3-1/2 rear, standard equipment 1909-1925.

TECHNICAL: Planetary transmission. Speeds: 2F/1R. 3 pedal controls and 1 lever on floor. Multiple disk clutch. Torque tube drive. Straight bevel rear axle. Overall ratio: 3.63:1. Brakes: Contracting band in transmission. Hand-operated internal expanding in rear wheels. Foot brake stops driveshaft. Parking brake on two rear wheels.
Note: Additional technical details will be found in the 1909 "General Comments" box.

OPTIONS: The many options listed for 1909 were not available in 1910. Standard equipment for the open cars now included the windshield, gas headlamps and carbide generator, speedometer and top with side curtains.
Interestingly, the more expensive closed cars (Landaulet, Town Car and Coupe) were equipped with horn and oil lamps only. Headlamps and speedometer were $80 extra.

1910
Model T, 4-cyl.

	FP	5	4	3	2	1
Rbt	650	1400	4200	7000	9800	14,000
Tr	950	1500	4350	7250	10,150	14,500
Cpe	1050	1550	4500	7500	10,500	15,000
TwnC	1200	2000	5100	8500	11,900	17,000
C'ml Rds	900	1550	4500	7500	10,500	15,000

1911

1911 Ford, model T, town car, HAC

FORD — MODEL T: Approximately January 1911 the Model T was completely restyled. New fenders, a new but similar radiator, new wheels, new bodies, and during the year, a new engine, front axle and rear axle made the 1911 Ford almost a new beginning.
Bodies were now made with steel panels over a wood framework. A new standard color of dark blue was used on all models. *
Body types continued those offered in 1910. The Tourabout and Landaulet, while listed in the catalogs, were not produced in 1911. The Coupe was phased out; only forty-five being built.
Two new bodies were offered, the Open Runabout and the Torpedo Runabout, both of which differed considerably from the other models in that they had curved fenders, a longer hood, a lower seating arrangement and a lower and longer steering column. In addition, the gas tank was located on the rear deck, behind the seat. The two cars were similar; the Open Runabout not having doors while the Torpedo had one on each side.
Near the end of the year, and then called a "1912" model, a Delivery Car was offered.
Fender construction was also new, setting a general pattern for the bulk of Model T production (until 1926). The front fenders had larger "Gills" than did the 1910 style.
Lamps were all brass; gas headlights and oil (kerosene) side and tail lamps.
The rear axle housing was redesigned. The earlier pressed steel type had gone through a number of modifications in 1909, 1910 and early 1911 but in mid-year a new type with a cast-iron center section appeared. Axles were now taper-end (perhaps changed before the new housing) and the hub flanges were 6" in diameter.
The front axle now used spindles with separate steering arms, and the axle ends were modified to accept the new spindles. The front axle remained relatively unchanged in later years.
* See comments on black cars in 1909.

I.D. DATA: Serial number was behind the timing gear on the lower right side of the engine. Starting: 31533 (approx.). Ending: 70749 (approx.). (There is no "break" between the 1911 and 1912 cars. 70750 was the first number assembled in October 1911, the beginning of Ford's fiscal year 1912.) 1911 Calendar year engine numbers: 34901 to 88900 (approx.).
Car numbers were stamped on a plate on the fire wall and these might be the same as the engine numbers. Ford now used the engine number to identify all cars. Other numbers stamped on the body sills, etc. were manufacturer's numbers and not an identifying number.

Model No.	Body Type & Seating	Price	Weight	Prod. Total
T	Tr.-5P	780 (B)	1200	26,405 (C)
T	Trbt.-4P	725 (B)	NA	0 (E)
T	Rbt.-2P	680 (B)	NA	7845 (E)
T	Torp. Rbt.-2P	725 (B)	NA	(E)
T	Open Rbt.-2P	680 (B)	NA	(E)
T	Twn. Car-7P	960 (A)	NA	315 (C)
T	Lan.-7P	1100 (A)	NA	0 (C)
T	Cpe.-2P	840 (A)	NA	45 (C)
T	Chassis	NA	940	248 (D)

Note: 1200 pounds was the figure given for the Touring car, with "others in proportion." The bare chassis weighed about 940 pounds.
All body styles except the Roadster and the Tourabout had two doors; the front compartment being open and without doors on all but the Coupe. The Tourabout was similar to the Touring but had two roadster-like seat sections and no doors.
The Coupe, Landaulet and Tourabout were discontinued before calendar 1911.
(A) Prices for cars without headlamps!
(B) Prices effective October 1, 1910.
(C) Fiscal year, October 1, 1910 to September 30, 1911.
(D) Chassis not shown in catalogs.
(E) Runabouts not broken down by types in production figures.

1911 Ford, model T, touring, OCW

ENGINE: L-head. Four. Cast iron block. B & S: 3-3/4 in. x 4 in. Disp.: 176.7 cu. in. C.R.: 4.5:1 (approx.). Brake H.P.: 22 @ 1600 R.P.M. N.A.C.C. H.P.: 22.5. Main bearings: Three. Valve lifters: Solid. Carb.: Kingston 5-ball, Holley 4500, Holley H-1 4550. Torque: 83 lbs.-ft. @ 900 R.P.M.
Note: Thermo-syphon. Upper main bearings now babbitted. Valve chambers (2) now enclosed using steel doors held with one stud/nut each. Inspection plate in the crankcase.

CHASSIS: W.B.: 100 in. O.L.: 10 ft. 8 in. (Chassis) 11 ft. 2-1/2 in. (car). Frt/Rear Tread: 56 in. (60 in. optional until 1916). Tires: 30 x 3 front, 30 x 3-1/2 rear, standard equipment 1909-1925.

TECHNICAL: Planetary transmission. Speeds: 2F/1R. 3 pedal controls and 1 lever on floor. Multiple disk clutch. Torque tube drive. Straight bevel rear axle. Overall ratio: 3.63:1. Brakes: Contracting band in transmission. Hand-operated internal expanding in rear wheels. Foot brake stops driveshaft. Parking brake on two rear wheels.
Note: Additional technical details will be found in the 1909 "General Comments" box.

OPTIONS: All cars equipped with headlamps, horn, etc. with no options. Ford even said the warrantee would be voided if any accessories were added, although it's doubtful this ever happened.

1911
Model T, 4-cyl.

	FP	5	4	3	2	1
Rbt	680	1750	4800	8000	11,200	16,000
Tor Rds	725	1750	4800	8000	11,200	16,000
Tr	700	2800	5700	9500	13,300	19,000
Trbt	780	2300	5400	9000	12,600	18,000
Cpe	1050	1550	4500	7500	10,500	15,000
TwnC	1200	2800	5700	9500	13,300	19,000
C'ml Rds	680	1250	3900	6500	9100	13,000
Dely Van	700	1250	3900	6500	9100	13,000

1912

FORD — MODEL T: Approximately January, 1912 the Model T was again restyled, although the appearance was similar to the 1911 cars. The Touring car was now supplied with "fore doors" which enclosed the front compartment. These were removable and many have been lost over the years. The metal side panels of the Touring were now relatively smooth from top to bottom, eliminating the "step" under the seats which marked the 1911's.

The top support straps now fasten to the windshield hinge, rather than to the front of the chassis as they had in prior years.

The Torpedo Runabout was now based on the standard runabout, and the Open Runabout was discontinued. While retaining the curved rear fenders, the front fenders were now standard. The hood and steering column were also the same as those used on the other 1912 cars. The front compartment was enclosed in a manner similar to the 1911 Torpedo.

The "1912" style year lasted only about nine months; an all new "1913" car appeared about September.

The only color on record for 1912 was dark blue but the existence of black cars of the era seems to indicate that black was available as well.

I.D. DATA: Serial number was behind the timing gear on the lower right side of the engine until about 100,000, then just behind the water inlet on the left side of the engine. Also about this time the location was again changed to the standard position above the water inlet, with some mixture of locations for a time. Starting: 70750 (approx.) (Some records show 69877 built on September 30, 1911.) Ending: 157424 (approx.) (There is no "break" between the 1912 and 1913 cars. 157425 was the first number assembled on October 1912, the beginning of Ford's fiscal year 1913.) 1912 Calendar year engine numbers: 88901 to 183563. According to Ford records engines with numbers B1 and B12247 were built at the Detroit plant beginning October 1912 and October 1913 but no records

1912 Ford, model T, touring, OCW

exist as to the exact dates. Car numbers were stamped on a plate on the fire wall. Other numbers stamped on the body sills, etc. were manufacturer's numbers and not an identifying number. Car numbers no longer agreed with the motor numbers and Ford kept no records of them.

Model No.	Body Type & Seating	Price	Weight	Prod. Total
T	Tr.-5P	690	1200	50,598 (A)
T	Torp. Runabout-2P	590	NA	13,376 (B)
T	Comm. Rdstr.-2P	590	NA	(B)
T	Town Car-7P	900	NA	802 (A)
T	Delv. Car-2P	700	NA	1845 (A)
T	Cpe.-2P	NA	NA	19 (C)
T	Chassis	NA	940	2133 (C)

Note: 1200 pounds was the figure given for the Touring car, with "others in proportion." The bare chassis weighed about 940 pounds.
The Touring cars had three doors (none for the driver).
(A) Fiscal year, October 1, 1911 to September 30, 1912.
(B) Roadster production figures were combined. The total was 13,376.
(C) Coupes and the Chassis were not shown in the catalogs.

ENGINE: L-head. Four. Cast iron block. B & S: 3-3/4 in. x 4 in. Disp.: 176.7 cu. in. C.R.: 4.5:1 (approx.) Brake H.P.: 22 @ 1600 R.P.M. N.A.C.C. H.P.: 22.5. Main bearings: Three. Valve lifters: Solid. Carb.: Kingston 6-ball*, Holley H-1 4550. Torque: 83 lbs.-ft. @ 900 R.P.M.
Note: Thermo-syphon. Valve chambers (2) now enclosed using steel doors held with one stud/nut each. Inspection plate in the crankcase.
* Kingston carburetor used in limited quantities and does not appear in any of the Ford parts lists.

CHASSIS: W.B.: 100 in. O.L.: 10 ft. 8 in. (Chassis) 11 ft. 2-1/2 in. (car). Frt/Rear Tread: 56 in. (60 in. optional until 1916). Tires: 30 x 3 front, 30 x 3-1/2 rear, standard equipment 1909-1925.

TECHNICAL: Planetary transmission. Speeds: 2F/1R. 3 pedal controls and 1 lever on floor. Multiple disk clutch. Torque tube drive. Straight bevel rear axle. Overall ratio: 3.63:1. Brakes: Contracting band in transmission. Hand-operated internal expanding in rear wheels. Foot brake stops driveshaft. Parking brake on two rear wheels.
Note: Additional technical details will be found in the 1909 "General Comments" box.

OPTIONS: The basic equipment included three oil lamps. (Two side and one tail.)
Windshield. Headlamps. Tops. Horns. Top boots. Speedometers.

1912
Model T, 4-cyl.

	FP	5	4	3	2	1
Rds	590	1550	4500	7500	10,500	15,000
Tor Rds	590	1750	4800	8000	11,200	16,000
Tr	690	2000	5100	8500	11,900	17,000
TwnC	900	2300	5400	9000	12,600	18,000
Dely Van	700	1400	4200	7000	9800	14,000
C'ml Rds	590	1250	3900	6500	9100	13,000

1913

1913 Ford, model T, touring, HFM

FORD — MODEL T: About September 1912 Ford introduced the second new body in the year, the "1913" models. These were the first to set the "pattern" for the next 12 years. The metal side panels now extended from the firewall to the rear, with one door on the left side (Touring Car) at the rear, and two doors on the right.

The doors were unique with this new body; they extended clear to the splash apron. There was no metal support between the front and rear sections of the body and this proved to be a severe problem. The body could flex so much that the doors opened while underway. The initial solution to the problem was to add a steel reinforcement across the rear door sills; then heavier body sills, and then both the heavy sills and the steel reinforcement.

The bottom section of the windshield on the open cars now sloped rearwards; the top section being vertical and folding forward.

The fenders followed the pattern of the 1911-12 cars except that they no longer had the "Bills" at the front.

Side, tail and headlamps were still oil and gas but were now made of steel (painted black) except for the tops and rims which were still brass.

The rear axle housings were again redesigned. The center section was now larger (fatter) and the axle tubes were flared and riveted to it.

"Made in USA" now appeared on the radiator under the "Ford." The same notation appeared on many other parts as well and perhaps this was due to the Canadian production. 1913 was the first year in which Ford of Canada manufactured their own engines, etc.

According to Ford data, the 1913 cars were painted dark blue with striping on the very early models. As in earlier models, black is a possibility but it is not documented in any Ford literature.

Body styles offered were the Touring, Runabout and Town Car. The Torpedo with the rear deck mounted gas tank was discontinued. (Ford called the regular runabout a "torpedo" for several years after this.) The Delivery Car, which had proved to be a sales disaster, was also dropped.

I.D. DATA: Serial number was above the water inlet on the left side of he engine. Starting: 157,425 (approx.) October 1912. "1913" cars may have been built earlier. Ending: 248735. (There is no "break" between the 1913 and 1914 cars. The "1914" style Touring was introduced about August 1913, which could make the ending number around 320000 for "1913" cars.) 1913 Calendar year engine numbers: 183564 to 408347. According to Ford records engines with numbers B1 and B12247 were built at the Detroit plant between October 1912 and October 1913 but no records exist as to the exact dates. Numbers stamped on the body sills, etc. were manufacturer's numbers and not an identifying number.

Model No.	Body Type & Seating	Price	Weight	Prod. Total
T	3-dr. Tr.-5P	600 (A)	1200	126,715 (B)
T	2-dr. Rbt.-2P	525 (A)	NA	33,129 (B)
T	4-dr. Twn. Car-7P	800 (A)	NA	1,415 (B)
T	Delivery Car-2P	625 (A)	NA	513 (B)
T	2-dr. Cpe.-2P	NA	NA	1 (C)
T	Chassis	NA	960	8,438 (C)

Note: 1200 pounds was the figure given for the Touring car, with "others in proportion." The bare chassis weighed about 960 pounds.
(A) October 1, 1912.
(B) Fiscal year, October 1, 1912 to September 30, 1913.
(C) Coupes and the Chassis were not shown in the catalogs.

ENGINE: L-head. Four. Cast iron block. B & S: 3-3/4 in. x 4 in. Disp.: 176.6 cu. in. C.R.: 4.0:1 (approx.). Brake H.P.: 20 @ 1600 R.P.M. N.A.C.C. H.P.: 22.5. Main bearings: Three. Valve lifters: Solid. Carb.: Kingston Y (4400), Holley S (4450). Torque: 83 lbs.-ft. @ 900 R.P.M.
Note: Thermo-syphon. Valve chambers (2) now enclosed using steel doors held with one stud/nut each. Inspection plate in the crankcase.

Camshaft modified for less power (less overlap in timing). Modified cylinder head for slightly lower compression.

CHASSIS: W.B.: 100 in. O.L.: 10 ft. 8 in. (Chassis) 11 ft. 2-1/2 in. (car). Frt/Rear Tread: 56 in. (60 in. optional until 1916). Tires: 30 x 3 front, 30 x 3-1/2 rear, standard equipment 1909-1925. Chassis essentially identical except those after mid-1913 have a longer rear crossmember.

TECHNICAL: Planetary transmission. Speeds: 2F/1R. 3 pedal controls and 1 lever on floor. Multiple disk clutch. Torque tube drive. Straight bevel rear axle. Overall ratio: 3.63:1. Brakes: Contracting band in transmission. Hand-operated enternal expanding in rear wheels. Foot brake stops driveshaft. Parking brake on two rear wheels.
Note: Additional technical details will be found in the 1909 "General Comments" box.

OPTIONS: All cars equipped with headlamps, horn, etc. with no options. About 1915 the speedometer was discontinued (and the price reduced). Ford even said the warrantee would be voided if any accessories were added, although it's doubtful this ever happened.

1913
Model T, 4-cyl.

	FP	5	4	3	2	1
Rds	525	1550	4500	7500	10,500	15,000
Tr	600	2000	5100	8500	11,900	17,000
TwnC	850	1750	4800	8000	11,200	16,000

1914

1914 Ford, model T, touring, OCW

FORD — MODEL T: The 1914 models looked almost identical to the 1913's but the doors were now inset into the side panels, and the body metal extended across the rear door sills, solving the weakness at that point in the 1913's, and setting the pattern for doors until 1926 models.

The windshield, while similar in appearance to the 1913, now folded to the rear. The windshield support rods were given a bend to clear the folded section.

Fenders were modified and now had embossed reinforcing ribs across the widest part and, later, in the apron area of both front and rear fenders. Front fenders, had no "Bill" in most 1914 models but a "Bill" was added late in the year. The front fender iron bracket is secured to the fender with four rivets.

Black was now *the* Ford color, although Ford Archives records seem to indicate blue was still offered. Interestingly, Black was never listed as an available color prior to 1914; this in spite of the many seemingly original pre-1914 black Fords. It is possible black was a common color even in 1909 but there is nothing in the records to prove it.

Lamps continued in the pattern of the 1913's; black and brass.

The chassis frame was modified; now had a longer rear crossmember, eliminating the forged body brackets used since 1909.

A bare chassis was added to the Ford line in 1914. In the fall of the year a Sedan (commonly called a "centerdoor sedan") and a Coupelet (the first "convertible") were introduced but these were "1915 models."

I.D. DATA: Serial number was above the water inlet on the left side of the engine. Starting: 348736 (approx.) October 1913. "1914" cars were built as early as August, which could make the first "1914" cars about 320000. Ending: 670000 (Mid-January, 1915). The new "1915" Ford was introduced in January at the Highland Park plant, but the "1914" style continued for a time at the branches. There is no clear break point in the style years. 1914 Calendar year engine numbers: 408348 to 656063. Numbers stamped on the body sills, etc., were manufacturer's numbers and not an identifying number.

Model No.	Body Type & Seating	Price	Weight	Prod. Total
T	3-dr. Tr.-5P	550 (A)	1200	165,832 (B)
T	2-dr. Rbt.-2P	500 (A)	NA	35,017 (B)
T	4-dr. Twn. Car-7P	750 (A)	NA	1,699 (B)
T	Chassis	NA	960	119 (B)

Note: 1200 pounds was the figure given for the Touring car, with "others in proportion." The bare chassis weighed about 960 pounds.
(A) August 1, 1913.
(B) Fiscal year, October 1, 1913 to July 31, 1914.

ENGINE: L-head. Four. Cast iron block. B & S: 3-3/4 in. x 4 in. Disp.: 176.7 cu. in. C.R.: 4.0:1 approx. Brake H.P.: 20 @ 1600 R.P.M. N.A.C.C. H.P.: 22.5. Main bearings: Three. Valve lifters: Solid. Carb.: Kingston Y (4400), Holley G (6040 brass body). Torque: 83 lbs.-ft. @ 900 R.P.M.
Note: Thermo-syphon. Valve chambers (2) now enclosed using steel doors held with one stud/nut each. Inspection plate in the crankcase.

CHASSIS: W.B.: 100 in. O.L.: 10 ft. 8 in. (Chassis) 11 ft. 2-1/2 in. (car). Frt/Rear Tread: 56 in. (60 in. optional until 1916). Tires: 30 x 3 front, 30 x 3-1/2 rear, standard equipment 1909-1925.

TECHNICAL: Planetary transmission. Speeds: 2F/1R. 3 pedal controls and 1 lever on floor. Multiple disk clutch. Torque tube drive. Straight bevel rear axle. Overall ratio: 3.63:1. Brakes: Contracting band in transmission. Hand-operated internal expanding in rear wheels. Foot brake stops driveshaft. Parking brake on two rear wheels.
Note: Additional technical details will be found in the 1909 "General Comments" box.

OPTIONS: The basic equipment included three oil lamps. (Two side and one tail.) Windshield. Headlamps. Tops. Horns. Top boots. Speedometers.

1914
Model T, 4-cyl.

	FP	5	4	3	2	1
Rds	440	1400	4200	7000	9800	14,000
Tr	550	1550	4500	7500	10,500	15,000
TwnC	690	2000	5100	8500	11,900	17,000
Cpe	750	1000	2400	5000	7000	10,000

1915 & EARLY 1916

1915 Ford, model T, touring, AA

FORD — 1915-1916 — MODEL T: The 1915-style open cars were introduced at the Highland Park plant in January 1915 but the 1914 style continued in some of the branches until as late as April.

The bodies were essentially the same as the 1914 except for the front cowl section. Instead of the exposed wood firewall, the metal cowl curved "gracefully" inward to the hood former. The hood and radiator were the same as earlier (except for the louvres in the hood side panels).

The windshield is now upright, with the top section folding to the rear. Electric headlights were standard, these being of the "typical" size and shape of common Model T Fords until 1927.

Headlight rims were brass. Side lights were now of the rounded style, and interchangeable from side to side. The tail lamp was similar but with a red lens in the door, and a clear lens on the side towards the license plate. Side and tail lamps were still kerosene. Side and tail lamps had brass tops and rims but were otherwise painted black. The headlights were powered by the engine magneto.

Fenders in the front again had "Bills" and were the same as the later 1914's. While retaining the same style, later the fender iron bracket was revised and now held with three rivets. Rear fenders were now curved to follow the wheel outline. Neither front nor rear fenders were crowned.

The standard horn in 1915 was a bulb type, mounted under the hood. The hood now had louvres; perhaps so that the horn could be heard. Early in the year, though, Ford began using a magneto-powered horn on some production, and by October 1915 all had the new horn.

The Sedan was unique. Made of aluminum panels, it required special rear fenders and splash aprons. The gasoline tank was located under the rear seat and proved to be quite unsatisfactory because of the poor fuel flow. The body was redesigned during the year and made of steel panels, and the gasoline tank was relocated under the driver's seat.

The Coupelet had a folding top but differed from the Runabout in that the doors had windows and the windshield was like that in the Sedan. It also had a larger turtle deck.

The rear axle was redesigned again, for the last time except for minor modifications. The center section was cast iron and the axle tubes were straight and inserted into it.

The 1916 Fords were but an extension of the 1915's except for the deletion of the brass trim on the lamps. The hood was now made of steel, and all were equipped with the magneto horn.

"Port holes" were added to the side of the Coupelet in an effort to allow the driver a better side view.

The sedan body was redesigned to now use standard fenders and splash aprons, and for a new gas tank under the driver's seat. The new body was all steel.

Body styles offered in 1915 and 1916 were the Touring, Runabout, Sedan, Coupelet and Town Car, in addition to the bare chassis.

I.D. DATA: [1915] Serial number was above the water inlet on the left side of the engine. Starting: 670,000 approx. (January 1915.) the new "1915" Ford was introduced in January at the Highland Park plant, but the "1914" style continued for a time at the branches. There is no clear break point in the style years. Ending: 856,513 (July 24, 1915, end of fiscal 1915.) 1915 Calendar year engine numbers: 656,064 to 1,028,313. Numbers stamped on the body sills, etc. were manufacturer's numbers and not an identifying number. [1916] Serial number was above the water inlet on the left side of the engine. Starting: 856,514 (August 1, 1915.) Ending: 1,362,989 (July 25, 1916, end of fiscal 1916.) 1916 Calendar year engine numbers: 1,028,314 to 1,614,516. Numbers stamped on the body sills, etc. were manufacturer's numbers and not an identifying number.

1915 Ford, model T, runabout, OCW

Model No.	Body Type & Seating	Price	Weight	Prod. Total
1915				
T	3-dr. Tr.-5P	490 (A)	1500	244,181 (B)
T	2-dr. Rbt.-2P	440 (A)	1380	47,116 (B)
T	4-dr. Twn. Car-7P	690 (A)	NA	(B)
T	2-dr. Sed.-5P	975 (A)	1730	989 (B)
T	2-dr. Cpe.-2P	750 (A)	1540	2417 (B)
T	Chassis	410 (A)	980	13,459 (B)

(A) August 1, 1914.
(B) Fiscal year, August 1, 1914 to July 31, 1915.

Model No.	Body Type & Seating	Price	Weight	Prod. Total
1916				
T	3-dr. Tr.-5P	440 (A)	1510	363,024 (B)
T	2-dr. Rbt.-2P	390 (A)	1395	98,633 (B)
T	4-dr. Twn. Car-7P	640 (A)	NA	1972 (B)
T	2-dr. Sed.-5P	740 (A)	1730	1859 (B)
T	2-dr. Cpe.-2P	590 (A)	1540	3532 (B)
T	Chassis	360 (A)	1060	11,742 (B)
T	Ambulance	NA	NA	20,700 (C)

(A) Price effective August 1, 1915.
(B) Fiscal year 1916, August 1, 1915 to July 30, 1916.
(C) Built for military.

ENGINE: L-head. Four. Cast iron block. B & S: 3-3/4 in. x 4 in. Disp.: 176.7 in. C.R.: 4.0:1 approx. Brake H.P.: 20 @ 1600 R.P.M. N.A.C.C. H.P.: 22.5. Main bearings: Three. Valve lifters: Solid. Carb.: Kingston L (6100), Holley G (6040 brass body). Torque: 83 lbs.-ft. @ 900 R.P.M.
Note: Thermo-syphon. Valve chambers (2) now enclosed using steel doors held with one stud/nut each. Inspection plate in the crankcase.

CHASSIS: [1915-1916] W.B.: 100 in. O.L.: 10 ft. 8 in. (Chassis) 11 ft. 2-1/2 in. (car). Frt/Rear Tread: 56 in. Tires: 30 x 3 front, 30 x 3-1/2 rear, standard equipment 1909-1925.

TECHNICAL: Planetary transmission. Speeds: 2F/1R. 3 pedal controls and 1 lever on floor. Multiple disk clutch (26 disks 1909-1915). (25 disks 1915-1927). Torque tube drive. Straight bevel rear axle. Overall ratio: 3.63:1. Brakes: Contracting band in transmission. Hand-operated internal expanding in rear wheels. Foot brake stops driveshaft. Parking brake on two rear wheels.
Note: Additional technical details will be found in the 1909 "General Comments" box.

OPTIONS: The basic equipment included three oil lamps. (Two side and one tail.) Windshield. Headlamps. Tops. Horns. Top boots.

1916 Ford, model T, center door sedan, OCW

555

1915 & early 1916
Model T, 4-cyl., (brass rad.)

	FP	5	4	3	2	1
Rds	390	1400	4200	7000	9800	14,000
Tr	440	1550	4500	7500	10,500	15,000
Conv Cpe	590	2000	5100	8500	11,900	17,000
Ctr dr Sed	740	1150	3600	6000	8400	12,000
TwnC	640	1550	4500	7500	10,500	15,000

1916
Model T, 4-cyl., (steel rad.)

Rds	345	1250	3900	6500	9100	13,000
Tr	360	1150	3600	6000	8400	12,000
Conv Cpe	505	1000	2400	5000	7000	10,000
Ctr dr Sed	640	950	2100	4750	6650	9500
TwnC	595	1150	3600	6000	8400	12,000

1917 & 1918

1917 Ford, model T, runabout, HAC

FORD — 1917-1918 — MODEL T: The Model T for 1917 looked like an all-new car but was a rather simple evolution from the 1916. The brass radiator and the small hood were gone, as were all bits of brass trim.

New curved and crowned fenders, a new black radiator shell, and a new hood and hood former were the essential changes. The body itself was unchanged. Lamps were also the same as 1916.

The car continued with minor modifications, such as a different mounting base for the windshield, and new rectangular cross-section top sockets replacing the oval ones used since 1915.

Nickel plating on the steering gear box, hub caps and radiator filler neck replaced the earlier brass trim.

A new engine pan came out in 1917 which had a larger front section for a larger fan pulley. The pulley, however, was not enlarged until about 1920.

The "convertible" Coupelet was replaced with a "hard top" Coupelet. While the top could no longer fold, the side window posts could be removed (and stored under the seat) giving the car the hard-top look.

During 1917 the Ford Model TT truck chassis was introduced.

The Town Car was discontinued during the year.

I.D. DATA: [1917] Serial number was above the water inlet on the left side of the engine. Starting: 1362990 (August 1, 1916.) Ending: 2113501 (July 28, 1917, end of fiscal 1917.) 1917 Calendar year engine numbers: 1614517 to 2449179. Numbers stamped on the body sills, etc. were manufacturer's numbers and not an identifying number. [1918] Serial numbers was above the water inlet on the left side of the engine. Starting: 2113502 (August 1, 1917.) Ending: 2756251 (July 27, 1918, end of fiscal 1918.) 1918 Calendar year engine numbers: 2449180 to 2831426. Numbers stamped on the body sills, etc. were manufacturer's numbers and not an identifying number.

Model No.	Body Type & Seating	Price	Weight	Prod. Total
1917				
T	3-dr. Tr.-5P	360 (A)	1480	568,128 (B)
T	2-dr. Rbt.-2P	345 (A)	1385	107,240 (B)
T	4-dr. Twn. Car-7P	595 (A)	NA	2328 (B)
T	2-dr. Sed.-5P	645 (A)	1745	7361 (B)
T	2-dr. Cpe.-2P	505 (A)	1580	7343 (B)
T	Chassis	325 (A)	1060	41,165 (B)
T	Amb.	NA	NA	1452 (C)
TT	Truck Chassis	NA	1450	3 (D)

(A) Price effective August 1, 1916.
(B) Fiscal year 1917, August 1, 1916 to July 30, 1917.
(C) Built for military.
(D) Apparently a pilot run.

Model No.	Body Type & Seating	Price	Weight	Prod. Total
1918				
T	3-dr. Tr.-5P	360 (A)	450 (C)	432,519 (D)
T	2-dr. Rbt.-2P	345 (A)	435 (C)	73,559 (D)
T	4-dr. Twn. Car-7P	595 (A)	NA	2142 (D)
T	2-dr. Sed.-5P	645 (A)	1715	35,697 (D)
T	2-dr. Cpe.-2P	505 (A)	1580	14,771 (D)
T	Chassis	325 (A)	1060	37,648 (D)
T	Amb.	NA	NA	2136 (E)
TT	Truck Chassis	600 (B)	1450	41,105 (D)
T	Del.	NA	NA	399 (F)
T	Foreign	NA	NA	24,000 (G)

(A) Price effective August 1, 1917.
(B) Price effective October 6, 1917.
(C) Price effective February 21, 1918.
(D) Fiscal year 1918, August 1, 1917 to July 30, 1918.
(E) Built for military.
(F) Not indicated in catalog, perhaps for military.
(G) Cars built in foreign plants and Canada (no breakdown by types).

556

1918 Ford, model T, center door, sedan, HAC

ENGINE: L-head. Four. Cast iron block. B & S: 3-3/4 in. x 4 in. Disp.: 176.7 cu. in. C.R.: 3.98:1. Brake H.P.: 20 @ 1600 R.P.M. N.A.C.C. H.P.: 22.5. Main bearings: Three. Valve lifters: Solid. Carb.: Kingston L2 (6100), Holley G (6040 iron body). Torque: 83 lbs.-ft. @ 900 R.P.M.
Note: Thermo-syphon. Valve chambers (2) enclosed using steel doors held with one stud/nut each. Inspection plate in the crankcase.
New cylinder head with slightly lower compression and much larger water jacket.

CHASSIS: [1917-1918] W.B.: 100 in. O.L.: 10 ft. 8 in. (Chassis) 11 ft. 2-1/2 in. (car). Frt/Rear Tread: 56 in. Tires: 30 x 3 front, 30 x 3-1/2 rear, standard equipment 1909-1925.

TECHNICAL: Planetary transmission. Speeds: 2F/1R. 3 pedal controls and 1 lever on floor. Multiple disk clutch. (25 disks 1915-1927). Torque tube drive. Straight bevel rear axle. Overall ratio: 3.63:1. Brakes: Contracting band in transmission. Hand-operated internal expanding in rear wheels. Foot brake stops driveshaft. Parking brake on two rear wheels.
Note: Additional technical details will be found in the 1909 "General Comments" box.

OPTIONS: The basic equipment included three oil lamps. (Two side and one tail.) Windshield. Headlamps. Tops. Horns. Top boots.

1917
Model T, 4-cyl.

	FP	5	4	3	2	1
Rds	345	1075	3000	5500	7700	11,000
Tr	360	1150	3600	6000	8400	12,000
Conv Cpe	505	1000	2400	5000	7000	10,000
TwnC	595	1125	3450	5750	8050	11,500
Ctr dr Sed	645	900	1900	4500	6300	9000
Cpe	550	700	1350	2800	4550	6500

1918
Model T, 4-cyl.

Rds	500	1075	3000	5500	7700	11,000
Tr	525	1150	3600	6000	8400	12,000
Cpe	650	700	1350	2800	4550	6500
TwnC	700	1075	3000	5500	7700	11,000
Ctr dr Sed	775	875	1700	4250	5900	8500

1919 & 1920

1919 Ford, model T, runabout, HAC

FORD — 1919-1920 — MODEL T: The body styling continued unchanged from 1918 but the Ford was finally given a battery and an electric starter. Beginning as standard equipment on the closed cars only, by mid-1919 it became an option on the open cars. This modification required a new engine block, transmission cover, flywheel, etc. but the general design of these items was unchanged except for the modifications needed to adapt the starter and generator.

Also available for the first time from Ford were wheels with demountable rims as standard equipment on the closed cars, and optional on the open models. When demountable wheels were used, all tires were the same size; 30 by 3-1/2.

With the electrical equipment came an instrument panel for the first time on a Model T (as factory equipment) on cars so equipped. Instrumentation consisted of an ammeter. Controls on the panel were the choke knob and the ignition/light switch. Speedometers were dealer installed options.

The Coupelet was restyled. While looking the same, the door posts were now integral with the doors; no longer removable.

The rear axle was modified slightly. The oil filler hole was lowered to reduce the amount of oil that could be put in, and thus help the oil leak problem at the rear axles. The center section was milled to accept a gasket between the two halves.

The front radius rod was redesigned and now fastened below the axle, adding strength to the assembly.

I.D. DATA: [1919] Serial number was above the water inlet on the left side of the engine. Starting: 2756252 (August 1, 1918.) Ending: 3277851 (July 30, 1919, end of discal 1919.) 1919 Calendar year engine numbers: 2831407 to 3659971. Numbers stamped on the body sills, etc. were manufacturer's numbers and not an identifying number. [1920] Serial number was above the water inlet on the left side of the engine. Starting: 3277852 (august 1, 1919.) Ending: 4233351 (July 31, 1920, end of fiscal 1920.) 1920 Calendar year engine numbers: 3659972 to 4698419. Numbers stamped on the body sills, etc. were manufacturer's numbers and not an identifying number.

1919 Ford, model T, touring, OCW

Model No.	Body Type & Seating	Price	Weight	Prod. Total
T	3-dr. Tr.-5P	525 (B)	1500	286,935 (E)
T	2-dr. Rbt.-2P	500 (B)	1390	48,867 (E)
T	2-dr. Sed.-5P	875 (A)	1875	24,980 (E)
T	2-dr. Cpe.-2P	750 (A)	1685	11,528 (E)
T	4-dr. Twn. Car-7P	NA	—	17 (G)
T	Chassis	475 (B)	1060	47,125 (E)
T	Amb.	NA	—	2227 (F)
TT	Truck Chassis	550 (C)	1477	70,816 (E)
T	Del.	590 (D)	—	5847 (G)

(A) Includes starter and demountable wheels.
(B) Price effective August 16, 1918.
(C) Price with solid rubber tires.
(D) Price with Pneumatic tires.
(E) Fiscal year 1919, August 1, 1918 to July 30, 1919.
(F) Built for military.
(G) Not indicated in catalog, perhaps for military.
Note: Starter was an option on the open cars at $75. Weight 95 lbs. Demountable rims were an additional $25. Weight 55 lbs.

1920

T	3-dr. Tr.-5P	575 (B)	1500	165,929 (E)
		675 (A)	1650	367,785 (E)
T	2-dr. Rbt.-2P	550 (B)	1390	31,889 (E)
		650 (A)	1540	63,514 (E)
T	2-dr. Sed.-5P	975 (A)	1875	81,616 (E)
T	2-dr. Cpe.-2P	850 (A)	1760	60,215 (E)
T	Chassis	525 (B)	1060	18,173 (E)
		620 (A)	1210	16,919 (E)
TT	Truck Chassis	660 (C)	1477	135,002 (E)
		640 (D)		

(A) Includes starter and demountable wheels.
(B) Price effective March 3, 1920.
(C) Price with solid rubber tires.
(D) Price with Pneumatic tires.
(E) Fiscal year 1920, August 1, 1919 to July 30, 1920.
Note: Starter was an option on the open cars at $75. Weight 95 lbs. Demountable rims were an additional $25. Weight 55 lbs.

ENGINE: L-head. Four. Cast iron block. B & S: 3-3/4 in. x 4 in. Disp.: 176.7 cu. in. C.R.: 3.98:1. Brake H.P.: 20 @ 1600 R.P.M. N.A.C.C. H.P.: 22.5. Main bearings: Three. Valve lifters: Solid. Carb.: Kingston L4 (6150). Holley NH (6200). Torque: 83 lbs.-ft. @ 900 R.P.M.
Note: Thermo-syphon. Valve chambers (2) enclosed using steel doors held with one stud/nut each. Inspection plate in the crankcase. New light-weight connecting rods.

CHASSIS: [1919-1920] W.B.: 100 in. O.L.: 10 ft. 8 in. (Chassis) 11 ft. 2-1/2 in. (car). Frt/Rear Tread: 56 in. Tires: 30 x 3 front, 30 x 3-1/2 rear, standard equipment 1909-1925. 30 x 3-1.2 all around with demountable rims 1919-1925.

TECHNICAL: [1919-1920] Planetary transmission. Speeds: 2F/1R. 3 pedal controls and 1 lever on floor. Multiple disk clutch. (25 disks 1915-1927). Torque tube drive. Straight bevel rear axle. Overall ratio: 3.63:1. Brakes: Contracting internal expanding in rear wheels. Foot brake stops driveshaft. Parking brake on two rear wheels.
Note: Additional technical details will be found in the 1909 "General Comments" box.

OPTIONS: All cars equipped with headlamps, horn, etc. Starter (75.00). Demountable rims (25.00).

1919
Model T, 4-cyl.

	FP	5	4	3	2	1
Rds	500	1000	2400	5000	7000	10,000
Tr	525	1025	2600	5250	7300	10,500
Cpe	650	650	1250	2400	4200	6000
TwnC	700	1150	3600	6000	8400	12,000
Ctr dr Sed	775	825	1600	4000	5600	8000

1920-1921
Model T, 4-cyl.

Rds	395	1000	2400	5000	7000	10,000
Tr	440	1025	2600	5250	7300	10,500
Cpe	745	700	1350	2800	4550	6500
Ctr dr Sed	795	875	1700	4250	5900	8500

1920, 1921 & 1922

1920 Ford, model T, roadster, JAC

FORD — MODEL T: Another new body appeared in the open cars in late 1920. It takes an expert to see the difference but different it was. Most noticeable was a new rear quarter panel, now an integral part of the side panel instead of the two-piece assembly used since 1913.

An oval-shaped gas tank (located under the driver's seat) had replaced the previous round type earlier in 1920, and this allowed the seat to be lowered. Seat backs were given a more comfortable angle and the result was a far more comfortable car.

The chassis frame was modified slightly; the running board support brackets were now pressed steel channels instead of the forged brackets with a tie rod used since 1909. Otherwise the basic car was like the previous models.

A new pinion bearing spool was used on the rear axle. The earlier type was an iron casting with enclosed mounting studs. The new spool was a forging and used exposed mounting bolts.

Body styles offered during this period were the Touring, Runabout, Coupelet and Sedan, in addition to the Chassis and the Truck Chassis.

1921 Ford, model T, touring, IMS

557

I.D. DATA: (1921) serial number was above the water inlet on the left side of the engine. Starting: 4233352 (August 2, 1920). Ending: 5223135 (July 30, 1921, end of fiscal 1921). 1921 Calendar year engine numbers: 4698420 to 5568071. Numbers stamped on the body sills, etc, were manufacturer's numbers and not an identifying number. (1922) serial number was above the water inlet on the left side of the engine. Starting: 5223136 (August 1, 1921). Ending: 6543606 (September 14, 1922; introduction of first "1923" model). 1922 Calendar year engine numbers: 5638072 to 6953071. Numbers stamped on the body sills, etc. were manufacturer's numbers and not an identifying number.

Model No. 1921	Body Type & Seating	Price	Weight	Prod. Total
T	3-dr. Tr.-5P	440 (A) 415 (B)	1500	84,970 (D)
T	3-dr. Tr.-5P	535 (A) 510 (B)	1650	647,300 (E)
T	2-dr. Rbt.-2P	395 (A) 370 (B)	1390	25,918 (D)
T	2-dr. Rbt.-2P	490 (A) 465 (B)	1540	171,745 (E)
T	2-dr. Sed.-5P	795 (A) 760 (B)	1875	179,734 (E)
T	2-dr. Cpe.-2P	745 (A) 695 (B)	1760	129,159 (E)
T	Chassis	360 (A) 345 (B)	1060	13,356 (D)
T	Chassis	455 (A) 440 (B)	1210	23,436 (E)
T	Truck Chassis	545 (C) 495 (B)	1477	118,583 (D)
T	Foreign & Canada	NA	NA	42,860 (D)

(A) Price effective September 22, 1920.
(B) Price effective June 7, 1921.
(C) Price with Pneumatic tires.
(D) August 1, 1920 to December 31, 1921 (Ford began calendar year figures in 1921).
(E) Includes starter and demountable wheels.
Note: Starter was an option on the open cars at $70. Weight 95 lbs. Demountable rims were an additional $25. Weight 55 lbs.

Model No. 1922	Body Type & Seating	Price	Weight	Prod. Total
T	3-dr. Tr.-5P	355 (A) 348 (B) 298 (C)	1500	80,070 (D)
T	3-dr. Tr.-5P	450 (A) 443 (B) 393 (C)	1650	514,333 (E)
T	2-dr. Rbt.-2P	325 (A) 319 (B) 269 (C)	1390	31,923 (D)
T	2-dr. Rbt.-2P	420 (A) 414 (B) 364 (C)	1540	133,433 (E)
T	2-dr. Sed.-5P	660 (A) 645 (B) 595 (C)	1875	146,060 (E)
T	4-dr. Sed.-5P	725 (C)	1950	4,286 (E)
T	2-dr. Cpe.-2P	595 (A) 580 (B) 530 (C)	1760	198,382 (E)
T	Chassis	295 (A) 285 (B) 235 (C)	1060	15,228 (D)
T	Chassis	390 (A) 380 (B) 330 (C)	1210	23,313 (E)
T	Truck Chassis	445 (A) 430 (B) 380 (C)	1477	135,629 (D)
T	Truck Chassis	475 (C)	1577	18,410 (E)

(A) Price effective September 2, 1921.
(B) Price effective January 16, 1922.
(C) Price effective October 17, 1922.
(D) January 1, 1922 to December 31, 1922. (Includes foreign production.)
(E) Includes starter and demountable wheels.
Note: Starter was an option on the open cars at $70. Weight 95 lbs. Demountable rims were an additional $25. Weight 25 lbs.

1921 Ford, model T, touring, OCW

ENGINE: [1920] L-head. Four. Cast iron block. B & S: 3-3/4 in. x 4 in. Disp.: 176.7 cu. in. C.R.: 3.98:1. Brake H.P.: 20 @ 1600 R.P.M. N.A.C.C. H.P.: 22.5. Main bearings: Three. Valve lifters: Solid. Carb.: Kingston L4 (6150). Holley NH (6200). Torque: 83 lbs.-ft. @ 900 R.P.M.
Note: Thermo-syphon. Valve chambers (2) enclosed using steel doors held with one stud/nut each. Inspection plate in the crankcase. New light-weight connecting rods.
[1921-1922] L-head. Four. Cast iron block. B & S: 3-3/4 in. x 4 in. Disp.: 176.7 cu. in. C.R.: 3.98:1. Brake H.P.: 20 @ 1600 R.P.M. N.A.C.C. H.P.: 22.5. Main bearings: Three. Valve lifters: Solid. Carb.: Kingston L4 (6150), Holley NH (6200). Torque: 83 lbs.-ft. @ 900 R.P.M.
Note: Thermo-syphon. Single valve chamber covered with one steel door helf with two stud/nuts or bolts. Beginning in 1922 (#5,530,000 — April, 1922)

1921 Ford, model T, center door sedan, JAC

CHASSIS: [1909-1925] W.B.: 100 in. O.L.: 10 ft. 8 in. (Chassis) 11 ft. 2-1/2 in. (car). Frt/Rear Tread: 56 in. (60 in. optional until 1916). Tires: 30 x 3 front, 30 x 3-1/2 rear, standard equipment 1909-1925. 30 x 3-1.2 all around with demountable rims 1919-1925. 4:40 x 21 optional in late 1925.
Note: Chassis essentially identical except those after mid-1913 have a longer rear crossmember.

TECHNICAL: Planetary transmission. Speeds: 2F/1R. 3 pedal controls and 1 lever on floor. Multiple disk clutch (25 disks 1915-1927). Torque tube drive. Straight bevel rear axle. Overall ratio: 3.63:1. Brakes: Contracting band in transmission. Hand-operated internal expanding in rear wheels. Foot brake stops driveshaft. Parking brake on two rear wheels.
Note: Additional technical details will be found in the 1909 "General Comments" box.

OPTIONS: No factory options were available.

1922 Ford, model T, coupe, OCW

1922-1923
Model T, 4-cyl.

	FP	5	4	3	2	1
Rds	364	1000	2400	5000	7000	10,000
'22 Tr	348	1075	3000	5500	7700	11,000
'23 Tr	395	1025	2600	5250	7300	10,500
Cpe	530	650	1250	2400	4200	6000
4 dr Sed	725	600	1200	2200	3850	5500
2 dr Sed	595	550	1150	2100	3700	5300

1923, 1924 & 1925

1923 Ford, model T, Fordor sedan, HAC

FORD — 1923 — MODEL T: The 1923 Model T open cars were again restyled. Using the same bodies as the 1921-1922 cars, a new windshield with a sloping angle, and a new "one man" top, the Touring and Runabout looked all new.

The 1923 model was introduced in the fall of 1922, and was to continue until about June 1923, when another "new" line of Model T's appeared.

About November 1922, a new "Fordor" Sedan was added to the line. The Fordor body was made of aluminum panels over a wood frame.

Instrument panels were now standard on all cars. Non-starter open cars had a blank plate where the ammeter would be.

The early 1923 cars continued the wooden firewall of all previous Fords until early calendar 1923, when the firewall was changed to sheet metal. (This before the styling change in June, mentioned above.)

The starter and generator were standard equipment on all closed cars, as were the demountable wheels. This equipment was optional on the Runabout and Touring cars.

1923 was the last year for the Centerdoor Sedan and the Coupe with the forward-opening doors. The "1924" Tudor Sedan and a new Coupe replaced them.

1924 Ford, model T, touring, HAC

FORD — 1923-1925 — MODEL T: In June of 1923 the Ford line was restyled again. While those cars built after June but before calendar 1924 are commonly called "1923's", Ford referred to them as 1924's.

The open cars continued the same body, windshield and top as the earlier 1923's, but a new higher radiator and larger hood altered the appearance noticeably. The front fenders were given a lip on the front of the apron to blend in wit a new valence under the radiator; these giving the car a more "finished" look.

Two new models replaced the Centerdoor Sedan and the Coupe. These were a new Coupe, now with an integral rear turtle back, and doors that now opened at the rear. A new Tudor Sedan was also introduced, with the doors at the front of the body instead of at the center.

The Fordor Sedan was the same as the earlier one except for the new hood and front fenders. Lower body panels were now steel instead of aluminum.

During 1924 the closed car doors were changed to all metal construction, eliminating the wood framing of previous Sedan and Coupe doors.

In 1924, for the first time Ford offered a "C" cab and a rear platform body on the truck chassis.

The 1924 line continued until about July of 1925 with no major changes except in upholstery material, and construction details.

About May 1925 the Roadster/Pickup and the Closed Cab Truck appeared.

"Balloon" tires (4:40 x 21") mounted on demountable-rim wooden wheels in either black or natural were added as optional equipment in late 1925.

I.D. DATA: [1923] Serial number was above the water inlet on the left side of the engine. Starting: 6,543,607 (September 22, 1922 introduction of 1923 model.) Ending: 7,927,374 (June 30, 1923; introduction of "1924" models.) 1923 Calendar year engine numbers: 6,953,072 to 9,008,371. Numbers stamped on the body sills, etc. were manufacturer's numbers and not an identifying number. [1924] Serial number was above the water inlet on the left side of the engine. Starting: 7,927,375 (July 2, 1923 introduction of 1924 models.) Ending: 10,266,471 (July 31, 1924 end of fiscal 1924.) 1924 Calendar year engine numbers: 9,008,372 to 10,994,033. Numbers stamped on the body sills, etc. were manufacturer's numbers and not an identifying number. [1925] Serial number was above the water inlet on the left side of the engine. Starting: 10,266,472 (August 1, 1924, start of fiscal 1925.) Ending: 12,218,728 (July 27, 1925; Start of "1926" models.) 1925 Calendar year engine numbers: 10,994,034 to 12,990,076. Numbers stamped on the body sills, etc. were manufacturer's numbers and not an identifying number.

Model No.	Body Type & Seating	Price	Weight	Prod. Total
1923				
T	3-dr. Tr.-5P	298 (A) 295 (B) 295 (C)	1500	136,441 (D)
	3-dr. Tr.-5P	393 (A) 380 (B) 380 (C)	1650	792,651 (E)
T	2-dr. Rbt.-2P	269 (A) 265 (B) 265 (C)	1390	56,954 (D)
	2-dr. Rbt.-2P	364 (A) 350 (B) 350 (C)	1540	238,638 (E)
T	2-dr. Sed.-5P	595 (A) 590 (B) 590 (C)	1875	96,410 (E)
T	4-dr. Sed.-5P	725 (A) 685 (B) 685 (C)	1950	144,444 (E)
T	2-dr. Cpe.-2P	530 (A) 525 (B) 525 (C)	1760	313,273 (E)
T	Chassis	235 (A) 230 (B) 230 (C)	1060	9443 (D)
	Chassis	330 (A) 295 (B) 295 (C)	1210	42,874 (E)
TT	Truck Chassis	380 (A) 370 (B) 370 (C)	1477	197,057 (D)
TT	Truck Chassis	475 (A) 435 (B) 455 (C)	1577	64,604 (E)
TT	Trk. w/body	490 (C)	NA	(F)

(A) Price effective October 17, 1922.
(B) Price effective October 2, 1923.
(C) Price effective October 30, 1923.
(D) January 1, 1923 to December 31, 1923. (Includes foreign production.)
(E) Includes starter and demountable wheels.
(F) Not listed separately from chassis figures.
Note: Starter was an option on the open cars at $65. Weight 95 lbs. Demountable rims were an additional $20. Weight 55 lbs. "C" type truck cab, $65. Truck rear bed, $55 if ordered separately.

Model No.	Body Type & Seating	Price	Weight	Prod. Total
1924				
T	3-dr. Tr.-5P	295 (A) 290 (B) 290 (C)	1500	99,523 (D)
	3-dr. Tr.-5P	380 (A) 375 (B) 375 (C)	1650	673,579 (E)
T	2-dr. Rbt.-2P	265 (A) 260 (B) 260 (C)	1390	43,317 (D)
	2-dr. Rbt.-2P	350 (A) 345 (B) 345 (C)	1540	220,955 (E)
T	2-dr. Sed.-5P	590 (A) 580 (B) 580 (C)	1875	223,203 (E)
T	4-dr. Sed.-5P	685 (A) 660 (B) 660 (C)	1950	84,733 (E)
T	2-dr. Cpe.-2P	525 (A) 520 (B) 520 (C)	1760	327,584 (E)
T	Chassis	230 (A) 225 (B) 225 (C)	1060	3921 (D)
	Chassis	295 (A) 290 (B) 290 (C)	1210	43,980 (E)
TT	Truck Chassis	370 (A) 365 (B) 365 (C)	1477	127,891 (D)
TT	Truck Chassis	435 (A) 430 (B) 430 (C)	1577	32,471 (E)
TT	Trk. w/body	490 (A) 485 (B) 485 (C)	NA	38,840 (D)
	Trk. w/body	555 (A) 550 (B) 550 (C)	NA	5649 (E)
TT	Trk. w/stake body	495 (C)	NA	(F)

1924 Ford, model T, coupe, JAC

(A) Price effective October 30, 1923.
(B) Price effective December 2, 1924.
(C) Price effective October 24, 1924.
(D) January 1, 1924 to December 31, 1924. (Includes foreign production.)
(E) Includes starter and demountable wheels.
(F) Not listed separately from body figures.
Note: Starter was an option on the open cars at $65. Weight 95 lbs. Demountable rims were an additional $20. Weight 55 lbs. "C" type truck cab, $65. Truck rear bed, $55 if ordered separately.

1925

T	3-dr. Tr.-5P	290 (A)	1500	64,399 (D)
		290 (B)		
		290 (C)		
	3-dr. Tr.-5P	375 (A)	1650	626,813 (E)
		375 (B)		
		375 (C)		
T	2-dr. Rbt.-2P	260 (A)	1390	34,206 (D)
		260 (B)		
		260 (C)		
	2-dr. Rbt.-2P	345 (A)	1536	264,436 (E)
		345 (B)		
		345 (C)		
T	2-dr. Pickup-2P	281 (B)	1471	33,795 (G)
		281 (C)		
	2-dr. Pickup-2P	366 (B)	1621	(G)
		366 (C)		
T	2-dr. Sed.-5P	580 (A)	1875	195,001 (E)
		580 (B)		
		580 (C)		
T	4-dr. Sed.-5P	660 (A)	1950	81,050 (E)
		660 (B)		
		660 (C)		
T	2-dr. Cpe.-2P	520 (A)	1760	343,969 (E)
		520 (B)		
		520 (C)		
T	Chassis	225 (A)	1060	6523 (D)
		225 (B)		
		225 (C)		
	Chassis	290 (A)	1210	53,450 (E)
		290 (B)		
		290 (C)		
TT	Truck Chassis	365 (A)	1477	186,810 (D)
		365 (B)		
		365 (C)		
TT	Truck Chassis	430 (A)	1577	62,496 (E)
		430 (B)		
		430 (C)		
TT	Trk. w/body	485 (A)	NA	192,839 (US
		485 (B)		
		485 (C)		
	Trk. w/body	550 (A)	NA	(E, F)
		550 (B)		
		550 (C)		
TT	Trk. w/stake body	495 (A)	NA	(F)
		495 (B)		
		495 (C)		

(A) Price effective October 24, 1924.
(B) Price effective March 4, 1925.
(C) Price effective December 31, 1925 (unchanged from March).
(D) January 1, 1925 to December 31, 1925. (Includes foreign production.)
(E) Includes starter and demountable wheels.
(F) Not listed separately from body figures. (U.S. production only.)
(G) Pickups not separate into starter/non-starter. Figure is for total of the two.
Note: Starter was an option on the open cars at $65. Weight 95 lbs. Demountable rims were an additional $20. Weight 55 lbs. 21'' tires and rims $25 extra. Weight 65 lbs. "C" type truck cab, $65. Truck rear bed, $55 if ordered separately. Pickup body for Runabout, $25.

ENGINE: [1923-1924-1925]L-head. Four. Cast iron block. B & S: 3-3/4 in. x 4 in. Disp.: 176.7 cu. in. C.R.: 3.98:1. Brake H.P.: 20 @ 1600 R.P.M. N.A.C.C. H.P.: 22.5. Main bearings: Three. Valve lifters: Solid. Carb.: Kingston L4 (6150). Holley NH (6200). Torque: 83 lbs.-ft. @ 900 R.P.M. Note: Thermo-syphon. Inspection plate in the crankcase. New light-weight connecting rods.

1925 Ford, model T, roadster, OCW

[1921-1922] L-head. Four. Cast iron block. B & S: 3-3/4 in. x 4 in. Disp.: 176.7 cu. in. C.R.: 3.98:1. Brake H.P.: 20 @ 1600 R.P.M. N.A.C.C. H.P.: 22.5. Main bearings: Three. Valve lifters: Solid. Carb.: Kingston L4 (6150), Holley NH (6200). Torque: 83 lbs.-ft. @ 900 R.P.M. Single valve chamber covered with one steel door held with two stud/nuts or bolts.

CHASSIS: [1923-1924-1925] W.B.: 100 in. O.L.: 10 ft. 8 in. (Chassis) 11 ft. 2-1/2 in. (car). Frt/Rear Tread: 56 in. Tires: 30 x 3 front, 30 x 3-1/2 rear, standard equipment 1909-1925. 30 x 3-1.2 all around with demountable rims 1919-1925. 4:40 x 21 optional in late 1925.

TECHNICAL: Planetary transmission. Speeds: 2F/1R. 3 pedal controls and 1 lever on floor. Multiple disk clutch (26 disks 1909-1915). (25 disks 1915-1927). Torque tube drive. Straight bevel rear axle. Overall ratio: 3.63:1. Brakes: Contracting band in transmission. Hand-operated internal expanding in rear wheels. Foot brake stops driveshaft. Parking brake on two rear wheels.
Note: Additional technical details will be found in the 1909 "General Comments" box.

OPTIONS: The basic equipment included three oil lamps only. (Two side and one tail.)
Options listed included: Windshield. Headlamps. Tops. Horns. Prestolite tanks (instead of the carbide tank). Robe rails. Tire chains. Top boots. Foot rests. Spare tire carriers. Speedometers. Bumpers. No prices were given.

1925 Ford, model T, touring, JAC

1924
Model T, 4-cyl.

	FP	5	4	3	2	1
Rds	265	1000	2400	5000	7000	10,000
Tr	295	1025	2600	5250	7300	10,500
Cpe	525	700	1350	2800	4550	6500
4 dr Sed	685	600	1200	2200	3850	5500
2 dr Sed	590	600	1200	2300	4000	5700
Rds PU	366	900	1900	4500	6300	9000

1925
Model T, 4-cyl.

Rds	260	1000	2400	5000	7000	10,000
Tr	290	1025	2600	5250	7300	10,500
Cpe	520	700	1350	2800	4550	6500
2 dr	580	600	1200	2200	3850	5500
4 dr	660	650	1250	2400	4200	6000

1926 & 1927

FORD — 1926-1927 — MODEL T: About July 1925 the "Improved Ford" marked the first major restyling of the Model T since 1917. New fenders, running boards, bodies (except for the Fordor), hoods and even a modified chassis made these Fords unique during the era of the Model T.

1926 Ford, model T, touring, OCW

*Most records show 15007032 or 15007033 as the last car but the factory records indicate these numbers were built on May 31, 1927, five days after the car assembly line was stopped. Ford continued building engines through 1927 and at a considerable rate until January 1931 (as many as 12,000 per month after the end of the Model T!). Production averaged about 100 per month in 1931, then dropped to less than ten and ended, finally, on August 4, 1941 with number 15176888.

The Touring was given a door on the driver's side for the first time since 1911 (in U.S. cars; Canadian-built Fords had a driver's side door). The Tudor Sedan and the Coupe were all new, though similar in style to the 1925's. The Fordor Sedan continued the same basic body introduced in late 1922 except for the new cowl, hood, fenders, etc.

The chassis had a new longer rear cross-member, and with a modification of the springs and front spindles, the car was lowered about an inch.

While basically the same running gear as earlier models, the 1926-27 cars had 11-inch rear wheel brake drums, although they were only operated by the "emergency brake" lever. The foot pedals for the low speed and the brake were larger, and the internal transmission brake was made wider for better life and operation.

Initially offered in black, the Coupe and the Tudor were later painted a dark green, while the Fordor Sedan came in a dark maroon, as standard colors. The open cars sontinued in black until mid-1926.

In 1926, perhaps as "1927" models (Ford didn't name yearly models consistantly), colors were added for the open cars: Gunmetal blue or Phoenix brown. Closed cars were offered in Highland green, Royal maroon, Fawn gray, Moleskin and Drake green. By Calendar 1927, any body could be ordered in any standard Ford color. Black could be had on special order on the pickup body, although Commercial Green was the standard color. Fenders and running boards were black on all models.

When introduced in 1925, standard wheels on the closed cars were the 30 by 3-1/2'' demountables, and 30 by 3-1/2 non-demountables on the open cars. By calendar 1926, the 21'' balloons were standard on all models.

Wire wheels were offered as an option beginning January 1926. By early 1927, many Ford branches were supplying wire wheels as standard equipment on closed cars.

The gasoline tank was now located in the cowl on all models except the Fordor Sedan, which continued to have it under the driver's seat.

Model T production ended in May 1927 although Ford continued building engines through the year, then a few at a time until August 4, 1941!

I.D. DATA: [1926] Serial number was above the water inlet on the left side of the engine. Starting: 12218729 (July 27, 1925; Start of "1926" models.) Ending: 14049029 (July 30, 1926; end of fiscal 1926.) 1926 Calendar year engine numbers: 12990077 to 14619254. Numbers stamped on the body sills, etc. were manufacturer's numbers and not an identifying number. [1927] Serial number was above the water inlet on the left side of the engine. Starting: 14,049,030 (August 2, 1926 start of fiscal 1927.) Ending: 15006625 (May 25, 1927) (End of Model T Ford car production.)* 1927 Calendar year engine numbers: 14619255 to 15076231.* Numbers stamped on the body sills, etc. were manufacturer's numbers and not an identifying number.

1926 Ford, model T, Tudor sedan, HAC

Model No. 1926	Body Type & Seating	Price	Weight	Prod. Total
T	4-dr. Tr.-5P	290 (A)	1633 (D)	—
T	4-dr. Tr.-5P	375 (A) 380 (B) 380 (C)	1738	364,409 (F)
T	2-dr. Rbt.-2P	260 (A)	1550 (D)	—
T	2-dr. Rbt.-2P	345 (A) 360 (B) 360 (C)	1655	342,575 (F)
T	2-dr. Pickup-2P	281 (A)	NA (D)	N/L (E)
T	2-dr. Pickup-2P	366 (A) 381 (B) 381 (C)	1736	75,406 (F)
T	2-dr. Sed.-5P	580 (A) 495 (B) 495 (C)	1972	270,331 (F)
T	4-dr. Sed.-5P	660 (A) 545 (B) 545 (C)	2004	102,732 (F)
T	2-dr. Cpe.-2P	520 (A) 485 (B) 485 (C)	1860	288,342 (F)
T	Chassis	225 (A)	1167 (D)	—
T	Chassis	290 (A) 300 (B) 300 (C)	1272	58,223 (F)
TT	Truck Chassis	365 (A) 325 (B) 325 (C)	1477	228,496 (G)
TT	Truck Chassis	430 (A) 375 (B) 375 (C)	1577	(F)

Truck Bodies Only

TT	Open Cab	65 65	NA	142,852 (U.S)
TT	Closed Cab	85 85	NA	— (G)
TT	Express Body	55 55	NA	— (G)
TT	Platform Body	50 50	— —	(G)
TT	Expr. w/roof & screen	110 110	— —	(G)

(A) Price effective January 1, 1926.
(B) Price effective June 6, 1926.
(C) Price effective December 31, 1926 (unchanged from June).
(D) Early models with 30 x 3-1/2 non-demountable wheels and no starter. Available only on special order by calendar 1926.
(E) January 1, 1926 to December 31, 1926. (Includes foreign production.)
(F) Includes starter and 21'' demountable wheels.
(G) Chassis production figures are for U.S. and foreign. Body figures are for U.S. only and are included in the chassis count. Starter production is not listed separately.
Note: Starter and demountable wheels are standard on all cars. Starter is optional on the truck. Early 1926 cars with 30 by 3-1/2'' demountables are 10 pounds lighter.
Pickup body for Runabout, $25.

Model No. 1927	Body Type & Seating	Price	Weight	Prod. Total
T	4-dr. Tr.-5P	380	1738	81,181 (A)
T	2-dr. Rbt.-2P	360	1655	95,778 (A)
T	2-dr. Pickup-2P	381	1736	28,143 (A)
T	2-dr. Sed.-5P	495	1972	78,105 (A)
T	4-dr. Sed.-5P	545	2004	22,930 (A)
T	2-dr. Cpe.-2P	485	1860	69,939 (A)
T	Chassis	300	1272	19,280 (A)
TT	Truck Chassis	325	1477	83,202 (C)
TT	Truck Chassis	375	1577	(B)

Truck Bodies Only

TT	Open Cab	65	NA	41,318 (U.S.)
TT	Closed Cab	85	NA	(C)
TT	Express body	55	NA	(C)
TT	Platform Body	50	NA	(C)
TT	Expr. w/roof & screen	110	NA	(C)

(A) January 1, 1927 to December 31, 1927. (Includes foreign production.)
(B) Includes starter and demountable wheels.
(C) Chassis production figures are for U.S. and foreign. Body figures are for U.S. only and are included in the chassis count. Starter production is not listed separately.
Note: Starter and demountable wheels are standard on all cars. Starter is optional on the truck.
Pickup body for Runabout, $25.
Automobile production ended May 26, 1927 but trucks continued for some time.

ENGINE: L-head. Four. Cast iron block. B & S: 3-3/4 in. x 4 in. Disp.: 176.7 cu. in. C.R.: 3.98:1. Brake H.P.: 20 @ 1600 R.P.M. N.A.C.C. H.P.: 22.5. Main bearings: Three. Valve lifters: Solid. Carb.: Kingston L4 (6150B), Holley NH (6200C), Holley Vaporizer (6250), Kingston Regenerator. Torque: 83 lbs.-ft. @ 900 R.P.M.
Note: Thermo-syphon. Single valve chamber covered with one steel door helf with two stud/nuts or bolts.
Transmission housing now bolts to the rear of the cylinder. Fan mounted on the water outlet. Later production used nickel plated head and water connection bolts.

CHASSIS: W.B.: 100 in. O.L.: 10 ft. 8 in. (chassis). 11 ft. 2-1/2 in. (car). Frt/Rear Tread: 56 in. Tires: 30 x 3-1/2 all around in early 1926 models. 4:40 x 21 optional in early 1926 and standard in later production. Note: Chassis essentially identical to 1913-1925 except for a much longer rear crossmember. Chassis lowered about an inch by the use of a different front spindle and spring, and a deeper crown in the rear crossmember. In mid-1926 the rear crossmember was made with a flanged edge and the chassis was of heavier steel.

TECHNICAL: Planetary transmission. Speeds: 2F/1R. 3 pedal controls and 1 lever on floor. Multiple disk clutch (25 disks 1915-1927). Torque tube drive. Straight bevel rear axle. Overall ratio: 3.63:1. Brakes: Contracting band in transmission. Hand-operated internal expanding in rear wheels. Foot brake stops driveshaft. Parking brake on two rear wheels.

In January, 1926 optional 21" wire wheels became available, and these became standard on some closed cars in calendar year 1927.

In mid 1925 (1926 models) the transmission brake was made about a half-inch wider, and the rear wheel brakes were enlarged to 11" with lined shoes.

Note: Additional technical details will be found in the 1909 "General Comments" box.

1927 Ford, model T, roadster, OCW

OPTIONS: All cars equipped with headlamps, horn, starter and 21" demountable rims after by January 1926. Windshield wiper (hand operated) (.50).* Windshield wiper (vacuum operated) (3.50) (2.00 in 1927). Windshield wings (open cars) (6.50 pr.) (2.50 in 1927). Gipsy curtains (open cars) (3.00 pr.) (1.10 in 1927). Top boot (open cars) (5.00) (4.00 in 1927). Bumpers (front and rear) (15.00). Wire wheels, set of 5 (50.00) (35.00 later 1926). Rear view mirror (open cars) (.75).* Dash lamp (open cars) (.60).* Stop light and switch (2.50). Shock absorbers (9.00 set).
* Standard on closed cars.

1926
Model T, 4-cyl.

	FP	5	4	3	2	1
Rds	360	1075	3000	5500	7700	11,000
Tr	380	1150	3600	6000	8400	12,000
Cpe	485	700	1350	2800	4550	6500
2 dr	495	700	1350	2800	4550	6500
4 dr	545	600	1200	2200	3850	5500

1927
Model T, 4-cyl.

	FP	5	4	3	2	1
Rds	360	1075	3000	5500	7700	11,000
Tr	380	1150	3600	6000	8400	12,000
Cpe	485	700	1350	2800	4550	6500
2 dr	495	600	1200	2200	3850	5500
4 dr	545	650	1200	2300	4100	5800

1928

FORD — MODEL A — FOUR: The reverting to a Model A designation for the new Ford symbolized the impact this automobile had upon the Ford Motor Company. A far more complex automobile than the Model T, the Model A contained approximately 6800 different parts as compared to the less than 5000 components that comprised the Model T. There were however, similarities. Both cars had 4 cylinder L-head engines and semi-elliptic front and rear transverse springs. But beyond this point the Model A moved far away from the heritage of the Model T. Its engine with a water pump displaced just over 200 cubic inches and with 40hp was virtually twice as powerful as the Model T's and provided a 65mph top speed. Superseding the old magneto ignition was a contemporary battery and ignition system. The Model T's planetary transmission gave way to a three-speed sliding gear unit. Other technical advancements found in the Model A included the use of 4-wheel mechanical brakes and Houdaille, double-action hydraulic shock absorbers.

The styling of the Model A maintained a link with that of the Model T but with a 103-1/2 inch wheelbase, 4.50 x 21 tires and a high belt line the influence of the Lincoln automobile upon the appearance of the new Ford was unmistakable. Full crown fenders were used and the bodywork of each of the five models initially offered had their body surrounds outlined in contrasting body colors and pin striping. The Model A's 2-piece front and rear bumpers were similar to those used on the 1927 Model T but its

1928 Ford, model A, roadster, AA

new radiator shell with its gentle center V-dip and moderately curved crossbar for the headlights made it impossible to confuse the two Fords.

The first Model A engine was completed on October 20, 1927 and the following day it was installed in the first Model A assembled. From that day (May 25, 1927) Ford announced it would produce a successor to the Model T, public interest had steadily increased to a level that was finally satisfied on December 2, 1927 when the nationwide introduction of the Model A took place. While many industry observers recognized the passing of the Model T as the end of an era, there was equal appreciation for the extraordinary value the Model A represented and an awareness that it was in all ways more than a worthy successor to the Tin Lizzie.

I.D. DATA: Serial numbers were located on top side of frame near clutch pedal. Starting: Oct. 20-Dec. 31, 1927 - A1; Jan. 1-Dec. 31, 1928 - A5276. Ending: Oct. 20-Dec. 31, 1927 - A5275; Jan. 1-Dec. 31, 1928 - A810122. Engine numbers were located on boss placed on center of left side of block directly below the cylinder head. A prefix letter A was used and a star is found on either end. Starting: Oct. 20-Dec. 31, 1927 - A1; Jan. 1-Dec. 31, 1928 - A5276. Ending: Oct. 20-Dec. 31, 1927 - A5275; Jan. 1-Dec. 31, 1928 - A810122. Model Numbers: 1928 models have a date when the body was manufactured stamped on the upper left side of the firewall.

1928 Ford, model A, Fordor sedan, JAC

Model No.	Body Type & Seating	Price	Weight	Prod. Total
A	2-dr. Rds. R/S-2/4P	480	2106	Note 1
A	4-dr. Phae.-4P	460	2140	Note 1
A	2-dr. Bus. Cpe.-4P	550	2225	Note 1
A	2-dr. R/S Cpe.2/4P	550	2265	Note 1
A	2-dr. Std. Bus. Rds.	480	2050	Note 1
A	2-dr. Spt. Bus. Cpe.-2P	525	NA	Note 1
A	2-dr. Tudor-4P	550	2340	Note 1
A	4-dr. Fordor-4P	585	2386	Note 1
A	4-dr. Taxi Cb.	600	NA	Note 1

Note 1: Body style production was recorded only by calendar year. See list at end of Model A section.

ENGINE: Inline. L-head. Four. Cast iron block. B & S: 3-7/8 in. x 4-1/4 in. Disp.: 200.5 cu. in. C.R.: 4.22:1. Brake H.P.: 40 @ 2200 R.P.M. SAE H.P.: 24.03. Main bearings: Three. Valve lifters: Mechanical. Carb.: Zenith or Holley double venturi. Torque: 128 lbs.-ft. @ 100 R.P.M.

CHASSIS: W.B.: 103.5 in. Frt/Rear Tread: 56. Tires: 4.50 x 21.

TECHNICAL: Sliding gear transmission. Speeds: 3F/1R. Floor shift controls. Dry multiple disc clutch. Shaft drive. 3/4 floating rear axle. Overall ratio: 3.7:1. Mechanical internal expanding brakes on four wheels. Welded wire wheels. Wheel size: 21.

OPTIONS: Single sidemount. External sun shade. Radiator ornament. Wind vanes. Rear view mirror. Rear luggage rack. Radiator stone guard. Spare tire lock.

HISTORICAL: Introduced December 2, 1927. Innovations: Safety glass installed in all windows. Calendar year production: 633,594. The president of Ford was Edsel Ford.

1928 Ford, model A, phaeton, JAC

1928
Model A, 4-cyl.
(Add 20 percent avg for early 'AR' features)

	FP	5	4	3	2	1
Rds	480	3000	6000	10,000	14,000	20,000
Phae	460	3150	6300	10,500	14,700	21,000
Cpe	550	1000	2400	5000	7000	10,000
Spec Cpe	525	1125	3450	5750	8050	11,500
Bus Cpe	525	1150	3600	6000	8400	12,000
Spt Cpe	550	1250	3900	6500	9100	13,000
2 dr	550	775	1500	3750	5250	7500
4 dr	585	825	1600	4000	5600	8000

1929

1929 Ford, model A, sport coupe, AA

FORD — MODEL A — FOUR: The most apparent change made in the Model A's appearance, aside from brighter trim and body paint were the exterior door handles on open models. With production rapidly increasing more body styles became available. A Town Car model was introduced on December 13, 1928 following during 1929 by a wood-bodied station wagon on April 25. Other new styles included a Convertible Cabriolet, several new four door sedans and a Town Sedan. As in 1928 the Model A's base price included many standard equipment features such as a combination tail and stop light, windshield wiper, front and rear bumpers and a Spartan horn.

I.D. DATA: Serial numbers were located on top side of frame, near clutch pedal. Starting: A 810,123. Ending: A 2742695. Engine no. location: Boss placed on center of left side of block directly below the cylinder head. Starting: A 810120. Ending: A 2724695.

Model No.	Body Type & Seating	Price	Weight	Prod. Total
A	4-dr. Sta. Wag.-4P	650	2500	Note 1
A	2-dr. RS Conv.-2-4P	670	2339	Note 1
A	2-dr. RS Spt. Cpe.-2/4P	550	2250	Note 1
A	Mur. Std. Fordor Sed.-4P	625	2497	Note 1
A	Brgg. Std. Fordor Sed.-4P	625	2497	Note 1
A	Brgg. 2W Std. Fordor Sed.-4P	625	2419	Note 1
A	Brgg. Std. Fordor Sed.-4P	625	2497	Note 1
A	Brgg. L.B. Fordor Sed.-4P	625	2500	Note 1
A	2-dr. Tudor Sed.-4P	525	2348	Note 1
A	4-dr. Mur. Twn. Sed.-4P	695	2517	Note 1
A	4-dr. Brgg. Twn. Sed.-4P	695	2517	Note 1
A	2-dr. Std. RS Rds.-2/4P	450	2106	Note 1
A	2-dr. Std. Rds. R/S-2/4P	450	2161	Note 1
A	2-dr. Std. Bus. Cpe.	525	2216	Note 1
A	4-dr. Std. Phae.-4P	460	2203	Note 1
A	4-dr. Std. Cpe.-2P	550	2248	Note 1
A	4-dr. Twn. Cr.-4P	1400	2525	Note 1
A	4-dr. Taxi-4P	800	NA	Note 1

Note 1: Body style production was recorded only by calendar year. See list at end of Model A section.

1929 Ford, model A, taxicab, JAC

1929 Ford, model A, Fordor sedan, JAC

ENGINE: Inline. L-head. Four. Cast iron block. B & S: 3-7/8 in. x 4-1/4 in.. Disp.: 200.5 cu. in. C.R.: 4.22:1. Brake H.P.: 40 @ 2200 R.P.M. N.A.C.C. H.P.: 24.03. Main bearings: Three. Valve lifters: Mechanical. Carb.: Zenith or Holley double-venturi. Torque: 128 lbs.-ft. @ 1000 R.P.M.

CHASSIS: W.B.: 103.5 in. Frt/Rear Tread: 56 in. Tires: 4.50 x 21.

TECHNICAL: Sliding gear. Speeds: 3F/1R. Floor shift controls. Dry multiple disc. Shaft drive. 3/4 floating rear axle. Overall Ratio: 3.7:1. Mechanical internal expanding brakes on four wheels. Welded wire wheels. Wheel Rim Size: 21''.

OPTIONS: Single Sidemount. External Sun Shade. Radiator ornament (3.00). Wind vanes. Rear view mirror. Rear luggage rack. Radiator stone guard. Spare tire lock.

HISTORICAL: Introduced January, 1929. Calendar year sales: 1,310,147 (registrations). Calendar year production: 1,507,132. The president of Ford was Edsel Ford. Production of the first million Model A Fords was completed on February 4, 1929. The 2-millionth Model A Ford was constructed on July 24, 1929.

1929 Ford, model A, town car, JAC

1929
Model A, 4-cyl.

	FP	5	4	3	2	1
Rds	450	3000	6000	10,000	14,000	20,000
Phae	460	3150	6300	10,500	14,700	21,000
Cabr	670	2800	5700	9500	13,300	19,000
Cpe	550	1000	2400	5000	7000	10,000
Bus Cpe	525	975	2200	4850	6800	9700
Spec Cpe	525	1150	3600	6000	8400	12,000
Spt Cpe	550	1250	3900	6500	9100	13,000
2 dr Sed	525	950	2100	4750	6650	9500
3W 4 dr Sed	625	1000	2400	5000	7000	10,000
5W 4 dr Sed	625	950	2100	4750	6650	9500
DeL 4 dr Sed	625	900	1900	4500	6300	9000
Twn Sed	695	1150	3600	6000	8400	12,000
Taxi	800	1550	4500	7500	10,500	15,000
TwnC	1400	3750	7500	12,500	17,500	25,000
Sta Wag	695	1750	4800	8000	11,200	16,000

1930

1930 Ford, model A, coupe, JAC

ENGINES: In line, L-head. Four. Cast iron block. B. x S.: 3-7/8 in. x 4-1/4 in. Disp.: 200.5 cu. in. C.R.: 4.22:1. Brake H.P. 40 @ 2200 R.P.M. Taxable horsepower: 24.03. Main bearings: Three. Valve lifters: Mechanical. Carb.: Zenith or Holley double-venturi. Torque: 128 lbs.-ft. at 1000 R.P.M.

CHASSIS: W.B.: 103.5 in. Frt/Rear Tread: 56 in. Tires: 4.75 x 19.

TECHNICAL: Transmission: Sliding gear. Speeds: 3F/1R. Floor shift controls. Dry multiple disc clutch. Shaft drive. 3/4 floating rear axle. Overall ratio: 3.77:1. Mechanical internal expanding brakes on four wheels. Welded wire wheels. Wheel size: 19.

OPTIONS: Single sidemount (20.00). External sun shade. Radiator ornament. Wind vanes. Rear view mirror. Rear luggage rack. Radiator stone guard. Spare tire lock.

HISTORICAL: January, 1930. Calendar year sales: 1055097 (registrations). Calendar year production: 1,155,162. The president of Ford was Edsel Ford.

1930 Ford, model A, roadster, AA

FORD — MODEL A — FOUR: The Model A was given a substantial face lift for 1930 and it was very effective. Larger 4.75 tires on smaller 19 inch wheels resulted in an overall height reduction which along with wider fenders, a deeper radiator shell and the elimination of the cowl stanchion all were contributors to the Model A's fresh new look. Replacing the older nickel finish for the Ford's exterior brightwork was both nickel and stainless steel trim. During the year a new Victoria model was introduced along with a deluxe version of the phaeton.

I.D. DATA: Top side of frame near clutch panel. Starting: A 2742696. Ending: A4237500. Boss placed on center of left side of block, directly below the cylinder head. Starting Engine No: 1 2742696. Ending: A 4237500.

Model No.	Body Type & Seating	Price	Weight	Prod. Total
35-B	4-dr. Std. Phae-2P	440	2212	Note 1
40-B	2-dr. Std. Rds.	435	2155	Note 1
40-B	2-dr. Del. Rds. R/S-2-4P	495	2230	Note 1
45-B	2-dr. Std. Cpe.	500	2257	Note 1
45-B	2-dr. Del. Cpe.	550	2265	Note 1
50-B	2-dr. Spt. Cpe. R/S-2-4P	530	2283	Note 1
55-B	2-dr. Tudor Sed.	490	2372	Note 1
68-B	2-dr. Cab.	645	2273	Note 1
150-B	4-dr. Sta. Wag.-4P	650	2482	Note 1
155-C	4-dr. Mu'ry Twn. Sed.-4P	640	2495	Note 1
155-D	4-dr. Briggs Twn. Sed.-4P	650	2495	Note 1
165-C	Std. Mu'ry Fordor Sed.-4P	580	2462	Note 1
165-D	Std. Briggs Fordor Sed.-4P	590	2462	Note 1
170-B	Std. Briggs Fordor 2W Sed.-4P	590	2488	Note 1
170-B	Briggs Fordor 2W Sed.-4P	650	2488	Note 1
180-A	4-dr. Del. Phae-4P	645	2285	Note 1
190-A	2-dr. Vict.-4P	580	2375	Note 1

Note 1: Body style production was recorded only by calendar year. See list at end of Model A section.

1930 Ford, model A, town sedan, JAC

1930
Model A, 4-cyl.

	FP	5	4	3	2	1
Rds	435	3150	6300	10,500	14,700	21,000
DeL Rds	495	3300	6600	11,000	15,400	22,000
Phae	440	3600	7200	12,000	16,800	24,000
DeL Phae	625	3750	7500	12,500	17,500	25,000
Cabr	645	3150	6300	10,500	14,700	21,000
Cpe	500	1000	2400	5000	7000	10,000
DeL Cpe	550	1125	3450	5750	8050	11,500
Spt Cpe	530	1250	3900	6500	9100	13,000
Std 2 dr	490	875	1700	4250	5900	8500
DeL 2 dr	525	950	2100	4750	6650	9500
3W 4 dr	590	900	1900	4500	6300	9000
5W 4 dr	590	875	1700	4250	5900	8500
DeL 4 dr	650	1150	3600	6000	8400	12,000
Twn Sed	640	1075	3000	5500	7700	11,000
Vic	580	1750	4800	8000	11,200	16,000

1931

FORD — MODEL A — FOUR: The final year of Model A production brought revised styling, several new body types and on April 14th production of the 20-millionth Ford, a Fordor sedan. Heading the list of styling changes was a radiator shell with a relief effect, plus running boards fitted with single piece slash aprons. In addition to the 2 and 4 door sedans introduced with a smoother roofline, a revamped cabriolet model was also introduced during 1931. However the star attraction was the convertible sedan which had fixed side window frames over which the top rode up or down on a set of tracks. Standard equipment on the convertible sedan included a side mount.

I.D. DATA: Serial numbers were located on top side of frame, near clutch pedal. Starting: A4237501. Ending: A4849340. Engine numbers were located on boss placed on center of left side of block, directly below the cylinder head. Starting: A4327501. Ending: A4849340.

1930 Ford, model A, phaeton, JAC

1931 Ford, model A, victoria coupe, AA

ENGINE: Inline. L-head. Four. Cast iron block. B & S: 3-7/8 in. x 4-1/4 in. Disp.: 200.5 cu. in. C.R.: 4.22:1. Brake H.P.: 40 @ 2200 R.P.M. Taxable H.P.: 24.03. Main bearings: Three. Valve lifters: Mechanical. Carb.: Zenith or Holley double venturi. Torque: 128 lbs.-ft. @ 1000 R.P.M.

CHASSIS: W.B.: 103.5. Frt/Rear Tread: 56 in. Tires: 4.75 x 19.

TECHNICAL: Sliding gear transmission. Speeds: 3F/1R. Floor shift controls. Dry multiple disc clutch. Shaft drive. 3/4 floating rear axle. Overall Ratio: 3.77:1. Mechanical internal expanding brakes on four wheels. Welded wire wheels. Wheel size: 19.

OPTIONS: Single sidemount. External sun shade. Radiator ornament. Wind vanes. Rear view mirror. Rear luggage rack. Radiator stone guard. Spare tire lock.

HISTORICAL: Introduced January, 1931. Calendar year sales 528581 (registrations). Calendar year production: 541615. The president of Ford was Edsel Ford.

Model No.	Body Type & Seating	Price	Weight	Prod. Total
A	4-dr. Std. Phae.-4P	435	2212	Note 1
A	2-dr. Std. Rds.	430	2155	Note 1
A	2-dr. Del. Rds.	475	2230	Note 1
A	2-dr. Std. Cpe.	490	2257	Note 1
A	2-dr. Del. Cpe.	525	2265	Note 1
A	2-dr. Spt. Cpe.	500	2283	Note 1
A	2-dr. Std. Tudor Sed.-4P	490	2462	Note 1
A	2-dr. Del. Tudor Sed.-4P	525	2488	Note 1
A	2-dr. Cab	595	2273	Note 1
A	4-dr. Sta. Wag.-4P	625	2505	Note 1
A	4-dr. Mu'ry Twn. Sed.-4P	630	2495	Note 1
A	4-dr. Briggs Twn. Sed.-4P	630	2495	Note 1
A	4-dr. Std. Fordor Sed.-4P	590	2462	Note 1
A	4-dr. Twn. Sed.-4P	630	2495	Note 1
A	4-dr. Del. Fordor Sed.-4P	630	2488	Note 1
A	Mu'ry Std. Fordor Sed.-4P	590	2462	Note 1
A	Briggs STd. Fordor Sed.-4P	590	2462	Note 1
A	Briggs De. Fordor 2W Sed.-4P	630	2488	Note 1
A	2-dr. Del. Phae.-4P	580	2265	Note 1
A	2-dr. Vic. Cpe.-4P	580	2375	Note 1
A	2-dr. Conv. Sed.-4P	640	2335	Note 1

Note 1: Body style production was recorded only by calendar year. See list at end of Model A section.

1931 Ford, model A, roadster, JAC

1931 Ford, model A, Fordor sedan, JAC

1931
Model A, 4-cyl.

	FP	5	4	3	2	1
Rds	430	3150	6300	10,500	14,700	21,000
DeL Rds	495	3300	6600	11,000	15,400	22,000
Phae	435	3600	7200	12,000	16,800	24,000
DeL Phae	580	3750	7500	12,500	17,500	25,000
Cabr	595	3150	6300	10,500	14,700	21,000
SW Cabr	595	3300	6600	11,000	15,400	22,000
Conv Sed	640	3900	7800	13,000	18,200	26,000
Cpe	490	1150	3600	6000	8400	12,000
DeL Cpe	525	1200	3750	6250	8750	12,500
Spt Cpe	590	1250	3900	6500	9100	13,000
Tudor	490	875	1700	4250	5900	8500
DeL Tudor	525	900	1900	4500	6300	9000
Fordor	590	1075	3000	5500	7700	11,000
DeL Fordor	630	1150	3600	6000	8400	12,000
Twn Sed	630	1200	3750	6250	8750	12,500
Vic	580	1750	4800	8000	11,200	16,000
Sta Wag	625	1400	4200	7000	9800	14,000

FORD
Model A Domestic Production Figures
(Calendar Year)

	1927	1928	1929	1930	1931	Totals
Phaeton						
standard	221	47,255	49,818	16,479	4076	117,849
deluxe	—	—	—	3946	2229	6175
Roadster						
standard	269	81,937*	191,529	112,901	5499	392,135
deluxe	—	—	—	11,318	52,997	64,315

*Of these, 51,807 were produced without rumble seat.

	1927	1928	1929	1930	1931	Totals
Sport Coupe	734	79,099	134,292	69,167	19,700	302,992
Coupe						
standard	629	70,784	178,982	226,027	79,816	556,238
deluxe	—	—	—	28,937	23,067	52,004
Bus. Coupe	—	37,343	37,644	—	—	74,987
Conv. Cabr.	—	—	16,421	25,868	11,801	54,090
Tudor						
standard	1948	208,562	523,922	376,271	148,425	1,259,128
deluxe	—	—	—	—	21,984	21,984
Fordor (2-window)						
standard	—	82,349	146,097	5279	—	233,725
deluxe	—	—	—	12,854	3251	16,105
Fordor (3-window)						
standard	—	—	53.941	41,133	18,127	113,201
town sedan	—	—	84,970	104,935	55,469	245,374
Conv. Sedan	—	—	—	—	4864	4864
Victoria	—	—	—	6306	33,906	40,212
Town Car	—	89	913	63	—	1065
Station Wagon	—	5	4954	3510	2848	11,317
Taxicab	—	264	4576	10	—	4850

1932

1932 Ford V-8, DeLuxe 3-window coupe, AA

FORD — MODEL 18 — EIGHT: Once again Henry Ford made automotive history when, on March 31, 1932 he announced the Ford V-8. This type of engine wasn't a novelty by that time but when offered at traditional Ford low prices this new engine was a true milestone. Henry Ford had this 221 cubic inch displacement engine developed in traditional Ford style — extreme secrecy — a small work force operating under relative primitive conditions — under Henry Ford's close personal supervision.

Its early production life was far from tranquil. Hastily rushed into assembly, many of the 1932 engines experienced piston and bearing failures plus overheating as well as block cracking. However, these problems were soon overcome and for the next 21 years this V-8 would be powering Ford automobiles.

The new Ford was extremely handsome. Both front and rear fenders were fully crowned. The soon-to-be classic radiator shell was slightly V'eed and carried vertical bars. Positioned in the center of the curved headlight tie-bar was Ford's timeless V-8 logo. Apparently sensitive that most of its competitors had longer wheelbases, Ford measured the distance from the center position of the front spring to the center of the rear and claimed it as the V-8's 112 inch wheelbase. Actually its wheelbase was 106 inches.

The new Ford's dash carried all instruments and controls within an engine-turned oval placed in the center of a mahogany colored (early) or walnut (late) grained panel. An anti-theft device was incorporated into the key and ignition switch which was mounted on a bracket attached to the steering column. During the model year Ford incorporated many changes into the design of its new model. One of the most obvious, intended to improve engine cooling was a switch from a hood with 20 louvers to one with 25.

FORD — MODEL B — FOUR: Somewhat overwhelmed by the public's response to Model 18, the four-cylinder Model B shared the same body as the V-8, minus V-8 emblems on the headlamp tie bars and with Ford rather than V-8 lettering on its hub caps.

Both types had single transverse leaf springs front and rear. The locating of the rear spring behind the differential and the use of 18 inch wheels gave the Fords a lower overall height than previous models.

I.D. DATA: Top side of frame, near clutch pedal. Starting: [Model B] AB 5000,001 & up. [Model 18] 18-1. Ending: [Model 18] 18-2031126. Prefix ''C'' indicates Canadian built. Boss placed on center of left side of block, directly below the cylinder head [Model B]. Starting Engine No.: [Model B] AB 5000,005 & up. [Model 18] 18-1. Ending: [Model 18] 18-2031,126.

1932 Ford V-8, sport coupe, JAC

Model No.	Body Type & Seating	Price	Weight	Prod. Total
Ford V-8				
18	2-dr. Rds.	460	2203	520
18	2-dr. Del. Rds.	500	2308	6893
18	4-dr. Phae.	495	2369	483
18	4-dr. Del. Phae.	545	2375	923
18	2-dr. Cpe.	490	2398	28,904
18	2-dr. Spt. Cpe.	535	2405	1982
18	2-dr. Del. Cpe.	575	2493	20,506
18	2-dr. Tudor Sed.-4P	500	2508	57,930
18	2-dr. Del. Tudor Sed.-4P	550	2518	18,836
18	4-dr. Fordor Sed.-4P	590	2538	9310
18	4-dr. Del. Fordor Sed.-4P	645	2568	18,880
18	2-dr. Cab. R/S-2-4P	610	2398	5499
18	2-dr. Vic.-4P	600	2483	7241
18	2-dr. Conv. Sed.-4P	650	2480	842
Ford 4-cyl.				
B	2-dr. Rds.	410	2095	948
B	2-dr. Del. Rds.	450	2102	3719
B	4-dr. Phae.	445	2238	593
B	4-dr. Del. Phae.	495	2268	281
B	2-dr. Cpe.	440	2261	20,342
B	2-dr. Spt. Cpe.	485	2286	739
B	2-dr. Del. Cpe.	425	2364	968
B	2-dr. Tudor Sed.-4P	450	2378	36,553
B	2-dr. Del. Tudor Sed.-4P	500	2398	4077
B	4-dr. Fordor Sed.-4P	540	2413	4116
B	4-dr. Del. Fordor Sed.-4P	595	2432	2620
B	2-dr. Cab.-4P	560	2295	427
B	2-dr. Vic.-4P	550	2344	521
B	2-dr. Conv. Sed.-4P	600	2349	41

ENGINE: [Model B] In line, L-head. Four. Cast iron block. B x S: 3-7/8 in. x 4-1/4 in. Disp.: 200.5 cu. in. C.R.: 4.6:1. Brake H.P.: 50. Taxable H.P.: 30. Main bearings: Three. Valve lifters: Mechanical. Carb.: Zenith or Holley double-venturi. [Model 18] 90° V, L-head. Eight. Cast iron block. B x S: 3-1/16 in. x 3-3/4 in. Disp.: 221 cu. in. C.R.: 5.5:1. Brake H.P. 65 @ 3400 R.P.M. SAE H.P.: 30. Main bearings: Three. Valve lifters: Mechanical. Carb.: Special Ford Detroit lubricator downdraft, single barrel, 1-1/2'' throat. Torque: 130 lbs.-ft. @ 1250 R.P.M.

CHASSIS: Model 18 & B. W.B.: 106 in. O.L.: 165-1/2. Height: 68-5/8. Frt/Rear Tread: 55.2/56.7. Tires: 5.25 x 18.

TECHNICAL: Transmission: Sliding gear. Speeds: 3F/1R. Floor shift controls. Single dry plate, molded asbestos lining clutch. Shaft drive. 3/4 floating rear axle. Overall ratio: 4.11:1 (early cars - 4.33:1). Mechanical, rod activated brakes on four wheels. Welded wire, drop center rim wheels. Wheel size: 18.

OPTIONS: Single sidemount. Dual sidemount. Clock. Trunk rack. Leather upholstery. Mirror. Twin tail lamps. Bedford cord upholstery. Cowl lamps (Std. models).

HISTORICAL: Introduced: April 2, 1932. Mass production of a low-priced one-piece 90° V-8 engine block. Calendar year sales: 2581927 (registrations). Calendar year production: 287,285. The president of Ford was Edsel Ford.

1932
Model B, 4-cyl.

	FP	5	4	3	2	1
Rds	410	3400	6900	11,500	16,100	23,000
Phae	445	3750	7500	12,500	17,500	25,000
Cabr	560	3300	6600	11,000	15,400	22,000
Conv Sed	495	3400	6900	11,500	16,100	23,000
Cpe	440	1250	3900	6500	9100	13,000
Spt Cpe	485	1300	4050	6750	9450	13,500
Tudor	450	1075	3000	5500	7700	11,000
Fordor	540	950	2100	4750	6650	9500
Vic	550	3000	6000	10,000	14,000	20,000
Sta Wag	600	2800	5700	9500	13,300	19,000

Model 18, V-8

	FP	5	4	3	2	1
Rds	460	4050	8100	13,500	18,900	27,000
DeL Rds	500	4200	8400	14,000	19,600	28,000
Phae	495	4050	8100	13,500	18,900	27,000
DeL Phae	545	4200	8400	14,000	19,600	28,000
Cabr	610	3600	7200	12,000	16,800	24,000
Conv Sed	650	3600	7200	12,000	16,800	24,000
Cpe	490	1550	4500	7500	10,500	15,000
DeL Cpe	575	1750	4800	8000	11,200	16,000
Spt Cpe	535	1650	4650	7750	10,850	15,500
Tudor	500	1250	3900	6500	9100	13,000
DeL Tudor	550	1300	4050	6750	9450	13,500
Fordor	590	1200	3750	6250	8750	12,500
DeL Fordor	645	1300	4050	6750	9450	13,500
Vic	600	3000	6000	10,000	14,000	20,000
Sta Wag	600	3300	6600	11,000	15,400	22,000

1933

1933 Ford V-8, victoria, OCW

FORD — MODEL 40 — EIGHT: In addition to a longer 112 inch wheelbase, X-member double-drop frame, the Model 40 Ford had valenced front and rear fenders, a new radiator design with vertical bars slanted back to match the rear sweep of the windshield and acorn-shaped headlight shells. Curvaceous one-piece bumpers with a center-dip were used at front and rear. Enhancing the Ford's streamlined appearance were the angled side hood louvers. All models regardless of body color were delivered with black fenders and 17 inch wire spoke wheels.

Accompanying these exterior revisions was a new dash arrangement with a reshaped engine-tuned panel enclosing the gauges placed directly in front of the driver. A similarly shaped glove box was placed on the passenger's side.

With its teething problems part of the past, the Ford V-8 by virtue of an improved ignition system, better cooling, higher compression ratio and aluminum cylinder heads developed 75 horsepower.

FORD — MODEL 40 — FOUR: As before the four-cylinder Fords were identical to the eight-cylinder models except for their lack of V-8 trim identification.

I.D. DATA: Serial numbers were located on top side of frame near clutch pedal also, left front pillar, foreward portion of left frame member, transmission housing. Starting: (V-8) 18-2031127 & up; (four-cylinder, with prefix "B") 5185849 & up. Engine numbers were located on boss placed on center of left side of block, directly below the cylinder head (four-cylinder); On top of clutch housing (V-8). Starting: (V-8) 18-2031127 & up; (four-cylinder) 5185849 & up.

Model No.	Body Type & Seating	Price	Weight	Prod. Total
Ford V-8				
40	2-dr. Del. Rds. R/S-2/4P	510	2461	4223
40	2-dr. Std. RS Rds.-2/4P	475	2422	126
40	2-dr. Cab R/S-2/4P	585	2545	7852
40	4-dr. Std. Phae.-4P	495	2520	232
40	4-dr. Del. Phae.-4P	545	2529	1483
40	2-dr. 3W Del. Cpe.-2P	540	2538	15894
40	2-dr. 3W Std. Cpe.-2P	490	2534	6585
40	2-dr. 5W Del. Cpe.-2P	540	2538	11244
40	2-dr. 5W Std. Cpe.-2P	490	2534	31797
40	2-dr. Vic.-4P	595	2595	4193
40	2-dr. Del. Tudor Sed.-4P	550	2625	48233
40	2-dr. Std. Tudor Sed.-4P	500	2621	106387
40	4-dr. Del. Fordor Sed.-4P	610	2684	45443
40	4-dr. Std. Fordor Sed.-4P	560	2675	19602
40	4-dr. Sta. Wag.-4P	640	2635	1654
Ford 4-cyl.				
40	2-dr. Del. Rds. R/S-2/4P	460	2278	101
40	2-dr. Std. RS Rds.-2/4P	425	2268	107
40	2-dr. Cab R/S-2/4P	535	2306	24
40	4-dr. Std. Phae.-4P	445	2281	457
40	4-dr. Del. Phae.-4P	495	2290	241
40	2-dr. 3W Del. Cpe.-2P	490	2220	24
40	2-dr. 3W Std. Cpe.-2P	440	2380	189
40	2-dr. 5W Del. Cpe.-2P	490	2299	28
40	2-dr. 5W Std. Cpe.-2P	440	2220	2148
40	2-dr. Vic.-4P	545	2356	25
40	2-dr. Del. Tudor Sed.-4P	500	2520	85
40	2-dr. Std. Tudor Sed.-4P	450	2503	2911
40	4-dr. Del. Fordor Sed.-4P	560	2590	179
40	4-dr. Std. Fordor Sed.-4P	510	2550	682
40	4-dr. Sta. Wag.-4P	590	2505	359

1933 Ford V-8, DeLuxe coupe, JAC

ENGINE: [Model B] Inline. L-head. Four. Cast iron block. B & S: 3-7/8 in. x 4-1/4 in. Disp.: 200.5 cu. in. C.R.: 4.6:1. Brake H.P.: 50. Taxable H.P.: 30. Main bearings: Three. Valve lifters: Mechanical. Carb.: Zenith or Holley double venturi. [Model 40] 90° V, L-head. Eight. Cast iron block. B & S: 3-1/16 in. x 3-3/4 in. Disp.: 221 cu. in. C.R.: 6.3:1. Brake H.P.: 75 @ 3800 R.P.M. Main bearings: Three. Valve lifters: Mechanical. Carb.: Detroit Lubricator downdraft, single barrel 1.25" throat.

CHASSIS: [Model 40] W.B.: 112 in. O.L.: 182-9/10 in. Height: 68 in. Frt/Rear Tread: 55-1/5 in./56-7/10 in. Tires: 5.50 x 17.

TECHNICAL: Sliding gear transmission. Speeds: 3F/1R. Floor shift controls. Single dry plate, woven asbestos lining clutch. Shaft drive. 3/4 floating rear axle. Overall Ratio: 4.11:1. Mechanical internal expanding brakes on four wheels. Welded spoke wheels, drop center rims. Wheel Size: 17 in.

OPTIONS: Radio. Heater. Clock. Radio antenna. Greyhound radiator ornament. Trunk. Trunk rack. Twin tail lamps. Cowl lamps (Std. models). Windshield wings. Dual horns (Std. models). Whitewalls. Leather seats. Dual wipers. Steel spare tire cover. Rumble seat (Coupes).

HISTORICAL: Introduced February 9, 1933. Calendar year sales: 311,113 (registrations). Calendar year production: 334,969. The president of Ford was Edsel Ford. During 1933 Ford conducted a number of economy runs with the Model 40. Under conditions ranging from the Mojave Desert to the Catskill Mountains the Fords averaged between 18.29 and 22.5mpg.

1933
Model 40, V-8

	FP	5	4	3	2	1
Phae	495	3900	7800	13,000	18,200	26,000
DeL Phae	545	4050	8100	13,500	18,900	27,000
Rds	475	3900	7800	13,000	18,200	26,000
DeL Rds	510	4050	8100	13,500	18,900	27,000
3W Cpe	490	1150	3600	6000	8400	12,000
3W DeL Cpe	540	1250	3900	6500	9100	13,000
5W Cpe	490	1150	3600	6000	8400	12,000
5W DeL Cpe	540	1250	3900	6500	9100	13,000
Cabr	585	3000	6000	10,000	14,000	20,000
Tudor	500	1150	3600	6000	8400	12,000
DeL Tudor	550	1250	3900	6500	9100	13,000
Fordor	560	1000	2500	5100	7100	10,200
DeL Fordor	610	1075	3000	5500	7700	11,000
Vic	595	2000	5100	8500	11,900	17,000
Sta Wag	640	3000	6000	10,000	14,000	20,000

Model 40, 4-cyl.
(All models deduct 20 percent avg from V-8 models)

1934

1934 Ford V-8, station wagon, AA

FORD — MODEL 40 — EIGHT: Visual changes for 1934 were minor. Different V-8 hub cap emblems (now painted rather than chrome-finished and without a painted surround) were used and the side hood louvers were straight instead of curved. Although the same grille form was continued for 1934 there were changes. The 1934 version had fewer vertical bars and its chrome frame was deeper and flatter. The V-8 grille ornament was placed within an inverted 60° triangle and carried a vertical divider. Other exterior alterations included smaller head and cowl light shells, two rather than one, hood handles and three instead of two body pin stripes. In addition fenders were painted in body color on all models. However, black fenders were available as an option. Closed body models featured front door glass that prior to lowering vertically into the door, moved slightly to the rear. This was usually referred to as "clear vision" ventilation.

The dash panel no longer had the engine-turned panel insert. For 1934 this surface was painted.

DeLuxe models were easily distinguished from their Standard counterparts by their pin-striping, cowl light, twin horns and two taillights.

The principle change in the design of the Ford V-8 consisted of a Stromberg carburetor in place of the Detroit Lubricator unit and a reshaped air cleaner.

Ford also offered its four-cylinder engine in all models at a price $50.00 below that of a corresponding V-8 design. This was the final year for this engine's use in a Ford automobile. The engine was designated Model B; the car was designated Model 40.

I.D. DATA: Serial numbers were on top side of frame, near clutch panel. Also left front pillar forward portion of left frame member transmission housing. Starting No.: 18-451478 & up. Engine numbers on top of clutch housing. Starting Engine No.: 18-457478 & up.

1934 Ford V-8, cabriolet, JAC

Model No. Ford V-8	Body Type & Seating	Price	Weight	Prod. Total
40 V-8	2-dr. Del. Rds.-2P	525	2461	—
40 V-8	4-dr. Phae.-4P	510	2520	373
40 V-8	4-dr. Del. Phae.-4P	550	2529	3128
40 V-8	2-dr. Cab.-2/4P	590	2545	14,496
40 V-8	2-dr. Std. 5W Cpe.-2P	515	2534	47,623
40 V-8	2-dr. Del. 3W Cpe.-2/4P	555	2538	26,348
40 V-8	2-dr. Del. 5W Cpe.-2/4P	555	2538	26,879
40 V-8	2-dr. Tudor-4P	535	2621	124,870
40 V-8	2-dr. Del. Tudor-4P	575	2625	121,696
40 V-8	4-dr. Fordor-4P	585	2675	22,394
40 V-8	4-dr. Del. Fordor-4P	625	2684	102,268
40 V-8	2-dr. Vic.-4P	610	2595	20,083
40 V-8	4-dr. Sta. Wag.-4P	660	2635	2905
Ford 4-cyl.				
40	2-dr. Del. Rds.-2P	475	2278	—
40	4-dr. Phae.-4P	460	2281	377
40	4-dr. Del. Phae.-4P	510	2290	412
40	2-dr. Cab.-2P	540	2306	12
40	2-dr. Std. 5W Cpe.-2P	465	2220	20
40	2-dr. Del. 3W Cpe.-2/4P	505	2220	7
40	2-dr. Del. 5W Cpe.-2/4P	505	2299	3
40	2-dr. Tudor-4P	485	2503	185
40	2-dr. Del. Tudor-4P	525	2520	12
40	4-dr. Fordor-4P	535	2590	405
40	4-dr. Del. Fordor-4P	575	2590	384
40	2-dr. Vic.-4P	560	2356	—
40	4-dr. Sta. Wag.-4P	610	2505	95

ENGINE: [Model B] Inline. L-head. Four. Cast iron block. B & S: 3-7/8 in. x 4-1/4 in. Disp.: 200.5 cu. in. C.R.: 4.6:1. Brake H.P.: 50. Taxable H.P.: 30. Main bearings: Three. Valve lifters: Mechanical. Carb.: Zenith or Holley double venturi. [Model 40] 90° V, L-head. Eight. Cast iron block. B & S: 3-1/16 in. x 3-3/4 in. Disp.: 221 cu. in. C.R.: 6.3:1. Brake H.P.: 85 @ 3800 R.P.M. Main bearings: Three. Valve lifters: Mechanical. Carb.: Stromberg EE-1 2bbl. downdraft. Torque: 150 lbs.-ft. @ 2200 R.P.M.

CHASSIS: W.B.: 112. O.L.: 182.9 in. Height: 68 in. Frt/Rear Tread: 55.2/56.7 in. Tires: 5.50 x 17.

TECHNICAL: Sliding gear. Speeds: 3F/1R. Floor shift controls. Single dry plate, woven asbestos lining. Shaft drive. 3/4 floating rear axle. Overall Ratio: 4.11:1. Mechanical internal expanding on four wheels. Welded spoke drop center rims. Wheel Size: 17"

OPTIONS: Radio (ash tray or glove box door mounted). Heater. Clock. Cigar Lighter. Radio Antenna. Seat Covers. Spotlight. Cowl lamps (std. models). Trunk. Whitewalls. Greyhound radiator ornament. Special steel spoke wheels. Oversize balloon tires. Bumper guards. Extra horn, black finish (std. models). Dual windshield wiper. Steel tire cover (std. models). Black painted fendors. Two taillights (std. models).

HISTORICAL: Introduced: January, 1934. Calendar year production: 563,921. The president of Ford was Edsel Ford. In April 1934 Clyde Barrow wrote his famous (infamous?) letter to Henry Ford in which he told Ford "what a dandy car you make." At the Ford press preview, held on December 6, 1933 Ford served alcoholic beverages for the first time.

For the first time since 1930 the Ford Motor Company reported a profit ($3,759,311) for 1934.

1934
Model 40, V-8

	FP	5	4	3	2	1
Rds	525	3900	7800	13,000	18,200	26,000
Phae	550	3900	7800	13,000	18,200	26,000
Cabr	590	3150	6300	10,500	14,700	21,000
SW Cpe	515	1075	3000	5500	7700	11,000
DeL 3W Cpe	555	1250	3900	6500	9100	13,000
DeL 5W Cpe	555	1150	3600	6000	8400	12,000
Tudor	535	875	1700	4250	5900	8500
DeL Tudor	575	1000	2400	5000	7000	10,000
Fordor	585	925	2000	4600	6400	9200
DeL Fordor	625	975	2200	4850	6800	9700
Vic	610	1750	4800	8000	11,200	16,000
Sta Wag	660	3000	6000	10,000	14,000	20,000

1935

1935 Ford V-8, convertible cabriolet, AA

FORD — MODEL 48 — EIGHT: Few Ford enthusiasts would dispute Ford's claim of "Greater Beauty, Greater Comfort, and Greater Safety" for its 1935 models.

The narrower radiator grille lost its sharply V'eed base and four horizontal bars helped accentuate the 1935 model's new, lower and more streamlined appearance. Fender outlines were now much more rounded and the side hood louvers received three horizontal bright stripes. In profile the Ford windshield was seen to be more sharply sloped then previously. No longer fitted were the old cowl lamps since the parking lamps were integral with the headlamps. The headlight shells were body color painted.

For the first time Ford offered a built-in trunk for its 2 and 4-door models and all Fords had front-hinged doors front and rear.

Both Standard and DeLuxe versions shared a painted dash finish with the latter Fords having a set of horizontal bars running down the center section. External distinctions were very obvious. DeLuxe models had bright windshield and grille trimwork as well as dual exposed horns and twin taillights.

Added to the Ford model line up was a Convertible Sedan. No longer available was the Victoria.

1935 Ford V-8, DeLuxe roadster, JAC

I.D. DATA: Serial numbers were located on left side of frame near firewall. Starting No.: 18-1234357. Ending: 18-2207110. Prefix "C" indicates Canadian built. Engine no. location on top of clutch housing. Starting Engine No.: 18-1234357. Ending: 18-2207110.

Model No.	Body Type & Seating	Price	Weight	Prod. Total
48	4-dr. Del. Phae.-4P	580	2667	6073
48	2-dr. Del. Rds. R/S-2/4P	550	2597	4896
48	2-dr. Del. RS Cab.-2/4P	625	2687	17,000
48	4-dr. Del. Conv. Sed.-4P	750	2827	4234
48	2-dr. Std. Cpe. 3W-2P	—	2647	
48	2-dr. Del. Cpe. 3W-2P	570	2647	31,513
48	2-dr. Std. Cpe. 5W-2P	520	2620	78,477
48	2-dr. Del. Cpe. 5W-2P	560	2643	33,065
48	2-dr. Std. Tudor-4P	510	2717	4,237,833
48	2-dr. Del. Tudor-4P	595	2737	84,692
48	4-dr. Std. Fordor-4P	575	2760	49,176
48	4-dr. Del. Fordor-4P	635	2767	75,807
48	4-dr. Sta. Wag.	670	2896	4536
48	Del. Tudor Sed.-4P	595	2772	87,336
48	Del. Fordor Sed.-4P	655	2787	105,157

ENGINE: 90° V, L-head. Eight. Cast iron block. B & S: 3-1/16 in. x 3-3/4 in. Disp.: 221 cu. in. C.R.: 6.3:1. Brake H.P.: 85 @ 3800 R.P.M. Main bearings: Three. Valve lifters: Mechanical. Carb.: Stromberg EE-1, 2 bbl downdraft. Torque: 144 lbs.-ft. @ 2200 R.P.M.

CHASSIS: W.B.: 112 in. O.L.: 182-3/4 in. Height: 64-5/8 in. Frt/Rear Tread: 55-1/2 / 58-1/4 in. Tires: 6.00 x 16.

TECHNICAL: Sliding gear trans. Speeds: 3F/1R. Floor shift controls. Single dry plate, woven asbestos lining clutch. Shaft drive. 3/4 floating rear axle. Overall Ratio: 4.33:1. Mechanical, internal expanding brakes on four wheels. Welded spoke, drop center rims on wheels. Wheel Size: 16"

1935 Ford V-8, Fordor sedan, JAC

OPTIONS: Radio. Heater. Clock. Cigar lighter. Radio antenna. Seat covers. Spotlight. Cowl lamps (std. models). Trunk. Luggage rack. Whitewalls. Greyhound radiator ornament. Special steel spoke wheels. Oversize balloon tires. Bumper guards. Extra horns black finish (std. models). Dual windshield wipers. Steel tire cover (std. models). Black painted fenders. Two taillights (std. models). Banjo type steering wheel. Rumble seat (coupes and roadsters).

HISTORICAL: Introduction: December, 1934. Calendar year registrations: 826,519. Calendar year production: 942,439. The president of Ford was Edsel Ford. Ford was America's best selling car for 1935. A Ford Convertible Sedan paced the 1935 Indianapolis 500. Ford produced its two-millionth V-8 engine in June 1935.

1935
Model 48, V-8

	FP	5	4	3	2	1
Phae	580	4050	8100	13,500	18,900	27,000
Rds	550	3900	7800	13,000	18,200	26,000
Cabr	625	3400	6900	11,500	16,100	23,000
Conv Sed	750	3600	7200	12,000	16,800	24,000
DeL 3W Cpe	595	1550	4500	7500	10,500	15,000
5W Cpe	520	1250	3900	6500	9100	13,000
DeL 5W Cpe	585	1400	4200	7000	9800	14,000
Tudor	510	875	1700	3900	6000	8600
DeL Tudor	595	900	1800	4450	6250	8900
Fordor	575	875	1700	4350	6050	8700
DeL Fordor	655	900	1900	4500	6300	9000
Sta Wag	670	2800	5700	9500	13,300	19,000
C'ham TwnC	2600	3300	6600	11,000	15,400	22,000

1936

1936 Ford V-8 DeLuxe, club cabriolet, AA

FORD — MODEL 68 — EIGHT: The 1936 Fords retained the same basic body of the 1935 models but carried a restyled front end and new rear fenders. The grille, consisting only of vertical bars extended further around the hood sides and the dual horns of the DeLuxe models were placed behind screens set into the fender catwalks.

The Convertible Sedan with its "flat-back" body was superseded by a version with a built-in luggage compartment or "trunk-back" style during the model year.

In place of wire wheels were new pressed steel, artillery wheels with large 12 inch painted hubcaps and chrome centers carrying a very narrow, stylized V-8 logo. The same design was used on the Ford's hood ornament.

Design changes for 1936 included a larger capacity radiator, better engine cooling via new hood side louvers and front vents, and helical-type gears for first and reverse gears. Previously only the second and third gears were of this design. The Ford V-8 now had domed aluminum pistons (replaced by steel versions during the year) and new insert main bearings.

DeLuxe models featured bright work around the grille, headlamps and windshield as well as dual horns and taillights. Those DeLuxe Fords produced later in the model year also had as standard equipment dual windshield wipers, wheel trim rings, clock and rear view mirror.

I.D. DATA: Serial numbers were located on left side of frame near firewall. Starting: 18-2207111. Ending: 18-3331856. Prefix "C" indicates Canadian built. Engine numbers were located on top of clutch housing. Starting: 18-2207111. Ending: 18-3331856.

Model No.	Body Type & Seating	Price	Weight	Prod. Total
68	2-dr. Del. Rds.-2P	560	2561	3862
68	4-dr. Del. Phae.-4P	590	2641	5555
68	2-dr. Cab-4P	625	2649	
68	2-dr. Clb. Cab.-4P	675	2661	4616
68	4-dr. Conv. Trk. Sed.-4P	780	2916	
68	4-dr. Conv. Sed.-4P	760	2791	5601
68	2-dr. Del. 3W Cpe.-2P	570	2621	21,446
68	2-dr. Std. 5W Cpe.-2P	510	2599	78,534
68	2-dr. Del. 5W Cpe.-2P	555	2641	29,938
68	2-dr. Std. Tudor Sed.-4P	520	2659	174,770
68	Std. Tudor Tr. Sed.-4P	545	2718	
68	2-dr. Del. Tudor Sed.-4P	565	2691	20,519
68	Del. Tudor Tr. Sed.-4P	590	2786	125,303
68	4-dr. Std. Fordor Sed.-4P	580	2699	31,505
68	Std. Fordor Tr. Sed.-4P	605	2771	
68	4-dr. Del. Fordor Sed.-4P	625	2746	42,867
68	Del. Fordor Tr. Sed.-4P	650	2816	159,825
68	4-dr. Sta. Wag.	670	3020	7044

1936 Ford V-8, Fordor sedan, JAC

ENGINE: 90° V, inline. Eight. Cast iron block. B & S: 3-1/16 in. x 3-3/4 in. Disp.: 221 cu. in. C.R.: 6.3:1. Brake H.P.: 85 @ 3800 R.P.M. Taxable H.P.: 30. Main bearings: Three. Valve lifters: Mechanical. Carb.: Ford 67-9510A Abb1 downdraft. Torque: 148 lbs.-ft. @ 2200 R.P.M.

CHASSIS: W.B.: 112 in. O.L.: 182-3/4 in. Height: 68-5/8 in. Frt/Rear Tread: 55-1/2 in./58-1/4 in. Tires: 6.00 x 16.

TECHNICAL: Sliding gear transmission. Speeds: 3F/1R. Floor shift controls. Single dry plate, moulded asbestos lining clutch. Shaft drive. 3/4 floating rear axle. Overall Ratio: 4.33:1. Mechanical, internal expanding brakes on four wheels. Pressed steel wheels, drop center rim. Wheel Size: 16.

OPTIONS: Radio (five versions from 44.50). Heater (14.00). Clock (9.75). Cigar lighter. Radio antenna. Seat covers. Spotlight. Rumble seat (coupes, roadster) (20.00). Luggage rack (7.50). Banjo steering wheel. "Spider" wheel covers (3.75 early). Wind wings (10.00). Combination oil-pressure, gas gauge (3.75). Dual windshield wipers (3.00). Leather upholstery. Electric air horns.

HISTORICAL: Introduced October, 1935. Ford was the overall winner of the 1936 Monte Carlo Rally. Calendar year registrations: 748,554. Calendar year production: 791,812. The president of Ford was Edsel Ford.

1936
Model 68, V-8

	FP	5	4	3	2	1
Rds	560	3900	7800	13,000	18,200	26,000
Phae	590	4050	8100	13,500	18,900	27,000
Cabr	625	3400	6900	11,500	16,100	23,000
Clb Cabr	675	3600	7200	12,000	16,800	24,000
Conv Trk Sed	780	3750	7500	12,500	17,500	25,000
Conv Sed	760	3600	7200	12,000	16,800	24,000
3W Cpe	595	1550	4500	7500	10,500	15,000
5W Cpe	535	1250	3900	6500	9100	13,000
DeL 5W Cpe	580	1400	4200	7000	9800	14,000
Tudor	520	875	1700	4350	6050	8700
Tudor Tr Sed	525	900	1900	4500	6300	9000
DeL Tudor	565	900	1900	4500	6300	9000
DeL Tr Sed	590	925	1900	4550	6350	9100
Fordor	580	925	1900	4550	6350	9100
Fordor Tr Sed	605	900	1900	4500	6300	9000
DeL Fordor	625	925	1900	4550	6350	9100
Sta Wag	670	2800	5700	9500	13,300	19,000

1937

1937 Ford V-8, 5-window coupe, AA

FORD — MODEL 78 — EIGHT: The 1937 models were the first Fords to have their headlights mounted in the front fenders and possess an all steel top. The 1937 Fords' styling reflected the strong influence of the Lincoln-Zephyr. The grille with horizontal bars and a center vertical bar cut a sharp V into the side hood area. As had been the case for many years the side hood cooling vents reflected the grille's general form.

Ford offered sedans with either a "slant-back" or "trunk-back" rear deck. All Ford sedans had access to the trunk area through an external lid.

In addition, a new coupe with a rear seat was introduced. All models had a rear-hinged alligator-type hood.

The operation of the 221 cid V-8 was further improved by the use of a higher capacity water pump, larger insert bearings and cast alloy steel pistons. Replacing the rod-operated mechanical brake system was a version using a cable linkage.

As in previous years Ford offered both Standard and DeLuxe models with the latter possessing interiors with walnut woodgrain window molding and exterior trim bright work. Standard models had painted radiator grilles and windshield frames. A burl mahogany woodgrain finish was applied to their interior window trim.

Ford introduced a smaller version of its V-8 with a 2-3/5 inch bore and 3-1/5 inch stroke. Its displacement was 136 cubic inches. This 60 hp engine was available only in the Standard Ford models.

1937 Ford V-8, Tudor sedan, AA

I.D. DATA: Left side of frame near firewall. Starting: [Model 74] 54-6602. [Model 78] 18-3331857. Ending: [Model 74] 54-358334. [Model 78] 18-4186446. Prefix "C" indicates Canadian built. Top of clutch housing. Starting Engine No.: [Model 74] 54-6602; [Model 78] 18-3331857. Ending: [Model 74] 54-358334; [Model 78] 18-4186446.

Model No.	Body Type & Seating	Price	Weight	Prod. Total
78	2-dr. Del. Rds.-2P	696	2576	1250
78	4-dr. Del. Phae.-5P	750	2691	3723
78	2-dr. Del. Cab.	720	2616	10,184
78	2-dr. Del. Clb. Cab.	760	2636	8001
78	2-dr. Del. Conv. Sed.	860	2861	4378
78	2-dr. Del. Cpe. 5W-3P	660	2506	26,738
78	Del. Clb. Cpe. 5W-4P	720	2616	16,992
78	2-dr. Del. Tudor Sed.-5P	675	2656	33,683
78	Del. Tudor Tr. Sed.-5P	700	2679	—
78	4-dr. Del. Fordor Sed.-5P	735	2671	22,885
78	Del. Fordor Tr. Sed.-5P	760	2696	98,687
78	4-dr. Sta. Wag.-5P	755	2991	9304
78	2-dr. Std. Tudor Sed.-5P	610	2616	308,446
78	Std. Tudor Tr. Sed.-5P	635	2648	—
78	4-dr. Std. Fordor Sed.-5P	670	2649	49,062
78	Std. Fordor Tr. Sed.-5P	695	2666	45,531
78	2-dr. Std. Cpe. 5W-3P	585	2496	90,347

Note 1: The five standard bodies when ordered with the 60 hp V-8 were designated as Model 74 Fords and weighed over 200 lbs. less.

1937 Ford V-8, station wagon, JAC

ENGINE: [Model 78] 90° V, inline. 8. Cast iron block. B & S: 3-1/16 in. x 3-3/4 in. Disp.: 221 cu. in. C.R.: 6.3:1. Brake H.P.: 85 @ 3800 R.P.M. Taxable H.P.: 30.01. Main bearings: Three. Valve lifters: Mechanical. Carb.: Stromberg 67-9510A 2bbl downdraft. Torque: 153 lbs.-ft. @ 2200 R.P.M. [Model 74] 90° V, inline. 8. Cast iron block. B & S: 2-3/5 in. x 3-1/5 in. Disp.: 136 cu. in. C.R.: 6.6:1. Brake H.P. 60 @ 3600 R.P.M. Taxable H.P. 21.6. Main bearings: Three. Valve lifters: Mechanical. Carb.: Stromberg 922A-9510A 2bbl. downdraft. Torque: 94 lbs.-ft. @ 2500 R.P.M.

CHASSIS: Model 74 & 78. W.B.: 112 in. O.L.: 179-1/2 in. Height: 68-5/8 in. Frt/Rear Tread: 55-1/2 / 58-1/4. Tires: 6.00 x 16 [Model 74-5.50 x 16].

TECHNICAL: Transmission: Sliding gear. Speeds: 3F/1R. Floor shift controls. Single dry plate, molded asbestos lining clutch. Shaft drive. 3/4 floating rear axle. Overall Ratio: 4.33:1. Mechanical, internal expanding brakes on 4 wheels. Pressed steel, drop center rim wheels. Wheel size: 16''.

OPTIONS: Fender skirts. Radio. Heater. Clock (mirror clock & glove box clock). Cigar lighter. Radio antenna. Seat covers. Side view mirror. Dual wipers. Sport light. Dual taillights (std. on DeLuxe models). Fog lamps. Locking gas cap. Glove box lock. Defroster. Draft deflectors. Vanity mirror. Wheel trim bands. DeLuxe hubcaps. White sidewall tires. Center bumper guard. DeLuxe steering wheel. Sliding glass panels (Sta. Wag.) (20.00).

HISTORICAL: Introduction: November, 1937. First year for 60 hp V-8, first year for rear fender skirts. Calendar year sales: 765,933 (registrations). Calendar year production: 848,608. The president of Ford was Edsel Ford.

1937
Model 74, V-8, 60-hp

	FP	5	4	3	2	1
Tudor	—	800	1550	3900	5450	7800
Tudor Tr Sed	635	825	1600	3950	5500	7900
Fordor	670	775	1500	3750	5250	7500
Fordor Tr Sed	695	800	1550	3850	5400	7700
Cpe	585	875	1700	4250	5900	8500
Cpe PU	635	900	1900	4500	6300	9000
V-8 DeLuxe						
Sta Wag	755	1300	4050	6750	9450	13,500
Model 78, V-8, 85-hp						
Rds	696	3150	6300	10,500	14,700	21,000
Phae	750	3300	6600	11,000	15,400	22,000
Cabr	720	3300	6600	11,000	15,400	22,000
Clb Cabr	760	3400	6900	11,500	16,100	23,000
Conv Sed	860	3600	7200	12,000	16,800	24,000
Cpe	660	900	1900	4500	6300	9000
Clb Cpe	720	950	2100	4750	6650	9500
Tudor	675	800	1550	3850	5400	7700
Tudor Tr Sed	700	825	1600	4000	5600	8000
Fordor	735	800	1550	3900	5450	7800
Fordor Tr Sed	760	850	1650	4100	5700	8200
Sta Wag	775	2300	5400	9000	12,600	18,000

1938

1938 Ford, V-8, DeLuxe, station wagon, AA

FORD — DELUXE — MODEL 81A — EIGHT: Ford adopted a new marketing strategy for 1938 in which its Standard models carried the same basic front sheet metal used in 1937 while the DeLuxe models were given a substantially revised appearance. A curved grille outline with horizontal bars and a separate set of side hood louvers distinguished the more costly DeLuxe models. Interior alterations consisted of a new instrument panel with a centrally located radio speaker grille and recessed control knobs. As before, the windshield opening knob was centered high on the dash.

FORD — STANDARD — MODEL 82A — EIGHT: The 60hp Ford V-8 engine was standard only in the three models offered in the Standard line. These Fords were also available with the 221cid V-8. The Standard Ford grille featured horizontal bars that extended into the side hood region for engine cooling.

I.D. DATA: Serial numbers were located on left frame side member near fire wall. Starting: 81A — 18-4186447; 82A — 54-358335 & up. Ending: 81A — 18-4661100. Engine numbers were located on top of clutch housing. Starting: 81A — 18-4186447; 82A — 54-358335 & up. Ending: 81A — 18-4661100.

Model No.	Body Type & Seating	Price	Weight	Prod. Total
81A	2-dr. Std. Cpe.-2P	625	2575	34,059
81A	2-dr. Std. Tudor Sed.-5P	665	2674	106,117
81A	4-dr. Std. Fordor Sed.-5P	710	2697	30,287
81A	4-dr. Sta. Wag.-5P	825	2981	6944
81A	4-dr. DeL. Phae.-5P	820	2748	1169
81A	2-dr. Del. Clb. Conv.-5P	800	2719	6080
81A	2-dr. DeL. Conv. Cpe.-3P	770	2679	4702
81A	4-dr. DeL. Conv. Sed.-5P	900	2883	2703
81A	2-dr. DeL. Cpe.-3P	685	2606	22,225
81A	2-dr. DeL. Clb. Cpe.-5P	745	2688	7171
81A	2-dr. DeL. Tudor Sed.-5P	725	2742	101,647
81A	DeL. Fordor Sed.-5P	770	2773	92,020

Note 1: The three Standard bodies when ordered with the 60hp V-8 were designated as Model 81A Fords.

1938 Ford, V-8, Standard coupe, HAC

ENGINE: [Model 81A] 90° V, inline. Eight. Cast iron block. B & S: 3-1/16 in. x 3-3/4 in. Disp.: 221 cu. in. C.R.: 6.12:1. Brake H.P.: 85 @ 3800 R.P.M. Taxable H.P.: 30. Main bearings: Three. Valve lifters: Mechanical. Carb.: Chandler-Groves and Stromberg 21A-9510A, 2bb1 downdraft. Torque: 146 lbs.-ft. @ 2000 R.P.M. [Model 82A] 90° V, inline. Eight. Cast iron block. B & S: 2-3/5 in. x 3-1/5 in. Disp.: 136 cu. in. C.R.: 6.6:1. Brake H.P.: 60 @ 3500 R.P.M. Taxable H.P.: 21.6. Main bearings: Three. Valve lifters: Mechanical. Carb.: Chandler-Groves and Stromberg 9221-95101, 2bb1 downdraft. Torque: 94 lbs.-ft. @ 2500 R.P.M.

CHASSIS: Models 81A & 82A. W.B.: 112 in. O.L.: 179-1/2 in. Height: 68-5/8 in. Frt/Rear Tread: 55-1/2 in./58-1/4 in. Tires: 6.00 x 16 (Model 82A — 5.50 x 16).

TECHNICAL: Sliding gear transmission. Speeds: 3F/1R. Floor shift controls. Single dry plate, molded asbestos lining clutch. Shaft drive. 3/4 floating rear axle. Overall Ratio: 4.33:1. Mechanical, internal expanding brakes on four wheels. Pressed steel wheels, drop-center rims. Wheel Size: 16''.

OPTIONS: Fender skirts. Bumper guards. Radio. Heater. Clock (mirror and glove box). Cigar lighter. Seat covers. Side view mirror. Dual wipers. Sportlight. Dual taillights (Std. models). Fog lights. Locking gas cap. Glove box lock. Defroster. Draft deflectors. Vanity mirror. Wheel trim bands. DeLuxe hub caps. White sidewall tires. DeLuxe steering wheel. License plate frame.

HISTORICAL: Introduced November, 1937. Ford secured its second victory in the Monte Carlo Rally. Calendar year registrations: 363,688. Calendar year production: 410,048. The president of Ford was Edsel Ford.

1938
Model 81A Standard, V-8

	FP	5	4	3	2	1
Cpe	625	875	1700	4250	5900	8500
2 dr	665	775	1500	3750	5250	7500
4 dr	710	800	1550	3800	5300	7600
Sta Wag	825	1300	4050	6750	9450	13,500

Model 81A DeLuxe, V-8

Phae	820	3400	6900	11,500	16,100	23,000
Conv	770	3300	6600	11,000	15,400	22,000
Clb Conv	800	3400	6900	11,500	16,100	23,000
Conv Sed	900	3600	7200	12,000	16,800	24,000
Cpe	685	950	2100	4750	6650	9500
Clb Cpe	745	1000	2400	5000	7000	10,000
2 dr	725	875	1700	4250	5900	8500
4 dr	770	875	1700	4350	6050	8700

NOTE: Deduct 10 percent avg. for 60 hp 82A Cord.

1939

1939 Ford, V-8, DeLuxe, coupe, AA

FORD — DELUXE — MODEL 91A — EIGHT: The 1939 Fords were again divided into Standard and DeLuxe models. The former carried the general styling of the 1938 DeLuxe Ford. Thus they had a sharply V'eed grille with horizontal bars, headlights mounted inboard of the fenders and small side hood louvers. The DeLuxe models had a much more modern appearance. Their teardrop-shaped headlights blended smoothly into the leading edges of the front fenders and a grille set lower in the hood than as previous models carried vertical bars. Simple chrome trim replaced the hood louvers and a more smoother body profile was featured. The most significant technical development was the adoption by Ford of Lockheed hydraulic brakes.

1939 Ford V-8, Fordor sedan, JAC

FORD — STANDARD — MODEL 922A — EIGHT: Only four body styles were offered in the Standard series. Customers could chose either the 60 hp or 85 hp engines.

Standard models were not equipped with the banjo steering wheel, glove box lock and clock found on DeLuxe Fords.

I.D. DATA: Serial numbers were located on the left side member near firewall. Starting No. Model: 91A — 18-4661001. Model 922A — 54-506501 & up. Ending: 91A-18-210700. Engine no. location was top of clutch housing. Starting Engine No.: Model 91A — 18-4661001. Model 922A — 54-506501 & up. Ending: Model 91A — 18-5210700.

Model No.	Body Type & Seating	Price	Weight	Prod. Total
922A	Std. 2-dr. Cpe.-3P	640	2710	38,197
922A	Std. 2-dr. Tudor Sed.-5P	680	2830	124,866
922A	Std. 2-dr. Fordor Sed.-5P	730	2850	
922A	Std. 4-dr. Sta. Wag.-5P	840	3080	3277
91A	2-dr. DeL. Conv. Cpe.-3P	790	2840	10,422
91A	4-dr. DeL. Conv. Sed.-5P	920	2935	3561
91A	2-dr. DeL. Cpe.-3P	700	2752	33,326
91A	2-dr. DeL. Tudor Sed.-5P	745	2867	144,333
91A	DeL. Fordor Sed.-5P	790	2898	
91A	4-dr. DeL. Sta. Wag.-5P	920	3095	6155

Note 1: The Standard models were available with the 60 hp or 85 hp engines.

1939 Ford, V-8, DeLuxe, station wagon, OCW

ENGINE: [85hp] 90° V, inline. Eight. Cast iron block. B & S: 3-1/16 in. x 3-3/4 in. Disp.: 221 cu. in. C.R.: 6.15:1. Brake H.P.: 90 @ 3800 R.P.M. Taxable H.P.: 30. Main bearings: Three. Valve lifters: Mechanical. Carb.: Stromberg 21A-951A, 2 bbl downdraft. Torque: 155 lbs-ft. @ 2200 R.P.M. [60 hp] 90° V, inline. Eight. Cast iron block. B & S: 2-3/5 in. x 3-1/5 in. Disp.: 136 cu. in. C.R.: 6.6:1. Brake H.P.: 60 @ 3500 R.P.M. Taxable H.P.: 21.6. Main bearings: Three. Valve lifters: Mechanical. Carb.: Stromberg 922A-9510A, 2 bbl downdraft. Torque: 94 lbs-ft. @ 2500 R.P.M.

CHASSIS: Series 91A-922A. W.B.: 112 in. O.L.: 179-1/2 in. Height: 68-5/8 in. Frt/Rear Tread: 55-1/2 / 58-1/4 in. Tires: 6.00 x 16. (60hp-5.50 x 16).

TECHNICAL: Sliding gear trans. Speeds: 3F/1R. Floor shift controls. Single dry plate, molded asbestos lining clutch. Shaft drive. 3/4 floating rear axle. Overall Ratio: 4.33:1. Lockheed hydraulic brakes on four wheels. Pressed steel, drop-center rim on wheels. Wheel Size: 16''.

OPTIONS: Bumper guards. Radio. Heater. Clock. Seat covers. Sideview mirror. Sport light. Fog lamps. Locking gas cap. Draft deflectors. Vanity mirror. Wheel dress up rings. DeLuxe hub caps. White sidewall tires. License plate frames. Fender skirts.

HISTORICAL: Introduced: November 4, 1938. Lockheed hydraulic brakes. Calendar year registrations: 481,496. Calendar year production: 532,152. The president of Ford was Edsel Ford.

1939
Model 922A Standard, V-8

	FP	5	4	3	2	1
Cpe	640	825	1600	4000	5600	8000
2 dr	680	750	1450	3300	4900	7000
4 dr	730	725	1400	3200	4850	6900
Sta Wag	840	2300	5400	9000	12,600	18,000

Model 91A DeLuxe, V-8

	FP	5	4	3	2	1
Conv	790	4050	8100	13,500	18,900	27,000
Conv Sed	920	4200	8400	14,000	19,600	28,000
Cpe	700	875	1700	4250	5900	8500
Tudor	745	825	1600	4000	5600	8000
Fordor	790	825	1600	3950	5500	7900
Sta Wag	920	2800	5700	9500	13,300	19,000

NOTE: Deduct 10 percent avg. for V-60 hp models.

1940

1940 Ford, V-8, DeLuxe, convertible coupe, AA

FORD — MODEL 01A — EIGHT: The 1940 Fords featured extremely handsome styling by Eugene Gregorie. All models were fitted with sealed beam headlights and a steering column-mounted shift lever. DeLuxe models had chrome headlight trim rings with the parking light cast into its upper surface. The DeLuxe grille combined a center section with horizontal bars and secondary side grids whose horizontal bars were subdivided into three sections by thicker molding. Hubcaps for these top level Fords featured bright red "Ford DeLuxe" lettering and trim rings finished in the body color. The DeLuxe instrument panel was given a maroon and sand two-tone finish which matched that of the steering wheel. Model 01A carried the 85 hp engine and was available in both Standard and DeLuxe versions.

FORD — MODEL 022A — EIGHT: Distinguishing the 60 hp Standard Fords was their grille and hood that were very similar to those of the 1939 DeLuxe models. Their headlight shells were finished in the body color and the integral parking lamp lacked the ribbed surround used on the DeLuxe model. The vertical grille bars were painted to match the body color. DeLuxe hubcaps had a series of concentric rings surrounding a blue V-8.

The Standard dash and steering wheel had a Briarwood Brown finish and the instrument panel had a larger speedometer face. Both Standard and DeLuxe Fords had front vent windows.

For the final year the Ford V-8 60 was available for Standard models.

1940 Ford V-8, DeLuxe station wagon, OCW

I.D. DATA: Left frame side member near firewall. Starting: [Model 01A] 18-5210701; [Model 022A] 54-506501 & up. Ending: [Model 01A] 18-5896294. Top of clutch housing. Starting Engine No.: [Model 01A] 18-5210701; [Model 022A] 54-506401 & up. Ending Engine No.: [Model 01A] 18-5896294.

Model No.	Body Type & Seating	Price	Weight	Prod. Total
022A	2-dr. Std. Cpe.-3P	660	2763	33,693
022A	2-dr. Std. Tudor Sed.-5P	700	2909	150,933
022A	4-dr. Std. Fordor Sed.-5P	750	2936	25,545
022A	4-dr. Std. Sta. Wag.-5P	875	3249	4469
022A	2-dr. Std. Bus. Cpe.-5P	680	2801	16,785
01A	2-dr. Del. Conv. Cpe.-5P	850	2956	23,704
01A	2-dr. Del. Cpe.-3P	721	2791	27,919
01A	2-dr. Del. Tudor Sed.-5P	765	2927	171,368
01A	4-dr. Del. Fordor Sed.-5P	810	2966	91,756
01A	4-dr. Del. Sta. Wag.	950	3262	8730
01A	2-dr. Del. Bus. Cpe.-5P	745	2831	20,183

ENGINE: [85 hp Engine] 90° V, inline. Eight. Cast iron block. B & S: 3-1/16 in. x 3-3/4 in. Disp.: 221 cu. in. C.P.: 6.15:1. Brake H.P. 85 @ 3800 R.P.M. Taxable H.P.: 30. Main bearings: Three. Valve lifters: Mechanical. Carb.: Chandler-Groves 21A-9510A, 2bbl downdraft. Torque: 155 lbs.-ft. @ 2200 R.P.M. [60 hp Engine] 90° V, inline. Eight. Cast iron block. B & S: 2-3/5 in. x 3-1/5 in. Disp.: 135 cu. in. C.R.: 6.6:1. Brake H.P.: 60 @ 3500 R.P.M. Taxable H.P. 21.6. Main bearings: Three. Valve lifters: Mechanical. Carb.: Chandler-Groves 922A-9510A 2bbl downdraft. Torque: 94 lbs.-ft. @ 2500 R.P.M.

CHASSIS: 01A & 022A. W.B.: 112 in. O.L.: 188-1/4 in. Height: 68 in. Frt/Rear Tread: 55-3/4 / 58-1/4. Tires: 6.00 x 16. (60 hp - 5.50 x 16).

TECHNICAL: Transmission: Sliding gear. Speeds: 3F/1R. Steering column-mounted shift lever. Single dry plate, molded asbestos lining clutch. Shaft drive. 3/4 floating rear axle. Overall Ratio: 4.33:1. Lockheed hydraulic brakes on 4 wheels. Pressed steel, drop-center rims wheels. Wheel size: 16 in.

OPTIONS: Fender skirts. Bumper guards. Radio. Heater. Cigar lighter. Radio antenna. Seat covers. Sideview mirror. Right hand side mirror. Sport light. Fog lamps. Locking gas cap. Defroster. Vanity mirror. DeLuxe wheel rings. DeLuxe hubcaps. White sidewall tires. Gravel deflectors. License plate frame. Two-tone paint.

HISTORICAL: Introduction: October 1940. Calendar year sales: 542,755 (registrations). Calendar year production: 599,175. The president of Ford was Edsel Ford.

1940
Model 022A, V-8

	FP	5	4	3	2	1
Conv	850	4200	8400	14,000	19,600	28,000
Cpe	680	1150	3600	6000	8400	12,000
DeL Cpe	721	1250	3900	6500	9100	13,000
Tudor	700	800	1550	3850	5400	7700
DeL Tudor	765	825	1600	4000	5600	8000
Fordor	750	800	1550	3800	5300	7600
DeL Fordor	810	875	1700	4250	5900	8500
Sta Wag	875	3000	6000	10,000	14,000	20,000

NOTE: Deduct 10 percent avg. for V-8, 60 hp models.

1941

1941 Ford, Super DeLuxe, club coupe, AA

FORD — SUPER DELUXE — SIX or EIGHT: The 1941 Fords were with fresh styling and a revamped chassis easily recognized as new models. All versions were mounted on a longer by two inches wheelbase of 114 inches and by virtue of a wider body featured substantially increased interior dimensions. Emphasizing Ford's rounder, more curved body form was a new three-piece grille that consisted of a neo-traditional vertical center section with two auxillary units set low on either side. Running boards were continued but due to the body's greater width were far less noticeable than on earlier Fords. Further accentuating the lower and wider nature of the 1941 Ford was the position of the headlights, which were further apart in the fenders.

Super DeLuxe Fords were easily identified by the bright trim on their running board edges and chrome grille sections. The Super DeLuxe bumpers had ridges along their bottom edge. A mid-year (March) revision to Super DeLuxe models added bright trimwork to the front and rear fenders, windshield, rear and side windows. Super DeLuxe script was placed in the inboard position of the left front fender. Bright rear taillight surrounds were installed. In addition the standard features of the Super DeLuxe included a trunk light, glove box mounted clock, bright wheel trimmings, twin visors, wipers and plastic Kelobra grain dash trim. The wheels had either Vermillion or Silver Gray stripes. Seven body styles were offered in Super DeLuxe form.

FORD — DELUXE — SIX or EIGHT: DeLuxe series Fords lacked the trunk light, glove box clock, wheel trim rings and unique license plate guard found on the Super DeLuxe models. Their instrument panels were finished in Ebony grain and among standard features were a glove box lock, dual wipers and sun visors. There was no striping in the DeLuxe Ford wheels which were painted black regardless of body color. Those on the Super DeLuxe models were painted to match the color of the body and fenders. Only the center grille portion was chromed on DeLuxe models.

Both Super DeLuxe and DeLuxe Fords were available with either Ford's V-8 engine, now rated at 90hp or for $15 less a new 26cid flathead six also credited with 90hp. Among its design features were four main bearings, a vibration damper, forged connecting rods, molybdenum-chrome alloy steel valve seat inserts and solid valve lifters. The six cylinder engine was a mid-year offering and its availability required new hood trim. Prior to the Sixes' introduction the molding was a plain trim piece with horizontal liner. With the availability of two engines it now carried either a V-8 or 6 identification with a blue background.

FORD — STANDARD — SERIES 11A — SIX: The three Standard models were offered only in a Harbor grey finish and without the V-8 engine option. In addition the windshield divider was a black, rather than stainless steel molding and like the DeLuxe Fords only the center grille section was chromed. In addition the Standard Fords were equipped with a single taillight, horn, windshield wiper and sun visor. Lacking from their interior were such appointments as arm rests, dome light, cigarette lighter and glove box lock.

1941 Ford, Super DeLuxe, 4-dr. sedan, OCW

I.D. DATA: Serial numbers were on left frame member directly behind front engine mount. Starting No.: 6 cyl-1GA-1 V-8 18-5986295. Ending: 6 cyl-1GA-34800 -8 18-6769035. Prefix "C" indicates Canadian built. Engine numbers located on top of clutch housing. Starting Engine No.: 6 cyl-1GA-1 V-8 18-5986295. Ending: 6 cyl-1GA-34800 V-8 18-6769035.

Model No.	Body Type & Seating	Price	Weight	Prod. Total
Sup. DeL.	2-dr. Conv.-6P	950	3187	30,240
Sup. DeL.	2-dr. Cpe.-3P	775	2969	22,878
Sup. DeL.	2-dr. Cpe.-4P	800	3001	10,796
Sup. DeL.	2-dr. Cpe. Sed.-6P	850	3052	45,977
Sup. DeL.	2-dr. Tudor-6P	820	3110	185,788
Sup. DeL.	4-dr. Fordor-6P	860	3146	88,053
Sup. DeL.	4-dr. Sta. Wag.-6P	1015	3419	9485
DeLuxe	2-dr. Cpe.-3P	730	2953	33,598
DeLuxe	2-dr. Cpe.-4P	750	2981	12,844
DeLuxe	2-dr. Tudor-6P	775	3095	177,018
DeLuxe	4-dr. Fordor-6P	815	3121	25,928
DeLuxe	4-dr. Sta. Wag.-6P	965	3412	6116
Special	2-dr. Cpe.-3P	706	2878	9823
Special	2-dr. Tudor-6P	735	2983	27,189
Special	4-dr. Fordor-6P	775	3033	3838

Note: Weights are for V-8 equipped models.

ENGINE: [V-8] 90° V Inline. Eight. Cast iron block. B & S: 3-1/16 in. x 3-3/4 in. Disp.: 221 cu. in. C.R.: 6.15:1. Brake H.P.: 90 @ 3800 R.P.M. Taxable H.P.: 30. Main bearings: Three. Valve lifters: Mechanical. Carb.: Ford 21A-9510A 2bbl. downdraft. Torque: 156 lbs.-ft. @ 2200 R.P.M. [6 Cylinder] Inline. L-head. Six. Cast iron block. B & S: 3-3/10 in. x 4-2/5 in. Disp.: 225.8 cu. in. C.R.: 6.7:1. Brake H.P.: 90 @ 3300 R.P.M. Taxable H.P.: 30. Main bearings: Four. Valve lifters: Mechanical. Carb.: Ford 1GA-9510A 1bbl. Torque: 180 lbs.-ft. @ 2000 R.P.M.

CHASSIS: Special, DeLuxe, Super DeLuxe. W.B.: 114 in. O.L.: 194.3 in. Height: 68.15 in. Frt/Rear Tread: 55.75/58.25 in. Tires: 6.00 x 16.

TECHNICAL: Sliding gear transmission. Speeds: 3F/1R. Column controls. Semi-centrifugal, moulded asbestos linings. Shaft drive. 3/4 floating rear axle. Overall Ratio: 3.78:1. Hydraulic brakes on four wheels. Pressed steel, drop center rim wheels. Wheel Size: 16".

1941 Ford, Super DeLuxe, 2-dr. sedan, OCW

OPTIONS: Fender skirts (12.50). Radio. Heater (hot air 23.00, hot water 20.00). Clock. Seat covers. Side view mirror. Passenger side mirror. Sport light. Locking gas cap. Glove compartment lock. Defroster. Vanity mirror. Radio foot control. Wheel trim rings. DeLuxe hub caps. White sidewall tires. Center bumper guards - front (3.50) rear (2.50). Gravel deflector (1.50).

1941 Ford, DeLuxe, 2-dr. sedan, AA

HISTORICAL: Introduced September, 1941. Calendar year sales: 602013 (registrations). Calendar year production: 600,814. The president of Ford was Edsel Ford. On April 29, 1941 the 29 millionth Ford was constructed.

1941
Model 11A Special, V-8

	FP	5	4	3	2	1
Cpe	700	775	1500	3750	5250	7500
Tudor	735	650	1250	2400	4200	6000
Fordor	775	650	1250	2400	4150	5900
DeLuxe						
3P Cpe	730	825	1600	4000	5600	8000
4P Cpe	750	875	1700	4250	5900	8500
Tudor	775	675	1300	2500	4350	6200
Fordor	815	675	1300	2600	4400	6300
Sta Wag	965	3000	6000	10,000	14,000	20,000
Super DeLuxe						
Conv	950	3400	6900	11,500	16,100	23,000
3P Cpe	775	850	1650	4100	5700	8200
4P Cpe	800	900	1900	4500	6300	9000
Cpe Sed	850	875	1700	4350	6050	8700
Tudor	820	750	1450	3400	5000	7100
Fordor	860	750	1450	3300	4900	7000
Sta Wag	1015	3150	6300	10,500	14,700	21,000

NOTE: Deduct 10 percent average for 6-cyl.

1942

1942 Ford, DeLuxe, 4-dr. sedan (Army staff car), OCW

FORD — SUPER DELUXE — SIX or V-EIGHT: The 1942 Fords were redesigned with fully concealed running boards plus new front fenders and hood sheet metal. A new grille design featured a very narrow center section in conjunction with side grilles considerably larger and more squared off than previously. The Super Deluxe grille had its bright work accentuated by blue painted grooves. Used only on these top of the line Fords were front and rear bumpers with ridges along their upper surface. The Super DeLuxe script was now positioned just below the left headlight. The taillights on all models were now horizontally positioned but only those on the Super DeLuxe had bright trim plates. Also unique to Super DeLuxe Fords were bright trim surrounds for the windshield, rear window and side windows. Wheel covers were painted to match body color and carried three stripes. Trim rings were standard.

Interior features included an electric clock, left front door arm rests, a steering wheel with a full circle horn ring and crank-operated front vent windows. The instrument panel was finished in Sequoia Grain. Assist cords were installed on sedan and sedan coupe models.

1942 Ford, Super DeLuxe, coupe-sedan, HAC

FORD — DELUXE — SERIES 21A: Common to all 1942 Fords was a revised frame design that was lower by one inch than the 1941 version, lower and wider leaf springs, a two inch wider tread and dual lateral stabilizer bars. DeLuxe models were equipped with the bumpers used for the 1941 Super DeLuxe Ford models. Their grille frames were painted body color. Unique to the DeLuxe Ford was its center grille panel with "DeLuxe" spelled out vertically in bright letters before a blue background. Wheel covers were painted to match body color. The DeLuxe instrument panel was finished in Crackle Mohagany grain.

FORD — SPECIAL — SERIES 2GA — SIX: The three Special models shared their grille design and bumpers with the DeLuxe models but lacked the latter's bumper guards. Black wheel covers were standard and like those on all 1942 models carried blue Ford script.

The transition to a war time economy brought many material substitutes in the 1942 models. Among the more obvious was the use of plastic interior components and the replacement of nickel by molybdenum in valves, gears and shafts. The final 1942 model Fords were produced on February 10, 1942.

I.D. DATA: Serial numbers located on left frame member directly behind front engine mount. Starting: 6 cyl. — IGA-34801; V-8 — 18-6769036. Ending: 6 cyl. — IGA-227,523; V-8 — 18-6925878. Prefix "C" indicates Canadian built. Engine numbers were located on top of clutch housing. Starting: 6 cyl. — IGA-34801; V-8 — 18-6769036. Ending: 6 cyl. — IGA-227523; V-8 — 18-6925898.

Model No.	Body Type & Seating	Price	Weight	Prod. Total
2GA	2-dr. Cpe.-3P	780	2910	1606
2GA	2-dr. Tudor-6P	815	3053	3187
2GA	4-dr. Fordor-6P	850	3093	27,189
21A	2-dr. Cpe.-3P	810	2978	5936
21A	2-dr. Cpe. Sed.-5P	875	3065	5419
21A	2-dr. Tudor-6P	840	3141	27,302
21A	4-dr. Fordor-6P	875	3161	5127
21A	4-dr. Sta. Wag.-6P	1100	3460	567
Sup. DeL.	2-dr. Conv.-5P	1080	3238	2920
Sup. DeL.	2-dr. Cpe.-3P	850	3050	5411
Sup. DeL.	2-dr. Cpe. Sed.-5P	910	3120	13,543
Sup. DeL.	2-dr. Tudor-6P	885	3159	37,199
Sup. DeL.	4-dr. Fordor-6P	920	3200	24,846
Sup. DeL.	4-dr. Sta. Wag.-6P	1100	3468	5483

ENGINE: [V-8] 90° V, inline. Eight. Cast iron block. B & S: 3-1/16 in. x 3-3/4 in. Disp.: 221 cu. in. C.R.: 6.2:1. Brake H.P.: 96 @ 3800 R.P.M. Taxable H.P.: 30. Main bearings: Three. Valve lifters: Mechanical. Carb.: Ford 21A-9510A. Torque: 156 lbs.-ft. @ 2200 R.P.M. [6-cyl.] Inline. L-head. Six. Cast iron block. B & S: 3-3/10 in. x 4-2/5 in. Disp.: 225.8 cu. in. C.R.: 6.7:1. Brake H.P.: 90 @ 3300 R.P.M. Taxable H.P.: 30. Main bearings: Four. Valve lifters: Mechanical. Carb.: Ford IGA-9510A 1bb1. Torque: 180 lbs.-ft. @ 2000 R.P.M.

CHASSIS: Special, DeLuxe, Super DeLuxe. W.B.: 114 in. O.L.: 194.4 in. Height: 68.15 in. Frt/Rear Tread: 58 in./60 in. Tires: 6.00 x 16.

TECHNICAL: Sliding gear transmission. Speeds: 3F/1R. Column controls. Semi-centrifugal, molded asbestos lining clutch. Shaft drive. 3/4 floating rear axle. Overall Ratio: 3.78:1. Hydraulic brakes on four wheels. Pressed steel wheels, drop center rims. Wheel Size: 16".

OPTIONS: Fender skirts. Bumper guards (center). Radio (39.00). Heater (air-$23, water $20). Clock. Side view mirror. Passenger side mirror. Sport light. Locking gas cap. Fog lights. Seat covers. Defroster. Visor-vanity mirror. Radio foot control. Wheel trim rings. White sidewall tires (15.00). Bumper end guards (2.75 a pair). Oil filter (6.14). License plate frames.

HISTORICAL: Introduced September 12, 1941. Calendar year production: 43,407. Model year production: 160,211. The president of Ford was Edsel Ford.

1942
Model 2GA Special, 6-cyl.

	FP	5	4	3	2	1
3P Cpe	780	775	1500	3600	5100	7300
Tudor	815	600	1200	2300	4000	5700
Fordor	850	650	1200	2300	4100	5800
Model 21A DeLuxe, V-8						
Cpe	810	800	1550	3800	5300	7600
Cpe Sed	875	800	1550	3900	5450	7800
Tudor	840	700	1350	2900	4600	6600
Fordor	875	725	1400	3100	4800	6800
Super DeLuxe						
Conv	1080	3500	7050	11,750	16,450	23,500
3P Cpe	850	800	1550	3900	5450	7800
Cpe Sed	910	850	1650	4150	5800	8300
Tudor	885	725	1400	3000	4700	6700
Fordor	920	750	1450	3300	4900	7000
Sta Wag	1100	3000	6000	10,000	14,000	20,000

NOTE: Deduct 10 percent avg. for 6-cyl.

574

FORDHAM — The Fordham Company was organized in Rochester, New York during the early fall of 1912 with a capital stock of $3000 and a plan to manufacture and deal in automobiles. Involved in this venture were Gerald F. Cox, Eugene F. Reinke and Richard Stanton, all of Rochester. Manufacture is doubted.

FORDMOBILE — That was the projected name for the car, and it was advertised as thus even before production of the Model A began in 1903. By the time the car was introduced, however, Henry and company had decided to call it simply a Ford. Refer to Ford.

FORE-RIVER — The Fore-River Shipbuilding Company of Quincy, Massachusetts, has frequently been cited as producing a car in 1903. It did, but the car was the Lyman & Burnham and not one of either Fore-River's design or trademark. According to a Quincy automobile enthusiast who went to work for the company in 1911, Fore-River never produced an automobile of its own. The shipyard did build a piece of fire apparatus upon one occasion, however. Its powerplant was a marine engine so heavy that it went through the floor of the fire station.

FOREST — The Forest Automobile Company was organized in Jersey City, New Jersey early in 1901 with a capital stock of $250,000. Incorporators were John Lieban, Paul Erdreich, John H. Eendelken, Eugene C. Jones and Ephraim Berlowitz. The manufacture of automobiles was the plan, but this seems not to have been realized.

The Forest Automobile Company of St. Louis, Missouri evolved early in 1907 from the Union Automobile Company of St. Louis. Union had built a car of its own in 1905 though by the time of takeover had metamorphosed into a dealership. Despite occasional references to Forest as a manufacturer, it would appear that firm operated only as a dealership.

1905 Forest, touring, RNT

FOREST — Boston, Massachusetts — (1905-1906) — The Forest Motor Car Company was located at 257 Columbus Avenue in Boston. "It has been truly said of the automobile," the firm declared stoutly in its 1905 brochure, "that no difference how perfect the machine is built in all other respects, it is a complete failure without a perfect motor and transmission." Forest further declared that because of its "years of experience in the manufacture of gas and gasoline engines of every size from two to one hundred horsepower" that success was guaranteed for its Forest automobile. The Forest was a five-passenger touring car on an 86-inch-wheelbase chassis with three-speed sliding gear transmission. Its highly vaunted engine was a twin exceptionally long in stroke (4.5 by 7 inches) which generated 20 hp which was good for 40 mph on the road. The price was $1200 including lamps and horns. Forest's foray into automobile manufacture seems to have been a short one. The firm may have continued as a dealership.

FOREST CITY — Only the 1905 prototype of this car was called the Forest City. That happened to be the nickname of Cleveland, Ohio during this period, and the Forest City Motor Car Company had been organized there. When more attractive financial inducements arrived from Massillon, however, the venture moved to that Ohio city in 1906, and the car was renamed the Jewell. Refer to Jewell.

FORSYTH — Franklin, Minnesota — (c.1896) — George Forsyth was a flour miller from Franklin who journeyed to Chicago for the World's Columbian Exposition in 1893 with his friend Olaf Nelson, a blacksmith. Subsequently, the duo purchased gasoline engines and installed them in chassis that they devised themselves. Reportedly, Nelson never drove his machine because he feared its speed. The Forsyth machine served George Forsyth and his family for some time.

FORT — "It is reported that Col. Robert Fort, Illinois state senator from Lacon, is planning to engage in the manufacture of steam-driven motor vehicles," *The Motor Age* reported in January 1900. It does not appear the senator did, however.

FORTH — Mansfield, Ohio — (1910) — Clarence R. Forth was a graduate of M.I.T. who first tried to build an automobile in New York in 1905 when he organized the Forth Company which went nowhere, and again in 1908 with the aborted Blair-Forth Manufacturing Company in Boston. Apparently previous to all this, he had worked in the engineering department of the Packard company in Warren, Ohio and he returned to the Midwest after the Boston failure to work as a consulting engineer for Overland for a year. In 1909 he tried again to become a manufacturer, persuading O.V. Dibble, the president of the Buckeye Match Company to help him organize a corporation for the production of runabouts in Akron, Ohio. Nothing came of this either. And most probably he had not yet built a single car. Early in 1910 he did, however, procuring all component parts from various accessory companies and putting together a four-cylinder touring car prototype. Then he approached the Chamber of Commerce in Mansfield for support in his manufacturing proposition. At least enough financial assistance followed for him to organize the Forth Motor Car Company — with one S.J. Colwell as president — and to take over the Bucyrus Steam Shovel Company in Bucyrus for forthcoming production of the Forth car. But all further assistance ended quickly. In the fall of 1911 the Forth Motor Car Company of Mansfield was declared bankrupt, with liabilities estimated at $1000 and assets consisting of one automobile and a few parts. Thereafter, Clarence Forth went to work for Church-Field as sales manager.

FORTMAN — The Fortman Manufacturing Company was organized in Philadelphia, Pennsylvania late in 1912 with a capital stock of $100,000 to manufacture, sell and deal in automobiles and accessories. The incorporators were Leo Abelis, Jesse Drew and Frank E. Bidlack, all of Philadelphia. Maufacture of an automobile is doubted.

FORT PITT — Occasional trade press references to the contrary, the product of the Fort Pitt Motor Manufacturing Company was never marketed as the Fort Pitt. Built in New Kensington, Pennsylvania from 1908 to 1910, and in Pittsburgh in 1911, the car was always known as the Pittsburgh Six. Refer to Pittsburgh Six.

FORT WAYNE — The Fort Wayne Motor Sales Company was organized with $10,000 capital stock early in 1911 to "manufacture, sell or rent automobiles or parts thereof" in Fort Wayne, Indiana. Incorporators were C.R. Dancer, H.R. Fullenwider and H.S. Morrison. Manufacture of a car is doubted.
The Fort Wayne Automobile Manufacturing Company was organized with a capital stock of $20,000 during the summer of 1910 to manufacture automobiles in Fort Wayne, Indiana. Incorporators were L.J. Wilrath, G.T. Fox, W.H. Rohan and G.C. Dudenhofer. The firm proceeded into manufacture but of commercial vehicles only, remaining in that field into 1913.

FORT WAYNE — Fort Wayne, Indiana — (1903) — The Fort Wayne Automobile Company was organized in late 1903 by G.C. Dudenhofer, H.C. Bucker and H.W. Meyer. Meyer was the local Oldsmobile agent and the new superintendent of the Fort Wayne factory. But apparently that factory never got going. The Fort Wayne car was to be powered by an 8 hp two-cylinder opposed engine, shod with artillery wheels and three-inch tires, and selling for $800 or $900 with tonneau body. Plans called for the debut of the Fort Wayne at the Chicago Automobile Show in February 1904, but the car didn't make it. This venture died somewhere in the prototype stage. Eight years later Dudenhofer was among the backers of the Fort Wayne Automobile Manufacturing Company, but its products were commercial vehicles only.

FORT WORTH — The Fort Worth Automobile Company was organized with a capital stock of $10,000 late in 1905 for the manufacture of automobiles in Fort Worth, Texas. M.R. Sanguinet, A.B. Wharton, C.D. Rainers, W.W. Sloan, Jr. and F.R. Hedrick were the incorporators. Manufacture is doubted.

FOSS-HUGHES — The Foss-Hughes Motor Car Company of Philadelphia, Pennsylvania has been indicated on numerous rosters as the manufacturer of an automobile in 1908. This seems highly unlikely. At the time, the firm was acting as agents for Pierce-Arrow, Cadillac and Baker and that summer took on the agency for the Pope-Hartford. In 1911 Foss-Hughes completed its new facilities at 21st and Market streets, described by *Cycle and Automobile Trade Journal* as "the largest and most complete motor car building under one roof in Philadelphia." But the company remained a dealership only.

FOSTER — That a car called the Foster was built by the Improved Gasoline Motor & Automobile Company of Haverhill, Massachusetts has been noted in numerous auto rosters. Haverhill city directories indicate no such company in town during this period. A machinist named Mathew Foster lived at 100 Washington Street, however, and may have had grand ambitions. Documentation regarding a car he might have built is lacking, however.
Trade directory references indicate a Foster automobile from New Haven, Connecticut in 1906. There was such a company, the Foster Motor Company, Inc. at 31 Crown Street that year, but its city directory listing notes "yachts, machinery and gasoline motors" only.

FOSTER STEAM — Westbrook, Maine — (1896) — Foster & Brown were machinists, iron founders and manufacturers of safety elevators in Westbrook. This activity was enough to satisfy N.A. Brown, but his partner Thomas J. Foster was bitten by the horseless carriage bug. Early in 1896 he constructed a three-wheeled motor wagon using an Acme steam engine for its motive power. Foster was not at all impressed with that powerplant and planned to replace it with "a suitable oil motor," as *The Horseless Age* reported in its April 1896 issue. Whether he ever did is not known, but apparently Foster's focus of interest was chassis/running gear design in any case. He was particularly proud of his worm and worm wheel steering system. "This method is exactly like driving a horse," he advised,

"so that the operator has nothing new to learn." There is no evidence that he built another car. Subsequent city directories for Westbrook indicate that the Foster & Brown Company added gasoline engine and automobile repair to its work roster, however.

1896 Foster Motor Wagon, NAHC

1902 Foster, electric runabout, HAC

FOSTER — Rochester, New York — (1901-1904) — Pianos were the principal product of Foster & Company of Rochester when, in 1899, the firm built its first experimental steam carriage. Early in 1900 the Foster Automobile Company was incorporated with a capital stock of $100,000 for the purpose of manufacturing steam and electric vehicles, although almost immediately one Paul Densmore bought the company, the original stockholders withdrew, (except for G.G. Foster himself), and the firm was reorganized as the Foster Automobile Manufacturing Company. Both steam and electric cars followed, with production totalling 165 cars by the end of 1901. Foster promotion was predominantly geared to its chain drive steamers, one of which won a gold medal in the New York-Boston run of 1902. The company proudly declared this a victory over the internal combustion engine. Curiously Foster followed in 1903 with the marketing of a gasoline car, which may have been the result of a lawsuit instituted the previous year by the Whitney Steam Motor Wagon Company which alleged infringement of the Whitney patent. But this was the least of the Foster's problems. By the summer of 1903 the company was bankrupt, with assets of only $2000, debts of more than $40,000, and its president nowhere in sight. Forgery and grand larceny were the charges leveled at Paul Densmore; it was said that promissory notes totalling $30,000, in many cases made out to fictitious names, had been cashed by him at various Rochester banks. "There are ugly rumors afoot to the effect that Densmore is not the only culprit," *The Horseless Age* noted in reporting that a warrant for Densmore's arrest had been sent to Brooklyn, New York, "where he was last heard from." The last heard from the Foster was in 1904. In 1904, production of the steam car was taken over for a short while by the Artzberger Automobile Company of Allegheny, Pennsylvania.

1901 FOSTER Steam Surrey						
	FP	5	4	3	2	1
Electric Runabout	—					
1902 FOSTER						
Steam Light Roadster	—	—	—	—	—	—
Steam Touring Wagon	—	—	—	—	—	—
Steam Surrey	—	—	—	—	—	—
Steam Speed Wagon	—	—	—	—	—	—
Electric Runabout	—	—	—	—	—	—
1903 FOSTER						
Steam Light Roadster	1000	—	—	—	—	—
Gasoline Tour. (2-cyl, 9 hp)	1400	—	—	—	—	—
Gasoline Tour. (2-cyl, 12 hp)	2000	—	—	—	—	—

1904 Foster steam roadster, NAHC

1904 FOSTER

	FP	5	4	3	2	1
Steam Light Roadster	1000	—	—	—	—	—

FOSTER — Newton, Iowa — (1908) — In 1908, W.O. Foster & Company of Newton indicated that it was building a high-wheeled motor buggy for the market, an activity in which the firm did not long remain. By 1909 Foster had prospered sufficiently in the repair of automobiles, however, that a new two-story garage was erected which was also to serve as a car dealership.

FOSTLER — Chicago, Illinois — (1905) — The Chicago Motocycle Company produced a car called the Chicago in 1902 which was renamed the Caloric in 1903. Most unusual about these cars was the engine, a two- or three-cylinder unit which could be run on hot air in addition to the more common gasoline or kerosene fuels. That the Chicago-cum-Caloric was not particularly successful might be indicated by the fact that two of the cars on the company's stand at the Chicago Automobile Show in January 1905 were three years old. The third car, however, was a new one, a standard gasoline-powered runabout with single-cylinder vertical engine mounted in front of the dash, two-speed planetary transmission, and single chain drive. The car was called the Fostler, probably after the client who had commissioned its building. A few more examples may have been built that year, but by now automobile repair was the Chicago Motocycle Company's chief field of business.

FOSTORIA — Fostoria, Ohio — (1904) — The Fostoria Foundry and Machine Company was an Ohio manufacturer of gasoline engines. In 1904 the company is indicated to have built an automobile as well, which likely as not did not happen. By 1905, however, the firm had wholeheartedly returned to engine manufacture. Automobile production may have ended with but a single example.

FOSTORIA — Fostoria, Ohio — (1906-1907) — This Fostoria from Fostoria, Ohio was merely the Oxford from Oxford, Michigan renamed. When the Detroit-Oxford Manufacturing Company went to the wall in Michigan in 1906, Oxford automobile designer William H. Radford took the one thing he had left, his Oxford prototype, and moved to Fostoria where he convinced local townspeople to back its manufacture. The Fostoria Motor Car Company survived slightly more than a year. Thereon, Radford went to work for Hudson and later was responsible for the designs of the Warren-Detroit, the Pilgrim and the Balboa.

1906-1907 FOSTORIA
Two-Cylinder — 16 hp, 90" wb

	FP	5	4	3	2	1
Touring-5P	1500	2000	3000	4200	6500	14,000

1916 Fostoria, touring, WLB

FOSTORIA — Fostoria, Ohio — (1915-1916) — The incorporators were J.H. Jones, a local contractor; Ira Cadwallader, a local industrialist; Charles

Ash, a local banker; and A.O. George who talked them into it. During the summer of 1915 they got together as the Fostoria Light Car Company to produce four different models of a low-priced four-cylinder assembled car. Although initially locating in the old Seneca Lamp plant, by December of 1915 they had bought out the Storm Buggy Company and were making plans to move there. Approximately 2000 Fostorias were built by September of 1916 when the company found itself in trouble. Reportedly, the problem was the engines Fostoria had bought from Sterling Motors in Milwaukee. They were lemons. A call was made to Le Roi. Believing that a change of image would help too, the Fostoria people reorganized in December as the Seneca Motor Car Company for the manufacture of a new car called the Seneca.

1915-1916 FOSTORIA
Four — 17 hp, 108" wb

	FP	5	4	3	2	1
Model C Touring	675	2400	3400	4800	8000	17,000
Model B Roadster	615	2500	3500	5000	8500	18,000
Model G Speedster	495	2700	3600	5300	8800	19,000
Model F Coupe	825	2200	3200	4400	7000	15,000

1914 Fouch, roadster, NAHC

FOUCH — Los Angeles, California — (1914-1915) — James R. Fouch had a small machine shop at 2002 South Main Street in L.A., and the Fouch was built there for the whole of its life. No company was ever established for its manufacture. For what was obviously a shoestring operation, the Fouch was a remarkably fine little car. It was powered by a four-cylinder water-cooled engine set in a 100-inch wheelbase chassis, with tread the standard 56 inches. The engine was built in unit with a three-speed selective transmission; two Spicer universal joints with a tubular shaft between provided final drive. Forty-five miles an hour was the top speed; the price was $495. At 1000 pounds, the Fouch was a hefty little two-seater. James Fouch produced his car for a little more than a year. Prior to the Fouch, he had designed the Moro and the Perfex in Los Angeles. After the Fouch, he remained in L.A. and became a designer for the Bulkley-Rider Tractor Company. Perhaps it was as much racing as sunshine that had lured James Fouch and his brothers Harry and John to California from their native Minnesota. James had patented two types of disc wheels while in Minneapolis. In California he got behind the wheel (of a Staver usually) to compete in area races.

1914-1915 FOUCH
Light Car — 4-cyl., 100" wb

Roadster-2P		495	2000	3000	4200	6500	14,000

FOUR DRIVE — The Four Drive Auto Company was organized during the spring of 1908 with a capital stock of $250,000 to manufacture and sell automobiles in Springfield, Illinois. Incorporators were C.T. Murphy, A.P. Dewey and L.E. Hill. Manufacture is doubted.

FOUR TRACTION — In the early summer of 1908 Ernest Rosenberger of Mankato, Minnesota organized the Four Traction Automobile Company for the manufacture of four-wheel-drive automobiles and trucks that carried the name Kato. Refer to Kato.

FOUR WHEEL DRIVE — The Four Wheel Drive Automobile Company of Clintonville, Wisconsin used its initials to designate the cars it marketed from 1911-1912. Refer to F.W.D.

The Four Wheel Drive Motor Company was organized in Kansas City, Missouri during the summer of 1915 with a capital stock of $500,000 for the manufacture of automobiles. Theodore Ditmars, H.A. Dougherty and S.B. Gatewood were the incorporators. Manufacture is doubted.

The Four Wheel Drive Wagon Company was a $3 million Maine incorporation from early 1907 for the manufacture of automobiles. M.M. Spinney and E.J. Pike were among the people involved. Manufacture of a car is doubted. A company of this same name manufactured passenger and commercial vehicles in Milwaukee, Wisconsin from 1904-1906.

FOUR WHEEL DRIVE — Milwaukee, Wisconsin — (1904-1906) — In November of 1903, Charles Cotta of Rockford (Illinois) sold the patent rights to the four-wheel drive system he had devised for his Cotta Steam Runabout to a consortium of businessmen from Milwaukee. Principal among them were H. Theodore Hanson, Lyman G. Wheeler and Charles B.

Perry, who organized as the Four Wheel Drive Wagon Company with a whopping capitalization of one million dollars. Although "motor vehicles for business purposes" was the declared manufacturing purpose of the company, which located its factory at Vliet and 34th streets in Milwaukee, it would appear that at least a few pleasure cars were put together alongside the delivery wagons and trucks. These were four-cylinder 40 hp Rutenber-engined tourers on the long 132-inch wheelbase truck chassis. Early in 1906 the Four Wheel Drive Wagon Company announced that work would begin immediately on an enlargement to its factory. The company ceased production later that year. Bankruptcy was declared early in 1907.

FOURNIER-SEARCHMONT — Because of the celebrity of French race driver Henri Fournier, the Searchmont Motor Company of Philadelphia, with which he was associated in 1902, was renamed the Fournier-Searchmont Company that year. The cars were sometimes referred to as Fournier-Searchmonts as well. Refer to Searchmont.

FOWLER — The Fowler was to be a four-cylinder car built in Alexandria, Indiana by the Fowler Manufacturing Company. "The Alexandria Industrial Association is endeavoring to raise the necessary capital for the purpose," reported *The Horseless Age* in September 1910. "The company is now disposing of $10,000 worth of bonds to be used in building the factory," *Automobile Topics* reported a short while later. Then all reports stopped.

FOX — In December of 1904, Charles A. Fox of Syracuse, New York reported that he was organizing a company in that city to manufacture touring cars. There is no evidence he ever succeeded.

During the summer of 1908, the Fox Metallic Tire Belt Company was organized in New York City with a $100,000 capital stock for the manufacture of automobiles. Incorporators were W.A. Malone, A.E. Smith and W.H. Klock, all of New York City. There is no indication that Fox ever built a car.

1922 Fox, model A-1, 5-pass. touring, HAC

FOX — Philadelphia, Pennsylvania — (1921-1923) — The air-cooled Fox motorcar was the second good idea that Ansley H. Fox had. The first was the Fox shotgun, which he also invented, and which was produced by his A.H. Fox Gun Company from which he took leave near the close of World War I because he had decided to get into the automobile business. Initially he did this via his Fox Motor Company which built air-cooled engines only, but he was thinking automobile from the beginning. The Fox Motor Car Company was organized on November 21st, 1919, and the following year absorbed the Fox Motor Company. In March of 1921 announcement was made that Fox planned to produce 2000 cars its first year; in July came the news that Frank H. Golding, formerly general manager of the Holmes Automobile Company (the Canton, Ohio firm which manufactured an air-cooled car called the Holmes) had joined Fox as general manager and treasurer, and that H.O. Swanson, a veteran of the engineering department of H.H. Franklin in Syracuse (New York), had come aboard as chief engineer. The Fox was the only air-cooled car in America which gave the venerable Franklin even a semblance of a run for its money. It featured aluminum pistons and overhead valves actuated by an overhead camshaft. Advertisements indicated twenty miles per gallon of gasoline, up to a thousand miles on a gallon of oil, and two thousand miles on a set of tires. The Fox was a handsome car with luxurious appointments and coachwork by Derham. It was quiet, and it was speedy — rum runners fancied it nearly as much as they did the Pierce-Arrow. The Fox was a bigger car in both wheelbase (132 inches) and horsepower (50 bhp) than the Franklin; whether it was a better car is an issue hotly debated by Franklin adherents. What is not debatable is that the Fox did not long succeed in the marketplace. This may have been partly the result of birthing problems. It took a long time for the Fox to get into production. It was not until January of 1922 that the Fox toured the automobile show circuit, creating quite a stir in New York, Philadelphia, Chicago, Boston, Pittsburgh and Atlanta. And it was not until late May of 1922 that regular production was begun. "Impaired finances" was the reason given for the company's inability to continue production in January 1924. Reorganization under receivership failed. The company's liabilities were listed as $213,000; its assets including real estate, machinery and equipment as $529,920. The latter went to the auction block in late spring of 1924. Although estimates of total Fox production have been as high as 3000 cars, it is more likely that a figure of one-third that was the actual.

1921 FOX
Model A-1 — 6-cyl., 50 hp, 128" wb

	FP	5	4	3	2	1
Touring Prototype	3500	3100	4200	6300	10,500	22,000

1922 Fox, model A-1, touring, JAC

1922 FOX
Model A-1 — 6-cyl., 50 hp, 132" wb

	FP	5	4	3	2	1
Touring-5P	3900	3200	4300	6500	11,000	23,000
Sedan-5P	4900	2200	3200	4400	7000	15,000

1923 FOX
Model A-1 — 6-cyl., 50 hp, 132" wb

	FP	5	4	3	2	1
Touring-5P	3900	5300	10,650	17,700	24,800	35,000
Coupe-3P	4900	2400	3400	4800	8000	17,000
Sedan-5P	4900	2200	3200	4400	7000	15,000

FOXHALL-WILSON — The Foxhall-Wilson Company was organized in Passaic, New Jersey during the summer of 1908 to manufacture and sell bicycles, automobiles and hardware supplies. Capital stock was $5000, and the partners involved were Thomas Foxhall and Clarence A. Wilson. Manufacture of a car is doubted.

FOYE — Jersey City, New Jersey — (1901) — The Foye Hub Motor and Automobile Company of 539 Bergen Avenue in Jersey City was incorporated with a capital stock of $200,000 by G.A. Foye, A.C. Dieterle and F.W. Dieterle for the purpose of manufacturing an automobile designed and patented by company engineer Carl Bergman. The Foye was one of several steam cars of the turn of the century period distinguished by its use of a motor fitted to the hub of each driving wheel. Production of this car was minimal, and perhaps only the prototype was built. In announcing its steam car in April of 1901, the Foye company indicated that the next vehicle on its agenda was a gasoline hub motor car, but whether it was ever completed is not known.

F. & P. — The F. & P. Auto Transportation Company was organized in Brooklyn, New York early in 1913 with a capital stock of $70,000 to "manufacture and trade in vehicles propelled by gas, electricity, etc." Incorporators were W.O. Goddard, G.A. Logan and F.K. Fairchild. Manufacture of a car is doubted.

FRANCISCO-MARTIN — Newport, Michigan — (1915) — In late summer of 1915 the Francisco-Martin Motor Company was incorporated with a capital stock of $30,000 to manufacture automobiles in a new factory to be built in Newport, Michigan. The people involved were G.W. Francisco, L.J. Martin and F.B. Scholl. The company was not heard from again. It would appear that the new factory was never built, and the new Francisco-Martin car never produced, though a prototype may have been completed.

1904 Francke, touring, NAHC

FRANCKE — Milwaukee, Wisconsin — (1904) — George O. Francke was one of the legion of early automobile dealers who believed there was little more complication involved in the building of automobiles than in the selling of them. He proceeded rather farther than most. In 1904 he secured a two-cylinder water-cooled 12 hp engine which he mounted in a chassis of his own making which featured right-hand wheel steering and a demi-tonneau body. "Here is the touring car that you have been looking for," he advertised. "Will go anywhere the big fellows go, and yet the price is only $1,200." A few Franckes indeed were sold in the next year, but in 1905 the George O. Francke Auto Company at 534 Reed Street in Milwaukee returned to being a dealership exclusively.

FRANCO-AMERICAN — The Franco-American Auto Supply Company was organized during the early summer of 1906 in Chicago, Illinois with a capital stock of $25,000 to manufacture and deal in automobiles. William T. Church, Howard W. Lewis and Lloyd A. Wicks were the incorporators. Manufacture is doubted.

FRANCO-AMERICAN — Marion, New Jersey — (1902) — In September of 1902 the assets of the Automobile Company of America, erstwhile producer of the Gasmobile, were sold at public auction. High bidder was one Richard Currier who announced his intention to manufacture a licensed version of the French Rochet-Schneider in the former Gasmobile plant in Marion, New Jersey. The Franco-American Automobile Company was hastily organized for this purpose, and probably an equally hasty, and curious, decision was made to call the resulting car the Pedro. The Pedro never arrived, and the Franco-American company was stillborn. There is some evidence that Currier fitted Franco-American emblems to a few of the Gasmobile stanhopes which remained to be completed in the Marion factory. But in November 1902 Henry C. Cryder, trustee for the Automobile Company of America, announced that the Franco-American plan had fallen through. Apparently, in addition to acquiring the Automobile Company of America assets, Currier had also acquired its debts, and these he could not handle.

FRANCO-AMERICAN — Los Angeles, California — (1907) — C.C. Davis was president, Frank M. Bell general manager and Andrew M. Boulanger superintendent. Their firm was the Franco-American Car Company which had offices in the Chamber of Commerce Building and a factory at 1501-1523 East Seventh Street in Los Angeles. The car they advertised was described as "French type" with brakes both front and rear. A good deal of history would have to be rewritten if indeed the Franco-American was America's first production car with a four-wheel brake system. But documentation of this is wanting. The company was out of business within the year. Thereon Andrew Boulanger moved to the north side of Los Angeles, joined in partnership with Felix Merlo, and they advertised themselves as manufacturers of a new French-type car. Most probably, this venture was simply the putting together ot parts which had been left over when Franco-American went under.

FRANKFORD — The Frankford Taxi Company was a $10,000 Delaware incorporation from late 1917 for the purpose of manufacturing automobiles. Incorporators were Elizabeth S. Beddow, Harry A. Beddow and George Schlafer. Manufacture is doubted.

FRANKFORD — Philadelphia, Pennsylvania — (1922) — The Frankford was an all-Pennsylvania venture. Its suspension system came via the Sheldon Axle & Spring Company of Wilkes Barre, and featured the Laycock leaf spring developed by Arthur M. Laycock, Sheldon's chief engineer. Axles front and rear, in conjunction with four-wheel cable-operated brakes and disc wheels, were developed by the U.S. Axle Company of Pottstown and the Budd Wheel Company of Philadelphia. Lee Oldfield of Philadelphia was designer of the Frankford's six-cylinder engine, which featured an overhead camshaft. Phaeton coachwork would arrive from Fleetwood of Fleetwood. And the car would be produced and marketed by Frankford Motors Company of Philadelphia. Its price tag was slated to be "close to $10,000 complete." Alas, this ambitious effort never proceeded beyond the prototype stage. Interestingly, over a decade later, Lee Oldfield would be involved in designing a Pennsylvania car that was at the precise other end of the automotive marketing scale, when he went to work for American Bantam in Butler. Prior to the First World War, he had been a race driver of modest renown.

FRANKFORT — Frankfort, Indiana — (1917) — In 1917 the Frankfort Motor Company attempted to get into automobile manufacture in Frankfort, Indiana. The attempt failed before a car ever reached an assembly line. Possibly a prototype was completed, but wartime material shortages and undercapitalization stopped this venture in its tracks. In 1919 the Frankfort factory equipment was purchased by the Midwest Motor Company and moved to Kansas City, Missouri. Moving with it was former Frankfort president R.E. Stevenson who now took charge of production for the new Highlander car.

1902 Franklin, runabout, HAC

FRANKLIN — Syracuse, New York — (1902-1934) — Had John Wilkinson been paid for his work at the turn of the century, the Franklin might never have happened — and automobile history would be much the poorer. In addition to being the most long-lived and successful air-cooled automobile in America, the Franklin represents a fascinating and bittersweet saga of the automobile industry. The story began in 1901. By that time John Wilkinson, a recent Cornell engineering graduate, had completed two air-cooled prototype cars for the New York Automobile Company, whose promoters neglected the matter of recompense. Naturally, he was perturbed. Then Wilkinson met Alexander T. Brown, who was a big-time investor in numerous companies in Upstate New York — and who introduced Wilkinson and his car to Herbert H. Franklin, a former newspaper publisher and now a manufacturer of die castings in Syracuse. Franklin took a ride in one of the Wilkinson prototypes and decided that his H.H. Franklin Company should manufacture automobiles. Alexander Brown became a substantial investor in the Franklin venture, and that was that. Following some litigation, the New York Automobile Company was absorbed by Franklin, and the Franklin automobile was born. The first production car was sold to S.G. Averill of New York City on June 23rd, 1902 for $1200. A dozen more Franklins were built and sold that year. They were all runabouts, with their four-cylinder overhead valve engines mounted transversely, and featuring throttle control, float-feed carburetor, two-speed planetary transmission, full-elliptic springs and wooden frames. The car for 1903 remained a runabout, with wooden artillery replacing the original wire wheels. Some aspects of the Franklin, however, wouldn't change for decades or forever: the full-elliptic suspension, for example, which provided superior riding comfort and such stingy tire wear — the rubber on a Franklin was good for at least 20,000 miles — that the company didn't offer detachable rims as standard equipment until 1922. The Franklin wood frame endured through 1928, and Franklin engines were overhead valve to the end. That the car was robust and dependable was demonstrated early on, in 1904 when transcontinental driver L.L. Whitman, accompanied by Franklin representative C.S. Carris, drove a runabout from New York City to San Francisco in just under 33 days, which cut the previous Winton and Packard records by almost half. The engine of the Franklin moved up front under a barrel hood in 1905, with the Renault-type hood following in 1911, the horse collar in 1921. A fan had been deemed superfluous on the first Franklins, but

1904 Franklin, type B, light tonneau, HAC

by 1905 most models had one (front mounted and gear driven); in 1910 the fan was incorporated into the flywheel for a suction cooling system which remained until the 1923 Series 10 cars which introduced a Scirocco fan geared directly to the front of the crankshaft. Shaft drive and three-speed selective transmissions had arrived with the barrel-hood models of 1905; 1906 saw Franklins employing drive through the springs, one of numerous technical features pioneered in the industry by Franklin. The company's engineering budget — computed on a percentage of income basis — was among the highest in the industry. High quality with less weight was a guiding Wilkinson principle, and resulted in the company's pace-setting use of aluminum pistons in 1915. Franklin's first six, with seven bearing crankshaft, arrived in 1906, and a variety of four- and six-cylinder models on varying wheelbases followed. For 1914 Franklin went to sixes exclusively, and on a standardized 120-inch wheelbase chassis. Late in 1913 the first production model Franklin sedan was introduced, and the company remained ever after in the forefront in promoting that body style. In subsequent years, when asked which were his favorites of all the Franklins produced, Herbert Franklin chose that first little runabout and the Franklin sedan. Though competition was generally eschewed by the factory, the car enjoyed some estimable successes, Ralph Hamlin winning a hot one in 1912 over a 400-mile course from Los Angeles to Phoenix, a Franklin keeping its cool several years later when driven in low gear from San Francisco to Walla Walla in a promotional run, and beating a big 120 hp McFarlan in 1920 in a match race from New York City to Montreal. An economy run in 1917 saw 179 Franklins average 40.3 mpg; production that year was nearly 9000 cars, a new Franklin high. Matters at the factory remained salutary, until the summer of 1923. For years the Franklin had prospered with its unusual styling look, but now dealers were clamoring for a Franklin that was conventional. A contingent of them, led by Ralph Hamlin (since 1905 the Franklin distributor for southern California), descended upon Syracuse with an ultimatum: new car, or no car, the dealers were ready to give up their franchises. Herbert Franklin was persuaded; John Wilkinson was aghast. A Franklin with a false radiator was anathema to him. Form following function, which he ardently believed, meant a Franklin hood in a single assembly, hinged at the front and easily removable. He resigned from the company in protest. (Interestingly, in 1925, Wilkinson built another car, this one under his own name, and water cooled; while another disgruntled ex-Franklin employee named James Yarian tried on his own too with an air-cooled four which had been developed and rejected at the factory.) Designs for the new Franklin were sought from the Walter M. Murphy Company in Pasadena, California and from that brilliant and quite mysterious body designer from New York City named J. Frank de Causse. The de Causse ideas became the Series II Franklin, introduced in March of 1925; among the new cars was a long, low and racy boattail speedster. It is a wonderful irony that the company which had become famous for the sedan would be the first in America to catalog the sexiest body style of the era. A custom department was now established at Franklin, with de Causse at its head, and the years which followed saw an expanding custom line featuring coachwork by Holbrook, Brunn, Derham, Willoughby, Locke and Merrimac. Following the death of de Causse in 1928, Raymond Dietrich became the Franklin designer. In 1928, too, the inimitable Cannon Ball Baker took a Series 11B Franklin on an extended series of endurance runs which saw the two of them challenge the continent, the Union Pacific Limited and Pikes Peak. ''That old waffle iron was the greatest car I ever drove,'' Cannon Ball would remember later. ''That snub-nosed baby buggy would run forever.'' Another devoted Franklin driver was Charles Lindbergh, for whom the Airman series was named. It arrived in 1928, and featured Franklin's first use of front wheel brakes. Concealed running boards accompanied the Pirate models of 1930. But by now the effects of the stock market crash were weighing heavy in Syracuse. From production of over 14,000 cars in 1929, output plummeted to under 2000 in 1932. A banking syndicate was in control at Franklin, with Edwin McEwan in charge. Introduced that fall was a V-12 model that was the antithesis of previous Franklins. The prototype, developed by company engineers Edward Marks and Carl Doman, had been exemplary, but McEwan had dictated otherwise for production: a trucklike chassis that eliminated the traditional Franklin full-elliptic suspension and tubular axles. At a full three tons, it weighed a third more than the prototype. The LeBaron body styling was elegant, but this Franklin was clumsy. In October of 1932, there was another new Franklin, the Olympic, again an antithesis. It was, in fact, mostly Reo. From Lansing came the Reo chassis and body; in Syracuse, Franklin installed an Airman engine, a Franklin hood, and Franklin emblems for the hubcaps and the place on the Reo dash where a water temperature gauge would have been installed. (Engine temperature had never been a matter of concern at Franklin, and thus none of its cars ever had a gauge to reveal it.) The V-12 was a luxury car in the $4000 range (slashed to $3000 in 1934); the Olympic made more sense at the time as a $1500 car. In 1934 Franklin built 360 cars. They were the last. To the end, Herbert Franklin insisted that his company was, despite a large indebtedness, entirely solvent. But the banks won out, and the H.H. Franklin Manufacturing Company was wiped out. As legend has it, on the last day in the office from which he had guided Franklin fortunes for nearly three decades, Herbert Franklin simply got up from his chair, took his hat off the hook, walked out the door, left everything behind and never looked back. What an incredibly sad finale that was.

1904 Franklin, type A, runabout, OCW

1905 Franklin, type F, light touring, HAC

1903 Franklin, runabout, HAC

1906 Franklin, model D, limousine, HAC

1903
Four, 10 hp, 72" wb

	FP	5	4	3	2	1
Rbt	1300	4800	9600	16,000	22,400	32,000

1904
Type A, 4-cyl., 12 hp, 82" wb

2/4P Light Rbt	1500	4650	9300	15,500	21,700	31,000

Type B, 4-cyl., 12 hp, 82" wb

4P Light Ton	1650	4650	9300	15,500	21,700	31,000

Type C, 4-cyl., 30 hp, 110" wb

5P Side Entrance Ton	3500	4650	9300	15,500	21,700	31,000

Type D, 4-cyl., 20 hp, 100" wb

5P Light Tr	2500	4500	9000	15,000	21,000	30,000

Type E, 4-cyl., 12 hp, 74" wb

2P Gentleman's Rbt	1400	4350	8700	14,500	20,300	29,000

Type F, 4-cyl., 12 hp, 82" wb

4P Light Ton	1700	4500	9000	15,000	21,000	30,000

1905
Type A, 4-cyl., 12 hp, 80" wb

Rbt	1500	4050	8100	13,500	18,900	27,000
Detachable Ton	1650	4200	8400	14,000	19,600	28,000

Type B, 4-cyl., 12 hp, 80" wb

Tr	1650	4200	8400	14,000	19,600	28,000

Type C, 4-cyl., 30 hp, 107" wb

Tr	2500	4650	9300	15,500	21,700	31,000

Type D, 4-cyl., 20 hp, 100" wb

Tr	2500	4500	9000	15,000	21,000	30,000

Type E, 4-cyl., 12 hp, 80" wb

Rbt	1400	4050	8100	13,500	18,900	27,000

1906
Type E, 4-cyl., 12 hp, 81-1/2" wb

	FP	5	4	3	2	1
2P Rbt	1400	3750	7500	12,500	17,500	25,000

Type G, 4-cyl., 12 hp, 88" wb

5P Tr	1800	3900	7800	13,000	18,200	26,000

Type D, 4-cyl., 20 hp, 100" wb

5P Tr	2800	4050	8100	13,500	18,900	27,000
5P Limo (115" wb)	4000	3150	6300	10,500	14,700	21,000

Type H, 6-cyl., 30 hp, 114" wb

5P Tr	4000	4200	8400	14,000	19,600	28,000

1907
Model G, 4-cyl., 12 hp, 90" wb

2P Rbt	1800	4350	8700	14,500	20,300	29,000
4P Rbt	1850	4500	9000	15,000	21,000	30,000

Model D, 4-cyl., 20 hp, 105" wb

5P Tr	2800	4650	9300	15,500	21,700	31,000
2P Rbt	2800	4500	9000	15,000	21,000	30,000
5P Lan'let	4000	3750	7500	12,500	17,500	25,000

Model H, 6-cyl., 30 hp, 127" wb

7P Tr	4000	4800	9600	16,000	22,400	32,000
2P Rbt	4000	4650	9300	15,500	21,700	31,000
5P Limo	5200	3900	7800	13,000	18,200	26,000

1907 Franklin, model D, runabout, WLB

1908 Franklin, model G, runabout, OCW

1908
Model G, 4-cyl., 16 hp, 90" wb

	FP	5	4	3	2	1
Tr	1850	4200	8400	14,000	19,600	28,000
Rbt	1750	4350	8700	14,500	20,300	29,000
Brgm	2250	3150	6300	10,500	14,700	21,000
Lan'let	2500	3300	6600	11,000	15,400	22,000

Model D, 4-cyl., 28 hp, 105" wb

	FP	5	4	3	2	1
Tr	2850	4350	8700	14,500	20,300	29,000
Surrey-Seat Rbt	2850	4200	8400	14,000	19,600	28,000
Lan'let	4000	3400	6900	11,500	16,100	23,000

Model H, 6-cyl., 42 hp, 127" wb

	FP	5	4	3	2	1
Tr	4000	4650	9300	15,500	21,700	31,000
Limo	5200	4050	8100	13,500	18,900	27,000
Rbt	4000	4500	9000	15,000	21,000	30,000

1909 Franklin, model D, touring, OCW

1909
Model G, 4-cyl., 18 hp, 91-1/2" wb

	FP	5	4	3	2	1
4P Tr	1850	4200	8400	14,000	19,600	28,000
4P Cape Top Tr	1950	4350	8700	14,500	20,300	29,000
Brgm	2250	3150	6300	10,500	14,700	21,000
Lan'let	2500	3300	6600	11,000	15,400	22,000

Model D, 4-cyl., 28 hp, 106" wb

	FP	5	4	3	2	1
5P Tr	2800	4350	8700	14,500	20,300	29,000
5P Cape Top Tr	2950	4500	9000	15,000	21,000	30,000
Rbt, Single Rumble	2700	4650	9300	15,500	21,700	31,000
Rbt, Double Rumble	2700	4800	9600	16,000	22,400	32,000
Lan'let	4000	3400	6900	11,500	16,100	23,000

Model H, 6-cyl., 42 hp, 127" wb

	FP	5	4	3	2	1
7P Tr	3750	4500	9000	15,000	21,000	30,000
7P Cape Top Tr	3880	4650	9300	15,500	21,700	31,000
Limo	5000	4200	8400	14,000	19,600	28,000

1910 Franklin, model H, touring, OCW

1910
Model G, 4-cyl., 18 hp, 91-1/2" wb

	FP	5	4	3	2	1
5P Tr	1850	4950	9900	16,500	23,100	33,000
4P Rbt	1800	4800	9600	16,000	22,400	32,000
2P Rbt	1750	4650	9300	15,500	21,700	31,000

Model K, 4-cyl., 18 hp, 91-1/2" wb

	FP	5	4	3	2	1
Twn Car	4300	4500	9000	15,000	21,000	30,000
Taxicab	2850	4200	8400	14,000	19,600	28,000

Model D, 4-cyl., 28 hp, 106" wb

	FP	5	4	3	2	1
5P Tr	2800	5100	10,200	17,000	23,800	34,000
4P Surrey	2800	4500	9000	15,000	21,000	30,000
6P Limo(111-1/2"wb)	4000	4200	8400	14,000	19,600	28,000
Lan'let						
6P (111-1/2"wb)	4000	4350	8700	14,500	20,300	29,000

Model H, 6-cyl., 42 hp, 127" wb

	FP	5	4	3	2	1
7P Tr	3750	5250	10,500	17,500	24,500	35,000
4P Surrey	3600	4650	9300	15,500	21,700	31,000
7P Limo	5000	4350	8700	14,500	20,300	29,000

1911 Franklin, model M, touring, RM

1911
Model G, 4-cyl., 18 hp, 100" wb

	FP	5	4	3	2	1
5P Tr	1950	4800	9600	16,000	22,400	32,000
Torp Phae (108" wb)	1950	4950	9900	16,500	23,100	33,000

Model M, 4-cyl., 25 hp, 108" wb

	FP	5	4	3	2	1
5P Tr	2700	4950	9900	16,500	23,100	33,000
7P Limo	3500	4050	8100	13,500	18,900	27,000
7P Lan'let	3500	4200	8400	14,000	19,600	28,000

Model D, 6-cyl., 38 hp, 123" wb

	FP	5	4	3	2	1
4P Torp Phae	3500	5250	10,500	17,500	24,500	35,000
5P Tr	3500	5100	10,200	17,000	23,800	34,000
6P Limo	4400	4200	8400	14,000	19,600	28,000
6P Lan'let	4400	4350	8700	14,500	20,300	29,000

Model H, 6-cyl., 48 hp, 133" wb

	FP	5	4	3	2	1
7P Tr	4500	5250	10,500	17,500	24,500	35,000
Torp Phae (126" wb)	4500	5400	10,800	18,000	25,200	36,000

1912 Franklin, model M, touring, HAC

1912

Model G, 4-cyl., 18 hp, 100" wb

	FP	5	4	3	2	1
Rbt	1650	4800	9600	16,000	22,400	32,000

Model G, 4-cyl., 25 hp, 103" wb

Tr	2000	4800	9600	16,000	22,400	32,000

Model M, 6-cyl., 30 hp, 116" wb

Tr	2800	4950	9900	16,500	23,100	33,000
Torp Phae	2800	5250	10,500	17,500	24,500	35,000
Rds	2800	5100	10,200	17,000	23,800	34,000

Model K-6, 4-cyl., 18 hp, 100" wb

Taxicab	2850	4200	8400	14,000	19,600	28,000

Model D, 6-cyl., 38 hp, 123" wb

Tr	3500	5100	10,200	17,000	23,800	34,000
Torp Phae	3500	5400	10,800	18,000	25,200	36,000

Model H, 6-cyl., 38 hp, 126" wb

Tr	4000	5250	10,500	17,500	24,500	35,000
Limo	5000	4650	9300	15,500	21,700	31,000

1913 Franklin, model H, limousine, OCW

1913

Model G, 4-cyl., 18 hp, 100" wb

2P Rbt	1650	4650	9300	15,500	21,700	31,000

Model G, 4-cyl., 25 hp, 103" wb

5P Tr	2000	4650	9300	15,500	21,700	31,000

Model M, 6-cyl., 30 hp, 116" wb

5P Little Six Tr	2900	4800	9600	16,000	22,400	32,000
2P Little Six Vic	2900	4500	9000	15,000	21,000	30,000

Model D, 6-cyl., 38 hp, 123" wb

5P Tr	3600	5100	10,200	17,000	23,800	34,000
4P Torp Phae	3600	5250	10,500	17,500	24,500	35,000

Model H, 4-cyl., 38 hp, 126" wb

7P Tr	4850	5250	10,500	17,500	24,500	35,000
7P Limo	4850	4650	9300	15,500	21,700	31,000

1914 Franklin, Six-30, limousine, HAC

1915 Franklin, Six-30, roadster, HAC

1914

Model Six-30, 6-cyl., 31.6 hp, 120" wb

	FP	5	4	3	2	1
5P Tr	2300	4650	9300	15,500	21,700	31,000
Rds	2300	4950	9900	16,500	23,100	33,000
Cpe	2950	4050	8100	13,500	18,900	27,000
Sed	3200	3900	7800	13,000	18,200	26,000
Limo	3300	4350	8700	14,500	20,300	29,000
Berlin	3400	4650	9300	15,500	21,700	31,000

1915

Model Six-30, 6-cyl., 31.6 hp, 120" wb

2P Tr	2150	5100	10,200	17,000	23,800	34,000
5P Tr	2150	4950	9900	16,500	23,100	33,000
Cpe	2600	4050	8100	13,500	18,900	27,000
Sed	3000	3900	7800	13,000	18,200	26,000
Berlin	3200	4650	9300	15,500	21,700	31,000

1916 Franklin, Six-30, touring, HAC

1916

Model Six-30, 6-cyl., 31.6 hp, 120" wb

5P Tr	1950	5100	10,200	17,000	23,800	34,000
3P Rds	1900	5250	10,500	17,500	24,500	35,000
5P Sed	2850	4050	8100	13,500	18,900	27,000
4P Doctor's Car	2800	4200	8400	14,000	19,600	28,000
7P Berlin	3100	4800	9600	16,000	22,400	32,000

1917 Franklin, Series 9, touring, HAC

1917

Series 9, 6-cyl., 25.35 hp, 115" wb

5P Tr	1850	5250	10,500	17,500	24,500	35,000
4P Rds	1850	5400	10,800	18,000	25,200	36,000
2P Rbt	1800	4650	9300	15,500	21,700	31,000
7P Limo	3000	4050	8100	13,500	18,900	27,000
5P Sed	2750	4350	8700	14,500	20,300	29,000
7P Twn Car	3000	4350	8700	14,500	20,300	29,000
4P Brgm	2700	4800	9600	16,000	22,400	32,000
4P Cabr	2650	5100	10,200	17,000	23,800	34,000

1918 Franklin, Series 9, touring, HAC

1918

Series 9, 6-cyl., 25.35 hp, 115" wb

5P Tr	2050	5250	10,500	17,500	24,500	35,000
2P Rds	2000	5400	10,800	18,000	25,200	36,000
4P Rds	2050	5550	11,100	18,500	25,900	37,000
Sed	2950	4050	8100	13,500	18,900	27,000
Brgm	2900	4200	8400	14,000	19,600	28,000
Limo	3200	4200	8400	14,000	19,600	28,000
Twn Car	3200	4350	8700	14,500	20,300	29,000
Cabr	2850	4800	9600	16,000	22,400	32,000

1919 Franklin, Series 9, victoria, HAC

1919
Series 9, 6-cyl., 25.35 hp, 115" wb

	FP	5	4	3	2	1
5P Tr	2450	5250	10,500	17,500	24,500	35,000
Rbt	2400	5250	10,500	17,500	24,500	35,000
4P Rds	2450	5550	11,100	18,500	25,900	37,000
Brgm	3300	4200	8400	14,000	19,600	28,000
Sed	3350	4050	8100	13,500	18,900	27,000
Limo	3400	4350	8700	14,500	20,300	29,000

1920 Franklin, Series 9-B, touring, HAC

1920
Model 9-B, 6-cyl., 25.3 hp, 115" wb

5P Tr	2750	5250	10,500	17,500	24,500	35,000
4P Rds	2750	5400	10,800	18,000	25,200	36,000
2P Rds	2700	5250	10,500	17,500	24,500	35,000
5P Sed	3750	4050	8100	13,500	18,900	27,000
4P Brgm	3700	4200	8400	14,000	19,600	28,000

1921 Franklin, Series 9-B, sedan, HAC

1921
Model 9-B, 6-cyl., 25 hp, 115" wb

2P Rbt	2400	5250	10,500	17,500	24,500	35,000
4P Rds	2500	5400	10,800	18,000	25,200	36,000
5P Tr	2600	5250	10,500	17,500	24,500	35,000
2P Conv Rbt	2750	5400	10,800	18,000	25,200	36,000
5P Conv Tr	2950	5550	11,100	18,500	25,900	37,000
4P Brgm	3500	4200	8400	14,000	19,600	28,000
5P Sed	3600	3900	7800	13,000	18,200	26,000

1922
Model 9-B, 6-cyl., 25 hp, 115" wb

2P Rds	2300	5250	10,500	17,500	24,500	35,000
5P Tr	2350	5100	10,200	17,000	23,800	34,000
2P Demi Cpe	2650	4350	8700	14,500	20,300	29,000
5P Demi Cpe	2750	4050	8100	13,500	18,900	27,000
4P Brgm	3200	4200	8400	14,000	19,600	28,000
5P Sed	3350	3900	7800	13,000	18,200	26,000
5P Limo	3800	4200	8400	14,000	19,600	28,000

582

1922 Franklin, Series 9-B, demi-sedan, JAC

1923 Franklin, Series 10, all-weather touring, HFM

1923
Model 10, 6-cyl., 25 hp, 115" wb

	FP	5	4	3	2	1
5P Tr	1950	4650	9300	15,500	21,700	31,000
2P Rds	1900	4950	9900	16,500	23,100	33,000
5P Demi Sed	2250	4200	8400	14,000	19,600	28,000
4P Brgm	2750	4350	8700	14,500	20,300	29,000
4P Cpe	2750	4350	8700	14,500	20,300	29,000
5P Sed	2850	3900	7800	13,000	18,200	26,000
5P Tr Limo	3150	4350	8700	14,500	20,300	29,000

1924 Franklin, Series 10-B, sedan, HAC

1924
Model 10-B, 6-cyl., 25 hp, 115" wb

5P Tr	1950	4650	9300	15,500	21,700	31,000
5P Demi Sed	2250	4200	8400	14,000	19,600	28,000
4P Cpe	2750	4350	8700	14,500	20,300	29,000
5P Brgm	2850	4200	8400	14,000	19,600	28,000
5P Sed	2850	3900	7800	13,000	18,200	26,000
Tr Limo	2950	4350	8700	14,500	20,300	29,000

1925
Model 10-C, 6-cyl., 32 hp, 115" wb

5P Tr	1950	4650	9300	15,500	21,700	31,000
5P Demi Sed	2850	4200	8400	14,000	19,600	28,000
4P Cpe	2750	4350	8700	14,500	20,300	29,000
4P Brgm	2850	4200	8400	14,000	19,600	28,000
5P Sed	2850	3900	7800	13,000	18,200	26,000

NOTE: Series II introduced spring of 1925.

1925 Franklin, Series 11-A, sport runabout, HAC

1926 Franklin, Series 11-A, sedan, HAC

1926
Model 11-A, 6-cyl., 32 hp, 119" wb

	FP	5	4	3	2	1
5P Sed	3090	3900	7800	13,000	18,200	26,000
5P Spt Sed	3225	4000	7950	13,250	18,550	26,500
4P Cpe	2700	4200	8400	14,000	19,600	28,000
5P Encl Dr Limo	3275	4350	8700	14,500	20,300	29,000
4P Cabr	4400	4650	9300	15,500	21,700	31,000
5P Tr	2635	4800	9600	16,000	22,400	32,000
2P Spt Rbt	2750	4950	9900	16,500	23,100	33,000
5P Cpe Rumble	—	4400	8850	14,750	20,650	29,500

1927 Franklin, Series 11-B, tandem sport, JAC

1927
Model 11-B, 6-cyl., 32 hp, 119" wb

4P Vic	2740	4200	8400	14,000	19,600	28,000
2P Spt Cpe	3050	4300	8550	14,250	19,950	28,500
4P Tandem Spt	3150	4650	9300	15,500	21,700	31,000
5P Sed	2790	3900	7800	13,000	18,200	26,000
5P Spt Sed	2910	4000	7950	13,250	18,550	26,500
3P Cpe	2490	4200	8400	14,000	19,600	28,000
5P Encl Dr Limo	2940	4650	9300	15,500	21,700	31,000
5P Cabr	4400	6750	13,500	22,500	31,500	45,000
5P Tr	2635	6300	12,600	21,000	29,400	42,000
2P Spt Rbt	2690	7050	14,100	23,500	32,900	47,000
5P Cpe Rumble	2565	4800	9600	16,000	22,400	32,000

1928
Airman, 6-cyl., 46 hp, 119" wb

3P Cpe	2490	4350	8700	14,500	20,300	29,000
4P Vic	2740	4400	8850	14,750	20,650	29,500
5P Sed	2740	4050	8100	13,500	18,900	27,000
5P Oxford Sed	2815	4100	8250	13,750	19,250	27,500
5P Spt Sed	2910	4200	8400	14,000	19,600	28,000
3/5P Conv	2925	7050	14,100	23,500	32,900	47,000

Airman, 6-cyl., 46 hp, 119" wb

Spt Rbt	2975	7200	14,400	24,000	33,600	48,000
Spt Tr	2975	7050	14,100	23,500	32,900	47,000
7P Sed	2980	3900	7800	13,000	18,200	26,000
Oxford Sed	3015	4050	8100	13,500	18,900	27,000
7P Tr	3060	6750	13,500	22,500	31,500	45,000
7P Limo	3080	4200	8400	14,000	19,600	28,000

1928 Franklin, Airman sedan, JAC

1929 Franklin, Series 135, sport sedan, Derham, JAC

1929 Franklin, Series 135, sedan, HAC

1929
Model 130, 6-cyl., 46 hp, 120" wb

	FP	5	4	3	2	1
3/5P Cpe	2160	4350	8700	14,500	20,300	29,000
5P Sed	2180	3900	7800	13,000	18,200	26,000
Model 135, 6-cyl., 60 hp, 125" wb						
3P Cpe	2510	4400	8850	14,750	20,650	29,500
5P Sed	2485	4000	7950	13,250	18,550	26,500
3/5P Conv Cpe	2610	6000	12,000	20,000	28,000	40,000
4P Vic Brgm	2595	4200	8400	14,000	19,600	28,000
5P Oxford Sed	—	4050	8100	13,500	18,900	27,000
5P Spt Sed	2625	4200	8400	14,000	19,600	28,000
Model 137, 6-cyl., 60 hp, 132" wb						
5P Spt Tr	2785	6900	13,800	23,000	32,200	46,000
4P Spt Rbt	2785	7200	14,400	24,000	33,600	48,000
7P Tr	2870	6150	12,300	20,500	28,700	41,000
7P Sed	2775	4200	8400	14,000	19,600	28,000
7P Oxford Sed	—	4350	8700	14,500	20,300	29,000
7P Limo	2970	4500	9000	15,000	21,000	30,000

1930 Franklin, Series 147, convertible speedster, HAC

1930 Franklin, Series 147, Pirate touring, HAC

1930
Model 145, 6-cyl., 87 hp, 125" wb

	FP	5	4	3	2	1
Sed	2485	3900	7800	13,000	18,200	26,000
Cpe	2510	4350	8700	14,500	20,300	29,000
Club Sed	2575	4050	8100	13,500	18,900	27,000
DeL Sed	2585	4100	8250	13,750	19,250	27,500
Vic Brgm	2595	4200	8400	14,000	19,600	28,000
Conv Cpe	2610	6750	13,500	22,500	31,500	45,000
Tr Sed	2625	4050	8100	13,500	18,900	27,000
Pursuit	2670	4050	8100	13,500	18,900	27,000

Model 147, 6-cyl., 87 hp, 132" wb

	FP	5	4	3	2	1
Rds	2785	7800	15,600	26,000	36,400	52,000
Pirate Tr	2795	7050	14,100	23,500	32,900	47,000
Pirate Phae	2870	7200	14,400	24,000	33,600	48,000
5P Sed	2600	4200	8400	14,000	19,600	28,000
7P Sed	2775	4300	8550	14,250	19,950	28,500
Limo	2970	4350	8700	14,500	20,300	29,000
Sed Limo	3050	4500	9000	15,000	21,000	30,000
Spds	3375	8100	16,200	27,000	37,800	54,000
Conv Spds	3625	8250	16,500	27,500	38,500	55,000
Deauville Sed	5000	6300	12,600	21,000	29,400	42,000
Twn Car	5100	4800	9600	16,000	22,400	32,000
Cabr	6000	5400	10,800	18,000	25,200	36,000
Conv Sed	7500	7350	14,700	24,500	34,300	49,000

1931 Franklin, Series 15, deluxe victoria brougham, JAC

1931
Series 15, 6-cyl., 100 hp, 125" wb

	FP	5	4	3	2	1
Pursuit	2495	4050	8100	13,500	18,900	27,000
5P Sed	2295	3900	7800	13,000	18,200	26,000
Cpe	2345	4350	8700	14,500	20,300	29,000
Oxford Sed	2345	4000	7950	13,250	18,550	26,500
Vic Brgm	2345	4200	8400	14,000	19,600	28,000
Conv Cpe	2395	7200	14,400	24,000	33,600	48,000
Twn Sed	2425	4350	8700	14,500	20,300	29,000

Series 15, 6-cyl., 100 hp, 132" wb

	FP	5	4	3	2	1
Rds	2345	9300	18,600	31,000	43,400	62,000
7P Sed	2475	4350	8700	14,500	20,300	29,000
Spt Salon	2595	4500	9000	15,000	21,000	30,000
Limo	2725	4800	9600	16,000	22,400	32,000

Series 15 DeLuxe, 6-cyl., 100 hp, 132" wb

	FP	5	4	3	2	1
5P Tr	2695	9000	18,000	30,000	42,000	60,000
7P Tr	2695	8850	17,700	29,500	41,300	59,000
Spds	3345	9900	19,800	33,000	46,200	66,000
5P Sed	2695	4500	9000	15,000	21,000	30,000
Club Sed	2745	4650	9300	15,500	21,700	31,000
Conv Cpe	2765	8850	17,700	29,500	41,300	59,000
Twn Sed	2775	4800	9600	16,000	22,400	32,000
7P Sed	2895	4500	9000	15,000	21,000	30,000
Limo	2995	4950	9900	16,500	23,100	33,000

1932
Airman, 6-cyl., 100 hp, 132" wb

	FP	5	4	3	2	1
Spds	2545	8700	17,400	29,000	40,600	58,000
5P Sed	2345	4200	8400	14,000	19,600	28,000
Cpe	2345	4350	8700	14,500	20,300	29,000
Club Sed	2395	4350	8550	14,250	19,950	28,500
Vic Brgm	2445	4350	8700	14,500	20,300	29,000
Conv Cpe	2390	7500	15,000	25,000	35,000	50,000
7P Sed	2545	4350	8700	14,500	20,300	29,000
Limo	2695	4500	9000	15,000	21,000	30,000
Sed Oxford	2395	4200	8400	14,000	19,600	28,000

1932 Franklin, Airman club sedan, HAC

1933 Franklin, Twelve, club brougham, JAC

1933 Franklin, Twelve, sedan, HAC

1933
Olympic, 6-cyl., 100 hp, 118" wb

	FP	5	4	3	2	1
5P Sed	1385	3150	6300	10,500	14,700	21,000
4P Cpe	1385	3400	6900	11,500	16,100	23,000
4P Conv Cpe	1500	5550	11,100	18,500	25,900	37,000

Airman, 6-cyl., 100 hp, 132" wb

	FP	5	4	3	2	1
4P Spds	2545	7500	15,000	25,000	35,000	50,000
5P Sed	2345	3600	7200	12,000	16,800	24,000
5P Cpe	2345	3900	7800	13,000	18,200	26,000
5P Club Sed	2395	3750	7500	12,500	17,500	25,000
5P Vic Brgm	2445	3900	7800	13,000	18,200	26,000
7P Sed	2545	3400	6900	11,500	16,100	23,000
6P Oxford Sed	2395	3600	7200	12,000	16,800	24,000
7P Limo	2695	3750	7500	12,500	17,500	25,000

Twelve, V-12, 150 hp, 144" wb

	FP	5	4	3	2	1
5P Sed	3885	4200	8400	14,000	19,600	28,000
5P Club Brgm	3885	4350	8700	14,500	20,300	29,000
7P Sed	3985	4050	8100	13,500	18,900	27,000
7P Limo	4185	4500	9000	15,000	21,000	30,000

1934 Franklin, Airman sedan, JAC

584

1934
Olympic, 6-cyl., 100 hp, 118" wb

	FP	5	4	3	2	1
Sed	1435	3150	6300	10,500	14,700	21,000
Cpe	1435	3400	6900	11,500	16,100	23,000
Conv Cpe	1550	5550	11,100	18,500	25,900	37,000

Airman, 6-cyl., 100 hp, 132" wb

Sed	2185	3600	7200	12,000	16,800	24,000
Club Sed	2285	3750	7500	12,500	17,500	25,000
Sed	2385	3650	7350	12,250	17,150	24,500
Oxford Sed	2245	3800	7650	12,750	17,850	25,500
Limo	2535	4500	9000	15,000	21,000	30,000

Twelve, V-12, 150 hp, 144" wb

Sed	2885	4050	8100	13,500	18,900	27,000
Club Brgm	2885	4200	8400	14,000	19,600	28,000
Sed	2995	3900	7800	13,000	18,200	26,000
Limo	3185	4650	9300	15,500	21,700	31,000

1902 Frantz Steamer, auto-buggy, NAHC

FRANTZ STEAM — Cherryville, Pennsylvania — (1901-1902) — Hiram Frantz was an inventor whose patented efforts ran a gamut from a sewing machine motor to a can opener to a burner for steam automobiles to a device for hanging brooms. He was also a minister of the gospel and in 1901 he decided to become an automobile manufacturer. "The Frantz Automobile Company is presided over by a preacher who combines theology and mechanics thoroughly," noted *The Motor Age* in its May 30th, 1901 edition. Already the Rev. Frantz's company had completed its fourth steam carriage, and stood ready to build gasoline cars to order. A larger factory was contemplated which when completed would afford a wider range of models, but for the present only a $700 steam runabout would be the output. The runabout featured Rev. Frantz's patented burner, of course, which had been tested in stormy weather; "he declares the wind will not affect it in the least." Although success of the enterprise might have seemed assured — there were potential stockholders aplenty in his congregation, as *Motor Age* commented brightly — the Rev. Frantz had returned to preaching exclusively by the end of 1902.

FRAWLEY — The Frawley Taxi Company was organized during the fall of 1908 with a capital stock of $100,000 to "manufacture, rent, sell and store motor cars" in New York City. Behind this venture were Patrick J. Frawley of 922 East 167th Street, Henry Kellersholm of 1025 Lexington Avenue, and Paul L. Kiernan of 142 East 40th Street. Manufacture is doubted.

1904 Frayer-Miller, touring, OCW

FRAYER-MILLER — Columbus, Ohio (1904-1907)/Springfield, Ohio — (1907-1909) — In 1902 Lee A. Frayer and William J. Miller working jointly, and Oscar S. Lear working independently, completed designs for air-cooled engines. When the three got together two years later to pool their efforts for an automobile, it was as the Oscar Lear Automobile Company

to produce the Frayer-Miller car, thus providing equal billing and gaining the advantage of combining the best features of both designs into one new engine. (The Buckeye Motor Company that Oscar Lear had established following his building of an experimental car at the turn of the century was also brought into the combine.) A rotary blower forcing air through aluminum jackets around the cylinders distinguished the Frayer-Miller's method of air cooling, and that it worked well was indicated by the number of twenty-four-hour and other endurance contests on the East Coast in which the four-cylinder car performed so well "during the hottest weather" in the summer of 1905. That fall a Frayer-Miller made news as the first six-cylinder automobile known to be sold in America, the Frayer-Miller six delivered to William Monypeny of Columbus on November 1st. Thereafter Frayer-Millers were available as both fours and sixes in touring, runabout and limousine models, in addition to a truck introduced in 1907 and the agricultural Farmobile in 1908. Although a team of three special-built Frayer-Miller four-cylinder race cars failed to bring glory in the 1906 Vanderbilt Cup, the stock cars invariably finished all speed contests they started. The company moved operations from Columbus to Springfield in 1907. Passenger car manufacture was discontinued in the early fall of 1909 in order for the firm (now renamed Buckeye National Motor Car Company) to devote full attention to the commercial field. Early Seagrave fire trucks, incidentally, were built on Frayer-Miller chassis. In 1910 E.S. Kelly, producer of the Kelly-Springfield tire and the founder of the Kelly Motor Truck Company, took over the Buckeye factory.

1905 Frayer-Miller, touring, HAC

1904-1905 FRAYER-MILLER
Four — 24 hp, 96" wb

	FP	5	4	3	2	1
Touring-5P	2500	2300	3300	4600	7500	16,000

1906 Frayer-Miller, touring, WLB

1906 FRAYER-MILLER
Four — 24 hp, 100" wb

Touring-5P	3000	2300	3300	4600	7500	16,000

Six — 36 hp, 120" wb

Touring-5P	4000	2400	3400	4800	8000	17,000

1907 FRAYER-MILLER
Six — 36 hp, 120" wb

Touring-5P	4000	2600	3600	5200	8700	18,500

Four — 24 hp, 100" wb

Runabout-2P	2500	2500	3500	5000	8500	18,000
Touring-5P	3000	2400	3400	4800	8000	17,000
Limousine-4P	4000	2300	3300	4600	7500	16,000

Four — 50 hp, 122" wb

Touring-7P	4000	2700	3600	5300	8800	19,000
Limousine-7P	6000	2500	3500	5000	8500	18,000

1907 Frayer-Miller, runabout, HAC

1908 Frayer-Miller, town car, OCW

1908 FRAYER-MILLER
Four — 24 hp, 100" wb

	FP	5	4	3	2	1
Model B Touring	2500	2400	3400	4800	8000	17,000
Model D Taxicar	2500	2200	3200	4400	7000	15,000
Philadelphia Rbt.	2250	2300	3300	4600	7500	16,000
Combination Rbt.	2500	2350	3400	4700	7800	16,500

1909 Frayer-Miller, touring, HAC

1909 FRAYER-MILLER
Four — 24 hp, 107" wb

Model D Runabout		2500	2300	3300	4600	7500	16,000
Model D Combination Rbt.		2500	2400	3400	4800	8000	17,000
Model D Touring		2500	2500	3500	5000	8500	18,000
Model D Landaulet		2500	2450	3500	4900	8300	17,500

FRAZEE — Osage, Iowa — (1903) — The Frazee was a pretty little jewel of a runabout built by a jeweler from Osage. In 1901 George T. Frazee set up a shop in the back of his home and designed and built every part of the Frazee himself, with the exception of its wheels and tires. His engine was an overhead valve twin, some parts of which he had cast at the Kelly-Morgan Iron Foundry in town. Final drive was by sprocket and chain, steering by tiller. Since his car-building venture was extracurricular, George Frazee did not complete his automobile until 1903. He drove it for many years thereafter. It was the tenth car registered in the state of Iowa. The car remains extant, and is owned by a collector in Osage.

1903 Frazee, runabout, OCW

FRAZIER — Only the prototype of this cyclecar was so named. When W.S. Frazier & Company of Aurora, Illinois began to market its car later in 1914, the name was changed to Sprite. Refer to Sprite.

FRAZIER-ELKHART — Elkhart, Indiana — (1915) — "Pneumatic Control Valveless Car Runs on Acetylene," the headline read, but one might wonder whether it ever did. The Frazier-Elkhart was the idea of Orville Z. Frazier of Elkhart, and he verily bristled with innovative notions. His car was to be a seven-passenger touring with a six-cylinder valveless engine offered in three horsepower sizes of 186, 90 and 60. The depression of a crank on the dashboard started the dynamo and generated the spark, doing away with the necessity for storage battery, dry cells, or electric starter. Power was provided by acetylene gas. Both the transmission and brakes were controlled at the steering wheel by air. In May of 1915 Orville Frazier announced that he had completed the blueprints for his car. The prototype does not appear to have been very successful. Frazier was not heard from again.

FRECH — Early in 1900, Albert Frech purchased the gasoline engine business of W.E. Watkins and A.J. Short of Phelps, New York which he removed to nearby Newark, New York where his intention was the manufacture of launches and automobiles. Subsequent details regarding his automotive activity is lacking.

1914 Frederickson, 2-pass. tandem cyclecar, OCW

FREDERICKSON — Chicago, Illinois — (1914) — The Frederickson Patents Company of Chicago built its cyclecar to demonstrate a new type of two-stroke engine. "The motor uses no crankcase compression, but compresses the mixture on the lower side of the piston, the motor being built with a crosshead like a steam engine," reported *The Automobile* in January 1914. "This makes a very high motor, but the one on this car started on the first kick, on magneto, ran very slowly without missing, and was very low on fuel consumption." Aside from its engine, the Frederickson was a typical cyclecar with friction transmission and final drive by belt. A top speed of 55 mph was claimed "even with the wind resistance of side-by-side seating," according to the company. The Frederickson Patents Company planned to market its motor as well as license its manufacture, in addition to production of the cyclecar itself. None of these ventures lasted very long. The man behind them, however, Clayton E. Frederickson, continued developing his small car ideas — and in 1929 tried again with the Littlemac.

1914 FREDERICKSON
Cyclecar — 2-cyl., 15 hp, 96" wb

	FP	5	4	3	2	1
Tandem Rds.-2P	375	2000	3000	4200	6500	14,000
Staggered Seat Rds.-2P	375	2200	3400	4400	7000	15,000

1903 Fredonia Gas Carriage, NAHC

FREDONIA — Youngstown, Ohio — (1902-1904) — The Fredonia Manufacturing Company of Youngstown built its first car in 1895, followed by a few more later that year, one of which the company claimed was the first sale of a gasoline vehicle to a physician in the U.S. The doctor entered his car in the Cosmopolitan race of 1896. The company continued experimentation, occasionally selling one of its efforts, but did not proceed into manufacture until September of 1902. During that year a Fredonia won a gold medal in the New York to Boston Reliability Contest. The Fredonia's engine was a single-cylinder hydro-carbon unit in which fuel was pre-compressed in an annular chamber prior to introduction in the cylinder, a system which the company said prolonged valve life, lowered cylinder temperature and ameliorated "disagreeable odors." Also noteworthy about the Fredonia was its use of Sarven wooden wheels during a period when most small runabouts like it sported flimsy wire wheels. Although the Fredonia Manufacturing Company was in the hands of the receiver in early summer of 1904 the plant remained in operation until the final disposition of the property that fall.

1902-1903 FREDONIA

	FP	5	4	3	2	1
Rbt. (1-cyl., 9 hp, 72" wb)	1000	1600	2700	3800	5800	12,000
Tonneau (1-cyl., 10 hp, 87" wb)	1250	1800	2800	4000	6200	13,000

1904 Fredonia, touring, KM

1904 FREDONIA
1-cyl., 10/12 hp, 84" wb

Runabout-2P	1000	2000	3000	4200	6500	14,000
Touring-5P	1250	2100	3100	4300	6800	14,500

FREEMAN — Joplin, Missouri — (1901) — John W. Freeman was the proprietor of the Freeman Foundry and Machine Works at 14th and Main in Joplin. He dabbled in steam cars on the side. Most of this activity he kept to himself, but in mid-1901 he was proud enough of his latest endeavor to inform the trade press. "The engine is about 12 inches long and half as wide," he wrote *Cycle and Automobile Trade Journal*. "It is completely encased in a gun metal casing, and all the working parts are submerged in oil." It was a two-cylinder unit generating five horsepower. The asbestos-covered boiler was sixteen inches in diameter and eighteen inches high, and was fitted directly under the seat. This would seem to have been less than a desirable location. It would seem, too, that John Freeman never regarded his steam-car activity as other than a leisure-time pursuit.

FREEMAN — Omaha, Nebraska — (1920) — H.O. Stonebreaker was president, Paul Reiff the vice-president, George H. Reiff the secretary-treasurer and F.L. Freeman the general manager of the new Freeman Motor Car Company of Omaha which announced in early spring of 1920 that fifty passenger cars and five hundred trucks would be built that year in Cleveland. The firm's present headquarters were indicated to be in Cleveland's Whitney Power Block building in which Freeman said "space has been leased for an assembly room." This venture never reached production status, but it appears a prototype was built.

1921 Fremont, Six, touring, WLB

FREMONT — Fremont, Ohio — (1920-1922) — To say the history of the Fremont Motors Corporation was checkered is rather like saying the Empire State Building is tall. The company was organized with a capital stock of $2,000,000 in September of 1919 to build a four-passenger car selling for $1285. Fred M. Guy, the former designer of the rotary valve Ace, was noted as sales manager; C.W. Whitmore, formerly of Packard, had charge of the factory. The new Fremont car had been perfected, following $50,000 worth of experimentation, and its manufacture was to begin in sixty days at the plant of the Taylor Motor Truck Company which Fremont had purchased. (The Taylor plant itself had a checkered past, having been the home earlier for the Burford, Fremont-Mais and Lauth-Juergens trucks.) Sixty days passed. Then another four months. Finally, in April of 1920, Fremont made news again with the announcement that it would produce a six-cylinder assembled car (Falls engine) to sell for $1850. R.T. Walsh, the former advertising manager of the King Motor Car Company, now headed up the Fremont enterprise. The complete output of Fremont cars for 1920 was slated for export. Truck manufacture also remained on the company's agenda. Probably few passenger or commercial vehicles ever saw the assembly line. The Fremont Model R-6 touring car was introduced at the Cleveland Automobile Show in February of 1921. Horizontal hood louvers distinguished what was otherwise a conventional car. There was another price tag, $1685, which was lowered to $1450 in 1922. The Fremont disappeared thereafter. During the summer of 1922, Fremont had acquired the All American Truck Company, but it soon disappeared too. In November of 1924 when the receivership of Fremont Motors was announced because of creditor's claims aggregating $500, high cost of materials and lack of working capital were given as the reasons for the company's failure. And it was noted that for the previous two years, work had been "more or less suspended."

1921 FREMONT
Model R-6 — 6-cyl., 37 hp, 116" wb

	FP	5	4	3	2	1
Touring-5P	1685	2700	3600	5300	8800	19,000

1922 FREMONT
Model R-6 — 6-cyl., 37 hp, 116" wb

		5	4	3	2	1
Touring-5P	1450	2700	3600	5300	8800	19,000

FRENCH STEAM — Andover & Rumford, Maine — (1899-1900) — Tom French was an engineer from Andover, and John Stevens a jeweler from Rumford. French supplied the know-how, Stevens supplied the money; a steam car was designed in 1899 and completed in 1900. Subsequently, capitalists in both Andover and Rumford took an interest in the vehicle, and there were attempts to organize a company for its building. The Rumford venture was called United States Carriage Company, the Andover version the U.S. Motor Carriage Company — and both these firms died aborning.

FRENCH — Clinton, Massachusetts — (1905) — The good people of Clinton were right the first time around. Initially, when C.L. French arrived asking for a $15,000 stock subscription in exchange for bringing his new automobile venture to town, the Clinton Board of Trade was sufficiently skeptical to investigate and discovered that the assets of the French Automobile Company — machinery, prototypes, et al., which French valued at $15,000 — were encumbered by a mortgage of several thousand dollars. The firm had been incorporated in Maine, but whence its pilot models and equipment came is not known. The French Automobile Company did come to Clinton, however, that October, following an apparent change of mind on the part of some townspeople, and perhaps against the advice of the Board of Trade. The firm moved into the factory formerly occupied by the Clinton Wall Trunk Company to begin the manufacture of "runabouts, touring cars, jobbing trucks and marine gas engines." Almost as quickly, the company moved out. Most probably production had never begun.

FRENCH — Washington, D.C. — (1913-1914) — "Still another cyclecar is announced," *Automobile Topics* reported on November 8th, 1913. "It comes from Washington, D.C. where Earl French is startling the citizens with his diminutive car." French's car was powered by a two-cylinder 12 hp Spacke engine, fitted in a 75-inch wheelbase chassis, with 36-inch tread. Friction transmission and final drive by chain to a live rear axle were featured, the chassis being supported by a mortgage of several thousand dollars. tics in the rear. Two passengers sat side-by-side in the 600-pound roadster which Earl French planned to sell for about $400. He drove his demonstrator extensively, and in a few months put up 4100 miles. There is no indication, however, that he was ever able to secure the financial backing necessary to go into production.

FRENCH-AMERICAN — The French-American Automobile Company was organized in Brooklyn, New York early in 1910 with a capital stock of $4000 to "manufacture, repair and store motor cars." Joseph B. Marquette, Benedict Mandelberg and Robert W. Ferguson were the backers of this venture. Manufacture is doubted.

FRENCH-AMERICAN — **Cleveland, Ohio** — **(1907-1908)** — The French-American Motor Company was organized in Cleveland during the fall of 1907 for the manufacture of a water-cooled 45 hp four-cylinder car. A building on East Fortieth Street was secured for that purpose. Behind this venture were M.B. White as president, W.B. White as vice-president, J.J. Carroll as secretary-treasurer, W.B. Brown as general manager and G.R. Graham as factory superintendent. No further news followed of this venture until January 1908 when it was announced that Will B. White had taken over the Auto Parts Company of Cleveland, had installed W.D. Brown as manager, and was setting up for business on Euclid Avenue and East Eighteenth. The same announcement indicated that the automobile being built by the French-American Motor Company, which was referred to as the F.A.M. car, would be handled by Auto Parts. Manufacture of a French-American or F.A.M. car cannot be documented with certainty. Any production would have been minimal, all parties involved concluding by year's end that their fortunes were better served in the parts business.

FRENIER — **Rutland, Vermont** — **(1912)** — Wilfred A. Frenier established his automobile dealership in Rutland in 1909. Various references have indicated the building of a Frenier car in 1912 in Rutland, and this was probably a prototype to test the waters of potential manufacture. Wilfred Frenier decided not to dive in. Directories for the city of Rutland indicate that the Frenier Automobile Company remained an automobile dealership and branched later into the automobile supply business.

FRICTION DRIVE — **Worcester, Massachusetts** — **(1905)** — The Friction Drive Automobile Company was a case of the Far West meeting the Midwest and proceeding East for automobile manufacture. James A. Dorr of Oakland (California) and G.B. Londerbach of St. Louis (Missouri) were the promoters of this friction-drive car. By early 1905 they were in Worcester announcing the lease they had just signed for the Coes Wrench Company building at Main and Mill streets — and their expectation to begin "turning out cars by June 1." There is no evidence, however, that manufacture ever began.

FRIDDLE — In September of 1915 the Friddle Motor Car Company of Tacoma, Washington announced its intention to build a factory for the manufacture of automobiles. President J.A. Friddle declared that it would cost about $50,000. Apparently he never came up with the money.

1903 Friedman, runabout, WLB

FRIEDMAN — **Chicago, Illinois** — **(1900-1903)** — Oscar J. Friedman was a Chicago florist who, with his friend Walter W. Robinson, bought the old Sterling Cycle Works on Carroll Avenue in order to experiment with automobiles. Their first gasoline three-wheeler was complete in 1900, and the partners incorporated as the Friedman Automobile Company that year to build cars with four wheels and also "airships as a sideline." Obviously, ambition overrode them, because the Friedman Company didn't have the wherewithal to set up shop for either its land or air vehicles. Instead the airship remained a dream, and Friedman contracted with the National Sewing Machine Company in Belvidere in 1902 to build 525 Friedman cars. "She has a good front," Friedman advertised. "Sound as a Dollar. Well Gaited. Safe...Try It and You Will Buy It." Alas, Belvidere failed to provide enough cars for anyone to try. In April of 1903, Friedman sued National Sewing Machine Company for $100,000, claiming that his business had been damaged by the latter's failure to provide vehicles in the quantity contracted for. That deal was off. National Sewing Machine proceeded to build its own car called the Eldredge instead. And Friedman began looking for his own factory. At the same time, he and Robinson decided to rename their enterprise the Ideal Motor Vehicle Company. All succeeding vehicles would be known as Ideals, but they survived less than a year.

1900-1901 FRIEDMAN

	FP	5	4	3	2	1
Three-Wheeler (2-cyl., 3 hp)	—					

1902-1903 FRIEDMAN

	FP	5	4	3	2	1
Four-Wheeler (2-cyl., 6 hp)	750					

1921 Friend, roadster, WLB

FRIEND — **Pontiac, Michigan** — **(1921)** — Early in 1920 Otis C. Friend, who had begun in the automobile business selling Locomobiles in Chicago and who later was sales manager and president for Mitchell in Racine (Wisconsin), took over the Olympian Motor Company in Pontiac. His plan, he said, was to continue the manufacture of the Olympian car until such time as his own line of motorcars was ready. Three new Friends were on display at the New York Automobile Show in January 1921. Like the Olympian, the Friend was a four, differing mainly in its higher price tags. A six was promised, but Friend Motor Corporation went under before it made it to the assembly line. Operations ceased later in 1921. On May 1st, 1922 Otis Friend filed a bankruptcy petition as an individual from his home in Racine. He gave the assets of his company as $50,000, liabilities as $288,364. Lack of working capital and the "general industrial conditions" were noted as the reason for failure. The sale of the Friend factory in Pontiac, which had seen production of the Cartercar prior to the Olympian, was ordered on a mortgage foreclosure. Later that year Otis Friend showed up in Warren, Ohio with a plan to organize another firm called Colonial Motors Company for the manufacture of yet another car called the Colonial Six. That venture died a quick death too.

1921 FRIEND
Four — 31 hp, 112" wb

	FP	5	4	3	2	1
Touring-5P	1585	—	—	—	—	—
Roadster-3P	1585	—	—	—	—	—
Coupe-3P	2485	—	—	—	—	—
Sedan-5P	2585	—	—	—	—	—

1895 Fries, steam surrey, HAC

FRIES — **Reading, Pennsylvania** — **(1895)** — Around 1895 Frederick Fries of 15th and Perkohman Avenues in Reading decided he wanted a horseless carriage. In those days, of course, one had to build one's own, and Fries did. Not surprisingly, it was a steamer since boilers and engines were readily available for purchase. What could not be bought, Fries made himself. All accounts indicate the car served the Fries family well.

1901 Frisbie, roadster, OCW

FRISBIE — Cromwell & Middletown, Connecticut — (1901 et seq.)/**FRIS-BIE-HOEFT** — Cromwell & Middletown, Connecticut — (1909) — Russell Abner Frisbie was born in Middletown in 1874, as a small boy moved with his family to nearby Cromwell, and later returned to Middletown to establish a factory. In 1900 he was in Cromwell operating a bicycle shop when he built his first car. By September that year he had nearly completed it, reporting same to the trade press. Rumors followed that Frisbie was contemplating automobile manufacture, but he denied it in December. The vehicle he produced was for his own use, he said, and his plan was only "to furnish engines to other companies." This Russell Frisbie would do for the next two decades, following his establishing of a factory in Middletown in 1902, with most of his engine output slated for marine use. An occasional vehicle followed, as well. Frisbie is believed to have built a second car, probably powered by a four-stroke twin as his first had been, around 1902. According to *The Motor Age* in April 1905, Frisbie had by then just completed building two six-cylinder engines, "one of which has been installed in a large touring car, while the other is about to be dropped into Captain A. Bruce Tucker's new high-speed launch. It is expected that both the car and motor boat will be extremely fast." It is known that earlier during this period Frisbie's engine-building talents had come to the attention of the Pope-Hartford Company, and he was offered a job there at what was described as "an exorbitant salary." Frisbie refused, and the Pope-Hartford people made it quite clear to him that he could not produce cars for sale himself without a lawsuit resulting. This, of course, was during the height of the Selden Patent litigation. Frisbie did indeed build a few more cars, however, his total perhaps being as many as six. The last was in 1909, by which time his Frisbie Motor Company had evolved into the Frisbie-Hoeft Company. This car was a four-cylinder which was road-tested that June. The first car Russell Frisbie built remains extant, the final destiny of the others is unknown. The last year he registered a Frisbie (28 hp) was 1913; he was issued the same number in 1914 for a Model T Ford. During World War I, Frisbie converted his factory to the manufacture of aircraft components. After the war he sold his business to "go fishing" — though he continued to service the Frisbie motors with which half of the area fishing boats were equipped. During the Twenties he launched a new career: the design of mechanical toys. He died in 1968 at the age of ninety-four. The Frisbie name would become immortal via the family's Frisbie Pie Company of Bridgeport. Yale undergraduates discovered that the firm's pie plates were so aerodynamically fine that they flew very well. A new industry was in the making.

1908 Fritchle, victoria roadster, HAC

FRITCHLE ELECTRIC — Denver, Colorado — (1905-1919) — Oliver P. Fritchle, a young chemical engineer in Denver, began experimenting with storage batteries in 1897, perfected a new design after the turn of the century, and patented it in 1903. Shortly thereafter he organized the Fritchle Electric Storage Battery Company and proceeded into manufacture. Building an electric car was a natural progression, and by 1905 Oliver Fritchle had begun producing electrics in small numbers for a local clientele. In 1908 the Fritchle came to national prominence when its maker challenged other electric manufacturers to a long-distance speed contest. Racing an electric was virtually unheard of, and there were no takers. Consequently, Oliver Fritchle made the trip himself, 2140 miles from Lincoln (Nebraska) to New York City, with publicity accrued all along the way. The trek proved that a Fritchle Electric could travel 100 miles on a single battery charge, which was a remarkable performance. Fritchle began advertising his product as the 100 Mile Electric, changed the name of his company to the Fritchle Automobile & Electric Storage Battery Company, expanded his line and moved into manufacture in earnest. In the spring of 1909 he leased a mammoth roller skating rink in Denver with plans to convert it into a factory. His prices were high (the $2000-$3000 range), but his sales were good for a number of years following. With the electric vehicle itself waning in popularity, the Fritchle Company introduced a gas-electric model in 1916, similar to the Woods Dual Power from Chicago. Very few of these were sold. The Fritchle Electric was continued in production for several years thereafter, and then just quietly faded from the scene.

1905-1908 FRITCHLE ELECTRIC

	FP	5	4	3	2	1
Electric Stanhope	2300	2700	3600	5300	8800	19,000
Electric Vict.	2000	2500	3500	5000	8500	18,000

1909 Fritchle, 100-mile electric roadster, HAC

1909 FRITCHLE ELECTRIC
100 Mile Electric — 80" wb

Stanhope	2300	2700	3600	5300	8800	19,000
Victoria	2000	2500	3500	5000	8500	18,000
Stanhope	1900	2400	3400	4800	8000	17,000
Roadster (96" wb)	2500	2450	3500	4900	8300	17,500
Coupe (84" wb)	2600	2200	3200	4400	7000	15,000

1910 Fritchle, 100-mile electric roadster, NAHC

1910 FRITCHLE ELECTRIC
100 Mile Electric

Victoria Phae. (80" wb)	3000	2400	3400	4800	8000	17,000
Roadster (100" wb)	2000	2500	3500	5000	8500	18,000
Coupe (84" wb)	2800	2200	3200	4400	7000	15,000

1911 Fritchle, 100-mile electric roadster, HAC

1911 FRITCHLE ELECTRIC
100 Mile Electric

	FP	5	4	3	2	1
Coupe (86″ wb)	3000	2200	3200	4400	7000	15,000
Victoria (84″ wb)	2000	2400	3400	4800	8000	17,000
Roadster(100″ wb)	2400	2500	3500	5000	8500	18,000

1912 Fritchle, touring, HAC

1912 FRITCHLE ELECTRIC

	FP	5	4	3	2	1
Vict. Chain Drive(86″ wb)	2000	2500	3500	5000	8500	18,000
Vict. Shaft Drive(86″ wb)	2100	2500	3500	5000	8500	18,000
Torpedo Rdstr. Shaft Drive (88″ wb)	2100	2700	3600	5300	8800	19,000
Tour. Chain Drive (100″ wb)	2400	2700	3600	5300	8800	19,000
Tour. Shaft Drive (100″ wb)	2500	2700	3600	5300	8800	19,000
Extension Cpe. Shaft Drive (88″ wb)	3000	2400	3400	4800	8000	17,000
Colonial Cpe.	3600	2500	3500	5000	8500	18,000

1913 Fritchle, colonial coupe, HAC

1913-1915 FRITCHLE ELECTRIC

	FP	5	4	3	2	1
Brougham-5P (103″ wb)	3600	2300	3300	4600	7500	16,000
Colonial Cpe.-4P (88″ wb)	3000	2400	3400	4800	8000	17,000
Rbt.-4P(104″ wb)	2500	2500	3500	5000	8500	18,000
Rdstr.-2P (96″ wb)	2400	2600	3600	5200	8700	18,500

1916 FRITCHLE ELECTRIC

	FP	5	4	3	2	1
Torpedo Rdstr.(104″ wb)	2400	2500	3500	5000	8500	18,000
Colonial Cpe. (96″ wb)	3200	2300	3300	4600	7500	16,000
Gas-Electric Car	3000	2400	3400	4800	8000	17,000

1914 Fritchle, roadster, HAC

1917-18 Fritchle, coupe, HAC

1917 FRITCHLE ELECTRIC

	FP	5	4	3	2	1
100 Mile Coach(104″ wb)	3000	2400	3400	4800	8000	17,000

1918 FRITCHLE ELECTRIC

	FP	5	4	3	2	1
100 Mile Cpe. (104″ wb)	3000	2500	3500	5000	8500	18,000

1919 FRITCHLE ELECTRIC

	FP	5	4	3	2	1
100-Mile Brgm.(100″ wb)	3200	2700	3600	5300	8800	19,000

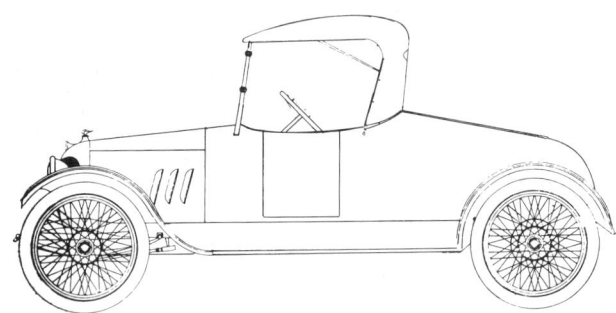

1917 Frontaway, roadster, NAHC

FRONTAWAY — Chicago, Illinois — (1917) — Early in 1917 the Millington Auto Engineering Company of Chicago, which had been producing attachments to convert rear-drive trucks into four-wheel drive, was superseded by the Millington Motor Car Company, a $500,000 incorporation. Its principal product was to be a 1000-pound $675 delivery wagon which was described as ''a radical departure from previous designs in that it drives through the front axle and carries its frame unusually low.'' A drawing, which remains extant, indicates that a ''business runabout'' was also produced by the company, most likely on the same chassis as the delivery. Production did not survive 1917.

FRONT DRIVE — The Front Drive Automobile Company was incorporated early in 1911 with a capital stock of $50,000 for the manufacture of automobiles in New York City. Incorporators were J.F. Denison, F.E. Collier and H. Roth. Manufacture is doubted.

The Front Drive Motor Car Company was organized in April of 1908 for the manufacture of taxicabs especially for the theatre district in Manhattan. Millionaire automobile enthusiast W. Gould Brokaw and Morris Gest (of the theatrical firm of Comstock & Gest) were the backers of this project, the car for which was to be designed by Walter Christie. This venture as well as the Front Drive Motor Company (organized in Hoboken, New Jersey in 1912) were but two of a number of ill-fated enterprises in which front-drive pioneer Walter Christie was involved during this period. Refer to Christie.

A Front Wheel Drive car purportedly was built in 1926 in Brookline, Massachusetts by the Positive Traction Motors Corporation. Refer to Positive Traction.

1905 Front-Drive, chassis, NAHC

FRONT-DRIVE — St. Louis, Missouri — (1905) — During the fall of 1905 the Auto Front-Drive Manufacturing Company of St. Louis began production of a front-drive axle which had been tested for the several months past in a car the firm had built for that purpose. During this period, of course, rear drive was the norm in the industry; there were few cars sporting four-wheel drive, fewer yet with front-wheel drive. The Auto Front-Drive Manufacturing Company was convinced a lucrative market awaited and proposed to sell its front-drive axle as an attachment for any make of car. The firm also planned to market a car fitted with the axle to be called the Front-Drive. It does not appear this happened, nor that production of the front-drive axle unit itself was significant. The ungainly-looking prototype that had been built was fitted with a 16 hp Streite engine (purchased from Cincinnati, Ohio) and solid tires, pictures indicating its chain drive to the front wheels to be remarkably crude. Charles Hall, inventor of the front-drive attachment, took the editor of *The Motor Review* for a test drive in it, during which a speed of 30 mph was claimed to have been reached. *The Motor Review* editor was impressed. Apparently few others were.

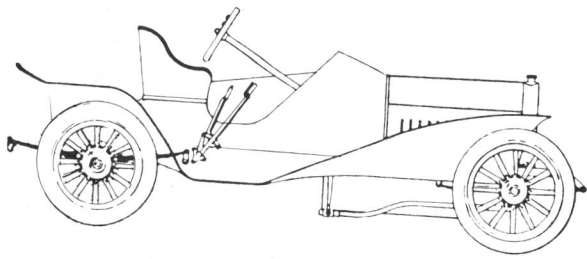

1907 Frontenac, model D, runabout, HAC

FRONTENAC — Newburgh, New York — (1906-1913) — For forty years previous, the Abendroth and Root Manufacturing Company of Newburgh had produced spiral riveted pipe, water tube boilers and other high grade ironware. With its own foundry, machine, pattern, forge and sheet metal shops, A & R believed itself well equipped to produce a motorcar. And, not surprisingly, the motorcars produced were big, impressive machines with four-cylinder 45 hp engines, sliding gear transmissions, shaft drive, and wheelbases of at least 123 inches. Racy runabouts, sturdy tourers and commodious limousines were built, all of them expensive. About a dozen cars were manufactured in 1906, approximately 100 in 1907. Production ebbed thereafter, and ultimately Abendroth and Root returned to ironware exclusively.

1906-1907 FRONTENAC
Four — 40-45 hp, 123'' wb

	FP	5	4	3	2	1
Touring-5P	3500	4300	8500	14,250	20,000	28,500
Runabout-2P	3500	4200	8400	14,000	19,500	27,500

1908 Frontenac, model D, runabout, HAC

1908 FRONTENAC
Four — 40/45 hp, 124'' wb

	FP	5	4	3	2	1
Touring-7P	4000	4300	8500	14,250	20,000	28,500
Limousine-7P	5000	3150	6300	10,500	14,700	21,000
Runabout-2P	4000	4200	8400	14,000	19,500	27,500

1909 Frontenac, model C, touring, NAHC

1909 FRONTENAC
Four — 40/45 hp, 124'' wb

	FP	5	4	3	2	1
Model C Tour.-7P	4000	4300	8500	14,500	21,000	29,000
Model D Rbt.-3P	4000	4200	8400	14,000	19,700	28,000
Model E Limo.-7P	5000	3150	6300	10,500	14,700	21,000

1910 Frontenac, model C, touring, HAC

1910 FRONTENAC
Four — 45 hp, 124'' wb

	FP	5	4	3	2	1
Model C Tour.-7P	3500	4300	8500	14,500	21,000	29,000
Model D Rbt.-3P	3500	4200	8400	14,000	19,700	28,000
Model E Limo.-7P	4500	3200	6400	10,700	15,000	21,500

1911 FRONTENAC
Four — 45 hp, 124'' wb

	FP	5	4	3	2	1
Model C Tour.-7P	3500	4300	8500	14,500	21,000	29,000

1912 Frontenac, model E, touring, HAC

1912 FRONTENAC
Four — 45 hp, 124" wb

	FP	5	4	3	2	1
Model C Tour.-7P	3500	4300	8500	14,500	21,000	29,000
Model D Rdstr.-2P	3000	4200	8400	14,000	19,700	28,000
Model E Limo.-7P	4000	3200	6400	10,700	15,000	21,500

1913 FRONTENAC
Four — 45 hp, 124" wb

	FP	5	4	3	2	1
Model C Tour.-7P	3500	4300	8500	14,500	21,000	29,000
Model D Rdstr.-2P	3500	4200	8400	14,000	19,700	28,000
Model E Limo.-7P	4500	3150	6300	10,500	14,700	21,000

1924 Frontenac, touring, NAHC

FRONTENAC — Indianapolis, Indiana — (1921-1925) — The Frontenac from Indianapolis was designed by noted engineer Cornelius Van Ranst (whose talents would later contribute handsomely to the development of the L-29 Cord) and equally noted engineer-driver Louis Chevrolet (who had been building race cars under the Frontenac name since 1916). It was a remarkably advanced four-cylinder motorcar with single overhead camshaft, thermo-syphon cooling, four-wheel brakes, and front and rear bumpers constructed as an integral part of the frame. The wheelbase was 120 inches, and developed horsepower was 60. According to Chevrolet, the prototype reached speeds of 75 mph in Indianapolis track tests in the late fall of 1921. The Frontenac Motor Company was incorporated soon after for one million dollars, and the former factory of the Empire Motor Car Company was secured for manufacture in Indianapolis. Initially, the Frontenac venture had represented an alliance among Allan A. Ryan, who was manipulating Stutz stock in New York City; William N. Thompson, who was president of Stutz in Indianapolis; and Louis Chevrolet. But Ryan was in the midst of engineering his infamous corner on Stutz stock, and within eight months he was broke. The Indianapolis end of the old alliance immediately reorganized, with Thompson making pointed mention that the new plans did not "include any New York men in the financial scheme." Louis Chevrolet was the company's new president. The Frontenac made its official debut at the Indianapolis 500 race on May 30th, 1922. Unfortunately, the economic climate at the time resulted in this very advanced motorcar never reaching the production stage. The following May, Frontenac Motor Company, through president Chevrolet, filed a bankruptcy petition in Indianapolis court, listing assets of $425 and liabilities of $88,163. There was another Frontenac motorcar, however, and it arrived soon after bankruptcy. Louis Chevrolet designed this one by himself; it was on a 140-inch wheelbase chassis featuring four-wheel hydraulic brakes and powered by an 80 hp eight-cylinder single-sleeve-valve Burt-type (based on Argyll principles) engine the option to which Chevrolet had acquired. Unfortunately, Chevrolet was unable to obtain financing for manufacture prior to the expiration of the option — and so this car too was built only as a prototype. Interestingly, during this period, Frontenac also promoted an export car called the Anahuac, of which four examples are known to have been produced.

1917 Frontmobile, roadster, AA

FRONTMOBILE — Greenloch, New Jersey — (1917-1918) — "The Car Built on Correct Principles" had front drive and "low down construction," the frame dropping precipitously nine inches aft of the engine. Patents were pending on virtually everything in a Frontmobile: its unit powerplant (four-cylinder Le Roi engine embodying transmission, clutch, differential, worm drive, radiator, gearshift and control levers), the transmission gears mounted on differential housing and revolving at axle speed, the driveshaft connected to wheels by special design universal located within ball and socket joint, the control lever connected to rocker shaft in front of transmission and passing through instrument board to right of steering wheel column. The Frontmobile bristled with ingenuity; it was also hopelessly

complicated. The car was produced by the Safety Motor Company of Greenloch, a subsidiary set up for the purpose by the Bateman Manufacturing Company, producers of farm, garden and orchard equipment since 1836. Everyone involved returned to agriculture very soon — except for C.H. Blomstrom, whose idea the Frontmobile had been. Blomstrom's previous automotive efforts had included the Queen in 1904, the Blomstrom in 1907, the Gyroscope in 1908 and the Rex in 1914. The year following his failure with the Frontmobile in Greenloch, he showed up in Camden with plans to manufacture it as Camden Motors Corporation. That venture was liquidated in 1922, probably before the production of a single car. Possibly as many as five Frontmobiles had been built in Greenloch, one of which — a 1918 model for which year the engine was a GB&S — survives.

1918 Frontmobile, roadster, WLB

1917-1918 FRONTMOBILE
Four — 26 hp, 112" wb

	FP	5	4	3	2	1
Roadster	1000	4500	5800	9500	18,000	32,000
Touring	1200	4300	5400	8700	16,500	30,000

1915 F.R.P., model 45, Series C, touring, HAC

F.R.P. — Port Jefferson, New York — (1914-1916) — F.R.P. was Finley Robertson Porter, whom history has immortalized as the designer and engineer of the legendary T-head Mercer. With the Mercer decision to go to an L-head design for its 1915 models, Porter departed. That he did not recall his Mercer experience fondly may be indicated by his reference to it in subsequent F.R.P. promotion only as "my association with a well known Automobile Company from 1910 to 1914." When he left the company he chose not to name, he immediately began his own, the Finley Robertson Porter Company on Long Island in New York. His initial plan of producing a Knight-engined automobile resulted in three race cars built for the Indianapolis 500 in 1914 which never made it to the starting line because of motor problems. It was then he decided to build a better Mercer, and the chassis was ready in late 1914. Its engine was a single-overhead-camshaft four producing at least 100 hp. A powerful high-class automobile, it combined features of efficiency and gasoline economy as well. The F.R.P. was good for about 12 mpg, which was remarkable for a car of its size. Road speeds of up to 80 mph were easily delivered. Only touring and sporting two-seater models were built, and very few of them, in the former Metropol plant in Port Jefferson. Production estimates vary from a high of twelve F.R.P. cars to a low of three. Parts for at least ten cars are known

1916 F.R.P., model 45, Series B, runabout, WLB

to have been ordered, however, prior to America's entry into World War I when the F.R.P. plant was taken over by the government. Finley Robertson Porter worked for the Division of Military Aeronautics for the duration of the war, and after the Armistice was appointed chief engineer of the Curtiss Engineering Corporation in Garden City, Long Island. After the Armistice, too, the decision was made to resume manufacture of the F.R.P., but now the name would be changed to Porter.

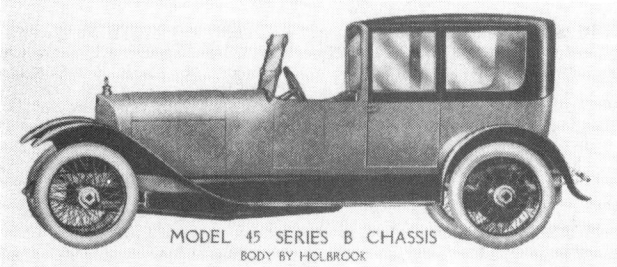

1916 F.R.P., model 45, Series B, town car, HAC

1914-1916 F.R.P.
Model A — 4-cyl., 100 hp, 110'' wb

	FP	5	4	3	2	1
Raceabout	5000	4000	5000	8000	15,000	28,000

Model B — 4-cyl., 100 hp, 130'' wb

Runabout	6500	4200	5200	8400	15,700	29,000

Model C — 4-cyl., 100 hp, 140'' wb

Touring-7P	6800	3900	4800	7700	14,300	27,000

1909 Frykman, runabout, JB

FRYKMAN — Souris, North Dakota — (1908-1909) — In 1908 August Frykman was the proprietor, with his brother Victor, of the Souris Blacksmith and Machine Shop and became an important man in town for the second time. In 1904 he had been the first automobile owner in Souris (a Rambler); in 1908 he built the first car in town. His achievement made the front page of the *Souris Messenger* on May 15th, 1908. The Frykman was a high-wheeled runabout powered by a two-cylinder water-cooled 12 hp engine and fitted with a friction transmission and double chain drive. Frykman used the car regularly, and the year following was asked by the local butcher, Tom Nichol, to build one for him too. That second Frykman, virtually identical to the first, was also the last. No doubt, his machine shop work kept him busy enough, and establishing an automobile factory on the prairies of North Dakota didn't make logistic good sense. August Frykman was the first automobile dealer in Souris, however, and remained in the dealership business (after 1926 in nearby Bottineau) until his death in 1954.

1912 F.S., runabout, NAHC

F.S. — Milwaukee, Wisconsin — (1911-1912) — The initials represented Filer and Stowell, a firm highly regarded in Wisconsin as builders of the Corliss steam engine. The new F.S. Motors Company represented the move by this old firm into gasoline automobile production, which was accomplished by the simple expedient of Filer and Stowell absorbing two other Wisconsin companies already well known in the automotive industry: the automobile producing Petrel Motor Car Company and the gasoline engine producing Beaver Manufacturing Company. Part and parcel of both were moved to an extensive new factory just outside the city limits of Milwaukee, where manufacture of engines, cars and trucks was embarked upon immediately in a rather confusing welter of models, each with its own engine and chassis. The new F.S. did not survive longer than a year.

1912 F.S., torpedo, NAHC

1911-1912 F.S.

	FP	5	4	3	2	1
Parcel Car (12 hp, 90'' wb)	600	2000	3000	4200	6500	14,000
Runabout (22 hp, 98'' wb)	850	2200	3200	4400	7000	15,000
Runabout (30 hp, 115'' wb)	1500	2300	3300	4600	7500	16,000
Torpedo (40 hp, 118'' wb)	1600	2500	3500	5000	8500	18,000

FUJIOKA — Los Angeles, California — (1922-1923) — In 1922 two veterans of the Pierce-Arrow Motor Car Company, Earl B. Spencer and George B. Morrow, decided to build a small automobile for the Japanese market. Spencer designed the car to be easily assembled of standard components, and Morrow began securing contracts with various parts manufacturers in the United States. The name Fujioka was supplied by Fred J. Fujioka, proprietor of the F & K Garage in Los Angeles and officer in the Japanese Automobile Club of Southern California. The new Fujioka Motor Car Company was headquartered in Los Angeles, and assembly of the Fujioka was planned there as well as in Tokyo. Financing this venture was Sakai Shokai, Ltd., a company which purportedly had stores in China, Japan and New York City. What these stores sold was not indicated, but an automobile would not be among its products. No more than a few Fujiokas were built. Earl Spencer tried again with a car named for himself.

FULLER — The Fuller Electric Car Company was indicated in trade directories to be producing an automobile in Detroit, Michigan in 1914. There was no such company in town at that time, though a few Fullers were machinists and perhaps had grand ambitions.

1908 Fuller, Six-60, touring, NAHC

FULLER — Angus, Nebraska — (1908-1910) — The Fuller brothers — C.M., L.E. and C.E. — of Angus had been producers of wagons and buggies since the turn of the century. Their first automobile was realized when they bought a single-cylinder engine in St. Louis and simply fitted it to one of their horsedrawn carriages. The car found ready sale to a doctor in town, and the Fullers were embued with enthusiasm. By the time that full-scale manufacture was embarked upon in 1908, the Fuller had grown up into a four, with a big six-cylinder car also offered that first season. The Angus Automobile Company was established, and a new factory built in town. "The only car manufacture in Nebraska," the brothers advertised in 1908. In the three years following, approximately 400 Fullers were built. Early on, however, residents in the nearby town of Nelson had purchased a controlling stock in the Angus company. In late 1910 this majority ruled in favor of relocating Fuller operations to Nelson, and the car did not survive the move.

1908 FULLER
Four-30 — 22/26 hp, 96'' wb

Runabout	1500	2000	3000	4200	6500	14,000
Touring	1800	2200	3200	4400	7000	15,000

Four-40 — 35/40 hp, 106'' wb

Touring	2500	2400	3400	4800	8000	17,000

Six-60 — 60 hp, 118'' wb

Touring	3500	2700	3600	5300	8800	19,000
Gentleman's Roadster	2500	3000	4000	6000	9500	21,000

1909 FULLER
Four — 35/40 hp, 106" wb

	FP	5	4	3	2	1
Touring	2000	2400	3400	4800	8000	17,000
Roadster	2000	2500	3500	5000	8500	18,000

1910 Fuller, model A, runabout, WLB

1910 FULLER
Model A-2 — 4-cyl., 25/30 hp, 110" wb

Roadster	1500	2400	3400	4800	8000	17,000
Touring	1500	2300	3300	4600	7500	16,000

Model A — 4-cyl., 35.40 hp, 115" wb

Runabout	2000	2500	3500	5000	8500	18,000
Touring	2000	2400	3400	4800	8000	17,000

FULLER — Jackson, Michigan — (1909-1910) — This Fuller was born because George A. Matthews, one of the directors of the Jackson Automobile Company, wanted to see the name of his Fuller Buggy Company on an automobile. The resulting Fuller was offered as a double-chain-drive high-wheeler, as well as a shaft-drive standard car, all Fullers featuring full-elliptic springs. Ego gratification aside, there wasn't any business logic to producing the Fuller, and consequently by 1911 it was unceremoniously absorbed into the Jackson Automobile Company, with the highwheeler model discontinued and the remaining parts of the standard Fuller moved over to the assembly line of the Jackson.

1909-1910 FULLER
Highwheeler — 2-cyl., 22 hp, 100" wb

Model B Tour. (solid tires)	850	1800	2800	4000	6200	13,000
Model K Tour. (pneumatics)	950	2000	3000	4200	6500	14,000

Standard car — 4-cyl., 25/30 hp, 100" wb

Model Thirty Tour.	1165	2200	3200	4400	7000	15,000
Model Thirty Roadster	1065	2300	3300	4600	7500	16,000

FULTON — The Fulton Machine Works was indicated in trade directories as producing an automobile in Chicago, Illinois from 1900-1901. Further details are lacking. The company indicated itself only as "bicycle makers" in the Chicago city directory, with Arthur J. Adams, Benjamin Hampton and Alexander B. Luth the Fulton partners and the firm in two locations, 353 West 20th and 271 Wabash.

The Fulton Motor Car Company of New York City has been noted on car rosters as the manufacturer of an automobile in 1908-1909. This firm, which succeeded to the Revolving Cylinder Motor Company in July 1908, was in the truck field exclusively.

The Fulton Motor Exchange was organized in Atlanta, Georgia late in 1909 with a capital stock of $10,000 to manufacture and deal in automobiles and motorcycles. James J. Murphy, S.J. Pridgen and William A. Sims were the incorporators. Manufacture of a car is doubted.

FULTON — The Connecticut Automobile Works of New Haven was headquartered in the former factory of the National Folding Box & Paper Company. This was appropriate because the Fulton was a car that existed on paper only. John E. Fulton was the man behind this scam, and he claimed his son had devised a two-cylinder four-stoke air-cooled engine of 10/12 hp with combination flywheel/fan which could be built as a light touring car for a factory cost of $250 and sold for $350 for a nice and easy profit. Fulton advertised widely — under the nicely ironic headline of "The Robbers are on the Run" — and attracted a number of investors. "John Fulton . . . left town suddenly some time last night," *The Automobile* reported on January 20th, 1908, "and the police with an army of creditors are hot on his trail." It was revealed that New Haven creditors had an aggregate of about $5000 in claims. Not one car had been built, not one order taken. Whether Fulton was ever apprehended is not known.

FULTON — Farmingdale, New York — (1920) — The Fulton Motor Truck Company had been building commercial vehicles in Farmingdale, Long Island since 1917. One day in the fall of 1920 in New York City a four-cylinder, right-hand-drive automobile with a Fulton emblem was seen coursing the streets. A reporter from *Automobile Topics* called Fulton for a little information. "The company has been considering the manufacture of a car for export," the reporter was told, but "none had been turned out as far as was known." Obviously the Fulton was a prototype. And obviously too Fulton decided against its manufacture. Fulton trucks continued in production into 1923.

FULTON & WALKER — Philadelphia, Pennsylvania — (1899-1901) — The slogan of the Fulton & Walker Company of Philadelphia was "wagons for business" — and commercial vehicles seemed to have dominated the line, although a "businessman's" runabout was also featured. All Fulton & Walkers were electrics. At the 1901 Philadelphia Automobile Show, the

company exhibited an ambulance that was quite favorably received in the automotive press. "This vehicle is completely fitted up, and is so arranged that four patients may be accommodated at one time," *The Motor Age* commented. "Medicine chests, stretchers, inside and outside electric light and all needed appliances make it the acme of perfection in its particular sphere." Nonetheless, it would appear that Fulton & Walker was out of the ambulance and automobile business by 1902.

FURBISH — New Haven, Connecticut — (1908) — George H. Furbish was an instructor at the Boardman School in New Haven and the builder of at least two automobiles. His second was reported upon in the *New England Automobile Journal* in August 1908: "One of the improvements made by Mr. Furbish (over his first effort) is that of a pedal and emergency brake. The pedal brake acts independently, but when the emergency brake is thrown in by a lever it applies and locks both brakes without applying the foot lever."

FURGASON — Claude E. Furgason was the owner of a machine shop in Lansing, Michigan. In 1910 he allied himself with Frank Clark, producer of the former Clarkmobile, and together they launched into the manufacture of a second-generation version to be known as the Clark. Refer to Clarkmobile.

FURNER — The Furner Motor Car Company was organized in Chicago during the summer of 1910 with a capital stock of $25,000 for the manufacture and sale of motor cars. E. Furner, A.W. Eschert and W.J. Bell were the incorporators. Manufacture is doubted.

1912 FWD, touring, WLB

F.W.D. — Clintonville, Wisconsin — (1910-1912) — The F.W.D. evolved from the inventions of two machinists of Clintonville. In their small machine shop, Otto Zachow and his brother-in-law William Besserdich devised and patented a double-Y universal joint in a ball-and socket allowing for the front wheels of a vehicle to be powered and steered at the same time. In 1908 they fitted their invention into an experimental car of their own design. It was dubbed a Z&B, and was fitted with a cross-compound steam engine which did not work at all well. The partners substituted a 45 hp gasoline engine in their second automobile, a 3800-pound vehicle which they dubbed The Battleship. Neither of these cars was marketed. In the meantime, in order to secure necessary capital to continue their development work, Zachow and Besserdich talked Dr. W.H. Finney into backing their efforts and in 1909 the Badger Four Wheel Drive Automobile Company was organized to manufacture automobiles utilizing the Zachow-Besserdich patents, with the partners being given stock in exchange for manufacturing rights. The first cars from the company were called the Badger or Badger F.W.D. But that name was dropped quickly when Dr. Finney accepted the ill-advised advice of his financial advisors and opted out of the whole thing. Zachow and Besserdich returned the $1800 the doctor had invested, and had their patent rights back again. The cars for 1911 were referred to simply as F.W.D., and by now the firm's name had been shortened to Four Wheel Drive Automobile Company. Walter A. Olen was now company president and chief financial backer. By now, too, the first F.W.D. trucks had been built, and the passenger car was dropped after twelve units had been produced, to concentrate all effort on the commercial field. By 1913 a huge new plant was under construction next to the former Zachow-Besserdich machine shop, and Clintonville was on its way to becoming one of the most famous truck-producing towns in America.

1910 F.W.D.
Badger F.W.D. — 4-cyl., 55/60 hp, 128" wb

	FP	5	4	3	2	1
Model 100-F Tour.-7P	4500	—	—	—	—	—

1911-1912 F.W.D.
F.W.D. — 4-cyl., 45 hp, 134" wb

Model A Tour.-7P	4500	5400	7300	11,800	25,000	38,000
Model A Runabout	4500	5500	7500	12,000	26,000	39,000
Model A Roadster	4500	5800	8000	12,500	28,000	40,000

FWICK — The name is so amusing, one rather wishes it had been built. Alas, the Fwick which has appeared on numerous car rosters was merely the Fawick Flyer misspelled. Refer to Fawick Flyer.

1910 Gabriel, NAHC

GABRIEL — Cleveland, Ohio — (1910-1912) — The Gabriel Auto Company was an outgrowth of the W.H. Gabriel Carriage & Wagon Company which had been established in 1851. In March of 1910 Gabriel announced its forthcoming automobile and exhibited the prototype at the Cleveland Automobile Show that month. It was a four-cylinder 25/30 hp touring car on a 120-inch wheelbase, and it proceeded into production in April. In July a Gabriel was one of eighteen cars to complete the *Cleveland News* Reliability Run with a perfect score. The company's offices were at 478 Broadway S.E. in Cleveland, its factory at 1674 West Third Street. In announcing its entry into automotive ranks, Gabriel indicated that it would also act as the state agents for the K-R-I-T car and would soon add the Grabowsky truck to its line. Apparently the idea of commercial vehicle production proved more alluring for Gabriel, for with the introduction of a one-ton Gabriel truck for 1913, the company summarily dropped its touring car. Gabriel trucks were produced through the First World War.

GADABOUT — The Gadabout was one of two cars built by George T. Turner at the turn of the century in Philadelphia. Refer to Turner.

1914 Gadabout, roadster, WLB

GADABOUT — Newark, New Jersey — (1914-1915)/Detroit, Michigan — (1915-1916) — A wickerwork body on a wood frame was the most distinctive feature of the Gadabout, a cyclecar with side-by-side seating, a 46-inch tread and 86-inch wheelbase. Power was supplied by a four-cylinder water-cooled Sterling engine producing about 12 hp. Splash lubrication, a Schebler carburetor and magneto ignition were featured. Right-hand steering was fitted, and the solid rear axle came from the Detroit Axle Company. Philip Heseltine promoted the Gadabout venture, and Walter Greunberg designed the car. During the summer of 1914, Gadabout Motor Corporation announced that it had leased a building at the southwest corner of Badger Avenue and Runyon Street in Newark for manufacture. One year later the company moved to another factory, on Lafayette Street in Detroit, and continued production there. The Gadabout was shown at the Chicago Automobile Show in January 1916, by which time it had lengthened into a 104-inch wheelbase car and lost its distinctive wickerwork body. Surviving into 1916 was a rarity for a cyclecar, though the Gadabout didn't last out the year. By late summer the firm was succeeded by Heseltine Motor Corporation and a new car called the Heseltine.

1914 GADABOUT
Cyclecar — 4-cyl., 12 hp, 86" wb

	FP	5	4	3	2	1
Model G Rdstr.-2P	400	1800	2800	4000	6200	13,000

1916 Gadabout, roadster, WLB

1915 GADABOUT
Cyclecar — 4-cyl., 12 hp, 86" wb

Model G Rdstr.-2P	450	1800	2800	4000	6200	13,000

1916 GADABOUT
Cyclecar — 4-cyl., 12 hp, 104" wb

Model G Rdstr.-2P	485	2000	3000	4200	6500	14,000

1905 Gaeth, Triplex touring, HAC

GAETHMOBILE — Cleveland, Ohio — (1902-1904)/GAETH — Cleveland, Ohio — (1905-1910) — Paul Gaeth of Cleveland was a consummate tinkerer. He made bicycles and stationary engines and in 1898 built an experimental steam car, followed by a gasoline car. Though by 1900 he had sold his first gasoline car as well as another he had built, he allied himself with the People's Automobile Company in Cleveland that year and remained there as superintendent until the summer of 1902 when People's went bankrupt. Immediately thereafter, with the financial assistance of a local undertaker, druggist and wholesale meat dealer, he organized the Gaeth Automobile Company and began building cars to custom order. By the end of 1903, twenty-five customers had ordered. Gaethmobile was the name by which these cars were known, and they were small sturdy single-cylinder chain-drive runabouts with tiller steering and a 72-inch wheelbase. Gaeth began thinking bigger in late 1904. His first shaft-drive planetary-transmission cars had three-cylinder engines mounted under the front seat, with a false hood, and a model designation of Gaeth Triplex. The following year Gaeth put a four-cylinder engine in the front with shaft drive and sliding gear transmission. "Go with a Gaeth" was a company slogan. The cars performed extremely well in Glidden Tours, scoring 997 out of a possible 1000 points in 1907, and a perfect thousand in 1908. Brochures enthused that "Mr. Gaeth is a born mechanic — it's his bent — his hobby." Unfortunately, Paul Gaeth wasn't a born-businessman, and in November of 1910 the business that was his hobby was acquired by the Stuyvesant Motor Car Company of Cleveland. Stuyvesant already had announced its new six-cylinder car; the firm's new four would be the Gaeth modified and renamed. Until his death at age seventy-nine in 1952, Paul Gaeth remained in Cleveland operating out of a small shop and continuing his tinkering. His patented inventions ranged from a fuel mixing device in 1903 to a "fluid-meter" in 1915. As late as the Twenties, he was still driving his personal Gaeth as regular transportation, and he was servicing and making replacement parts for another Gaeth still on the road into the 1930's. After the Second World War, he was among the earliest restorers in the burgeoning antique car hobby.

1902-1904 GAETHMOBILE
Gaethmobile — 1-cyl., 6 hp, 72" wb

	FP	5	4	3	2	1
Runabout-2P		4000	5000	8000	15,000	28,000

1905 GAETH
Triplex — 3-cyl., 25/30 hp

Side Entrance Tonneau	2600	3700	4700	7300	13,700	26,000

1906 Gaeth, type G, King of Belgian touring, HAC

1906 GAETH
Model G — 4-cyl., 20/24 hp, 98" wb

Touring-5P	2000	3700	4700	7300	13,700	26,000

Model H — 4-cyl., 30/34 hp, 104" wb

Touring-5P	2500	4200	5000	8000	15,000	28,000

Model J — 4-cyl., 50/54 hp, 109" wb

Touring-5/6P	3500	4200	5200	8400	15,700	29,000

1907 Gaeth, type XII, touring, HAC

1907 GAETH
Type XII — 4-cyl., 35 hp, 112" wb

Touring-7P	3500	4000	5000	8000	15,000	28,000

1908 Gaeth, type XV, touring, HAC

1908 GAETH
Type XV — 4-cyl., 35/40 hp, 112" wb

Touring	3500	4200	5200	8400	15,700	29,000
Roadster	3500	4300	5300	8600	16,100	29,500
Limousine	3500	4000	5000	8000	15,000	28,000

1909 Gaeth, type XX, tourabout, HAC

1909 GAETH
Type XX — 4-cyl., 38 hp, 114" wb

	FP	5	4	3	2	1
Touring-7P	3500	4200	5200	8400	15,700	29,000
Cl. C. Tour.-5P	3500	4200	5200	8400	15,700	29,000
Tourabout-4P	3500	4000	5000	8000	15,000	28,000
Limousine-6P	3500	4000	5000	8000	15,000	28,000

1910 Gaeth, type XX, touring, HAC

1910 GAETH
Type XX — 4-cyl., 40/45 hp, 120" wb

Touring	3500	4500	5800	9500	18,000	32,000
Pony Tonneau	3500	4400	5600	9200	17,300	31,000
Limousine	4500	4200	5200	8400	15,700	29,000

GAGE — During the early fall of 1914, J.P. Gage of 237 West 57th Street in New York City announced his resignation as export manager for the Trumbull cyclecar in order to manufacture a "light runabout, touring and town car, especially designed for foreign trade." Manufacture does not appear to have followed, however.

GAGE STEAM — West Gardner, Massachusetts — (1900) — A.S. Gage of West Gardner lived on Summer Street and in 1900 built a steam carriage for his own use in the saw shop operated by his son Ernest. The vehicle weighed 800 pounds, used a direct spur-gear transmission and was powered by a 4 hp engine of Gage's own design. It was the only automobile A.S. Gage built.

GAGE — Los Angeles, California — (1914) — The news carried a March 14th, 1914 dateline from Los Angeles. The Gage Manufacturing Company had just been incorporated for $20,000 for the manufacture of cyclecars and had already contracted to produce 4500 of them for distribution on the Pacific Coast. With whom this contract was made was not revealed. Indeed, other than the fact that the Gage was a two-cylinder air-cooled 9/12 hp side-by-side two-seater runabout on a 104-inch-wheelbase chassis, very little was. The price was $300 — "the champagne car that fits the beer pocketbook" was the slogan. Chain drive and a differential were featured, the hood sloped in front a'la Renault, and the whole package weighed 650 pounds. The man behind this venture was Jay Gage, who boasted of his pioneering aircraft experience. By December, there was further news. The firm had changed its name to Union Car Company and had opted to discontinue the Gage. "Our company has decided to go heavier into car construction than planned when we put out Gage cyclecar," Union wrote *Carette* that month. "We became of the opinion the western public desired a heavier machine than our car and are now building along considerably different lines.'' The new car would be called the Permax. How long Jay Gage remained with the venture is not known. But probably not long. This new Union venture seems to have wiped the personnel slate clean.

GAGEMOBILE STEAM — Saratoga Springs, New York — (1902-1905) — During the summer of 1902, William M. Gage of Saratoga Springs announced that he stood ready to build cars to custom order based upon a steam carriage prototype of his own design. Orders would be taken for passenger, racing and commercial cars. How many orders were received is a mystery, though at least one car was built, which was revised from a gasoline car chassis designed by Charles Mayhew which was supposed to have been marketed by the Hudson Gas Motor & Vehicle Manufacturing Company of Saratoga Springs. Hudson gave up its automotive venture in 1902, though Hudson manager Lester E. Heath remained to assist William Gage in this new steam-car enterprise. The Gagemobile Company was located at 29-31 Excelsior Avenue, and a city directory listing indicated it to be in business in 1905. The listing was not repeated in 1906. William M. Gage is not to be confused, incidentally, with A.S. Gage of Massachusetts who built a steam car strictly for his own use in 1900. Conceivably, W.M. Gage may have produced no more cars than did A.S.

GAINESVILLE — The Gainesville Automobile Company was organized to manufacture and sell automobiles, motor boats and marine and stationary engines in Gainesville, Florida during the fall of 1905. Plans also included the company's bidding to supply power to the Gainesville and Green Cove Railway and Canal Company, the railroad of which was in the course of construction. To be constructed too was a new factory for the Gainesville Automobile Company, using ''the first steel structure in the city.'' Already the firm had leased premises across from the post office. The fellow promoting this venture was described only as a ''Mr. Lilienblum of New York.'' The venture was shortly not heard from again.

GAITHER — The Gaither Auto Company was organized in Columbus, Ohio during the fall of 1913 with a capital stock of $10,000 to manufacture and deal in motor cars. Incorporators were William Gaither, Allen Leamy, Jesse J. Brown, William B. Leamy and L.E. Andrews. Manufacture is doubted.

GALE STEAM — Albion, Michigan — (1901) — The Gale Manufacturing Company had been in the hardware business in Albion since 1861, branching into farm implement manufacture two years later. For a short while at the turn of the century it appeared that Gale might branch into automobile production as well. The reason was W.D. Brundage, the superintendent of the firm from 1898 to 1904. During the winter of 1900-1901, he built a steam runabout. The car was successfully tested the following spring. ''The operation of starting the fire is the same as in the common gasoline stove, and requires no more skill,'' *The Albion Evening Recorder* reported enthusiastically in its May 23rd, 1901 edition. ''. . . The fire can be left burning for days without any attention whatever.'' By late summer the Gale Manufacturing Company announced to the automotive trade press its intention to manufacture automobiles. Second thoughts were quickly experienced, however, and production did not follow. Probably the only Gale steamer built was the prototype Brundage completed in the spring of 1901. It was Albion's first automobile.

1907 Gale, model G-7, runabout, NAHC

GALE — Galesburg, Illinois — (1905-1907) — D.W. Cook was an employee of a machine shop in Chicago who spent his evenings and other spare time building an automobile of his own design which attracted the attention of a Mr. Hayden and George Clark of Chicago's Crane company. Cook's shop was across the street from the mail-order house of Sears, Roebuck and Company, and Crane's president was a neighbor of Sears' president Rosenthal. Rosenthal at the time was looking for an automobile

to include in his catalog, and agreed to take a demonstration ride in the Cook vehicle. Impressed with the results, Rosenthal arrived at the machine shop the next morning with his body guard, anxious to conclude a deal. ''For how much under two hundred dollars can you supply these for us?,'' he asked. With that, Hayden backed up to a work bench, grabbed a large wrench and chased both Rosenthal and his bodyguard out of the shop, and out of the future of D.W. Cook's car. Thus it was that Rosenthal had to look elsewhere for a car to market in his Sears catalog, and the Cook-Hayden-Clark triumvirate had to look elsewhere for a place to build the Cook car. A place was found in Galesburg, the old Brown Corn Planter building which was secured by the Western Tool Works. Western Tool's Percy Robson was the man who backed the project. The car would be called the Gale. Five single-cylinder Model A's were built in 1905; the Gale really got rolling the following year, with a vast expansion of its line, and the sale of more than 100 cars at the Chicago Automobile Show. In addition to automobiles, Western Tool Works also produced screw machines, wall safes and emery wheel dressers, and its dealership network was an international one which worked to the advantage of the Gale. A number of Gale cars were sold in Europe, as well as Australia, New Zealand and Borneo. Over 600 single-cylinder cars and about 140 of the twins were produced before financial difficulties at Western Tool resulted in the cessation of Gale manufacture. Subsequently Percy Robson reorganized and took the car to market again as the Robson.

1905 GALE						
Model A — 1-cyl., 8 hp, 80'' wb						
	FP	5	4	3	2	1
Runabout-2P	500	1800	2800	4000	6200	13,000
1906 GALE						
Model E — 2-cyl., 18/20 hp, 92'' wb						
Touring-5P	1250	1800	2800	4000	6200	13,000
Model F — 2-cyl., 18/20 hp, 92'' wb						
Touring-5P	1325	2000	3000	4200	6500	14,000
Model G — 2-cyl., 18/20 hp, 92'' wb						
Runabout-2P	1000	2000	3000	4200	6500	14,000
Model C — 1-cyl., 8/10 hp, 73'' wb						
Runabout-2P	600	1800	2800	4000	6200	13,000
Model D — 1-cyl., 8/10 hp, 73'' wb						
Runabout w/top	650	2000	3000	4200	6500	14,000
1907 GALE						
Model K-7 — 2-cyl., 24/26 hp, 95'' wb						
Touring-5P	1250	2000	3000	4200	6500	14,000
Model G-7 — 2-cyl., 14 hp, 86'' wb						
Runabout	900	1800	2800	4000	6200	13,000
Model C-7 — 1-cyl., 8/10 hp, 73'' wb						
Runabout	600	1600	2700	3800	5800	12,000

GALE FOUR — Indianapolis, Indiana — (1920) — The Gale Four was a new prototype designed by Garde Gale and introduced at the Indianapolis Automobile Show in 1920. Impressed with it there was Lynn McCurdy, son of Colonel William H. McCurdy, the founder of Hercules Corporation of Evansville, Indiana. Garde Gale couldn't afford production himself, but Lynn McCurdy's father could. The Gale Four thus evolved into the McCurdy Six. Garde Gale, who had previously been the distributor for the Dort car in Canada among other automotive affiliations, became the general sales manager for the automobile department of Hercules Corporation.

GALLIA ELECTRIC — The Gallia Electric has frequently been cited on rosters of American cars. It was marketed in this country certainly, its New York headquarters located at 152-154 West 38th Street. But the car was imported from France and not manufactured here. During the summer of 1905, in full-page advertisements in the automotive press, Bernard Maurice Dufresne and Count Armand de Gontaut Biron officially announced their establishment of the American agency for Gallia Electric Carriages. The cars continued to be imported into this country as late as 1908.

1911 Galloway, dual purpose car, NAHC

597

GALLOWAY — Waterloo, Iowa — (1908-1911) — The William Galloway Company of Waterloo scoffed that feeding horses "corn worth 75¢ a bushel and oats worth 35¢ to 40¢, and hay worth $14 to $20 per ton" was a waste of hard-earned money better spent on buying automotive transport by Galloway. Agricultural products had been the mainstay of the William Galloway Company from its founding in 1906 until 1908 when Galloway decided also to offer a two-cylinder, solid-tired, chain-drive $570 highwheeler that could take a large family to church on Sunday and become a heavy load carrier during the week. With just 14 hp and an 85-inch-wheelbase chassis, how heavy the loads could be was questionable. During the summer of 1910 William Galloway persuaded Fred Maytag of Des Moines to bring his Maytag-Mason Motor Car Company to town by offering to buy a substantial interest in the venture. The 1911 Galloway, which was the last year for the marque, was nothing more than a re-emblemed Maytag. Thereafter William Galloway turned his attention to the Dart Manufacturing Company which he had brought to town from Anderson and which was enjoying considerably more commercial success with the Dart truck. In 1915 Galloway returned to automobile manufacture briefly with a new car called the Arabian.

GARDNER — The Gardner-Matthews Automobile Manufacturing Company was organized in New York City during the summer of 1911 to manufacture motors and motor vehicles. Capital stock was $100,000; the incorporators were R.E. Matthews and M.D. Schneer of Manhattan, and J.W. Pascom of Brooklyn. Manufacture of an automobile is doubted.

The Gardner Taxicab Company was organized in Maplewood, New York with a capital stock of $50,000 during the spring of 1916 to manufacture and deal in motor cars. Incorporators were William W. Jones, Warren Gardner and Isabel S. Miller. Manufacture is doubted.

GARDNER STEAM — Hingham, Massachusetts — (1865) — Technical details regarding the steam car invented by John C. Gardner of Hingham are lacking, but the vehicle is known to have been built and successfully tested. "It runs upon the common road, goes up hill and down, and moves at a two-forty gait without the least apparent difficulty," reported *The Hingham Journal* on September 15th, 1865. "All that is required is to keep its insides well filled with suitable rations, and it will give full evidence of its capacities and power of speed." The car was exhibited at the local Agricultural Fair that year. Its further adventures are unknown.

GARDNER — New Orleans, Louisiana — (1896) — In 1896 an engine invented by Levi S. Gardner was put into production by the newly-formed Gardner Motor Company, Ltd. at 215 Carondalet Street in New Orleans. The president of the firm was Jefferson C. Wenck. The Gardner motor was a single-cylinder vertical unit with 3-by-5-inch bore-stroke dimensions; its height was 28 inches, its weight 150 pounds, and it was claimed to develop 6 hp at 600 rpm. Distinctive features were lightness and simplicity; the engine's only moving parts were the connecting rod, piston and crankshaft. The Gardner company is believed to have constructed an automobile using this engine, but this was merely for experimental purposes and was not publicized. In 1900, when Adolph Peteler built his gasoline car in New Orleans, it was reported in the local *Times-Democrat* to be the first in the city. At that time Gardner remained in the engine-producing field, and reportedly had one of the largest factories of this kind in the South. During the summer of 1901 the Gardner plant was struck by lightning and burned to the ground. Apparently the firm moved thereafter to Biloxi, Mississippi.

1910 Gardner, runabout, OCW

GARDNER — New London, Connecticut — (1910) — The Brown Cotton Gin Company of New London has appeared in numerous rosters as an automobile manufacturer. The company did experiment with a steam vehicle in 1902, but whether it was ever completed has not been documented. The company produced automobile parts awhile beginning in

1908, as well as the six-cylinder models of the Cameron for Everett S. Cameron from 1908-1910. In 1910, too, at Brown Cotton Gin, a one-off effort was produced by an employee, M.G. Gardner, entirely for his own use and that of his large family. Although begun in 1910, the car may not have been completed until 1912. A surviving photograph indicates that a wagon bed was used for the body; the motive power was a gasoline engine. Apparently the car was wholly successful, Gardner driving it on one occasion all the way to Detroit and back. He did not, however, build another car.

1921 Gardner, model G, roadster, HAC

GARDNER — St. Louis Missouri — (1920-1931) — In 1879 Russell E. Gardner left his native Tennessee for St. Louis without a dollar to his name. Three-and-a-half decades later, when he turned the management of his business over to his sons Russell, Jr. and Fred, he was a millionaire several times over. Russell Gardner had made it big in St. Louis. He had begun manufacturing Banner buggies before the turn of the century and, unlike many wagonbuilders, was well aware of what the automotive age meant to his business. Initially, and probably wisely, he elected not to enter the field with a car of his own, instead tip-toeing in by building bodies for the new Chevrolet alongside his wagons. By 1915, this had led to assembly of the complete Chevrolet in St. Louis, and to Russell Gardner controlling all Chevrolet trade in the Mississippi River states. When his sons entered the Navy during World War I, the Gardners sold their Chevrolet business to General Motors — and after the Armistice established the Gardner Motor Company. All three Gardners were involved, Russell E. Gardner, Sr. as chairman of the board, Russell, Jr. as president, Fred Gardner as vice-president. Since their previous experience had been in the assembling of cars, the Gardner was, not surprisingly, an assembled car — Lycoming engines were used throughout — and a very good one. A medium-sized and medium-priced four on a 112-inch wheelbase. Gardners sold well from the beginning. The car was introduced in late 1919 as a 1920 model. Sales in 1921 were 3800 cars, increased in 1922 to 9000, with preparation begun then for expansion of both the distributorship network and the product line. Plant capacity was 40,000 cars annually, and by 1925 these included both sixes and eights. The fours were dropped after 1925; sixes and eights were produced in 1926 and 1927, eights only in 1928 and 1929. In early 1924 Cannon Ball Baker established a new mid-winter transcontinental record (New York to Los Angeles in 7 days 17 hours 8 minutes) in a Gardner, and in 1928 the Gardner company built a racing balloon as the St. Louis entry for the International James Gordon Bennett Cup races. Promotional stunts like these were rare, however; the company tended to avoid pyrotechnics or deviations from the norm in the automobile industry. Except for its exit from the field. For 1930, when many other manufacturers were adding cylinders, Gardner subtracted, returning a six to the line. And in January that year, the company announced a front wheel drive car that was quite sensational. An 80 hp six on a 133-inch wheelbase, its Baker-Raulang body sported a long hood and distinctive low-slung lines. Lockheed hydraulic internal expanding brakes — rare in America — and two-way hydraulic shock absorbers were featured. "The only Front Wheel Drive in the $2000 field," the brochures said — and, alas, although that was true, the reality was that only prototypes would be built. Gardner was now in a death struggle, but the company did not give up without a terrific fight. During the summer of 1929, Gardner had announced two "very important" automobile contracts. One was with Sears, Roebuck and Company for development of a new car to be sold by the mail order house. The other was with New Era Motors for manufacture

1922 Gardner, Four, touring, HAC

of its front wheel drive Ruxton. The stock market crash resulted in Sears' immediate disinterest in pursuing its car idea further. And it resulted too in playing havoc with Archie Andrews' plans for his New Era empire which he had been nurturing since his acquisition of Moon of St. Louis. Both deals were off for Gardner. The 1931 models of the Gardner were the 1930 models updated and marketed during the company's phaseout. In mid-1931 Russell E. Gardner, Jr. solicited the permission of his stockholders to abandon the manufacture of automobiles. The reasons he gave for his company's failure — Gardner had been profitable until 1927 — was the fierce competition of the major producers and their control of many sources of parts supplies. The Gardner funeral car was built into 1932, but then the Gardner was dead. In addition to a longevity surpassing most assembled car manufacturers in America, the Gardner venture was distinguished also by a product exceptional for its type — the 1928 model line had been so beautifully and strikingly styled that it still looked new in 1930, which could be said of few automobiles of that era. And rare too was the fact that in liquidating their automobile business, the Gardners actually made money rather than losing it. Ned Jordan managed this, as did J. Dallas Dort, but few others.

1920
Model G, 4-cyl., 35 hp, 112" wb

	FP	5	4	3	2	1
5P Tr	1125	3600	7200	12,000	16,800	24,000
3P Rds	1125	4050	8100	13,500	18,900	27,000
5P Sed	2145	1550	4500	7500	10,500	15,000

1921
Model G, 4-cyl., 35 hp, 112" wb

3P Rds	1195	2000	5100	8500	11,900	17,000
5P Tr	895	3600	7200	12,000	16,800	24,000
5P Sed	1595	1550	4500	7500	10,500	15,000

1922 Gardner, five-passenger coach, Willoughby, HAC

1922
Four, 35 hp, 112" wb

3P Rds	1095	4050	8100	13,500	18,900	27,000
5P Tr	1095	3600	7200	12,000	16,800	24,000
5P Sed	1795	1550	4500	7500	10,500	15,000

1923 Gardner, model 5, sedan, HAC

1923
Model 5, 4-cyl., 43 hp, 112" wb

5P Tr	965	3600	7200	12,000	16,800	24,000
2P Rds	965	4050	8100	13,500	18,900	27,000
2P Cpe	1115	2800	5700	9500	13,300	19,000
5P Sed	1365	1550	4500	7500	10,500	15,000

1924
Model 5, 4-cyl., 43 hp, 112" wb

3P Rds	995	4050	8100	13,500	18,900	27,000
5P Tr	995	3600	7200	12,000	16,800	24,000
5P Spt Tr	1045	3750	7500	12,500	17,500	25,000
3P Cpe	1145	2800	5700	9500	13,300	19,000
5P Brgm	1335	1750	4800	8000	11,200	16,000
5P Sed	1445	1550	4500	7500	10,500	15,000

1924 Gardner, model 5, roadster, HAC

1925 Gardner, model 5, deluxe touring, HAC

1925
Model 5, 4-cyl., 44 hp, 112" wb

	FP	5	4	3	2	1
5P Tr	995	3600	7200	12,000	16,800	24,000
3P Rds	945	4050	8100	13,500	18,900	27,000
5P Std Tr	1045	3750	7500	12,500	17,500	25,000
5P DeL Tr	1145	3900	7800	13,000	18,200	26,000
5P Sed	1475	1550	4500	7500	10,500	15,000
4P Cpe	1275	2800	5700	9500	13,300	19,000
5P Radio Sed	1595	1750	4800	8000	11,200	16,000

Six, 57 hp, 117" wb

5P Tr	1395	3750	7500	12,500	17,500	25,000

Line 8, 8-cyl., 65 hp, 125" wb

5P Tr	1995	3900	7800	13,000	18,200	26,000
5P Brgm	1995	2000	5100	8500	11,900	17,000

1926 Gardner, Line 8, roadster, HAC

1926
Six, 57 hp, 117" wb

5P Tr	1395	4200	8400	14,000	19,600	28,000
4P Rds	1595	4800	9600	16,000	22,400	32,000
4P Cabr	1845	4050	8100	13,500	18,900	27,000
5P 4 dr Brgm	1595	2300	5400	9000	12,600	18,000
5P Sed	1595	1750	4800	8000	11,200	16,000
DeL Sed	1795	2000	5100	8500	11,900	17,000

Line 8, 65 hp, 125" wb

5P Tr	1995	5700	11,400	19,000	26,600	38,000
4P Rds	1995	6300	12,600	21,000	29,400	42,000
4P Cabr	2245	5550	11,100	18,500	25,900	37,000
5P 4 dr Brgm	1995	4200	8400	14,000	19,600	28,000
5P Sed	1995	3900	7800	13,000	18,200	26,000
5P DeL Sed	2495	4050	8100	13,500	18,900	27,000

599

1927 Gardner, roadster, JAC

1927
Model 6-B, 6-cyl., 55 hp, 117" wb

	FP	5	4	3	2	1
5P Tr	1545	4200	8400	14,000	19,600	28,000
4P Rds	1545	4800	9600	16,000	22,400	32,000
4P Cabr	1845	4350	8700	14,500	20,300	29,000
5P 4 dr Brgm	1695	2300	5400	9000	12,600	18,000
5P Sed	1745	1750	4800	8000	11,200	16,000

Model 8-80, 8-cyl., 70 hp, 122" wb

	FP	5	4	3	2	1
4P Rds	1395	6000	12,000	20,000	28,000	40,000
5P Sed	1695	3900	7800	13,000	18,200	26,000
Vic Cpe	1695	4350	8700	14,500	20,300	29,000

Model 8-90, 8-cyl., 84 hp, 130" wb

	FP	5	4	3	2	1
4P Rds	1995	6300	12,600	21,000	29,400	42,000
5P Sed	2295	2000	5100	8500	11,900	17,000
5P Brgm	2295	2800	5700	9500	13,300	19,000
5P Vic	2295	3000	6000	10,000	14,000	20,000

1928 Gardner, 4-dr. sedan, OCW

1928
Model 8-75, 8-cyl., 65 hp, 122" wb

	FP	5	4	3	2	1
4P Rds	1195	6150	12,300	20,500	28,700	41,000
Vic	1295	4350	8700	14,500	20,300	29,000
Cpe	1295	4200	8400	14,000	19,600	28,000
5P Club Sed	1395	4050	8100	13,500	18,900	27,000
5P Sed	1495	3750	7500	12,500	17,500	25,000

Model 8-85, 8-cyl., 74 hp, 125" wb

	FP	5	4	3	2	1
4P Rds	1695	6300	12,600	21,000	29,400	42,000
5P Brgm	1875	4350	8700	14,500	20,300	29,000
5P Sed	1895	3900	7800	13,000	18,200	26,000
4P Cus Cpe	2095	4500	9000	15,000	21,000	30,000

Model 8-95, 8-cyl., 115 hp, 130" wb

	FP	5	4	3	2	1
4P Rds	2095	6750	13,500	22,500	31,500	45,000
5P Brgm	2275	4500	9000	15,000	21,000	30,000
5P Sed	2295	4050	8100	13,500	18,900	27,000
4P Cus Cpe	2495	4650	9300	15,500	21,700	31,000

1929 Gardner, model 120, sport sedan, HAC

1929 Gardner, coupe, JAC

1929
Model 120, 8-cyl., 65 hp, 122" wb

	FP	5	4	3	2	1
4P Rds	1395	6300	12,600	21,000	29,400	42,000
5P Spt Sed	1295	4350	8700	14,500	20,300	29,000
4P Cpe	1495	4650	9300	15,500	21,700	31,000
5P Sed	1595	3900	7800	13,000	18,200	26,000

Model 125, 8-cyl., 85 hp, 125" wb

	FP	5	4	3	2	1
4P Rds	1695	6450	12,900	21,500	30,100	43,000
4P Cabr	1795	5700	11,400	19,000	26,600	38,000
5P Brgm	1875	4350	8700	14,500	20,300	29,000
5P Sed	1895	4050	8100	13,500	18,900	27,000
4P Vic	1895	4200	8400	14,000	19,600	28,000
Cpe	—	4650	9300	15,500	21,700	31,000

Model 130, 8-cyl., 115 hp, 130" wb

	FP	5	4	3	2	1
4P Rds	2195	6600	13,200	22,000	30,800	44,000
4P Cpe	2295	4800	9600	16,000	22,400	32,000
5P Brgm	2375	4500	9000	15,000	21,000	30,000
5P Sed	2395	4350	8700	14,500	20,300	29,000
5P Vic	2395	4800	9600	16,000	22,400	32,000

1930 Gardner, phaeton, OCW

1930
Model 136, 6-cyl., 70 hp, 122" wb

	FP	5	4	3	2	1
Rds	1245	6450	12,900	21,500	30,100	43,000
5P Spt Phae	1245	6150	12,300	20,500	28,700	41,000
7P Spt Phae	1545	6300	12,600	21,000	29,400	42,000
Spt Sed	1195	4500	9000	15,000	21,000	30,000
Cpe	1245	4800	9600	16,000	22,400	32,000
Brgm	1245	4350	8700	14,500	20,300	29,000
5P Sed	1295	3900	7800	13,000	18,200	26,000
7P Sed	1595	4050	8100	13,500	18,900	27,000

Model 140, 8-cyl., 90 hp, 125" wb

	FP	5	4	3	2	1
Rds	1645	6750	13,500	22,500	31,500	45,000
5P Spt Phae	1695	6300	12,600	21,000	29,400	42,000
7P Spt Phae	1945	6450	12,900	21,500	30,100	43,000
Spt Sed	1595	4650	9300	15,500	21,700	31,000
Cpe	1645	4950	9900	16,500	23,100	33,000
Brgm	1645	4500	9000	15,000	21,000	30,000
5P Sed	1695	4050	8100	13,500	18,900	27,000
7P Sed	1995	4200	8400	14,000	19,600	28,000

Model 150, 8-cyl., 126 hp, 130" wb

	FP	5	4	3	2	1
Rds	1995	7050	14,100	23,500	32,900	47,000
5P Spt Phae	2045	6750	13,500	22,500	31,500	45,000
7P Spt Phae	2295	6900	13,800	23,000	32,200	46,000
Spt Sed	1945	4800	9600	16,000	22,400	32,000
Cpe	1995	5100	10,200	17,000	23,800	34,000
Brgm	1995	4650	9300	15,500	21,700	31,000
5P Sed	2045	4200	8400	14,000	19,600	28,000
7P Sed	2345	4350	8700	14,500	20,300	29,000

1931 Gardner, model 150, sedan, JAC

1931
Model 136, 6-cyl., 70 hp, 122" wb

	FP	5	4	3	2	1
Rds	1320	6600	13,200	22,000	30,800	44,000
Spt Sed	1270	4650	9300	15,500	21,700	31,000
Cpe	1320	4800	9600	16,000	22,400	32,000
Sed	1370	4200	8400	14,000	19,600	28,000

Model 148, 6-cyl., 100 hp, 125" wb

	FP	5	4	3	2	1
Rds	1795	6750	13,500	22,500	31,500	45,000
Phae	1845	6600	13,200	22,000	30,800	44,000
Spt Sed	1795	4950	9900	16,500	23,100	33,000
Cpe	1795	5100	10,200	17,000	23,800	34,000
Brgm	1795	4950	9900	16,500	23,100	33,000
Sed	1845	4350	8700	14,500	20,300	29,000

Model 150, 8-cyl., 126 hp, 130" wb

	FP	5	4	3	2	1
Rds	2120	6900	13,800	23,000	32,200	46,000
Cpe	2120	5250	10,500	17,500	24,500	35,000
Brgm	2120	5100	10,200	17,000	23,800	34,000
Sed	2170	4500	9000	15,000	21,000	30,000

GARFIELD — Chicago, Illinois — (1904-1905) — The Garfield Automobile Company at State Street and Garfield Boulevard in Chicago operated principally as a repository for automobiles and as a repair station. The men behind this venture were N.E. McDaniels, George Schein and Justus Chancellor, and they had incorporated with a modest capital stock of $15,000 in October 1904. For a short while the company also produced a limited number of two- and three-cylinder air-cooled runabouts, but the firm was undercapitalized for any major manufacturing effort and soon returned to garage work exclusively.

GARFIELD PARK — The Garfield Park Automobile Garage was organized in Chicago, Illinois late in 1911 with a capital stock of $5000 to manufacture and deal in motor cars and accessories. Incorporators were H.E. Halbert, A.F.W. Seibel and Augustus Binswanger. Manufacture of an automobile is doubted.

1908 Garford, model A, runabout, WLB

GARFORD — Elyria, Ohio — (1908; 1911-1913) — The Garford Company of Elyria grew out of the Federal Manufacturing Company which had begun manufacture of component parts for automobiles in 1903. Garford took this venture one step further and began supplying the industry with complete chassis. Among companies using Garford chassis were Ardsley, Gaeth, Cleveland, Royal, Rainier — and, most notably, Studebaker. The

Garford of Garford was Arthur L., who had begun his career in banking and was subsequently treasurer of the American Bicycle Company prior to establishing Federal Manufacturing. Interestingly, Garford as an automobile marque name did not exist as early as commonly thought, at least not legally. The contract Garford signed with Studebaker prevented that; a 1910 brochure noted that "the termination this year of its obligation to Studebaker enables the Garford Company at last to realize the long deferred hope of presenting its product under its own name." Actually, that long deferred hope had been realized earlier when Garford introduced four-cylinder Models A and B at the Grand Central Palace Show in October 1907 as Garford cars. They were sold in 1908 and entered in the Glidden Tour and other competitive events as Garfords as well. Most likely, Studebaker objected because subsequently the cars were referred to, as they had always been, only as Studebaker-Garfords or Studebakers. With the Studebaker takeover of E-M-F, the South Bend company no longer needed Garford, and the Elyria company was now on its own at last. Unfortunately, the years of alliance with Studebaker meant that Garford had never developed a distribution network of its own. The Garford that was really a Garford was introduced at the New York Automobile Show in January 1911. One year later the Garford automobile-building enterprise was absorbed by Willys-Overland. For 1913 one of the new sixes featured a single headlight recessed flush with the radiator, and became popularly known as the "One-Eyed Garford." Nineteen thirteen was the marque's curtain call as an automobile. The Garford truck-producing venture which had begun in 1909 was not part of the Willys-Overland deal, and the Garford marque name was thereafter continued on commercial vehicles.

1908 GARFORD
Model A — 4-cyl., 30 hp, 104" wb

	FP	5	4	3	2	1
Touring	3500	3700	4700	7300	13,700	26,000
Town Car	4200	3500	4500	7000	13,000	25,000
Runabout	—	3300	4400	6700	12,000	24,000
Landaulet	3700	4700	7300	13,700	26,000

Model B — 4-cyl., 40 hp, 114" wb

	FP	5	4	3	2	1
Touring	4000	4000	5000	8000	15,000	28,000
Runabout	—	3700	4700	7300	13,700	26,000
Limousine	—	3900	4800	7700	14,300	27,000
Landaulet	—	4000	5000	8000	15,000	28,000

1911 GARFORD
Model G-7 — 4-cyl., 40 hp, 117-1/2" wb

	FP	5	4	3	2	1
Touring-4/5P	3500	4000	5000	8000	15,000	28,000
Touring-7P	3500	4200	5200	8400	15,700	29,000
Limousine (123" wb)	4750	3700	4700	7300	13,700	26,000

1912 Garford, touring, AA

1912 Garford, model G-14 touring, FR

1912 GARFORD
Model G-12 — 4-cyl., 30 hp, 119" wb

	FP	5	4	3	2	1
Limousine	4000	3700	4700	7300	13,700	26,000
Landaulet	4100	3900	4800	7700	14,300	27,000
Touring-4/5P	3200	4000	5000	8000	15,000	28,000
Roadster-2P	3200	4200	5200	8400	15,700	29,000

601

Model G-8 — 4-cyl., 40 hp, 119" wb

	FP	5	4	3	2	1
Limousine	4800	3900	4800	7700	14,300	27,000
Landaulet	4900	4000	5000	8000	15,000	28,000
Touring-5/6/7P	3750	4200	5200	8400	15,700	29,000
Roadster-2P	3750	4300	5400	8700	16,500	30,000

Model G-14 — 6-cyl., 50 hp, 138-3/4" wb

Limousine	5600	4200	5200	8400	15,700	29,000
Landaulet	5750	4300	5400	8700	16,500	30,000
Touring-4/6P	4500	4500	5800	9500	18,000	32,000
Roadster-2P	4500	4700	6100	9900	19,000	33,000

1913 Garford, model G-12 limousine, HAC

1913 GARFORD

Model G-12 — 4-cyl., 30 hp, 118" wb

Limousine-5P	4000	3900	4800	7700	14,300	27,000
Landaulet-5P	4100	4000	5000	8000	15,000	28,000

Model G-15 — 6-cyl., 50 hp, 128" wb

Touring-5P	2750	4000	5000	8000	15,000	28,000
Roadster-2P	2750	4200	5200	8400	15,700	29,000
Town Car	3750	3900	4800	7700	14,300	27,000

Model G-14 — 6-cyl., 60 hp, 135" wb

Touring-5P	4500	4200	5200	8400	15,700	29,000
Touring-7P	4500	4000	5000	8000	15,000	28,000
Limousine-7P	5600	3700	4700	7300	13,700	26,000
Landaulet-7P	5750	3900	4800	7700	14,300	27,000
Berlin Limousine	6000	4000	5000	8000	15,000	28,000

GARICAR — Aberdeen, South Dakota — (1909) — Early in 1909 W.M. Pease of Aberdeen completed the prototype of a gasoline automobile he called a Garicar. Then he began tramping around the Midwest to find a community willing to back him in its manufacture. In March he was in Minneapolis talking with the Commercial Club about locating in that city "provided conditions are to his liking," as *The Motor World* reported. "Mr. Pease plans to erect a plant to cost $100,000," *The Horseless Age* informed readers, "and to employ 200 men at the start." Whether the conditions in Minneapolis were not to Pease's liking, or whether Pease's Garicar was not to Minneapolis' is not known. Although he may have tried other communities thereafter, Pease does not appear ever to have manufactured his Garicar.

GARLAND — The Garland Automobile Company was organized in New York City with a capital stock of $25,000 during the late summer of 1909 for the manufacture of automobiles and motors. Incorporators were G.W. Garland, Jr., G.P. Strobel and J.A. Garland. Manufacture was decided against almost immediately, and instead the firm took on the local agencies for the Velie and Speedwell, locating at 1657 Broadway.

GARNY — The Garny-Mehserle Machine & Auto Company was organized in Rochester, New York during the spring of 1909 with a capital stock of $2000 to "manufacture motors, engines, wagons, cars and vehicles of all kinds." The partners involved were George Garny and Henry Mehserle. Manufacture of an automobile is doubted.

GARRETT — Although three separate automotive manufacturing ventures were established in Garrett, Indiana during the years 1907-1910, it appears little actual manufacturing was done.
The Garrett Automobile Company was organized early in 1907 with a capital stock of $10,000 by C.J. Rollins, W.F. Mitchell and C.E. Colegrove. Manufacture was intended, but probably not realized.
The Garrett Machine Works Company at King and Guilford Streets built a highwheeler in 1909, according to the Ware yearbook of the industry that year. Details regarding it are lacking.
In early 1910 in Garrett, the Hoosier Auto Company was organized with a capital stock of $80,000 by J.A. Moore, T.C. Little, J.B. Mager, Leigh Hunt, A.C. Widmer, I.A. Gingery, W.W. Sharpless and E.C. Reyher. Again, manufacture was intended but does not seem to have been realized.

GARRISON — Dayton, Ohio — (1914) — High-grade tools, dies and special machinery represented the products of the Garrison Machine Works of Dayton, to which the firm briefly considered adding a cyclecar in 1914. A prototype is known to have been built, though details of its specifications are lacking. Garrison almost immediately decided to forgo manufacture, however.

GARSTANG — Alton, Illinois — (1899) — Ira Garstang of Alton completed his gasoline car in December of 1899. Its body was a phaeton, and Garstang claimed speeds of 30 mph and up. "Local enthusiasts and friends of the builder predict great things for the Alton production," reported *The Autobain*. But, alas, the great things would not include manufacture.

GARVIN — New York, New York — (1901) — The Garvin Machine Company at Spring and Varick streets in Lower Manhattan grew out of a bicycle emporium. Beginning in 1898 the firm refocused its activity to milling and screw machines and special and automatic machinery for automobile production. In June of 1899 *The Horseless Age* commended Garvin for its "characteristic foresight" in preparing "for the motor vehicle industry." Garvin also opened a store in Philadelphia and established a branch in Berlin, Germany. Its New York premises were advertised extensively as the perfect place for a budding inventor to perfect his invention — "Privacy If Desired," the headline read — and a good many early automobile builders took advantage of the Garvin facilities. In 1901 the Garvin people built an automobile themselves, but it was strictly an experimental project to test some of the firm's new machinery.

GARY — Muskegon, Michigan — (1909) — Alfred C. Gary, nephew of Judge Elbert Henry Gary of U.S. Steel fame, was the organizer during the summer of 1909 in Muskegon of the Gary Motor Car Company. Associated with him in this venture were James L. Maloney and William L. Simonton of Chicago. As *The Motor World* reported in July, "the company, which was secured for Muskegon by a bonus of a site and factory building, plans to produce the first of its touring cars by October and later to make motor trucks." This venture seems to have died at the prototype stage.

1909 Gary, landaulet taxi, NAHC

GARY — Chicago, Illinois — (1909) — The Gary that was built in Chicago in 1909 was a taxi. "We Build Nothing But . . .," the Gary Taxicab Company boasted in advertisements. "It's a taxicab that a professional cab driver or hackman can understand and operate as readily as he can drive a horse knowing what to do when the horse needs attention." That had to have been something of an exaggeration, though the Gary was provided with an interchangeable powerplant (18 hp gasoline engine) which presumably could be removed and a new one installed in less than twenty minutes. The coachwork of the Gary was attractive, though the stylish landaulet body provided for enclosed comfort only for the taxi occupants, not the driver. The Gary Taxicab Company's offices were at 1256 Michigan Avenue. Where the taxis themselves were built, and for precisely how long, is not known.

GARY SIX — Gary, Indiana — (1914) — During the early summer of 1914, the Gary Automobile Manufacturing Company announced its intention to manufacture a six-cylinder speedster with wire wheels and a family touring car for six passengers. Apparently the company did do just that, but for a short time only. Although *Scientific American* listed the Gary in its January 1915 issue, the car was out of production by that time. Its 135-inch wheelbase was a commodious one, and the $2300 price tag was attractive. The venture must have been dreadfully underfinanced. The people behind it were Dr. G. Pass, C.J. Flannigan and D.C. Throckmorton. Consulting engineer was E.T. Birdsall of Detroit; the prototype of the Gary had been built in that city under his direction, the small production which followed having been seen to in Gary. The Gary Motor Truck Company which was organized in Gary in 1915 probably was not related, since the officers of the two firms were dissimilar. Gary trucks were built until 1927.

1914 GARY SIX
Six — 34 hp, 135" wb

	FP	5	4	3	2	1
Touring-6P	2300	4200	5200	8400	15,700	29,000
Speedster-2P	2300	4400	5600	9200	17,300	31,000

1905 Gas-Au-Lec, touring, WLB

GAS-AU-LEC — Peabody, Massachusetts — (1905-1906) — The word Gas-au-lec was coined from "gasoline," "auxiliary" and "electric" and was, the Vaughn Machine Company of Peabody said, to be pronounced with the accent on the first and last syllables. The Gas-au-lec was a big 40/45 hp T-head four claimed to combine all advantages of gasoline, steam and electric vehicles, though it "primarily is a gasoline car." An ancillary electric motor geared to the propeller shaft was used for starting, reverse, slow speeds through traffic and added hill climbing power. Valves were electromagnetically operated and their timing could be varied by the driver. This simple engine, the Vaughn company, said, "works perfectly without a starting crank, without cam shafts, cams or tappets, and their accompanying mechanism, and without change gears." Apparently not. In 1906 Vaughn president Hamilton S. Corwin reorganized as Corwin Manufacturing Company and revised the car's name to Gasaulec. Alas, removing the hyphens didn't move sales. Total production was no more than four cars and possibly only one. The designer of the Gas-au-lec was Ralph Hood who earlier had designed the Hood/Simplex Steamer in Danvers.

1905-1906 GAS-AU-LEC
Gas-au-lec — 4-cyl., 40/45 hp. 108" wb

Touring-5P	5000	—	—	—	—	—

1928 Gas-Electric Taxicab

GAS-ELECTRIC — Philadelphia, Pennsylvania — (1928) — Gas-Electric was the only name given this experimental taxicab developed by Mitten Management engineers in 1928 for the Philadelphia Rapid Transit Company. The chassis was a Willys-Knight Model 70-A into which General Electric motors similar to those used in the P.R.T. gas-electric buses were fitted and coupled to the Knight sleeve valve engine. The special-design body featured one door on the right side and two doors on the left. Smoother and quicker acceleration and lower maintenace were among the advantages seen for this hybrid taxicab. "The new cab, demonstrated on Tam-O-Shanter hill in Fairmount Park," reported *The Commercial Car Journal*, "gained speed on the ascent with five passengers and driver on a grade on which other taxicabs were shifted into second gears." The car is not believed to have been put into production, however.

GAS ENGINE — The Gas Engine and Appurtenance Company was organized in Cleveland, Ohio during the summer of 1910 with a capital stock of $10,000 for the manufacture of gas engines, motor vehicles, motor boats and accessories. Incorporators were Andrew B. Nichols, Edward H. Sherbourne, Florence A. Lautermilch, Rob Roy Alexander and J.M. Bing. Manufacture of an automobile is doubted.

1901 Gasmobile, phaeton, HAC

GASMOBILE — New York, New York — (1899-1900)/Marion, New Jersey — (1900-1902) — The Automobile Company of America had introduced its first cars and trikes in 1899 under the names of American or American (Automobile) Voiturette, but switched to Gasmobile the year following because president John H. Flagler believed it more descriptive. In addition to Flagler, Robert L. Stevens, E.P. Kimball and Albert T. Otto were involved in this venture, as was Frederick R. Blount of the American Motor Company. The latter firm had discontinued production of its motor vehicle and now supplied the Automobile Company of America with its engine under contract. The Automobile Company of America also purchased the American rights to the French Decauville automobile, and consequently there would be both French and American influence in the Gasmobile. Alexander Fischer was the car's designer, and also the inventor of the automatic starting-device that was featured on the cars at the turn of the century. Ambition seems to have been the company's undoing. A plethora of models ensued, three-cylinder rear mounted, four-cylinder front mounted, with horsepower ranging from 9 to 25 bhp. By November 1901 a total of 140 cars had been produced. At the New York Automobile Show in January 1902, the company exhibited a six-cylinder automobile (designed by Fischer) which, if it would have been marketed, would have been the first six sold commercially in the United States. The car was produced on custom order for C.V. Brokaw, however, and was probably the only one built. In March of 1902 the company was declared in the hands of a receiver "for the purpose of adjusting its affairs." Production purportedly was in full operation. By August, alas, the Automobile Company of America plant and all property was ordered to be sold at public auction. It was, the month following, and the high bidder was one Richard Currier for $100,000, subject to two mortgages amounting to $65,000 and unpaid taxes of $3000. The Automobile Company of America's liabilities at that time were assessed at $210,000. The company's failure was not the fault of its product; by all accounts, the Gasmobile was among the more meritorious of American pioneer cars. In November 1900 it had won all contests staged for gasoline vehicles at the Automobile Club of America's show at Madison Square Garden, and in 1901 a Gasmobile won first prize in the Long Island Endurance Contest. It may not have been "the finest road carriage built in America," as the ads averred, bu the Gasmobile was assuredly one of the finer of the period. Richard Currier's plans to continue production as the Franco-American Automobile Company did not succeed. By December of 1902

1901 Gasmobile, runabout, WLB

the machinery and stock of the Automobile Company of America was purchased by the Pan-American Motor Company and was moved to Mamaroneck, New York to be used in the production of the Panam. John Flagler was a member of Pan-American's board of directors.

1899-1900 GASMOBILE
American/American Voiturette (1-cyl., 3 hp)

	FP	5	4	3	2	1
Runabout	—	—	—	—	—	—
Phaeton	—	—	—	—	—	—

1900-1901 GASMOBILE
Gasmobile — 1-cyl., 3 hp

Phaeton	—	—	—	—	—	—
Delivery	—	—	—	—	—	—
Surrey	—	—	—	—	—	—
Racer	—	—	—	—	—	—

1902 Gasmobile, Special, phaeton, WLB

1902 GASMOBILE
Three-Cylinder Chassis

Stanhope (9 hp, 71" wb)	2000	2000	3000	4200	6500	14,000
Sthp. (12 hp, 78" wb)	2500	2100	3100	4300	6800	14,500
Surrey (20 hp, 78" wb)	2500	2200	3200	4400	7000	15,000

Four-Cylinder Chassis — 88-1/2" wb

Model 4-C Touring (25 hp)	5000	2300	3300	4600	7500	16,000

Six-Cylinder Chassis — 35 hp, 88-1/2" wb

New York Show Car	—	—	—	—	—	—

GASPORT — The Gasport Motor Company was organized with a capital stock of $20,000 during the summer of 1910 to manufacture gasoline engines and motor vehicles in Gasport, New York. Incorporators were Charles W. Day, Ellis S. Button and Frances R. Day. Manufacture of an automobile is doubted.

GATE CITY — The Gate City Motor Car Company was organized in Keokuk, Iowa early in 1904 with a capital stock of $10,000 for the manufacture of automobiles. Incorporators were J.E. Baker, L.H. Ayer and E.R. Baker. Manufacture is doubted.

The Gate City Automobile Company of Fargo, North Dakota was organized during the fall of 1911 with a capital stock of $50,000 to manufacture and deal in automobiles. Incorporators were Joseph E. Fields, Fred R. Schofield and M.L. Feckler. Manufacture is doubted.

GATES — The A.J. Gates Company of Detroit, Michigan has been indicated on various car rosters as an automobile builder from 1928-1930. City directory listings indicate an A.J. Gates & Company at 616 West Milwaukee Avenue during this period, but note its activity as "electric truck manufacturers." There is no evidence of an automobile being built.

GATTS — Bethel, Ohio — (1905) — Alfred Parmer Gatts was born and died in Bethel, Ohio. His was a farming family, and he seems to have been the only member not interested in agriculture. Instead he opened a machine shop on the Gatts farm, which evolved into a garage with the advent of the automotive age. He built his first car in 1905, a high-wheeled buggy with its single-cylinder engine cranked from the rear which he sold to Leonard Moon of Mount Orab for $100. His second car he sold for $350 to Mose Brooks of Greenbush, his third to William Burkel of Amelia for $150. He built two further cars, which he kept for himself. Family members recall that he was still tinkering with automobiles in the 1950's. The garage business remained his livelihood, inventing things his source of pleasure. Alfred Parmer Gatts died in 1963 at the age of eighty. The car he built for William Burkel remains extant.

1905 Gatts, runabout, GR

GAUNTT — In 1908 Newton C. Gauntt, an architect from Yakima, Washington, built an automobile which he called the Flying Dutchman. Refer to Flying Dutchman.

GAWLEY — Aurora, Nebraska — (1895) — T.R. Gawley was a grocer from Aurora who built a two-cylinder 6 hp gasoline car in 1895. Ball bearings were used in the vehicle, which was set in a 66-inch wheelbase chassis. The front wheels measured 36 inches, the rear wheels 42 inches. "The back wheels are on a stiff axle going ahead," reported *The Horseless Age*, "but are so constructed that they can turn back, by means of a ratchet. On the back axle the ball bearings are set under the spring blocks." Gawley planned to enter the car in the Chicago Times-Herald Contest of 1895, but could not complete it on time. He also advertised for "a capitalist to take hold of his invention," stating that he guaranteed "to sell fifty machines in his own state of Nebraska, just as soon as they can be put on the market." This plan apparently went awry too.

1911 Gaylord, tourister, WLB

GAYLORD — Gaylord, Michigan — (1911-1913) — "All Roads Are Easy to the Gaylord" was the slogan of the Gaylord Motor Car Company which was incorporated during late spring of 1910 and which put its car on the market in late fall. Initially, the Gaylord was offered in one model only, a four-passenger touring car that was quickly convertible to a utility car for transporting packages or to a depot-type wagon for transporting up to eight people. Thermo-syphon cooling, a multiple disc clutch and Schlebler carburetor were featured. Though Gaylord's claim as the "Pioneer Utility Car Builders" was dubious, the company was certainly among the most ardent promoters of the idea. As many as 350 such cars may have been sold. For 1912, however, Gaylord decided to expand its line, adding three new models on a common wheelbase but with overhead-valve four-cylinder engines of varying horsepower. Conceivably the company should have stuck exclusively with its first idea. Gaylord was out of business before the end of 1913. Guy Hamilton had been the chief promoter of the Gaylord venture. In 1914 he moved to Plymouth, Michigan and tried again with the Alter.

1911 GAYLORD
Utility — 4-cyl., 35 hp, 112" wb

	FP	5	4	3	2	1
Touring-4/6/8P	1250	2200	3200	4400	7000	15,000

1912-1913 GAYLORD
Utility — 4-cyl., 35 hp, 112" wb

Touring-4/6/8P	1250	2200	3200	4400	7000	15,000

Model R — 4-cyl., 20/25 hp, 106" wb

	FP	5	4	3	2	1
Roadster-2P	1000	2300	3300	4600	7500	16,000

Model D — 4-cyl., 28/30 hp, 106" wb

	FP	5	4	3	2	1
Demi-Tonneau-4P	1150	2400	3400	4800	8000	17,000

Model S — 4-cyl., 30 hp, 106" wb

	FP	5	4	3	2	1
Roadster-2P	1250	2500	3500	5000	8500	18,000

GEARHART — Houston, Texas — (1911-1912) — Glenn D. Gearhart was the general manager of the Southern Motor Sales Company which was located at 2811 Preston Avenue and served as the Houston agency for the McIntyre automobile. For those of his clients desiring more minimal transport, Gearhart offered a gasoline-powered three-wheeler of his own design. The car was sold locally, and from 1911 to 1912 only.

1907 Gearless, touring, NAHC

GEARLESS — Rochester, New York — (1907-1909) — The Gearless Transmission Company was organized in Rochester with a capital stock of a half-million dollars in the fall of 1905 by I.L. Fairbanks, John W. Breyfogle and L.A. Burleigh. Automobile production began late in 1906. The Gearless began life as a big four-cylinder car of 50, 60 and 75 hp — with high-powered price tags to match. Friction transmission and double chain drive were common to all the cars. A 75 hp Great Six model followed for the 1908 model year, and as a Greyhound roadster, it was an impressively formidable machine. More than half its length was hood, two hoods as a matter of fact ("with the motor under one and the gearset under the other, so that either of these essentials is very accessible") and with four straps holding them down. But the Gearless Transmission Company found that its high-power, high-price policy was not producing a profit. And the firm began wondering if friction drive might not be part of its marketing problem. Consequently, in the spring of 1908, the firm was reorganized to Gearless Motor Car Company with William Bausch (of the Bausch & Lomb Optical Company), W.H. Rogers (president of the Rochester Tile & Brick Company) and George F. Roth (described as "collector of customs" in Rochester) providing additional financing. The same management remained intact. For the 1909 model year lower-powered and lower-priced fours were added to the line, with "Olympic" versions being made available with a conventional transmission. Gearless never had a chance to find out if its new marketing policy would prove workable. The company was bankrupt by the fall of 1909.

1907 GEARLESS
Model 50 — 4-cyl., 50 hp, 124" wb

	FP	5	4	3	2	1
Touring-5P	3000	3100	4200	6300	10,500	22,000

Model 60 — 4-cyl., 60 hp, 124" wb

	FP	5	4	3	2	1
Touring-7P	3250	3200	4300	6500	11,000	23,000

Model 75 — 4-cyl., 75 hp, 128" wb

	FP	5	4	3	2	1
Touring-7P	4000	3300	4400	6700	12,000	24,000

1908 GEARLESS
Four — 60 hp, 126" wb

	FP	5	4	3	2	1
Touring-5P	3500	3300	4400	6700	12,000	24,000
Greyhound Rdstr.	3500	3500	4500	7000	13,000	25,000

Great Six — 75 hp, 126" wb

	FP	5	4	3	2	1
Touring-7P	4000	3500	4500	7000	13,000	25,000
Greyhound Rdstr.	4000	3900	4800	7700	14,300	27,000

1909 GEARLESS
Four — 32/35 hp, 119" wb

	FP	5	4	3	2	1
Touring-5P	1500	3300	4400	6700	12,000	24,000
Roadster-3/4P	1500	3500	4500	7000	13,000	25,000
Olympic Tour.-5P	1650	3500	4500	7000	13,000	25,000
Olympic Rdstr.-3/4P	1650	3700	4700	7300	13,700	26,000

Four — 50 hp, 124" wb

	FP	5	4	3	2	1
Touring-7P	2750	3500	4500	7000	13,000	25,000
Cl. C. Tour.-5P	2750	3700	4700	7300	13,700	26,000
Roadster-3/4P	2750	3900	4800	7700	14,300	27,000
Olympic Tour.-7P	2750	3700	4700	7300	13,700	26,000
Olympic Cl. C. Tour.-5P	2750	3900	4800	7700	14,300	27,000
Olympic Rdstr.-3/4P	2750	4000	5000	8000	15,000	28,000

Six — 30/60 hp, 114" wb

	FP	5	4	3	2	1
Touring-7P	3250	3500	4500	7000	13,000	25,000
Cl. C. Tour.-5P	3250	3700	4700	7300	13,700	26,000
Roadster-3/4P	3250	3900	4800	7700	14,300	27,000
Olympic Tour.-7P	3250	3700	4700	7300	13,700	26,000
Olympic Cl. C. Tour.-5P	3250	3900	4800	7700	14,300	27,000
Olympic Rdstr.-3/4P	3250	4000	5000	8000	15,000	28,000

GEARLESS STEAM — Pittsburgh, Pennsylvania — (1919-1922) — Gearless Motors Corporation of Pittsburgh was organized in November of 1919 to manufacture steam cars under patents acquired by Duncan MacDonald, who became Gearless president. Chief engineer was William H. Edmundson. Also involved in the venture were Raymond R. Stearns, Frank

1922 Gearless, steam, roadster, WLB

E. McClintock, S.H. Smith and Paul Moscou. A five-passenger touring car at $2600 and a three-passenger roadster at $2650 represented the Gearless line. Either wood or wire wheels were optional. The Gearless had two individual double-acting side-valve two-cylinder steam engines. Five prototype cars had been built by November of 1920 when Duncan MacDonald resigned abruptly and moved to Garfield, Ohio to begin manufacture on his own and under his own name. Gearless was gone by 1922. Production had been minimal, but a lot of stock in the company had been parlayed. In May of 1923 four officers of Gearless were indicted for conspiracy and using the mails to defraud. A total of $1,360,000 in stock was alleged to have been sold under false representation. In January of 1924, three of the four officials were found guilty. Duncan MacDonald was among them.

1919-1923 GEARLESS STEAM
Model 4-36 — 4-cyl., 65 hp, 126" wb

	FP	5	4	3	2	1
Touring-5P	2600	—	—	—	—	—
Roadster-3P	2650	—	—	—	—	—

GEARLESS STEAMER — This was one of several designations used in 1918-1919 to refer to the steam car built in Denver, Colorado by the Peterson-Culp Gearless Steam Automobile Company. A brochure indicates the vehicle was planned to be marketed as the Super-Steamer. Refer to Super-Steamer.

GEBER — Two automobile ventures named Geber have appeared on various car rosters, and it appears that in neither case was a car ever produced.

The Geber Automobile Manufacturing Company of Pittsburgh was the first in 1904, this listing the result of the mention in *The Horseless Age* that December that the company's "automobile factory at Beatty Street and Penny Avenue . . . was destroyed by fire last week." What may have been produced there is not known, but it seems certainly not to have been an automobile. The Geber firm does not appear in the 1904 Pittsburgh and Allegheny city directory.

During the summer of 1913 the Edward F. Geber Company was organized in Wilmington, Delaware with a capital stock of $500,000 to manufacture and deal in automobiles. No Geber automobile followed.

GEER — St. Louis, Missouri — (1901) — Though in 1901 he indicated himself to be a "manufacturer and dealer in automobiles, motor cycles and bicycles," Harry R. Geer of St. Louis used four wheels only for an occasional experimental car. "The Motor Cycle Man" was how he liked to advertise himself, and his small factory at 1017 Pine Street was a thriving one. Geer brochures of the period include reference to motorcycle parts only, though the resourceful Harry was willing to "build a duplicate of the Mitchell or Indian" motorcycles for anybody desiring one. Geer was also a pretty good motorcycle racer. "He is a hard rider," *Cycle and Automobile Trade Journal* commented in 1903, "and holds the State records for 1 to 10 miles."

1919 Geiger, NAHC

GEIGER — Covington, Indiana — (1919) — The Geiger was a rakish little speedster built in 1919 by Ray Geiger of Covington. Its wheelbase was 98 inches, its tread 48 inches, its engine a Ford, its carburetor a Schebler, its front axle tubular and its rear axle purloined from a Buick. Ray Geiger built the car purely for his own enjoyment.

GEM — The Duryea GEM was the final car built by Charles E. Duryea. No more than a half-dozen were produced in 1917. Refer to Duryea.

1917 Gem, model A, touring, NAHC

GEM — Grand Rapids, Michigan — (1917-1919) — The Gem Motor Car Corporation was incorporated in December of 1917. In early January the announcement was made that authorized capitalization was $250,000, of which $150,000 was yet to be issued. The Gem would use a four-cylinder G.B.&S. engine. Initially, the company's intention was to buy the chassis (from Pontiac) and bodies (possibly from Hayes) complete and to perform only final assembly in Grand Rapids. Ultimately, Gem planned to manufacture some parts itself. Probably that point was never reached. A five-passenger touring car at $845 and a light delivery truck represented the Gem's complete model line.

1917-1919 GEM

	FP	5	4	3	2	1
Gem Four Touring	845	2500	5000	10,000	15,000	19,000
Gem Four Light Delivery	—	2000	4000	8000	12,000	14,500

GENERAL — A number of companies called General announced the forthcoming production of an automobile, but do not appear to have followed through on the promise.

The General Accumulator and Battery Company of Milwaukee, Wisconsin, organized with a capital stock of $25,000 late in 1906 to "manufacture electric automobiles and machinery." Incorporators were R.J. Fleisher, A.J.F. Uchitil and H.G. Decker.

The General Auto Company of Camden, New Jersey, organized during the summer of 1912 with a capital stock of $50,000 to manufacture and deal in automobiles. Incorporators were Frank A. Kuntz, F. Stanley Sauerman and Frank S. Mussey.

The General Automobile Company of Jersey City, New Jersey, organized in 1900 to build motor vehicles. T.J. Ryan, C.W. Hamill and A.W. Hewitt were the incorporators.

The General Automobile Company of Pittsburgh, Pennsylvania, organized early in 1911 with a capital stock of $10,000 to manufacture and deal in automobiles and other vehicles. Harry Silverman, Aaron De Roy and E.A. Burchfield were the incorporators.

The General Automobile & Repair Company which was in operation in Chicago, Illinois in 1911 and engaged in the repair of cars and other garage work, but never manufactured an automobile despite the presence of this firm on various car rosters.

The General Carriage Company of Camden, New Jersey, listed as an automobile manufacturer with the address "c/o Guaranty and Trust Company" in the Hiscox book, Horseless Vehicles, Automobiles, Motor Cycles published in 1900.

The General Carriage Company of Trenton, New Jersey, incorporated in May of 1899 with a $20 million capital stock. "The company is reputed to be backed by Richard Croker of New York," reported The Hub, "and his business partners of the New York Auto-Truck Company and the International Power Company."

The General Industrial and Manufacturing Company of Indianapolis, Indiana, capitalized at $1,000,000 early in 1912 to manufacture automobiles and motor trucks. Incorporators were T.B. Laycock, C.E. Coffin and W.J. Mooney.

The General Vehicle Company of Kerhonkson, New York, organized with a capital stock of $1,750,000 during the summer of 1906 to manufacture automobiles. B.L. Mason of East Orange (New Jersey), M.J. Duffy of Jersey City (New Jersey), C.S. Batt of Tarrytown (New York), and Philip S. Hill, Frank M. Van Wagenen, Charles H. Clark and Edward F. Magoffin of New York City were the incorporators.

The General Vehicle Company of Rotterdam, New York, organized with a capital stock of $10 million late in 1912. Incorporators were A.E. Jackson, S.L. Whitestone and J.F. Zoller.

GENERAL — New York, New York — (1900) — The General Power Company of 100 William Street in New York City was the manufacturer of the Secor kerosene engine at the turn of the century. "This engine differs from most kerosene engines in that the oil is sprayed in liquid form into the air supply, somewhat as gasoline is," noted The Horseless Age in 1900. "Combustion is said to be perfect, with no tarry deposits on the cylinder walls or head." General Power did build an automobile that year, but its purpose was to demonstrate the effectiveness of its power unit. Manufacture was not envisioned.

1903 General, runabout, NAHC

GENERAL — Cleveland, Ohio — (1902-1903) — The General Automobile and Manufacturing Company of Cleveland succeeded the Hansen Automobile Company of Cleveland simply because Rasmus Hansen wanted to expand and needed to reorganize to do it. The former single-cylinder Hansen runabout was pepped up to 8 hp, a new two-cylinder 14 hp tonneau model was added. Prices were $900 and $1000 respectively, the wheelbase was 78 inches, and the final drive by chain. General boasted that each chain was tested to a lifting capacity five times the vehicle's weight which "prevents the bare possibility of defective chains, and helps to insure a safe journey." General survived no longer than had Hansen. The new company was ready for business in September 1902. By the summer of 1903 production was up to a car a day, but dealers were complaining of slow deliveries. The necessary money to expand, which had been Hansen's reason for beginning General in the first place, went wanting because company stockholders feared retaliation by the Association of Licensed Automobile Manufacturers from whom General had tried and failed to receive a license for manufacture. The A.L.A.M. petulance in not granting the license was absurd; the General was a fine little car, and the organization a sound one. When the company went bankrupt in September 1903, twenty-five Generals remained to be completed. They were finished prior to the October sale of the General assets, which were bought by the wagon-producing Studebaker brothers of Indiana. The last Generals were immediately shipped to South Bend. Rasmus Hansen subsequently went into the construction business.

1902 GENERAL

	FP	5	4	3	2	1
General Runabout	900	2500	5000	9000	12,500	16,000
General Detachable Tonneau	1000	2800	5400	9500	13,500	17,000

1903 General Electric, touring, NAHC

GENERAL ELECTRIC — Lynn, Massachusetts — (1894-1898)/Schenectady, New York — (1902-1903) — The gigantic General Electric Company built automobiles at two different times before and after the turn of the century, these being experimental models, with production never considered. The purpose the first time around, according to the company, was to obtain "engineering data on the problem of traction over all kinds of roads." An electric carriage with a 3 hp motor was first in 1894, followed by several single-cylinder gasoline vehicles, and an electric wagonette in 1897, all of them designed by Prof. Elihu Thomson and built at the G.E. works at Lynn, Massachusetts. Electric cars were also built to the patents of Hermann Lemp of Lynn. In 1902, at the company's Schenectady, New York plant and in association with the Grant-Ferris Company of Troy, a combination gas-electric car was developed, featuring a four-cylinder gasoline engine and equipped with two electric motors so that each of the rear wheels was driven independently without the use of a differential gear. Lemp patents were also involved in this design. Early in 1903 this vehicle was given a test run between the cities of Troy and Schenectady, the driver being none other than William S. Howard, who seemed to get himself involved with most of the cars built in the Troy area. In addition, General Electric experimented with steam vehicles (usually referred to by Prof. Thomson's name) and even with liquid air propulsion during this period. At least nine, and possibly as many as eighteen, General Electric experimental cars were built, one of which (a four-cylinder steamer) remains extant.

1897 General Electric, Wagonette, NAHC

GENERAL ELECTRIC — Manyunck, Pennsylvania — (1898-1900) — On June 3rd, 1898, the General Electric Automobile Company of Philadelphia was organized, with factory in Manyunck. Chief instigator of the organization was John A. Brill of the trolley and electrical-equipment producing J.G. Brill Company. The chief feature of the General Electric was a very light battery (700 pounds, instead of the usual thousand) the patent rights to which the company secured and which allowed for a thirty-mile range between charges, a commendable distance for this early period. A doctor's dos-a-dos, a brougham and a delivery wagon were put into production. John Wanamaker was the selling agent in Philadelphia and New York, and early in 1900 was reported to be ''selling a fair number.'' Unfortuna-

1900 General Electric, runabout, MVMA

tely, within months, Brill found himself in financial hot water. In June of 1900 the reorganization committee of the company, of which Brill was not a member, announced that it was about to issue a circular calling for an assessment of four dollars a share on 50,000 shares of capital stock. ''The company owes $50,000,'' reported *The Horseless Age*, ''so that if all the shareholders pay up there will be $150,000 left for working capital.'' The shareholders didn't pay up. In July the patents of General Electric were sold at auction for $29,000 in order to satisfy the claims of creditors. James W. Cunningham of 41 Wall Street, New York City, was the purchaser. This car and company should not be confused with the far-better-known General Electric Company which also produced cars during this period, though only experimentally.

GENESEE — Batavia, New York — (1911) — The Genesee was a big car. Indeed, its producers bragged in 1911 that its 148-inch wheelbase made it the longest car in America by some two inches. Its wheels were 48 inches in diameter; its six-cylinder 564-cubic-inch engine developed 96 horsepower. The Genesee was a seven-passenger touring car, painted and upholstered in black with gold trimming and, according to the Batavia *Daily News* of September 18th, 1911, was fitted with ''$200 worth of leather alone.'' In road tests in the Batavia area, the Genesee put up a speed of 75 mph. ''It is possible that the automobile will be placed on exhibition at the County Fair,'' the *Daily News* advised. ''If there is a demand for such automobiles, the manufacture may be begun in Batavia.'' There

1912 Genesee, 8-pass. torpedo touring, WLB

was no such demand, the Genesee was really too big and cumbersome to be practical. The automotive trade press was informed of the impending organization of a Genesee Motor Company, and announcement was made of five varying body styles to be provided with price tags of from $7000 to $10,000, but the only Genesee ever built was the first one. The men behind the car were O.E. Bray and Dr. Harvey Burkhart of Batavia and fre-mont Clemens of Pavilion. Dr. Burkhart was a young dentist who had set up his office in Batavia following graduation from dental school. In 1915, when Batavia became a city, he was its first mayor. Dr. Burkhart drove the Genesee for a number of years. The car remains extant, owned by a collector in the Midwest.

GENESSEE — Rochester, New York — (1904) — E.A. Keenan was a member of the law firm of Murphy, Keenan & Keenan in Rochester, and in January 1904 he established the Genessee Auto Company for the manufacture of a 12 hp touring car and light runabout to sell for $500. Engines were supplied by Henry Trebert, across town in Rochester. By 1905, it appears, Keenan had decided that the practice of law was considerably more profitable than the manufacture of automobiles.

GENEVA — The Geneva Automobile Company was organized during the summer of 1906 with a capital stock of $15,000 to manufacture automobiles in Geneva, New York, Incorporators were A.G. Lewis, L.G. Hoskins and John W. Mellen, all of Geneva.

Although initially the name Geneva was considered for the taxi built in the Geneva, Ohio factory which formerly had seen the production of the Geneva steam car, the cab which was ultimately built there from 1908-1911 was marketed under the name of Ewing. Refer to Ewing.

1901 Geneva, steam runabout, HAC

GENEVA STEAM — Geneva, Ohio — (1901-1904) — The Geneva Automobile & Manufacturing Company stood ready ''to demonstrate to any unbiased mind'' that its steam car was the best that ''inventive genius and mechanical skill can produce.'' Its two-cylinder marine-type engine connected directly to the differential, and there was a combination water tube and tubular boiler. The Geneva Automobile & Manufacturing Company was an outgrowth of the Geneva Cycle Company which had been established in 1894. J.A. Carter was president, one A. Thompson the chief engineer. The first Geneva steamer rolled out of the factory on May 9th, 1901, the car later that year taking part in the New York to Buffalo run that was cut short by the assassination of President McKinley, and being exhibited at Madison Square Garden in New York City in December. In October of 1902 the Geneva venture was given a terrific publicity boost when a special-built Geneva racer, which looked rather like a Franklin stove on wheels, was raced at Grosse Pointe, Michigan and in varying events won sprints against a White Steamer and proved faster than a Winton, being bettered that day only by the Ford 999 driven by Barney Oldfield. Thereafter the Geneva store in Cleveland (which also marketed the Rambler and Yale gasoline cars) sold thirty of its steamers within the next six months. This attracted considerable attention in Cleveland, and there seemed to be the promise of additional financing available from wealthy Cleveland circles. The town of Geneva had a population of about 2342 people at that time and could not itself support a major manufacturing effort. With new backing from Cleveland financiers, Geneva's commercial success seemed assured, but unfortunately assurances deceived because the financing didn't come through. The Geneva was exhibited at Macy's Exhibition Hall at Herald Square in New York City in January 1904, but the marque simply disappeared soon after that. Later in 1904 the plant and machinery of the Geneva Automobile and Manufacturing Company were sold to the Colonial Brass Company. Probably no more than twenty to thirty Geneva steamers were built in any single year, at least one of which survives, in the collection of the Henry Ford Museum.

1901-1902 GENEVA STEAM

	FP	5	4	3	2	1
Model A Steam Runabout	—	2300	3300	4600	7500	16,000
Model B Steam Runabout	—	2300	3300	4600	7500	16,000
Model C Steam Runabout	—	2300	3300	4600	7500	16,000
Model D Steam Touring	—	2350	3400	4700	7800	16,500
Steam Dos-a-Dos	—	2350	3400	4700	7800	16,500
Steam Light Delivery	—	2200	3200	4400	7000	15,000

1903 Geneva, steam runabout, NAHC

1903 GENEVA STEAM

Steam Runabout (4/6 hp)	900	2300	3300	4600	7500	16,000
Steam Surrey (4/6 hp)	1200	2350	3400	4700	7800	16,500
Steam Tonneau (10 hp)	—	2350	3400	4700	7800	16,500

1904 GENEVA STEAM

Style G Runabout	1250	2400	3400	4800	8000	17,000
Syle F Tonneau	1750	2400	3400	4800	8000	17,000

1903 Geneva, steam tonneau, NAHC

GENEVA — Geneva, Indiana — (1914) — In 1914 the Geneva Auto Specialty & Repair Company built a cyclecar to the designs of W.B. Hey, also of Geneva, which subsequently became a familiar sight on the roads of Adams and Jay counties. "It has regular automobile wheels, and weighs about 800 pounds," *The American Cyclecar* reported that summer. "The motor was taken from a Cadillac automobile and placed in the new frame. The tread is narrow, and the wheelbase is shorter than that of other machines. The bed is low, and the seats are of the tandem style." With the Cadillac engine, the Geneva cyclecar must have been among the speediest built in 1914. The Geneva company and Hey indicated plans to collaborate on the building of several more cyclecars that year, but whether they did indeed do so has not been documented.

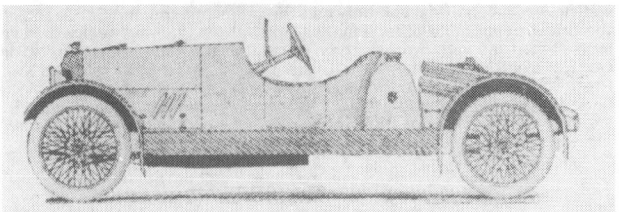

1917 Geneva, 2-pass. roadster, WLB

GENEVA — Harvey, Illinois — (1916-1917) — Fresh from his failure with the New Era car in Joliet, Forrest J. Alvin showed up in Harvey to try again. His base this time was the Owen-Schoeneck Company of Chicago which had been organized in 1914 by John L. Owen and George Schoeneck to manufacture and sell automobiles. A few four-cylinder cars had followed for the 1914-1915 model years, marketed under the initials O-S, and a six had been developed as well for 1916, but by now John Owen had wearied of the business, leaving George Schoeneck bereft until Forrest Alvin came along. The venture was renamed the Schoeneck Company, Alvin was its president, and the six-cylinder car which had been planned as an O-S would now be marketed as a Geneva. Although Schoeneck's engineering credentials — including work with Renault in France and Palmer & Singer in New York — were widely bruited, the task he had designing the O-S-cum-Geneva had been a simple one. It was an assembled car throughout, with Herschell-Spillman engine, Brown-Lipe transmission and disc clutch, and Timken axle — and carried the same $2350 price tag as the O-S had. The Geneva did not survive 1917.

GENEVA — Geneva, New York — (1920-1921) — The Geneva Wagon Company was incorporated in 1894 and moved into the plant formerly occupied by the Pierce, Butler & Pierce Company. In 1899 the firm built its first experimental gasoline-powered road wagon, although the horsedrawn trade occupied the firm's production activity for the following decade. In 1910 the company took up truck manufacture. According to a history of the city of Geneva published in 1912, the Geneva Wagon Company was then producing "auto wagons, light and medium express wagons, panel top delivery wagons, ambulances and wagonettes." The officers of the firm were M.F. Blaine as president, C.G. Blaine as vice-president and R.M. Johnson as secretary-manager. Not until 1920 was a passenger car built. It was an assembled automobile, with a six-cylinder Herschell-Spillman engine, a four-speed transmission, and a floating rear axle. The wheelbase was 139 inches, the price $2300. The Geneva car may have represented a last-ditch effort to save the company. If it was, it failed. By early 1921 production of both the Geneva car and the Geneva truck ceased.

GENEVIEVE — The Genevieve was one of a number of kit cars produced by the Neustadt-Perry Company of St. Louis, Missouri during 1903. Refer to Neustadt.

GEOMETRIC — The Geometric Drill Company of Westville, Connecticut was indicated as an automobile manufacturer in the Hiscox book *Horseless Vehicles, Automobiles, Motor Cycles* published in 1900. Further documentation is lacking.

1909 George White, NAHC

GEORGE WHITE — Rock Island, Illinois — (1909) — The George White Buggy Company was one of the largest in the Middle West, and the fact that it decided to enter the automobile industry is not at all surprising, although that it waited until so late and then gave up so easily is. Initial announcement of the venture came in early spring of 1909 and, though a highwheeler was the product, the company initially decided that its market should be urban, nearby Chicago specifically. The George White (sometimes referred to simply as the White) was a two-seater buggy, powered by a two-cylinder engine, with friction transmission and 36-inch wheels in front, 38 in the rear. Shaft drive and magneto ignition were progressive features for a buggy type, but there could be no denying that the George White would have been more comfortably at home on country roads. Although in July of 1909 the company said that it "will take up and push this work vigorously," it would seem that the push ended before 1909 did. There is no evidence that the George White automobile was built in 1910.

GERDE — Sacred Heart, Minnesota — (1901) — Early in 1901 Albert Gerde of Sacred Heart purchased all the components necessary to build an automobile. "He wants the distinction of having made the first in the neighborhood as well as the experience he will gain in building it," reported *The Motor Age* in February. Having earned that distinction, Albert Gerde is not believed to have built another car.

1902 German-American, runabout, NAHC

GERMAN-AMERICAN — New York, New York — (1902-1903) — The German American Automobile Company was born on January 22nd, 1902 and died on January 21st, 1903. Its president was William N. Beach, who was also president of the Lawrenceville Cement Company. Its superintendent was John L. Schultz, an immigrant who had formerly worked for what was described as the "Daimler-Mercedes Company" in Germany. Its general manager was James MacNaughton. The first car was completed in February 1902. It followed German lines, but with special features designed especially for American drivers and American conditions. The four-cylinder engine developed 24 hp, a lever locking device was added to the transmission in order to make it "impossible to strip gears," and all chassis parts were made double-strength to endure pounding on the roads. The company was not six months old when internal management difficulties arose. Among the creditors petitioning German-American into insolvency in late September of 1902 were James MacNaughton for four months' back salary ($1708) and John Schultz for the two months he hadn't been paid ($425). Apparently the problems were ameliorated somewhat, for the company struggled on awhile. Following the declaration of irrevocable bankruptcy in January 1903, James MacNaughton made an attempt to resurrect the marque. He failed, though several years later, he did produce another car called the Hercules Electric in Buffalo. This German American Company is not to be confused, incidentally, with the German-American Motor Wagon Company of St. Louis, Missouri which was briefly in the commercial vehicle field prior to the turn of the century.

1918 Geronimo, touring, NAHC

GERONIMO — Enid, Oklahoma — (1917-1920) — The Geronimo Motor Company was Enid, Oklahoma's first sizable manufacturing plant, and it promised to be a fine success from the beginning. Capitalized at $500,000, the company was financed mostly by enthusiastic local bankers. Will C. Allen was president, Robert Clark vice-president, Guy E. Darland secretary and treasurer. To manage the factory, Allen invited J. Tom Brewer from Jones Motor Company in Wichita, Kansas. The Geronimo, named of course for the famous Indian chief, was introduced for 1917 as a Lycoming-engined four (not unlike the Tulsa Four that was also an Oklahoma product), but quickly following for 1918 was a Rutenber-engined six (which was similar to the Jones Six of Wichita). Also arriving from Geronimo was a worm-drive one-ton truck priced at $1195 and a four-wheel drive tractor that "will do the work of six horses." The Geronimo's initial problem was poor timing. At the stockholders' meeting in January 1919, the company officers lamented that, according to the next day's edition of *Enid Events*, "the factory was only able to manufacture a limited number of cars owing to the fact that the government restricted the number which they were permitted to manufacture, and also on account of the difficulty in getting materials on account of the various restrictions on the same." One E.J. Masemore replaced Darland as company secretary/treasurer at

that meeting, but this may have been because Guy Darland was anxious to take the Geronimo racing. In July 1919 he narrowly missed winning the 300-mile cross country endurance race at Stockton, California, a burnt-out bearing forty-two miles from the finish resulting in his finishing the event on five cylinders and in eighth place. Guy Darland was subsequently made sales manager, and undoubtedly it was he who was responsible for such catchy slogans as "Power to loan your neighbor" and "Speed you'll never dare to use." This was perhaps overdoing it, since a Geronimo's top speed was about 50 mph, but it was a durable automobile and a classy looking one too. All Geronimos were open cars, colorfully painted, some models sporting wire wheels (a $55 option). Although about a hundred Geronimos were exported to France, and bore emblems reading "Wing," most Geronimos stayed home and wore the Indian chief badge. Total Geronimo production may have been as many as 600 units. What stopped the Geronimo assembly line was a fire in August 1920. Just shortly before, Will Allen had borrowed money for the buying of parts and machinery to expand production. Plant loss was estimated to be $250,000. Will Allen sadly told reporters at the scene that the company was insured for only $65,000.

1917 GERONIMO
Model 4-A-40 — 4-cyl., 37 hp, 114" wb

	FP	5	4	3	2	1
Touring-5P	895	2500	3500	5000	8500	18,000

1918 GERONIMO
Model 6-A-45 — 6-cyl., 45 hp, 122" wb

Touring-7P	1295	3000	4000	6000	9500	21,000
Roadster-2P	1295	3100	4200	6300	10,500	22,000

1919 GERONIMO
Model 6-A-45 — 6-cyl., 45 hp, 122" wb

Touring-5P	1550	3000	4000	6000	9500	21,000
Touring-7P	1595	3000	4000	6000	9500	21,000
Chummy Rdstr.-4P	1550	3100	4200	6300	10,500	22,000
Roadster-2P	1550	3100	4200	6300	10,500	22,000

1920 GERONIMO
Model 6-A-45 — 6-cyl., 45 hp, 123" wb

Touring-5P	1995	3100	4200	6300	10,500	22,000
Touring-7P	1995	3000	4000	6000	9500	21,000
Roadster-2P	1995	3200	4300	6500	11,000	23,000
Speedster-2P	1995	3500	4500	7000	13,000	25,000

GERSIX — Although the Gersix has been indicated on various rosters as a West Coast built automobile circa 1920, no such car ever was built. Edward E. Gerlinger had organized a company for vehicle manufacture in Tacoma in 1916, but its sole product was to be a truck, the introduction of which wartime materials shortages delayed until 1920. Gersix truck production was limited. By 1921 Edward Gerlinger was a truck dealer in San Francisco.

GEYER — The Geyer Sales Company was organized early in 1911 in Dayton, Ohio with a capital stock of $75,000 to "manufacture and deal in automobiles and supplies and aeroplanes and accessories." Incorporators were Carl F. Geyer, Frank C. Vail, J. Carl Horton, Harry S. Snyder and F.S. Carnes. Manufacture of an automobile is doubted.

GEYLER — In 1909 the Louis Geyler Company was incorporated in Chicago with a capital stock of $60,000 for the manufacture of automobiles. Louis Geyler, L.R. Geyler and Joseph L. McNab were the people involved, and they set themselves up in business at 100 Washington Street. No manufacture followed, the firm instead becoming an agency for Stevens-Duryea, and adding Hudson to its line in 1910. Manufacture was contemplated again in 1915 when Louis Geyler moved to Peoria and reorganized there, though again only a dealership followed.

1917 Ghent, touring, WLB

GHENT — Chicago, Illinois — (1916-1917)/Ottawa, Illinois — (1917-1918) — The Ghent Motor Company was organized in Chicago in late 1916 by C.A. Ghent. Only prototypes were built in Chicago, with the firm moving to the corner of Lafayette and Clinton streets in Ottawa in 1917, by which time Ormus L. Brockett had become president. The Ghent was a typical assembled car of the period, though the company behind it was somewhat atypical in changing its mind so quickly about the engines that should power its automobile. For 1917 both a four and a V-8 were offered, for 1918 Ghent decided to split the difference and offer just a six. Neither plan worked very well. In January of 1919 the factory of the defunct Ghent Motor Company in Ottawa was sold for $5382.

609

Model 4-30 — 4-cyl., 23 hp, 120" wb

	FP	5	4	3	2	1
Touring-5P	750	—	—	—	—	—

Model 8-40 — 8-cyl., 22 hp, 120" wb

Touring-5P	1050	—	—	—	—	—

1918 GHENT
Model 6-60 — 6-cyl., 23.5 hp, 125" wb

Sedan-7P	2475	—	—	—	—	—
Touring-7P	1875	—	—	—	—	—

GIBBS — The American Tractor Company was organized in Newark, New Jersey during the early spring of 1901 and leased a plant formerly occupied by the Gates Carpet Works in Elizabethport. The company's stated purpose was the building of steam vehicles designed by William E. Gibbs, and it would appear that the few built were all heavy duty trucks.

GIBBS — **Glendale, New York** — **(1904)** — Although the Gibbs Engineering & Manufacturing Company of Long Island has frequently been cited as a producer of automobiles, it is doubtful that a car for less than forty passengers was ever built. Apparently the company was an outgrowth of the North American Air Motor Company which had been organized in 1899 to develop the automotive ideas of Lucius Gibbs, a New York mechanical engineer. In addition to the forty-passenger sight-seeing car produced for a Colorado touring company, Gibbs built a heavy-duty truck with drive to the rear wheels by double chain and the power unit mounted behind the rear wheels. But it would seem the company placed more hope for financial success in its 1500-pound "largest automobile cooler ever made" that was designed for a trackless train to be used for hauling borax out of Death Valley. In December 1904 Gibbs Engineering was forced into bankruptcy by an involuntary petition of creditors.

GIBSON — The John G. Gibson Company was organized in Buffalo, New York during the spring of 1909 with a $20,000 capital stock to manufacture automobiles and motors. Incorporators were J.N. Gregory, J.G. Gibson and George Roughead, Jr. Manufacture of an automobile is doubted.

The Gibson Motor Car Company was organized early in 1913 as a $3 million Delaware corporation to manufacture motor cars in Pittsburgh, Pennsylvania. Incorporators were C.E. Gibson, I.H. Mahoney and E.D. Johnson. Manufacture of an automobile is doubted. This incorporation had been preceded in 1910 by the Cecil E. Gibson Motor Car Company which planned to produce automobiles in Indianapolis. That venture went nowhere too.

1899 Gibson, NAHC

GIBSON — **Jersey City, New Jersey** — **(1899)** — No inventor could have asked for a more favorable review than that accorded Charles D.P. Gibson by the editors of *The Horseless Age*. Gibson was a chemist and mechanical engineer from Jersey City and he spent three years and, purportedly, thousands of dollars perfecting his "lightest engine of the power ever built." It was a two-cylinder unit, weighed only thirty-two pounds, developed twelve horsepower and ran on carbonic acid gas stored in batteries which were built for Gibson by the Cooper Chemical Company of Newark and were tested by him to a pressure of 6000 p.s.i. Because the patents he had applied for "in all foreign countries" had not yet been granted, Gibson was naturally loath to discuss his "most remarkable achievement." The vehicle in which he fitted his achievement was a two-place stanhope, which purportedly could travel sixty miles an hour. Had the car indeed been able to do that, probably more would have been heard of it. As it happened, although there was talk of a syndicate being formed for manufacture, the Gibson was out of the automotive picture almost as quickly as its alleged top speed. When last heard from later in 1899, Charles Gibson had taken his car to Rome, New York for further experimentation there.

GIDDINGS & STEVENS — **Rockford, Illinois** — **(1900-1901)** — G.M. Giddings and R.C. Stevens were mechanical engineers who built gasoline engines in Rockford. In 1900 they styled themselves as the Giddings & Stevens Motor Vehicle Company and announced their forthcoming entry into the automobile industry to the trade press. A runabout fitted with their two-cylinder gasoline engine was displayed at the Chicago Automobile Show that year. The year following, Giddings visited the De Mooy brothers in Cleveland, who were personal friends and who were also building their own automobile. The brothers pronounced the Giddings & Stevens' car "a success in every way except in a few minor details." Apparently these were the company's undoing. The Giddings and Stevens business appeared only once in the Rockford city directories of the period, in the 1900-1901 edition.

GIFFORD-PETTIT — **Chicago, Illinois** — **(1907-1908)** — Although the Gifford-Pettit Manufacturing Company of Chicago was organized with capital stock of $10,000 in May of 1907 for the purpose of building automobiles to the designs of A.F. Feldt, it would appear that Feldt had a quick change of mind regarding the vehicles he wanted to build. His first car was a truck, with a four-cylinder 35 hp engine and a three-ton capacity. It was designated the Model A. There was no Model B, either car or truck. The company was quickly out of business.

1902 Gilbert, runabout, NAHC

GILBERT — **St. Joseph, Missouri** — **(1902)** — The runabout built by C.S. Gilbert of St. Joseph was powered by a single-cylinder 6 hp engine noteworthy for its very short stroke (5½-inch bore, 4½-inch stroke). This permitted, he said, "high rotative speed without excessive piston speed." A three-speed selective transmission was fitted. All machinery of the Gilbert was attached to the angle iron frame, not to the body which was claimed removable in one minute "by taking off four nuts." Although C.S. Gilbert announced his intention to proceed into manufacture of this car, the evidence suggests that he was not able to do this.

GILBERTSON — **Milnor, North Dakota** — **(1912)** — In 1912 Ole B. Gilbertson of Milnor built an automobile for himself. Other than the fact that its gasoline engine developed 16 hp and its body style was described as a "Belfuse," nothing further is known about it.

GILL — **Portland, Oregon** — **(1908)** — "Building automobiles in Oregon did not pay," lamented A.J. Gill in the early fall of 1909 when he announced that he had sold out his A.J. Gill Company of Portland and joined an automobile dealership instead. The one car he built was a twelve-passenger machine for the Deschutes Irrigation Company which was produced at a loss to himself as well as a subsequent loss for Deschutes. The plan was to use the vehicle for transport on an 80-mile oiled road between Shanike and Bend. The problem was the road built by Deschutes over which the car was to travel. "The roadway made by the company proved a failure," Gill reported. "The sand was so deep that at many places the automobile was stalled, and it was impracticable to put enough oil on the roadway to make it hard." The Gill car was driven about 2000 miles before the Deschutes company gave up on the idea.

GILLETTE — The Gillette Athletic Goods Corporation was organized in Hartford, Connecticut early in 1903 with a capital stock of $3000 to manufacture and deal in motorcycles and automobiles. Company officers were Norman Gillette, Harrison B. Freeman, Jr. and John J. McKone as president/treasurer, vice-president and secretary respectively. Manufacture of an automobile is doubted.

GILLETTE — **Mishawaka, Indiana** — **(1916)** — In mid-1916 William Gillette strode into the factory in Mishawaka which had successively seen the production of the American Simplex and the Amplex. The purchase price of the Amplex assets included designs for a sleeve-valve-engined car which had been proposed for production in 1913 but had never made it. Gillette was intrigued — and bought. Possibly he did have a prototype car run up with the sleeve-valve-engine installed, but almost immediately decided to concentrate production on the engine alone, which was called a Wilmo after its inventor M.L. Williams of South Bend. The Gillette Motor Company was organized for production of the Wilmo engine, but by December of 1917 was bankrupt. Thereon William Gillette returned to the business he knew best: making razors.

GILLILAND — The D.C. Gilliland Manufacturing & Auto Supply Company was organized in St. Louis, Missouri early in 1915 with a capital stock of $8000 and the plan to ''manufacture, sell, repair and deal in automobiles.'' Incorporators were David C. Gilliland, Elmo P. Orner and F. Spoeneman. Manufacture of a car is doubted.

GILLINGHAM — The Gillingham Automobile and Supply Company was organized in Newark, New Jersey late in 1906 with a capital stock of $100,000 for the manufacture of automobiles and parts. Incorporators were G.O. Gillingham and F.W. Sanford of New York City, and G.W. Porter of Newark. Manufacture of an automobile is doubted.

GILLIS — The Gillis Strickland Motor Company was organized in Rochester, New York during the summer of 1909 for the manufacture of automobiles. Capital stock was $25,000. Incorporators were J.W. Gillis of Pittsford, New York, and S.M. Havens and R.H. Strickland of Rochester. Manufacture is doubted.

GILMORE — **Detroit, Michigan** — **(1904)** — In 1904 George A. Gilmore changed the name of his cycle shop at 1174 Fort Street West in Detroit to the Gilmore Motor Works. ''Manufacturers of automobiles and bicycles, models, tools, dies and general repairing'' read his new city directory advertisement. The number of cars he built must have been small, though conceivably his shop may have built them to customer order for a number of years following. In 1913 he incorporated the Gilmore Motor Manufacturing Company in Detroit with a capital stock of $35,000, but his venture was for engine building only.

GILMORE — **Philadelphia, Pennsylvania** — **(1908)** — In 1907 William Gilmore of 262 North Broad Street in Philadelphia secured the agency for the Deere car manufactured in Moline, Illinois. By the end of 1907 the John Deere people had decided to get out of the automobile-manufacturing business, which left William Gilmore without a car to sell. References from late 1907 indicate that Gilmore then moved into manufacture himself of a highwheeler. Details regarding the Gilmore motor buggy are lacking, but Gilmore obviously did not produce it long. Nor apparently did he acquire the agency for the Midland which succeeded the Deere.

GILMORE ELECTRIC — **Boston, Massachusetts** — **(1905)** — E.A. Gilmore operated a garage and machine shop on Columbus Avenue in Boston where he built a few electric cars in 1905. Most likely, these were to specific customer order. By 1906 he had removed his machine shop to Park Square where he continued in operation as a charging station and garage only.

1900 Githens, steam runabout, NAHC

GITHENS — **Cleveland, Ohio** — **(1900)/Chicago, Illinois** — **(1902)** — At the most, there were two automobiles built bearing the name Githens, and but a single example of each. The first was a steam car put together by former bicycle racer Herbert A. Githens in collaboration with C.M. Raymond in Cleveland in 1900. It used a two-cylinder reversible Mason steam engine and a water-tube boiler of the partners' own design. Although somewhat heavier and longer, the Githens steam runabout was typical for its day. Manufacture was not considered. Herbert Githens at the time was manager of the Cleveland branch store of the American Bicycle Company. In 1902, in Chicago, his brother Walter L. Githens organized Githens Brothers, Inc. with a capital stock of $30,000 for the manufacture of automobiles. Though brother Herbert was involved, he did not immediately move to Chicago, but remained with his job in Cleveland. Among the other people associated in the Chicago company was James Levy, formerly of the Electric Vehicle Company. It is possible that a prototype electric car was completed, but Walter Githens quickly concluded that dealing in automobiles was preferable to manufacturing them. Agencies for Cook County were secured for the Waverley electric and the Toledo steam and gasoline automobiles. Subsequently the full line of the International Motor Car Company was taken on, and by the end of 1903 brother Herbert had joined Walter L. Githens at their dealership at 1412 Michigan Avenue in Chicago.

G & J — The initials represent R. Phillip Gormully and Thomas B. Jeffery. The cars their company produced in Chicago prior to the turn of the century were designed by Jeffery and his son and were referred to as G & J only in the trade press. Jeffery himself preferred the name Rambler, the designation used for the bicycles manufactured by the Gormully-Jeffery partnership. Refer to Rambler.

1912 G.J.G., Junior, runabout, WLB

G.J.G. — **White Plains, New York** — **(1909-1914)** — The initials stood for George John Grossman who was the designer of the car and the president of the G.J.G. Motor Car Company of White Plains which grew out of the Mammoth Garage (which was that) he had built there in 1907 when he was New York agent for Cadillac sales. The G.J.G. venture was apparently launched in order for Grossman to provide his two sons something interesting to do; Grossman's wife Matilda was among the firm's incorporators, so obviously she approved as well. The G.J.G. was a four-cylinder automobile for the whole of its life, and it was offered in a variety of body styles with such catchy designations as Pirate, Scout, Comfort and Carryall. Styling was rather imaginative too. A cone clutch and three-speed selective transmission was standard throughout the line, and the speedster model was said to be capable of 65 mph. In 1910, G.J.G. also produced the Allen-Kingston Junior (a virtual copy of the G.J.G. Junior) for Walter J. Allen of New York City. In September of 1913, George Grossman revealed to *The Motor World* that ''there are better places than White Plains for the manufacture of motor cars'' and indicated that he had leased his factory there to a publishing company and was about to seek a new location for his firm in the Midwest. He also indicated that he had never made any money in his automobile-building venture, which was no surprise to *The Motor World* because, as the magazine commented, it had been a matter of speculation for some time ''how much longer he would continue to pour money into the enterprise.'' Ultimately, he changed his mind about continuing in the automobile manufacturing business altogether, and instead of searching out an amenable location in the Midwest, he used a small corner of the White Plains plant to finish up parts on hand with the assembly of a few speedster models in early 1914.

1909-1911 G.J.G.
Four — 26 hp, 104" wb

	FP	5	4	3	2	1
Junior Tour.-5P	1000	3100	4200	6300	10,500	22,000
Four — 36.1 hp, 121" wb						
Pirate Rdstr.-2P	2500	3500	4500	7000	13,000	25,000
Scout Tour.-4P	2500	3400	4500	6900	12,500	24,500
Comfort Tour.-5P	2500	3500	4500	7000	13,000	25,000
Carryall Tour.-7P	2750	3200	4300	6500	11,000	23,000
1912 G.J.G.						
Junior — 4-cyl., 26 hp, 104" wb						
Raceabout-2P	1000	3000	4000	6000	9500	21,000
Runabout-2P	1125	2900	3700	5600	9100	20,000
Fore-Door Rbt.-2P	1175	3100	4200	6300	10,500	22,000
Touring-5P	1250	3100	4200	6300	10,500	22,000

Senior — 4-cyl., 42 hp, 121" wb

	FP	5	4	3	2	1
Speedster-2P	2500	3500	4500	7000	13,000	25,000
Pirate Rbt.-2P	2500	3300	4400	6700	12,000	24,000
Scout Gunboat-4P	2500	3300	4400	6700	12,000	24,000
Comfort Tour.-5P	2500	3500	4500	7000	13,000	25,000

1913 G.J.G.
Junior — 4-cyl., 26 hp, 104" wb

Raceabout-2P	1000	3000	4000	6000	9500	21,000
Runabout-2P	1125	3000	4000	6000	9500	21,000
Fore-Door Rbt.-2P	1175	3100	4200	6300	10,500	22,000
Touring-5P	1250	3100	4200	6300	10,500	22,000

Senior — 4-cyl., 42 hp, 121" wb

Speedster	2500	3500	4500	7000	13,000	25,000
Pirate Rbt.	2500	3300	4400	6700	12,000	24,000
Scout Gunboat-4P	2500	3300	4400	6700	12,000	24,000
Comfort Tour.-5P	2500	3500	4500	7000	13,000	25,000

1914 G.J.G.
Four — 36 hp, 121" wb

Speedster-2P	2500	3500	4500	7000	13,000	25,000

1910 Gleason, touring, NAHC

GLEASON — Kansas City, Missouri — (1909-1913) — The Gleason followed the automobiles named Caps and Kansas City into the same Missouri factory. The firm building the Gleason was called Kansas City Vehicle Company, and it was among the last highwheeler manufacturers to enter the field. A shaft-drive, two-cylinder motor buggy with a lovely brass radiator was designed and put on the production line in 1909 where it was built unchanged for the next four years. A truck also was manufactured. Although pneumatic tires were later made available, the company stuck with the highwheeler idea to the end. When the end came for the Gleason, the Kansas City Vehicle Company sold out to Bauer Machine Works whose founders thought they had a better idea for success. It was a cyclecar.

1909-1913 GLEASON
Gleason — 2-cyl., 20 hp, 95" wb

Model K High Wheel Buggy	950	2000	3000	4200	6500	14,000
Model L High Wheel Rbt.	970	2100	3100	4300	6800	14,500
Model M High Wheel Baby Tonneau	1000	2100	3100	4300	6800	14,500
Model Q Baby Tonneau	1125	2200	3200	4400	7000	15,000

GLENS FALLS — The Glens Falls Automobile Company was organized during the spring of 1908 for the manufacture of motor cars and motors in Glens Falls, New York. Behind this $20,000 venture were W. Irving Griffing, Edward F. Irish and Winifred S. Harris. A three-story garage was to be built on Glens Street, according to *The Motor Age*, "on the site now occupied by Arthur Denton's second-hand store." Manufacture of an automobile is doubted.

GLENWOOD — Youngstown, Ohio — (1922) — The Glenwood Motor Car Company was a five-million-dollar corporation organized in early 1922 and backed by a number of prominent Cleveland businessmen. Among them was B.J. Cline (formerly of Pierce-Arrow and Chandler) as president, T.D. Lamb (president of the Hess Body Company) as treasurer, Capt. R.L. Queisser as secretary. Another director of the firm was William H. Graham, who was described as "a well known florist." By March a fifteen-acre tract of land in Youngstown had been purchased, upon which a factory was to be erected. According to an article in *Motor Age* that month, "The company has under control an engine, which has developed what are said to be unusual features, but for the present Cline had no announcement to make about the car." Apparently, he never did. Possibly the prototype was completed.

GLIDE — Peoria, Illinois — (1903-1920) — J.B. Bartholomew was a producer of peanut and coffee roasters from Peoria who built his first gasoline automobile in 1901 which he named for himself. He tinkered with it for the two years following but upon deciding to go into manufacture, he changed his vehicle's name to Glidemobile. By 1904 it had become simply the Glide. It looked rather like Henry Leland's Cadillac. Motorized peanut roasters and popcorn poppers became a lucrative sideline business to the Glide passenger cars, and in 1905 *Automobile Review* extolled J.B. Bartholomew at length as the first in the industry "to provide an independent mounting of the power plant from the body for the purpose of disconnecting the vibration of the machinery from the seat for carrying the passengers." Like many manufacturers beginning in business with a single-cylinder runabout, the Bartholomew Company quickly added a two of its own manufacture, then supplemented with four- and six-cylinder models powered by Rutenber engines. Production for 1908 was 200 cars, a high

mark for the company; from 1916 all Glides were sixes. Although output was never high by mass-production standards, the Glide was distinguished by comparative longevity in the automobile industry, and reportedly the Bartholomew Company was responsbile for launching Wheeler-Schebler into business by giving that company its first carburetor order. (Bartholomew was a heavy investor in the Avery Company, a major producer of farm machinery, too.) Catchy slogans were a mark of the Glide. J.B.'s brother O.Y. Bartholomew, who had charge of sales and advertising from the beginning, was largely responsible for that. "Ride in a Glide and Then Decide" and similar word-play with the marque name was rife. Especially effective, one suspects, was "The Chauffeur's Choice, the Owner's Pride, the Dealer's Opportunity." But one wonders about the merit of "A Hill Climber Built in the Hills," especially anyone aware of the terrain in Peoria. Though many of its streets have a fair amount of tilt, Peoria is not the Catskills nor the Berkshires from whence came other automobile companies using similar slogans considerably more effectively.

1903 Glidemobile, runabout, NAHC

1903 GLIDE
Glidemobile — 1-cyl., 6 hp, 72" wb

	FP	5	4	3	2	1
Runabout-2P	750	2450	3500	4900	8300	17,500

"THE GLIDE" With Stanhope Seat and Top

1904 Glide, style A, runabout, HAC

1904 GLIDE
Glide — 1-cyl., 8 hp, 72" wb

Style A Rbt.-2P	750	2500	3500	5000	8500	18,000
Style A Tonneau-5P	850	2500	3500	5000	8500	18,000
Style B Rbt.-3P	750	2500	3500	5000	8500	18,000

1905 GLIDE
Style A - 1-cyl., 8 hp, 74" wb

Runabout-2P	850	2500	3500	5000	8500	18,000
Tonneau-5P	900	2500	3500	5000	8500	18,000

Style D - 2-cyl., 14 hp, 80" wb

Side Entrance T.	1125	2600	3600	5200	8700	18,500

1905 Glide, style A, tonneau, HAC

1906 Glide, model E, touring, HAC

1906 GLIDE
Model C — 1-cyl., 10 hp, 84" wb

	FP	5	4	3	2	1
Runabout-2P	800	2400	3400	4800	8000	17,000
Model F — 2-cyl., 18 hp, 86" wb						
Touring-5P	1250	2500	3500	5000	8500	18,000
Model E — 4-cyl., 36 hp, 103" wb						
Touring-5P	3000	3300	4400	6700	12,000	24,000

1907 Glide, model H, touring, HAC

1907 GLIDE
Model E — 4-cyl., 30/35 hp, 103" wb

Touring-5P	2250	2700	3600	5300	8800	19,000
Model G — 4-cyl., 36/40 hp, 120" wb						
Touring-5P	2500	2900	3700	5600	9100	20,000
Limousine-5P	3700	2500	3500	5000	8500	18,000
Model H — 6-cyl., 50/60 hp, 132" wb						
Touring-7P	3500	6750	13,500	22,500	31,500	45,000

1908 GLIDE
Model G — 4-cyl., 40 hp, 120" wb

Touring	2500	3500	4500	7000	13,000	25,000
Special Touring (45 hp)	3000	3700	4700	7300	13,700	26,000
Model H — 6-cyl., 54/60 hp, 132" wb						
Touring-7P	5000	6750	13,500	22,000	31,500	45,000

1908 Glide, model H, touring, WLB

1909 Glide, model G, special touring, HAC

1909 GLIDE
Model G — 4-cyl., 45 hp, 120" wb

	FP	5	4	3	2	1
Special Tour.-5/7P	2500	3700	4700	7300	13,700	26,000
Model R — 4-cyl., 45 hp, 126" wb						
Cl. C. Tonneau-4P	2250	3900	4800	7700	14,300	27,000
Single Seat Rbt.-2P	2250	3500	4500	7000	13,000	25,000

1910 Glide, model 45, touring, HAC

1910 GLIDE
Model 45 — 4-cyl., 45 hp, 122" wb

Roadster-3P	2400	3900	4800	7700	14,300	27,000
Scout Touring-5P	2500	3700	4700	7300	13,700	26,000
Special Tour.-7P	2500	3700	4700	7300	13,700	26,000

1911 Glide, model 45, Scout, HAC

613

1911 GLIDE
Model 45 — 4-cyl., 45 hp, 120'' wb

	FP	5	4	3	2	1
Touring-7P	2000	3900	4800	7700	14,300	27,000
Touring-5P	2000	3700	4700	7300	13,700	26,000
Roadster-4P (122'' wb)	2000	4000	5000	8000	15,000	28,000
Scout-5P (122'' wb)	2000	3900	4800	7700	14,300	27,000
Fore-Door Tour.-7P	2150	3300	4400	6700	12,000	24,000

1912 Glide, model 36, touring, HAC

1912 GLIDE
Model 36 — 4-cyl., 36 hp, 114'' wb

Roadster-2P	1550	3900	4800	7700	14,300	27,000
Fore-Door Tour.-5P	1550	3700	4700	7300	13,700	26,000

Model 45 — 4-cyl., 45 hp, 120'' wb

Roadster-2P	2000	4000	5000	8000	15,000	28,000
Roadster-4P	2000	4000	4900	7900	14,800	27,500
Touring-5P	2150	3700	4700	7300	13,700	26,000
Touring-7P	2250	3800	4800	7500	14,000	26,500

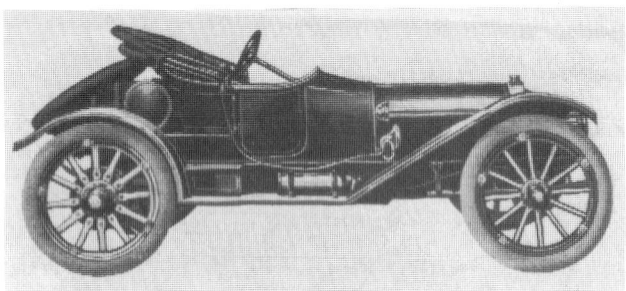

1913 Glide, model 45, Scout, HAC

1913 GLIDE
Model 36 — 4-cyl., 36 hp, 118'' wb

Roadster-2P	1690	3900	4800	7700	14,300	27,000
Touring-5P	1690	3700	4700	7300	13,700	26,000

Model 45 — 4-cyl., 45 hp, 120'' wb

Scout-2P	2000	3900	4800	7700	14,300	27,000
Torpedo-4P	2150	3900	4800	7700	14,300	27,000
Touring-5P	2250	3900	4800	7700	14,300	27,000

1914 Glide, model 36-42, touring, HAC

1914 GLIDE
Model 36-42 — 4-cyl., 36 hp, 118'' wb

Touring-5P	1840	3900	4800	7700	14,300	27,000
Roadster-2P	1840	4000	5000	8000	15,000	28,000

1915 GLIDE
Model 30 — 4-cyl., 30 hp, 116'' wb

Touring-5P	1195	3700	4700	7300	13,700	26,000
Roadster-2P	1195	3900	4800	7700	14,300	27,000

1915 Glide, model 30, touring, HAC

1916 Glide, model 6-40, touring, HAC

1916 GLIDE
Model 6-40 — 6-cyl., 40 hp, 119'' wb

	FP	5	4	3	2	1
Touring-5P	1095	3700	4700	7300	13,700	26,000
Sedan-5P	1295	2500	3500	5000	8500	18,000

1917 Glide, model 40, light six touring, HAC

1917 GLIDE
Model 40 — 6-cyl., 40 hp, 119'' wb

Touring-5P	1195	3700	4700	7300	13,700	26,000
Sedan-5P	1395	2500	3500	5000	8500	18,000
Roadster-4P	1195	3900	4800	7700	14,300	27,000

1918-19 Glide, model 40, touring, HAC

1918 GLIDE
Model 40 — 6-cyl., 45 hp, 119" wb

	FP	5	4	3	2	1
Touring-5P	1495	4000	5000	8000	15,000	28,000
Roadster-4P	1495	4200	5200	8400	15,700	29,000
Sedan-5P	1695	2500	3500	5000	8500	18,000

1919 GLIDE
Model 40 — 6-cyl., 45 hp, 119" wb

	FP	5	4	3	2	1
Touring-5P	1655	4000	5000	8000	15,000	28,000
Roadster-4P	1655	4200	5200	8400	15,700	29,000

1920 Glide, model 40, touring, HAC

1920 GLIDE
Model 40 — 6-cyl., 45 hp, 119" wb

	FP	5	4	3	2	1
Touring-5P	1695	4000	5000	8000	15,000	28,000
Roadster-4P	1695	4200	5200	8400	15,700	29,000

GLOBE — The Globe Motor Car Company was organized in Detroit, Michigan during the summer of 1910 with a capital stock of $50,000 to manufacture and deal in automobiles. Robert S. Milhollen spearheaded this venture, remarking at the time that the firm "will build pleasure cars, starting in at once." Evidence of manufacture is lacking, however.

The Globe Power Company was organized in Buffalo, New York during the summer of 1903 with a capital stock of $200,000 for the manufacture of "power machinery and automobiles." Incorporators were William F. Hoffman, Elmer E. Hoover and George H. Hoover. Manufacture of an automobile is doubted.

The Globe Motor Car Company was organized early in 1915 in Canton, Ohio. Incorporators were C.S. Lochemer, E.M. Raber, G.A. Marks, J.R. Rober and J.R. Bodine. The presence of this company on rosters of automobile manufacturers is in error, because the firm's plan from the beginning was to operate as a dealership.

1921 Globe, Four, sport roadster, WLB

GLOBE FOUR — Cleveland, Ohio — (1920-1922) — Charles H. Davies had been one of the founders of Supreme Motors Corporation and had served as vice-president and general manager of that Ohio-based engine-producing company. Therefore, when he left Supreme to begin his own car-manufacturing firm, it was to no one's surprise that he selected the 39 hp four-cylinder Supreme engine as the powerplant for his new product. Globe Motors Company was incorporated in September 1920, its factory sited on Euclid Avenue, not far from the Stearns-Knight plant. The Globe was set on a 115-inch wheelbase and was priced at $1800. It was a conventional assembled car of the period, but with two illumination features that were rather nice extras offered as standard equipment. Up front, under the hood, was a light for the engine; inside, for the convenience of passengers, was a lamp on an extension cord. Neither of these fillips, however, was sufficient to make a commercial success of an automotive venture introduced in the midst of the postwar depression. The final cars, built in 1922, were leftover 1921 models.

1920-1922 GLOBE FOUR
Four — 39 hp, 115" wb

	FP	5	4	3	2	1
Touring-5P	1800	4400	5600	9200	17,300	31,000
Roadster	1800	4700	6100	9900	19,000	33,000
Sport Rdstr.	1800	5000	6500	11,000	22,000	35,000

GLORIA — Gloria Motors Corporation was a $5 Delaware incorporation from early 1920 for the manufacture and sale of automobiles. Incorporators were Edward S. Napolis, Edgar H. Napolis and Frances E. Jaffe, all of Philadelphia. Manufacture is doubted.

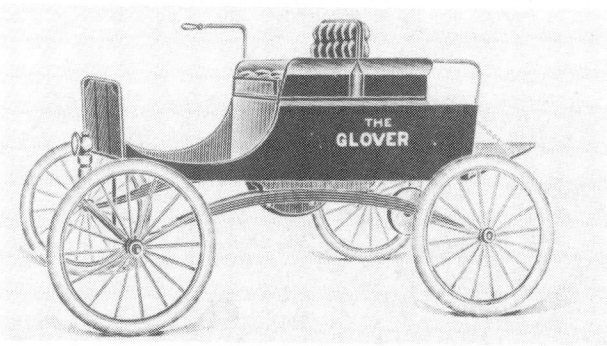

1902 Glover, auto-buggy, NAHC

GLOVER STEAM — Chicago, Illinois — (1902) — In 1902 George T. Glover of Chicago produced a two-passenger steam car for $750 and a four-passenger for $1200 which were undistinguished except for their "winter use" equipment. This consisted of a traction wheel mounted midship which was hollow and filled with hot water from the engine boiler. Ostensibly, this wheel served to melt snow under the vehicle and render it usable in wintry conditions. Rather quickly, Glover concluded that his idea was better applicable elsewhere, and the Glover Steam Tractor followed. One of these, incidentally, was bought in 1903 by Packard official Russell A. Alger for use in his logging camp in northern Michigan. By 1911 Glover was extending his ideas into the bus and truck field; including a fifth-wheel "flexible traction truck" which could be utilized to convert a horsedrawn wagon into a motorized one. In 1913 he was among the incorporators of the C.A. Martin Manufacturing Company in Chicago, though that venture is not believed to have produced any cars.

GLOVER — New York, New York — (1920-1921) — The Glover was an export only car, produced in this country by the Glover Motor Company of New York, and sold in England by Glover's Motors Ltd. of Leeds, Yorkshire. An assembled car throughout, it was no doubt manufactured for Glover by one of the established American manufacturers who specialized in this sort of service. Possibly this might have been Seneca in Fostoria, Ohio, although the Glover was not simply a Seneca in chassis or disassembled form shipped overseas as has occasionally been thought; the *Automobiles of the World* yearbook published in 1921 by Aeroplane & General Publishing Company, Ltd. of England belies that. The Glover was powered by a four-cylinder 27 hp Le Roi engine and was fitted into a 114-inch wheelbase chassis with wire wheels. It was rather attractive.

1920 GLOVER
Four — 27 hp, 114" wb

	FP	5	4	3	2	1
Roadster-2P	£ 550	—	—	—	—	—

1921 GLOVER
Four — 27 hp, 114" wb

	FP	5	4	3	2	1
Touring-4P	£ 595	—	—	—	—	—

GOABOUT — Kokomo, Indiana — (1901-1902) — Simply put, the Goabout didn't. It was the product of the Standard Manufacturing Company of Kokomo which was incorporated on December 4th, 1901. Among the people involved were Watson Irvin, a former employee of the Haynes-Apperson company of Kokomo, and Edwin Shortride, a former traveling salesman who was an old friend of Elwood P. Haynes. Incorporation papers indicate that Standard would "manufacture, sell and deal" in mill supplies, tools, engines, motor vehicles and general machinery. In addition, a general foundry and repair business was to be operated. After building just one automobile — a 6 hp 1000-pound gasoline runabout — and putting a Goabout nameplate on it, the Standard people decided to confine themselves to their other pursuits. The firm was reorganized as the Standard Motor Company in 1902; stationary engines became the principal manufacture.

GOBY — Cleveland, Ohio — (1914) — G.S. Goby was a mechanical engineer from Cleveland who designed and built a most unusual cyclecar, one of the few to provide seating for three people. "Great care has been exercised in the production of a car of unusual stability, pleasing lines and general efficiency," reported *The Cyclecar Age* in April 1914. "The motor, a four-cylinder water-cooled engine, designed by Mr. Goby, is said by experts to be excellent in quality." The Goby was to be priced in the $400 range, and "several well-known capitalists" in Cleveland were reported about to organize a company for manufacture. Purportedly, too, the Motor Engineering Company, also in Cleveland, was "now building the first installment of these cars." That was the last heard of the Goby.

GODDARD — Akron, Ohio — (1904) — That this gasoline car was completed has been documented, that it was "practically useless" was subsequently alleged by the man for whom it was built. The Williams Foundry & Machine Company of Akron constructed the car for Frank C. Goddard, and then took Goddard to court when he refused to pay up completely. Goddard countersued that Williams had promised a May 1st delivery date for a car that would cost between $500 and $600 — and that he had given the company $497.02, and because of the Williams' failure to complete the car on time and the fact that it wasn't any good anyway, he had been "damaged to the extent of $500." That the Akron man behind the Williams Foundry was Harry A. Williams who attempted to produce a car under his own name in 1906 is likely.

1908 Goddard, NAHC

GODDARD — **Conneaut, Ohio** — **(1908)** — "The problem of raising sufficient cash to purchase an automobile, even a one-lunger, second-hand, sold out cheap, looked too long a task for a couple of fifteen-year-old boys," explained *The Automobile.* Consequently, the Goddard twins — Wilford and Winfred — built their own, and they didn't do too bad a job of it. The single-cylinder engine they saved up to buy, the wheels were purloined from a carriage and shod with bicycle tires; two lengths of wood and suitable cross sections of same provided the rest.

1898 Goddeu, four-wheel tandem, FR

GODDEU — **Winchester, Massachusetts** — **(1898)** — Louis Goddeu was a Canadian who emigrated to the United States and made his fortune. In Winchester, Massachusetts he rose to the top of the McKay Metal Fastener Company, and when that firm was absorbed by United Shoe

Machinery Company, he quickly became a member of the executive suite there too. Possessed of an extraordinarily inventive mind, he patented over 300 devices. Among these was a small tandem-seated four-wheeled automobile in 1898 powered by denatured alcohol. Although this invention of Louis Goddeu's was never marketed, many of his others were. The preponderance of these revolved around shoe machinery, but mass production also followed his invention of a warship gun turret and his tiniest invention of all, the small piece of formed wire which when used in a device called a stapler allowed the effective joining together of two or more pieces of paper. Louis Goddeu built at least four other cars after the turn of the century, but they all seem to have been for family and friends. The inventor apparently regarded automobiles strictly as a hobby.

GODSHALL — Although William H. Godshall of Philadelphia, Pennsylvania indicated his intention to build automobiles during the fall of 1911, it appears that the $15,000 company he organized at the time proceeded to operate as a dealership only.

GODWIN & WRENN — **Norfolk, Virginia** — **(1901)** — In 1901 in Norfolk two companies got together to build one car. Godwin & Company provided the machinery, A. Wrenn & Son the body. No further automobiles ensued from this partnership.

GOETHE — The Goethe, which various car rosters indicate was built from 1900 to 1902, is a further example of misspelling. These turn of the century automobiles were built by Paul Gaeth of Cleveland, Ohio. Refer to Gaeth.

1915 Golden, touring, WLB

GOLDEN — **Chicago, Illinois** — **(1915)** — The Golden Motor Car Company of Chicago was not in the automobile business long, and a picture of a car produced probably provides much of the reason for that. The Golden was a thoroughly ordinary five-passenger touring with wire wheels and a frontal aspect that looked rather like it was sucking a lemon.

GOLDEN ARROW — Golden Arrow was the name of the car proposed to be built in Los Angeles, California by the Curtis-Shea-Cox Company. In December of 1911 representatives of that San Francisco firm were in L.A. "endeavoring to sell stock" in order to build a factory there. Their endeavors apparently weren't rewarded.

GOLDEN GATE — **San Francisco, California** — **(1893)** — This pioneer vehicle from San Francisco has been referred to as both a Golden Gate and a Schilling. It was a gasoline-powered tricycle produced by A. Schilling & Sons of San Francisco, manufacturers of the Golden Gate gasoline engine. One of the company's 2 hp units was naturally used in the vehicle, "placed in front of the seat in full view." The trike carried two passengers at a speed of 10 to 12 mph and was built on order for the Messrs. Doane and Thornburghs, local purveyors of farm implements. The Doanes and Thornburghes were pioneering families in the Santa Maria area. It is not believed that Schilling built another car.

GOLDEN STATE — **San Jose, California** — **(1902-1903)** — H.M. Barngrover was president, George H. Voss secretary and H.W. Lupton manager of the Golden State Automobile Company which moved into the 86-88 East San Fernando Street factory in San Jose which had previously seen production of the Christman runabout. Though Charles Christman had sold out his Christman Motor Carriage Company, he remained on at the factory overseeing manufacture of the Christman Silent Muffler he had invented. In addition to this, Golden State also indicated itself to be "sole manufacturers" of the Lupton friction transmission. The Golden State automobile the firm produced was perhaps an even more primeval vehicle than the Christman had been. Powered by a two-cylinder 8 hp Brennan engine, it was a typical two-seater buggy with wire wheels, right-hand tiller steering, two cone-shaped flywheels, a rawhide pinion and iron gear. Friction transmission by Lupton and silent muffler by Christman were also featured, naturally. Production of the car seems to have ceased sometime in 1903, although the firm continued awhile in gear cutting, machine work and automobile repairing.

1904 Golden State, runabout, JHV

GOLDEN STATE — Los Angeles, California — (1904-1906) — The second car called Golden State was quite possibly the first car ever designed by a policeman. Having wearied of inventing holsters and other weapons accessories as an adjunct to his work as a member of the Los Angeles police force, Ross M.G. Phillips resigned in 1902 to devote his time to inventions of a more mechanical sort. The first automobile he devised probably never left the blueprint stage, but his second was built with the help of a machinist friend in L.A. It was a two-passenger runabout powered by an air-cooled engine with transmission built in unit, and it was completed in 1904. Every part of the car was of Phillips' own design, and he patented numerous of its features, including the flexible driveshaft. Until the patents were awarded, Phillips was reluctant to talk much about his car. By January 1906, however, he felt sufficiently protected to begin soliciting assistance for manufacture. The Golden State Motor Car Company was organized that month, but never got off the ground, perhaps because of the sudden death of one of Phillips' principal financial angels during the stock promotion period. Thereafter Phillips moved east, where his forthcoming inventions were in the field of kitchen stoves.

GOLDEN WEST — Sacramento, California — (1914-1915) — "A factory for the manufacturing of four-wheel-drive, four-wheel-steer pleasure and commercial cars is being erected at Sacramento," *Automobile Topics* announced in January 1914. "The company is called the Golden West Motors Company, with Fred A. Sloss as moving spirit." The building of a few prototypes was as far as this venture proceeded for more than a year, *Automobile Topics* further reporting in July 1915 that the selling of Golden West stock had "struck a decided snag" and there was a fight in progress "between hostile factions among the stockholders." When the air finally cleared in 1916, Golden West was reorganized, with the new company assuming the debts of the old and electing to concentrate energies in the commercial field only.

GOODNOW — Natick, Massachusetts — (1905) — At the turn of the century James E. Belger built a steam automobile in collaboration with fellow Natickian Samuel Bowker. Only a single example was produced before the Belger and Bowker partnership was dissolved. A half decade later, in 1905, James Belger built another automobile, entirely on his own this time, in his machine shop on North Main street across from the Natick Beef Company. He called it the Goodnow, and again only one was produced, though it does have the distinction of being the first gasoline car built in Natick.

GOODRICH — Hartford, Connecticut — (1903) — Raymond Goodrich built a steam car in the Hartford factory of Mansury & Smith in 1903. He was assisted by Christopher M. Spencer who had already built a number of steam cars himself. The Goodrich was a tonneau seating six passengers and built to resemble a gasoline touring car, with both boiler and engine up front under a hood. Most probably, Goodrich — who was an officer of the Hartford & New York Transportation Company — envisioned the vehicle as a prototype for a line of passenger-carrying cars to be operated between the two cities. Only the one car appears to have been built, however.

1922 Goodspeed, phaeton, WLB

GOODSPEED — Joliet, Illinois — (1922) — When Leland F. Goodspeed joined the Commonwealth Motors Company late in 1921, rumor had it that the reason was the impending production of a new car called the Goodspeed. For the five years previous, Goodspeed had been vice-president in charge of engineering for the Barley Motor Car Company, that firm's Roamer motorcar was renowned, and Goodspeed's credentials impeccable. Moreover, Goodspeed had recently proved his name delightfully appropriate by driving the Roamer to several world's records for stock cars at Daytona Beach. Fuel was added to the fire of rumor when a Goodspeed was shown at the New York Automobile Show in January 1922. It was a sporty car with a six-cylinder engine designed by Goodspeed. "The engine is unusual in that it employs piston valves," said *Automotive Industries*, "producing a silent running mechanism, free from the clatter often resulting from the use of poppet valves and strong valve springs." The 124-inch wheelbase frame incorporated integral brackets for the mounting of bumpers. Dual ignition and individual step-plates were featured. The price tag attached read $5400. Production of the car was announced to be limited. It was. The first Goodspeeds were also the last. (Another car had been built for the Chicago show, possibly there was a third, but that was it.) During this same period, Commonwealth Motors had merged with the Markin Auto Body Corporation. Morris Markin was now the new Commonwealth president, and he had another idea. It was a taxi-cab that he would choose to call the Checker. Leland F. Goodspeed would be Checker's chief engineer.

GOODSPEED-DETROIT — Detroit, Michigan — (1913) — In 1913 the Goodspeed-Detroit Manufacturing Company, Ltd. was organized at 272 Harper Avenue in Detroit for "making automobiles and doing machinery work on automobiles on contract." A few totally Goodspeed-Detroit-built automobiles may have followed, but the firm's work was predominantly in the repair and rebuilding fields.

GOODWIN — The Goodwin Car & Manufacturing Company of Poughkeepsie, New York has been frequently indicated as building an automobile in 1923. The firm had been a producer of steel railroad dump cars for years, and in October of 1922 announced its formation of an automotive department. What followed was not an automobile, however, but a thirty-passenger bus called the Goodwin-Guilder. The Goodwin-Guilder evolved into the Guilder by 1924. Guilder trucks and buses were built in Poughkeepsie into the mid-Thirties. A passenger car was never built.

GOODWIN — Chicago, Illinois — (1913-1914) — In 1913 the Goodwin Car Company revealed that it was erecting a one-story factory at 10 South LaSalle Street in Chicago. William H. Taylor was the president, James T. Gilman the vice president and William H. Safford the secretary of this venture, which survived into 1914. Documentation regarding the cars produced is lacking.

GORE — Brattleboro, Vermont — (circa 1837) — John Gore was a native of Vermont who spent the beginning years of his career building stationary steam engines and boilers. During the early 1830's he began work on an automotive vehicle which was completed by 1837. He spent about $600 in its construction, a princely figure in those days. The Gore steam wagon was powered by a two-cylinder engine which with two large wood-burning vertical boilers occupied approximately three-quarters of the space in the vehicle, leaving room for only a driver and a passenger. John Gore drove the automobile frequently for more than a decade. It was not a quiet machine, however, and its approach often frightened horses and other livestock for blocks around. For this reason, the selectmen of Brattleboro allowed it to be driven only if a boy ringing a warning bell preceded the vehicle. Ultimately, this restriction, and probably complaints from neighbors, tried John Gore's patience. On his last trip with the vehicle, from Bernardston (Massachusetts) back to Brattleboro, he inadvertently swerved into a ditch, climbed out and said that, as far as he was concerned, the thing could stay there. Evidently it did, though the engine purportedly was removed for a local bakery.

GORMULLY & JEFFERY — The partners' names were R. Phillip Gormully and Thomas B. Jeffery, manufacturers of the Rambler bicycle in Chicago. The cars produced at the company's plant prior to the turn of the century are properly referred to by the tradename of the partners' bicycle. Refer to Rambler.

GOSHEN — Goshen, Indiana — (1905-1907) — Capitalization of $50,000 and an addition to their Goshen Motor Works at Ninth and Lincoln was the announced intention of the Ihrig brothers during the fall of 1905 when they declared their impending entrance into the automotive field. The 1906-1907 Goshen city directory indicates the Ihrigs as builders of "automobiles, launches, marine and stationary engines," but although a prototype car is known to have been built and others may have followed to custom order, the principal activity of the Goshen Motor Works was engine building.

GOSPER — Harry Gosper of Mumford, New York was indicated as a manufacturer of an automobile in the Hiscox book *Horseless Vehicles, Automobiles, Motor Cycles* published in 1900. Further documentation is lacking.

GOTHAM — The Gotham Transportation Company was organized in New York City during the fall of 1916 with a capital stock of $50,000 to manufacture "motor driven vehicles, parts and accessories." J.F. Wiggin of 59 West 65th Street was behind this venture. Manufacture of a car is doubted.

GOTHAM — New York, New York — (1910-1915) — The Gotham Motor Car Company was organized in New York City during the summer of 1910 with a capital stock of $25,000. William Schuette and Robert W. Schuette of Long Island, and Daniel W. Bluck of Manhattan, were the people involved. For years the Gotham has been assumed to be a bona-fide automobile manufacturer, with estimates of as many as fifty Gothams built, this the number of cars so indicated in East Coast motor vehicle department registration lists. It appears almost certain, however, that Gotham operated principally as a dealership, which on occasion may have specially outfitted one of the cars it sold upon specific customer order. Among the cars for which Gotham held an agency was the S.G.V. built in Reading, Pennsylvania from 1911 to 1915. Cornelius Tangemann was both a director of the S.G.V. Company as well as Gotham. Examination of the "Gotham" serial numbers in numerous cases on the registration lists indicate that the cars were undoubtedly S.G.V.'s. That a car might be registered under the dealer and not the manufacturer's name was not an unusual occurrence during this period. The Gotham Motor Car Company operated at 1853 Broadway from 1911-1912, moving to 236 West 54th Street for 1913-1914. The Gotham business was dissolved in 1915, at the same time that S.G.V. was going to the wall in Reading. Thereafter, Robert Schuette became the U.S. dealer for Rolls-Royces imported from England.

GOULD — The Gould Automobile Company was organized in Watertown, New York to manufacture automobiles and accessories early in 1910. Capital stock was $500; the incorporators were A.W. and W.L. Gould of Watertown and W.S. Rice of Adams, Jefferson County. Manufacture of a car is doubted.

That a steamer was built in 1900 by the Gould Manufacturing Company of Seneca Falls, New York has been indicated on various car rosters. It is unknown in Seneca Falls, both to historians there and to Gould's Pump Corporation, the international headquarters for which remain in Seneca Falls.

The Gould Motor & Manufacturing Company was organized in Marion, Indiana during the spring of 1917 with a capital stock of $100,000 to manufacture automobiles, aeroplanes and "a new type of gasoline engine." Incorporators were J.S. Hardman, O.M. Scarborough and Frank Barr. Manufacture of a car is doubted.

The Gould Motor Parts Company was organized in York, Pennsylvania during the summer of 1917 with a $2 million capital stock for the manufacture of automobiles, automobile differentials and airplanes. Behind this venture were Walter O. Lum, Thomas B. Baird, G. Brewer Griffin, John F. Blanchard, H.T.E. Beardsley, James A. Kline and W.E. Lennon. Manufacture of a car is doubted. Among the incorporators, James A. Kline was already in the car-manufacturing business with his Kline Kar, which had originated in York, though by now it was being built in Richmond, Virginia.

1921 Gove, touring, NAHC

GOVE — Pocatello, Idaho — (1921-1922)/Detroit, Michigan — (1921-1922) — The likelihood of there having been two Gove Motor Car Company ventures in two different states during the same period of the Twenties is so remote that these two efforts are included together. Trade press references from the period indicate Detroit as the location of manufacture. The stock prospectus for the firm indicates Pocatello, Idaho (the corner of Oak Street and Pocatello Avenue) with a full-page map provided to demonstrate that Pocatello indeed was the "Hub of the North West." Behind this venture were H.E. Gove, whose previous experience in the automobile industry remains elusive, and O.J. Howick, a Detroit engineer who had worked for Packard, Lozier, Republic, Ford and Premier, among others. Possibly the prototypes of the Gove were produced in Detroit (or in nearby Brighton, Michigan), with grand plans for locating a grand factory in Pocatello once enough stock had been sold. Undoubtedly, the Gove never made it to Pocatello. Nor to Reno, Nevada nor Denver, Colorado, where the Gove people had also shown up briefly. A 1½-ton four-cylinder Gove truck priced at $2250 was slated for production, the Gove car was to be priced $100 less. A prototype of the latter, is known to have been built using a six-cylinder 45 hp Falls engine; the wheelbase was 114 inches, the body style a five-passenger touring with wood wheels. The Gove mentioned in the Pocatello prospectus differs only in indicating a 110-inch wheelbase, and its picture has the look of a car that had previously been something else with maybe a new radiator tacked on. General sales manager for the Gove venture was announced as E.M. Beauchamp, who previously had sold such varied cars as the Locomobile, the Stearns and the Chalmers. Undoubtedly his assignment with Gove was a short one.

GRAHAM — The Graham Differential Gear Company was organized in Chicago, Illinois with a capital stock of $50,000 during the spring of 1910 to manufacture automobiles, accessories and machinery. Incorporators were Percival Steele, J.T. Tyrell and G.J. Jeffries. Manufacture of a car is doubted.

Graham & Goodman, Inc. was organized in New York City early in 1906 with a capital stock of $10,000 to make automobiles. C.W. Graham, J.M. Graham and F.T. Goodman were the principals involved. The firm is known to have moved into a large garage at 53 West 93rd Street which bristled with new features, including a "club room for chauffeurs," but manufacture was not embarked upon.

GRAHAM STEAM — Boston, Massachusetts — 1899 — In September of 1899 the Graham Equipment Company of Boston announced that it had ten steam carriages on hand ready for delivery. According to J. Hector Graham, these had been built according to the general design of the Whitney steam carriage being produced elsewhere in Massachusetts, except that the engine was mounted by means of the Graham "Leaf and Spiral Suspension" system and that the vehicle used anthracite coal as fuel. How many more complete carriages Graham might have built is not known. The following month, however, J. Hector Graham changed his firm's name to Graham Equipment-Motor Company, sold out his former heavy wagon business, and declared that henceforth he would confine activity to outfitting light carriages and deliveries with the special Graham spring suspension system. This activity appears to have been short-lived.

1903 Graham Electric, runabout, NAHC

GRAHAM ELECTRIC — Chicago, Illinois — (1903) — This product of the Graham Automobile & Launch Company of 145 LaSalle Street in Chicago was a small electric roadster on a 78-inch wheelbase powered by a Westinghouse motor and featuring an angle-iron frame, reachless running gear, chain drive, and artillery wooden wheels. The price tag was $850. The Graham Electric arrived on the market in the early spring of 1903, and departed before the end of the year. If the engineers behind it were as skilled in their profession as the Graham Electric ad writers were in the rudiments of grammar, one would know immediately why this car failed. "The Swellest Electric Vehicle Made," the ads said. The Graham Automobile & Launch Company promised an 8 hp single-cylinder gasoline car on the same chassis, but it did not arrive before the company departed.

1903 Graham-Fox, touring, WLB

GRAHAM-FOX — The prototype show car displayed at the New York Automobile Show in 1903 carried the name Graham-Fox, but when the car was put into production the year following, it was as the Compound. The Compound was built in Middletown, Connecticut from 1904 to 1908. Refer to Compound.

GRAHAM MOTORETTE — Brooklyn, New York — (1902-1903) — The Graham Motorette was a small 450-pound piano-box buggy powered by a single-cylinder 3 hp air-cooled engine which was started from the seat. Chain drive and tiller steering were featured. The car was produced in Brooklyn beginning in 1902 by the Graham Automobile Company. In 1903

Charles Sefrin of Brooklyn bought out Graham, though the only change he made in the company product that year was the substitution of a Thomas engine (supplied from Buffalo) which provided an extra half horsepower. Early in 1904 Charles Sefrin & Company was reorganized as the Charles Sefrin Motor Carriage Company, and the firm's model line was expanded with the addition of a 9 hp touring car which, together with the runabout, would now be called the Sefrin.

1903 Graham Motorette, runabout, NAHC

1928 Graham, model 614, opera coupe, AA

GRAHAM-PAIGE — Dearborn, Michigan — (1928-1930)/**GRAHAM** — (1930-1941) — The Graham brothers were back, and spectacularly. Their new Graham-Paige automobile was introduced during New York Automobile Show week in January 1928 with a lavish luncheon at the Hotel Roosevelt where the speakers included Gene Tunney and Knute Rockne — and was followed by a complete gravure section, eight full pages, in the Detroit *Free Press* of January 22nd devoted to the new Graham-Paige Motors Corporation, whose emblem was a stylized profile rendering of Joseph B., Robert C. and Ray A. Graham, the brothers coiffed in knightly helmeted splendor. The Grahams had just reentered America's most formidable jousting arena — the automobile industry. Formerly a power in the truck field, the brothers had joined commercial vehicle ranks following the Armistice ending World War I, allying themselves with Dodge Brothers in 1921 and ultimately selling out to Dodge in April 1926. In June of 1927 they had put themselves back into business by buying out the faltering Paige-Detroit Motor Car Company. The Paige was continued as a 1928 model. The new Graham-Paige was introduced in a line of fours, sixes and a single eight, all models featuring L-head engines (aluminum pistons with Invar struts, water jackets running the full length of cylinders), hydraulic brakes (internal or external expanding, depending upon model) and four-speed Warner Gear transmission (save the least expensive six). First year production totaled 73,195 cars. This eclipsed the maiden-year record set by Pontiac in 1926, though it would be exceeded the year following by DeSoto. The Grahams were riding high. Plant expansion (including purchase of the former Harroun factory in Wayne, Michigan) followed, as did a second line of eights for 1929 and the sixes now on longer wheelbases. Through the first series of 1931, several custom cars — with coachwork by LeBaron — would be offered as standard catalog models. The first series of 1930 was the last for the car as a Graham-Paige; the name became simply Graham thereafter, with Paige being used for the firm's new commercial vehicles until Chrysler Corporation reminded the Grahams that in selling out to the Dodge Brothers they had agreed not to manufacture trucks for at least five years. The Grahams' Paige truck had sold dismally anyway, so probably the brothers didn't mind discontinuing it after the 1932 model year. By now the full force of the Great Depression was being felt, and simply selling the Graham car was arduous task enough. Production for 1930 had been 33,560 cars, less than half that of 1929; in 1931 it fell to 20,428. But the brothers really were trying, and boldly for 1932 with the introduction of the Blue Streak Eight, with body styling by Amos Northup of Murray and detailing by Raymond Dietrich. A

thoroughly handsome car with full skirted fenders (a feature widely copied by the rest of the industry a year later), the Blue Streak was miniaturized by the Tootsietoy Company in a model car that sold by the millions. But only 12,967 Grahams including Blue Streaks were sold in 1932. Ray Graham committed suicide in August that year. His two brothers struggled on. Supercharging was introduced on the second series Custom Eight of 1934, the Graham blower a centrifugal unit designed by company assistant chief engineer F.F. Kishline, and unabashedly patterned after that of the Duesenberg. Supercharging raised the eight's horsepower from 95 to 135 bhp, and made the Graham, always a fine-performing car, into a genuine 90-mph-plus machine. Production increased some: to 15,745 cars in 1934. In 1935 it increased again, to 18,466 units, but the Grahams that year had another less favorable distinction; they were the homeliest cars yet built by the company. The decision was made that year to confine Graham production henceforth only to sixes, in three series for '36; Crusader, Cavalier and Supercharger. No longer did Grahams feature the expensive banjo frame that had been a hallmark of the marque since 1932, and their bodies now arrived courtesy of Reo. There had been merger talks between the two companies (amid a flurry of others) that year, but the only definitive result had been the agreement for Graham to use the Reo Flying Cloud bodies on a royalty basis. Earlier years had seen a Graham emphasis on performance, with the car setting records at Brooklands Track in England in the late Twenties, in the early Thirties in America establishing a new record up Mount Washington, and with Graham-powered banjo-framed race cars even contesting Indy, qualifying at 109 mph in 1932, and finishing tenth with a 95.9 mph average in 1934. But now the competition news from Graham was economy, and three consecutive victories in the Gilmore-Yosemite Economy Run. Abroad, Graham chassis were used by Lammas, Ltd. for a run of sports touring cars in England, and in France supercharged Graham engines found their way into the Type C-30 Voisins. At home, for 1938, the company believed that a new body design termed the "Spirit of Motion" and a new radiator design that came to be known as the sharknose would regain for the Graham the styling leadership it had enjoyed with the introduction of the Blue Streak a half-dozen years before. But the sharknose did a nosedive. Public reaction was that it was too radical, or too ugly, or both. Desperate now, Graham tried again in 1940 with the Hollywood, which used the Cord 810/812 dies that Hupp had purchased from the receivers of E.L. Cord's moribund automotive empire. The Hupmobile company was in even more dire straits than Graham, and the deal done involved Graham building the Cord-derived Skylark for Hupp, and receiving rights to build its own similarly-styled Hollywood. For 1940 the sharknose Grahams were continued, redesignated Senior, and the new Hollywood arrived as a four-door supercharged sedan at $1250. A few months later, the sharknose was dropped — and only the Hollywood was continued, now in both supercharged and unsupercharged models. But it was not built long; in September of 1940 the Graham company announced the temporary closing of its automobile plant. A total of 2859 Grahams had been built in 1940; they were the last of the line. Graham-Paige Motors Corporation turned its major effort thereafter to military production for the war effort. In August of 1944 controlling interest in the Graham-Paige company was acquired by the former president of Willys-Overland, Joseph W. Frazer. After the war the Graham-Paige organization would produce another car, but it would be called a Frazer. In February of 1947 all automotive assets of the Graham-Paige Motors Corporation were transferred to the new automotive venture styled the Kaiser-Frazer Corporation. In 1950 the word "motors" was dropped from the Graham-Paige company name, and it became a closed investment corporation. Among the investments acquired following its move of headquarters from Michigan to New York City was Madison Square Garden. Graham-Paige Corporation became Madison Square Garden Corporation in 1962 and is now a Gulf & Western subsidiary. The company which had begun its life building cars today continues its life, and considerably more profitably, as the sponsor of sporting events and circuses, and as the owners of the basketball-playing New York Knicks, and the New York Rangers hockey team.

1928 Graham, model 629, 4-dr. sedan, AA

1928
Model 610, 6-cyl., 111" wb

	FP	5	4	3	2	1
Cpe	860	775	1500	3750	5250	7500
4 dr Sed	875	675	1300	2600	4400	6300

Model 614, 6-cyl., 114" wb

Cpe	1275	725	1400	3000	4700	6700
4 dr Sed	1295	700	1350	2800	4550	6500

Model 619, 6-cyl., 119" wb

Cpe	1575	725	1400	3200	4850	6900
4 dr Sed	1595	700	1350	2800	4550	6500
DeL Cpe	1725	750	1450	3300	4900	7000
DeL 4 dr Sed	1745	700	1350	2900	4600	6600

Model 629, 6-cyl., 129" wb	FP	5	4	3	2	1
Cpe 2 Pas	2185	725	1400	3200	4850	6900
Cpe 5 Pas	2085	750	1450	3400	5000	7100
Cabriolet	2185	2800	5700	9500	13,300	19,000
4 dr 5 Pas Sed	1985	825	1600	4050	5650	8100
4 dr Twn Sed	2085	850	1650	4100	5700	8200
4 dr 7 Pas Sed	2110	850	1650	4150	5800	8300
Model 835, 8-cyl., 137" wb						
Cpe 2 Pas	2485	875	1700	4250	5900	8500
Cpe 5 Pas	2385	900	1900	4500	6300	9000
Cabriolet	2485	2900	5850	9750	13,650	19,500
4 dr 5 Pas Sed	2285	850	1650	4150	5800	8300
4 dr 7 Pas Sed	2410	850	1650	4200	5850	8400
4 dr Twn Sed	2385	850	1650	4150	5800	8300
Limo	2560	875	1700	4350	6050	8700

1929 Graham-Paige, roadster, WLB

1929
Model 612, 6-cyl., 112" wb						
Rdst	970	4000	7950	13,250	18,550	26,500
Tour	970	4050	8100	13,500	18,900	27,000
Cpe	955	825	1600	4000	5600	8000
Cabriolet	1025	2800	5700	9500	13,300	19,000
2 dr Sed	855	825	1600	3950	5500	7900
4 dr Sed	955	825	1600	4000	5600	8000
Model 615, 6-cyl., 115" wb						
Rdst	1195	4050	8100	13,500	18,900	27,000
Tour	1195	4100	8250	13,750	19,250	27,500
Cpe	1195	850	1650	4100	5700	8200
Cabriolet	1295	2900	5850	9750	13,650	19,500
2 dr Sed	1155	825	1600	4000	5600	8000
4 dr Sed	1195	825	1600	4050	5650	8100
Model 621, 6-cyl., 121" wb						
Rdst	1795	4100	8250	13,750	19,250	27,500
Tour	1865	4200	8400	14,000	19,600	28,000
Cpe	1595	850	1650	4100	5700	8200
Cabriolet	1810	2950	5950	9900	13,800	19,800
4 dr Sed	1595	850	1650	4150	5800	8300
Model 827, 8-cyl., 127" wb						
Rdst	2125	4500	9000	15,000	21,000	30,000
Tour	2195	4650	9300	15,500	21,700	31,000
Cpe	2125	1075	3000	5500	7700	11,000
Cabriolet	2145	4500	9000	15,000	21,000	30,000
4 dr Sed	1925	1000	2400	5000	7000	10,000
Model 837, 8-cyl., 137" wb						
Tour	2195	5250	10,500	17,500	24,500	35,000
Cpe	2355	1550	4500	7500	10,500	15,000
4 dr 5 Pas Sed	2355	1400	4200	7000	9800	14,000
4 dr 7 Pas Sed	2425	1500	4350	7250	10,150	14,500
4 dr Twn Sed	2355	1400	4200	7000	9800	14,000
Limo	2495	3000	6000	10,000	14,000	20,000
Le Barron Limo	4430	3300	6600	11,000	15,400	22,000
Le Barron Twn Car	4180	3400	6900	11,500	16,100	23,000

1930 Graham Six, coupe, JAC

1930
Standard, 6-cyl., 115" wb						
Rdst	995	5250	10,500	17,500	24,500	35,000
Phae	1015	5100	10,200	17,000	23,800	34,000
Cpe	895	900	1900	4500	6300	9000
Cabriolet	1065	3750	7500	12,500	17,500	25,000
2 dr Sed	895	800	1550	3850	5400	7700
4 dr Sed	895	800	1550	3900	5450	7800
DeL 4 dr Sed	995	825	1600	4000	5600	8000
4 dr Twn Sed	845	825	1600	3950	5500	7900
DeL Twn Sed	945	825	1600	4050	5650	8100
DeL Cpe	945	875	1700	4250	5900	8500

1931 Graham, Prosperity, 4-dr. sedan, AA

Special, 6-cyl., 115" wb	FP	5	4	3	2	1
Cpe	1195	825	1600	4050	5650	8100
4 dr Sed	1225	825	1600	4000	5600	8000
Standard, 8-cyl., 122" and *134" wb						
Cpe	1445	950	2100	4750	6650	9500
4 dr Sed	1445	925	2000	4650	6500	9300
Conv Sed	1985	5250	10,500	17,500	24,500	35,000
*4 dr 7 Pas Sed	1745	950	2100	4750	6650	9500
Special, 8-cyl., 122" and *134" wb						
Cpe	1595	1000	2400	5000	7000	10,000
4 dr Sed	1595	950	2100	4750	6650	9500
Conv Sed	2085	5550	11,100	18,500	25,900	37,000
*4 dr 7 Pas Sed	1845	1000	2400	5000	7000	10,000
Custom, 8-cyl., 127" wb						
Rdst	2225	5700	11,400	19,000	26,600	38,000
Phae	2295	5550	11,100	18,500	25,900	37,000
Cpe	2225	1025	2600	5250	7300	10,500
Cabriolet	2245	5250	10,500	17,500	24,500	35,000
4 dr Sed	2025	1250	3900	6500	9100	13,000
Custom, 8-cyl., 137" wb						
Phae	2295	6000	12,000	20,000	28,000	40,000
4 dr 5 Pas Sed	2455	1400	4200	7000	9800	14,000
4 dr Twn Sed	2455	1400	4200	7000	9800	14,000
4 dr 7 Pas Sed	2525	1550	4500	7500	10,500	15,000
Limo	2595	3000	6000	10,000	14,000	20,000
Le Barron Limo	4505	3300	6600	11,000	15,400	22,000
Le Barron Twn Car	4255	3000	6000	10,000	14,000	20,000

1931

First Series
Standard, 6-cyl., 115" wb						
Rdst	995	4350	8700	14,500	20,300	29,000
Phae	1015	4200	8400	14,000	19,600	28,000
Bus Cpe	845	800	1550	3850	5400	7700
Cpe	895	825	1600	4000	5600	8000
Sport Cpe	1045	825	1600	4050	5650	8100
2 dr Sed	895	775	1500	3600	5100	7300
4 dr Twn Sed	845	775	1500	3700	5200	7400
4 dr Univ Sed	895	775	1500	3750	5250	7500
DeL 4 dr Sed	995	800	1550	3850	5400	7700
DeL 4 dr Twn Sed	945	800	1550	3900	5450	7800
Special, 6-cyl., 115" wb						
Bus Cpe	1195	825	1600	4050	5650	8100
Cpe	1225	850	1650	4100	5700	8200
4 dr Sed	1225	775	1500	3700	5200	7400
Model 621, 6-cyl., 121" wb						
Rdst	1795	4500	9000	15,000	21,000	30,000
Phae	1865	4350	8700	14,500	20,300	29,000
Victoria	1595	800	1550	3900	5450	7800
Cpe	1795	850	1650	4150	5800	8300
4 dr Sed	1595	775	1500	3750	5250	7500
Standard, 8-cyl., 122" and *134" wb						
Cpe	1445	1000	2400	5000	7000	10,000
4 dr Sed	1445	950	2100	4750	6650	9500
Conv Sed	1635	4500	9000	15,000	21,000	30,000
*4 dr 7 Pas Sed	1745	950	2100	4750	6650	9500
*4 dr 5 Pas Sed	1695	950	2100	4750	6650	9500
*Limo	1945	1075	3000	5500	7700	11,000
Special 822, 8-cyl., 122" and *134" wb						
Cpe	1595	1125	3450	5750	8050	11,500
4 dr Sed	1635	1000	2400	5000	7000	10,000
Conv Sed	1985	4800	9600	16,000	22,400	32,000
*4 dr 7 Pas Sed	1845	1075	3000	5500	7700	11,000
*4 dr 5 Pas Sed	1795	1075	3000	5500	7700	11,000
*Limo	2045	1150	3600	6000	8400	12,000
Custom, 8-cyl., 127" wb						
Rdst	2225	5250	10,500	17,500	24,500	35,000
Phae	2295	5100	10,200	17,000	23,800	34,000
Victoria	2025	1150	3600	6000	8400	12,000
Cabriolet	2245	4800	9600	16,000	22,400	32,000
4 dr Sed	2025	1125	3450	5750	8050	11,500
Custom, 8-cyl., 137" wb						
7 Pas Phae	2595	7200	14,400	24,000	33,600	48,000
4 dr Sed	2455	1400	4200	7000	9800	14,000
Le Barron Limo	4505	3000	6000	10,000	14,000	20,000

Second Series
Prosperity, 6-cyl., 113" wb						
Cpe	785	800	1550	3850	5400	7700
Cpe 2-4	825	825	1600	4000	5600	8000
4 dr Sed	825	775	1500	3600	5100	7300
4 dr Twn Sed	795	775	1500	3750	5250	7500
Standard, 6-cyl., 115" wb						
Rdst	895	4650	9300	15,500	21,700	31,000
4 dr Sed	955	800	1550	3850	5400	7700
Bus Cpe	845	825	1600	4050	5650	8100
Cpe 2-4	895	850	1650	4150	5800	8300
4 dr Twn Sed	895	825	1600	3950	5500	7900

Special, 6-cyl., 115" wb

	FP	5	4	3	2	1
Bus Cpe	925	850	1650	4100	5700	8200
Cpe 2-4	975	850	1650	4200	5850	8400
4 dr Sed	1035	825	1600	3950	5500	7900
4 dr Twn Sed	975	825	1600	4050	5650	8100

Special 820, 8-cyl., 120" wb

Bus Cpe	1155	950	2100	4750	6650	9500
Cpe 2-4	1195	1000	2400	5000	7000	10,000
4 dr Spt Sed	1195	950	2100	4750	6650	9500
4 dr Sed	1245	900	1900	4500	6300	9000

Custom 834, 8-cyl., 134" wb

4 dr Sed	1845	950	2100	4750	6650	9500
4 dr 7 Pas Sed	1895	1000	2400	5000	7000	10,000
Limo	2095	1150	3600	6000	8400	12,000

1932 Graham, Bluestreak 8, 4-dr. sedan, AA

1932 Graham, Bluestreak 8, convertible coupe, AA

1932

Prosperity, 6-cyl., 113" wb

	FP	5	4	3	2	1
Cpe	785	800	1550	3850	5400	7700
Cpe 2-4	825	825	1600	4000	5600	8000
4 dr Sed	825	775	1500	3600	5100	7300
4 dr Twn Sed	795	775	1500	3750	5250	7500

Graham, 6-cyl., 113" wb

Bus Cpe	825	825	1600	3950	5500	7900
Cpe 2-4	875	825	1600	4050	5650	8100
Cabriolet	895	3300	6600	11,000	15,400	22,000
4 dr Sed	—	775	1500	3750	5250	7500

Standard, 6-cyl., 115" wb

Rdst	945	3750	7500	12,500	17,500	25,000
Bus Cpe	945	800	1550	3800	5300	7600
Cpe 2-4	985	850	1650	4150	5800	8300
4 dr Sed	995	800	1550	3850	5400	7700
4 dr Twn Sed	975	825	1600	3950	5500	7900

Special, 6-cyl., 115" wb

Rdst	985	4800	9600	16,000	22,400	32,000
Bus Cpe	985	850	1650	4100	5700	8200
Cpe 2-4	1025	850	1650	4200	5850	8400
4 dr Sed	1035	800	1550	3900	5450	7800
4 dr Twn Sed	1015	825	1600	3950	5500	7900

Model 57, 8-cyl., 123" wb

Cpe	1095	950	2100	4750	6650	9500
Cpe 2-4	1145	1000	2400	5000	7000	10,000
4 dr Sed	1145	900	1900	4500	6300	9000
DeL Cpe	1170	1025	2600	5250	7300	10,500
DeL Cpe 2-4	1220	1075	3000	5500	7700	11,000
Conv Cpe	1270	4500	9000	15,000	21,000	30,000
DeL 4 dr Sed	1220	950	2100	4750	6650	9500

Special 820, 8-cyl., 120" wb

Bus Cpe	1185	1000	2400	5000	7000	10,000
Cpe 2-4	1225	1075	3000	5500	7700	11,000
4 dr Spt Sed	1235	950	2100	4750	6650	9500
4 dr Sed	1285	925	2000	4650	6500	9300

Special 822, 8-cyl., 122" wb

4 dr Sed	1635	950	2100	4750	6650	9500
Conv Sed	1635	6150	12,300	20,500	28,700	41,000

Custom 834, 8-cyl., 134" wb

4 dr Sed	1895	1400	4200	7000	9800	14,000
4 dr 7 Pas Sed	1945	1500	4350	7250	10,150	14,500
Limo	2145	3000	6000	10,000	14,000	20,000

1933

Graham, 6-cyl., 113" wb

	FP	5	4	3	2	1
4 dr Sed	710	750	1450	3400	5000	7100
4 dr Twn Sed	680	775	1500	3600	5100	7300

Model 65, 6-cyl., 113" wb

Bus Cpe	745	800	1550	3800	5300	7600
Cpe 2-4	795	825	1600	3900	5450	7800
Conv Cpe	835	3000	6000	10,000	14,000	20,000
4 dr Sed	795	775	1500	3700	5200	7400

Graham, 6-cyl., 118" wb

Bus Cpe	825	825	1600	3950	5500	7900
Cpe 2-4	875	825	1600	4050	5650	8100
Cabriolet	895	3600	7200	12,000	16,800	24,000
4 dr Sed	875	775	1500	3750	5250	7500

Model 64, 8-cyl., 119" wb

Bus Cpe	845	825	1600	4050	5650	8100
Cpe 2-4	895	850	1650	4150	5800	8300
Conv Cpe	935	3750	7500	12,500	17,500	25,000
4 dr Sed	895	800	1550	3850	5400	7700

Model 57A, 8-cyl., 123" wb

Cpe	925	875	1700	4250	5900	8500
Cpe 2-4	975	900	1900	4500	6300	9000
4 dr Sed	975	825	1600	3950	5500	7900
DeL Cpe	1000	925	2000	4600	6400	9200
DeL Cpe 2-4	1050	950	2100	4750	6650	9500
DeL Conv Cpe	1070	4050	8100	13,500	18,900	27,000
DeL 4 dr Sed	1050	850	1650	4100	5700	8200

Custom 57A, 8-cyl., 123" wb

Cpe	1045	950	2200	4800	6700	9600
Cpe 2-4	1095	1000	2400	5000	7000	10,000
4 dr Sed	1095	875	1700	4250	5900	8500

1934 Graham, Standard 8, convertible coupe, AA

1934

Model 65, 6-cyl., 113" wb

	FP	5	4	3	2	1
Cpe	745	800	1550	3850	5400	7700
Cpe 2-4	795	825	1600	3950	5450	7900
Conv Cpe	835	3150	6300	10,500	14,700	21,000
4 dr Sed	795	775	1500	3700	5200	7400

Model 64, 6-cyl., 119" wb

Cpe	845	825	1600	3950	5500	7900
Cpe 2-4	895	825	1600	4050	5650	8100
Conv Cpe	935	3300	6600	11,000	15,400	22,000
4 dr Sed	895	775	1500	3750	5250	7500

Model 68, 6-cyl., 116" wb

Bus Cpe	805	825	1600	4000	5600	8000
Cpe 2-4	855	850	1650	4150	5800	8300
Conv Cpe	845	3750	7500	12,500	17,500	25,000
4 dr Sed	855	800	1550	3800	5300	7600
4 dr Sed Trunk	890	800	1550	3850	5400	7700

Model 67, 8-cyl., 123" wb

Bus Cpe	965	875	1700	4250	5900	8500
Cpe 2-4	1015	900	1900	4500	6300	9000
Conv Cpe	995	3900	7800	13,000	18,200	26,000
4 dr Sed	1015	825	1600	4000	5600	8000
4 dr Sed Trunk	1050	850	1650	4100	5700	8200

Model 69, 8-cyl., 123" wb

Bus Cpe	1245	900	1800	4400	6150	8800
Cpe 2-4	1295	925	2000	4600	6400	9200
Conv Cpe	1295	4050	8100	13,500	18,900	27,000
4 dr Sed	1295	850	1650	4100	5700	8200
4 dr Sed Trunk	1330	850	1650	4200	5850	8400

Custom 8-71, 8-cyl., 138" wb

4 dr 7 Pas Sed	1695	875	1700	4350	6050	8700
4 dr 7 Pas Sed Trunk	1730	900	1900	4500	6300	9000

1935 Graham, Special 8, sedan, JAC

1935

Model 74, 6-cyl., 111" wb

	FP	5	4	3	2	1
2 dr Sed	595	750	1450	3500	5050	7200
4 dr Sed	635	775	1500	3600	5100	7300
DeL 2 dr Sed	645	775	1500	3600	5100	7300
DeL 4 dr Sed	685	775	1500	3700	5200	7400

Model 68, 6-cyl., 116" wb

Bus Cpe	695	775	1500	3750	5250	7500
Cpe 3-5	765	800	1500	3900	5450	7800
Conv Cpe	845	3000	6000	10,000	14,000	20,000
4 dr Sed	775	775	1500	3700	5200	7400
4 dr Sed Trunk	810	775	1500	3750	5250	7500

Model 67, 8-cyl., 123" wb

Cpe	875	825	1600	4000	5600	8000
Cpe 3-5	925	875	1700	4250	5900	8500
Conv Cpe	995	3150	6300	10,500	14,700	21,000
4 dr Sed	925	800	1550	3850	5400	7700
4 dr Sed Trunk	960	800	1550	3900	5450	7800

Model 72, 8-cyl., 123" wb

Cpe	925	850	1650	4100	5700	8200
Cpe 2-4	975	875	1700	4350	6050	8700
Conv Cpe	1045	3400	6900	11,500	16,100	23,000
4 dr Sed	975	800	1550	3900	5450	7800

Custom Model 69, Supercharged, 8-cyl., 123" wb

Cpe	1245	875	1700	4250	5900	8500
Cpe 3-5	1295	900	1900	4500	6300	9000
Conv Cpe	1295	3600	7200	12,000	16,800	24,000
4 dr Sed	1295	825	1600	4000	5600	8000
4 dr Sed Trunk	1330	825	1600	4050	5650	8100

Model 75, Supercharged, 8-cyl., 123" wb

Cpe	1095	850	1650	4200	5850	8400
Cpe 2-4	1145	875	1700	4250	5900	8500
Conv Cpe	1215	3400	6900	11,500	16,100	23,000
4 dr Sed	1145	825	1600	3950	5500	7900

1936 Graham, Standard 6, coupe, HAC

1936 Graham, custom convertible victoria, Vanden Plas, AA

1936

Crusader Model 80, 6-cyl., 111" wb

2 dr Sed	635	750	1450	3400	5000	7100
2 dr Sed Trunk	665	750	1450	3500	5050	7200
4 dr Sed	665	750	1450	3500	5050	7200
4 dr Sed Trunk	695	775	1500	3600	5100	7300

Cavalier Model 90, 6-cyl., 115" wb

Bus Cpe	765	775	1500	3600	5100	7300
Cpe 2-4	795	775	1500	3750	5250	7500
2 dr Sed	765	750	1450	3500	5050	7200
2 dr Sed Trunk	795	775	1500	3600	5100	7300
4 dr Sed	795	775	1500	3600	5100	7300
4 dr Sed Trunk	825	775	1500	3700	5200	7400

Model 110, Supercharged, 6-cyl., 115" wb

Cpe	865	800	1550	3850	5400	7700
Cpe 2-4	895	825	1600	4000	5600	8000
2 dr Sed	865	775	1500	3700	5200	7400
2 dr Sed Trunk	895	775	1500	3750	5250	7500
4 dr Sed	895	775	1500	3750	5250	7500
4 dr Sed Trunk	925	800	1550	3900	5450	7800
Cus 4 dr Sed	1170	825	1600	4000	5600	8000

1937 Graham, Cavalier, coupe, AA

1937

Crusader, 6-cyl., 111" wb

	FP	5	4	3	2	1
2 dr Sed	690	750	1450	3300	4900	7000
2 dr Sed Trunk	720	750	1450	3400	5000	7100
4 dr Sed	770	750	1450	3400	5000	7100
4 dr Sed Trunk	795	750	1450	3500	5050	7200

Cavalier, 6-cyl., 116" wb

Bus Cpe	850	775	1500	3750	5250	7500
Cpe 3-5	900	800	1550	3850	5400	7700
Conv Cpe	945	3150	6300	10,500	14,700	21,000
2 dr Sed	875	750	1450	3400	5000	7100
2 dr Sed Trunk	905	750	1450	3500	5050	7200
4 dr Sed	905	750	1450	3500	5050	7200
4 dr Sed Trunk	935	775	1500	3600	5100	7300

1937 Graham, Series 116, 4-dr. sedan, AA

Series 116, Supercharged, 6-cyl., 116" wb

Bus Cpe	1015	825	1600	4000	5600	8000
Cpe 3-5	1045	850	1650	4150	5800	8300
Conv Cpe	1080	3300	6600	11,000	15,400	22,000
2 dr Sed	1020	775	1500	3750	5250	7500
2 dr Sed Trunk	1050	800	1550	3800	5300	7600
4 dr Sed	1050	800	1550	3800	5300	7600
4 dr Sed Trunk	1080	800	1550	3850	5400	7700

Series 120, Custom Supercharged, 6-cyl., 116" and 120" wb

Bus Cpe	1105	850	1650	4100	5700	8200
Cpe 3-5	1135	875	1700	4250	5900	8500
Conv Cpe	1170	3600	7200	12,000	16,800	24,000
4 dr Sed	1160	825	1600	4000	5600	8000
4 dr Sed Trunk	1190	850	1650	4100	5700	8200

1938 Graham, Supercharger, combination coupe, HAC

1938

Standard Model 96, 6-cyl., 120" wb

4 dr Sed	1025	725	1400	3100	4800	6800

Special Model 96, 6-cyl., 120" wb

4 dr Sed	1075	750	1450	3300	4900	7000

Model 97, Supercharged, 6-cyl., 120" wb

4 dr Sed	1198	775	1500	3600	5100	7300

Custom Model 97, Supercharged, 6-cyl., 120" wb

4 dr Sed	1320	800	1550	3850	5400	7700

1939 Graham-Paige, "sharknose," 2-dr. sedan, OCW

1939 Graham, sedan, HAC

1939
Special Model 96, 6-cyl., 120" wb

	FP	5	4	3	2	1
Cpe	940	750	1450	3300	4900	7000
2 dr Sed	940	725	1400	3000	4700	6700
4 dr Sed	965	725	1400	3100	4800	6800

Custom Special 96, 6-cyl., 120" wb

Cpe	1070	750	1450	3400	5000	7100
2 dr Sed	1070	725	1400	3100	4800	6800
4 dr Sed	1095	725	1400	3200	4850	6900

Model 97, Supercharged, 6-cyl., 120" wb

Cpe	1070	875	1700	4350	6050	8700
2 dr Sed	1070	925	1900	4550	6350	9100
4 dr Sed	1095	925	2000	4650	6500	9300

Custom Model 97, Supercharged, 6-cyl., 120" wb

Cpe	1200	950	2200	4800	6700	9600
2 dr Sed	1200	925	2000	4650	6500	9300
4 dr Sed	1225	875	1700	4250	5900	8500

1940
DeLuxe Model 108, 6-cyl., 120" wb

Cpe	1020	775	1500	3700	5200	7400
2 dr Sed	995	725	1400	3200	4850	6900
4 dr Sed	1015	750	1450	3300	4900	7000

Custom Model 108, 6-cyl., 120" wb

Cpe	1160	775	1500	3750	5250	7500
2 dr Sed	1135	750	1450	3300	4900	7000
4 dr Sed	1160	750	1450	3500	5050	7200

DeLuxe Model 107, Supercharged, 6-cyl., 120" wb

Cpe	1160	950	2100	4750	6650	9500
2 dr Sed	1135	925	2000	4600	6400	9200
4 dr Sed	1160	950	2100	4700	6600	9400

Custom Model 107, Supercharged, 6-cyl., 120" wb

Cpe	1295	900	1900	4500	6300	9000
2 dr Sed	1265	875	1700	4250	5900	8500
4 dr Sed	1295	875	1700	4350	6050	8700

1941 Graham, model 109, Hollywood, 4-dr. sedan, OCW

1941
Custom Hollywood Model 113, 6-cyl., 115" wb

	FP	5	4	3	2	1
4 dr Sed	968	1075	3000	5500	7700	11,000

Custom Hollywood Model 113, Supercharged, 6-cyl., 115" wb

4 dr Sed	1065	1150	3600	6000	8400	12,000

GRAMM STEAM — Chillicothe, Ohio — (1902) — In 1902 Benjamin A. Gramm, general manager of the Motor Storage & Repair Company of Chillicothe, announced his forthcoming manufacture of steam carriages in the $750 to $900 range. The Gramm steamers were built for one season only. In 1903 Benjamin Gramm switched to a gasoline surrey that he called the Buckeye. The year following he remained with gasoline cars, but switched their name again to Logan.

GRAND — The Grand Center Motor Car Company was organized in St. Joseph, Missouri late in 1913 with a capital stock of $5000 to manufacture and deal in automobiles. Incorporators were W.J. Hendler, H.R. Lewis and Louis Seigel. Manufacture is doubted.

The Grand Rapids Motor Truck Company of Detroit, Michigan is indicated on various car rosters as producing an automobile in 1912. The firm is known to have been organized in March that year with a capital stock of $600,000. Manufacture is doubted, however.

The Grand St. Louis Auto Company was organized with a capital stock of $4000 during the summer of 1913 to manufacture, buy, sell, deal in and repair automobiles in St. Louis, Missouri. Incorporators were Leon B. and John J. Scherrer, E.A. Stosberg and A.W. Michaels. Manufacture is doubted.

The Grand Ridge Automobile Company was organized in Grand Ridge, Illinois during the spring of 1907 "to build and assemble cars, the model to be a five-passenger rig fitted with a 36-40-horsepower four-cylinder engine." Dr. W.E. Smith was president of the company, with F.K. Hook vice-president, Charles Turner treasurer, G.L. Dearth secretary. Subsequent manufacture has not been documented.

The Grand X Garage was organized in Chicago, Illinois early in 1914 with a capital stock of $2000 for the manufacture of automobiles. Frank L. Johnson, John Farr and Elof W. Johnson were the incorporators. Manufacture is doubted.

GRANE — The Grane Brothers at 640 West Third Street in Cincinnati, Ohio were indicated to be building automobiles in pre-World War I editions of the Ware yearbook of the industry. The brothers involved were Henry and Hermann. Further documentation is lacking.

GRANGER — The Granger Motor Works of Chicago, Illinois has appeared on various car rosters as the manufacturer of an automobile in 1909. City directories of the period make no reference to such a company in town.

GRANITE FALLS — The cars built from 1902 to 1909 in Granite Falls, Minnesota are properly referenced under the name of the man who built them. Refer to Lende.

GRANT — That the Grant Brothers of Boston, Massachusetts were building a car in 1900 was noted in a trade publication that year. There was no company of that name in Boston, but the two Grants in town who may have been responsible were Charles G. at 360 Dorchester and George A. at 73 Shawmut.

The Grant Square Automobile Company was organized in New York City during the spring of 1906 with a capital stock of $20,000 to manufacture motor vehicles and parts. Three Brooklynites were behind this venture: C.F. Batt, F. Wilson and W. Weston. Manufacture of a car is doubted.

GRANT STEAM — Cleveland, Ohio — (1864) — John J. Grant of Cleveland was among the pioneers in steam car development during the Civil War period. Details regarding the steamer he built in 1864 are lacking, but it is known that the vehicle did run and also that it ran into a woman and child during one trial, whereupon Grant never used it again. The turn of the century found John J. Grant working with the Cleveland Machine Screw Company, where he had the reputation, so *The Motor Age* said, of knowing "more about steel balls than any other man in the country." Subsequently he formed his own Grant Machine Tool Company in Franklin, Pennsylvania. The 1864 steamer was the only car he built.

GRANT — Brooklyn, New York — (1897) — The first gasoline car to be called a Grant was built in Brooklyn. W. Wallace Grant was its inventor, and his runabout boasted such advances for this early period as three-quarter elliptic springs in front, and canted half elliptics in the rear — and a wheel for steering. For whatever the reason, and probably it was lack of financing, the Grant was never produced, though it was exhibited for a number of years thereafter as "The Oldest Car on Long Island." Its whereabouts today are not known.

1897 Grant, runabout, WLB

1913 Grant, roadster, WLB

GRANT — **Detroit, Michigan** — **(1913)/Findlay, Ohio** — **(1913-1916)/Cleveland, Ohio** — **(1916-1922)** — Of all the new automobile ventures establishing themselves in business in 1913, the Grant Motor Company of Detroit certainly seemed to be the most solidly based for future success in the industry. George D. Grant and his brother Charles A., president and vice-president respectively, had established their automobile dealership at 1000 Woodward Avenue soon after the turn of the century and owned a successful machine foundry as well. Secretary-treasurer David A. Shaw had been treasurer for the Simplex Motor Car Company in Indiana. Chief engineer James M.L. Howe, a Cornell graduate, had held high positions in the engineering departments of Thomas, Cunningham and Selden in New York State, and Studebaker in Indiana. Factory manager George S. Salzman had built his first experimental gasoline car in Boston in 1897 and thereafter had been production manager for Thomas and Simplex. General sales manager George S. Waite had served in that same sales position for Thomas and Simplex too, having learned his trade with Alvan T. Fuller, the dynamic Boston dealer for Packard. As the *Automobile Trade Journal* pointed out, "this group of men constitutes a galaxy of automobile experts whose experience cannot but guarantee the excellence of the product they are turning out." The car had been designed by Salzman and refined by Howe — and was, as its makers rather modestly put it, "a thoroughly good low-priced car." The Grant's problem was that it arrived during the cyclecar frenzy and although the company and knowledgeable reporters insisted the vehicle was a "miniature motor car" they had little luck in convincing the general populace of this. The Grant was a natty little two-seater roadster on a 90-inch wheelbase with standard 56-inch tread. It was powered by a four-cylinder 12 hp water-cooled engine. It featured shaft drive, a sliding gear transmission, drop forged front axle, and a three-point suspension arrangement of full elliptic springs at the front, semi-elliptic at the rear placed crosswise back of the rear axle. It had perky drum headlamps, nicely curved full fenders and sprightly but substantial wire wheels. And its price tag was $495. As a sports car, which the Grant really was (in the much later M.G. TC tradition), it was really a honey. After a small production run in temporary headquarters in Detroit in 1913, the firm moved into the plant of the defunct Findlay Motor Com-

1914 Grant, roadster, HAC

pany of Ohio in November of 1913. In 1914 a total of 3000 of these little Grants was produced, but with the cyclecar onus hanging heavy, the line was expanded in 1915 to include a larger six-cylinder car. Production increased to 2100 that year. An even larger six was introduced in 1916, and the wonderful little four was dropped, but Grant quality remained high, and Grant prices attractively low. Grant was reorganized as Grant Motor Car Corporation that year, and a new plant said to have a 35,000 annual production capacity was opened in Cleveland that fall. Optimism reigned. Production for 1916 totaled a few more than 4000 cars; in 1917 in Cleveland it shot up to 12,000. That year, too, in an exchange of stock, Grant acquired the Denneen Motor Company of Cleveland, makers of the Denmo truck. Manufacture of Denmo-Grant trucks was continued in the Denneen factory until an addition to the Grant factory in Cleveland was completed. Grant car production was 10,000 units for 1918 and 1919; the Cleveland plant made ordnance trailers for the war effort, the Findlay plant was reactivated for munitions production. Grant entered the postwar market loaded for bear. David Shaw, now Grant president, announced that 21,000 orders had been received for the company's new Model H, introduced in October 1919. The following March the firm bought controlling interest in the engine-producing H.J. Walker Manufacturing Company of Cleveland. Then Grant was hit with the postwar depression. Orders no longer necessarily translated into sales. Production for 1920 totaled just 5400 cars. The company desperately tried to retrench, but the vast quantities of parts ordered for the hoped-for boom year continued to arrive at the factory. Soon the company had a half-million-dollar inventory — and sales continued to plummet. One of the last Grant brochures noted that "the financial resources of the company are an assurance of permanence and stability." But there were no financial resources left, nor even the working capital to cover basic operating expenses. Grant sold off the Walker engine company, but it didn't help. Receivership arrived in October 1922. Some truck production continued under receivership, but the cars were immediately discontinued. It was all over in June 1923 when the Grant factory in Cleveland was sold to the Lincoln Electric Company for $425,000.

1913-1914 GRANT
Four — 12 hp, 90" wb

	FP	5	4	3	2	1
Roadster-2P	495	2300	3300	4600	7500	16,000

1915 Grant, model M, roadster, HAC

1915 GRANT
Model M — 4-cyl., 12 hp, 90" wb

Roadster-2P	425	2300	3300	4600	7500	16,000

Model S — 6-cyl., 20 hp, 106" wb

Touring-5P	795	2400	3400	4800	8000	17,000
Roadster-2P	795	2450	3500	4900	8300	17,500

1916 Grant, model V, touring, HAC

1916 GRANT
Model V — 6-cyl., 22 hp, 112" wb

Touring-5P	795	2400	3400	4800	8000	17,000
Roadster-2P	795	2500	3500	5000	8500	18,000
Cabriolet	1025	2300	3300	4600	7500	16,000

1917 GRANT
Model K — 6-cyl., 22 hp, 112" wb

Touring-5P	825	2400	3400	4800	8000	17,000
Cabriolet	1050	2300	3300	4600	7500	16,000
Tour. Sedan-5P	1000	2500	3500	5000	8500	18,000
Roadster-2P	960	2500	3500	5000	8500	18,000

1917 Grant, model K, roadster, HAC

1918 Grant, model G, sedan touring, HAC

1918 GRANT
Model G — 6-cyl., 22 hp, 114" wb

	FP	5	4	3	2	1
Touring-5P	1055	2500	3500	5000	8500	18,000
Roadster-3P	1055	2700	3600	5300	8800	19,000
Sedan Touring	1595	2500	3500	5000	8500	18,000
Sedan Roadster	1575	2500	3500	5000	8500	18,000

1919 Grant, model G, touring, HAC

1919 GRANT
Model G — 6-cyl., 22 hp, 114" wb

		5	4	3	2	1
Touring-5P	1220	2500	3500	5000	8500	18,000
Roadster-3P	1220	2700	3600	5300	8800	19,000
Detachable Sed.-5P	1500	2500	3500	5000	8500	18,000
All-Weather Sed.	1745	2400	3400	4800	8000	17,000
All-Weather Cpe.	1725	2300	3300	4600	7500	16,000

1920-21 Grant, model H, touring, HAC

1920 GRANT
Model H — 6-cyl., 35 hp, 116" wb

Touring-5P	1495	2700	3600	5300	8800	19,000
Roadster-2P	1495	2800	3700	5500	9000	19,500
Sedan-5P	2450	1600	2700	3800	5800	12,000
Coupe-3P	2450	2000	3000	4200	6500	14,000

1921 GRANT
Model HX — 6-cyl., 45 hp, 116" wb

	FP	5	4	3	2	1
Touring-5P	1550	2800	3700	5500	9000	19,500
Roadster-2P	1550	2900	3700	5600	9100	20,000
Coupe-4P	2450	2000	3000	4200	6500	14,000
Sedan-5P	2450	1600	2700	3800	5800	12,000

1922 Grant, touring, HAC

1922 GRANT
Six — 45 hp, 116" wb

Touring-5P	1550	2800	3700	5500	9000	19,500
Roadster-2P	1550	2900	3700	5600	9100	20,000
Coupe-4P	2450	2000	3000	4200	6500	14,000
Sedan-5P	2450	1600	2700	3800	5800	12,000

1912 Grant Six

GRANT SIX — Cleveland, Ohio — (1912-1913) — The Grant Six from Cleveland was born as the Elmer Six from Elkhart (Indiana). When it was not possible for Harry Elmer to move his car into production in Elkhart, he simply moved it to Cleveland. There the Grant-Lees Machine Company provided the necessary backing, organizing the Grant Motor Car Company as a department of the parent organization. Harry Elmer was manager of this new department, and he brought along all of the people who had been with him in the Elmer venture from the beginning, except for one lawyer who had largely been the reason he had not been able to get into production in Elkhart. While a new factory building was being built, Grant Six production began in other Grant-Lees facilities. The car was introduced in April 1912, and it was a 50 hp six like the Elmer prototype, though cowl lines and the sweep of the front fender were somewhat modified. "The Pioneer Semi-Assembled Car" was a Grant Six slogan, and its price was $2750. It was not manufactured for long. For reasons which history has obscured, Harry Elmer resigned from the company in November of 1912. The Grant Six may have been produced for a short while thereafter, but by early 1913, it was gone, just about the same time that Grant-Lees was also unloading Stuyvesant, another car company it had bought when Harry Elmer came to town.

GRASBERGER — The J.A. Grasberger Manufacturing Company was organized in Richmond, Virginia late in 1910 with a capital stock of $60,000 to manufacture and sell "motor cars, buggies and flying machines." Joining J.A. Grasberger in this venture were E.P. Foote, A.W. Foote and John B. Welsh. The firm was reincorporated with a capital stock of $50,000 during the fall of 1911, with J.E. Sorg and Robert N. Wildbore joining Grasberger this time. Manufacture of a car is doubted.

GRAVES & CONGDON — The cars produced by the machine shop of Graves & Congdon from 1908 to 1910 in Amesbury, Massachusetts were usually marketed under the tradename of Crown. Refer to Crown.

GRAY — The Gray Auto & Supply Company was organized early in 1912 in Portland, Maine with a capital stock of $10,000 to "manufacture, sell, export and import automobiles." Incorporators were H.P. Sweetser, W.J. Hardy and H.H. Sweetser. Manufacture of a car is doubted.

The Gray Automobile Company was organized late in 1905 in Salt Lake City, Utah with a capital stock of $5000 to manufacture, buy, sell, rent and repair automobiles. William H. Gray was president, Sidney M. Bamberger vice-president, Joshua B. Bean treasurer. Manufacture of a car is doubted.

The Gray & Couch Motor Vehicle Company of Stoneham, Massachusetts has occasionally appeared as a manufacturer on car rosters. No documentation of this has been discovered. The Couch of this partnership was undoubtedly Stillman A. Crouch. Refer to Crouch.

The Gray & Davis Factory Corporation was organized in Cambridge, Massachusetts with a capital stock of $50,000 early in 1913 for the manufacture of motor vehicles. J.H. Maxwell and H.W. Taplin were the principals involved. Manufacture of an automobile did not follow, Gray & Davis remaining in the automobile accessory field.

The Gray Specialty Company was organized in Newark, New Jersey during the fall of 1911 with a capital stock of $125,000 for the manufacture of automobiles and supplies. E. Gray, E. Gray, Jr. and T.F.N. Gray were the people involved. Manufacture of a car is doubted.

The Gray Manufacturing Company was organized in Burlington, New Jersey early in 1902 to manufacture bicycles, automobiles and machinery. Behind this venture were Michael J. Gray, A.L. Hildaman, John Gray, Oliver Van Wagoner, William R. Conrad, Daniel C. Bayer. Manufacture of a car is doubted.

1908 Gray, NAHC

GRAY — New York, New York — (1908) — In 1908 H. Liggett Gray of New York City wrote the editors of *The Automobile* about the steam car he had just completed. Its engine was two-cylinder, double-acting and placed under the seat, with boiler and water tank mounted up front under a hood, and the gasoline tank to the rear. The frame was angle iron, with three-quarter elliptic springs in front, quarter elliptics in the rear. "I can make between 25 and 30 miles per hour," Gray explained. "Even with high gearing, it has sufficient power to carry three persons, and is a good hillclimber." The Gray seemed to be an altogether admirable homemade car. "P.S. — I am fourteen years old," H. Liggett Gray wrote.

GRAY — Sunnyvale, California — (1916) — On Christmas Eve of 1915, Robert P. Matches and Gilbert M. Anderson announced the establishment of a factory to build taxis for their Gray Taxicab Company, the partners having operated a taxi service in Los Angeles and San Francisco for the several years past and now having been awarded "exclusive taxicab rights on the entire Southern Pacific system." No other company thereafter would be allowed to solicit taxicab business at any station or depot on the Southern Pacific Railroad. What a Christmas present that was. Immediately the partners purchased the property of the Goldy Machine Company (earlier that year home to the Elbert cyclecar) in Sunnyvale which lay adjacent to the main line of the Southern Pacific, and in its complex of buildings began making plans for the manufacture of seven-to-eight taxis a day. But this good deal was quickly undone, and shenanigans and quarreling among the partners seems to be the reason. In May 1916 Anderson informed the press that he had dismissed Matches because of his diversion of Gray Taxicab profits into other business ventures, including the Hydromotor amphibian project. From New York City, Matches replied that he had "resigned voluntarily to give my entire attention to aeroplane interests." And he denied any wrongdoing. During all this time, Anderson had been otherwise engaged too, as "Broncho Billy" of silent film fame. And, in collaboration with George Spoor, Anderson had his own studio as well — Essanay in Niles, which produced some of Charlie Chaplin's earliest films. By 1916, however, Chaplin had wearied of the primitive conditions in Niles and left for Hollywood. And at the same time, Spoor and Anderson had a falling out, and the Niles studio was closed. All this and the fracas with Matches combined to make 1916 a very bad year for "Broncho Billy." How many taxis were produced by the Andermat Machine Company (as the partners had combined their names when they were friends) is unclear. Most probably operations came to a quick halt after Matches left for New York. Even the Gray Taxicab Company was in receivership by now, although its passenger-ferrying operations continued into 1918 when even that phase of the business was kaput. Among Matches' subsequent involvements in the automotive industry was a turn with Emerson Motors Company. Matches was among those indicted in that firm's collapse. Perhaps "Broncho Billy" had been right about his Gray Taxicab partner all along.

GRAY — Detroit, Michigan — (1922-1926) — When initially announced during the spring of 1920, the Gray Motor Corporation was a venture capitalized at $4 million which took over the plant and equipment of the Gray Motor Company, builders of engines in Detroit, for the purpose of manufacturing a medium-priced four-cylinder car. Spearheading the project were Frank F. Beall, former vice-president of the Packard Motor Car Company, and William H. Blackburn, former Cadillac superintendent. A year

1922 Gray, touring, HAC

later Frank L. Klingensmith resigned as vice-president and treasurer of the Ford Motor Company, took on the presidency of the Gray Motor Corporation and, though official announcements continued to talk of a medium-priced car, a few savvy reporters in the trade press wondered. The new Gray did not arrive until November of 1921, being delayed, Gray said, "for a more satisfactory market condition," but those same savvy reporters were aware they had wondered correctly. The new Gray turned out to be a $500 range car designed to compete with the Model T Ford head-on. Its engine was a 20 hp four, like the T's, and on a 100-inch wheelbase too — but its chassis featured a three-speed selective transmission and single cantilever springs in front, double cantilevers in the rear. In the fall of 1922 a stock Gray touring car was driven from San Francisco to New York, averaging 33.8 miles per gallon in 4819 miles of travel. An official observer of the American Automobile Association had accompanied the car the entire distance, and the gas mileage realized set a new transcontinental mark. The "Aristocrat of Small Cars," the company advertised, "offers you World Record Economy." Gray predicted annual sales in the quarter of a million range. They never happened. A total of 14,772 Grays had been built by the end of June 1923. Beating Henry Ford at his own game was not as easy as envisioned. For the 1925 model year the wheelbase of the Gray was increased to 104 inches but by now its price had been increased too; another inch in wheelbase and front wheel brakes were offered in 1926, but then it was all over. In January of 1925 Frank Klingensmith resigned from the company and took an extended vacation in Australia. That summer the firm announced plans to produce the British Tilling-Stevens Gas-Electric bus under patent. The following summer the Gray Motor Corporation factory and equipment went to the auction block.

1922 Gray, touring, WLB

1923 Gray, roadster, HAC

1922-1923 GRAY
Four — 20 hp, 100" wb

	FP	5	4	3	2	1
Touring-5P	520	2400	3400	4800	8000	17,000
Roadster-2P	490	2500	3500	5000	8500	18,000
Coach-5P	785	1600	2700	3800	5800	12,000
Coupe-2P	685	2300	3300	4600	7500	16,000
Sedan-5P	835	1800	2800	4000	6200	13,000

The GRAY Coupe

1924 Gray, coupe, HAC

1924 GRAY
Four - 20 hp, 100" wb

	FP	5	4	3	2	1
Roadster-2P	510	2500	3500	5000	8500	18,000
Touring-5P	520	2400	3400	4800	8000	17,000
Sport Touring-5P	625	2500	3500	5000	8500	18,000
Coupe-2P	685	2300	3300	4600	7500	16,000
Coach-4P	785	1600	2700	3800	5800	12,000
Sedan-5P	835	1800	2800	4000	6200	13,000

1925 Gray, touring, HAC

1925 GRAY
Four — 20 hp, 104" wb

Touring-5P	630	2700	3600	5300	8800	19,000
Coupe-2P	750	2300	3300	4600	7500	16,000
Coupe-3P	845	2200	3200	4400	7000	15,000
Sedan-5P	895	1800	2800	4000	6200	13,000
Sport Sedan-5P	995	1900	2900	4100	6400	13,500

1926 Gray, sedan, HAC

1926 GRAY
Four — 21 hp, 105" wb

Touring-5P	595	2700	3600	5300	8800	19,000
Sedan-5P	845	1800	2800	4000	6200	13,000

GRAY LIGHT CAR — Denver, Colorado — (1920) — Apparently no one was fooled into believing that the Gray was anything other than a cyclecar, which it was, fully a half decade after the cyclecar fad had died in the United States. Two pilot models of the Gray were built, with power provided by Harley-Davidson (one a single-cylinder engine, the other a twin) and wheels that were strictly motorcycle. Projected price range was $350-$450. The Gray Light Car Corporation of Denver made grand plans to launch manufacture in a new factory to be sited in Longmont. But potential investors stayed away in droves. Only the two pilot models were ever built, though as late as January 1921 H.A. Gray was still announcing that as soon as "steel prices stabilize," he planned to get on with the business.

GRAYGOOD — The Graygood Company was organized in New York City during the summer of 1907 with a capital stock of $5000 for the manufacture of automobiles. Incorporators were C.W. Graham, J.H. Graham and H.D. Thorp. Manufacture is doubted.

GREAT — A number of companies prefaced with "Great" seemingly weren't so, announcing intended manufacture of an automobile but apparently never following through on it.

The Great American Automobile Company of Philadelphia, Pennsylvania, organized with a $1.5 million capital stock during the summer of 1910 for the manufacture of automobiles and trucks. Samuel Quinn, Charles N. Lee, L.H. Van Briggle and H.W. Davis were the incorporators.

The Great American Truck & Tractor Company of Philadelphia, Pennsylvania, organized during the summer of 1917 to manufacture and sell automobiles, trucks and tractors. Incorporators were H. Theobald, E. Franklin and G. King Franklin.

The Great Central Electric Company of Chicago, Illinois, organized with $25,000 capital stock late in 1908 to manufacture and deal in automobiles, motors and machinery. John S. Crowell, J.E. Haschke and F.L. Harford were the incorporators. Haschke was a storage battery manufacturer who had built a car under his own name in 1904.

The Great Eagle Motor Devices Company, a $130,000 Delaware incorporation from early 1912 for the manufacture and sale of automobiles, motor boats and "self-propelled vehicles of all kinds." The incorporators were G. Hagstrom, I. Hagstrom and H.W. Davis.

The Great Northern Motors Company of Minneapolis, Minnesota, organized during the summer of 1917 with a $100,000 capital stock to "manufacture and assemble automobiles, tractors and other motor vehicles." Incorporators were Jerome Landauer and A.M. Choate of Minneapolis, and Thomas J. Clifford of St. John, North Dakota.

The Great Western Manufacturing Company of Chicago, Illinois, incorporated with a capital stock of $200,000 during the fall of 1899 for the manufacture of bicycles and motor vehicles. Incorporators were Henry L. Stern, Henry Frantzen and Henry A. Gardner.

The Greater New York & Suburban Transportation Company, organized late in 1908 in New York City with a $25,000 capital stock to build "taximeter motor vehicles, engines, etc." Incorporators were H. Lauterbach and C.E. Volz of Brooklyn, and C.A. Conner of Manhattan.

GREAT ARROW — Great Arrow was the designation decided upon by George N. Pierce for the four-cylinder car he introduced as a companion to his line of twins in 1904. Great Arrow continued as a marque or model designation until 1909. From that time forward, all the cars from this Buffalo, New York company were known simply as Pierce-Arrows. Refer to Pierce-Arrow.

1910 Great Eagle, limousine, NAHC

GREAT EAGLE — Columbus, Ohio — (1910-1915) — In October of 1909 the United States Carriage Company of Columbus announced its intention to engage in the manufacture of touring cars, runabouts, motor hearses, cabs and ambulances, and promised its new cars would be on the market early the following year. Not until they arrived in February was the public made aware of what they would be called. The cars were appropriately named. Great Eagles were huge automobiles. Interestingly, although a runabout had been promised from the beginning, it did not arrive until nearly the end. The Great Eagles inbetween were mainly seven-passenger cars, on wheelbases often stretching beyond 140 inches, which leads to the suspicion that the principal focus of the company was conveyances for one's final ride. Fred C. Myers was the company president, and by 1912 he had added a six-cylinder model to the Great Eagle's original line of fours. Receivership for United States Carriage Company arrived in an interesting way. It was requested by Katherine Myers, wife of the president, who held a note of $6000 against the company and feared her money would be lost if other creditors, who were threatening, were permitted to take action. The company went into receivership in February of 1915. Interestingly, too, in 1918 the Great Eagle was reported to be flying again, with the same two models announced for that model year as had been last built in early 1915. This could have been wishful thinking, since the evidence suggests the Great Eagle had been grounded permanently by then.

1910-1911 GREAT EAGLE
Four — 40 hp, 126" wb

	FP	5	4	3	2	1
Model 1215 Limo.-7P	3500	3000	4000	6000	9500	21,000
Model 1217 Landaulet-7P	3500	3100	4200	6300	10,500	22,000

1912 GREAT EAGLE
Model 4-50 — 4-cyl., 36 hp, 135" wb

Limousine-7P	3500	3000	4000	6000	9000	21,000
Landaulet-7P	3500	3100	4200	6300	10,500	22,000

Model 6-60 — 6-cyl., 41 hp, 138" wb

	FP	5	4	3	2	1
Limousine-7P	3500	3200	4300	6500	11,000	23,000
Landaulet-7P	3500	3300	4400	6700	12,000	24,000

1913 GREAT EAGLE
Model B — 4-cyl., 50 hp, 135" wb

Touring-7P	3500	4700	6100	9900	19,000	33,000
Limousine-7P	4000	3100	4200	6300	10,500	22,000
Landaulet-7P	3750	3200	4300	6500	11,000	23,000
Limousine-10P (142" wb)	4750	3300	4400	6700	12,000	24,000

Model C — 6-cyl., 60 hp, 142" wb

Touring-7P	4000	5000	6500	11,000	22,000	35,000
Limousine-7P	4500	3300	4400	6700	12,000	24,000
Landaulet-7P	3750	3500	4500	7000	13,000	25,000
Limousine-10P (147" wb)	5250	3700	4700	7300	13,700	26,000

1914-1915 GREAT EAGLE
Model 4-50 — 4-cyl., 50 hp, 138" wb

Model A Roadster-2P	—	5200	6800	11,300	23,000	36,000
Model B Touring-7P	—	5000	6500	11,000	22,000	35,000

Model 6-60 — 6-cyl., 60 hp, 142" wb

Model C Touring-7P	—	5200	6800	11,300	23,000	36,000

GREAT SIX — The Great Six was a model of the Gearless from Rochester, New York introduced in 1908. Refer to Gearless.

GREAT SMITH — The Great Smith produced in Topeka, Kansas from 1907 to 1911 was the linear successor to the Smith produced by the same factory for the four years previous. Refer to Smith.

1913 Great Southern, model 30, roadster

GREAT SOUTHERN — Birmingham, Alabama — (1912-1914) — The Great Southern Automobile Company was organized with a capital stock of $100,000 in October of 1909. E.F. Enslen was president; Ike Adler, vice-president; John J. Kyser, secretary-treasurer; E.F. Enslen, Jr., general manager. The new company had already secured property formerly used as a cotton mill, it was announced, and would engage anon in the manufacture and repair of automobiles. Nothing further was heard from Great Southern until February of 1911. "Although it has done but little in the way of turning out cars," *The Horseless Age* noted pointedly then, the company had just increased its capitalization to $500,000. E.F. Enslen, Jr. was quoted as remarking that Great Southern "has met with rare success thus far." One cannot imagine what that would have been. The first Great Southern automobiles were introduced to the public in January of 1912. Two four-cylinder models of varying horsepower and wheelbase were offered. The Great Southern line was curtailed to a single model for 1914, and it does not appear to have been built into 1915. During that year Great Southern turned its attention completely to the manufacture of commercial vehicles, in which pursuit it continued until going bankrupt in 1917.

1912-1913 GREAT SOUTHERN
Thirty — 4-cyl., 30 hp, 113" wb

Fore-Door Touring-5P	1400	3100	4200	6300	10,500	22,000
Fore-Door Roadster-2P	1400	3200	4300	6500	11,000	23,000

Forty — 4-cyl., 45/55 hp, 128" wb

Fore-Door Touring-6P	2100	3500	4500	7000	13,000	25,000

1914 GREAT SOUTHERN
Fifty — 4-cyl., 50 hp, 128" wb

Touring-7P	1750	3500	4500	7000	13,000	25,000

GREAT WESTERN — La Porte, Indiana — (1902-1905) — The Great Western Manufacturing Company, a longtime bicycle establishment in La Porte, began experimenting with a steam vehicle in 1902, as the Great Western people said, "with a view to manufacturing carriages of that class." They were still experimenting two years later when, in December 1904, finally word came that a light steam touring car and delivery wagon would be placed on the market for 1905. There is no evidence it ever was, but apparently Great Western continued experimenting into 1905.

GREAT WESTERN — San Diego, California — (1907-1908) — The Great Western Motor Car Company was incorporated in the late fall of 1907 with a capital stock of $200,000 for the manufacture of an automobile with a two-stroke four-cylinder engine with sheet-metal water jackets. The principals involved were Charles L. Brimhall and I.C. Brimhall — and the Hunt brothers, William H. and Clarence, who would later build their own car in San Diego. For the Great Western venture, the Hunts were to provide two-stroke engines of their own design, and they moved to National City (a

suburb of San Diego) to set up shop. Meanwhile the Brimhalls were announcing to the press the acquisition of a two-story brick building at Twenty-Fourth Street and National Avenue which had formerly been a carriage manufactory and which "covers a city block and has switching facilities to three railroad lines." This was grandiose boasting, or city blocks were smaller in those days — the two-story building measured 40 by 60 feet, the machine shop alongside 30 by 100. By March of 1908 the first prototype Great Western car had been completed. It was also the last. As the Hunt brothers quickly learned, the Brimhalls were rather short in the cash department. In addition to their grand plans for the Great Western, however, they had also established a Mason agency, repaid the Hunts for the two-stroke engines they had built by giving them two Masons, and then vanished into the Great Western sunset.

1910 Great Western, Thirty, touring, WLB

GREAT WESTERN — Peru, Indiana — (1910-1916) — The notice of incorporation, dated September 8th, 1909, indicated that the purpose of the Great Western Automobile Company was "to manufacture, buy, sell, barter and otherwise dispose of automobiles and other propelled vehicles." Actually, the real purpose of the Great Western incorporation was to avoid embarrassment. E.A. Myers was the manufacturer of complete cars, as well as engines, transmissions and clutches available to other manufacturers to make complete cars, and he had been selling both under the name of Model since 1902. In 1907 he called his automobile a Star, produced by Model. But by 1909 discretion prompted him to rename both his car and the company producing it. The Great Western initially was not otherwise different from the automobiles previously produced, but by 1911 the firm had settled on a one-model policy, a fine 40 hp four available in a wide range of models, including a sprightly roadster painted "Chrome Yellow Orange." Management of the new enterprise was placed in the hands of Milton Kraus. In 1912 Myers sold his Model Gas Engine Works to interests in Pittsburgh and established a residence there to supervise the operation. Thereafter he was a frequent Peru-Pittsburgh commuter, particularly after 1913. In August that year, a problem developed at Great Western. "Owing to lack of orders during the past few months," the company announced with surprising candor, either additional time had to be secured from creditors or the business would have to be discontinued. During the receivership that followed, E.A. Myers took control of the company, with the retirement of Kraus. A good many mistakes began to be made now. In 1914 Great Western experimented with a model carrying a Carter piston valve engine. In 1915 the company contracted with the Rayfield people in Chrisman, Illinois to build their cars for them, and were subsequently sued for failure to carry out the contract. For the 1916 model year Great Western abandoned its four and went over to a lower-priced light six. Early in 1916 it was all over. The trade press blamed Great Western's failure on faulty engines made by the Model company in Pittsburgh. In Peru the last few cars were assembled from parts on hand by loyal employees, including Myers himself, and were then driven out into the countryside to be sold door-to-door.

1910 GREAT WESTERN
Thirty — 4-cyl., 30 hp, 106" wb

	FP	5	4	3	2	1
Model 20 Touring-5P	1600	3000	4000	6000	9500	21,000
Model 20A Runabout-3/4P	1600	3100	4100	6200	10,000	21,500

Forty — 4-cyl., 40 hp, 114" wb

Model 21 Touring-5P	2500	3100	4200	6300	10,500	22,000

Fifty — 4-cyl., 50 hp, 122" wb

Model 22 Touring-7P	4000	3300	4400	6700	12,000	24,000

1911 Great Western Forty, semi-torpedo, HAC

1911 GREAT WESTERN
Forty — 4-cyl., 40 hp, 114" wb

	FP	5	4	3	2	1
Touring-5P	1600	3000	4000	6000	9500	21,000
Demi-Tonneau Roadster-4P	1600	3100	4100	6200	10,000	21,500
Semi-Torpedo- 5P	1650	3100	4200	6300	10,500	22,000
Roadster-3P	1600	3200	4300	6500	11,000	23,000
Full-Torpedo-5P	1750	3200	4300	6500	11,000	23,000

1912 Great Western Forty, touring, HAC

1912 GREAT WESTERN
Forty — 4-cyl., 40 hp, 114" wb

Detachable 4-Dr. Tr.-5P	1750	3100	4200	6300	10,500	22,000
Semi-Torpedo-5P	1650	3000	4000	6000	9500	21,000
Touring-5P	1600	3100	4200	6300	10,500	22,000
Torpedo-Roadster-2P	1600	3200	4300	6500	11,000	23,000
Demi-Tonneau Roadster-4P	1600	3200	4300	6500	11,000	23,000

1913 Great Western Forty, roadster, HAC

1913 GREAT WESTERN
Forty — 4-cyl., 40 hp, 118" wb

Torpedo Roadster-2P	1585	3300	4400	6700	12,000	24,000
Semi-Torpedo-4P	1585	3200	4300	6500	11,000	23,000
Touring-5P	1585	3300	4400	6700	12,000	24,000
Sedan-5P	2250	2300	3300	4600	7500	16,000

1914 Great Western Forty, touring, HAC

1914 GREAT WESTERN
Forty — 4-cyl., 40 hp, 118" wb

Touring-5P	1710	3300	4400	6700	12,000	24,000
Touring-4P	1710	3300	4400	6700	12,000	24,000
Runabout-2P	1710	3500	4500	7000	13,000	25,000

1915 GREAT WESTERN
Forty — 4-cyl., 40 hp, 122" wb

Touring-6P	2500	3700	4700	7300	13,700	26,000
Touring-4P	2250	3500	4500	7000	13,000	25,000
Touring-5P	2250	3500	4500	7000	13,000	25,000
Touring-7P	2500	3700	4700	7300	13,000	26,000
Roadster-2P	2200	3900	4800	7700	14,300	27,000
Convertible Coupe-2P	3200	3300	4400	6700	12,000	24,000
Sedan Limousine-4P	3200	3100	4200	6300	10,500	22,000
Berlin Limousine-6P	3800	3300	4500	7000	13,000	25,000

1916 GREAT WESTERN
Six — 21.6 hp, 118" wb

Touring-5P	1185	3500	4500	7000	13,000	25,000

1915 Great Western Forty, touring, HAC

1916 Great Western, touring, MVMA

1903 Greeley, runabout, NAHC

GREELEY — Greeley, Colorado — (1902-1903) — This car seems to have been referred to as the Miller as frequently as it was by the town in which it was built, and a controversy raged in the *Greeley Tribune* in 1903 about which Miller was responsible for its design. E.N. Miller was a local machinist with a shop on Sixth Avenue; W.L. Miller was a local physician with a thriving practice in town. The car was a water-cooled two-cylinder 8hp runabout with wheel steering, two-speed planetary transmission and make-and-break ignition. The debate erupted in January 1903 when E.N. Miller provided a *Tribune* reporter with a story about the car and how he had designed it. This prompted W.L. Miller to reply that he had designed the car, that E.N. Miller had merely put it together for him under explicit instructions, and that he (W.L.) had organized the Miller Automobile Company with offices on Ninth Street for its manufacture. E.N. Miller immediately responded that perhaps Dr. Miller had organized a company for manufacture, but what he would be manufacturing was the car that he (E.N.) had designed and sold to W.L. The force of the argument definitely appears to be E.N.'s. He cited the many townspeople who visited his shop when he was building the car. "I doubt the doctor's ability to run the auto," the machinist said, to "say nothing of the building of it" — and he offered as proof the fact that W.L. Miller had not used the vehicle since its purchase and that when he took the machine from the shop, "it was behind a dray, the doctor seated in the auto tooting the horn." Because some residents of Greeley assumed the controversy was a family quarrel, E.N. Miller took pains to insist that "Dr. W.L. Miller is positively no relative of mine." Dr. Miller never did get his automobile company going, E.N. Miller continued awhile to advertise the building of automobiles to customer order, although perhaps memory of his experience with his first customer was among the reasons he soon chose to concentrate on machine work exclusively.

GREEN — The Green Auto Company was organized in Danbury, Connecticut during the summer of 1910 with a capital stock of $30,000 to manufacture automobiles and parts. Incorporators were John W. Green, Samuel E. Ryder and Clayton G. Haviland. Manufacture of a car is doubted.

The Green Engineering Company of Dayton, Ohio produced a car in 1920 called the C.R.G. Special. Refer to C.R.G. Special.

The Green Manufacturing Company of Cobleskill, New York has been indicated on various rosters as producing a car in 1913. There is no documentation that this ever happened.

R.G. Green, Inc. was organized during the summer of 1910 with a capital stock of $500 to "manufacture, repair, paint and deal in motor cars, carriages, motor cycles and to store motor cars" in New York City. Incorporators were R. Granville Green, Mabel L. Kirkham and I. Cleveland Kirkman. Manufacture is doubted.

W.H. Green was the designer of an engine and car promoted by the Hassall Iron Works of Colorado Springs, Colorado in late 1907. Refer to Hassall.

GREEN BAY — **Wequiock, Wisconsin** — **(1878)** — The State of Wisconsin could legitimately claim itself to be the first of the then thirty-seven to subsidize the development of the automobile in America. Spurred on by the success of the steam car designed by J.W. Carhart of Racine in 1871, the Wisconsin legislature in Madison enacted a law in 1875 that provided for a $10,000 prize for any citizen of the state who invented "a cheap and practical substitute for use of horses and other animals on the highway and farm." A trial of 200 miles was necessary to capture the prize, and the summer of 1878 was the time selected for the trial. Of the seven inventors who said they would enter, only two showed up at the starting line on July 16th. Both were steam cars. The Green Bay was built by E.P. Cowles of Wequiock, a community near Green Bay. It was powered by a two-cylinder engine, had three speeds forward and one reverse, and weighed a formidable 14,255 pounds. In addition to the wagon itself, the Green Bay pulled its own "tender" for fuel and water. Although his car was acknowledged to be faster than the other entrant, the Oshkosh, E.P. Cowles drove his Green Bay into a culvert early in the event and lost valuable time in repairs. Although the prize was not his, Cowles retains the distinction of being the first second-place finisher in any automobile race in America.

GREENE — **Newark & Paterson, New Jersey** — **(1916)** — Although the Greene Motor Car Company had been organized in 1905 presumably to manufacture automobiles, the firm proceeded to operate as a dealership only, handling the Smith & Mabley imports (Panhard, Mercedes and Renault) and the Locomobile. (The company did exhibit an electric truck at 1908 automobile shows but manufacture did not follow.) By 1916 Raymond A. Greene had earned a good reputation in Newark, which he came close to ruining in 1916 when he became involved with a monstrosity. It had three axles, six wheels, a 200-inch wheelbase and a turning radius of 32 feet. The invention of one M.A. Mackay, who was described as a "Maine backwoodsman," the car's front and rear wheels were controlled by the steering gear, with the center wheels fixed. For some reason, businessmen in Paterson became intrigued with the idea of producing this vehicle, in both large touring car and delivery van guise. The trade press remained skeptical. "R.A. Greene . . . is connected with the enterprise, which lends it a credibility it would not otherwise possess," reported *Automobile Topics* that September. The other two principals were textile men: William A. Arnold of the American Silk Dyeing & Finishing Company and William H. Fletcher of the Peerless Plush Company. Whether this car would have carried Greene's name if produced is not known. The prototype of this six-wheeled goliath is as far as the venture proceeded.

1902 Greenleaf, surrey, NAHC

GREENLEAF — **Lansing, Michigan** — **(1902)** — H.S. and Smith T. were Clawson & Son of Lansing in 1898, and in 1900 they reorganized themselves as the Greenleaf Cycle Company. Their activity revolved principally around the manufacture and repair of bicycles and sundries related thereto. In 1902, however, Smith T. Clawson made one short foray into the manufacture of automobiles. According to the November 13th issue of the *Lansing Journal*, he showed up at the National Grange Meeting with two automobiles of his own design. They were both exactly the same, and may have represented the total Greenleaf automobile production. The Greenleaf was a surrey with a two-cylinder horizontally opposed engine placed under the front seat with the cylinders facing forward, the crankshaft crosswise. A three-speed transmission and wood wheels were featured. The wheelbase was 78 inches. The Greenleaf weighed 1750 pounds,

and was priced at a dollar a pound. A price tag of $1750 was exorbitant for a car with such a simple specification, which is probably the reason the Greenleaf Cycle Company had returned full-time to the manufacture of two-wheelers by 1903. Although Smith T. Clawson was listed in the Lansing city directory as an automobile garage owner in 1904, and in 1906 as engaging in automobiles and repairs, bicycles remained the mainstay of the family business.

GREENSBORO — The Greensboro Motor Car Company was organized late in 1911 with a capital stock of $25,000 to make and sell automobiles in Greensboro, North Carolina. Incorporators were H.M. Chamblee, W.M. Fowler and W.J. Sherrod. Manufacture is doubted.

GREENVILLE — The Greenville Steel Car Company of Greenville, Pennsylvania produced the Fay of 1912 and the Empire from 1912-1914. Refer to Fay and Empire.

GREER — The H.R. Greer indicated as an automobile manufacturer in St. Louis in 1901 on various automobile rosters was in reality Harry R. Geer who operated a cycle emporium at 1017 Pine Street in St. Louis. Refer to Geer.

GREER — **Chicago, Illinois** — **(1916-1917)** — The Greer Motor Car Company had been organized in Chicago in 1904 by three Greers — Robert, Joseph H. and Frederick — as an automobile dealership, the Greer College of Motoring following in late 1915. Any Greer automobiles built were strictly as a classroom assignment, and were not marketed. By 1918 the Greer motoring school venture had evolved into the Greer College of Automobile, Tractor & Aeroplane Engineering, and the school was endorsed that year by the Chicago Automobile Trade Association.

GREGG — In early 1909 the trade press reported that application for a charter had been made by the Gregg Carriage Company of Philadelphia which planned to manufacture and deal in carriages and motor cars. Most likely, this venture never left the paper stage because by 1911 the man behind it, Elmore Gregg, was sales manager for the Penn from Pittsburgh. That a Gregg car was manufactured in Pittsburgh in 1916 has been indicated on various car rosters, and is in error. When Penn went to the wall in New Castle, Pennsylvania in 1912, Elmore Gregg returned to Pittsburgh to try the manufacturing field on his own. The car which resulted in 1916 was the Pennsy.

GREGORY — **Bellows Falls, Vermont** — **(1909)** — Two Vermont schoolboys named Charles Gregory and Burt Vreeland began building an automobile in 1907 and completed it in June 1909. The car had cost them practically nothing, being constructed from the remains of four automobiles which had suffered fortuitous wrecks near Bellows Falls.

1922 Gregory, roadster, AA

GREGORY — **Kansas City, Missouri** — **(1920-1922)** — Ben F. Gregory was a front-wheel-drive enthusiast. In 1920 he completed an experimental car, based on a Scripps-Booth chassis, fitted with a de Dion front axle, and with the engine placed conventionally between the frame rails but the flywheel mounted at the front. He spent the next two years trying to find the wherewithal to produce it. In the meantime he barnstormed dirt tracks in the Middle West with a single-seater racing version powered initially by a Curtiss OX-5 engine, later an Hispano-Suiza aviation motor. Purportedly, some of Gregory's ideas would later be borrowed by Harry A. Miller for his front-wheel-drive race cars. Although Gregory exhibited a front-wheel-drive touring car at the Kansas City Automobile Show in 1921, manufacture still lay beyond his reach. Early in 1922 the Front Drive Motor Company was grandly capitalized ($1.5 million) in Kansas City, although this enterprise did not move very far from the paper upon which the incorporation notice was written. The company did place an order for roadsters to be built by the O.E. Szekely Company in Moline, Illinois, and some cars were indeed built. Total Gregory production, prototypes and race cars included, has been estimated as high as thirty automobiles but was probably closer to ten. Following the Second World War, Ben Gregory again attempted the marketing of a front-wheel-drive production car, to no avail. Ultimately he turned his talents to the design of military vehicles.

1920-1922 GREGORY
Front Drive — 4-cyl., 22 hp, 110" wb

	FP	5	4	3	2	1
Roadster-2P	1550	—	—	—	—	—

GREINER — Late in 1914 in Chicago, Illinois, the A.W. Greiner Auto Sales Company was organized with a capital stock of $25,000 for the manufacture of automobiles and accessories. Incorporators were A.W. Greiner, Michael Feinberg and C.E. Becker. Manufacture of a car is doubted.

1916 Gremel, roadster, NAHC

GREMEL — Detroit, Michigan — (1916) — H.G. Gremel of Detroit liked to boast that the car he built in 1916 was made up of the parts of 102 different automobiles. He was not exaggerating. Gremel was the manager of the Puritan Machine Company of Detroit which was in the business of buying up defunct car companies and providing parts to the owners whose automobiles had so quickly become orphans. Gremel had carefully totted up the 102 cars that made up his effort, the largest single part of which was the body, which had been destined for a Krit. "It is a striking monument to the standardization of the American automobile," *Motor World* commented of Gremel's work, "indicating how well the parts of various cars can be made to work together."

GREN — The Gren Motor Car Company was organized in Chicago, Illinois during the summer of 1913 with a capital stock of $25,000 for the manufacture of automobiles and engines. Incorporators were G.H. Wilkins, R.C. Steel and T.S. McCoy. Manufacture of an automobile is doubted.

1901 Grensfelder, runabout, NAHC

GRENSFELDER — Herculaneum, Missouri — (1901) — In 1901 Dr. J.M. Grensfelder put together a car in Herculaneum, Missouri. Literally. Every part of the vehicle he had purchased from one source or another, and he frankly admitted that this was purely an assembly job. The car's engine was a two-cylinder, with chain drive to the rear wheels. The body was a dos-a-dos. Dr. Grensfelder is known to have motored often in the car, including a trip from Herculaneum to Festus, "where a large crowd soon collected to see the wonderful horseless vehicle that came over the large hill into their town."

GREUTER — Holyoke, Massachusetts — (1898) — In 1898 Charles R. Greuter built two experimental gasoline cars, subsequently setting up shop as the Holyoke Motor Works in Holyoke, Massachusetts. The Holyoke was produced from 1899 to 1903. Several decades later, Greuter became famous as chief engineer for Stutz and the man most responsible for engine development of the legendary DV-32.

GREYHOUND — In 1904 the H.H. Buffum Company of Abington, Massachusetts included in its catalog an eight-cylinder race car called the Greyhound. This was the first eight-cylinder car offered for regular sale in America. Refer to Buffum.

The 1909 Greyhound from Eau Claire, Wisconsin was slated to be a special 85 hp model of the Burdick, built by Ralph Burdick's American Motor Company. Refer to Burdick.

The 1918 Greyhound was a slightly larger roadster marketed alongside the juvenile car built in Lafayette, Indiana by the American Motor Vehicle Company. Refer to American Junior.

The Greyhound Motor Works was organized in Buffalo, New York late in 1909 with a capital stock of $100,000 to manufacture automobiles and motorcycles. F.P. Fox, W.C. Overman and J.W. Van Allen were the incorporators. Manufacture of a car is doubted.

1914 Greyhound Cyclecar, runabout, NAHC

GREYHOUND — Toledo, Ohio — (1914-1915) — Kalamazoo, Michigan — (1915-1916) — "The Aristocrat of Cyclecars" had a 14/18 hp water-cooled four-cylinder engine, cone clutch, 104-inch wheelbase, 40-inch tread, sliding gear transmission, shaft drive and electric starting. Designed by E.J. Cooke, it was a tandem two-seater with back-seat drive, priced at $385. The Greyhound Cyclecar Company of Toledo announced this car early in 1914 and declared itself "prepared to deliver 2400 cars" that year. When 2400 orders did not arrive in Toledo, the company decided to try again the following year in Kalamazoo, and now the story becomes confusing. The company — whose officers included W.D. Smith of Toledo and Dr. F.C. Bonine and James H. Johnson of Michigan — was reorganized, but to what it was reorganized is puzzling. Initial references from Kalamazoo indicate that the firm's name was Crown Automobile Manufacturing Company and that it had taken over the factory and assets of the former Michigan Buggy Company. But the Crown name disappeared almost immediately thereafter. By March of 1915 all references indicate that the firm was called the States Motor Car Company. The States' product continued to be called a Greyhound, however, though now it was a light car of 30 hp on a 106-inch wheelbase. And thus it remained into early 1916. Then in April a whole new set of people arrived in the old Michigan Buggy plant in Kalamazoo and joined with James H. Johnson to take over the States venture. They reorganized the firm yet again as the States Motor Car Manufacturing Company and introduced a slightly bigger car as the States. It was finished by the end of 1918.

1914-1915 GREYHOUND
Cyclecar — 4 cyl., 14/18 hp, 104" wb

	FP	5	4	3	2	1
Tandem Roadster-2P	385	2000	3000	4200	6500	14,000

1916 Greyhound, Light Car, roadster, NAHC

631

1915-1916 GREYHOUND
Light Car — 4-cyl., 30 hp, 106" wb

	FP	5	4	3	2	1
Roadster-2P	600	2200	3200	4400	7000	15,000
Touring-5P	600	2300	3300	4600	7500	16,000

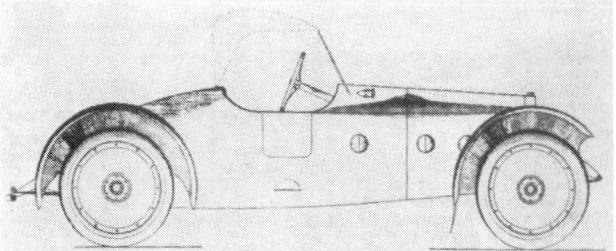

1919 Greyhound, speedster, KM

GREYHOUND — East Warren, Rhode Island — (1919-1920) — This venture began as Greyhound Motors Corporation of Five Columbus Circle in New York City. Prospectus drawings of the Greyhound car indicate a racy little speedster with a ''Trinca Patent Body,'' round hood louvers and artfully shaped fenders. ''Just as Good as It Looks'' was the headline, and the car looked rather like it might have been an attempt to make a sporting vehicle of the Model T Ford. Prettying-up the Tin Lizzie was a sometimes lucrative proposition in those days. Greyhound apparently was serious in this effort. Early in 1920, when its name changed to Greyhound Motor Car Company, the firm purchased fifteen acres in East Warren, Rhode Island to erect a plant. Prior to its completion, Greyhound planned to lease a factory in the area for the making of parts. Whether either of its plans bore fruit is not known. The Greyhound promoters had been M.L. Rogers, L.A. Irwin and W.G. Singer.

1909 Griffin, auto-buggy, NAHC

GRIFFIN — Fredonia, Kansas — (1909) — Although a photograph exists of the Griffin car that was made by the Fredonia Iron Works in Kansas, little further is known about it, except that it sold for $500 and was marketed in 1909.

GRIFFIN — San Diego, California — (1930) — Three wheels (two in the front, one in the rear) and three doors (one in the front, two on the sides) were the distinguishing features of the car built by R.A. Griffin of San Diego in 1930. Suspension was on rubber-band principles, and most parts, including four-cylinder engine, had originated on a motor bike. Overall, Griffin's car had the look of a postwar Messerschmitt, but unlike the Messerschmitt, Griffin's three-wheeler was not put into manufacture.

GRIFFITH — In early 1914 Nicolas M. Griffith of Chicago incorporated with a capital stock of $50,000 for the manufacture and sale of automobiles in Illinois. Joining him in the venture were C.U. Martin and L.L Cowan. Manufacture is doubted.

GRIFFITHS — Boston, Massachusetts — (1899-1900) — A machinist in Boston named W.H. Griffiths built himself a steam carriage during the winter of 1899-1900. Preferring ease of access to more commodious accommodations, he placed his boiler and small two-cylinder double-acting steam engine in front of the seat rather than under it. Power transmission from engine to axle was via expanding pulleys, Griffiths claiming this to provide a more economical application of power. This is believed to be the only car he built.

1899 Griffiths Steamer, runabout, WLB

1912 Grinnell Electric, coupe, WLB

GRINNELL ELECTRIC — Detroit, Michigan — (1912-1915) — The Grinnell Electric Automobile Company followed the breakup of the partnership which had seen production of the Phipps-Grinnell in 1911. Ira and C.A. Grinnell simply bought out Joel G. Phipps, and were now on their own. The electric car they produced from 1912 through 1915 does not seem to have differed markedly from the electric Phipps had designed for them in 1911. It enjoyed a modest success initially, but as electric car sales in general began to wane, the Grinnells decided to forgo the pleasure of being automobile manufacturers at a loss and concentrate instead on their chain of piano and music stores in Detroit which were operating at a very nice profit. The Grinnells placed a small obituary notice for the Grinnell Electric in automotive trade publications of January 1916 — and that was that.

1912 GRINNELL

	FP	5	4	3	2	1
Model H Brgm. (90" wb)	3000	3300	4400	6700	12,000	24,000
Model K Coupe (92" wb)	3000	3100	4200	6300	10,500	22,000
1913 GRINNELL						
Model K Coupe (94" wb)	2800	3100	4200	6300	10,500	22,000
Model M Coupe (96" wb)	2800	3100	4200	6300	10,500	22,000
Model H Coupe (90" wb)	2800	3100	4200	6300	10,500	22,000
1914 GRINNELL						
Model R French Brgm. (105" wb)	3400	3200	4300	6500	11,000	23,000
Model S Brgm. (100" wb)	3000	3100	4200	6300	10,500	22,000
Model K Coupe (94" wb)	2800	3100	4200	6300	10,500	22,000
1915 GRINNELL						
Model R French Brgm. (105" wb)	3400	3200	4300	6500	11,000	23,000
Model S Brgm. (100" wb)	3000	3100	4200	6300	10,500	22,000

GRISWOLD — Quincy, Massachusetts — (1905-1906) — Robert G. Griswold was a draftsman and toymaker from Quincy who issued a press release to trade publications in late September of 1905 indicating that he had just organized the Griswold Manufacturing Company with a capital stock of $25,000 for the manufacture of automobiles. He listed himself as the president and treasurer of the firm. Evidently the company never got off the ground. Quincy city directory references from this period do not mention the company nor the manufacture by Robert Griswold of anything other than toys. Conceivably, however, he might have built a prototype automobile but then decided not to go into manufacture.

1906 Griswold, runabout (Troy), KM

GRISWOLD — **Troy, New York** — **(1906)** — In 1906 George W. Griswold began building an automobile. Precisely when he completed it is not known, but he was still driving it in early 1911 when he and his car hit the pages of the *Troy Times*. Griswold's car was a primeval machine, an exemplary example of early minimal transport. As described in the Troy newspaper, its most unique feature was undoubtedly its braking system "which consists of a pair of shoes which lift the rear wheels off the ground to stop the vehicle."

1907 Griswold, runabout, NAHC

GRISWOLD — **Detroit, Michigan** — **(1907)** — This Griswold was one of several cars designed by the ubiquitous J.P. La Vigne — and perhaps it was the most curious of all his efforts. The reason for specifying a tread of 55 inches — one inch less than the standard — defies easy explanation. The Griswold's engine was a four-stroke water-cooled two-cylinder unit, which was conventional, but its placement in the car was not. The power-plant was mounted with the flywheel down, the cylinders lengthwise under the hood. The crankshaft was vertical, and a friction transmission was featured. The Griswold was offered as a 10 hp runabout on a 90-inch wheelbase, a 15 hp runabout on a 100-inch wheelbase, and a 20 hp runabout on a 110-inch wheelbase. Prices were in the $1500 range. Organization of the Griswold Motor Company was announced in mid-summer of 1907, with note made that the first Griswold car had been on the road since May. Very few others followed it. Griswold was out of business by the end of the year. Thereupon, the equally ubiquitous C.H. Blomstom stepped in and marketed the Griswold as the Gyroscope.

GROFF & RUNKLE — **Columbus, Ohio** — **(1901)** — Charles W. Groff and J. Frank Runkle were the partners behind this venture, and were joined in the $50,000 incorporation of the Groff-Runkle Motor Vehicle Company in late 1901 by George W. Groff, Frank Burkholder and Barton Griffiths. The venture located itself at 272-278 Kimball Street in Columbus, and its purpose was the manufacture of motor vehicles using the "Runkle patent speed gear." Already the first vehicle had been completed, under the supervision of Frank Burkholder of Wooster, and had undergone a 200-mile round trip between Columbus and Wooster with no problems encountered. By the time manufacture began the year following, however, the decision had been made to change the firm's name to Columbus Motor Vehicle Company and to name the car after the renowned French balloonist Santos Dumont. The Santos Dumont was produced in Columbus from 1902 until the fall of 1904.

GROSSMAN — In early 1909 the Emil Grossman Company was organized in New York City with a capital stock of $100,000 for the manufacture of automobiles. Joining Grossman in this venture were J.A. Vesey and J. Silverman. Manufacture of a car is not believed to have resulted. Emil Grossman was a prominent figure in New York City automobile circles, incidentally, as publisher of *The Motor Review* at the turn of the century and subsequently, as manufacturer of the Red Head spark plug and other automobile accessories.

GROUT — **Orange, Massachusetts** — **(1900-1912)** — Few automobiles in American history had as frenetic an existence as the Grout. Company brochures frequently made reference to the fact that in 1896 the Grout brothers built the first automobile factory in the United States, which was blatantly untrue. Presumably an experimental steam car was produced that year. The next reference to the Grouts' activity was late 1898, when they were reported to be building an automobile for their own use fitted with a Haynes-Apperson gasoline engine. Not until 1899 was it reported that the brothers had secured a factory and were preparing for manufacture. And the story becomes even more complicated now. The Grout boys — Carl, Fred and C.B. — were the sons of William L. Grout who in the late 1850's had pooled his resources with Thomas H. White and, with a joint capital of $400, had put themselves into the sewing machine business. Thereafter White settled in Cleveland, Ohio to make his fortune in the White Sewing Machine Company. And Grout settled in Orange, Massachusetts to prosper with the New Home Sewing Machine Company. Because his sons had no interest whatsoever in the family business, William Grout set them up as the Grout Brothers Automobile Company. (Interestingly, the sons of Thomas H. White were also automotively inclined, and they too were backed by their father.) The Grout brothers began experimenting in 1899, and built several gasoline cars and perhaps a steam car prototype by year's end. When production began the following summer, however, just the light steam car was manufactured. New models followed in 1901, all of them steamers. Cars exported to England were marketed under the name of Weston; the domestic cars were referred to as the Grout "New Home" through 1901, the coupe version being so much taller than it was long as to resemble a sentry box. Subsequent Grouts were considerably more handsome though equally as distinctive, with hoods that were a perfect circle, and a single headlight placed smack in the center. One rather unfortunate model, however, arrived complete with cowcatcher and resulted in what was the only American production automobile to look identical to a steam locomotive. By 1904 the Grout business was doing splendidly, with eighteen steam cars a week being produced. Later that year a gasoline car was added, and from 1906 on only gasoline automobiles were produced, all of them fours. Gasoline car production never approximated the commercial success enjoyed by the Grout steamers, but this had nothing to do with the quality of the automobile. In 1907 William L. Grout, dissatisfied with the manner in which his sons were conducting the business, served a $200,000 attachment on the factory. The sons retaliated, asking that a conservator be appointed for their father because of his advanced age. He was seventy-four. William L. Grout did succeed in taking over the company, his sons taking leave to settle in other parts of the country. On April 20th, 1908 William Grout died, and the company was in chaos again. The business was reorganized as the Grout Automobile Company in 1909 by a triumvirate of Orange businessmen headed by Walter J. Gould. But the other two businessmen died suddenly, leaving Gould alone with the company — and short of funds. Production ceased in 1912, and in September of 1913 the plant was sold at auction. In August of 1914 Grout made news again, when the old factory was leased by the new Red Arrow Automobile Company.

1900 GROUT

	FP	5	4	3	2	1
Steam "New Home" Sthp.	750	—	—	—	—	—

1901 Grout, steam "New Home" stanhope, HAC

1901 GROUT

Steam "New Home" Sthp.	570	3100	4200	6300	10,500	22,000
Steam "New Home" Delivery	900	3000	4000	6000	9500	21,000
Steam "New Home" Coupe	1500	3200	4300	6500	11,000	23,000
Steam Fire Chief's Wagon	—	3200	4300	6500	11,000	23,000

633

1902 Grout, steam runabout, HAC

1902 GROUT

	FP	5	4	3	2	1
Model B Steam Runabout	825	3000	4000	6000	9500	21,000
Model E Steam Runabout	950	3000	4000	6000	9500	21,000
Model C Steam Stanhope	875	2900	3700	5600	9100	20,000
Model H Steam Runabout	850	2900	3700	5600	9100	20,000
Model I Steam Touring	1000	3000	4000	6000	9500	21,000
Model G Steam Delivery	1000	2900	3700	5600	9100	20,000

1903 Grout, steam tonneau, HAC

1903 GROUT

Model H Steam Rbt.-2P	775	3000	4000	6000	9500	21,000
Model J Steam Rbt.-4P	1200	3100	4200	6300	10,500	22,000
Grout Steam Tonneau-5P	2500	3200	4300	6500	11,000	23,000

1904 Grout, steam runabout, HAC

1904 GROUT
Steam — 1-cyl., 7 1/2 hp, 76" wb

Runabout	650	3700	4700	7300	13,700	26,000
Surrey-4P	700	3900	4800	7700	14,300	27,000

Steam — 2-cyl., 12 hp, 86" wb

Touring-5P	2000	4000	5000	8000	15,000	28,000

1905 Grout, steam tonneau, HAC

1905 GROUT
Steam — 2-cyl., 12/18 hp, 86" wb

	FP	5	4	3	2	1
Side Entrance Tonneau	1500	3900	4800	7700	14,300	27,000

Gasoline — 4-cyl., 20 hp, 102" wb

Side Entrance Tonneau	2000	4000	5000	8000	15,000	28,000

1906 Grout, touring, HAC

1906 GROUT
Four — 30/35 hp, 102" wb

Runabout-2P	2400	3700	4700	7300	13,700	26,000
Touring-5P	2500	3900	4800	7700	14,300	27,000

1907-08 Grout, touring, HAC

1907-1908 GROUT
Four — 35 hp, 108" wb

Touring-5P	2500	3700	4700	7300	13,700	26,000
Runabout-2/3P	2400	3900	4800	7700	14,300	27,000

1909 GROUT
Four — 35 hp, 116" wb

Touring-5P	2500	4000	5000	8000	15,000	28,000
Close-Coupled Tonneau-4P	2500	3900	4800	7700	14,300	27,000
Roadster-2/3/4P	2400	3700	4700	7300	13,700	26,000

1909-10 Grout, touring, HAC

1910 GROUT
Four — 40/45 hp, 123" wb

	FP	5	4	3	2	1
Touring-5P	2500	4000	5000	8000	15,000	28,000
Baby Tonneau-4P	2500	3900	4800	7700	14,300	27,000
Sport-4P	2500	3900	4800	7700	14,300	27,000
Runabout-3P	2500	3700	4700	7300	13,700	26,000

1911 Grout, model 35-H, touring, HAC

1911 GROUT
Model 35 — 4-cyl., 35 hp, 116" wb

Touring-5P	1850	3700	4700	7300	13,700	26,000
Tonneauette-4P	1850	3700	4700	7300	13,700	26,000

Model 45 — 4-cyl., 45 hp, 123" wb

Touring-5P	2500	3900	4800	7700	14,300	27,000
Tonneauette-4P	2500	3900	4800	7700	14,300	27,000
Fore-Door Touring-7P	2850	4000	5000	8000	15,000	28,000
Touring-7P	2750	3700	4700	7300	13,700	26,000

1912 Grout, model 45, touring, HAC

1912 GROUT
Model 35 — 4-cyl., 35 hp, 116" wb

Touring-5P	2000	3700	4700	7300	13,700	26,000
Touring-2P	2000	3700	4700	7300	13,700	26,000

Model 45 — 4-cyl., 45 hp, 123" wb

Fore-Door Touring-7P	2850	4000	5000	8000	15,000	28,000
Fore-Door Touring-5P	2750	3900	4800	7700	14,300	27,000
Fore-Door Roadster-2P	2500	4000	5000	8000	15,000	28,000
Fore-Door Roadster-4P	2500	4200	5200	8400	15,700	29,000

GROVE PARK — The Grove Park Motor Car Company was organized in Asheville, North Carolina early in 1912 with a capital stock of $20,000 to manufacture, repair and deal in automobiles. Incorporators were E.W. Grove of St. Louis, Missouri, and W.F. Randolph and John S. Adams of Asheville. Manufacture is doubted.

GRUBB — William I. Grubb was the man behind the Light Cycle Company of Pottstown, Pennsylvania. Although his company's product line was automobile and airplane parts, Grubb did build a few cars at the turn of the century. Refer to Light Steamer.

GRUBE — Rahway, New Jersey — (1900-1902) — Charles Grube headed the Grube Carriage Works in Rahway at the turn of the century, and apparently added an electric motor and the further necessities to some of his usual products to become an automobile manufacturer. In this venture he did not remain long.

GUARANTY — Cambridge, Massachusetts — (1917-1918) — Guaranty Motors Corporation of Cambridge has appeared on several American automotive rosters. The company was organized during the summer of 1917 by Samuel W. Prussian, who was described as a "furniture man." At that time, its product was stated to be a truck attachment for use on Model T Fords and other cars. A complete truck later was to be built, although it would appear Guaranty specialized in making truck attachments, truck frames and gear drive units. There is no documented evidence that Guaranty ever manufactured an automobile, although the firm may have experimented in the field. The company remained in business in Cambridge until approximately 1922.

1901 Guenther, electric juvenile, NAHC

GUENTHER — New York, New York — (1901) — The Guenther was an electric children's car built by New York machinist E.B. Guenther for his ten-year-old son Charles. Its body was three-and-a-half feet long, its front wheels measured sixteen inches in diameter, the rear twenty inches. "Seen on the street, the little machine seemed to operate as satisfactorily and to be under as perfect control as the more pretentious carriages driven by adult chauffeurs," commented *The Motor Age* admiringly in 1901 of young Charles' motoring expertise.

GUICHARD & PECK — Walla Walla, Washington — (1899) — That Guichard & Peck of Walla Walla, Washington built a gasoline-powered runabout in 1899 was reported in *The Autobain* that December. That the car would prove a "commercial success" was expected. Further details are lacking.

GULLIFORD — "It is reported that George Gulliford will open an automobile factory at Findlay, Ohio," reported *The Horseless Age* during the summer of 1903. There is no evidence he ever did, however.

1924 Gumher, NAHC

635

GUMHER — Hampton Roads, Virginia — (1924) — The Gumher from Hampton Roads weighed 460 pounds, developed a tenth of a horsepower and was capable of six miles an hour. It was built in 1924 by Sergeant T.G. Gumher for his daughter.

GUNN — Utica, New York — (1910) — On paper, the Gunn from Utica had success written all over it. The car was the idea of John K. Gunn of the Utica Pipe Foundry. He developed a compact eight-cylinder engine which he installed in his Thomas car, which performed well in that application. A second engine was built, and it was tested running the lights at the pipe foundry. In June of 1910, the Gunn Motor Company was organized with many prominent members of the Utica community coming aboard, among them William T. Baker of the *Utica Saturday Globe*, William H. Roberts of the Roberts Hardware Company, W.L. Taber of the Citizens' Trust Company and George L. Wood of the Utica Fine Yarn Company. As the *Utica Daily Press* reported on June 1st, 1910, one-quarter of the intended $200,000 capital stock was subscribed in the hour and a half after its availability was announced. The Gunn engine was said to generate 52 hp and "will not only propel the car, but will also operate a pump for inflating tires." John Gunn had already designed the chassis and body. "The car is to be high grade," the paper reported, "and will resemble the Packard, perhaps, as much as any in appearance." Commercial vehicles were also planned. For whatever the reason, the Gunn automobile died aborning.

1901 Gurley, NAHC

GURLEY — Meyersdale, Pennsylvania — (1899-1901) — In addition to being a jeweler and the owner of a book shop, Tom W. Gurley had been the Meyersdale agent for Columbia and Hartford bicycles for years before the advent of the automotive age. Since he ran a bicycle repair shop too, he saw no reason why he could not become a manufacturer of automobiles which, after all, were only two wheels and one motor more complicated than a bicycle. And so he did. Wheels and steering devices he secured from Weston-Mott, tires from Hartford Rubber, tubing from Shelby Steel, engines from Milne & Killam, body and upholstery from Jerry J. Livengood, a local carriage builder. All this he put together in his bicycle store, offering a choice of either steam or gasoline motor, and trap or runabout coachwork. "Any ordinarily well-equipped repair shop can build carriages like these," he wrote enthusiastically in a letter published in *Cycle and Automobile Trade Journal's* January 1900 issue. "This carriage costs me complete about $500, and I can sell all I can turn out for $600." Unfortunately he raised his price to $1000 in 1901. Maybe Tom Gurley should have kept quiet. In 1902 he discontinued manufacture of his car and, in partnership with his brother Oscar, established Meyersdale's first automobile garage and dealership. The Gurleys prospered in this venture. In April 1915 the Meyersdale Automobile Company reported the sale of a dozen cars in a dozen days: two Franklins, five Hupmobiles and five Maxwells.

GURLITT — In New York City, late in 1911, the Gurlitt-Braun-Davis Corporation was organized with a capital stock of $25,000 to manufacture and deal in motor vehicles. Incorporators were H. Gurlitt, D.S. Davis, Jr. and V.C. Bogardus. Manufacture of a car is doubted.

GUY VAUGHAN — Although occasionally referred to as the Guy Vaughan, this car built in Kingston, New York from 1910-1914 was more usually simply the Vaughan. Refer to Vaughan.

G.V. — Long Island City, New York — 1907 — The G.V. rose from the ashes of the V.E. In 1907 the Vehicle Equipment Company of Long Island City was reorganized under receivership as the General Vehicle Company, and carried on from there. An electric "Ladies Phaeton" and roadster were marketed that year, but commercial vehicles were the company's sole focus thereafter. General Vehicle built electrics for a wide variety of applications — and in 1913 began building gasoline trucks as well under license from the Daimler company in Germany. Late in 1915 the General Vehicle Company merged with the truck-building department of Peerless in Cleveland, though both firms retained their own identity. G.V. commercial vehicles were built into 1920.

GYREX — The Gyrex Manufacturing Company was organized in New York City early in 1910 with a $25,000 capital stock to manufacture and deal in engines, automobiles, motor boats and aeroplanes. Edward H. Stickels, Charles A. Wardle (both of New York City) and H.W. Webb (of Cresskill) were the incorporators. Manufacture of an automobile is doubted.

GYROSCOPE — Gyroscope was a designation occasionally given for two cars produced in Chicago at the turn of the century. Refer to Holson and Trimoto.

1909 Gyroscope, touring, WLB

GYROSCOPE — Detroit, Michigan — (1908-1909) — C.H. Blomstrom, doyen of the Blomstrom Manufacturing Company, was never without ideas. Earlier these had included the Blomstrom, Queen and De Luxe automobiles, and now he added the Griswold, a car that had died aborning in 1907. Designed by J.P. La Vigne, whose earlier work had included the La Petite, the Griswold had featured a vertical crankshaft and a horizontal flywheel mounted under the engine. Blomstrom concluded that this arrangement, which was not an entirely new one in the industry, caused a gyroscopic effect which enhanced stability and prevented skidding — and thus renamed the car the Gyroscope. It was described in the press as an "improved" Griswold, but the only apparent improvement Blomstrom made was an increase of an inch to the car's tread for the standard 56 inches. Initial advertising in 1908 indicated the car's prices in the $1300 range, for 1909 the figure was slashed below $1000. Very few Gyroscopes were produced. Among the reasons was that Blomstrom, who had acquired patent rights to the La Vigne design, had decided that there might be a better business in selling the Gyroscope engines than the Gyroscope cars. In mid-1909 he proceeded to do just this. He sold first to the Page company in Adrian, which promptly went nowhere. He sold next to the Lion company, also in Adrian, but that concern quickly decided to build another car without a "gyroscopic" engine. In 1914, by which time the Blomstrom company was in receivership and the Lion company defunct, the receiver for the former sued officials of the latter charging breach of contract. Blomstrom had delivered a number of engines to Lion before that company decided to use another powerplant. A $60,000 loss was claimed. The court ruled in favor of the plaintiff; the Blomstrom receiver was awarded a judgment of $46,000.

1908 GYROSCOPE
Gyroscope — 2-cyl., 16.2 hp, 95" wb

	FP	5	4	3	2	1
Runabout	1250	—	—	—	—	—
Touring	1350	—	—	—	—	—

1909 GYROSCOPE
Gyroscope — 2-cyl., 16.2 hp, 95" wb

	FP	5	4	3	2	1
Touring	800	—	—	—	—	—
Runabout	750	—	—	—	—	—

1904 Haase, phaeton, NAHC

HAASE — Milwaukee, Wisconsin — (1902-1904) — In 1902 the Northwestern Furniture Company of 271 North Water Street in Milwaukee built two experimental cars which were given their public debut during the Labor Day parade in Milwaukee. Encouraged by the reception received, the company decided to enter the automotive field, with its cars to carry the name of Northwestern president Haase. A single wheelbase chassis of 72 inches was used, with a pair of two-cylinder-engined models (a 6 hp Model A and an 8 hp Model B) available. The Haase was offered as a runabout only, with the fuel tank under the seat and the engine to the rear, the radiator slanting in front of the dash. There was a left-hand tiller, and the Haase cranked from the left-hand seat. A curiosity was the method of speed control, actuated by a lifting of the inlet valves. By December of 1902, a total of fifteen Haase cars were sold. The Northwestern Furniture Company's slogan to potential dealers of "Sure Sellers, Quick Sellers, Easy Sellers" was something of an exaggeration, however. By mid-1904, with sales ebbing, Haase prices were slashed — from $1000 to $600 for the Model A, from $1200 to $750 for the Model B. The evidence suggests that Northwestern did not build the production Haase cars itself, but rather the cars were built for the company by H. Brothers of Chicago, who later built their own car called the H.B. In late 1906 the Northwestern Furniture Company announced that it would again market an automobile; if indeed the company did so, however, it was simply as an agency for an established manufacturer.

HABERER — Haberer & Company was the former carriagemaker in Cincinnati, Ohio which produced the Cino car from 1910-1913. Refer to Cino.

1921 Habig, MVMA

HABIG — Cincinnati, Ohio — (1921) — The Habig used an air-cooled motorcycle engine, standard motorcycle wheels and tires, and a good many of the after-high-school hours of Harry Habig of Cleveland. His speedster weighed less than 500 pounds and was good for 60 mph and 30-40 mpg. According to the *American Automobile Digest* in 1921, as a cellar-built car, "the finished product is a marvel of mechanical genius and skill."

1917 Hackett, touring, WLB

HACKETT — Jackson & Grand Rapids, Michigan — (1917-1919) — Mansell Hackett was an Englishman, the owner of the Disco Starter Company of Detroit, and the founder of an ancillary enterprise in 1914 to buy up bankrupt automobile companies. In September of 1916 he decided to get into the "living" automobile business as a manufacturer and bought out Benjamin Briscoe's Argo Motor Company in Jackson to do it. The first Hacketts were fours with G.B.&S. power units, introduced later that year as 1917 models. Though subsequently chief engineer Fred M. Guy developed a rotary valve engine for the car, the product of the Hackett Motor Car Company remained a conventional four for the rest of its life, which was a short one. Early on Mansell Hackett demoted himself to general manager of his company, placing in its presidency one J.S. Johnston of the shipbuilding Johnston Brothers of Ferrysburg, who had invested in the Hackett car venture. For a time in 1918 operations ceased because of the unavailability of materials during the First World War. During this period the company moved its factory to Grand Rapids. There production resumed in 1919 at the rate of twelve cars a week, but not for long. In October 1919 there was a try at reorganization. It failed. Total Hackett production is believed to have been 118 cars. Thereafter a car called the Lorraine was built in the Hackett factory, but Mansell Hackett does not seem to have been involved in this subsequent venture. Conceivably, he went back to starters and dead companies. Meanwhile chief engineer Fred Guy took his rotary valve engine to Ypsilanti where finally it was produced in the Ace automobile.

1917 HACKETT
Four — 4-cyl., 22.5 hp, 112" wb

	FP	5	4	3	2	1
Touring-5P	888	2700	3600	5300	8800	19,000
Roadster-4P	888	2800	3700	5500	9000	19,500

1918-1919 HACKETT
Four — 4-cyl., 22.5 hp, 112" wb

Touring-5P	—	2700	3600	5300	8800	19,000
Roadster-2P	—	2800	3700	5500	9000	19,500
Roadster-3P	—	2900	3700	5600	9100	20,000
All-Seasons Tour.-5P	—	2900	3700	5600	9100	20,000

HACKLEY — Los Angeles, California — (1905) — In 1905 a Los Angeles patent attorney named George T. Hackley built a roller clutch transmission incorporating the link valve motion of a locomotive rather than the more usual gears or friction disc for speed changing. He installed the device in a Winton for testing and later patented it. By 1907 he had formed the Direct Drive Power Transmission Company for marketing the device. A lot of success does not seem to have followed.

HAFEMEISTER — The G.H. Hafemeister Motor Company was organized in Watertown, Wisconsin early in 1912 for the manufacture of automobiles. Capital stock was $10,000. The incorporators were G.H. Hafemeister, R.P. Hafemeister and W.M. Wegeman. Manufacture is doubted.

HAFER ELECTRIC — Los Angeles, California — (1903-1904) — There were four Hafer brothers: Levi, Gaylord, Clyde L. and Walter B. They were carriage builders in Los Angeles, and apparently it was Levi's idea in 1903 to supply the company's vehicles with electric power. The business was renamed Electric Carriage Works, and it remained at the same 302 East Seventh Street address. In 1905 the company moved to Central Avenue, only brother Walter joining Levi in moving with it and the Hafer product thereafter was supplied only as a horsedrawn vehicle. Whether any Hafer Electric cars were sold has not been documented.

HAGAMAN — Adrian, Michigan — (1895) — J.D. Hagaman of 52 Riverside Avenue in Adrian entered the Chicago Times-Herald Contest of 1895 with plans to drive an automobile of his own design. At the starting line of the event, however, Hagaman was a no-show — and whether he ever did successfully complete his car has not been documented.

1896 Hagenlocher, runabout, WLB

HAGENLOCHER — Erie, Pennsylvania — (1896) — This pioneer gasoline vehicle was begun in 1895 and completed in 1896 by Henry Hagenlocher of Erie. Whether Hagenlocher built more than one example is not known, but it is certain that Charles LeJeal, who later built an automobile of his own in Erie, contributed to its building. A Hagenlocher remains extant.

HAGMANN & HAMMERLY — Chicago, Illinois — (1902-1905) — The grand-sound name of this very obscure car resulted from the two Chicago partners who saw to its building. Both a steamer and a gasoline car were produced. The steamer was first, Dr. L.W. Sheppard driving one of the partners' vehicles in a one-mile race for stock steam cars sponsored by the Chicago Automobile Club in October 1902. The Hagmann & Hammerly's competition in the event comprised two Locomobiles, one of which caught fire during the race which, according to *The Automobile*, pleased the crowd immensely, with ''prospects of a blazing car rushing toward victory and destruction.'' Instead, the Locomobile's fire was put out, and the Hagmann & Hammerly motored on to a non-blazing victory. How many further steamers might have been built is not known. By 1904 the Hagmann & Hammerly Automobile Station had moved from its original quarters at 931 Van Buren Street to what was described by *Cycle and Automobile Trade Journal* as ''perhaps the largest garage and repair shop in Chicago'' on Harrison Street near Oakley Boulevard. There in 1905 a gasoline car was produced. It featured a water-cooled two-cylinder 20 hp engine. Planetary transmission and chain drive were featured, with the wheelbase 88 inches, steering by wheel, and a double-side-entrance tonneau the sole body style. The Hagmann & Hammerly gasoline car seems to have been produced only in 1905. Thereafter the partners returned to their repair work and subsequently became automobile dealers.

HAHN — Pueblo, Colorado — (1902) — Charles Hahn designed the car, with David Klein and B. Greenwood providing the financing. The result was the Hahn Automobile Company, organized during the summer of 1902 in Denver, with Hahn, Klein and Greenwood taking the firm's presidential, secretarial and treasurer chairs respectively. Already machinery had arrived at the company's plant at 1023 Abriendo Avenue in Pueblo, and the expectation was the manufacture of two Hahn cars a week. The firm also expected to promote an automobile line between Pueblo and Beulah. The venture seems to have folded during the prototype stage.

HAIN — Mishawaka, Indiana & Los Angeles, California — (1898-1902) — Ralph B. Hain built the first bicycle to appear on the streets of Grand Rapids, Michigan and organized the Clipper cycle company there which he later sold at a considerable profit. When next heard from, he was in Mishawaka, Indiana building boats full time and putting together a one-cylinder gasoline automobile in his spare time. In 1898 Hain drove his car around neighboring South Bend, showing it to the wagon-producing Studebaker brothers among others. At some point he returned to Grand Rapids with hopes to manufacture his gasoline car in collaboration with F.J. Lamb who had just built an electric in town. Those hopes quickly dashed, Hain left town for the West Coast. His car was also shipped to Los Angeles, where he established a machine shop. During much of 1901, Hain attempted to produce another automobile and searched for partners for a car-building venture. The Auto Vehicle Company was the result in 1902. His partner was Carroll S. Hartman. Of the $250,000 capitalization, Hain put up his share in cash, an inkling of how successful he had been as a bicycle producer. Alas, as an automobile designer, he was considerably less so. His prototype for the car that would be called the Tourist was an overweight 6 hp one-lunger. It was not produced. Instead a young man from Pasadena named Waldemar Hansen was called in, and his horizontally-opposed two-cylinder engine was fitted into the early production Tourists. That Ralph Hain was not entirely sanguine about this turn of events is indicated by his selling out his share of the Auto Vehicle Company at its annual meeting in late 1902 and becoming an automobile dealer.

1917 HAL-Twelve, touring, WLB

HAL — Cleveland, Ohio — (1916-1918) — ''Only an accident . . . prevented the formation of my company last summer,'' Harry A. Lozier announced from Detroit in June of 1915. The accident preventing an earlier organization of the H.A. Lozier Company was the First World War. Disgruntled that stockholders of the Lozier Motor Company had decided to turn his high-priced Lozier into a popularly-priced car, Harry Lozier had already resigned from that firm, determined to build the automobile he wanted. Like Ransom Eli Olds with his Reo and Harry C. Stutz with his H.C.S., Lozier chose his initials for his new car. The prototype was shown at the New York Automobile Show in January 1916. It was powered by the Weidely V-12 engine. Production began that summer in Cleveland, to which city Lozier had moved shortly after announcing his HAL-Twelve. Although he had indicated its price as $1750 initially, by now it had risen to $2100 — and would become more expensive still in succeeding years. Others, however, would be responsible for the upward pricing. In September 1916, Lozier left the enterprise, reportedly for reasons of ''continued ill health.'' The new president of the newly-renamed Hal Motor Car Company was A. Ward Foote of Foote-Burt Machine Company of Cleveland. Brochures proclaimed that, although the HAL-Twelve was rated at 40 hp, it actually developed over 70 at 2000 rpm, 100 at 3000 rpm. Two hundred HAL-Twelves had been built by October 1916, with production now at ten cars per day. The continuing war in Europe played havoc with company plans. Materials were hard to come by. In October 1917 there were rumors of a forthcoming merger with the Abbott Corporation which had just recently moved from Detroit to Cleveland, but Abbott was bankrupt by January 1918. The Hal Motor Car Company hung on for another month. Frank B. Willis, who had succeeded Foote as president in late 1917, introduced the HAL-Twelve line at the Chicago Automobile Show in late January 1918. Willis resigned as president shortly thereafter, and in early February involuntary bankruptcy proceedings were requested upon creditors' claims of only $1500. The Hal Motor Car Company assets, including ten finished but unsold cars, were sent to the auction block in April. (Among earlier purchasers, incidentally, had been Warren G. Harding, although he would switch allegiance to Locomobile by the time he became president of the United States). The Hal factory, which earlier had seen the production of the Royal Tourist automobile, had been leased from F.B. Stearns Company which had purchased it when Royal went under. Stearns had the factory back now.

1916 HAL
Twelve — 40 hp, 135'' wb

	FP	5	4	3	2	1
Model 12 Touring-7P	2100	5300	7000	11,500	24,000	37,000
Model 12 Roadster-2P	2100	5400	7300	11,800	25,000	38,000

1917 HAL
Twelve — 40 hp, 135'' wb

	FP	5	4	3	2	1
Model 21 Roadster-2P	2385	5400	7300	11,800	25,000	38,000
Model 21 Limousine-7P	4250	4200	5200	8400	15,700	29,000
Model 21 Brougham	4250	4000	5000	8000	15,000	28,000
Model 21 Cloverleaf Rds.-4P	2385	5500	7500	12,000	26,000	39,000
Model 21 Touring-7P	2385	5300	7000	11,500	24,000	37,000

1918 HAL, shamrock roadster, KM

1918 HAL
Twelve — 40 hp, 135'' wb

	FP	5	4	3	2	1
Model 25 Sedan-7P	3500	3900	4800	7700	14,300	27,000
Model 25 Limousine-7P	4500	4200	5200	8400	15,700	29,000

	FP	5	4	3	2	1
Model 25 Town Car-7P	4500	4300	5400	8700	16,500	30,000
Model 25 Touring-7P	2600	5300	7000	11,500	24,000	37,000
Model 25 Roadster-2P	2600	5400	7300	11,800	25,000	38,000
Model 25 Shamrock Rds.-4P	2600	5500	7500	12,000	26,000	39,000

HALE — Charles E. Hale & Sons was a $500,000 incorporation from Boston, Massachusetts during the summer of 1912 for the manufacture and sale of automobiles. R.J. Cram was president and A.N. Hunt (of Braintree) treasurer. Manufacture is doubted.

The Hale Motor & Machine Company was organized in Detroit, Michigan during the summer of 1910 with a capital stock of $125,000 for the manufacture of automobiles and parts. Incorporators included S.E. Hale, Charles Ritter and J.L. Hudson. Manufacture of a car does not seem to have followed. J.L. Hudson, of course, was the principal financial angel behind the Hudson Motor Car Company which had been organized the year previous.

HALEY — Hartford, Connecticut — (1899) — In 1899, at the back of his home at 34 Elm Street in Hartford, Jeremiah Haley, with a little help from his friends, built a carriage powered by compressed air. Further details regarding the vehicle are lacking, but it is believed Haley did not build another.

HALF BREED — McCraken, Kansas — (1916) — In 1916 one Wiley Griffin of McCraken built an automobile composed of the parts of two existing production cars which in the years since has consistently appeared on rosters of cars manufactured in the United States. The reason is that Griffin was an adept press agent for himself, and wrote numerous letters to editors of automobile publications of the era announcing his feat. Probably the car received more publicity than was its due because editors were charmed or amused by the name Wiley Griffin chose for his vehicle. Actually, it was charming, and amusing, and wonderfully apt. Griffin did announce that he was "looking for capital to start an assembling company," but it would appear his first Half Breed was also his last.

HALL — The Hall Car Company was organized in New York City during the summer of 1909 with a capital stock of $20,000 for the manufacture of "engines, cars, locomotives and vehicles of all kinds." H.P. Hall, B.H. Howell and T.M. May were the incorporators. The venture was reincorporated as the Hall Development Company in early 1910, with a capital stock of $100,000. Manufacture of a car is doubted.

Hall & Mitchell, Inc. was organized in Springfield, Massachusetts early in 1913 with a capital stock of $3000 to manufacture automobiles and parts. James Mitchell was president; John Hall, Jr. was treasurer, and C.F. Walsh secretary. Manufacture of a car is doubted.

The Hall-Seeley Motor Corporation was organized in Baltimore, Maryland early in 1913 with a $1 million capital stock for the manufacture of automobiles. Milan W. Hall, C. Ford Seeley and Leo S. Meyer were the principals involved. Manufacture is doubted.

1905 Hall, touring, HAC

HALL — St. Louis, Missouri — (1905) — This St. Louis car of 1905 was built at 2821 Easton Avenue. Its engine was an opposed two-cylinder, its wheels were wood shod with solid rubber tires, its body was a rear-entrance tonneau. All of this was the usual for the period, but the fact that the car was also front wheel drive was not. Its inventor was Charles Hall; Henry Specht and Nicholas A. Kuntz supplied him the money for the car's building, and for the building of one further model similar to it. It was the partner's intention to go into manufacture, but the capital necessary to do that eluded them.

HALL — Abington, Massachusetts — (1907) — In October of 1907, Bicknell Hall of Taunton purchased the factory of the bankrupt H.H. Buffum Company of Abington and announced to the trade press that he would continue production of the former Buffum eight-cylinder car. This he appears to have done, but only to complete the automobiles for which parts remained on hand. His venture, which he named the Hall Manufacturing Company, survived no longer than the Buffum parts did.

1904 Hall, rear entrance tonneau, NAHC

HALL — Dover, New Jersey — (1903-1904) — This two-cylinder 20 hp touring car began its life with a $3500 price tag and as the product of the Hall Motor Carriage Company of Dover. An aluminum body was featured. The Hall was weighty at 2400 pounds, and advertising was honest in declaring a comfortable cruising speed of 20 mph. Obviously the first year did not go well for Hiram P. Hall. For 1904 he changed his firm's name to Hall Motor Vehicle Company, and slashed $500 from the Hall's price. His company was no longer in the automobile business in 1905. Its subsequent effort, announced in November 1904, was a line of traction engines. In December Hiram P. Hall also joined in the establishment of the Dover Garage.

1903 HALL

Hall Touring-4P	3500	2200	3200	4400	7000	15,000

1904 HALL

Hall Touring-4P	3000	2200	3200	4400	7000	15,000

1914 Hall, cyclecar, roadster, OCW

HALL — Waco, Texas, (1914-1915) — Lawrence Hall operated the Hall Cycle & Plating Company of Waco in association with John B. Fisher. In 1914 he designed a cyclecar which featured an underslung frame with a special hole through which the front axle passed in order to secure rigidity. Although one cannot imagine this working well, Hall did drive his prototype on a test run from Waco to Dallas, covering the 104-mile distance in a little over six hours and with a gasoline consumption of only two-and-a-half gallons. Shaft drive was also featured in the Hall cyclecar, as was a two-speed transmission. The prototype's engine was a two-cylinder Spacke, but the production car had a Perkins 18 hp four. Wheelbase was 100 inches, tread 36 inches. The enterprise was initially organized as the Hall Cyclecar Manufacturing Company in 1914, but was reorganized in 1915 as the Hall Motor Car Company. There were no further reorganizations. Production had been minimal, but this venture had been ambitious. A coupe version of the Hall cyclecar was even built. Subsequently Lawrence Hall moved to Los Angeles. His activities there are not known.

639

1915 Hall, cyclecar, roadster, WLB

1914-1915 HALL
Cyclecar — 4-cyl., 18 hp, 100" wb

	FP	5	4	3	2	1
Roadster	425	1600	2700	3800	5800	12,000
Speedster	395	1800	2800	4000	6200	13,000
Coupe	650	1100	2200	3200	4900	9000
Light Delivery	435	1000	2000	3000	4600	8000

1895 Hall, motor trap, NAHC

HALL GASOLINE TRAP — Jacksonville, Illinois — (1895) — John W. Hall & Sons was a carriage manufacturing company in Jacksonville. In 1895 the firm built a gasoline carriage weighing 700 pounds which provided accommodations for four passengers who had the option of sitting dos-a-dos or all facing forward. As a Nineteenth Century automobile, the Hall Gasoline Trap was a good-looking vehicle. There is no evidence that the company ever built more than the one car, however. Initially, it was powered by a Kane-Pennington engine, which didn't work at all well, whereupon it was dispatched the following year to Decatur for refitting with two Walls engines of the Decatur Gasoline Engine Company.

HALLADAY — Illinois & Ohio — (1905-1922) — The origins of the Halladay began in Anderson, Indiana with the Erie Motor Carriage & Manufacturing Company, a going-nowhere business bought out in late 1902 by L.P. Halladay and moved to Streator, Illinois. There Halladay spent a year rounding up stockholders and $30,000 capital, and the Streator Automobile & Manufacturing Company was the result. The first Halladay automobile was built in great secrecy in 1904 and was placed on the market in 1905. It was a touring car powered by a 40 hp four from Rutenber, the company which would supply the Halladay its engines for the whole of its life. Although an assembled car, the Halladay was very well built. It was the only competitor to finish without a stop in the 250 Mile Free for All race at Atlanta in 1910; a Halladay served as the press car for the Glidden Tour of 1911. And the Streator Motor Car Company, as the firm had by now been renamed, proudly advertised that a Halladay had been purchased by the prestigious Armour Institute of Technology in Chicago for experimental use in its Mechanical Engineering Laboratory. Production stood at about 900 cars a year, and counted among Halladay's early workforce were such later industry notables as Eddie Rickenbacker and three of the Fisher brothers (Frederick, Charles and Lawrence). "Every Day a Halladay" punned the company rather cleverly in 1911, if not appropriately — for the firm was in trouble. On September 23rd that year the Streator Motor Car Company fell into receivership. "Internal strife" was the reason given. The firm's liabilities were $250,000, its assets $200, and its problem the attempt "to operate on credit and not enough cash." In January 1913 the personal property of the Streator company was sold for $56,000 to the Merchants' Realization Company of Chicago, which in turn sold the firm to Albert C. Barley, secretary of the Rutenber Motor Company. Barley reorganized as Barley Manufacturing Company, reopened the factory and resumed Halladay production. Things proceeded splendidly for awhile, until Albert Barley lost interest. His lack of enthusiasm for the Halladay was prompted by another car he decided to launch in 1916 called the Roamer. It would be produced in Kalamazoo, Michigan, to which city Bar-

ley immediately moved. He sold the Halladay organization to a group of investors headed by T.E. Huth, Y.F. Stewart, J.N. Horne, George B. Stacey and E.D. Baxter. This quintet reorganized as the Halladay Motor Car Company and moved operations out of Illinois and into Ohio in early 1917. The Halladay spent the rest of its life moving around the Buckeye state. Among the towns planned and announced for Halladay manufacture were Mansfield, Warren, Lexington, Attica and Newark. It would appear that real production was seen only in Warren, Attica and Newark. The Halladay arrived in Newark with the first roar of the Twenties, by which time the company name had changed to Halladay Motors Corporation. Its latterday schizophrenic existence preordained ultimate failure for the Halladay. And in 1922 it came. The Halladay line was entirely composed of sixes now, though there was an attempt to produce a companion four under the marque name of Falcon, that car was introduced at the New York Automobile Show in January of '22. In March, however, Halladay Motors Corporation was in receivership. The proceedings were instituted by the Barber Asphalt Paving Company of Pennsylvania which had completed the work around the Newark factory for which it had been contracted, but had never been paid.

1907 Halladay, model B, touring, HAC

1905-1907 HALLADAY
Four — 35/40 hp, 108" wb

	FP	5	4	3	2	1
Model B Tour.-5P	3000	3100	4200	6300	10,500	22,000

1908 HALLADAY
Four — 35/40 hp, 118" wb

Model C Tour.-5P	3000	3100	4200	6300	10,500	22,000
Model C Rbt.-3P	3000	3200	4300	6500	11,000	23,000
Model C Limousine	3500	2700	3600	5300	8800	19,000

1909 Halladay, model D, touring, HAC

1909 HALLADAY
Four — 24 hp, 100" wb

	FP	5	4	3	2	1
Model G Tourabout-4P	1200	2700	3600	5300	8800	19,000
Model F Surrey-4P	1100	2700	3600	5300	8800	19,000
Model E Rbt.-3P	1050	2500	3500	5000	8500	18,000

Four — 35/40 hp, 118" wb

Model D Tour.-5P	2500	3100	4200	6300	10,500	22,000
Model D Rbt.-3P	2500	3200	4300	6500	11,000	23,000
Model D Limousine	2500	2700	3600	5300	8800	19,000

1910 HALLADAY
Four — 24/28 hp, 104" wb

Model E-10 Rdst.-2P	1100	2700	3600	5300	8800	19,000
Model F-10 Surrey-3P	1150	2500	3500	5000	8500	18,000
Model G-10 Tour.-5P	1250	2700	3600	5300	8800	19,000

Four — 30 hp, 110" wb

Model J-10 Rdstr.-2P	1500	3000	4000	6000	9500	21,000
Model J-10 Toy Tonneau-4P	1500	2700	3600	5300	8800	19,000
Model J-10 Tour.-5P	1500	2900	3700	5600	9100	20,000

Four — 40 hp, 123" wb

| Model D-10 Tour.-7P | 2500 | 3000 | 4000 | 6000 | 9500 | 21,000 |
| Model D-10 Toy Tonneau-5P | 2500 | 2900 | 3700 | 5600 | 9100 | 20,000 |

1910 Halladay, model G-10, touring, HAC

1911 Halladay, model 40, roadster, HAC

1911 HALLADAY
Model G-30 — 4-cyl., 30 hp, 106" wb

	FP	5	4	3	2	1
Touring-5P	1250	2700	3600	5300	8800	19,000
Surrey-4P	1150	2700	3600	5300	8800	19,000
Roadster-2/3P	1100	2900	3700	5600	9100	20,000
Model J-30 — 4-cyl., 30 hp, 110" wb						
Touring-5P	1540	2800	3700	5500	9000	19,500
Roadster-2P	1540	2900	3700	5600	9100	20,000
Model 40 — 4-cyl., 40 hp, 118½" wb						
Toy Tonneau-4P	1700	2700	3600	5300	8800	19,000
Touring-5P	1700	3000	4000	6000	9500	21,000
Roadster-3P	1700	3100	4200	6300	10,500	22,000
Winter Front Tour.	1800	3000	4000	6000	9500	21,000
Limousine	3000	2500	3500	5000	8500	18,000
Model 50 — 4-cyl., 50 hp, 128" wb						
Touring-7P	2650	3500	4500	7000	13,000	25,000
Toy Tonneauette-4P	2650	3300	4400	6700	12,000	24,000
Winter Front Tour.-7P	2750	3500	4500	7000	13,000	25,000
Limousine-7P	4000	2700	3600	5300	8800	19,000

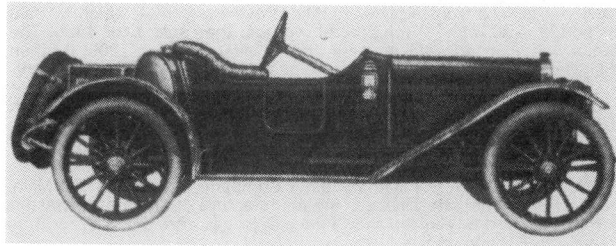

1912 Halladay, model 30, roadster, HAC

1912 HALLADAY
Model 30 — 4-cyl., 30 hp, 112" wb

Touring-5P	1100	2900	3700	5600	9100	20,000
Roadster-2P	1100	3000	4000	6000	9500	21,000
Model 40 — 4-cyl., 40 hp, 118" wb						
Touring-5P	1800	3000	4000	6000	9500	21,000
Toy Tonneau-4P	1800	2900	3700	5600	9100	20,000
Roadster-2P	1800	3100	4200	6300	10,500	22,000
Model 6-50 — 6-cyl., 50 hp, 128" wb						
Toy Tonneau-4P	3000	3300	4400	6700	12,000	24,000
Touring-5P	3000	3500	4500	7000	13,000	25,000
Tour.-7P (134" wb)	3000	3300	4400	6700	12,000	24,000

1913-1914 HALLADAY
Model 32 — 4-cyl., 32 hp, 112" wb

Touring-5P	1200	2900	3700	5600	9100	20,000
Roadster-2P	1200	3000	4000	6000	9500	21,000
Model 40 — 4-cyl., 40 hp, 118" wb						
Touring-5P	1800	3000	4000	6000	9500	21,000
Roadster-2P	1800	3100	4200	6300	10,500	22,000
Model 6-50 — 6-cyl., 50 hp, 134" wb						
Touring-5P	3000	3500	4500	7000	13,000	25,000
Toy Tonneau-4P	3000	3300	4400	6700	12,000	24,000

1915 Halladay Light Six, touring, HAC

1915-1916 HALLADAY
Light Six — 122" wb

	FP	5	4	3	2	1
Touring-5P	1385	3000	4000	6000	9500	21,000
Big Six — 50 hp, 134" wb						
Touring-5P	2285	3500	4500	7000	13,000	25,000
1917-1919 HALLADAY						
Model S — 6-cyl., 118" wb						
Touring-5P	1085	2900	3700	5600	9100	20,000
Model R — 6-cyl., 122" wb						
Touring-5P	1385	3000	4000	6000	9500	21,000
Roadster-3P	1385	3100	4200	6300	10,500	22,000
Model O — 6-cyl., 136" wb						
Touring-7P	2285	3700	4700	7300	13,700	26,000
1920-1921 HALLADAY						
Six — 46 hp, 116" wb						
Touring-5P	1985	3100	4200	6300	10,500	22,000
Roadster-2/3P	1985	3200	4300	6500	11,000	23,000
Coupe-4P	2385	2500	3500	5000	8500	18,000
Sedan-5P	2485	2200	3200	4400	7000	15,000
1922 HALLADAY						
Six — 46 hp, 115" wb						
Touring-5P	1595	3100	4200	6300	10,500	22,000
Roadster-2P	1595	3200	4300	6500	11,000	23,000
Victoria-5P	1695	2500	3500	5000	8500	18,000
Touring-5P	1795	3200	4300	6500	11,000	23,000
Roadster-2P	1795	3300	4400	6700	12,000	24,000
Cabriolet-2P	1795	3100	4200	6300	10,500	22,000

HALLER — **Louisville, Kentucky** — **(1910)** — Like many carriage and wagon makers in America, George Haller of Louisville thought the building of an automobile would be an easy matter. In 1910 he outfitted one of his buggies with a two-cylinder air cooled 14 hp engine which he planned to manufacture as a "convertible pleasure and business machine." The vehicles would be fitted with low wheels, but solid tires. In the July 14th, 1910 issue of *Motor World*, George Haller announced that his Haller Brothers company intended "to commence building cars next month." This activity was not continued long.

HALLETT — **Casselton, North Dakota** — **(1914)** — North Dakota's entry into cyclecar ranks was built by Chester P. Hallett. Details regarding its construction are lacking, but the two-passenger vehicle is known to have developed 10 hp. Manufacture did not follow.

HALLOCK — The Hallock Engineering Company was organized in Cleveland, Ohio during the spring of 1915 with a capital stock of $25,000 for the manufacture of automobiles and accessories. Incorporators included T.P. Hallock, R.H. Bosley, R.E. Kimmel, William H. Chapman and Olga E. Schultz. Manufacture of a car is doubted.

HALSEY — The Halsey Automobile Company was organized in St. Louis, Missouri during the summer of 1902 with a capital stock of $30,000 for the manufacture of automobiles. Oscar L. Halsey, Augustus C. Halsey and Edward J. Snowden were the people involved. Manufacture is doubted.

HALSEY STEAM — **Philadelphia, Pennsylvania** — **(1901-1907)** — James T. Halsey was a New York engineer who, *The Horseless Age* said in introducing him, "endeavored to construct a steam wagon that would be free from odors, have no ashes to be taken care of, no dangerous gasoline lamp, require no stoking, be simple in construction and operation, so as to require no skilled operator, and to decrease the possibility of repair, and to accomplish this on a wagon of the ordinary horsedrawn type, with steel tires and solid axles." Whether James Halsey was able to accomplish all this is doubtful, but the Halsey he designed was virtuous enough to remain in production for more than a half decade. The Halsey Motor Vehicle Company was organized in Philadelphia in 1901, with its factory located at Twenty-seventh and Brown streets. Most Halseys were trucks, although the company built omnibuses as well, and an occasional large touring car.

HALVERSON — **New York, New York** — **(1908)** — The press said at the time that it was probably the smallest gasoline-powered automobile ever built. Its wheelbase was 46 inches, its tread but 26, and it weighed 223 pounds. The engine was a four-cylinder air-cooled F.N., and its top speed was said to be 40 mph, though doubtless its owners were not allowed to approach that. The car was built by A. Halverson to the special order of John Lurie as a gift to his sons George and Herbert, aged thirteen and eleven respectively. Halverson produced a miniature masterpiece, the car's specifications including pressed-steel frame, artillery wheels, selective transmission, I-beam front axle and semi-elliptic springs. Few full-size

1908 Halverson, juvenile, NAHC

automobiles of that period were built so well. When not in use by the youngsters, the car was displayed at the Auto Supply Company at 1733-1737 Broadway in New York City.

HAMBLET — Lawrence, Massachusetts — (c.1909) — George W. Hamblet, proprietor of the Hamblet Machine Company of Lawrence, built an automobile for himself in about 1909. Coachwork was provided by the Amesbury Metal Body Company, but the rest of the car was Hamblet's doing. The wheelbase was 126 inches, with full floating axles, full elliptical springs in front, semi-elliptics in the rear, and a three speed selective transmission. Hamblet also built the car's original air-cooled engine, but replaced it in 1912 with a Palmer & Singer six-cylinder T-head combined with Stevens-Duryea radiator. The Hamblet remains extant.

HAMBRICK — Huntington, West Virginia — (1905-1906) — Apparently J.W. Hambrick built the prototype of his gasoline car in his native Covington, Kentucky in 1905. To manufacture it, however, he went first to Huntington, West Virginia, where he organized his Hambrick Motor Car Company, then proceeded to Parkersburg. Then he gave up on West Virginia altogether. Early in 1906 he reported that his company would move to Washington, Indiana "for a $25,000 inducement." Later in 1906 he was purportedly "looking for a site" there. Whether he ever found it is not known, but it is unlikely that the Hambrick ever proceeded into manufacture. One reference from 1908 indicates that he was still in Washington and still looking. Probably in addition to a factory site, Hambrick remained waiting for the "inducement."

HAMILTON — Although occasionally referred to as the Hamilton, the product of the Columbia Carriage Company of Hamilton, Ohio in 1909 was more often designated the Columbia. The reason possibly was that in 1907 another venture styling itself the Hamilton Motor Car Company had come to town to build automobiles as well, and had died aborning. Refer to Columbia Motor Buggy.
   The Hamilton Auto Company was organized in Weehawken, New Jersey during the summer of 1910 with a $6000 capital stock to manufacture and deal in automobiles and parts. Incorporators were Hans C. Schultze, William Ihmken and Herman Mutz. Manufacture of an automobile is doubted.
   The Hamilton Garage and Motor Company was organized during the spring of 1907 in Weehawken, New Jersey with a capital stock of $15,000 for the manufacture of automobiles. Behind this venture were Thomas Oldcorn Whitfield P. Pressinger and Richard S. Newcombe. Manufacture is doubted, but the firm is known to have operated a garage and blacksmith shop, and undoubtedly was the basis for the Hamilton Auto Company organized three years later.
   The Hamilton Vehicle Company was organized in Hamilton, Ohio during the fall of 1912 with a capital stock of $50,000 for the manufacture of automobiles. Behind this venture were A.A. Dornbush, Louis J. Brenig and William Kloeb. Manufacture is doubted.

HAMILTON — York, Pennsylvania — (1917) — Early in 1917 the automotive press reported the forthcoming manufacture of a four-cylinder automobile in York to be built by the Hamilton Motor Car Company. Whether this car ever saw an assembly line is not known. No further references from 1917 survive. The Hamilton Motor Car Company was heard from again a half decade later, however. Its president Adolph Pricken, who was also president of Coastwise Warehouses, Inc., was reportedly taken to trial in Brooklyn, New York though he was subsequently discharged when the court ruled no jurisdiction. Purportedly, Pricken returned all monies to his dissatisfied investors — and that was that.

642

HAMILTON — Grand Haven, Michigan — (1917) — Almost immediately after bankruptcy was declared for his Alter Motor Car Company, Guy Hamilton tried again with his new Hamilton Motors Company organized in Grand Haven and capitalized at $500,000. The new Hamilton was very much like the old Alter, a four on medium wheelbase offered at a lowish price. A six was promised, but never delivered. The car was produced a single season only. In 1918, the H.A. Oswald Engineering Company which had served as consulting engineers to Guy Hamilton's venture tried to resurrect the Hamilton as an Oswald, but didn't succeed. Hamilton's truck-building department was longer lived, the Alter truck being succeeded by the Panhard and then the Apex, which was produced into 1921.

1917 HAMILTON
Model A-14 — 4-cyl., 28 hp, 112" wb

	FP	5	4	3	2	1
Touring-5P	745	2700	3600	5300	8800	19,000

HAMILTONIAN — Greensburg, Indiana — (1909) — There was just one example of the six-cylinder Hamiltonian built. It was designed by Harry Hamilton, with the assistance of Lon Powell and Frank McCracken and was slated to sell for $1700. Announcement of its forthcoming manufacture was made in the trade press during early fall 1909. The Hamilton Motor Car Company was organized at that time, and a total of $50,000 was raised to launch the enterprise. President of the firm was W.W. Bonner, the vice-president was Harry Woodfill; C.P. Corbett was secretary and treasurer. According to the *History of Decatur County, Indiana,* "some steps were taken toward opening a factory, and then the entire matter was dropped." Total Hamiltonian production was the single prototype. Thereafter Harry Hamilton returned to the usual work of his Hamilton Garage.

1901 Hamlin, runabout, JHV

HAMLIN — Los Angeles, California — (1901) — In 1901, in the Los Angeles shop where he sold bicycles and repaired motors, Ralph Hamlin completed his first car, using a 3¼ hp Aster engine, bicycle parts and pieces of metal that he found around the shop. Drive to the countershaft was by belt, from there by chain to the rear axle. Subsequently, he installed a geared transmission. Hamlin drove the car — which he said was good for 30 mph — for several months, then sold it for $450. The Hamlin was reportedly still in use in the Pasadena area in 1906. By then Ralph Hamlin was on his way to becoming famous in West Coast motorcycle and automobile racing circles; later he would enjoy considerable repute, and considerable influence in company affairs, as a Franklin dealer.

HAMLIN-FOSTER — The Hamlin-Foster Company was a $100,000 Maine incorporation from late 1911 for the manufacture of automobiles. Arthur D. Hamlin, Albert S. Ventrea and Charles C. Briggs were the incorporators. Manufacture is doubted.

1919 Hamlin-Holmes, touring, WLB

HAMLIN-HOLMES — Chicago & Harvey, Illinois — (1919-1929)/**HAMLIN** — Chicago & Harvey, Illinois — (1930) — According to the press release issued in September 1919, the idea was to produce a front-wheel-drive car that was the "equivalent of Dodge at 10% less than Ford." The Hamlin-Holmes Motor Company never did manage that, indeed Hamlin-Holmes never really got into production, but somehow the company hung around for better than a decade assembling a few prototypes and accumulating a lot of publicity. Hamlin was F.B., a Chicago promoter; Holmes was E.R., an engineer. The first car was built in Denver, with subsequent development taking place in a "small experimental factory" in Detroit, but by 1920 Hamlin-Holmes forsook Colorado and Michigan to settle in Illinois, with headquarters in Chicago, the plant in nearby Harvey. The first Hamlin-Holmes, which looked more like a Ford than a Dodge, was powered by a four-cylinder Lycoming engine set in a 114-inch wheelbase chassis with the differential on the front axle. It appeared more ungainly than the Model T. In 1926, when Hamlin-Holmes went racing at Indianapolis, it was with a front-drive special built on a Model T chassis, with a Fronty Ford engine, and sponsored by the Chevrolet brothers. It did not exactly cover itself with glory in the 500, qualifying 25th out of 28 entrants, and being retired after 23 laps with a broken connecting rod. Undeterred, Hamlin-Holmes soldiered on, though without seriously trying racing again. Because the company bought bodies from several established manufacturers of the period — Cleveland and Moon, among them — there never was an identity of its own to the look of a Hamlin-Holmes. The last car

1930 Hamlin, 4-dr. sedan, WLB

looked rather like a Gardner; it was built in 1929 for the 1930 model year, and was called a Hamlin. By now F.B. had eased E.R. out of the organization, for brochures read "The Hamlin Motor Company, America's Pioneer Builders of Front Wheel Drive Cars" — which was a convenient forgetting of such other pioneers as Walter Christie, not to mention E.R. Holmes. The heart of the Hamlin-Holmes was its twin-axle drive, the car's weight carried on a lower dead axle, the front drive moving through a smaller upper axle. A low center of gravity was a Hamlin-Holmes hallmark, and the car was said to handle quite well. "Motordom's Sensation Beckons You To Fortune!" glowed a prospectus issued shortly before the stock market crash. Interestingly, had it not been for Wall Street, the last car built — a good-looking club sedan — just might have made it to an assembly line. Instead, the new front-drive cars that arrived with the Depression were the L-29 Cord and the Ruxton.

HAMMER — The E.A. Hammer Company was organized in Cleveland, Ohio early in 1912 with a capital stock of $15,000 to manufacture, buy, sell and deal in automobiles, motor boats and accessories. Incorporators included E.A. Hammer, W.J. Mahon, J. Miller, C. Murman and J. Bushea. Manufacture of a car is doubted.

1905 Hammer, touring, JB

HAMMER — Maddock, North Dakota — (1905) — In 1905, in Maddock, Julius Hammer and his brother Simon built a two-cylinder four-passenger gasoline touring car. Alas, the brothers had scant time to enjoy the vehicle. It was destroyed by fire in October the following year.

HAMMER-SOMMER — Detroit, Michigan — (1903-1904)/**HAMMER** — Detroit, Michigan — (1905) — The Hammer-Sommer Auto Carriage Company, Ltd. of Detroit produced a two-cylinder 12 hp car on an 80-inch wheelbase chassis with a Renault-type hood and a detachable tonneau body. Several varieties of single-cylinder 6.7 hp runabouts were manufactured too. The Hammer-Sommer appears to have been a substantially well-built automobile, but unfortunately substantial too was the bickering among the partners building it. In late spring of 1904, the company and the partnership were dissolved. Herman A. and William J. Sommer went off to build their Sommer which was very much like the Hammer-Sommer, and Henry F. Hammer went off to build his Hammer which had double the cylinders, double the horsepower and double the price of the Hammer-Sommer — and may have been the reason for all the arguing. Hammer did interest Detroit investors Leon J. Paszski, Foster W. Allen and Harry W. Nichols into putting money into his venture, and the Hammer was introduced for the 1905 model year. By the fall of 1905, however, the coffin was nailed shut on the new Hammer Motor Company. The Sommers didn't fare much better independently either. Another of the brothers — L.A. Sommer — would subsequently be involved with the Allen car in Ohio.

1904 Hammer-Sommer, runabout, GR

1903-1904 HAMMER-SOMMER
Hammer-Sommer — 2-cyl., 12 hp, 80" wb

	FP	5	4	3	2	1
Touring-5P	1250	1600	2700	3800	5800	12,000

Hammer-Sommer — 1-cyl., 6.7 hp

Runabout, Model A	900	1500	2500	3600	5500	11,000
Runabout, Model B	800	1500	2500	3600	5500	11,000
Runabout, Model C	700	1500	2500	3600	5500	11,000

1905 Hammer, touring, WLB

1905 HAMMER
Hammer — 4-cyl., 24 hp, 100" wb

Touring-5P	2500	2500	3500	5000	8500	18,000

HAMMETT STEAM — Boston, Massachusetts — (1900) — H.M. Hammett was a machinist at 4 Blue Hill Avenue in Boston and in 1900 he constructed a steam carriage of what he said was "extreme lightness." If its total weight was the 300 pounds he claimed, he was not exaggerating.

1914 Hammett, cyclecar, NAHC

HAMMETT — Lincoln, Nebraska — (1914) — In 1914 E.A. Hammett of Lincoln built himself a cyclecar. It was a tandem two-seater on a long 118-inch wheelbase with a tread of 46 inches. The engine was a four-cylinder bought by Hammett from the American Floor Surfacing Machinery Company of Toledo, Ohio. A cone clutch was fitted, as was a two-speed selective transmission. The front springs were quarter elliptics, with cantilevers at the rear. "A test has proven it is capable of traveling 40 miles to the gallon of gasoline with my wife and son as passengers," Hammett wrote *Motor Age* in October of 1914. "We drove on country roads a distance of 43 miles on 9 pints of gasoline and 1 pint of oil and the time for the trip was 2 hours 15 minutes, all the hills being negotiated on high gear." A top speed of 50 mph was claimed, as were the exceptional riding qualities of the vehicle because of the long wheelbase. But one wonders what would have resulted if the car ever hit a decent-sized pothole. E.A. Hammett never considered production.

1901 Hampden, runabout, NAHC

HAMPDEN — Springfield, Massachusetts — (1900-1901) — Following the break-up of his partnership with his brother Charles and his designing of the American for a New York City company, J. Frank Duryea — in collaboration with A.M. Green of Holyoke, Massachusetts and W.D. Eaton of Portland, Maine — organized the Hampden Automobile & Launch Company in September 1900 in Springfield for the manufacturer of motor vehicles and motor launches. The Hampden was a small 750-pound runabout the two-cylinder four-stroke engine of which could be cranked from the seat. "The engine starts with the least possible exertion," *The Motor Vehicle Review* noted in June 1901, "and the vehicle can be operated by a woman or child." Only pilot models of the Hampden were built in Springfield, however. By the fall of 1901, Duryea's car had come to the attention of the J. Stevens Arms & Tool Company of Chicopee Falls, and the entire operation was moved there. The famous Stevens-Duryea was the result. Meanwhile, the Hampden business was taken over by Homer R. Burton and R.A. McKee and turned into a repair station and garage.

HANAUER — Cincinnati, Ohio — (1901) — "Mr. Hanauer is one of the shrewdest merchants in the city and his judgement is highly valued by wheelman and dealers alike," reported *The Motor Vehicle Review* in December 1900 in announcing the entrance of the Charles Hanauer Cycle Company into the automotive field. In addition to operating as a repair shop, the firm also built motorcycles and steam cars to order during 1901. During that year, too, Hanauer moved from Seventh and Walnut streets to a new three-story building at 619 Main Street. Hanauer vehicle production was minimal, but the company did operate successfully thereafter as a dealership.

HANCHETT — New York, New York — (1900) — George T. Hanchett of 123 Liberty Street in New York City was indicated to be an automobile manufacturer in the Hiscox book *Horseless Vehicles, Automobiles, Motor Cycles* published in 1900. He is known to have been a mechanical engineer at that address, with his home in Hackensack, but details regarding the car he produced are lacking.

HANCOCK — Concord, Massachusetts — (1901) — William C. Hancock was an English-born machinist who emigrated to this country prior to the turn of the century and set himself up in business on Lexington Road in Concord, engaging initially in the grinding of lawn mowers and the repairing and building to order of bicycles. In 1901 his city directory advertisement added "automobiles built to order and repaired" to the aforementioned services. Local lore indicates that William Hancock built at least a few automobiles, and that they were all electrics.

HAND — The Hand Corporation was organized in Grand Rapids, Michigan during the fall of 1912 with a capital stock of $30,000 for the manufacture of automobiles and accessories. George H. Hand, H.C Cornelius and George G. Whitworth were among the people involved. Manufacture of a car is doubted.

HANDLEY-KNIGHT — Kalamazoo, Michigan — (1921-1922)/**HANDLEY** — (1923) - The Handley-Knight Company of Kalamazoo was a million-dollar corporation organized in January of 1920 to manufacture an automobile using the four-cylinder Knight sleeve valve engine. J.I. Handley, whose previous automotive affiliations included American (Indianapolis), Marion and Willys-Overland, was the man behind the venture, and the firm's president; W.E. Upjohn and C.S. Campbell were principal investors and vice-presidents; W.O. Otis was secretary-treasurer. The first experimental Handley-Knight was completed on July 1st, 1920; production began that October 1. Handley-Knight declared itself "America's Finest Knight-Motored Car." Its Knight motors were provided by the Willys plant in Elyria, Ohio. In November of 1922 Elyria was notified that no further Knight engines would be needed, because J.I. Handley had decided to go conventional with his powerplant. He reorganized in early December as Handley Motors, Inc. and bought a poppet-valve 60 hp six from Midwest and a 40 hp six from Falls. The new Handley was introduced in January 1923. The larger six had a flat radiator, the smaller a "European" vee-type; both models featured small handle attachments on the tops of their headlamps. Though Reo also sported same, the company nonetheless advertised that "if it carries handles, it's a Handley." But it wasn't a Handley for long. In early spring of 1923, the Checker Cab Manufacturing Company bought the Handley plant in Kalamazoo (as well as the Dort body plant) and moved its operations to town. Although at the time, J.I. Handley announced that "an arrangement probably will be worked out whereby the Checker company will continue the manufacture of the Handley car," this did not ensue. J.I. Handley's subsequent death was listed as suicide.

1921 HANDLEY-KNIGHT
Handley-Knight — 4-cyl., 54 hp, 125" wb

	FP	5	4	3	2	1
Model A Touring-7P	2985	3700	4700	7300	13,700	26,000
Model A Sedan-7P	3750	2300	3300	4600	7500	16,000
Model A Sedan-Coupe-4P	3750	2500	3500	5000	8500	18,000

1922 Handley-Knight, sedan, WLB

1922 HANDLEY-KNIGHT
Handley-Knight — 4-cyl., 54 hp, 125" wb

Model B Touring-7P	2450	3700	4700	7300	13,700	26,000
Model B Deluxe Touring-7P	2650	3900	4800	7700	14,300	27,000
Model B Sedan-7P	3750	2300	3300	4600	7500	16,000
Model B Sedan-Coupe-4P	3750	2500	3500	5000	8500	18,000
Model B Touring-5P	2250	3500	4500	7000	13,000	25,000

1923 Handley, touring, JAC

1923 HANDLEY
Handley — 6-cyl., 125" wb

Standard Touring-7P(60 hp)	2450	5200	6800	11,300	23,000	26,000
Deluxe Touring-7P (60 hp)	2650	3900	4800	7700	14,300	27,000
Coupe-4P (60 hp)	3450	2500	3500	5000	8500	18,000
Sedan-7P (60 hp)	3450	2300	3300	4600	7500	16,000
Standard Tr.-5P (40 hp)	2000	3500	4500	7000	13,000	25,000

HANN — The Hann Automobile Company was organized in Bridgeton, New Jersey with a capital stock of $50,000 during the spring of 1910 for the manufacture of automobiles. H.L. Howell, C.D. Stowell and C.A. Hann were the principals involved. Manufacture is doubted.

HANNA — The Hanna Motor Manufacturing Company was organized in Kansas City, Missouri early in 1913 with a capital stock of $60,000 for the manufacture of automobiles. Behind this venture were John M. Frank and Roy J. Hanna. Manufacture is doubted.

HANOVER — The Hanover Automobile Company was organized in Hanover, Pennsylvania early in 1905 with a capital stock of $10,000 to manufacture, buy, sell and repair automobiles. Behind this venture were Charles H. Heindel and W.F. Kintzing. Manufacture of a car is doubted.

1923 Hanover, roadster, WLB

HANOVER — Pennsylvania & New York — (1921-1927) — The Hanover arrived about a half-decade after the cyclecar debacle in the United States, and was what the cyclecar should have been all along. A lightweight miniature of a full-size car with a 12/15 hp air-cooled vee-twin engine, it featured a no-nonsense pressed steel 92-inch frame and two-seater racing type body, and a guarantee of 50 mpg and 20,000 miles per set of tires. Priced at $345, a detachable delivery case was available for $25 extra and quick conversion to commercial service. An unusual feature was the choice of right- or left-hand steering. The reason for this was that the Hanover Motor Car Company envisioned export from the beginning. Indeed, most of its cars ended up in Japan. Determining how many cars were built and for how long is difficult. The company was organized in Hanover, Pennsylvania in 1921, and 133 cars were produced that year. Twenty-five cars followed in 1922, and so did a projected move of the company to Buffalo, New York. In June Hanover purchased the factory of the defunct Parenti Motors Corporation for $225,000 at the receiver's sale. Whether Hanover ever shuffled off to Buffalo is problematical. Surviving company records in Hanover, Pennsylvania indicate further production of five cars in 1924 and a half-dozen in 1927, the last being water-cooled versions. Previously published references to a total Hanover output of 800 cars seem wildly inflated.

1927 Hanover, roadster, MC

HANSEN — An automobile called the Hansen has been indicated on various rosters to have been built by the Four Wheel Drive Wagon Company of Milwaukee, Wisconsin in 1906. One H. Theodore Hansen was among the people behind this venture, but proof of a Hansen automobile is lacking. The firm's purpose was manufacture of a four-wheel-drive truck. When the company went bankrupt in early 1907 with assets of $115,000 and liabilities of $190,000, *The Motor World* revealed that "although some $200,000 is said to have been expended in the effort, no very substantial progress was made."

HANSEN — Chicago, Illinois — (1895) — In 1895, C.O. Hansen, representing the Chicago Carriage Motor Company of 342 Center Street in Chicago, entered the Chicago Times-Herald Contest with a gasoline vehicle of his own design. Although not completed in time for the event, the Hansen was subsequently finished and successfully tested. Hansen's company did not, however, move into manufacture of the car.

1902 Hansen, gasoline runabout, NAHC

HANSEN — Cleveland, Ohio — (1902) — Rasmus Hansen was a Dane who had arrived in Cleveland at age eighteen. He was a man who knew precisely the automobile he wanted to build, but not what he wanted to call it. The result was a car that was most often referred to as the Cleveland, but occasionally referred to as the Hansen as well. It was a single-cylinder 6 hp runabout with a flanged radiator, a choice of wood or wire wheels, and a steering lever positioned in the center or at the right side. The Hansen Automobile Company — and the firm name was never other than that — entered one of its runabouts in the Cleveland Automobile Club's race at Glenville Track in September 1902. It finished second to an Elmore. Later that month, because he wished to expand his line, Rasmus Hansen reorganized as the General Automobile and Manufacturing Company. All subsequent cars had but one name, and that was General.

HANSEN-BUSCH — The Hansen-Busch Automobile Company was organized in Chicago, Illinois during the spring of 1908 with a $5000 capital stock to manufacture and deal in automobiles and operate a machine shop. Arnold Hansen and Herman Busch were the partners involved. Manufacture of a car is doubted, but the partners are known to have opened a garage at 1006 Ashland for the repair of automobiles.

1907 Hansen-Whitman, runabout, GR

HANSEN-WHITMAN — Pasadena, California — (1907) — The Hansen Auto & Machine Works produced a number of cars in Pasadena in 1907. Two-cylinder, two-stroke, water-cooled engines were used, with friction transmission and chain drive fitted. A nicely finished two-passenger roadster is known to have been built, and as many as ten five-passenger touring cars have also been claimed.

HANSON — Hanson's Auto Works was organized in Chicago, Illinois during the summer of 1904 with a capital stock of $1500 to build, repair and store automobiles. Incorporators were John Hanson, Charles O. Mueller and Louis A. Mueller. Manufacture is doubted.

HANSON — Sharon, North Dakota — (1908) — John G. Hanson of Sharon built himself a 20 hp gasoline roadster in 1908. Whether he hoped for manufacture is not known, but it did not happen in any case.

HANSON — Atlanta, Georgia — (1918-1925) — Shortly after the turn of the century, finding work in a local cotton mill less than challenging, George Washington Hanson opened a bicycle store in Griffin, Georgia and soon took on the local agency for Franklin. He was a natural salesman. Word of his talent reached Atlanta, and by 1907 Hanson was regional distributor for E-M-F there. When Studebaker took over control of E-M-F,

1921 Hanson, roadster, WLB

1923 Hanson, touring, HAC

1925 Hanson, touring, HAC

Hanson took on the Atlanta agency for Saxon — and it was during this period that he got his idea to build a small, light and low-priced car for the Southern market. With fellow Georgian Don M. Ferguson (a former E-M-F engineer), Hanson tore apart a Packard touring car for the good ideas it might give him, and in February 1917 the partners traveled north to Detroit where they assembled the prototype of the Hanson car in the Puritan Machine Company plant in Detroit. The new Hanson was introduced at the Southeastern Automobile Show in Atlanta on February 27th that month. Already a $50,000 factory was being constructed for manufacture, but by the time it was completed that spring the United States had declared war on Germany and the government commandeered the plant for military purposes. Hanson proceeded with his plans anyway. The Hanson Motor Company was formally organized in December of 1917, the government released his factory the following May, and that June the first Hanson rolled off the assembly line. Like all those which followed, it was an assembled car with engine by Continental. A 45 hp six on a 119-inch wheelbase and sold only as a $1685 touring car through 1919, the Hanson was increased in horsepower (to 55), wheelbase (to 121 inches) and price (three open and closed body styles from $1265-$2885) for 1920. "Tested and Proved in the South" and "Made in Dixie" were company slogans. For a while during 1921, George W. Hanson toyed with the idea of a torque-converter type of automatic transmission suggested to him by Roy Evans of Atlanta, but they never could get it to work right. (Roy Evans later became the man behind the American Bantam.) For a while, too, Hanson gave thought to producing a small export-type car and imported a Moller from Lewistown, Pennsylvania for experimental purposes. He also pondered a Hanson at the other end of the automotive scale, and ran up a prototype of a Super Sports model with Duesenberg eight-cylinder engine. But these projects came to naught after the boll weevil hit the South in 1921, and all of America was struck with the postwar economic recession. In 1922 George W. Hanson slashed his prices and introduced a Little Six (50 hp Continental engine) bargain-basement priced at $995. In March that year, he absorbed the American Motors Export Company, the Jacksonville, Florida automotive venture which was to have produced the Innes car, but which had collapsed with the death of Henry Innes. The Little Six had become the Special Six by 1923 and was higher priced, and the larger car was higher powered at 66 bhp. But George W. Hanson's struggle to survive was nearing an end. Sometime during 1925, he closed his factory doors. Total Hanson production had been approximately 850 cars. Subsequently, George W. Hanson manufactured baby nursing bottles in Pennsylvania. He returned to Atlanta in the mid-Thirties and was a sales agent for the Gulf Life Insurance Company when he died, at age sixty-five, in 1940.

1918-1919 HANSON
Six — 45 hp, 119" wb

	FP	5	4	3	2	1
Touring-5P	1685	3700	4700	7300	13,700	26,000

1920 HANSON
Six — 55 hp, 121" wb

Touring-5P	2165	3900	4800	7700	14,300	27,000
Roadster-2P	2885	4000	5000	8000	15,000	28,000
Sedan-5P	2885	2300	3300	4600	7500	16,000

1921 HANSON
Six — 55 hp, 121" wb

Roadster-2P	2365	4000	5000	8000	15,000	28,000
Sport-4P	2465	4200	5200	8400	15,700	29,000
Sedan-5P	3165	2300	3300	4600	7500	16,000
Touring-5P	2365	3900	4800	7700	14,300	27,000

1922 HANSON
Little Six — 50 hp, 112" wb

Touring-5P	995	3100	4200	6300	10,500	22,000

Six — 55 hp, 121" wb

Touring-5P	1795	3900	4800	7700	14,300	27,000
Touring-7P	1995	3700	4700	7300	13,700	26,000
Roadster-2P	1795	4000	5000	8000	15,000	28,000
Sport-4P	1895	4200	5200	8400	15,700	29,000
Coupe-4P	2775	2700	3600	5300	8800	19,000
Sedan-5P	2885	2300	3300	4600	7500	16,000

1923 HANSON
Special Six — 50 hp, 115" wb

Touring-5P	1195	3100	4200	6300	10,500	22,000

Six — 66 hp, 121" wb

Touring-5P	1595	3900	4800	7700	14,300	27,000
Roadster-2P	1595	4000	5000	8000	15,000	28,000
Sport-4P	1695	4200	5200	8400	15,700	29,000
Touring-7P	1795	3700	4700	7300	13,700	26,000
Sedan-5P	1795	2300	3300	4600	7500	16,000
Coupe-4P	2475	2700	3600	5300	8800	19,000

1924-1925 HANSON
Six — 66 hp, 121" wb

	FP	5	4	3	2	1
Roadster-2P	1395	4000	5000	8000	15,000	28,000
Touring-5P	1395	3900	4800	7700	14,300	27,000
Sport-4P	1495	4000	5000	8000	15,000	28,000
Sedan-5P	2195	2300	3300	4600	7500	16,000

HARBER — Bloomington, Illinois — (1904) — The Harber brothers of Bloomington have been cited as the manufacturers of an automobile in 1904. That there were brothers named Harber in Bloomington at that time can be documented. They were E.D., J.W., and B.F., and they were wholesalers in farm machinery, vehicles and binder twine. The automobile they built that year was for family use only. Manufacture was not contemplated.

HARDIE — Whether the company ever indeed did so has not been documented, but in November 1900 *The Horseless Age* reported that the Hardie-Lynes Foundry & Machine Company of Birmingham, Alabama "will soon put a line of vehicles on the market."

HARDIE — New York, New York — (1896) — Robert Gordon Hardie was the designer for the American Air Power Company of 160 Broadway in New York City. In 1896 he built an automobile for experimental purposes. Details regarding it are lacking; manufacture did not follow.

HARDING — Nashville, Tennessee — (1899) — The Harding Manufacturing Company was indicated as an automobile manufacturer in the Hiscox book *Horseless Vehicles, Automobiles, Motor Cycles* published in 1900. References from 1899 indicate the building of an automobile by the company that year, but further details are lacking.

1915 Harding, roadster, OCW

HARDING — Oshkosh, Wisconsin — (c. 1919) — Considerable mystery surrounds the Harding despite the fact that one of these cars exists, a roadster on display at Reynold's Museum in Alberta, Canada. Among the mysteries is where the car was built, when and by whom. Oshkosh has long been believed to be the place, but cannot be documented with certainty. A 1915 date has been suggested as well, but does not square with the dated shock absorbers on the vehicle itself. Thirteen Hardings were supposed to have been built, but the reality is more likely four or five. The Harding which remains extant was discovered in a storage shed in Pamperin Park, west of Green Bay, during the 1950's. It had arrived there during the Great Depression when Samuel B. Harding was hired by the W.P.A. to supervise the construction of a shelter and bandshell on the park land donated by the Pamperin family. The Pamperins lent Samuel Harding money, and Harding provided his vehicle as collateral. He later abandoned it. The Harding automobile was long in wheelbase and rakish in design, and no doubt was a swift performer with its 60 hp six-cylinder Wisconsin engine. The car was right-hand drive and included a large hub attached to each of the front wheels and dubbed the "Harding Steersafe." This caster hub was probably the feature which Samuel Harding believed would make his automobile stand out among its brethren, but whether it worked well is open to debate. T.A. Pamperin, whose grandfather had donated the park land and who as a teenager attempted to get the Harding back on the road, has commented that the "Steersafe" front hub design was poor, one wheel taking leave of the car during a test drive. Pictures of Harding cars with somewhat different bodies were provided to Ted Pamperin when he wrote Samuel Harding's widow during the 1950's. He believes the Harding was built in Kenosha, and that total production was less than a half-dozen. As for Samuel B., there was a Harding so named in Oshkosh during the World War I period. He was proprietor of a foundry producing boilers and steam engine equipment. But there was another Samuel B. Harding in Wisconsin during that same period, as historian William T. Cameon has discovered, and he was president of the Modern Steel Structural Company of Waukesha. As a construction engineer, this Harding might have been more likely to have been hired by the W.P.A. for the shelter/bandshell work in the Pamperin Park. At this point, whether the Harding mystery will ever be completely solved is problematical.

1916 Harding, Twelve, touring, WLB

HARDING TWELVE — Cleveland, Ohio — (1915-1916) — It was a well-kept secret. Sometime during 1914, Frank I. Harding resigned his position as secretary of the Peerless Motor Car Company, and took along with him Nathan Wyeth of the Peerless engineering staff. In rented space in a Cleveland factory, they proceeded to build a prototype of a twelve cylinder automobile. It was completed sometime during 1915, and was among the earliest twelve-cylinder cars in America. The engine was an L-head, cast in two blocks each mounted on a separate crankcase. Displacement was 356.4 cubic inches. A common crankshaft was used, and a single camshaft with twenty-four integral cams was fitted. The wheelbase was 132-inches, the body style a seven-passenger touring with khaki top. The projected price tag was $2000. Not until 1916 was the automotive press made aware of the car, announcement of the new Harding Motor Car Company arriving that January. Included in the venture now was one W.C. Spaulding, who was described as the "former president of a large knitting company." In February the company took a temporary showroom at 1824 Euclid Avenue and said it expected "to close negotiations for its permanent sales quarters and factory site in the near future." But the future for Harding was a quick demise. Since the company had been casually organized, with no stock issued, bankruptcy did not follow. The problem of obtaining materials in the midst of the war production effort ultimately convinced Harding that the time was not right to launch the enterprise, and so he simply disbanded it. Reportedly, Nathan Wyeth took the Harding prototype with him when he moved east to Boston. He drove it for a number of years thereafter, at some point substituting a six-cylinder engine for the twelve.

HARDINGE — The 1903 six-wheeler designed by Albert P. Broomell and produced in the shops of the Hardinge Company in York, Pennsylvania was named the Pullman. Refer to Pullman Six-Wheeler.

HARDY — The car produced by the Flint Automobile Company of Flint, Michigan from 1902 to 1904 occasionally carried the name of the man who had designed it — A.B.C. Hardy — but more often was called the Flint Roadster. It was always referred to as the latter in advertising. Refer to Flint Roadster.

HARE — Hare & Chase, Inc. was a million-dollar Delaware incorporation from late 1917 to manufacture and deal in automobiles and supplies. Incorporators were R.F. Hansell, J. Vernon Pimm and S.C. Seymour. Manufacture of a car did not follow.

Shortly after the First World War, an entrepreneur named Emlen S. Hare acquired control of the Mercer, Locomobile and Simplex automobile companies. No car, however, was produced under his name.

1903 Harkness, racer, NAHC

HARKNESS — Flushing, New York — (1903) — Harry Harkness of Flushing was an American millionaire and a sportsman who liked fast cars. He was both a patron of racing and an occasional racer himself. Like others of similar financial resources, he seemed to prefer Mercedes machinery. In 1903 he designed a car for himself fitted with a Mercedes four-cylinder engine tweaked to 120 hp. It was fifteen feet long, most of that distance being hood and cowl. The reinforced wood chassis was underslung, and the coachwork was aluminum. The transmission was a three-speed sliding gear, with 34 mph promised in first, 71 mph in second, 107 mph in third. Following completion of the car in the machine shop of Phillip Gill & Son in Brooklyn, Harkness immediately took it to France for testing on the roads of that country. The November 6th, 1903 edition of *L'Automobile* featured a long article on the car: *"une voiture automobile fantastique"* was that magazine's assessment of the Harkness vehicle. Harkness admitted to the *L'Automobile* reporter that his top speed in the car was 87 mph, though this was attributable to road conditions and not performance potential. Later that month Harkness returned to the United States with the car. In May 1904 he announced the formation in Flushing of the Harkness Automobile Company for the manufacture of automobiles. He thought better of it almost immediately. The only Harkness cars ever built were strictly for Harry Harkness.

1906 Harmer, roadster, NAHC

HARMER — Columbus, Ohio — (1906-1907) — Frederick S. Harmer was an employee of the Hoster-Columbus Associated Breweries Company in 1906, but among his places of previous employment had been the Oscar Lear Automobile Company, where he had worked as a draftsman and had learned a good deal about the air cooling of automobile engines via Lear's product, the Frayer Miller motorcar. Precisely when he decided to build an automobile of his own is not known, but he applied for a patent on various features of its overhead valve air-cooled engine in December 1905. By June of 1906, *The Automobile* reported that Columbus capitalists stood ready to invest in the Harmer project "if the new car proves a success when completed." By October, according to Columbus newspapers, the Harmer prototype had proved itself successful. Its engine was a 24 hp four mounted in a 96-inch wheelbase chassis with shaft drive and a three-speed selective transmission. That month announcement was made that among the capitalists to invest in the project were Carl J. Hoster (Harmer's old boss), C. Edward Born (another breweries magnate), and Thomas Curtin, who previously had organized the Curtin-Williams Automobile Company in Columbus which would now serve as the sponsoring organization for the new Harmer car. Apparently the ardor of these people cooled rather quickly, because the following year (July 5th, 1907) the Harmer Automobile Company was incorporated, and none of them were listed among the principals. The new Harmer angels were P. Scott Stafford, E.H. Holterman, J.E. Ward, W.M. Parsons and B.N. Zigler. Their ardor must have cooled quickly as well. Both touring and runabout models of 40 hp, and a five-ton truck, were projected for manufacture. None of these vehicles ever saw a production line. Possibly among the problems the Harmer company faced was potential litigation by Oscar Lear. Because Harmer's air-cooling patents applied for in 1905 were not granted until 1911, it might be that Frederick Harmer used too many ideas learned at

Lear in his Harmer design. Meanwhile the Curtin-Williams Automobile Company was enjoying considerable success as a repair agency, and two years later would receive recognition in the series published in *The Horseless Age* that was a sort of *House Beautiful* approach to the nation's garages.

HARMON — The Harmon Manufacturing & Distributing Company was organized in Chicago, Illinois late in 1904 with a capital stock of $50,000 for the manufacture and sale of automobiles. Henry Harmon, Theodore Stensland and H.W. Hering were the principals involved. Manufacture of an automobile is doubted.

HARPER — The Harper Automobile Company was organized in Lancaster, Pennsylvania early in 1911 to manufacture and deal in motor cars. Ira B. Jones, R.S. Harper, William Jones, J.F. Moore and E.C. Mabry were the principals involved. Manufacture of an automobile is doubted.

The Harper Engineering Company was organized in New York City during the summer of 1910 with a $50,000 capital stock to manufacture and deal in engines, automobiles and motor boats. Behind this venture were E.R. Berkeley, W. Harper, Jr. and A.J. Clayton. Manufacture of an automobile is doubted.

1908 Harper, gasoline runabout, NAHC

HARPER — Columbia City, Indiana — (1907-1908) — In January of 1907 the Harper Buggy Company of Columbia City announced its forthcoming entrance into the gasoline automobile field, with two models to be built, "one of which will be of the auto buggy type with a 4 horse power engine." The other car Harper declined to comment upon at all. When the Harper car finally made it to market later that year, it would appear that the company had changed its mind about offering two models and instead offered a heftier version of the one car announced at the outset. The new Harper was a two-cylinder two-stroke water-cooled runabout on a 76-inch wheelbase with a two-speed planetary transmission and an $800 price tag. Harper did not build the car long, returning soon to its horsedrawn vehicle business. In 1916 the Harper Buggy Company added the manufacture of trailers to its repertoire.

HARRIGAN — The Harrigan Auto Company was organized in Oak Park, Illinois late in 1914 with a capital stock of $5000 to manufacture, lease, repair and deal in automobiles. Incorporators were George von Moos and Thomas J. Harrigan. Manufacture of a car is doubted.

1922 Harrigan Six, touring, KM

HARRIGAN — Jersey City, New Jersey — (1922) — According to the prospectus, Harrigan Motors Corporation was a million-dollar company with its head offices in Jersey City, and its factory temporarily in Cleveland, though a permanent site was planned for Jersey City. The fact was there was never any factory anywhere. The president and chief engineer of Harrigan Motors was one William C. Harrigan, who said he had worked on the engineering staffs of Locomobile and Packard in the United States, as well

as Isotta-Fraschini in Milan. The Italian connection was a shade removed from the truth. Harrigan never worked at Isotta, but he did visit the factory to check out the company's four-wheel braking system while on a trip to Europe. Conceivably he had worked for Locomobile and Packard, though not very high up on their engineering department rosters. In later years Harrigan would claim to have exported 200 Harrigan cars and sold 300 more domestically, all of them the Model 51X, a six-cylinder (Continental engine) 55 hp touring car on a 126-inch wheelbase with a $1490 price tag. But this would be several shades further removed from the truth. The only photograph extant of a Harrigan indicates it to be a 1922 Case with a Harrigan emblem and a new radiator that did not fit very well. It is quite possible this was the only Harrigan built.

HARRIS — C.R. Harris of Williamsport, Pennsylvania built a car he called the Luxor in 1900. Refer to Luxor.

The Harris Automatic Press Company of Niles, Ohio was reported "about to engage in the manufacture of automobiles" during the summer of 1901. The evidence is lacking that the firm followed through on this.

The Harris Car Company was a $10,000 Maine incorporation from the spring of 1909 to manufacture and deal in automobiles. A.F. Dunham, M.S. Wells and F. Hale were the incorporators. Manufacture is doubted.

HARRIS STEAM — Baltimore, Maryland — (1891, 1896) — George T. Harris patented his steam vehicle in 1890 and tested it for the first time on the streets of Baltimore in 1891. It ran under its own power, but not very well. The axles overheated, and its gears were quickly rendered *hors de combat*. Whether its odor or its noise were the more objectionable was debatable. A mammoth bolide with accommodation for fifteen passengers, the Harris cracked the roads on which it was driven. Most probably, its first test run was its last. The vehicle was subsequently destroyed when the District of Columbia repository in which it was stored burned to the ground. George Harris built another steam car in 1896 which apparently was not the terror his first one had been. Thereafter his interest shifted to gasoline and electric propulsion. In December 1899 he applied for a patent on a gas-electric he had designed, though whether he ever built it has not been documented.

1899 Harris, NAHC

HARRIS STEAM — Manchester, New Hampshire — (c.1899) — This Harris has the distinction of being the first rubber-tired automobile in the state of New Hampshire. It was a two-passenger runabout powered by a two-cylinder steam engine and a boiler made up from bicycle frame tubing. Soft coal and wood were used for fuel, and the Harris was said to travel from Manchester to the halfway house in Hooksett "on one fire." A tiller provided for steering, and the entire front axle turned when the wheels did. When the car was completed, it was exhibited for a time in the window of the Manchester shoe store owned by William P. Farmer. Thereafter the Harris was driven on a routine basis for at least three years. Some controversy exists as to just who was responsible for this car's building. Official Manchester history indicates it as the creation solely of Peter Harris and his son Leander. But George A. Harris, brother to Peter and a resident of Springfield, insisted to a representative of *The Motor Vehicle Review* that he had been equally responsible. Although an 1896 date has been given for the car's completion, 1899 is more likely. "Just completed" was the phrase used by George Harris in the December 1899 *MVR* article about the car. "Boston people . . . expressed a wish to purchase it and all rights of manufacture," the article went on. "Mr. Harris declined the offer and said that if the carriage fulfills his present expectations he will either form a company or turn out the vehicles solely under his name." There is no evidence either Harris proceeded into manufacture, however.

HARRIS — Chicago, Illinois — (1904) — Yet another claimant for honors as America's youngest automobile builder was Stanley Harris of Chicago. He was thirteen years old when he built his automobile in 1904. It was a three-wheeler, the two rear wheels carrying the weight, the front wheel doing the steering. A 1¾ hp gasoline engine weighing just 35 pounds was placed under the seat. "The entire machine is the work of his own hands," reported *Automobile Review*. Young Stanley claimed his car would travel 30 mph. Presumably his parents had taught him never to lie.

1910 Harris, runabout, WLB

HARRIS — Chicago, Illinois — (1910) — The Harris from Chicago used a two-cylinder four-stroke ("It is air cooled and we thoroughly cool it") 12 hp engine fitted into a 74-inch wheelbase chassis featuring a planetary transmission and shaft drive. It was available as a two-passenger runabout in a solid-tired Model C or a pneumatic-tired Model D. And the price for either was only $395. "The Greatest Innovation in the Automobile World," the company said. The firm producing this world-beater was, of all things, the Chicago House Wrecking Company at 35th and Iron Streets. Had the Harris been as good a car as purported, the firm probably would have left the demolition business to challenge Henry Ford head-on. Instead it was the Harris that the company left, after only a year of trying.

1937 Harris, sporting one-seater, MVMA

HARRIS — Chicago, Illinois — (1936) — Benjamin F. Harris III was an industrial designer from Chicago who spent his spare hours over the course of three years designing and building a most unusual one-passenger automobile. It was powered by a 92-cubic-inch 32 hp V-8 which was set in an 86-inch wheelbase chassis with a 50-inch tread. Harris was obviously a student of Jaray aerodynamics and German Grand Prix design because his car reflected both. Concealed pop-up headlights, a broad, smooth-lined body capped by a centrally-mounted fin on the rear deck made for aerodynamic efficiency capable of propelling this single-seater sporting car at a claimed speed of 110 mph. The car was completed in 1936. Harris never had any plans for marketing it.

1923 Harris Six, touring, KM

HARRIS SIX — Menasha, Wisconsin — (1923) — In the spring of 1919 the U.S. Tractor Company moved from Chicago to Menasha where production of its Uncle Sam Tractor was continued, the firm's name was changed to U.S. Tractor & Machinery Company, and the firm's vice-president G.D. Harris decided to build an automobile. To do so, Harris negotiated the purchase of patterns from the Winther Motor Company of Kenosha which had decided to forgo automobile production to concentrate on its trucks. The April 30th, 1923 edition of the *Menasha Record* heralded the advent of the new Harris Six in a splendid advertisement complete with a drawing of the new car which looked, not surprisingly, rather like the Winther. It was a Touring Phaeton complete with disc wheels and a $1485 price tag. Also advertised were a Touring at $1275 and an All-Year

Touring at $1675. These cars were not pictured. In August of 1923 announcement was made in the national automotive press of the reorganization of U.S. Tractor & Machinery Company into the Wisconsin Automotive Corporation. The principals of the company remained the same, and bus manufacture was now intended as well. It would appear that the first step the Wisconsin Automotive Corporation took was into bankruptcy court. Thus far the Harris Six had not left the drawing board. Under court decree such automobiles as could be built from parts ordered were put together. This represented over six to ten cars, all of them the Touring Phaeton with disc wheels. The next venture embarked upon by G.D. Harris was the manufacture of snowplows. He did get into genuine production this time, and was quite successful.

HARRISON — The H.O. Harrison Company was organized in Los Angeles, California during the spring of 1906 with a capital stock of $50,000 for the manufacture and sale of automobiles. Incorporators included Ray D. Robinson, J.W McAlister and H.O. Harrison. Manufacture is doubted.

1906 Harrison, model C, touring, NAHC

HARRISON — Grand Rapids, Michigan — (1906-1907) — The Harrison Motor Company was a department of Harrison Wagon Works of Grand Rapids and the producer of a large touring car which featured a device that was part better mousetrap, part Rube Goldberg. "The Car Without a Crank," as the Harrison was known, provided on-the-spark starting by a press of a push-button which activated an air pump and sent a measured acetylene mixture into the appropriate cylinder. But this was not all; the device could also be used, the company said, for the testing of coils and plugs, and the lighting of lights, as well as the pumping of tires and the dusting off of the entire car. Apparently the only thing it did not do was windows. The price for all this, including the car, was $5000. The Harrison had been designed by Albert C. Menges, an engine builder from Memphis, Tennessee who had been lured west by William H. Harrison. It was introduced at the Chicago Automobile Show in February 1906. Almost immediately, there were problems. Certainly this early self-starting device could not have worked satisfactorily; in November Albert Menges left the company to begin another named for himself. In March of 1907, *The Motor World* reported internal dissension and the realization of the Harrison people that "motor cars and wagons minus motors do not mix as readily as may appear possible." A separate company to take over the "crankless car" was planned and a reorganization committee assembled. The latter was composed of James R. Wiley, Clay H. Hollister, Maurice Shanahan and Mark Norris (all of Grand Rapids) and Henry W. Marsh of Manistee. Instead of reorganizing, however, these gentlemen decided to simply turn the automobile business over to its creditors. This was done in March 1907. On January 17th, 1908 Harrison Wagon Works itself was adjudged bankrupt. After more than a half-century in business, the "crankless car" had done in one of Grand Rapids' oldest vehicle builders. There was an attempt to resuscitate the Harrison automobile venture as the Anthony-Hatcher Company, but it failed.

1906-1907 HARRISON
Model C — 4-cyl., 40 hp, 106" wb

	FP	5	4	3	2	1
Touring-7P	5000	—	—	—	—	—

HARROLDS — New York, New York — (1905 et seq.) — The Harrolds Motor Car Company was organized with a capital stock of $30,000 late in 1903 for the purpose of dealing in motorcars. Harry Unwin, formerly secretary of the National Association of Automobile Manufacturers, was the president and general manager, though he had left by 1905 when the company elected to confine itself exclusively to the sale of Pierce-Arrows and Robert D. Garden (who had come to prominence in Colonel Albert Pope's bicycle empire) took over as general manager. That Harrolds was a thriving success was unquestioned; *The Automobile Review* noted that it was the only New York City company with the exception of John Wanamaker to occupy an entire Broadway block (from 58th-59th streets). That Harrolds was an automobile manufacturer in the strictest sense is in doubt. Most probably, the firm provided custom cars to specific client request using the Pierce-Arrow chassis, or purchased electric running gear for the making of small town cars for driving around Manhattan. Registration lists indicate that a Harrolds was in the William Rockefeller garage in New York City, and that Howard J. Dietz owned both a Harrolds and a Pierce-Arrow, both no doubt purchased from the Broadway emporium.

HARROUN — Chicago, Illinois — (1905) — Ray W. Harroun built his first automobile in 1905 and promptly forgot it in 1906 when he was given the opportunity to become a riding mechanic for the Buick factory racing team. Motor sports occupied his total efforts in the years following, Har-

1905 Harroun, Aerial, racer, NAHC

roun becoming AAA National Champion in 1910 and retiring that year to join the engineering staff of Marmon. The year following Marmon persuaded Harroun to "unretire" long enough to race in the new 500-mile Memorial Day inaugural at Indianapolis. Six years later Ray Harroun entered the automobile industry as a bone-fide manufacturer.

1917 Harroun, model A-1, touring, NAHC

HARROUN — Wayne, Michigan — (1917-1922) — Although cars bearing celebrated names are not uncommon in the United States, it has not been common for the celebrity to contribute much more than his name and promotional efforts. Ray Harroun, however, designed the Harroun entirely by himself, and it was introduced six years after he became famous as the winner of the first Indianapolis 500. The Harroun was a good little car with a quite efficient ohv four-cylinder engine rated at 16.9 hp but developing 43.1 hp at 2400 rpm. Three-speed transmission and cone clutch were combined in unit with the engine, and the wheelbase was a trim 107 inches. Roadsters for three and five passengers were offered at $595, a sedan at $850. The Harroun gave every indication of becoming a sterling success. Harroun Motors Corporation was incorporated for $10,000,000 on September 14th, 1917. Serving as its president was John Guy Moniham, formerly of Premier and Marion. Construction of a factory in Wayne with a 24,000-unit-per-year capacity was immediately begun. In the meantime, Harroun went into production at the Wayne plant of the former Prouty & Glass Carriage Company. Approximately 500 cars were produced prior to April of 1918 when the company received a large government contract for the manufacture of munitions. A half million dollars in new machinery was installed by Harroun to produce them, and after the Armistice the company had more than a little difficulty settling with the government on its war claims. This delayed the return to full-time automobile production and represented the death knell for Harroun Motors Corporation. Although an improved Model AA-2 was readied by Ray Harroun for 1922 model year introduction, it was built in very small numbers. Having exhausted working capital in wartime production, and discovering new investors hard to come by in the wake of the postwar recession, Harroun Motors Corporation found itself in receiver's hands in June 1922. Its factory was purchased by Gotfredson Truck Corporation.

1918 Harroun, model A-1, roadster, WLB

1917-1918 HARROUN
Model A-1 — 4-cyl., 43 hp, 107" wb

	FP	5	4	3	2	1
Roadster-3P	595	2300	3300	4600	7500	16,000
Roadster-5P	595	2300	3300	4600	7500	16,000
Sedan-5P	850	1600	2700	3800	5800	12,000

1919-1921 HARROUN
Model 18 — 4-cyl., 43 hp, 107" wb

	FP	5	4	3	2	1
Touring-5P	1195	2400	3400	4800	8000	17,000
Military Roadster-3P	1195	2400	3400	4800	8000	17,000

1922 HARROUN
Model AA-2 — 4-cyl., 41 hp, 106" wb

	FP	5	4	3	2	1
Touring-5P	995	2300	3300	4600	7500	16,000

1930 Harruff, sedan, NAHC

HARRUFF — Toledo, Ohio — (1930) — The Harruff was, as the *Automobile Trade Journal* headlined, a "One-Man Car," the magazine explaining that this referred not to seating capacity but to the number of men required to build it. The one man was J.W. Harruff of 193 Woodruff Avenue in Toledo. His car was an example of downsizing in an era not noted for same. It was powered by a 20 hp engine, had an 80-inch wheelbase and was 60 inches high. It looked rather like a Whippet. Manufacture did not follow, and doubtless had never been envisioned.

HART — The Hart Motor Car Company was organized early in 1912 in Chicago, Illinois with a capital stock of $10,000 to manufacture automobiles and accessories. Incorporators were F.P. Hart, K. Bylington and C.G. Stroher. Manufacture of a car is doubted.

HART — Detroit, Michigan — (1898) — Hart & Company of Detroit manufactured cabinet hardware, though the man behind the firm, Henry C. Hart, described himself as "a motor student of many years' standing." In 1898 he built several carriages into which he fitted gasoline engines of his own invention. This seems to have been strictly a sideline activity, and concerted manufacture was never embarked upon.

HART STEAM — Poughkeepsie, New York — (1903-1904) — "The constructor is a consulting mechanical engineer, and the car, built entirely at his laboratories, shows in every detail a thorough comprehension of all the conditions involved in the problem, and a systematic attack from an engineering standpoint." Thus reported *The Horseless Age* regarding the steam carriage built by Frederick Hart in Poughkeepsie. It was powered by a double-cylinder vertical engine with multi-tubular boiler, and while not avant-garde, represented, at least in reporter N.B. Pope's point of view, state of the art in steam car design for that period. The car had been successfully operated on the road for over 3,000 miles, already, Hart told Pope, "over rough and hilly roads without any serious failures in any part of its mechanism." No mention was made in the extensive article about the car regarding any intention of Frederick Hart to manufacture it.

HARTFORD — Hartford, Connecticut was the site of a variety of automotive ventures carrying the city's name in the years prior to World War I.
In 1900 the Hartford Accumulator Company built a prototype car which demonstrated the new storage battery system invented by Frederick W. Barhoff and the general lines of which followed the design of Halsey B. Philbrick. Refer to Barhoff and Philbrick.
The Hartford-Apperson Motor Company has been indicated on various car rosters as the manufacturer of an automobile in 1916. The firm instead was a dealer for the Apperson built in Kokomo, Indiana.
The Hartford Automobile & Boat Supply Company was organized in January 1910 to manufacture and sell automobiles, motor boats and motorcycles. T. Edward Oakes, William J. Rabbit and George Stoner, all of Hartford, were the principals involved. Of the $50,000 capital stock, just $4 was reported paid in at the time of incorporation. Manufacture did not follow.
The Hartford Motor Car Company has been indicated on various car rosters as the manufacturer of an automobile in 1914. This is highly unlikely. There was such a company at 410 Main Street, but it operated as a dealership during this period.
The Hartford Motor Machine Company at 902 Main Street was listed as an automobile manufacturer in the *New England Business Directory and Gazette* for 1902. The firm purportedly built a steam car called the Collins that year. Further documentation is lacking.
The Hartford Motor Vehicle Company was organized in early 1903 to "make motor vehicles of all descriptions." Capital stock was $50,000; the incorporators were Albion R. Wilson, Lucius Rumson and Frank A. Hagarty, all of Hartford. Manufacture of an automobile is doubted.

650

1895 Hartley Steam, motor trap, NAHC

HARTLEY — Chicago, Illinois — (1895-1899) — The Hartley Steam Trap was among the more handsome of the myraid cars planned for entry in the Chicago Times-Herald Contest of 1895, one of the few that made it to the starting line — and the Hartley Power Supply Company continued building automotive vehicles for a good time longer than most of the other entrants as well. Its Times-Herald car was powered by a steam engine of the company's own design, "a combination of the rotary and automatic cut-off principles," Hartley said. Fuel could be either gasoline, wood or coal, "a small grate being carried along to be substituted for the oil burner should it be impossible to obtain oil." In December 1895 the Hartley Power Supply Company indicated that it planned henceforth to engage in the manufacture of steam traps, delivery wagons, tricycles and heavy trucks. Whether commercial vehicle production was ever embarked upon is not known, but Hartley was building a compressed-air passenger car in 1897 and a gasoline-engined three-wheeler in 1899.

HARTMAN — In 1900 *The Horseless Age* reported that W.G. Hartman of Portland, Oregon had built a steam carriage to his own design. Further details are lacking.

1915 Hartman, roadster, GR

HARTMAN — Red Bluff, California — (1914-1918) — George V. Hartman was creator of this car. Its engine was a four produced by the Model Gas Engine Works, that unit being chosen because Model was in the process of moving its plant from Peru, Indiana to Pittsburgh and was disposing of its stock at closeout prices. The Model engine purchased was built in unit with the crankcase and three-speed transmission. The 110-inch-wheelbase chassis designed by Hartman featured a semi-floating rear axle and suspension by semi-elliptics at the front, cantilever at the rear. In four years he may have built as many as twenty cars. With the entrance of the United States into World War I, George Hartman closed up shop and entered the Army. He did not resume manufacture after the Armistice although he did return home to Red Bluff.

HART-PARR — Charles City, Iowa — (1908) — The Hart-Parr Company of Charles City manufactured gasoline tractors. The two-cylinder runabout that has been listed through the years on various car rosters was indeed built by Hart-Parr, but for internal use only. Rather than purchase automobiles for its traveling salesmen, Hart-Parr decided to produce the cars themselves in 1908. Subsequently, Hart-Parr salesmen drove in automobiles of other manufacturers and the Hart-Parr Company built only tractors.

HARVARD — That a car called the Harvard was produced by the Pioneer Motor Car Company in York, Pennsylvania has been indicated on various car rosters. There is no evidence of this. Possibly the venture was confused with the Harvard produced by the Pioneer Motor Car Company of Troy, New York in 1915.

1915 Harvard, model 4-20, roadster, HAC

HARVARD — New York & Maryland — (1915-1921) — Shortly after disposing of his Herreshoff Motor Company of Detroit, Charles Herreshoff announced that he had organized the Herreshoff Light Car Company in Troy, New York for the manufacture of another car he had designed which was smaller and lighter than his Detroit Herreshoff. But it didn't happen that way. There indeed was a Herreshoff Light Car Company in Troy; it was owned by Northrup R. Holmes, a successful young Troy attorney, and it had served as an agency for the selling of the original Detroit Herreshoff cars. The new car designed by Herreshoff was certainly built in Troy, but it would not be called a Herreshoff. Instead it was the Harvard. The story is confusing. When Herreshoff moved to Troy following his Detroit adventure, he brought with him the prototype of his new light car. Doubtless Herreshoff knew Holmes previously through his Herreshoff Light Car Company dealership, and the two men now became friends. Herreshoff suggested to Holmes that the new car be produced in Troy, for the seemingly lucrative export market (New Zealand specifically), but preliminary plans for manufacture were abruptly halted when Herreshoff suddenly took off for South America, taking the prototype with him. Holmes remained interested and, fortunately, still had the plans for the car locked in his office safe. Thereon he approached Theodore Litchfield, a Troy mechanic and local agent for the Herff-Brooks automobile. Holmes offered Litchfield the same proposition that Herreshoff had offered him. Build the car, Holmes said, and Litchfield promptly completed the chassis, fitted with a small four-cylinder engine from Model. Meantime, Holmes had decided on the name Harvard for the car, and Pioneer Motor Car Company for its manufacturing firm, though he soon changed the latter to Harvard-Pioneer Motor Car Company. Several cars were built during the winter of 1915-1916. Among the distinctive features of the Harvard were its rear compartment for a hidden spare tire (one of the first, and possibly *the* first, in this country) and the mounting of the headlights to supports that were bolted directly to the radiator shell. Early in 1916 Northrup Holmes approached George N. Nay, a lawyer in nearby Hudson Falls who also operated a dealership for Overland, Saxon, Cole and Mitchell cars. Nay's facilities were more extensive than Holmes', and so assembly of the Harvard now moved to the top floor of Nay's Adirondack Motor Car Company. As many as 80 cars may have been built there. Seeing to their supervision was Walter Bulow who had previously worked for Lozier and American Fiat. In 1919, Bulow redesigned the Harvard and built a demonstrator touring car larger and with a more highly rounded radiator than previous Harvards. The Holmes-Nay partnership resulted in the incorporation of a new Harvard Motor Car Company on October 18th, 1919, but it was very short-lived. Onto the scene now strode Henry R. Carroll of Washington, D.C. — together with the Carter Brothers — who bought up the entire operation and moved it to Hyattsville, Maryland. There several of the new Bulow-designed chassis were completed, but there too the Harvard died, a victim of the postwar depression.

1915-1919 HARVARD
Model 4-20 — 4-cyl., 14.3 hp, 100" wb

	FP	5	4	3	2	1
Roadster-2P	750	2400	3400	4800	8000	17,000
Coupe-2P	850	2200	3200	4400	7000	15,000

1920-1921 HARVARD
Four — 35 hp, 108" wb

	FP	5	4	3	2	1
Touring-4P	850	2500	3500	5000	8500	18,000

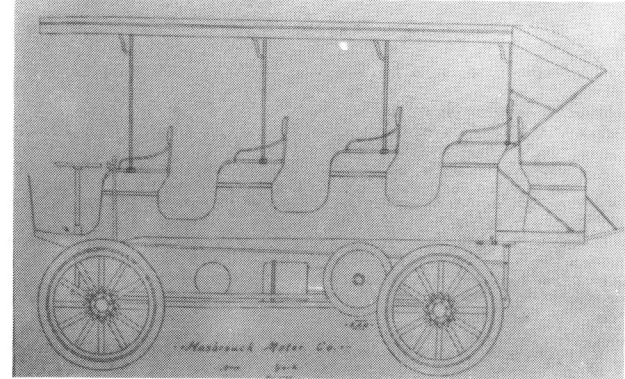

1901 Hasbrouck, gasoline stage, WLB

HASBROUCK — Piermont, New York — (1900-1902) — Hasbrouck Motor Works was incorporated in Newark, New Jersey in March of 1899 for the building of marine engines. In May of 1900 the firm moved to Piermont, New York, and there began experimentation with motor vehicles, principally omnibuses and delivery trucks. In 1901 the company built a two-passenger phaeton featuring a single-cylinder 6 hp engine, planetary transmission and chain drive. It was successfully tested in April, but by November the company was in receivership. Apparently, its financial problems were quickly resolved because in March of 1902 Hasbrouck reported shipping two gasoline runabouts to South America and the building to customer order of others. The firm remained in the vehicle-manufacturing business only for a short while, however. By the end of 1902 Hasbrouck had relocated to Yonkers, and a few years later moved again, to New London, Connecticut. Only in Piermont does it appear that the company built cars. Repair and general garage work was its activity in Yonkers and New London. The people behind the Hasbrouck venture were Stephen A. Hasbrouck, William H. Burchell, Joseph Hasbrouck, Carl F. Hermann, Lemuel F. Dickerson, William H. Hassett, F.O. Matthiessen and E.J. Collins.

1904 Haschke, electric touring, WLB

HASCHKE ELECTRIC — Chicago, Illinois — (1904) — J.E. Haschke of Chicago was a long-time storage battery maker who was described by *Motor Age* in 1904 as "devoting considerable attention to the study of electric vehicles for touring." Since mileage between charges generally rendered the electric car as a short-range vehicle, Haschke's idea obviously was a good one. In 1904 he revised a five-passenger Waverley into a touring car outfitted with one of his 70-volt multiple series batteries weighing 950 pounds and having a capacity of 180 ampere-hours. He tested the vehicle extensively in the Chicago area. Although its top speed of 25 mph was nothing to brag about, its between-charge range of 100 miles was. Indeed, one test run demonstrated 103 miles. Haschke never envisioned automobile manufacture, however. He continued in the storage battery business for some years thereafter.

HASSALL — Colorado Springs, Colorado — (1907) — In late 1907 the Hassall Iron Works at 31 West Cimarron Street in Colorado Springs announced expansion plans which included a plant addition of 4500 square feet for the manufacture of automobiles to carry the engine invented by W.H. Green, also of Colorado Springs. Green's unit was claimed to "develop more power than the general order of engines." Possibly this automotive venture did not make it through the prototype stage.

1917 Hassler, roadster, WLB

HASSLER — Indianapolis, Indiana — (1917) — Robert H. Hassler of Indianapolis built his first experimental motor buggy in 1898. The car was not marketed, however. In 1904 Hassler was among the people who organized the Marion Motor Car Company in Indianapolis, and subsequently he went into business himself making shock absorbers, transmissions and other automobile components as Robert H. Hassler, Inc. But the automotive bug bit him again in 1917. Early in the spring of that year he organized the subsidiary Hassler Motor Company to manufacture an automobile. The Hassler was offered as a $1650 two-passenger stagger-seat 112-inch wheelbase roadster only. It featured a four-cylinder Buda engine, Auto-Lite ignition, Brown-Lipe gears, Houk wire wheels and a suspension system very like the Marmon's. "The Restful Riding Car" was a slogan. Several Hasslers were shown during the automobile show in Chicago that summer. They might have represented the total production. In early fall the Hassler Motor Company filed a certificate of dissolution, its founder having decided, as reported in the press, that "it is not the time to place a new car on the market."

HASTINGS STEAM — New York, New York — (1902) — T.K. Hastings of 385 East Sixteenth Street in the Flatbush section of Brooklyn built himself a steam touring car in 1902 that was quite modern for the period. Both its engine and boiler were mounted up front under a hood, with "nearly every working part," Hastings boasted, "in view of the operator." Manufacture was not considered.

HASTINGS — Detroit, Michigan — (1910) — An automobile with a six-cylinder rotary valve engine was the idea of the Hastings Motor Car Company of Detroit, but it is doubted that the idea was ever put into production. Formation of the company was announced in the trade press during the summer of 1910, and then Hastings vanished from view.

HATFIELD — The Hatfield Company of Cornwall-on-the-Hudson was organized early in 1910 with a capital stock of $125,000 to manufacture, deal in and repair automobiles in New York. Incorporators were D.H. McConnell, G.C. Brown and G.W. Blanchard. Manufacture of an automobile is doubted, but the firm did produce trucks for several years, moving to Elmira in 1911.

1907 Hatfield, buggyabout, NAHC

HATFIELD — Miamisburg, Ohio — (1907-1908) — The Hatfield of Ohio was born in Cortland, New York. There, late in 1906, Charles B. Hatfield, Sr. and Jr., incorporated their Hatfield Motor Vehicle Company to manufacture a highwheeler they alternately called a Buggyabout or a Unique. By spring of 1907 they had relocated in Miamisburg, however, and production began there. The Hatfield sported an air-cooled two-cylinder four-cycle engine, friction transmission, double chain drive, large wheels (38 inches front, 40 inches rear) with solid tires. It was a car that was almost primevally simple, but there was a Madison Avenue flair to its advertising. The Hatfield was, so the slogan said, "an automobile without an expense account" — with little more outlay required for it than the low purchase price, and the cost of gas and oil. Running gear and bodies for the Hatfield were produced by the Kauffman Buggy Company across town in Miamisburg. In the early spring of 1908, as receivership loomed for the Hatfield venture, that firm was merged with Kauffman, and in June the Advance Motor Vehicle Company was organized to carry on manufacture under the Kauffman name. As for the Hatfields, they returned to Upstate New York to build the Hatfield truck in Elmira. Charles B. Hatfield, Sr. had formerly been associated with George Selden. Charles B. Hatfield, Jr. would subsequently design a cyclecar named O-We-Go.

1907 HATFIELD
Model B — 2-cyl., 12 hp, 74" wb

	FP	5	4	3	2	1
Buggyabout-4P	600	2000	3000	4200	6500	14,000
Model C — 2-cyl., 14 hp, 101" wb						
Buggyabout-4P	750	2100	3100	4300	6800	14,500
1908 HATFIELD						
Model B — 2-cyl., 12 hp, 78" wb						
Buggyabout-2P	650	2000	3000	4200	6500	14,000

1917 Hatfield, model B, speedster-roadster, HAC

HATFIELD — Sidney, New York — (1916-1924) — The Hatfield family of Sidney had been producers of carriages and sleighs since the late Nineteenth Century, and spent a good many years squabbling among themselves — and with W.T. Sherwood who was a major stockholder — on the matter of whether to enter the horseless arena. Finally L.I. Hatfield prevailed, although reluctant members of the organization insisted that the firm's name not be changed from Cortland Cart & Carriage Company, and it would not be, despite its distinctly old-fashioned sound by 1916. Hatfields were medium-priced fours and sixes (engines either from G.B.&S. or Herschell-Spillman) offered in the usual complement of body styles, including a delivery car. Two interesting offerings for 1917 were the Model I Suburban, an early station wagon, and the Model B Roadster-Speedster, a rakish proposition with two specially fitted suitcases mounted behind the gasoline tank. Sporting models in the 1920's featured individual step-plates and wire wheels. When bankruptcy arrived in the summer of 1924, business was reported to be continued by the receiver. Doubtless this was simply to complete cars already on the assembly line.

1916 HATFIELD
Four — 4-cyl., 23 hp, 106" wb

	FP	5	4	3	2	1
Model H Roadster-2P	795	2500	3500	5000	8500	18,000

1917 Hatfield, model I, suburban, HAC

1917 HATFIELD
Four — 4-cyl., 23 hp, 106" wb

Model A Touring-5P	875	2500	3500	5000	8500	18,000
Model H Roadster-2P	875	2700	3600	5300	8800	19,000
Model B Rds.-Spdstr.-2P	875	2900	3700	5600	9100	20,000
Model I Suburban-5P	800	2400	3400	4800	8000	17,000

1918 HATFIELD
Four — 4-cyl., 23 hp, 115" wb

Touring-5P	1080	2700	3600	5300	8800	19,000
Roadster-2P	950	2900	3700	5600	9100	20,000
Runabout-2P	950	2700	3600	5300	8800	19,000
Sociable Roadster-4P	1090	3000	4000	6000	9500	21,000

1919 HATFIELD
Four — 4-cyl., 23 hp, 115" wb

Touring-5P	1250	2700	3600	5300	8800	19,000
Roadster-4P	1260	2900	3700	5600	9100	20,000

1920 HATFIELD
Model A-42 — 4-cyl., 42 hp, 115" wb

Roadster-2P	1125	2900	3700	5600	9100	20,000
Speedster-2P	1125	3000	4000	6000	9500	21,000
Suburban-4P	1020	2500	3500	5000	8500	18,000
Touring-5P	1695	2700	3600	5300	8800	19,000
Roadster-4P	1695	3000	4000	6000	9500	21,000
Sedan-5P	3500	2200	3200	4400	7000	15,000
Brougham-5P	3500	2300	3300	4600	7500	16,000

1921 Hatfield, model A-42, roadster, MVMA

1921-1922 HATFIELD
Model A-42 — 4-cyl., 35 hp, 115" wb

Roadster-4P	1695	3000	4000	6000	9500	21,000
Touring-5P	1695	2900	3700	5600	9100	20,000
Sedan-5P	2595	2200	3200	4400	7000	15,000

1923 HATFIELD
Model A-42 — 4-cyl., 35 hp, 115" wb

Touring-5P	1345	2900	3700	5600	9100	20,000
Sport-4/5P	1495	3000	4000	6000	9500	21,000
Sedan-5P	1950	2300	3300	4600	7500	16,000
Coupe-4P	1950	2500	3500	5000	8500	18,000

1924 HATFIELD
Model 55 — 6-cyl., 55 hp, 121" wb

Touring-5P	1775	3100	4200	6300	10,500	22,000
Sport Touring-5p	1975	3200	4300	6500	11,000	23,000
Coupe-4P	2175	2700	3600	5300	8800	19,000
Sedan-5P	2350	2600	3600	5200	8700	18,500

1922 Hatfield, model A-42, coupe, HAC

1923 Hatfield, model A-42, 4-dr. sedan, WLB

1914 Hathorn, cyclecar, NAHC

HATHORN — Davenport, Iowa — (1914) — C.E. Hathorn built a cyclecar with a Spacke engine, a 100-inch wheelbase, 36-inch tread and a long, long belt drive. It was a tandem two-seater with a metal body and leather seats. Although not underslung, it appeared low to the ground because of the fitting of quarter-elliptic springs. As an example of the cyclecar genre, Hathorn's effort was as meritorious as most. "Recently the car was taken out in a severe snowstorm," *The American Cyclecar* reported in early 1914, "and negotiated a notoriously steep hill near Davenport on high gear, overtaking a roadster which had considerable difficulty in making the grade." That showed effective power for a two-cylinder 9/13 hp engine. Quantity production of the Hathorn was promised soon. It never arrived.

HAUSER — The Hauser Machine & Manufacturing Company, Inc. was organized in Rochester, New York during the spring of 1917 for the manufacture of automobiles, machinery and engines. Capital stock was $50,000; the incorporators were J. Hauser, W. Hauser and G.J. Dash. Manufacture of an automobile is doubted.

HAUSHALTER — Milwaukee, Wisconsin — (1910) — This automobile, which appeared in chassis form at the Milwaukee Automobile Show in February 1910, was invented, patented, designed and built by one Dr. H.P. Haushalter. What Haushalter was a doctor of was not revealed, but he admitted to being neither an engineer nor a mechanic, but "merely a jack-of-all trades." The Haushalter's engine was an air-cooled twin, its underslung frame was wood; friction transmission and four-wheel-drive were featured, the last named seen to by an assortment of pulleys. Large-diameter spring wheels with solid tires were purportedly "of such efficiency that not even riding springs are required." An inverted glass bottle constituted the gasoline supply tank; lubrication was handled by a belt-driven mechanical oiler. Remaining specifications of the Haushalter were the usual. Its inventor declared at the show that he was not quite finished with the car, and did not plan to exhibit it formally before spring. Probably he did eventually body his Haushalter chassis. But no one ever provided him the money to proceed into manufacture.

1910 Haushalter, NAHC

HAVANA — Paterson, New Jersey — (1905) — During the late spring of 1905 the Havana Automobile Company was organized in Paterson with a capital stock of $500,000 to manufacture automobiles and to operate an automobile freighting business in the Caribbean. William Schek, Jr. of West Nyack, New York; and Louis H. Pink and Walter Moffet of New York City were behind this venture. There were some Havana vehicles built — both trucks and large touring cars — though they were not produced by the Havana Automobile Company. Instead, they were manufactured by the Mack Brothers Motor Car Company of Allentown, Pennsylvania. A news release from October 1905 indicated that ten Havana passenger cars built by Mack were being shipped to Havana, Cuba to be put in service there by the Havana Automobile Company.

HAVENS — Denver, Colorado — (1906) — Herbert Havens was a Denver machinist who built himself a car in 1906. Initially its engine was a 35 hp four, with the completed vehicle, according to *Motor Field*, being "flatteringly commented on by friends of the builder, who also know a few practical things about gasoline motor engines and automobiles." But Havens wasn't satisfied with the power of his car, and so dismantled the engine with plans to beef it up to a 60 hp. "The perfected Havens will be ready in about six weeks for the inspection of Centennial State automobilists and friends of home industry," reported *Motor Field* that April. Manufacture did not follow.

1911 Havers Six, roadster, HAC

HAVERS — Port Huron, Michigan — (1911-1914) — The Havers Motor Car Company was organized in Port Huron in the early spring of 1910. Two Havers were involved: Fred, who served as president, and Ernest, who designed the six-cylinder car the company would market. Production began in December 1910. Initially the Havers was manufactured in the plant of the Port Huron Engine and Thresher Company, but in 1912 another factory in town which had been used for E-M-F production was secured. Two hundred Havers were built in 1912, and the company seemed to be moving along nicely. To the original 44 hp six of 1911-1912, a 55 hp was added in 1913, beefed up to 60 hp for 1914, including the racy "Speed Car" version. On July 8th, 1914 the Havers factory was destroyed by fire. Although the Havers immediately announced plans to rebuild, they did not have the financial resources to do so. In November a bankruptcy suit was filed against the company. Two receiver's sales of the Havers assets were required. At the first, in January 1915, the bids were so low none were accepted. The equipment was sold then for $7500. What remained of Havers was acquired by the Puritan Machine Company at the second sale the following October.

1911 HAVERS
Six — 44 hp, 115" wb

	FP	5	4	3	2	1
Roadster-2P	1500	3000	4000	6000	9500	21,000
Touring-4P	1650	2900	3700	5600	9100	20,000

1912 Havers, model Six-44, touring, HAC

1912 HAVERS
Model Six-44 — 36/44 hp, 122" wb

	FP	5	4	3	2	1
Fore-Door Touring-5P	1850	3100	4200	6300	10,500	22,000
Fore-Door Roadster-2P	1850	3100	4200	6300	10,500	22,000

1913 Havers, model Six-55, touring, GR

1913 HAVERS
Model Six-44 — 44 hp, 122" wb

	FP	5	4	3	2	1
Fore-Door Touring-5P	1850	3000	4000	6000	9500	21,000
Fore-Door Roadster-2P	1850	3100	4200	6300	10,500	22,000

Model Six-55 — 55 hp, 128" wb

	FP	5	4	3	2	1
Fore-Door Touring-5P	2250	5500	10,900	18,200	25,500	36,000
Speed Car-2P	2250	5700	11,400	19,000	26,600	38,000

1914 Havers, model Six-44, touring, HAC

1914 HAVERS
Model Six-44 — 44 hp, 122" wb

	FP	5	4	3	2	1
Touring-5P	1985	3000	4000	6000	9500	21,000
Roadster-2P	1985	3100	4200	6300	10,500	22,000

Model Six-60 — 60 hp, 128" wb

	FP	5	4	3	2	1
Touring-5P	2485	5700	11,400	19,000	26,600	38,000
Roadster-2P	2485	5500	10,900	18,200	25,500	36,000
Speed Car-2P	2485	5800	11,500	19,200	26,900	38,500

HAVILAND — New York, New York — (1895-1896) — Dr. Frank M. Haviland was a physician residing at 210 West 123rd Street in Manhattan who told *The Horseless Age* in 1895 that he had come up with an automotive idea which he believed would be a "sensation when it is fully perfected." Unfortunately, he could not perfect his vehicle in time for the Chicago Times-Herald Contest that November, but he had attached his device to a 200-pound buggy which he fitted with a single-cylinder American motor. The whole package weighed 400 pounds. The doctor's device, which he sought to patent, was the Haviland Vehicle Driving Gear. It was described in *The Horseless Age* in November 1896 as follows: "The object of the independent propelling wheel is to provide a friction surface with the ground that will not slip and that will utilize the weight of the wagon and road as friction power, thus doing away with the necessity of either serrated or rubber tires. By having power applied to both front and rear, the inventor claims the propelling power is always exerted in the direction of the rotation of the wheels, thus overcoming any difficulties in turning round." The inventor had returned to his medical practice exclusively before the turn of the century.

HAVOC — Rochester, New York — (1914) — That the Havoc Cyclecar Manufacturing Company was planning to enter manufacturing ranks was indicated in a one-line reference in a cyclecar magazine during 1914. There is no evidence the company ever did so but a prototype is believed to have been built.

HAWK — Detroit, Michigan — (1914) — The Hawk Cyclecar Company of Detroit was organized by Frank S. Salter, Duane Tibbetts and W.W. McIntyre. The company's product differed from the cyclecar norm in its Frenchified cascading hood line which was complemented by a similar slope of the rear quarter, and made for a certainly interesting looking car. Only one body style, a side-by-side two-seater, was made available, at $390. The Hawk was powered by a two-cylinder air-cooled engine of 9/13 hp. Final drive was by belt, the wheelbase was 100 inches, tread the standard 56 inches. The frame was white ash, reinforced by steel. Hawk cyclecar advertised its product, perhaps too apologetically, as "neither Toy nor Freak." The company factory was at 256 Harmon Avenue in Detroit where, according to the February 1914 issue of *Cyclecar Age*, president Frank Salter was "literally 'on the job' morning, noon and night." By 1915 he was looking for another job.

1914 Hawk, cyclecar, WLB

1920 Hawk, touring, HAC

HAWK — Detroit, Michigan — (1919) — That a Hawk was built is documented by photographs extant, showing a handsome touring car with disc wheels. The car was made in 1919 for a hoped-for 1920 model year introduction, with a roadster to be available as well. Abruptly, however, this venture stalled. Nothing is known about the Hawk Motor Company of Detroit which built the prototype. Alas, it wasn't in town long enough to have made the city directory.

HAWKEYE — The Hawkeye Motor Car Company was organized in Burlington, Iowa during the summer of 1912 with a capital stock of $15,000 for the manufacture of automobiles. Incorporators were H.L. Madison, E.L. Horsford and L.H. Vahle. Manufacture is doubted. A subsequent incorporation in Sioux City, Iowa did result in the Hawkeye truck, built there from 1916 into the early Thirties.

HAWKINS — The Hawkins Automobile & Gas Engine Company was organized in Houston, Texas in late 1902 with a $20,000 capital stock with the plan to deal in automobiles and engines. George W. Hawkins was the man behind this venture. Several car rosters have indicated this company as an automobile manufacturer several years later, but the evidence is lacking that Hawkins ever strayed from its original intention of operating as a dealership.

The Hawkins Cyclecar Company of Xenia, Ohio produced an automobile in 1914 that was marketed under the tradename of Xenia. Refer to Xenia.

The William W. Hawkins Engineering Company was organized in Brooklyn, New York during the spring of 1911 with a capital stock of $25,000 to "manufacture, repair, store and deal in motor cars and motors." Behind this venture were P.J. McDonald, Alex Bernardik and Richard F. Woodward. Manufacture is doubted.

HAWKINS — Seattle, Washington — (1910) — Howard Hawkins was a young Seattle lad who built himself an automobile in 1910. "The materials he had to work with were such as naturally accumulate in spareroom and cellar," *Motor Field* commented. The Hawkins' frame was fashioned from an iron bedstead, its wheels came from an old coaster, its seat from an old cart, its springs from an abandoned wagon, its radiator from the tubes of a refrigerator, its chain from a motorcycle, its lamp from a bike, its steering handle from a baby carriage. A local machine shop supplied the belt-and-pulley transmission and the small two-horsepower engine, the countershaft was from a sewing machine, and the gasoline tank was a former syrup can. Amazingly, it all worked. "This home-made product is attracting much attention," said *Motor Field*.

HAWLEY — The William J. Hawley Auto Company was organized early in 1912 in Canandaigua, New York for the manufacture of automobiles, with Hawley joined in partnership for this venture by Edson T. Case. Manufacture is doubted.

HAWLEY — Paxton, Illinois — (1902) — T.G. Hawley was a machinist from Paxton who built a three-seated gasoline automobile in 1902 for a resident in town named C.H. Langford. Conceivably, Hawley may have built further automobiles for Paxtonites, but this has not been documented.

HAWLEY — Constantine, Michigan — (1906-1907) — Mendon, Michigan — (1907-1908) — The Hawley Automobile Company, Ltd. was organized in the summer of 1906 in Constantine to manufacture cars according to patents owned by one R.B. Hawley. Because the Hawley specifications were standard throughout, one presumes the patented features of the vehicle to be of minor import. The Hawley was powered by a two-cylinder two-stroke water-cooled 16 hp engine. Single chain drive and friction transmission were fitted. The car was available in two models — a runabout on an 84-inch wheelbase at $450 and a touring on a 96-inch wheelbase at $700. Top speed was a claimed 45 mph. The company moved rather quickly too, in late 1907 to Mendon. It died there soon after. Thereon the Hawley people moved back whence they had begun and established the Constantine Motor Car Company, which was an even shorter entry in automotive ranks than the Hawley had been.

1898 Hay & Hotchkiss, stanhope, NAHC

HAY & HOTCHKISS — New Haven, Connecticut — (1898-1899) — Walter Hay was a mechanical engineer from Seville, Ohio who interested E.M. Hotchkiss of Waterbury, Connecticut in his proposition — and thus the Hay & Hotchkiss Company was born in September of 1898. Hay's proposition was an internal combustion engine he had designed and named the "Hay Frictionless Gasolene Motor." It had four cylinders, generated 5 hp and weighed 240 pounds, which Hay said in 1898 was "more than is necessary." Presumably he meant this as a plus for his design, because he subsequently refined the engine, and it weighed 250 pounds. In October 1898 the new Hay & Hotchkiss partnership secured the New Haven, Connecticut factory of the former Manville Carriage Company, together with the services of L.S. Manville. The price was $30,000, probably most of that supplied by Hotchkiss. About a dozen hands were immediately hired to take on the design of the first Hay carriage. It was enthusiastically reviewed the following year in *The Horseless Age* as one of the most original motor carriages thus far built in the United States. "The most remarkable feature about it," the magazine said, "is the inventor's claim that no oil or water is required in the operation of the motor, the motor simply running a trifle harder when no oil is used." The engine was described as an "eight-cycle, four-cylinder horizontal, giving an explosion in each of the four cylinders every fourth turn . . . A few radiating ribs are used over the explosion chamber, but aside from this no cooling devices are needed." The comparative efficacy of the Hay engine notwithstanding, the Hay-designed body in which it was fitted was a handsome stanhope phaeton, a very good-looking rig. For whatever the reasons, and probably flaws in engine design was among them, the Hay & Hotchkiss Company had faded from sight by the turn of the century. Walter Hay immediately began looking for further "capitalists wishing to engage in the business." It does not appear he found them.

1908 Hay-Berg, 3-seat roadster, NAHC

HAY-BERG — Milwaukee, Wisconsin — (1907-1908) — The purpose of the Hay-Berg Motor Car Company of Milwaukee, so it was said, was "to purchase components of the best makers and assemble them in a harmonious design, carefully suited to the best service of the selected elements." The engine of the Hay-Berg was an air-cooled 20 hp four from

Carrico, its pressed steel 100-inch frame was from A.O. Smith, its axles from Timken, its transmission from Brown-Lipe. The whole package was put together very well. During the late summer of 1907, veteran automotive journalist Hugh Dolnar of *Cycle and Automobile Trade Journal* journeyed to Wisconsin to report on the car. During its first test run, about seventeen miles out of Milwaukee, its overanxious operator drove the Hay-Berg off the road while running at about 28 mph. No one was hurt except the Hay-Berg, with a burst right rear tire and a big bend in the front axle. The car was driven to Menominee Falls on the wheel rim, which ruined it of course as well. A second run was made following repairs, the driver this time being Mr. Sternberg, one of the two company owners who, Dolnar noted, "has had only a limited experience driving." He too came to momentary grief in a ditch, and the Hay-Berg was repaired again. By the time Dolnar's sojourn in Milwaukee had ended, some 200 miles had been put on the Hay-Berg. As Dolnar sagely noted in his subsequent report, "if the Hay-Berg roadster had not been very well put together," it would certainly not have survived so well the accidents of its drivers. Apparently it was the inexperience of the Hay-Berg people in the automobile business itself which killed the Hay-Berg car. Although a 40 hp seven-passenger touring car was announced by the company, it would seem that only the 20 hp roadster was ever produced. It was a good-looking car. It faded from sight in 1908.

HAYDEN — The Hayden-Croninger Automobile Company was organized in Chicago, Illinois during the fall of 1903 with a capital stock of $10,000 for the manufacture of automobiles and parts. John A. Hayden and R. Harry Croninger were the partners involved. Manufacture of a car did not follow.

The Hayden Automobile Company was a Chicago incorporation from early 1904 with Howard W. Hayes, Robert W. Dunn and James B. Devitt indicated as the incorporators. Again, $10,000 was the capital stock and manufacture was intended. Probably there was a connection with the earlier Hayden-Croninger venture (which by this time was serving as an agency for the National electric) but, again, manufacture does not seem to have followed.

HAYDOCK — Although the highwheeler introduced in 1907 by the D.W. Haydock Motor Car Manufacturing Company of St. Louis, Missouri initially bore the name Haydock Front-Drive, it was quickly changed to Cosmopolitan and became a rear-drive like all other highwheelers. Refer to Cosmopolitan.

The Haydock Motor Car Company of Cincinnati has been indicated on rosters as producing an automobile in 1915-1916. A firm of that name did announce forthcoming production of a $750 four that year, but was never heard from again. There was a T.T. Haydock Carriage Company in town at that time at the corner of Richmond and Carr, but its activity was noted only as "wholesale manufacturing of high grade vehicles." That any of these vehicles may have been horseless has not been documented.

1901 Hayn, gasoline carriage, NAHC

HAYN — **Mishawaka, Indiana** — **(1901)** — R.B. Hayn was an employee of the Western Gas Engine Company of Mishawaka. In 1901, during his spare time, he built a two-cylinder gasoline vehicle for his own use. This was an extracurricular activity completely. The Western Gas Engine Company never contemplated manufacture.

HAYNE — The Hayne Motor Company was incorporated in Plainfield, New Jersey with a capital stock of $25,000 to manufacture and deal in motor vehicles. Incorporators were Harrison Coddington, Charles F. Fulmer, Charles F. Hayne and William B. Harsel. Manufacture of a car is doubted.

HAYNES-APPERSON/ — **Kokomo, Indiana** — **(1898-1904)** / **HAYNES** — **(1904-1925)** — One day during the fall of 1893 the field superintendent of the Indiana Natural Gas and Oil Company visited the Riverside Machine Works in Kokomo and asked for assistance. Elwood P. Haynes had just purchased a little single-cylinder two-stroke Sintz marine engine, and he wanted to build a car. The Apperson brothers, who owned the machine shop, said sure. The car which resulted had a spur gear transmission with

1894 Haynes-Apperson, auto-buggy, HAC

three forward speeds (but no reverse), a friction differential, tiller steering and a foot throttle — and it was first run on the streets of Kokomo on July 4th, 1894. The story of this car was never told quite that way again, at least by Elwood Haynes. A few years later, when he decided to market the vehicle and had learned in the meantime of the gasoline car built by John Lambert in 1891, he visited Lambert and extracted from him a promise not to object if Haynes referred to his automobile as America's first. He also dated the car from its conception (1893) and not its birth. Furthermore, he tended to disregard the Appersons' part in the whole thing. None of this presented an insuperable problem in the beginning. The Haynes and Apperson partnership was a casual one at first; Haynes kept his gas company job, the Appersons continued their machine work, and a few Haynes-Apperson cars were turned out betweentimes. It was not until 1898 that the Haynes-Apperson Automobile Company was organized and the Riverside Machine Works turned into an automobile factory with a production capacity of one car every two or three weeks. By that fall a new factory was secured which raised output to two cars a week, offered in three models for two, four or six passengers. By the summer of 1899 the company was working two shifts and twenty-four hours a day to keep up with the demand. That year a Haynes-Apperson was driven from Kokomo to New York (which Elwood Haynes advertised as the "first 1000 mile run made in America," though Kokomo to New York is less than that) and in 1901 the trip was made again in 73 hours (which Haynes said was a speed record). There was no doubt, however, that the Haynes-Apperson was a fine automobile; it won a blue ribbon in the Long Island Endurance Run and two first prizes in the New York-Rochester Endurance Contest in 1901.

1897 Haynes Apperson, motor carriage, HFM

Later that year the Appersons and Elwood Haynes parted, none too amicably. In July of 1902 the first Apperson arrived. Elwood Haynes continued the Haynes-Apperson name until June of 1904 when his car became simply the Haynes. In September 1905 the firm became the Haynes Automobile Company. Neither Haynes nor the Appersons referred much to their previous partnership thereafter, and Haynes subsequently wrote various treatises along the "How I Built the First Automobile" line. Though his 1903 runabout retained a tiller, the phaeton and surrey now sported a wheel, and on the left-hand side, which was most unusual. In 1904 his car's horizontally opposed twin-cylinder engine moved from under the seat to under a hood up front. In 1905, with a good deal of panoply, Elwood Haynes presented the car he had built with the Appersons in 1893-1894 to the Smithsonian Institution. The Appersons were not mentioned in the press release. Haynes cars for 1904 had included a four-cylinder

1900 Haynes-Apperson, motor carriage, OCW

model, and fours became the company's sole product in 1906. All models featured shaft drive and selective sliding gear transmissions. A Haynes was entered in the 1906 Vanderbilt Cup, placed third in the elimination trials and was still running at the end, but well out of the money, in the race itself. A Vanderbilt Speedster model was offered in 1907, and Haynes advertised that his 50 hp touring model was the highest-powered shaft drive car in America. A six joined the Haynes line for 1913, and later that year the Vulcan electric gearshift was introduced for a short run on all models. The 365.3-cubic-inch V-12 Haynes made its debut at the New York Automobile Show in January 1916, though production did not begin until that August. In an elaborately promoted contest, one of the first V-12's off the line was offered in exchange for the oldest Haynes extant; E.J. Howard of Jeffersonville, Indiana received the V-12 when he presented the car he had bought in 1897 to the factory. That it was really a Haynes-Apperson went unmentioned. The Haynes V-12, or Light Twelve, was continued in production through 1922, though less than 650 were built in all. Haynes sixes remained the mainstay of production from 1915 (when the four was dropped) to the end. Though Elwood Haynes could scarcely be accused of conservatism in promoting his cars, Haynes cars themselves were simply good, if conventionally styled, automobiles. A rather nice sport speedster with individual aluminum step-plates arrived for 1921, but so by now had financial troubles for the company. A merger among Haynes, Winton and Dorris was rumored in 1923, but came to nothing. Instead, Elwood Haynes began slashing his prices, advertising his $1295 Model 60 touring car for 1924·as the lowest-priced Haynes ever built — and he began the retelling of his ''first car'' story with a vengeance, even taking to the radio waves with it. But it didn't help. In September of 1924, petitions by creditors to have the Haynes Automobile Company declared bankrupt were filed in the United States District Court in Indianapolis. Production ceased. By January of 1925, it had resumed but only on a temporary basis to use up stock on hand. About 200 broughams and sedans were the last Haynes cars built. On April 13th, 1925 Elwood Haynes died of

pneumonia at his home in Kokomo. Though one might have wished more modesty in the man behind the car, the demise of the Haynes was a sad day in the history of the American industry.

1898-1901 HAYNES-APPERSON
Two-Cylinder — 7/8 hp

	FP	5	4	3	2	1
Carriage-2P	1350	2000	3000	4200	6500	14,000
Carriage-4P	1500	2000	3000	4200	6500	14,000
Carriage-6P	—	2100	3100	4300	6800	14,500

1902 Haynes-Apperson, runabout, HAC

1902-1903 HAYNES-APPERSON
Two-Cylinder — 8 hp

Runabout	1200	4500	9000	15,000	21,000	30,000

Two-Cylinder — 12 hp

Phaeton	1500	4700	9500	15,500	22,000	31,000
Surrey	1800	4600	9300	15,200	21,500	30,500

1903 Haynes-Apperson, runabout, HAC

1901 Haynes-Apperson, HAC

1904 Haynes-Apperson, touring, KM

1904 HAYNES-APPERSON/HAYNES
Two-Cylinder — 12 hp, 76" wb

Touring-2P	1400	4700	9500	15,500	22,000	31,000
Folding Top Touring-2P	1450	4750	10,000	16,000	23,000	32,000

Four-Cylinder — 93" wb

Touring-4P	2450	4750	10,000	16,000	23,000	32,000
Canopy Top Touring-4P	2550	5000	10,500	16,500	24,000	33,000

1905 Haynes, model K, touring, HAC

1905 HAYNES
Model L — 2-cyl., 16/18 hp, 82" wb

	FP	5	4	3	2	1
Stanhope	1350	4600	9300	15,200	21,500	30,500
Model M — 2-cyl., 16/18 hp, 82" wb						
Detachable Tonneau	1500	4000	7950	13,250	18,550	26,500
Model K — 4-cyl., 35/40 hp, 108" wb						
King of Belgium Touring	3000	4100	8250	13,750	19,250	27,500

1906 Haynes, model O, touring, HAC

1906 HAYNES
Model O — 4-cyl., 30/35 hp, 97" wb

Touring-5P	2250	4300	8550	14,250	19,950	28,500
Runabout-2P	2250	4200	8400	14,000	19,600	28,000
Model R — 4-cyl., 45/50 hp, 108" wb						
Touring-5P	3500	4400	8850	14,750	20,650	29,500

1907 Haynes, model S, touring, HAC

1907 HAYNES
Model S — 4-cyl., 30 hp, 103" wb

Runabout-2P	2400	4200	8400	14,000	19,600	28,000
Touring-5P	2500	4300	8550	14,250	19,950	28,500
Limousine-5P	3500	4000	8250	13,750	19,250	27,500

Model V — 4-cyl., 50 hp, 106" wb

	FP	5	4	3	2	1
Vanderbilt Speedster	3500	4600	9150	15,250	21,350	30,500
Model T — 4-cyl., 50 hp, 108" wb						
Touring-7P	3500	4500	9000	15,000	21,000	30,000
Limousine-7P	4500	4100	8250	13,750	14,250	27,500

1908 Haynes, model U, touring, WLB

1908 HAYNES
Model S — 4-cyl., 30 hp, 102" wb

Touring-5P	2500	4400	8850	14,750	20,650	29,500
Model W — 4-cyl., 45 hp, 108" wb						
Touring-5P	3000	4500	9000	15,000	21,000	30,000
Model U — 4-cyl., 60 hp, 118" wb						
Touring-7P	3750	4900	9750	16,250	22,750	32,500
Roadster	3750	4800	9600	16,000	22,400	32,000
Limousine	4750	4400	8850	14,750	20,650	29,500

1909 Haynes, model X, runabout, HAC

1909 HAYNES
Series X — 4-cyl., 36 hp, 112" wb

Touring-5/7P	3000	3200	4300	6500	11,000	23,000
X1 Runabout-3P	2900	3300	4400	6700	12,000	24,000
X2 Baby Tonneau-4P	3000	3100	4200	6300	10,500	22,000
X3 Double-Seated Rds.-4P	3000	3300	4400	6700	12,000	24,000
X4 Hiker-2P	2900	3200	4300	6500	11,000	23,000

1910 Haynes, model 19, touring, HAC

1910 HAYNES
Model 19 — 4-cyl., 36 hp, 110-1/2" wb

Touring-5P	2000	3300	4400	6700	12,000	24,000
Runabout-3P	2000	3200	4300	6500	11,000	23,000

1911 HAYNES
Model Y — 4-cyl., 40 hp, 125" wb

Touring-7P	3000	3700	4700	7300	13,700	26,000
Model 20 — 4-cyl., 28 hp, 114" wb						
Suburban-4P	2100	3100	4200	6300	10,500	22,000
Touring-5P	2000	3200	4300	6500	11,000	23,000
Fore-Door Touring-5P	2100	3300	4400	6700	12,000	24,000
Roadster-2P	2000	3500	4500	7000	13,000	25,000

1911 Haynes, model Y, touring, HAC

1912 Haynes, model 21, colonial coupe, HAC

1912 HAYNES

Model 20 — 4-cyl., 30 hp, 114" wb

	FP	5	4	3	2	1
A Speedster	1650	3900	4800	7700	14,300	27,000
A Open Touring	1650	3300	4400	6700	12,000	24,000
B Roadster	1800	3700	4700	7300	13,700	26,000
B Fore-Door Touring	1800	3500	4500	7000	13,000	25,000
B Suburban	1800	3500	4500	7000	13,000	25,000

Model 21 — 4-cyl., 40 hp, 120" wb

A Touring	2100	4000	5000	8000	15,000	28,000
A Close-Coupled Touring	2100	4000	5000	8000	15,000	28,000
B Coupe	2450	2500	3500	5000	8500	18,000
C Limousine	2750	2700	3600	5300	8800	19,000

Model Y — 4-cyl., 60 hp, 127-1/2" wb

A Touring-7P	3000	4650	9300	15,500	21,700	31,000
A Close-Coupled Touring	3000	4200	5200	8400	15,700	29,000
B Newport Limousine	3800	2900	3700	5600	9100	20,000
C Berlin Limousine	3900	3000	4000	6000	9500	21,000

1913 Haynes, model 24, touring, HAC

1913 HAYNES

Model 24 — 4-cyl., 35 hp, 118" wb

Touring-5P	1785	3700	4700	7300	13,700	26,000

Model 22 — 4-cyl., 40 hp, 120" wb

Touring-5P	2250	4000	5000	8000	15,000	28,000
Touring-4P	2250	4000	5000	8000	15,000	28,000
Roadster	2250	4200	5200	8400	15,700	29,000
Coupe	2750	2700	3600	5300	8800	19,000
Limousine-7P	3400	3000	4000	6000	9500	21,000
Berlin Limousine-7P	3500	3100	4200	6300	10,500	22,000

Model 23 — 6-cyl., 50 hp, 130" wb

Touring-5P	2500	4650	9300	15,500	21,700	31,000

1914 HAYNES

Model 28 — 4-cyl., 35 hp, 118" wb

Touring-5P	1985	3700	4700	7300	13,700	26,000
Touring-7P	1985	3700	4700	7300	13,700	26,000
Roadster-2P	1985	3900	4800	7700	14,300	27,000
Coupe-4P	2700	2700	3600	5300	8800	19,000

Model 26 — 6-cyl., 50 hp, 130" wb

	FP	5	4	3	2	1
Touring-4P	2700	4650	9300	15,500	21,700	31,000
Roadster-2P	2700	4000	5000	8000	15,000	28,000
Touring-5P	2700	3900	4800	7700	14,300	27,000
Coupe-4P	3200	2900	3700	5600	9100	20,000

Model 27 — 6-cyl., 50 hp, 136" wb

Touring-6P	2785	4800	9600	16,000	22,400	32,000
Touring-7P	2785	4900	9750	16,250	22,750	32,500
Limousine-7P	3850	3100	4200	6300	10,500	22,000

1914 Haynes, model 27, limousine, HAC

1915 Haynes, model 32, touring, HAC

1915 HAYNES

Model 32 — 6-cyl., 48 hp, 121" wb

Touring	1660	3700	4700	7300	13,700	26,000
Coupe	2500	2500	3500	5000	8500	18,000

Model 30 — 6-cyl., 55 hp, 121" wb

Touring-5P	1485	4800	9600	16,000	22,400	32,000
Roadster-2P	1485	4000	5000	8000	15,000	28,000
Touring-7P	1550	4900	9750	16,250	22,750	32,500
Cabriolet-3P	1750	3700	4700	7300	13,700	26,000

Model 31 — 6-cyl., 65 hp, 121" wb

Touring	2250	5000	10,050	16,750	23,450	33,500
Coupe	3000	2700	3600	5300	8800	19,000

1916 Haynes, model 41, touring, HAC

1916 HAYNES

Model 34 — 6-cyl., 55 hp, 121" wb

Roadster-3P	1485	4000	5000	8000	15,000	28,000
Light Six Touring-5P	1385	3900	4800	7700	14,300	27,000

Model 35 — 6-cyl., 55 hp, 127" wb

Kokomo Six Touring	1495	4000	4900	7900	14,700	27,500

Model 40/41 — 12-cyl., 60 hp, 127" wb

Roadster	1595	4400	5600	9200	17,300	31,000
Touring-5P	1885	5000	10,050	16,750	23,450	33,500
Touring-7P	1985	5100	10,200	17,000	23,800	34,000

1917 HAYNES

Light Six-36 — 6-cyl., 29.4 hp, 121" wb

Touring-5P	1485	3700	4700	7300	13,700	26,000
Roadster-4P	1585	3900	4800	7700	14,300	27,000
Touring-7P	1585	3700	4700	7300	13,700	26,000
Sedan-5P	2150	2200	3200	4400	7000	15,000
Sedan-7P	2250	2300	3300	4600	7500	16,000

Light Six-37 — 6-cyl., 29.4 hp. 127" wb

	FP	5	4	3	2	1
Roadster-4P	1485	4000	5000	8000	15,000	28,000
Touring-7P	1585	5100	10,200	17,000	23,800	34,000
Sedan-5P	2150	2300	3300	4600	7500	16,000
Sedan-7P	2250	2400	3400	4800	8000	17,000

Light Twelve — 12-cyl., 36.3 hp, 127" wb

Touring-7P	2085	4500	5800	9500	18,000	32,000
Touring-5P	1985	4500	5800	9500	18,000	32,000
Roadster-4P	2085	4700	6100	9900	19,000	33,000
Sedan-5P	2650	2900	3700	5600	9100	20,000
Sedan-7P	2750	3000	4000	6000	9500	21,000

1917 Haynes Light Twelve, touring, HAC

1918 Haynes Light Twelve, town car, HAC

1919 Haynes Light Six, sedan, HAC

1918-1919 HAYNES
Light Six, Model 38 — 6-cyl., 29.4 hp, 121" wb

Touring-5P	1725	3700	4700	7300	13,700	26,000
Touring-7P	1825	3700	4700	7300	13,700	26,000
Sedan-7P	2585	2300	3300	4600	7500	16,000
Coupe-4P	2535	2700	3600	5300	8800	19,000
Town Car-5P	3250	3100	4200	6300	10,500	22,000
Fourdore Roadster-4P	1825	3900	4800	7700	14,300	27,000

Light Six, Model 39 — 6-cyl., 29.4 hp, 127" wb

Fourdore Roadster-4P	1825	4000	5000	8000	15,000	28,000
Touring-5P	1725	3900	4800	7700	14,300	27,000
Touring-7P	1825	3900	4800	7700	14,300	27,000
Sedan-7P	2585	2400	3400	4800	8000	17,000
Coupe-4P	2535	2900	3700	5600	,9100	20,000
Town Car-5P	3250	3200	4300	6500	11,000	23,000

Light Twelve — 12-cyl., 36.3 hp, 127" wb

Town Car-5P	3985	4000	5000	8000	15,000	28,000
Fourdore Roadster-4P	2785	4700	6100	9900	19,000	33,000
Sedan-7P	3385	3700	4700	7300	13,700	26,000
Coupe-4P	3335	3900	4800	7700	14,300	27,000
Touring-5P	2785	4400	5600	9200	17,300	31,000

660

1920 Haynes Light Twelve, limousine, HAC

1920 HAYNES
Light Six, Model 45 — 51 hp, 127" wb

	FP	5	4	3	2	1
Touring-7P	2685	3900	4800	7700	14,300	27,000
Roadster-4P	2685	4000	5000	8000	15,000	28,000
Coupe-4P	3300	2700	3600	5300	8800	19,000
Sedan-7P	3550	2300	3300	4600	7500	16,000
Limousine-7P	4200	3000	4000	6000	9500	21,000

Light Twelve, Model 46 — 62 hp, 127" wb

Touring-7P	3450	4500	5800	9500	18,000	32,000
Roadster-4P	3450	4700	6100	9900	19,000	33,000
Coupe-4P	4000	4200	5200	8400	15,700	29,000
Sedan-7P	4200	4000	5000	8000	15,000	28,000
Limousine-7P	4950	4300	5400	8700	16,500	30,000

1921 Haynes, Light Six, speedster, HAC

1921 HAYNES
Light Six, Model 47 — 50 hp, 132" wb

Touring-7P	2935	3900	4800	7700	14,300	27,000
Tourister-4P	2935	4000	5000	8000	15,000	28,000
Speedster-2P	3500	4300	5400	8700	16,500	30,000
Brougham-5P	3950	3100	4200	6300	10,500	22,000
Sedan-7P	4250	2900	3700	5600	9100	20,000
Suburban-7P	4250	3700	4700	7300	13,700	26,000

Light Twelve, Model 48 — 70 hp, 132" wb

Touring-7P	3635	4400	5600	9200	17,300	31,000
Tourister-4P	3635	4500	5800	9500	18,000	32,000
Speedster-2P	4200	4700	6100	9900	19,000	33,000
Coupe-4P	4350	4000	5000	8000	15,000	28,000
Brougham-5P	4650	4400	5600	9200	17,300	31,000
Suburban-7P	4950	4300	5400	8700	16,500	30,000

1922 Haynes, model 55, 4-dr. sedan, OCW

1922 HAYNES
Model 55 — 6-cyl., 50 hp, 121" wb

Touring-5P	1785	4000	5000	8000	15,000	28,000
Roadster-2P	1835	4200	5200	8400	15,700	29,000
Sedan-5P	2835	2300	3300	4600	7500	16,000

Model 75 — 6-cyl., 75 hp, 132" wb					
	FP	5	4	3	2	1
Touring-7P	2485	4200	5200	8400	15,700	29,000
Tourister-4P	2485	4400	5600	9200	17,300	31,000
Speedster-2P	2685	4300	5400	8700	16,500	30,000
Brougham-5P	3185	2700	3600	5300	8800	19,000
Sedan-7P	3485	2400	3400	4800	8000	17,000
Suburban-7P	3485	3500	4500	7000	13,000	25,000

Model 48 — 12-cyl., 70 hp, 132" wb					
Touring-7P	3635	4700	6100	9900	19,000	33,000
Tourister-4P	3635	4900	6300	10,300	21,000	34,000
Speedster-2P	4200	5000	6500	11,000	22,000	35,000
Brougham-5P	4650	3000	4000	6000	9500	21,000
Sedan-7P	4950	2900	3700	5600	9100	20,000
Suburban-7P	4950	3900	4800	7700	14,300	27,000

1923 Haynes, model 57, sports touring, HAC

1923 HAYNES
Model 57 — 6-cyl., 55 hp, 121" wb

	FP	5	4	3	2	1
Touring-5P	1595	4000	5000	8000	15,000	28,000
Sedan-5P	2595	2300	3300	4600	7500	16,000
Sport Touring-5P	1850	4200	5200	8400	15,700	29,000
Sport Sedan-5P	2695	2400	3400	4800	8000	17,000
Sport Brougham-5P	2395	2500	3500	5000	8500	18,000

Model 77 — 6-cyl., 70 hp, 132" wb

	FP	5	4	3	2	1
Touring-7P	2395	4200	5200	8400	15,700	29,000
Brougham-5P	3095	2700	3600	5300	8800	19,000
Sedan-7P	3395	2400	3400	4800	8000	17,000
Sport Touring-7P	2550	4300	5400	8700	16,500	30,000
Blue Ribbon Speedster	3250	4900	6300	10,300	21,000	34,000
Suburban-7P	3395	4400	5600	9200	17,300	31,000

1924 Haynes, model 60, sedan, HAC

1924 HAYNES
Model 60 — 6-cyl., 50 hp, 121" wb

	FP	5	4	3	2	1
Touring-5P	1295	4000	5000	8000	15,000	28,000
Special Touring-5P	1395	4200	5200	8400	15,700	29,000
Roadster-2P	1695	4300	5400	8700	16,500	30,000
Sedan-5P	1895	2300	3300	4600	7500	16,000
Special Sedan-5P	1945	2400	3400	4800	8000	17,000

1925 Haynes, model 60, touring, HAC

1925 HAYNES
Model 60 — 6-cyl., 50 hp, 121" wb

	FP	5	4	3	2	1
Touring-5P	1600	4000	5000	8000	15,000	28,000
Brougham-5P	2200	2400	3400	4800	8000	17,000
Sedan-5P	2300	2300	3300	4600	7500	16,000

HAYS-SCHOEPFLIN — The Hays-Schoepflin Company of Buffalo, New York was organized late in 1910 with a capital stock of $10,000 for the manufacture of "automobiles and auto trucks." The partners involved were Walter Hays and Louis G. Schoepflin. Manufacture is doubted.

HAZARD — Rochester, New York — (1913-1915) — The Hazard Motor Manufacturing Company has frequently been cited as the producer of automobiles from 1913 to 1915. No evidence has been found to confirm this. Hazard certainly was in business in Rochester during this period, however, and doing quite well with sales of the various four-cylinder engines that were marketed under the name Ergon (which the company explained was Greek for "strength or work"). Indeed, by October of 1913 Hazard had discontinued manufacture of the change-speed gears it had previously produced in order to concentrate all efforts on the Ergon engines. Any automobiles produced by the company would have been for demonstration only. The Hazard Motor Manufacturing Company had been organized in 1910 to take over the former Hazard Engineering Company. Involved in this venture were E.C. Hazard, John F. Alden, George R. Coates, Willett E. Hazard and George E. Hazard.

HAZEL — The Hazel Machine Company in Chicago, Illinois was organized during the fall of 1906 with a capital stock of $2500 for the manufacture of motor cars and parts. Rush C. Butler, L.M. Goodhue and Ernest C. Best were the principals involved. Manufacture of a car is doubted.

1908 Hazelton, NAHC

HAZLETON — Oneonta, New York — (1908) — In 1908 M.W. Hazleton of Oneonta built a coal-burning steam car with a very long wheelbase and shod with steel tires. Its inventor claimed that 100 pounds of steam could be raised from cold water in six minutes. Hazleton drove the car frequently in Upstate New York. "I would like to correspond with parties interested in this car with a view of manufacturing it," he wrote the editor of *The Automobile* in the fall of 1908. "The cost of a two-seated car, all of the best possible material, would be about $700, and it will last longer than any $2,000 car on the market. The tires will last ten years." Whether he was contacted by any interested parties is not known. But any interest generated did not result in manufacture of the Hazleton steam car.

1908 H.B., high-wheeled, runabout, WLB

H.B. — Chicago, Illinois — (1908) — H. Brothers of 232-236 LaSalle Street in Chicago was an oldtime carriage making concern whose first foray into the automotive field happened in 1903 when the company produced Haase cars for the Northwestern Furniture Company of Milwaukee. Not until 1908 did H. Brothers again approach the automobile idea, and this time it was with a highwheeler to carry the name H.B. It featured an air-cooled two cylinder 10 hp engine, a reinforced 76-inch oak frame, friction drive, rack and pinion steering and full elliptic springs. By this time, H. Brothers had also begun the manufacture of motor buggy parts, to which activity the company returned after discontinuing the H.B. at the end of the 1908 model year. Its price had been $500.

H-C — Detroit, Michigan — (1916) — According to the listing of automobile manufacturers in the January 1916 issue of *Scientific American,* the H-C Motor Car Company of Detroit was engaged in the production of a four-cylinder 28 hp car that was being sold as a $600 roadster and a $650 touring. Further documentation is lacking.

H.C.S. — Indianapolis, Indiana — (1920-1925) — Following his resignation from the company bearing his name, Harry C. Stutz almost immediately announced a new company bearing his initials and located in the same town as the Stutz. The H.C.S. Motor Car Company was a million-dollar incorporation, with Stutz as president, Samuel T. Murdock as vice-president, H.G. Campbell as treasurer and Gordon Murdock as secretary. First news of Harry Stutz's new venture arrived in late fall of 1919; the first ten H.C.S. cars were shipped to distributors in May 1920. Not surprisingly, the new H.C.S. was rather akin the old Stutz, an expensive car, with an accent on the sporting. The first H.C.S.'s were 50 hp fours (Weidely engines); in 1923 an 80 hp six (from Midwest) was added to the line. The H.C.S. Special which Tommy Milton drove to victory in the Indianapolis 500 in 1923 was more Miller than Stutz — but it provided great publicity for the company. Slogans like "The Car Born with a Reputation" played on the celebrity which had come Harry's way with his Stutz, and taglines like "We Know of No Better Motor Cars" provided a calculated dig at his old company. H.C.S. automobiles sold quite well in their early years. But in October of 1924 Harry Stutz announced the formation of his H.C.S Cab Manufacturing Company, another million-dollar incorporation, which succeeded the H.C.S. Motor Car Company. Now the H.C.S. emphasis would be placed on taxicabs, with manufacture of passenger cars to be relegated to the sidelines. This proved a disaster. The last H.C.S. production cars were built in 1925. The H.C.S. Cab Manufacturing Company went into receivership in 1927. Harry C. Stutz died in 1930.

1921 H.C.S., Series II, touring, HFM

1920-1921 H.C.S.
Series II — 4-cyl., 50 hp, 120" wb

	FP	5	4	3	2	1
Touring-4P	2975	4400	5600	9200	17,300	31,000
Roadster-2P	2925	4500	5800	9500	18,000	32,000

1922 H.C.S.
Series III — 4-cyl., 50 hp, 120" wb

Touring-4P	2775	4400	5600	9200	17,300	31,000
Roadster-2P	2725	4500	5800	9500	18,000	32,000
Coupe-3P	3450	2700	3600	5300	8800	19,000
Sedan-5P	3650	2300	3300	4600	7500	16,000

1922 H.C.S., Series III, touring, HAC

1923-1925 H.C.S.
Series IV — 4-cyl., 52 hp, 120" wb

Model 4 Tour. 5P	2200	4500	5800	9500	18,000	32,000
Model 4 Rdst. 2P	2200	4700	6100	9900	19,000	33,000
Model 4 Brougham	2950	3000	4000	6000	9500	21,000
Model 4 Coupe	2750	2700	3600	5300	880	19,000

Series VI — 6-cyl., 80 hp, 126" wb

Model 6 Touring	2650	5000	6500	11,000	22,000	35,000
Model 6 Sedan 5P	3350	2900	3700	5600	9100	20,000

1923 H.C.S., Series IV, roadster, HAC

1924 H.C.S., Series VI, touring, HAC

1925 H.C.S., taxicab, HAC

H.E. — H.E. Motors, Inc. was organized during the summer of 1927 in Winston-Salem, South Carolina to manufacture and deal in automobiles. Capital stock was $50,000; the incorporators were A.T. Lewallen, L.D. Moore and G.S. Clark. Manufacture is doubted.

HEADLAND — Freedom, Pennsylvania — (1895) — During the late spring of 1895 Harry Headland of Freedom announced to the automotive press that he was building a two-seated motor carriage. Details regarding the car were not forthcoming, but most probably it was an electric, and most probably its inventor left Freedom soon after. In 1899 a patent for an electric motor for automobiles was granted to one Henry William Headland of London, England. Likely as not, Harry and Henry were the same people.

HEALEY — New York, New York — (c.1905-c.1916) — Inclusive dates for the automobiles produced by the renowned coachbuilding house of Healey & Company of New York City are difficult to determine. The first vehicle thus far known to have been built by Healey was an electric coupe for inventor W.H. Douglas of Belleville, New Jersey in 1905. Thereafter electrics of various styles seem to have been produced intermittently by the firm, with possibly even a gasoline car in 1910. Most likely, Healey purchased the chassis outside, confining its efforts to coachwork. Total production is a mystery, though at least twenty cars called Healey were registered in New York City in 1914. Healey doubtless built the cars at the request of its elite clientele, and among those who are known to have requested Healey cars are Mrs. George S. Bowdoin and John D. Rockefeller, Sr., the latter puchasing one each in 1912, 1914 and 1916.

1888 Healy, steam carriage, WLB

HEALY STEAM — New London, Ohio — (1888) — In 1887 Caleb E. Healy of New London invented a steam engine that was small but obviously powerful. In April of the following year, he fitted it into a carriage and sent out invitations to seventy-five people in New London to join him for a ride. Newspaper accounts of the event indicate that everyone who was invited showed up. It was quite a procession. Healy hitched several gaily-decorated following wagons to his steam carriage, and spent the entire afternoon driving the streets of town at a speed estimated at three miles an hour. The day's outing was marred, unfortunately, by the death of a young boy who fell under the wheels of one of the procession wagons, an accident described in grisly detail in the *New London Record*. Manufacture of the steam vehicle did not interest Caleb Healy. He continued development of his steam engine, however, and began to promote it for street-car and motor-boat use. Moving to Detroit in 1892 to expand his business, Healy was drowned in Lake St. Clair two years later while enjoying an afternoon's excursion in a yacht powered by one of his engines.

HEALY — Madera, California — (1900) — The Healy brothers of Madera described themselves as "sons of a wealthy rancher of that part of San Joaquin Valley and graduates of Ann Arbor" — and in 1900 they completed a motor vehicle of their own invention. Its "triple system" of brakes, they declared, was the best yet devised for a horseless carriage and absolutely foolproof. "There is absolutely no way for the machine to get beyond the control of the operator," the Healy brothers boasted, "even on the steepest mountain grades."

HEARNE — The Hearne Motor Company was organized late in 1910 in Wheeling, West Virginia with a capital stock of $20,000 to manufacture and deal in automobiles and fire engines. Julian A. Hearne and Thomas Hearne of Wheeling, together with Leech K. Cricraft of Elm Grove, were the principals involved. Manufacture of a car is doubted.

HEATH — The Heath Dry Gas Company of Saratoga Springs, New York was organized during the spring of 1906 with a capital stock of $100,000 for the manufacture of automobiles. E.L. Heath and S.C. Brown of Saratoga Springs, in association with F.A. Heath of Jersey City, New Jersey, were the principals involved. Manufacture is doubted.

The Mark W. Heath Company was organized in Chicago, Illinois during the fall of 1913 with a capital stock of $2500 for the manufacture and sale of automobiles. John Schott was Heath's partner. Manufacture is doubted.

HEATHERMAN — During the fall of 1911 the Heatherman-Solliday Motor Company was organized in Dayton, Ohio with a capital stock of $20,000 to manufacture and deal in motor cars, parts and accessories. The partners involved were Frank B. Heatherman, Charles H. Solliday, Zora G. Solliday and Joseph D. Chamberlain. Manufacture of a car is doubted.

1919 Heifner, roadster, NAHC

HEIFNER — Chester, Pennsylvania — (1919-1920) — Geneva, Ohio — (1920-1921) — Lambert M. Heifner was the Philadelphia distributor for Bethlehem trucks but when he decided to become a manufacturer he chose passenger cars and farm tractors as his products. The L.M. Heifner Manufacturing Company was organized in June of 1919 with a capital stock of $1.5 million. Heifner took an option on a large factory in Chester, Pennsylvania and announced his plans to begin manufacture by August 15th. He didn't. Instead, the summer of 1920 found him in Geneva, Ohio — and still not manufacturing. Selling stock occupied most of his time for the remainder of that year, with $50,000 purportedly having been put up by five Akron businessmen, and a mere $10,000 needed from residents of Geneva to proceed ahead. An option was obtained on the Geneva Canning Company plant, which was to be converted into a worker's paradise complete with 180-foot swimming pool, bowling alley and billiard room. Obviously, despite a grandiose prospectus and grand promotion, Genevans weren't buying, because by January 1921 the company was offering a free share of common for every share of preferred stock bought. This didn't work either, and the company folded in April. Total Heifner production was at most two cars. Reputedly, $100,000 had been spent on research and development work. Lambert Heifner thought big. The Heifner was to use a four-cylinder 81 hp Wisconsin engine (a 70 hp Continental six was also announced) with wheelbases of 138 inches for the sports model, 148 for the touring. The car's sharp vee-shaped radiator grille had a European look, and purportedly a four-wheel hydraulic brake system was to be imported from abroad. A prototype of the touring car was begun, though possibly not completed. The roadster was finished, though not without an argument. As legend has it, the mechanic hired to assemble the car refused to make it operable until he was paid. One month after the Heifner venture was kaput, the H.B. Young Motor Truck Company moved into the Geneva Canning Company plant and produced the Little Giant there for a short while.

HEIGHTS — The Heights Garage & Storage Company was organized in New York City during the fall of 1906 with a $42,000 capital stock to manufacture and store automobiles. Incorporators were William J. Weller, P.N. Fowler and Wilbert Garrison. Manufacture is doubted.

1907 Heilman, runabout, NAHC

HEILMAN — Cincinnati, Ohio — 1907 — John C. Heilman of Cincinnati built a small gasoline runabout in 1907. Whether he contemplated manufacture is not known. It is known that early in 1908 Heilman established an automobile dealership in Cincinnati which traded under the name of Heilman Motor Car Company.

1921 Heine-Velox, touring, WLB

HEINE-VELOX — San Francisco, California — (1906) (1921-1923) — The Heine Piano Company of San Francisco was a thriving enterprise with an automobile enthusiast at its helm. In 1903 Gustav Otto Heine was among the earliest Ford dealers on the West Coast. In 1904 he announced that he had secured the San Francisco agency for the Queen car, and that

663

he planned to produce a car of his own as well, which had been designed for him by Victor Emerson and would be built in Cincinnati. Heine had a quick change of mind both about Ohio and the designer of his car. He decided to take on the job himself back home. The Heine Motor Car Company was immediately established, but the Heine car was two years in the making, and when it arrived it was newly christened the Heine-Velox. This was early February 1906. Three four-cylinder 35/45 Heine-Velox motorcars were now coursing the streets of San Francisco, and others were under construction in the factory. Ultimately it was planned to establish a plant elsewhere in the United States (Cincinnati and Milwaukee being mentioned), but for the Heine-Velox's maiden year of 1906 a production of fifty cars was scheduled in San Francisco. They were never built. The earthquake on April 18th wiped out the Heine Motor Company, as well as the Heine Piano Company. In the aftermath of this disaster, Gustav Heine of necessity concentrated his efforts on restoring his well-established piano business. But he never forgot about the car he wanted to build, and in 1921 he tried again. And he really went all-out this time. The second-generation Heine-Velox was to be the most expensive automobile in America, offered as a sedan, runabout and sport model at $17,000 and with custom-built versions scaling up to $25,000. Its V-12 engine was built by Weidely to Heine-Velox specifications. The wheelbase was a long, long 148 inches. Lockheed supplied the hydraulic brakes, the Heine-Velox being one of the first cars in America to utilize them. The Heine-Velox was a curious-looking automobile, with its radiator resembling the Italian Fiat, its headlights perched atop the front fenders. The inclined windshield glass was set in rubber. Manufacturing plans were discarded early. Only five cars were built — a sporting victoria, three sedans and an unfinished limousine. Gustav Heine gave away the cars he didn't keep himself. Not one Heine-Velox was sold. In 1923 his Heine-Velox Engineering Company was dissolved. Gustav Heine returned ever after to the piano field.

HEINZ — Ypsilanti, Michigan — (1921) — In April of 1921, O.W. Heinz left the presidency of the Apex Motor Car Company, producers of the Ace in Ypsilanti, and in August he declared himself at work on a new car to be offered as both a four and a six and to be named after himself. He was uncertain at that point whether he would manufacture the car in Ypsilanti or nearer to Detroit, but ultimately he did neither, forgoing production of a Heinz car to join his old Apex partner Fred M. Guy to establish the Guy Disc-Valve Motor Company for development and manufacture of the Guy engine.

HEINZELMAN — Belleville, Illinois — (1908) — The Heinzelman Brothers Carriage Company of Belleville declared itself the "builders of fine vehicles" since 1857, and its first motorized version was a gasoline-powered highwheeler shod with Firestone tires that was on the road in 1908. In a testimonial letter written to Firestone in March that year, R.L. Merkin of Heinzelman commented that the car "has gone over some very rough roads, clay hills and you may know that they get pretty bad when the wheels have sunk so low in the mud that the running boards drag and push the mud along like a snow plow, for 50 feet at a time." Merkin declared that his company looked forward to "a large trade in the high wheeled auto" and would "use the Firestone tire exclusively." The extent of subsequent Heinzelman manufacture is not known.

HEMSTREET — Niobrara, Nebraska — (1901) — One C. Hemstreet, proprietor of the Hubbard House in Niobrara, built an 18 hp steam car in 1901. "I am an engineer and a lover of steam," he wrote The Motor Age, "and, having studied the matter carefully, would advise steam power in all cases." The vehicle was entirely designed by Hemstreet and he did all work except for the installation of the engine which he farmed out to the Scott Automobile Company of St. Louis. Because his touring car afforded accommodations for fifteen passengers, no doubt he built the vehicle for use in ferrying guests of Hubbard House.

1910 Hendee, torpedo runabout, NAHC

HENDEE — Springfield, Massachusetts — (1910) — This experimental car from 1910 was built in the shops of the Hendee Manufacturing Company in Springfield to the design of James H. Jones, formerly an engineer for the Knox Automobile Company. Its engine was a six, cast in blocks of three and with detachable cylinder heads. The chassis weighed but 1600 pounds, complete with spare tire on the back. The wire wheels were English Rudge-Whitworth type. An altogether appealing torpedo runabout, the Hendee was never produced, but was instead one of a number of development cars built through the years by this Springfield company which was famous for its manufacture of the Indian motorcycle. Most of the other automotive ventures of Hendee carried the Indian name, although apparently there were at least two others that were called Hendee. This 1910 torpedo runabout remained the property of George M. Hendee for some time. Its final disposition is not known.

1904 Hendel, runabout, NAHC

HENDEL — Red Wing, Minnesota — (1903-1904) — "Red Wing is becoming well known as a manufacturing center, but few people are aware that an automobile factory is developing in our midst." The quote is from the April 22nd, 1903 edition of the Red Wing Daily Republican. And the story which followed announced that the wagon-building firm of William Hendel & Company was building a "fine machine for a Minneapolis physician" that was priced at $1000. By the time the car was completed in July, the price had risen to $1200. The Hendel was powered by a one-cylinder 8 hp engine and featured jump spark ignition, a Baldwin muffler and a Brown-Lipe compensating gear. Its top speed was 35 mph. The car, with its French front bonnet, was painted in light maroon, with brass trimmings, and upholstered in maroon trimming leather. It must have been handsome because the newspaper commented in July that "quite a number of people were astonished that such an elegant vehicle could be built in Red Wing." Most probably the problem encountered by this budding automotive enterprise was the decision by William Hendel to ally himself with a new company recently incorporated in Minneapolis with whom he contracted in October for the building of a demonstrator car. The Hoffman Motor Company of Minneapolis never did get off the ground. And apparently William Hendel & Company did not have the wherewithal to go it alone.

HENDERSON STEAM — Decatur, Illinois — (1905) — "I began my experience with steam by purchasing a second-hand car that proved to be less of a 'snap' than I had expected," George A. Henderson wrote the editors of The Automobile in July 1905. "I came near becoming involved in litigation with the firm that sold me the outfit, but concluded that the same money that would pay for a course of law might possibly pay for a course of study in steam, and so took up the work of reconstructing the car." The vehicle that resulted was sold by Henderson and with the proceeds he built a steam car all his own. It had two cylinders, a tubular boiler and used kerosene for fuel. It appeared an altogether praiseworthy machine, and Henderson's description of its design and building indicate him to be remarkably articulate for a backyard mechanic. He did not subsequently build cars, except for his own pleasure.

1913 Henderson, touring, HAC

HENDERSON — Indianapolis, Indiana — (1912-1914) — The Henderson brothers of Indianapolis were employees of the Cole Motor Car Company who took leave of that firm early in 1912 in order to begin their own, the Henderson Motor Car Company being organized with a paid-up capital of $100,000 and the plan to produce a low-priced Cole-type automobile. Chester Ricker, until now best known as a technical writer, was the Henderson's designer. (He would subsequently become better known as the Indianapolis 500 chief timer and scorer for several decades — and also was Duesenberg's general manager in 1923-1924.) C.P. Henderson served as the company's president and sales manager, R.P. Henderson as vice-president and general manager. The Henderson car was introduced prior to the Indianapolis 500 in 1912 with a police-escorted parade through the city streets to Monument Place where Mayor Lew Shank gave a short address and, according to The Automobile, formally christened the car and autographed its hood with a huge pencil. "The Car of Your Dreams," as the Henderson company put it, was initially offered only as a four; for 1914 a six was added to the line. Nineteen fourteen was also the Henderson's final year, sufficient working capital having been the company's problem from the beginning. The Hendersons chose to liquidate, converting all assets to cash and apportioning same to creditors. No court action was required. Thereon Chester Riker organized the Bicar Company in Indianapolis for the manufacture of a cyclecar which was advertised but never produced, and Riker returned to his technical writing. As for the Hendersons, they were welcomed back by the Cole Motor Car Company, C.P. as sales head, R.P. as his asistant. The Henderson family later became famous in the motorcycle field.

1912-1913 HENDERSON
Four — 4-cyl., 44 hp, 116" wb

	FP	5	4	3	2	1
Model 44 Roadster-2P	1385	3100	4200	6300	10,500	22,000
Model 46 Touring-5P	1485	3000	4000	6000	9500	21,000
Model 48 Touring-7P	1685	2700	3600	5300	8800	19,000
Model 56 Roadster-3P	1585	3200	4300	6500	11,000	23,000

1914 Henderson, roadster, WLB

1914 HENDERSON
Light Four — 4-cyl., 27 hp, 116" wb

Touring-5P	1585	2900	3700	5600	9100	20,000
Roadster-2P	1585	3000	4000	6000	9500	21,000

Deluxe Four — 4-cyl., 27 hp, 116" wb

Touring-5P	1785	3000	4000	6000	9500	21,000
Roadster-2P	1785	3100	4200	6300	10,500	22,000
Coupe-3P	2285	2500	3500	5000	8500	18,000

Six — 6-cyl., 34 hp, 126" wb

Touring-5P	2285	3200	4300	6500	11,000	23,000
Roadster-2P	2885	3300	4400	6700	12,000	24,000

1902 Hendrickson, touring, JHC

HENDRICKSON — Chicago, Illinois — (1902) — In his native Sweden, Magnus Hendrickson learned mechanics in a machine shop established by his uncles and during a year of service with the Corps of Engineers in the Swedish Army. Emigrating to the United States in 1887, Hendrickson initially had charge of maintaining the steam engine driving the sewing machines in a brother's garment factory in Chicago. Following work at a mill producing potato starch and at a logging camp in Wisconsin, Hendrickson returned to the Windy City and began a bicycle manufactory, experimenting with gasoline engines during his off hours. In 1900, in association with a brother-in-law he formed the Hendrickson-Danielson Machine Shop at 62nd and Morgan. (Whether this Danielson was the Frank who made two attempts to get into the automobile business in Chicago cannot be confirmed with certainty, but the partnership was short-lived in any case). At the turn of the century, Hendrickson had built his first motor truck and, in 1902, now at his own machine shop at 59th and Racine, he built his first automobile. A one-lunger with solid rubber tires, the car was purchased by a Chicago doctor later that year. In 1903 Hendrickson designed a clutch (which is still produced) and built several experimental friction-drive cars and trucks. By now his talent had come to the attention of Jacob Lauth of Chicago who suggested Hendrickson move his shop part and parcel into the Lauth tanning plant and join him in his automotive venture. This Hendrickson did, serving as chief engineer of the subsequent Lauth-Juergens Motor Car Company until 1913 when he left to establish his own commercial vehicle manufacturing enterprise. In the three decades that followed, the Hendrickson name became famous for innovation in the motor truck field. Magnus Hendrickson died in 1944. His sons carried on the family tradition.

HENLEY — That the Henley-Kimball Company of Boston, Massachusetts built a steam car in 1899 has been indicated on various rosters. This has not been confirmed. Boston city directories of the turn-of-the-century period do not list such a company. Much later a firm of that name was organized as a distributorship for Hudson.

1908 Hennegin, model F, physician's car, NAHC

HENNEGIN — Chicago, Illinois — (1908) — This highwheeler from Chicago was the product of the Commercial Automobile Company. It was offered as a Physician's Car and as a Family/Utility, the latter resembling a light truck. The firm's title would seem to indicate that commercial vehicle production was planned. Initial promotion was aimed at the passenger car market, however, and when it failed, so did the company.

1908 HENNEGIN
Model G — 2-cyl., 12/14 hp, 87" wb

	FP	5	4	3	2	1
Family/Utility	725	—	—	—	—	—

Model F — 2-cyl., 12/14 hp, 75" wb

Physician's Car	650	—	—	—	—	—

1921 Henney, touring, WLB

HENNEY — Freeport, Illinois — (1921-1931) — The Henney family had been in the wagon and buggy building business in Freeport since the late 1870's and by the early 1920's the Henney name was among America's best known in the funeral car trade. In the decade which followed, the company produced approximately thirty limousine and sedan passenger cars to custom order, as well as a production run of fifty sport phaetons designed by Herman Earl (whose previous credits included work with Haynes-Apperson, Schacht and Halladay) which were marketed on the West Coast. The Henney passenger cars were, like the Henney hearses, powered by six-cylinder Continental or eight-cylinder Lycoming engines. The sport phaeton run had occurred during the early Twenties. In 1929 Henney produced 100 taxicabs on stretched Model A Ford chassis — and in 1930-1931 came the Henney passenger car *piece-de-resistance*. It happened principally because John W. Henney, Jr. — who had followed in his father's footsteps in the family business in 1912 — was a good friend of Errett Lobban Cord's and was challenged to come up with a car equally as classy as those Cord was purveying in Indiana. The convertible sedan which resulted was a handsome thing, powered by a Lycoming straight-eight and set on a 137 1/2-inch wheelbase chassis, just like the new L-29 Cord. Only four examples were built and sold to friends or undertaking clients of Henney's. The last one was delivered in October 1931, and it was the final Henney passenger car as well. Henney Motor Company remained in the funeral car business (in addition to providing limousine bodies to Packard and producing a special run of Lincolns for the U.S. Government) until ceasing operations in 1954 and closing its doors forever the following year.

HENRICO — The Henrico Car Company was organized in Richmond, Virginia during the fall of 1913 with a capital stock of $50,000 for the manufacture of automobiles. Behind this venture were A.C. Nelson, J.A. Reams and George Preston. Manufacture is doubted.

1901 Henrietta Steam, carriage, NAHC

HENRIETTA STEAM — New York, New York — (1901) — The Henrietta Motor Company of New York City built a steam car in 1901 which featured a four-cylinder single-acting steam engine. The vehicle sported wire wheels, and weighed 1100 pounds. Whether more than a single example was built is not known, but the Henrietta steam car had disappeared by 1902.

HENRY ELECTRIC — Denver, Colorado — (1899) — In 1899, in Denver, John C. Henry, who was described as a "well-known electrical engineer," built an electric carriage and applied for patents on many of its features. A one-lever control for steering and acceleration was among these, and so was the electrical steering system itself. As explained by *The Horseless Age*, "the motors will be so arranged that by a simple turn . . . the machine can be steered around a corner, or zigzag with more accuracy and rapidity than mechanical steering would permit." Henry is not believed to have proceeded into manufacture of his car.

1911 Henry, touring, WLB

HENRY — Muskegon, Michigan — (1910-1912) — In 1909 the Muskegon Chamber of Commerce built a factory for an automotive venture styling itself as the Gary Motor Car Company. This firm failed before even taking possession of the plant, and thus it was nicely unoccupied in November 1909 when the Henry Motor Car Company moved in. Capitalized at $200,000, the Henry organization included W.L. Simonton as president, Charles F. Latimer as vice-president, Charles H. Latimer as treasurer, and P.H. DeMange as secretary. The car would be named for David W. Henry, its designer, who came to Michigan following ten years' working experience with the Columbia company in Hartford, Connecticut. For 1910 a single 35 hp four was offered, but the Henry line blossomed in 1911 into an array of four-cylinder models of varying horsepower and body styles numbering no less than nine, including the perky Roadstar, the name for which had been chosen in a Muskegon newspaper contest. By now the man for whom the car was named had departed, David Henry leaving for Iowa to design the Colby after what appears to have been a substantial argument. Internal problems seemed to haunt the Henry company. In September 1911, W.L. Simonton resigned, his place taken by John Q. Rose who was also the Lieutenant Governor of Michigan. But the principal dilemma of insufficient working capital remained. By early spring of 1912, after producing approximately 600 cars, the company was in receivership. Charles Latimer made an attempt to reorganize, but his bid for the company assets was not accepted by the courts. Instead the Henry company was sold for $9000 to a Philadelphia firm specializing in buying up bankrupt automotive ventures.

1910 HENRY
Model 35 — 4-cyl., 35 hp, 116" wb

	FP	5	4	3	2	1
Model L Touring-4P	1750	3000	4000	6000	9500	21,000
Model D Touring-5P	1750	2900	3700	5600	9100	20,000

1911-1912 HENRY
Twenty-Four — 4-cyl., 24 hp, 106" wb

	FP	5	4	3	2	1
Model K Roadster	900	2900	3700	5600	9100	20,000

Thirty — 4-cyl., 30 hp, 112" wb

	FP	5	4	3	2	1
Model A Touring-5P	1100	2700	3600	5300	8800	19,000

Forty — 4-cyl., 40 hp, 116" wb

	FP	5	4	3	2	1
Model M Touring-5P	1750	3000	4000	6000	9500	21,000
Model F Fore-Dr. Touring-5P	1850	3100	4200	6300	10,500	22,000
Model H Fore-Dr. Demi-Tonneau	1800	3000	4000	6000	9500	21,000
Model T Torpedo Tourist	1850	3200	4300	6500	11,000	23,000
Model B Demi-Tonneau-4P	1800	3000	4000	6000	9500	21,000
Model E Fore-Dr. Roadster	1800	3200	4300	6500	11,000	23,000
Model P Roadstar	1750	3100	4200	6300	10,500	22,000

HENRY GREY — Los Angeles, California — (1912) — Henry Grey was a Los Angeles architect who drew himself a car in 1910 and completed building it in 1914. Its engine was a 20 hp four with copper water jackets built by Grey himself though incorporating a 1910 Ford crankshaft; likewise the transmission was Ford design, but with a Grey transmission housing. Originally the body sported two bucket seats, a round gasoline tank and no fenders, but in 1919 Grey restyled the car into a rather spindly-looking roadster. Purportedly, Henry Grey would have enjoyed becoming an automobile manufacturer, but no one was forthcoming with the necessary capital. Grey drove the car until 1927, claiming to have put over 175,000 miles on it by that time. The vehicle remains extant.

HENSHAW — Boston, Massachusetts — (1914) — Charles Henshaw of Boston was a former bicycle racer who, together with another Boston cyclist named Fred Graves, decided to enter the cyclecar field in 1914. "Work is being pushed . . . on the first model" declared *The American Cyclecar* in April that year. The work was never pushed far enough, however, for this car to have been put into manufacture.

HENSLEY — San Diego, California — (1901) — Every part of the three-wheeler built by George A. Hensley of San Diego was of his own making. The engine was an air-cooled one-lunger that weighed but 75 pounds. Belt drive from engine to countershaft was featured. "The complete machine weighs 283 pounds with tank filled," Hensley reported in July 1901, "and it will go between 10 and 12 miles per hour on a good road." The Hensley was a spare-time project; its inventor did not consider manufacture.

HERBY — Oakland, California — (1903-1904) — In the Oakland city directory, Nels J. Herby referred to himself as an "automobile manufacturer" and it is known that he "manufactured" at least one car because the person to whom it was sold took Herby to court over it. Specifications regarding the Herby are scant, but it was priced at $700 for a Mr. Blake who requested that the body be "about the same as a Knox mobile with a low seat in front," that the finish be "black piano," and that the transmission be a three-speed. The car was completed on November 15th, 1903 and delivered to Blake along with Herby's assurance that 30 mph was possible. Blake could only manage 24 mph, and the car just didn't run well. Hence the lawsuit, which was settled in Blake's favor, the court ordering Herby to return all advance money received less the value of the car (which was set at $250). Herby may have built an automobile for himself as well during this period, but it does not appear that he built any more for customers. By 1905 Nels Herby was working as a machinist with the Stearns Brothers Spraying Machine Company in Oakland. Stearns is believed to have built an experimental automobile that year but how involved Herby was with it is not known.

HERCULES — According to *Automobile Topics* during the summer of 1905, Hercules was the name chosen by Joseph Moon for the new car he was soon to be producing in St. Louis, Missouri. Almost immediately, however, Moon decided to name it for himself. Refer to Moon.

Although frequently cited in rosters as an automobile manufactured around 1902 by the A.O. Smith Company of Milwaukee, Wisconsin, the Hercules instead was merely the tradename under which the firm sold its running gear for both electric and gasoline vehicles. From 1916-1919, A.O. Smith did produce and market a small buckboard. Refer to Smith Flyer.

The Hercules Taxicab and Motor Delivery Company was organized in Trenton, New Jersey early in 1911 with a capital stock of $2000 for the manufacture of automobiles. Behind this venture were H.O. Coughlan, L.H. Gunther and John R. Turner. Manufacture is doubted.

1914 Hercules, 4-pass. touring, NAHC

HERCULES — New Albany, Indiana — (1914-1915) — In June of 1914 the plant of the Ohio Falls Motor Company of New Albany was sold to the Louisville, Kentucky firm called the Crown Motor Car Company which had produced a cyclecar bearing that name in 1913. Shortly after moving to New Albany, the Crown company was reorganized as the Hercules Motor

Car Company, although all the principals involved remained the same: B.F. Lambert, as president, A.B. Lambert as vice-president, and C.H. Lambert as secretary-treasurer. The new car would be called the Hercules and though its $495 price was cyclecar-like, the Hercules was not a cyclecar. It was a touring car on a 100-inch wheelbase with a standard 56-inch tread. Its engine was a 20 hp four; shaft drive and a two-speed selective transmission were featured. The car was designed by R.W. Fiskback who, the Hercules company boasted, had ''brought to perfection the Fiskback motor and car in Europe.'' Scarcely had the Hercules made it to the assembly line than big trouble arrived. ''Hercules and Crown Company Officials Charged With Taking Deposits and Not 'Making Good' '' screamed the *Motor World* headline in November. C.H. Lambert and his son A.B. were indicted. (B.F. was not named at this time.) The indictment revolved around machinations attendant to the Crown company being reorganized into Hercules. As Crown, the Lamberts had sold about 400 distributing agencies (for $100 deposits each) and had manufactured about a dozen or so Crown cars. With the reorganization to Hercules, 300 former Crown dealers were invited to transfer their contracts to the new organization which over 200 of them did. (The remaining agents had received their money back.) When some of the Crown-cum-Hercules dealers failed to receive cars, they complained to postal authorities. The indictment followed. Hercules company auditor, I.C. Soper, who was also a Hercules stockholder, objected vigorously, stating that ''the company never refused a single demand for the return of the deposit money and that this money is at present being held and will be returned if cars are not delivered.'' Approximately 100 Hercules cars had been manufactured thus far. The brouhaha continued for approximately a year, and the sensationalized stories in the press effectively killed whatever chance the Hercules car had for survival. Late in 1915 the Hercules assets were sold to Kentucky Wagon Manufacturing Company of Louisville, Kentucky (where the Lamberts had begun with the Crown). The new car from Kentucky Wagon would be called the Dixie Flyer. As for the Lamberts, who were weary of the contretemps, they entered technical pleas of guilty to a charge of using the mails to defraud and each of them (B.F. Lambert included now) was fined $500 in October of 1915. In 1917 the New Albany factory of the old Hercules was demolished in a cyclone. That same year in Anderson, Indiana production of the Lambert car, in which some of the Hercules Lamberts had been involved, was discontinued.

1914-1915 HERCULES
Twenty — 4-cyl., 20 hp, 100' wb

	FP	5	4	3	2	1
Touring-4P	495	2300	3300	4600	7500	16,000

HERCULES ELECTRIC — In 1919 the Hercules Corporation of Evansville, Indiana built a single example of an electric car. It was never produced. But a few years later, a car called the McCurdy (named after the son of the company president) was. Refer to McCurdy.

1907 Hercules, model 140, electric, HAC

HERCULES ELECTRIC — Buffalo, New York — (1907) — Although he had failed several years before to resurrect the defunct German-American, James MacNaughton, a carriage maker from Buffalo, tried again in 1907 with an electric car called Hercules. High priced, as were most electrics, it was available as a runabout or landaulet, and was rather pretty. A commercial vehicle was built as well. The James MacNaughton Company produced its electric for one year only, however, and then returned to carriage making and serving as an agency for the electric cars of other manufacturers.

1907 HERCULES ELECTRIC

Model 140 Rbt.-2/4P	2350	2700	3600	5300	8800	19,000
Model 141 Landaulet-2P	2500	2700	3600	5300	8800	19,000

HERFF-BROOKS — Indianapolis, Indiana — (1915-1916) — The Herff-Brooks Corporation was initially organized in August of 1913 to handle the national sales of the Marathon Motor Works of Nashville, Tennessee. H.H. Brooks was the former sales manager of the Marathon company, and there were several Herffs — George, Herbert and Jacob — who had been the local Indianapolis distributors for the same car. Subsequently, Herff-Brooks produced, in addition to selling, some models of the Marathon — and, consequently, when Marathon went into receivership in Tennessee, the Herffs and Brooks went into the automobile manufacturing business themselves in Indianapolis. Both fours and sixes were produced in the

1915 Herff-Brooks, touring, WLB

medium-priced range, but Herff-Brooks quickly discovered the reality that Marathon had awakened to earlier. Competition in the automobile industry was now very keen. The Herff-Brooks automobile was discontinued by 1917. H.H. Brooks was also allied during this period with the Pontiac Chassis Company in Michigan.

1915 HERFF-BROOKS
Model 4-40 — 4-cyl., 32 hp, 118'' wb

	FP	5	4	3	2	1
Touring-5P	1100	3000	4000	6000	9500	21,000
Roadster-2P	1100	3100	4200	6300	10,500	22,000
Model 6-50 — 6-cyl., 38 hp, 124'' wb						
Roadster-2P	1375	3200	4300	6500	11,000	23,000
Touring-5P	1375	3100	4200	6300	10,500	22,000
1916 HERFF-BROOKS						
Model 4-35 — 4-cyl., 26 hp, 110'' wb						
Touring-5P	885	3000	4000	6000	9500	21,000
Roadster-2P	885	3100	4200	6300	10,500	22,000
Model 6-50 — 6-cyl., 38 hp, 120 wb						
Touring-5P	1095	3100	4200	6300	10,500	22,000
Roadster-2P	1095	3200	4300	6500	11,000	23,000

HERFURTH — The R.W. Herfurth Company was organized in Hartford, Connecticut early in 1908 with a capital stock of $125,000 for the manufacture of machinery, tools, motor cars and bicycles. ''It will take over and use the various patents and rights owned by R.W. Herfurth,'' reported *The Motor Age*. Joining Herfurth in this venture were George Surand and B.S. Morehouse of New York City. Manufacture of an automobile is doubted.

HERKIMER — Herkimer, New York — (1903-1904, 1910) — In the July 15th, 1903 issue of *The Horseless Age*, it was reported that the James A. Clark Company had completed its first two-cylinder 18 hp touring car known as the Herkimer and had driven the vehicle to Schenectady to be delivered to its new owner. The firm — whose address was alternately given as Herkimer and Utica — was already at work on other machines to specific customer order, and that October announced that the Herkimer was now officially on the market. It did not remain there long. What James Clark occupied himself with in the meantime is not known, but in 1910 he was back in the automotive news as ''General Clark'' and announcing that he had purchased the Herkimer Manufacturing Company plant which was being outfitted with new machinery for the manufacture of a four-cylinder car of his own design. ''The company that will handle the car will be a family affair,'' revealed *Automobile Topics*. This venture does not appear to have passed the prototype stage.

HERMAN — The Herman Motor Truck Company was organized in Chicago, Illinois during the spring of 1911 with a capital stock of $50,000 to manufacture and deal in ''automobiles, motor trucks and other motor vehicles. Incorporators were Paul W. Herman, Carmi P. Williams and Daniel G. Ramsay. Manufacture of a car is doubted.
The Herman Motor Company was organized in Cincinnati, Ohio early in 1913 with capital stock of $30,000 for the manufacture of automobiles. Charles Eissen spearheaded this venture. Manufacture of an automobile is doubted.

HERMAN — Harrisburg, Pennsylvania — (1900) — ''About the first of next month Harrisburgers can look for a handsome new motor vehicle on the streets, almost every bit of which was made at home by Harrisburg mechanics,'' *The Motor Vehicle Review* revealed in January 1900. ''M.P. Herman, who is well known in mechanical circles, is building it for J.N. McCulloch, manufacturer of Hickok bicycles, who will use it as a pleasure vehicle.'' The car Herman built was steam powered, with a small 60-pound 2½ hp engine using gasoline for fuel. The frame was seamless steel, and the 28-inch wire wheels were rubber-tired. I.W. Dill furnished the body. The car was expected to be capable of 30 mph.

HERMES — Cincinnati, Ohio — (1913) — In January of 1913, Albert Kleybolte organized the Hermes Motor Car Company in Cincinnati with a capital stock of $30,000. The prototype Hermes was completed that month and tested in the Cincinnati area into April. Designated Model 6-50, it had a Beaver six-cylinder engine fitted into a 124-inch wheelbase chassis. Electric starting and wire wheels were featured. The projected price tag was $1700. It does not appear any manufacture resulted. The most interesting aspect of the brief Hermes company history was the presence on its roster of incorporators of Powel Crosley, Jr., who had tried to build a six himself called the Marathon in 1909, was about to try again with a cyclecar called DeCross, but who really wouldn't begin making a name for himself until he entered the refrigerator business which would make him enough money to try the automotive field again in 1939 with more lasting success.

HERMES — **New York, New York** — **(1920)** — The Hermes featured a four-cylinder Buda engine, Bosch magneto, Westinghouse electrics, Zenith carburetor and Hotchkiss drive. At the press conference in New York City in August 1920 to announce the car, one A. Lucand described the Hermes and described himself as a member of the Society of Automotive Engineers. The Hermes was an export-only car being promoted by Demos Tsaconas for sale to Greece, Tsaconas having "attempted to meet the Greek demands for a trustworthy car highly finished and equipped." Presumably, adequate illumination was deemed a Greek requirement, because the Hermes had lots of lights: thirteen of them, two double lamps in front, two side lamps, two engine lights, two dash lights, two back seat lights and one back light. Two touring car models were to be built, of five- and seven-passenger capacity, both on a 125-inch wheelbase. A diminutive statue of "that ancient character . . . the old Greek god of speed," as the press put it, adorned the radiator cap, and the car's name was spelled in the Greek letters EPMΣ on the emblem. In September, one month following the press conference and the press story, Mr. Lucand — while still admitting to being a member of the SAE — demurred that he was not the designer of the Hermes, but had been "merely describing the car for Mr. Demos, the constructor, who has sailed for Greece. Mr. Demos has not announced the name of the designer." Perhaps not in the United States. But in Europe the August 25th, 1920 issue of the French *La Vie Automobile* had revealed the Hermes' designers as A.G. Herreshoff and C.F. Drumm. Two Hermes chassis were shipped in June to Athens. That would appear to represent the total Hermes production. Sometime thereafter the Greek government banned the importation of automobiles. Demos Tsaconas probably returned full-time efforts to the garage he operated at 225 West 65th Street in Manhattan where he specialized in the repair and maintenance of Packards and Cadillacs.

HERMITAGE — The Hermitage Automobile Company was organized in Nashville, Tennessee late in 1911 with a capital stock of $10,000 to deal in automobiles and make repairs and to conduct a livery service. Among the incorporators were L.W. Jacobs, E.L. Holt, James Clough and Thomas White. Although this firm has been indicated as a manufacturer on various rosters, there is no evidence that it ever operated as other than originally intended.

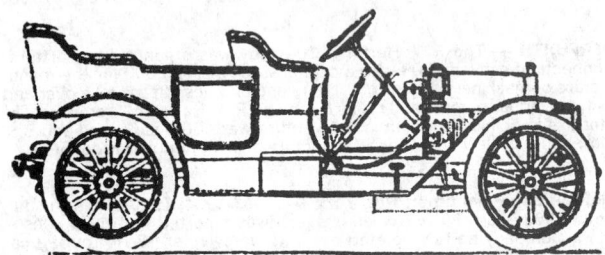

1909 Herreshoff, model 20-A, touring, HAC

HERRESHOFF — **Detroit, Michigan** — **(1909-1914)** — The famed boat-building Herreshoff family counted a number of automobile enthusiasts among its ranks. Around 1880 the Herreshoff Company in Bristol (Rhode Island) produced a light coal-burning steam buggy that made one trip from Bristol to Barrington (just two towns away) and then was unceremoniously retired. It was not until September of 1908 that a member of the family made a serious attempt at automotive manufacture, and the Herreshoff involved was Charles Frederick. He organized the Herreshoff Motor Company in Michigan that month, taking as temporary factory headquarters the old Thomas-Detroit plant in Detroit. The first Herreshoffs, introduced as 1909 models, were small 24 hp fours, the engines of which had been originally designed by Charles Herreshoff as marine powerplants. A piquant Colonial Coupe was among the body styles offered, and a stripped roadster won the five-mile stock chassis race at Indianapolis Speedway in 1910. For 1911 Herreshoff made two fours available, and a 40 hp T-head six was an offering for 1913. "As on blue water so on dry land pin your faith to Herreshoff," Charles Herreshoff said, not too cleverly. Trouble plagued the company early on. In September 1911 ground was broken in Detroit for a new plant on Woodward Avenue between Belmont and Trowbridge. Area residents objected vigorously. Nor was this the only dilemma. Not all of the engines fitted into latterday Herreshoffs were of Herreshoff design. Proprietary units from Lycoming were used, and in March of 1914 when Herreshoff left his company, he blamed defective Lycoming motors as the reason for the financial straits of the firm. In May the Herreshoff Motor Company was sold to Ernst C. and Otto Kern, drygoods merchants of Detroit. All parts, jigs and tools for the car were later purchased by J.C. Gorey & Company of New York City, and the last few cars assembled were marketed by that firm. Meanwhile, in April of 1914, Charles Herreshoff had announced his new Herreshoff Light Car Company of Troy (New York). But the car built there would be called a Harvard. Several years later another family automotive enthusiast, Sidney DeWolf Herreshoff, would build an automobile called the Novara in the company boatbuilding plant in Bristol, Rhode Island. And A.G. Herreshoff was one of the designers of the 1920 Hermes.

1909 HERRESHOFF
Model 20-A — 4-cyl., 24 hp, 100" wb

	FP	5	4	3	2	1
Touring-5P	1500	2500	3500	5000	8500	18,000
Roadster-2P	950	2700	3600	5300	8800	19,000
Colonial Coupe	1400	2300	3300	4600	7500	16,000

1910 HERRESHOFF
Model 20-A — 4-cyl., 24 hp, 100" wb

Runabout-2P	1650	2500	3500	5000	8500	18,000
Tourabout-4P	1650	2700	3600	5300	8800	19,000
Touring-5P	1650	2700	3600	5300	8800	19,000

1910 Herreshoff, model 20-A, runabout, WLB

1911 Herreshoff, model 25, runabout, HAC

1911 HERRESHOFF
Model 25 — 4-cyl., 25 hp, 98" wb

	FP	5	4	3	2	1
Touring-5P	950	2500	3500	5000	8500	18,000
Light Delivery	950	2200	3200	4400	7000	15,000
Model 30 — 4-cyl., 30 hp, 110" wb						
Touring-5P	1350	2700	3600	5300	8800	19,000
Fore-Door Touring-5P	1350	2900	3700	5600	9100	20,000
Demi-Tonneau	1350	2900	3700	5600	9000	20,000
Limousine	—	2400	3400	4800	8000	17,000

1912 Herreshoff, model 25, touring, HAC

1912 HERRESHOFF
Model 25 — 4-cyl., 25 hp, 100" wb

Runabout	950	3150	6300	10,250	14,350	20,500
Roadster	950	3200	6450	10,750	15,050	21,500
Coupe	1400	2300	3300	4600	7500	16,000
Touring (110" wb)	1150	3300	6600	11,000	15,400	22,000

1913 Herreshoff, model 6-36, touring, HAC

1913 HERRESHOFF
Model 30 — 4-cyl., 30 hp, 110" wb

	FP	5	4	3	2	1
Touring-5P	1350	3200	6400	10,750	15,050	21,500
Runabout-2P	1250	3150	6300	10,250	14,350	20,500

Slx-36 — 6-cyl., 40 hp, 124" wb

	FP	5	4	3	2	1
Touring-5P	1850	3800	7650	12,750	17,850	23,300
Roadster-2P	1850	3750	7500	12,500	17,500	25,000

1914 Herreshoff, model 4-30, runabout, HAC

1914 HERRESHOFF
Model 4-30 — 4-cyl., 30 hp, 100" wb

	FP	5	4	3	2	1
Roadster-2P	1250	3150	6300	10,250	14,350	20,500
Touring-5P	1350	3200	6400	10,750	15,050	21,500

Model 6-40 — 6-cyl., 40 hp, 124" wb

	FP	5	4	3	2	1
Roadster-2P	1850	3100	4200	6300	10,500	22,000
Touring-7P	1900	3900	7800	13,000	18,200	26,000
Touring-5P	1850	3750	7500	12,500	17,500	25,000
Touring-6P	1850	3750	7500	12,500	17,500	25,000

HERRICK — The William Herrick Company was organized in Chicago, Illinois late in 1904 with a capital stock of $50,000 for the manufacture of automobiles and parts. Joining Herrick in this venture were Frank E. Drake and Robert Pringle. Manufacture of a car is doubted.

HERRING — A.W. Herring of St. Joseph, Missouri was listed as an automobile manufacturer in the Hiscox book *Horseless Vehicles, Automobiles, Motor Cycles* published in 1900. Further documentation is lacking.

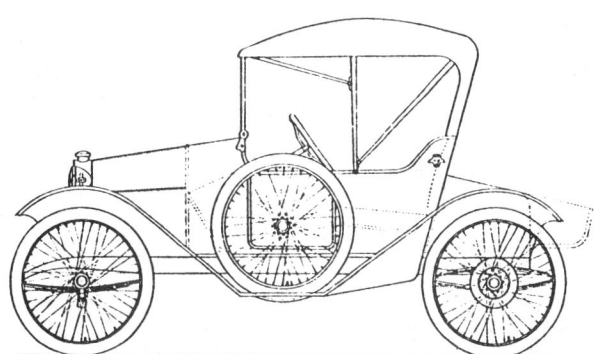

1914 Herrmann, cyclecar

HERRMANN — Tell City, Indiana — (1905) — In 1905 a Tell City mechanic by the name of Herman Gloor built an automobile in the washing machine factory in town for Charles Herrmann. It was fitted with a two-cylinder motorcycle engine and friction transmission, and it did not have sufficient power to run well at all. Although it had been Charles Herrmann's intention to organize an automobile company for manufacture, he quickly became disenchanted with his Herrmann and so purchased a Kenosha-built Rambler from a Louisville agency instead. Actually, it would appear that Herrmann's prime interest was a car in which he could commute from his home to the U.S. Brick Plant which he managed. The Rambler was the first automobile in Tell City to run properly, but there was no one in town in 1905 well-versed enough in mechanics to keep it running. So Herrmann put the car in his garage and forgot about it, subsequently selling it in 1910. Meanwhile, his old Herrmann had come into the possession of a dentist in town named Clark who was determined to get the thing running properly. With the aid of two mechanics, a two-cylinder air cooled engine from Monarch and a planetary transmission, the car did successfully make it to the roads. It was thereafter rechristened the Clark Special. But, again, manufacture did not follow.

HERSCHELL-SPILLMAN — North Tonawanda, New York — (1901-1904, 1907) — The Herschell-Spillman name is well known as the proprietary engine purchased by myriad assembled car manufacturers in America. Less well known is that Herschell-Spillman built an automobile, and even less well known than that is the fact that most of the "horses" the company produced during its lifetime were not for the automobile industry at

1904 Herschell-Spillman, touring, WLB

all. The Armitage-Herschell Company was established in 1880 for the manufacture of merry-go-rounds, and by 1892 production was up to one complete carousel per day. Around the turn of the century, Armitage-Herschell metamorphosed into Herschell-Spillman, Inc. The partners were Allan Herschell and Edward Spillman, and it was the latter who was most interested in the automotive scene and who moved the company into that field. Company announcements in the trade press late in 1900 indicate the firm's original intention was the building of automobiles. In the fall of 1901, Herschell-Spillman reported the successful completion of its first car and its willingness to "build to order" thereafter. A further press reference to the Herschell-Spillman car — a four-cylinder 18 hp tonneau featuring chain drive — was late 1904. By the spring of 1905 the company was reported to be building gasoline engines only. In 1907, however, one further prototype — a 60 hp touring car — was designed for Herschell-Spillman by L.C.Kenen of New York (who later produced the Kenen truck on the West Coast). The Herschell family today recalls the total number of cars built as four. Disagreements over management of the engine-building division of the company caused a split between Herschell and Spillman in 1915, though both names remained on the engines until 1923 when the last one was produced. Although mergers and splits altered the name of the carousel-producing firm in the years to follow, Herschell-Spillman remained the name for the amusement-ride side of the business throughout as well. The last Herschell-Spillman merry-go-round was produced in the early 1960's.

HERSCHMANN — Brooklyn, New York — (1901-1903) — Arthur J. Herschmann was a mechanical engineer from Brooklyn and the designer of the Herschmann Steamer. Although an example or two of an automobile may have been built, the Herschmann was marketed only as a truck, a big three-ton steam wagon rather resembling the British Thornycroft. The vehicles were built for Herschmann by the Columbia Engineering Works in Brooklyn. Production was minimal, but patented features of the Herschmann were reportedly utilized by English lorry maufacturers as late as 1907.

1899 Hertel, runabout, HAC

HERTEL — Greenfield, Massachusetts — (1895-1900) — Max Hertel was an engineer with the American Biscuit Company and an entrant in the 1895 Chicago Times-Herald Contest. His was the smallest gasoline car entered in the event, powered by a two-cylinder two-horsepower engine of Hertel's own design. The car was lever steered, the front wheels set on bicycle forks connected by a bar. Unfortunately, Hertel broke the steering gear en route to the starting line, and thus did not compete. Undeterred by this failure, Max Hertel returned to his native East Coast, continued his experimentation and organized the Oakman Motor Vehicle Company in Greenfield. He began producing his small 500-pound $750 two-seater runabouts in 1899. These cars were very similar to Hertel's Times-Herald Contest car, which was a problem. Although the automobile industry in America was not yet very sophisticated, the motoring public still desired a vehicle more progressive than two bicycle-type frames with an engine and body perched between them. Max Hertel printed a lot more catalogues than he ever produced cars. A creditors' meeting closed his factory door on November 8th, 1900. Although often referred to as Oakmans now, incidentally, these cars were marketed only under the Hertel name at the turn of the century.

1926 Hertz, 4-dr. sedan, WLB

HERTZ — Chicago, Illinois — (1924-1927) — The Hertz was successor to the Ambassador which was produced by the Walden W. Shaw Livery Corporation of Chicago, a firm controlled by John Hertz. In late October of 1924 Hertz had abandoned the idea of selling the Ambassador as a big 75 hp six in a flurry of body styles, electing instead to offer a six-cylinder 25 hp version in either sedan or touring form and to make the car available both for sale and for lease. His idea was described in *Automobile Topics* as "a system designed after the old livery stable plan . . . where a man might go hire a 'rig' for a day's pleasure or business traveling." He renamed the Ambassador the Hertz, and continued it in production into 1927. Then he decided the "system" was a winner, but manufacturing the cars for it was not. The Hertz was discontinued late in 1927, and John Hertz thereafter provided his "drive it yourself" service in cars produced by other manufacturers. Total Hertz production had been 51 cars in 1924, 1672 cars in 1925, 2303 cars in 1926 and just 35 in 1927. Conceivably some of the 1924 and 1925 production may have carried the Ambassador name.

1926-1927 HERTZ
Model D-1 — 6-cyl., 25 hp, 114" wb

	FP	5	4	3	2	1
Drive-It-Yourself Sedan	1675	2500	3500	5000	8500	18,000
Drive-It-Yourself Touring	1675	3500	4500	7000	13,000	25,000

HERVEY — The Hervey Corporation was organized in New York City during the fall of 1912 with a capital stock of $100,000 to manufacture and deal in motor vehicles. W.J. Hervey was behind this venture. Manufacture of an automobile is doubted.

1917 Heseltine, 4-pass. roadster, WLB

HESELTINE — Buffalo, New York — (1916-1917) — In late summer of 1916 the Heseltine Motor Corporation of Buffalo succeeded the Gadabout Motor Corporation of Detroit, with Philip Heseltine remaining onboard as president, Walter Greunberg as chief engineer. The Gadabout had been a cyclecar, the Heseltine represented a step up to light car ranks. Powered by a four-cylinder 27 hp engine, the Heseltine was offered as a two-seater roadster only, though in two wheelbase sizes. It survived less long than had the Gadabout.

1916-1917 HESELTINE
Shamrock — 4-cyl., 27 hp, 106" wb

Roadster-4P	695	2700	3600	5300	8800	19,000

HESS — Philadelphia, Pennsylvania — (1902) — In 1901 Henry K. Hess of 729 Filbert Street in Philadelphia was granted a patent on a steam-propelled vehicle using charcoal as fuel. Later that year he established the Hess Steam Vehicle Company for manufacture of the charcoal burner, claiming that "sufficient fuel may be readily carried to insure ample steam for at least sixty miles. The fire is regulated by draft, requiring no air under pressure and once lighted it is possible to let it go without having to relight for a day or more." In order to demonstrate the efficiency of his unit, Hess

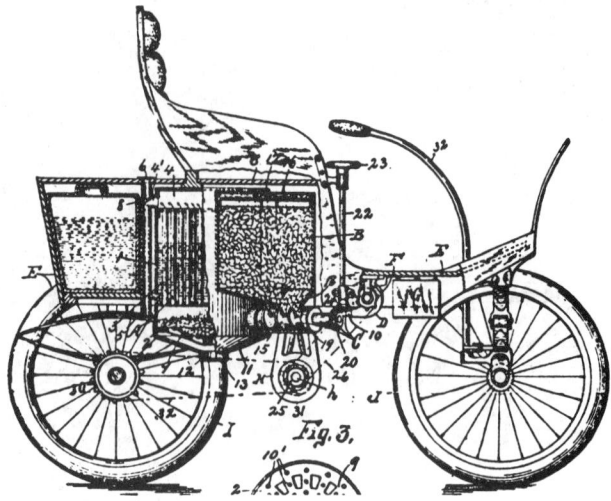

1902 Hess Steamer, NAHC

purchased a Mobile steamer and revised it for fitting of his charcoal burner and charcoal bin (which rather resembled a backyard barbecue grille). There is no evidence that he ever produced more than this one demonstrator car. Its first demonstration, in early March 1902, created a sensation, however. As reported in *The Motor Review*, Hess "showed the machine's paces to the best advantage — and it could go like a streak, too. When stopping occasionally, the machine was instantly surrounded by curious crowds, who fired questions by the hundreds at the occupants. The charcoal machine has very little visible exhaust, absolutely no odor, and gets up steam in a remarkably short time."

HESSE — New York, New York — (1895) — G. Emil Hesse was a mechanical engineer operating out of a shop at 35 Broadway in Manhattan with his home at 21 Strong Place in Brooklyn, and in 1895 he is reported to have built an automobile. No doubt it was for experimental purposes only. In 1906 a Hesse Automobile Company was organized in Brooklyn by Emanuel Hesse, John J. Hesse and Herman Hesse. Their relationship to G. Emil is not known, but their capital stock was a mere $1200, and manufacture of a Hesse automobile did not follow.

HESSE — Santa Rosa, California — (1901) — During the summer of 1901, Fred Hesse of Santa Rosa and his partner Harry Duckworth were in the process of completing their first automobile with the full expectation, as *The Motor Age* said, of being able "to interest capital and build and operate a factory there." This expectation was not realized.

HEWALL — The Hewall Manufacturing Company was organized in New York City during the spring of 1907 with a capital stock of $35,000 for the manufacture of automobiles. Behind this venture were H.C. Messimer, E.B. Jackson and D. Campbell, all of New York City. Manufacture is doubted.

1907 Hewitt, touring, NAHC

HEWITT — New York, New York — (1906-1907) — In June of 1905 the Hewitt Motor Company secured office space on East 31st just off Fifth Avenue, factory quarters on the West Side at 64th and Tenth, and bought the Selden Patent license owned by the Standard Motor Construction Company which had elected to retire from the automobile field in Jersey City. Edward Ringwood Hewitt was now in business. His first production cars arrived in 1906, a cute one-lunger offered as town car, limousine and "Little Touring Car" for two passengers, and a rather ordinary four offered as a touring car and limousine. For the single-cylinder car, Hewitt allied himself with the Adams Manufacturing Company of London, and the cars sold in England were called the Adams-Hewitt. France, and the Antoinette aviation engine, seems to have been the derivation of the new Hewitt offering to replace the Hewitt four in 1907. Edward Hewitt claimed that the Hewitt V-8 was America's first, but this was an honor he possibly shared with the Buffum. Commercial vehicle production had played a prominent role in Hewitt's manufacturing plans from the beginning, and in 1907 when Hewitt was absorbed by the Metzger Motor Car Company (builders of the Everett car), Hewitt production became confined thereafter to trucks. In 1912 the Hewitt enterprise became part of a consortium also including Mack and American Saurer. Edward Hewitt remained a consulting engineer for Mack trucks into the World War II years.

1906 HEWITT
1-cyl., 8 hp, 84" wb

	FP	5	4	3	2	1
Town Car-4P	2600	2300	3300	4600	7500	16,000
Limousine-4P	2600	2000	3000	4200	6500	14,000
"Little Touring Car"-2P	1500	2200	3200	4400	7000	15,000

4-cyl., 20/30 hp, 112" wb

	FP	5	4	3	2	1
Touring-5P	4000	2400	3400	4800	8000	17,000
Limousine-5P	4500	2200	3200	4400	7000	15,000

1907 HEWITT
1-cyl., 10 hp, 84" wb

	FP	5	4	3	2	1
Touring-5P	1900	2400	3400	4800	8000	17,000
"Little Touring Car"-2P	1000	2300	3300	4600	7500	16,000
Town Car-5P	2600	2000	3000	4200	6500	14,000
Limousine	2500	2200	3200	4400	7000	15,000
Runabout-2/3P (72" wb)	1000	2300	3300	4600	7500	16,000

8-cyl., 50/60 hp, 112" wb

	FP	5	4	3	2	1
Touring-5P	4500	2500	3500	5000	8500	18,000
Landaulet (chassis price)	4000	—	—	—	—	—
Limousine (chassis price)	4000	—	—	—	—	—

1900 Hewitt-Lindstrom, coach, GR

HEWITT-LINDSTROM — Chicago, Illinois — (1900-1902) — The Hewitt-Lindstrom Motor Company was located at 75 North Clinton Street in Chicago. John Hewitt was president and treasurer, and also the proprietor of the Miehle Company, one of Chicago's largest printing firms. Charles A. Lindstrom was a Swedish emigre and described as the "mechanical genius of the institution." All Hewitt-Lindstroms were electric-powered, and in July of 1900 the company announced its intention not only to manufacture vehicles but "to sell licenses to carriage manufacturers or others who contemplate entering the automobile field." Already a number of Hewitt-Lindstrom models were in production, including a 2500-pound four-passenger brake which would travel forty miles on a charge and was capable of climbing a twenty-two percent grade, and a 1600-pound two-seater stanhope which had a forty-one-mile range and a sixteen-percent-grade climbing ability. Lindstrom's thirteen-year-old daughter was pronounced perfectly capable of operating the latter vehicle. Its maximum speed was 16 mph. Commercial vehicle production included a light delivery wagon and a twenty-passenger omnibus (equipped with two of the company's 4-1/2 hp motors) which was given its first outing that year when John Hewitt took twenty of his friends to the races on Derby Day. The distance traveled was thirty-eight miles, which was deemed "remarkable on a first trip." Hewitt-Lindstrom exhibited at the Chicago Automobile Show in March 1902. The company does not appear to have remained in business long thereafter. Meanwhile, Charles Lindstrom had shuffled off to Buffalo in December 1901 to build another electric called the Niagara.

HEXTER — The Hexter Taximeter Company of Manhattan was organized during the spring of 1908 with a capital stock of $100,000 to manufacture and operate motor cars. Behind this venture were P.K. Hexter, T.F. McDermott and E.L. Ansell. Manufacure is doubted.

HEYER — The A.P. Heyer Company was organized in Denver, Colorado during the spring of 1911 to manufacture "motor cars and electric vehicles." Capital stock was $50,000. Joining Heyer in this venture were G.D. Smith and W.W. Crane. Manufacture is doubted.

HEYMANN — Melrose, Massachusetts — (1898-1907) — The Heymann Motor Vehicle and Manufacturing Company was organized with a capital stock of $250,000 in the late summer of 1898. The Heymanns involved were Edward and F.W., electrical engineers of Boston. Company president

1898 Heymann, gasoline carriage, NAHC

was R.M. Fogg; treasurer was C.H. Pratt. Construction was immediately begun on a factory located in Melrose, seven miles from Boston. There production began later that year on a three-cylinder four-cycle water-cooled 6 hp stanhope with tiller steering, wooden wheels and solid tires. Fifty cars were reported to be in the building stage prior to year's end. In November of 1900 the company was reorganized with a capital stock of $350,000, but very little was heard from it thereafter, until 1904 that is, when the Heymann became another car altogether. Now it was a five-cylinder 40 hp rotary-engined touring car featuring the "Gearless Variable Speed Controller," a variation on the friction transmission theme which in theory provided an infinite number of ratios, although "for convenience we have provided 20 positions for the controlling lever, thus 20 speeds." There may have been a number of problems involved in this Heymann's design, because no reports of production followed. The car did appear at the Boston Automobile Show early in 1907, however, and thereafter disappeared completely.

1898-1903 HEYMANN

	FP	5	4	3	2	1
Stanhope (3-cyl., 6 hp, 56" wb)	—	3000	4000	6000	9500	21,000

1904 Heymann, HAC

1904-1907 HEYMANN

	FP	5	4	3	2	1
Rotary (5-cyl., 40 hp, 102" wb)	4000	3200	4300	6500	11,000	23,000

H.F. — The H.F. Construction Company of New London, Connecticut has been indicated on various rosters as the manufacturer of an automobile in 1902. This is highly unlikely. Such a company was not in existence in New London for an entire decade following the turn of the century.

H & F ELECTRIC — Detroit, Michigan — (1910) — Frank H. Hovey of Detroit and F.E. Foulke of Kansas City got together to design an electric limousine with a cast aluminum body and a claimed mileage between charges of 140 miles. The car weighed 2200 pounds, it was priced at $3000, and it was displayed at the Detroit Exposition during the summer of 1910. At that time Hovey and Foulke mentioned that orders for fully 1500 cars had already been secured, that they were considering four sites in town as a possible factory location, and that they were in the process of organizing a company which, the press said, "will, doubtless, be capitalized at $1,000,000." Much of this must have been wishful thinking. Hovey's and Foulke's H & F Electromobile Company died aborning. Thereafter Frank Hovey probably returned to managing the Eldorado Apartments which he owned in Detroit.

H & H — The H & H Auto Company was organized in Cleveland, Ohio during the summer of 1913 with a capital stock of $10,000 for the manufacture and sale of automobiles. Incorporators were F.M. Fogarty, J.O. Fordyce, A.B. Brackenridge, H.M. Reidel and C.M. Dolan. Manufacture of a car is doubted.

The H & H Motor Car Company was organized in New York City early in 1910 with a capital stock of $12,000 for the manufacture and sale of gasoline and electric cars and engines. Incorporators were Charles L. Holden, John H. Hershfield and Solomon Wall. Manufacture of a car is doubted.

HIAWATHA — Hiawatha, Kansas — (1904) — Incubators and washing machines were the principal products of the Hiawatha Manufacturing Company, whose officer roster included Charles Knabb as president, George R. Adams as vice-president, William Knabb as treasurer and Eaton S. Edgerton as secretary and general manager. For a short while during 1904 the company also manufactured a single-cylinder 4 hp motor buggy. Production began on May 1st. It was probably discontinued several months later when the Hiawatha people concluded that profitability was better served by sticking to the products they knew best.

HIBBARD & BUSH — Fond du Lac, Wisconsin — (1902) — A 5½ hp run-about that would be a "cheap machine to manufacture" and could sell for $650 was the idea W.L. Hibbard and W.J. Bush submitted to the Fond du Lac Advancement Association. A prototype had been built, to Bush's designs, and the partners claimed to already have "one order for 100 machines besides several smaller orders." No factory in Fond du Lac followed, however. It is known that Hibbard subsequently opened a dealership in Milwaukee, which was dissolved in 1909, and that thereafter he became an agent for the Rapid truck.

HICKS — Chicago, Illinois — (1899-1900) — John C. Hicks was the proprietor of the Hicks Motocycle Company of Chicago. During the winter of 1899-1900, he built a gasoline car with four wheels at the furthermost corners as was the usual practice whether a vehicle was horseless or horse-drawn. However, the Hicks was driven by yet another wheel mounted in the center of the rear axle. One cannot imagine this arrangement working well, but it may have been the industry's first example of fifth-wheel drive.

HICKS — San Francisco, California — (1899) — That J.L. Hicks of 667 Mission Street in San Francisco was advertising himself in 1899 as a manufacturer of "motor vehicles of all kinds" has been documented, but what those vehicles might have been has not been determined, nor how many he might have built. It is known that in 1897, J.A. Meyer, the foreman of the J.L. Hicks Gas Engine Company, built an automobile in the company shops.

HICKS — Waycross, Georgia — (1905) — "Waycross Has Corporation with Big Money," *The Motor World* headline read. The money — some $180,000 in cash, as reported from Georgia — was for the organization of the Hicks Gas Motor Company whose purpose was the manufacture of gasoline engines and motor cars to the patents of J.B. Hicks. Hicks purportedly had been "making the motors in a small way for years." Engine manufacture followed, but motor cars did not. A prototype was as far as the Hicks automobile proceeded.

HICO — Bond C. Hico of Howard Avenue in Chicago, Illinois was listed as an automobile manufacturer in the Hiscox book *Horseless Vehicles, Automobiles, Motor Cycles* published in 1900. Further documentation is lacking. No one by that name appears in the Chicago city directories during the turn of the century period.

HIDLEY — Troy, New York — (1901-1902) — In February of 1901, J.H. Hidley, a well-known and popular bicycle dealer in Troy, began building a steam automobile in the window of his store at 257 Broadway. He made all parts of the vehicle himself, and in the months to follow crowds of people watched him work. The automobile was for Hidley's personal use, though as *The Motor Vehicle Review* commented, it was also providing him "an unlimited amount of advertising." Apparently the crowd reaction to Hidley's window workmanship encouraged him to build further cars. By the fall of 1901 he had established the Hidley Automobile Company for manufacture of 8 hp steamers to be sold as runabouts for $750, traps for $800 and delivery wagons for $900. The Hidley used gasoline for fuel, with the feed automatic. The hand brake worked both in ascending and descending inclines, and was accompanied by a steam power brake for use in emergencies. An electric device informed the driver of steam pressure, with an adjustment to warn him when the water supply was low. "In case any of the levers fail to perform their functions a steam controller promptly shuts off the steam from the engine," *Cycle and Automobile Trade Journal* reported. "Every emergency likely to occur seems to have been provided for, and the Hidley automobile ought to be a winner." The car does not seem to have been produced beyond 1902, however.

1896 Higdon, NAHC

HIGDON — St. Louis, Missouri — (1896) — John C. Higdon was one-half of the St. Louis law partnership of Higdon & Higdon. In 1896 he built a high-wheeled surrey powered by a 7 hp gasoline engine designed by George C. Weber (who subsequently founded the Weber Gas Engine Company) with final drive to the rear axle by means of a single sprocket and chain. "Horseless Carriage," said a large sign on the side of the vehicle, "Higdon & Higdon, Patent Lawyers." It was splendid advertising, and at the time the only car planned. "Although we are patent lawyers, there is no patent on this vehicle, and everyone is perfectly free to copy it . . .," the Messrs. Higdon and Higdon wrote *The Horseless Age* that year. "We do not propose to build the vehicles, as it is entirely out of our line. We use our vehicle much the same as the owner of a common carriage uses it, with the exception that ours has no animals to get frightened and run away." Amusingly, a number of years later John C. Higdon changed his mind on both counts. First, he established the Success Auto-Buggy Manufacturing Company and proceeded into production of a highwheeler. Second, Success subsequently sued several other highwheeler manufacturers for patent infringement. Amusingly, too, his 1896 car does not appear to have been much good "Higdon rode alone mostly," it was said, "friends and family gave the freak vehicle a wide berth and commented disrespectfully on its many failings."

1919 Highlander, NAHC

HIGHLANDER — Kansas City, Missouri — (1919-1922) — The Midwest Motor Company of Kansas City had originally been organized in 1917 by B.P. Bagby for production of a car to be called the Kay-See. The First World War halted that venture at the prototype stage, and following the Armistice, Bagby was out, a new set of backers — P.M. Crone, J.A. Fullerton, E.J. Short and R.L. Cleveland — moved in, and the car's name was changed to Highlander. Early in 1919 Midwest announced its purchase of equipment from the defunct Frankfort Motor Company of Indiana which had failed in 1917 before a car ever made it to the assembly line. Coming along to take charge of the Highlander's production was former Frankfort president R.E. Stevenson; and he brought along O.C. White, the former president of the Princess Motor Car Company of Detroit, as the Highlander's new sales manager. The Midwest Motor Company displayed the prototype of its new Highlander at the Kansas City Automobile Show in March 1919 and mentioned that although a few cars were on the assembly line, quantity production was still to come. It never arrived. The Highlander, or Hylander as it was occasionally misspelled, was an assembled automobile powered by a Continental six-cylinder 55 hp engine. Only open cars were built and, though a four-cylinder sport model was promised, it does not appear to have been marketed. Only small quantities of the Highlander Six were produced before the company went under.

1919-1922 HIGHLANDER
Six — 55 hp, 120" wb

	FP	5	4	3	2	1
Roadster	—	2700	3600	5300	8800	19,000
Six — 55 hp, 125" wb						
Touring-5P	1975	2900	3700	5600	9100	20,000
Touring-7P	—	2700	3600	5300	8800	19,000

HIGHWAY — The Highway Motors Company was organized with a capital stock of $1.5 million early in 1920 for the manufacture of passenger cars in Defiance, Ohio. Among the incorporators were such industry luminaries as Charles F. Kettering, E.H. Belknap and J.W. Schwartz. The venture took over the business of the engine-producing Golden, Belknap & Schwartz Company as well as the Trucking Machine Company of Detroit. Apparently the idea of passenger car manufacture was decided against early on. Engines only continued to be built. This firm should not be confused, incidentally, with the Highway Motors Company of Chicago which produced the Highway-Knight truck from 1919-1921.

HILDEBRAND — That one J.A. Hildebrand in association with the R.F. McMullin Company of Chicago, Illinois built automobiles in 1895 and 1897 has been indicated on various car rosters. This has not been confirmed. There was a McMullin Motive Power and Construction Company in Chicago during the turn-of-the-century period, presided over by F.R. McMullin. This firm built stationary engines and a few cars in 1900-1901.

HILL — That the C.C. Hill Automobile Company of Chicago, Illinois built an automobile in 1900 has been indicated on car rosters. This is not the case. C.C. Hill did build automobiles in Chicago, however. Refer to Hill Locomotor.

In 1901 the J.J. Hill Company of Knightsville, Rhode Island was acquired by the Rhode Island Auto Carriage Company of Olneyville and for a short period the Hughes & Atkin steam car was produced there. Refer to Hughes & Atkin.

HILL STEAM — Fleetwood, Pennsylvania — (1868) — James Hill of Fleetwood was a farmhand, cabinetmaker, carriage builder and portrait painter. All this, he decided, was not enough. In 1868 he built his first steam car; it ran but not very well, and he tinkered with it for decades thereafter, until the town council finally enjoined him from testing the vehicle on city streets because it frightened the horses. Ultimately, he replaced its steam powerplant with a gasoline engine, but manufacture never followed. Apparently Hill could not interest his brother Charles in the idea, and so employed himself instead as a stationary engineer in the family-owned Hill Granite Works. The Hill car survives in a private collection in Berks County.

1904 Hill, touring, HS

HILL — Haverhill, Massachusetts — (1904-1908) — George S. Hill established his Hill Motor Car Company in 1904 at 108 Merrimack Street in Haverhill. The prototype of his car had been built in the shops of Gilman W. Brown on Main Street in West Newbury, but all subsequent Hills were assembled in Haverhill. The cars were air cooled, an $1850 two-cylinder touring car being the first offering, joined by a $3000 four in 1907. That the local newspaper was wholeheartedly behind the venture is evident: "a perfect type of the highest standard on the market," the *Haverhill Evening Gazette* enthused in December 1904. "The air-cooling device . . . is a novel arrangement of aluminum pins which throw off the heat generated by the engine in remarkably quick time, so that within a very few minutes from the time the engine is stopped there is not the slightest trace of heat to denote that the car had been operated." Engines for the cars were built for Hill by Upton in Beverly, with coachwork arriving from Bryant in Amesbury. According to Hill's widow, though the air cooling device (a porcupine-type) might have been effective, there were problems with the aluminum pins: "These sometimes fell out," she reminisced in the early 1950's. Her husband's automobile-building venture ended in 1908, after the production of ten cars. Though he had wished to expand his efforts with better equipment and a more suitable location, he was unable to convince anyone in Haverhill to back him financially. In the fall of 1908 George Hill sold out his business to Elmer C. Bassett, who retained the Hill Motor Car Company title but confined activity to repair and service, and to serving as an agency for Maxwell and Buick cars.

1904 HILL
Twin — 16/18 hp, 90" wb

	FP	5	4	3	2	1
Touring-5P	1850	2000	3000	4200	6500	14,000

1905-1906 HILL
Twin — 20/22 hp, 90" wb

	FP	5	4	3	2	1
Touring-5P	1850	2000	3000	4200	6500	14,000

1907 Hill, touring, HAC

1907-1908 HILL
Twin — 20/22 hp, 90" wb

	FP	5	4	3	2	1
Touring-5P	1850	2000	3000	4200	6500	14,000

Four — 35 hp, 90" wb

	FP	5	4	3	2	1
Touring-5P	3000	2200	3200	4400	7000	15,000

HILL CLIMBER — San Francisco, California — (1904-1905) — The Hill Climbing Automobile Manufacturing Company was organized late in 1904 with P.J. Leharbach as president, A.B. Cameron as vice president, M. Mackowitz as treasurer, and T.J. Henderson as ultimately disgruntled employee. How many Hill Climbers were built is unknown, but the fate of the last one is. It was a custom job built for one E. Holler in town who had paid $600 in advance for it. The car was completed, but before Holler could take delivery, the company failed. Thereupon T.J. Henderson, whose position at the firm had been as machinist, appropriated the vehicle, claiming Hill Climbing owned him $150 in back wages. Holler objected to this, and Henderson was arrested on a charge of grand larceny.

1895 Hill's Locomotor, motor carriage, NAHC

HILL LOCOMOTOR — Chicago, Illinois — (1895; 1901) — C.C. Hill was an inveterate tinkerer from Chicago whose first automotive effort was financed in 1895 by a Chicagoan named Cummings. At a small machine shop at 232 Clinton Street, Hill built his Locomotor which was a gasoline powered canopy-top surrey he proposed to manufacture as a $350 vehicle for two passengers, a $500 vehicle for four. The two-cylinder engine developed 6 hp at 700 rpm, and a "possible" speed of 28 mph was claimed. The complete rig weighed but 600 pounds. It would appear that a few of these cars were produced in the year that followed. Production does not appear to have been the case for C.C. Hill's second automotive effort, however. This one arrived at the turn of the century and it was described by Hill as a "Closed Circuit Steam Carriage." The January 9th, 1901 edition of *The Horseless Age* reported this vehicle nearing completion, soon to be "ready for trial." Although C.C. Hill attempted to organize a company for its manufacture, he never succeeded.

HILLSDALE — Hillsdale, Michigan — (1908) — The Hillsdale Motor Company was organized in January 1908 by George W. Gardner, C.S. Wolcott, Fred C. Thatcher and John W. Raymond. Two low-priced models — one at $450, the other at $850 — were slated to be built. A prototype of the $450 car — a runabout powered by a single-cylinder 15 hp engine — had been completed in the machine shop of the Reek Brothers the previous fall. Designer of both cars was John Raymond, who formerly had been with the Buckeye Manufacturing Company in Anderson, Indiana. In addition to engineering the new Hillsdale, Raymond was also to be secretary and general manager of the company. By summer the Hillsdale venture was kaput. In October Raymond was back, however, with a new organization in Hillsdale called the Mercury Motor Car Company, capitalized at $50,000. Raymond was the president and general manager this time, and the company's first cars were reported to be under construction in late October. Whether these were prototypes begun under the Hillsdale Motor Company is not known, but Mercury is not believed to have made it into production either.

HILLSIDE — The Hillside Motor Car Company was organized in New York City with a capital stock of $40,000 late in 1907 to manufacture and deal in automobiles. Joseph A. Jones, Marion S. Sears and Robert Robinson were behind this venture. Manufacture is doubted.

HILSENDEGEN — Detroit, Michigan — (1899) — "George Hilsendegen, the Woodward Avenue bicyclist, is getting in line on these new-fangled machines," *The Motor Vehicle Review* noted brightly in September 1899. "He says that in about two weeks he will show the boys something in the way of a motor tricycle and also a motor vehicle. He has these machines under construction and will spring them in due time." Spring them he may have, but the results never led to manufacture.

HILTON — Riverton, New Jersey — (1920-1921) — The company's name was Motor Sales & Service Corporation, the company's founder was Hilton W. Sofield, the company's product was known as the Hilton. Though Sofield headquartered his venture at 1714 North Broad Street in Philadel-

1920 Hilton, coupe, WLB

phia, he located his Hilton factory at Riverton, New Jersey on the Delaware River. The Hilton Four (Herschell-Spillman engine) was offered only as a closed coupe with wire wheels and a very large rear deck. Three people could be accommodated in the front seat, with the driver ''set sufficiently forward so that in turning the wheel the other occupants of the car do not hinder (his) movements.'' Almost immediately after launching the Hilton Four at a dinner-dance for employees at the Philadelphia Rifle Club on August 13th, 1920, Sofield went off to design a truck (his previous employment had included serving as vice-president of the Keystone Truck Company) and organize yet another company (Pennsylvania Motors Corporation) for its manufacture. The burning to the ground of his Riverton factory in June 1921 spelled finis for his Hilton car as well as his truck which does not appear ever to have been given a proper name.

1920-1921 HILTON
Four — 4-cyl., 19.6 hp, 114'' wb

	FP	5	4	3	2	1
Coupe-3P	2375	2200	3200	4400	7000	15,000

HINCKLEY — Hinckley Motors Corporation was organized in 1914 at Ecorse, Michigan and built engines for the government during World War I. Carl C. Hinckley, a former chief engineer for Olds and Chalmers, was the man behind this venture. Although briefly during the 1920's the manufacture of an automobile was contemplated, this never followed. Instead, after liquidation of his firm in 1926, Carl Hinckley joined the Buda Company in Harvey, Illinois.

1908 Hines, 5-pass. touring, NAHC

HINES — Cleveland, Ohio — (1908-1910) — The car was designed by and named for William R. Hines, the chief engineer of the National Screw & Tack Company of Cleveland. It was built, however, by the Moehlhauser Machine Company across town. Hines had built his first automobile, a single-cylinder four-stroke, in 1902, and had followed it with a number of others, all experimental, all now with two-stroke engines. The Hines that was produced from 1908 until early 1910 was a two-stroke as well, a water-cooled four. Shaft drive and a three-speed sliding gear transmission were featured. Only one model was offered, a five-passenger touring on a 106-inch wheelbase. Presumably this car — which was also called the Hinescar its final year — finally got the automotive bee out of William Hines' bonnet. He is not known to have built another. Production of the Hines was not large. When the car was discontinued, most probably its designer returned to the engineering of screw and tack machines.

HINMAN — (1906) — Where Jay A. Hinman built his car is not known, but the description and picture of it that he submitted to *The Horseless Age* in 1906 reveal it to be a substantially constructed vehicle. A two-cylinder 16 hp Brennan engine was fitted into 108-inch wheelbase chassis riding on thirty-inch wheels shod with three-inch solid tires. ''Motor wagon builders claim it is impossible to use solid tires, as the vibration will rattle the engine to pieces,'' Hinman wrote, ''With a suitable set of springs such as I had made for me, which are of special design, that trouble is entirely overcome. The springs are of the full elliptic pattern, but of a different shape than the ordinary ones. Instead of the springs lengthening out when under

1906 Hinman, NAHC

load, both the top and bottom halves work with an up and down motion at the same time, and the spring remains the same length.'' Hinman claimed a speed of 35 mph for his car.

HIPWELL — Pittsburgh, Pennsylvania — (1901) — In announcing its plans during the summer of 1901, the Hipwell Manufacturing Company of Pittsburgh bragged that it would be ''the pioneer builder in this city, as none of the firms now handling motor vehicles ever built more than two or three, and those only on request.'' Two or three probably proved the total extent of Hipwell production as well, all of them prototypes. Although gasoline, electric and steam automobiles were envisioned, the evidence would suggest that only the latter two were tried. The Hipwell company had long been in the electric field in Pittsburgh, and Harry Hipwell was at work at that time on a steam wagon. Hipwell's subsequent activity in the automobile field seems to have been as an agency for the products of the National Automobile & Electric Company of Indianapolis.

HITCHCOCK — Warren, Ohio — (1907-1908) — The Hitchcock Motor Car Company was organized in Warren, Ohio during the summer of 1907 with a capital stock of $20,000. Involved in the venture were J.A. Hitchcock, W.H. Creahen, Herbert E. Craig, T.M. Burton and S.E. Wannamaker. Immediately after the New Year, the firm (now calling itself the Hitchcock Motor Car Company) announced the completion of its first car which featured a two-cylinder two-stroke 20 hp Speedwell air-cooled engine and friction transmission. If any manufacture followed, it was minimal. The Warren company almost immediately faded from sight.

H. & N. — The H. & N. Manufacturing Company, Inc. was organized in New York City late in 1917 with a $225,000 capital stock for the manufacture of automobiles, airplanes and engines. Incorporators were W.G. Decker, J.B. Mooney and J.B. Mackie. Manufacture of a car is doubted.

HOAGLAND-THAYER — The Hoagland-Thayer Company was organized in Newark, New Jersey during the spring of 1911 with a capital stock of $25,000 for the manufacture of automobiles and engines. Involved in the venture were Alger M. Hoagland, George H. Thayer and Edward B. Thayer. Manufacture of a car is doubted.

1908 Hobbie Accessible, NAHC

HOBBIE ACCESSIBLE — Hampton, Iowa — (1908-1910) — Leslie Hobbie's father had been a pioneer blacksmith in Hampton. The son continued this trade, and soon after the turn of the century established the Hobbie Automobile Company, one of Iowa's very early car dealerships. The lure to manufacture was apparently irresistible and in 1908 Leslie Hobbie introduced a typical tiller-steered, solid-tired highwheeler known alternately as the Hobbie, the Hobbie Accessible, or the Accessible. Production of the highwheeler was discontinued in 1910, and Hobbie continued instead as a dealer, subsequently marketing Willys-Overland cars, Chrysler cars from the early 1930's and in 1939 the Crosley car as well.

1908-1909 HOBBIE ACCESSIBLE

Model A — 2-cyl., 10/12 hp, 82" wb

	FP	5	4	3	2	1
Road Wagon-2P	750	1400	2400	3500	5300	10,000

Model B — 2-cyl., 14 hp, 88" wb

	FP	5	4	3	2	1
Piano Box Buggy-4P	850	1500	2500	3600	5500	11,000

1910 Hobbie Accessible, KM

1910 HOBBIE ACCESSIBLE

Model A — 2-cyl., 12/14 hp, 82" wb

	FP	5	4	3	2	1
Runabout-2P	650	1500	2500	3600	5500	11,000

HOBBS — Chicago, Illinois — (1903) — John O. Hobbs of Chicago had been tinkering with his automotive ideas since the turn of the century, and in 1903 built a car to demonstrate them. Not until 1907, however, were his ideas put into an automobile for manufacture. In that year the Lorraine Automobile Manufacturing Company was organized, and the Hobbs ideas found their way into the Lorraine which was produced into 1908.

HODGETTS — Wallingford, Connecticut — (1908) — The only garage in Wallingford in 1908 was the one operated by W.J. Hodgetts in association with his son E.R. Before joining his father, young E.R. had worked with the Locomobile Company during its steam-car producing days. Now, at the Hodgetts garage, he built five cars himself. When he began building them is not known, but they were described in a September 1908 issue of *New England Automobile Journal*. Of the five, three were steamers and two gasoline powered. And all had been sold, except for Hodgetts' latest effort. It was a big seven-passenger touring car on a 120-inch-wheelbase chassis with sliding gear transmission and double chain drive. Its four-cylinder engine developed 40 horsepower. "Since the car has been built a distance of eight to ten thousand miles has been covered," the magazine said, "and the vehicle has always been satisfactory in operation, and compares favorably with that produced by the best manufacturers."

HODGKINS STEAMER — Gloucester, Massachusetts — (1913) — The Hodgkins Steamer was rather a hodge-podge, but it worked out well. The chassis was a Prescott, the steam engine was a Mason, the boiler and burner was a Stanley and the steering wheel a Model T Ford. Pierce N. Hodgkins of Gloucester fashioned most of the rest of the machine himself, registered it as a Hodgkins Steamer, drove the car for about two years, then sold it to a chauffeur from Topsfield.

1903 Hodgson, runabout, NAHC

HODGSON — Waukesha, Wisconsin — (1902) — After visiting the Chicago Automobile Shows of 1901 and 1902, and observing the defects of the cars on display, Dr. A.J. Hodgson set about to build his own. His speci-

fications were the following: two-cylinder vertical motor cast en bloc, jump spark, "no chain whatever, everything geared . . . no universal joints to transmit power," artillery wooden wheels, detachable tonneau unattached to machinery, irreversible wheel steering, all running parts enclosed in dust-proof casing. Dr. Hodgson purchased the motor, but built the rest of the car himself. It weighed 1860 pounds complete. He also built a garage for it. Dr. Hodgson was an advocate of winter motoring, and his apparel for such occasions included, from inside out, a union suit, a suit of perforated buckskin, a heavy business suit, a pair of slicker overalls and jumper, two pairs of socks and one of felt shoes, yarn mittens over kid gloves and a cap with ears. "If some brother medico will let me know how to keep my nose warm — it is a large, long, sharp organ, and the jacket water don't seem to circulate to the end —," Dr. Hodgson wrote *The Horseless Age* in 1903, "financial dyspepsia and flatulence of the pocketbook could be as easily borne as minor ills."

HOFFMAN — William G. Hoffman of 79 Bolivar Street in Cleveland, Ohio was listed as an automobile manufacturer in the Hiscox book *Horseless Vehicles, Automobiles, Motor Cycles* published in 1900. The extent of his automotive activity is not known; a turn-of-the-century Cleveland city directory reference to his business indicates him as the "manufacturer of fine delivery wagons."

Jacob Hoffman of 41 Michigan Street in Cleveland, Ohio was indicated to be "experimenting" with an automobile in 1902, as revealed in a February issue of the *Automobile & Motor Review*.

The Hoffman Brothers Motor Company was organized with a capital stock of $1 million early in 1919 in Omaha, Nebraska for the manufacture of automobiles. William L. Hoffman, Ralph S. Willnent and Verne G. Cawley were the incorporators. Manufacture is doubted.

1902 Hoffman Steam Carriage, runabout, NAHC

HOFFMAN — Cleveland, Ohio — (1901-1904) — Louis E. Hoffman was president of the Hoffman Bicycle Company of Cleveland, and he went automotive initially with a light 700-pound 6 hp chain-drive steam car the boiler of which was wound with piano wire and tested to 600 pounds cold water pressure. The experimental model of 1900 was followed by a small production in 1901 which provided sufficient encouragement for its inventor to organize the Hoffman Automobile and Manufacturing Company in January 1902. In September that year Louis Hoffman himself drove one of his cars to finish third (behind a White and a Geneva) in the steam class at the first annual races at Glenville Track sponsored by the Cleveland Automobile Club. Four months later, in January 1903, the first Hoffman gasoline car was introduced. There was popular demand, Hoffman said, for a "compact, strong, but light and tasty Gasoline Runabout." Hoffman supplied it with a single-cylinder 7 1/2 hp tourer that he referred to rather cumbersomely as the Hoffman General Utility Gasoline Car. About this time, in order to secure necessary capital to expand, Hoffman had reorganized his company, retaining its general managership but passing the presidency on to Edward D. Shurmer. Some friction may have developed because in late 1903 Hoffman was reported to have resigned from his company to "go into other business." (The other business turned out to be the Reliance Motor Car Company in Detroit the executive staff of which he joined. Hoffman was subsequently killed in an automobile accident in 1912.) Production in 1903 was approximately 100 cars. The Hoffman name for both car and company remained through the end of that year, and into early 1904 for the steam cars. Thereon the steam cars were discontinued, and the Hoffman company was reorganized as the Royal Motor Car Company to manufacture the gasoline car called the Royal Tourist.

1901 HOFFMAN

	FP	5	4	3	2	1
Steam Stanhope (6 hp)	750	3100	4200	6300	10.500	22.000

1902 HOFFMAN

	FP	5	4	3	2	1
Steam Stanhope (6 hp)	1200	3100	4200	6300	10,500	22,000

1903 HOFFMAN

	FP	5	4	3	2	1
Steam Stanhope (6 hp)	950	3100	4200	6300	10,500	22,000
Gasoline Tr (7 1/2 hp, 72" wb)	950	2500	3500	5000	8500	18.000

1904 HOFFMAN

	FP	5	4	3	2	1
Steam Stanhope (6 hp)	1000	3100	4200	6300	10,500	22,000

1903 Hoffman Gasoline, touring, HAC

1931 Hoffman, 4-dr. sedan, WLB

HOFFMAN — Detroit, Michigan — (1931) — The Hoffman attempted to succeed where Hamlin-Holmes had failed after a decade of trying. The Hoffman failed too, and it required just a year to do it. This front-wheel-drive car was designed by Roscoe C. Hoffman, a consulting engineer from Detroit. It was introduced to the automobile trade press in March of 1931. Like the Hamlin of the year previous, it featured a dual-axle system. Unlike the Hamlin, it had an outward look very much its own, with four-door sedan body by Baker-Raulang. The engine was a Lycoming straight-eight. Independent rear wheel suspension was complemented by conventional semi-elliptic springs at the front in a torque arm arrangement that Hoffman said was similar to that used on the Bugatti, Austro Daimler and Alfa Romeo. Two prototypes were built and tested, but Hoffman could not find the financing necessary to proceed into manufacture. His car arrived just about the time America had awakened to the fact that what it was experiencing was a depression. There was no money to be had anywhere for Hoffman.

1909 Hofmann, touring, NAHC

HOFMANN — Aiken, South Carolina — (1909) — In addition to being one of the most acclaimed concert pianists of the Twentieth Century, Josef Hofmann displayed a good bit of dexterity and talent in automobile deisgn. He built his first car in Europe in 1902, and followed with another in the United States which was begun in 1908. (European born, Hofmann had married an American in 1905 and subsequently became a U.S. citizen.) The U.S.-built car was fitted with a 50/60 hp six-cylinder engine, which Hofmann doubtless purchased, set into a long-wheelbase chassis that Hofmann built himself with the assistance of his chauffeur at his American home in Aiken, South Carolina. The body, which he designed as a demi-limousine that could be converted into an open touring car, was built for him by the Springfield Metal Body Company. The car was completed in Massachusetts and shipped from there on May 24th, 1909 to Havre, France whence Hofmann drove it himself to his villa in Switzerland. Presumably the car remained in Europe.

HOFWEBER — LaCrosse, Wisconsin — (1913) — Whether this car would have been known as the Hofweber or the Hoff had it seen production is not known. It was the idea of the Hofweber brothers — Joseph E. and August H. — who organized the Hoff Motor Company in February of 1913. Fours and sixes to sell in the $800 range were projected, and prototype models they had designed were then being tested. Because construction of a factory in LaCrosse would take time to complete, initial production was to take place at the Wahl Motor Car Company in Detroit, Joseph Hofweber being involved in that venture too. The Hofweber never proceeded beyond prototype; the Wahl saw only a small production before bankruptcy arrived in 1914. Thereon the Hofweber brothers returned to their father's automobile agency on Main Street in LaCrosse and got back to work. The Hofweber family remained in the dealership business for several decades thereafter.

HOLBROOK-ARMSTRONG — Racine, Wisconsin (1912) — The Holbrook-Armstrong Iron Company was located at Junction Avenue N.W. at the corner of 16th in Racine, right across the street from the carriage-building Racine-Sattley Company. In 1910 Holbrook-Armstrong built the engines for the new Racine-Sattley cars, and it was this experience which provided the impetus for Holbrook-Armstrong to venture further into the automotive field. In 1911 the company's capital stock was increased from $150,000 to $300,000 in order to increase production of its four-cylinder engines. Charles Buehner was president of the firm, Arthur Buehner was vice-president and J.A. Armstrong was secretary-treasurer. And they soon began trying to put a stop to rumors. There was no question that Holbrook-Armstrong was building three chassis in November from designs submitted by a Chicago firm but, as *The Automobile* noted that month, "reports that the company will engage in the business of building complete cars are denied although practically all parts are now being made." The reason for the Holbrook-Armstrong reluctance to publicity is curious. During 1912 there indeed was a small production of four-cylinder Holbrook-Armstrong cars, though company officers remained loath to talk about them.

HOLBROOK-SINGER — Early in 1908 in Larchmont, New York, the Holbrook-Singer Company was incorporated for the manufacture of motors and vehicles. Henry F. Holbrook and Charles Singer, Jr. of New York City, together with David J. Levitt of Larchmont, were the principals involved. This venture seems to have proceeded little further than incorporation. In 1909 Charles Singer, Jr. was made general sales manager for the Palmer & Singer Manufacturing Company, his father being half of the partnership producing the Palmer-Singer automobile.

HOLCOMB — During the fall of 1903 the Holcomb Manufacturing Company was organized with a capital stock of $50,000 in Hartford, Connecticut to take over the business of H.C. Holcomb, who was described at the time as having "been manufacturing automobiles in a small way." Incorporators of the new venture included H.C. Holcomb and Henry W.B. Manson. Further details are lacking.

A car called the Holcomb has been indicated on various rosters as having been built in 1913 by the American Box Ball Company of Indianapolis, Indiana. There was such a firm at Draper and Van Buren engaged in the manufacture of "box ball alleys" and headed by J.F. Hoke and his son Fred. Conceivably, they may have built an automobile for their own use, or had one built for them. Certainly manufacture was not contemplated.

HOLDEN — Boston, Massachusetts — (1914) — George B. Holden was the Boston agent for the Indian motorcycle and in 1914 he purloined, with permission, three Indian motorcycle engines from the Springfield factory in order to build himself three cyclecars. The cars were tandem two-seaters with friction transmission and chain drive — and Holden reported them to be "successful performers." Whether he entertained notions of persuading the Hendee Manufacturing Company, makers of the Indian motorcycle, into manufacturing his car is not known. But Hendee did not do so. The company had built an experimental Indian cyclecar itself that year, which it also had no intention of manufacturing.

HOLDEN — Comanche, Texas — (1915) — C. Clarence Holden of Comanche produced one of the more unusual three-wheelers ever built in America. At first glance, it looked a four-wheeler which had lost its right front wheel and front axle. A glance to the rear revealed that the two wheels back there were not aligned, but staggered, with the drive taken only to the furthermost (left) wheel. The reason for this unusual configuration, Holden commented, was motoring comfort. "As no two wheels strike a cross obstruction, such as a railroad track, at once, much bounce is done away with, and instead there is an easy tipping, rocking motion, in connection with which considerable virtue is attributed to the underslung frame," *Automobile Topics* said. Tread was the standard fifty-six inches. "Because the driving and steering wheels are in line with each other," Holden claimed, "the car can climb about anywhere, in and over and through ruts, leaving the idler wheel (the staggered right) to take care of itself." Holden took his car to Dallas with hopes of securing capital for manufacture. It does not appear he ever found it. Nor does it seem that the 60 hp racing version he was planning to build ever made it to a race track.

1915 Holden Three-Wheeler, HAC

HOLDS — The Holds Tractor Company was a Delaware incorporation from the spring of 1917 with a capital stock of $250,000 and the plan to "manufacture and sell tractors, automobiles and vehicles of all kinds." Herbert E. Latter, C.L. Rimlinger and Clement M. Egner were the incorporators. Manufacture of a car is doubted.

HOLL — The Holl Motor Carriage Service Company was organized in Camden, New Jersey early in 1914 with a capital stock of $125,000 for the manufacture of automobiles and motorcycles. A.H. and L.E. Holl, in association with H.C. Henry, were the principals involved. Manufacture of a car is doubted.

1900 Holland, runabout, JB

HOLLAND — Park River, North Dakota — (1898-1908) — The total number of cars built, as well as the inclusive dates of their manufacture, is difficult to determine because Sam Holland didn't brag much, nor did he bother informing the trade press of his exploits. He was a blacksmith in Park River, and he seems to have built the cars for employees in his shop or friends in the neighborhood. There were at least six Hollands built. The first was a steam car which he began around 1898, which was fol-

lowed by a gasoline highwheeler. Two low-wheeled runabouts were next, one of which remains extant today. These were interesting cars, powered by a 4 hp single-cylinder engine of Holland's own design and fitted with two radiators, one to cool the water in the head, the other the water in the block. Chain drive, two-speed planetary transmission and tiller steering were typical for the period. The Holland's frame was a box perimeter of angle iron with only the engine, clutch and transmission serving as structural bracing. The wheelbase was 67 inches, tread 55, and the vehicle sat two comfortably. Most probably, further cars followed these turn of the century runabouts, but this cannot be documented. In 1908, however, two more Holland cars were known to have been built. These were air-cooled cars of four cylinders, and a short notice appearing in an issue of the *Grand Forks* (North Dakota) *Herald* that year suggested that Sam Holland was all set for manufacture. This never followed, although possibly a few more cars did from Sam Holland's blacksmith shop.

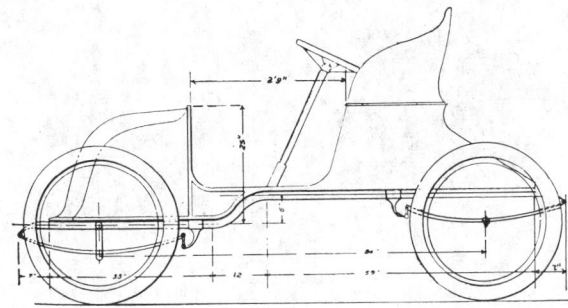

1902 Holland, runabout, NAHC

HOLLAND — Jersey City, New Jersey — (1902-1903) — The Holland Automobile Company of Jersey City was successor to the firm which had built the Boisselot gasoline car in 1901. The Hollands that were built as complete cars were steamers, though most of the company's efforts seem to have been concentrated on the sale of components for the building of gasoline cars by do-it-yourselfers. Both air- and water-cooled motors of 1-1/4 to 12 hp, twelve varied chassis, a "combination mixer, air heater and air regulator" in small and large size, and steering wheels of manganese bronze, aluminum and cast steel were offered in the Holland catalog. The body was up to the do-it-yourselfer.

HOLLAND — Holland, Michigan — (1910) — Fred W. Jackson was the president, G.Y. Courtney the vice president and A. Leenhauts the secretary-treasurer of the Holland Automobile Manufacturing Company, a firm which was indicated in the Ware yearbook of the industry in 1910 as a producer of automobiles. Documentation regarding the automobiles built is lacking.

HOLLE — Whether the Holle Automobile and Manufacturing Company manufactured any cars is not known. The firm shared quarters with the Sunset Automobile Company at 1814 Market Street in San Francisco in 1904 and 1905, however. Sunset did indeed manufacture automobiles there. In 1906 the San Francisco earthquake destroyed the Sunset factory. Joseph Holle, who prior to the earthquake had also operated a bicycle and automobile dealership at 20th and Folsom streets in San Francisco, remained in town, continuing in business as an automobile/bicycle dealer. Meanwhile Sunset moved to San Jose to continue automobile manufacture.

1904 Holley, runabout, WLB

HOLLEY — Bradford, Pennsylvania — (1900-1904) — George M. Holley of Bradford built his first automobile in 1897, and organized the Holley Motor Company at the turn of the century to build it. His runabout looked rather French, with a coil radiator, and lots of brass. Holley was one of the few manufacturers who chose not to guess at horsepower, nor exaggerate it; his single-cylinder engine, tests revealed, developed 5.27 hp. Though wheel steering was advanced for the day, and the price was attractive, George Holley couldn't make a go of it with his Holley, nor with the motorized bicycles which were built for him by the Olive Wheel Company in Syracuse, New York. But he was also sole U.S. agent for the French

Longuemare carburetor, and in 1904 decided to get into carburetor manufacture. He sold the Holley Motor Company to a group of businessmen who styled themselves as the Bradford Motor Works and sold the leftover parts of the Holley as a kit car under the marque name of Bradford. The whole Holley had been priced at $650. The sum of its parts could be put together as the Bradford for only $277.50.

1900-1904 HOLLEY
Holley — 1-cyl., 5.27 hp, 60" wb

	FP	5	4	3	2	1
Touring Rbt.	650	1600	2700	3800	5800	12,000

1915 Hollier Eight, touring, HAC

HOLLIER — Jackson & Chelsea, Michigan — (1915-1921) — Produced by Charles Lewis, former president of the Jackson Automobile Company, and built in the two Michigan factories of his Lewis Spring and Axle Company, the Hollier was equipped with a 40 hp V-8 of the company's own design, supplemented in 1917 with a Falls-engined six. It was a completely conventional car, distinguished only perhaps by Charles Lewis' insistence in providing open models only despite the industry trend toward providing at least a few closed cars. Sales were only minimally satisfactory, and the eight was discontinued when materials shortages became critical during World War I. Production, which in the early years had peaked at 3000 units, never approached that figure when manufacture was fully resumed following the Armistice. Lewis finally decided that a change of name to Hollier Automobile Company from Lewis Spring and Axle might better indicate the complete nature of his production. The name change came in 1921, and it was too late.

1915 HOLLIER
Eight — 40 hp, 112" wb

Touring	985	3100	4200	6300	10,500	22,000

1916 Hollier Eight, roadster, HAC

1916 HOLLIER
Eight — 40 hp, 112" wb

Model 158 Rdst.-3P	985	3200	4300	6500	11,000	23,000
Model 168 Tour.-5P	985	3100	4200	6300	10,500	22,000

1917 Hollier Eight, touring, HAC

1917 HOLLIER
Six — 21.6 hp, 116" wb

	FP	5	4	3	2	1
Model 186 Tour.-5P	895	3000	4000	6000	9500	21,000

Eight — 40 hp, 116" wb

Model 178 Tour.-5P	1185	3300	4400	6700	12,000	24,000
Model 178 Rdst.-4P	1185	3500	4500	7000	13,000	25,000

1918 Hollier Eight, touring, HAC

1918 HOLLIER
Six — 25.35 hp, 116" wb

Model 206 Tour.-5P	1085	3000	4000	6000	9500	21,000

Eight — 40 hp, 116" wb

Model 188 Tour.-5P	1285	3300	4400	6700	12,000	24,000

1920 Hollier Six, touring, HAC

1919-1921 HOLLIER
Six — 55 hp, 120" wb

Model 206 Touring	1785	3000	4000	6000	9500	21,000
Model 206-B Touring	1985	3100	4100	6200	10,000	21,500

HOLLIS ELECTRIC — Tiffin, Ohio — (1921-1922) — The first Hollis was a tractor. It was the invention of Otis A. Hollis of Pittsburgh (Pennsylvania) who interested a number of investors in Tiffin (Ohio) in its manufacture. The Hollis Tractor Company was the result, and plans were made to convert the Strawboard building in Tiffin into a factory. Meantime Hollis was busy in Pittsburgh, with his chief mechanical engineer Walter H. Roe, trying to simplify his tractor design and reduce the number of parts from 700 to 200. All the foregoing happened between May of 1919 and February of 1921. On August 27th, 1921 Tiffin investors in the Hollis project were informed that a Hollis automobile was also in the works, but it was being built in Hollywood, California. "The auto, which is said to eliminate gears and transmission, will run from power furnished by a dynamo," reported the Tiffin *Daily Advertiser*. " . . . it will be taken on a transcontinental trip as a test and for demonstration purposes . . . the car will visit Tiffin, en route to Pittsburgh. President Hollis has been in Hollywood the past several months supervising construction of the car." Three days later, Tiffinites were informed that the car had been tested in Hollywood, had attained a speed of 25 mph, and had required no adjustments. Two weeks after that, it was revealed that the transcontinental trek was off, and that the car would be shipped by rail to Pittsburgh and following testing there would be driven to Tiffin. On October 4th the Hollis car arrived in Pittsburgh. It remained there into the new year. In March of 1922, however, the car finally showed up in Tiffin, and its operation was explained to 100 of the town's stockholders in the Hollis Tractor Company. The last heard of this entire venture was in July. In three years just one Hollis tractor and one Hollis electric car were built. Reconstruction of the Strawboard building in Tiffin into a factory for the Hollis was never completed.

HOLLISTER — The Hollister Standard Motor Company, Inc. was organized in New York City late in 1912 with a capital stock of $675,000 "to construct and sell motor vehicles and supplies." Incorporators were W.H. Langford, Learned White and H.H. Sevier. Manufacture of a car is doubted.

1914 Holly, model A-Six, 6-pass. touring, WLB

HOLLY SIX — Mount Holly, New Jersey — (1913-1915) — The Holly Motor Company succeeded the bankrupt Otto Gas Engine Company and after continuing production of the Otto-designed Ottomobile for the 1912 season launched the Holly Six for 1913. A 38 hp car on a 130-inch wheelbase, the Holly was offered as a touring car only during its maiden season, though a roadster was added in 1914 and continued through 1915, the last year of the Holly Six's existence. Like many small enterprises of that era, the Holly Motor Company came onto the scene quietly, and left it just as quietly, with no one paying particular attention in the meantime.

1913 HOLLY SIX
Model A-Six — 6-cyl., 38 hp, 130" wb

	FP	5	4	3	2	1
Touring-5P	2500	3500	4500	7000	13,000	25,000
Touring-7P	2750	3300	4400	6700	12,000	24,000

1914 HOLLY SIX
Model A-Six — 6-cyl., 38 hp, 130" wb

Touring-5P	2750	3500	4500	7000	13,000	25,000
Touring-6P	2750	3500	4500	7000	13,000	25,000
Touring-7P	2750	3300	4400	6700	12,000	24,000
Roadster-2P	2750	3700	4700	7300	13,700	26,000

1915 HOLLY SIX
Model A-Six — 6-cyl., 38 hp, 130" wb

Touring-5P	2750	3500	4500	7000	13,000	25,000
Roadster-2P	2750	3700	4700	7300	13,700	26,000

HOLMES — The Holmes Automobile, Engineering and Power Company was a $200,000 incorporation from Chicago, Illinois in early 1903 for the manufacture of cars. Iowa had been selected as the manufacturing site. Incorporation seems to have been as far as this venture proceeded.

The Holmes & Childs Motor Company was organized in Camden, New Jersey during the fall of 1905 with a capital stock of $25,000 for the manufacture of "motor vehicles of every description." William H. Childs and Frank C. Holmes were the partners involved. Manufacture of a car is doubted.

The Holmes Motor Company was a $500,000 Maine incorporation from the summer of 1911 "to manufacture, contract for, deal in and repair gas engines, motor cars, motor boats, flying machines and any and every other vehicle requiring or using motive power." L.B. Swett and G.E. Burnham were the incorporators. Manufacture of a car is doubted.

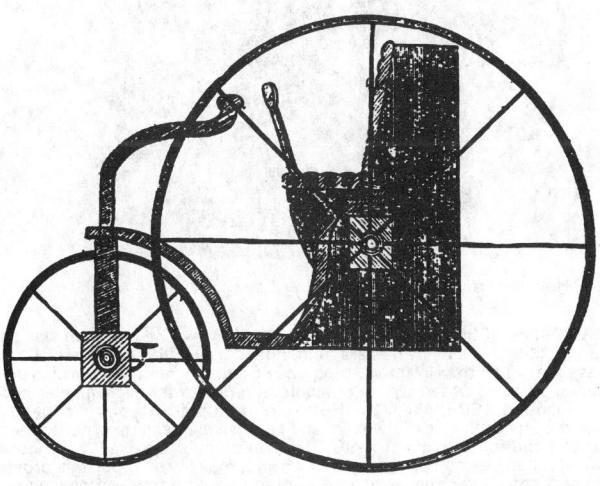

1895 Holmes, NAHC

HOLMES — Gloversville, New York — (1895) — In 1895 Lyman S. Holmes of Gloversville fitted a three-horsepower rotary gasoline engine of his own design into a three-wheeled vehicle he had run up as well. Its single front wheel was three feet in diameter, its two rear wheels (between which the two-passenger seat was centered) were a full six feet high. One cannot imagine the car having performed well, but Holmes insisted that it did run. He is not known to have built another.

HOLMES — San Jose, California — (1900) — In 1900 at his farm near San Jose, Frank H. Holmes built an automobile for his own use. Its gasoline engine is believed to have been a two-stroke. Apparently Holmes was just practicing, because he soon became involved with the Sunset Automobile Company which did manufacture automobiles.

HOLMES — Binghamton, New York — (1900)/Virginia City, Nevada — (1902) — Frank C. Holmes ran a bicycle repair shop from his home at 486 Chanango Street in Binghamton from 1897 to 1899. In 1900 he allied himself with one E.F. Gilmore and opened a shop at 74 State Street. There bicycles were built and repaired, and apparently a few gasoline automobiles were produced. By the end of 1900 the Holmes and Gilmore partnership had disbanded. In 1901 Frank Holmes allied himself with C.S. Millard and together they went into the automobile supply business on Sturges Street. No automobiles at all were produced of this partnership. References from Binghamton indicate that Frank Holmes left town for parts unknown about 1902. The parts unknown probably was Virginia City, Nevada where a man named Frank Holmes had established the Automobile Supply Company by the summer of 1902 and had also built himself a dos-a-dos steam carriage.

HOLMES STEAM — Danville, Illinois — (1902) — In 1884, after arriving initially in Danville as a serviceman for Huber Threshing Machines of Marion (Ohio), Robert Holmes elected to settle down in that town and in 1884 he began a small shop specializing in the sales of threshing machines and other farm machinery. His younger brother Grant joined him in 1893; a mine and mill supply store, and a bicycle agency and repair shop, followed. With the advent of the automotive age, so did the selling of automobiles. In 1902 Robert Holmes & Brother announced itself as "manufacturers and dealers in everything on wheels," and among the company's products that year was a steam car of the brothers' own design. It was marketed for one year only, and thereafter the company confined its selling to everything "else" on wheels. A third brother, Sherman Holmes, joined the company in 1905; Robert Holmes & Brothers, Inc. bought out the Danville Foundry and Machine Company in 1915, and the firm has prospered in the decades since. But never following 1902 did this company attempt automobile manufacture.

1906 Holmes, touring, HAC

HOLMES — Cambridgeport, Massachusetts — (1906-1907) — The Charles Holmes Machine Company offered a five-seater with a choice of either air-cooled ($1365, 30 mph top speed) or water-cooled ($1400, 40 mph) four-cylinder engine, plus two-cylinder water-cooled and four-cylinder air-cooled runabouts at $650 and $750. Charles Holmes designed the car's friction transmission, and the device which allowed him to advertise that a Holmes "starts from the seat." He did not bother to explain this device in his 1906 brochure, nor in 1907 when his car was marketed under the aegis of the Holmes Motor Vehicle Company. During the summer of 1907 Holmes Motor Vehicle went into bankruptcy following claims against it totaling $571. Chief among the creditors was the Charles Holmes Machine Company.

1907 Holmes, touring, WLB

1906-1907 HOLMES

	FP	5	4	3	2	1
Model H (4-cyl., air cooled, 100" wb)	1365	2000	3000	4200	6500	14,000
Model G (4-cyl., water cooled, 100" wb)	1400	2100	3100	4300	6800	14,500
Model D (2-cyl., water cooled, 80" wb)	650	1900	2900	4100	6400	13,500
Model E (4-cyl., air cooled, 80" wb)	750	1800	2800	4000	6200	13,000

1919 Holmes, touring, HAC

HOLMES — Canton, Ohio — (1918-1923) — Arthur Holmes was a vice-president and, for seven years, chief engineer of the H.H. Franklin Company. Not surprisingly, when he launched his Holmes Automobile Company of Canton, it was for manufacture of an air-cooled car. The Holmes was a six, which sold in the $2950-$4150 range, slightly more than the Franklin, though it was a larger car on a 126-inch wheelbase — "the world's only full-sized air-cooled car," the company said. The Holmes was also advertised as "America's Most Comfortable Car" — for reasons of its longer wheelbase, flexible chassis and full-elliptic springs — and was quite possibly America's ugliest at the time as well. From the front, it was variously said to resemble a caterpillar's head or the lungs of a patient who had died horribly. Although 4000 units were planned for 1918, production generally hovered around the 500 mark annually. A four-cylinder companion car had been planned, but the company was out of business before it could be produced. In December of 1921 a warrant was issued for the arrest of the vice-president of the Holmes company; the charge was larceny and embezzlement. In 1922 the Holmes Automobile Company was in receivership. The attempt to reorganize and refinance under receivership failed, and the Holmes was no more by May of 1923.

1918-1919 HOLMES
Series A — 6-cyl., 29.4 hp, 126" wb

	FP	5	4	3	2	1
Touring-5P	2900	4000	5000	8000	15,000	28,000

1920 Holmes, 4-pass. touring car, WLB

1920 HOLMES
Model I — 6-cyl., 29.4 hp, 126" wb

Touring-6P	2900	4000	5000	8000	15,000	28,000
Roadster-4P	2900	4200	5200	8400	15,700	29,000
Sedan 2-door-5P	3900	2000	3000	4200	6500	14,000
Sedan 4-door-5P	4000	2200	3200	4400	7000	15,000
Sedan-7P	4000	2100	3100	4200	6800	14,500
Sport Coupe-3P	3500	2300	3300	4600	7500	16,000

1921 Holmes, touring, HAC

1921 HOLMES
Series 4 — 6-cyl., 31.5 hp, 126" wb

Touring-7P	3350	3900	4800	7700	14,300	27,000

680

	FP	5	4	3	2	1
Roadster-4P	3350	4000	5000	8000	15,000	28,000
Artcraft-5P	3900	3900	4800	7700	14,300	27,000
Coupe-4P	4250	2300	3300	4600	7500	16,000
Sedan-6P	4550	2000	3000	4200	6500	14,000

1922 Holmes, coupe, HAC

1922 HOLMES
Series 4 — 6-cyl., 32 hp, 126" wb

Touring-7P	2950	3900	4800	7700	14,300	27,000
Roadster-4P	2950	4000	5000	8000	15,000	28,000
California Sedan-5P	3200	3900	4800	7700	14,300	27,000
Coupe-4P	3850	2300	3300	4600	7500	16,000
Sedan-6P	4150	2000	3000	4200	6500	14,000

1923 HOLMES
Series 4 — 6-cyl., 32 hp, 126" wb

Touring-7P	2500	3900	4800	7700	14,300	27,000
Roadster-2P	2500	4000	5000	8000	15,000	28,000
Artcraft-7P	2600	3900	4800	7700	14,300	27,000
Coupe-4P	3300	2300	3300	4600	7500	16,000
Sedan-7P	3600	2000	3000	4200	6500	14,000

HOLMES-SCHMIDT — Chicago, Illinois — (1906) — In November of 1906 the Holmes-Schmidt Motor Company of Chicago announced its forthcoming entry into the automobile industry. Its product was to be a four-cylinder 24 hp car offered as a runabout complete with detachable tonneau. The Holmes-Schmidt was to be introduced shortly as a 1907 model. It does not appear the car ever went into manufacture, though a prototype was built.

1903 Holsman, runabout, JAC

HOLSMAN — Chicago, Illinois — (1903-1910) — The Holsman was the grand-daddy of all highwheelers, and indeed it was the commercial success enjoyed by the Holsman Automobile Company of Chicago which persuaded so many other Midwest manufacturers into the highwheeler business around 1906, the year Holsman sextupled its plant capacity, increased its capital stock twofold, and put on a nightshift in order to meet the demand for its piquant if primitive two-cylinder carriage automobile. Initially, the Holsman drive was by 7/8-inch manila rope, but this proved unsatisfactory after sustained wet-weather use, so Henry K. Holsman and associate C.H. Bryan devised a chain braided over with manila and steel wire at first, later a naked chain alone. Primeval brakes acted directly against the steel tires and were hand-operated because, as the company said, "in emergencies and under excitement the foot cannot be relied upon to act sub-consciously or automatically, and to do the right thing instantly." Ultimately, Henry K. Holsman did not do the right thing either. Unlike other highwheeler manufacturers who added pneumatic-tired standard models to their lines, Holsman stuck with the highwheeler idea to the end. When his company in Chicago went into receivership in 1910, he relocated fifty miles west in Plano and produced a Holsman lookalike that he called, not very imaginatively, the Independent Harvester.

1903 HOLSMAN
Highwheeler — 2-cyl., 5hp

Runabout	650	2300	3300	4600	7500	16,000

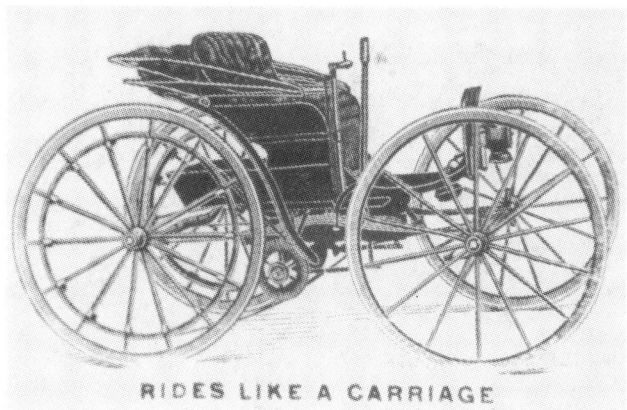

1904 Holsman, model 3, runabout, HAC

1904 HOLSMAN
Highwheeler — 2-cyl., 7hp

	FP	5	4	3	2	1
Model 3 Runabout-2P	650	2300	3300	4600	7500	16,000
Model 4 Runabout-4P	700	2350	3400	4700	7800	16,500
Model 5 Runabout-2P	600	2300	3300	4600	7500	16,000

1905 HOLSMAN
Highwheeler — 2-cyl., 10 hp, 66'' wb

	FP	5	4	3	2	1
Model 3 Piano Body-2P	650	2300	3300	4600	7500	16,000
Model 6 Surrey	800	2400	3400	4800	8000	17,000
Model 8 Folding Front Seat	800	2400	3400	4800	8000	17,000

1906 Holsman, model 6, runabout, HAC

1906 HOLSMAN
Highwheeler — 2-cyl., 10 hp, 65'' wb

	FP	5	4	3	2	1
No. 3 Runabout-2P	650	2300	3300	4600	7500	16,000
No. 6 Runabout-4P	800	2350	3400	4700	7800	16,500

1907 Holsman, model 3, runabout, OCW

1907 HOLSMAN
Highwheeler — 2-cyl., 10 hp, 65'' wb

	FP	5	4	3	2	1
No. 3 Runabout	650	2300	3300	4600	7500	16,000
No. 9 Runabout	700	2350	3400	4700	7800	16,500
No. 10 Runabout	750	2400	3400	4800	8000	17,000
No. 11 Touring (76'' wb)	800	2500	3500	5000	8500	18,000

1908 Holsman, model 11, surrey, HAC

1908 HOLSMAN
Highwheeler — 2-cyl., 4/5 hp, 75'' wb

	FP	5	4	3	2	1
No. 5 Runabout	650	2300	3300	4600	7500	16,000
No. 9 Runabout	700	2350	3400	4700	7800	16,500
No. 10 Runabout	750	2400	3400	4800	8000	17,000
No. 11 Surrey	800	2500	3500	5000	8500	18,000

1909 Holsman, model 15-K, couplette, GR

1910 Holsman, model 10-K, coupe, HAC

1909 HOLSMAN
Highwheeler — 2-cyl., 4/5 hp

	FP	5	4	3	2	1
No. 4-K Piano Box Buggy (66 1/2" wb)	500	2200	3200	4400	7000	15,000
No. 9-K Runabout (80" wb)	625	2300	3300	4600	7500	16,000
No. 10-K Sthp. (80" wb)	675	2300	3300	4600	7500	16,000
No. 11-K Surrey (92" wb)	740	2400	3400	4800	8000	17,000
No. 15-K Coupe (80" wb)	800	2000	3000	4200	6500	14,000

Highwheeler — 4-cyl., 26 hp

	FP	5	4	3	2	1
No. 9-H Runabout (80" wb)	850	2300	3300	4600	7500	16,000
No. 10-H Sthp. (80" wb)	900	2400	3400	4800	8000	17,000
No. 11-H Surrey (92" wb)	965	2500	3500	5000	8500	18,000
No. 15-H Coupe (80" wb)	1000	2200	3200	4400	7000	15,000

1910 HOLSMAN
Highwheeler — 2-cyl., 12 hp

	FP	5	4	3	2	1
Model 10-K Rbt. (80" wb)	725	2400	3400	4800	8000	17,000
Model 10-K Coupe (80" wb)	850	2000	3000	4200	6500	14,000
Model 4 Runabout (65" wb)	550	2300	3300	4600	7500	16,000
Model 9 Runabout (65" wb)	650	2400	3400	4800	8000	17,000
Model 10 Rbt. (80" wb)	725	2450	3500	4900	8300	17,500
Model 6 Roadster (75" wb)	600	2500	3500	5000	8500	18,000

Highwheeler — 4-cyl., 26 hp, 80" wb

	FP	5	4	3	2	1
Model H-15 Coupe	1000	2300	3300	4600	7500	16,000
Model H-11 Touring-4P	965	2400	3400	4800	8000	17,000

1901 Holson, MVMA

HOLSON — Chicago, Illinois — (1901-1904) — In a May 1903 issue of *Motor Age*, A.B. Holson of Chicago was described as a "genial genius" and "one of the most untiring among persistent inventors." He was most assuredly the latter, because he had been trying to get into production with his automotive idea (an electric motor which could be incorporated in the traction wheel hub) since the turn of the century when he was working for the Helios-Upton Company days and moonlighting with his invention nights. He had a two-wheeler with his hub-motor ready to demonstrate at the Chicago Automobile Show in early 1901. "The vehicle certainly moved, although not at what one would term a 'hot pace'," commented *The Motor Vehicle Review* at the time. "He has not yet perfected the steering arrangements, hence he has difficulties in that direction." Holson was not discouraged. For the 1904 Chicago Automobile Show, he had a three-wheeler ready, driven by a half-horsepower hub motor in the front wheel. It didn't move at a "hot pace" either, but at least it steered admirably. Because Holson believed its power application to have gyroscopic qualities, he sometimes referred to the vehicle as a Gyroscope, and he seemed anxious to have it produced. Production never was forthcoming, however. Meantime, A.B. Holson had happened upon another promoter, one M.B. Church who organized the Holson Motor Patents Company in Grand Rapids (Michigan) to exploit the Holson invention. Since Holson had thus far proceeded from two wheels to three, it was not illogical that he would try four next. And he did so, but with a truck. The Holson Gyroscope Truck also appeared at the Chicago Automobile Show of 1904. And Holson was now envisioning adaptation of his idea to an electro-gasoline automobile because, according to promoter Church, "of the readiness with which it can be applied to the gasoline motor flywheel, there to act both as a motor and generator." Autolet was proposed as the name for such a vehicle. It never arrived. But finally, late in 1904, the Holson hub-wheel idea did see production in Grand Rapids, in the Couple-Gear truck, which was built into the early Twenties. The Couple-Gear was not known for a "hot pace" either, but it steered fine. The available evidence indicates that A.B. Holson never applied his hub-motor idea to a four-wheeled automobile.

HOLT — Stockton, California — (1899) — That Holt Brothers, manufacturers of agricultural machinery in Stockton, ever proceeded into automobile manufacture is doubtful, but the firm did have that intention, and probably a prototype was built. "They have engaged a prominent mechanic and inventor of their city as chief engineer," *The Horseless Age* revealed in April that year, "and he has a new type of gasoline motor under construction."

1908 Hol-Tan, roadster, WLB

HOL-TAN — New York, New York — (1908) — G.P. and C.H. Tangeman and E.R. Hollander established the Hol-Tan Company in New York City in January of 1906 as a motor vehicle dealership. The partnership had been casually importing Italian Fiats into this country since 1902. The $100,000 incorporation simply made it official. Not quite two years later, in mid-November, the Hol-Tan Company announced that it had given up the Fiat agency and would "hereafter sell American cars only." The truth was that Fiat in Italy had taken the agency away from Hol-Tan, pursuant to the manufacture of the American Fiat in Poughkeepsie. The American car that Hol-Tan would now sell was a four-cylinder 25 hp Moon built in St. Louis, shipped to New York and cloaked there with new standard coachwork or special bodies by Locke, Quinby and Demarest. The resulting Hol-Tans were expensive automobiles, in the $3000-plus range, and were produced for one year only. Apparently the company had visions of improving the breed by racing, but didn't manage that at all. Although Hol-Tan was the first American company to sign up for the epic New York to Paris race of 1908, it never produced a car for the event; and though the Hol-Tan was entered in the AAA Reliability Run that summer, the company made an eleventh hour substitution and sent a Shawmut instead, Hol-Tan being the New York agency for that Massachusetts-built car. In 1909 Hol-Tan returned to being a dealership exclusively, adding the Delaunay-Belleville and the Lancia as its new imports following the failure of Shawmut.

1908 HOL-TAN
Hol-Tan — 4-cyl., 25 hp chassis

	FP	5	4	3	2	1
Standard Tour. (110" wb)	3000	2300	3300	4600	7500	16,000
Standard Rds. (110" wb)	3000	2400	3400	4800	8000	17,000
Roadster Special (121" wb)	3750	2500	3500	5000	8500	18,000
Touring Special (121" wb)	3750	2400	3400	4800	8000	17,000

1919 Holtom, touring, NAHC

HOLTOM — Clyde, Ohio — (1919)/New York, New York — (1934) — Hal Holtom was a British-born automotive consultant whose principal work was in the commercial vehicle field. In 1919, however, he designed and built a most unusual touring car. Its headlamps were shrouded with "eyelids," and there were concealed lights in the radiator grille to illuminate the grille bars. The instrument panel was cleverly designed, with a rear-view mirror of periscope type. The vehicle had a low angular look, enhanced by a two-piece windshield that folded to reinforce the snug-to-the-ground appearance. All seats and backs were air cushions. Apparently, taxi service had been among the *raisons d'etre* of the design, because the driver's seat was elevated for maximum visibility and the rear doors were controlled from the driver's compartment. Only the prototype was built, and indications are that it was put together in the shops of the Clyde Cars Company, builders of the Clydesdale trucks in Clyde, Ohio. The radiator cap design of the Holtom and the Clydesdale were identical. It would seem likely that Hal Holtom was serving as a consultant to Clyde Cars during this period. Later, in 1925, he is known to have worked on designs for a new Selden truck. In 1934 Hal Holtom again assayed the passenger-car field with a new taxicab that was dramatically streamlined and with an equally dramatic and striking grille design. Though production was announced, with New York City to be the streets upon which the new Holtom taxi would course, this venture never passed the prototype stage.

1934 Holtom, MVMA

1892 Holtzer-Cabot Elec. Carriage

HOLTZER-CABOT — **Brookline, Massachusetts** — **(1892, 1895)** —
Charles W. Holtzer emigrated to the United States from Karlsruhe, Germany in 1866, spending his first years in New York and Boston engaged in experimental work on artillery ammunition and in making tower clocks. In 1875 he moved to Brookline where he began the manufacture of electric devices, incorporating his enterprise under the name of the Holtzer-Cabot Electric Company. (George E. Cabot was his partner.) During this period Charles Holtzer operated the first telephone exchange outside of Boston, with fourteen subscribers and one toll line to the big city. In 1892 he built his first automobile, an eight-passenger electric brake custom built for Fiske Warren, the president of the paper-manufacturing S.D. Warren & Company of Boston. Its components had been purchased by Fiske Warren in London during a trip abroad, and the Holtzer-Cabot Company put them together splendidly. The car served Warren very well, and he drove it frequently, with only one minor mishap which apparently was sensationalized in the press. "The newspaper accounts of this accident that I have seen were evidently written by those who neither knew the truth about it nor wanted to," wrote Fiske Warren in an angry letter to the *Brookline Chronicle* which was printed in its June 17th, 1893 edition. Two years later, Holtzer-Cabot built another electric for Fiske Warren. A handsome machine designed by Edward C. Newcomb (who later became well known for carburetors), this Holtzer-Cabot again an English brake, though its components were of American manufacture entirely. It was a solid 5100 pounds and sat six to seven people. The electric motor weighed 450

1895 Holtzer-Cabot Electric, brake, NAHC

pounds and developed 7-1/2 hp at 250 rpm. Speed could be varied from 4 to 15 mph. The good-looking upholstery and coachwork were seen to by Chauncey Thomas & Company, a carriage-building firm in Boston. Charles Holtzer announced in November 1895 that he stood ready to build electric cars to special order of other clients, but most probably few orders resulted. His obituaries in 1927 do not mention his automotive activity. The Holtzer-Cabot Electric Company by that time had relocated in Jamaica Plain, and had entered the radio field. His will indicated that Charles Holtzer died a wealthy man.

1900 Holyoke, gasoline trap, NAHC

HOLYOKE — **Holyoke, Massachusetts** — **(1899-1903)** — Charles R. Greuter was a mechanical engineer at the Columbia Stoker Works in Holyoke when he built his first two experimental gasoline cars in 1898. In 1899 he resigned from Columbia and set himself up in a small shop as Holyoke Motor Works. His first production car was a trap, powered by a two-cylinder 7 hp gasoline engine and featuring "helical emergency springs" on the wheel axles which supplemented the full-elliptic leaf springs. In April 1899 Greuter announced that he planned to build ten vehicles a month, and also make semi-steel castings for the trade on the side. Greuter's venture became more serious the following year when people with money in Holyoke offered to invest same, and the Holyoke Automobile Company was organized in April 1900 with a capitalization of $200,000. "Won second prize in brake and obstacle contests at Madison Square Garden with a 2800 lb. Surrey against 1500 lb. Phaetons" was the rubber-stamped addition made to Holyoke brochures following the first automobile show in New York City later that year. Charles Greuter believed in building big and strong. Another of his stanhopes, produced in 1901 and dubbed the "baby elephant," scaled 3000 pounds and would have finished the Long Island Endurance Contest in fine fettle except for an unfortunate encounter with a stone wall. Somehow Greuter seemed happier experimenting than manufacturing. In August of 1903 his Holyoke shop consolidated with the Matheson Motor Car Company of Grand Rapids, Michigan. Thereafter engines and transmissions were built at Holyoke, and the cars assembled in Grand Rapids — and they were called Mathesons. Charles Greuter remained as chief engineer for the Matheson company following its move to Wilkes Barre, Pennsylvania in 1906, but left two years later to attempt the marketing of a new car of his own design, called the C.R.G. He became an engineering consultant subsequently. In 1923 he was employed by the Excelsior Motor Manufacturing Company of Chicago when his work was noticed by Fred Moskovics of Stutz in Indianapolis. Charles Greuter was on the engineering team at Stutz from that date until the end, serving as chief engineer for the company and the man most responsible for engine development of the famed DV-32.

HOMAN & SCHULTZ — The Homan & Schultz Company was organized in New York City early in 1904 with a capital stock of $20,000 for the manufacture of automobiles. Behind this venture were Frank D. Homan of Jersey City and Theo E. Schultz of New York City. Manufacture is doubted.

HOME — The Home Manufacturing Company was organized in Chicago, Illinois during the spring of 1916 with a capital stock of $36,000 to manufacture and deal in motor cars and motor vehicles. B.F. Bartel, L.B. Jacobs and W.F. Heineman were the incorporators. Manufacture of a car is doubted.

HOMER LAUGHLIN — **Los Angeles, California** — **(1916)** — Homer Laughlin, Sr. was one of the largest importers of china in the United States and in 1897 he moved from the East Coast to the West, settling in Los Angeles where he engaged very lucratively in real estate development. His son Homer Laughlin, Jr. was responsible for turning the family name into an automobile. In 1913 he established Homer Laughlin Engineers Corporation in L.A. and began development work on a new automobile to be powered by a V-8 engine (rated at 16 hp) of his own design. The fitting of front wheel drive was certainly a forward thinking notion on Laughlin's part, the fitting of a friction transmission certainly was not. Curiously, final drive to the front wheels was by chain; and the rear suspension was a curious (and patented) combination of twin cantilever springs. In a news story dated June 28th, 1916, Homer Laughlin Engineers Corporation announced the completion of three pilot 112-inch-wheelbase roadster models. "The factory is now turning out ten machines on order," the com-

1916 Homer Laughlin, roadster, WLB

pany advised. The sales price of the car was to be $1050. The new Homer Laughlin roadster was pictured in all of the automotive trade publications during the fall of 1916. But the car vanished from sight and news of it from press columns by early 1917. In 1918 Homer Laughlin Engineers Corporation reported that its new business would be the "auxiliary transmission for Ford cars" formerly known as the Langbein and now to be known as the Laughlin-Langbein auxiliary transmission.

HOMESTEAD — Joseph Doyle was a physician in West Homestead, Pennsylvania who designed an automobile in 1900 which was built for him in the wagon shop of Al Leuschner. Thereafter Doyle decided to get into the automobile business as the Homestead Motor Vehicle Company, but quickly changed his mind. Refer to Doyle.

1900 Hood Simplex Steamer, HS

HOOD STEAMER — Danvers, Massachusetts — (1899-1901; 1908-1910) — Ralph Otho Hood may not have been responsible for a large total production of automobiles, but he built a variety of different ones. The first was the Hood Steamer, also called the Electronomic Steamer and was occasionally referred to as the Simplex Steamer as well. Ralph Hood had built his first steam-powered car in 1899. In April 1900 he incorporated the Simplex Motor Vehicle Company for its manufacture. He built his second steamer in 1901. It was also his last. Although outwardly conventional, the Hood Steamer brimmed with ingenuity inside. The engine had four single acting cylinders and was made in a single casting with the steam chest. The intake valves were electro-magnetically operated by three small dry cell batteries. The flash boiler was good for 1000 p.s.i. The water tank was good for fifty miles, the kerosene fuel tank for seventy-five. One thousand dollars was the asking price, and 30 mph the comfortable cruising speed. Although his failure to secure financial backing resulted in his car never making it to production, the two Hood Steamers he did build remain to this day in the hands of family descendants. Following the Hood Steamer, Ralph Otho Hood designed the Gas-au-lec in Peabody, Massachusetts of which only a handful were made. And following the Gas-au-lec, Hood built another car he called the Otho which he began in 1908 and completed in 1910. This car's special feature was an electrical flywheel starter, which Ralph Hood later claimed was the first practical electric starter. Only the one Otho was built.

1908 Hood Otho Gasoline Car, HS

HOOPER — The A.H. Hooper Company of Detroit, Michigan was indicated as the builder of a cyclecar in the March 1914 issue of *Motor Print*. Further details are lacking, a company of such name not being listed in Detroit city directories of the period.

The Hooper Hoffer Company of New Haven, Connecticut was organized during the summer of 1917 for the manufacture of automobiles and wagons. Capital stock was $4000; Charles B. Hoffer and Maurice S. Hooper were the principals involved. Manufacture of a car is doubted.

HOOSIER LIMITED — The Hoosier Limited was a model of the Decatur of Decatur, Indiana, which was the automotive venture of Lembert W. Coppock. Refer to Decatur.

1914 Hoosier Scout, cyclecar, WLB

HOOSIER SCOUT — Indianapolis, Indiana — (1914) — The Hoosier Scout was one of the snazziest cyclecars produced in America. "It is built somewhat like a racer," *The Automobile* said, "and has good wind-cutting lines." Its racer appearance was a calculated one, since the car's designers — E.A. Shelley and Theodore A. Meyer — freely acknowledged that Bob Burman's Blitzen Benz had been their inspiration. Tandem seating was provided for two passengers, the frame was underslung, and there was a boattail in the back. Wheelbase was 96 inches, tread 36. The powerplant was a Spacke vee-twin, the transmission was friction disc, the final drive by belt. Forty to sixty miles to a gallon of gasoline was promised, and 200 miles to a quart of oil. The Hoosier Scout was built by the Warren Electric & Machine Company of Indianapolis.

1914 HOOSIER SCOUT
Cyclecar — 2-cyl., 9/13 hp, 96" wb

	FP	5	4	3	2	1
Tandem Roadster-2P	375	1000	1600	2700	4000	6500

HOOVER — St. Louis, Missouri — (1913-1914) — In mid-October of 1913, H.H. Hoover announced that he was organizing a company to manufacture a cyclecar of his own design. It featured a single-cylinder 5 hp air-cooled engine, sprocket chain drive, an underslung frame and wire wheels. Fenders were not fitted, and the car was cranked from the side. The Hoover cyclecar weighed 350 pounds, was placed on an 84-inch wheelbase, with 36-inch tread, and was priced at $375. If production proceeded beyond the prototype, it was at best minimal. H.H. Hoover never did find the wherewithal to form a company, though he tried manfully to do so in St. Louis.

1913-1914 HOOVER
Cyclecar — 1-cyl., 5 hp, 84" wb

Tandem Roadster-2P	375	950	1400	2500	3700	6000

HOPEWELL — Newton, Massachusetts — (1911) — The Hopewell was a Christmas present for the three-year-old son of Frank Hopewell of Newton. The elder Hopewell designed and built the entire car. Its wheelbase was 48 inches, its motive power was an electric motor with power transmitted "to a direct shaft by foot pressure, the brakebands on the rear axle . . . operated by a lever conveniently situated at the driver's right hand." The Hopewell arrived fully equipped with a set of tools, electric lights, clock, speedometer — and liability insurance policy.

684

HOPKINS — Wellington, Massachusetts — (1902) — Just before spring of 1902 the Hopkins Motor Carriage Company of 187 Middlesex Avenue in Wellington announced its presence on the automotive scene, stating its willingness to build gasoline automobiles to order and the happy circumstance that orders were on hand for two months. "They are at present working on light touring wagons for four persons and some skeleton rigs for speed work," *Cycle and Automobile Trade Journal* revealed. "They make both air and water cooled gasoline engines." Nothing further was heard of the Wellington Hopkins in 1903.

1902 Hopkins, gas runabout, NAHC

HOPKINS — New York, New York — (1902) — In December 1902, E.P. Hopkins of 143 West 103rd Street in New York City reported that he had built and intended to manufacture a light runabout powered by a single-cylinder two-stroke engine placed in a 58-inch wheelbase chassis, with chain drive and tiller steering, and a total package weight of 700 pounds. Hopkins stated that he had tested his machine for about three months and had covered about 1000 miles. This Hopkins was not heard from again in 1903 either.

1935 Hoppe & Streur, streamliner, MVMA

HOPPE & STREUR — Hollywood, California — (1935) — Yet another experimental car in the vogueish streamlining mode of the mid-Thirties was this creation of Allen M. Hoppe and Allyn F. Streur of Hollywood. The chassis was a six-cylinder (unidentified make) which the partners redesigned into a rear-engine configuration. The body structure was aluminum, and the car was sixteen feet long and seven feet wide. The rather sketchy bodywork may have been filled in later. A further source indicates that one E.F. Hunter, Jr. collaborated on the design as well.

HOPPER — The Hopper Automobile Sales Company, Inc. was organized in New Rochelle, New York early in 1918 for the manufacture of "automobiles, boats, locomotives and flying machines." Incorporators were Thomas T. Hopper of Pelham Manor, C.M. Thorne of New York City and Donald C. Muhleman of Orange, New Jersey. Manufacture of a car is doubted.

HORNECKER — The Hornecker Motor Manufacturing Company was organized in Geneseo, Illinois during the spring of 1908 for the manufacture of motor vehicles and accessories. Capital stock was $25,000; the incorporators were G.J. and George M. Hornecker and G. Blankenheim. Manufacture of an automobile is doubted.

HORSELESS — The Horseless Carriage Company of Barberton, Ohio has been cited on rosters as having built a car in 1901. The community of Barberton was incorporated in 1891 and thereafter published complete directories of the businesses in town into the early 1930's. In none of these listings does a Horseless Carriage Company appear. There was an automobile built in Barberton in 1901, however. Refer to Huene.

The Horseless Vehicle Company was organized in Pittsburgh, Pennsylvania during the fall of 1896 to manufacture a gasoline automobile invented by L. Hisig. An experimental car is known to have been built.

The Horseless Vehicle Company of New York City was organized in early 1899 with a capital stock of $150,000 for the manufacture of gasoline and electric vehicles. Directors of this venture were F.W. Dunton of Hollis, John H. Eldert and H.G. Fleck of Staten Island, and Abraham Booth and Harold D. Bernstein of Manhattan. Manufacture has not been confirmed.

The Horseless Wagon Company of Jamaica, New York is listed as an automobile manufacturer in the Hiscox book *Horseless Vehicles, Automobiles, Motor Cycles* published in 1900. Further documentation is lacking.

1899 Horsey Horseless, carriage, NAHC

HORSEY HORSELESS — Battle Creek, Michigan — (1899) — Uriah Smith of Battle Creek was sure he had the answer. The only reason the automotive idea had not thus far made better progress in America was the fact that a horseless carriage scared horses. This he believed could be solved by the simple expedient of placing a sculpted horse's head on the front of the automobile. "It would have all the appearance of a horse and carriage," he reasoned, "and hence raise no fears in any skittish animal; for the live horse would be thinking of another horse, and before he could discover his error and see that he had been fooled, the strange carriage would be passed, and then it would be too late to grow frantic and fractious." He recommended that the horse's head be made hollow, and thus it could also serve as a gasoline tank. Uriah Smith drew up his idea and submitted it to *The Horseless Age*, whose editors printed it, with a straight face. Whether Smith successfully motored in his Horsey Horseless Carriage in the Battle Creek area is not known.

HORTON — The Horton Boat, Engine and Supply Company was organized in Rochester, New York during the spring of 1908 with a capital stock of $75,000 for the manufacture of "boats, engines and automobiles." Incorporators were L. La V Horton, C.D. Larabee and M.A. Brush. Manufacture of a car is doubted.

HORTON AUTOETTE — Detroit, Michigan — (1910) — In October of 1910 the Horton Autoette Manufacturing Company was organized in Detroit with a capital stock of $100,000 for the manufacture of a diminutive vehicle invented by Allen Horton and J.J. Chapin. Also involved were A.J. Potter and H.B. Schantz. "In addition to two 30-inch wheels, set far apart, there is a pair of smaller auxiliary wheels, directly under the seat, which may be raised or lowered at will," reported *The Motor Age*. This venture seems to have stalled at the prototype stage. There is no discernible connection between the Horton Autoette and the Autoette built in Manistee (Michigan) or the Auto-Ette built in Chrisman (Illinois) a couple of years later.

HOSKINS — Los Angeles, California — (1920) — The Hoskins was built in Los Angeles of American components (Beaver engine) but its principle feature was Australian. So were the two men who built it. George J. Hoskins was the engineer, his son Leslie Hoskins the body designer. It was the elder Hoskins, a prominent member of the Sydney steel industry, who was

1920 Hoskins, touring, NAHC

responsible for the vehicle's front wheel drive. In the Hoskins, the differential attached to the front axle with the power applied by ''a new discovery in tooth gear.'' This gear, which Hoskins had patented in Australia, was so placed in the center of the wheel ''that it enables one to drive and steer at the same time.'' Front wheel wobble, a criticism of some earlier f.w.d. designs, was therefore theoretically eliminated. ''After long and severe testing,'' the elder Hoskins said, ''this gear has proved wear-resisting, prevents skidding and gives greater power and mileage on tires and gasoline.'' The body styled by Leslie Hoskins was designed ''to give the public something good to look at.'' It was interesting, with a shortish radiator grille and a large-ish cow-catcher of the sort not seen since the Grout steamer. Immediately upon completion of the prototype, Leslie Hoskins took the car to the top of Mt. Wilson, arriving at the apex with a motor he said was ''as cool as the proverbial cucumber.'' Thereafter he took off on a transcontinental trek, which was successfully completed too. One more test car was built, but manufacture did not follow.

1920 Hoskins, touring (father & son onboard), WJL

HOUGH — Chester, South Carolina — (1910) — The Hough Automobile Company was formed in 1910 of a partnership between D.P. Crosby and F.M. Hough. Crosby was president of the Chester Machine Company in town, and the new car designed by Hough was to be manufactured in its foundry on Gadsden Street. All Houghs were to be four-cylinder cars, offered as 22 hp runabouts and 40 hp tourers. The initial intent was for an assembled car, with the company branching into manufacture of all parts save engines later. Neither reality followed, however, this venture ending at the prototype stage.

HOUGHTON — Norwalk, Connecticut — (1897) — In 1897 W.C. Houghton of Norwalk built an electric automobile for himself with, as the *Norwalk Bulletin* put it, ''some assistance on the wood work from his manual training boys.'' Forty-pound half-horsepower motors were attached to either side of the carriage placed on steel springs attached at right angles to the rear axles. Houghton needed both hands to drive his car, the right for the steering handle, the left for the controller. The car's body was carriage-type painted black with red running gear. Houghton was hoping for speeds of 10 or 12 mph with a forty-mile range between charge-ups, but whether this was ever realized is not known.

HOUGHTON — West Newton, Massachusetts — (1900-1901) — In December of 1900, ''after experiments and study covering a period of five years,'' as *The Motor Vehicle Review* said, the Houghton Automobile Company of West Newton was at last into manufacture. Since the Houghton was a quite typical steamer of the era, with a two-cylinder engine and boiler heated by either kerosene or gasoline, and no distinctive engineering features at all, one is pressed to understand the reason for the long development period — unless of course it had been exaggerated, which was not unusual either. Houghton did have grand plans for a lavish production, but managed only to sell a few example of its $800-$850 stan-

hopes and $1100 surrey before going out of business later in 1901. The Houghton responsible for the car's design had been William C., with George S. Houghton presiding over the company and H.R. Houghton over its treasury.

1900 Houghton, stanhope, NAHC

HOUK — In late 1913 George W. Houk organized his Houk Manufacturing Company in Buffalo, New York with a capital stock of $900,000. Although he indicated a plan to produce automobiles, there is no evidence that he ever did so. The Houk wheel became famous, of course.

1910 Houpt, touring, NAHC

HOUPT — Bristol, Connecticut — (1909)/HOUPT-ROCKWELL — (1910) — Harry S. Houpt and Albert F. Rockwell were friends and very well known in the motor trade on the East Coast. Houpt was the New York City agent for the popular Thomas car built in Buffalo, and in January of 1909 he announced that he would now handle the Herreshoff car and would also build one of his own design in the fall. Rockwell was the inventor of a signal bell and coaster brake for bicycles, both of which were manufactured by his New Departure Manufacturing Company, makers of ball bearings in Bristol, Connecticut. In the summer of 1908 he had spun off another enterprise from New Departure called Bristol Engineering Corporation. Its purpose was the manufacture of taxicabs (the Rockwell would be introduced in 1909) and automobiles. Regarding the latter, Rockwell would build a few for Allen-Kingston, but more for Harry S. Houpt. In mid-August of 1909 Houpt organized the H.S. Houpt Manufacturing Company in New York, with a capitalization of $60,000, for the manufacture of ''cars, motor boats and aviation machinery.'' A week later, on August 27th-28th, his new car made its debut, at Brighton Beach for the twenty-four-hour race. Though the car did not finish, it had been fielded by the renowned Vanderbilt winner George Robertson, and considerable publicity accrued. Interestingly, the car had been entered in the event as the Houpt-Rockwell. It would appear that the name Houpt alone for the production cars was very short-lived. The advance catalog for 1910 indicated both names. ''You can't go by a Houpt-Rockwell so go buy one'' was the frontispiece slogan. These were big, powerful cars (a 60 hp four and a 90 hp six) and very expensive. Any question of what they were properly called was solved by April 1910 when the official announcement came that the H.S. Houpt Manufacturing Company had been absorbed by the New Departure Manufacturing Company, which itself had absorbed the Bristol Engineering Corporation the previous fall. Now Albert F. Rockwell was president of these three companies which had become one. The Houpt-Rockwell did not survive 1910. Internal dissension would appear to be one of the reasons. In October New Departure announced its discontinuation of automobile manufacture; Harry Houpt departed to become the sales manager for Alco; soon thereafter Albert F. Rockwell, who was described by a detractor on the New Departure board of directors as a ''will-of-the-wisp dreamer,'' was ousted from his own company. Although there was a landaulet, touring car and Rockwell taxi, on exhibit at the Houpt-Rockwell stand at the New York Automobile Show at Grand Central Palace in late December/early January 1911, it was the marque's swan song. Approximately 100 Houpt-Rockwells had been built. Ultimately New Departure became a subsidiary of General Motors.

1909-1910 HOUPT/HOUPT-ROCKWELL
Four - 60 hp, 127'' wb

	FP	5	4	3	2	1
Touring	5000	2700	3600	5300	8800	19,000
Toy Tonneau	5000	2500	3500	5000	8500	18,000
Runabout	5000	2500	3500	5000	8500	18,000

	FP	5	4	3	2	1
Limousine	6500	2300	3300	4600	7500	16,000
Landaulet	6500	2400	3400	4800	8000	17,000
Six — 90 hp, 140" wb						
Touring	6000	2900	3700	5600	9100	20,000
Toy Tonneau	6000	2700	3600	5300	8800	19,000
Runabout	6000	2700	3600	5300	8800	19,000
Limousine	7500	2400	3400	4800	8000	17,000
Landaulet	7500	2500	3500	5000	8500	18,000

1909 Houpt, toy tonneau, OCW

HOUSE — Cheyenne, Wyoming — (1906) — A seventeen-year old by the name of Harry House built himself a car in 1906 powered by a motorcyle engine and built from odds and ends gathered in his father's bicycle repair shop in Cheyenne. "On its trial trip, the machine worked to perfection until the vibration of the engine and the rough roads caused the bicycle wheels with which it was equipped to collapse, all four wheels going down at the same instant," reported *Motor Field*. "The motor car will be equipped with heavier wheels, and young House then expects to use it in running about the streets of the city. The boy had no aid whatever in constructing the machine, and worked out the details of gearing, etc., along original lines."

1867 House Steamer, MVMA

HOUSE STEAM — Bridgeport, Connecticut — (1867 et seq.) — In 1866 the House brothers — Joseph A. and Henry A. — were working to help Wheeler & Wilson in Bridgeport to perfect their sewing machine. In 1867 they were building a steam car featuring double side chain drive from a jackshaft. The vehicle weighed a hefty 5000 pounds, was shod with wooden wheels with iron tires, and carried three men, a stoker, engineer and helmsman. S.A. Nickerson assisted in the final construction of the House, which was operated on the public streets of Bridgeport though a special permit was required from the city fathers to do so. Ultimately, Henry House turned the coachwork of the vehicle into a horsedrawn wagon for use on his Connecticut farm; Joseph House used the boiler to heat his home and greenhouse; and Nickerson was given the engine which he installed in a boat. Subsequently the House brothers turned their talents to the invention of machinery for corset manufacture. Most probably, the Steam Car Company which was organized in Bridgeport around the turn of the century was a House brothers venture, though it does not appear Nickerson was involved. Henry A. House enjoyed considerably more success on the other side of the Atlantic, as the designer of Lifu steam automobiles and trucks in England. S.A. Nickerson became a Pierce-Arrow dealer.

HOUSE & ROHLE — St. Louis, Missouri — (1908) — The House & Rohle Carriage Company of St. Louis advertised itself as the manufacture of both horsedrawn vehicles and automobiles and early in 1908 revealed that a new one-story brick-and-stone building was in the course of construction at 3958-3962 Laclede Avenue. Such automobile building as the firm did undoubtedly was to customer order.

HOUSEL — The Housel Manufacturing Company was organized in Rochester, New York late in 1913 with a capital stock of $25,000 for the manufacture of automobiles. William E. Housel of 1 Cornell Street in Rochester spearheaded this venture, in association with William H. Cole of Pittsford. Manufacture is doubted.

HOUSER — Chillicothe, Ohio — (1906) — Orville E. Houser operated an automobile repair shop at 101 N. Mulberry in Chillicothe, just a few houses down from his residence at 150. In 1906 he built an automobile in his shop, but it does not appear he ever contemplated manufacture.

HOWARD — The Howard Automobile Company of San Francisco, California was a $2 million venture from the fall of 1923 backed by A.B. Mason, H.A. Black, H.D. Costigan, E.S. Pillsbury and J.D. Adams. Manufacture of an automobile is doubted.

The Thomas Howard Company of Brooklyn, New York built a car called the Flyer in 1913-1914. Refer to Flyer.

1895 Howard, gasoline carryall, NAHC

HOWARD — Trenton, New Jersey — (1895-1903) — William L. Howard apparently began thinking about horseless carriages in the late 1880's while apprenticing in the McCardell & West workshops in Trenton. His first attempts were failures, but quite possibly he may have had his first gasoline car on the road, if haltingly, in the late fall of 1893, just a few months after the Duryea brothers had their car running up in Massachusetts. The first completely documented Howard car arrived in 1895, however, by which time William Howard had established his Howard Cycle Company. This vehicle had three bench seats to accommodate six large people (or nine medium-sized ones) and was powered by two 3 hp Wing motors. "Either gasoline, kerosene or city gas can be used as fuel," said William Howard. He experimented with several other automotive ideas prior to the turn of the century, including a steam car with a double-acting engine and a twenty-eight-inch diameter boiler with 1400 half-inch copper tubes. By now a Howard "Carryall" was being used for public transport around the Trenton Fair Grounds. In 1900 William Howard secured local financing and organized the Howard Automobile Company. President was George B. Yard; secretary was Frank W. Williams; treasurer was Frank W. Muschert. William Howard served as vice-president. Another of the Carryalls produced by Howard was used in 1903 as public transport from Philadelphia to Atlantic City. Nineteen-three would appear to be the last year a William

1902 Howard, steamer runabout, NAHC

Howard-designed automobile was produced. Howard's brother, John Howard, had been building automobiles during this same period too, incidentally, but his efforts were confined to special racers which he contested at Brighton Beach and other tracks on the East Coast. Conceivably, the steam car he raced at Newport in August 1901 may have been designed by his brother William. Among William Howard's later inventions was a demountable rim for automobile and bicycle wheels.

1903 Howard, tonneau, NAHC

HOWARD — New York State — (1895, 1901-1904, 1908) — William S. Howard got around a lot. He built his first experiment gasoline car, a surrey, in 1895 in his native Troy. His first production car, a single-cylinder 5 hp gasoline runabout introduced in 1901, was initially built for him by the Grant-Ferris Company, marine engine manufacturers in Troy. Howard soon launched his own Trojan Launch and Automobile Works, however, to build the Howard (and later Trojan) cars, as well as gasoline engines and motor launches. It would appear that most of his production was of the last named. When he moved to Yonkers in 1903 as the Howard Automobile Company, he reordered his priorities, emphasizing motorcars, although "auto-boats" continued to be featured in his catalog. The Howard was offered in two, three and four cylinders and in runabout, touring and delivery models. His prices were rather high for medium-sized machines, and in November 1904 he sold out his automobile business to Charles L. Seabury of Morris Heights, who continued production of the largest Howard for a few months as the new Seabury. (Budd D. Gray, a mechanical engineer from the LaFrance Fire Engine Company was called in by Seabury to see to the few design revisions necessary. Meanwhile Howard, who had assisted the General Electric Company in Schenectady during their early car experimentation period, moved to Morris Heights too for a short period to serve as chief engineer for the Gas Engine and Power Company. But he was back in Yonkers by 1905 to design the new Ardsley — and when it failed at the end of 1906, he opened a small engine works at 17 Nepperhan Avenue and played a part in the development of the Colt, which failed quickly too. Relentlessly he pressed on, and in 1908 decided to produce a Colt-like six himself which he sold either assembled or unassembled. He didn't sell many, and though there are references extant to his plans to move his Howard Motor Works to Albany or Athens, this does not appear to have happened. Instead he remained in Yonkers to help out a friend named C.P. Munch who had a new car to build but no place to build it. Howard produced thirty cars for Munch who in the meantime found a factory in Pennsylvania and moved there to continue production under the marque name of Keystone. William S. Howard remained in Yonkers and turned his attention to the development of a rotary sleeve valve engine which was produced for a short period beginning in 1912 by the New York Motor Works, Inc. He never built another car.

1904 Howard Three-Cylinder, touring, HAC

1903-1904 HOWARD

	FP	5	4	3	2	1
No. 1 Rbt. (2-cyl., 8 hp, 84" wb)	800	2300	3300	4600	7500	16,000
No. 1 Tonneau (2-cyl., 8 hp, 84" wb)	1000	2300	3300	4600	7500	16,000

	FP	5	4	3	2	1
No. 2 Delivery (2-cyl., 12 hp, 84" wb)	1500	2200	3200	4400	7000	15,000
No. 3 Touring (3-cyl., 12 hp, 84" wb)	2000	2400	3400	4800	8000	17,000
No. 4 Touring (4-cyl., 24 hp, 90" wb)	3000	2500	3500	5000	8500	18,000
No. 4 Coupe (4-cyl., 24 hp, 96" wb)	5000	2300	3300	4600	7500	16,000
No. 4 Tonneau (4-cyl., 24 hp, 105" wb)	5000	2400	3400	4800	8000	17,000

(Note: It was the No. 4 Tonneau which was continued as the Seabury.)

HOWARD — Jackson, Michigan & Macon, Georgia — (1911) — The Howard Automobile Company was organized in Michigan during the early spring of 1911. By early summer $50,000 worth of machinery had been installed in a new factory, and the first ten cars on the assembly line were nearing completion. Then the trouble began. Dissension arose, and many of the founding officers departed. Company president J.E. Keith immediately got an idea — and headed south. In Macon, he talked to local businessmen and bankers about relocating his factory in Georgia. The outcome of the Macon negotiations is not known, nor is the final destiny of those ten cars on the Jackson assembly line.

1914 Howard, Six, touring, WLB

HOWARD — Connersville, Indiana — (1913-1914) — Early use of a dual exhaust system distinguished this Howard, a big 132-inch-wheelbase car designed by H.P. Tuttle and J.C. Moore and announced under the aegis of the Central Car Company in Connersville. Powered by a six-cylinder 60 hp Continental engine, the $2075 Howard was introduced at the New York Automobile Show at Grand Central Palace in December 1913, the Howard Motor Car Company by now having been organized in Chicago for its distribution. For its manufacture the Howard firm contracted with E.W. Ansted, the Central director who had just acquired the Lexington Motor Car Company in Connersville. He proceeded to build the new Howard alongside the continued Lexington. Rather logically, this whole enterprise evolved into the Lexington-Howard Company. When the people in Chicago did not renew their contract with Lexington, the Howard was simply discontinued.

HOWARD — Galion, Ohio — (1911, 1916-1917, 1919) — In 1911 an organization called the Howard Motor Car Company was established for the manufacture of automobiles. Adam Howard, who had been building horsedrawn carriages in Galion for a quarter century, was behind this venture, though he selected one H. Gottfiener as its president. Stock was sold, and within months no one was happy. "The Howard Motor Company, which aroused high hopes . . . has dashed them to earth," *The Motor World* reported in July. "The stockholders, who once expected to become coupon-clippers and to hear the hum of industry, have decided that the prospects do not justify further investment, and accordingly the plant will be disposed of. It had not yet commenced to produce cars." How many of the people involved with the Howard-that-never-was were involved with the Howard-that-came-to-be a half decade later is not known, but probably they were few. On September 16th of '16, Adam Howard announced the $500,000 incorporation of his A. Howard Company to take over his buggy business, with Howard himself as vice-president, R.W. Johnson as vice-president and A.W. Monroe as secretary-treasurer, new people all. The new Howard quickly made it to the production line. It was a 50 hp six on a 120-inch wheelbase and offered as an $1800 touring car only. "The company will start without a penny of indebtedness," Adam Howard announced in September 1916, "and will practically have $500,000 with which to begin operations." Despite a half million dollars, the Howard car survived but a year. Following the war, a comeback was tried with a 50 hp six-cylinder (Supreme engine) sport touring being built in 1919 for the New York Automobile Show. But just that one car, which remains extant, is believed to have been produced.

1916-1917 HOWARD
Six — 50 hp, 120" wb

	FP	5	4	3	2	1
Touring-5P	1800	3200	4300	6500	11,000	23,000

HOWARD — Detroit, Michigan — (1928-1929) — This Howard was grandiosely promoted as the "Morning Star" or the "Silver Morn," these titles presumably to personify the new dawn the Howard heralded in low-cost motoring. The venture was sponsored by John Howard Rees, who had built the Rees car in Ohio in 1921 and who announced the formation of Howard Motors Corporation in '28 following his acquisition of the former Acme Brass Works factory in Detroit. Joining him were L.P. Chittenden as vice-president; H.B. Trix as director; R.E. Fremont as secretary-treasurer. The Howard idea was an assembled car for export only. Four chassis models were offered, two sixes and two eights on four different wheelbase sizes, with tourers, roadsters and sedans made in each size. The sixes were 15 and 20 hp, the eights 24 and 29 hp; wheelbases were respectively 103, 110, 120 and 134 inches. Price range was $615 to $2485. Rees announced that production was expected to begin on April 5th, 1928, with 100 cars scheduled that month. The schedule was not met. Truck manufacture was slated to begin "as soon as passenger car production is well under way." It never began at all. How many Howards left the country is not known. Perhaps none at all. It would appear that this Howard died very quickly on the assembly line of the old Acme Brass Works factory.

HOWE — The Howe Engine Company of Indianapolis, Indiana has appeared on various rosters as an automobile builder. The firm is known to have produced a 32 hp gasoline fire engine in late 1905, but this would appear to have been the extent of its vehicle-building activity.
The Howe Motor Car Company was organized in Newark, New Jersey with a capital stock of $125,000 to manufacture and deal in automobiles late in 1907. Incorporators included Albert F. Howe, Michael F. O'Neil and John Howe. Manufacture is doubted.

HOWELL — **Racine, Wisconsin** — **(1900)** — The Howell was a single gasoline car built to order for L.A. Howell by the Wisconsin Wheel Works of Racine in 1900. At the turn of the century, Wisconsin Wheel Works was engaged principally as a bicycle manufacturer, though the company did begin producing a motorized bicycle that year, and in 1903 proceeded into formal manufacture of an automobile called the Mitchell.

HOWELL — **Atlantic City, New Jersey** — **(1909)** — Technical details are lacking regarding the amphibious automobile built in 1909 by Rear Admiral J.A. Howell, U.S. Navy, retired, though one reporter suggested it resembled a runaway submarine. "Every bar in Atlantic City felt a distinct slackening in trade as the result of the machine's visual impression on the citizens and visitors when it came out the first time recently," he remarked. Howell, who was assisted in the car's building by his son, a young engineer, admitted that he had spent $7000 on the vehicle thus far and hoped "to perfect it soon to practical capabilities." Most probably, perfection was never realized.

HOWELL — **New York, New York** — **(1914)** — In April 1914, C.W. Howell of the Son Typewriter Company in New York City declared that his company was just completing its experimental work on a cyclecar that would contain no "freak" developments. "The efforts of the company will be to provide an individual type of motorcar construction suitable for light car work, and at the same time incorporating material and construction from a standpoint of durability and efficiency," stated C.W. Howell verbosely. Verbosity seems to have been the limit to which this cyclecar progressed. Production did not follow.

1907 Howey, auto-buggy, GR

HOWEY — **Kansas City, Missouri** — **(1907-1908)** — "A frail car can go thirty miles an hour, but not long" was the contention of the Howey Motor Car Company of Kansas City. The Howey was a highwheeler powered by a 10 hp engine, with hub, sprocket and brake of one-piece steel, and an ungainly wagon body of the same material. "We Lead Them All in Strength" read a company advertisement, which was belied by a photograph of the Howey underneath indicating double chain drive from a very flimsy jackshaft. The Howey was sold for $600 f.o.b. the factory; the company had no dealers. Previously published references to the lifespan of the Howey being a half decade are in error. The company appears to have been in business for two years at best.

HOWICK — Oscar J. Howick designed two automobiles in Fenton, Michigan in 1913-1914 and although the experimental version of the second was announced under his name, it was produced as the Elgin. Refer to Fenton and Elgin.

HOWSE — The Howse Commercial Car Company was organized in Detroit, Michigan during the summer of 1910 with a capital stock of $50,000 for the manufacture of both pleasure and commercial cars, and parts and accessories. Charles F. Howse, Edward P. Newton, August J. Steiber, Frank P. Mullin and Albert McClatchey were the incorporators. Manufacture of an automobile is doubted.

HOYT — Hoyt & DeMallie, Inc. was organized in New York City early in 1907 with a capital stock of $75,000 for the manufacture of electric vehicles. P.V. Hoyt and J.M. DeMallie were the partners involved. Manufacture of an automobile is doubted.

HOYT — **Penacook, New Hampshire** — **(1900-1901)** — Adrian Hazen Hoyt received a medical degree from Dartmouth College in 1887 and thereon returned to his native Magog (in the Province of Quebec) to begin his practice. But he was soon bored. As a genealogical history put it, the practice of medicine was "not congenial to his bent of mind," and he hastened below the border again to engage in a business that was. Initially he entered the employ of the Standard Electric Company in St. Johnsbury, Vermont, but he later joined the Whitney Electric Instrument Company in Manchester, New Hampshire, and followed that firm to Penacook when it moved there. During his employment with Whitney, he built his first experimental car, in 1900, and curiously it was a steamer. He prided himself on being the first owner and user of an automobile in the state of New Hampshire. He built another that year, and a couple more the year following. By 1905 he had begun his own shop for the manufacture and repair of electrical instruments and automobiles. He was also an instructor in manual training and electrics at St. Paul's School. Although he may have put together another automobile or two during this period, the thought of serious manufacture was never broached. Among his twenty-five patented inventions were an alternating current ammeter and a number of other devices for automotive use.

HOYT — **Cleveland, Ohio** — **(1909)** — In late 1913, when the Falcon Cyclecar Company was being organized, Francis R. Hoyt retroactively declared himself the designer of the first cyclecar built in the United States. His 1909 effort, if properly a cyclecar, would indeed have been America's first. But a blurred photo of that vehicle indicates that it really should have been termed a juvenile. The little girl behind the wheel probably had not reached puberty.

H.P.M. — H.P.M. Motors, Inc., with executive offices at 30 Church Street in New York City, marketed an automobile during the early Twenties, though the car was not an H.P.M. but a Moller instead. Refer to Moller.

H. & R. — **Ridgewood, New Jersey** — **(1915)** — In 1915, in Ridgewood, the H. & R. Machine & Garage Company built a 1200-pound runabout on a 96-inch wheelbase with 42-inch tread. Its engine was a 20hp water-cooled four built in unit with a three-speed selective sliding gear transmission. Its pressed steel chassis used a tubular front axle, and a semi-floating rear with driveshaft enclosed in a torsion tube. As described in the August issue of *Carette* that year, the H. & R. effort seemed an altogether admirable one. But manufacture, apparently, was not envisioned.

HUB — The Hub Auto-Carriage Company was organized in Brookings, South Dakota during the summer of 1900 with a capital stock of $100,000 for the manufacture of automobiles. Incorporators included William H. Ashley, James A. Kilburn, Louis N. Fuller, T. Arthur Fuller, J.P. Cheever, Philo Hall, George P. Hall and Frederick E. Lusk. Manufacture of an automobile is doubted.
The Hub Twenty-Second Street Garage Company was organized in Camden, New Jersey during the fall of 1912 with a capital stock of $100,000 to manufacture and sell automobiles. Incorporators included F.R. Hansell, George H.B. Martin and I.C. Clow. Manufacture is doubted.

HUB — **Dorchester, Massachusetts** — **(1907)** — The Hub Motor Car Exchange was a dealership at 195 Freeport Street in Boston which purchased the factory of the defunct Crestmobile in Dorchester in 1906. Produced there that year was a small primeval runabout called the Dorchester. Few were sold and, believing a more sophisticated car might fare better, the company came up with another small runabout for 1907, introducing this one under its own name. The new Hub was powered by a single-cylinder, air-cooled 10 hp engine mounted under a hood, with shaft drive and planetary transmission featured. The car was exhibited at the Boston Automobile Show in early 1907. It did not reappear in 1908.

HUB ELECTRIC — **Chicago, Illinois** — **(1899-1900)** — Charles Berg was a Chicago real estate man and H.L. Irwin was a lawyer — and between them they didn't know much about automobiles. But they were quite adept at borrowing and adapting, their ideas and plans largely being derived from those of Fred J. Newman and the Hungarian-born engineer Joseph Ledwinka. The Hub Electric was so called because it had an electric motor in each wheel, encased in the hub. The Hub Motor Company survived but two years. In 1901 its patents were bought by Westinghouse in Pittsburgh, that company announcing that it would build forty buses with the hub-motor principle. All of the vehicles marketed by the Hub Motor Company in Chicago apparently were small two or four-passenger carriages.

1900 Hub Electric, MVMA

HUBER — Detroit, Michigan — (1903-1907) — Prior to the turn of the century, in their native Oxford (Michigan), Edmund Sprung and Henry G. Ide built an experimental car which was never produced though the partners informally announced an Ide-Sprung-Huber Automobile Company. After the turn of the century, the partners relocated in Detroit and were joined by Mersden Burch. In 1903, the Huber Automobile Company was organized with a capital stock of $100,000 and Sprung as the firm's president. Manufacture of automobiles was the stated purpose of the venture, but when production began attention was devoted almost exclusively to large sight-seeing buses. In later years the focus of the firm drifted from marketing its vehicles for sale to leasing them for hire. The Huber venture ended dismally in August of 1907 when Burch and Ide attempted to secure a chattel mortgage on all company property, for the purpose, as *The Motor World* related, "of protecting the interests held by them and their wives." Ide was described as secretary-treasurer of the firm, while Burch purportedly was "connected with the treasury department in Washington." Sprung fought back, alleging that the company's books had been doctored. The final outcome of this spat is not known. Emil Huber seems to have held himself above the fracas. He left for Meteor in Iowa.

HUBER — Davenport, Iowa — (1909) — In 1909, just before the firm folded, Emil Huber left the Meteor Motor Car Company of Bettendorf, Iowa intent upon becoming a manufacturer of his own. He proceeded as far as building a prototype — a runabout with four-cylinder engine, 100-inch wheelbase and underslung frame — which he drove that summer in the Glidden Tour, probably hoping to find potential investors enroute. He did not, however, and his plans to organize a company for manufacture in his native Davenport fell through. Emil Huber subsequently went on to a distinguished career as an engineer for Hudson.

HUBERS — The Hubers Machine Company was organized during the summer of 1917 with a capital stock of $50,000 to manufacture and deal in automobiles and wagons in Newark, New Jersey. Spearheading this venture was Herman W. Hubers of Newark, in association with Milton Bierman and Joseph Korn of East Orange. Manufacture is doubted.

HUDDLESTON — Louisville, Kentucky — (1899) — The only specific regarding the automobile built in 1899 by M.L. Huddleston of 406 Fifth Street in Louisville is that most of its parts came from two bicycles. Most likely its engine was a small gasoline unit.

HUDFORD — The Hudford Company was organized in New York City during the spring of 1916 for the manufacture of automobiles and equipment. Capital stock was $10,000; the incorporators were W.C. Hunter, R. Vollbracht and H.A. Demarest. Manufacture of a car is doubted but truck production did follow.

HUDSON — The number of Hudsons which might have been are many. The ventures following indicated that a Hudson car would be forthcoming, but apparently the automobiles never arrived.

The Hudson Auto Engineering company of Passaic, New Jersey, organized early in 1919 with a capital stock of $200,000. Incorporators were the brothers Hudson — Arthur, Fred and Christopher.

The Hudson Automobile Company of New York City, organized during the fall of 1905 with a capital stock of $5000. Incorporators were Ferdinand Schussler, Harold A. Wright, Estelle Schussler and Moses G. Wright.

The Hudson County Automobile Company of Guttenberg, New Jersey, organized early in 1910 with a $10,000 capital stock. Incorporators were Stuart J. Lebach, George W. and Henry H. Kern.

The Hudson County Auto Supply Company of Jersey City, New Jersey, organized in June of 1917 with a $25,000 capital stock. Incorporators were John Moran and Frank W. Meixsell.

The Hudson-Phillips Motor Car Company of St. Louis, Missouri, organized with a capital stock of $10,000 in early 1913. C.F. Phillips, J.H. Phillips and J.E. Stewart were the incorporators.

The Hudson-Stuyvesant Motor Company of Cleveland, Ohio, organized with a capital stock of $25,000 during the summer of 1914. This venture, which ultimately did produce automobile accessories, was headed by Frank E. Stuyvesant who earlier had built the Stuyvesant car in Cleveland.

W.H. Hudson of Detroit, Michigan apparently wished to organize a company for the manufacture of cyclecars in 1914. *Motor Print* that March indicated his experimental building of a car.

The Hudson Valley Automobile Company of New York City, organized with a capital stock of $10,000 during the summer of 1911. Incorporators were Alfred M. Keene and Harry L. Twine.

A steam car purportedly was built in Covington, Georgia in 1904 by one C.J. Hudson. Documentation of this is lacking.

1901 Hudson, touring, LC

HUDSON — Saratoga Springs, New York — (1899-1902) — The Hudson Gas Motor & Vehicle Manufacturing Company of Saratoga Springs was incorporated in the early fall of 1899 with $100,000 capitalization. It evolved out of the Mayhew Gas Engine Company at 31 Geneva Street, which was the new firm's address as well. Charles Mayhew was Hudson's chief designer and machinist. Others involved with the company included William P. Tarrant as president, William S. Robertson as treasurer and H. Allison Rood as secretary. This original incorporation notice appeared in the October 4th, 1899 issue of *The Horseless Age*. Then the firm dropped from the public print for one year. In the November 14th, 1900 issue of *The Horseless Age*, there appeared yet another reference to a $100,000 incorporation of the Hudson Gas Motor & Vehicle Company. It was probably at this time that the officers changed to William Martin as president, E.D. Starbuck as treasurer and Lester E. Heath as manager. Charles Mayhew was the only member of the original company still on board. It would seem that this Saratoga Springs automotive venture spent most of its time incorporating and none of it manufacturing. Fred Tarrant, son of Hudson's first president, has recalled that only two cars were constructed. The first "ran fitfully and cracked like a rifle, and could only be driven evenings when most horses were off the streets," he said in an interview in 1982. "The second was improved. It vibrated badly, but it did run and could climb hills." The two cars built were put together on the second floor of the Van Raalte wallpaper factory. Charles Mayhew designed both of them and ran into some difficulty with his backers when he patented a clutch he had developed at company expense and then sold it to a competitor. In 1903 the 31 Geneva Street address of the Hudson company was occupied by the Saratoga Waste and Metal Company. Meantime, another resident of Saratoga Springs took possession of the chassis of the second Mayhew-designed car, converted it to a steamer called the Gagemobile, and tried to get into the automobile business himself.

HUDSON

HUDSON — Detroit, Michigan — (1910-1942 et. seq.) — The first advertisement appeared in *The Saturday Evening Post* on June 19th, 1909, the first car left the factory on July 8th, by the following July more than 4000 Hudsons had been sold for the biggest first-year business yet recorded in the automobile industry. It was an auspicious beginning. But it wasn't really surprising. The men behind the Hudson were Roy D. Chapin and Howard E. Coffin, veterans of Olds Motor Works who had just recently built the Thomas-Detroit and the Chalmers-Detroit. Joining them in partnership in 1908 were George W. Dunham and Roscoe B. Jackson, also graduates of Olds. Putting up the money was Joseph L. Hudson, probably the only member of the venture who had any misgivings, but his niece was Roscoe Jackson's wife, and gentle family pressure combined with the fact that $90,000 wasn't an outlandish sum for the man who owned Detroit's most successful department store proved ultimately persuasive. On February 24th, 1909, the Hudson Motor Car Company had been organized with a capital stock of $100,000, by spring the firm had bought up the Selden patent license of the defunct Northern and had moved into the factory of the defunct Aerocar, and by summer the company was in business. The car which enjoyed that record-breaking first year success was a 20 hp four good for 50 mph, priced at $900 and offered only as a racy and brassy little roadster on a 110-inch wheelbase. It was introduced as a 1910 model. Though it carried the soon-to-be-famous Hudson triangle, the emblem was brass on the Model 20. It turned white with the introduction of the Model 33 for 1911, a larger monobloc four on a 114½-inch wheelbase with prices now edging upwards of $1000 and with a spartan but speedy new two-seater called the Mile-a-Minute Roadster — and guaranteeing that — available in 1912. All this was but prelude, however, for already Coffin (the engineering genius of the Hudson group) was working on the car that would transform Hudson's auspicious beginning into a long-term solid industry success. By now the company had moved into its brand-new Albert Kahn-designed factory at the corner of Jefferson and Conner avenues in Detroit, and it was there that the prototype of the first Hudson six was completed in July of 1912. It was introduced for the 1913 model year, promising 65 mph in touring trim for $2450, and was followed in 1914 by a lightweight six offering similar performance for only $1550. Prior to Hudson, fast-paced sixes had primarily been the preserve of luxury car manufacturers. By 1914 all Hudsons were sixes, with over 10,000 built that year, over 12,000 the year following as the company began advertising itself as the "world's largest manufacturer of six-cylinder cars." At the New York Automobile Show in January 1916, the Super Six arrived — and it was that, an entirely new L-head engine with improved cylinder head design for a 5.0:1 compression ratio on standard fuel and a puissant 76 bhp at 3000 rpm. In April at Daytona, Ralph Mulford drove a Super Six to a new one-mile straightaway stock speed record of 102.5 mph; in May at Sheepshead Bay the 24-hour stock speed record was taken at a 75.8 mph average, a mark that would stand for fifteen years; in August Mulford's climb up Pikes Peak in 18 minutes 25 seconds represented a new class record to stand for eight; in September Mulford with co-drivers Vincent and Patterson got into a Super Six seven-passenger touring car in San Francisco, 5 days 3 hours 31 minutes later were in New York City to break the Marmon's previous cross-country record, then they turned around and drove back to San Francisco to establish America's first ever double-transcontinental. Hudson sales doubled that year too: to more than 25,000 cars. The Super Six would remain the solid rock around which Hudson fortunes revolved for a decade, followed in 1928 by the 91 hp Special Six, an F-head that was an amalgam of the meritorious engineering features of the Essex four-and six-cylinder engines as well as the venerable Hudson unit. The Essex, introduced for 1918, was Hudson's low-priced companion car and by the mid-Twenties had forcefully carried forward the Hudson focus on closed car production (begun in 1916 when the company sold more sedans then either Ford or Chevrolet) with the offering of a closed coach for less than a touring car, heretofore unheard of in the industry. Be they open or closed models, some Hudsons of the later Twenties and early Thirties carried custom bodies, initially from Biddle & Smart, later Murray, Briggs and occasionally LeBaron. In 1930 the chassis on which these — and all Hudsons — were built was a straight-eight, which was essentially the Essex six with two cylinders added. It was called the Great Eight, though at 80 hp, it was less powerful than the big six. It became heftier in horses subsequently, and a big six was soon returned to the line. In 1931 Frank Spring, formerly of Murphy, joined the company as styling director. By now most of the original team members who had started Hudson had retired or died, save for Roy Chapin who had a short sojourn in Washington as President Hoover's Secretary of Commerce but who returned to Hudson in '33. His company's hottest car now was the Terraplane, which would spur sales immeasurably, but like every other business in America, Hudson's financial outlook was lukewarm at best. The strain of keeping the company afloat hastened his death at age fifty-six in February 1936. Taking over now were A.E. Barit as president, who had begun as a stenographer for the company in 1910; and Stuart G. Baits as engineering vice-president, who had entered Hudson as a draftsman in 1915. Hudsons for 1934 had seen introduction of "Axle-Flex," a semi-independent front suspension; and 1935 brought the "Electric Hand," a vacuum-powered automatic gearshift built by Bendix and not a particularly good idea. Though beauty be in the proverbial beholder's eye, the look of the '36 and later Hudsons was perhaps not a good idea either, though the appearance of the 1940 line ("symphonic styling," the company said) was nice and tidy. Tidy too were records resulting at Bonneville by a stock 1940 model — now with fully independent front suspension — driven by John Cobb to capture virtually every AAA Class C closed car record from one mile to 3000 kilometers, and from one hour to twelve, the half-day completed at a terrific 91.29 mph. Despite the vagaries of the Depression, the Hudson Motor Car Company had survived the Thirties in good order. In 1941 the company made a profit of $3,756,000. On February 5th, 1942 Hudson ceased building cars, for the duration of the war its factories turning out machine guns and aircraft components. Hudson's best prewar year had been 1929, with over 300,000 cars produced, a figure the company would never approach again. Although there would be some very interesting and spirited cars built postwar, the glory years of the Hudson were already behind it.

Hudson Data Compilation
by Robert C. Ackerson

1910

HUDSON — MODEL 20 — FOUR: The Model Twenty Rds. was an extremely handsome automobile that Hudson advertised as "Strong — Speedy — Roomy — Stylish". In the first public announcement the Twenty was touted as an automobile that was far and away superior to its competitors.

Included in its initial price were two headlamps, generator, side oil lamps, a tool set and a horn. Both the Hudson's appointments and design belied its low $900 price. The early models were finished in maroon with black striping and fenders. The interior was blue-black leather. The radia-

1910 Hudson, model 20, touring, JAC

tor, steering column, side lamp brackets, hub caps and side control levers were finished in brass and the entry step plate was of aluminum.

Hudson pointed with pride to the features the Twenty shared with far more expensive automobiles. For example, its sliding gear transmission was "such as you find on the Packard, Peerless, Pierce, Lozier and other high grade cars." The Hudson engine was described as "the Renault type and Renault Motors are the pride of France."

The larger 110 inch wheelbase Fore-Door Rds. and Tr. models were less graceful than the Rds. but their body styles enabled Hudson to expand its share of the market. By the end of 1910 it ranked seventeenth in U.S. automobile sales.

1910 Hudson, model 20, touring, WRG

I.D. DATA: Serial numbers found in two locations, on plate on front seat riser and on right side of frame. Starting: 1. Ending: 7100. Engine No. Location: NA. Starting Engine No.: NA. Ending Engine No.: NA

Note: Initially the Twenty was powered by an engine supplied by the Atlas Motor Company of Indianapolis. As production increased the Buda company of Harvey, Ill. also supplied engines.

Model No.	Body Type & Seating	Price	Weight	Prod. Total
20	Open Rds.-3P	900	1800	4000
20	2-dr. Rds.-3P	1200	1800	1000
20	2-dr. Tr. Car-5P	1150	2000	2099

Note 1: Beginning in Jan., 1910 the price of the Model 20 Open Rds. was increased to $1000.
Note 2: The Model 20 2-dr. Rds. differed from the Open Rds. by having 2 small drs. However that on the right side was not operational due to the position of the outside controls!
Note 3: Production total on Model 20 Open Rds. included approximately 1100 cars built in 1909 but announced as 1910 models by Hudson.
Note 4: Price on the Model 20 2-dr. Tr. included 3 oil lamps, 2 gas lamps, generator, horn, tire repair kit, tools and jack.

ENGINE: Inline Four. Cast iron block. B & S: 3-3/4 x 4-1/2 in. Disp. 198.8 cid. Brake H.P.: 20. A.L.A.M./ H.P.: 22.5. Main bearings: 2. Valve lifters: mechanical. Carb. Holley, Mayer and Stromberg Model B carburetors were used.

CHASSIS: [Model 20 Rds.] W.B.: 100 in. Tires: 32 x 3 front 32 x 3-1/2 rear. [Model 20 Fore-Door Rds.] W.B.: 110 in. Tires: 32 x 35. [Model 20 Tr.] W.B.: 110 in. Tires: 32 x 35.

*Note — There was only one series — Model 20, but the 3 different body types warrant identification. After January 1910 the 20 designation was abandoned and the 3 Hudsons were advertised as either the Rds., Tr. car or Fore-Door Rds.

TECHNICAL: Sliding gear transmission. Speeds: 3F/1R. Floor shift controls. Leather-faced cone clutch. Shaft drive. Semi-floating rear axle. Overall Ratio: NA. Mechanical brakes on two wheels. Wooden wheels. Rim size: 32 in.

OPTIONS: Bosch magneto, top, Presto-O-Lite tank, rumble seat available as a group option for the Rds., priced at $150.00. "Zig-Zag" windshield ($40). Rumble seat or 25 gallon fuel tank (Fore-Door Rds.) (NA).

HISTORICAL: Introduced June 1909. Oct. 1909 preliminary (10 lap Massapequa Cup) to Vanderbuilt Cup race. Set fastest lap, finished 4th. Hudson offered a competition model, the Express which won a 24 hour race held at Seattle, WA. From July 1909 thru Dec. 1909 — 1108 cars shipped. Calendar year production 7100 cars. Hudson made 4556 shipments to dealers during the 1910 calendar year. Model year production approximately 8200. The president of Hudson was Roy D. Chapin.

1909
Model 20, 4-cyl.

	FP	5	4	3	2	1
Rds	—	1550	4500	7500	10,500	15,000

1910
Model 20, 4-cyl.

Rds	—	1400	4200	7000	9800	14,000
Tr	—	1400	4200	7000	9800	14,000

1911

1911 Hudson, model 33, phaeton, OCW

HUDSON — MODEL 33 — FOUR: The Model 33 was an entirely new Hudson designed by Howard E. Coffin. As such it is usually accepted as the first of the true Hudson automobiles. Its monobloc engine had its intake and exhaust valves on opposite sides of the cylinder head and they were completely enclosed. The Model 33's clutch with its cork facings was enclosed in an oil filled unit along with its disc. This was expensive to manufacture but it soon gave the Model 33 a deserved reputation for smooth operation.

The Model 33's styling was conventional with high crowned fenders, exposed controls and suspension components. However the distinctive shape of its radiator with the already well-known triangular Hudson crest and the large letter spelling HUDSON across its surface made it easy to pick out a Model 33 from the competition.

HUDSON — MODEL 20 — FOUR: No changes were made in the Model 20 for 1911.

I.D. DATA: Car number on front seat riser plate and on right side of frame: Starting: Model 20 7101, Model 33 7501. Ending: Model 20 9000, Model 33 15,000. Engine numbers on right front of cylinder block. Starting Engine No.: NA. Ending Engine No.: NA.

Note: Model 20 engine built by Buda Company. The Model 33 engine was manufactured by the Continental Motor Manufacturing Company of Muskegan, Michigan. During 1911 a new plant was built by Continental in Detroit and it then became Hudson's only supplier of engines.

Model No.	Body Type & Seating	Price	Weight	Prod. Total
20	Rds.	1000	1800	400
20	Fore Dr. Rds.-3P	1200	1800	NA
33	2-dr. Tr. 5P	1250	2250	1500
33	3-dr. Fore Dr. Tr. 5P	1600	2250	500
	2-dr. Pony Ton.	1300	2360	3500
	3-dr. Torpedo Tr. 5P	1350	2460	2000

ENGINE: [Model 20] Inline Four. Cast iron block. B & S: 3-3/4 x 4-1/2 in. Disp. 198.8 cu. in. Brake H.P.: 26. N.A.C.C. H.P.: 22.5. Main bearings: 2. Valve lifters: mechanical. Carb.: Stromberg Model B. [Model 33] Inline Four. Cast iron block. B & S: 4 x 4-1/2 in. Disp. 226 cu. in. Brake H.P.: 33. N.A.C.C. H.P.: 26.6. Main bearings: 2. Valve lifters: mechanical. Carb.: Stromberg.

CHASSIS: [Model 20] W.B.: 110 in. Tires: 32 x 3-1/2. [Model 33] W.B.: 114 in. Tires: 34 x 3-1/2.

TECHNICAL: Sliding gear transmission. Speeds: 3F/1R. Floor shift controls. Leather-faced clutch (Model 20) cork insert, wet clutch (Model 33). Shaft drive. Semi-floating rear axle. Overall ratio: NA. Mechanical brakes on two wheels. Wood wheels. Rim size: [Model 20] 32 in. [Model 33] 34 in.

OPTIONS: Front bumper. Rear bumper. Double rumble seat — Model 20. 25 gallon fuel tank.

HISTORICAL: Introduced Oct. 1910. Hudson made 6486 shipments to dealers during the 1911 calendar year. Model year production was approximately 7900. The president of Hudson was Roy D. Chapin.

1911
Model 33, 4-cyl.

	FP	5	4	3	2	1
Rds	—	1200	3750	6250	8750	12,500
Tor Rds	—	1300	4050	6750	9450	13,500
Pony Ton	—	1300	4050	6750	9450	13,500
Tr	—	1150	3600	6000	8400	12,000

1912

1912 Hudson, model 33, touring, FSA

HUDSON — MODEL 33 — FOUR: The Model 20 was dropped from the 1912 line and all Hudsons were Model 33s. There were no major mechanical or styling changes but a total of seven body types were available including the 60 mph, Mile-A-Minute Roadster. Unlike the standard roadster this two-seater was fitted with 32 inch wheels and was not equipped with doors or a windshield. An interesting piece of standard equipment was a 100 mph speedometer. Hudson continued to tout the engineering virtues of the Model 33 in 1912. Potential customers were warned to "Beware of unsafe motor car purchases" that were out of date due to rapid engineering advances. In contrast the Model 33 was depicted as a car that possessed more advanced features than any other automobile. In mid-model year the Disco self starter built by the Disco Company of Grand Rapids, Michigan became standard equipment for the Model 33. With a weight of just 4-1/2 pounds and only 12 moving parts it was an appropriate addition to the Model 33 which Hudson claimed had "approximately 1,000 fewer parts" than the average car.

I.D. DATA: Car number on front seat riser plate and right side of frame. Starting: 15001. Ending: 27200 upward. Engine number on left side of front motor mount.

Note: Hudson continued to use Continental built engines.

Model No.	Body Type & Seating	Price	Weight	Prod. Total
NA	3-dr. Tr.-5P	1600	2757	NA
NA	3-dr. Torp.-4P	1600	2737	NA
NA	Mile-A-Minute Rds.-2P	1600	NA	NA
NA	2-dr. Comm. Rds.-2P	1600	2631	NA
NA	4-dr. Limo.-7P	2750	NA	NA
NA	2-dr. Cpe.-2P	2250	NA	NA
NA	3-dr. Torp.-5P	1600	2737	NA

ENGINE: Inline. Four cyl. Cast iron block. B & S: 4 x 4-1/2 in. Disp. 226 cu in. Brake H.P.: 33. N.A.C.C. H.P.: 26.6. Main bearings: 2. Valve lifters: mechanical. Carb. Stromberg.

CHASSIS: [Model 33] W.B.: 144-1/2 in. Frt./Rear Tread: 56 in. Tires: 34 x 4.

TECHNICAL: Sliding gear transmission. Speeds: 3F/1R. Floor shift controls. Cork inserts, wet clutch. Shaft drive. Semi-floating rear axle. Mechanical brakes on two wheels. Wood wheels. Rim size: 34 in.

OPTIONS: Front bumper. Rear bumper. All Model 33's with exception of the Mile-A-Minute Roadster were delivered with a top, windshield, Bosch dual ignition Prest-O-Lite gas tank or generator as standard equipment.

1912 Hudson, model 33, limousine, WRG

HISTORICAL: Introduced July 1911. Hudson made 5708 shipments to dealers during the 1912 calendar year. The president of Hudson was Roy D. Chapin.

1912
Model 33, 4-cyl.

	FP	5	4	3	2	1
Rds	—	1550	4500	7500	10,500	15,000
Tor Rds	—	1400	4200	7000	9800	14,000
Tr	—	3150	6300	10,500	14,700	21,000
Cpe	—	1900	5000	8350	11,700	16,700
Limo	—	2300	5400	9000	12,600	18,000

1913

1913 Hudson, model 37, coupe, WRG

HUDSON — MODEL 37 — FOUR: 1913 Hudsons were easily identified by their lack of an externally mounted crank. However, a crank was packed in with the Hudson's standard equipment tool kit. In addition, the longer wheelbase of the Model 37 set it apart from the older Model 33. The most stylish Hudson in either the Model 37 or Model 54 lines was the Torpedo. Compared to the Touring Car body its cowl was extended slightly and a shorter windshield was installed. The front seat and steering wheel were also repositioned slightly further back.

HUDSON — MODEL 54 — SIX: The Model 54 introduced Hudson's new 6-cylinder engine. Its success enabled Hudson to both proclaim itself "the world's largest producer of six-cylinder automobiles" and declare in Aug. 1913 a stock dividend of 100%. The 6-cylinder Hudson's top speed was approximately 65 mph and it could reach 58 mph in 30 seconds. With the 127 inch wheelbase the Model 54 was easily set apart from the Model 37 line. Both Model 37 and Model 54 were equipped with a Delco starting system in place of the older and less-efficient Disco acetylene-gas unit.

I.D. DATA: Car number on front seat riser plate and on right side of frame. Starting: Model 37 30001, Model 54 45001. Ending: Model 37 39200, Model 54 56000. Engine number on left side of cylinder block (Model 54), right front of cylinder block (Model 37).

Note 1: The Model 37 engine was supplied by Continental which gave it a Model C designation.

1913 Hudson, model 54, torpedo, OCW

Model No.	Body Type & Seating	Price	Weight	Prod. Total
37	2-dr. Rds.-2P	1875	3173	NA
37	3-dr. Torpedo-5P	1875	3350	NA
37	3-dr. Tr. Car-5P	1875	3390	NA
37	2-dr. Cpe.-3P	2350	3408	85
37	3-dr. Limo.-7P	3250	3680	41
54	2-dr. Rds.-2P	2450	3588	NA
54	3-dr. Torpedo-5P*	2450	3748	NA
54	3-dr. Tr. Car-7P	2600	3870	NA
54	3-dr. Tr. Car-5P	2450	3823	NA
54	3-dr. Limo.7P	3750	4110	59
54	2-dr. Cpe.-3P	2950	3933	15

* Re-designated the Phaeton in Feb 1913.

ENGINE: [Model 54] Inline. Six cyl. Cast iron block. B & S: 4-1/8 x 5-1/4 in. Disp.: 421 Cu. in. Brake H.P.: 54 @ 1500 R.P.M. N.A.C.C. H.P.: 40.84. Main bearings: 3. Valve lifters: mechanical. [Model 37] Inline. Four cyl. Cast iron block. B & S: 4-1/8 x 5-1/4. Disp. 280.6 cu. in. Brake H.P.: 37 @ 1500 R.P.M. N.A.C.C. H.P.: 27.23. Main bearings: 3. Valve lifters: mechanical.

CHASSIS: [Model 37] W.B.: 118 in. Frt/Rear Tread: 56 in. Tires: 34 x 4. [Model 54] W.B.: 127 in. Frt/Rear Tread: 56 in. Tires: 36 x 4-1/2.

TECHNICAL: Sliding gear transmission. Speeds: 3F/1R. Floor shift controls. Cork insert, wet clutch. Shaft drive. Semi-floating rear axle. Mechanical brakes on two wheels. Wooden wheels. Rim size: 34 in. [Model 37] 36 in. [Model 54].

OPTIONS: Front bumper. Rear bumper. Standard equipment both of the Model 37 and Model 54 was very extensive, including electric starting and lights, illuminated dash, mohair top, side curtains, "rain vision" windshield, speedometer, clock and demountable rims. Jump seats for Tr. car models $40.

HISTORICAL: Introduced July 1912 — Model 37, Aug. 1912 — Model 54. Innovations: Delco starting system. Hudson made 6404 shipments to dealers during the 1913 calendar year. The president of Hudson was Roy D. Chapin.

1913 HUDSON
Model 37, 4-cyl.

	FP	5	4	3	2	1
Rds	—	1650	4650	7750	10,850	15,500
Tor Rds	—	1750	4800	8000	11,200	16,000
Tr	—	2000	5100	8500	11,900	17,000
Cpe	—	1400	4200	7000	9800	14,000
Limo	—	1900	5000	8350	11,700	16,700

Model 54, 6-cyl.

	FP	5	4	3	2	1
2P Rds	—	1650	4650	7750	10,850	15,500
5P Rds	—	1750	4800	8000	11,200	16,000
Tor Rds	—	1800	4950	8250	11,550	16,500
Tr	—	2000	5100	8500	11,900	17,000
7P Tr	—	2200	5250	8750	12,250	17,500
Cpe	—	1650	4650	7750	10,850	15,500
Limo	—	2000	5100	8500	11,900	17,000

1914

HUDSON — MODEL SIX—40 — SIX: Hudson was strictly a manufacturer of 6-cylinder automobiles in 1914 and while the new Six-40 Series was larger than the 4-cylinder models they replaced, their prices were reduced. The new engine's dimensions of 3-1/2 inch bore and 5 inch stroke pointed towards future American practice and offered both better fuel economy and more power than the old 4. Appearance changes included enclosed hinges on all models and a reshaped radiator with smooth curves.

HUDSON — MODEL SIX-54 — SIX: Hudson's senior six series, the Six-54 now had a long 135 inch wheelbase and featured, along with the Six-40, new styling. The Hudson grille still carried the familiar triangular logo but its rounded form joined the more gently curved fenders and the smooth lines of the cowl as clear indicators that the Hudson was abandoning the angular appearance of earlier models. Also adding to the Hudson's visual appeal was its windshield, which for the first time was designed as a fully integrated part of its body.

693

1914 Hudson, model 40, landau, WRG

1914 Hudson, model 46, touring, WRG

I.D. DATA: Car number on front seat riser plate and on right side of frame. Starting: [Six-40] 63001, [Six-54] 565001. Ending: [Six-40] 77,201, [Six-54] 62500. Engine number on left side of cylinder block.

Note: The Six-54 engine was a Continental 6C model. The Six-40 engine was designated 7N by Continental.

Model No.	Body Type & Seating	Price	Weight	Prod. Total
Six-40	2-dr. Rds.-2P	1750	2822	NA
Six-40	4-dr. Phae.-6P	1750	2977	NA
Six-40	2-dr. Cabr.-2P	1950	2976	NA
Six-40	4-dr. Tr.-5P	1750	2968	NA
Six-40	4-dr. Tr.-5P (right hand drive)	1750	2974	NA
Six-40	4-dr. Phae.-7P	2250	3939	NA
Six-54	2-dr. Sed.-5P	3100	4100	NA

ENGINE: [Model Six-40] Inline. Six cyl. Cast iron block. B & S: 3-1/2 x 5 in. Disp. 288.5 cu. in. Brake H.P.: 40. S.A.E. H.P.: 29.4. Main bearings: 3. Valve lifters: mechanical. [Model Six-54] Inline. Six cyl. Cast iron block. B & S: 4-1/8 x 5-1/4 in. Disp.: 421 cu. in. Brake H.P.: 54 @ 1500 R.P.M. N.A.C.C. H.P.: 40.84. Main bearings: 3. Valve lifters: mechanical.

CHASSIS: [Model Six-40] W.B.: 123 in. Frt/Rear Tread: 56 in. Tires: 34 x 4. [Model Six-54] W.B.: 135 in. Frt/Rear Tread: 56 in. Tires: 36 x 4-1/2.

1914 Hudson, model 54, sedan, JAC

TECHNICAL: Sliding gear transmission. Speeds: 4F/1R, 3F/1R (Model Six-40). Floor shift controls. Cork insert, wet clutch. Shaft drive. Semi-floating rear axle. Mechanical brakes on two (rear) wheels. Artillery type wood wheels. Rim size: 36 in., 34 in. (Model Six-40).

OPTIONS: Front bumper. Rear bumper. Wire wheels, radiator cap with Hudson triangle I.D.

HISTORICAL: Introduced Aug. 1913 — Six-54, Nov. 1913 — Six-40. Hudson made 10,261 shipments to dealers during the 1914 calendar year. The president of Hudson was Roy D. Chapin.

1914

Model 40, 6-cyl.

	FP	5	4	3	2	1
Rbt	1750	1250	3900	6500	9100	13,000
Tr	1750	1400	4200	7000	9800	14,000
Cabr	1950	1300	4050	6750	9450	13,500
Model 54, 6-cyl.						
7P Tr	2250	1650	4650	7750	10,850	15,500

1915

1915 Hudson, model 40, 7-pass. touring, OCW

HUDSON — MODEL SIX-40 — SIX: The new Hudson models were externally identified by their honey-comb type radiators (previous models were fitted with horizontal-finned versions) and higher mounted headlamp tie-bar. All models also had a smoother radiator/hood line. Open cars (Roadster and Phaeton) had a new non-folding 2-piece windshield design whose upper portion pivoted from the top of the side brackets. On the Six-40 models a revamped interior arrangement placed the gas pedal between the brake and clutch pedals. A new electric horn was activated by the steering wheel center mounted button. Mechanically the Six-40 for 1915 had a new tubular driveshaft and a tapered frame that allowed for a slightly shorter turning radius. Other improvements to the Six-40 for 1915 included a horsepower increase to forty-two, a cast on bloc manifold, more efficient pre-heating of carburetor air and a hollow rather than solid driveshaft.

HUDSON — MODEL SIX-54 — SIX: Changes in the Six-54 were limited to the use of the honeycomb radiator and smoother radiator/hoodline as adopted by the Six-40.

I.D. DATA: Car number on front seat riser plate and on right side of frame. Starting: Six-40 73501, Six-54 59001. Ending: Six-40 90000, Six-54 62000. Engine number on left side of cylinder block.

1915 Hudson, model 40, coupe, WRG

Model No.	Body Type & Seating	Price	Weight	Prod. Total
Six-40	2-dr. Rds.-3P	1550	2772	NA
Six-40	4-dr. Phae.-7P	1550	2922	NA
Six-40	2-dr. Cabr.-3P	1750	2946	NA
Six-40	2-dr. Cpe.-4P	2150	3162	NA
Six-40	4-dr. Limo. Landaulet-7P	2700	3432	NA
Six-40	4-dr. Limo.-7P	2550	3362	NA
Six-40	4-dr. R.H. Phae.-7P	1550	2922	NA
Six-54	4-dr. Phae.-7P	2350	3965	NA
Six-54	2-dr. Sed.-5P	3100	NA	NA
Six-54	4-dr. Limo.-7P	3500	4226	NA

ENGINE: [Model Six-40] Inline. Six cyl. Cast iron block. B & S: 3-1/2 x 5 in. Disp.: 288.5 cu. in. Brake H.P.: 42. N.A.C.C. H.P.: 29.4. Main bearings: 4. Valve lifters: mechanical.[Model Six-54] Inline. Six cyl. Cast iron block. B & S: 4-1/2 x 5-1/4 in. Disp.: 421 cu. in. Brake H.P.: 55 @ 1500 R.P.M. N.A.C.C. H.P.: 40.84. Main bearings: 3. Valve lifters: mechanical.

CHASSIS: [Model Six-40] W.B.: 123 in. Frt/Rear Tread: 56 in. Tires: 34 x 4. [Model Six-54] W.B. 135 in. Frt/Rear Tread: 56 in. Tires: 36 x 4-1/2.

TECHNICAL: Sliding gear transmission. Speeds: 4F/1R, 3F/1R [Model Six-40]. Floor shift controls. Cork insert, wet clutch. Shaft drive. Semi-floating rear axle. Mechanical brakes on two rear wheels. Artillery-type wood wheels. Rim size: 36 in., 34 in. (Model Six-40).

OPTIONS: Front bumper. Rear bumper. Wire wheels.

HISTORICAL: Introduced June 1914. Hudson made 12,864 shipments to dealers during the 1915 calendar year. The president of Hudson was Roy D. Chapin.

1915
Model 40, 6-cyl.

	FP	5	4	3	2	1
Rds	1550	1750	4800	8000	11,200	16,000
Phae	1550	1800	4950	8250	11,550	16,500
Tr	1550	1550	4500	7500	10,500	15,000
Cabr	1750	1200	3750	6250	8750	12,500
Cpe	2150	1025	2600	5250	7300	10,500
Limo	2550	1125	3450	5750	8050	11,500
Lan Limo	2700	1150	3600	6000	8400	12,000

Model 54, 6-cyl.

Phae	2350	2200	5250	8750	12,250	17,500
7P Tr	2350	2000	5100	8500	11,900	17,000
Sed	3100	1150	3600	6000	8400	12,000
Limo	3500	1400	4200	7000	9800	14,000

1916

1916 Hudson, Super Six, touring victoria, OCW

HUDSON — MODEL SIX-40 — SERIES G-SIX: The Six-40's model run was a short one, lasting from June, 1915 to January, 1916 when it, as well as the unchanged Six-54, was replaced by the Super Six. The Six-40 featured both styling and engineering changes. The beltline was given a gentle curve to further enhance the "yacht-line" styling that had been an advertised feature since 1913, and both entry into and riding in a Hudson became a bit more enjoyable due to wider doors and a roomier interior. On open models the upper portion of the beltline was leather-covered. Hudson also touted its new "Ever-Lustre" finish which in a veiled reference to rust and corrison, it noted "combats as never before the main cause of depreciation." In preparation for the new Super Six and a change of philosophy regarding annual model changes Hudson identified the last of the Six-40s as Series G.

I.D. DATA: Car number on front seat riser plate and on right side of frame. Starting: G10001. Ending: G40000. Engine number on left side of cylinder block.

Model No.	Body Type & Seating	Price	Weight	Prod. Total
Series G	2-dr. Rds.-3P	1350	2900	NA
Series G	4-dr. Phae.-7P	1350	3033	NA
Series G	2-dr. Cabr.-3P	1650	3009	NA
Series G	2-dr. Cpe.-4P	2000	3240	NA
Series G	2-dr. Tr.Sed.-7P	1875	3330	NA
Series G	4-dr. Limo.-7P	2450	3535	NA
Series G	4-dr. Twn. Car-7P	—	3370	NA

ENGINE: Inline. Six cyl. Cast iron block. B & S: 3-1/2 x 5 in. Disp.: 288.5 cu. in. C.R.: 5.0:1. Brake H.P.: 42. N.A.C.C. H.P.: 29.4. Main bearings: 4. Valve lifters: mechanical.

CHASSIS: [Model Six-40] W.B.: 123 in. Frt/Rear Tread: 56 in. Tires: 34 x 4.

TECHNICAL: Sliding gear transmission. Speeds: 3F/1R. Floor shift controls. Cork insert, wet clutch. Shaft drive. Semi-floating rear axle. Mechanical brakes on two (rear) wheels. Artillery-type wood wheels. Rim size: 34 in.

OPTIONS: Front bumper. Rear bumper. Wire wheels.

HISTORICAL: Introduced June 1916. Hudson made 25,772 shipments to dealers during the 1916 calendar year. The president of Hudson was Roy D. Chapin.

1916 Hudson, Super Six, touring, WRG

HUDSON — SUPER SIX — SERIES H — SIX: Hudson made motoring history with the introduction of the Super Six. Not only was this car powered by the first Hudson-built engine but it established a new benchmark by which the performance of production automobiles would be measured. The Super Six four-bearing crankshaft was fitted with eight counterweights, for which Hudson received a patent. Other notable advancements included larger valves, a high 5.0:1 compression ratio and excellent porting. With considerable justification Hudson called the Super-Six "the greatest motor built." In production until 1926 it established Hudson as a manufacturer whose 6-cylinder engines made a mockery of performance claims made by producers of far more expensive automobiles.

I.D. DATA: Car numbers on front seat riser plate and on right side of frame. Starting: Series H H-1. Ending: Series H H-99999. Engine number on left side of cylinder block.

Model No.	Body Type & Seating	Price	Weight	Prod. Total
Series H	2-dr. Rds.-2P	1375	3170	NA
Series H	4-dr. Phae.-7P	1375	3385	NA
Series H	2-dr. Cabr.-3P	1675	3310	NA
Series H	4-dr. Tr. Sed.-7P	1900	3600	NA
Series H	4-dr. Limo.-7P	2500	3750	NA
Series H	4-dr. Limo.-Landaulet-7P	2750	—	NA
Series H	4-dr. Twn. Car-7P	2500	3660	NA
Series H	4-dr. Twn. Car Landaulet-7P	2750	—	NA
Series J	4-dr. Phae.-4P	1750	3180	NA

ENGINE: Inline. Six cyl. Cast iron block. B & S: 3-1/2 x 5 in. Disp.: 289 cu. in. C.R.: 5.00:1. Brake H.P.: 76 @ 2450 R.P.M. N.A.C.C. H.P.: 29.4. Main bearings: 4. Type of Valve lifters: mechanical. Carb. Hudson-built, side draft.

CHASSIS: [Series H] W.B.: 125-1/2 in. Frt/Rear Tread: 56 in. Tires: 35 x 4-1/2.

TECHNICAL: Sliding gear transmission. 3F/1R. Floor shift. Cork inserts, wet clutch. Shaft drive. Semi-floating rear axle. Mechanical brakes on two (rear) wheels. Artillery-type wood wheels. Rim size: 34 in.

OPTIONS: Front bumper. Rear bumper. Wire wheels, spare tire. The Series H Phaeton had disc wheels and Moto-Meter as standard equipment.

HISTORICAL: Introduced Jan. 16, 1916 following a series of Super Six speed runs made on a Long Island (New York) track in December 1915. Series H shipments to dealers were included in the 25,772 total for the 1916 calendar year. The president of Hudson was Roy D. Chapin. The Super Six set a new, transcontinental, San Francisco-New York record of 5 days, 3 hours, 31 minutes. After an 8-hour rest, the car, a stock touring car and its four-man crew headed back and arrived in San Francisco 5 days, 17 hours and 32 minutes later. At Daytona Beach on April 10, 1916 Ralph Mulford drove a Super-Six with a competition body to a new stock car chassis speed record of 102.53 mph. Mulford also set a new Pikes Peak record with a Super-Six of 18 minutes, 24 seconds. Mulford's Daytona Beach Record car also established a 24 hour mark for stock chassis automobiles at Sheepshead Bay, New York. His average of 74.8 mph for 1819 miles stood for 15 years before it was beaten by a 16-cylinder Marmon.

1916
Super Six, 6-cyl.

	FP	5	4	3	2	1
Rds	1475	1550	4500	7500	10,500	15,000
Cabr	1675	1650	4650	7750	10,850	15,500
Phae	1475	1750	4800	8000	11,200	16,000
Tr Sed	2000	1075	3000	5500	7700	11,000
TwnC	2750	1100	3300	5650	7900	11,300
Model 54, 6-cyl.						
7P Phae	2350	1550	4500	7500	10,500	15,000

1917

1917 Hudson, Super Six, touring, JAC

1917 Hudson, Super Six, coupe, WRG

HUDSON — SUPER SIX — SERIES J — SIX: Beginning on December 1, 1916 the Series H Super Six was superseded by the Series J and 4J with a built-in radiator shutters and a Boyce Moto-Meter radiator cap. In addition, a different upholstery pattern was used on open phaetons, and the limousine version had a straight, instead of curved front door line and squared off window edges.

I.D. DATA: Car numbers on front seat riser plate and on right side of frame. Starting: Series J J-1, Series 4J 4J-75000. Ending: Series J J-96499, Series 4J 4J-97999. Engine number on left side of cylinder block.

Model No.	Body Type & Seating	Price	Weight	Prod. Total
Series J	4-dr. Phae.-4P	1750	3180	NA
Series J	4-dr. Phae.-7P	1650	3220	NA
Series J	4-dr. Tr. Sed.-7P	2175	3450	NA
Series J	2-dr. Cabr.-3P	1950	3195	NA
Series J	4-dr. Limo.-7P	2925	3715	NA
Series J	4-dr Limo. Lan.-7P	3025	3760	NA
Series J	4-dr. Twn. Car-7P	2925	3530	NA
Series J	4-dr. Twn. Car Lan.-7P	3025	3585	NA
Series J	2-dr. Tr. Sed.-5P	NA	NA	NA
Series J	2-dr. Rbt. Lan.	2350	3250	NA
Series 4J	4-dr. Sed.-7P	NA	3700	NA
Series 4J	4-dr. Tr. Limo.-4P	3150	3655	NA
Series 4J	4-dr. Full-Folding Lan.-4P	NA	NA	NA

ENGINE: Inline. Six cyl. Cast iron block. B & S: 3-1/2 x 5 in. Disp.: 289 cu. in. C.R.: 5.00:1. Brake H.P.: 76 @ 2450 R.P.M. N.A.C.C. H.P.: 29.4. Main bearings: 4. Type of Valve lifters: mechanical. Carb. Hudson-built, side draft.

CHASSIS: [Series J] W.B.: 125-1/2 in. Frt/Rear Tread: 56 in. Tires: 35 x 4-1/2.

TECHNICAL: Sliding gear transmission. 3F/1R. Floor shift. Cork inserts, wet clutch. Shaft drive. Semi-floating rear axle. Mechanical brakes on two (rear) wheels. Artillery-type wood wheels. Rim size: 34 in.

OPTIONS: Front bumper. Rear bumper. Wire wheels, spare tire.

HISTORICAL: Introduced December 1, 1916. The president of Hudson was Roy D. Chapin. The Super Six continued its winning ways, a four-car team enjoying numerous racing victories during 1917.

696

1917 Hudson, Super Six, limousine, WRG

1917
Super Six, 6-cyl.

	FP	5	4	3	2	1
Rds	1650	1200	3750	6250	8750	12,500
Cabr	1950	1250	3900	6500	9100	13,000
7P Phae	1650	1200	3750	6250	8750	12,500
Tr Sed	2175	1000	2400	5000	7000	10,000
TwnC	2925	1200	3750	6250	8750	12,500
Twn Lan	3025	1250	3900	6500	9100	13,000
Limo Lan	3025	1200	3750	6250	8750	12,500

1918

1918 Hudson, Super Six, touring limousine, JAC

HUDSON — SUPER SIX — SERIES M — SIX: Changes in the Super Six format were very limited. The rear doors on phaeton models now were rear hinged and closed models were not equipped with external windshield visors.

I.D. DATA: Car number on front seat riser plate and on right side of frame. Starting: M5000. Ending: M97499. Engine number on left side of cylinder block/motor mount.

Model No.	Body Type & Seating	Price	Weight	Prod. Total
NA	4-dr. Phae.-4P	2050	3180	NA
NA	4-dr. Phae.-7P	1950	3400	NA
NA	2-dr. Rbt. Lan.-2P	2350	3250	NA
NA	2-dr. Cabr.-3P	2650	3500	NA
NA	2-dr. Cpe.-4P	2850	3450	NA
NA	4-dr. Sed.-7P	2750	3700	NA
NA	4-dr. Limo.-7P	3400	3715	NA
NA	4-dr. Limo. Lan.-7P	3500	3760	NA
NA	4-dr. Twn. Car-7P	3400	3605	NA
NA	4-dr. Full-Folding Lan.-4P	4250	3765	NA
NA	4-dr. Tr.Limo.-7P	3150	NA	NA
NA	4-dr. Twn.Car Lan.-7P	3500	NA	NA

ENGINE: Inline. Six cyl. Cast iron block. B & S: 3-1/2 x 5 in. Disp.: 289 cu. in. C.R.: 5.0:1. Brake H.P.: 76 @ 2450 R.P.M. N.A.C.C. H.P.: 29.4. Main bearings: 4. Valve lifters: mechanical. Carb: Hudson-built, side draft.

CHASSIS: [Series M] W.B.: 125-1/2 in. Tires: 35 x 4-1/2*
*4P Phae. and Rbt. Lan. used 32 x 4-1/2 tires. The Twn Car Lan. Twn Car and Limo. Lan. were fitted with 33 x 5 tires.

TECHNICAL: Sliding gear transmission. 3F/1R. Floor shift. Cork inserts, running in oil. Shaft drive. Semi-floating rear axle. Mechanical brakes on two (rear) wheels. 10 spoke, wooden front, 12 spoke wooden rear. Rim size: 34 in.

OPTIONS: Front bumper. Rear bumper. Wire wheels. Windshield mounted spot light. Running board mats. Leather top for Rbt. Lan.

1918 Hudson, Super Six, full-folding landau, WRG

HISTORICAL: Introduced Dec. 1917. Hudson made 12,526 shipments to dealers during the 1918 calendar year. The president of Hudson was Roy D. Chapin. The Hudson racing team was disbanded in Aug. 1917.

1918
Super Six, 6-cyl.

	FP	5	4	3	2	1
Rds	1650	1250	3900	6500	9100	13,000
Cabr	1950	1300	4050	6750	9450	13,500
4P Phae	2050	1150	3600	6000	8400	12,000
5P Phae	1950	1200	3750	6250	8750	12,500
4P Cpe	2000	900	1900	4500	6300	9000
Tr Sed	2175	950	2100	4750	6650	9500
Sed	2750	950	2100	4750	6650	9500
Tr Limo	3150	1150	3600	6000	8400	12,000
TwnC	3400	1150	3600	6000	8400	12,000
Limo	3400	1150	3600	6000	8400	12,000
Twn Limo	3500	1200	3750	6250	8750	12,500
Limo Lan	3500	1150	3600	6000	8400	12,000
F F Lan	4250	1200	3750	6250	8750	12,500

1919

HUDSON — SUPER SIX — SERIES O — SIX: All closed body Series O Hudsons had large external sun visors, and their front doors were now rear-hinged. Common to all Hudsons were new 12 spoke front wheels. Major chassis revision included larger 7 inch side frame rails, a larger and sturdier rear axle plus brakes with measurements of 2-1/2 x 15 inches. The Hudson's single taillight was moved from its left rear fender location on Series M to the rear cross member on Series O. Also identifying the Series O Hudsons were their higher gear shift and 4 hinge doors. The Model M doors had 3 hinges.

Note 1: Hudson regarded the Series M Super Six as a 1919 model until the Series O was introduced in May 1919.

I.D. DATA: Car number on front seat riser plate and on right side of frame. Starting: 5000. Ending: 90999. Engine number of left side of cylinder block/motor mount.

Model No.	Body Type & Seating	Price	Weight	Prod. Total
NA	4-dr. Phae.-4P	2075	3320	NA
NA	4-dr. Phae.-7P	1975	3475	NA
NA	2-dr. Cabr.-3P	2450	3500	NA
NA	2-dr. Cpe.-4P	2950	3530	NA
NA	4-dr. Sed.-7P	2775	3775	NA
NA	4-dr. Tr. Limo.-7P	3300	3730	NA
NA	4-dr. Limo.-7P	3650	3800	NA
NA	4-dr. Limo. Lan.-7P	NA	NA	NA
NA	4-dr. Twn. Car-7P	NA	NA	NA
NA	4-dr. Twn. Car Lan.-7P	NA	NA	NA

1919 Hudson, Super Six, special sedan, WRG

ENGINE: Inline. Six cyl. Cast iron block. B & S: 3-1/2 x 5 in. Disp. 289 cu. in. C.R.: 5.0:1. Brake H.P.: 76 @ 2450 R.P.M. N.A.C.C. H.P.: 29.4. Main bearings: 4. Valve lifters: mechanical. Carb. Hudson-built, side draft.

CHASSIS: [Series O] W.B.: 125-1/2 in. Frt/Rear Tread: 56 in. Tires: 34 x 4-1/2.

TECHNICAL: Sliding gear transmission. 3F/1R. Floor shift. Cork inserts, running in oil. Shaft drive. Semi-floating rear axle. Mechanical brakes on two (rear) wheels. Wooden spoke wheels. Rim size: 34 in.

OPTIONS: Front bumper. Rear bumper. Wire wheels. Windshield mounted spotlight. Running boat mats. Leather top for Runabout Landau.

HISTORICAL: Introduced May 1919. Hudson made 18,175 shipments to dealers during the 1919 calendar year. The president of Hudson was Roy D. Chapin. Six old Hudson racers attempted to qualify for the 1919 Indianapolis 500. Ira Vail's Hudson qualified at 94.1 mph and finished eighth. Just behind was Car #21, a Hudson driven by Denny Hickey who averaged 80.22 mph for the 50 miles. Another Hudson, driven by Ora Haibe started in 26th position and was credited with 14th place at the race's end. Car #5, which was powered by a modified Hudson engine was, with a qualifying average of 99.80 mph, placed in the 14th position for the race's start. However it was out on lap 14 with a broken connecting rod.

1919
Super Six Series O, 6-cyl.

	FP	5	4	3	2	1
Cabr	2000	1150	3600	6000	8400	12,000
4P Phae	2100	1200	3750	6250	8750	12,500
7P Phae	—	1250	3900	6500	9100	13,000
4P Cpe	—	875	1700	4250	5900	8500
Sed	—	775	1500	3750	5250	7500
Tr Limo	—	950	2100	4750	6650	9500
TwnC	—	1075	3000	5500	7700	11,000
Twn Lan	—	1125	3450	5750	8050	11,500
Limo. Lan.	—	1150	3600	6000	8400	12,000

1920

1920 Hudson, Super Six, coupe, OCW

HUDSON — SUPER SIX — 10-O, 11-O, 12-O — SIX: Hudson produced the Super Six in three series yet they were little changed from 1919. Most models were slightly heavier than their year-old counterparts. Although not used throughout the entire model run, a new front tiebar was introduced that positioned the headlights notably higher.

I.D. DATA: Car number on front seat riser plate and on right side of frame. Starting: 5000. Ending: 91999. Engine number on left side of cylinder block/motor mount.

Model No.	Body Type & Seating	Price	Weight	Prod. Total
NA	4-dr. Phae.-4P	2600	3405	NA
NA	4-dr. Phae.-7P	2600	3575	NA
NA	2-dr. Cabr.-2P	NA	3550	NA
NA	2-dr. Cpe.-4P	3575	3620	NA
NA	4-dr. Tr.Limo.-7P	3925	3840	NA
NA	4-dr. Limo.-7P	4275	3860	NA
NA	4-dr. Sed.-7P	3400	3815	NA

Note: During the year Hudson made substantial price cuts.

ENGINE: Inline. Six cyl. Cast iron block. B & S: 3-1/2 x 5 in. Disp.: 289 cu. in. C.R.: 5.0:1. Brake H.P.: 76 @ 2450 R.P.M. N.A.C.C. H.P.: 29.4. Main bearings: 4. Valve lifters: mechanical. Carb.: Hudson built, side draft.

CHASSIS: [Series 10-O] W.B.: 125-1/2 in. Frt/Rear Tread: 56 in. Tires: 34 x 4-1/2. [Series 11-O] W.B.: 125-1/2 in. Frt/Rear Tread: 56 in. Tires: 34 x 4-1/2. [Series 12-O] W.B.: 125-1/2 in. Frt/Rear Tread: 56 in. Tires: 34 x 4-1/2.

TECHNICAL: Sliding gear transmission. 3F/1R. Floor shift. Multiple disc, cork inserts, running in oil. Shaft drive. Semi-floating rear axle. Mechanical brakes on two (rear) wheels. Wooden spoke wheels with detachable rims.

OPTIONS: Front bumper. Rear bumper. Wire wheels. Spot light. Running board mats.

1920 Hudson, Super Six, limousine, WRG

HISTORICAL: Introduced Dec. 1919. Hudson made 22,268 shipments to dealers during the 1920 calendar year. The president of Hudson was Roy D. Chapin.

1920
Super Six Series 10-12, 6-cyl.

	FP	5	4	3	2	1
4P Phae	—	1200	3750	6250	8750	12,500
7P Phae	—	1150	3600	6000	8400	12,000
Cabr	31800	1250	3900	6500	9100	13,000
Cpe	—	875	1700	4250	5900	8500
Sed	—	775	1500	3750	5250	7500
Tr Limo	—	900	1900	4500	6300	9000
Limo	—	950	2100	4750	6650	9500

1921

1921 Hudson, Super Six, 4-pass. coupe, OCW

HUDSON — SUPER SIX — SIX: From 1921 through 1923 Hudson annually produced, in effect 2 separate lines of automobiles. For example the initial 1921 models were essentially carry overs from 1920. Then in September revamped models also regarded as 1921 models were introduced. In turn these became 1922 models until May 1922 when new versions, also regarded as of 1922 vintage debuted. The second run of 1921 models were identified by a revamped interior featuring a new steering wheel and instrument panel which placed all the instruments in a panel center mounted on the dash. In addition the classic H-shaped shifting gate was replaced with a rotating ball arrangement. Hudson also rearranged its foot controls by moving the accelerator from its position between the clutch and brake to the more logical location adjacent to the right side of the brake.

External styling revisions of the second series Hudsons included heavier fenders with a more pronounced overlap and the installation of splash shields beneath the radiator.

I.D. DATA: Car number on front frame channel, dash and frame side. Starting: 100000. Ending: 499999 (serial number range 1921-23). Engine number on left side of cylinder block/motor mount.

Model No.	Body Type & Seating	Price	Weight	Prod. Total
NA	4-dr. Phae.-4P	NA	3405	NA
NA	4-dr. Phae.-7P	NA	3575	NA
NA	2-dr. Cabr.-2P	NA	3550	NA
NA	2-dr. Cpe.-4P	3275	3620	NA
NA	4-dr. Tr. Limo.-7P	3625	3840	NA
NA	4-dr. Limo.-7P	4000	3860	NA
NA	4-dr. Sed.-7P	3400	3815	NA

Note 1: Hudson reduced the prices of its automobiles twice during 1921, in June and Aug.

ENGINE: Inline. Six cyl. Cast iron block. B & S: 3-1/2 x 5 in. Disp.: 289 cu. in. C.R.: 5.0:1. Brake H.P.: 76 @ 2450 R.P.M. N.A.C.C. H.P.: 29.4. Main bearings: 4. Valve lifters: mechanical. Carb.: Hudson-built, side draft.

CHASSIS: No series identification used during 1921-23. W.B.: 125-1/2 in. Frt/Rear Tread: 56 in. Tires: 34 x 4-1/2.

TECHNICAL: Sliding gear transmission. 3F/1R. Floor shift. Multiple disc, cork inserts, running in oil. Shaft drive. Semi-floating rear axle. Mechanical brakes on two (rear) wheels. Wood spoke wheels with detachable rims.

OPTIONS: Front bumper. Rear bumper. Spotlight. Wire wheels. Running board mats. Radiator shutters.

1921 Hudson, Super Six, 7-pass. touring, JAC

HISTORICAL: Introduced Dec. 1, 1920, revamped models introduced Sept. 1921. Hudson made 13,721 shipments to dealers during the 1921 calendar year. The president of Hudson was Roy D. Chapin. A competition-prepared Hudson won the Penrose trophy at the Pikes Peak hill climb with a time of 19 minutes, 16.1 seconds.

1921
Super Six, 6-cyl.

	FP	5	4	3	2	1
4P Phae	—	1200	3750	6250	8750	12,500
7P Phae	—	1150	3600	6000	8400	12,000
Cabr	—	1250	3900	6500	9100	13,000
4P Cpe	—	875	1700	4250	5900	8500
Sed	—	825	1600	4000	5600	8000
Tr Limo	—	900	1900	4500	6300	9000
Limo	—	950	2100	4750	6650	9500

1922

HUDSON — SUPER SIX — SERIES 9 — SIX: Hudson moved out of the post war sales depression in a strong fashion. In July price reductions ranging from $50 to $100 were announced and company president Roy D. Chapin reported that "the volume of shipment is now so great that certain savings have been effected in costs, and the public is to be given the benefit." Stockholders also received a share of Hudson's renewed prosperity since in Sept. a dividend of 50¢ per share in non-par and $2.50 per share on par capital stock was declared. Although the new Essex coach captured the bulk of the public's attention, Hudson also introduced this new body style. During the first portion of the model year new drum shaped headlights were adopted. Among the second line of Super Sixes for 1922 which debuted in May 1922 was a sedan with a Biddle & Smart body. Its styling, far more elegant than the Fisher-built body it replaced pointed toward the classic Biddle & Smart-bodied Hudsons yet to come. Improvements to Hudson's long-lived Super-Six included the adoption of aluminum pistons and a Morse timing chain in place of the older helical gear drive. Second series Hudsons had their batteries placed under the front seat.

1922 Hudson, Super Six, phaeton, HAC

I.D. DATA: Car number on front frame channel, dash and frame side. Starting: 100,000. Ending: 499999 (series numbers range 1921-23). Engine number on left side of cylinder block/motor mount.

Model No.	Body Type & Seating	Price	Weight	Prod. Total
NA	4-dr. Phae.-4P	1695	3395	NA
NA	4-dr. Phae.-7P	1745	3445	NA
NA	2-dr. Cabr.-2P	2295	3550	NA
NA	2-dr. Cpe.-4P	2570	3620	NA
NA	2-dr. C'ch.-5P	1625	3435	NA
NA	4-dr. Sed.-7P	2650	3785	NA
NA	4-dr. Tr. Limo.-5P	2920	3870	NA
NA	4-dr. Limo.-7P	3495	3860	NA
NA	4-dr. Spds.-4P	1525	3310	NA
NA	4-dr. Phae.-7P*	1575	3455	NA
NA	4-dr. Sed.-7P*	2295	3720	NA

Note 1: *4-dr. Sed.-7P: Biddle & Smart body.

ENGINE: Inline. Six cyl. Cast iron block. B & S: 3-1/2 x 5 in. Disp. 289 cu. in. C.R.: 5.0:1. Brake H.P.: 76 @ 2450 R.P.M. N.A.C.C. H.P.: 29.4. Main bearings: 4. Valve lifters: mechanical. Carb. Hudson-built, side draft.

CHASSIS: No series identification used 1921-23. W.B. 125-1/2 in. Frt/Rear Tread: 56 in. Tires: 34 x 4-1/2.

TECHNICAL: Sliding gear transmission. Speeds: 3F/1R. Floor shift controls. Multiple disc, cork inserts, running in oil. Shaft drive. Semi-floating rear axle. Mechanical brakes on two (rear) wheels. Wooden spoke wheels with detachable rims.

OPTIONS: Front bumper. Rear bumper. Wire wheels. Running board mats. Radiator shutters.

HISTORICAL: Introduced Dec. 1921, 2nd version — May 1922. Hudson made 28,242 shipments to dealers during the 1922 calendar year. The president of Hudson was Roy D. Chapin. Hudsons finished first at Pikes Peak in hill climb with a time of 20 minutes, 5 seconds.

1922
Super Six, 6-cyl.

	FP	5	4	3	2	1
Spds	—	1250	3900	6500	9100	13,000
Phae	—	1300	4050	6750	9450	13,500
Cabr	—	1400	4200	7000	9800	14,000
Cpe	—	800	1550	3850	5400	7700
2 dr Sed	—	775	1500	3750	5250	7500
Sed	—	750	1450	3400	5000	7100
Tr Limo	—	900	1900	4500	6300	9000
Limo	—	950	2100	4750	6650	9500

1923

1923 Hudson, Super Six, coach, JAC

HUDSON — SUPER SIX — SIX: Except for minor detail modifications which were incorporated as running changes during the year the 1923 Hudsons were virtually identical to the 1922 models. Among these revisions were the use of McKee "Spreadlight" headlight lenses, plus an extended length, 28" gear shift. This was an extremely profitable year for Hudson. Its fiscal year profits totalled nearly $14.5 million, up from the $12.6 million level of the previous year. Twice during the year the company declared an extra 25¢ dividend in addition to the regular 50¢ dividend. The Hudson Motor Car Company also made some significant changes in its top level management structure. Roy D. Chapin, after serving as president for 13 years became chairman of the board. His successor was Roscoe B. Jackson. Replacing Jackson as vice-president and treasurer was William J. McAneeny.

I.D. DATA: Car number on front frame channel, dash and frame side. Starting: 100000. Ending: 499999 (serial number range 1921-23). Engine number on left side of cylinder block.

Model No.	Body Type & Seating	Price	Weight	Prod. Total
NA	4-dr. Spds.-4P	1295	3395	NA
NA	4-dr. Phae.-7P	1350	3445	NA
NA	2-dr. Cch.-5P	1375	3433	NA
NA	2-dr. Cpe.	2570	3620	NA
NA	4-dr. Sed.-5P	1895	3620	NA
NA	4-dr. Sed.-7P	2095	3720	NA

Note 1: 4-dr. Sed.-5P: Biddle & Smart body.
Note 2: 2-dr. Cpe. and 4-dr. Sed.-7P: These two bodies were phased out of production during 1922.

ENGINE: Inline. Six cyl. Cast iron block. B & S: 3-1/2 x 5 in. C.R.: 5.0:1. Brake H.P.: 76 @ 2450 R.P.M. N.A.C.C. H.P.: 29.4. Main bearings: 4. Valve lifters: mechanical. Carb.: Stewart Warner.

CHASSIS: No series identification used 1921-23. W.B.: 125-1/2 in. Frt/Rear Tread: 56 in. Tires: 34 x 4-1/2.

TECHNICAL: Sliding gear transmission. Speeds: 3F/1R. Floor shift controls. Multiple disc, cork inserts, running in oil. Shaft drive. Semi-floating rear axle. Mechanical brakes on two (rear) wheels. Wooden spoke wheels with detachable rims.

1923 Hudson, Super Six, limousine, WRG

OPTIONS: Front bumper. Rear bumper. Spotlight. Steel disc wheels (25.00) Spare wheel. Under seat heater. Radiator shutters.

HISTORICAL: Introduced Dec. 1922. Hudson made 46,337 shipments to dealers during the 1923 calendar year. The president of Hudson was Roscoe B. Jackson.

1923
Super Six, 6-cyl.

	FP	5	4	3	2	1
Spds	—	1400	4200	7000	9800	14,000
Phae	—	1250	3900	6500	9100	13,000
2 dr Sed	—	775	1500	3750	5250	7500
Sed	—	825	1600	4000	5600	8000
7P Sed	—	875	1700	4250	5900	8500
Cpe	—	900	1900	4500	6300	9000

1924

1924 Hudson, Super Six, 5-pass. sedan, JAC

HUDSON — SUPER SIX — SIX: The initial line of Hudson Super-Six automobiles were virtually unchanged from those offered in the latter part of 1923. In mid-June they were replaced by significantly altered models. Styling changes included windshields with a curved lower edge and a raised hood line from radiator to cowl. A new fender crease line began to take Hudson away from the more rigid look of the early twenties. A longer, 127.5 inch wheelbase also contributed to this effect. Mechanical changes were also extensive. New, smaller 33 inch wheels were fitted with new "balloon" type, 33 x 6.20 tires. To accommodate this change the Hudson's steering and suspension were modified. Although its horsepower rating of 76 remained unchanged the Super Six engine now had a separate intake manifold mounted on the right side. Previously the manifold had been on the opposite side of the engine and cast integrally with the block. The Hudson-made side draft carburetor was also replaced by a Detroit Lubrication model.

I.D. DATA: Car number on front frame channel, dash and frame side. Starting: 500001. Ending: 562016. Engine number on left side of cylinder block.

Model No.	Body Type & Seating	Price	Weight	Prod. Total
NA	4-dr. Sed.-5P	1895	3590	NA
NA	4-dr. Sed.-7P	2145	3675	NA
NA	4-dr. Sed.-5P	2145	3605	NA
NA	4-dr. Spds.-4P	1400	3275	NA
NA	4-dr. Phae.-7P	1500	3400	NA
NA	4-dr. Sed.-5P	2150	3585	NA
NA	2-dr. C'ch.-5P	1395	3385	NA
NA	4-dr. Sed.-7P	2250	3640	NA

Note: 4-dr. Sed.-5P and 4-dr. Sed.-7P: Biddle & Smart body

1924 Hudson, Super Six, 7-pass. phaeton, WRG

ENGINE: Inline. Six cyl. Cast iron block. B & S: 3-1/2 x 5 in. Disp. 289 cu. in. C.R.: 5.0:1. Brake H.P. 76 @ 2450 R.P.M. N.A.C.C. H.P.: 29.4. Main bearings: 4. Valve lifters: mechanical. Carb.: Detroit Lubrication.

CHASSIS: No series designation used. W.B. 127-1/2 in. Tires: 33 x 6.20.

TECHNICAL: Sliding gear transmission. Speeds: 3F/1R. Floor shift controls. Multiple disc, cork inserts, running in oil. Shaft drive. Semi-floating rear axle. Mechanical brakes on two (rear) wheels. Wooden spoke wheels with detachable rims.

OPTIONS: Front bumper. Rear bumper. Spotlight. Auxiliary seats & carpeting (Sed.) (115.00). Steel Tuarc disc wheels. Wire wheels. Radiator shutters.

HISTORICAL: Introduced Dec. 1923 — new models introduced June 1924. Hudson made 59,427 shipments to dealers during the 1924 calendar year. The president of Hudson was Roscoe B. Jackson.

1924
Super Six, 6-cyl.

	FP	5	4	3	2	1
Spds	—	1300	4050	6750	9450	13,500
Phae	—	675	1300	2600	4400	6300
2 dr Sed	—	775	1500	3750	5250	7500
Sed	—	825	1600	4050	5650	8100
7P Sed	—	875	1700	4250	5900	8500

1925

1925 Hudson, Super Six, brougham, WRG

HUDSON — SUPER SIX — SIX: Hudson did not make any significant changes in the appearance of its automobiles for 1925. However, beginning in June, 1925 a very handsome Biddle & Smart bodied Brougham model became available and proved to be the most popular Biddle & Smart Hudson ever offered. Hudson also revised its Coach model during 1925 by reshaping its body to accept thinner side pillars and a windshield with a curved lower edge. In January a shift from 33 x 6.20 to 33 x 6.00

tires was announced. A total output of 269,474 Hudson and Essex automobiles put the Hudson Motor Car Company in third position behind Chevrolet and Ford for the 1925 calendar year.

I.D. DATA: Car number on front frame channel, dash and frame side. Starting: 562017. Ending: 672227. Engine number on left side of cylinder block/motor mount.

Model No.	Body Type & Seating	Price	Weight	Prod. Total
NA	2-dr. C'ch.-4P	1345	3385	NA
NA	2-dr. C'ch.-4P (A)	1165	3385	NA
NA	4-dr. Sed.-5P (B)	1695	3585	NA
NA	4-dr. Sed.-7P (B)	1650	3640	NA
NA	4-dr. Brgm.-4P (B)	1450	3425	NA
NA	4-dr. Phae.-7P	1200	3400	NA

Note 1: (A) This C'ch replaced the older C'ch in March 1925. Its Biddle & Smart body was constructed of aluminum.
Note 2: (B) Biddle & Smart body.

1925 Hudson, Super Six, 7-pass. sedan, WRG

ENGINE: Inline. Six cyl. Cast iron block. B & S: 3-1/2 x 5 in. Disp. 289 cu. in. C.R.: 5.0:1. Brake H.P.: 76 @ 2450 R.P.M. N.A.C.C. H.P.: 29.4. Main bearings: 4. Valve lifters: mechanical. Carb.: Detroit Lubrication.

CHASSIS: No series designations assigned. W.B. 127-1/2 in. Tires: 33 x 6.20 — replaced by 33 x 6.00 starting Jan. 1925.

TECHNICAL: Sliding gear transmission. Speeds: 3F/1R. Floor shift controls. Multiple disc, cork inserts, running in oil. Shaft drive. Semi-floating rear axle. Mechanical brakes on two (rear) wheels. Wooden spoke wheels with detachable rims.

OPTIONS: Front bumper. Rear bumper. Auxiliary seats and carpeting (Sedan). Steel Tuarc disc wheels. Wire wheels. Radiator shutters.

HISTORICAL: Introduced Dec. 1924. Hudson made 109,840 shipments to dealers during the 1925 calendar year. The president of Hudson was Roscoe B. Jackson.

1925
Super Six, 6-cyl.

	FP	5	4	3	2	1
Spds	—	1400	4200	7000	9800	14,000
Phae	—	1300	4050	6750	9450	13,500
2 dr Sed	1165	775	1500	3750	5250	7500
Brgm	1450	900	1900	4500	6300	9000
Sed	1650	775	1500	3750	5250	7500
7P Sed	1695	825	1600	4000	5600	8000

1926

1926 Hudson, Super Six, phaeton, WRG

HUDSON — SUPER SIX: Although Hudson carried the style and design of its 1925 models in 1926, it was nonetheless an important year for Hudson. Recognition of the role Hudson had played in automotive history in developing the Essex Coach came from *The New York Times* (Jan 10, 1926) which noted, "The flood of new, small closed sixes is one of the outstanding features of the year . . . That the light, economical six makes a definite and potent appeal cannot be doubted. Indeed the Hudson and Essex organization has one of the most remarkable achievements of 1925 to its credit in the production of 250,000 cars both makes, almost entirely closed models." Hudson also moved boldly to expand its corporate base in 1926 with the opening of its new, $3 million body plant whose first product was a revised coach for both Hudson and Essex. Mechanical changes consisted of revamped carburetor and intake manifold that Hudson said would improve fuel consumption by 2 mpg.

I.D. DATA: Car number on front frame channel, dash and frame side. Starting: 672228. Ending: 713809*. Engine number on left side of cylinder block/motor mount.

* In a letter to its dealers dated Sept 10, 1926 Hudson explained that it was instituting a yearly model classification starting with definite serial numbers. Thus the following cars were considered 1927 models, Hudson Coach beginning with serial number 713810, Sedans starting with serial number 714674 and Broughams starting with serial number 716440.

Model No.	Body Type & Seating	Price	Weight	Prod. Total
NA	4-dr. Brgm.-4P	1450	3425	—
NA	4-dr. Brgm.-5P	1395	3495	—
NA	4-dr. Sed.-7P	1650	3640	—
NA	4-dr. Tr. Car-7P	1300	3395	—
NA	2-dr. C'ch.-4P	1165	3470	—
NA	2-dr. C'ch. Sp.	1150	3440	—

Note 1: 4-dr. Brgm.-5P: Biddle & Smart body replaced the older Brgm mid-way through the model year.
Note 2: The 4-dr. Tr. Car-7P had the Biddle & Smart body.
Note 3: The 2-dr. C'ch. Sp. was fitted with a Hudson-built body approximately 2" lower than the older version.

1926 Hudson, Super Six, brougham, WRG

ENGINE: L-head. Inline. Six cyl. Cast iron block. B & S: 3-1/2 x 5 in. Disp.: 289 cu. in. C.R.: 5.0:1. Brake H.P.: 76 @ 2450 R.P.M. N.A.C.C. H.P.: 29.4. Main bearings: 4. Valve lifters: mechanical. Carb.: Detroit Lubrication.

CHASSIS: No series designation used. W.B.: 127-1/2 in. Tires: 33 x 6.00.

TECHNICAL: Sliding gear transmission. Speeds: 3F/1R. Floor shift controls. Multiple disc, cork inserts, running in oil. Shaft drive. Semi-floating rear axle. Mechanical brakes on two (rear) wheels. Wooden spoke wheels with detachable rims.

OPTIONS: Front bumper. Rear bumper. Spotlight. Radiator shutters.

HISTORICAL: Introduced Dec. 1925. Hudson made 70,261 shipments to dealers during the 1926 calendar year. The president of Hudson was Roscoe B. Jackson.

1926
Super Six, 6-cyl.

	FP	5	4	3	2	1
Phae	1150	2300	5400	9000	12,600	18,000
2 dr Sed	1095	775	1500	3750	5250	7500
Brgm	1395	950	2100	4750	6650	9500
7P Sed	1550	825	1600	4000	5600	8000

1927

HUDSON — MODEL O & S — SIX: Hudsons for 1927 were radically changed automobiles. They were fitted with new 18 inch wheels, four wheel brakes, new rear suspension and styling that featured a higher radiator-hood line and fenders of full crown design. Head lamps were bullet shaped and contributed along with a four-inch reduction in height to Hudson's very attractive styling. Hudson also offered new exterior color choices to take full advantage of its new look and on models offered after late June a full-length beltline molding painted in a contrasting body color dramatically improved Hudson's appearance. The Model S Hudsons were mounted on a 118 inch wheelbase, while the Model O cars continued the 127-3/8 inch wheelbase. A startling development was the replacement of the Veteran Super Six engine with a six cylinder engine of F-head design.

Also breaking with previous practice was the adoption of a single-plate clutch in place of the older multi-disc unit. Hudson had spent some $7 million to expand output of its factory to 1800 cars per nine-hour day and Hudson chairman Roy D. Chapin understandably looked to the future with optimism. He noted however that "Buyers are now insistent that cars shall excel in appearance and convenience as well as in the fundamental qualities. The demand for improved performance is widespread and is being met by better design, material and workmanship.

1927 Hudson, roadster, WRG

I.D. DATA: Car numbers on front frame channel, dash and frame side. Starting: Model O 750000, Model S 1001. Ending: Model O 803568, Model S 12269. Starting: 713810 (carry over 1926 cars sold as 1927 models) Engine numbers on left side of cylinder block/motor mount. Starting: 438,230. Ending: NA.

Model No.	Body Type & Seating	Price	Weight	Prod. Total
O	Standard 2-dr. C'ch.-5P	1285	3505	NA
O	Standard 4-dr. Sed.-5P	1385	3620	NA
O	Custom 2-dr. Rds.-2P	1500	3480	NA
O	Custom 4-dr. Sed.-5P	1750	3755	NA
O	Custom 4-dr. Phae.-7P	1600	3565	NA
O	Custom 4-dr. Sed.-7P	1850	3870	NA
O	Custom 4-dr. Brgm.-4P	1575	3660	NA
S	Standard 2-dr. C'ch.-5P	1175	3510	NA
S	Standard 4-dr. Sed.-5P	1285	3590	NA

Note 1: All Model O Custom Hudsons had Biddle & Smart bodies.

1927 Hudson, victoria, Murphy, WRG

ENGINE: F-head. Inline. Six cyl. Cast iron block. B & S: 3-1/2 x 5 in. Disp. 288.5 cu. in. C.R.: 5.0:1. Brake H.P.: 92 @ 3200 R.P.M. N.A.C.C. H.P.: 29.4. Main bearings: 4. Valve lifters: mechanical. Carb.: Marvel 1-1/4 in.

CHASSIS: [Model O] W.B. 127-3/8 in. O.L.: 188 in. Tires: 31 x 6.00. [Model S] W.B. 118 in. O.L.: 178-1/2 in. Tires: 31 x 6.00.

TECHNICAL: Sliding gear transmission. Speeds: 3F/1R. Floor shift controls. Single disc, cork inserts, running in oil. Shaft drive. Semi-floating rear axle. Overall Ratio: 4.09:1-Model S, 4.45:1-Model O. Bendix mechanical brakes on four wheels. Wooden spoke wheels with detachable rims. Rim size: 19 x 4-1/2 in.

OPTIONS: Trunk. Bumpers — front and rear. Radiator shutters.

HISTORICAL: Introduced Jan. 1927. Innovations: new F-head engine, four wheel brakes. Hudson made 66,034 shipments to dealers during the 1927 calendar year. The president of Hudson was Roscoe B. Jackson. The Hudson's F-head official rating of 92 hp has been regarded as very conservative by Hudson historians. This is especially true of a revised version which became available in July 1927 which had new manifolding, altered head design and relocated spark plugs and intake valves. Claims of a 100 mph top speed for the 1927 Hudson were not uncommon and Barney Oldfield drove a 1927 Coach for 1,000 miles at the Culver City, CA track at a speed in excess of 76 mph.

1927
Standard Six, 6-cyl.

	FP	5	4	3	2	1
Phae	1300	2600	5500	9250	12,950	18,500
2 dr Sed	1095	750	1450	3500	5050	7200
Spec 2 dr Sed	1150	775	1500	3750	5250	7500
Brgm	1395	875	1700	4250	5900	8500
7P Sed	1495	875	1700	4250	5900	8500
Super Six						
Cus Rds	1600	5250	10,500	17,500	24,500	35,000
Cus Phae	1600	5400	10,800	18,000	25,200	36,000
2 dr Sed	1285	875	1700	4250	5900	8500
Sed	1385	1000	2400	5000	7000	10,000
Cus Brgm	1575	1800	4950	8250	11,550	16,500
Cus Sed	1850	2000	5100	8500	11,900	17,000

1928

1928 Hudson, roadster, JAC

HUDSON — MODEL O & S — SIX: The 1928 Hudsons were handsome automobiles. The use of a higher and more slender radiator, vertical engine louvers and larger, parabolically shaped headlights gave them a stately, almost aristocratic appearance. With the Motometer moved to the dash a sculptured hood ornament took its place and small "saddle lamps" were now mounted on the cowl.

An industry first was Hudson's new steering wheel constructed of a hard rubber shell and a solid steel core. Formed with finger scallops it was colored ebony black to match the finish of the instrument panel. The spark, throttle, light and horn controls were placed at the steering wheel's center. In place of the transmission lock previously used, the Hudson was now equipped with an Electrolock ignition system. Although the Hudson's basic chassis structure was unchanged, two tubular cross members were added.

During 1928 a number of Hudsons were fitted with custom-built bodies by Murphy Body of Pasadena, CA that were extremely handsome. Murphy was also responsible for the basic design of two of the most attractive Hudson production models, the Victoria and Landau Sedan.

The Model S line Hudsons were mounted on a 118 1/2" wheelbase and were available in standard and custom form. The Model O versions also had standard and custom styles and a 127 3/8" wheelbase.

1928 Hudson, convertible landau sedan, WRG

I.D. DATA: Car numbers on front frame channel, dash and frame side. Starting: [Model S] 12270, [Model O] 803569. Ending: [Model S] NA, [Model O] 825406. Engine numbers on left motor mount, side of cylinder block.

Model No.	Body Type & Seating	Price	Weight	Prod. Total
S	Standard 2-dr. Cpe.-2P	1295	3525	NA
S	Standard 2-dr. C'ch.-5P	1250	3575	NA
S	Standard 4-dr. Sed.-5P	1325	3645	NA
S	Custom 2-dr. Rds.-3P	1295	3355	NA
O	Standard 4-dr. Sed.-5P	1450	3720	NA
O	Custom 4-dr. Phae.-7P	1650	3630	NA
O	Custom 2-dr. Vic.-4P	1650	3710	NA
O	Custom 4-dr. Lan. Sed.-5P	1650	3780	NA
O	Custom 4-dr. Sed.-7P	1950	3945	NA

ENGINE: F-head. Inline. Six cyl. Cast iron block. B & S: 3-1/2 x 5 in. Disp.: 288.5 cu. in. C.R.: 5.0:1. Brake H.P.: 92 @ 3200 R.P.M. N.A.C.C. H.P.: 29.4. Main bearings: 4. Valve lifters: mechanical. Carb.: Marvel, 1-1/4".

CHASSIS: [Model O] W.B.: 127 3/8 in. O.L.: 188 in. Tires: 31 x 6.00. [Model S] W.B.: 118 1/2 in. O.L.: 178 1/2 in. Tires: 31 x 6.00.

TECHNICAL: Sliding gear transmission. Speeds: 3F/1R. Floor shift controls. Single disc, cork inserts, running in oil. Shaft drive. Semi-floating rear axle. Overall Ratio: 4.09:1-Model S, 4.45:1-Model O. Bendix Mechanical brakes on four wheels. Wooden spoke wheels with detachable rims. Rim size: 18 in.

OPTIONS: Front bumper. Rear bumper. Leather upholstery. Triplex shatterproof windshield glass. Trunk. Radiator shutters. Sidemounts (single & dual).

HISTORICAL: Introduced Jan. 1928. Hudson made 52,316 shipments to dealers during the 1927 calendar year. The president of Hudson was Roscoe B. Jackson.

1928 Hudson, coupe, Murphy, WRG

1928
First Series, 6-cyl., (Start June. 1927)

	FP	5	4	3	2	1
Std 2 dr Sed	1175	750	1450	3500	5050	7200
Std Sed	1285	775	1500	3700	5200	7400
2 dr Sed	1250	800	1550	3850	5400	7700
Sed	1325	875	1700	4250	5900	8500
Rds	1500	3300	6600	11,000	15,400	22,000
Cus Phae	1600	3750	7500	12,500	17,500	25,000
Cus Brgm	1575	1650	4650	7750	10,850	15,500
Cus Sed	1850	1800	4950	8250	11,550	16,500
Second Series, 6-cyl., (Start Jan. 1928)						
2 dr Sed	1250	825	1600	4000	5600	8000
Sed	1325	875	1700	4250	5900	8500
RS Cpe	1325	1200	3750	6250	8750	12,500
Rds	1295	3350	6750	11,250	15,750	22,500
Ewb Sed	1450	800	1550	3850	5400	7700
Lan Sed	1650	825	1600	4000	5600	8000
Vic	1650	850	1650	4100	5700	8200
7P Sed	1950	875	1700	4250	5900	8500

1929

1929 Hudson, model R, coupe, WRG

HUDSON — MODEL L — SIX: The 139" wheelbase Model L chassis was used exclusively for custom-built bodies supplied by Biddle & Smart. All Model L Hudsons were fitted with five wire wheels as standard equipment. All Hudsons had a higher radiator, cowl and hoodline plus larger diameter headlights. Included in the list of 64 improvements Hudson claimed for 1929 were hydraulic, double-action shock absorbers, self-energizing brakes and "silenced roof construction". Hudsons were delivered with a long list of standard equipment such as an electric gas and oil gauge, windshield wiper, rear view mirror and the electrolock anti-theft device.

HUDSON — MODEL R — SIX: In a move which undoubtedly upset old line Hudson fans but apparently did not harm sales, Hudson abandoned the time-honored "Super-Six" label and instead identified its 1929 offering "The Greater Hudson". All Hudsons had bodies approximately 4 inches longer with the Model R versions having a 122.5" wheelbase. Among Hudson's 1929 styling highlights were larger windshields of shatter-proof glass and narrower cornerposts. The Landau Sedan and Victoria Model R Hudsons had Biddle & Smart bodies.

1929 Hudson, model L, club sedan, Biddle & Smart, WRG

HUDSON — MODEL L — SIX: The 139" wheelbase Model L chassis was used exclusively for custom-built bodies supplied by Biddle & Smart. All Model L Hudsons were fitted with five wire wheels as standard equipment. All Hudsons had a higher radiator, cowl and hoodline plus larger diameter headlights. Included in the list of 64 improvements Hudson claimed for 1929 were hydraulic, double-action shock absorbers, self-energizing brakes and "silenced roof construction". Hudsons were delivered with a long list of standard equipment such as an electric gas and oil gauge, windshield wiper, rear view mirror and the electrolock anti-theft device.

I.D. DATA:: Car numbers on front frame channel, dash and frame side. Starting: Model R 825407, Model L 41384. Ending: Model R 893401, Model L 46598. Engine numbers on left side of cylinder block/motor mount.

1929 Hudson, model L, limousine, Murphy, WRG

Model No.	Body Type & Seating	Price	Weight	Prod. Total
R	2-dr. Phae.-5P	1350	3495	NA
R	2-dr. Conv. Cpe.-3P	1450	3580	NA
R	4-dr. Std. Sed.-5P	1175	3785	NA
R	2-dr. Cpe.-3P	1195	3610	NA
R	2-dr. C'ch.-5P	1095	3680	NA
R	4-dr. Twn. Sed.-5P	1375	3795	NA
R	2-dr. Vic.-5P	1500	3795	NA
R	4-dr. Lan. Sed.-5P	1500	3825	NA
R	2-dr. Rds.-2P	NA	NA	NA
L	4-dr. Clb. Sed.-5P	1850	4140	NA
L	4-dr. Limo.-7P	2100	4290	NA
L	4-dr. Sed.-7P	2000	4260	NA
L	4-dr. Spt. Phae.-4P	2200	3795	NA
L	4-dr. Phae.-7P	1600	3760	NA

ENGINE: F-head. Inline. Six cyl. Cast iron block. B & S: 3-1/2 x 5 in. Disp. 288.5 cu. in. Brake H.P.: 92 @ 3200 R.P.M. Taxable/A.L.A.M./N.A.C.C. H.P.: 29.4. Main bearings: 4. Valve lifters: mechanical. Carb.: Marvel 1-1/4 in.

CHASSIS: [Model R] W.B.: 122.5 in. Frt/Rear Tread: 56/57.5 in. Tires: 31 x 6.50. [Model L] W.B.: 139 in. Frt/Rear Tread: 56/57.5 in. Tires: 31 x 6.0. Rim size: 19 in.

TECHNICAL: Sliding gear transmission. Speeds: 3F/1R. Floor shift controls . Single disc, cork insert, running in oil. Shaft drive. Semi-floating rear axle. Bendix mechanical brakes on four wheels. Wooden spoke wheels with detachable rims. Rim size: 19 in.

OPTIONS: Front bumper. Rear Bumper. Eight-day clock. Cigar Lighter. Spotlight. 5 wire wheels. 12 spoke demountable wood wheels (10 spoke standard). Radiator shutters. Trunk. Special trunk with fitted luggage. Ball-jointed tire mount mirrors. Protectahood. Lap robes. Spring covers. Window awnings. Spare tire locks. Sidemounts (single & dual).

1929 Hudson, model L, sport phaeton, Biddle & Smart, WRG

HISTORICAL: Introduced Jan. 1929. Hudson made 71,179 shipments to dealers during the 1929 calendar year. 139" wheelbase models with Biddle & Smart bodies only. The president of Hudson was William J. McAneeny.

1929
Series Greater Hudson, 6-cyl., 122" wb

	FP	5	4	3	2	1
RS Rds	1295	4500	9000	15,000	21,000	30,000
Phae	1650	4800	9600	16,000	22,400	32,000
Cpe	1295	1250	3900	6500	9100	13,000
2 dr Sed	1250	900	1900	4500	6300	9000
Conv	1450	4350	8700	14,500	20,300	29,000
Vic	1650	950	2100	4750	6650	9500
Sed	1325	900	1900	4500	6300	9000
Twn Sed	1375	950	2100	4750	6650	9500
Lan Sed	1500	950	2100	4750	6650	9500

Series Greater Hudson, 6-cyl., 139" wb

	FP	5	4	3	2	1
Spt Sed	2000	2600	5500	9250	12,950	18,500
7P Sed	1950	3300	6600	11,000	15,400	22,000
Limo	2100	3600	7200	12,000	16,800	24,000
DC Phae	1350	6300	12,600	21,000	29,400	42,000

1930

1930 Hudson, model T, roadster, WRG

HUDSON — MODEL T — EIGHT: Styling changes for 1930 were limited to details such as the use of hood doors instead of louvers and a thinner radiator shell with a simulated cap. In addition the headlights were now mounted on a curved bar. The Model T Hudsons were mounted on a 119" wheelbase and were highlighted by the new Sunsedan body which provided the open-air motoring pleasure of a phaeton with the comfort of a two-door, 5 passenger closed car. Its interior featured special upholstery without pleats. Common to all 1930 Hudsons were wider fenders, chrome-plated trim, beaded body beltline, a lower overall height and running board shields.

1930 Hudson, model U, close coupled sedan, LeBaron, OCW

HUDSON — MODEL U — EIGHT: The Model U wheelbase at 126'' was a full 13'' shorter than that of the 1929 Model L. But far more controversial was Hudson's decision to drop its F-head six and replace it with an L-head straight eight. This engine was to be the only eight-cylinder engine ever offered by Hudson and it would remain in production until 1952. Perhaps in anticipation of the controversy this move would cause Hudson to call its 1930 offering the Hudson Great Eight. Although with 80 hp it was less powerful than the old F-head six it was installed in an automobile that was significantly lighter. Thus explained Hudson, "It strikes off the shackles of bulk and useless weight."

I.D. DATA: Car numbers on front frame channel, dash and frame side. Starting: [Model T] 893402, [Model U] 46599. Ending: [Model T] 914292, [Model U] 57114. Engine numbers on left side of cylinder block.

Model No.	Body Type & Seating	Price	Weight	Prod. Total
T	2-dr. Cpe.-2P	885	3010	NA
T	4-dr. Phae.-5P	965	2940	NA
T	2-dr. Rds.-4P	995	2870	NA
T	2-dr. Cpe. w/R/S-4P	925	3060	NA
T	4-dr. Std.Sed.-5P	1025	3200	NA
T	2-dr. Sun.Sed.-5P	1045	3100	NA
T	2-dr. C'ch.-5P	895	3080	NA
U	4-dr. Phae.-7P	1160	3080	NA
U	4-dr. Brgm.-5P	1195	3210	NA
U	4-dr. Tr. Sed.-5P	1145	3270	NA
U	4-dr. Sed.-7P	1295	3385	NA

Note: During 1930 Hudson made significant price reductions in an effort to spur sales, the prices cited represent the lowest levels reached.

ENGINE: L-head. Inline. Eight cyl. Cast iron block. B & S: 2-3/4 x 4-1/2 in. Disp.: 213.8 cu. in. C.R.: 5.78:1. Brake H.P.: 80 @ 3400 R.P.M. N.A.C.C. H.P.: 24.2. Main bearings: 5. Valve lifters: mechanical. Carb.: Marvel 10-776.

CHASSIS: [Model T] W.B.: 119 in. Tires: 18 x 5.50. [Model U] W.B.: 126 in. Tires: 18 x 5.50.

TECHNICAL: Sliding gear transmission. Speeds: 3F/1R. Floor shift controls. Single disc, cork insert, running in oil. Shaft drive. Semi-floating rear axle. Bendix mechanical brakes on four wheels. Wooden spoke wheels with steel rims.

OPTIONS: Spotlight. Sidemounts (single & dual). Trunk. Spare tire. Radiator shutters.

HISTORICAL: Introduced Jan. 1930. A car known as the Marr Special, consisting of an Essex chassis and a Hudson Eight engine qualified for the 1930 Indianapolis 500 at a speed of 106.185 mph. Its driver was Chet Miller. Starting in 15th position, Miller finished a respectable 10th, averaging 89.58 mph. This was the last Hudson-engined car to complete the 500-mile Indianapolis Race. A Hudson also won the 1930 Tour de France. Hudson made 36,674 shipments to dealers during the calendary year. The president of Hudson was William J. McAneeny.

1930
Great Eight, 8-cyl., 119" wb

	FP	5	4	3	2	1
Rds	1200	4950	9900	16,500	23,100	33,000
Phae	1300	5100	10,200	17,000	23,800	34,000
RS Cpe	1100	1550	4500	7500	10,500	15,000
2 dr Sed	1050	900	1900	4500	6300	9000
Sed	1150	950	2100	4750	6650	9500
Conv Sed	1335	4500	9000	15,000	21,000	30,000

Great Eight, 8-cyl., 126" wb

	FP	5	4	3	2	1
Phae	1500	5250	10,500	17,500	24,500	35,000
Tr Sed	—	1125	3450	5750	8050	11,500
7P Sed	1650	1500	2500	3600	5500	000
Brgm	1295	1025	2600	5250	7300	10,500

1931

1931 Hudson, Series T, sport roadster, WRG

HUDSON — SERIES T — EIGHT: The Series T version of the "Hudson Greater Eight" as the 1931 Hudsons were advertised had a 119'' wheelbase. Although styling changes were not extensive they were sufficient to represent another evolutionary step away from the severe angular lines characteristic of the nineteen twenties. The grille insert was now a very fine mesh and a new front headlight tie-rod gave the headlights both a free-standing appearance and a lower position. The fenders were more deeply flanged and at the front swept downward to further enclose the

wheels. Also redesigned for 1931 were the Hudson's bumpers, hubcaps, running boards and exterior hardware. At the rear a new rectangular window was used. Also identifying the 1931 Hudson were belt moldings that extended the full length of the hood to the radiator shell and at the rear, were positioned higher than previously.

HUDSON — SERIES U — EIGHT: The Series U Hudson had a 126'' wheelbase and was easily identified by its standard left front fender spare tire well. The hood louvers on all models were placed higher than in 1930. A sure sign of the times was Hudson's decision to discontinue standard radiator shutters. They were still available as an accessory where there were extremely cold winters. However, Hudson noted that they had "been virtually useless, as evidenced by the fact that few and particularly the newer members of the Hudson family ever made use of them."

Interior revisions common to all 1931 Hudsons included a handbrake lever with a pawl and ratchet design that Hudson promised was "rattle-proof". Hudson offered new choices of Bedford cord, flat fabrics, mohairs and velour interiors and all models had walnut finishes on the dash and side garnish moldings. Rear seat occupants enjoyed at least 2 inches of additional leg room in the 1931 Hudsons with some sedan models offering as much as 5 more inches.

Free-wheeling was introduced as a $35 option in June and was operated by a small lever placed just behind the gearshift.

I.D. DATA: Car numbers on front frame channel, dash and frame side. Starting: Series T 914293, Series U 57115. Ending: Series T 930769, Series U 62883. Engine numbers on left side of cylinder block.

Model No.	Body Type & Seating	Price	Weight	Prod. Total
T	4-dr. Phae.-5P	1095	2865	NA
T	2-dr. Cpe.-2P	875	2865	NA
T	2-dr. Cpe. R/S-2/4P	925	2955	NA
T	2-dr. Sp. Cpe. R/S-2/4P	1065	3145	NA
T	2-dr. C'ch.-5P	895	2975	NA
T	4-dr. Twn. Sed.-5P	945	3055	NA
T	4-dr. Std. Sed.-5P	995	3115	NA
815	2-dr. Spt. Rds.-2P	995	2675	NA
815	2-dr. Rds. R/S-2/4P	NA	NA	NA
U	4-dr. Phae.-7P	1295	3055	NA
U	4-dr. Tr. Sed.-5P	1145	3190	NA
U	4-dr. Family Sed.-7P	1195	3230	NA
U	4-dr. Sp. Sed.-5P	1325	3430	NA
U	4-dr. Sed.-7P	1450	3375	NA
U	4-dr. Clb. Sed.-5P	1445	3235	NA
U	4-dr. Brgm.-5P	1225	3190	NA
U	4-dr. Brgm. Del.-5P	1375	3480	NA

ENGINE: L-head. Inline. Eight cyl.. Cast iron block. B & S: 2-7/8 x 4-1/2 in. Disp.: 233.7 cu. in. C.R.: 5.8:1. Brake H.P.: 87 @ 3600 R.P.M. N.A.C.C. H.P.: 26.4. Main bearings: 5. Valve lifters: mechanical. Carb.: 1-1/2'' Marvel 10-951.

CHASSIS: [Series T] W.B.: 119 in. Tires: 18 x 5.50. [Series U] W.B.: 126 in. Tires: 18 x 5.50.

1931 Hudson, Series U, brougham, OCW

TECHNICAL: Sliding gear transmission. Speeds: 3F/1R. Floor shift controls. Single disc, cork insert, running in oil. Shaft drive. Semi-floating rear axle. Bendix mechanical brakes on four wheels. Wooden spoke wheels. Free-Wheeling (35.00). Startix.

OPTIONS: Heater. Chrome windshield frame. Dual windshield wipers. Twin taillights. White sidewall tires. Spare tire cover. Wire wheels. Sidemounts (single & dual).

HISTORICAL: Introduced Nov. 1930. In August 1931 the Hudson and Essex became the first American cars available with Startix. This device automatically started and if needed restarted the car after the driver turned the ignition key to the "on" position. Cluth plate now constructed from duralumin. Hudson made 17487 shipments to dealers during the 1931 calendar year. The president of of Hudson was William J. McAneeny. The Marr Special average 89.58 mph to finish 10th, at Indy. The driver was Chet Miller.

1931
Greater Eight, 8-cyl., 119" wb

	FP	5	4	3	2	1
Rds	995	6000	12,000	20,000	28,000	40,000
Phae	1095	6300	12,600	21,000	29,400	42,000
Cpe	875	1075	3000	5500	7700	11,000
Special Cpe	1065	1150	3600	6000	8400	12,000
RS Cpe	925	1125	3450	5750	8050	11,500
2 dr Sed	895	825	1600	4000	5600	8000
Sed	995	875	1700	4250	5900	8500
Twn Sed	945	800	1550	3900	5450	7800

Great Eight, l.w.b., 8-cyl., 126" wb

	FP	5	4	3	2	1
Spt Phae	1295	6750	13,500	22,500	31,500	45,000
Brgm	1225	1150	3600	6000	8400	12,000
Fam Sed	1195	1025	2600	5250	7300	10,500
7P Sed	1450	1150	3600	6000	8400	12,000
Clb Sed	1445	1025	2600	5250	7300	10,500
Tr Sed	1145	900	1900	4500	6300	9000
Special Sed	1325	1000	2400	5000	7000	10,000

1932

1932 Hudson, Series T, coupe, WRG

HUDSON — SERIES T (STANDARD) — EIGHT: The 1932 "Greater Eight" Hudsons were easily identified by their elegant V-shaped grille with prominent vertical bars, single-piece bumper and triangular-shaped head, cowl and taillights. Frank Spring who was to influence the appearance of virtually every future Hudson gave the 1932 models a fresh look by the use of gracefully sweeping fenders and gentler body curves. All new Hudsons had a new instrument panel with larger gauges and a knob allowing the driver to adjust the ride control of the shock absorbers. The Standard models had a 119 inch wheelbase and were equipped with a single windshield wiper and taillight. A choice of either painted wood or wire wheels was offered.

1932 Hudson, Series U, 7-pass. sedan, OCW

HUDSON — SERIES U (STERLING) — EIGHT: Sterling Series Hudsons were mounted on a 126 inch wheelbase and were equipped with standard dual wipers, taillights, and white sidewall tires.

1932 Hudson, Series L, phaeton, WRG

HUDSON — SERIES L (MAJOR) — EIGHT: The 132 inch wheelbase Hudson had the same standard features of the Series U. Thus customers had a choice of either natural-finish wood wheels or wire wheels.

I.D. DATA: Car numbers on front frame channel, dash and frame side. Starting: [Series U] 62884, [Series L] 25001. Ending: [Series T] 936702, [Series U] 68332, [Series L] 25116. Engine numbers on left side of cylinder block.

Model No.	Body Type & Seating	Price	Weight	Prod. Total
Series T	Std. 2-dr. Sp. Cpe. R/S-4P	1115	3215	NA
Series T	Std. 4-dr. Twn. Sed.-5P	1050	3270	NA
Series T	Std. 2-dr. Conv. Cpe.-2P	1195	3085	NA
Series T	Std. 2-dr. C'ch.-5P	1025	3190	NA
Series T	Std. 4-dr. Std. Sed.-5P	1095	3285	NA
Series T	Std. 2-dr. Cpe.-2P	995	—	NA
Series T	Std. 2-dr. Cpe. R/S-4P	1045	—	NA
Series U	Sterling 2-dr. Sub.-5P	1275	3350	NA
Series U	Sterling 4-dr. Sp. Sed.-5P	1295	3415	NA
Series L	Major 4-dr. Tr. Sed.-5P	1445	3475	NA
Series L	Major 4-dr. Clb. Sed.-5P	1495	3555	NA
Series L	Major 4-dr. Brgm.-5P	1495	3560	NA
Series L	Major 4-dr. Sed.-7P	1595	3590	NA

ENGINE: Inline. Eight cyl. Cast iron block. B & S: 3 x 4-1/2 in. Disp.: 254.4 cu. in. C.R.: 5.8:1. Brake H.P.: 101 @ 3600 R.P.M. Main bearings: 5. Valve lifters: mechanical. Carb.: 1-1/2'' Marvel 10-996.

CHASSIS: [Series T] W.B. 199 in. [Series U] W.B.: 126 in. Tires: 17 x 6.00. [Series L] W.B.: 132 in. Tires: 17 x 6.50.

TECHNICAL: Sliding gear transmission. Speeds: 3F/1R. Floor shift controls. Single disc, cork inserts, running in oil. Shaft drive. Semi-floating rear axle. Overall Ratio: 4.64 (5-1 opt.). Bendix mechanical brakes on four wheels. Wooden artillery wheels. Drivetrain Options: Free-wheeling and selective automatic clutch.

OPTIONS: Sidemount cover(s) metal, fabric. Clock. Radio Antenna. Wire wheels. Chrome grille cover. Chrome hood doors. Shatter proof glass. Leather upholstery. Locking glove box. Whitewall tires. Trunk (and trunk rack). Double stop and tail lights. Side and center rear armrests. Sidemounts (single & dual).

HISTORICAL: Introduced Jan. 1932. Hudson made 7,777 shipments to dealers during the 1932 calendar year. The president of Hudson was William J. McAneeny. Two Hudson Specials were entered at Indy. Chet Miller's car qualified at 111.053 mph, Al Miller's at 110.129. Neither car finished. The Chet Miller car was out on lap 125, that of Al Miller on lap 66.

1932
(Standard) Greater, 8-cyl., 119" wb

	FP	5	4	3	2	1
2P Cpe	995	875	1700	4250	5900	8500
4P Cpe	1045	900	1900	4500	6300	9000
Spec Cpe	1115	1150	3600	6000	8400	12,000
Conv	1195	3300	6600	11,000	15,400	22,000
2 dr Sed	1025	900	1900	4500	6300	9000
5P Sed	1095	950	2100	4750	6650	9500
Twn Sed	1050	900	1900	4500	6300	9000

(Sterling) Series, 8-cyl., 132" wb

	FP	5	4	3	2	1
Spec Sed	1295	1000	2400	5000	7000	10,000
Sub	1275	950	2100	4750	6650	9500

Major Series, 8-cyl., 132" wb

	FP	5	4	3	2	1
Phae	1395	3750	7500	12,500	17,500	25,000
Tr Sed	1445	1050	2800	5400	7500	10,800
Clb Sed	1495	1125	3450	5750	8050	11,500
Brgm	1495	1200	3750	6250	8750	12,500
7P Sed	1595	1025	2600	5250	7300	10,500

1933

1933 Hudson, Series E, sedan, WRG

HUDSON — SUPER SIX — SERIES E — SIX: The Super Six Hudson was essentially the 1932 Essex Pacemaker. Distinguishing them from other Hudsons for 1933 were their triangular-shaped headlights and single row of hood louvers. The first 6-cylinder Hudson since 1923 featured a two-piece aluminum and iron cylinder head with either a 6.2:1 or 7.1:1 compression ratio.

HUDSON — STANDARD EIGHT — SERIES T — EIGHT: The Standard Eight Hudson was mounted on a 119 inch wheelbase and retained door-type hood ventilators.

1933 Hudson, Series L, brougham, OCW

HUDSON — MAJOR EIGHT — SERIES L — EIGHT: Production of Hudsons reached its nadir in 1933. Only 2,401 were assembled in spite of more attractive styling and significant engineering improvements. The Series L on a 132" wheelbase had a more luxurious interior than the Standard Eight. Aside from their greater length the Major Eight Hudsons were distinguished from the Standard Eights by their wide running board trim, and dual chromed horns mounted on each side of the grille. After losing $5,429,350 in 1932 Hudson experienced another loss of $4,409,903 on sales of $23,521,458 in 1933.

I.D. DATA: Car number on dash, right rear frame cross member. Starting: [Series E] 1300501, [Series T] 936703, [Series L] 251117. Ending: [Series E] 1301462, [Series T] 938029, [Series L] 251679. Engine number on left side of cylinder block opposite number one cylinder.

Model No.	Body Type & Seating	Price	Weight	Prod. Total
Series E — Hudson Super Six				
Series E	2-dr. Cpe.-4P	735	2845	NA
Series E	2-dr. Bus. Cpe.-2P	695	2780	NA
Series E	2-dr. C'ch.-5P	695	2900	NA
Series E	4-dr. Sed.-5P	765	2980	NA
Series E	2-dr. Conv. Cpe. R/S-4P	845	2800	NA
Series E	4-dr. Phae.-5P	835	—	NA
Series T — Hudson Pacemaker Std Eight				
Series T	2-dr. Cpe. R/S-4P	995	3190	NA
Series T	2-dr. C'ch.-5P	975	3245	NA
Series T	4-dr. Sed.-5P	1045	3345	NA
Series T	2-dr/ Conv. Cpe. R/S-4P	1145	3145	NA
Series L — Hudson Pacemaker Major Eight				
Series L	4-dr. Tr. Sed.-5P	1250	3485	NA
Series L	4-dr. Clb. Sed.-5P	1350	3630	NA
Series L	4-dr. Sed.-7P	1350	3605	NA
Series L	4-dr. Brgm.-5P	1350	3650	NA

Series T and L
ENGINE: Inline. Eight cyl. Cast iron block. B & S: 3 x 4-1/2 in. Disp.: 254.4. C.R.: 5.8:1. Brake H.R.: 101 @ 3600 R.P.M. Main bearings: 5. Valve lifters: mechanical. Carb.: updraft Marvel 10-1535. Optional Engine: Inline. Eight cyl. Cast iron block. B & S: 3 x 4-1/2 in. Disp. 254.4. C.R.: 7.1:1. Brake H.P.: 110 @ 3600 R.P.M. Main bearings: 5. Valve lifters: mechanical. Carb.: updraft Marvel 10-1535.

Super Six
ENGINE: Inline. Six cyl. Cast iron block. B & S: 2-15/16 x 4-3/4 in. Disp.: 193.1 cu. in. C.R.: 6.2:1. Brake H.P.: 73 @ 3200 R.P.M. Main bearings: 3. Valve lifters: mechanical. Carb.: updraft Marvel 10-1532. Optional Engine: Inline. Six cyl. Cast iron block. B & S: 2-15/16 x 4-3/4 in. Disp.: 193.1 cu. in. C.R.: 7.1:1. Brake H.P.: 80 @ 3200 R.P.M. Main bearings: 3. Valve lifters: mechanical. Carb.: updraft Marvel 10-1532.

CHASSIS: [Series E] W.B.: 113 in. Tires: 18 x 5.25. (17 x 5.50 opt). [Series L] W.B.: 132 in. Tires: 17 x 6.50. [Series T] W.B.: 119 in. Tires: 17 x 6.00.

1933 Hudson, Series L, sedan, WRG

TECHNICAL: Sliding gear transmission. Speeds: 3F/1R. Floor mounted shift controls. Single plate, cork inserts, running in oil. Shaft drive. Semi-floating rear axle. Overall ratio: 4.64 (5.1 opt.). Bendix mechanical on four wheels. Wire spoke wheels. Rim size: Super Six - 18", Std Eight - 17", Major Eight - 17". Drivetrain options were automatic clutch [Super Six]. 17 x 5.50 tires, 17" wheels [Super Six].

OPTIONS: Wirewheels. Chrome grille cover. Chrome hood doors. Shatter proof glass. Leather upholstery. Locking glove box. White wall tires. Trunk, trunk rack. Double stop and taillights. Side and center rear armrests. Sidemounts (single & dual).

HISTORICAL: Introduced Jan. 1933. Innovations: std equipment on all Hudsons was free-wheeling, Startix and adjustable steering column. Hudson made 2401 shipments to dealers during the 1933 calendar year. The president of Hudson was William J. McAneeny. Four cars powered by Hudson engines qualified at Indianapolis. Car No. 29 driven by Gene Haustein qualified in 28th position. It retired after 197 laps and was credited with a 15th place finish. Car No. 28 was driven by Chet Miller. Qualifying at 112.025 mph it began the race in 32nd position. Just after Miller was relieved by Shorty Cantlon it fell by the wayside with a broken connecting rod. Al Miller's Car No. 19 started 24th and also retired with a blown connecting rod on lap 161. It was placed 20th in the final standing. A fourth Hudson-powered car, No. 59 was qualified by Ray Campbell at 108.65 mph. Starting the race in 37th position it retired after 24 laps with an oil leak.

1933
Pacemaker Super Six, 6-cyl., 113" wb

	FP	5	4	3	2	1
Conv	845	3000	6000	10,000	14,000	20,000
Phae	765	3300	6600	11,000	15,400	22,000
Bus Cpe	695	700	1350	2800	4550	6500
RS Cpe	735	750	1450	3300	4900	7000
2 dr Sed	695	650	1250	2400	4200	6000
Sed	765	700	1350	2800	4550	6500
Pacemaker Standard, 8-cyl., 119" wb						
Conv	1145	3300	6600	11,000	15,400	22,000
RS Cpe	995	825	1600	4000	5600	8000
2 dr Sed	975	700	1350	2800	4550	6500
Sed	1045	875	1700	4250	5900	8500
Pacemaker Major, 8-cyl., 132" wb						
Phae	1250	3750	7500	12,500	17,500	25,000
Tr Sed	1250	750	1450	3300	4900	7000
Brgm	1350	750	1450	3500	5050	7200
Clb Sed	1350	775	1500	3750	5250	7500
7P Sed	1350	775	1500	3600	5100	7300

1934

HUDSON — STANDARD EIGHT — SERIES LL (123" wheelbase models) EIGHT: The 1934 Hudsons had all new styling with wide flowing fenders, longer hoods and in sedans and coaches a reverse curve rear section that allowed the spare tire to be stored within the body. Hudson described this new look as "Streamlined in Wind-Sculptured Steel." For the first time Hudson offered a factory-installed radio and a no-cost option the "Axle-Flex", semi-independent front suspension. Other improvements included a new dash panel which placed the instruments closer to the driver, an improved interior ventilation system and an improved synchromesh for the 3-speed transmission. An interesting innovation was the use of three-beam headlights. The third beam was intended to serve as a cornering light and was controlled along with the usual high and low beams by a toe switch. Although sales rebounded strongly during 1934 Hudson reported a loss of $3,239,201 for the year. Hudson Standard Eight models in the LL series had Bedford cord interiors.

HUDSON — DeLUXE EIGHT — SERIES LLU — EIGHT: The LLU models were distinguished from the LL versions by their broadcloth upholstery, and front fender side lamps. Both types had six hood doors, fender striping, bright-work trim around the windshield and front door vent panes.

1934 Hudson, Series LT, coupe, WRG

HUDSON — EIGHT — SERIES LT — EIGHT: The LT models lacked front fender parking lights. Their windshields were given bright molding trim and front door vent panes were fitted. The Sport Roadster model was equipped with dual horns and taillights in a chrome finish. In addition they had two windshield wipers while other models carried a single wiper for the driver.

1934 Hudson, Series LU, DeLuxe sedan (with Lowell Thomas), WRG

1934 Hudson, Series LT, convertible, OCW

HUDSON — DeLUXE EIGHT — SERIES LU — EIGHT: The DeLuxe models were equipped with dual front fender side-lamps, dual chrome-finish tail-lights, dual windshield wipers and horns.

HUDSON — CHALLENGER — SERIES LTS — EIGHT: These ultra-low priced models were introduced in June. They were identified by their 3 hood doors and lack of front door vent panes. They were fitted with a manual rather than automatic clutch and lacked such features as an interior sun visor.

I.D. DATA: Car numbers on firewall, right rear frame cross member. Starting: [Series LT & LU] 950000, [Series LTS] 964463, [Series LL & LLU] 252000. Ending: [Series LT & LU] 968679, [Series LTS] 968679, [Series LL & LLU] 256158. Engine numbers on left side of cylinder block opposite number one cylinder.

Model No.	Body Type & Seating	Price	Weight	Prod. Total
Series LT	2-dr. Cpe.-4P	775	2795	NA
Series LT	2-dr. Bus. Cpe.-2P	695	2720	NA
Series LT	2-dr. Cpe.-2P	725	2750	NA
Series LT	2-dr. Conv. Cpe. R/S-4P	835	2815	NA
Series LT	2-dr. Spt. Rds. R/S-4P	—	2845	NA
Series LT	2-dr. C'ch.-5P	745	2855	NA
Series LT	2-dr. Vic.-5P	785	2850	NA
Series LT	4-dr. Sed.-5P	805	2905	NA
Series LT	2-dr. Compartment Sed.-5P	845	2930	NA
Series LT	2-dr. C'ch. with built-in trunk-5P	745	—	NA
Series LT	2-dr. Sed. with built-in truck-5P	805	—	NA
Series LTS — 116" wheelbase				
Series LTS	4-dr. Sed.-5P	765	2910	NA
Series LTS	2-dr. Cpe.-2P	685	2720	NA
Series LTS	2-dr. Cpe. R/S-4P	735	2765	NA
Series LTS	2-dr. Conv. Cpe.-4P	800	2785	NA
Series LTS	2-dr. C'ch-5P	705	2800	NA

Note 1: Series LTS 4-dr. Sed.-5P was manufactured after Aug. with built-in trunk at no price change.

Series LL	4-dr. Tr. Sed.-5P	970	2950	NA
Series LL	4-dr. Compartment Tr. Sed.-5P	1000	2975	NA
Series LLU	4-dr. Clb. Sed.-5P	1070	3080	NA
Series LLU	4-dr. Compartment Clb. Sed.-5P	1125	3110	NA
	4-dr. Brgm.-5P	1145	3075	NA
Series LU	2-dr. Cpe. R/S-4P	855	2850	NA
Series LU	2-dr. Cpe.-2P	815	2805	NA
Series LU	2-dr. Conv. Cpe. R/S-4P	900	2835	NA
Series LU	4-dr. Sed.-5P	895	2930	NA
Series LU	4-dr. Compartment Sed.-5P	935	2955	NA
Series LU	2-dr. C'ch.-5P	835	2870	NA
Series LU	2-dr. Compartment Vic.	875	2895	NA
Series LU	4-dr. Sed. w/built-in trunk	895	—	NA
Series LU	2-dr. C'ch. w/built-in trunk	835	—	NA

Note 1: Production ceased June 1935 for Series LTS 4-dr. Sed.-5P and 2-dr. C'ch.-5P: Series LU 4-dr. Compartment Sed.-5P and 2-dr. Compartment Vic.
Note 2: Series LU 4-dr. Sed. w/built-in trunk and 2-dr. C'ch. w/built-in trunk were introduced in Aug. 1935.

ENGINE: [Series LL & LLU] L-head. Straight. Eight cyl. Chrome alloy block. B & S: 3 x 4-1/2 in. Disp. 254.4 cu. in. C.R.: 6.25:1. Brake H.P. 113 @ 3800 R.P.M. Taxable/A.L.A.M./N.A.C.C. H.P.: 28.8. Main bearings: 5. Valve lifters: mechanical. Carb.: Carter downdraft 1 barrel 2825. Optional Engine: L-head. Straight. Eight cyl. Chrome alloy block. B & S: 3 x 4-1/2 in. Disp. 254.4. C.R.: 7.0:1. Brake H.P. 121 @ 3800 R.P.M. Taxable/A.L.A.M./N.A.C.C. H.P.: 28.8. Main bearings: 5. Valve lifters: mechanical. Carb.: Carter Downdraft 1 barrel 2825.

ENGINE: [Series LT, LTS, & U] Straight L-head. Inline. Eight cyl. Chrome alloy block. B & S: 3 x 4.5 in. Disp.: 254.4. C.R.: 5.75:1. Brake H.P.: 108 @ 3800 R.P.M. Taxable H.P.: 28.8. Main bearings: 5. Valve lifters: mechanical. Carb.: Carter downdraft 1 barrel 2825. Optional Engine: Straight L-head. Inline. Eight cyl. Chrome alloy block. B & S: 3 x 4.5 in. Disp. 254.4. C.R.: 7.0:1. Brake H.P. 121 @ 3800 R.P.M. Taxable/A.L.A.M./N.A.C.C. H.P.: 28.8. Main bearings: 5. Valve lifters: mechanical. Carb. Carter downdraft 1 barrel 2825.

CHASSIS: [Series LL] W.B.: 123 in. O.L.: 197 in. Frt/Rear Tread: 56/57.5 in. Tires: 16 x 6.50. [Series LT] W.B.: 116 in. O.L.: 194 in. Frt/Rear Tread 56/56 in. Tires: 16 x 6.25. [Series LU] W.B.: 116 in. O.L.: 194 in. Frt/Rear Tread 56/56 in. Tires: 16 x 6.25. [Series LLU] W.B.: 123 in. O.L.: 197 in. Frt/Rear Tread 56/57.5 in. Tires: 16 x 6.50. [Series LTS] W.B.: 116 in. O.L.: 194 in. Frt/Rear Tread 56/56 in. Tires: 16 x 6.25.

TECHNICAL: Sliding gear transmission. Speeds: 3F/1R. Floor shift controls. Single plate, cork insert, running in oil. Shaft drive. Semi floating rear axle. Overall Ratio: 4.11:1. Bendix mechanical brakes on four wheels. Steel artillery wheels. Rim size: 16 in. Drivetrain options: Hill-holder. Automatic clutch.

OPTIONS: Dual Sidemount (except for Challenger). Bumper guards front & rear (2.15 pr.). Radio. Heater (std 12.50, DeL 15.50). Electric clock (13.50). Cigar lighter (1.25, 2.00). Stainless steel wheel moldings (5) (9.00). Underhood battery charger (9.75). Chrome plated exhaust extension (1.95). Luggage rack (9.50). Rightside tail & stop light (6.00). Twin horns (10.00 pr). Dual windshield wipers (10.00). Inside right side visor. Trunk light. Fender skirts (9.50 pr in primer). Hill hold (32.50). Fitted luggage (9.75 to 22.50). Vacuum clutch (15.00). 7:1 cylinder head (18.00).

HISTORICAL: Introduced Jan. 1934. Innovations: Axle-flex 3 beam headlights. Hudson made 27,130 shipments to dealers during the 1934 calendar year. The president of Hudson was Roy D. Chapin. Freewheeling was discontinued. The Martz Special powered by a 257 cid Hudson engine was qualified for the Indianapolis 500 by Gene Haustein at 109.426 mph. The car started in 31st position and was credited with finishing in 30th place after being wrecked in an accident in lap 13. Another Hudson-powered car, Number 13, was the first alternate to the qualifiers but it didn't race.

1934
Special, 8-cyl., 116" wb

	FP	5	4	3	2	1
Conv	855	3000	6000	10,000	14,000	20,000
Bus Cpe	695	675	1300	2500	4350	6200
Cpe	735	700	1350	2800	4550	6500
RS Cpe	785	750	1450	3300	4900	7000
Comp Vic	785	725	1400	3000	4700	6700
2 dr Sed	755	700	1350	2800	4550	6500
Sed	815	650	1250	2400	4200	6000
Comp Sed	845	750	1450	3300	4900	7000

DeLuxe Series, 8-cyl., 116" wb

2P Cpe	815	700	1350	2700	4500	6400
RS Cpe	855	725	1400	3200	4850	6900
Comp Vic	875	775	1500	3750	5250	7500
2 dr Sed	835	725	1400	3100	4800	6800
Sed	895	675	1300	2500	4350	6200
Comp Sed	935	700	1350	2800	4550	6500

Challenger Series, 8-cyl., 116" wb

2P Cpe	685	700	1350	2800	4550	6500
RS Cpe	735	750	1450	3300	4900	7000
Conv	800	3600	7200	12,000	16,800	24,000
2 dr Sed	705	700	1350	2800	4550	6500
Sed	765	725	1400	3000	4700	6500

Major Series, 8-cyl., 123" wb
(Special)

Tr Sed	970	775	1500	3750	5250	7500
Comp Trs	1000	800	1550	3850	5400	7700
(DeLuxe)						
Clb Sed	1070	800	1550	3900	5450	7800
Brgm	1145	800	1550	3800	5300	7600
Comp Clb Sed	1125	775	1500	3750	5250	7500

1935

1935 Hudson, Series GH, convertible, OCW

HUDSON CUSTOM EIGHT — HHU — EIGHT: Although the styling of the 1935 Hudson was very similar to the 1934 model, there were many improvements that have prompted Hudson historians to regard the 1935's as the first modern Hudsons. The most dramatic advancement was the industry's first all steel body which Hudson introduced prior to General Motor's Turret Top. The most predominant external changes aside from the steel roof were the new bullet-shaped headlight shells, larger rear windows and narrow hood louver panels. The use of flatter rear leaf springs enabled overall height to be lowered 1.5 inches. On July 8, 1935 the Hudson Motor Car company celebrated its 26th anniversary with the production of its 2,262,810th automobile. Also during 1935, Roy Chapin established the "Twenty Year Club" for Hudson employees with that number of years of service. Members received a solid gold pin with a Hudson 20 engraved on one side and their name on the other. January 5, 1935 was the 25th anniversary of Roy D. Chapin's election to the presidency of Hudson. The Custom Eight had the exterior features of the DeLuxe Eights plus chrome trim for the running boards and three chrome stripes on the trailing edge of the front fenders. Interior trim appointments were also upgraded. Standard equipment included the Electric Hand transmission.

HUDSON SPECIAL EIGHT — HT — EIGHT: The Special 8 was Hudson's lowest priced line of 8 cyl. models and had a 117" wheelbase. They had painted headlights shells and single windshield wipers.

HUDSON DELUXE EIGHT — SERIES HU — EIGHT: The DeLuxe 8 models shared the 117" chassis with the Special 8 series. However they were equipped with dual windshield wipers and chrome plated headlight shells.

SPECIAL COUNTRY CLUB EIGHT — SERIES HTL — EIGHT: This series combined the painted headlight shells and single windshield wiper of the Special Eight series with the long, 124" wheelbase of the DeLuxe Eight models. Wood spoke wheels were optional at no extra cost.

DELUXE COUNTRY CLUB EIGHT — SERIES HUL — EIGHT: The HUL series shared their chromed headlight shells with the HU models but were given a higher quality interior. Wire wheels were standard, wood spoke wheels optional at no extra cost.

HUDSON BIG SIX — SERIES GH — SIX: The Hudson Six was easily identified by its grille mesh with its horizontal inserts.

I.D. DATA: Car numbers on dash, right rear frame cross member. Starting: [Ser. GH] 53101, [Ser. HHU] 56101, [Ser. HT] 54101, [Ser. HU] 55101, [Ser. HTL] 57101, [Ser. HUL] 58101. Ending: [Ser. GH] 537724, [Ser. HHU] 561560, [Ser. HT] 547250, [Ser. HU] 553197, [Ser. HTL] 571066, [Ser. HUL] 58221. Canadian built cars inserted a "C" between series and serial number (i.e., 53C60432). Engine numbers on left rear side of cylinder block. Starting: 70000. Ending: 78999.

Model No.	Body Type & Seating	Price	Weight	Prod. Total
Ser. HHU	4-dr. Clb. Sed.-5P	1025	3130	720
Ser. HHU	4-dr. Sub. Sed.-5P	1057	3145	720
Ser. HHU	4-dr. Brgm.-6P	1095	3055	720*
Ser. HHU	4-dr. Tr. Brgm.-6P	1127	3070	720
Ser. HU	2-dr. C'ch.-5P	875	2880	3096
Ser. HU	2-dr. Tr. Brgm.	907	2895	3096
Ser. HU	Sed.	935	2945	3096
Ser. HU	4-dr. Sub. Sed.-5P	967	2960	3096
Ser. HU	Bus. Cpe.-2P	845	2790	3096*
Ser. HU	Cpe. R/S-4P	895	2855	3096
Ser. HU	2-dr. Conv. Cpe. R/S-2P	955	2805	3096
Ser. HTL	2-dr. Tr. Brgm.-5P	812	2855	965
Ser. HTL	2-dr. C'ch.-5P	780	2840	965
Ser. HTL	4-dr. Sed.-6P	840	2890	965
Ser. HTL	4-dr. Sub. Sed.-6P	872	2905	965*
Ser. HUL	4-dr. Sub. Sed.-5P	1007	3030	9923
Ser. HUL	4-dr. Clb. Sed.-5P	975	3015	9923
Ser. HUL	4-dr. Brgm.-5P	1025	3055	9923
Ser. HUL	4-dr. Tr. Brgm.-5P	1052	3070	9923*
Ser. GH	2-dr. Cpe. R/S-3P	740	2665	7623
Ser. GH	2-dr. Bus. Cpe.-2P	695	2600	7623
Ser. GH	4-dr. Sed.-5P	770	2780	7623
Ser. GH	2-dr. C'ch.-5P	710	2720	7623
Ser. GH	4-dr. Sub. Sed.-5P	802	2795	7623
Ser.GH	2-dr. Conv. Cpe.	790	2640	7623*
Ser. GH	2-dr. Tr. Brgm.	742	2735	7623

Model No.	Body Type & Seating	Price	Weight	Prod. Total
Ser. HT	2-dr. C'ch.-5P	780	2840	7149
Ser. HT	2-dr. Tr. Brgm.	812	2855	7149
Ser. HT	Sed.	840	2890	7149
Ser. HT	4-dr. Sub. Sed.-5P	872	2905	7149
Ser. HT	Bus. Cpe.-2P	760	2740	7149
Ser. HT	Cpe. R/S-4P	810	2810	7149
Ser. HT	2-dr. Conv. Cpe. R/S-2P	860	2765	7149*

Note: * applies to total series production not model production.

1935 Hudson, Series HUL, custom brougham, WRG

ENGINE: [Hudson Eight] (This engine used for all Hudson Eight models). L-head. Inline. Eight cyl. Chrome alloy block. B & S: 3 x 4.5. Disp.: 254. C.R.: 6.0:1. Brake H.P.: 113 @ 3800 R.P.M. Taxable H.P.: 28.8. Main bearings: 5. Valve lifters: mechanical. Carb.: Carter 330S. Optional Engine: L-head. Straight Eight. Chrome alloy block. B & S: 3 x 4.5 in. Disp.: 254 cu. in. C.R.: 7.0:1. Brake H.P.: 124 @ 4000 R.P.M. Main bearings: 5. Valve lifters: mechanical. Carb.: Carter 330S.

ENGINE: [Hudson Six] L-head. Inline. Six cyl. Chrome alloy block. B & S: 3 x 5 in. Disp.: 212 cu. in. C.R.: 6.25:1. Brake H.P.: 93 @ 3800 R.P.M. Taxable H.P.: 21.6. Main bearings: 3. Valve lifters: mechanical. Carb.: Carter 329S. Optional Engine: L-head. Inline. Six cyl. Chrome alloy block. B & S: 3 x 5 in. Disp.: 212. C.R.: 7.0:1. Brake H.P.: 100 @ 3800 R.P.M. Main bearings: 3. Valve lifters: mechanical. Carb.: Carter 329S.

CHASSIS: [Series HHU] W.B.: 124 in. Tires: 16 x 6.50. [Series HU] W.B.: 117 in. Tires: 16 x 6.25. [Series HTL] W.B.: 124 in. Tires: 16 x 6.50. [Series HUL] W.B.: 124 in. Tires: 16 x 6.50. [Series HT] W.B.: 117 in. Tires: 16 x 6.25. [Series GH] W.B.: 116 in. Tires: 6.00 x 16.

TECHNICAL: Manual, sliding gear transmission. Speeds: 3F/1R. Floor shift controls. Single disc, cork insert, running in oil. Shaft drive. Semi-floating rear axle. Overall Ratio: 4.19:1. Mechanical, "Rotary Equalizer" brakes on four wheels. Steel wheels. (Wooden spokes on 124" wheelbase models). Drivetrain Options: Electric hand (std. on Custom Eights, opt on all other Hudsons & Terraplanes) (20.42). Axelflex independent front suspension. Adjustable steering column. Automatic clutch (10.21). Automatic clutch and Electric Hand (28.08).

OPTIONS: Radio (51.81). High compression cylinder head (6 cyl.) (18.50). High compression cylinder head (8 cyl.) (22.00). Startix (8.50). Luggage carrier (10.00). Tune up kit (4.50). Zenith radio (44.00). Twin air horns (11.50). Front & rear seat covers (7.50). Leather upholstery (18.81). Side-mounts (single & dual).

HISTORICAL: Introduced Dec. 1934. Rotary-Equalized brakes. Opt. Electric Hand. Pre-selector shifting mechanism. Hudson made 29,476 shipments to dealers during the 1935 calendar year. The president of Hudson was Roy D. Chapin. 2 Hudson powered cars were entered in the Indy but neither qualified. In Feb. 1935, Sir Malcolm Campbell set 7 new records at Daytona Beach with a Hudson sedan. These included the flying mile at 88.207 mph, flying kilometer at 88.207 mph, flying 5 miles at 88.051 mph, flying 5 kilometers at 88.105 mph and the standing start one mile at 68.18 mph. In April, 36 new AAA records were captured by a Hudson 8 sedan at Muroc Dry Lake in California. Among these records set by Wilbur Shaw, Babe Stapp and Al Gordon was a 93.03 mph speed for 5 miles and an average of 85.8 mph for 1,000 miles. In addition the Hudson captured every record in its engine displacement up to 3000 kilometers as well as 4 unlimited class records for closed cars.

1935

Big Six, 6-cyl., 116" wb	FP	5	4	3	2	1
Conv	790	3750	7500	12,500	17,500	25,000
Cpe	695	775	1500	3750	5250	7500
RS Cpe	740	825	1600	4000	5600	8000
Tr Brgm	742	650	1250	2400	4200	6000
2 dr Sed	710	600	1200	2200	3850	5500
Sed	770	650	1250	2400	4200	6000
Sub Sed	802	700	1350	2700	4500	6400
Eight Special, 8-cyl., 117" wb						
Conv	860	3900	7800	13,000	18,200	26,000
Cpe	760	725	1400	3000	4700	6700
RS Cpe	810	775	1500	3750	5250	7500
Tr Brgm	812	675	1300	2500	4350	6200
2 dr Sed	780	675	1300	2500	4300	6100
Sed	840	700	1350	2900	4600	6600
Sub Sed	872	725	1400	3000	4700	6700

Eight DeLuxe
Eight Special, 8-cyl., 124" wb

	FP	5	4	3	2	1
Brgm	930	700	1350	2900	4600	6600
Tr Brgm	962	725	1400	3000	4700	6700
Clb Sed	880	650	1250	2400	4200	6000
Sub Sed	912	700	1350	2800	4550	6500

Eight DeLuxe, 8-cyl., 117" wb

2P Cpe	845	725	1400	3100	4800	6800
RS Cpe	895	800	1550	3800	5300	7600
Conv	955	4050	8100	13,500	18,900	27,000
Tr Brgm	907	675	1300	2600	4400	6300
2 dr Sed	875	675	1300	2500	4350	6200
4 dr Sed	935	725	1400	3000	4700	6700
Sub Sed	967	725	1400	3100	4800	6800

Eight Custom, 8-cyl., 124" wb

Brgm	1095	725	1400	3000	4700	6700
Tr Brgm	1127	725	1400	3100	4800	6800
Sed	1025	700	1350	2800	4550	6500
Sub Sed	1057	725	1400	3100	4800	6800

Late Special, 8-cyl., 124" wb

Brgm	930	675	1300	2500	4350	6200
Tr Brgm	962	675	1300	2600	4400	6300
Club Sed	880	675	1300	2500	4300	6100
Sub Sed	912	725	1400	3100	4800	6800

Late DeLuxe, 8-cyl., 124" wb

Brgm	1025	675	1300	2600	4400	6300
Tr Brgm	1057	700	1350	2700	4500	6400
Club Sed	975	675	1300	2500	4350	6200
Sub Sed	1007	725	1400	3200	4850	6900

1936

1936 Hudson, Series 63, coupe, OCW

HUDSON — CUSTOM SIX — SERIES 63 — SIX: A new styling motif for Hudson with rounded surfaces, highly domed fenders and an ornate front grille design was introduced in 1936. All series had longer wheelbases and body widths. An important technical advance was Hudson's adoption of a hydraulic braking system that incorporated a mechanical unit operating on the rear wheels. If the front pedal traveled beyond the 3/4 point of its maximum distance this system would function. Replacing the Axleflex system as Hudson's answer to General Motors' independent front suspension system was Radial Safety Control. A solid front axle was continued but two radius arms attached to the axle and pivoted to the frame side members controlled its movement. This allowed softer leaf springs to be used and the result was steady steering and a smooth ride. Net profits for the year totalled $3,305,616. All Custom models (6 or 8 cylinder) had chrome wheelcovers and front fender medallions. Standard upholstery texture was worsted boucle with a green-gray color.

HUDSON — CUSTOM EIGHT — SERIES 65 & 67 — EIGHT: With the exception of their wheelbases these two series of Custom Eight Hudson were identical. Full size wheelcovers with Hudson Eight lettering were standard. Standard equipment on the Custom Eight included a radio with its antenna positioned under the car.

1936 Hudson, Series 64, convertible coupe, WRG

HUDSON — DELUXE EIGHT — SERIES 64 & 66 — EIGHT: The DeLuxe Eight shared both of its 120 and 127 inch wheelbase chassis with the Custom Eight Series. Their small standard hubcaps made them easy to identify.

I.D. DATA: Car number on dash, right rear frame cross member. Starting: [Ser. 63] 63101, [Ser. 64] 64101, [Ser. 66] 66101. Ending: [Ser. 63] 639820, [Ser. 64] 645456, [Ser. 66] 663543. Engine number on left side of cylinder block. Car number on plate mounted on firewall. Starting: [Series 65] 65101, [Ser. 67] 67101. Ending: [Ser. 65] 652514, [Ser. 67] 675004. Engine numbers on left side of cylinder block. Starting: 79000 - 6 cyl. 1008 - 8 cyl. Ending: 89999 - 6 cyl. 17634 - 8 cyl. Canadian-built cars included letter "C".

Model No.	Body Type & Seating	Price	Weight	Prod. Total
Series 63	2-dr. Cpe. R/S-3-5P	755	7810	NA
Series 63	2-dr. Bus. Cpe.-3P	710	2730	NA
Series 63	2-dr. Conv. Cpe.-3P	810	2870	NA
Series 63	2-dr. Brgm.-6P	730	2830	NA
Series 63	2-dr. Tr. Brgm.-6P	755	2830	NA
Series 63	4-dr. Sed.-6P	785	2880	NA
Series 63	4-dr. Tr. Sed.-6P	810	2880	NA
Series 64	2-dr. Bus. Cpe.-3P	760	2865	NA
Series 64	2-dr. Cpe. R/S-3-5P	810	2965	NA
Series 64	2-dr. Conv. Cpe.-3P	875	3000	NA
Series 64	2-dr. Brgm.-6P	790	2985	NA
Series 64	2-dr. Tr. Brgm.-6P	815	2985	NA
Series 64	4-dr. Sed.-6P	830	3045	NA
Series 64	4-dr. Tr. Sed.-6P	855	3045	NA
Series 66	4-dr. Sed.-6P	855	3110	NA
Series 66	4-dr. Tr. Sed.-6P	880	3110	NA
Series 65	2-dr. Bus. Cpe.-3P	845	2915	NA
Series 65	2-dr. Cpe. R/S-3-5P	895	3000	NA
Series 65	2-dr. Conv. Cpe.-3-5P	970	3045	NA
Series 65	2-dr. Brgm.-6P	885	3030	NA
Series 65	2-dr. Tr. Brgm.-6P	910	3030	NA
Series 65	2-dr. Sed.-6P	925	3075	NA
Series 65	4-dr. Tr. Sed.-6P	950	3075	NA
Series 67	4-dr. Sed.-6P	950	3140	NA
Series 67	4-dr. Tr. Sed.-6P	975	3140	NA

1936 Hudson, Series 65, touring sedan (with Malcolm Campbell), WRG

ENGINE: This engine used for all Hudson 8 cyl. models. L-head. Inline. Eight cyl.. Chrome alloy block. B & S: 3 x 4.5 in. Disp. 254. C.R.: 6.0:1. Brake H.P.: 113 @ 3800 R.P.M. Taxable H.P.: 28.8. Main bearings: 5. Valve lifters: mechanical. Carb.: Carter 330S. Optional Engine: L-head. Straight. Eight cyl. Chrome alloy block. B & S: 3 x 4.5 in. Disp. 254 cu. in. C.R.: 7.0:1. Brake H.P.: 124 @ 4000 R.P.M. Main bearings: 5. Valve lifters: mechanical. Carb.: Carter 330S. [Custom Six] L-head. Inline. Six cyl. Chrome alloy block. B & S: 3 x 5 in. Disp. 212 cu. in. C.R.: 6.25:1. Brake H.P. 93 @ 3800 R.P.M. Taxable H.P.: 21.6. Main bearings: 3. Valve lifters: mechanical. Carb.: Carter 329S. Optional Engine: L-head. Inline. Six cyl. Chrome alloy block. B & S: 3 x 5 in. Disp. 212 cu. in. C.R.: 7.0:1. Brake H.P. 100 @ 3800 R.P.M. Main bearings: 3. Valve lifters: mechanical. Carb.: Carter 329S.

CHASSIS: [Series 63] W.B.: 120 in. Tires: 16 x 6.00. [Series 64] W.B.: 120 in. Tires: 16 x 6.25 in. [Series 65] W.B.: 120 in. Tires: 16 x 6.25. [Series 66] W.B.: 127 in. Tires: 16 x 6.25. [Series 67] W.B.: 127 in. Tires: 16 x 6.25.

TECHNICAL: Sliding gear transmission. Speeds: 3F/1R. Floor shift controls. Single disc, cork insert, running in oil. Shaft drive. Semi-floating rear axle. Overall ratio: 4.19:1. Hydraulic brakes on four wheels. Pressed steel wheels. Rim size: 16 in. Drivetrain Options: Electric hand preselector transmission.

OPTIONS: Bumper Guards. Radio. Heater. Mohair upholstery. Fender skirts. Full wheel covers. High compression cylinder heads. Startix. Luggage carrier. Tune up kit. Zenith radio. Twin air horns. Front and rear seat covers. Leather upholstery. Sidemounts (single & dual).

HISTORICAL: Introduced Nov. 1935. Innovations: radial safety control front suspension, hydraulic brakes. Hudson made 25,409 shipments to dealers during the 1936 calendar year. The president of Hudson was A. Edward Barit (elected president, Feb. 1936 following death of Roy D. Chapin).

1936
Custom Six, 6-cyl., 120" wb

	FP	5	4	3	2	1
Conv	810	4050	8100	13,500	18,900	27,000
Cpe	710	700	1350	2800	4550	6500
RS Cpe	755	750	1450	3300	4900	7000
Brgm	730	650	1250	2400	4200	6000
Tr Brgm	755	675	1300	2500	4300	6100
Sed	785	650	1250	2400	4200	6000
Tr Sed	810	700	1350	2800	4550	6500

DeLuxe Eight, Series 64, 8-cyl., 120" wb

	FP	5	4	3	2	1
Conv	875	4200	8400	14,000	19,600	28,000
Cpe	760	725	1400	3000	4700	6700
RS Cpe	810	775	1500	3700	5200	7400
Brgm	790	675	1300	2500	4350	6200
Tr Brgm	815	675	1300	2500	4350	6200

DeLuxe Eight, Series 66, 8-cyl., 127" wb

Sed	855	725	1400	3000	4700	6700
Tr Sed	880	750	1450	3300	4900	7000

Custom Eight, Series 65, 120" wb

2P Cpe	845	725	1400	3100	4800	6800
RS Cpe	895	775	1500	3750	5250	7500
Conv	960	4200	8400	14,000	19,600	28,000
Brgm	885	675	1300	2600	4400	6300
Tr Brgm	910	700	1350	2700	4500	6400

Custom Eight, Series 67, 127" wb

Sed	850	700	1350	2900	4600	6600
Tr Sed	975	725	1400	3000	4700	6700

1937

1937 Hudson, Series 74, convertible coupe, WRG

HUDSON CUSTOM SIX — SERIES 73 — SIX: The Custom Six wheelbase was extended to 122 inches for 1937. Appearance of the Custom Six was identical to that of the DeLuxe and Custom Eight models. The only exception was the Hudson 6 identification on the Custom Six grille.

All the restyled Hudsons were described by their manufacturer as possessing "useful beauty" with interiors of "Drawing room luxury." Overall body width was increased by 5 inches and wheelbases of all series was lengthened by 2 inches, while overall height was reduced by the same amount. These new dimensions were accompanied by the use of a stronger 7-1/4 inch deep double drop frame.

In addition to their greater size, the 1937 Hudsons were set apart from previous models by their front hinged front doors, reshaped hood louvers and simpler grille design. In place of the rumble seat on Coupe models was a transversely-mounted jump seat. Detail changes included placement of the battery within the engine compartment and improvements in Hudson's Radial Safety front suspension and Electric Hand gear shift mechanism.

The downturn in the nation's economy had a negative impact upon Hudson sales and at year's end Hudson's profit was a slim $670,716.

HUDSON DELUXE EIGHT — SERIES 74 & 76 — EIGHT: DeLuxe Eight models carried front fender medallions, running board trim strips and Hudson 8 identification on the front grille.

The Series 74 Hudsons had a 122 inch wheelbase while that of the Series 76 models extended to 129 inches.

HUDSON CUSTOM EIGHT — SERIES 75 & 77 — EIGHT: Custom Eight models were externally identical to DeLuxe Eights. However their interiors differed significantly. That of the Custom Eight had a knobby twist upholstery (leather was used for all Hudson convertible interiors), standard equipment radio, cigarette lighter and electric clock.

With the exception of its 129 inch wheelbase, the Series 77 Hudson was identical to the Series 75.

1937 Hudson, Series 77, sedan, WRG

I.D. DATA: Car numbers on plate mounted on firewall. Starting: [Ser. 73] 73101, [Ser. 74] 74101, [Ser. 75] 75101, [Ser. 76] 76101, [Ser. 77] 77101. Ending: [Ser. 73] 766913, [Ser. 74] 745728, [Ser. 75] 753374, [Ser. 76] 761197, [Ser. 77] 773752. Canadian-built chassis serial number have a C after the first 2 digits which identify the Series. Engine numbers on left side of cylinder block. Starting: 90000 — 6 cyl., 18000 — 8-cyl. Ending: 97082 — 6 cyl., 31693 — 8 cyl. Canadian-built cars included letter "C".

Model No.	Body Type & Seating	Price	Weight	Prod. Total
Series 73	2-dr. Vic. Cpe.-4P	765	2865	—
Series 73	2-dr. Bus. Cpe.-3P	695	2760	—
Series 73	2-dr. Cpe.-3P	720	2805	—
Series 73	2-dr. Brgm.-5P	740	2925	—
Series 73	2-dr. Tr. Brgm.-5P	765	2925	—
Series 73	2-dr. Conv. Cpe.-4P	820	2870	—
Series 73	4-dr. Sed.-6P	790	2990	—
Series 73	4-dr. Tr. Sed.-6P	815	2990	—
Series 73	2-dr. Conv. Brgm.-6P	900	2945	—
Series 74	2-dr. Conv. Brgm.-6P	965	3125	—
Series 74	2-dr. Conv. Cpe.-4P	885	3020	—
Series 74	2-dr. Brgm.-5P	800	3105	—
Series 74	2-dr. Tr. Brgm.	825	3105	—
Series 74	2-dr. Tr. Sed.-6P	865	3135	—
Series 74	4-dr. Sed.-6P	840	3135	—
Series 74	2-dr. Cpe.-3P	770	3010	—
Series 74	2-dr. Vic. Cpe.-4P	820	3055	—
Series 74	4-dr. Sed.-6P	865	3205	—
Series 74	4-dr. Tr. Sed.	890	3205	—
Series 76	4-dr. Sed.-6P	865	3205	—
Series 76	4-dr. Tr. Sed.-6P	890	3205	—
Series 77	4-dr. C.C. Sed.-6P	965	3260	—
Series 77	4-dr. C.C. Tr. Sed.-6P	990	3260	—
Series 75	2-dr. Vic. Cpe.-4P	905	3085	—
Series 75	2-dr. Conv. Cpe.-4P	980	3070	—
Series 75	2-dr. Cpe.-3P	855	3055	—
Series 75	2-dr. Conv. Brgm.-6P	1060	3160	—
Series 75	2-dr. Brgm.-6P	895	3135	—
Series 75	2-dr. Tr. Brgm.-6P	920	3135	—
Series 75	4-dr. Tr. Sed.-6P	965	3195	—
Series 75	4-dr. Sed.	940	3195	—

Note: Prices increased later in the model year.

ENGINE: [Custom Six] L-head. Inline. Six cyl. Chrome alloy block. B & S: 3 x 5 in. Disp.: 212 cu. in. C.R.: 6.25:1. Brake H.P.: 101 @ 4000 R.P.M. Taxable H.P.: 21.6. Main bearings: 3. Valve lifters: mechanical. Carb.: 2 barrel Carter. Option Engine: L-head. Inline. Six cyl. Chrome alloy block. B & S: 3 x 5 in. Disp.: 212 cu. in. C.R.: 7.0:1. Brake H.P.: 107 @ 4000 R.P.M. Taxable H.P.: 21.6. Main bearings: 3. Valve lifters: mechanical. Carb.: 2 barrel Carter.

[This engine used in all DeLuxe and Custom Eight models.] L-head. Straight. Eight cyl. Chrome alloy block. B & S: 3 x 4-1/2 in. Disp.: 254.47 cu. in. C.R.: 6.25:1. Brake H.P.: 122 @ 4200 R.P.M. Taxable H.P.: 28.8. Main bearings: 5. Valve lifters: mechanical. Carb.: 2 barrel Carter.

CHASSIS: [Series 73] W.B.: 122 in. O.L.: 199 in. Tires: 16 x 6.00 (15 x 7.00 opt.) [Series 74] W.B.: 122 in. O.L.: 199 in. Tires: 16 x 6.25. (15 x 7.00 opt.) [Series 76] W.B.: 129 in. O.L.: 203 in. Tires 16 x 6.25. (15 x 7.00 opt.) [Series 75] W.B.: 122 in. O.L.: 199 in. Tires: 16 x 6.25 (15 x 7.00 opt.). [Series 77] W.B.: 129 in. O.L.: 203 in. Tires: 16 x 6.25 (15 x 7.00 opt.)

TECHNICAL: Manual synchromesh transmission. 3F/1R. Floor shift. Single plate, cork inserts, running in oil. Shaft drive. Semi-floating rear axle. Overall Ratio: 4.11:1. Hydraulic brakes on four wheels. Steel drop center type wheels. Drivetrain Options: "Hydraulic Hill Hold". The Electric Hand (pre-selector).

OPTIONS: Single sidemount. Dual sidemount. Fender skirts. Bumper guards. Radio. Heater. Clock (standard on Custom Eight). Cigar lighter. Seat covers. Spotlight. Twin air horns. Vacuum assist fuel pump.

HISTORICAL: Introduced Nov. 1937. Under AAA supervision Hudson broke all existing Class C, closed stock car records from 10 to 2000 miles and from one to twenty-four hours. In addition new records were set in the unlimited class for all distances from 500 to 2000 miles and from six to twenty-four hours. In the latter run the Hudson DeLuxe Eight Brougham covered 2,104.22 miles in 24 hours at an average speed of 87.67 mph. The Hudson's speed of 93.03 mph across the Muroc Dry Lake was the fastest speed a closed, Class C car had ever attained in a five mile run. In addition to the 38 new stock car records set on this outing, Hudson had earlier claimed 7 additional new marks in speed at Daytona Beach. Hudson made 19,848 shipments to dealers during the 1937 calendar year. The president of Hudson was Abraham Edward Barit.

1937
Custom Six, Series 73, 6-cyl., 122" wb

	FP	5	4	3	2	1
Conv	1005	4050	8100	13,500	18,900	27,000
Conv Brgm	1090	4200	8400	14,000	19,600	28,000
Bus Cpe	865	600	1200	2200	3850	5500
3P Cpe	905	650	1250	2400	4200	6000
Vic Cpe	950	700	1350	2800	4550	6500
2 dr Brgm	930	600	1200	2200	3850	5500
2 dr Tr Brgm	955	600	1200	2300	4000	5700
Sed	980	650	1250	2400	4200	6000
Tr Sed	1005	675	1300	2500	4300	6100

DeLuxe Eight, Series 74, 8-cyl., 122" wb

Cpe	950	750	1450	3300	4900	7000
Vic Cpe	1015	775	1500	3750	5250	7500
Conv	1080	4200	8400	14,000	19,600	28,000
2 dr Brgm	1000	700	1350	2900	4600	6600
2 dr Tr Brgm	1025	725	1400	3000	4700	6700
Sed	1040	725	1400	3000	4700	6700

	FP	5	4	3	2	1
Tr Sed	1065	725	1400	3100	4800	6800
Conv Brgm	1165	4350	8700	14,500	20,300	29,000
DeLuxe Eight, Series 76, 8-cyl., 129" wb						
Sed	1065	825	1600	4000	5600	8000
Tr Sed	1090	875	1700	4250	5900	8500
Custom Eight, Series 75, 8-cyl., 122" wb						
Cpe	1050	750	1450	3300	4900	7000
Vic Cpe	1100	750	1450	3500	5050	7200
Conv Cpe	1175	4350	8700	14,500	20,300	29,000
2 dr Brgm	1090	725	1400	3100	4800	6800
2 dr Tr Brgm	1115	750	1450	3300	4900	7000
Sed	1145	725	1400	3100	4800	6800
Tr Sed	1165	725	1400	3200	4850	6900
Conv Brgm	1260	4500	9000	15,000	21,000	30,000
Custom Eight, Series 77, 8-cyl., 129" wb						
Sed	1165	750	1450	3300	4900	7000
Tr Sed	1190	750	1450	3500	5050	7200

1938

1938 Hudson, Series 89, 112 coach, OCW

HUDSON 112 — SERIES 89 — SIX: The Hudson 112 was introduced in Jan 1938, Standard and DeLuxe models were available on a 112 inch wheelbase. The more expensive DeLuxe version had a walnut grain finish on the dash and window moldings, in place of the painted finishes found on the Standard models. In addition stainless steel trim was used for the DeLuxe interior. A more attractive upholstery with a pleated surface was also used. Both versions were powered by a 175cid 6 cylinder engine. At Bonneville the Hudson 112, which was also the pace car for the Indianapolis 500, set numerous Class D records including 80.50 mph for one hour and a 12-day, 20,327 mile run at 70.58 mph.

HUDSON CUSTOM SIX — SERIES 83 — SIX: All 1938 Hudsons featured a new grille with larger horizontal bars divided by a single vertical bar. This arrangement was less complicated than the form used in 1937. The Custom Six displayed a new front bumper with a center indentation that gave it a 2 piece appearance.

HUDSON CUSTOM EIGHT — SERIES 85 & 87 — EIGHT: The Custom Eight was with the exception of its engine identical to the Custom Six. The only difference was represented by the 2 Custom Eight Series 87 Country Club models that used a 129 rather than 122 inch wheelbase.

1938 Hudson, Series 84, coupe, WRG

HUDSON DELUXE EIGHT — SERIES 84 — EIGHT: The DeLuxe Eight shared its 122 inch chassis with the Custom Six and Eight Series. In addition its interior appointments were those of the Custom Six.

I.D. DATA: Hudson 112: Car numbers on plate mounted on firewall. Starting: 8928566. Ending: 8956040. Engine numbers on left side of cylinder block. Starting: same as serial numbers. Hudson Six: Car numbers on right front door post. Starting: 83131. Ending: 8356040. Engine numbers on top right side of cylinder block. Starting: same as serial numbers. Hudson DeLuxe Eight: Car numbers on right front door post. Starting: 84101. Ending: 8456040. Engine numbers on top right side of cylinder block. Starting: same as serial numbers. Hudson Custom Eight Country Club: Car numbers on right front door post. Starting: 87161. Ending: 8756040.

Engine numbers on top right side of cylinder block. Starting: same as serial numbers. Note: Starting engine numbers were 360000 for all series until car number 11630 when engine number began matching serial number.

Model No.	Body Type & Seating	Price	Weight	Prod. Total
Series 89				
Std.	2-dr. Cpe.-3P	694	2500	NA
Std.	2-dr. Vic. Cpe.-4P	740	2540	NA
Std.	2-dr. Conv. Brgm.-6P	886	2610	NA
Std.	4-dr. Sed.-6P	755	2620	NA
Std.	4-dr. Tr. Sed.-6P	775	2625	NA
Std.	2-dr. Conv. Cpe.-3P	835	2545	NA
Std.	2-dr. Brgm.-6P	724	2595	NA
Std.	2-dr. Tr. Brgm.-6P	743	2600	NA
DeLuxe	2-dr. Cpe.-3P	704	2500	NA
DeLuxe	2-dr. Vic. Cpe.-4P	750	2540	NA
DeLuxe	2-dr. Conv. Brgm.-6P	891	2610	NA
DeLuxe	4-dr. Sed.-6P	765	2620	NA
DeLuxe	4-dr. Tr. Sed.-6P	785	2625	NA
DeLuxe	2-dr. Conv. Cpe.-3P	840	2545	NA
DeLuxe	2-dr. Brgm.-6P	734	2595	NA
DeLuxe	2-dr. Tr. Brgm.-6P	753	2600	NA

Note 1: The Standard models comprised the initial 112 offerings. After May 1 they were designated as "Standard" models when the DeLuxe version with walnut grain finished instrument panels and interior trim were introduced.

Model No.	Body Type & Seating	Price	Weight	Prod. Total
Custom Six — Series 83				
Series 83	2-dr. Cpe.-3P	909	2825	NA
Series 83	2-dr. Conv. Cpe.-3P	1041	2895	NA
Series 83	2-dr. Vic. Cpe.-5P	995	2880	NA
Series 83	2-dr. Conv. Brgm.-6P	1104	2975	NA
Series 83	2-dr. Brgm.-6P	948	2935	NA
Series 83	2-dr. Tr. Brgm.-6P	968	2940	NA
Series 83	4-dr. Sed.-6P	984	3005	NA
Series 83	4-dr. Tr. Sed.-6P	1005	3010	NA
DeLuxe Eight — Series 84				
Series 84	2-dr. Vic. Cpe.-5P	1031	3060	NA
Series 84	2-dr. Cpe.-3P	990	3010	NA
Series 84	2-dr. Conv. Cpe.-3P	1121	3060	NA
Series 84	2-dr. Conv. Brgm.-6P	1185	3140	NA
Series 84	4-dr. Sed.-6P	1060	3155	NA
Series 84	4-dr. Tr. Sed.-6P	1080	NA	NA
Series 84	2-dr. brgm.-6P	1028	3115	NA
Series 84	2-dr. Tr. Brgm.-6P	1049	3120	NA
Custom Eight — Series 85				
Series 85	2-dr. Cpe.-3P	1080	3020	NA
Series 85	2-dr. Vic. Cpe.-5P	1131	3080	NA
Series 85	2-dr. Brgm.-6P	1134	3140	NA
Series 85	2-dr. Tr. Brgm.-6P	1155	3145	NA
Series 85	4-dr. Sed.-6P	1171	3190	NA
Series 85	4-dr. Tr. Sed.-6P	1191	3195	NA
Custom Eight Country Club — Series 87				
Series 87	4-dr. Sed.-6P	1199	3270	NA
Series 87	4-dr. Tr. Sed.-6P	1219	3275	NA

1938 Hudson, Series 87, touring sedan, WRG

ENGINE: [All Hudson Eights used this engine.] L-head. Straight. Eight cyl. Chrome alloy block. B & S: 3 x 4.5 in. Disp.: 254 c.i.d. C.R.: 6.25:1. Brake H.P.: 122 @ 4200 R.P.M. Taxable H.P.: 28.8. Main bearings: 5. Valve lifters: mechanical. Carb.: 2 barrel, downdraft Carter WDO 402S. [Hudson 112] L-head. Inline. Six cyl. Chrome alloy block. B & S: 3 x 4-1/8 in. Disp.: 175 cu. in. C.R.: 6.50:1. Brake H.P.: 83 @ 4000 R.P.M. Taxable H.P.: 21.6. Main bearings: 3. Valve lifters: mechanical. Carb.: Carter 411S (early, 417S (late). [Hudson Six] L-head. Six cyl. Chrome alloy block. B & S: 3 x 5 in. Disp.: 212 cu. in. Comp.: 6.25:1. Brake H.P.: 101 @ 4000 R.P.M. Taxable H.P.: 21.6. Main bearings: 3. Valve lifters: mechanical. Carb.: 2 barrel Carter WDO downdraft. Optional Engine: L-head. Six cyl. Chrome alloy block. B & S: 3 x 5 in. Disp.: 212 cu. in. C.R.: 7.0:1. Brake H.P.: 107. Main bearings: 3. Valve lifters: mechanical. Carb.: Dual Downdraft Carter WDO 397S.

CHASSIS: [Series 89 (112)] W.B.: 112 in. O.L.: 186 in. Height: 70 in. Frt/Rear Tread: 56/59 in. Tires: 16 x 5.50. [Series 85 (Hudson Custom Eight)] W.B.: 122 in. O.L.: 197-3/4 in. Frt/Rear Tread: 56/59 in. Tires: 16 x 6.00 (15 x 7.00 opt.). [Series 83 (Hudson Custom Six)] W.B.: 122 in. O.L.: 197-3/4 in. Frt/Rear Tread: 56/59 in. Tires: 16 x 6.00 (15 x 7.00 opt.). [Series 84 (Hudson DeLuxe Eight)] W.B.: 122 in. O.L.: 197-3/4 in.

Frt/Rear Tread: 56/59 in. Tires: 16 x 6.00 (15 x 7.00 opt.). [Series 87 (Hudson Custom Eight Country Club)] W.B.: 129 in. Frt/Rear Tread: 56/59 in. Tires: 16 x 6.00 (15 x 7.00 opt.).

TECHNICAL: Sliding gear, synchromesh transmission. 3F/1R. Floor shift. Single disc cork insert, running in oil. Shaft drive. Semi-floating rear axle. Overall Ratio: 4.11:1. Bendix Hydraulic brakes on four wheels. Steel disc wheels. Drivetrain Options: Selective Automatic shift. Automatic clutch.

OPTIONS: DeLuxe heater. Custom radio (7 tubes) Hudson-RCA Victor DB-38. DeLuxe radio (6 tubes) Hudson-RCA Victor SA-38. Custom hot water heater. Hydraulic hill-hold. Dual sidemounts (last year at availability). Fender skirts. Fog and spot lights. 15x7.00 tires.

HISTORICAL: Introduced Jan. 1938. Hudson made 51,078 shipments to dealers during the 1938 calendar year. Terraplanes carried the Hudson name in sales literature and on hubcaps (see Terraplane section). The president of Hudson was A.E. Barit.

1938
Standard Series 89, 6-cyl., 112" wb

	FP	5	4	3	2	1
Conv	835	3900	7800	13,000	18,200	26,000
Conv Brgm	886	4050	8100	13,500	18,900	27,000
3P Cpe	695	400	1000	1600	3100	4400
Vic Cpe	740	550	1150	2100	3800	5400
Brgm	724	550	1150	2100	3800	5400
Tr Brgm	743	600	1200	2200	3850	5500
Sed	755	600	1200	2200	3900	5600
Tr Sed	775	600	1200	2300	4000	5700

Utility Series 89, 6-cyl., 112" wb

Cpe	724	300	900	1350	2700	3900
2 dr Sed	697	300	900	1250	2650	3800
2 dr Tr Sed	716	300	900	1350	2700	3900

DeLuxe Series 89, 6-cyl., 112" wb

Conv	840	4050	8100	13,500	18,900	27,000
Conv Brgm	891	4200	8400	14,000	19,600	28,000
3P Cpe	704	675	1300	2500	4350	6200
Vic Cpe	750	700	1350	2800	4550	6500
Brgm	734	650	1250	2400	4150	5900
Tr Brgm	753	600	1200	2200	3900	5600
Sed	765	600	1200	2300	4000	5700
Tr Sed	785	650	1200	2300	4100	5800

Custom Series 83, 6-cyl., 122" wb

Conv	1041	4200	8400	14,000	19,600	28,000
Conv Brgm	1104	4350	8700	14,500	20,300	29,000
3P Cpe	909	750	1450	3300	4900	7000
Vic Cpe	955	775	1500	3750	5250	7500
Brgm	948	700	1350	2700	4500	6400
Tr Brgm	968	675	1300	2500	4350	6200
Sed	984	650	1200	2300	4100	5800
Tr Sed	1005	650	1250	2400	4150	5900

DeLuxe Series 84, 8-cyl., 122" wb

Conv	1121	4200	8400	14,000	19,600	28,000
Conv Brgm	1185	4350	8700	14,500	20,300	29,000
3P Cpe	990	750	1450	3300	4900	7000
Vic Cpe	1031	775	1500	3750	5250	7500
Brgm	1028	725	1400	3200	4850	6900
Tr Brgm	1049	650	1250	2400	4150	5900
Tr Sed	1080	650	1250	2400	4200	6000

Custom Series 85, 8-cyl., 122" wb

3P Cpe	1080	775	1500	3750	5250	7500
Vic Cpe	1131	825	1600	4000	5600	8000
Brgm	1134	775	1500	3700	5200	7400
Tr Brgm	1155	825	1600	3950	5500	7900
Sed	1171	675	1300	2500	4300	6100
Tr Sed	1191	675	1300	2600	4400	6300

Country Club Series 87, 8-cyl., 129" wb

Sed	1199	675	1300	2500	4300	6100
Tr Sed	1219	675	1300	2600	4400	6300

1939

1939 Hudson, Series 90, 112, convertible, OCW

HUDSON 112 — SERIES 90 — SIX: The Hudson 112 was the only Hudson model for 1939 that retained the side-hood mounted headlights of earlier years. Artifical catwalk grille panels were new as was the steering column mounted shift lever.

HUDSON PACEMAKER — SERIES 91 — SIX: The Pacemaker Series was introduced in March 1939 and is often regarded as the successor to the Terraplane. As were other Hudsons, the Pacemaker's suspension was equipped with Auto-Poise Control. This consisted of a bar attached to the frame across the front of the chassis. Its ends were angled backward to form arms that attached to the wheel spindles. The result was a torsional effect that pulled the wheels back to a center location whenever they moved away from a straight-ahead position.

HUDSON SIX — SERIES 92 — SIX: Interior and dash appointments of the Series 92 were of a highter quality than those of the Series 91. Both Series shared painted catwalk grilles, narrow body beltline trim and a relatively short hood ornament. In common with all Hudsons, the Six was equipped with the forward hinged hood introduced in 1938 on the Hudson 112.

HUDSON COUNTRY CLUB SIX — SERIES 93 — SIX: Standard equipment on all Country Club and convertible models were Airfoam latex rubber cushions. Exterior appointments included chrome catwalk grilles, front fender chrome spears placed above the headlights, wider beltline molding and small arrowhead shaped lights in the leading edge of the side hood trim.

1939 Hudson, Series 95, convertible brougham, WRG

HUDSON COUNTRY CLUB EIGHT — SERIES 95 — EIGHT: These Hudsons were identical to the Series 93 versions with the exception of their front bumper center section which carried a plate reading "Hudson Eight". Those on the Series 93 read "Hudson."

HUDSON COUNTRY CLUB EIGHT — SERIES 97 — EIGHT: The 2 models in this series were mounted on 109 inch wheelbase chassis and were distinguished by their taupe cashmere cloth interiors.

I.D. DATA: Car number on plate mounted on firewall. Starting: [Series 90] 90101, [Series 91] 9132576, [Series 92] 92101. Ending: [Series 90] 9054902, [Series 91] 9154902, [Series 92] 9254902. Engine numbers on right side of cylinder block. Starting: same as serial numbers. Car numbers on plate mounted on firewall. Starting: [Series 93] 93101, [Series 95] 95101, [Series 97] 97101. Ending: [Series 93] 9354902, [Series 95] 9554902, [Series 97] 9754902. Engine numbers on right side of cylinder block. Starting: same as serial numbers. Canadian-built cars included letter "C".

Model No.	Body Type & Seating	Price	Weight	Prod. Total
Series 90	2-dr. Cpe.-3P	745	2587	NA
Series 90	2-dr. Conv. Cpe.-3P	886	2627	NA
Series 90	2-dr. Conv. Brgm.-6P	936	2732	NA
Series 90	2-dr. Tr. Brgm.-6P	775	2682	NA
Series 90	4-dr. Tr. Sed.-6P	806	2712	NA
Series 90	2-dr. Vic. Cpe.-4P	791	2622	NA
Series 90	2-dr. Util. Cpe.-3P*	750	2714	NA
Series 90	2-dr. Trav. Cpe.-3P*	695	2544	NA
Series 90	2-dr. Util. C'ch.-6P*	725	2634	NA
Series 90	4-dr. Sta. Wag.-6P	931	2880	NA

Note 1: The 2-dr. Util. Cpe.-3P, 2-dr. Trav. Cpe.-3P, 2-dr. Util. C'ch.-6P, and 4-dr. Sta. Wag.-6P were classified as Series 90 — Business Car.

Model No.	Body Type & Seating	Price	Weight	Prod. Total
Series 91	4-dr. Tr. Sed.-6P	854	2867	NA
Series 91	2-dr. Tr. Brgm.-6P	823	2832	NA
Series 91	2-dr. Vic. Cpe.-4P	844	2752	NA
Series 91	2-dr. Cpe.-3P	973	2717	NA
Series 92	2-dr. Cpe.-3P	823	2757	NA
Series 92	2-dr. Vic. Cpe.-5P	869	2787	NA
Series 92	2-dr. Conv. Cpe.-3P	972	2782	NA
Series 92	2-dr. Conv. Brgm.-6P	1032	2892	NA
Series 92	2-dr. Tr. Brgm.-6P	856	2847	NA
Series 92	4-dr. Tr. Sed.-6P	898	2897	NA
Series 93	2-dr. Cpe.-3P	919	2848	NA
Series 93	2-dr. Vic. Cpe.-5P	967	2893	NA
Series 93	2-dr. Conv. Cpe.-3P	1052	2898	NA
Series 93	4-dr. Tr. Sed.-6P	995	3023	NA
Series 93	2-dr. Conv. Brgm.-6P	1115	2983	NA
Series 93	2-dr. Tr. Brgm.-6P	960	2968	NA
Series 95	2-dr. Vic. Cpe.-5P	1051	3053	NA
Series 95	2-dr. Conv. Cpe.-3P	1138	3033	NA

Model No.	Body Type & Seating	Price	Weight	Prod. Total
Series 95	2-dr. Conv. Brgm.-6P	1201	3123	NA
Series 95	2-dr. Tr. Brgm.-6P	1049	3138	NA
Series 95	4-dr. Tr. Sed.-6P	1079	3193	NA
Series 97	4-dr. Cust. 6p. Sed.-6P	1175	3268	NA
Series 97	4-dr. Cust. 7p. Sed.-7P	1430	3378	NA

1939 Hudson, Series 90, 112, sedan, WRG

ENGINE: [Series 95 and 97] L-head. Straight. Eight cyl. Chrome alloy block. B & S: 3 x 4-1/2 in. Disp.: 254 cu. in. C.R.: 6.25:1. Brake H.P.: 122 @ 4200 R.P.M. Taxable H.P.: 28.8. Main bearings: 5. Valve lifters: mechanical. Carb.: Carter 2 barrel, downdraft WDO 402S. [Series 93] L-head. Straight. Six cyl. Chrome alloy block. B & S: 3 x 5 in. Disp.: 212 cu. in. Comp.: 6.25:1. Brake H.P. 96 @ 3600 R.P.M. Main bearings: 3. Valve lifters: mechanical. Carb.: 2bbl Carter downdraft WDO. [Series 91] L-head. Straight Six. Chrome alloy block. B & S: 3 x 5 in. Disp. 212 cu. in. C.R.: 6.25:1. Brake H.P.: 96 @ 3900 R.P.M. Main bearings: 3. Valve lifters: mechanical. Carb.: 1bbl Carter. [Series 92] L-head. Straight Six. Chrome alloy block. B & S: 3 x 5 in. Disp. 212 cu. in. C.R.: 6.25:1. Brake H.P. 96 @ 3900 R.P.M. Main bearings: 3. Valve lifters: mechanical. Carb.: 1bbl Carter. Optional Engine: L-head. Straight Six. Chrome alloy block. B & S: 3 x 5 in. Disp. 212 cu. in. C.R.: 6.25:1. Brake H.P. 101. Main bearings: 3. Valve lifters: mechanical. Carb.: 2bbl Carter WDO downdraft. [Series 90] L-head. Straight Six. Chrome alloy block. B & S: 3 x 4-1/2 in. Disp.: 175 cu. in. C.R.: 6.5:1. Brake H.P.: 86 @ 4000 R.P.M. Taxable H.P.: 21.6. Main bearings: 3. Valve lifters: mechanical. Carb.: 1bbl Carter WDO.

CHASSIS: [Series 90] W.B.: 112 in. O.L.: 187-7/8 in. Frt/Rear Tread: 50/59-1/2 in. Tires: 6.00 x 16. [Series 91] W.B.: 118 in. O.L.: 193-7/16 in. Frt/Rear Tread: 56/59-1/2 in. [Series 93] W.B.: 122 in. O.L.: 199 in. Frt/Rear Tread: 56/59-1/2 in. Tires: 6.25 x 16. [Series 92] W.B.: 118 in. Frt/Rear Tread: 56/59-1/2 in. [Series 95] W.B.: 122 in. O.L.: 199 in. Frt/Rear Tread: 56/59-1/2 in. Tires: 6.50 x 16. [Series 97] W.B.: 129 in. O.L.: 206 in. Frt/Rear Tread: 56/59-1/2 in. Tires: 6.50 x 16.

TECHNICAL: Sliding gear transmission. Speeds: 3F/1R. Steering column controls. Single disc, cork inserts, running in oil. Shaft drive. Semi-floating rear axle. Overall ratio: 4.11:1. Bendix hydraulic brakes on four wheels. Steel, drop center type wheels. Rim size: 16 in. Selective automatic shift. Automatic clutch.

OPTIONS: Single sidemount. Heater (custom and deluxe). Custom radio. DeLuxe radio. Foglights. Air electric horns. Side mirrors. Seat covers.

HISTORICAL: Introduced Nov. 1938. Innovations: Airform seat cushions, Auto-Poise Control, interior hood release. Hudson made 82161 shipments to dealers during the 1939 calendar year. The president of Hudson was A.E. Barit.

1939
DeLuxe Series 112, 6-cyl., 112" wh

	FP	5	4	3	2	1
Conv	886	3600	7200	12,000	16,800	24,000
Conv Brgm	936	3750	7500	12,500	17,500	25,000
Trav Cpe	695	700	1350	2700	4500	6400
Utl Cpe	750	675	1300	2600	4400	6300
3P Cpe	745	700	1350	2700	4500	6400
Vic Cpe	791	700	1350	2900	4600	6600
2 dr Utl Sed	725	600	1200	2200	3850	5500
Tr Brgm	775	650	1250	2400	4150	5900
Tr Sed	806	650	1250	2400	4200	6000
Sta Wag	—	825	1600	3950	5500	7900

Pacemaker Series 91, 6-cyl., 118" wb

	FP	5	4	3	2	1
3P Cpe	793	700	1350	2800	4550	6500
Vic Cpe	844	725	1400	3000	4700	6700
Tr Brgm	823	675	1300	2500	4300	6100
Tr Sed	854	675	1300	2500	4300	6100

Series 92, 6-cyl., 118" wb

	FP	5	4	3	2	1
Conv	982	3750	7500	12,500	17,500	25,000
Conv Brgm	1042	3900	7800	13,000	18,200	26,000
3P Cpe	833	700	1350	2900	4600	6600
Vic Cpe	879	725	1400	3100	4800	6800
Tr Brgm	866	675	1300	2600	4400	6300
Tr Sed	903	675	1300	2500	4350	6200

Country Club Series 93, 6-cyl., 122" wb

	FP	5	4	3	2	1
Conv	1052	3900	7800	13,000	18,200	26,000
Conv Brgm	1115	4050	8100	13,500	18,900	27,000
3P Cpe	819	725	1400	3100	4800	6800
Vic Cpe	967	750	1450	3300	4900	7000
Tr Brgm	960	700	1350	2800	4550	6500
Tr Sed	995	675	1300	2600	4400	6300

Big Boy Series 96, 6-cyl., 129" wb

	FP	5	4	3	2	1
6P Sed	884	700	1350	2900	4600	6600
7P Sed	1114	725	1400	3200	4850	6900

Country Club Series 95, 8-cyl., 122" wb

	FP	5	4	3	2	1
Conv	1138	4050	8100	13,500	18,900	27,000
Conv Brgm	1201	4200	8400	14,000	19,600	28,000
3P Cpe	1009	750	1450	3300	4900	7000
Vic Cpe	1051	750	1450	3500	5050	7200
Tr Brgm	1049	725	1400	3200	4850	6900
Tr Sed	1079	700	1350	2700	4500	6400

Custom Series 97, 8-cyl., 129" wb

	FP	5	4	3	2	1
5P Tr Sed	1199	725	1400	3200	4850	6900
7P Sed	1219	775	1500	3700	5200	7400

1940

1940 Hudson, Series 41, coupe, OCW

HUDSON — OVERVIEW FOR ALL 1940 MODELS — Hudson's styling was extensively revised for 1940. The almond shaped head lights of 1939 gave way to circular sealed beam units although the shape of the headlight frame and the positioning of the parking lights directly below the main lamps gave both arrangements a similar appearance. The Hudson's grille form which had been steadily evolving towards a strictly horizontal design for several years took another strong step in that direction as a two section arrangement with horizontal bars was adopted. Additional horizontal bars ran the length of the body adding an impression of low built and fleetness. At the rear a larger, single piece window was adopted. All models were offered with or without running boards at no extra cost. Leading the list of Hudson mechanical and technical improvements was a full independent front suspension consisting of coil springs, unequal length A-arms and hydraulic shock absorbers. Also new were longer by 5 inches, rear semi-elliptic springs with a total length of 60" and as an option, the semi-electric Warner overdrive feature which replaced Selective Automatic Shift. Hudson's "Fluid Cushioned" automatic clutch was available with or without overdrive. The Hudson 112 series was dropped for 1940 with a new line of four Hudson Six Travelers taking its place. Hudson produced 86,865 automobiles but losses still totalled $1,507,780.

HUDSON SUPER-SIX — SERIES 41 — SIX: Super-Six models carried Hudson lettering on the sides of their hood along with the small triangular lights of the Series 43 and 44 models. In addition their greater length made it easy to separate them from the Series 40T and 40P.

HUDSON SIX TRAVELER SIX — SERIES 40T — SIX: As did all Hudsons the Series 40T models were equipped with sealed beam headlamps. Since this line was Hudson's least expensive it was fitted with sliding glass. Its interior featured taupe worsted boucle. The Traveler was easily set apart from other Hudsons by its lack of front vent-panes.

HUDSON DELUXE SIX — SERIES 40P — SIX: The higher price of the Series 40P compared to the Traveler Six was justified by its higher quality brown taupe stripe broadcloth upholstery and roll-down windows.

HUDSON EIGHT — SERIES 44 — EIGHT: The Series 44 Hudsons were identical in appearance to the Series 41, Super Six models.

HUDSON EIGHT DELUXE — SERIES 45 — EIGHT: The two models in this series had a higher quality interior than the Series 44.

HUDSON COUNTRY CLUB EIGHT — SERIES 47 — EIGHT: These Hudsons were identified by their added length, wider door (front) and distinctive front grille with a rectangular opening in its center section. The front fenders were crowned with chrome strips and the taillights were given added chrome trim. Included as standard equipment were directional signals.

HUDSON COUNTRY CLUB SIX — SERIES 43 — SIX: These three Hudsons were with the exception of their engine and running gear identical to the Country Club Eight. Interior features included a std. 2-tone brown and tan Hockanum woolen upholstery. Door panels were fitted with chrome scruff plates and the pleated sections of the seats and door panels had horizontal dividers.

I.D. DATA: Car numbers on plate mounted on firewall. Starting: [Series 40] 40101, [Series 41] 41250, [Series 43] 43370, [Series 44] 44294, [Series 45] 451752, [Series 47] 47167. Ending: [Series 40] 4089192, [Series 41] 4189192, [Series 43] 4389192, [Series 44] 4489192, [Series 45] 4589192, [Series 47] 4789192.

* Includes 40T, 40P and 40C (commercial cars).
Engine numbers on right side of cylinder block. Starting: Series 40 same as serial numbers, [Series 41 & 43] 43101, [Series 44 & 45] 45101. Ending: Series 40 same as serial numbers, [Series 41 & 43] 4389192, [Series 44 & 45] 4589192. Canadian-built cars included letter "C".

Model No.	Body Type & Seating	Price	Weight	Prod. Total
Series 40T	2-dr. Cpe.-3P	670	2800	NA
Series 40T	2-dr. Vic. Cpe.-4P	750	2830	NA
Series 40T	2-dr. Tr. Sed.-6P	735	2895	NA
Series 40T	4-dr. Sed.-6P	763	2940	NA
Series 40P	2-dr. Cpe.-3P	745	2840	NA
Series 40P	2-dr. Vic. Cpe.-4P	791	2865	NA
Series 40P	2-dr. Conv. Cpe.-5P	930	2860	NA
Series 40P	2-dr. Tr. Sed.-6P	775	2930	NA
Series 40P	2-dr. Conv. Sed.-6P	955	2920	NA
Series 40P	4-dr. Tr. Sed.-6P	806	2965	NA
Series 41	2-dr. Cpe.-3P	809	2950	NA
Series 41	2-dr. Vic. Cpe.-5P	860	2980	NA
Series 41	2-dr. Conv. Cpe.-5P	1087	2980	NA
Series 41	2-dr. Conv. Sed.-6P	1030	3020	NA
Series 41	2-dr. Tr. Sed.-6P	839	3020	NA
Series 41	4-dr. Tr. Sed.-6P	870	3050	NA
Series 43	4-dr. Tr. Sed.-6P	1018	3240	NA
Series 43	4-dr. Sp. Tr. Sed.-6P	1044	3240	NA
Series 43	4-dr. Sed.-8P	1230	3355	NA
Series 44	2-dr. Cpe.-3P	860	3040	NA
Series 44	2-dr. Vic. Cpe.-4P	942	3075	NA
Series 44	2-dr. Conv. Sed.-6P	1122	3130	NA
Series 44	2-dr. Conv. Cpe.-5P	1087	3065	NA
Series 44	2-dr. Tr. Sed.-6P	942	3185	NA
Series 44	4-dr. Tr. Sed.-6P	952	3185	NA
Series 45	2-dr. Tr. Sed.-6P	942	3185	NA
Series 45	4-dr. Tr. Sed.-6P	976	3215	NA
Series 47	4-dr. Tr. Sed.-6P	1118	3285	NA
Series 47	4-dr. Sp. Tr. Sed.-6P	1144	3285	NA
Series 47	4-dr. Sed.-8P	1330	3400	NA

1940 Hudson, Series 47, sedan, WRG

ENGINE: [Series 40T and 40P] L-head. Straight. Six cyl. Chrome alloy block. B & S: 3 x 4-1/8 in. Disp.: 175 cu. in. C.R.: 6.5:1. Brake H.P.: 92 @ 4000 R.P.M. Main bearings: 3. Valve lifters: mechanical. Carb.: Carter 430 SV (early) 461S (late). Optional Engine: L-head. Straight. Six cyl. Chrome alloy block. B & S: 3 x 5 in. Disp.: 212 cu. in. C.R.: 6.5:1. Brake H.P.: 102 @ 4000 R.P.M. Main bearings: 3. Valve lifters: mechanical. Carb.: Carter 430SV (early) 461S (late). [Series 41 and 43] L-head. Inline. Six cyl. Chrome alloy block. B & S: 3 x 5 in. Disp.: 212 cu. in. C.R.: 6.5:1. Brake H.P.: 102 @ 4000 R.P.M. Main bearings: 3. Valve lifters: mechanical. Carb.: 2bb Carter 454S. [Series 44, 45 and 47] L-head. Inline. Eight cyl. Chrome alloy block. B & S: 3 x 4-1/2 in. Disp.: 254.4 cu. in. C.R.: 6.5:1. Brake H.P.: 128 @ 4200 R.P.M. N.A.C.C. H.P.: 28.8. Main bearings: 5. Valve lifters: mechanical. Carb.: 2bb Carter 455S. Note: cars with the 3x5 engine were designated by the letter "L" placed between series and serial number.

CHASSIS: [Series 40T, 40P] W.B.: 113 in. O.L.: 190-3/8 in. Height: 70.5 in. Frt/Rear Tread: 56-1/4 / 59-1/2 in. Tires: 16 x 5.50 — 40T, 16 x 6.00 — 40P, 15 x 7.00 opt. [Series 41] W.B.: 118 in. O.L.: 195-3/8 in. Height: 70.5 in. Frt/Rear Tread: 56-1/4 / 59-1/2 in. Tires: 16 x 6.00, 15 x 7.00 opt. [Series 43] W.B.: 125 in. O.L.: 202-3/8 in. Height: 70.5 in. Frt/Rear Tread: 56-1/4 / 59-1/2 in. Tires: 16 x 6.25, 15 x 7.00 opt. [Series 44] W.B.: 118 in. O.L.: 195-3/8 in. Height: 70.5 in. Frt/Rear Tread: 56-1/4 / 59-1/2 in. Tires: 16 x 6.00, 15 x 7.00 opt. [Series 45] W.B.: 118 in. O.L.: 195-3/8 in. Height: 70.5 in. Frt/Rear Tread: 56-1/4 / 59-1/2 in. Tires: 16 x 6.00, 15 x 7.00 opt. [Series 47] W.B.: 125 in. O.L.: 202-3/8 in. Height: 70.5 in. Frt/Rear Tread: 56-1/4 / 59-1/2 in. Tires: 16 x 6.50, 15 x 7.00 opt.

TECHNICAL: Sliding gear transmission. 3F/1R. Column controls. Single disc, cork inserts, running in oil. Shaft drive. Semi-floating rear axle. Overall Ratio: Series 40T & 40P — 4.55 all others 4.11. Bendix hydraulic brakes on four wheels. Steel, drop center type wheels. Drivetrain Options: Overdrive. Automatic clutch.

OPTIONS: Turn signals (standard only on Country Club models). Airfoam cushions (optional on Hudson Six models — standard in all others). Weather-Master Fresh Air and Heat Control.

HISTORICAL: Introduced Sept. 1939. 1940 was the first year for Hudson's fully independent suspension. Hudson made 87,900 shipments to dealers during the 1940 calendar year. The president of Hudson was A.E. Barit. From August 23 to August 27, just prior to the introduction date of the

714

1940 Hudson both the Hudson Six and Hudson Eight set numerous new AAA speed records. The Hudson Six established 58 new Class D endurance marks plus 23 unlimited records for stock cars regardless of size or price. Equipped with overdrive and the optional 3.88:1 rear axle the Hudson averaged 70.5 mph for 10,000 miles. The Hudson Eight with the optional 7.0:1 cylinder head, overdrive and 3.88:1 rear axle was used by John Cobb to set additional Class D records including a 10 mile run at 92.89 and a flying mile record of 93.89. Both cars also participated in economy runs. The Hudson Six finished a 1,000 mile run at an average of 29.88 mph with a fuel consumption of 32.66 mpg. The Hudson Eight averaged 27.12 mpg for one thousand miles at a constant speed of 29.31 mph.

1940

	FP	5	4	3	2	1
Traveler Series 40-T, 6-cyl., 113" wb						
Cpe	670	700	1350	2700	4500	6400
Vic Cpe	750	725	1400	3200	4850	6900
2 dr Tr Sed	38000	650	1250	2400	4150	5900
4 dr Tr Sed	763	650	1250	2400	4150	5900
DeLuxe Series, 40-P, 6-cyl., 113" wb						
Conv 6 Pass	930	3000	6000	10,000	14,000	20,000
Cpe	745	700	1350	2900	4600	6600
Vic Cpe	791	750	1450	3300	4900	7000
2 dr Tr Sed	775	650	1250	2400	4200	6000
4 dr Sed	806	675	1300	2500	4300	6100
Super Series 41, 6-cyl., 118" wb						
Conv 5 Pass	995	3150	6300	10,500	14,700	21,000
Conv 6 Pass	1030	3300	6600	11,000	15,400	22,000
Cpe	809	725	1400	3100	4800	6800
Vic Cpe	860	750	1450	3400	5000	7100
2 dr Tr Sed	839	675	1300	2500	4300	6100
4 dr Tr Sed	870	675	1300	2500	4350	6200
Country Club Series 43, 6-cyl., 125" wb						
6P Sed	1044	675	1300	2500	4350	6200
7P Sed	1230	700	1350	2700	4500	6400
Series 44, 8-cyl., 118" wb						
Conv 5 Pass	1087	3300	6600	11,000	15,400	22,000
Conv 6 Pass	1122	3400	6900	11,500	16,100	23,000
Cpe	860	750	1450	3300	4900	7000
Vic Cpe	942	775	1500	3700	5200	7400
2 dr Tr Sed	918	675	1300	2500	4350	6200
4 dr Tr Sed	952	675	1300	2600	4400	6300
DeLuxe Series 45, 8-cyl., 118" wb						
2 dr Tr Sed	942	675	1300	2600	4400	6300
4 dr Tr Sed	976	700	1350	2700	4500	6400
Country Club Eight Series 47, 8-cyl., 125" wb						
Tr Sed	1144	700	1350	2900	4600	6600
7P Sed	1330	725	1400	3200	4850	6900
Big Boy Series 48, 6-cyl., 125" wb						
C-A Sed	989	700	1350	2800	4550	6500
7P Sed	1095	700	1350	2900	4600	6600

1941

HUDSON — GENERAL DESCRIPTION: The 1941 Hudsons were substantially redesigned automobiles, sharing only the front fender sheet metal and drive line components with the 1940 models. All wheelbases were increased three inches and overall height was reduced by two inches thanks to a flatter roof line. Overall body length was extended by 5½ inches. The handsome, horizontal grille format was continued from 1940 but 9 rather than 7 grille bars were used and their greater length reduced the size of the center grille divider. Rear deck changes included taillights moved from the fenders to the quarter panels and externally mounted chrome trunk hinges.

Convertible models were now equipped with a power top and a new 3 speed synchromesh transmission with helical-cut gears was also introduced.

In a break with tradition, Hudson introduced Symphonic Styling for 1941 which at no extra cost offered the customer a wide selection of interior color combinations that harmonized with the car's exterior color.

Although shipments to dealers dropped to 79,529, Hudson's profit was a respectable $3,756,418.

HUDSON TRAVELER, SIX DELUXE — SERIES 10T, 10P — SIX: The 10T and 10P shared the same chassis, wheelbase and engine. Both series were equipped with a single taillight and sunvisor but the 10P was fitted with many other features. These included larger 16 x 6.00 standard tires, gray or tan colored broadcloth upholstery (in place of the 10T's taupe worsted worsted bouclé) wood grained dash and garnish moldings, front window vent panes, rear anti-sway bar, spring covers, bumper guards, rear seat ash trays and assist plus front arm rests.

1941 Hudson, Series 11, station wagon, OCW

HUDSON SUPER SIX — SERIES 11 — SIX: The Super Six was powered by the same cylinder engine as the Commodore Six and shared the 121 inch wheelbase chassis with both the Commodore Six and Eight. Externally it was identified by the Super Six name plates positioned on each side of the hood near the windshield's base. Its standard equipment was identical to that of the DeLuxe Six but the Super Six interior featured Hockanum Tweed in either tan, gray or green and the instrument panel and garnish molding was painted to match one of these colors.

HUDSON COMMODORE SIX — SERIES 12 — SIX / COMMODORE EIGHT — SERIES 14 — EIGHT: The Commodore Six and Commodore Eight were, except for their engine and accompanying mechanical modifications, identical automobiles. The only exceptions were their hood identifications which read either Commodore Six or Commodore Eight. Both cars had a 121 inch wheelbase and crowning their front fenders were long chrome bars that trailed away from the parking lights. The front bumpers had large "guard wings" at either end with similar gravel deflectors mounted on the rear bumpers.

The Commodore interior featured Hockanum Twill Cord upholstery in gray, tan, or green and the finish of the instrument panel matched that of the upholstery. The front and rear seat backs and arm rests were leather finished and a deluxe, 18 inch steering wheel with a chrome horn ring was fitted. Among the Commodore's standard equipment were airfoam seats, twin horns and taillights, large hubcaps and on sedans a rear dome light. In addition, the Commodores were offered in special, two-tone exterior color combinations.

HUDSON COMMODORE CUSTOM EIGHT — SERIES 15 & 17 — EIGHT: The Commodore Custom Eights were offered in either coupe (121 inch wheelbase) or sedan (128 inch wheelbase) models. They were identified by such external features as the center bar placed between the front bumper guards, wheel trim rings, hood ID script, inward pointed, triangular taillights and similarly shaped rear deck emblem.

In addition to the equipment supplied to the Commodore Series the Custom Eight's standard appointments included two cigarette lighters, radio and front and rear center armrests. Their Hockanum Fancy Bedford Cord upholstery in green, gray or tan covered double thickness airfoam cushions. Additional leather trim was also installed on the interior door edges and front seat corners.

I.D. DATA: Car numbers on plate positioned on right front door hinge pillar post. Starting: [Series 10T] T10,101, [Series 10P & 10C] P10,101, [Series 11 & 12] 11,101, [Series 14 & 15] 14,101, [Series 17] 17,101. Ending: [Series 10T] T1,092,988, [Series 10P & 10C] P1,092,988, [Series 11 & 12] 1,192,988, [Series 14 & 15] 1,492,988, [Series 17] 1,792,988. Engine number on stamping on top of the cylinder block between numbers one and two exhaust manifold flanges. Starting: [Series 10T] T10,101, [Series 10P & 10C] C10,101, [Series 11 & 12] 12,101, [Series 14 & 15] 15,101, [Series 17] NA. Ending: [Series 10T] T1,092,988, [Series 10P & 10C] C1,092,988, [Series 11] & 12 1,292,988, [Series 11 & 12]1,292,988, [Series 14 & 15] 1,592,988, [Series 17] NA. "C" included in Canadian cars.

Model No.	Body Type & Seating	Price	Weight	Prod. Total
Series 10T	2-dr. Clb. Cpe.-6P	788	2840	NA
Series 10T	2-dr. Cpe.-3P	695	2790	NA
Series 10T	2-dr. Tr. Sed.-6P	765	2850	NA
Series 10T	4-dr. Tr. Sed.-6P	793	2900	NA
Series 10P	2-dr. Clb. Cpe.-6P	848	2895	NA
Series 10P	2-dr. Cpe.-3P	801	2840	NA
Series 10P	2-dr. Tr. Sed.-6P	822	2900	NA
Series 10P	4-dr. Tr. Sed.-6P	856	2950	NA
Series 10P	2-dr. Conv. Sed.-6P	1063	2980	NA
Series 11	2-dr. Clb. Cpe.-6P	936	2980	NA
Series 11	2-dr. Cpe.-3P	881	2935	NA
Series 11	2-dr. Tr. Sed.-6P	901	3000	NA
Series 11	4-dr. Tr. Sed.-6P	932	3050	NA
Series 11	2-dr. Conv. Sed.-6P	1156	3125	NA
Series 11	4-dr. Sta. Wag.-8P	1383	3400	NA
Series 12	2-dr. Clb. Cpe.-6P	997	3045	NA
Series 12	2-dr. Cpe.-3P	935	3000	NA
Series 12	2-dr. Conv. Sed.-6P	1204	3160	NA
Series 12	2-dr. Tr. Sed.-6P	966	3050	NA
Series 12	4-dr. Tr. Sed.-6P	994	3100	NA
Series 14	2-dr. Clb. Cpe.-6P	1040	3210	NA
Series 14	2-dr. Cpe.-3P	978	3135	NA
Series 14	2-dr. Conv. Sed.-6P	1254	3350	NA
Series 14	2-dr. Tr. Sed.-6P	1003	3210	NA
Series 14	4-dr. Tr. Sed.-6P	1035	3260	NA
Series 14	4-dr. Sta. Wag.-8P	1383	3400	NA
Series 15	2-dr. Clb. Cpe.-6P	1127	3235	NA
Series 15	2-dr. Cpe.-3P	1064	NA	NA
Series 17	4-dr. Tr. Sed.-6P	1232	3400	NA
Series 17	4-dr. Sed.-8P	1438	3440	NA

ENGINE: [Series 11 and 12] L-head. Inline. Six cyl. Chrome alloy block. B & S: 3 x 5 in. Disp.: 212 cu. in. C.R.: 6.25:1. Brake H.P.: 102 @ 4000 R.P.M. Taxable H.P.: 21.6. Main bearings: 3. Valve lifters: mechanical. Carb.: Carter Duplex Down Draft 501S. [Series 10T and 10P] L-head. Inline. Six cyl. Chrome alloy block. B & S: 3 x 4-1/2 in. Disp.: 175 cu. in. C.R.: 7.25:1. Brake H.P.: 92 @ 4000 R.P.M. Taxable H.P.: 21.6. Main bearings: 3. Valve lifters: mechanical. Carb.: Carter Single Down-draft. Optional Engine: L-head. Inline. Six cyl. Chrome alloy block. B & S: 3 x 5 in. Disp.: 212 cu. in. C.R.: 6.5:1. Brake H.P.: 102 @ 4000 R.P.M. Taxable/A.L.A.M./N.A.C.C. H.P.: 21.6. Main bearings: 3. Valve lifters: mechanical. Carb.: Carter Duplex Down-Draft. [Series 14 and 15 and 17] L-head. Inline. Eight cyl. Chrome alloy block. B & S: 3 x 4-1/2 in. Disp. 254.4 cu. in. C.R.: 6.5:1. Brake H.P.: 128 @ 4200 R.P.M. Taxable H.P.: 28.8. Main bearings: 5. Valve lifters: mechanical. Carb.: 2bb Carter 502S.

1941 Hudson, Series 14, Commodore coupe, WRG

CHASSIS: [Series 10T] W.B.: 116 in. O.L.: 195-1/4 in. Height: 68 in. Frt/Rear Tread: 56-1/4 / 59-1/2 in. Tires: 16 x 5.50 (16 x 6.00 optional). [Series 10P] W.B.: 116 in. O.L.: 195-1/4 in. Height: 68 in. Frt/Rear Tread: 56-1/4 / 59-1/2 in. Tires: 16 x 6.00. [Series 11] W.B.: 121 in. O.L.: 200-1/4 in. Height: 68-3/4 in. Frt/Rear Tread: 56-1/4 / 59-1/2 in. Tires: 16 x 6.00 (16 x 6.50 or 15 x 7.00 optional). [Series 12] W.B.: 121 in. O.L.: 203-1/4 in. Height: 68-3/4 in. Frt/Rear Tread: 56-1/4 / 59-1/2 in. Tires: 16 x 6.25 (16 x 6.50 or 15 x 7.00 optional). [Series 14] W.B.: 121 in. O.L.: 203-1/4 in. Height: 68-3/4 in. Frt/Rear Tread: 56-1/4 / 59-1/2 in. Tires: 16 x 6.25 (16 x 6.50 or 15 x 7.00 optional). [Series 15] W.B.: 121 in. O.L.: 203-1/4 in. Height: 68-3/4 in. Frt/Rear Trend: 56-1/4 / 59-1/2 in. Tires: 16 x 6.25 (16 x 6.50 or 15 x 7.00 optional). [Series 17] W.B.: 128 in. O.L.: 210-1/4 in. Height: 68-3/4 in. Frt/Rear Tread: 56-1/4 / 59-1/2 in. Tires: 16 x 6.50 (15 x 7.00 optional).

TECHNICAL: Sliding gear transmission. Speeds: 3F/1R. Column controls. Single disc, cork inserts, running in oil. Shaft drive. Semi-floating rear axle. Overall ratio: 4.11, 4.55 optional - except series 10T and 10P. Standard axle with overdrive 4.55, 4.11 optional. Bendix hydraulic brakes on four wheels. Steel wheels. Rim size: 16 in. (15 in. optional). Vacumotive Drive (automatic clutch) (27.50). Overdrive (62.50).

OPTIONS: DeLuxe radio (49.75). Custom heater (includes defroster) (26.00). Clock (13.50). Spotlight (17.00). Junior radio (29.50). Custom radio (67.50). Power radio antenna (6.75). Weathermaster heater and defroster (36.00). Directionals (17.50, 19.50). Seat covers (7.25). Chrome outside window mouldings (7.25, 13.00). DeLuxe 18" steering wheel (13.95). Special running board mouldings (2.25). Air foam seats. Large hub caps (6.75). Twin horn.

HISTORICAL: Hudson made 79,529 shipments to dealers during the 1941 calendar year. The president of Hudson was A.E. Barit.

Hudson emphasized its economic operation rather than performance in 1941. In the Gilmore Oil Grand Canyon a DeLuxe Six was a class winner with a 24.6mpg. mark. Also a class champion was the Commodore Eight at 20.18mpg. *Safety Engineering Magazine* persented Hudson with its Safety Engineering Trophy for the 1941 models' safety and engineering excellence. In each of 14 categories the Hudson received a perfect score.

1941 Hudson, Series 14, Commodore, sedan, OCW

1941
Utility Series 10-C, 6-cyl., 116" wb

	FP	5	4	3	2	1
Cpe	840	650	1250	2400	4200	6000
2 dr Sed	780	600	1200	2300	4000	5700

Traveler Series 10-T, 6-cyl., 116" wb

	FP	5	4	3	2	1
Cpe	754	675	1300	2500	4300	6100
Clb Cpe	847	675	1300	2500	4350	6200
2 dr Sed	824	650	1250	2400	4200	6000
4 dr Sed	852	650	1250	2400	4200	6000

DeLuxe Series 10-P, 6-cyl., 116" wb

	FP	5	4	3	2	1
Conv	1132	3000	6000	10,000	14,000	20,000
Cpe	870	650	1200	2300	4100	5800
Clb Cpe	917	650	1250	2400	4150	5900
2 dr Sed	891	600	1200	2300	4000	5700
4 dr Sed	925	650	1200	2300	4100	5800

Super Series 11, 6-cyl., 121" wb						
	FP	5	4	3	2	1
Conv	1230	3300	6600	11,000	15,400	22,000
Cpe	955	650	1250	2400	4150	5900
Clb Cpe	1011	675	1300	2500	4300	6100
2 dr Sed	973	600	1200	2200	3900	5600
4 dr Sed	1007	600	1200	2300	4000	5700
Sta Wag	1298	850	1650	4200	5850	8400
Commodore Series 12, 6-cyl., 121" wb						
Conv	1297	3400	6900	11,500	16,100	23,000
Cpe	1028	650	1250	2400	4200	6000
Clb Cpe	1090	675	1300	2500	4350	6200
2 dr Sed	1059	600	1200	2300	4000	5700
Sed	1087	600	1200	2300	4100	5800
Commodore Series 14, 8-cyl., 121" wb						
Conv	1347	3600	7200	12,000	16,800	24,000
Cpe	1071	675	1300	2500	4350	6200
Clb Cpe	1133	700	1350	2700	4500	6400
2 dr Sed	1096	650	1250	2400	4150	5900
Sed	1132	650	1250	2400	4200	6000
Sta Wag	1385	850	1650	4200	5850	8400
Commodore Custom Series 15, 8-cyl., 121" wb						
Cpe	1162	725	1400	3200	4850	6900
Clb Cpe	1225	775	1500	3700	5200	7400
Commodore Custom Series 17, 8-cyl., 128" wb						
Sed	1537	700	1350	2700	4500	6400
7P Sed	1330	725	1400	3200	4850	6900
Big Boy Series 18, 6-cyl., 128" wb						
C-A Sed	1094	675	1300	2500	4350	6200
7P Sed	1223	700	1350	2700	4500	6400

Model No.	Body Type & Seating	Price	Weight	Prod. Total
Series 22	2-dr. Clb. Cpe.-6P	1239	3090	NA
Series 22	2-dr. Cpe.-3P	1176	2995	NA
Series 22	2-dr. Clb. Sed.-6P	1216	3090	NA
Series 22	4-dr. Sed.-6P	1246	3145	NA
Series 22	2-dr. Conv. Sed.-6P	1481	3280	NA
Series 24	2-dr. Clb. Cpe.-6P	1282	3205	NA
Series 24	2-dr. Cpe.-3P	1220	3130	NA
Series 24	2-dr. Clb. Sed.-6P	1252	3230	NA
Series 24	4-dr. Sed.-6P	1291	3280	NA
Series 24	2-dr. Conv. Sed.-6P	1533	3400	NA
Series 25	2-dr. Clb. Cpe.-6P	1380	3235	NA
Series 25	2-dr. Cpe.-3P	1318	3160	NA
Series 27	4-dr. Sed.-8P	1510	3395	NA
Series 20T	2-dr. Clb. Cpe.-6P	965	2845	NA
Series 20T	2-dr. Cpe.-3P	893	2795	NA
Series 20T	2-dr. Clb. Sed.-6P	945	2895	NA
Series 20T	4-dr. Sed.-6P	973	2940	NA
Series 20P	2-dr. Clb. Cpe.-6P	1034	2900	NA
Series 20P	2-dr. Cpe.-3P	981	2845	NA
Series 20P	2-dr. Clb. Sed.-6P	1012	2935	NA
Series 20P	4-dr. Sed.-6P	1045	2975	NA
Series 20P	2-dr. Conv.-6P	1292	3140	NA
Series 21	2-dr. Clb. Cpe.-6P	1159	3010	NA
Series 21	2-dr. Cpe.-3P	1102	2950	NA
Series 21	2-dr. Clb. Sed.-6P	1132	3035	NA
Series 21	4-dr. Sed.-6P	1162	3080	NA
Series 21	2-dr. Conv. Sed.-6P	1414	3200	NA
Series 21	4-dr. Sta. Wag.-6P	1486	3315	NA

1942

1942 Hudson, Series 21, Super-Six, club coupe, OCW

HUDSON — ALL SERIES OVERVIEW: The last of the pre-war Hudsons received a fairly substantial face lift. The lower body section now flared out to conceal the remnants of the running board and pointing the way to the full width grille arrangements common to most postwar American cars were the chrome strips running full width of the body and extending around the first few inches of the front fender. Also given greater width was the Hudson's grille. To accommodate these changes new front and rear fenders were used. Overall height was reduced by 1.5 inches due to altered rear spring and frame design. The Hudson's profile also carried new trim consisting of a single long bright strip with shorter stripes at either extremity. However, Dec. 31, 1941 was the end of chrome plating trim for U.S. cars with the only external components exempt being bumpers. After that date Hudson's trim consisted of metal pressings covered with plastic.

Hudson's production of its 1942 models began on July 21, 1941 and by Feb. 5, 1942 when it came to an end, a total of 40,661 were assembled.

I.D. DATA: Car numbers on plate mounted on firewall. Starting: [Series 20T] T-20101, [Series 20P] P-20101, [Series 21] 21,101, [Series 22] 22101. Ending: [Series 20T] T2,041,232, [Series 20P] P2,041,232, [Series 21] 2,141,232, [Series 22] 2,241,232. Engine numbers stamped on top of the cylinder block between numbers one and two exhaust manifold flanges. Starting: same as serial numbers. Car numbers on plate mounted on firewall. Starting: [Series 24] 24101, [Series 25] 25101, [Series 27] 27101. Ending: [Series 24] 2,441,232, [Series 25] 2,541,232, [Series 27] 2,741,232. Engine number staped on top of the cylinder block between numbers one and two exhaust manifold flanges. Starting: same as serial numbers. Canadian-built cars included letter "C".

1942 Hudson, Series 24, Commodore Eight, sedan, OCW

ENGINE: [Series 24, 25, 27] L-head. Inline. Eight cyl. Chrome alloy block. B & S: 3 x 4-1/2 in. Disp.: 254.4 cu. in. C.R.: 6.5:1. Brake H.P.: 128 @ 4200 R.P.M. Taxable H.P.: 28.8. Main bearings: 5. Valve lifters: mechanical. Carb.: 2bbl Carter 502S downdraft. [Series 21, 22] L-head. Inline. Six cyl. Chrome alloy block. B & S: 3 x 5 in. Disp.: 212 cu. in. C.R.: 6.25:1. Brake H.P.: 102 @ 4000 R.P.M. Taxable H.P.: 21.6. Main bearings: 3. Valve lifters: mechanical. Carb.: Carter Duplex Downdraft 501S. [Series 20T, 20P] L-head. Inline. Six cyl. Chrome alloy block. B & S: 3 x 4-1/2 in. Disp.: 175 cu. in. C.R.: 7.25:1. Brake H.P.: 92 @ 4000 R.P.M. Taxable H.P.: 21.6. Main bearings: 3. Valve lifters: mechanical. Carb.: Carter Single Downdraft 454S. Optional Engine: L-head. Inline. Six cyl. Chrome alloy block. B & S: 3 x 5 in. Disp.: 212 cu. in. C.R.: 6.5:1. Brake H.P.: 102 @ 4000 R.P.M. Taxable H.P.: 21.6. Main bearings: 3. Valve lifters: mechanical. Carb.: Carter Duplex Downdraft 501S.

CHASSIS: [Series 20T] W.B.: 116 in. O.L.: 198-1/4 in. Frt/Rear Tread: 56-5/16 / 59-1/2 in. Tires: 16 x 5.50 (16 x 6.00 optional). [Series 20P] W.B.: 116 in. O.L.: 200-1/2 in. Frt/Rear Tread: 56-5/16 / 59-1/2 in. Tires: 16 x 6.00 (16 x 6.50 optional). [Series 21] W.B.: 121 in. O.L.: 207-3/8 in. Frt/Rear Tread: 56-5/16 / 59-1/2 in. Tires: 16 x 6.00 (16 x 6.50, 15 x 7.00 optional). [Series 22] W.B.: 121 in. O.L.: 207-3/8 in. Frt/Rear Tread: 56-5/16 / 59-1/2 in. Tires: 16 x 6.00 (16 x 6.50, 15 x 7.00 optional). [Series 24] W.B.: 121 in. O.L.: 207-3/8 in. Frt/Rear Tread: 56-5/16 / 59-1/2 in. Tires: 16 x 6.25 (16 x 6.50, 15 x 7.00 optional). [Series 25] W.B.: 121 in. O.L.: 207-3/8 in. Frt/Rear Tread: 56-5/16 / 59-1/2 in. Tires: 16 x 6.25 (16 x 6.50, 15 x 7.00 optional). [Series 27] W.B.: 128 in. O.L.: 214-3/8 in. Frt/Rear Tread: 56-5/16 / 59-1/2 in. Tires: 15 x 6.50 (15 x 7.00 optional).

TECHNICAL: Sliding gear transmission. Speeds: 3F/1R. Steering column controls. Single disc, cork inserts, running in oil. Shaft drive. Semi-floating rear axle. Overall Ratio: Series 20T & 20P 4.55, all others 4.11. With over drive: Series 20T, 20P — 4.87, all others 4.55. Bendix hydraulic brakes on four wheels. Steel drop center type wheels. Drivetrain Options: Drive-Master transmission. Overdrive.

1942 Hudson, Series 21, Super-Six, sedan, WRG

OPTIONS: White sidewall tires. Full chrome hub caps. Bumper wing guards (standard on Commodore). Sleeper kit.

HISTORICAL: Introduced Aug. 1941. Innovations: Drive-Master, which was a combination of vacumotive plus an additional power unit which shifted gears by intake manifold vacuum. Cars with this feature had an instrument panel switch with 3 push buttons. The Off button allowed the car to function in the conventional manner. The "VAC" button put Vacumotive Drive into action. For full Drive-Master operation, the "HDM" button was pushed. Model Year production: 40,661 cars. The president of Hudson was A.E. Barit.

1942
Traveler Series 20-T, 6-cyl., 116" wb

	FP	5	4	3	2	1
Cpe	828	675	1300	2500	4350	6200
Clb Cpe	897	700	1350	2700	4500	6400
2 dr Sed	877	675	1300	2500	4300	6100
4 dr Sed	3-850	675	1300	2500	4350	6200

DeLuxe Series 20-P, 6-cyl., 116" wb

Conv	1212	3300	6600	11,000	15,400	22,000
Cpe	916	700	1350	2700	4500	6400
Clb Cpe	967	725	1400	3200	4850	6900
2 dr Sed	945	675	1300	2500	4350	6200
4 dr Sed	977	700	1350	2700	4500	6400

Super Series 21, 6-cyl., 121" wb

Conv	1332	3400	6900	11,500	16,100	23,000
Cpe	1036	725	1400	3000	4700	6700
Clb Cpe	1090	750	1450	3400	5000	7100
2 dr Sed	1064	675	1300	2600	4400	6300
Sed	1092	700	1350	2900	4600	6600
Sta Wag	1412	900	1800	4450	6250	8900

Commodore Series 22, 6-cyl., 121" wb

Conv	1402	3600	7200	12,000	16,800	24,000
Cpe	1115	700	1350	2800	4550	6500
Clb Cpe	1175	725	1400	3100	4800	6800
2 dr Sed	1152	700	1350	2700	4500	6400
Sed	1181	700	1350	2800	4550	6500

Commodore Series 24, 8-cyl., 121" wb

Conv	1451	3750	7500	12,500	17,500	25,000
Cpe	1156	725	1400	3100	4800	6800
Clb Cpe	1186	750	1450	3300	4900	7000
2 dr Sed	1215	700	1350	2900	4600	6600
Sed	1223	725	1400	3000	4700	6700

Commodore Custom Series 25, 8-cyl., 121" wb

Clb Cpe	1311	750	1450	3300	4900	7000

Commodore Series 27, 8-cyl., 128" wb

Sed	—	725	1400	3000	4700	6700

1901 Hudson Steamer, MVMA

HUDSON STEAMER — Hudson, Michigan — (1901-1902) — The Bean-Chamberlain Manufacturing Company of Hudson commenced the manufacture in 1901 of a steam car with a two-cylinder double-reversing engine, the cylinders being a one-piece casting. That novel construction aside, the Hudson Steamer produced by Bean-Chamberlain was otherwise the usual chain-drive tiller-steered light steam runabout being built by dozens of other steam cars manufacturers in the United States. Production limped through 1902, and halted there. Interestingly, in early spring of 1903, some businessmen in the city of Hudson banded together with Roscoe Bean to take up where Bean-Chambelain left off, organizing themselve as the Hudson Motor Vehicle Company, capitalized at $150,000 for the manufacture of steam automobiles and motorcycles. Almost immediately, they changed their minds to the Hudson Auto-Vehicle Company and decided to build light gasoline cars and motorcycles instead. They did neither, though they were still trying to get their enterprise going as late as December of 1904.

HUEBNER — Brooklyn, New York — (1914) — O.E. Huebner, a Brooklyn engineer who gave his address as 131 Sumpter Street, might be said to have provided a gimmick for a fad. The cyclecar he designed in 1913 was an electric, and Huebner claimed it to be the first such cyclecar developed in the United States. Whether this was true is problematical — there was another developed in the Midwest during this period — but certainly Huebner's was the first three-wheeled electric cyclecar in America. Its wheelbase was 96 inches, the tread 54, just two inches short of the standard. The single driving wheel was at the rear of the prototype he built, but he also designed on paper another version with the single wheel in front, and front wheel drive. He envisioned his vehicle principally as a light delivery; the prototype had a box mounted up front between the two front wheels for the carrying of a 200-pound load. Apparently, Huebner lent his prototype to a local Brooklyn laundry for test purposes. In eight months of steady delivery duty, the car put up 2500 miles and averaged 23 miles for each charge. Operating costs, including depreciation, Huebner calculated at four cents a mile. Immediate manufacture was contemplated, and also the addition of a "four-wheeled cyclecar with one driving wheel," which

would have been interesting. But none of these things came to pass. Probably the prototype was the only Huebner built.

HUENE — Barberton, Ohio — (1901) — E.A. Huene had been an enthusiast of the steam automobile since before the turn of the century, purchasing several and tinkering with them perpetually. In 1901 he built his own steam car, which was driven by bevel gears acting on each of the rear wheels, and that spring he journeyed to Cleveland to see what he could do in the way of arranging for equipment in order to go into manufacture in Barberton. His cart was before his horse, however, because no one back home was willing to support him financially in setting up a factory. No company was ever organized for production of the Huene.

HUENE — Barberton, Ohio — (1901) — E.A. Huene had been an enthusiast of the steam automobile since before the turn of the century, purchasing several and tinkering with them perpetually. In 1901 he built his own steam car, which was driven by bevel gears acting on each of the rear wheels, and that spring he journeyed to Cleveland to see what he could do in the way of arranging for equipment in order to go into manufacture in Barberton. His cart was before his horse, however, because no one back home was willing to support him financially in setting up a factory. No company was ever organized for production of the Huene.

1921 Huffman, touring, WLB

HUFFMAN — Elkhart, Indiana — (1920-1925) — In early September of 1919, the Huffman Brothers Motor Company of Elkhart announced its intention to add a line of six-cylinder passengers cars to the Huffman trucks which had been introduced the year previous. The Model R Touring, with 55 hp Continental engine, followed for the 1920 season. And so did a good deal of trouble in the next half decade that the Huffman Six was produced. The first receivership request arrived during the summer of 1920, brought by stockholders who claimed Huffman officers had not been duly elected and were conspiring to defraud them. That action was summarily thrown out of court. In October of 1921, Huffman creditors (Goshen Buggy Top Company, Ligonier Automobile Body Company, Marion Malleable Iron Works and Woonsocket Manufacturing Company) brought suit, claiming debts aggregating $14,845. Upon payment of those claims, that suit too was dismissed. Another one followed in April of 1923 which treasurer and general manager Earl R. Huffman explained was not "due to present conditions" but dated back to the previous receivership during which the company had become delinquent in its payments on an outstanding bond issue of $165,000. "We have not yet caught up," rued Huffman president W.L. Huffman. And so it went for the Huffmans. Finally, it would appear, they just gave up. The Huffman Six for 1925 sported four-wheel hydraulic brakes and disc wheels and fresh new body styling — and was the last Huffman passenger car built. Huffman trucks were continued awhile. In early June 1926 it was announced that the Valley Motor Truck Company had succeeded the Huffman Brothers Motor Company.

1920 HUFFMAN
Model R — 6-cyl., 55 hp, 120" wb

	FP	5	4	3	2	1
Touring-5P	1895	3000	4000	6000	9500	21,000

1921-1922 HUFFMAN
Model 7-R — 6-cyl., 55 hp, 120" wb

Touring-5P	1250	3000	4000	6000	9500	21,000

1923-1924 HUFFMAN
Model K — 6-cyl., 55 hp, 120" wb

Touring-5P	1395	3000	4000	6000	9500	21,000
Roadster-2P	1395	3100	4200	6300	10,500	22,000
Spt. Tour.-5P	1495	3100	4200	6300	10,500	22,000
Sedan-7P	2295	2300	3300	4600	7500	16,000

1925 HUFFMAN
Model L — 6-cyl., 50 hp, 115" wb

Phaeton-5P	1395	3000	4000	6000	9500	21,000
Spt. Rdstr.-2P	1395	3100	4200	6300	10,500	22,000
Semi-Sed.	—	2400	3400	4800	8000	17,000
Bus. Cpe.-3P	—	2500	3500	5000	8500	18,000
Artcraft Sed.-5P	—	2300	3300	4600	7500	16,000

717

1925 Huffman Artcraft, sedan, NAHC

1899 Hughes & Atkin, runabout, WLB

HUGHES & ATKIN — Olneyville, Rhode Island — (1899-1901) — William Hughes and his partner, a man named Atkin whose first name appears lost to history, built their first steam car in the machine shop they shared in Providence, Rhode Island in 1899. Soon thereafter they moved into a small factory in Olneyville to begin manufacture as the newly organized Rhode Island Auto Carriage Company. The steam cars they built were powered by two-cylinder double-acting engines, featured tiller steering and buggy wheels, and were offered as a single- or double-seat runabout and a delivery wagon. Early in 1901 the partners bought out the J.J. Hill Company of Knightsville, and a few cars were produced there as well. A total of eighteen Hughes & Atkins were built before the partners split up later in 1901. The further activity of Atkin is not known. Hughes subsequently became one of the first Reo dealers in New England.

HUMA-SWAN — Early in 1914 the Huma-Swan Company was organized with a capital stock of $100,000 in Chicago, Illinois to "manufacture, buy and sell cyclecars, automobiles and machinery of all kinds." Charles G. Georges, F.T. Huma and Willis A. Swan were the incorporators. Manufacture of a car is doubted.

HUMBERT — George J. Humbert was the president of the Rolling Mill Company of America and in 1904 announced his plans to begin a factory for the manufacture of automobiles in Morgantown, West Virginia. He did not do so.

HUMMINGBIRD — Hummingbird was the model name of the car produced in Philadelphia, Pennsylvania in 1913 by the Baker-Bell Motor Company. Refer to Baker-Bell.

HUMPHREY — That a John D. Humphrey of New Britain, Connecticut built an automobile in 1899 has been indicated on various car rosters. Documentation of this has not been discovered.

HUNGERFORD ROCKET — Elmira, New York — (1929) — The Hungerford brothers of Elmira built what was most probably the only rocket car in America ever to be licensed for travel on public roads. Capable of being powered by either the usual internal combustion system or by a rocket installed at the rear of the machine, the vehicle was of course operated in only the former mode on the highway. That Daniel and Floyd Hungerford were expert mechanics was well known in the Elmira area, that they were somewhat eccentric was well known too. The works of Jules Verne, together with the automotive experiments in rocketry of Fritz von Opel and Max Valier in Europe, provided the inspiration for the Hungerford Rocket car which was built in the brothers' machine shop at 823 West Second Street where their usual work was the repair of airplanes and gliders. A 1921 Chevrolet chassis formed the basis for the car, with its clutch and three-speed gearbox operational for both engine or rocket mode. The

1929 Hungerford Rocket Car, KM

body devised by the Hungerfords was a virtual thesis for the aerodynamic teardrop school. Daniel Hungerford later lamented that a Duesenberg or Locomobile chassis would have allowed for the cutting in of two, three or perhaps four rockets — with the small Chevy chassis, only one rocket was utilized, and the car achieved 70+ mph rocket-propelled. First tested in October 1929, the car was driven thousands of miles thereafter as the brothers attempted vainly to promote the concept of land rocketry. They seriously planned to manufacture their rocket car but never obtained necessary financing. The highpoint of their car's career was probably the reading of a Hungerford letter about it on a "Buck Rogers in the 25th Century" radio show in 1934. The Hungerford Rocket remains in existence.

1939 Hunt, house car, JHV

HUNT — Los Angeles, California — (1939) — This pioneer R.V. — or "house-car," as its maker called it — was unusual in being a steamer. Built by J. Roy Hunt of Los Angeles, it was powered by two high-pressure cylinders coupled to a flash boiler of Hunt's own design. The wheelbase was 121 inches, the overall length of the body 18-1/2 feet. Inside were seats for five passengers and sleeping accommodations for two, plus electric refrigerator, hot water, shower and bathroom facilities. Hunt built the vehicle as an experiment, but sold it before he finished testing. A steam car devotee since 1908, he converted at least one of his private cars to his favorite power as well.

HUNT & OSEN — San Jose, California — (1900-1901) — The firm of Osen & Hunt operated a bicycle emporium at 69 South Second Street in San Jose, though when the company produced an automobile, the partners names were reversed. Most likely this was because W.F. Hunt, who had lived a number of years in France, was the more instrumental in the vehicle's design. The Hunt & Osen (often misspelled Olsen) was a runabout powered by a 2-1/2 hp Crest engine. Though belt drive was used in the first car, chain drive was substituted thereafter. In March of 1901 the company announced that a recent run of 98 miles in the Hunt & Osen had been made "on 2-1/4 gallons of gasoline, 51 miles being made without stop in three hours and forty minutes." Apparently four cars in all were produced. Then George H. Osen and W.F. Hunt elected to continue in business as dealers for Locomobile and Winton.

1910 Hunt Special, NAHC

HUNT SPECIAL — San Diego, California — (1910) — William H. Hunt and his brother Clarence were machinists in San Diego and, following a visit by a representative of the Ford Motor Company in 1904, became the first automobile dealers in town. Hunt and Hunt Automobile Specialists, as their new firm was called, sold only one car in the next two years, but the brothers built a delivery van for a local baker in 1905, established a livery service, designed and built the two-stroke engines for an ill-fated San Diego automotive venture called Great Western, and developed a lively automobile repair business. Among their best customers in the last-named endeavor was Arnie Babcock, a rancher in Ensenada, Mexico whose business and medical appointments (he had contracted tuberculosis) in San Diego meant frequent trips between the two cities. The cars he had purchased for this commuting were not robust enough for the lamentable roads, which resulted in perpetual repairs by the Hunt brothers, and finally the commissioning by Babcock of a special car to be built with those conditions specifically in mind. It was called the Hunt Special, and nicknamed "Alkali Ike." A powerful overhead valve four was its engine, with double-chain drive and a three-speed selective transmission fitted into a 108-inch wheelbase chassis. The tread was 60 inches (the same as the wheel ruts in the roads) and its center clearance was 18 inches (out of harm's way of most rocks in the roadway). The body style was a five-passenger touring, and the wheels were a huge 33 inches in diameter. Clarence Hunt was killed in an automobile accident in October 1909, soon after work had begun; and Arnie Babcock, who paid $16,000 for the car to be built, died before ever riding in it. His widow subsequently sold the car. The new owners, who were hellions on the road, wrecked the Hunt Special on occasion, but William Hunt always managed to put it back together. During World War I, the car was stored — and it remains extant to this day.

HUNTER — The Hunter built in Fulton, New York in 1900 has appeared on numerous rosters of automobiles built in the United States. Like such other armaments manufacturers as Stevens-Duryea and Remington, it was assumed that the Hunter Arms Company of Fulton also gave the automobile industry a try. It did not. Hunter manufactured guns and bicycles, but never a car. "At one time the company installed a Parker transmission in a Cadillac," notes Virna Hunter Wadsworth, a direct descendant of the family still living in Fulton. "As far as I know, this is as near as the Hunter Arms ever came to producing a car."

HUNTER — Harrisburg, Pennsylvania — (1920) — In the early summer of 1920, the Hunter Motor Car Company announced its purchase of twenty-one acres at White Hill on the Gettysburg State Highway. To be constructed there was a factory for the manufacture of a moderately priced ($2250) six-cylinder car on a 121-inch wheelbase. C.H. Hunter and Simon E. Miller were the men-behind this venture. By November the first prototype Hunter Six was being tested. Conceivably, it might also have been the last. Although the company was listed in both the 1920 and 1921 editions of Boyd's Harrisburg City Directory, production of the Hunter Six has not been documented.

HUNTER ELECTRIC — Philadelphia, Pennsylvania — (1899-1903) — How many cars Rudolph M. Hunter may have built himself is not known, but all of them would have been strictly experimental. He was a Philadelphia lawyer and electric vehicle inventor with offices at 926 Walnut Street. In 1899 he was granted his first patents (for an electric vehicle and an electric controller), followed in 1901 by a patent for an electric tractor. This last design was produced in small numbers in 1903 by the Electric Vehicle Company of Philadelphia for use by the postal service.

HUNTER-HAMMOND — The Hunter-Hammond Auto Company was organized in Indianapolis, Indiana late in 1912 with a capital stock of $12,000 for the manufacture of automobiles and accessories. F.E. Hunter and H.L. Hammond were the partners involved. Manufacture of an automobile is doubted.

1901 Huntingburg, runabout, WLB

HUNTINGBURG — Huntingburg, Indiana — (1901-1903) — The Huntingburg Wagon Works was a typical Midwestern horsedrawn vehicle enterprise which, typically, entered the horseless age with caution. Around the turn of the century Huntingburg motorized a few of its buggies, mounting a single-cylinder gasoline engine under the seat, with a carriage-type body on top. Amusingly, the car was sold with a leather whip and an iron anchor as standard equipment. Lest abject naivete be thought, it should be mentioned that the whip was useful for chasing away dogs. The iron anchor was probably not a bad idea either, since brakes on all turn-of-the-century cars were notoriously ineffective. One Huntingburg is known to exist today.

HUNTINGTON — From 1906 to 1907, the Huntington Automobile Company from the Long Island, New York town of the same name produced a car which it chose to market under the name of Merciless. Refer to Merciless.

HUNTINGTON — San Francisco, California — (1889) — Quite possibly, Frank A. Huntington was the first inventor on the West Coast to patent an automobile. This he did on September 17th, 1889. His vehicle was a steamer. Huntington was a manufacturer of mining and industrial machine equipment in San Francisco — and, although it cannot be confirmed with certainty, it would appear likely that he built an automobile to his patents. He remained active in automotive pursuits into the turn of the century, patenting a steam generator as late as 1903.

HUPMOBILE — Detroit, Michigan — (1909-1941) — By November 1st, 1908, Robert Craig Hupp's career in the automotive industry included stints with Olds, Ford and Regal — in addition to the experimental model of a new car of his own which was completed that day. It was cute and it had moxie. A little two-passenger runabout with gasoline tank mounted behind the seat, power was provided by a water-cooled, four-cylinder, four-stroke engine pushing out 16.9 hp. Its two-speed sliding gear transmission and high tension magneto were unusual for a car planned for the lower-price class, which usually made do with a planetary gearset and dry cell ignition. This first little Hupmobile was designated the Model 20, was priced at $750, was introduced in February 1909 at the Detroit Automobile Show, and was put into production in March by the Hupp Motor Car Company, which had been organized in Detroit one week (November 8th, 1908) after the experimental model had been finished. Involved in the Hupp organization during its borning years were J. Walter Drake (as president), Edward Denby (who would later become Secretary of the Navy), Charles Hastings (formerly of Thomas-Detroit), and engineers Otto von Bachelle (who had built the Bachelle electric in Chicago at the turn of the century) and Emil Nelson (who would build the Nelson in Detroit from 1917 to 1921). Nelson was the man most responsible for the engineering design of the car, Hastings was the workaholic who might be largely credited with its phenomenal early sales success. In 1909 a total of 1618 Hupmobiles were built and sold; in 1910 the figure was 5340 cars; in 1911, 6079. On November 10th, 1910, one of the first new Model D four-passenger touring cars off the assembly line left Detroit on a round-the-world promotional trek (prompted by the success of the 1908 New York to Paris contest) which would see the little Hupmobile travel 48,600 miles to twenty-six different countries, and return to Detroit in triumph on January 24th, 1912 — though to a company which had been through a revolution in the meantime. In September 1911 Robert C. Hupp left the Hupp Motor Car Company following a dispute with Drake and Hastings. Like Ransom Eli Olds with his Reo, Hupp's next new car venture would carry his initials, though the R.C.H. would not be a success, nor would his further adventures with the Hupp-Yeats electric, nor the Monarch, nor the Emerson. Meanwhile the Hupmobile moved from success to success. The Model 32 — a more powerful car on a 106-inch wheelbase — was introduced in 1912; in 1913, 11,649 of them were sold. By now Emil Nelson had left, Otto van Bachelle was about to — and Frank E. Watts (who previously had worked for the Electric Vehicle Company and Eisenhuth) arrived as Hupmobile's new chief engineer, a position he would hold for the next twenty-six years. In 1915, Hupp acquired the American Gear and Manufacturing Company of Jackson, Michigan and with it the services of DuBois ("Pink") Young, who would ultimately rise to the presidency of Hupp Motor Car Corporation, as the firm was renamed following the American Gear takeover. Becoming president in 1917, however, was Charles Hastings who had ostensibly retired three years earlier for the California sunshine but who now returned at the behest of the Hupp board of directors. His verve and his leadership had been missed, and the Hupp board may have been dismayed, too, by Drake's direction of the company which had seen the Hupmobile expand into a flurry of models, including a couple of seven-passenger versions on 134-inch wheelbases. In any case, year's end in 1917 saw the introduction of the Series R, a smaller Hupmobile in the Model 20 tradition which would remain the mainstay of the company through 1924. Model R production reached its peak in 1923, with 38,279 units built. Interestingly, for a company which had produced only four-cylinder cars from the beginning, Hupp's first automobile providing more was an eight, a 60 hp L-head straight-eight introduced in 1925 as Series E. It was joined by a six in 1926, and the venerable Hupp four was now forever gone. In August that year Charles Hastings became Hupp's chairman of the board, and DuBois Young moved into the presidency. Four-wheel hydraulic brakes, together with balloon tires, had arrived with the straight-eight in 1925, the six came with four-wheel mechanical braking in 1926. Hupp found itself happy with neither. Thus for 1928 the Hupmobile was provided four-wheel Steeldraulics (a one-piece internal-expanding brake band in lieu of separate brake shoes). But the biggest news from Hupmobile was not how the car stopped, but how it looked. Styling heretofore had never been given more than passing notice by the company, now it came to the fore, courtesy of Murray's talented designer, Amos Northup. Sales in 1928 leapt to 65,862 cars. In November that year Hupp bought Chandler-Cleveland Motors Corporation of Ohio, its facilities needed for expanded production. Alas, the public fancy being fickle, the Hupmobile lagged in sales in 1929. Production totaled 50,579, half of the hoped-for 100,000. Even before the stock market crashed, the company was headed for trouble. Hupmobile took to free-wheeling in 1931, a notion discarded a few years later. Nineteen thirty-two saw the advent of fenders that Hupp called "form-fitting," but which most people remember as the cycle-fendered Hupps — as well as chrome-plated wheel discs, for five dollars extra. Both the fenders and the discs were the work of industrial designer Raymond Loewy, whom DuBois Young had hired to dress up the Hupmobile product. A Hupmobile was entered in the Indianapolis 500 in 1932 — the Hupp Comet driven by Russell Snowberger — and it finished fifth. The Aerodynamic Hupmobiles arrived in 1934 — again courtesy of Raymond Loewy, though, as with the cycle-fendered cars, Amos Northup had kibitzed some. They were splendid looking cars, with faired-in headlights, three-piece windshields, and tire-carrying fastback models. But arriving now as well was a furious battle for control of the Hupp company itself, and the man who was waging it was Archie Andrews. Through an associate, he sent a letter to all Hupp stockholders charging gross mismanagement; the result was the resignation of DuBois Young and the sequential taking of the Hupmobile presidential chair by several others, though it was obvious that Andrews was calling all the shots, as chairman of the board for a short while. When the smoke cleared, however, J. Walter Drake and other members of the Hupp old guard (save for Hastings, who retired irrevocably early on in the fracas) had won their company back, but there was little left of it. Production was suspended in late December 1935; Hupp was down, but not quite out. A Federal Reserve loan was denied, and so the company began selling off some of its plants to raise money. There was no new 1937 Hupmobile, but a new six and eight did arrive for 1938. The Hupp Super-Drive, an overdrive transmission introduced as an option in '36, was continued, but the former Aerodynamic styling was gone. A conservative caution seemed the answer for calamity, but it didn't help either. In August of 1938, Samuel L. Davis became the Hupp president, and he brought in as general manager a man with a new idea. This was Norman de Vaux whose DeVaux and DeVo had failed earlier in the Thirties, and who believed another recently defunct car could be the Hupmobile's salvation. For $45,000 the dies, tools, jigs et al. used for the front-drive 810/812 Cord were purchased and converted for use in a rear-drive Hupmobile. John Tjaarda, whose aerodynamic experimental cars for Briggs had brought him fame among industry insiders and whose Lincoln Zephyr had been widely hailed, was assigned the job of revising the Cord coffin nose into a front end distinctively Hupmobile. The result was called the Skylark. In 1938 four Skylarks were built for show purposes, thirty-one more assembled in 1939 for display at major Hupp dealerships. Then the roof fell in — again. A company request to the city of Detroit for relief on the payment of delinquent taxes was refused. The taxes were paid, but Hupp was broke. There was another stockholder lawsuit; Samuel Davis left the Hupp presidency, and that chair was taken again by J. Walter Drake, who had assumed it the first time two decades before. Norman de Vaux remained, however, and he went back to see the man who had turned him down on the Cord-dies proposition before he approached Hupp. This time Joseph Graham was receptive, and the result was an agreement whereby Graham-Paige would manufacture the Skylark for Hupp, and Hupp would grant Graham-Paige the right to use the Cord for a similar car of its own (the Hollywood). But Graham-Paige's financial plight by now was little better than Hupp's, and the plan was doomed. Graham-Paige couldn't afford the financing required for necessary tool revision; Hupp couldn't even afford to pay for all of the 319 Skylarks that Graham-Paige produced in 1940. There is a wistful sadness to the fact that the final Hupmobiles, which had begun with the pertness and the promise of the Model 20's, were produced in someone else's factory and wearing coachwork makeshifted from someone else's body. During the second week of July 1940 the last Hupmobile Skylark was built in the Graham-Paige plant. Hupmobile did not even own it; of the 319 Skylarks produced, 239 were sold to Hupp distributors by Graham-Paige, the last of them in 1941. On November 1st, 1940 the Hupp Motor Car Corporation began reorganization under bankruptcy. As Hupp, Inc., it remains today as a Cleveland subsidiary of White Consolidated Industries. Its products now are industrial heating and air conditioning units.

1909
Model 20, 4-cyl., 16.9 hp, 86" wb

	FP	5	4	3	2	1
2P Rbt	750	1400	4200	7000	9800	14,000

1910 Hupmobile, model 20, runabout, OCW

1910
Model 20, 4-cyl., 18/20 hp, 86" wb

2P B Rbt	750	1400	4200	7000	9800	14,000

1911
Model 20, 4-cyl., 20 hp, 86" wb

2P C Rbt	750	1400	4200	7000	9800	14,000
2P T Torp	850	1500	4350	7250	10,150	14,500
4P D Tr	900	1550	4500	7500	10,500	15,000
4P F Cpe	1100	1150	3600	6000	8400	12,000

1911 Hupmobile, model 20, torpedo, HAC

1912 Hupmobile, model 20, runabout, HAC

1912
Model 20, 4-cyl., 20 hp, 86" wb

	FP	5	4	3	2	1
2P Rbt	750	1400	4200	7000	9800	14,000
2P Rds	850	1550	4500	7500	10,500	15,000
2P Cpe	1100	1150	3600	6000	8400	12,000

Model 32, 4-cyl., 32 hp, 106" wb

4P Torp Tr	900	1550	4500	7500	10,500	15,000

1913 Hupmobile, model 32, coupe, HAC

1914 Hupmobile, model 32, touring, OCW

1913
Model 20-C, 4-cyl., 20 hp, 86" wb

	FP	5	4	3	2	1
2P Rbt	750	1400	4200	7000	9800	14,000

Model 20-E, 4-cyl., 20 hp, 110" wb

Rds	850	1550	4500	7500	10,500	15,000

Model 32, 4-cyl., 32 hp, 106" wb

5P H Tr	975	1550	4500	7500	10,500	15,000
2P H Rds	975	1750	4800	8000	11,200	16,000
H L Cpe	1350	1150	3600	6000	8400	12,000

Model 32, 4-cyl., 32 hp, 126" wb

6P Tr	1175	2000	5100	8500	11,900	17,000

1914
Model 32, 4-cyl., 32 hp, 106" wb

6P HM Tr	1200	1550	4500	7500	10,500	15,000
2P HR Rds	1050	1800	4950	8250	11,550	16,500
5P H Tr	1050	1750	4800	8000	11,200	16,000
3P HAK Cpe	1350	1250	3900	6500	9100	13,000

1915 Hupmobile, model K, touring, HAC

1915
Model 32, 4-cyl., 32 hp, 106" wb

4P Tr	1050	1550	4500	7500	10,500	15,000
2P Rds	1050	1750	4800	8000	11,200	16,000

Model K, 4-cyl., 36 hp, 119" wb

2P Rds	1200	2000	5100	8500	11,900	17,000
5P Tr	1200	1750	4800	8000	11,200	16,000
2P Cpe	1325	1250	3900	6500	9100	13,000
Limo	1365	1400	4200	7000	9800	14,000

1916 Hupmobile, model N, limousine, HAC

1916
Model N, 4-cyl., 22.5 hp, 119" wb

5P Tr	1085	2300	5400	9000	12,600	18,000
2P Rds	1085	2800	5700	9500	13,300	19,000
5P Sed	1365	1550	4500	7500	10,500	15,000
5P Year-'Round Tr	1185	2000	5100	8500	11,900	17,000
Year-'Round Cpe	1165	1750	4800	8000	11,200	16,000

Model N, 4-cyl., 22.5 hp, 134" wb

7P Tr	1225	3000	6000	10,000	14,000	20,000
7P Limo	2365	2300	5400	9000	12,600	18,000

1917 Hupmobile, model N, touring, HAC

1917
Model N, 4-cyl., 22 hp, 119" wb

	FP	5	4	3	2	1
5P Tr	1185	1750	4800	8000	11,200	16,000
6P Rds	1185	2000	5100	8500	11,900	17,000
5P Year-'Round Tr	1385	2000	5100	8500	11,900	17,000
2P Year-'Round Cpe	1370	1250	3900	6500	9100	13,000
5P Sed	1735	1150	3600	6000	8400	12,000

Model N, 4-cyl., 22.5 hp, 134" wb

7P Tr	1340	2800	5700	9500	13,300	19,000

NOTE: Series R introduced October 1917.

1918-19 Hupmobile, series R, roadster, HAC

1918
Series R-1, 4-cyl., 16.9 hp, 112" wb

5P Tr	1250	1150	3600	6000	8400	12,000
2P Rds	1250	2300	5400	9000	12,600	18,000

1919
Series R-1,2,3, 4-cyl., 16.9 hp, 112" wb

5P Tr	1500	2000	5100	8500	11,900	17,000
2P Rds	1500	2300	5400	9000	12,600	18,000
5P Sed	2135	1150	3600	6000	8400	12,000
4P Cpe	—	1400	4200	7000	9800	14,000

1920 Hupmobile, series R, coupe, HAC

1920
Series R-3,4,5, 4-cyl., 35 hp, 112" wb

5P Tr	1450	2000	5100	8500	11,900	17,000
2P Rds	1450	2300	5400	9000	12,600	18,000
4P Cpe	2185	1400	4200	7000	9800	14,000
5P Sed	2185	1150	3600	6000	8400	12,000

1921 Hupmobile, series R, sedan, HAC

1921
Series R-4,5,6, 4-cyl., 35 hp, 112" wb

5P Tr	1685	2000	5100	8500	11,900	17,000
2P Rds	1685	2300	5400	9000	12,600	18,000
4P Cpe	2775	1400	4200	7000	9800	14,000
5P Sed	2800	1150	3600	6000	8400	12,000

1922 Hupmobile, touring, OCW

1922
Series R-7,8,9,10, 4-cyl., 35 hp, 112" wb

	FP	5	4	3	2	1
5P Tr	1250	2000	5100	8500	11,900	17,000
2P Rds	1250	2300	5400	9000	12,600	18,000
2P Cpe	1485	1400	4200	7000	9800	14,000
4P Cpe	2100	1500	4350	7250	10,150	14,500
5P Sed	2150	1150	3600	6000	8400	12,000

1923 Hupmobile, series R, touring, HAC

1923
Series R-10,11,12, 4-cyl., 35 hp, 112" wb

	FP	5	4	3	2	1
5P Tr	1150	2300	5400	9000	12,600	18,000
5P Spl Tr	1250	2800	5700	9500	13,300	19,000
2P Rds	1150	3000	6000	10,000	14,000	20,000
Spl Rds	1250	3150	6300	10,500	14,700	21,000
5P Sed	1785	1150	3600	6000	8400	12,000
4P Cpe	1635	1550	4500	7500	10,500	15,000
2P Cpe	—	1400	4200	7000	9800	14,000

1924 Hupmobile, series R, special touring, HAC

1924
Series R-12,13, 4-cyl., 39 hp, 115" wb

	FP	5	4	3	2	1
5P Tr	1175	2800	5700	9500	13,300	19,000
5P Spl Tr	1195	3000	6000	10,000	14,000	20,000
2P Spl Rds	1195	3150	6300	10,500	14,700	21,000
2P Cpe	1445	1400	4200	7000	9800	14,000
4P Cpe	1595	1550	4500	7500	10,500	15,000
5P Sed	1750	1150	3600	6000	8400	12,000
5P Clb Sed	1425	1250	3900	6500	9100	13,000

1925
Model R-14,15, 4-cyl., 39 hp, 115" wb

	FP	5	4	3	2	1
5P Tr	1225	2800	5700	9500	13,300	19,000
2P Rds	1225	3000	6000	10,000	14,000	20,000
2P Cpe	1350	1400	4200	7000	9800	14,000
5P Clb Sed	1375	1250	3900	6500	9100	13,000
5P Sed	1800	1150	3600	6000	8400	12,000

Model E-1, 8-cyl., 60 hp, 118-1/4" wb

	FP	5	4	3	2	1
5P Tr	1975	3600	7200	12,000	16,800	24,000
2P Rds	1975	3750	7500	12,500	17,500	25,000
4P Cpe	2325	1550	4500	7500	10,500	15,000
5P Sed	2375	1250	3900	6500	9100	13,000

1925 Hupmobile, series R, sport roadster, AA

1926 Hupmobile, model A-1, 4-dr. landau sedan, AA

1926 Hupmobile, model E-2, 4-dr. sedan, AA

1926
Model A-1, 6-cyl., 50 hp, 114" wb

	FP	5	4	3	2	1
5P Tr	1225	2800	5700	9500	13,300	19,000
5P Sed	1285	1150	3600	6000	8400	12,000

Model E-2, 8-cyl., 63 hp, 118-1/4" wb

	FP	5	4	3	2	1
4P Rds	1895	3750	7500	12,500	17,500	25,000
5P Tr	1795	3600	7200	12,000	16,800	24,000
2P Cpe	2095	1550	4500	7500	10,500	15,000
4P Cpe	2095	1750	4800	8000	11,200	16,000
5P Sed	2195	1250	3900	6500	9100	13,000

1927 Hupmobile, model E-3, roadster, AA

1927
Series A, 6-cyl., 50 hp, 114" wb

	FP	5	4	3	2	1
5P Tr	1325	3000	6000	10,000	14,000	20,000
2P Rds	1385	3150	6300	10,500	14,700	21,000
5P Sed	1385	1075	3000	5500	7700	11,000
4P Cpe	1385	1400	4200	7000	9800	14,000
5P Brgm	1250	3900	6500	9100	13,000	

Series E-3, 8-cyl., 67 hp, 125" wb

	FP	5	4	3	2	1
4P Rds	2045	3600	7200	12,000	16,800	24,000
5P Tr	1945	3400	6900	11,500	16,100	23,000
5P Spt Tr	2045	3600	7200	12,000	16,800	24,000
2P Cpe	2345	1550	4500	7500	10,500	15,000
7P Tr	2045	3300	6600	11,000	15,400	22,000
5P Sed	2345	1150	3600	6000	8400	12,000
7P Sed	2495	1200	3750	6250	8750	12,500
5P Berl	2445	1250	3900	6500	9100	13,000
5P Brgm	2245	1200	3750	6250	8750	12,500
5P Vic	2345	1250	3900	6500	9100	13,000
Limo Sed	2595	1400	4200	7000	9800	14,000

1928 Hupmobile, Century Six, coach, AA

1928 Hupmobile, Century Eight, 7-pass., sedan, HAC

1928 Hupmobile, Century Eight, roadster, AA

1928
Century Series A, 6-cyl., 57 hp, 114" wb

	FP	5	4	3	2	1
5P Phae	1425	3600	7200	12,000	16,800	24,000
7P Phae	1455	3400	6900	11,500	16,100	23,000
4P 4 dr Cpe	1385	1400	4200	7000	9800	14,000
5P 4 dr Sed	1395	1150	3600	6000	8400	12,000
5P 2 dr Sed	1345	1075	3000	5500	7700	11,000

Century Series M, 8-cyl., 80 hp, 120" wb

	FP	5	4	3	2	1
Rds	—	4200	8400	14,000	19,600	28,000
5P Tr	—	4050	8100	13,500	18,900	27,000
7P Tr	—	3900	7800	13,000	18,200	26,000
2P Cpe	—	2300	5400	9000	12,600	18,000
Brgm	—	1750	4800	8000	11,200	16,000
Vic	—	2000	5100	8500	11,900	17,000
5P Sed	—	1250	3900	6500	9100	13,000
7P Sed	—	1150	3600	6000	8400	12,000
Sed-Limo	—	1400	4200	7000	9800	14,000

Century Series 125 (E-4), 8-cyl., 80 hp, 125" wb

	FP	5	4	3	2	1
R.S. Rds	1895	4350	8700	14,500	20,300	29,000
5P Tr	1795	4200	8400	14,000	19,600	28,000
7P Tr	1895	4050	8100	13,500	18,900	27,000
R.S. Cpe	2195	3000	6000	10,000	14,000	20,000
5P Brgm	2095	2000	5100	8500	11,900	17,000
5P Sed	2195	1400	4200	7000	9800	14,000
7P Sed	2345	1250	3900	6500	9100	13,000
Vic	2195	2300	5400	9000	12,600	18,000
Sed-Limo	2520	1750	4800	8000	11,200	16,000

NOTE: Series A and Series E-3 of 1927 carried over as 1928 models. Both Century Series A and M available in custom line.

1929 Hupmobile, Century Six, coach, AA

1929
Series A, 6-cyl., 57 hp, 114" wb

	FP	5	4	3	2	1
5P Tr	1425	4200	8400	14,000	19,600	28,000
4P Rds	1435	4350	8700	14,500	20,300	29,000
7P Tr	1485	4050	8100	13,500	18,900	27,000
5P Brgm	1345	1750	4800	8000	11,200	16,000
4P Cpe	1385	2000	5100	8500	11,900	17,000
5P Sed	1395	1250	3900	6500	9100	13,000
2P Cabr	1475	3900	7800	13,000	18,200	26,000
4P Cabr	1550	4050	8100	13,500	18,900	27,000

Series M, 8-cyl., 80 hp, 120" wb

	FP	5	4	3	2	1
5P Tr	1905	4350	8700	14,500	20,300	29,000
4P Rds	1915	4500	9000	15,000	21,000	30,000
7P Tr	1935	4200	8400	14,000	19,600	28,000
5P Brgm	1825	2000	5100	8500	11,900	17,000
4P Cpe	1865	2300	5400	9000	12,600	18,000
5P Sed	1875	1400	4200	7000	9800	14,000
5P Cabr	1955	4200	8400	14,000	19,600	28,000
5P Twn Sed	—	1750	4800	8000	11,200	16,000
7P Sed (130" wb)	2345	2000	5100	8500	11,900	17,000
7P Limo (130" wb)	2475	3750	7500	12,500	17,500	25,000

NOTE: Both series available in custom line models.

1930 Hupmobile, Century Eight, town sedan, AA

1930 Hupmobile, Century Eight, 4-dr. sedan, AA

1930

Model S, 6-cyl., 70 hp, 114" wb

	FP	5	4	3	2	1
Phae	1100	5100	10,200	17,000	23,800	34,000
Cpe	995	2300	5400	9000	12,600	18,000
Sed	1060	1400	4200	7000	9800	14,000
Conv Cabr	1075	4650	9300	15,500	21,700	31,000

Model C, 8-cyl., 100 hp, 121" wb

	FP	5	4	3	2	1
Cpe	1595	2800	5700	9500	13,300	19,000
Sed	1595	1550	4500	7500	10,500	15,000
Cabr	1670	4950	9900	16,500	23,100	33,000
Tr Sed	1670	1750	4800	8000	11,200	16,000

Model H, 8-cyl., 133 hp, 125" wb

	FP	5	4	3	2	1
Sed	2125	2000	5100	8500	11,900	17,000
Cpe	1985	3000	6000	10,000	14,000	20,000
Cabr	2060	5100	10,200	17,000	23,800	34,000
Tr Sed	2145	2000	5100	8500	11,900	17,000

Model U, 8-cyl., 133 hp, 137" wb

	FP	5	4	3	2	1
Sed	2495	2800	5700	9500	13,300	19,000
Sed Limo	2645	3900	7800	13,000	18,200	26,000

NOTE: All models available in custom line.

1931 Hupmobile, Century Six, roadster, AA

1931

Century Six, Model S, 70 hp, 114" wb

	FP	5	4	3	2	1
Phae	1050	5400	10,800	18,000	25,200	36,000
2P Cpe	995	2300	5400	9000	12,600	18,000
4P Cpe	995	2800	5700	9500	13,300	19,000
Rds	1075	5550	11,100	18,500	25,900	37,000
Sed	995	1400	4200	7000	9800	14,000
Cabr	1050	4650	9300	15,500	21,700	31,000

Century Eight, Model L, 90 hp, 118" wb

	FP	5	4	3	2	1
Phae	1350	5700	11,400	19,000	26,600	38,000
Rds	1375	5850	11,700	19,500	27,300	39,000
2P Cpe	1295	3000	6000	10,000	14,000	20,000
4P Cpe	1295	3150	6300	10,500	14,700	21,000
Sed	1295	1550	4500	7500	10,500	15,000
Cabr	1350	4800	9600	16,000	22,400	32,000

Model C, 8-cyl., 100 hp, 121" wb

	FP	5	4	3	2	1
Spt Phae	1685	6300	12,600	21,000	29,400	42,000
4P Cpe	1595	3300	6600	11,000	15,400	22,000
Sed	1595	1750	4800	8000	11,200	16,000
Vic Cpe	1615	3150	6300	10,500	14,700	21,000
Cabr	1595	4950	9900	16,500	23,100	33,000
Twn Sed	1705	2300	5400	9000	12,600	18,000

Model H, 8-cyl., 133 hp, 125" wb

	FP	5	4	3	2	1
Cpe	1895	3400	6900	11,500	16,100	23,000
Sed	1895	2000	5100	8500	11,900	17,000
Twn Sed	2005	2300	5400	9000	12,600	18,000
Phae	2005	6750	13,500	22,500	31,500	45,000
Vic Cpe	1915	3300	6600	11,000	15,400	22,000
Cabr	1915	5100	10,200	17,000	23,800	34,000

Model U, 8-cyl., 133 hp, 137" wb

	FP	5	4	3	2	1
Vic Cpe	2295	3600	7200	12,000	16,800	24,000
Sed	2295	2300	5400	9000	12,600	18,000
Sed Limo	2295	3750	7500	12,500	17,500	25,000

NOTE: All models available in custom line.

1932 Hupmobile, Six 216, coupe AA

1932

Series S-214, 6-cyl., 70 hp, 114" wb

	FP	5	4	3	2	1
Rds	—	5700	11,400	19,000	26,600	38,000
Cpe		2800	5700	9500	13,300	19,000
Sed	795	1550	4500	7500	10,500	15,000
Cabr	—	5400	10,800	18,000	25,200	36,000

Series B-216, 6-cyl., 75 hp, 116" wb

	FP	5	4	3	2	1
Phae	1050	6000	12,000	20,000	28,000	40,000
Rds	1075	6150	12,300	20,500	28,700	41,000

	FP	5	4	3	2	1
2P Cpe	995	3000	6000	10,000	14,000	20,000
4P Cpe	995	3150	6300	10,500	14,700	21,000
Sed	995	1750	4800	8000	11,200	16,000
Conv Cabr	1050	5850	11,700	19,500	27,300	39,000

Series L-218, 8-cyl., 90 hp, 118" wb

	FP	5	4	3	2	1
Rds	—	5850	11,700	19,500	27,300	39,000
Cpe		3150	6300	10,500	14,700	21,000
Sed		2000	5100	8500	11,900	17,000
Cabr		5700	11,400	19,000	26,600	38,000

Series C-221, 8-cyl., 100 hp, 121" wb

	FP	5	4	3	2	1
Sed		2300	5400	9000	12,600	18,000
Vic		3300	6600	11,000	15,400	22,000
Twn Sed		2800	5700	9500	13,300	19,000

1932 Hupmobile, Eight 222, 4-dr. sedan, AA

Series F-222, 8-cyl., 93 hp, 122" wb

	FP	5	4	3	2	1
Cabr	1395	6000	12,000	20,000	28,000	40,000
Cpe	1295	3300	6600	11,000	15,400	22,000
Sed	1295	3000	6000	10,000	14,000	20,000
Vic	1360	3400	6900	11,500	16,100	23,000

Series H-225, 8-cyl., 133 hp, 125" wb

	FP	5	4	3	2	1
Sed	—	3150	6300	10,500	14,700	21,000

Series I-226, 8-cyl., 103 hp, 126" wb

	FP	5	4	3	2	1
Cpe	1595	3400	6900	11,500	16,100	23,000
Cabr Rds	1695	6150	12,300	20,500	28,700	41,000
Sed	1595	3150	6300	10,500	14,700	21,000
Vic	1660	3600	7200	12,000	16,800	24,000

Series V-237, 8-cyl., 133 hp, 137" wb

	FP	5	4	3	2	1
Vic	—	3750	7500	12,500	17,500	25,000
Sed		3300	6600	11,000	15,400	22,000

NOTE: Series S-214, L-218, C-221, H-225 and V-237 were carryovers of 1931 models. Horsepower of Series F-222 raised to 96 mid-year.

1933 Hupmobile, Eight 322, cabriolet, AA

1933

Series K-321, 6-cyl., 90 hp, 121" wb

	FP	5	4	3	2	1
4P Cpe	995	2000	5100	8500	11,900	17,000
5P Sed	995	1400	4200	7000	9800	14,000
5P Vic	1060	1750	4800	8000	11,200	16,000
3P Cabr	1095	5700	11,400	19,000	26,600	38,000

Series KK-321A, 6-cyl., 90 hp, 121" wb

	FP	5	4	3	2	1
4P Cpe	895	2300	5400	9000	12,600	18,000
5P Sed	895	1550	4500	7500	10,500	15,000
5P Vic	960	2000	5100	8500	11,900	17,000

Series F-322, 8-cyl., 96 hp, 122" wb

	FP	5	4	3	2	1
4P Cpe	1195	2800	5700	9500	13,300	19,000
5P Sed	1195	1750	4800	8000	11,200	16,000
5P Vic	1260	2300	5400	9000	12,600	18,000
3P Cabr	1245	5850	11,700	19,500	27,300	39,000

Series I-326, 8-cyl., 109 hp, 126" wb

	FP	5	4	3	2	1
4P Cpe	1445	3000	6000	10,000	14,000	20,000
5P Sed	1445	2000	5100	8500	11,900	17,000
5P Vic	1510	2800	5700	9500	13,300	19,000
3P Cabr	1545	6000	12,000	20,000	28,000	40,000

1934

Series 417-W, 6-cyl., 80 hp, 117" wb

	FP	5	4	3	2	1
Cpe	795	1750	4800	8000	11,200	16,000
Sed	795	1150	3600	6000	8400	12,000

Series KK-421A, 6-cyl., 90 hp, 121" wb

	FP	5	4	3	2	1
DeL Sed	845	1400	4200	7000	9800	14,000
Sed	795	1250	3900	6500	9100	13,000
Tr Sed	845	1400	4200	7000	9800	14,000
Cpe	795	2800	5700	9500	13,300	19,000
Cabr	845	6000	12,000	20,000	28,000	40,000
Vic	860	2300	5400	9000	12,600	18,000

1934 Hupmobile, Six 417, 4-dr. sedan, AA

1934 Hupmobile, Eight 427, 4-dr. sedan, AA

Series K-421, 6-cyl., 90 hp, 121" wb

	FP	5	4	3	2	1
Cpe	895	1250	3900	6500	9100	13,000
Sed	895	1150	3600	6000	8400	12,000
Vic	960	1400	4200	7000	9800	14,000
Cabr	995	5400	10,800	18,000	25,200	36,000

Series 421-J, 6-cyl., 93 hp, 121" wb

Cpe	—	2800	5700	9500	13,300	19,000
Sed		1550	4500	7500	10,500	15,000
Vic		2800	5700	9500	13,300	19,000

Series F-442, 8-cyl., 96 hp, 122" wb

Cpe	1045	3000	6000	10,000	14,000	20,000
Sed	1045	1750	4800	8000	11,200	16,000
Vic	1110	3000	6000	10,000	14,000	20,000
Cabr	1145	5550	11,100	18,500	25,900	37,000

Series I-426, 8-cyl., 109 hp, 126" wb

Cpe	1145	3150	6300	10,500	14,700	21,000
Sed	1145	2000	5100	8500	11,900	17,000
Vic	1210	3150	6300	10,500	14,700	21,000
Cabr	1245	5700	11,400	19,000	26,600	38,000

Series 427-T, 8-cyl., 115 hp, 127" wb

Cpe	—	3300	6600	11,000	15,400	22,000
Sed		2300	5400	9000	12,600	18,000
Vic		3300	6600	11,000	15,400	22,000

NOTE: Series KK-421A, K-421, F-422, I-426 were carryover 1933 models.

1935 Hupmobile Aerodynamic, sedan, MVMA

1935
Series 517-W, 6-cyl., 91 hp, 117" wb

Sed	695	875	1700	4250	5900	8500
Sed Tr	745	900	1900	4500	6300	9000

Series 518-D, 6-cyl., 91 hp, 118" wb

Sed	—	900	1900	4500	6300	9000

Series 521-J, 6-cyl., 101 hp, 121" wb

Sed	1905	950	2100	4750	6650	9500
Cpe	1195	1075	3000	5500	7700	11,000
Vic	1115	1075	3000	5500	7700	11,000

Series 521-O, 8-cyl., 120 hp, 121" wb

Cpe	1195	1075	3000	5500	7700	11,000
Vic	1195	1075	3000	5500	7700	11,000
Vic Tr	1195	1125	3450	5750	8050	11,500
Sed	1195	950	2100	4750	6650	9500
Sed Tr	1195	1000	2400	5000	7000	10,000

Series 527-T, 8-cyl., 120 hp, 127-1/2" wb

	FP	5	4	3	2	1
Sed	1395	1150	3600	6000	8400	12,000
Cpe	1395	1400	4200	7000	9800	14,000
Vic	1395	1400	4200	7000	9800	14,000

NOTE: All series except 517-W available in deluxe models.

1936 Hupmobile Eight, touring sedan, MVMA

1936
Series 618-D, 6-cyl., 101 hp, 118" wb

4 dr Sed	795	825	1600	4000	5600	8000
4 dr Tr Sed	845	875	1700	4250	5900	8500

Series 618-G, 6-cyl., 101 hp, 118" wb

Bus Cpe	795	1000	2400	5000	7000	10,000
5P Cpe	840	1075	3000	5500	7700	11,000
6P 4 dr Sed	855	900	1900	4500	6300	9000
6P 2 dr Sed	815	825	1600	4000	5600	8000
6P 4 dr Tr Sed	890	950	2100	4750	6650	9500
6P 2 dr Tr Sed	850	875	1700	4250	5900	8500

Series 621-N, 8-cyl., 120 hp, 121" wb

5P Cpe	1035	1150	3600	6000	8400	12,000
6P 2 dr Sed	995	900	1900	4500	6300	9000
6P 4 dr Sed	1035	950	2100	4750	6650	9500
6P 4 dr Tr Sed	1075	1000	2400	5000	7000	10,000
6P 2 dr Tr Sed	1035	950	2100	4750	6650	9500

Series 621-O, 8-cyl., 120 hp, 121" wb

5P Cpe	1195	1250	3900	6500	9100	13,000
5P 4 dr Vic	1195	1400	4200	7000	9800	14,000
5P 4 dr Tr Vic	1195	1500	4350	7250	10,150	14,500
5P 4 dr Sed	1195	1000	2400	5000	7000	10,000
5P 4 dr Tr Sed	1195	1025	2600	5250	7300	10,500

NOTE: Series 618-G and 621-N available in custom models. Series 618-D and 621-O available in deluxe models.
1937
Although ostensibly there were no 1937 Hupmobiles, beginning July 1937, some 1936 style 618-G and 621-N models were run off to use up parts. Some of these cars may have been sold in the U.S. as 1937 models.

1938 Hupmobile, Six, 4-dr. sedan, AA

1939 Hupmobile, Skylark, 4-dr. sedan, MVMA

1938

Series 822-ES, 6-cyl., 101 hp, 122" wb

	FP	5	4	3	2	1
Std Sed	1045	500	1100	1900	3500	5000

Series 822-E, 6-cyl., 101 hp, 122" wb

Sed	1180	600	1200	2200	3850	5500
DeL Sed	1223	650	1250	2400	4200	6000
Cus Sed	1340	700	1350	2800	4550	6500

Series 825-H, 8-cyl., 120 hp, 125" wb

Sed	1325	650	1250	2400	4200	6000
DeL Sed	1365	700	1350	2800	4550	6500
Cus Sed	1485	750	1450	3300	4900	7000

1939

Model R, 6-cyl., 101 hp, 115" wb

Spt Sed	—	650	1250	2400	4200	6000
Cus Sed	—	675	1300	2500	4350	6200

Model E, 6-cyl., 101 hp, 122" wb

DeL Sed	995	700	1350	2800	4550	6500
Cus Sed	1095	725	1400	3000	4700	6700

Model H, 8-cyl., 120 hp, 125" wb

DeL Sed	1145	750	1450	3300	4900	7000
Cus Sed	1245	750	1450	3500	5050	7200

NOTE: The first pilot models of the Skylark were built April, 1939.

1940 Hupmobile, Skylark, 4-dr. sedan, AA

1940 Hupmobile, Skylark Corsair, prototype, convertible, AA

1940

Skylark, 6-cyl., 101 hp, 115" wb

5P Sed	1145	825	1600	4000	5600	8000

1941

Series 115-R Skylark, 6-cyl., 101 hp, 115" wb

5P Sed	1095	875	1700	4250	5900	8500

HUPP-YEATS — Detroit, Michigan — (1911-1919) — Although Hupp Corporation was initially announced to be the producer of the new Hupp-Yeats electric car in 1911, it did not long remain so. Robert C. Hupp had not left the Hupp Motor Car Company he had founded very pleasantly, and the people who were now producing his Hupmobile were not anxious to memorialize the association through any reference to Hupp's new venture which might benefit him and detract from the Hupp Motor Car Company. The court agreed. Thus Robert C. Hupp was disallowed use of the Hupp Corporation name which was to build his new gasoline car called the R.C.H. as well as the electric called Hupp-Yeats. Both would now be produced by the R.C.H. Corporation. The Hupp-Yeats was a fine example of the second-generation of American electrics. It was a good-looking car, and between 75 to 90 miles was claimed per charge, a good figure. Unfortunately, the R.C.H. Corporation was not a similar success, and by 1913 Robert C. Hupp had left to try again with the Monarch Motor Car Company. Approximately 1000 Hupp-Yeats electrics had been built thus far; a final twenty were made up from parts on hand in May of 1914. In July the assets of the Hupp-Yeats and the R.C.H. were purchased for $100,000 by a group of Detroit investors. They discontinued the R.C.H. and revived the Hupp-Yeats, reorganizing as the Hupp-Yeats Electric Car Company to do so. Sales were modest in the three years following, but the electric car itself was on the wane in America, and finally in 1919, the car was simply discontinued. Robert C. Hupp died in 1931.

1911 Hupp-Yeats, landaulet, RM

1911 HUPP-YEATS

	FP	5	4	3	2	1
Three-Passenger Landaulet	1750	2300	3300	4600	7500	16,000

1912 Hupp-Yeats, Regent, torpedo, HAC

1912 HUPP-YEATS

Regent Cpe. (86" wb)	1750	2400	3400	4800	8000	17,000
Regent Torpedo (86" wb)	1650	2500	3500	5000	8500	18,000
Patrician Cpe.	3000	2700	3600	5300	8800	19,000
Patrician Torpedo	2150	2700	3600	5300	8800	19,000
French DeLuxe-4P	4000	3000	4000	6000	9500	21,000
Imp. Lim.	5000	2900	3700	5600	9100	20,000
Regina Rdstr.-4P	2500	3000	4000	6000	9500	21,000

1913 Hupp-Yeats, Regent, brougham, HAC

1913-1915 HUPP-YEATS
Regent Brougham (86" wb)

	1750	2400	3400	4800	8000	17,000

1916 HUPP—YEATS

Model 3-A Regent Cpe. (86" wb)	1500	2400	3400	4800	8000	17,000
Model 4-B Reg. Cpe. (86" wb)	1750	2500	3500	5000	8500	18,000
Model 5 Patrician Cpe. (100" wb)	2000	2700	3600	5300	8800	19,000

1917 HUPP-YEATS

Model 4 Regent-4P	1500	2400	3400	4800	8000	17,000
Model 4 Cpe.-4P	1500	2400	3400	4800	8000	17,000
Model 4 Cpe.-5P	1750	2500	3500	5000	8500	18,000
Model 5 Patrician-5P	1750	2500	3500	5000	8500	18,000
Model 5 Cpe.-4P	1500	2400	3400	4800	8000	17,000

1918-1919 HUPP-YEATS

Model 5 Patrician-5P	1750	2400	3400	4800	8000	17,000
Model 4 Regent-4P	1500	2300	3300	4600	7500	16,000

1916 Hupp-Yeats, model 3-A, Regent, coupe, HAC

1917-19 Hupp-Yeats, model 5, Patrician, coupe, HAC

HURLBUT — The Hurlbut Company was a $400,000 Maine incorporation from late 1908 for the manufacture and sale of automobiles "and carriages of all kinds." Clarence E. Eaton was president of this venture. Manufacture of a car is doubted.

HURON — The Huron Motor Car Company of Detroit, Michigan has been indicated as an automobile manufacturer in 1915 in various rosters. Detroit city directories reveal the existence of no such company during this period. Possibly it was confused with the earlier Huron Motor Company.
    The Huron River Manufacturing Company of Ann Arbor, Michigan produced a car called the Ann Arbor in 1911-1912. Refer to Ann Arbor.

HURON — Detroit, Michigan — (1911) — The Huron Motor Company was successor to the ventures which had produced the Detroit-Dearborn and Vernon 30 cars in 1910. In March of 1911 Huron took over the Vernon assets and the Detroit-Dearborn factory, intent upon automobile manufacture. President of this new venture was J.F. Burns, vice-president was J.W. Reynolds, the secretary-treasurer was J.F. Sughrow. "The company is now turning out touring cars and roadsters in preparation for a promising season," *Motor Age* reported that month. The promise went unfulfilled. Indeed, most likely, the only cars turned out by Huron were those assembled from Detroit-Dearborn and Vernon 30 parts remaining on hand. Eight Hurons were registered in Michigan in 1915.

HUSELTON — Butler, Pennsivania — (1911-1914) — Edgar C. Huselton was Butler County's first automobile dealer. He handled Reliance, Maxwell and Reo cars, but when he decided to build an automobile of his own, his ideas became loftier. The body of the Huselton 40 was designed unabashedly along the lines of the Packard Thirty, and its radiator flattered the Pierce-Arrow by imitation. "To follow in the footsteps of high grade manufacturers as Pierce, Packard and Peerless" was the way E.C. Huselton described what he was trying to do. The Huselton was an assembled car, but its component parts were exemplary. Front and rear axles were Timken, the magneto was by Bosch, Hess-Bright bearings abounded in the four-speed transmission, the 36-inch wheels were fitted with Continental demountable rims. The maker of his four-cylinder 40 hp engine was not specified. The wheelbase of his car was 123 inches. Edgar Huselton began building his prototype in 1909, but his dealership business and other delays postponed its completion and first road test until September of 1911. Immediately thereafter he wrote a letter to friends and acquaintances to come visit the car and perhaps join him as a stockholder in the Huselton Automobile Company he was hoping to organize. Whether a manufacturing firm was ever officially incorporated is not known, but a

1912 Huselton, touring, NAHC

total of thirteen Huseltons were built, roadsters and tourers mostly. In 1913-1914 Huselton also built a three-quarter-ton truck called the Butler using the Huselton's engine. He seems to have given up manufacture of both his cars and trucks by 1915. One of the Huselton cars remains extant, owned today by the grandson of the man who built it.

1903 Hussey, runabout, NAHC

HUSSEY — Detroit, Michigan — (1902-1903) — The Hussey runabout was produced to show off and promote the Hussey tilting steering wheel. In December of 1902 the Hussey Automobile & Supply Company of Detroit announced completion of the car, and its availability complete with single-cylinder 7 hp engine, or without power. Apparently a small production of Hussey runabouts followed in the next few months, but by mid-1903 Hussey had returned simply to promoting and selling its tilting steering wheel.

HUSSON — The Husson Motor Car Company of America was organized in New York City during the summer of 1909 with a capital stock of $12,000 for the manufacture of "gas engines, motors, machines, motor cars, aerial vehicles, motor boats, etc." Incorporators were John Husson, J.J. Hogan and W.E. Young. Manufacture of a car is doubted.

HUTCHCROFT — The D.G. Hutchcroft & Sons Company was organized in Cleveland, Ohio early in 1912 with a capital stock of $10,000 to manufacture and deal in automobiles and parts. Incorporators were D.G. Hutchcroft, Glidden W. Hutchcroft, Thornton Hutchcroft, William Mertz and S.H. Meacham. Manufacture of a car is doubted.

HUTTO — Jacksonville, Florida — (1905) — Formerly one of the incorporators of the Florida Automobile and Acetylene Gas Company and later the manager of the East Coast Automobile Company, M.C. Hutto opened a repair shop in 1905 on the waterfront in Jacksonville. There he put together a four-cylinder 24 hp touring car featuring shaft drive and weighing about 1700 pounds. He sold the first one he built for $1500, and he built and sold a few more as well. "Jacksonville, Florida now boasts an automobile factory," *Motor Age* announced that November. But undoubtedly that "factory" was simply Hutto's repair shop, and it seems evident that he never proceeded into any sustained manufacture of automobiles. In 1907, together with Claude Nolan, Hutto bought out the Clarke Automobile & Launch Company of Jacksonville. "This combined equipment will give the firm one of the most extensive repair shops and supply stores in the South," *The Automobile* reported.

727

H.W.O. — Hugo W. Ogren built cars in Chicago and Waukegan, Illinois from 1915 to 1917, and in Milwaukee, Wisconsin from 1920 to 1923. Previous to this, beginning in 1914, he had produced one-off race cars which were designated by his initials, and occasionally H.W.O. was used informally thereafter. The cars he marketed were properly referred to as Ogrens, however. Refer to Ogren.

HYATTSVILLE — The Hyattsville was a 30 hp four-cylinder roadster and touring car planned as a companion make to the Independence of 1912. The Independence Motor Car Company was another of the ventures of the Carters brothers of Hyattsville, Maryland. Refer to Independence.

HYDE — Milwaukee, Wisconsin — (1904) — In the announcement heralding his new car, W.W. Hyde was described as "an erecting engineer of thirteen years' experience . . . who has a number of practical ideas he desires to exploit." Precisely what they were was not amplified upon. The Hyde was powered by an air-cooled 8 hp engine mounted in a lightweight touring car chassis. It would appear that a prototype was built, but that production did not begin. The W.W. Hyde Company of Milwaukee was not heard from again following its initial announcement. "Several new features in engine appliance and other parts will be worked in," W.W. Hyde had said. But his whole automotive adventure just did not work out.

HYDRAULIC — The Hydraulic Motor Car Company of Los Angeles was headed by Harwood Robbins and headquartered at 940 South Los Angeles Street, an address it shared with the Model Motor Company. Hydraulic advertised itself as an automobile manufacturer that year, as did Model. Further details are lacking. Both firms had exited the scene by the year following.
The Hydraulic Motor Vehicle Company was organized in Madison, Wisconsin early in 1912 with a capital stock of $15,000 for the manufacture of automobiles. August Baltzer, W.M. Stewart and W.B. Brown were the incorporators. Manufacture is doubted.

HYDRO — Cincinnati, Ohio — (1919) — The Hydro Engineering Company of Cincinnati was a one-million dollar venture to build a one-thousand-dollar steam car which went nowhere fast. G.W. Evans was spokesman for the firm which planned to purchase a 300-acre site within fifteen miles of Cincinnati and there to build a factory and "1000 residences for the use of employees, somewhat after the plan adopted by the Firestone Tire & Rubber Company." This model industrial community was never built, and probably not many examples of the Hydro either.

1901 Hydro-Car, runabout, NAHC

HYDRO-CAR — Chicago, Illinois — (1901-1902) — A left-hand-drive $1000 runabout, the Hydro-Car was powered by a two-cylinder 7 hp motor that was mounted up front (unusual for 1901), and that used ordinary stove gasoline (rather unusual too). It was the successor to the car built at the turn of the century by Thomas B. Jeffery and R. Phillip Gormully, which was alternately called the G. & J. or the Rambler. Gormully and Jeffery were at the time the proprietors of a bicycle factory in Chicago, and Rambler was the trade name of the bicycle they produced. In 1900 the partners sold out their business to the American Bicycle Company and moved to Kenosha, Wisconsin where in 1902 they launched themselves spectacularly into the automobile field with their new Rambler. Meanwhile the car they left behind in Chicago was produced for one season by the American Bicycle Company as the Hydro-Car. Its manufacture was discontinued in 1902, by which time the American Bicycle conglomerate had moved into serious production of the Toledo steam car in its Ohio factory.

HYDROCAR — Canton, Ohio — (1917) — "The car is designed to run backward on water by means of special propellers," *Automobile Trade Journal* said in its February 1917 issue. "When land is reached the land wheels take a firm grip." The Hydrocar was the idea of George Monnot, an erstwhile bicycle builder who in 1905 had become a successful Canton automobile dealer. His Monnot & Sacher agency dealt in Fords, Ramblers, Jefferys, Oaklands and Paiges. It may be safely said that none of these cars influenced Monnot's design of the Hydrocar in the slightest. It was not an attractive vehicle, but it did appear to be part boat, part automobile — which of course was precisely what it was. Monnot envisioned his vehi-

1917 Hydrocar, amphibian, HAC

cle to have both passenger car and truck potential and, because World War I was ongoing, military application as well. The Hydrocar was powered by a Hercules four-cylinder engine, and had two steering wheels at opposite ends, since the car was driven forward on land, backward on water. The propeller was mounted upfront under the radiator grille. If extended water travel was planned, the removal of axles and wheels for better speed was advised. Tests in the surrounding area, and at Meyers Lake near Canton, revealed speeds of 25 mph on land, 8-9 mph on sea. And testing was as far as the Hydrocar project ever proceeded. Two prototypes were built in the old livery barn behind the Women's Christian Temperence Union in Canton. Offices for the new Hydro Motor Car Company, incorporated with $100,000 capital, were taken at 302 Walnut Avenue N.E. Joining Monnot in this venture were Oliver Light (president), Ralph E. Hay (vice-president), Harry O. Myers (secretary) and Roy W. Oats (treasurer). In the fall of 1917 the two prototypes were driven through Pennsylvania to Washington, D.C. where demonstrations were provided the U.S. Army on the Potomac River. The Army was only mildly interested; the Armistice in November 1918 quashed military application in any case. The idea of a land-water vehicle that could be used both as car and truck remained an interesting one, but unfortunately there was not any money left to pursue it further.

HYDRO-CARBON — Although occasionally referred to by this generic designation, the products of the Friedman Automobile Company which marketed cars in Chicago, Illinois from 1901 to 1903 were properly designated as Friedman. Refer to Friedman.

HYDROMOBILE — Winchester, Ohio — (1902) — Joe Smith was his name, and he ran a small factory in Winchester that supplied power from the dam which provided lighting for the town. He was the congenial sort, and if a Winchester resident was planning a party to last late into the evening Joe Smith would keep the lights on past the usual shut-off hour. In 1902 he built an automobile in which he provided free rides to neighbors around two or three blocks in town. Very little is known about the car; a native of Winchester has recalled that it had four cylinders, buggy wheels and was driven by chain. In 1902 Joe Smith grandly announced the formation of the American Hydromobile Company. But he never built another car. In January of 1903 he elected to enter another field and renamed his firm the O.K. Gas Engine Company.

1917 Hydromotor, amphibian, WLB

HYDROMOTOR — Los Angeles & Seattle — (1914-1917) — This West Coast amphibious car was designed by William Massei and William F. Purcell of Los Angeles and ultimately was agreed to be built by the Automobile Boat Manufacturing Company, Inc. of Seattle. Although a Haynes engine powered the prototype, a Continental was planned for production. The Hydromotor had 42-inch wire wheels and a 16-inch propeller, and looked rather like a bloated German Hanomag. Unlike the Hydrocar from Canton, Ohio, the Hydromotor drove in the same direction whether on land or water. A single steering wheel operated both the front wheels and the rudder, which was mounted at the rear with the propeller. The car was tested extensively during the Panama-Pacific Exposition in San Francisco in 1915. Speeds of 60 mph on land and 25 in water were claimed, but undoubtedly exaggerated. At that time, a manufacturing site in Los

Angeles was contemplated, with further testing and demonstrations to ensue at "the various southern California beach resorts." Roadster, touring, limousine and light delivery versions were planned in a $2000-$3000 price range. Apparently testing continued for the two following years, as the partners shopped for a manufacturing site. In 1916 the Hydromotor showed up on a beach near San Francisco, where it was touted as the Delia by one Michael de Cosmo. About that same time Robert P. Matches of the Gray Taxicab Company was getting himself into trouble with partner Gilbert Anderson for purportedly diverting taxicab profits into the amphibian project. Not until late in 1917 was the Hydromotor heard from again. By that time the Seattle boat factory had been selected for production. Probably very few of the cars were built. A rumored move of the newly-styled Hydromotor Car Manufacturing Company to Indianapolis later in 1917 did not materialize.

HYGRADE — The Hygrade Motor Car Company was organized in Newark, New Jersey during the summer of 1907 with a capital stock of $10,000 for the manufacture of gasoline engines and motor cars. Incorporators were J. Hardman, Jr. and A.H. Osborne. Manufacture of a car is doubted.

HYLANDER — The Highlander was produced by the Midwest Motor Company from 1919 to 1922 in Kansas City, Missouri. Occasionally, it was misspelled Hylander in the trade press, and it appears the company itself might have considered taking up that spelling at one point. Predominantly, however, the car was the Highlander. Refer to Highlander.

HYLE — The Hyle Spring Hub Company was organized in Buffalo, New York late in 1908 with a capital stock of $150,000 for the manufacture of "motors, engines, machinery, cars, carriages, boats and motor vehicles." Behind this venture were W.A. Hyle and Blum Yates of Buffalo, and V.E. Peckham of Jamestown. Manufacture of a car is doubted.

HYNE — Plainfield, New Jersey — (1904) — The Hyne Motor Company was organized during the summer of 1904 by Harrison Coddington, Charles P. Fulmer, Charles F. Hyne and William B. Harsel, all of the Plainfield area. Capital stock was $25,000, and the plan was production of a three-cylinder two-stroke 14 hp car that would retail for $700. The Hyne engine, which was to be offered on the market as well, was this venture's particular point of pride. A small and compact unit (just 20 inches long, 20 inches high and weighing 300 pounds), it was described as "so constructed that it is to all effects and purposes three engines combined in one. For example, it is possible to remove one or two cylinders and the engine will run just as though all were in place." No doubt the Hyne people were unjustifiably proud. This venture was stalled at the prototype stage.

HYSLOP — Toledo, Ohio — (1914) — In September of 1914 W.S. Hyslop and H.W. Clark of Toledo formed a partnership to manufacture a cyclecar with a vee-shaped radiator grille and a four-cylinder water-cooled Farmer engine. The price they decided upon for their vehicle was $425. Whatever further decisions they may have made are not known. No company was organized for manufacture. A prototype probably was built, and the Hyslop died soon thereafter.

IDEAL • IZZER

IDEAL — The Ideal Auto Company of Fort Wayne, Indiana was organized with a capital stock of $25,000 late in 1909 for the manufacture of motorcars. The firm did proceed into production the year following but of commercial vehicles only, in which field it remained until 1915.

The Ideal Commercial Car Company of Akron, Ohio was incorporated with a capital stock of $200,000 during the summer of 1912 for the manufacture of "motor cars, engines and trucks." This was a reorganization of the firm which had built the Ideal truck in Detroit the year previous. The marque name was now changed to Akron, but although automobiles were planned the firm did not enter the passenger car market. Akron trucks were built into 1914.

The Ideal Electric Vehicle Company was organized in New York City with a capital stock of $250,000 early in 1911 to "manufacture motor cars, mechanical and electrical appliances, devices, etc." Incorporators were H.A. Tufel, R.G. Chase and C.A. Elliott. Manufacture of a car is doubted.

The Ideal Garage Company was organized in Frederick, Maryland late in 1911 with a capital stock of $30,000 to manufacture and deal in automobiles and accessories and to maintain a garage. Behind this venture were Grayson H. Staley, Elias B. Ramsburg, Samuel G. Duvall, Charles H. Conley, Thomas O. White and J. Windsor Williams. Manufacture of an automobile is doubted.

The Ideal Manufacturing Company of Portsmouth, Ohio was organized in 1907 for manufacture of motor vehicles. Only a truck was built, and apparently it proceeded no further than the prototype stage.

The Ideal Motor Car Company was organized in June of 1912 for the manufacture in Indianapolis, Indiana of the automobile designed by Harry C. Stutz. Refer to Stutz.

The Ideal Motor Car Company of Cleveland, Ohio has appeared on various rosters as the manufacturer of an automobile in 1905-1906. This is in error. Such a company was organized, but its product was announced as an electric truck.

The Ideal Motor Vehicle Company was the name to which the Friedman Automobile Company of Chicago was changed in 1903. Refer to Friedman.

IDEAL — New Castle, Indiana — (1902) — In late November of 1901, the Ideal Automobile Manufacturing Company of New Castle announced that it was hard at work in temporary quarters at the Burk & Saffel buggy shop and that it had already expended $3000 for machinery for its new plant. H.H. Hennigen, who was described as "an expert from St. Louis," was seeing to the building of the Ideal prototype, which was a gasoline-powered runabout subsequently completed in January 1902. Manufacture did follow, the first car sold to a John E. Cramer of St. Louis, but production was not long-lived.

IDEAL — Milwaukee, Wisconsin — (1902-1903) — An automobile made entirely of metal was the distinctive feature of the Ideal produced by the B. & P. Company of Milwaukee. As explained in *The Horseless Age*, "the whole vehicle is constructed and coupled together on an angle iron frame, which not only holds the engine in place, but attaches to the springs and makes possible a reachless running gear." The Ideal was powered by a single-cylinder 5 hp water-cooled engine set in a 68-inch wheelbase chassis and was fitted with a tilting runabout body so that "at any time or place the owner may open his car, thereby getting at all working parts without covering himself with grease." Prior to coming up with the Ideal, the B. & P. Company manufactured several varieties of gasoline engine, and it was probably to this activity that the company returned full-time after discontinuing the Ideal in 1903.

IDEAL — Bethlehem, Pennsylvania — (1907-1908) — The entrance and exit of the Bethlehem Automobile Company was typical for this period. In February of 1907 the venture was organized for the manufacture of a car patterned after the English Napier to be called the Ideal. In November came the announcement that the first example had been completed and was about to be demonstrated. On July 6th, 1908 the local sheriff took over the Bethlehem property. A few weeks later the machinery of the Bethlehem Automobile Company was sold. How many cars were produced between the demonstrator and the sheriff is not known. The value of the machinery Bethlehem had installed for manufacture was indicated to be approximately $15,000. The men behind this short-lived Ideal were M.S. Heim and W.S. Stoltz, former general manager and superintendent respectively of the Duryea Power Company of Reading.

IDEAL — Stanton, Nebraska — (1908) — Godfrey Lund of Stanton called his car Ideal because he said it was. He built it himself, for the rutty roads of Nebraska. "Mud has no terrors for this machine," he said. "I have traveled in mud up to the rear sprockets, going on high gear on level roads. I have no tire troubles, using solid tires which ride as easy as any pneumatic tire machine selling for $1250." Lund's Ideal car used a two-cylinder opposed water-cooled engine, and whenever he found a good road, he said he could speed it along at 40 mph.

1908 Ideal, auto-buggy (Stanton), NAHC

IDEAL — Buffalo, New York — (1914) — The Buffalo firm producing this two-cylinder 9/13 hp Spacke-engined cyclecar was known simply as the Ideal Shop. A two-speed planetary transmission and belt drive from a countershaft to the rear wheels were featured. The wheelbase was 96 inches, the tread 36 inches. Interestingly, on this one chassis, a total of three body styles were offered: single-seater, tandem two-seater, side-by-side two-seater. It cannot be imagined that the last named would have been very commodious. Conceivably, the Ideal cyclecar may not have proceeded far beyond the prototype stage. The last word in the press from the company, before it faded into oblivion, was "experimental work indicates that the cars are a success."

IDEAL — Allentown, Pennsylvania — (1920) — This Ideal was planned for the export market only and was built by the Bethlehem Motor Truck Corporation of Allentown. The car was a four-passenger sporting type with four-cylinder 40 hp Bethlehem-built engine, Timken axles, and a price tag in the $3000 range. It was built in 1920 only. Bethlehem moved into receivership later that year, and a special stockholders committee reported the financial situation of the company as "discouraging, but . . . not without hope" in early 1921. All hopes for the Ideal export car were dashed, however, and it was discontinued immediately. A new management team arrived later in 1921, and the last few Ideal cars were disposed of for under $1000 apiece. Bethlehem remained in the truck business, if haltingly, into 1926.

1910 Ideal Electric, coupe, NAHC

IDEAL ELECTRIC — Chicago, Illinois — (1910-1911) — The Ideal Electric Vehicle Company of 444 West Indiana Street in Chicago produced a chain-drive electric brougham on a 92-inch wheelbase which sold for $1875 in 1910 and $2200 in 1911. John H. Ryerson was president, S.H. Peterson vice-president and Carl J. Holdredge secretary and manager of the firm. Five hundred cars had been slated to be produced during 1910, but whether they were in the wake of early tragedy is not known. On May 16th that year John Ryerson jumped from the thirteenth story of the Chamber of Commerce Building in Chicago. "The reason for his action is unknown."

The Horseless Age commented. "A memorandum book found on the body indicates that Ryerson had advanced $35,500 to finance the company, which was apparently in good condition, with much ready cash in the bank." In January 1912 Bruce Borland took over the firm. Both the company and the car name were changed to Borland.

1910 IDEAL ELECTRIC

	FP	5	4	3	2	1
Chain-Drive Brougham	1875	2700	3600	5300	8800	19,000

1911 IDEAL ELECTRIC

	FP	5	4	3	2	1
Chain-Drive Brougham	2200	2900	3700	5600	9100	20,000

IDEAL LIGHT CAR — Columbus, Ohio — (1915-1916) — The Ideal Light Car Company was organized in early fall of 1915 to manufacture a four-cylinder roadster on a 110-inch wheelbase to sell for $750. Capitalization was set at $100,000, and the firm's officers were J. Herman Axline (president and general manager), Fred B. Hill (secretary and treasurer) and Samuel C. Hill (vice president). A prototype is believed to have been built. In early May of 1916, however, there followed the announcement that the idea of Ideal manufacture had been abandoned. "Materials and parts are too high in cost," the company said, though it was hoped "when conditions improve" to place the car on the market. This never happened.

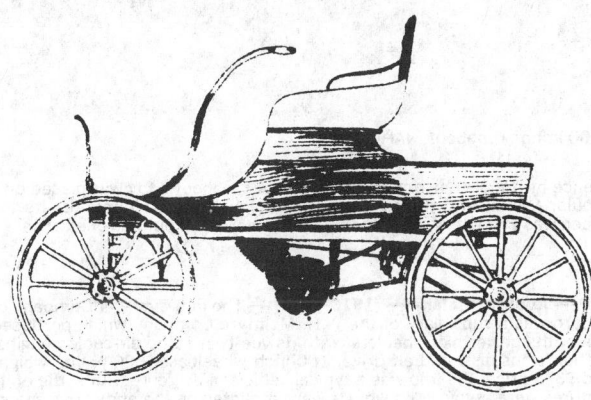

1907 Ideal Runabout, NAHC

IDEAL RUNABOUT — Buffalo, New York — (1907) — In March of 1907 the Ideal Runabout Manufacturing Company advertised in the trade press the availability of its little one-cylinder 5 hp two-seater which provided speeds up to 25 mph for only $400. In July of 1907 the Ideal Runabout Manufacturing Company reported an increase in its capital stock from $10,000 to $100,000. That was the last heard from the Ideal Runabout Manufacturing Company of Buffalo. George P. Askin, Arthur C. Whittemore and Anna G. Whittemore had been behind this Ideal.

IDEAL STEAMER — On July 10th, 1906, F.A. Hobbs incorporated the Ideal Steam Auto Company in South Berwick, Maine. A reference in the August 30th, 1906 edition of *Motor Age* that the company's purpose was "to manufacture gas and electric generators" is either in error — or most peculiar. It would seem unlikely that any significant, or possibly any, automobile production resulted. Later the firm's name was changed to Mitchell-Mainland Steam Company. In 1909 its charter was suspended.

IDLE HOUR — The Idle Hour Auto Company was organized in Paterson, New Jersey during the summer of 1910 with $100,000 capital stock "to construct and deal in automobiles." C.A. Isleib, A. Naab and A. Schmid were the incorporators. Manufacture is doubted.

I. & F. — The I. & F. Motor Car Company was organized in Branford, Connecticut late in 1910 to manufacture and deal in automobiles and parts. Incorporators were Charles Bunnell, Richard Bradley and H.F. Jordan. Manufacture is doubted.

IGNITION — The Ignition Manufacturing Company was organized in Newark, New Jersey with a capital stock of $100,000 during the summer of 1911 for the manufacture of "automobiles, motor vehicles, and automobile and motor supplies." P.G. Rode, A. Markowsky and W.L. Rader were the incorporators. Manufacture of a car is doubted.

I.H.C. — The International Harvester Company built a highwheeler from 1907 to 1911 which was known by its initials only from 1910. Refer to International (I.H.C.). The highwheeler produced by the Independent Harvester Company was also occasionally designated by its initials. Refer to Independent Harvester.

IHRIG — During the fall of 1905 the Ihrig brothers, proprietors of the Goshen Motor Works in Goshen, Indiana, announced their impending entrance into the automotive field. Refer to Goshen.

ILLINOIS — The Illinois Cyclecar Company has been indicated as a manufacturer in Kankakee, Illinois in 1914 on various car rosters. There is no evidence of a car having been built in Kankakee in 1914, though there had been thwarted plans. Possibly, too, some of the same people involved were among those trying again in 1916 with a venture to build a car called the Kankakee.

The Illinois Electric Motors Manufacturing Company was organized in Chicago during the summer of 1912 with a $5000 capital stock for the manufacture of electric vehicles. Incorporators were Abe F. Richman, James R. Semple and Edgar E. Benedict. Manufacture of a car is doubted.

The Illinois Motor Car Company was organized early in 1904 in Chicago with a capital stock of $5000 for the manufacture of automobiles and parts. Among the incorporators were John C. Zimmerman, John W. Clark and Hiram I. Keck. Manufacture of a car is doubted.

The Illinois Motor Patents Corporation was organized in Chicago during the spring of 1912 with a $5000 capital stock for the manufacture of automobiles and parts. Incorporators were William D. Kirk, Edward C. Marsh and George E. Daniels. Manufacture of an automobile is doubted.

1899 Illinois Electric, hansom, NAHC

ILLINOIS ELECTRIC — Chicago, Illinois — (1897-1901) — The Illinois Electric Vehicle and Transportation Company announced in October of 1899 that it had thirty vehicles available for hire in Chicago. These included stanhopes, runabouts, broughams and hansom cabs. The hansoms and broughams were steered by their rear wheels, the motors and gearing being mounted on the front wheels. The stanhopes and runabouts were precisely the opposite. Apparently, Illinois Electric considered itself more in the leasing than the selling business. Whichever, the company was out of it by the end of 1901. The cars it did build were put together in the plant of the Siemens-Halske Electric Company in Cicero.

ILLINOIS ELECTRIC — Chicago, Illinois — (1899) — The Illinois Automobile Company was located at 120 Michigan Avenue in Chicago and in late 1899 announced that its engineer J.M. Hirsh had "perfected an electric carriage with a motor in the hub of each of the four wheels." The hub-motor idea would enjoy a short-lived vogue among a few manufacturers, but it would appear that the Illinois Automobile Company did not proceed into production.

ILLINOIS — Chicago, Illinois — (1905) — William Landshaft was the president, George J. Blum the vice-president and Francis J. Bloom the secretary-treasurer of the Illinois Auto-Motor Company of 1938 Milwaukee Avenue in Chicago. In October of 1905 they announced their ongoing construction of a touring car with an eight-cylinder 35/40 hp engine. Had it arrived on the marketplace, it would have rivaled the Buffum as America's first automobile with that many cylinders. Because Illinois Auto-Motor was not heard from in 1906, one would suspect that the car was not a success.

ILLINOIS — Moline, Illinois — (1907) — In January of 1907 the Moline Pump Company exhibited its new line of gasoline engines at the Chicago Automobile Show. In February the firm announced its plans for manufacture of a $650 12 hp runabout and an $850 20 hp runabout, using its new engines. The cars would carry the trade name of Illinois. Production would begin, Moline Pump said, as soon as a number of old sheds were razed and an addition made to its present factory. Six weeks was the estimated completion time. It appears the company marketed its gasoline engines for several seasons, but its cars in 1907 only.

1910 Illinois, baby tonneau, NAHC

ILLINOIS — Galesburg, Illinois — (1909-1912) — Ed Overholt changed his mind a lot. Secure in his position as secretary-treasurer of the Wenzelmann Manufacturing Company, farm machinery and equipment manufacturers in Galesburg, he concluded in late 1908 that the automobile industry held more promise. Consequently, he resigned from Wenzelmann and began The Overholt Company. For 1909 he brought to market a small air-cooled two-cylinder 12 hp runabout on an 86-inch wheelbase which he designed himself, save for the body which was the work of fellow townsman A.L. Nelson, who would design the coachwork for all subsequent cars as well. He built ten of these cars in 1909. Initially he referred to them as Overholts, but by year's end he had decided he preferred Illinois as a marque name. He also decided that he preferred a bigger car. For 1910, therefore, he marketed a 30 hp four (air cooled Reeves engine) on a 110-inch wheelbase with a price tag of $1350 that was double his first offering. He built fifteen of these cars in 1910. For 1911 he decided to become bigger yet (35/40 hp four on a 120-inch wheelbase), and he also switched to water-cooling (Waukesha engine) and raised his prices again. Ed Sundell of Oneida raced some of these cars to fine success in local events. For 1912 Overholt concluded that two fours were better than one, and made a 25 hp model on a 107-inch wheelbase available too — and he lowered prices this time. After approximately fifty of the 1911-1912 cars were produced, he concluded that he didn't want to manufacture automobiles any longer. In August that year he bought the patterns and parts for the air-cooled engine he had used in 1910 from the Reeves Pulley Company in Indiana, and it would appear that he subsequently purchased all of the Reeves assets. Thereafter he manufactured engines, automobile horns, spring-powered starters for the Model T Ford, and other sundries in his Overholt factory in Galesburg, until it burned down in 1914. A few years later Ed Overholt moved to California where he put himself into the business of making "fiddles" and novelties. He died in 1958. "The Cars That Are" was Ed Overholt's slogan for the Illinois, which begs the question "are what?" — and could be seen to indicate that Ed Overholt hadn't made his mind up about that either. The evidence certainly indicates, however, that, whatever his cars were, Ed Overholt built them well. The Illinois was a fine automobile.

1909 Illinois (Overholt), roadster, NAHC

1909 ILLINOIS
Overholt — 2-cyl., 12 hp, 86" wb

	FP	5	4	3	2	1
Roadster-2P	600	2000	3000	4200	6500	14,000
Roadster-4P	650	2000	3000	4200	6500	14,000

1910 ILLINOIS
Illinois — 4-cyl., 30 hp, 110" wb

Touring-5P	1350	2000	3000	4200	6500	14,000
Baby Tonneau-4P	1350	2200	3200	4400	7000	15,000

1911 ILLINOIS
Illinois — 4-cyl., 35/40 hp, 120" wb

Touring-5P	2000	2000	3000	4200	6500	14,000
Toy Tonneau-4P	2000	2200	3200	4400	7000	15,000
Semi-Torpedo-5P	2000	2200	3200	4400	7000	15,000

1912 ILLINOIS
Illinois — 4-cyl., 25.6 hp, 107" wb

Model K Tour.-5P	1250	2200		3200	4400	7000	15,000

Illinois — 4-cyl., 35/40 hp, 120" wb

Model G Tour.-5P	1750	2400	3400	4800	8000	17,000
Model G Rdstr.-2P	1750	2500	3500	5000	8500	18,000
Model G Rdstr.-4P	1750	2500	3500	5000	8500	18,000
Model G Coupe	2700	1800	2800	4000	6200	13,000
Model G Limo.	3600	2000	3000	4200	6500	14,000

IMHOF — Racine, Wisconsin — (1900) — John Imhof was a machinist, his wife Mary was a dressmaker, and they operated both businesses from their home at 1647 Howe Street in Racine. There, in 1900, John Imhof built an automobile powered by a two-cylinder 3 hp water-cooled engine of his own design. Power transmission was by belt to countershaft, and

1900 Imhof, runabout, NAHC

thence by double chain to the rear axle. A runabout body was placed on a tubular frame, and the rig complete weighed but 310 pounds. Its top speed was 15 mph. Most probably, John Imhof built but this one car.

IMP — Auburn, Indiana — (1913-1914) — The Imp Cyclecar Company of Auburn was a subsidiary of the W.H. McIntyre Company which produced one of the better highwheelers. With its vee-twin 15 hp air-cooled engine, friction transmission, belt drive, 100-inch wheelbase, 600-pound weight and $375 price, the Imp was a typical vehicle of its genre. But some of its features were atypical. Its wheels were mounted on the end of transverse springs; the Imp had no axles. The Imp could be started from the driver's seat by inserting a crank into the center of the steering column which connected with a ratchet on the crankshaft through bevel gears. Its braking system was a hardwood block which passed into the pulley grooves on the rear wheels. In November of 1913 one of the first Imps off the line was taken from its Auburn factory and driven over the roads to Fort Wayne, a trip made difficult because of recent heavy rains — but the Imp made it with facility. "Imp cyclecars are produced in larger quantities probably than any other manufacturer in the same line," *Automobile Trade Journal* announced in July 1914. That was probably true. Imp cyclecar production had begun at ten cars a month in 1913; by now it was up to fifty cars a month. Ten Imp cyclecars were even sold in Nome, Alaska where sled runners in front and the car's lightness were expected to make traversing the snow crust a breeze. Imp advertising promotion emphasized the car's sporting pretensions: "Everyone has Speed Protoplasms in his Blood and Motor Car Driving is the Universal Symtomic (sic) Manifestation." A four-cylinder model followed for the 1914 model year and was claimed capable of 50 mph and 50 mpg. The Imp was designed by William B. Stout who earlier had tried and failed to market a cyclecar under his own name in Chicago. In late 1914 he left Imp in Auburn to join Scripps-Booth in Detroit. Meanwhile, in Auburn, by the end of 1914 the W.H. McIntyre Company went to the wall and took the Imp with it. William Stout later estimated that total Imp production had been several hundred units — and that the cars had had a lot of problems.

1913 Imp, cyclecar, HAC

1913 IMP
Cyclecar — 2-cyl., 15 hp, 100" wb

	FP	5	4	3	2	1
Tandem Two-Seater	375	1400	2400	3500	5300	10,000

1914 Imp, cyclecar, JAC

1914 IMP
Cyclecar — 2-cyl., 15 hp, 100" wb

	FP	5	4	3	2	1
Tandem Two-Seater	375	1400	2400	3500	5300	10,000
Model 11 — 4-cyl., 23 hp, 105" wb						
Roadster-2P	695	1600	2700	3800	5800	12,000

IMPERIAL — The Imperial Automobile Company of Chicago, Illinois was organized in 1900 and in November that year announced its plans for construction of a factory costing $30,000 for the production of automobiles. The company was not heard from again. Most probably the factory was not built, nor was this Imperial.

The Imperial Garage Company was a $25,000 Delaware incorporation from the fall of 1912 to "deal in and manufacture cars, construct and operate a garage." Manufacture is doubted.

The Imperial Garage and Supply Company was organized in Waco, Texas during the summer of 1910, incorporating the former Evans Bell Auto Company. L.B. McCulloch was president, S.H. McCulloch vice-president, and L.E. Boren general manager. The building of automobiles at the firm's garage at 114-116 South Eighth Street was planned but does not seem to have been realized.

The Imperial Motor Car Company of Hamilton, Ohio was organized in July of 1909. Both the company name and the name of its car had been changed to Republic by January 1910. Refer to Republic.

The Imperial Motor Vehicle Company was organized in New York City during the summer of 1909 with a capital stock of $10,000 for the manufacture of automobiles and engines. Incorporators were C.S. Waeder, G.W. Mead and H.E. Tunnell. Manufacture of a car is doubted.

1900 Imperial, runabout, MVMA

IMPERIAL — Philadelphia, Pennsylvania — (1900-1901) — "Mr. J.C. Nichols is a moving spirit in the enterprise and is the general sales manager of the company, and under his experienced guidance a large and increasing business should be worked up." The name of the business was the Philadelphia Motor Vehicle Company, and the name of its product was the Imperial. It was a very substantially-built runabout with pneumatic-tired 32-inch wheels. A single-cylinder 4 hp engine propelled it, and speeds were claimed to reach the 12-16 mph range. A single lever took care of stopping, starting and steering. "The company starts out with bright prospects," said *The Automobile Review* in June 1900, the same source as the flattering quote about Mr. Nichols, "their product will certainly meet with approval and ready acceptance of the vehicle-using public." Not enough members of the vehicle-using public bought this Imperial to keep it in business beyond 1901. What was described as a "big batch" of cars was ready for the market by the summer of 1900, and J.C. Nichols declared himself "kept busy attending to the immense amount of correspondence in regard to their machines." Although the company was later said to be equipping a large factory in Camden, New Jersey, it would appear the Imperial venture never moved out of its 204 North Broad Street facilities in Philadelphia.

1904 Imperial, model A, runabout, WLB

IMPERIAL — Columbus, Ohio — (1903-1904) — The cars built by Rodgers & Company of Columbus were occasionally referred to as Rodgers. The company, however, seemed to prefer the name Imperial, though it was perhaps too tony a designation for such a piquant little car. Its engine was an air-cooled 8 hp twin, its wheelbase but 78 inches. Although four models were initially announced for 1903, only three were produced: runabout, coupe and light delivery. It was not until 1904 that the fourth arrived, a surrey with a two-cylinder air-cooled engine from the Buckeye Motor Company and shaft drive replacing the usual bevel gear. Imperial production was discontinued by 1905.

1903 IMPERIAL
Imperial — 2-cyl., 8 hp, 78" wb

	FP	5	4	3	2	1
Model A Runabout	950	2300	3300	4600	7500	16,000
Model D Physician's Cpe.	1350	2400	3400	4800	8000	15,000
Model C Light Delivery	1150	2200	3200	4400	7000	15,000
1904 IMPERIAL						
Imperial — 2-cyl., 8 hp, 78" wb						
Model A Runabout	950	2300	3300	4600	7500	16,000
Model D Physician's Cpe.	1350	2400	3400	4800	8000	17,000
Model C Light Delivery	1150	2200	3200	4400	7000	15,000
Shaft-Drive Surrey	—	2300	3300	4600	7500	16,000

1908 Imperial, Second, roadster, WLB

IMPERIAL — Williamsport, Pennsylvania — (1907-1908) — The history of the Imperial Motor Car Company of Williamsport was short but somewhat complicated. It grew out of a garage established in town by one N. Burrows Bubb in October of 1905. In November Bubb's sons — Harry A. and Nathan B. — persuaded their father to rent them the facility to use as a car dealership, which they organized that month as the Williamsport Automobile Exchange. By the spring of 1906 the Bubb brothers were doing a brisk business in Reos, Whites and Premiers, and by the fall they had begun construction of a prototype automobile of their own, designed by a Dutchman named C.P. Van Ferls, who was manager of the dealership. It was compiled and given its first road test early the following spring. "The Imperial roadster, as it will be called, is strictly a gentleman's machine, built for hill climbing and absolutely easy riding over the mountainous Pennsylvania roads," reported the Williamsport *Gazette and Bulletin* on April 3rd, 1907. "The car is so constructed that the center of gravity will be in the center of the car, a point striven for but not reached by many of the manufacturers." The Imperial was among the first cars in America to feature a double-dropped frame. Meantime, another firm, the Williamsport Engineering Company, had been organized to secure capital for the building of the prototype, and Harry C. Bubb — the Bubb brothers' uncle and a wholesale grocer in Williamsport — assisted in this and was named that company's president. On August 6th, 1907, Williamsport Engineering and the Exchange evolved into the Imperial Motor Car Company — and all of the Bubbs were now involved, as well as a number of other prominent businessmen in town. Five new Imperial roadsters were ready for the New York Automobile Show which opened in late October. Interestingly, in introducing their new car, the Bubbs referred to it as the "second imperial," and magazine editors blithely went along. Actually, the second Imperial was merely the production version of the first. It was a very handsome and rakish car, available as a $2500 roadster with two bucket seats, or a $2650 folding-rumble-seat roadster for four. It featured a four-cylinder 35 hp engine by Milwaukee, shaft drive and, of course, the double-dropped frame. Had the car been introduced at a time other than the wake of the Panic of '07, it might have fared better than it did. Undercapitalization was a problem as well. Probably not more than fifty cars were produced before September 4th, 1908 when N. Burrows Bubb requested receivership and his sons' Imperial adventure was over.

733

1907-1908 IMPERIAL
Four — 35 hp, 108" wb

	FP	5	4	3	2	1
Roadster-2P	2500	2500	3500	5000	8500	18,000
Rumble-Seat Rdstr.-4P	2650	2700	3600	5300	8800	19,000

1910 Imperial, model 36, roadster, HAC

IMPERIAL — Jackson, Michigan — (1908-1916) — T.A. and George N. Campbell were brothers and the proprietors of the Jackson Carriage Company. In 1908 they added motorcars to their line, calling them Imperials. In 1909 the Imperial Automobile Company succeeded the Jackson Carriage Company. The Imperials produced by the Campbells were medium-sized fours produced in roadster and touring variations. In the spring of 1912 the Imperial factory burned down, but by the summer the Campbells had purchased the old Buick truck plant in town, and they were in operation there by the fall. In 1914 a six was added to the line. In 1915 the Campbells had another idea, however. They rid themselves of their company by the simple expedient of merging Imperial with Marion of Indianapolis and leaving the result to a new combine called Mutual Motors Corporation in which they had absolutely no interest, financial or otherwise. That left the Campbell brothers free to join with Robert C. Hupp to venture forth with their new idea, the "lowest priced five-passenger car in the world," which would be called the Emerson. Meanwhile Mutual Motors moved to Jackson, discontinued the Imperial, and went on to produce the Marion-Handley.

1908-1909 IMPERIAL
Four — 30/35 hp, 108" wb

Roadster-4P	2650	2400	3400	4800	8000	17,000
Roadster-Runabout-2/3P	2500	2500	3500	5000	8500	18,000

1910 IMPERIAL
Model 30 — 4-cyl., 30 hp, 106" wb

Touring-5P	1350	2400	3400	4800	8000	17,000

Models 35 & 36 — 4-cyl., 35 hp, 112" wb

Touring-5P	1650	2500	3500	5000	8500	18,000
Roadster-4P	1650	2700	3600	5300	8800	19,000

Models 45 & 46 — 4-cyl., 45 hp, 117" wb

Touring-5P	2000	2700	3600	5300	8800	19,000
Roadster-4P	2000	2900	3700	5600	9100	20,000

1911 Imperial, model 38, roadster, HAC

1911 IMPERIAL
Model 30 — 4-cyl., 30 hp, 106" wb

Touring-5P	1350	2500	3500	5000	8500	18,000

Series 35 — 4-cyl., 45 hp, 112" wb

Model 37 Fore-Dr. Tr.-7P	1700	3300	6600	11,000	15,400	22,000
Model 38 Fore-Dr. Rds.-4P	1650	2900	3700	5600	9100	20,000
Model 35 Touring-5P	1650	3200	6450	10,750	15,000	21,500
Model 35 Roadster-3P	1650	2700	3600	5300	8800	19,000

Series 40 — 4-cyl., 45 hp, 115" wb

Model 44 Semi-Torpedo-5P	1600	2900	3700	5600	9100	20,000
Model 43 Roadster-2P	1500	3000	4000	6000	9500	21,000
Model 42 Touring-7P	1500	3400	6900	11,500	16,100	23,000

Series 50 — 4-cyl., 50 hp, 118" wb

Model 50 Fore-Dr. Tr.-5P	2000	3500	7000	11,750	16,450	23,500
Model 51 Fore-Dr. Rds.-5P	2000	3100	4200	6300	10.500	22.000

1912 IMPERIAL
Models 32 & 33 — 4-cyl., 35 hp, 114" wb

Semi-Torpedo-5P	1250	2700	3600	5300	8800	19,000
Torpedo-2P	1250	2900	3700	5600	9100	20,000

Model 34 — 4-cyl., 40 hp, 116" wb

Semi-Torpedo Touring-5P	1400	3000	4000	6000	9500	21,000

Model 44 — 4-cyl., 45 hp, 120" wb

Semi-Torpedo Touring-5P	1750	3100	4200	6300	10,500	22,000

Models 50 & 51 — 4-cyl., 50 hp, 118" wb

Touring-5P	1850	3300	4400	6700	12,000	24,000
Roadster-4P	1850	3500	4500	7000	13,000	25,000

734

1912 Imperial, model 33, torpedo, HAC

1913 Imperial, model 44, touring, HAC

1913 IMPERIAL
Model 32 & 33 — 4-cyl., 30 hp, 114" wb

	FP	5	4	3	2	1
Touring-5P	1285	3100	4200	6300	10,500	22,000
Roadster-2P	1285	3200	4300	6500	11,000	23,000

Model 34 — 4-cyl., 40 hp, 118" wb

Touring-5P	1650	3200	4300	6500	11,000	23,000

Model 44 — 4-cyl., 45 hp, 122" wb

Touring-5P	1875	3300	4400	6700	12,000	24,000

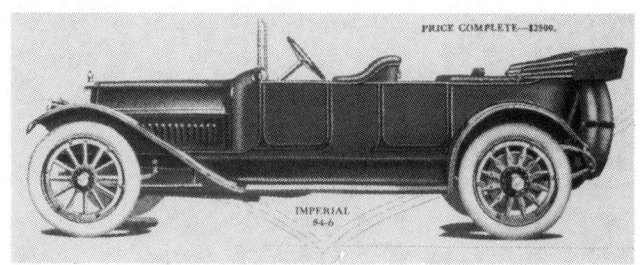

1914 Imperial, model 54, touring, HAC

1914 IMPERIAL
Model 32-33 — 4-cyl., 28.9 hp, 114" wb

32 Touring-5P	1500	3300	4400	6700	12,000	24,000
33 Roadster-2P	1500	3500	4500	7000	13,000	25,000

Model 34 — 4-cyl., 32.4 hp, 118" wb

Touring-5P	1650	3500	4500	7000	13,000	25,000

Model 44-6 — 6-cyl., 33.7 hp, 126" wb

Touring-5P	2000	3700	4700	7300	13,700	26,000

Model 54 — 6-cyl., 40.9 hp, 137" wb

Touring-7P	2500	3900	4800	7700	14,300	27,000

1915 Imperial, model 64, touring, HAC

1915 IMPERIAL
Model 64 — 4-cyl., 22.5 hp, 115" wb

Roadster-2P	1085	3500	4500	7000	13,000	25,000
Touring-5P	1085	3300	4400	6700	12.000	24.000

	FP	5	4	3	2	1
Model 56 — 6-cyl., 34 hp, 130" wb						
Touring-7P	2200	3700	4700	7300	13,700	26,000
1916 IMPERIAL						
Model 64 — 4-cyl., 22.5 hp, 115" wb						
Touring-5P	995	3500	4500	7000	13,000	25,000

IMPERIAL — Houston, Texas — (1910) — The Imperial Motor Car Company was located at 1117-1119 Prairie Avenue in Houston. Its president was George W. Collier, its vice-president Jonathon Lane, its manufacturing manager John H. Bright. Sales manager was Bright's brother, J.D., and he was probably kept busier vending the wares of other manufacturers than in selling the Imperial car of Houston. The Imperial was a high-wheeled motor buggy produced for a local clientele, and in 1910 only. The Imperial company was also a dealership for the Pullman and the Baker electric, which was its main focus of activity. "The company intends to practice something which is a new venture in the south," *Motor Age* reported late in 1909, "— to carry a complete line of samples of its entire line on its salesrooms floors at all time, eliminating the uncertainty of factory shipments."

1903 Imperial Electric, runabout, NAHC

IMPERIAL ELECTRIC — Detroit, Michigan — (1903-1904) — The Imperial Automobile Company was organized in Detroit late in 1902 for the manufacture of a single light two-passenger electric buggy priced at $950. After a year and a half of struggling the company gave up. Although manufacture ceased in 1904, Imperial Electric did not file notice of dissolution until early spring of 1905. This venture is interesting principally because of two names which appeared among the company's officers: D.J. Campau and J.B. Book, both members of prominent "first families" of Detroit. Consulting engineer was Joseph Ledwinka, later an experimental engineer with the Edward G. Budd Manufacturing Company.

1903-1904 IMPERIAL ELECTRIC

Runabout	950	2400	3400	4800	8000	17,000

IMPROVED — The Improved Gasoline Motor & Automobile Company is presumed to have built a car called the Foster in Haverhill, Massachusetts in 1901. Refer to Foster.

INDEPENDENCE — Hyattsville, Maryland — (1912) — During the early spring of 1912 the Independence Motor Company was organized by the Carter brothers of Hyattsville to take over the assets of their Washington Motor Car Company. The Washington had been a 40 hp four in the $1750 price range. Planned for production now were a variety of cars named Independence: a two-cylinder 16 hp roadster for $650, a six-cylinder 40 hp roadster ($1250) and touring ($1350), a 50 hp six sedan ($1500) and touring ($1600). A 30 hp four-cylinder car ($850 roadster, $900 touring) was slated to be called the Hyattsville. A $650 Atlantic delivery van was also planned for the line. Only prototypes followed. The Independence Motor Company did not survive 1912. A handwritten note on the Independence prospectus belonging to one investor in the venture read, "I have kissed my cash goodby." He was right.

INDEPENDENCE — Detroit, Michigan — (1914) — The Independence Motor Car Company of Detroit, Michigan was indicated in the March 1914 issue of *Motor Print* to be building a cyclecar. Manufacture did not follow.

INDEPENDENCE — Lima, Ohio — (1915) — W.A. Williams was a former Buick dealer in Lima who decided he could design a better medium-priced automobile for America, and so he established his Independence Motor Car Company in Ohio. Almost immediately thereafter, however, he decided to move south, to Atlanta, Georgia. In announcing his relocation in the summer of 1915, he also said something else. "The company will build two machines," he boasted, "one of which will be the same $1000 machine which the plant has been putting out for a number of years, and another that will be sold for much lower price." He should have been ashamed of himself. W.A. Williams had built one prototype only, earlier in 1915, and he assembled it in the Gramm-Bernstein truck plant in Lima. The Independence Motor Car Company never had a factory. And it certainly never moved to Atlanta.

INDEPENDENT — The Independent Auto Repair Company was organized in Omaha, Nebraska during the spring of 1904 with a capital stock of $25,000 for the manufacture of automobiles and engines. The incorporators were Henry J. Galarneau, Ezra P. Beechler and Thaddeus E. Smith. Manufacture of a car is doubted.

The Independent Automobile Manufacturing Company was organized in Sioux Falls, South Dakota late in 1903 with a capital stock of $100,000 for the manufacture of cars. Manufacture does not appear to have followed.

INDEPENDENT HARVESTER — Plano, Illinois — (1910-1911) — Henry K. Holsman really should have known better. As the man responsible for introducing the highwheeler type of automobile to American roads, it was scarcely to his credit, and not characteristic of him, to be so imitative in naming his new car. True, it was to be built by the agricultural-implement-producing Independent Harvester Company of Plano, but Holsman was given carte blanche in its new automobile department and could have named the car anything he liked. Instead he chose Independent Harvester, and the vehicle was even referred to on occasion as an I.H.C. The car was basically a Holsman with detail refinements, priced at $750, and it lasted less than a year; indeed there is evidence no more than the pilot models made it down the production line. Interestingly, International Harvester discontinued production of its highwheeler car during 1911 as well.

INDIAN — The Indian Motor Car Company was organized in Upper Sandusky, Ohio early in 1911 with a capital stock of $10,000 to manufacture and sell "motor cars, motor trucks and accessories." Incorporators were S.W. Martin, M.M. Stoneburner, William Olpp and Thomas O'Brien. Manufacture is doubted.

1927 Indian, town car delivery, WLB

1929 Indian, roadster, KM

INDIAN — Springfield, Massachusetts — (1905 et seq.) — The Hendee Manufacturing Company of Springfield was famous for years as the producers of the celebrated Indian motorcycle. Hendee marketed a three-wheeled Indian Tricar in 1905, and occasionally the firm built a four-wheeler as well, the first very soon after the turn of the century. But such vehicles were experimental, and most were referred to by the Indian name, though a 1910 runabout was called a Hendee. In 1914 there appeared published rumors that Hendee planned to enter the cyclecar field. George M. Hendee, president of the company, immediately fired off a letter to editors stating "emphatically" that the Hendee Manufacturing Company had no intention of becoming an automobile producer. "While it is a fact that we have built a model car, that is as far as it will ever go with us," he said, "and we trust that you will not fall for any rumor, as our plant is devoted entirely and solely to the manufacture of Indian motorcycles." In 1916 *The Automobile* reported that five cars were registered in Massachusetts under the Hendee name. And at least one experimental Indian cyclecar had been sold to a private party. Interestingly, during the 1920's, by which time the firm name had changed to Indian Motorcycle Company, there was more serious investigation of the possibility that three- and four-wheelers as well as two-wheelers would bear the Indian emblem. Indian even began construction of a factory for automobile manufacture, but when the plant was finished, it was sold — and soon thereafter Rolls-Royces were on the assembly line there. Around 1927 Indian built four quite interesting small four-wheeled cars, two of them with bodies by Merrimac, one with LeBaron coachwork. Some $65,000 was expended in their development. (Three of these cars remain extant.) A quick halt was called to all this in 1929 when Charles A. Levine took control of the Indian company and immediately curtailed all activity that was not profitable. (Levine was at that time still basking in the publicity of being the world's first transatlantic airplane passenger, having accompanied Clarence Chamberlain overseas in his June 1927 flight, a month after Lindbergh.) Ironically, in May of 1930, when the Indian Motorcycle Company was acquired by Paul du Pont, some of the last du Pont automobiles were built in its plant.

INDIANA — The Indiana Bicycle Company, a branch of the American Bicycle "trust," produced the Waverley Electric in Indianapolis at the turn of the century. Refer to Waverley Electric.

The Indiana Liquid Air, Power and Automobile Company was organized in Indianapolis during the fall of 1900 with a $500,000 capital stock by T.V. Page, E.J. Richards, W.W. Carter, W.P. Herod and E.M. Elliott. Manufacture of an automobile is doubted; most likely this venture was allied with the Liquid Air company on the East Coast.

Although the car to be produced by the Indiana Motor & Manufacturing Company went unnamed throughout its entire formative period, a name was finally decided upon shortly before reaching the market. It was the Continental, produced in Franklin, Indiana from 1910 to 1914. Refer to Continental.

The Indiana Scale & Truck Company was organized in 1904 with a capital stock of $100,000 for the manufacture of trucks, scales, automobiles and bicycles in Bluffton, Indiana. An automobile never was built, the company's product line consisting entirely of hand-trucks to be operated by manpower for the moving of grain and of platform scales to weigh it.

1901 Indiana, brake, NAHC

INDIANA — Indianapolis, Indiana — (1901) — The Indiana was simply a continuation of the Black, and was produced by the Indiana Motor & Vehicle Company which acquired rights to the motor vehicle patents of Charles H. Black in 1900. Black had built the first gasoline car ever seen on the streets of Indianapolis in 1893 and had become quite a local celebrity since. Nonetheless, the new people building his car were out of business within a year.

INDIANAPOLIS — Between 1897 and 1900, Charles H. Black, who had built his first gasoline car in 1893 in Indianapolis, produced a refined version of that automobile for sale locally. Although occasionally referred to as the Indianapolis, the car more often bore his own name. Refer to Black.

The Indianapolis Automobile Clearing House was organized in Indianapolis during the fall of 1912 with a capital stock of $50,000 for the manufacture and sale of automobiles. The incorporators were E.J. Kane, F.E. Barrett and T.E. Byrne. Manufacture is doubted.

The Indianapolis Transfer Company was listed as the manufacturer of an automobile at 215 North Delaware Street in the Hiscox book *Horseless Vehicles, Automobiles, Motor Cycles* published in 1900. Details are lacking. Turn of the century Indianapolis city directory references confirm the firm's existence at 215 North Delaware, and with J.E. Morand as president and general manager. The Indianapolis Transfer ad read: "The Official Company for Theatrical Hauling. Only Up to Date Passenger and Baggage Transfer Company in the City. All Passenger Service Rubber Tired."

INDUSTRIAL — The Industrial Automobile Company at Elkhart, Indiana built the final Federal cars in 1909. Refer to Federal.

The Industrial Investment & Development Company of New York City promoted the Lewis B. White car beginning in October 1898. Refer to New Power.

The Industrial Machine Company was reorganized in Phoenix, New York early in 1902 for promotion of a car designed by George E. De Long. Refer to De Long.

The Industrial Motor Car Company was organized in Middletown, New York during the summer of 1912 for the manufacture and sale of automobiles and parts. Capital stock was $350,000. The incorporators were William A. Courtland, Cuthbert W. Jewell, M.G. Crawford, Harris H. Rayl and Montecelle A. Bonneford. Manufacture of a car is doubted.

INGERSOLL — That the Ingersoll-Rand Company produced an automobile during its early years has been rumored for a number of years. Archivists for the firm indicate that no Ingersoll-Rand car was ever built, but there is

a likelihood that the man who was among the founding fathers of the firm did build an automobile. This was Simon Ingersoll, who founded the Ingersoll Rock Drill Company in 1871, but who sold out about 1880 to get on with his other inventions, among which was a steam engine which he had developed and patented and which he may have fitted into a car of his own construction for testing purposes. Manufacturing an automobile probably never entered his mind. Instead, following his steam development he simply moved his inventiveness into other fields.

INGERSOLL MOORE — Bloomington, Illinois — (1888-1895) — Ingersoll Moore must have been a fascinating person to talk to. Born in Ohio in 1837, he apprenticed as a carpenter and mill worker there, and then moved south to Mississippi where he followed his trade and married Miss Lucy A. Colony. When the Civil War came, he was conscripted into the Confederate army, though he was known to be a Union sympathizer. When several Union soldiers were captured in his home, things became rather dicey for Ingersoll Moore. He arranged to be captured by the North, and returned to the Midwest with a number of paroled Union prisoners in 1863. His wife joined him when peace came. Settling in Bloomington, Illinois, Ingersoll Moore continued his former trade, and for more than a quarter of a century worked as the planing mill foreman for the Chicago & Alton Railroad. Throughout this period he invented things, none of which he bothered to patent. Among his inventions were several steam automobiles, which he sometimes referred to as Moorespring Steamers. The first was a four-wheeler in 1888. Three-wheeled and six-wheeled automobiles followed in 1889. Though he designed an entry for the 1895 Chicago Times-Herald Contest, he didn't finish it in time for the event. Among other creations of his imagination were a device to make sure electric lights stayed on in railroad cars, and a large curious gadget that had two functions: it pumped well water and mowed grass. It does not appear that any of Ingersoll Moore's inventions saw widespread practical application or reaped him any financial reward. One suspects that this did not bother him much.

INGOT — Calumet, Michigan — (1915) — In a short news story dateline April 12th, 1915, it was revealed that a four-cylinder touring car to be known as the Ingot was on the way. "The new concern intends to make the price of its car between $700 and $1,000 and employ 200 men the first year," *The Automobile* revealed. The Ingot was to be an assembled automobile, its parts and accessories purchased principally in Detroit. The factory was planned for either Calumet or Houghton. It would appear that the only subsequent decision the Ingot Automobile Company made was for Calumet as the site for a factory that was never built. Quite possibly, the prototype of the Ingot proved a dismal failure.

1915 Ingram-Hatch, chassis, HAC

INGRAM-HATCH — Staten Island, New York — (1917) — The Ingram-Hatch Motor Corporation had its offices in lower Manhattan, its factory on Staten Island, and a display chassis ready for the Brooklyn Automobile Show in January 1917. Promotion of the car centered on the negative: the Ingram was boasted to have "no clutch, no radiator, no magneto, no gearshift, no water system, no central controlled shaft, no fan, no carburetor, no water jackets, no timers, no selective transmission and no need for gasoline." What the Ingram-Hatch had was a four-cylinder, overhead camshaft, air-cooled 40 hp four-cylinder engine which used kerosene for fuel. Friction transmission was employed, and drive was by twin shafts, one for each axle half. But the soul of the Ingram-Hatch was its wheels, which featured heart-shaped mechanical springs instead of spokes, with compressed air cushions in between and designed to absorb road shock. The tires for these wheels were also unique, made of leather and steel and in easily removable sections. "It is not necessary to discard a whole tire because one little spot becomes badly worn or is damaged," advertising said, "that particular section can be discarded and a new one inserted in less time than it takes to tell about it." Joseph A. Ingram and William P. Hatch had been reluctant during development of their car to talk much about it, preferring a big publicity splurge at automobile show time. Some members of the trade press were enthusiastic: "Quite the most novel car that America has seen in many years," reported *The American Chauffeur*. Others were not. "That such important news could have been kept secret for six months shows the existence of a highly efficient censorship on Staten Island," commented *Automobile Topics*. "But the automobile industry is going to be revolutionized — wait and see! And in the meantime stock certificates of the company are available for the stroke of a fountain pen..." Obviously not many signed up. The Brooklyn show chassis is believed to be the total extent of Ingram-Hatch automobile production. Thereafter the Messrs. Ingram and Hatch returned to their Staten Island factory — which was a converted steam laundry — and continued in the building of two-and four-stroke engines (which used gasoline for fuel) for stationary, marine and automotive use.

INLAND — The Inland Auto Company was organized in Harrington, Lincoln County, Washington during the spring of 1906 with a capital stock of $10,000 for the manufacture and sale of automobiles and motor boats. O.M. Graves and H. Conger were the principals involved. Manufacture of an automobile is doubted.

The Inland Motor Parts Company was organized in Chicago, Illinois during the summer of 1910 with a capital stock of $2500 for the manufacture and sale of motors, motor vehicles and accessories. Incorporators were F.M. Lindgren, H.W. Carter and C.A. Garner. Manufacture of an automobile is doubted.

1921 Innes, roadster, WLB

INNES — Jacksonville, Florida — (1920-1921) — The Innes was an attempted revival of the Simms automobile idea, which had just ended its brief existence in Atlanta. The two cars were similar, both light fours on a 114-inch wheelbase, though the Innes used a Supreme 40 hp engine and sported wood wheels. (The Simms engine had been an in-house design, and its wheels were disc.) A Canadian, Henry L. Innes had been associated with a number of automotive-related companies in the North (Dodge in Detroit, Chevrolet in Flint, Parrish and Bingham in Cleveland, among them) when he decided to make the South his home. During the fall of 1920, following his short sojourn as production manager for the ill-fated Simms Motor Car Corporation in Atlanta, he moved to Florida and established the American Motors Export Company. Having spent the whole of his career in the employ of others, it was his dream to head his own manufacturing establishment and to have an automobile named for himself. The Innes was planned to be an export car predominantly. Construction of a $180,000 factory was ongoing at a site northwest of Jacksonville, and the half-dozen pilot Innes motorcars were being tested, when tragedy struck. After an illness of two weeks, Henry Innes died on August 16th, 1921 at the age of forty-six. His dream died with him. The following year his venture was absorbed by the Hanson Motor Company of Atlanta.

INTERBOROUGH — The Interborough Auto Repair & Supply Company was organized in Cold Spring, New York early in 1909 with a capital stock of $15,000 to build automobiles and electric cars. Incorporators were Frederick A. Verdon, Daniel McElroy and John McRoberts. Manufacture is doubted.

INTERNATIONAL — Although organized as the International Automobile Company of Boston, Massachusetts, this company name was changed in July of 1899 to the Strathmore Automobile Company to avoid confusion with other companies bearing the International name. Refer to Strathmore.

The International Automobile Company was organized in Charleston, West Virginia during the fall of 1899 to manufacture and sell automobiles. Capital stock was $500,000, and the incorporators — H.A. La Paugh, Rebecca La Paugh, R.H. Hepner, D.B. Luckey and J. Story — were all New Yorkers. Manufacture is doubted.

The International Automobile Construction Company was organized in Portland, Maine early in 1900 with a capital stock of $100,000. Incorporators were R.M. Gray, W.H. Ricker, C.E. Fay and H.L. Cram. Manufacture is doubted.

The International Automobile & Engine Company was a $10 million Delaware incorporation from late 1910 to manufacture automobiles, airships, motorcycles and motor boats. Incorporators were William D. Yarnall of Yeadon, Pennsylvania, Elwood H. James of Sharon Hill, Pennsylvania and S.C. Seymour of Camden, New Jersey. Manufacture is doubted.

The International Automobile League was organized in Buffalo, New York during the summer of 1908 with a capital stock of $50,000 for the manufacture of motorcars. A.C. Bidwell and C.H. Bowe were the incorporators. This venture was followed in the summer of 1910 by the International Automobile League Tire & Rubber Company, a million-dollar incorporation by Bidwell and Bowe to "manufacture automobiles and rubber." Manufacture of a car is doubted.

The International Cyclecar Company of New York City had its factory in Providence, Rhode Island and there in 1914 produced the Economycar cyclecar. Refer to Economycar.

The International Generator Company was organized in Hoboken, New Jersey with a capital stock of $100,000 during the spring of 1908 for the manufacture of machinery, engines, automobiles and motor boats. J.E. Whiting, Willard P. Jessup and Frank C. Pringle were the incorporators. Manufacture of a car is doubted.

The International Manufacturing Company was organized in Washington, D.C. with a capital stock of $100,000 during the spring of 1911 to manufacture automobiles and other vehicles. Incorporators were John Ebersole, John B. Flick, Henry F.M. Cunningham, Ross C. Barrett and Howard P. Meldrum, all of the District of Columbia. Manufacture of a car is doubted.

The International Motor Company was a $10 million Delaware incorporation from late 1911 for the manufacture of motor vehicles. The incorporators were R.A. Aldrich, G. Foster and J.A. Bennett, all of New York City. Manufacture is doubted.

The International Motor Company from the summer of 1912 was a $10 million Delaware incorporation for the manufacture and sale of automobiles. C.P. Coleman, F.C. Richardson and Vernon Monroe were behind this one. Manufacture is doubted.

The International Motor Car Company of Toledo, Ohio built the Toledo steamer from 1901-1903. Refer to Toledo.

The International Motor Car Company of Chicago, Illinois was organized during the spring of 1906 with a capital stock of $150,000 to manufacture "a six-cylinder touring car which will not weigh more than 1500 pounds and have a wheelbase of 112 inches." H.G. Moore, formerly with the McDuffee Automobile Company, was the sales manager for this venture. He announced that the firm was "looking for a factory site and would like to hear from towns or cities which have a proposition to offer" and that the "first car will be out about the 15th of August." This venture was not heard from again.

The International Motor Car Manufacturing Company was organized in Springfield, Illinois early in 1908 with a capital stock of $250,000 to "manufacture motor cars of all kinds." W.P. and H.S. Dixon, together with E.M. Dixon, were the incorporators. Manufacture is doubted.

The International Motor Service Association was organized in New York City late in 1911 with a capital stock of $100,000, for the manufacture of automobiles. W.H. Brearley, W.W. Friend and I.A. Monsees were the incorporators. Manufacture is doubted.

The International Motor Vehicle Company at 2158 Broadway in New York City was listed as an automobile manufacturer in the Hiscox book *Horseless Vehicles, Automobiles, Motor Cycles* published in 1900. Further documentation is lacking. A company of that name does not appear in the New York City directories of the turn of the century.

The International Motor Wheel Company of 302 West 53rd Street in New York City was organized during the fall of 1899 to promote the automotive idea of Julius M. Walters. Refer to Walters.

The International Power Company at 253 Broadway in New York City was listed as an automobile manufacturer in the Hiscox book *Horseless Vehicles, Automobiles, Motor Cycles* published in 1900. Further documentation is lacking. This firm is known to have taken over the Stamford, Connecticut factory of the Klock at the end of 1901. References from as late as the summer of 1903 indicate the firm issuing descriptive catalogs, regarding its "kerosene oil engines and motor cars," but actual manufacture of automobiles cannot be documented with certainty.

The International Power Company of Providence, Rhode Island has appeared on various car rosters as a manufacturer during the turn of the century years. This is in error. The firm built "auto trucks" and locomotives beginning in 1899, selling out in 1902 to the American Locomotive Company and organizing the Equipment Motor Company at that time for the manufacture of engines only.

The International Sales Corporation was organized in New York City in early 1907 with a capital stock of $5000 to manufacture and deal in motorcars. Emil Grossman, Carl Kauffman and Frank Lowe were the incorporators. Manufacture of a car is doubted. This was one of several automobile ventures of Emil Grossman during this period.

1900 International, stanhope, MVMA

INTERNATIONAL — New York, New York — (1900) — The International Motor Carriage Company was organized with a capital stock of $200,000 in the early fall of 1900 by Percy L. Klock, Robert S. Rudd and Langdon Greenwood. The Astor Court Building in New York City was officially the firm's address, but the cars were produced in Percy Klock's factory in Stamford, Connecticut. The International was a two-cylinder 5 hp $1200 car sold as a phaeton or physician's stanhope, and marketed only for a short period under the International name. Most of the vehicles built by the company were sold as Klocks.

INTERNATIONAL — Toledo, Ohio — (1901) — The International Motor Car Company was organized in 1901 as the automobile department of the American Bicycle Company of Toledo. Only in 1901, however, was the steam car produced known as an International too. By 1902 Toledo had become its name, and a gasoline car was added as well. Toledo steam and gasoline vehicles were produced through 1903, when they were superseded by the Pope-Toledo.

1936 International, airport limousine, AA

INTERNATIONAL (I.H.C.) — Akron, Ohio — (1907-1911, 1930's) — Although the International Harvester Company of Chicago built its first experimental motor buggy in 1899, the firm did not venture into production until eight years later, and the approach was ingenuous. "It is built as nearly as possible like a buggy," International Harvester said. "This type of vehicle has been serving country-town and rural people for years, and there is no reason why a simple motor vehicle of this type cannot serve them in the future." Thus did the company introduce its automotive product in 1907, in words it would have to eat several years later when a standard car with pneumatic tires was added to the line. The first production International highwheeler was completed in February 1907 at I.H.C.'s McCormick Works in Chicago. In October, after 100 units had been built, production was transferred to the Akron factory. The International was a two-cylinder, friction-transmission, solid-tired vehicle available as a passenger-carrying car or light delivery truck. It was probably the most rugged highwheeler built in America and among the most popular, some 4500 units being built. The initials I.H.C. were not widely used until 1910. Four-cylinder standard models, either air or water cooled, joined the line that year. After 1911 the automobile department was shut down and only trucks were produced thereafter, though Sunday-go-to-meetin' seats were available for the back of highwheeler truck models as late as 1916. Later, in the Thirties, an occasional passenger car was built to order on the smallest truck chassis.

1907 International, model A, runabout, HAC

1907 INTERNATIONAL
Highwheeler — 2-cyl., 14/16 hp, 84" wb

	FP	5	4	3	2	1
Model A Runabout-2P	600	2400	3400	4800	8000	17,000
Model B Farmer's Auto-4P	600	2450	3500	4900	8300	17,500

1908 International, model A, runabout, OCW

1909 International, model A, runabout, JAC

1908-1909 INTERNATIONAL
Model A — 2-cyl., 14 hp, 84" wb

	FP	5	4	3	2	1
Runabout-2/4P	850	2400	3400	4800	8000	17,000

1910 International I.H.C., roadster, JAC

1911 International I.H.C., touring, JAC

1910-1911 INTERNATIONAL (I.H.C.)
International — 2-cyl., 14 hp, 84" wb

Auto Buggy-4P	800	2500	3500	5000	8500	18,000

I.H.C. — 2-cyl., 18/20 hp, 92" wb

Model 19 Roadster-4P	1000	2700	3600	5300	8800	19,000

Model F — 4-cyl., 18/20 hp, 92" wb

I.H.C. Roadster-2P	—	2500	3500	5000	8500	18,000

Model J — 4-cyl., 26/30 hp, 110" wb

I.H.C. Touring-5P	—	2700	3600	5300	8800	19,000

INTERNATIONAL — Chicago, Illinois — (1909) — The International Automobile Company of 1243-1245 Wabash Avenue in Chicago approached advertising in a way that can only be likened to that practiced decades later by late-night TV hucksters selling vegetable slicers. Though International's were print ads, they came at you in a torrent of words and verily shouted. The company's product was a quite ordinary highwheeler offered in several body styles and guaranteed for a year, though one scarcely thinks seriously. International also advertised itself as jobbers in all kinds of other automobiles and declared that "250 rebuilt, slightly used cars" were always in stock and "we guarantee like new." The International Automobile Company was around no longer in 1910. The firm had been a $20,000 incorporation in November 1908 by E.C. Haynes, C.E. Hall and J.W. McDaniel.

1909 International, type 16, surrey, NAHC

1909 INTERNATIONAL

Type 14 — 12/14 hp, 72" wb

	FP	5	4	3	2	1
Surrey	500	1800	2800	4000	6200	13,000

Type 16 — 16/18 hp, 84" wb

Surrey	650	2000	3000	4200	6500	14,000

Type 10 — 12 hp, 70" wb

Runabout	475	1600	2700	3800	5800	12,000

Little Giant — 12 hp

Delivery	450	1500	2500	3600	5500	11,000

Little Giant — 18/20 hp

Delivery	650	1600	2700	3800	5800	12,000

INTERSTATE — The Interstate Supply Company was organized in Toledo, Ohio during the spring of 1911 with a capital stock of $10,000 for the manufacture and sale of motorcars and supplies. Incorporators were Clarence D. Pettingell, James Samsen, Fred H. Kruse, Mark Winchester and William J. Frische. Manufacture of a car is doubted.

1909 Inter-State, model 28, single-rumble roadster, HAC

INTER-STATE — Muncie, Indiana — (1909-1919) — The Inter-State had two lives. The first began in October of 1908 when Thomas F. Hart of Muncie announced the winner of the contest he had staged to name his new car, and the Inter-State Automobile Company was born. Production began soon after at 142 Willard Street, and Hart proclaimed to the local press that he was building "the best automobile made in America, even though everyone doesn't know it." Everyone in Muncie did, and indeed in 1910 the *Muncie Press* suggested that Inter-State might spread the fame of Muncie, Indiana throughout the world. That, alas, did not happen. The first Inter-States were medium-sized and medium-priced fours, followed by a six for 1913, and trouble in the company soon after. In October of '13 Thomas Hart requested receivership, citing internal dissension and his inability to secure working capital because of disagreement among stockholders. The problems were not worked out, and involuntary bankruptcy proceedings followed before year's end. On February 5th, 1914 the Inter-State factory and real estate were sold to F.C. Ball, whose usual line was the manufacture of glass jars but who had been among the investors in Inter-State from the beginning. He paid the firm's debts and reorganized as the Inter-State Motor Company. An all-new Inter-State, a low-priced four (Beaver engine) on a 110-inch wheelbase, followed for 1915. In May of 1918 Inter-State became one of the first American companies to discontinue automobile production for the duration of World War I. The factory was converted to war work; peace arrived six months later. Although F.C. Ball announced in late February of 1919 that he was completing government orders and was planning the resumption of passenger car production, he had changed his mind by the month following. In March he sold his Inter-State factory to General Motors for the production of the Sheridan automobile.

1909 INTER-STATE

Four — 35/40 hp, 112" wb

Touring-5P	1750	2500	3500	5000	8500	18,000
Runabout-4P	1750	2400	3400	4800	8000	17,000
Demi-Tonneau	1750	2500	3500	5000	8500	18,000

1910 Inter-State, model 30, touring, WLB

1910 INTER-STATE

Forty — 4-cyl., 40 hp, 118" wb

	FP	5	4	3	2	1
Model 30 Touring-5P	1750	2500	3500	5000	8500	18,000
Model 31 Demi-Tonneau-4P	1750	2400	3400	4800	8000	17,000
Model 32 Roadster-3P	1750	2500	3500	5000	8500	18,000
Model 33 Roadster-4P	1750	2600	3600	5200	8700	18,500
Model 34 Torpedo	2000	2700	3600	5300	8800	19,000

1911 Inter-State, model 34, torpedo, HAC

1911 INTER-STATE

Forty — 4-cyl., 40 hp, 118" wb

Model 31-A Demi-Tonneau-4P	1750	2500	3500	5000	8500	18,000
Model 30-A Touring-5P	1750	2700	3600	5300	8800	19,000
Model 32-A Roadster-3P	1750	2900	3700	5600	9100	20,000
Model 33-A Roadster-4P	1750	3000	3900	5800	9300	20,500
Model 34-A Torpedo-5P	2000	3000	4000	6000	9500	21,000

Fifty — 4-cyl., 50 hp, 124" wb

Model 35 Touring-7P	2700	4200	8400	14,000	19,600	28,000

1912 Inter-State, model 42, roadster, HAC

1912 INTER-STATE

Thirty — 4-cyl., 30 hp, 118" wb

Model 30-A Fore-Door Tour.-5P	1750	2900	3700	5600	9100	20,000
Model 32-B Roadster-3P	1700	3000	4000	6000	9500	21,000

Forty — 4-cyl., 40 hp, 118" wb

Model 40 Fore-Dr. Tr.-5P	2400	3000	4000	6000	9500	21,000
Model 41 Fore-Dr. Demi-Tonneau-4P	2400	2900	3700	5600	9100	20,000
Model 42 Fore-Dr. Rds.	2400	3100	4200	6300	10,500	22,000

Fifty — 4-cyl., 50 hp, 124" wb

Model 50 Fore-Dr. Tr.-7P	3400	4300	8500	14,250	20,000	29,000
Model 51 Fore-Dr. Demi-Tonneau	3400	3000	4000	6000	9500	21,000
Model 52 Fore-Dr. Rds.	3400	4200	8400	14,000	19,600	28,000

1913-1914 INTER-STATE

Model 45 — 6-cyl., 38.4 hp, 132" wb

Touring-5P	2750	3500	4500	7000	13,000	25,000

1913 Inter-State, model 45, touring, HAC

1914 Inter-State, model 45, touring, HAC

1915 Inter-State, model T, touring, HAC

1915 INTER-STATE
Model T — 4-cyl., 19.6 hp, 110" wb

	FP	5	4	3	2	1
Touring-5P	1000	3000	4000	6000	9500	21,000

1916 Inter-State, model T, touring, HAC

1916 INTER-STATE
Model T — 4-cyl., 19.6 hp, 110" wb

	FP	5	4	3	2	1
Touring-5P	850	3100	4200	6300	10,500	22,000
Roadster-2P	850	3200	4300	6500	11,000	23,000
Sedan-5P	1050	2000	3000	4200	6500	14,000
Coupe-2P	1050	2300	3300	4600	7500	16,000

1917 Inter-State, model T, touring sedan, HAC

1917 INTER-STATE
Model T — 4-cyl., 19.6 hp, 110" wb

	FP	5	4	3	2	1
Touring-5P	850	3100	4200	6300	10,500	22,000
Roadster-2P	850	3200	4300	6500	11,000	23,000
Divided Seat Touring-5P	895	3200	4300	6500	11,000	23,000
Roadster-4P	895	3300	4400	6700	12,000	24,000
Sedan-5P	1250	2000	3000	4200	6500	14,000
Deluxe Delivery	850	1800	2800	4000	6200	13,000

1918 Inter-State, model T, touring, HAC

1918 INTER-STATE
Model T — 4-cyl., 19.6 hp, 110" wb

	FP	5	4	3	2	1
Touring-5P	925	3100	4200	6300	10,500	22,000
Roadster-4P	950	3300	4400	6700	12,000	24,000
Roadster-2P	875	3200	4300	6500	11,000	23,000
Touring Sedan-5P	1325	2000	3000	4200	6500	14,000
Delivery Wagon	875	1800	2800	4000	6200	13,000

INTER-URBAN — The Inter-Urban Motor Company was organized in Ithaca, New York early in 1910 with a capital stock of $8000 to manufacture and deal in vehicles of all kinds. Incorporators were O.L. Stewart, G.C. Mowry and W.H. Arden. Manufacture of a car is doubted.

INTERURBAN — Chicago, Illinois — (1905) — The Interurban bristled with ingenuity. It was a runabout the body of which was its frame. It was front drive, the steering accomplished by the pivoting of the entire front axle. And, although ostensibly an electric, it could be quickly converted — in ten minutes, its inventor said — to an 8 hp two-cylinder gasoline car, all that was required being the substitution of the entire front axle. The Interurban was the idea of Francis A. Woods of Chicago, and in practical terms was no doubt more ingenuous than ingenious. The F.A. Woods Auto Company never moved into production, and probably only the single Interurban was built. A decade later, Francis Woods was considerably more successful with his Woods Mobilette, and at that time made no reference at all to the Interurban.

INTREPID — Boston, Massachusetts — (1903-1905) — Intrepid it was not. Its engine was an 8 hp single-cylinder with two connecting rods on the one piston rotating two shafts in opposite direction, this configuration presumably rendering the unit vibrationless. The Rotary Motor Vehicle Company of Boston had been trying to get its car on the market since 1900, not succeeding until 1903. Although advertisements indicate the firm's penchant for calling its product the Intrepid, that was not an officially registered trademark. The shaft-drive car, which was sold as a $2150 wire-wheeled runabout and $1500 wooden-wheeled tonneau, is more properly called a Rotary.

INVENTS — The Invents Tri-Cycle Car Company of Peoria, Illinois was indicated as building a cyclecar in the March 1914 issue of *Motor Print*. Manufacture did not follow.

INVINCIBLE — The Invincible Storage Battery Company was organized in Chicago, Illinois late in 1907 with a capital stock of $5000 to ''manufacture and deal in electric generating machinery, motor vehicles and also furnish electricity.'' Manufacture of a car is doubted.

IOWA — In 1907 Jesse O. Wells of Des Moines organized the Iowa Motor Car Company for the manufacture of automobiles. Although that firm did not get off the ground, Wells did build a number of vehicles in Des Moines from 1904-1910. Refer to Wells.

IRON CITY — The Iron City Vehicle Company was organized in Pittsburgh, Pennsylvania during the spring of 1904 with a capital stock of $10,000 to ''manufacture, sell, buy and repair carriages, wagons and automobiles.'' Directors of the firm were John A. Hawkins, George A. Urling, Harry W. Urling and Robert Y. McKinnon. Manufacture of a car is doubted.

1905 Iroquois, runabout, NAHC

IROQUOIS — Syracuse & Seneca Falls, New York — (1903-1907) — The Leggett Carriage Company in Syracuse had been building bodies for automobile manufacturers since the turn of the century, and in February 1903 J.S. Leggett decided to build complete cars called Iroquois too. He reorganized as the J.S. Leggett Manufacturing Company that month but was in receivership ten months later, complaining that stockholders had failed to put up sufficient capital ''to conduct a large enough business to yield profits.'' Production virtually ceased during 1904, one merchanic remaining at the factory to finish up ''a few machines.'' In December that year Leggett finally found more willing stockholders, Charles A. Fox most prominently. The Iroquois Motor Car Company capitalized at $450,000, succeeded the Leggett company and moved to Seneca Falls where it took over the factory formerly occupied by the National Yeast Company. The basic design of the Iroquois — including sliding gear transmission and shaft drive — remained the same, though the four-cylinder engine was beefed up a bit for 1905, and even more so for 1906-1907. But the money problems remained. In February 1907 the Iroquois Motor Car Company property and business were sold under mortgage foreclosure. Later that year J.S. Leggett tried to reorganize yet again as the Iroquois Motor Vehicle Company, with plans to return to Syracuse, but he never made it.

1903 Iroquois, runabout, NAHC

1903-1905 IROQUOIS
(4-cyl., 15 hp)

	FP	5	4	3	2	1
Iroquois Runabout	—	2000	3000	4200	6500	14,000
Iroquois Tonneau	—	2000	3000	4200	6500	14,000
1905 IROQUOIS						
Side-Entrance Tonneau (4-cyl., 20 hp, 100'' wb)	2500	2200	3200	4400	7000	15,000
Rear-Entrance Tonneau (4-cyl., 20 hp, 90'' wb)	2500	2000	3000	4200	6500	14,000
1906 IROQUOIS						
Type D — 4-cyl., 25/30 hp, 100'' wb						
Touring-5P	2600	2300	3300	4600	7500	16,000
Type E — 4-cyl., 40 hp, 100'' wb						
Touring-7P	3000	2400	3400	4800	8000	17,000

1907 Iroquois, model D, touring, NAHC

1907 IROQUOIS
Type C — 4-cyl., 25/30 hp, 104'' wb

	FP	5	4	3	2	1
Touring-5P	2400	2400	3400	4800	8000	17,000
Type D — 4-cyl., 35/40 hp, 108'' wb						
Touring-7P	2800	2500	3500	5000	8500	18,000

IROQUOIS STEAMER — Although this 1902 car was built in the shops of the Iroquois Iron Works in Buffalo, New York, it is more appropriately referred to by the name of the man who built it. Refer to King Steamer.

ITHACA — The Ithaca Import Company was organized in Ithaca, New York during the spring of 1906 with a capital stock of $50,000 ''to manufacture and repair automobiles, steam and electric, gasoline, etc.; carriages, vehicles, etc.'' H.S. Velsor of Huntington, Long Island, J.H. Demarest of Saranac Lake and R. Condon of New York City were the incorporators. Manufacture of a car is doubted.

IVERSON — The Iverson Manufacturing Company was organized in Pittsburgh, Pennsylvania with a capital stock of $100,000 during the summer of 1908 to manufacture automobiles and accessories. S. Iverson, J.C. Conley and W.D. Rowan were the incorporators. Manufacture of a car is doubted.

IVERSON — Milwaukee, Wisconsin — (1902) — In January of 1902, U.W. Iverson of Milwaukee announced his plans for the future. He had, he said, been building automobiles to order for some time but now decided to manufacture a vehicle for the market as well. He planned to use a ''valveless gasoline engine'' of three or six horsepower, the latter simply being two of the 3 hp units coupled together on a main shaft. Apparently, he wished to manufacture the engines and bodies only, purchasing running gear and other components outside. ''He wants to hear from manufacturers of parts,'' *Cycle and Automobile Trade Journal* advised. No doubt he did, but the available evidence indicates that he did not become a bona-fide manufacturer. No standard line of Iverson automobiles was ever announced in any case. He may have continued to build cars to custom order for several years thereafter.

IZZER — A man by the name of Irvington Izzer purportedly built an automobile in Irvington, New York in 1910, according to various car rosters. Documentation of this is lacking.

1911 Izzer, runabout, NAHC

IZZER — Peru, Indiana — (1911) — The Izzer was so named because the man who ordered it wanted an up-to-date custom-made car with all modern improvements, not the ''was-ers'' or ''has-beens'' that populated American roads of the day. Dr. H.H. Bissell of Watseka (Illinois) obviously had a great sense of humor. He took his order for this specially-designed car to E.A. Myers of the Model Gas Engine Company in Peru, the Indiana firm which formerly had manufactured the Model car and was now engaged in the engine-building business. Myers was so enthused with the idea that he built two more Izzers, one for himself, the other for Model office manager James Littlejohn. A Model four-cylinder engine was featured in the Izzer; most drivetrain components were secured from Great Western, another automobile manufacturer in town. The three-passenger roadster body resembled the Great Western's as well. The wheelbase was 99 inches. Interestingly, for a client who demanded the up-to-date, Dr. Bissell insisted on solid tires. Of the three cars built, the Myers Izzer was destroyed in 1912 following a plunge down a 450-foot bluff, the ultimate destiny of the Littlejohn car is not known, but the Bissell car remains extant. A delightful footnote to history, the Izzer still is.

1903 Jack Frost, auto-buggy, NAHC

JACK FROST ELECTRIC — Chicago, Illinois — (1903) — The Jack Frost was a three-seated electric roadster on an 86-inch wheelbase with an aluminum wagon-box-type body, left-hand lever steering and solid tires on tubular steel wheels. Pneumatic cushions were provided for the seats. They were probably necessary. This was a quite crude machine, which is probably the reason it was built for less than one year by the Kammann Manufacturing Company of Chicago. This firm probably evolved out of the Kammann Electric Company of Minneapolis which had been organized in 1897 to build electric vehicles and launches under the patents of W.T. Kammann. Manufacture of automobiles is not believed to have followed in Minnesota, however.

JACK RABBIT — The most famous of the early Appersons from Kokomo, Indiana was the racing runabout model called the Jack Rabbit introduced in 1907. The Jack Rabbit was widely raced thereafter, and the fame it won resulted in the Apperson company taking promotional advantage by calling all of its cars Apperson Jack Rabbits from 1911 through 1913. Refer to Apperson.

1900 Jacks, roadster, NAHC

JACKS — Napa, California — (1899-1900) — Fred S. Jacks was the proprietor of the Elk Cyclery at 139 Main Street in Napa and in 1899 he took time away from his bicycle dealership — where he also sold phonograph records — to build a gasoline automobile. It was completed before year's end. The engine he used was a 2 hp single-cylinder unit from St. Louis, though Jacks indicated that he planned to build his own motors in the future. "The transmission is an invention of my own, same is a friction clutch, works satisfactorily, giving several speeds," he wrote *Cycle and Automobile Trade Journal* in a letter published in its January 1900 issue. ". . . Have used tubing in the running gear, wire wheels, 2-inch tires, pneumatic; would recommend 4-inch for practical purposes. Have a muffler of my design. This is a perfect silencer and does not throttle motor percepti-

bly. One lever steers vehicle and starts motor." Jacks was intent upon manufacture, and chose a name for his venture as winsome as the one for his bicycle shop. Jacks Autobain Company he called it. Unfortunately, it never got off the ground. Jacks built a second car in 1900, however, a steamer considerably more heavy than his first effort. Because heftier pneumatics were now required, he wrote the Goodrich company in Ohio asking that special ones be made. Goodrich agreed, so long as Jacks paid for the mold. A few months later, another automotive pioneer from Michigan requested larger pneumatics as well, and Goodrich asked Jacks if his mold could be used. Jacks said sure, if the fellow from Michigan would split the cost of the mold with him. Ransom Olds did. In 1906 Fred Jacks was among the organizers of the Bay Cities Automobile Company in Oakland, but that firm seems to have operated only as a dealership.

JACKSON — The Jackson Carriage Company of Jackson, Michigan produced a car called the Imperial in 1908. Refer to Imperial.

During the summer of 1910 the Jackson Carriage Company of Jackson, Tennessee announced its forthcoming entry into the automobile manufacturing field and its takeover of the automobile factory of the Southern Motor Works, which had recently moved operations from Jackson to Nashville, Tennessee. That fall the Jackson Motor Car Company was organized with a capital stock of $5000. Incorporators were H.C. Gillespie, H.D. Canfield, E.L. Bowne, W.H. Weakley, W.C. Sandifeur. What stalled this venture thereafter is not known, but manufacture does not seem to have followed.

The Jackson Motor Car Company was organized in New York City late in 1906 with a capital stock of $20,000 for the manufacture of automobiles. Charles M. Herring of Manhattan and Henry W. and Frank H. Palmer of Brooklyn were the incorporators. Manufacture is doubted.

JACKSON STEAM — San Francisco, California — (1897) — Byron Jackson was the proprietor of the Byron Jackson Machine Works at 625 Sixth Street in San Francisco and in 1897 he devised a double-acting vertical steam engine using kerosene as fuel. He also built a carriage in which he fitted the engine, but this is believed to be the only car he built.

1905 Jackson, model C, touring, HAC

JACKSON — Jackson, Michigan — (1903-1923) — Byron J. Carter of Jackson was a steam-driven press printer and rubber stamp manufacturer who went into partnership with his father, Squire B. Carter, in a bicycle store in 1894 and started his own U.S. Tag Company in 1896. He built his first automobile in 1899, a gasoline car, but thereafter put his steam printing experience to work. The Carter steam stanhope he built in 1901 was produced as the Michigan by the Michigan Automobile Company in Grand Rapids. In 1902 Carter invented an improved three-cylinder 6 hp steam engine which he patented, and in July that year he returned home and persuaded fellow Jackson residents George A. Matthews (owner of the Fuller Buggy Company and director of the Jackson City Bank) and Charles Lewis (president of Lewis Spring and Axle Company and Union Bank of Jackson director) to help him incorporate the Jackson Automobile Company for the manufacture of both steam and gasoline cars. The steamer was spelled Jaxon, and was built in 1903 only. Jackson gasoline cars continued in manufacture thereafter, but without Byron Carter who left the company early on because his partners did not wish to pursue the friction-drive idea he had which he would go off on his own to build as the Carter-car. Without the inventive Mr. Carter, Jacksons were conventional if well-built and durable automobiles. "No Hill Too Steep, No Sand Too Deep," advertisements said. The original single-cylinder runabout, a curved-dash Olds lookalike, was followed by a twin in 1904 and a four in 1906. A high-wheeler was produced under the marque name of Fuller from 1909 to 1911. A six-cylinder Jackson arrived courtesy of the Northway engine company in 1913, a Ferro-supplied V-8 was available beginning in 1916. Later cars bore a distinct Rolls-Royce appearance: "The Car with the Keystone Radiator" was a slogan. The only real tries at ingenuity from Jackson were a companion car in 1904 called the Orlo which was distinguished by the under-front-of-the-hood mounting of its finned coil radiator, and a model called the Duck in 1913 which was known more descriptively as the Jackson Back Seat Steer, which it literally was, the rear-seat passenger doing the driving. In 1910 George Matthews had bought out the financial interest of Charles Lewis, though Lewis remained on a while longer before taking off to build the Hollier car. Matthews thereafter provided gainful employment to his three sons by appointing them company president, secretary and treasurer. Jacksons for 1917 and 1918 were marketed as Wolverine models. In 1919 no Jackson automobiles were produced, as the factory was turned over to truck manufacture exclusively. Passenger cars returned to the line in 1920. But apparently they weren't very good; one man who worked on the assembly line at the time commented that the engineer responsible "should have raised chickens instead." In 1923 the Jackson, together with the Dixie Flyer of Louisville (Kentucky) and the National of Indianapolis, were merged into a new combine called Associated Motor Industries. The Dixie Flyer and the Jackson Six survived a year as the National 4-H and 6-51. All three marques were gone by the end of 1924, as was Associated Motors.

1903 JACKSON
Jaxon Steam — 3-cyl., 6 hp.

	FP	5	4	3	2	1
Model A Runabout (72" wb)	975	2700	3600	5300	8800	19,000
Model B Runabout (65" wb)	800	2500	3500	5000	8500	18,000

Jackson Gasoline — 1-cyl., 7 hp, 72" wb

Runabout-2P	750	2400	3400	4800	8000	17,000

1904 JACKSON
Model A — 1-cyl., 6 hp, 72" wb

Runabout-2P	650	2700	3600	5300	8800	19,000

Model B — 2-cyl., 12 hp, 82" wb

Surrey-4P	1100	2800	3700	5500	9000	19,500

1905 JACKSON
Model A — 1-cyl., 7 hp, 72" wb

Runabout-2P	650	2700	3600	5300	8800	19,000

Model B — 2-cyl., 16 hp, 86" wb

Side Entrance Tonneau	1125	2800	3700	5500	9000	19,500

Model C — 2-cyl., 18 hp, 90" wb

King of Belgium Touring	1250	2900	3700	5600	9100	20,000

1906 Jackson, model D, touring, HAC

1906 JACKSON
Model C — 2-cyl., 20/24 hp, 90" wb

Touring-5P	1250	2300	3300	4600	7500	16,000

Model D — 2-cyl., 20/24 hp, 100" wb

Touring-5P	1500	2400	3400	4800	8000	17,000

Model G — 4-cyl., 40/45 hp, 108" wb

Touring-5P	2500	2500	3500	5000	8500	18,000

1907 Jackson, touring, JAC

1907 JACKSON
Model C — 2-cyl., 20/24 hp, 96" wb

	FP	5	4	3	2	1
Touring-5P	1250	2300	3300	4600	7500	16,000

Model D — 2-cyl., 20/24 hp, 106" wb

Touring-5P	1500	2400	3400	4800	8000	17,000

Model G — 4-cyl., 40/45 hp, 111" wb

Touring-5P	2500	2500	3500	5000	8500	18,000

1908 Jackson, model E, touring, HAC

1908 JACKSON
Model F — 2-cyl., 16 hp, 90" wb

Runabout	850	2000	3000	4200	6500	14,000

Model C — 2-cyl., 24 hp, 96" wb

Touring-5P	1250	2200	3200	4400	7000	15,000

Model D — 2-cyl., 24 hp, 106" wb

Touring-5P	1500	2300	3300	4600	7500	16,000

Model E — 4-cyl., 35 hp, 111" wb

Touring-5P	2000	2400	3400	4800	8000	17,000
Gentleman's Roadster	2000	2500	3500	5000	8500	18,000

1909 Jackson, touring, HAC

1909 JACKSON
Model R — 2-cyl., 15/18 hp, 96" wb

Runabout	850	2000	3000	4200	6500	14,000

Model C — 2-cyl., 20/24 hp, 104" wb

Touring-5P	1250	2200	3200	4400	7000	15,000

Model H — 4-cyl., 30 hp, 110-1/2" wb

Touring-5P	1600	2300	3300	4600	7500	16,000
Tourabout-4P	1600	2300	3300	4600	7500	16,000

Model E — 4-cyl., 36/40 hp, 111" wb

Touring-5P	2000	3000	6000	10,000	14,000	20,000
Tourabout-4P	2000	3000	6000	10,000	14,000	20,000

1910 Jackson, model 50, touring, HAC

1910 JACKSON
Model C — 2-cyl., 22 hp, 103" wb

	FP	5	4	3	2	1
Touring-5P	1250	2400	3400	4800	8000	17,000

Model 30 — 4-cyl., 25.6 hp, 105" wb

	FP	5	4	3	2	1
Touring-5P	1250	2500	3500	5000	8500	18,000

Model H — 4-cyl., 30 hp, 110" wb

	FP	5	4	3	2	1
Touring-5P	1600	2700	3600	5300	8800	19,000

Model 40 — 4-cyl., 32.4 hp, 110" wb

	FP	5	4	3	2	1
Touring-5P	1700	3750	7500	12,500	17,500	25,000

Model 50 — 4-cyl., 36 hp, 120" wb

	FP	5	4	3	2	1
Touring-7P	2350	3850	7700	12,750	17,800	27,000
Tourabout	2350	3800	7600	12,600	77,600	26,000

1911 Jackson, model 51, touring, HAC

1911 JACKSON
Twin — 2-cyl., 20 hp, 100" wb

	FP	5	4	3	2	1
Model K Touring	950	2400	3400	4800	8000	17,000
Model B Surrey	850	2400	3400	4800	8000	17,000

Model 25 — 4-cyl., 26 hp, 100" wb

	FP	5	4	3	2	1
Roadster-2P	1000	2500	3500	5000	8500	18,000

Model 30 — 4-cyl., 26 hp, 105" wb

	FP	5	4	3	2	1
Convertible Torpedo	1250	2700	3600	5300	8800	19,000

Model 38 — 4-cyl., 30 hp, 115" wb

	FP	5	4	3	2	1
Full Torpedo-4P	1650	2900	3700	5600	9100	20,000

Model 41 — 4-cyl., 32 hp, 110" wb

	FP	5	4	3	2	1
Tourabout	1700	3100	4200	6300	10,500	22,000
Convertible Torpedo	1700	3000	4000	6000	9500	21,000

Model 51 — 4-cyl., 36 hp, 120" wb

	FP	5	4	3	2	1
Touring-5P	2200	3750	7500	12,500	17,500	25,000

1912 Jackson, touring, WLB

1912 JACKSON
Models 26, 28 & 32 — 4-cyl., 30 hp, 110" wb

	FP	5	4	3	2	1
26 Runabout-2P	1100	2500	3500	5000	8500	18,000
28 Runabout-2P	1000	2500	3500	5000	8500	18,000
32 Touring-5P	1100	2700	3600	5300	8800	19,000

Model 42 — 4-cyl., 40 hp, 118" wb

	FP	5	4	3	2	1
Touring-5P	1500	2900	3700	5600	9100	20,000

Model 52 — 4-cyl., 50 hp, 124" wb

	FP	5	4	3	2	1
Touring-5P	1800	3900	7800	13,000	18,200	27,500

1913 Jackson, Majestic touring, HAC

1913 JACKSON
Olympic — 4-cyl., 27.2 hp, 115" wb

	FP	5	4	3	2	1
Touring-5P	1500	2500	3500	5000	8500	18,000

Majestic — 4-cyl., 32.4 hp, 124" wb

	FP	5	4	3	2	1
Touring-5P	1975	2700	3600	5300	8800	19,000

Sultanic — 6-cyl., 40 hp, 138" wb

	FP	5	4	3	2	1
Touring-7P	2650	2900	3700	5600	9100	20,000
Touring-5P	2500	3000	4000	6000	9500	21,000
Duck (Jackson Back Seat Steer)	—	2700	3600	5300	8800	19,000

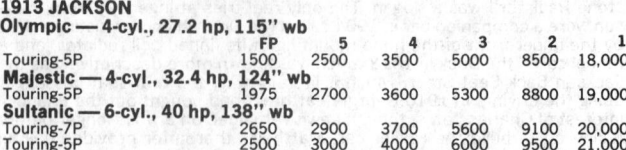

1914 Jackson, Olympic Forty, roadster, HAC

1914 JACKSON
Olympic Forty — 4-cyl., 27.2 hp, 115" wb

	FP	5	4	3	2	1
Touring-5P	1385	2200	3200	4400	7000	15,000

Majestic — 4-cyl., 32.4 hp, 124" wb

	FP	5	4	3	2	1
Touring-5P	1885	2300	3300	4600	7500	16,000

Sultanic — 6-cyl., 40.9 hp, 132" wb

	FP	5	4	3	2	1
Touring-5P	2250	3400	6900	11,500	16,100	23,000
Roadster-2P	2250	2700	3600	5300	8800	19,000
Touring-7P	2300	3500	7050	11,750	16,450	23,500

1915 Jackson, model 48-Six, touring, HAC

1915 JACKSON
Model 44 — 4-cyl., 27.2 hp, 115" wb

	FP	5	4	3	2	1
Touring-5P	1250	2200	3200	4400	7000	15,000
Roadster-3P	1250	2300	3300	4600	7500	16,000

Olympic Model 46 — 4-cyl., 32 hp, 117" wb

	FP	5	4	3	2	1
Touring-5P	1375	2300	3300	4600	7500	16,000
Roadster-3P	1375	2400	3400	4800	8000	17,000

Model 48-Six — 6-cyl., 125" wb

	FP	5	4	3	2	1
Touring-5P	1650	3500	7050	11,750	16,450	23,500

1916 Jackson, model 34, touring, HAC

1916 JACKSON
Model 34 — 4-cyl., 19.6 hp, 112" wb

	FP	5	4	3	2	1
Touring-5P	985	2900	3700	5600	9100	20,000
Touring Sedan-5P	1195	3000	4000	6000	9500	21,000
Roadster-3P	985	3100	4200	6300	10,500	22,000

Model 348 — 8-cyl., 26.45 hp, 112" wb

	FP	5	4	3	2	1
Touring-5P	1195	4200	5200	8400	15,700	29,000
Touring Sedan-5P	1405	4300	5400	8700	16,500	30,000
Roadster-3P	1195	4400	5600	9200	17,300	31,000

Model 68 — 8-cyl., 39.2 hp, 124" wb

	FP	5	4	3	2	1
Touring-7P	1685	4300	5400	8700	16,500	30,000
Touring Sedan-7P	1925	4400	5600	9200	17,300	31,000

1917 Jackson Wolverine, model 349, touring, HAC

1917 JACKSON
Wolverine, Model 349 — 8-cyl., 28.8 hp, 118" wb

	FP	5	4	3	2	1
Touring-5P	1295	4400	5600	9200	17,300	31,000
Roadster-2P	1295	4700	6100	9900	19,000	33,000
Cruiser-4P	1395	4500	5800	9500	18,000	32,000
Sedan-5P	1505	3300	4400	6700	12,000	24,000

1918 Jackson Wolverine VIII Flyer, HAC

1918 JACKSON
Wolverine VIII — 8-cyl., 28.8 hp, 118" wb

	FP	5	4	3	2	1
Flyer-4P	1575	4400	5600	9200	17,300	31,000
Touring-5P	1495	4200	5200	8400	15,700	29,000
Cruiser-4P	1495	4500	5800	9500	18,000	32,000
Roadster-2P	1495	4700	6100	9900	19,000	33,000
Touring-7P	1570	4300	5400	8700	16,500	30,000
Sedan-7P	2195	3300	4400	6700	12,000	24,000

Note 1: No cars were manufactured in 1919.

1920 Jackson, model 6-38, touring, HAC

1920 JACKSON
Model 6-38 — 6-cyl., 55 hp, 121" wb

		5	4	3	2	1
Touring-5P	1885	3000	4000	6000	9500	21,000
Sport Model-4P	2500	3100	4200	6300	10,500	22,000
Sedan-5P	2850	2000	3000	4200	6500	14,000

1921 JACKSON
Model 6-38 — 6-cyl., 55 hp, 121" wb

		5	4	3	2	1
Touring-5P	1950	3000	4000	6000	9500	21,000
Semi-Sport-5P	2350	3100	4200	6300	10,500	22,000
California Special Sport-4P	2785	3300	4400	6700	12,000	24,000
Broadway Special Sport-4P	2685	3200	4300	6500	11,000	23,000
Princess Coupe-4P	3760	2700	3600	5300	8800	19,000
Hollywood Sedan-5P	3760	2200	3200	4400	7000	15,000

1922 JACKSON
Model 6-38 — 6-cyl., 55 hp, 121" wb

		5	4	3	2	1
Touring-5P	1635	3000	4000	6000	9500	21,000
Semi-Sport-5P	1885	3100	4200	6300	10,500	22,000
Broadway Special Sport-4P	2285	3200	4300	6500	11,000	23,000
California Special Sport-5P	2285	3300	4400	6700	12,000	24,000
Princess Coupe-4P	2985	2700	3600	5300	8800	19,000
Hollywood Sedan-5P	2985	2200	3200	4400	7000	15,000

1921 Jackson, model 6-38, "Broadway" Special, HAC

1922-23 Jackson, model 6-38, semi-sport, HAC

1923 JACKSON
Model 6-38 — 6-cyl., 55 hp, 121" wb

	FP	5	4	3	2	1
Touring-5P	1485	3000	4000	6000	9500	21,000
Semi-Sport-5P	1585	3100	4200	6300	10,500	22,000
Broadway Special Sport-4P	1685	3200	4300	6500	11,000	23,000
California Special Sport-5P	1885	3300	4400	6700	12,000	24,000
Princess Coupe-4P	2985	2700	3600	5300	8800	19,000
Hollywood Sedan-5P	2985	2200	3200	4400	7000	15,000

JACOBSON — The Jacobson Motor Company was organized in Jamestown, New York during the fall of 1906 with a capital stock of $100,000 for the manufacture of automobiles. Incorporators were Charles and Jacob Jacobson and G.F. Selstram. Manufacture is doubted.

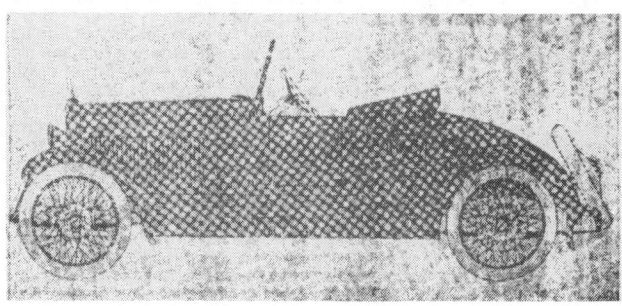

1920 Jacquet Flyer

JACQUET FLYER — Belding, Michigan — (1920) — Infighting killed the Jacquet Flyer before it ever had a chance to become successful. In January 1920 Jacquet Motors Corporation of America was organized with a capitalization of $100,000 for the purpose of manufacturing a high-priced, high-powered sport-roadster that Alfred J. Jackson said would be "the fastest in the world, absolutely barring none." Jackson, whose previous credits had included stints with Napier in England and Pierce-Arrow and Republic trucks in this country, had designed the car and was president of the company. As general manager he brought in L.W. Wilson, formerly superintendent of Timken Axle; Charles Marquet, who had worked for H.H. Franklin and for American Motors in Battle Creek, was placed in charge of experimental work and production. The name for the marque was a coinage derived from Jackson and Marquet. The first car was expected to be completed by March. Designed to out-Bearcat the Stutz, the Jacquet Flyer was powered by a four-cylinder engine generating 82 hp and placed in a 130-inch wheelbase chassis. A sporty two-seater aluminum body and wire wheels were featured. The town of Belding, Michigan was enthusiastic and lent its support; the former Belding Shoe Company building was secured, and the Jacquet people moved in. The first car did not arrive as promised in March. Instead, in June, Alfred Jackson was booted out of his own company; a "vote of confidence" was extended to L.W. Wilson, and Jacquet was reorganized with the citizens of Belding providing more working capital in a new stock subscription. Subsequently, Jackson showed up in Manitowoc (Wisconsin), where he said the Jacquet Flyer would now be built. Wilson immediately denied that rumor, commenting that Jackson had been dismissed by the Jacquet board of directors and no longer had anything to do with the company, but admitting as well that not a single Jacquet Flyer had yet been built. One was soon after, and it was introduced at the Labor Day parade in Belding where it was described as "moving along...like a prince among automobiles." Its sporting potential was "a dog trot gait of between 90 and 100" mph, with higher speeds at the ready. Four more cars were said to be in various stages of construction. The price tag was to be $4000. Meanwhile in a mass meeting of the Belding citizenry the company advised that $50,000 was needed to commence production and invited Belding townspeople to provide it by purchasing further stock. On December 22nd, Jacquet announced that it had "temporarily sidelined" car production to manufacture the B.J. Steam Gas Generator. By March of 1921 the Jacquet Company was producing the Little Giant cement mixer. In August of 1921 Jacquet decided to forget automobile manufacturing altogether. The one Jacquet Flyer which had been completed was turned over to the merchants of Belding who raffled it off. A farmer near Parnell was the winner. He later sold it. What happened to the Jacquet Flyer thereafter is not known.

1933 Jaeger, sport coupe, WLB

JAEGER — Belleville, Michigan — (1932-1933) — In a two-lap trial sprint around a half-mile dirt track in Michigan one day in the early Thirties, a Jaeger Six won handily over a Ford V-8 and a Chevrolet Six. Superior handling in the corners was credited for the performance, this the result of the Jaeger's novel suspension system, two coils in tandem at each wheel separated by the axle mounting. It was an idea patented by Charles F. Jaeger, a Michigan man who spent a lifetime coming up with good ideas. Among his earliest was putting lard, peanut butter, coffee and other products into packages for a food store chain so they could be sold from the shelf rather than over the counter. Later he organized a traveling baseball team (the legendary Satchel Paige was his pitcher), then invented portable power takeoff units for cars and trucks, portable saws and generators, portable water pumps for fire engines — and he even got himself into the adding machine business with Burroughs. All these enterprises made him a fortune. Purportedly, he sold his holdings before the Wall Street crash, which left him with money and time to venture into a field that had always fascinated him. He developed a rotary engine, though it was not as successful as he had hoped. But his novel suspension system held promise. Rather than merely market it, Charles Jaeger decided to market a car on which it would be based. The first prototype, a coupe, was put together in a two-car garage with the help of his sons. In August of 1932 the Jaeger Motor Car Company was incorporated in Belleville, and in November Jaeger announced that he planned small assembly plants all over the country with his Jaeger Six to sell direct to the customer at a price under $700. By October three production cars — all sport coupes on a 113-inch wheelbase — had been built. Surviving invoices indicate a $587 base price, and with a few accessories, license, title and excise tax, a total price tag of $650. Manufacturing cost — including 70 hp Continental engine — was a little over $275. The Jaeger Six gave every promise of being a smashing commercial success. But Charles Jaeger's personal funds were running low, and this was the Great Depression. Securing additional financing was impossible. The Jaeger Six did not survive 1933. Total production, including the prototype, was five cars. Their whereabouts today is not known. Thereafter, Charles Jaeger attempted to sell his suspension set-up to an established manufacturer, but General Motors and Chrysler were by now all set to introduce their own variations on 1934 cars, and Henry Ford wasn't interested. By 1936 Charles Jaeger had another idea and established the Red Arrow Trailer Corporation in East Detroit.

JAFFRAY & BRIGGS — Jaffray & Briggs, Inc., was organized in Rochester, New York early in 1919 with a capital stock of $10,000 for the manufacture, sale and repair of automobiles and motorcycles. Charles L. Briggs and James Jaffray were the partners involved. Manufacture is doubted.

JAMES — The James Auto Company was organized in Syracuse, New York during the fall of 1910 with a capital stock of $25,000 "to deal in accessories and supplies, to manufacture, sell and rent automobiles." F.H. Plumb, F.E. Welch and W.D. Andrews, all of Syracuse, were behind this venture. Manufacture is doubted.

JAMES STEAM — New York, New York — (1829-1830) — In 1829 William T. James demonstrated a wagon powered by steam on the streets of Manhattan. Its engine was a two-cylinder reciprocating unit, but James' subsequent steam engines would be rotaries. The year following he tested a three-wheeled steamer in New York. In 1831 he entered this vehicle in a contest staged by the Baltimore and Ohio Railroad. Though he didn't capture first prize, he did catch the interest of B & O railway executives who offered him an engineering job, which he accepted, utilizing his talents thereafter in the cause of rail and not road transportation.

JAMES — La Crosse, Wisconsin — (1904) — Alfred James was the proprietor of the Pioneer Foundry at Front and King streets in La Crosse. During the summer of 1904 he announced that he would soon begin the manufacture of automobiles. Perhaps a small production did follow, but this has not been documented. The Alfred James Company remained in business at the same address into the 1930's, however.

1909 James, model A, roadster, NAHC

JAMES — Lawrenceburg, Indiana — (1909-1911) — On April 2nd, 1909 a Model A James Roadster made a test run from Lawrenceburg to New Castle about 100 miles away. The trip commenced at high noon; arrival in New Castle, after a stop for supper, was at 8:00 p.m.; a reporter for *Cycle and Automobile Trade Journal* was along. "The James will climb any ordinary hill with two or four passengers and will run easily through mud or sand or, in fact, on any road where the wheels can find a bottom," he said. "The car certainly rides fine and takes the crossings with no jar or bump and negotiates nearly everything on high gear." A highwheeler with 36-inch wheels front and 38-inch in the rear, the James was powered by a two-cylinder air cooled engine, was fitted with a planetary transmission and shaft drive, and was offered in three body styles in a $700-$800 range. It was the product of the J & M Motor Car Company of Lawrenceburg. H.K. James was president and general manager. The name of the James engineer was not recorded, but perhaps there wasn't one. The evidence suggests that the James was as close to a De Tamble as possible without actually being one. Conceivably, Lawrenceburg simply bought chassis from the Anderson, Indiana company and badge-engineered the car into the James. Production in the next year and a half was minimal, and for 1911 J & M decided to market a standard four-cylinder car at more than twice the price. Occasionally, and curiously, this car was referred to as the "Dearborn" model. It was not produced beyond 1911.

1909-1910 JAMES
Highwheeler — 2-cyl., 14/16 hp, 90" wb

	FP	5	4	3	2	1
Model A Rdstr.	700	2300	3300	4600	7500	16,000
Model B Surrey	800	2400	3400	4800	8000	17,000
Model C Rbt.	700	2200	3200	4400	7000	15,000

1911 JAMES
Dearborn — 4-cyl., 35 hp, 108" wb

Touring-5P	1850	2400	3400	4800	8000	17,000

JAMES — Los Angeles, California — (1914) — Irving James of Los Angeles built two cyclecars early in 1914, both with air-cooled T-head engines, one a tandem two-seater with a 36-inch tread, the other a side-by-side "sociable" with a 42-inch tread. In May he stated his "intention of quantity production later on" — but most certainly he never realized it.

JAMESVILLE — The Jamesville Manufacturing Company was organized in Jamesville, New York early in 1904 with a capital stock of $20,000 for the manufacture of bicycles and automobiles. Behind this venture were Albert Spencer and J.H. Olcott of Jamesville, and Herbert Hotaling of Syracuse. No car was forthcoming, though the firm did move into manufacture of bicycles and accessories. In October of 1909 *Motor Field* reported that Jamesville was "making ready to produce motor cars; they will mount a two-cycle, air-cooled engine." Manufacture does not seem to have followed.

JAMIESON STEAM — Rochester, New York — (1899) — Robert W. Jamieson built a steam carriage in 1899 specifically to demonstrate the efficacy of the steering system he had invented and for which he was seeking patents. Most crucial to his device was its self-locking mechanism which, he said, eliminated "the action of the steering lever, commonly expressed as jiggering, and the whipping of the lever from the hand." The Rochester inventor is not known to have built another car.

1899 Jamieson, steam runabout, NAHC

1902 Jamieson, gasoline runabout, FR

JAMIESON — Warren, Pennsylvania — (1902) — Mark W. Jamieson was an industrialist and merchant in Warren and a dabbler in automobiles on the side. In 1902 he built a two-cylinder 7 hp gasoline runabout fitted with double chain drive, tiller steering, high wire wheels and pneumatic tires. He built seven further cars more or less like the first one. But he never contemplated manufacture, building them was simply his hobby. One of these cars remains extant, discovered during the early Fifties in a dairy barn on the old Jamieson property and acquired at that time by D. Cameron Peck. The car has passed through several hands since.

JANNEY — Janney, Steinmetz & Company of Philadelphia has been indicated as an automobile producer at the turn of the century on numerous car rosters. There was such a firm in Philadelphia at the time, located at 4th and Market streets, but it did not manufacture an automobile. Instead, the components field was the focus of its activity. For at least a decade beginning in 1899, Janney, Steinmetz produced gasoline storage tanks, boiler shells, malleable iron castings, tire iron and tubing, et cetera.

JANNEY — Flint, Michigan — (1907) — Though his first name appears lost to history, Janney the man was a naval armaments engineer who had designed large coastal defense guns and who had a yen to build an automobile. Janney the automobile's main claim to fame was its engine, even if it was a failure. William C. Durant, head of the Buick Motor Company, had brought Janney to town with the hope that the automobile he designed might be produced in the Jackson plant he (Durant) had acquired and which he had promised his Flint investors that he would phase out as a Buick factory. The Janney Motor Company was accordingly organized, and Janney designed two models of a light four-cylinder car, two prototype examples of each being built. Its engine had problems, however, and the whole matter was quickly forgotten, the Janney company simply being absorbed by Buick. Thereupon, Buick engineers Walter Marr and Enos DeWaters redesigned the engine. It would power the famous Model 10 Buick. As for Janney, if he was E. Stanton Janney, he would move next to Muncie, Indiana and then Toledo, Ohio where, with Thomas W. Warner, he would try and fail again with an automobile venture called Warner.

1912 Jarvis-Huntington, model M, 8-pass. touring, WLB

JARVIS-HUNTINGTON — Huntington, West Virginia — (1912) — The Jarvis-Huntington Automobile Company was a $100,000 incorporation evolving out of the Jarvis Machinery & Supply Company of Huntington, West Virginia. The incorporators were Mrs. R.J. Poster, G.G. Poster, R.D. Seaman, T.L. Millard and F.C. Pifer. The new venture was organized "to manufacture and sell automobiles and motor trucks and operate a garage." First to arrive was the Jarvis-Huntington car; it was huge and available in two models: a $4000 45 hp six on a 128-inch wheelbase and a $5000 70 hp six on a 142-inch wheelbase. Final drive was by double chain: the transmission was a three-speed selective. The Jarvis-Huntington automobile was on the market for the 1912 model year only. The company's truck building venture was equally short. The record does not indicate how long the garage survived.

1912 JARVIS-HUNTINGTON
Model 6-45 — 6-cyl., 45 hp, 128" wb

	FP	5	4	3	2	1
Fore-Door Touring-7P	4000	3100	4200	6300	10,500	22,000
Fore-Door Roadster	4000	3200	4300	6500	11,000	23,000
Fore-Door Limousine	4000	2500	3500	5000	8500	18,000
Model 6-70 — 6-cyl., 70 hp, 142" wb						
Fore-Door Touring-8P	5000	3500	4500	7000	13,000	25,000
Fore-Door Limousine	5000	2900	3700	5600	9100	20,000

1902 Jaszkowiak, gasoline wagon, JB

1908 Jaszkowiak, gasoline runabout, JB

JASZKOWIAK — Bismarck, North Dakota — (1902-1908) — The first automobile in Bismarck was built by Frank Jaszkowiak. It was a two-seat motor buggy powered by a two-cylinder two-stroke 3 hp engine purchased from Palmer Brothers in Mianus, Connecticut. An article on the car appeared in the April 7th, 1902 edition of the *Bismarck Daily Tribune* which revealed that Jaszkowiak's car was "capable of making eight to ten miles an hour on good level road." Two other cars followed, the last a two-cylinder 20 hp roadster completed in 1908. Frank Jaszkowiak never contemplated manufacture. The cars he built were for family use.

747

1903 Jaxon, surrey, NAHC

JAXON STEAM — Jackson, Michigan — (1903) — The Jackson Automobile Company was organized in Jackson, Michigan in 1902 for the manufacture of both steam and gasoline automobiles. Production began in 1903, and during that year only a steam car was built. Powered by a three-cylinder 6 hp engine, it was available as a $975 Model A runabout on a 72-inch wheelbase and an $800 Model B runabout on a 65-inch wheelbase. The steamer was marketed under the name of Jaxon. The company's gasoline cars, which would be manufactured for two decades, were called Jackson. Designer of both the Jaxon and the early Jacksons was Byron J. Carter, who became more famous as the man behind the friction-drive Cartercar.

1903 JAXON STEAM
Model B — 3-cyl., 6 hp, 65" wb

	FP	5	4	3	2	1
Runabout	800	2200	3200	4400	7000	15,000

Model A — 3-cyl., 6 hp, 72" wb

	FP	5	4	3	2	1
Runabout	975	2300	3300	4600	7500	16,000

JAY STEAM — Frank Jay and his brother, race driver Webb Jay, built a steam car in 1908 which was marketed as the Webb Jay in Chicago. Refer to Webb Jay.

JAY-EYE-SEE — The designation Jay-Eye-See was initially used for a racing special produced by the J.I. Case Threshing Machine Company in 1914. From 1923 through 1927 this phonetic spelling of the company's initials was used to designate varying models of the Case car. Refer to Case.

1908 Jeannin, runabout, WLB

JEANNIN — St. Louis, Missouri — (1908) — H.W. Jeannin claimed that nothing under his car would ever require any attention. Though the Jeannin was a very simple highwheeler with a two-cylinder air-cooled engine, direct shaft bevel gear drive and solid rubber tires, one might imagine something going wrong on occasion. Certainly, something very quickly went wrong for the Jeannin Automobile & Manufacturing Company which was incorporated in 1908 for the car's manufacture. It did not survive into 1909. The car that "Goes and Comes" was the company slogan. The reverse would have been more appropriate.

1908 JEANNIN

Jeannin Runabout	625	2000	3000	4200	6500	14,000
Jeannin Doctor's Car	675	1800	2800	4000	6200	13,000
Jeannin Light Delivery	750	1500	2500	3600	5500	11,000
Jeannin Closed Top Del.	800	1600	2700	3800	5800	12,000

JEFFERSON — The Jefferson Automobile Company was organized in Peoria, Illinois during the fall of 1912 with a capital stock of $30,000 to "manufacture, repair and deal in automobiles and to operate a garage." R.C. Uckena, Frank E. Howland, F.I. Archdale, W.C. Ronneberg and Cedric Howland were behind this venture. Manufacture is doubted.

The Jefferson Four was a single prototype made up of F.R.P. parts in the Port Jefferson, New York factory of the Finlay Robertson Porter Company. It was an attempt by a small group of Long Islanders to carry on the F.R.P. idea after the F.R.P. people had given up on it in 1916. The venture failed almost immediately, however, and the Port Jefferson factory was taken over by the government for war work.

1914 Jeffery, roadster, WLB

JEFFERY — Kenosha, Wisconsin — (1914-1917) — "To the end that his name may remain in the memories of men, we have named our new car the Jeffery." Charles Jeffery was speaking of his father, Thomas Jeffery, the man who had brought the Rambler to Wisconsin and who, as a local historian put it, changed Kenosha "from a prairie to a city." In the years since 1902, Thomas Jeffery had also constructed the largest automobile factory in the United States and had built the Rambler into one of the most respected and successful American automobiles. In 1910 he had died suddenly of a heart attack. Most likely, the principal motivating factor behind Charles Jeffery's decision to rename the car was sentiment; certainly discarding a name as revered as Rambler was a gutsy decision. The Jeffery was a new car, a 40 hp monobloc four on a 118-inch wheelbase and a 48 hp six on a 128-inch chassis. Both models featured left-hand drive, a feature of the first experimental cars built by Charles Jeffery at the turn of the century, but which Thomas Jeffery had decided against for all production Ramblers. New for the Thomas B. Jeffery Company, too, was a truck called the Quad. Production for 1914 totaled 10,417 Jeffery cars and 3096 Jeffery Quads. In 1915 the four was refined, and the six was revised with worm drive — but with the war in Europe, and the likelihood that America would be drawn into it, Charles Jeffery chose to concentrate his company's efforts on trucks, some 7600 of them being produced, with only half that number of the Jeffery cars. In May that year Charles Jeffery embarked upon a trip which would forever change his life. The ship on which he set sail for what was expected to be yet another of his routine fact-finding treks on the Continent was the *Lusitania*. He was one of the 761 survivors of the torpedoes, but the memory of the four harrowing hours he spent in the icy water before being picked up by a trawler remained horrifically in his mind. Conceivably, too, the memory of his father's sudden death brought to him a vivid realization of his own mortality. During the summer of 1916, at the age of forty, he decided to retire, to spend the rest of his life in personal pursuits. Charles Jeffery sold his company to another Charles . . . whose last name was Nash.

1914 JEFFERY
Four, 40 hp, 116" wb

	FP	5	4	3	2	1
5P Tr	1550	1750	4800	8000	11,200	16,000
5P Sed	2350	1075	3000	5500	7700	11,000

Four, 27 hp, 120" wb

2P Rds	1875	2300	5400	9000	12,600	18,000
4P/5P/7P Tr	1875	2000	5100	8500	11,900	17,000

Six, 48 hp, 128" wb

5P Tr	2250	3000	6000	10,000	14,000	20,000
6P Tr	2300	2800	5700	9500	13,300	19,000
7P Limo	3700	1750	4800	8000	11,200	16,000

1915 Jeffery Chesterfield Six, roadster, JAC

1915 JEFFERY
Four, 40 hp, 116" wb

5P Tr	1450	2800	5700	9500	13,300	19,000
2P Rds	1450	3000	6000	10,000	14,000	20,000
2P All-Weather	1750	3150	6300	10,500	14,700	21,000
7P Limo	2900	2000	5100	8500	11,900	17,000
4P Sed	2250	1250	3900	6500	9100	13,000

Chesterfield Six, 48 hp, 122" wb

5P Tr	1650	3150	6300	10,500	14,700	21,000
2P Rds	1650	3300	6600	11,000	15,400	22,000
2P All-Weather	1950	3400	6900	11,500	16,100	23,000

1916 Jeffery Four, touring, JAC

1916 JEFFERY
Four, 40 hp, 116" wb

	FP	5	4	3	2	1
7P Tr	1035	3300	6600	11,000	15,400	22,000
5P Tr	1000	3400	6900	11,500	16,100	23,000
7P Sed	1200	1250	3900	6500	9100	13,000
5P Sed	1165	1150	3600	6000	8400	12,000
3P Rds	1000	3600	7200	12,000	16,800	24,000

Chesterfield Six, 48 hp, 122" wb

| 5P Tr | 1350 | 4050 | 8100 | 13,500 | 18,900 | 27,000 |

1917 Jeffery, touring, JAC

1917 JEFFERY
Model 472, 4-cyl., 40 hp, 116" wb

7P Tr	1095	3150	6300	10,500	14,700	21,000
2P Rds	1065	3300	6600	11,000	15,400	22,000
7P Sed	1260	1150	3600	6000	8400	12,000

Model 671, 6-cyl., 48 hp, 125" wb

7P Tr	1465	3400	6900	11,500	16,100	23,000
3P Rds	1435	3600	7200	12,000	16,800	24,000
5P Sed	1630	1250	3900	6500	9100	13,000

JEM — New York, New York — (1922) — The Jem or Jem Special was built by John E. Meyer of New York City. It carried a six-cylinder 55 hp Continental 7R engine in a 128-inch wheelbase chassis. According to a 1923 edition of the *Automobile Reference Manual*, the car's body style was a two/four-passenger "camping phaeton." Meyer affixed the designation Model A and a price tag of $2500 to his car. Certainly there was no Model B, and possibly only one example of the Model A was built.

JENKINS — Washington, D.C. — (1900-1901) — C. Francis Jenkins was the man behind the Jenkins Automobile Company of 1325 F Street N.W. in Washington, D.C. His principal activity was in the steamer field. In 1900 he produced a small runabout powered by a 2 1/2 hp double-acting steam engine that weighed but 320 pounds dry and was good for a run of twenty miles between stops for water. In addition, he built a steam-powered sixteen-foot-long freight truck and a large passenger-carrying coach. Most likely the electric car he designed in 1901 became better known. With a 24-inch tread and 24-inch wheelbase, this "littlest automobile ever built," as Jenkins claimed it was a victoria specially made for a Cuban midget named Chiquita who was 26 inches tall. Chiquita drove the car as personal transport and in his carnival act. Both he and his vehicle performed during the Pan American Exposition of 1901. The Jenkins Automobile Company appears to have died early in 1902.

1901 Jenkins, electric runabout, NAHC

JENKINS — Rochester, New York — (1907-1912) — J. William Jenkins was a shoe manufacturer from Rochester who moved into the automobile field in 1907 as the Jenkins Motor Car Company. The car he produced was a four with cone clutch, selective transmission and shaft drive. Other than changing wheelbase sizes virtually every model year, the Jenkins remained much the same for the whole of its life. In July of 1912, Jenkins decided he didn't want to be an automobile manufacturer any longer, and he sold out to his chief engineer, Fred J. Decker, who turned the Jenkins plant into a dealership agency for the Cole car.

1908 Jenkins, Special, touring, NAHC

1907 JENKINS
Four — 40/45 hp, 107" wb

	FP	5	4	3	2	1
Touring-5P	3000	2200	3200	4400	7000	15,000

1908 JENKINS
Four — 40/45 hp, 112" wb

Touring-5P	3000	2300	3300	4600	7500	16,000
Town Car	4200	2000	3000	4200	6500	14,000

1909-1910 JENKINS
Four — 40/45 hp, 116" wb

| Touring-5P | 2750 | 2300 | 3300 | 4600 | 7500 | 16,000 |

1911 JENKINS
Four — 40/45 hp, 118" wb

Touring-5P	2750	2400	3400	4800	8000	17,000
Roadster-5P	2750	2500	3500	5000	8500	18,000
Touring-7P	2850	2300	3300	4600	7500	16,000

1912 JENKINS
Four — 38 hp, 119" wb

Touring-7P	2550	2400	3400	4800	7000	17,000
Touring-5P	2500	2500	3500	5000	8500	18,000

JENNEY — New Bedford, Massachusetts — (1899) — Of the automobile built in 1899 by J.A. Jenney of New Bedford, it is known that the motive force was compressed air. And it is probable that the result was not very satisfactory.

JENNINGS — The Jennings Automobile & Manufacturing Company was organized in Jersey City, New Jersey late in 1903 with a capital stock of $500,000 for the manufacture of automobiles. John J. Curtis, Jr. of Honesdale, Pennsylvania; Russell Bonnell of Philadelphia and Edward W. Ward of New York City backed this venture. Manufacture is doubted.

The people behind the Jennings Motor Car Company of Michigan were described only as "influential Detroit businessmen." During the summer of 1910 they were reported to be "dickering with the town officials" of Ecorse "over a site for buildings, with fair prospects of coming to an amiable agreement shortly." It would appear no amiable agreement followed.

1903 Jennis, touring, GR

1908 Jewel, model 40, roadster, NAHC

JENNIS — Flourtown, Pennsylvania — (1903-1905) — The Jennis was something. A large five-passenger touring car powered by a four-cylinder 48 hp engine with automatic intake valves, it featured a three-speed selective transmission, double chain drive, Kells radiator and coachwork by Quinby which included flamboyantly flared aluminum fenders, headlamps imported from France, and enough brass to give an onlooker eyestrain. Only two cars were built, by Peter Jennis, a mechanic from Flourtown. The project required two years; "1903" was stamped on the underside of the chassis, and it is known that the Quinby bodies were fitted in 1905. Financing for the construction of these two cars had been provided by a wealthy Philadelphia businessman, and they were to be the prototypes for the new Jennis, an automobile to take its place among the Locomobile, Pope-Hartford, Peerless and the finest of the European imports. Reportedly, these grand plans came to a sudden halt when the Philadelphia businessman died of a heart attack during the prototype testing period, which apparently was an extensive one. According to an April 1907 issue of *Automobile Topics*, the Jennis Company was only then being formed, and Peter Jennis was described as having built "a few cars for himself and friends ever since 1902." Of the two Jennis cars produced, one remains extant.

JENSEN — C. Jensen, Inc. was organized in New York City during the fall of 1908 with a capital stock of $10,000 for the manufacture of automobiles. Behind this venture were Charles Jensen, Edward B. Wilson and Franklin Lockwood. Manufacture is doubted.

JERSEY CITY — The Argonne was built in Jersey City, New Jersey from 1919 to 1920. An occasional reference has designated the car by the name of the town in which it was manufactured. This has been in error. Refer to Argonne.

JEWEL — The Jewel Carriage Company of Carthage, Ohio produced a car called the Breeze in 1910. Refer to Breeze.

The Jewel Electric Company was organized in Chicago, Illinois during the spring of 1909 with a capital stock of $15,000 to manufacture and deal in automobiles and electrical supplies. Incorporators were Robert K. Phillips, M.C. St. John and M.C. Diller. Manufacture is doubted.

JEWELL — Massillon, Ohio — (1906-1907) / JEWEL — (1908-1909) — In September of 1905, in Cleveland which was known as the "Forest City" a venture called the Forest City Motor Car Company was organized by W.E. Stone, George J. Weitz, Philip Lehr, Frank R. Wall and Charles Eby. A prototype automobile was built, and investors were sought. The latter arrived from Massillon, and so the Forest City Motor Car Company moved out of the "Forest City" and sixty miles to the south. In Massillon the decision was made to call the car a Jewell. It was a single-cylinder highwheeler with rope drive. Its seat and rear deck were hinged so the body could be tilted up for owner ease in maintenance work, the sort of arrangement subsequently popular in truck design. Neither this feature nor the Jewell highwheeler proved popular, so Forest City dropped an "l" from the name of its product and added a new car to its line, a 40 hp four-cylinder (Rutenber) standard model. Early in 1909 the firm's name changed to Jewel Motor Car Company. Late in 1909 the company changed altogether. Herbert A. Croxton who had invested heavily in the firm in 1907, gaining its presidency thereby, was joined by Forrest M. Keeton. Their partnership resulted in the Croxton-Keeton Motor Company and a new car bearing that name.

1906 JEWELL
Jewell — 1-cyl., 8 hp, 60" wb

	FP	5	4	3	2	1
Model B Runabout	400	1800	2800	4000	6200	13,000
Model C Runabout w/top	500	2000	3000	4200	6500	14,000

1907 JEWELL
Jewell — 1-cyl., 8 hp, 68" wb

	FP	5	4	3	2	1
Model D Runabout	600	1800	2800	4000	6200	13,000
Model E	800	1900	2900	4100	6400	13,500

1908 JEWEL
Highwheeler — 1-cyl., 10 hp, 70" wb

	FP	5	4	3	2	1
Model D Runabout	500	2000	3000	4200	6500	14,000
Model E Stanhope	750	2100	3100	4300	6800	14,500

Model 40 — 4-cyl., 40 hp, 120" wb

	FP	5	4	3	2	1
Touring-5P	3000	2500	3500	5000	8500	18,000

1909 JEWEL
Four — 4-cyl., 20/30 hp, 111" wb

	FP	5	4	3	2	1
Jewel-Keeton Taxicab-5P	3450	2000	3000	4200	6500	14,000
Jewel-Keeton Landaulet/Brgm.-4P		2300	3300	4600	7500	16,000
Jewel-Keeton Suburban-5P	2800	2200	3200	4400	7000	15,000

Four — 4-cyl., 40 hp, 120" wb

	FP	5	4	3	2	1
Model G Tour.-5P	3000	2500	3500	5000	8500	18,000
Model K Rds.-3P	3000	2700	3600	5300	8800	19,000
Model H Limo.-7P	4000	2300	3300	4600	7500	16,000

JEWETT — In December 1901 in Columbus, Ohio, the Jewett Motor Carriage Company was incorporated with a capital stock of $25,000 for manufacture of automobiles in Harrison County near Jewett. Incorporators were S.F. Switzer, O.A. Schweitzer, A.G. Messe, Burton S. Moore and F.B. Schlafly. The following summer the firm announced its relocation from Jewett to Beach City. Manufacture has not been documented.

1922 Jewett, touring, HAC

JEWETT — Detroit, Michigan — (1922-1927) — Jewett Motors, Inc. was a wholly-owned subsidiary of the Paige-Detroit Motor Car Company and was organized in December of 1921 for the manufacture of a popularly priced six-cylinder car that would be built in the Paige-Detroit factory and sold through the Paige dealership network. Like the Erskine built by Studebaker, the Jewett built by Paige-Detroit was named after the parent company's president. "In beauty, in comfort and in performance, we feel that the new car will be a real and pleasant surprise," Harry M. Jewett commented at the press introduction, and the Jewett was that. A handsome automobile, it proved popular immediately, and body styles proliferated quickly. With the arrival of hydraulic four-wheel brakes for 1926, Jewett declared a "New Day" for his car, and that designation was used thereaf-

1906 Jewell, model B, runabout, JAC

ter. But the New-Day Jewett also represented the last days for the marque. In January 1927, after the production of 40,000 Jewetts, the name was dropped, and the car became simply another model of the Paige, the 6-45.

1922 JEWETT
Six — 50 hp, 112" wb

	FP	5	4	3	2	1
Touring-5P	1065	2500	3500	5000	8500	18,000
Sedan-5P	1395	2000	3000	4200	6500	14,000

1923 JEWETT
Six — 50 hp, 112" wb

Touring-5P	995	2500	3500	5000	8500	18,000
Roadster-2P	995	2700	3600	5300	8800	19,000
Sedan-5P	1465	1800	2800	4000	6200	13,000
Coupe-4P	1445	2200	3200	4400	7000	15,000

1924 Jewett, touring, HAC

1924 JEWETT
Six — 50 hp, 112" wb

Touring-5P	1065	2500	3500	5000	8500	18,000
Special Roadster-3P	1195	2700	3600	5300	8800	19,000
Brougham-5P	1325	2000	3000	4200	6500	14,000
Sedan-5P	1495	1800	2800	4000	6200	13,000
Special Sedan-5P	1695	1900	2900	4100	6400	13,500
Special Touring-5P	1220	2700	3600	5300	8800	19,000

1925 Jewett, 2-dr. sedan, WLB

1925 JEWETT
Six — 50 hp, 112" wb

Special Touring-5P	1315	2500	3500	5000	8500	18,000
Standard Touring Rds.-5P	1135	2700	3600	5300	8800	19,000
Special Sedan-5P	1770	1800	2800	4000	6200	13,000
Standard Sedan-5P	1570	1600	2700	3800	5800	12,000
Special Brougham-5P	1550	1800	2800	4000	6200	13,000
Standard Brougham-5P	1410	1600	2700	3800	5800	12,000
Coupe-3P	1335	2200	3200	4400	7000	15,000

1926 Jewett, sedan, HAC

1926-1927 JEWETT
New-Day — 6-cyl., 40 hp, 112" wb

	FP	5	4	3	2	1
Deluxe Touring-5P	1095	2700	3600	5300	8800	19,000
Standard Sedan-5P	995	1800	2800	4000	6200	13,000
Deluxe Sedan-5P	1095	2000	3000	4200	6500	14,000

J.H.N. — **St. Louis, Missouri** — **(1903)** — The J.H.N. was one of a number of kit cars produced by J.H. Neustadt's Neustadt-Perry Company of St. Louis. A touring car with a Renault-type front and a removable rear seat, it was advertised during 1903. J.H. Neustadt was in the kit car business from 1901 through 1907, offering other varieties under catchy designations like Bluff Climber, and also under the Neustadt name.

JILEK — **Devils Lake, North Dakota** — **(1903)** — In 1903 Joseph Jilek of Devils Lake completed the automobile he had begun building the year before. Details regarding its construction are lacking, but Jilek did apply for three patents for various aspects of its design.

J.L.B. — The J.L.B. Motor Car Company was the linear successor to the Dayton Electric Car Company of Dayton, Ohio and was established in 1915 to complete cars for which parts remained in stock and to handle the business of supplying parts for the Dayton electric. Refer to Dayton.

JOERNS-THIEM — **St. Paul, Minnesota** — **(1910)** — Early in 1910 Fred Joerns and Edward A. Thiem joined together as the Joerns-Thiem Motor Car Company of St. Paul and moved into the plant formerly occupied by the Brace Furniture Company at 2237 Hampden Avenue. Thiem was an engine producer who had marketed a few motor buggies under his own name at the turn of the century and who later had run up a few motorcycles too. Joerns most likely put up the capital for this venture which was organized to manufacture cars and trucks. Production of both was minimal, and probably consisted entirely of small runabouts and light deliveries. The Joerns-Thiem did not reappear in the 1911 model year.

JOHANNES — Jacob Johannes was a carriagemaker in St. Paul, Minnesota who announced during the summer of 1909 that he planned to build automobiles alongside his traditional product. Documentation that he indeed did do this is lacking.

JOHN BERRY — The John Berry Automobile Company was organized in St. Louis, Missouri early in 1913 with a capital stock of $20,000 to manufacture, rebuild and repair automobiles. John Berry was joined in this venture by Louis J. Koenigstein and Albert Bommer. Manufacture is doubted.

JOHNSON — C.F. Johnson was city engineer for Stephen, Minnesota in 1908 during which year, according to *The Horseless Age*, he built a "motor runabout" and gave it a trial. Further details are lacking.
The Charles M. Johnson Company was organized in Chicago, Illinois during the fall of 1906 with a capital stock of $2000 for the manufacture of automobiles. Johnson does not seem to have proceeded into production.
Daniel E. Johnson of Hartford, Connecticut purportedly built an automobile in 1913. Documentation is lacking.
Elmer F. Johnson of Kalkaska, Michigan built a total of seven automobiles in his Cedar Street bicycle shop from 1898-c.1906. Refer to Elmer.
The Iver Johnson Arms & Cycle Works of Fitchburg, Massachusetts announced early in 1900 its plans to enter the steam automobile field. Fred I. Johnson visited Boston in March to check out the equipment available on the market. "The company intends to build steam vehicles of all descriptions and is well supplied with machinery to make most of the parts required," reported *The Motor Age*. "At first it is the intention to purchase boilers and engines in the open market, but ultimately nearly every factor of their carriages will be made in Fitchburg." Manufacture of a car does not seem to have followed, although the company did enter the components building field.
The Johnson Brothers Motor Company was organized in Terre Haute, Indiana early in 1913 with a capital stock of $70,000 for the manufacture of automobiles, motors and aeroplanes. Demas Deming and Charles Minall, who were described as "two well-known financiers," were backing this venture. Manufacture is doubted.
The Johnson Motor Car Company at 326 North Broad Street in Philadelphia, Pennsylvania was an automobile dealership and a family affair, with James H. Johnson as president, C.R. Johnson as treasurer and J. Howard Johnson as secretary. In 1911 the Johnson brothers purportedly built themselves a steam car, but for their own amusement only, with no intention of manufacture.
In 1902 at the Johnson-Jennings Company in Cleveland, Ohio, one T.J. Calhoun experimented with the building of an automobile. Further details are lacking.

JOHNSON STEAM — **Philadelphia, Pennsylvania** — **(c.1828)** — "An oddly arranged and rudely constructed machine" was the description given to the steam carriage built by Nicholas and James Johnson in Philadelphia circa 1828. It was powered by a horizontal single-cylinder engine with a boiler that looked like a big beer bottle. The Johnson brothers tested their car in Philadelphia on at least several occasions, and it ran — but once it ran away from them. According to a book published in 1872 entitled *The Locomotive Engine and Philadelphia's Share in Its Improvement*, after the car had turned up Brown Street, "its course could not be changed quick enough, and before it could be stopped it had mounted the curbstone, smashed the awning posts, and had make a demonstration against the bulk window of a house at the southwest corner of Brown and Oak Streets." This was probably America's first automobile accident. Following it, the vehicle was not seen again on the streets of Philadelphia.

JOHNSON STEAM — Uniontown, Pennsylvania — (1896) — The first and only automobile built in the city of Uniontown was a steamer designed and constructed by Charley Johnson in 1896. Although he never built another automobile, it was Charley Johnson who was subsequently the man most responsible for the building of the famous Uniontown Speedway.

1918 Johnson Special, Hayden Shepley

JOHNSON — Beverly, Massachusetts — (1903, 1918) — Ingenuity was Ernest Johnson's forte. The first car he built, in 1903, was made up of a marine engine, four bicycle wheels and divers parts from mowing machines and plows. His second, a cyclecar in 1918, used more sophisticated components: a Chevrolet 490 transmission, Timken bearings, and an air-cooled engine later replaced with an Argo four, and still later with a Willys four. Its hood was from a 1908 Simplex, gas and spark controls from a Pierce of the same year; and the gas tank was fashioned from a piece of metal from the roof of a building at M.I.T. For most of his life, Ernest Johnson was, in one way or another, in the business of cars: He worked in the Cameron factory when it was in Beverly, and later he was a chauffeur. The Johnson cyclecar is believed to remain extant.

1906 Johnson, steam auto-carriage, HAC

JOHNSON — Milwaukee, Wisconsin — (1905-1912) — In the 1880's, while teaching at Wisconsin's Whitewater State College, natural science professor Warren S. Johnson become bored with the necessity of ringing a bell down to the furnace room whenever his students complained of being too hot or too cold. So he connected electrodes to a mercury thermometer — and invented the electric thermostat. Years later H.L. Mencken called Johnson "one of the great benefactors of humanity," likening him to Marconi, Edison and Bell. Though he has not enjoyed the historical renown of that trio, Warren Johnson's thermostats earned him worldwide acclaim and a healthy fortune by the turn of the century. By then he had become an enthusiast of the automotive age as well. In 1901 his Johnson Service Company of Milwaukee built a one-ton steam truck which served the firm well until a careless driver loaded it with about two tons of sheet iron. Heavier axles for his second truck solved that problem, and Johnson followed with a third (a three-ton moving van) and a fourth (a coal-hauling steamer for the Pfister-Vogel tannery). Subsequently, in collaboration with D.C. Owen, the Milwaukee postmaster, a steamer was designed for mail collection. Eight such vehicles were produced, and these were among the first ever specifically contracted for by the U.S. Postal Service. The Pabst Brewing Company bought a steam truck as well. Success in the commercial field prompted Warren Johnson to expand in 1905 into the manufacture of passenger cars for "touring in civilized countries by civilized tourists." Ten steam limousines were produced in the next two years, their amenities including an arrangement by which the tourists could cook their meals on the boiler. Ten touring car steamers followed. In 1908 Johnson turned to gasoline automobile manufacture, selling the cars under such model designations as Empress and Elite. He called his entire line for 1911 the Silent Johnson. These were big cars of 30, 40 and 50 hp, and many were custom built to order. Commercial production now included a fire

truck, a trolley-wire maintenance wagon, a sightseeing bus, portable stone crushers, ambulances, hearses and street-cleaning equipment. On December 4th, 1911, Warren Johnson died, and the Johnson motorcar building adventure died with him. Probably because a Minneapolis company (eventually to become Honeywell) was now providing stiff competition with its version of a thermostat (invented, like the Johnson, in 1885), all efforts of the Milwaukee firm returned to the field of automatic temperature control systems.

1905-1906 JOHNSON
Steam — 4-cyl., 30 hp, 108" wb

	FP	5	4	3	2	1
Auto-Carriage Limousine	5000	3300	4400	6700	12,000	24,000

1907 Johnson, steam touring, HAC

1907 JOHNSON
Steam — 4-cyl., 30 hp, 112" wb

Touring-5P	2500	3200	4300	6500	11,000	23,000

1908 Johnson, gasoline touring, HAC

1909 Johnson, gasoline limousine, HAC

1908-1909 JOHNSON
Four — 25 hp, 102" wb

Special Runabout-2P	1475	2300	3300	4600	7500	16,000
Special Touring-4P	1500	2400	3400	4800	8000	17,000
"Solid Comfort Car"-5P	2500	2500	3500	5000	8500	18,000
Four — 35 hp, 112" wb						
Elite Tonneau-5P	2500	3000	4000	6000	9500	21,000
Limousine	3500	2500	3500	5000	8500	18,000
Landaulet	3500	2700	3600	5300	8800	19,000
Four — 50 hp, 122" wb						
Limousine-8P	4000	2700	3600	5300	8800	19,000
Landaulet-7P	4000	2900	3700	5600	9100	20,000
Elite Tonneau-7P	3000	3100	4200	6300	10,500	22,000

1910 Johnson, Empress touring, WLB

1910 JOHNSON
Four — 30 hp, 112" wb

	FP	5	4	3	2	1
Special Touring-5P	1500	2400	3400	4800	8000	17,000
Elite Touring-5P (40 hp)	2500	2500	3500	5000	8500	18,000
Empress — 4-cyl., 50 hp, 124" wb						
Touring-7P	3000	3400	6900	11,500	16,100	23,000

1911 Johnson, Silent Four special touring, HAC

1911 JOHNSON
Silent Four — 30 hp, 112" wb

Fore-Door Touring	3100	2700	3600	5300	8800	19,000
Touring	1600	2400	3400	4800	8000	17,000
Silent Four — 40 hp, 112" wb						
Touring-5P	2500	2500	3500	5000	8500	18,000
Limousine	3500	2200	3200	4400	7000	15,000
Silent Four — 50 hp, 124" wb						
Touring-7P	3000	3600	7200	12,000	16,800	24,000
Fore-Door Touring-7P	3100	2900	3700	5600	9100	20,000
Limousine	4000	2300	3300	4600	7500	16,000

1912 Johnson, model B, touring, HAC

1912 JOHNSON
Model A — 4-cyl., 30 hp, 112" wb

Open Touring	1600	2300	3300	4600	7500	16,000
Fore-Door Touring	1600	2400	3400	4800	8000	17,000
Runabout	1600	2300	3300	4600	7500	16,000
Model B — 4-cyl., 40 hp, 112" wb						
Open Touring	2500	2400	3400	4800	8000	17,000
Fore-Door Touring	2500	3300	6600	11,000	15,400	22,000
Model C — 4-cyl., 50 hp, 124" wb						
Fore-Door Touring	3100	3400	6750	11,250	16,100	23,000
Open Touring-7P	3000	3500	7000	11,750	16,500	24,000

JOHNSTON — Manchester, New Hampshire — (1902 et seq) — James H. and Carl D. Johnston were the proprietors of the Johnston Gasoline Motor Company located at West Auburn and the corner of Canal in Manchester. Although they advertised themselves as producing "stationary, portable, marine and automobile engines, motor carriages, running gears...supplies and repairing," it would appear that repair and mainte-

nance work was the crux of their operation. No doubt, a few automobiles were built by the Johnstons for local clients, but this was strictly a sideline activity. References extant indicate that the company may have been in business through 1907.

JOHNSTOWN — That automobiles were planned to be made in Johnstown, Pennsylvania was revealed late in 1905 when *The Motor Way* reported the granting of a charter to the Johnstown Automobile Company which had been capitalized at $10,500 for the purpose of locating its factory there. Manufacture did not follow. In the early 1920's the Wharton Motors Company of Dallas, Texas considered Johnstown as an automobile manufacturing site, but again plans fell through.

JOLIET — The Joliet Automobile and Garage Company was organized early in 1904 with a capital stock of $25,000 to "manufacture and repair automobiles and horseless vehicles" in Joliet, Illinois. Backing this venture were H.A. Fisher, L.D. Fisher and C.S. Munroe. Manufacture is doubted.

JONAS — "A disastrous fire broke out in the warehouse of the Jonas Automobile Company, Milwaukee, Wisconsin on May 20th," reported *The Motor World* in 1904. "Fifteen automobiles and two buggies were destroyed, causing a loss of $17,000. Of this $14,000 is covered by insurance." The Jonas company dropped from sight soon after, and some question remains whether the cars in the fire had been built by Jonas or by another manufacturer.

JONES — That C.H. Jones of Columbus Grove, Ohio had automotive ambitions was revealed by *The Motor Vehicle Review* during the fall of 1899 in its report that Jones was organizing a $25,000 company for automobile manufacture. Manufacture did not follow, however.

The J.W. Jones Sons Company was organized in Watervliet, New York early in 1911 with a capital stock of $100,000 for the manufacture of automobiles and railroad cars. Incorporators were John H. Jones, James H. McLeese, Floyd R. Jones and Paul R. Jones. Manufacture of a car is doubted.

The Jones Taximeter Company of Chicago, Illinois was organized late in 1909 with a capital stock of $20,500 to manufacture and deal in taxicabs and other vehicles. Incorporators were A.R. Hurburt, S.S. Gorham and H.H. Wales. Manufacture of a car is doubted.

JONES STEAM — New York, New York — (1899) — In 1899, in the shop in which he worked on Houston Street on the Lower East Side of Manhattan, Joseph W. Jones completed the steam automobile he had begun the year before. A runabout with dos-a-dos seats, it was fitted with an automatic reversible valve engine, a kerosene burner and a flash boiler. Although Jones patented some of the car's features, he was not destined to consider manufacture. Something better came along. On one of the drives in his steamer, his wife happened to ask him how fast they were going. Jones couldn't tell her, whereupon she suggested that he make a device that could. Thus it was that Joseph W. Jones invented the first speedometer to be used on an automobile. His further inventions in the automobile accessory field included the "Jones Live Map" and the Jones taximeter. But it was the Jones speedometer (and he coined that word, incidentally) which made him rich and famous.

JONES — Xenia, Ohio — (1899) — Although the Baldner brothers of Xenia have frequently been cited as the builders of the first automobile in that Ohio town, the first automobile in Xenia was in fact the work of Isaac B. Jones of 31 Trumbull Street. Jones was a prolific inventor whose inventions included a cultivator and riding plow, a power ditching machine, a patented buck saw, a cutting box for feed or stock and a potato digger. Shortly before the turn of the century, he designed and built a gasoline automobile which did run but had two difficulties. According to a resident of Xenia, who was an eyewitness and who was interviewed by the *Evening Gazette* of Xenia in 1946, "One [difficulty] was that his engine was not large enough and second his transmission of power from the engine to the rear axle was accomplished by means of two cones and a leather belt made up in the form of a ring which ran between them. By this means he was able to vary the speed of the automobile." But not very well, apparently. Isaac Jones' principal problem, however, was his inability to secure the capital necessary to develop his automobile. Although the Baldners did proceed into production with their Baldner, Isaac Jones was not able to do the same with his car. He died in 1904.

JONES — Bridgeport, Connecticut — (1902) — Early in 1902, A.B. Jones of Lebanon, Pennsylvania traveled to Bridgeport, Connecticut and there, according to *The Motor Age*, "designed and had set up under his personal supervision a complete automobile." The car was built in the shops of L.E. Longevir, with he and A.B. Jones doing all the work to finish the machine themselves.

JONES — Philadelphia, Pennsylvania — (1905) — Lewis Jones was a machinist in Philadelphia who built a gasoline automobile in 1905 in his shop on North Edgewood at the corner of Media. Experimental reasons only lay behind its building; manufacture was not contemplated. Lewis Jones seems to have been an inveterate tinkerer. His earliest automotive patent was in 1900, an "igniter for explosive engines."

JONES — New England, North Dakota — (1910) — This Jones car was a two-seater with a 5 hp engine driven by belt and chain. W.N. Jones completed it in New England in 1910. Further details are lacking.

753

1913 Jones, roadster, NAHC

JONES — Leslie, Georgia — (1913) — J.L. Jones operated an automobile garage out of his barn in Leslie and in December 1913 finished building what he believed was a better cyclecar. Probably he was right. For its chassis, he used an old Demotcar which he revised with a two-cylinder 9 hp DeLuxe engine and two-speed planetary transmission. He retained the 80-inch wheelbase of the Demotcar but shortened the tread to 36 inches, and built his own sprightly little roadster body. The car complete weighed 980 pounds and was good for 30 mph. J.L. Jones believed a good market existed for a car like his, though he hadn't the wherewithal for manufacture, since the total workforce of his garage consisted of one young black man. But he offered advice to potential cyclecar builders whom he believed were making an error in removing so many essentials of commodious motoring in designing their cars. "An automobile is a good deal like a watch," he wrote. "If a watch could keep good time with only half the number of wheels as a standard watch, it would prove beyond a doubt that the standard watch had too many wheels, for what the buyer wants is 'time' and not wheels, but he recognizes the fact that in order to get 'good time' he is compelled to buy a certain number of wheels." And that was a very nice bit of down-home philosophy.

1917 Jones, touring, WLB

JONES — Wichita, Kansas — (1914-1920) — John J. Jones was an Iowa farm boy who labored in the oil fields of Oklahoma and Kansas before settling down in Wichita shortly after the turn of the century to make his fortune. A furniture store was his first business, but it was quickly replaced by the Jones-Sparks Auto Exchange, a used car emporium which prospered and paved the way for Jones becoming the Ford dealer for Wichita in 1910. He made over $125,000 selling Model T's, and in 1914 was ready to strike out on his own. With the help of a Wichita mechanic named Carl Evans, who earlier had assisted him in used car restorations, Jones came up with a medium-priced six (Continental Red Seal engine) that he thought sure would be a best-seller. His Jones Motor Car Company was established in 1914, largely with his own funds. His car proved so successful immediately that in October of 1915 money men from the East became interested, and the firm was capitalized at $500,000. In October of 1917 this figure was increased to $2,500,000. In six years approximately 3000 Jones Sixes were built. Peak employment was 985 workers, a goodly number of whom worked on the Jones truck which also proved popular. In one corner of John Jones' plant, a man named Clyde Cessna built his first airplane. Although Jones vehicles were sold worldwide, it was the domestic market which received the emphasis. In 1919 Jones introduced the Oil Field Special, a roadster-pickup with a drill bit rack on the rear deck. He also sold a number of flamboyantly painted custom cars to oil-rich Oklahoma Indians. A few more special-built Joneses found their way into Hollywood garages. Things were moving along splendidly for John J. Jones until February 20th, 1920 when a fire broke out at his factory. Fourteen completed cars and 100 bodies were destroyed. Operations resumed the following week, but the Jones Motor Car Company was mortally wounded. The fire, combined with the postwar recession, killed the firm. In August creditors asked for a receiver.

1914-1915 JONES
Six — 21.6 hp, 118" wb

	FP	5	4	3	2	1
Touring-5P	995	2500	3500	5000	8500	18,000

1916 JONES
Six — 21.6 hp, 118" wb

	FP	5	4	3	2	1
Touring-5P	1150	2500	3500	5000	8500	18,000

1917 JONES
Six — 29 hp, 125" wb

	FP	5	4	3	2	1
Touring-5P	1475	2500	3500	5000	8500	18,000
Roadster-2P	1475	2700	3600	5300	8800	19,000
Touring Sedan-5P	2350	1600	2700	3800	5800	12,000

1918 Jones Six, victoria touring, HAC

1918 JONES
Six — 29 hp, 125" wb

	FP	5	4	3	2	1
Touring-5P	1675	2500	3500	5000	8500	18,000
Roadster-4P	1675	2700	3600	5300	8800	19,000
Sedan-7P	2550	1600	2700	3800	5800	12,000
Victoria-4P	1775	2000	3000	4200	6500	14,000

1919 JONES
Six — 29.6 hp, 126" wb

	FP	5	4	3	2	1
Roadster-4P	2100	2700	3600	5300	8800	19,000
Touring-7P	2100	2500	3500	5000	8500	18,000
Speedster-4P	2350	3000	4000	6000	9500	21,000
Oil Field Special	2000	2400	3400	4800	8000	17,000

1920 Jones Six, speedster type, HAC

1920 JONES
Six — 29.6 hp, 126" wb

	FP	5	4	3	2	1
Touring-5P	2250	2900	3700	5600	9100	20,000
Touring-7P	2250	2700	3600	5300	8800	19,000
Speedster-4P	2350	3100	4200	6300	10,500	22,000
Victoria-5P	2350	2200	3200	4400	7000	15,000
Victoria-7P	2350	2000	3000	4200	6500	14,000
Roadster-5P	2250	2900	3700	5600	9100	20,000
Roadster-2P	2250	3000	4000	6000	9500	21,000
Oil Field Special	2000	2500	3500	5000	8500	18,000

1903 Jones-Corbin, model A, runabout, NAHC

JONES-CORBIN — Philadelphia, Pennsylvania — (1903-1907) — George H. Jones and E.O. Corbin, Jr. unabashedly acknowledged their debt to Europe in the manufacture of their cars. Single- and two-cylinder "genuine De Dion" engines were featured, as well as the "latest Mercedes cooling device" and a "large size imported horn." Jones and Corbin contributed their own amusingly-named "Neverout dash lamps and rear signal." From $1000 in 1903, prices soared to the $4500 range in 1906 with the introduction of a more powerful four-cylinder car. In late 1903 the Jones-Corbin Company had declared bankruptcy and promptly reorganized as the Jones-Corbin Automobile Company. By 1907 Jones-Corbin had sold out to Matthews Motor Company of Camden (New Jersey), and from this firm came a new car called the Sovereign.

1903 JONES-CORBIN
Model A — 1-cyl., 8 hp, 78" wb

	FP	5	4	3	2	1
Runabout-2P	1000	2000	3000	4200	6500	14,000

1904 Jones-Corbin, model A, runabout, HAC

1904-1905 JONES-CORBIN
Model A — 1-cyl., 8 hp, 78" wb

Runabout-2P	1250	2000	3000	4200	6500	14,000

Model B — 2-cyl., 14 hp, 78" wb

Runabout-2P	1350	2200	3200	4400	7000	15,000
Tonneau-4P	1500	2300	3300	4600	7500	16,000
Canopy Top Touring-5P	1650	2400	3400	4800	8000	17,000

1906-1907 JONES-CORBIN
Model L — 4-cyl., 45 hp, 110" wb

Side Entrance Tonneau	4500	2400	3400	4800	8000	17,000
Limousine	5000	2500	3500	5000	8500	18,000

1909 Jonz, Three, roadster, NAHC

JONZ — Beatrice, Nebraska & New Albany, Indiana — (1909-1912) — Chester Charles Jones was a Nebraska automobile dealer who was arrested on the streets of Beatrice in 1906 for exceeding the town's 6 mph speed limit and who in 1908 applied for a patent on a two-stroke gasoline engine that he described as "new and useful" because of its mere five movable parts and the fact that it was air cooled from inside the cylinder. With his brother Ellsworth, a local druggist, he organized the Jonz Automobile Company later during 1908. A three-cylinder Jonz runabout was reportedly ready for the Chicago Automobile Show early in 1909, but already the Jones brothers were in financial trouble. They allied themselves with another automobile dealership and a lawnmower company in Beatrice, but still there wasn't enough money available locally to get the enterprise going. Outside capital arrived in late 1910 from Berton B. Bales of Louisville, Kentucky. The American Automobile Manufacturing Company resulted, and all Jonz machinery was moved from Beatrice to a new factory in New Albany, Indiana, just across the river from Louisville. And stock subscriptions were sought. "The prospectus issued was one of the most elaborate and most extravagant that ever has seen the light," *The Motor World* commented in 1912. "Among other things it contained the portraits of everyone connected with the company, from the president almost to the office boy . . . While the portraits of at least some of the officials were handsome to look upon, the letterpress of the book was its chief charm; it was a masterpiece of word-juggling." An estimated eight to nine thousand people bought what it said and invested in the company.

The chief selling point of the Jonz was its "vapor-cooled" engine. Promotion extolled that it "has no valves, no cams, no gears, no push-rods, no rollers, no rocker arms, no pumps, no radiator and no water." The car in which it was fitted was dubbed "The Tranquil Jonz." Apparently, it was too tranquil. One New Albany man who witnessed a test demonstration at the factory reported that the Jonz refused to run more than a hundred yards or so before serenely coming to a halt. This may have been an extreme, or isolated case, but it was obvious the Jonz engine was something of a lemon. Reportedly, Continental engines were imported, and the few cars that were produced in New Albany before the company went into receivership in March 1912 were shipped out of town. At least one Beatrice Jonz is known to exist, but the number of cars which may survive from the Indiana operation is not known. In January 1913 what was left of Jonz was purchased by Fred Kahler who built the Pilgrim in the same factory.

1909 JONZ
Three — 3-cyl., 30/35 hp, 96" wb

	FP	5	4	3	2	1
Roadster-4P	1000	2300	3300	4600	7500	16,000
Touring-5P	1000	2200	3200	4400	7000	15,000

Three — 40/45 hp, 111" wb

Touring-5P	1650	2500	3500	5000	8500	18,000

Twin — 2-cyl., 20/25 hp, 111" wb

Runabout-2P	850	2300	3300	4600	7500	16,000

1910 JONZ
Twin — 2-cyl., 20 hp, 80" wb

Model J Runabout-2P	750	2200	3200	4400	7000	15,000
Model O Roadster-4P	1000	2400	3400	4800	8000	17,000
Model N Touring-5P (105" wb)	1500	2300	3300	4600	7500	16,000

1911 Jonz, model A, runabout, JAC

1911 JONZ
Model A — 2-cyl., 20 hp, 90" wb

Runabout-2P	825	2200	3200	4400	7000	15,000

Model B — 3-cyl., 30 hp, 104" wb

Demi-Tonneau	1150	2400	3400	4800	8000	17,000
Taxicab	1150	1800	2800	4000	6200	13,000
Light Delivery	1250	1600	2700	3800	5800	12,000

Model C — 4-cyl., 40 hp, 120" wb

Toy Tonneau	1750	2500	3500	5000	8500	18,000
Touring-5P	1850	2700	3600	5300	8800	19,000
Touring-7P	2000	2500	3500	5000	8500	18,000
Coupe	2000	2200	3200	4400	7000	15,000
Limousine	2500	2300	3300	4600	7500	16,000

1912 JONZ
Model A — 2-cyl., 20 hp, 96" wb

Runabout	750	2300	3300	4600	7500	16,000

Model B — 3-cyl., 30 hp, 104" wb

Touring-5P	1200	2400	3400	4800	8000	17,000
Demi-Tonneau	1200	2500	3500	5000	8500	18,000
Taxicab	1500	2000	3000	4200	6500	14,000

Model D — 4-cyl., 40 hp, 120" wb

Touring-5P	2000	2500	3500	5000	8500	18,000

Model C — 4-cyl., 40 hp, 120" wb

Touring	2500	2700	3600	5300	8800	19,000
Torpedo	2500	2800	3700	5500	9000	19,500
Limousine	2500	2300	3300	4600	7500	16,000
Coupe	2250	2200	3200	4400	7000	15,000

JOO — The Raymond S. Joo Company was organized in Newark, New Jersey early in 1907 with a capital stock of $25,000 for the manufacture of automobiles. Joining Joo in this venture was Julius Koch. Manufacture is doubted.

JORDAN — Cleveland, Ohio — (1917-1931) — There had to be a Jordan, if for no other reason than to allow Ned Jordan unfettered license in the prose he chose to extol it. And how the man could write, lyrically, romantically, emotionally. Never before had automobiles been written about thusly. Somehow one gets the idea Jordan knew this was what he wanted to do long before he had the chance to do it. Edward S. Jordan was born in 1882 in Merrill, a Wisconsin lumber town; he worked his way through the University of Wisconsin as a newspaper reporter, and soon thereafter met one of the Jeffery girls from Kenosha. Though she was old enough to be his mother, he married her and became advertising manager of the Thomas B. Jeffery Automobile Company in 1906. Both his marriage and his sojourn at Jeffery provided him the opportunity to make enough friends with enough capital for him to strike out on his own. And in January 1916 the Jordan Motor Car Company was duly established in Cleveland, Ohio — and Ned Jordan was all set to go. His idea was an assembled car (mechanics never interested him much) with the look of a custom car and the highest quality standard components in the industry: Continental

1917 Jordan, roadster, AA

engine, Bosch ignition, Stromberg carburetion, Fedders radiator, Bijur electrics, Gemmer steering, Brown Lipe clutch, Stewart-Warner vacuum fuel feed, Sparton electric horn. All this made for a nice package, but probably it was the racy wire wheels provided as standard equipment on the first Jordans that Ned liked best. Production began September 1916; 1788 Jordans were sold during the marque's maiden year; by 1918 the annual output was well over the 5000 mark. In 1919 came the Playboy, the most celebrated Jordan model of all, offering what Ned Jordan would call the promise of happy days: "Some day in June, when happy hours abound, a wonderful girl and a wonderful boy will leave their friends in a shower of rice — and start to roam . . . Give them a Jordan Playboy, the blue sky overhead, the green turf flying by and a thousand miles of open road." That was decorous enough, but his famous "Port of Missing Men" advertisement (with light emanating from just one upstairs window of the house in front of which a Playboy was parked, and accompanied by suggestive prose) didn't make it past the Society for the Prevention of Vice. "They were squeamish then about those things," Ned Jordan would reminisce; the light was airbrushed out of the upstairs window. A few years later, in 1923, while traveling by private railroad car to San Francisco, Jordan happened to notice a beautiful girl on a magnificent horse outside the window and asked a lawyer friend accompanying him where they were. "Oh, somewhere west of Laramie" came the reply. Ned Jordan finished the ad in minutes, his immortality was assured, and so was his significant place in the history of American advertising. Late 1925 saw the introduction of Lockheed hydraulic brakes throughout the Jordan line, as well as the introduction of a Jordan-designed Continental-built straight eight, the Model A Line Eight. Nineteen twenty-six was the company's best year, with a production of over 11,000 cars. Nineteen twenty-seven was a disaster. Of the 10,000 cars he built, he sold only 6258. Among the reasons was the introduction that year of his Little Custom (with bodies by Murray, as were most of his big cars); Ned Jordan was simply too far ahead of his time with the idea of a luxury compact. Late in 1927 both his health and his marriage were failing. He recovered then and started picking up the pieces, hiring Edward Ver Linden away from Peerless to take over as Jordan president. For 1928 the Cross-Country Six (a cheaper Little Custom) was in, but by fall Ver Linden was out. Jordan returned to the presidency and brought in Chrysler veteran John McArdle to help. Just as a lightbulb burns its brightest during the moments before it is forever dimmed, Ned Jordan's greatest car was his last. For 1929 all Jordan sixes were discontinued, all hopes placed on the Great Line Eighty and Ninety. For 1930 came the Model Z Speedway Ace, with a hefty 85 hp engine, aircraft dashboard, four-speed gearbox, sporty low-slung coachwork and Woodlite headlamps. An easy 100 mph was promised for $5500, an agreeable price tag for the Roaring Twenties. But introducing such a car in the wake of the stock market crash spelled disaster. And the less expensive models in the Jordan line were selling scarcely better. Reorganization as Jordan Motors Corporation, Inc. was tried in December 1930. Receivership arrived in April 1931; from spare parts on hand 262 further cars were built before final liquidation in 1932. Of the more than 65,000 cars produced during the Jordan's lifetime, better than 50,000 of them were still on the road the year the company died. Though the name Jordan shall forever be synonymous with Playboy, it should not be forgotten that the cars had virtues beyond their dash and elan, and the evocative prose written about them.

1917 JORDAN
Four — 29.4 hp, 127" wb

	FP	5	4	3	2	1
Touring	1650	3900	4800	7700	14,300	27,000
Roadster	1650	4000	5000	8000	15,000	28,000

1918 Jordan, touring, AA

1918 JORDAN
Four — 29.4 hp, 127" wb

	FP	5	4	3	2	1
Touring-7P	1995	3900	4800	7700	14,300	27,000
Touring-4P	1995	4000	5000	8000	15,000	28,000
Sedan-7P	2650	2000	3000	4200	6500	14,000
Brougham	2900	2200	3200	4400	7000	15,000
Town Car	3100	2300	3300	4600	7500	16,000
Sport Marine-4P	2375	2500	3500	5000	8500	18,000
Limousine-7P	3500	2900	3700	5600	9100	20,000

1919 Jordan, touring, AA

1919 JORDAN
Six — 29.4 hp, 127" wb

Suburban Seven Touring	1995	3900	4800	7700	14,300	27,000
Sport Marine	1995	2500	3500	5000	8500	18,000
Town Sedan	2650	2200	3200	4400	7000	15,000
Brougham	2900	2300	3300	4600	7500	16,000
Town Car	3100	2400	3400	4800	8000	17,000
Limousine	3300	2700	3600	5300	8800	19,000

1920 Jordan Silhouette, touring, HAC

1920 JORDAN
Model M — 6-cyl., 56 hp, 120" wb

Silhouette-5P	2550	3700	4700	7300	13,700	26,000
Playboy	2550	3900	4800	7700	14,300	27,000
Silhouette Brougham	3600	3100	4200	6300	10,500	22,000
Silhouette Sedan	3600	3000	4000	6000	9500	21,000

Model F — 6-cyl., 56 hp, 127" wb

Silhouette Touring-7P	2775	4000	5000	8000	15,000	28,000
Town Sedan-7P	3800	2400	3400	4800	8000	17,000
Silhouette-4P	2775	3900	4800	7700	14,300	27,000
Brougham	3800	3200	4300	6500	11,000	23,000
Playboy	2775	4200	5200	8400	15,700	29,000

1921 Jordan, Locke bodied landaulet, AA

1921 JORDAN
Model M — 6-cyl., 56 hp, 120" wb

	FP	5	4	3	2	1
Silhouette Touring-5P	2650	3900	4800	7700	14,300	27,000
Silhouette Playboy	2650	4000	5000	8000	15,000	28,000
Silhouette Sedan-5P	3700	3100	4200	6300	10,500	22,000

Model F — 6-cyl., 60 hp, 127" wb

	FP	5	4	3	2	1
Silhouette Touring-7P	2875	4200	5200	8400	15,700	29,000
Silhouette Brougham-7P	3700	3200	4300	6500	11,000	23,000

1922 Jordan, 4-dr. sedan, AA

1922 JORDAN
Model MX — 6-cyl., 56 hp, 120" wb

	FP	5	4	3	2	1
Touring-5P	2095	3500	4500	7000	13,000	25,000
Playboy	2095	3900	4800	7700	14,300	27,000
Silhouette Touring	2095	3700	4700	7300	13,700	26,000
Custom Landaulet-2P	2995	3200	4300	6500	11,000	23,000
Silhouette Brougham-4P	3200	3100	4200	6300	10,500	22,000
Silhouette Sedan-5P	3200	3000	4000	6000	9500	21,000

Model F — 6-cyl., 56 hp, 127" wb

	FP	5	4	3	2	1
Touring-7P	2475	3700	4700	7300	13,700	26,000
Sedan-7P	3500	3100	4200	6300	10,500	22,000

1923 Jordan, 4-dr. brougham, OCW

1923 JORDAN
Model MX — 6-cyl., 54-1/2 hp, 120" wb

	FP	5	4	3	2	1
Touring-5P	1795	3500	4500	7000	13,000	25,000
Playboy	1895	3700	4700	7300	13,700	26,000
Silhouette Sedan-5P	2485	3000	4000	6000	9500	21,000
Silhouette Brougham-4P	2485	3100	4200	6300	10,500	22,000
Landaulet-2P	2485	3200	4300	6500	11,000	23,000

Model H — 6-cyl., 54-1/2 hp, 124-1/2" wb

	FP	5	4	3	2	1
Sport-4P	2150	4000	5000	8000	15,000	28,000

1924 Jordan, 2-dr. brougham, AA

1924 JORDAN
Model MX — 6-cyl., 54 hp, 120" wb

	FP	5	4	3	2	1
Touring-5P	1675	3700	4700	7300	13,700	26,000
Playboy	1750	4000	5000	8000	15,000	28,000
Blueboy	1995	3900	4800	7700	14,300	27,000
Brougham-5P	2285	3100	4200	6300	10,500	22,000
Victoria-4P	2285	3000	4000	6000	9500	21,000

Models H & L — 6-cyl., 54 hp, 124-1/2" wb

	FP	5	4	3	2	1
Sport-4P	1995	4000	5000	8000	15,000	28,000
Sedan-5P	2585	3200	4300	6500	11,000	23,000
Sedan-7P	2785	3100	4200	6300	10,500	22,000

1925 Jordan, 2-dr. sedan, AA

1925 JORDAN
Models K & L — 6-cyl., 56 hp, 124-1/2" wb

	FP	5	4	3	2	1
Blueboy-4P	2095	3900	4800	7700	14,300	27,000
Brougham-5P	2385	3200	4300	6500	11,000	23,000
Victoria-5P	2385	3100	4200	6300	10,500	22,000

Line Eight — 8-cyl., 74 hp, 125-1/2" wb

	FP	5	4	3	2	1
Playboy-4P	2575	4200	5200	8400	15,700	29,000
Touring-5P	2575	4000	5000	8000	15,000	28,000
Victoria-4P	2775	3200	4300	6500	11,000	23,000
Brougham-5P	2865	3300	4400	6700	12,000	24,000
Cabriolet-3P	2875	3700	4700	7300	13,700	26,000
Sedan-5P	2975	3100	4200	6300	10,500	22,000

1926 Jordan, 4-dr. sedan, AA

1926 JORDAN
Line Eight — 8-cyl., 74 hp, 125-1/2" wb

	FP	5	4	3	2	1
Sedan-5P	1845	3000	4000	6000	9500	21,000
Roadster-4P	1695	4400	5600	9200	17,300	31,000

Great Line Eight — 8-cyl., 74 hp, 125-1/2" wb

	FP	5	4	3	2	1
Touring-5P	2275	4200	5200	8400	15,700	29,000
Brougham-5P	2575	3200	4300	6500	11,000	23,000
Sedan-5P	2675	3100	4200	6300	10,500	22,000
Sedan-7P	2925	3000	4000	6000	9500	21,000

1927 Jordan, 4-dr. sedan, AA

1927 Jordan, Playboy, roadster, HFM

1927 JORDAN
Line Eight — 8-cyl., 74 hp, 116" wb

	FP	5	4	3	2	1
Sedan-5P	1945	3000	4000	6000	9500	21,000
Playboy Roadster-4P	1845	4900	6300	10,300	21,000	34,000
Victoria-4P	1945	3100	4200	6300	10,500	22,000
Custom Style Sedan-5P	2195	3200	4300	6500	11,000	23,000
Custom Style Victoria-4P	2195	3300	4400	6700	12,000	24,000
Sport Coupe-4P	2195	3700	4700	7300	13,700	26,000

Great Line Eight — 8-cyl., 74 hp, 125-1/2" wb

	FP	5	4	3	2	1
Custom Style Sedan-5P	2495	3300	4400	6700	12,000	24,000
Custom Style Victoria-4P	2495	3500	4500	7000	13,000	25,000

1928 Jordan, Cross Country, 2-dr. sport sedan, AA

1928 Jordan, 4-dr. sedan, AA

1928 JORDAN
Model R — 6-cyl., 62 hp, 107" wb

Blueboy-4P	1745	3700	4700	7300	13,700	26,000
Sedan-5P	1595	3000	4000	6000	9500	21,000
Sport Salon-4P	1595	3100	4200	6300	10,500	22,000
Tomboy-4P	1595	3500	4500	7000	13,000	25,000

Air Line Eight — 8-cyl., 80 hp, 116" wb

Playboy Coupe-4P	2195	3900	4800	7700	14,300	27,000
Sedan-5P	2195	3100	4200	6300	10,500	22,000
Victoria-5P	2195	3200	4300	6500	11,000	23,000

1929 Jordan, model 80, 4-dr. sedan, AA

758

1929 Jordan, model 90, 4-dr. sedan, AA

1929 JORDAN
Model 6RE — 6-cyl., 66 hp, 107" wb

	FP	5	4	3	2	1
Blueboy-4P	1495	4500	5800	9500	18,000	32,000
Sport Salon-4P	1295	3500	4500	7000	13,000	25,000
Tomboy-4P	1395	4000	5000	8000	15,000	28,000
Sedan-5P	1395	3300	4400	6700	12,000	24,000

Model 8JE — 8-cyl., 85 hp, 116" wb

Coupe-4P	1995	3700	4700	7300	13,700	26,000
Sedan-5P	1995	3000	4000	6000	9500	21,000
Victoria-5P	1995	3100	4200	6300	10,500	22,000
Landau Brougham-5P	1995	3500	4500	7000	13,000	25,000

1930 Jordan, Speedway Ace, 4-dr. sedan, AA

1930 JORDAN
Model 8T — 8-cyl., 80 hp, 120" wb

Sedan	2095	3100	4200	6300	10,500	22,000
Coupe	2095	3900	4800	7700	14,300	27,000

Model 8G — 8-cyl., 85 hp, 125" wb

Phaeton	2895	5400	7300	11,800	25,000	38,000
Coupe	2395	4000	5000	8000	15,000	28,000
Sedan-5P	2395	3200	4300	6500	11,000	23,000
Convertible Coupe	2595	4500	5800	9500	18,000	32,000
Sport Sedan	2695	3300	4400	6700	12,000	24,000
Sedan-7P	2795	3200	4300	6500	11,000	23,000

Model 8G — 8-cyl., 85 hp, 131" wb

Roadster	2695	5800	8000	12,500	28,000	40,000
Touring	2995	5500	7500	12,000	26,000	39,000
Limousine	2795	3500	4500	7000	13,000	25,000

1931 Jordan, model 90, Speedboy sport phaeton, HAC

1931 JORDAN
Model 80 — 8-cyl., 80 hp, 120" wb

Coupe	1795	4200	5200	8400	15,700	29,000
Sedan	1795	3500	4500	7000	13,000	25,000

Model 90 — 8-cyl., 85 hp, 125" wb

Speedboy	2795	5400	7300	11,800	25,000	38,000
Sedan-5P	2295	3700	4700	7300	13,700	26,000
Coupe	2295	4300	5400	8700	16,500	30,000
Convertible Coupe	2495	4700	6100	9900	19,000	33,000
Sport Sedan	2595	3900	4800	7700	14,300	27,000
Sedan-7P	2595	3700	4700	7300	13,700	26,000

Model 90 — 8-cyl., 85 hp, 131" wb

Touring	2495	5800	8000	12,500	28,000	40,000
Playboy	2595	6400	9300	14,500	33,000	45,000
Limousine	2695	4200	5200	8400	15,700	29,000

JOSLYN — The Joslyn Automobile Company was organized in Rockford, Illinois during the spring of 1908 with a capital stock of $5000 to "engage in the manufacture of motor cars and accessories." J.S. Joslyn, H.B. Sivwright and K.M. Chambers were behind this venture. Manufacture is doubted.

JPL — This was J.P. La Vigne's cyclecar built in Detroit in 1913-1914. Brochures variously refer to the JPL of the JPL Cyclecar Company and the La Vigne of the La Vigne Cyclecar Company. They were the same car. Refer to La Vigne.

J.R. — The initials represent John J. Rascob, Jr., and this car built in Lockport, New York in 1924 is more properly referred to as the Junior R. Refer to Junior R.

JUDD — New York, New York — (1900-1901) — The Judd Motor Vehicle and Carriage Company was incorporated with a capital stock of $500,000 in December of 1900. The men behind the venture were D.J. Newland, F.A. Camp, H. Motley, F.B. Carpenter, W.E. Knight, all of New York City. The man they were backing was Silas C. Judd, also a New Yorker, who had invented a three-wheeled electric runabout. The automotive press was not nearly so enthused with the inventor's efforts as were his backers. "Mr. Judd has a queer machine," reported *The Motor Age* in April 1901. "It mainly comprises a storage battery, motor and seat frame mounted on the axle of the two traction wheels, and a third wheel trailer behind for steering purposes." It was not so much the components of Judd's machine — storage battery, motor, et cetera were of standard design — but the arrangement of its parts that distressed the magazine. As the editors pointed out: "The body being rigidly mounted on the traction wheels, the middle portion of the seat is made separate from the rim portion and is mounted on a spring standard so that it may rise and fall. Just what degree of comfort such an affair would afford in a rough country is a questionable point." Questionable, too, is whether this venture ever got off the ground. Probably not. The Judd Motor Vehicle and Carriage Company had been preceded, incidentally, in the summer of 1899 by the Judd-Comiskey Motor Vehicle Company, a $100,000 incorporation which hadn't seen a single vehicle built. Within months Frank W. and Archibald Comiskey had opted out of the project. Only Frederick A. Camp and Amzi Camp among the Judd-Comiskey people followed with the second company launched that December.

JUDSON — In early 1906, W.L. Judson of Chicago was down south in New Orleans endeavoring to begin a factory to manufacture automobiles in Louisiana. The New Orleans *Picayune* reported that "automobiles of the 'Mud King' variety will be manufactured in addition to gasoline engines for multiple uses." Judson said that his sons were engine manufacturers back in Chicago, and that half of the necessary $100,000 to get things going in New Orleans had been subscribed. The venture stalled soon after though perhaps not before the building of a prototype car. Refer to New Orleans.

A car called the Judson has appeared on various car rosters as having been produced by the Judson Motor Car Company in Detroit, Michigan in 1915. No such company is listed in Detroit city directories during this period. Possibly the Judson was simply a typographical error for Hudson, or possibly it was W.L. Judson of Chicago trying, and failing, again.

JUERGENS — That an automobile was built by the Juergens Motor Car Company of Chicago, Illinois in 1908 is indicated on various car rosters. This has not been documented. Chicago city directories of the period do not include a listing for the company of that name.

In 1932 *Automotive Abstracts* reported that Edwin C. Juergens of Detroit was experimenting with an "aeromobile," the concept of a car that could fly too enjoying a certain currency during this period. Further details are lacking.

1922 Julian, coupe, GR

JULIAN — Syracuse, New York — (1918, 1925) — Marching to a different drummer is the mark of a self-confirmed eccentric. Julian S. Brown of Syracuse didn't march, however, he cantered. He also earned for himself legendary status as a playboy in upstate New York. The son of millionaire Alexander T. Brown, whose automotive affiliations included the Brown, Lipe Gear Company and H.H. Franklin, Julian Brown entered the automobile industry initially as an engine builder. In 1913 he boasted that the latest product (a six) of his Julian Motor Company was the highest priced engine in America. He declined to mention the price. He was out of business within a year. In 1918 Brown designed his first automobile, a V-6 (he called the engine a "Twin Three") set in a chassis that was unusual. "The car sets low, the frame being only 21 inches from the ground," explained *Automobile Topics*. "This is because of the spring suspension and the radically new method of applying the

driving power. The drive is through the rear springs, these springs being shackled in front instead of being pushed along." An attempt was made to organize the Julian Motor Car Company in Detroit for its manufacture, but the project never proceeded beyond the prototype. In 1925 Julian Brown built an even more unusual car which paid little heed to anything the rest of the industry was then doing. First, like the Adams-Farwell of a generation previous, it featured a rear-mounted radial engine. (A large cooling fan attached to an eight-inch long vertical crankshaft directed air over the six finned cylinders.) Second, the frame was a platform-backbone type anticipating the Volkswagens of a generation in the future. Admittedly, the aluminum body by Fleetwood and the four disc wheels seemed somewhat in the mode of the day, but the upholstery inside was strictly Victorian. And the seating arrangement — the driver centrally located in front, with a two-passenger seat behind him and accommodation for two more passengers on folding seats on either side — was a bit bizarre. So were the brakes, which were on the rear wheels only, but adjustable from the driver's seat. Ostensibly, adjustment was possible while the car was in motion but since this required the manipulation of thumb screws on the adjusting mechanism (located on the pedal levers), its practical application was questionable. The Julian Brown Development Company was organized to secure financing to put the vehicle into production, and *Motor World* reported in 1925 that among those interested were Alexander Meldrum, Stewart F. Hancock, Charles G. Hanna, Carl Gabrielson and Ray L. Caldwell. Apparently, they were not interested enough. Although six cars were reported to have been produced, it is more likely that only the prototype was built. It was Julian Brown's last car.

1924 Junior R, touring, KM

JUNIOR R — Lockport, New York — (1924) — John J. Raskob was a native of Lockport and a vice-president of General Motors. The Junior R was perfectly named; it was a special touring car that Raskob ordered to be built as a gift for his son, John J. Raskob, Jr. The father's hometown of Lockport happened also to be the home of the Harrison Radiator Division, a GM subsidiary. On one of his visits to home and Harrison during 1923, Raskob asked Wellington W. Muir, a Harrison research engineer, to design and build the Junior R. The car's engine, an L-head four, was produced in the Harrison plant, though the crankshaft and connecting rods were from Chevrolet, the valve tappets and steering gear from Cadillac. Oakland supplied the rear axle, Chevrolet the front. The radiator was pure Harrison, however, the famous Harrison "Hexagon." The body was all aluminum, on a 111-inch wheelbase, with sporty disc wheels and lines that had a GM look, though not of any specific GM car. Following its completion in 1924, the Junior R was driven by Raskob Junior for approximately two years. Then Raskob Senior presented it to Wellington Muir as a gift. Muir drove it until 1971, when he donated it to the Harrison Radiator Division in Lockport. The car remains on display there to this day. This Junior should not be confused, incidentally, with the car of the same name which was a model of the Locomobile during the mid-Twenties.

JUNKERS-BURDICK — The Junkers-Burdick Company was organized in Chicago, Illinois during the summer of 1910 with a capital stock of $25,000 for the manufacture of automobiles and accessories. Otto Junkers and Winthrop Burdick were the partners involved. Manufacture of a car is doubted.

JUNO — Juneau, Wisconsin — (1912-1914) — The Juno Motor Truck Company was organized in 1912 by L.C. Pautsch, Henry Henning, Martin Lueck, Peter Peters, Theodore P. Hemmy and Ferd Lindeman — all businessmen of Juneau. They took over the Brodesser Motor Truck Company, which had been begun about 1909 by Peter H. Brodesser as a sideline business to his P.H. Brodesser & Company, which manufactured such diverse products as cable-operated elevators, coal and bark conveyors, and lawn mowing and rolling machines. Both the Brodesser and the Juno have occasionally, and erroneously, found their way into rosters of automobiles built in the United States. Both companies built motor trucks only. One owner did convert his truck into a fifteen-passenger jitney bus for use during the summer tourist season, but every winter the seats were replaced with a body for hauling furniture — and this was as close as either a Juno or a Brodesser came to being a passenger car.

JURUICK — The Juruick Auto Company was organized in Brooklyn, New York early in 1909 with a capital stock of $5000 for the manufacture of automobiles. Incorporators were M.F. Juruick, L.R. Smith and A.F. Juruick. Manufacture is doubted.

JUVENILE ELECTRIC — This child's car built in Toledo, Ohio from 1906-1907 by the American Metal Wheel & Auto Company was more often designated the American Juvenile Electric. Refer to American Juvenile Electric.

KADOW — During the summer of 1912, E.C. Kadow & Company was organized in Chicago, Illinois with a capital stock of $25,000 for the manufacture of automobiles. Indicated incorporators were Benjamin Gordon and Simon LaGrou. Manufacture of a car is doubted.

KAESTNER — Chicago, Illinois — (1903-1906) — In May of 1903 the trade press reported the organization with a capital stock of $50,000 of the Charles Kaestner Manufacturing Company in Chicago for the production of automobiles. In February of 1906 the firm's plant was disposed of at a receiver's sale. No documentation has surfaced regarding what production the factory might have seen, nor was this specific company listed in Chicago city directories during this period. There was a machinery-producing firm called Kaestner & Company which apparently was related to but independent of the auto-making venture, and which survived the 1906 receivership.

KAHN-STERN — During the summer of 1904 the Kahn-Stern Company was organized in Jersey City, New Jersey with a capital stock of $15,000 to ''engage in the manufacture of and deal in carriages, wagons, automobiles, motorcycles and conveyances of every kind; also in horses, cows and all animals whatsoever.'' Louis J. Kahn, Emmanuel J. Stern and Faerber Goldenhorn were the incorporators. Manufacture of a car is doubted.

KALAMAZOO — In 1904 the Michigan Buggy Company, of Kalamazoo motorized one of its carriages and began marketing it locally under either the name Kalamazoo or Michigan. Serious manufacture did not begin until 1911, however, and at that time the Michigan name was used exclusively. Refer to Michigan.

In late 1902 the Kalamazoo Cycle Company announced its building of a ''$400 automobile weighing 300 pounds.'' Documentation regarding subsequent manufacture is lacking, but the evidence suggests a minimal production at best.

KAMMANN — The Kammann Electric Company of Minneapolis was organized in 1897 to build electric vehicles and launches under the patents of W.T. Kammann. No manufacture of automobiles is believed to have followed in Minnesota, however. By 1903 the firm was in Chicago, and that year produced a three-seated electric roadster that was marketed as the Jack Frost. Refer to Jack Frost.

KANE — The Kane-Champlin Company was organized in Buffalo, New York during the summer of 1905 with a capital stock of $250,000 to manufacture and deal in automobiles. Incorporators were Oliver P. Champlin, Charles R. Ham and Gertrude R. Kane. Manufacture is doubted.

Kane-Pennington was the partnership of Thomas Kane, a furniture manufacturer from Racine, Wisconsin, and Edward Joel Pennington, one of the earliest and most flamboyant flim-flam artists in the history of the American automobile. A few cars were built of this collaboration in Wisconsin prior to the turn of the century. Refer to Pennington.

KANKAKEE — The Kankakee Automobile Manufacturing Company was organized early in 1908 with a capital stock of $250,000 for the manufacture of motor cars and accessories in Kankakee, Illinois. The Dixon family — W.P., H.S. and E.M. — backed this venture. Manufacture of an automobile is doubted.

KANKAKEE — Kankakee, Illinois — (1916) — In 1914, in Kankakee, there was an attempt to market a cyclecar called the Illinois. The project went nowhere, and while it cannot be determined with certainty, probably the Chiniquy brothers were involved. In 1916 they tried again, with a full-sized standard car this time, organizing the Kankakee Automobile Company with another automobile enthusiast in town named R.E. Parker. R.L. Chiniquy was elected president of the new company, with his brother O.L. serving as secretary, and Parker as general manager. E. Betourne and E.C. Chabot were vice-president and treasurer respectively. The Kankakee company was incorporated for $500,000, Chiniquy announcing that summer that over $300,000 of the stock had already been subscribed. The Kankakee car was to be a six and offered as a touring car only, in both a light car and a larger version. It is known that by late summer the light six prototype had been completed and tested, with the larger six then ''being worked out in the shop.'' *The Automobile* reported that ''the company has been corresponding with manufacturers of engines and other supplies and contracts are now being written to cover a good-sized output.'' *Motor Age* indicated that ''should the business prove profitable, it will be enlarged from time to time.'' Obviously the Kankakee business did not so prove; indeed possibly the car was never built in other than pilot models.

1906 Kansas City, victoria touring, NAHC

KANSAS CITY — Kansas City, Missouri — (1906-1908)/KANSAS CITY WONDER — (1909) — In October of 1905 the Kansas City Motor Car Company moved into the Missouri plant vacated by the Caps brothers who had had the devil's own time in trying to get into manufacture of their two-seater runabout. J.C. Caps remained behind to design the new Kansas City car which for 1906 was introduced as a pair of twins and a small four. He did not remain with the company long. In mid-September of 1906 Kansas City president F.E. Wear announced that the firm's new chief engineer was one L.M. De Dieterich of Detroit. ''The prefix 'De' seems to be a recent improvement of Mr. Dieterich's name, as when with the Waltham, Cadillac and Aerocar companies he was plain 'Dieterich' without prefix,'' *The Horseless Age* noted archly. ''The change is likely to be confusing, as a well known foreign car is manufactured and sold under the name of De Dieterich.'' Maybe that was precisely the point; indeed some trade publications obligingly misspelled the engineer's name exactly like the French car. In any case, De Dieterich designed two big fours of 55/60 hp, and they were produced the following year. So was a motor truck which bore the Dieterich name. The company was in receivership by December. Six months later, in late June 1908, a valiant effort to reorganize the firm was announced by president Wear. Now the plan was production of a four-cylinder 18 hp motor buggy designed by A.R. Walton, who had formerly been with Dorris. The last-gasp effort of this venture came in early 1909 when it was renamed the Wonder Motor Car Company, for the marketing of a two-cylinder 16 hp motor buggy called the Kansas City Wonder. This car had been designed by Charles F. Ettwein, its chief claim to fame being the performance its inventor achieved in the prototype in September 1908; as *Motor Age* noted, he ''made two-thirds the distance in the 1000-mile southwest reliability tour.'' Joining him now was his brother L.A. Ettwein, and H.N. Strait, who was building Corliss steam engines in Kansas City. Finally, in late 1909, all the Kansas City/Wonder people decided to give up altogether. Into the factory now strode the Kansas City Vehicle Company which would produce another car called the Gleason.

1906 KANSAS CITY
Two-Cylinder — 20 hp

	FP	5	4	3	2	1
Runabout	—	2300	3300	4600	7500	16,000
Two-Cylinder — 25 hp						
Touring	—	2500	3500	5000	8500	18,000
Four-Cylinder — 90'' wb						
Touring	—	2900	3700	5600	9100	20,000
1907 KANSAS CITY						
Four-Cylinder — 55/60 hp						
Touring	—	4000	5000	8000	15,000	28,000
Four-Cylinder — 75 hp						
Touring	—	4300	5400	8700	16,500	30,000
1908 KANSAS CITY						
Motor Buggy — 4-cyl., 18 hp						
Motor Buggy	—	2300	3300	4600	7500	16,000
1909 KANSAS CITY WONDER						
Wonder — 2-cyl., 16 hp, 90'' wb						
Model E Rbt.-2P	850	2400	3400	4800	8000	17,000
Model F Rbt.-3P	870	2450	3500	4900	8300	17,500
Model H Tour.-4P	900	2500	3600	5200	8700	18,000

KANSAS CITY HUMMER — Kansas City, Kansas — (1904-1905) — Little is known about the car called the Kansas City Hummer. It was a motor buggy powered by an air-cooled two-cylinder opposed engine mounted up front under a hood. Planetary transmission and single chain drive were featured. The car was produced by the Hummer Motor Car Company, which was in business but two years.

KAPPE — Quincy, Illinois — (1895) — William J.H. Kappe was one of the many backyard inventors who were lured to build an automobile both for its own sake and for the possibility of winning a prize in the contest sponsored on Thanksgiving Day by the Chicago Times-Herald. Kappe built a three-cylinder 4 hp wagon-type car which was wheel steered and which he hoped would attain a top speed of 20 mph. Instead it never ran at all, and probably never left the second floor of the Sturhahn wagon shop in Quincy where it was built. When his second attempt to make the vehicle operational proved fruitless, Kappe simply abandoned it. Later he moved to Los Angeles.

KARBACH — Omaha, Nebraska — (1905-1908) — P.J. Karbach & Sons was a large carriage-building firm in Omaha. In 1901 the company built a passenger-carrying wagon propelled by a 10 hp motor purchased from the St. Louis Motor Carriage Company. It was driven from Omaha to Sheridan (Wyoming) to be put into service there on the stage line. Karbach returned to horsedrawn vehicles exclusively thereafter until 1905 when the firm was reorganized as Karbach Automobile & Vehicle Company, with a capitalization of $75,000 and Arthur P. Karbach, Richard L. Karbach, H. Wheelock and A.T. Cajacob as the incorporators. Although the company announced its intention to build "automobiles," none of these turned out to be passenger cars, except for a runabout for personal use. Instead, Karbach produced commercial vehicles exclusively. The company's first effort was a 1 1/2-ton truck which proved unsatisfactory, so it was converted into a twenty-passenger sightseeing bus. "It was run until cold weather with apparent success," *The Motor Way* noted in January 1907, "but the Karbach people, though they do not state the reason, have not put out any more machines." Subsequent advertisements from later in 1907 and 1908 indicate that the Karbachs did continue to offer their "seeing Omaha" bus for sale, and apparently had set matters right with their truck because it was marketed as well.

KARNS — Everett, Pennsylvania — (1905) — A.M. Karns was a carriage builder in Everett whose son was an avid automobile enthusiast. Young Chester Karns built his first automobile in 1898 but could not persuade his father to produce it. In 1905 he built another one, a small 12 hp gasoline runabout, and he was obviously more persuasive this time. In September of that year, A.M. Karns announced that he was about to undertake the manufacture of automobiles "on a small scale." This was the final press reference to this venture. No doubt the cars were built as orders were received, and when orders ceased so did the Karns car.

KASSONY — The Kassony Motor Sales Corporation was organized in New York City during the fall of 1920 with a capital stock of $12,500 for the manufacture of automobiles. Incorporators were M.K. Kassony, C.G. Keutgen and G.E. Merrifield. Manufacture of a car is doubted.

KATO — Mankato, Minnesota — (1907-1913) — Ernest Rosenberger was a candy-maker from Mankato who concluded that four-wheel drive was a fine expedient for negotiating Minnesota hills. "March 19th was a proud day for Mankato," *The Motor World* reported in 1907, for on that day Rosenberger " 'pressed the button' that set his automobile factory in operation." With three men working, five cars were produced by early 1908 and, with the financial assistance of A.G. Wasson and J.W. Schmitt, the Four Traction Automobile Company was organized. By the end of 1908, twenty-five vehicles (all using two-stroke Brennan engines) were in the process of construction, that number including trucks. The first cars were referred to simply as Four Traction, but succeeding vehicles carried the names Mankato or Kato, the latter most often being used for a delivery wagon. Early in 1913 Four Traction sold out completely — stock, drawings and production in progress — to the Nevada Manufacturing Company of Nevada, Iowa. Truck production only was planned following the move to Iowa, but despite a government contract for 500 commercial vehicles, it seems that Nevada closed its doors before an assembly line was ever opened. Production in Mankato is estimated to have been about a dozen cars and perhaps as many as thirty trucks.

1910 Kauffman, model C, roadster, WLB

KAUFFMAN — Miamisburg, Ohio — (1909-1912) — For three years previous, the Kauffman Buggy Company of Miamisburg had produced running gear and bodies for the Hatfield Motor Vehicle Company also of that city. In 1909 the two firms pooled their resources and reorganized as the Advance Motor Vehicle Company. The word "advance" may have been used to indicate progress; the Hatfield had been a high-wheeler, the Kauffman would be a standard car. It was a four-seater roadster utilizing a refined version of the Hatfield's four-cylinder air-cooled engine. After a year or two as Advance Motor Vehicle, the company name changed to Kauffman Motor Car Company, but the car did not long survive.

1909-1912 KAUFFMAN
Model C — 4-cyl., 20 hp, 104" wb

	FP	5	4	3	2	1
Roadster-4P	1250	2400	3400	4800	8000	17,000

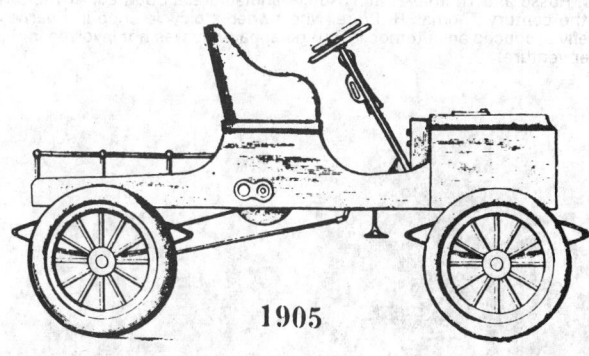
1905 Kavan, runabout, GR

KAVAN — Chicago, Illinois — (1905) — In 1905 the Kavan Manufacturing Company of Chicago submitted to the automotive trade press a drawing of the light runabout it planned to produce and sell to the public for $200. Its coachwork was a wooden box with single bench seat under which a motor was fitted. A friction transmission and a right-hand steering wheel were featured. This vehicle would have been extremely simple to manufacture, but whether the Kavan Manufacturing Company ever did so is not known. The company had disappeared from public print by 1906. Some references indicate that Kavan planned to call this vehicle a Light. Probably only a prototype was built.

KAY-SEE — Kansas City, Missouri — (1917) — The Kay-See was designed by B.P. Bagby, who had previously designed the Ben Hur from Willoughby, Ohio. Bagby was also the president of the Midwest Motor Company which was incorporated, with a capital stock of $1,000,000, for manufacture in Kansas City. A prototype was built, but the war delayed its production. By the time the Armistice was signed, Bagby had run out of money. A new set of backers took over, and the Kay-See was ultimately produced as the Highlander, without Bagby.

KAYTON — The Kayton Taxicar and Garage Company was organized in New York City during the fall of 1908 with a capital stock of $100,000 to manufacture and deal in automobiles. Incorporators were E.M. Leventritt, J.F. Jacobs, W.F. Tracy, F.G. Braun and C.J. Heermance. Manufacture is doubted.

1913 K-D, touring, WLB

K-D — Brookline, Massachusetts — (1912-1913) — If for no other reason than the fact that it had been designed by two women, the K-D would be a noteworthy car. But the K-D is significant for reasons other than the sex of its inventors. Its engine featured solid crescent-shaped slide valves, the inlet and exhaust forming together a complete sleeve with but 1/16th-inch between the two halves. This differed markedly from the Charles Yale Knight version which featured double concentric sleeves. The K-D engine was a six developing a hefty 90 hp. The designers were Miss Margaret E. Knight (who claimed no relation to C.Y. Knight) in association with Mrs. A.M. (Beatrice) Davidson (who claimed to be his aunt). Their chassis design was developed into production format by the ubiquitous Charles R. Greuter, who had been engineering automobiles since the turn of the century. The K-D's body design was a rakish proposition for the period which was refined for the women by coachbuilders Moore and Munger of New York. In mid-summer of 1912 the K-D Motor Company was organized in Brookline with a capitalization of $100,000. The car was introduced at the 1913 Boston Automobile Show, where it bore a $6000 price tag. Probably it was the only K-D built. In October 1914 Margaret E. Knight died. Her obituary indicated no fewer than 87 patents to her credit. These ranged from a machine for manufacturing square-bottomed paper bags which she invented shortly after the Civil War to devices for use in fabric and shoe production, and the crescent-valve automobile engine.

1912-1913 K-D
K-D — 6-cyl., 90 hp, 128" wb

	FP	5	4	3	2	1
Touring	6000	4500	5800	9500	18,000	32,000

KEARNEY — The Kearney Foundry, Machine & Automobile Company was organized during the fall of 1907 with a capital stock of $25,000 for the purpose of "manufacturing, repairing, storing automobiles, and carrying a general line of supplies for same" in Kearney, Nebraska. Incorporators were C.M. Kuhn, F.P. Kuhn, A.M. Franks, Harry Black, Frank Mott, Amos F.C. Rosso and Thomas Hutchinson. Manufacture is doubted. At the turn of the century Thomas H. Bolte, who owned a bicycle shop in Kearney, briefly produced an automobile, but he apparently was not involved in this later venture.

1909 Kearns, high-wheeled motor buggy, HAC

KEARNS — Beavertown, Pennsylvania — (1909-1916) — The Kearns Motor Buggy Company took over the premises occupied by the Eureka in Beavertown. Initially, two- and three-cylinder Speedwell two-stroke engines were featured in highwheeler models which Kearns advertised as "not a 'made-over' buggy hastily assembled to meet the popular demand." This was partly true, since the Kearns — unlike many high-wheelers — sported a conventional hood, though it was of virtually the same configuration as the former Eureka. When the popular demand for highwheelers ebbed, Maxwell Kearns moved his company into the manufacture of a light four-cylinder standard car. During the summer of 1913, six months before Henry Ford introduced the $5 day, Kearns announced a program by which every Kearns employee became a company stockholder. In 1914 company automobile production centered on a cyclecar called the Lulu, though occasionally also referred to as the Kearns-Kar. In mid-1915 Kearns introduced the Trio, which was in essence three cars in one. Available as a runabout, touring or light delivery, any of these bodies could be fastened to the same frame by use of only four bolts. After 1916 Kearns discontinued automobile production to consolidate manufacture of trucks and fire engines, the commercial vehicle side of its business having begun with a brewery wagon pilot model in 1909, manufacture in earnest following in 1911, reorganization of the firm to Kearns Motor Truck Company soon after. Kearns remained in the commercial vehicle business until 1928, moving to Danville, Pennsylvania as Kearns-Dughie Motor Company in late 1920.

1909 KEARNS
Two — 12 hp, 80" wb

	FP	5	4	3	2	1
Storm Queen Doctor's Special	700	2500	3500	5000	8500	18,000

1910 Kearns, model L, roadster, NAHC

1910 KEARNS
Two — 12/14 hp

Model K Roadster	650	2450	3500	4900	8300	17,500
Model N Storm Queen	850	2500	3500	5000	8500	18,000
Model D Roadster	950	2700	3600	5300	8800	19,000
Model F Surrey	875	2600	3600	5200	8700	18,500

Three — 20 hp

Model L Roadster	750	2500	3500	5000	8500	18,000
Model G Roadster	850	2600	3600	5200	8700	18,500

762

1911 Kearns, model F, surrey, HAC

1911 KEARNS
Three — 20 hp, 110" wb

	FP	5	4	3	2	1
Model R Roadster	1350	2500	3500	5000	8500	18,000
Model K Tourabout	1350	2500	3500	5000	8500	18,000
Model F Surrey (100" wb)	875	2400	3400	4800	8000	17,000

1912 KEARNS
Four — 32 hp, 115" wb

Model H Runabout-2P	1100	2600	3600	5200	8700	18,500
Model J Tourabout-4P	1100	2600	3600	5200	8700	18,500

1913 Kearns Senior, surrey, HAC

1913 KEARNS
Three — 26.4 hp, 100" wb

Senior Surrey-2P	950	2450	3500	4900	8300	17,500

1914-1915 KEARNS
Cyclecar/LuLu — 4-cyl., 12 hp, 96" wb

Roadster-2P	450	1800	2800	4000	6200	13,000
Speedster-2P	450	1800	2800	4000	6200	13,000

1916 Kearns, model L, roadster, KM

1916 KEARNS
Trio — 4-cyl., 12 hp, 90" wb

Roadster-2P	650	2300	3300	4600	7500	16,000
Touring-4P	700	2300	3300	4600	7500	16,000
Light Delivery	750	2200	3200	4400	7000	15,000

KEATING — During the summer of 1908 the Keating Garage and Engine Company was organized in Oswego, New York with a capital stock of $10,000 for the manufacture of motorcars and motorcycles. Behind this venture were P.R. Keating, Jr., James Dunlap, Jr. and A.C. Coon. Manufacture is doubted.

KEATING — Middletown, Connecticut — (1899-1901) — The Keating people of Middletown seem to have spent much of their time renaming their company. In the October 24th, 1899 issue of *Motor Age*, the transmogrification of the Keating Wheel Company into the Keating Automobile Company was announced, with the company indicating it would manufacture steam delivery wagons only. Shortly thereafter the firm was referred to as the Keating Bicycle & Automobile Company, and shortly after that (April of 1901), the R.M. Keating Motor Company was grandly incorporated at $500,000 capitalization. Now the company indicated it would build single-cylinder gasoline runabouts and electric cars. But by year's end the whole Keating business had been taken over by the Eisenhuth Horseless Vehicle Company then in development of a car that would eventually be marketed as the Compound. How many vehicles, either steam, gas or electric, were ever produced by Keating is not known. It is known that in August of 1902 Keating placed an attachment on Eisenhuth to satisfy a $30,000 claim. If the claim was satisfied, it doubtless represented more profit to the company than it had ever seen in vehicle production.

c.1942 Keen Steamliner (photographed in 1947), JB

KEEN STEAMLINER — Madison, Wisconsin — (1870's, 1940 et. seq.) — Charles Keen came by his love of steam naturally, following in the footsteps of his father, grandfather and great-grandfather. The last named had built the first steam power plant in the Allegheny Mountains and was involved in the production of early steam locomotives as well. The family moved themselves and their entire machine shop west on the *Katie Keen* steamboat they had built. In the early 1870's Charles Keen's father and an uncle produced a small steam-powered carriage. Decades later the son took up the steam cause. Charles Keen began work on his first Steamliner in 1940, mating a 10 hp Stanley Model 60 engine and rear axle to a Willys frame. Historian Jim Benjaminson has researched this car assiduously. Under its hood was a Keen- and Doble-designed steam generator with flash oiler and electrically-ignited atomizing burners. The controls, pumps and exhaust turbine were also designed by the two men, the result being a "baby Doble" for those familiar with the cars produced by that illustrious steam car engineer. Keen's adaptation of the Willys brakes to the rear axle of the Stanley was his vehicle's Achilles' heel and the major complaint of the many who owned or drove the car. The coachwork was an amalgam: hood and front fenders from a 1942 Plymouth; cowl, doors and dash from a 1939 Chevrolet (the instrument board filled with Stanley valves and gauges), the rear body courtesy of a 1940 Plymouth. To hide the splices, the roof was a fabric non-folding convertible-type top hand-formed over tubing. Keen's Steamliner was on the road by 1944. Experimentation continued after the war, and a second car, with V-4 engine and sleek sports roadster body, was built. Again, Abner Doble was involved in the project until his death in 1961. Charles Keen died later that decade. His Steamliner dreams died with him. His first car remains extant.

KEENE STEAMOBILE — Keene, New Hampshire — (1900-1901) — In July of 1900 the Trinity Cycle Manufacturing Company of Keene announced its forthcoming entry into automotive ranks. Trinity superintendent Reynold Janney (father of Russell Janney, the playwright and novelist) was the designer of the company's steam car which was introduced that fall as the Keene Steamobile. It was powered by a two-cylinder double-acting 7/9 hp engine, with a water-tube boiler of 420 copper pipes and an 8 1/2-gallon fuel tank good for a 60-mile run in hilly country and 100 miles on level road. "No torch is needed to generate the gasoline vapor in the combustion chamber," noted *The Motor Age* in November 1900, "and the flame regulating diaphragm does not merely slow down the flame when the steam pressure becomes excessive but shuts it off entirely with the exception of the pilot burner." This was regarded as a considerable safety feature. "Just one Little Wagon made by One Little Factory in One Little New Hampshire town" was the homey way Trinity advertising put it. The price was $850. Early in 1901 Trinity restyled itself as the Keene Automobile Company, but this enterprise was very short-lived because in February a Delaware firm acquired the Trinity rights and patents and moved to Keene as the Steamobile Company of America. All subsequent cars were called Steamobiles.

1912 Keeton Four, touring, HAC

KEETON — Detroit, Michigan — (1912-1914) — In 1908, Forrest M. Keeton, whose previous credits had included stints with Pope-Toledo and DeLuxe, designed a taxicab in Detroit and organized the Keeton Town Car Works. Soon thereafter the Jewel Motor Car Company in Massillon (Ohio) purchased the taxi, which went into production in Ohio as the Jewel-Keeton. The man behind the Jewel company was Herbert A. Croxton, and in 1909 he joined forces with Forrest Keeton to reorganize Jewel as the Croxton-Keeton Motor Car Company. The partnership was very short-lived, the partners said quite nasty things about each other, and Keeton promptly returned to Detroit. There, in March of 1912, he organized, with a modest capital stock of $10,000, the Keeton Motor Car Company which soon moved into the former plant of the Seitz Auto & Transmission Company. Production of fours and sixes very like the former "French" Croxton-Keeton followed, and the initial public response was satisfying enough to prompt Keeton to purchase the Oliver Motor Truck Company factory in Detroit in January of 1913. That Memorial Day Bob Burman drove a Keeton in the Indianapolis 500, but unfortunately the car caught on fire on the 55th lap. A few weeks later the Keeton company posted a check for $10,000 to the *New York World* as a challenge to Frenchman Jules Goux, winner of the 500 on a Peugeot, for a rematch with Bob Burman on the Keeton, although since Goux was already back in Europe preparing for the French Grand Prix, it was regarded as doubtful that he would accept. He didn't for which Keeton was probably grateful. By now the company was in financial trouble anyway. Forrest M. Keeton got the cash he needed to remain solvent, but he had to give up control of his company to get it. Charles S. Shaffer, who was president of the American Voiturette Company (manufacturer of the Car-Nation), bought a majority of the Keeton stock and became company president. In January of 1914 Keeton was absorbed by American Voiturette, both the Car-Nation and the Keeton being produced by the same company now. By September American Voiturette was in receivership. Liquidation proceedings included the sale of some 600 Car-Nations (a cyclecar) at $250 each, and 100 Keetons at $1000 each. What was left afterwards was purchased by Sam Winternitz for $100,000 in November 1914. Interestingly, about three months later, Forrest M. Keeton bought back the Keeton assets from Winternitz with the intention of furnishing repairs and continuing to manufacture in a small way. He only had money enough for the repair business. The Keeton was never again produced. Forrest Keeton remained anxious to return to the manufacturing field, however, and as late as 1923 was attempting, without success, to promote a company for the building of taxicabs.

1913 Keeton Six, roadster, HAC

1914 Keeton Six, Riverside, touring, NAHC

1912-1913 KEETON
Four — 22 hp, 120" wb

	FP	5	4	3	2	1
Touring-5P	2100	3500	4500	7000	13,000	25,000

Six — 48 hp, 136" wb

	FP	5	4	3	2	1
Riverside Touring-7P	2750	4000	5000	8000	15,000	28,000
Meadowbrook Roadster-2P	2750	4000	5000	8000	15,000	28,000
Tuxedo Coupe-3P	3000	3300	4400	6700	12,000	24,000

1914 KEETON
Six — 34 hp, 136" wb

	FP	5	4	3	2	1
Riverside Touring-7P	3250	4200	5200	8400	15,700	29,000
Overbrook Roadster-2P	3250	4200	5200	8400	15,700	29,000
Convertible-3P	3350	3900	4800	7700	14,300	27,000
Convertible-5P	3450	3900	4900	7900	14,700	27,500
Coupe-3P	3500	3300	4400	6700	12,000	24,000
Limousine-7P	3975	3500	4500	7000	13,000	25,000

KELLER — E.E. Keller and Fred Dagenhardt were two of the three electric vehicle proponents (Clyde J. Coleman the third) who proposed to provide motorized transport for visitors to the World's Columbian Exposition in Chicago in 1893. Three vehicles resulted. Refer to Columbia Electric.

J.M. Keller of Goshen, Indiana built an automobile for his own use in 1901, according to the February issue that year of *The Motor Vehicle Review*. Further details are lacking.

KELLER ELECTRIC — **Canton & Cleveland, Ohio** — **(1899, 1903)** — Though attempts to get into manufacture took place in two Ohio cities, the Keller never did move very far. The first try, in 1899, was in Canton where the Keller Electrical Shops were in the process of building an electric carriage, as reported in *The Autobain* that October. Probably only the single vehicle was produced at that time. By 1903 the company was in Cleveland as the J. Keller Electric Works. There, in August, a small piano-box electric runabout with its motor hung on the rear axle and a 12 cell Willard battery good for a 40-mile driving radius was placed on the market. Perhaps a small production followed, but the Keller seems to have withdrawn from view by year's end.

1914 Keller-Kar, cyclecar, WLB

KELLER-KAR — **Chicago, Illinois** — **(1914)** — The Keller Cyclecar Corporation was capitalized at $250,000 and incorporated in the state of Delaware by a group of people who were described only as Wilmington lawyers. The Keller Company itself was headquartered in Chicago. Interestingly, the initial plan was to power the Keller-Kar with a mini version of the Knight sleeve-valve engine which would certainly have made this cyclecar among the more unique in America. As it happened, however, the powerplant finally chosen was a two-cylinder air-cooled Wilson. Final drive by vee belt, transmission by friction set, a wheelbase of 96 inches and a tread of 36 inches completed the Keller-Kar's very typical cyclecar specifications. The price for the tandem two-seater was $375. The company was finished by the end of 1914.

1914 KELLER-KAR
Cyclecar — 2-cyl., 10 hp, 96" wb

	FP	5	4	3	2	1
Tandem Rdstr.-2P	375	1800	2800	4000	6200	13,000

KELLEY — The Kelley-Bridgett Company was organized in Danville, Illinois during the summer of 1904 with a capital stock of $50,000 for the manufacture of automobiles. Edward J. Kelley, William M. Bridgett and George Buckingham were the incorporators. Manufacture is doubted.

The Kelley-Hunter Company of Chicago, Illinois was organized during the fall of 1905 with a capital stock of $15,000 for the manufacture of automobiles. Incorporators were Gordon L. Gray, George P. Rowell and Henry A. Ritter. Manufacture is doubted, but subsequently this venture took on the dealership for the Northern car.

KELLY — Ernest R. Kelly of Wilmington, Delaware produced a small gasoline runabout which he marketed under the name of Acadia in 1903-1904. Refer to Acadia.

H.B. Kelly & Son of Topeka, Kansas announced its intention to establish an automobile factory at Salina early in 1909. This did not follow.

The Kelly-Field Company was organized in New York City during the summer of 1912 with a capital stock of $10,000 for the manufacture of automobiles. Charles F.U. Kelly and Harry E. Field were the partners involved. Manufacture is doubted.

KELLY — **Detroit, Michigan** — **(1895, 1901)** — Little is known about the experimental automobile built by William E. Kelly in 1895 other than the fact that, in his words, it did not "come up to my expectations." Another experimental gasoline car followed in 1901, which probably didn't either, though Kelly continued development work. Subsequently he was among the founders of the Wayne Automobile Company which produced a refined version of his car as the Wayne from 1904 to 1908. But he was most satisfied with the next car he designed, the E-M-F built from 1908 to 1912, and which he said was for him the realization of "a long cherished ambition."

KELLY STEAM — **Springfield, Ohio** — **(1901-1902)** — The O.S. Kelly Company manufactured steam traction engines in Springfield, and in 1901 O.W. Kelly of that firm built a steam carriage to test out a new engine of his invention featuring a rotary valve with a positive cut-off. He was so pleased with the results that he built a steam delivery wagon next, which was completed and successfully tested in 1902. There is no evidence, however, that either O.W. Kelly or the O.S. Kelly Company proceeded into manufacture of the steam car, though it would appear a few examples of the delivery wagon were built into 1903.

KELSEY — The Kelsey Car Corporation has been indicated on various car rosters as building a cyclecar in Connersville, Indiana in 1914. There was no such car built, nor any such company in town. Possibly this car-that-wasn't was confused with the prototype cyclecar built by the Connersville Buggy Company that year.

1897 Kelsey & Tilney, runabout, GR

KELSEY — **Philadelphia, Pennsylvania** — **(1897-1902)/KELSEY** — **Newark, New Jersey** — **(1920-1924)** — Cadwallader Washburn Kelsey was born into a well-to-do family living in the Chestnut Hill section of Philadelphia. He preferred being called Carl. In 1897, at age seventeen, he built his first car, a four-wheeler — and, when he entered Haverford College the year following, he constructed his second with a school chum named Sheldon Tilney. It was powered by a single-cylinder 5 hp Buffalo engine, had two wheels in front and one in the rear, and was dubbed an Autotri. The boys decided to proceed into manufacture and got as far as designing an emblem, when their respective fathers intervened and sent their progeny back to their studies because the automobile was an "instrument of the devil." (The Kelsey and Tilney Autotri is on display at the Smithsonian Institution.) By 1901 Carl Kelsey was consorting with the devil again, building a car with one more wheel and one more cylinder than the Autotri. This four-wheeler had an interesting two-cylinder engine: two one-cylinders mounted on either side of the differential housing. Graduating from college, Kelsey sold Autocars awhile in Philadelphia, until finally his father, though still no devotee of the automobile, relented sufficiently to put up the capital for a service and repair agency in Germantown. Looking after the cars of other manufacturers, he reasoned, might not leave his son the time to build any more of his own. Carl Kelsey found the time, building his fourth car, a monstrous four-cylinder bolide, in 1902. He would not build another for eight years, however, happening now upon a new car called the Maxwell, which he thought would go places and he wanted to go along. He wrote Maxwell-Briscoe in Tarrytown (New York) requesting the agency in Philadelphia, and Benjamin Briscoe said he could have it for $5000. Kelsey sold his Germantown garage and bought. He proved a salesman extraordinaire. Very shortly there were more Maxwells being sold in Philadelphia than anywhere else in the country, Tarrytown noticed, and Carl Kelsey was the Maxwell-Briscoe company's new sales manager. It was largely his efforts which resulted in Maxwell's ranking number three in the industry in 1909 (behind Ford and Buick), and largely Briscoe's efforts in trying to emulate Billy Durant's General Motors with his own United States Motor Company which convinced Kelsey to leave and become an automobile manufacturer himself. And he decided to challenge not Billy Durant, but Henry Ford. Two cars followed: the four-wheeled Spartan in 1910, which was built only as a prototype, and the three-wheeled Motorette of which about 210 were produced from 1911 until 1914. Then Carl Kelsey announced his retirement from the automobile industry, and went into banking awhile to make ends meet. But he couldn't stay away. In 1916 he designed another novelty: a friction-transmission, shaft-drive automobile. World War I intervened, and it was not until 1920 that the Kelsey Motor Company was organized in Newark (New Jersey) with a factory in Belleville to produce it. "You can actually coast one mile in three...," ads ballyhooed. "Think of the savings in gasoline, oil and tires this means." One of his new Kelseys pulled a seven-ton steam roller through the streets of Newark in the spring of 1921. But though a coterie of former Cartercar and Metz owners remained enamoured of the friction-transmission idea, the rest of America did not. Standard selective-transmission taxis were introduced, and by September of 1922 production cars as well. By now several hundred Kelseys had been built, the company had undergone a voluntary receivership and been reorganized, and Carl Kelsey thought everything was going well. But one day early in 1924 Kelsey was visited by the "Bankruptcy Gang," a group of infamous New Jersey attorneys who inveigled a company's receivership (persuading someone on the inside to swear mismanagement) in order to take advantage of the subsequent

1902 Kelsey, runabout, WLB

drop in a firm's stock prices. Enough was quite enough, Kelsey concluded, he was through with the automobile industry, this time for good. But he was not through with tinkering. In his late eighties he designed a two-man Skycar "helicopter" that he thought he could produce for use as a crop-duster to sell for about $2500. Shortly thereafter, in May 1970, he died.

1921 Kelsey, coupe, WLB

1920-1921 KELSEY
Model GW — 6-cyl., 46 hp, 116" wb

	FP	5	4	3	2	1
Touring-5P	1800	3700	4700	7300	13,700	26,000
Sedan-5P	2700	2300	3300	4600	7500	16,000
Runabout-2P	1750	3300	4400	6700	12,000	24,000

1922 KELSEY
Model GW — 6-cyl., 46 hp, 118-1/2" wb

Touring-5P	1800	3900	4800	7700	14,300	27,000
Roadster-3P	1800	4000	5000	8000	15,000	28,000
Coupe-4P	2700	2500	3500	5000	8500	18,000
Sedan-5P	2700	2300	3300	4600	7500	16,000

1923-1924 KELSEY
Model G — 4-cyl., 35 hp, 111" wb

Phaeton-5P	1150	4000	5000	8000	15,000	28,000
Sedan-5P	1450	2200	3200	4400	7000	15,000

KEMP — Quincy, Massachusetts — (1907) — John Kemp of Water Street in Quincy was a builder of two-stroke marine engines of one, two and three cylinders. In 1907 he built an automobile but it was strictly for his own use. Its components, save for the opposed two-cylinder four-stroke engine, were purchased from outside sources.

KENDALL — The Kendall Carriage Company was incorporated in Camden, New Jersey during the fall of 1897 for the manufacture of electric vehicles. Capital stock was $50,000 of which *The Motocycle* reported, a total of $10,000 was paid in. Manufacture is doubted.

KENDALLVILLE — Kendallville, Indiana — (1910) — Early in 1910 the Kendallville Buggy Company owned by the Rupp brothers, Fred and R.C., built a five-passenger touring car with a four-cylinder Waukeska engine. "This simple car is being turned out with a view of going extensively into automobile manufacture," the company announced to the press. There is no evidence, however, that this indeed did happen. Possibly the only Kendallville was the sample car.

KENDEL — The Kendel Motor Car Company was organized in Philadelphia, Pennsylvania late in 1910 with a capital stock of $500,000 to manufacture and deal in automobiles. Incorporators were C.F. Black, J.K. Allen and F. Mettler. During the summer of the following year, the firm announced its purchase of a two-acre plot in Lansdale upon which a factory would be built. Lansdale businessmen Howard Mitchell and J.F. Zane were also now involved in the project. This venture seems to have ended soon after.

1912 Kenmore, touring, WLB

KENMORE — Chicago, Illinois — (1910-1912) — "If you are in a position to take the agency for the Kenmore and can do us justice in your vicinity, we are prepared to offer you a proposition that you cannot afford to overlook. We intend to start an aggressive selling campaign which will cover the entire country and will back it up with some extensive advertising. This will create a big demand for our 1910 output, and as we have a limited number of cars ready for immediate delivery, you should make your arrangements with us as soon as possible in order to get the full benefit of this publicity. Send in your application for territory at once. Our policy is 'first come first served' and a square deal for all." Thus wrote the Kenmore Manufacturing Company of Chicago to the Flatrock Automobile Company of Flatrock, Indiana on February 3rd, 1910. The Kenmore offices were located at 234 La Salle Street, its factory and salesroom at Sangamon and 14th Place, and this venture was the idea of the F.A. and J.D. Meidinger. Little more is known about this automotive enterprise than the fact that the Meidinger brothers could not decide precisely what they wished to build. Their product had 32-inch wheels shod with pneumatic tires, which placed it at least philosophically out of the highwheeler genre, but the car had an unattractive motor-buggy look about it anyway. A two-speed planetary transmission was offered initially, though a three-speed selective followed for 1911, when the line also was supplemented with a larger four. The Kenmore quietly faded from the scene after 1912. The Sears, Roebuck and Company's later use of the Kenmore name for household appliances is believed to have followed the Sear's purchase of the Kenmore assets.

1910 KENMORE
Model A — 2-cyl., 14 hp, 82" wb

	FP	5	4	3	2	1
Runabout-2P	500	1800	2800	4000	6200	13,000
Roadster-3P	600	2000	3000	4200	6500	14,000

Model B — 2-cyl., 18 hp, 82" wb

Roadster-3P	650	2100	3100	4300	6800	14,500
Surrey-4P	675	2200	3200	4400	7000	15,000

1911 KENMORE
Model A — 2-cyl., 14 hp, 87" wb

Runabout-2/3P	550	1800	2800	4000	6200	13,000

Model C — 2-cyl., 18 hp, 87" wb

Surrey-4P	675	2000	3000	4200	6500	14,000
Roadster-2P	650	2000	3000	4200	6500	14,000

Model 30 — 4-cyl., 30 hp, 114" wb

Touring-5P	1250	2200	3200	4400	7000	15,000

1912 KENMORE
Model C — 2-cyl., 16/18 hp, 100" wb

Runabout	625	2000	3000	4200	6500	14,000
Roadster	650	2200	3200	4400	7000	15,000
Tourabout	675	2250	3300	4500	7300	15,500

Model D — 4-cyl., 20 hp, 100" wb

Runabout	700	2200	3200	4400	7000	15,000
Roadster	725	2300	3300	4600	7500	16,000
Touring	750	2350	3400	4700	7800	16,500

KENNEDY — Cortland, New York — (1900, 1905) — Kennedy Brothers of Cortland built a gasoline automobile in 1900 which, according to *The Autobain*, "has stood some very satisfactory tests," and according to *Cycle and Automobile Trade Journal*, would be offered "to the trade the coming season." There is no evidence that it ever was. One of the Kennedy brothers, Thomas J., did build another car, however, which was completed and tested on the streets of Cortland in the early fall of 1905. It was painted green, had two bench seats, and a number of novel features, among them that the car could be run on either one, two or three-cylinders. The engine lacked cams, oil cups or valves. Just one control lever took care of everything with regard to operation. The October 12th, 1905 issue of *The Motor Age* reported the forthcoming formation of a $150,000 stock venture. "The company will probably buy the plant of the Ellis Omnibus and Cab Company and begin the manufacture of automobiles on a large scale," *The Motor Age* noted. That was the last press reference to this venture. And this was probably the last automobile built by the Kennedy brothers.

KENNEDY STEAM — Cambridge, Massachusetts — (1901) — Details regarding its construction are lacking, but it is known that F. Lowell Kennedy, who described himself as "an instructor in the scientific school of Harvard University," built a steam car in 1901. Its purpose was experimental; manufacture did not follow.

KENNEDY — Los Angeles, California — (1915-1917) — The Kennedy from Los Angeles was a small gasoline-powered car with a Renault-type hood that was offered only as a coupe and was occasionally called the Petite. Its short wheelbase and tall body gave it the look of an electric. The car was built in small numbers until the shortage of materials in the wake of World War I brought the venture to a close. Various sources indicate the Kennedy involved as either G.M. or W.J. But it may have been one G.L. Kennedy instead. Guy L. Kennedy was president of the Model Motor Company at 940 South Los Angeles Street at the time and purported to be an automobile manufacturer.

1898 Kennedy Electric, NAHC

KENNEDY ELECTRIC — Philadelphia, Pennsylvania — (1898-1903) — The Kennedy Electric Carriage was introduced to the public on June 1st, 1898 at the Philadelphia Electrical Exhibition. It was named for C.W. Kennedy, who was described in *The Horseless Age* as "an electrical engineer of thirty years' experience." Kennedy was principally responsible for the storage batteries which he invented for the car and which purportedly had a number of advantages, to wit, "the small space they occupy, impossibility of buckling, large area of surface exposed, extraordinarily heavy charge and discharge rates, no slopping of the acid, and small weight." Other factors related to the design of the carriage were credited to Kennedy's associates F.A. Pocock and R. Ashley. The vehicle was a two-seater with drive to the front wheels. "The carriage does not 'weave,' as the rear steering machines do," its designers boasted. Although no formal company was ever incorporated for manufacture, it would appear that the Kennedy Electric was sold quietly and in small numbers as late as 1903.

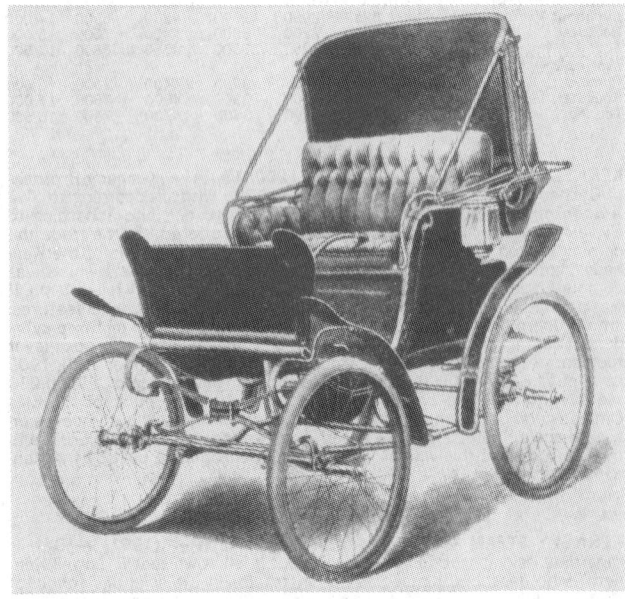

1900 Kensington, electric stanhope, NAHC

766

KENSINGTON — Buffalo, New York — (1899-1904) — In August of 1899 the Kensington Bicycle Company of Buffalo announced the successful completion of its first electric automobile. In October the company announced that it would close out its bicycle business and concentrate on electric car production. By early spring of 1901, Kensington had added a steam car to its line; by mid-summer of 1902, Kensington had mortgaged its factory for $25,000, which was not a good sign. Earlier that year the Kensington Automobile Company, as it was now known, had indicated its arrangement with the French Darracq company for production of the Darracq in the United States, but this plan apparently fell through. A gasoline car did follow in 1902, but though it had a French look it was not a Darracq built under license. Its engine was a two-cylinder air-cooled Kelecom imported from Belgium. In 1903 Kensington advised its clients that the gasoline car was "receiving our exclusive attention and taxing the entire capacity of our factory." Not for long, however; the year after that Kensington was out of business. Kensington president William Knowles tried again later in 1904 with the Knowles Automobile Manufacturing Company and a car named for himself, but whether any production at all was realized is problematical. Interestingly, in 1906 what was called at the time a "unique decision" was handed down in an Indianapolis court when it was ruled that a former Kensington owner did not have to repay a $2000 note he had borrowed from a bank to purchase a Kensington. The car had been worthless, he had claimed, and he had returned it to the company.

1899-1900 KENSINGTON

	FP	5	4	3	2	1
Small Electric Stanhope	1500	2700	3600	5300	8800	19,000

1901 Kensington, electric stanhope, HAC

1901 KENSINGTON

Small Electric Stanhope	1500	2700	3600	5300	8800	19,000
Steam Runabout	750	3100	4200	6300	10,500	22,000

1902 Kensington, gasoline, tonneau, NAHC

1902 KENSINGTON

Small Electric Stanhope	1500	2700	3600	5300	8800	19,000
Steam Vehicle No. 1 Rbt.	800	3100	4200	6300	10,500	22,000
Steam Vehicle No. 3 Surrey	1000	3200	4300	6500	11,000	23,000
Gasoline Tonneau (2-cyl., 12 hp, 72" wb)	2500	2500	3500	5000	8500	18,000

1903 Kensington, gasoline, tonneau, HAC

1903-1904 KENSINGTON

	FP	5	4	3	2	1
Gasoline Tonneau (2-cyl., 12 hp, 72" wb)	2500	2500	3500	5000	8500	18,000

KENT — A.W. Kent is indicated on some car rosters as having built a steam car in Marietta, Ohio in 1901. This has not been confirmed. There is documentation, however, regarding the steamer he built in Boston, Massachusetts from 1899-1901. Refer to Kent's Pacemaker.

The Kent Motor Car Company was organized in Grand Rapids, Michigan in early 1901 with a capital stock of $2000 to manufacture and deal in automobiles. Incorporators were Fred B. Clark, Roy L. Leigh and Nelson M. Abernethy. Manufacture is doubted.

1917 Kent, 5-pass., touring, WLB

KENT — Newark, New Jersey — (1916-1917) — Kent Motors Corporation was originally a dealership operating at 1704 Broadway in New York City, and specializing in the export of cars to Latin America. Among the grand plans envisioned when the firm decided to enter automobile manufacture was the construction of a factory in Havana, Cuba — but for the moment Kent contented itself with the purchase of 16 1/2 acres along the Passaic River in the Belleville section of Newark upon which land a plant was begun. The new Kent Motors Company was incorporated for $200,000 in September 1916. Among the people involved were F.H. Clarke, Dr. H.F. Clarke, R.J. Cosgrove, Lloyd H. Foster, Wallace A. Hood, F.J. Nagel and J.H. Simpson. Stock in this new venture was offered for sale in January 1917, three months after the Kent automobile was introduced. The Kent was a quite ordinary assembled car with a four-cylinder Continental engine and standard components throughout, though it did come fully equipped with such niceties as a robe carrier, footrail and eight-day clock. The Kent's principal problem seems to have been some of the people behind it. In May 1917 an involuntary petition in bankruptcy was filed against Kent Motors. In July several officials of the company were indicted by a federal grand jury for fraud in stock promotion. They were convicted in November.

1916-1917 KENT
Four — 40 hp, 116" wb

		5	4	3	2	1
Touring-5P	985	2700	3600	5300	8800	19,000
Club Roadster-4P	985	2900	3700	5600	9100	20,000

1900 Kent's Pacemaker, runabout, NAHC

KENT'S PACEMAKER — Boston, Massachusetts — (1899-1901) — Kent's Pacemaker was a steam car named for its designer, A.W. Kent. It sported a single steering wheel in front and three rear wheels, the center one of which did the driving, the other two "for stability only" and so arranged that they could be raised to allow the vehicle to coast like a bicycle. In the early fall of 1899 the automotive press was informed that George N. March was organizing the Colonial Automobile Company at 32 Hawley Street in Boston for manufacture of cycle boats, felt-edged rims for pneumatic tires, and A.W. Kent's car. Apparently production of a few Kent's Pacemakers followed. The last reference to this car and company was September 1901, when both were declared defunct. An unconfirmed reference from 1901 has A.W. Kent in Marietta, Ohio and building a steam car there. If indeed it was built, it was never manufactured.

KENTUCKY — Kentucky Electric and Kentucky Kar were initially announced as names for the new cars of the Kentucky Wagon Works in Louisville, Kentucky. When an automobile did finally arrive from the company in 1916, however, it was called the Dixie Flyer. Refer to Dixie Flyer.

The Kentucky Thoroughbred was a model of the Ames from Owensboro, Kentucky which was marketed in 1914 and 1915. The first Ames car had been produced in 1910. Refer to Ames.

1921 Kenworthy, Line-O-Eight, touring, WLB

KENWORTHY — Mishawaka, Indiana — (1920-1921) — In November of 1919, Cloyd Y. Kenworthy exchanged his vice-presidential chair at Roamer for a presidential seat in his own new company. Kenworthy Motors Corporation was organized with a capital stock of $400,000 that month, and a factory site at Mishawaka, Indiana was chosen. In January of 1920 the Kenworthy venture became considerably more grandiose as capitalization was raised to $6 million, and S.C. Wood, L.B. Phillips and Harry McDonald, Jr. — monied capitalists all — joined the enterprise. The Kenworthy idea was "A Car with No Superior" — and initially this was provided in a big four and six. But in December of 1920 Kenworthy announced its *piece-de-resistance:* the "Line-O-Eight" which featured four-wheel brakes and which, with the Duesenberg Model A, was America's first production automobile to do so. The engine powering the Kenworthy four was a Rochester-Duesenberg, the six was a Continental, the straight-eight was of Cloyd Kenworthy's own design. The car was magnificent. Its body design was by Karl H. Martin, designer also of the Wasp. Perhaps it was the Kenworthy timing that was wrong. Introducing a very expensive new motorcar in the midst of the postwar recession was a risky venture at best, and Kenworthy Motors Corporation quickly failed. In March of 1921 there was a try at reorganization. In August Kenworthy formally admitted bankruptcy.

1920-1921 KENWORTHY
Model 4-80 — 4-cyl., 80 hp, 130" wb

	FP	5	4	3	2	1
Touring-5P	5000	4000	5000	8000	15,000	28,000
Model 6-55 — 6-cyl., 55 hp, 130" wb						
Touring-5P	3900	4300	5400	8700	16,500	30,000
Model 8-90 — 8-cyl., 90 hp, 130" wb						
Touring-5P	5550	4500	5800	9500	18,000	32,000

KEPLER-BEERY — Dayton, Ohio — (1903-1904) — The Kepler-Beery Motor Car Company of Dayton was organized during the summer of 1903. Its officers were C. Carlisle Beery (president), Jesse S. Kepler (vice-president and general manager), and Herman R. Scammon (secretary). Their product was a single-cylinder 10 hp light touring car. "This company has several machines in service at present and they are giving good service," *The Automobile Review* reported in October 1903. The magazine also reported the Kepler-Beery intention to produce engines for the trade as well, but it would appear the entire venture had ended by early in 1904.

KEQUA — In an August 1901 issue, *The Motor Age* reported that Kequa & Sons of Springfield, Ohio were about "to engage in the manufacture of automobiles." So far as has been recorded, this did not follow.

KERMATH — Detroit, Michigan — (1907) — The Kermath Motor Car Company of Detroit decided that specialization was its key to success. It would offer just one model, what in those days was known as a "gentleman's roadster," though Kermath preferred the term "Speedaway" to describe it. It was a high-powered, high-quality four which featured shaft drive, a tubular front axle and a semi-floating rear axle. Timken bearings were used throughout. The Kermath's most distinctive feature, however, was its radiator design, which resembled a heraldic shield in configuration and which Kermath was attempting to patent. The Kermath Speedaway was introduced at the Detroit Automobile Show in February of 1907. In March the company announced that it was negotiating for a new factory in the city because its present East Fort Street quarters were inadequate. Alas, more inadequate than that was the Kermath treasury. The company quickly folded. The Detroit show car is the only Kermath Speedaway believed to have been built.

1907 Kermath, Speedaway, roadster, NAHC

1907 KERMATH
Speedaway — 4-cyl., 26 hp, 103" wb

	FP	5	4	3	2	1
Roadster-3P	2000	3100	4200	6300	10,500	22,000

KERN — The Kern Automobile Transportation Company was organized during the spring of 1900 with a capital stock of $25,000 to "rent, construct and purchase motor vehicles and to operate the same" in Kern County, California. Behind this venture were H.E. Sweetser, L.F. Champion, L.J. Whyers, G.G. Hutchings, J. Sanderson, W.F. Matlock, J.W. Shaffer, all of the foregoing from Kern; and Alvin Fay, from Bakersfield. Manufacture of a car is doubted.

KERNODLE-McDANIEL — The Kernodle-McDaniel Manufacturing Company was organized in Frankfort, Indiana during the summer or 1912 with a capital stock of $10,000 for the manufacture of automobiles and parts. The partners involved were W.T. Kernodle and P. McDaniel. Manufacture of a car is doubted.

KERO-CAR — Dayton, Ohio — (1909) — The Kero-Car Motor Company was organized in late November 1909 by a group of Dayton businessmen. As the name indicates, its product was to be driven by a kerosene engine. "The new engine is said not to be a freak, either in appearance or operation," *The Automobile* noted in its December 2nd issue. "It will burn, however, either gasoline, kerosene or alcohol." A prototype car was built, but the company's manufacturing plans died aborning.

KEROMOBILE — Brooklyn, New York — (1902) — The Keromobile was so named because of its use of kerosene as fuel. But it was called that for five months only, beginning in March 1902 when the car was advertised by B.H. Pomeroy of Brooklyn, and ending in July when Pomeroy decided to rename the car for himself. All subsequent production was marketed under the name of Pomeroy. The Keromobile-cum-Pomeroy was a small runabout powered by a two-cylinder two-stroke 8 hp engine weighing only 85 pounds. The price was $650.

KEROMOTOR — The Keromotor Development Company was organized in Newark, New Jersey during the fall of 1900 with a capital stock of $100,000 to deal in motors and engines. This incorporation was followed several months later by the Keromotor Company of Newark which announced plans to "manufacture a steam carriage using kerosene as fuel." By year's end, Keromotor indicated that it was "about to start business." Subsequent manufacture of a car has not been documented.

KEROSENE MOTOR — In November of 1901 the Kerosene Oil Automobile Company of New York City announced its plans to begin the manufacture of kerosene-fueled automobiles. There is no evidence this ever followed.

KERSTON — Detroit, Michigan — (1917) — In April of 1917 Harry Kerston left his engineering post with Studebaker in South Bend, Indiana and traveled to Detroit where he opened an office in the Kresge Building. There he announced that, in association with J. William Barnes, he was preparing to organize a company for the manufacture of the Kerston gas-electric car he had designed. Kerston was described in the press as an Englishman who had worked with the Daimler and Meteor companies abroad and who had come to the United States in 1914. In the three short years that followed, he had worked for Hupmobile and Packard in addition to Studebaker. "He is somewhat of an inventive turn of mind," *Automobile Topics* reported, "and owns the patent covering the radiator shutters used on the Hudson and Columbia cars, made by the Harrison Radiator Company under an arrangement with the Detroit Motor Appliance Company." Whether Harry Kerston was everything he purported to be is not known. Neither is the existence of any Kerston car except that on his drawing board. Possibly a prototype was built; certainly manufacture never followed.

KESSELL — Massillon, Ohio — (1899) — In the woodshed at the Coxey residence at Millport where he was employed, Frank E. Kessell built an automobile in 1899 all parts of which he fashioned himself. The result was not exactly state of the art, even for this early period. The steering mechanism, for example, was seen to by running a cable over two shive wheels at the rear and one up front. The Kessell traveled five feet on its first test run, and then stopped. Subsequently, Kessell made a few changes, and his car performed more admirably, with a top speed of fifteen miles an hour. Hills required some pushing, however.

1921 Kessler, touring, WLB

KESSLER — Detroit, Michigan — (1920-1921)/**KESS-LINE** — (1922) — Martin C. Kessler designed his first automobile engine in 1907 for the Chalmers Motor Company of Detroit, and he served various automotive firms in a consulting capacity for a decade thereafter. After a few abortive attempts, he began his own Kessler Motor Company in 1917 for the manufacture of aircraft engines, and war contracts kept that enterprise going nicely for awhile. In January of 1920 Kessler Motor Company announced its forthcoming entrance onto the automotive scene; the month following the Kessler made its debut at the Detroit Automobile Show. Its chassis was of standard components throughout, the vehicle distinguished by its Kessler-designed supercharged 70 hp four-cylinder engine. Available only as a $1995 touring car, the Kessler Super-Charge Four went into production later that year. In 1921 another car was developed, and another company formed for its production, in September that year Kess-Line Motors being announced as an offspring to Kessler Motor Company. The former factory of the Liberty Motor Car Company in Detroit was leased, and Kess-Line's officers were indicated as Martin Kessler, president; W.H. Radford, vice-president; H.H. Scott, formerly of Fisher Body, as secretary-treasurer. The new Kess-Line Eight (a supercharged overhead cam 100 hp straight-eight) was introduced at the Detroit Automobile Show in early 1922 with a $2150 price tag. There is some controversy as to whether its engine was designed by Kessler or Radford. Both subsequently claimed it. Probably only the prototype Kess-Line car was ever built. Subsequently the Kess-Line engine was reworked and fitted into the Balboa, a California automotive venture of the mid-Twenties in which W.H. Radford was prominently involved. What Kessler was doing following the failure of the Kess-Line venture is not precisely known, though his Kessler Motor Company was in business at least as late as 1927 when a claims judgment was awarded in its favor for World War I operational expenses. During the mid-Thirties Martin Kessler was reported to have gone broke trying to develop a ten-cylinder car.

1922 Kess-Line, touring, WLB

1920-1921 KESSLER
Super-Charge Four — 70 hp, 117" wb

	FP	5	4	3	2	1
Touring	1995	3300	4400	6700	12,000	24,000

1922 KESS-LINE
Eight — 100 hp, 119" wb

	FP	5	4	3	2	1
Touring	2150	3700	4700	7300	13,700	26,000

KEYS — Council Bluffs, Iowa — (1914) — "That it would be practicable to manufacture automobiles in Council Bluffs has been proven within the last few weeks at the Keys Bros.' Carriage factory at Twenty-Eighth Street and First Avenue," *The Automobile* announced during the summer of 1914. Two sample Keys cars had just been completed and "a thorough test has shown them to be equal to any make of the same size." The Keys was a 40 hp four-cylinder touring car on a 112-inch wheelbase. The engine was a Buda, coachwork was via Michigan Body Company. Possibly the first two Keys were also the last; there is no evidence of sustained manufacture following.

KEYSTONE — The Keystone Automobile Exchange, Inc. was organized in Lancaster, Pennsylvania during the summer of 1912 with a capital stock of $100,000 to manufacture and deal in motor cars. James W. White, Clarence J. Jacobs and H.W. Davis were the principals involved. Manufacture is doubted.

The Keystone Automobile and Garage Company was organized in Brooklyn, New York during the spring of 1906 with a capital stock of $20,000 for the manufacture and sale of automobiles and machinery. Incorporators were H.M. Norwood, H.E. Gates and W.W. Lansing, all of Brooklyn. Manufacture of a car is doubted.

The Keystone Motor Car Company was organized in Camden, New Jersey during late 1903 with a capital stock of $12,500 for the manufacture of automobiles. Incorporators were E.H. Godshalk, C.A. Godshalk and John F. Joline, all of Camden. Manufacture is doubted.

The Keystone Motor Supply Company was organized in Pittsburgh, Pennsylvania during late 1911 with a capital stock of $12,000 to "manufacture, sell, trade and repair motor cars and vehicles of all kinds." Incorporators were R.V. Campbell, C.H. McDonald and E.H. Biedringhas. Manufacture of a car is doubted.

The Keystone Vehicle Company was organized in Columbus, Ohio early in 1914 with a capital stock of $15,000 to manufacture and deal in motor vehicles. Incorporators were H.E. Sullivan, Earl C. Bates, S.L. McMillin, W.H. Bates, W.D. Sullivan.

1900 Keystone, Autocycle, runabout, WLB

KEYSTONE — Philadelphia, Pennsylvania — (1900) — The Keystone Motor Company of Philadelphia went to market during the summer of 1900 with a gasoline car powered by a single-cylinder 5 hp water-cooled engine which was offered as the Autocycle and the Wagonette two-passenger models, and a Parcel Delivery with accommodation for only the driver. The cars were designed by Edward B. Gallaher. The company also made the motor available independently. In August 1900 Keystone boasted sales of seventy-one motors, five Autocycles and four Wagonettes in the first month of business. Sales continued to improve. In their fifth month of business, however, the Keystone people found the offer of a group of high-powered Philadelphia businessmen too good to resist, and sold out. By November the Keystone had become the Searchmont.

1900 Keystone, Wagonette, runabout, NAHC

1900 KEYSTONE

	FP	5	4	3	2	1
Autocycle (1-cyl., 5 hp, 52" wb)	750	1600	2700	3800	5800	12,000
Wagonette (1-cyl., 5 hp, 52" wb)	750	1800	2800	4000	6200	13,000
Parcel Delivery (1-cyl., 5 hp, 52")	750	1500	2500	3600	5500	11,000

KEYSTONE — Pittsburgh, Pennsylvania — (1914-1915) — The Keystone from Pittsburgh probably didn't survive six months. It featured a six-cylinder 55 hp Rutenber engine, four-speed selective transmission, electric lighting and starting, and a longish 138-inch wheelbase. The chassis was designed by Charles C. Snodgrass and the vehicle was built by H. Cook & Brothers. The car was announced in the October 1914 issue of *Cycle and Automobile Trade Journal*, and disappeared soon thereafter.

1910 Keystone Six, touring, WLB

KEYSTONE SIX — Yonkers, New York & Du Bois Pennsylvania — (1909-1910) — Early in 1909 C.P. Munch of Yonkers bought out the W.S. Reed Company which had begun manufacture of the Massillon in Ohio only to go under within months. The Reed factory was not part of the deal, which left Munch with a car but no place to build it. He found a partner in Pennsylvania named R.M. Allen, and a factory was begun for the new Munch-Allen Motor Car Company in the town of Du Bois for the manufacture of the Pennsylvania six. In the meantime, Munch talked a neighbor, W.S. Howard, into building the first batch of cars for him in the Howard Motor Works plant now at liberty in Yonkers because W.S.'s Howard car had just failed. Howard produced thirty cars for Munch, by which time the Du Bois factory was ready, and the operation moved to Pennsylvania, although the partners now decided they preferred to call the car the Keystone. Available as a two-seater roadster and two touring cars, all models carried the same $2250 price tag. The Keystone Six-Sixty featured a four-speed gearbox with direct on third *and* fourth — which seems to be the only deviation from the specifications of the former Massillon. Things did not go well in Du Bois. In 1910 C.P. Munch returned home to build the Keystone in Yonkers, quite possibly the old Howard plant again, as the Munch Motor Car Company. Though he now added a $1950 light six to his line, he fared no better back home either.

1909 KEYSTONE SIX
Six-Sixty — 6-cyl., 60 hp, 122" wb

	FP	5	4	3	2	1
Roadster-2P	2250	3300	4400	6700	12,000	24,000
Baby Tonneau-4P	2250	3300	4400	6600	11,500	23,500
Touring-5P	2250	3200	4300	6500	11,000	23,000

1910 KEYSTONE SIX
Light Six — 6-cyl., 30/35 hp, 116" wb

	FP	5	4	3	2	1
Touring-5P	1950	3200	4300	6500	11,000	23,000
Baby Tonneau-4P	1950	3300	4400	6600	11,500	23,500
Roadster-2P	1950	3300	4400	6700	12,000	24,000

Six-Sixty — 6-cyl., 60 hp, 122" wb

	FP	5	4	3	2	1
Roadster-2P	2250	3500	4500	7000	13,000	25,000
Baby Tonneau-4P	2250	3400	4500	6900	12,500	24,500
Touring-5P	2250	3300	4400	6700	12,000	24,000

1899 Keystone Steamer, runabout, NAHC

KEYSTONE STEAMER — Lebanon, Pennsylvania — (1899-1900) — The Keystone Match & Machine Company was, as its name implies, the manufacturer of matches and match-making machines. It had begun in business in Lebanon in 1894, and added bicycles to its line in 1896. By 1899 Keystone had a steam car as well. "The application of steam is through small cylinders in the hub of the wheel, each of the rear wheels being supplied with three small engines of that type," *The Horseless Age* said in December. "The construction of the motors is such that they dispense with the use of sprockets, chains and compensating gears, each wheel being independent of the other on a stationary axle." Twenty miles an hour was the car's speed, and Keystone M & M (as the company frequently abbreviated itself) declared that it would be in a position to supply "both light vehicles and trucks for delivery purposes at an early day." Keystone returned exclusively to matches and the machines for making them soon after the turn of the century. Meanwhile J.G. Xander, an engineer with the company, took off for Reading to get into the automobile business on his own.

1907 Kiblinger, surrey, HAC

KIBLINGER — Auburn, Indiana — (1907-1909) — The W.H. Kiblinger Company of Auburn called its highwheeler the "lowest priced successful automobile on the road." And that may not have been too far from the truth at the time, since the price was as low as $250 for a sturdy runabout, and Kiblinger was selling as many of its two-cylinder air-cooled buggies as it could make. "All the machines are carefully crafted," the company said. "When you receive your car, simply attach wheels and top and it is ready to roll." One satisfied customer called the Kiblinger a "Hercules in hill climbing," and the superintendent of the Apperson factory in Kokomo gave it high praise as well. What ended life for the Kiblinger was a court case. When the people building the Success (a highwheeler from St. Louis also sold for as low as $250) sued for patent infringement, the manager of the Kiblinger factory, one W.H. McIntyre, found a convenient solution for the Kiblinger board of directors by buying them out and continuing in production with a Kiblinger that was revised out of harm's way of the lawsuit and renamed the McIntyre.

1908 Kiblinger, runabout, GR

1907-1909 KIBLINGER
Highwheeler — 2-cyl., 65" wb

	FP	5	4	3	2	1
Model A (4 hp)	250	2200	3200	4400	7000	15,000
Model B (6 hp)	300	2250	3300	4500	7300	15,500
Model C (6 hp)	320	2300	3300	4600	7500	16,000
Model D (10 hp)	375	2400	3400	4800	8000	17,000
Model E (10 hp)	395	2400	3400	4800	8000	17,000
Model F (10 hp)	450	2450	3500	4900	8300	17,500

KIDDER — New Haven, Connecticut — (1899-1903) — Wellington P. Kidder of Jamaica Plain, Massachusetts was the inventor of the Kidder press and the Wellington and Franklin typewriters. In 1899 he built two steam cars, the second of which was successful and prompted him to go into manufacture the following year as the Kidder Motor Vehicle Company. Most of the money behind this venture came from T. Attwater Barnes, who became the Kidder president. The plant of the former New Haven Chair Company on Audubon Street in New Haven, Connecticut was selected for manufacture. Although Kidder had also come up with a gasoline car he called the Petromobile, it was not produced. The Kidder was offered only as a steamer: a $1000 Model 2 runabout and $1600 Model B delivery wagon. The twin cylinders of its motor were placed on each side of the boiler at the back of the vehicle with direct drive to the rear axle.

1901 Kidder, steam carriage, NAHC

The car looked to be quite sturdily built, but the price was high. In November 1900, thirty-five Kidder steamers were reported to be under construction. In April 1903, according to *The Automobile*, the Kidder Motor Vehicle Company simply "voted to discontinue its corporate existence." Most likely the reason for this was the death of T. Attwater Barnes and Wellington P. Kidder's interest now in pursuing experiments with gasoline and electric vehicles. "He himself is worth a fortune," *The Motor Age* had commented regarding Kidder, though it appears he did not wish to risk any of it by going into sustained manufacture. The Kidder Motor Vehicle Company was sold to John H. Springer of New York, who subsequently built the Springer automobile. Wellington P. Kidder did produce at least a half-dozen more cars by 1907, but these appear to have been for family and friends in Jamaica Plain and environs.

1901 Kidder, model 2, light runabout, HAC

1899-1903 KIDDER

	FP	5	4	3	2	1
Model 2 Runabout	1000	2400	3400	4800	8000	17,000
Model B Delivery	1600	2300	3300	4600	7500	16,000

KIEL — "Kiel, a town in Manitowoc County, Wisconsin, is a little bit of a place but Frederick Thiessen, Philip Juenheimer and William Drucker believe it is big enough to support an automobile factory of at least modest proportions," reported *The Motor World* in November 1911. "Accordingly, they have organized and incorporated the Kiel Motor Car Company, with capital stock of $14,000 and it is not improbable that the citizens of the town will supply the factory building necessary to keep the town on the automobile map." Apparently the town of Kiel had second thoughts about its desire to be on the automobile map at all. This venture died aborning.

KILBOURN — Kilbourn, Wisconsin — (1909) — What this car might have been called had it proceeded into manufacture is not known, but the prototype was built in the Marshall machine shop in Kilbourn. It used a two-cylinder air-cooled 18 hp engine with double disc friction transmission and 36-inch solid rubber tires. A two-million-dollar water power dam had recently been completed in Kilbourn, and apparently businessmen in town believed their community now ready for a brand-new industry. About $12,000 was raised for a new factory, but when it was gone so were the hopes of Kilbourn for getting into the car business. The town of Kilbourn (named for Bryan Kilbourn; the founder of what is now the Chicago, Milwaukee, St. Paul and Pacific Railroad) no longer exists, incidentally, though its remnants are among the points of interest sighted when riding the "Ducks" in the Wisconsin Dells.

1888 Kimball, tricycle, NAHC

KIMBALL — Boston, Massachusetts — (1888) — In 1888, in Boston, Fred M. Kimball built a tricycle with its passenger seat perched loftily between two gigantic wire wheels, the smaller driving wheel in front, and power supplied by a six-cell lead storage battery. This unusual pioneer electric could travel at about 5 mph and was good for 10 miles on level road between battery charges. The vehicle accommodated but one passenger and was built by Kimball for P.W. Pratt of Boston.

1910 Kimball Electric, runabout, WLB

KIMBALL ELECTRIC — Chicago, Illinois — (1910-1912) — C.P. Kimball & Company of Chicago was famous as the maker of quality pianos, and by the turn of the century had launched a sideline coachbuilding business, specializing by 1905 in the transformation of old-style rear-entrance tonneau bodies into the more modish side-entrance versions. The automobiles which the company also built were electrics. Precisely when Kimball built its first is not known, but it may have been even before 1900. Possibly cars to custom order were produced thereafter, but it was not until 1910 that the firm offered a standard production line. These Kimballs featured final drive by double chain, cushion tires and left-hand wheel steering. In May of 1912 Kimball announced that production henceforth would be to custom order only. This offer was repeated in 1913, and Kimballs may have been offered on this basis for a while thereafter.

1911 Kimball Electric, landaulet, HAC

1910-1911 KIMBALL ELECTRIC

	FP	5	4	3	2	1
Model E-8 Victoria Phae. (72'' wb)	2000	2700	3600	5300	8800	19,000
Model E-7 Extension Cpe. (72'' wb)	3000	2400	3400	4800	8000	17,000
Model F-10 Landaulet (100'' wb)	3800	2500	3500	5000	8500	18,000

1912 KIMBALL ELECTRIC

	FP	5	4	3	2	1
George IV Phaeton (82'' wb)	3000	3000	4000	6000	9500	21,000
Special Design Cpe. (82'' wb)	3000	2500	3500	5000	8500	18,000

KIMPEL — Cleveland, Ohio — (1914) — Using the facilities of a local blacksmith shop, George W. Kimpel of Cleveland built himself a cyclecar in 1914. Its engine was an air-cooled 10 hp vee-twin, which he fitted in a 100-inch wheelbase chassis with 48-inch tread and two-speed transmission. All components of the car were made by Kimpel, and he envisioned marketing the vehicle at $375. No company was ever organized for manufacture, however, and his total production was possibly the single vehicle.

KINDALL — Bluffton, Indiana — (1903) — That the 10 hp steam car he built in 1903 was fitted with seats in the back for the carrying of six passengers and would do double-duty as a produce carrier is the extent of knowledge regarding the automobile of A.J. Kindall. He is believed to have built the one car only.

KING — A steam car was purportedly built in Osgood, Indiana by a Mr. King circa 1904. Further details are lacking.

In 1921 W.A. King, whose previous effort had been with the Southern Six from Memphis, Tennessee, was in Los Angeles, California arranging to begin manufacture of his new idea. "He will form a company . . . and has plans completed for a car to suit Coast conditions particularly," reported *Motor West* that April. No doubt this venture ended as dismally as the Southern Six had, and probably before the building of a single prototype.

The King Auto Company was organized during the fall of 1910 in Trenton, New Jersey with a capital stock of $3000 to manufacture and deal in motor vehicles. Incorporators were Hugh Grant King and William Holt Apgar. Manufacture is doubted.

The King Cyclecar Company is indicated on various car rosters as producing the Ambler cyclecar in Cleveland, Ohio in 1914. Documentation is lacking. No such firm is listed in Cleveland city directories of the period.

KING — Chicago, Illinois — (1899-1900) — A.W. King was a machinist at 71 West Jackson Street in Chicago who ran a sideline business of building gasoline-powered runabouts at the turn of the century. Details regarding the cars are lacking, but it is known that in November 1899 King received an order for six cars and, in order to produce them in the time specified, leased floor space for their assembly at George E. Lloyd & Company.

1896 King, runabout, NAHC

KING — Detroit, Michigan — (1896, 1911-1923)/Buffalo, New York — (1923-1924) — Charles Brady King had planned to enter the Chicago Times-Herald Contest of 1895 with a four-cylinder gasoline automobile he was then in the process of building. Unable to complete it in time, he served instead as umpire for the Mueller-Benz entry and drove the car for the last hour of the event to finish second to the Duryea. Back home in Detroit, he finished his car, and on March 6th, 1896 it became the first gasoline automobile to be successfully driven on the streets of that city. Henry Ford followed him on a bicycle. Already in the manufacturing business — "King Patent Gas Engines for Vehicles and Launches," the ads said — King helped Ford secure the parts for his first car. Then he went off to fight the Spanish-American War, as chief machinist on the U.S.S. *Yosemite*. Returning home in 1899, he sold his engine business to Olds Motor Works, though remaining on the Olds engineering staff until that company suffered its famous fire. Thereafter he allied himself with another Olds veteran, Jonathan D. Maxwell, to establish the Northern Manufacturing Company which produced the Northern car from 1902-1908. Early in 1908, when he saw the fortunes of that company flagging, he left with plans to build another car, first spending two years in Europe to study the art of

771

1911 King, model A, touring, HAC

automobile design there, then returning to Detroit to put together his new King, which like the 1896 King was a four-cylinder. It was tested in 1910, and in February 1911 the King Motor Car Company was incorporated with a capital stock of $500,000 for its manufacture. Among the progressive features of the new King were its en bloc engine, cantilever springs, centrally-located gearshift and left-hand drive. Initially, the King organization — H.K. White, Jr. was its president — worked out of a rented factory at 1559 West Jefferson, but had outgrown that premises by year's end and early in 1912 moved into the old Hupp plant at Jefferson and Concord when the Hupmobile operation was relocated. Possibly this expansion had been too hasty, since the King company went into receivership within months. The firm was bought by Artemus Ward, an advertising man from New York City, who installed J.G. Bayerline as the new president in the spring of 1913. Two years later, following a dispute, Bayerline was out and Ward was King's new president. Meanwhile, in December of 1914, two months after Cadillac announced its V-8, the King Motor Car Company was on the market with one too. At $1350, it was advertised as "the world's first popular-priced Eight." King's biggest years were 1915 and 1916, with an output of 3000 cars each year. During the latter year, Charles B. King went off to war again, serving with the Signal Corps of the U.S. Army, for whom he directed the design of the King-Bugatti aero engine. In addition to being an engineer, King was an architect, musician, artist, writer, painter and yachtsman. Business acumen seems to have been his failing, which he shared with the people in executive control of the company bearing his name. From 1916 onward, the King automobile was produced only as an eight, and there were fewer of them as year passed year. In the fall of 1920 Artemus Ward led a group of five King directors in a request for dissolution. Failure to be granted bank loans and a lack of working capital were cited as the reasons behind the company's problems. Inefficient management was the conclusion reached by the trade press. Early in 1921, the King assets were sold for $500,000 to Charles A. Finnegan of Buffalo. He also assumed the King debts of approximately $1,000,000. The claims were paid off by late 1922, receivership was lifted, and for a while it appeared the company might make it. In October of 1923 the King Motor Car Company moved into a much smaller plant in Buffalo. A total of 240 cars was built that year. Considerably less than that were produced before the company entered final bankruptcy in 1924. During the King's good years, export had been healthy, with King motorcars sold throughout Europe, in additon to South America, South Africa, Australia and Russia. The last Kings were sold in England in 1925.

1912 King, model A, coupe, WLB

1911-1912 KING
Model A — 4-cyl., 35 hp, 115" wb

	FP	5	4	3	2	1
Touring-5P	1565	2500	3500	5000	8500	18,000
Roadster-2P	1565	2700	3600	5300	8800	19,000
Coupe-3P	2165	2000	3000	4200	6500	14,000

1913 KING
Model B — 4-cyl., 30 hp, 112" wb

	FP	5	4	3	2	1
Touring-5P	1095	2400	3400	4800	8000	17,000

Model A — 4-cyl., 35 hp, 115" wb

	FP	5	4	3	2	1
Touring	1565	2500	3500	5000	8500	18,000
Roadster-2P	1565	2700	3600	5300	8800	19,000
Coupe-3P	2165	2000	3000	4200	6500	14,000

1914 KING
Model B — 4-cyl., 30 hp, 112" wb

	FP	5	4	3	2	1
Touring-5P	1095	2400	3400	4800	8000	17,000
Roadster-2P	1095	2500	3500	5000	8500	18,000

1913 King, model B, touring, HAC

1914 King, model B, touring, HAC

1915 King, model C, cabriolet, HAC

1915 KING
Model C — 4-cyl., 30 hp, 113" wb

	FP	5	4	3	2	1
Touring-5P	1075	2500	3500	5000	8500	18,000
Roadster-2P	1075	2700	3600	5300	8800	19,000
Cabriolet-2P	1490	2400	3400	4800	8000	17,000

Model D — 8-cyl., 40/50 hp, 120" wb

	FP	5	4	3	2	1
Touring-5P	1350	3000	4000	6000	9500	21,000

1916 King, model D, touring, HAC

1916 KING
Model D — 8-cyl., 40/50 hp, 120" wb

	FP	5	4	3	2	1
Corsair-5P	1350	3100	4200	6300	10,500	22,000
Reliance-5P	1150	3000	4000	6000	9500	21,000
Challenger Touring-7P	1350	3200	4300	6500	11,000	23,000
Challenger Roadster	1350	3300	4400	6700	12,000	24,000
Challenger Sedan-5P	1900	2300	3300	4600	7500	16,000

1917 King, model E, roadster, HAC

1917 KING
Model E — 8-cyl., 40/50 hp, 120" wb

	FP	5	4	3	2	1
Touring-7P	1585	3200	4300	6500	11,000	23,000
Foursome	1585	3200	4300	6500	11,000	23,000
Roadster-3P	1585	3300	4400	6700	12,000	24,000
Sedan-7P	2150	2300	3300	4600	7500	16,000

1918 King, model F, foursome, HAC

1918 KING
Model F — 8-cyl., 40/50 hp, 120" wb

Touring-7P	2150	3200	4300	6500	11,000	23,000
Foursome	2300	3200	4300	6500	11,000	23,000
Roadster-3P	2150	3300	4400	6700	12,000	24,000
Sedan-7P	2900	2300	3300	4600	7500	16,000

1919 King, model G, foursome, HAC

1919 KING
Model G — 8-cyl., 40/50 hp, 120" wb

Touring-7P	2170	3200	4300	6500	11,000	23,000
Foursome	2370	3200	4300	6500	11,000	23,000
Sedan-7P	2950	2000	3000	4200	6500	14,000

1920 King, model H, touring, HAC

1920-1921 KING
Model H — 8-cyl., 60 hp, 120" wb

	FP	5	4	3	2	1
Touring-7P	2585	3300	4400	6700	12,000	24,000
Road King	2600	3500	4500	7000	13,000	25,000
Foursome	2585	3300	4400	6700	12,000	24,000
Limoudan-7P	2985	2300	3300	4600	7500	16,000

1922 King, model J, touring, OCW

1922 KING
Model D — 8-cyl., 40/45 hp, 113" wb

Touring-5P	1350	3100	4200	6300	10,500	22,000
Roadster-2P	1350	3200	4300	6500	11,000	23,000

Model J — 8-cyl., 69 hp, 120" wb

Touring-7P	2125	3300	4400	6700	12,000	24,000
Sport Foursome-4P	2125	3500	4500	7000	13,000	25,000
Road King Roadster-2P	2140	3700	4700	7300	13,700	26,000
Coupe-4P	3125	2500	3500	5000	8500	18,000
Sedan-7P	3125	2300	3300	4600	7500	16,000

1923 King, model L, sedanette, HAC

1923-1924 KING
Model L — 8-cyl., 60 hp, 124" wb

Touring-7P	1795	3500	4500	7000	13,000	25,000
Sport Foursome-4P	1795	3700	4700	7300	13,700	26,000
Road King Roadster-2P	1795	3900	4800	7700	14,300	27,000
Sedanette-5P	1995	2500	3500	5000	8500	18,000
Coupe-4P	2400	2700	3600	5300	8400	19,000
Sedan-7P	2550	2300	3300	4600	7500	16,000

KING — Auburn, Indiana — (1908) — The King Motor Vehicle Company was among the shortest-lived automotive enterprises in Auburn, that town bristling with automotive activity during this period. Ralph King was the man behind the company, and the designer of its product, which he described as "a motor buggy especially designed for use of rural mail carriers." Rural mail carriers apparently weren't interested. King's enterprise didn't survive into 1909.

1909 King-Remick, runabout, WLB

773

KING-REMICK — Detroit, Michigan — (1910) — Undoubtedly there was a King and a Remick involved in this venture, but their first names appear lost to history. The King-Remick was a six with shaft drive, three-speed selective transmission and left-hand steering. It was a sporty two-seater runabout with an oval fuel tank mounted at the rear. The prototype had a 115-inch wheelbase, but this was slated to be raised to 123 inches for the production version. The car was built for King and Remick by A.O. Dunk of the Autoparts Manufacturing Company in Detroit. "Plans for the quantity manufacture of this roadster are not yet complete," *The Horseless Age* announced on November 23rd, 1910, "but will be announced shortly." They never were. Probably only the 115-inch wheelbase prototype was built. Because A.O. Dunk was famous during this period for buying up defunct automobile companies, the King-Remick was probably realized by an amalgam of parts which had previously been run up for other cars.

KING STEAMER — Buffalo, New York — (1902) — At the turn of the century, W. Grant King was the manager of the Iroquois Iron Works in Buffalo. In 1902, believing as he said that the available steam cars on the market were "fragile, complicated and generally unsatisfactory," he built one for himself. It was a runabout which he used for four years before selling it to a local farmer. During 1905-1906, Iroquois Iron Works built two commercial vehicles which reportedly were intended for motor stagecoach use in Utah. In 1909 *Motor* magazine published its "Historical Table of the American Motor Car Industry," and in it listed the Iroquois Iron Works as an automobile manufacturer from 1906-1908. The error has been perpetuated to this day. The only vehicles produced, however, were the steam runabout of 1902 built by W. Grant King at the Iroquois Iron Works and the two commercial vehicles of 1905-1906 which were built by the company under King's supervision. W. Grant King, incidentally, later went on to manufacture the King sewing machine and King radio.

KING STEAMER — Providence, Rhode Island — (1904) — The Providence machine shop which built the car for him is not known, but Gilbert M. King's steamer in 1904 was reputed to be "the largest automobile in New England." King was a wealthy sportsman who held the state speed record for both the mile and five miles. His new car developed 46 hp, accommodated eight passengers and was constructed entirely of steel and aluminum. Its wheelbase was 120 inches, with an overall length of nearly 14 feet. Its boiler was 24 inches in diameter, and its water tank had a 45-gallon capacity, this allowing for a run of 250 miles between fill-ups. King was intent upon some serious touring in the car.

KINGSBURY — The Kingsbury-Leahy Company, Inc. was organized in Albany, New York during the spring of 1912 with a capital stock of $40,000 to "manufacture automobiles and carriages." The partners involved were Edward W. Leahy and S. Kingsbury. Manufacture of a car is doubted.

KINGSBURY — Keene, New Hampshire — (1900) — On December 28th, 1900 Harry T. Kingsbury tested his first naptha-fueled automobile on the streets of Keene. He had finished it just the day before in the shop of his Wilkins Toy Company. "The motor forms a part of the forward axle having two-cylinders opposite each other on either end with the crankshaft in the center," the Keene newspaper reported the next day. "The crankshaft runs at right angles to the forward axle and extends back to the rear axle to which power is transmitted by a compensating reversible gear of three speeds, designed by Mr. Kingsbury and controlled by a single lever." This was the only automobile Harry T. Kingsbury built. Thereafter he turned his talent to inventions pursuant to the New England Cycle Company which he had established in 1898 in conjunction with his toy factory. Among the devices he patented for bicycle riders and repairers were a semi-automatic rim drill, the Keene universal repair jack, the Keene crank and axle straightener and the Apollo home trainer.

KINGSBURY — Great Falls, Montana — (1915) — In January 1915 the Kingsbury Gas-Electric Motor Car Company was organized in Great Falls to build and demonstrate an automobile invented by a local electrical engineer named J. McLean Kingsbury. The company was very much a civic venture, with fifty-four Great Falls business and professional men as stockholders. The directors were Kingsbury himself, Fred A. Fligman and Edwin L. Norris. "We have formed this company simply to provide the money for Mr. Kingsbury to go ahead and build a car after his plans," Fred Fligman told the *Great Falls Daily Tribune.* "We are not in the promotion business and we have no stock to sell. Mr. Kingsbury's automobile, we believe, will prove to be a remarkable and successful thing. He has submitted his plans to half a dozen expert engineers and they have called the design practical and with several distinct advantages over other motor cars." Kingsbury's car was an electric carrying its own generating plant, with each wheel driven by a separate electric motor, any one of which or all of which might be in operation at the same time. This principle was seen as applicable to large trucks as well as small broughams, a considerable saving in power being effected by driving only so many wheels as the load demanded. "We haven't felt it was sensible to consider a manufacturing plant yet, but we don't see why it couldn't be here," Fred Fligman said. "Mr. Woodbury of the Great Falls Iron Works told us that iron and steel could be gotten here cheap enough to be practical." It's rather a pity that this venture did not succeed, because in an era when flim-flam was so frequently a part of new automobile enterprises, this one was decidedly earnest and sincere. Because the money had already been subscribed for the building of a prototype, it is likely that the Kingsbury was begun and perhaps even finished. But the car did not go into production. J. McLean Kingsbury's name does not appear in the city directory of Great Falls after 1916.

KINGS COUNTY — The Kings County Automobile Company was organized in Brooklyn, New York late in 1903 with a capital stock of $10,000 for the manufacture of automobiles. Henry Aufderheide, Henry W. Palmer and Paul Schissel were the incorporators. Manufacture is doubted.

KINGSTON — Although this venture was initially organized as the Kingston Motor Car Company in 1907, Walter C. Allen changed its name to Allen-Kingston Motor Car Company early in 1908. Refer to Allen-Kingston.

KINNEAR — Columbus, Ohio — (1913) — The Kinnear Manufacturing Company of Columbus had been in business since the turn of the century and only occasionally dabbled in automobiles. The production of components and accessories was its standard line. Most probably, the firm's experience in 1913 was sufficient to dissuade it from further automobile experimentation. A front-drive touring car the firm produced that year was responsible for the death of Harry C. Knight, and because the accident happened during a Columbus race event it was widely reported. A Kinnear spokesman insisted that the car had not been at fault. "The fact of the matter was that there was a slow leak in the tire, which bore indications of rim cutting," he wrote the editors of *The Automobile.* "This would seem to be a sign that Knight went twice around the track on a flat tire." Still, the consequences were fatal, and Kinnear seems not to have produced further automobiles.

KINNER — Bert Kinner was well-known on the West Coast in aviation circles, both as an engine manufacturer and the builder of Amelia Earhart's first plane. For a short period following the First World War, he also dabbled in the automobile business, building custom cars for movie folk particularly. Details are lacking, but this venture unquestionably was just a sideline activity.

KINSEY — The Kinsey Motor Company was organized in Detroit, Michigan early in 1911 with a capital stock of $150,000 for the manufacture of automobiles. Incorporators were S.W. Kinsey, Thomas Mottaram, A.G. Schlee, E.H. Ziegler, F.T. McGlinnon, R.D. Richards, W.H. Graham and F.A. Gies. Manufacture is doubted.

KINSLER-BENNETT — The Kinsler-Bennett Company was organized in Hartford, Connecticut during the summer of 1907 with a capital stock of $40,000 to "manufacture automobiles, auto parts, special machinery and firearms." Incorporators were Joseph A. Bennett, E.D. Seymour, G.B. Kinsler and C.S. Lyons. Manufacture of a car is doubted.

KIRBY — The Kirby Motor Car Company was organized in Detroit, Michigan with a capital stock of $300,000 early in 1911 to deal in and manufacture motor vehicles. Incorporators were Mark W. Allen, Walter G. May, O.F Hawley and Frank A. Kirby, all of Detroit. Manufacture of a car is doubted.

KIRCHEN STEAM — Lansing, Michigan — (1921) — In early summer of 1921, Otto J. Kirchen of the Kirchen Machine Company of Lansing announced the completion of the pilot model of his new steam car. Manufacture was on the way. "It will be similar in some respects to the Stanley but will weigh less and probably not cost so much," Kirchen advised. He also indicated that the cost of running his steam car would be a quarter that of a contemporary gasoline car, and that its speed would be greater; "150 miles can easily be attained in a quick getaway." One would tend to doubt that, and also that this automotive venture ever got off the ground.

KIRK — In 1899 the Kirk Manufacturing Company of Toledo, Ohio announced plans to add automobiles to its product line of bicycles. A car from Kirk did ultimately arrive in 1902, and its name was the Yale, produced into 1905. Refer to Yale.

The Kirk-Hall Company of Toledo, Ohio was organized during the fall of 1903 with a capital stock of $10,000 to "manufacture, deal in, repair and store automobiles." Incorporators were Edward A. Kirk, Charles M. Hall, Edwin J. Marshall, Harold W. Fraser and George C. Bryce. Manufacture of a car is doubted. Whether Edward A. Kirk was related to Ezra E. Kirk of the Kirk Manufacturing Company in Toledo is not known, but seems probable.

KIRKHAM — Bath, New York — (1903 et seq.) — In 1903 Glenn Curtiss of Hammondsport disposed of the cycle motor branch of his business to Charles Kirkham of Bath, the latter organizing the Kirkham Motor Manufacturing Company. Although Kirkham built an occasional automobile, this was merely for demonstration purposes, to try out the latest model engine the company would be producing. For a while, Kirkham was modestly profitable in the engine business, providing the power units for the Kline Kar of Richmond (Virginia) from 1912 and introducing a small two-cylinder air-cooled 9 hp engine during the cyclecar craze. Most of its output, however, was destined for aviation use. Kirkham went broke late in 1913. At the trustees' sale the following March, the Kirkham building was sold for $5010 to Dr. Douglas H. Smith of Bath who said he planned to use it "for hospital purposes." Kirkham's machinery and tools brought another $8000. Of the total realized in the sale, the preponderance was slated to meet an outstanding bond issue, leaving $1705 to be apportioned among general creditors whose claims aggregated more than $60,000.

KIRK-LATTY — Cleveland, Ohio — (1903) — The Kirk-Latty Manufacturing Company of Cleveland manufactured bolts and rivets, and wagons and tricycles for children. In *Motor Age's* February 26th, 1903 issue, announcement was made that after experimental work for some months past Kirk-Latty now had its first two-cylinder gasoline touring car in operation in the city. "The company is almost ready to commence manufacturing these cars on an extensive scale," *Motor Age* said. Something must have gone wrong somewhere, because production never commenced on any scale whatsoever — and Kirk-Latty quickly returned its attention to bolts and rivets and children's things.

KIRKSEL — Aurora, Illinois — (1907) — Dr. James Selkirk, bored with the management problems of the Aurora Motor Works of which he was part owner, reversed the syllables of his name and came up with the Kirksel. It was a four-cylinder 50 hp touring car, two examples being built by the C.C. Hinckley Machine Shop located near the Chicago & North Western Railway tracks in Aurora. One of the cars was for himself; the other was for Albert J. Denney, president of Denney & Denney Furniture & Undertaking Company, who had supplied the bright red upholstery for the cars. The Kirksel exterior was painted a gleaming white. Dr. Selkirk planned to market this car for $3000 and tried organizing a Kirksel Motor Car Company to do it. His efforts came to naught, and he returned to his medical and surgical practice. Dr. Selkirk was not the first physician to build an automobile in Aurora, however. That honors belongs to Dr. Courtney L. Smith, who put together a steam car for himself in 1901. Unlike Dr. Selkirk, Dr. Smith built only the one car — and then bought a curved dash Oldsmobile.

KIRK-SNELL — Although the automobile built in 1902 in Toledo, Ohio by the merger of the Kirk Manufacturing Company and the Snell Cycle Fittings Company was occasionally referred to as a Kirk-Snell in the trade press, it was marketed under the tradename of Yale. Refer to Yale.

KIRSCH — Decatur, Indiana — (1905/1908-1916) — Born in Heidelberg, Germany in 1863, Peter Kirsch arrived in the United States as a young boy, his family settling in Adams County, Indiana. Apprenticing as a carpenter, he established a wood planing mill in Decatur in 1893. In 1905 he built his first automobile, in 1908 his second. "The automobile has all of the latest appliances, including a new brake, which was invented by Mr. Kirsch, and which does away with the spring," the *Decatur Democrat* reported on June 11th, 1908. "Two seats have been arranged in the auto and the bed which was made by Mr. Kirsch is of up to the minute style." Peter Kirsch indicated that he planned to build ten more, and the newspaper indicated that the quality of his machine and his reasonable prices would make for a ready market in the area. Kirsch's total production is not known, though a car he built in 1913 remains in existence. Most likely, he simply built his machines as Adams County residents requested them. An advertisement from 1916 for his Kirsch Planing Mill includes the phrase "automobiles built to order." Conceivably, he may have built a few more cars following that date.

1907 Kissel Kar, model A, touring, HAC

KISSEL KAR — Hartford, Wisconsin — (1907-1918) / KISSEL — (1919-1931) — The car was known as the Kissel Kar for over a decade, the "Kar" ultimately being dropped for 1919 because, in the wake of the First World War, it was deemed too forbiddingly German. Whatever it was called, the vehicle that was born and died in Hartford, Wisconsin was a good car "from the early beginning," as one of the company brochures put it. Like many German immigrant families in Wisconsin, the Kissels initially were farmers, expanding into the hardware and grocery businesses, then into lumber, quarries, sand pits, real estate and homebuilding. By 1906 there was a quartet of companies under the umbrella of the parent firm L. Kissel & Sons, and the newest that year was the Kissel Motor Car Company, which was the idea of sons George and Will. These young men, in their twenties, had built their first experimental car in 1905, a shaft-drive four-cylinder runabout, rather ambitious for a maiden effort. Production in earnest began in 1906 for the 1907 model year. Initially bodies came from the sleigh-manufacturing Zimmerman Brothers in nearby Waupun, and Beaver engines were used in the next several cars run up, but soon Kissels would be virtually all Kissel made. An order for 100 cars from a Chicago distributor named W.A. McDuffee who wanted a car as good as the Stoddard-Dayton he was selling, but lower priced, helped get the business started. And two fortuitous personnel additions really got things rolling. The first was Herman Palmer. Though a university-educated engineer, he was playing cello in a small orchestra passing through Hartford when he saw the Kissel factory from the train window and got a job doing what he had wanted to do all along. The second was J. Friedrich Werner, a German coachbuilder with impeccable credentials, including a stint with Opel Motor Works in Russelsheim. By 1909 there were Kissel Kars in wheelbases from 107 to 128 inches at prices from $1350 to $3000, a six-cylinder model being added for good measure, as well as several truck variations. In 1911 Kissel introduced a double-drop frame (kick-up over both front and rear wheels), and the company's use of three dash lamps under a steel cornice in 1914 gave credence to the Kissel claim of pioneering indirect illumination of dashboard instruments. In August 1913 the company began advertising its "All Year Car" with detachable top. Packard's success with the Twin Six prompted a Kissel version (with Weidley V-12 engine) called the Double-Six in 1917, but it lasted just two seasons. Kissel fortunes were far better served with its own L-head long-stroke six which

1908 Kissel Kar, model A9, roadster, HAC

endured with only minor changes from June 1915 until August 1928. The sportiest Kissels of this era were designed with New York distributor Conover T. Silver, which for a while carried his name in addition to Kissel's and which were refined by the factory into a full line of models. Among these was a speedster featuring the innovative use of an outrigger seat neatly folding into a drawer on each side of the body and nicknamed the Gold Bug, the winning entry among some 500 received in a contest to name the car. The Staggered-Door Sedan introduced for 1918 (one front driver's door, one rear door on the opposite side) was an unusual body style, but the company's Speedsters and Toursters, as well as the sprightly razor-edge 1922 Coach Sedan, proved popular. Production of 2123 units in 1923 was a healthy sign after several years of wallowing in the postwar recession, but then dipped to 803 units in 1924 when retooling and other problems delayed delivery of the new 1925 Kissel straight-eight companion line. The new engine was engineered from a Lycoming block and crankshaft; the new bodies revived the "Custom-Built" appellation previously used after the World War I years. Though the new Kissels had the look of it, they were not of course fully custom built, though this apparently mattered not a whit to the long list of celebrity purchasers ranging from Fatty Arbuckle and Al Jolson to Amelia Earhart and Ralph De Palma. For many years the Kissel mounted its radiator emblem offset on the radiator core itself rather than the more usual radiator shell location. Then came the change eliminating the emblem in favor of a wide eagle pressing in a black panel above the radiator core. Bodies for this 1929 White Eagle Series (still the Lycoming-derived straight-eights, and no smaller sixes)

1909 Kissel Kar, model G-9, coupe, HAC

were all-new. But the company's production figures tell the story: 1925, 2122 units; 1926, 1972 units; 1927, 1147 units; 1928, 1068 units; 1929, 881 units — and of the totals for 1928 and 1929, 200 each year were "National-Kissel" funeral cars to be distributed through the National Casket Company. Another ominous sign. In 1930, with bank credit shut off and the business mortgaged to the hilt, George Kissel nailed the coffin shut on the Kissel automotive enterprise by entering into an agreement with Archie Andrews, who promised to obtain $250,000 in new loans to the company for a commitment to build 1500 of his Ruxton front-drive cars alongside the five White Eagles, one funeral car and one taxicab slated to be the daily production of Kissel vehicles for the remainder of 1930. But Archie Andrews' financial contributions stopped at $100,000. The Kissels could not continue and, rather than have their company fall into Andrews' hands, George Kissel requested a friendly creditor to bring on receivership in September 1930. Bankruptcy was declared. Production that year was 93 Kissels (16 of them 1931 models), 77 funeral cars, 2 trucks, 49 taxis. (There had been 285 taxis built in 1929.) The fine old name of Kissel was heard no more in the automobile industry. Subsequently, in 1932, a successor, Kissel Industries, took on a contract to adapt two Lever engines in leftover cars for the A.L. Powell Power Company of Wheaton, Illinois, which brought less good fortune than had the Andrews deal. Finally, entering other fields (mainly marine outboard motors), the plant saw prosperity return with war production in 1942, the year George Kissel died. Two years later his widow sold the business.

775

1907 KISSEL KAR
Model A — 4-cyl., 30 hp, 96" wb

	FP	5	4	3	2	1
Touring	1850	3000	4000	6000	9500	21,000

1908 KISSEL KAR
Four — 4-cyl., 40 hp, 108" wb

D9 Touring	2000	3000	4000	6000	9500	21,000
A9 Roadster	—	3100	4200	6300	10,500	22,000
Inside Drive Limousine	—	2500	3500	5000	8500	18,000

1909 KISSEL KAR
Model LD9 — 4-cyl., 30 hp, 107" wb

Touring-5P	1500	3000	4000	6000	9500	21,000
Roadster-2P	1350	3100	4200	6300	10,500	22,000
Baby Tonneau-4P	1500	3100	4200	6300	10,500	22,000

Model D9 — 4-cyl., 40 hp, 115" wb

Touring-5/7P	2000	3100	4200	6300	10,500	22,000
Roadster-4P	2000	3200	4300	6500	11,000	23,000
Baby Tonneau-4/5P	2000	3200	4300	6500	11,000	23,000

Model G-9 — 6-cyl., 60 hp, 128" wb

Touring-7P	3000	3200	4300	6500	11,000	23,000
Roadster-4P	3000	3300	4400	6700	12,000	24,000
Baby Tonneau-7P	3000	3300	4400	6700	12,000	24,000

1910 Kissel Kar, model LD, touring, HAC

1910 KISSEL KAR
Model LD10 — 4-cyl., 30 hp, 112" wb

Touring-5P	1500	3000	4000	6000	9500	21,000
Toy Tonneau-4P	1500	3100	4200	6300	10,500	22,000

Model D10 — 4-cyl., 50 hp, 112" wb

Touring-5P	2000	3100	4200	6300	10,500	22,000
Toy Tonneau-4P	2000	3200	4300	6500	11,000	23,000

Model F10 — 4-cyl., 50 hp, 124" wb

Touring-7P	2500	3200	4300	6500	11,000	23,000
Toy Tonneau-4P	2500	3300	4400	6700	12,000	24,000

Model G10 — 6-cyl., 60 hp, 132" wb

Touring-7P	3000	3300	4400	6700	12,000	24,000
Toy Tonneau-4P	3000	3500	4500	7000	13,000	25,000

1911 Kissel Kar, model F-11, touring, HAC

1911 KISSEL KAR
Model LD11 — 4-cyl., 30 hp, 116" wb

Touring-5P	1500	3000	4000	6000	9500	21,000
Baby Tonneau-4P	1500	3100	4200	6300	10,500	22,000
Semi-Racer	1600	3200	4300	6500	11,000	23,000
Fore-Door Touring-5P	1600	3100	4200	6300	10,500	22,000

Model D11 — 4-cyl., 50 hp, 124" wb

Touring-5P	2000	3100	4200	6300	10,500	22,000
Baby Tonneau-4P	2000	3200	4300	6500	11,000	23,000
Semi-Racer	2100	3300	4400	6700	12,000	24,000
Fore-Door Touring-5P	2100	3200	4300	6500	11,000	23,000
Limousine-7P	3200	2500	3500	5000	8500	18,000

Model F11 — 6-cyl., 60 hp, 132" wb

Touring-7P	2500	3200	4300	6500	11,000	23,000
Baby Tonneau-7P	2500	3300	4400	6700	12,000	24,000
Fore-Door Touring-7P	2600	3300	4400	6700	12,000	24,000
Semi-Racer	2600	3500	4500	7000	13,000	25,000

Note: This Kissel truck line was introduced this year.

1912 KISSEL KAR
Thirty — 4-cyl., 30 hp, 116" wb

Model A Touring	1500	3000	4000	6000	9500	21,000
Model B Semi-Touring	1500	3000	4000	6000	9500	21,000
Model C Semi-Racer	1500	3100	4200	6300	10,500	22,000
Model D Coupe	2100	2300	3300	4600	7500	16,000

Forty — 4-cyl., 40 hp, 118" wb

Model A Semi-Touring	1850	4400	8850	14,750	20,650	29,500
Model B Semi-Racer	1850	3200	4300	6500	11,000	23,000
Model C Coupe	2300	2400	3400	4800	8000	17,000
Model D Limousine	2900	2700	3600	5300	8800	19,000

1912 Kissel Kar, model A, touring, AA

Fifty — 4-cyl., 50 hp, 124" wb

	FP	5	4	3	2	1
Model A Touring	2350	4650	9300	15,500	21,700	31,000
Model B Semi-Touring	2350	3200	4300	6500	11,000	23,000
Model C Semi-Racer	2350	3300	4400	6700	12,000	24,000
Model D Coupe	2800	2500	3500	5000	8500	18,000
Model E Limousine	3550	2900	3700	5600	9100	20,000

Sixty — 6-cyl., 60 hp, 132" wb

Model A Touring-7P	3000	4800	9600	16,000	22,400	32,000
Model B Semi-Touring	3000	3300	4400	6700	12,000	24,000
Model C Semi-Racer	3000	3500	4500	7000	13,000	25,000
Model D Coupe	3500	2700	3600	5300	8800	19,000
Model E Limousine	4200	3000	4000	6000	9500	21,000

1913 Kissel Kar, model H-13, touring, HAC

1913 KISSEL KAR
Thirty — 4-cyl., 28.9 hp, 116" wb

LD13 Semi-Touring-5P	1700	3100	4200	6300	10,500	22,000
LD13 Semi-Racer-2P	1700	3200	4300	6500	11,000	23,000

Forty — 4-cyl., 32.4 hp, 121" wb

H13 Semi-Touring-5P	2000	3200	4300	6500	11,000	23,000
H13 Limousine-5P	2000	2500	3500	5000	8500	18,000

Fifty — 4-cyl., 38.02 hp, 132" wb

D13 Semi-Touring-6P	2500	3300	4400	6700	12,000	24,000
D13 Limousine-6P	2500	2700	3600	5300	8800	19,000

Sixty — 6-cyl., 48.6 hp, 140" wb

F13 Semi-Touring-6P	3150	4350	8700	14,500	20,300	29,000
F13 Semi-Touring-7P	3150	4400	8850	14,750	20,650	29,500

1914 Kissel Kar, model 48-Six, limousine, HAC

1914 KISSEL KAR
Model 40-Four — 4-cyl., 32 hp, 121" wb

Coupe	2850	2500	3500	5000	8500	18,000
Touring-5P	1850	3200	4300	6500	11,000	23,000
Roadster-2P	1850	3300	4400	6700	12,000	24,000

Model 48-Six — 6-cyl., 34 hp, 132" wb

Touring-5P	2350	2900	3700	5600	9100	20,000
Limousine-6P	3850	2700	3600	5300	8800	19,000
Berlin-6P	4100	2500	3500	5000	8500	18,000

Model 60-Six — 6-cyl., 49 hp, 142" wb

Touring-7P	3150	4000	7950	13,250	18,550	26,500
Roadster	3150	3300	4400	6700	12,000	24,000
Low Fore-Door Limousine	3900	2900	3700	5600	9100	20,000
Full Fore-Door Limousine	4000	3000	4000	6000	9500	21,000
Detachable Sedan	—	2500	3500	5000	8500	18,000

1915 Kissel Kar, model 4-36, detachable town car, HAC

1917 Kissel Kar, 7-pass. sedan, AA

1915 KISSEL KAR
Model 4-36 — 4-cyl., 28.9 hp, 121" wb

	FP	5	4	3	2	1
Touring-5P	1450	2500	3500	5000	8500	18,000
Detachable Sedan	1800	1800	2800	4000	6200	13,000
Touring-7P	1550	2400	3400	4800	8000	17,000
Roadster	1450	2900	3700	5600	9100	20,000
Cabriolet	1750	2300	3300	4600	7500	16,000
Coupe	2100	2200	3200	4400	7000	15,000

Model 6-42 — 6-cyl., 31.6 hp, 126" wb

	FP	5	4	3	2	1
Touring-5P	1650	2700	3600	5300	8800	19,000
Detachable Sedan	2000	2000	3000	4200	6500	14,000
Touring-7P	1850	2500	3500	5000	8500	18,000
Cabriolet	1950	2400	3400	4800	8000	17,000
Coupe	2300	2300	3300	4600	7500	16,000

Model 6-42 — 100 Point — 6-cyl., 31.54 hp

	FP	5	4	3	2	1
Two-Door Tour.-5P	—	3100	4200	6300	10,500	22,000
Four-Door Tour.-5P	—	3200	4300	6500	11,000	23,000
Three-Door Tour.-7P	—	3200	4300	6400	10,800	22,500
Roadster-2P	—	3300	4400	6600	11,500	23,500
All-Year Sed.-5/7P	—	2200	3200	4400	7000	15,000
Coupelet-2P	—	2400	3400	4800	7000	15,000
Coupe-3P	—	2500	3500	5000	8500	18,000
Limousine-5P	—	2700	3600	5300	8800	19,000

Double Six — 12-cyl., 39.7 hp

	FP	5	4	3	2	1
Gibraltar Tour.-7P	—	3100	4200	6300	10,500	22,000
Roadster-4P	—	3200	4300	6500	11,000	23,000
Coupe-4P	—	2700	3600	5300	8800	19,000
Sedan-5/7P	—	2300	3300	4600	7500	16,000
Sedan-4P	—	2400	3400	4800	8000	17,000
Sedan Tour.-4P	—	3300	4400	6700	12,000	24,000

1916 Kissel Kar, model 4-32, touring, HAC

1916 KISSEL KAR
Model 4-32 — 4-cyl., 24.03 hp, 115" wb

		5	4	3	2	1
Two-Door Touring-5P	—	2900	3700	5600	9100	20,000
Four-Door Touring-5P	—	3000	4000	6000	9500	21,000
Roadster-4P	—	3200	4300	6500	11,000	23,000
Coupe-4P	—	2500	3500	5000	8500	18,000

Model 6-38 — 6-cyl., 25.35 hp, 117" wb

		5	4	3	2	1
Town Car-5P	—	2700	3600	5300	8800	19,000
All-Year Sedan-5/7P	—	1800	2800	4000	6200	13,000
All-Year Coupe-4P	—	2200	3200	4400	7000	15,000
All-Year Sedan-4P	—	2000	3000	4200	6500	14,000
Sedan Touring-4P	—	2500	3500	5000	8500	18,000
Staggered Door Sed.-5/7P	—	1800	2800	4000	6200	13,000
Touring-7P	—	2700	3600	5300	8800	19,000
Gibraltar Touring-7P	—	2900	3700	5600	9100	20,000
Roadster-3P	—	3000	4000	6000	9500	21,000
Gibraltar Roadster	—	3100	4200	6300	10,500	22,000

Model 6-42 — 6-cyl., 31.54 hp, 126" wb

		5	4	3	2	1
Touring-5P	—	3000	4000	6000	9500	21,000
Roadster-2P	—	3100	4200	6300	10,500	22,000
Sedan-5/7P	—	2000	3000	4200	6500	14,000
Coupelet-2P	—	2200	3200	4400	7000	15,000
Coupe-3P	—	2300	3300	4600	7500	16,000
Limousine-5P	—	2700	3600	5300	8800	19,000

Note: Models 6-38 and 6-42 designated "Hundred Point Six."

1918 Kissel Kar, 7-pass. town car, AA

1918 Kissel Kar, Double Six, 7-pass. sedan, AA

1917 KISSEL KAR
Model 6-38 100 POINT — 6-cyl., 25.35 hp

		5	4	3	2	1
Touring-5/7P	—	3000	4000	6000	9500	21,000
Gibraltar Tour.-5/7P	—	3100	4100	6200	10,000	21,500
Roadster-3P	—	3100	4200	6300	10,500	22,000
Gibraltar Rdstr.-4P	—	3200	4300	6400	10,800	22,500
Town Car-5P	—	2500	3500	5000	8500	18,000
All-Year Sed.-5/7P	—	2200	3200	4400	7000	15,000
All-Year Cpe.-4P	—	2400	3400	4800	8000	17,000
Sed. Tour.-4P	—	2000	3000	4200	6500	14,000
All-Year Sedan-4P	—	3000	4000	6000	9500	21,000
Staggered Door Sed.-5/7P	—	1800	2800	4000	6200	13,000

1918 KISSEL KAR
Custom Silver Special — 6-cyl., 26.33 hp

		5	4	3	2	1
Touring-7P	—	3100	4200	6300	10,500	22,000
Tourster-4P	—	3200	4300	6500	11,000	23,000
Speedster-4P	—	4300	5400	8700	16,500	30,000
Gibraltar Tour.-5/7P	—	3500	4500	7000	13,000	25,000
All-Year Sed.-5/7P	—	3000	4000	6000	9500	21,000

Model 6-38 100 POINT — 6-cyl., 25.35 hp

		5	4	3	2	1
Touring-5/7P	—	3200	4300	6500	11,000	23,000
Gibraltar Tour.-5/7P	—	3700	4700	7300	13,700	26,000
Roadster-3P	—	3900	4800	7700	14,300	27,000
Gibraltar Rdstr.-4P	—	4000	5000	8000	15,000	28,000
Town Car-5P	—	2500	3500	5000	8500	18,000
All-Year Sed.-5/7P	—	2300	3300	4600	7500	16,000
All-Year Cpe.-4P	—	2400	3400	4800	8000	17,000
All-Year Sed.-4P	—	2200	3200	4400	7000	15,000
Sed. Tour.-4P	—	3100	4200	6300	10,500	22,000
Staggered Door Sed.-5/7P	—	2000	3000	4200	6500	14,000

1918 Kissel Kar, 7-pass. touring, AA

Double Six — 12-cyl., 39.7 hp

	FP	5	4	3	2	1
Gibraltar Tour.-7P	—	3900	4800	7700	14,300	27,000
Roadster-4P	—	4200	5200	8400	15,700	29,000
Coupe-4P	—	2700	3600	5300	8800	19,000
Sedan-5/7P	—	2200	3200	4400	7000	15,000
Sedan-4P	—	2000	3000	4200	6500	14,000
Sed. Tour.-4P	—	3900	4800	7700	14,300	27,000
Sedan-4P	—	2300	3300	4600	7500	16,000
Staggered Door Sed.-5/7P	—	2000	3000	4200	6500	14,000
Stnd. Tour.-5/7P	—	3900	4800	7700	14,300	27,000
Coupe-4P	—	2500	3500	5000	8500	18,000
De Luxe Sed.-6P	—	2200	3200	4400	7000	15,000
Urban Sed.-6P	—	2300	3300	4600	7500	16,000
Coach Sed.-6P	—	2000	3000	4200	6500	14,000

1919 Kissel, tourster, AA

1919 Kissel Silver Special, speedster, AA

1919 KISSEL
Custom-Built — 6-cyl., 26.33 hp

	FP	5	4	3	2	1
Touring	—	4200	5200	8400	15,700	29,000
Tourster	—	4300	5400	8700	16,500	30,000
Speedster	—	6000	8500	13,000	30,000	42,000
Gibraltar Tour.	—	4400	5600	9200	17,300	31,000
All-Year Sed.	—	2200	3200	4400	7000	15,000
Sedan	—	2000	3000	4200	6500	14,000
Town Car	—	2300	3300	4600	7500	16,000
Staggered Door Sed.	—	1800	2800	4000	6200	13,000
Stnd. Tour.	—	4000	5000	8000	15,000	28,000
Coupe	—	2300	3300	4600	7500	16,000
De Luxe Sed.	—	2100	3100	4300	6800	14,500
Urban Sed.	—	1800	2800	4000	6200	13,000
Coach Sed.	—	1600	2700	3800	5800	12,000

778

Model 6-38 100 Point — 6-cyl., 25.35 hp

	FP	5	4	3	2	1
Touring-5/7P	—	4300	5400	8700	16,500	30,000
Gibraltar Tour.-5/7P	—	4500	5800	9500	18,000	32,000
Roadster-3P	—	4900	6300	10,300	21,000	34,000
Gibraltar Rdstr.-4P	—	5000	6500	11,000	22,000	35,000
Town Car-5P	—	2400	3400	4800	8000	17,000
All-Year Sed.-5/7P	—	2300	3300	4600	7500	16,000
All-Year Cpe.-4P	—	2400	3400	4800	8000	17,000
All-Year Sed.-4P	—	2300	3300	4600	7500	16,000
Sed. Tour.-4P	—	4200	5200	8400	15,700	29,000
Staggered-Door Sed.-5/7P	—	2200	3200	4400	7000	15,000

1920 Kissel, Custom-Built, 4-pass. tourster, HAC

1920 KISSEL
Custom-Built — 6-cyl., 61 hp

	FP	5	4	3	2	1
Stnd. Open Tour.-7P	—	4000	5000	8000	15,000	28,000
Touring-7P	—	4200	5200	8400	15,700	29,000
Tourster-4P	—	4300	5400	8700	16,500	30,000
Speedster-2P	—	6000	8500	13,000	30,000	42,000
Staggered Door Sed.	—	2200	3200	4400	7000	15,000
Coupe	—	2400	3400	4800	8000	17,000
Sedan-6P	—	2000	3000	4200	6500	14,000
Urban Sedan	—	1800	2800	4000	6200	13,000

1921 Kissel, Custom-Built, coupe, AA

1921 KISSEL
Custom-Built — 6-cyl., 61 hp

	FP	5	4	3	2	1
Speedster-2P	—	6800	10,300	16,000	35,500	48,000
Tourster-4P	—	5200	6800	11,300	23,000	36,000
Touring-7P	—	4900	6300	10,300	21,000	34,000
Coupe-4P	—	2500	3500	5000	8500	18,000
Sedan-6P	—	2000	3000	4200	6500	14,000
Urban Sed. Limited	—	2200	3200	4400	7000	15,000
Coach Sed-6P	—	1800	2800	4000	6200	13,000
Stnd. Open Tour.-7P	—	4700	6100	9900	19,000	33,000

1922 Kissel, Deluxe, tourster, AA

1922 Kissel, Deluxe, tourster with Gould winter top, HAC

1922 KISSEL
Custom-Built — 6-cyl., 61 hp

	FP	5	4	3	2	1
Stnd. Tour.-5P	—	5000	6500	11,000	22,000	35,000
De Luxe Spdstr.-4P	—	7000	10,800	16,900	37,100	49,000
De Luxe Tourstr.-4P	—	5300	7000	11,500	24,000	37,000
De Luxe Tour.-7P	—	5200	6800	11,300	23,000	36,000
De Luxe Cpe.-4P	—	2700	3600	5300	8800	19,000
De Luxe Sed.-6P	—	2200	3200	4400	7000	15,000
De Luxe Coach Sed.-6P	—	2000	3000	4200	6500	14,000
De Luxe Urban Sed.-6P	—	2300	3300	4600	7500	16,000

1923 Kissel, all-year coupe-roadster, HAC

1923 KISSEL
Model 45 — 6-cyl., 61 hp

	FP	5	4	3	2	1
Touring-5/7P	—	5000	6500	11,000	32,000	35,000
Tourster-4/7P	—	5200	6800	11,300	23,000	36,000
Speedster-2/4P	—	6800	10,300	16,000	35,500	48,000
Coupe-4P	—	2700	3600	5300	8800	19,000
De Luxe Sed.-6P	—	2200	3200	4400	7000	15,000
Brougham-6P	—	2300	3300	4600	7500	16,000
Urban Sed.-6P	—	2200	3200	4400	7000	15,000
Coach Sed.-5P	—	2000	3000	4200	6500	14,000

Model 55 — 6-cyl., 50 hp

	FP	5	4	3	2	1
Stnd. Phae.-5P	—	5200	6800	11,300	23,000	36,000
Stnd. Sed.-5P	—	2400	3400	4800	8000	17,000
De Luxe Phae.-5P	—	5400	7300	11,800	25,000	38,000
De Luxe Brougham Sed.-5P	—	2500	3500	5000	8500	18,000
Coupe-4P	—	2700	3600	5300	8800	19,000
Speedster-2P	—	6000	8500	13,000	30,000	42,000
Tourster-4P	—	5500	7500	12,000	26,000	39,000

1924 Kissel, model 55, brougham sedan, HAC

1924 KISSEL
Model 55 — 6-cyl., 48 hp

	FP	5	4	3	2	1
Stnd. Phae.-5P	—	5200	6800	11,300	23,000	36,000
Stnd. Sed.-5P	—	2000	3000	4200	6500	14,000
De Luxe Phae.-5P	—	5400	7300	11,800	25,000	38,000
De Luxe Brougham Sed.-5P	—	2200	3200	4400	7000	15,000
Coupe-4P	—	2700	3600	5300	8800	19,000
Speedster-2P	—	7000	10,800	16,900	37,100	49,000
Tourster-4P	—	5400	7300	11,800	25,000	38,000

1925 Kissel, enclosed speedster, HAC

1925 KISSEL
Model 55 Standard — 6-cyl., 53 hp

	FP	5	4	3	2	1
Phaeton-5P	1685	5500	7500	12,000	26,000	39,000
Touring-7P	1785	5400	7300	11,800	25,000	38,000
Speedster-2P	1895	6800	10,300	16,000	35,500	48,000
Speedster-4P	1895	7000	10,800	16,900	37,100	49,000
Tourster-4P	1895	5900	8300	12,800	29,000	41,000
Coupe-4P	2185	2700	3600	5300	8800	19,000
Two-Door Brougham-5P	1795	2300	3300	4600	7500	16,000
Brougham Sed.-5P	1995	2400	3400	4800	8000	17,000
Enclosed Spdstr.-2P	2385	4400	5600	9200	17,300	31,000
Enclosed Spdstr.-4P	2185	4500	5800	9500	18,000	32,000
Victoria-5P	2285	2900	3700	5600	9100	20,000

Model 55 DeLuxe — 6-cyl., 53 hp

	FP	5	4	3	2	1
Phaeton-5P	1885	5800	8000	12,500	28,000	40,000
Touring-7P	1985	5500	7500	12,000	26,000	39,000
Speedster-2P	2185	7000	10,800	16,900	37,100	49,000
Speedster-4P	2185	7200	11,300	17,700	38,700	50,000
Tourster-4P	2085	6000	8500	13,000	30,000	42,000
Coupe-4P	2585	2900	3700	5600	9100	20,000
Brougham Sed.-6P	2685	2500	3500	5000	8500	18,000
Enclosed Spdstr.-2P	2785	4500	5800	9500	18,000	32,000
Sedan-7P	3285	2500	3500	5000	8500	18,000
Victoria-6P	2635	3000	4000	6000	9500	21,000
Ber. Sed.-7P	3385	2700	3600	5300	8800	19,000

Model 75 Standard — 8-cyl., 71 hp

	FP	5	4	3	2	1
Three-Door Brougham-5P	2095	2400	3400	4800	8000	17,000
Phaeton-5P	1985	5500	7500	12,000	26,000	39,000
Touring-7P	2085	5400	7300	11,800	25,000	38,000
Speedster-2P	2195	7300	11,600	18,100	39,600	51,000
Speedster-4P	2295	7300	11,800	18,400	40,400	52,000
Tourster-4P	2195	6400	9300	14,500	33,000	45,000
Coupe-4P	2485	2500	3500	5000	8500	18,000
Brougham Sed.-5P	2395	2300	3300	4600	7500	16,000
Encl. Spdstr.-2P	2485	4400	5600	9200	17,300	31,000
Encl. Spdstr.-4P	2585	4500	5800	9500	18,000	32,000

Model 75 DeLuxe — 8-cyl., 71 hp

	FP	5	4	3	2	1
Victoria-5P	2585	2700	3600	5300	8800	19,000
Phaeton-5P	2585	6400	9300	14,500	33,000	45,000
Phaeton-5P	2185	6000	8500	13,000	30,000	42,000
Touring-7P	2285	5800	8000	12,500	28,000	40,000
Speedster-2P	2485	7300	11,800	18,400	40,400	52,000
Speedster-4P	2585	7500	12,300	19,100	41,700	54,000
Tourster-4P	2585	5800	8000	12,500	28,000	40,000
Coupe-4P	2885	2900	3700	5600	9100	20,000
Brougham Sed.-5P	2935	2700	3600	5300	8800	19,000
Encl. Spdstr.-2P	2985	4400	5600	9200	17,300	31,000
Encl. Spdstr.-4P	3085	4500	5800	9500	18,000	32,000
Sedan-7P	3485	2400	3400	4800	8000	17,000
Victoria-5P	2885	2500	3500	5000	8500	18,000
Ber. Sed.-7P	3585	2700	3600	5300	8800	19,000

1926 Kissel, model 75, deluxe brougham sedan, HAC

1926 KISSEL
Model 55 Standard — 6-cyl., 61 hp

	FP	5	4	3	2	1
Phaeton-5P	1585	5500	7500	12,000	26,000	39,000
Touring-7P	1685	5400	7300	11,800	25,000	38,000
Speedster-2P	1795	6800	10,300	16,000	35,500	48,000
Speedster-4P	1895	7000	10,800	16,900	37,100	49,000
Tourster-4P	1795	5900	8300	12,800	29,000	41,000
Coupe-4P	2085	2700	3600	5300	8800	19,000
Two-Door Brougham-5P	1695	2300	3300	4600	7500	16,000
Brougham Sed.-5P	1995	2400	3400	4800	8000	17,000
Encl. Spdstr.-2P	2085	4400	5600	9200	17,300	31,000
Encl. Spdstr.-4P	2185	4500	5800	9500	18,000	32,000
Victoria-5P	2185	2900	3700	5600	9100	20,000

Model 55 DeLuxe — 6-cyl., 61 hp

	FP	5	4	3	2	1
Phaeton-5P	1785	5800	8000	12,500	28,000	40,000
Touring-7P	1885	5500	7500	12,000	26,000	39,000
Speedster-2P	2085	7000	10,800	16,900	37,100	49,000
Speedster-4P	2185	7200	11,300	17,700	38,700	50,000
Tourster-4P	1985	6000	8500	13,000	30,000	42,000
Coupe-4P	2485	2900	3700	5600	9100	20,000
Brougham Sed.-5P	2485	2500	3500	5000	8500	18,000
Encl. Spdstr.-2P	2485	4500	5800	9500	18,000	32,000
Encl. Spdstr.-4P	2585	4700	6100	9900	19,000	33,000
Sedan-7P	3085	3000	4000	6000	9500	21,000
Victoria-5P	2485	3000	4000	6000	9500	21,000
Ber. Sed.-7P	3185	2700	3600	5300	8800	19,000

Model 75 Standard — 8-cyl., 71 hp

	FP	5	4	3	2	1
Two-Door Brougham-5P	2095	2400	3400	4800	8000	17,000
Phaeton-5P	1985	5500	7500	12,000	26,000	39,000
Touring-7P	2085	5400	7300	11,800	25,000	38,000
Speedster-2P	2195	7300	11,600	18,100	39,600	51,000
Speedster-4P	2295	7300	11,800	18,400	40,400	52,000
Tourster-4P	2195	6400	9300	14,500	33,000	45,000
Coupe-4P	2485	2500	3500	5000	8500	18,000
Brougham Sed.-5P	2395	2300	3300	4600	7500	16,000
Encl. Spdstr.-2P	2485	4400	5600	9200	17,300	31,000
Encl. Spdstr.-4P	2585	4500	5800	9500	18,000	32,000
Victoria-5P	2585	2700	3600	5300	8800	19,000

Model 75 DeLuxe — 8-cyl., 71 hp

	FP	5	4	3	2	1
Phaeton-5P	2185	6400	9300	14,500	33,000	45,000
Touring-7P	2285	6000	8500	13,000	30,000	42,000
Speedster-2P	2385	7300	11,800	18,400	40,400	52,000
Speedster-4P	2485	7400	12,100	18,800	41,100	53,000
Tourster-4P	2385	5800	8000	12,500	28,000	40,000
Coupe-4P	2835	2900	3700	5600	9100	20,000
Brougham Sed.-5P	2985	2700	3600	5300	8800	19,000
Encl. Spdstr.-2P	2985	4400	5600	9200	17,300	31,000
Encl. Spdstr.-4P	3085	4500	5800	9500	18,000	32,000
Sedan-7P	3485	2400	3400	4800	8000	17,000
Victoria-5P	2885	2500	3500	5000	8500	18,000
Ber. Sed.-7P	3585	2700	3600	5300	8800	19,000

1927 Kissel, model 75, speedster, AA

1927 Kissel, model 75, all-year coupe-roadster, HAC

1927 KISSEL
Model 55 — 6-cyl., 61 hp

Two-Door Brougham-5P	1695	2700	3600	5300	8800	19,000
Four-Door Brougham-5P	1895	2900	3700	5600	9100	20,000
Cpe. Rdstr.-2P	1795	5400	7300	11,800	25,000	38,000
Cpe. Rdstr.-4P	1895	5500	7500	12,000	26,000	39,000
Encl. Spdstr.-2P	2085	5000	6500	11,000	22,000	35,000
Encl. Spdstr.-4P	2185	5200	6800	11,300	23,000	36,000
Speedster-2P	1795	7200	11,300	17,700	38,700	50,000
Phaeton-5P	1685	6700	9900	15,500	34,800	47,000
Touring-7P	1785	6400	9300	14,500	33,000	45,000
Two-Door Brgm. Spec.-5P	1795	2900	3700	5600	9100	20,000
Four-Door Brgm. Spec.-5P	2095	3000	4000	6000	9500	21,000
Open Spdstr.-4P	1895	7300	11,800	18,400	40,400	52,000
Tourster-4P	1595	6500	9500	15,000	34,000	46,000
DeLuxe Sed.-7P	3085	2900	3700	5600	9100	20,000
DeLuxe Brougham-5P	3685	3000	4000	6000	9500	21,000
DeLuxe Ber. Sed.-7P	3185	3100	4200	6300	10,500	22,000
All-Year Brougham-5P	2295	3200	4300	6500	11,000	23,000
Sedan-7P	2295	2700	3600	5300	8800	19,000

Model 75 — 8-cyl., 71 hp

Two-Door Brougham-5P	2195	2900	3700	5600	9100	20,000
Four-Door Brougham-5P	2395	3000	4000	6000	9500	21,000
Cpe. Rdstr.-2P	2195	5500	7500	12,000	26,000	39,000
Cpe. Rdstr.-4P	2295	5800	8000	12,500	28,000	40,000
Encl. Spdstr.-2P	2485	5200	6800	11,300	23,000	36,000
Encl. Spdstr.-4P	2585	5300	7000	11,500	24,000	37,000
Phaeton-5P	1985	6800	10,300	16,000	35,500	48,000
Touring-7P	2085	6500	9500	15,000	34,000	46,000
Tourster-4P	2195	6700	9900	15,500	34,800	47,000
Two-Door Brgm. Spec.-5P	2295	3000	4000	6000	9500	21,000
Four-Door Brgm. Spec.-5P	2595	3100	4200	6300	10,500	22,000
Open Spdstr.-4P	2295	7400	12,100	18,800	41,100	53,000
DeLuxe Brougham-5P	2985	3200	4300	6500	11,000	23,000
DeLuxe Sed.-7P	3495	3000	4000	6000	9500	21,000
All-Year Cpe.-4P	2395	5200	6800	11,300	23,000	36,000
Sedan-7P	2795	2900	3700	5600	9100	20,000

Model 8-65 — 8-cyl., 65 hp 125" wb

	FP	5	4	3	2	1
Two-Door Brougham-5P	1995	3100	4200	6300	10,500	22,000
Four-Door Brougham-5P	2095	3200	4300	6500	11,000	23,000
All-Year Cpe. Rdstr.-5P	2095	5300	7000	11,500	24,000	37,000
All-Year Brougham-5P	2495	—	—	—	—	24,000
Speedster-4P	2095	7500	12,300	19,100	41,700	54,000
Four-Door Brgm. Spec.-5P	2295	3300	4400	6700	12,000	24,000
Sedan-7P	2495	3000	4000	6000	9500	21,000

Model 8-65 — 8-cyl., 65 hp, 132" wb

Touring-7P	1985	7000	10,800	16,900	37,100	49,000
Tourster-4P	2095	7200	11,300	17,700	38,700	50,000
Phaeton-5P	1885	7300	11,800	18,400	40,400	52,000

1928 Kissel, straight-eight speedster, HAC

1928 KISSEL
Model 70 — 6-cyl., 52 hp

Four-Door Brgm. Sed.-5P	1495	2700	3600	5300	8800	19,000
All-Year Cpe. Rdstr.-5P	1595	5000	6500	11,000	22,000	35,000
Four-Door Sed.-5P	1595	2500	3500	5000	8500	18,000
Victoria-5P	1595	2700	3600	5300	8800	19,000

Model 55 — 6-cyl., 61 hp

Two-Door Brougham-5P	1795	2900	3700	5600	9100	20,000
Four-Door Brgm. Sed.-5P	1895	3000	4000	6000	9500	21,000
All-Year Cpe. Rdstr.-4P	1895	5200	6800	11,300	23,000	36,000
All-Year Brougham-5P	2295	4000	5000	8000	15,000	28,000
Speedster-4P	1895	7200	11,300	17,700	38,700	50,000
Phaeton-5P	1685	6700	9900	15,500	34,800	47,000
Four-Door Brgm. Spec.-5P	2095	3100	4200	6300	10,500	22,000
Sedan-7P	2295	2700	3600	5300	8800	19,000
Touring-7P	1785	6000	8500	13,000	30,000	42,000
Tourster-4P	1895	6200	8800	13,500	31,000	43,000

Series 8-80 — 8-cyl., 70 hp, 125" wb

Four-Door Brougham-5P	1895	2900	3700	5600	9100	20,000
Four-Door Sed.-5P	1995	2700	3600	5300	8800	19,000
Cpe. Rdstr.-4P	1995	6400	9300	14,500	33,000	45,000
Victoria-5P	1995	3000	4000	6000	9500	21,000

Series 80 — 8-cyl., 70 hp, 125" wb

All-Year Brougham-5P	2495	3000	4000	6000	9500	21,000
Speedster-4P	2095	7300	11,800	18,400	40,400	52,000
Phaeton-5P	1895	6800	10,300	16,000	35,500	48,000
Four-Door Brougham Spec.	2295	3100	4200	6300	10,500	22,000

Series 80 — 8-cyl., 70 hp, 132" wb

Sedan-7P	2495	2700	3600	5300	8800	19,000
Touring-7P	1985	6800	10,300	16,000	35,500	48,000
Tourster-4P	2095	7000	10,800	16,900	37,100	49,000

Series 8-90 — 8-cyl., 85 hp, 131" and 139" wb

Two-Door Brgm. Sed.-5P	2295	3300	4400	6700	12,000	24,000
Two-Door Brgm. Sed.-5P	2395	3500	4500	7000	13,000	25,000
All-Year Cpe. Rdstr.-4P	2395	5300	7000	11,500	24,000	37,000
All-Year Brougham-5P	2795	4200	5200	8400	15,700	29,000
Speedster-4P	3395	7600	12,500	19,400	42,400	55,000
Phaeton-5P	2185	7000	10,800	16,900	37,100	49,000
Four-Door Brougham Spec.	2595	3500	4500	7000	13,000	25,000
Sedan-7P	2795	3000	4000	6000	9500	21,000
Touring-7P	2285	6800	10,300	16,000	35,500	48,000
Touring-4P	2395	7000	10,800	16,900	37,100	49,000
DeLuxe Brougham Sed.-5P	2985	3700	4700	7300	13,700	26,000
DeLuxe Sed.-7P	3495	3100	4200	6300	10,500	22,000
DeLuxe Ber. Sed.-7P	3585	3300	4400	6700	12,000	24,000

Series 8-90 — 8-cyl., 85 hp

Cpe. Rdstr.-4P	3185	6700	9900	15,500	34,800	47,000
Victoria-5P	3185	3100	4200	6300	10,500	22,000
Speedster-4P	3275	7700	12,700	19,700	43,000	56,000
Tourster-4P	3275	7200	11,300	17,700	38,700	50,000
Brougham-5P	3275	3500	4500	7000	13,000	25,000
Sedan-7P	3785	3000	4000	6000	9500	21,000
Ber. Sed.-7P	3885	3700	4700	7300	13,700	26,000

NOTE: This was the White Eagle Series, with wheelbases of 132 and 139 inches, as well as a few on a 142-inch wheelbase.

1929 Kissel, series 8-126, White Eagle coupe-roadster, HAC

1929 KISSEL
Series 6-73 — 6-cyl., 52 hp, 117" wb

Four-Door Brgm. Sed.-5P	1595	3100	4200	6300	10,500	22,000
Four-Door Long Sed.-5P	1695	3000	4000	6000	9500	21,000
All-Year Cpe. Rdstr.-4P	1695	7000	10,800	16,900	37,100	49,000
Cpe. Rdstr. (Solid Top)-4P	1695	4200	5200	8400	15,700	29,000

1929 Kissel, series 8-95, coupe-roadster, AA

1929 Kissel, series 8-126, White Eagle, 7-pass. sedan, AA

Series 8-95 — 8-cyl., 95 hp, 125" wb

	FP	5	4	3	2	1
Four-Door Brgm. Sed.-5P	1995	3200	4300	6500	11,000	23,000
All-Year Cpe. Rdstr.-4P	2095	7200	11,300	17,700	38,700	50,000
Four-Door Long Sed.-5P	2095	3100	4200	6300	10,500	22,000
Cpe. (Solid Top)-4P	2095	4300	5400	8700	16,500	30,000
All-Year Brougham-5P	2595	3500	4500	7000	13,000	25,000
New Sed.-7P	2595	3200	4300	6500	11,000	23,000
Touring-7P	2095	5400	7300	11,800	25,000	38,000
Speedster-4P	2195	7200	11,300	17,700	38,700	50,000
Tourister-4P	2195	5800	8000	12,500	28,000	40,000

Series 8-126 — 8-cyl., 126 hp, 132" and 139" wb

Four-Door Brougham-5P	3275	3300	4400	6700	12,000	24,000
All-Year Cpe. Rdstr.-4P	3185	7300	11,600	18,100	39,600	51,000
Cpe. Rdstr. (Solid Top)	3185	3300	4400	6700	12,000	24,000
All-Year Brougham-5P	3185	3700	4700	7300	13,700	26,000
Sedan-7P	3785	3300	4400	6700	12,000	24,000
Ber. Sed.-7P	3885	3500	4500	7000	13,000	25,000
Speedster-4P	3275	7300	11,800	18,400	40,400	52,000
Tourster-4P	3275	6000	8500	13,000	30,000	42,000
Victoria-4P	3185	3200	4300	6500	11,000	23,000

1930-31 Kissel, series 6-73, sedan, HAC

1930 KISSEL
Series 6-73 — 6-cyl., 73 hp, 117" wb

Four-Door Brgm. Sed.-5P	1695	3200	4300	6500	11,000	23,000
Four-Door Long Sed.-5P	1695	3100	4200	6300	10,500	22,000
All-Weather Cpe. Rdstr.-4P	1695	7200	11,300	17,700	38,700	50,000
Cpe. Rdstr. (Solid Top)-4P	1695	4300	5400	8700	16,500	30,000

Series 8-95 — 8-cyl., 95 hp, 125" and 132" wb

Four-Door Brgm. Sed.-5P	1995	3300	4400	6700	12,000	24,000
All-Year Cpe. Rdstr.-4P	2095	7300	11,600	18,100	39,600	51,000
Four-Door Long Sed.	2095	3200	4300	6500	11,000	23,000
Cpe. (Solid Top)-4P	2595	4400	5600	9200	17,300	31,000
All-Year Brougham	2595	3700	4700	7300	13,700	26,000
New Sed.-7P	2595	3300	4400	6700	12,000	24,000
Touring-7P	2095	5500	7500	12,000	26,000	39,000
Speedster-4P	2195	7300	11,600	18,100	39,600	51,000
Touuister-4P	2195	5900	8300	12,800	29,000	41,000

Series 8-126 — 8-cyl., 126 hp, 132" and 139" wb

	FP	5	4	3	2	1
Four-Door Brougham-5P	3275	3500	4500	7000	13,000	25,000
All-Year Cpe. Rdstr.-4P	3185	7300	11,800	18,400	40,400	52,000
Cpe. Rdstr. (Solid Top)-4P	3185	4000	5000	8000	15,000	28,000
All-Year Brougham-5P	3185	3900	4800	7700	14,300	27,000
Sedan-7P	3785	3500	4500	7000	13,000	25,000
Ber. Sed.-7P	3885	3700	4700	7300	13,700	26,000
Speedster-4P	3275	7400	12,100	18,800	41,100	53,000
Tourster-4P	3275	6200	8800	13,500	31,000	43,000
Victoria-4P	3185	3300	4400	6700	12,000	24,000

1931 KISSEL
Series 6-73 — 6-cyl., 73 hp, 117" wb

Four-Door Brgm. Sed.-5P	1595	3200	4300	6500	11,000	23,000
Four-Door Long Sed.-5P	1695	3100	4200	6300	10,500	22,000
All-Year Cpe. Rdstr.-4P	1695	7200	11,300	17,700	38,700	50,000
Cpe. Rdstr. (Solid Top)-4P	1695	4300	5400	8700	16,500	30,000

Series 8-95 — 8-cyl., 95 hp, 125" and 132" wb

Four-Door Brgm. Sed.-5P	1995	3300	4400	6700	12,000	24,000
All-Year Cpe. Rdstr.-4P	2095	7300	11,600	18,100	39,600	51,000
Four-Door Long Sed.-5P	2095	3200	4300	6500	11,000	23,000
Cpe. (Solid Top)-4P	2095	4400	5600	9200	17,300	31,000
All-Year Brougham-5P	2595	3700	4700	7300	13,700	26,000
New Sed.-7P	2595	3300	4400	6700	11,000	24,000
Touring-7P	2095	5500	7500	12,000	26,000	39,000
Speedster-4P	2195	7300	11,600	18,100	39,600	51,000
Tourster-4P	2195	5900	8300	12,800	29,000	41,000

Series 8-126 — 8-cyl., 126 hp, 132" and 139" wb

Four-Door Brougham-5P	3275	3500	4500	7000	13,000	25,000
All Year Cpe. Rdstr.-4P	3185	7300	11,800	18,400	40,400	52,000
Cpe. Rdstr. (Solid Top)	3185	4000	5000	8000	15,000	28,000
All-Year Brougham-5P	3185	3900	4800	7700	14,300	27,000
Sedan-7P	3785	3500	4500	7000	13,000	25,000
Ber. Sed.-7P	3885	3700	4700	7300	13,700	26,000
Speedster-4P	3275	7400	12,100	18,800	41,100	53,000
Tourster-4P	3275	6200	8800	13,500	31,000	43,000
Victoria-4P	3185	3300	4400	6700	12,000	24,000

KITE — Fort Scott, Kansas — (1903) — The Kite brothers were Milton T. and John D., and in 1903 they were reported to have built an automobile in Fort Scott. Most probably, they never built another. The year following Milton Kite was working as a machinist at the Fort Scott Syrup Manufacturing Company. A half decade later the brothers were in partnership in a machine shop at 501 East Wale Street in Fort Scott.

KITTO — Connecticut, Iowa & Ohio — (1903-1911) — There was never an automobile in America called the Kitto. But there was a man named W.H. Kitto. Since he promoted at least three different vehicles in three different states under three different names, it seems appropriate to include them all under the name of the man who perpetrated them, because the documented total production of all these efforts appears to be just one car. William H. Kitto was an English car dealer who was first mentioned in the American press in February 1903 when he exhibited a car purportedly of U.S. manufacture under his own name at the Crystal Palace Automobile Show in London. Thereafter he visited this country to arrange for the exportation of cars to his London agency. Obviously he found these shores more congenial to his get-rich plans, because by October of 1904 he returned to stay, but not in any one place for long. Initially, he settled in Middletown, Connecticut where he organized the Simplicities Automobile Company for manufacture of a four-cylinder 24 hp touring car "of English-French style." He promoted this car early in 1905, and managed to extract a loan of $1000 from the Warwick Cycle and Automobile Company of Springfield (Massachusetts). He also sold a good deal of stock. In September 1905 Warwick sued Kitto, whereupon Kitto announced the closing of his plant and the discharge of all his employees. There could not have been many, since only one Simplicities had been built. Kitto immediately left Middleton and next was heard from in Des Moines, Iowa where he formed the Motor Components Manufacturing Company which he reorganized in early 1907 as the Criterion Motor Company and announced the forthcoming manufacture of a $2750 four-cylinder 40 hp touring car. After selling stock in Des Moines, he moved Criterion over to Kent (Ohio) and sold some more stock. A good many members of the Kent citizenry put up money, while others delayed paying their subscriptions — and all, as time went by, lost faith. Meantime, in August of 1910, Kitto turned up in Lisbon (Ohio) where he promoted the Lisbon Auto Truck Company and sold some more stock. There is no documented evidence that a single example of either the Criterion or the Lisbon was ever built. The Criterion caper lingered on for some time, however. A full four years following his promotion of the Criterion company in Kent, suits and countersuits still raged through the courts. In what might be viewed sublime audacity, W.H. Kitto sued several Criterion stock subscribers who had never paid for their subscriptions. The irony is that, in late April of 1911, he won. His contention was that if all subscriptions were paid, he would have had the necessary capital to open the Criterion factory. The 129 delinquent subscribers immediately appealed the decision. The Criterion factory was never opened.

1925 Kleiber, all-weather, touring, OCW

KLEIBER — San Francisco, California — (1924-1929) — Paul Kleiber was a native San Franciscan who began experimenting with horseless carriages in the 1890's, became the distributor for the Gramm truck after the turn of the century, and in November 1913 organized the Kleiber Motor Truck Company for the manufacture of commercial vehicles of his own design. A decade later he decided to add passenger cars to his line. Their marketing was confined to the three Pacific Coast states, and a new plant was built for their manufacture which San Francisco mayor James Rolph opened ceremonially in early April of 1925. Apparently production had begun the previous year, however, because in November of 1925 *Motor West* reported the production of thirty Kleibers in 1924 with 175 thus far for 1925. "Aristocratic in Appearance" was a Kleiber slogan and a misnomer because the car was absolutely undistinguished. It was powered by the six-cylinder Continental Red Seal engine, and used standard components throughout. Production never was very large, and ebbed during the later Twenties. An 85 hp Continental straight-eight was announced for 1929, but only two prototypes were built. The Kleiber was discontinued following the stock market crash, although the Kleiber Motor Truck Company continued in the commercial field for another eight years.

1924-1925 KLEIBER
Six — 60 hp, 128" wb

	FP	5	4	3	2	1
Sport Touring-5P	1885	4500	5800	9500	18,000	32,000
California Top Touring-5P	2285	4200	5200	8400	15,700	29,000
Coach-4P	2285	1600	2700	3800	5800	12,000
Sedan-5P	2350	1800	2800	4000	6200	13,000

1926 KLEIBER
Six — 60 hp, 128" wb

Sport Touring-5P	1885	4500	5800	9500	18,000	32,000
California Top Touring-5P	2285	4200	5200	8400	15,700	29,000
Coach-4P	2285	1600	2700	3800	5800	12,000
Sedan-5P	2350	1800	2800	4000	6200	13,000
Coupe-4P	2575	2300	3300	4600	7500	16,000
Brougham-5P	2350	2000	3000	4200	6500	14,000

1927 KLEIBER
Six — 60 hp, 122" wb

Standard Touring-5P	1885	3900	4800	7700	14,300	27,000
California Top Touring-5P	2150	4200	5200	8400	15,700	29,000
California Top Touring-7P	2250	4000	5000	8000	15,000	28,000
Coupe-4P	2575	2300	3300	4600	7500	16,000
Coach-5P	2575	1600	2700	3800	5800	12,000
Brougham-5P	2350	2000	3000	4200	6500	14,000
Sedan-5P	2675	1800	2800	4000	6200	13,000

1929 Kleiber, straight eight, prototype, KM

1928-1929 KLEIBER
Six — 60 hp, 122" wb

Standard Touring-5P	1885	3900	4800	7700	14,300	27,000
California Top Touring-5P	2150	4200	5200	8400	15,700	29,000
California Top Touring-7P	2250	4000	5000	8000	15,000	28,000
Coupe-4P	2575	2300	3300	4600	7500	16,000
Coach-5P	2575	1600	2700	3800	5800	12,000
Brougham-5P	2350	2000	3000	4200	6500	14,000
Sedan-5P	2675	1800	2800	4000	6200	13,000

KLEMM — E.R. Klemm of Chicago has frequently been cited on rosters as the manufacturer of an automobile. There is no evidence that he was. He is indicated to have built a truck, however, in both the 1917 and 1918 editions of *Motor Trucks of America*, published by the B.F. Goodrich Company.

KLEMP — The Carl Klemp Company of Chicago, Illinois was organized with a capital stock of $2100 for the manufacture of automobiles and accessories early in 1909. Carl Klemp, H.T. Kett and T.H. Rooney were the incorporators. Manufacture of a car is doubted.

KLENKE — The Klenke Pneumatic Suspension Company was organized early in 1911 in New York City with a capital stock of $150,000 for the manufacture and repair of vehicles, cars and engines. Incorporators were W.H. Klenke, T.A. Klenke and M.S. Brown. Manufacture of a car is doubted.

KLEPFER — Depew, New York — (1912-1914) — The Klepfer brothers of Depew were Matthew, John and Frank, the last named having established a Buick agency in town in 1905. From 1912 to 1914 the brothers constructed two prototype cars with the intention of following this with a small series of a half-dozen production examples. Their inability to secure parts because of materials shortages concomitant to the onset of World War I thwarted their plans. Only the two prototypes were completed, some parts of one of them remaining with the Klepfer family to this day.

KLINE — The Kline Company was organized in Chicago, Illinois late in 1906 with a capital stock of $15,000 for the manufacture of automobiles and parts. Incorporators were F.L. Kline, George H. McCune and Samuel Hals. Manufacture of a car is doubted.

KLINE — Harrisburg, Pennsylvania — (1900) — James A. Kline of the Kline Cycle and Automobile Company of Harrisburg believed in a wide repertoire: "Automobiles, Bicycles, Sporting Goods, Fishing Tackle, Live Bait, Phonographs and Records, Machine Work a Specialty" read his ads. In addition to becoming Harrisburg's first automobile dealer in 1900 with the acquisition of a Locomobile franchise, he also built a gasoline motor buggy for himself, which he may have copied in a few more examples for a local clientele. He moved into the big time a decade later with the Kline Kar.

1910 Kline Kar, model 4-24, touring, HAC

KLINE KAR — York, Pennsylvania — (1910-1912)/Richmond, Virginia — (1912-1923) — James A. Kline was born in 1877 on a farm near Hummelstown, Pennsylvania and left there as a teenager for the nearest big city. In Harrisburg he worked awhile as an optician before establishing a machine shop and bicycle dealership in 1899; the following year he built his first gasoline car and became Harrisburg's first automobile dealer with the acquisition of a Locomobile franchise. Subsequently he secured the agencies for the curved dash Oldsmobile and the Franklin. In 1905 he was enticed to York by Samuel E. Baily to redesign a car then known as the York, but subsequently to be called the Pullman. In 1909, after being eased out of the Pullman organization, Kline went into partnership with Baily and Joseph C. Carrell to establish the B.C.K. Motor Company, locating its factory in Baily's carriage works in York. The new Kline Kar was in production for the 1910 season; the six-cylinder model was almost immediately sent into competition. Two dirt track racing specials named "Jimmy" and "Jimmy, Jr." (after their designer and his son) brought the Kline name to national prominence and to the attention of a group of businessmen in Richmond, Virginia who had also noticed how well the Kline Kar was selling in that state. In the spring of 1911 the B.C.K. Motor Company was sold lock, stock, and James A. Kline to the Virginia consortium. The firm was reorganized as the Kline Motor Car Corporation, and a large new factory was begun in Richmond. By November 1912 the Richmond factory was ready, and the Kline Kar became a product of Dixie, save for its engines which were built in the North to Kline's design by the Kirkham Machine Company of Bath, New York. Probably this farming out of engine production was for the purpose of moving into quantity manufacture quickly. Before long nearly a thousand cars a year were leaving the Kline Kar factory, a meritorious figure for an automobile that was never inexpensive and was always promoted as a quality vehicle. "Jimmy Kline is one of the recognized masters of the business," enthused the Richmond folk, and the $2585 Model 6-50 runabout was advertised as "one of the classiest roadsters brought out for several seasons . . . for a physician or a young man of fastidious taste." In 1915 Kline Motor Car Corporation survived a receivership. In 1917 the company produced 1399 cars and appeared well grounded to enter a prosperous postwar market forcefully. Unfortunately the postwar recession arrived instead. The Kline Kar became an assembled automobile (Continental engine), which could not have pleased James Kline much. Shortly before the company went to the wall in early 1924, he was quoted in reference to his Kline Kars as saying that "I would rather see my children dead than prostituted to cheapness and inferior workmanship."

1910 KLINE KAR
Model 4-24 — 4-cyl., 24/30 hp, 110" wb

	FP	5	4	3	2	1
Roadster-4P	1575	2500	3500	5000	8500	18,000

Model 6-40 — 6-cyl., 40 hp, 123" wb

Touring-5P	2500	2400	3400	4800	8000	17,000
Toy Tonneau-4P	2500	2400	3400	4800	8000	17,000
Runabout-2P	2500	2300	3300	4600	7500	16,000
Limousine	3750	2000	3000	4200	6500	14,000
Landaulet	3750	2200	3200	4400	7000	15,000
Meteor Roadster (108" wb)	2500	2500	3500	5000	8500	18,000

1911 KLINE KAR
Model 4-24 — 4-cyl., 24 hp, 110" wb

Meteor Roadster-2P	1500	2500	3500	5000	8500	18,000

Model 4-30 — 4-cyl., 30 hp, 112" wb

Toy Tonneau-4P	1675	2300	3300	4600	7500	16,000
Touring-5P	1675	2300	3300	4600	7500	16,000
Runabout	1625	2000	3000	4200	6500	14,000

1911 Kline Kar, model 6-50, touring, HAC

Model 4-40 — 4-cyl., 40 hp, 117" wb

	FP	5	4	3	2	1
Toy Tonneau	2250	2400	3400	4800	8000	17,000
Touring-5P	2250	2400	3400	4800	8000	17,000
Runabout	2225	2500	3500	5000	8500	18,000

Model 6-50 — 6-cyl., 50 hp, 124" wb

Touring-5P	2700	3200	6450	10,750	15,050	21,500
Toy Tonneau-4P	2700	2500	3500	5000	8500	18,000
Meteor Roadster	2650	2700	3600	5300	8800	19,000

1912 Kline Kar, model 6-60, touring, JAC

1912 KLINE KAR
Model 4-30 — 4-cyl., 30 hp, 114" wb

Touring-5P	1750	2500	3500	5000	8500	18,000
Toy Tonneau-4P	1750	2500	3500	5000	8500	18,000
Runabout-2P	1700	2400	3400	4800	8000	17,000

Model 4-40 — 4-cyl., 40 hp, 118" wb

Touring-5P	2250	3200	6450	10,750	15,050	21,500
Toy Tonneau-4P	2250	2700	3600	5300	8800	19,000
Runabout-2P	2000	2500	3500	5000	8500	18,000

Model 6-50 — 6-cyl., 50 hp

Roadster (110" wb)	2850	3000	4000	6000	9500	21,000
Speed Car (110" wb)	2850	3100	4200	6300	10,500	22,000
Touring-4P (126" wb)	2850	3400	6900	11,500	16,100	23,000
Touring-5P (126" wb)	2850	3500	7050	11,750	16,450	23,500

Model 6-60 — 6-cyl., 60 hp, 130" wb

Touring-7P	3500	3750	7500	12,500	17,500	25,000
Semi-Torpedo-4P	3500	3200	4300	6500	11,000	23,000
Semi-Torpedo-6P	3500	3100	4200	6300	10,500	22,000
Meteor (110" wb)	3200	3000	4000	6000	9500	21,000

1913 Kline Kar, model 6-50, runabout, HAC

1913 KLINE KAR
Model 4-30 — 4-cyl., 30 hp, 115" wb

Touring	1750	2500	3500	5000	8500	18,000
Toy Tonneau	1750	2500	3500	5000	8500	18,000
Runabout	1750	2400	3400	4800	8000	17,000

Model 4-40 — 4-cyl., 40 hp, 118" wb

	FP	5	4	3	2	1
Touring	1985	2700	3600	5300	8800	19,000
Toy Tonneau	1985	2700	3600	5300	8800	19,000
Runabout	1985	2400	3400	4800	8000	17,000
Meteor Speed Car	1935	2900	3700	5600	9100	20,000

Model 6-50 — 6-cyl., 50 hp, 126" wb

Touring	2585	3900	7800	13,000	18,200	26,000
Toy Tonneau	2595	3800	7600	12,750	17,500	25,000
Runabout	2585	2500	3500	5000	8500	18,000
Coupe	3200	2400	3400	4800	8000	17,000
Limousine	3785	2500	3500	5000	8500	18,000
Meteor Speed Car	2535	3300	4400	6700	12,000	24,000

Model 6-60 — 6-cyl., 60 hp, 132" wb

Touring	3500	4300	8550	14,250	19,950	28,500
Toy Tonneau	3500	4000	8000	14,000	19,000	27,500
Runabout	3250	2700	3600	5300	8800	19,000
Coupe	3650	2300	3300	4600	7500	16,000
Limousine	4700	2700	3600	5300	8800	19,000
Meteor Speed Car	3200	3900	4800	7700	14,300	27,000

1914 Kline Kar, model 4-30, touring, HAC

1914 KLINE KAR
Model 4-30 — 4-cyl., 33 hp, 115" wb

Touring-5P	1685	2500	3500	5000	8500	18,000
Toy Tonneau-4P	1685	2500	3500	5000	8500	18,000

Model 4-40 — 4-cyl., 30 hp, 120" wb

Touring-5P	1985	2700	3600	5300	8800	19,000
Roadster-2/4P	1985	2900	3700	5600	9100	20,000

Model 6-50 — 6-cyl., 41 hp, 128" wb

Touring-5P	2585	2900	3700	5600	9100	20,000
Runabout-2P	2585	2900	3700	5600	9100	20,000

Model 6-60 — 6-cyl., 44 hp, 133" wb

Touring-7P	2985	4300	8550	14,250	19,950	28,500
Toy Tonneau	2985	4000	8000	14,000	19,000	27,500
Runabout-2P	2985	2900	3700	5600	9100	20,000

1915 Kline Kar, model 6-42-A, touring, HAC

1915 KLINE KAR
Model 6-42 — 4-cyl., 41 hp, 123" wb

Touring-5P	1750	2700	3600	5300	8800	19,000
Roadster-2P	1750	2900	3700	5600	9100	20,000
Toy Tonneau-4P	1750	2700	3600	5300	8800	19,000
Detachable Coupe-2P	2400	2300	3300	4600	7500	16,000

Model 6-42A — 6-cyl., 44 hp, 127" wb

Touring-7P	1850	2900	3700	5600	9100	20,000
Limousine-5/7P	2850	2500	3500	5000	8500	18,000

1916 Kline Kar, model 6-36, touring, HAC

1916 KLINE KAR
Model 6-36 — 6-cyl., 44 hp, 120" wb

Touring-5P	1095	2700	3600	5300	8800	19,000
Roadster-2P	1095	2900	3700	5600	9100	20,000

1917 Kline Kar, model 6-38, touring, HAC

1917 KLINE KAR
Model 6-38 — 6-cyl., 25.35 hp, 120" wb

	FP	5	4	3	2	1
Touring-5P	1195	2500	3500	5000	8500	18,000
Shamrock Roadster-4P	1195	2700	3600	5300	8800	19,000
Roadster-2P	1175	2900	3700	5600	9100	20,000
Roadster-3P	1175	3000	4000	6000	9500	21,000

1918 Kline Kar, model 6-38, touring, HAC

1918 KLINE KAR
Series 6-38 — 6-cyl., 25.35 hp, 120" wb

Touring-5P	1495	2500	3500	5000	8500	18,000
Sport Touring-4P	1495	3100	4200	6300	10,500	22,000
Shamrock Roadster-4P	1495	2900	3700	5600	9100	20,000
Roadster-2P	1495	3000	4000	6000	9500	21,000
Roadster-3P	1495	3100	4200	6300	10,500	22,000
Sedan-5P	2220	1800	2800	4000	6200	13,000

1919 Kline Kar, model H-6-42, touring, HAC

1919 KLINE KAR
Series H 6-42 — 6-cyl., 25.35 hp, 121" wb

Touring-5P	1865	2700	3600	5300	8800	19,000
Sport-Touring-4P	1865	3000	4000	6000	9500	21,000
Shamrock Roadster-4P	1865	3100	4200	6300	10,500	22,000
Roadster-2P	1865	3100	4200	6300	10,500	22,000
Roadster-4P	1865	3200	4300	6500	11,000	23,000
Sedan-5P	2590	1800	2800	4000	6200	13,000

1920 KLINE KAR
Model 6-55-J — 6-cyl., 25.4 hp, 121" wb

Roadster-3P	1865	3000	4000	6000	9500	21,000
Sport-4P & 5P	1865	3100	4200	6300	10,500	22,000
Touring-5P & 7P	1990	2900	3700	5600	9100	20,000
Sedan-5P & 7P	2790	2000	3000	4200	6500	14,000
Coupe-2P & 4P	2750	2300	3300	4600	7500	16,000

1921 KLINE KAR
Model 6-55-K — 6-cyl., 55 hp, 121" wb

Roadster-3P	2290	3000	4000	6000	9500	21,000
Sport-5P	2290	3100	4200	6300	10,500	22,000
Auxiliary-7P	2290	2900	3700	5600	9100	20,000
Coupe-4P	3250	2300	3300	4600	7500	16,000
Sedan-7P	3290	2000	3000	4200	6500	14,000

1920-21 Kline Kar, model 6-55, sport touring, HAC

1922 KLINE KAR
Model 6-55-K — 6-cyl., 55 hp, 121" wb

	FP	5	4	3	2	1
Special Sport Touring-5P	1990	3100	4200	6300	10,500	22,000
Sport Touring-5P	1890	3000	4000	6000	9500	21,000
Sedan-7P	3090	2000	3000	4200	6500	14,000
Roadster-3P	1890	3500	4500	7000	13,000	25,000
Coupe-4P	3050	2400	3400	4800	8000	17,000

1923 Kline Kar, special sport phaeton, HAC

1923 KLINE KAR
Model 6-60-L — 6-cyl., 60 hp, 121" wb

Touring-5P	1690	2900	3700	5600	9100	20,000
Sport-5P	1690	3000	4000	6000	9500	21,000
Roadster-3P	1690	3200	4300	6500	11,000	23,000
Special Sport Phaeton-5P	1890	3300	4400	6700	12,000	24,000
Coupe-3P	2750	2300	3300	4600	7500	16,000
Sedan-7P	2790	2000	3000	4200	6500	14,000

1924 KLINE KAR
Model 6-60-L — 6-cyl., 55 1/2 hp, 121" wb

Sport-5P	1590	3100	4200	6300	10,500	22,000
Touring-7P	1590	3000	4000	6000	9500	21,000
Coupe-3P	2550	2300	3300	4600	7500	16,000
Sedan-7P	2590	2000	3000	4200	6500	14,000

KLINGBERG — Elmo, Kansas — (1921) — The Klingberg was a contraption but apparently it served Dr. W.A. Klingberg well during those months when Kansas roads were excessively muddy. The good doctor designed the car himself, using a Model T chassis, a buggy top and wheels from an old farm wagon. "A country blacksmith put the contraption together," Motor Age reported, "and the doctor does the chauffeuring."

1907 Klink, touring, NAHC

KLINK — Dansville, New York — (1907-1910) — John F. Klink was a photograher in Dansville who was something of a showman and a promoter as well. In 1906 he asked a handyman and bicycle repairer in town named Harvey Toms to build a car for him, which he drove for the first time on

July 8th, 1906 and was so impressed that he decided to go into manufacture. With another Dansville native, Charles Day, he sold enough stock to organize the Klink Motor Car Manufacturing Company in March 1907. Most of the stock went to local residents, though a relative in California was enticed into the venture too. Fifteen workmen moved into the vacant factory of a former chair manufacturer, with Charles Day as general superintendent of the operation and Harvey Toms as foreman — and in May the first Klink car rolled out and was shipped the following month to the company's stockholder in California, who apparently had put up more money than anyone else. In October John Klink took three cars to the New York Automobile Show, and the car received a very good press, with more fulsome praise accorded it than the usual which no doubt was the result of Klink's prowess in promotion. The Klink was an assembled car, with bodies arriving from Buffalo, rear axles and transmissions from Brown-Lipe in Syracuse. The engines were Continental, fours initially, supplemented by a six in 1909. Such parts manufacture as was required locally was handled by the Sweet Foundry, which specialized in farm implements and steam generating equipment. At a hillclimb in Hornell in 1908, a Klink finished third out of twenty-five entrants. Except for an occasionally obstinate clutch, the car was considered a good performer. But obviously there was some obstinacy brewing in the company as well. In July 1909 Charles Day walked out after an argument with Klink. (He had plans to produce another car called the Day's Messenger Six, but that never came to be.) Severely short of cash, John Klink closed his factory's doors on September 25th, 1909. He made one last valiant effort early in 1910 to get back into manufacture, assembling two six-cylinder cars from parts on hand but nobody wanted to buy an automobile from a company that was in the throes of death, (Those two cars were stored in a building behind the Klink Photo Studios until 1934, when they were junked without ever having been driven.) Total Klink production has been estimated at twenty cars. John Klink went back to his photography business, though he tried being an entrepreneur again some years later in promoting the manufacture of a coffee substitute in soluble form. This venture failed more quickly than the Klink car. John Klink died in Dansville at age seventy-one, in November 1940, of injuries sustained when he was struck down by an automobile.

1907 KLINK
Model 30 — 4-cyl., 30 hp, 108" wb

	FP	5	4	3	2	1
Touring-5P	2000	2000	3000	4000	6500	14,000
Roadster-4P	2000	2200	3200	4400	7000	15,000

1908 KLINK
Model 30 — 4-cyl., 30 hp, 112" wb

Touring-5P	2000	2200	3200	4400	7000	15,000
Roadster-4P	2000	2300	3300	4600	7500	16,000

Model 40 — 4-cyl., 40 hp, 120" wb

Touring-7P	2500	2500	3500	5000	8500	18,000

1909 Klink, Six, touring, WLB

1909 KLINK
Model 30 — 4-cyl., 30 hp, 110" wb

Touring-5P	1750	2300	3300	4600	7500	16,000
Roadster-3P	1750	2400	3400	4800	8000	17,000

Model 35 — 6-cyl., 35 hp, 119" wb

Roadster-4P	2250	2700	3600	5300	8800	19,000
Touring-5P	2250	2500	3500	5000	8500	18,000

1910 KLINK
Model 35 — 6-cyl., 35 hp, 119" wb

Touring-5P	2000	2900	3700	5600	9100	20,000

1900 Klock, gasoline stanhope, WLB

KLOCK. — Stamford, Connecticut — (1900-1901) — Percy L. Klock began advertising his new car under his own name in August 1900. "The Most Perfect Gasoline Carriage in Use," he said, and his ad stated that the car was being built under Duryea patents. Within weeks, however, Percy Klock had a change of mind regarding his marketing approach, as the subsequent October advertisement revealed. During his experimental stage prior to the turn of the century, he had casually organized himself as the National Motor Carriage Company which was a grandiloquent designation for an automotive venture that had not been born yet. How could he top that now that he was on the road to production? Easy. He simply called himself the International Motor Carriage Company. He also dropped the reference to Duryea. His new advertisement otherwise was exactly the same, save for changing "elegant in design" to "excellent in design" and admitting that the horsepower of his two-cylinder engine was five instead of six. The illustration of his Stanhope Phaeton remained the same and so did the reference to the convenient "foot lever for starting from the seat." It did appear that Percy Klock was going places. His new office address for the International Motor Carriage Company in New York City was the Astor Court Building adjoining the Waldorf Astoria. His address as just plain Percy L. Klock had been Broadway and 100th Street. The factory remained in Stamford, Connecticut. *The Horseless Age* pronounced the car that Klock built as "one of the neatest in outside appearance among the gasoline vehicles at the show" following its formal debut at New York City's Madison Square Garden in November 1900. Why Percy Klock's car survived but a year is something of a mystery. It could have been the high price: $1200. Or it could have been that Percy Klock moved too fast for his own good in leasing those new offices near the Waldorf. He dropped from the automotive press the following year. Whether he was involved with the International (or United) Power Vehicle Company which took over his factory is not known for certain, but seems doubtful.

c.1917 Klondike, touring, OCW

KLONDIKE — Logansville, Wisconsin — (1916-1920) — Total Klondike car production was either six or eight units, all seven-passenger touring cars save for one four-door sedan. The Klondike was built by Fred Kohlmeyer & Sons of Logansville, and although the output was small, the firm remained active in the field longer than most. Six-cylinder 65 hp Wisconsin engines were used, the price tag was usually $1650, and the car's color always was black. In addition to automobiles, Kohlmeyer also built trucks and continued doing so for nine years after the last Klondike car was produced. Approximately 25 trucks were eventually built. Fred Kohlmeyer had selected the Klondike name in memory of the gold prospecting trip he had taken to Alaska in the 1890's.

1905 K & M, transformable highwheelers, NAHC

K & M — Lancaster, Pennsylvania — (1905) — An automobile that was easily convertible from pleasure car to delivery wagon was an idea that numerous manufacturers of highwheelers tried during the early years of the industry, but Enos H. Kreider of the Kreider Machine Company of Lancaster carried the convertible concept quite a bit further. Not only could this K & M highwheeler take produce to the market during the week and the family to church on Sunday, but the vehicle was quickly transformable as well to "a stationary power plant for driving such farm essentials as wood saw, water pump, corn grinder, churn, root-cutter or washing machine." As a pleasure car, the K & M accommodated four passengers on two bench seats, its two-cylinder 18 hp engine being carried in the center of the car, its wheelbase being 102 inches. Solid rubber tires were fitted, and a canopy top with side curtains was provided. Removal of the back seat turned the car into a delivery wagon, with the canopy left in place to protect the produce. Enos Kreider described his K & M's final metamorphosis as follows: "In effecting the transformation to a stationary engine the vehicle is run to the spot where the power is required and stopped. By lifting the right step to the rear seat a shaft is disclosed and onto the end of this is slipped a pulley. A belt is run from this pulley to the piece of machinery." Although the K & M seemingly carried the multi-use idea of the automobile to new heights, it was in production for less than a year. A few years later Kreider established the Lancaster Automobile Company, which was a garage and repair shop, and a dealership for such diverse automobiles as Buick, Winton, Packard, Pope-Toledo and Pope-Waverley. By 1913 Enos Kreider had discontinued both his Kreider Machine Company and Lancaster Automobile Company and had become an instructor at the Stevens Industrial School.

KNAPP — The A.C. Knapp Company was organized in Detroit, Michigan early in 1912 with a capital stock of $20,000 for the manufacture of automobiles. Joining A.C. Knapp in this venture were L.A. Droelle and W.S. Harrison. Manufacture is doubted.

The Knapp Motor Corporation was organized in New York City during the summer of 1914 with a capital stock of $10,000 to manufacture and deal in automobiles, engines and hardware. Incorporators were H.L. Hughes, T.G. Jenkins and E.S. McKeller. Manufacture of a car is doubted.

KNAPP — San Jose, California — (1906) — In 1906, following the dissolution of the partnership of Rolls A. Morton and Bert E. Knapp which had resulted in the Morton automobile of 1904, Bert Knapp seems to have attempted to continue in the car business in concert with his brother Rollin Knapp. The Knapp Manufacturing Company, whose address was the same 31 South Third Street as the former Morton Automobile and Motor Works, noted its principal activity in the machining field. But that at least one Knapp automobile was produced is indicated by the local reputation is earned as a hill climber. Following the San Francisco earthquake in 1906, Knapp Manufacturing joined the Sunset Automobile Company to form the Victory Motor Car Company which continued the Sunset in production in a new factory in San Jose.

1905 Knecht, steam touring, NAHC

KNECHT — West Salisbury, Pennsylvania — (1905) — In 1905 John Knecht and his brother Harry F. Knecht built two steam automobiles. Except for the wheels, the cars were built completely of components devised by the brothers. Assembly was done in the family M. Knecht & Son Foundry. There was certainly a backyard look to the vehicles, but they were reported to have been operated successfully for a considerable period.

KNICKERBOCKER — The Knickerbocker Automobile Company was organized in Wilmington, Delaware during the spring of 1909 with a capital stock of $100,000 for the manufacture of motorcars. R.L. Squire, G.W. Dorsey and A. Bird were the incorporators. Manufacture is doubted.

The Knickerbocker Friction Drive Automobile Company was organized with a capital stock of $50,000 during the spring of 1905 to manufacture automobiles in Worcester, Massachusetts. Incorporators were James Dorr, George B. Louderback, John P. Ashley, James F. Dorr and Charles G. Milton. Manufacture is doubted.

The Knickerbocker-Havers Company was organized in New York City during the spring of 1912 with a capital stock of $50,000 for the manufacture of motor vehicles. Incorporators were Erastus M. Cravath, Burnwell M. Crosthwait and Fredrick E. Grant. Manufacture of a car is doubted.

KNICKERBOCKER — Bronxville, New York — (1901-1903) — The Knickerbocker was the second car introduced by the Ward Leonard Electric Company of Bronxville. First, in February 1901, was the Century Tourist, a 3-1/2 hp runabout with a $1000 price tag. The Knickerbocker, which followed a few months later, was larger (at 5 hp) and was available as a

1901 Knickerbocker, model 1, runabout, HAC

$1400 runabout and $1700 tonneau. Both the Century Tourist and the Knickerbocker carried single-cylinder De Dion engines. By July the Century Tourist name was dropped, the car becoming, retroactively, the Knickerbocker Model 1. The Ward Leonard-designed cars looked very French, which was not surprising since H. Ward Leonard had initially considered securing a license to manufacture the Darracq in this country; the car he came up with himself was a model of modernity, shaft drive and wheel steering being very progressive features for the turn of the century period. Three of the four Knickerbockers entered in the Long Island Endurance Contest of 1902 finished splendidly, two of them with perfect scores. In the New York-Boston reliability run that year, the Knickerbocker again acquitted itself admirably, the plaque it won remaining in the archives of the Ward Leonard Company today. By 1903 Knickerbockers were available with both single- and two-cylinder engines (these remaining De Dions), as well as a 24 hp four (Bouchet). Also introduced that year was the largest car yet from the company, a 30 hp four that was marketed as a Ward Leonard. Citing difficulty in obtaining materials, the Ward Leonard Electric Company abandoned the car-making field at the end of 1903. H. Ward Leonard's subsequent contributions to the industry included an electric lighting system for automobiles. When he died in 1915, there were more than a hundred Ward Leonard patents in commercial use. His company moved to Mount Vernon, New York the following year, where it remains today.

1901-1902 KNICKERBOCKER
Model 1 — 1-cyl., 3-1/2 hp

	FP	5	4	3	2	1
Runabout	1000	3000	4000	6000	9500	21,000
Model 2 — 1-cyl., 5 hp						
Runabout	1400	3100	4200	6300	10,500	22,000
Tonneau	1700	3300	4400	6700	12,000	24,000
1903 KNICKERBOCKER						
Model 1 — 1-cyl., 10 hp						
Runabout	—	3100	4200	6300	10,500	22,000
Model 2 — 2-cyl., 15 hp						
Runabout	—	3200	4300	6500	11,000	23,000
Tonneau	—	3100	4200	6300	10,500	22,000
Model 3 — 4-cyl., 24 hp						
Tonneau	—	3300	4400	6700	12,000	24,000

KNIGHT — The partners were Miss Margaret E. Knight and Mrs. A.M. Davidson, and the car they built in Brookline, Massachusetts in 1912 carried their initials. Refer to K-D.

The car which resulted from the partnership of Charles Y. Knight and L.K. Kilbourne which was built in Chicago in 1905-1907 was called the Silent Knight. Refer to Silent Knight.

The Knight Equipment Company of Chicago, Illinois was organized during the spring of 1910 with a capital stock of $2500 to "manufacture and deal in motor cars, motor boats, aeroplanes, et cetera." Incorporators were Vincent Bendix, W.D. Jones and R.J. Jacker. Manufacture of a car is doubted. During this period Vincent Bendix was involved in a variety of automotive enterprises in the Midwest, including a highwheeler manufactured under his own name.

KNIGHT STEAM — Hudson, Massachusetts — (1901-1902) — In 1899 Frank D. Knight, who for many years had operated a machine shop in Hudson specializing in work for local shoe factories, sold out his business and took off for Alaska. Less than two years later he returned from the Gold Rush "broke but game," as his younger son later remembered. With his older son, George H. Knight, who had graduated from M.I.T. in 1897, the father decided to build a steam automobile. He borrowed $2000, bought machine tools and set up a little factory in a barn in Hudson. In preparation for his Alaskan venture, Knight had invented an earth-boring device, a porcupine water-tube boiler and a two-cylinder steam engine, so consequently the first Knight Steam Carriage was put together quickly. George Knight designed it, Frank Knight did all the machine work, the younger son helped after high school classes every day. The vehicle was completed in the spring of 1901. A marvelous picture of what it was like to be a small-town steam car builder at the turn of the century has been provided by the younger Knight: "Fuel and water required constant attention and frequent replenishment. Kerosene was available in every country store, and watering troughs were in every town. We had a steam ejector for drawing water from the trough to the tank but sometimes had to fall back to using a pail or folding bucket. Backfires and explosions occurred infrequently but a 'good one' would blow off the rear deck, chimney and the sheet asbestos insulation. Once my father got badly burned around his face by a backfire

1901 Knight Steamer, runabout, NAHC

from the burner while he was on his knees looking under the body at the main jet. That was 'early in the game' and was a good reason for changing from gasoline to kerosene." A little company called F.D. Knight & Son was informally organized, brochures were printed and about eight examples of the Knight Steam Carriage, a small stanhope priced at $800, were produced. The venture ended there. The Knights had hoped to establish a viable factory, but they could not raise capital. This they attributed to the lamentable demise of the Marlboro steam car produced by Orrin Walker a few towns away in Massachusetts for which stock had been sold throughout the area: "The failure of this venture raised so much doubt that my father was unable to get the necessary backing for his plan." Thereafter Frank Knight operated an automobile repair shop in Hudson.

1917 Knight Special, touring, NAHC

KNIGHT SPECIAL — New York, New York — (1917) — The Knight Special had a four-cylinder Moline-Knight engine, Entz magnetic transmission, and worm gear drive. Its wheelbase was a long 132 inches, its cantilever springs an extra-long 61 inches. The universal joints were leather, the axles by Timken. One car was built. It was a five-passenger touring with what *Motor Life* described as an "oddly placed" toolbox; it was designed as a drawer into the long stepplate. Chassis price was to be $4000, with custom bodies built to order. The New York City firm of Watson & Stoekle was behind this venture which ended with the building of the prototype. Among other factors, America's entrance into the First World War played havoc with the firm's plan for manufacture.

KNIGHTSTOWN — In late 1900 the Knightstown Buggy Company incorporated with a capital stock of $30,000 in order to add the manufacture of automobiles to the horsedrawn vehicles already being produced in its Knightstown, Indiana factory. The Knightstown directors were Robert Silver, Mason Walters and Robert Logan. Documentation regarding any subsequent car manufacture is lacking.

KNOTTS — The Knotts Taxicab Company was organized in Wilmington, Delaware during the summer of 1914 with a capital stock of $25,000 to "manufacture automobiles, cyclecars, etc." Incorporators were J.T. Knotts, J.W. Brady and E. Krause. Manufacture is doubted.

KNOW — The Know Automobile Company of New York City is indicated to have built an automobile in 1900, according to various car rosters. New York City directories of the turn-of-the-century period do not reveal such a company in town. Probably this car was simply a misspelling of Knox. On a number of occasions from 1900 through 1908 references appeared in automobile trade journals to the presence of a "Know" at a particular automobile show. Invariably the car turned out to be a Knox.

KNOWLES — Buffalo, New York — (1904) — The Knowles Automobile Manufacturing Company of 1904 was an attempt by William Knowles to stay in the automobile business after his Kensington Automobile Company had failed earlier that year. A special modified model of the Kensington from 1901 had been marketed as the Knowles Khaki Flyer, and now in 1904 the last of the Kensingtons were marketed under the Knowles name as well. They were $2500 72-inch-wheelbase touring cars powered by two-cylinder 12 hp air-cooled Kelecom engines imported from Belgium.

KNOX — The Knox Automobile Company of Chicago, Illinois was organized late in 1906 with a capital stock of $5000 to manufacture and repair automobiles. Incorporators were Theodore C. Robinson, William W. Hodge and E. Rising. Manufacture is doubted.

The Knox Motor Car Company of Camden, New Jersey was organized late in 1906 to "manufacture automobiles, vehicles, electric and other motors." Incorporators were F.P. Wilcox and G.W. Kritler of Philadelphia, and W.L. Hurley of Camden. Manufacture of a car is doubted.

1900 Knox, three-wheeler runabout, HPN

KNOX — Springfield, Massachusetts — (1900-1914) — Harry A. Knox was encouraged to build an automobile by his next-door neighbor J. Frank Duryea. A graduate of the Springfield Technical Institute and an apprentice with the Elektron Company which manufactured elevators in Springfield, Knox left his apprenticeship in 1895 to take on a job with the Overman Wheel Company of Chicopee Falls. At Overman he built three experimental gasoline cars, then left abruptly in 1898 when A.H. Overman decided he'd rather manufacture a steamer. Returning to Springfield, he joined with his former Elektron boss, E.H. Cutler, to organize the Knox Automobile Company. Its first factory was the Waltham Watch Company. Fifteen three-wheeler runabouts were produced in 1900, 100 in 1901. Production increased to 250 cars in 1902, when a four-wheeler runabout was added to the line. Early cars had been called Knoxmobile; the Waterless Knox became a popular designation in 1903. "Old Porcupine" was the car's affectionate nickname, however, and rather apt since Harry Knox effected his air cooling by using two-inch pins stuck into the cylinder barrel rather than the more usual fins. "The Car That Never Drinks" was a slogan. Late in 1904 Harry Knox resigned from his company and set up shop across town to build the Atlas air-cooled car and later the sleeve-valve Atlas-

1901 Knox, three-wheeler runabout, HAC

787

Knight. The parting of Knox from Knox apparently was not a pleasant one, though for a little while the company continued handsomely without him. In 1906 a Knox completed the Glidden Tour without the loss of a single penalty point. In 1907 the company survived the receivership brought on principally by its expansion efforts to meet an ever-increasing business. Knox creditors were in virtual control of the company, which was described early in 1908 as "on the fair road to recovery." The first four-cylinder Knox had been introduced in 1906; shaft drive replaced the former chain in 1907; the first water-cooled Knox was introduced in 1908. By now the Knox automobile had changed significantly from the car that Harry had built. From a thousand-dollar price range, the Knox had crept up above $2500 in 1908, and some of the larger limousine models would later sell for as much as $6400. From 1910 onward, all Knoxes were water-cooled, with a six added to the line in 1911. That these were fine cars there was no doubt, but the Knox had lost the personality of the "Old Porcupine." Late in 1912 the company began operating under a trusteeship, which was reported to have been occasioned "due to technicalities" caused by the death of Knox treasurer A.N. Mayo. The company's affairs were finally sorted out by May of 1914 when its entire assets were purchased for $631,090 by Edward O. Sutton, who reorganized as the Knox Motors Company. Knox had entered the commercial field early on, and would now continue in the manufacture of tractor-trailer and fire apparatus units. The Knox passenger car was phased out in 1914. In 1919 Knox merged with Militor Corporation of Springfield, and announced continuing manufacture of the Militor motorcycle as well as reentry into the passenger-car field. A Militor automobile was never marketed, however, and during the early Twenties Knox irrevocably went under in the wake of the postwar economic upheaval.

1900-1901 KNOX
Model A — 1-cyl., 5 hp

	FP	5	4	3	2	1
Three-Wheeler Runabout	750	2500	3500	5000	8500	18,000

1902 Knox, model B, runabout, HAC

1902 Knox, model C, runabout, HAC

1902 KNOX
Model A — 1-cyl., 5 hp

Three-Wheeler Runabout	750	2500	3500	5000	8500	18,000
Three-Wheeler Delivery	—	2400	3400	4800	8000	17,000

Model B — 1-cyl., 8 hp, 69" wb

Runabout	1000	2500	3500	5000	8500	18,000

Two-Cylinder — 8 hp

Runabout	1100	2700	3600	5300	8800	19,000

1903 Knox, model C, runabout, HAC

1903 KNOX
Model C — 1-cyl., 8 hp, 72" wb

	FP	5	4	3	2	1
Runabout	1200	2700	3600	5300	8800	19,000

1904 Knox, surrey, HAC

1904 Knox, surrey, OCW

1904 KNOX
One-Cylinder — 8/10 hp, 72" wb

Runabout	1350	2700	3600	5300	8800	19,000
Davis Delivery	1500	2400	3400	4800	8000	17,000
Lenox Touring	1500	2900	3700	5600	9100	20,000
Leroy Touring	1500	2900	3700	5600	9100	20,000
Lorraine Runabout	1400	2700	3600	5300	8800	19,000
Murray Delivery (84" wb)	1600	2400	3400	4800	8000	17,000

Two-Cylinder — 16/18 hp, 84" wb

Tuxedo Touring	2200	2400	3400	4800	8000	17,000
Tudor Surrey	2200	2300	3300	4600	7500	16,000
Touraine Runabout	2000	2400	3400	4800	8000	17,000
Adams Delivery	2500	2000	3000	4200	6500	14,000

1905 Knox, model F, surrey, HAC

1905 KNOX

Model E — 1-cyl., 8/10 hp, 72" wb

	FP	5	4	3	2	1
Runabout-4P	1335	2500	3500	5000	8500	18,000

Model F — 2-cyl., 14/16 hp, 90" wb

Tonneau	1900	3000	4000	6000	9500	21,000

Model F-1 — 2-cyl., 14/16 hp, 81" wb

Closed Top Runabout-4P	1615	3100	4200	6300	10,500	22,000
Open Top Runabout-4P	1600	3000	4000	6000	9500	21,000

Model F-3 — 2-cyl., 14/16 hp, 87" wb

Closed Top Surrey	1865	3200	4300	6500	11,000	23,000
Open Top Surrey	1850	3100	4200	6300	10,500	22,000

1906 Knox, model G, tonneau, HAC

1906 KNOX

Model F-1 — 2-cyl., 14/16 hp, 81" wb

Runabout-2/4P	1500	3100	4200	6300	10,500	22,000

Model F — 2-cyl., 14/16 hp, 90" wb

Tonneau-5P	1900	3200	4300	6500	11,000	23,000

Model F-4 — 2-cyl., 14/16 hp, 81" wb

Tourist-2P	1400	3000	4000	6000	9500	21,000

Model F-3 — 2-cyl., 14/16 hp, 87" wb

Surrey	1750	3200	4300	6500	11,000	23,000

Model G — 4-cyl., 35/40 hp, 112" wb

Limousine-6P	5000	2700	3600	5300	8800	19,000
Tonneau-7P	4000	3000	4000	6000	9500	21,000

1907 KNOX

Model F-4 — 2-cyl., 14/16 hp, 81" wb

Tourist-2P	1400	3100	4200	6300	10,500	22,000

Model H — 4-cyl., 25/30 hp, 102" wb

Stanhope-2P	2500	3200	4300	6500	11,000	23,000
Touring-5P	2500	3300	4400	6700	12,000	24,000

Model G — 4-cyl., 35/40 hp, 112" wb

Touring-7P	4000	3500	4500	7000	13,000	25,000
Limousine-6P	5000	2700	3600	5300	8800	19,000

1908 KNOX

Model H (air cooled) — 4-cyl., 30 hp, 102" wb

Touring-5P	2600	3100	4200	6300	10,500	22,000
Landaulette	3500	2500	3500	5000	8500	18,000
Tourist-3P	2500	3000	4000	6000	9500	21,000
Tourist-4P	2600	3100	4200	6300	10,500	22,000
Stanhope	2500	2700	3600	5300	8800	19,000
Sportabout	2500	2900	3700	5600	9100	20,000
Limousine	3500	2700	3600	5300	8800	19,000

1907 Knox, model F-4, tourist, HAC

1908 Knox, touring, WLB

Model L (water cooled) — 4-cyl., 30 hp, 102" wb

	FP	5	4	3	2	1
Touring-5P	2700	3300	4400	6700	12,000	24,000
Landaulette	3600	2900	3700	5600	9100	20,000
Tourist-3P	2650	3200	4300	6500	11,000	23,000
Tourist-4P	2700	3300	4400	6700	12,000	24,000
Stanhope	2600	2900	3700	5600	9100	20,000
Sportabout	2600	3000	4000	6000	9500	21,000
Limousine	3600	2900	3700	5600	9100	20,000

Model G (air cooled) — 4-cyl., 40 hp, 112" wb

Touring-7P	4000	3200	4300	6500	11,000	23,000
Limousine	5000	3100	4200	6300	10,500	22,000

1909 Knox, model O, tonneauette, HAC

1909 KNOX

Model H (air cooled) — 4-cyl., 30 hp, 102" wb

Touring-5P	2600	3000	4000	6000	9500	21,000

Model O (water cooled) — 4-cyl., 38 hp, 102" wb

Double Rumble Sportabout-4P	2900	3300	4400	6700	12,000	24,000
Single Rumble Sportabout-3P	2850	3200	4300	6500	11,000	23,000

Model O (water cooled) — 4-cyl., 38 hp, 114" wb

Tonneauette-4P	2950	3900	4800	7700	14,300	27,000
Touring-5P	3000	4000	5000	8000	15,000	28,000
Landaulet-5P	3750	3900	4800	7700	14,300	27,000
Limousine-5P	3750	3700	4700	7300	13,700	26,000

Model M (water cooled) — 4-cyl., 48 hp, 127" wb

Touring-7P	5000	3900	4800	7700	14,300	27,000
Limousine-7P	6000	3500	4500	7000	13,000	25,000
Sportabout	4700	3700	4700	7300	13,700	26,000

1910 Knox, model S, six, tonneau, HAC

1910 KNOX
Model R — 4-cyl., 40 hp, 117" wb

	FP	5	4	3	2	1
Touring-5P	3250	4000	5000	8000	15,000	28,000
Tourabout-4P	3150	3900	4800	7700	14,300	27,000
Tonneauette-4P	3150	3900	4800	7700	14,300	27,000
Raceabout	3150	4300	5400	8700	16,500	30,000
Limousine	4000	2700	3600	5300	8800	19,000
Landaulet	4000	2900	3700	5600	9100	20,000

Model M — 4-cyl., 48 hp, 127" wb
Touring-7P	5000	4000	5400	8700	16,500	30,000
Runabout	4700	3100	4200	6300	10,500	22,000
Limousine	6000	2900	3700	5600	9100	20,000

Model S — 6-cyl., 60 hp, 134" wb
Touring-7P	5000	4400	5600	9200	17,300	31,000
Tonneau	4800	4300	5400	8700	16,500	30,000
Limousine	6000	3000	4000	6000	9500	21,000

1911 Knox, model R, double-rumble runabout, HAC

1911 KNOX
Model R — 4-cyl., 40 hp, 104" wb
Raceabout-2P	3200	3900	4800	7700	14,300	27,000

Model S — 6-cyl., 60 hp, 106" wb
Raceabout-4P	4790	4200	5200	8400	15,700	29,000

Model R, Series A — 4-cyl., 40 hp, 117" wb
Tonneauette-5P	3350	4200	5200	8400	15,700	29,000
Touring-5/7P	3300	4000	5000	8000	15,000	28,000
Raceabout	3300	4300	5400	8700	16,500	30,000

Model R, Series B — 4-cyl., 40 hp, 122" wb
Fore-Door Touring-7P	3500	4400	5600	9200	17,300	31,000
Limousine-5/7P	4400	2900	3700	5600	9100	20,000
Landaulet-5/7P	4250	3000	4000	6000	9500	21,000

Model S — 6-cyl., 60 hp, 134" wb
Touring-5/7P	5000	4500	5800	9500	18,000	32,000
Fore-Door Touring-5/7P	5000	4700	6100	9900	19,000	33,000
Torpedo-6P	5000	5000	6500	11,000	22,000	35,000
Tonneauette-5P	4900	4900	6300	10,300	21,000	34,000
Limousine-7P	6250	3100	4200	6300	10,500	22,000
Fore-Door Limousine-7P	6400	3200	4300	6500	11,000	23,000
Double Rumble Raceabout-4P	4800	4900	6300	10,300	21,000	34,000

1912 Knox, model S, series B, touring, HAC

1912 KNOX
Model R — 4-cyl., 40 hp, 122" wb

	FP	5	4	3	2	1
Raceabout-2P	3200	2400	3400	4800	8000	17,000
Roadster-4P	3300	2700	3600	5300	8800	19,000
Tonneauette	3350	2900	3700	5600	9100	20,000
Torpedo-4P	3400	3100	4200	6300	10,500	22,000
Touring-5P	3450	3000	4000	6000	9500	21,000
Touring-7P	3500	2900	3700	5600	9100	20,000
Limousine	4400	2500	3500	5000	8500	18,000

Model R-45 — 4-cyl., 40 hp, 126" wb
Limousine	4700	2700	3600	5300	8800	19,000
Touring	3800	3100	4200	6300	10,500	22,000
Torpedo	3700	3200	4300	6500	11,000	23,000
Tonneauette	3650	3000	4000	6000	9500	21,000
Raceabout-2P	3500	2700	3600	5300	8800	19,000
Raceabout-4P	3600	2900	3700	5600	9100	20,000

Model S — 6-cyl., 60 hp, 134" wb
Tonneau	5000	3000	4000	6000	9500	21,000
Limousine	6400	2900	3700	5600	9100	20,000
Torpedo	5000	3500	4500	7000	13,000	25,000
Tonneauette	4900	3300	4400	6700	12,000	24,000
Raceabout-2P	4700	3000	4000	6000	9500	21,000
Roadster-4P	4800	3100	4200	6300	10,500	22,000

1913 Knox, model 45, landaulette, HAC

1913 KNOX
Model 44 — 4-cyl., 40 hp, 122" wb
Raceabout-2P	3500	3000	4000	6000	9500	21,000
Torpedo-4P	3550	2900	3700	5600	9100	20,000
Torpedo-5P	3600	3000	4000	6000	9500	21,000
Touring-5P	3650	3100	4200	6300	10,500	22,000

Model 45 — 4-cyl., 40 hp, 126" wb
Raceabout-2P	3800	3100	4200	6300	10,500	22,000
Torpedo-4P	3800	3000	4000	6000	9500	21,000

Model 46-Six — 6-cyl., 46 hp, 130" wb
Touring-6P	4350	3200	4300	6500	11,000	23,000
Torpedo-7P	4350	3300	4400	6700	12,000	24,000
Raceabout	4350	3200	4300	6500	11,000	23,000
Limousine	5350	2700	3600	5300	8800	19,000
Berline	5350	2900	3700	5600	9100	20,000
Landaulet	5400	3000	4000	6000	9500	21,000

Model 66-Six — 6-cyl., 60 hp, 134" wb
Touring-7P	5000	4200	5200	8400	15,700	29,000
Raceabout-2P	4800	3900	4800	7700	14,300	27,000
Torpedo-4P	5000	4000	5000	8000	15,000	28,000

1914 Knox, model 44, touring, HAC

1914 KNOX
Model 44 — 4-cyl., 40 hp, 117" wb
Touring-5P	3400	3200	4300	6500	11,000	23,000

Model 45 — 4-cyl., 40 hp, 126" wb
Extension Limousine-7P	4700	2900	3700	5600	9100	20,000

Model 46 — 6-cyl., 46 hp, 134" wb
Touring-5P	4500	3900	4800	7700	14,300	27,000

KNUDSEN ELECTRIC — Chicago, Illinois — (1899) — Karsten Knudsen was a Chicago electrical engineer who built an electric carriage at his shop at 1545 Michigan Avenue in 1899. Details are lacking, but manufacture did not follow.

1906 Kobusch, model A, limousine, NAHC

KOBUSCH — **St. Louis, Missouri** — **(1906)** — The Kobush Automobile Company was organized in the spring of 1906 as a million-dollar concern. George J. Kobusch owned all but three of the 10,000 shares of Kobusch stock. The other three were in the hands of H.J. Vogel, George H. Mills and W.S. Miller. All of these men were associated with the St. Louis Car Company, which had long been famous as the builder of railroad cars. Kobusch, in fact, was president of that firm — and the Kobusch venture was in reality the St. Louis Car Company's automobile department masquerading under another name. In 1905 St. Louis had attempted to enter the field with a light two-cylinder runabout which was announced as the St. Louis and was not a success. This time, soon after incorporation, the Kobusch company announced that it would manufacture an exact reproduction of the famous French Mors. Three different four-cylinder models were offered, each as close a copy of the Mors as Kobusch engineers could fashion. The cars were not very successful, and by late summer the St. Louis Car Company decided to do things the proper way. The U.S. license for Mors manufacture was secured, together with plans and blueprints. The Kobusch was dead. The American Mors was born.

1906 KOBUSCH
Model A — 4-cyl., 20 hp, 102" wb

	FP	5	4	3	2	1
Touring-5P	4500	3300	4400	6700	12,000	24,000
Demi-Limousine	4700	2900	3700	5600	9100	20,000
Model B — 4-cyl., 35 hp, 106" wb						
Limousine	6000	3100	4200	6300	10,500	22,000
Model C — 4-cyl., 50 hp, 120" wb						
Landaulette	7000	3300	4400	6700	12,000	24,000

KOCH — Early in 1910 it appeared that a pair of automobile entrepreneurs called the Koch Brothers were about to descend upon Ann Arbor, Michigan. "A $50,000 company has been organized," *The Motor World* reported, "and $31,000 worth of the stock is represented as having been disposed of already." An automobile factory near North Main Street was planned. It never resulted.

1910 Koeb-Thompson, touring, NAHC

KOEB-THOMPSON — **Springfield, Ohio** — **(1901-1902)** / **Leipsig, Ohio** — **(1910)** — Emil Koeb and Ralph P. Thompson of Springfield built their first experimental gasoline vehicle in 1902. Details are lacking, but it is known that the car used a two-stroke engine mounted up front, make and break ignition, chain drive and was fitted with a touring tonneau body. The partners followed this vehicle with a 40 hp race car when they contested in local Ohio events. Automobile repair work occupied much of their time in the ensuing years although by 1910 Koeb and Thompson had completed development work on a novel lever suspension system which *The Motor World* spent several pages describing in its February 3rd, 1910 issue. A touring car to test the suspension was built for the partners by the American Foundry Company in Leipsig, and was demonstrated extensively. American Foundry was so impressed with the vehicle that the company decided to back its manufacture. Further money was offered by Leipsig businessmen, and the Koeb-Thompson Motor Company, capitalized at

$300,000, was the result. Automobile production was short-lived, however, and probably did not remain into 1911. A 1916 catalog indicates that the firm continued in the suspension business as the Koeb-Thompson Lever Spring Company.

KOEHLER ELECTRIC — **Detroit, Michigan** — **(1897)** — H.W. Koehler was a carriagemaker at 115 St. Aubin Avenue in Detroit and in 1897 he built an electric carriage. The driver sat in front, and there were two seats behind for three passengers. Koehler claimed his electric car to be state of the art, or beyond, "far ahead of anything hitherto seen," he said. The Detroit *Journal* reported on several of its advances that summer: "One new feature is an attachment which throws the outside wheel out of gear when the vehicle is turning a corner, allowing it to revolve independently of its mate. As the outside wheel always travels farther than the inside one on a curve, the benefit of this appliance can be readily seen. As the motive shaft is attached directly to the wheels, Mr. Koehler expects to be able to attain a speed, with safety, which has never been accomplished by carriages depending on a chain or cog connection." H.W. Koehler did not proceed into manufacture.

1911 Koehler, 40, touring, WLB

KOEHLER — **Bloomfield, New Jersey** — **(1910-1912)** — The H.J. Koehler Sporting Goods Company of New York City had sold automobiles in its stores since 1898, among them the Rider-Lewis and the Hupmobile. In 1910, deciding it could do equally as well, the Koehler company ventured into both motorcar and truck manufacture itself, locating its new factory in Bloomfield, New Jersey. A 40 hp four-cylinder touring car on a 112-inch wheelbase was introduced early in 1910 and was sold at a $1650 price tag for the two years following. In 1913 Koehler decided to confine its manufacturing efforts to the commercial field. Koehler trucks were produced until 1923.

KOEN — The James B. Koen Company was organized in Buffalo, New York early in 1908 with a capital stock of $10,000 for the manufacture of automobiles. Fellow Buffalo residents joining Koen in this venture were John Van Arsdale and James Griffin. Manufacture is doubted.

KOHL — The John Kohl Carriage & Automobile Company was organized in Mason, Ohio early in 1912 with a capital stock of $10,000 for the manufacture of horsedrawn and horseless vehicles. John Kohl, George Kohl, A.H. Bennett, G.A. Moon and F. Ward were the incorporators. Manufacture of an automobile is doubted.

KOHL — **Cleveland, Ohio** — **(1900-1902)** / **Whitney Point, New York** — **(1902)** — Edward Kohl might have been better advised to stay in Cleveland. There, in 1900, he took over the complete business of the Kohl & Gates Motor Company and began building gasoline carriages which appeared to be quite substantial. Their engines were single-cylinder and four-stroke and developed about six horsepower. Two forward speeds were provided, the vehicle complete weighed 900 pounds, and Edward Kohl claimed 35 mph on the road. In Cleveland he built at least a dozen or more of these cars from 1900 into 1902. Then in September of 1902, having moved to New York State in the meantime, Kohl announced that he had completed the first pilot model of his new gasoline car which was to sell for $700, the entire year's output having been contracted for by one New York dealer named Gates, who conceivably may have been his former partner. But the Kohl Automobile Company which Edward Kohl organized in Whitney Point did not survive into 1903. Possibly Gates did not renew his contract, or perhaps he just reneged.

KOKOMO — "Kokomo, Indiana is to have still another automobile factory," reported *The Motor World* late in 1901. This one was a $50,000 venture organized by E.G. Shortridge, W.A. Sellers and W.D. Irvin for production of a $500 Kokomo car. And this one died aborning.
 The Kokomo Six, although indicated on some car rosters as a make of car, was instead simply a model of the Haynes introduced for the 1916 model year. Refer to Haynes.

KOLBE — The Kolbe Auto Company was organized in Syracuse, New York during the spring of 1908 with a capital stock of $7500 for the manufacture of motor vehicles. Incorporators were R.E. Kolbe, J.D. Buckmaster and F.L. Buckmaster. Manufacture is doubted.

KOMET — The Elkhart Motor Car Company produced cars from 1909 to 1911 in Elkhart, Indiana. They were marketed under the name Sterling from the beginning, though the same car was also called a Komet on occasion during 1911. Refer to Sterling.
 A Komet built by the Keith Brothers in Elkhart, Indiana in 1898 has been an entry on various car rosters. Documentation has not been discovered.

791

KONIGSLOW — From 1902 to 1904 in Cleveland, Ohio, Otto Konigslow produced gasoline cars which were occasionally referred to by his last name but more often were marketed under the trade name of Ottokar. Refer to Ottokar.

KONOLLMAN — **Philadelphia, Pennsylvania** — **(1900)** — H. Konollman of 1328 Fairmount Avenue in Philadelphia was a bicycle machinist who built a two-passenger gasoline runabout in 1900 which he planned to market at around $350. Its powerplant, transmission and drive train were entirely of his own design. The engine developed not quite two horse-power, but Konollman stated this was more than sufficient "to carry a load of 300 pounds as fast as desirable." The reason was the lightness of his carriage — just 250 pounds — which was accountable through his extensive use of ordinary bicycle parts throughout. Konollman planned both to manufacture himself and to license other manufacturers under his patents. He apparently followed with a small production of Konollman run-abouts, but there is no evidence that his licensing plan proved profitable.

1914 Koppin, roadster, WLB

KOPPIN — **Fenton, Michigan** — **(1914)** — The Koppin was the Fenton renamed. In the spring of 1914 the Fenton Cyclecar Company, which had begun in business the year before, was acquired by H.S. Koppin following the death of George Jenks, the man behind the Fenton. Koppin owned the former A.J. Phillips plant in town which had been vacant for two years and which would provide a handy place for manufacture of the new Koppin. The price of the Fenton cyclecar was raised ten dollars under its new name, but that appears to have been the most significant change made by the newly organized Koppin Motor Company. A modest production seems to have followed before Koppin decided to get out of the automobile business at the end of 1914.

1914 KOPPIN
Cyclecar — 2-cyl., 10 hp, 96" wb

	FP	5	4	3	2	1
Model A Roadster-2P	385	—	—	—	—	—

KORN & BREIDING — **Sterling, Illinois** — **(1901)** — "Korn & Breiding of Sterling have built and tested an automobile," reported *The Motor Age* in July 1901. "They expect to make others." Breiding was one A.H., who had built himself a car the year before. Korn's identity has not been documented. How well the partners' expectation was fulfilled is not known, but no doubt few automobiles were produced.

KOSMATH — This marque's inclusion in various automobile rosters is in error. Indeed there was a Kosmath Company in Detroit, but it produced trucks only. In 1916 Kosmath was taken over by the Pennsy Motors Company of Pittsburgh, and the last few trucks were manufactured there prior to being discontinued in January 1917 in order that Pennsy could concentrate all its production facilities upon manufacture of the Pennsy car.

KOSMOS ELECTRIC — **New York, New York** — **(1909)** — The KosMos Electric Runabout Company planned to motorize transport on the board-walk at Atlantic City and on the beaches in Florida. The KosMos idea of an electric three-wheeler with wicker chair and driver riding behind the passengers at the rear was an old one, first tried at the World's Columbian Exposition in Chicago in 1893 by the Columbia Perambulator Company. The KosMos company, which was based in New York, announced plans to locate its factory in Detroit, but the evidence suggests it never arrived there.

KRAFT STEAM — **St. Louis, Missouri** — **(1896, 1901)** — J.F. Kraft built two cars at 4229 North Broadway in St. Louis, both of them steamers. The first, completed in 1896, burned charcoal, its two-cylinder engine and fire-tube boiler located behind the passenger seat. Kraft drove the vehicle successfully, though his picking up of two hitchhikers on one occasion resulted in grief; one of his passengers panicked, grabbed Kraft's arm and the vehicle ended upside down in a water-filled ditch with the three men pinned under it and only narrowly escaping drowning. In 1901 Kraft built his second car, which featured an improved steam engine, Bunsen gasoline burner and copper-tube boiler. Its body was a stanhope with leather dash and lever steering. Kraft drove this car about a year and then sold it.

1901 Kraft, steam runabout, HAC

KRAJEWSKI-PESANT — **Brooklyn, New York** — **(1898-1900)** — Krajewski, Pesant & Company owned the Erie Basin Iron Works in Brooklyn and in the early fall of 1898 reported to *The Horseless Age* that it was "putting the finishing touches on a gasoline vehicle representing several years of study and experiment." A few further vehicles followed, and the company was indicated in the "List of Automobile Manufacturers" published in the 1900 edition of the Hiscox reference book, but its automotive activity seems to have ended shortly thereafter.

KRAMER — The Kramer Auto & Carriage Company of Lancaster, Pennsylvania has frequently been indicated on rosters to have manufactured an automobile in 1915. The company never did so. The firm was organized in December 1914 by carriagemakers I. Newton Kramer and Edward McLaughlin and their business was the repairing, remodeling, reupholstering and repairing of both carriages and automobiles initially, and the building of bodies soon after. But a car was never produced.

KRAMER STEAM — **Peoria, Illinois** — **(1920)** — E.M. Kramer of Peoria invented a kerosene-fueled steam automobile engine which he believed to be a world-beater, capable of thirty miles on a gallon of kerosene. "The mechanism is without transmission of gears, the engine shaft connected directly with the wheels," *Automobile Trade Journal* noted in September 1920. "The inventor claims he uses less than half the usual number of parts, and stows engine, coil and water supply under the hood. The pilot light and ignition are automatic. Ten gallons of water are carried and used over and over, and the car can stand in zero temperature without freezing." Kramer planned manufacture on "an exclusive scale" but no manufacture at all resulted.

KRASS — Although the Detroit machine shop of J.H. Krass was used for the building of this 1913 car, it is more appropriately referred to by the name of its designer, George W. Meredith. Refer to Meredith.

KRASTIN — **Cleveland, Ohio** — **(1902-1904)** — The Krastin Automobile Manufacturing Company was organized November 20th, 1901 to produce a water-cooled two-cylinder 10 hp chain-drive car designed by August Krastin. Krastin had been working on the car for years, and nine features were patented, the most unusual of which was the control lever. It looked like an ordinary steering wheel, but instead of turning the wheel left or right to guide the car on the road, one tilted it instead. Turning the wheel performed other functions: a short turn to the right disengaged the clutch, a further right turn shifted the transmission to low, a further turn yet engaged high. Turning the wheel to the left provided reverse. Krastin's patented carburetor was said to be smokeless, his "screw-type" muffler noiseless. A detachable tonneau was provided the Krastin to afford the carrying of parcels or an extra two or four passengers. The price was

1903 Krastin, runabout, HAC

$2500. The first production Krastin was built and sold in October 1902. Charles S. Beardslee, who was also secretary of the Cleveland Gas Light and Coke Company, was president of the firm; August Krastin was its general manager. Although the factory had a four-car-per-day capacity, it is doubtful that production ever reached that pace. The company was bankrupt early in 1904, and was in even more trouble that summer when suit was brought by the attorney general to recover $22,000 due in excise taxes. Actually, the tax was only $50, but the $100-per-day penalty had rather mounted up.

1902-1904 KRASTIN
Krastin — 2-cyl., 10 hp, 72" wb

	FP	5	4	3	2	1
Tonneau-2/4/6P	2500	2400	3400	4800	8000	17,000

KREBS — "A Mr. Krebs of Ottawa, Ohio has built an automobile in his machine shop," reported *The Motor Age* during the summer of 1901, offering no further details.

Early in 1912, in Clyde, Ohio, the Krebs Commercial Car Company was organized with a capital stock of $100,000 to "manufacture and sell trucks, pleasure cars and accessories." J.C.L. Krebs was the man behind this venture, and may have been the Ottawa Krebs as well. The Krebs Commercial Car Company did proceed into manufacture in Clyde, but of trucks only. No Krebs automobile was built. Krebs commercial vehicles continued in production into 1917.

KREEB — The firm of John Kreeb's Sons was organized in New York City during the summer of 1911 with a capital stock of $5000 for the manufacture of automobiles. John Kreeb, Jr. and George Kreeb were the partners involved. Manufacture is doubted.

KREHBIEL — In 1897-1898, in Moundridge, Kansas, Charles Krehbiel is reported to have built an automobile. Details are lacking.

KREIDER — The automobile produced in 1905 in Lancaster, Pennsylvania by the Kreider Machine Company was marketed under the name of K & M. Refer to K & M.

KREIGSHABER — From Atlanta, Georgia, during the summer of 1909, came word from V.H. Kreigshaber of his plans for the establishment of an automobile factory there. "Runabouts and light touring cars ranging in price up to $1,400 are to be made," he said, and he expected to have his first examples ready in two months. V.H. Kreigshaber was not heard from again.

KRESS — Lawrence, Massachusetts — (1900) — The Kress Brothers Carriage Company was the largest builder of horsedrawn vehicles in Lawrence. Franz Schneider was proprietor of the largest jewelry store in town. In 1900 Kress built a two-seater motor carriage for Schneider. The evidence suggests that this might have been the only car the carriage company ever built. Apparently, Franz Schneider had been trying for two years to build a successful automobile himself, and finally asked someone else to have a go at it.

KRIT — Detroit, Michigan — (1910-1915) — The Krit Motor Car Company of Detroit was organized during the summer of 1909 to manufacture cars designed by Kenneth Crittenden, formerly of Ford and Regal. Claude S. Briggs and W.S. Piggins were among the people involved in the venture, though Briggs left early on for Brush and subsequently Detroiter. In early fall the erstwhile plant of the Blomstrom company was secured, and the first Krit cars (spelled K-R-I-T during the early years, and left-hand-drive from the beginning) were introduced as 1910 models. During 1910 the cars proved very effective hillclimbers, winning a half-dozen events from Georgia to Kansas to New Jersey. Krits were four-cylinder cars for the whole of their lives, except for 1913 when a Krit Six was introduced at the Chicago Automobile Show and was marketed for that single year only. The company was in financial trouble most of the time. In 1911 ownership changed hands as Walter S. Russel (of the Russel Wheel and Foundry Company) led a syndicate which purchased control, and increased capitaliza-

1910 K-R-I-T, model A, runabout, HAC

tion from $100,000 to $250,000. Crittenden remained on as vice-president and head of the engineering department. The former Owen plant now became the new Krit factory, and former Owen factory manager Alwin A. Gloetzner now served in the same capacity for Krit. Poor crop weather in the West (where many Krits were sold) was given as the reason, so *The Horseless Age* said in September 1913, "for the necessity of the creditors of the Krit Motor Car Company stepping in and taking a hand in the conduct of the affairs of the company." It was believed at the time that the creditors could "adjust matters so that the company will not be engulfed in more serious trouble." But it was anyway. In January 1914 a separate Krit Sales Company was organized with a capitalization of $100,000 in order to bear the brunt of Krit's factory expenses. This didn't work either. Nor had badge-engineering Krits to be sold under other names elsewhere (i.e., the M.C.C. Six). The onset of the war in Europe hurt the company further, because it had enjoyed a healthy export trade. By January 1915 both the Krit Motor Car Company and the Krit Sales Company were petitioned into bankruptcy. One final reorganization was tried in February, but following that, defeat was finally admitted. The Krit assets went to the auction block that spring, to be purchased by a salvage company which completed the final cars from parts on hand. Interestingly, the Krit's swastika trademark had been selected, according to the company, "to insure favor of auspicious gods."

1910 KRIT
Four — 22.5 hp, 96" wb

	FP	5	4	3	2	1
Model A Runabout-2P	800	2700	3600	5300	8800	19,000
Model B Roadster-3P	825	3100	4200	6300	10,500	22,000
Model C Surrey-4P	850	3200	4300	6500	11,000	23,000

1911 K-R-I-T, model U, underslung, roadster, WLB

1912 K-R-I-T, model U, underslung roadster, HAC

1911 KRIT
Four — 22.5 hp, 96" wb

	FP	5	4	3	2	1
Model A Runabout-2P	800	2900	3700	5600	9100	20,000
Model A Roadster-3P	825	3200	4300	6500	11,000	23,000
Model A Surrey-4P	850	3300	4400	6700	12,000	24,000
Model U Underslung Rbt.	1200	3000	4000	6000	9500	21,000

1912 KRIT
Four — 22.5 hp

	FP	5	4	3	2	1
Model A Roadster (96" wb)	800	3100	4200	6300	10,500	22,000
Model K Touring (106" wb)	900	3300	4400	6700	12,000	24,000
Model M Torpedo (98" wb)	1000	3100	4200	6300	10,500	22,000
Model U Underslung Rdstr.	1200					

1913 Krit, model A, roadster, HAC

1913 KRIT
Four — 25 hp, 106" wb

	FP	5	4	3	2	1
Model KR Roadster-2P	900	3200	4300	6500	11,000	23,000
Model KT Touring-5P	900	3300	4400	6700	12,000	24,000
Model A Rds.-2P (96" wb)	800	3100	4200	6300	10,500	22,000

Six — 36 hp, 120" wb

	FP	5	4	3	2	1
Model M.C.C. Touring-5P	—	3500	4500	7000	13,000	25,000

1914 Krit, model L, touring, HAC

1914 KRIT
Model L — 4-cyl., 22.5 hp, 108" wb

	FP	5	4	3	2	1
Touring-5P	1050	3300	4400	6700	12,000	24,000
Roadster-3P	1050	3500	4500	7000	13,000	25,000
Delivery Car	1000	2300	3300	4600	7500	16,000

1915 Krit, model O, touring, HAC

1915 KRIT
Model O — 4-cyl., 22.5 hp, 108" wb

	FP	5	4	3	2	1
Touring-5P	850	3200	4300	6500	11,000	23,000
Roadster-3P	850	3300	4400	6700	12,000	24,000

Model M — 4-cyl., 22.5 hp, 108" wb

	FP	5	4	3	2	1
Deluxe Touring-5P	995	3300	4400	6700	12,000	24,000
Cabriolet-3P	1295	3100	4200	6300	10,500	22,000
Roadster-3P	995	3700	4700	7300	13,700	26,000

KROHN KAR — Oakland, California — (1916) — Louis J. Krohn was an Oakland bicycle dealer who had a short fling in the car business in 1916. Like the Kissels in Wisconsin, he liked the look of a double ''K'' although Krohn's Kar was not nearly as estimable as the Hartford product. His pro-

totype — a small 18 hp roadster — was completed in late December of 1915. It featured shaft drive and a three-speed transmission, and was announced with a price tag of $435. Krohn indicated that he would offer a small 22 hp four-passenger touring car as well. The attractive price apparently resulted in a goodly quantity of orders because by May 13th, 1916 Krohn reported that his shop at 128 Twelfth Street was inadequate to the production task and he was looking for a larger factory. Thus far the budding manufacturer had noted his firm's name variously as simply his own, L.J. Krohn and Company and the Krohn Light Car Company. Selecting a permanent name from among them proved unnecessary because after announcing his search for a new factory Krohn was not heard from again.

KROPP — Lansing, Michigan — (c.1908) — James A. Kropp of Lansing built an automobile for himself in about 1908. So far as is known, it was his first and last. For the remainder of his career, he worked as a research engineer for Continental Engineering and Aviation Company.

KROTZ ELECTRIC — Springfield, Ohio — (1903-1904)/KROTZ GAS-ELECTRIC — Defiance, Ohio — (1908-1911) — In March of 1903 Alvaro S. Krotz announced from Springfield that he was building two electric cars, and in June he said that he was ''now about ready'' to market them. Several machines were produced for sale the following year under the Krotz Manufacturing Company name in Springfield. Their condensed storage battery and solid tires appear to have been of Krotz' own design, the rest of the machine was standard electric practice. When the Springfield operation fizzled, Krotz moved to Chicago where he talked Sears, Roebuck into cataloguing a highwheeler and continued puttering with various automotive inventions, finally coming up with a gas-electric buggy that he thought would be a winner. Since Sears wasn't enamoured, he returned to Ohio, to his hometown of Defiance this time, and convinced a number of townspeople to join him in his new venture. In February 1908 the Krotz-Defiance Auto Buggy Company was incorporated with a $50,000 capitalization to build ''a vehicle which can be sold at a price that will appeal to the farm trade and others desirous of a cheap machine.'' Among the company's incorporators were J.A. Deindoerfer, August Martin, D.F. Krotz, John Diehl, C.P. Harley and W.G. Lehman. ''It is the intention of the men promoting the enterprise to operate it along very conservative lines,'' reported the *Daily Crescent-News* on February 4th. Apparently, this happened. The Krotz Gas-Electric Buggy was produced very quietly and in small numbers until 1911.

KROYER — The Kroyer Motors Company was a five-million-dollar Delaware incorporation whose announced intention in 1920 was the manufacture of automobiles. John M. Kroyer was the man involved. Founder of the Samson Iron Works (later Samson Sieve-Grip Tractor Company) of Stockton, California, Kroyer had sold out to William C. Durant in 1917, staying on to manage the plant until it was closed by General Motors. Kroyer then designed a new tractor, formed Kroyer Motors Company and thought awhile about automobile manufacture as well. The last named did not follow.

KRUEGER — From 1905 to 1906, the Krueger brothers of Milwaukee, Wisconsin produced a gasoline automobile. Most of these cars were marketed under the name of Eclipse, although the last cars bore the brother's name. Refer to Eclipse.

KRUPP — In January of 1912, the Krupp Motor Works of Ambridge, Pennsylvania reported that it planned the building of a factory for the manufacture of pleasure cars, trucks and engines. Land was purchased near Beaver Falls by early April, but in late April news stories indicated that Krupp Motor Works had been enjoined by the Krupp interests in Essen, Germany from use of the Krupp name. This would appear to have ended the venture. No evidence has been found of another company being organized thereafter in the area.

1896 Kulage, motor vehicle, NAHC

KULAGE — St. Louis, Missouri — (1896-1897) — It was certainly an unusual looking vehicle. Four passengers could ride between its gigantic agricultural wheels and under a fringed canopy. Among the advantages claimed for the Kulage were the safety of knowing that it could not possibly turn over, the convenience of being able to turn on so small a radius as the distance between its wheels, the effortlessness of full foot power (the hand was needed neither for steering nor braking), and the simplicity of its "scientific principles which . . . prevent the slipping of the wheels in ascending hills or in mud or snow, and . . . the propulsion of the vehicle with less power than is required in the ordinary style of motor vehicle." Joseph Kulage of 1435 College Avenue in St. Louis invented this novelty. First mention of it appeared in the automotive press in 1896, when it was noted that Kulage intended to organize a company to begin manufacture at once. He was still advertising for potential backers for his company in the classifieds in the spring of 1897.

KULL — In 1906 in New York City A.L. Kull of 1659 Broadway organized with a capital stock of $50,000 the A.L. Kull Automobile Company for the manufacture of motorcars. No manufacture followed. By 1908 Kull had taken on the job of sales manager and vice president for the Dragon Motor Company which, if briefly, produced the Dragon car in Detroit and Philadelphia.

KUNKEL — The Kunkel-Lebman Company was organized in Brooklyn, New York early in 1909 with a capital stock of $3000 for the manufacture of "carriages, wagons, motor cars, et cetera." J. Kunkel, C.F. Lebman and K.K. Kunkel were the incorporators. Manufacture of an automobile is doubted.

1903 Kunz, Speedwell runabout, NAHC

KUNZ — Milwaukee, Wisconsin — (1902-1905) — John L. Kunz was born in Appleton, Wisconsin in 1866 and had his first car on the road there in 1897. It was sold the following year, though Kunz would not build another until 1902. In the meantime, he relocated to Milwaukee and began a successful machine shop. The Kunz Automobile Company was organized in late 1901, and the Kunz automobile of 1902 was a handsome single-cylinder runabout with suction intake over exhaust valves, and a three-speed transmission which was called "a sliding wedge" and probably did not work well. Sometime during that year he changed the name of his firm to Kunz Automobile & Motor Company, and a few months later he changed it yet again, to Speedwell Automobile Company. In 1903 his car was renamed the Speedwell too, and it differed from its predecessor only in increased horsepower and the fitting of a two-speed planetary transmission. By November 1904, however, he changed everything again, reincorporating for $75,000 as the J.L. Kunz Machine Company and deciding to call his car a Kunz once again. "This season we have built twelve cars, three of which are being used in Milwaukee and Wauwatosa," he told *The*

1905 Kunz, runabout, NAHC

Automobile. "During the winter we will build 100 cars for spring delivery." Most probably, not nearly that many were built, and these were the last Kunz cars. Thereafter John Kunz concentrated all efforts on his machine business. In 1917 he reorganized one final time, as the Kunz Wheel Company, and spent the rest of his career in the manufacture of resilient sheet steel wheels of his own design for automobiles and trucks.

1902 KUNZ	FP	5	4	3	2	1
Kunz Rbt. (1-cyl., 4 1/2 hp)	1000	2000	3000	4200	6500	14,000
1903-1904 KUNZ						
Speedwell Rbt. (1-cyl., 8 hp, 68" wb)	1000	2200	3200	4400	7000	15,000
1905 KUNZ						
Kunz Rbt. (1-cyl., 8 hp, 72" wb)	675	1800	2800	4000	6200	13,000

KUPFER — Los Angeles, California — (1914) — The A.M. Kupfer Corporation was a motorcycle dealership in Los Angeles which boasted that its sales of motorcycles were the equal of all the cars sold in the state of California. Among the Kupfer salesmen was Ray Johnson, who was described as "formerly an aeroplane operator located at Cleveland," and who designed a four-cylinder cyclecar with 96-inch wheelbase, 36-inch tread, and side-by-side seating for two passengers. In April 1914, *The American Cyclecar* reported that the "vehicle will be placed in the market by the Kupfer Cyclecar Co., for two years." A price tag of $450 had been decided upon. Already Kupfer had a "traveling man" in Southern California whipping up business, and the company was preparing to send a number of cars on order to the Antipodes. Five hundred cars was the expected output for 1914, and Kupfer was already making plans for a "big 1915 season." The Kupfer Cyclecar Company was no longer around when it arrived.

KUQUA — Springfield, Ohio — (1901) — Kuqua & Sons were carriage-makers in Springfield who decided to go automotive soon after the turn of the century. "They have commenced the manufacture of motor vehicles and will build steam and electric types," announced *The Motor Review* in August 1901. Further details are lacking, but this automotive venture was undoubtedly a short one.

1921 Kurtz Automatic, touring, WLB

KURTZ AUTOMATIC — Cleveland, Ohio — (1920-1925) — Cyrus B. Kurtz was a native of Cleveland, a graduate of the Case School of Applied Science, and an automobile enthusiast since his school days. While at Case he built his first two cars in a makeshift machine shop he converted from his father's chicken coop on the family farm. Following graduation, he worked for a number of Midwest automobile and truck manufacturers, including Spaulding in Grinnell, Iowa. Inventive since his youth, Kurtz was continually patenting various of his ideas for devices to make motoring easier. In 1916 he interested a group of Cleveland businessmen in his ideas, and the Kurtz Syndicate was the result. With this financial backing behind him, he developed the Kurtz Automatic, a preselector gearshift. Shifting in a Kurtz was done at the steering wheel, via a ring with shifting levers superimposed on the wheel. A move of the lever to the proper notched position, a quick manipulation of the clutch pedal, and the Kurtz automatically changed gear. During the summer of 1920 the Kurtz Motor Car Company was incorporated, with a capitalization of $525,000, in Cleveland. The first Kurtz Automatic automobile also arrived that year. It was powered by a six-cylinder Herschell-Spillman engine and used standard components throughout. Two wheel brakes were featured. Subsequently, in 1924, a Lycoming-engined eight with four-wheel brakes was offered, on a mammoth 139-inch wheelbase and probably on a custom basis only since the Kurtz never included it in their roster of production cars. In 1922 the Kurtz Motor Car Company indicated that it would produce 600 cars that year. That proved to be wishful thinking. An estimated 250 Kurtz Automatics were built from 1920 until 1924. During the latter year, aware that he needed considerably more financing to continue in production, Cyrus Kurtz chose to discontinue his car. Initially he had considered getting the money he needed from Wall Street, but he had been warned by his local backers that to do so would mean the Cleveland operation would be under the dictates of New York money. This he could not countenance. Fliers had been printed for the 1925 model year but only pilot models were built prior to Cyrus Kurtz's decision. Among automobile manufacturers who bought the Kurtz preselector gearshift idea was Apperson of Kokomo, who offered it as an option in the early Twenties.

1920-1922 KURTZ AUTOMATIC
Model A — 6-cyl., 55 hp, 122" wb

	FP	5	4	3	2	1
Touring-5P	1845	3500	4500	7000	13,000	25,000
Roadster-2P	1845	3700	4700	7300	13,700	26,000
Coupe-3P	2250	3100	4200	6300	10,500	22,000
Sport Sedan-4P	2250	3000	4000	6000	9500	21,000
Sedan-5P	2350	2500	3500	5000	8500	18,000

1923 KURTZ AUTOMATIC
Model 65 — 6-cyl., 75 hp, 122" wb

Touring-5P	1845	4000	5000	8000	15,000	28,000
Roadster-2P	1845	4200	5200	8400	15,700	29,000
Touring-7P	1895	3900	4800	7700	14,300	27,000
Brougham-4P	2925	2500	3500	5000	8500	18,000
Sedan-5P	2925	2400	3400	4800	8000	17,000

1924 KURTZ AUTOMATIC
Model 65 — 6-cyl., 75 hp, 122" wb

Touring-5P	1845	3700	4700	7300	13,700	26,000
Roadster-2P	1845	3900	4800	7700	14,300	27,000
Two-Door Sedan-5P	2250	2300	3300	4600	7500	16,000
Four-Door Sedan-5P	2250	2400	3400	4800	8000	17,000
Sedan-7P	2350	2300	3300	4600	7500	16,000

1925 Kurtz Automatic, sedan, KM

LACKAWANNA — Buffalo, New York — (1904) — The Lackawanna Motor Company of Buffalo was an attempt to pick up the pieces of the defunct Conrad Motor Carriage Company, which had built both steam and gasoline cars from 1900 into 1903. Lackawanna chose the gasoline field exclusively, building engines of one to four cylinders, as well as transmissions, for both automotive and marine use. At the New York Automobile Show in January 1904, the company exhibited a combination runabout-surrey powered by one of its two-cylinder two-stroke engines. How many further cars might have been built before the firm went under is not known. But Lackawanna failed quickly. In November its assets were sold for $2010. The firm may have come back the year following as the Lackawanna Valveless Motor Company, but its sole product now was a gasoline engine principally for marine use.

LACONIA — Laconia, New Hampshire — (1900, 1912) — The Laconia Car Company was in the business of providing coachwork for steam railroads and traction lines, and on two occasions contemplated entry into the automobile manufacturing field. The first announcement came in 1900, the second in 1912 from the firm's headquarters in Boston. Both these efforts appear to have ended at the prototype stage. Certainly no viable manufacture was ever realized.

1914 Laconia, cyclecar, MVMA

LACONIA — Laconia, New Hampshire — (1914) — The second automotive effort of H.H. Buffum who had built a car named for himself in Abington, Massachusetts from 1901 to 1907, the Laconia was first shown at the Boston Automobile Show in early 1914. As a cyclecar, it was particularly well built. Its frame was ash reinforced with steel, the body was aluminum, the upholstery leather. Wheelbase was 90 inches, tread 40, with staggered seating provided for two passengers. A two-cylinder 7 hp motor powered the Laconia, with transmission by universal worm gear friction drive. The car was center slung with double cantilever springs coupled over the tubular axle in front and the solid one at the rear. Total weight was 400 pounds, the price $450. The Laconia was New Hampshire's first cyclecar. It was also its last. "This is not a case of hurry with me," Buffum told *The American Cyclecar* in April 1914, "for I am entering this field to stay . . . and feel that much may be lost by a too hurried entry with a large product into a new and untried field." His plan was for production of 100 cars in 1914, with a healthy increase in 1915. Probably considerably fewer than 100 Laconias resulted in all. H.H. Buffum never formally organized a company for manufacture.

1914 Lad's Car, runabout, WLB

LAD'S CAR — Niagara Falls, New York — (1912-1914) — The Niagara Motor Car Corporation was a rather lofty designation for a firm which produced juvenile cars only, occasionally under the Niagara name but more usually Lad's Car. The company stated its purpose as providing "mechanically minded children a 'sure-enough' motor vehicle, with a 'sure-enough' engine, the possession of which is calculated to teach a great deal about the rudiments of automobilism, while at the same time the machine is so designed that even quite small children cannot come seriously to grief when handling it." The Lad's Car was cute as a bug. It was powered by a tiny single-cylinder 4 hp air cooled engine, and was sold as a two seater roadster on a 72-inch wheelbase, with choice of Renault or American style hood. The price complete was $170 with vee belt, $160 with flat belt, and it was available in ready-to-assemble form at twenty dollars off those prices.

LAFAYETTE — The Lafayette Auto Company of Detroit, Michigan was organized in September of 1903 to produce a car designed by Oliver Barthel. Refer to Barthel.

The Lafayette Motor Car Company, Ltd. was organized in Lafayette, Indiana early in 1911, incorporated with a capital stock of $25,000 in Louisiana, for the purpose of manufacturing and dealing in automobiles. Incorporators were Charles D. Caffery, S.R. Parkerson, T.M. Blossat, Jr., L.O. Clark and J.E. Trahan. Manufacture is doubted.

The Lafayette Motor Car Company of Easton, Pennsylvania was organized in early 1912 with a capital stock of $30,000 to manufacture and deal in automobiles. R.N. Fulton, R.W. Bowlby and F.C. Rockafellow were the incorporators. Manufacture is doubted.

LAFAYETTE — Indianapolis & Milwaukee — (1921-1924) — At first no one mentioned who the president of the new company was. There were a good many Cadillac people involved, including chief engineer D. McCall White and his assistant J.W. Applin, sales manager Earl C. Howard and advertising manager Leo Burnett. Jim Storrow and Lee Higginson, stalwart financial men of General Motors, were putting up much of the money. But who was behind it all? The LaFayette Motors Company of Mars Hill, Indianapolis was founded in October of 1919. In January of 1920, when the new LaFayette was introduced, the man whose idea it was came out of the closet. It was Charles W. Nash, the automotive King of Kenosha, who had purloined the Cadillac people in order to produce a luxury car of his own. The LaFayette venture was entirely separate from Nash Motors. D. McCall White told the press, with a blatant slap at his former employer, that the LaFayette was "far ahead of any previous automobile built under (my) supervision." The car was powered by a 90 hp V-8, and was offered in a variety of open and closed body styles on a 132-inch wheelbase, with price tags beginning in the $5000 range. Production began in August of 1920, with the LaFayette introduced as a 1921 model, and meeting the postwar depression head-on. "There have been far better times to introduce a motorcar," Charlie Nash rued in the fall of 1921 as he announced the sale of just 700 LaFayettes thus far. In April of 1922 there were rumors that LaFayette and Pierce-Arrow would merge, with Nash to become chairman of the board of the combined companies, but neither LaFayette nor Pierce-Arrow could come to terms. In July LaFayette announced its forthcoming move from the Mars Hill factory (which had been used by the government to produce hand grenades during World War I) to Milwaukee for the declared dual reason of "desire for a closer geographical coordination of Nash activities and the need for greater factory space." Only the former reason was really valid. By now the venture had been reorganized into LaFayette Motors Corporation, with Nash Motors as the largest stockholder. Only about 1000 cars had thus far been sold. By now, too, D. McCall White had left, as had Leo Burnett who remained in Indianapolis to work for an advertising agency there and to begin thinking about starting his own. Former Packard engineer Earl G. Gunn became LaFayette's chief engineer by January of '23, when the company was installed in its new factory in Milwaukee. But the end was near. In August a letter to LaFayette stockholders bearing the signatures of Jim Storrow and Charlie Nash announced that "the company has not been able to overcome the difficulty of unprofitable operation" and advised that they agree to the sale of LaFayette to Ajax Motors Company for $225,000. The stockholders did. Ajax was a new organization owned entirely by Nash Motors. Ajax would be a new car at the precise opposite end of the automotive scale from the LaFayette. But no one knew that at the time. Charlie Nash was playing cat-and-mouse again. After pouring $2 million of Nash Motors money into the LaFayette, he gave up on it. Never again would Nash produce an all-out luxury car. The last of the 2267 LaFayettes were built in early 1924. Soon thereafter the machinery from the LaFayette plant was shipped to the old Mitchell plant in Racine which Charlie Nash had just bought for the building of the new Ajax. Interestingly, Nash would resurrect the LaFayette name in 1934, but this time it would be for a lower-priced Nash.

1921 LAFAYETTE
Model 134 — 8-cyl., 90 hp, 132" wb

	FP	5	4	3	2	1
Touring-7P	5025	4500	5800	9500	18,000	32,000
Torpedo-4P	5025	4500	5800	9500	18,000	32,000
Coupe-4P	7200	2900	3700	5600	9100	20,000
Sedan-7P	7400	2400	3400	4800	8000	17,000
Limousine-7P	7500	2700	3600	5300	8800	19,000

1922 LAFAYETTE
Model 134 — 8-cyl., 90 hp, 132" wb

Touring-7P	4850	4400	5600	9200	17,300	31,000
Torpedo-4P	4850	4500	5800	9500	18,000	32,000
Roadster-2P	4850	4700	6100	9900	19,000	33,000
Coupe-4P	6250	2900	3700	5600	9100	20,000
Sedan-7P	6500	2400	3400	4800	8000	17,000
Limousine-7P	6750	2700	3600	5300	8800	19,000

1921 LaFayette, model 134, roadster, JAC

1922 LaFayette, model 134, sedan, JAC

1923 LaFayette, model 134, coupe, JAC

1923 LAFAYETTE
Model 134 — 8-cyl., 100 hp, 132" wb

	FP	5	4	3	2	1
Touring-7P	4400	4400	5600	9200	17,300	31,000
Roadster-2P	3985	4700	6100	9900	19,000	33,000
Torpedo-4P	4300	4500	5800	9500	18,000	32,000
Sedan-7P	5500	2000	3000	4200	6500	14,000
Coupe-4P	5500	2400	3400	4800	8000	17,000
Limousine-7P	5750	2700	3600	5300	8800	19,000
Vestibule Sedan-7P	6250	3000	4000	6000	9500	21,000

1924 LaFayette, model 134, touring, HAC

798

1924 LAFAYETTE
Model 134 — 8-cyl., 100 hp, 132" wb

	FP	5	4	3	2	1
Touring-7P	5000	4400	5600	9200	17,300	31,000
Roadster-2P	5000	4700	6100	9900	19,000	33,000
Torpedo-4P	5000	4500	5800	9500	18,000	32,000
Coupe-4P	6300	2400	3400	4800	8000	17,000
Limousine-7P	6500	2700	3600	5300	8800	19,000
Sedan-7P	6500	2000	3000	4200	6500	14,000
Imperial Limousine-7P	6750	3100	4200	6300	10,500	22,000

1903 LaFrance, touring, NAHC

LA FRANCE — Elmira, New York — (1903-1905) — In 1903 approximately ten to fifteen automobiles built by the International Fire Engine Company in Elmira were marketed and sold through Sidney Bowman of New York City. Their look was very French (a Renault-type hood with fin-tube coil radiator slung below the front of the frame), and the body style was a rear entrance tonneau. The engine was a four, final drive was chain, steering was right-hand wheel, and the price tag in the $5000 range. The cars were called La France. Later in 1903 International was reorganized into the American-La France Fire Engine Company. Although a 1905 shaft-drive roadster is believed to have carried the La France name, all subsequent automobiles from the firm used the full American-La France designation.

LAGERQUIST — Des Moines, Iowa — (1909) — "Divining more profits in the manufacture of automobiles than of carriages," as *The Motor World* put it, the Lagerquist Carriage Company of 209 West Grand Avenue in Des Moines began construction in November of 1909 on a new two-story factory at West Second and Chestnut streets. Part of the building would be used to establish an automobile repair facility, while the company continued its experimentation with various designs of automobiles before hitting the market. Lagerquist had been building a high-wheeled motor buggy (including delivery versions called Hawkeye) for the few months past, and apparently felt ready for bigger and better things. Apparently, too, the company was not ready. Although motor buggy production for a local clientele may have continued, Lagerquist never entered the market with any sustained automobile production.

LAIDLAW ELECTRIC — Jersey City, New Jersey — (1903) — James Laidlaw of Jersey City built himself an electric motor sleigh which was completed in time for the winter of '03. The storage battery was located under the seat. Tiny cog wheels were fitted to the runners which, so *The Automobile Review* reported, enabled "the sled to be propelled at a rapid rate over ice or snow."

LAIRD — Hanford, California — (1899) — Among the pioneer cars from the West Coast was one built in 1899 by Robert Laird, an electrician from Hanford. Other than the fact that the vehicle was, logically, electric powered, little is known about it nor any other automobiles that Laird may have built subsequently.

LAKEDEL — The Lakedel Automobile Company was organized in St. Louis, Missouri during the fall of 1906 with a capital stock of $15,000 to manufacture and deal in automobiles. W.J. Rea, J.A. Prescott and G.B. O'Reilly were the incorporators. Manufacture is doubted.

LAKE VIEW — The Lake View Automobile Company was organized in Chicago, Illinois during the fall of 1907 with a capital stock of $15,000 to manufacture and deal in automobiles. Incorporators were F.A. Croft and C.K. Samuels. Manufacture is doubted.

LAKEWOOD — New York, New York — (1920) — The Lakewood Engineering Company was headquartered in New York City, with its factory in Cleveland, Ohio. Charles F. Lang was president, E.S. Hough vice-president and A.W. Stone secretary. The firm manufactured industrial cars and concrete mixers. In 1920 Lakewood announced from New York its building of a two-passenger electric coupe with wire wheels and on a 104-inch-wheelbase chassis. Details are lacking, but a logical assumption is that Lakewood briefly considered entering what was thought during this period to be the lucrative automobile export business. Most probably only the prototype was built, and Lakewood then concluded that the idea wasn't so lucrative after all.

LALOR — The Lalor Wagon Company was organized in Chicago, Illinois early in 1911 with a $200,000 capital stock to manufacture and deal in "automobiles, wagons, carriages and other vehicles." M.W. Lalor, D.K. Lindout and J.C.K. Lindout were the incorporators. Manufacture of a car is doubted.

LAMAR — The H.J. Lamar Company was organized in Macon, Georgia late in 1917 with a capital stock of $25,000 to manufacture and sell automobiles. Incorporators were H.J. Lamar, F.A. Goss and J.L. Evans. Manufacture is doubted.

1920 LaMarne, touring, NAHC

LA MARNE — **Cleveland, Ohio** — **(1919-1920)** — So far as is known, the La Marne was the last major automotive design of Francois Richard, whose previous efforts had included the Only, the Metropol and the RiChard. Indeed, the La Marne Motor Company (some advertisements indicated LaMarne Motor Car Company) followed the Ri Chard Automobile Manufacturing Company into the same Finney Avenue plant in Cleveland. The La Marne was among America's earliest straight-eights, its 364.5-cubic-inch engine developing 85 hp. (Bore-stroke dimensions of 3-1/2 by 5 were out of the ordinary for Richard, who had previously been an ultra-long-stroke advocate.) The one body style available was termed a "Semi Enclosed Car" which was rather accurate since the rear quarter of the long, long passenger compartment had a victoria-type enclosure which swept in a hard top to the visored windshield. Disappearing headlamps were another feature of the La Marne. The price was $1485. Production in Cleveland was minimal. Plans were made for the car to be manufactured in Trenton, Ontario by Anglo-American Motors Ltd., although possibly only one car was built there. La Marne production on both sides of the border had ceased by the end of 1920. Thereafter Francois Richard went freelance as a design consultant to a variety of automobile manufacturers. He remained a resident of Cleveland until his death in 1960.

1919-1920 LA MARNE
La Marne — 8-cyl., 85 hp, 128" wb

	FP	5	4	3	2	1
Semi Enclosed Car	1485	2700	3600	5300	8800	19,000

LAMB — **Chicopee Falls, Massachusetts** — **(1899)** — Early in 1899 the Lamb Manufacturing Company completed prototype models of a two-passenger gasoline carriage for the well-known sporting goods house of A.G. Spaulding & Brothers. For a number of years Spaulding had sold the bicycles made by the Lamb Company, this new venture being embarked upon because, as a Lamb official said, both companies were "confident the motor carriage is to have a large place in transportation in the future." Lamb's future in the industry was short-lived, however. Whether the Lamb-built cars were sold as Lambs or as Spauldings, or whether indeed any cars were built beyond the prototypes, is not known. Shortly after the turn of the century, Spaulding was heartily into the car business, but as dealers of established makes only.

LAMB ELECTRIC — **Grand Rapids, Michigan** — **(1901-1902)** — Lamb & Company at Kent and Lyon streets in Grand Rapids had been in the business of producing electric motors and controllers since before the turn of the century. In 1901 F.J. Lamb reported his completion of an 800-pound electric runabout, and began soliciting stock subscriptions. "This city aspires to become an automobile manufacturing center of as great importance as it once was in the cycle trade" was the news from Grand Rapids that December. "We are threatened with both electric and gasoline vehicles." In addition to the electric built by F.J. Lamb, there was a new gasoline car in town built by Ralph B. Hain, who earlier had produced the first bicycle in Grand Rapids and who had organized the Clipper bicycle company. It was the plan of Lamb and Hain to join forces in this new automobile venture, with Lamb producing the electrics, Hain the gasoline cars. "The two would not interfere with each other in the market," *The Motor Age* revealed, "as they each appeal to different classes of customers." Hain was not heard from again. Lamb was, in February 1902, with the news that his electric would be on the market soon. Thereafter all news stopped. Any manufacture was minimal.

LAMB — **Clinton, Iowa** — **(1905)** — In 1905 the Lamb Boat and Engine Company of Clinton evolved into the Lamb Automobile Company. In February the firm broke ground for its new garage from which it was also planned to conduct an automobile livery. J.D. Lamb, V.A. Bonney and F.B. King were the men behind this venture, and they secured dealerships for the Thomas, Pope-Tribune, Cadillac and Pope-Waverley cars. The appearance of the Lamb on numerous automobile rosters is a puzzlement, since all available references indicate the company never had any intention to

manufacture an automobile. An experimental car appears to have been built but with the death of J.D. Lamb later in 1905, the decision was made to return the firm to its first area of activity, though marine engines only (and not motor boats) would be the focus of production.

LAMB & VEDDER — **Adrian, Michigan** — **(1901)** — H.R. Lamb was the secretary of the Lamb Wire Fence Company and Walter F. Vedder was a wagonmaker, and together they built a 4 1/2 hp experimental gasoline runabout in 1901. Though trade press directories that year indicated the existence of a Lamb & Vedder Company, it does not appear that the partners' experiments ever resulted in production.

LAMBERT — Late in 1916, H. Jerome Lambert, formerly vice-president of the Calumet Motors Corporation and now president of the Lambert Engineering Company of Chicago, Illinois, announced his plans for manufacture of a six-cylinder, five-passenger roadster. What happened next is not known, but production did not follow.

The Lambert-Marion Company has been indicated on various car rosters as producing an automobile in St. Louis, Missouri in 1903. This cannot be documented. The St. Louis city directory for 1903 indicates no such company, though there was a Marion L.J. Lambert whose business was the Lambert Pharmacal Company on Hortense Place. Conceivably he may have built an automobile for his own use that year. There were automobile companies in the field with similar names to the nonexistent Lambert-Marion, incidentally: the Lambert-Morin Motor Vehicle Company of Lawrence, Massachusetts which attempted to enter the commercial car field in 1912, and the Lammert & Mann Company of Chicago which built the Ehrlich Electric experimental car in 1918.

1891 Lambert, gasoline buggy, NAHC

LAMBERT — **Anderson, Indiana** — **(1891, 1906-1917)** — In 1891 John William Lambert was the proprietor of a grain elevator, lumber yard and hardware store in Ohio City (just across the Indiana state line in Ohio) and had some rather nice real estate holdings in town too, including the local opera house, town hall and jail. That year he successfully tested a three-wheeled surrey-top gasoline-powered runabout of his own design, though he was unsuccessful in attempting to market it, despite his printing up of a sales brochure and attaching a price of $550 to the car. A few years later, Elwood P. Haynes, who had successfully tested his first gasoline car in Kokomo (Indiana) on July 4th of 1894, visited Lambert and announced that he planned to get into manufacture and to bill his product as "America's First Car." Haynes was conveniently forgetting the gasoline car experimentation of the Duryeas and others which also had predated his own, but nonetheless he extracted a promise from John Lambert that he would not dispute Haynes' claim. And he never did, though when Lambert did get into manufacture, frequent reference was made by him to the fact of the 1891 gasoline car; he simply did not say he was the first. Automobile manufacture was a long time in coming, however. After failing to market his car in the early 1890's, Lambert turned attention to stationary gasoline engine manufacture, organizing the Buckeye Manufacturing Company in Anderson, Indiana. In 1895 he announced that he would "soon have a gasoline vehicle on the market" to be called the Buckeye. The picture he sent to the press was that of the three-wheeler he had built four years before. It didn't get into production this time either. Instead, Lambert returned to experimentation, devised the friction transmission that would be the feature of all cars he marketed, and put together a four-wheeler in 1898. Still, manufacture eluded him. Finally, in 1902, production of a Lambert-designed car arrived, though it was called neither a Lambert nor a Buckeye. Instead it was the Union, which he built in Union City, Indiana following favorable overtures from that town's chamber of commerce. Most of the Union's components were built in Lambert's Buckeye Manufacturing Company, however, and by 1905 the Union moved to Anderson as well. It was discontinued later that year and was followed by the new Lambert car for the 1906 model year. The Lambert's smaller two-cylinder models were virtually the old Union renamed, but now Lambert was building much larger fours as well. The engines on Lamberts moved around some during the early years, from the back of the car to midships to upfront. Early engines were built in-house, later by such proprietary manufacturers as Buda, Rutenber, Continental, Trebert and Davis. Although shaft drive was provided an occasional model, most Lamberts were chain drive. Friction transmission remained a constant. Commercial vehicle production had been embarked upon by the Buckeye Manufacturing Company soon after the turn of the century, and the firm continued in the truck field for a year after phasing out the Lambert car in 1917.

1906 Lambert, model A, runabout, HAC

1906 LAMBERT
Model A — 1-cyl., 16 hp, 78" wb

	FP	5	4	3	2	1
Runabout-2P	900	1800	2800	4000	6200	13,000
Model 4 — 2-cyl., 16 hp, 94" wb						
Touring-5P	1050	2000	3000	4200	6500	14,000
Model 5 — 2-cyl., 16 hp, 94" wb						
Touring-5P	1200	2100	3100	4300	6800	14,500
Model 6 — 2-cyl., 18 hp, 84" wb						
Touring-5P	1500	2200	3200	4400	7000	15,000
Model 7 — 4-cyl., 34 hp, 98" wb						
Touring-5P	2000	2250	3300	4500	7300	15,500
Model 8 — 4-cyl., 34 hp, 98" wb						
Touring-5P	3000	2300	3300	4600	7500	16,000

1907 Lambert, model F, touring, HAC

1907 LAMBERT
Model L — 2-cyl., 16 hp, 94" wb

Touring-5P	1200	2300	3300	4600	7500	16,000
Model J — 4-cyl., 40 hp, 105" wb						
Runabout-2p	1800	2500	3500	5000	8500	18,000
Model G — 4-cyl., 40 hp, 106" wb						
Touring-7P	2500	2700	3600	5300	8800	19,000
Model F — 4-cyl., 40 hp, 106" wb						
Touring-5P	3000	2900	3700	5600	9100	20,000
Model H — 4-cyl., 40 hp, 106" wb						
Touring-5P	2000	3000	4000	6000	9500	21,000

1908 Lambert, model 18, runabout, WLB

800

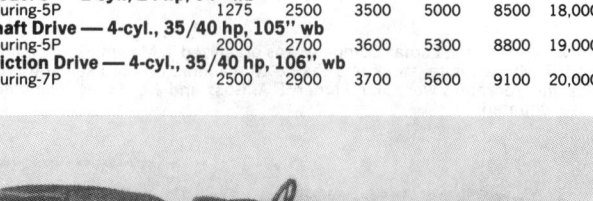

1908 LAMBERT
Model 18 — 2-cyl., 18 hp, 95" wb

	FP	5	4	3	2	1
Runabout	800	2300	3300	4600	7500	16,000
Model S — 2-cyl., 24 hp, 94" wb						
Touring-5P	1275	2500	3500	5000	8500	18,000
Shaft Drive — 4-cyl., 35/40 hp, 105" wb						
Touring-5P	2000	2700	3600	5300	8800	19,000
Friction Drive — 4-cyl., 35/40 hp, 106" wb						
Touring-7P	2500	2900	3700	5600	9100	20,000

1909 Lambert, model 30, touring, HAC

1909 LAMBERT
Model A1 — 2-cyl., 20 hp, 95" wb

Surrey-4P	875	2400	3400	4800	8000	17,000
Roadster-3P	800	2500	3500	5000	8500	18,000
Model 27 — 4-cyl., 28 hp, 110" wb						
Roadster-4P	1250	2700	3600	5300	8800	19,000
Model 30 — 4-cyl., 28 hp, 110" wb						
Touring-5P	1250	2900	3700	5600	9100	20,000
Model B2 — 4-cyl., 40 hp, 117" wb						
Touring-7P	2000	3000	4000	6000	9500	21,000
Touring-5P	1750	3100	4200	6300	10,500	22,000

1910 Lambert, model 36, touring, HAC

1910 LAMBERT
Model 17 — 4-cyl., 28 hp, 100" wb

Runabout	900	2300	3300	4600	7500	16,000
Model 21 — 4-cyl., 28 hp, 100" wb						
Surrey	975	2500	3500	5000	8500	18,000
Model 28 — 4-cyl., 35 hp, 105" wb						
Toy Tonneau-4P	1200	2700	3600	5300	8800	19,000
Model 36 — 4-cyl., 35 hp, 110" wb						
Touring-5P	1275	2400	3400	4800	8000	17,000
Model 47 — 4-cyl., 49 hp, 115" wb						
Touring-5P	1700	2500	3500	5000	8500	18,000

1911 LAMBERT
Model 44 — 4-cyl., 35 hp, 100" wb

Runabout-2P	1000	2300	3300	4600	7500	16,000
Model 55 — 4-cyl., 35 hp, 100" wb						
Surrey-4P	1075	2500	3500	5000	8500	18,000
Model 77 — 4-cyl., 35 hp, 107" wb						
Tonneau-4P	1250	2400	3400	4800	8000	17,000
Model 88 — 4-cyl., 35 hp, 112" wb						
Touring-5P	1350	2500	3500	5000	8500	18,000
Model 101 — 4-cyl., 40 hp, 112" wb						
Torpedo-4P	1600	2700	3600	5300	8800	19,000
Model 100 — 4-cyl., 40 hp, 117" wb						
Touring-5P	1700	2900	3700	5600	9100	20,000

1912 LAMBERT
Model 66 — 4-cyl., 35 hp, 112" wb

Touring-4P	1400	2500	3500	5000	8500	18,000
Touring-5P	1500	2500	3500	5000	8500	18,000
Model 99-C — 4-cyl., 40 hp, 112" wb						
Roadster	1650	2700	3600	5300	8800	19,000
Model 99 — 4-cyl., 40 hp, 117" wb						
Touring-5P	1700	2900	3700	5600	9100	20,000
Torpedo-4P	1700	2900	3700	5600	9100	20,000

1912 Lambert, model 99-C, roadster, HAC

1913 LAMBERT
Model 9 — 4-cyl., 20 hp, 102" wb

	FP	5	4	3	2	1
Roadster-2P	930	2400	3400	4800	8000	17,000
Model 10 — 4-cyl., 20 hp, 107" wb						
Touring-5P	930	2700	3600	5300	8800	19,000
Model 40 — 3-cyl., 16.8 hp, 112" wb						
Touring-5P	1030	2900	3700	5600	9100	20,000
Model 50 — 4-cyl., 40 hp, 112" wb						
Touring-5P	1185	3000	4000	6000	9500	21,000
Model 99 — 4-cyl., 40 hp, 117" wb						
Touring-5P	1250	3100	4200	6300	10,500	22,000
Roadster-3P	1250	3200	4300	6500	11,000	23,000

1914 Lambert, model 46-C, touring, HAC

1914 LAMBERT
Model 46-C — 4-cyl., 23 hp, 112" wb

Touring-4P	1200	2500	3500	5000	8500	18,000
Model 60-C — 4-cyl., 27 hp, 115" wb						
Touring-5P	—	2700	3600	5300	8800	19,000

1915 Lambert, model 48-C, touring, HAC

1915 LAMBERT
Model 48-C — 4-cyl., 23 hp, 112" wb

Touring-5P	1200	2500	3500	5000	8500	18,000
Model 68-C — 4-cyl., 27 hp, 115" wb						
Touring-5P	1565	2700	3600	5300	8800	19,000
Roadster-5P	1565	2900	3700	5600	9100	20,000
1916 LAMBERT						
Model 76 — 4-cyl., 23 hp, 112" wb						
Touring-5P	685	2700	3600	5300	8800	19,000
Roadster-2P	685	2900	3700	5600	9100	20,000
1917 LAMBERT						
Model 90 — 4-cyl., 35 hp, 115" wb						
Touring-5P	850	2900	3700	5600	9100	20,000

LAMPKIN — At the turn of the century, a machinist named C.L. Lampkin built himself a car, which he described fully in a letter to *The Horseless Age* a few years later though he didn't mention where he had built it. Presumably the area was rural, however, because he indicated he had never seen an automobile before he started his. He made all the parts himself. Its engine was a one-lunger, its transmission a two-speed planetary, and the runabout body with folding seat in front was mounted on full elliptic springs. ''The wheelbase is 80 inches, and the tread is standard, and while 'Betsy' isn't as beautiful as some of the new touring cars, she has many redeeming features, most important of which is accessibility,'' Lampkin wrote. ''Circulation is by positive rotary pump of my own make, driven by a short chain, though I believe in direct drive, but space, or rather want of it, makes us do things of which we do not exactly approve, though my pump never gives me any trouble and can be packed without getting under the rig, by using an ordinary monkey wrench.'' All in all, Lampkin was satisfied with his effort, but it hadn't been easy. ''It amuses me to hear some people tell how they would build a machine,'' he said, ''when I think of the snags that they would encounter.''

LAMPO — New York, New York — (1915) — The Adams & Montant Company of New York City was an automobile dealership which specialized in importing European cars, the Lancia during this period most particularly. The Lampo — Italian for ''lightning'' — was planned as a small Lancia-like car to sell in the $800 range and to be built in the United States, saving hefty import duties. Adams & Montant also planned to build a larger car that year to be called the RomeR. The evidence suggests, however, that neither of these cars proceeded beyond the prototype stage.

LANCAMOBILE — New York, New York — (1900-1901) — The James H. Lancaster Company of 95-97 Liberty Street in New York City produced a 7 hp two-cylinder car with engine under the seat, tiller steering, chain drive and vis-a-vis body. To this quite standard specification for a turn-of-the-century gasoline car, James Lancaster added an unusual starting device the operation of which was described as follows: ''an independent air-motor starts the gas motor, when the latter is running, the air motor becomes a compressor and stores air in the tubular frame of the vehicle.'' Had this device worked effectively, the Lancamobile would have been produced for more than the short year that it was. James H. Lancaster was described in the press at that time as ''the well-known manufacturer of acetylene gas plants.''

1900 Lancamobile, runabout, HAC

LANCASTER — The Lancaster Motor Company of Pittsburgh, Pennsylvania was listed as an automobile manufacturer in the Hiscox book *Horseless Vehicles, Automobiles, Motor Cycles* published in 1900. Documentation of this is lacking. Turn of the century city directories for Pittsburgh reveal no such company.

The Lancaster Motor Company of Lancaster, New York was organized during the summer of 1910 with a capital stock of $2000 to manufacture automobiles, engines and accessories. Incorporators were George A. Davis, Frederick Howard and Odell R. Blair. Manufacture is doubted.

LANCIA — Late in 1927, Lancia Motors of America, Inc. was organized in New York with a $1 million capital stock for the manufacture of a Lancia in the United States. Plans called for the building of the engines, transmissions and differentials at Lancia's factory in Turin, Italy, with the remainder of the parts being produced and the entire car assembled in America. The general lines of the Lancia Lambda were to be followed, but this was to be a distinctively American car, with its own V-8 engine and 128-inch-wheelbase chassis. The price was to be in the $3500 range, ''representing an enormous saving under the cost of importing a complete car,'' the company said. Prototypes were built in Italy. Ultimately the plans fell through, however, and the American Lancia factory was never built.

LAND YACHT — Philadelphia, Pennsylvania — (1920) — The Land Yacht was a custom-made car produced for Dale B. Fitler, who was described as ''one of Philadelphia's wealthiest young sportsman.'' Its chassis was that of a 1-1/2-ton (140-inch wheelbase) White truck, the car designed by an architect named C.E. Schermerhorn and built by the Dunbar Automobile Body Company. Unquestionably, it was one of the most luxurious of the pioneer R.V.-type vehicles. The body was hand-hammered aluminum over a skeleton ash frame. Inside were seating accommodations for six, sleeping accommodations for four. The "galley" included a small refrigerator and cooking equipment, plus hunting, fishing and general camping paraphernalia. All this cost Dale Fitler approximately $7500.

LANDMANN-GRIFFITH — The Landmann-Griffith is a mystery. All that is known of it is that it was a cyclecar and that it was exhibited at the automobile show in Toledo, Ohio in February 1914.

LANDON — Whether he ever indeed did sell any cars is unknown, but in the 1926 Los Angeles, California city directory, Jack Landon of 5250 West Hollywood Boulevard indicated himself to be an automobile manufacturer. He was missing entirely from the directory after 1927. Landon seems to have been involved in West Coast racing in the late Twenties, and conceivably may have built some competition machines.

LANDRY — The J.A. Landry Motor Car Company was organized in New Orleans, Louisiana late in 1912 with a capital stock of $25,000 for the manufacture of automobiles. J.A. Landry, J.B. Avergo and Roger J. Montrose were the incorporators. Manufacture is doubted.

LANDSHAFT — W. Landshaft & Son of 2336 Milwaukee Avenue in Chicago, Illinois was indicated as an automobile manufacturer in the 1909 Ware yearbook of the industry. Documentation is lacking.

LANE — The Lane Auto Association, Inc. was organized in Syracuse, New York during the summer of 1911 with a capital stock of $10,000 to manufacture and deal in motor vehicles and maintan a garage. The incorporators were Bradley J. Lane, Anna L. Lane and Earl R. Elmer. Manufacture is doubted.

"Lane & Lay of Kalamazoo, Michigan are forming a company of local capitalists to build light gasoline runabouts," *The Motor Age* reported early in 1903. Possibly this venture evolved out of the Kalamazoo Cycle Company's attempt to get into manufacture late the year previous, but it seems to have gone nowhere as well.

1900 Lane, runabout, HAC

LANE STEAM — Poughkeepsie, New York — (1900-1911) — The Lane brothers of Poughkeepsie — William J., George and John M. — were successful producers of hardware specialties at the turn of the century when they began looking for an automobile to buy, and decided they could build a better one themselves. Ultimately the Lanes became among the most successful producers of steam cars and among the most vociferous proponents of steam power. "It propels our great ships, pulls our railway trains, runs our factories," they said and, managing all that, obviously it was most eminently suited to the horseless carriage. The first Lane steamer was on the road during the sumer of 1900, with five more built and sold by the end of the year. The Lane Motor Vehicle Company was incorporated shortly thereafter. The Lane car was ruggedly built, its engine compact but powerful, and the entire vehicle guaranteed for a year. "This does not mean a free repair shop," one of the brothers explained, "but only applies to defective materials, flaws, cracks or checks, or work that was clearly improperly performed by us." The Lanes were quite convinced of the superiority of their workmanship, and probably rightly so. Lane steam cars were regularly awarded first-class certificates in Automobile Club of America endurance events, and in a decade about two dozen different models were made available. Production in 1908 was 89 cars; in 1909 the 150 mark was approached. The Lane Company began to sputter only with the falling from favor of the steam car itself. Thereafter the Lane Brothers turned to the manufacture of barn door rollers.

1900 LANE STEAM

	FP	5	4	3	2	1
No. 1 Steam Rbt.	1100	2700	3600	5300	8800	19,000

1901 LANE STEAM

	FP	5	4	3	2	1
No. 1 Steam Rbt.	1100	2700	3600	5300	8800	19,000
No. 2 Dos-a-Dos	1150	2900	3700	5600	9100	20,000
No. 0 Light Steam Rbt.	750	2500	3500	5000	8500	18,000
No. 4 Surrey	—	3000	4000	6000	9500	21,000
No. 3 Surrey	1400	3000	4000	6000	9500	21,000

1902 LANE STEAM

	FP	5	4	3	2	1
No. 4 Steam Surrey	—	3000	4000	6000	9500	21,000
No. 2 Steam Rbt.	750	2900	3700	5600	9100	20,000
No. 3 Steam Rbt.	1150	3100	4200	6300	10,500	22,000
No. 1 Steam	1000	2900	3700	5600	9100	20,000
No. 0 Light Steam Rbt.	750	2700	3600	5300	8800	19,000

1903-1904 LANE STEAM

	FP	5	4	3	2	1
No. 0 Light Steam Rbt.	750	3000	4000	6000	9500	21,000
No. 1 Steam Rbt.	1100	3100	4200	6300	10,500	22,000
No. 2 Steam Rbt.	—	3200	4300	6500	11,000	23,000
No. 4 Steam Tour.	1500	3300	4400	6700	12,000	24,000

1905 Lane, style 6, runabout, HAC

1906 Lane, style 6, tonneau, HAC

1905-1906 LANE STEAM

	FP	5	4	3	2	1
Style 6 Tonneau	2250	3100	4200	6300	10,500	22,000
Style 6 Rbt.	2100	3000	4000	6000	9500	21,000

1907 LANE STEAM

	FP	5	4	3	2	1
Model 75 Tour. (30 hp, 112" wb)	3400	2700	3600	5300	8800	19,000
Model 75 Rbt. (30 hp, 112" wb)	3000	2400	3400	4800	8000	17,000
Model 7 Tour. (20 hp, 97" wb)	2500	2500	3500	5000	8500	18,000
Model 7 Victoria (20 hp, 97" wb)	2650	2300	3300	4600	7500	16,000

1908 Lane, model 11, touring, HAC

1908 LANE STEAM

	FP	5	4	3	2	1
Model 11 Tour. (20 hp)	2000	2700	3600	5300	8800	19,000
Model 10 Rbt. (20 hp)	1800	2400	3400	4800	8000	17,000
Model 9 Tour. (30 hp)	3100	2900	3700	5600	9100	20,000
Model 8 Rdstr. (30 hp)	2800	3100	4200	6300	10,500	22,000

1909 LANE STEAM

	FP	5	4	3	2	1
Model 10 Tour. (20 hp, 101"wb) Tour.	2000	2700	3600	5300	8800	19,000
Model 14 Rbt. (20 hp, 98" wb)	1800	2900	3700	5600	9100	20,000
Model 18 Rdstr. (30 hp, 112" wb)	2800	3200	4300	6500	11,000	23,000
Model 15 Tour. (30 hp, 119" wb)	3100	3000	4000	6000	9500	21,000
Model 12 Close-Coupled (30 hp, 126" wb)	3000	2500	3500	5000	8500	18,000

1910 Lane, model 26, touring, HAC

1910 LANE STEAM

	FP	5	4	3	2	1
Model 21 Tour. (20 hp, 125" wb)	2400	3100	4200	6300	10,500	22,000
Model 19 Rbt. (20 hp, 99" wb)	1250	2400	3400	4800	8000	17,000
Model 20 Tour. (20 hp, 103" wb)	1500	2700	3600	5300	8800	19,000
Model 22 Tour. (20 hp, 119" wb)	2500	3000	4000	6000	9500	21,000
Model 24 Rbt. (20 hp, 100" wb)	—	2500	3500	5000	8500	18,000
Model 25 Tour. (20 hp, 110" wb)	1600	2900	3700	5600	9100	20,000
Model 26 Tour. (20 hp, 125" wb)	—	3100	4200	6300	10,500	22,000

1911 Lane, model 25, touring, NAHC

1911 LANE STEAM

	FP	5	4	3	2	1
Model 25 Tour. (20 hp, 110" wb)	1600	2500	3500	5000	8500	18,000

1915 Lane, light car, NAHC

LANE — Wichita Falls, Texas — (1915) — This Lane was a light car built in Wichita Falls. Its wheelbase was 108 inches, its tread 44 inches, its engine a two-cylinder air-cooled Spacke, its transmission a planetary, its final drive by belt. At 1000 pounds, the Lane was considerably heavier than the usual cyclecars on the market, and pictures indicate that it was probably more substantially built. The prototype purportedly had been on the road since November of 1913. "No previous publicity of this car has been given to speak of owing to the fact that the company wished to subject the car to all manner of testing," reported *Carette* in January 1915. The truth was that the prototype tested around Thanksgiving of 1913 was the Wichita Falls, Theodore F. Lane's first cyclecar effort which had fared none too well in the marketplace. It is to be doubted that the Lane Light Car Manufacturing Company which he organized to produce his new Lane fared much better.

1902 Lane & Daley, steam carriage, NAHC

LANE & DALEY STEAM — Barre, Vermont — (1901-1902) — For a short time the Lane & Daley Company of Barre produced a steam vehicle with two cylinders, two boilers, two tanks and two driving speeds. Among its safety features was a self-closing throttle, in case the driver fell out or lost control. Shod with solid rubber tires over wooden wheels, the Lane & Daley was usable either as a three-seat passenger car or delivery wagon. Fifteen miles an hour was its speed on the level, and the vehicle could haul a two-ton load up a modest hill. Both W.A. Lane and F.A. Daley were machinists. Lane was also a dealer in granite, and Daley apparently had been the first of the duo to experiment with an automobile, building his first before the turn of the century. Production of the Lane & Daley was discontinued at the end of 1902. Thereupon Daley left for Everett, Massachusetts for a try at commercial vehicle production. And Lane relocated his shops in Montpelier where his company became famous for the manufacture of tools for the granite industry. The brick buildings of the Lane factory remain and in recent years were renovated into low-income housing units.

LANG — C.W. Lang was one-half of the partnership that attempted to promote an air-cooled car called the Elliott in Dayton, Ohio in 1925. Refer to Elliott.

John S. Lang's Sons & Company was organized in New York City early in 1907 with a capital stock of $100,000 for the manufacture of bicycles and automobiles. Incorporators were G.E. Relyea, J.H. Richards and A.G. Cross. Manufacture of a car is doubted.

LANG & SCHARMANN — Marshfield, Wisconsin — (1907-1909) — George J. Lang and Otto T. Scharmann were two of the three partners in the machine shop at 206 South Central Avenue known initially as the Marshfield Iron Works, later as Kliner, Lang and Scharmann. Kliner apparently wasn't interested in automobiles, but Lang and Scharmann certainly were. Their first venture was a two-cylinder 24 hp gasoline car, the engine for which was built entirely at Marshfield Iron Works. This Lang & Scharmann was announced to the press in January 1907 as strictly an experimental job. In February 1908 the partners revealed that they were building a 40 hp automobile for a local doctor named K.W. Dodge. That this car was completed and successfully operated has been documented by I.W. Wendt, a lifelong resident of Marshfield and three times the mayor of the city, who recalls having been a passenger in the car. Lang & Scharmann subsequently built further vehicles, their total production believed to be six cars.

1898 Langan, runabout, NAHC

LANGAN — St. Louis, Missouri — (1898) — In 1898 the editor of *The Horseless Age* commented that, as far as he knew, Louis Langan was the only builder of motor carriages in St. Louis. The year previous Langan had visited Europe to investigate the state of the art there, and on his return through New York he purchased a number of single-cylinder 1-3/4 hp American motors. Back in St. Louis, at his shop at 1015 Morgan Street, Langan completed his first horseless carriage during the summer of 1898. It was a light 390-pound runabout mounted on a frame of steel tubing with 32-inch wire wheels shod with 2 1/2-inch pneumatic tires. Its top speed was 18 mph. A subsquent 570-pound wagon he built was given a test run of twenty miles on good roads "at a cost of a cent and a half for the entire distance," according to Louis Langan. He reported that his next effort would be a motor tricycle, but all subsequent activity seems to have been directed toward the organization of the St. Louis Gasoline Motor Company which was incorporated in November of 1898. Though a few St. Louis cars were built, that firm's focus was engine and components manufacture, though not for long. Following a substantial order from a purported automobile company in Elgin, Illinois for 100 motors, transmission and chassis, Louis Langan ordered full speed ahead at his small factory. Unfortunately the promised check from Elgin never arrived, and the St. Louis firm was forced to shut its doors. Later in 1899 Louis Langan ventured to the East Coast again, where he secured employment in Upstate New York with the Buffalo Gasoline Engine Company. Although various car rosters have indicated Louis Langan to be building automobiles as late as 1905, that appears to be in error.

LANGE — The Charles Lange & Brothers Company was organized in Chicago, Illinois early in 1910 with a capital stock of $5000 for the manufacture of "buggies, wagons, sleighs, motor cars, etc." Incorporators were Adolph C. Gresen, Anton Pinger and Alvah T. Martin. Manufacture of a car is doubted.

The Lange-Smith Motor Company was organized in Springfield, Illinois during the summer of 1907 with a capital stock of $2500 for the manufacture of automobiles and engines. Ohmer G. Smith, Fred H. French and William E. Ward were the incorporators. Manufacture of a car is doubted.

LANGFORD — The Langford Company of America was a million-dollar Maine incorporation from the fall of 1916 for the purpose of "manufacturing, buying, selling and dealing in automobiles and accessories." Langford president was M.E. Hegarty; the company directors were John J. Shay, Walter T. Hannigan, Daniel J. O'Keefe, Norman L. Bassett, Frank G. Farrington, Sarah Miller. Manufacture of a car is doubted.

LANICH — Baraboo, Wisconsin — (1908) — Arthur S. Lanich of Baraboo built an experimental highwheeler in 1908 which he sold that summer to a Dr. J.E. English who purportedly was set to "promote its commercial manufacture." Lanich also indicated his interest in manufacture, but did not follow through. Dr. English was not heard from again. In 1909, however, Arthur Lanich was. This time he had invented a railway motor runabout which was being successfully used by the Madison division of the Chicago & Northwestern Railroad. It featured a two-stroke 3 hp engine and was equipped with solid rubber tires on flanged wheels. In 1910 Arthur Lanich became the western Wisconsin agent for the Halladay car. In 1918 he disposed of his retail business and garage in order to turn his energies to the manufacture of a number of automobile-related specialties, including a device to automatically open and close garage doors.

1910 Lanpher, model L, motor buggy, NAHC

LANPHER — Carthage, Missouri — (1906-1916) — From Carthage came the Lanpher, a prototypical highwheeler with a two-cylinder air-cooled engine, planetary transmission, double chain drive and solid rubber tires. The price of $550 for the standard two-seater buggy was attractive, and other body styles were available on request. That the Lanpher Motor Buggy Company survived as long as it did in the production of a vehicle fast becoming obsolete was doubtless due to the low-key aspect of this enterprise. The men behind it were Earl and Norman Lanpher, the former seeing to the horsedrawn aspect of their business (the Lanpher Brothers Carriage Works), the latter to the automobiles. Both vehicles were produced side by side, and were sold in the surrounding area. The brothers never advertised nationally, nor locally for that matter, which was probably the reason their enterprise seldom made the news columns. A rare exception was a story in the October 12th, 1905 edition of the *Carthage Democrat* which read: "The Lanpher Carriage Shop on South Grant Street was entered sometime during Tuesday night by someone unknown. Three hammers and two chisels are missing. The shop was entered by breaking the latch on the front door." The Lanpher family appears to have left Carthage late in 1916.

1910 LANPHER
Highwheeler — 2-cyl., 12/14 hp, 76" wb

	FP	5	4	3	2	1
Model L Buggy-2P	550	2000	3000	4200	6500	14,000

1907 Lansden Electrette, runabout, NAHC

LANSDEN ELECTRIC — Birmingham, Alabama — (1901-1903)/Newark, New Jersey — (1906-1910) — In 1901 John M. Lansden and William M. Little announced their organization of the Birmingham Electric Manufacturing Company for the production of electric vehicles. Experimentation followed until the summer of 1903 when the partners announced the "approaching completion" of two Lansden electric cars which were to be used as demonstrators prior to the onset of quantity production. Lansden did indeed move into manufacture, though not in Birmingham, Alabama. By 1904, as the Lansden Company, the venture had moved to Newark, New Jersey where commercial vehicle production was embarked upon, the firm selling its first electric truck to the Adams Express Company that year. In 1906 passenger cars were added to the line, an Electrette Runabout on a 90-inch wheelbase and a Limousine on an 88-inch wheelbase, with a larger touring and limousine models being added the year following. The Lansden sported a long snout wherein were housed its batteries; instrumentation consisted of a clock and odometer, and steering was by wheel. Twenty-five miles an hour was guaranteed and sixty miles between charges. Prices began in the $2000 range, and rose to twice that. Although the Lansden Company officially discontinued its passenger-car department in 1908, the firm reported its building of "a few pleasure cars to order" as well as an electric taxicab as late as 1910. But by then production was turning exclusively to the commercial vehicle field, in which manufacture continued for two decades, for a short while under the aegis of Maccar, a company set up by one of the Mack brothers. John M. Lansden left the firm in 1911 to manage General Motors Corporation's electric truck division.

1906 LANSDEN

	FP	5	4	3	2	1
Type 56 Electrette Rbt. (90" wb)	1850	2300	3300	4600	7500	16,000
Type 40-CC Limo. (88" wb)	4000	2500	3500	5000	8500	18,000

1907-1908 LANSDEN

	FP	5	4	3	2	1
Type 56 Electrette Rbt. (90" wb)	2250	2300	3300	4600	7500	16,000
Type 40-CC Limo. (88" wb)	4000	2500	3500	5000	8500	18,000
Type 38C Touring (91" wb)	3400	2900	3700	5600	9100	20,000
Type 98CC Limo. (108" wb)	4000	2700	3600	5300	8800	19,000

1905 LaPetite, runabout, NAHC

LA PETITE — Detroit, Michigan — (1905) — J.P. La Vigne built his first car in Detroit in 1898 and a new one thereafter each year, though the only person who rode much in these experimental three-wheelers was his daughter Olive. She grew up so well versed in engineering matters that she became his technical advisor. La Vigne's first four-wheeler arrived in 1903, followed in turn by a second experimental four-wheeler and the idea of going into manufacture of a car to sell for $375. In 1905, at the Detroit Automobile Show, La Vigne exhibited a four-wheeler with a 5 hp single-cylinder engine under the hood, a three-speed planetary transmission and shaft drive. He called it La Petite and placed it under a large banner reading "Within the Reach of All." As La Vigne told the story a few years later, one Henry Ford approached him at the show and said, "You have my idea, and that is what I am going to build." Apocryphal though the tale might be, La Petite did not become the car of the masses in any case. The Detroit Automobile Manufacturing Company was hastily organized to build the vehicle, and an engine-building firm was contracted to produce the La Vigne engine. According to the inventor, the engines supplied were abysmal so he gave up on the La Petite idea after production of a claimed 200 cars "to take up other and more important matters." This left the Detroit Automobile Manufacturing Company people rather in a lurch, but they recovered quickly enough to offer another car called the Paragon in 1906. As for J.P. La Vigne, he went on to design the Griswold and later the La Vigne cyclecar.

1905 LA PETITE
Model A — 1-cyl., 5 hp

	FP	5	4	3	2	1
Runabout-2P	375	2000	3000	4200	6500	14,000
Delivery Car (65" wb)	425	1600	2700	3800	5800	12,000

LA POINTE SIMPLEX — Hancock, Michigan — (1903) — The La Pointe Simplex was built in Hancock by the Hodge Iron Company, makers of brass and iron castings. It had been designed by C.J. Costelle and N.M. Benson of Chicago. Charles J. Hodge put up the money for the building of the prototype. It was a small 8 hp runabout with shaft drive, selective sliding gear transmission, wood wheels and a Mercedes-type radiator. Its projected price tag was $750. Local Houghton County capitalists were interested in the project, and it was announced that if the "sample proves satisfactory," Charles Hodge would organize a company for manufacture. No such company ensued, and no reason ever was given for the curious name of the car.

LA PORTE — La Porte, Indiana — (1895) — In 1895 the La Porte Carriage Company announced its entry with a vehicle of its own design for the Chicago Times-Herald Contest. The car was not completed in time for the event, nor did the La Porte company subsequently begin the manufacture of automobiles.

LARCHMONT — Newark, Delaware — (1920) — Larchmont Motors Corporation was organized in the spring of 1920 for the manufacture of cars and trucks. Walter H. Schimpf headed the company, and he was described as having been in the "auto game" since 1899 when he was plant superintendent for the Mobile Company of America at Tarrytown, New York. He moved west thereafter, and sold White Steamers, Wintons and Stanleys in Denver, Colorado — and later handled district sales in the West for Cadillac, Oldsmobile and Paige. His chief engineer and vice-president was Joseph Anglada, designer of the Liberty cyclecar of New York City and subsequently the Anderson of Rock Hill, South Carolina. Two basic models of the Larchmont were slated to be built: a six (Beaver engine) to be sold as a $2600 sporting car (128-inch wheelbase), $1850 touring, $2850 five-passenger sedan and $3450 seven-passenger sedan (all on 120-inch wheelbases), and an export version also on a 120-inch wheelbase to use a four-cylinder Supreme engine and to be sold as a $1700 sporting car. Pilot models only were produced before Larchmont Motors Corporation, which had been incorporated at $5 million, went under. Walter Schimpf immediately found other work as sales manager for A.H. Lyons & Company, storage battery makers in Philadelphia.

LA ROCHE — The La Roche Automobile Company of Philadelphia was organized with a capital stock of $50,000 during the summer of 1905 to manufacture, repair and deal in motor cars. Behind this venture were M.F. La Roche, W.J. Thoroughgood, G.H. Walker and W.H. Brines. Though the firm did proceed into the business of repair and as a dealership, no manufacture is believed to have followed. This Pennsylvania venture should not be confused, incidentally, with the activities of F.A. La Roche, who was well known at the time for contesting the French-built Darracq in match races and other competitions and who was the head of the American Darracq Company. F.A. La Roche died early in 1905, before the La Roche Automobile Company was organized.

LARSEN — From 1907 to 1909, in Chicago, an ice-machine maker named John M. Larsen built automobiles as a sideline activity. He marketed them under the name Falcon. Refer to Falcon.

LASALLE — The LaSalle Garage Company was organized during the fall of 1908 with a capital stock of $6000 to manufacture and repair automobiles in LaSalle, Illinois. E.M. Lawrence, William Kinder and William W. Griffing were the people involved. Manufacture is doubted.

LASALLE

LASALLE — Detroit, Michigan — (1927-1940) — It was named for the French adventurer who explored the Mississippi River valley in 1682, and it was a companion to the car named for the French explorer who discovered Detroit about twenty years later. That the LaSalle built by Cadillac was a commercial failure is a reality, but that reality pales in the light of the LaSalle's historic significance. Because of the LaSalle, automobile styling at General Motors moved out of engineering and into a department of its own — Art and Colour as it was called then, "a sissy name" according to Harley Earl who headed it, though that was perhaps the only negative in this very positive move by GM. The LaSalle's genesis dated back to the early Twenties, as Alfred P. Sloan, Jr. noticed a price gap which needed filling between the Buick and the Cadillac. When Lawrence P. Fisher took over Cadillac's presidency in 1924, a massive expansion program was inaugurated to raise Cadillac's production capability, and Harley Earl, whose work as chief designer for Don Lee Corporation in California had attracted Fisher's attention, was invited to submit design proposals, as he later related, not "quite as conservative as the Cadillac." Inspired by one of the most sensational-looking cars on the Continent, the Hispano-Suiza, Earl came up with the LaSalle which was introduced on March 5th, 1927 to a reception equally sensational. Art and Colour almost immediately followed. Though built by Cadillac to Cadillac standards, the LaSalle initially was its own car and even a pacesetter for Cadillac. Its 303-cubic-inch 75 hp V-8 engine and its overall look were adapted to the new 341 Series Cadillac introduced for 1928. That the new LaSalle could hold its own in a performance vein too was demonstrated in mid-1927 when Bill Rader drove a stripped stock model at the GM Proving Ground a total of 951.0 miles for a 95.3 mph average, which was only a couple of miles an hour less than the Duesenberg had required the month before to win the famous Memorial Day race of 500 miles at Indianapolis. In 1928, with LaSalle's help, Cadillac production climbed above 40,000 cars for the first time in history. By the end of 1929 nearly 50,000 LaSalles had been sold. With Cadillac as doting parent, the LaSalle received synchromesh (on second and high), safety glass and chrome in '29. But then the stock market crashed, and the Great Depression began. Fewer than 3500 LaSalles were sold in each of the 1932 and 1933 model years. By 1934 the LaSalle no longer enjoyed favorite-child status, but instead hand-me-downs from the parts bins of other GM cars, the Olds straight-eight engine among them. The new styling was superb, a tall and skinny vee radiator, artfully designed porthole louvers, pontoon fenders — and the chassis was fine, with independent front suspension and hydraulic brakes. But as the economy began to recover, the LaSalle did not, at least commensurately: 7195 cars in 1934, 8651 in 1935, 13,004 in 1936. Meanwhile the Packard One-Twenty had been introduced for 1935, and had taken off like a rocket. For 1937 Cadillac made the LaSalle its own again, giving it the L-head V-8 of the Series 60, nice new styling, a lower price range and a heavy promotion campaign emphasizing that the car was completely Cadillac built. But it was too late. Model year production of 32,000 LaSalles was a terrific leap forward, but the LaSalle remained leagues behind the Junior Packards. Interestingly, in Packard circles, the fact that the marque's lower-priced cars were designated Packard is thought by many to have ultimately resulted in the ruination of the company. In LaSalle's case, that it wasn't a Cadillac was probably the ruinous factor. People do tend to buy prestige, and a Cadillac was prestige; LaSalle did not have the time to develop a prestigious name before the onset of the Depression, and did not have the opportunity after. Competition from the Lincoln Zephyr in the later Thirties didn't help either. The LaSalle was discontinued following the 1940 model after a total of 205,000 cars had been built in thirteen largely unlucky years. In 1941 the spot filled by the LaSalle in the Cadillac lineup was taken by a new Series 61 model called a Cadillac. That year GM's premiere division sold more cars than ever before in its history.

LaSalle Data Compilation
by Philip S. Dumka

1927

1927 LaSalle, roadster, AA

LASALLE — **SERIES 303** — **EIGHT:** LaSalle — A new line to fill the gap between Buick and Cadillac in the General Motors lineup of prices. Billed as a "Companion Car to Cadillac," the LaSalle boasted Cadillac quality and dependability in a smaller package, at a lower price. Styling stood equal alongside function in the design.

Bodies: The initial offering in March, 1927 consisted of Roadster, Phaeton, Coupe, Convertible Coupe, Victoria, and five passenger Sedan by Fisher plus Coupe, Sedan, and Town Cabriolet by Fleetwood. A dual cowl Sport Phaeton was soon available, followed by midyear offerings of Town Sedan, seven passenger Sedan, and five and seven passenger Imperials by Fisher plus a Transformable Town Cabriolet by Fleetwood ("Transformable" indicates that the front compartment can be totally enclosed, with windows in the doors, not that the rear quarter can be lowered). Body features included: High, slim radiator set low in the frame. Twelve louvers, centered in hood panels. Twin cowl vents on Roadster and Phaeton. Bullet shaped head and cowl lights. Posts under headlights to conduct wiring. Monogram rod between headlights. On Roadster and Phaetons the cut-down effect of the belt line was accentuated by double molding curving upward onto the cowl. Rear window in Coupe and rear curtain in Convertible Coupe could be opened for communication with rumble seat passengers. The four door Town Sedan was close-coupled, with no rear quarter windows.

Chassis: Similar to Cadillac; scaled to LaSalle size and power. Differences as follows: Fuel feed by manifold vacuum, assisted by engine driven vacuum pump. Mechanical brakes with fourteen inch drums on all wheels. Rear semi-elliptic springs shackled at both ends, rear shackle with ball and socket joint. Front wheels run on ball bearings. Watson stabilators.

Drive line: Multiple (eleven) disc clutch, three speed selective transmission, torque tube drive, 3/4 floating rear axle with helical bevel gear and pinion.

Engine: The compensated two-plane crankshaft in the V-63 engine and the separate starter and generator on the 314 engine had been major changes, but the basic engine remained the Type 51 design. The 303 engine was a new basic design, with offset blocks and side by side connecting rods (babbitted). The outward appearance was the same as the final version of the 314 engine except that the 303 starter was horizontal, mounted behind the flywheel on the right side. The oil filter was mounted on the engine rather than the firewall. The carburetor was similar to Cadillac but reversed. The oil level indicator was mounted behind the right hand block. A common manifold, connecting the two exhaust manifolds at the front of the engine, fed to a single muffler at the left side of the chassis.

I.D. DATA: Serial numbers were not used. Engine numbers were stamped on plate on front face of dash and on crankcase just below the water inlet on the right side. Starting: 200001. Ending: 212000.

1927 LaSalle, phaeton, JAC

Style No.	Body Type & Seating	Price	Weight	Prod. Total
Fisher — 125 in. Wheelbase				
1168	4-dr. Phae.-4P	2495	3770	NA
1168-B	4-dr. Spt. Phae.-4P	2975	4190	NA
1169	2-dr. Rds.-2/4P	2525	3755	NA
7410	2-dr. Cpe.-2/4P	2585	3770	NA
7400	2-dr. Conv. Cpe.-2/4P	2635	3770	NA
7390	2-dr. Vic.-4P	2635	3985	NA
7380	4-dr. Sed.-5P	2685	4090	NA
7420	4-dr. Twn. Sed.-5P	2495	4065	NA
Fisher — 134 in. Wheelbase				
8090	4-dr. Imp.-5P	2775	4315	NA
8060	4-dr. Sed.-7P	2775	4345	NA
8070	4-dr. Imp.-7P	2875	4570	NA
Fleetwood — 125 in. Wheelbase				
3110	2-dr. Cpe.-2P	4275	5000	NA
3120	4-dr. Sed.-5P	4475	5100	NA
3130	4-dr. Twn. Cab.-5/7P	4500	5100	NA
3051	4-dr. Trans. Twn. Cab.-5/7P	4700	5100	NA

Note: Weight of the four Fleetwood models is approximate.

ENGINE: Ninety Degree V-8, L-head. Eight. Cast iron block of four, offset on copper/aluminum crankcase. B & S: 3-1/8 x 4-15/16 in. Disp.: 303 cu. in. C.R.: 4.8:1 std, 5.3:1 opt. H.P. 75 plus advertised. SAE/N.A.C.C. H.P.: 31.25. Main bearings: Three. Valve lifters: Mechanical, with rollers riding on cam. Carb.: mfg by Cad under C.F. Johnson patents. Compression: 90-92 PSI at 1000 R.P.M.; 105-107 PSI at 1000 R.P.M. with hi-comp heads.

CHASSIS: [Series] 303 W.B.: 125 in. O.L.: 185 in. Frt/Rear Tread: 56 in. Tires: 32 x 6.00 (6.00-20). W.B.: 134 in. O.L.: 196-5/8 in. Frt/Rear Tread: 56 in. Tires: 32 x 6.20 (6.50-20).

TECHNICAL: Selective sliding gear transmission, in unit with engine. Speeds: 3F/1R. Left drive, center controls (rhd opt.). Multiple disc clutch, 11 discs. Shaft drive (Torque tube). 3/4 floating rear axle, helical bevel drive. Overall ratio: 4.54 std, 4.07, 4.91 opt. Mechanical brakes, 14 in. drums on four wheels. Artillery wheels (wire and disc opt.). Wheel size: 20 in.

806

1927 LaSalle, sedan, JAC

OPTIONS: Wire wheels, fender wells, 2 spare tires (250.00). Disc wheels, fender wells, 2 spare tires (150.00). Wood wheels, fender wells, 2 spare tires (140.00). Folding trunk rack (35.00). 5 wire wheels without spare tire (95.00).

HISTORICAL: Introduced March, 1927. Calendar year sales: 16,850. Calendar year production: 16,850. Model year sales: 12,000. Model year production: 12,000. President & general manager was Lawrence P. Fisher.

On June 20, 1927 at the General Motors Proving Ground, Milford, Michigan, Willard Rader and Gus Bell drove a LaSalle Roadster on a remarkable endurance test run. In ten hours, the car covered 951 miles at an average speed of 95.2 miles per hour, the fastest of 252 laps having been run at an average speed of 98.8 miles per hour (the winner at the Indy 500 in 1927 averaged 97.5 miles per hour for 500 miles). The test was terminated when an oil suction line fractured.

The LaSalle was a production roadster with windshield, lamps, fenders, running boards, and muffler removed. The camshaft had been altered, and a 3.5:1 rear axle and high compression heads had been installed. No mechanical adjustments were required during the entire run. The nine stops, taking a total of 7 min., 24.7 sec., were for tire changes, water, oil, and gasoline.

1927
Series 303. V-8. 125" wb

	FP	5	4	3	2	1
RS Rds	2525	12,000	24,000	40,000	60,000	80,000
Phae	2495	12,300	24,600	41,000	62,000	82,000
Spt Phae	2995	13,500	27,000	45,000	70,000	90,000
2P Conv Cpe	2635	11,400	22,800	38,000	56,000	76,000
RS Cpe	2585	6300	12,600	21,000	29,400	42,000
4P Vic	2635	6000	12,000	20,000	28,000	40,000
Sed	2685	4650	9300	15,500	21,700	31,000
Twn Sed	2650	4950	9900	16,500	23,100	33,000
Series 303, V-8, 134" wb						
Imp Sed	2820	5400	10,800	18,000	25,200	36,000
7P Sed	2820	5400	10,800	18,000	25,200	36,000
7P Imp Sed	2920	5550	11,100	18,500	25,900	37,000

1928

1928 LaSalle, sedan, AA

LASALLE — SERIES 303 — EIGHT: The bodies were a continuation of 1927 LaSalle line. Fisher Business Coupe, five passenger Family Sedan on 125 in. wheelbase, five passenger Cabriolet Sedan, seven passenger Family Sedan on 134 in. wheelbase added. Fleetwood Coupe and Sedan dropped; Transformable Town Cabriolet on 134 in. wheelbase added in midyear. The five passenger Standard Sedan came with leather or metal back. The five and seven passenger Family Sedans were "economy" versions of the Standard Sedans. The five passenger Family Sedan and the Business Coupe were offered at the new low price of $2350. Details remained the same except for added side ventilators in the cowl on closed cars and twenty eight louvers toward the rear of the hood panels on all body styles. The number of louvers might have signified the year, but Cadillac for 1928 had thirty louvers.

Chassis, drive line, and engine: Similar to 1927 LaSalle except — Shock absorbers changed to Lovejoy hydraulic. Clutch changed to twin disc. Many detail changes made to brakes and brake linkage, including 16 in. drums on front wheels only.

I.D. DATA: There were no serial numbers used. Engine numbers were stamped on plate on front face of dash and on crankcase just below the water inlet on the right side. Starting: 212,001. Ending: 226,806.

Style No.	Body Type & Seating	Price	Weight	Prod. Total
Fisher — 125 in. Wheelbase				
1168	4-dr. Phae.-4P	2485	3770	NA
1168-B	4-dr. Spt. Phae.-4P	2975	4190	NA
1169	2-dr. Rds.-2/4P	2485	3755	NA
8140	2-dr. Cpe.-2/4P	2450	3770	NA
7400	2-dr. Conv. Cpe.-2/4P	2550	3770	NA
8130	2-dr. Vic.-4P	2550	3985	NA
8120	4-dr. Std. Sed.-5P	2495	4090	NA
8110	4-dr. Sed.-5P	(2450)	(4070)	NA
7420	4-dr. Twn. Sed.-5P	2495	4065	NA
8140-A	2-dr. Bus. Cpe.-2/4P	2350	3935	NA
8110-A	4-dr. Family Sed.-5P	2350	4060	NA
Fisher - 134 in. Wheelbase				
8090	4-dr. Imp.-5P	2775	4315	NA
8060	4-dr. Std. Sed.-7P	2775	4345	NA
8070	4-dr. Imp.-7P	2875	4570	NA
8050	2-dr. Cpe.-5P	2625	4050	NA
8080	4-dr. Cabr. Sed.-5P	2675	4060	NA
8060-A	4-dr. Family Sed.-7P	2575	4300	NA
Fleetwood — 125 in. Wheelbase				
3051	4-dr. Trans. Twn. Cab.-5/7P	4700 5100 app		NA
3130	4-dr Twn. Cabr.-5/7P	4500 5100 app		NA
Fleetwood — 134 in. Wheelbase				
3751	4-dr Trans. Twn. Cab.-5/7P	4900 5100 app		NA

1928 LaSalle, 2-pass. coupe, JAC

ENGINE: Ninety Degree V-8, L-Head. Eight. Cast iron blocks of four, offset on copper/aluminum crankcase. B & S: 3-1/8 in. x 4-15/16 in. Disp.: 303 cu. in. C.R.: 4.8:1 std., 5.3:1 opt. Taxable/N.A.C.C. H.P.: 31.25. Main bearings: Three. Valve lifters: Mechanical, with rollers riding on cams. Carb.: Mfg. by Cad under C.F. Johnson patents. (Compression) 90-92 PSI @ 1000 R.P.M., 105-107 PSI @ 1000 RPM with hi-comp. heads.

CHASSIS: [Series: 303] W.B.: 125 in. O.L.: 185 in. Frt/Rear Tread: 56 in. Tires: 32 x 6.00 (6.00-20) [Series: 303] W.B.: 134 in. O.L.: 196-5/8 in. Frt/Rear Tread: 56 in. Tires: 32 x 6.20 (6.50-20)

TECHNICAL: Selective sliding gear transmission, in unit with engine. Speeds: 3F/1R. Left drive, center controls (rhd opt). Twin disc clutch. Shaft drive (Torque tube). 3/4 floating rear axle, helical bevel drive. Overall ratio: 4.54:1 std.; 4.07:1, 4.91:1 opt.* Mechanical brakes on four wheels. 14 in. rear drums, 16 in. front drums. Artillery wheels (wire and disc opt). Wheel size: 20 in.
*; 4.91:1 may have been used on some 134 in. wheelbase cars.

OPTIONS: Natural wood wheels (10.00). 5 disc wheels (20.00). 6 disc wheels, fender wells, 2 spare tires (175.00). 5 wire wheels (95.00) 6 wire wheels, fender wells, 2 spare tires (250.00) Fender wells for wood wheels (140.00). Folding trunk rack (25.00).

HISTORICAL: Introduced as a continuation of 1927 line. (Minor changes Sept. '27). Calendar year sales: 9,956. Calendar year production: 9,956. Model year sales: 14,806. Model year production: 14,806. President & General Manger was Lawrence P. Fisher.

1928 LaSalle, phaeton, JAC

1928
Series 303. V-8. 125" wb

	FP	5	4	3	2	1
Rds	2485	12,000	24,000	40,000	60,000	80,000
Phae	2485	12,300	24,600	41,000	62,000	82,000
Spt Phae	2975	12,900	25,800	48,200	66,000	86,000
Conv	2550	11,400	22,800	38,000	56,000	76,000
Bus Cpe	2350	6150	12,300	20,500	28,700	41,000
RS Cpe	2450	6300	12,600	21,000	29,400	42,000
Vic	2550	6000	12,000	20,000	28,000	40,000
5P Sed	2495	5550	11,100	18,500	25,900	37,000
Fam Sed	2350	5250	10,500	17,500	24,500	35,000
Twn Sed	2495	5400	10,800	18,000	25,200	36,000
Series 303, V-8, 134" wb						
5P Cpe	2625	6750	13,500	22,500	31,500	45,000
Cabr Sed	2675	11,400	22,800	38,000	56,000	76,000
Imp Sed	2775	6750	13,500	22,500	31,500	45,000
7P Sed	2775	6750	13,500	22,500	31,500	45,000
Fam Sed	2575	6900	13,800	23,000	32,200	46,000
Imp Fam Sed	2775	7050	14,100	23,500	32,900	47,000
Series 303, V-8, 125" wb						
Fleetwood Line						
Bus Cpe	3000	7050	14,100	23,500	32,900	47,000
Sed	3200	5550	11,100	18,500	25,900	37,000
Twn Cabr	4500	11,700	23,400	39,000	58,000	78,000
Trans Twn Cabr	—	12,000	24,000	40,000	60,000	80,000

1929

1929 LaSalle, roadster, OCW

LASALLE — SERIES 328 — EIGHT: Similar to 1928 LaSalle Series 303 except:
Bodies: Victoria and Business Coupe dropped. Landau Cabriolet added. Fleetwood 134 in. wheelbase Transformable Town Cabriolet available with collapsible quarter. Convertible Imperial Sedan (All Weather Phaeton) available on order. All Fisher bodies except Roadster and Phaetons on 134 in. wheelbase. Parking lights moved to fenders. Brightwork chrome plated. Security-Plate glass in all windows and windshields. Closed body interiors 2-1/2 in. wider, 1 in. higher. Adjustable front seat on closed bodies with no division. Electric tandem windshield wipers. Oval panel on rear of body, formed by quarter molding.
Chassis: Duplex-mechanical brakes — all shoes inside drums.
Drive line: Synchro-mech transmission.
Engine: Piston pins pressure lubricated. Midyear change to Metric spark plugs.

I.D. DATA: Serial numbers were not used. Engine numbers were stamped on plate on front of dash and on crankcase just below the water inlet on the right side. Starting: 400001. Ending: 422961.

Style No.	Body Type & Seating	Price	Weight	Prod. Total
Fisher — 125 in. Wheelbase				
1186	2-dr. Rds.-2/4P	2345	3990	NA
1185	4-dr. Phae.-4P	2295	4140	NA
1185-B	4-dr. Spt. Phae.-4P	2875	4405	NA
Fisher — 134 in. wheelbase				
8590	2-dr. Cpe.-2/4P	2495	4310	NA
8580	2-dr. Conv. Cpe.-2/4P	2595	4135	NA
8555	4-dr. Family Sed.-5P	2450	4550	NA
8550	4-dr. Sed.-5P	2595	4490	NA
8610	4-dr. Twn. Sed.-5P	2675		NA
8615	4-dr. Imp. Twn. Sed.-5P	—	—	NA
8530	4-dr. Sed.-7P	2775	4615	NA
8540	4-dr. Imp.-7P	2875	4760	NA
8570	2-dr. Cpe.-5P	2625	4335	NA
8600	4-dr. Lan. Cab.-5P	2725	4635	NA
8605	4-dr. Imp. Land. Cab.-5P	—	—	NA
Fleetwood — 125 in. Wheelbase				
3051	4-dr. Trans. Twn. Cab.-5/7P	4800 5100 app		NA
3130	4-dr. Twn. Cab.-5/7P	4500		NA
Fleetwood — 134 in. Wheelbase				
3751	4-dr. Trans. Twn. Cab.-5/7P	4900 5125 app		NA
3751-C	4-dr. Tr. Coll. Twn. Cab.-5/7P	—	—	NA
3780	4-dr. Conv. Imp. Sed.-5P	—	—	NA

1929 LaSalle, sedan, JAC

ENGINE: Ninety Degree, V-8, L-head. Eight. Cast iron blocks of four, offset on copper/aluminum crankcase. B & S: 3-1/4 x 4-15/16 in. Disp.: 328 cu. in. C.R.: 5.3:1 std, 4.8:1 opt. SAE/Taxable/N.A.C.C. H.P.: 33.8. Main bearings: Three. Valve lifters: Mechanical, with rollers riding on cams. Carb.: mfg. by Cad under C.F. Johnson patents. Torque (Compression): 105-107 P.S.I. at 1000 R.P.M.; 90-92 P.S.I. at 1000 R.P.M. with lo-comp heads.

CHASSIS: [Series 328] W.B.: 125 in. O.L.: 185 in. Frt/Rear Tread: 56/58 in. Tires: 6.50-19 (31 x 6.20). W.B.: 134 in. O.L.: 196-5/8 in. Frt/Rear Tread: 56/58 in. Tires: 6.50-19 (31 x 6.20).

TECHNICAL: Selective transmission with synchro-mesh. Speeds: 3F/1R. Left drive, center control (rhd opt). Twin disc clutch. Shaft drive (torque tube). 3/4 floating rear axle, helical bevel drive. Overall ratio: 4.54:1 std; 4.91:1, 4.07:1 opt. Duplex-mechanical brakes on four wheels, all shoes internal, 15 in. drums on all wheels. Artillery wheels (wire and disc optional). Wheel size: 19 in.

OPTIONS: Tire cover(s) (5.00-12.00). "LaSalle" radiator ornament (12.00). Heater (40.00). Tonneau windshield (185.00). Seat covers (30.00-230.00). Trunks (60.00-100.00). Fender wells. Colored fenders. Wire wheels. Disc wheels.

HISTORICAL: Introduced August, 1928. Innovations: Synchro-mesh transmission. Safety glass. Model year sales: 22,961. Model year production: 22,961. President & General Manager of LaSalle was Lawrence P. Fisher.

1929
Series 328, V-8, 125" wb

	FP	5	4	3	2	1
Rds	2345	13,500	27,000	45,000	70,000	90,000
Phae	2295	13,800	27,600	46,000	73,500	92,000
Spt Phae	2875	14,400	28,800	48,000	76,000	96,000
Trans FW Twn Cabr	4800	12,000	24,000	40,000	60,000	80,000

Series 328, V-8, 134" wb

	FP	5	4	3	2	1
Conv	2595	11,400	22,800	38,000	56,000	76,000
RS Cpe	2625	7500	15,000	25,000	35,000	50,000
5P Cpe	2495	7050	14,100	23,500	32,900	47,000
Sed	2595	6750	13,500	22,500	31,500	45,000
Fam Sed	2450	6750	13,500	22,500	31,500	45,000
Twn Sed	2675	6900	13,800	23,000	32,200	46,000
7P Sed	2775	6900	13,800	23,000	32,200	46,000
7P Imp Sed	2875	7050	14,100	23,500	32,900	47,000
Conv Lan Cabr	2725	11,400	22,800	38,000	56,000	76,000
FW Trans Twn Cabr 1	4900	12,300	24,600	41,000	62,000	82,000

1930

1930 LaSalle, 5-pass. coupe, AA

LASALLE — SERIES 340 — EIGHT: Slight changes from Series 328 LaSalle. Becoming more and more like Cadillac (Series 353); differences being mainly in size, weight, and power.
Bodies: Fisher line decreased to seven closed bodies, including Convertible Coupe. Fleetwood line increased to six. Styling same as Cadillac, with size scaled to six inch shorter wheelbase. LaSalle line includes Fleetwood seven passenger Touring and four passenger Phaeton, not included in Cadillac line. These two, plus Roadster, are distinguished by louvers in side of cowl. With battery under front seat, LaSalle has no hatches in splash pans. Headlights have 10-1/2" lens, are 11" overall. Single rear light is mounted on left rear fender.

Chassis, drive line: All bodies on 134" wheelbase. Front tread increased from 56 to 57-1/2 in. Rear tread increased from 58 to 59-1/2 in. Rear springs are underslung. Brake system same as Cadillac Series 353, but drums are still 15 in. Exhaust ends in straight pipe. Standard final drive ratio remains at 4.54:1.
Engine: Bore increased by 1/16 in., making displacement same as Series 341-B Cadillac. No cover over sparkplugs or intake header. Cover plate on intake header changed in midyear from Aluminum to Cast Iron to eliminate problem with leaking cover plate gaskets.

1930 LaSalle, convertible coupe, JAC

I.D. DATA: Serial numbers were not used. Engine numbers were stamped on crankcase just below the water inlet on the right hand side. Starting: 6000001. Ending: 614995.

Style No.	Body Type & Seating	Price	Weight	Prod. Total
Fisher				
30252	4-dr. Twn. Sed.-5P	2590	4705	NA
30258	2-dr. Cpe.-2/4P	2490	4510	NA
30259	4-dr. Sed.-5P	2565	4690	NA
30262	4-dr. Sed.-7P	2775	4790	NA
30263	4-dr. Imp.-7P	2925	4865	NA
30268	2-dr. Conv. Cpe.-2/4P	2590	4480	NA
30272	2-dr. Cpe.-5P	2590	4530	NA
Fleetwood				
4002	2-dr. Rds.-2/4P	2450	4385	NA
4057	4-dr. Tr.-7P	2525	4480	NA
4060	4-dr. Phae.-4P	2385	4425	NA
4080	4-dr. All-Weath Phae.-5P	3995	4715	NA
4081	4-dr. Sednet. Cab.-5P	3725	4645	NA
4082	4-dr. Sedanette-5P	3825	4645	NA
4151	4-dr. Stat. Trans. Twn. Cab.	Built to order		
3351	Trans. Cab.-5P	—	—	NA
3364	Brougham-5P	—	—	NA

ENGINE: Ninety degree V-8, L-head. Cast iron block on silicon/aluminum crankcase. B & S: 3-5/16 in. x 4-15/16 in. Disp.: 340 cu. in. C.R.: 5.05:1 std., 4.92:1 opt. Brake H.P.: 90 @ 3000 R.P.M. SAE/Taxable H.P.: 35.1. Main bearings: Three. Valve lifters: Mechanical, with rollers riding on cams. Carb.: mfg. by Cad under C.F. Johnson patents.

CHASSIS: W.B.: 134 in. O.L.: app. 201-3/4 in. Frt/Rear Tread: 57-1/2/59-1/2 in. Tires: 6.50-19 w/wood art, 7.00-18 w/all others.

TECHNICAL: Selective, synchro-mesh transmission. Speeds: 3F/1R. Left drive, center controls (rhd opt). Twin disc clutch. Shaft drive (torque tube). 3/4 floating rear axle, spiral bevel gears. Overall ratio: 4.54:1 std.; 4.07:1, 4.91: 1 opt. Safety-mechanical brakes on four wheels (15 in. drums). Wood artillery wheels (disc, wire, wood demountable opt). Wheel size: 19 in. w/wood artillery, 18 in. all others.

OPTIONS: Tire cover(s) (5.50-30.00). Wind wings (25.00-55.00). Tonneau shield (185.00). Radio (175.00). Heater (42.50). Radiator ornament (25.00). Trunks (80.00-115.00). Seat covers (26.75-230.25). Spotlight/Driving lights (15.50-80.00). Tire mirrors (32.00/pair). 5 wire wheels (60.00). 6 wire wheels w/fender wells, trunk rack (190.00). 5 demountable wood wheels (50.00). 6 dem. wood wheels w/fender wells, trunk rack (190.00). 5 disc wheels (50.00). 6 disc wheels w/fender wells, trunk rack (190.00).

1930 LaSalle, all-weather phaeton, JAC

HISTORICAL: Introduced September, 1929. Innovations: radio available; most bodies prewired for radio, with aerial built into top. Model year sales: 11,005. Model year production: 11,005. President & General Manager was Lawrence P. Fisher. Since 1926, Cadillac Series designation had been based on cubic inches of engine displacement. For 1930, the dimensions of the LaSalle engine were identical to the 1928/1929, 341-A, -B Cadillac engine. To avoid confusion, the 1930 LaSalle was designated Series 340.

1930
Series 340, V-8, 134" wb
Fisher Line

	FP	5	4	3	2	1
Conv	2590	14,400	28,800	48,000	76,000	96,000
RS Cpe	2590	8250	16,500	27,500	38,500	55,000
Cpe	2490	7500	15,000	25,000	35,000	50,000
Sed	2565	6750	13,500	22,500	31,500	45,000
Imp Sed	2590	6900	13,800	23,000	32,200	46,000
7P Sed	2775	7050	14,100	23,500	32,900	47,000
7P Imp Sed	2925	7500	15,000	25,000	35,000	50,000

Series 340, V-8, 134" wb
Fleetwood Line

	FP	5	4	3	2	1
RS Rds	2450	14,700	29,400	49,000	78,000	98,000
Fleetcliffe						
Phae	2385	17,100	31,800	53,000	85,000	106,000
7P Tr	2525	14,400	28,800	48,000	76,000	96,000
Fleetlands						
A/W Phae	3995	15,000	30,000	50,000	80,000	100,000
Fleetway						
S'net Cabr 4081	3725	13,500	27,000	45,000	70,000	90,000
Fleetwind						
S'net Cabr 4082	3825	14,400	28,800	48,000	76,000	96,000

1931

1931 LaSalle, Fleetwood roadster, OCW

LASALLE — SERIES 345-A — EIGHT: Similar to Series 340 except as follows:
Bodies: No basic changes as with Series 355. Straight sill retained. Hood louvers retained until mid-model. When louvers were replaced by doors, cowl doors did not match hood doors. Radiator screen optional extra. New oval instrument panel, with different grouping than 355. Single bar bumper becomes only fast way to differentiate between 340 and early 345 from a distance.
Chassis and drive line: Metal covers on springs. Radiator positioned vertical instead of sloping to rear.
Engine: Displacement now same as 353 and 355. Series designation on V-8's no longer matches displacement. Intake muffler used. Three point engine mounting retained. Distributor 1-1/2 inches lower than on 355.

I.D. DATA: There were no serial numbers used. Engine numbers were stamped on crankcase just below the water inlet on the right hand side. Starting: 900001. Ending: 910103.

Style No. Fisher	Body Type & Seating	Price	Weight	Prod. Total
31652	4-dr. Twn. Sed.-5P	2345	4665	NA
31658	2-dr. Cpe.-2/4P	2195	4470	NA
31659	4-dr. Sed.-5P	2295	4650	NA
31662	4-dr. Sed.-7P	2475	4750	NA
31663	4-dr. Imp. Sed.-7P	2595	4825	NA
31668	2-dr. Conv. Cpe.-2/4P	2295	4440	NA
31672	2-dr. Cpe.-5P	2295	4490	NA
Fleetwood				
4602	2-dr. Rds.-2/4P	2245	4345	NA
4657	4-dr. Tr.-7P	2345	4440	NA
4680	4-dr. All. Wthr. Phae.-5P	3245	4675	NA
NA	Sedanette-5P	3245	4650	NA
NA	Sednet. Cab.-5P	3245	4675	NA

ENGINE: Ninety degree L-head. Eight. Cast iron block on aluminum crankcase. B & S: 3-3/8 in. x 4-15/16 in. Disp.: 353 cu. in. C.R.: 5.35:1 std., 5.26:1 opt. Brake H.P.: 95 plus @ 3000 R.P.M. SAE/Taxable H.P.: 36.45. Main bearings: Three. Valve lifters: Mechanical. Carb.: Cad/Johnson, with intake silencer.

CHASSIS: [Series: 345-A] W.B.: 134 in. O.L.: 202 in. H.: 72-1/2 in. Frt/Rear Tread: 57-1/4/59-1/2 in. Tires: 6.50 x 19 (7.00 x 18 opt. on 7P Sedan).

1931 LaSalle, sedan, JAC

TECHNICAL: Selective, synchro transmission. Speeds: 3F/1R. LHD center control, RHD opt. Twin disc clutch. Shaft drive, torque tube. 3/4 floating rear axle, spiral bevel drive. Overall ratio: 4.75:1 std.; 4.07:1, 4.54:1 opt. Mechanical brakes on four wheels (15 in. drums). Wood artillery wheels. Wheel size: 19 in.

OPTIONS: Trunks (100.00-119.00). Tonneau windshield (185.00). Wind wings (25.00-47.50). Tire cover(s) (5.00-40.00). Mirrors (10.00-32.00/pair). Radio (price on application). Heater (41.00-55.00). Auxiliary lights (37.50-75.00). Seat Covers (26.75-73.50). Heron or Goddess (20.00). Radiator screen (33.00).

HISTORICAL: Introduced August, 1930. Model year sales: 10,103. Model year production: 10,103. President & general manager was Lawrence P. Fisher.

1931
Series 345A, V-8, 134" wb
Fisher Line

	FP	5	4	3	2	1
RS Cpe	2295	9000	18,000	30,000	42,000	60,000
Cpe	2195	8550	17,100	28,500	39,900	57,000
Sed	2295	6900	13,800	23,000	32,200	46,000
Twn Sed	2345	6900	13,800	23,000	32,200	46,000
7P Sed	2475	6900	13,800	23,000	32,200	46,000
7P Imp Sed	2595	7050	14,100	23,500	32,900	47,000

Series 345A, V-8, 134" wb
Fleetwood Line

	FP	5	4	3	2	1
RS Rds	2245	17,100	31,800	53,000	85,000	106,000
Conv	2295	13,500	27,000	45,000	70,000	90,000
Tr	2345	14,700	29,400	49,000	78,000	98,000
A/W Phae	3245	18,500	33,000	55,000	88,000	110,000
S'net Cabr 4081	3245	15,000	30,000	50,000	80,000	100,000
S'net Cabr 4082	3245	17,100	31,800	53,000	85,000	106,000

1932

1932 LaSalle, coupe, JAC

LASALLE — SERIES 345-B — EIGHT: Engine and mechanical features same as V-8 Cadillac except for shorter wheelbase (130, 136 in. vs 134, 140 in.). Overall styling and appearance identical to V-8 Cadillac except for: Seven body styles, all by Fisher. LaSalle emblems. Five hood ports on shorter hood. Continued use of 1931 (-A) lights. No fender tie bar used, but monogram bar retained. Dual horns, projecting thru headlight stanchions, have right angle trumpets. Dual rear lights used.

I.D. DATA: Serial numbers were not used. Engine numbers were stamped on crankcase near the water inlet on the right hand side. Starting: 1100001. Ending: 1103290.

Style No. Fisher — 130 in. Wheelbase	Body Type & Seating	Price	Weight	Prod. Total
32-678	2-dr. Cpe.-2/4P	2395	4660	NA
32-668	2-dr. Conv. Cpe.-2/4P	2545	4630	NA
32-672	2-dr. Twn. Cpe.-5P	2545	4695	NA
32-659	4-dr. Sed.-5P	2495	4840	NA
Fisher — 136 in. wheelbase				
32-652	4-dr. Twn. Sed.-5P	2645	4895	NA
32-662	4-dr. Sed.-7P	2645	5025	NA
32-663	4-dr. Imp. Sed.-7P	2795	5065	NA

ENGINE: Ninety degree L-head. Eight. Cast iron block on aluminum crankcase. B & S: 3-3/8 x 4-15/16 in. Disp.: 353 cu. in. C.R.: 5.38:1 std; 5.70:1, 5.20 opt. Brake H.P.: 115 @ 3000 R.P.M. SAE/Taxable H.P.: 36.45. Main bearings: Three. Valve lifters: Mechanical. Carb.: Cad/Johnson.

1932 LaSalle, sedan, JAC

CHASSIS: [Series 345-B] W.B.: 130, 136 in. O.L.: 204, 210 in. Frt/Rear Tread: 59-7/8 / 61 in. Tires: 7.00 x 17.

TECHNICAL: Selective, synchro transmission. Speeds: 3F/1R. LHD center controls, RHD opt. Twin disc clutch — selective vacuum-activation. Shaft drive, torque tube. 3/4 floating rear axle, spiral bevel drive. Overall ratio: 4.36:1, 4.60:1. Mechanical brakes on four wheels (15" drums). Wire wheels std, demountable wood opt. Wheel size: 17 in. drop center.

OPTIONS: Tire cover(s) (5.00 — 20.00 each). Trunks (100.00 — 180.00). Heron or Goddess (20.00). Radio (price on application). Heater (37.50 — 47.50). Auxiliary lights (37.50 — 57.50). Wind wings (25.00 — 47.50). Tonneau shield (185.00). Seat covers (26.50 — 73.50). Mirrors (8.00 — 16.00 each). Full covers for wire wheels (10.00 each). 6 wire wheels w/fender wells and trunk rack (130.00). 5 demountable wood wheels (30.00). 6 demountable wood wheels w/wells and rack (166.00). Colored fender set (50.00).

HISTORICAL: Introduced January, 1932. Model year sales: 3290. Model year production: 3290. President & General Manager was Lawrence P. Fisher.

1932 LaSalle, convertible coupe, JAC

1932
Series 345B, V-8, 130" wb

	FP	5	4	3	2	1
Conv	2540	14,400	28,800	48,000	76,000	96,000
RS Cpe	2395	8250	16,500	27,500	38,500	55,000
Twn Cpe	2545	7500	15,000	25,000	35,000	50,000
Sed	2495	6000	12,000	20,000	28,000	40,000

Series 345B, V-8, 136" wb

	FP	5	4	3	2	1
7P Sed	2645	6000	12,000	20,000	28,000	40,000
7P Imp Sed	2645	6300	12,600	21,000	29,400	42,000
7P Twn Sed	2645	6300	12,600	21,000	29,400	42,000

1933

1933 LaSalle, town sedan, OCW

LASALLE — SERIES 345-C — EIGHT: The 1933 LaSalle had most of the new features of the Cadillac line, including new radiator grill/shell, skirted fenders, no-draft ventilation, and vacuum assisted brakes. To provide distinction, the LaSalle had four hood doors and retained the bumper and

light system of the "B" Series. The new, hidden fender tie-bar was used but the monogram bar was dropped. Respective body styles had four inch shorter wheelbase and an average $500 lower price.

I.D. DATA: There were no serial numbers used. Engine numbers were stamped on crankcase near the water inlet on the right hand side. Starting: 2000001. Ending: 2003381.

Style No.	Body Type & Seating	Price	Weight	Prod. Total
Fisher — 130 in. Wheelbase				
33-659	4-dr. Sed.-5P	2245	4805	NA
33-668	2-dr. Conv. Cpe.-2/4P	2395	4675	NA
33-672	2-dr. Twn. Cpe.-5P	2395	4695	NA
33-678	2-dr. Cpe.-2/4P	2245	4730	NA
Fisher — 136 in. Wheelbase				
33-652	4-dr. Twn. Sed.-5P	2495	4915	NA
33-662	4-dr. Sed.-7P	2495	4990	NA
33-663	4-dr. Imp. Sed.-7P	2645	5020	NA
Fleetwood — 136 in. Wheelbase				
5281	2-dr. Twn. Cpe.-5P	—	—	NA

ENGINE: Ninety degree L-head. Eight. Cast iron block on aluminum crankcase. B & S: 3-3/8 x 4-15/16 in. Disp.: 353 cu. in. C.R.: 5.4:1 std., 5.7:1 opt. Brake H.P.: 115 @ 3000 R.P.M. SAE/Taxable H.P.: 36.45. Main bearings: Three. Valve lifters: Mechanical. Carb.: Cad/Johnson.

CHASSIS: [Series 345-C] W.B.: 130, 136 in. O.L.: approx. 204-210 in. Frt/Rear Tread: 59-7/8, 61 in. Tires: 7.00 x 17.

TECHNICAL: Selective synchro transmission. Speeds: 3F/1R. LHD center control, RHD optional. Twin disc clutch. Shaft drive, torque tube. 3/4 floating rear axle, spiral bevel drive. Overall ratio: 4.36:1, 4.60:1. Mechanical brakes on four wheels with vacuum assist (15" drums). Wire wheels std; demountable wood opt. Wheel size: 17 in. drop center.

OPTIONS: Sidemount covers. Wheel discs (chrome 10.00 each/ body color 12.50 each). Radio (Standard 64.50, Imperial 74.50). Heater: hot air or hot water. Draft deflector for Conv. Cpe. (35.00/pair). Luggage sets (37.00 — 110.00). Trunks w/luggage (104.00 — 180.00). Seat covers (10.00/seat). Mirrors. Spotlight (Lorraine 24.50). Dual pilot ray lights (44.50). "Torpedo" ornament (20.00). Six wire wheels with fender wells. Five demountable wood wheels. Six demountable wood wheels with fender wells.

HISTORICAL: Introduced January, 1933. Innovations: Fisher no-draft individually controlled ventilation (I.C.V.) (Vent windows). Model year sales: 3381. Model year production: 3381. President & General Manager was Lawrence P. Fisher.

1933
Series 345C, V-8, 130" wb

	FP	5	4	3	2	1
Conv	2395	10,500	21,000	35,000	49,000	70,000
RS Cpe	2395	6750	13,500	22,500	31,500	45,000
Twn Cpe	2245	6300	12,600	21,000	29,400	42,000
Sed	2245	5700	11,400	19,000	26,600	38,000

Series 345C, V-8, 136" wb

	FP	5	4	3	2	1
Twn Sed	2495	6450	12,900	21,500	30,100	43,000
Sed	2495	6150	12,300	20,500	28,700	41,000
7P Imp Sed	2495	6450	12,900	21,500	30,100	43,000

1934

1934 LaSalle, convertible coupe, DW

LASALLE — SERIES 50 — MODEL 350 — EIGHT: By 1933, LaSalle had become a Cadillac, discounted $500; and Cadillac had become a highly individualized luxury product. The early Thirties economy would not support this combination. The General Motors alternative to dropping the Cadillac Division was to produce the 1934 LaSalle, with the hope that LaSalle sales would bring the division out of the red. The 1934 LaSalle was presented as an entirely new car, backed by the prestige of Cadillac/Fleetwood, but not a Cadillac, and priced $1000 less than the least expensive Cadillac, to compete for buyers in the upper medium price range. Cost was reduced by using off-the-shelf components from other GM divisions and outside suppliers.

Bodies: Body style selection reduced to four, all by Fleetwood. "Bodies by Fleetwood" may have sounded incongruous, but it was a selling point and likely filled a gap in the work load at Fleetwood. Styling emphasized streamlining and concealment of the chassis. Slender Vee radiator grill sloped steeply to the rear. Teardrop lamps filleted to radiator housing. Hood, with circular ports, extended nearly to the 25 degree sloping windshield. Cowl vent door opened at the rear. All doors hinged at the rear. Beaver tail rear deck completely covered the chassis and concealed luggage and spare-wheel compartment. Air-foil type front fenders arched low in the front to cover the chassis and blended into the radiator housing to eliminate splash shields. Biplane bumpers mounted on concealed coil springs.

Chassis: Entirely new X type frame designed so as to reduce the overall height of the car by four inches. Entirely new A-frame type independent front suspension with coil springs and center point steering. Semi-elliptic rear springs to accomodate the Hotchkiss drive. Double acting shock absorbers, rear shocks being combined with a ride stabilizer bar. Bendix hydraulic brakes were Cadillac's first departure from mechanicals and were used only on LaSalle in 1934.

Drive Line: Single plate dry disc clutch. Three speed synchro-mesh transmission with helical cut spline shaft and gears. Rear axle semi-floating, with spiral bevel gears. Hotchkiss drive was a departure from Cadillac's long use of torque tube drive.

Engine: Eight cylinder in-line L-head of conventional design. 3x4¼, developing 95 horsepower at 3700 R.P.M. Five main bearings, Aluminum pistons, dual downdraft carburetor.

I.D. DATA: Serial numbers were on top surface of frame side bar, left side, just ahead of dash. Starting no.: 2100001. Serial number same as engine number. Ending: 2107218 (includes Jan, Feb, Mar, 1935). Engine numbers were on left side of cylinder block, at front, just below cylinder head. Starting engine no.: 2100001. Ending: 2107218 (includes Jan, Feb, Mar, 1935).

1934 LaSalle, 4-dr. sedan, HAC

Style No.	Body Type & Seating	Price	Weight	Prod. Total
6330-S	4-dr. Sed.-5P	1695	3960	—
6333-S	4-dr. Club Sed.-5P	1695	3960	—
6335	2-dr. Conv. Cpe.-2/4P	1695	3780	—
6376	2-dr. Cpe.-2P	1595	3815	—
6380	4-dr. Conv. Sed.-5P (probably none built)	—	—	—

ENGINE: In-line. L-head. Eight. Cast iron block (block integral with upper crankcase). B & S: 3 in. x 4-1/4 in. Disp.: 240.3 cu. in. C.R.: 6.5:1 std., 5.5:1 opt. Brake H.P.: 95 @ 3700 R.P.M. Taxable H.P.: 28.8. Main bearings: Five. Valve lifters: Mechanical. Carb.: Stromberg EE-23 Duplex downdraft.

CHASSIS: [Series 50] W.B.: 119 in. O.L.: 202-1/4 in. Frt/Rear Tread: 58-15/16 / 60-1/2 in. Tires: 7.00 x 16.

TECHNICAL: Selective synchro transmission. Speeds: 3F/1R. Left drive, center control (rhd. opt.). Single plate clutch. Shaft drive, Hotchkiss. Semi-floating rear axle, spiral bevel drive. Overall ratio: 4.78:1. Hydraulic brakes on four wheels (emergency mechanical on rear wheels). Steel wheels with disc cover. Wheel size: 16 in. drop center.

OPTIONS: Dual sidemount. Sidemount cover(s) (20.00 ea.). Fender skirts (wheel shields) (25.00 pair). Radio (std. 64.50, master 74.50). Heater (hot air, hot water, steam) (steam heater 44.50). Mirrors (8.00-10.00 ea.). Luggage racks, trunks (85.00-195.00). Seat covers. Spotlight (24.50). Torpedo ornament (20.00). Four spoke flexible strg wheel.

HISTORICAL: Introduced: January, 1934. Calendar year production: 6169. Model year sales: 7218. Model year production: 7218. The president & general manager was Lawrence P. Fisher to May 31, 1934; Nicholas Dreystadt general manager after June 1, 1934.

A 1934 LaSalle Convertible Coupe was the Indy pace car in 1934.

Much has been written to the effect that the straight eight LaSalle engine was in fact an Oldsmobile engine or was built by Oldsmobile for Cadillac. Contemporary factory information to Cadillac/LaSalle salesmen stated that the car was designed and developed by Cadillac engineers and the engine was built in the Cadillac factory. The suggestion was made that salemen invite prospects to visit the Cadillac factory to see the LaSalle being built. The carefully chosen wording used by the factory leaves open the possibility that Cadillac started with raw or semi-finished Oldsmobile parts and finished/assembled the parts to special Cadillac tolerances. The similarities between Oldsmobile and LaSalle engine, transmission, rear end, brakes, etc. are too obvious to go unnoticed. The salemen's information sheets list the following LaSalle parts sources: A.C. fuel pump, air cleaner, ammeter; Delco battery; Delco-Remy ignition, horn; Guide lights; Harrison radiator, themostat; New Departure and Hyatt bearings; Stromberg carburetor; Lynite (Alcoa) pistons; Whitney timing chain and sprockets; Thompson valves; Oldberg muffler; Alemite-Zerk chassis lubrication; Automotive Fan & Bearing Co. fan; Borg & Beck clutch; Spicer universal joints; Brown Lipe differential; Motor Wheel wheels; Saginaw steering gear, Bendix brakes; and A.O. Smith frame.

1934
Series 350, 8 cyl., 119" wb

	FP	5	4	3	2	1
Conv	1695	9300	18,600	31,000	43,400	62,000
Cpe	1595	5700	11,400	19,000	26,600	38,000
Clb Sed	1695	4650	9300	15,500	21,700	31,000
Sed	1695	4500	9000	15,000	21,000	30,000

1935

1935 LaSalle, 2-dr. sedan, AA

LASALLE — SERIES 35-50 — EIGHT: No major changes from 1934, but many detail improvements and a price reduction of approximately $400. Performance improved thru detail changes in the engine and a 9% weight reduction.

Bodies: Now made by Fisher, featuring new all steel turret roof. Four door town sedan replaced by two door sedan. New Vee windshield and two division moldings in rear window. Wipers below windshield. Cowl ventilator opens forward. Gasoline filler neck moved to right rear fender. Built-in trunk on sedans. New, bar-type bumpers. Controls moved from steering wheel to instrument panel.

Chassis: Wheelbase increased to 120 in. Bore increased to 4-3/8 in. New carburetor with electric choke. New generator with charging rate controlled by electrical load and battery condition.

I.D. DATA: Serial numbers were located on top surface of frame side bar, left side, just ahead of dash. Starting no.: 2200001. Serial number same as engine number. Ending: 2208653. Engine numbers were located on left side of cylinder block, at front, just below cylinder head. Starting engine no.: 2200001. Ending: 2208653.

Style No. Fisher 120 in. w.b.	Body Type & Seating	Price	Weight	Prod. Total
35-5077	2-dr. Cpe.-2P	1225	3475	—
35-5067	2-dr. Conv. Cpe.-2/4P	1325	3510	—
35-5019	4-dr. Sed.-5P	1295	3650	—
35-5011	2-dr. Sed.-5P	1255	3620	—

ENGINE: Inline. L-head. Eight. Cast iron block (block integral with upper crankcase). B & S: 3 in. x 4-3/8 in. Disp.: 248 cubic in. C.R.: 6.25:1 std.; 5.75:1 opt. Brake H.P.: 105 @ 3600 R.P.M. SAE/Taxable H.P.: 28.8. Main bearings: Five. Valve lifters: Mechanical. Carb.: Stromberg EE-15 Duplex Downdraft.

1935 LaSalle, 4-dr. sedan, JAC

CHASSIS: W.B.: 120 in. O.L.: 200 in. Height: 64-1/2 — 67-1/2 in. Frt/Rear Tread: 58-1/8 in. /59-1/16 in. Tires: 7.00 x 16.

TECHNICAL: Selective, synchro transmission. Speeds: 3F/1R. Left drive, central control (rhd opt). Single plate dry disc clutch. Shaft drive, Hotchkiss. Semi-floating rear axle, spiral bevel drive. Overall ratio: 4.55:1. Hydraulic brakes on four wheels (emergency mechanical on rear wheels). Disc wheels. Wheel size: 16 in. drop center.

OPTIONS: Dual sidemount. Sidemount cover(s) (35.00/pair). Radio (Master/Standard) (89.50/54.50). Heater (35.00). Clock (14.50). Seat covers. Flexible steering wheel (16.00). Wheel shields (25.00/pair).

HISTORICAL: Introduced March, 1935. Innovations: All steel Turret Tops. Model year sales: 8653. Model year production: 8653. The general manager was Nicholas Dreystadt.

1935
Series 50, 8 cyl., 120 wb

	FP	5	4	3	2	1
Conv	1545	9000	18,000	30,000	42,000	60,000
Cpe	1445	5250	10,500	17,500	24,500	35,000
2 dr Sed	1545	3900	7800	13,000	18,200	26,000
4 dr Sed	1545	4050	8100	13,500	18,900	27,000

1936

1936 LaSalle, convertible coupe, OCW

LASALLE — SERIES 36-50 — EIGHT: Changed little from the 1935 LaSalle. The new "Convex-Vee" grill retains the shape but has less slope than the old. New hood port treatment partially conceals the ports under a rounded canopy. The hand brake lever is moved to the left of the driver, under the instrument panel. The exhaust system has two mufflers, in series. Vacuum advance has been added to the distributor.

I.D. DATA: Engine numbers were on the left side of the engine block at the forward end, just below the cylinder head. Starting: 2210001. Ending: 2223004.

Style No.	Body Type & Seating	Price	Weight	Prod. Total
36-5077	Cpe.-2P	1175	3460	—
36-5067	Conv. Cpe.-2P	1255	3540	—
36-5011	2-dr. Tr. Sed.-5P	1185	3605	—
36-5019	4-dr. Tr. Sed.-5P	1225	3635	—

1936 LaSalle, 4-dr. sedan, JAC

ENGINE: Inline, L-head. Eight. Cast iron (block integral with upper half of crankcase). B & S: 3 x 4-3/8 in. Disp.: 248 cu. in. C.R.: 6.25:1 std. 5.75:1 opt. Brake H.P.: 105 @ 3600 R.P.M. SAE/Taxable H.P.: 28.8. Main bearings: Five. Valve lifters: Mechanical. Carb.: Stromberg EE-15.

CHASSIS: W.B.: 120 in. O.L.: 200 in. H.: 65-1/2 - 67-1/2 in. Frt/Rear Tread: 58-1/2 / 59-1/16 in. Tires: 7.00 x 16.

TECHNICAL: Selective synchro transmission. Speeds: 3F/1R. Left drive, center control (rhd opt.) Hand brake at left, under panel. Single plate clutch. Shaft drive, Hotchkiss. Semi-floating rear axle, spiral bevel drive. Overall ratio: 4.55:1. Hydraulic brakes on four wheels. (Emergency mechanical on rear wheels). Disc wheels. Wheel size: 16 in. drop center.

OPTIONS: Sidemount cover(s) (17.50). Radio (master/standard 89.50/54.50). Heater (18.50). Clock (14.50). Seat covers. Flexible steering wheel (16.00). Trim rings (1.50 each).

HISTORICAL: Introduced: October, 1935. Model year sales: 13004. Model year production: 13004. The general manager was Nicholas Dreystadt.

1936
Series 50, 8 Cyl., 120" wb, LaSalle

	FP	5	4	3	2	1
Conv	1255	7050	14,100	23,500	32,900	47,000
RS Cpe	1175	4200	8400	14,000	19,600	28,000
2 dr Sed	1185	3000	6000	10,000	14,000	20,000
4 dr Sed	1225	3150	6300	10,500	14,700	21,000

1937

1937 LaSalle, 4-dr. sedan, HAC

LASALLE — SERIES 37-50 — EIGHT: Body styling changes were minor: Die cast eggcrate grill; hood louver treatment featuring rectangular lines; headlights attached lower on the radiator casing; new front fenders with higher rear halves and a lengthwise crease along the top surface; bumpers carrying the LaSalle insignia; entire rear quarter window pivoted; and windshields with a 39 degree slope and a deeper Vee. 1937 LaSalle bodies were constructed entirely of steel. The line now included a Convertible Sedan. The big change for 1937 was the return to a V-8 engine — the 322 cu. in. unit as used in the 1936 Cadillac Series 60. This engine shared all the changes made in other 1937 V-8's. Unique to the LaSalle and the Cadillac Series 60 was the relocation of the exhaust down-pipe to the front of the right hand cylinder block and the use of a single muffler. Chassis changes, common to LaSalle and Cadillac Series 60 included use of hypoid rear axle, addition of front stabilizer bar, new steering box with shaft out of bottom. A LaSalle Commercial Chassis with 160-3/8 in. wheelbase was offered. This, and all Cadillac Commercial Chassis featured one-piece side rails in the frame.

I.D. DATA: Engine numbers were on the crankcase, just behind the left cylinder group, parallel to the dash. Starting: 2230001. Ending: 2262005.

Style No.	Body Type & Seating	Price	Weight	Prod. Total
37-5011	2-dr. Tr. Sed.-5P	1105	3780	—
37-5019	4-dr. Tr. Sed.-5P	1145	3810	—
37-5049	Conv. Sed.-5P	1485	3850	—
37-5067	Conv. Cpe.-2P	1175	3715	—
37-5027	Spt. Cpe.-2P	995	3675	—

1937 LaSalle, convertible sedan, OCW

ENGINE: Ninety degree, L-head. Eight. Cast iron block (blocks cast enbloc with crankcase). B & S: 3-3/8 x 4-1/2 in. Disp.: 322 cu. in. C.R.: 6.25:1 std.; 5.75:1 opt. Brake H.P.: 125 @ 3400 R.P.M. SAE/Taxable H.P.: 36.45. Main bearings: Three. Valve lifters: Hydraulic. Carb.: Stromberg AA-25, Carter WDO-374S.

CHASSIS: [Series 37-50] W.B.: 124 in. O.L.: 201-1/4 in. Frt/Rear Tread: 58/59. Tires: 7.00 x 16. [Series 37-50 Commercial Chassis] W.B.: 160-3/8 in. O.L.: 237-7/8 in. Tires: 7.00 x 16.

TECHNICAL: Selective, synchro transmission. Speeds: 3F/1R. LHD, center control, emerg at left under panel (RHD opt.). Single disc clutch. Shaft drive Hotchkiss. Semi-floating rear axle, Hypoid gearing. Overall ratio: 3.92:1. Hydraulic brakes on four wheels. Disc wheels. Wheel size: 16 in.

OPTIONS: Sidemount cover(s) (15.00 - 17.50). Radio (master/standard 79.50/59.50). Heater (19.50 - 60.00). Seat covers (7.50 per seat). Wheel discs (4.00 each). Trim rings (1.50 each). Flexible steering wheel (15.00).

HISTORICAL: Introduced: November, 1936. Model year sales: 32005. Model year production: 32005. The general manager was Nicholas Dreystadt.

1937
Series 50, V-8 124" wb, LaSalle

	FP	5	4	3	2	1
Conv	1350	7500	15,000	25,000	35,000	50,000
Conv Sed	1680	6900	13,800	23,000	32,200	46,000
4P Cpe	1155	3900	7800	13,000	18,200	26,000
2 dr Sed	1275	3600	7200	12,000	16,800	24,000
4 dr Sed	1320	3750	7500	12,500	17,500	25,000

1938

1938 LaSalle, coupe, OCW

LASALLE — SERIES 38-50 — EIGHT: The 1938 LaSalle remained much the same as the 1937 models. Along with many refinements, there were a few notable changes. LaSalle used the front-opening "Alligator" hood and the column gear shift common to the full Cadillac line. The grille remained eggcrate style but was two inches wider. Hood louvers were longer and more visible, due to the fact that the headlights were mounted low, on the sheet metal between the fenders and the grille. Chevrons were deleted from the nose of the front fenders. If used, sidemount covers were hinged on the fenders. Horns were mounted just behind the grille. The battery was under the hood on the right hand side but was removed from under the fender.

I.D. DATA: Serial numbers were located on left frame side bar, at the rear of the left front motor support. Starting: Same as engine number. Ending: Same as engine number. Engine numbers were on crankcase, just behind left cylinder block. Starting Engine No.: 2270001. Ending: 2285501.

1938 LaSalle, 4-dr. sedan, OCW

Style No.	Body Type & Seating	Price	Weight	Prod. Total
38-5027	Cpe.-2P	1295	3745	—
38-5067	Conv. Cpe.-2P	1415	3735	—
38-5049	Conv. Sed.-5P	1820	3870	—
38-5011	2-dr. Tr. Sed.-5P	1340	3800	—
38-5019	4-dr. Tr. Sed.-5P	1380	3830	—

ENGINE: Ninety degree. L-Head. Eight. Cast iron block (blocks cast enbloc with crankcase). B & S: 3-3/8 in. x 4-1/2 in. Disp.: 322 cu. in. C.R.: 6.25:1. Brake H.P.: 125 @ 3400 R.P.M. SAE/Taxable H.P.: 36.45. Main bearings: Three. Valve lifters: Hydraulic. Carb.: Stromberg AAV-25; Carter WDO 392s.

CHASSIS: [Series 38-50] W.B.: 124 in. O.L.: 201 in. Frt/Rear Tread: 58/59 in. Tires: 7.00 x 16. [Series 38-50 Commercial Chassis] W.B.: 160 in.

TECHNICAL: Selective synchro manual transmission. Speeds: 3R/1R. LHD; gearshift on column; handbrake at left (RHD opt.). Single disc clutch. Shaft drive, Hotchkiss. Semi-floating rear axle. Hypoid gears. O.R.: 3.92:1. Hydraulic brakes on four wheels. Disc wheels. Wheel size: 16 in.

OPTIONS: Radio (Master/Standard) (79.50/65.00). Heater (26.50-42.50). Clock (12.50). Seat covers (7.50 per seat). Spotlight (18.50). Automatic Battery Filler (7.50). Flexible steering wheel (15.00). Fog lights (17.50 pair). Wheel Discs (4.00 each). Trim rings (1.50 each).

HISTORICAL: Introduced October, 1937. Model year sales and production: 15501. The general manager was Nicholas Dreystadt.

1938
Series 50, V-8, 124" wb, LaSalle

	FP	5	4	3	2	1
Conv	1420	7650	15,300	25,500	35,700	51,000
Conv Sed	1680	6900	13,800	23,000	32,200	46,000
4P Cpe	1155	3900	7800	13,000	18,200	26,000
2 dr Sed	1275	3600	7200	12,000	16,800	24,000
4 dr Sed	1320	3750	7500	12,500	17,500	25,000

1939

1939 LaSalle, coupe, OCW

LASALLE — SERIES 39-50 — EIGHT: The 1939 LaSalle was characterized by a new tall, narrow grille plus side grilles; all fine-pitch diecast units. A new louver panel was set to the rear of the hood side panels. Headlights were once more fixed to the sides of the radiator casing. Glass area was increased by more than twenty five percent. Closed sedans were available with "Sunshine Turret Top". Chrome reveals appeared on all windows and the windshield. All but the lower front door hinge were concealed. Runningboards had become a no-cost option. Chassis changes included: Tube and fin in place of cellular radiator core; vacuum for crankcase ventilation generated by motion of the car rather than by engine intake system; new cross-link steering hookup.

I.D. DATA: Serial numbers were on the left frame side bar, opposite the steering gear. Starting: Same as engine number. Ending: Same as engine number. Engine numbers were on the crankcase, just behind the left cylinder block, parallel to the dash. Starting Engine No.: 2290001. Ending: 2313028.

Style No. Fisher Series 39-50, 120" wb	Body Type & Seating	Price	Weight	Prod. Total
39-5027	Cpe.-2P	1323	3635	—
39-5067	Conv. Cpe.-2P	1475	3715	—
39-5011	2-dr. Tr. Sed.-5P	1358	3710	—
39-5011-A	2-dr. Tr. Sed. (STT)-5P	1398	—	—
39-5029	Conv. Sed.-5P	1895	3780	—
39-5019	4-dr. Tr. Sed.-5P	1398	3740	—
39-5019-A	4-dr. Tr. Sed. (STT)-5P	1438	—	—
39-5019-F	4-dr. Tr. Sed. (Div)-5P	—	—	—

Note: (STT) Sunshine Turret Top.

ENGINE: Ninety degree. L-head. Eight. Cast iron block (blocks cast enbloc with crankcase). B & S: 3-3/8 in. x 4-1/2 in. Disp.: 322 cu. in. C.R.: 6.25.1. Brake H.P.: 125 @ 3400 R.P.M. SAE/Taxable H.P.: 36.45. Main bearings: Three. Valve lifters: Hydraulic. Carb.: Carter WDO 423s.

CHASSIS: [Series 39-50] W.B.: 120 in. O.L.: 202-1/2 in. Frt/Rear Tread: 58/59 in. Tires: 7.00 x 16. [Series 39-50 Commercial Chassis] W.B.: 156-1/2 in. O.L.: 239 in. Tires: 7.00 x 16.

1939 LaSalle, convertible sedan, JAC

TECHNICAL: Selective synchro manual transmission. Speeds: 3F/1R. LHD; gearshift on column; handbrake at left. Single disc clutch. Shaft drive Hotchkiss. Semifloating rear axle. Hypoid gears. O.R.: 3.92:1. Hydraulic brakes on four wheels. Slotted disc wheels. Wheel size: 16 in.

OPTIONS: Radio (69.50). Heater (31.50). Seat covers (8.25 per seat). Spotlight (18.50). Windshield washer (5.75). Automatic battery filler (7.50). Fog lights (14.50 pair.

HISTORICAL: Introduced: October, 1938. Model year sales and production: 23,028. The general manager was Nicholas Dreystadt.

1939
Series 50, V-8, 120" wb

	FP	5	4	3	2	1
Conv	1395	7350	14,700	24,500	34,300	49,000
Conv Sed	1800	7500	15,000	25,000	35,000	50,000
Cpe	1240	4500	9000	15,000	21,000	30,000
2 dr Sed	1280	2800	5700	9500	13,300	19,000
2 dr SR Sed	—	3000	6000	10,000	14,000	20,000
4 dr Sed	1320	3000	6000	10,000	14,000	20,000
4 dr SR Sed	—	3150	6300	10,500	14,700	21,000

1940

1940 LaSalle, Special convertible coupe, OCW

LASALLE — SERIES 40-50, 40-52 — EIGHT: LaSalle ended, as it began, with distinctive body styles; the Series 52 "Torpedo" or "Projectile" bodied "Specials". Introduced as Coupe and Sedan, the 52 line was expanded in mid-year with Convertible Coupe and Convertible Sedan. The "Torpedo" styles featured forty five degree sloping windshield, curved rear window, no belt molding, and rounder, smoother line down rear of body and trunk. A vacuum powered top was used on the Series 52 Convertible Coupe.

Body changes on Series 50 and 52 included: Wider spacing of center and side grille bars; triple vents on hood side panels; fenders flowing without a valley into the hood; sealed beam headlights built into the fenders; and parking lights on top of the headlights.

I.D. DATA: Serial numbers were on the left frame side bar, opposite the steering gear. Starting: Same as engine number. Ending: Same as engine number. Engine numbers were on the crankcase, just behind the left cylinder block, parallel to the dash. Starting Engine No.: [Series 40-50] 2320001; [Series 40-52] 4320001. Ending: [Series 40-50] 2330382; [Series 40-52] 4333751.

Style No.	Body Type & Seating	Price	Weight	Prod. Total
Fisher Series 40-50 123 in. w.b.				
40-5027	Cpe.-2P	1240	3700	—
40-5067	Conv. Cpe.-2P	1395	3805	—
40-5011	2-dr. Tr. Sed.-5P	1280	3760	—
40-5011-A	2-dr. Tr. Sed. (STT)-5P	—	—	—
40-5029	Conv. Sed.-5P	1800	4000	—
40-5019	4-dr. Tr. Sed.-5P	1320	3790	—
40-5019-A	4-dr. Tr. Sed. (STT)-5P	—	—	—
40-5019-F	4-dr. Tr. Sed. (Div)-5P	—	—	—
Note: (STT) Sunshine Turret Top				
Fisher Series 40-52 123 in. w.b.				
40-5227C	Cpe.-2P	1380	3810	—
40-5219	Tr. Sed.-5P	1440	3900	—
40-5229	Conv. Sed.-5P	1895	4110	—
40-5267	Conv. Cpe.-2P	1535	3915	—

ENGINE: Ninety degree. L-Head. Eight. Cast iron block (blocks case enbloc with crankcase). B & S: 3-3/8 in. x 4-1/2 in. Disp.: 322 cu. in. C.R.: 6.25:1. Brake H.P.: 130 @ 3400 R.P.M. SAE/Taxable H.P.: 36.45. Main bearings: Three. Valve lifters: Hydraulic. Carb.: Carter WDO 460s.

CHASSIS: [Series 40-50] W.B.: 123 in. O.L.: 206-3/4 in. Frt/Rear Tread: 58/59 in. Tires: 7.00 x 16. [Series 40-52] W.B.: 123 in. O.L.: 210-1/2 in. Frt/Rear Tread: 58/59 in. Tires: 7.00 x 16. [Series 40-50 Commercial Chassis] W.B.: 159 in. O.L.: 244-7/8 in. Tires: 7.00 x 16.

1940 LaSalle, 4-dr. sedan, JAC

TECHNICAL: Selective synchro manual transmission. Speeds: 3R/1R. LHD; gearshift on column; handbrake at left (RHD opt.). Single disc clutch. Shaft drive, Hotchkiss. Semi-floating rear axle. Hypoid gears. O.R.: 3.92:1. Hydraulic brakes on four wheels. Slotted disc wheels. Wheel size: 16 in.

OPTIONS: Radio (69.50). Heater (26.50-52.50). Seat covers (8.25 per seat). Spotlight (18.50). Automatic battery filler (7.50). Flexible steering wheel (15.00). Fog lights (14.50 pair). Windshield washer (6.50). Grille guard. Wheel discs (4.00 each). Trim rings (1.50 each).

HISTORICAL: Introduced October, 1939. Model year sales and production: [Series 40-50] 10382; [Series 40-52] 13751. The general manager was Nicholas Dreystadt.

1940
Series 50, V-8, 123" wb

	FP	5	4	3	2	1
Conv	1395	7350	14,700	24,500	34,300	49,000
Conv Sed	1800	7500	15,000	25,000	35,000	50,000
Cpe	1240	4500	9000	15,000	21,000	30,000
2 dr Sed	1280	2800	5700	9500	13,300	19,000
2 dr SR Sed	1440	3000	6000	10,000	14,000	20,000
4 dr Sed	1320	3000	6000	10,000	14,000	20,000
4 dr SR Sed	1440	3150	6300	10,500	14,700	21,000
"Special" Series 52 LaSalle V-8, 123" wb						
Conv	1795	7500	15,000	25,000	35,000	50,000
Conv Sed	2195	7650	15,300	25,500	35,700	51,000
Cpe	1685	4650	9300	15,500	21,700	31,000
4 dr Sed	1745	3000	6000	10,000	14,000	20,000

1906 LaSalle-Niagara, model B, touring, NAHC

LASALLE-NIAGARA — Niagara Falls, New York — (1905-1906) — The LaSalle-Niagara Automobile Company was the idea of E.A. Kinsey of Niagara Falls who took the assets and equipment of the Wilson Automobile Manufacturing Company which had been producing a small runabout called the Niagara in Wilson, New York since 1903. The LaSalle-Niagara was not, however, merely a continuation of the former Niagara. It was a brand-new car built under the patents of George E. Whiteside and offered as a chain-drive twin and a shaft-drive four at $1250 and $2250 respectively. The LaSalle-Niagara plant, at 91st and Schantz, was the former home of a button factory. This automotive venture was a short one. Although an occasional advertisement referred to this car simply as the Niagara, it would appear LaSalle-Niagara was used more often.

1905-1906 LASALLE-NIAGARA
Model A — 4-cyl., 26/30 hp, 100" wb

Tour.-5P	2250	2300	3300	4600	7500	16,000
Model B — 2-cyl., 16/18 hp, 90" wb						
Tour.-4P	1250	2200	3200	4400	7000	15,000

LASHER — In 1895, R.E. Lasher of 2732 South Third Street in St. Louis, Missouri entered the Chicago Times-Herald Contest. The car he was building for the event was not completed in time, however, and documentation that he subsequently finished and successfully tested the car is lacking.

LATHROP — That Mystic, Connecticut marine engine builder James W. Lathrop planned becoming an automobile manufacturer was revealed in a November 1902 issue of *The Automobile and Motor Review*. Already he had purchased an automobile to experiment upon, and he had bought the building next door to his engine shop for development purposes and, ultimately, automobile production. Further details are lacking.

LAUER — Detroit, Michigan — (1894) — John Lauer has been credited with the building of an automobile in Detroit in 1894. He was reputed at the time to be the ablest mechanic in town, and his machine shop was a busy, thriving place, though it would appear that his automotive activity was largely confined to lending an assisting hand to others. In the mid-1890's Charles B. King worked out of his shop developing the motor vehicle that was tested on March 6th, 1896 and which has since been generally acknowledged as being Detroit's first gasoline car. While employed by the Edison Illuminating Company, a young Henry Ford often brought work there. Oliver Barthel worked at the shop, and in 1903 Jonathan D. Maxwell built the prototype of the car bearing his name there. But whether John Lauer ever built a complete automobile himself has not been adequately documented, although it seems likely.

LAUGHLIN — In 1916 Homer Laughlin, Jr. built an automobile in Los Angeles, California. Although trade press references occasionally called it a Laughlin, it would appear that Homer preferred his full name being used. Refer to Homer Laughlin.

1917 Laurel, model 35, 5 pass. touring, WLB

LAUREL — Richmond & Anderson, Indiana — (1916-1920) — In July of 1916 the Laurel Motor Car Company of Richmond announced its new automobile, a four-cylinder touring car at $795 which was marketed for the remainder of that year. In 1917 Laurel raised its prices and expanded its line — and in November the company was reorganized and relocated. Laurel Motors Corporation took over the earlier firm and moved to Anderson. The reason for this was the presence in that city of the Roof Auto Specialty Company which was also brought into the fold. Robert M. Roof, who had become famous in Ford speed circles as the designer of a sixteen-valve head for the Model T, had completed his design of an all-new sixteen-valve four-cylinder engine. The Laurel, it was announced in October of 1917, would be fitted with the Roof-designed engine. A new factory was built in Anderson, but the new Laurel was built for a few years only. Some cars carried the Laurel name in script above the louvers on both sides of the hood. After 1920 Laurel devoted its attention exclusively to the very lucrative business of manufacturing accessories to make the Model T go faster.

1916 LAUREL
Model 35 — 4-cyl., 23 hp, 112" wb

	FP	5	4	3	2	1
Touring-5P	795	2300	3300	4600	7500	16,000

1917 LAUREL
Model 35 — 4-cyl., 23 hp, 112" wb

Roadster-4P	895	2500	3500	5000	8500	18,000
Touring-5P	850	2300	3300	4600	7500	16,000
Touring-7P	885	2400	3400	4800	8000	17,000

1918-1920 LAUREL
Model 50 — 4-cyl., 50 hp, 116" wb

Touring-5P	1095	2400	3400	4800	8000	17,000
Roadster-4P	1095	2500	3500	5000	8500	18,000

1908 Lauth-Juergens, touring, NAHC

LAUTH — Chicago, Illinois — (1905)/LAUTH-JUERGENS — (1908-1909) — Jacob Lauth of Chicago owned a tanning company which he found boring. In 1905 he built two gasoline engines, both fours, one an in-line overhead valve, the other a T-head. He fitted them into two demonstrator models and spent the next two years looking for financial backing, which he ultimately found via Theodore Juergens. The new Lauth-Juergens made its debut at the Chicago Automobile Show in December of 1907, and was one of the most powerful newcomers on display. The Lauth engines developed up to 50 hp and, placed in a 118-inch-wheelbase chassis, promised a potent performance. The Lauth-Juergens Motor Car Company failed to live up to its promise in the passenger-car market, however, and soon switched over to the commercial field, moving to Fremont (Ohio) in 1910 and continuing to build trucks there until 1915.

1908-1909 LAUTH
Model D — 4-cyl., 45 hp, 118" wb

Touring-5P	3250	3500	4500	7000	13,000	25,000

Model C — 4-cyl., 50 hp, 118" wb

Tourist-5/7P	2800	3700	4700	7300	13,700	26,000

LA VIGNE — Detroit, Michigan — (1913-1914) — J.P. La Vigne was back. After his failure with the La Petite and the Griswold in the early years of the century, he gave up automobile manufacturing awhile to develop some of the 224 patents — many of them of the Rube Goldberg variety — which would be credited to his name. In 1913, however, he returned to the automobile field with two cars: a standard four called the Traveler and a cyclecar he named for himself. The La Vigne was one of the best of its genre. It had a four-cylinder air-cooled engine built in unit with the sliding

1914 La Vigne, runabout, NAHC

gear transmission, a multiple disc clutch, worm drive to the rear axle, and attractive body styling available as a two-passenger roadster ($425) or cabriolet ($650). Apparently La Vigne had trouble deciding what to call both his car and his company, because brochures variously refer to the JPL of the JPL Cyclecar Company and the La Vigne of the La Vigne Cyclecar Company. Both were in Detroit, and the factory address, at Commonwealth Avenue and Grand Trunk Railroad, was the same. During 1913 the La Vigne suffered, unfairly, from the dismal reputation earned by cyclecars in general. In 1914 the enterprising Mr. La Vigne marketed his cyclecar as a light car under the aegis of the new La Vigne Motor Company. The factory remained the same and so did the fate of the car. During the summer of 1914 the Pullman Motor Company of York, Pennsylvania considered building the La Vigne awhile, but decided against it.

1913-1914 LA VIGNE
Cyclecar — 4-cyl., 15 hp, 96" wb

	FP	5	4	3	2	1
Roadster-2P	425	2000	3000	4200	6500	14,000
Cabriolet-2P	650	1600	2700	3800	5800	12,000

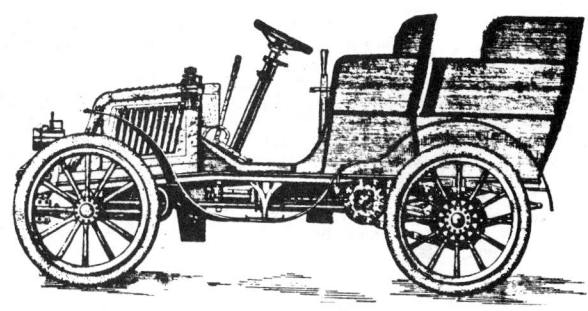

1902 Law, touring, NAHC

LAW — Bristol, Connecticut — (1905-1907) — Frederick A. Law of Hartford built his first gasoline car in 1902 with the financial help of Frederick Newton Manross. Rights to the design were quickly sold to the Electric Vehicle Company, many of the ideas therein subsequently finding their way into various of the Pope motorcars, with Law serving as a consulting engineer for the Pope empire. In October 1904 he again allied himself with Manross whose money saw to the establishment of the Law Auto Manufacturing Company with a capital stock of $50,000. The Law car was a four-cylinder 20 hp machine in the $2000 price range. "Practically all of them will find local owners," *The Motor Age* reported, and undoubtedly most of them did. Production was minimal, and by 1907 the firm slid from the manufacture of automobiles into the manufacture of an automobile's component parts for general trade sale. In 1917 Frederick Law was chief engineer of the Eastern Motors Syndicate which produced the Charter Oak.

LAWRENCE — The Lawrence Stamping Company of Toledo, Ohio built a car called the Odelot in 1915. Refer to Odelot.

LAWRENCE & HOLLISTER — New Haven, Connecticut — (1902) — T.R. Lawrence was a carriage and wagon maker in New Haven in 1902, and Frederick H. Hollister was a machinist. Together they built an automobile that year. Manufacture did not follow.

LAWSON — Though Samuel Lawson designed the engine, the 1895 New York City car into which it was fitted is more properly designated under the firm's name. Refer to Welch & Lawson.
The Lawson Motor Car & Garage Company was organized early in 1910 in Peekskill, New York with a capital stock of $75,000 to manufacture and deal in automobiles. W.A. and M.S. Lawson were the partners involved. Manufacture is doubted.

LAWTER — New Castle, Indiana — (1909) — Two cars were designed by Benjamin Lawter, both with two-cylinder engines, one a 16 hp, the other a 20 hp. The more powerful car on a 94-inch wheelbase, four inches longer than the 16 hp. A multiple disc clutch, three-speed planetary transmission and double chain drive were featured. Lawter made arrangements with the Safety Shredder Company of New Castle to build his cars for him, pending his organization of a company and the securing of his own factory

1909 Lawter, touring, NAHC

site. He went broke before he had a chance to do either. There had been a modest production of Lawter cars at the Safety Shredder factory, however.

1909 LAWTER
Sixteen — 2-cyl., 16 hp, 90" wb

	FP	5	4	3	2	1
Baby Tonneau-4P	950	2200	3200	4400	7000	15,000

Twenty — 2-cyl., 20 hp, 94" wb

	FP	5	4	3	2	1
Touring-5P	1350	2300	3300	4600	7500	16,000

LAYMAN-LOWY — New York, New York — (1916) — "The car will be made in radical design; the axle is to be new, while the transmission will have only five parts," reported *Automobile Trade Journal* in October 1916. "The price of $8000 is set for the chassis alone." M.C. Mayer, Winthrop S. Horton and George B. Rubenstein were the New York businessmen behind the newly incorporated Layman-Lowy Motor Car Company. Layman and Lowy remain a mystery, though presumably the latter was the more significant engineer since a Lowy Patent Corporation was also formed at the same time "to hold the patent rights to the various constructions of the new car." Given its very high price, had the Layman-Lowy ever been marketed, it would doubtless have made news. Since it did not, one might assume this project died on the drawing board or at the prototype stage.

LAZENBY — Early in 1899, Allen Lazenby of Lazenby & Penby in Baltimore, Maryland patented a gasoline motor carriage in which a group of local businessmen headed by James E. Hopper were reported to be interested. Whether the Lazenby car was ever built has not been determined.

L.C.E. — Waterloo, Iowa — (1915-1916) — L.C. Erbes was a very rich man from St. Paul, Minnesota and an automobile enthusiast who had his fingers in a good many pies. He was the financial backer of race driver Bob Burman and the owner of the Peugeot race car that Burman drove to victory all across the country. In October 1913 he purchased the assets of the Clarke-Carter Company which had built the Cutting car in Jackson, Michigan, and consolidated it with his components-producing Bull Moose Company in St. Paul. When the Duesenberg brothers moved their automotive venture to St. Paul in 1914, Erbes was their first landlord and he produced a limited run of race cars for Bob Burman that year too. He decided to manufacture a car bearing his initials as well. The L.C.E. was a four, available as a touring car at $1650, a roadster at $1550, and a gentleman's speedster guaranteed to do 80 mph. For this venture, he allied himself with both Bob Burman and with Walter T. Rice, the importer of Peugeot automobiles in Chicago who was having problems getting deliveries from France because of the war situation in Europe. Although pilot models of the L.C.E. were built in the former Cutting plant in Michigan, production did not begin there, Erbes moving operations instead to Waterloo, Iowa before the end of 1914. There, in the factory of the nearly defunct Mason (the Duesenberg brothers' former home), manufacture began, and the L.C.E. was introduced as a 1915 model. Burman and Rice meantime formed a partnership and established the L.C.E. sales agency in Chicago. Production in Waterloo was hampered almost immediately by materials shortages, and the L.C.E. never did establish a solid footing. Although Erbes had briefly tried before with a commercial delivery called the Van-L, his plan now to build a passenger car called the Van died aborning. The L.C.E. soon followed it. Probably the death of Bob Burman in a race in California in April 1916 dimmed the Erbes' enthusiasm for the L.C.E. In the fall of that year Erbes announced the forthcoming removal of all operations to the Duesenberg plant in St. Paul which the brothers had recently vacated following the relocation of their venture to Elizabeth, New Jersey. Although L.C. Erbes remained in the automobile business, it was now in another area entirely. "New Parts for Orphan Cars," he advertised, servicing owners of Cuttings and Masons, among others. Louis C. Erbes died in St. Paul during the early Twenties.

1915-1916 L.C.E.

	FP	5	4	3	2	1
Touring	1650	2700	3600	5300	8800	19,000
Roadster	1550	2900	3700	5600	9100	20,000
Gentleman's Spdstr.	—	3000	4000	6000	9500	21,000

L.C.S. — Fort Wayne, Indiana — (1910) — Charles La Due, J.M. Carmer and C.C. Snyder were the people behind the L.C.S. Motor Company which was organized in the late fall of 1910. Previously each had worked in New York as agents for what was described as "three makes of unlicensed cars." Unlicensed cars during this period were those not being built under Selden Patent. The L.C.S. was to be a 40 hp $1560 car built in the partners' new factory in Fort Wayne. The evidence is that this project did not proceed beyond a prototype. Ironically, if it had, there would have been no necessity for La Due, Carmer and Snyder to apply for a license for their L.C.S. In January 1911 a court decision rendered the Selden Patent unenforceable.

1928 L & E, prototype, KM

L & E — Los Angeles, California — (1924-1934) — Lundelius & Eccleston of Los Angeles formed their partnership in 1922, introduced their first car in 1924, built six more in the next eight years, and never did get into production. The L & E was promoted as the "car without axles." "Four transverse springs are used at both front and rear to support the wheels," noted *MoToR*. "Each rear wheel is driven by a short shaft having two universal joints, the shaft connecting with a bevel gear and differential unit hung from cross members on the frame." Initially, and at least officially, manufacture was contemplated. During the spring of 1924 the car was heavily promoted in Long Beach, and during its ten-day exhibition in that city its story was told extensively in news columns and advertisements, including announcement of a proposed "giant" factory in Long Beach, and a blurb touting the honesty and virtue of the promoters. The L & E on dis-

1931 L & E, prototype, MVMA

play was a touring car with a six-cylinder Franklin air-cooled engine set in a 132-inch wheelbase chassis. None of the ensuing cars looked quite like it, or like each other for that matter. It would appear that Lundelius & Eccleston, following their failure to attract sufficient investors in Long Beach to embark upon manufacture, decided to take a different tack. The prototypes which followed were geared more to selling the axleless concept than the car, and thus tended to resemble the product of whatever manufacturer L & E was wooing at the time. One resembled a Cadillac, another was outright Studebaker, yet another Ford based. The penultimate L & E, announced in October of 1931, was a Franklin-ish sedan with wire wheels, a Lycoming eight-cylinder engine, L & E hubcaps and, of course, no axles. Lundelius & Eccleston produced their last automobile in 1934 but remained in business with commercial chassis and miscellaneous design work until World War II. Of the L & E cars produced, the first Franklin-based car of 1924 is known to exist.

LEACH STEAM — Everett, Massachusetts — (1899-1901) — The Leach Motor Vehicle Company was the title selected by John M. Leach in 1899 when he chose to turn his Everett Cycle Company automotive. The Leach car was both described in the news columns and advertised in the trade press from October through December of 1899. It was a steamer built on a frame of steel tubing with suspension by three elliptical springs. The boiler was fed automatically, and the fuel was gasoline, "utilized in a burner that is provided with safety attachments and automatic diaphram." The Leach was a runabout providing accommodations for either two or four passengers. In October of 1900 announcement was made of the formal organization of the Leach Motor Vehicle Company, its capitalization said to be $50,000, which clearly proved illusory. In January of 1901 John Leach announced to the trade press that "a New York capitalist who undertook to raise funds failed to connect, and the works have been closed until the necessary capital can be secured." It never was.

816

1900 Leach Steam Carriage, MVMA

LEACH — Lima, Ohio — (1909) — In early fall of 1909, Charles Leach announced from Lima his organization of the Leach Automobile Company and his intention to build an air-cooled two-cylinder motorcar. He indicated at the time that he might locate his factory in Columbus. No Leach car arrived on the market in either Lima or Columbus. Conceivably, a prototype might have been completed, however.

1922 Leach, all-weather touring, WLB

LEACH — Los Angeles, California — (1920-1923) — Martin Andrew Leach was a native of Detroit who propelled himself into the automobile field on the West Coast by serving as front man for the Leach Motor Car Company, a wholesale/retail dealership wholly owned by an Oklahoma oilman. That was in late 1916. Within two years Leach was in the sideline business of customizing cars for the Hollywood community, and the year following that he became a bona fide manufacturer after leaving the Oklahoma oilman's venture which had been reorganized and renamed the Security Motor Corporation. The Leach Biltwell Motor Company was a million-dollar organization established during the fall of 1919 by Leach in association with Leon G. Martin. By December the company announced its purchase, for $250,000, of the former Republic Truck Company plant in Los Angeles and introduced its Leach Power Plus Six motorcar. Leach (occasionally referred to as Leach-Biltwell) automobiles were expensive, with price tags beginning about $5000. Continental engines were used throughout, though a new powerplant was added in mid-1921 when Leach Biltwell was reorganized and recapitalized at $5 million following the acquisition of the Miller Engine and Foundry Works of Los Angeles. Harry A. Miller now became a director and vice-president of the new concern, as well as the designer of its new six-cylinder 100 hp engines. These featured overhead valves and an overhead cam, in addition to early use of a counterbalanced crankshaft. Leach popularized the California top (historically, America's first "hardtop"), and in 1923 introduced a companion car called the California. This was a smaller four to complement the bigger Leach six, its 50 hp engine also designed by Miller. By now, however, Leach Biltwell was in serious financial trouble. The Leach cars introduced for 1923 were simply the 1922 models with a thousand dollars slashed off their price tags. Operations moved from 4800 S. Santa Fe Avenue to a smaller facility at 112 West 9th Street. Production of the expensive Leach, which had been a favorite among silent film folk, was discontinued shortly thereafter. Total Leach output may have been as high as several hundred cars. The California seems to have continued in manufacture into 1925.

1920 LEACH
Series 20 — 6-cyl., 60 hp, 126-1/2" wb

	FP	5	4	3	2	1
Touring-5P	5200	4000	5000	8000	15,000	28,000
Touring-7P	5950	4200	5200	8400	15,700	29,000

1921 LEACH
Series 20 — 6-cyl., 60 hp, 128" wb

	FP	5	4	3	2	1
Model A Tour.-5P	5200	4000	5000	8000	15,000	28,000
Model B Tour.-7P	5700	4200	5200	8400	15,700	29,000
Model C Rdstr.-3P	5700	4300	5400	8700	16,500	30,000

1922 LEACH
Leach Six — 6-cyl., 100 hp, 134" wb

	FP	5	4	3	2	1
Touring-5P	6500	4200	5200	8400	15,700	29,000
Touring-7P	6500	4300	5400	8700	16,500	30,000
Roadster-3P	6500	4400	5600	9200	17,300	31,000
Sport-4P	6500	4500	5800	9500	18,000	32,000
Coupette-4P	6500	2700	3600	5300	8800	19,000

1923 LEACH
Leach Six — 6-cyl., 100 hp, 134" wb

	FP	5	4	3	2	1
Touring-5P	5500	4200	5200	8400	15,700	29,000
Touring-7P	5500	4300	5400	8700	16,500	30,000
Roadster-3P	5500	4400	5600	9200	17,300	31,000
Sport-4P	5500	4500	5800	9500	18,000	32,000
Coupette-4P	5500	2700	3600	5300	8800	19,000
California Four prototype	—	—	—	—	—	—

LEADER — The Leader Automobile Company of 2442 Lisbon Avenue in Milwaukee, Wisconsin was indicated as the manufacturer of a gasoline automobile in the January 1906 edition of *Cycle and Automobile Trade Journal*. Further details are lacking.

The Leader Manufacturing Company was organized during the spring of 1908 with a $150,000 capital stock for the manufacture of automobiles in St. Louis, Missouri. Incorporators were Frank D. Gildersleeve, Augustus Ross, John E. Tackabury and Henry W. Allen. Manufacture is doubted.

1905 Leader, model B, runabout, HAC

LEADER — McCordsville, Indiana — (1905-1907)/Knightstown, Indiana — (1907-1912) — There are several curiosities about the Leader of Indiana. First, it was a gasoline car built by the Columbia Electric Company. (Various trade press references indicate a change of the firm's name to Leader Manufacturing Company, but this does not appear to have happened; Indiana newspaper advertisements from as late as 1911 refer to the Columbia Electric Company.) Second, although through the years a veritable plethora of Indiana towns were indicated as manufacturing sites for the Leader, the car was actually built in only two: McCordsville from 1905 through 1906, with the move to Knightstown occuring in early 1907 following the securing of expanded facilities and fresh capital there. Prior to making the Leader automobile, Columbia Electric manufactured telephones. The driving force behind the Leader automobile was Luther Frost, an engineering graduate of Purdue University. Columbia Electric management changed hands several times during the Leader's lifetime, most significantly in mid-1909 when Luther Frost, together with his brother Earl, and Alonzo Thomas, bought complete control from Columbia Electric owner Moses Vanderbark. Previous Leaders had been small two-cylinder

1906 Leader, model B, touring, HAC

planetary-transmission cars exclusively, the new Leader leaders introduced fours with more horsepower and sliding gear transmissions. Production was modest but ever on the rise, from twenty-five in 1905 to a 100-unit-per-year average during the early years to about three times that by 1911. Contemporary accounts indicate the Leader was a fine and sturdy automobile. "The Honest Built Car" was an early slogan, later changed to the grammatically correct "Honestly Built." Ironically, the reason for the Leader's demise was largely due to the bad health of Luther Frost. His respiratory problems were aggravated by the fumes and dust in his automobile factory. When Luther Frost was forced to leave the company, the Leader did not long survive. Sometime during 1912 the factory was shut down.

1905 LEADER
Model B — 2-cyl., 16 hp, 84" wb

	FP	5	4	3	2	1
Runabout	800	1800	2800	4000	6200	13,000

1906 LEADER
Model B — 2-cyl., 16 hp, 84" wb

	FP	5	4	3	2	1
Runabout	800	1800	2800	4000	6200	13,000

Model B — 2-cyl., 18 hp, 84" wb

Touring	1000	2000	3000	4200	6500	14,000

1907 Leader, model B, runabout, HAC

1907-1909 LEADER
Model B — 2-cyl., 16 hp, 84" wb

Runabout	850	2300	3300	4600	7500	16,000

Model C — 2-cyl., 16 hp, 90" wb

Touring-4P	1000	2400	3400	4800	8000	17,000

Model D — 2-cyl., 20 hp, 90" wb

Touring-4P	1050	2500	3500	5000	8500	18,000

1910 Leader, model L-30, touring, NAHC

1910 LEADER
Model E — 2-cyl., 20 hp, 98" wb

Touring-4P	850	2300	3300	4600	7500	16,000

Model L-30 — 4-cyl., 30/35 hp, 107" wb

Touring-5P	1250	2400	3400	4800	8000	17,000

1911 Leader, model R-35, touring, HAC

1911 LEADER
Model R-35 — 4-cyl., 40 hp, 116" wb

	FP	5	4	3	2	1
Demi-Torpedo-4P	1625	2300	3300	4600	7500	16,000
Touring-5P	1825	2400	3400	4800	8000	17,000

1912 LEADER
Model R-35 — 4-cyl., 30/35 hp, 116" wb

Semi-Torpedo	1600	2300	3300	4600	7500	16,000

Model 40 — 4-cyl., 40 hp, 124" wb

Four-Door Touring	1800	2400	3400	4800	8000	17,000

LEAR — From 1904-1909 the Oscar Lear Automobile Company of Columbus, Ohio produced a car called the Frayer-Miller. Refer to Frayer-Miller.

LEBANON — During the summer of 1905 the Lebanon Motor Works superseded the Upton Motor Company of Lebanon, Pennsylvania. The car, which was produced into 1907, continued to be designated an Upton, however. Refer to Upton.

LEBLANC — The Leblanc Carburetor Company was organized in Trenton, New Jersey during the spring of 1907 with a capital stock of $2000 to manufacture carburetors, motor cars and motor boats. J. Casraight and Jean Leblanc of Guttenburg, New York, and Henry Cryder of New York City, were the incorporators. Manufacture of a car is doubted.

1897 Leck, gasoline wagon, JHV

LECK — Santa Ana, California — (1897) — Probably the automobile built by John Leck was the first to travel the roads of Orange County. It did so at a speed of approximately five miles an hour. Leck arrived at his car by the simple expedient of fitting a one-cylinder stationary engine to an ordinary wagon. Primitive it was. Chain and sprocket carried power to one rear wheel, and a disc clutch was a later addition. Apparently the Leck remained the only automobile in Santa Ana until 1902, when its inventor upgraded to a curved dash Oldsmobile. Subsequently, Leck turned his talents to the production of self-powered bean harvesters which he sold to growers in the area.

LECKIE — The firm of James Leckie & Son was organized in Camden, New Jersey during the summer of 1908 with a capital stock of $250,000 to "manufacture gas and gasoline engines, automobiles and bakers' machines." Incorporators were F.R. Hansell, John A. MacPeak and George H.B. Martin. Manufacture of a car is doubted.

1906 Lecklider, runabout, WLB

LECKLIDER — Toledo, Ohio — (1902, 1906) — A.E. Lecklider was a plumber from Toledo who began building his first car in 1898, a spare-time project he completed in 1902. "It did the business," reported *The Motor Way* in 1906, "but a year later the little car met the fate of a fire which completely annihilated the machine." Thereafter, Lecklider built another, similar to it but improved. Its engine was a 6 hp gasoline-powered one-lunger made of cast iron, as were all other mechanical parts. The cooling was thermo-syphon, the transmission a two-speed sliding gear, the wheelbase 40 inches, the tread 38 inches. "A horse will cost at least $15 a month for its keep, while, counting my time at 50 cents an hour, my motor wagon doesn't cost me an average of more than $2 a month," boasted A.E. Lecklider. "Outside of the cost of replacing a 'rattled out' bolt, now and then, I have not paid out one cent for repairs."

LE COMPTE — New York, New York — (1913-1914) — George W. Le Compte was a mechanical engineer with offices at 65 Murray Street in Lower Manhattan. In 1913 he designed a cyclecar and interested enough people on Wall Street — Lee S. Higgins, H.R. Buckingham and Godfrey Goldmark among them — to back him in the incorporation, with a capital stock of $60,000 of the Le Compte Cycle Car Corporation. Either he or his backers had quick second thoughts, however, and the car was never put into production. The Le Compte company rechanneled its efforts into the manufacture of automobile hardware and later into the production of accessories for the lucrative Model T Ford market.

LEE — An automobile called the Lee has been indicated on various car rosters as being built in 1910 by the Diamond Manufacturing Company of Detroit, Michigan. This has not been documented. The Diamond company manufactured plumbing supplies, automobile parts, and copper and brass specialities at its factory on Summit Avenue north of West Jefferson in Detroit. Dwight B. Lee was Diamond's general manager, and no doubt the man behind the car. Most probably it was built for Lee's personal use; certainly it was not put into manufacture.

LEE & LARNED — Despite appearances on rosters of American-built cars, Lee & Larned was never a passenger automobile producer, though the firm is well known historically for having built three self-propelled steam fire engines during the Civil War period.

LEE & PORTER — In October of 1903 S.E. Lee and H.H. Porter announced their incorporation of the Lee & Porter Manufacturing Company, with headquarters in Dowagiac, factory in Buchanan, where the firm owned a power dam. Capitalization of this Michigan company was $200,000, and the stated purpose was the manufacture of automobiles, or so was reported in the trade press. In November the partners advised that the report was "due to a misunderstanding," and instead of automobiles their new firm would engage in the manufacture of axles. Apparently the writing of concise and correct press releases was somewhat beyond the ken of this duo, or at least legible ones. Earlier releases had indicated the company's name as Lee & Perkins.

LEECH — The Leech Automobile Company was organized in Trenton, New Jersey during the fall of 1909 with a capital stock of $500,000 for the manufacture of automobiles. Behind this venture were C.A. Bliss of Toledo, Ohio; J.P. Le Fevre of Dover, Delaware; C.H. Le Fevre of Smyrna, Delaware. Manufacture is doubted.

LEEPER — The Leeper Automobile Company was organized during the summer of 1911 in St. Louis, Missouri with a capital stock of $2000 to manufacture and deal in motor cars. Oscar W. Schmidt spearheaded this venture. Manufacture is doubted.

LEGGETT — The Leggett Carriage Company of Syracuse, New York was involved in the building of two automobiles at the turn of the century. Refer to De Long and Iroquois.

LEHNERT — E.R. and W. Lehnert were Lehnert & Son at 221 North Street in Baltimore, Maryland. From approximately 1908-1910, they indicated themselves to be builders of "custom to order" automobiles. Further details are lacking.

LEHR — Fremont, Ohio — (1905-1908) — The Lehr Agricultural Company, founded by Nicholas P. and Joseph W. Lehr in 1873, was one of Fremont's most important and prosperous manufacturing firms at the turn of the century. In the October 27th, 1905 edition of the *Fremont Weekly Messenger,* the company announced its plans to enter the automobile industry with manufacture of gasoline touring cars of 20 to 45 hp. "E. Williams of Toledo has charge of the automobile department and he is at present making patterns for engines and various parts of the machines they will turn out," the newspaper revealed, adding, "The Lehr company show that they have faith in Fremont by starting this new industry here without asking for a bonus which so many factories are securing for locating their plants. Just a few days ago an automobile factory was secured for Fostoria but the citizens had to subscribe for $25,000 of the $100,000 of stock in the concern." Despite the integrity of their plans, it does not appear the Lehrs succeeded in their automotive venture, at least beyond the building of pilot models. Certainly the firm did not begin manufacture in 1905. In 1908 the Lehr Agricultural Company again announced its plans to enter the automobile field — but again only prototypes resulted. There was never any sustained manufacture of a Lehr car.

LEICHER — The Leicher Brothers of Lu Verne, Iowa announced their new automobile factory in December of 1903. "Their plan is to buy the parts and assemble them," *The Motor Age* reported. "They believe they can make a more suitable machine for the western country at a lower price than eastern manufacturers can furnish them." Whether they were able to do it is not known.

LEIGHTON — Syracuse, New York — (1902)/Brockton, Massachusetts — (1910) — In 1902 H.J. Leighton, a marine engine builder from Syracuse, announced that he was building an experimental automobile using a three-cylinder two-stroke 8 hp engine of his own design. "If it is a success he may go into the business," *The Automobile and Motor Review* reported that June. "Mr. Leighton has every facility for making a good machine and has had many years of experience in the marine motor line." No further word was heard from H.J. Leighton, but quite possibly he was the Leighton involved in the establishment seven years later in Brockton, Massachusetts of a garage which traded under the name of Leighton Auto Company and which in 1910 purportedly built a few automobiles to custom order.

LEIST — Michigan City, Indiana — (1911) — The Leist Automobile Manufacturing Company of Michigan City was listed as an automobile producer in the Ware yearbook of the industry for 1911. No doubt, Charles Leist had wonderful plans for a healthy production, but like so many small-town builders, he was not able to manage it. Family descendants recall that he built at least one car, and perhaps a few more.

1902 LeJeal Steamer, runabout, NAHC

LeJEAL — Erie, Pennsylvania — (1900-1906) — The LeJeal Cycle & Mobile Works was located at 1721 Sassafras Street in Erie. Charles H. LeJeal was the young man behind the operation, and he experimented through the years with electric, steam and gasoline power. At the age of sixteen, he devised a 110 volt electric motor which he sold locally to a number of businesses, including the beauty parlor where it generated heat for the hair dryers. Prior to the turn of the century he assisted Henry Hagenlocher in building his automobile. His own first car was a steamer that he finished in 1900 and drove to Buffalo for the Pan American Exposition that year. From 1902 to 1905 he built three air-cooled four-cylinder runabouts one of which he kept for himself (driving it until 1921); the other two he sold for $750 apiece. Although he produced yet another runabout in 1906, he never proceeded into manufacture. He became very well known in Erie, however, as the first Bosch magneto repairman in town and also for his deft servicing of automotive speedometers. The outsized speedometer in the window of his LeJeal's Automotive Service, as his company later was named, had become a landmark in Erie by the 1950's. At that time, Charles LeJeal was also a member of the Erie Philharmonic Orchestra.

1898 Lemp Electric, HS

819

LEMP ELECTRIC — Lynn, Massachusetts — (1897 et seq.) — Hermann Lemp of Lynn was a pioneer in the electric car field who began experimenting in the mid-1890's and to whom by 1900 the U.S. Patent Office had granted no fewer than thirteen patents. Lemp assigned most of his patents to his employer, the General Electric Company which built at least four experimental electrics to Lemp's designs prior to 1900, one of them demonstrated in Chicago that year. A subsequent Lemp patent from 1905 and assigned to General Electric was for a gasoline-electric car, Lemp's developments in this area also having found their way into experimental vehicles produced by General Electric after the turn of the century.

1904 Lenawee, tonneau, WLB

LENAWEE — Adrian, Michigan — (1904) — The Lenawee was the successor to the Murray and was built by the Church Manufacturing Company of Adrian, Lenawee County, Michigan. A single-cylinder five-passenger $1000 touring car, it was designed by Andrew Bachle, a gasoline engine builder from Detroit. The Lenawee was produced only in 1904, with a total of about fifteen built, one of which remains extant.

1909 Lende, 30 hp, touring, NAHC

LENDE — Granite Falls, Minnesota — (1902-1909) — Olaus Lende had emigrated to the United States as a teenager with his parents, the family settling in the farming country of Minnesota. Young Olaus' first work was as a smithy for S. Olander, and in June 1901 he associated himself with John Iverson in the Iverson foundry in Granite Falls. He became interested in automobiles when he was called upon to repair an aborted effort in automobile design that had been brought to him by its owner. His own first car was a two-cylinder chain-drive tourer he nicknamed "Betsey." After selling "Betsey" to Ole Swenson, a Granite Falls painter, he built two more cars similar to it, and sold them readily as well. Soon thereafter he completed his design of a four-cylinder air-cooled engine which featured an ignition system with a single coil (rather than the usual four) and distributor. He sold a number of cars with this engine as well. His use of a generator to charge a storage battery for ignition and lights was progressive. A Lende won its first race at the Yellow Medicine County Fair at Canby in 1908, and a Lende car was sold as far away as Watertown, South Dakota. In 1907 Olaus Lende made an attempt to launch himself into serious manufacture, securing an office in Minneapolis and promoting the formation of the Lende Automobile Manufacturing Company. He did receive some national press attention with announcement of the Lende for 1909, a four-cylinder 30 hp, shaft-drive, planetary-transmission touring car that he placed on the market for $1800. But his attempt to begin an automobile company failed, and ultimately Lende returned to his machine work and establishing a dealership to handle, variously, the Studebaker, Star and Saxon automobiles. Total Lende production was seventeen cars, and each of them had been custom-built to individual customer order.

LENGERT — In 1896 the Lengert Company of Philadelphia acquired a license to manufacture the electric car designed by Charles Barrows which had been produced in New York City beginning the year previous. Refer to Barrows Electric.

LENOX — The Lenox Motor Car Company was organized in Newark, New Jersey late in 1911 with a capital stock of $25,000 for the manufacture of automobiles and accessories. Incorporators were L. Lippman, J.M. Shreffler, M. Lippman and C. Shreffler. Manufacture of a car is doubted.

1912 Lenox, model D, speedster, WLB

LENOX — Jamaica Plain, et al., Massachusetts — (1911-1917) — The Lenox Motor Car Company succeeded the Martell Motor Car Company which had spent two years trying to get organized in Jamaica Plain and never succeeding. The first Lenox, a 27 hp four, was introduced at the Boston Automobile Show in early 1911. It was designed by Chester T. Bates, who had designed the Morse the year previous. Production began in Jamaica Plain, but almost immediately the company began scouting other factory sites. "The Only Car Made in Boston" became a Lenox slogan, but that was hedging the truth. A plant in that city was secured later in 1911, but by the fall of 1912 it was turned over to service functions only when a factory in Hyde Park became available. In 1913 a 40 hp four and a 60 hp six made up the Lenox line, the cars being built in both Jamaica Plain and Hyde Park. A move to Lawrence followed in 1915 as a result of the Lenox decision to enter the commercial vehicle field. By now Daniel N. Emerson of the Emerson Shoe Company was at the helm of the Lenox enterprise. Fall River was also purported to be the site of yet another Lenox factory. A three-ton truck was introduced for the 1916 model year, and tractors were added to the line by October. Conceivably, the decision to enter the commercial vehicle field may have been the Lenox car's undoing. A good deal of money was spent tooling up for trucks and tractors, and soon there was no money left at all. Although Lenox bravely announced a Model 6-33 touring car to sell for $2650 for the 1918 model year, that was cockeyed optimism pure and simple. The Lenox assembly line had shut down by January of 1917, and it was never started up again. Ajax Motors Corporation, which was organized in Boston in 1920 for the manufacture of both cars and trucks, may have been a postwar attempt to revive the business.

1911-1912 LENOX
Four — 4-cyl., 27 hp, 114" wb

	FP	5	4	3	2	1
Model A Roadster-2P	1800	2500	3500	5000	8500	18,000
Model A Roadster-4P	1800	2600	3600	5200	8700	18,500
Model A Touring-5P	1800	2400	3400	4800	8000	17,000
Model D Speedster	1800	2700	3600	5300	8800	19,000
Model E Limousine	2750	2300	3300	4600	7500	16,000

1913 Lenox, model 4-40, touring, HAC

1913 LENOX
Model 4-40 — 4-cyl., 40 hp, 118" wb

Runabout-2P	2000	2400	3400	4800	8000	17,000
Touring-5P	2000	2500	3500	5000	8500	18,000
Speedster-2P	2100	2900	3700	5600	9100	20,000
Limousine-5P	3250	2400	3400	4800	8000	17,000

Model 6-60 — 6-cyl., 60 hp, 130" wb

Touring-7P	2750	4000	5000	8000	15,000	28,000
Limousine-7P	4050	2900	3700	5600	9100	20,000

1914 Lenox, model 4-40, speed car, HAC

1914 LENOX
Model 4-40 — 4-cyl., 40 hp, 118" wb

	FP	5	4	3	2	1
Model A Touring-5P	2000	2700	3600	5300	8800	19,000
Model C Roadster	2000	3100	4200	6300	10,500	22,000
Model D Speed Car	2000	3200	4300	6500	11,000	23,000
Model B Touring-4P	2100	3000	4000	6000	9500	21,000

Model 6-60 — 6-cyl., 60 hp, 130" wb

	FP	5	4	3	2	1
Model MC Touring-7P	2750	4000	5000	8000	15,000	28,000
Model NC Limousine-7P	4050	2900	3700	5600	9100	20,000
Model AC Touring-5P	2000	4200	5200	8400	15,700	29,000
Model DC Rds.-2/3/4P	2000	4500	5800	9500	18,000	32,000
Model EC Torp. Speed Car-2P	2100	4400	5600	9200	17,300	31,000
Model FC Limousine-5P	3300	2900	3700	5600	9100	20,000
Model HC Touring-4P	2000	3100	4200	6300	10,500	22,000

1915 LENOX
Four — 4-cyl., 40 hp, 118" wb

	FP	5	4	3	2	1
Touring-5P	2000	3100	4200	6300	10,500	22,000

Six — 6-cyl., 50 hp, 130" wb

	FP	5	4	3	2	1
Touring-5P	2465	3700	4700	7300	13,700	26,000

1916-1917 LENOX
Four — 4-cyl., 50 hp, 118" wb

	FP	5	4	3	2	1
Model D Speed Car	2000	4000	5000	8000	15,000	28,000

Six — 6-cyl., 130" wb

	FP	5	4	3	2	1
Model O Touring-5P (50 hp)	1965	3500	4500	7000	13,000	25,000
Model M Touring-7P (60 hp)	2465	3700	4700	7300	13,700	26,000

LENOX — New York, New York — (1920) — In October of 1920 Arthur G. Delamater announced that he had designed a four-cylinder car on a 120-inch wheelbase which he intended to market as the Lenox for export only. His intentions did not become reality. Possibly a prototype was built.

LENOX ELECTRIC — Lenox Electric was the alternative name decided upon by Hiram Percy Maxim and T.W. Goodridge for the electric car they planned to build in Hartford, Connecticut in 1907. Refer to Maxim-Goodridge Electric.

1923 Leon Rubay, all-weather touring, WLB

LEON RUBAY — Cleveland, Ohio — (1923) — Leon Rubay was a Parisian who emigrated to this country shortly after the turn of the century. Initially he worked in Manhattan for the French automobile accessory firm of J. La Costa et Cie, but by 1908 he had involved himself with several New York custom coachbuilders, Rothschild and Holbook among them. In 1915 he was enticed to Cleveland by the White Company to be its pleasure vehicle department's general manager. The following year Leon Rubay launched himself into his own business, that of manufacturing high-class coachwork. His former employer was among his clients, as was H.A. Lozier: Rubay bodies graced both White and HAL-Twelve chassis. Following the First World War, Rubay coachwork appeared on both Franklins and Duesenbergs — as well as a line of automobiles designed and marketed under the Leon Rubay name. These were exceptionally fine cars. The Rubay engine — a modification of the Belgian SAVA — was designed by A.M. Dean, former chief engineer for Templar. A small overhead cam four, it displaced 97.5 cubic inches and developed 36 hp at 3000 rpm. Four wheel brakes were a progressive feature. Paul Bastien had assisted in overall design. Five closed body styles were offered on a common 118-inch wheelbase, with price tags in the $5000 range. The Leon Rubay was introduced in December of 1922 and was produced for less than a year. Total output was less than 75 cars. Undoubtedly, the Leon Rubay's principal problem was its compact and efficient sophistication. Generally speaking, in those days anyone paying $5000 for a car wanted more cylinders, more cubic inches, more horsepower and more wheelbase. Contributing to the car's demise as well was the decision of Leon Rubay later in 1923 to retire and return to France. In January 1924 the Rubay Company real estate was purchased by Baker-Raulang.

1923 LEON RUBAY
Four — 32 hp, 118" wb

	FP	5	4	3	2	1
Berlin	5300	3300	4400	6700	12,000	24,000
Sedan	5200	2500	3500	5000	8500	18,000
Coupe	5100	2900	3700	5600	9100	20,000
Town Car	5250	3100	4200	6300	10,500	22,000
Cabriolet	5250	3500	4500	7000	13,000	25,000

LEPPO — The Leppo Brothers of Belleville, Ohio announced their entry in the Chicago Times-Herald Contest of 1895, but were a no-show at the starting line. Whether they ever completed their car has not been documented.

LeROUX — A steam car called the LeRoux has been indicated on various car rosters as being built by the Marquette Motor Sales Company of Chicago, Illinois in 1918. This has not been documented. No company of that name is listed in Chicago city directories of this period.

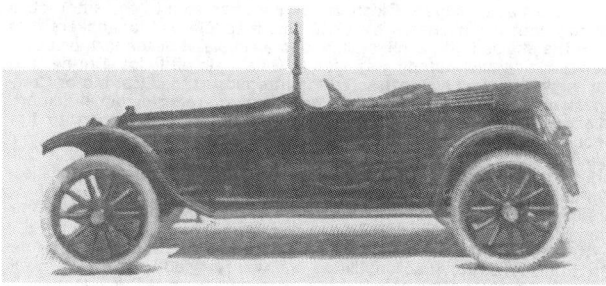

1916 Lescina, model A, utility roadster, WLB

LESCINA — Newark, New Jersey — (1916) — The Lescina Automobile Company obviously believed in the theory of there being safety in numbers. At the New York Automobile Show at the Grand Central Palace in January 1916, the company exhibited several of its new cars and promised to be in production soon on a total of ten different body types on three different chassis. The show cars had been built in Chicago, but Lescina's new factory in Newark, New Jersey was all set to go, with an additional assembling plant to be set up at 76th and Wallace in the Windy City. The cars would be built of standard components throughout, with quantity manufacture the key to keeping prices down. Lescina was at the time in the process of establishing a countrywide dealership network, offering as enticement to pay all freight costs for deliveries to dealers. What went wrong is not known, but something did, and quickly. The Lescina Automobile Company did not last out the year. How many cars were produced is a mystery as well. Quite possibly the six-cylinder chassis never made it to the assembly line at all, though Lescina did exhibit one of the sixes at Grand Central Palace. The firm's demise was recorded in January 1917.

1916 LESCINA
Model V — 6-cyl., 125" wb

	FP	5	4	3	2	1
Model E Touring-7P	1288	3700	4700	7300	13,700	26,000
Model I Touring-7P	—	3900	4800	7700	14,300	27,000

Model W — 4-cyl., 30 hp, 112" wb

	FP	5	4	3	2	1
Model C Cabriolet	1288	3300	4400	6700	12,000	24,000
Model D Touring-5P	888	3500	4500	7000	13,000	25,000
Model F Roadster DeLuxe	888	3700	4700	7300	13,700	26,000
Model G Combination Express Car	888	2900	3700	5600	9100	20,000
Model H Delivery DeLuxe	990	2500	3500	5000	8500	18,000
Model J Cloverleaf Rds.	888	2700	3600	5300	8800	19,000

Model X — 4-cyl., 25 hp, 106" wb

	FP	5	4	3	2	1
Model A Utility Roadster	555	3000	4000	6000	9500	21,000
Model B Touring-5P	666	2900	3700	5600	9100	20,000

LESLIE — The Leslie Motor Car Company of Detroit, Michigan has been indicated on various car rosters as an automobile manufacturer in 1916. No evidence of this has been discovered. Detroit city directories of this period do not include a Leslie company.

L'ESPERANCE — The L'Esperance Motor Car Company was organized in Detroit, Michigan during the summer of 1911 with $10,000 capital stock to manufacture and deal in automobiles. Manufacture is doubted.

LESTER — Newton, Kansas — (1901) — L.P. Lester of Newton built himself an automobile in 1901 the details of which are lacking although obviously Lester had great faith in the machine. *The Motor Age* reported in July that year that Lester was enroute to Walla Walla, Washington in his car. "When last heard from he was progressing without trouble," the magazine advised.

1930 Lever (Elcar), roadster, HAC

LEVER — Elkhart, Indiana — (1930)/Hartford, Wisconsin — (1930-1933) — The word Lever described the engine: an otherwise standard internal combustion unit to which an oscillating lever was interposed between piston and crankshaft. It was the idea of a Southern minister named Alvah A. Powell, who spent most of the Twenties variously in Oak Park, Illinois and Quapaw, Oklahoma trying to break into the automobile industry with it. The result by 1930 was a couple of Studebakers into which the engine had been installed, and a couple of dozen further Lever engines which saw pumping service in Oklahoma oil fields. During that year, however, the Lever attracted the attention of the Elcar Motor Company, which was in the throes of proceeding into receivership in Elkhart, Indiana. This, the Elcar people thought, might be their salvation. In July announcement was made that Lever Motors Corporation, an independent organization but allied to Elcar, would give up its general offices in Oak Park and its plant in Quapaw, and move to Elkhart. There several Elcar 8-95 chassis were transformed with six-cylinder Lever engines, one of the cars being shown at the 1930 New York Automobile Show. But then the Elcar company chose to cast its fading fortunes with Harry Wahl and a revival of the Mercer instead, which left Lever Motors Corporation homeless, so it moved to Wheaton, Illinois and was restyled as the A.L. Powell Power Company, a designation it had enjoyed earlier in the Twenties. In 1933 Kissel Industries (as the Kissel Motor Car Company had been designated following bankruptcy) beckoned from Hartford, Wisconsin. Kissel built several Lever engines — straight eights this time for which 110 bph was claimed — and tested them in two different Kissel chassis. An attempt was made to install the Lever in a front-drive Ruxton chassis, Kissel having been involved with that car venture as well during its early stages, but it just didn't work. Both the Elcar and the Kissel periods of the Lever project resulted in promotion or advertising indicating the forthcoming production of Lever-engined cars. But no more than the aforementioned prototypes ever were built. Thereafter the Lever venture was revised into development of stationary engines principally, though not very successfully; after the expenditure of more than two million dollars, the Lever project was ultimately abandoned in the early Fifties in Addison, Illinois, not far from Wheaton.

LEVY — The Levi (sic) electric is being built by S.M. Levy (sic) of Cleveland, Ohio and the output will be handled by the Squires Company," reported *Motor Vehicle Review* during the summer of 1901. Further word of the Levi from Levy has not been discovered.

The James Levy Company was organized with a capital stock of $35,000 during the fall of 1907 to manufacture and deal in automobiles in Chicago, Illinois. Eugene H. Garnett, Clarence Morse and John F. Finnerty, Jr. were the incorporators. Manufacture is doubted.

LEWIS — I.H. Lewis built an automobile called the Superior in Cleveland, Ohio in 1902. Refer to Superior.

Although Paul M. Lewis of Denver, Colorado was the man with the idea, he always referred to his 1937 automobile as simply the Aeromobile and not the Lewis Aeromobile. Refer to Aeromobile.

Although Ralph Lewis was the designer of the car built between 1908 and 1911 in Muncie and Anderson, Indiana, it was marketed only as the Rider-Lewis, George D. Rider having put up most of the money for its manufacture. Refer to Rider-Lewis.

The Lewis Automobile Company was organized in New York City during the spring of 1903 with a capital stock of $1000 to manufacture "automobiles and self-propelling vehicles." Directors were Lewis M. Bloomingdale and Leo Jacobson of Manhattan, and Charles D. Clark of Brooklyn. Manufacture is doubted.

The Lewis Motor & Engineering Company was a $200,000 Delaware incorporation from early 1913 for the manufacture of automobiles and parts. G.D. Hopkins, G.W. Dillman and S.M. Crawl were the incorporators. Manufacture of a car is doubted.

The Lewis Power Company was organized in New York City with a capital stock of $40,000 during the summer of 1906 for the manufacture of automobiles and railroad cars. Incorporators were H. Oppenheim, F. Kopper, Jr., E.A. Weed and F.P.V. Lewis. Manufacture of an automobile is doubted.

The Lewis Spring & Axle Company produced a car called the Hollier in Jackson and Chelsea, Michigan from 1915-1921. Refer to Hollier.

The Lewis Strong Supply Company was organized in New York City during the spring of 1908 with a capital stock of $50,000 to "manufacture cars, carriages, wagons and boats." Incorporators were H.H. Pennock, Joseph Brewster and R.M. Farris. Manufacture of an automobile is doubted.

1899 Lewis, NAHC

1894 Lewis, NAHC

1900 Lewis, runabout, NAHC

LEWIS — Chicago & Philadelphia — (1894-1900) — A friction-drive device he had invented first brought George W. Lewis to prominence in his native Chicago. In 1894 he built an automobile to demonstrate its efficiency (the flywheel acted as a disc for the friction transmission) and he won a prize for the device in the Chicago Times-Herald Contest of 1895. By now, however, he had turned his talents to engine design and came up with a small 2 to 5 hp single-cylinder gasoline unit which he marketed as the Lewis engine. His claim to have built 800 of them by the end of 1895 is dubious, but it is known that a Lewis powered the Brown Touring Cart of 1898. By that time George Lewis had built another automobile himself, and was in the process of convincing Philadelphia capitalists to invest in its manufacture. The new Lewis was a 3 hp runabout with tiller steering, and it was introduced in the fall of 1899. Production must have been minimal. By October of 1900 the Lewis Motor Vehicle Company announced from Philadelphia that it was decreasing capital stock from $10 million to $90,000 to avoid payment of corporation taxes. Shortly thereafter the company decided to avoid manufacture as well, and simply distributed the assets that were left among stockholders.

LEWIS — Brooklyn, New York — (1901-1902) — Very little is known about the automotive product of the Lewis Cycle Company of 338 Lewis Avenue in Brooklyn save for the fact that it was a two-cylinder 4 1/2 hp $750 gasoline runabout and that it was built for two short seasons only. City directory references indicate the company remained in the two-wheeler bicycle business after discontinuation of its four-wheeler runabout.

LEWIS — Racine, Wisconsin — (1914-1916) — The initials of the L.P.C. Motor Company translated to William Mitchell Lewis, Rene M. Petard and James M. Cram. Initially, in November of 1913, this new venture had been termed the Lewis Motor Company, but this had been changed before year's end to L.P.C. in order to avoid any confusion with the Mitchell-Lewis Motor Company across town in Racine. All three L.P.C. partners were alumni of the Mitchell-Lewis company, builders of the Mitchell car. The trio got together because, in their words, "we really have done something to advance automobile design." Actually, engineer Rene Petard, a Frenchman who had worked for Itala, Unic, Darracq and Fiat on the Continent before being brought to this country by William Mitchell Lewis, had done it. He had come up with one of America's first long-stroke engines — a 3-1/2-inch bore, 6-inch stroke six which developed better than 60 bhp. (A few months earlier Moline had introduced a shorter long-stroke; the year following Metropol would carry the long-stroke idea to unheard of lengths.) The Lewis was offered at first only as a six-passenger touring car, though a roadster variation was added for 1915. The Vulcan electric gearshift (produced by Cutler-Hammer in Milwaukee) was also introduced that year. More than any other single factor, the outbreak of World War I

1914 Lewis, VI, touring, WLB

1893 Lewis Electric, runabout, HAC

spelled the end for the Lewis automobile. Shortly after its introduction, Rene Petard was called back to France to serve in the Army engineering corps. (He would be seriously wounded in the Battle of the Marne.) His absence was sorely missed by his associate and friend William Mitchell Lewis, who finally concluded that he could not make a go of the venture without him. Lewis wound up the affairs of the L.P.C. Motor Company with dignity and integrity. All 280 workers in the plant were paid in full and relocated to other jobs in Racine, Kenosha and neighboring cities. William Mitchell Lewis pledged to pay all creditors' claims at 100 percent of value, and following the sale of company assets, he did just that, although much of the money came from his own pocket. This fine though short-lived marque, incidentally, was officially designated Lewis VI, and its slogan was "Monarch of the Sixes." Someone at L.P.C. had a wonderfully wry sense of humor.

1914 LEWIS
Lewis VI — 6-cyl., 60 hp, 135" wb

	FP	5	4	3	2	1
Touring-6P	1600	3000	4000	6000	9500	21,000

1915 Lewis, VI, touring, HAC

1915 LEWIS
Lewis VI — 6-cyl., 60 hp, 135" wb

Touring-6P	1600	3000	4000	6000	9500	21,000
Roadster-2P	1600	3100	4200	6300	10,500	22,000

1916 Lewis, VI, roadster, HAC

1916 LEWIS
Lewis VI — 6-cyl., 60 hp, 135" wb

Touring-6P	1390	3000	4000	6000	9500	21,000
Roadster-2P	1390	3100	4200	6300	10,500	22,000

LEWIS ELECTRIC — St. Louis, Missouri — (1893-1895) — J.D. Perry Lewis built his first electric car in 1893, and it was the first in St. Louis as well. Admittedly crude, and made up of an assortment of available parts, the Lewis car did run successfully at speeds up to 8 mph, though Perry Lewis never drove it far from home lest he'd have to push it back. His second effort was more ambitious, and brought national attention, *The Horseless Age* reporting in November 1895 that Lewis had introduced an electric carriage in St. Louis which "he conducted around the streets of that city with considerable eclat." The chassis and body of the vehicle were the work of a local carriage maker, but the rest of the car was Perry's doing.

Lewis called his motor a "quadrupler" — a large armature surrounded by four secondary coils. The thirty-cell storage batteries were of the chloride type. Ten hours was required to charge the batteries, and once charged they were capable of propelling the vehicle at 12 mph for approximately four hours. Although this performance approached state of the art for electric vehicles at this early date, the car cost Lewis $1500 to build. He never considered manufacture. At the turn of the century he became an automobile salesman at a local dealership, and in 1912 he established his own dealership, handling Chandler cars.

1909 Lexington, touring, HAC

LEXINGTON — Lexington, Kentucky & Connersville, Indiana — (1909-1927) — The Lexington Motor Company was founded in 1909 by Kinsey Stone, a Kentucky race horse promoter, but by the summer of 1910 it had left the city for which it was named and moved to Connersville. Two years later the firm was bought by E.W. Ansted, who manufactured springs and axles in Connersville, and who now found himself with two cars to produce: the four-cylinder Lexington and the six-cylinder Howard, the latter having been contracted for by a Chicago distributor. The result was a company renamed Lexington-Howard. The Howard was produced only until 1914, however, and there was an eventual reorganization of the firm into Lexington Motor Company again in 1918. From the beginning, the Lexington was an assembled car, and John C. Moore was its chief engineer for the seventeen years it was in Connersville. For a long time Lexingtons were popular cars offered in a variety of four- and six-cylinder models, among them the Thoroughbred Six (an allusion to the car's origins that was probably lost on most) and the Minute Man Six (which was appropriate to the Lexington name if not this one's origins). A Concord model was later available to further drive home the historical reference, and the Lexington emblem for a while sported a minute man with musket. There was a certain whimsy to this since during the Revolutionary War era, Connersville was strictly frontier territory. But there was nothing whimsical about the Lexington. In 1920 Lexingtons placed first and second in the famous Pikes Peak Hill Climb. The cars during the Twenties were smart looking. Many of them sported Ansted engines, and a few of them were badge engineered and marketed under the marque name of Ansted. Six thousand Lexingtons were produced in 1920, production reached nearly a thousand cars a month in 1921. In 1920 E.W. Ansted had corralled all his various enterprises together under the umbrella of the United States Automotive Corporation. But then everything seemed to fall apart. Late in 1921 Alanson P. Brush sued the company, alleging that the Ansted engine infringed a number of his patents. The publicity hurt. Then the postwar recession hit Lexington as it did so many other small producers, and the Jacques Manufacturing Company (makers of automobile bodies in Wilmington, Delaware) filed suit in Indianapolis court claiming that Lexington was insolvent. Production in 1922, it was revealed, had plummeted to 3500 cars. Lexington struggled on under receivership awhile, operating at half capacity and issuing optimistic pronouncements for the future. On May 23rd, 1927 the Lexington factory was taken over by Auburn, and Auburn's new president, Errett Lobban Cord, promptly phased out the Lexington.

1909-1910 LEXINGTON
Model C — 4-cyl., 40/50 hp, 116" wb

	FP	5	4	3	2	1
Runabout-2P	2500	2500	3500	5000	8500	18,000
Model D — 4-cyl., 30/35 hp, 116-1/2" wb						
Touring-5P	1650	2700	3600	5300	8800	19,000
Model A — 4-cyl., 40/50 hp, 120" wb						
Touring-5/7P	2500	4500	9600	15,000	21,000	30,000
Model B — 4-cyl., 40/50 hp, 120" wb						
Close-Coupled-4P	2500	2500	3500	5000	8500	18,000

1910 Lexington, touring, JAC

1911 Lexington, model F, touring, HAC

1911 LEXINGTON
Four-40 — 4-cyl., 40 hp, 117" wb

	FP	5	4	3	2	1
Model E Torpedo-4P	1775	2400	3400	4800	8000	17,000
Model E Roadster	1650	2700	3600	5300	8800	19,000
Model D Touring-5P	1650	2500	3500	5000	8500	18,000
Model F Foredoor Tour. (122" wb)	1850	2700	3600	5300	8800	19,000
Four-45 — 4-cyl., 45 hp, 122" wb						
Model A Touring-5P	2500	2700	3600	5300	8800	19,000
Model A Fore-Door Tour.-5P	2500	2900	3700	5600	9100	20,000
Model A Limousine	3550	2400	3400	4800	8000	17,000

1912 Lexington, model F, touring, HAC

1912 LEXINGTON
Model DF — 4-cyl., 40 hp, 117" wb

	FP	5	4	3	2	1
Touring	1175	2400	3400	4800	8000	17,000
Roadster	1175	2500	3500	5000	8500	18,000
Model F — 4-cyl., 45 hp, 122" wb						
Touring	1975	2500	3500	5000	8500	18,000
Demi-Tonneau	1975	2500	3500	5000	8500	18,000
Coupe	2500	2200	3200	4400	7000	15,000

1913 LEXINGTON
Six — 55/60 hp, 128" wb

	FP	5	4	3	2	1
Roadster	2500	3100	4200	6300	10,500	22,000
Touring	2500	4650	9300	15,500	21,700	31,000

1914 LEXINGTON
Model 4-24 — 4-cyl., 24 hp, 115" wb

	FP	5	4	3	2	1
Touring	1335	3000	4000	6000	9500	21,000
Model 6-41 — 6-cyl., 41 hp, 130" wb						
Touring	2500	3100	4200	6300	10,500	22,000

1915 Lexington Light Six, Thoroughbred, touring, HAC

1915 LEXINGTON
Famous — 4-cyl., 24 hp, 115" wb

	FP	5	4	3	2	1
Touring-5P	1375	3000	4000	6000	9500	21,000
Coupe-2P	1375	2400	3400	4800	8000	17,000
Coupe-3P	2050	2400	3400	4800	8000	17,000
Light Six — 29 hp, 128" wb						
Touring-6P	1875	3000	4000	6000	9500	21,000
Touring-5P	1875	3100	4200	6300	10,500	22,000
Roadster-3P	1875	3200	4300	6500	11,000	23,000
Sedan-6P	2750	2000	3000	4200	6500	14,000
Supreme — 6-cyl., 41 hp, 130" wb						
Touring-7P	2675	3100	4200	6300	10,500	22,000
Touring-5P	2575	3200	4300	6500	11,000	23,000
Limousine-7P	3550	2500	3500	5000	8500	18,000

1916 Lexington, model 6, touring, HAC

1916 LEXINGTON
Model 4-KA — 4-cyl., 24 hp, 115" wb

	FP	5	4	3	2	1
Touring-5P	1375	3000	4000	6000	9500	21,000
Model 6-LA — 6-cyl., 29 hp, 128" wb						
Clubster w/Coupe Top-3P	2125	2200	3200	4400	7000	15,000
Touring-6P	1875	3100	4200	6300	10,500	22,000
Clubster-3P	1875	2300	3300	4600	7500	16,000
Sedan-6P	2175	2000	3000	4200	6500	14,000

1917 Lexington Minute Man Six, touring, HAC

1918 Lexington Clubster, roadster, HAC

1917 LEXINGTON
Series 6 — 6-cyl., 25/35 hp, 116" wb

	FP	5	4	3	2	1
Touring-5P	1185	3000	4000	6000	9500	21,000
Clubster	1185	2200	3200	4400	7000	15,000
Convertible Sedan	1350	2500	3500	5000	8500	18,000
Convertible Coupe	1350	2400	3400	4800	8000	17,000
Touring-7P (144" wb)	2875	2900	3700	5600	9100	20,000

1918 LEXINGTON
Series 6 — 6-cyl., 25/35 hp, 116" wb

Clubster-4P	1385	2200	3200	4400	7000	15,000
Convertible Coupe-4P	1545	2400	3400	4800	8000	17,000
Touring-7P	1585	2900	3700	5600	9100	20,000
Convertible Sedan-7P	1785	2500	3500	5000	8500	18,000
Sport-Tour-4P	1585	3100	4200	6300	10,500	22,000

1919 Lexington, model R-19, touring, HAC

1919 LEXINGTON
Model R-19 — 6-cyl., 25/35 hp, 122" wb

Touring-5P	1785	3000	4000	6000	9500	21,000
Tourabout-4P	1785	3100	4200	6300	10,500	22,000
Convertible Sedan	1985	2500	3500	5000	8500	18,000
Coupelet	2450	2200	3200	4400	7000	15,000
Sedanette	2550	1800	2800	4000	6200	13,000
Coupe	2650	2000	3000	4200	6500	14,000
Salon Sedan	2750	1800	2800	4000	6200	13,000
Limousine-Brougham	3250	2300	3300	4600	7500	16,000

1920 Lexington Minute Man Six, sedanette, HAC

1920 LEXINGTON
Series S — 6-cyl., 47 hp, 120" wb

Touring-5P	1885	3700	4700	7300	13,700	26,000
Thorobred-4P	1985	3900	4800	7700	14,300	27,000
Lex-Sedan-5P	2285	2200	3200	4400	7000	15,000
Coupe-4P	2850	2400	3400	4800	8000	17,000
Sedanette	2850	2300	3300	4600	7500	16,000

1921 Lexington Minute Man Six, touring, HAC

1922 Lexington Thoroughbred, touring, HAC

1921-1922 LEXINGTON
Series S — 6-cyl., 47 hp, 122' wb

	FP	5	4	3	2	1
Thorobred Sport	2285	4000	5000	8000	15,000	28,000
Touring-5P	2285	3700	4700	7300	13,700	26,000
Lex-Sedan-5P	2785	2300	3300	4600	7500	16,000
Coupe-4P	3250	2500	3500	5000	8500	18,000
Sedan-5P	3350	2200	3200	4400	7000	15,000

Series T — 6-cyl., 60 hp, 128" wb

Touring-7P	2985	4200	5200	8400	15,700	29,000
Sedanette-4P	4150	2900	3700	5600	9100	20,000
Salon Sedan-7P	4250	2500	3500	5000	8500	18,000

1923 Lexington Skylark, roadster, HAC

1923 LEXINGTON
Model 23 — 6-cyl., 65 hp, 123" wb

Touring-5P	1695	4000	5000	8000	15,000	28,000
Roadster-2P	1695	4200	5200	8400	15,700	29,000
Touring-7P	1795	3900	4800	7700	14,300	27,000
California-5P	1995	3700	4700	7300	13,700	26,000
Lark-5P	2045	2300	3300	4600	7500	16,000
California-7P	2095	3500	4500	7000	13,000	25,000
Coach-5P	2145	2200	3200	4400	7000	15,000
Coupe-4P	2345	2300	3300	4600	7500	16,000
Sedan-5P	2545	1800	2800	4000	6200	13,000
Brougham	2645	2200	3200	4400	7000	15,000

1924 Lexington Concord Six, touring, HAC

1924 Lexington Minute Man, Lark, sport touring, HAC

1924 LEXINGTON
Concord — 6-cyl., 65 hp, 119" wb

	FP	5	4	3	2	1
Touring-5P	1395	3100	4200	6300	10,500	22,000
Sedan-5P	1845	2000	3000	4200	6500	14,000

Minute Man — 6-cyl., 72 hp, 123" wb

Touring-5P	1795	3200	4300	6500	11,000	23,000
Skylark Roadster-2P	1895	3500	4500	7000	13,000	25,000
Touring-7P	1895	3100	4200	6300	10,500	22,000
Lark Sport Touring-5P	2145	3300	4400	6700	12,000	24,000
Royal Coach-5P	2245	2000	3000	4200	6500	14,000
Brougham-5P	2345	2300	3300	4600	7500	16,000
Sedan-5P	2645	2200	3200	4400	7000	15,000

1925 Lexington Concord Six, touring, HAC

1925 LEXINGTON
Concord — 6-cyl., 65 hp, 119" wb

Touring-5P	1595	3200	4300	6500	11,000	23,000
Enclosure-5P	1695	3200	4300	6500	11,000	23,000
Special Touring-5P	1795	3100	4200	6300	10,500	22,000
Sedan-5P	2185	1800	2800	4000	6200	13,000
Special Sedan-5P	2445	2000	3000	4200	6500	14,000

Minute Man — 6-cyl., 72 hp, 123" wb

Touring-5P	2095	3200	4300	6500	11,000	23,000
Roadster-2P	2145	3500	4500	7000	13,000	25,000
Touring-7P	2195	3300	4400	6700	12,000	24,000
Lark Sport Touring-5P	2345	3500	4500	7000	13,000	25,000
California-5P	2395	3300	4400	6700	12,000	24,000
California-7P	2495	3200	4300	6500	11,000	23,000
Royal Coach-5P	2495	1800	2800	4000	6200	13,000
Brougham-5P	2595	2200	3200	4400	7000	15,000
Sedan-5P	2895	2000	3000	4200	6500	14,000

1926 Lexington, model 6-50, sedan, HAC

1926-1927 LEXINGTON
Model 6-50 — 6-cyl., 65 hp, 119" wb

Phaeton-5P	1795	3700	4700	7300	13,700	26,000
Roadster-4P	1745	3900	4800	7700	14,300	27,000
Sedan-5P	2185	2200	3200	4400	7000	15,000
Landau Sedan-5P	2285	2300	3300	4600	7500	16,000
Landaulet-4P	2445	2400	3400	4800	8000	17,000

LIBERTY — The Liberty was a projected new model for 1910 of the Belmont automobile that was built in divers locations of New York and Connecticut from 1909-1910. Refer to Belmont.

The Liberty Motor Service Association was a $25,000 Delaware incorporation from late 1918 to manufacture and sell automobiles and trucks. Incorporators were C.L. Rimlinger, M.M. Clancy and P.B. Drew. Manufacture of a car is doubted.

The Liberty Tractor Company was organized in Dubuque, Iowa during the summer of 1918 with a capital stock of $300,000 to manufacture "gasoline and kerosene tractors, engines, motor trucks and automobiles." Incorporators were L. Edgar Jerome, Paul Klumb and W.J. Klumb. Manufacture of a car is doubted.

LIBERTY — New York, New York — (1914) — Joseph A. Anglada was a freelance automobile engineer with offices in the Wall Street section of New York City. In January 1914 he announced that the pilot model of his new Liberty Cyclecar was completed. It featured an air-cooled vee-twin engine, friction drive to a countershaft, and final drive by double belt. The wheelbase was 92 inches, the tread 42, and two passengers could sit side

1914 Liberty Cyclecar, runabout, NAHC

by side in the roadster body. The price tag Anglada placed on the car was $375, and the Liberty Motor Company he organized to build it was out of business before it was in. Thereupon, Anglada went south to Rock Hill, South Carolina where he designed a six-cylinder car for the Anderson Motor Company that was eminently more successful. During his New York City period, Anglada had been head of the Metropolitan section of the Society of Automotive Engineers.

1917 Liberty, touring, WLB

LIBERTY — Detroit, Michigan — (1916-1923) — The Liberty Motor Car Company was organized in February of 1916 with a capital stock of $400,000 and the stated purpose of producing a "medium-priced car with body refinements as a most attractive feature." The men behind it were prominent in the industry, headed by Percy Owen, the former vice-president and sales manager for Saxon, who brought two former Saxon men into the venture with him: R.E. Cole as engineer and H.M. Wirth as purchasing agent. Owen's vice-president was James F. Bourquin, formerly of Paige-Detroit and Chalmers. The Liberty, which was introduced in the lobby of the Hotel Pontchartrain in Detroit during the summer of 1916, was a six for the whole of its life, Continental engines being used initially, followed by a unit of the company's own design in 1921. During its maiden year, the firm produced 733 cars, a remarkable beginning. By 1919 production was up to 6000 cars, and in 1921 production crested at 11,000 units. Originally the company had operated out of the plant formerly occupied by the R-C-H Corporation in Detroit, but with success came the move to new and larger quarters — and financial trouble. When receivership arrived in January 1923, Percy Owen declared that it was result of his company's "inability to take advantage of the facilities" of its new plant, this occasioned "by the failure of large parts makers to make deliveries in the quantity ordered." Reorganization, attempted both before and during receivership, failed. In September of 1923 the assets of the Liberty Motor Car Company were acquired by Columbia Motor Car Company. Columbia declared its intention to continue the Liberty in production, but the cars it sold as 1924 models were simply leftover 1923 cars for which sufficient parts remained on hand for assembly. When those parts were gone, so was the Liberty. Fewer than 100 cars had been built in 1923. Columbia followed Liberty to the wall later in 1924, and the Liberty plant was bought in early 1925 by the Budd Wheel Company.

1918 Liberty Six 10-B, touring, HAC

1916 LIBERTY
Model 10-A — 6-cyl., 23 hp, 115" wb

	FP	5	4	3	2	1
Touring-5P	1095	2700	3600	5300	8800	19,000
Roadster-4P	1095	2900	3700	5600	9100	20,000
Town Car-5P	2350	2300	3300	4600	7500	16,000
Touring Sedan-5P	1295	2400	3400	4800	8000	17,000

1917 LIBERTY
Model 10-B — 6-cyl., 25 hp, 123" wb

Roadster-4P	1195	3300	4400	6700	12,000	24,000
Touring-5P	1195	3200	4300	6500	11,000	23,000
Coupe-4P	1795	2500	3500	5000	8500	18,000
Touring Sedan-5P	1395	2300	3300	4600	7500	16,000
Roadster Coupe	1795	2700	3600	5300	8800	19,000
Brougham	2450	2400	3400	4800	8000	17,000

1918 LIBERTY
Model 10-B — 6-cyl., 25 hp, 115" wb

Touring-5P	1350	3300	4400	6700	12,000	24,000
Roadster-2P	1350	3500	4700	7000	13,000	25,000
Roadster-4P	1350	3700	4700	7300	13,700	26,000
Sedan-5P	1925	2000	3000	4200	6500	14,000
Town Car	2700	2300	3300	4600	7500	16,000
Landaulet	2700	2400	3400	4800	8000	17,000

1919 Liberty Six 10-B, touring, HAC

1919 LIBERTY
Model 10-B — 6-cyl., 25 hp, 115" wb

Touring-5P	1570	3300	4400	6700	12,000	24,000
Roadster-2P	1570	3500	4500	7000	13,000	25,000
Sport Touring-4P	1720	3700	4700	7300	13,700	26,000
Touring Limousine	2640	2500	3500	5000	8500	18,000
Brougham	3000	2700	3600	5300	8800	19,000
Coupe	2640	2400	3400	4800	8000	17,000

1920 Liberty Six 10-B, touring, HAC

1920 LIBERTY
Model 10-B — 6-cyl., 25 hp, 115" wb

Touring-5P	1695	3200	4300	6500	11,000	23,000
Sport-4P	1785	3300	4400	6700	12,000	24,000
Roadster-2P	1695	3500	4500	7000	13,000	25,000
Coupe-4P	2495	2300	3300	4600	7500	16,000
Sedan-5P	2595	2000	3000	4200	6500	14,000
Town Car-6P	3225	2300	3300	4600	7500	16,000
Landaulette-6P	3325	2500	3500	5000	8500	18,000

1921 Liberty, model 10-C, touring, HAC

1921 LIBERTY
Model 10-C — 6-cyl., 56 hp, 117" wb

	FP	5	4	3	2	1
Touring-5P	1795	3200	4300	6500	11,000	23,000
Roadster-2P	1795	3300	4400	6700	12,000	24,000
Speedster-4P	1885	3500	4500	7000	13,000	25,000
Coupe-4P	2825	2300	3300	4600	7500	16,000
Sedan-5P	2850	2000	3000	4200	6500	14,000

1922 Liberty, model 10-C, coupe, HAC

1922 LIBERTY
Model 10-C — 6-cyl., 56 hp, 117" wb

Touring-5P	1595	3200	4300	6500	11,000	23,000
Sport-4P	1675	3300	4400	6700	12,000	24,000
Roadster-2P	1595	3500	4500	7000	13,000	25,000
Special Touring-5P	2250	3500	4500	7000	13,000	25,000
Special Sport-4P	2250	3500	4500	7000	13,000	25,000
Coupe-4P	2400	2300	3300	4600	7500	16,000
Sedan-5P	2495	2000	3000	4200	6500	14,000

1923 Liberty, model 10-D, coupe, JAC

1923 LIBERTY
Model 10-D — 6-cyl., 56 hp, 117" wb

Standard Touring	1395	3200	4300	6500	11,000	23,000
Cavalier Roadster	1575	3500	4500	7000	13,000	25,000
Cavalier Four-Passenger	1575	3300	4400	6700	12,000	24,000
Cavalier Touring-5P	1575	3500	4500	7000	13,000	25,000
Commander Coupe	1695	2300	3300	4600	7500	16,000
Cavalier Coupe	1995	2400	3400	4800	8000	17,000
Cavalier Sedan	2095	2200	3200	4400	7000	15,000

LIBERTY BRUSH — Detroit, Michigan — (1912) — The Liberty Brush of 1912 was merely the Brush Runabout of 1911 stripped of amenities and reduced to essentials in order to be offered at the low price of $350. Previous Brush Runabouts had been priced at $450 to $500.

1912 LIBERTY BRUSH
Model F — 1-cyl., 10 hp, 80" wb

	FP	5	4	3	2	1
Runabout	350	1800	2800	4000	6200	13,000

LIBERTY LIGHT CAR — New York, New York — (1920-1921) — The Liberty Manufacturing Company was a New York City operation which announced in 1920 that production of a light five-passenger $1250 touring car on a 105-inch wheelbase would begin for the 1921 model year in the Stratford (Connecticut) factory of the Cameron company. The Liberty Light Car's engine was to be the new air-cooled Cameron six. Because Cameron itself was phasing out of automobile production at this time, it seems unlikely that any meaningful manufacture resulted, though perhaps a few cars were put together with available engines. Most of the new Cameron sixes, however, would be used in farm tractors.

LIGHT — For a short while during 1905, it appeared the Kavan Manufacturing Company of Chicago might call its new car a Light. Most references indicate Kavan, however. Refer to Kavan.

LIGHT SIX — Detroit, Michigan — (1914) — Little imagination was shown by the Light Motor Car Company of Detroit either in the naming of its product or its design. The Light Six was an L-head with cylinders cast in pairs. It featured a wet disc clutch, splash and plunger-pump lubrication, and a three-speed selective transmission. The wheelbase was 115 inches, and body styles placed on it included a $1050 roadster, an $1150 demi-tonneau and a $1250 touring car. The car was introduced in October of 1913 for the 1914 model year, and did not live it out.

1914 LIGHT SIX

	FP	5	4	3	2	1
Light Six Roadster	1050	2400	3400	4800	8000	17,000
Light Six Demi-Tonneau	1150	2500	3500	5000	8500	18,000
Light Six Touring	1250	2300	3300	4600	7500	16,000

LIGHT STEAMER — Pottstown, Pennsylvania — (1901-1902) — During the height of the bicycle craze in the 1880's, William I. Grubb set up the Light Cycle Company on Union Alley near Evans Street in Pottstown. Business was good, and in 1895 local capitalists became interested. A new factory was erected at Union and Queen streets, and the firm was reorganized into the Light Manufacturing and Foundry Company. Among the company's products through the years were automobile gears, airplane parts, and a variety of aluminum and brass castings. At the turn of the century especially, the firm was prominent in supplying builders in the nascent automobile industry. William Grubb built himself two automobiles during this period. Both were steamers, and he was assisted in their development by John Xander, who also built a car of his own. "When your representative called one evening last week he found Mr. Grubb on his knees, not in an attitude of prayer, but closely inspecting the machinery of a new steam automobile which he had just tested," *The Motor Age* reported in May 1901. "Grubb said that if a machine stood the roads of Pennsylvania it could be accepted without fear in any other part of the country." Grubb never planned manufacture. Indeed a report that the Light Cycle Company was planning entry into auto building ranks was immediately denied by the firm because, as was said, it "has caused unpleasantness with people to whom it supplies parts." There was some manufacture, however, of a motorcycle called the Merkel Light. Interestingly, the Light company did later take over the factory in Pottstown that had seen the production of the town's most famous car, and one of the finest of the pre-World War I era, the estimable Chadwick. Light continued in business until felled by the Great Depression.

LIGHTNING — The Lightning Electric Accessories Company was organized in Chicago, Illinois during the spring of 1909 with a capital stock of $2500 to manufacture and deal in automobiles. Samuel Breakstone, Isadore Breakstone and H.M. Fisher were the incorporators. Manufacture is doubted.

LILIPUTIAN — The Liliputian was one of two cars built by George T. Turner at the turn of the century in Philadelphia. Refer to Turner.

LILLY — The Lilly Engine Company was organized in Jamestown, New York early in 1910 with a capital stock of $150,000 to manufacture and deal in automobiles, engines and motorcycles. C.H. Henderson and J.R. Graves were the people behind this venture. Manufacture of a car is doubted.

LIMA — Lima, Ohio — (1915) — C.E. Miller and F.E. McGraw were the men behind the Lima Light Car Company, and they organized their venture in April of 1915 with a capital stock of $50,000. Initial plans called for the production of ten cars a day in three models: speedster, roadster and light delivery. Four-cylinder 18 hp engines were used throughout the line; the common wheelbase was 100 inches, and the common price $500. Experimental cars were on the road later that month, but whether any production cars followed them is problemmatical. The Lima Light Car Company disappeared from view later that year.

1915 LIMA
Lima Four — 18 hp, 100" wb

	FP	5	4	3	2	1
Speedster	500	2500	3500	5000	8500	18,000
Roadster	500	2700	3600	5300	8800	19,000
Light Delivery	—	1800	2800	4000	6200	13,000

LIMA ROADSTER — Lima, Ohio — (1912) — William Townsend Marsh was the president of the American Motor Company, a motorcycle-manufacturing business operated by the four Marsh brothers of Brockton, Massachusetts. The firm had also produced a $750 runabout called the Marsh from 1905 to 1906. In 1910 Alonzo R. Marsh attempted to build a car called the Eastern in Brockton, and in 1912 William T. Marsh got the idea for a new low-priced ($550) runabout to be called the Lima Roadster. Like his brother's Eastern, the Lima Roadster did not proceed beyond a prototype. Its name had been selected because Marsh had hoped to convince the Lima Progressive Association of Lima, Ohio to make it financially attractive for him to set up a factory there. In mid-January arrangements were said to be "almost, but not quite, concluded." The negotiations fell apart soon after that. In 1915 the Marsh brothers had another go at the automobile industry with a new car called the Sterling, produced back home in Brockton.

LINACE — Boulder, Colorado — (1909) — In February of 1909, the American Machine & Manufacturing Company of Boulder announced its forthcoming entry into the automotive field. The men backing the project were J.H. Wallace, W.E. Whitacre and R. Lindemann. Whitacre appears to have been the least significant member of the trio. The car was to be

called the Linace, which was most likely derived from the first syllable of Lindemann's name and the last of Wallace's. There are no references to this venture getting off the ground, although a prototype may have been built.

LINCOLN — That there might have been three more cars called Lincoln was indicated by the incorporations of the three companies following, although in each case a car is not believed to have been produced.

The Lincoln Auto Company of Jersey City, New Jersey, organized during the summer of 1908 with a capital stock of $12,000 to "engage in the manufacture of motor cars." S. Newman and E. Alexander were the incorporators.

The Lincoln Carriage & Automobile Company of New York City, organized early in 1905 with a capital stock of $5000 "to make automobiles." Incorporators were A.M. Lasser, L. Lasser and W.R. Ecker.

The Lincoln Square Garden Company of Mineola, Long Island, New York, organized with a capital stock of $5000 for the manufacture and sale of motor cars and motorcycles. Incorporators were L.B. Sharpe, J.H. Vernon and J.F. Cronin.

1908 Lincoln, runabout, NAHC

LINCOLN — Lincoln, Illinois — (1908-1909) — In early fall of 1907 the Lincoln Automobile Company declared that it had completed several cars in its temporary quarters at George Kate's machine shop on Clinton and Logan streets, that the cars were now running, and that the company was "looking for capital." Apparently the money was found because the Lincoln was in production early the following year. The car was a highwheeler made available with a choice of shaft or chain drive. This was unusual for a buggy manufacturer, but the company was otherwise conventional in its specification: air-cooled two-cylinder engine, solid tires, planetary transmission, right-hand wheel steer. Lincoln was also typical in not surviving long in the marketplace. By the spring of 1909 the company was bankrupt and its plant was sold at an auction. The men behind this venture had been L.W. Walker, William Bates, Robert M. Berry and William Fogarty, Jr.

1908-1909 LINCOLN

	FP	5	4	3	2	1
Model A Buggy (2-cyl., 10/12 hp, 72" wb)	550	1600	2700	3800	5800	12,000
Model B Runabout (2-cyl., 16/18 hp, 82" wb)	700	1800	2800	4000	6200	13,000
Model C Surrey (2-cyl., 16/18 hp, 82" wb)	800	2000	3000	4200	6500	14,000

1912 Lincoln, runabout, WLB

LINCOLN — Chicago, Illinois — (1912-1913) — The Lincoln Motor Car Works at 1348 Harrison Street in Chicago enjoyed a brisk business for the half decade that Sears, Roebuck elected to include an automobile in its catalog. Lincoln produced components for the Sears, and when the mail order house elected to discontinue the Sears Motor Buggy, Lincoln manufactured virtually the same car under its own name as the Model 24 Runabout. It featured an air-cooled L-head two-cylinder engine, friction transmission, single chain drive, 32-inch tires and a 72-inch wheelbase. A tiller was fitted on the left side for steering. The price was $585. Unlike Sears, however, Lincoln seemed to place more emphasis on its light touring model, which carried a $650 price tag. Though various sources have indicated production continuing into 1914, trade press references from the period suggest that manufacture had ceased in 1913.

1913 Lincoln, 3-pass. touring, WLB

1912-1913 LINCOLN

	FP	5	4	3	2	1
Model 24 Runabout	585	1800	2800	4000	6200	13,000
Light Touring	650	1500	2500	3600	5500	11,000

LINCOLN

LINCOLN — Detroit, Michigan — (1920-1942 et. seq.) — He named the company for the President for whom he had first voted in 1864; initially, it was not intended for automobile manufacture at all, and its organization was the product of circumstance. In early 1917 Henry Martyn Leland had walked out of Cadillac following unpleasant words both he and his son Wilfred had with William C. Durant of General Motors. A lot of people left GM that way, the confrontation in this case being, according to the Lelands, the reluctance of Durant to convert Cadillac to Liberty aviation engine production for the war effort. Already Henry Leland was seventy-four years old, but his stature in the industry and his passionate patriotism resulted in his new Lincoln Motor Company being given a government contract to build some 6000 Liberty engines and a $10,000,000 advance to do it. But the Armistice came quickly, too quickly for the Lelands to have established a solid footing with their new company. Faced with a huge factory, a workforce of about 6000 men and mounting debts, they made a quite logical decision. The man who had given America the Cadillac motorcar would now provide the country with the Lincoln. Capital stock for the venture — $6.5 million of it — was subscribed within three hours of being placed on sale. This was a terrific beginning; unfortunately, it would prove to be one of only two high points the Lelands would enjoy during their short tenure with the car. The other was the trade press response to the engineering of the Lincoln itself. Like any Leland product, the Lincoln was precision built. Its 60° V-8 engine with its characteristic fork-and-blade connecting rods, was rugged and compact, developed 81 bhp and ensured a 70 mph performance. Full-pressure lubrication and a massive torque tube drive highlighted the chassis. But two factors convened to make the Lincoln less appealing. First, its coachwork had been assigned to Leland's son-in-law whose previous speciality seems to have been ladies millinery. The Lincoln look was strictly old-hat, dowdy even, with styling reminiscent of the prewar era past, not a breath of the flapper flamboyance that would mark the Twenties. Second, because of late supplier deliveries and Leland's penchant for engineering perfection, the car was delayed, arriving in the marketplace in September 1920 — not the planned January — which missed an entire selling season and hit the postwar recession. The Lelands were convinced they could set matters right, and contacted Brunn in Buffalo about coachwork. But still, the Lincoln board directors could only see the figures — 3407 cars produced by February 4th, 1922 vis-a-vis the projected 6000 for the first year alone — and on that day, over the vigorous objection of the Lelands, they put the company into receivership and up for sale. It was bought for $8 million by Henry Ford. Though the car hadn't appealed to many customers, Ford took a fancy to the Lincoln for several intertwined reasons. His Model T was America's best-selling cheap car by leagues; offering a luxury automobile at over ten times the price (the Lincoln was introduced as a $5000 range car) probably tweaked his interest, and certainly that of his son Edsel whose refined sense of the aesthetic was certainly not satisfied with his father's "Tin Lizzie." Moreover, in 1902, Henry Leland had made his Cadillac out of the frazzled remains of a company Henry Ford himself had started and which he left in disgust after, among other vexations, listening to Leland's uncomplimentary comments about his car. Buying out Leland now must have been a splendid satisfaction. It may have been further vengeance, or the genuine admiration Ford had for Henry Leland, but initially the plan was for the Lelands to remain with the company. This was a marriage made in hell, however, and the Lelands left after four months, seeing Henry Ford thereafter only in court during the lawsuit they instituted regarding reimbursement to original creditors and stockholders. Meanwhile, Edsel Ford became the president of the Lincoln Motor Company. By December 1922, just ten months after the Ford purchase of the company, 5512 Lincolns had been sold, over two thousand more cars than the Lelands had delivered in seventeen months. The Leland fears to the con-

trary, the product had not been compromised; indeed it had been improved, with aluminum pistons and better cylinder head cooling immediately, and an increase in wheelbase to 136 inches (from 130) for 1923. Sales that year rose to 7875. Under Ford aegis, the Lincoln remained a robust car, favored by the Detroit Police Flying Squad amongst other progressive law enforcement agencies, the cars for the police sometimes being provided four-wheel brakes which production versions wouldn't have until 1927. Perhaps more importantly, under Edsel Ford's direction, the Lincoln became a beautiful car, with series production of designs from the masters of America's coachbuilding craft. By 1929 the Model L Lincoln was up to 90 hp and 90 mph, and leading it down the road was a graceful greyhound mascot, selected by Edsel and produced by Gorham. In 1931 the Model K (that designation having been used on Henry Ford's first foray into the luxury car field in 1908, incidentally) replaced the L, a refined V-8 offering 120 hp, 145-inch wheelbase and duo-servo brakes. Clearly, it was an interim model. In 1932 the Ford became a V-8, and though the Lincoln Model K V-8 was continued that year, the Lincoln grabbing the headlines was the new V-12 Model KB with 447.9 cubic inches, 150 hp and 95+ mph performance. Interestingly, the more expensive and custom-built KB (with price tags ranging from $4300 to $7200) fared rather well against the V-8 Model K (at $2900 to $3350) that year, with 1641 of the former built, 1765 of the latter. In 1933 the V-8 was replaced by a smaller 382-cubic-inch 125 hp V-12 designated KA and set in a 136-inch wheelbase chassis as opposed to the KB's 145. But that depth-of-depression year brought sales of only 587 KB's and 1420 KA's. Building two different engines for a plummeting luxury car market didn't make a great deal of sense, and in 1934 both were dropped and replaced with a 414-cubic-inch 150 hp unit with aluminum cylinder heads. All Lincolns into the early postwar years would be V-12 powered, though precious few of them would be the K series as sales of these big Lincolns continued to dwindle while the Thirties wore on. Just 120 of the big K's would be built in 1939-1940, the most famous of which was President Roosevelt's "Sunshine Special," FDR carrying forth a Presidential preference for Lincolns which had begun with Calvin Coolidge and which would endure to the present day. But prestige was not what made Lincoln financially respectable in the later Thirties. The Zephyr did, and when it arrived for 1936, Lincoln sales soared from the under 4000 cars in '35 to over 22,000. Originally intended to use a modified version of the Ford V-8, the Zephyr instead, at Edsel Ford's direction, became a 75° 267-cubic-inch 110 hp V-12 with aluminum alloy heads, cast steel pistons and a reputation for sluggishness and unreliability it has had ever to live with, not always fairly. (The engine was used in England in the Allard, Atalanta and Brough Superior.) The chassis with its transverse springs and mechanical four-wheel brakes represented a specification only to be whispered about, but the synchromesh gearbox was fine and the unitized construction was worthy of a shout, as was the very fresh (and later imitated) styling courtesy of John Tjaarda and Briggs, and refined for production by E.T. "Bob" Gregorie of Lincoln. With some models listing under $1500, the Zephyr was the lowest-priced V-12 offered on the American market since Errett Lobban Cord's Auburn of the early Thirties. It didn't change appreciably in the years to follow, though 1938 saw the gearshift lever spring from the dashboard, 1939 at last brought hydraulic brakes, and in 1940 the by-now-popular column-mounted gearshift arrived on the Zephyr. With the demise of the big K in 1940 — the last cars carrying prophetic black cloisonne emblems replacing the former red or blue — there was room for a new car in the Lincoln lineup, though the one which arrived did so rather by accident. It was in September of 1938 that, returning from a trip to Europe, Edsel Ford asked Bob Gregorie to design a special custom job for him that would be "strictly continental." Whether a Lincoln or Ford would be used, or the chassis of the company's new car called Mercury, was a matter decided in favor of the first named. And thus it was that the Continental was born of the Zephyr. Ford's personal car engendered such comment wherever he took it that production seemed a good and viable idea. On October 2nd, 1939, the new Contiental cabriolet was introduced at the Ford Rotunda in Dearborn as a model of the Lincoln Zephyr. A coupe followed in May 1940, and in September that year the word "Zephyr" was dropped and the car became simply the Lincoln Continental. A total of 1990 Continentals were built before the war put an end to all automobile production. Postwar the Continental would return, but without Edsel Ford. Henry's son, whose unerring good taste had made a ravishing beauty of the Lincoln, died on May 26th, 1943.

Lincoln Data Compilation
by Robert C. Ackerson

1921

1921 Lincoln, model L, coupe, AA

829

LINCOLN — MODEL L — EIGHT: The styling of the first Lincoln was conservative to the point of being uninspired. However in terms of its design the Lincoln was an automobile of grandeur. Rightly identified in automotive history as the "Master of Precision" its creator, Henry M. Leland, was 75 years old when the company he and his son founded produced its first automobile. Leland had already made his mark in the automotive industry as a supplier of engines to Ransom E. Olds, the creator of the first Cadillac in 1903 and the prime force behind their quality. Under Leland's presidency Cadillac won the 1908 Dewar Trophy in England, introduced its self-starter and all-electric system in 1912 and two years later the first American 90° V-8 automobile engine.

After breaking with William Durant in 1917 Leland proceeded to form the Lincoln Motor Company to produce Liberty aircraft engines for the U.S. government. However this effort came to a close after 6500 engines had been delivered. The next step in Leland's career was the development and production of the Lincoln automobile, of which its engine and chassis design attracted considerable attention. Key engine features included a 60° instead of 90° Vee and fork and blade connecting rods. The chassis was noted for its strong torque-tube drive and Alemite lubrication fittings.

I.D. DATA: Serial numbers were on right side of cowl, top of clutch housing and transmission case. Starting: 1 (1920), 835 (1921). Ending: 834 (1920), 3151 (1921). Engine numbers were on left side of crankcase between cylinders 1 and 2. Starting: 1 (1920), 835 (1921). Ending: 834 (1920), 3151 (1921).

Model No.	Body Type & Seating	Price	Weight	Prod. Total
101	4-dr. Tr. (perm top)-7P	4600	—	1015
102	2-dr. Rds.-3P	—	—	78
103	4-dr. Phae.-5P	—	—	278
104	2-dr. Cpe.-4P	—	—	451
105	4-dr. Sed.-5P	—	—	352
106	4-dr. Limo. gls. part-7P	6600	—	101
107	4-dr. Twn. Brgm.-7P	6600	—	10
108	4-dr. Sed.-7P	—	—	26
109	4-dr. Twn. Car-7P	6600	—	19
110	4-dr. Berl. gls. part-7P	—	—	6
111	2-dr. Brun. Rds.-3P	—	—	68
112	2-dr. Brun. Phae. Del.-7P	—	—	196
113	4-dr. Sed.-4P	—	—	50
114	4-dr. Jud. Sed. gls. part-7P	—	—	29
115	4-dr. Jud. Berl. gls. part-5P	—	—	25
122	Chassis only	4000	—	253

ENGINE: 60° V, L-head. Eight. Cast iron block. B & S: 3-3/8 in. x 5 in. Disp.: 357.8 cu. in. C.R.: 4.8:1. Brake H.P.: 81 @ 2600 R.P.M. Main bearings: Three. Valve lifters: Mechanical. Carb.: Stromberg updraft.

CHASSIS: [Types 101-105 and 107] W.B.: 130 in. Frt/Rear Tread: 60 in. Tires: 33 x 5. [Types 106, 108-115, 122] W.B.: 136 in. Frt/Rear Tread: 60 in. Tires: 33 x 5.

TECHNICAL: Sliding gear transmission. Speeds: 3F/1R. Floor shift controls. Multiple disc, dry plate clutch. Shaft drive. Full floating rear axle. Overall Ratio: 4.58:1. Mechanical brakes on two rear wheels. Twelve spoke wooden artillery wheels, demountable rims. Wheel Size: 23 in.

OPTIONS: Front bumper. Rear bumper. Dual sidemount. Sidemount cover(s).

HISTORICAL: Introduced: September, 1920. A Lincoln won a Los Angeles to Phoenix race in April 1921. Innovations: circuit breaker electrical system, Alemite pressure gun lubrication, automatic tire pump, thermostatic radiator shutters, sealed cooling system with condenser tank. Calendar year production: 2957 (1920 and 1921). Model year sales: 674. Model year production: 2957*. The president of Lincoln was Henry Martyn Leland. Considerable discrepancies exist in early production and sales records for the Lincolns. Thus these and subsequent figures should be considered only approximate levels.

1921
Lincoln, V-8, 130" - 136" wb

	FP	5	4	3	2	1
3P Rds	—	6000	12,000	20,000	28,000	40,000
5P Phae	—	6300	12,600	21,000	29,400	42,000
7P Tr	—	6150	12,300	20,500	28,700	41,000
4P Cpe	—	4350	8700	14,500	20,300	29,000
4P Sed	—	4050	8100	13,500	18,900	27,000
5P Sed	—	4200	8400	14,000	19,600	28,000
Sub Sed	—	4200	8400	14,000	19,600	28,000
TwnC	—	4500	9000	15,000	21,000	30,000

1922

LINCOLN — MODEL L — EIGHT: The postwar depression that overwhelmed William Durant's best efforts to retain control of General Motors and put Henry Ford to a severe test forced the Lincoln Motor Company into receivership in November 1921. Subsequently the firm was purchased by Henry Ford for $8 million on February 4, 1922.

Changes in the Lincoln's design were minor. The acquisition of Lincoln by Ford was made evident by a new radiator badge that had the Lincoln name sandwiched by "Ford Detroit" and placed within an oval shell. The older more ornate, version had carried the words "Leland Built". Design changes included an improved cylinder head for better engine cooling (on cars after serial number 7820) and the use of aluminum in place of the older cast iron versions. Also phased in after car number 8500 was a new timing chain and sprockets.

In June 1922 both Henry Leland and his son acrimoniously left Lincoln and Edsel Ford became the company's president. Under total Ford control the above noted engineering changes were made as well as a price reduc-

tion of $1000 on all models with non-custom bodies. Aided by the economy's recovery these moves caused a major reversal in Lincoln sales which after totalling only 150 cars in January and February reached 5512 for the remaining ten months of 1922.

1922 Lincoln, model L, touring, OCW

I.D. DATA: Serial numbers were located on right side of cowl, top of clutch housing and transmission case. Starting: 3152. Ending: 8709. Engine numbers were located on left side of crankcase between cylinder 1 and 2. Starting: 3152. Ending: 8709.

Model No.	Body Type & Seating	Price	Weight	Prod. Total
101	4-dr. Tr. (perm top)-7P	3800	—	483
102	2-dr. Rds.-3P	—	—	6
103	4-dr. Phae.-5P	—	—	37
104	2-dr. Cpe.-4P	3900	—	441
105	4-dr. Sed.-5P	4200	—	344
107	4-dr. Twn. Brgm.-7P	—	—	2
109	4-dr. Twn. Car-7P	—	—	12
111	2-dr. Brun. Rds.-3P	3800	—	178
112	4-dr. Brun. Phae. Delx.-4P	3800	—	771
113	4-dr. Sed.-4P	3800	—	353
114	4-dr. Jud. Sed. gls. part-7P	—	—	22
115	4-dr. Jud. Berl. gls. part-5P	—	—	29
116	4-dr. FW Sed.-7P	—	—	6
117	4-dr. Brun. Sed.-7P	4900	—	718
118	4-dr. Brun. Limo. gls. part.-7P	—	—	554
119	4-dr. FW Limo. gls. part.-7P	5800	—	20
120	4-dr. Brun. Twn. Car-7P	7200	—	6
121	4-dr. Brun. Limo. gls. part.-7P	5100	—	2
122	Chassis	3400	—	287
124A	4-dr. Tr.-7P	3300	—	1136
125	4-dr. Sed.-4P	5200	—	59
126	2-dr. Brun. Cpe.-2P	4400	—	1
127	4-dr. Jud. Sed.-4P	—	—	104
128	4-dr. Jud. Berline-4P	5200	—	74
129	4-dr. Brun. Sed.-5P	4700	—	1
702	2-dr. Jud. Cpe.-2P	—	—	1

1922 Lincoln, model L, 4-pass. sedan, HAC

ENGINE: 60° V, L-head. Eight. Cast iron block. B & S: 3-3/8 in. x 5 in. Disp.: 357.8 cu. in. C.R.: 4.8:1. Brake H.P.: 90 @ 2800 R.P.M. Main bearings: Three. Valve lifters: Mechanical. Carb.: Stromberg updraft.

CHASSIS: [Series 101-105] W.B.: 130 in. Frt/Rear Tread 60 in. Tires: 33 x 5. [All others] W.B.: 136 in. Frt/Rear Tread: 60 in. Tires: 33 x 5.

TECHNICAL: Sliding gear transmission. Speeds: 3F/1R. Floor shift controls. Multiple disc, dry plate clutch. Shaft drive. Full floating rear axle. Overall Ratio: 4.58:1. Mechanical brakes on two rear wheels. Twelve spoke wooden artillery wheels, demountable rims. Wheel Size: 23 in.

OPTIONS: Front bumper. Rear bumper. Dual sidemount. Sidemount cover(s).

HISTORICAL: Introduced: January, 1922. Calendar year production: 5512. The president of Lincoln was Edsel Ford - after June 1922.

1922
Lincoln, V-8, 130" wb

	FP	5	4	3	2	1
3P Rds	—	6450	12,900	21,500	30,100	43,000
5P Phae	—	6150	12,300	20,500	28,700	41,000
7P Tr	—	6000	12,000	20,000	28,000	40,000
Conv Tr	—	6150	12,300	20,500	28,700	41,000
4P Cpe	—	4500	9000	15,000	21,000	30,000
5P Sed	—	4350	8700	14,500	20,300	29,000

Lincoln, V-8, 136" wb

	FP	5	4	3	2	1
Spt Rds	—	6300	12,600	21,000	29,400	42,000
DeL Phae	—	6450	12,900	21,500	30,100	43,000
DeL Tr	—	6150	12,300	20,500	28,700	41,000
Std Sed	—	4500	9000	15,000	21,000	30,000
Jud Sed	—	4650	9300	15,500	21,700	31,000
FW Sed	—	4650	9300	15,500	21,700	31,000
York Sed	—	4650	9300	15,500	21,700	31,000
4P Jud Sed	—	4650	9300	15,500	21,700	31,000
7P Jud Sed	—	4800	9600	16,000	22,400	32,000
Sub Limo	—	5250	10,500	17,500	24,500	35,000
TwnC	—	5250	10,500	17,500	24,500	35,000
FW Limo	—	5400	10,800	18,000	25,200	36,000
Std Limo	—	5400	10,800	18,000	25,200	36,000
FW Cabr	—	5700	11,400	19,000	26,600	38,000
FW Coll Cabr	—	5850	11,700	19,500	27,300	39,000
FW Lan'let	—	5850	11,700	19,500	27,300	39,000
FW TwnC	—	5400	10,800	18,000	25,200	36,000
Holbrk Cabr	—	6000	12,000	20,000	28,000	40,000
Brn TwnC	—	5550	11,100	18,500	25,900	37,000
Brn OD Limo	—	5550	11,100	18,500	25,900	37,000

1923

1923 Lincoln, model L, touring, OCW

LINCOLN — MODEL L — EIGHT: After the Ford takeover, the Lincoln Motor Company became an independent operation whose stock was 100 percent owned by the Ford Motor Company. However, with the Lelands completely out of the picture, it was absorbed into Ford.

Principle changes for 1923 were headlined by the elimination of the 130 inch wheelbase chassis. During the model year a number of changes occurred, including the use of Houdaille hydraulic shock absorbers.

I.D. DATA: Serial numbers were located on the right side of cowl, top of clutch housing and transmission case. Starting: 8710. Ending: 16,434. Engine numbers were located on left side of crankcase between cylinders 1 and 2. Starting Engine No.: 8710. Ending: 16,434.

Model No.	Body Type & Seating	Price	Weight	Prod. Total
111	2-dr. Brun. Rds.-2P	3800	NA	54
112	4-dr. Brun. Del. Phae.-4P	3800	—	15
117	4-dr. Brun. Sed.-7P	4900	—	971
118	4-dr. Brun. Limo.-7P	—	—	563
120	4-dr. Brun. Fwn. Car-6P	—	—	50
121	4-dr. Brun. Limo. gls. part-7P	—	—	18
122	Chassis	—	—	177
123A	4-dr. Brun. Phae.-4P	—	—	1061
124A	4-dr. Tr.-4P	—	—	1182
125	4-dr. Jud. Sed.-4P	—	—	365
126	2-dr. Brun. Cpe.-4P	—	—	816
127	4-dr. Jud. Sed. 3W-4P	—	—	532
128	4-dr. Jud. Ber. gls. part-4P	—	—	238
129	4-dr. Brun. Sed.-5P	—	—	1195
130	2-dr. Brun. Rds.-3P	—	—	48
131	4-dr. Brun. Cab.-6P	—	—	14
132	4-dr. Jud. Sed. 2W-4P	—	—	93
133	4-dr. Jud. Sed. 3W-4P	—	—	269
	4-dr. FW Cab. Coll. Tp.-7P	6200	—	—

ENGINE: 60° V, L-head. Eight. Cast iron block. B & S: 3-3/8 in. x 5 in. Disp.: 357.8 cu. in. C.R.: 4.8:1. Brake H.P.: 90 @ 2800 R.P.M. Taxable H.P.: 39.2. Main bearings: Three. Valve lifters: Mechanical. Carb.: Stromberg 03 updraft.

1923 Lincoln, model L, 5-pass. coupe, HAC

CHASSIS: W.B.: 136 in. Frt/Rear Tread: 60 in. Tires: 33 x 5.

TECHNICAL: Sliding gear transmission. Speeds: 3F/1R. Floor shift controls. Multiple disc, dry plate clutch. Shaft drive. Full floating rear axle. Overall Ratio: 4.58:1; opt. 4.90:1. Mechanical brakes on two rear wheels (Lincolns for police use had 4 wheel brakes). 12 spoke wooden artillery wheels with demountable rims. Wheel Size: 23 in.

OPTIONS: Front bumper. Rear bumper. Dual sidemount. Sidemount cover(s). Drum headlights.

HISTORICAL: Introduced: January, 1923. Calendar year registration: 7875. Calendar year production: 7875. The company president was Edsel Ford.

1923
Model L, V-8

	FP	5	4	3	2	1
Tr	—	6000	12,000	20,000	28,000	40,000
Phae	—	6150	12,300	20,500	28,700	41,000
Rds	—	6000	12,000	20,000	28,000	40,000
Cpe	—	4800	9600	16,000	22,400	32,000
5P Sed	—	4650	9300	15,500	21,700	31,000
7P Sed	—	4500	9000	15,000	21,000	30,000
Limo	—	5400	10,800	18,000	25,200	36,000
OD Limo	—	5550	11,100	18,500	25,900	37,000
TwnC	—	5700	11,400	19,000	26,600	38,000
4P Sed	—	4650	9300	15,500	21,700	31,000
Berl	—	4800	9600	16,000	22,400	32,000
FW Cabr	—	5850	11,700	19,500	27,300	39,000
FW Limo	—	5700	11,400	19,000	26,600	38,000
FW TwnC	—	5700	11,400	19,000	26,600	38,000
Jud Cpe	—	4950	9900	16,500	23,100	33,000
Brn TwnC	—	5850	11,700	19,500	27,300	39,000
Brn OD Limo	—	5850	11,700	19,500	27,300	39,000
Jud 2W Berl	—	5700	11,400	19,000	26,600	38,000
Jud 3W Berl	—	5700	11,400	19,000	26,600	38,000
Holbrk Cabr	—	5850	11,700	19,500	27,300	39,000

1924

1924 Lincoln, model L, touring, OCW

LINCOLN — MODEL L — EIGHT: Although there was no single styling change in the Lincoln's appearance that could even remotely be regarded as revolutionary the sum total of the revisions made for 1924 resulted in a more modern and decidedly more attractive appearance. All models had as standard equipment the nickel-plated drum-style headlights that had been optional in 1923. A higher radiator with a nickel-plated shell enabled a smoother hoodline to be used. The radiator shutters were now vertical instead of horizontal. The Lincoln's oval grille emblem no longer carried the "Ford Detroit" lettering. On all models except type 702 (a Judkin-bodied coupe) new fenders with a smoother and wider design were installed.

Although no changes were made in the Lincoln's engine's basic specifications a new cam reshaped for smoother valve operation was installed.

I.D. DATA: Serial numbers were located on right side of cowl, top of clutch housing and transmission case. Starting: 16435. Ending: 23614. Engine numbers were located on left side of crankcase between cylinders 1 and 2. Starting: 16435. Ending: 23614.

Model No.	Body Type & Seating	Price	Weight	Prod. Total
117	4-dr. Brun. Sed.-7P	—	—	271
118	4-dr. Brun. Limo.-7P	5100	—	128
120	4-dr. Brun. Twn. Car-6P	—	—	12
121	4-dr. Brun. Limo.-7P	—	—	8
122	Chassis	3600	—	79
123A	4-dr. Brun. Phae.-4P	4000	—	829
124A	4-dr. Tr.-7P	4000	—	601
126	2-dr. Brun. Cpe.-4P	4600	—	424
127	4-dr. Jud. Sed. 3W-4P	4800	—	2
128	4-dr. Jud. Ber.-4P	5400	—	111
129	4-dr. Brun. Sed.-5P	4900	—	351
130	2-dr. Brun. Rds.-3P	4000	—	188
131	2-dr. Brun. Cab-6P	—	—	13
132	4-dr. Jud. Sed. 2W-4P	—	—	358
133	4-dr. Jud. Sed. 3W-4P	—	—	889
134	4-dr. Jud. Sed.-7P	—	—	846
135	4-dr. Brun. Limo.-7P	6400	—	482
136	4-dr. Brun. Sed.-5P	—	—	928
137	4-dr. Brun. Cab-5P	—	—	6
138	4-dr. Brun. Twn. Car-5P	6400	—	8
139	4-dr. FW Limo.-7P	6000	—	29
140	4-dr. Jud. Ber.-4P	5400	—	20
140	4-dr. Brun. Open Drive Limo.-5P	6400	—	—

ENGINE: 60° V, L-head. Eight. Cast iron block. B & S: 3-3/8 in. x 5 in. Disp.: 357.8 cu. in. C.R.: 4.8:1. Brake H.P.: 90 @ 2800 R.P.M. Taxable H.P.: 39.2. Main bearings: Three. Valve lifters: Mechanical. Carb.: Stromberg 03 updraft.

CHASSIS: W.B.: 136 in. Frt/Rear Tread: 60 in. Tires: 33 x 5.

TECHNICAL: Sliding gear transmission. Speeds: 3F/1R. Floor shift controls. Multiple disc, dry plate clutch. Shaft drive. Full floating rear axle. Overall Ratio: 4.58:1, Opt. 4.90:1. Mechanical brakes on two rear wheels (Lincolns for police use had 4 wheel brakes). 12 spoke wooden artillery wheels, demountable rims. Wheel Size: 23 in.

OPTIONS: Front bumper. Rear bumper. Dual sidemount. Sidemount cover(s). Natural wood finish wheels. Disc wheels. Rudge-Whitworth wire wheels. Painted radiator shell.

HISTORICAL: Introduced: January, 1924. Calendar year registrations: 5672. Calendar year production: 7,053. The president of Ford was Edsel Ford. The 1924 models were the first Lincolns to have a spark setting mark on the clutch ring and fly wheel.

1924 V-8

	FP	5	4	3	2	1
Tr	—	6000	12,000	20,000	28,000	40,000
Phae	—	6150	12,300	20,500	28,700	41,000
Rds	—	6000	12,000	20,000	28,000	40,000
Cpe	—	4650	9300	15,500	21,700	31,000
5P Sed	—	4350	8700	14,500	20,300	29,000
7P Sed	—	4200	8400	14,000	19,600	28,000
Limo	—	4800	9600	16,000	22,400	32,000
4P Sed	—	4500	9000	15,000	21,000	30,000
TwnC	—	5250	10,500	17,500	24,500	35,000
Twn Limo	—	5550	11,100	18,500	25,900	37,000
FW Limo	—	5400	10,800	18,000	25,200	36,000
Jud Cpe	—	4800	9600	16,000	22,400	32,000
Jud Berl	—	4950	9900	16,500	23,100	33,000
Brn Cabr	—	5850	11,700	19,500	27,300	39,000
Brn Cpe	—	4800	9600	16,000	22,400	32,000
Brn OD Limo	—	5550	11,100	18,500	25,900	37,000
Leb Sed	—	5700	11,400	19,000	26,600	38,000

1925

1925 Lincoln, model L, touring, OCW

LINCOLN — MODEL L — EIGHT: The absence of cowl lights made it easy to identify the 1925 Lincoln. Also giving them a distinctive appearance was the Gorham-produced greyhound radiator ornament. Initially this was an option but during the year it was included in the Lincoln's standard equipment. Other changes included a longer and smoother operating emergency brake lever plus factory installed front and rear bumpers for all models. Early in the model year run a steering ratio of 15:1 replaced the older 12-2/3:1 ratio.

I.D. DATA: Serial numbers were located on right side of cowl, top of clutch housing and transmission case. Starting: 23615. Ending: 32029. Engine numbers were located on left side of crankcase between cylinder 1 and 2. Starting Engine No.: 23615. Ending: 32029.

Model No.	Body Type & Seating	Price	Weight	Prod. Total
122	Chassis	3800	—	121
123A	4-dr. Brun. Phae.-4P	4000	—	689
123B	4-dr. Brun. Spt. Phae.-4P	—	—	25
123C	4-dr. Brun. Spt. Phae. TC-4P	—	—	1
124A	4-dr. Tr.-7P	4000	—	418
124B	4-dr. Brun. Spt. Tr. TC-7P	4200	—	324
124C	4-dr. Brun. Spt. Tr.-7P	—	—	3
126	2-dr. Brun. Cpe.-4P	4600	—	204
128	4-dr. Jud. Berl.-4P	5600	—	31
130	2-dr. Brun. Rds.-2P	4000	—	126
132	4-dr. Jud. Sed. 2W-4P	—	—	146
133	4-dr. Jud. Sed. 3W-4P	—	—	548
134	4-dr. Brun. Sed.-7P	—	—	829
135	4-dr. Brun. Limo. gls. part.-7P	—	—	443
136	4-dr. Brun. Sed.-5P	—	—	541
137	4-dr. Brun. Cab.-5P	6600	—	58
138	4-dr. Brun. Twn. C.-7P	—	—	18
139	4-dr. FW Limo.-7P	—	—	297
140	4-dr. Jud. Berl. gls. part. 2W-4P	—	—	248
141	2-dr. LeB. Cpe. Rds.-2P	—	—	95
142	4-dr. Holbrk. Coll. Cab-7P	7200	—	11
143	2-dr. Brun. Cpe.-4P	—	—	470
144A	4-dr. LeB. Trk. Sed. 2W-4P	—	—	159
144B	4-dr. LeB. Trk. Sed. 3W-4P	—	—	433
145A	4-dr. Brun. Brgm. gls. part.-7P	—	—	15
146	4-dr. Diet. Sed.-5P	—	—	1095
147A	4-dr. Diet. Sed.-7P	—	—	398
147B	4-dr. Diet. Berl.-7P	—	—	214
148A	4-dr. Diet. Brgm.-6P	6800	—	3
149A	4-dr. Diet. Coll. Cab	—	—	12
150A	Burial C'ch.	—	—	1
702	2-dr. Jud. Cpe.-2P	5100	—	345
2557	Special	—	—	2
2686	Special Rds.	—	—	11
123D	4-dr. Spt. Phae.-4P	—	—	106
	4-dr. Brun. Twn. C.-5P	6400	—	—
	4-dr. Brun. Open-D Limo.	6400	—	—
	4-dr. FW Limo.	6000	—	—
	4-dr. Jud. Berl. 3W-4P	5400	—	—

1925 Lincoln, model L, limousine, JAC

ENGINE: 60° V, L-head. Eight. Cast iron block. B & S: 3-3/8 in. x 5 in. Disp.: 357.8 cu. in. C.R.: 4.8:1. Brake H.P.: 90 @ 2800 R.P.M. Taxable H.P.: 39.2. Main bearings: Three. Valve lifters: Mechanical. Carb.: Stromberg 03 updraft.

CHASSIS: W.B.: 136 in. Frt/Rear Tread: 60 in. Tires: 33 x 5.

TECHNICAL: Sliding gear transmission. Speeds: 3F/1R. Floor shift controls. Multiple disc, dry plate clutch. Shaft drive. Full floating rear axle. Overall Ratio: 4.58:1; opt. 4.90:1. Mechanical brakes on two rear wheels (Lincolns for police use had 4 wheel brakes). 12 spoke wooden artillery wheels with demountable rims. Wheel Size: 23 in.

HISTORICAL: Introduced: January, 1925. Calendar year registrations: 6808. Calendar year production: 8451. The company president was Edsel Ford.

1925
Model L, V-8

	FP	5	4	3	2	1
Tr	4000	6300	12,600	21,000	29,400	42,000
Spt Tr	4200	6750	13,500	22,500	31,500	45,000
Phae	4000	6900	13,800	23,000	32,200	46,000
Rds	4000	6300	12,600	21,000	29,400	42,000
Cpe	4600	5100	10,200	17,000	23,800	34,000
4P Sed	4800	4350	8700	14,500	20,300	29,000
5P Sed	4900	4200	8400	14,000	19,600	28,000
7P Sed	5100	4200	8400	14,000	19,600	28,000
Limo	5300	5100	10,200	17,000	23,800	34,000
FW Limo	6000	5250	10,500	17,500	24,500	35,000
Jud Cpe	5100	4500	9000	15,000	21,000	30,000
Jud Berl	5600	4650	9300	15,500	21,700	31,000
Brn Cabr	6600	6600	13,200	22,000	30,800	44,000
FW Coll Clb Rds	4500	6450	12,900	21,500	30,100	43,000
FW Sed	—	5700	11,400	19,000	26,600	38,000
FW Brgm	—	5850	11,700	19,500	27,300	39,000
FW Cabr	—	6300	12,600	21,000	29,400	42,000
Jud 3W Berl	5400	5850	11,700	19,500	27,300	39,000
Jud 4P Cpe	5100	5850	11,700	19,500	27,300	39,000
Jud Brgm	4800	5700	11,400	19,000	26,600	38,000
Mur OD Limo	—	6300	12,600	21,000	29,400	42,000
Holbrk Brgm	—	6000	12,000	20,000	28,000	40,000
Holbrk Coll	7200	6150	12,300	20,500	28,700	41,000
Brn OD Limo	6400	6150	12,300	20,500	28,700	41,000
Brn Spt Phae	—	7050	14,100	23,500	32,900	47,000
Brn Lan Sed	—	6150	12,300	20,500	28,700	41,000
Brn TwnC	6400	6300	12,600	21,000	29,400	42,000
Brn Pan Brgm	—	6150	12,300	20,500	28,700	41,000
Hume Limo	—	6450	12,900	21,500	30,100	43,000
Hume Cpe	—	5850	11,700	19,500	27,300	39,000
5P Leb Sed	—	6300	12,600	21,000	29,400	42,000
4P Leb Sed	—	6000	12,000	20,000	28,000	40,000
Leb DC Phae	—	9000	18,000	30,000	42,000	60,000
Leb Clb Rds	—	7500	15,000	25,000	35,000	50,000
Leb Limo	—	6000	12,000	20,000	28,000	40,000
Leb Brgm	—	6150	12,300	20,500	28,700	41,000
Leb Twn Brgm	—	6300	12,600	21,000	29,400	42,000
Leb Cabr	—	6750	13,500	22,500	31,500	45,000
Leb Coll Spt Cabr	—	7500	15,000	25,000	35,000	50,000
Lke Cabr	—	7200	14,400	24,000	33,600	48,000
Dtrch Coll Cabr	7200	7350	14,700	24,500	34,300	49,000

1926

1926 Lincoln, model L, Dietrich coupe roadster, OCW

LINCOLN — MODEL L — EIGHT: Exterior changes were virtually non-existent in the Lincoln's appearance but a number of interior revisions and engine modifications contributed to the best sales year yet for Lincoln. During the model year a non-movable 19 inch wheel with a smaller cross section and molded to form finger grips on its lower surface replaced the older tilt-type 18 inch unit. The headlight tilting lever was now located below the horn button on the hub and both the wheel and spokes were of black walnut construction.

Beneath the Lincoln hood, a new centrifugal-type carburetor air cleaner was readily noticeable. A new distributor cam that Lincoln said provided more efficient high-speed operation was standard.

I.D. DATA: Serial numbers were located on right side of cowl, top of clutch housing and transmission case. Starting: 32030. Ending: 39899. Engine numbers were located on left side of crankcase between cylinders 1 and 2. Starting: 32030. Ending: 39899.

Model No.	Body Type & Seating	Price	Weight	Prod. Total
122	Chassis	—	—	154
123A	4-dr. Phae.-4P	4000	—	147
123B	4-dr. Spt. Phae.-4P	4500	—	283
123C	4-dr. Brun. Spt. Phae. TC-4P	—	—	41
124A	4-dr. Tr.-7P	—	—	93
124B	4-dr. Brun. Spt. Tr. TC-7P	4500	—	324

Model No.	Body Type & Seating	Price	Weight	Prod. Total
124C	4-dr. Brun. Spt. Tr.-7P	—	—	12
130	2-dr. Brun. Rds.-3P	—	—	99
136	4-dr. Brun. Sed.-5P	6400	—	3
137	4-dr. Brun. Cab-5P	6600	—	52
139	4-dr. FW Limo.-7P	6000	—	60
140	4-dr. Jud. Berl 2W gls. part.-4P	5400	—	273
141	2-dr. Leb. Cpe. Rds. Aux. St.-2P	—	—	150
142	4-dr. Holbrk. Coll. Cab-7P	7200	—	13
143	2-dr. Brun. Cpe.-4P	—	—	308
144A	4-dr. Leb. Trk. Sed. 2W-4P	4800	—	513
144B	4-dr. Leb. Trk. Sed. 3W-4P	4800	—	1350
145A	4-dr. Brun. Brgm. gls. part.-7P	6400	—	42
145B	4-dr. Brun. Open Limo.	—	—	3
146	4-dr. Diet. Sed.-5P	6800	—	558
147A	4-dr. Diet. Sed.-7P	—	—	1590
147B	4-dr. Diet. Berl.-7P	6800	—	1180
148A	4-dr. Diet. Brgm.-6P	6800	—	2
149A	4-dr. Diet. Coll. Cab-5P	7200	—	2
150A	Burial C'ch.	—	—	8
150B	150'' wb Chassis	—	—	37
151	2-dr. Lke. Rds.-2P	—	—	101
152	4-dr. Diet. Sed.-5P	—	—	653
153A	4-dr. Holbrk. Coll. Cab-5P	7200	—	10
154	2-dr. Diet. Cpe. R/S-2P	—	—	263
155	4-dr. Leb. Coll. Spt. Cab-5P	—	—	7
157	4-dr. Wilby Land.-6P	6700	—	10
702	2-dr. Jud. Cpe.-2P	5300	—	371

1926 Lincoln, model L, 7-pass. sedan, JAC

ENGINE: 60° V, L-head. Eight. Cast iron block. B & S: 3-3/8 in. x 5 in. Disp.: 357.8 cu. in. C.R.: 4.8:1. Brake H.P.: 90 @ 2800 R.P.M. Taxable H.P.: 39.2. Main bearings: Three. Valve lifters: Mechanical. Carb.: Stromberg 03 updraft.

CHASSIS: W.B.: 136 in. Frt/Rear Tread: 60 in. Tires: 33 x 5.

TECHNICAL: Sliding gear transmission. Speeds: 3F/1R. Floor shift controls. Multiple disc, dry plate clutch. Shaft drive. Full floating rear axle. Overall Ratio: 4.58:1. Opt. 4.90:1. Mechanical brakes on two rear wheels (Lincolns for police use had 4 wheel brakes). 12 spoke wooden artillery wheels, demountable rims. Wheel Size: 23 in.

OPTIONS: Dual sidemount. Sidemount cover(s). Natural wood finish wheels. Disc wheels. Buffalo wire wheels. 7.00 x 21 balloon tires. Monogram (5.00). Tonneau cowl & rear windshield (400.00).

HISTORICAL: Introduced: January, 1926. Calendar year registrations: 7711. Calendar year production: 8787. The president of Lincoln was Edsel Ford

1926 Lincoln, model L, Locke sport roadster, JAC

1926
Model L, V-8

	FP	5	4	3	2	1
Tr	4000	7050	14,100	23,500	32,900	47,000
Spt Tr	4500	7650	15,300	25,500	35,700	51,000
Phae	4000	7500	15,000	25,000	35,000	50,000
Rds	4000	7200	14,400	24,000	33,600	48,000
Cpe	4600	4350	8700	14,500	20,300	29,000
4P Sed	4800	4200	8400	14,000	19,600	28,000
5P Sed	4900	4200	8400	14,000	19,600	28,000
7P Sed	5100	4050	8100	13,500	18,900	27,000
Limo	5300	4500	9000	15,000	21,000	30,000
FW Limo	6000	4650	9300	15,500	21,700	31,000
Jud Cpe	5100	5550	11,100	18,500	25,900	37,000
Jud Berl	5400	5400	10,800	18,000	25,200	36,000
Brn Cabr	6600	6900	13,800	23,000	32,200	46,000
Holbrk Coll Cabr	7200	7050	14,100	23,500	32,900	47,000
Hume Limo	—	5400	10,800	18,000	25,200	36,000
W'by Limo	—	5400	10,800	18,000	25,200	36,000
W'by Lan'let	—	5550	11,100	18,500	25,900	37,000
Dtrch Sed	6800	5100	10,200	17,000	23,800	34,000
Dtrch Coll Cabr	7200	7200	14,400	24,000	33,600	48,000
Dtrch Brgm	6800	5700	11,400	19,000	26,600	38,000
Dtrch Cpe Rds	7000	7050	14,100	23,500	32,900	47,000
Jud 3W Berl	5600	5250	10,500	17,500	24,500	35,000
Jud Brgm	—	5100	10,200	17,000	23,800	34,000
Brn Phae	—	6900	13,800	23,000	32,200	46,000
Brn Sed	6400	4950	9900	16,500	23,100	33,000
Brn Brgm	6400	5100	10,200	17,000	23,800	34,000
Brn Semi-Coll Cabr	—	6900	13,800	23,000	32,200	46,000
Leb 2W Sed	—	4950	9900	16,500	23,100	33,000
Leb 3W Sed	—	4950	9900	16,500	23,100	33,000
Leb Cpe	—	5250	10,500	17,500	24,500	35,000
Leb Spt Cabr	—	7050	14,100	23,500	32,900	47,000
Leb A-W Cabr	—	6750	13,500	22,500	31,500	45,000
Leb Limo	—	5550	11,100	18,500	25,900	37,000
Leb Clb Rds	—	7200	14,400	24,000	33,600	48,000
Lke Rds	—	7500	15,000	25,000	35,000	50,000
Lke Semi-Coll Cabr	—	6750	13,500	22,500	31,500	45,000
Lke Cabr	—	7200	14,400	24,000	33,600	48,000
Leb Conv Phae	—	7500	15,000	25,000	35,000	50,000
Leb Conv	—	7350	14,700	24,500	34,300	49,000

Model No.	Body Type & Seating	Price	Weight	Prod. Total
144A	4-dr. Leb. Trk. Sed. 2W-4P	4600	—	400
144B	4-dr. Leb. Trk. Sed. 3W-4P	4800	—	926
145A	4-dr. Brun. Brgm.-7P	6800	—	63
146	4-dr. Diet. Sed.-5P	5100	—	3
147A	4-dr. Diet. Sed.-7P	5300	—	1193
147B	4-dr. Diet. Ber.-7P	—	—	1005
150B	150" wb Chassis	3700	—	22
151	2-dr. Lke. Rds.-2P	4600	—	178
152	4-dr. Diet. Sed.-5P	—	—	917
153A	4-dr. Holbrk. Coll. Cab-5P	7200	—	7
154	2-dr. Diet. Cpe. R/S-2P	—	—	580
155	4-dr. Leb. Coll. Spt. Cab-5P	7300	—	7
156	2-dr. Leb. Cpe.-4P	—	—	293
157	4-dr. Wilby Ber.-6P	—	—	12
158	4-dr. Jud. Ber.-5P	—	—	100
159	4-dr. Brun. Cab-5P	—	—	54
160	4-dr. Wilby Limo.-7P	6000	—	164
161	4-dr. Jud. Ber.-5P	—	—	352
162A	4-dr. Leb. Cab 2W-5P	—	—	—
162B	4-dr. Leb. Lan. 3W-5P	—	—	Note 1
162C	4-dr. Leb. Brgm. 3W-5P	—	—	Note 1
	4-dr. Brun. Cab-7P	—	—	—
	4-dr. Brun. Brgm.-7P	—	—	—
	4-dr. Jud. Ber. 2W-4P	5500	—	—
	4-dr. Holbrk. Cab-7P	7400	—	—
	4-dr. Lab. Cab-7P	7600	—	—
	4-dr. Wilby Ber. Land.-6P	6500	—	—
163A	4-dr. Lke. Spt. Phae.-4P	—	—	167
163B	4-dr. Lke. Dbl. Cwl. Spt. Phae.-4P	—	—	90
164A	4-dr. Lke. Spt. Tr.-7P	—	—	173
702	2-dr. Jud. Cpe.-2P	5300	—	205
Cus. Jobs		—	—	72

Note 1: Total combined production for the Leb. Lan. and Leb. Brgm. was 20.

ENGINE: 60° V, L-head. Eight. Cast iron block. B & S: 3-3/8 in. x 5 in. Disp.: 357.8 cu. in. C.R.: 4.8:1. Brake H.P.: 90 @ 2800 R.P.M. Taxable H.P.: 39.2. Main bearings: Three. Valve lifters: Mechanical. Carb.: Stromberg 03 updraft.

CHASSIS: W.B.: 136 in. Frt/Rear Tread: 60 in. Tires: 32 x 6.75.

1927

1927 Lincoln, model L, 3-window sedan, OCW

LINCOLN — MODEL L — EIGHT: Identifying the 1927 Lincolns were bullet-shaped headlight shells enclosing new lamps with dual filaments providing high and low beams in place of the older tilting beam arrangement. Also updated were the Lincoln's rear lights which now consisted of a red lens-taillight, amber lens-brake light and a white lens-backup light. Another revision taking place during 1927 was the use of running boards with black-ribbed rubber rather than a linoleum covering. Although not easily detected, the 1927 Lincolns were one inch lower than previously, due to new 32 x 6.75 tires and a 1/2 inch reduction in spring camber. A new instrument panel placed all instruments within an oval surface.

After offering front wheel brakes for police use since 1923, Lincoln installed mechanical 4-wheel brakes on all its 1927 models. This was described as a "six brake system" in reference to the hand brake control over the rear brakes and the operation of the front and rear brakes by the foot pedal.

The technical changes for 1927 included a new lighter weight clutch system with fewer parts plus a standard equipment "coincidental lock" for the ignition and steering wheel.

I.D. DATA: Serial numbers were located on right side of cowl, top of clutch housing and transmission case. Starting: 39900. Ending: 47499. Engine numbers were located on left side of crankcase between cylinders 1 & 2. Starting: 39900. Ending: 47499.

Model No.	Body Type & Seating	Price	Weight	Prod. Total
122	Chassis	3500	—	83
123B	4-dr. Brun. Spt. Phae.-4P	4700	—	8
123C	4-dr. Brun. Spt. Phae. TC-4P	—	—	1
124A	4-dr. Tr.-7P	—	—	2
124B	4-dr. Brun. Spt. Tr. TC-7P	—	—	6
143	2-dr. Brun. Cpe.-4P	—	—	46

1927 Lincoln, model L, Locke dual cowl phaeton, HAC

TECHNICAL: Sliding gear transmission. Speeds: 3F/1R. Floor shift controls. Multiple disc, dry plate clutch. Shaft drive. Full floating rear axle. Overall Ratio: 4.58:1, Opt. 4.90:1. Mechanical internal expanding brakes on four wheels. 12 spoke wooden artillery wheels, demountable rims. Wheel Size: 20 in.

OPTIONS: Dual sidemount. Sidemount cover(s). Natural wood finish wheels. Steel disc wheels. Buffalo wire wheels. Monogram. Tonneau cowl and rear windshield.

HISTORICAL: Introduced: January, 1927. Innovations: four wheel mechanical brakes, dual filament headlights. Calendar year registrations: 6460. Calendar year production: 7149. The president of Lincoln was Edsel Ford.

1927
Model L, V-8

	FP	5	4	3	2	1
Spt Rds	4600	7650	15,300	25,500	35,700	51,000
Spt Tr	4600	7500	15,000	25,000	35,000	50,000
Phae	4800	7350	14,700	24,500	34,300	49,000
Cpe	4600	5250	10,500	17,500	24,500	35,000
2W Sed	4800	4800	9600	16,000	22,400	32,000
3W Sed	4800	4650	9300	15,500	21,700	31,000
Sed	5000	4500	9000	15,000	21,000	30,000
FW Limo	5200	5700	11,400	19,000	26,600	38,000
Jud Cpe	5000	5550	11,100	18,500	25,900	37,000
Brn Cabr	6600	7650	15,300	25,500	35,700	51,000
Holbrk Cabr	7200	8250	16,500	27,500	38,500	55,000
Brn Brgm	6400	6900	13,800	23,000	32,200	46,000
Dtrch Conv Sed	—	8550	17,100	28,500	39,900	57,000
Dtrch Conv Vic	—	8700	17,400	29,000	40,600	58,000

		5	4	3	2	1
Brn Conv	6600	8100	16,200	27,000	37,800	54,000
Brn Semi-Coll Cabr	6600	8250	16,500	27,500	38,500	55,000
Holbrk Coll Cabr	7200	8550	17,100	28,500	39,900	57,000
Leb A-W Cabr	7300	8700	17,400	29,000	40,600	58,000
Leb A-W Brgm	7300	8700	17,400	29,000	40,600	58,000
W'by Semi-Coll Cabr	6500	8250	16,500	27,500	38,500	55,000
Jud Brgm	5500	6900	13,800	23,000	32,200	46,000
Clb Rds	4600	7500	15,000	25,000	35,000	50,000
Jud 2W Berl	5500	5250	10,500	17,500	24,500	35,000
Jud 3W Berl	5500	5250	10,500	17,500	24,500	35,000
7P E d Limo	5200	5850	11,700	19,500	27,300	39,000
Leb Spt Cabr	7300	8550	17,100	28,500	39,900	57,000
W'by Lan'let	6500	7500	15,000	25,000	35,000	50,000
W'by Limo	6000	6000	12,000	20,000	28,000	40,000
Leb Cpe	7000	5700	11,400	19,000	26,600	38,000
Der Spt Sed	—	5550	11,100	18,500	25,900	37,000
Lke Conv Sed	—	8550	17,100	28,500	39,900	57,000
Dtrch Cpe Rds	6500	8400	16,800	28,000	39,200	56,000
Dtrch Spt Phae	6500	8700	17,400	29,000	40,600	58,000

Model No.	Body Type & Seating	Price	Weight	Prod. Total
165	2-dr. Clb. Rds. R/S-2P	—	—	347
166	4-dr. Brun. Brgm.-7P	—	—	86
167	4-dr. Diet. Conv. Sed.-5P	—	—	38
168A	4-dr. Sed.-7P	—	—	1
168B	4-dr. Limo.-7P	—	—	1
169A	4-dr. Twn. 2W Sed.-5P	—	—	88
169B	4-dr. Twn. 3W Sed.-5P	—	—	140
170	2-dr. Jud. Cpe.-2P	—	—	14
171	4-dr. Diet. Conv. Cpe.-4P	6500	—	6
172	4-dr. Jud. Ber.-5P	—	—	1
702	2-dr. Jud. Cpe.-2P	5000	—	110
Custom				59

Note 1: Total combined production of the Leb. Cab., Leb. Lan. and Leb. Brgm. was 66.

1928

1928 Lincoln, model L, Locke sport roadster, OCW

1928 Lincoln, model L, club roadster, HAC

LINCOLN — MODEL L — EIGHT: Lincoln did not endorse the concept of model years, explaining, ''There are no yearly or periodic Lincoln models; the Lincoln has reached such a state of development that drastic changes are neither necessary or desirable. Whenever it is possible to achieve an improvement in the Lincoln, it is made interchangeable with previous design.'' This philosophy was illustrated by the use of new mufflers during 1928 that dealers were able to retrofit to earlier Lincolns.

Of greater importance was the use of a larger engine that began very late in 1927 and was carried over into 1928. By virtue of a 1/8'' bore increase the Lincoln V-8 now displaced 384.8 cubic inches. Other changes occurring at this time included a slight boost in compression ratio to 4.81:1, larger 1-7/8 inch rather than 1-3/4 inch intake valves, a reshaped combustion chamber and the use of counterweights on the crankshaft. Also debuting in 1928 was an engine oil filter and conical valve springs. Other technical changes included new steering tube bearings and lighter-weight rear axle.

Appearance revisions consisted of cowl lights shaped in the form of Lincoln's front and rear lamps, chrome-plated bumpers and five-stud, steel spoke wheels.

I.D. DATA: Serial numbers were located on right side of cowl, top of clutch housing and transmission case. Starting: 47500. Ending: 54500. Engine numbers were located on left side of crankcase between cylinders 1 and 2. Starting: 47500. Ending: 54500.

Model No.	Body Type & Seating	Price	Weight	Prod. Total
122	Chassis	—	—	105
144A	4-dr. LeB. Trk. Sed. 2W-4P	4800	—	263
144B	4-dr. LeB. Trk. Sed. 3W-4P	4800	—	529
145A	4-dr. Brun. Brgm.-7P	6400	—	3
147A	4-dr. Diet. Sed.-7P	5000	—	1023
147B	4-dr. Diet. Ber.-7P	5200	—	709
150B	150'' wb Chassis	—	—	24
151	2-dr. Lke. Rds.-2P	4600	—	65
152	4-dr. Diet. Sed.-5P	4800	—	835
153A	4-dr. Holbrk. Coll. Cab.-5P	7200	—	8
154	2-dr. Diet. Cpe. R/S-2P	4600	—	54
155	4-dr. LeB. Coll. Spt. Cab.-5P	7300	—	9
156	2-dr. LeB. Cpe.-4P	4600	—	230
157	4-dr. Wilby Ber.-6P	6500	—	6
159	4-dr. Brun. Cab.-5P	6600	—	12
160	4-dr. Wilby Limo.-7P	6000	—	483
161	4-dr. Jud. Ber.-7P	5500	—	348
162A	4-dr. LeB. Cab. 2W-5P	7350	—	Note 1
162B	4-dr. LeB. Lan. 3W-5P	7350	—	Note 1
162C	4-dr. LeB. Brgm.-3W-5P	—	—	Note 1
163A	4-dr. Lke. Spt. Phae.-4P	4600	—	226
163B	4-dr. Lke. Dbl. Cwl. Spt. Phae.-4P	—	—	150
164A	4-dr. Lke. Spt. Tr.-7P	4600	—	323

ENGINE: 60° L-head. Eight. Cast iron block. B & S: 3-1/2 in. x 5 in. Disp.: 384.8. C.R.: 4.81:1. Brake H.P.: 90 @ 2800 R.P.M. Taxable H.P.: 39.2. Main bearings: Three. Valve lifters: Mechanical. Carb.: Stromberg 03 updraft.

CHASSIS: W.B.: 136 in. Frt/Rear Tread: 60 in. Tires: 32 x 6.75. Opt. 20 x 7.00.

TECHNICAL: Sliding gear transmission. Speeds: 3F/1R. Floor shift controls. Multiple disc, dry plate clutch. Shaft drive. Full floating rear axle. Overall Ratio: 4.58:1 opt. 4.90:1. Mechanical internal expanding brakes on four wheels. Steel spoke wheels. Wheel Size: 20 in.

OPTIONS: Dual Sidemount. Sidemount cover(s). Wooden artillery wheels. Steel disc wheels (all-welded ''safety wheels''). Buffalo wire wheels. Monogram. Tonneau cowl and windshield.

HISTORICAL: Introduced: January, 1928. Innovations: standard oil filter, counter balanced crankshaft. Calendar year registrations: 6039. Calendar year production: 6362. The president of Lincoln was Edsel Ford.

1928
Model L. V-8

	FP	5	4	3	2	1
164 Spt Tr	4600	8250	16,500	27,500	38,500	55,000
163 Lke Spt Phae	4600	9000	18,000	30,000	42,000	60,000
151 Lke Spt Rds	4600	8250	16,500	27,500	38,500	55,000
154 Clb Rds	4600	8100	16,200	27,000	37,800	54,000
156 Cpe	4600	5100	10,200	17,000	23,800	34,000
144A 2W Sed	4800	4650	9300	15,500	21,700	31,000
144B Sed	4800	4650	9300	15,500	21,700	31,000
152 Sed	4800	4500	9000	15,000	21,000	30,000
147A Sed	5000	4500	9000	15,000	21,000	30,000
147B Limo	5200	5100	10,200	17,000	23,800	34,000
161 Jud Berl	5500	5400	10,800	18,000	25,200	36,000
161C Jud Berl	5500	5400	10,800	18,000	25,200	36,000
Jud Cpe	5000	5700	11,400	19,000	26,600	38,000
159 Brn Cabr	6600	8400	16,800	28,000	39,200	56,000
145 Brn Brgm	6400	7800	15,600	26,000	36,400	52,000
155A Hlbrk Coll Cabr	7200	9000	18,000	30,000	42,000	60,000
155 Leb Spt Cabr	7300	10,500	21,000	35,000	49,000	70,000
157 W'by Lan'let Berl	6500	9000	18,000	30,000	42,000	60,000
160 W'by Limo	6000	9900	19,800	33,000	46,200	66,000
162A Leb A-W Cabr	7350	9300	18,600	31,000	43,400	62,000
162 Leb A-W Lan'let	7350	8550	17,100	28,500	39,900	57,000
Jud Spt Cpe	5000	9300	18,600	31,000	43,400	62,000
Leb Cpe	6900	7500	15,000	25,000	35,000	50,000
Dtrch Conv Vic	6500	7950	15,900	26,500	37,100	53,000
Dtrch Cpe Rds	6300	7800	15,600	26,000	36,400	52,000
Dtrch Conv Sed	6500	9900	19,800	33,000	46,200	66,000
Holbrk Cabr	7200	9000	18,000	30,000	42,000	60,000
W'by Spt Sed	6500	6300	12,600	21,000	29,400	42,000
Der Spt Sed	6500	6300	12,600	21,000	29,400	42,000
Brn Spt Conv	6600	10,200	20,400	34,000	47,600	68,000

1929

LINCOLN — MODEL L — EIGHT: The 1929 Lincoln's appearance was highlighted by a higher, narrower and somewhat squarer radiator shell topped by a larger filler cap. In addition, the old leather windshield visor was replaced by a dark glass version. Many models had laminated safety glass and all 1928 Lincolns had twin windshield wipers.

Interior changes consisted of a new engine temperature gauge, (which corresponded with the repositioning of the cigar lighter to the dashboard from its previous instrument panel location) and an electric rather than spring-wound clock.

Technical changes were not extensive consisting of the use of rubber engine mounts, increased (from 30 to 50 pounds), oil pressure and a stronger starter-generator.

I.D. DATA: Serial numbers were located on right side of cowl, top of clutch housing and transmission case. Starting: 54501. Ending: 61699. Engine numbers were located on left side of crankcase between cylinders 1 and 2. Starting: 54501. Ending: 61699.

1929 Lincoln, model L, roadster, AA

Model No.	Body Type & Seating	Price	Weight	Prod. Total
122	Chassis	3300	—	75
150B	150" wb Chassis	3500	—	43
151	2-dr. Lke. Rds.-2P	4650	—	7
153A	4-dr. Holbrk. Coll. Cab.-5P	6800	—	2
155	4-dr. LeB. Coll. Spt. Cab.-5P	7400	—	3
156	2-dr. LeB. Cpe.-4P	5300	—	138
157	4-dr. Wilby Ber.-6P	—	—	5
160	4-dr. Wilby Limo.-7P	6200	—	155
162A	4-dr. LeB. Cab. 2W-5P	7400	—	Note 1
162B	4-dr. LeB. Lan. 3W-5P	—	—	Note 1
162C	4-dr. LeB. Brgm. 3W-5P	—	—	Note 1
163A	4-dr. Lke. Spt. Phae.-4P	4650	—	88
163B	4-dr. Lke. Dbl. Cwl. Spt. Phae.-4P	—	—	58
164A	4-dr. Lke. Spt. Tr.-7P	—	—	88
164B		—	—	18
165	2-dr. Clb. Rds. R/S-2P	4900	—	225
166	4-dr. Brun. Brgm.-7P	7400	—	78
167	4-dr. Diet. Conv. Sed.-7P	6900	—	60
168A	4-dr. Sed.-7P	5100	—	1380
168B	4-dr. Limo.-7P	5300	—	837
169A	4-dr. Twn. 2W Sed.-5P	4900	—	658
169B	4-dr. Twn. 3W Sed.-5P	—	—	1513
170	2-dr. Jud. Cpe.-2P	5200	—	270
171	4-dr. Diet. Conv. Cpe.-4P	6000	—	69
172	4-dr. Jud. Ber.-5P	5800	—	360
173A	4-dr. Sed. 2W-5P	4900	—	22
173B	4-dr. Sed. 3W-5P	4900	—	436
174	4-dr. Wilby Limo.-7P	6200	—	228
175	4-dr. Brun. Brgm.-5P	7200	—	50
176A	4-dr. Spt. Phae.-4P	4650	—	92
176B	4-dr. Spt. Phae. Dbl. Cwl.-4P	5050	—	42
177	4-dr. Spt. Tr.-7P	4650	—	174
178	4-dr. LeB. Spt. Sed.-5P	—	—	42
179	2-dr. Cpe.-4P	4800	—	209
180	4-dr. Brun. Brgm. 2W-7P	7200	—	24
181	2-dr. Diet. Conv. Cpe.-4P	6500	—	8
182	4-dr. Diet. Conv. Sed.-5P	6900	—	10
183	4-dr. Sed.-5P	5000	—	27
184	4-dr. LeB. Brgm.-5P	—	—	2

Note 1: Total combined production of the Leb. Cab., Leb. Land. and Leb. Brgm. was 74.

1929 Lincoln, model L, town sedan, JAC

836

ENGINE: 60° V, L-head. Eight. Cast iron block. B & S: 3-1/2 in. x 5 in. Disp.: 384.8 cu. in. C.R.: 4.81:1. Brake H.P.: 90 @ 2800 R.P.M. Taxable H.P.: 39.2. Main bearings: Three. Valve lifters: Mechanical. Carb.: Stromberg 03 updraft.

CHASSIS: [Model L] W.B.: 136 in. Frt/Rear Tread: 60 in. Tires: 32 x 6.75. Opt. 20 x 7.00.

TECHNICAL: Sliding gear transmission. Speeds: 3F/1R. Floor shift controls. Multiple disc, dry plate clutch. Shaft drive. Full floating rear axle. Overall Ratio: 4.58:1 opt. 4.90:1. Mechanical external expanding brakes on four wheels. Steel spoke wheels. Wheel Size: 20 in.

OPTIONS: Dual Sidemount. Sidemount cover(s). Wooden artillery wheels. Steel disc wheels. Buffalo wire wheels. Monogram. Tonneau cowl and windshield.

HISTORICAL: Introduced: January 1, 1929. Calendar year sales: 6399 (6151 registrations). Calendar year production: 7672. Model year production: 7641. The president of Lincoln was Edsel Ford.

1929 Lincoln, model L, phaeton, JAC

1929
Model L, V-8
Standard Line

	FP	5	4	3	2	1
Lke Spt Rds	4650	11,400	22,800	38,000	56,000	76,000
Clb Rds	4900	11,100	22,200	37,000	52,000	74,000
Lke Spt Phae	4650	11,400	22,800	38,000	56,000	76,000
Lke TWS Spt Phae	4890	12,000	24,000	40,000	60,000	80,000
Lke Spt Phae TC & WS	5000	12,900	25,800	48,200	66,000	86,000
Lke Spt Tr	4650	11,400	22,800	38,000	56,000	76,000
4P Cpe	4800	6450	12,900	21,500	30,100	43,000
Twn Sed	4900	6300	12,600	21,000	29,400	42,000
5P Sed	5000	6150	12,300	20,500	28,700	41,000
7P Sed	5100	6300	12,600	21,000	29,400	42,000
7P Limo	5300	6750	13,500	22,500	31,500	45,000
2W Jud Berl	4900	7050	14,100	23,500	32,900	47,000
3W Jud Berl	5000	6900	13,800	23,000	32,200	46,000
Brn A-W Brgm	7400	9000	18,000	30,000	42,000	60,000
Brn Cabr	7400	9900	19,800	33,000	46,200	66,000
Brn Non-Coll Cabr	7400	9900	19,800	33,000	46,200	66,000
Holbrk Coll Cabr	6800	10,500	21,000	35,000	49,000	70,000
Leb A-W Cabr	7400	9900	19,800	33,000	46,200	66,000
Leb Semi-Coll Cabr	7400	10,500	21,000	35,000	49,000	70,000
Leb Coll Cabr	7400	10,800	21,600	36,000	50,500	72,000
W'by Lan'let	6100	8250	16,500	27,500	38,500	55,000
W'by Limo	6200	7800	15,600	26,000	36,400	52,000
Dtrch Cpe	6000	9000	18,000	30,000	42,000	60,000
Dtrch Sed	6000	8700	17,400	29,000	40,600	58,000
Dtrch Conv	—	12,000	24,000	40,000	60,000	80,000
Leb Spt Sed	5300	9000	18,000	30,000	42,000	60,000
Leb Aero Phae	7400	12,900	25,800	48,200	66,000	86,000
Leb Sal Cabr	7400	10,500	21,000	35,000	49,000	70,000
Brn Spt Conv	7400	11,400	22,800	38,000	56,000	76,000
Dtrch Conv Sed	6900	12,000	24,000	40,000	60,000	80,000
Dtrch Conv Vic	6500	12,300	24,600	41,000	62,000	82,000
Lke Clb Rds	4900	11,700	23,400	39,000	58,000	78,000

1930

1930 Lincoln, model L, roadster, DW

LINCOLN — MODEL L — EIGHT: With the L series Lincoln scheduled for replacement in 1931 only minor changes were to be found in the Lincoln's format for 1930. The Brunn seven-passenger brougham, Willoughby six-passenger landaulet and the seven-passenger cabriolets by Brunn and Holbrook were no longer available. An open, convertible model took the place of the club roadster. Lincoln made a concession to modern tastes by offering fenders painted to match body colors for the first time. More precise control was now provided by the adoption of worm and roller type steering.

I.D. DATA: Serial numbers were located on right side of cowl, top of clutch housing and transmission case. Starting: 61700. Ending: 66000. Engine numbers were located on left side of crankcase between cylinders 1 and 2. Starting: 61700. Ending: 66000.

1930 Lincoln, model L, 7-pass. sedan, JAC

Model No.	Body Type & Seating	Price	Weight	Prod. Total
122	Chassis	—	—	30
165	2-dr. Clb. Rds. R/S-2P	—	—	12
172	4-dr. Jud. Ber.-5P	5600	—	72
174	4-dr. Wilby Limo.-7P	—	—	244
175	4-dr. Brun. Brgm.-5P	—	—	44
176A	4-dr. Spt. Phae.-4P	—	—	53
176B	4-dr. Spt. Phae. Dbl. Cwl.-4P	—	—	90
177	4-dr. Spt. Tr.-7P	—	—	79
178	4-dr. Leb. Spt. Sed.-5P	5300	—	8
179	2-dr. Cpe.-4P	—	—	275
180	4-dr. Brun. Brgm. 2W-7P	—	—	68
181	2-dr. Diet. Conv. Cpe.-4P	—	—	42
182	4-dr. Diet. Conv. Sed.-5P	—	—	40
183	4-dr. Sed.-5P	—	—	541
184	4-dr. Leb. Brgm.-5P	—	—	49
185	2-dr. Leb. Conv. Rds.-2P	6900	—	100
186	4-dr. Jud. Ber.-5P	5600	—	100
187	4-dr. Wilby Panel Brgm.-4P	7000	—	5
188	2-dr. Der. Conv. Rds.-2P	—	—	1
189	4-dr. Der. Conv. Phae.-5P	6000	—	21
190	2-dr. Jud. Cpe.-2P	5000	—	25
191	2-dr. Lke. Spt. Rds.-2P	4500	—	15

ENGINE: 60° V, L-head. Eight. Cast iron block. B & S: 3-1/2 in. x 5 in. Disp.: 384.8 cu. in. C.R.: 4.81:1. Brake H.P.: 90 @ 2800 R.P.M. Taxable H.P.: 39.2. Main bearings: Three. Valve lifters: Mechanical. Carb.: Stromberg 03 updraft.

CHASSIS: W.B.: 136 in. Frt/Rear Tread: 60 in. Tires: 32 x 6.75; Opt. 20 x 7.00.

TECHNICAL: Sliding gear transmission. Speeds: 3F/1R. Floor shift controls. Multiple disc clutch. Shaft drive. Full floating rear axle. Overall Ratio: 4.58:1; Opt. 4.90:1. Mechanical external expanding brakes on four wheels. Steel spoke wheels. Wheel Size: 20 in.

1930 Lincoln, model L, LeBaron convertible roadster, JAC

OPTIONS: Dual sidemount. Sidemount cover(s). Wooden artillery wheels. Steel disc wheels. Buffalo wire wheels. Monogram. Tonneau cowl and windshield.

HISTORICAL: Introduced: January, 1930. Calendar year registrations: 4356. Calendar year production: 3515. Model year production: 3212. The president of Lincoln was Edsel Ford.

1930 Lincoln, model L, Judkins two-window berline, JAC

1930
Model L, V-8
Standard Line

	FP	5	4	3	2	1
Conv Rds	4500	11,400	22,800	38,000	56,000	76,000
5P Lke Spt Phae	4200	11,700	23,400	39,000	58,000	78,000
5P Lke Spt Phae TC & WS	4400	12,900	25,800	48,200	66,000	86,000
7P Lke Spt Phae	4200	12,000	24,000	40,000	60,000	80,000
Cpe	4400	5850	11,700	19,500	27,300	39,000
Twn Sed	4400	5550	11,100	18,500	25,900	37,000
5P Sed	4500	5700	11,400	19,000	26,600	38,000
7P Sed	4600	5700	11,400	19,000	26,600	38,000
7P Limo	4900	6000	12,000	20,000	28,000	40,000
Custom Line						
Jud Cpe	5000	6750	13,500	22,500	31,500	45,000
2W Jud Berl	5600	8250	16,500	27,500	38,500	55,000
3W Jud Berl	5600	8250	16,500	27,500	38,500	55,000
Brn A-W Cabr	7200	9000	18,000	30,000	42,000	60,000
Brn Non-Coll Cabr	7200	8700	17,400	29,000	40,600	58,000
Leb A-W Cabr	7100	13,500	27,000	45,000	70,000	90,000
Leb Semi-Coll Cabr	7100	12,900	25,800	48,200	66,000	86,000
W'by Limo	5900	8250	16,500	27,500	38,500	55,000
Dtrch Cpe	6000	7800	15,600	26,000	36,400	52,000
Dtrch Sed	6000	6150	12,300	20,500	28,700	41,000
2W W'by Twn Sed	4400	6300	12,600	21,000	29,400	42,000
3W W'by Twn Sed	4400	6450	12,900	21,500	30,100	43,000
W'by Pan Brgm	7000	7050	14,100	23,500	32,900	47,000
Leb Cpe	5300	7650	15,300	25,500	35,700	51,000
Leb Conv Rds	6900	12,900	25,800	48,200	66,000	86,000
Leb Spt Sed	5300	9900	19,800	33,000	46,200	66,000
Der Spt Conv	6200	11,700	23,400	39,000	58,000	78,000
Der Conv Phae	6200	12,900	25,800	48,200	66,000	86,000
Brn Semi-Coll Cabr	7200	11,400	22,800	38,000	56,000	76,000
Dtrch Conv Cpe	6600	12,000	24,000	40,000	60,000	80,000
Dtrch Conv Sed	6600	12,300	24,600	41,000	62,000	82,000
Wolf Conv Sed	—	12,000	24,000	40,000	60,000	80,000
Lke Rds	4500	12,300	24,600	41,000	62,000	82,000

1931

1931 Lincoln, model K, Murphy dual cowl phaeton, OCW

LINCOLN — SERIES 201 — MODEL K — EIGHT: The Model K represented a dramatic shift away from the confines of the Model L design, although that car's great engine in updated form was continued.

The use of a new 145 inch wheelbase frame with six cross members and cruciform braces plus 7.00 x 19 tires gave the new Lincoln a low, sleek profile. Accentuating this look were numerous other styling changes. A new peaked radiator shape, a longer hood plus higher windows were key contributors. Only slightly less dramatic were the new bowl-shaped headlight shells and imposing dual trumpet horns with town and country settings. The graceful flow of the Lincoln fenders plus the rounded form of the front and rear bumpers were further examples of a well-coordinated design.

Both free wheeling and synchromesh on 2nd and 3rd gears were introduced on the 1931 models. In addition, a new double dry disc clutch was installed. Lincoln retained both a floating rear axle and torque tube drive with slight revisions. The old steel rod and Perrot braking system was replaced by a cable operated Bendix Duo-Servo system. Also introduced in 1931 were double acting Houdaille hydraulic shock absorbers at all four wheels.

In addition to a new Stromberg carburetor and more efficient manifolding, the Lincoln V-8 was now fitted with 5 main bearings plus separate generator and starter units. A mechanical fuel pump replaced the obsolete vacuum system.

1931 Lincoln, model K, Judkins two-pass. coupe, JAC

1931 Lincoln, model K, town sedan, JAC

I.D. DATA: Serial numbers were located on the right side of cowl, top of clutch housing and transmission case. Starting: 66001. Ending: 70000. Engine numbers were located on left side of crankcase between cylinders 1 and 2. Starting: 66001. Ending: 70000.

Model No.	Body Type & Seating	Price	Weight	Prod. Total
201	Chassis	—	—	61
202A	4-dr. Dbl. Cwl. Spt. Phae.-5P	4600	5245	77
202B	4-dr. Spt. Phae.-5P	4400	5175	60
203	4-dr. Spt. Tr.-7P	4400	5250	45
204-A	4-dr. Twn. Sed. 2W-5P	4600	5205	211
204-B	4-dr. Twn. Sed. 3W-5P	4600	5205	447
205	4-dr. Sed.-5P	4700	5440	552
206	2-dr. Cpe.-5P	4600	5235	225
207-A	4-dr. Sed.-7P	4900	5420	521
207-B	4-dr. Limo.-7P	5100	5370	387
207-C	4-dr. Limo.-7P	5100	5370	14
208-A	4-dr. All. W. Non-Clp. Brun. Cab-5P	7400	5340	30
208-B	4-dr. All W. Semi-Clp. Brun. Cab-5P	7400	5440	—
209	4-dr. All. W. Brgm. Brun.-5P	7200	5370	34
210	4-dr. Diet. Conv. Cpe.-4P	6400	5220	25
211	4-dr. Diet. Sed.-5P	6800	5250	65
212	4-dr. Der. Phae.-4P	6200	5040	11
213-A	4-dr. Jud. Ber. 2W-4P	5800	5420	—
213-B	4-dr. Jud. Ber. 3W-4P	5800	5460	171
214	2-dr. LeB. Conv. Cpe.-2/4P	4700	5070	275
215	4-dr. Wilby Limo.-6P	6100	5370	151
216	4-dr. Wilby Panel Brgm.-7P	7400	5400	15
217-A	4-dr. All W. Non-Up Leb. Cab-7P	7100	5320	Note 1
217-B	4-dr. All W. Semi-Clp. Leb. Cab-7P	7300	5420	Note 1
218	2-dr. Jud. Cpe.-2P	5200	5180	86
219	2-dr. Diet. Cpe.-2P	—	—	35
220	150" wb Chassis	—	—	3
221	155" wb Chassis	—	—	3
	Special	—	—	26
	RHD	—	—	21

Note 1: Total combined production of the All W. Non-Up Leb. Cab. and All W. Semi-Clp. Leb. Cab. was 21.

ENGINE: 60° V, L-head. Eight. Cast iron block. B & S: 3-1/2 in. x 5 in. Disp.: 384.8 cu. in. C.R.: 4.95:1. Brake H.P.: 120 @ 2900 R.P.M. N.A.C.C. H.P.: 43. Main bearings: Five. Valve lifters: Mechanical. Carb.: Stromberg DD3 downdraft 2bbl.

CHASSIS: W.B.: 145 in. Frt/Rear Tread: 60 in. Tires: 19 x 7.00.

TECHNICAL: Sliding gear transmission. Speeds: 3F/1R. Floor shift controls. Double dry disc clutch. Shaft drive. Full floating rear axle. Overall Ratio: 4.58:1, 4.90:1, 4.23:1 (standard). Bendix Duo-Servo mechanical brakes on four wheels. Steel spoke wheels. Wheel Size: 19 in.

OPTIONS: Dual sidemount.

838

HISTORICAL: Introduced: January, 1931. Innovations: First American use of a two-barrel down-draft carburetor. Free wheeling was introduced on the 1931 Lincolns. Calendar year registrations: 3466. Calendar year production: 3592. Model year production: 3540. The president of Lincoln was Edsel Ford.

1931
Model K, V-8
Type 201, V-8, 145" wb

	FP	5	4	3	2	1
202B Spt Phae	4400	12,300	24,600	41,000	62,000	82,000
202A Spt Phae	4600	12,900	25,800	48,200	66,000	86,000
203 Spt Tr	4400	12,600	25,200	42,000	64,000	84,000
214 Conv Rds	4700	12,900	25,800	48,200	66,000	86,000
206 Cpe	4600	6000	12,000	20,000	28,000	40,000
204 Twn Sed	4600	5700	11,400	19,000	26,600	38,000
205 Sed	4700	5850	11,700	19,500	27,300	39,000
207A Sed	4900	5850	11,700	19,500	27,300	39,000
207B Limo	5100	6300	12,600	21,000	29,400	42,000
212 Conv Phae	6200	12,900	25,800	48,200	66,000	86,000
210 Conv Cpe	6400	12,600	25,200	42,000	64,000	84,000
211 Conv Sed	6800	13,200	26,400	44,000	68,000	88,000
216 W'by Pan Brgm	7400	8250	16,500	27,500	38,500	55,000
213A Jud Berl	5800	7500	15,000	25,000	35,000	50,000
213B Jud Berl	5800	7500	15,000	25,000	35,000	50,000
Jud Cpe	5200	7350	14,700	24,500	34,300	49,000
Brn Cabr	7400	12,000	24,000	40,000	60,000	80,000
Leb Cabr	7100	12,000	24,000	40,000	60,000	80,000
W'by Limo	6100	7500	15,000	25,000	35,000	50,000
Lke Spt Rds	4700	13,200	26,400	44,000	68,000	88,000
Der Conv Sed	6200	13,500	27,000	45,000	70,000	90,000
Leb Conv Rds	4700	13,500	27,000	45,000	70,000	90,000
Mur DC Phae	6800	14,700	29,400	49,000	78,000	98,000
Dtrch Conv Sed	6800	13,800	27,600	46,000	73,50	92,000
Dtrch Conv Cpe	6400	13,500	27,000	45,000	70,000	90,000
Wtrhs Conv Vic	—	14,400	28,800	48,000	76,000	96,000

1932

1932 Lincoln, model KA, coupe, AA

LINCOLN — SERIES 501 — MODEL KA — EIGHT: Lincoln significantly altered its marketing stance in 1932. The KA series models were priced lower than previous K models and was offered in seven standard body styles. On a 136 inch wheelbase chassis the KA Lincoln featured a sharply pointed front grille, one-piece front and rear bumpers and thermostatically-operated hood shutters.

LINCOLN — SERIES 231 — MODEL KB — TWELVE: The KB shared the modern appearance of the medium-priced KA but since it represented a new peak of Lincoln excellence the KB had many distinctive features. Its cloisonne' emblem was blue (that of the KA was red), its radiator shell was noticeably thinner and of course its wheelbase was 145 inches. As was the case with the 1931 Model K, the KA was available in nine standard and fourteen factory custom bodies. Of even greater interest was the KA's new V-12 engine. The terms "massive" and "rugged" have often been applied to this engine with good reason. Displacement was 447.9 cubic inches, installed weight exceeded a ½ ton and the valves measured 2 inches in diameter. The forged-steel crankshaft was carried in 7 main bearings.

I.D. DATA: Serial numbers were located on the right side of cowl, top of clutch housing and transmission case. Starting: KA-70001; [KB] KB1. Ending: KA-72041; [KB] KB1666. Engine numbers were located on left side of crankcase between cylinders 1 and 2. Starting: KA-70001; [KB] KB1. Ending: KA-72041; [KB] KB1666.

1932 Lincoln, model KB, 7-pass. sedan, JAC

Model No.	Body Type & Seating	Price	Weight	Prod. Total
Series 501 KA				
501	Chassis	—	—	7
502	2-dr. Cpe.-2P	3200	5220	—
502	2-dr. Cpe.-2/4P	3245	5090	86
503				40
504	4-dr. Twn. Sed.-4P	3100	5450	147
505	4-dr. Sed.-5P	3200	5430	921
506	2-dr. Vict.-5P	3200	5345	265
507-A	4-dr. Sed.-7P	3300	5435	508
507-B	4-dr. Limo.-7P	3350	5520	122
508	4-dr. Phae.-4P	3000	5145	29
510	2-dr. Rds.-2P	2900	4925	—
	RHD			5
Series 231 KB				
231	Chassis	—	—	18
232-A	4-dr. Mphy. Dbl. Cwl. Spt. Phae.-4P	4500	5625	30
232-B	4-dr. Mphy. Spt. Phae.-4P	4300	5600	13
233	4-dr. Spt. Tr.-7P	4300	5720	24
234-A	4-dr. Twn. Sed. 2W-5P	4500	5740	123
234-B	4-dr. Twn. Sed. 3W-5P	4500	5740	200
235	4-dr. Sed.-5P	4600	5750	216
236	2-dr. Cpe.5-P	4400	5750	83
237-A	4-dr. Sed.-7P	4700	5855	266
237-B	4-dr. Limo.-7P	4900	5885	41
237-C	4-dr. Limo.-7P	4900	5885	135
238	4-dr. Brun. all w. Cab.-5P	7200	5585	14
239	4-dr. Brun. all w. Brgm.-7P	7000	5920	13
240	4-dr. Diet. Spt. Ber.-5P	6500	5605	8
241	4-dr. Diet. Conv. Sed.-5P	6400	5720	20
242-A	2-dr. Diet. Cpe.-2/4P	5150	5710	—
242-B	2-dr. Diet. Cpe.-2P	5000	5710	17
243-A	4-dr. Jud. Ber. 2W-5P	5700	5860	—
243-B	4-dr. Jud. Ber. 3W-5P	5700	5860	74
244-A	2-dr. Jud. Cpe.-2/4P	5350	5610	—
245	4-dr. Wilby Limo.-7P	5900	5950	64
246	4-dr. Wilby Pan. Brgm.-4P	7100	5855	4
247	4-dr. Waths Conv. Vict.-5P	5900	5470	10
248	2-dr. Conv. Rds.-2/4P	4600	5535	112
249	2-dr. Muphy Spt. Rds.	6800	5605	3
250	150'' wb Chassis	—	—	1
	Specials	—	—	3
	RHD	—	—	10

ENGINE: [Series KA] 60° V, L-head. Eight: Cast iron block. B & S: 3-1/2 in. x 5 in. Disp.: 384.8 cu. in. C.R.: 5.23:1. Brake H.P.: 125 @ 2900 R.P.M. Main bearings: Five. Valve lifters: Mechanical. Carb.: Stromberg DD3 downdraft 2bhl. [Series KB] 60° V, L-head. Twelve. Cast iron block. B & S: 3-1/4 in. x 4-1/2 in. Disp.: 447.9 cu. in. C.R.: 5.25:1. Brake H.P.: 150 @ 3400 R.P.M. Main bearings: Seven. Valve lifters: Mechanical. Carb.: Stromberg DD downdraft 2bbl. Torque: 292 lbs.-ft. @ 1200 R.P.M.

CHASSIS: [Series KA] W.B.: 136 in. Frt/Rear Tread: 60 in. Tires: 18 x 7.00. [Series KB] W.B.: 145 in. O.L.: 214 in. Frt/Rear Tread: 60 in. Tires: 18 x 7.50.

TECHNICAL: Sliding gear transmission. Speeds: 3F/1R. Floor shift controls. Double dry disc clutch. Shaft drive. Full floating rear axle. Overall Ratio: 4.58:1; 4.90:1; 4.23:1 (standard). Bendix Duo-Servo mechanical brakes on four wheels. Steel spoke wheels. Wheel Size: 18 in.

OPTIONS: Dual sidemount.

HISTORICAL: Calendar year registrations: 3179. Calendar year production: 3388. Model year production: Series 501 (KA)-2132, Series 231 (KB)-1515. The company president of Lincoln was Edsel Ford.

1932
Model KA, V-8, 8-cyl., 136" wb

	FP	5	4	3	2	1
Rds	2945	13,200	26,400	44,000	68,000	88,000
Phae	3000	13,200	26,400	44,000	68,000	88,000
Twn Sed	3100	6750	13,500	22,500	31,500	45,000
Sed	3200	6600	13,200	22,000	30,800	44,000
Cpe	3245	6900	13,800	23,000	32,200	46,000
Vic	3200	6750	13,500	22,500	31,500	45,000
7P Sed	3300	6600	13,200	22,000	30,800	44,000
Limo	3350	7200	14,400	24,000	33,600	48,000

Model KB, V-12
Standard, 12-cyl., 145" wb

	FP	5	4	3	2	1
Phae	4300	13,500	27,000	45,000	70,000	90,000
Spt Phae	4500	14,100	28,200	57,000	74,000	94,000
Cpe	4400	7200	14,400	24,000	33,600	48,000
2W Tr Sed	4600	6900	13,800	23,000	32,200	46,000
3W Tr Sed	4600	6900	13,800	23,000	32,200	46,000
5P Sed	4606	6900	13,800	23,000	32,200	46,000
7P Sed	4700	7050	14,100	23,500	32,900	47,000
Limo	4900	7500	15,000	25,000	35,000	50,000
Custom, 145" wb						
Leb Conv Cpe	4600	12,000	24,000	40,000	60,000	80,000
2P Dtrch Cpe	5100	7800	15,600	26,000	36,400	52,000
4P Dtrch Cpe	5150	7500	15,000	25,000	35,000	50,000
Jud Cpe	5350	7950	15,900	26,500	37,100	53,000
Jud Berl	5700	6750	13,500	22,500	31,500	45,000
W'by Limo	5900	7050	14,100	23,500	32,900	47,000
Wtrhs Conv Vic	5900	12,000	24,000	40,000	60,000	80,000
Dtrch Conv Sed	6400	18,500	33,000	55,000	88,000	110,000
Mur Spt Rds	6800	15,000	30,000	50,000	80,000	100,000
W'by Twn Brgm	7100	9000	18,000	30,000	42,000	60,000
Brn Brgm	7000	8700	17,400	29,000	40,600	58,000
Brn Non-Coll Cabr	7200	10,500	21,000	35,000	49,000	70,000
Brn Semi-Coll Cabr	7200	12,000	24,000	40,000	60,000	80,000
Leb Twn Cabr	4600	12,300	24,600	41,000	62,000	82,000
Dtrch Spt Berl	5150	9000	18,000	30,000	42,000	60,000
5P Rlstn TwnC	—	10,500	21,000	35,000	49,000	70,000
7P Rlstn TwnC	—	10,500	21,000	35,000	49,000	70,000
Brn Phae	7200	15,000	30,000	50,000	80,000	100,000
Brn dbl-entry Spt Sed						
	7000	10,800	21,600	36,000	50,500	72,000
Brn A-W Brgm	7000	10,500	21,000	35,000	49,000	70,000
Brn Clb Sed	—	10,200	20,400	34,000	47,600	68,000
Mur Conv Rds	6800	15,000	30,000	50,000	80,000	100,000

1933

1933 Lincoln, model KB, Brunn convertible victoria, AA

LINCOLN — SERIES 511 — MODEL KA — TWELVE: Lincoln concluded the era of the classic V-8 engine with its fork and blade connecting rods by introducing a new 67° V-12 for the KA series. Its displacement was 381.7 cubic inches. Aluminum pistons were installed and the crankshaft was carried in four bearings. The detachable cylinder heads were constructed of cast iron. This engine while based upon the KB V-12 was simpler and less expensive to produce.

A total of 12 models were available in KA form and their styling was once again substantially revised. Lincoln adopted hood louvers rather than shutters for both KA and KB models and an elegant chrome mesh grille sloped backward for a more streamlined profile. Early models continued to use the older clamshell type fenders but mid-way through the model year valanced-type versions were adopted and Lincoln agreed to retro-fit them to the early 1933 models at no cost to owners.

LINCOLN — SERIES 251 — MODEL KB — TWELVE: The KB had the same basic styling of the KA but its considerably larger size and available custom bodywork left no chance of being mistaken for a KA. A new double-drop frame was introduced for 1933.

1933 Lincoln, model KB, coupe, HAC

I.D. DATA: Serial numbers were located on right side of cowl, top of clutch housing and transmission case. Starting: [KA] KA1; [KB] KB2001. Ending: [KA] KA1140; [KB] KB2604. Engine numbers were located on left side of crankcase between cylinders 1 and 2. Starting: [KA] KA1; [KB] KB2001. Ending: [KA] KA1140; [KB] KB2604.

Model No.	Body Type & Seating	Price	Weight	Prod. Total
Series 511 KA				
511	Chassis	—	—	7
512-A	2-dr. Cpe.-2/4P	3145	5210	Note 1
512-B	2-dr. Cpe.-2P	3100	5190	Note 1
513	2-dr. Conv. Rds.-2/4P	3200	5050	85
514	4-dr. Twn. Sed.-5P	3100	5235	201
515	4-dr. Sed.-5P	3200	5270	320
516	2-dr. Vict.-5P	3200	5200	109
517-A	4-dr. Sed.-7P	3300	5440	190
517-B	4-dr. Limo.-7P	3350	5465	111
518-A	4-dr. Dbl. Cwl. Phae.-5P	3200	5040	12
518-B	4-dr. Phae.-5P	3000	5030	12
519	4-dr. Phae.-7P	3200	5040	10
520-A	2-dr. Rds.-2/4P	2745	5030	Note 2
520-B	2-dr. Rds.-2P	2700	5020	Note 2
	Specials	—	—	1
	RHD	—	—	4
Series 251 KB				
251	Chassis	—	—	4
252-A	2-dr. Dbl. Cwl. Spt. Phae.-4P	4400	5500	9
252-B	4-dr. Spt. Phae.-4P	4200	5410	6
253	4-dr. Spt. Tr.-7P	4300	5500	6
254-A	4-dr. Twn. Sed. 2W-5P	4400	5590	39
254-B	4-dr. Twn. Sed. 3W-5P	4400	5590	41
255	4-dr. Sed.-5P	4500	5790	52
256	4-dr. Vict. Cpe.-5P	4300	5710	18
257-A	4-dr. Sed.-7P	4600	5820	110
257-B	4-dr. Limo.-7P	4800	5840	105
258-C	4-dr. Brun. Non. Clp. Cab.-7P	6900	5685	—
258-D	4-dr. Brun. Smi. Clp. Cab.-5P	6900	5685	8
14	4-dr. Brun. Brgm.-7P	6900	5730	13
260	2-dr. Brun. Conv. Cpe.-5P	5700	5470	—
260	2-dr. Diet. Spt. Ber.-5P			15
261	4-dr. Diet. Conv. Sed.-5P	6100	5600	15
263-A	4-dr. Jud. Ber. 2W-4P	5500	5710	Note 3
263-A	4-dr. Jud. Ber. 3W-4P	5500	5710	Note 3
264-D	2-dr. Jud. Cpe.-2P	5000	5720	12
265-B	4-dr. Wilby Limo.-7P	5700	5840	40
266-B	4-dr. Wilby Pnl. Brgm.	7000	5840	2
267-B	2-dr. LeB. Conv. Rds.-2/4P	4500	5490	37
2197	2-dr. Diet. Cpe.-2P	4900	—	8
1308	4-dr. Jud. Sed. Limo.-7P	5800	—	—
	155'' wb Chassis	—	—	1
	Specials	—	—	16
	RHD	—	—	3

Note 1: Total combined production of the Series 511 KA 2-dr. coupes was 44.
Note 2: Total combined production of the Series 511 KA 2-dr. rdsts. was 12.
Note 3: Total combined production of the Series 251 KB 4-dr. Jud. Ber. (2W and 3W) was 36.

ENGINE: [KA] 67° V, L-head. Twelve. Cast iron block. B & S: 3 in. x 4-1/2 in. Disp.: 381.7. Brake H.P.: 125 @ 3400 R.P.M. N.A.C.C. H.P.: 43.2. Main bearings: Four. Valve lifters: Mechanical. Carb.: Stromberg EE22 downdraft, 2bhl. [KB] 65° V, L-head. Twelve. Cast iron block. B & S: 3-1/4 in. x 4-1/2 in. Disp.: 447.9. C.R.: 5.25:1. Brake H.P.: 150 @ 3400 R.P.M. N.A.C.C. H.P.: 50.7. Main bearings: Seven. Valve lifters: Mechanical. Carb.: Stromberg DD downdraft 2bbl. Torque: 292 lbs.-ft. @ 1200 R.P.M.

CHASSIS: [Series KA] W.B.: 136 in. Frt/Rear Tread: 60 in. Tires: 18 x 7.00. [Series KB] W.B.: 145 in. O.L.: 214 in. Frt/Rear Tread: 60 in. Tires: 18 x 7.50.

TECHNICAL: Sliding gear transmission. Speeds: 3F/1R. Floor shift controls. Double dry disc clutch. Shaft drive. Full floating rear axle. Overall Ratio: 4.58:1, 4.90:1, 4.23:1 (std.). Bendix Duo-Servo mechanical brakes on four wheels. Steel spoke wheels. Wheel Size: 18 in. Drivetrain Options: Free-wheeling std. on KB, opt. on KA.

OPTIONS: Dual sidemount.

HISTORICAL: Calendar year production: 2007. Model year production: 1647 (1114-KA, 533-KB). The president of Lincoln was Edsel Ford.

1933
Model KA, V-12, 12-cyl., 136" wb

	FP	5	4	3	2	1
512B Cpe	3100	7050	14,100	23,500	32,900	47,000
512A RS Cpe	3145	7500	15,000	25,000	35,000	50,000
513A Conv Rds	3200	12,000	24,000	40,000	60,000	80,000
514 Twn Sed	3100	6150	12,300	20,500	28,700	41,000
515 Sed	3200	6000	12,000	20,000	28,000	40,000
516 Cpe	3200	7200	14,400	24,000	33,600	48,000
517 Sed	3300	6000	12,000	20,000	28,000	40,000
517B Limo	3350	6600	13,200	22,000	30,800	44,000
518A DC Phae	3200	14,700	29,400	49,000	78,000	98,000
518B Phae	3000	14,400	28,800	48,000	76,000	96,000
519 7P Tr	3200	12,900	25,800	48,200	66,000	86,000
520A RS Rds	2745	14,400	28,800	48,000	76,000	96,000
520B Rds	2700	14,100	28,200	57,000	74,000	94,000

Model KB, V-8
12-cyl., 145" wb

	FP	5	4	3	2	1
252A DC Phae	4400	15,000	30,000	50,000	80,000	100,000
252B Phae	4200	14,400	28,800	48,000	76,000	96,000
253 7P Tr	4300	13,500	27,000	45,000	70,000	90,000
Twn Sed	4400	6750	13,500	22,500	31,500	45,000
255 5P Sed	4500	6750	13,500	22,500	31,500	45,000
256 5P Cpe	4300	7200	14,400	24,000	33,600	48,000
257 7P Sed	4600	6750	13,500	22,500	31,500	45,000
257B Limo	4800	7050	14,100	23,500	32,900	47,000
258C Brn Semi-Coll Cabr	6900	15,000	30,000	50,000	80,000	100,000
258d Brn Non-Coll Cabr	6900	15,000	30,000	50,000	80,000	100,000
259 Brn Brgm	6900	9000	18,000	30,000	42,000	60,000
260 Brn Conv Cpe	5700	14,700	29,400	49,000	78,000	98,000
Dtrch Conv Sed	6100	15,000	30,000	50,000	80,000	100,000
2P Dtrch Cpe	4900	7950	15,900	26,500	37,100	53,000
4P Dtrch Cpe	4900	7800	15,600	26,000	36,400	52,000
Jud Berl	5500	7500	15,000	25,000	35,000	50,000
2P Jud Cpe	5000	8100	16,200	27,000	37,800	54,000
4P Jud Cpe	5500	7950	15,900	26,500	37,100	53,000
Jud Limo	5800	8250	16,500	27,500	38,500	55,000
Leb Conv Rds	6200	15,000	30,000	50,000	80,000	100,000
W'by Limo	5700	8550	17,100	28,500	39,900	57,000
W'by Brgm	7000	9000	18,000	30,000	42,000	60,000

1934

1934 Lincoln, model KB, Willoughby sport sedan, AA

LINCOLN — SERIES 521 — MODEL KA — TWELVE: In effect there was only a single Lincoln series for 1934. However the use of KA and KB prefixes for serial numbers as well as the use of different series numbers for the 136 inch and 145 inch wheelbase chassis warrants their separation into KA and KB series.

Lincoln styling was little changed for 1934. Radiator shells in both series were now painted body color instead of being chrome plated and all models had hood shutters rather than louvers. Smaller headlights further enhanced the Lincoln's refined front end appearance.

1934 Lincoln, model KB, touring, JAC

LINCOLN — SERIES 271 — MODEL KB — TWELVE: The Senior Lincoln shared a draftless ventilation system with the KA models. In addition, all 1934 Lincolns were fitted with asymmetric headlights which had an additional passing feature in which only the left headlight would be lowered. Powering these 145 inch wheelbase Lincolns was a larger version of the KA V-12. Among its features were aluminum cylinder heads providing a 6.28:1 compression ratio and an engine oil cooler.

I.D. DATA: Serial numbers were located on right side of cowl, top of clutch housing and transmission case. Starting: 136'' wheelbase KA1501, 145'' wheelbase KB3001. Ending: 136'' wheelbase KA3176, 146'' wheelbase KB3744. Engine numbers were located on left side of crankcase between cylinders 1 and 2. Starting: 136'' wheelbase KA1501, 145'' wheelbase KB3001. Ending: 136'' wheelbase KA3176, 145'' wheelbase KB3744.

Model No.	Body Type & Seating	Price	Weight	Prod. Total
Series 521 (136" wheelbase)				
521	Chassis	—	—	21
522-A	2-dr. Cpe.-2/4P	3250	4959	Note 1
522-B	2-dr. Cpe.-2P	3200	4929	Note 1
523	2-dr. Conv. Rds.-2/4P	3400	3934	75
524	4-dr. Twn. Sed.-5P	3450	5044	450
525	4-dr. Sed.-5P	3400	5044	425
526	2-dr. Vict.-5P	3400	5029	115
527-A	4-dr. Sed.-7P	3500	5203	275
527-B	4-dr. Limo.-7P	3550	5228	175
531	4-dr. Conv. Sed. Phae.	3900	5029	75
	RHD			8
Series 271 (145" wheelbase)				
271	Chassis	—	—	12
272-A		—	—	2
272-B		—	—	—
273	4-dr. Tr.-7P	4200	5125	20
277-A	4-dr. Sed.-7P	4500	5510	210
277-B	4-dr. Limo.-7P	4700	5570	215
278-A	4-dr. Brun. Semi-Clp. Cab-5P	6800	5335	—
278-B	4-dr. Brun. Non-Clp. Cab-5P	6800	5315	13
279	4-dr. Brun. Brgm.-7P	6800	5480	15
280	2-dr. Brun. Conv. Cpe.-5P	5600	5045	Note 2
280-?	2-dr. Diet. Conv. Rd.	—	—	Note 2
281	4-dr. Diet. Conv. Sed.-5P	5600	5330	25
282	4-dr. Jud. Sed. Limo.-7P	5700	5605	Note 3
282-?	2-dr. Diet. Cpe.-2P	—	—	Note 3
283-A	4-dr. Jud. Ber. 2W-4P	5400	5495	37
283-B	4-dr. Jud. Ber. 3W-4P	5400	5520	17
285	4-dr. Wilby Limo.-7P	5600	5605	77
287	2-dr. Leb. Conv. Rds.-2/4P	4400	5085	45
	Special	—	—	7
	RHD	—	—	5

Note 1: The total combined production of the Series 521 2-dr. coupes was 60.
Note 2: The total combined production of the Series 271 Brunn conv. cpe. and Dietrich conv. rds. was 25.
Note 3: The total combined production of the Series 271 Judkins sed. limo. and Dietrich coupe was 27.

1934 Lincoln, model KB, LeBaron roadster, JAC

ENGINE: 67° V, L-head. Twelve. Cast iron block. B & S: 3-1/8 in. x 4-1/2 in. Disp.: 414 cu. in. C.R.: 6.38:1. Brake H.P.: 150 @ 3800 R.P.M. Taxable H.P.: 46.8. Main bearings: Four. Valve lifters: Mechanical. Carb.: Stromberg EE22 downdraft 2bb1.

CHASSIS: [Series 521] W.B.: 136 in. Frt/Rear Tread: 60 in. Tires: 18 x 7.00. [Series 271] W.B.: 145 in. O.L.: 214 in. Height: 72 in. Frt/Rear Tread: 60 in. Tires: 18 x 7.50.

1934 Lincoln, model KB, Judkins two-window berline, JAC

TECHNICAL: Sliding gear transmission. Speeds: 3F/1R. Floor shift controls. Double dry disc clutch. Shaft drive. Full floating rear axle. Overall Ratio: 4.58:1, 4.90:1, 4.23:1 (Standard). Bendix Duo-Servo mechanical brakes on four wheels. Steel spoke wheels. Wheel Size: 18 in.

OPTIONS: Dual sidemount.

HISTORICAL: Calendar year registrations: 3024. Model year production: 2411 (1671 - 136" wheelbase, 740 - 145" wheelbase). The president of Lincoln was Edsel Ford.

1934
Series K, V-12
12-cyl., 136" wb

	FP	5	4	3	2	1
4P Conv Rds	3400	11,400	22,800	38,000	56,000	76,000
4P Twn Sed	3450	6300	12,600	21,000	29,400	42,000
5P Sed	3400	6150	12,300	20,500	28,700	41,000
7P Sed	3500	6600	13,200	22,000	30,800	44,000
7P Limo	3550	7350	14,700	24,500	34,300	49,000
2P Cpe	3200	7050	14,100	23,500	32,900	47,000
5P Conv Phae	3900	12,000	24,000	40,000	60,000	80,000
4P Cpe	3250	7200	14,400	24,000	33,600	48,000
V-12, 145" wb						
Tr	4200	10,500	21,000	35,000	49,000	70,000
Sed	4500	6900	13,800	23,000	32,200	46,000
Limo	4700	7500	15,000	25,000	35,000	50,000
2W Jud Berl	5400	7200	14,400	24,000	33,600	48,000
3W Jud Berl	5400	7050	14,100	23,500	32,900	47,000
Jud Sed Limo	5700	7800	15,600	26,000	36,400	52,000
Brn Brgm	6800	8250	16,500	27,500	38,500	55,000
Brn Semi-Coll Cabr	6800	9900	19,800	33,000	46,200	66,000
Brn Conv Cpe	6800	12,000	24,000	40,000	60,000	80,000
W'by Limo	5600	7500	15,000	25,000	35,000	50,000
Leb Rds	4400	12,900	25,800	48,200	66,000	86,000
Dtrch Conv Sed	5600	13,200	26,400	44,000	68,000	88,000
Brn Conv Vic	6800	13,200	26,400	44,000	68,000	88,000
Leb Cpe	4000	7500	15,000	25,000	35,000	50,000
Dtrch Conv Rds	5600	14,400	28,800	48,000	76,000	96,000
W'by Spt Sed	5500	7350	14,700	24,500	34,300	49,000
Leb Conv Cpe	4400	12,900	25,800	44,000	66,000	86,000
Brn Conv Sed	5600	13,500	27,000	45,000	70,000	90,000
Brn Cus Phae	—	14,400	28,800	48,000	76,000	96,000
Brwstr Non-Coll Cabr	—	7500	15,000	25,000	35,000	50,000

1935

1935 Lincoln, model K, LeBaron convertible coupe, AA

LINCOLN — SERIES 301 — MODEL K — TWELVE: The long wheelbase Lincolns were available in three factory body styles for 1935. Other configurations were offered as in earlier years by Brunn, LeBaron, Judkins and Willoughby. Whereas the new bodies were moved forward 4½ inches on the 136 inch wheelbase models, those for the 145 inch wheelbase version were moved a full 9 inches to the front. In either case Lincoln claimed the result was an improved ride and a lower center of gravity.

Technical changes while less dramatic than the Lincoln's new appearance were still noteworthy. A new cam provided a smoother level of operation and along with a new exhaust system contributed to improved performance and a lower overall noise level.

Transmission changes included the use of helical cut gears for 2nd and 3rd plus the use of needle roller bearings in the clutch. A fully automatic spark control was also a first-time feature for the Lincoln.

LINCOLN — SERIES 541 — MODEL K — TWELVE: Lincoln limited the use of the 136 inch wheelbase chassis in 1935 to its two-door factory custom and five-passenger standard bodies. The exceptions to this policy was the availability of the LeBaron coupe, sedan, phaeton and convertible roadster plus a Brunn convertible Victoria with this wheelbase.

Regardless of their wheelbase all Lincolns had new styling dominated by a more rounded, softer appearance. A sloping rear deck, similar to that of the 1934 Willoughby Sport Sedan was adopted as was a honeycomb mesh radiator grille. With the radiator cap now placed under the hood, the Lincoln's greyhound hood ornament was permanently mounted. Other changes enabling the 1935 Lincolns to be quickly perceived as new models were their one-piece bumpers with twin vertical bars, horizontal hood ventilators extending nearly to the windshield and smaller headlights that were further elongated to add another element of fleetness. Their shells were now body-color painted.

Interior changes were highlighted by a new dash with two large dials containing the instruments and a placement was provided for a radio. The glove box was also enlarged.

I.D. DATA: Serial numbers were located on right side of cowl, top of clutch housing and transmission case. Starting: K 3501. Ending: K 4919. Engine numbers were located on left side of crankcase between cylinders 1 and 2. Starting: K 3501. Ending: K 4919.

1935 Lincoln, model K, 4-dr. sedan, JAC

Model No.	Body Type & Seating	Price	Weight	Prod. Total
Series 541 (136" wb)				
541	Chassis	—	—	1
542	2-dr. Leb. Conv. Rds.-2/4P	4600	5335	30
543	4-dr. Sed. 2W-5P	4300	5690	170
544	4-dr. Sed. 3W-5P	4300	5680	278
545	2-dr. Cpe.-5P	4200	5535	44
546	2-dr. Leb. Conv. Sed. Phae.-5P	5000	5665	20
547	2-dr. Brun. Conv. Vict.-5P	5500	5440	15
548	2-dr. Leb. Cpe.-2P	4600	5335	23
	RHD	—	—	5
Series 301 (145" wb)				
301	Chassis	—	—	8
302	4-dr. Tr.-7P	4200	5155	15
303-A	4-dr. Sed.-7P	4600	5840	351
303-B	4-dr. Limo.-7P	4700	5935	282
304-A	4-dr. Brun. Semi-Clp. Cab-5P	—	—	13
304-B	4-dr. Brun. Non-Clp. Cab-5P	—	—	13
305	4-dr. Brun. Brgm.-7P	—	—	10
307	4-dr. Leb. Conv. Sed.-5P	5500	5965	20
308	4-dr. Jud. Limo.-7P	—	—	18
309-A	4-dr. Jud. Ber. 2W-5P	—	—	34
309-B	4-dr. Jud. Ber. 3W-5P	—	—	13
310	4-dr. Wilby Limo.-7P	—	—	40
311	4-dr. Wilby Spt. Sed.-5P	—	—	5
8	Specials	—	—	8
	RHD	—	—	18

1935 Lincoln, model K, LeBaron convertible sedan, JAC

ENGINE: 67° V, L-head. Twelve. Cast iron block. B & S: 3-1/8 in. x 4-1/2 in. Disp.: 414 cu. in. C.R.: 6.38:1. Brake H.P.: 150 @ 3800 R.P.M. Taxible H.P.: 46.8. Main bearings: Four. Valve lifters: Mechanical. Carb.: Stromberg EE22 downdraft 2bbl.

CHASSIS: [Series 541] W.B.: 136 in. Frt/Rear Tread: 60 in. Tires: 17 x 7.50. [Series 301] W.B.: 145 in. O.L.: 214. Frt/Rear Tread: 60 in. Tires: 17 x 7.50.

TECHNICAL: Sliding gear transmission. Speeds: 3F/1R. Floor shift controls. Double dry disc clutch. Shaft drive. Full floating rear axle. Overall Ratio: 4.58:1, 4.90:1, 4.23:1 (Std.). Bendix Duo-Servo mechanical brakes on four wheels. Steel spoke wheels. Wheel Size: 17 in.

OPTIONS: Dual sidemount. Radio. Heater. Clock.

HISTORICAL: Model year production: 1411 (Series 541-581, Series 301-830). The president of Lincoln was Edsel Ford.

1935
Series K, V-12
V-12, 136" wb

	FP	5	4	3	2	1
Leb Conv Rds	4600	10,500	21,000	35,000	49,000	70,000
Leb Cpe	4600	7500	15,000	25,000	35,000	50,000
Cpe	4200	7200	14,400	24,000	33,600	48,000
Brn Conv Vic	5500	10,500	21,000	35,000	49,000	70,000
2W Sed	4300	6300	12,600	21,000	29,400	42,000
3W Sed	4300	6150	12,300	20,500	28,700	41,000
Leb Conv Phae	5000	11,400	22,800	38,000	53,200	76,000
V-12, 145" wb						
7P Tr	4200	10,800	21,600	36,000	50,500	72,000
7P Sed	4600	6450	12,900	21,500	30,100	43,000
7P Limo	4700	7350	14,700	24,500	34,300	49,000
Leb Conv Sed	5500	12,900	25,800	48,200	66,000	86,000
Brn Semi-Coll Cabr	6700	13,200	26,400	44,000	68,000	88,000
Brn Non-Coll Cabr	6600	12,000	24,000	40,000	60,000	80,000
Brn Brgm	6700	7500	15,000	25,000	35,000	50,000
W'by Limo	5700	7500	15,000	25,000	35,000	50,000
W'by Spt Sed	6800	7350	14,700	24,500	34,300	49,000
2W Jud Berl	5500	7650	15,300	25,500	35,700	51,000
3W Jud Berl	5500	7800	15,600	26,000	36,400	52,000
Jud Sed Limo	5700	7500	15,000	25,000	35,000	50,000

1936

1936 Lincoln-Zephyr, 4-dr. sedan, OCW

LINCOLN-ZEPHYR — TWELVE: The Lincoln-Zephyr was both one of the most handsome American cars of the thirties and one of the most revolutionary. The word teardrop was applicable to its overall form, taillights, fender skirts and grille emblem. The sloping rear deck, curved side window corners, simple grille form with horizontal bars in combination with headlights fully molded into the front fenders were successfully coordinated in an appearance that gave life to the expression ''streamlined''

The dramatic exterior appearance of the Zephyr was mirrored by its interior motif. Twin circular dials containing the oil temperature, fuel, battery gauges and the speedometer was reminiscent of earlier Lincolns. In the dash center was a circular ash tray and directly beneath two large dials were the controls for the instrument panel light, throttle, choke and cigarette lighter. The dual windshield wipers were operated by a button just above the ash tray. The starter button was to the driver's left while the steering wheel hub contained the switch controlling the exterior lights. A steering wheel/ignition lock was installed on the steering column.

The Zephyr's pleated upholstery was available in taupe broadcloth or tan bedford cord. Leather was offered as an option.

The engineering design format of the Zephyr was headed by its integral body-frame construction and all-steel roof, the first offered by Ford Motor Company. Suspension was by transverse springs with solid front and rear axles.

To power the Lincoln-Zephyr a V-12 was developed from the Ford V-8 design. In essence the Zephyr engine was a 75 degree version of the Ford V-8 with four additional cylinders. Twin water pumps were used as was a single down-draft carburetor. Other key features included alloy steel pistons, aluminum cylinder heads and a one piece block casting.

I.D. DATA: Serial numbers were located on right side of cowl, top of clutch housing and transmission case. Starting: H1. Ending: H15528. Engine on left side of crankcase between cylinder 1 and 2. Starting: H1. Ending: H15528.

Model No.	Body Type & Seating	Price	Weight	Prod. Total
902	4-dr. Sed.-6P	1320	3349	12,272
902	4-dr. Sed. RHD-6P	—	—	908
903	2-dr. Sed.-6P	1275	3289	1814

ENGINE: 75° V, L-head. Twelve. Cast iron block. B & S: 2-3/4 in. x 3-3/4 in. Disp.: 267.3 cu. in. C.R.: 6.7:1. Brake H.P.: 110 @ 3900 R.P.M. Taxable H.P.: 36.3. Main bearings: Four. Valve lifters: Mechanical. Carb.: Stromberg downdraft 2bbl. Torque: 186 lbs.-ft. @ 2000 R.P.M.

CHASSIS: W.B.: 122 in. O.L.: 202.5 in. Height: 69 in. Frt/Rear Tread: 55.5/58.25 in. Tires: 16 x 7.00

TECHNICAL: Sliding gear transmission. Speeds: 3F/1R. Floor shift controls. Single dry plate, centrifugal clutch. Shaft drive. 3/4 floating rear axle. Overall Ratio: 4.44:1. Mechanical brakes on four wheels. Pressed steel, drop-center rims wheels. Wheel Size: 23 in. Drivetrain Options: Columbia two-speed rear axle.

OPTIONS: Clock. Leather upholstery. Fitted luggage.

HISTORICAL: Introduced: November, 1935. Innovations: Aerodynamic design, low priced V-12 motoring, float indicator for oil level. Model year production; 14,994. The president of Lincoln was Edsel Ford.

1936 Lincoln, model K, LeBaron coupe AA

LINCOLN — SERIES 300 — MODEL K — TWELVE: All Lincolns, regardless of wheelbase carried the K label and a 300 series model number. Changes in the year-old body shell consisted of a more sharply (27 degrees instead of 20 degrees) rearward sloping windshield, a grille with more prominent horizontal bars and fenders with smoother and more rounded edges. Substantially changing the Lincoln's front end appearance was the lowering of the headlights. Standard pressed steel wheels with larger hubcaps replaced the older wire version. A new interior feature was the under-dash placement of the handbrake.

Technical changes included the use of dual windshield wiper motors, a five rather than four engine mount system and an all-helical gear transmission.

I.D. DATA: Serial numbers were located on right side of cowl, top of clutch housing and transmission case. Starting: K 5501. Ending: K 7014. Engine numbers were located on left side of crankcase between cylinders 1 and 2. Starting: K 5501. Ending: K 7014.

Model No.	Body Type & Seating	Price	Weight	Prod. Total
321	145" wheelbase Chassis	—	—	9
322	136" wheelbase Chassis	—	—	6
323	4-dr. Tr.-7P	4200	5276	8
324-A	4-dr. Sed. 2W-5P	4300	5426	103
324-B	4-dr. Sed. 3W-5P	4300	5476	297
326	2-dr. Cpe.-5P	4200	5266	36
327-A	4-dr. Sed.-7P	4600	5591	368
327-B	4-dr. Limo.-7P	4700	5641	370
328	2-dr. Brun. Conv. Vict.-5P	5500	5176	10
329-A	4-dr. Brun. Non Clp. Cab.-5P	—	—	10
329-B	4-dr. Brun. SC Cab.-5P	—	—	10
330	2-dr. LeB. Conv. Rds.-2/4P	4700	5136	20
331	4-dr. Brun. Brgm.-7P	—	—	20
332	2-dr. LeB. Cpe.-2/4P	4700	5126	25
333	4-dr. LeB. Conv. Sed. Phae.-5P	5000	5296	30
334	4-dr. LeB. Conv. Sed.-5P	5500	5381	15
335	4-dr. Jud. Sed. Limo.-7P	—	—	26
337-A	4-dr. Jud. Ber. 2W-5P	—	—	51
337-B	4-dr. Jud. Ber. 3W-5P	—	—	13
339	4-dr. Wilby Limo.-7P	—	—	62
341	4-dr. Wilby Spt. Sed.-5P	—	—	11
	RHD (136" wb)	—	—	4
	RHD (145" wb)	—	—	15
	Specials	—	—	15

ENGINE: 67° V, L-head. Twelve. Cast iron block. B & S: 3-1/8 in. x 4-1/2 in. Disp.: 414 cu. in. C.R.: 6.38:1. Brake H.P.: 150 @ 3800 R.P.M. Taxable H.P.: 46.8: Main bearings: Four. Valve lifters: Mechanical. Carb.: Stromberg EE22 downdraft 2bbl.

CHASSIS: W.B.: 136/145 in. Frt/Rear Tread: 60 in. Tires: 17 x 7.50.

TECHNICAL: Sliding gear transmission. Speeds: 3F/1R. Floor shift control. Double dry disc clutch. Shaft drive. Full floating rear axle. Overall Ratio: 4.58:1, 4.90:1, 4.23:1 (std.). Bendix Duo-Servo mechanical brakes on four wheels. Pressed steel disc wheels. Wheel Size: 17 in.

OPTIONS: Dual sidemount. Radio. Heater. Clock.

HISTORICAL: Model year production: 1515. The president of Lincoln was Edsel Ford.

1936
Zephyr, V-12, 122" wb

	FP	5	4	3	2	1
4 dr Sed	1320	4800	9600	16,000	22,400	32,000
2 dr Sed	1275	4950	9900	16,500	23,100	33,000
12-cyl., 136" wb						
Leb Rds Cabr	4700	9000	18,000	30,000	42,000	60,000
2P Leb Cpe	4700	6000	12,000	20,000	28,000	40,000
5P Cpe	4200	5700	11,400	19,000	26,600	38,000
Brn Conv Vic	5500	9300	18,600	31,000	43,400	62,000
2W Sed	4300	4650	9300	15,500	21,700	31,000
3W Sed	4300	4500	9000	15,000	21,000	30,000
Leb Conv Sed	5000	9000	18,000	30,000	42,000	60,000
V-12, 145" wb						
7P Tr	4200	9000	18,000	30,000	42,000	60,000
7P Sed	4600	6000	12,000	20,000	28,000	40,000
7P Limo	4700	6750	13,500	22,500	31,500	45,000
Leb Conv Sed W/part	5500	10,200	20,400	34,000	47,600	68,000
Brn Semi-Coll Cabr	6700	9900	19,800	33,000	46,200	66,000
Brn Non-Coll Cabr	6600	9600	19,200	32,000	44,800	64,000
Brn Brgm	6700	6450	12,900	21,500	30,100	43,000
W'by Limo	5700	7050	14,100	23,500	32,900	47,000
W'by Spt Sed	6800	6600	13,200	22,000	30,800	44,000
Jud 2W Berl	5500	6900	13,800	23,000	32,200	46,000
Jud 3W Berl	5600	7050	14,100	23,500	32,900	47,000
Jud Limo	5800	7200	14,400	24,000	33,600	48,000

1937

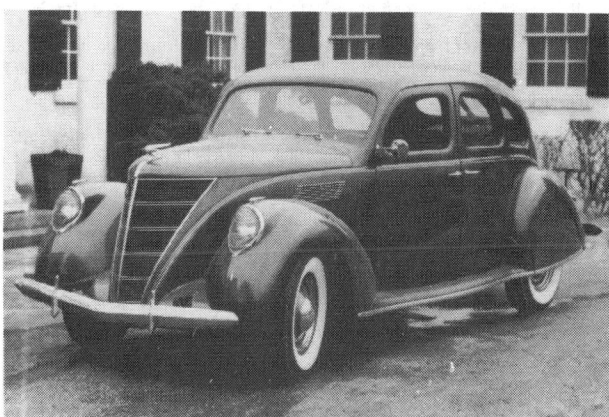

1937 Lincoln-Zephyr, 4-dr. sedan, OCW

LINCOLN-ZEPHYR — TWELVE: The positive public reaction to the original Lincoln-Zephyr was underscored by a doubling of its popularity in 1937. As expected of a new car beginning its second year the Zephyr wasn't radically changed for 1937. However a new instrument panel with twin glove compartments bracketing a center console carrying the controls and instruments was featured. The speedometer was placed within a large circular dial with a smaller unit positioned directly below contained the clock. On either side were vertical dials with the fuel and oil level gauges placed in the unit to the left. The right side unit enclosed the temperature and battery gauges.

Easier access to the trunk was provided by a revised spare tire bracket which now folded outward when the trunk lid was opened.

Styling changes while limited in scope made it easy to identify a 1937 Lincoln-Zephyr. The grille now carried 5 pairs of vertical bars and a new side molding swept upward from the grille bar prior to extending along the upper belt line in its way to the rear deck. In addition, the front bumper was slightly less V'eed than previously and a more ornate set of hood vents were used which matched the grille texture.

I.D. DATA: Serial numbers were located on right side of cowl, top of clutch housing and transmission case. Starting: H 15529. Ending: H 45529. Engine numbers were located on left side of crankcase between cylinders 1 and 2. Starting: H 15529. Ending: H 45529.

Model No.	Body Type & Seating	Price	Weight	Prod. Total
700	2-dr. Cpe. Sed.-6P	1245	3329	1500
720	2-dr. Cpe.-6P	1165	3214	5199
730	4-dr. Sed.-6P	1265	3369	23159
737	4-dr. Twn. Limo.-6P	1425	3398	139

ENGINE: 75° V, L-head. Twelve. Cast iron block. B & S: 2-3/4 in. x 3-3/4 in. Disp.: 267.3 cu. in. C.R.: 6.7:1. Brake H.P.: 110 @ 3900 R.P.M. N.A.C.C. H.P.: 36.3. Main bearings: Four. Valve lifters: Mechanical. Carb.: Stromberg downdraft 2bbl. Torque 186 lbs.-ft. @ 2000 R.P.M.

CHASSIS: W.B.: 122 in. O.L.: 202.5 in. Height: 69 in. Frt/Rear Tread: 55.5/58.25. Tires: 16 x 7.00.

TECHNICAL: Sliding gear transmission. Speeds: 3F/1R. Floor shift controls. Single dry plate, centrifugal clutch. Shaft drive. 3/4 floating rear axle. Overall Ratio: 4.44:1. Mechanical brakes on 4 wheels. Pressed steel wheels, drop center rims. Wheel Size: 16 in. Drivetrain Options: Columbia two-speed rear axle.

OPTIONS: Radio. Heater. Leather upholstery. Fitted luggage.

HISTORICAL: Calendar year production: 29293. Model year production: 29997. The company president was Edsel Ford.

1937 Lincoln, model K, Brunn convertible sedan, JAC

LINCOLN — MODEL K — TWELVE: Lincoln continued to place a priority on custom body styles with a total of 17 versions available, along with 4 standard body types in 1937. For the first time the Lincoln V-12 was fitted with hydraulic valve lifters. Other technical changes for 1937 included a positioning of the V-12 further forward on the chassis as well as the use of altered engine mounts.

New styling that blended the headlights into the front fender form and gave the Lincolns even more of a rounded, smooth appearance represented the last major changes that would be made in the design of the K Lincoln.

I.D. DATA: Serial numbers were located on right side of cowl, top of clutch housing and transmission case. Starting: K 7501. Ending: K 8490. Engine numbers were located on left side of crankcase between cylinders 1 and 2. Starting: K 7501. Ending: K 8490.

1937 Lincoln, model K, LeBaron convertible sedan, AA

Model No.	Body Type & Seating	Price	Weight	Prod. Total
353	4-dr. Wilby Tr.-7P	5550	—	7
354-A	4-dr. Sed. 2W-5P	4450	5492	48
354-B	4-dr. Sed. 3W-5P	4450	5522	136
356	2-dr. Wilby Cpe.-5P	5550	—	6
357-A	4-dr. Sed.-7P	4750	5697	212
357-B	4-dr. Limo.-7P	4850	5647	248
358	2-dr. Brun. Conv. Vict.-5P	5550	5346	13
359-A	4-dr. Brun. Non-Clp. Cab-5P	6650	—	10
359-B	4-dr. Brun. Semi-Clp. Cab	6750	5646	7
360	2-dr. Leb. Conv. Rds.-2/4P	4950	—	15
361	4-dr. Brun. Brgm.-7P	6750	5681	29
362	2-dr. Leb. Cpe.-2P	4950	5172	24
363-A	4-dr. Leb. Conv. Sed. part.-5P	5650	—	12
363-B	4-dr. Leb. Conv. Sed.-5P	5450	5547	37
365	4-dr. Jud. Sed. Limo.-7P	5950	5732	27
367-A	4-dr. Jud. Ber. 2W-5P	5650	5622	47
367-B	4-dr. Jud. Ber. 3W-5P	5750	5682	19
369	4-dr. Wilby Limo.-7P	5850	5801	60
371	4-dr. Wilby Spt. Sed.-5P	6850	—	6
373	4-dr. Wilby Pnl. Brgm.-5P	7050	—	4
375	4-dr. Brun. Tr. Cab-5P	6950	—	10

ENGINE: 67° V, L-head. Twelve. Cast iron block. B & S: 3-1/8 in. x 4-1/2 in. Disp.: 414 cu. in. C.R.: 6.38:1. Brake H.P.: 150 @ 3800 R.P.M. Taxable H.P.: 46.8. Main bearings: Four. Valve lifters: Hydraulic. Carb.: Stromberg EE22 downdraft 2bb1.

CHASSIS: W.B.: 136 in./145 in. Frt/Rear Tread: 60 in. Tires: 17 x 7.50.

TECHNICAL: Sliding gear transmission. Speeds: 3F/1R. Floor shift controls. Double dry disc clutch. Shaft drive. Full floating rear axle. Overall Ratio: 4.58:1, 4.90:1, 4.23:1 (Std.). Bendix Duo-Servo mechanical brakes on four wheels. Pressed steel disc wheels. Wheel Size: 17 in.

OPTIONS: Dual sidemount. Radio. Heater. Clock. Cigar lighter.

HISTORICAL: Model year production: 977. The president of Lincoln was Edsel Ford.

1937
Zephyr, V-12

	FP	5	4	3	2	1
3P Cpe	1165	5100	10,200	17,000	23,800	34,000
2 dr Sed	1245	4650	9300	15,500	21,700	31,000
4 dr Sed	1265	4500	9000	15,000	21,000	30,000
Twn Sed	1425	4650	9300	15,500	21,700	31,000
Conv Sed	1790	7500	15,000	25,000	35,000	50,000
Series K, V-12						
V-12, 136" wb						
Leb Conv Rds	4950	9000	18,000	30,000	42,000	60,000
Leb Cpe	4950	6000	12,000	20,000	28,000	40,000
W'by Cpe	5550	6300	12,600	21,000	29,400	42,000
Brn Conv Vic	5550	8850	17,700	29,500	41,300	59,000
2W Sed	4450	4800	9600	16,000	22,400	32,000
3W Sed	4450	4650	9300	15,500	21,700	31,000
V-12, 145" wb						
7P Sed	4750	5400	10,800	18,000	25,200	36,000
7P Limo	4850	5700	11,400	19,000	26,600	38,000
Leb Conv Sed	5450	9900	19,800	33,000	46,200	66,000
Leb Conv Sed W/part	5650	9900	19,800	33,000	46,200	66,000
Brn Semi-Coll Cabr	6750	9600	19,200	32,000	44,800	64,000
Brn Non-Coll Cabr	6650	8700	17,400	29,000	40,600	58,000
Brn Brgm	6750	7050	14,100	23,500	32,900	47,000
Brn Tr Cabr	6950	9300	18,600	31,000	43,400	62,000
Jud 2W Berl	5650	6750	13,500	22,500	31,500	45,000
Jud 3W Berl	5750	6750	13,500	22,500	31,500	45,000
Jud Limo	5950	7350	14,700	24,500	34,300	49,000
W'by Tr	5550	8250	16,500	27,500	38,500	55,000
W'by Limo	5850	7350	14,700	24,500	34,300	49,000
W'by Spt Sed	6850	6750	13,500	22,500	31,500	45,000
W'by Cpe	5500	7050	14,100	23,500	32,900	47,000
W'by Pan Brgm	7050	7200	14,400	24,000	33,600	48,000
Jud Cpe	5600	7050	14,100	23,500	32,900	47,000

1938

1938 Lincoln-Zephyr, convertible sedan, AA

LINCOLN-ZEPHYR — TWELVE: The Lincoln-Zephyr received a major styling revision utilizing new front sheet metal and rear fenders as well as a longer, 125 inch wheelbase. The grille now was divided and consisted of very thin, horizontal chrome bars. This design set the theme for the rest of the Lincoln-Zephyr's exterior body trim. The narrow belt line molding enhanced the low profile of the Zephyr which was further accentuated by the four side hood bars. Furthering the integration of the Zephyr's various body trim components into an extremely coherent styling format was the unobtrusive hood ornament which flowed downward to accentuate the 2-piece grille design. At the rear the fenders were like those up front, larger and more elongated than previously. The teardrop shaped headlights were incorporated into the smooth form of the fenders.

Following up on the construction of 3 prototype convertible sedans were two production open models, a convertible coupe and convertible sedan.

Interior revisions were numerous. The metal surrounds for the seats used in 1936 and 1937 were removed, a larger banjo-type, 18 inch steering wheel was installed and a new biscuit upholstery pattern was introduced. Closed model seats were available in striped tan broadcloth or tan bedford cloth as well as tan leather. The convertible models were upholstered in tan leather and whipcord. Lincoln once again rearranged the Zephyr's dash gauges for gas, oil, temperature and battery functions. Pointing the way to the column-mounted shift lever which Lincoln would introduce in 1940, was a convoluted shift handle that protruded from the center console.

I.D. DATA: Serial numbers were located on right side of cowl, top of clutch housing and transmission case. Starting: H 45530. Ending: H 64640. Engine numbers were located on left side of crankcase between cylinders 1 and 2. Starting: H 45530. Ending: H 64640.

Model No.	Body Type & Seating	Price	Weight	Prod. Total
700	2-dr. Cpe. Sed.-6P	1355	3409	800
720	2-dr. Cpe.-6P	1295	3294	2600
730	4-dr. Sed.-6P	1375	3444	14,520
737	4-dr. Twn. Limo.-6P	1550	3474	130
740	4-dr. Conv. Sed.-6P	1790	3724	461
760-B	2-dr. Conv. Cpe.-6P	1650	3489	600

ENGINE: 75° V, L-head. Twelve. Cast iron block. B & S: 2-3/4 in. x 3-3/4 in. Disp.: 267.3 cu. in. Overall Ratio: 6.7:1. Brake H.P.: 110 @ 3900 R.P.M. Taxable H.P.: 36.3. Main bearings: Four. Valve lifters: Hydraulic. Carb.: Chandler Gloves AA1 downdraft 2bbl. Torque: 186 lbs.-ft @ 2000 R.P.M.

CHASSIS: W.B.: 125 in. O.L.: 210 in. Height: 63-1/4 in. Frt/Rear Tread 55-1/2 / 58-1/4. Tires: 16 x 7.00.

TECHNICAL: Sliding gear transmission. Speeds: 3F/1R. Floor located controls. Single dry plate clutch. Shaft drive. 3/4 floating rear axle. Overall Ratio: 4.44:1. Mechanical brakes on 4 wheels. Pressed steel wheels, drop center rim. Wheel size: 16 in. Drivetrain options: Columbia 2-speed rear axle.

OPTIONS: Bumper guards. Radio. Heater. Leather upholstery. Wind wings. Whitewall tires. Fitted luggage.

HISTORICAL: Calendar year production: 19751. Model year production: 19111. The president of Lincoln was Edsel Ford. A Zephyr sedan was second among 26 entrants in the 1938 Gilmore Economy run with a 23.47 MPG.

1938 Lincoln, model K, 4-dr. sedan, JAC

LINCOLN — MODEL K — TWELVE: The 1938 K Lincoln's grille was given a new look via the use of 18 rather than 30 horizontal bars as used previously. Due to the elimination of thermostatically controlled hood shutters the side engine louvers were also revised. Built-in trunks were found on all standard sedan models and both the side belt line molding and exterior door handles were of stainless steel construction.

Minor changes to the Lincoln's upholstery plus rheostat dash-panel lighting highlighted the Lincoln's interior.

Technical changes consisted of improved synchomesh and brakes with a greater resistance to fading.

I.D. DATA: Serial numbers were located on right side of cowl, top of clutch housing and transmission case. Starting: K 9001. Ending: K9450. Engine numbers were located on left side of crankcase between cylinders 1 and 2. Starting: K 9001. Ending: K 9450.

Model No.	Body Type & Seating	Price	Weight	Prod. Total
403	4-dr. Wilby Tr.-7P	5900	—	5
404.A	4-dr. Sed. 2W-5P	4900	5527	9
404-B	4-dr. Sed. 3W-5P	4900	5532	49
406	2-dr. Wilby Cpe.-5P	5900	5407	4
407-A	4-dr. Sed.-7P	5100	5672	78
407-B	4-dr. Limo.-7P	5200	5762	91
408	4-dr. Brun. Conv. Vict.-5P	5900	5322	8
409-A	4-dr. Brun. Sm. Clp. Cab.-5P	7000	5716	6
409-B	4-dr. Brun. Non. Clp. Cab.-5P	6900	5696	5
410	2-dr. Leb. Conv. Rds.-2-4P	5300	—	8
411	4-dr. Brun. Brgm.-5P	7000	5806	13
412	2-dr. Leb. Cpe.-2P	5300	5227	12
413-A	4-dr. Leb. Conv. Sed.-5P	5800	5462	15

ENGINE: 67° V, L-head. Twelve. Cast iron block. B & S: 2-1/8 in. x 4-1/2 in. Disp.: 414 cu. in. C.R.: 6.38:1. Brake H.P. 150 @ 3800 R.P.M. Taxable H.P. 46.8. Main bearings: Four. Valve lifters: Hydraulic. Carb.: Stromberg EE1 downdraft 2bbl.

CHASSIS: W.B.: 136/145 in. O.L.: 213 in. Frt/Rear Tread: 60 in. Tires: 17 x 7.50.

TECHNICAL: Sliding gear transmission. Speeds: 3F, 1R. Floor shift controls. Double dry disc clutch. Shaft drive. Full floating rear axle. Overall Ratio: 4.58:1. Bendix Duo-Servo mechanical brakes on 4 wheels. Pressed steel disc wheels. Wheel Size: 17 in.

OPTIONS: Dual sidemount. Sidemount cover(s). Radio. Heater. Clock. Cigar lighter.

HISTORICAL: Model year production: 416. The president of Lincoln was Edsel Ford.

1938
Zephyr, V-12

	FP	5	4	3	2	1
3P Cpe	1295	5250	10,500	17,500	24,500	35,000
3P Conv Cpe	1700	6750	13,500	22,500	31,500	45,000
4 dr Sed	1375	3750	7500	12,500	17,500	25,000
2 dr Sed	1355	3900	7800	13,000	18,200	26,000
Conv Sed	1790	7050	14,100	23,500	32,900	47,000
Twn Sed	1550	4200	8400	14,000	19,600	28,000

Series K, V-12
V-12, 136" wb

	FP	5	4	3	2	1
Leb Conv Rds	5300	8250	16,500	27,500	38,500	55,000
Leb Cpe	5300	5700	11,400	19,000	26,600	38,000
W'by Cpe	5900	5850	11,700	19,500	27,300	39,000
2W Sed	4900	4800	9600	16,000	22,400	32,000
3W Sed	4900	4650	9300	15,500	21,700	31,000
Brn Conv Vic	5900	8550	17,100	28,500	39,900	57,000

V-12, 145" wb

	FP	5	4	3	2	1
7P Sed	5100	5100	10,200	17,000	23,800	34,000
Sed Limo	5100	5250	10,500	17,500	24,500	35,000
Leb Conv Sed	5800	8550	17,100	28,500	39,900	57,000
Leb Conv Sed W/part	6000	9000	18,000	30,000	42,000	60,000
Jud 2W Berl	6000	5400	10,800	18,000	25,200	36,000
Jud 3W Berl	6100	5550	11,100	18,500	25,900	37,000
Jud Limo	6300	6000	12,000	20,000	28,000	40,000
Brn Tr Cabr	7200	8700	17,400	29,000	40,600	58,000
W'by Tr	5900	8400	16,800	28,000	39,200	56,000
W'by Spt Sed	7000	6000	12,000	20,000	28,000	40,000
Brn Non-Coll Cabr	6900	8100	16,200	27,000	37,800	54,000
Brn Semi-Coll Cabr	7000	8550	17,100	28,500	39,900	57,000
Brn Brgm	7000	6000	12,000	20,000	28,000	40,000
W'by Pan Brgm	7400	6150	12,300	20,500	28,700	41,000
W'by Limo	6200	6000	12.000	20.000	28.000	40,000

1939

1939 Lincoln-Zephyr, convertible coupe, AA

LINCOLN-ZEPHYR — TWELVE: The use of hydraulic brakes highlighted the Lincoln-Zephyr's technical changes for 1939. The other change of any consequence was the use of a voltage-regulator rather than a generator cut-out. This feature was also found on Zephyrs produced towards the end of the 1938 model run.

Among styling changes found on the 1939 Lincoln-Zephyr was a larger grille shape with vertical bars, two rather than four side hood bars and a more vertical front prow. The lower body panels now enclosed the running boards. Both the front and rear bumpers were reshaped. The front unit had a two-part center section while at the rear the bumper was less pointed than previously.

The Zephyr's dash continued to feature symmetrically positioned dual glove boxes and ash trays plus the centrally located speedometer. For 1939 this circular panel also contained the gauges for battery oil, fuel and engine temperature. A battery-condition gauge replaced the ammeter.

Once again a new upholstery scheme was used with vertical pleats and the optional leather option was offered in tan, red, gray and brown. In addition a new custom interior option (standard on the Town Limousine) was offered.

I.D. DATA: Serial numbers were located on right side of cowl, top of clutch housing and transmission case. Starting: H 64641. Ending: H 85640. Engine numbers were located on left side of crankcase between cylinders 1 and 2. Starting: H 64641. Ending: H 85640.

Model No.	Body Type & Seating	Price	Weight	Prod. Total
H-70	2-dr. Cpe. Sed.-6P	1330	3600	800
H-72	2-dr. Cpe.-6P	1320	3520	2500
H-73	4-dr. Sed.-6P	1360	3620	16,663
	4-dr. Tun.-Limo.-6P	1700	3670	95
H-74	4-dr. Conv. Sed.-6P	1790	3900	302
H-76	2-dr. Conv. Cpe.-6P	1700	3790	640

ENGINE: 75° V, L-head. Twelve. Cast iron block. B & S: 2-3/4 in. x 3-3/4 in. Disp.: 267.3 cu. in. C.R.: 6.7:1. Brake H.P. 110 @ 3900 R.P.M. Taxable H.P. 36.3. Main bearings: Four. Valve lifters: Hydraulic. Carb.: Stromberg downdraft 2bbl. Torque: 186 lbs.-ft. @ 2000 R.P.M.

CHASSIS: W.B.: 125 in. O.L.: 210 in. Height: 69-1/2 in. Frt/Rear Tread: 55-1/2/58-1/4 in. Tires: 16 x 7.00.

TECHNICAL: Sliding gear transmission. Speeds: 3F/1R. Floor shift controls. Single dry disc plate clutch. Shaft drive. 3/4 floating rear axle. Overall Ratio: 4.44:1. Bendix hydraulic internal expanding brakes on four wheels. Pressed steel, dropped center wheels. Wheel Size: 16 in. Drivetrain Options: Columbia 2-speed rear axle.

OPTIONS: Bumper guards. Radio. Heater. Leather upholstery. Wind wings. Whitewall tires. Fitted luggage. Custom interior.

HISTORICAL: Calendar year production: 22578. Model year production: 21000. The president of Lincoln was Edsel Ford.

LINCOLN — MODEL K — TWELVE: Changes in the Lincoln K were limited to the use of a different model Stromberg carburetor and wider steel wheel rims with steel spokes added to the back side for greater strength.

Specific production figures for the last of the K Lincoln are unavailable. If any were built in 1940 they were unchanged from the 1939 version.

I.D. DATA: Serial numbers were located on right side of cowl, top of clutch housing and transmission case. Starting: K 9451. Ending: K 9674. Engine numbers were located on left side of crankcase between cylinder 1 and 2. Starting: K 9451. Ending: K 9674.

1939 Lincoln, model K, Willoughby, limousine, OCW

Model No.	Body Type & Seating	Price	Weight	Prod. Total
403	4-dr. Tr.-7P	—	—	1
404-A	4-dr. Sed. 2W-5P	4800	5735	2
404-B	4-dr. Sed. 3W-5P	4800	5740	12
406	2-dr. Wilby Cpe.-5P	5800	5615	1
407-A	4-dr. Sed.-7P	5000	5880	25
407-B	4-dr. Limo.-7P	5100	5970	58
408	2-dr. Brun. Conv. Vict.-5P	5800	5530	2
409-A	4-dr. Brun. Non. Clp. Cab.-5P	6800	6010	1
409-B	4-dr. Brun. Smi. Cpl. Cab.-5P	6900	6030	1
410	2-dr. LeB. Conv. Rds.-2/4P	5200	5505	2
411	4-dr. Brun. Brgm.-7P	6900	6120	2
412	2-dr. LeB. Cpe.-2P	5200	5425	4
413-A	4-dr. LeB. Conv. Sed.-5P	5700	5670	3
413-B	4-dr. LeB. Conv. Sed. Part.-5P	5900	5780	6
415	4-dr. Jud. Limo.-7P	6200	5950	2
417-A	4-dr. Jud. Ber. 2W-5P	5900	5770	2
417-B	4-dr. Jud. Ber. 3W-5P	6000	5840	1
419	4-dr. Wilby Limo.-7P	6100	6140	4
421	4-dr. Wilby Spt. Sed.-5P	6900	6030	1
423	4-dr. Wilby Pnl. Brgm.-5P	—	—	1
425	4-dr. Brun. Tr. Cab.-5P	7100	5870	2

ENGINE: 67° V, L-head. Twelve. Cast iron block. B & S: 3-1/8 in. x 4-1/2 in. Disp.: 414 cu. in. C.R.: 6.38:1. Brake H.P.: 150 @ 3800 R.P.M. Taxable H.P.: 46.8. Main bearings: Four. Valve lifters: Hydraulic. Carb.: Stromberg downdraft 2bbl.

CHASSIS: W.B.: 136/145 in. Frt/Rear Tread: 60 in. Tires: 17 x 7.50

TECHNICAL: Sliding gear transmission. Speeds: 3F/1R. Floor shift controls. Double dry disc clutch. Shaft drive. Full floating rear axle. Overall Ratio: 4.58:1; 4.90:1; 4.23:1 (std.) Bendix Duo-Servo mechanical brakes on four rear wheels. Wheel size: 17 in.

OPTIONS: Dual sidemount. Sidemount cover(s). Radio. Heater. Clock. Cigar lighter.

HISTORICAL: Model year production: 133. The president of Lincoln was Edsel Ford.

1939
Zephyr, V-12

	FP	5	4	3	2	1
3P Cpe	1358	4500	9000	15,000	21,000	30,000
Conv Cpe	1747	6300	12,600	21,000	29,400	42,000
2 dr Sed	1368	3600	7200	12,000	16,800	24,000
5P Sed	1399	3750	7500	12,500	17,500	25,000
Conv Sed	1839	6900	13,800	23,000	32,200	46,000
Twn Sed	1747	3900	7800	13,000	18,200	26,000
Series K, V-12						
V-12, 136" wb						
Leb Conv Rds	5313	7950	15,900	26,500	37,100	53,000
Leb Cpe	5313	5700	11,400	19,000	26,600	38,000
W'by Cpe	5926	5850	11,700	19,500	27,300	39,000
2W Sed	4905	5100	10,200	17,000	23,800	34,000
3W Sed	4905	5100	10,200	17,000	23,800	34,000
Brn Conv Vic	5926	7800	15,600	26,000	36,400	52,000
V-12, 145" wb						
Jud 2W Berl	6028	5400	10,800	18,000	25,200	36,000
Jud 3W Berl	6130	5400	10,800	18,000	25,200	36,000
Jud Limo	6334	5700	11,400	19,000	26,600	38,000
Brn Tr Cabr	7253	8250	16,500	27,500	38,500	55,000
7P Sed	5109	5400	10,800	18,000	25,200	36,000
7P Limo	5211	5850	11,700	19,500	27,300	39,000
Leb Conv Sed	5823	8250	16,500	27,500	38,500	55,000
Leb Conv Sed W/part	6028	8400	16,800	28,000	39,200	56,000
W'by Spt Sed	7049	5250	10,500	17,500	24,500	35,000
V-12, 145" wb, 6 wheels						
Brn Non-Coll Cabr	6947	6750	13,500	22,500	31,500	45,000
Brn Semi-Coll Cabr	7049	7350	14,700	24,500	34,300	49,000
Brn Brgm	7049	5250	10,500	17,500	24,500	35,000
W'by Limo	6232	5700	11,400	19,000	26,600	38,000

1940

LINCOLN-ZEPHYR — TWELVE: The use of a redesigned body shell for the Zephyr which was to remain in use until 1949 cushioned the demise of the K Lincolns and buoyed the Lincoln-Zephyr into the mainstream of Lin-

1940 Lincoln-Zephyr, 4-dr. sedan, JAC

coln's marketing strategy. The major styling-features for 1940 consisted of larger, by 22% glass area, front window vent windows and the inboard positioning of the taillight. In addition, the one-piece rear window, lack of running boards and the use of sealed-beam headlights made it easy to identify the 1940 Lincoln-Zephyr.

Once again a rearranged instrument panel was introduced for the Lincoln-Zephyr. The circular case for the speedometer and instruments was now located directly behind the steering column (which for the first time carried the "Finger-Tip Gearshift") and a single, large glove box was placed in front of the passenger seat. The optional radio was installed on the upper dash panel just above the centrally located radio grille. To the left of the speaker was the clock.

All interior appointments had a mahogany metal finish and a two-spoke steering wheel was installed.

By virtue of a large 2-7/8 inch bore the Zephyr's engine now displaced 292 cubic inches and was rated at 120hp.

In addition to the production model Lincoln-Zephyrs, a small number of custom-built versions were constructed during 1940. Three of these carried Brunn Town car bodies. In addition three Custom series limousines were completed.

1940 Lincoln-Zephyr, coupe, AA

CONTINENTAL — TWELVE: The outstanding nature of the Lincoln-Zephyr's styling was further demonstrated by its transformation into one of America's most beautiful classics, the Continental. Compared to the Zephyr, the Continental was 3 inches lower and had a longer, by 7 inches, hood. During the 1940 model run many styling developments took place. These included the installation of a spare tire cover, rear bumper splash shields and rubber rear fender gravel shields. Also changed was the location of the license bracket which was moved from the body to the bumper. Continentals were fitted with the instrument panel of the Lincoln-Zephyr Town Limousine and featured a gold colored finish for the interior trim and hardware.

With the exception of a side-mounted engine air cleaner the Continental's mechanical composition was essentially that of other Lincoln-Zephyrs. However Continental engines had polished aluminum heads and manifolds and chromed acorn cylinder head nuts.

1940 Lincoln, Zepher, sedan coupe, OCW

1940 Lincoln, Continental, coupe, AA

I.D. DATA: Serial numbers were located on right side of cowl, top of clutch housing and transmission case. Starting: H 85641. Ending: H 107687. Engine numbers were located on left side of crankcase between cylinders 1 and 2. Starting: H 85641. Ending: H 107687.

Model No.	Body Type & Seating	Price	Weight	Prod. Total
72A	2-dr. Cpe.-2P	1360	3375	1256
72AS	2-dr. Cpe.-4P	1400	3465	316
73	4-dr. Sed.-6P	1400	3535	15764
	4-dr. Twn. Sed.-7P	1740	3575	98
76	2-dr. Conv. Cpe.-6P	1770	3635	700
77	2-dr. Clb. Cpe.-6P	1400	3465	3500
H-32	4-dr. Limo.-7P	—	—	4
H-36	4-dr. Brun. Twn. Car-5P	—	—	4
56	2-dr. Cont. Cab.-5P	2840	3615	350
57	2-dr. Cont. Cpe.-5P	—	—	54

ENGINE: 75° V, L-head. Twelve. Cast iron block. B & S: 2-7/8 in. x 3-3/4 in. Disp.: 292 cu. in. C.R.: 7.2:1. Brake H.P.: 120 @ 3500 R.P.M. Taxable H.P.: 39.3. Main bearings: Four. Valve lifters: Hydraulic. Carb.: Holley downdraft 2bbl. Torque: 220 lbs.-ft. @ 2000 R.P.M.

CHASSIS: W.B.: 125 in. O.L.: 209-1/2 in. Height: 69-1/2 (Continental 63). Frt/Rear Tread: 55-1/2 / 58-1/4 in. Tires: 16 x 7.00.

TECHNICAL: Sliding gear transmission. Speeds: 3F/1R. Column shift controls. Single dry plate clutch. Shaft drive. 3/4 floating rear axle. Overall Ratio: 4.44:1. Bendix hydraulic internal expanding brakes on four wheels. Pressed steel, dropped center wheels. Wheel Size: 4-1/2 K - 16. Drivetrain Options: Columbia 2 speed rear axle.

1940 Lincoln, Continental, cabriolet, JAC

OPTIONS: Bumper guards. Radio. Heater. Leather upholstery. Wind wings. Whitewall tires. Fitted luggage. Custom interior.

HISTORICAL: Introduced October 2, 1939. Calendar year production: 24021. Model year production: 22046. The president of Lincoln was Edsel Ford.

1940
Zephyr, V-12

	5	4	3	2	1
3P Cpe	1399	4200	8400	14,000	19,600	28,000
OS Cpe	1429	4350	8700	14,500	20,300	29,000
Clb Cpe	1439	4500	9000	15,000	21,000	30,000
Conv Clb Cpe	1818	5700	11,400	19,000	26,600	38,000
6P Sed	1547	3750	7500	12,500	17,500	25,000
Twn Limo	1787	4350	8700	14,500	20,300	29,000
Cont Clb Cpe	2783	5400	10,800	18,000	25,200	36,000
Cont Conv Cabr	2916	6300	12,600	21,000	29,400	42,000

Series K, V-12
Available on special request, black emblems rather than blue.

1941

LINCOLN — ZEPHYR — TWELVE: Lincolns for 1941 were available as either Zephyr, Custom or Continental models with the Zephyr providing the basic styling — engineering platform for all three versions.

The new Zephyrs had a wide grille outline molding, front fender mounted parking lights, more heavily chromed and reshaped taillights and a com-

bined trunk lid and rear deck light. The front and rear bumpers were also slightly altered and a new hubcap design was introduced.

Interior alterations were similarly of a minor nature. The clock and ash tray were now circular in shape as were the door handles. Additional upholstery fabrics were also available.

For the first time Borg-Warner overdrive was optional and a power top was standard on the convertible model.

1941 Lincoln-Zephyr, 4-dr. sedan, AA

1941 Lincoln, Continental, cabriolet, HFM

LINCOLN — CONTINENTAL — TWELVE: Since the Continental had used the Zephyr's new styling for its 1940 debut, only superficial appearance changes distinguished the 1941 version, although separate tooling was now used for the Continental. Both interior and exterior door handles were of the push-button type and the same styling changes found of the 1941 Zephyr models were also carried over to the Continental. Lincoln Continental script was found both on the hood and spare tire hubcap of the 1941 model. Road hubcaps carried Lincoln V-12 inscriptions. During the 1941 model run minor refinements took place in the appearance of the Continental's hood ornament, V-12 emblem and taillight form. Both turn signals and vacuum window lifts were standard. Interior selection consisted of blue cord/leather, green cord/leather and tan cord matched with either tan or red leather. All-leather upholstery was available in colors of green, black, blue, red or tan. The instrument panel had a mahogany finish.

LINCOLN — CUSTOM — TWELVE: With a wheelbase 13 inches longer than the other 1941 Lincolns and a more luxurious interior the Custom series represented a reasonable reincarnation of the K Lincoln spirit. The Custom carried a Continental hood ornament and Zephyr club coupe front doors. The Custom's side hood molding had previously been used on the 1940 Lincoln Zephyr.

Custom interiors were of a very high quality. A pinstripe broadcloth upholstery was available in blue, green and tan-brown. A cord pattern was offered in tan-brown. Optional custom interiors were also available.

I.D. DATA: Serial numbers were located on right side of cowl, top of clutch housing and transmission case. Starting: H 107688. Ending: H 129690. Engine numbers were located on left side of crankcase between cylinders 1 and 2. Starting: H 107688. Ending: H 129690.

Model No.	Body Type & Seating	Price	Weight	Prod. Total
Lincoln-Zephyr				
72A	2-dr. Cpe.-3P	1432	3560	972
72B	2-dr. Cpe.-5P	1464	3580	178
73	4-dr. Sed.-6P	1493	3710	14,469
76	2-dr. Conv. Cpe.-6P	1801	3840	725
77	2-dr. Clb. Cpe.-6P	1493	3640	3750
36	4-dr. Brun. Twn. Cr.-5P	—	—	5
Lincoln-Continental				
56	2-dr. Cab.-5P	2778	3860	400
57	2-dr. Cpe.-5P	2727	3890	850
Lincoln-Custom				
31	4-dr. Sed.-7P	2622	4250	355
32	4-dr. Limo.-7P	2751	4270	295

ENGINE: 75° V, L-head. Twelve. Cast iron block. B & S: 2-7/8 in. x 3-3/4 in. Disp.: 292 cu. in. C.R.: 7.2:1. Brake H.P.: 120 @ 3500 R.P.M. Taxable H.P.: 39.3. Main bearings: Four. Valve lifters: Hydraulic. Carb.: Holley downdraft 2bbl. Torque: 220 lbs.-ft. @ 2000 R.P.M.

CHASSIS: [Zephyr] W.B.: 125 in. O.L.: 210 in. Height: 69-1/2 in. Frt/Rear Tread: 55-1/2 in./60-3/4 in. Tires: 16 x 7.00. [Custom] W.B.: 138 in. O.L.: 225.3 in. Height: 70.5. Frt/Rear Tread: 55-1/2 in./60-3/4 in. Tires: 16 x 7.00. [Continental] W.B.: 125 in. O.L.: 209-8/10 in. Height: 63 in. Frt/Rear Tread: 55-1/2 in./60-3/4 in. Tires: 16 x 7.00.

TECHNICAL: Sliding gear transmission. Speeds: 3F/1R. Column shift controls. Single dry plate clutch. Shaft drive. 3/4 floating rear axle. Overall Ratio: 4.44:1. Bendix Hydraulic, internal expanding brakes on four wheels. Pressed steel, dropped center wheels. Wheel Size: 5K-16. Drivetrain Options: Columbia 2-speed rear axle. Borg-Warner overdrive.

1941 Lincoln, Continental, coupe, OCW

OPTIONS: Bumper guards. Radio. Heater. Custom interior (100.00). Leather upholstery. Wind wings. Whitewall tires. Fitted luggage.

HISTORICAL: Calendar year production: 17756 (Lincoln-Zephyr: 20094, Lincoln-Continental: 1250, Lincoln-Custom: 650). Model year production: 21994. The president of Lincoln was Edsel Ford. In the 1941 Gilmore Economy Run the first place winner was a Lincoln Custom with a ten-miles-per-gallon average of 57.827 or 21.03 mpg. The second place car was a Lincoln Zephyr at 57.749 t.m.p.g. or 22.96 mpg. Both cars had Columbia 2-speed rear axles and Borg-Warner overdrive.

1941
Zephyr, V-12

	FP	5	4	3	2	1
3P Cpe	1478	4200	8400	14,000	19,600	28,000
OS Cpe	1508	4350	8700	14,500	20,300	29,000
Clb Cpe	1541	4500	9000	15,000	21,000	30,000
Conv Cpe	1858	5700	11,400	19,000	26,600	38,000
Cont Cpe	2812	5400	10,800	18,000	25,200	36,000
Cont Conv Cabr	2865	6300	12,600	21,000	29,400	42,000
6P Sed	1541	3750	7500	12,500	17,500	25,000
Cus Sed	2704	3900	7800	13,000	18,200	26,000
8P Limo	2836	4350	8700	14,500	20,300	29,000

1942

1942 Lincoln-Zephyr, 4-dr. sedan, AA

LINCOLN-ZEPHYR — TWELVE: The 1942 Lincoln-Zephyr was longer, wider and lower. A two-part grille with horizontal bars accentuated the Lincoln's more massive form. Adding to the popular horizontal-line styling theme common to so many 1942 automobiles were the new headlight trim plates containing the parking and directional lights. Common to all 1942 Lincolns were exterior push-button door latches.

Although chassis revisions included longer front springs and a wider front tread, the big technical news was the availability of the Liquimatic 2-speed automatic transmission. This complex and ultimately unsuccessful venture combined overdrive, a fluid coupling and a semi-automatic transmission.

CONTINENTAL — TWELVE: Common to all 1942 Lincolns was a larger, 306 cubic inch V-12 rated at 130 hp. A lower 7.0:1 compression ratio was specified and cast iron heads replaced the aluminum versions. The Continental also shared the Zephyr's new styling format.

1942 Lincoln, Continental, cabriolet, AA

CUSTOM — TWELVE: The Custom shred a rearranged dashboard with the Zephyr. The circular speedometer was placed just to the right of the steering column with a panel containing fuel, temperature, oil and battery gauges to its immediate left. A very large radio speaker grille occupied the center section. A clock, whose size and shape matched that of the speedometer plus a Lincoln plaque provided design symmetry on the right side of the dash.

I.D. DATA: Serial numbers were located on right side of cowl, top of clutch housing and transmission case. Starting: H 129691. Ending: H 136254. Engine numbers were located on left side of crankcase between cylinders 1 and 2. Starting: H 129691. Ending: H 136254.

Model No.	Body Type & Seating	Price	Weight	Prod. Total
Lincoln-Zephyr				
72-A	2-dr. Cpe.-3P	1748	3790	Note 1
72-B	2-dr. Cpe.-5P	—	3790	Note 1
73	4-dr. Sed.-6P	1801	3980	4418
76	2-dr. Conv. Cpe.-6P	2274	4190	191
77-A	2-dr. Clb. Cpe.-6P	1801	3810	253
Lincoln Continental				
56	2-dr. Cab.-5P	3174	4020	136
57	2-dr. Cpe.-5P	3174	4060	200
Lincoln Custom				
31	4-dr. Sed.-7P	3117	4380	47
32	4-dr. Limo.-7P	3248	4400	66

Note 1: The total combined production of these models was 1236.

1942 Lincoln, Continental, coupe, OCW

ENGINE: 75° V, L-head. Twelve. Cast iron block. B & S: 2-15/16 in. x 3-3/4 in. Disp.: 292 cu. in. C.R.: 7.0:1. Brake H.P.: 130 @ 4000 R.P.M. Taxable H.P.: 39.9. Main bearings: Four. Valve lifters: Hydraulic. Carb.: Holley downdraft 2bbl. Torque 220 lbs.-ft. @ 2000 R.P.M.

CHASSIS: [Zephyr] W.B.: 125 in. O.L.: 218.7 in. Height: 68-1/2. Frt/Rear Tread: 59/60-3/4. Tires: 15 x 7.00. [Custom] W.B.: 138 in. Frt/Rear Tread 59/60-3/4. Tires: 15 x 7.00. [Continental] W.B.: 125 in. O.L.: 217 in. Height: 63-1/10 (Cabriolet). Frt/Rear Tread: 59/60-3/4. Tires: 15 x 7.00.

TECHNICAL: Sliding gear transmission. Speeds: 3F/1R. Column shift controls. Single dry plate clutch. Shaft drive. 3/4 floating rear axle. Overall Ratio: 4.22:1. Bendix hydraulic, internal expanding brakes on 4 wheels. Pressed steel, dropped center wheels. Drivetrain Options: Columbia 2-speed rear axle. Borg-Warner overdrive. Liquimatic (189.00).

OPTIONS: Bumper guards. Radio. Heater. Clock. Custom interior (95.00). Leather upholstery. Wind wings. Whitewall tires. Fitted luggage.

HISTORICAL: Introduced: September 30, 1942. Innovations: Liquimatic transmission. Calendar year production: 1276. Model year production: 6547 (Zephyr: 6098, Continental: 336, Custom: 113). The president of Lincoln was Edsel Ford. 1942 model year production ended January 31, 1942.

1942
Zephyr, V-12

	FP	5	4	3	2	1
3P Cpe	1650	1550	4500	7500	10,500	15,000
Clb Cpe	1700	1750	4800	8000	11,200	16,000
Conv Clb Cpe	2150	5700	11,400	19,000	26,600	38,000
Cont Cpe	3000	4650	9300	15,500	21,700	31,000
Cont Conv Cabr	3000	6150	12,300	20,500	28,700	41,000
6P Sed	1700	1400	4200	7000	9800	14,000
Cus Sed	2950	1550	4500	7500	10,500	15,000
8P Limo	3075	2800	5700	9500	13,300	19,000

1900 Lincoln Electric, runabout, NAHC

LINCOLN ELECTRIC — Cleveland, Ohio — (1900) — The Lincoln Electric Company of Cleveland produced an attractive little runabout equipped with a 2-1/2 hp motor and Willard batteries weighing 420 pounds. The vehicle complete weighed 1175 pounds, and was priced at $800. A special "Lincoln Controller" which was elaborately but not very understandably described in a lengthy article about the car appearing in *Motor Age's* September 6th, 1900 edition was said to "give an increase of from ten to twenty-five percent in the battery radius of the carriage, according to the roads." Notwithstanding this ringing endorsement by *Motor Age*, the Lincoln Electric did not survive into 1901, though the company behind it remained in the electric-components-producing field awhile thereafter.

1914 Lincoln Highway, touring, WLB

LINCOLN HIGHWAY — Detroit, Michigan — (1914) — The Lincoln Motor Car Company of Detroit was the successor to the American Motorette Company which had been the idea of several former Keeton officials and which had died before it was born in the same city. This Lincoln was a cycle/light car with a four-cylinder engine, cone clutch, two-speed progressive transmission, a Renault-type front end, and a rather peculiar seating arrangement. The steering wheel was in the rear seat which provided accommodations for two; a third folding seat was placed forward. The price was $500. The first Lincoln prototype, which was designed by H.D.W. Mackaye, was being tested on Detroit streets on January 5th, 1914. Very few more followed before the company went under.

1914 LINCOLN HIGHWAY
Highway Model — 4-cyl., 100'' wb

	FP	5	4	3	2	1
Roadster-2/3P	500	2300	3300	4600	7500	16,000

LINSCOTT — J.W. Linscott & Company of Boston, Massachusetts was among the most prominent automobile dealers in the city during the pre-war years, but at no time did the firm manufacture an automobile, despite the Linscott presence in various car rosters.

LINDSAY — Indianapolis, Indiana — (1902-1903) — In November of 1902 T.J. Lindsay Automobile Parts Company bought out an obscure little business in Dayton, Ohio and moved both it and the man behind it to Indianapolis. The business was a machine shop that specialized in building gasoline engines, and the man behind it was Harry C. Stutz. The Lindsay Company had previously devoted itself exclusively to the manufacture of electric running gear and other parts for electric cars and wished to enter into the gasoline automobile field. Harry Stutz headed that department. Most Lindsays, either gasoline or electric, would be sold in kit form: "This

1903 Lindsay, runabout, NAHC

is the Proposition, We Have to Make Manufacturers" was the headline of a full-page ad in *Motor Age*. But Lindsay also offered to put all parts together if the purchaser wished. The company's announced intention to build 500 to 1000 complete cars during 1903 was probably not realized. Those which were built were runabouts on a 68-inch wheelbase. In 1903, too, the company's name was changed to Lindsay-Russell Axle Company, with a fresh infusion of capital from Harley Russell, a threshing machine manufacturer and a millionaire. By 1904 the firm's products were automotive components only. Harry C. Stutz didn't remain at the Lindsay Company long, though he did stay in Indianapolis where he later entered the automobile industry himself, quite spectacularly. T.J. Lindsay did try the vehicle-building field himself again briefly in 1907 but the product this time was a gasoline delivery wagon.

1908 Lindsley, runabout, NAHC

LINDSLEY — Dowagiac, Michigan — (1908-1909) — J. Victor Lindsley was the son of a wealthy Dowagiac lumberman who traveled to Chicago to make his own fortune. Establishing J.V. Lindsley & Company there, he designed a highwheeler and then discovered that it took money to get into manufacture. Almost immediately he returned home where, with his father's financial assistance, he bought out the Dowagiac Automobile Company which had just recently been organized by two local machinists, Frank Lake and Doras Neff. Initially, the Lindsley idea was to offer a chassis only at $250 to which the purchaser could add his own buggy body and thus have a complete motorcar at a price that couldn't be beat. He put this plan into action as the J.V. Lindsley Auto Chassis Company. When chassis sales amounted to a mere handful, Lindsley had another idea, provided his chassis with his own bodies and marketed the result as the Lindsley for $475. On the face of it, this should have resulted in a fine profit, since the Lindsley chassis was a simple affair with planetary transmission, double chain drive, solid tires and power provided by a two-cylinder air-cooled engine. There was a choice of tiller or wheel steering, and the body was a simple box-type on a 78-inch-wheelbase frame. Unfortunately, amid the fine press reports of local-boy-makes-good was a telling interview with Lindsley in which he indicated that it required two men two weeks to build one car. Efficient auto production obviously was not his forte. In December 1908 the automotive trade press reported that Lindsley had disappeared and the shop had been closed down. Ultimately, he resurfaced to revive the family lumber business and become a millionaire, but for the moment Lindsley's father paid off his debts and the Lindsley enterprise was bought by a group of Dowagiac residents, including Frank Lake who had sold the shop to Lindsley in the first place. The fifteen cars which remained to be completed were put together by the newly formed Dowagiac Motor Car Company (or Dowagiac Auto-Car Company, references conflict) and were sold as Dowagiacs. Apparently, the new firm planned to continue production in the commercial field only, manufacturing a light delivery to carry the name Dowagiac and a larger vehicle to be marketed under the phonetic spelling of Doe-Wah-Jack. Before this happened, however, Frank Lake was killed in July 1909 in an accident which also took the life of another Dowagiac official — and the life out of this

849

borning company as well. Subsequently, the assets of the firm were sold to the Tulsa Auto Manufacturing Company which had moved the whole works to Oklahoma by 1912.

1908-1909 LINDSLEY

	FP	5	4	3	2	1
Lindsley/Dowagiac High-wheeler	475	2000	3000	4200	6500	14,000

1908 LINDSLEY
Lindsley — 2-cyl., 10 hp, 78" wb

	FP	5	4	3	2	1
Runabout-2P	475	1800	2800	4000	6200	13,000

1909 LINDSLEY
Dowagiac — 2-cyl., 10 hp, 78" wb

	FP	5	4	3	2	1
Model B Rbt.	550	1800	2800	4000	6200	13,000
Model C Stnhpe.	750	2000	3000	4200	6500	14,000

LINKROUM — The Linkroum Automobile Company was organized in Newark, New Jersey during the summer of 1909 with a capital stock of $20,000 to manufacture and deal in automobiles and engines. Incorporators were Courtlandt Linkroum, William H. Linkroum and C.R. Erith. Manufacture of a car is doubted.

1911 Lion, touring, WLB

LION — Adrian, Michigan — (1910-1912) — The Lion Motor Car Company of Adrian was organized with $300,000 capitalization in September of 1909. The principals involved were Henry Bowen, formerly of Page-Adrian, and Fred Postal, the proprietor of the Hotel Griswold in Detroit. Austin E. Morey of Detroit was president. Initially, the Lion idea was to produce automobiles using the "gyroscopic" engine which the Blomstrom Manufacturing Company of Detroit had promoted in its Gyroscope car. But that idea was quickly abandoned, and the new Lion for the 1910 model year was powered by a quite typical 40 hp four. "The Lion Forty runs like Sixty" was the clever company slogan. The cars were medium priced in the $1600 range, were well built and enjoyed a fine success. On June 2nd, 1912 the factory of the Lion Motor Car Company burned to the ground. It was the most catastrophic fire in the city's history. One fireman was killed, and more than 150 cars inside were destroyed. So, too, was the prototype of the Model Thirty, a new $890 four being readied for the 1913 model year. As plant manager Humphrey told a reporter afterward, "We finally got the testers out of the sheds, but failed to rescue the Lion Thirty which we wanted worse than anything." A mass meeting of Adrian's citizenry was called the following day, and the city pledged its support in a rebuilding program. A booster campaign in July raised $8000 in an hour for Lion. Company machinery and other manufacturing property saved in the fire were stored in the local toy factory, and temporary headquarters were leased in the Wing & Parsons Company plant across town. But the fire had already killed the Lion company. In mid-October of 1912 receivership came. The Lion assets were sold in December to A.O. Dunk who specialized in buying moribund companies and who got a particularly good buy on this one. The Lion property was appraised at $32,000, Dunk's winning auction bid was only $7000, and it was initially rejected as being ridiculously low. Further problems visited Lion the following year. Blomstrom Manufacturing sued Fred Postal and Henry Bowen for breach of contract with regard to the "gyroscopic" engine commitment they had made. The $46,000 court-awarded judgment was in Blomstrom's favor.

1910 LION
Forty — 4-cyl., 40 hp, 112" wb

	FP	5	4	3	2	1
Model A Runabout	1500	2500	3500	5000	8500	18,000
Model A Touring	1600	2700	3600	5300	8800	19,000

1911 LION
Forty — 4-cyl., 40 hp, 112" wb

	FP	5	4	3	2	1
Model C Roadster-2P	1450	2700	3600	5300	8800	19,000
Model D Fore-Door Tour.-5P	1600	2500	3500	5000	8500	18,000
Model A Touring-5P	1500	2400	3400	4800	8000	17,000
Model B Touring-4P	1475	2300	3300	4600	7500	16,000

1912 LION
Forty — 4-cyl., 40 hp, 116" wb

	FP	5	4	3	2	1
Model K Touring-5P	1600	2400	3400	4800	8000	17,000
Model L Roadseter-2P	1600	2700	3600	5300	8800	19,000

LIPMAN — Beloit, Wisconsin — (1901, 1911) — Carl Lipman of Beloit built two cars a decade apart. The first, at the turn of the century, was a small gasoline runabout that he called the Motormobile. It was not marketed, however, and Lipman subsequently moved into the manufacture of

speedometers and other auto accessories. In 1909 he announced his intention to produce six-cylinder cars under the name Rocoit (that strange appellation combining Rockford and Beloit, since manufacture was planned also for Rockford, Illinois). The Rocoit car never arrived at all. The second Lipman automobile followed in 1911 and was a six-cylinder 35 hp touring car on a 122-inch wheelbase. In mid-summer that year, Lipman announced that it was "highly probable" that he would organize a company for manufacture, with the car to be priced at $1500. But he never did follow through on this. Instead, his Lipman Manufacturing Company moved out of speedometers and into the refrigerator business. In 1918 the firm was renamed the Lipman Refrigerator Car and Manufacturing Company, which evolved ultimately into the General Refrigeration Corporation of Beloit.

1900 Liquid Air, runabout, WLB

LIQUID AIR — Boston, Massachusetts & New York City — (1899-1900) — "Of all the magic words (in the automobile industry), 'liquid air' is today the strongest," a reporter for *The Motor Age* wrote in September 1899. "It draws into a charmed circle of hasheesh-laden atmosphere all the smart gentry who have succeeded in getting a little money ahead at the cost of fellow-beings and whose idea it is to get something for nothing." The object of the reporter's derision was the Liquid Air Power and Automobile Company, with offices in Boston and New York City. The men behind it were George Code of Boston, Milton Chase of Haverhill, and Hans Knudsen of Vamdrup, Denmark — the "genius of two continents," as the stock prospectus put it. The trio was selling stock all over the country, and advertising widely, though never explaining very well just how liquid air would propel an automobile. In December of 1899 *The Carriage Monthly* noted that an unexplained device could raise horsepower from two to five by the "mere turning of a screw, and without additional cost." *The Motor Review* published several pages of descriptive material from the stock prospectus which made no engineering sense at all. When the *Motor Age* reporter asked to see the completed demonstration carriage at the company offices in Boston, he was told it was not possible. He was also told the factory was in Cambridge. But not precisely where. A drawing of the car — which was occasionally referred to as the Peerless — was a rather silly exercise in demure flamboyance. The Liquid Air scam continued into the turn of the century as the American Liquid Air Company which gave its address as 1 Broadway in New York City. Ultimately a prototype car, a quite ordinary-looking runabout, was built. In 1901, when receivership arrived, this company whose capital stock was a declared $1.5 million had assets totaling about $7500.

LIQUID AIR — Indianapolis, Indiana — (1900) — Following hard upon the establishment of the Liquid Air Power and Automobile Company on the East Coast was a venture styling itself the Liquid Air Company in Indianapolis. Behind this one were J.E. Pierce as president, W.P. Herod as secretary, E.J. Richards as general manager — and an unnamed Cleveland industrialist who was supposed to furnish this trio with $100,000 worth of machinery. "The chief business will be the manufacture of motor vehicles, and, as steam and liquid air operate on the same principle, the company will make machines to be operated by both motive powers," *The Motor Vehicle* review reported in September 1900. Apparently, pilot models were in the process of being built, but "a slight hitch in the arrangements" with the Cleveland industrialist ultimately rendered this manufacturing venture asunder before it began.

LISTMAN — The H.E. Listman Company was organized in Troy, New York during the spring of 1917 with a capital stock of $100,000 for the manufacture of motor vehicles and accessories. Incorporators were E. Bailey, J.H. Broderick and H.E. Listman. Manufacture of a car is doubted.

LITTLE — The Little & Congdon Company of Amesbury, Massachusetts was organized during the summer of 1900 with a capital stock of $100,000 for the manufacture and sale of automobiles. Incorporators were J.H. Little, S.W. Congdon, J. Joyce, J.F. Finn and C.S. Mayo, all of Amesbury. Manufacture is doubted.

The Little Giant Motor Car Company was organized in Camden, New Jersey late in 1911 with a capital stock of $125,000 to manufacture and deal in motor cars. W.C. Davis and D. Cooney were among the incorporators. Manufacture of an automobile is doubted.

The Little Motor Kar Company has been indicated on various lists as an automobile manufacturer in Arlington, Texas in 1911. No documentation of this has been discovered. Possibly this company was confused with the venture of the same name which produced the Texmobile in Grand Prairie, Texas in 1920.

1912 Little, roadster, WLB

LITTLE — Flint, Michigan — (1912-1913) — The Little was one of two cars William C. Durant decided to build following his first ouster from General Motors. It was the first announced, on October 30th, 1911 — and the first to arrive, during late summer of 1912. The Little Motor Car Company was named for a huge bear of a man, William H. Little, Durant's former general manager at Buick. The car was more appropriately named than the man: it was little and cute as a button. A 20 hp $690 four on a 90-inch wheelbase, it was "simple to the point of innocence," according to Alex Hardy, the Durant man in charge of Little production. The car was produced at the Flint Wagon Works, which had previously seen manufacture of the Whiting. Meantime Bill Little himself was in Detroit, assigned as liaison to hurry Louis Chevrolet along in the design of the other car Billy Durant was planning to build. The new Chevrolet had been announced November 8th, 1911, a week after the Little, but Louis was taking his time finishing it. When finally during the summer of 1912 the prototype Chevrolet was completed, Durant was displeased. The car was too big, too heavy, too expensive; he knew he couldn't sell it for less than $2150. But at least it was a car to sell, so he ordered the Chevrolet into production. Meantime, aware of the costly direction the Chevrolet was taking, Durant had also decided to build a Little Six to sell for $1285, which was closer to his desired price range for the Chevrolet. Both cars arrived in the marketplace at the same time, which was unfortunate since each was a Durant car and tended to be confused or compared in the automotive press. This was to the benefit of neither, since the Chevrolet was sturdily built and expensive, and the Little was hastily built and inexpensive, Durant aware that it would be "driven to its death in less than 25,000 miles." A road test of that duration that Durant had ordered for the Little had proved it. Naturally, since the public was unaware of this, the Little's sales figures were far better than the Chevrolet's. Durant thus found himself with two cars, one that could be driven forever and wasn't selling, one that couldn't and was selling. His solution was to take the individual virtues of each car and combine them into one new car. Chevrolet was to be the one car. Among other factors, as Alex Hardy pointed out, the Little's name would ultimately have proved a negative, few people buying a small, inexpensive car wishing to be so pointedly reminded of it. And so the Little was discontinued without regrets in May of 1913 after approximately 3500 were built. All efforts now were focused on the Chevrolet. It appeared to be a wise decision.

1912 LITTLE
Four — 4-cyl., 20 hp, 90" wb

	FP	5	4	3	2	1
Roadster-2P	690	2000	3000	4200	6500	14,000

1913 Little Six, touring, HAC

1913 LITTLE
Four — 4-cyl., 20 hp, 90" wb

	FP	5	4	3	2	1
Roadster-2P	690	2000	3000	4200	6500	14,000
Six — 6-cyl., 26.4 hp, 106" wb						
Touring-5P	1285	2300	3300	4600	7500	16,000

LITTLE DETROIT — Two cars built in Detroit were occasionally referred to by the name Little Detroit. The first was the Demotcar of 1909-1910, which ultimately evolved into the Ritter. Refer to Demotcar. The second was the Detroit Cyclecar of 1914, which later became the Saginaw Speedster. Refer to Detroit Cyclecar.

LITTLE FOUR STEAM — Detroit, Michigan — (1904) — The Little Four steam car was exhibited at the Detroit Automobile Show in early 1904. It was a small two-passenger runabout with a three-cylinder 6/8 hp single-acting steam engine. The Little Automobile Manufacturing Company was organized soon thereafter, but did very little manufacturing. Wyatt L. Brown, J.D. McLachlan and Fred L. Brown were the men behind this short-lived enterprise.

LITTLE KAR — The product of the Little Motor Kar Company which was organized in Grand Prairie, Texas in 1920 was called the Texmobile. Refer to Texmobile.

1942 Littlemac, coupe, KM

LITTLEMAC — Muscatine, Iowa — (1930-1932) — Herbert and Ralph Thompson were brothers and lawyers in Muscatine; Herbert was also mayor of the town, and Ralph a state senator, in November of 1929 when they organized the Thompson Motor Corporation for production of a car to be called the Littlemac. Involved in this venture with them were Joseph W. Valentine and Harry H. Hoban, both of Rock Island, Illinois. Involved as well was Clayton E. Frederickson, whose idea the Littlemac was and who had been experimenting with the small-car idea since 1914 when his Fredrickson cyclecar failed to make it in Chicago. The Littlemac was indeed a small car, fitted with a four-cylinder Star engine and other modified Star components, all of them placed in an 80-inch wheelbase chassis (40-inch tread) to be sold at $350 as a coupe and $500 as a light delivery. William C. Durant undoubtedly was happy to provide the Star parts; he had phased out the Star car in 1928 (replacing it with the Durant 4-40) and probably needed the money since his second automobile empire was in financial distress. So was the Littlemac for all of its life. Initially, Frederickson had been given only money enough to build a prototype, which he completed in a plant in Moline, Illinois in August 1929. It was the coupe model, and it created sufficient interest to encourage the Thompsons to organize the million-dollar company. A total of about a dozen cars was built during all of 1930. "The Fastest Small Automobile in the World," brochures said — with a 55 mph cruising speed and up to 75 mph available if needed. Fuel economy was 35 mpg. But thus far the Littlemac was strictly a local product, and the Thompsons believed that to survive they had to go national. The Littlemac was introduced at the Chicago Automobile Show in January 1931. The venture really ended soon after that, although precisely when the last nail closed the Littlemac coffin is difficult to determine. Total production of over 200 Littlemacs has been estimated, but that obviously was a wild guess by somebody. Undoubtedly the final figure wasn't much more than the approximate dozen of 1930. The light delivery, or "Truckette," was not built until August of 1931, and a new one is known to have been sold as late as February of 1934. When production of the coupe ceased cannot be determined. The company ceased to exist in 1935. Among the Littlemac's problems, in addition to its introduction as the Great Depression was about to take hold, was the Littlemac's looks. Its body styling, which was the work of Oscar P. Eklund, was rather high and boxy, and didn't have the piquant charm of the American Austin or, ironically, Billy Durant's American version of the French Mathis, both of which had also appeared at the Chicago Automobile Show of 1931. The Littlemac venture, though it might have been ill advised, was not a flim-flam operation of dubious character as were so many in automobile history. It was an honest effort. It simply didn't work.

LITTLE MYSTERY — Detroit, Michigan — (1929) — The Little Mystery was small but not much of a mystery. Its builder, Kenneth L. Morehouse, promoted it — and himself — with a fury, even taking his new bride and

For the Lilliputs

1929 Little Mystery, NAHC

the wee car on a much publicized honeymoon. Morehouse built the Little Mystery nights while working days in the engineering department at Ford. It took him three years to complete, and $9000. Its engine was an eight with twin ignition and two carburetors, and self-starter, which was snugged into a small 52-inch wheelbase chassis fitted with four-wheel brakes and four-speed transmission. Morehouse claimed a top speed of 130 mph; the Little Mystery is known to have traveled 91.2 mph to a small-car record at Indy. The car also traveled to myriad department stores across the country where it and Morehouse were put on prominent display. Morehouse's reason for building the car was principally to tout its engine, in which he hoped to interest aero manufacturers.

1914 Little Princess, runabout, WLB

LITTLE PRINCESS — Detroit, Michigan — (1913-1914) — The Little Princess was unique among cyclecars in having a Renault-type hood and specifications rather more sophisticated than the general run of vehicles of that genre. It boasted a four-cylinder engine rather than a two, shaft instead of belt drive, a planetary rather than a friction transmission. Moreover, two people could sit side by side comfortably, instead of staggered or in tandem. "You will not be ashamed to have the Little Princess in front of your residence," its makers said, a tacit admission of the ill repute most cyclecars suffered. That this admirable example suffered the same is indicated by the fact that after a year of trying the Princess Cyclecar Company metamorphosed into the Princess Motor Car Company, and the Little Princess grew up to become the Princess.

1913-1914 LITTLE PRINCESS
4-cyl., 14/16 hp, 88" wb

	FP	5	4	3	2	1
Two-Seater Cyclecar	395	1800	2800	4000	6200	13,000

1904 Little Red Devil, runabout, LC

LITTLE RED DEVIL — St. Louis, Missouri — (1904) — The St. Louis lad who built the car he called a Little Red Devil is not known, but Percy Megargel, the well-known Reo transcontinentalist, was so impressed that he forwarded a letter and picture of it to the trade press in 1905. The car's engine was a 1-1/2 hp air-cooled unit that had previously seen service in the boy's Thomas Auto-Bi. "The entire outfit, ready to run, weighs 225 pounds," wrote Megargel. "The wheelbase is 5 feet 6 inches and the tread 30 inches. It carries one person nicely and can carry two at a speed of from 18 to 20 miles an hour. The drive is direct from the engine through the clutch."

1902 Little Steamer, runabout, NAHC

LITTLE STEAMER — Salem, Massachusetts — (1900-1903) — At the turn of the century in Salem, David M. Little, with the help of Frank Cook, built at least two steam vehicles. The cars were constructed at Little's boatyard on the wharf off Derby Street. A single-cylinder engine, 30-gallon water tank and 10-gallon gasoline tank were fitted. The frame was tubular, and steering was by tiller. A simple box delivery wagon and a two-seater bench wagon have been documented in photographs. Manufacture was not embarked upon, however.

LIVESEY — The Livesey Pionnis Motor Car Company was organized in Newark, New Jersey early in 1907 with a capital stock of $25,000 for the manufacture of automobiles. H. Livesey and A.J. Giommer were the incorporators. Manufacture is doubted.

LIVINGSTON — The Livingston & Van Epps Company was organized in Syracuse, New York early in 1909 with a capital stock of $5000 to manufacture engines, boats, motor cars, machinery and tools. T.E. Lanback, B.B. Parsons and E.P. Van Epps were the incorporators. Manufacture of an automobile is doubted.

L.M. — Just two L.M.'s were built in 1912, one for Charles L. Lawrence, the other for Andrew Moulton. They were two members of the triumvirate which had produced the B.L.M. in Brooklyn, New York from 1906-1907. But the L.M. was not an American car, its presence on U.S. lists to the contrary. Both examples were built in Paris, France.

The L. & M. Manufacturing Company was organized in Chicago, Illinois during the summer of 1914 with a $10,000 capital stock to manufacture automobiles and accessories. Charles A. Larson, Louis Teuber and Ivan Thorsell were the incorporators. Manufacture of a car is doubted.

LOCKE — From 1902 to 1905, in Salem, Massachusetts, the Locke Regulator Company produced a car which it marketed under the tradename of Puritan. Refer to Puritan Steam.

LOCOMOBILE — Watertown, Massachusetts — (1899-1900) / Bridgeport, Connecticut — (1900-1929) — The Locomobile Company of America was incorporated in June of 1899 by John Brisben Walker, editor and publisher of *Cosmopolitan* magazine, and Amzi Lorenzo Barber, who had made a fortune in asphalt. Earlier that year Walker had talked the Stanley brothers in Watertown, Massachusetts into selling out their steam car business for $250,000, and Walker had talked Barber into putting up precisely that figure for a half-interest in their new venture. Production of a run of 100 Stanley cars had been begun in the Watertown factory the year previous, and now production continued there with the car renamed Locomobile. Within months Walker and Barber quarreled, however, and the partnership broke up, with Barber retaining the Locomobile name and Watertown factory, and Walker taking off for Tarrytown, New York to build the same car as the Mobile. Late in 1899 Barber also acquired plants for Locomobile production in Worcester and Westboro, Massachusetts, though in 1900 he secured a factory in Bridgeport, Connecticut which he vastly preferred and into which he moved all production by early 1901. By May of 1902 more than 4000 Locomobiles had been built. In truth, though they were nicely fitted out, they weren't very good cars. Chain driven and tiller steered, these early Locomobiles were none too sturdy with their welded bicycle-like frames, and were incredibly thirsty, using up all their water in a 20-mile run. In January 1902 a specially built Locomobile steam racer was driven a mile in 1 minute 15 seconds by S.T. Davis, Jr., and the year following Davis was appointed Locomobile's president, succeeding his father-in-law Amzi Barber who could now tend to his asphalt and other pursuits. A civil engineering graduate of Rensselaer Polytechnic Institute, Davis had joined Locomobile as treasurer in 1900, the year he had been instrumental in organizing the National Association of Automobile Manufacturers and was made its first president. Now, as Locomobile's president, he had a big job to do. By 1902 the Stanley brothers were heartily back in the steam car business with a newly designed and refined car — and latterday Locomobile steamers were improved as well, with larger boilers and better water pumps, the latter supplied by the Overman Wheel Company which built the Victor steamer in Chicopee Falls. In October of 1902 Overman merged with Locomobile, moving all its machinery to Bridgeport. It was in the Overman plant in Chicopee Falls, however, that Andrew Lawrence Riker designed the first Locomobile gasoline car in 1902, with heavy secrecy being maintained largely for the practical business reason that potential Locomobile steam car customers might be reluctant to purchase an automobile seemingly, and in fact, destined to be withdrawn from the market. The Victor steamer was discontinued early in 1903, the Locomobile steamer was continued into early 1904, then the Locomobile Company of America became a gasoline car producer exclusively. The Riker-designed Locomobile was an exemplary automobile. Offered initially as a twin and a four (with automatic inlet valves), its body was pressed steel, and it was steered by wheel from the right side. T-head fours only were produced from 1904, as Locomobile settled down to its long career of building exceptionally fine and very expensive motorcars. "Easily the Best Built Car in America" was a company slogan. For a short period, the Locomobile was a major factor in motor sport as well. Although victory never was his, Joe Tracy drove Locomobiles spiritedly in the 1905

1899 Locomobile, steam runabout, OCW

Gordon Bennett in France, and the Vanderbilt Cups on Long Island that year and in 1906, finishing third in the 1905 race. European cars had overwhelmed American opposition in most contests during this period, but finally in 1908 a car built in the United States won a world-class event when George Robertson piloted the Locomobile that would ever after be famous as "Old 16" to victory in the 1908 Vanderbilt Cup. Robertson won a few more races for Locomobile that year; the year following the company decided to rest on its racing laurels and entered no further contests. In 1911 the renowned six-cylinder T-head Locomobile Model 48 was introduced; it would endure as long as the Locomobile itself, models in the late Twenties developing more than 100 bhp. Late in 1914 a special custom department was set up at the factory headed by the brilliant designer J. Frank de Causse, and thereafter custom-built Locomobiles found their way into the garages of William Wrigley, Lawrence Copley Thaw, William Carnegie, Reggie Vanderbilt, Lolita Armour and William K. Vanderbilt. General John J. "Black Jack" Pershing took his overseas. In 1916 de Causse designed a Locomobile for Rodman Wanamaker which was probably the world's first dual cowl phaeton. (It was subsequently catalogued by Locomobile as the Sportif, though not all Sportifs would carry the dual cowl feature, the name becoming virtually synonymous with Locomobile's four-passenger close-coupled phaeton). During this period, lamps and metal work for some Locomobile bodies was designed by the Tiffany studios, and noted actress/interior decorator Elsie De Wolf lent her hand in devising super-elegant interiors for Locomobile closed cars. Locomobile was riding high, in prestige and popularity, but trouble lay ahead. In the fall of 1915, S.T. Davis, Jr. died suddenly of a cerebral hemorrhage. Those who took over his reins elected to expand the company's efforts, purchasing huge quantities of materials on credit, and in 1919 finding their loans called but no money to pay for them. Receivership followed. In 1920 the Locomobile company became one-third of the disaster known as Hare's Motors, the other two-thirds being Mercer and Simplex. This attempt at empire building by former Packard vice-president Emlen S. Hare was in disarray within a year, and in 1922 another empire builder stepped in. "From the midst of a somewhat opaque cloud of rumor there emerged this week the personally unauthorized assertion that William C. Durant is negotiating for the purchase of the Locomobile Company of America," reported *Automobile Topics* guardedly in July 1922. *Automobile Topics* got the story right. Durant immediately announced that "no radical change is contemplated either in the policy or design" of the Locomobile except that which might be dictated for "greater elevation of standards." He didn't exactly follow through on this. True, the magnificent Model 48 was continued, and the Model 90 he introduced for 1926 (with L-head monobloc engine) was a luxury car only a tad smaller and less expensive than the mighty 48. But the year previous Durant had put the Locomobile name on a Junior Eight (ohv engine) which sold for as low as $1785, and had an abortive go at a Junior Six that was nothing more than a fancy Flint. And the year following

he introduced a straight-eight with a Lycoming engine. A proprietary engine in a Locomobile was virtual heresy. Although the luxury models remained on the Locomobile agenda, most of the cars sold in 1928 were the Model 8-70 (the former Junior) or the Lycoming-engined 8-80. The new 88 for 1929, with 115 hp Lycoming engine, was announced proudly as the first Locomobile ever to wear a crest, and was claimed "to outperform any other Locomobile ever built." Probably no one believed that, not even Billy Durant himself. Fortunately, at least a few of the Model 48 and 90 Locomobiles were also built in 1929, the company's last year. William C. Durant was mortally wounded in the stock market crash. Of all the cars in his second empire — the Flint, the Star, the Durant, the Locomobile — only the Durant survived into the Thirties, and it succumbed in 1932.

1900 Locomobile, steam runabout, HAC

1899-1900 LOCOMOBILE

	FP	5	4	3	2	1
Steam Runabout	600	—	4	3	2	1

1901 Locomobile, steam surrey, JAC

1901

	FP	5	4	3	2	1
Style 2 Steam Rbt	750	3150	6300	10,500	14,700	21,000
Style 02 Steam Rbt	850	3300	6600	11,000	15,400	22,000
Style 3 Buggy Top Rbt	900	3400	6900	11,500	16,100	23,000
Style 03 Vic Top Rbt	900	3400	6900	11,500	16,100	23,000
Style 003 Vic Top Rbt	1000	3400	6900	11,500	16,100	23,000
Style 5 Locosurrey	1200	3600	7200	12,000	16,800	24,000
Style 05 Locosurrey	1400	3750	7500	12,500	17,500	25,000

1901 Locomobile, steam victoria, HAC

1902 Locomobile, steam runabout, HAC

1902

	FP	5	4	3	2	1
4P Model A Steam Tr	1600	3600	7200	12,000	16,800	24,000
2/4P Model B Steam Tr	2400	3750	7500	12,500	17,500	25,000
2P Steam Vic	1400	3300	6600	11,000	15,400	22,000
Style No. 2 Std Steam Rbt	900	3000	6000	10,000	14,000	20,000
Style No. 02 Steam Rbt	950	3150	6300	10,500	14,700	21,000

1903 Locomobile, gasoline touring, HAC

854

1902

	FP	5	4	3	2	1
4P Style No. 5 Steam Locosurrey	1200	3400	6900	11,500	16,100	23,000
4P Style No. 05 Steam Locosurrey	1400	3600	7200	12,000	16,800	24,000
Style No. 3 Steam Physician's Car	950	3000	6000	10,000	14,000	20,000
Style No. 03 Steam Stanhope	950	2800	5700	9500	13,300	19,000
Style No. 003 Stanhope	1100	3150	6300	10,500	14,700	21,000
Steam Locotrap	1200	3150	6300	10,500	14,700	21,000
Steam Locodelivery	2000	3300	6600	11,000	15,400	22,000

1903 Locomobile, gasoline touring, JAC

1903
Steam Cars

	FP	5	4	3	2	1
Dos-a-Dos	1600	3400	6900	11,500	16,100	23,000
Locosurrey	1200	3600	7200	12,000	16,800	24,000
Rbt	950	3150	6300	10,500	14,700	21,000
Gasoline Car, 2-cyl., 9 hp, 76" wb						
5P Ton	3300	3300	6600	11,000	15,400	22,000
Gasoline Car, 4-cyl., 16 hp, 86" wb						
5P Ton	4500	3750	7500	12,500	17,500	25,000

1904 Locomobile, type D, tonneau, HAC

1904
Steam Cars

	FP	5	4	3	2	1
Tr, 85" wb	1800	3600	7200	12,000	16,800	24,000
Tr, 79" wb	2400	3750	7500	12,500	17,500	25,000
Stanhope, 79" wb	1500	3150	6300	10,500	14,700	21,000
Dos-a-Dos, 79" wb	1800	3400	6900	11,500	16,100	23,000
Long Wb Rbt	750	3300	6600	11,000	15,400	22,000
Locosurrey, 75" wb	1200	3750	7500	12,500	17,500	25,000
Spl Surrey, 93" wb	1800	3900	7800	13,000	18,200	26,000
Gasoline Model C, 2-cyl., 9/12 hp, 76" wb						
5P Ton	2100	3600	7200	12,000	16,800	24,000
5P Canopy Top Ton	2325	4200	8400	14,000	19,600	28,000
Gasoline Model D, 4-cyl., 16/22 hp, 86" wb						
6/8P Limo	5000	3400	6900	11,500	16,100	23,000
6P King of Belgian Ton	5100	3600	7200	12,000	16,800	24,000
6P Ton DeL	4000	3300	6600	11,000	15,400	22,000

1905

	FP	5	4	3	2	1
Model E, 4-cyl., 15/20 hp, 92" wb						
5P Tr	2800	3750	7500	12,500	17,500	25,000
5P Lan'let	3300	3400	6900	11,500	16,100	23,000
Model D, 4-cyl., 20/25 hp, 96" wb						
7P Tr	3700	3900	7800	13,000	18,200	26,000
Model H, 4-cyl., 30/35 hp, 106" wb						
7P Tr	5000	4200	8400	14,000	19,600	28,000
7P Limo	6000	3600	7200	12,000	16,800	24,000
Model F, 4-cyl., 40/45 hp, 110" wb						
7P Limo	8000	3750	7500	12,500	17,500	25,000

1905 Locomobile, type E, touring, HAC

1906 Locomobile, type H, touring, HAC

1906
Model E, 4-cyl., 15/20 hp, 93" wb

	FP	5	4	3	2	1
5P Tr	3130	3750	7500	12,500	17,500	25,000
2P Fishtail Rbt	2900	3600	7200	12,000	16,800	24,000
5P Limo	3700	2800	5700	9500	13,300	19,000

Model H, 4-cyl., 30/35 hp, 106" wb

5/7P Tr	5000	4050	8100	13,500	18,900	27,000
5/7P Limo	6200	3000	6000	10,000	14,000	20,000

Special, 4-cyl., 90 hp, 110" wb

Vanderbilt Racer	18,000	12,000	24,000	40,000	60,000	80,000

1907 Locomobile, type E, touring, HAC

1907
Model E, 4-cyl., 20 hp, 96" wb

5P Tr	2800	3900	7800	13,000	18,200	26,000
2P Fishtail Rbt	2700	3750	7500	12,500	17,500	25,000
5P Limo	3800	3000	6000	10,000	14,000	20,000

Model H, 4-cyl., 35 hp, 120" wb

7P Tr	4500	4200	8400	14,000	19,600	28,000
7P Limo	5700	3150	6300	10,500	14,700	21,000

Special, 4-cyl., 90 hp, 120" wb

Vanderbilt Racer	15,000	12,300	24,600	41,000	62,000	82,000

1908
Model E, 4-cyl., 20 hp, 102" wb

Std Tr	2900	4050	8100	13,500	18,900	27,000

Model E, 4-cyl., 20 hp, 116" wb

6P Limo	4200	2300	5400	9000	12,600	18,000
6P Lan'let	4300	2800	5700	9500	13,300	19,000

Model I, 4-cyl., 40 hp, 123" wb

3P Rbt	4750	4350	8700	14,500	20,300	29,000

1908 Locomobile, type E, touring, HAC

1908 Locomobile, type E, limousine, KM

1909 Locomobile, model 30, runabout, HAC

1910 Locomobile, model 40, type I, limousine, HAC

855

1909
Model 30, 4-cyl., 32 hp, 120" wb

	FP	5	4	3	2	1
5P Tr	3500	4200	8400	14,000	19,600	28,000
4P Rbt	3500	4050	8100	13,500	18,900	27,000

Model 40, 4-cyl., 40 hp, 123" wb

	FP	5	4	3	2	1
7P Tr	4500	4500	9000	15,000	21,000	30,000
4P Baby Ton	4500	4650	9300	15,500	21,700	31,000
7P Limo	5900	2800	5700	9500	13,300	19,000

1910
Model 30(L), 4-cyl., 30 hp, 120" wb

	FP	5	4	3	2	1
4P Rds	3500	4350	8700	14,500	20,300	29,000
4P Baby Ton	3500	4200	8400	14,000	19,600	28,000
5P Tr	3500	4050	8100	13,500	18,900	27,000
Limo	4700	2800	5700	9500	13,300	19,000

Model 40(I), 4-cyl., 40 hp, 123" wb

	FP	5	4	3	2	1
7P Tr	4500	4350	8700	14,500	20,300	29,000
Rbt	4500	4200	8400	14,000	19,600	28,000
7P Limo	5900	3000	6000	10,000	14,000	20,000
7P Lan'let	6000	3300	6600	11,000	15,400	22,000
4P Baby Ton	4500	4200	8400	14,000	19,600	28,000

1911 Locomobile, model 30, type L, torpedo, HAC

1911
Model 30(L), 4-cyl., 32 hp, 120" wb

	FP	5	4	3	2	1
5P Tr	3500	4500	9000	15,000	21,000	30,000
4P Baby Ton	3500	4800	9600	16,000	22,400	32,000
4P Torp	3700	4950	9900	16,500	23,100	33,000
6P Limo	4600	3300	6600	11,000	15,400	22,000
6P Lan'let	4600	3750	7500	12,500	17,500	25,000

Model 48(M), 6-cyl., 48 hp, 125" wb

	FP	5	4	3	2	1
7P Tr	4800	4800	9600	16,000	22,400	32,000
4P Baby Ton	4800	5250	10,500	17,500	24,500	35,000
7P Limo	6050	3600	7200	12,000	16,800	24,000
7P Lan'let	6150	4050	8100	13,500	18,900	27,000

1912 Locomobile, model 30, type L, touring, JAC

1912
Model 30(L), 4-cyl., 30 hp, 120" wb

	FP	5	4	3	2	1
Tr	3500	4500	9000	15,000	21,000	30,000
Baby Ton	3500	4800	9600	16,000	22,400	32,000
Torp	3600	4950	9900	16,500	23,100	33,000
Limo	4600	3300	6600	11,000	15,400	22,000
Berl	4800	3600	7200	12,000	16,800	24,000
Lan'let	4700	3400	6900	11,500	16,100	23,000

Model 48(M), 6-cyl., 48 hp, 135" wb

	FP	5	4	3	2	1
Tr	4800	4800	9600	16,000	22,400	32,000
4P Torp	4800	5100	10,200	17,000	23,800	34,000
5P Torp	4800	5250	10,500	17,500	24,500	35,000
Limo	6050	3400	6900	11,500	16,100	23,000
Berl	6250	3750	7500	12,500	17,500	25,000
Lan'let	6150	3600	7200	12,000	16,800	24,000

1913
Model 30(L), 4-cyl., 32.4 hp, 120" wb

	FP	5	4	3	2	1
4P Torp	3600	4800	9600	16,000	22,400	32,000
5P Tr	3600	4650	9300	15,500	21,700	31,000
Rds	3600	5250	10,500	17,500	24,500	35,000

Model 38(R), 6-cyl., 43.8 hp, 128" wb

	FP	5	4	3	2	1
4P Torp	4300	6600	13,200	22,000	30,800	44,000
5P Tr	4300	6450	12,900	21,500	30,100	43,000
Rds	4300	7050	14,100	23,500	32,900	47,000
Limo	5350	3300	6600	11,000	15,400	22,000
Lan'let	5450	3400	6900	11,500	16,100	23,000
Berl Limo	5550	3600	7200	12,000	16,800	24,000
Berl Lan'let	5650	3750	7500	12,500	17,500	25,000

1913 Locomobile, model 38, little six, roadster, HAC

1914 Locomobile, touring, OCW

1914
Model 38, 6-cyl., 43.8 hp, 132" wb

	FP	5	4	3	2	1
4P Torp	4400	9600	19,200	32,000	44,800	64,000
5P Tr	4400	9900	19,800	33,000	46,200	66,000
2P Rds	4400	10,200	20,400	34,000	47,600	68,000
7P Limo	5400	4800	9600	16,000	22,400	32,000
7P Lan'let	5500	4950	9900	16,500	23,100	33,000
7P Berl	5700	5250	10,500	17,500	24,500	35,000

Model 48, 6-cyl., 48.6 hp, 136 & 140" wb

	FP	5	4	3	2	1
7P Tr	5100	9900	19,800	33,000	46,200	66,000
6P Torp	5100	10,200	20,400	34,000	47,600	68,000
2P Rds	5100	10,500	21,000	35,000	49,000	70,000
7P Limo	6200	5250	10,500	17,500	24,500	35,000
7P Lan'let	6300	5550	11,100	18,500	25,900	37,000
7P Berl	6500	5850	11,700	19,500	27,300	39,000

1915 Locomobile, model 48, touring, HAC

1916 Locomobile, model 38, touring, HAC

856

1915
Model 38, 6-cyl., 43.3 hp, 132" wb

	FP	5	4	3	2	1
5P Tr	4400	10,800	21,600	36,000	50,500	72,000
2P Rds	4400	11,100	22,200	37,000	52,000	74,000
4P Torp	4400	10,800	21,600	36,000	50,500	72,000
7P Limo	5400	5550	11,100	18,500	25,900	37,000
7P Lan'let	5500	5700	11,400	19,000	26,600	38,000
7P Berl	5700	5850	11,700	19,500	27,300	39,000

Model 48, 6-cyl., 48.6 hp, 140" wb

	FP	5	4	3	2	1
7P Tr	5100	11,100	22,200	37,000	52,000	74,000
2P Rds	5100	11,400	22,800	38,000	56,000	76,000
6P Torp	5100	11,100	22,200	37,000	52,000	74,000
7P Limo	6200	5700	11,400	19,000	26,600	38,000
7P Lan'let	6300	5850	11,700	19,500	27,300	39,000
7P Berl	6500	6000	12,000	20,000	28,000	40,000

1916
Model 38, 6-cyl., 43.35 hp, 140" wb

	FP	5	4	3	2	1
7P Tr	4400	11,700	23,400	39,000	58,000	78,000
6P Tr	4400	12,000	24,000	40,000	60,000	80,000
7P Limo	5400	5550	11,100	18,500	25,900	37,000
7P Lan'let	5500	5700	11,400	19,000	26,600	38,000
7P Berl	5700	5850	11,700	19,500	27,300	39,000

Model 48, 6-cyl., 48.6 hp, 143" wb

	FP	5	4	3	2	1
6P Tr	5100	14,400	28,800	48,000	76,000	96,000
7P Tr	5100	13,200	26,400	44,000	68,000	88,000
7P Lan'let	6300	6150	12,300	20,500	28,700	41,000
7P Berl	6500	6300	12,600	21,000	29,400	42,000
7P Limo	6200	6000	12,000	20,000	28,000	40,000

1917
Model 38, 6-cyl., 43.34 hp, 139" wb

	FP	5	4	3	2	1
7P Tr	4600	13,800	27,600	46,000	73,500	92,000
6P Tr	4600	14,400	28,800	48,000	76,000	96,000
4P Tr	4750	14,700	29,400	49,000	78,000	98,000
7P Limo	5600	6000	12,000	20,000	28,000	40,000
7P Lan'let	5700	6150	12,300	20,500	28,700	41,000
7P Berl	5900	6450	12,900	21,500	30,100	43,000

Model 48, 6-cyl., 48.6 hp, 142" wb

	FP	5	4	3	2	1
Sportif	—	31,100	58,000	88,000	114,000	150,000
6P Tr	5400	14,700	29,400	49,000	78,000	98,000
7P Tr	5400	14,400	28,800	48,000	76,000	96,000
7P Lan'let	6600	6450	12,900	21,500	30,100	43,000
7P Berl	6800	6750	13,500	22,500	31,500	45,000
7P Limo	6500	6300	12,600	21,000	29,400	42,000

1918 Locomobile, model 38, four passenger model, HAC

1918
Model 38, Series Two, 6-cyl., 43.35 hp, 139" wb

	FP	5	4	3	2	1
7P Tr	5000	13,800	27,600	46,000	73,500	92,000
6P Tr	5000	14,100	28,200	57,000	74,000	94,000
4P Tr	5150	14,400	28,800	48,000	76,000	96,000
7P Lan'let	6300	6000	12,000	20,000	28,000	40,000
7P Berl	6400	6450	12,900	21,500	30,100	43,000
7P Limo	6200	5850	11,700	19,500	27,300	39,000

Model 48, Series Two, 6-cyl., 48.6 hp, 142" wb

	FP	5	4	3	2	1
Sportif	—	31,100	58,000	88,000	114,000	150,000
7P Tr	5950	14,400	28,800	48,000	76,000	96,000
6P Tr	5950	14,700	29,400	49,000	78,000	98,000
4P Tr	6050	14,700	29,400	49,000	78,000	98,000
7P Limo	7200	6300	12,600	21,000	29,400	42,000
7P Lan'let	7300	6450	12,900	21,500	30,100	43,000
7P Berl	7400	6750	13,500	22,500	31,500	45,000

1919 Locomobile, model 48, touring, HAC

1919
Model 48, 6-cyl., 48.6 hp, 142" wb

	FP	5	4	3	2	1
7P Tr	6600	14,700	29,400	49,000	78,000	98,000
Torp	6600	14,700	29,400	49,000	78,000	98,000
Sportif	6700	31,100	58,000	88,000	114,000	150,000
Limo	7700	7500	15,000	25,000	35,000	50,000
Lan'let	7800	7800	15,600	26,000	36,400	52,000
Berl	7900	8250	16,500	27,500	38,500	55,000

1920 Locomobile, model 48, touring, HAC

1920
Model 48, 6-cyl., 142" wb

	FP	5	4	3	2	1
4P Spl Tr	9600	15,000	30,000	50,000	80,000	100,000
4P Tr	8200	14,400	28,800	48,000	76,000	96,000
7P Tr	8100	13,500	27,000	45,000	70,000	90,000
7P Limo	9600	8250	16,500	27,500	38,500	55,000
7P Lan'let	9600	8550	17,100	28,500	39,900	57,000
7P Sed	11,300	4800	9600	16,000	22,400	32,000
4P Cabr	11,000	6750	13,500	22,500	31,500	45,000
5P Semi-Tr	11.500	8250	16,500	27,500	38,500	55,000

1921 Locomobile, model 48, cabriolet, HAC

1921
Model 48, 6-cyl., 95 hp, 142" wb

	FP	5	4	3	2	1
7P Tr	7550	13,500	27,000	45,000	70,000	90,000
Sportif	7650	30,300	57,000	86,000	112,000	145,000
7P Limo	9150	8250	16,500	27,500	38,500	55,000
7P Lan	9150	8550	17,100	28,500	39,900	57,000

1922
Model 48, 6-cyl., 95 hp, 142" wb

	FP	5	4	3	2	1
7P Tr	7600	13,500	27,000	45,000	70,000	90,000
4P Sportif	7600	30,300	57,000	86,000	112,000	145,000
6P Limo	9150	8250	16,500	27,500	38,500	55,000
Lan'let	9150	8550	17,100	28,500	39,900	57,000
Dual Cowl Phae	9500	29,500	55,000	84,000	110,000	140,000
Cpe-Limo	10,500	9000	18,000	30,000	42,000	60,000
Cabr	10,700	9900	19,800	33,000	46,200	66,000
Sed	11,000	6750	13,500	22,500	31,500	45,000

1922 Locomobile, model 48, sportif, HAC

1925 Locomobile, model 48, limousine, OCW

1923 Locomobile, model 48, limousine, HAC

1923
Model 48, 6-cyl., 95 hp, 142" wb

	FP	5	4	3	2	1
7P Tr	7600	13,500	27,000	45,000	70,000	90,000
4P Tr	7600	14,400	28,800	48,000	76,000	96,000
7P Limo	9150	9000	18,000	30,000	42,000	60,000
4P Dual Cowl Phae	9500	29,500	55,000	84,000	110,000	140,000
5P Cpe	10,500	6750	13,500	22,500	31,500	45,000
5P Cabr	10,700	9900	19,800	33,000	46,200	66,000
7P Sed	11,000	6000	12,000	20,000	28,000	40,000

1925 Locomobile, model 48, limousine, OCW

1924 Locomobile, model 48, town car, OCW

1924
Model 48, 6-cyl., 95 hp, 142" wb

	FP	5	4	3	2	1
4P Sportif	7900	29,500	55,000	84,000	110,000	140,000
7P Tr	7900	14,400	28,800	48,000	76,000	96,000
7P Tr Limo	9000	9900	19,800	33,000	46,200	66,000
5P Brgm	10,600	9000	18,000	30,000	42,000	60,000
Encl Dr Limo	11,000	9300	18,600	31,000	43,400	62,000
Vic Sed	11,000	6750	13,500	22,500	31,500	45,000
5P Cabr	11,200	10,500	21,000	35,000	49,000	70,000

1925
Junior 8, 8-cyl., 66 hp, 124" wb

	FP	5	4	3	2	1
5P Tr	1785	11,400	22,800	38,000	56,000	76,000
5P Sed	2285	5250	10,500	17,500	24,500	35,000
5P Brgm	2285	6750	13,500	22,500	31,500	45,000
4P Rds	2150	12,000	24,000	40,000	60,000	80,000
4P Cpe	2265	6000	12,000	20,000	28,000	40,000

Model 48, 6-cyl., 103 hp, 142" wb

	FP	5	4	3	2	1
4P Sportif	7400	29,500	55,000	84,000	110,000	140,000
7P Tr	7400	14,400	28,800	48,000	76,000	96,000
7P Tr Limo	9000	9900	19,800	33,000	46,200	66,000
6P Brgm	9990	9000	18,000	30,000	42,000	60,000
5P Vic Sed	9990	6750	13,500	22,500	31,500	45,000
7P Encl Limo	9990	9300	18,600	31,000	43,400	62,000
7P Cabr	10,250	10,500	21,000	35,000	49,000	70,000

1926 Locomobile Junior Eight, brougham, HAC

1926
Junior 8, 8-cyl., 66 hp, 124" wb

	FP	5	4	3	2	1
5P Tr	1785	11,700	23,400	39,000	58,000	78,000
5P Sed	2285	5250	10,500	17,500	24,500	35,000
5P Brgm	2285	6000	12,000	20,000	28,000	40,000
4P Rds	2150	12,000	24,000	40,000	60,000	80,000
4P Cpe	2265	6300	12,600	21,000	29,400	42,000

Model 90, 6-cyl., 86 hp, 138" wb

	FP	5	4	3	2	1
4P Sportif	5500	25,500	45,000	73,000	100,000	130,000
4P Rds	5900	24,100	42,000	68,000	98,000	126,000
5P Vic Cpe	6950	6300	12,600	21,000	29,400	42,000
5P Vic Sed	7300	6000	12,000	20,000	28,000	40,000
5P Vic Div Sed	7450	6750	13,500	22,500	31,500	45,000
7P Brgm	7500	7050	14,100	23,500	32,900	47,000
7P Sub Limo	7500	7200	14,400	24,000	33,600	48,000
7P Cabr	7500	9600	19,200	32,000	44,800	64,000

Model 48, 6-cyl., 103 hp, 138" wb

	FP	5	4	3	2	1
4P Sportif	7460	27,900	51,000	79,000	106,000	136,000
7P Tr	7460	14,400	28,800	48,000	76,000	96,000
7P Cabr	10,300	9900	19,800	33,000	46,200	66,000
5P Vic Sed	10,050	6750	13,500	22,500	31,500	45,000
7P Encl Dr Limo	10,050	8250	16,500	27,500	38,500	55,000
7P Tr Limo	9500	7500	15,000	25,000	35,000	50,000
6P Twn Brgm	10,050	7350	14,700	24,500	34,300	49,000

1927
Junior 8, 8-cyl., 66 hp, 124" wb

	FP	5	4	3	2	1
5P Tr	1785	12,900	25,800	48,200	66,000	86,000
5P Sed	2285	6750	13,500	22,500	31,500	45,000
5P Brgm	2285	8250	16,500	27,500	38,500	55,000
4P Rds	2150	12,300	24,600	41,000	62,000	82,000
4P Cpe	2265	8550	17,100	28,500	39,900	57,000

Model 8-80, 8-cyl., 90 hp, 130" wb

	FP	5	4	3	2	1
5P Sed	2850	6000	12,000	20,000	28,000	40,000

1927 Locomobile, model 48, sportif, HAC

1927
Model 90, 6-cyl., 86 hp, 138" wb

	FP	5	4	3	2	1
4P Tr	5500	13,500	27,000	45,000	70,000	90,000
4P Sportif	5500	25,500	45,000	73,000	100,000	130,000
4P Rds	5900	14,700	29,400	49,000	78,000	98,000
5P Vic Cpe	6950	9000	18,000	30,000	42,000	60,000
5P Sed	7300	7500	15,000	25,000	35,000	50,000
5P Divided Sed	7450	7800	15,600	26,000	36,400	52,000
7P Sed	7500	7650	15,300	25,500	35,700	51,000
7P Brgm	7500	9000	18,000	30,000	42,000	60,000
7P Cabr	7500	10,500	21,000	35,000	49,000	70,000

Model 48, 6-cyl., 103 hp, 138" wb

	FP	5	4	3	2	1
4P Sportif	7460	27,900	51,000	79,000	106,000	136,000
7P Tr	7460	13,800	27,600	46,000	73,500	92,000
4P Rds	9660	15,000	30,000	50,000	80,000	100,000
5P Cabr	10,300	11,400	22,800	38,000	56,000	76,000
5P Vic Sed	10,050	6750	13,500	22,500	31,500	45,000
7P Encl Dr Limo	10,050	8250	16,500	27,500	38,500	55,000
7P Tr Limo	9500	7800	15,600	26,000	36,400	52,000
6P Twn Brgm	10,400	9000	18,000	30,000	42,000	60,000

1928 Locomobile, model 8-70, roadster, HAC

1928
Model 8-70, 8-cyl., 70 hp, 122" wb

	FP	5	4	3	2	1
5P Sed	1975	5250	10,500	17,500	24,500	35,000
5P Brgm	1975	5550	11,100	18,500	25,900	37,000
5P DeL Brgm	2550	5850	11,700	19,500	27,300	39,000
4P Vic Cpe	2100	6300	12,600	21,000	29,400	42,000

Model 8-80, 8-cyl., 90 hp, 130" wb

	FP	5	4	3	2	1
5P Spt Phae	3300	9900	19,800	33,000	46,200	66,000
5P Sed	3850	5550	11,100	18,500	25,900	37,000
5P Brgm	2900	5850	11,700	19,500	27,300	39,000
4P Vic Cpe	2975	6750	13,500	22,500	31,500	45,000
Spl Rds	3500	10,200	20,400	34,000	47,600	68,000
4P Collegiate Cpe	3350	7200	14,400	24,000	33,600	48,000
7P Tr	3500	9900	19,800	33,000	46,200	66,000
Vic Sed	5250	5850	11,700	19,500	27,300	39,000
7P Sed, 140" wb	3350	5550	11,100	18,500	25,900	37,000
7P Sub, 140" wb	3500	5850	11,700	19,500	27,300	39,000

Model 90, 6-cyl., 86 hp, 138" wb

	FP	5	4	3	2	1
4P Sportif	5900	12,900	25,800	48,200	66,000	86,000
4P Rds	5900	11,400	22,800	38,000	56,000	76,000
7P Tr	6000	11,100	22,200	37,000	52,000	74,000
Cpe	6950	7050	14,100	23,500	32,900	47,000
5P Vic Sed	7300	6300	12,600	21,000	29,400	42,000
5P Divided Vic Sed	7450	6750	13,500	22,500	31,500	45,000
7P Sub	7500	6900	13,800	23,000	32,200	46,000
7P Twn Brgm	7500	6900	13,800	23,000	32,200	46,000
7P Cabr	7500	9900	19,800	33,000	46,200	66,000
7P Semi-Collapsbl.Cabr	7750	9600	19,200	32,000	44,800	64,000

Model 48, 6-cyl., 103 hp, 142" wb

	FP	5	4	3	2	1
4P Sportif	9600	13,500	27,000	45,000	70,000	90,000
7P Tr	9600	12,900	25,800	48,200	66,000	86,000
Rds	11,000	13,200	26,400	44,000	68,000	88,000
7P Cabr	12,500	10,200	20,400	34,000	47,600	68,000
5P Vic Sed	12,500	10,200	20,400	34,000	47,600	68,000
7P Encl Dr Limo	12,500	9900	19,800	33,000	46,200	66,000
7P Tr Limo	12,500	10,500	21,000	35,000	49,000	70,000
6P Twn Brgm	12,500	10,500	21,000	35,000	49,000	70,000

1929
Model 88, 8-cyl., 115 hp, 130" wb

	FP	5	4	3	2	1
4P Phae	3350	11,400	22,800	38,000	56,000	76,000
5P Sed	2650	6000	12,000	20,000	28,000	40,000
Vic Cpe	2650	8250	16,500	27,500	38,500	55,000
5P Brgm	2700	7500	15,000	25,000	35,000	50,000
4P Collegiate Cpe	3150	8550	17,100	28,500	39,900	57,000
7P Sed	3150	5700	11,400	19,000	26,600	38,000
7P Sub	3500	5850	11,700	19,500	27,300	39,000
7P All Weather Cabr	7200	9000	18,000	30,000	42,000	60,000

1929
Model 90, 6-cyl., 86 hp, 138" wb

	FP	5	4	3	2	1
4P Sportif	5900	12,900	25,800	48,200	66,000	86,000
4P Rds	5900	12,900	25,800	48,200	66,000	86,000
7P Tr	6000	11,700	23,400	39,000	58,000	78,000
5P Vic Sed	7300	8250	16,500	27,500	38,500	55,000
5P Vic Div Sed	7450	9000	18,000	30,000	42,000	60,000
6P Twn Brgm	7500	9300	18,600	31,000	43,400	62,000
7P Cabr	7500	10,500	21,000	35,000	49,000	70,000
Semi-Collapsible Cabr	7750	10,200	20,400	34,000	47,600	68,000

Model 48, 6-cyl., 103 hp, 142" wb

	FP	5	4	3	2	1
4P Sportif	9600	13,800	27,600	46,000	73,500	92,000
7P Tr	9600	12,900	25,800	48,200	66,000	86,000
Rds	11,000	13,500	27,000	45,000	70,000	90,000
7P Cabr	12,500	11,400	22,800	38,000	56,000	76,000
5P Vic Sed	12,500	9000	18,000	30,000	42,000	60,000
7P Encl Dr Limo	12,500	9600	19,200	32,000	44,800	64,000
7P Tr Limo	12,500	9900	19,800	33,000	46,200	66,000
6P Twn Brgm	12,500	9900	19,800	33,000	46,200	66,000

LOCOMOTIVE — Though an occasional production car (like the Grout from Massachusetts) might sport a cow-catcher on the front, two custom-made cars were designed and built to resemble an entire steam locomotive as closely as possible. Refer to the Owens of Minneapolis, Minnesota (1922) and the Sternad of Chicago, Illinois (1917).

1902 Locomotor, runabout, OCW

LOCOMOTOR — Connellsville, Pennsylvania — (1900-1901) The Locomotor was the Baldwin renamed, and sold under the aegis of the American Locomotor Manufacturing Company instead of the Baldwin Automobile Company, which had been in financial trouble in Connellsville virtually since its doors were opened in 1899. The Locomotor-nee-Baldwin was a two-passenger steam car built under the patents of L.F.N. Baldwin of Rhode Island. Its engine was a two-cylinder double-acting vertical unit with its condenser mounted up front. Undoubtedly the change to Locomotor was at the request of the Baldwin receiver who was anxious to sell off the leftover cars in stock and thought a new name might help.

LOGAN — The Logan Carriage and Automobile Company of Parkersburg, West Virginia was organized early in 1912 with a capital stock of $25,000 to build and repair automobiles and conduct a general manufacturing business. Incorporators were Henry Logan, Thomas Page, Henry Huffman, Sherman Dils and B.F. Stout. Manufacture of a car is doubted.

The Logan Square Automobile Company was organized in Chicago, Illinois during the summer of 1910 with a capital stock of $50,000 to manufacture motor cars and accessories. Incorporators were F. Ginnor, C.F. Moremac and G.N. Harmon. Manufacture of a car is doubted.

1904 Logan, touring, HAC

LOGAN — Chillicothe, Ohio — (1904-1908) — Like the Gramm and the Buckeye, the Logan from Chillicothe was the invention of Benjamin A. Gramm and was originally produced by his Motor Storage & Manufacturing Company. Because this was a designation that was not particularly impressive, Gramm's previous manufacturing having been in the plumbing and electrical supply business, he soon changed the firm's name to Logan Construction Company, which was not particularly informative. The cars were introduced in January 1904. Both water- and air-cooled versions were offered initially, though by 1907 the Logan was air-cooled only. Most of the output consisted of two-cylinder cars that the company said were perfectly balanced and vibrationless — "one may easily write a letter in the car" — but a very appealing model was the four-cylinder 20/25 hp Blue Streak Semi-Racer Runabout which "could feed its dust to most anything on wheels" for only $1750. Truth in advertising was not a Logan virtue. The Logan slogan of "That Car of Quality" was more apt, because the car was well built. Interestingly, in 1907 Benjamin Gramm sued Premier of Indianapolis for infringement of his slogan; Gramm was awarded priority of claim, and Premier could no longer call itself a quality car. This is interesting because dozens of cars in America were being referred to in terms of quality in those days, but apparently B.A. Gramm hadn't noticed any of the others. Logan produced trucks as well from the beginning, and by 1907 had begun concentrating on this aspect of the business. The Logan company was bankrupt by early summer of 1908. Benjamin Gramm immediately relocated to Bowling Green where he established the Gramm-Logan Motor Car Company and henceforth concentrated exclusively on truck manufacture. Under varying designations, Gramm trucks were built until the Second World War.

1904 LOGAN

	FP	5	4	3	2	1
Tour.-5P (2-cyl., 10 hp)	1200	2000	3000	4200	6500	14,000

1905 Logan, model D, touring, HAC

1905 LOGAN
Model D — 2-cyl., 20 hp, 90" wb

Touring-5P	1600	2200	3200	4400	7000	15,000

1906 Logan, model F, runabout, HAC

1906 LOGAN
Model G — 4-cyl., 20 hp, 90" wb

Touring-5P	1500	2000	3000	4200	6500	14,000

Model H — 4-cyl., 30 hp, 100" wb

Touring-5P	2000	2300	3300	4600	7500	16,000

Model F — 2-cyl., 10 hp, 90" wb

Runabout-2P	900	1800	2800	4000	6200	13,000

1907 Logan, runabout, WLB

1908 Logan Blue Streak, semi-racer runabout, HAC

1907-1908 LOGAN
Four — 20/24 hp, 86" wb

	FP	5	4	3	2	1
Model O Rdstr.	1500	2000	3000	4200	6500	14,000
Blue Streak Semi-Racer Rdstr.	1750	2300	3300	4600	7500	16,000

LOGAN — Chicago, Illinois — (1914) — The Logan cyclecar was the product of the Northwestern Motorcycle Works of Chicago. It featured a two-cylinder air-cooled 9/13 hp Spacke engine, friction transmission, final drive by vee-belt, an underslung steel frame of 102-inch wheelbase, and a metal roadster body which provided side by side seating. Since the tread of the Logan was just 40 inches, this made for rather cozy accommodations for two passengers. The Logan's wheels were wire, its weight complete was 500 pounds, and its price was $375. Production was minimal.

1914 LOGAN
Cyclecar — 2-cyl., 9/13 hp, 102" wb

	FP	5	4	3	2	1
Roadster-2P	375	1800	2800	4000	6200	13,000

1911 Lohr, touring, NAHC

LOHR — Elkhart, Indiana — (1911) — Seeing the handwriting on the wall during the summer of 1911, the Elkhart Motor Car Company, makers of the Sterling in Elkhart, quickly disposed of its plant before creditors could file an involuntary petition in bankruptcy against it. Initially, when petition was filed, Elkhart claimed solvency and asked for a jury trial. Later this application was withdrawn, and by October the firm had been adjudged bankrupt. In the meantime, Harry H. Elmer and a number of other veterans of the Haynes Automobile Company in Kokomo had organized the

Elmer Auto Corporation and moved into the Elkhart factory, declaring in August that a new six-cylinder car to be called the Lohr was "almost ready for the market." Charles Lohr had been a designer at Haynes, and was a member of Elmer's group, but the new car was named for him less than a month. Then it became the Elmer.

LOHSE — The Lohse Automobile Improvement Company was organized in Cleveland, Ohio late in 1914 with a capital stock of $25,000 to manufacture motor cars and accessories. Incorporators were B. Ryder, W.G. Rauder, M. Reitz, R. Lohse and K.C. Wehrmeyer. Manufacture of an automobile is doubted.

LOMAX — An automobile called the Lomax Flint has been indicated on various rosters as being built in Denver, Colorado in 1905. The car was actually the Flintlo, the product of the firm of Flint & Lomax. Refer to Flintlo.

LOMAX — Lomax, Illinois — (1913-1914) — The Lomax Motor Car Company was a million-dollar incorporation organized late in 1913 for the manufacture of automobiles. Lomax exhibited at both the New York and Chicago automobile shows in 1913-1914, though reporters of both events ignored the car completely. Years later residents of Lomax, Illinois recalled that the Lomax was a light car and that it was not a heavy success.

LOMBARD — References to the building of an automobile by Alvin O. Lombard of Waterville, Maine have been in error. But in a loose sense of the term, Lombard did build an automotive vehicle. Lombard conceived the idea for an endless caterpillar tread (which he patented on May 21st, 1901) and his Lombard log hauler proved to be a predecessor of the endless-tread machine which would revolutionize agriculture, industry and, most dramatically, warfare in years to come. The first Lombard Log Hauler was horsedrawn; subsequent versions were steam-powered. One of the latter remains in existence, and is being restored with the support of the Waterville Historical Society.

LONDON — The London Auto Supply Company was organized in Chicago, Illinois during the summer of 1905 with a capital stock of $10,000 for the manufacture of motor vehicles. Incorporators were W.B. Jones, Fred G. Smith and Max Weiss. Manufacture of an automobile has not been documented.

1920 Lone Star, touring, WLB

LONE STAR — San Antonio, Texas — (1919-1922) — The Lone Star represented an absolutely exemplary case of badge engineering. It was marketed by the Lone Star Motor Truck and Tractor Association of San Antonio, but it was neither manufactured nor assembled in Texas. Instead the Lone Star was put together in Lynchburg, Virginia by the Piedmont Motor Car Company. The only difference between a Lone Star and a Piedmont was the emblem. Like the Piedmont, the Lone Star was available with either a four- (Lycoming) or six-cylinder (Continental) engine. In April 1919 the Lone Star office in San Antonio was opened ceremonially, with San Antonio's mayor on hand for a welcoming speech. When the Piedmont Motor Car Company went out of business in Lynchburg in 1922, the only thing left of the Lone Star in San Antonio was its radiator badge. Interestingly, earlier in 1922, H.G. Blumberg, who had previously sold a lot of stock (and little else) as major domo of the Blumberg Motor Manufacturing Company, became Lone Star's president.

1919-1921 LONE STAR
Beauty Four — 4-cyl., 35 hp, 116" wb

	FP	5	4	3	2	1
Touring-5P	1395	2400	3400	4800	8000	17,000

Beauty Six — 6-cyl., 57 hp, 122" wb

	FP	5	4	3	2	1
Touring-5P	1595	3350	6750	11,250	15,750	22,500

1922 LONE STAR
Model 4-35 — 4-cyl., 35 hp, 116" wb

	FP	5	4	3	2	1
Touring-5P	1595	2400	3400	4800	8000	17,000

LONG — Aneta, North Dakota — (1908) — Apparently two cars were built by Harry Long of Aneta, one for himself, another for his brother. The first developed 12 hp, the second 14 hp — and it's likely Harry kept the more powerful one. Neither of the cars exist today but several of the snow machines that Harry Long subsequently produced do survive.

1939 Long, roadster, MVMA

LONG — Spartanburg, South Carolina — (1939) — This tiny roadster with a wheelbase of 68 inches and a tread of 44 was built by Long's Motor Service of Spartanburg in 1939. Engine and chassis components were an amalgam of Model T Ford and Whippet, but the car's body was entirely Long's own. Complete, the Long weighed 1840 pounds and had a maximum speed of over 80 mph, it was claimed, and could travel 40 to 45 miles on a gallon of gas.

1880 Long Steam Tricycle, SI

LONG STEAM — Hartford, Connecticut — (circa 1880) — Though his patent application for a "steam-road-vehicle" was submitted to the U.S. Patent Office in 1882, it would appear that George Alexander Long had built his vehicle's engine three years earlier in his Northfield (Massachusetts) home, then journeyed down to Hartford (Connecticut) the following year to put together the frame and running gear in the Columbia bicycle plant of Albert Pope. The result was a two-seater tricycle with a two-cylinder gasoline-burning steam engine and a two-pulley crankshaft. The steel plate to which the engine was attached was operated by a lever in front of the seats. The five-foot single rear wheel drove the vehicle, one of the pulleys coming into contact with it when the engine plate proceeded rearward. The larger crankshaft pulley was splined and moved lengthwise along the shaft, with the disparity in pulley diameters providing two driving ratios. Spoon brakes on the front wheels took care of stopping. The delicate appearance of the 350-pound Long was deceiving. For best results, two operators were needed to drive it, two handlebars as well as two brake levers being provided. Although George Long apparently never built more than this one vehicle, he was luckier than most Nineteenth Century pioneers because his car survives. It is on display at the Smithsonian Institution in Washington, D.C.

LONG DISTANCE — Jersey City, New Jersey — (1901-1903) — Although the U.S. Long Distance Automobile Company was organized in early 1900 by Lewis Nixon, Lt. John C. Fremont and D.J. Newland, production initially centered on marine engines only. Not until April 1901 was the Long Distance automobile introduced. It was offered in a variety of body styles and with water-cooled engines of one, two or three cylinders. C.C. Riotte, who had already earned a considerable reputation for himself in the field of marine engine design, was the designer of the car, and apparently he had come up with a very good one. "We were especially pleased with the absence of noise and vibration while in motion," *The Automobile Magazine* reported in June of 1901 following a test ride. "She glided along with very little fuss indeed....The mechanism is the embodiment of simplicity and, what is more, is very easy to get at, a matter of no little importance in the modern automobile." Final drive by chain, and a planetary transmission of either two or three speeds was fitted. In November of 1901 the company announced its plans to produce at the rate of 10 to 12 cars a week. That appears to have been achieved. A brochure from late 1901 indicates that the U.S. Long Distance Automobile Company was willing to build racing machines to order, and also that its complete model line had been made ready by that time. A wheel replaced the former tiller in the runabout in late 1902. There seem to have been few other deviations during the two-plus years Long Distance automobiles were produced. By January of 1904, however, the firm had changed its name to the Standard Motor Construction Company, and all succeeding cars to come from the factory at 307 Whiton Street in Jersey City were called the Standard.

1902 Long Distance, type A, runabout, HAC

1903 Long Distance, type D, tonneau, HAC

1901-1903 LONG DISTANCE
Type A — 1-cyl., 7 hp, 74" wb

	FP	5	4	3	2	1
Runabout	1000	2000	3000	4200	6500	14,000
Type B — 2-cyl., 10 hp, 80" wb						
Tonneau	2500	2200	3200	4400	7000	15,000
Type C — 2-cyl., 12 hp, 80" wb						
Runabout	2500	2300	3300	4600	7500	16,000
Type D — 3-cyl., 20 hp, 80" wb						
Tonneau	4000	2400	3400	4800	8000	17,000
Type E — 2-cyl., 10 hp, 80" wb						
Delivery Wagon	2000	1800	2800	4000	6200	13,000

Note: The Type A was raised in price to $1250 in January 1903.

LONGEST — Louisville, Kentucky — (1906) - W.B., T.F. and C.F. were the Longest Brothers of Louisville, and in September 1906 they organized their Longest Brothers Company with a capital stock of $10,000 "to deal in automobiles and gasoline motors." Stoddards were the cars dealt in, but how many Longest automobiles followed cannot be confirmed. Almost immediately the company elected to concentrate its manufacture in the commercial vehicle field. Longest trucks were produced until 1912, when H.J. Edwards and C.G. Stoddard (formerly of Stoddard-Dayton) took over the Longest enterprise and incorporated the Edwards Motor Car Company to carry on commercial vehicle manufacture. Edwards announced that trucks would be this new venture's sole production.

LONG ISLAND — The Long Island Garage Company was organized in Glen Cove, New York early in 1907 with a capital stock of $25,000 "to maintain a garage and manufacture motor cars." Incorporators were W.J. Blair of 67 Quincy Street in Brooklyn, Arthur J. Farrell of Glen Cove, and C.A. Vostock of 1907 Washington Avenue in the Bronx. Manufacture of a car is doubted.

LONG ISLAND — Brooklyn, New York — (1901-1904) — The Long Island Motor Company was established at 32 Hanson Place in Brooklyn in October 1901. The capital stock was $100,000 and the people involved were Charles Rockliff, A.R. Pardington and F.G. Webb. The company's principal

activity was as a garage for the repair of vehicles, but it stood ready to fill any orders from customers desiring to have an automobile built. Early in 1902 Charles Rockliff, who served as the firm's general manager, reported that two such cars were then being built: both four-cylinder touring cars, one of 15 hp for a "prominent member of the Long Island Automobile Club," the other of 24 hp for "a well-known businessman of Brooklyn." Conceivably, further cars to customer order may have followed. The firm continued to list itself as an automobile builder in the 1904 Brooklyn directory. In addition to the Long Island venture, Charles Rockliff was also building trucks under his own name at 446 Hudson Avenue in Brooklyn.

LONG SILENT — The Long Silent Motor Company was organized in Hannibal, Missouri late in 1911 with a capital stock of $12,000 "to make automobiles and engines." Incorporators were Elmer C. Long, Frank R. Tate and Theodore Moreno. Manufacture of a car is doubted.

1900 Loomis, model no. 1, Park Wagon, HAC

LOOMIS — Westfield, Massachusetts — (1900-1904) — Gilbert J. Loomis of Westfield built his first car in 1896, a steamer which he did not market, then came up with a carburetor which he did. In 1900 he incorporated his Loomis Automobile Company to manufacture air-cooled gasoline cars of two-cylinders, 5 hp and varying models differentiated by the width of their tracks. Model No. 1, for example, was designed for urban use, its 40-inch tread too narrow to follow in carriage grooves on country roads but making for a vehicle that could be "stored in a very small place"; Model No. 3 was 4 feet 8-1/2 inches so that it could ride along street car tracks "where very rough pavements are encountered." Loomis also offered to sell all necessary components to anyone desiring to build their own car. Bloomingdale's department store in New York City was interested in the purchase of a fleet of Loomis commercial vehicles — which was a marvelous opportunity and one Loomis immediately accepted. Unfortunately, the contract which he willingly signed dictated delivery of 500 units in two months — an impossible deadline — and when he didn't come through, Bloomingdale's called the whole thing off. His cars for 1903 were called Bluebirds, but they didn't bring him commercial happiness either. That year he took one of his cars to Pittsburgh and tried to interest Andrew Carnegie in investing in his venture. Carnegie declared, "I wouldn't ride in one of those things." This was not a derogation of Loomis' car specifically, but an automobile generally, and Carnegie would later change his mind. In 1904 Loomis sold his company to Samuel Squires, a hotel owner in Westfield, and thereafter plied his trade as an engineer for such automobile manufacturers as Pope-Tribune, Payne Modern and Speedwell. Gilbert Loomis was not a very good businessman. He was an excellent engineer. He also holds the distinction of having purchased the first automobile liability insurance in the United States, in 1897, a $1000 policy for an annual premium of $7.50.

1902 Loomis, runabout, HAC

1900-1901 LOOMIS

	FP	5	4	3	2	1
Model 1 Gasoline Park Wagon	750	1800	2800	4000	6200	13,000
Model 2 Gasoline Road Wagon	850	2000	3000	4200	6500	14,000
Model 3 Gasoline Light Del.	1200	1600	2700	3800	5800	12,000

1902 LOOMIS

	FP	5	4	3	2	1
Model 1 Gasoline Park Wagon	750	1800	2800	4000	6200	13,000
Model 2 Gasoline Road Wagon	850	2000	3000	4200	6500	14,000
Model 3 Gasoline Light Del.	1200	1600	2700	3800	5800	12,000
Model 4 Gasoline Rbt.	850	1800	2800	4000	6200	13,000
Model 5 Gasoline Trap	900	2000	3000	4200	6500	14,000

1903 Loomis Bluebird, touring, HAC

1904 Loomis, touring, WLB

1903-1904 LOOMIS

	FP	5	4	3	2	1
Bluebird Gasoline Tour.	—	2300	3300	4600	7500	16,000

LOOS — Grafton, North Dakota — (1907) — In 1907 in Grafton one George Loos built himself a 12-14 hp runabout. Details regarding the vehicle are lacking, and he is not known to have built another.

LORAIN — The Lorain Motor Carriage Company of Lorain, Ohio was listed as an automobile manufacturer in the Hiscox book *Horseless Vehicles, Automobiles, Motor Cycles* published in 1900. Further documentation is lacking.

The Lorain Automobile Company of Lorain, Ohio was a newly organized venture from early 1905 which announced that its new touring car would be ready for the Cleveland Automobile Show that year. The car didn't make it.

The Lorain Steel Motor Company was organized in Newark, New Jersey early in 1901 with a capital stock of $600,000 for "making and dealing in all manner of electrical appliances, machines and vehicles." Manufacture of a car is doubted.

LORD BALTIMORE — Baltimore, Maryland — (1913) — The Lord Baltimore Motor Car Company was organized in 1910 to build a truck designed by John Luntz, Jr., whose father was the treasurer of the Davison Chemical Company and probably set his son up in business. The first Lord Baltimore truck was tested in April of 1911, with production of the three-ton Model A following almost immediately, subsequently one- and two-ton versions and a light delivery. For one season only did Lord Baltimore elect to build a passenger car as well. Two four-cylinder models were offered: a 35 hp touring at $2200 and a 40 hp raceabout at $2500, both on a 125-inch

1913 Lord Baltimore, touring, WLB

wheelbase. Apparently the passenger car experience was not a pleasant one for Lord Baltimore. The prototype had been completed sometime in 1912. The new car was announced in February 1913, and in May the company declared it would be discontinued. Production of Lord Baltimore trucks continued through 1915. The 1916 Baltimore directory indicates John Luntz, Jr. as the proprietor of The Service Company, which was a sales emporium for tires and accessories.

1913 LORD BALTIMORE
Model T-3 — 4-cyl., 35 hp, 125" wb

	FP	5	4	3	2	1
Touring-5P	2200	2500	3500	5000	8500	18,000

Model TR-4 — 4-cyl., 40 hp, 125" wb

	FP	5	4	3	2	1
Raceabout-2P	2500	2700	3600	5300	8800	19,000

LORRAINE — The Lorraine Motor Company was organized in Camden, New Jersey during the summer of 1910 with a capital stock of $60,000 for the manufacture of automobiles and motorcycles. Incorporators were F.H. Hansell, J.A. McPeak and W.E. Eidell. Manufacture of a car is doubted.

1908 Lorraine, touring, NAHC

LORRAINE — Chicago, Illinois — (1907-1908) — The Lorraine Automobile Manufacturing Company was incorporated in Chicago in 1907 to exploit the motorcar inventions of one John O. Hobbs. Among these was an elastic shaft drive, which was not very well explained. But the Hobbs-Renault compressed air self-starter was, described by the company as being "situated between the clutch and the gear-set, air being stored in a tank and maintained automatically at a pressure of 60-80 pounds, so that the apparatus is always capable of starting the motor from sixteen to twenty times." The pressure pump of the starter could also be used to inflate the tires. The short life of the Lorraine would indicate that it did not work well. Two models were offered: a 50/55 hp four on a 124-inch wheelbase and a 25/30 hp four on a 110-inch wheelbase. The car was introduced at the Chicago Automobile Show in December of 1907. It disappeared sometime during 1908.

1907-1908 LORRAINE
Model L — 4-cyl., 50/55 hp, 124" wb

	FP	5	4	3	2	1
Touring-7P	4500	3500	4500	7000	13,000	25,000

Model M — 4-cyl., 25/30 hp, 110" wb

	FP	5	4	3	2	1
Touring-5P	3000	3000	4000	6000	9500	21,000
Limousine-5P	3750	2500	3500	5000	8500	18,000
Gentleman's Rdstr. (Model N)	3000	2700	3600	5300	8800	19,000

1920 Lorraine, touring, WLB

863

LORRAINE — Grand Rapids, Michigan — (1920-1922) — The Lorraine took up where the Hackett left off in the same Grand Rapids factory. Organized in 1920 as Lorraine Motors Corporation, the firm initially launched into production with a four-cylinder (Herschell-Spillman engine) assembled car on a 114-inch wheelbase with a $1695 price tag for the touring model. It went nowhere quickly and in June of 1921 a new group took over, headed by David Dunbar Buick, who had left the car and the company he had founded in 1908 and who had foundered in a number of ill-advised enterprises thereafter. Joining him in this new venture were A.H. Wyatt and John J. Larkin, the former sales manager for Haynes. A new lower-priced ($1200) Lorraine was planned, to be fitted with an engine of Buick's own design, on the valve-in-head principle that he had made so famous with his first car. A prototype was built, but it does not seem this new Lorraine proceeded any further than that. A few of the old Lorraines continued to straggle out of the factory until August of 1922. At that time, and after production of about 200 cars at best, Lorraine announced its departure from the automobile manufacturing scene. Plans now called for relocation in Beverly, Michigan with production to concentrate on automobile parts and equipment. By December, however, Lorraine Motors filed a voluntary petition in bankruptcy. The year following David Buick was in Walden, New York, where an automobile called the Dunbar was being planned.

1920-1922 LORRAINE
Four — 35 hp, 114" wb

	FP	5	4	3	2	1
Touring-5P	1695	3000	4000	6000	9500	21,000
Sedan-5P	2590	2000	3000	4200	6500	14,000
Roadster-2P	1665	3100	4200	6300	10,500	22,000
Coupe-3P	2590	2300	3300	4600	7500	16,000

LORRAINE — Richmond, Indiana — (1920-1921) — D.H. Cummings launched the Lorraine Car Company in Richmond in 1917 with $200 in cash and a blueprint. The blueprint was of a hearse, and the funeral car trade was the focus of Cummings' new business. For a while it prospered, and in 1920 the company also offered a line of large limousines. The cars were placed on a 122-inch wheelbase chassis, and were fitted with the 55 hp six-cylinder Continental 7R engines. This activity was strictly a sideline to the principal Lorraine business, and passenger-car production was minimal. In 1921 the Lorraine Car Company hit the postwar depression head-on. "Few people understand how hard the undertakers of the country have been hit by the unusual conditions," D.H. Cummings lamented to a Richmond reporter when Lorraine went into receivership in September 1921. "It has been calculated that the number of funerals, the country over, have been only two-fifths of normal, since last October." Subsequently, Lorraine was taken over by the Pilot Motor Car Company of Richmond, which continued to market the Lorraine, but as a hearse only.

1920-1921 LORRAINE
Six — 55 hp, 122" wb

Limousine-7P		2850	2700	3600	5300	8800	19,000

LOS ANGELES — Compton, California — (1914) — In 1913 L.E. French, a former writer for *The Horseless Age*, designed a cyclecar he called the California, for the manufacture of which the California Cycle Car Company was organized in Los Angeles. It went nowhere. Subsequently, later in 1913, French found new financial backers, and a new company was established, the Los Angeles Cycle Car Company, to which French assigned the rights to the California body style which he had patented. The two-cylinder 10 hp $395 California was now to be called the Los Angeles, with a 12/15 hp four-cylinder version to be produced alongside it which would sell for $475. Chassis specifications for both cars were the same: friction transmission, double vee belt drive, 102-inch wheelbase, 44-inch tread, an underslung frame boasting a nine-inch ground clearance. Model designations of Angelus (sic) and Pacific were to differentiate the two- and four-cylinder Los Angeles cars respectively. The body of the latter model was redesigned from French's patented California style to resemble the stern of a boat from the rear. A factory site on sixteen acres of land was leased in nearby Compton, as well as a plant in Buffalo, New York which had formerly been occupied by the E.R. Thomas Motor Car Company. The latter facility was to be used as a branch factory for the East Coast trade. On neither coast, however, was the trade very brisk. By early 1914 both models of the air-cooled Los Angeles reportedly were to be phased out in favor of an 18 hp water-cooled four to be placed on a brand-new 100-inch-wheelbase chassis and cloaked in a brand-new body. How many of any of the Los Angeles variations were built is anyone's guess. The Los Angeles Cycle Car Company did not survive into 1915.

LOS ANGELES ELECTRIC — The Los Angeles Electric Vehicle Company was organized during the summer of 1911 with a capital stock of $200,000 to manufacture and deal in electric vehicles. Incorporators were S. Hendricks, P.L. Lindley, W.K. Crawford, C.E. Nester, J.A. Lightipe. No manufacture seems to have resulted from this venture, and there seems to be no connection between it and the Volney Beardsley Company which did move into electric car production in Los Angeles, California a few years later.

LOSURE — Van Buren, Indiana — (1906) — Whenever he could spare time from his planing mill business, Zan Losure was working on his automobile. By late summer of 1906 he was ready to go public with his plans — at least in the local Van Buren paper. Zan used a 10 hp Galesburg engine in his Losure car, "the same engine that is used in the Gale automobile which sells at $1000," he said proudly. His pride was due to the fact that he expected to sell his car for $400, "upholstered in leather, finely painted ... and with all the accessories that go with any machine." At this point, Zan was about to test drive his first prototype and "if the auto meets expectations he has orders for twelve similar machines for Van Buren people." Whether the dozen Losures were ever produced is not known.

LOTZ — The Lotz Automobile Company was organized early in 1910 in Detroit, Michigan with a capital stock of $30,000 for the manufacture of "three types of cars and a new rubber tire." Behind this venture were J.A. Lotz, George Christianson and George Cooley. Cooley, a Grand Rapids man, was the inventor of the new tire. "Property for the new plant has been secured on Harper Avenue," *Motor Age* announced in late January. Whether a factory was built and production begun has not been documented. The Lotz venture dropped from sight soon after.

LOUIS — The Louis J was a roadster model of the Bergdoll offered in 1911 and 1912. The Bergdoll was produced in Philadelphia from 1910 to 1913. Refer to Bergdoll.
The J.H. Louis Automobile Company was organized in Cincinnati, Ohio early in 1911 with a capital stock of $75,000 to manufacture and repair automobiles. The incorporators were J.H. Louis, Peter Reiter, M.Y. Cheval, Thomas S. Danks and Edward Y. Schultz. Manufacture of a car is doubted.

LOUISIANNE — The 1921 Louisianne is one of the more amusing automobiles that never was which has been perpetuated on automotive car rosters for a number of years. "Name this automobile and it is yours," said the full-page advertisement in *The Shreveport Times*. The ad was placed by the Louisiana Motor Car Company as a promotion for its product, the Bour-Davis, an example of which would be awarded the person submitting the "most appropriate and euphonious name" for the car. Second, third and fourth finishers would receive stock in the Louisiana company. Louisiana warned contestants not to submit the likes of "Pelican, Caddo, Caddoa, Loumocar and such trite names as Premier, Excelsior, etc." for the Bour-Davis. The winner of the competition was a Mrs. A.R. Kilgore of Cedar Grove, which was the Shreveport suburb in which the car was built. "Louisianne" was her choice, and the Bour-Davis was her prize. Whether the Louisianne was ever subsequently used in any Bour-Davis promotion is not known, but it never became the name of either a car or a standard Bour-Davis model.

LOUISVILLE — The Louisville Carriage Company of Louisville, Kentucky was listed as an automobile manufacturer in the Hiscox book *Horseless Vehicles, Automobiles, Motor Cycles* published in 1900. Further documentation is lacking.
The Louisville Motor Vehicle Company was organized in Louisville, Kentucky during the fall of 1899 with a capital stock of $10,000 for the manufacture of horseless vehicles. "They will be adaptable for handling freight and passengers," *The Hub* reported in August "Light vehicles will also be furnished for pleasure riding . . . The company is to start operations immediately." Behind this venture were John E. Roche, George G. Briggs and George E. Roche. Whether manufacture actually resulted has not been determined.
Louisville Electric was to be the name of the car from the Electric Vehicle Company which was organized in Louisville, Kentucky late in 1910 with a capital stock of $10,000. H.B. Hewitt, P.E. Allison and E.M. Drammond were the incorporators. Manufacture is doubted. The Louisville Electric was not exhibited at the Louisville Automobile Show in March 1911, nor did it appear in 1912.

1914 Los Angeles Cyclecar, runabout, NAHC

1895 Lovejoy, horseless carriage, GR

LOVEJOY — Laramie, Wyoming — (1895) — Elmer Floyd Lovejoy built the first automobile in the state of Wyoming, and one of the first in the West when it was still wild and woolly. He seems to have been an inveterate tinkerer, though considerably more sophisticated than the usual backyard inventor. His family was engaged in the draying business in Laramie, and young Lovejoy learned the carpenter's trade in the contracting firm of Cook and Callahan at age seventeen. After working briefly in the Laramie Post Office, Lovejoy began a repair shop in town. "We fix things and any old thing" was his slogan. In 1895 he built his automobile, powered by a single-cylinder, two-stroke marine engine mounted in a wagon chassis and steered by a tiller. He drove it and tinkered with it for two years, substituting balloon tires of his own invention in 1896. This was among the earliest uses of balloon tires in the automotive field. Because guiding his vehicle presented some problems, he invented a steering knuckle the rights for which he later sold to the Locomobile company for $800 and a Locomobile motorcar. By now he had named his shop the Lovejoy Novelty Works. He became an agent for Franklin automobiles, and in 1917 patented the Lovejoy Automatic Door Opener. During the 1930's, the Works was converted into an automobile repair shop, and the business was turned over to his son in 1936. Elmer Floyd Lovejoy died in 1960 at the age of eighty-seven.

LOVELACE-THOMPSON — The Lovelace-Thompson Aeroplane & Motor Works was organized in New York City during the late fall of 1910 with a capital stock of $100,000 for the manufacture of automobiles, motors and aeroplanes. R.L. Offett, N.A. Egbert and M. Ogg were the incorporators. This venture succeeded the Lovelace Aeroplane and Motor Company which had been organized two months earlier with a capital stock of $25,000. Manufacture is doubted.

LOVELL-McCONNELL — The Lovell-McConnell Manufacturing Company was a $2 million Delaware incorporation from the spring of 1913 for the manufacture of automobiles. Lovell-McConnell was already well-known in the industry as manufacturers of such components as the Klaxon horn, Raiswell jack and Conover Safe-guard bumper, but this plan to expand the products which emanated from its Newark, New Jersey factory seems to have been thwarted early on. No Lovell-McConnell car ever arrived in the marketplace.

LOW — The Low Speed Turbine Company was organized in Camden, New Jersey late in 1910 with a capital stock of $100,000 for the manufacture of automobiles, airships and motorcycles. Among the incorporators were J.H. Gaul and H.L. Reese. Manufacture of a car is doubted.

LOWA — Lowa's Garage was organized in Yonkers, New York during the summer of 1911 with a capital stock of $30,000 to manufacture and deal in automobiles, supplies and accessories. The Lowas behind this venture were three — W., C.W. and W. Jr., all of Yonkers. Manufacture of an automobile is doubted.

LOWE-HOWARD — The Lowe-Howard Company was organized in Boston, Massachusetts with a capital stock of $10,000 late in 1910 for the manufacture of automobiles. Involved in this venture were George H. Lowe, Frank J. Howard and George E. Tufts. Manufacture is doubted.

1909 Lowell American, runabout, WLB

LOWELL-AMERICAN — Lowell, Massachusetts — (1908-1909) — The Lowell Motor Company had been supplying engines to the general trade since the turn of the century and during the late spring of 1908 decided to get into the automobile manufacturing business itself. That summer the Lowell-American Automobile Company was organized by John F. Spaulding, Moses Lahue and Jesse G. Hanson for production of four-, six- and eight-cylinder automobiles priced in the $1250-$2500 range. Only the four seems to have arrived, however, and it remained on the scene a short time only. A three-speed selective transmission and shaft drive were employed, with the Lowell-American placed on a 98-inch wheelbase and carrying a $1250 price tag.

1908 LOWELL-AMERICAN
Four — 16/20 hp, 98" wb

	FP	5	4	3	2	1
Runabout	1250	1800	2800	4000	6200	13,000

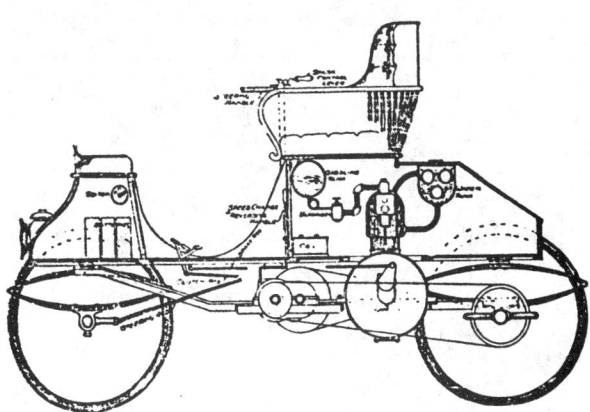

1902 Lowell Automotor, runabout, NAHC

LOWELL AUTOMOTOR — Lowell, Massachusetts — (1902) — Perhaps the Lowell Model Company put together only one of these vehicles itself, just to prove that it would work. The Lowell Automotor was a small runabout powered by a single-cylinder 3 1/2 hp engine, weighing about 500 pounds and capable of speeds up to 18 mph on level roads. It was offered as a kit car only. "Those who wish to construct such a vehicle can obtain all necessary material for the motor, running gear, transmission differential gear, etc., in either a rough or finished state from this concern," *The Gas Engine* reported in March 1902. "Complete working blueprints of the different parts are furnished by which construction may be readily understood."

LOWER — Syracuse, New York — (1899) — "C.E. Lower of the Syracuse Chilled Plow Company, has built an automobile having a twin cylinder 4 hp gasoline motor," *Cycle and Automobile Trade Journal* reported in December 1899. Undoubtedly, the car was for Lower's own use.

LOWERY — V.L.D. Lowery of Eaton, Illinois was yet another no-show at the starting line of the Chicago Times-Herald Contest. Whether he ever successfully completed and tested the vehicle he had entered in the event has not been documented.

LOWY — Lowy was one-half of the partnership behind the projected Layman-Lowy car from New York in 1916. Refer to Layman-Lowy.

1901 Lozier, steam runabout, RD

LOZIER — Plattsburgh, New York — (1898, 1901, 1905-1910)/Detroit, Michigan — (1910-1918) — In 1897 Henry Abram Lozier became bored with it all. His large bicycle works in Toledo, Ohio was turning out Cleveland two-wheelers in record-breaking numbers, but Lozier was weary of the enterprise and set his factory superintendent George R. Burwell and his engineer John G. Perrin to investigating what next they might do. In 1898 these two go-getters built a steam car employing a flash tube boiler of Serpollet type, as well as a Rochet-type tricycle using a De Dion gasoline engine. Producing 100 of the latter was decided upon, but before an assembly line could be cranked up, Lozier had sold the four bicycle factories of his Lozier Manufacturing Company to the American Bicycle Company in a deal that included the tricycle design as part of the package. Since the deal was a cool four million dollars, there was certainly enough now in the kitty to investigate just about anything else. In 1900, as A.B.C. began marketing the Lozier trike as the Cleveland Three-Wheeler, the Lozier Motor Company was established in Plattsburgh, New York to manufacture marine engines and launches. Neither Burwell nor Perrin, however, could get the automotive idea out of their heads, and they convinced Henry Lozier of its continuing merit. In 1901 another steamer and a gaso-

1905 Lozier, model B, touring, HAC

line car were tried experimentally but Burwell and Perrin remained unsatisfied. During 1902 J.M. Whitbeck, another engineer in the firm, was dispatched to Europe to look at what the Continent had to offer, no one at Lozier being particularly impressed with American efforts at the time. In January 1903 John Perrin left the company, or so it seemed. Actually he was still very much with it, indulging in a little industrial espionage, his rent and expenses being paid by Burwell as he made his way up and down the East Coast poking around the repair shops of foreign car dealers. When millionaire sportsman James L. Breese cracked up his Mercedes, Burwell told Perrin to offer to repair it, at no cost to the owner. Lozier Senior died in May 1903, but his son Harry A. Lozier took over, and the project proceeded. Perrin returned to Plattsburgh, his notebooks teeming with meticulous drawings of Mercedes, Panhard, Mors, Darracq and Charron, Giradot & Voight motorcars. The best engines in Europe were imported for further study, as was Krupp steel and Bosch magnetos from Germany, ignition apparatus and carburetors from France. In January 1905 the Lozier automobile made its debut at the New York Automobile Show at Madison Square Garden. The word at the factory was that John Perrin had designed a better Mercedes. Production in 1905 was twenty-five units, raised to fifty-six the following year. In 1907 Lozier went racing, most memorably with Ralph Mulford as driver. No other car of its time would break so many world's twenty-four-hour records or win so many twenty-four-hour races. In 1910 Lozier also won the famous Elgin road race, in 1911 it took the Vanderbilt Cup and placed second in the Indianapolis 500. The Lozier prowess in racing was not because it was the biggest and fastest; it was neither of those, but there was no car anywhere that had its stamina and durability. If anything ever broke on a Lozier, it was a major news story. In an era when braking systems were scarcely meritorious, Lozier declared its brakes "impossible to burn out." The drums were hollow and, at the driver's command, carried water from a supply tank under air pressure for cooling, a feature Briggs Cunningham would adopt on his Le Mans cars a half century later. Before going over to shaft drive in 1908, Lozier pioneered a casing for its double chain drive. Its first body was all aluminum, and Lozier introduced the foredoor torpedo style in 1909 and crown fenders in 1912. What most people thought was bronze striping on the cars was gold, as J.M. Quinby (one of Lozier's New York coachbuilders) advised, "24-carat — like everything else on a Lozier car." Naturally it was among the most expensive automobiles in America, and it was also one of the best. Production in Plattsburgh was never high, of necessity, the plant having an annual capacity of 600 cars. And the demand for Loziers was soon outstripping that. Meantime, in the Midwest, some entrepreneurs were scouting around for something to compete with Detroit's prestige car, the Packard. They convinced Harry Lozier on a reorganization of the company which was effected in February of 1910, with a large new factory built in the Motor City. It was a decision Harry Lozier regretted because by July of 1912 he was eased out of his own company (he would subsequently build the H.A.L. car), the presidency taken over by Harry M. Jewett, also president of the Paige-Detroit Motor Car Company at the time. A Light Six to sell in the $3250 range was introduced. Things began going very badly. Sales manager Fred C. Chandler, who had been with Lozier since its bicycle days (as foreign representative in Hamburg, Germany), left with four other members of the Lozier old guard (including Whitbeck) to form another company to build a medium-price Lozier lookalike to be called the Chandler. Perrin wanted to join them (Burwell had retired some time previous), but the contract he had negotiated with Jewett still had two years to run. Instead it was Jewett who left in another managerial shake-up. The new head of Lozier was Joseph M. Gilbert, former general manager of the United States Tire Company. Things began going worse. Perrin was assigned the design of a $2100 four-cylinder car to compete with the popular Cadillac four that Henry Leland was marketing. The resulting Lozier four, introduced as the Type 84 in April of 1914, could run rings around Leland's four, but in about six months it didn't matter, as Cadillac came out of hiding with its V-8 in the $2000 price range. And Lozier was in receivership. Perrin left to become chief engineer of the Timken Detroit Axle Company, and some banking people organized themselves as the Associated Lozier Purchasers and took over in mid-March 1915, slashing prices and announcing the continuation of production. The Plattsburgh plant was sold, as was the large Mack Avenue factory in Detroit, with residency now taken up in a smaller Detroit facility. By mid-1917 this reorganization effort fizzled, and three more Detroit businessmen decided to try. They incorporated as the Lozier Motor Company and leased the former plant of the Standard Auto Truck Company. In March 1918 a trade periodical noted that production was about five cars a day and that the company had orders for six months. That must have been an unduly optimistic pronouncement because six months later the lease on the Standard plant was up for renewal. It was not renewed. The Lozier story had ended, and not in the blaze of glory this stellar American marque deserved.

1905 LOZIER
Model B — 4-cyl., 30/35 hp, 115 1/2" wb

	FP	5	4	3	2	1
Touring-5P	4500	5800	8000	12,500	28,000	40,000

1906 Lozier, model D, limousine, HAC

1906 LOZIER
Model C — 4-cyl., 35 hp, 117" wb

Landaulet-5P	4500	5400	7300	11,800	25,000	38,000

Model D — 4-cyl., 40 hp, 117" wb

Touring-7P	5500	6400	9300	14,500	33,000	45,000
Limousine-7P	6500	5300	7000	11,500	24,000	37,000

Model E — 4-cyl., 60 hp, 120" wb

Touring-7P	7000	6800	10,300	16,000	35,500	48,000

1907 Lozier, model F, touring, HAC

1907 LOZIER
Model F — 4-cyl., 40 hp, 117" wb

Runabout-3P	5000	6400	9300	14,500	33,000	45,000
Limousine-7P	6000	5500	7500	12,000	26,000	39,000
Touring-7P	5000	6800	10,300	16,000	35,500	48,000
Landaulet-7P	6000	5500	7500	12,000	26,000	39,000

Model E — 4-cyl., 60 hp, 120" wb

Touring-7P	7000	7200	11,300	17,700	38,700	50,000
Limousine-7P	8000	6000	8500	13,000	30,000	42,000

1908 Lozier, type G, limousine, HAC

1908 LOZIER
Type G — 4-cyl., 40 hp, 117" wb

Touring	4000	6400	9300	14,500	33,000	45,000
Runabout	—	6000	8500	13,000	30,000	42,000
Limousine	5000	5400	7300	11,800	25,000	38,000

Type H — 4-cyl., 45 hp, 124" wb

	FP	5	4	3	2	1
Touring-7P	5000	6700	9900	15,500	34,800	47,000
Runabout	5000	6400	9300	14,500	33,000	45,000
Limousine	6000	5800	8000	12,500	28,000	40,000

Type I — 6-cyl., 51 hp, 131" wb

	FP	5	4	3	2	1
Touring-7P	6000	7200	11,300	17,700	38,700	50,000
Runabout	6000	6800	10,300	16,000	35,500	48,000
Limousine	7000	6000	8500	13,000	30,000	42,000

1909 Lozier, type H, Briarcliff, HAC

1909 LOZIER

Model G — 4-cyl., 33 hp, 116" wb

Touring-7P	3500	6800	10,300	16,000	35,500	48,000
Briarcliff	3500	7200	11,300	17,700	38,700	50,000
Limousine/Landaulet	4200	6000	8500	13,000	30,000	42,000

Type H — 4-cyl., 45 hp, 124" wb

Touring-7P	5000	7200	11,300	17,700	38,700	50,000
Briarcliff	5000	7400	12,100	18,800	41,100	53,000
Limousine/Landaulet	6000	6400	9300	14,500	33,000	45,000

Type I — 6-cyl., 50 hp, 131" wb

Touring-7P	6000	7800	13,300	20,300	44,000	60,000
Briarcliff-7P	6200	8000	13,900	20,900	44,800	63,000
Limousine/Landaulet	7000	6700	9900	15,500	34,800	47,000

1910 Lozier, model I, Briarcliff, HAC

1910 LOZIER

Model J — 6-cyl., 33 hp, 116" wb

Touring-5P	3500	7600	12,500	19,400	42,400	55,000
Limousine-5P	4200	6700	9900	15,500	34,800	47,000
Briarcliff	3500	7800	13,300	20,300	44,000	60,000

Model H — 4-cyl., 45 hp, 124" wb

Touring-7P	5000	7900	13,700	20,700	44,500	62,000
Limousine-7P	6000	7000	10,800	16,900	37,100	49,000
Briarcliff	5000	8200	14,500	21,500	45,800	65,000
Lakewood	5000	7900	13,700	20,700	44,500	62,000

Model I — 6-cyl., 50 hp, 124" wb

Touring-7P	6000	8200	14,500	21,500	45,800	65,000
Limousine-7P	7000	7200	11,300	17,700	38,700	50,000
Briarcliff	6000	8500	16,000	23,000	48,000	68,000
Lakewood	6000	8300	15,000	22,000	46,500	66,000

1911 Lozier, touring, OCW

1911 LOZIER

Model 46 — 6-cyl., 46 hp, 131" wb

	FP	5	4	3	2	1
Touring	4600	9400	18,800	26,500	53,800	75,000
Briarcliff	4600	10,000	20,000	30,000	60,000	80,000
Limousine	6000	7600	12,500	19,400	42,400	55,000
Landaulet	6000	7800	12,900	19,900	43,300	57,000
Limousine/Touring	6750	7800	13,200	20,200	43,800	59,000

Model 51 — 6-cyl., 51 hp, 131" wb

Touring	5500	10,000	20,000	30,000	60,000	80,000
Briarcliff	5500	11,300	21,300	32,500	65,000	85,000
Lakewood	5500	10,800	20,800	31,500	63,000	83,000
Limousine	5500	7800	12,900	19,900	43,300	57,000
Landaulet	5500	7800	13,200	20,200	43,800	59,000
Limousine/Touring	7750	7900	13,700	20,700	44,500	62,000

1912 Lozier, type 51, Lakewood, HAC

1912 LOZIER

Type 46 — 4-cyl., 46 hp, 124" wb

Touring-7P	4600	9400	18,800	26,500	53,800	75,000

Type 51 — 6-cyl., 51 hp, 131" wb

Lakewood Torpedo-5P	5000	18,500	32,000	51,000	88,000	110,000
Briarcliff Toy Tonneau-5P	5000	18,500	32,000	51,000	88,000	110,000
Riverside Touring-7P	5000	13,800	23,800	37,500	75,000	95,000
Meadowbrook Runabout-3P	5000	15,000	25,000	40,000	80,000	100,000
Knickerbocker Berlin	6500	18,500	32,000	51,000	88,000	110,000

1913 Lozier, type 72, Meadowbrook, HAC

1913 Lozier, type 72, Briarcliff, HAC

1913 LOZIER

Type 77 — 6-cyl., 31.6 hp, 127 1/2" wb

Montclair Touring-5P	3250	13,800	23,800	37,500	75,000	95,000
Fairmont Runabout	3250	12,500	22,500	35,000	70,000	90,000
Touraine Coupe	3850	9400	18,800	26,500	53,800	75,000
Metro. Encl. Limo.-5P	4450	7600	12,500	19,400	42,400	55,000
Coronado Limousine-6P	4450	7600	12,500	19,400	42,400	55,000

Type 72 — 6-cyl., 51.6 hp, 131" wb

Riverside Touring-7P	5000	18,500	32,000	51,000	88,000	110,000
Lakewood Torpedo	5000	22,000	37,000	62,000	93,000	120,000
Larchmont Touring-5P	5000	20,300	34,500	56,000	90,500	115,000
Briarcliff Toy Tonneau	5000	22,000	37,000	62,000	93,000	120,000
Meadowbrook Runabout	5000	18,500	32,000	51,000	88,000	110,000
Knickerbocker Berlin	6500	23,800	41,000	67,000	97,500	125,000

1914 Lozier, touring, WLB

1914 LOZIER
Type 84 — 4-cyl., 28.9 hp, 120" wb

	FP	5	4	3	2	1
Touring-7P	2100	13,800	23,800	37,500	75,000	95,000
Runabout-2P	2100	12,500	22,500	35,000	70,000	90,000

Type 77 — 6-cyl., 36.06 hp, 127 1/2" wb

Touring-5P	3250	15,000	25,000	40,000	80,000	100,000
Enclosed Limousine-5P	4450	7600	12,500	19,400	42,400	55,000
Runabout-2P	3250	13,800	23,800	37,500	75,000	95,000
Fore-Door Limousine-6P	4450	7600	12,500	19,400	42,400	55,000
Coupe-3P	3850	6400	9300	14,500	33,000	45,000

1915 Lozier, type 82, limousine, HAC

1915 LOZIER
Type 82 — 6-cyl., 36 hp, 132" wb

Touring-7P	3250	14,300	24,300	38,500	77,000	97,000

1916 Lozier, type 82, touring, HAC

1916 LOZIER
Type 82 — 6-cyl., 36 hp, 132" wb

Touring-7P	3250	14,300	24,300	38,500	77,000	97,000

1917-1918 LOZIER
Model 84 — 4-cyl., 29 hp, 120" wb

Touring-7P	1695	11,800	21,800	33,500	67,000	87,000
Roadster-2P	1695	12,500	22,500	35,000	70,000	90,000
Limousine-7P	3500	7200	11,300	17,700	38,700	50,000
Sedan-5P	3500	5000	6500	11,000	22,000	35,000

Model 82 — 6-cyl., 36.04 hp, 132" wb

Touring-7P	2775	12,500	22,500	35,000	70,000	90,000
Limousine-7P	4450	7300	11,800	18,400	40,400	52,000

LOZIER — New York, New York — (1922) — The 1922 Lozier, the availability of which was indicated in trade press specification rosters that year, is something of a mystery, though educated conjecture would be that the car was simply leftover from the aborted 1918 attempt to continue the Lozier in production. Theodore Friedburg, Leopold Landsberger and W.S. Grant, all of New York City, had been behind the $200,000 reincorporation of the defunct Lozier organization as the Lozier Motor Company in March 1918. It is known that some Loziers were built by this group in the plant of the Standard Auto Truck Company in Detroit in 1918. Possibly the Loziers

1922 Lozier, touring, HAC

offered for sale in the early 1920's were simply those cars which remained unsold when manufacture ceased in Detroit. The "1922" Lozier was indicated as a Model 92 six-cylinder car on a 142-inch wheelbase offered as a $8500 seven-passenger touring car and a $10,000 limousine. The last Lozier sixes sold in Detroit had been designated Model 82, with 132 inches designated as their wheelbase length and with price tags of $2775 and $4450 for seven-passenger touring and limousine respectively. Quite possibly the difference in wheelbase could have been a typographical error. Certainly there is no evidence that by 1922 Lozier was a going concern.

L.P.C. — The initials translated to William Mitchell Lewis, Rene M. Petard and James M. Cram — and, although their venture was initially organized as the L.P.C. Company, it was changed very soon to the Lewis Motor Company. The Lewis was built in Racine, Wisconsin from 1914 to 1916. Refer to Lewis.

LUBECK — The Lubeck Automobile Company was organized in Grand Rapids, Michigan during the spring of 1906 with a capital stock of $15,000 to "manufacture, buy, sell, rent or otherwise deal in automobiles." J. Oakley Carson, Philip H. Travis, Benjamin P. Merrick were behind this venture. Manufacture is doubted.

LUCE — The Luce Auto Power Company was a $1 million Delaware incorporation from early 1917 to manufacture and sell automobiles and parts. Incorporators were G.M. Brooks, L.P. Van Duzer and M.F. Barr, all of New York City. Manufacture of a car is doubted.

LUCEY — The Lucey Motor Car Company was organized in Troy, New York early in 1907 with a capital stock of $10,000 for the manufacture of automobiles. This venture evolved out of the Lucey-Taylor Automobile Company which had been established in Troy in 1903 as a dealership. The idea of automobile manufacture was a brief one, however, and no doubt did not leave the paper stage. The Lucey company remained one of the biggest dealerships in Troy into the early 1930's.

c.1912 Luck Utility, roadster, DJK

LUCK UTILITY — Cleburne, Texas — (1911-1914) — Harry Eugene Luck was a Texas preacher who made his rounds in an old 1903 Cadillac Model A, which he found a fine car except for continual problems with its pneumatic tires. Settling in Cleburne around 1908, he continued to drive the Cadillac — and, in his words, began to build a machine to "overcome obstacles in a country where there are no piked roads to run on." This translated to a touring car with solid rubber tires complemented with a soft spring suspension so the pleasant riding qualities of pneumatics would not be lost. The car was completed in July of 1910, and the Reverend Luck was pleased with it. So, it seemed, was everyone else in Cleburne. An "automobile committee" began looking into the possibilities of manufacture — and in May 1911 the car, which by now had been nicknamed Chaparral, was taken on a three-day test run during the Cleburne Trade Excursion, which served to further excite the populace. The Cleburne Auto Car Manufacturing Company was organized shortly thereafter with the Reverend as president, R.H. Crank as secretary, E.N. Brown as first vice-president, and F.L. Deal as second vice-president. The idea now was not to build the Chaparral, however, but another car to be called the Luck Utility, this because it was convertible from roadster to light delivery, and was a much more practical affair. "The first car has not been run much this week on account of the sloppy conditions of the road," the *Morning Review* of

Cleburne reported on December 20th, 1911. "However, as soon as it fairs off, it will be brought out where the people can see it." Already the Cleburne Company was behind schedule, since it had been hoped that the Luck Utility would have been completed in time for the Dallas State Fair in October. That deadline had not been achieved, but the Reverend Luck had traveled north the month previous to visit car factories in Michigan and to get pointers on how this whole business should be operated. By August of 1912 the Cleburne Auto Car Manufacturing Company was in production. Four cars were under construction, two of them the Luck Utility roadster, one a touring car and one a light delivery. "Mr. Luck stated that the Utilities were beginning to attract attention all over the state," the *Morning Review* reported enthusiastically. Nine cars were sold in the following year. A heftier commercial vehicle followed in May 1913 which the president of the company said would be called the "Luck Truck" — but only one was built. By now sales of the Luck Utility were ebbing as well. The Reverend Luck's principal problem was that his product was just a mite after its time. Slogans like "never runs away or kicks the wagon to pieces" would have been cute and catchy at the turn of the century, but were strictly passe by 1911. And the Model T Ford was cheaper than the Luck Utility, and could serve the rural community equally as well. After a total production of about twenty cars, the Luck Utility assembly line was closed down in 1914. Harry Eugene Luck remained in the automobile business, however, as a garage owner — and he continued preaching until his death in 1934. Today his first car is affectionately recalled at Six Flags Over Texas, the large recreation and amusement park near Dallas. One of the rides there is called the Chaparral.

1911-1914 LUCK UTILITY
Utility — 4-cyl., 25/30 hp, 115" wb

	FP	5	4	3	2	1
Roadster/Delivery	950	2500	3500	5000	8500	18,000

LUDWIG — During the spring of 1907, Jacob Ludwig of Newark, New Jersey incorporated under his own name with a capital stock of $100,000 to manufacture "wagons, carriages, trucks motor vehicles, etc." Joining Ludwig in this venture were F.A. Nott and E. Tinton. Manufacture of a car is doubted.

The Ludwig Motor Car Company has been indicated on various rosters as producing a car in Detroit, Michigan in 1914. This has not been documented. Detroit city directories of the period do not list a Ludwig company.

LUETH — During the summer of 1903, Lueth Brothers of Kankakee, Illinois announced their forthcoming entry into the automobile field. The Lueths intended to be assemblers of cars rather than builders of the component parts. "They will make their own bodies," *The Horseless Age* reported. Subsequent manufacture has not been documented.

1891 Lugo Electric, high-wheeled runabout, NAHC

LUGO ELECTRIC — Boston, Massachusetts — (1891) — Two electric cars are known to have been built at the Electric Road Carriage Company of Boston, both of them designed by Dr. Orazio Lugo. The first was a small tricycle, the second a four-wheeled carriage which featured front wheel drive. Storage batteries weighing 360 pounds were placed under the rear seat of this latter vehicle, and the horsepower developed was three. A speed of 10 mph and a between-charge driving range of 60 miles was claimed; the former is probable, the latter extremely doubtful for this early date.

LUGREEN — Wilmington, Delaware — (1920) — Lugreen Motors Corporation was a three-million-dollar company that produced a single prototype of a four-cylinder car on a 114-inch wheelbase that was planned to be marketed in vast quantities in the $1000 price range. H.E. Knox and S.E. Dill were among the people behind this venture, which died very soon after it began in 1920 in Wilmington.

LUITWIELER — Rochester, New York — (1909) — The Luitwieler Pumping Engine Company was organized in Rochester with a capital stock of $300,000 during the summer of 1909 for the manufacture of "engines, automobiles and other vehicles." S.W. Luitwieler, W.C. Smith, J.G. Haap and G.W. Rich were behind this venture. Fire-fighting apparatus was the firm's specialty, of course, but during that first season among its offerings was an "Auxiliary Squad Auto." It was built on a 126-inch wheelbase, was powered by a four-cylinder 55/60 hp engine, was fitted with three seats for the carrying of nine men, and featured two lanterns and two extinguishers. It was the sort of vehicle one would wish to take only to a fire.

1914 Lulu, 2-pass. roadster, WLB

LULU — Beavertown, Pennsylvania — (1914-1915) — The Lulu was a cyclecar produced by the Kearns Motor Truck Company of Beavertown. Although initially announced to sell for $398, the firm was unable to bring the car in at that figure and thus the Lulu was introduced at $450. Occasionally it was also referred to as the Kearns-Kar. A snappy little two-seater, it was powered by a four-cylinder 12 hp Farmer engine placed in a 96-inch-wheelbase chassis. A 44-inch tread was standard, though a 56-inch version was available optionally at no extra charge. The chassis was channel steel, the body metal, the transmission a three-speed selective, with final drive by shaft to a bevel-gear differential rear axle. For a cyclecar, the Lulu was extraordinarily well built. By November of 1914 approximately twenty-five Lulus a week were being produced, and manufacture continued into 1915 for a longevity enjoyed by few cyclecars. The Lulu was followed in 1916 by the new Kearns Trio.

1914-1915 LULU
Cyclecar — 4-cyl., 12 hp, 96" wb

	FP	5	4	3	2	1
Roadster-2P	450	1600	2700	3800	5800	12,000
Speedster-2P	450	2000	3000	4200	6500	14,000

LUMUND — The Lumund Motor Car Company was organized early in 1910 in Rutherford, New Jersey with a capital stock of $150,000 for the manufacture of automobiles. This firm was listed in the Ware yearbook of the industry as a producer, but further details are lacking.

LUND — Woodhaven, New York — (1914) — In December 1914 — one month after the Metropol Motors Corporation factory in Port Jefferson was turned over the manufacture of the F.R.P. car — C.H. Lund, who had been Metropol's superintendent, announced that he was building a prototype of a car that he would now manufacture under his own name. Like the Metropol, the Lund was a long stroke, its four-cylinder T-head engine measuring 3-inch bore by 6-inch stroke and developing 30 hp. "Three point suspension is to be used," Lund advised, "the front end being supported by a bronze bushing which will allow the frame to twist without disturbing the motor." Lund further advised that he would announce his manufacturing plans shortly. He never did.

1902 Lunkenheimer, touring, NAHC

LUNKENHEIMER — Cincinnati, Ohio — (1902) — In 1862, in Cincinnati, Frederick Lunkenheimer began manufacture of industrial valves. Although at the turn of the century the family name was shortened to Lunken, the family business remained Lunkenheimer Brass Works. In 1902 Edmund

Lunken, son of Frederick, built two experimental automobiles. The first was a rather primeval buckboard, the second a quite handsome touring car powered by a two-cylinder gasoline engine and distinguished by an unusual grate-type radiator and a heavy cast-iron wheel purportedly purloined from an iron gate valve. Though the Lunkenheimer Motor Vehicle Company was organized with a thought to production, the thought quickly passed. Lunkenheimer went on to serve the industry, however, with manufacture of priming cups, grease cups and a variety of lubrication devices. In later years, the Lunkenheimer Company became noted as among the foremost makers of industrial valves in America. Today it is part of Condec Corporation.

LUSK — Cicero, Illinois — (1942) — Bill Lusk of Cicero built his "cycle bus" in five months from the spare parts of other vehicles. A three-wheeler and unrelievedly ugly, the Lusk carried six passengers and delivered 50 miles to the gallon of gasoline. Lusk's timing in building the vehicle in 1942 was fortuitous, since the materials he used were the sort subsequently sacrificed to the war effort.

LUTZ STEAM — San Antonio, Texas — (1898)/Buffalo, New York — (1917) — In 1898 George H. Lutz of San Antonio built a steam car. Nothing more was heard of him or the car until 1917 when his name headed the directorate of the newly capitalized (at $100,000) Lutz Motor Car Company of Buffalo, New York. The other directors included Orman H. Lutz of San Antonio (probably a brother) and three businessmen — John H. McLean, George B. Hurd and Levi R. Lupton — from Upstate New York. The directors were said to be looking for a factory site in Buffalo to build steam cars. There is no evidence that the company ever got into manufacture. Probably the 1898 car and a possible prototype in 1917 were the only Lutzes produced.

1905 Luverne, touring, JAC

LUVERNE — Luverne, Minnesota — (1904-1916) — "We were engaged in making buggies," Fenton A. Leicher remembered in the mid-1950's, "and when we saw that autos would likely displace buggies, and as we had a good working force, we began in 1904 to build autos to order on a very limited scale, and we continued until the year 1916 when it became evident that competition of the larger producers would eventually eliminate such small concerns as ourselves." That's a disarmingly modest summation for the history of Minnesota's most distinguished motorcar. It all began when Fenton Leicher, with his brother Ed, put together their first automobile in late 1903 from a kit they had ordered from A.L. Dyke in St. Louis. Manufacture of their own car, a two-cylinder highwheeler, followed, with engines supplied initially by Buick. Subsequently, Rutenber and Beaver powerplants would be used. Late in 1906 the Luverne Automobile Company was formally established, with a capitalization of $50,000, $25,000 of that paid in. A standard four joined the highwheeler twins in 1909, and from 1910 the company concentrated on large touring cars. One of these became known as the Montana Special. It was a Model Fifty which had been displayed at the 1913 St. Paul Automobile Show and had been judged as just the car to transport the wealthy financiers, Northern Pacific's James Hill among them, from the rail depot to the posh hotel they owned in the mountains of Montana. It performed so capably that the hotel's manager wrote an enthusiastic letter of endorsement to Luverne, and the company began calling its Model Fifty the Montana Special thereafter. But its popularity was dimmed by the most famous of all the Luvernes: the six-cylinder Big Brown Luverne with its solid German silver radiator, its many coats of "Luverne Brown" paint, its upholstery of "Old Spanish brown leather with all hair filling. In 1912 Luverne produced its first fire engine, and truck manufacture followed. Passenger car production came to an end late in 1916, with the company devoting itself exclusively to the assembly of farm trucks for the war effort after America's entrance into World War I. The Luverne Motor Truck Company evolved into the Luverne Fire Apparatus Company during the mid-Twenties. Corporate control of the firm passed from the Leicher family in 1970; the firm remains today as the Luverne Fire Equipment Company.

1905-1906 LUVERNE
Two-Cylinder — 20 hp

	FP	5	4	3	2	1
Side Entrance Tour.	—	2700	3600	5300	8800	19,000
Surrey		2900	3700	5600	9100	20,000
Two-Cylinder — 10 hp						
Runabout		2500	3500	5000	8500	18,000

870

1907 Luverne, touring, WLB

1907 LUVERNE
Model A — 2-cyl., 20 hp, 94" wb

	FP	5	4	3	2	1
Touring-5P	1250	3000	4000	6000	9500	21,000
Runabout-3P	1250	3100	4200	6300	10,500	22,000
Surrey-2/4P (78" wb)						
Surrey-2/4P	950	2700	3600	5300	8800	19,000

1908 Luverne, touring, JAC

1908 LUVERNE
Model C — 2-cyl., 12 hp, 78" wb

	FP	5	4	3	2	1
Runabout-2P	650	2900	3700	5600	9100	20,000
Model A — 2-cyl., 20 hp, 94" wb						
Runabout-3P	1250	3000	4000	6000	9500	21,000
Touring-5P	1250	3100	4200	6300	10,500	22,000

1909 Luverne, surrey, JAC

1909 LUVERNE
Highwheeler — 2-cyl., 24 hp, 100" wb

	FP	5	4	3	2	1
Model A Tour.-5P	1250	3200	4300	6500	11,000	23,000
Model B Tour.-5P	900	3100	4200	6300	10,500	22,000
Model C Surrey-4P	800	2700	3600	5300	8800	19,000
Model D Rbt.-2P	750	2500	3500	5000	8500	18,000
Four — 4-cyl., 40 hp, 108" wb						
Model 40 Tour.-7P	2000	3300	4400	6700	12,000	24,000

1910 LUVERNE
Model 530 — 4-cyl., 30 hp, 108" wb

	FP	5	4	3	2	1
Touring-5P	1400	2700	3600	5300	8800	19,000

Model 535 — 4-cyl., 35 hp, 120" wb

	FP	5	4	3	2	1
Touring-5P	1600	3000	4000	6000	9500	21,000

Four-40 — 4-cyl., 40 hp, 120" wb

	FP	5	4	3	2	1
Model 540 Tour.-5P	2000	3100	4200	6300	10,500	22,000
Model 740 Tour.-7P	2250	3000	4000	6000	9500	21,000

1911 Luverne Forty, touring, JAC

1911 LUVERNE
Thirty — 4-cyl., 30 hp, 110" wb

		5	4	3	2	1
Model 530 Tour.-5P	1500	3000	4000	6000	9500	21,000

Forty — 4-cyl., 40 hp, 122" wb

		5	4	3	2	1
Model 740 Tour.-7P	2500	3200	4300	6500	11,000	23,000

1912 Luverne, touring, JAC

1912 LUVERNE
Forty — 4-cyl., 40 hp, 124" wb

		5	4	3	2	1
Model 540 Tour.-5P	1850	3100	4200	6300	10,500	22,000

Fifty — 4-cyl., 50 hp, 126" wb

		5	4	3	2	1
Model 750 Tour.-7P	2600	3600	7200	12,000	16,800	24,000

Sixty — 6-cyl., 60 hp, 128" wb

		5	4	3	2	1
Model 260 Rdstr.-2P	2750	3650	7350	12,250	17,150	24,500
Model 460 Rdstr.-4P	2750	3650	7350	12,250	17,150	24,500

1913 LUVERNE
Forty — 4-cyl., 40 hp, 124" wb

		5	4	3	2	1
Model 540 Tour.-5P	1850	3100	4200	6300	10,500	22,000

Sixty — 6-cyl., 60 hp, 130" wb

		5	4	3	2	1
Model 760 Tour.-7P	2850	3800	7600	12,750	17,800	25,500

1914 Luverne, "Big Brown Luverne" roadster, HAC

1914 Luverne, "Big Brown Luverne" touring, JAC

1914-1916 LUVERNE
Big Brown Luverne — 6-cyl., 60 hp, 130" wb

	FP	5	4	3	2	1
Touring-7P	2500	3500	4500	7000	13,000	25,000
Roadster-2P	2250	3700	4700	7300	13,700	26,000

LUXAMORE — With the intention of supplying "luxurious cars to discriminating buyers," the Luxamore Motor Company of New York was incorporated with a capital stock of $750,000 during the spring of 1915. The principals involved were Joseph F. Curtin, Samuel B. Howard and S.A. Anderson, all residents of New York City. Where they planned to produce the Luxamore was not indicated. The name was dreadful. The car did not proceed into manufacture.

LUXFORD — **New York, New York** — **(1928)** — The Luxford was a taxicab on the Model A Ford chassis the coachwork for which was designed by Edsel Ford. Its lines were low and rakish, its paint scheme being green with a belt of yellow and red striping and the spoke wheels in red. The side lights were miniature replicas of the front headlights, with two signal lights on the roof. The upholstery inside was blue mohair, and there were accommodations for three passengers. The Luxford was shown for the first time on March 13th, 1928 at the Ford showroom at 1710 Broadway in New York City. The extent of production is not certain.

1900 Luxor, gasoline chariot, MVMA

LUXOR — **Williamsport, Pennsylvania** — **(1900)** — Undoubtedly, it was the closest approximation realized in 1900 to a Roman chariot. As *Cycle and Automobile Trade Journal* grossly understated, "its design and appearance are a broad departure from all existing models." C.R. Harris of Williamsport was the man behind the Luxor, and he envisioned considerable fame and fortune, the former because of the unique look of his vehicle, the latter because its design simplicity meant production costs of half the norm. The Luxor was powered by a 4 hp engine, with a tiller for steering, and a lever for all other operations. The body was fitted on pneumatic springs which, Harris said, took care of easy riding and dispensed with the need for troublesome (and expensive) pneumatic tires. "The frame construction is light, strong and elastic." Harris commented, "and will withstand the severest usage under the most adverse and trying conditions." Unfortunately, Harris discovered the conditions involved in securing capital for manufacture quite trying, and the result adverse. The Luxor was never put into manufacture.

1925 Luxor Taxicab, HAC

LUXOR — Hagerstown, Maryland — (1924)/Framingham, Massachusetts — (1924-1927) — In the early Twenties, King Tut's tomb was discovered in Egypt, which led to large headlines in U.S. newspapers and the naming of a taxicab in 1924 after the city near which the emtombed pharoah's riches had been found. The Luxor was planned as the *ne plus ultra* of metered travel. It was the idea of New York City entrepreneurs Allie S. Freed and Mickey Heidt, who approached M.P. Moller, the builder of the Dagmar in Hagerstown, Maryland with their proposal. A few Luxors were produced in Hagerstown early in 1924 by the newly organized Luxor Cab Manufacturing Company — in which Moller held a substantial interest — but by the spring of that year arrangements had been made to move the Luxor operation to Framingham, Massachusetts where the taxis would be assembled alongside the Bay State cars in the factory of the R.H. Long Motor Car Company. Though the Luxor's four-cylinder Buda engine and 114-inch wheelbase were typically taxicab, the car's commodious leather-upholstered interior and its color scheme — cream, yellow and black with red striping — were distinctive. Indeed, early on Luxor sued a taxicab operating company in New York City for effecting the same colors, and the Supreme Court of New York awarded Luxor exclusive rights to the paint scheme. The decision in this important test case was widely reported. "The taxicab industry and even some lawyers who should know better," Luxor attorney and vice-president Joseph Sapinsky explained, "seemed to have been of the opinion that a taxicab manufacturer could acquire no property right on a color combination and that everyone was free to appropriate a competitor's good will. This mistaken idea was due to a misreading of the Yellow Cab cases." In November of 1925, Luxor bought the Bay State machinery and plant in Framingham, following the failure of the R.H. Long automotive venture. During the summer of the following year, Luxor itself proceeded into receivership, though production of both the $2693 Luxor limousine and $2795 landaulet continued into late 1927. Luxor also built a private passenger car called the Standish during 1924-1925.

1924-1927 LUXOR
Taxi — 4-cyl., 114" wb

	FP	5	4	3	2	1
Limousine	2695	3000	4000	6000	9500	21,000
Landaulet	2795	3100	4200	6300	10,500	22,000

L.W.C. — St. Louis, Missouri — (1915-1917) — During the summer of 1916 the Columbia Taxicab Company of St. Louis, which previously had purchased the cabs it used, announced that now it would manufacture them as well. One hundred of the small cabs heretofore in the Columbia fleet were retired and replaced with larger four-cylinder 27 hp seven-passenger cars. "The new machine is finished in ultra-fashionable style," Columbia boasted, "is upholstered in gray whipcord, and has the appearance more of a high-priced family car than of a taxicab." The L.W.C. was also available for sale to the general public for $3500. In 1917 Columbia announced that it had fitted a taxi body to a Stanley steam car and was testing it "for street service" to compare its effectiveness with the L.W.C. By 1918, it appears, the Columbia Taxicab Company had returned to purchasing its vehicles.

LYBE — Sidney, Iowa — (1895) — A spring motor said to store up power while the vehicle was coursing downhill and to utilize it on a level or upgrade was the idea of D.I. Lybe of Sidney. The device was priced at $120 and could be adapted for both automotive and marine vehicles. In a four-seater carriage the motor was capable of running 2000 feet itself, with a maximum speed of 30 mph. Arm and foot power would also have to be employed on occasion with a Lybe. Its inventor believed that his machine would "afford a mild and pleasing form of exercise, in addition to its speed advantages." He didn't find too many people who agreed with him.

LYKKE — Grand Island, Nebraska — (1901) — Albert Lykke was a mechanic who operated a foundry and built gasoline engines in Grand Island. In 1901 he built a gasoline car, which performed admirably. "Mr. Lykke was, and, indeed is yet to be complimented for it," a Grand Island chronicler recalled some years later. "But the muffler cut-out was not then perfected and the vehicle naturally did some quite audible 'chug-chuggin'." So much so, in fact, that local residents complained to the press and the town council. Restrictive legislation was passed. Earlier Albert Lykke had informed the automotive trade press that he planned to start a "small auto factory." The town apparently persuaded him not to. His son recalls today that only the one car was ever built.

1904 Lyman, touring, WLB

LYMAN — Boston, Massachusetts — (1904) — The Lyman was a very expensive automobile — $6250 — that was offered as a five-passenger touring car with a rear-entrance tonneau and a removable limousine top. It featured a four-cylinder 30/35 hp engine, a 100-inch wheelbase chassis, three-speed sliding gear transmission, shaft drive, and right-hand steering. The desire of its builder, C.F. Lyman, to name the car for himself was understandable. It may not have been wise, however, since there was already another, and considerably cheaper, car in town bearing the same first name. C.F. Lyman introduced his expensive car early in 1904, its production did not survive the year. John Appleton Burnham does not seem to have been involved with this car. Both the Lyman and the Lyman & Burnham ventures were located in Kirby street in Boston, although the addresses were not the same.

1903 Lyman & Burnham, touring, NAHC

LYMAN & BURNHAM — Boston, Massachusetts — (1903-1905) — Following the dissolution of the Binney & Burnham partnership in January 1903, James Binney departed for endeavors unknown, and John Appleton Burnham found himself a new partner named C. Frederick Lyman. Although the Binney & Burnham had been a steam car, the Lyman & Burnham was gasoline powered. The new partners leased Room 92 at 70 Kilby in Boston. The cars were built for them by the Fore River Ship & Engine Company of Quincy. Only one model was offered, a tourer with rear-entrance tonneau making provision for five passengers. Its engine was a water-cooled twin of 12/15 hp; the 78-inch-wheelbase frame was angle steel, the body wood with aluminum panels. A two-speed sliding gear transmission, shaft drive, and right-hand wheel steering were featured. The price for all this was $2000. Early in 1905 Lyman and Burnham announced they were quitting the automobile business.

LYNDON — The Lyndon Manufacturing Company was organized in Chicago, Illinois early in 1913 with a capital stock of $25,000 for the manufacture of automobiles. Incorporators were S. Donahue, F.M. Donahue and W.E. Lyons. Manufacture is doubted.

LYNN — Lynn, Massachusetts — (1903) — The Lynn Automobile Company was initially organized in Springfield, Massachusetts in 1902. The venture seems to have stalled there until, early in 1903, when Lynn took over the faltering Malden Automobile Company which was building a steam car in Malden, Massachusetts. The Malden operation was moved to 306 Broad Street in Lynn, where a few of the Malden steamers, now renamed Lynn, were produced. A gasoline car was also promised, but it never arrived. The Lynn Automobile Company was out of business before year's end.

LYNN — Everett, Massachusetts — (1908) — The Lynn Car Company on Orient Avenue in Everett seems to have operated principally as a dealership, but it is known that the firm experimented with a highwheeler. In February 1908 Lynn wrote the Firestone Tire & Rubber Company of its complete satisfaction with the solid rubber Firestone tires which had been fitted to the experimental car. "We have given our machine some very hard usage," the company commented, "and these tires have proved to be all you represented them to be." Whether manufacture of the Lynn highwheeler followed has not been documented.

LYON — Despite various roster references, there was no Lyon Motor Car Company in Adrian, Michigan in 1911. There was, however, a Lion Motor Car Company. Refer to Lion.

The Lyon Motor Car Company of Columbia, South Carolina was organized during the summer of 1912 with a capital stock of $50,000 for the manufacture of automobiles. Incorporators were E.B. Lyon, J.M. Black and J.E. Johnson. Manufacture is doubted.

LYON STEAM — New York, New York — (1902) — He had been driving automobiles, he said, since one had to be a licensed engineer to do so, and he still held his "engineer's ticket" to prove it. It was his experience with other steam automobiles which led E.H. Lyon of 453 West 24th Street in Manhattan, with an assist from his chauffeur William Conklin, to build his own car in 1902. The wide separation and inaccessibility of engine and boiler, and the exposure of the machinery to dust and dirt, were disadvantages of other steam cars which he sought to correct in his own. Thus, the engine of the Lyon was, to quote its builder, "stuck on" the front of the hood and completely covered with a removable sheet metal casing. In

1902 Lyon Steamer, NAHC

back of it was the 14-inch fire-tube boiler, the rear bulkhead of which formed the dashboard. Transmission of power to the rear axle was via a long chain running the entire length of the car. The results of road tests were completely successful. No patents were applied for on any of the Lyon's features, however, because its inventor's sole purpose had been to satisfy his own requirements. Having done that, he said he planned to build another car along the same general principles, with a slightly longer wheelbase, a more attractive hood, and prettier body lines.

LYONS — The Lyons was an export car distributed in England by London & Midland Motors in 1920. Its engine was a 35 hp Herschell-Spillman four, its wheelbase was 115 inches, its body style was a five-passenger touring with Rolls-Royce-ish radiator, and its price was £725. The car definitely was built in the United States, what is not known is who built it. The possibilities, of course, are limitless. But, given that New York City was the source of many of the postwar export automobile ventures and that the man behind the car might have wished to name it for himself, the possibilities are reduced to two. The 1920 *Trow's Directory of New York* reveals two Lyons who indicated their occupation as "automobiles": Herbert on West 176th Street and Howard on Morningside Drive. That either of these Lyons was the man behind this Lyons remains a guess however.

LYONS-KNIGHT — Indianapolis, Indiana — (1913-1915) - In October of 1912 the Lyons brothers of Indianapolis — James W., William P. and George W. — bought out the Atlas Engine works in town and organized themselves as the Lyons-Atlas Company. Both James W. and William P. Lyons had been associated with the Atlas Company, a pioneer builder of two-stroke gasoline engines and diesel stationary units which had recently developed a line of Knight sleeve-valve engines. (The Atlas Company had

tried automobile manufacture once, a highwheeler in 1909, but that venture never got off the ground.) Immediately upon organization, the new Lyons-Atlas Company announced that it would produce complete cars in addition to the Knight engine. This created "quite a stir in the industry," as *The Horseless Age* put it, until it was also revealed that Harry Knox was coming to town. The Atlas-Knight motorcar he had been producing in Springfield, Massachusetts had recently been discontinued because of a problem called bankruptcy, which left him free to join the Lyons people in Indianapolis and help them build their Knight engined car. The Lyons-Knight, which arrived in late 1913 was, unremarkably, quite similar to the Atlas-Knight that Harry Knox had built in Massachusetts. In Indiana, however, a six-cylinder model was added (the Atlas-Knight had been a four exclusively), although it was dropped for 1915, which was the Lyons-Knight's last year. In August of 1915 the announcement of Harry Knox's resignation from the company was accompanied by an announcement that Lyons-Atlas would discontinue the manufacture of automobiles. During World War I, Lyons-Atlas built Standard marine engines for British government use in submarine chasers.

1913-1914 LYONS-KNIGHT
Model K-4 — 4-cyl., 50 hp, 130" wb

	FP	5	4	3	2	1
Touring-5P	2900	3300	4400	6700	12,000	24,000
Touring-7P	2980	3200	4300	6500	11,000	23,000
Sedan	3900	2000	3000	4200	6500	14,000
Berline	4300	2300	3300	4600	7500	16,000

Model K-6 — 6-cyl., 50 hp, 130" wb

	FP	5	4	3	2	1
Touring-5P	3100	3500	4500	7000	13,000	25,000
Touring-7P	3200	3300	4400	6700	12,000	24,000

1915 Lyons-Knight K-4, touring, HAC

1915 LYONS-KNIGHT
Model K-4 — 4-cyl., 50 hp, 130" wb

Touring-7P	2980	3300	4400	6700	12,000	24,000
Touring-5P	2900	3500	4500	7000	13,000	25,000
Roadster-2P	2900	3700	4700	7300	13,700	26,000
Limousine-7P	4300	2700	3600	5300	8800	19,000
Berline-7P	4300	2700	3600	5300	8800	19,000
Sedan-5P	3900	2000	3000	4200	6500	14,000

MACBETH — The MacBeth Brothers Company was organized in New York City with a capital stock of $10,000 late in 1905 for the manufacture of automobiles and wagons. Incorporators were John Robison, Magnus Eriksen, Elisha T. Halse and George MacBeth. Manufacture of a car is doubted.

MACDONALD — "D.J. MacDonald of Anaconda, Montana has about completed a steam automobile," reported *The Horseless Age* in August of 1902. Details are lacking, and whether "D.J." was the "Duncan MacDonald" behind the MacDonald steam car of the early Twenties is not known.

James B. MacDonald, Inc. was organized in New York City early in 1917 with a capital stock of $2000 for the manufacture of automobiles and carriages. Behind this venture were James B. MacDonald of 650 East 17th Street and John Gabbo of 433 East 65th Street. Manufacture of a car is doubted.

1923 MacDonald, steam roadster, GR

1924 MacDonald, steam sedan, KM

MACDONALD STEAM — **Garfield, Ohio** — **(1920-1923)** — "Practically unlimited capital is behind the invention," the inventor said. It was a "gearless" steamer, the same vehicle Duncan MacDonald had been promoting the year before as the Gearless in Pittsburgh. Leaving the Gearless Company in 1920, MacDonald hastened to Garfield, Ohio where he organized the MacDonald Steam Automotive Corporation. Initially announcing steam trucks, tractors and buses to be his products, MacDonald subsequently decided to market a roadster called the Bobcat as well. It was a three-cylinder two-seater on a 106-inch wheelbase. Most probably, only the prototype was built. Possibly there were not even prototypes of the commercial vehicles. Not until the spring of 1923 did MacDonald announce manufacture was about to begin. Where the "unlimited capital" was that he boasted of in 1920 is anyone's guess, but a reasonable conclusion might be that it was all on paper — or back in Pittsburgh, with Gearless. In May 1923 Duncan MacDonald was among the four Gearless officials indicted for stock fraud, and in January 1924 he was one of the three convicted. Interestingly, that same month MacDonald was advertising in the trade press for "district distributors," noting that 1924 output of 1000 units would include touring cars, sedans and coupes. Again, probably only prototypes resulted. MacDonald production in Garfield had been almost exclusively devoted to conversion kits to render gasoline cars into steamers. A reference from *MoToR* in 1936 indicates that he was by then doing the same once again, but his company was now in Los Angeles. In 1930, in Chicago, he had also seen to the conversion of a gasoline car to a steam car called the Cardon with Jeffery Carqueville.

MACDUFF — **Brooklyn, New York** — **(1903)** — Initially, this experimental car built by J.B. MacDuff of Brooklyn was equipped with an 8 hp engine but, as he expressed it, "the water-cooling abomination, with its pumps, et

1904 MacDuff Aeropinion, runabout, NAHC

cetera" robbed the vehicle of half its horsepower, so he decided to go "aeropinion" instead. His air propeller achieved only 4 hp, but managed 16 mph on its first test run. The vehicle was put together at the automobile repair shop of A.K. Schaap at 1740 Fulton Street in Brooklyn, and MacDuff christened it a "pneumoslito," which translated to air sled ("slito" being the German term for sled). On its second trial run on Cypress Hill Lake near Ridgewood, Long Island, the vehicle achieved 25 mph. "It runs faster going into the eye of the wind than when running with it," *The Motor World reported*, "...attested by four witnesses besides the inventor." MacDuff next planned a bigger vehicle with a more powerful engine, "a car made to run over the roads to the shore and go right on over the water," MacDuff explained. Whether he ever completed it is not known. More than likely, he returned to his principal occupation. J.B. MacDuff sold real estate in Brooklyn.

MACINNIS ELECTRIC — **Toledo, Ohio** — **(1909-1911)** — MacInnis Brothers of Toledo produced a small electric coupe priced at $2400 beginning in 1909 and ending about 1911. Late in 1910 the MacInnis Brothers believed they had found more profitable activity in the body-building business, most specifically remodeling 1910 cars into the fore-door bodies that would become all the rage in 1911. They may have remained in the coachbuilding business for a while after discontinuing the MacInnis.

MACK — Prior to their move to Allentown, Pennsylvania where the first Mack truck was built, the Mack Brothers Company was in Brooklyn, New York where in 1903-1904 they produced what they called "Big Cars." Refer to Manhattan.

The S. Mack Motor Company was a $50,000 Delaware incorporation from late 1910 to "manufacture, sell and operate motor vehicles of all kinds" in Baltimore, Maryland. Incorporators were Joseph J. Smith of Baltimore, and Harry C. Yarrow, Jr., George Yarrow and W.K. Yarrow of Philadelphia. Manufacture of a car is doubted.

MACK — **Milwaukee, Wisconsin** — **(1908)** — In 1908 in Milwaukee a machinist by the name of Perry Mack built himself an automobile using an air-cooled engine and friction transmission of his own devising. The car was still running some six years later by which time Perry Mack was heartily in the automobile business, as the designer of the air-cooled Mack engine being built by the Universal Machinery Company of Milwaukee.

MACKAY — The three-axle six-wheeled behemoth built by M.A. Mackay in 1916 interested Raymond A. Greene of the Greene Motor Car Company of Newark, New Jersey sufficiently to become involved in its proposed manufacture. Refer to Greene.

MACKENZIE — H. Jordan MacKenzie of New Orleans, Louisiana was reported to have built a cyclecar, according to the March 1914 edition of *Motor Print*. Details are lacking.

MACKENZIE & MCARTHUR — **New Haven, Connecticut** — **(1895)** — After experimenting for three years with various kinds of motors, MacKenzie & McArthur, who operated a machine shop at 65 Orange Street in New Haven, announced that they had come up with the optimal motive force for vehicles: compressed air. As announced by *The Horseless Age* in

November 1895, "they propose, while the vehicle is in motion, to pump air into a tank under a pressure of about 300 pounds, and then carry it to a pair of compound engines of the marine type, weighing about 50 pounds apiece. The engines will be geared direct to the axle." The partners saw commercial vehicle production as the most viable avenue they might travel and planned to build light (800-pound) delivery wagons using their engine. Whether they ever produced more than a prototype is open to question.

MACKER — Westborough, Massachusetts — (1902) — During mid-summer of 1902, Melvin A. Macker and his brother Clarence announced to the automotive trade press that their first light gasoline runabout had been under test on the streets of Westborough since June 8th. Subsequent announcements from the brothers that summer indicated that they had "closed a contract to build a number of autos" and that the Macker Automobile Company was being established. The first was true, the second was not. The Mackers did build a few automobiles for a man named Whitcomb in Worcester. "It has been supposed by some people that Mr. Macker was engaged in automobile building on his own hook, which is a mistake," the *Westborough Chronotype* reported on August 23rd, 1902. Instead, Melvin Macker finished up the contract and then "secured a good situation with the Worcester Automobile Company and will probably commence there next Monday."

MACKEY — John C. Mackey tried twice but appears to have succeeded neither time. In 1910 in his native Newark, New Jersey he organized the Mackey Motor Company with a capital stock of $300,000 for the manufacture of automobiles. In 1917 he was in Akron, Ohio with another company of the same name, incorporated for $250,000 this time and with plans for the manufacture of four-wheel-drive automobiles. That even a prototype resulted from either of these ventures has not been documented.

1903 Mackle-Thompson, runabout, NAHC

MACKLE-THOMPSON — Elizabeth, New Jersey — (1903) — In the early spring of 1903 Frederick Mackle of Elizabeth and Andrew Thompson of Newark formed a partnership and established the Mackle-Thompson Automobile Company at 855 Magnolia Avenue in Elizabeth. It was to serve as an agency for the Olds, and also the venue in which the Mackle-Thompson would be built and marketed. The partners' car was a light runabout with a single-cylinder engine, shaft drive, two-speed sliding gear transmission and right-hand wheel steering. It was said to be "the result of five years of building gas and electric automobiles," but one would suspect the Messrs. Mackle and Thompson exaggerated. They both previously seem to have been engaged primarily as mechanics, though Thompson had enjoyed a brief fling in 1901 producing an electric car under his own name. The Mackle-Thompson runabout was produced for one season only. Thereafter the partners continued in business as dealers and repairmen.

1903 MACKLE-THOMPSON

	FP	5	4	3	2	1
Model B Rbt. (1-cyl., 3 1/2 hp)	500	1800	2800	4000	6200	13,000
Model C Rbt. (1-cyl., 5 hp)	600	2000	3000	4200	6500	14,000

1895 MacLeod, surrey, NAHC

MacLEOD — New York, New York — (1895) — Walter MacLeod was a British mechanical engineer who took up residence in New York City in 1895 to promote and sell his version of the horseless carriage idea. "The motor, which is capable of 4 horse power, employs kerosene as fuel and is of the automatic type, no flame being required after four or five minutes," *The Horseless Age* noted. "It is enclosed in a box at the rear of the vehicle to protect it from the dust which arises on even good roads and from the interference of thoughtless persons who might wish to tamper with it." About a half-gallon of kerosene was required per hour of driving, and speeds of up to 15 mph were claimed. The body style was a surrey, accommodating six passengers. How many clients MacLeod garnered for his car is not known, though it can be documented that the Alliance Carriage Company of Cincinnati built at least one.

MACLAREN — The Maclaren Company of Cleveland, Ohio was organized during the summer of 1911 with a capital stock of $10,000 to manufacture and deal in automobiles. Incorporators were Don P. Maclaren, Harry H. Hamilton, W.R. Godfey and R.W. Sanborn. Manufacture is doubted.

MacNAUGHTON — Buffalo, New York — (1906) — Late in 1905 James MacNaughton and F. Louis DuBroy organized the MacNaughton & DuBroy Company in Buffalo with a capital stock of $10,000. Its purpose was the manufacture of engines and automobiles. In 1906 some automobiles did follow, all of them electrics. Although these cars often carried the MacNaughton name, MacNaughton did not build them. Instead they were produced by the coachbuilding Brunn company in Buffalo, MacNaughton being the sole selling agent for these Brunn-built electrics. MacNaughton did produce an electric of his own, however, called the Hercules. DuBroy seems to have been a short-time partner, incidentally; by 1906 the firm was called the James MacNaughton Motor Car Company.

MACOMBER — The Macomber engine was a rotary five-cylinder air-cooled unit designed by Walter G. Macomber. From 1914-1915 it powered the Eagle cyclecar built in Los Angeles and Chicago, and from 1917-1918 the Eagle-Macomber produced in Sandusky, Ohio. Refer to Eagle.

1916 Macon, touring, WLB

MACON — Macon, Missouri — (1915-1917) — Early trade press references to this car from Missouri refer to it as the Alstel or All-Steel. But neither name was ever formally applied by the company. Macon was the only trade name given to this ill-starred automobile. In June of 1915 the All-Steel Motor Car Company was organized in St. Louis. Charles L. Smith was the designer of its car, which had a conventional four-cylinder engine and unconventional chassis/body construction. The body was electrically welded, attached to the chassis at three points, and was easily removable. The frame was a narrow platform backbone in which the propeller shaft and gearbox were enclosed. Hunter Woodson, F.V. Smith and E.J. Spencer were the promoters of the car, though Spencer resigned in 1916. Later that year the two remaining partners, after surveying several communities in the Midwest, decided on Macon as the site for manufacture. The Macon Merchants Association promised support in the conversion of the Blees-McVicker Carriage Company into a first-rate automobile factory. Sanitary facilities ("toilets and lavatories of the best and modern type . . . eighty-four men may wash in comfort") and creature comforts (a game room with billiard tables and well-stocked book shelves) were prominent in the plans. Maconites were told that not only would this be "the largest automobile factory in the world," but also the most sanitary and comfortable. Stock in the company was sold, and construction was begun. The Macon was to be a light four on a 114-inch wheelbase selling for about $350 as a roadster, $400 as a touring car. W.E. Duerston was imported from Hudson in Detroit to serve as production manager. On December 30th, 1916 the All-Steel Motor Car Company metamorphosed into the Macon Motor Car

1917 Macon, touring, WLB

Company. This followed charges by the Missouri state's attorney of "irregularities in the conduct" of All-Steel's affairs. On May 17th, 1917 the former carriage factory burned to the ground. Although prototypes of the Macon car "for the masses as well as the classes" may have been built, production had not begun. Receivership immediately followed, and receiver Ives B. Jones immediately sued the Wabash Railroad for the $250,000 fire loss, alleging that the conflagration had been begun by a passing train which threw a spark igniting first the railway depot and then the factory adjacent. The case was finally decided in May 1920, and the by-now defunct Macon Motor Car Company was awarded $60,000. Its insurance settlement had been $20,000.

MACY-ROGER — The Macy-Roger of 1895 was promoted by Emile Roger, a Frenchman who was attempting to market his cars in America, and it was bought by Macy's department store of New York City. Refer to Roger-American.

MADDEN — Mechanicsburg, Pennsylvania — (1896) — Dutton Madden's automotive idea was a three-wheeler which he said could be adapted to any size from cycle up to streetcar. "The motive power is applied separately to the two rear wheels running loose on the axle," he explained. "The front wheel is connected with the frame or carriage body to run automatically on the caster principle, adapting itself to go in any direction required by the movement of the vehicle. There is to be a separate motor for each wheel, and the operator is to have a hand on each handle bar to regulate the speed of each wheel, running each at the same speed to make a straight course and to change the course, changing the speed of the wheel. If one wheel is stopped and the other is in motion the vehicle will make a complete turn around on its own length." Electric motors would power the Madden, the number of them necessary depending on the size of the vehicle. Madden built just one example, a small one. Presumably, he found his principle didn't work at all well.

MADDOCKS — The H. Ross Maddocks Company was organized in Boston, Massachusetts early in 1914 with a capital stock of $25,000 to manufacture and deal in motor vehicles. H.R. Maddocks, Charles West and J.A. Maddocks were the incorporators. Manufacture of a car is doubted. Earlier Maddocks had been a Twombly dealer. In 1915 he became an agent for Stewart cars and trucks.

MADISON — The Madison Auto Company was organized during the summer of 1919 with a capital stock of $25,000 to manufacture and deal in automobiles in Jersey City, New Jersey. Walter W. Stewart, William S. Rowland and Charles W. Grant, all of Jersey City, were the incorporators. Manufacture is doubted.

MADISON — The Madison of 1878 from Madison, Wisconsin was a valiant try, but a no-succeed. Prompted by the offering of a $10,000 prize by the Wisconsin State Legislature to any resident of the state who could come up with a cheap and practical alternative to the horse, Wisconsin inventors everywhere put themselves to the task in the late 1870's. Two succeeded in building automotive vehicles which are documented to have run successfully. These were the Green Bay and the Oshkosh. The Madison is one that didn't make it.

1916 Madison, model 6-40, 5-pass. touring, WLB

MADISON — Anderson, Indiana — (1915-1919) — "The plant has been closed several months, but has now been overhauled, and ample capital has been secured. It is reported a light, popular-priced car will be the product," *The Automobile* announced in March of 1915. Henry Nyberg whose Nyberg automobile had died in Anderson the year previous was ready to try again. This time he allied himself with Cecil Gibson, who had formerly been associated with the Empire from Indianapolis. Their new car, a light six with Rutenber engine, would initially be called the Dolly (sic) Madison, but by 1916 the partners decided that was a bit too cute and shortened it to simply Madison. The Madison Motor Company had been incorporated in 1915 with $500,000 capitalization. In October 1916 it was reorganized as the $2 million Madison Motors Corporation. The money obviously was predominantly on paper, because this venture never did become very well established. In the early spring of 1919 Madison was taken over by the Bull Tractor Company, which announced its intention to manufacture both the tractor and the car in the Bull factory in Minneapolis and the Madison factory in Anderson. When receivership was announced in July of 1920, reference was made that the Anderson plant had been used "only for general repair work" for the last year.

1915 MADISON
Dolly Madison — 6-cyl., 22 hp, 120" wb

	FP	5	4	3	2	1
Touring-7P	1685	3100	4200	6300	10,500	22,000
Touring-5P	985	3200	4300	6500	11,000	23,000
Roadster-2P	985	3200	4300	6500	11,000	23,000

1916 MADISON
Model 6-40 — 6-cyl., 22 hp, 120" wb

	FP	5	4	3	2	1
Touring-7P	1085	3100	4200	6300	10,500	22,000
Touring-5P	985	3200	4300	6500	11,000	23,000
Roadster-2P	985	3200	4300	6500	11,000	23,000
Foreign-Type Tour.	1025	3200	4300	6400	10,800	22,500

1917 Madison, model 5, touring, HAC

1917 MADISON
Model 5 — 6-cyl., 24 hp, 115" wb

	FP	5	4	3	2	1
Touring-5P	1050	3000	4000	6000	9500	21,000
Deluxe Tour.-5P	1150	3100	4200	6300	10,500	22,000

Model 7 — 6-cyl., 24 hp, 124" wb

	FP	5	4	3	2	1
Touring-7P	1150	3200	4300	6500	11,000	23,000
Deluxe Tour.-7P	1250	3300	4400	6700	12,000	24,000

Model 4 — 6-cyl., 24 hp, 120" wb

	FP	5	4	3	2	1
Roadster-4P	—	3200	4300	6500	11,000	23,000

1918 MADISON
Light Six — 24 hp, 115" wb

	FP	5	4	3	2	1
Touring-5P	1485	3000	4000	6000	9500	21,000
Touring-7P	1485	3100	4200	6300	10,500	22,000
Roadster-4P	1485	3200	4300	6500	11,000	23,000

1919 MADISON
Model 6-19 — 24 hp, 115" wb

	FP	5	4	3	2	1
Touring-5P	1550	3100	4200	6300	10,500	22,000

MADSEN — Council Bluffs, Iowa — (1901) — L.P. Madsen of 329 Broadway in Council Bluffs produced an automobile in 1901 noteworthy for two special features. Its fenders, which were hollow, served to carry the cooling water for the engine. And the wood wheels, with reinforced steel-flanged hubs, had a double row of rivets which allowed use of extra high mitered spokes which Madsen claimed could not become loose and which he offered to the trade separate from his vehicle. The Madsen car was a chain-drive 700-pound runabout powered by a two-cylinder 10 hp engine. Though he may have sold his wheels longer, Madsen offered his car for one season only.

MAGIC — The Magic was a sliding-valve engine invented by Swiss engineer Martin Fischer. It saw use in this country in the Mondex Magic car built by the Aristos Company of New York City in 1914-1915. And it was projected to be used in a special model of the Premocar of Birmingham, Alabama in 1921, though it did not see production in that case.

MAGNETIC — Magnetic refers to an electric transmission developed by Justus B. Entz which was utilized in the Owen Magnetic built from 1915 to 1921 in New York City, Cleveland and Wilkes Barre, Pennsylvania. An export version carried the name Crown Magnetic. No cars were ever marketed as simply the Magnetic, however. Refer to Entz and Owen Magnetic.
Magnetic Motor Car Company was a $3 million Delaware incorporation from the fall of 1917 for the manufacture of automobiles. Incorporators were W.S. Randall, F.A. Armstrong and C.M. Egner. Manufacture is doubted.

1903 Magnolia, runabout, NAHC

MAGNOLIA — Riverside, California — (1902-1903) — Around the turn of the century, Watt Moreland was dispatched by his boss in Cleveland, one Alexander Winton, to trek west to California and see to repairs on a Winton automobile owned by a Riverside orange grower. The car wasn't running at all well, and whether Moreland was able to set it right history has not recorded. His efforts, however, attracted the attention of Albert W. Miller, a planing mill operator in Riverside. Miller persuaded Moreland to stay in town and help him in the formation of the Magnolia Automobile Company. Moreland readily agreed. The company was named after the flowering trees which graced the most beautiful boulevard in Riverside. The car was a single-cylinder runabout which, not surprisingly, resembled the Winton. Its price was to be $750. Miller put up the money for a large factory for its production. According to the May 4th, 1903 edition of the *Riverside Daily Press*, the Magnolia appeared on the streets of Riverside for the first time that day. It was the only Magnolia ever produced. A history of the area published in 1915 indicates the reason for the company's failure as the lawsuit brought against it by the holders of the Selden Patent. A mechanic who had worked on the car remembered the matter differently; in the early Fifties he stated that the Magnolia had "flubbed a trial run" when a connecting rod broke and pierced the crankcase. A local carriage maker built two bodies for Magnolia, but apparently only the one car was completed. Albert Miller lost about $28,000 in the venture. The fine factory he had built was later converted into an apartment building. Watt Moreland remained in California. His next two automotive ventures were the Tourist and the Durocar automobiles. Subsequently he enjoyed his greatest success with the Moreland truck which was produced in Burbank until the Second World War.

MAGNOLIA — Magnolia, Minnesota — (c. 1908) — Magnolia was the name given to the third car built by a Magnolia blacksmith named Tom Dean. The precise date of its construction is not known, but Dean's blacksmith shop had produced its first car in 1907, followed quickly by a second, these initial cars bearing the name Minnesota Special. The columnist and radio personality Cedric Adams learned to drive in the Magnolia.

MAGNOLIA — Houston, Texas — (1910-1911) — Gaeton A. Alessandra headed the Magnolia Carriage Company at 310 Austin Street in Houston which in 1910 changed its name to Magnolia Motor Car Company. Apparently, a small production of cars to specific customer order followed, but by 1911 the company changed its name back again to Magnolia Carriage, and automobile building was discontinued.

MAGUIRE — Chicago, Illinois — (1895) — The Maguire Power Generating Company, which had its offices at 709 Masonic Temple in Chicago, entered a vehicle of its design in the 1895 Chicago Times-Herald. The car wasn't completed in time for the event, however, and whether it was ever successfully tested has not been documented.

MAHANA — Poultney, Vermont — (1910) — The automobile invented in 1910 by J.B. Mahana of Poultney used a four-cylinder 16 hp engine that was produced in town and installed in a four-wheel drive chassis of Mahana's own devising. According to the inventor, the Mahana would "plow, harrow, mow, haul loads of three tons, carry the family to the country fair and do other useful things, all at the initial cost of less than $1000." Whether Mahana built more than the one car is not known.

1905 Mahoning, touring, OCW

MAHONING — Youngstown, Ohio — (1904-1905) — W.P. Williamson was part owner of the Youngstown Carriage & Wagon Company and Charles T. Gaither was the mechanical engineer for the Fredonia. In 1904 they interested a man named Mahoning in putting up the money for an automobile factory. The Mahoning Motor Car Company was organized in April with a capital stock of $25,000. Its first car arrived in September. Production began later that year. The Mahoning was offered as a small single-cylinder machine in three body styles at a common $950 price, and a larger four for which the price was not disclosed. The cars were built for one year only. Then the company opted out. Following rumors in December 1905 of

an intention to quit the business, an official statement from Mahoning in January 1906 revealed that "exorbitant demands of labor" was the reason for discontinuation of motorcar manufacture. Charles Gaither acquired control of the patents he had secured with regard to the Mahoning and announced that he would go into business for himself. It does not appear that he did. Among the Mahoning's problems, other than a recalcitrant labor force, might have been the product itself. The four-cylinder model was reportedly so feeble in power that upon approaching any sizable hill all passengers had to disembark and walk, leaving only the driver aboard to make it up the grade.

1904-1905 MAHONING
Mahoning — 1-cyl., 9 hp, 82" wb

	FP	5	4	3	2	1
Side Entrance Tonneau	950	1600	2700	3800	5800	12,000
Stanhope	950	1600	2700	3800	5800	12,000
Delivery Car	950	1500	2500	3600	5500	11,000
Mahoning Four — 24/28 hp, 100" wb						
Touring	—	2300	3300	4600	7500	16,000

MAHS — Detroit, Michigan — (1903-1904) — William H. Mahs was an alderman for the city of Detroit and produced automobiles and bicycles at his shop on 1389 Jefferson Avenue. His total production of the former is not known, but that he began building five cars in October of 1903 has been documented. These vehicles were for a specific purpose, it being Mahs' intention to begin an automobile service around Belle Isle to ferry passengers across the bridge from the city to the island. The cars were large tourers with three seats accommodating nine passengers.

1917 Maibohm, roadster, WLB

MAIBOHM — Racine, Wisconsin & Sandusky, Ohio — (1916-1922) — Peter C. Maibohm was a blacksmith, wagonmaker and real estate man from Racine whose Maibohm Wagon Company had been successfully plying its trade since 1886. His son H.C. Maibohm had worked awhile for Locomobile, and was the man responsible for reorganizing the family business into Maibohm Motors Company in the early spring of 1916. The Maibohm was announced as a four during that summer and was in production by fall. A Falls-engined six joined the line for 1918, and a fire swept through the Racine factory on December 4th that year. Initially continuing manufacture in a small wing which had escaped the conflagration, Maibohm announced plans to rebuild in Racine but decided instead to relocate in Sandusky by the spring of the following year. Production there was up to thirty cars a day by late 1920, but Maibohm was not around to see many of them built. Perhaps had he not chosen to meddle in the affairs of the East Coast company building the Biddle, he might have fared better with his Maibohm in Ohio. Soon after he had helped march Biddle into receivership in New York, however, he returned to Sandusky to find his Maibohm Motors Company in similar straits. In April 1922 he believed he might salvage his operation by acquiring the rights to the former Simplex which earlier had been absorbed into Emlem Hare's aborted automotive empire. But that failed to materialize. In May his creditors bought the Maibohm company for $110,000 and turned it over to Arrow Motors, a new concern which planned to market a refined Maibohm as the Courier. The Courier was introduced for 1923, but failed soon after. H.C. Maibohm meanwhile had gone into the radio manufacturing business.

1916-1917 MAIBOHM
Model A — 4-cyl., 17 hp, 105" wb

	FP	5	4	3	2	1
Roadster-2P	595	3000	4000	6000	9500	21,000
Roadster-Coupe-2P	865	3200	4300	6500	11,000	23,000
Coupe-2P	1095	2500	3500	5000	8500	18,000
1918 MAIBOHM						
Model A — 4-cyl., 17 hp, 105" wb						
Roadster-2P	795	3100	4200	6300	10,500	22,000
Roadster-Coupe-2P	865	3200	4300	6500	11,000	23,000
Coupe-2P	1095	2500	3500	5000	8500	18,000
Model B — 6-cyl., 46 hp, 115" wb						
Touring-4P	975	3200	4300	6500	11,000	23,000
Roadster-2P	975	3300	4400	6700	12,000	24,000
Coupe-2P	1375	2700	3600	5300	8800	19,000
Sedan-4P	1375	2300	3300	4600	7500	16,000
Roadster-Coupe-2P	1095	3500	4500	7000	13,000	25,000
1919 MAIBOHM						
Model B-6 — 6-cyl., 46 hp, 116" wb						
Brougham	1890	2400	3400	4800	8000	17,000
Sedan	1890	2300	3300	4600	7500	16,000
Phaeton	1290	3100	4200	6300	10.500	22,000
1920 MAIBOHM						
Model B-6 — 6-cyl., 46 hp, 116" wb						
Phaeton-5P	1395	3100	4200	6300	10,500	22,000
Brougham-4P	1995	2400	3400	4800	8000	17,000
Sedan-5P	1995	2300	3300	4600	7500	16,000

1921 MAIBOHM
Model B-6 — 6-cyl., 46 hp, 116" wb

	FP	5	4	3	2	1
Phaeton-5P	1575	3100	4200	6300	10,500	22,000
Roadster-3P	1575	3200	4300	6500	11,000	23,000
Sport-4P	1750	3500	4500	7000	13,000	25,000
Coupe-4P	2395	2700	3600	5300	8800	19,000
Sedan-5P	2395	2300	3300	4600	7500	16,000

1922 MAIBOHM
Model B-6 — 6-cyl., 46 hp, 116" wb

	FP	5	4	3	2	1
Phaeton-5P	1395	3200	4300	6500	11,000	23,000
Roadster-3P	1395	3300	4400	6700	12,000	24,000
Sport-4P	1595	3500	4500	7000	13,000	25,000
Coupe-4P	2295	2700	3600	5300	8800	19,000
Sedan-5P	2295	2300	3300	4600	7500	16,000
Sport Roadster-3P	1395	3700	4700	7300	13,700	26,000

MAINE — The Maine Machine Works built a car called the Hartman in Los Angeles, California from 1914-1918. Refer to Hartman.

The Maine Motor Carriage Company was organized in Portland, Maine late in 1903 with a capital stock of $10,000 "to make and deal in carriages of all kinds." Incorporators were A.W. Coombs, C.H. Tolman and S.I. Gould. Manufacture of a car is doubted.

c.1912 Mais, roadster, MVMA

MAIS — Indianapolis, Indiana — (c.1912) — The Mais Motor Truck Company built commercial vehicles in its Indianapolis factory at South LaSalle and the Belt Railroad from 1911 into 1916. Company officers were Charles A. Bookwalter (president), Albert F. Mais (vice-president), A.W. Markham (secretary-treasurer) and Edward Robison (general manager). Mais trucks were variously of 1 1/2-, 2 1/2- and 5-ton capacity, and until recently it had not been thought the company ever strayed into the passenger car field. Apparently, it did, however, even though briefly. A Model engine catalog circa 1912 included a photograph of a Mais roadster, equipped (naturally) with a Model engine. The car had been tested at the Indianapolis Motor Speedway at 57 mph, and had been put to two longer-distance tests: Indianapolis to Cleveland (350 miles in 12-1/2 hours) and Cleveland to Buffalo and return (380 miles). How many of these cars were produced is not known. In 1916 the Mais company was taken over by Premier.

MAJA — The Maja has frequently been cited on American car rosters, but it was never produced here. It was built in Austria at the Austro-Daimler factory, and was named after the younger daughter of Emil Jellinek, a wealthy European who had earlier persuaded the Daimler company to build a high-performance sporting car that he named after his elder daughter Mercedes. The Maja was produced in Austria for two years only, 1907-1908, and a very few may have been imported into this country. Many more Mercedes arrived on this shores, of course, and that car was in production in the United States as the American Mercedes from 1905 until a fire destroyed its plant in 1907.

MAJERUS — Goodhue, Minnesota — (1909) — "J.B. Majerus ... is building a motor-propelled road wagon," reported *The Horseless Age* in January 1909. Details are lacking.

MAJESTIC — The Majestic Automobile Company was organized in New York City during the summer of 1905 with a capital stock of $5000 for the manufacture of automobiles. George H. Mulligan and William J. Greene were the partners involved. Manufacture is doubted.

MAJESTIC — Milwaukee, Wisconsin — (1909) — Announcement of the completion of the prototype of its new six-cylinder car to be called the Majestic was made by the Milwaukee Auto and Engine Supply Company in October of 1909. According to the *Motor Age* that month, the company intended to enter into manufacture on a large scale "as soon as it can obtain larger quarters, for which it is now negotiating." The firm was then located at 706-708 Winnebago Street in Milwaukee, and it remained there for the two years following. Roster indications that the Majestic was built through 1911 appear to be in error. Perhaps a few cars were built, but Milwaukee Auto Engine and Supply most likely continued predominantly with auto engines and supplies.

MAJESTIC — Chicago, Illinois — (1916) — The Majestic Motor Car Company of Chicago produced a four-cylinder 30 hp touring car at $1075 and a 45 hp six at $1530 — but not for long. The car was mentioned and described in the annual automobile edition of *Scientific American* in January 1916. It appeared at the Chicago Automobile Show and maybe a few others. In August 1916, when receivership arrived, mismanagement was given as the reason for the company's failure.

1917 Majestic, landau touring, WLB

MAJESTIC — New York, New York — (1917) — This venture began as the Monitor Motor Company, Inc., the name change to Majestic Motor Company, Inc. following the decision to make the product a little grander. The firm was located at 1790 Broadway in New York City, and Harry Kitzinger, Frank A. Kateley, Samuel Fein and Max Monfried were the men behind it. Kateley was the only one of them with automobile experience, having previously been sales manager for the Remington Motor Company. The new Majestic had a V-8 engine, 125-inch wheelbase, and was offered in four body styles priced from $1650 to $3500. The more expensive models included as standard equipment such niceties as a folding table, lunch boxes, a custom-built thermos bottle and vacuum ice box. The Majestic also enjoyed one of the most pretentious pieces of promotion in the history of the American automobile. "The subtle element of personal charm is so strong in these designs that no description can convey a fair impression," the catalog read. Unfortunately, the catalog also included illustrations. The Majestic was a completely ordinary looking car with a Fiat-like radiator; its charm was obviously too subtle, and a custom-built thermos bottle was not sufficient inducement to buy. The car was first shown at the New York Automobile Show in January 1917. It did not survive the year.

1917 MAJESTIC
Eight — 125" wb

	FP	5	4	3	2	1
Touring-7P	1650	4200	5200	8400	15,700	29,000
Club Rdstr.	1650	4300	5300	8600	16,100	29,500
Stuyvesant Vict.	2500	2700	3600	5300	8800	19,000
Conv. Tour. Sed.	3500	4000	5000	8000	15,000	28,000

1926 Majestic, taxi, NAHC

MAJESTIC — Binghamton, New York — (1925-1927) — The Majestic was a Buda-engined taxicab and the only passenger car produced by the Larrabee-Deyo Motor Truck Company of Binghamton. These taxis, which were quite attractive, were destined for service in New York City, and several hundred were built. Larrabee trucks were manufactured from 1916 into 1932.

MALCOLM — The Malcolm Motor Car Company was organized in Philadelphia, Pennsylvania during the spring of 1916 with a $1 million capital stock to manufacture passenger cars and trucks. Incorporators were F.D. Buck, G.H. Dillman and M.L. Horty. Manufacture is doubted.

MALCOLM — Oxford, Michigan — (1900) — C.P. Malcolm & Company manufactured two-stroke gasoline engines in Oxford which were claimed to provide twice the horsepower of a similarly-sized four-stroke and which were "more reliable under an overload than any other." Units of one, two and four cylinders were produced, with horsepower ranging from 2-1/2 to 12. In 1900 Malcolm offered an automobile as well, in three models: a runabout fitted with the company's 5 hp twin, and two light touring cars, a two-seater and a three-seater, powered by an 8 hp twin. Prices ranged from $800 to $1000. The cars were produced for one season only.

1914 Malcolm, runabout, NAHC

MALCOLM — Detroit, Michigan — (1914-1915) — In late November of 1913 the Malcolm-Jones Cyclecar Company was launched into business as the thirtieth new venture in the United States organized to produce a cyclecar. Stockholders included E. Malcolm Jones, C.H. Lawrence and Charles H. Bennett. Their product was to be a two-cylinder tandem two-seater with provision for a third passenger if desired and a single headlight mounted atop the radiator. The price was projected as $395. Only prototypes were built. During the summer of 1914 there was an interim attempt to reorganize as the Malcolm Cyclecar Company and move to another factory in Plymouth, Michigan. Ultimately, however, the decision was made to remain in Detroit and reorganize as the Malcolm Motor Company, since the very word "cyclecar" by now had a negative connotation. For 1915 the Messrs. Jones, Lawrence and Bennett provided their earlier car with two headlights, two more cylinders, a longer wheelbase, and shaft drive instead of the former belt. This Malcolm was called a light roadster, and its price was $425. Memories in Detroit, unfortunately, were not quite as short as the Malcolm people might have wished them to be.

1914 MALCOLM
Cyclecar — 2-cyl., 10/15 hp, 100" wb

	FP	5	4	3	2	1
Roadster	395	2000	3000	4200	6500	14,000

1915 MALCOLM
Four — 18 hp, 106" wb

Roadster	425	2200	3200	4400	7000	15,000

MALCOLMSON — Detroit, Michigan — (1905-1906) — "Hotter than sunshine" was one of the slogans of Alexander Young Malcolmson. He was a coal merchant by trade and so successful in that endeavor that he had the resources to invest substantially in the borning automobile industry. An enthusiast of the automobile since his purchase of a Winton at the turn of the century, Malcolmson is remembered today for his early backing of a maverick automobile builder in Detroit by the name of Henry Ford. Without Malcolmson, there might never have been a production car called the Ford; he had faith in Henry when very few other people did. In 1905 Malcolmson again decided to invest substantially in the automobile industry. Initially, this new car was announced as a Malcolmson. By the time the production version arrived on the market in 1906, however, its name had been changed to Aerocar.

1902 Malden Steamer, runabout, NAHC

MALDEN STEAM — Malden, Massachusetts — (1898/1902) — Although the Malden Automobile Company of Middlesex Court in Malden built its first experimental steam car in 1898, it does not appear the car was marketed until 1902. Among the features claimed for the Malden were a pilot light guaranteed not to burn out and a gasoline tank which could be filled "while the fire is burning." The automatic boiler was fitted with a "fusible plug" also guaranteed not to burn out. Speeds of up to 40 mph were promised. Whether the Malden delivered on all this is very much open to question. What cannot be disputed is that the firm was taken over by the Lynn Automobile Company of Lynn, Massachusetts in early 1903.

1900 Malden Steamer, runabout, FR

MALLEY — The Malley Motor Company was organized in New York City during the spring of 1910 with a capital stock of $500 to manufacture and repair motor vehicles. Thomas Malley of Brooklyn, and W.H. Pumphrey and M.G. Crawford of Manhattan, were the incorporators. Manufacture of a car is doubted.

The Malley Motor Vehicle Company was organized in Boston, Massachusetts during the summer of 1911 with a capital stock of $50,000 to manufacture and deal in automobiles. Manufacture is doubted, but the firm subsequently became dealers for the Warren and the Flanders Electric.

1901 Maltby Gasoline Runabout, NAHC

MALTBY — Brooklyn, New York — (1900-1901)/Matawan, New Jersey — (1901-1902) — Frank D. Maltby was a trick cycle rider who moved into the bicycle business at 10-12 Clinton Street in Brooklyn during the 1890's and at the turn of the century took up the automobile, initially serving as a storage and charging station for electrics and as a dealership for the Mobile steamer. His new Maltby Automobile & Motor Company became a manufacturer later in 1900 following a grand million-dollar incorporation. The new Maltby was a light wire-wheeled buggy with two-cylinder 4 hp engine and right-hand tiller steering. The Maltby gasoline engine was offered for sale independently, and Frank Maltby also offered to produce "any style of carriage built to order" from an owner's drawings. C.C. Hoge, C.A. Mackenzie, P.R. Brooks and E.L. Maltby were among the people involved with Frank Maltby in this venture, and they seem not to have been able to agree on anything. During 1901 the company was described as "wracked with internal dissension" — and later that year Frank Maltby reincorporated with a much more modest capital stock of $20,000 and moved to Matawan, New Jersey. A few Maltby cars were built in Matawan in 1902, but by year's end Frank Maltby had decided to continue in business as an automobile dealer only.

MALTERNER — Canton, New York — (1903) — The first automobile seen on the streets of Canton in Upstate New York was a steamer built by Silas Malterner in 1903. "While it cannot be said that he has built every part of it himself," the local paper reported, "he has, nevertheless done the most important portions and now has the machine perfect and in use." An engine maker, Malterner did most of the work on the gasoline-fueled 8 hp steam unit himself. The boiler was a Salamandrine. The car was tested successfully at speeds of up to 20 mph. "Mr. Malterner has perfected arrangements so that when passing teams the steam exhaust goes through the water tank, thus practically avoiding any noise in the exhaust," the newspaper said. This was the only automobile built by Silas Malterner who remained a resident of Canton until his death into his late eighties.

MANEXALL — The Manexall of 1920 was a $475 longer-wheelbase version of the Cyclomobile built in Toledo. Its name was derived from Manufacturers' & Exporters' Alliance, Inc., the New York City company at 438 Broadway which was to handle distribution of both the Cyclomobile and the Manexall. Refer to Cyclomobile.

MANHATTAN — The Manhattan High Powered Car Company was organized in New York City during the spring of 1908 with a capital stock of $300,000 for the manufacture of automobiles. F.W. Barker, J.F. Brandenburg and F.C. Bonney were the incorporators. Manufacture is doubted.

MANHATTAN — **New York, New York** — **(1901)** — During the late fall of 1900, the Manhattan Automobile Company was organized by J. Overton Paine, James A. Hands and Arthur B. Paine. The capital stock was $150,000, and the ambitious idea was both the manufacture of electric vehicles and the operation of electric motor bus lines. Things did not work out as planned. The company did produce a few light $1200 electric runabouts, said to resemble the well-known Baker and the construction for which was contracted out to a factory in Jersey City. The Manhattan Automobile Company was soon attached by creditors, however, and in October of 1901 the firm's building at 502 West 38th Street was ordered sold. The price realized was $5500 of which $2000 went to pay off creditors. The new owner of the Manhattan building was another automotive entrepreneur with plans to build a gasoline car called the Stratton.

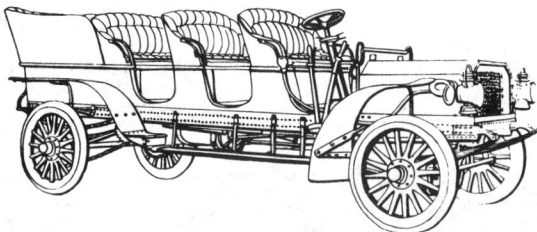

1904 Manhattan, touring bus, NAHC

MANHATTAN — **Brooklyn, New York** — **(1903-1904)** — Prior to the turn of the century, the wagon-building Mack Brothers of Brooklyn purportedly put together a steam car (in 1894) and an electric (in 1896). By 1903 the Mack Brothers Company was in the automotive repair and rebuilding field, and from its shops at 532-540 Atlantic Avenue emanated a number of vehicles called Manhattan. These the Mack Brothers built in "Wagonette, Tonneau or Tally-ho type" — and although, properly, they might have been called buses, the brothers tended to refer to them as "Big Cars," and the automotive press went along with them. "The Mack Brothers Company enjoy the distinction of showing the largest gasoline pleasure car at the show," *The Automobile* reported in January 1904 following the event at Madison Square Garden, "the passenger capacity being seventeen, two seats being arranged across the car, with a double tonneau at the back." Mack offered these vehicles in passenger-carrying capacities of from ten to thirty, though the company could be flexible. "As we build them to order only we can give you just what you want," the brothers advertised. "Tell us what you want and we will let you know what it will cost." By 1905 Mack Brothers moved to Allentown, Pennsylvania where the first Mack-built truck was constructed. The tradename Manhattan was continued awhile, but by 1911 all products of the Mack Brothers were called Macks.

MANHEIM — **Manheim, Pennsylvania** — **(1902)** — The Manheim Automobile Company in Pennsylvania was not in the automobile business long, but in 1902 is known to have marketed a high-wheeled electric stanhope equipped with a "Porter No. 19 battery and a recharging motor."

1902 Manistee runabout, LC

MANISTEE — **Manistee, Michigan** — **(1902)** — Otto and Henry Brugman operated a jewelry, gun and bicycle shop at 344 River Street in Manistee and in 1899 began construction of an automobile which was completed in 1902. The brothers called it the Manistee. Powered by a single-cylinder engine located under the seat, the vehicle was started by a crank at the side. The car ran, and apparently ran well, because the brothers thereafter built a number of others for local residents. According to Otto Brugman's son, G.E. Brugman, these additional cars were not built at the family business but instead "at a different location known as the American Garage & Motor Company and finally at a manufacturing plant situated at River and Smith streets in Manistee." The Brugman brothers' Manistee should not be confused, incidentally, with the cyclecar built a decade later in that city by the Manistee Auto Company. That car was sold under the tradename of Autoette.

MANKATO — From 1908 to 1913, the Four Traction Automobile Company built automobiles in Mankato, Minnesota. Most of these vehicles were marketed under the tradename of Kato. Refer to Kato.

1910 Manlius, roadster, NAHC

MANLIUS — **Manlius, New York** — **(1910)** — Very little is known about the Manlius Motor Company of Manlius except that it was organized during the summer of 1909 in Syracuse by G.A. Fowler, M.J. Topp and W.H. Topp. Capital stock was $20,000. The Manlius car arrived for the 1910 model year. The Messrs, Fowler, Topp and Topp must have been sporting blades. Only two models were offered: a two-cylinder 12 hp rumble-seat runabout on a 86-inch wheelbase at $725 and a four-cylinder 28 hp two-passenger roadster on a 108-inch wheelbase at $1250. Both cars featured shaft drive, but the runabout had a planetary transmission, while the roadster had selective sliding gear. The Manlius did not survive into 1911. Occasionally it was referred to by its initials, M.M.C.

MANN — **Gladbrook, Iowa** — **(1895)** — Lee Count Mann was a school teacher in Gladbrook. He was also a partner with his brother Thomas Erly Mann in the manufacture and sale of printing presses. He dabbled in the oil business and in horseless carriages too, building an internal combustion engine of his own design, and an automobile. His letters to *The Horseless Age* regarding his car indicate that among the subjects he taught in school one must have been English. His grammar was excellent. Most probably, his car was not. He never ventured into automobile manufacture.

MANNING — **Lewiston, Maine** — **(1901)** — That George Manning of Lewiston had "already made one automobile [and] is now at work on two more" was reported in the May 1901 issue of *The Motor Age*. Manning, who operated a local machine shop, did not proceed into formal manufacture, however.

1932 Manning, midget, NAHC

MANNING — **Lockport, Illinois** — **(1932)** — This midget car was the work of Don Manning of Lockport, most of its parts courtesy of an Overland Model 91. The complete vehicle weighed 1275 pounds, its wheelbase was 61 inches, its tread 40 inches. "It is said to be sufficiently roomy for two persons, although much, probably, would depend upon the size of the persons," reported *Automobile Trade Journal* in February 1932.

MANROSS — Bristol, Connecticut — (1908) — In 1908 Frederick New-ton Manross, with the assistance of his son Robert, built a gasoline touring runabout for his own use. In a photo caption appearing in the *Bristol Press* of March 29th, 1908, reference is made to the fact that this was the fifth machine built by Manross. Conceivably this total included the Bristol and Law cars which had earlier been produced and promoted by Manross.

MANSEN — The Mansen Motor Company was a million-dollar Maine incorporation from the fall of 1916 for the purpose of "manufacturing, exporting and importing automobiles and motor trucks." Ernest O. Hiler was president, Howard F. Kingsley treasurer. Manufacture is doubted.

MANSFIELD — Although for a short period late in 1901, the Mansfield Motor Company was the designation for the venture which had begun as the Beardsley & Hubbs Manufacturing Company, no cars were ever produced under that name. Instead the cars were called Darling in Mansfield, Ohio — and were joined in 1903 by the Shelby in Shelby, Ohio. Refer to Darling and Shelby.

MANSURY & SMITH — In 1903 Raymond Goodrich built a steam car in the Hartford, Connecticut factory of Mansury & Smith. Refer to Goodrich.

MANTON STEAM — Providence, Rhode Island — (1866) — A steam car was built by Joseph P. Manton of Providence in 1866. Its top speed was 15 mph, and Manton used the vehicle for several months, long enough to prove his point that it was a feasible mode of transport, though not very efficient. Coal stored under the seat of the vehicle was its energy source, which made the carriage very heavy and short runs the only possibility. "Insurmountable fuel arrangements, which precluded the carriage from being practical for everyday use" was the way Manton put it.

1907 Maplebay, runabout, NAHC

MAPLEBAY — Crookston, Minnesota — (1907) — The Maplebay-Wind-stacker Company was an implement-manufacturing firm in Crookston. In 1907 the company produced a runabout with a four-cylinder 22 hp air-cooled Reeves engine, friction transmission, wheel steering and runabout body with a quite-long hood. According to *The Horseless Age*, experimen-tation had begun in December of '06; *Motor World* announced in July 1907 that the first car had been completed, and several others were underway. Whether they were ever finished is not known. In April of 1908, the *Crookston Daily Times* noted the visit to town of several North Dako-tans to look over the car "made last year" by the Maplebay-Windstaker Company. Possibly the first Maplebay was also the last.

MAPLE LEAF — The Maple Leaf Electric Automobile & Manufacturing Company has been indicated on various car rosters as the producer of an automobile in London, Connecticut in 1905. This does not appear to be the case. A company of that name was incorporated that year, one refer-ence indicating a capital stock of $5000 and London, Connecticut — and another indicating a $50,000 capital stock, a London, Ontario location, and a plan to build "electrical appliances, dynamos and engines" only.

MARATHON — The Marathon was planned as an export version of the Crow-Elkhart, but its name was quickly changed after an English automo-bile agent named F.E. Morriss contracted with the Crow-Elkhart company for a large order. The cars were built circa 1919-1920. Refer to Morriss-London.

1909 Marathon, model C, roadster, NAHC

MARATHON — Jackson & Nashville, Tennessee — (1908-1914) — The Marathon was a medium-priced four sold in several different horsepower sizes and chassis lengths and at least a half-dozen different body styles. It was a conventional motorcar, deviating interestingly only in its latter-day use of the engine's flywheel to serve as an oil pump. The Marathon was originally produced by Southern Motor Works of Jackson (occasionally the car was referred to as a Southern as well), but in 1910 the company became Marathon Motor Works soon after its move to Nashville. This relo-cation allowed the nice promotional touch of using a photograph of Nash-ville's famous architectural re-creation of the Greek Parthenon in the Mar-athon catalog together with references to Athenian supremacy and the historic relevance of the word Marathon in Olympiad history. None of this served the company well in the sales market, though. Marathon was declared bankrupt in early summer 1914, a situation it initially tried to fight. Before the year ended, however, the fight was over and Herff-Brooks of Indianapolis, which had both sold and produced some cars for the Mar-athon company, took over and built a Marathon-like car of its own called the Herff-Brooks in Indiana for a couple of years.

1908-1909 MARATHON
Model C — 4-cyl., 30/35 hp, 108" wb

	FP	5	4	3	2	1
Touring-5P	1500	2400	3400	4800	8000	17,000
Tourabout-4P	1500	2500	3500	5000	8500	18,000
Roadster-3/4P	1500	2700	3600	5300	8800	19,000

1910 Marathon, model M-10, touring, HAC

1910 MARATHON
Four — 30 hp, 112" wb

Model M-10 Tour.	1500	2500	3500	5000	8500	18,000
Model L-10 Rdstr.	1500	2700	3600	5300	8800	19,000

1911 Marathon Four, touring, HAC

1911 MARATHON
Four — 35 hp, 116" wb

Touring	1500	2700	3600	5300	8800	19,000
Roadster	1500	2900	3700	5600	9100	20,000
Fore-Door Tour.	1550	3000	4000	6000	9500	21,000
Torpedo Rdstr.	1500	3200	4300	6500	11,000	23,000
Torpedo Tour. (120" wb)	1700	3500	4500	7000	13,000	25,000

1912 Marathon, model M-40, roadster, HAC

1912 MARATHON
Model K-20 — 4-cyl., 20 hp

Roadster (90" wb)	685	3100	4200	6300	10,500	22,000
Fore-Door Rdstr. (96" wb)	850	3200	4300	6500	11,000	23,000

Model L-30 — 4-cyl., 30 hp, 116" wb

	FP	5	4	3	2	1
Fore-Door Tour.	1200	3200	4300	6500	11,000	23,000
Torpedo Rdstr.	1000	3300	4400	6700	12,000	24,000

Model M-40 — 4-cyl., 35 hp, 120" wb

Torpedo	1600	3300	4400	6700	12,000	24,000
Fore-Door Tour.	1500	3500	4500	7000	13,000	25,000
Roadster	1400	3700	4700	7300	13,700	26,000

Model N-50 — 4-cyl., 45 hp, 123½" wb

Fore-Door Tour.	1800	3500	4500	7000	13,000	25,000
Roadster	1800	3700	4700	7300	13,700	26,000
Limousine	2000	2700	3600	5300	8800	19,000

1913 Marathon Runner, roadster, HAC

1913 MARATHON
Runner Series — 4-cyl., 25 hp, 104" wb

Light Delivery	850	2400	3400	4800	8000	17,000
Roadster-2P	875	3200	4300	6500	11,000	23,000
Touring-5P	950	3100	4200	6300	10,500	22,000
Coupe-2P	1050	2700	3600	5300	8800	19,000

Winner Series — 4-cyl., 35 hp, 116" wb

Roadster-2P	1275	3300	4400	6700	12,000	24,000
Touring-5P	1350	3200	4300	6500	11,000	23,000
Coupe-3P	1600	2800	3700	5500	9000	19,500

Champion Series — 4-cyl., 45 hp, 123" wb

Roadster-2P	1675	3500	4500	7000	13,000	25,000
Touring-5P	1750	3300	4400	6700	12,000	24,000
Touring-7P	1800	3200	4300	6500	11,000	23,000

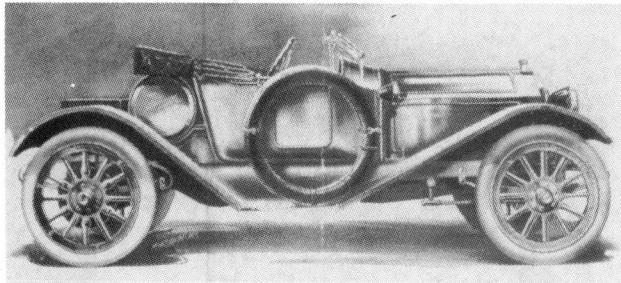

1914 Marathon Champion, roadster, HAC

1914 MARATHON
Runner Series — 4-cyl., 25 hp, 106" wb

Touring	975	3100	4200	6300	10,500	22,000
Roadster	925	3200	4300	6500	11,000	23,000

Winner Series — 4-cyl., 35 hp, 118" wb

Touring	1325	3200	4300	6500	11,000	23,000
Roadster	1300	3400	4400	6700	12,000	24,000

Champion Series — 4-cyl., 45 hp, 123" wb

Touring	1495	3300	4400	6700	12,000	24,000
Roadster	1470	3500	4500	7000	13,000	25,000

MARATHON SIX — Cincinnati, Ohio — (1909) — The Marathon Six was the first automobile built by an enthusiast named Powel W. Crosley, Jr. It was slated to be an inexpensive car on a 114-inch wheelbase. A prototype was completed, and the Marathon Automobile Company was casually organized. About six orders were taken, which may or may not have been filled. The company was quickly bankrupt. Powel Crosley tried again in 1913 with the DeCross cyclecar which survived no longer. Thereafter he ventured into the radio and refrigerator businesses, and made a fortune. His third automobile, the Crosley, was introduced in 1939. It enjoyed a considerable success.

MARBLE-SWIFT — Chicago, Illinois — (1903-1905) — "The Marble-Swift Automobile Company . . . are establishing themselves in a new factory having a floor space of 12,000 square feet, and are putting through 100 rigs," *The Horseless Age* announced in July of 1903. The Marble of the partnership was George W., who previously had manufactured wood rims in Plymouth, Indiana but who had earlier sold out to the American Bicycle Company. The Swift was George P., a mechanic from the Windy City. Together they had come up with a friction transmission described by *Motor Age* as consisting "of two large metal disks attached to short cross

1904 Marble-Swift, runabout, WLB

shafts attached to the frame, each of which carries a driving sprocket." Initially, they had considered manufacture of this transmission gear only, but ultimately they chose to produce an entire motorcar. From 1903-1904, the Marble-Swift was a two-cylinder 16 hp runabout on an 83-inch wheelbase selling for $1050; for 1905 it became an 18/22 hp four on a 90-inch wheelbase with a $1500 price tag. By August of 1905 the Marble-Swift Automobile Company had been succeeded by the Windsor Motor Car Company.

1903-1904 MARBLE-SWIFT
Two — 16 hp, 83" wb

	FP	5	4	3	2	1
Runabout-2P	1050	2000	3000	4200	6500	14,000

1905 MARBLE-SWIFT
Four — 18/22 hp, 90" wb

Touring-5P	1500	2200	3200	4400	7000	15,000

MARINETTE — In late 1907 the Marinette Iron Manufacturing Company of Marinette, Wisconsin announced its plans to enter the automobile manufacturing business. Harry Thayer was the man behind this venture. Refer to Thayer-Isham.

MARION — Marion, Ohio — (1901) — In May of 1901 the Marion Automobile Company announced that it had four automobiles under construction: one electric, two steamers and one gasoline car. Apparently, none of these proved very satisfactory because manufacture was never embarked upon. The Marion Automobile Company remained in business, however. City directories indicate that in 1905 Fred S. Titus was proprietor and the business was "garage, repairs, automobiles, supplies and electric charging." In 1907 H.T. Love was proprietor and the business remained the same, likewise in 1910 though ownership had once again changed, to Willis and W.C. Kenable.

1904-05 Marion Four, tonneau, HAC

MARION — Indianapolis, Indiana — (1904-1915)/MARION-HANDLEY — Jackson, Michigan — (1916-1918) — "The Car That Has Set Men to Thinking" was a Marion slogan. Early purchasers might have thought about the resemblance the Marion bore to the Premier being built across town in Indianapolis, or the Franklin built in Syracuse. Like those cars, the Marion was air-cooled, initially by a four-cylinder 16 hp unit from Reeves. Later, water-cooled models were added. A special straight-eight race car called the Comet was built in the Marion shops in 1904, and George Schebler used a Marion chassis to build a V-12 roadster in 1908, but the best-known sporting car from Marion was the Bobcat roadster of 1913, a rakish machine. What the people behind the Marion Motor Car Company, which was organized in January 1904, had to think about mostly was staying in business. And this was not easy, the firm having been badly undercapitalized. Early alumni of the Marion venture later went on, with varying degrees of success, to build their own cars — Robert Hassler, Fred Tone and Harry C. Stutz among them — as Marion struggled on vainly attempting to make ends meet. In June of 1912, according to *Motor Field*, the problem of undercapitalization ostensibly had been solved with a reorganization which raised capital stock from $100,000 to $1,125,000 and put J.I. Handley into the Marion presidency. Handley was also president of the American Motors Company in Indianapolis, builders of the American Underslung. In 1914 the Standard Brass Foundry attempted to block the sale of the Marion company to Handley by suing for a $4000 judgment and appointment of a receiver, but Handley won out by November and purchased the assets of the Marion company for $120,000. John North Willys, who had bought a controlling interest in Marion in 1909 and whose Willys-Overland company had handled Marion sales through 1910, was now out completely. In December 1914 Handley organized Mutual Motors Corporation, acquired Imperial of Jackson, Michigan, and moved the Marion to Jackson as well. The cars remained independent, however, each marketed through its own sales organization. The Imperial was discontinued by the end of 1915. The Marion-Handley, as it was now called, struggled on for a few more years. By now it was a typical assembled car, fitted with a Continental six-cylinder engine. In October of 1917 there was a report that Mutual Motors was planning to reorganize. In January 1919 *Motor Age* noted that the company was "believed out of business." That it was; the Jackson plant had gone to the auction block in February 1918. It brought $212,000.

1904-1905 MARION
Four — 16 hp, 96" wb

	FP	5	4	3	2	1
Side Entrance Detachable Tonneau	1500	2400	3400	4800	8000	17,000

1906 Marion, model 5, touring, HAC

1906 MARION
Model 2 — 4-cyl., 16 hp, 96" wb

	FP	5	4	3	2	1
Touring-5P	1500	2500	3500	5000	8500	18,000

Model 5 — 4-cyl., 28 hp, 108" wb

	FP	5	4	3	2	1
Touring-5P	2500	2700	3600	5300	8800	19,000

1907 Marion, model 7, touring, JAC

1907 MARION
Model 7 — 4-cyl., 22/24 hp, 100" wb

	FP	5	4	3	2	1
Runabout-2P	2000	2400	3400	4800	8000	17,000
Touring-5P.	3000	—	—	—	—	—

1908 Marion, model 8, runabout, HAC

1908 MARION
Model 8 — 4-cyl., 22/24 hp, 104" wb

	FP	5	4	3	2	1
Roadster	2250	2500	3500	5000	8500	18,000

Model 9 — 6-cyl., 30/35 hp, 104" wb

	FP	5	4	3	2	1
Roadster	2750	2700	3600	5300	8800	19,000

1909 Marion, model 9, Flyer, touring, HAC

1909 MARION
Model 8 — 4-cyl., 24 hp, 102" wb

	FP	5	4	3	2	1
Touring-4P	2250	3000	4000	6000	9500	21,000
Roadster-2/3P	2250	3100	4200	6300	10,500	22,000

Model 9 — 4-cyl., 32/35 hp, 112" wb

	FP	5	4	3	2	1
Flyer Touring-5P	1850	3100	4200	6300	10,500	22,000
Flyer Toy Tonneau	1850	3000	4000	6000	9500	21,000

1910 Marion, model 10, Flyer, touring, HAC

1910 MARION
Model 10 — 4-cyl., 35 hp, 112" wb

	FP	5	4	3	2	1
Touring-5P	1850	3200	4300	6500	11,000	23,000
Close-Coupled-4P	1850	3000	4000	6000	9500	21,000

1911 Marion, model 40, coupe, JAC

1911 MARION
Model 30 — 4-cyl., 30 hp, 110" wb

	FP	5	4	3	2	1
Model A Roadster	1000	3200	4300	6500	11,000	23,000
Model B Torpedo	1050	3100	4200	6300	10,500	22,000
Model C Touring	1150	3000	4000	6000	9500	21,000
Model D Fore-Door Touring	1200	3200	4300	6500	11,000	23,000

Model 40 — 4-cyl., 40 hp, 115" wb

	FP	5	4	3	2	1
Roadster	1600	3300	4400	6700	12,000	24,000
Touring-4P	1600	3200	4300	6500	11,000	23,000
Torpedo	1650	3200	4300	6500	11,000	23,000

	FP	5	4	3	2	1
Touring-5P	1650	3300	4400	6700	12,000	24,000
Coupe	2000	2800	3700	5500	9000	19,500
Limousine	2500	3000	4000	6000	9500	21,000
Fore-Dr. Touring (118" wb)	1700	3500	4500	7000	13,000	25,000

1912 Marion, model 33, roadster, WLB

1912 MARION
Four — 30 hp, 111" wb

	FP	5	4	3	2	1
Model 33 Roadster-2P	1150	3300	4400	6700	12,000	24,000
Model 35 Touring-5P	1285	3200	4300	6500	11,000	23,000

Four — 45 hp, 120" wb

Model 46 Torpedo Roadster	1750	3500	4500	7000	13,000	25,000
Model 47 Touring-4P	1750	3300	4400	6700	12,000	24,000
Model 48 Touring-5P	1750	3200	4300	6500	11,000	23,000

1913 Marion, model 48-A, touring, HAC

1913 MARION
Model 37-A — 4-cyl., 30/40 hp, 112" wb

	FP	5	4	3	2	1
Bobcat Roadster-2P	1425	4000	5000	8000	15,000	28,000
Touring-5P	1475	3700	4700	7300	13,700	26,000
Fore-Door Roadster	1475	3900	4800	7700	14,300	27,000

Model 48-A — 4-cyl., 48 hp, 120" wb

Touring-5P	1850	4000	5000	8000	15,000	28,000

1914-15 Marion, model G, touring, HAC

1914 MARION
Model B — 4-cyl., 25.6 hp, 117" wb

	FP	5	4	3	2	1
Touring-5P	1650	3900	4800	7700	14,300	27,000
Roadster-2P	1650	4000	5000	8000	15,000	28,000
Coupe-4P	2150	2500	3500	5000	8500	18,000

Model G — 6-cyl., 33.7 hp, 124" wb

Touring-5P	2150	4000	5000	8000	15,000	28,000
Roadster-2P	2150	4200	5200	8400	15,700	29,000
Coupe-4P	2650	2700	3600	5300	8800	19,000
Sedan-5P	2950	2400	3400	4800	8000	17,000

884

1915 MARION
Model G — 6-cyl., 33.7 hp, 124" wb

	FP	5	4	3	2	1
Touring-5P	2150	4300	5400	8700	16,500	30,000
Roadster-2P	2150	4500	5800	9500	18,000	32,000
Coupe-4P	2650	2700	3600	5300	8800	19,000
Sedan-5P	2950	2400	3400	4800	8000	17,000

1916 MARION-HANDLEY
Model K — 6-cyl., 21.6 hp, 120" wb

Touring-5P	1090	4400	5600	9200	17,300	31,000
Roadster-2P	1090	4500	5800	9500	18,000	32,000

1917 Marion-Handley, Six-60, touring roadster, WLB

1917 MARION-HANDLEY
Model 6-40 — 6-cyl., 23.44 hp, 120" wb

	FP	5	4	3	2	1
Touring-7P	1275	4700	6100	9900	19,000	33,000
Roadster-4P	1275	5000	6500	11,000	22,000	35,000

Model 6-60 — 6-cyl., 29.4 hp, 125" wb

Touring-7P	1575	5000	6500	11,000	22,000	35,000
Touring Roadster-4P	1575	5300	7000	11,500	24,000	37,000

1918 MARION-HANDLEY
Model 6-60 — 6-cyl., 29.4 hp, 125" wb

Touring-7P	1575	5200	6800	11,300	23,000	36,000

MARION FLYER — Marion, Indiana — (1910) — John I. Rennaker, Charles Rennaker and Clifford G. Rust were the men behind the Marion Flyer, which was a simple motorized buggy that these gentlemen hoped the people of Marion, Indiana would go for. "Invitations are to be extended to the public of Marion to invest in the Marion Automobile & Manufacturing Company" reported *The Motor World* in February 1910. It would seem that sufficient invitations were not accepted. The Messrs. Rennaker, Rennaker and Rust leased quarters in a livery at Third and Nebraska streets in town, but this venture went no further than that. The Marion company in Indianapolis used the designation Flyer on some of its models as well, which is probably the reason this car has appeared to have a longer life on some automotive rosters.

MARK — That Harry J. Mark of New York City built an electric car in 1902 has been indicated on various car rosters. This has not been confirmed. City directories for the turn-of-the-century period do not note a Harry J. Mark as being a New York City resident.

MARKERT — F.G.R. Markert of Mount Healthy, Ohio was indicated to be a manufacturer of automobiles in his shop on Main Street, according to the 1906 Ware yearbook of the industry. Documentation is lacking.

MARKLE — The L. Markle Company was organized in Springfield Illinois during the fall of 1913 with a capital stock of $40,000 for the manufacture of motor vehicles, parts and accessories. Incorporators were E.C. Wetten, J.E. Rommell and H.M. Doyle. Manufacture of a car is doubted.

MARKOWSKY — The Markowsky Inventions Company was organized in Newark, New Jersey early in 1910 with a $50,000 capital stock for the manufacture of "automobiles, motor vehicles, mechanical devices, etc." Incorporators were W.M. Brown and H.C. Beecher of Newark, and Alfred Markowsky of Jersey City. Manufacture of a car is doubted.

MARLBORO — Marlboro, Massachusetts — (1900-1903) — In March of 1900 the Marlboro Automobile & Carriage Company announced the completion of its first automobile. Initially, president Orrin P. Walker named it after himself, but upon proceeding into manufacture several months later he decided to call his car by his company's name. The Marlboro was fitted with a Mason engine, seamless steel copper tube boiler, automatic pressure regulator, tubular running gear, full elliptic spring, and single chain drive. In two-passenger form, its wheelbase was 62 inches, in four passenger 67 inches. The price range was $700-$1000. By January of 1901 Walker had built and sold thirty of his steam cars, and perhaps ambition overrode him. He stepped up production and in July of 1902 regretfully announced that he had accumulated a "stock of cars" and had temporarily shut down the Marlboro plant. People who had bought stock in the company were chagrined, needless to say. Early in 1903 the Marlboro Automobile & Carriage Company sold out to the Videx Automobile & Carriage Company. This may have been an expediency to quell stockholder dissatisfaction, because Orrin Walker remained as president of the new firm. No Videx automobile was ever produced, and the Videx company closed its doors in September 1903 after several attachments had been served against the firm.

1901 Marlborough, stanhope, NAHC

1900-1901 MARLBORO

	FP	5	4	3	2	1
Steam Stanhope-2P	700	2700	3600	5300	8800	19,000
1902-1903 MARLBORO						
Model A Curved-Dash Carriage-2P	750	2500	3500	5000	8500	18,000
Model C Straight-Dash Carriage-2P	750	2400	3400	4800	8000	17,000
Model B Carriage-4P	1000	2700	3600	5300	8800	19,000

1905 Marmon, model B, touring, HAC

MARMON — Indianapolis, Indiana — (1902-1933) — In the mid-1890's Howard C. Marmon graduated from the University of California at Berkeley with a degree in mechanical engineering and, as had his elder brother Walter, immediately joined the family business. The Nordyke & Marmon Company of Indianapolis was already a half century old and prospering in the manufacturing of flour milling machinery which was sold under the tradename of Marmon. By 1902, at age twenty-three, Howard Marmon was chief engineer of the firm, though nepotism was not the only reason for his appointment. He was a brilliant engineer, as evidenced by his first automobile which he completed that year. It was strictly experimental and remarkably progressive: an overhead valve air-cooled two-cylinder engine in 90° vee configuration, multiple disc clutch in the flywheel, three-speed selective sliding gear transmission, a subframe carrying engine and transmission with single three-point suspension, force feed lubrication, shaft drive. For the second car he built the following year, a V-4 replaced the former twin, a three-speed planetary the former sliding gear; lubrication was now full force feed, and the suspension layout a double-three-point, an early attempt approaching the independent front suspension of a generation hence. Six of these cars were built and sold — mostly to friends — in 1904. Although his brother Walter, the businessman of the two, would have been content in confining Nordyke & Marmon manufacturing efforts to flour milling machinery, Howard Marmon championed the automobile cause — and production in earnest was begun in 1905. Twenty-five cars were sold that year. In 1905 too he built an experimental V-6 engine which was installed in the original V-twin chassis, and the year following came up with a 65 hp V-8 in a new chassis of 128-inch wheelbase, formidably longer than the production Marmon's 90-inch. This car was exhibited at the New York Automobile Show in December 1906 as the Model M-37 with $5000 price tag attached, but no one appeared interested and so the car was never put into production. Instead, Marmon concentrated on the air-cooled V-4 car and in introducing as much light alloy construction as possible to it. By now this included the entire body and much of the running gear. Although the principal business of the Nordyke & Marmon Company was going great guns — in 1904 it had produced more flour mill machinery than any other firm in the world — the automobile division was pretty much small caliber. Marmons simply weren't selling well. Deriving sufficient power from his air-cooled engines became increasingly difficult as Marmons grew larger, and the double-three-point suspension system was too complicated and costly. In 1908 Marmon's first water-cooled engine was offered; from 1909 all Marmons used water cooling. The engines now were conventional in-line T-heads, and the chassis was conventional too, even to a rear-axle transmission mounting, which was rather

a step backwards. Nonetheless, the Model 32 (one of several new cars introduced for 1909, and the longest lived) was a fine automobile, and a racing variation of it dubbed the Marmon Wasp (it was bright yellow, and with a long stinger tail) was driven by Ray Harroun to win the first Indianapolis 500 in 1911. A six-cylinder Marmon, loosely based on the Wasp and designated Model 48, as well as a smaller companion Model 41 six, were produced thereafter — but no doubt Howard Marmon himself was far happier with the Model 34 six which followed for 1916. An advanced overhead valve design, its cylinder block and most engine components (including pushrods) were aluminum, as was the entire body and radiator shell. Assisting Howard Marmon in its development were new company employees Fred Moskovics (who would leave in 1923 for Stutz) and Alanson Brush; assisting the Marmon company in its promotion was Samuel B. Stevens who headed the contingent which took a Model 34 cross-country in 1916 in less than six days, beating the record made by Cannon Ball Baker in a V-8 Cadillac by forty-one hours. The Model 34 was continued in production through 1928, in refined versions designated Models 74 and 75 in the later years. Prices generally were $3000 and up. Meanwhile, there had been considerably more activity behind the scenes at Nordyke & Marmon. In May 1924 George M. Williams, former president of the Wire Wheel Corporation of American, purchased a substantial block of stock in the Indianapolis company and became its president. Walter Marmon moved up to the board chairmanship, Howard Marmon remained as chief engineer and vice-president. It was hoped that Williams might infuse new prosperity into a venture that was losing money. Sales of 2597 Marmons in 1924 rose to nearly 4500 in both 1925 and 1926, but Williams was convinced that low production of a high quality, high priced car as Marmons had been from the beginning was no longer sufficient to make it in the automobile industry. Since more space was needed to build more cars, Nordyke & Marmon sold out its flour mill machinery business to Allis-Chalmers in 1926 and the firm was reorganized as the Marmon Motor Car

1906 Marmon, model C, touring, HAC

Company. The Little Marmon arrived in 1927, a straight-eight in the $1795-$1895 price range, which was designed by former Locomobile engineer Barney Roos, who left Marmon for Studebaker before the car even made it to the marketplace. The Little Marmon survived there but a single season, and was followed in 1928 by two eight-cylinder models, one priced as low as $1395. All this was prelude, however, to Williams' grand plan of eights straight across the board, which came in 1929 courtesy of former Lincoln chief engineer Thomas J. Litle who had been hired by Williams to manage the straight-eight program, which included an entirely new car called the Roosevelt with prices starting at an incredibly low $995. The Roosevelt presence in the Marmon company lineup resulted in a vast

1907 Marmon, model F, touring, JAC

increase in sales: from 14,770 cars in 1928 to 22,323 in 1929. But Williams hadn't reckoned with the stock market crash, and when it happened, Marmon fortunes plummeted: 12,369 cars in 1930, 5687 in 1931, 1365 in 1932, 86 in 1933. To the everlasting glory of history, however, the Marmon went out like it came in, with an advanced motorcar of utter magnificence. While Williams was producing Marmons of the bread-and-butter sort, Howard Marmon was designing a sixteen-cylinder $5000-plus Marmon that was strictly caviar. It displaced nearly 500 cubic inches, developed a full 200 hp and was good for 100 mph. And it was gorgeous. But it was also too late. Cadillac's sixteen arrived first, and although the Marmon was introduced at the Chicago Automobile Show in November of 1930, deliveries did not begin until the following April. Eight-cylinder Marmons were built alongside the Sixteen through 1932; for 1933 the company announced that the Sixteen would be its sole product. And so it was, until May of that year when the Marmon Motor Car Company moved into receivership. The month previous Howard Marmon had completed, entirely at his own expense, a V-12 Marmon with independent front suspension, tubular backbone frame, De Dion rear axle, and ultra-modern styling by Walter Dorwin Teague, Jr. With his company gone, and the Great Depression at its worst, he could find no one to produce it. His brother Walter Marmon had in the meantime allied himself with Arthur W. Herrington in the production of four-wheel-drive trucks which were manufactured under the Marmon-Herrington name into the early 1960's. Although the Marmon automobile became a memory in the early Thirties, it has been a memory that has lingered on, and always the Marmon is remembered as a very fine car.

1908 Marmon, model G, touring, HAC

1909 Marmon, model 45, coupe, HAC

1910 Marmon, model 32, touring, HAC

NOTE: Marmon production started in 1902, but the earliest car known to exist is a 1909 speedster. Therefore "ballpark values" on pre-1909 models are inestimable.

1909-1912
Model 32, 4-cyl., 32 hp, 120" wb

	FP	5	4	3	2	1
Rds	2750	3400	6900	11,500	16,100	23,000
4P Tr	2750	3600	7200	12,000	16,800	24,000
5P Tr	2750	3600	7200	12,000	16,800	24,000
Spds	2500	4500	9000	15,000	21,000	30,000
Limo	—	3750	7500	12,500	17,500	25,000

1911 Marmon, model 32, roadster, HAC

1912 Marmon, model 32, roadster, OCW

1913 Marmon, model 48, touring, HAC

1913
Model 32, 4-cyl., 32 hp, 120" wb

	FP	5	4	3	2	1
Rds	3000	3400	6900	11,500	16,100	23,000
5P Tr	3000	3600	7200	12,000	16,800	24,000
7P Tr	3000	3600	7200	12,000	16,800	24,000
Spds	2750	4500	9000	15,000	21,000	30,000
Limo	—	3750	7500	12,500	17,500	25,000

Model 48, 6-cyl., 48 hp, 145" wb

	FP	5	4	3	2	1
Rds	5000	4350	8700	14,500	20,300	29,000
4P Tr	5000	4500	9000	15,000	21,000	30,000
5P Tr	5000	4500	9000	15,000	21,000	30,000
7P Tr	5000	4650	9300	15,500	21,700	31,000
Spds	4500	5400	10,800	18,000	25,200	36,000
Limo	—	4650	9300	15,500	21,700	31,000

1914 Marmon, model 48, touring, HAC

1914
Model 32, 4-cyl., 32 hp, 120" wb

	FP	5	4	3	2	1
Rds	2900	3400	6900	11,500	16,100	23,000
4P Tr	3000	3600	7200	12,000	16,800	24,000
5P Tr	3000	3600	7200	12,000	16,800	24,000
Spds	2850	4500	9000	15,000	21,000	30,000
Limo	4000	3750	7500	12,500	17,500	25,000

Model 41, 6-cyl., 41 hp, 132" wb

Rds	3250	3750	7500	12,500	17,500	25,000
4P Tr	3250	3900	7800	13,000	18,200	26,000
5P Tr	3250	3900	7800	13,000	18,200	26,000
7P Tr	3300	4200	8400	14,000	19,600	28,000
Spds	3000	4800	9600	16,000	22,400	32,000

Model 48, 6-cyl., 48 hp, 145" wb

Rds	5000	4350	8700	14,500	20,300	29,000
4P Tr	5000	4500	9000	15,000	21,000	30,000
5P Tr	5000	4500	9000	15,000	21,000	30,000
7P Tr	5000	4650	9300	15,500	21,700	31,000
Spds	4500	5400	10,800	18,000	25,200	36,000
Limo	6250	4650	9300	15,500	21,700	31,000
Ber Limo	6450	5250	10,500	17,500	24,500	35,000

1915 Marmon, model 41, touring, HAC

1915
Model 41, 6-cyl., 41 hp, 132" wb

Rds	3250	3750	7500	12,500	17,500	25,000
4P Tr	3250	3900	7800	13,000	18,200	26,000
5P Tr	3250	3900	7800	13,000	18,200	26,000
7P Tr	3350	4200	8400	14,000	19,600	28,000
Spds	3250	4800	9600	16,000	22,400	32,000

Model 48, 6-cyl., 48 hp, 145" wb

7P Tr	5000	4650	9300	15,500	21,700	31,000

1916 Marmon, model 34, 4-pass. custom victoria roadster, AA

1916
Model 41, 6-cyl., 41 hp, 132" wb

Rds	3250	3600	7200	12,000	16,800	24,000
4P Tr	3250	3750	7500	12,500	17,500	25,000
5P Tr	3250	3750	7500	12,500	17,500	25,000
7P Tr	3350	4050	8100	13,500	18,900	27,000
Spds	3250	4650	9300	15,500	21,700	31,000

Model 34, 6-cyl., 34 hp, 136" wb

Clb Rds	2950	3000	6000	10,000	14,000	20,000
5P Tr	2900	2800	5700	9500	13,300	19,000
7P Tr	2950	3000	6000	10,000	14,000	20,000
Limo	4550	2300	5400	9000	12,600	18,000
Lan'let	4650	3150	6300	10,500	14,700	21,000
Sed	4100	1400	4200	7000	9800	14,000
Twn Car	5500	2200	5250	8750	12,250	17,500

1917 Marmon, model 34, touring, HAC

1917
Model 34, 6-cyl., 34 hp, 136" wb

	FP	5	4	3	2	1
5P Tr	3100	3000	6000	10,000	14,000	20,000
4P Rds	3100	3000	6000	10,000	14,000	20,000
7P Tr	3100	3000	6000	10,000	14,000	20,000
Limo	4550	2300	5400	9000	12,600	18,000
Lan'let	4650	3300	6600	11,000	15,400	22,000
Sed	4100	1400	4200	7000	9800	14,000
Twn Car	5500	2200	5250	8750	12,250	17,500

1918 Marmon, model 34, limousine, AA

1918
Model 34, 6-cyl., 34 hp, 136" wb

5P Tr	3700	3000	6000	10,000	14,000	20,000
4P Rds	3750	3000	6000	10,000	14,000	20,000
7P Tr	3750	3000	6000	10,000	14,000	20,000
Sed	5150	1400	4200	7000	9800	14,000
Limo-Twn Car	5250	2300	5400	9000	12,600	18,000
Lan'let	5350	3300	6600	11,000	15,400	22,000
Rubay Twn Car	5700	3600	7200	12,000	16,800	24,000
Rubay Limo	5750	3750	7500	12,500	17,500	25,000

1919 Marmon, model 34, New Series, 6-pass. sedan, AA

1919
Model 34, 6-cyl., 34 hp, 136" wb

5P Tr	3950	3000	6000	10,000	14,000	20,000
4P Rds	4000	3000	6000	10,000	14,000	20,000
7P Tr	4000	3000	6000	10,000	14,000	20,000
Sed	5550	1400	4200	7000	9800	14,000
Limo	5650	2300	5400	9000	12,600	18,000
Twn Car	5650	2300	5400	9000	12,600	18,000
Lan'let	5750	3300	6600	11,000	15,400	22,000

1920 Marmon, model 34, New Series, touring, AA

1920
Model 34, 6-cyl., 34 hp, 136" wb

	FP	5	4	3	2	1
4P Rds	—	3150	6300	10,500	14,700	21,000
4P 4 dr Tr	—	3100	6150	10,250	14,350	20,500
4P Cpe	—	1750	4800	8000	11,200	16,000
7P Sed	—	1550	4500	7500	10,500	15,000
Twn Car	—	2000	5100	8500	11,900	17,000
7P Tr	—	3150	6300	10,500	14,700	21,000

1921 Marmon, model 34, New Series, export touring, AA

1921
Model 34, 6-cyl., 34 hp, 136" wb

	FP	5	4	3	2	1
4P Rds	—	3150	6300	10,500	14,700	21,000
7P Tr	—	3150	6300	10,500	14,700	21,000
2P Spds	—	3750	7500	12,500	17,500	25,000
4P Cpe	—	1750	4800	8000	11,200	16,000
4P Tr	—	3000	6000	10,000	14,000	20,000
7P Sed	—	1550	4500	7500	10,500	15,000
Limo	—	1750	4800	8000	11,200	16,000
Twn Car	—	2000	5100	8500	11,900	17,000

1922 Marmon, model 34, New Series, 7-pass. 4-dr. sedan, AA

1922
Model 34, 6-cyl., 34 hp, 136" wb

	FP	5	4	3	2	1
4P Rds	—	3150	6300	10,500	14,700	21,000
4P Tr	—	3300	6600	11,000	15,400	22,000
7P Tr	—	3150	6300	10,500	14,700	21,000
2P Spds	—	4500	9000	15,000	21,000	30,000
4P Spds	—	3600	7200	12,000	16,800	24,000
W'by Cpe	—	2300	5400	9000	12,600	18,000
N & M Cpe	—	1550	4500	7500	10,500	15,000
7P N & M Sed	—	1550	4500	7500	10,500	15,000
Rubay Limo	—	3750	7500	12,500	17,500	25,000
4P N & M Sed	—	1250	3900	6500	9100	13,000
7P Sub	—	1250	3950	6600	9200	13,200
Spt Sed	—	1300	4050	6750	9450	13,500
N & H Sed	—	1750	4800	8000	11,200	16,000
Rubay Twn Car	—	3600	7200	12,000	16,800	24,000
W'by Limo	—	4350	8700	14,500	20,300	29,000
W'by Twn Car	—	3750	7500	12,500	17,500	25,000

NOTE: N & M bodies by Nordyke & Marmon Co. (factory custom).

1923 Marmon, model 34, 4-pass. speedster, AA

1923
Model 34, 6-cyl., 34 hp, 132" wb

	FP	5	4	3	2	1
4P Phae	—	3150	6300	10,500	14,700	21,000
2P Rds	—	3000	6000	10,000	14,000	20,000
4P Rds	—	3200	6450	10,750	15,050	21,500
7P Phae	—	3300	6600	11,000	15,400	22,000
4P Tr	—	3300	6600	11,000	15,400	22,000
2P Spds	—	4500	9000	15,000	21,000	30,000
4P Spds	—	3750	7500	12,500	17,500	25,000
4P Cpe	—	1550	4500	7500	10,500	15,000
4P Sed	—	1250	3900	6500	9100	13,000
7P Sed	—	1300	4050	6750	9450	13,500
7P Limo	—	3600	7200	12,000	16,800	24,000
Twn Car	—	3500	7050	11,750	16,450	23,500
Sub Sed	—	1250	3900	6500	9100	13,000

1924 Marmon, model 34, 4-pass. sedan, AA

1924
Model 34, 6-cyl., 34 hp, 132" wb

	FP	5	4	3	2	1
Spt Spds	3395	4500	9000	15,000	21,000	30,000
4P Spds	3295	3750	7500	12,500	17,500	25,000
4P Phae	3095	3150	6300	10,500	14,700	21,000
4P Conv Phae	—	4200	8400	14,000	19,600	28,000
4P Phae	3095	3200	6450	10,750	15,050	21,500
7P Conv Phae	—	3400	6900	11,500	16,100	23,000
4P Cpe	3585	1650	4650	7750	10,850	15,500
4P Sed	3985	1250	3900	6500	9100	13,000
7P Sed	3985	1400	4200	7000	9800	14,000
Sub Sed	4285	1250	3900	6500	9100	13,000
Limo	4285	3600	7200	12,000	16,800	24,000
Twn Car	4285	3500	7050	11,750	16,450	23,500

NOTE: The Phaeton (Phae) is a touring car; the convertible Phaeton (Conv Phae) is a convertible sedan with glass slide-in windows.

The following Marmon models are authentic Classic Cars: all 16-cyl., all Models 74 (1925-26); all Models 75 (1927); all Models E75 (1928), 1930 "Big Eight" and 1931 Model "88" and "Big Eight".

1925 Marmon, model 74, touring, AA

1925
Model D-74, 6-cyl., 34 hp, 136" wb

	FP	5	4	3	2	1
R/S Rds	3165	7050	14,100	23,500	32,900	47,000
5P Phae	3165	7350	14,700	24,500	34,300	49,000
7P Tr	3165	6000	12,000	20,000	28,000	40,000
Std Sed	3295	2300	5400	9000	12,600	18,000
Brgm Cpe	3295	2600	5500	9250	12,950	18,500
DeL Cpe	3455	2800	5700	9500	13,300	19,000
DeL Sed	3775	2600	5500	9250	12,950	18,500
7P DeL Sed	3850	2800	5700	9500	13,300	19,000
5P Sed Limo	3900	2800	5700	9500	13,300	19,000
7P Sed Limo	3975	2800	5700	9500	13,300	19,000
7P Std Sed	—	2600	5500	9250	12,950	18,500
4P Vic Cpe	—	2900	5850	9750	13,650	19,500
2P Std Cpe	—	2800	5700	9500	13,300	19,000

1926
Model D-74, 6-cyl., 34 hp, 136" wb

	FP	5	4	3	2	1
2P Spds	3295	7050	14,100	23,500	32,900	47,000
5P Phae	3295	7350	14,700	24,500	34,300	49,000
7P Tr	3295	6000	12,000	20,000	28,000	40,000
Std Cpe	3295	2800	5700	9500	13,300	19,000
Std Sed	3370	2300	5400	9000	12,600	18,000
5P Del Sed	3775	2600	5500	9250	12,950	18,500
7P Del Sed	3850	2800	5700	9500	13,300	19,000
Std Vic	3295	2900	5850	9750	13,650	19,500
Std Brgm	3295	2600	5500	9250	12,950	18,500
5P DeL Limo	3900	2900	5850	9750	13,650	19,500
7P DeL Limo	3975	3000	6000	10,000	14,000	20,000
Spl Brgm	3395	2800	5700	9500	13,300	19,000
7P Spl Sed	3470	2800	5700	9500	13,300	19,000
5P Spl Sed	3395	2600	5500	9250	12,950	18,500

1926 Marmon, model 74, 7-pass. phaeton, AA

1927 Marmon, Little Eight, Locke 2-window sedan, AA

1927
Little Marmon Series, 8-cyl., 24 hp

	FP	5	4	3	2	1
2P Spds	1895	3300	6600	11,000	15,400	22,000
4P Spds	1965	2800	5700	9500	13,300	19,000
4 dr Sed	1895	1075	3000	5500	7700	11,000
2 dr Sed	1795	1025	2600	5250	7300	10,500
R/S Cpe	1895	1250	3900	6500	9100	13,000
Coll Rds Cpe	1995	3000	6000	10,000	14,000	20,000
4P Brgm	1895	1125	3450	5750	8050	11,500

1927 Marmon, model 75, custom sedan, HAC

E-75 Series (Factory-body), 6-cyl., 34 hp, 136" wb

5P Sed	3565	2900	5850	9750	13,650	19,500
7P Sed	3640	3000	6000	10,000	14,000	20,000
5P Brgm	3565	3100	6150	10,250	14,350	20,500
R/M Cpe	3565	3150	6300	10,500	14,700	21,000
Twn Cpe	3195	3200	6450	10,750	15,050	21,500
Vic	3485	3300	6600	11,000	15,400	22,000
4P Spds	3485	6750	13,500	22,500	31,500	45,000
2P Spds	3485	7500	15,000	25,000	35,000	50,000

E-75 Series (Custom Body), 6-cyl., 136" wb

7P Sed	4075	3750	7500	12,500	17,500	25,000
5P Sed	3960	3600	7200	12,000	16,800	24,000
Limo	4175	3650	7350	12,250	17,150	24,500
7P Sods	3565	9000	18,000	30,000	42,000	60,000

1928 Marmon, model 78, coupe, HAC

1928
Series 68, 8-cyl., 24 hp, 114" wb

	FP	5	4	3	2	1
Sed	1395	1125	3450	5750	8050	11,500
Cpe	1395	1300	4050	6750	9450	13,500
Vic	1450	1400	4200	7000	9800	14,000

Series 78, 8-cyl., 28 hp, 120" wb

Cpe	1895	1550	4500	7500	10,500	15,000
Sed	1895	1200	3750	6250	8750	12,500
Rds	1895	4500	9000	15,000	21,000	30,000
Spds	1965	4650	9300	15,500	21,700	31,000
Coll Cpe	1995	3150	6300	10,500	14,700	21,000
Vic Cpe	1995	1750	4800	8000	11,200	16,000

Series 75 Standard Line, 6-cyl., 34 hp

Twn Cpe	3195	3150	6300	10,500	14,700	21,000
2P Spds	3485	5250	10,500	17,500	24,500	35,000
Cpe	3485	2800	5700	9500	13,300	19,000
Vic	3485	3000	6000	10,000	14,000	20,000
Cpe Rds	3565	3600	7200	12,000	16,800	24,000
Brgm	3565	2800	5700	9500	13,300	19,000
5P Sed	3565	2300	5400	9000	12,600	18,000
7P Sed	3640	2600	5500	9250	12,950	18,500

Series 75 Custom Line, 6-cyl., 34 hp

4P Spds	3485	7500	15,000	25,000	35,000	50,000
7P Spds	3565	7350	14,700	24,500	34,300	49,000
5P Sed	3960	2300	5400	9000	12,600	18,000
7P Sed	4075	2800	5700	9500	13,300	19,000
Limo	4175	2900	5850	9750	13,650	19,500

1929 Marmon, model 68, roadster, HAC

1929
Series 68, 8-cyl., 28 hp, 114" wb

Sed	1465	1150	3600	6000	8400	12,000
Coll Cpe	1565	3150	6300	10,500	14,700	21,000
Cpe	1465	1400	4200	7000	9800	14,000
Rds	1565	4500	9000	15,000	21,000	30,000
Vic Cpe	1520	1500	4350	7250	10,150	14,500

Series 78, 8-cyl., 28 hp, 120" wb

Sed	1965	1200	3750	6250	8750	12,500
Cpe	1965	1550	4500	7500	10,500	15,000
Vic Cpe	2065	1750	4800	8000	11,200	16,000
Coll Cpe	2065	3750	7500	12,500	17,500	25,000
Rds	1965	4800	9600	16,000	22,400	32,000
6P Spds	2065	5400	10,800	18,000	25,200	36,000

Marmon Roosevelt, 8-cyl., 24 hp, 112.75" wb

Sed	995	1075	3000	5500	7700	11,000
Cpe	995	1125	3450	5750	8050	11,500
Vic Cpe	1065	1150	3600	6000	8400	12,000
Coll Cpe	1095	2300	5400	9000	12,600	18,000

1930 Marmon, model 79, 5-pass. sedan, AA

1930
Model 8-79, 8-cyl., 32.5 hp, 125" wb

Sed	2020	1150	3600	6000	8400	12,000
R/S Cpe	1995	1550	4500	7500	10,500	15,000
Phae	2020	6300	12,600	21,000	29,400	42,000
Conv	2120	6000	12,000	20,000	28,000	40,000
Brgm	2070	1200	3750	6250	8750	12,500
Clb Sed	2070	1125	3450	5750	8050	11,500

Model "Big Eight", 8-cyl., 34 hp, 136" wb

5P Sed	2720	3600	7200	12,000	16,800	24,000
R/S Cpe	2850	4500	9000	15,000	21,000	30,000
7P Tr	3170	7350	14,700	24,500	34,300	49,000
Conv Sed	3895	9000	18,000	30,000	42,000	60,000
7P Sed	2920	3650	7350	12,250	17,150	24,500
Limo	3120	3750	7500	12,500	17,500	25,000
Brgm	2770	3650	7350	12,250	17,150	24,500
Clb Sed	2770	4050	8100	13,500	18,900	27,000

Model 8-69, 8-cyl., 25.5 hp, 118" wb

	FP	5	4	3	2	1
Sed	1520	1125	3450	5750	8050	11,500
Cpe	1495	1200	3750	6250	8750	12,500
Phae	1610	6000	12,000	20,000	28,000	40,000
Conv	1610	5700	11,400	19,000	26,600	38,000
Brgm	1565	1150	3600	6000	8400	12,000
Clb Sed	1565	1150	3600	6000	8400	12,000

Marmon Roosevelt, 8-cyl., 24 hp, 112.75" wb

	FP	5	4	3	2	1
Sed	1075	1075	3000	5500	7700	11,000
R/S Cpe	995	1125	3450	5750	8050	11,500
Vic Cpe	1145	1150	3600	6000	8400	12,000
Conv	1175	3750	7500	12,500	17,500	25,000

1931 Marmon, Sixteen, LeBaron, close-coupled sedan, AA

1931
Model "Big Eight" (First Series), 8-cyl., 33.8 hp, 136" wb

	FP	5	4	3	2	1
5P Sed	2720	3600	7200	12,000	16,800	24,000
Cpe	2850	4500	9000	15,000	21,000	30,000
Tr	3170	6150	12,300	20,500	28,700	41,000
Conv Cpe	3895	8250	16,500	27,500	38,500	55,000
Weyman Sed	—				value inestimable	
7P Sed	2920	3650	7350	12,250	17,150	24,500
Limo	3120	3750	7500	12,500	17,500	25,000
Brgm	2770	3650	7350	12,250	17,150	24,500
Clb Sed	2770	4050	8100	13,500	18,900	27,000

Model 8-79 (First Series), 8-cyl., 32.5 hp, 125" wb

	FP	5	4	3	2	1
5P Sed	2020	1150	3600	6000	8400	12,000
Cpe	1995	1550	4500	7500	10,500	15,000
Phae	2020	5850	11,700	19,500	27,300	39,000
Conv Cpe	2120	5100	10,200	17,000	23,800	34,000
Brgm	2070	1200	3750	6250	8750	12,500
Clb Sed	2070	1125	3600	5750	8050	11,500

Model 8-69 (First Series), 8-cyl., 25.3 hp, 118" wb

	FP	5	4	3	2	1
Sed	1520	1075	3000	5500	7700	11,000
Cpe	1495	1250	3900	6500	9100	13,000
Phae	1610	5400	10,800	18,000	25,200	36,000
Conv Cpe	1610	4950	9900	16,500	23,100	33,000
Brgm	1565	1150	3600	6000	8400	12,000
Clb Sed	1565	1150	3600	6000	8400	12,000

Marmon Roosevelt (First Series), 8-cyl., 25.3 hp, 112.75" wb

	FP	5	4	3	2	1
Sed	985	1075	3000	5500	7700	11,000
Cpe	950	1125	3450	5750	8050	11,500
Vic Cpe	995	1150	3600	6000	8400	12,000
Conv Cpe	1045	3750	7500	12,500	17,500	25,000

Model 70 (Second Series), 8-cyl., 25.3 hp, 112.75" wb

	FP	5	4	3	2	1
Sed	995	1000	2400	5000	7000	10,000
Cpe	950	1075	3000	5500	7700	11,000
Vic Cpe	995	1125	3450	5750	8050	11,500
Conv Cpe	1045	3650	7350	12,250	17,150	24,500

NOTE: Effective with release of the Second Series on January 1, 1931 the Roosevelt became the Marmon Model 70.

Model 88 (Second Series), 8-cyl., 33.8 hp, 130"-136" wb

	FP	5	4	3	2	1
5P Sed	2220	3800	7650	12,750	17,850	25,500
Cpe	2275	3900	7800	13,000	18,200	26,000
Conv Cpe	2395	7500	15,000	25,000	35,000	50,000
Spl Sed	1895	3900	7800	13,000	18,200	26,000
Clb Sed	2345	3750	7500	12,500	17,500	25,000
Tr	2375	6750	13,500	22,500	31,500	45,000
Spl Cpe	2395	4300	8550	14,250	19,950	28,500
7P Sed	2495	3800	7650	12,750	17,850	25,500
Limo	2595	4050	8850	14,750	20,650	29,500

Series 16 (Second Series), 16-cyl., 62.5 hp, 145" wb

	FP	5	4	3	2	1
5P Sed	5200	9900	19,800	33,000	46,200	66,000
2P Cpe	5220	10,200	20,400	34,000	47,600	68,000
5P Cpe	5270	10,200	20,400	34,000	47,600	68,000
Conv Cpe	5370	29,500	55,000	84,000	110,000	140,000
Conv Sed	5420	32,700	60,000	92,000	118,000	160,000
7P Sed	5400	10,500	21,000	35,000	49,000	70,000
Limo	5500	10,800	21,600	36,000	50,500	72,000
C.C. Sed	5270	10,800	21,600	36,000	50,500	72,000

1932 Marmon, model 8-125, sedan, HAC

1932
Series 70, 8-cyl., 25.3 hp, 112.75" wb

	FP	5	4	3	2	1
Sed	995	1125	3450	5750	8050	11,500
Cpe	950	1150	3600	6000	8400	12,000

Series 125, 8-cyl., 33.8 hp, 125" wb

	FP	5	4	3	2	1
Sed	1395	1250	3900	6500	9100	13,000
Cpe	1395	1550	4500	7500	10,500	15,000
Conv Cpe	1445	6300	12,600	21,000	29,400	42,000

Series 16, 16-cyl., 62.5 hp, 145" wb

	FP	5	4	3	2	1
Sed	5700	10,200	20,400	34,000	47,600	68,000
Cpe	5700	10,200	20,400	34,000	47,600	68,000
2 dr Cpe	5800	10,200	20,400	34,000	47,600	68,000
Conv Cpe	5850	30,300	57,000	86,000	112,000	145,000
Conv Sed	5950	34,300	62,000	96,000	122,000	170,000
Sed	5900	10,800	21,600	36,000	50,500	72,000
Limo	6100	10,800	21,600	36,000	50,500	72,000
C.C. Sed	5800	10,800	21,600	36,000	50,500	72,000

1933 Marmon, Sixteen, custom-bodied 4-dr. sedan, OCW

1933
Series 16, 16-cyl., 62.5 hp, 145" wb

	FP	5	4	3	2	1
Sed	4825	10,200	20,400	34,000	47,600	68,000
2P Cpe	4825	10,500	21,000	35,000	49,000	70,000
5P Cpe	4925	10,800	21,600	36,000	50,500	72,000
Conv Cpe	4975	31,100	58,000	88,000	114,000	150,000
Conv Sed	5075	35,900	64,000	100,000	126,000	180,000
Sed	4975	11,100	22,200	37,000	52,000	74,000
Limo	5175	11,400	22,800	38,000	56,000	76,000
C.C. Sed	4925	10,800	21,600	36,000	50,500	72,000

NOTE: Marmon discontinued after close of 1933 model year.

MARQUETTE — In 1904 the Berwick Auto Car Company of Grand Rapids, Michigan produced an electric car which was occasionally referred to as a Marquette. More often, however, the vehicle was called by the company name. Refer to Berwick.

1912 Marquette, model 24, 4-pass. tourabout, WLB

MARQUETTE — Saginaw, Michigan — (1912) — Marquette resulted from the buying binge that William C. Durant embarked upon after founding General Motors in 1908. Two among the myriad companies he purchased were the Rainier of Saginaw and the Welch-Detroit of Detroit. The Marquette Motor Company was organized in 1909 with headquarters in Saginaw to continue production of the Rainier and to produce parts for the Welch-Detroit, both of these cars surviving under their own names into 1911. The Marquette name did appear in 1909-1910 hyphenated as Marquette-Buick when Billy Durant decided to take Buick racing, and, in order to follow the letter of the prevailing race regulations, needed another name to do it. Marquette-Buicks were formidable contenders in a number of competition events, with Bob Burman and Louis Chevrolet usually driving. The Marquette production car, which was designed by Durant man A.B.C. Hardy, was introduced late in 1911 as "the outgrowth of two well-established and favorably known cars, the Rainier and the Welch-Detroit." It was a T-head four offered in two horsepower and wheelbase sizes and priced in the $3000-$4000 range. Marquette Motor Car Company was the firm's new designation, but it did not remain long. In late February of 1912 it was announced the Marquette had changed its name to Peninsular Motor Company. Officially, this was to avoid confusion with the Marquette company which had been established in Detroit late in 1911 to handle the output of the Saginaw factory's production. The reasoning was curious, but there was confusion aplenty by this time. In September of 1910 Billy Durant had lost control of General Motors, and the syndicate in charge now was trying to pick up the pieces of what he had left behind. The Marquette seems to have been an attempt to consolidate losses of the Rainier and the Welch-Detroit and turn them into a profit with one new car. There was a quick change of syndicate mind on that, however. In September of 1912 General Motors announced the discontinuation of the Marquette automobile. Some of the last cars produced seem to have carried the Peninsular name. Although this cannot be substantially documented, two Peninsular cars were subsequently registered in the state of Michigan.

1912 MARQUETTE
Four - 40 hp, 122" wb

	FP	5	4	3	2	1
Model 22 Rbt.-2P	3000	3000	4000	6000	9500	21,000
Model 24 Tourabout-4P	3000	3000	4000	6000	9500	21,000
Model 25 Tour.-5P	3000	3100	4200	6300	10,500	22,000
Model 27 Tour.-7P	3000	3200	4300	6500	12,000	23,000

Four - 45 hp, 119" wb

	FP	5	4	3	2	1
Model 28 Tour.-7P	4000	3300	4400	6700	12,000	24,000

1930 Marquette, rumble-seat coupe, OCW

MARQUETTE — Flint, Michigan — (1930) — The Marquette was introduced by Buick in the wake of the success that Oakland had discovered with its Pontiac and Cadillac with its LaSalle. It was a companion car, a distinct marque of its own, but produced and marketed under the aegis of the Buick Motor Company. A smaller car on a 114-inch wheelbase, the Marquette was powered by an L-head six, unlike the Buick's famous valve-in-head engine. It was offered in six body styles in the $1000 price range, and was rushed into production on June 1st, 1929, nearly two months before the introduction of Buick's 1930 model line. Promotion was vigorous, and press reaction was favorable. Although the car looked Oldsmobile-like, one admiring reporter saw it as "a small edition of the Cadillac." Its herringbone-pattern radiator core set it apart from other GM cars. If it shone in neither styling nor engineering, the Marquette acquitted itself admirably in performance. Maximum speed approached 70 mph, and a Marquette was driven from Death Valley to the top of Pikes Peak with no problem at all. The Marquette's biggest problem appears to have been the stock market crash, and the Buick Motor Company's impatience with its initial lackluster sales. After 35,007 Marquettes were built (all of them designated 1930 models), the car was abruptly dropped. Just a few months earlier, 4000 Marquette service signs had been dispatched to Buick dealer/service stations. (See Buick section for further details.)

1930 MARQUETTE
Series 30 - 6-cyl., 67 hp, 114" wb

	FP	5	4	3	2	1
Model 30 Two-Door Sed.	1000	1000	2000	3000	4600	8000
Model 34 Sport Rds.	1020	3600	4200	6300	10,500	22,000
Model 35 Phae.	1020	3200	4300	6500	11,000	23,000
Model 36 Business Cpe.	990	1500	2500	3600	5500	11,000
Model 36S Spe. Cpe.	1020	2000	3000	4200	6500	14,000
Model 37 Sedan	1060	1000	2000	3000	4600	8000

1903 Marr Autocar, runabout, WLB

MARR — Detroit, Michigan — (1902-1904) — Late in 1902 Walter L. Marr secured a job with Detroit automobile dealer J.P. Schneider and, with Schneider's blessing, embarked immediately upon the building of an experimental one-cylinder gasoline runabout. The vehicle had its first demonstration on Christmas night of 1902, and was put through a test run of 1000 miles early the following year. The Marr Autocar Company was immediately formed, and the partners contracted with the Fauber Manufacturing Company of Elgin, Illinois for the building of 100 units while they searched the Detroit area for a proper factory for manufacture. How many of the 100 units were built is not known, but on August 11th, 1904 the Fauber plant in Elgin burned to the ground in a fire resulting in $325,000 damages. Included in that loss were fourteen Marr Autocars inside, which were entirely consumed. The Elgin plant was not rebuilt, although by now this probably didn't matter much to Walter Marr anyway. In the meantime he had returned to work for a former employer with whom he had earlier had difficulty dealing. It was David Dunbar Buick. Together they improved the Buick valve-in-head engine, and launched the Buick automobile. Among the features of the first Buick was the tilting steering wheel that had first appeared on the Marr.

1902-1904 MARR
Autocar - 1-cyl., 6½ hp, 66" wb   800 — — — — —

1914 Marr, cyclecar, SM

MARR — Detroit, Michigan — (1914) — Following his retirement from the Buick Motor Company, Walter L. Marr continued to serve the company as a consulting engineer. Among his assignments, in 1914, was the design of a cyclecar. As an example of the genre, Marr's cyclecar was one of the best, and perhaps even the most substantial ever built. Seating was tandem, but the car sported a four-cylinder, water-cooled engine fitted into a 100-inch wheelbase chassis, with a channel frame, I-beam axle, shaft drive and standard gearshift. An interesting feature was an adjustable steering wheel which could be raised or lowered by moving the wheel up or down on a spindle protruding from the steering column. Buick was pleased with Marr's efforts, but a cost analysis proved that his cyclecar would have been almost as expensive to manufacture as a small production Buick. Only the one prototype was built, and it is on display today at the Sloan Museum in Flint. Buick embarked upon no further development of the cyclecar type of vehicle simply because by the end of 1914 the cyclecar idea was virtually dead.

1899 Marsh, runabout, HAC

1901 Marsh, runabout, WLB

891

1905 Marsh, runabout, WLB

1920 Marshall, four, touring, NAHC

MARSH — Brockton, Massachusetts — (1899-1905) — There were four Marsh brothers in Brockton and they spent three years building one steam car which was completed in 1899. The older brothers (Alonzo R. and William T.) were the steamrollers behind this project, but the younger boys (George R. and Clifton) assisted as well. Although two separate organizations (the Marsh Motor Carriage Company and the Atlantic Automobile Manufacturing Company) were incorporated to produce the car, the brothers almost immediately thought better of the idea. After assembling perhaps three more steam carriages, all of them light runabouts which were sold locally, they proceeded to manufacture only motorcycles instead through another firm they called American Motor Company. But the Marsh brothers were back in the automotive field in 1905 when the American Motor Company introduced a 785-pound $750 Marsh Runabout on an 80-inch wheelbase with a two-cylinder 10 hp air-cooled engine mounted up front. Right-hand wheel steering and an acetylene cyclops headlight fitted permanently into the front of the grille were featured. Once again, however, the Marsh brothers had quick second thoughts. "They will stick to their original business," *The Motor World* announced in November 1905, "the manufacture of motor bicycles." Their automobile business was sold to Charles H. Metz with whom the brothers had been associated in their motorcycle operation. But the Marshes weren't finished with cars yet. In 1910 Alonzo T. attempted to market a new car in Brockton called the Eastern, then left Massachusetts to build the Vulcan in Painesville, Ohio. Meanwhile, his brother William T. had an abortive go with the Lima Roadster in 1912, also in Ohio. Back home in Brockton, in 1915, the brothers collaborated on the Sterling; and in 1920 were in Cleveland, Ohio with yet another new automobile, this one again called the Marsh.

MARSH — Detroit, Michigan — (1907-1908) — Frederick D. and Winfred Marsh were machinists whose shop was located at 26 Sylvester Avenue in Detroit. During 1907-1908 they built a few highwheelers at that location. This was strictly a sideline activity. Although they never formally incorporated, the brothers did refer to themselves as the Marsh Motor Buggy Company during those years.

MARSH — Cleveland, Ohio — (1920-1923) — During World War I, the Marsh brothers of Brockton, Massachusetts occupied themselves principally in the lucrative production of munitions for the war effort. Together, and independently, the brothers had thus far been responsible for five automotive ventures — the 1905 Marsh runabout, the Eastern, the Lima Roadster, the Vulcan and the Sterling — and following the Armistice, Alonzo R. Marsh was anxious to return to the automobile industry. He convinced his brother William to join him, as well as two younger Marsh sons, David and Bennett. The new Marsh was to be built in Cleveland. Equipment from the brothers' old Sterling automobile factory in Brockton and usable munitions machinery was freighted to Ohio in 135 railway cars. The new Marsh was aimed to be a bigger and better Model T Ford. At least six cars were built, all of them prototypes as the brothers sought to improve their offering. Collaborating with them during the later days was Forrest Cameron. Four of the six Marsh cars had four-cylinder engines on 114-inch wheelbase chassis, two had sixes on a 117-inch wheelbase. All of the engines were Continentals. Only one Marsh was an open car, the remainder were closed. A projected price tag was $1450. But there was not enough ready cash in the wake of the postwar depression to get the Marsh enterprise going. The Marsh Motors Company, which had been capitalized at $3.5 million in 1919, went into receivership in June of 1923. The total investment in the venture had been about $1.5 million; stockholders were ultimately paid fifty cents on the dollar, a surprisingly high figure for the period. Alonzo Marsh never tried the automobile field again, though he remained at the site of his Marsh factory in Cleveland where he dealt in used machinery until his death in 1940.

MARSHALL — In 1909, in Kilbourn, Wisconsin, a prototype car was built in the Marshall machine shop. Refer to Kilbourn.
The firm of William Marshall, Inc. was organized in White Plains, New York late in 1911 with a capital stock of $20,000 for the manufacture of automobiles. Joining William Marshall in this venture was John Hamilton. Manufacture is doubted.

MARSHALL — Chicago, Illinois — (1920-1922) — The Marshall Motor Car Company was an automobile agency in Chicago. The Marshall car was simply a Norwalk sold by that Windy City distributor. During its early years, the Norwalk had been built in Martinsburg, West Virginia, but by now its cars were being manufactured in Lynchburg, Virginia by Piedmont. When Piedmont went out of business in Virginia in 1922, Norwalk promptly went out of business in West Virginia, which rather effectively also put the Marshall out of business in Illinois. "Built on a Promise that's right clear thru, Sold on a guarantee that our promise is true" had been the Marshall's slogan.

1920 MARSHALL
Model K — 4-cyl., 35 hp, 116" wb

	FP	5	4	3	2	1
Beauty Touring-4P	1295	3000	4000	6000	9500	21,000

MARSHALLTOWN — Marshalltown, Iowa — (1909) — L.M. Osborne was the president and treasurer, Ray R. East the secretary and Joseph Lempe the superintendent of the Marshalltown Buggy Company at the corner of Third and Church streets. That the firm was an automobile manufacturer was indicated in the 1910 edition of the Ware yearbook of the industry, though the car being manufactured is not known. During the summer of 1909, L.M. Osborne had announced ongoing negotiations "for the purchase of the manufacturing rights of a car now in successful operation." Whatever it was, Marshalltown didn't produce it long. By 1911 the company was confining its industry activity to the manufacture of automobile tops.

MARSHFIELD — The Marshfield Iron Works of Marshfield, Wisconsin was the predecessor company to Kliner, Lang and Scharmann. George J. Lang and Otto T. Scharmann did build a number of cars during the years 1907 to 1909, but these are correctly referred to by their names. Refer to Lang & Scharmann.

MARTEL — Elkhart, Indiana — (1925-1927) — The Martel was a taxicab built by the Elcar company for taxi entrepreneur Jules Martin. Details regarding it are obscure, since Elcar was at the time building taxis under its own name as well. Both a Martel and Royal Martel were produced, the addition of bumpers and shock absorbers to the latter perhaps being the difference between them. Apparently the Royal Martel was destined principally for the New York City market, Martin incorporating the Royal Martel Taxi Corporation there in 1925. Total Martel and Royal Martel production has been estimated in the 200-unit range.

MARTELL — The Martell Motor Car Company of Jamaica Plain, Massachusetts was organized in 1908 and spent the next two years trying to get into manufacture. When this was not successful, the firm was taken over by the Lenox Motor Car Company, which proceeded to the assembly line with its Lenox automobile. Refer to Lenox.

M'ARTHUR — Rockford, Illinois — (1895) — A.W. M'Arthur, president of the Rockford Foundry Company, was another of the entrants in the Chicago Times-Herald Contest who did not make it to the starting line. The likelihood is that he eventually completed the car.

MARTIN — That a car called the Martin was built by Palmer & Christie of New York City in 1905 has been indicated on various rosters. There was no such car. Instead the car involved was the Martini, which was imported from Switzerland. Later that year the firm of Palmer & Christie was succeeded by the Martini Import Company.
The Martin Auto Company of 208 Broad Street in Elizabeth, New Jersey was organized during the summer of 1904 with a capital stock of $50,000 to manufacture and deal in "automobiles and auto-boats." Incorporators were D. Mooney, William Bryan and George D. Willinger. Manufacture of a car is doubted.
The C.A. Martin Manufacturing Company was organized in Chicago, Illinois late in 1913 with a capital stock of $2000 to manufacture and sell motor vehicles. Incorporators were C.A. Martin, George T. Glover and William Schulze. Manufacture is doubted. George T. Glover had built a car under his own name in Chicago in 1902.

MARTIN — Buffalo, New York — (1898-1900) — In early 1898 the Martin Motor Wagon Company of Buffalo bought an engine for $275 from Charles B. King in Detroit. Obviously, this was for the purpose of study because that fall the company announced it would soon put a wagonette on the market powered by a gasoline motor designed by A.J. Martin. The Martin company continued to build its motor wagonette into the turn of the century. Whether A.J. Martin was related to Dr. Truman J. Martin who used his Columbia Electric in 1899 for the first motorized delivery of mail in Buffalo — and purportedly the United States — is not known.

MARTIN — Grand Rapids, Michigan — **(1903)** — Details regarding the gasoline automobile built by M.B. Martin of Grand Rapids are lacking, but trade press references from the period indicate that he produced a few of them beginning during the summer of 1903. Late that fall he moved his shop from 145 Monroe Street to 592 Cherry and continued the operation there awhile.

MARTIN — Atlanta, Georgia — **(1907)** — Al Martin was certain he had the makings of an automobile manufacturer, and in order to interest potential investors he built a single-cylinder 6 hp runabout which he completed in early 1907 and in which he decided to make a test trip to his hometown of Portland, Indiana. He waved good-bye to everyone in Atlanta, and nine harrowing months later he arrived in Portland . . . on a train. Twenty miles from home, after numerous accidents had turned the vehicle into "the beginning of a junkyard," both Martin and his car had given up. The car had cost him $725. He sold the remains for $15, and decided against becoming an automobile manufacturer.

1910 Martin, runabout, WLB

MARTIN — York, Pennsylvania — **(1910)** — In 1909 the Martin Carriage Works of York went automotive with a highwheeler powered by a two-cylinder 16 hp engine and fitted with planetary transmission and chain drive. The company's sole offerings that year and for all years after 1910 were commercial vehicles. In 1910, however, Martin also offered a six-passenger touring car on the same chassis. Martin trucks were produced through 1915, succeeded that year by the Atlas which was produced through 1923.

1921 Martin Scootmobile, runabout, NAHC

MARTIN — Springfield, Massachusetts — **(1921-1922)** — This Martin was a three-wheeler powered by a two-cylinder air-cooled engine. Its wheelbase was 60 inches, its weight 150 pounds, and its price 250 dollars. The car was made almost entirely of aluminum. It was designed by Charles H. Martin, the inventor of a device by which a truck could be converted into a tractor who had organized the Martin Rocking Fifth Wheel Company in Springfield for its manufacture in 1915. In September of 1921 the Martin Motor Company in Springfield was organized to produce Charles Martin's little three-wheeler. This new firm made more news than otherwise it would have because of the man who financed it: none other than Charles J. Glidden, famous in the automobile world as the donor of the Glidden trophy and the originator of the Glidden tours. The Martin company, of which he was president, marked Glidden's return to the automobile field and business life. He might have chosen more wisely. In November it was

announced that the third Martin prototype — with steel body and Henderson motorcycle engine — was undergoing tests in Springfield, and that the most successful of the three cars thus far built would be put into production early in 1922. By April of 1922 the Martin was declared not yet ready for manufacture. More than likely, it never was. The Martin three-wheeler venture failed before the end of 1922. Had it been brought to market, most probably the car would have carried the tradename Scoutmobile, Scootamobile or Scootmobile, references to these designations appearing on occasion during the development period.

1928 Martin Dart, coupe, FP

MARTIN — Garden City, New York — **(1928-1932)** — Two hundred dollars for a car with garage included. What a buy that would have been. The idea belonged to James V. Martin of Garden City, New York, who called in a Long Island neighbor, Miles H. Carpenter, the man behind the Phianna, to engineer it into reality. The Martin idea was, in his words, "the smallest motor car for practical purposes ever made." It had a 60-inch wheelbase, a four-cylinder 29 hp Cleveland motorcycle engine, and suspension by elastic airplane cord. The entire package in coupe form weighed 600 pounds, was capable of 40-50 mpg and the same mph — and would arrive in a packing crate that could double as its garage. Three prototype Martin Darts (as they were designated then) were completed and tested by March of 1928. For three years thereafter James Martin sought financing to get into manufacture; for a while it appeared he might have it. One James William Bryan, a promoter from Washington, D.C., entered the Martin picture in 1929, talked to Sears, Roebuck, and began rumors that a "prominent mail order house" would market the car. Sears immediately denied the rumor. The announcement of Martin Motors, Inc. was almost immediately followed by announcement of the Martin Motor Truck Company, for manufacture of a $450 baby truck on the same chassis as the coupe. A prototype of it was built and tested. Then virtually nothing happened for a year. In 1931 the M.P. Moller Motor Car Company in Hagerstown, Maryland strode onto the scene. Production of both the baby car and truck was now all set to start there. Possibly a few vehicles were built — by now the wheelbase was 70 inches, the weight 750 pounds, the price $250 — but no assembly line was ever started up. The Dart designation had by now been dropped in favor of Midget — and in 1931, shortly before defeat was admitted, the car's name was changed to Victory. At the 1932 National Automobile Show in New York, James V. Martin displayed two experimental rear-engined cars of his own design — a four-wheeler and a three-wheeler — which were streamlined along Jaray principles and which incorporated numerous airplane design features. But the Great Depression was raging by now. Not even a prayer of producing these latest Martin vehicles followed. After the Second World War, James Martin produced the Martinette and Stationette, but neither of them for very long. He died in 1956.

1932 Martin, rear-engined experimental, KM

1928-1930 MARTIN
Dart — 4-cyl., 29 hp, 60" wb

	FP	5	4	3	2	1
Coupe-2/3P	200	2000	3000	4200	6500	14,000

1931 MARTIN
Midget/Victory — 4-cyl., 29 hp, 70" wb

	FP	5	4	3	2	1
Coupe-2/3P	250	2100	3100	4300	6800	14,500

MARTIN WASP — From 1919 to 1924 the Martin Wasp Corporation produced automobiles in Bennington, Vermont which were sold under the tradename of Wasp. Refer to Wasp.

MARTINDALE & MILLIKAN — The names refer to F.N. Martindale and Frank M. Millikan. The car which resulted from the collaboration was called the Continental, built in Franklin, Indiana from 1910-1914. Only in 1914 was the car referred to by the partners' names. Refer to Continental.

MARTINE — The Martine Motor Car Company was organized in Westfield, New Jersey during the spring of 1910 with a capital stock of $25,000 for the manufacture of automobiles. Incorporators were Levi D. and Harry C. Darby and George W. Frederick. Manufacture is doubted.

MARVEL — The first car to be produced by the Duesenberg brothers was initially planned to be called the Marvel. But when Edward R. Mason, a local attorney, offered to assist financially, the name was quickly changed. The Mason was subsequently built from 1906 to 1910 in Des Moines, and from 1912 to 1915 in Waterloo, Iowa. Refer to Mason.

1907 Marvel, runabout, WLB

MARVEL — Detroit, Michigan — (1907)— The Marvel followed Paragon into the same Rivard and Mullett street factory in Detroit. It was a runabout as well, with twice the cylinders and twice the horsepower of its predecessor, but a life equally as short. There was no connection between the two firms. The new Marvel Motor Car Company was announced late in 1906; J.C. Foster was its general manager, William A. Phister its superintendent, and the plan was for the production of 325 cars in 1907. The Marvel sported shaft drive, thermo-syphon cooling, full elliptic springs and an $800 price tag. In the early fall of 1907 the company building it declared bankruptcy, its liabilities about $40,000, its assets about $4000. But the Marvel was not quite dead yet. Another group of entrepreneurs arrived, bought the company assets, and declared itself ready to resume production of the car as the Crescent. The Crescent didn't last long either.

1907 MARVEL
Model A — 2-cyl., 14 hp, 84" wb

Runabout-2P	800	—	—	—	—	—

1900 Maryland Steamer, runabout, WLB

894

MARYLAND STEAM — Luke, Maryland — (1900-1901) — The Maryland Automobile & Manufacturing Company was incorporated during the spring of 1900 with a capital stock of $5000 and by the fall had moved into the foundry and machine shops of the Twin Towns Manufacturing Company in Luke. (References to the firm's earlier location in the town of Cumberland appear to be in error.) In December the factory was blown down by gale force winds. "An interesting thing in connection with the accident," *The Motor World* reported, "is that the owners of the plant were the only holders of a tornado policy in the entire county, and are by their foresight thus amply protected against loss." When the plant was put back together, production resumed. The Maryland company's products included tubular shell boilers of various sizes (a specialty of the firm) and a variety of steam vehicles fitted with two-cylinder engines and single chain drive. The model list was a long one and the price range was $900-$2500. Production was short lived, however. By May 15th of 1901, *The Horseless Age* reported that receivership had been requested. In 1902 Maryland's vacated factory was turned over to a local beverage bottling company. Three of the cars produced were in use by the local Piedmont Foundry for some years thereafter, and at least one of the runabouts is known to be extant. The backers of the Maryland had been S.B. Harcom, Joseph Borrow, Alexander S. Stern, Milton Jacobi and John C. Bossel.

1900-1901 MARYLAND STEAM
Maryland Steam — 2-cyl.

	FP	5	4	3	2	1
Tourist Carriage	1400	3000	4000	6000	9500	21,000
Surrey	1200	2900	3700	5600	9100	20,000
Phaeton	1000	2900	3700	5600	9100	20,000
Runabout	900	2700	3600	5300	8800	19,000
Omnibus-14P	1800	3100	4200	6300	10,500	22,000
Omnibus	2500	2900	3700	5600	9100	20,000
Delivery Wagon	1500	2500	3500	5000	8500	18,000
Racing Machine	—	3000	4000	6000	9500	21,000

1908 Maryland, runabout, NAHC

MARYLAND — Baltimore, Maryland — (1907-1910) — This Maryland was the Ariel reborn, and it was probably reborn simply because the Sinclair-Scott Company of Baltimore wished to recoup its investment in parts supplied to Ariel for which it had not been paid prior to that company's quick dash into financial distress. Sinclair-Scott had been a manufacturer of canning factory machinery and hardware specialities for over seven decades, and with the advent of the automotive age had begun producing automobile parts under contract for a number of car manufacturers. When Ariel's past-due invoices remained unpaid, Sinclair-Scott simply took over. The name Maryland replaced Ariel on the radiator script, and the new car was introduced at the Baltimore Automobile Show in January 1907. The incorporation charter of the Ariel company was officially dissolved that April. Detail changes in the car's design followed, though these were not significant. What was significant was the Maryland's lackluster sales. In four years only 871 cars were built, and Sinclair-Scott purportedly lost money on every one of them. By the end of 1910 the company had returned wholeheartedly to the manufacture of food processing machinery.

1907 MARYLAND
Four — 26/28 hp, 100" wb

Touring-5P	2500	3200	4300	6500	11,000	23,000
Roadster	2500	3300	4400	6700	12,000	24,000

1908 MARYLAND
Four — 36 hp

Roadster (106" wb)	2500	3300	4400	6700	12,000	24,000
Touring (112" wb)	2500	3200	4300	6500	11,000	23,000
Limousine (112" wb)	3450	2500	3500	5000	8500	18,000

1909 MARYLAND
Four — 30 hp, 114" wb

Touring-5P	2500	3500	4500	7000	13,000	25,000
Roadster-4P	2350	3700	4700	7300	13,700	26,000
Town Car-4P	3200	2700	3600	5300	8800	19,000

1910 MARYLAND
Four — 28 hp, 116" wb

Model H Touring-5P	2750	3300	4400	6700	12,000	24,000
Model H Toy Tonneau-4P	2750	3500	4500	7000	13,000	25,000

MARYLAND ELECTRIC — Baltimore, Maryland — (1914) — The Maryland Electric Vehicle & Manufacturing Company was organized in Baltimore in March of 1914 for the production of electric commercial vehicles of up to 10,000 pounds capacity. Few of the large electrics were built, but the firm manufactured a number of small 1000-pound vehicles selling for $1250, and references indicate Maryland planned to use this chassis for a passenger car too. Perhaps a prototype was built, but the company was out of business before it could be sent to market. The only known catalog issued by Maryland Electric Vehicle & Manufacturing deals with commercial vehicles exclusively.

MARYLAND — Frederick, Maryland — (1922) — C.H. Kehne, W.C. Cadle, D.F. Davis and R.D. Zimmerman were the people behind the Maryland Motor Machine Company of Frederick. Theirs was an ambitious $250,000 corporation organized to deal in automobiles, tires and accessories and to act as an agency for the Nash car and "transport trucks." Early in 1922 the company also made known its intention to manufacture a medium-priced car. Work on a prototype was begun. By mid-July of 1922, however, the Maryland company in receivership. According to a report in *Automotive Industries* that month, no cars had been manufactured.

MARYSVILLE — Marysville, Ohio — (1905) — The Marysville Motor Car Company was organized late in 1905 to manufacture automobiles in Marysville. Prominent among the official staff were Harry Tarkington (who previously had been superintending the manufacture of the Sommer, which had recently died in Detroit), H.A. Stephenson, George Rausch and Dr. L.T. Henderson. Both the prototype and the early production cars were slated to be built in the machine shop of Thomas Brown on Plum Street pending the construction of a permanent factory. No permanent factory was built, however; this venture died at the prototype stage. "Although a car was completed some time ago and found to have good features," *The Motor Way* reported in June 1906, "lack of capital made it impossible for the Marysville Motor Company to actually begin manufacture. Local papers are appealing to the townspeople to help the company financially."

MASCOTTE — Although various car rosters have included it as a make, the Mascotte was instead a model of the Maxwell introduced for the 1912 model year. Refer to Maxwell.

MASON — The Mason Motor Car Company was organized in New York City during the spring of 1916 with a capital stock of $30,000 for the manufacture of engines and automobiles. Incorporators were N.N. Mason, J. Ward and A.W. Logan. Manufacture of a car is doubted.

The Mason-Harvey Company was organized in Chicago, Illinois during the fall of 1904 with a capital stock of $2500 to manufacture and repair automobiles. W.W. Harvey and W.R. Mason were the partners involved. Manufacture is doubted, but the firm is known to have taken on the agencies for the Austin and Baker Electric.

The Mason-Richardson Corporation was organized in Brooklyn, New York early in 1919 with a capital stock of $25,000 for the manufacture of automobiles and machinery. Incorporators were R.W. and F.J. Richardson and C.J. Mason. Manufacture of a car is doubted.

MASON STEAM — Dorchester, Massachusetts — (1898-1899) — William B. Mason was a Massachusetts inventor who built a steam car of his own design in 1898. The reason for the car was to demonstrate the governing regulator he had devised; consequently he did not build another, but turned his attention to manufacture of the device, as well as the engines for Locomobile initially and for the Stanley Steamer until 1903. He died in February 1911 at the age of fifty-eight. According to his obituary in *The Milton Record*, "the reducing valve perfected by him [was] used on three-quarters of the locomotives in the country." The firm he founded survived him. The Mason Steam Regulator Company evolved into the Mason-Neilan Regulator Company. About twenty years ago, it moved to Norwood, Massachusetts, where it remains in operation to this day.

1907 Mason, runabout, HAC

MASON — Des Moines, Iowa — (1906-1910)/Waterloo, Iowa — (1910-1914) — The Mason Motor Car Company was incorporated early in 1906 in Des Moines. It was named for Edward R. Mason, a local attorney who supplied the money. Supplying the two-cylinder car to be built was Fred S. Duesenberg, who with his brother August had opened a garage in town in 1903 where the following year they built their first automobile. Initially they had planned to call it the Marvel, but when Mason arrived with the money, the brothers quickly agreed to the name change. "The Fastest and Strongest Two-Cylinder Car in America" was the Mason's slogan in 1906, and it quickly proved itself adept as a hill-climber and, after 1907, as a race car. Late in 1908 the firm was reorganized as the Mason Automobile Company, and early in 1909 Mason indicated that a new addition was being built to the Des Moines factory. In June, however, F.L. Maytag and his son Elmer H., who built washing machines and agricultural machinery in Newton, purchased a controlling interest in the Mason company and moved it to the former plant of the Waterloo Motor Works in Waterloo.

There, early in 1910, the firm was reorganized as the Maytag-Mason Motor Car Company. The announced plan was to continue the two-cylinder car as the Mason and to introduce a new four to be called the Maytag. The four was indeed introduced as a Maytag for the 1910 season, with the two continuing as the Mason. For 1911, both lines carried the Maytag name. "It was because Senator Maytag, with the eye of the mechanical expert, appreciated the mechanical excellencies of the Mason that he was willing to invest a large sum of money in the building of and lend his name to the 'Premier Hill Climber' and was glad to sacrifice other important interests that he might devote more of his time and attention to its greater development" was the way the point was belabored in a brochure that year. The implication was that Maytag had improved upon and refined the Duesenbergs' design. Whether the Duesenbergs objected to this inference is not known, but they reclaimed the Mason name which they used for their own four-cylinder racing cars which performed admirably in numerous contests and which barely missed qualifying for the 1912 Indianapolis 500. By then the Maytags were out of Mason. Apparently, they had bought huge quantities of parts and had been unable to sell their cars fast enough to pay their bills. A creditors' committee brought suit for notes due and contracts unfulfilled. The Maytags opted out of the whole venture, and on January 12th, 1912 the firm was reorganized yet again as the Mason Motor Company — and Edward R. Mason again had control. Mason-Maytag creditors agreed to a settlement, and Mason carried on. All cars were once more known as Masons. Although a Knight-engined Mason was announced to be built in January 1912, it never arrived. In 1913 the Duesenbergs left Iowa to establish their Duesenberg Motor Company in St. Paul, Minnesota. They still retained some ties with Edward Mason in Waterloo, however. In mid-summer of 1913 a new car for the 1914 model year was announced: the $3000 Mason-Mohler with a four-cylinder 65 hp Duesenberg engine mounted on a 128-inch wheelbase chassis that was underslung in the front and overslung at the rear. By now the Mason Motor Company was in receivership, its creditors having refused to grant an extension and the firm having met neither its bonds at maturity nor the overdue interest thereon. "Despite the black outlook, E.R. Mason . . . has not entirely lost hope of saving the property," *Motor World* reported on October 16th, 1913. Production struggled along under receivership, but by the end of 1914 Mason finally admitted defeat. In September of 1915 the Mason factory in Waterloo was sold for $35,000. Edward Mason never produced another car. The Duesenberg brothers did.

1906 Mason, touring, NAHC

1906-1908 MASON
Two - 24 hp, 90" wb

	FP	5	4	3	2	1
Tour.-5P	1350	2700	3000	5300	8800	19,000
Rbt.-2P	1285	2900	3700	5600	9100	20,000

1909 Mason, tourabout, HAC

1909 MASON
Two - 24 hp, 96" wb

Tour.-5P	1350	2900	3700	5600	9100	20,000
Tourabout-4P	1250	3000	4000	6000	9500	21,000

1910 MASON
Two - 24 hp, 96" wb

Tourabout-2/4P	1250	2700	3600	5300	8800	19,000
Toy Tour.-4P	1300	3000	4000	6000	9500	21,000
Tour.-5P	1350	2900	3700	5600	9100	20,000

1910 Mason, touring, HAC

1912 Mason, model H, roadster, HAC

1912 MASON
Two - 20 hp, 96" wb

	FP	5	4	3	2	1
Model A Tour.	1050	2900	3700	5600	9100	20,000
Model B Torpedo	1050	3000	4000	6000	9500	21,000
Model C Rdst.	1050	3000	4000	6000	9500	21,000
Four - 30 hp, 116" wb						
Model D Rdst.	1750	3100	4200	6300	10,500	22,000
Model E Tour.	1000	3000	4000	6000	9500	21,000
Model F Tour.	1150	3100	4200	6300	10,500	22,000
Model G Tour.	1250	3200	4300	6500	11,000	23,000
Model H Rdst.	1650	3300	4400	6700	12,000	24,000

1913 Mason, model C, touring, HAC

1913 MASON
Model C - 2-cyl., 20 hp, 96" wb

Fore-Door Tour.-5P	900	3000	4000	6000	9500	21,000

Model K - 4-cyl., 30 hp, 116" wb

Fore-Door Tour.-5P	1290	3100	4200	6300	10,500	22,000

1914 Mason-Mohler, coupe, WLB

896

1914 MASON
Model K - 4-cyl., 30 hp, 116" wb

	FP	5	4	3	2	1
Tour.-5P	1350	3000	4000	6000	4500	21,000
Mason-Mohler - 4-cyl., 65 hp, 128" wb						
Rdst.	3000	3200	4300	6500	11,000	23,000
Cpe.	3150	2500	3500	5000	8500	18,000

MASON — Boston, Massachusetts — (1907) — That a car called the Mason was exhibited at the Boston Automobile Show in 1907 by a company called Puritan has been documented. Details regarding it are lacking. In January 1907 a firm called the Puritan Motor Company was indicated in the trade press as a recent incorporation in the field. Probably this was an offshoot venture of the Puritan Engine Company which had been producing gasoline engines at its plant at 95 Milk Street in Boston for a few years already. The idea of automobile manufacture was discarded almost immediately; after the Boston show the Mason car was not heard from again. The Puritan Engine Company was still in business on Milk Street in 1909.

MASON-MOHLER — The Mason-Mohler was introduced during the summer of 1913 as a 1914 model of the Mason then being built in Waterloo, Iowa. Refer to Mason.

MASON-SEAMAN — New York, New York — (1914) — In 1914, Albert F. Rockwell, who had been described as a "will-o-the-wisp dreamer" a few years earlier during his Rockwell and Houpt-Rockwell ventures, was dreaming again. His idea this time was a gas-electric taxicab which he had designed and which he planned to build in association with W.H. Barnard of the Mason-Seaman Transportation Company. This venture does not seem to have proceeded any further than the prototype stage. This was rather a pity, because the Rockwell taxi had been one of the finest in New York City.

c.1918 Mason Tourist King, phaeton, KM

MASON TOURIST KING — Newark, New Jersey — (c. 1918) — Very little is known about the Mason Tourist King, save for the fact that it was built and that it still exists. A big phaeton with wire wheels and six-cylinder Continental Red Seal engine, it was produced with a specific idea in mind: sale to the government as a military staff car. Among its unusual features was the design of the right front passenger seat which was fitted to and swung out with the front door. The body lines of the car were interesting, with nothing of the homemade or backyard look to the design. Although a building date of 1915 has been suggested, 1918 seems more likely, and Newark, New Jersey the place. What killed the Mason Tourist King was the Armistice.

MASSACHUSETTS — Lynn, Massachusetts — (1899) — In 1899 John C. Welch completed a vehicle powered by an engine he had purchased from the St. Louis Gas Motor Company. During the late summer that year, he reported its successful testing and the organizing of the Massachusetts Motor Vehicle Company in Lynn for its manufacture. "Twenty different styles of automobiles are reported to be completed or in process of construction in and around Lynn," reported *The Motor Age* in September. Conceivably, a few of these might have been Welch's Massachusetts car, but the evidence suggests that his manufacturing venture did not survive into the turn of the century.

MASSACHUSETTS STEAM — Pittsfield, Massachusetts — (1901) — Whether the Massachusetts Steam Wagon Company ever had time to build more than a prototype of its steam vehicle is doubtful. In May of 1901 the firm announced its intention to manufacture in Pittsfield. In June the Massachusetts Steam Wagon Company reported that reorganization was now ongoing and the decision had been made to locate the factory elsewhere than Pittsfield. Massachusetts Steam Wagon was not heard from again. So far as is known, its sole completed effort was one big beer truck.

MASSIE — Quincy, Illinois — (1903) — Samuel B. and Edwin S. Massie were a father-son team operating a machine shop at 219 North Fourth Street in Quincy. In 1903 the Massies built an automobile called the Massie to custom order, but manufacture was never comtemplated. Instead Massie & Son confined efforts thereafter to automobile repair.

MASSILLON — The Massillon Developing Company was organized during the summer of 1917 with a capital stock of $5000 for the manufacture and sale of automobiles in Massillon, Ohio. Among the incorporators were S. Bert Hankins, Grace A. Snyder, Mary R. Yohe, Charles E. Nickles and Carl N. Nickles. Manufacture is doubted.

1909 Massillon, Six, roadster, NAHC

MASSILLON — Massillon, Ohio — (1909) — In March of 1909 W.S. Reed announced his intention to build thirty-five cars that year under the name of Massillon, the W.S. Reed Company being capitalized at $10,000 for that purpose. Allied with him in this venture were Melville Schworm (who had built a steam car in Massillon in 1888), F.O. Shoemaker and H. McYost. The Massillon was a 60 hp six-cylinder shaft-drive car which as a 118-inch wheelbase roadster was to sell for $1750, as a 124-inch touring for $2000. Scarcely had the assembly line been started than W.S. Reed was in financial trouble. Before the year's end he sold out to C.P. Munch who ultimately produced the car as the Keystone in both Pennsylvania and New York.

1909 MASSILLON
Six — 60 hp, 118" wb

	FP	5	4	3	2	1
Roadster-2/3/4P	1750	3100	4200	6300	10,500	22,000
Six — 60 hp, 124" wb						
Touring-5/7P	2000	3500	4500	7000	13,000	25,000

MASSNICK-PHIPPS — Detroit, Michigan — (1914-1915) — "Contracting machinists and auto parts" was the phrase used by Frederick C. Massnick and Walter Phipps to describe the work of their Massnick-Phipps Manufacturing Company at 1091 Champlain in Detroit. Although no car was built carrying the firm's name, Massnick-Phipps did build the Robie in 1914 and, purportedly, the Perkins during that same period. The firm was most famous for its production of the Perkins four and eight-cylinder engines used by several car manufacturers, including Remington, during this period. In 1915 Massnick-Phipps moved into the plant of the former Wahl Motor Company on East Congress where it would be possible to increase engine production from fifty to one hundred units a day.

MASTER — Cleveland, Ohio — (1917-1918) — The Master Motor Car Company of Cleveland was incorporated with a capital stock of $200,000 for the purpose of manufacturing motorcars in early 1917. Principals involved were Alfred Whiteworth, Milton R. Slocum, Fred G. Theuer, Perry J. Eubanks and S.J. Kornhauser. The Master was a six-cylinder 100 hp car with a $5000 price tag produced as runabout, touring car and limousine. The company was short-lived, and the production minimal. Although some commercial vehicles may have been built, this Master is not to be confused with the Chicago company producing the better-known Master trucks from 1917 to 1929.

1926 Masterbilt Six, sedan, HAC

MASTERBILT SIX — Detroit, Michigan — (1926) — The Masterbilt Six was produced by the Govreau-Nelson Engineering Company of Detroit. Victor Govreau had been chief engineer of the Pan Motor Company of St. Cloud, Minnesota, although he had not been involved in the fraud that had resulted in Pan promoter Sam Pandolfo's taking up residence in Leavenworth. Several other blameless officers of the Pan operation joined him in this effort to produce a new motorcar capitalizing on the current popularity of the air-cooled Franklin. "Heat Controlled" was the term Govreau preferred. At least one chassis and one complete car were built. The latter was a four-door sedan which resembled a number of other cars of the period, Reo, Packard, Hupmobile, Peerless and Willys-Knight among them. The double-belt molding offered an appreciative nod to the styling of Ray Dietrich. The absence of hood louvers was, of course, Franklin-like. Possibly the Pan association worked against Govreau and his associates. The capital necessary for production was never forthcoming, and the prototypes eventually were scrapped. The Govreau-Nelson company, later anglicized to Govro-Nelson, remains in existence to this day in Detroit as the manufacturers of drilling units. In 1929 it had become a subsidiary of Ex-Cell-O Aircraft and Tool Corporation of Detroit.

1904 Matheson, touring, HAC

MATHESON — Grand Rapids, Michigan — (1903)/Holyoke, Massachusetts — (1904-1905)/Wilkes-Barre, Pennsylvania — (1906-1912) — Frank F. and Charles W. Matheson were employed by the Fred Macey Company in their hometown of Grand Rapids at the turn of the century. The Macey firm was in the mail order business dealing in office furniture, which did not interest the mechanically-inclined brothers much. After initial negotiations with Grand Rapids engine builder Clark Sintz came to naught, they traveled to Holyoke, Massachusetts to talk to Charles G. Greuter whose Holyoke Motor Works had recently been put up for sale. The Mathesons bought both Holyoke and the services of Greuter, who would remain as chief engineer of the company until 1908. Actually, the Mathesons had been more interested in the overhead valve engine Greuter had designed than in the Holyoke company itself. Initially, production of engines and transmissions only was conducted in the Holyoke shop, with the cars assembled in Grand Rapids. The entire operation moved to Holyoke early in 1904, however, but this was strictly an interim expediency while the Mathesons shopped around for a permanent location. Meantime, late in 1903, the Matheson Motor Car Company, Ltd. had been organized. Sixty Matheson cars were produced during the company's first fiscal year, which was a splendid beginning, because at $5000 the Matheson obviously was not a car for the masses. Late in 1905 the Wilkes-Barre (Pennsylvania) Board of Trade invited Matheson to town, and the company relocated there in March of 1906. Now the Matheson really got going. In competition the big Mathesons were formidable competitors, with such famous drivers as Louis Chevrolet, Ralph De Palma, Frank Lescault and Ralph Mongini driving them. A Matheson touring car with seven passengers aboard established a world's record of a mile in fifty seconds at Atlantic City in September 1906. In New York, Charles A. Singer and H.V. Palmer were the Matheson agents; they subsequently went on to build the Palmer-Singer. William Randolph Hearst owned two Mathesons, and Harlan W. Whipple, former president of the American Automobile Association, wrote the company in 1908 that "my Matheson has come nearer being the ideal touring car that I have been eight years hunting for than anything else I have ever had." With the departure of Charles Greuter, the Matheson engineering department secured the services of French engineer L.D. Kenan, and later A.M. Dean. A six-cylinder Matheson joined the traditional fours for the 1909 model year. By now nearly 400 workers were employed in the Wilkes Barre plant. Although chain drive was fitted to some of the Matheson fours until as late as 1910, the six was shaft-drive from the beginning. It was improved into the Silent Six for 1911, the year in which the slogan "Have You Tried to Hear It Run?" was adopted. But by now the company was in financial trouble. Its first receivership arrived in July of 1910 and was lifted in November with a reorganization as the Matheson Automobile Company. Its second receivership arrived in December of 1912, and the company did not survive that one. The announced date for the sale of the Matheson assets was April 21st, 1913. Frank Matheson remained at the factory until 1914, however, supervising the parts business until the plant was taken over by a New York concern for the manufacture of munitions for the war effort. After the Armistice Matheson and the munitions people joined Raymond Owen in the production of the Owen-Magnetic car. With the failure of the Owen-Magnetic in 1921, Frank Matheson bought his old plant back to use as a distributorship for Oakland (and later Pontiac), Dodge and GMC trucks. His brother Charles Matheson, meantime, became vice-president of sales for Dodge Brothers and later served in the same capacity at Oakland when the Pontiac was introduced. Still later he was the man who launched the sales effort for the new DeSoto. When he died in 1940, he was general sales manager for Graham.

1903-1904 MATHESON
Four — 24 hp, 96" wb

	FP	5	4	3	2	1
Touring-7P	5000	2700	3600	5300	8800	19,000

1905 Matheson, touring, HAC

1905 MATHESON
Four — 24 hp, 106" wb

	FP	5	4	3	2	1
Touring-7P	5000	3100	4200	6300	10,500	22,000
Four — 40 hp, 106" wb						
Limousine-7P	6000	2900	3700	5600	9100	20,000

1906 Matheson, runabout, HAC

1906 MATHESON
Four — 40/45 hp, 112" wb

Touring-7P	6000	3500	4500	7000	13,000	25,000
Four — 60/65 hp, 118" wb						
Touring-7P	7500	4700	6100	9900	19,000	33,000

1907 Matheson, touring, HAC

1907 MATHESON
Four — 35 hp, 123" wb

Runabout-2P	4000	3300	4400	6700	12,000	24,000
Touring-7P	4500	3200	4300	6500	11,000	23,000
Limousine-7P	5500	2700	3600	5300	8800	19,000
Landaulet-7P	5500	2900	3700	5600	9100	20,000
Four — 50 hp, 129" wb						
Runabout-2P	5000	4500	5800	9500	18,000	32,000
Touring-7P	5500	4400	5600	9200	17,300	31,000
Limousine-7P	6500	3000	4000	6000	9500	21,000
Landaulet-7P	6500	3100	4200	6300	10,500	22,000

1908 MATHESON
Four — 50 hp, 128" wb

Touring-7P	5500	5000	6500	11,000	22,000	35,000
Runabout-2P	5250	4900	6300	10,300	21,000	34,000
Limousine-7P	6500	3000	4000	6000	9500	21,000
Landaulette-7P	6500	3100	4200	6300	10,500	22,000

1909 MATHESON
Six — 50 hp, 125 1/2" wb

Touring-5/7P	3000	4900	6300	10,300	21,000	34,000
Four — 50 hp, 128" wb						
Touring-7P	4500	5000	6500	11,000	22,000	35,000
Roadster-2P	4350	5200	6800	11,300	23,000	36,000
Limousine-7P	5500	3000	4000	6000	9500	21,000

1908 Matheson, touring, HAC

1909 Matheson, touring, JAC

1910 Matheson, touring, WLB

1910 MATHESON
Model E — 4-cyl., 50 hp, 128" wb

	FP	5	4	3	2	1
Touring-7P	5000	5200	6800	11,300	23,000	36,000
Limousine-7P	5750	3100	4200	6300	10,500	22,000
Model M — 6-cyl., 50 hp, 125 1/2" wb						
Toy Tonneau-4/5P	3000	4900	6300	10,300	21,000	34,000
Touring-5P	3500	4700	6100	9900	19,000	33,000
Limousine-7P	4200	2900	3700	5600	9100	20,000

1911 Matheson, limousine, HAC

898

1911 MATHESON
Silent Six — 6 cyl., 50 hp, 125 1/2" wb

	FP	5	4	3	2	1
Model 18 Touring-5P	3500	4700	6100	9900	19,000	33,000
Model 18 Toy Tonneau-4P	3500	5000	6500	11,000	22,000	35,000
Model 23 Limousine-6P	4700	3000	4000	6000	9500	21,000
Model 18 Tour. (135" wb)	4000	5400	7300	11,800	25,000	38,000

Big Four — 4-cyl., 50 hp, 128" wb

Touring-7P	5000	5000	6500	11,000	22,000	35,000
Toy Tonneau-7P	5000	5000	6500	11,000	22,000	35,000
Limousine-7P	5750	3000	4000	6000	9500	21,000
Landaulet-7P	5750	3100	4200	6300	10,500	22,000

1912 Matheson, touring, HAC

1912 MATHESON
Silent Six — 6-cyl., 50 hp, 125 1/2/135" wb

Open Touring	3500	5200	6800	11,300	23,000	36,000
Fore-Door Touring-5P	3750	5300	7000	11,500	24,000	37,000
Fore-Door Touring-7P	4000	5400	7300	11,800	25,000	38,000
Toy Tonneau-4P	3500	5300	7000	11,500	24,000	37,000
Speedster-2P	3500	5800	8000	12,500	28,000	40,000
Limousine-6P	4700	3100	4200	6300	10,500	22,000
Landaulet-6P	4700	3200	4300	6500	11,000	23,000
Fore-Door Demi-Limo.-7P	6500	3900	4800	7700	14,300	27,000
Fore-Door Berlin Limo.-7P	6500	4000	5000	8000	15,000	28,000
Roadster-2P	4500	5000	6500	11,000	22,000	35,000
Cruiser-4P	4000	5200	6800	11,300	23,000	36,000
Limousine-7P	6700	3700	4700	7300	13,700	26,000

MATHEWS — Lidgerwood, North Dakota — (1912-1914) — J.L. Mathews of Lidgerwood is known to have built two cars during the pre-World War I era. The first, a 40/45 hp two-passenger that was nicknamed the "Bull Moose Racer," was licensed in 1912. The second was a 30 hp roadster licensed in 1914.

1931 Mathis, HAC

MATHIS — Lansing, Michigan — (1931) — The French Mathis, a little car which sold in big numbers on the Continent, was one of the last-ditch efforts of William C. Durant to save his second empire. In the summer of 1930 Durant Motors announced plans to build an American version under license in Lansing. Huge quantities of brochures for the $455 "Wonder Car" were printed up, carefully designating the vehicle as a light car not a small car, the latter anathema on the American market by now. Although a company called American Mathis, Inc. was organized for its production, the car itself was always officially referred to as the Mathis, and occasionally spelled phonetically in promotion as "May-theece," which wasn't quite the way the French pronounced it. Among the people involved with the Mathis project was Edward Ver Linden, the former Peerless president who had recently rejoined the Durant organization. (Ver Linden had been among the people instrumental in the management of Durant Motors in the early twenties.) The Mathis was introduced at the New York Automobile Show in January 1931, and showed out afterwards at the Chicago show. In addition to the $455 coupe, a $445 light delivery car was shown, and a roadster was promised anon. All versions carried the same four-cylinder 12 hp engine in a 96-inch-wheelbase chassis. Sources vary as to the quantity of Mathis cars produced in this country in the next short months though it would seem that at least a few were. But by April 1931 receivers were removing the fixtures from Billy Durant's offices in New York City, and any ongoing Mathis production in Lansing ceased then too.

MATRIX — The Matrix Automobile Company was organized in Joliet, Illinois during the summer of 1912 for the manufacture of motorcars. Behind this venture were Earl D. Fuller and William O. Dayton of Joliet, and J.T. Wilcox of Fairbury. Manufacture is doubted. W.O. Dayton, incidentally, was involved in four other automobile ventures which did result in production: Reliable Dayton, Dayton, Crusader and New Era.

MATTHEWS — From 1906-1907 in Camden, New Jersey, the Matthews Motor Company manufactured a four-cylinder car which was marketed under the tradename of Sovereign. Refer to Sovereign.

MAUMEE — Dundee, Michigan — (1906) — In May of 1906 the newly organized Maumee Motor Car Works took over the Dundee factory of the defunct Wolverine Automobile Company. Company organizers were J.G. Swindeman, W.K. Terry and Frank Blair, all of Toledo, in which city the firm's offices would be located. The new car from this venture was to be named the Maumee, or Maumee-Craig, the name under which it had been introduced at the Grand Central Palace Automobile Show in New York the preceding January. By late fall, however, the announcement came that the Maumee Motor Car Works had been succeeded by the Craig-Toledo Motor Company. All production cars were known as Craig-Toledos.

MAX — The Max Motor Car Company was organized in Providence, Rhode Island early in 1907 with a capital stock of $20,000 "to manufacture automobiles, acquire letters patent, etc." Incorporators were Albert Curtis Tingley, Leonard C. Tingley and Walter C. Suesman, all of Providence. Manufacture of a car is doubted.

1913 Maxen Electric, roadster, WLB

MAXEN ELECTRIC — Cedar Rapids, Iowa — (1904, 1913) — In 1904 in Cedar Rapids a man named Roy McCartney built an electric car he called the Maxen. It featured an underslung frame and a sloping Renault-type hood. McCartney definitely planned manufacture but could not secure the necessary financial backing. Still, he was able to complete three cars, one of which remains extant, before giving up. Approximately a decade later, in 1913, a Maxen Motors Company of Cedar Rapids announced its intention to enter the automobile field for the production of an underslung electric runabout. A brochure was printed up, and a prototype built, but that was it. No doubt Roy McCartney was behind this venture as well.

MAXIM — "C.W. Maxim of Middleboro, Massachusetts is about to engage in the manufacture of automobiles at that place," reported *The Horseless Age* in August 1902. Whether he ever did is not known.

1908 Maxim-Goodridge Electric, victoria, NAHC

MAXIM MOTOR TRICYCLE — Hartford, Connecticut — (1895)/MAXIM-GOODRIDGE ELECTRIC — (1908) — Hiram Percy Maxim was a big name in the automobile field at the turn of the century. He had built his first car five years earlier, a trike devised from a Columbia bicycle and fitted with a three-cylinder four-cycle gasoline engine with two flywheels. Thereafter Maxim allied himself with the Pope interests, and subsequently the Electric Vehicle Company, manufacturers of the Columbia in Hartford. He was the firm's chief engineer, and much in the news, since the people behind the Columbia were also the people who owned the Selden Patent. During the summer of 1907, however, Maxim resigned his position, and late that fall emphasized that he had severed all connections with his former employer. Now he allied himself with T.W. Goodridge, formerly general manager for the Studebaker Brothers in Indiana, and together they com-

899

pleted plans for a new electric car to be put on the market. A prototype of the one body style to be offered was built. It was a victoria phaeton that was comely if a bit old-fashioned. Worm drive and left-hand tiller steering were featured, and fifty miles to a battery charge and 18 mph were guaranteed. The car's price tag was to be $1800. At first the partners decided to call the vehicle a Maxim-Goodridge, though ultimately they decided Lenox Electric had a nicer ring to it. By the time they decided that, however, they also decided to break up their partnership. This apparently was Maxim's idea. He had developed his ''silent gun'' and launched into its manufacture instead. The Maxim-Goodridge project was dropped after the building of just the prototype. Its worm-drive feature, which had been patented by Maxim, was sold to the Waverley Company of Indianapolis. In 1910 T.W. Goodridge joined the Matheson Automobile Company in its sales agency office.

1911 Maxim Tri-Car, runabout, NAHC

MAXIM TRI-CAR — Thompsonville, Connecticut — (1911-1912)/Port Jefferson, New York — (1913-1914) — The Maxim Tri-Car was jointly designed by a Frenchman named Maxim Karminski and a German named George Peters who cribbed rather liberally from the Phanomen that had been designed by Gustav Hiller of Zittau (Germany) and was now enjoying considerable success on the Continent. Karminski and Peters thought the same success might be theirs in this country, and convinced the G.H. Bushnell Press Company of Thompsonville, Connecticut of the merit of their notion. Bushnell sold all of its cottonseed oil machinery to the American Machine & Manufacturing Company of Greenville, South Carolina during the summer of 1911 and was in the automobile manufacturing business that fall. The Maxim Tri-Car, which was introduced as a 1912 model, was designed for pleasure or business use, although its configuration certainly better adapted it for the latter. A tiller-steered tricycle with its motor perched atop the single front wheel, it was a try to garner the same market that Charles Duryea was attempting to lure with his light delivery tri-cars and that C.W. Kelsey was attempting to entice with his Motorette. The market was a very small one. The prototype Maxim Tri-Car had a single-cylinder engine; the production cars which followed were fitted with a two-cylinder 8 hp unit. The car's wheelbase was 96 inches, final drive was by chain, and the price was $395. The front bench seated two comfortably, and the delivery box was said to be easily removable for replacement by a second seat for two more passengers. Ten thousand cars in the next twelve months had been the projected output when the car was first announced by Karminski and Peters late in 1910. Undoubtedly that figure was not even approached. In July of 1913 the Maxim Tri-Car Manufacturing Company (as the organization was now restyled, Bushnell having opted out, and two officials of the company having resigned) announced its purchase of the Jefferson, Long Island factory that had until recently been devoted to production of the Only car. The Only had just moved into bankruptcy, the same situation in which the Maxim Tri-Car found itself the following year. Interestingly, during the early Twenties another Tri-Car called the Peters was produced in Philadelphia. The Peters this time was Karl R., but the car looked so much like a Maxim that there must have been a relationship between the two.

MAXTON — The Maxton Auto Company was organized early in 1913 with a capital stock of $50,000 to manufacture and deal in automobiles in Maxton, North Carolina. Behind this venture were A.J. McKinnon, R.M. Williams, Byron McCallum and Ernest Williams. Manufacture is doubted.

MAXWELL — The Maxwell Motor Car Company was organized in Lawrenceville, Illinois during the fall of 1914 with a capital stock of $200,000 to ''manufacture, buy, sell and repair automobiles.'' Behind this venture were Andrew L. Maxwell, Casper L. Lewis and Noah M. Tehill. Manufacture is doubted.

MAXWELL — Tarrytown, New York — (1905-1913)/New Castle, Indiana — (1906-1916)/Pawtucket, Rhode Island — (1905-1913) / Auburn, New York — (1908-1913)/Cranston, Rhode Island — (1909-1913) / Detroit, Michigan — (1913-1925) — The Maxwell resulted because Benjamin Briscoe was convinced that the automobile David Dunbar Buick was trying to build, with the help of Briscoe's money, would never amount to anything.

1905 Maxwell, model H, touring, HAC

Briscoe, whose sheet metal manufacturing plant in Detroit was a prosperous one, was anxious to get into the automobile business, and thus in 1903 when he happened upon Jonathan D. Maxwell, an engineer with experience at both Olds and Northern, he sold out his investment in the Buick project and formed a new partnership. Ben Briscoe always thought big; since he didn't have sufficient money himself to launch the new Maxwell in a big way, he entrained to the East and talked J.P. Morgan into providing two-thirds of the $150,000 investment which launched the Maxwell-Briscoe Motor Company. The factory in Tarrytown, New York in which John Brisben Walker had built his Mobile Steamer was leased for manufacture. And Jonathan D. Maxwell came up with a splendid little car featuring, a two-cylinder water-cooled engine (with mechanically operated inlet valves) mounted up front under a hood, a honeycomb radiator with thermo-syphon cooling, a two-speed planetary gearset, shaft drive and right-hand steering wheel. At $750 for the two-passenger tourabout and $1400 for the five-passenger touring, the Maxwell was a fine buy and sold well from the beginning. A pilot production run in Tarrytown produced 10 cars in 1904; 823 more followed the next year. All of these Maxwells were designated 1905 models. A four-cylinder model joined the Maxwell line in 1906, and twins and fours were produced through 1912. A particularly popular model was the ''Dr. Maxwell'' runabout, a car designed and promoted especially for physicians. By now thinking even bigger, Benjamin Briscoe had begun establishing branch factories in Auburn, New York and in Indiana and Rhode Island. Maxwell sales continued on the increase: 3785 cars in 1907, 4455 in 1908, 9460 in 1909. In addition to the efforts

1906 Maxwell, model M, touring limousine, HAC

of Maxwell and Briscoe, contribution to this sterling success was also made by the company's indefatigable sales manager, Cadwallader Washburn Kelsey whose penchant for thinking up publicity stunts was practically unparalleled. Most of these — teeterboard riding, chases with police, driving up steps to venerable buildings including churches, et al. — he captured on film for use in nickelodeons. And he proved the Maxwell's performance in more dignified ways too. The car won its class at Mount Washington, participated commendably in the Glidden Tours, and in 1908 a team of five Maxwells finished sixth through tenth in the light car race preceding the Grand Prize, a super performance for such a presumably underpowered car. In 1909 he persuaded Alice Huyler Ramsey and three of her lady friends to trek cross-country, from Hell's Gate in New York to the Golden Gate in San Francisco, in a Maxwell. In that era, the idea of women even comtemplating such a trek was preposterous; that they succeeded brought more press coverage than even Kelsey could have hoped for. In 1910 approximately 20,500 Maxwells were sold. Unfortunately, that year too, Ben Briscoe launched his United States Motor Company, com-

1907 Maxwell, model R, tourabout, JAC

bining Maxwell-Briscoe and Columbia (and ultimately others like Stoddard-Dayton and Brush). Kelsey thought he was crazy, believing that Maxwell-Briscoe (which now ranked number three in the industry behind Ford and Buick) should battle for first place a la Henry Ford with one car. Briscoe preferred the General Motors approach. Kelsey abruptly left the company to produce another car of his own, though Jonathan Maxwell (who had long been dismayed at Briscoe's expansionist policies too) stayed on, taking over Maxwell-Briscoe's presidency from Ben Briscoe, who preoccupied himself with U.S. Motor until its collapse later in 1912. Thereon Briscoe went off to try again with a new car named for himself, and Jonathan Maxwell sought to pick up the pieces of Maxwell-Briscoe. Most of the factories in which the car had been built were sold off, including the main Tarrytown plant in 1914 to William C. Durant for production of his new Chevrolet. By that time, however, Jonathan Maxwell had reorganized as the Maxwell Motor Company and had removed himself and his car to Detroit. There a refined version of his four (with the three-speed sliding gear transmission introduced in 1907) was continued, and a six was added to the line, but for the 1914 model year only. Maxwell fours continued to the end. Truck and bus production which had begun in 1905 was continued as well. In 1917 the 100,000th Maxwell was built. The crunch came about 1920, when hit by the postwar recession, Maxwell dealers found themselves hopelessly overstocked. At one point there were 17,000 unsold Maxwells. The company's 1922 marriage with Chalmers did not work out at all well, and by 1923 an industry wizard named Walter Percy Chrysler arrived to help. An engineering weakness in recent models had blemished the Maxwell name, which Chrysler sought to undo by recalling and repairing vehicles in the field gratis — and facelifting the car into a new model widely advertised as the Good Maxwell. By 1924 Chrysler had become president of the Maxwell-Chalmers organization. He introduced his new Chrysler in January that year. In mid-1925 the Chrysler Corporation was born. The last Maxwell was built in 1925. For the 1926 model year it was revamped into a new four-cylinder Chrysler. Jonathan D. Maxwell died in 1928 at the age of sixty-three.

1905 MAXWELL
Model L - 2-cyl., 8/12 hp, 72" wb

	FP	5	4	3	2	1
Tourabout-2P	750	2400	3400	4800	8000	17,000
Model H - 2-cyl., 16 hp, 88" wb						
Tour.-5P	1400	2500	3500	5000	8500	18,000

1906 MAXWELL
Model L - 2-cyl., 10 hp, 72" wb

	FP	5	4	3	2	1
Tourabout-2P	780	2400	3400	4800	8000	17,000
Model S - 2-cyl., 10 hp, 72" wb						
Gentlemen's Spdstr.	800	2500	3500	5000	8500	18,000
Model N - 2-cyl., 20 hp, 85" wb						
Dr. Maxwell Rbt.	1375	2300	3300	4600	7500	16,000
Model H - 2-cyl., 20 hp, 85" wb						
Tour.-5P	1450	2400	3400	4800	8000	17,000
Model M - 4-cyl., 36/40 hp, 104" wb						
Tour.-5P	3000	2700	3600	5300	8800	19,000

1907 Maxwell, model H.B., "Doctor Maxwell", HAC

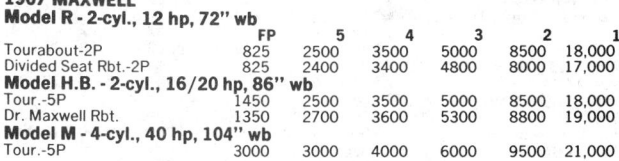

1907 MAXWELL
Model R - 2-cyl., 12 hp, 72" wb

	FP	5	4	3	2	1
Tourabout-2P	825	2500	3500	5000	8500	18,000
Divided Seat Rbt.-2P	825	2400	3400	4800	8000	17,000
Model H.B. - 2-cyl., 16/20 hp, 86" wb						
Tour.-5P	1450	2500	3500	5000	8500	18,000
Dr. Maxwell Rbt.	1350	2700	3600	5300	8800	19,000
Model M - 4-cyl., 40 hp, 104" wb						
Tour.-5P	3000	3000	4000	6000	9500	21,000

1908 Maxwell, model M, touring, HAC

1908 MAXWELL
Model LC - 2-cyl., 14 hp, 72" wb

	FP	5	4	3	2	1
Rbt.	825	2300	3300	4600	7500	16,000
Model K - 4-cyl., 20/22 hp, 97¼" wb						
Rbt.	1750	2400	3400	4800	8000	17,000
Model D - 4-cyl., 20/22 hp, 97¼" wb						
Tour.	1750	2200	3200	4400	7000	15,000
Model HC - 2-cyl., 18/20 hp, 90" wb						
Rbt.	1450	2400	3400	4800	8000	18,000
Tour.	1450	2300	3300	4600	7500	16,000
Model M - 4-cyl., 36/40 hp, 114" wb						
Tour.	3000	2900	3700	5600	9100	20,000

1909 Maxwell, model LD, runabout, HAC

1910 Maxwell, model DA, touring, OCW

1909 MAXWELL

Model A - 2-cyl., 10 hp, 82" wb

	FP	5	4	3	2	1
Rbt.-2P	500	2300	3300	4600	7500	16,000

Model LD - 2-cyl., 14 hp, 84" wb

	FP	5	4	3	2	1
Rbt.-2/3P	825	2400	3400	4800	8000	17,000

Model HD - 2-cyl., 20 hp, 96" wb

	FP	5	4	3	2	1
Tour.-5P	1450	2400	3400	4800	8000	17,000
Dr. Maxwell Rbt.-2P	1350	2500	3500	5000	8500	18,000

Model DA - 4-cyl., 30 hp, 104" wb

	FP	5	4	3	2	1
Tour.-5P	1750	2500	3500	5000	8500	18,000

Model KA - 4-cyl., 30 hp, 104" wb

	FP	5	4	3	2	1
Rdst.-2/4P	1750	2700	3600	5300	8800	19,000

1910 MAXWELL

Model AA - 2-cyl., 12 hp, 86" wb

	FP	5	4	3	2	1
Rbt.	600	2400	3400	4800	8000	17,000

Model Q - 4-cyl., 22 hp, 93" wb

	FP	5	4	3	2	1
Rdst.	900	2900	3700	5600	9100	20,000
Surrey	950	2500	3500	5000	8500	18,000
Tour.-4P	1000	2700	3600	5300	8800	19,000

Model E - 4-cyl., 30 hp, 110" wb

	FP	5	4	3	2	1
Tonneau-5P	1500	2900	3700	5600	9100	20,000

Model G - 4-cyl., 30 hp, 110" wb

	FP	5	4	3	2	1
Tour.-5P	1575	3000	4000	6000	9500	21,000

1911 Maxwell, model GA, roadster, HAC

1911 MAXWELL

Model AA - 2-cyl., 22 hp, 86" wb

	FP	5	4	3	2	1
Rbt.	600	2400	3400	4800	8000	17,000

Model Q - 4-cyl., 22 hp, 93" wb

	FP	5	4	3	2	1
Tour.-4P	1000	2700	3600	5300	8800	19,000
Tourabout-4P	950	2900	3700	5600	9100	20,000
Rdst.-3P	925	3000	4000	6000	9500	21,000
Std. Rdst.-2P	900	2700	3600	5300	8800	19,000
Sportsman-2P	1000	3100	4200	6300	10,500	22,000

Model I - 4-cyl., 25 hp, 104" wb

	FP	5	4	3	2	1
Tour.	1100	2700	3600	5300	8800	19,000
Rbt.	1100	2500	3500	5000	8500	18,000
Surrey	1100	2700	3600	5300	8800	19,000

Model EA - 4-cyl., 30 hp, 110" wb

	FP	5	4	3	2	1
Tour.	1500	2900	3700	5600	9100	2000

Model GA - 4-cyl., 30 hp, 110" wb

	FP	5	4	3	2	1
Tour.	1600	2700	3600	5300	8800	19,000
Rdst.	1600	2900	3700	5600	9100	20,000

1912 Maxwell "Mascotte" Family, touring, HAC

1912 MAXWELL

Messenger - 2-cyl., 16 hp, 86" wb

		5	4	3	2	1
Vestibuled Rdst.-2P	625	3000	4000	6000	9500	21,000

Mascotte - 4-cyl., 25 hp, 104" wb

		5	4	3	2	1
Fore-Door Rdst.-2P	950	3200	4300	6500	11,000	23,000

Mercury - 4-cyl., 30 hp, 110" wb

		5	4	3	2	1
Fore-Door Rdst.-2P	1150	3300	4400	6700	12,000	24,000

Special - 4-cyl., 36 hp, 114" wb

		5	4	3	2	1
Fore-Door Tour.-5P	1480	3500	4500	7000	13,000	25,000

902

1913 Maxwell, model 40, roadster, HAC

1913 MAXWELL

Model 22 - 4-cyl., 22.5 hp, 93" wb

	FP	5	4	3	2	1
Rdst.-2P	785	3000	4000	6000	9500	21,000

Model 30 - 4-cyl., 30 hp, 111" wb

	FP	5	4	3	2	1
Tour.-5P	1145	3000	4000	6000	9500	21,000
Rdst.-2P	1110	3100	4200	6300	10,500	22,000

Model 40 - 4 cyl., 40 hp, 115" wb

	FP	5	4	3	2	1
Tour.-5P	1675	3100	4200	6300	10,500	22,000
Rdst.-2P	1625	3200	4300	6500	11,000	23,000

Six - 38.4 hp, 130" wb

		5	4	3	2	1
Model I Tour.-7P	2250	2700	3600	5300	8800	19,000
Model D Tour.-4P	2200	2900	3700	5600	9100	20,000

Six - 31.54 hp, 118" wb

		5	4	3	2	1
Model J Tour.	—	3100	4200	6300	10,500	22,000

1914 Maxwell, model 50-6, touring, HAC

1914 MAXWELL

Model 25-4 - 4-cyl., 21 hp, 103" wb

		5	4	3	2	1
Tour.-5P	750	2700	3600	5300	8800	19,000

Model 35-4 - 4-cyl., 26 hp, 110" wb

		5	4	3	2	1
Tour.-5P	1225	2900	3700	5600	9100	20,000

Model 50-6 - 6-cyl., 41 hp, 130" wb

		5	4	3	2	1
Tour.-7P	1975	3100	4200	6300	10,500	22,000
Tour.-4/5P	1975	3000	4000	6000	9500	21,000

1915 Maxwell, model 25, town car, HAC

1915 MAXWELL

Model 25 - 4-cyl., 21 hp, 103" wb

		5	4	3	2	1
Tour.-5P	695	3000	4000	6000	9500	21,000
Rdst.	670	3100	4200	6300	10,500	22,000
Cabr.	840	2900	3700	5600	9100	20,000
Twn. Car	920	2700	3600	5300	8800	19,000

1916 Maxwell, model 25, cabriolet, HAC

1916 MAXWELL
Model 25 - 4-cyl., 21 hp, 103" wb

	FP	5	4	3	2	1
Tour.-5P	655	3000	4000	6000	9500	21,000
Rdst.	635	3100	4200	6300	10,500	22,000
Cabr.	865	2900	3700	5600	9100	20,000
Sed.	935	1400	2400	3500	5300	10,000
Twn. Car	915	2700	3600	5300	8800	19,000

1917 Maxwell, model 25, cabriolet, AA

1917 MAXWELL
Model 25 - 4-cyl., 21.03 hp, 103" wb

Tour.	635	2900	3700	5600	9100	20,000
Rdst.	620	3000	4000	6000	9500	21,000
Cabr.	865	2700	3600	5300	8800	19,000
Twn. Car	915	1200	2300	3300	5100	9500
Sed.	985	1100	2200	3200	4900	9000
Limo.	985	2000	3000	4200	6500	14,000

1918 Maxwell, model 25, sedan, HAC

1918 MAXWELL
Model 25 - 4-cyl., 21.03 hp, 108" wb

Tour.	745	2900	3700	5600	9100	20,000
Rdst.	745	3000	4000	6000	9500	21,000
Sed.	1195	1100	2200	3200	4900	9000
Ber.	1095	1600	2700	3800	5800	12,000
All-Weather Top Tour.	855	3100	4200	6300	10,500	22,000
Spe. Top Rdst.	830	3000	4000	6000	9500	21,000

1919 Maxwell, model 25, coupe, AA

1919 MAXWELL
Model 25 - 4-cyl., 21.03 hp, 108" wb

	FP	5	4	3	2	1
Tour.	895	2900	3700	5600	9100	20,000
Rdst.	895	3000	4000	6000	9500	21,000
Cpe.	1520	1500	2500	3600	5500	11,000
Sed.	1565	1100	2200	3200	4900	9000
All-Weather Tour.	1005	3000	4000	6000	9500	21,000
All-Weather Rdst.	980	3100	4200	6300	10,500	22,000

1920 Maxwell, model 25, touring, AA

1920 MAXWELL
Model 25 - 4-cyl., 33.8 hp, 109" wb

Tour.-5P	1055	2900	3700	5600	9100	20,000
Sed.-5P	1795	1100	2200	3200	4900	9000
Cpe.-3P	1695	1500	2500	3600	5500	11,000
Rdst.-2P	1055	3000	4000	6000	9500	21,000

1921 Maxwell, model 25, touring, HAC

1921 MAXWELL
Model 25 - 4-cyl., 33.8 hp, 109" wb

Tour.-5P	995	3000	4000	6000	9500	21,000
Rdst.-2P	935	3100	4200	6300	10,500	22,000
Cpe.-3P	1595	1600	2700	3800	5800	12,000
Sed.-5P	1695	1400	2400	3500	5300	10,000

1922 MAXWELL
Model 25 - 4-cyl., 33.8 hp, 109" wb

Tour.-5P	885	3100	4200	6300	10,500	22,000
Rdst.-2P	885	3200	4300	6500	11,000	23,000
Cpe.-4P	1385	1800	2800	4000	6200	13,000
Sed.-5P	1485	1500	2500	3600	5500	11,000
Club Sed.-5P	1175	1600	2700	3800	5800	12,000
Club Cpe.-2P	1120	2000	3000	4200	6500	14,000

903

1922 Maxwell, model 25, roadster, AA

1922 Maxwell, model 25, 4-pass. coupe, HAC

1923 Maxwell, model 25, sport touring, AA

1924 Maxwell, model 25, coupe, AA

1923 MAXWELL
Model 25 - 4-cyl., 30 hp, 109" wb

	FP	5	4	3	2	1
Tour.-5P	885	3100	4200	6300	10,500	22,000
Rdst.-2P	885	3200	4300	6500	11,000	23,000
Spt. Rdst.-2P	960	3500	4500	7000	13,000	25,000
Spt. Tour.-5P	985	3300	4400	6700	12,000	24,000
Club Cpe.-2P	985	1600	2700	3800	5800	12,000
Cpe.-4P	1235	1800	2800	4000	6200	13,000
Sed.-5P	1335	1500	2500	3600	5500	11,000

1924 MAXWELL
Model 25 - 4-cyl., 34 hp, 109" wb

	FP	5	4	3	2	1
Tour.-5P	795	3200	4300	6500	11,000	23,000
Rdst.-2P	795	3500	4500	7000	13,000	25,000
Spt. Rdst.-2P	895	3700	4700	7300	13,700	26,000
Spt. Tour.-5P	960	4000	5000	8000	15,000	28,000
Spe. Spt. Tour.-5P	975	3500	4500	7000	13,000	25,000
Club Cpe.-2P	985	3900	4800	7700	14,300	27,000
Club Sed.-5P	1045	1800	2800	4000	6200	13,000
Cpe.-4P	1195	1600	2700	3800	5800	12,000
Sed.-5P	1295	2000	3000	4200	6500	14,000
Traveler Sed.	1585	1400	2400	3500	5300	10,000

1925 Maxwell, model 25-C, club coupe, AA

1925 MAXWELL
Model 25-C - 4-cyl., 38 hp, 109" wb

Tour.-5P	975	3500	4500	7000	13,000	25,000
Club Cpe.-2P	1025	2000	3000	4200	6500	14,000
Club Sed.-5P	1185	1500	2500	3600	5500	11,000
Sed.-5P	1465	1500	2500	3600	5500	11,000
Rdst.	965	4200	5200	8400	15,700	29,000
Spt. Tour.	1140	4000	5000	8000	15,000	28,000

MAXWELL-FITCH — Rome, New York — (1905, 1909) — The Maxwell & Fitch Company was organized in Rome, New York during the summer of 1904 with a capital stock of $12,000. Harry B. Maxwell and Lauren M. Fitch were the partners involved, and their plan was to "make and sell gas and gasoline engines, vapor gas and automobile parts." In October of 1905 the firm announced its building of a prototype car which was planned to be put on the market soon. Most likely it was not, and plans for entry into the passenger car market were shelved thereafter until January of 1909 when word came from the Fitch Gear Company in Rome that a new venture was to be organized for the manufacture of motor vehicles. "All types of cars are to be made," reported *The Horseless Age*, "and a special feature of the construction will be the possibility of interchanging large diameter wheels with solid tires and small diameter wheels with pneumatic tires." The cars were to be assembled and the bodies built at the Fitch company plant on South James street, while a salesroom and finishing department was to be located at the plant of the Maxwell & Fitch Company on West Dominick Street. Again, however, it would appear that the firm's automotive venture did not pass the prototype stage.

1900 Mayer, runabout, HAC

904

MAYER — Chicago, Illinois — (1899-1901) — Simon Mayer was a member of the Chicago Police Department and since he was given top billing in the Mayer, Corey & Paulson triumvirate which produced this car, presumably he was the gentleman who had put up most of the money. References indicate that Paulson, formerly of Gormully & Jeffery, designed the car; Corey's background is not known. The Mayer was a two-cylinder runabout which was air cooled by a "forced blast" from a centrifugal engine-driven fan. The first car apparently was completed sometime late in 1899. At the 1901 Chicago Automobile Show it was exhibited under a sign reading "Our First Machine — has run over 4,000 miles." Mayer and Paulson were quoted at the time as saying that they were "now looking for capital to build these machines." Any production which resulted had to have been minimal, because the Mayer disappeared from the public prints by 1902.

MAYER SLOTKIN — The Mayer Slotkin Manufacturing Company was organized in New York City during the fall of 1909 to "engage in the manufacture of cars, wagons, boats, motors, engines and machinery of various kinds." Incorporators were S. Slotkin, S. Goldstein and Jacob Burnstone. Manufacture of a car is doubted.

MAYER SPECIAL — Mankato, Minnesota — (1903-1907) — The Mayer Special was an early V-8, which Louis Mayer of Mankato began planning in 1903, completed some time later and ultimately tested in 1907. The engine was unusual, its iron cylinders cast in pairs, with the remainder of the unit being aluminum. Minnesota historian Alan Ominsky interviewed Mayer's son, Aloys Mayer, during the early 1970's regarding the car. The son described the car in considerable detail. "Modern V-8 construction practice attaches each piston rod to the crankshaft journal," Alan Ominsky wrote. "Mayer, however, accomplished this connection by hinging four rods from their mates on the opposite bank of cylinders just above the crankshaft." The Mayer Special was fitted with a two-speed transmission and a seven-passenger touring body, which was subsequently updated in 1912. Having proved he could build the car, Louis Mayer returned to the usual work of the Mankato machine shop which he operated in partnership with his brother Lawrence. Subsequently he did construct a tractor and two more vee-type engines which were mounted in a boat. Louis Mayer drove his V-8 Mayer Special for more than a decade until, in 1922, his wife insisted that he junk it.

1925 Mayfair, 4-dr. sedan, WLB

MAYFAIR — Boston, Massachusetts — (1925) — The Mayfair painted the lily of the Ford. In essence, it was a rebuilt Model T, and unabashedly so. The car was introduced at the Boston Automobile Show in March of 1925, and the principals in the new Mayfair Manufacturing Company were introduced as Frank L. Hamilton, W.S. Carruthers and M.K. Coates. The Boston banking firm of A.W. Lincoln & Company backed the project. "In the manufacture of the Mayfair extensive use is made of parts obtained from discarded Ford cars," Automotive Industries reported. "Such parts are inspected and tested before being used and new parts used wherever necessary. The cylinder blocks are reground and fitted with oversize pistons. New bearings are used throughout the car." The fitting of a disc clutch and three-speed sliding gear transmission represented the most noteworthy engineering departures from the Model T norm. On the outside, the radiator configuration was of new design, the overall height was lowered five-and-a-half inches by relocating the gas tank to the rear, and the rear quarter of the three-door sedan body was covered in fabric, with ventilated oval windows on each side. An annual production of 3000 cars was contemplated, all of them to be sold in the Boston area. The price was $485. A site in nearby Jamaica Plain was selected for the factory, and apparently production did commence there. Not long thereafter it ceased, however, as the Mayfair Manufacturing Company quickly went to the wall. Obviously there were not enough people in Boston who wanted to buy a used Model T that had been refined and prettified into a new Mayfair. Jesse T. Billington, who worked for the company, later reported that about ten cars had been produced.

1925 MAYFAIR
Mayfair — 4-cyl., 20 hp, 100" wb

	FP	5	4	3	2	1
Three-Door Sedan-5P	485					

MAYTAG — Waterloo, Iowa — (1910-1911) — Despite references to the contrary, it does not appear that the Maytag name appeared on the cars of the perpetually trouble-plagued Iowa company that was responsible for its production for more than two seasons. The Maytag had its origins in

Des Moines where the initial Mason company was founded in 1906 to produce a car designed by the Duesenberg brothers. Edward R. Mason was the principal backer. In June 1909 Senator Fred L. Maytag and his son Elmer H. decided to add automobiles to the line of products they produced (agricultural machinery and washing machines) and purchased controlling interest in Mason to do so. They reorganized the firm as Maytag-Mason Motor Car Company, and moved it to Waterloo in early 1910. A new four-cylinder car was introduced that year as the Maytag, the former two-cylinder Mason being continued under its own name. For 1911 all cars of the company were called Maytags, however. But that appears to have been the end of it. Although the company remained in Waterloo, the Maytags exited in January 1912 — and Edward R. Mason was once again in control. The firm had been in trouble under the Maytags, and it continued to be under Mason until finally in September 1915, the Waterloo plant was sold at auction. Interestingly, that factory had formerly been the home of the Waterloo Motor Works which was owned by William Galloway who built a highwheeler under his own name there from 1908. The car he offered as a Galloway in 1911, however, was simply a Maytag with a new radiator emblem. William Galloway had been the man responsible for luring the Maytags from Des Moines to Waterloo, and had purchased a controlling interest in the Maytag-Mason Motor Car Company during the summer of 1910, about six months before control reverted back to Edward R. Mason.

1910 Maytag, 5-pass. touring, MC

1910 MAYTAG
Four — 32/35 hp, 114" wb

	FP	5	4	3	2	1
Touring-5P	1800	3000	4000	6000	9500	21,000

1911 Maytag, 7-pass. touring, WLB

1911 MAYTAG

Two — 20 hp, 96" wb						
Model A Runabout	1250	2700	3600	5300	8800	19,000
Model B Toy Tonneau	1300	2900	3700	5600	9100	20,000
Model C Touring	1350	2900	3700	5600	9100	20,000
Four — 35 hp, 114" wb						
Model D Roadster	1750	3100	4200	6300	10,500	22,000
Model E Toy Tonneau	1750	3000	4000	6000	9500	21,000
Model F Touring	1750	3000	4000	6000	9500	21,000
Model G Torpedo	1750	3100	4200	6300	10,500	22,000
Model H Boattail Roadster	1650	3500	4500	7000	13,000	25,000

M.B. — Minneapolis, Minnesota — (1908-1911) — The Motor Buggy Manufacturing Company of the Columbia Heights section of Minneapolis chose the tradename of Acme Roadster to introduce its highwheeler. It was a 1600-pound four-seater with 22 hp, a 12-gallon gasoline tank, a 25 mph top speed, and a 17-inch road clearance. By removing the rear seat, a delivery box could be fitted to carry loads of 500 pounds or more. When sales of the car as an Acme did not prove lucrative after one season, the Motor Buggy company decided to use its initials instead and marketed the vehicle as the M.B. beginning in 1909. Sales did not improve, despite the addition of a larger touring body style. Late in 1910 Motor Buggy introduced another even larger car with four cylinders, pneumatic tires and a less buggy-like appearance. This car was marketed as the Renville and lasted less than a season. Interestingly, Renville was the name of the town in Minnesota from which the Hoffman brothers came, and it was the Hoffmans who took over the factory of the Motor Buggy Manufacturing Company in 1912. Arnold Hoffman had previously been company treasurer; Nels Nelson was president, M.J. Jacobson general manager. When the Hoffman brothers went into production under their own name for the 1913 season, however, it was for the manufacture of commercial vehicles. Offered only as a single three-ton model, the Hoffman truck survived little over a year.

1908 M.B.

	FP	5	4	3	2	1
Acme Roadster (2-cyl., 22 hp, 97" wb)	—	2000	3000	4200	6500	14,000

1910 M.B., touring, NAHC

1909-1910 M.B.

	FP	5	4	3	2	1
M.B. Roadster (2-cyl., 22 hp, 97" wb)	—	2000	3000	4200	6500	14,000
M.B. Touring (2-cyl., 22 hp, 97" wb)	—	1800	2800	4000	6200	13,000

1911 M.B.

	FP	5	4	3	2	1
M.B. Roadster (2-cyl., 22 hp, 97" wb)	—	2000	3000	4200	6500	14,000
M.B. Touring (2-cyl., 22 hp, 97" wb)	—	1800	2800	4000	6200	13,000
Renville touring (4-cyl., 45 hp, 102" wb)	—	2200	3200	4400	7000	15,000

McADAMS — Middletown, Ohio — (1903) — In December of 1902, the local paper in Middletown announced that John McAdams had been hired as the manager of a new company financed by local businessmen for the manufacture of automobile engines. These plans apparently came to naught, but John McAdams did build a car for himself the following year. It was a small buggy with single-cylinder engine and chain drive, which he drove regularly to his mechanic's job at a paper mill. There is no evidence that he built another.

McAULIFFE — McAuliffe & Company was organized in New York City during the summer of 1909 with a $25,000 capital stock to manufacture automobiles and carriages. Incorporators were J.J. McAuliffe, D.H. McAuliffe and H. Feltman. Manufacture of a car is doubted.

McCAN — New York, New York — (1902) — D.C. McCan was a Frenchman in New York who leased a two-story building at 58-62 Broadway in July of 1902 and announced to the press that he was altering it for the manufacture of gasoline and electric vehicles. That October D.C. McCan was heard from again. This time he was in Buffalo, and he had just opened his new shop, but it was for the repair of automobiles only. Perhaps he had built a car or two, but certainly not more than that.

McCLINTOCK — Kansas City, Missouri — (1904) — Capital stock of $375,000 was the heady figure reported by the McClintock Automobile & Engine Company when it was incorporated in October of 1904 in Kansas City. D.L. McClintock was described as the "leading spirit" behind the venture, and he was joined by Hiram Landrus, Edwin Bond and Fred J. Close. "Non-exhaust steam and gasoline machines" were to be the company's products, both varieties featuring McClintock's invention of "an adjustment by which the propelling power can be attached to either the front or rear axle." A prototype seems to have been completed, but the company does not appear to have proceeded into any viable manufacture.

McCLUER — Spring Lake, Michigan — (1891) — Marshall McCluer lived in Spring Lake and in 1891 built a motor buggy that reportedly achieved speeds of up to 20 mph. Documentation of this, however, is lacking. If the vehicle was, as reports suggest, powered by gasoline, it would have been among the earliest in the United States.

1891 McCluer, runabout, WLB

McCOOLE-MERCER — The McCoole-Mercer Motor Company was organized in Oklahoma City, Oklahoma during the summer of 1910 with a capital stock of $10,000 for the manufacture and sale of automobiles and engines. Incorporators were M.F. McCoole, B.B. Mercer and M.L. Mercer. Manufacture of a car is doubted.

1913 McCord, touring, WLB

McCORD — Chicago, Illinois — (1913) — One wonders how they thought they could get away with it. During the summer of 1913 a small group of Chicago people organized the McCord Automobile Company, claiming an association with the McCord Manufacturing Company, a well-known Detroit maker of radiators. The radiators maker immediately denied any involvement. The McCord Automobile Company never got off the ground. A prototype was built, however, a light four-cylinder (Rutenber engine) touring car on a 110-inch wheelbase. It was a completely straightforward proposition, more than can be said of its makers' attempt to link their effort with the McCord radiator.

McCORMACK — Birmingham, Alabama — (1921-1922) — The McCormack Brothers Motor Company was located at 2021 Fourth Avenue South in Birmingham. P.R. McCormack was president, H.J. McCormack was vice-president and W.H. Chambers was the general manager. A steam car purportedly was built by this firm during the early Twenties. Documentation is lacking, and the likelihood is that this venture proceeded little further than the prototype stage.

McCRARY — The McCrary Motor Company was organized during the spring of 1910 with a capital stock of $5100 to manufacture and deal in automobiles and accessories in Detroit, Michigan. Incorporators were C.R. McCrary, John G. Staling, Jay F. Pool and George W. Edson. Manufacture of a car is doubted.

1913 M.C.C. Six, touring, WJL

M.C.C. SIX — Detroit, Michigan — (1913) — The M.C.C. Six was a badge-engineered Krit produced by the Detroit company during receivership. All specs — including 250-cubic-inch 36 hp engine, 120-inch wheelbase and even the hubcaps — were the same. Presumably a new M.C.C. radiator badge was conjured. Very frequently during receivership a manufacturer would dump leftover cars overseas but, in this case, Krit "exported" to the Deep South. So far as is known, the M.C.C. Six was sold only in Louisiana, the initials perhaps representing the name of a Krit dealership there.

1909 McCue, model C, touring, HAC

McCUE — Hartford, Connecticut — (1909-1911) — The McCue Company of Hartford had been in the business of manufacturing carriage fittings since shortly after the turn of the century. Its reputation in this field was a fine one. By 1908 the company had extended its manufacture into frames, hoods and varying accessories for the automobile trade as well. Though Charles T. McCue steadfastly denied that year that he would build a complete automobile too, he did precisely that in 1909, moving his factory from Capitol Avenue to a new plant on Pliny Street. Many of the component parts of the new McCue were supplied by the Billings & Spencer Company, F.C. Billings being a vice-president of McCue. The McCue was a medium-powered four in the medium-priced range, featuring a three-speed selective transmission, shaft drive and a pressed steel floating rear axle. The car did not sell well. In late summer of 1911 C.T. McCue merged with the Superior Axle & Forge Company of Buffalo, and both his Hartford plant and the Buffalo facility were turned over to the manufacture of axles for cars and trucks. The combined firms carried the name McCue Manufacturing Company. During the spring of 1913 C.T. McCue resigned from the presidency following difficulties with his board of directors which included, *Automobile Topics* said, "a matter of correspondence that it is alleged was burned, when, according to the directors, it should have been retained in the company's files as the company's own property." In late summer of 1913 the McCue company was acquired by George W. Houk of the Houk Wire Wheel Company.

1909 McCUE
Model F — 4-cyl., 30 hp, 108" wb

	FP	5	4	3	2	1
Runabout	2000	2200	3200	4400	7000	15,000
Model D — 4-cyl., 30 hp, 117" wb						
Gentlemen's Roadster	2200	2300	3300	4600	7500	16,000
Model C — 4-cyl., 30 hp, 116" wb						
Touring	2250	2400	3400	4800	8000	17,000

1910 McCue, model 6, roadster, WLB

1910-1911 McCUE
Model XXX — 4-cyl., 40 hp, 123" wb

Touring-5P	2750	2500	3500	5000	8500	18,000
Model 6 — 4-cyl., 40 hp, 123" wb						
Torpedo-4P	2450	2700	3600	5300	8800	19,000

McCULLOUGH — Boston, Massachusetts — (1899-1900) — W.T. McCullough was the proprietor of the Back Bay Cycle & Motor Company at 122 Massachusetts Avenue in Boston, and in early 1899 he completed an experimental automobile with two twin-cylinder engines, each of them driven to a rear wheel by chain and sprocket. This novel car could not have worked very well, because McCullough immediately built another with but a single engine, this one a 4½ hp twin. Possibly he produced a few more examples of this car since he advertised himself in the 1899 Boston city directory as possessing "motor carriages to rent with competent instructors." He did not proceed into sustained manufacture, however. By 1900 he had sold the patent rights to his vehicles to the United States Motor Vehicle Company of New York City.

1899 McCullough, NAHC

1922 McCurdy, touring, WLB

McCURDY — Evansville, Indiana — (1922) — In 1922 the Hercules Corporation of Evansville produced 84,000 buggies, 62,000 gasoline engines, 40,000 trucks and automobile bodies — and a handful of cars called McCurdy. The company had been founded in 1891 (in Cincinnati) and had previously given only cursory thought to automobile manufacture. Before the First World War, Hercules founder Colonel William H. McCurdy persuaded his personal friend General Robert E. Wood, the president of Sears, Roebuck and Company, into getting into the automobile business. Prior to the completion of Sears' own factory in Chicago, the Sears motor buggy was built in the Hercules plant. Interestingly, that experience did not persuade Colonel McCurdy into manufacture himself. Following the First World War, Hercules ran up a single example of an electric. A few years later the McCurdy followed. It represented not so much a corporate venture as the whim of the Colonel's son, Lynn McCurdy. While attending the 1920 Indianapolis Automobile Show, young McCurdy had been impressed by a new prototype shown there called the Gale Four, designed by Garde Gale. Gale was unable to secure financing for production, and consequently the Gale Four evolved into the McCurdy Six (Continental engine), with the announcement made in December of 1921 that Hercules would enter the automobile field early in 1922. Garde Gale became general sales manager of the new automobile department at Hercules Corporation. Bodies for the McCurdy were built in the company's shops, the engine and chassis parts arrived from various accessory manufacturers in the field. Wheelbase was 127 inches. The exact number of McCurdys built is in dispute. One reference indicates five begun and only two completed. Another source (a former employee) recalled seven built, with five of these experimental, and two cars sold. The two cars which are definitely known to have been built were purchased (for $2500 apiece) by executives of Hercules Corporation. They are also known to have provided a good many problems. Hercules Corporation subsequently became the Service Manufacturing Company, makers of Servel refrigerators.

McDOWELL — The McDowell County Automobile Company was organized in Keystone, West Virginia early in 1911 with a capital stock of $5000 to manufacture automobiles. Incorporators were J.K.F. Steele, I.L. Shor, H.B. Reynolds, F.T. Hutson and F.B. Steel. Manufacture is doubted.
 The McDowell Motor Vehicle Manufacturing Company was organized in Auburn, Indiana early in 1908 with a capital stock of $20,000 for the manufacture of automobiles and motor vehicles. Incorporators were Willis McDowell, Wheeler McDowell and A.W. McDowell. Manufacture of a car is doubted.

McDUFFEE — That the McDuffee Automobile Company of Dayton, Ohio built an automobile in 1905 has been indicated on various car rosters. This apparently was an error arising from a trade publication mention that year noting that the Dayton company expected "to open a salesroom at 1449 Michigan Avenue in Chicago." Such a salesroom was opened, but it was not for a McDuffee car. Instead the Royal and Stoddard-Dayton were sold there, and by the McDuffie Automobile Company which had been earlier incorporated by J.H. McDuffie.

McELROY — "George E. McElroy, 340 East Market Street, Elmira, New York has patented an automobile and will manufacture it," reported *The Horseless Age* in October 1899. There is no evidence McElroy ever did, however.

1913 McEwen, cyclecar, HAC

McEWEN — Nashville, Tennessee — (1913) — The McEwen was a backyard-built cyclecar which was perhaps a better effort than many such cars that were manufactured. It was begun in October 1913 in the backyard at 111 Louise Avenue in Nashville by Norman S. McEwen, the high school lad giving the car its first road test that Christmas Eve. Its engine was a 7 hp air-cooled Yale motorcycle unit which was incorporated with a standard motorcycle clutch. Final drive was by vee belt. The frame and body of the car were hickory wood, with full elliptic springs front and rear. A tandem two-seater, its tread was 30 inches, and young McEwen stated that "no vibration is felt up to 30 miles an hour, while even on the most slippery streets no tendency to skid is apparent." The first report of his car appeared in an early 1914 issue of *The American Cyclecar*. Approximately one year later, McEwen wrote *Carette* that his cyclecar had now put up about 3000 miles and "still appears to be in the best of condition."

McFADDEN — The McFadden Auto Company was organized in Rock Hill, South Carolina during the fall of 1912 with a capital stock of $3500 for the manufacture of automobiles. Incorporators were V.B. McFadden and D.B. McFadden. Manufacture is doubted.

1910 McFarlan Six, pony tonneau, HAC

McFARLAN — Connersville, Indiana — (1910-1928) — The initial announcement was, in retrospect, startingly innocuous. The McFarlan Carriage Company of Connersville, the trade press reported during the summer of 1909, "will soon manufacture a motor buggy." What followed was a large, prestigious motorcar that was produced always in small numbers (about 200 units annually) and always with an engine of no fewer than six cylinders (with an eight joining the line in 1926). It was the product of one of Connersville's most prominent enterprises, the carriage works which British-born John B. McFarlan had organized in 1856 and around which, three decades later, he had established one of this nation's first industrial parks. (Lexington and Ansted, and even E.L. Cord, would later stroll into that park.) The McFarlan car was the idea of John B. McFarlan's grandson, Harry McFarlan, and — sadly — the grandfather would die, at age eighty-seven, two weeks before the first experimental car was completed. The McFarlan was introduced late in 1909. The first cars were road tested on a track, literally, the one at the Indianapolis Motor Speedway during Labor Day Weekend of 1910, McFarlan finishing third and fifth and fourth and fifth in two races there. It was super publicity for a brand-new automobile. In 1913 the McFarlan Motor Car Company superseded the McFarlan Carriage Company. A variety of proprietary engines (Wisconsin, Buda, Brownell, Continental) were used in the early McFarlans, with a Teetor-Hartley being settled upon in 1916. Having begun as a $2000 car, the McFarlan steadily rose in price, until by 1920 some models passed the $6000 mark. They were to zoom even higher, however, for 1921 saw the introduction of the formidable Twin-Valve Six, with triple ignition, 18 spark plugs and 120 hp. McFarlan built that engine itself. The Knickerbocker Cabriolet, at $9000, was the priciest McFarlan then, though in 1922 — MacFarlan's best year, with 235 cars sold — the company also built a special version with all exposed and usually-nickel-plated hardware finished in 24 carat gold. It was exhibited at the 1923 Chicago Automobile Show and then delivered — after the exchange of $25,000 — to a lady from Oklahoma City whose family was in oil. For 1924 the McFarlan company set its sights lower, with introduction of the Single-Valve model, a Wisconsin-engined six that was lesser powered, and lesser priced by several thousand dollars — and a dismal failure in the marketplace. It was discontin-

ued during 1926, during which year another try at a lower-priced McFarlan was made with a Lycoming-engined straight-eight. It sold somewhat better, but still the end was near. Partly, this was due to the car itself; certainly the small annual production had been spread thin over the flurry of models offered, and by the late Twenties the car, which had enjoyed no significant restyling since 1921, was long overdue for one. This arrived in 1928 with a McFarlan that was lower and more lithe, but by then it was too late — and for another reason unrelated to the car. Since 1924 Harry McFarlan had been in ill health, operating management of his company having fallen at that time to his long-time associate Burton Barrows. In 1928 Burt Barrows died suddenly. So did the McFarlan. Later that year the McFarlan assets were purchased by Errett Lobban Cord, who had already arrived in town and begun his empire building.

1910 McFARLAN
Six — 35/40 hp, 120" wb

	FP	5	4	3	2	1
Touring-5P	2000	2700	3600	5300	8800	19,000
Baby Tonneau-4P	2000	2900	3700	5600	9100	20,000
Roadster-2/3P	2000	3000	4000	6000	9500	21,000

1911 McFarlan, model 35/40, runabout, HAC

1911 McFARLAN
Model 35-40 — 6-cyl., 35/40 hp, 120" wb

Runabout-2P	2100	2900	3700	5600	9100	20,000
Torpedo-4P	2100	3000	4000	6000	9500	21,000
Touring-5P	2100	3000	4000	6000	9500	21,000

Model 50-60 — 6-cyl., 50/60 hp, 128" wb

Touring-7P	2500	4000	5000	8000	15,000	28,000
Runabout-2P	2500	3900	4800	7700	14,300	27,000
Torpedo-4P	2500	4200	5200	8400	15,700	29,000

1912 McFarlan, model 55/60, touring, HAC

1912 McFARLAN
Model 40-45 — 6-cyl., 40/45 hp, 124" wb

Roadster-2P	2100	2900	3700	5600	9100	20,000
Torpedo-4P	2100	3000	4000	6000	9500	21,000
Touring-5P	2100	3000	4000	6000	9500	21,000

Model 55-60 — 6-cyl, 55/60 hp, 128" wb

Roadster-2P	2750	4200	5200	8400	15,700	29,000
Torpedo-4P	2750	4000	5000	8000	15,000	28,000
Touring-5P	2750	3900	4800	7700	14,300	27,000
Touring-7P	2750	4300	5400	8700	16,500	30,000

1913 McFarlan Six, 4-pass. roadster, HAC

1913 McFARLAN
Six — 57 hp, 124" wb

	FP	5	4	3	2	1
Roadster-4/5P	2300	4000	5000	8000	15,000	28,000
Coupe-2P	3100	2700	3600	5300	8800	19,000
Coupe-3P	3300	2800	3700	5500	9000	19,500
Six — 63 hp, 124" wb						
Roadster-4/5P	2500	4200	5200	8400	15,000	29,000
Touring-6P	2600	4000	5000	8000	15,000	28,000
Coupe-2P	—	2900	3700	5600	9100	20,000
Coupe-3P	—	3000	4000	6000	9500	21,000
Limousine-7P	—	3300	4400	6700	12,000	24,000
Six — 66 hp, 128" wb						
Speedster-4/5/6P	2750	4400	5600	9200	17,300	31,000
Limousine-7P	4050	4000	5000	8000	15,000	28,000

1914 McFarlan, series T, touring, HAC

1914 McFARLAN
Series T — 6-cyl., 38.4 hp, 132" wb

	FP	5	4	3	2	1
Touring-7P	2590	4000	5000	8000	15,000	28,000
Touring-4P	2590	3900	4800	7700	14,300	27,000
Touring-5P	2590	3700	4700	7300	13,700	26,000
Touring-6P	2590	3700	4700	7300	13,700	26,000
Roadster-2P	2590	4000	5000	8000	15,000	28,000
Coupe-4P	3300	2700	3600	5300	8800	19,000
Limousine-7P	4000	2900	3700	5600	9100	20,000

1915 McFarlan, series T, touring, HAC

1915 McFARLAN
Series T — 6-cyl., 38.4 hp, 132" wb

	FP	5	4	3	2	1
Touring-7P	2590	3700	4700	7300	13,700	26,000
Touring-4P	2590	3500	4500	7000	13,000	25,000
Touring-5P	2590	3500	4500	7000	13,000	25,000
Touring-6P	2590	3600	4600	7200	13,400	25,500
Roadster-2P	2590	4000	5000	8000	15,000	28,000
Coupe-4P	3300	2700	3600	5300	8800	19,000
Limousine-7P	4000	3000	4000	6000	9500	21,000
Series X — 6-cyl., 48.6 hp, 132" wb						
Touring-5P	2900	4000	5000	8000	15,000	28,000
Touring-7P	2900	4200	5200	8400	15,700	29,000
Roadster-2P	2900	4300	5400	8700	16,500	30,000

1916 McFarlan, series T, roadster, HAC

1916 McFARLAN
Series X — 6-cyl., 48.6 hp, 132" wb

	FP	5	4	3	2	1
Touring-7P	2990	4300	5400	8700	16,500	30,000
Touring-6P	2990	4200	5200	8400	15,700	29,000
Touring Roadster	2990	4400	5600	9200	17,300	31,000
Submarine-4P	3140	4500	5800	9500	18,000	32,000
Semi-Touring	4400	4400	5600	9200	17,300	31,000
Sedan-6P	4000	2000	3000	4200	6500	14,000
Town Car	4000	2300	3300	4600	7500	16,000

	FP	5	4	3	2	1
Coupe	3600	2500	3500	5000	8500	18,000
Berline	4300	2700	3600	5300	8800	19,000
Limousine	4200	3000	4000	6000	9500	21,000
Landaulet	4200	3100	4200	6300	10,500	22,000
Series T — 6-cyl., 38 hp, 132" wb						
Touring	2680	4200	5200	8400	15,700	29,000
Roadster	2680	4300	5400	8700	16,500	30,000
Submarine	2830	4400	5600	9200	17,300	31,000

1917 McFarlan, type 135, sedan, HAC

1917 McFARLAN
Type 127 — 6-cyl., 48.6 hp, 136" wb

	FP	5	4	3	2	1
Touring-7P	3500	4500	5800	9500	18,000	32,000
Roadster	3700	4700	6100	9900	19,000	33,000
Submarine	3650	4400	5600	9200	17,300	31,000
Pasadena-5P	3500	4000	5000	8000	15,000	28,000
Touring-6P	3500	4400	5600	9200	17,300	31,000
Type 135 — 6-cyl., 48.6 hp, 136" wb						
Sedan-5P	4750	2000	3000	4200	6500	14,000
Town Car	4600	2300	3300	4400	7500	16,000
Knickerbocker Cabriolet	5300	5000	6500	11,000	22,000	35,000
Sedan-7P	4600	2200	3200	4400	7000	15,000
Philadelphia Berline	4900	2300	3300	4600	7500	16,000
Limousine	4650	2700	3600	5300	8800	19,000
Continental Landaulet	4900	3100	4200	6300	10,500	22,000
Country Club Coach	5300	3300	4400	6700	12,000	24,000

1918 McFarlan, type 138, limousine, HAC

1918 McFARLAN
Type 127 — 6-cyl., 48.6 hp, 136" wb

	FP	5	4	3	2	1
Touring-7P	3500	4500	5800	9500	18,000	32,000
Roadster-2P	3500	4700	6100	9900	19,000	33,000
Roadster-4P	3500	4900	6300	10,300	21,000	34,000
Destroyer-4P	3750	5200	6800	11,300	23,000	36,000
Sport-5P	3700	5400	7300	11,800	25,000	38,000
Touring-6P	3500	5500	7500	12,000	26,000	39,000
Type 138 — 6-cyl., 48.6 hp, 136" wb						
Limousine	4650	3500	4500	7000	13,000	25,000
Town Car	4600	3300	4400	6700	12,000	24,000
Knickerbocker Cabriolet	5250	5200	6800	11,300	23,000	36,000
Philadelphia Berline	4900	4000	5000	8000	15,000	28,000
V Front Sedan	4600	2700	3600	5300	8800	19,000
Continental Landaulet	4900	3000	4000	6000	9500	21,000

1919 McFarlan, type 127, touring, HAC

1919 McFARLAN
Type 127 — 6-cyl., 48.6 hp, 136" wb

	FP	5	4	3	2	1
Touring-7P	4300	4200	5200	8400	15,700	29,000
Roadster-2P	4300	4300	5400	8700	16,500	30,000
Roadster-4P	4300	4400	5600	9200	17,300	31,000
Destroyer-4P	4500	4300	5400	8700	16,500	30,000
Sport-5P	4500	4500	5800	9500	18,000	32,000
Touring-6P	4300	4300	5400	8700	16,500	30,000

Type 138 — 6-cyl., 48.6 hp, 136" wb

Limousine-7P	5450	2700	3600	5300	8800	19,000
Town Car	5400	2900	3700	5600	9100	20,000
Knickerbocker Cabriolet	6000	5200	6800	11,300	23,000	36,000
Philadelphia Berline	5700	4000	5000	8000	15,000	28,000
V Front Sedan	5400	3700	4700	7300	13,700	26,000
Continental Landaulet	5700	3900	4800	7700	14,300	27,000
Sport Sedan	5600	3500	4500	7000	13,000	25,000

1920 McFarlan, model 90, touring, HAC

1920 McFARLAN
Model 90 — 6-cyl., 80 hp, 136" wb

Destroyer Touring-4P	5050	5400	7300	11,800	25,000	38,000
Touring-4P	4800	5000	6500	11,000	22,000	35,000
Touring-7P	4800	5300	7000	11,500	24,000	37,000
Town Car	5900	4400	5600	9200	17,300	31,000
Sport-4P	5000	5200	6800	11,300	23,000	36,000
Roadster-2P	5000	5300	7000	11,500	24,000	37,000
Sport Sedan	6100	4200	5200	8400	15,700	29,000
Knickerbocker Cabt.-7P	6550	5400	7300	11,800	25,000	38,000
Sloping Vee Sedan	5900	4000	5000	8000	15,000	28,000
Straight Front Sedan	5900	3900	4800	7700	14,300	27,000
Limousine	5950	4300	5400	8700	16,500	30,000
Continental Landaulet	6200	4400	5600	9200	17,300	31,000

1921 McFarlan, TV-Six, touring, JAC

1921 McFARLAN
Twin-Valve Six — 120 hp, 140" wb

Touring-7P	6300	5200	6800	11,300	23,000	36,000
Roadster-2P	6300	5400	7300	11,800	25,000	38,000
Sport-4P	6300	5400	7300	11,800	25,000	38,000
Touring Sedan-7P	7500	2900	3700	5600	9100	20,000
Town Car-7P	7500	3000	4000	6000	9500	21,000
Coupe-4P	7500	3200	4300	6500	11,000	23,000
Sedan-5P	7500	2700	3600	5300	8800	19,000
Limousine-7P	7500	3100	4200	6300	10,500	22,000
Sedan-5P	7800	2900	3700	5600	9100	20,000
Landau-5P	8500	3100	4200	6300	10,500	22,000
Knickerbocker Cabriolet-7P	9000	5400	7300	11,800	25,000	38,000

1922 McFarlan, type 157, Suburban sedan, KM

910

1922 McFarlan, type 154, Knickerbocker Cabriolet, HAC

1922 McFARLAN
Twin-Valve Six — 120 hp, 140" wb

	FP	5	4	3	2	1
Touring-7P	6300	4700	6100	9900	19,000	33,000
Sport-4P	6300	4900	6300	10,300	21,000	34,000
Roadster-2P	6300	5000	6500	11,000	22,000	35,000
Sport Sedan-4P	7500	3700	4700	7300	13,700	26,000
Touring Sedan-7P	7500	3900	4800	7700	14,300	27,000
Limousine	7500	4200	5200	8400	15,700	29,000
Suburban Sedan	7800	4000	5000	8000	15,000	28,000
Continental Landaulet	8500	4200	5200	8400	15,700	29,000
Town Car	7500	4400	5600	9200	17,300	31,000
Coupe	7500	3900	4800	7700	14,300	27,000
Knickerbocker Cabriolet-7P	9000	5400	7300	11,800	25,000	38,000

1923 McFarlan, type 154, Knickerbocker cabriolet, HAC

1923 McFARLAN
Twin-Valve Six — 120 hp, 141" wb

Touring-7P	6300	5200	6800	11,300	23,000	36,000
Roadster-2P	6300	5300	7000	11,500	24,000	37,000
Sport-4P	6300	5400	7300	11,800	25,000	38,000
Suburban-7P	7800	3900	4800	7700	14,300	27,000
Touring Sedan-7P	7500	2300	3300	4600	7500	16,000
Sport Sedan-4P	7500	2400	3400	4800	8000	17,000
Cabriolet-7P	9000	5200	6800	11,300	23,000	36,000

1924 McFarlan TV-Six, roadster, HAC

1924 McFARLAN
Single-Valve Six — 75 hp, 140" wb

Roadster-2P	2600	4500	5800	9500	18,000	32,000
Touring-5P	2600	4300	5400	8700	16,500	30,000
Coupe-4P	3100	2200	3200	4400	7000	15,000
Sedan-5P	3100	2000	3000	4200	6500	14,000
Sedan-6P	3200	2100	3100	4300	6800	14,500
Limousine-7P	3450	2500	3500	5000	8500	18,000
Town Car-7P	4600	2900	3700	5600	9100	20,000

Twin-Valve Six — 120 hp, 140" wb

Roadster-2P	5400	5300	7000	11,500	24,000	37,000
Sport-4P	5600	5400	7300	11,800	25,000	38,000
Touring-7P	5700	5200	6800	11,300	23,000	36,000
Sport Sedan-5P	6600	2300	3300	4600	7500	16,000
Coupe	6720	2500	3500	5000	8500	18,000
Touring Sedan-4P/6P/7P	6720	2400	3400	4800	8000	17,000
Limousine	6900	2700	3600	5300	8800	19,000
Suburban Sedan	7000	2900	3700	5600	9100	20,000
Knickerbocker Cabriolet-7P	7300	5300	7000	11,500	24,000	37,000

1925 McFarlan TV-Six, sport touring, HAC

1925 McFarlan TV-Six, sport touring, HAC

1925 McFARLAN
Single-Valve Six — 75 hp, 140" wb

	FP	5	4	3	2	1
Roadster-2P	2600	4500	5800	9500	18,000	32,000
Touring-5P	2600	4300	5400	8700	16,500	30,000
Touring-7P	2700	4400	5600	9200	17,300	31,000
Coupe-4P	3100	2700	3600	5300	8800	19,000
Sedan-5P	3100	2400	3400	4800	8000	17,000
Sedan-6P	3200	2300	3300	4600	7500	16,000
Limousine-7P	3450	2700	3600	5300	8800	19,000
Brougham-5P	4500	3000	4000	6000	9500	21,000
Coach Brougham-5P	3450	3200	4300	6500	11,000	23,000
Suburban Sedan-5P	3400	3000	4000	6000	9500	21,000
Sedan-7P	3500	2300	3300	4600	7500	16,000
Town Car-7P	4600	3300	4400	6700	12,000	24,000

Twin-Valve Six — 120 hp, 140" wb

	FP	5	4	3	2	1
Roadster-2P	5400	5200	6800	11,300	23,000	36,000
Sport Touring-4P	5600	5400	7300	11,800	25,000	38,000
Touring-7P	5700	5300	7000	11,500	24,000	37,000
Coupe-4P	6720	3000	4000	6000	9500	21,000
Touring Sedan-4P	6720	2500	3500	5000	8500	18,000
Sedan-5P	6720	2300	3300	4600	7500	16,000
Touring Sedan-6P	6720	2400	3400	4800	8000	17,000
Sedan-7P	6810	2350	3400	4700	7800	16,500
Limousine-7P	7300	3200	4300	6500	11,000	23,000
Town Car-7P	9000	3900	4800	7700	14,300	27,000

1926 McFarlan Eight-in-Line, town coupe, HAC

1926 McFARLAN
Single-Valve Six — 75 hp, 127" wb

	FP	5	4	3	2	1
Roadster-2P	2650	4400	5600	9200	17,300	31,000
Touring-5P	2650	4300	5400	8700	16,500	30,000
Touring-7P	2750	4500	5800	9500	18,000	32,000
Brougham-5P	3180	2500	3500	5000	8500	18,000
Sedan-7P	3280	2000	3000	4200	6500	14,000
Coupe-4P	3180	2700	3600	5300	8800	19,000
Coach-5P	3180	1800	2800	4000	6200	13,000
Sedan-5P	3180	2000	3000	4200	6500	14,000
Brougham-5P	3180	2200	3200	4400	7000	15,000
Suburban Sedan-7P	3280	2300	3300	4600	7500	16,000
Suburban Sedan-7P	3480	2200	3200	4400	7000	15,000

Line-8 — 70 hp, 131" wb

	FP	5	4	3	2	1
Roadster-2P	2650	4500	5800	9500	18,000	32,000
Touring-5P	2650	4400	5600	9200	17,300	31,000
Touring-7P	2750	4700	6100	9900	19,000	33,000

	FP	5	4	3	2	1
Brougham-5P	3180	2700	3600	5300	8800	19,000
Sedan-7P	3280	2200	3200	4400	7000	15,000
Coupe-4P	3180	2900	3700	5600	9100	20,000
Coach-5P	3180	2000	3000	4200	6500	14,000
Sedan-5P	3180	2200	3200	4400	7000	15,000
Brougham-5P	3180	2400	3400	4800	8000	17,000
Suburban Sedan-7P	3280	2300	3300	4600	7500	16,000
Sedan-7P	3480	2400	3400	4800	8000	17,000
Suburban Sedan-7P	4600	2500	3500	5000	8500	18,000

Twin-Valve Six — 120 hp, 140" wb

	FP	5	4	3	2	1
Roadster-4P	5400	4700	6100	9900	19,000	33,000
Sport Touring-5P	5600	4500	5800	9500	18,000	32,000
Touring-7P	5700	4400	5600	9200	17,300	31,000
Sedan-5P	6720	2400	3400	4800	8000	17,000
Coupe-4P	6720	2700	3600	5300	8800	19,000
Suburban Sedan-7P	6810	2500	3500	5000	8500	18,000
Berline-7P	7300	2700	3600	5300	8800	19,000
Town Car-7P	9000	3000	4000	6000	9500	21,000

1927 McFarlan TV-Six, town car, HAC

1927 McFARLAN
Line 8 — 79 hp, 131" wb

	FP	5	4	3	2	1
Roadster-2P	2650	4700	6100	9900	19,000	33,000
Touring-5P	2650	4500	5800	9500	18,000	32,000
Touring-7P	2750	5000	6500	11,000	22,000	35,000
Brougham-5P	3180	3900	4800	7700	14,300	27,000
Sedan-7P	3280	3300	4400	6700	12,000	24,000
Coupe-4P	3180	3700	4700	7300	13,700	26,000
Coach-5P	3180	3500	4500	7000	13,000	25,000
Sedan-5P	3180	3200	4300	6500	11,000	23,000
Brougham-5P	3180	3700	4700	7300	13,700	26,000
Suburban Sedan-7P	3280	3400	4800	7700	14,300	27,000
Sedan-7P	3480	4000	5000	8000	15,000	28,000
Suburban Sedan-7P	4600	4200	5200	8400	15,700	29,000

Twin Valve Six — 120 hp, 140" wb

	FP	5	4	3	2	1
Roadster-4P	5400	5200	6800	11,300	23,000	36,000
Sport Touring-5P	5600	4000	5000	8000	15,000	38,000
Touring-7P	5700	5300	7000	11,500	24,000	37,000
Sedan-5P	6720	3300	4400	6700	12,000	24,000
Coupe-4P	6720	3900	4800	7700	14,300	27,000
Suburban Sedan-7P	6810	4000	5000	8000	15,000	28,000
Berline-7P	7300	4200	5200	8400	15,700	29,000
Town Car-7P	9000	4400	5600	9200	17,300	31,000

1928 McFarlan, Line 8, brougham, HAC

1928 McFARLAN
Line 8 — 8-cyl., 79 hp, 131" wb

	FP	5	4	3	2	1
Touring-5P	2650	5300	7000	11,500	24,000	37,000
Touring-7P	2750	5400	7300	11,800	25,000	38,000
Roadster-4P	3050	5200	6800	11,300	23,000	36,000
Sport Phaeton-4P	3180	5500	7500	12,000	26,000	39,000
Sedan-5P	3180	3300	4400	6700	12,000	24,000
Coupe-3P	3180	3500	4500	7000	13,000	25,000
Brougham-4P	3180	3500	4500	7000	13,000	25,000
Coupe-5P	3180	3700	4700	7300	13,700	26,000
Suburban Sedan-5P	3380	3900	4800	7700	14,300	27,000
Sedan-7P	3680	4000	5000	8000	15,000	28,000
Suburban Sedan-7P	3780	4100	5100	8200	15,400	28,500
Town Car-4P	4600	4200	5200	8400	15,700	29,000

Twin-Valve Six — 120 hp, 140" wb

	FP	5	4	3	2	1
Town Car-4P	4600	4400	5600	9200	17,300	31,000
Sport Touring-5P	5600	6000	8500	13,000	30,000	42,000
Touring-7P	5700	5800	8000	12,500	28,000	40,000
Roadster-4P	5800	5500	7500	12,000	26,000	39,000
Touring Sedan-5P	6720	3500	4500	7000	13,000	25,000
Coupe-3P	6720	3700	4700	7300	13,700	26,000
Suburban Sedan-7P	6720	3900	4800	7700	14,300	27,000
Berline Sedan-7P	6920	4200	5200	8400	15,700	29,000
Town Car-6P	9000	4500	5800	9500	18,000	32,000

McGIEARNAN — "A company is being formed in Clinton, Missouri to manufacture a low-priced car designed by Charles McGiearnan," reported *The Horseless Age* in early 1905. This was a typographical error. The fellow in question was Charles A. McKiernan. Refer to McKiernan.

1922 McGill, model 5-6, touring, WLB

McGILL — Fort Worth, Texas — (1921-1922) — "Style and beauty with the pep" and "power and efficiency with a business dash" was the way the McGill Motor Car Company of Fort Worth put it. The McGill was an attempt to sell four-wheel-drive to the American public in the Twenties. It didn't work. George A. McGill — who had tried with the Falcon in Tennessee in 1916 — presided over the venture, assisted by L.B. Davis as vice-president and N.B. Sawyer as secretary-treasurer. One prototype and one brochure seem to have been the company's entire output. The brochure was a single-page leaflet printed in pink on one side, blue on the other; the prototype was a 1920 Model D Elcar Six with McGill radiator emblem and hubcaps and the four-wheel-drive mechanism fitted. The car was driven around the streets of Fort Worth for about a year, its backers searching for someone willing to finance its manufacture. No one was ever found. Interestingly, in 1921 the McGill was the only four-wheel-drive passenger car in America. In 1922 it was joined by the Cla-Holme from Denver. That one never proceeded beyond the prototype stage either. There is a slight possibility, incidentally, that two McGill prototypes were built. The car pictured in the brochure has a decided Lexington look to it, but the illustration was highly retouched and this McGill might only have seen reality via an artist's pen. Apparently, George McGill had begun four-wheel-drive experimentation in Mississippi during World War I. A prototype built in a blacksmith shop — which remains extant — carries a 1917 date.

McGLASHAN — In December of 1899 *The Autobain* reported that William McGlashan of East Otto, New York had completed the building of an automobile and expected to engage in its manufacture. Details are lacking.

McGOWEN — Vincennes, Indiana — (1913) — Following the publication in a 1920 issue of *MoToR* of a technical article about the no-axle Parenti car from Buffalo, there came to the magazine's editorial office a letter on the stationery of the Peoples Tire Store of Vincennes written by one W.H. McGowen. McGowen took exception to *MoToR's* designation of the no-axle principle as new, since he had built a light car with neither front nor rear axle way back in 1913. His letter showed the backhanded but wonderful good humor of someone who had tried and failed to make it in the automobile industry: "All who rode in it expressed wonder at its marvelous riding qualities. Notwithstanding I received thousands of inquiries and orders from every civilized point of the world [doubtless McGowen was exercising poetic license] no one would assist in putting the car on the market. Even the local papers refrained from printing a word about it. After going broke fooling with the thing I gave up in disgust. I drove this model over 20,000 miles, disposing of it in 1917 when I enlisted in the World War. After my return I redesigned the job, and felt that I had the niftiest small car imaginable but because of lack of capital I chucked the whole business away and have since been devoting my crippled energies to a one-horse tire business."

McHARDY — The McHardy-Peterson Motor Car Works was incorporated in Detroit, Michigan during the summer of 1904 with a capital stock of $100,000 for the manufacture of automobiles. James H. McHardy spearheaded this venture. Manufacture is doubted.

McHARG — Edgewater, New Jersey — (c. 1900) — "To the funny side of automobiling I want to add my own little story of pioneer effort in the whizwagon industry," wrote A.V.A. McHarg regarding the first, and last, automobile he built. Reports of Alexander Winton's trailblazing trip to New York prior to the turn of the century had persuaded McHarg that he could build an automobile too. "Reasoning that if one horse pulled a wagon satisfactorily, a one-horsepower motor should be able to do as much," he purchased a small farm motor and ruined two good bicycles in "trying to

adapt their running gear to my needs." Ultimately, the McHarg was finished and taken to the curb outside the family home in Edgewater for its first test run — to cries from neighbors of "What are you going to keep in it?," "Whose dog have you got in there?," and "Which way will it run if it goes?" The McHarg ran in the right direction, but never at a pace faster than a walk, and hills of any gradient were utterly beyond it. A.V.A. McHarg purchased all the ensuing automobiles he drove.

McINTOSH — Cleveland, Ohio — (1903) — The McIntosh Brothers were machinists and bicycle manufacturers in Cleveland, and decided to become automobile producers in 1903. After several months of experimentation, they reported to *The Automobile* in October that they had "perfected a gasoline car which appears satisfactory," and that they planned to enter the automotive field the following year. That was the last heard from the McIntosh Brothers on the subject, so it may be assumed that their car had not really been perfected, nor was it even satisfactory for that matter. This venture, incidentally, should not be confused with that of the McIntosh Iron & Wood Works which produced the Bjella car in McIntosh, Minnesota in 1906.

1909 McIntyre, model NN, runabout, HAC

McINTYRE — Auburn, Indiana — (1909-1915) — The McIntyre was successor to the Kiblinger highwheeler, Kiblinger factory manager W.H. McIntyre buying out the company in 1909 in the midst of a patent-infringement lawsuit. Manufacture of a slightly revised, non-patent-infringing McIntyre commenced in the old Kiblinger factory in Auburn, the firm now renamed W.H. McIntyre Company. McIntyre produced highwheelers of two and four cylinders, in four various horsepower sizes and no fewer then nine different body styles. In 1909 McIntyre claimed to be the only highwheeler manufacturer to offer a complete line of vehicles, and this is likely to have been true. In addition, McIntyre contracted with the Tudhope company of Ontario for manufacture in Canada, one of the rare highwheeler builders in the United States to do so. In 1913-1914 McIntyre built a cyclecar called the Imp. The company introduced a line of standard vehicles as well, in 1911 taking over the America produced by the Motor Car Company (New York City) which was thereafter marketed as the McIntyre Special. These cars did not sell well. Like most highwheeler producers, McIntyre could not overcome the stigma of having been a motor buggy builder, and its unfortunate marketing of a cyclecar too meant that the firm never was taken seriously in the conventional car field. The company was in receivership by January 1915. At the end of that year it was succeeded by the DeKalb Manufacturing Company of Ft. Wayne.

1909 McIntyre, model K, buggy, NAHC

1909 McINTYRE
Two — 12/14 hp, 69-1/2 wb

	FP	5	4	3	2	1
Model H Buggy-2P	450	2300	3300	4600	7500	16,000
Model K Buggy-2P	475	2300	3300	4600	7500	16,000
Model F Surrey-4P	500	2400	3400	4800	8000	17,000
Model I Limo.-2P	525	2500	3500	5000	8500	18,000
Two — 16 hp, 75" wb						
Model G Surrey-4P	575	2500	3500	5000	8500	18,000
Model GG Surrey-4P	600	2500	3500	5000	8500	18,000
Two — 18.2 hp, 75" wb						
Model NN Runabout-4P	650	2450	3500	4900	8300	17,500
Model T Surrey-4P	775	2600	3600	5200	8700	18,500

Four — 24/26 hp, 111" wb	FP	5	4	3	2	1
Model M Runabout-4P	750	2500	3500	5000	8500	18,000

1910 McINTYRE
Two — 14 hp, 80" wb

	FP	5	4	3	2	1
Model B-1 Runabout-2P	600	2500	3500	5000	8500	18,000

Two — 20 hp, 90" wb

Model A-1 Runabout-2P	750	2500	3500	5000	8500	18,000

Four — 30 hp, 112" wb

Model M-3 Touring-4P	1500	2700	3600	5300	8800	19,000
Model M-4 Touring-5P	1500	2700	3600	5300	8800	19,000
Model M-2 Runabout-3P	1400	2600	3600	5200	8700	19,500

Four — 40 hp, 115" wb

Model M-10 Runabout	1750	3000	4000	6000	9500	21,000
Model M-15 Roadster	1750	3100	4200	6300	10,500	22,000
Model M-20 Touring	1750	3000	4000	6000	9500	21,000

1911 McINTYRE
Two — 20 hp, 97" wb

Model A-4 Tonneau	850	2700	3600	5300	8800	19,000

Four — 35 hp, 110" wb

Model A-5 Touring-4P	1350	3100	4200	6300	10,500	22,000
Model T-5 Torpedo-2P	1350	3200	4300	6500	11,000	23,000

Four — 35 hp, 115" wb

Model C-5 Touring-5P	1400	3200	4300	6500	11,000	23,000

Four — 40 hp, 125" wb

Model M-5 Touring-5P	1650	3500	4500	7000	13,000	25,000
Model M-5 Fore-Dr. Tour.-5P	1700	3700	4700	7300	13,700	26,000
Model T-1 Torpedo-4P	1850	3900	4800	7700	14,300	27,000

1912 McINTYRE
Model F-12 — 4-cyl., 26 hp, 114" wb

Touring-5P	1125	3500	4500	7000	13,000	25,000

1913 McIntyre, model 6-40, Limited touring, JAC

1913-1914 McINTYRE
Model 6-40 — 6-cyl., 40 hp, 120" wb

Limited Touring-5P	1485	3900	4800	7700	14,300	27,000

1915 McIntyre, model 4-25, touring, GR

1915 McINTYRE
Model 4-25 — 4-cyl., 25 hp, 106" wb

Touring-5P	695	3000	4000	6000	9500	21,000

Model 6-40 — 6-cyl., 40 hp, 120" wb

Limited Touring-5P	1275	3900	4800	7700	14,300	27,000

McKAIG — Although this venture began as the McKaig Friction Drive Vehicle Company in 1903, it went nowhere quickly. One of the partners to the venture, however, went on the year following to produce vehicles in North Milwaukee, Wisconsin. Refer to Meiselbach.

McKAY STEAM — Lawrence, Massachusetts — (1899-1902) — The McKay was a steam car produced by the Stanley Manufacturing Company of Lawrence. Frank F. Stanley was head of the company, and he was no relation to the well-known Stanley twins of Newton, who had already built a steam car of their own. Frank Stanley did not design his car, rather he

1900 McKay Steamer, surrey, HAC

built it under license from steam car inventor George E. Whitney. For a short time in 1899, the car bore the name of Stanley-Whitney. Later that year Frank Stanley announced the forthcoming name change to McKay, in honor of "the well-known inventor, whose machines we have manufactured for many years." That the McKay invention spoken of was a sewing machine was not noted. "The McKay carriages have several notable features," *Motor Age* remarked in August 1900. "The gasoline tank is immersed in the water tank. The engine is simple or compound and has a super-heating device." The price tag was $1800. The McKay was shown at America's first automobile show at Madison Square Garden in New York in 1900, and twenty-five cars are known to have been built by the end of that year. Most probably, production ended sometime early in 1902. Subsequent production of McKays seem to have been exclusively sewing machines.

1902 McKay Steamer, runabout, GR

McKEAGUE — The Joseph B. McKeague Company was organized in Chicago, Illinois early in 1908 with a capital stock of $5000 for the manufacture of automobiles and accessories. Incorporators were James B. Leahy, K. Neale and J. McCarthy. Manufacture of a car is doubted.

McKEEN — The McKeen Motor Car Company was organized with a million-dollar capital during the summer of 1908, its stated purpose being the manufacture of motor cars and engines in Omaha. What McKeen actually manufactured, however, was a motor car for railroad use. The man behind this venture was W.R. McKeen, Jr., formerly superintendent of motive power for the Union Pacific. E.H. Harriman reportedly had provided the financing for his railroad car company.

McKELLAR — Grafton, North Dakota — (1904) — Robert McKellar of Grafton believed in the "fail-safe" approach. The automobile he built in 1904 had two engines, the second to be used for added power or "if the first engine goes bump..."

McKENNEY — Chicago, Illinois — (1900) — In a July 1900 issue of *The Motor Vehicle Review*. James S. McKenney was described as "a manufacturer of motor vehicles at 333 Wabash Avenue" in Chicago. At the time he was declaring bankruptcy with debts of $155,469 and assets of $15,350. And it would appear he was less a manufacturer than a purveyor of automobiles left over when the Elgin Sewing Machine and Bicycle Company went under during the fall of 1899. McKenney had been a large stockholder in the Elgin venture, perhaps acquiring the Elgin Electric cars in a vain attempt to retrieve something from his investment.

McKENNEY-DEVLIN — The McKenney-Devlin Company was organized in Detroit, Michigan during the summer of 1914 with a capital stock of $10,000 to manufacture and sell automobiles. Incorporators were George A. and Lyle A. Devlin and Paul R. McKenney. Manufacture is doubted.

McKIERNAN — Clinton, Missouri — (1905)/Carthage, Missouri — (1908) — Charles A. McKiernan first attempted to enter the automobile field in Clinton in 1905. Failing there, he tried again in 1908 in Carthage, announcing his new car that August. The McKiernan was to be a lightweight, moderately-priced runabout and light delivery. "Control will be entirely by a single lever in the center of the rig," *Cycle and Automobile Trade Journal* reported. "The mechanism is said to be exceptionally simple and the machine can be operated by a 15-year-old boy, as there are no complications either in the mechanism or in the operation and control of the car." So far as is known, McKiernan didn't make it to market this time either.

McKINLEY — The McKinley Motor Car Company was organized in Rochester, New York late in 1905 with a capital stock of $20,000 for the manufacture of automobiles. Incorporators were Stanley R. Snook, Alfred H. Sowers, Elwood H. Lapp and George H. Smith, all of Rochester. Manufacture is doubted.

The McKinley Square Auto Company was organized in New York City with a capital stock of $1000 "to construct autos and supplies." Incorporators were G. Herrmann, O.A. Green, M. Hermann and K. Green. Manufacture is doubted.

1926 McLaughlin, NAHC

McLAUGHLIN — Bangor, Maine — (1926) — The full name for this automotive oddity was McLaughlin Maine Mobile. It was built by George McLaughlin of Bangor, and it was designed to run on roads, over water and atop snow. Speeds as high as 106 mph were promised on good roads; 30 mph was possible through fresh water, 35 mph through salt water. Snow speed was not mentioned. Power was provided by a 72 hp specially-built airplane motor and propeller which was started with the turn of a switch: "When that is done the propeller begins going around immediately . . . as she 'gets the gas' the big blade whirls faster until the car starts off." The McLaughlin was no beauty. As the *Bangor Daily Commercial* reported, if the car "has any forty-second cousins, then the small war tank, it seems, would be the nearest relative." Built into the McLaughlin, beneath the steps on either side, were steel air compartments, presumably a safety device to keep the vehicle afloat on water. (It was a light machine, incidentally, weighing but 1580 pounds.) The disc wheels with balloon tires purportedly served as rudders. A toboggan device provided for snow travel. His 1926 vehicle was not McLaughlin's first such attempt. He built a similar machine four years earlier, but on a smaller scale. The disposition of that one is not known. The 1926 McLaughlin, however, was sold that year to Alfred Wilson who operated a campground at Moosehead Lake. George McLaughlin had high hopes for his vehicle, commenting that he planned to be "turning 'em out in big lots" in the near future once the public became aware of the machine's commercial value and possibilities. Public awareness never arrived. No mention was made of the Maine Mobile in George McLaughlin's obituary following his death in 1961.

McLAUGHLIN & ASHLEY — The McLaughlin & Ashley Motor Cycle Company was organized in New York City early in 1909 with a capital stock of $10,000 to "manufacture motor cars, motor cycles and motor boats." Incorporators were J.F. McLaughlin, G.A. Ashley and Dwight Patterson. Manufacture of a car is doubted.

McLEAN — C.H. McLean proceeded far enough to organize his McLean Motor Car Company and to lease a plant at South Port Huron, Michigan "to serve at present as an experimental station," according to *Automobile Trade Journal*'s October 1923 issue. McLean's plan was to manufacture a "new type of automobile next Spring." It does not appear he made it.

McLELLEN — The McLellen Auto Shop was organized in Indianapolis, Indiana during the fall of 1912 with a capital stock of $1000 to manufacture and sell automobiles. Incorporators were F.P. McLellen, F.E. Barrett and J.M. Milne. Manufacture is doubted.

1900 McMullin, phaeton, NAHC

McMULLIN — Chicago, Illinois — (1900-1901) — The McMullin Motive Power and Construction Company of Chicago manufactured stationary engines and during 1900 to 1901 adapted one of them to a carriage. Steering was by hand wheel, the change-speed mechanism was a single handle. The vehicle was low-slung for the period, and was reported to be a very easy riding machine. F.R. McMullin promised speeds "forward, zero to 12 miles" and "back, zero to 6 miles per hour." In April 1900 he moved his factory's quarters to the Royal Insurance Building on Jackson Boulevard, and announced he had perfected his car. "The public will before long be able to place orders for this machine," *The Automobile Review* reported in April, "as Mr. McMullin is known as an energetic hustler." But obviously his machine had not yet been perfected. No McMullin cars had been placed on the market at all by January 1901 when *The Horseless Age* noted that the company preferred "to do their experimenting at home and at their own expense — a very praiseworthy idea." Possibly a few cars ultimately were sold — $1000 was the price tag — but the McMullin company soon reverted full attention to the gasoline engine field.

McMURTRY — Chester, Pennsylvania — (1896) — In late summer of 1896, A.L. McMurtry of Chester reported to *The Horseless Age* that he had just completed building a "steam pleasure carriage for a party in Allegheny." Two single-acting 3/4 hp engines were fitted under the seat, with the boiler placed to the rear. The fuel was gasoline, the tank holding enough for a four-hour run. Two levers — one for steering, the other for speed changing — operated the vehicle. McMurtry emphasized that the car was experimental, and that he planned to replace the engines with two 1 hp compound units. "Mr. McMurtry intends to make 'the one' next spring," the magazine noted. Whether he ever did has not been recorded.

McNABB — In 1910 the McNabb Iron Works of Atlanta, Georgia produced a little gasoline runabout named the Billy Four. Refer to Billy Four.

McNABB & CHAPMAN — Basic City, Virginia — (1900) — In December 1900 *The Motor Age* reported that McNabb & Chapman of Basic City had just begun to build their first automobile. "They have a splendid factory," the report said brightly, "and expect to build in numbers later on." That expectation does not appear to have been fulfilled. Interestingly, the year previous in Basic City, George Dawson had the distinction of building the first automobile in the state of Virginia.

McNUTT — Early in 1902, John McNutt, who had previously operated a machine shop in Warren, Ohio, purchased the Brenning Brothers' larger machine shop in Springfield, Ohio and announced that he would at once "take up the manufacture of automobiles" there. The evidence suggests that he did not, however.

McOMBER — Late in 1913, J.E. McOmber of 5501 Cates Avenue in St. Louis, Missouri announced that his new factory for the manufacture of cyclecars would be "in operation early in 1914." E.L. McBride was associated with this venture, and they declared themselves "anxious to hear from the parts manufacturers." Manufacture does not seem to have followed.

McPHAIL STEAM — Boston, Massachusetts — (1906) — John N. McPhail was a reporter for the Boston *Globe* who built himself a steam car in 1906 and subsequently reported to readers of the *Globe* how easy it had been

1906 McPhail, runabout, NAHC

and how to do it themselves. Most of the components had been purchased from outside suppliers, McPhail having earlier taken measurements of the "different parts from the machines I saw in the streets and at the different exhibitions where they were to be seen." The car he built was absolutely standard in all respects, which is precisely the machine McPhail desired. "Such a carriage can be built for $300, not counting labor," he said. "It is one of the most satisfactory investments of time and money I ever made, and I am well satisfied with the results of my labors."

McPHERSON — The McPherson Automobile Company was organized in Camden, New Jersey late in 1899 with a capital stock of $20,000 for the manufacture and sale of automobiles. Incorporators were S.C. Woodhull, Harry F. Carr and D. Truman Stackhouse. Manufacture is doubted.

1934 McQuay Norris, MVMA

McQUAY-NORRIS — St. Louis, Missouri — (1933-1934) — Six of these cars were built on Ford chassis to serve as a rolling laboratory and sales promoter for the McQuay-Norris Manufacturing Company, which had been in the business of producing engine and chassis components in St. Louis since 1910. In 1932 McQuay-Norris contracted their building to the Hill Auto Body Metal Company of Cincinnati, and from 1934 to 1940 the cars toured the country, visiting auto repair shops and wholesale distributors and other McQuay-Norris customers. "The cars are not only of interest because of their unusually handsome lines but also because they carry what is probably the most complete list of testing apparatus ever installed in an automobile," *MoToR* reported in 1935. "Except for a roomy opening for the driver's feet the instrument board is carried all the way to the floor." Among the instruments were a clock, speedometer, ammeter, "Moto Vita combustion indicator," and other gauges indicating exhaust temperature, compression pressure, oil level, pressure, temperature, viscosity and water temperature. The car's teardrop shape was reminiscent of the Arrow Plane which the Hill company had built earlier in 1932 for Lyman Voelpel.

McQUESTEN STEAM — Boston, Massachusetts — (1901) — George B. McQuesten was a well-known New England lumberman for whom Binney & Burnham constructed a steam car in 1901. This vehicle was probably the first built by the B/B partnership and ultimately led to the others produced for a short while under the Binney & Burnham name. An enthusiastic motorist, McQuesten had, incidentally, been the guiding light in the establishment of the Automobile Club of New England in December 1900. The McQuesten family lumber business remains extant.

McTEAGUE — The Joseph McTeague Company was organized in Chicago, Illinois early in 1908 for the manufacture of automobiles and accessories. James J. Leahy and K. Neale were the incorporators. Manufacture of a car is doubted.

M & C ELECTRIC — That a car called the M & C Electric was built by the National Contracting Company of New York City in 1913 has been indicated on various car rosters. This has not been confirmed. The National Contracting Company was at 107 Hudson Street in Manhattan; its city directory listing during this period indicates the firm only as "agents."

M.C.M. — The M.C.M. Motor Company was organized in Bedford, Indiana during the summer of 1914 with a capital stock of $10,000 to manufacture and sell automobiles and engines. The M.C.M. people were Walter M. Mathes, L. Cobb and E.L. Morris. Manufacture of a car is doubted.

MEAD — Chicago, Illinois — (1902-1907) — The Mead Cycle Company was one of Chicago's leading mail order bicycle houses at the turn of the century. Although it never became an automobile manufacturer, Mead did serve as a used car dealership which specialized in the reconditioning of vehicles which it then resold under whatever name a prospective purchaser might wish. When offering new cars (imported Benzes and a few American makes), the firm usually traded under the name Mead Motor Company. Mead was in the automobile business from 1902 until at least 1907.

MEAD — Dayton, Ohio — (1912) — In 1912 the Mead Engine Company of Dayton built an experimental car to demonstrate its rotary valve engine. The car was not produced as a Mead, however, but as a Speedwell, the Mead people having effectively insinuated themselves onto the board of directors of the Speedwell Motor Car Company.

1916 Mecca, model 30, 5-pass. touring, WLB

MECCA — New York, New York — (1915-1916) — The Times Square Automobile Company in New York City was a firm dealing principally in rebuilt and used cars. When it decided to market an automobile of its own, the name chosen for the marque was whimsically appropriate; the Broadway area surrounding Times Square in Manhattan had long been referred to as the "mecca" of the theatre world. The first Mecca was a four-cylinder $450 cyclecar that was shown at the automobile show sponsored by the Manufacturers' and Dealers' Cyclecar Association in Boston in October 1914. Times Square was to produce the car itself in Teaneck, New Jersey as the Mecca Motor Car Company, but the car probably never saw an assembly line. By 1915 Times Square had concluded that building of the Mecca might best be left to someone else, and that the Mecca should not be a cyclecar. Consequently, the Princess Motor Car Company of Detroit was contacted to build a version of its four-cylinder Model 30 with Mecca trim and nameplate. This car was introduced by Times Square in mid-1915 as a 1916 model. A reference from *Motor Age* dated January 4th, 1917 indicates that the Mecca did not survive into that new year.

	FP	5	4	3	2	1
1915 MECCA						
Mecca Cyclecar	450	1400	2400	3500	5300	10,000
1916 MECCA						
Mecca Thirty — 4-cyl., 23 hp, 104" wb						
Touring-5P	695	1800	2800	4000	6200	13,000
Roadster-2P	695	1900	2900	4100	6400	13,500
Runabout-2P	695	1800	2800	4000	6200	13,000

1903 Mechaley, touring, NAHC

MECHALEY — Stamford, Connecticut — (1903) — Mechaley Brothers of Stamford stored, repaired and supplied automobiles of all kinds, were the East Coast agents for the Rambler built in Kenosha (Wisconsin) and also marketed the Brennan gasoline motor produced in Syracuse (New York). In 1903 the brothers put one of the two-cylinder 12 hp Brennan engines into an experimental chassis they had run up and liked the result so well that they tried to market it as Mechaleys' Touring Car. Its price was $1500 "delivered anywhere in the U.S.A." Probably no Mechaley car ever found its way out of Connecticut, however, and after dismal sales of one season, the brothers returned full time to storing, repairing, supplying and selling the cars manufactured by others.

1903 MECHALEY
Two — 12 hp, 75" wb

	FP	5	4	3	2	1
Touring-5P	1500	1500	2500	3600	5500	11,000

MECKY — Philadelphia, Pennsylvania — (1901-1902) — A. Mecky lived in Tioga, Pennsylvania but operated his small (and unnamed) automobile enterprise from a little shop at 3635 Smedley Street in Philadelphia. There he produced a number of two- and four-passenger runabouts powered by single-cylinder De Dion engines. "Prices vary according to size of motor," A. Mecky informed the trade press, "and will be cheerfully given upon application." He also invited potential customers to come to his works for a test drive. His automotive venture seems to have ended by late 1902.

1901-1902 MECKY

Mecky	—	—	—	—	—	—

MED-BOW — The name was a constriction of the two partners involved: Harry C. Medcraft and George B. Bowersox. The Med-Bow Automobile Company was initially the name of this venture, but was changed by the fall of 1907 to the H.C. Medcraft Automobile Company, which may indicate George Bowersox was no longer around. The cars produced were built in Springfield, Massachusetts from 1907-1908 and in Springfield, Illinois from 1909-1910. Although frequently appearing on Massachusetts registration lists as Med-Bow or Medcraft, the cars were marketed in both that state and in Illinois under the tradename of Springfield. The confusion was the fault of the Massachusetts Motor Vehicle Department which for years requested not "make of car" or "name of car" but instead "maker's name." Refer to Springfield.

1900 Media, electric runabout, MVMA

MEDIA — Media, Pennsylvania — (1899-1900) — Ten men were employed by the Media Carriage Works during its inaugural year of 1895, but the workforce had risen to thirty by the turn of the century and business was booming. W.W. Johnson, H.J. Hipple and E.L. Cunningham were the men behind Media, and their factory was a four-story building at State and Radnor streets. Media's foray into the automobile field was a short one, instigated principally by Cunningham. The company's first car, an electric, was built to order for a Dr. W.A. Davis of Camden, New Jersey in 1899. The result being salutary, Media decided to market the car in 1900 and allied itself with the Pullen Battery & Electrical Manufacturing Company of Philadelphia. The Pullen storage battery was used in the Media car, a 900-pound runabout being delivered to Pullen in January for demonstration purposes. Media offered versions of this vehicle for sale at $1100. Its running range was thirty-five miles on a single charge, and its top speed was approximately 12 mph. Although an occasional car may have been built later, it would appear the bulk of the Media car production occurred during 1900, with the company electing to confine its major effort to the carriage trade thereafter.

MEEKER — The Meeker Manufacturing Company of Dayton, Ohio was indicated as an automobile manufacturer in the Hiscox book *Horseless Vehicles, Automobiles, Motor Cycles* published in 1900. Further documentation is lacking. Turn-of-the-century Dayton city directories show the company's product only as rubber tires. The firm was located at Linden Avenue south of Huffman; Herman Rogge was president, Henry Zwich was secretary.

1924 Meisenhelder, roadster, WFOR

MEISENHELDER — York, Pennsylvania — (1919-1924) — Roy M. Meisenhelder of York never built a complete automobile of his own, but when he was finished with those he rebuilt, it wasn't easy to ascertain what they had been in the first place. His business was sheet metal and auto repairs, but his sideline was customizing. He would have been right at home at any contemporary custom car show. His first known creation was in 1919 and based on a Paige; he is documented to have created three more in 1924 (which remain extant) — and his creativity probably didn't end there. The number of customs by Meisenhelder will probably always remain a mystery, but a surviving photograph of one, which looks to have as many gee-gaws and gadgets as a dentist's chair, indicates that he must have had a great deal of fun in his sideline.

MEISELBACH — North Milwaukee, Wisconsin — (1904-1909) — Initially this venture began in Washington, D.C. as the McKaig Friction Drive Vehicle Company which was incorporated for $350,000 in 1903 by several natives of that city as well as three Chicagoans including E.T. McKaig and August D. Meiselbach. McKaig was an engineer with some patents, Meiselbach was known as the largest builder of cheap bicycles in Chicago and the chief promoter of the Meiselbach Typewriter Company. Announcement of this new McKaig venture was made in August of 1903, together with plans to "manufacture vehicles of all kinds," and to locate a factory in the Chicago area. Almost immediately, McKaig and Meiselbach had a falling out, and all plans were off. In mid-1904, Meiselbach was back, however, incorporating the A.D. Meiselbach Motor Vehicle Company with a capital stock of $50,000. Apparently by this time, Meiselbach had reconciled sufficiently with McKaig to acquire the use of his patents, though McKaig was not officially involved in this new venture. New York and Chicago capital — and A.N. Miller, Fred D. Clinton and Byron R. Godfrey — backed the Meiselbach company. A factory in North Milwaukee was acquired and there production began in late fall. The first Meiselbach was a one-ton truck, followed later by two- and three-ton capacity models. The company did not build automobiles on a regular basis, but is believed to have produced a few for in-house use or as salesman's cars. All Meiselbachs were highwheelers.

MEL SPECIAL — Ohio & Pennsylvania — (1918-1924) — Mel Stringer was a dirt-track racing car driver and builder who moonlighted at various other jobs to make ends meet. Brooklyn born, he operated a garage in that New York City borough beginning in late 1912; 1917 found him in Chicago as general sales manager for Keller Engineering & Sales Service, that company having arranged to market the cars produced by Harry Miller of Los Angeles. Conceivably this experience may have given him the idea to market an automobile of his own. In April of 1918 *Motor Age* carried the announcement that Mel Stringer had begun to build sport-type cars for the trade, in addition to all-out racing cars for the competition enthusiast. He produced a number of these in Cleveland, Ohio where he remained until at least 1920 and where he also manufactured automobile speed accessories. Subsequently he moved to Pottstown, Pennsylvania where he built a few more specials through 1924. His production for the entire period was quite small, however, and entirely to order. Doubtless most of his orders were for dirt-track racing cars. The price quoted in 1924 for one of his four-cylinder chassis was $4250.

MEMPHIS — Memphis, Tennessee — (1904-1905) — The two most important figures in the Memphis Motor Carriage Company were its president W.T. Watson, the head of Watson's Business College in Memphis, and its general manager Herbert H. Pilcher, who designed the Memphis steam car. The flash-tube generator in the Memphis was similar to that of the White, because as Pilcher unabashedly admitted, "the White people have come as near perfection in generators as anyone is liable to get, and I do not ask for a better steam generator than theirs." The Memphis engine, however, was pure Pilcher: "It is a tandem compound, in which the high and low pressure cylinders are combined. This feature enables me to dispense with cross heads and consequent friction and it does away with long piston rods." Both commercial and passenger vehicles with the Pilcher compound engine were planned, and the first prototypes were completed late in 1904. Construction of a factory in Memphis was ongoing, and by

April of 1905 was nearing completion. Whether the Memphis Motor Carriage Company ever moved into it is problematical, but full production of the Memphis steam vehicles was not reached before this venture, which had been severely undercapitalized, failed.

1907 Menges, touring, NAHC

MENGES — Grand Rapids, Michigan — (1907) — Albert C. Menges was a native of Memphis, Tennessee who organized the Menges Engine & Manufacturing Company in that city in 1902. A few years later he was lured to Michigan by William H. Harrison of Grand Rapids who wished to move his Harrison Wagon Works into the automotive age. Menges provided him the car with which to do it, which was introduced at the Chicago Automobile Show in February 1906 under the Harrison name as "The Car Without a Crank." Internal dissension arose within the Harrison company soon thereafter and in November Menges departed, announcing that he would begin again on his own in Grand Rapids. The Menges Motor Company followed, as did the Menges car. Like the Harrison, the Menges had no crank, being started by a clutch-operated electric motor which was not totally effective. It was a much larger car than the Harrison, an eight-passenger tourer on a 122-inch wheelbase powered by a four-cylinder engine with overhead valves "in cages" developing a purported but very doubtful 100 hp. The prototype was completed, and a $5000 price tag was put on it. But there was no manufacture in Grand Rapids. By October of 1907 it was reported that the Sterling-Hudson Whip Company of Elkhart, Indiana had bought the rights to the Menges car. A prototype was built there, but manufacture did not follow, that firm deciding to enter the market with a lower-priced Sterling instead. In February of 1908 it was revealed that Beck & Clausel in Menges' hometown of Memphis would produce his car, but manufacture did not follow there either. Most likely the only Menges cars built were the prototypes in Grand Rapids and Elkhart. In 1920 Albert Menges surfaced in Greenville, Mississippi as a hopeful truck maker. He fared no better there.

1937 Menkenns, MVMA

MENKENNS — Hillsboro, Oregon — (1937) — An airplane propellor, a motorcycle engine, three wheels and an automobile's steering wheel represented just about the toto of what Willie Menkenns required to build his strange little automobile in 1937. "This one wins the fur-lined cylinder block," commented *Motor Age*. The Menkenns was purportedly capable of 55 mph.

MENOMINEE ELECTRIC — Menominee, Michigan — (1902, 1915) — The Menominee Electric Company controlled the Dudly Tool Company, and H.F. Tideman was president of both. In 1914 Dudly Tool introduced a cyclecar called the Dudly Bug, while Menominee continued on in its usual manufacturing activity of electric motors, telephones and electric goods. In 1902 the firm had built an experimental electric to test its storage battery and in 1912 had experimented with a light electric car for children's use, but tests had proven unsatisfactory and the project was abandoned. Now, with the experience gained with the Dudly Bug cyclecar, Menominee

decided to try an electric again, this time for adults. Built as a cabriolet only on a 108-inch wheelbase, the Menominee Electric's top speed was 20 mph, with a 50-60 mile range per charge. A recharging outfit was included as standard equipment, and the price for the whole package was $1250. A small run of these cars was off the line in July of 1915, but manufacture had been discontinued by year's end. By now the Dudly Bug was gone too.

MENUS-VAN HORN — The Menus-Van Horn Motor Company was indicated in a 1902 trade journal as the manufacturer of an automobile. This probably was in error. The firm was in the auto accessories field. Early in 1903 Menus-Van Horn moved from its original location at 11 High Street in Boston to 49 Galen Street in Waterloo, Massachusetts.

MERCANTILE — The Mercantile Motor Company was organized in Jersey City, New Jersey during the summer of 1905 with a capital stock of $200,000 for the manufacture of automobiles, engines and trucks using both steam and gasoline power. Albert H. Overman, Ward B. Chamberlin and Albert W. Chamberlin were the incorporators. Manufacture of a car is doubted.

MERCEDES — From 1905 until February 1907, when a disastrous fire destroyed its Long Island City, New York factory, the German Mercedes was produced under license in this country by the Daimler Manufacturing Company. Refer to American Mercedes.

The Mercedes Realty Company of New York City was organized during the summer of 1909 with a capital stock of $10,000 for the manufacture of motor cars and engines. Incorporators were A.C. Beckert, H. Hitchback and W. Luttgen. Manufacture of an automobile is doubted.

1910 Mercer, model 30, toy tonneau, HAC

MERCER — Trenton, New Jersey — (1910-1926)/Elkhart, Indiana — (1931) — For many people the Mercer was a hairy, thundering machine with monocle windshield in front, round gasoline tank in the rear, and two bucket seats inbetween. Its coachwork consisted of a hood and fenders usually painted a yellow vivid enough to blind, and if that didn't, the abundance of brass would. This was the Raceabout, the most famous of Mercers though but one of varied models produced by the company during the two-plus decades of its peripatetic existence. In May of 1909 the Mercer Automobile Company was born in Trenton, Mercer County, New Jersey. It evolved from the Walter Automobile Company which had built the Walter and Roebling-Planche cars in the former factory of a brewery into which the new Mercer moved. Behind the Mercer venture were the monied Roebling and Kuser families, who had been involved in the building of another engineering tour de force called the Brooklyn Bridge. The first Mercer cars arrived in 1910. Whether Etienne Planche, who had designed the final Walter cars, was substantially involved in their design has not been documented; press references credit A.R. Kingston and E.T. George, with a healthy assist from C.G. Roebling. Available as a speedster, toy tonneau and touring, the first Mercers were powered by four-cylinder L-head Beaver engines. The T-head Raceabout was announced late in 1910 for the 1911 model year, this car the idea of C.G. Roebling's son, Washington A. Roebling II, which had been translated into reality by the brilliant engineer, Finley Robertson Porter. Although not a particularly large (300 cubic inches) or puissant (about 34 bhp) engine, the T-head in the spartan Raceabout body made for a very light machine which was quick and nimble, the latter assisted by an exemplary three-speed, (four-speed in 1913-14), selective transmission and an oil-immersed multiple-disc clutch which assured a smooth — for that period — gear change. In 1911 Mercer Raceabouts were entered in six major races, and won five of them. In 1912, at the Los Angeles Speedway, Ralph De Palma established eight new class world records with a Raceabout, and that year too Spencer Wishart took one of the cars off an Ohio showroom floor and won a 200-mile race with it in Columbus, setting four new world's dirt-track records in the process. The Mercer was a phenomenon, and its competition successes through 1916, set amid a furious rivalry with Stutz and the headline-grabbing antics of sometime Mercer driver Barney Oldfield, placed the company in the forefront of American motor sport. Mercers were relatively expensive cars with a median price of about $2500; no more than 500 were built in a single year, no more than 150 of these being the Raceabout. "The Mercer is the Steinway of the automobile world," an advertisement from 1914 read. "It is possible to thread a needle while travelling 60 mph." But already the Mercer company had begun to travel a rocky road. In 1912 Washington A. Roebling II died in the disaster of the *Titanic*. In 1914 Finley Porter resigned from the firm, his place taken by Eric H. Delling, who designed the new L-head cars. Like the T-head, the Mercer L-head was a four, nominally rated at 22.5 hp but developing at least 70 bhp. Delling was considerably more concerned with creature comforts than Porter had been; now even sporting Mercers had full-length

917

1911 Mercer, model 35, raceabout, HAC

windshields, bench seats and enclosed coachwork, as well as Houdaille shock absorbers. But Delling's sojourn at Mercer was even shorter than Porter's; he resigned in 1916. (Both Porter and Delling later built cars under their own names.) In 1917 F.W. Roebling died, followed the year after by C.G. Roebling. The Mercer Automobile Company was in disarray now, though production continued with varying models of the Delling-designed four. In October of 1919 a Wall Street syndicate calling itself the Mercer Motors Company acquired control of Mercer. A former Packard vice-president named Emlen S. Hare was put in charge, and in December the new Mercer organization acquired a substantial interest in Locomobile, and the following January absorbed Simplex. Hare's Motors resulted from all this, and was a disaster. Among other of Emlen Hare's ideas was increasing Mercer production to 50,000 cars a year. By August of 1921, however, Hare's Motors collapsed, and control of Mercer passed back to old-guard Mercer people, John Kuser among them. A tangled web, and receivership, followed. For 1923 an overhead valve six (Rochester engine) was introduced with three-speed Brown & Lipe gearbox, joining the four-speed Mercer four. The old Mercer people held onto their factory, although in 1924 the other assets of the company were sold to Curran-McDevitt, the Philadelphia Mercer dealership. Production, which had ceased altogether during the spring of 1924, was resumed late in the year though new cars (mostly from parts on hand) merely trickled out of the factory. In 1926 even the trickle stopped, and the Mercer Motors Company closed its doors to all but service work. Though dead, the company remained in existence — If that not be a contradiction in terms — and in 1928 was sold to a New York investment group headed by a former Durant man named Harry M. Wahl, who believed in the magic of the Mercer name and in the marketability of a Mercer car. But all Wahl could buy was rights to the name and a few parts, because the Mercer factory in Trenton had in the meantime been sold to a roller bearing company. To get the revived Mercer produced, Wahl turned to the Elcar Motor Company in Elkhart, Indiana, a firm in rather precarious circumstances itself. Elcar's chief engineer, Mike Graffis, served in the same capacity for the new Mercer which was to be powered by a 140 hp Continental straight-eight set into a 135-inch wheelbase chassis and offered in five body styles (with coachwork by Merrimac) in a price range of $2640-$4000. But the Mercer revival collided head-on with the stock market crash. One car and one chassis (which remain extant) were completed and shown at the Hotel Montclair during New York Automobile Show week in January 1931. Then the Mercer Motors Corporation, which had been incorporated by Wahl on November 21st, 1929, died — and ceased to exist as well. Mercer now was a memory.

1910 MERCER
Model 30 — 4-cyl., 30 hp, 116" wb

	FP	5	4	3	2	1
A Touring-5P	1950	6400	9300	14,500	33,000	45,000
B Toy Tonneau	1950	6700	9900	15,500	34,800	47,000
C Speedster	1950	18,500	33,000	55,000	88,000	110,000

1911 MERCER
Model 30 — 4-cyl., 30 hp, 116" wb

	FP	5	4	3	2	1
M Touring-5P	2400	6400	9300	14,500	33,000	45,000
C Toy Tonneau-4P	2150	6700	9900	15,500	34,800	47,000
C Limousine	3250	5400	7300	11,800	25,000	38,000

Model 35 — 4-cyl., 34 hp, 116" wb

	FP	5	4	3	2	1
R Raceabout-2P	2250	18,500	33,000	55,000	88,000	110,000
Toy Tonneau-4P	2750	7600	12,500	19,400	42,400	55,000

1912 Mercer, model 35C, raceabout, OCW

918

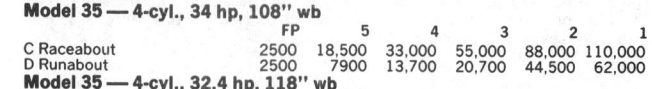

1912 MERCER
Model 35 — 4-cyl., 34 hp, 108" wb

	FP	5	4	3	2	1
C Raceabout	2500	18,500	33,000	55,000	88,000	110,000
D Runabout	2500	7900	13,700	20,700	44,500	62,000

Model 35 — 4-cyl., 32.4 hp, 118" wb

	FP	5	4	3	2	1
A Touring-4P	2750	6700	9900	15,500	34,800	47,000
B Touring-5P	2750	6800	10,300	16,000	35,500	48,000
Limousine	3800	5400	7300	11,800	25,000	38,000

1913 Mercer, model 35J, raceabout, HFM

1913 Mercer, model 35G, touring, HAC

1913 MERCER
Model 35 — 4-cyl., 34 hp, 108" wb

	FP	5	4	3	2	1
J Raceabout-2P	2600	18,500	33,000	55,000	88,000	110,000
K Runabout	2700	6000	8500	13,000	30,000	42,000

Model 35 — 4-cyl., 32.4 hp, 118" wb

	FP	5	4	3	2	1
G Touring-4P	2900	6700	9900	15,500	34,800	47,000
H Touring-5P	2900	6800	10,300	16,000	35,500	48,000

1914 Mercer, model J, raceabout, OCW

1914 MERCER
Model J — 4-cyl., 34 hp, 108" wb

	FP	5	4	3	2	1
Raceabout-2P	2600	18,500	33,000	55,000	88,000	110,000

Model M — 4-cyl., 32.4 hp, 124" wb

	FP	5	4	3	2	1
Touring-5P	3000	6800	10,300	16,000	35,500	48,000

Model O — 4-cyl., 32.4 hp, 118" wb

	FP	5	4	3	2	1
Roadster-2P	2900	7200	11,300	17,700	38,700	50,000

Model H — 4-cyl., 32.4 hp, 118" wb

	FP	5	4	3	2	1
Touring-5P	2900	7000	10,800	16,900	37,100	49,000

1915 MERCER
Model 22-70 — 4-cyl., 70 hp, 130" wb

	FP	5	4	3	2	1
Sporting-4P	3000	8400	15,500	22,500	47,300	67,000
Touring-6P	3000	8200	14,500	21,500	45,800	65,000

Model 22-70 — 4-cyl., 70 hp, 115" wb

	FP	5	4	3	2	1
Raceabout-2P	2750	22,000	36,000	60,000	93,000	120,000
Runabout	2900	8200	14,500	21,500	45,800	65,000

1915 Mercer, model 22-70, sport touring, HAC

1916 Mercer, model 22-72, sporting, OCW

1916 MERCER
Model 22-72 — 4-cyl., 70 hp, 132" wb

	FP	5	4	3	2	1
Touring-6P	3000	8200	14,500	21,500	45,800	65,000
Sporting-4P	3000	8500	16,000	23,000	48,000	68,000
Limousine	—	6800	10,300	16,000	35,500	48,000
Town Car	—	7000	10,800	16,900	37,100	49,000

Model 22-72 — 4-cyl., 70 hp, 115" wb

Runabout-2P	2900	8500	16,000	23,000	48,000	68,000
Raceabout-2P	2750	22,000	36,000	60,000	93,000	120,000

1917 Mercer, model 22-73, runabout, HAC

1917 MERCER
Model 22-73 — 4-cyl., 70 hp, 132" wb

Touring-6P	3500	8500	16,000	23,000	48,000	68,000
Sporting-4P	3500	8800	17,000	24,000	49,000	70,000

Model 22-73 — 4-cyl., 70 hp, 115" wb

Runabout-2P	3400	8800	17,000	24,000	49,000	70,000
Raceabout-2P	3250	22,000	36,000	60,000	93,000	120,000

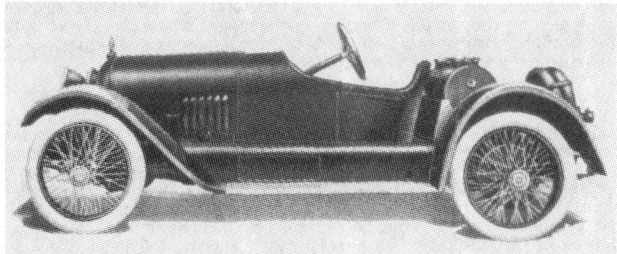

1918 Mercer, model 22-73, raceabout, HAC

1918 Mercer, model 22-73, sporting, HAC

1918 MERCER
Model 22-73 — 4-cyl., 70 hp

	FP	5	4	3	2	1
Sporting-4P (132" wb)	3850	8500	16,000	23,000	48,000	68,000
Runabout-2P (115" wb)	3750	8800	17,000	24,000	49,000	70,000
Raceabout-2P (115" wb)	3600	22,000	36,000	60,000	93,000	120,000

1919 Mercer, series 4, raceabout, HAC

1919 MERCER
Series 4 — 4-cyl., 70 hp, 132" wb

Sporting-4P		8500	16,000	23,000	48,000	68,000
Runabout-2P	4350	8800	17,000	24,000	49,000	70,000
Raceabout-2P (115" wb)	4200	22,000	36,000	60,000	93,000	120,000

1920 Mercer, series 5, raceabout, OCW

1922 Mercer, series 5, raceabout, HAC

1920 MERCER
Series 5 — 4-cyl., 70 hp, 132" wb

	FP	5	4	3	2	1
Raceabout-2P (115" wb)	4200	8800	17,000	24,000	49,000	70,000
Touring-6P	4500	7800	13,300	20,300	44,000	60,000
Sportabout-4P	4500	7900	13,700	20,700	44,500	62,000
Runabout-4P	4500	22,700	38,000	64,000	95,000	122,000
Limousine-6P	5750	7200	11,300	17,700	38,700	50,000

1921 MERCER
Series 5 — 4-cyl., 70 hp, 132" wb

	FP	5	4	3	2	1
Raceabout-2P (115" wb)	3675	22,700	38,000	64,000	95,000	122,000
Touring-6P	3950	7800	13,300	20,300	44,000	60,000
Sport-4P	3950	8500	16,000	23,000	48,000	68,000
Roadster-4P	3950	8200	14,500	21,500	45,800	65,000
Coupe-4P	5150	7600	12,500	19,400	42,400	55,000
Touring Limousine-7P	5650	7800	13,300	20,300	44,000	60,000

1922 MERCER
Series 5 — 4-cyl., 70 hp, 132" wb

	FP	5	4	3	2	1
Raceabout-2P	3950	22,700	38,000	64,000	95,000	122,000
Runabout-4P	3950	8200	14,500	21,500	45,800	65,000
Sport-5P	3950	8500	16,000	23,000	48,000	68,000
Coupe-4P	4850	7600	12,500	19,400	42,400	55,000
Limousine-7P	5250	7800	13,300	20,300	44,000	60,000
Touring-5P	3950	8400	15,500	22,500	47,300	67,000

1923 Mercer, series 6, sporting, HAC

1923 MERCER
Series 6 — 6-cyl., 84 hp, 132" wb

	FP	5	4	3	2	1
Touring-6P	3750	8200	14,500	21,500	45,800	65,000
Sporting-4P	3750	8500	16,000	23,000	48,000	68,000
Runabout-4P	3750	8400	15,500	22,500	47,300	67,000
Touring Limousine-6P	5000	7600	12,500	19,400	42,400	55,000
Sedan-6P	5000	5800	8000	12,500	28,000	40,000
Sport Sedan	4700	6000	8500	13,000	30,000	42,000

1924 MERCER
Series 6 — 6-cyl., 84 hp, 132" wb

	FP	5	4	3	2	1
Touring-6P	3750	8200	14,500	21,500	45,800	65,000
Sporting-4P	3750	8500	16,000	23,000	48,000	68,000
Runabout-4P	3750	8400	15,500	22,500	47,300	67,000
Touring Limousine-6P	5000	7600	12,500	19,400	42,400	55,000
Sedan-6P	5000	5800	8000	12,500	28,000	40,000
Sport Sedan	4700	6000	8500	13,000	30,000	42,000

1925 Mercer, series 6, sport sedan, KM

1931 Mercer, convertible victoria, HAC

1925 MERCER
Series 6 — 6-cyl., 84 hp, 132" wb

	FP	5	4	3	2	1
Raceabout-2P	3900	24,100	42,000	68,000	98,000	12,600
Runabout-4P	4500		15,500	22,500	47,300	67,000
Sportabout-4P	4500	8700	16,500	23,500	48,500	69,000
Touring-5P	4500	8200	14,500	21,500	48,000	65,000
Coupe-4P	6250	7600	12,500	19,400	42,400	55,000
Sport Sedan	6250	6400	9300	14,500	33,000	45,000
Touring Limousine-6P	6500	7800	12,900	19,900	43,300	57,000

MERCHANTS — Several ventures with the Merchants name indicated a plan to manufacture automobiles but appear to have not done so.

The Merchants' Automobile Company of Chicago, Illinois, organized early in 1909 with a capital stock of $50,000 to "manufacture and deal in vehicles and mechanical specialties." Incorporators were John C. Cumpper, John W. Wikgren and Andrew J. Burkman.

The Merchants Motor Car Company of Newark, New Jersey, organized with a capital stock of $500,000 during the fall of 1911 to manufacture automobiles. Anthony Del Rago, Benjamin Orange and George Hubschmitt were the incorporators.

The Merchants Motor Service Corporation of Philadelphia, Pennsylvania, organized during the spring of 1912 with a capital stock of $100,000 "to construct lease and hire pleasure and commercial automobiles." Incorporators were George B. Teaz, George W. O'Day and Nathan W. Buzby.

MERCILESS — Huntington, New York — (1906-1907) — As strange as it might seem, the name was purposely chosen. It was, its makers believed, as close an approximation to Mercedes as might be conjured without fear of a lawsuit. Likewise, the Merciless itself was as near a copy of the German car as legally comfortable without license. A 70 hp six on a 127-inch wheelbase, it was designed by John F. McMulkin, an engineer who had formerly been associated with the American Mercedes company. The Huntington Automobile Company was organized for manufacture of the Merciless, and one August Heckscher, said to be a member of the "Zinc Trust," was reportedly among the potential big investors. A factory in Huntington on Long Island was secured, and several cars purportedly were built before the company went into receivership in December of 1907.

1904 Mercury, runabout, NAHC

MERCURY — Philadelphia, Pennsylvania — (1903-1904) — The Mercury Machine Company of 1328 Olive Street in Philadelphia produced a medium-sized, medium-priced gasoline car with a look much heavier and more expensive than it was. The car was a 1250-pound runabout on a 78-inch wheelbase powered by a single-cylinder 7 hp engine. The engine together with the three-speed planetary transmission were mounted "exactly in the lateral center," according to *The Automobile*, "to assure good balance." The car's frame was angle iron, the entire mechanism and body being attached to it, with no perches used to connect front and rear axles, on which were mounted the semi-elliptic springs. Sturdy wood wheels were shod with three-inch double tube tires. The vehicle was wheel steered, and final drive was by shaft. At $925, the Mercury was a fine buy, and the car quite progressive for the period. That it failed so quickly was most probably due to undercapitalization of the venture by the machine shop producing it.

MERCURY — Hillsdale, Michigan — (1908) — The Mercury Motor Car Company of Hillsdale was the successor to the Hillsdale Motor Company. The latter was organized in January 1908, the former followed that fall when Hillsdale failed. Involved with both ventures was John W. Raymond, formerly an engineer with the Buckeye Manufacturing Company in Anderson, Indiana. He had been secretary and general manager of the Hillsdale company; he was president and general manager of Mercury. From both these efforts, probably only a single prototype resulted. Whether it was more properly a Hillsdale or a Mercury is debatable.

MERCURY — Detroit, Michigan — (1913-1914) — The Mercury Cyclecar Company was organized in early November of 1913 by W.J. Marshall and R.C. Albertus and moved into the Detroit factory at 807 Scotten recently vacated by the defunct Tribune. A pilot model of the Mercury was on the streets within a week, and the first Mercury was sold on November 15th. The company later bragged that its cyclecar was the first to be sold in Detroit, which it probably was, but history would prove the distinction was not really one to brag about. Mercury boasted too that its product was "the first distinctively American cyclecar" and that may have been true as

1914 Mercury, model A, 2-pass. tandem cyclecar, WLB

well. In a way, the Mercury was a very early example of unit body construction, a transverse half-elliptic spring under the front axle carrying the torpedo body's forward end, two quarter elliptics underneath the rear axle supporting the back end. The wheelbase of this chassis-less car was 100 inches. The engine was De Luxe's 9.8 hp twin, a friction transmission was employed, and final drive was by copper-riveted vee belt. The Mercury was offered as the usual tandem two-seater and light delivery; a rather unusual body style was the monocar for one passenger, this one designed for a salesman's use. Probably the company's greatest success was the selection of its cyclecar as the driver training vehicle by the Michigan State Automobile School, that institution obviously impressed by the car. Indeed, after a bankruptcy proceeding was filed against the company in August of 1914, the Michigan Cyclecar Company was bought out by the driving school which announced that it would continue to manufacture and sell the car for $200, a considerable savings over the former $375 price tag. The school thought better of the idea, however. When Mercury went under, William J. Marshall moved up a few doors to 815 Scotten Avenue where he became general manager for H. Collier Smith, a manufacturer of special sheet metal machinery. Mr. Albertus' subsequent employment is not known. An electric cyclecar called the Storms moved into the Mercury factory in 1915.

1920 Mercury, touring, (Hollis, New York), WLB

MERCURY — Hollis, New York — (1918-1920) — The Mercury from Hollis was introduced at the Hotel Astor in New York City during January of 1918. It was powered by a four-cylinder 243-cubic-inch Weidely engine set in a 114-inch wheelbase. A small, lightweight automobile, it was simple in construction and designed with owner convenience and ease of maintenance in mind. The space under the cowl was lighted and ventilated; two small trap doors in the floorboard provided ready access to the service brake mechanism and the storage battery. The price range was $2750-$2959 for open models, $3600-$3900 for closed models. Bodies were semi-stock, but trim and color were strictly to customer preference. "The company has established a factory of limited size at Hollis, Long Island," *Automotive Industries* announced in January 1918, "and plans to enlarge this long before active production of cars is commenced, which probably will be mid-summer of this year." Significant enlargement probably was not necessary because the output of Mercury Cars, Inc. remained a small one for the whole of its life. Indications are that the company was out of business sometime during 1920. The Serrifile from Hollis in 1921 appears to have been this venture's successor.

MERCURY — Cleveland, Ohio — (1920) — The Mercury Motor Car Company was organized in Cleveland to produce expensive cars fitted with the four-cylinder 381.6-cubic-inch 81 hp Rochester-Duesenberg engine. A common wheelbase of 138 inches was to be used for all body styles, which were to be open cars only, and with a common price tag of $6750. That the company produced a few advertisements is known. How many cars it produced is not, but there could not have been many.

MERCURY — Belfast, New York — (1922) — Mercury Motors Company was organized in Belfast, near Rochester, New York and announced its entry into the automobile field with two closed coupe models, a four and a six, of 72 hp and 128-inch wheelbase, and 96 hp and 132-inch wheelbase respectively. Price tags were slated to be $4875 for the former, $5625 for the latter, but how many of these were affixed to any cars is not known. The company's exit from the automobile field followed later in 1922.

1922 MERCURY

Model A — 4-cyl., 72 hp, 128" wb	FP	5	4	3	2	1
Coupe-3P	4875	—	—	—	—	—
Model B — 6-cyl., 96 hp, 132" wb						
Coupe-4P	5625	—	—	—	—	—

MERCURY — Dearborn, Michigan — (1939-1942) — "The car that dares to ask 'Why?'," some ads said, and though the question referred to dealt with why a big car couldn't be an economical car too, another question might have been why the Ford Motor Company hadn't introduced the Mercury sooner. The answer to that one undoubtedly was that it had taken that long for Edsel Ford to convince his father to build it. The Mercury was priced in the thousand-dollar range, several hundred dollars more than the Ford V-8, several hundred less than the Lincoln Zephyr — and about the same as the upper-range Olds and Dodges and the lower-range Buicks and Chryslers, sales from all of which, it was hoped, the new Mercury would usurp. Its engine was a 95 hp version of the flathead Ford V-8, its styling was inspired by the Zephyr, and it had hydraulic brakes from the beginning. With a wheelbase of 116 inches (increased to 118 in '40) and an overall length of 196 inches, the Mercury was a good-sized car, which fact the Ford company advertised extensively, together with its up-to-20 mpg performance — "few cars of *any* size can equal such economy." By 1941 Ford could also headline that "It's made 150,000 owners change cars!" — and that year another 80,000 Mercurys were produced, plus a total of 4430 more in 1942 before the production shutdown for the duration of World War II. Although its prewar history was short, the Mercury had already earned for itself the image of being a fine performer in mph as well as mpg, this "hot car" image quite in keeping with its name, chosen by Edsel Ford, that of the fleet-footed messenger of the gods of Roman mythology. The Mercury was strongly identified as an upmarket Ford during this period; in 1945 the Lincoln-Mercury Division would be established to change that.

1939 Mercury, convertible coupe, AA

1939 Mercury, town sedan, JAC

1940 Mercury, coupe, AA

1939
Series 99A, V-8, 116" wb

	FP	5	4	3	2	1
Conv	1018	4700	9450	15,750	22,050	31,500
Cpe	957	1300	4000	6650	9300	13,300
2 dr Sed	916	925	2000	4600	6400	9200
4 dr Sed	957	925	2000	4650	6500	9300

1940
Series O9A, V-8, 116" wb

Conv	1079	4700	9450	15,750	22,050	31,500
Conv Sed	1272	4300	8550	14,250	19,950	28,500
Cpe	987	1050	2800	5400	7500	10,800
2 dr Sed	946	925	2000	4650	6500	9300
4 dr Sed	987	950	2100	4700	6600	9400

1941 Mercury, town sedan, AA

1941
Series 19A, V-8, 118" wb

	FP	5	4	3	2	1
Conv	1100	4600	9150	15,250	21,350	30,500
Bus Cpe	910	900	1800	4400	6150	8800
5P Cpe	936	925	2000	4650	6500	9300
6P Cpe	977	975	2300	4900	6850	9800
2 dr Sed	946	900	1800	4400	6150	8800
4 dr Sed	987	900	1900	4500	6300	9000
Sta Wag	1141	1900	5050	8400	11,750	16,800

1942 Mercury, station wagon, OCW

1942
Series 29A, V-8, 118" wb

Conv	1215	4000	7950	13,250	18,550	26,500
Bus Cpe	995	925	2000	4600	6400	9200
6P Cpe	1055	950	2200	4800	6700	9600
2 dr Sed	1030	850	1650	4150	5800	8300
4 dr Sed	1065	850	1650	4200	5850	8400
Sta Wag	1260	1550	4400	7400	10,400	14,800

NOTE: Add 10 percent for liquamatic drive models.

MEREDITH — Despite his entry in the Chicago Times-Herald of 1895, Edwin Meredith of Batavia, Illinois was a no-show at the starting line. Whether he ever completed and successfully tested his car has not been documented.

MEREDITH — Detroit, Michigan — (1913-1914) — "As yet unnamed, a new small car has appeared on the streets of Detroit," *Automobile Topics* announced in September of 1913. Built by George W. Meredith at the machine shop of J.H. Krass, it was fitted with a GB&S four-cylinder 23 hp engine, friction drive transmission and weighed about 2000 pounds. "Indianapolis capital is said to be behind the new car," said. Obviously not substantially enough. *The American Cyclecar*, in its May 1914 issue, indicated Samuel E. Jones, William E. Canfield, Charles F. Thomas, Walter G. Quick and a whole bunch of people named Valade — M.G., Charles C., Victor C., William I. and Thomas A. — as among the organizers of a yet unnamed company for the manufacture of George Meredith's car. "The initial capital is $25,000, all paid up," the magazine revealed. "With the completion of the experimental and test work this capital will be increased probably to $150,000." There is no evidence that it ever was, or that this venture ever moved out of the Krass machine shop at 451-543 Gratiot Avenue in Detroit.

922

MERIT — The Merit Motor Car Manufacturing Company was organized in New York City during the fall of 1910 with a capital stock of $50,000 for the manufacture of engines and automobiles. Incorporators were E.H. Knight, J.H. Riviere and E.C. Billings. Manufacture of a car is doubted.

1922 Merit, touring, WLB

MERIT — Cleveland, Ohio — (1921-1922) — The Merit resulted from a partnership between a department store owner and a pharmacist in Cleveland. The department store owner was Henry J. Berger who, with his brother William, had long been an enthusiast of the automobile. The pharmacist was Bert F. Landefeld, whose drug store was just up the block from the Berger emporium. Bert's brother Al served as the Merit's sales manager. This venture was a family affair. The Merit Motor Company was incorporated in 1920 with a $5 million capitalization. Plans were made to introduce the car at the New York Automobile Show in January 1921 — and the car was ready, except for varnishing, just before the show. Unfortunately, in their hurry to get ready, the Bergers used a coal-oil heater to speed up drying, the varnish ignited, and the car burned. So the Merit was introduced at the Cleveland Automobile Show instead, where it was warmly received. Among the special features of the Merit was a brake system (Jacobson patent) which expanded and contracted in simultaneous operation. Bodies were hardwood covered with non-rusting aluminum. For 1921 the Merit engine was a Walker six, replaced with a Continental Red Seal six the following year. A coupe and a four-passenger touring were the two models offered in '21; a roadster was added for '22. The reason for the Merit's failure might be indicated by its price fluctuations. The car was introduced at $2245, reduced in September of '21 to $1985, and further reduced in March of '22 to $1895. The Merit had hit the postwar depression head-on. Total production through 1922 has been estimated at between fifty and seventy-five cars. Then the Bergers returned to their department store, the Landefelds to the pharmacy business.

1921 MERIT
Model B - 6-cyl., 119" wb

	FP	5	4	3	2	1
Cpe.-2P	2245	1600	2700	3800	5800	12,000
Tour.-4P	2245	3000	4000	6000	9500	21,000

1922 MERIT
Model B-C - 6-cyl., 119" wb

Cpe-2P	1985	1600	2700	3800	5800	12,000
Tour.-5P	1985	3000	4000	6000	9500	21,000
Rdst.-2P	1985	2100	4200	6300	10,500	22,000

1906 Merkel, runabout, NAHC

MERKEL — Milwaukee, Wisconsin — (1905-1907) — Early in 1901 Joseph F. Merkel bought out the Layton Park Manufacturing Company in Milwaukee and moved his Merkel Manufacturing Company into the premises. Production of motors, bicycles and the "Flying Merkel" motorcycle followed — in September of 1904 he changed his firm's name to Merkel Motor Company and moved his enterprise into the automotive field. Three different models — he preferred the term "forms" — were offered in three different horsepower and wheelbase sizes. Air- or water-cooled engines were optional; shaft drive was used throughout. Prices ranged from $1500 to $3500. Production on a small scale may have continued into early 1907. Thereafter Joe Merkel produced only his water- and air-cooled engines, bicycles and motorcycles . . . until 1914 when he tried the automobile industry again with a cyclecar in Middletown, Ohio.

1906 Merkel, touring, NAHC

1905-1907 MERKEL
Small Four - 14/16 hp, 86" wb

	FP	5	4	3	2	1
Rbt.-2P	1500	1800	2800	4000	6200	13,000
Form P - 4-cyl., 20/24 hp, 98" wb						
Tour.-4P	2250	2000	3000	4200	6500	14,000
Form N - 4-cyl., 35/40 hp, 106" wb						
Tour.-5P	3500	2200	3200	4400	7000	15,000

MERKEL — Middletown, Ohio — (1914) — Joseph F. Merkel had made his name in Milwaukee as the designer and builder of the ''Flying Merkel'' motorcycle. Following his move to Middletown in 1911, he tried the automobile field once again, as he had in Milwaukee. The new Merkel was a cyclecar, with a four-cylinder 12 hp water-cooled engine and a tandem two-seater roadster body. At 1060 pounds, it was considerably heavier than most cyclecars, and Merkel's projected price tag of $520 was heftier than most as well. But this car never made it to market. He built two of them in his basement, and tried unsuccessfully to generate investment interest in the local business community. When this did not arrive, he returned wholeheartedly to motorcycle and bicycle manufacture, under the aegis of the Miami Cycle and Manufacturing Company in Middletown which produced about ten thousand of his motorcycles annually and about a hundred thousand bicycles until late 1917 when the factory was turned over to war work. Neither motorcycle nor bicycle production was resumed after the Armistice.

MERRILL — Frank Merrill of Plainfield, New Jersey built his first gasoline engine in 1892 and his first gasoline car in mid-1904. When he decided to market the vehicle the following year, he chose Veerac as its name. Refer to Veerac.

MERRILL — Londonderry, New Hampshire — (1906) — In the year 1906 there were three automobiles and one motorcycle registered in the town of Londonderry: a 14/16 hp Merrill, a 4 hp Waltham, an 8 hp St. Louis, and a 3 hp American motorbike. The Waltham had been manufactured in Massachusetts, the St. Louis in Missouri. The Merrill was built in Londonderry by one Oliver Merrill. Aside from documented evidence of its building, nothing further is known about the Merrill or its inventor. Probably only the one car was built.

1914 Merz, cyclecar, WLB

MERZ — Indianapolis, Indiana — (1914) — Charles Merz was a former racing driver who had earned a good deal of renown piloting Nationals and Stutzes in competition. Searching for something to do following his retirement from the sports world, he decided to build a cyclecar. Although he finished the prototype in time for the Chicago Automobile Show in January of 1914, he arrived too late at the Coliseum and was unable to secure space to exhibit it inside. He told a *Cyclecar Age* reporter that never before had he seen such enthusiasm for a motor vehicle as the cyclecar

was generating. ''They are the popular cars of the future,'' he said, ''and no mistake.'' Among the special features of Charles Merz' version was a one-piece body and hood ''giving the most sought-for straight-line effect from front to rear of tonneau.'' The single headlamp was mounted almost flush with the hood front, a wire screen fitted below for circulation of air to the two-cylinder De Luxe 9 hp engine. The wheelbase was 84 inches, tread 40 inches, and the seating two-passenger tandem. Transmission was friction disc, final drive vee belt. Merz said that extended road tests had demonstrated an operating expense of less than a cent a mile for gasoline, oil and tires. ''The Merz is probably the highest-priced cyclecar built in America,'' he advertised. Actually, at $450, it wasn't, but he must have figured lending a ''luxury'' air to a budget product had a certain sales appeal. It did not. Whether his Merz Cyclecar Company in Indianapolis ever really got down to the matter of volume production is not known. Probably not. Receivership arrived during the summer of 1914. Assets were indicated as $30,000, liabilities at $12,000. In January of 1915, the business was disposed of for $1200.

1914 MERZ
Cyclecar - 2-cyl., 9 hp, 84" wb

	FP	5	4	3	2	1
Tandem Rdstr.-2P	450	1600	2700	3800	5800	12,000
Light Dly.	485	1500	2500	3600	5500	11,000

1904 Meserve, touring, NAHC

MESERVE — Canoble Lake, New Hampshire — (1901-1904) — William Forest Meserve began his experimentation with gasoline engines in the mid-1890's, and built his first automobile at the turn of the century. It was a gasoline car powered by a single-cylinder two-stroke engine that he had ordered by mail from New York City. The car was subsequently sold to Harry Wilson, a grocer in Derry. His second vehicle was a steam-powered motor truck built later in 1901 which was sold locally as well. Apparently Meserve harbored some entrepreneural thoughts because in February of 1902, the Meserve Auto Truck Company was casually organized in Canobie Lake (where the Meserve family summered), though nothing further of it was ever heard. William Meserve continued building vehicles, however, whenever anyone in the area asked for one. His most ambitious effort was in 1904, a car for West Derry lawyer B.T. Bartlett. Its four-cylinder two-stroke engine was of Meserve's own design, and developed 32 hp. *The Horseless Age* remarked that this Meserve was the ''first vehicle of large power ever constructed in this country propelled by a two-cycle engine.'' A three-speed transmission was used, and a compressed air self-starter was fitted. The wheelbase was 108 inches, and the touring car body carried five passengers easily. Speeds up to 40 mph were possible. Meserve announced that he stood ready to build further cars ''after designs suited to the individual taste of purchasers,'' but whether anyone took him up on it is not known. He is not mentioned in the automotive press after 1904. The steam truck he built in 1901 was used for some twenty years by Pemberton Mills in Lawrence. Among his later endeavors was the assembly of jail cells in Derry and the invention of a rotary snow remover for the city of Lawrence.

MESSENGER — The Messenger was one of several models of the Brasie produced in Minneapolis, Minnesota from 1914 to 1916. Refer to Brasie.

MESSERER — Newark, New Jersey — (1899-1901) — Stephen Messerer was a watchmaker and jeweler whose shop was at 15 Springfield Avenue at the foot of Centre Street in Newark. In the rear of his store, he outfitted an experimental studio where he and other inventors could perfect their ideas. He built his first automobile there in 1897, having casually organized the S. Messerer Motor Wagon Company. This firm did no manufacturing of vehicles. By the fall of 1899, however, Messerer had secured sufficient capital from Newark businessmen (Joseph Fisch, Julius E. Seitz and Adolph Goldfinger) to incorporate the Messerer Automobile Company with a capital stock of $300,000. Initial production focused on large delivery wagons with hefty four-cylinder engines and a combined belt and gear drive. For the 1901 season, the company also offered a belt-drive, high-wheeled stanhope powered by a single-cylinder 4 hp engine which provided for a speed of 12 mph. The company did not survive into 1902.

1901 Messerer, stanhope, NAHC

METCALFE — Patchogue, New York — (1902) — In 1902 R.H. Metcalfe of Patchogue, Long Island built himself a 3 hp gasoline-engined runabout weighing 250 pounds for which he modestly, though probably accurately, claimed a top speed of only eight miles an hour. "A new feature is a funnel underneath the vehicle," reported *The Motor Age*, "designed to catch the wind and direct it to the motor for cooling purposes."

METEOR — The Meteor Automobile Company was organized in Mt. Vernon, New York late in 1911 with a capital stock of $50,000 for the manufacture of engines and motor vehicles. Incorporators were F.A. Kateley, A.F. Gescheidt and J. Emmeluth. Manufacture of a car is doubted.

The Meteor Motor Car Company was organized in Anderson, Indiana during the summer of 1911 with a capital stock of $100,000 to manufacture automobiles and aeroplanes. F.H. Brock and Ernest Oswalt were the incorporators. Manufacture of a car is doubted.

1901 Meteor, runabout, (Springfield, Massachusetts), HAC

METEOR — Springfield, Massachusetts — (1900-1901) — Meteor proved to be one of the more popular names affixed to an American automobile, and the first company to use it was Springfield Cornice Works in Massachusetts. Springfield's Meteor was designed by Hinsdale Smith and was a fragile-looking runabout with single-cylinder De Dion or Aster engine mounted in front and a long single chain driving to the rear axle. "The most accurate brief description that could be given of it would be that it looks like a French 'voiturette' disrobed of visible mechanism," *The Motor Age* commented in November 1900. "It is low and the floor is flat from end to end, carrying the seat at its rear and a small motor and attachments box in front. With the exception of the steering wheel there are no visible running parts, the driving gear being well encased and hung so close to the under side of the floor as to be not noticeable from the level of the eye." The price range was $800-$850. The Meteor was shown at the first National Automobile Show at Madison Square Garden in New York City in November of 1900. After one year in production as the Meteor, however, both the car and the company name was changed to Automotor.

METEOR STEAM — Reading, Pennsylvania — (1902-1903) — This Meteor was a bigger and higher priced ($2000 vis-a-vis $800) version of the Reading Steamer. For a while both cars were built on the same assembly line. The Meteor Engineering Company was organized in September of

1903 Meteor, steam touring, (Reading, Pennsylvania), NAHC

1902, with L.W. Alexander as president, to take over the assets of the bankrupt Steam Vehicle Company of America, erstwhile producers of the Reading. Late in 1902 a Philadelphia firm placed an order with the new Meteor company, apparently unaware that the firm's only experience was steamers. Meteor was all set to buy De Dion engines to fill the order, but the now-aware Philadelphia company had doubts about Meteor's ability to build a gasoline car well when it had never before produced one. The contract was cancelled. With this experience in mind, perhaps, the Meteor people decided that its cars for the New York Automobile Show in January 1903 had best be discreet. The two Meteor steamers on display, with their wheel steering and conventional hoods, looked valorously like gasoline-engined cars. Alas, no orders were taken. Meteor then ran up a gasoline touring car, but most probably it was never marketed. The Meteor Engineering Company was bankrupt by early fall. E.S. Youse of Reading purchased the firm's assets and announced that he would continue to make parts to keep both the Meteor and Reading steamers in service.

1905 Meteor, touring, (New York City & Cleveland), WLB

METEOR — New York City & Cleveland, Ohio — (1904-1905) — In 1904 C.C. Worthington of New York City bought out the Berg Automobile Company of Cleveland. Production of the Berg was continued by the new Worthington Automobile Company, and a new car called the Meteor was introduced, to be built by Federal Manufacturing Company in Cleveland. "The first of the Meteor cars . . . have reached their destination in New York," *The Motor Age* announced in August 1904, "and are continuing to arrive at the rate of four or five a week." The Meteor was a four-cylinder 18 hp touring car selling for $2750 with wood coachwork, $2950 with aluminum body fittings. A three-speed transmission, bevel gear drive and pressed steel frame were featured. Steering was right-hand wheel, and a canopy top was featured. The Meteor price tag dropped to $2500 for 1905, and early that year the cars began carrying the tradename of Cleveland. This followed the exit of Worthington from the venture in December 1904 and the arrival of William L. Colt (former general sales manager of Federal) who reorganized as the Cleveland Motor Car Company.

1904 METEOR
Four — 18 hp, 91" wb

	FP	5	4	3	2	1
Touring, wood body-5P	2750	3000	4000	6000	9500	21,000
Touring, aluminum body-5P	2950	3100	4200	6300	10,500	22,000

1905 METEOR
Four — 18 hp, 91" wb

	FP	5	4	3	2	1
Touring, wood body-5P	2500	3000	4000	6000	9500	21,000

METEOR — St. Louis, Missouri — (1904-1905) — One can understand why the Lemon Automobile and Manufacturing Company of St. Louis chose a name other than its own for the car it produced. Among all the possibilities in the cosmos, however, Meteor was hardly the most imaginative. This Meteor was a highwheeled surrey which sat four passengers on two bench seats, and was produced for only a short period. Conceivably, it had proved to be a vehicle more befitting the company's name.

1909 Meteor, touring, (Bettendorf, Iowa), NAHC

METEOR — Bettendorf, Iowa — (1908-1909) — Arno Petersen of Bettendorf was the son of the owner of the largest department store in nearby Davenport and had a friend by the name of Bodo Liebert. The young men were automobile enthusiasts and in early fall of 1906 casually established the Meteor Auto Works in Bettendorf to get themselves into the automobile game. Apparently their enthusiasm overran them because although they priced and announced three models to the automotive press in 1907, the cars never arrived. Perhaps family financial backing did soon after, however, because by March of 1908 the Meteor Motor Car Company was formally established, its first car was completed in May, with twelve more already in the works. That summer the company announced full production "after three years' experimental work." The Meteor was a 50 hp four of sturdy construction and shaft drive. Prices were in the $3000-$4000 range. Though total production is not known, surviving factory photographs indicate the Meteor company to be a going concern. What stopped it was a fire at the factory during the summer of 1909. Though drawings, jigs and patterns were saved, the loss to the company was too heavy for it to continue. In January of 1910 the Bettendorf Axle Company acquired the Meteor plant and land. The Twin Bridges Motel is located there today. Bettendorf's city hall and fire station are now on the site of the Meteor company's offices. Ironically, in 1912, a Meteor passenger car had been remodeled by the Bettendorf volunteer fire department as its first piece of motorized fire equipment. Following the fire there had been an attempt to relocate the Meteor factory in Davenport, but it failed almost immediately.

1908 METEOR
Four — 50 hp, 120" wb

	FP	5	4	3	2	1
Model C Runabout	3000	5400	7300	11,800	25,000	38,000
Model D Touring Car	3000	5500	7500	12,000	26,000	39,000
Model E Limo.	4000	4300	5400	8700	16,500	30,000

1909 METEOR
Four — 50 hp, 120" wb

Type C Limo.-9P	4000	4300	5400	8700	16,500	30,000
Type D Tour.-5P	3000	5500	7500	12,000	26,000	39,000
Type F Tour-7P	3750	5800	8000	12,500	28,000	40,000
Type F-1 Baby Tonneau-4P	3750	5500	7500	12,000	26,000	39,000

1915 Meteor, roadster, (Piqua, Ohio), WLB

METEOR — Piqua, Ohio — (1915-1930) — From Minneapolis, Minnesota where he gave his efforts and his name to the four-cylinder Wolfe produced by the H.E. Wilcox Company, Maurice Wolfe traveled to Shelbyville, Indiana in 1912, where he bought out the foundering Clark Motor Car Company ($26,000 for the plant, $11,219 for the personal property) and set up shop as the Meteor Motor Car Company. Almost immediately, however, he decided to move part and parcel to Piqua, Ohio, where the facilities of the former Sprague-Smith Furniture Company offered a fourteen-car-a-day production capacity as opposed to Shelbyville's three-car-a day. Wolfe continued to produce and sell a few Clark automobiles during the factory changeover, but once settled into the Piqua plant in early 1914, all subsequent vehicles were called Meteors. Most of them would be hearses, the first in 1914 in collaboration with A.J. Miller for a vehicle combining Miller body and Meteor chassis. Passenger cars were offered on Meteor chassis for the 1915 model year as tourers and roadsters with six-cylinder Continental or Model engines. For 1916 a V-12 Meteor touring (Weidely engine) was also listed as available but probably few if any were built. By now Wolfe was convinced his fortunes could be better served by serving the professional car trade. Although pleasure cars would be available on special order from 1917 until 1930, factory production was concentrated on funeral cars and ambulances. Maurice Wolfe must have had a wicked sense of humor. As a smaller companion to his Meteor funeral car, he introduced a vehicle called the Mort, which is French for "dead." By 1920

1920 Meteor, sedan, (Piqua, Ohio), KM

he had developed a sideline business of phonographs and phonograph records, with a civic parade in Piqua that year including a float from Meteor combining examples of both the company's enterprises. The banner read, "Kills 'em with Music and Hauls 'em Away," a slogan that was not officially adopted. Meteor ultimately evolved into Miller-Meteor Division of Divco-Wayne Corporation, which survived into late 1979.

1919 Meteor, sport touring, (Philadelphia, Pennsylvania), HAC

METEOR — Philadelphia, Pennsylvania — (1919-1922) — The officers of Meteor Motors, Inc. of Philadelphia were E.A. Schoen as president, W.D. Morton as vice-president and general manager, S.L. Bader as secretary and A.M. Hooven as treasurer. Of that quartet, W.D. Morton possessed the most automotive expertise, having previously worked for both Mercer and Biddle. The Meteor was aimed to be a car in that high quality class. It was fitted with a Rochester-Duesenberg engine with aluminum pistons, two valves per cylinder, and a claimed output of 80 bhp at 2200 rpm. Carburetor was by Zenith, magneto by Simms, clutch by Borg and Beck, but the four-speed transmission (direct on third) was of Meteor's own design. The deep vee of the car's radiator was a distinguishing characteristic. Fleetwood supplied the bodies. Meteor prices were in the $5000 range. Although a sport touring and a runabout were announced during the summer of 1919, the runabout did not arrive on the market until the summer of 1920. A town car was added for 1921, and the Meteor chassis was now available at $4000 for customers who preferred coachwork of their own choosing. The Meteor factory was at 36th and Lancaster Avenue in Philadelphia. Production of this luxury car continued there until sometime during 1922, when Meteor Motors, Inc. found it could no longer fight the effects of the postwar depression.

1920 Meteor, runabout, (Philadelphia, Pennsylvania), NAHC

1919 METEOR
Four — 80 hp, 129" wb

	FP	5	4	3	2	1
Sport Tourin-4P	4850	6400	9300	14,500	33,000	45,000

1920 METEOR
Four — 80 hp, 129" wb

	FP	5	4	3	2	1
Sport Touring-4P	5000	6400	9300	14,500	33,000	45,000
Runabout-2P	5500	6200	8800	13,500	31,000	43,000

1921-1922 METEOR
Four — 80 hp, 129" wb

	FP	5	4	3	2	1
Sport Touring-4P	5500	7000	10,800	16,900	37,100	49,000
Runabout-2P	5500	6400	9300	14,500	33,000	45,000
Town Car	—	5400	7300	11,800	25,000	38,000
Chassis	4000					

1914 Metropol, gentlemen's roadster, WLB

METROPOL — Port Jefferson, New York — (1913-1914) — Metropol Motors Corporation of Port Jefferson was the new sponsoring organization for a car which had begun life as the Only. The Metropol was a sporty speedster with no doors, gas tank mounted in the rear and very high hood in front. The reason for the very high hood was "The Real Long Stroke Motor," as Metropol described its 4¼ by 7-⅞-inch T-head four, which was rated at 30 hp but developed a claimed 90 bhp. A top speed of 75 mph was guaranteed, as was an admirable fuel consumption of 25 mpg. All this for $1475. The Metropol was designed by Francois Richard and was produced by the same people who had backed the Only. If the Metropol had been half of what it advertised, with that price and that specification, every sporting blade on Long Island would have beat a path to the factory door. This did not happen. Further models were added for the 1914 model year, but few of them were produced. In April 1914 *Automobile Topics* reported that a judgment had been served against the Metropol company for an advertising bill of $136 that had not been paid. In November *Horseless Age* announced that Finlay Robertson Porter had acquired the old Metropol plant for production of his F.R.P. Francois Richard was heard from next in Cleveland, with a new car bearing his own name.

1913 METROPOL
Four — 90 hp, 115" wb

	FP	5	4	3	2	1
Speedster-2P	1475	5400	7300	11,800	25,000	38,000

1914 METROPOL
Four — 90 hp, 115" wb

	FP	5	4	3	2	1
Model C Roadster-2P	1475	4500	5800	9500	18,000	32,000
Model E Racer-2P	2250	5000	6500	11,000	22,000	35,000
Model D Touring-5P	1650	4300	5400	8700	16,500	30,000

METROPOLIS — The Metropolis Taxicab Company was organized in New York City during the summer of 1910 with a capital stock of $500 to manufacture, rent and deal in motor cars. Incorporators were S.J Quinn, John D. Ashton and George M. Brooks. Manufacture is doubted.

METROPOLITAN — The following ventures named Metropolitan indicated an intention to build an automobile but apparently failed to follow through on it.

The Metropolitan Auto Company of New York City, organized with a capital stock of $25,000 late in 1905 to manufacture automobiles and autoboats. Incorporators were S.F. Randolph, J.M. Belin and H.H. Colbath.

The Metropolitan Automobile Company, a $25,000 Maine incorporation from late 1906 for the manufacture of motorcars. Horace Mitchell of Kittery was president, S.J. Morrison of Portsmouth (New Hampshire) was treasurer.

The Metropolitan Garage Company of Cleveland, Ohio, organized with a capital stock of $5000 during the fall of 1913 to manufacture and deal in automobiles and to conduct a garage. Incorporators were C. Mulvahy, H.C. Quigley, H. Loeb, W.I. Quigley and M. Schwab.

The Metropolitan Mercantile Motors Company of New York City, organized late in 1910 with a capital stock of $50,000 to "manufacture, sell and repair carriages and motor vehicles." Incorporators were D. Campbell, F.G. Lyon and H.S. Reynolds.

The Metropolitan Motors Corporation of Kansas City, Missouri did produce a car, but it was marketed as the Severin in 1921. Refer to Severin.

The Metropolitan Taxicab and Auto Service Company of New York City, organized early in 1908 with a capital stock of $100,000 to manufacture and deal in motor cars and vehicles. Incorporators were J.W. Cummin, L.G. Hall and E. True, all of New York City.

METROPOLITAN — Kansas City, Missouri — (1922-1923) — Metropolitan Motors, Inc. was organized in Kansas City in late November of 1921. H.D. Taylor was president; G.H. Clevidence, vice-president; Ross H. Rheem, treasurer; Robert H. Campbell, purchasing agent and chief engineer. Campbell's dual function would not tax him severely, at least initially, because the new Metropolitan company had simply taken over the old Severin; Severin parts on hand would suffice for the first year's production of the Metropolitan Model M-61. By the time the parts were

1922 Metropolitan, touring, MVMA

depleted, Metropolitan was ready with its own car, the Model M-41, a four which it could sell at half the price of the Severin six. The company proceeded to do so the following year. Apparently, a Model M-81, an eight for the higher-priced market, was also on the Metropolitan drawing boards, but it never got off. The Metropolitan M-41 was finished by the end of 1923.

1922 METROPOLITAN
Model M-61 — 6-cyl., 60 hp, 122½" wb

	FP	5	4	3	2	1
Touring-5P	1500	5000	6500	11,000	22,000	35,000
Sedan-5P	2000	2500	3500	5000	8500	18,000

1923 METROPOLITAN
Model M-41 — 4-cyl., 40 hp, 108" wb

	FP	5	4	3	2	1
Touring-5P	600	3500	4500	7000	13,000	25,000
Roadster-2P	600	4000	5000	8000	15,000	28,000
Sedan-5P	700	2000	3000	4200	6500	14,000
Coupe-2P	700	2300	3300	4600	7500	16,000

1909 Metz Plan, runabout, HAC

METZ — Waltham, Massachusetts — (1909-1921) — Charles Herman Metz won the New York State High Wheel Bicycle Championship at the 1885 State Fair at Syracuse, joined the Union Cycle Manufacturing Company of Highlandville (Massachusetts) as designer in 1899, and organized his own Waltham Manufacturing Company in 1893 for the production of Orient bicycles. By 1897 annual output was up to 15,000 units, he built the ten-seater Oriten that year which was the largest bicycle yet produced, and the year following motorized a tandem which was acknowledged at the time to be America's first motorcycle. In 1898, too, his Waltham company began building automobiles. At the turn of the century, in order to obtain the financing necessary to expand, he brought in two investors who thought their large blocks of stock allowed them a say regarding the direction in which Waltham Manufacturing should proceed. Because C.H. Metz did not agree, he left the Waltham company in December of 1901 to take on the technical editorship of *Cycle and Automobile Trade Journal*. He continued independently to build motorcycles, first under his own name, and from late 1905 in association with the Marsh brothers of Brockton as the Marsh-Metz motorcycle. During the summer of 1908 he got his old company back. Waltham Manufacturing was, by now, in a state of financial disrepair, with a large quantity of debts and an even larger inventory of parts. Metz offered the latter in packages selling for $25 each. Fourteen packages made for one car. The "Metz Plan," as it was known,

1910 Metz Plan, runabout, HAC

1911 Metz, runabout, HAC

provided for the graduated payment on the part of a purchaser of both his financial outlay and his time in assembling his own car. By the time he finished putting together the components in Parts Group One, Parts Group Two arrived. A new owner thus paid for his new car as he was building it. The idea was an immediate hit. By late summer of 1909 C.H. Metz had paid off all of Waltham's debts — and reorganized as the Metz Company. The per-package price of a Metz was raised to $27 that December but it remained a very good deal. Metz cars also began to be offered factory assembled. From a 12 hp twin, the Metz grew to a 22 hp four for 1912, which carried a $495 price tag, and in a "Special" stripped-down version was bargain-basement priced at $395. A three-car Metz team won the 1913 Glidden as the only entries to finish with a perfect score. Their performance convinced C.H. Metz of the efficacy of chain drive and friction transmission, which had been Metz car features from the beginning, although because of the pejorative image the latter had now acquired, Metz preferred the term "pressure drive" for his system. In 1915 Metz produced 7200 cars, its best year ever. In 1917 the company entered the commercial vehicle field. Production was suspended during the 1918 war year; Metz returned in 1919 with a new car, the 45 hp Master 6 with a geared transmission and shaft drive. But already the company was in trouble. Rumors had persisted throughout 1918 that Metz would have to sell its large plant in order to pay its debts, but the company struggled on awhile without being forced to do that. In December of 1921 announcement was made of the firm's reorganization to Waltham Motor Manufacturers, Inc., and the marque name was changed to Waltham too. It was a last-ditch effort which survived less than a year. In August 1922 the Metz company was petitioned into bankruptcy by three creditors, the Johns-Manville Company among them. In its obituary on the company shortly thereafter, *MoToR* magazine noted that Metz was one of the few automobile manufacturers ever to fail for reasons of conservatism rather than overextension.

1909 METZ
Two — 10 hp, 81" wb

	FP	5	4	3	2	1
Plan Runabout-2P	350	2300	3300	4600	7500	16,000

1910 METZ
Two — 12 hp, 81" wb

Plan Runabout-2P	378	2300	3300	4600	7500	16,000
Assembled Runabout-2P	475	2700	3600	5300	8800	19,000

1911 METZ
Two — 12 hp, 81" wb

Runabout	485	2400	3400	4800	8000	17,000
Special Delivery	500	2000	3000	4200	6500	14,000

1912 Metz, model 22, roadster, HAC

1912 METZ
Model 22 — 4-cyl., 22 hp, 90" wb

Plan Roadster-2P	495	2300	3300	4600	7500	16,000
Assembled Roadster-2P	600	2700	3600	5300	8800	19,000

1913 Metz, model 22, runabout, HAC

1913 METZ
Model 22 — 4-cyl., 22 hp, 90" wb

	FP	5	4	3	2	1
Runabout-2P	495	2400	3400	4800	8000	17,000
Special Runabout-2P	395	2300	3300	4600	7500	16,000

1914 Metz, model 22, runabout, HAC

1914 METZ
Model 22 — 4-cyl., 22 hp, 90" wb

Roaster-2P	475	2500	3500	5000	8500	18,000
Speedster-2P	500	3000	4000	6000	9500	21,000
Torpedo-2P	475	2900	3700	5600	9100	20,000

1915 Metz, roadster, OCW

1915 METZ
Model 22 — 4-cyl., 22 hp, 96" wb

Roadster-2P	495	2700	3600	5300	8800	19,000
Speedster-2P	500	3100	4200	6300	10,500	22,000

Model 25 — 4-cyl., 25 hp, 105" wb

Roadster-2P	600	3000	4000	6000	9500	21,000
Touring-5P	600	2900	3700	5600	9100	20,000

1916 METZ
Model 25 — 4-cyl., 25 hp, 108" wb

Touring-5P	600	3000	4000	6000	9500	21,000
Roadster-2P	600	3100	4200	6300	10,500	22,000

1916 Metz, model 25, roadster, HAC

1917 Metz, model 25, touring, HAC

1917 METZ
Model 25 — 4-cyl., 25 hp, 108" wb

	FP	5	4	3	2	1
Touring	600	3000	4000	6000	9500	21,000
Roadster	600	3100	4200	6300	10,500	22,000

Note: no manufacturing in 1918.

1919 METZ
Master 6 — 45 hp, 117" wb

Touring-5P	1495	3300	4400	6700	12,000	24,000

1920 Metz Master 6, touring, HAC

1920 METZ
Master 6 — 45 hp, 120" wb

Touring-5P	1895	3300	4400	6700	12,000	24,000
Roadster-3P	1895	3500	4500	7000	13,000	25,000
Coupe-4P	2695	2500	3500	5000	8500	18,000

1921 METZ
Master 6 — 45 hp, 120" wb

Touring-5P	1995	3300	4400	6700	12,000	24,000
Roadster-2P	1995	3500	4500	7000	13,000	25,000
Coupe-4P	2795	2500	3500	5000	8500	18,000
Sedan-5P	2895	2000	3000	4200	6500	14,000

METZGER — The Metzger Motor Car Company was organized in Detroit in mid-1909 for the production of an automobile to be called the Everitt. William Metzger and Barney Everitt were the two men involved. Refer to Everitt.

METZLER — The J. Metzler & Sons Company was organized in Chicago, Illinois during the spring of 1907 with a capital stock of $10,000 for the manufacture of automobiles. The Metzlers involved in this venture were Jacob, Clyde J. and Robert E. Manufacture is doubted.

MEYER — Sometime around the turn of the century J.A. Meyer of San Francisco, California built several gasoline cars which he called by the name of Pioneer. Refer to Pioneer.

The A.J. Meyer Motor Car Company was organized in Cedarburg, Wisconsin during the summer of 1912 with a capital stock of $25,000 and a plan to manufacture automobiles. Incorporators were John Armbruster,

928

Jacob Dietrich and John F. Bruss. Manufacture is doubted, but the firm is known to have opened a garage. A.J. Meyer tried again in Chicago in 1919, and at least one car followed that venture.

The Meyer Motor Car Company was organized in Buffalo, New York late in 1913 with a $50,000 capital stock to manufacture and deal in automobiles. Behind this venture were Arthur C. Meyer, Clayton H. Meyer and Franklin B.L. Stone. Manufacture is doubted.

1919 Meyer, touring, NAHC

MEYER — Chicago, Illinois — (1919) — Whether many of these cars were built is questionable, but the A.J. Meyer Corporation of Chicago obviously believed in trying to please everybody. It is difficult to pinpoint what a Meyer was supposed to be, since it could be virtually anything. Available engines ranged from two to twelve cylinders, and any style of body was offered to accommodate whatever the passenger number the purchaser desired. Prices ranged up to $7000. An automatic gearshift was said to be a feature. But the patented Meyer wheel was the company's touted selling point. It was of pressed steel which was welded to the hub with sections of rubber wedged between shell and collar. The Meyer tire was unique too, consisting of two hollow sections, presumably providing flexibility and driving ease. A large Meyer touring car with the distinctive wheel and tire (and a large bird hood ornament) was pictured in *Motor Age* in March 1919. It may have been the only Meyer.

1931 Meyers, roadster, NAHC

MEYERS — Just where he built it is not known, but the automotive idea of Roy J. Meyers in 1931 was a runabout driven by compressed air, a concept that had enjoyed a limited vogue at the turn of the century. "The powerplant resembles a rotary aircraft engine and is mounted in an upright position in a standard automotive chassis," *Automobile Trade Journal* reported. "An air valve is the only control necessary. One thing's sure, there won't be any trouble with fouled spark plugs." Meyers claimed that one filling of the compressed air tanks would carry the car for 600 miles.

M.H.C. — Grand Rapids, Michigan — (1917) — During the summer of 1917 the Michigan Hearse & Motor Company of Grand Rapids, Michigan announced its intention to "erect a plant for the manufacture of limousines on a large scale." Possibly some M.H.C. automobiles for the living followed, but the predominant focus of Michigan Hearse & Motor remained on vehicles for the recently departed.

MIAMI — The steam cars built from 1901-1902 in Middletown, Ohio by the Miami Cycle and Manufacturing Company bore the Indian name Ramapaugh. Refer to Ramapaugh Steamer.

MICHAELSON — Minneapolis, Minnesota — (1914) — A motorcycle was the progenitor of this cyclecar from Minnesota. The former had been designed in 1909 by Joseph M. Michaelson and was produced thereafter by the Minneapolis Motorcycle Company. In 1912 Michaelson, together with his brother Walter E. Michaelson, left the Minneapolis company, but remained in town to begin their own firm — the Michaelson Motor Company, which by 1914 had evolved into the Shapiro-Michaelson Motor Car Company. Presumably this reorganization was to bring fresh money into the firm in order to add the Michaelson cyclecar to the existing company product line of motorcycles and engines. An air-cooled Michaelson motorcycle engine was beefed up to 15 hp and used in the car. The cyclecar's price tag was $400, and it was exhibited for the first time at the Minneapolis Automobile Show in January 1914. Precisely what happened next is not known. But in April, Lee W. Oldfield, a racing driver whose renown suffered because of a last name that was the same as the flamboyant Barney's, took over the presidency of the company. Joseph Michaelson left for the Brasie Motor Car Company where he became sales manager. Walter Michaelson resigned, saying he planned to manufacture the cyclecar in another location. There is no evidence that he ever did, nor is there evidence that Lee Oldfield ever moved into viable production. Only the Minneapolis Automobile Show prototype can be verified with certainty to have been built. Two decades later Lee Oldfield was involved in another small car venture: the American Bantam.

MICHIGAN — In addition to the Michigans that were, there were a number that weren't apparently, despite announced intentions of automobile manufacture.

The Michigan Automobile and Carriage Company of Detroit, organized during the spring of 1903 to "make automobiles." Incorporators were James H. Harwick, Henry Wright, George Everhart, Frank Bryan and Don Waldeck.

The Michigan Motor Car Company organized in Washington, D.C. late in 1910 with $10,000 for the manufacture of automobiles. Incorporators were J.H. Stuart, T. Oliver Probey, George R. Stuart, E.G. Powell and F.C. Sibbald.

The Michigan Motor & Machine Company of Detroit was indicated as an automobile manufacturer in trade directory listings from 1904. Documentation is lacking. By August of 1905 the firm, which was then noted to be in Niles, Michigan was undergoing reorganization, with Daniel McHenry (of South Bend, Indiana) taking the presidency, and W.F. Koeller as superintendent. George Brown and H.H. Hutson of Niles were also reported as directors of the company.

The Michigan Steel Boat Works of Detroit, with Hugo Scherer as president and F.E. Wadsworth as secretary, which announced during the late summer of 1910 the intention to erect a three-story plant at Jefferson and Bellevue for the manufacture of a $1000 car.

The Michigan Steam Motor Company of Pontiac, which evolved from the Belknap Motor Company of Detroit during the spring of 1907, and apparently produced a truck only.

1901 Michigan Steamer, stanhope, MVMA

MICHIGAN STEAM — **Grand Rapids, Michigan** — **(1901)** — The Michigan was a steam car, and the first car designed by Byron J. Carter that was put on the market. Alternately called the Carter steam stanhope, it was a graceful little car with a victoria top, a tufted leather seat and grained leather dash. Lever steered, it sported 32-inch wire wheels, and the price complete was $1000. The car was built by the Michigan Automobile Company at 45 Monroe Street in Grand Rapids, and in 1901 only. By 1902 Byron Carter had returned to his native Jackson, Michigan where he persuaded local businessmen to back him in the production of an improved steam car design. The Jaxon followed, as did Carter's new gasoline car called the Jackson. But Carter would be best remembered for the next automobile he designed, the famous friction-drive Cartercar. Meanwhile the Michigan steamer he had designed in 1901 was continued for a short while in Grand Rapids where it was marketed as the Clipper in 1902.

MICHIGAN — **Kalamazoo, Michigan** — **(1903-1907)** — Washboards and other things made of wood were the products of the Kalamazoo manufacturing company called Fuller Brothers. The brothers were Charles D. and Frank D., and when they decided to enter the automobile business, they contacted another pair of brothers in town, the Bloods, who were the proprietors of the Kalamazoo Cycle Company and astute mechanics. The result, on December 30th, 1902, was the Michigan Automobile Company,

Ltd., with Charles Fuller as chairman, Frank Fuller as secretary and general manager, Maurice Blood as treasurer and Charles Blood as superintendent. The Bloods' first prototype car was a 3 1/2 hp one-lunger on a 48-inch wheelbase, which was lengthened to 54 inches for the production version. About 100 of these runabouts were sold by the end of 1904, by which time the line had been expanded to include a light touring twin of which thirty were produced before year's end. The Bloods had designed two more two-cylinder models by now for the 1905 season, but they would not be around to see them built. Late in 1904 they quarreled with the Fullers and left the Michigan organization to set up shop across town and to produce the same car that was being marketed as the Michigan under their own name. Had this situation long endured, it might have become confusing. As it was, the Bloods elected to quit the automobile manufacturing business after 1906 and produce universal joints instead. The Michigan survived one year longer, but in 1908 the Fullers too elected to leave automobile manufacturing to others and to focus their attention on producing automobile components. A few years later they changed their firm's name to Fuller & Sons Manufacturing company to avoid confusion with the new Michigan Motor Car Company.

1903 Michigan, model A, runabout, HAC

1903 MICHIGAN
Model A — 1-cyl., 3 1/2 hp, 54" wb

	FP	5	4	3	2	1
Runabout	450	1600	2700	3800	5800	12,000

1904 Michigan, model C, light touring, NAHC

1904 MICHIGAN
Model A — 1-cyl., 3 1/2 hp, 54" wb

Runabout	475	1600	2700	3800	5800	12,000
Model C — 2-cyl., 12 hp, 78" wb						
Light Touring	900	2000	3000	4200	6500	14,000
1905 MICHIGAN						
Model C — 2-cyl., 12 hp, 78" wb						
Light Touring	900	200	300	4200	6500	14,000
Model D — 2-cyl., 12 hp, 80" wb						
Demi-Tonneau	1100	2300	3300	4600	7500	16,000
Model E — 2-cyl., 16 hp, 90" wb						
Side Entrance Tonneau	1250	2500	3500	5000	8500	18,000
1906-1907 MICHIGAN						
Model E — 2-cyl., 16 hp, 90" wb						
Side Entrance Tonneau	1500	2500	3500	5000	8500	18,000

MICHIGAN — **Kalamazoo, Michigan** — **(1904 et seqq., 1911-1913)** — The Michigan Buggy Company of Kalamazoo motorized one of its standard products in 1904 and offered the result for $450. The car was powered by a single-cylinder 3 1/2 hp engine, the wheelbase was 54 inches, the tread 36 inches — and the car was provided with a two-speed transmission which had no reverse. Backing up had to be accomplished by pushing. The firm continued to offer its motor buggy on a limited basis through the years, occasionally under the name of Kalamazoo, but more often as the Michigan. Serious production of a standard automobile did not begin until 1911 with the formation of the Michigan Motor Car Company. Involved in

1911 Michigan, model B, touring, HAC

1913 Michigan, model S, roadster, HAC

this new venture were company officials Victor L. Palmer, Frank B. Lay, Jr., M. Henry Lane and George T. Lay. W.H. Cameron, whose previous credits included being chief engineer for both Willys-Overland and the Flanders Manufacturing Company, was imported to engineer Michigan's new 40 hp four; and John A. Campbell, an East Coast coachwork designer whose previous assignments included "equipages for the late King of England, also for the Sultan of Turkey," as Michigan advertising put it, was enlisted to style the body. The result was nicknamed the Mighty Michigan and its slogan of "A Mechanically Right and Right Priced Car Supreme in the Forty Field" may have been awkward but was not unwarranted. The car's specification, plus its leather upholstery and 22-coat paint finish of "Michigan, golden auto brown," indicate it to be a fine buy in the $1500 price range. The Michigan's problem was in the front office. Advertising was budgeted at a hefty $350,000; "6,125 sold . . . With 300 Improvements — Is This Year's Wanted Car" blared ad headlines in 1913. Alas, by that time, a few officials in the company were wanted too. In October Kalamazoo County had its first grand jury case in forty-two years, as newspapers headlined "one of the worst business deals in Michigan financial history." Though the company had grandly announced that its labor force had risen from 348 in 1909 to 553 in 1913, it would appear that a lot of these people were on paper only. Four officials of the Michigan firm were said to have earned an extra $100,000 each from what the press called the "velvet payroll." Another official was found to have lost substantial company funds at the racetrack. Yet another was sentenced to a two-year prison term for using the mails to defraud in the sale of stock. There was an attempt by Edward F. Gerber, the Michigan distributor in Pittsburgh, to buy the company and continue manufacture, but this plan fell through. Hugh Chalmers was asked to take time away from building his Chalmers in Detroit to assume charge of the company and get it back on its feet, but the taint of scandal had doomed the Michigan by now, and his efforts were unavailing. In 1915 the Michigan plant was sold and the States Motor Car Company moved in to build its Greyhound light car there.

1904 et seq. MICHIGAN

	FP	5	4	3	2	1
Motor Buggy	450	3200	4300	6500	11,000	23,000

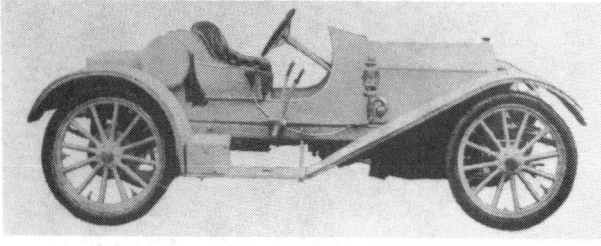

1911 Michigan, model B, roadster, WLB

1911 MICHIGAN
Model B — 4-cyl., 40 hp, 112" wb

	FP	5	4	3	2	1
Touring-5P	1750	3300	4400	6700	12,000	24,000
Roadster-2P	1650	—	—	—	—	—

1912 Michigan, model 40-M, runabout, HAC

1912 MICHIGAN
Four-33 — 4-cyl., 33 hp, 112" wb

	FP	5	4	3	2	1
Model D Roadster-2P	1150	3300	4400	6700	12,000	24,000
Model E Roadster-2P	1150	3300	4400	6700	12,000	24,000
Model H Tour.-5P	1250	3200	4300	6500	11,000	23,000
Model H Torpedo Touring-5P	1400	3400	4500	6900	12,500	24,500
Four-40 — 4-cyl., 40 hp, 116" wb						
Model 40-K Touring-5P	1500	3400	4500	6900	12,500	24,500
Model 40-M Runabout-2P	1500	3500	4500	7000	13,000	25,000

1913 MICHIGAN
Model L — 4-cyl., 33 hp, 114" wb

	FP	5	4	3	2	1
Touring-5P	1400	3700	4700	7300	13,700	26,000
Models R/S — 4-cyl., 40 hp, 118" wb						
Touring-5P	1585	4000	5000	8000	15,000	28,000
Roadster-2P	1585	4200	5200	8400	15,700	29,000

1910 Michigan Six, roadster, GR

MICHIGAN SIX — Detroit, Michigan — (1910) — The Michigan Motor Car Manufacturing Company, Ltd. was organized in Detroit late in 1909 and showed its first car at the Detroit Automobile Show in January 1910. It was a 30 hp six-cylinder roadster on a 123-inch wheelbase, with a $1550 price tag. In February the company announced that it would relocate in a new factory in Rochester — the former Ayres gasoline engine works — and production for 1910 would be 500 cars. All this was window dressing. In March *Motor World* revealed that the factory in Rochester was a small shed, and the Michigan Motor Car Manufacturing Company, Ltd. was a stock-selling scheme. This one was found out more quickly than a lot of others. The first Michigan Six was also the last.

MICK — Mick's Automobile Company of 58 North Second Street in Camden, New Jersey was organized early in 1907 with a capital stock of $5000 for the manufacture of automobiles. Joining J.R. Mick in this venture were E.S. Dickerson and G.P. Williams. Manufacture is doubted.

1909 Middleby, roadster, CCC

MIDDLEBY — Reading, Pennsylvania — (1909-1913) — After failing to locate a suitable home for his automobile company on the East Coast, Charles M. Middleby found Reading, Pennsylvania and the ready-made factory formerly occupied by Charles E. Duryea's Duryea Power Company. In addition to using the Duryea equipment left there, Middleby also borrowed the Duryea idea of air cooling, which he had admired in the Franklin from New York as well as the Corbin from his native state of Connecticut. The Middleby was placed on a 108-inch wheelbase, was priced in the thousand-dollar range, and by 1910 was available in six body styles, the most appealing of them the runabout in which the high peaked hood that was a styling feature of the marque was particularly effective. In 1911 Charles Middleby changed his mind on just about everything. His engines remained four-cylinders, but they were now water-cooled, and the Middleby wheelbase was increased to 122 inches. For dramatic effect, the runabout was given huge 36-inch wheels. Bigger did not prove better in the marketplace, however, and the Middleby Automobile Company which had enjoyed a modest success early on — production of about 400 cars yearly, including a companion marque called the Reading — was out of business entirely by October of 1913. In November the plant was sold to J.E. Conant & Company of Lowell, Massachusetts, that firm announcing that it planned to export the machinery. Several Middlebys are known to be extant; one of the snappy runabout models is in the collection of Car & Carriage Caravan in Luray Caverns, Virginia.

1909 MIDDLEBY
Four — 25 hp, 108" wb

	FP	5	4	3	2	1
Model A Runabout-2P	850	3000	4000	6000	9500	21,000
Model B Surrey-4P	1000	3100	4200	6300	10,500	22,000
Model C Touring-5P	1250	3200	4300	6500	11,000	23,000

1910 Middleby, touring, WLB

1910 MIDDLEBY
Four — 25 hp, 108" wb

Touring	1250	3200	4300	6500	11,000	23,000
Toy Tonneau	1250	3300	4400	6700	12,000	24,000
Runabout	850	3100	4200	6300	10,500	22,000
Double Rumble Roadster	1100	3300	4400	6700	12,000	24,000
Single Rumble Roadster	1000	3200	4300	6500	11,000	23,000
Surrey	1000	3200	4300	6500	11,000	23,000

1911-1913 MIDDLEBY
Four — 40 hp, 122" wb

Touring-5P	1250	4350	8700	14,500	20,300	29,000
Roadster-2P	1250	3700	4700	7300	13,700	26,000

MIDDLESEX — The Middlesex Motor Company was organized in New Brunswick, New Jersey during the fall of 1905 to manufacture automobiles and construct garages. Incorporators were H.C. Saunders, L.A. Voorhees and Charles White. Manufacture is doubted.

MIDDLETON — The Middleton Manufacturing Company was organized in Milwaukee, Wisconsin early in 1905 with a capital stock of $200,000 for the manufacture of automobiles and parts. Incorporators were William C. Middleton, Frederick S. Middleton and Albert S. Schrewe. Manufacture of a car is doubted.

MIDDLETOWN — **Middletown, Ohio** — **(1905)** — In 1905 the Middletown Machine Company, which had established itself in business at the turn of the century, employed sixty mechanics and produced six engines a day. Most of these were intended for industrial use, though a few may have found their way into buggies which were sold to a local clientele. The Middletown engines, which were sold under the tradenames of Miami and Woodpecker, were apparently not very sophisticated, however. The Middletown Machine Company went out of business during 1906.

MIDDLETOWN — **Middletown, Ohio** — **(1909-1911)** — In 1901, Harry H. Elwood moved his Decatur Buggy Company of Greensburg, Indiana to Ohio following attractive offers from the Middletown business community. There it was reorganized as the New Decatur Buggy Company, and a plant double the size of the Indiana facility was erected. Soon the company employed over 200 workers, was producing 20,000 buggies a year and was among the best-equipped horsedrawn factories in the United States. New Decatur's failure to recognize the importance and competition of the motor vehicle industry, however, resulted in the company moving into bankruptcy court in April 1908. Thereon Harry Elwood hired on as manager of the Middletown Buggy Company and moved into the automotive age, though not very progressively, because four-cylinder Rutenber engines were simply purchased and fitted to the standard Middletown product. In 1911 both the Middletown buggy and motor buggy operations were bankrupt too, and soon thereafter the company's factory was remodeled into the first large apartment building in Middletown. Undaunted,

Harry Elwood leased part of his old New Departure factory, commenced to build the Crescent truck there — and went bankrupt again around 1914. His failure to remain in business this time seems to have had nothing to do with the product, however, the Crescent being favorably compared with the well-known Packard truck. Harry Elwood's continuing problem was his old New Departure company which was still in bankruptcy court after five years.

MIDGET — **Springfield, Massachusetts** — **(1915)** — Midget, of course, was a perfect name for a cyclecar — and this was one built by C.S. Root and L.E. Bartlett of Springfield. It featured a two-cylinder, four-stroke, water-cooled engine of 12 hp, a friction transmission, and a special spring arrangement which did away with the need for either front or rear axle. The wheelbase was 102 inches, the tread 36 inches, the total weight 600 pounds, and the price $325. The U.S. Post Office was envisioned by the Midget's makers as their principal purchasing source; a specially constructed "mail delivery" body was featured on the prototype. Possibly it was the only car built. The Midget Cyclecar Company never got off the ground.

MIDGLEY — **Columbus, Ohio** — **(1901-1905)** — The Midgley Manufacturing Company was organized in Columbus in the late fall of 1900, with a capital stock of $10,500, for the manufacture of automobiles and automobile parts. By 1903 capital stock had been increased to $200,000, and the Midgley factory was employing over 200 men. They were making tubular steel wheels, this manufacturing focus having been decided upon by Thomas Midgley. Although Midgley apparently did put together a few cars, these were for experimental purposes only. The Midgley wheel was the sole product manufactured, and very successfully during this period. Among other automobiles, Midgley built wheels for Olds, Glide, Crest, Dumont, Dawson, Premier, Mitchell, Bramwell, National and Autocar.

MIDLAND — The Midland Motor Company was organized in Jersey City, New Jersey during the summer of 1917 with a $1 million capital stock for the manufacture and sale of automobiles and airplanes. Incorporators were Harry B. Davis, Louis H. Gunther and Arthur W. Britton. Manufacture of a car is doubted.

The Midland New York Company was organized with a capital stock of $50,000 during the fall of 1909 for the manufacture of "motor car engines, cars, carriages, boats and vehicles" in New York City. Incorporators were M. Boyle, A.F. Britton and E.M. Boyle. Manufacture of a car is doubted.

1908 Midland, model G-9, roadster, HAC

MIDLAND — **Moline, Illinois** — **(1908-1913)** — Early in 1908 the Midland Motor Car Company succeeded the Deere-Clark Motor Car Company in Moline. Capital stock in this new venture was $100,000, and the man behind it was Charles H. Pope. The first 30/35 hp four was introduced later that year, with a companion 25/30 hp line ushered in for 1909. For 1910 horsepower was up to 40 and 50 hp, though prices remained very nicely in the $2000 range. "Demonstrated worth is one thing that counts in these days of keen competition and the people of Moline have followed the Midland run with deep interest," reported the *Moline Dispatch* in July of 1911 following the conclusion of the transcontinental trek of a Midland from Moline to San Francisco. The Midland factory, which actually was geographically sited on First Street in East Moline, was seemingly prosperous, with every right to be so. The Midland product was a good one; "Unusual Cars at Common Prices" was an apt slogan, and the company's logo with a large British pound-sterling sign substituting for the "L" and centering the name was most striking. C.H. Pope retired as president in 1911, and the Deere estate took over control. Production for 1912 was 200 cars. In 1913 Midland became the largest bankruptcy case thus far ever handled in the Central Illinois district court. Company liabilities totalled $450,000. In March of 1914 court action disclosed that Midland had been solvent at the time of receivership, but gross irregularities in the firm's operations were everywhere. Payroll discrepancies and overdrafts appeared. Company books and papers had mysteriously disappeared, as had forty to fifty cars, surreptitiously from the factory, without serial numbers. Much of the blame for the shenanigans was placed at the feet of C.H. Pope, who had died in the meantime. The fine Midland car was now dead too. A proposed merger with Colby in Mason City, Iowa fell through. The Midland factory equipment was sold to John McLaughlin for $22,000 in January 1914. The Midland real estate was purchased for the same price that March by Harry M. Schriver, the mayor of nearby Rock Island.

1908 MIDLAND
Model G-9 — 4-cyl., 30/35 hp, 118" wb

	FP	5	4	3	2	1
Touring-5/7P	2250	—	—	—	—	—

1909 Midland, model E, touring, HAC

1909 MIDLAND
Model E — 4-cyl., 25/30 hp, 112" wb

	FP	5	4	3	2	1
Roadster-4P	1800	3700	4700	7300	13,700	26,000
Touring-5P	1800	3500	4500	7000	13,000	25,000

Model G-9 — 4-cyl., 30/35 hp, 118" wb

Touring-5/7P	2250	3700	4700	7300	13,700	26,000

1910 Midland, model L, touring, HAC

1910 MIDLAND
Model L — 4-cyl., 40 hp, 115" wb

Touring-5P	1800	3500	4500	7000	13,000	25,000
Roadster-4P	1800	3700	4700	7300	13,700	26,000
Tonneau-4P	1800	3700	4700	7300	13,700	26,000

Model K — 4-cyl., 50 hp, 120" wb

Touring-5/7P	2250	3900	4800	7700	14,300	27,000

1911 Midland, model L, toy tonneau, HAC

1911 MIDLAND
Model L-1 — 4-cyl., 40 hp, 115" wb

Touring-5P	2000	3500	4500	7000	13,000	25,000
Roadster-4P	1950	3700	4700	7300	13,700	26,000
Toy Tonneau-4P	2000	3700	4700	7300	13,700	26,000
Fore-Door Touring-5P	2100	3700	4700	7300	13,700	26,000

Model K — 4-cyl., 50 hp, 118" wb

Touring-5/7P	2250	3700	4700	7300	13,700	26,000

1912 Midland, model L-111, touring, HAC

1912 MIDLAND
Model L-III — 4-cyl., 40 hp, 115" wb

	FP	5	4	3	2	1
Touring	2100	3900	4800	7700	14,300	27,000
Toy Tonneau	2100	4000	5000	8000	15,000	28,000
Roadster	2000	4000	5000	8000	15,000	28,000
Colonial Coupe	2500	2500	3500	5000	8500	18,000

Model R — 4-cyl., 40 hp, 118" wb

Touring-5P	2750	4200	5200	8400	15,700	29,000

Model O — 6-cyl., 46 hp, 118" wb

Roadster-2P	3000	4000	5000	8000	15,000	28,000

1913 Midland, model T-4, touring, WLB

1913 MIDLAND
Model T-4 — 4-cyl., 40 hp, 122" wb

Touring-5P	1685	4500	5800	9500	18,000	32,000
Roadster-2/3P	1685	4700	6100	9900	19,000	33,000
Speedster-2P	1685	5200	6800	11,300	23,000	36,000
Coupe-2P	2350	3000	4000	6000	9500	21,000

Model T-6 — 6-cyl., 50 hp, 134" wb

Touring-5P	2385	4900	6300	10,300	21,000	34,000
Touring-7P	2450	5000	6500	11,000	22,000	35,000
Roadster-2P	2385	5200	6800	11,300	23,000	36,000
Napoleon Coach-5P	3250	3300	4400	6700	12,000	24,000

MIDLAND — Muskogee, Oklahoma — (1909-1912) — H.A. Von Unwerth was the proprietor of the Midland Machine Works located at 118 Times Place in Muskogee. Manufacture of the Muskogee Water Filter was the firm's principal preoccupation, but a few cars were assembled to local customer order as well. This was strictly a sideline activity, and had been discontinued by 1913.

MIDLAND — Oklahoma City, Oklahoma — (1918-1919) — The Midland Motor Car and Truck Company was a million-dollar incorporation organized in Oklahoma City in 1918 by James M. Aydelotte, Floyd Thompson, George L. Cooke and Robert P. Inglis. According to *The Daily Oklahoman* of June 9th that year, the firm planned "to be making battleplanes next year; first cars to go out in July." Whether any battleplanes resulted is not known, but no Midland automobile appeared on the market. The company did build a 2-1/2-ton truck into 1919, however.

MIDWAY — A car called the Midway has been indicated on various rosters to have been built by the Mountain Brothers Company of Los Angeles, California in 1910. This is in error. George E. and William F. Mountain were in business at 416 South Spring Street in Los Angeles at that time but conducted an automobile livery and dealership. At the Los Angeles Dealers' Association automobile show in February 1910 the Mountain Brothers exhibited a Royal Tourist and a Midland. Obviously the Midway was a typographical error.

MIDWEST — Midwest Motor Company was the firm's name, but the cars produced were never called that. This Kansas City automobile of the World War I era was planned as the Kay-See in 1917 and produced as the Highlander from 1919-1922. Refer to Kay-See and Highlander.
  The Midwest Motor Supply Company was organized in Camden, New Jersey late in 1910 with a capital stock of $100,000 for the manufacture of automobiles and engines. Incorporators were F.R. Hansell, William F. Eidell and John A. McPeak. Manufacture is doubted.
  The Mid-West Steam Motor Company of 305 Second Street in Laramie, Wyoming was indicated as the producer of both a steam passenger car and a steam truck in a Chilton Automobile Directory for 1925. Manufacture is doubted.

1908 Mier, model A, runabout, NAHC

MIER — **Ligonier, Indiana** — **(1908-1909)** — The Mier Carriage & Buggy Company had the distinction of erecting the first three-story building in Ligonier, and the Miers were prominent citizens of the town. Indeed, Solomon Mier was an early settler of the region. His son A.B. Mier joined him at the turn of the century in their buggy business, which was a thriving one. The Miers' foray into the automobile field was a short one. In 1908 they added a two-cylinder engine, friction transmission and double-chain drive to one of their standard buggy models, provided wheel steering, fitted solid tires — and sold about 100 of the motorized buggies that resulted. A longer wheelbase buggy was motorized the following year, but thereafter the Miers returned to horsedrawn buggy manufacture exclusively, surviving in this field until the 1920's.

1908 MIER
Mier — **2-cyl., 10/12 hp, 86" wb**

	FP	5	4	3	2	1
Model A Runabout	575	1800	2800	4000	6200	13,000
Model B Rbt. (square stern)	575	1800	2800	4000	6200	13,000

1909 MIER
Mier — **2-cyl., 12 hp, 86" wb**

Model A Runabout 2P	575	1800	2800	4000	6200	13,000
Model B Doctor's Stanhope	575	1900	2900	4100	6400	13,500

Mier — **2-cyl., 18 hp, 96" wb**

Model C Runabout- 2P	650	2000	3000	4200	6500	14,000
Model D Runabout-4P	700	2100	3100	4300	6800	14,500
Model D Surrey-4P	700	2200	3200	4400	7000	15,000

MIERLEY — **Davenport, Iowa** — **(1902)** — A.W. Mierley of Davenport was among the many American physicians who built an automobile for his own use at the turn of the century. Unlike most of the others, however, Dr. Mierley attempted to organize a company for its manufacture. He did not succeed.

MIEUSSET — Although the Mieusset often appears on rosters of American-made cars, its presence is in error. The car was built by Ateliers de Construction Mecanique et d'Automobiles Mieusset in Lyons, France from 1903 through 1914. From 1906 to 1907 the company did launch a concerted drive in the United States, but the cars were never built here, but imported instead. J.P. Bruyere was the man in charge. Importation seems to have been discontinued by 1908.

MIGHTY MICHIGAN — Mighty Michigan was the often advertised name for the Michigan that was built in Kalamazoo from 1911 to 1913. The venture had begun as the Michigan Buggy Company in 1904, with serious production following in 1911 with the firm's reorganization to the Michigan Motor Car Company. Refer to Michigan.

1916 Milac, racer, RBB

MILAC — **Los Angeles, California** — **(1916)** — The Milac was "made in Los Angeles, California," hence the name, by the Linthwaite-Hussey Motor Company. Although the firm tried to subdue its sporting image, insisting that "L.&H. Motors are not necessarily racing motors," the eight cars it built in 1916 were no doubt destined for go-fast devotees. Milacs were raced at Ascot and Corona among other venues. The two engines fitted into the cars were tweaked to fit just under the prevailing regulations. Both were sixteen-valve high-revving fours, the Model C displacing 199 cubic inches and developing 90 hp at 4000 rpm, the Model D displacing 299 cubic inches and developing 110 hp at 3800 rpm. "Terrible" Teddy Tetzlaff drove one of the 199-cubic-inch Milacs to victory at Ascot in March of 1916. The cars continued to be raced into 1918. Of the two partners, the first name of Hussey is not known, though presumably he put up the money. Owen C. Linthwaite was the engineer. In 1910 he had worked for Volney Beardsley's California Automobile Company. Subsequently he was an engineer for the Columbus Buggy Company, producers of the Firestone-Columbus, until that Ohio firm folded in 1915 and Linthwaite returned to the West Coast to begin his Milac adventure.

MILBURN ELECTRIC — **Toledo, Ohio** — **(1914-1923)** — The Milburn Wagon Company, which had been in the vehicle-building business in Toledo since 1848, announced its entry into the automotive field in late September of 1914. One thousand cars were built in 1915; fifteen hundred in 1916. The Milburn product was a lightweight electric with a speed of 19

1916 Milburn Electric, coupe, HAC

mph in roadster form, 15 mph as a coupe. Initially, a Milburn had to be recharged every 60 to 75 miles, but by 1918 the company had eliminated the delay that recharging usually involved. "In the Milburn the batteries are now on rollers that operate on tracks," advertising stated. "Simply roll out the discharged ones and roll in the freshly charged set . . . It makes charging as easy as driving." Although the Milburn Electric Charger did help to spur sales, the electric vehicle as a genre was on a decline by this time. The Light Delivery that had been an early offering was discontinued early as well; a taxicab was offered in 1920. In December of 1919 a disastrous fire at the Milburn plant resulted in losses totaling $900,000, including thirty completed electrics and even more automobile bodies. Production continued in January 1920 in the building on the grounds of Toledo University which had been used to train Motor Transport Corps recruits during the First World War. In 1921 Milburn Wagon Company capitalization was increased to $1 million, and it was revealed that of the 800-man workforce, 200 were building the cars, 600 were building automobile bodies (for Oldsmobile most prominently). In February of 1923 the Milburn plant was purchased by General Motors for $2 million. Milburn workers remained in the plant for the two months following, finishing up cars and bodies contracted for — but then Buick moved in. And the Milburn Electric was no more.

1914-1916 MILBURN ELECTRIC

	FP	5	4	3	2	1
Light Coupe (100" wb)	1485	1800	2800	4000	6200	13,000
Light Roadster (100" wb)	1285	2000	3000	4200	6500	14,000
Light Delivery (100" wb)	985	1600	2700	3800	5800	12,000

1917 Milburn Electric, brougham, HAC

1917 MILBURN ELECTRIC

	FP	5	4	3	2	1
Light Electric Brgm (105" wb)	1685	2000	3000	4200	6500	14,000
Town Car (105" wb)	1995	2300	3300	4600	7500	16,000

1918 Milburn Electric, sedan, KM

1918 MILBURN ELECTRIC

	FP	5	4	3	2	1
Light Electric Brgm (105" wb)	1885	2300	3300	4600	7500	16,000
Sedan (105" wb)	2685	1800	2800	4000	6200	13,000
Limousine (105" wb)	2785	2500	3500	5000	8500	18,000

1919 MILBURN ELECTRIC

	FP	5	4	3	2	1
Light Electric Brgm (105" wb)	2185	2400	3400	4800	8000	17,000

1920 Milburn Electric, brougham, WLB

1920 MILBURN ELECTRIC

	FP	5	4	3	2	1
Model 27L Brougham (105" wb)	2485	2500	3500	5000	8500	18,000
Taxicab (111" wb)	—	1800	2800	4000	6200	13,000

1921 Milburn Electric, brougham, HFM

1921 MILBURN ELECTRIC

	FP	5	4	3	2	1
Model 27L Brgm. (105" wb)	2685	2500	3500	5000	8500	18,000

1922-23 Milburn Electric, brougham, HAC

1922-1923 MILBURN ELECTRIC

	FP	5	4	3	2	1
Model 27L Brgm. (105" wb)	2385	2700	3600	5300	8800	19,000

MILITAIRE — In 1912 the Militaire Company of Cleveland, Ohio introduced a two-wheel scooter with a single-cylinder engine, friction transmission, underslung frame and wheel steering. The company was in the hands of the receiver by the summer of 1913, with liabilities of $20,000. In 1916 the Militaire Autocycle Company of America, located in Buffalo, New York, introduced its Militaire which the company referred to as a two-wheeled automobile. Although both these vehicles have found their way into occasional rosters of American-built cars, they cannot be regarded as such. They were motorcycles, plain and simple.

MILITARY — Cincinnati, Ohio — (1907) — In January of 1904, Victor L. Emerson, who had built two cars under his own name prior to the turn of the century, announced that he planned to establish a factory in Baltimore for the manufacture of yachts, motors and automobiles. He did not move to Maryland. Instead, late in 1904, he advertised himself as general manager of the American Motor Company in Cincinnati. This firm apparently never built anything. The next news from Emerson arrived in 1907, and it would seem that he might have managed a prototype this time. He called it the Military, a six boasting 60/70 hp with a touring body on a 96-inch wheelbase. His price tag was $8000. Probably he didn't sell one. No company was ever incorporated for the Military's manufacture. Four years later, Emerson was in Philadelphia trying again with the S.S.E.

MILLBURN — The Millburn Motor Car Company was organized early in 1911 with a capital stock of $50,000 to manufacture automobiles in Millburn, New Jersey. Incorporators were the brothers Wittkop, Julius, Charles and Henry. Manufacture is doubted.

MILLER — The Colorado car of 1902-1903 which has occasionally been referred to as a Miller is more correctly referred to as a Greeley. Refer to Greeley.

The Charles Miller Cycle Shop of Anderson, Indiana purportedly built a three-wheeler in 1898. Documentation is lacking.

The Miller Centrifugal Motor Company was organized in Brooklyn, New York during the summer of 1915 for the manufacture of engines and automobiles. Capital stock was $600,000; Martin Lippman, Emanuel L. Meyer and Emma Ullmann were the incorporators. Manufacture of a car is doubted.

The Miller Machine Company of Defiance, Ohio announced its entry into autombile ranks during the summer of 1909 with a car called the Defiance. Refer to Defiance.

The Miller-Sprague-Waldo Manufacturing Company was organized in Detroit, Michigan early in 1910 with a capital stock of $25,000 for the manufacture of automobiles and accessories. Incorporators were Lewis C. Waldo, John R. Waldo, George Miller, H.B. Ransom and Edwin W. Sprague. Manufacture of a car is doubted.

MILLER — Cincinnati, Ohio — (1900) — In 1900 the George C. Miller Sons' Carriage Company of Cincinnati built an automobile to custom order for one of its former horsedrawn clients. The firm did not embark upon manufacture, however, becoming the local dealers for the Mobile car instead in 1901.

MILLER ELECTRIC — Kenton, Ohio — (1900, 1902) — George J. Miller was an electrician from Kenton who invented a dry battery and an electric motor and installed same in an experimental car he built in 1900. The result, he claimed, was "noiseless and much lighter" than electrics then in use, the mechanism was simple, and the speed attained satisfactory. Although capitalists from Columbus were purportedly interested in the Miller car, nothing seems to have come of that. In 1902, by which time Miller had secured a patent on his storage battery, he also built a second experimental car — and this time money arrived from Bellefontaine, Ohio for manufacture. The Miller Storage Battery & Electric Company produced only the Miller storage battery, however; the only Miller cars were the two experimental jobs. This Miller, incidentally, is not to be confused with the George C. Miller Sons' Carriage Company of Cincinnati.

1901 Miller Steamer, surrey, NAHC

MILLER STEAM — Meyersdale, Pennsylvania — (1901) — Tom Gurley can be credited with building the first automobile in the town of Meyersdale. Milton D. Miller built the second, though it was the first steamer. Miller made the boiler, engine, wheels and seats himself in his Meyersdale machine shop. The car was tiller steered, and used gasoline for fuel. The one car was Milton Miller's total production. He built it strictly for family use.

MILLER — Trail & Orrville, Ohio — (1901-1902) — J.W. Miller was a mechanic who built several gasoline vehicles on a shoestring in Trail in 1901 and who thought he was on the verge of making it big in 1902 when a number of businessmen from Orrville — including S.M. Brenneman, S.P. Eshelman and H.M. Bechtel — agreed to furnish him backing for experimentation. Apparently that backing was short-lived, however, because the evidence suggests that no viable manufacture followed.

MILLER — Amesbury, Massachusetts — (1902) — The Miller Brothers — John, Thomas, Robert and William — were carriage builders in Amesbury who completed their first automobile in the spring of 1902 and gave it a test run on May 16th. Its engine was a two-cylinder 8 hp gasoline unit purchased from H.A. Spiller who was getting ready to market his Boston-Amesbury across town. Although the Millers indicated at the time that they might form a company for automobile manufacture, they never did do so. Instead, later that year, they joined Cullen B. Small in the manufacture of Climax spark plugs and they remained in the carriage business until 1915.

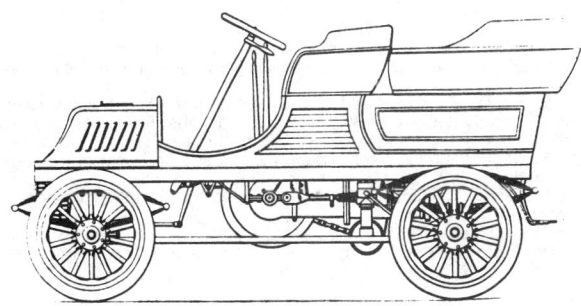

1902 Miller, gasoline tonneau, (New York City), NAHC

MILLER — New York, New York — (1902-1903) — Although Charles E. Miller of 97 Reade Street in New York City occasionally had a gasoline or steam automobile built to his own design either for himself or a special customer, his principal production was running gear and other components, and he carried on a lively sideline business as an automotive jobber. "He is just in receipt of a large shipment of genuine French imported spark plugs from France," *Cycle and Automobile Trade Journal* reported in March 1902, "and is in a position to quote the very largest buyers on this style of plug in any quantity. It would pay the users to get his quotation before buying." He had also reduced the retail price of his automobile kid leather gauntlets to $2.00 a pair, and offered them for a whole lot less wholesale. His business obviously was thriving, because later that year he designed for himself a spacious gasoline tonneau — 84-inch wheelbase, 60-inch tread, 16 hp Binate engine — that was built for him by an unnamed company in the South. Within a few years Charles Miller was the biggest automobile parts dealer in New York City.

MILLER — Goshen, New York — (1905) — "The first automobile ever constructed in Orange County, New York is awaiting its finishing touch — namely, a coat of paint," reported *The Motor World* in November 1905. The car, a 30 hp gasoline machine, was being built as an experiment by the Miller factory in Goshen, whose usual activity was the manufacture of carts for sulky horse racing. "If it goes," *The Motor World* commented regarding the Miller car, "the cart company will doubtless change its name." The cart company did not. The placing of the Miller company in Goshen, Indiana — as it appears in numerous rosters — is in error, incidentally, the result of *The Horseless Age* having mistaken the state in its report of the Miller experimental car. There was no Miller company in Goshen, Indiana during this period, though the Goshen Motor Works was in the automobile business there at that time.

MILLER — Bridgeport, Connecticut — (1907) — The Miller Garage Company, Inc. of Bridgeport was organized in late 1906 for the manufacture of trucks and buses. For the 1907 season the firm decided first to change its name to Miller Motor Company, and second to include a passenger car in its line. It was called the Model H, a 24/30 hp surrey on a 115-inch wheelbase. Its dash was mahogany, its hood aluminum, its radiator honeycomb. The Miller Motor Company was no longer around for the 1908 season.

MILLER — Detroit, Michigan — (1911-1914) — The Miller Car Company of Detroit was organized in the fall of 1911 with a capital stock of $50,000. Theodore Miller was president; associated with him were E.L. McMillan from the Continental Can Company and J.C. Hallock whose Detroit Excelsior Works would provide the quarters for the Miller venture. The Miller car was soon in production. A 30 hp four, it was offered as a roadster on a 110-inch wheelbase for $1250 and a touring on a 116-inch wheelbase at

1912 Miller, touring, NAHC

$1350. In 1912 Guy Sintz, the former gasoline engine maker, joined the firm as factory manager, and in 1913 a 1000-pound delivery wagon was added to the line. By January of 1914, the company was in receivership, with assets of $8000, liabilities of $10,500. In February the Kosmath company bought what was left of Miller and continued production of the delivery wagon. The Miller automobile design ended up in Pittsburgh where it was refined into the Pennsy automobile. Total production of Miller cars is not known; thirty-six were reported to be registered in the state of Michigan in 1916.

1912 Miller, roadster, HAC

1928 Miller, speedster, MVMA

MILLER — Los Angeles, California — (1928, 1932) — The first inkling that renowned race car builder Harry Armenius Miller was considering entering the passenger car field arrived during the summer of 1923 with announcement from Los Angeles that plans had been drawn up for use of Miller's racing 122-cubic-inch eight-cylinder in a built-to-order car for customers able and willing to spend over $10,000 — and that plans were ongoing for a new Miller four-cylinder engine to be used in a quantity-produced car to sell in the less rarefied realm of $2000. But, the announcement also said, "there will be no production this year as Miller will devote all his time to racing." And so he did — and would. Not until 1928 did he again contemplate building a passenger automobile, and the car he designed that year — in collaboration with Leo Goossen and Fred Offenhauser — was a one-off four-wheel-drive open speedster, with body by Kirchoff, powered by a 310-cubic-inch V-8 engine which had been designed especially for it. When finished, the car was delivered to the wealthy Santa Barbara sportsman (Phillip Chancellor) who had ordered it. The second Miller road-going car, commissioned by a U.S. diplomat from New York (William A.M. Burden), was also a speedster, but powered by a 303-cubic-inch V-16 supercharged engine and fitted with front-wheel-drive (as were Miller's most recent Indy cars). It cost Burden about $35,000, and he wasn't particularly happy with it. Although in January 1933, *Automotive Industries* reported that "Harry Miller likes the front-wheel drive and is turning over in his mind the possibility that some day in the not too distant future he may be building a sizeable quantity of them for those who want something different," the race car genius ultimately decided to stick with what he knew best. The two one-off speedsters were the only production cars which carried his name. Neither is believed to survive.

935

MILLER-PETERS — Newport, Kentucky — (1907) — Very little is known about the Miller-Peters Motor Car Company of Newport except that it began building automobiles in small numbers in 1907 and had grand plans to move across the river to Cincinnati (Ohio) later that year where it would reorganize as Miller & Peters Company. "Ther first step in that direction was taken last week," *The Motor World* announced in April 1907, "when a two-acre site on Mitchell Avenue, Cincinnati, was purchased and on which will be erected a one-story factory 2000 feet in length, the idea being not only to obtain light but to begin work on the cars at one end and send them out completed and crated from the other end." An increase in capitalization to $500,000 was necessary to accomplish this, and it does not appear that Miller-Peters ever got it.

MILLER-QUINCY — Quincy, Illinois — (1922-1924) — The E.M. Miller Company manufactured hearses in Quincy, and for a few years in the early Twenties a few large sedans and limousines as well. These carried the Continental 8R six-cylinder 50 hp engine and were on the same 130-inch wheelbase chassis as the funeral cars. Disc wheels were featured, and the price for a sedan was quoted as $2780.

MILLERSVILLE — Millersville, Ohio — (1910) — In April of 1910 the Millersville Machine Company announced that the automobile marketplace was now being graced by the addition of a 25 hp Millersville runabout. According to a reference in *The Automobile* that month, a new plant was being erected for its manufacture. Whether the facility was ever finished is not known. Millersville was not heard from again in 1911.

MILLINGTON — (1913) — In late 1913 Theodore H. Millington pronounced himself at work on a one-seater cyclecar with parcel carrier body, that he called the Spider. Friction drive was featured, the tread was 36 inches, and Millington indicated his intention to sell the car for $300. There is no evidence, however, that the vehicle was ever produced. Possibly Theodore Millington was associated with the Millington Auto Engineering Company of Chicago which did produce a car called the Frontaway in 1917.

MILLION — Monticello, Indiana — (1896) — In 1896, in Monticello, Robert J. Million built a gasoline motor buggy for his own use. Its special feature was the direct transmission of power from motor shaft to rear axle, eliminating the need for belts, chains, friction pulleys or cog gears, and adjusting itself automatically to the load. As Million explained, "for a hard pull speed is reduced to one-third of the high-speed limit, while three times the power is developed." Million believed his transmission principle would be applicable to all sizes of vehicle, but evidence is lacking that he ever built another car.

MILLIONAIRE'S CAR — Millionaire's Car, or Banker's Car, was the probably-not-always-appreciated nickname the trade press gave to the Orson which was promoted in New York City from 1910-1912. Most probably, the Millionaire Auto Company which was incorporated in Manhattan late in 1912 with a capital stock of $300,000 was an attempt to carry this venture forward. A.W. Pritchett, F.A. Vanderlip, H.M. Kilborn, S. McRoberts, J.A. Stillman, P.A. Rockefeller and H. Hammond were the Millionaire company's incorporators.

MILNE STEAMER — Everett, Massachusetts — (1901) — The Milne Steamer of 1901 was the lineal successor to the Everett Steamer of 1898-1899. Following the sale of his Everett Motor Carriage Company to a group of Boston entrepreneurs, Frank Milne built another steam car under his own name and announced his readiness to build others to custom order. No formal company was established, and Frank Milne undoubtedly didn't continue in his steam-car-building venture long.

MILLS — The Mills Traction Company was organized in Sacramento, California late in 1906 with a capital stock of $75,000 to manufacture and deal in automobiles. Incorporators were A. Mills, D.D. Baker, W.A. Gauge, B.F. Driver and E.F. Smith. Manufacture is doubted.

MILLS STEAM — Pittsburgh, Pennsylvania — (1876) — The steam vehicle built by Isaac Mills, Jr. in 1876 was a cumbersome affair, but undoubtedly the first automobile in Pittsburgh. A small wagon powered by a steam engine under the bed, the vehicle was used by Mills for several months in his business as a building supply tradesman, but ultimately he gave it up because "it was too much trouble to keep out of the way of other wagons." Mills died in 1902 in Braddock, Pennsylvania. His father had been the first burgess of the borough of Braddock in 1867.

MILLS — Chicago, Illinois — (1895) — "A well-known inventor in the pneumatic line" was the phrase used by *The Horseless Age* to describe M.B. Mills, whose shop was at 125 LaSalle Street in Chicago. In 1895 he announced his entry in the Chicago Times-Herald Contest with a three-wheeled vehicle propelled by compressed air or gas. The vehicle resembled a dogcart, with its bicycle origins (tubular steel frame, all wheels being forked) plain to see. Though he did not make it to the starting line, he did subsequently complete and test his machine.

MILLS ELECTRIC — Lafayette, Indiana — (1917) — In May of 1917 the Mills Electric Company of Lafayette announced its intention to begin the manufacture of electric motor-driven cars for use on boardwalks and at

pleasure resorts. Involved in this venture were Byron J. Mills, Herbert A. Keller and Eldon L. Lewis. In addition to resort use, the partners believed their small electric would be marketable as a light car for women and, in specially designed versions, also for invalids. The small 3 hp motor was placed up front under a hood, with the battery under the seat. The car was provided a canopy top, as well as side curtains. "The company says it has orders for 100 cars this summer," *The Automobile* reported, "and expects to sell 200 this year." How long the Mills Electric Company remained in the car business is not known.

MILLS & SEARLS — The Mills & Searls Company of Chicago, Illinois was another entry in the Chicago Times-Herald Contest of 1895 that did not make the starting line. Whether the firm's car was subsequently completed and tested has not been documented.

MILOMETER — The Milometer Company was organized in Chicago, Illinois with a capital stock of $100,000 during the spring of 1915 to manufacture and deal in all kinds of motor-driven vehicles. Incorporators were O.E. Joseph, A.H. Joseph and James Callahan. Manufacture of a car is doubted.

MILTON — Los Angeles, California — (1914) — How many cars the Milton Manufacturing Company of Los Angeles manufactured is questionable but that was the activity in which it was reported to have been engaged during 1914. The firm, which was located at 610 East First Street, had vacated those premises by 1915, however, and president Charles Milton was purportedly now a mining engineer.

MILWAUKEE — Although announced as the Milwaukee, the car produced in 1902-1903 by the B & P Company was sold under the name of Ideal. Refer to Ideal.

Although originally projected to be called the Milwaukee, the Eagle Automobile Company decided on the Eagle name by the time its first car was completed during the summer of 1906. Refer to Eagle.

The Milwaukee Auto & Engine Supply Company produced a car called the Majestic in 1909. Refer to Majestic.

The Milwaukee Cyclecar Company marketed its car under the name of Billiken. Refer to Billiken.

The Milwaukee Motor Manufacturing Company produced its cars in 1903-1904 and marketed them under the tradename of Monarch. Refer to Monarch.

1900 Milwaukee Steamer, stanhope, HAC

MILWAUKEE STEAM — Milwaukee, Wisconsin — (1900-1902) — The Milwaukee Automobile Company was located at Nineteenth Street and St. Paul Avenue in the old Milwaukee Engineering Company plant. The firm was organized with a capital stock of $100,000 in December of 1899 by W.H. Starkweather, Herman Pfiel and W.G. Smith. "Thoroughly efficient" was the company's slogan, and its product was described as one that was not a "radical departure from all other types" and would not "revolutionize the whole automobile industry." It was a steam car because "steam is our oldest artificial power," and it had no ball bearings because "their value is uncertain, while bronze bearings are a known quantity." Having thus stated its case, this conservative Milwaukee company did not alter from its course for the two years following, except to raise prices. "The company's factory is now taxed to its limit," *Cycle and Automobile Trade Journal* enthused in March of 1902, "with the double task of filling back orders and providing for prompt deliveries when the selling season is at its height." When the end for Milwaukee came that May, *Motor Review* reported that overproduction was the reason, the market not being "so favorable as expected." In June the company was adjudged bankrupt, with liabilities of $41,993.48; in July its property was sold at auction. In August George Whitney in Boston sued Milwaukee Automobile Company for infringement of his steam patent of 1900. He was just a little too late.

Among the Milwaukee employees, incidentally, was W.H. McIntyre who later built the McIntyre highwheeler in Auburn, Indiana.

1900 MILWAUKEE STEAM

	FP	5	4	3	2	1
Steam Stanhope	750	2300	3300	4600	7500	16,000
Steam Surrey	900	2400	3400	4800	8000	17,000
Steam Delivery	900	2200	3200	4400	7000	15,000

1901 MILWAUKEE STEAM

Steam Surrey	1000	2400	3400	4800	8000	17,000
Steam Delivery	1000	2200	3200	4400	7000	15,000
Steam Truck	1000	2500	3500	5000	8500	18,000

1902 Milwaukee Steamer, touring, HAC

1902 MILWAUKEE STEAM

Steam Runabout	750	2300	3300	4600	7500	16,000
Steam Surrey	1300	2400	3400	4800	8000	17,000
Steam Delivery	1000	2200	3200	4400	7000	15,000

MILWAUKEE — Milwaukee, Wisconsin — (1901-1902) — In a two-story factory on Broadway just south of Biddle Street in Milwaukee, three gasoline cars — an $825 phaeton, a $750 runabout and a $1000 delivery wagon — were produced by the Milwaukee Automobile and Brass Specialty Company. The firm, organized with a capital stock of $15,000, was headed by William Spence, Frederick D. Bergman and George A. Rosenbauer, the last named having designed the car and briefly sold it under his own name. About forty men were employed by the company, but unfortunately not for long. Production began on the runabouts in September of 1901, with a few phaetons and delivery wagons following, before this undercapitalized venture failed early in 1902.

MILWAUKEE — Milwaukee, Wisconsin — (1903) — The Milwaukee Moto Company of 128 Ferry Street in Milwaukee was a turn-of-the-century gasoline engine builder. Apparently at least a few cars were produced too. "This company has also met with considerable success in building automobiles," *The Automobile Review* noted in a brief mention of the Milwaukee firm's activities in September 1903. "They report a ready sale for their product." Further details are lacking.

1903 Milwaukee Star, tonneau, WLB

MILWAUKEE STAR — Milwaukee, Wisconsin — (1903) — Bernard Amann was the president, John P. McCabe the secretary-treasurer and Fred Lederer the superintendent of the Milwaukee Auto Engines and Supply Company. In addition to their usual products, in 1903 they also built five 13 hp touring cars that they called Milwaukee Star. In 1904 they returned to the business of auto engines and supplies.

MILWAUKEE STEAMER — Although a car called the Milwaukee Steamer was purportedly built in Sun Prairie in 1878, it does not appear to have been either completed or successfully tested. The vehicle was commissioned to be built by one Dr. Karouse who wished to enter it in the contest being staged that summer by the State of Wisconsin to discover a "cheap

and practical" alternative to horses for motive transport. According to a mid-July 1878 edition of the *Evening Wisconsin*, "owing to a failure of the contractor to finish it in time and according to specifications," the Milwaukee Steamer did not make it to the starting line of the contest. Two other cars did, however: the Oshkosh and the Green Bay.

MINCH — Cleveland, Ohio — (1909) — In 1909 Captain Philip J. Minch completed a prototype of a four-passenger shaft-drive electric roadster on a lengthy 122-inch wheelbase. That August *The Horseless Age* reported Minch seeking a location to manufacture, adding "he is said to be looking favorably upon Springfield, Ohio." Apparently Springfield, Ohio did not look favorably upon him. There is no evidence the Minch car was ever put into manufacture.

MINERVA — The Minerva was one of two models produced by the Detroit-Dearborn Motor Car Company in 1910. Refer to Detroit-Dearborn.

MINNEAPOLIS — The Minneapolis Automobile Manufacturing Company was organized during the spring of 1906 with a capital stock of $10,000 to manufacture and deal in motor cars. Apparently, Minnie was the name chosen for the car to be produced. Behind this venture were J.M. Johnson, Thomas A. Barrett and James M. Crozier. Manufacture is doubted.

The Minneapolis Motor Company manufactured motorcycles in Minnesota and for a short time during the fall of 1913 was on the verge of getting into the automobile business too, via a merger with the Colby Motor Company of Mason City, Iowa. The "largest automobile manufacturing plant in the west" was planned for Minneapolis but, as reported by *Motor World* on January 1st, 1914, "at the eleventh hour, that deal fell through." There never was a Minneapolis built during this brief period, and the Colby was doomed thereafter as well.

The Minneapolis Motor Cycle Manufacturing Company announced its intention to build an automobile in 1914. One R.M. Page was superintendent. Most probably, this purported Minneapolis car did not reach even the prototype stage. It never appeared in local automobile shows, nor in the state automobile census. The same firm did produce a motorcycle called the Minneapolis, however, and a 300-pound delivery tri-car variation that sold for $375 in 1912-1913.

MINNESOTA — Minnesota Specials No. 1 and 2 were the names given to the first two cars built by Tom Dean, a blacksmith from Magnolia, Minnesota circa 1907. Refer to Magnolia.

MINO — New Orleans, Louisiana — (1914) — The New Orleans Cyclecar Company, Ltd. was organized early in 1914 by Julius C. Weiner, I.T. Rhea and W.S. Campbell to produce a $375 cyclecar. It was powered by a two-cylinder air-cooled engine, its wheelbase was 96 inches with 42-inch tread, a two-speed planetary transmission and vee-belt final drive were fitted. Initially, the car was to be called the New Orleans Cyclecar but by the time it arrived on the market its name had been changed to Mino, for reasons which history has obscured. Its price was also raised to $465. Production had to have been minimal; the company was out of business by year's end.

1914 Mission, MVMA

MISSION — Los Angeles, California — (1914) — Yancio R. del Valle was the distributor of the Detroiter on the West Coast. In January of 1914, *Motor World* announced, somewhat ominously, that "although no previous effort of the sort has succeeded, he has undertaken to produce Mission cars for the Pacific Coast trade." Supporting him in his Mission Motor Car Company venture were Garland P. Fallis as president, Alfred Barstow as vice-president and J.W. Kays as treasurer. The company's secretary, Henry L. Palmer, was also the Mission car's designer, and he was reported to have been "identified with Eastern automobile factories, the Ford and Studebaker among the number." The Mission was slated to be a low-priced car, made available as a roadster called the Angelus (four-cylinder, four-stroke engine, $475 price tag) and a 1000-pound delivery car to sell for $850, the same chassis to be available at $825 to purchasers who might want to add their own automotive touring coachwork. "Work has already started on the Angelus roadster," president Fallis told a *Motor West* reporter that August, "and a number of these cars will be ready for delivery in a short time. It is in every way a real automobile and not a cycle car." California registration lists of the period, however, indicate thirteen Mission trucks and just one automobile, a touring car. The Mission's factory was at 1310-12 South Grand Avenue in Los Angeles. The venture failed within a year.

MISSION — Los Angeles, California — (1921, 1923) — The West Coast Automobile Manufacturing Company was organized in Los Angeles during the summer of 1921 for the production of passenger cars, trucks, tractors and trailers. The firm elected to bring out its car first, under the trade-name of Mission. Theodore F. Ruhland was the West Coast president, Hargreaves Thompson the sales manager and Alexander N. Roberts the secretary-treasurer. Serving as vice president, general manager and designing engineer was W. Augustus King whose patents would be used for the "design of the car above the frame." Below the frame the Mission would be a typical assembled car of the period, offered either as a six (Continental engine) or straight-eight. The West Coast company's capital stock was $1.5 million, most of which must have remained on paper. There is no evidence of this venture reaching the manufacturing stage. Indeed, in 1923 in Los Angeles, there was another venture ongoing to also produce a car called the Mission. George A. Troutt, who said he had helped Ransom Olds install machinery at Olds Motor Works in 1896, was behind this one. Troutt's Mission was to be a $2000 car built by the Mission Motors Company that he was organizing. His Mission does not seem to have been accomplished either.

MISSISSIPPI — The Mississippi Valley Automobile Transportation Company of East St. Louis, Missouri was listed as an automobile manufacturer in the Hiscox book *Horseless Vehicles, Automobiles, Motor Cycles* published in 1900. Documentation is lacking.

MISSOURI — The Missouri Motor Car Company has been indicated on various car rosters as producing the Missouri in St. Louis in 1913. There is no evidence of such a firm in the automobile field in St. Louis at that time.

1903 Mitchell, model IV, runabout, HAC

MITCHELL — Racine, Wisconsin — (1903-1923) — William Turnor Lewis was a native of Utica, New York who served as a telegrapher during the Civil War and who joined the wagon works of Henry Mitchell in Racine when peace came. He married the boss' daughter and eventually came into control of the Mitchell & Lewis Wagon Company, which by the 1890's spun off the bicycle manufactory known as Wisconsin Wheel Works. By 1901 the latter firm was producing the Mitchell motorcycle which was equipped with a 1-3/4 hp gasoline engine and which, according to a Lewis descendant, was not a success because it was so slow any able-bodied bicyclist could pass it. Wisconsin Wheel Works would enjoy considerably more renown with its automobile. Although some experimental models preceded, production of the new Mitchell was not begun until 1903; in February of 1904 the Mitchell Motor Car Company succeeded Wisconsin Wheel Works. The bicycle business was disposed of to an Indiana concern in 1903; the wagon business would remain until mid-1917 when it was sold to Deere & Company of Moline, Illinois. The first Mitchells were chain-drive runabouts powered by water-cooled two-cylinder engines, a four-stroke 4 hp with left-hand tiller steering, a two-stroke 7 hp with right-hand wheel steer, and both with a two-speed planetary transmission. The cars were designed by John W. Bates, a Chicago engineer whose experimentation in automobiles had begun prior to the turn of the century. Nineteen four brought air-cooling and the addition of a four-cylinder touring model, both the twins and fours fitted with three-speed sliding gear transmissions. In 1905 Mitchells were offered with a choice of air- or water-cooling. By 1907 fours only were produced, with shaft drive on all models, all engines water-cooled. In 1910, upon the retirement of William T. Lewis, the Mitchell Car Company and the Mitchell & Lewis Company (now a prominent manufacturer of farm machinery in addition to wagons) merged as the Mitchell-Lewis Motor Company, with Lewis' son William Mitchell Lewis taking over as president. The 1910 line of Mitchells included two fours and the company's first six, all models with cylinders cast in pairs, a three-bearing crankshaft on the fours, a five-bearing on the six. Mitchell production through the years had risen handsomely: 82 cars in 1904, 315 in 1905, 666 in 1906, 1377 in 1907, 2166 in 1908, 2946 in 1909, 5614 in 1910. In 1912 the company broke the 6000 unit mark. In addition, the company had a short fling (1905-1908) with a small production of trucks and buses. Mitchell took particular pride in the fact that virtually all of the components in its car were made in Racine, and the company enjoyed a reputation as a quality builder of medium-priced cars. Apparently some structural problems arose in the Mitchells introduced in 1910, however, for French engineer Rene Petard was imported to design a new series of T-head engines which were introduced for the 1913 model year. And apparently, too, some financial problems had arisen as well because in 1913 William Mitchell Lewis retired from the company and, with Rene Petard, began another one across town in Racine for production of a new car called the Lewis. Succeeding him as president was Joseph Winterbottom,

1904 Mitchell, model B-2, runabout, HAC

Jr., who represented the banking interests which had financed Mitchell for the two years previous. The firm was reorganized as Mitchell Motors Company, Inc. In 1916 Mitchell sales manager Otis Friend took over the presidency of the company, though he was short term too, resigning by January of 1918 and subsequently building a car of his own called the Friend in Pontiac, Michigan. A General Electric executive named D.C. Durland now took over Mitchell. Meanwhile, for the 1916 model year, the four-cylinder Mitchell was dropped, and a V-8 was built that year, as well as the six, which the advertising department designated the "Six of '16." From 1917 to the end, only sixes were produced. With the first roar of the Twenties, alas, Mitchell made a real blooper. Purportedly, there were warring factions in the design department at the time, and the wrong faction won. The Mitchell introduced in 1920 had a sloping radiator configuration which gave rise to the epithet of "drunken Mitchell." This styling faux pas was immediately corrected with a vertical radiator the year following, and in 1922 a million-mile test was put up by 109 Mitchell "White Streaks" which resulted in some good publicity, but not enough to counter the losses incurred with the Mitchell which looked inebriated. Output had plummeted from 6400 cars in 1920 to less than 2500 in both 1920 and 1921. The company's best production years had been 1917 and 1919 (10,000 cars each), the company's last production year was 1923 when a mere 100 cars left the factory. Mitchell's schedule in bankruptcy, filed in June 1923, revealed assets of $3.7 million and liabilities of $3.9 million. Finished and unfinished automobiles, and raw materials, represented the company's largest asset ($1.6 million). Disposing of them took about a year. "Factories of the old Mitchell Motor Company are now entirely dismantled," *Automobile Topics* reported in January 1924, "and consequently there passes from the industry a name that was once familiar to everyone, and a concern that in the early days was a real factor in the business." The month following the Mitchell factory was sold to Nash. It would next be used for the building of the Ajax.

1903 MITCHELL
Model VI — 1-cyl., 4 hp

	FP	5	4	3	2	1
Runabout	600	2000	3000	4200	6500	14,000

Model IV — 1-cyl., 7 hp

Runabout	—	2200	3200	4400	7000	15,000

1904 MITCHELL
Model B-2 — 2-cyl., 7 hp, 72" wb

Runabout-2P	750	2200	3200	4400	7000	15,000

Model B-4 — 4-cyl., 16 hp, 90" wb

Touring-5P	1500	2400	3400	4800	8000	17,000

1905 Mitchell, model B-2, runabout, HAC

1905 MITCHELL
Model B-2 — 2-cyl., 7 hp, 76" wb

Runabout-2P	750	2400	3400	4800	8000	17,000

Model B-4 — 4-cyl., 18/20 hp, 90" wb

Light Tour.-5P	1500	2700	3600	5300	8800	19,000

1906 Mitchell, model B-4, touring, HAC

1906 MITCHELL
Model B-2 — 2-cyl., 9/10 hp, 76" wb

	FP	5	4	3	2	1
Runabout-2P	750	2000	3000	4200	6500	14,000
Model C-4 — 4-cyl., 14/18 hp, 86" wb						
Runabout-2P	1000	2300	3300	4600	7500	16,000
Model B-4 — 4-cyl., 18/20 hp, 90" wb						
Touring-5P	1500	2400	3400	4800	8000	17,000
Model D-4 — 4-cyl., 24/30 hpm 100" wb						
Touring-5P	1800	3300	4400	6700	12,000	24,000

1907 Mitchell, model F, touring, HAC

1907 MITCHELL
Model E — 4-cyl., 20 hp, 90" wb

Runabout-2P	1000	2300	3300	4600	7500	16,000
Model D — 4-cyl., 24/30 hp, 100" wb						
Touring-5P	1800	2400	3400	4800	8000	17,000
Model F — 4-cyl., 35 hp, 108" wb						
Touring-5P	2000	3300	4400	6700	12,000	24,000

1908 Mitchell, model G, runabout, HAC

1908 MITCHELL
Model H — 4-cyl., 20 hp, 92" wb

	FP	5	4	3	2	1
Runabout	1000	2400	3400	4800	8000	17,000
Model G — 4-cyl., 20 hp, 92" wb						
Runabout	1250	2500	3500	5000	8500	18,000
Model I — 4-cyl., 35 hp, 112" wb						
Touring	2000	3300	4400	6700	12,000	24,000

1909 Mitchell, model K, touring, HAC

1909 MITCHELL
Model J — 4-cyl., 20 hp, 92" wb

Runabout-2P	1000	2400	3400	4800	8000	17,000
Model K — 4-cyl., 30 hp, 105" wb						
Touring-5P	1500	2700	3600	5300	8800	19,000
Model L — 4-cyl., 40 hp, 117" wb						
Touring-7P	2000	3500	4500	7000	13,000	25,000
Limousine-5P	2500	2500	3500	5000	8500	18,000

1910 Mitchell, model T, touring, JB

1910 MITCHELL
Model R — 4-cyl., 30 hp, 100" wb

Runabout-2P	1100	2700	3600	5300	8800	19,000
Runabout-3P	1100	2800	3700	5500	9000	19,500
Rbt. Surrey	1100	2900	3700	5600	9100	20,000
Model T — 4-cyl., 30 hp, 112" wb						
Touring-4/5P	1350	3300	4400	6700	12,000	24,000
Model S — 6-cyl., 50 hp, 130" wb						
Touring-5/7P	2000	6400	9300	14,500	33,000	45,000

1911 Mitchell, model T, touring, HAC

1911 MITCHELL
Model R — 4-cyl., 30 hp, 100" wb

Runabout-2P	1200	2700	3600	5300	8800	19,000
Runabout-3P	1200	2800	3700	5500	9000	19,500
Rbt. Surrey	1250	2900	3700	5600	9100	20,000
Model T — 4-cyl., 30 hp, 112" wb						
Touring-4/5P	1500	3300	4400	6700	12,000	24,000
Model S — 6-cyl., 50 hp, 130" wb						
Touring-5/7P	2250	6400	9300	14,500	33,000	45,000

1912 Mitchell, model 5-4, limousine, HAC

1912 MITCHELL
Model 2-4 — 4-cyl., 25 hp, 100" wb

	FP	5	4	3	2	1
Roadster-2P	950	2900	3700	5600	9100	20,000

Model 4-4 — 4-cyl., 25 hp, 100" wb

Touring-4P	1150	3200	4300	6500	11,000	23,000

Model 5-4 — 4-cyl., 30 hp, 112" wb

Touring-5P	1350	3500	4500	7000	13,000	25,000
Limousine	2500	2500	3500	5000	8500	18,000

Model 5-6 Baby Six — 34 hp, 125" wb

Touring-5P	1750	3900	4800	7700	14,300	27,000
Roadster	1750	4000	5000	8000	15,000	28,000

Model 7-6 — 6-cyl., 48 hp, 135" wb

Touring-7P	2250	6700	9900	15,500	34,800	47,000

1913 Mitchell Big Six, touring, HAC

1913 MITCHELL
Model 5-4 — 4-cyl., 30 hp, 120" wb

Touring-5P	1500	3700	4700	7300	13,700	26,000
Roadster-2P	1500	3900	4800	7700	14,300	27,000

Model 5-6 — 6-cyl., 38.4 hp, 132" wb

Touring-5P	1850	3900	4800	7700	14,300	27,000
Roadster-2P	1850	4000	5000	8000	15,000	28,000

Model 7-6 — 6-cyl., 43.8 hp, 144" wb

Touring-7P	2500	7200	11,300	17,700	38,700	50,000

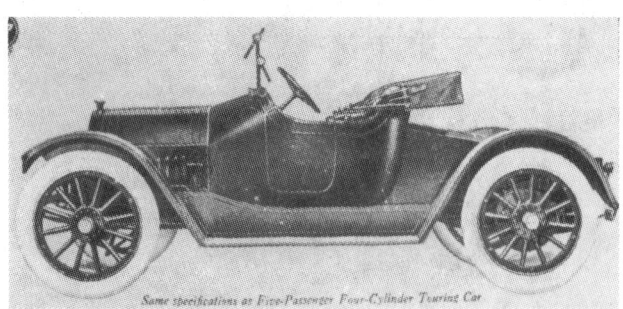

1914 Mitchell Four, roadster, HAC

1914 MITCHELL
Four — 4-cyl., 28.9 hp, 120" wb

Touring-5P	1595	4200	5200	8400	15,700	29,000
Touring-4P	1595	4000	5000	8000	15,000	28,000
Touring-7P	1695	4300	5400	8700	16,500	30,000
Roadster-2P	1595	4400	5600	9200	17,300	31,000

Little Six — 6-cyl., 43.8 hp, 132" wb

Touring-5P	1895	5000	6500	11,000	22,000	35,000
Touring-4P	1895	4900	6300	10,300	21,000	34,000
Touring-7P	1995	5800	8000	12,500	28,000	40,000
Roadster-2P	1895	5900	8300	12,800	29,000	41,000

Big Six — 6-cyl., 43.8 hp, 144" wb

Touring-7P	2350	7200	11,300	17,700	38,700	50,000

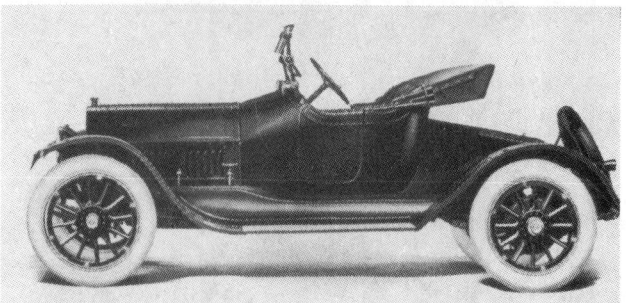

1915 Mitchell Special Six, roadster, HAC

1915 MITCHELL
Light Four — 26 hp, 116" wb

	FP	5	4	3	2	1
Touring-5P	1250	6400	9300	14,500	33,000	45,000
Touring-6P	1300	6700	9900	15,500	34,800	47,000
Roadster-2P	1250	6500	9500	15,000	34,000	46,000

Light Six — 38.4 hp, 128" wb

Touring-5P	1585	6500	9500	15,000	34,000	46,000
Touring-6P	1585	6800	10,300	16,000	35,500	48,000
Roadster-2P	1585	6700	9900	15,500	34,800	47,000

Special Six — 43.3 hp, 132" wb

Touring-5P	1895	7300	11,800	18,400	40,400	52,000
Touring-6P	1995	7500	12,300	19,100	41,700	54,000
Roadster-2P	1895	7400	12,100	18,800	41,100	53,000

Deluxe Six — 43.3 hp, 144" wb

Touring-7P	2350	7600	12,500	19,400	42,200	55,000

1916 Mitchell Eight, touring, HAC

1916 MITCHELL
The Six of '16 — 29.4 hp, 125" wb

Touring-5P	1250	6400	9300	14,500	33,000	45,000
Touring-7P	1285	6700	9900	15,500	34,800	47,000
Roadster-3P	1250	6500	9500	15,000	34,000	46,000

Eight — 29 hp, 125" wb

Touring-5P	1450	6700	9900	15,500	34,800	47,000
Touring-7P	1450	6800	10,300	16,000	35,500	48,000
Roadster-3P	1450	6700	9900	15,500	34,800	47,000

1917 Mitchell Junior, coupe, HAC

1917 MITCHELL
Model D-40 Junior — 6-cyl., 25.35 hp, 120" wb

Touring-5P	1150	6400	9300	14,500	33,000	45,000
Roadster-2P	1150	6300	9000	14,000	32,000	44,000

Model C-42 — 6-cyl., 29.4 hp, 127" wb

Touring-7P	1460	6700	9900	15,500	34,800	47,000
Touring-5P	1425	6500	9500	15,000	34,000	46,000
Cabriolet-4P	1895	6200	8800	13,500	31,000	43,000
Coupe-4P	1995	4000	5000	8000	15,000	28,000
Sedan-7P	2175	3100	4200	6300	10,500	22,000
Limousine-7P	2785	4200	5200	8400	15,700	29,000

1918 Mitchell, model C-7-42, seven passenger touring, HAC

1918 MITCHELL
Model D-5-40 — 6-cyl., 25.35 hp, 120" wb

	FP	5	4	3	2	1
Touring-5P	1250	6400	9300	14,500	33,000	45,000
Roadster-2P	1250	6300	9000	14,000	32,000	44,000
Tr.-5P (Demountable Top)	1550	6700	9900	15,500	34,800	47,000
Club Rdstr.-5P	1280	6500	9500	15,000	34,000	46,000
Coupe-3P	1850	3100	4200	6300	10,500	22,000
Tour. Sed.-5P	1950	2300	3300	4600	7500	16,000

Model C-7-42 — 6-cyl., 29.4 hp, 127" wb

	FP	5	4	3	2	1
Touring-7P	1525	7000	10,800	16,900	37,100	49,000
Speedster-4P	1660	7300	11,800	18,400	40,400	52,000
Roadster-3P	1490	7200	11,300	17,700	38,700	50,000
Club Rdstr.-5P	1560	7300	11,600	18,100	39,600	51,000
Touring-5P	1510	7200	11,300	17,700	38,700	50,000
Tour.-7P (Demountable Top)	1825	7300	11,800	18,400	40,400	52,000
Cabriolet-4P	1960	6800	10,300	16,000	35,500	48,000
Coupe-4P	2135	3300	4400	6700	12,000	24,000
Club Sed.-5P	2185	3200	4300	6500	11,000	23,000
Tour. Sed.-7P	2275	3500	4500	7000	13,000	25,000
Limousine-7P	2850	4000	5000	8000	15,000	28,000
Town Car-7P	2850	4200	5200	8400	15,700	29,000

1919 Mitchell, model C-7-42, sedan, HAC

1919 MITCHELL
Model D-5-40 — 6-cyl., 25.35 hp, 120" wb

	FP	5	4	3	2	1
Touring-5P	1275	4300	5400	8700	16,500	30,000
Roadster-3P	1275	4200	5200	8400	15,700	29,000
Coupe-3P	1950	3100	4200	6300	10,500	22,000

Model C-7-42 — 6-cyl., 29.4 hp, 127" wb

	FP	5	4	3	2	1
Touring-7P	1525	5200	6800	11,300	23,000	36,000
Club Rdstr.-5P	1525	4900	6300	10,300	21,000	34,000
Touring-5P	1675	5000	6500	11,000	22,000	35,000
Surrey-4P	1550	4300	5400	8700	16,500	30,000
Cabriolet-4P	1960	4500	5800	9500	18,000	32,000
Coupe-4P	2135	3500	4500	7000	13,000	25,000
Tour. Sed.-7P	2275	3200	4300	6500	11,000	23,000
Sed. DeL.-7P	2425	3300	4400	6700	12,000	24,000
Limousine-7P	2850	3900	4800	7700	14,300	27,000
Town Car-7P	2850	4200	5200	8400	15,700	29,000

1920 Mitchell, model E-40, coupe, HAC

1920 MITCHELL
Model E-40 — 6-cyl., 40 hp, 120" wb

	FP	5	4	3	2	1
Roadster-3P	1690	4500	5800	9500	18,000	32,000
Touring-5P	1690	4400	5600	9200	17,300	31,000
Touring-7P	1875	4700	6100	9900	19,000	33,000
Sedan-5P	2600	2000	3000	4200	6500	14,000
Coupe-4P	2600	2300	3300	4600	7500	16,000

1921 Mitchell, model F-40, sedan, HAC

1921 MITCHELL
Model F-40 — 6-cyl., 40 hp, 120" wb

	FP	5	4	3	2	1
Touring-5P	1750	4400	5600	9200	17,300	31,000
Roadster-3P	1750	4500	5800	9500	18,000	32,000
Coupe-4P	2800	2300	3300	4600	7500	16,000
Sedan-5P	2900	2000	3000	4200	6500	14,000

Model F-42 — 6-cyl., 48 hp, 127" wb

	FP	5	4	3	2	1
Touring-7P	—	5000	6500	11,000	22,000	35,000
Special-4P	—	4900	6300	10,300	21,000	34,000

1922 MITCHELL
Model F-50 — 6-cyl., 50 hp, 120" wb

	FP	5	4	3	2	1
Touring-5P	1490	4400	5600	9200	17,300	31,000
Roadster-3P	1490	4500	5800	9500	18,000	32,000
Sport-4P	1790	4700	6100	9900	19,000	33,000
Coupe-4P	2290	2300	3300	4600	7500	16,000
Sedan-5P	2440	2000	3000	4200	6500	14,000
Tour.-7P (12" wb)	1795	5200	6800	11,300	23,000	36,000

1923 Mitchell, model F-50, phaeton deluxe, HAC

1923 MITCHELL
Model F-50 — 6-cyl., 50 hp, 120" wb

	FP	5	4	3	2	1
Stnd. Phae.-5P	1590	4300	5400	8700	16,500	30,000
DeL. Rdstr.-3P	1750	4700	6100	9900	19,000	33,000
DeL. Phae.-5P	1790	4500	5800	9500	18,000	32,000
Stnd. Phae.-7P	1790	4400	5600	9200	17,300	31,000
DeL. Sport-4P	1850	4500	5800	9500	18,000	32,000
DeL. Phae.-7P	1990	5000	6500	11,000	22,000	35,000

MITCHELL — Chicago, Illinois — (1914) — The Mitchell Automobile Company was located at 2334 South Michigan Avenue in Chicago. H.L. Hall was president, A.C. Bieghler was secretary. Mitchell operated as a dealership, though briefly in 1914 the firm considered entering the ranks of cyclecar producers. The Stephens Engineering Company of Chicago is known to have built a cyclecar prototype that year for an undisclosed client. Conceivably, it may have been Mitchell. Manufacture did not follow, however.

MITCHELL — Topeka, Kansas — (1916) — There was only one Mitchell produced in Topeka, and its designer was the precocious fourteen-year-old son of Mr. and Mrs. Frank Mitchell of 1607 Western Avenue. The car built by young Donald Mitchell was a buckboard affair with large bicycle wheels which he fashioned of parts purloined from derelict vehicles. Whether the boy ever built another car is not known.

M.J.G. — The M.J.G. was a projected new model for 1910 of the Allen-Kingston produced in Kingston, New York from 1907 to 1910. Refer to Allen-Kingston.

M.M.C. — The Manlius Motor Company of Manlius, New York produced both two- and four-cylinder automobiles in 1910. Although occasionally the car was referred to by the company initials, more often it was designated the Manlius. Refer to Manlius.

M & L — **West Hampton, New York** — **(1911)** — The initials represented William B. Monger and G.H. Liedtke whose ambition it was to build cars and trucks in the Hamptons on Long Island. Already they had a garage at West Hampton Beach, which they planned to enlarge for manufacture. An 18 hp five-passenger touring car as well as a light delivery for $700 was the projected M & L line, but prototypes only followed — and very soon Monger and Liedtke had returned full-time to their garage business.

MOAKLER — The Moakler Automobile Company of Washington, D.C. was organized during the spring of 1903 with a $300,000 capital stock for the purpose of manufacturing automobiles. Incorporators were John W. Moakler, Alfred Gould, John McClintock, William B. Dashiel and John J. Nelligan. Manufacture is doubted. Among those who purchased stock in the venture was Harold S. Vanderbilt.

1900 Mobile Steamer, runabout, JC

MOBILE STEAM — **Tarrytown, New York** — **(1900-1903)** — Although it was John Brisben Walker who negotiated the sale, it was Amzi Lorenzo Barber who ended up with the company. Walker was the editor and publisher of *Cosmopolitan* magazine, an automobile enthusiast, and the sponsor of the Cosmopolitan Race of 1896. In April 1899 he talked the Stanley twins who had begun production of their steamer in the Boston suburb of Watertown into selling out their entire business for $250,000, and then began a search for financial backing. He found all he needed in one man, Barber, the captain of the American asphalt industry, who after a spin in the Stanley agreed to invest $250,000 for a half-interest in the new venture. In June 1899 the two partners incorporated as the Automobile Company of America, quickly discovered there had been a previous incorporation under that name, reincorporated as the Locomobile Company of America, and then almost immediately quarreled over a matter the nature of which has never been made clear. The partnership broke up, and the separation agreement was indisputably in Barber's favor. In addition to the

1901 Mobile Steamer, victoria runabout, NAHC

rights to produce the Stanley, he acquired the Watertown factory, the name Locomobile, and most of the steamers already under construction. Walker received only the rights to produce the Stanley, with an undeveloped piece of land in Tarrytown on which to produce it. During the summer of 1899 he organized as the Mobile Company of America and called in New York architect Stanford White to design a factory for him. While it was being built, Barber of course got a splendid head start with his Locomobile. All previous and current orders for Stanley steam vehicles were turned over to him to be produced and marketed as Locomobiles. The first Mobile didn't arrive until March 1900. The partners had become competitors, and Barber had essentially won the competition before it started. Walker did offer a good many more body styles, but Barber sold more cars. By the end of 1903 Walker had produced 600 Mobiles, Barber 5000 Locomobiles. John Brisben Walker gave up. In May 1904 he sold his Mobile plant in Tarrytown to Maxwell-Briscoe. There had been a couple of notable high spots in the short Mobile history, however. Around 1903, Virginia Earle, starring in *The Belle of Bohemia* on Broadway, sang one of the earliest American motoring songs, "My Mobile Gal." And three years earlier one Frank Lambkin had driven his Mobile from Tarrytown to Chicago "without breakage, interruption, or perceptible wear and tear of any kind." After putting 4000 miles on the car, he then sold it for the full price of a new Mobile. This must establish Lambkin as America's number one used-car salesman of the period.

1902 Mobile, model no. 4, runabout, HAC

1900-1903 MOBILE

	FP	5	4	3	2	1
Model 22 Steam Wagonette	2000	2000	3000	4200	6500	14,000
Model 9 Dos-a-Dos	1100	1600	2700	3800	5800	12,000
Model 8 Dos-a-Dos	1100	1600	2700	3800	5800	12,000
Model 7 Victoria Runabout	1000	1800	2800	4000	6200	13,000
Model 13 Touring Wagon	—	2000	3000	4200	6500	14,000
Model 10 Surrey	1325	2100	3100	4300	6800	14,500
Model 16 Light Delivery	1350	1500	2500	3600	5500	11,000
Special Runabout	550	1600	2700	3800	5800	12,000
Model 42 Merchant's Dly.	2000	1550	2600	3700	5700	11,500
Model 23 Touring-6P	1800	2000	3000	4200	6500	14,000
Model 50 Coupe-9P	3000	2200	3200	4400	7000	15,000
Model 31 Sold Top Rapid Transit Wagonette	2150	1800	2800	4000	6200	13,000
Model 30 Canopy Top Rapid Transit Wagonette	2150	2000	3000	4200	6500	14,000
Model 11 Std. Dos-a-Dos	1000	1600	2700	3800	5800	12,000
Model 20 Light Surrey	1275	1500	2500	3600	5500	11,000
Model 22 Extension Top Surrey	1800	1550	2600	3700	5700	11,500
Model 36 Rapid Transit Omnibus	3000	2000	3000	4200	6500	14,000
Model 40 Light Delivery	1085	1600	2700	3800	5800	12,000
Model 46 Heavy Truck	3000	2200	3200	4400	7000	15,000
Model 41 Heavy Delivery	1800	1600	2700	3800	5800	12,000
Model 12 Victoria Stanhope	1400	1600	2700	3800	5800	12,000
Model 7 Std. Rbt. Victoria	825	1500	2500	3600	5500	11,000
Model 3 Spindle Seat Rbt.	725	1400	2400	3500	5300	10,000
Model 4 Solid Seat Rbt.	750	1400	2400	3500	5300	10,000
Model 5 Buggy Top Rbt.	800	1450	2450	3600	5400	10,500
Model 6 Goddard Top Rbt.	825	1450	2450	3600	5400	10,500

MODEL — A steamer called the Model has been indicated on various car rosters as having been built in 1902 by the Steam Vehicle Company of America in New York City. The firm was indicated in a trade directory that year as a manufacturer, but obviously in error. Steam Vehicle Company of America advertisements in 1902 pictured a Reading steamer, for which the firm was the New York dealer.

The Model Automobile and Garage Company was organized in Belleville, Illinois late in 1908 with a capital stock of $2000 to manufacture automobiles and accessories and to operate a garage. I.H. Wangelin, Joseph Schwarz and E.L. Schwarz were the incorporators. Manufacture of a car is doubted.

The Model Motor Company of Los Angeles, California advertised itself as an automobile manufacturer in 1915. Guy L. Kennedy was Model's president, Nelson G. Douglas its vice-president. Documentation of manufacture is lacking.

1904 Moline, touring, HAC

and portable gasoline engines. Four years later Root and Vandervoort incorporated the Moline Automobile Company and proceeded into manufacture of medium-sized two- and four-cylinder cars. Rather like Walter Chrysler, whose claim to world's tallest skyscraper honors with his Chrysler Building would be quickly overshadowed by the Empire State, the Moline brochure headline late in 1911 that announced its new 4-1/8th by 6-inch 40 hp four as "The Longest Stroke Motor Made in America" was soon obsolete with the announcement of the even longer-stroke engine of the Metropol from Port Jefferson, New York. Though the wind was taken from its sales, the Moline was a sturdy machine, "The Car of Unfailing Service," as the slogan said, which won the Chicago Reliability run and other endurance contests with regularity. As a result the cars were proudly referred to as Dreadnought Molines. In 1914 Vandervoort became the president of the Society of Automotive Engineers, succeeding Henry Martyn Leland. That year, too, the Moline's battleship emblem was replaced by a medallion featuring Sir Galahad, "the most perfect of King Arthur's Knights." This served less-than-subtle notice that the Moline people believed their new four-cylinder sleeve-valve-engined car was superior to any other Knight in America. The Moline version was the only sleeve-valve with cylinders cast en bloc, and the only one to feature thermo-syphon cooling. At $2400 it was at the time the lowest-priced Knight-engined motorcar on the market. Sales proved to be very fine; from a peak pre-Knight output of 782 cars in 1912, Moline-Knight production began averaging 1000 cars a year by 1915. In 1920 the Moline-Knight was continued in production under the new marque name of R&V Knight.

1904 MOLINE
Two — 12 hp, 74" wb

	FP	5	4	3	2	1
Touring Runabout	1000	2000	3000	4200	6500	14,000

1905 Moline, touring, HAC

1906 Moline, touring, WLB

1905 MOLINE
Model D — 2-cyl., 12 hp, 86" wb

	FP	5	4	3	2	1
Surrey	1000	2000	3000	4200	6500	14,000
Model B — 4-cyl., 18/20 hp, 105" wb						
Surrey	1600	2200	3200	4400	7000	15,000

1906 MOLINE
Model G — 2-cyl., 16 hp, 86" wb

	FP	5	4	3	2	1
Touring	1000	2100	3100	4300	6800	14,500
Model C — 4-cyl., 18/20 hp, 100" wb						
Touring	1750	2300	3300	4600	7500	16,000
Model A — 4-cyl., 30/35 hp, 110" wb						
Touring	2500	2500	3500	5000	8500	18,000

1907 Moline, model A, touring, HAC

1907 MOLINE
Model H — 2-cyl., 18 hp, 92" wb

	FP	5	4	3	2	1
Touring-5P	1250	2200	3200	4400	7000	15,000
Model C — 4-cyl., 20 hp, 100" wb						
Runabout-2/3P	1800	2400	3400	4800	8000	17,000
Model S — 4-cyl., 25 hp, 110" wb						
Touring-5P	2000	2700	3600	5300	8800	19,000
Model A — 4-cyl., 35 hp, 110" wb						
Touring-5P	2500	3000	4000	6000	9500	21,000

1908 Moline, model S, touring, HAC

1908 MOLINE
Model H — 2-cyl., 20 hp, 96" wb

	FP	5	4	3	2	1
Touring	1250	2200	3200	4400	7000	15,000
Model S — 4-cyl., 24 hp, 100" wb						
Touring-5P	2000	2400	3400	4800	8000	17,000
Model A — 4-cyl., 35 hp, 110" wb						
Touring-5P	2500	2700	3600	5300	8800	19,000

1909 Moline, model K, touring, HAC

945

1909 MOLINE
Model M — 4-cyl., 25/30 hp, 105" wb

	FP	5	4	3	2	1
Touring-5P	1500	2400	3400	4800	8000	17,000

Model K — 4-cyl., 40 hp, 116" wb

	FP	5	4	3	2	1
Touring-7P	2500	2700	3600	5300	8800	19,000
Baby Tonneau-4/5P	2500	2500	3500	5000	8500	18,000

1910 Moline, model M, touring, HAC

1910 MOLINE
Model M — 4-cyl., 30 hp, 110" wb

Roadster	1500	2400	3400	4800	8000	17,000
Toy Tonneau	1500	2500	3500	5000	8500	18,000
Touring	1500	2500	3500	5000	8500	18,000

Model K — 4-cyl., 40 hp, 116" wb

Toy Tonneau	2500	2700	3600	5300	8800	19,000
Touring	2500	2900	3700	5600	9100	20,000

1911 Moline, model M-35, toy tonneau, HAC

1911 MOLINE/MOLINE-KNIGHT
Model M-35 — 4-cyl., 35 hp, 112" wb

Touring	1650	3000	4000	6000	9500	21,000
Fore-Door Touring	1700	2900	3700	5600	9100	20,000
Toy Tonneau	1600	2900	3700	5600	9100	20,000

1912 Moline, model M-35, Dreadnought roadster, HAC

1912 MOLINE
Model M-35 — 4-cyl., 35 hp, 114" wb

Dreadnought Touring-5P	1700	3000	4000	6000	9500	21,000
Dreadnought Touring-4P	1700	2900	3700	5600	9100	20,000
Dreadnought Torpedo-2P	1700	2900	3700	5600	9100	20,000
Dreadnought Roadster-4P	1600	2700	3600	5300	8800	19,000

1913 Moline, model M-40, Dreadnought, touring, HAC

1913 MOLINE
Model M-40 — 4-cyl., 40 hp

	FP	5	4	3	2	1
Dreadnought Rds.-2P (114" wb)	1950	2900	3700	5600	9100	20,000
Dreadnought Tour.-5P (124" wb)	1950	3100	4200	6300	10,500	22,000

1914 Moline-Knight, touring, HAC

1914 MOLINE-KNIGHT
Model M-40 — 4-cyl., 40 hp, 124" wb

Touring-5P	1950	3500	4500	7000	13,000	25,000

Knight — 4-cyl., 50 hp, 128" wb

Touring-5P	2400	4000	5000	8000	15,000	28,000

1915 Moline-Knight, roadster, HAC

1915 MOLINE-KNIGHT
Knight — 4-cyl., 50 hp, 128" wb

Roadster-2P	2500	3700	4700	7300	13,700	26,000
Touring-5P	2500	4000	5000	8000	15,000	28,000
Limousine	3800	3300	4400	6700	12,000	24,000
Sedan	3250	2400	3400	4800	8000	17,000

1916 Moline-Knight, 40, roadster, WLB

1916 MOLINE-KNIGHT
Knight. Model 40 — 4-cyl., 40 hp, 118" wb

	FP	5	4	3	2	1
Touring-7P	1450	3100	4200	6300	10,500	22,000
Roadster-2P	1450	3000	4000	6000	9500	21,000

Knight, Model 50 — 4-cyl., 50 hp, 128" wb

Touring-7P	2500	4000	5000	8000	15,000	28,000
Roadster	2500	3700	4700	7300	13,700	26,000
Limousine	3800	3300	4400	6700	12,000	24,000
Sedan	3250	2400	3400	4800	8000	17,000

1917 Moline-Knight, model-50, touring, HAC

1917 MOLINE-KNIGHT
Knight, Model 40 — 4-cyl., 40 hp, 118" wb

	FP	5	4	3	2	1
Touring-5P	1450	3100	4200	6300	10,500	22,000
Roadster-4P	1450	3000	4000	6000	9500	21,000

Knight, Model 50 — 4-cyl., 50 hp, 122" wb

Touring-7P	1840	3700	4700	7300	13,700	26,000
Roadster-4P	1840	3500	4500	7000	13,000	25,000
Touring Sedan	2350	2300	3300	4600	7500	16,000
Coupe-4P	2400	2500	3500	5000	8500	18,000

1918 Moline-Knight, model C, touring, HAC

1918 MOLINE-KNIGHT
Knight, Model C — 4-cyl., 40 hp, 118" wb

Touring-5P	1650	3700	4700	7300	13,700	26,000
Roadster-4P	1650	3500	4500	7000	13,000	25,000
Touring Sedan-5P	2280	2000	3000	4200	6500	14,000

Knight, Model G — 4-cyl., 50 hp, 122" wb

Touring-7P	2250	4000	5000	8000	15,000	28,000
Roadster-4P	2250	3900	4800	7700	14,300	27,000
Coupe-4P	2490	2500	3500	5000	8500	18,000

1919 MOLINE-KNIGHT
Knight, Model L — 4-cyl., 40 hp, 118" wb

Touring-5P	2000	3900	4800	7700	14,300	27,000
Sedan-5P	2500	2000	3000	4200	6500	14,000
Roadster-4P	2000	3700	4700	7300	13,700	26,000
Touring Standard-7P	2250	4000	5000	8000	15,000	28,000
Touring Deluxe-7P	2500	4200	5200	8400	15,700	29,000
Roadster Standard-4P	2250	3900	4800	7700	14,300	27,000
Roadster Deluxe-4P	2500	4000	5000	8000	15,000	28,000

MOLLENHOUR — A.T. Mollenhour of Mentone, Indiana was indicated as an automobile manufacturer in the "Buyer's Guide" section of *Cycle and Automobile Trade Journal*'s January 1908 issue. Documentation is lacking.

MOLLER — Lewistown, Pennsylvania — (1920-1922) — Prior to emigrating to the United States, Wilhelm and Holgar Moller had experimented in the light car field in their native Denmark, although production never resulted. Arriving in America and settling in Lewistown, the Mollers had launched themselves into the motor accessory business by 1909. In early 1920 they secured sufficient backing to establish the Moller Motor Company and to open an automobile factory in town. The Moller was a perky little four-cylinder roadster very much in the European light car idiom. It was on a 100-inch wheelbase, weighed 1000 pounds and was priced in the $1000 range. The car was announced to the trade press in January 1920 and was marketed locally that year. National exposure for the Moller arrived the following January when the car was introduced at the 1921 New York Automobile Show. By now the price had risen to a hefty $1500, for the chassis alone. Apparently, the Mollers considered the export mar-

1920 Moller, roadster, WLB

ket to be the most viable one for their car. Although a firm called H.P.M. Motors, Inc. represented the Moller domestically, Associated Motors Corporation, which handled the foreign business for a number of American manufacturers, was contracted to handle the Moller export trade. Neither domestic nor foreign sales kept the Mollers in business long. Interesting, and unwittingly, the Moller brothers were responsible for providing a good deal of confusion to automotive historians. First, they introduced a gussied-up Moller called the Falcon late in 1921 just about the same time as Halladay introduced its new car with that same name. And, just prior to going out of business, the brothers moved their operation to Hagerstown, Maryland, the town in which another fellow named Moller was producing a car called the Dagmar.

1920 MOLLER
Four — 20 hp, 100" wb

	FP	5	4	3	2	1
Sport-2P	1100	2200	3200	4400	7000	15,000
Roadster-4P	1150	2300	3300	4600	7500	16,000

1921-1922 MOLLER
Four — 20 hp, 100" wb

Roadster-2P	2000	2300	3300	4600	7500	16,000

MONARCH — The Monarch Metal Company was organized in Chicago, Illinois early in 1905 to manufacture and repair automobiles. Capital stock was $2500. Incorporators were Godfrey Johnson, Charles C. Stilwell and C.C. Bowersock. Manufacture is doubted.

The Monarch Motor Company was organized in Salt Lake City, Utah during the summer of 1905 for the manufacture of a steam car to be called the Autocrat. Refer to Autocrat.

The Monarch Motor Company was organized in New York City early in 1909 with a capital stock of $25,000 to "manufacture, rent and operate for hire motor vehicles of all kinds." Incorporators were A.C. Rader, E.H. Fritchmann and F.J. Griffin. Manufacture is doubted.

1903 Monarch, runabout, (Milwaukee, Wisconsin), WLB

MONARCH — Milwaukee, Wisconsin — (1903-1904) — The Milwaukee Motor Manufacturing Company was one of the first firms in the city to enter the automotive field. Production centered on engines, although automobiles were tried for two seasons. A runabout with right-hand lever steer, single-cylinder engine, planetary transmission and single chain drive seems to have been the sole model offered. In 1903 the car was called the Monarch, and forty-eight were built; in 1904 it was called the New Monarch, and twelve were produced. In November of the latter year, company secretary-treasurer Marner announced that "we have decided to confine our product to engines and other parts, because we do not think that the profit is great enough for a factory which cannot turn out a large number." The company stuck to its word. No further cars were built.

MONARCH — Aurora, Illinois — (1905-1908) — This Monarch was a single-cylinder 7 hp air-cooled runabout with planetary transmission and a $500 price tag. "Body Rides on One Set of Springs, Machinery on Another," advertising boasted, and its speed range was 4 to 22 miles an

1905 Monarch, runabout, (Aurora, Illinois), NAHC

1906 Monarch, racer, (Cleveland, Ohio), MVMA

hour. The car was supposed to have been built in Chicago; P.J. Dasey began advertising it in 1903, but the company never could supply him any cars. Early in 1905, after two years of trying to get into production in Chicago, Monarch moved out to the suburbs to be built by the new Monarch Automobile Company in Aurora. E.B. Overshiner drove out from Chicago with the car and remained as president. Vice-president and treasurer were D.W. Simpson and William George, both officers of the Old Second National Bank of Aurora. Frank Doussang was secretary and A.B. McCord was general manager. Whether George and McCord had misgivings about the Monarch venture is not known, but in 1906 both of them became involved in another automotive enterprise in town building a two-cylinder car called the Aurora. This may have occurred about March, when after only a year in business, Monarch went into receivership. Somehow the company sailed through the bankruptcy proceedings, however, and reopened later that year. The final foreclosure sale was in the summer of 1908.

would change their company's name because they had discovered another Monarch was already being built in Illinois. The venture failed before a new name was selected. Possibly the only Monarch ever built was the racer that W.D. Drown had crashed at Gates Mills.

1906 Monarch, runabout, (Aurora, Illinois), HAC

1905-1908 MONARCH

	FP	5	4	3	2	1
Rbt. (1-cyl., 7 hp, 68" wb)	500	1600	2700	3800	5800	12,000

MONARCH — New York, New York — (1906) — Joseph S. Heller worked as a secretary in a broker's office on William Street in Manhattan. His home was uptown at 108 West 75th Street and probably it was there that he built his Monarch. It was a small runabout powered by a single-cylinder 7 hp air-cooled engine and featured a three-speed epicyclic transmission. How serious Heller was about manufacture is anyone's guess, but he attached a price tag of $500 to his Monarch and may have sold a few.

MONARCH — Cleveland, Ohio — (1906) — W.D. Drown was an electrician from Cleveland who had a penchant for speedy automobiles. Early in 1906 he built himself a 90 hp racer which he entered in the Gates Mills Hill Climb on Memorial Day. Though he crashed the car there, his performance had been sufficiently impressive to have attracted the attention of two Clevelanders named Irwin G. Guthrie and Bernard Guthrie. By October these three men got together to organize the Monarch Motor Car Company with a capital stock of $25,000. The plan was to produce a version of the racer (upped in horsepower to 125), as well as a more sedate four-cylinder car of 40/45 hp which would be offered as a tourer and a turtle-back runabout. A common wheelbase of 120 inches would be used for all Monarchs, but while the racer would have the purchaser's choice of chain or shaft drive, the tourer and runabout would be available only with shaft, and at a $4500 price tag. Fifty of the latter cars were planned to be built in the year following, ten of the racers. Space in the Broc Carriage Company in Cleveland was rented, race driver Fred Crum was enlisted to campaign the racer for the 1907 sporting season — and that appears to be as far as plans proceeded. In December the Monarch people announced that they

1908 Monarch, touring, (Chicago Heights, Illinois), WLB

MONARCH — Franklin Park & Chicago Heights, Illinois — (1907-1909) — The Monarch Motor Car Company was organized by T.A. Quinlan, Jr. and James A. Ward during the spring of 1906 in Chicago. Capital stock was $150,000. That summer a factory for manufacture was secured in nearby Franklin Park. The company already knew what it would build there: a two-cylinder runabout designed by J.J. Boucher of Chicago. Boucher had already designed a one-cylinder runabout called the Monarch that was now being built in Aurora, so why these people decided to call their car the same thing is something of a mystery. In any case, four of these new cars were on display at the Chicago Automobile Show in January 1907 and the Monarch was in production in Franklin Park shortly thereafter. On May 2nd the factory and 176 runabouts inside were destroyed by fire. This sent the Monarch people scurrying to find a new site for production, and by August they were reporting "rapid progress" in getting their new Chicago Heights factory in order. By the time production resumed late in 1908, Monarch had changed its mind about what it wanted to build, and its car now was a much larger and much more expensive four. The company was bankrupt by the summer of 1909. Early in 1910 the machinery used to build the Monarch was sold to Velie and moved downstate to Moline.

1907 Monarch, stanhope, (Franklin Park, Illinois), WLB

1907 MONARCH
Two — 12/14 hp, 76" wb

	FP	5	4	3	2	1
Model A Runabout-2P	600	1800	2800	4000	6200	13,000
Model B Stanhope-2P	750	1600	2700	3800	5800	12,000
Two — 12/14 hp, 88" wb						
Model E Runabout-2P	900	2000	3000	4200	6500	14,000

948

1908 MONARCH
Four — 40 hp, 112" wb

	FP	5	4	3	2	1
Model G Touring	2500	2000	3000	4200	6500	14,000
Model F Gentleman's Rds.	2500	1800	2800	4000	6200	13,000

1909 MONARCH
Four — 40 hp, 111" wb

	FP	5	4	3	2	1
Model F Roadster-3P	2500	2200	3200	4400	7000	15,000

Four — 45 hp

	FP	5	4	3	2	1
Model H Tourabout-4P (112" wb)	2750	2300	3300	4600	7500	16,000
Model J Tour.-7P (124" wb)	3000	2500	3500	5000	8500	18,000

MONARCH — Des Moines, Iowa — (1908) — The Monarch Machine Company was located on East First Street in Des Moines and produced gasoline engines. Although the company may have motorized an occasional buggy for random customers earlier, production was not embarked upon until 1908. The product remained a motorized buggy, with two-cylinder 20 hp engine, planetary transmission, double chain drive, and the option of wheel or lever steering. Priced at $750, it was dubbed the Road King. Its reign was less than a year.

1908 Monarch, model D, motor buggy, (Des Moines, Iowa), NAHC

1908 MONARCH
Road King — 2-cyl., 20 hp, 84" wb

	FP	5	4	3	2	1
Model D Motor Buggy-4P	750	2700	3600	5300	8800	14,000

1914 Monarch, touring, (Detroit, Michigan), NAHC

MONARCH — Detroit, Michigan — (1913-1916) — In early spring of 1913 Joseph Bloom saw to the details of organizing the Monarch Motor Car Company in Detroit and then began looking for factory space which he found by August in the vacant Carhartt Motor Car Company plant in town. Meantime, Bloom's brother-in-law Robert C. Hupp had finished the details of the car to be built there. It was a small 16 hp four on a 110-inch wheelbase to sell in the thousand-dollar range. It moved into production later that year. By May of 1914 approximately 150 Monarchs had been built, and they were joined in a few months by a smaller $675 four. Now Robert Hupp began thinking bigger and designed a V-8 that he planned to sell at $1500. This required more money and in May of 1915 the *Automobile Journal* reported "new capital of large proportions" had been placed behind the Monarch Motor Car Company. Apparently, the investors were all Detroit people, and apparently too they didn't come through with the money promised. The Monarch V-8 did go into production, but for only a short time. By early spring of 1916 the Monarch Motor Car Company was adjudged bankrupt, with assets of $20,833 and liabilities of $5753. All rights to the Monarch were acquired that November by the Carter Brothers of Hyattsville, Maryland. Carter reported at the time that the Robert Hupp-designed V-8, as well as the twelve he had designed which was ready in prototype form, would be continued under the Monarch name. When the cars arrived on the market in 1917, however, they were called C.B.'s. Interestingly, Hupp's brother Louis G. Hupp had tried to build his own car in Detroit during this period. It was called the Tribune, and failed even more quickly than the Monarch. Meanwhile, the Hupmobile which had been the Hupps' first automotive effort, was prospering elsewhere in Detroit.

1913 MONARCH
Four — 16 hp, 110" wb

	FP	5	4	3	2	1
Touring-5P	1050	2400	3400	4800	8000	17,000
Runabout-2P	1050	2300	3300	4600	7500	16,000

1914-1915 MONARCH
Four — 16 hp, 103" wb

	FP	5	4	3	2	1
Touring-4P	675	2400	3400	4800	8000	17,000

Four — 16 hp, 110" wb

	FP	5	4	3	2	1
Touring-5P	1050	2500	3500	5000	8500	18,000
Runabout-2P	1050	2400	3400	4800	8000	17,000

1916 MONARCH
Eight — 29 hp, 125" wb

	FP	5	4	3	2	1
Touring-5P	1500	3300	4400	6700	12,000	24,000

1901 Moncrief Steamer, NAHC

MONCRIEF STEAM — Pawtucket, Rhode Island — (1901) — In 1901 James A. Moncrief of Pawtucket designed a steam car with a double-cylinder engine, vertical tube boiler, tubular steel frame, wood wheels with solid rubber tires, and chain drive. The engine and mechanical parts were made for him by the Pawtucket Steamboat Company. The Moncrief steamer, which its maker also called the King Bee, was a fine looking vehicle which impressed the Pawtucket Steamboat Company so much that the car was put into production by that firm as the Pawtucket. Moncrief came aboard as the company's general manager.

MONDEX MAGIC — New York, New York — (1914-1915) — Swiss engineer Martin Fischer invented a slide-valve engine in which the sleeves had both an oscillating and reciprocating motion. It was first shown at the Berlin Automobile Show in 1911, and Fischer began granting licenses for its manufacture thereafter. The Aristos Company of 250 West 54th Street in New York City secured a U.S. license. Aristos produced the Mondex Shock Preventer, in addition to the Mondex Helix mixer (to improve carburetion), and a Mondex body polish. The Fischer engine was called the Magic, hence Aristos chose the marque name Mondex-Magic for its expensive ($4500-$6500) six-cylinder car offered in 40 and 60 hp versions and built for the company by Palmer and Singer. The Mondex Magic was produced for one season only, whereupon Aristos returned to the manufacture of Mondex products exclusively, although perhaps for not long. In January 1915 Aristos was reported to have been invited to a meeting of its creditors.

1914-1915 MONDEX MAGIC

	FP	5	4	3	2	1
Six Touring (40 hp)	4500	3900	4800	7700	14,300	27,000
Six Touring (60 hp)	6500	4200	5200	8400	15,700	29,000

MONITOR — Although initially organized late in 1916 as the Monitor Motor Company, Inc., this New York City firm's name had been changed to Majestic Motor Company by early 1917. Refer to Majestic.

1909 Monitor, runabout, HAC

949

MONITOR — Chicago, Illinois & Janesville, Wisconsin — (1909-1911) — The two-passenger highwheeler produced by the Monitor Automobile Works of Chicago looked more like an electric car than any other motorized buggy on the market. Although its engine was under the seat, it had a hood in front and a deck in the back. "Cars That Run, Stand Up and Make Good" was the Monitor slogan. William Westerlund and J.E. Norling were the principals behind the company, and J. Frank Waters was general manager and designer. Late in 1910 Monitor relocated in Janesville, moving into a big warehouse previously used largely for the storing of tobacco. For the 1910 season Waters had designed a larger four-passenger surrey model, which he modified into a dual-purpose "Milk Wagon/Pleasure Car." In the endurance contest held January 21st, 1910 in Kansas City, a dual-purpose Monitor with a 1600-pound load traveled forty miles in three hours, winning the event by a full forty-five minutes over the second-place finisher. It was perhaps this performance which prompted the Monitor people to concentrate on the commercial field exclusively. After 1911 all Monitors were trucks. "Designed Right, Priced Right, Built Right, All Right" was their slogan. Monitor trucks were built into 1916.

1909 MONITOR
Model B — 2-cyl., 18/20 hp, 86" wb

	FP	5	4	3	2	1
Stanhope	875	2000	3000	4200	6500	14,000
Runabout	875	1800	2800	4000	6200	13,000

1910 Monitor, surrey, NAHC

1910 MONITOR
Model B — 2-cyl., 18/20 hp, 86" wb

Stanhope	875	2000	3000	4000	6500	14,000
Runabout	875	1800	2800	4000	6200	13,000
Surrey	850	2200	3200	4400	7000	15,000

1911 MONITOR
Model B — 2-cyl., 18/20 hp, 86" wb

Dual Purpose Car	900	2200	3200	4400	7000	15,000

1921 Monitor, touring, WLB

MONITOR — Columbus, Ohio — (1915-1922) — In 1915 the Cummins Auto Sales Company, a multi-car dealership in Columbus, evolved into the Cummins-Monitor Company. Charles C. Cummins, H.P. Jeffers and E.S. Cummins were the principals behind the firm. Their plan initially was to offer a Monitor V-8 to sell for $1275 and a Monitor Junior four to sell for $675. In March, when the Monitor arrived, however, it was a four only; a six was added for the 1916 model year. Monitors were assembled cars, with GB&S, Herschell-Spillman and Continental engines being variously used. The company was reorganized in December 1916 as the Monitor Motor Car Company, and the venture went public in the spring of 1917 offering a large block of preferred stock for sale in order to enlarge the factory. Some 3000 cars were produced in 1917, and in 1919 Monitor acquired the much larger Columbus factory formerly occupied by the Scioto Rubber Company. Monitor prices wildly escalated in the wake of the postwar depression, and Monitor sales just as wildly de-escalated. By August of 1921 the company was in the hands of receivers. Debts were everywhere. Herschell-Spillman sued; Monitor had contracted for 1000 of its engines, and had accepted and paid for only forty-two. In January of 1922 liquidation was ordered. In August the Monitor factory was sold to the Clark Grave Vault Company which moved in immediately. The Monitor was dead.

1915 MONITOR
Model 4-30 — 4-cyl., 30 hp, 108" wb

	FP	5	4	3	2	1
Touring-5P	795	2400	3400	4800	8000	17,000
Roadster	795	2300	3300	4600	7500	16,000

1916 MONITOR
Four — 30 hp, 108" wb

Touring-5P	795	2400	3400	4800	8000	17,000
Roadster	795	2300	3300	4600	7500	16,000

Six — 55 hp, 115" wb

Touring	895	3300	4400	6700	12,000	24,000
Roadster	895	3100	4200	6300	10,500	22,000

1917 MONITOR
Four — 30 hp, 108" wb

Touring	895	2500	3500	5000	8500	18,000
Roadster	895	2400	3400	4800	8000	17,000

Six — 55 hp, 115" wb

Touring	1095	3500	4500	7000	13,000	25,000
Roadster	1095	3300	4400	6700	12,000	24,000

1918 MONITOR
Four — 30 hp, 108" wb

Touring	1295	2500	3500	5000	8500	18,000
Roadster	1295	2400	3400	4800	8000	17,000

Six — 55 hp, 115" wb

Touring	1295	3500	4500	7000	13,000	25,000
Roadster	1295	3300	4400	6700	12,000	24,000

1919 MONITOR
Six — 55 hp, 115" wb

Touring	1495	3500	4500	7000	13,000	25,000
Roadster	1495	3300	4400	6700	12,000	24,000

1920 MONITOR
Six — 55 hp, 117" wb

Touring	2475	3700	4700	7300	13,700	26,000
Tu-or-Four Roadster	2475	3500	4500	7000	13,000	25,000
Sedan	3475	1800	2800	4000	6200	13,000

1921-1922 MONITOR
Six — 55 hp, 121" wb

Roadster	2475	3700	4700	7300	13,700	26,000
Touring	2475	3900	4800	7700	14,300	27,000
Sedan	3475	2000	3000	4200	6500	14,000

MONMOUTH RACEABOUT — The Monmouth Raceabout of 1914 was a model of the Brown produced by the Brown Cyclecar Company of Asbury Park, New Jersey. Refer to Brown Cyclecar.

MONO — The Mono Motor Car Company was organized in Elizabeth, New Jersey during the fall of 1909 with a capital stock of $300,000 for the manufacture of motor cars, motor boats and aeroplanes. Incorporators were W.H. Wood, H.T. Eaton and C. Roberts. Manufacture of a car is doubted.

MONROE — "A company is being formed in Amesbury, Massachusetts to manufacture a 15 hp car from the designs of Charles H. Monroe," reported *The Horseless Age* in August 1905. Subsequent production is doubted.

MONMOUTH RACEABOUT — The Monmouth Raceabout of 1914 was a model of the Brown produced by the Brown Cyclecar Company of Asbury Park, New Jersey. Refer to Brown Cyclecar.

MONO — The Mono Motor Car Company was organized in Elizabeth, New Jersey during the fall of 1909 with a capital stock of $300,000 for the manufacture of motor cars, motor boats and aeroplanes. Incorporators were W.H. Wood, H.T. Eaton and C. Roberts. Manufacture of a car is doubted.

MONROE — "A company is being formed in Amesbury, Massachusetts to manufacture a 15 hp car from the designs of Charles H. Monroe," reported *The Horseless Age* in August 1905. Subsequent production is doubted.

1915 Monroe, model M-2, roadster, WLB

MONROE — Flint, Michigan — (1914-1916) / Pontiac, Michigan — (1916-1918) / Indianapolis, Indiana — (1918-1923) — Initially, the Monroe was a collaboration. R.F. Monroe headed the Monroe Body Com-

1917 Monroe, model M-3, roadster, WLB

pany in Pontiac, William C. Durant was the man behind the Chevrolet in Flint. Although the Monroe Motor Company, which was organized in Flint in August of 1914, was separate and distinct from Chevrolet, there were a good many ties that bound. Monroe's president was R.F. Monroe; its vice-president was Durant. All of the stockholders of the Monroe company were also stockholders of Chevrolet, manufacture of the Monroe was begun in a plant formerly used by Chevrolet in Flint, and distribution of the Monroe was through the Chevrolet sales organization. The Monroe-Durant collaboration was short-lived, however. In April of 1916 Durant resigned his Monroe vice-presidency, and Monroe moved his company into the former Welch plant in Pontiac. Capital stock in the reorganized Monroe Motor Car Company was increased to $1 million, and R.F. Monroe announced that henceforth he would sell his cars himself. This he did for the two years following, and then went bankrupt. In the fall of 1918, the Monroe assets were purchased by the William Small Company of Indianapolis, the former distributor for Monroes in that city. The plant at Pontiac was leased to General Motors for production of its Samson tractors, and Monroe now moved to Indianapolis. Monroe had begun as a small light car fitted with a proprietary engine and offered in open body styles only. Now it sported an engine of its own make, a sedan was added — and Louis Chevrolet was recruited by William Small as a consulting engineer to "work out designing problems for the Monroe car." There was a nice irony in this, Chevrolet long since having disassociated himself from William C. Durant. The extent of Chevrolet's influence on the Monroe production car was limited, but he did move into the Small premises in Indianapolis where, with the help of Cornelius Van Ranst, he put together seven race cars, four of them to be campaigned under the Monroe name, three as Frontenacs. His brother Gaston Chevrolet drove a Monroe to victory in the 1920 Indianapolis 500, the first win by an American car at the Brickyard since 1912. Unfortunately, three months later, in August of 1920 William Small went into receivership. Refinancing schemes were tried thereafter, but ultimately in January of 1922 the Monroe assets were acquired at the receiver's sale for $175,000 in cash by the Fletcher American National Bank in Indianapolis. By March of 1923, Monroe had a new owner: Strattan Motors Corporation which had just been organized by Frank E. Strattan, who was also reported to have his eye on purchase of the Premier plant in town. Strattan announced that he would continue the Monroe and introduce a new lower-priced car to be called the Strattan. By June, however, he had sold his interest in the Monroe in order to concentrate all energies on the new low-priced Strattan, which didn't survive the year. Meanwhile, Monroe had been bought from Strattan by Frederick Barrows of Premier. Initially, he organized this venture as Monroe Motors, Inc., but rather quickly the Monroe was simply absorbed into the Premier company. The last Monroes were sold as the Premier Model B.

1914-1915 MONROE
Model M-2 — 4-cyl., 14 hp, 96" wb

	FP	5	4	3	2	1
Roadster-2P	460	2300	3300	4600	7500	16,000

1916 MONROE
Model M-2 — 4-cyl., 15 hp, 96" wb

Roadster-2P	495	2300	3300	4600	7500	16,000
Runabout-2P	495	2200	3200	4400	7000	15,000

1917 MONROE
Model M-3 — 4-cyl., 15 hp, 96" wb

Roadster-2P	565	2300	3300	4600	7500	16,000
Cloverleaf Roadster	635	2400	3400	4800	8000	17,000
Sedan-5P	965	1600	2700	3800	5800	12,000

Model M-4 — 4-cyl., 35 hp, 115" wb

Touring-5P	985	2400	3400	4800	8000	17,000
Cloverleaf Roadster	985	2500	3500	5000	8500	18,000

1918 Monroe, model M-6, sedan, HAC

1918-1919 MONROE
Model M-6 — 4-cyl., 35 hp, 115" wb

	FP	5	4	3	2	1
Touring-5P	995	2500	3500	5000	8500	18,000
Roadster-2P	995	2400	3400	4800	8000	17,000
Sedan-5P	1850	1800	2800	4000	6200	13,000

1920 Monroe, model S, touring, HAC

1920 MONROE
Model S — 4-cyl., 35 hp, 115" wb

Touring-5P	1295	2400	3400	4800	8000	17,000
Roadster-2P	1295	2300	3300	4600	7500	16,000

1921 Monroe, model S, touring, JAC

1921 MONROE
Model S — 4-cyl., 35 hp, 115" wb

Touring-5P	1440	2400	3400	4800	8000	17,000
Roadster-2P	1440	2300	3300	4600	7500	16,000

1922 Monroe, model S, roadster, HAC

1922 MONROE
Model S — 4-cyl., 35 hp, 115" wb

Touring-5P	1295	2400	3400	4800	8000	17,000
Roadster-2P	1295	2300	3300	4600	7500	16,000
Coupe-3P	2075	2000	3000	4200	6500	14,000
Sedan-5P	2175	1600	2700	3800	5800	12,000

1923 MONROE
Model S — 4-cyl., 35 hp, 115" wb

Touring-5P	950	2500	3500	5000	8500	18,000
Roadster-2P	950	1600	2700	3800	5800	12,000
Sedan-5P	1520	1600	2700	3800	5800	12,000

MONSEN — Chicago, Illinois — (1908-1910) — Adolph Monsen ran an automobile garage at 329 Clark Street in Chicago. Directory listings from 1908 and 1909 indicate that he built a few cars at that address as well during those years. This was strictly a small-scale operation, and remained so in 1910 when Monsen formally incorporated the Monsen Auto Garage with a capital stock of $10,000. A decade later, however, Adolph Monsen moved into the big time as one of the men behind the ReVere.

MONTANA SPECIAL — The Montana Special was a model of the Luverne, which was built in Luverne, Minnesota from 1904 to 1916. Refer to Luverne.

MONTGOMERY — The Montgomery Garage Company was organized in Jersey City, New Jersey early in 1911 with a capital stock of $125,000 for the manufacture of aeroplanes, motor cars and motorcycles. Incorporators were C.N. King, Jr., M.A. Cox and G.H. Russel. Manufacture of a car is doubted.

1896 Montgomery Ward Electric, runabout, GR

MONTGOMERY WARD — Chicago, Illinois — (1896) — In 1896 Montgomery Ward & Company commissioned the building of two electric cars by the American Electric Vehicle Company of Chicago. The cars carried four passengers at speeds of up to a claimed 14 mph, but not for any distance. Instead, the vehicles were sent by rail to various cities where they were paraded around town for advertising purposes. This early Montgomery Ward electric was neither marketed nor catalogued. A decade later the mail order house did make a brief incursion into the automobile field (as did its rival Sears, Roebuck) with a car called the Modoc. Another Montgomery Ward car to be called the Wardway was a stillborn. During the 1930's the mail order house again considered the idea of cataloging an automobile, as did Sears, but both companies decided against it at that time.

MOODY — Elgin, Illinois — (1903-1905) — Victor Moody has been credited as being Elgin's first automobile driver. The year was 1899 and, although the car he drove is not known, it has been documented that he caused Sheriff Sherwood's horse to stampede. Moody did not build his own car until 1903, and he did so at that time in collaboration with his brothers Charles, Andrew and Axel in their machine shop on North Grove. Five cars were built in the two years following. Although the bodies were made by Charles Stowe, a local patternmaker, all other parts of the cars were fabricated by the Moody brothers, including the engines. The first was a one-lunger, the last a four. One of the cars was driven by Victor Moody into the early Twenties; "Old Silver" was its nickname. Formal manufacture was never embarked upon.

MOOERS — New Haven, Connecticut — (1900-1901) / New York, New York — (1911) — Louis P. Mooers is a perfect example of an excellent engineer who was a dreadful businessman. At the turn of the century, he produced a gasoline car but was not able to find the necessary financial backing for manufacture. He went to Peerless in Cleveland instead and became that company's chief engineer, subsequently serving as same for the Moon Company in St. Louis. In 1908 he resigned from Moon and returned to the East Coast with plans to manufacture a six-cylinder car of his own design. After three years of trying, he did manage to incorporate his Mooers Automobile Company in 1911, and produced a prototype, but the financial backing he had found proved ephemeral quickly. By 1912 he had joined the engineering department of Herschell-Spillman. No automobile with the Mooers name ever proceeded beyond the prototype stage.

MOOERS — Goodwin Mills, Maine — (1902-1903) — W.E. Mooers of Goodwin Mills claimed to have built the first motor sleigh in upper New England. Its engine was a 2 hp water-cooled gasoline unit which drove a two-speed gear with separate friction clutches from which power was transmitted by Baldwin block chain to a spur wheel behind the sleigh. The spur wheel was held down in the snow by means of a lever worked by the foot. The vehicle weighed only 410 pounds, and with calcium chloride used in the cooling water, Mooers said there was no freezing even at tem-

1903 Mooers Motor Sleigh, NAHC

peratures of twenty below. The inventor's only dissatisfaction with the sleigh was its low speed potential, which he improved upon with the building of a more powerful version in 1903. He never went into manufacture, however.

1906 Moon, model A, touring, HAC

MOON — St. Louis, Missouri — (1905-1929) — Joseph W. Moon was one of five brothers of an Ohio farming family each of whom at age twenty-one was given the same stake — a horse, a saddle and a bridle — to make their own way into the world. Joseph Moon made his way to St. Louis where he set himself up in the buggy business. At a carriagemakers' convention in Detroit in 1902, he first became aware of the potential of the automobile industry, though he took his time before deciding to enter it. Unlike most builders of horsedrawn vehicles, Moon did not begin by motorizing a buggy. The first Moon car, introduced in 1905, was a five-passenger touring with 30/35 hp Rutenber engine, three-speed sliding gear transmission and shaft drive. It was designed by Louis P. Mooers, formerly of Peerless in Cleveland. Although not quite as upper echelon as the Peerless, "The Ideal American Car," as the Moon was called, was introduced as a $3000 automobile. Mooers did not remain Moon's chief engineer long, however, returning to Ohio by 1908 to design the Ewing. Nor did the Moon remain quite so expensive. Lower-priced lines in the $1500 and $2000 range were introduced in 1910. Production in 1906 had been 45 cars; by 1913 it was 1540 units. Moon's first six arrived that year, and for more

1907 Moon, model C, touring, HAC

than a decade beginning in 1916 all Moons were six-cylinder cars. Although an ohv Falls engine would be used in an export model (6-42) in 1921, most Moon powerplants were L-head Continentals. In 1919 Joseph Moon died, and the presidency of the Moon Motor Car Company passed to his son-in-law Stewart MacDonald. Despite being an assembled automobile, the Moon was a fine, well-built car boasting such refinements by the Twenties as demountable rims on detachable wheels, balloon tires (introduced in 1923), Lockheed hydraulic brakes (which followed for '24). Its square Rolls-Royce-like radiator was a distinguishing feature. The company's peak production year was 1925, with approximately 13,000 units built. Included in that number was a brand-new car from the company called the Diana, powered by a Continental straight-eight. The Moons were continued as sixes only until 1928, when the Diana was phased out and revised into the Aerotype 8-80 model of the Moon which, together with the Aerotype 6-72, reached a production of just 3000 units that year. Clearly the Moon Company was in trouble. Purportedly, reliability problems with the early Dianas, which were resolved though memory of them had lingered in the marketplace, represented the reason for discontinuation of that car. And now Moon elected to retire the long-lived Moon name as well. Introduced in January 1929 was another brand-new straight-eight called the Windsor. In April that name was given to all cars produced by the company. The Moon automobile was no more. And the Moon Company entered its final days. Prior to 1929 the company's history had been a relatively placid one, with its only foray into other automobile manufacture being the Hol-Tan which was built in the St. Louis factory in 1908 for a New York dealership. Now the Moon Company history became a raging one, as the firm decided to build another car called the Ruxton. The man behind the Ruxton, a canny promoter named Archie Andrews, inveigled and insinuated himself into control of the firm. The Moon old guard barricaded themselves in the factory, but the new regime broke in and took over. This was high-intrigue drama. It was also the end of Moon. The Ruxton and the Windsor did not survive 1930. The Moon Company did; though moribund, its tangled affairs would require more than two decades to finally resolve. Meanwhile the Moon factory, which had been appraised at $1,250,000, was sold during the early Thirties for $72,500 cash to the Cupples Company which would use it largely for the production of matches.

1905-1906
Model A, 4-cyl., 30/35 hp, 106" wb

	FP	5	4	3	2	1
5P Tr	3000	1550	4500	7500	10,500	15,000

1907
Model C, 4-cyl., 30/35 hp, 110" wb

5P Tr	3500	1550	4500	7500	10,500	15,000
Rbt	3500	1400	4200	7000	9800	14,000
Limo	3800	1250	3900	6500	9100	13,000

1908 Moon, model C, roadster, HAC

1908
Model C, 4-cyl., 30/35 hp, 110" wb

5P Tr	3000	1550	4500	7500	10,500	15,000
Rds	3000	1400	4200	7000	9800	14,000

Model D, 4-cyl., 30/35 hp, 121" wb

| 7P Tr | 3750 | 2000 | 5100 | 8500 | 11,900 | 17,000 |

1909 Moon, model D, landaulet, HAC

1909
Model C, 4-cyl., 32.3 hp, 112" wb

	FP	5	4	3	2	1
5P Tr	3000	1750	4800	8000	11,200	16,000
4/5P Baby Ton	3000	2000	5100	8500	11,900	17,000
3/4P Rds	3000	1550	4500	7500	10,500	15,000
6P Limo	3850	1250	3900	6500	9100	13,000

Model D, 4-cyl., 32.2 hp, 121" wb

| 7P Tr | 3500 | 2300 | 5400 | 9000 | 12,600 | 18,000 |
| 6P Lan'let | 3850 | 1750 | 4800 | 8000 | 11,200 | 16,000 |

1910 Moon, model 30, toy tonneau, HAC

1910
Model 30, 4-cyl., 30 hp, 110" wb

3P Rbt	1500	1550	4500	7500	10,500	15,000
5P Tr	1500	1750	4800	8000	11,200	16,000
4P Toy Ton	1500	2000	5100	8500	11,900	17,000

Model C, 4-cyl., 32.2 hp, 112" wb

5P Tr	2000	2300	5400	9000	12,600	18,000
4/5P Toy Ton	2000	2800	5700	9500	13,300	19,000
3/4P Rbt	2000	2000	5100	8500	11,900	17,000

Model 45, 4-cyl., 45 hp, 120" wb

3P Rbt	3000	3900	7800	13,000	18,200	26,000
7P Tr	3000	4050	8100	13,500	18,900	27,000
5P Baby Ton	3000	3750	7500	12,500	17,500	25,000

1911 Moon, model 45, torpedo, HAC

1911
Model 30, 4-cyl., 30 hp, 114" wb

5P Tr	1500	3400	6900	11,500	16,100	23,000
5P Toy Ton	1500	3600	7200	12,000	16,800	24,000
7P Limo	2750	3000	6000	10,000	14,000	20,000
4P Torp	1600	3750	7500	12,500	17,500	25,000
5P 4 dr Tr	1600	3900	7800	13,000	18,200	26,000
2/3P Cpe	2150	1750	4800	8000	11,200	16,000
3P Rds	1500	3600	7200	12,000	16,800	24,000

Model 45, 4-cyl., 45 hp, 121" wb

5/7P Tr	3000	4050	8100	13,500	18,900	27,000
5P Torp	3100	4200	8400	14,000	19,600	28,000
5P Toy Ton	3000	3900	7800	13,000	18,200	26,000
7P Limo	4000	2300	5400	9000	12,600	18,000
5/7P 4 dr Tr	3100	4200	8400	14,000	19,600	28,000

1912 Moon, model 30, runabout, HAC

953

1912

Model 30, 4-cyl., 32.4 hp, 116" wb

	FP	5	4	3	2	1
5P Tr	1600	3300	6600	11,000	15,400	22,000
Torp	1600	3400	6900	11,500	16,100	23,000
Rds	1600	3400	6900	11,500	16,100	23,000
Limo	2750	2300	5400	9000	12,600	18,000

Model 40, 4-cyl., 32.4 hp, 120" wb

5P Tr	1800	3400	6900	11,500	16,100	23,000
Torp	1800	3600	7200	12,000	16,800	24,000
Rds	1800	3600	7200	12,000	16,800	24,000
Cpe	3000	1750	4800	8000	11,200	16,000

Model 45, 4-cyl., 45 hp, 123" wb

7P Tr	3000	4350	8700	14,500	20,300	29,000
Torp	3000	4200	8400	14,000	19,600	28,000
Rds	3000	4200	8400	14,000	19,600	28,000
Limo	4000	3150	6300	10,500	14,700	21,000

1913 Moon, model 48, torpedo, HAC

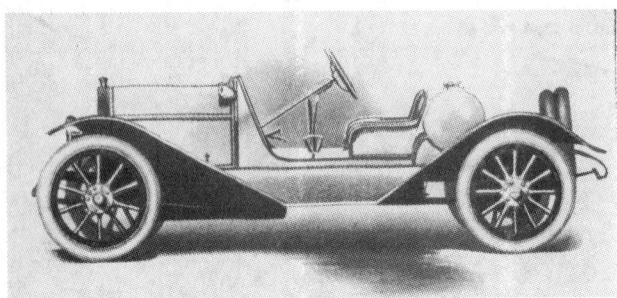

1913 Moon, model 39, Gentleman's Speedster, HAC

1913

Model 39, 4-cyl., 25.6 hp, 116" wb

4P Tr	1650	3300	6600	11,000	15,400	22,000
5P Tr	1650	3400	6900	11,500	16,100	23,000
Rds	1650	3300	6600	11,000	15,400	22,000
Spds	1650	4350	8700	14,500	20,300	29,000
Brgm Cpe	1900	2300	5400	9000	12,600	18,000

Model 48, 4-cyl., 32.4 hp, 121" wb

4P Torp	1985	4050	8100	13,500	18,900	27,000
5P Tr	1985	3900	7800	13,000	18,200	26,000
Rds	1985	3750	7500	12,500	17,500	25,000
Spds	1985	4650	9300	15,500	21,700	31,000
Brgm Cpe	2250	2800	5700	9500	13,300	19,000
Limo	3000	3150	6300	10,500	14,700	21,000

Model 65, 6-cyl., 38.4 hp, 132" wb

5P Tr	2500	4350	8700	14,500	20,300	29,000

1914 Moon, model 6-50, streamline touring, HAC

1914 MOON

Model 42 — 4-cyl., 32.4 hp, 118" wb

Torpedo	1750	3300	4400	6700	12,000	24,000
Roadster	1750	3300	4400	6700	12,000	24,000
Speedster	1750	4000	5000	8000	15,000	28,000

Model 6-50 — 6-cyl., 33.7 hp, 128" wb

Steamline Tour.-6P	2225	3900	4800	7700	14,300	27,000
Torpedo-4P	2150	3700	4700	7300	13,700	26,000
Touring-5P	2150	3500	4500	7000	13,000	25,000
Touring-7P	2224	3900	4800	7700	14,300	27,000

954

1914

Model 42, 4-cyl., 32.4 hp, 118" wb

	FP	5	4	3	2	1
Torp	1750	3600	7200	12,000	16,800	24,000
Rds	1750	3600	7200	12,000	16,800	24,000
Spds	1750	4200	8400	14,000	19,600	28,000

Model 6-50, 6-cyl., 33.7 hp, 128" wb

6P Steamline Tr	2225	4050	8100	13,500	18,900	27,000
4P Torp	2150	3900	7800	13,000	18,200	26,000
5P Tr	2150	3750	7500	12,500	17,500	25,000
7P Tr	2224	4050	8100	13,500	18,900	27,000

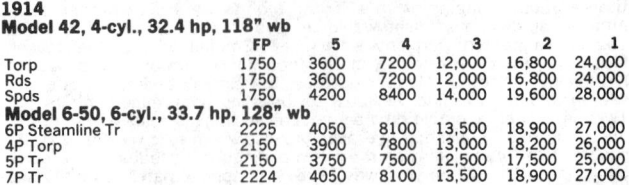

1915 Moon, model 6-40, touring, HAC

1915

Model 4-38, 4-cyl., 23 hp, 120" wb

5P Tr	1350	3900	7800	13,000	18,200	26,000
3P Rds	1350	3750	7500	12,500	17,500	25,000
3P Rbt	1350	3600	7200	12,000	16,800	24,000

Model 6-40, 6-cyl., 29 hp, 120" wb

6P Tr	1575	4050	8100	13,500	18,900	27,000
5P Tr	1575	3900	7800	13,000	18,200	26,000
3P Rds	1575	3750	7500	12,500	17,500	25,000
3P Rbt	1575	3600	7200	12,000	16,800	24,000
Limo	2250	2800	5700	9500	13,300	19,000
Cabr	2250	3300	6600	11,000	15,400	22,000

Model 6-50, 6-cyl., 34 hp, 130" wb

6P Tr	2250	4200	8400	14,000	19,600	28,000
5P Tr	2150	4050	8100	13,500	18,900	27,000
3P Rds	2150	4050	8100	13,500	18,900	27,000
3P Rbt	2150	3900	7800	13,000	18,200	26,000
Limo	2750	3000	6000	10,000	14,000	20,000
Cabr	2950	3400	6900	11,500	16,100	23,000

1916 Moon, model 6-30, touring, HAC

1916

Model 6-30, 6-cyl., 30 hp, 118" wb

5P Tr	1195	3400	6900	11,500	16,100	23,000
3P Rds	1195	3300	6600	11,000	15,400	22,000

Model 6-40, 6-cyl., 40 hp, 123" wb

7P Tr	1475	4200	8400	14,000	19,600	28,000
Rds	1475	3900	7800	13,000	18,200	26,000

Model 6-50, 6-cyl., 50 hp, 132" wb

7P Tr	2250	4350	8700	14,500	20,300	29,000

1917 Moon, model 6-66, club roadster, HAC

1917
Model 6-43, 6-cyl., 40 hp, 118" wb

	FP	5	4	3	2	1
5P Tr	1295	3400	6900	11,500	16,100	23,000
4P Clb Rds	1295	3300	6600	11,000	15,400	22,000
4P Cabr	1950	3150	6300	10,500	14,700	21,000

Model 6-66, 6-cyl., 66 hp, 125" wb

	FP	5	4	3	2	1
7P Tr	1690	3900	7800	13,000	18,200	26,000
4P Clb Rds	1690	3750	7500	12,500	17,500	25,000
4P Cpe	2250	2300	5400	9000	12,600	18,000
7P Sed	2350	1250	3900	6500	9100	13,000
4P Cabr	2250	3150	6300	10,500	14,700	21,000

1918 Moon, model 6-36, touring, HAC

1918
Model 6-36, 6-cyl., 35 hp, 114" wb

	FP	5	4	3	2	1
5P Tr	1095	3600	7200	12,000	16,800	24,000
2P Rds	1095	3400	6900	11,500	16,100	23,000

Model 6-45, 6-cyl., 45 hp, 125" wb

	FP	5	4	3	2	1
4P Cpe	2150	2300	5400	9000	12,600	18,000
7P Tr	1575	3900	7800	13,000	18,200	26,000
4P Rds	1575	3750	7500	12,500	17,500	25,000
4P Cabr	2050	3150	6300	10,500	14,700	21,000

Model 6-66, 6-cyl., 66 hp, 125" wb

	FP	5	4	3	2	1
7P Sed	2450	1400	4200	7000	9800	14,000
7P Tr	1850	4200	8400	14,000	19,600	28,000
7P Vic	2025	3000	6000	10,000	14,000	20,000
4P Rds	1850	3900	7800	13,000	18,200	26,000
4P Cpe	2450	2300	5400	9000	12,600	18,000

1919 Moon, model 6-36, touring, HAC

1919
Model 6-36, 6-cyl., 36 hp, 114" wb

	FP	5	4	3	2	1
5P Tr	1395	3600	7200	12,000	16,800	24,000

Model 6-66, 6-cyl., 66 hp, 125" wb

	FP	5	4	3	2	1
5P Sed	2950	1400	4200	7000	9800	14,000
Cabr	2750	3150	6300	10,500	14,700	21,000
Vic	2425	3000	6000	10,000	14,000	20,000
Clb Rds	2250	3900	7800	13,000	18,200	26,000

1920 Moon, model 6-68, touring, HAC

1920
Victory 6-48, 6-cyl., 48 hp, 118" wb

	FP	5	4	3	2	1
5P Tr	1885	3600	7200	12,000	16,800	24,000
3P Rds	1985	3400	6900	11,500	16,100	23,000
5P Sed	2885	1400	4200	7000	9800	14,000
4P Cpe	2885	1750	4800	8000	11,200	16,000

Model 6-68, 6-cyl., 68 hp, 124" wb

	FP	5	4	3	2	1
7P Tr	2750	3750	7500	12,500	17,500	25,000
7P Sed	3450	1500	4350	7250	10,150	14,500
4P Cpe	3650	1800	4950	8250	11,550	16,500
3P Rds	2750	3600	7200	12,000	16,800	24,000

1921 Moon 6-58, sport touring, JAC

1921
Model 6-42, 6-cyl., 37 hp, 115" wb

	FP	5	4	3	2	1
5P Tr	1885	3300	6600	11,000	15,400	22,000

Model 6-48, 6-cyl., 53 hp, 122" wb

	FP	5	4	3	2	1
5P Tr	1985	3600	7200	12,000	16,800	24,000
2P Rds	2085	3400	6900	11,500	16,100	23,000
4P Cpe	2985	1750	4800	8000	11,200	16,000
5P Sed	2985	1400	4200	7000	9800	14,000

Model 6-68, 6-cyl., 55 hp, 125" wb

	FP	5	4	3	2	1
7P Tr	2485	3750	7500	12,500	17,500	25,000

1922 Moon, model 6-40, touring, OCW

1922
Model 6-40, 6-cyl., 50 hp, 115" wb

	FP	5	4	3	2	1
5P Tr	1295	3300	6600	11,000	15,400	22,000

Model 6-48, 6-cyl., 53 hp, 122" wb

	FP	5	4	3	2	1
5P Tr	1785	3400	6900	11,500	16,100	23,000
2P Rds	1785	3300	6600	11,000	15,400	22,000
4P Cpe	2785	2000	5100	8500	11,900	17,000
5P Sed	2785	1550	4500	7500	10,500	15,000
5P Brgm	2785	1750	4800	8000	11,200	16,000

Model 6-75, 6-cyl., 70 hp, 135" wb

	FP	5	4	3	2	1
7P Tr	2285	4200	8400	14,000	19,600	28,000
7P Sed	2485	1400	4200	7000	9800	14,000

1923
Model 6-40, 6-cyl., 50 hp, 115" wb

	FP	5	4	3	2	1
5P Tr	1295	3600	7200	12,000	16,800	24,000
5P Tourlux	1445	3750	7500	12,500	17,500	25,000
4P Cpe	1585	1750	4800	8000	11,200	16,000
5P Sed	1695	1400	4200	7000	9800	14,000

Model 6-58, 6-cyl., 58 hp, 128" wb

	FP	5	4	3	2	1
7P Tr	1785	4050	8100	13,500	18,900	27,000
4P Spt	1985	4200	8400	14,000	19,600	28,000
7P Sed	2485	1550	4500	7500	10,500	15,000
5P Tr Sed	2585	1750	4800	8000	11,200	16,000

1924
Model 6-40, 6-cyl., 50 hp, 115" wb

	FP	5	4	3	2	1
2P Rds	1295	3600	7200	12,000	16,800	24,000
5P Tr	1295	3750	7500	12,500	17,500	25,000
5P Spt Tr	1495	4200	8400	14,000	19,600	28,000
4P Cpe	1685	2000	5100	8500	11,900	17,000
5P Sed	1695	1400	4200	7000	9800	14,000
5P Spt Sed	1895	1550	4500	7500	10,500	15,000

Model 6-50, 6-cyl., 50 hp, 112" wb

	FP	5	4	3	2	1
2P Rds	1495	3750	7500	12,500	17,500	25,000
5P Tr	1495	3900	7800	13,000	18,200	26,000
5P Spt Tr	1595	4350	8700	14,500	20,300	29,000
4P Cpe	1885	2300	5400	9000	12,600	18,000
5P Sed	1885	1550	4500	7500	10,500	15,000
5P Spt Sed	2095	1750	4800	8000	11,200	16,000

Model 6-58, 6-cyl., 58 hp, 128" wb

	FP	5	4	3	2	1
7P Tr	1785	4350	8700	14,500	20,300	29,000
7P Spt Phae	1995	4500	9000	15,000	21,000	30,000
5P Spt Tr	2150	4650	9300	15,500	21,700	31,000
7P Sed	2485	1750	4800	8000	11,200	16,000
4P Spl Sed	2585	2000	5100	8500	11,900	17,000

1924 Moon, model 6-40, standard touring, AA

1924 Moon, model 6-50, sedan, NAHC

1925 Moon, series A, cabriolet roadster, HAC

1925
Series A, 6-cyl., 50 hp, 113" wb

	FP	5	4	3	2	1
5P Tr	1195	3400	6900	11,500	16,100	23,000
5P Rds	1295	3300	6600	11,000	15,400	22,000
5P 2 dr Sed	1495	1400	4200	7000	9800	14,000
5P 4 dr Sed	1695	1400	4200	7000	9800	14,000

Model 6-40 Newport, 6-cyl., 50 hp, 115" wb

5P Tr	1495	3600	7200	12,000	16,800	24,000
4P Cpe	1815	2000	5100	8500	11,900	17,000
5P Sed	1815	1550	4500	7500	10,500	15,000
5P Petite Sed	1915	1650	4650	7750	10,850	15,500

Model 6-50, Metropolitan, 6-cyl., 52 hp, 115" wb

5P Tr	1525	3750	7500	12,500	17,500	25,000
5P Sed	1995	1650	4650	7750	10,850	15,500
5P Petite Sed	2095	1750	4800	8000	11,200	16,000

Model 6-58 London, 6-cyl., 56 hp, 128" wb

5P Tr	1985	3900	7800	13,000	18,200	26,000
5P Petite Sed	2540	1800	4950	8250	11,550	16,500

1926 Moon, series A, cabriolet roadster, HAC

956

1926 Moon, series A Deluxe, 4-dr. sedan, AA

1926
Series A, 6-cyl., 50 hp, 113" wb

	FP	5	4	3	2	1
5P Tr	1195	3300	6600	11,000	15,400	22,000
4P Rds	1395	3150	6300	10,500	14,700	21,000
5P Coach	1395	1250	3900	6500	9100	13,000
5P 2 dr DeL Sed	1495	1300	4050	6750	9450	13,500
5P Sed	1545	1400	4200	7000	9800	14,000
4P Cabr Rds	1595	3000	6000	10,000	14,000	20,000
5P DeL Sed	1695	1500	4350	7250	10,150	14,500

London, 6-cyl., 56 hp, 128" wb

5P Tr	1985	3600	7200	12,000	16,800	24,000
5P Petite Sed	2540	1550	4500	7500	10,500	15,000

1927 Moon, model 6-60, Deluxe roadster, HAC

1927
Model 6-60, 6-cyl., 47 hp, 110" wb

	FP	5	4	3	2	1
5P Tr	995	3300	6600	11,000	15,400	22,000
5P Std Rds	995	3150	6300	10,500	14,700	21,000
5P DeL Rds	1095	3300	6600	11,000	15,400	22,000
5P Coach	995	1250	3900	6500	9100	13,000
5P Sed	1195	1250	3900	6500	9100	13,000
5P Brgm	1095	1400	4200	7000	9800	14,000
5P Cabr	1195	3000	6000	10,000	14,000	20,000

Series A, 6-cyl., 50 hp, 113" wb

5P Tr	1195	3400	6900	11,500	16,100	23,000
4P Rds	1395	3300	6600	11,000	15,400	22,000
5P Brgm	1395	1550	4500	7500	10,500	15,000
5P Sed	1545	1400	4200	7000	9800	14,000
4P Cabr Rds	1595	3150	6300	10,500	14,700	21,000

1928 Moon, model 6-72 Royal, roadster, AA

1928
Aerotype Model 6-72, 6-cyl., 66 hp, 120" wb

	FP	5	4	3	2	1
5P Royal Rds	1395	4000	7900	13,250	18,550	26,500
5P Royal Cabr Rds	1445	3900	7800	13,000	18,200	26,000
5P Sed	1395	1800	2800	4000	6200	13,000
5P Royal Sed	1445	2000	3000	4200	6500	14,000
5P Sed	1445	1900	2900	4100	6400	13,500
5P Royal Sed	1545	2100	3100	4300	6800	14,500

Aerotype Model 8-80, 8-cyl., 85 hp, 125-1/2" wb

5P Sed	2195	1550	4500	7500	10,500	15,000
Cl C Cpe	—	2000	5100	8500	11,900	17,000
Royal Rdst. 2-4	—	4100	8250	13,750	19,250	27,500

1928 Moon, model 8-80 Royal, roadster, AA

1929 Moon, model 6-72, Petite, sedan, AA

1929 Moon, model 8-80 Royal, 4-dr. sedan, AA

1929
Model 6-72, 6-cyl., 66 hp, 120" wb

	FP	5	4	3	2	1
5P Cabr	1495	3300	6600	11,000	15,400	22,000
5P Petite Sed	1495	1750	4800	8000	11,200	16,000
5P Sed	1495	1550	4500	7500	10,500	15,000
4P Vic Cpe	2000	5100	8500	11,900	17,000	

Model 8-80, 8-cyl., 85 hp, 125" wb

5P Cabr	1845	3400	6900	11,500	16,100	23,000
5P Petite Sed	1845	2000	5100	8500	11,900	17,000
5P Sed	1845	1750	4800	8000	11,200	16,000
4P Vic	1845	2300	5400	9000	12,600	18,000
7P Sed	—	2000	5100	8500	11,900	17,000

MOORE — Despite numerous roster mentions of an automobile called the Moore from Cleveland, there was never a car marketed under that name. There were two men named Moore who were marketing vehicles in Cleveland during that period, however. One was A.L. Moore, whose Cleveland Automobile Company built a gasoline runabout called the Cleveland. The other was Harry S. Moore, who had an automobile called the Auburn-Moore built especially for himself and who bought the assets of the Star Automobile Company in Cleveland in late 1903, continuing production of that car under the Star name.

MOORE — Walla Walla, Washington — (1906) — This Moore was a protest car. It had a four-cylinder engine and was built by a small work-force of eight men in Walla Walla beginning in the summer of 1906. The Moore Automobile Company had been organized shortly before to rebuild, assemble and repair cars, and to take over the Franklin agency from the Gilbert Hunt Company. Only the frame of the Moore car was produced in Walla Walla, the remainder of its parts being purchased. The Moore was built for a single reason: to force Eastern automobile manufacturers to supply the state of Washington with cars having a track of 60 inches to conform to the standard width of that state's roads. (Most American roads were 56 inches.) By December of 1906, Franklin among others having in the meantime capitulated, the Moore Automobile Company announced the shutting down of its automobile manufacturing department. "The purpose for which the company was formed has been accomplished," declared president Moore triumphantly.

1907 Moore, runabout, NAHC

MOORE — Bridgeport, Connecticut — (1906-1907) — The Moore Automobile Company had its offices in New York City and its factory in Bridgeport. Its product was a very expensive 40 hp four with manganese bronze crankcase and ball bearings used everywhere. "The Ball Bearing Car" was the Moore slogan; the chassis price was $5000, and rose as high as $8000 with coachwork fitted. It didn't survive two years. W.J.P. Moore and F.D. Howe had been the designers of the car, Moore having formerly been manager of the Worthington Automobile Company, producers of the Berg and the Meteor.

1906-1907 MOORE
Four — 40 hp, 116" wb

	FP	5	4	3	2	1
Touring-7P	7000	2700	3600	5300	8800	19,000
Runabout-3P	6500	2500	3500	5000	8500	18,000
Limousine-7P	8000	2300	3300	4600	7500	16,000

1918 Moore, model 30, touring, WLB

MOORE — Minneapolis, Minnesota — (1916-1918) / Danville, Illinois — (1919-1920) — George L. Moore was a Ford dealer in Minneapolis who organized the Moore Motor Vehicle Company on a shoestring in 1916 for the production of a four-cylinder 30 hp touring car to compete with the Model T. An assembled vehicle, the Moore's frame and running gear arrived from Pontiac Chassis Company, its body from Wayne Works in Indiana, its engines from Golden, Belknap & Schwartz. The price tag was $550. In January 1918 former race driver Louis Disbrow arrived in Minneapolis to become chief engineer, but he found himself with little to engineer and quickly departed. By 1919 the Moore company had departed Minneapolis as well, relocating in Danville, Illinois. Price tags rose into the thousand-dollar range. In August 1919, George L. Moore resigned the company presidency, as did his vice-president, A.C. Leonard. E.K. Gallagher and J.H. Vickers took over those respective posts. Receivership followed in 1920; negotiations with the Marwin Motor Truck Company to take over fell through; the company was auctioned off for $54,807 that December. Scandal followed in 1921, as six Moore officials, including George L. Moore, were convicted of misrepresentation in the sale of stock. A total of 612 Moores had been built. Most of the efforts of the company had been devoted to stock selling. The car has been described by a Danville resident who remembers it as "a little horror with corners on the body sharp enough to cut your finger."

1916-1918 MOORE
Model 30 — 4-cyl., 30 hp, 106" wb

Touring-5P	550	2400	3400	4800	8000	17,000

1919 MOORE
Model 30 — 4-cyl., 30 hp, 106" wb

Touring-5P	850	2400	3400	4800	8000	17,000
Sport Model-5P	875	2500	3500	5000	8500	18,000

1920 MOORE
Model 30 — 4-cyl., 30 hp, 106" wb

Touring-5P	1095	2500	3500	5000	8500	18,000

1919 Moore, model 30, touring, HAC

MOORE AUTOPLANE — Los Angeles & Glendale, California — (1925-1933) — Inclusive dates of this venture are difficult to determine, but it is known that Virgil B. Moore applied for a patent on his flying car in June of 1925 and that it was granted in June of 1928. Throughout this period, and possibly before, Moore was located at 411 South Main Street in Los Angeles where as the Moore Autoplane Company, Inc., he was trying to get his project off the ground. He never succeeded. The early Thirties found him in Glendale as the manager of a new company called Autoplane Development Corporation which had leased space at Grand Central Air Terminal. But now one L. Morton Bach was the engineer in charge, most probably there having been a few snags in the original Moore design which seems to have been considerably revised by Bach. "A high-wing monoplane which can be driven as an automobile with the wing folded or detached and the rear of the fuselage detached is in the mock-up stage," *Western Flying* reported in January of 1933." . . . A clutch and gear shift will enable the pilot-driver to direct the power to the wheels or to a push propeller at will." Whether this version of the Autoplane ever got off the ground is not known.

1917 Moore-Car, NAHC

MOORE-CAR — Indianapolis, Indiana — (1917) — W.G. Moore insisted upon referring to his creation as an automobile, a point he emphasized by calling it the Moore-Car, but in reality this was a motorcycle with a pair of steadying auxiliary wheels which were raised and lowered with a touch of a button. The engine was a Sinclair, the transmission was three-speed, and shaft drive was featured. "The car is the product of the best engineering skill in America, and the steel stamping art is here shown in its perfection," enthused the *Commerce of Greater Indianapolis* in June 1917. "The Moore-Car, instead of a combination of castings and forgings, is an engineering triumph in pressed steel. A man or woman may ride the Moore-Car without fear of soiling their garments and an elderly man can handle and control this machine with a minimum of exertion." Moore, who indicated an experience in the automobile industry which dated back to helping Ransom Olds build his first cars, was the president of the Moore Car Corporation of America, a hefty five-million-dollar organization. Joining him were F.D. Hill as secretary, B.G. Hewitt as treasurer and I.E. Wemple as vice-president. The company's offices and factory were at 916-918 North Illinois Street in Indianapolis. The venture was short-lived.

MOORESPRING — Moorespring has been the occasional designation used for one of the automobiles built by Ingersoll Moore in Bloomington, Illinois during the years 1888 to 1895. The inventor's name was the more usual reference, however. Refer to Ingersoll Moore.

MOORE STEAMER — Charles J. Moore built his first steam car at the turn of the century, but when he began marketing the car in Westfield, Massachusetts in 1901, it was as the Westfield. Refer to Westfield.

MORA — Newark, New York — (1906-1910) — "Mora Makes Good," the company said in announcing that one of its cars had been driven over 8000 miles on the East Coast and in the Midwest during 1907 without its hood once being raised. The Mora Motor Car Company thereafter adver-

1906 Mora Racytype, roadster, HAC

tised its product as the "World's Record Sealed Bonnet Hero." Moras were produced with four- and six-cylinder engines, and with developed horse-power as high as sixty. The company's favorite model was the four-cylinder Racytype, which was grandly announced as a limited production car of which only a hundred units would be built annually. Probably not many more units of any Mora model were ever made in a single year. Sam H. Mora, who had formerly been sales manager for Kodak, was the man behind the company, and William H. Birdsall was his chief engineer. Birdsall designed the Browniekar juvenile auto also built by Mora under the anagram of Omar. Trouble arrived in July 1910. "The creditors of the company have been restive for many weeks," *The Motor World* reported that month, "and the company has frankly told them that it could not pay at present and that if matters were pressed the creditors would have to take their chances in whatever a bankruptcy action might yield." When Mora refused its creditors request for a complete statement of its financial condition, the company was petitioned into involuntary bankruptcy. The property sale which followed on November 15th, 1911 brought $120,000 for the Mora plant, real estate, parts and fifty as-yet-unsold cars. Meantime Sam H. Mora had relocated in Cleveland, where he formed the Mora Power Wagon Company for the manufacture of commercial vehicles.

1907 Mora, tourer, HAC

1906-1907 MORA
Four — 24 hp, 103″ wb

	FP	5	4	3	2	1
Tourer-5P	2200	3300	4400	6700	12,000	24,000
Racytype Roadster-2P	2300	3100	4200	6300	10,500	22,000
Four — 24 hp, 98″ wb						
Roadster-2P	1800	3300	4400	6700	12,000	24,000
Surrey-4P	1925	3100	4200	6300	10,500	22,000

1908 Mora, tourer, HAC

1908 MORA
Four — 24 hp, 103″ wb

Tourer-4P	2500	3300	4400	6700	12,000	24,000
Racytype-3P	2350	3100	4200	6300	10,500	22,000
Six — 42/50 hp, 115″ wb						
Tourer-5P	3600	4200	5200	8400	15,700	29,000
Racytype-3P	3500	4000	5000	8000	15,000	28,000

1909 Mora Racytype, roadster, HAC

1909 MORA
Four — 24/28 hp, 110" wb

	FP	5	4	3	2	1
Roadster-4P	1850	3500	4500	7000	13,000	25,000
Racytype Roadster-3/4P	1850	3300	4400	6700	12,000	24,000
Limousine-5/7P	3250	3300	4400	6700	12,000	24,000
Six — 42/50 hp, 115" wb						
Tourer-5P	3600	4300	5400	8700	16,500	30,000
Roadster-3P	3750	4200	5200	8400	15,700	29,000
Limousine-5/7P	5000	3500	4500	7000	13,000	25,000
Racytype Rds. (105" wb)	3500	4500	5800	9500	18,000	32,000
Large Four — 60 hp, 124" wb						
Touring-7P	2750	5000	6500	11,000	22,000	35,000
Racytype Roadster-3/4P	2750	4900	6300	10,300	21,000	34,000

1910 Mora, model 20, runabout, NAHC

1910 MORA
Model 20 — 4-cyl., 20 hp, 84" wb

	FP	5	4	3	2	1
Roadster-2P	1050	3100	4200	6300	10,500	22,000
Light Four — 40 hp, 112" wb						
Tourer-5P	2500	4000	5000	8000	15,000	28,000
Roadster-2P	2500	3900	4800	7700	14,300	27,000
Tourer-7P	2650	3900	4800	7700	14,300	27,000
Limousine-5/7P	3500	2500	3500	5000	8500	29,000
Racytype Roadster	2500	4200	5200	8400	15,700	29,000

MORE — The More Automobile Company was organized in St. Louis, Missouri late in 1914 with a capital stock of $15,000 to manufacture, sell, deal in and repair motor cars and accessories. Incorporators were Edward A. More, John B. Strauch, John T. Salisbury and Cyrus B. More. Manufacture of a car is doubted.

MOREHOUSE — Naples, New York — (1902) — Fisher Morehouse was a carriagebuilder in Naples who built himself a single-passenger gasoline car in 1902. It weighed 160 pounds and had an estimated speed of 8 mph.

MORELAND — Burbank, California — (1909, 1912, 1916 et seq.) — Following his resignation from the Durocar Manufacturing Company of Los Angeles, Watt Moreland moved to Burbank to do what his board of directors at Durocar had not allowed him to do: build a four-cylinder automobile. His Moreland prototype was a water-cooled L-head with cylinders cast in pairs. A four-speed transmission and cone clutch were featured. And the Moreland Motor Car Company was organized for its manufacture. The Moreland automobile was never produced, in quantity, however, because in the meantime Watt Moreland had another idea. It was the Moreland Motor Truck Company which became one of the most innovative and important truck-producing firms on the West Coast. At the end of 1912, the firm announced its output as 203 trucks and six touring cars, the latter for factory use. That Watt Moreland found it difficult to forgo the automobile is evidenced by the number of occasions in which he subsequently announced that his thriving truck company would produce a car. In 1916 this new Moreland was to be equipped with a magnetic transmission which Moreland declared would "revolutionize the cost and control of pleasure cars"; in 1917 the new Moreland automobile would feature the distillate "gassifier" used on the Moreland trucks; in 1924 the new Moreland was to be a deluxe sedan. None of these efforts ever reached the production stage, however. Moreland trucks were built until 1941.

MORGAN — The Morgan Manufacturing Company was organized in Detroit, Michigan late in 1910 with a capital stock of $10,000 to manufacture and deal in motor vehicles. Incorporators were H.S. Morgan and C.S. Morgan. Manufacture of a car is doubted.

The Morgan Motor Car Company was a $500,000 Delaware incorporation from late 1908 for the purpose of manufacturing and dealing in motor cars and supplies. Incorporators were E.L. Squier and K.M. and J.A. Byrne. Manufacture of a car is doubted.

The Morgan Manufacturing Company was organized in Chester, Pennsylvania during the summer of 1920 for the manufacture of automobiles. Capital stock was $3 million, and James L. Morgan of Overbook (who had formerly been associated with the Adair-Heyl Motors Company of Philadelphia) spearheaded this venture. "A site for the erection of buildings to contain improved machinery for the manufacture of automobiles has been secured in the western section of Chester and operations to improve the tract will begin in a few days." *Motor Age* reported in August. The venture was not heard from again.

1897 Morgan, steam carriage, HAC

MORGAN STEAM — Worcester, Massachusetts — (1897) — Although the year 1894 has been advanced as the date Ralph L. Morgan built his first automobile in Worcester, it would seem that 1897 is accurate. The vehicle was rather ungainly, with a small gas-burning boiler situated under a seat fastened on a shaky body and riding on four flimsy bicycle wheels. The car did run successfully, however, and Morgan followed it with a steam truck which he produced in Worcester from 1902 to 1903, though not very successfully. His efforts did catch the eye of the American Bicycle Company, however, which sent him to Toledo (Ohio) where he was responsible for much of the engineering of the Pope-Toledo. Subsequently, he returned to the East Coast, joining the Thomas company in Buffalo and being part of the engineering team responsible for the famous Thomas Flyer. In 1908 he was back home in Worcester where he began making gasoline trucks under his own name, an activity in which he continued until late 1912 when he sold out to William M. Steele.

MORGAN — Brooklyn, New York — (1900-1902) — The Morgan Motor Company of Brooklyn manufactured motorized bicycles and tricycles as well as rough castings of its various gasoline motors, running gear and other automotive parts. In 1900 the company also built a light runabout, which seems not to have been marketed. During the fall of 1901, however, Morgan announced that orders were being booked for both steam and gasoline automobiles, every part of which save for the wheels and lamps would be built in the company's Brooklyn shops at 50-54 Columbia Heights. A small production of cars followed in 1902.

MORGAN — Worcester, Massachusetts — (1913) — William M. Steele had been in charge of all machine work at the truck-building Morgan company in Worcester since 1908, and in December of 1912 he bought control of the firm from Ralph L. Morgan. Finding himself in the position of entrepreneur now, he flirted with the idea of entering the cyclecar field and had a prototype built in late 1913. Quite possibly this was the car which had been announced earlier by Frank O. Woodland. Rather quickly, however, Steele decided that the fortunes of the Morgan Motor Truck Company were better served in the commercial field only, and the cyclecar project was abandoned. Through 1913 Steele marketed trucks under the Morgan name, switching to his own beginning in 1914. Steele trucks were built in Worcester into 1919.

MORLOCK — Buffalo, New York — (1903) — In the spring of 1903, J.F. Morlock bought the old Spaulding automobile plant in Buffalo at the receiver's sale and organized the Morlock Automobile Manufacturing Company. Included in the deal were a few unsold Spaulding cars. The Morlocks which followed out of the same factory were lookalikes, sold as runabouts or dos-a-dos four-seaters with their 6 hp single-cylinder engines mounted under the seat. Wheelbases for both versions were 72 inches, the prices $650 and $700 respectively. In early October operations were shut down "pending action to increase capital." In late October the factory doors were closed by the sheriff, and the company assets seized. In November a court order was issued restraining any sale of property as Morlock creditors searched for ten cars which purportedly had been

1903 Morlock, runabout, NAHC

spirited away somewhere by J.F. Morlock. Whether the cars were ever found is not known, but in January of 1904 the Morlock Automobile Manufacturing Company was declared irrevocably defunct.

MORO — Los Angeles, California — (1911-1912) — Details regarding the makeup of the Moro are lacking, but at least a few prototypes were built. The venture was the idea of J.B. Morrow and James R. Fouch. Morrow headed a local Los Angeles automobile emporium called Morrow, Loomis & Company; Fouch was the proprietor of a machine shop in town. The first Moro was completed in late 1911, the Morrow-Mercury Motor Car Company being incorporated with a capital stock of $20,000 early in 1912 for its manufacture. The venture was soon abandoned, however, with J.B. Morrow returning to his dealership activity exclusively. James Fouch, however, went on to design the Perfex for another L.A. company, and subsequently the Fouch.

MORRELL & HIGGINS — The Morrell & Higgins Motor Company was organized in Portland, Maine late in 1911 with a capital stock of $10,000 for the manufacture and sale of automobiles and accessories. Fred S. Higgins, of Grey, Maine, was the firm's president and treasurer. Manufacture of a car is doubted.

1895 Morris & Salom, Electrobat, runabout, OCW

MORRIS & SALOM ELECTRIC — Philadelphia, Pennsylvania — (1894-1897) — Henry G. Morris was a mechanical engineer who had been born in Philadelphia in 1840; Pedro G. Salom was an electrician who had been born in the same city in 1856. On January 19th, 1894, they applied for a patent on their first electric car. They called it the Electrobat, as they did many of their subsequent vehicles. Although the partners brought three electric cars to the 1895 Chicago Times-Herald Contest, their official entry was the Electrobat II, undoubtedly the most sophisticated electric vehicle in the United States at the time. Two 1½ hp Lundell motors powered it, with the batteries furnished by the Electric Storage Battery Company of Philadelphia. The twin motors were attached to the front axle and were geared directly to the front wheels. Two smaller wheels to the rear saw to the steering. Electrobat II weighed 1650 pounds, could turn in a circle of twenty feet, could travel twenty miles a day and one work week without a charge. Morris and Salom were vociferous exponents of electric power. "All the gasoline motors we have seen belch forth from their exhaust pipe a continuous stream of partially unconsumed hydrocarbons in the form of a thick smoke with a highly noxious odor," Salom wrote in 1896 in the *Journal of The Franklin Institute.* "Imagine thousands of such

vehicles on the streets, each offering up its column of smell." The partners' Electric Carriage & Wagon Company was in business almost immediately after the Chicago Times-Herald Contest and soon had fleets of electric cabs in service in both Philadelphia and New York. The firm's name was changed to Electric Vehicle Company, and financing was provided by Isaac Rice. Around the turn of the century, Electric Vehicle was bought out by the people who were subsequently responsible for both building the Columbia automobiles (both electric and gasoline) and for enforcing the Selden patent.

MORRISON — Fred Morrison of 45 Bayne Street in Cleveland, Ohio was reported to have been experimenting with an automobile, according to the *Automobile & Motor Review* in February 1902. Details are lacking.
The Morrison Motor Car Company was organized in Chicago, Illinois with a capital stock of $20,000 during the summer of 1909 to manufacture motors, motor cars and accessories. Incorporators were said to be Bastrup and O'Neill. Manufacture of a car is doubted.

1895 Morrison Electric, Times-Herald car, NAHC

MORRISON ELECTRIC — Des Moines, Iowa — (1888-1895) — The first successful four-wheeled electric car in America was produced in Des Moines by William Morrison in either 1888 or 1890, the exact date remaining in some dispute. The car was Morrison's second effort, the first completed six months earlier in the shops of the Des Moines Buggy Company not having performed to Morrison's satisfaction. The Shaver Carriage Company of East Des Moines built Morrison's second car for him, and it made its public debut at the Seni Om Sed (Des Moines spelled backwards) parade. Power was furnished by twenty-four storage battery cells underneath the seat; the motor was four horsepower, of street car type with a Siemens armature, fitted beneath the carriage and geared to the rear axle. Steering was via a hand bar which connected to a pivot on each front wheel, the wheels linked with a yoke bar that turned on a rack-and-pinion device. This feature, and virtually every other one in the Morrison Electric, was patented by its inventor. Morrison patented eighty-seven of his ideas during his lifetime. News of the Morrison Electric's test run was picked up by the Associated Press, as well as *Scientific American.* Within months the Des Moines Post Office was deluged with 16,000 letters from all over the world. Then the Morrison Electric hit the road. Harold Sturges of the American Battery Company of Chicago purchased the car for $3600, demonstrated it at the World's Columbian Exposition, entered it in Chicago Times-Herald contest of 1895 (slightly modified for that event), and displayed it at fairs across the country. Although reportedly Morrison later built other electric cars, he was not really interested in the automobile other than as a demonstration of his battery design. "I wouldn't give ten cents for an automobile for my own use," he told the Des Moines *Register & Leader* in 1907. "But, of course, by this I'm not belittling their usefulness by any means." His subsequent inventions included the first motor boat on the Des Moines River, an electric gearshift and various battery improvements. When he died in 1927 he was working on a new invention to make gold mining easier.

1935 Morrison, sedan, MVMA

MORRISON — Buchanan, Michigan — (1935) — Willard L. Morrison was the manager of the Clark Equipment Company which manufactured air-conditioning components in Buchanan. In 1935 he built an automobile for himself which used a Ford V-8 engine, though all other parts of the vehicle were of his own design. The body was steamlined, wide in the front and tapering toward the rear, accommodating three people in the front seat, two in the back. "The windshield is set higher and farther back than in the conventional car, and is close up to the face of the driver, which gives him a greater field of vision," *Automotive Industries* reported in August 1935. "The steering wheel is under the cowl and forward of the windshield, which is considered a safety measure. An overhead mirror is provided with a reflector (periscope) and gives a wide field of vision toward the rear, without the possibility of obstruction by rear-seat passengers. The rear seat is set so low that it is impossible for the occupants to look through the high windshield except up into the air." Among other safety features incorporated by Morrison into the car were a spare wheel so arranged that it would absorb most of the shock in a rear-end collision and a gasoline filler cap which could be opened only from the inside of the car.

1923 Morriss-London, saloon, KM

MORRISS-LONDON — Elkhart, Indiana — (1919-1923) — In essence, the Morriss-London was a Crow-Elkhart that was sent overseas. This export car was originally to have been called the Marathon, but a seemingly good deal with automobile agent F.E. Morriss of 64 Piccadilly in London saw to the quick name change. Chassis only were shipped to England, where British coachwork was fitted to the cars. Further chassis presumably also found their way to the colonies; shipments to Australia are known to have been made. Unfortunately, Morriss went broke in London around 1920, which put a damper on the transatlantic arrangement. An estimated 100 chassis were consigned to a warehouse from which they were ultimately retrieved by Saunders Motors Ltd., that company bodying a few for sale and using the remainder for parts. Crow-Elkhart's demise in the United States in 1923 spelled the ultimate end for the entire venture. Century Motors Company was the Crow-Elkhart subsidiary under which the Morriss-London was built, and the evidence suggests that leftover cars may have been sold as late as 1925.

MORRISSEY — Despite its presence on car rosters, the Morrissey Motor Car Company of Bridgeport, Connecticut did not build an automobile. Its product line included trucks and buses marketed under the tradename of Bridgeport.

MORRISTOWN — The Morristown Garage Company was organized early in 1906 with a capital stock of $50,000 to manufacture and repair automobiles in Morristown, New Jersey. Behind this venture were Thomas B. Reid, John V. Wise and Alexander Reid. Manufacture is doubted, but the firm is known to have become the local agents for the Rainier and the Maxwell.

MORROW-MERCURY — The Morrow-Mercury Motor Car Manufacturing Company was incorporated in Los Angeles, California in 1912 for production of a car called the Moro. Refer to Moro.

MORSE STEAM — Milwaukee, Wisconsin — (1902) — In 1902 Frank, H. Morse built a four-wheel-drive steam car in Milwaukee which he sold for $550. Very few were produced. In 1903 Morse joined the Four Wheel Drive Wagon Company of Milwaukee where his efforts were concentrated in the commercial vehicle field. In 1907 he began the Wisconsin Motor Manufacturing Company, which was followed by three years (1909-1912) at Kissel, Morse taking charge of that Hartford, Wisconsin company's truck department. In April 1912 he moved east to design the Duquesne in Pittsburgh, and following its demise remained in town to produce a cyclecar bearing his own name.

MORSE — Newton, Massachusetts — (1901) — In 1901 J.S. Morse of Newton completed the steam automobile he had begun building the year previous. Aside from the fact that light weight was among its attributes, according to Morse, very little is known about it. He does not appear to have begun manufacture.

1904 Morse, kerosene-engined, runabout, NAHC

MORSE — Newark, New Jersey — (1903-1904) — In 1903 William W. Morse of Newark invented a kerosene engine which he tested for six months thereafter in a launch and a runabout. Early in 1904 a reporter from *The Automobile* was taken along by Morse on a drive in the runabout. "The machine was put through all its paces, made to climb hills, start and stop, and run at various speeds, all of which it did satisfactorily, and without the odor of kerosene being at any time noticeable," he commented. The necessity of using a plumber's torch to start the engine was viewed as a "serious objection," but once that was no longer required, the reporter thought the result would be "an automobile engine of satisfactory character." Perhaps William Morse was unable to come up with any other method of starting his engine than the plumber's torch. He was not heard from again in the trade press again.

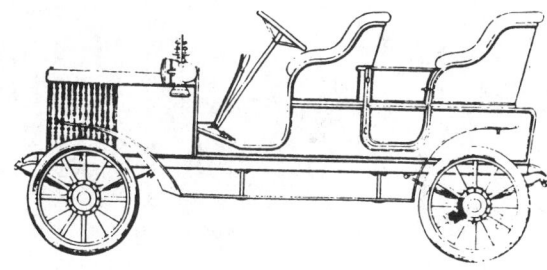

1905 Morse, steam touring, NAHC

MORSE STEAM — Springfield, Massachusetts — (1905-1906) — Sewell Morse built the prototype of his steam car in his native Detroit, but was unable to find anyone to back him there in its manufacture. Heading to the East Coast, which he did during the summer of 1904, was a logical move, since there were considerably more steam cars built in that area than in the Midwest. In Springfield, Massachusetts, Morse found a number of enthusiastic backers — F.H. Young, J. Frank Drake, A.E. Snow, Edward H. Cullen, Charles L. Hoyt, J. Douglas Law, Clinton Gowdy — who joined him in organizing the Morse Motor Vehicle Company. Capital stock was stated to be $250,000. Most of that must have remained on paper. Production of the Morse began early in 1905. It was powered by a three-cylinder single-acting 20 hp engine with flash generator and kerosene burner. A five-passenger touring car on a 103-inch wheelbase seems to have been the company's only model. References that this Morse may have been in production as late as 1909 seem wildly exaggerated. More than likely, manufacture had ceased before the end of 1906.

MORSE — South Easton, Massachusetts — (1910-1916) — The Easton Machine Company was established in 1904, during which year its founder, Alfred G. Morse, built his first experimental car. In August of 1905 he declared himself ready to get into automobile manufacture, although if he did he kept it quiet. A brochure from 1910, if carefully read between the lines, indicates that all previous work had been experimental. But now at last the Morse was ready for the world. It was a four, a rather expensive one in the $4000 range. It was designed by Chester T. Bates, who left almost immediately to join Lenox in Jamaica Plain. And that was only the first problem. The second arrived in 1911, when Easton Machine sued Providence Engineering Company in Rhode Island for defective castings which had resulted in the recall of a number of Morse cars. Nonetheless, Morse struggled on for a few years longer, and the car he built was a good one. By the end of 1913, unfortunately, the demise of the Morse was a foregone conclusion, though it would seem a few cars straggled out of the Easton Machine Company shops as late as 1916. In January of 1917, however, Alfred Morse announced that the Easton Machine Company was out of the automobile business. References placing this car or company in Beverly, Massachusetts have been in error, although there appears to have been a sales agency in Brookline trading under the name of Morse Motor Car Company.

1910 Morse, model B, touring, HAC

1910 MORSE
Model B — 4-cyl., 24 hp, 112" wb

	FP	5	4	3	2	1
Runabout-3P	3900	3900	4800	7700	14,300	27,000
Touring-5P	4000	4000	5000	8000	15,000	28,000
Torpedo-4P	4000	4000	5000	8000	15,000	28,000

1911 Morse, model D, runabout, OCW

1911 MORSE
Model D — 4-cyl., 34 hp, 127" wb

Touring-5/7P	4000	4200	5200	8400	15,700	29,000
Torpedo-4P	4200	4300	5400	8700	16,500	30,000
Limousine-7P	5200	2700	3600	5300	8800	19,000
Runabout-2P (112" wb)	4000	4000	5000	8000	15,000	28,000

1912 Morse, model D, touring, HAC

1912 MORSE
Model D — 4-cyl., 34 hp, 127" wb

Touring-5P	4200	4200	5200	8400	15,700	29,000
Touring-7P	4200	4300	5400	8700	16,500	30,000
Torpedo-5P	4200	4400	5600	9200	17,300	31,000

962

1913 Morse, model D, touring, HAC

1913 MORSE
Model D — 4-cyl., 34 hp, 127" wb

	FP	5	4	3	2	1
Touring-5/7P	4200	4200	5200	8400	15,700	29,000
Roadster-4/5P	4200	4000	5000	8000	15,000	28,000
Sedan-5P	5400	2000	3000	4200	6500	14,000

1914-1916 MORSE
Model D — 4-cyl., 34 hp, 127" wb

Touring-5/7P	3600	4200	5200	8400	15,700	29,000

1914 Morse, cyclecar, WLB

MORSE — Pittsburgh, Pennsylvania — (1914-1916) — By 1914 Frank H. Morse's resume of work in the automotive field was a lengthy one, beginning with a steam car he built in his native Milwaukee in 1902, followed by work for the Four Wheel Drive Wagon Company, Wisconsin Motor Manufacturing and Kissel in Wisconsin, and subsequently a chief engineer stint in Pittsburgh for Duquesne. When Duquesne went under in 1913, Morse remained in town. His next effort was a tandem-seater cyclecar which at first glance looked like many another of the genre, until one noticed the chain drive, and where the chain went. The Morse cyclecar drove from the front wheels. "There are no untried schemes in this drive," Frank Morse told *Cyclecar and Motorette*, "it is merely placing the universal joint in here, with the steering pivots in each wheel. Ninety-five percent of the time, the joints are running straight, and in fact in ordinary running the wheels are steered at such a small angle that the joints have no hard work to do." A two-cylinder Spacke engine powered the Morse, and the transmission was a two-speed planetary. The wheelbase was a long 105 inches. Frank Morse spent most of 1914 refining his prototype. He drove it 6000 miles and told *Carette* magazine that he could "beat any car on hills in Pittsburgh." In 1915 he established the Morse Cyclecar Company, but did not move into production until sometime that summer. Within a year production had ceased.

1914-1916 MORSE
Cyclecar — 2-cyl., 9 hp, 105" wb

Tandem Roadster	350	1600	2700	3800	5800	12,000
Light Delivery	350	1500	2500	3600	5500	11,000

1909 Morse-Readio, roadster, LC

MORSE-READIO — Springfield, Massachusetts — (1909-1910) — Glenn E. Morse and George N. Readio were the partners behind the Morse-Readio Auto Company at Mill and South Main streets in Springfield. Their car was a very stylish 110-inch-wheelbase roadster with a removable rumble seat. It was powered by an L-head 36 hp four-cylinder engine, and its performance was a sprightly 55 mph. "The car is more than ordinarily easy of control and it is very steady," remarked a reporter for the *New England Automobile Journal* in July 1909 after being taken for a test drive. At that time several cars had already been sold to residents of Springfield. The

Morse-Readio price tag was $2500. Proper production began shortly thereafter, but was concluded within a year. Morse and Readio had built a good car; they simply did not have the financial backing necessary to make it in the marketplace. In 1911 the Morse-Readio Auto Company became dealers for General Motors trucks, subsequently taking on agencies for the Alco in 1913 and the Velie in 1914. Prior to the Morse-Readio, George Readio had been responsible for the design of the Springfield built in 1907-1908 in that Massachusetts city.

MORT — Piqua, Ohio — (1917-1924) — The Mort was built by the Meteor Motor Car Company of Piqua, and was a smaller companion to the Meteor. Like most Meteors, the Mort was a funeral car. The man behind the Meteor company, Maurice Wolfe, had a devilish, if somewhat macabre, wit. Mort is French for dead. Refer to Meteor.

MORTON — San Jose, California — (1904-1905) — Raleigh A. Morton, who seemed to have preferred the nickname Rolla, completed his first automobile in the spring of 1904. Proprietor of the Morton Motor Works at 31 South Third Street in San Jose, he was the inventor of the Morton "center fire balance gas engine," and his shop specialized in pumping and marine powerplants. His hope to establish himself as a manufacturer of automobiles was short-lived, however. Associated with him in the venture was Bert E. Knapp, who continued in business under his own name following the dissolution of their partnership in 1906.

MOSEHART & KELLER — Houston, Texas — (1908-1909) — The Mosehart & Keller Company of Houston built horsedrawn buggies and sold such popular automobiles of that day as the Buick and the Ford. During 1908 and 1909 the firm also produced a few highwheeled motor buggies, but this was strictly a sideline to its principal activity.

MOSHER — Charles D. Mosher of 1 Broadway in New York City claimed himself to be the designer of the lightest and most powerful marine engines in the world. In late 1898 *The Horseless Age* reported him to be "making the plans for a steam carriage which he says will weigh only 90 pounds and yet be a practical machine." One wonders. Charles Mosher was not heard from again.
    The Mosher Automobile Company was organized in Anderson, Indiana during the fall of 1909 with a capital stock of $6000 for the manufacture of motor cars. Incorporators were A.T. Mosher, J.E. Van Deventer and E.E. Young. Manufacture is doubted.

MOSSBERG — Attleboro, Massachusetts — (1899-1901) — The Frank Mossberg Company manufactured bicycle bells in a factory in Attleboro which employed 200 workers and turned out a quarter of a million bells a year. In 1900 the company announced its plans to enter the automobile industry with an electric car. "They will have a new motor with revolving field and armature, and will dispense with compensating gear," *Cycle and Automobile Trade Journal* reported in April. "They say this new motor has double the starting torque, and weighs only half the amount of any other good make of the same power." Frank Mossberg had built the prototype of this car in 1899, and it remained the only electric he built. In 1900 and 1901 he built two gasoline cars, one of which he sold for $1500. But there was no sustained manufacture of any car bearing the Mossberg name. The United States Automobile Company which he had helped to establish in 1899, and the United States Auto-Car Company organized in 1903, were ventures in which, he lamented in 1904, he had been left "holding the bag" into which he had put his own savings. His bicycle business was prosperous, however, and he was a prolific inventor, who ultimately held 200 patents.

MOTOBLOC — The MotoBloc Import Company was organized in New York City late in 1908 with a capital stock of $5000 to manufacture, deal in and rent automobiles. Behind this venture were H.M. Brown, F.W. Mills and E.J. Forham. Manufacture is doubted.

MOTOR — Prefacing one's company designation with the word Motor was a very common occurrence in the automobile industry during the years preceding the First World War. The following companies thusly named either indicated forthcoming manufacture but apparently failed to follow through — or did proceed into manufacture but of a car that was sold under another name.
    The Motor Company, Ltd. of New Orleans, Louisiana, organized early in 1905 with a capital stock of $25,000 to manufacture and deal in motors and vehicles. Incorporators were Bishop C. Perkins, William P. Lusk and Thomas S. Witherspoon.
    The Motor Appliances Company of Chicago, Illinois, organized late in 1908 with a capital stock of $2500 to manufacture and deal in automobiles, engines and accessories. Incorporators were J. William Lindgren, E.H. Tillson and Al Ringo.
    The Motor Cab Company of New York City, organized during the fall of 1906 to manufacture vehicles of all kinds. H.P.C. Browne, H.J. Craig and H.F. Carson were the incorporators.
    The Motor Car Company of America, organized in 1911 in New York City which chose America as the tradename for its product. Refer to America.
    The Motor Car Company of Jackson, Michigan, organized in 1905 to produce the Cartercar. Refer to Cartercar.
    The Motor Car Company of Boston, Massachusetts, organized during the summer of 1911 with a capital stock of $25,000 to manufacture and deal in automobiles. Incorporators were W.H. Vinal and S.S. Anderson.
    The Motor Car Appliance Company of New York City, organized early in 1912 with a capital stock of $5000 to manufacture and deal in automobiles. Incorporators were R.J. Randolph, Jr., A.L. Smith, Jr. and J.B. Spencer.
    The Motor Car Conveyance Company of New York City, organized early in 1910 with a capital stock of $100,000 to manufacture and deal in motor

vehicles and taxicabs. Incorporators were C.E. Lockwood of East Orange (New Jersey), A. Lee of Brooklyn and J.W. Chapman of Manhattan.
    The Motor Car Fixture Company of New York City, organized during the summer of 1910 with a capital stock of $10,000 to manufacture automobiles, motor boats and accessories. Incorporators were John H. Dale, Walter I. Hess and Christian P. Roen, all of Manhattan.
    The Motor Car Livery of Philadelphia, Pennsylvania, organized during the summer of 1906 to manufacture, sell, store, repair and rent automobiles. Incorporators were Clarence W. Rowe, Frank G. Kennedy, Jr., R.P.H. Rile, William M. Jones and E.L. Kennedy.
    The Motor Car Manufacturing Company of Indianapolis, Indiana, organized in 1911 for manufacture of the Pathfinder automobile. Refer to Pathfinder.
    The Motor Car and Storage Company of Paterson, New Jersey, organized with a capital stock of $10,000 early in 1906 to manufacture and repair automobiles. Hatter A. Berry, H. Caulson and Alfreda Fairchild, all of Passaic, were the incorporators.
    The Motor Car Supply Company of East Orange, New Jersey, organized early in 1908 with a capital stock of $25,000 for the manufacture of "motor vehicles, engines, motor car apparatus, etc." Incorporators were C.O. Geyer, F.C. Ferguson and F.E. Ruggle.
    The Motor Carette Company of Buffalo, New York, organized late in 1913 with a capital stock of $30,000 for the manufacture of automobiles. Incorporators were Henry J. Carrigan, C.J. Kern and A.M. Pearsall, all of Buffalo.
    The Motor and Carriage Company of Boston, Massachusetts, listed as an automobile manufacturer in the Hiscox book *Horseless Vehicles, Automobiles, Motor Cycles* published in 1900.
    The Motor Carriage Company of 107 Main Street in Brockton, Massachusetts, also listed in the Hiscox book.
    The Motor Components Manufacturing Company of Des Moines, Iowa, which promoted the Des Moines Dazzler in 1906. Refer to Des Moines Dazzler.
    The Motors, Engineering & Sales Company of New York City, organized late in 1910 with a capital stock of $200,000 to manufacture and deal in motor vehicles and engines. Incorporators were C. Griswold, W.S. Jewell and J.L. Breese, Jr.
    The Motor Finance Company of New York City, organized during the spring of 1911 with a $100,000 capital stock to manufacture and deal in automobiles and accessories. Incorporators were H.S.J. Flynn, S. Friedlander and T.E. Flynn.
    The Motor League of America, organized in Syracuse, New York during the spring of 1909 with $100,000 capital stock to manufacture automobiles and engines. Incorporators were A.A. Schlachter, E. Woods and T.A. Levy.
    The Motor Machine and Manufacturing Company of Chicago, Illinois, organized late in 1907 with a capital stock of $2500 to manufacture motor cars and accessories. Incorporators were S. Williams and J.G. Finkbeiner.
    The Motor Mechanism Company of Cleveland, Ohio, organized late in 1912 with a capital stock of $25,000 for the manufacture of motor cars and parts. Incorporators were E. Younger, F. Castle, H.O. Evans, H.E. Gray and S.E. Sackerman.
    The Motor Products Company of Chelsea, Michigan, organized in late 1913 with a capital stock of $100,000 to manufacture motor vehicles. Joseph S. McDowell was behind this venture.
    The Motor Sales Company of Boston, Massachusetts, organized in late 1914 with a capital stock of $50,000 for the manufacture of automobiles. Incorporators were A.L. West, R.F. Tift and W.J. Cronin.
    The Motor Sales & Service Corporation of Riverton, New Jersey, which built the Hilton in 1920-1921. Refer to Hilton.
    The Motor Specialty Makers of Chicago, Illinois, organized during the summer of 1911 with a capital stock of $2500 to manufacture and deal in automobiles and accessories. Incorporators were C.B. MacDowell, R.A. Love and I.H. Kessler.
    The Motor Specialities Company of Oswego, New York, organized during the fall of 1911 with a capital stock of $175,000 for the manufacture of engines and automobiles. Incorporators were Arthur Lovell, Howard H. Williams and H.V. Walsh.
    The Motor Taximeter Cab Company of New York City, organized during the summer of 1908 with a capital stock of $150,000 to manufacture, operate and rent vehicles. Incorporators were H.C. Kibber and J.P. Murray.
    The Motor Touring Car Company of New York City, organized during the spring of 1905 with a capital stock of $25,000 to manufacture and rent automobiles. C.A. Sheehan, F.A. Fox and Florence M. Fox were the incorporators.
    The Motor Vehicle Company of Newark, New Jersey, organized late in 1905 with a capital stock of $5000 for the manufacture of automobiles. Alfred A. Walsh, William F. Kimber and William P. Howe were the incorporators.
    The Motor Vehicle Company of Savannah, Georgia, organized in late 1912 with a capital stock of $200,000 for the manufacture of automobiles. Incorporators were S. Myers, S.T. Stewart and W.A. Collins.
    The Motor Vehicle & Marine Construction Company of Sewaren, New Jersey, organized late in 1911 with a capital stock of $15,000 for the manufacture of automobiles. Incorporators were Henry E. Acker, Albert B. Boynton and William C. Muir.
    The Motor Vehicle Power Company of Philadelphia, Pennsylvania, organized during the spring of 1901 for the manufacture of running gear and complete vehicles.

MOTOR-BOB — Buffalo, New York — (1914) — The Motor-Bob was a juvenile car designed by E.N. Bowen of Buffalo and sold unassembled for $125. The instruction booklet had to be purchased separately for a quarter, and large working blueprints were another thirty-five cents. Only one engine — a 2 1/2 hp single-cylinder — was available but for thirty dollars a shaft-drive, worm-gear, friction-transmission setup was offered as an option to the standard belt drive. The completed car was 96 inches long, 31 inches wide and weighed 150 pounds. Speeds of up to 15 mph were claimed. Bowen made all the parts of the Motor-Bob himself, though his

1911 Motor-Bob, runabout, WLB

casting work was done for him by the J.W. Pohlman Company of Buffalo. Whether E.N. Bowen was any relation to the George B. Bowen who built a gasoline runabout in Buffalo at the turn of the century is not known, but seems likely.

MOTOR BUGGY — The Motor Buggy Company of Fort Wayne, Indiana was noted in trade directories of 1908 as the manufacturer of a highwheeler. Details regarding its car are lacking. In November 1908 the firm announced plans to move from Fort Wayne to Joliet, Illinois. That move apparently was never made, and the Fort Wayne operation had ceased by 1909.

The product of the Motor Buggy Manufacturing Company of Minneapolis, Minnesota was most often referred to as an M.B. Refer to M.B.

1916 Motor Chair, NAHC

MOTOR CHAIR — Chicago, Illinois — (1915-1916) — The Motor Chair Sales and Operation Company of Chicago introduced its motorized chair car at the Panama-Pacific Exposition in San Francisco in 1915 and introduced it on the market the year following. Battery powered, the Motor Chair was mounted on a substantial running gear with solid-tired wheels suspended on ball bearings. Bodies of metal or oak and rattan were available, and the company offered to build custom chairs to order.

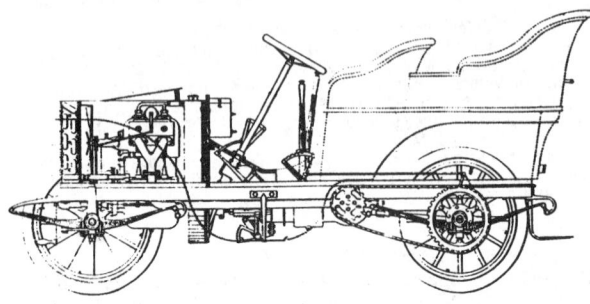

1903 Motor & Gear, tourer, LC

MOTOR & GEAR — New York, New York — (1903) — The Motor & Gear Manufacturing Company of 136 Liberty Street in New York City exhibited at Madison Square Garden in January of 1903 and declared itself ready to enter the automotive field as a producer. Although the vehicle talked about at the Garden was a two-cylinder 16 hp tourer, the firm also planned

to fit single- and four-cylinder engines to its basic chassis, and to adapt that chassis to carry commercial vehicle bodies as well. Probably some problems developed with the prototype, since Motor & Gear announced in March that it would give up the manufacture of complete cars and concentrate only on parts manufacture henceforth.

MOTOR HORSE — This was the mechanical horse that was the idea of Joseph Barsaleaux of Sandy Hill, New York in 1897. Refer to Barsaleaux. Uriah Smith of Battle Creek, Michigan had an idea along similar lines two years later. Refer to Horsey Horseless.

MOTORETTE — The cars produced by the George N. Pierce Company in 1901 and 1902 were called simply Motorette. They were the forerunner of the famous Pierce-Arrow. Refer to Pierce-Arrow.

1911 Motorette, model B, runabout, KM

MOTORETTE — Hartford, Connecticut — (1911-1914) — "Motorette is not a general word descriptive of all three-wheel motor vehicles," *Cycle and Automobile Trade Journal* announced in October 1911, "but has been registered as a trademark by the C.W. Kelsey Manufacturing Company of Hartford, Connecticut for their own product." Carl Kelsey had been building cars since his schoolboy days before the turn of the century, following graduation from college had begun selling them, ultimately becoming the sales manager for Maxwell-Briscoe and the man most responsible for the phenomenal rise in popularity that the Maxwell enjoyed. In 1910 he left that company following a disagreement with Benjamin Briscoe, intent now on becoming a manufacturer himself, and intent as well on competing with Henry Ford. His first effort was a four-wheeler called the Spartan, which didn't proceed beyond the prototype stage, principally because while Carl Kelsey was roadtesting it for production, Henry Ford slashed a couple of hundred dollars off his Model T's price tag, and Kelsey recognized that he could not afford to manufacture the car as a T competitor. If he couldn't compete with Ford, Kelsey reasoned next, he would undersell him. And he didn't think anyone would mind if to do that required the elimination of one wheel, and accommodations for only two passengers, since his price would be $385, about half that of a Model T. Just about everybody else in America had given up on the three-wheeler idea, but Kelsey was convinced he could do better. His three-wheeler might lean, but it would never tip over. He invented a cross bar and a system of links and levers so connecting the front axle with the frame that both the full-elliptic springs were forced to act together. (There was a truss connection over the rear wheel as well.) Kelsey called this a stabilizer; others when they adopted the same system preferred the term anti-sway bar. Kelsey's tiller-steered Motorette was introduced at Grand Central Palace in New York City on New Year's Eve of 1910. A little car, it was built like a big one: a pressed steel frame like Packard's, an I-beam front axle like Pierce-Arrow's, vanadium springs like Locomobile's, a tubular radiator like Alco's. This big-name dropping in which Kelsey freely indulged was designed to negate the Motorette's being thought sleazy, and the stunting in which he indulged was aimed at demonstrating the piquant little car's durability. During the dead of winter, he sent one Motorette across the continent, another pulled a 5700-pound Alco truck through the streets of Philadelphia, yet another was among the only three cars (a Stanley Steamer and Napier Special the other two) that made it to the top of Mt. Washington one afternoon. The car showed well in a Glidden Tour. Speed contests weren't tried because the Motorette's top was 25 mph. Commercial versions, with package carriers mounted on the front, were offered, and a rickshaw was designed for use in the Orient. The initial reception was terrific; it appeared America could be convinced of the efficacy of a three-wheeler, certainly as a family's second car, if not the first. Initially, Motorettes were air-cooled, then water-cooled, first two-strokes, then four-strokes; they were always two-cylinders. In 1911, Carl Kelsey made the mistake of contracting his engine building to Lycoming so he could concentrate on chassis improvements. A strike at Lycoming brought production to a halt, and when it was settled the arriving engines were quickly installed in the Kelsey-built chassis and sent out immediately to patiently waiting customers. They were all returned, their motors frozen. Upon investigation, sand was found in the crankcase of each one, apparently put there by still disgruntled Lycoming workers. That finished the C.W. Kelsey Manufacturing Company. In 1912 Kelsey reorganized as the Kelsey Motor Company and announced that electric Motorettes "fitted with motors in accordance with suggestions furnished by Thomas A. Edison" would be forthcoming, but they never were, in any great number anyway. Approximately 210 Motorettes had been built by late September of 1913, when Carl Kelsey announced his retirement from the automobile manufacturing field. Unofficially, he continued putting together a few Motorettes in his Hartford factory into 1914, and later that year thought for a short while of revising the Motorette into a four-cylinder, four-wheeled cyclecar, but only a prototype was built. By 1915 he was in the banking business, though within a year he had designed another car which would be introduced after the First World War as a Kelsey.

1911 MOTORETTE
Motorette — 2-cyl., 10 hp, 74" wb

	FP	5	4	3	2	1
Model M Rbt.	385	1500	2500	3600	5500	11,000

1912 MOTORETTE
Motorette — 2-cyl., 10 hp, 74" wb

	FP	5	4	3	2	1
Model A Rbt.	335	1500	2500	3600	5500	11,000
Model L Conv. Delivery	400	1600	2700	3800	5800	12,000
Model N Light Delivery	500	1400	2400	3500	5300	10,000

1913 Motorette, model R-1, Rickshaw, HAC

1913-1914 MOTORETTE
Motorette — 2-cyl., 10 hp, 72" wb

	FP	5	4	3	2	1
Model M-1 Rbt.-2P	350	1600	2700	3800	5800	12,000
Model R-1 Rickshaw-2P	500	1800	2800	4000	6200	13,000

MOTORMOBILE — The Motormobile of 1901 was one of two cars built a decade apart by Carl Lipman of Beloit, Wisconsin. Refer to Lipman.

MOTORMOBILE — Passaic, New Jersey — (1901) — The Motormobile Company of Passaic was organized early in 1901 to manufacture automobiles to the designs of an inventor named S.D. Mott. "The boiler is intermediate between the instantaneous or flash generator and the fire tube boiler now common in carriages," *The Horseless Age* reported that summer. "The water feed is automatic, on the gravity system, which dispenses with the use of pumps and injectors. The generator is built up of ½ inch copper tubing and weighs 110 pounds." A kerosene burner was fitted, and the engine had a universal joint suspension. The driving mechanism of the vehicle was fully enclosed. If any production of this vehicle resulted, it was minimal. The Motormobile Company had departed the automotive field by 1902.

MOTT — The Mott Wheel Works of Utica, New York was organized early in 1907 with a capital stock of $25,000 "to engage in the manufacture of bicycles, whole or in parts, wagons, carriages, motor cars and other vehicles, agricultural implements and various other things." So far as is known, however, Mott never built an automobile.

MOTZ — Akron, Ohio — (1900) — In December of 1900 Charles A. Motz of Akron completed his motor carriage, which had a single-cylinder engine with largish bore-stroke dimensions of six-and-a-half by seven inches. There is no indication that he ever built another.

MOULTON-JORDAN — The Moulton-Jordan Motor Car Company was organized in Minneapolis, Minnesota early in 1905 with a capital stock of $120,000 for the manufacture of automobiles. The partners involved were E.H. Moulton, Jr. and Theodore C. Jordan. Manufacture is doubted, but the firm did establish a garage and became dealers for the Franklin, Peerless, Locomobile and Corbin automobiles. In late 1906 Moulton-Jordan was succeeded by the Jordan Automobile Company.

MOUND CITY — The Mound City Automobile Company was organized in St. Louis, Missouri during the spring of 1904 with a capital stock of $10,000 to manufacture and deal in automobiles. John N. Bissell and Anderson M. Robertson of St. Louis were joined in this venture by James A. Scott of Alton, Illionis; Wilkinson C. Morse of Chillicothe, Illinois; and Edward W. Bissell of Poplar Bluff, Missouri. Manufacture is doubted.

MOUNT — Red Bank, New Jersey — (1908) — The only factor documented regarding the automotive venture of John W. Mount of Red Bank was his fire on June 12th, 1908. Apparently both carriages and automobiles had been built in his small shops. Damages estimated at $60,000 were sustained in the fire. John Mount was insured for only $8000.

MOUNT CLEMENS — The Mount Clemens Motor Car Manufacturing Company was organized early in 1910 with a capital stock of $200,000 for the manufacture of automobiles in Mount Clemens, Michigan. Robert Klagge, Fred Breitmeyer and Charles Lonsby of Mount Clemens were joined in this venture by H.H. Thorpe of Detroit. Attention was planned to be focused principally on the production of a delivery wagon. Manufacture is doubted.

MOUNT MORRIS — The Mount Morris Garage Company was organized during the summer of 1906 with a capital stock of $5000 to manufacture, maintain and repair motor vehicles in Mount Morris, New York. Incorporators were A.G. Ibbekem, F.W. Cuttrell and E.L. Barney. Manufacture is doubted.

MOUNT PLEASANT — Mount Pleasant, Michigan — (1915) — Only the prototype used this name. In 1915 the Mount Pleasant Motor Company staged a contest for the naming of its car, offering a five-dollar prize for something "short and catchy." The result was the M.P.M., and all subsequent cars were sold as such.

MOUNT WOLF — The Mount Wolf Car Company was organized in York, Pennsylvania during the spring of 1915 for the manufacture of both touring and convertible cars. Capital stock was $50,000, and a manufacturing site in Mount Wolf was selected. J.C. Krout was to manage the factory. C.J. Eisenhower was president of this venture, Henry S. Kohn was secretary. Among others of the interested were Albert Hoff, A.H. Diehl, Stephen A. Korh, Eli Hoff, George Sensabaugh and J.F. Buser. The venture is believed to have died aborning.

MOUNTAIN CITY — During the fall of 1910, S.W. Reams of the Mountain City Machine Works in Greenville, South Carolina announced his intention to begin the manufacture of 30 hp low-priced runabouts within two months. Associated with him in this venture was George Ledbetter, who was described as having had "experience in the automobile business in the North." Manufacture is doubted.

MOVER — The B & F Mover Company of Chicago, Illinois was indicated in 1902 trade directories as the manufacturer of an automobile. Documentation is lacking.

1903 Moyea, touring, WLB

MOYEA — Middletown, Ohio & Rye, New York — (1903-1904) — The Moyea Automobile Company was organized in January of 1903, and it was explained at the time that the name derived from the Indian word meaning "swift running." Henry Cryder, receiver for the Automobile Company of America, was responsible for both the name and the incorporation of this new company. Moyea headquarters were at 3 West 29th Street in New York City. Initially, Moyea cars would be built in Middletown, Ohio, prior to the completion of the Moyea factory in Rye, New York. The Moyea was a legitimate copy of the French Rochet-Schneider, the company having acquired the U.S. license for its manufacture. It was an expensive car. In January 1904 Moyea changed its firm's name to Consolidated Motor Company. Because the Rye factory was not yet complete and because detail changes in the 1903 car were found to be necessary from the French design (European roads being much better than American during this period, doubtless the chassis needed strengthening), the building of the prototype 1904 model was entrusted to the Alden Sampson Machine Company in Pittsfield, Massachusetts. The body for the car was built by the Springfield Metal Body Company in nearby Springfield. Apparently, Alden Sampson was most impressed with the result. Sampson himself drove a Moyea from Pittsfield to New York, a distance of 190 miles, in just eight hours. By the end of 1904, the Alden Sampson company had bought out Consolidated Motor and began production itself. All subsequent cars were called Alden Sampsons.

1903 MOYEA
Four — 12/16 hp, 88" wb

	FP	5	4	3	2	1
Tonneau-5P	5000	2300	3300	4600	7500	16,000

1904 MOYEA
Four — 25 hp, 91" wb

	FP	5	4	3	2	1
Touring-5P	4000	2400	3400	4800	8000	17,000

MOYER — Syracuse, New York — (1911-1915) — "All Roads Are Level to a Moyer" was the company slogan, but it would appear that the road was not easy for Harvey Allen Moyer. He was a native of Clay, New York who had established himself as a wagon builder in Cicero in 1875, moving to Syracuse in 1880, and building himself a fine reputation by the turn of the century. The horseles age did not apparently interest him much prior to 1908 when he built his first experimental automobile, and although he announced during the summer of 1909 that he was all set to produce 200 cars, it is unlikely that manufacture even began more than a few months prior to 1911. Moyer built big cars, and he built them well. Prices were in the $2000-$3000 range, and full-pressure lubrication was a progressive feature. Both fours and sixes were produced. Though he intended to introduce a lighter and less expensive version of the latter for the 1916 model year, Harvey Moyer did not have the capital to do so. Indeed, by the end of 1915 he found it necessary to discontinue his automobile business, after the production of about 400 cars. No company had ever been incorporated for their manufacture, incidentally. The Moyer was strictly a one-man operation. Most of the Moyer promotional material was written in first-person singular.

1911 Moyer, model B, touring, OCW

1911 MOYER
Four — 28.9 hp, 116" wb

	FP	5	4	3	2	1
Model A Runabout	—	2300	3300	4600	7500	16,000
Model B Touring	—	2500	3500	5000	8500	18,000

1912 Moyer, model C, runabout, OCW

1912 MOYER
Four — 28.9 hp, 116" wb

	5	4	3	2	1
Model B Touring	2350	2500	3500	5000	8500	18,000
Model C Runabout	2200	2300	3300	4600	7500	16,000

Six — 38.4 hp, 121" wb

Model D Touring	3000	3300	4400	6700	12,000	24,000

1914 Moyer, model E, runabout, WLB

1913-1915 MOYER
Four — 32 hp, 121" wb

Model E Touring/Runabout	2500	2500	3500	5000	8500	18,000

Six — 49 hp, 135" wb

Model G Touring-7P	3250	3300	4400	6700	12,000	24,000

M.P.M. — These initials have occasionally been represented to be a car built by M.P. Moller during the early 1920's. In addition to a plethora of taxicabs, Moller did indeed build a car during this period, but it was the Dagmar. M.P.M. was never a designation considered for the cars of Mathias P. Moller. The error may have simply been a typographical one. During this same period, a firm called H.P.M. Motors marketed an automobile called the Moller. It was produced by Wilhelm and Holgar Moller and another company altogether.

1916 M.P.M., model 44, touring, WLB

M.P.M. — Mount Pleasant, Michigan — (1915) — A five-dollar prize for a "short and catchy" name for the car resulted in the M.P.M. from Mount Pleasant, Michigan. The initials also stood for Mount Pleasant Motor Company. The car was the idea of Louis J. Lampke of New Jersey, but he had been unable to secure financing for it on the East Coast. Initially, it seemed the Michigan town was enthusiastic. The Mount Pleasant Motor Company was organized with $5000 capital stock; and a board composed of prominent members of Mount Pleasant, including Mayor Deuel, urged Lampke into full speed ahead. Lampke came up with a 44 hp V-8 tourer and a smaller four roadster — priced at $1095 and $1085 respectively — and production commenced. Ten cars were built and sold by late spring of 1915, but then Lampke ran out of money and asked for $10,000 more. Suddenly, the Mount Pleasant citizenry grew cool to the idea of automobile manufacturing. In July an offer from the Board of Trade in Saginaw seemed to augur an M.P.M. move to that city, but the plan fell through in December. The company just faded away after that. Its first ten cars were also its last. Several years later the M.P.M. factory in Mount Pleasant was sold for $3750. Meanwhile, Louis J. Lampke remained in Saginaw to build the Yale 8.

1915 M.P.M.
Eight — 44 hp, 113" wb

	FP	5	4	3	2	1
Touring-5P	1095	3200	4300	6500	11,000	23,000

Four — 112" wb

	FP	5	4	3	2	1
Roadster-3P	1085	2500	3500	5000	8500	18,000

1897 Mueller Motor Carriage, NAHC

MUELLER — Decatur, Illinois — (1896-1899) — Hieronymus Mueller founded his Mueller Manufacturing Company in Decatur in 1861. He had six sons — Robert, F.B., Philip, Adolph, Henry and Oscar — all of whom were brought into the family business. The Muellers manufactured water plumbing and gas meters, valves and other devices. In 1895 they imported a German Benz, which they modified and entered in the Chicago Times-Herald Contest that year and which they used as a basis for all their subsequent development work. In 1896 their first car was given an official road test, from Decatur to Bloomington, and their arrival in the latter city caused a considerable stir, the Mueller's being the first horseless carriage ever seen there. The car was demonstrated at the fair grounds. "The machine has but one cylinder which makes it a matter of difficulty to climb steep hills," a Bloomington reporter wrote. "The firm has just completed a strictly American motor carriage which will carry four persons, both seats facing forward, and which will have a double-cylinder motor." Hieronymous Mueller was careful to credit the Mueller automotive efforts to his entire family, and he hinted that they just might go into automobile manufacture. The Muellers never did, however. Possibly not more than four vehicles were built in all, with the name Mercury attached to at least one of them. References to Mueller-built cars in automobile publications of the day end at the turn of the century. In January 1901 the entire gasoline vehicle business of the Mueller company (including blueprints, patents and all equipment) was put up for sale.

MUELLER — Milwaukee, Wisconsin — (1909-1910) — At the turn of the century, as the Automobile Construction Company, Herman C. Mueller declared himself ready to build whatever car a purchaser might desire, either from one of myriad stock designs he had on hand or from designs and/or parts provided by the client. The catch-as-catch-can aspect of this business obviously didn't appeal to Mueller because he remained in it for a short time only. He stayed in Milwaukee, however, to become an automobile dealer, and at this he was successful. Beginning in 1909 his Mueller Motor Car Company also offered a standard motor buggy of its own for sale. Again, Mueller found being a manufacturer not particularly appealing, and he shortly returned to dealing in cars exclusively.

MUGGE — During the summer of 1910 Robert Mugge of Tampa, Florida announced his intention to construct a building for the manufacture and repair of automobiles which would measure 80 by 250 feet, by three stories high and would be "the largest factory in town." Mugge was described as "heavily interested" in the Sunlight Manufacturing Company in Tampa. His automobile venture, however, seems not to have seen the light of day.

MUIR — Norfolk, Connecticut — (1900) — John S. Muir of South Norfolk quit his job at the Edison Electrical Company prior to the turn of the century because he was convinced he was on to something big — in his own phrase, "how to make something of nothing, or, in other words, how to run an automobile without expense." His solution was compressed air. The automobile he built to test his idea had two tanks each with a capacity for 1000 pounds of compressed air. "Filled up," the car could run 100 miles without recharging. His plan was to have the tanks filled initially by factory machine, but to provide a hand-compressor device with each car sold so that the owner could easily "fill up" himself. Few people were sold on the idea.

MUIER — The Muier Company was a $100,000 Delaware incorporation from the summer of 1913 for the manufacture and sale of automobiles. Incorporators were S.E. Roberson, C.J. Jackobs and H.W. Davis. Manufacture is doubted.

MULFORD — Brooklyn, New York — (1915, 1922) — An automobile race driver of the first rank, Ralph K. Mulford might have enjoyed the same renown as an automobile builder except for his ingenuous trust in people which invariably resulted in his losing vast sums of money in business deals that were nothing more than stock swindles. In all, he built seven automobiles, the first two as the Ralph K. Mulford Company in 1915. They were prototypes for production, but the two bankers backing him simply took the cars for themselves and closed up his shop. He tried again as Mulford Motors Company in 1922, but again he was hoodwinked. In later years he could not remember much about the cars at all, except that he designed and built — or rebuilt — every part of them himself. His favorite was powered by a four-cylinder engine with four valves per cylinder which he said he patterned after the Duesenberg engine. He had worked with the Duesenberg brothers prior to the First World War, and Duesenberg engines were modified by him for use in several of his cars. Ralph Mulford died a poor man during the late Seventies. None of the cars he built are believed to survive, but the wonderful image of the great racing driver who built them will live forever.

MULHOLLAND — The Mulholland Company of Dunkirk, New York announced during the summer of 1906 its intention to manufacture electric cars in 1907. That this happened is doubted.

MULLER — The front-wheel-drive prototype built by William J. Muller in Philadelphia during the late Twenties, and which he nicknamed Alligator, ultimately saw production in St. Louis (Missouri) and Hartford (Wisconsin) as the Ruxton. Refer to Ruxton.

MULTI — The Multi Manufacturing Company was organized in Chicago, Illinois late in 1910 with a capital stock of $100,000 to manufacture and deal in automobiles, parts and accessories. Incorporators were George W. Beyers, M.M. Freiberg and H.A. Caperton. Manufacture is doubted.

1913 Multiplex, touring, WLB

MULTIPLEX — Berwick, Pennsylvania — (1912-1913) — The Multiplex Manufacturing Company of Berwick produced a roadster, raceabout and touring car on a big 134-inch wheelbase chassis with power supplied by a 50 hp four-cylinder engine from Waukesha. The price range was $3125 to $3600. Multiplex said its cars represented "the highest expression of touring luxury." Either few people agreed, or could afford to so express them-

selves, because total sales of the Multiplex after two years of trying was only fourteen cars. The designer of the Multiplex was one F. Bingaman, who apparently also ran up a short 85-inch wheelbase sporting job that weighed but 980 pounds and was claimed to do 126 mph. It was slated to sell for $4000, but the company failed before it could be produced. The high point in the Multiplex history, perhaps, was its fine first-place win in the "sealed bonnet" road test conducted by the Philadelphia Automobile Club in the spring of 1913.

1912-1913 MULTIPLEX
Four — 50 hp, 134" wb

	FP	5	4	3	2	1
Touring	3600	3100	4200	6300	10,500	22,000
Roadster	3175	3000	4000	6000	9500	21,000
Raceabout	3125	3100	4200	6300	10,500	22,000

MUNCH-ALLEN — Although the car was initially planned to carry the name of the partners involved, by the time it was produced in 1909 to 1910 (first in Yonkers, New York, subsequently in DuBois, Pennsylvania), the name had been changed to Keystone Six. Refer to Keystone Six.

MUNCIE — In 1903 the Muncie Wheel & Jobbing Company of Muncie, Indiana introduced a new car named for factory superintendent Hugh L. Warner. Refer to Warner.

MUNSING — The Munsing Motor Car Company was organized in Hoboken, New Jersey early in 1909 with a capital stock of $1 million to manufacture motor cars, engines and trucks. Incorporators were W.H. Buresmith, J.P. Franklin and C.H. Bellows, Jr. In 1910 the venture was reincorporated in New York City for $500,000, with motor boats added to the manufacturing scheme. Evidence of any automobile manufacture is lacking, however. A Munsing Tractor Company followed in New York City in 1912, with the same apparent lack of results.

1900 Munson, gas-electric runabout, NAHC

MUNSON — La Porte, Indiana — (1896-1900) — John W. Munson of Chicago was the man behind the Munson Company, but it would appear that he did not know a great deal about cars. The first Munson Electric was built in Chicago and was taken to La Porte, Indiana when the company moved there. "This vehicle was used to give demonstration rides to prominent citizens of La Porte, but to the best of my knowledge the engine never drove the motor as a generator," remembered P.M. Heldt. "It had been bought from an outside manufacturer, and no one connected with the organization seemed to know how to start it." P.M. Heldt was the engineer brought to La Porte to set things right, and get things going. The Munson he designed was most likely the first viable gas-electric car to be built in America. As described by Heldt, "All of the machinery was carried on a frame extending between the front and rear axles, the frame being pivotally connected to the front axle at its middle, to enable the wheels to freely follow road surface inequalities. Adjacent to the generator there was a two-speed gear of the individual (friction) clutch type, and from the secondary shaft of this transmission there was direct drive by spur gears to the live rear axle, which had an exposed differential gear." Four vehicles — including an eleven passenger omnibus — were built for testing purposes, and both passenger cars and commercial vehicles were envisioned from the outset. A splendid brochure was printed up, and company promotion noted that ten gallons of gasoline and a charged battery would propel a Munson "100 miles or more over ordinary well-traveled country roads at the rate of five to fifteen miles per hour." Properly organized now, the Munson Company listed William Niles as president, Meinrad Rumely as vice-president, Dr. C.S. Fahnestock as secretary-treasurer, and W.H. Phelps as superintendent. One wonders what had become of John Munson, who was not listed at all, and why manufacture did not follow. Entries from a La Porte citizen's diary at the turn of the century indicate that John Munson remained in town, and that the Munson vehicles were often tested locally. On May 7th, 1900 the Munson was in Chicago being shown to prospective Chicago and New York capitalists, with the Munson Safety Automobile Company being organized in the latter city. But the venture seems to have ended shortly thereafter "for reasons which it is not necessary to go into," as P.M. Heldt later noted. Some of the Munson assets were subsequently sold to the Oil Well Supply Company of Pittsburgh. Among other accomplishments, P.M. Heldt went on to a distinguished career as an automotive technical writer.

1901 Murdaugh, runabout, NAHC

MURDAUGH — Oxford, Pennsylvania — (1901-1903) — Burton Murdaugh operated a bicycle shop at the corner of Third and Locust Streets in the business district of Oxford. At the turn of the century, three automobiles were produced in his shop. The first two were built by Murdaugh himself. And they were marvelously described to Oxford historian Frank Peters by Ira W. Terry in an interview conducted for this book in 1982. Ira Terry was an apprentice barber in a shop nearby where the Murdaugh vehicles were built. "The first one proved not satisfactory, and a second one a little larger was built," Ira Terry related at age ninety-four. "Each had a chain-drive, one-cylinder gasoline engine with bicycle wheels...and with a straight rear, having no differential; as a result they were hard to steer, having a tiller for that purpose. Each was built with a seat for two with the gas tank underneath along with the motor. A bicyclist could out run the car on most occasions. The second car performed better than the first one but still had problems in that Mr. Murdaugh who drove the car up North Third Street most every day had to walk back, the car either pushed or hauled back too. One Memorial Day parade the car was forced out by some problem. Needless to say, the cars made problems for the other modes of transportation, horse-power." Mr. Terry was given a ride through the local cemetery one day in the Murdaugh. The third, and final, car was built by George Butcher, a black employee at the bicycle shop, and although it performed better than the other two, manufacture was not embarked upon. Burton Murdaugh did describe himself as the "Murdaugh Automobile Company" to the automotive trade press in 1901, and he indicated $600 as the selling price for his car. But whether he sold any of the three he built Mr. Terry could not recall. Subsequently, Burton Murdaugh went on to a fine career of thirty-one years with the Bell Telephone Company, serving as district plant superintendent in the West Chester district. His obituary in 1944 noted in the first paragraph that he had built the first automobile in Oxford.

1901-1903 MURDAUGH
Rbt. (1-cyl., 3-1/4 hp, 57" wb)

	FP	5	4	3	2	1
Runabout	600	—	—	—	—	—

MURILLO — Although the Murillo Manufacturing Company of Marion, Indiana announced its plans to enter the automotive field in 1906, it never did so. This rather irked Lembert W. Coppock who had joined the firm precisely for that reason. He moved to Decatur, Indiana where the Decatur Utility Car was introduced in 1910. Refer to Decatur.

MURLOCK — The Murlock which presumably was built by the Murlock Automobile Manufacturing Company of Buffalo, New York in 1903 was merely a typographical error appearing in the trade press that year. The car instead was the ill-fated Morlock. Refer to Morlock.

MURPHY SPECIAL — Minneapolis, Minnesota — (1906) — James M. Murphy and Charles Dennis were the men behind the Auto Construction Company of Minneapolis which was located at 1401 Hennepin Avenue from 1905 to 1906, and at 619-1/2 First Avenue South in 1907. During the middle year of the firm's existence, Auto Construction reportedly built a car called the Murphy Special. Documentation of this is lacking.

MURRAY — The Murray Manufacturing Company was organized in Pittsburgh, Pennsylvania early in 1912 for the purpose of manufacturing and selling motor cars, motor trucks and motor boats. The Murrays involved were James E., Frank P. and Thomas, and they were joined in the venture by John L. Howder and W.D. McBryar. Manufacture of a car is doubted.

MURRAY ELECTRIC — Boston, Massachusetts — (1897) — P.A. Murray was a Boston machinist who built a two-seater electric carriage in 1897 for clients who were identified only as the "Stanley Bros." Possibly they were Francis E. and Freelan O., who were then in the process of beginning their steam adventures in Watertown and who might have desired an example of their potential competition. "The carriage will be propelled by a chain and sprocket running from the motor, which will be supplied by power from a set of storage batteries in the rear of the body of the vehicle," the *Boston Herald* reported that year. "The wheels will be of the regular pneumatic sulky pattern." So far as is known, this electric was the only car built by P.A. Murray. The Stanleys built their steamer into the World War I years, and the car steamed on for another decade following their retirement.

1899 Murray, runabout, GR

MURRAY — Homer, New York — (1899) — Oliver Murray of Homer built himself a car in 1899. It was a quite ordinary high-wheeled gasoline buggy but apparently it proved sufficient to carry Murray into the Twentieth Century and the automotive age.

1902 Murray, runabout, NAHC

MURRAY — Adrian, Michigan — (1902-1903) — In 1899 Willis Grant Murray was a traveling salesman for the Arc Welding Company in Detroit. Entering the automotive field at the turn of the century, he was manager of the automobile department at Olds Motor Works in March 1901, when that company suffered its now famous fire. He left Detroit soon thereafter, anxious to strike out on his own. September found him in Adrian talking to Walter Clement, president of the Church Manufacturing Company. Incorporated in 1891, Church produced water pumps, steel land rollers and other products which now included gasoline engines. Murray sold Clement on his automobile idea. Clement offered him a $200-a-month salary, and a share in the profits; and Murray was given the green light to produce and find a market for the new Murray car. The prototype was completed and tested by January of 1902 and was exhibited at the Chicago Automobile Show in March. Not surprisingly, the car was a runabout of decidedly Olds resemblance. With a reported 14 hp engine (doubtless more hyperbole than horsepower), the Murray was claimed to be "the most powerful car of its kind in America." At $600, it was a good buy. Production began in

April, and that summer two Murrays were among 27 of the 80 entrants to finish a 100-mile race in Chicago. Clement gambled that the Murray car would be a big winner in the marketplace too, and virtually ceased manufacture of the usual Church company products to concentrate all effort on Murray production. But an attempt to secure needed capital for the factory change-over to quantity automobile assembly failed, and by September Willis Murray was handed a slip of paper announcing that his services were no longer needed. He took off for Chicago and joined the Standard Motor Vehicle Company. The Church automobile department was closed down temporarily, but it soon reopened, and production of the Murray (now renamed the Church) limped along. In December 1903 Walter Clement announced that his Church company was now in the wire-fence manufacturing business, emphasizing that automobile production had not been abandoned but instead simply curtailed pending the acquisition of additional financing. The Murray/Church had been abandoned, however. The new automobile from the company was a $1000 five-passenger touring car designed by Andrew Bachle, a gasoline engine builder from Detroit, and called the Lenawee after the county in which Adrian was located. It was produced only in 1904. Although the Church Manufacturing Company indicated itself as continuing to build automobiles into 1905, most probably this was a mere assembling of final vehicles from parts on hand. A single prototype called the Wilcox-Bachle was also built in 1905. In 1906 the old Church factory was taken over by the Page Woven Wire Fence Company, which immediately announced its intention to enter the automotive field, which it did but with even less luck than Church had enjoyed. Of the 225 Murrays built, four are known to survive; of the dozen Lenawees one remains extant.

1917 Murray Eight, roadster, WLB

MURRAY — Pittsburgh, Pennsylvania — (1916-1920) / Newark, New Jersey — (1920-1921) / MURRAY-MAC — Boston, Atlantic, Massachusetts — (1921-1929) — William M. Murray claimed he drove the first car in Pittsburgh (a De Dion tricycle before the turn of the century) and in 1916 was associated with the Packard distributorship in that city when he decided to build a car of his own. Joining him in the new Murray Motor Car Company organized in April of 1916 were J.W. Pontefract and W.W. Bensel. Fred Berger was chief engineer and Joseph Gardham production manager, though Berger left early on and was replaced by E.R. Fried. The first Murray was shown at the New York Automobile Salon in December 1916. It sported a Herschell-Spillman V-8 engine and a Rolls-Royce-like radiator. A roadster soon joined the touring car seen at the show, but the $2450 price tag did not long remain. By 1918 prices were up, a smaller open and a closed model added. Murray exhibited at both the New York Automobile Salon in November 1917 and the National Automobile Show in January 1918. A special touring car built to order for William C. Carnegie, outlandishly styled in the Cubist idiom, had received a good amount of attention at the Salon — and Murrays were widely regarded as very modish motorcars during this period. In January 1920, Murray announced the removal of its machinery from Pittsburgh to a new factory in Newark, New Jersey, though it would appear William N. Murray was no longer around, the Hon. Patrick J. Dolan being indicated as president. His tenure was decidedly brief, the Murray company being forced into receivership by its creditors that April. The Murray receiver subsequently reported that he could find no trace of manufacture in Newark, John J. McCarthy strode onto the Murray scene, hence the name change to Murray-Mac, though the car would not always be referred to thusly. Just who engineered it for him is not known, but it wasn't E.R. Fried because he strode out in 1921 to become chassis engineer for Pierce-Arrow. The Murray or Murray-Mac was now a six, and the handful built were fitted with whatever proprietary engine McCarthy could lay his hands on. References to the use of a Rochester-Duesenberg unit proved to be wishful thinking on McCarthy's part, as did extensive listings of models available which he occasionally supplied to the automotive trade press. A Murray-Mac sedan was built in 1926, but its two-wheel brakes indicate that it was probably run up on an old Murray chassis. Indeed, most of McCarthy's new cars used previous-generation Murray chassis. A roadster is known to have been built in 1927. Precisely where these cars were put together is something of a mystery, though the locale was somewhere in Massachusetts. At one point McCarthy said he was manufacturing in a marine engine plant in the Atlantic section of Quincy, but employees who were working for the Quincy company at that time insist that no car was ever built there. In early 1929 McCarthy attempted to reorganize the Murray Motor Car Company, proposing to build a $6500+ motorcar, and issuing a roster of 29 past Murray owners which included the aforementioned Carnegie, a Vanderbilt, a couple of Harrimans, Pliny Fisk, Mrs. William Thaw, movie star Mae Murray and novelist Mary Roberts Rinehart. Presumably this roster was meant to persuade prospective investors on the viability of financially backing the company; possibly the 29 owners mentioned had purchased the total production of Murray cars. A short notice in the April 1929 issue of *MoToR* revealed that "Murray Motor Car Company, formerly of Pittsburgh, has acquired a factory site at Everett, Mass., and announces that it will resume production of the Murray car. John J. McCarthy is president and manager." Murray production was never resumed, although the cars were being promoted as late as 1931. Subsequently, McCarthy turned his attention to diesel aviation engines.

1917 MURRAY
Eight — 34 hp, 128" wb

	FP	5	4	3	2	1
Tour.-7P	2450	3900	4800	7700	14,300	27,000
Rdst.-2P	2450	3700	4700	7300	13,700	26,000

1918 Murray Eight town car, KM

1918 MURRAY
Eight — 34 hp, 128" wb

Tour.-4P	2800	3900	4800	7700	14,300	27,000
Rdst.-2P	2800	3700	4700	7300	13,700	26,000
Sed.-5P	4000	2000	3000	4200	6500	14,000

1921 MURRAY / MURRAY-MAC
Superb Six - 52 hp, 129" wb

Rdst.-2P	2850	4000	5000	8000	15,000	28,000

1926 Murray-Mac, sedan, KM

1926-1927 MURRAY / MURRAY-MAC
Six — 52 hp, 129" wb

Sed.-5P	—	2000	3000	4200	6500	14,000
Rdst.-2P	—	3900	4800	7700	14,300	27,000

MUSKEGON — The Muskegon Motor Company was organized during the summer of 1905 to manufacture automobiles, motorcyles and gasoline engines in Muskegon, Michigan. Dr. C.J. Dove was president of this venture, Milo Pray was secretary-treasurer. Manufacture of a car is doubted.

MUTUAL — The Mutual Automobile Association was organized in New York City during the summer of 1909 with a capital stock of $50,000 for the manufacture of motor vehicles. Incorporators were F. Haasters, G.L. Clarke and O.B. Bachmann. Manufacture of a car is doubted.

The Mutual Garage Company was organized in New York City during the spring of 1909 with a capital stock of $10,000 for the manufacture of engines and automobiles and the operation of a garage. Incorporators were F.D. Searles, A.J. Moran and W. Holmes. Manufacture is doubted.

The Mutual Motor Car Company of Buffalo, New York was one of several firms involved in the building of the Niagara Four of 1915-1916. Refer to Niagara Four.

The Mutual Motor Service, Inc. was organized in Indianapolis, Indiana with a capital stock of $10,000 early in 1914 for the manufacture and sale of automobiles. Incorporators were Carl P. Lenz, C.B. Glick and W.C. Rutherford. Manufacture is doubted.

The Mutual Taxicab Company was organized in Pittsburgh, Pennsylvania during the fall of 1913 with a capital stock of $10,000 to manufacture and deal in taxicabs. Incorporators were Antonio Floecker, C.E. Meyer and M.J. Dain. Manufacture is doubted.

MYERS — New York, New York — (1901) — Thomas Myers was a machinist operating a small shop at 144 East 14th Street in Manhattan. There in 1901 he built himself a gasoline automobile. He is not believed to have built another.

MYERS — Berwick, Pennsylvania — (1907) — In 1907 in Berwick a young man who had to travel through life with the formidable name of Willie Westinghouse Edison Myers built an automobile. Specifications are lacking, but it is known that this enterprising lad realized his car by trading marbles for knives, the knives for a nanny goat, goats for a pony, the pony for a horse, and finally the horse for a gasoline motor. "The machine is now on the streets," *The Motor World* reported during the summer of 1907, "and its speedy careenings are giving all other traffic the shivers."

1911 Myers, roadster, RBB

MYERS — Atlanta, Georgia — (1911) — In 1910 the building at 38-40 Auburn Avenue in Atlanta was occupied by the Maxwell-Briscoe Southern Company, and in 1912 the Atlanta Automobile Brokerage Company moved in. But in 1911 the Myers was built there. It was named for F.M. Myers, Jr., who was listed in the Atlanta City Directory in 1910 as a clerk for the Southern Bell Telephone Company, and would be again in 1912, but in 1911 was indicated to be president of the Commercial Loan and Trust Company, which doubtless had been set up to provide financing for this automotive venture. The Myers was produced by another organization, the Consolidated Motor Car Company. Its president was Fletcher J. Spratling, an Atlantic merchandise broker; vice president was the afore-mentioned Mr. Myers; secretary was Francis H. Knauff, a civil engineer with Southern Bell; treasurer was James T. Knight, a traveling salesman. Robert C. Howard was general manager; all that is known about him is that he resided at the Majestic Hotel. The Myers was a four-cylinder assembled car offered as a roadster, tourer and light delivery. Production during its short life must have been minimal. By 1912 everyone involved in the Myers adventure was doubtless back doing what they had done before it began.

MYSTERY CAR — Chicago, Illinois - (1925) — That's what it was called, and it was exhibited at the Auditorium Hotel during Chicago Automobile Show week in 1925. "This car bore no name," *Motor Age* reported, "and those in charge of it studiously avoided revealing the name of the manu-facturer, although giving the impression that persons well known in the industry are back of it and have developed plans to produce the new car on a quantity basis." The car shown was a disc-wheeled five-passenger phaeton on a 103-inch wheelbase chassis, powered by a four-cylinder engine which one reporter guessed was "in the neighborhood of 150 cubic inches." A tantalizingly low price tag "in the neighborhood of $500" was

1925 Mystery Car, NAHC

bruited about. "This one, apparently, is going to cut a big dash in our auto-motive scheme of things," the *American Motorist* reporter opined. He had heard that "one of the most spectacular merchandising geniuses in the country, a man who has been strangely silent for several months" was behind the venture. Just who he was has not been determined. And the Mystery Car remains one.

1935 Mystery Car Electric, MVMA

MYSTERY CAR ELECTRIC — Oakland, California — (1935) — This Mys-tery Car from Oakland in 1935 is not one. A three-wheeled electric, it was built by Earl Clifford to advertise his battery supply house. The car was 4½ feet high, 8 feet long and cost about a cent a mile to operate.

NACHTWEY — Fond du Lac, Wisconsin — (1906) — During the winter of '06, James Nachtwey and Charles Schultz of Fond du Lac announced their building of a vehicle perfect for coursing wintry Wisconsin roads. Its body was that of a normal automobile, as was its three-speed transmission and 10 hp air-cooled engine. But this car was a sleigh. "The mode of propulsion will be by means of a steel wheel, four inches wide, to which prongs are attached," explained *The Horseless Age*. "This wheel is chain driven by the engine, and the prongs are of sufficient length to get a good purchase on snow or ice and propel the car."

1893 Nadig, gasoline carriage, NAHC

NADIG — Allentown, Pennsylvania — (1891-1896) — Although Henry Nadig neither patented his vehicle nor retained any records to verify the date of its building, his first car still exists. It was powered by a one-cylinder gasoline engine developing 2 hp at 600 to 800 rpm, with two flywheels, and set in a wagon-style chassis with belt drive, wooden wheels and steel rim tires. Nadig was among the early inventors called to testify in the Selden patent case. In his testimony, taken October 5th, 1905, he claimed the vehicle ran "under its own power when it was first finished on Fourth Street probably a dozen times in 1891." According to an article in *The Automobile* in 1901, the vehicle was used by the Nadigs until 1900. With his sons Charles and Lawrence, Henry Nadig later developed a two-cylinder engine developing between 12 and 14 hp, and this was placed in a new car of their design during the winter of 1895-1896. The Nadigs also built a gasoline truck around the turn of the century. Their automotive efforts, however, remained a sideline to their gasoline-engine building business. Manufacture was never contemplated.

1911 Nance, Six, touring, WLB

NANCE — Philadelphia, Pennsylvania — (1911) — The Nance Motor Car Company was organized by Harold B. Larzelere, former sales manager for the Chadwick from Pottstown, in September of 1910. Production began in early 1911. The Nance was a 35 hp six on a 122-inch wheelbase with a $1900 price tag, but it didn't remain the Nance for long. Larzelere quickly found himself another Philadelphian with more money to spend than backer Nance (also an ex-Chadwick man), and the same car was renamed the Touraine for model year 1912. A Nance roadster and touring car registered in California during World War I bore serial numbers 79 and 1004 respectively.

1911 NANCE
Six — 35/40 hp, 122" wb

	FP	5	4	3	2	1
Fore-Door Touring-5P	1900	3100	4200	6300	10,500	22,000
Fore-Door Roadster-2P	1900	3000	4000	6000	9500	21,000

NAPIER — In addition to being imported, the English Napier was manufactured in this country from 1904-1905 in Boston and from 1905-1911 in Jamaica Plain, Massachusetts. Refer to American Napier.

1917 Napoleon, 5-pass. touring, WLB

NAPOLEON — Napoleon, Ohio — (1916-1917)/Traverse City, Michigan — (1917-1919) — The Napoleon Motor Car Company was organized in the spring of 1916 in Napoleon, Ohio. The men behind the project were A.O. George, formerly chief engineer of the Fostoria Light Car Company; G.W. Russell, also of Fostoria; and F.N. McGrew, who had last worked for Auburn in Indiana. Malcolm Hall Ayer was general manager. "The new Napoleon is a daisy," reported the *Henry County Signal* on June 15th, "and a car that every citizen of this town can and should feel very proud of. The factory, while very young, managed with unusual effort to have the first machine ready for the arrival of the Dayton Boosters just to let them know that there were other towns able to show a mighty fine manufactured product. The local company deserves praise and encouragement from our people." Unfortunately, it didn't get it, or not enough of it anyway. Meanwhile, Traverse City in Michigan was anxious to welcome an automobile manufacturer to town because it was about to lose one of its two major industries, the Oval Wood Dish Company, to Tupper Lake, New York. The offer Traverse City made to Napoleon was $75,000 in working capital and rent-free use of the old Williams flooring factory for three years. Napoleon promptly moved to Michigan. The Traverse City Motor Car Company was formed with W.J. Chase as president, C.E. Culver as vice-president, Frank Trude as secretary-treasurer — and Leon Gauntlett, the Traverse City resident who had discovered Napoleon's availability for the move, as general manager and chief seller of stock. The car's name remained as Napoleon, and it remained a small 30 hp four with a $795 price tag as well for the remainder of the 1917 model year. The first six cars had been completed in Traverse City by November that year. For 1918 the four was beefed up to 37 hp, and a six was added. Capitalization was increased to $500,000 that summer, and the firm was reorganized as Napoleon Motors Company, with the intention now to enter the commercial vehicle field. Napoleon's first truck arrived in early 1919, and by year's end the company announced that trucks only would be the Napoleon product from now on. Total passenger car production had probably been in the 300-unit range. Napoleon trucks continued to be manufactured until 1923, although production had ground to a practical halt two years earlier when Napoleon began to feel the effects of the postwar depression. In the fall of '23 the Napoleon plant was sold to the Zapf Fruit Package Company. Three years later Zapf went broke, and Traverse City bought the old factory for $15,000 to use as a municipal garage.

1917 NAPOLEON
Model 30 — 4-cyl., 17 hp, 110" wb

	FP	5	4	3	2	1
Touring-5P	795	2700	3600	5300	8800	19,000
Touring-7P	795	2900	3700	5600	9100	20,000

1918-1919 NAPOLEON
Model 4-37 — 4-cyl., 37 hp

Roadster-3P	—	2500	3500	5000	8500	18,000
Touring-5P	—	2700	3600	5300	8800	19,000

Model 6-45 — 6-cyl., 45 hp

Touring-6P	—	2900	3700	5600	9100	20,000

NASH — The Nash Auto-Car Company has been indicated on various rosters as the producer of an automobile in Detroit for the years 1906 through 1911. Such a company was in existence in Detroit during the latter years, with its address at 12-13 Buhl Block. References from the summer of 1907 announced Nash Auto-Car's development of a four-cylinder two-stroke air-cooled motor. It seems likely that this firm produced engines only.

NASH

NASH — Kenosha, Wisconsin — (1917-1942 et. seq.) — Born in 1864 in Illinois and abandoned by his parents at age six, Charles W. Nash was "bound out" by a district court to work for a Michigan farmer from whom he was to receive room, board and three months of schooling a year until age twenty-one when $100, a new suit of clothes and freedom would be his. But Charlie Nash ran away at age twelve, got a paying job on another Michigan farm, learned the carpenter's trade, clerked in a grocery store in Flint, and by the early 1890's was the fastest cushion stuffer at the Flint Road Cart Company owned by William C. Durant and J. Dallas Dort. By 1895 he was managing the Durant-Dort Carriage Company, by 1910 he was heading the Buick Motor Car Company, by 1912 he was the president of General Motors. Rags to riches was a popular theme in novels of this period; Charlie Nash had managed to out-Alger Horatio. His career at General Motors ended in June 1916 like many did, in resignation following a policy dispute with Billy Durant. His next step was a logical one. He traveled to Kenosha and, with former GM man James Storrow, bought the Thomas B. Jeffery Company, former producers of the Rambler, the producers now of the Jeffery, and one of the oldest, best-known and largest automobile companies in the industry. The purchase price purportedly was $9 million. On July 29th, 1916, Nash Motors Company was born. The Jeffery was continued awhile in production, with Nash nameplates appearing on the cars from the summer of 1917. Indeed, the first Nash introduced remained a badge-engineered Jeffery. The first "Nash" Nash arrived on April 18th, 1918. It was a six designed by Erik Wahlberg, whom Nash had hired away from Oakland as his chief engineer; that the engine was overhead valve was no surprise given Nash's Buick experience, that both it and the Nash chassis (which featured Hotchkiss drive and semi-elliptic suspension all around) were formidably clean and tidy was commented upon with considerable favor in the trade press. Charlie Nash was a stickler for a conservative neatness, in car design and company management. Sales of 10,000+ cars in 1918 more than doubled, to 27,000, in 1919. In its first fifteen months of operation, Nash Motors netted over $2 million. Prior to the Armistice, the four-wheel-drive truck begun as the Jeffery was continued as the Nash Quad, alongside a standard Nash truck, but Charlie Nash began phasing out commercial vehicle manufacture by the Twenties, as he launched a several-pronged attack in the production car field. Introduced in 1920 was a brand-new car in the $5000 price range called the LaFayette, and built initially in Indianapolis; and that November

1917 Nash, model 674, sedan, JAC

in Kenosha, the Nash assembly line began humming with a new 35 hp four, in effect the 67 hp Nash six minus two cylinders and nine inches in wheelbase (or 112 inches) which Nash could sell for several hundred dollars less than his standard medium-priced product. For 1922 the four was provided rubber engine mounting and a "Carriole" sedan model at $1350, which was five dollars more expensive and introduced a few weeks after the Essex coach, forever after allowing the Hudson company to legitimately claim honors in pioneering the closed car in the popular-price field. Still, a net profit of $7.6 million for '22 had to make Charlie Nash feel good, as did sales for '23 which passed the 50,000 mark for the first time, for a net profit of $9.3 million. The LaFayette venture, which had moved into a new factory in Milwaukee by January of 1923, had proved a commercial disaster, however, and after pouring $2 million into it, Charlie Nash abandoned LaFayette manufacture early in 1924, moving the machinery from Milwaukee into the old Mitchell plant in Racine which he had just managed to outbid Hupp for. There from 1925 into 1926 he produced another new car at the opposite end of the scale from the LaFayette, the $865-$995 Ajax. He wasn't particularly thrilled with the less-than 25,000 Ajaxes sold during its first year, however, since more than 85,000 Nashes were delivered during the same period. But that was easily solved. The L-head Ajax six became the Nash Light Six during 1926, joining the Special and the Advanced ohv sixes, names having replaced the former numerical designations in 1925, the year Nash went six-cylinder across the board. In June of 1928 twin ignition arrived in Kenosha on the big Nashes, which increased horsepower measurably and made the Advanced a genuine 80 mph car, the Special good for 75 mph. The single-ignition Standard Six (former Light Six) shared its bigger brothers' invar-strutted aluminum pistons and compression ratio (5.0:1 from the former 4.5) for a car now capable of an easy 70 mph. These new Nashes were extremely fine cars with handsome Seaman bodies and price tags of $885-$2190, which made for some of the greatest bargains in the industry that year. More than 138,000 Nashes were produced in 1928, and Nash Motors made over $20 million. Charlie Nash was sixty-five years old when the stock market crashed. Already he had introduced for the 1930 model year one of the most splendid Nashes of all — the Twin-Ignition Eight, an ohv straight eight with nine main bearings, 298.6 cubic inches, 100 hp at 2900 rpm: "80 Miles an Hour in 3 Blocks," the billboards would say, and the price range was just $1675 to $2385. Because, unlike many manufacturers, Charlie Nash had not run wild during the Twenties, he was better prepared for the Thirties. His assets-to-liabilities ratio was by far the most exemplary in the automobile

1918 Nash, model 681, touring, JAC

industry; in 1931 when most companies lost money, Nash Motors turned a profit of $4.8 million. For 1932 Wahlberg and crew came up with even nicer Nashes boasting ride control, free wheeling, five-point rubber-insulated engine suspension and "synchro-shift." Nineteen thirty-two was an awful year in America, with industrywide automobile production a mere thirteen percent of the pre-Depression figure, but in Kenosha Charlie Nash's company made a million dollars. That year, in order to allow himself more time for long-range planning, he elevated associate Earl McCarty to Nash's presidency, retaining the chairmanship of the board which he had assumed after James Storrow's death in 1926. In 1933 he marked time with cars not noticeably different from '32, and for the first time in history Nash Motors lost money, a situation repeated in '34 though for a different reason, Charlie Nash had spent a fortune retooling for the new 1934 cars. The LaFayette name was revived for a car which now carried Nash into the low-priced ($595-$695) field. It used the L-head engine of the former Big Six, and although promoted under its own name until 1937, it was really a Nash model, just as the big Ambassador — and it was big, with wheelbases up to 142 inches — was at the opposite end of the Nash scale. In July of 1936 Charlie Nash purchased Seaman Body Corporation of Milwaukee (in which firm he had bought a half interest in 1919). In August Nash Motors was twenty years old, and Charlie Nash — now seventy-two — was growing tired. When Earl McCarty retired, Nash invited George W. Mason, the vice-president of Kelvinator Corporation, to become Nash president, to which Mason agreed so long as Nash bought Kelvinator. And so the deal was done. This provided comedians of the day with fodder for bad jokes: ice cube trays would now become standard equipment for Nash cars, Kelvinator refrigerators would get four-wheel brakes. But when the laughter died down, Nash had sold nearly 86,000 cars in 1937 (the best year of the decade) for a $3.5 million profit. The recession year of 1938 was bad for both cars and refrigerators, and the Nash-Kelvinator marriage had a $7.5 million loss. Under Mason's direction, Nash continued to build fine cars, however, with such interesting features from 1938 as the Weather-Eye controlled ventilation system and the option of overdrive first offered in 1936, 1940 saw a twenty-car production run of a nifty Ambassador Eight cabriolet styled by Alexis de Sakhnoffsky (who earlier had kibitzed with chief engineer Wahlberg on the 1934 Nash line) and the availability in England of a Perkins diesel-engined Nash. Since 1936 a Nash had been offered with a rear seat which converted into a bed. But it was 1941 which brought the biggest news from Nash; the Ambassador 600 which replaced the LaFayette and which boasted unitized body construction, torque tube drive, 75 bhp, 25-30 mpg and $750-$850 price tags. The public response was terrific; in 1941 sales topped 80,000 cars. Following Pearl Harbor, Nash cars ceased to be built in Kenosha, with Pratt & Whitney aviation engines manufactured instead for the duration of World War II. With the coming of peace, Nash was in a solid position as an independent. Nineteen forty-eight would mark the beginning of a new era for the company. In that year Charlie Nash died at age eighty-four on June 6th. Two months earlier, on April 1st, George Romney had arrived with a new idea of what a Nash should be.

Nash Data Compilation
by Arch Brown

1918

NASH — 680 — SIX: The 1918 Nash had a low hood line; short, vertical hood louvres; a painted radiator shell that was somewhat rounded on top; a slanted windshield on open models and shell headlamps.

I.D. DATA: Serial numbers on left front cross member, just in back of radiator. Starting: 100101. Engine numbers on right front of flywheel housing just behind starting motor.

Model No.	Body Type & Seating	Price	Weight	Start. Ser. No.
681	4-dr. Tr.-5P	1295	2930	100101
682	4-dr. Tr.-7P	1545	3040	111601
683	2-dr. Rds.-4P	1295	2930	121001
684	2-dr. Sed.-5P	1985	3455	100108
685	2-dr. Cpe.-4P	2085	3225	94501

Note: Models 681 and 683 have a 121 in. wheelbase. Other models have a 127 in. wheelbase.

ENGINE: Inline. OHV. Cast en bloc. Six. Cast iron block. B & S: 3-1/4 x 5 in. Disp.: 248.9 cu. in. Brake H.P. 55 @ 2400 R.P.M. N.A.C.C. H.P.: 25.35. Main bearings: Three. Valve lifters: Solid. Carb.: Marvel.

CHASSIS: W.B.: 121 in; 127 in. Frt/Rear Tread: 56 in./56 in. Tires: 34 x 4.

TECHNICAL: Selective, sliding gear transmission. Speeds: 3F/1R. Floor shift controls. Single dry plate clutch. Spiral bevel rear axle. Overall ratio: 4.50:1. Two-wheel external mechanical brakes. Artillery wheels.

HISTORICAL: Introduced: September 1, 1917. Enclosed overhead valve mechanism. Calendar year production: 10,283. The president of Nash was C.W. Nash. First Nash automobile. In its first full year of production, Nash accounted for 1.1% of all new car production in the U.S.

1918
Series 680, 6-cyl.

	FP	5	4	3	2	1
7P Tr	1465	1250	3900	6500	9100	13,000
5P Tr	1395	1250	3900	6500	9100	13,000
4P Rds	1395	1400	4200	7000	9800	14,000
7P Tr	1545	1250	3900	6500	9100	13,000
Sed	2085	900	1900	4500	6300	9000
Cpe	2085	925	2000	4600	6400	9200

1919

1919 Nash, model 681, touring, JAC

NASH — 680 — SIX: The 1919 Nash was identical to the 1918 model.

I.D. DATA: Serial number on left front cross member, just behind of radiator. Starting: 106430. Engine numbers on right front of flywheel housing behind starting motor.

Model No.	Body Type & Seating	Price	Weight	Start. Ser. No.
681	4-dr. Tr.-5P	1395	2930	106430
682	4-dr. Tr.-5P	1545	3040	111769
683	2-dr. Tr.-4P	1395	2930	121910
684	2-dr. Sed.-5P	2085	3455	120118
685	2-dr. Cpe.-4P	2085	3225	44035
686	2-dr. Rds.-2P	1490	2800	131851
687	4-dr. Spt. Tr.-4P	1595	2950	133351

Note 1: Models 681, 683, 686, and 687 have 121 in. wheelbase. Others have 127 in. wheelbase.

ENGINE: Inline. OHV. Cast en bloc. Six. Cast iron block. B & S: 3-1/4 x 5 in. Disp.: 248.9 cu. in. Brake H.P. 55 @ 2400 R.P.M. NACC H.P.: 25.35. Main bearings: Three. Valve lifters: Solid. Carb.: Marvel.

CHASSIS: W.B.: 121 in. & 127 in. Frt/Rear Tread: 56 in./56 in. Tires: 33 x 4. (34 x 4-1/2 on 127 w.b. models).

TECHNICAL: Selective, sliding gear transmission. Speeds: 3F/1R. Floor shift controls. Single dry plate clutch. Spiral bevel rear axle. Overall ratio: 4.50:1. Two-wheel external mechanical brakes. Artillery wheels.

HISTORICAL: Introduced: September 1, 1918. Calendar year production: 27,081. The president of Nash was C.W. Nash. Virtually unchanged from the previous year. Nash accounted for 1.6 percent of U.S. new car production for 1919. Nash also built 4,090 trucks during 1919, and during this year purchased a half-interest in the Seaman Body Corp., Milwaukee.

1919
Series 680, 6-cyl.

	FP	5	4	3	2	1
Rds	1295	1150	3600	6000	8400	12,000
Spt	1395	1150	3900	6500	9100	13,000
5P Tr	1395	1150	3600	6000	8400	12,000
7P Tr	1545	1250	3900	6500	9100	13,000
4P Rds	1395	1250	3900	6500	9100	13,000
Sed	2085	825	1600	4000	5600	8000
Cpe	2085	875	1700	4250	5900	8500

1920

1920 Nash, model 681, touring, JAC

NASH — 680 — SIX: The 1920 Nash was identical to the 1918-19 models.

I.D. DATA: Serial numbers on right rear engine girder at transmission base (effective 7/1/20. Earlier cars, on left front cross member, just back of radiator). Starting: 139330. Engine numbers on right front of flywheel housing just behind starting motor.

Model No.	Body Type & Seating	Price	Weight	Start. Ser. No.
681	4-dr. Tr.-5P	1490	2930	139330
682	4-dr. Tr.-7P	1640	3040	113661
684	4-dr. Sed.-7P	2575	3455	144334
685	2-dr. Cpe.-4P	2350	3225	144985
686	2-dr. Rds.-2P	1490	2800	132580
687	4-dr. Spt. Tr.-4P	1545	2950	134276

Note: Models 681, 686 and 687 had 121 in. wheelbase, other models have 127 in. wheelbase.

ENGINE: Inline. OHV. Cast en bloc. Six. Cast iron block. B & S: 3-1/4 x 5 in. Disp.: 248.9 cu. in. Brake H.P. 55 @ 2400 R.P.M. NACC H.P.: 25.35. Main bearings: Three. Valve lifters: Solid. Carb.: Marvel.

CHASSIS: W.B. 121 in. and 127 in. Frt/Rear Tread: 56 in./56 in. Tires: 33 x 4. (34 x 4-1/2 on 127'' w/b models).

TECHNICAL: Selective, sliding gear transmission. Speeds: 3F/1R. Floor shift controls. Single dry plate clutch. Spiral bevel drive. Semi-floating rear axle. Overall Ratio: 4.50:1. Two-wheel external mechanical brakes. Artillery wheels.

HISTORICAL: Introduced Sept. 1, 1920. Calendar year production was 35,084. The president of Nash was C.W. Nash. Nash Motors earned $7,007,471 during 1920. Nash accounted for 1.9 percent of U.S. auto production, 1920 essentially unchanged from 1918-1919 models. A new assembly plant was opened in Milwaukee.

1920
Series 680, 6-cyl.

	FP	5	4	3	2	1
5P Tr	1395	1250	3900	6500	9100	13,000
Rds	1395	1150	3600	6000	8400	12,000
7P Tr	1640	1400	4200	7000	9800	14,000
Cpe	2250	875	1700	4250	5900	8500
Sed	2575	825	1600	4000	5600	8000
Spt	1595	875	1700	4350	6050	8700

1921

1921 Nash, model 682, 7-pass. touring, JAC

NASH — 680 — SIX: The 1921 Nash 680 was identical to 1918-1920 models.

I.D. DATA: Serial numbers on right rear engine girder at transmission base. Starting: 175874. Engine numbers on right front of flywheel housing just back of starting motor.

Model No.	Body Type & Seating	Price	Weight	Start. Ser. No.
681	4-dr. Tr.-5P	1695	3068	175874
682	4-dr. Tr.-7P	1875	3198	167177
684	4-dr. Sed.-7P	2895	3708	178543
685	2-dr. Cpe.-4P	2650	3403	179003
686	2-dr. Rds.-2P	1695	2988	179551
687	4-dr. Spt. Tr.-4P	1850	3098	177655

Note: Models 681, 686 and 687 had a 121 in. wheelbase. Other models had a 127 in. wheelbase.

ENGINE: Inline. OHV. Cast en bloc. Six. Cast iron block. B & S: 3-1/4 x 5 in. Disp.: 248.9 cu. in. Brake H.P. 55 @ 2400 R.P.M. N.A.C.C. H.P.: 25.35. Main bearings: Three. Valve lifters: Solid. Carb.: Marvel.

CHASSIS: W.B.: 121 in.; 127 in. Frt/Rear Tread: 56 in./56 in. Tires: 33 x 4. (34 x 4-1/2 on 127 in. wheelbase models).

TECHNICAL: Selective sliding gear transmission. Speeds: 3F/1R. Floor shift controls. Single dry plate clutch. Spiral bevel drive. Semi-floating rear axle. Overall ratio: 4.50:1. Two-wheel mechanical brakes. Wood artillery wheels.

NASH — 40 — FOUR: The new 4-cylinder Nash models were similar in appearance to 680 series models except for their shorter stubbier hoods.

I.D. DATA: Serial numbers on front frame cross member just behind radiator on left side. Starting: 1000. Engine numbers on left side of crankcase just behind starting motor.

Model No.	Body Type & Seating	Price	Weight	Start. Ser. No.
41	4-dr. Tr.-5P	1395	2502	1000
42	2-dr. Rds.-2P	1395	2432	1000
43	2-dr. Cpe.-3P	1985	2732	1000
44	4-dr. Sed.-4P	2185	2942	1000
45	2-dr. Cabr.-2P	1545	2676	1000

ENGINE: OHV. Inline. Four. Cast iron block. B & S: 3-1/4 x 5 in. . Disp.: 165.9 cu. in. Brake H.P. 35 @ 2200 R.P.M. N.A.C.C. H.P.: 16.9. Main bearings: Two. Valve lifters: Solid. Carb. Schebler.

CHASSIS: W.B.: 112 in. Frt/Rear Tread: 56 in./56 in. Tires: 32 x 4.

TECHNICAL: Selective sliding gear transmission. Speeds: 3F/1R. Floor shift controls. Single dry plate clutch. Spiral bevel drive. Semi-floating rear axle. Overall ratio: 4.50:1. Two-wheel mechanical brakes. Wood artillery wheels.

HISTORICAL: Introduced: Sept. 1, 1920 (Series 680); Sept. 25, 1920 (Series 40). A new, four-cylinder series took Nash into a lower price range. Calendar year production: 20,850. The president of Nash was C.W. Nash. Severe postwar recession led to a sharp drop in production and sales. Nash accounted for 1.4 percent of U.S. auto production in 1921. On Feb. 14, 1921, the bore of the series "40" engine was increased to 3-3/8 in, raising the displacement to 178.9 cu. in. and the horsepower to 36.75 @ 2800 R.P.M. Starting serial no., cars with 178.9 c.i.d. engine: 1782.

1921
Series 680, 6-cyl.

	FP	5	4	3	2	1
5P Tr	1696	1075	3000	5500	7700	11,000
Rds	1695	1150	3600	6000	8400	12,000
Spt	1850	1250	3900	6500	9100	13,000
Tr	1696	1150	3600	6000	8400	12,000
Cpe	2650	875	1700	4250	5900	8500
Sed	2895	750	1450	3300	4900	7000

Series 40, 4-cyl.

	FP	5	4	3	2	1
Tr	1395	1000	2400	5000	7000	10,000
Rds	1395	1025	2600	5250	7300	10,500
Cpe	1985	725	1400	3100	4800	6800
Sed	2185	700	1350	2800	4550	6500
Cabr	1545	1000	2400	5000	7000	10,000

"THE NASH SIX" — SERIES 690 — SIX: Styling similar to 680 series of 1918-21, except taller radiator, drum headlamps.

"THE NASH FOUR" — SERIES 40 — FOUR: Identical to 1921 series 40.

I.D. DATA: [Series 690] Serial numbers on right rear engine girder at transmission base. Starting: 195754. Engine numbers on right front of flywheel housing just back of starting motor. [Series 40] Serial numbers on front frame cross member just back of radiator, left side. Starting: 4511. Engine numbers on left side of crankcase just back of starting motor.

Model No.	Body Type & Seating	Price	Weight	Prod. Total
691	4-dr. Tr.-5P	1545	2930	195754
692	4-dr. Tr.-7P	1695	2950	208441
693	4-dr. Sed.-5P	2040	3430	217938
694	4-dr. Sed.-7P	2695	3455	198240
695	2-dr. Vic.-4P	2395	3255	200013
696	2-dr. Rds.-2P	1525	2805	207559
697	4-dr. Spt. Tr.-4P	1695	3037	205729
41	4-dr. Tr.-5P	1045	2502	4511
42	2-dr. Rds.-2P	1025	2432	4511
43	2-dr. Cpe.-3P	1645	2732	4511
44	4-dr. Sed.-5P	1835	2942	4511
45	2-dr. Cabr.-5P	1245	2676	4511
46	2-dr. Carriole-5P	1350	2824	4511

ENGINE: [Nash 690] OHV. Inline. Six. Cast iron block. B & S: 3-1/4 in. x 5 in. Disp.: 248.9. C.R.: 4.2:1. Brake H.P.: 55 at 2400 R.P.M. Taxable H.P.: 25.35. Main bearings: Three. Valve lifters: Solid. Carb.: Marvel. [Nash 40] OHV. Inline. Four. Cast iron block. B & S: 3-3/8 in. x 5 in. Disp.: 178.9 cu. in. C.R.: 3.8:1. Brake H.P.: 36.75 @ 2800 R.P.M. Taxable H.P.: 18.23. Main bearings: Two. Valve lifters: Solid. Carb.: Schebler.

CHASSIS: [Series 690] W.B.: 121 in & 127 in. Frt/Rear Tread: 56 in./56 in. Tires: 33 x 4. (34 x 4-1/2 on 127" w/b models). [Series 40] W.B.: 112 in. Frt/Rear Tread: 56 in./56 in. Tires: 33 x 4.

TECHNICAL: Selective Sliding gear transmission. Speeds: 3F/1R. Floor shift controls. Single dry plate clutch. Spiral bevel. Semi-floating rear axle. Overall ratio: 4.50:1. Mechanical brakes on two wheels. Wood artillery wheels.

HISTORICAL: Introduced Oct. 5, 1921. Innovations: First use of rubber engine mountings (Series 40). Two-door Carriole (Series 40) brought closed-car comfort to a lower-priced field. Calendar year production: 41,652. The president of Nash was C.W. Nash. Production doubled the 1921 figure; Nash accounted for 1.7% of U.S. automobile production.* Nash claimed to manufacture a higher percentage of their components than any other automaker.
*8th in U.S. auto sales.

1922
Series 680, 6-cyl.

	FP	5	4	3	2	1
5P Tr	1545	1075	3000	5500	7700	11,000
7P Tr	1695	1150	3600	6000	8400	12,000
7P Sed	2695	825	1600	4000	5600	8000
Cpe	2395	775	1500	3750	5250	7500
Rds	1525	1200	3750	6250	8750	12,500
Spt	1695	1250	3900	6500	9100	13,000
5P Sed	2040	750	1450	3300	4900	7000

Series 40, 4-cyl.

	FP	5	4	3	2	1
Tr	1045	1025	2600	5250	7300	10,500
Rds	1025	1075	3000	5500	7700	11,000
Cpe	1645	750	1450	3300	4900	7000
Sed	1835	700	1350	2800	4550	6500
Cabr	1395	1000	2400	5000	7000	10,000
Ca'ole	1350	800	1550	3900	5450	7800

1923

1922 Nash, model 43, coupe, JAC

1923 Nash, series 690, sedan, OCW

"THE NASH SIX" — SERIES 690 — SIX: Identical to 1922 model, except disc wheels now optional, cowl ventilator used.

"THE NASH FOUR" — SERIES 40 — FOUR: Identical to 1921-22 series 40.

I.D. DATA: Series 690 serial numbers on right rear engine girder at transmission base. Starting: 226409. Engine numbers on right front of flywheel housing just back of starting motor. Series 40 serial numbers on front frame cross member just back of radiator, left side. Starting: 19436.

Model No.	Body Type & Seating	Price	Weight	Start Ser. No.
691	4-dr. Tr.-5P	1240	3030	226409
692	4-dr. Tr.-7P	1390	3150	226882
693	4-dr. Sed.-5P	2040	3430	218364
694	4-dr. Sed.-7P	2190	3580	232021
695	2-dr. Vic.-4P	1890	3330	232241
696	2-dr. Rds.-2P	1210	2930	232589
697	4-dr. Spt. Tr.-4P	1645	3530	227921
698	4-dr. Cpe.-5P	2090	3550	231401
41	4-dr. Tr.-5P	935	2720	19436
42	2-dr. Rds.-2P	915	2600	19436
46	2-dr. Carriole-5P	1275	2910	19436
47	4-dr. Sed.-5P	1445	3090	19436
48	4-dr. Spt. Tr.-5P	1195	2980	19436

ENGINE: Series 690 identical in all these respects to 1922 690 Series. Series 40 identical in all these respects to 1922 Series 40.

CHASSIS: Unchanged in these respects from 1922.

TECHNICAL: Identical to 1922 models except for overall drive ratio, series 40, as noted below. Overall ratio: 4.50:1 (690); 4.89:1 (40). Wood artillery wheels (disc optional).

HISTORICAL: Introduced: Oct. 17, 1922. Calendar year registrations: 41,838. Calendar year production: 41,652. The president of Nash was C.W. Nash. Nash accounted for 1.6% of U.S. auto production during 1923.

1923
Series 690, 6-cyl., 121" wb

	FP	5	4	3	2	1
Rds	1210	1150	3600	6000	8400	12,000
Tr	1240	1250	3900	6500	9100	13,000
Spt	1645	1400	4200	7000	9800	14,000
Sed	2090	800	1550	3900	5450	7800
Cpe	1890	825	1600	4000	5600	8000

Series 690, 6-cyl., 127" wb

Tr	1390	1250	3900	6500	9100	13,000
Sed	2040	825	1600	4000	5600	8000
Cpe	1990	875	1700	4250	5900	8500

Series 40, 4-cyl.

Tr	935	1075	3000	5500	7700	11,000
Rds	915	1150	3600	6000	8400	12,000
Spt	1195	1250	3900	6500	9100	13,000
Ca'ole	1275	1300	4050	6750	9450	13,500
Sed	1445	750	1450	3500	5050	7200

1924

1924 Nash, Carriole, sedan, OCW

"THE NASH SIX" — SERIES 690 — SIX: Identical to 1922-23 690 Series.

"THE NASH FOUR" — SERIES 40 — FOUR: Identical to 1921-23 Series 40.

I.D. DATA: Series 690 serial numbers on right rear engine girder at transmission base. Starting: 256987. Engine numbers on right front of flywheel housing just back of starting motor. Series 40 serial numbers on front frame cross member just back of radiator, left side. Starting: 34577.

Model No.	Body Type & Seating	Price	Weight	Start. Ser. No
691	4-dr. Tr.-5P	1240	3120	256987
692	4-dr. Tr.-7P	1390	3230	248120
693	4-dr. Sed.-5P	2040	3550	248526
694	4-dr. Sed.-7P	2190	3700	240423
695	2-dr. Vic.-4P	1990	3440	240778
696	2-dr. Rds.-2P	1240	3030	254852
697	4-dr. Spt. Tr.-4P	1645	3530	251417
698	4-dr. Cpe.-5P	2090	3550	259009
699	4-dr. Spt. Sed.-5P	1640	3400	269265

Model No.	Body Type & Seating	Price	Weight	Prod. Total
41	4-dr. Tr.-5P	935	2720	34577
42	2-dr. Rds.-2P	915	2600	34577
46	2-dr. Carriole-5P	1275	2910	34577
47	4-dr. Sed.-5P	1445	3090	34577
48	4-dr. Spt. Tr.-5P	1145	2800	34577
49	2-dr. Cpe.-2P	1165	2750	34577

ENGINE: [Series 690] Identical in all these respects to 1922-23 Series 690. [Series 40] Identical in all these respects to 1922-23 Series 40.

CHASSIS: Unchanged in these respects from 1922-23.

TECHNICAL: Unchanged except for another increase in overall drive ratio. Overall ratio: 4.50 (690); 5.50 (40).

HISTORICAL: Introduced: July 20, 1923. Innovations: Industry's first use of electric dashboard clock (optional). Calendar year registrations: 47,571. Calendar year production: 53,626. The president of Nash was C.W. Nash. Nash accounted for 1.7% of U.S. auto production in 1924. Last year for the Nash "Four". On Feb. 27, 1924 Nash purchased the Racine plant of the bankrupt Mitchell Motors Co.

1924
Series 690, 6-cyl., 121" wb

Rds	1275	1150	3600	6000	8400	12,000
Tr	1645	1075	3000	5500	7700	11,000
Spec DeL	1640	700	1350	2800	4550	6500
Cpe	2090	700	1350	4550	4550	6500
Spec Sed	2040	650	1250	2400	4200	6000

Series 690, 6-cyl., 127" wb

7P Tr	1425	1250	3900	6500	9100	13,000
7P Sed	2190	750	1450	3300	4900	7000
Vic	1990	725	1400	3200	4850	6900

4 cyl.

Tr	935	1250	3900	6500	9100	13,000
Rds	915	1300	4050	6750	9450	13,500
Cab	975	1350	4100	6850	9600	13,700
5P Sed	1195	700	1350	2800	4550	6500
Sed	1445	650	1250	2400	4200	6000
Spt	1195	1400	4200	7000	9800	14,000
Cpe	1165	700	1350	2700	4500	6400

1925

1925 Nash, roadster, OCW

NASH — ADVANCED "SIX" — SERIES 160 — SIX: Much updated from previous model: balloon tires; nickeled radiator shell; long, thin hood louvres; long visor, closed models; "boxy" configuration on closed models, particularly at the rear.

NASH — SPECIAL "SIX" — SERIES 130 — SIX: Similar in styling to 160 series, but smaller.

NASH — AJAX — SERIES 220 — SIX: "Vertical" styling similar to contemporary Nash models, but substantially smaller. Long visor on sedans; drum headlamps; low, flat hood.

I.D. DATA: Series 160 serial numbers on right side of front motor support. Starting: 288001. Engine numbers on engine block near starting motor. Series 130 serial numbers on top right side rear motor support or on left rear spring hanger. Starting: 51001. Engine numbers on engine block beside starting motor. Ajax serial numbers on right front spring hanger. Starting: 1001. Engine numbers on left side engine block, upper forward corner.

Model No.	Body Type & Seating	Price	Weight	Prod. Total
161	4-dr. Tr.-5P	1375	3400	288001
162	4-dr. Tr.-7P	1525	3480	290351
163	2-dr. Sed.-5P	1485	3550	308325
164	4-dr. Sed.-7P	2290	3830	290601
165	2-dr. Vic.-4P	2090	3640	297901
166	2-dr. Rds.-2P	1375	3320	290791
168	4-dr. Cpe.-4P	2190	3750	291281
169	4-dr. Sed.-5P	1695	3860	291571
131	4-dr. Tr.-5P	1095	2960	51001
132	2-dr. Rds.-2P	1095	2870	54573
133	2-dr. Sed.-5P	1225	3120	51001
134	4-dr. Sed.-5P	1545	3270	64990
21	4-dr. Sed.-5P	995	2410	
51	4-dr. Tr.-5P	865	2210	

ENGINE: Series 160 Engine: OHV. Inline. Six. Cast iron block. B & S: 3-1/4 in. x 5 in. Disp.: 248.9 cu. in. Brake H.P.: 60 @ 2400 R.P.M. Taxable H.P.: 25.35. Main bearings: Three. Valve lifters: Solid. Carb.: Marvel U4S. Series 130 Engine: OHV. Inline. Six. Cast iron block. B & S: 3-1/8 in. x 4-1/2 in. Disp.: 207.0 cu. in. Brake H.P.: 46 @ 2200 R.P.M. Taxable H.P.: 23.44. Main bearings: 3. Valve lifters: 3. Valve lifters: solid. Carb.: Marvel U3S. Ajax Engine: L-head. Inline. Six. Cast iron block. B & S: 3 in. x 4 in. Disp.: 169.6 cu. in. C.R.: 4.5:1. Brake H.P.: 40 @ 2400 R.P.M. Main bearings: 7. Valve lifters: solid. Carb.: Carter.

CHASSIS: [Series 160] W.B.: 121 in. & 127 in. Tires: 33 x 6.00. [Series 130] W.B.: 112-1/2 in. Tires: 31 x 5.25. [Series 220] W.B.: 108 in. Frt/Rear Tread: 56 in./56 in. Tires: 30 x 4.75.

TECHNICAL: Selective sliding gear transmission. Speeds: 3F/1R. Floor shift controls. Single dry plate clutch. Spiral bevel drive. Semi-floating rear axle. Overall ratio: 4.50:1 (160); 4.88:1 (130). Mechanical brakes on four wheels. Steel disc wheels. Ajax: Selective sliding gear transmission. Speeds: 3F/1R. Floor shift controls. Single dry plate clutch. Spiral bevel drive. Semi-floating rear axle. Overall ratio: 4.6:1. Mechanical brakes on four wheels. Steel disc wheels.

HISTORICAL: Introduced: Aug. 1, 1924. Innovations: Special ''Six'' replaced four-cylinder Nash. First use by Nash of four-wheel brakes. Calendar year registrations: 73,384. Calendar year production: 85,428. The president of Nash was C.W. Nash. Sales up 50% over 1924. Nash held 2.4% of new car registrations for the year. Ajax: Introduced May 1, 1925. Innovations: Nash's first entry in the ''$1,000-market''; first L-head engine; first 7-bearing crankshaft. At time of introduction, the Ajax was the only car in its price class with 4-wheel brakes. Calendar year production: 10,693 (1925 only). The president of Nash was C.W. Nash. About 20,000 AJax cars sold before name was changed (May 1, 1926) to ''Nash Light Six.''

1925 Nash Advanced Six, touring, AB

1925
Advanced models, 6-cyl.

Tr	1375	1200	3700	6200	8700	12,400
7P Tr	1525	1300	4050	6700	9400	13,400
4 dr Sed	1695	750	1450	3400	5000	7100
Vic Cpe	2090	850	1650	4200	5850	8400
7P Sed	2290	775	1500	3700	5200	7400
Rds	1375	1450	4300	7200	10,100	14,400
Cpe	2190	775	1500	3700	5200	7400
2 dr Sed	1485	700	1350	2700	4500	6400

Special models, 6-cyl.

Tr	1135	1200	3700	6200	8700	12,400
4 dr Sed	1545	650	1250	2400	4150	5900
Rds	1135	1300	4050	6700	9400	13,400
2 dr Sed	1265	650	1250	2400	4150	5900

Light six, (formerly Ajax), 6-cyl.

Tr	865	1025	2600	5200	7200	10,400
Sed	995	550	1150	2100	3800	5400

1926

NASH — ADVANCED ''SIX'' — SERIES 260 — SIX: Smoother, more rounded lines than 1925 models, particularly roof line at rear. Shorter visor than before.

NASH — SPECIAL ''SIX'' — SERIES 230 — SIX: Similar to 260 Series, but smaller.

NASH — LIGHT ''SIX'' — SERIES 220 — SIX: Identical but for name to 1925-26 Ajax.

I.D. DATA: Series 260 serial numbers on right side of front motor support. Starting: 330126. Engine numbers on engine block near starting motor. Series 230 serial numbers on top right side rear motor support or on left rear spring hanger. Starting: 75276. Engine numbers on engine block beside starting motor. Series 220 serial numbers on right frame member just ahead of rear spring rear bracket. Starting: 1001. Engine numbers on left side engine block, upper forward corner.

976

1926 Nash Light Six, sedan, OCW

Model No.	Body Type & Seating	Price	Weight	Start. Ser. No.
261	4-dr. Tr.-5P	1375	3400	330126
262	4-dr. Tr.-7P	1525	3480	330126
263	2-dr. Sed.-5P	1485	3550	330126
264	4-dr. Sed.-7P	2290	3830	336404
265	2-dr. Vic.-4P	2090	3640	336404
266	2-dr. Rds.-2P	1375	3320	337932
268	4-dr. Cpe.-4P	2190	3750	337932
269	4-dr. Sed.-5P	1525	3650	354114
231	4-dr. Tr.-5P	1135	2960	75276
232	2-dr. Rds.-2P	1115	2870	81509
233	2-dr. Sed.-5P	1265	3120	75276
234	4-dr. Sp. Sed.-5P	1545	3300	75276
235	2-dr. Cpe.-2P	1165	3030	92070
236	2-dr. Rds.-2/4P	1225	2980	A20247
239	4-dr. Sed.-5P	1315	3170	98405
221	4-dr. Tr.-5P	865	2210	1001
224	4-dr. Sed.-5P	995	2410	1001
225	2-dr. Cpe.-2P	925	2310	1001

ENGINE: [Series 260] OHV. Inline. Six. Cast iron block. B & S: 3-7/16 in. x 5 in. Disp.: 278.4 cu. in. Brake H.P.: 60 @ 2400 R.P.M. Taxable H.P.: 28.37. Main bearings: Seven. Valve lifters: Solid. Carb.: Marvel U4S. [Series 230] OHV. Inline. Six. Cast iron block. B & S: 3-1/8 in. x 4-1/2 in. Disp.: 207.4 cu. in. Brake H.P.: 47 @ 2200 R.P.M. Taxable H.P.: 23.44. Main bearings: Seven. Valve lifters: Solid. Carb.: Marvel U38. [Series 220] L-head. Inline. Six. Cast iron block. B & S: 3 in. x 4 in. Disp.: 169.6 cu. in. C.R.: 4.5:1. Brake H.P.: 40 @ 2400 R.P.M. Taxable H.P.: 21.6. Main bearings: Seven. Valve lifters: Solid. Carb.: Carter.

CHASSIS: [Series 260] W.B.: 121 in., 127 in. Tires: 33 x 6.00. [Series 230] W.B.: 112-1/2 in. Tires: 31 x 5.25. [Series 220] W.B.: 108 in. Frt/Rear Tread: 56 in./56 in. Tires: 30 x 4.75.

TECHNICAL: Selective sliding gear transmission. Speeds: 3F/1R. Floor shift controls. Single dry plate clutch. Spiral bevel drive. Semi-floating rear axle. Overall ratio: 4.5:1 (260); 4.9:1 (230); 4.6:1 (220). Mechanical brakes on four wheels. Steel disc wheels.

HISTORICAL: Introduced: June 1, 1925 [260], July 1, 1925 [230], May 1, 1926 [220]. Innovations: First use of 7-bearing crankshafts in Nash's OHV engines [Series 260 & 230], as well as L-head [Series 220]. Calendar year registrations: 98,804. Calendar year production: 135,520. The president of Nash was C.W. Nash. Light ''Six'' [Series 220] represented a continuation of the Ajax under a new name. Evidently as the result of the name change, sales took a great leap forward. 60% increase in Nash production for the year. Nash held 3.6% of new car registrations for the year.

1926 Nash Light Six, (Ajax), sedan, AB

1926
Advanced models, 6-cyl.

	FP	5	4	3	2	1
5P Tr	1340	1450	4300	7200	10,100	14,400
7P Tr	1490	1650	4600	7700	10,800	15,400
2 dr Sed	1425	725	1400	3200	4850	6900
4 dr Sed	1525	750	1450	3500	5050	7200
7P Sed	2090	775	1500	3700	5200	7400
4 dr Cpe	1990	750	1450	3500	5050	7200
Rds	1475	1650	4600	7700	10,800	15,400
Vic Cpe	1790	850	1650	4200	5850	8400

Special models, 6-cyl.

	FP	5	4	3	2	1
Rds	1115	1400	4150	6950	9750	13,900
2 dr Sed	1215	700	1350	2700	4500	6400
7P Sed	1445	750	1450	3400	5000	7100
Cpe	1165	725	1400	3200	4850	6900
4 dr Sed	1315	750	1450	3300	4900	7000
Spec Rds	1225	1450	4300	7200	10,100	14,400

Light six

	FP	5	4	3	2	1
Tr		865	1050	2700	5300	7400	10,600
Sed		995	550	1150	2100	3800	5400

1927

1927 Nash, 4-dr. sedan, OCW

NASH — ADVANCED "SIX" — SERIES 260 — SIX: Little change in styling from 1926 model.

NASH — SPECIAL "SIX" — SERIES 230 — SIX: Little changed in styling from 1926 model.

NASH — LIGHT "SIX" — SERIES 220 — SIX: Less boxy than 1926 model: styling similar to 230 series, but smaller.

I.D. DATA: Series 260 serial numbers on right side of front motor support. Starting: 386972. Engine numbers on engine block near starting motor. Series 230 serial numbers on top right side rear motor support or on left rear spring hanger. Starting: A26276. Engine numbers on engine block beside starting motor. Series 220 serial numbers on right frame member just ahead of rear spring bracket. Starting: R28374. Engine numbers on left side engine block, upper forward corner.

Model No.	Body Type & Seating	Price	Weight	Start. Ser. No.
260	2-dr. Cpe.-2/4P	1775	3580	419570
261	4-dr. Tr.-5P	1340	3400	386972
262	4-dr. Tr.-7P	1490	3480	386972
263	2-dr. Sed.-5P	1425	3550	386972
264	4-dr. Sed.-7P	2090	3830	386972
265	2-dr. Vic.-4P	1790	3640	386972
266	2-dr. Rds.-2/4P	1475	3390	386972
267	4-dr. Amb. Sed.-5P	2090	3800	408304
268	4-dr. Cpe.-4P	1990	3750	386972
269	4-dr. Sed.-5P	1525	3650	386972
270	4-dr. Sp. Sed.-5P	1695	3650	410709
271	4-dr. Spt. Tr.-5P	1540	3500	415998
231	4-dr. Tr.-5P	1135	2980	A26276
232	2-dr. Rds.-2P	1115	2900	A26276
233	2-dr. Sed.-5P	1215	3150	A26276
235	2-dr. Bus. Cpe.-2P	1165	3030	A26276
236	2-dr. Rds.-2/4P	1225	2980	A26276
237	4-dr. Cav. Sed.-5P	1695	3330	A42260
239	4-dr. Sed.-5P	1315	3170	A26276
240	4-dr. Sp. Sed.-5P	1485	3250	A44332
241	2-dr. Cabr.-2/4P	1290	3070	A46894
221	4-dr. Tr.-5P	865	2275	R28374
223	2-dr. Sed.-5P	925	2410	R46146
224	4-dr. Sed.-5P	995	2475	R28374
225	2-dr.Cpe.-2P	925	2310	R28374
227	4-dr. Del. Sed.-5P	1085	2550	R48852

ENGINE: [Series 260] OHV. Inline. Six. Cast iron block. B & S: 3-7/16 in. x 5 in. Disp.: 278.4 cu. in. C.R.: 4.6:1. Brake H.P.: 69 @ 2500 R.P.M. Taxable H.P.: 28.4. Main bearings: Seven. Valve lifters: Solid. Carb.: Marvel U4S. [Series 230] OHV. Inline. Six. Cast iron block. B & S: 3-1/4 in. x 4-1/2 in. Disp.: 224.0 cu. in. C.R.: 4.69:1. Brake H.P.: 52 @ 2600 R.P.M. Taxable H.P.: 25.3. Main bearings: Seven. Valve lifters: Solid. Carb.: Marvel U38. [Series 22]0 L-head. Inline. Six. Cast iron block. B & S: 3 in. x 4 in. Disp.: 169.6 cu. in. C.R.: 4.5:1. Brake H.P.: 40 @ 2400 R.P.M. Taxable H.P.: 21.6. Main bearings: Seven. Valve lifters: Solid. Carb.: 1 in. Carter 82S/89S.

CHASSIS: [Series 260] W.B.: 121 in. & 127 in. Tires: 33 x 6.00. [Series 230] W.B.: 112-1/2 in. Tires: 31 x 5.25. [Series 220] W.B.: 108 in. Tires: 30 x 4.75.

TECHNICAL: Selective sliding gear transmission. Speeds: 3F/1R. Floor shift controls. Single dry plate clutch. Spiral bevel drive. Semi-floating rear axle. Overall ratio: 4.5:1 [260]; 4.67:1 [230]; 4.77:1 [220] Mechanical brakes on four wheels. Steel disc wheels.

HISTORICAL: Introduced June 1, 1926 [260], July 6, 1926 [220], Aug. 1, 1926 [230]. Innovations: Larger bore, more power, series 260 and 230. Calendar year registrations: 109,979. Calendar year production: 122,606. The president of Nash was C.W. Nash. Two new premium-level sedans, the Ambassador [Series 260] and Cavalier [Series 230] featured more rounded rear contours, a styling feature picked up by all advanced and special "Six" Sedans for 1929. Nash held 4.2% of industry registrations for 1927.

1927 Nash, rumbleseat cabriolet, OCW

1927
Standard, 6-cyl.

	FP	5	4	3	2	1
Tr	865	1075	2900	5450	7600	10,900
Cpe	925	750	1450	3400	5000	7100
2 dr Sed	925	675	1300	2500	4350	6200
4 dr Sed	995	675	1300	2600	4400	6300
DeL Sed	1085	700	1350	2700	4500	6400

Special, 6-cyl.

(Begin September 1926)

	FP	5	4	3	2	1
Rds	1115	1550	4450	7450	10,400	14,900
Tr	1135	1300	4050	6700	9400	13,400
Cpe	1165	925	2000	4600	6400	9200
2 dr Sed	1215	875	1700	4300	6000	8600
4 dr Sed	1415	900	1900	4500	6300	9000

(Begin January 1927)

	FP	5	4	3	2	1
Cav Sed	1695	925	2000	4600	6400	9200
4 dr Sed	1485	900	1900	4500	6300	9000
RS Cab	1290	1450	4300	7200	10,100	14,400
RS Rds	1225	1650	4600	7700	10,800	15,400

Advanced, 6-cyl.

(Begin August 1926)

	FP	5	4	3	2	1
Rds	1470	1650	4600	7700	10,800	15,400
5P Tr	1340	1700	4750	7950	11,150	15,900
7P Tr	1490	1800	4900	8200	11,500	16,400
Cpe	1990	975	2300	4950	6900	9900
Vic	1790	950	2100	4700	6600	9400
2 dr Sed	1425	850	1650	4100	5700	8200
4 dr Sed	1525	850	1650	4200	5850	8400
7P Sed	2090	900	1800	4400	6150	8800

(Begin January 1927)

	FP	5	4	3	2	1
RS Cpe	1775	1025	2600	5200	7200	10,400
Spec Sed	1695	900	1800	4400	6150	8800
Amb Sed	2090	925	2000	4600	6400	9200

1928

1928 Nash Advanced Six, model 370, sedan, JAC

NASH — ADVANCED "SIX" — SERIES 360 — SIX: Similar in styling to 1927 model, but with taller radiator.

NASH — SPECIAL "SIX" — SERIES 330 — SIX: Similar in appearance to advanced (360) series, but smaller.

NASH — STANDARD "SIX" — SERIES 320 — SIX: Similar in styling to 360 and 330 series but much smaller.

I.D. DATA: Series 360 serial numbers on right side of front motor support. Starting: 423612. Ending: 452099. Engine numbers on engine block near starting motor. Series 330 serial numbers on top right side rear motor support or on left rear spring hanger. Starting: A58246. Ending: A87449. Engine numbers on engine block beside starting motor. Series 320 serial numbers on right frame member just ahead of rear spring rear bracket. Starting: R71557. Ending: R119558. Engine numbers on left side engine block, upper forward corner.

Model No.	Body Type & Seating	Price	Weight	Start. Ser. No.
360	2-dr. Cpe.2-/4P	1775	3650	423612
361	4-dr. Tr.-5P	1340	3400	423612
362	4-dr. Tr.-7P	1440	3500	423612
363	2-dr. Sed.-5P	1425	3620	423612
364	4-dr. Sed.-7P	1990	3830	423612
364-I	4-dr. Imp. Sed.-7P	2165	3900	440770
365	2-dr. Vic.4-P	1595	3640	423612
366	2-dr. Rds.-2/4P	1475	3400	423612
367	4-dr. Amb. Sed.-5P	1925	3820	422617
370	4-dr. Sed.-5P	1545	3650	423612
371	4-dr. Spt. Tr.-5P	1540	3500	423612
331	4-dr. Tr.-5P	1135	2980	A58246
333	2-dr. Sed.-5P	1215	3150	A58246
335	2-dr. Cpe.-2P	1165	3030	A58246
335R	2-dr. Cpe.-2/4P	1245	3030	A58246
336	2-dr. Rds.-2/4P	1225	2980	A58246
338	4-dr. Lan. Sed.-5P	1445	3380	A68271
340	4-dr. Sp. Sed.-5P	1335	3250	A58246
341	2-dr. Cabr.-2/4P	1290	3070	A58246
342	2-dr. Vic.-4P	1295	3170	A70804
320	4-dr. Sed.-5P	995	2500	R71557
321	4-dr. Tr.-5P	865	2325	R71557
322	2-dr. Cabr.-2/4P	995	2505	R91928
323	2-dr. Sed.-5P	895	2450	R71557
325	2-dr. Cpe.-2P	875	2345	R71557
328	4-dr. Lan. Sed.-5P	1085	2610	R71557

ENGINE: [Series 360] OHV. Inline. Six. Cast iron block. B & S: 3-7/16 in. x 5 in. Disp.: 279.0 cu. in. C.R.: 4.6:1. Brake H.P.: 70 @ 2400 R.P.M. Taxable H.P.: 28.35. Main bearings: Seven. Valve lifters: Solid. Carb.: Marvel U. [Series 330] OHV. Inline. Six. Cast iron block. B & S: 3-1/4 in. x 4-1/2 in. Disp.: 224.0 cu. in. C.R.: 4.69:1. Brake H.P.: 52 @ 2600 R.P.M. Taxable H.P.: 25.35. Main bearings: Seven. Valve lifters: Solid. Carb.: Marvel. [Series 320] L-head. Inline. Six. Cast iron block. B & S: 3-1/8 in. x 4 in. Disp.: 184.1 cu. in. C.R.: 4.5:1. Brake H.P.: 45 @ 2600 R.P.M. Main bearings: Seven. Valve lifters: Solid. Carb.: Carter DRHO.

CHASSIS: [Series 360] W.B.: 121 in. & 127 in. Tires: 32 x 6.00. [Series 330] W.B.: 112-1/2 in. Tires: 30 x 5.25. [Series 320] W.B.: 108 in. Tires: 30 x 5.00.

TECHNICAL: Selective, sliding gear transmission. Speeds: 3F/1R. Floor shift controls. Single dry plate clutch. Spiral bevel drive. Semi-floating rear axle. Overall ratio: 4.50:1 (360); 4.88:1 (330); 4.77:1 (320). Mechanical brakes on four wheels. Steel disc wheels.

OPTIONS: Single sidemount. Dual sidemount.

HISTORICAL: Introduced: June 29, 1927. Calendar year registrations: 115,172. Calendar year production: 138,137. The president of Nash was C.W. Nash. Introduction in June, 1928 of the stylish 1929 "400" series led to a sharp increase in sales for the calendar year. Nash's best year to date — not surpassed until 1949. (Nash held 3.67% of the 1928 automobile market.)

1928
Standard, 6-cyl.

Tr	865	1650	4600	7700	10,800	15,400
Cpe	875	750	1450	3400	5000	7100
Conv Cabr	995	1700	4750	7950	11,150	15,900
2 dr Sed	895	725	1400	3100	4800	6800
4 dr Sed	995	750	1450	3500	5050	7200
Lan Sed	1085	750	1450	3500	5050	7200

Special, 6-cyl.

Tr	1135	2100	5250	8700	12,200	17,400
RS Rds	1225	2100	5250	8700	12,200	17,400
Cpe	1165	950	2100	4700	6600	9400
Conv Cabr	1290	1800	4900	8200	11,500	16,400
Vic	1295	875	1700	4350	6050	8700
2 dr Sed	1215	875	1700	4300	6000	8600
4 dr Sed	1335	900	1800	4400	6150	8800
4 dr Cpe	1445	925	2000	4600	6400	9200

Advanced, 6-cyl.

Spt Tr	1340	2900	5800	9700	13,600	19,400
Tr	1440	2500	5500	9200	12,900	18,400
RS Rds	1475	2500	5500	9200	12,900	18,400
Cpe	1775	950	2100	4700	6600	9400
Vic	1595	950	2100	4750	6650	9500
2 dr Sed	1425	850	1650	4150	5800	8300
4 dr Sed	1545	875	1700	4300	6000	8600
4 dr Cpe	2165	975	2300	4950	6900	9900
7P Sed	1990	950	2100	4700	6600	9400

1929

NASH — ADVANCED "SIX" — SERIES 460 — SIX: Tall, narrow radiator; one-piece fenders; chromed, bowl-shaped headlamps with slight peak at top; tall, single row of vertical hood louvres; new "fish scale" radiator badge; double-bar bumpers.

978

1929 Nash Special Six, sedan, AB

NASH — SPECIAL "SIX" — SERIES 430 — SIX: Similar to advanced "six" except smaller; double row of vertical hood vents.

NASH — STANDARD "SIX" — SERIES 420 — SIX: Same general styling theme as advanced and special series, but considerably smaller. No "Peak" on bowl-shaped headlamps; single row of vertical hood louvres.

I.D. DATA: [Series 460] Serial numbers on right side front motor support. Starting: 452100. Ending: 496399. Engine numbers on engine block near starting motor. [Series 430] Serial numbers on top right side rear motor support or of left rear spring hanger. Starting: A87450. Ending: B37581. Engine numbers on engine block beside starting motor. [Series 420] Serial numbers on right frame member just ahead of rear spring rear bracket. Starting: R119559. Engine numbers on left side engine block, upper forward corner.

Model No.	Body Type & Seating	Price	Weight	Start. Ser. No.
460	2-dr. Cpe.-2/4P	1775	3710	452100
461	2-dr. Cabr.-2/4P	1660	3675	452100
462	4-dr. Phae.-7P	1550	3700	452100
463	2-dr. Sed.-5P	1480	3760	452100
464	4-dr. Sed.-7P	1990	3970	452100
465	4-dr. Limo.-7P	2190	4010	452100
467	4-dr. Amb. Sed.-5P	1925	3940	452100
470	4-dr. Sed.-5P	1550	3700	452100
431	4-dr. Phae.-5P	1250	3150	A87450
433	2-dr. Sed.-5P	1260	3400	A87450
434	2-dr. Cpe.-2/4P	1315	3250	A87450
435	2-dr. Cpe.-2P	1245	3250	A87450
436	2-dr. Rds.-2/4P	1345	3200	B18953
440	4-dr. Sed.-5P	1345	3400	A87450
441	2-dr. Cabr.-2/4P	1345	3260	A87450
442	2-dr. Vic.-4P	1345	3300	A87450
444	4-dr. Sed.-7P	1645	3530	B18339
420	4-dr. Sed.-5P	955	2725	R119559
421	4-dr. Phae.-5P	935	2500	R119559
422	2-dr. Cabr.-2/4P	955	2550	R119559
423	2-dr. Sed.-5P	885	2625	R119559
425	2-dr. Cpe.-2P	885	2500	R119559
428	4-dr. Lan. Sed.-5P	995	2725	R119559

ENGINE: [Series 460] OHV. Inline. Six. Cast iron block. B & S: 3-7/16 in. x 5 in. Disp.: 278.4 cu. in. C.R.: 5.1:1. Brake H.P.: 78 @ 2900 R.P.M. Taxable H.P.: 28.4. Main bearings: Seven. Valve lifters: Solid. Carb.: Marvel U 1-1/4 in. updraft. [Series 430] OHV. Inline. Six. Cast iron block. B & S: 3-1/4 in. x 4-1/2 in. Disp.: 224.0 cu. in. C.R.: 5.15:1. Brake H.P.: 65 @ 2900 R.P.M. Taxable H.P.: 25.3. Main bearings: Seven. Valve lifters: Solid. Carb.: Marvel U 1-1/4 in. updraft. [Series 420] L-head. Inline. Six. Cast iron block. B & S: 3-1/8 in. x 4 in. Disp.: 184.1 cu. in. C.R.: 5.0:1. Brake H.P.: 50 @ 2800 R.P.M. Taxable H.P.: 23.4. Main bearings: Seven. Valve lifters: Solid. Carb.: 1-1/8 in. Carter DRJH updraft.

CHASSIS: [Series 460] W.B.: 121 in. & 130 in. Tires: 32 x 6.00. [Series 430] W.B.: 116 in. & 122 in. Tires: 29 x 5.50. [Series 420] W.B.: 112-1/4 in. Tires: 30 x 5.00.

TECHNICAL: Selective sliding gear transmission. Speeds: 3F/1R. Floor shift controls. Single dry plate clutch. Spiral bevel drive. Semi-floating rear axle. Overall ratio: 4.5:1 (460); 4.8:1 (430); 4.7:1 (420). Mechanical brakes on four wheels. Wood artillery wheels. 20 in. [460, 420]; 19 in. [430].

1929 Nash, model 460, coupe, JAC

OPTIONS: Single sidemount. Dual sidemount (wires) (125.00). Leather upholstery (25.00). Wire wheels (5) (40.00).

HISTORICAL: Introduced June 1, 1928. Innovations: First year for "Twin Ignition" (OHV models only) - 2 spark plugs firing each cylinder. First use by Nash of chromed brightwork. Calendar year registration: 105,146. Calendar year production: 116,622. The president of Nash was C.W. Nash. Attractive new styling evidently inspired by LaSalle. Increased horsepower, all series. Longer wheelbases, standard and special series and most advanced models. Rumors were reported of a possible Nash-Packard merger. Nash held 2.7% of new car registrations.

1929
Standard, 6-cyl.

	FP	5	4	3	2	1
Sed	995	750	1450	3500	5050	7200
Tr	935	1450	4300	7200	10,100	14,400
Cabr	995	1300	4050	6700	9400	13,400
2 dr Sed	885	750	1450	3500	5050	7200
2P Cpe	885	750	1450	3400	5000	7100
4P Cpe	935	775	1500	3700	5200	7400
Lan Sed	995	725	1400	3200	4850	6900

Special, 6-cyl.

	FP	5	4	3	2	1
2 dr Sed	1260	775	1500	3700	5200	7400
2P Cpe	1245	825	1600	3950	5500	7900
4P Cpe	1315	850	1650	4200	5850	8400
Rds	1345	2900	5800	9700	13,600	19,400
Sed	1345	825	1600	3950	5500	7900
Cabr	1345	2500	5500	9200	12,900	18,400
Vic	1345	850	1650	4200	5850	8400

Advanced, 6-cyl.

	FP	5	4	3	2	1
Cpe	1775	950	2100	4750	6650	9500
Cabr	1660	2900	5800	9700	13,600	19,400
2 dr Sed	1480	850	1650	4200	5850	8400
7P Sed	1990	950	2100	4700	6600	9400
Amb Sed	1925	975	2300	4950	6900	9900
4 dr Sed	1550	875	1700	4350	6050	8700

1930

1930 Nash, model 498, dual cowl phaeton, OCW

NASH — "TWIN-IGNITION EIGHT" — SERIES 490 — EIGHT: Similar in styling to 1929 Series 460, but larger; narrower chrome band at top of radiator shell as seen from front; figure "8" with inverted wings above Nash badge; automatic shutters covering radiator. (Largest, heaviest Nash built to date.)

NASH — "TWIN-IGNITION SIX" — SERIES 480 — SIX: Similar to Series 490, but smaller.

NASH — "SINGLE SIX" — SERIES 450 — SIX: Similar in styling to 1929 Series 420, except for narrow chrome band at top of radiator shell as seen from front.

I.D. DATA: [Series 490] Serial numbers on frame near starting motor. Starting: 496400. Ending: 509200. Engine numbers on engine block near starting motor. [Series 480] Serial numbers on top right side rear motor support or on left rear spring hanger. Starting: B37582. Ending: B54927. Engine numbers on engine block beside starter motor. [Series 450] Serial numbers on right frame member just ahead of rear spring rear bracket. Starting: R216590. Ending: R249707. Engine numbers on left side engine block, upper forward corner.

1930 Nash Twin-Ignition Six, model 482R coupe, AB

Model No.	Body Type & Seating	Price	Weight	Start. Ser. No.
490	4-dr. Sed.-5P	1695	4000	496400
491	2-dr. Cabr.-2/4P	1775	3840	496400
492	2-dr. Cpe.-2P	1775	3900	496400
492R	2-dr. Cpe.2/4P	1845	3950	496400
493	2-dr. Sed.-5P	1625	3950	496400
494	4-dr. Sed.-5P	2085	4170	496400
495	4-dr. Limo.-7P	2260	4210	496400
497	4-dr. Amb. Sed.-5P	1995	4050	496400
498	4-dr. Phae.-7P	1845	3770	505422
498S	4-dr. Spt. Phae.-5P	1975	3840	505965
499	2-dr. Vic.-5P	1945	3950	496400
480	4-dr. Sed.-5P	1385	3535	B37582
481	2-dr. Cabr.-2/4P	1355	3350	B37582
482	2-dr. Cpe.-2P	1295	3400	B37582
482R	2-dr. Cpe.-2/4P	1345	3450	B37582
483	2-dr. Sed.-5P	1295	3535	B37582
484	4-dr. Sed.-7P	1695	3750	B37582
485	4-dr. Limo.-7P	1920	3760	B47085
486	2-dr. Rds.-2/4P	1415	3250	B37582
488	4-dr. Phae.-7P	1425	3450	B37582
488S	4-dr. Spt. Phae.-5P	1545	3720	B37582
489	2-dr. Vic.-4P	1385	3400	B37582
450	4-dr. Sed.-5P	985	2850	R216590
451	2-dr. Cabr.-2/4P	985	2600	R216590
452	2-dr. Cpe.-2P	915	2650	R216590
452R	2-dr. Cpe.-2/4P	955	2700	R216590
453	2-dr. Sed.-5P	915	2750	R216590
455	4-dr. Land. Sed.-5P	1125	2900	R216590
456	2-dr. Rds.-2/4P	945	2550	R216590
457	4-dr. Del. Sed.-5P	1075	2900	R216590
458	4-dr. Phae.-5P	975	2650	R216590

ENGINE: [Series 490] OHV. Straight eight. Cast iron block. B & S: 3-1/4 in. x 4-1/2 in. Disp.: 298.6 cu. in. C.R.: 5.25:1. Brake H.P.: 100 @ 3200 R.P.M. Taxable H.P.: 33.8. Main bearings: Nine. Valve lifters: Solid. Carb.: Marvel 2 in. [Series 480] OHV. Inline. Six. Cast iron block. B & S: 3-3/8 in. x 4-1/2 in. Disp.: 242.0 cu. in. C.R.: 5.0:1. Brake H.P.: 74-1/2 @ 2800 R.P.M. Taxable H.P.: 27.3. Main bearings: Seven. Valve lifters: Solid. Carb.: Marvel 1-1/4 in. [Series 450] -head. Inline. Six. Cast iron block. B & S: 3-1/8 in. x 4-3/8 in. Disp.: 201.3 cu. in. C.R.: 5.0:1. Brake H.P.: 60 @ 2800 R.P.M. Taxable H.P.: 23.4. Main bearings: Seven. Valve lifters: Solid. Carb.: Carter 1-5/16 in.

CHASSIS: [Series 490] W.B.: 124 in. & 133 in. Frt/Rear Tread: 56 in./58 in. Tires: 6.50 x 19. [Series 480] W.B.: 118 in. & 128-1/4 in. Frt/Rear Tread: 56-3/4 in./58-1/4 in. Tires: 5.50 x 19. [Series 450] W.B.: 114-1/4 in. Frt/Rear Tread: 56 in./57-1/4 in. Tires: 5.00 x 19.

TECHNICAL: Selective sliding gear transmission. Speeds: 3F/1R. Floor shift controls. Single dry plate clutch. Spiral bevel drive. Semi-floating rear axle. Overall ratio: 4.5:1 (490, 480); 4.7:1 (450). Mechanical brakes on four wheels. Wood artillery wheels. Wheel size: 19 in.

OPTIONS: Single sidemount. Dual sidemount (wire wheels) (87.00). 5 wire wheels (40.00).

HISTORICAL: Introduced Oct. 1, 1929. Innovations: [Series 490] was first Nash "eight", and largest Nash built to date. Longer wheelbases than corresponding 1929 models. First use by Nash of radiator shutters. Calendar year registrations: 51,086. Calendar year production: 54,605. The president of Nash was C.W. Nash. Nash held 1.95% of new car registrations for 1930.

1930
Single, 6-cyl.

	FP	5	4	3	2	1
Rds	975	2500	5500	9200	12,900	18,400
Tr	995	1650	4600	7700	10,800	15,400
2P Cpe	940	700	1350	2700	4500	6400
2 dr Sed	935	750	1450	3300	4900	7000
4P Cpe	980	850	1650	4200	5800	8400
Cabr	1005	1650	4600	7700	10,800	15,400
4 dr Sed	1005	750	1450	3400	5000	7100
DeL Sed	1095	775	1500	3600	5100	7300
Lan'let	1155	825	1600	3950	5500	7900

Twin-Ign, 6-cyl.

	FP	5	4	3	2	1
Rds	1365	3350	6750	11,250	15,750	22,500
7P Tr	1475	3650	7350	12,250	17,150	24,500
5P Tr	1595	3500	7050	11,750	16,450	23,500
2P Cpe	1345	825	1600	3950	5500	7900
4P Cpe	1395	850	1650	4200	5850	8400
2 dr Sed	1325	825	1600	3950	5500	7900
Cabr	1385	3200	6450	10,750	15,050	21,500
Vic	1410	1200	3700	6200	8700	12,400
4 dr Sed	1415	850	1650	4200	5850	8400
7P Sed	1745	875	1700	4350	6050	8700

Twin-Ign, 8-cyl.

	FP	5	4	3	2	1
2 dr Sed	1675	850	1650	4200	5850	8400
2P Cpe	1915	950	2100	4700	6600	9400
4P Cpe	1975	1025	2600	5200	7200	10,400
Vic	2045	1800	4900	8200	11,500	16,400
Cabr	1875	4400	8850	14,750	20,650	29,500
Sed	1795	900	1800	4450	6250	8900
Amb Sed	2095	1025	2600	5200	7200	10,400
7P Sed	2195	1025	2600	5200	7200	10,400
7P Limo	2385	1100	3400	5700	8000	11,400

1931

NASH — SERIES 890 — EIGHT: Nearly identical in styling to 480 series of 1930, but parking lamps mounted on fenders.

NASH — SERIES 880 — EIGHT: Similar in styling to 6-cylinder 480 series of 1930, but with longer hood to accommodate straight-8 engine.

979

1931 Nash, series 880, convertible sedan, HC

NASH — SERIES 870 — EIGHT: Similar in styling to 1930 "single six," series 450, but with longer hood to accommodate straight-8 engine. Figure "8" flanked by inverted wings above Nash radiator badge.

NASH — SERIES 660 — SIX: Identical in appearance except shorter hood, no "winged 8" radiator emblem.

I.D. DATA: [Series 890] Serial numbers on frame, adjacent to starting motor. Starting: 509201. Ending: 515399. Engine numbers on engine block right side, near starting motor. Starting: B70124. Ending: B74370. [Series 880] Serial numbers on frame adjacent to starting motor. Starting: B54928. Ending: B61757. Engine numbers on right side engine block near starting motor. Starting: B70124. Ending: B74370. [Series 870] Serial numbers on frame, adjacent to starting motor. Starting: X1001. Ending: X13116. Engine numbers on left side engine block next to generator. Starting: XE1000. Ending: XE13184. [Series 660] Serial numbers on frame, adjacent to starting motor. Starting: R249708. Ending: R261948. Engine numbers on left side engine block next to generator. Starting: E1000. Ending: E13290.

Model No.	Body Type & Seating	Price	Weight	Start. Ser. No.
890	4-dr. Sed.-5P	1565	4000	509201
891	2-dr. Cabr.-2/4P	1695	3840	509201
892	2-dr. Cpe.-2P	1695	3900	509201
892R	2-dr. Cpe.-2/4P	1745	3950	509201
894	4-dr. Sed.-7P	1925	4170	509201
895	4-dr. Limo.-7P	2025	4210	509201
897	4-dr. Amb. Sed.-7P	1825	4050	509201
898	4-dr. Phae.-7P	1595	3880	513589
899	2-dr. Vic.-5P	1765	3950	509201
880	4-dr. Sed.-5P	1295	3360	B54928
881	2-dr. Conv. Sed.-5P	1325	3275	B58597
882	2-dr. Cpe.-2P	1245	3200	B54928
882R	2-dr. Cpe.-2/4P	1285	3250	B54928
887	4-dr. Twn. Sed.-5P	1375	3400	B54928
870	4-dr. Sed.-5P	995	3000	X1001
871	2-dr. Conv. Sed.-5P	1075	2950	X8171
872	2-dr. Cpe.-2P	945	2870	X1001
872R	2-dr. Cpe.-2/4P	975	2920	X1001
877	4-dr. Sp. Sed.-5P	955	3000	X1001
660	4-dr. Sed.-5P	845	2800	R249708
662	2-dr. Cpe.-2P	795	2600	R249708
662R	2-dr. Cpe.-2/4P	825	2650	R249708
663	2-dr. Sed.-5P	795	2740	R249708
668	4-dr. Spt. Phae.-5P	895	2640	R249708

ENGINE: [Series 890] OHV Straight-"Eight". Cast iron block. B & S: 3-1/4 in. x 4-1/2 in. Disp.: 298.6 cu. in. C.R.: 5.25:1. Brake H.P.: 115 @ 3600 R.P.M. Taxable H.P.: 33.8. Main bearings: Nine. Valve lifters: Solid. Carb.: Stromberg UUR-2. [Series 880] OHV Straight "Eight". Cast iron block. B & S: 3 in. x 4-1/4 in. Disp.: 240.0 cu. in. C.R.: 5.25:1. Brake H.P.: 88-1/2 @ 3400 R.P.M. Taxable H.P.: 28.8. Main bearings: Nine. Valve lifters: Solid. Carb.: Marvel. Torque: 100 lbs.-ft. @ 200 R.P.M. [Series 870] L-head Straight "Eight". Cast iron block. B & S: 2-7/8 in. x 4-3/8 in. Disp.: 227.2 cu. in. C.R.: 5.0:1. Brake H.P.: 78 @ 3300 R.P.M. Taxable H.P.: 26.4. Main bearings: Nine. Valve lifters: Solid. Carb.: Stromberg E-2. Torque: 92 lbs.-ft. @ 1600 R.P.M. [Series 660] Inline. Six. Cast iron block. B & S: 3-1/8 in. x 4-3/8 in. Disp.: 201.3 cu. in. C.R.: 5.0:1. Brake H.P.: 65 @ 3200 R.P.M. Taxable H.P.: 23.4. Main bearings: Seven. Valve lifters: Solid. Carb.: Carter DRT-08. Torque: 92 lbs.-ft. @ 1600 R.P.M.

CHASSIS: [Series 890] W.B.: 124 in. & 133 in. Frt/Rear Tread: 56-1/4 in. x 4-1/2 in. Disp.: 298.6 cu. in. /58 in. Tires: 6.50 x 19. [Series 880] W.B.: 121 in. Frt/Rear Tread: 55-15/16 in./58-1/8 in. Tires: 5.50 x 18. [Series 870] W.B.: 116-1/4 in. Frt/Rear Tread: 56 in./58-3/8 in. Tires: 5.25 x 19. [Series 660] W.B.: 114-1/4 in. Frt/Rear Tread: 56 in./58-3/8 in. Tires: 5.00 x 19.

TECHNICAL: Selective sliding gear transmission. Speeds: 3F/1R. Floor shift controls. Single dry plate clutch. Spiral bevel drive. Semi-floating rear axle. Overall ratio: 4.5:1 (890), 4.72:1 (880), 5.1:1 (870, 660). Mechanical brakes on four wheels. Artillery wheels (wire opt., extra cost). Rim size: 18 in. (880), 19 in. (all others).

OPTIONS: Single sidemount. Dual Sidemount.

HISTORICAL: Introduced Oct. 1, 1930. Innovations: First Nash "Flathead Eight" (series 870) downdraft carburetors, 8-cyl. models. Calendar year registrations: 39,366. Calendar year production: 38,616. The president of Nash was E.H. McCarty. Despite falling sales, Nash earned $4,808,000 during fiscal 1931. Nash held 2.06% of new car registrations for the year.

1931
Series 660, 6-cyl.

	FP	5	4	3	2	1
5P Tr	895	1450	4300	7200	10,100	14,400
2P Cpe	795	725	1400	3200	4850	6900
4P Cpe	825	775	1500	3700	5200	7400
2 dr Sed	795	725	1400	3200	4850	6900
4 dr Sed	845	775	1500	3700	5200	7400
Series 870, 8-cyl.						
2P Cpe	945	900	1800	4450	6250	8900
4P Cpe	975	850	1650	4200	5850	8400
Conv Sed	1075	4100	8250	13,750	19,250	27,500
2 dr Sed	995	825	1600	3950	5500	7900
Spec Sed	955	850	1650	4200	5850	8400
Series 880 (Twin-Ign 8-cyl.)						
2P Cpe	1245	950	2100	4700	6600	9400
4P Cpe	1285	975	2300	4950	6900	9900
Conv Sed	1325	4300	8550	14,250	19,950	28,500
Sed	1295	950	2100	4700	6600	9400
Twn Sed	1375	975	2300	4950	6900	9900
Series 890 (Twin-Ign 8-cyl.)						
7P Tr	1595	3800	7650	12,750	17,850	25,500
2P Cpe	1695	975	2300	4950	6900	9900
4P Cpe	1745	1025	2600	5200	7200	10,400
Cabr	1695	3100	6150	10,250	14,350	20,500
Vic	1795	1200	3700	6200	8700	12,400
2 dr Sed	1565	950	2100	4700	6600	9400
Amb Sed	1825	975	2300	4950	6900	9900
7P Sed	1925	975	2200	4850	6800	9700
7P Limo	2025	1075	2900	5450	7600	10,900

1932

1932 Nash, model 1094, 7-pass. sedan, OCW

NASH — SERIES 990 — EIGHT: Basically a carry-over of the 1931 890 series, but with a vee'd grille instead of the shuttered flat radiator. Headlamps bullet-shaped. Single-bar bumpers.

NASH — SERIES 980 — EIGHT: Similar in appearance to 990 series, but smaller.

NASH — SERIES 970 — EIGHT: Similar in styling to 870 series of 1931, but with slightly vee'd grille instead of flat radiator front.

NASH — SERIES 960 — SIX: Virtually identical in appearance to 970 series, but hood 2" shorter.

NASH — AMBASSADOR & ADVANCED "EIGHTS" — SERIES 1090 — EIGHT: Second series 1932 car. Slanted windshield, visor eliminated; more sweeping lines, esp. fenders; semi-beavertail rear quarter. Ambassador models 1094-1099 were on the 142" wheelbase, longest ever offered by Nash. (These cars have been referred to by historian Dave Brownell as the "Kenosha Duesenbergs.") Advanced models similar, but shorter bodies on 133" wheelbase. Vertical, vee'd grille. Bullet-shaped, chrome-plated headlamps.

NASH — SPECIAL "EIGHT" — SERIES 1080 — EIGHT: Similar in appearance to 1090 series, but smaller; less brightwork on radiator shell.

NASH — STANDARD "EIGHT" — SERIES 1070 — EIGHT: Slanted windshield; vee'd, vertical grille; sweeping fender lines; semi-beavertail rear section.

NASH — "BIG SIX" — SERIES 1060 — SIX: Similar in appearance to 1070 series, but shorter hood and front fenders.

I.D. DATA: [Series 990] Serial numbers on frame, adjacent to starting motor. Starting: 515400. Ending: 519299. Engine numbers on right side engine block near starting motor. Starting: 398700. Ending: 402599. [Series 980] Serial numbers on frame, adjacent to starting motor. Starting: B61758. Ending: B66800. Engine numbers on right side engine block near starting motor. Starting: B74371. Ending: B79449. [Series 970] Serial numbers on frame, adjacent to starting motor. Starting: X13117. Ending: X21317. Engine numbers on left side engine block next to generator. Starting: XE13185. Ending: XE21416. [Series 960] Serial numbers on frame, adjacent to starting motor. Starting: R261949. Ending: R267735. Engine numbers on left side engine block next to generator. Starting: R261949. Ending: R267735. [Series 1090] Serial numbers on frame, adjacent to starting motor. Starting: 519300. Ending: 521190. Engine numbers on right side engine block near starting motor. [Series 1080] Serial numbers on frame, adjacent to starting motor. Starting: B66800. Ending: B70020. Engine numbers on right side engine block near starting motor. [Series 1070] Serial numbers on frame, adjacent to starting motor. Starting: X21318. Ending: X25386. Engine numbers on left side engine block next to generator. [Series 1060] Serial numbers on frame, adjacent to starting motor. Starting: R267736. Ending: R274299. Engine numbers on left side engine block next to generator.

Model No.	Body Type & Seating	Price	Weight	Start. Ser. No.
990	4-dr. Sed.-5P	1565	4000	515400
991	2-dr. Cabr.-2/4P	1695	3840	515400
992	2-dr. Cpe.-2P	1695	3900	515400
992R	2-dr. Cpe.-2/4P	1745	3950	515400
994	4-dr. Sed.-7P	1925	4170	515400
995	4-dr. Limo.-7P	2025	4210	515400
996	4-dr. Lwb. Sed.-5P	1825	4100	515400
997	4-dr. Amb. Sed.-5P	1825	4050	515400
998	4-dr. Phae.-7P	1595	3880	515400
999	2-dr. Vic.-5P	1765	3950	515400
980	4-dr. Sed.-5P	1295	3360	B61758
981	2-dr. Conv. Sed.-5P	1325	3275	B61758
982	2-dr. Cpe.-2P	1245	3200	B61758
982R	2-dr. Cpe.-2/4P	1285	3250	B61758
987	4-dr. Twn. Sed.-5P	1375	3400	B61758
970	4-dr. Sed.-5P	995	3000	X13117
971	2-dr. Conv. Sed.-5P	1075	2950	X13117
972	2-dr. Cpe.-2P	945	2870	X13117
972R	2-dr. Cpe.-2/4P	975	2920	X13117
977	4-dr. Sp. Sed.-5P	955	3000	X13117
960	4-dr. Sed.-5P	845	2800	R261949
962	2-dr. Cpe.-2P	795	2600	R261949
962R	2-dr. Cpe.-2/4P	825	2650	R261949
963	2-dr. Sed.-5P	795	2740	R261949
968	4-dr. Spt. Phae.-5P	895	2640	R261949
1090	4-dr. Sed.-5P	1595	4350	519300
1091	2-dr. Conv. Rds.-2/4P	1795	4270	519300
1092	2-dr. Cpe.-2P	1695	4210	519300
1092R	2-dr. Cpe.2/4P	1695	4300	519300
1093	4-dr. Conv. Sed.-5P	1875	4470	519300
1094	4-dr. Sed.-7P	1955	4600	519300
1095	4-dr. Limo.-7P	2055	4650	519300
1096	4-dr. Sed.-5P	1855	4510	519300
1097	4-dr. Brgm.-5P	1855	4470	519300
1099	2-dr. Vic.-5P	1785	4300	519300
1080	4-dr. Sed.-5P	1320	3870	B66800
1081	2-dr. Conv. Rds.-2/4P	1395	3750	B66800
1082	2-dr. Cpe.-2P	1270	3710	B66800
1082R	2-dr. Cpe.-2/4P	1320	3800	B66800
1083	4-dr. Conv. Sed.-5P	1475	4000	B66800
1089	2-dr. Vic.-5P	1395	3840	B66800
1070	4-dr. Sed.-5P	1015	3400	X21318
1071	2-dr. Conv. Rds.-2/4P	1055	3270	X21318
1072	2-dr. Cpe.-2P	965	3250	X21318
1072R	2-dr. Cpe.-2/4P	1015	3300	X21318
1073	2-dr. Conv. Sed.-5P	1095	3275	X21318
1077	4-dr. Twn. Sed.-5P	975	3400	X21318
1060	4-dr. Sed.-5P	840	3200	R267736
1061	2-dr. Conv. Rds.-2/4P	895	3120	R267736
1062	2-dr. Cpe.-2P	777	3050	R267736
1062R	2-dr. Cpe.-2/4P	825	3100	R267736
1063	2-dr. Conv. Sed.-5P	935	3125	R267736
1067	4-dr. Twn. Sed.-5P	825	3150	R267736

1932 Nash Ambassador Eight, sedan, JAC

ENGINE: [Series 990] OHV. Straight. Eight. Cast iron block. B & S: 3-1/4 in. x 4-1/2 in. Disp.: 298.6 cu. in. C.R.: 5.25:1. Brake H.P.: 115 @ 3600 R.P.M. Taxable H.P.: 33.8. Main bearings: Nine. Valve lifters: Solid. Carb.: Stromberg UUR.2. Torque: 100 lbs.-ft. at 1200 R.P.M. [Series 980] OHV. Straight. Eight. Cast iron block. B & S: 3 in. x 4-1/4 in. Disp.: 240.0 cu. in. C.R.: 5.25:1. Brake H.P.: 94 @ 3400 R.P.M. Taxable H.P.: 28.8. Main bearings: Nine. Valve lifters: Solid. Carb.: Stromberg UUR.2. Torque: 100 lbs.-ft. at 1200 R.P.M. [Series 970] L-head. Straight. Eight. Cast iron block. B & S: 2-7/8 in. x 4-3/8 in. Disp.: 227.2 cu. in. C.R.: 5.00:1. Brake H.P.: 78 @ 3200 R.P.M. Taxable H.P.: 26.4. Main bearings: Nine. Valve lifters: Solid. Carb.: Stromberg EE.2. Torque: 92 lbs.-ft. at 1600 R.P.M. [Series 960] L-head. Inline. Six. Cast iron block. B & S: 3-1/8 in. x 4-3/8 in. Disp.: 201.3 cu. in. C.R.: 5.00:1. Brake H.P.: 65 @ 3200 R.P.M. Taxable H.P.: 23.4. Main bearings: Seven. Valve lifters: Solid. Carb.: Carter 1-5/16 in. Torque: 92 lbs.-ft. at 1600 R.P.M. [Series 1090] OHV. Straight eight. Cast iron block. B & S: 3-3/8 in. x 4-1/2 in. Disp.: 322.0 cu. in. C.R.: 5.25:1. Brake H.P.: 125 @ 3600 R.P.M. Taxable H.P.: 36.4. Main bearings: Nine. Valve lifters: Solid. Carb.: Stromberg UUR.2. [Series 1080] OHV. Straight. Eight. Cast iron block. B & S: 3-1/8 in. x 4-1/4 in. Disp.: 260.8 cu. in. C.R.: 5.25:1. Brake H.P.: 100 @ 3400 R.P.M. Taxable H.P.: 31.2. Main bearings: Nine. Valve lifters: Solid. Carb.: Stromberg UUR.2. [Series 1070] L-head. Straight. Eight. Cast iron block. B & S: 3 in. x 4-3/8 in. Disp.: 247.4 cu. in. C.R.: 5.1:1. Brake H.P.: 85 @ 3200 R.P.M. Taxable H.P.: 28.8. Main bearings: Nine. Valve lifters: Solid. Carb.: Stromberg EE.22. [Series 1060] L-head. Inline. Six. Cast iron block. B & S: 3-1/8 in. x 4-3/8 in. Disp.: 201.3 cu. in. C.R.: 5.1:1. Brake H.P.: 70 @ 3000 R.P.M. Taxable H.P.: 23.4. Main bearings: Seven. Valve lifters: Solid. Carb.: Stromberg E.2.

CHASSIS: [Series 990] W.B.: 124 in. & 133 in. Frt/Rear Tread: 56-1/4 in./58 in. Tires: 6.50 x 19. [Series 980] W.B.: 121 in. Frt/Rear Tread: 55-15/16 in./58-1/8 in. Tires: 6.00 x 18. [Series 970] W.B.: 116-1/4 in. Frt/Rear Tread: 56 in./58-3/8 in. Tires: 5.25 x 19. [Series 960] W.B.: 114-1/4 in. Frt/Rear Tread: 56 in./58-3/8 in. Tires: 5.00 x 19. [Series 1090] W.B.: 133 in. & 142 in. Frt/Rear Tread: 57-1/4 in./58 in. Tires: 7.00 x 18. [Series 1080] W.B.: 128 in. Frt/Rear Tread: 58-3/4 in./60-3/4 in. Tires: 6.50 x 17. [Series 1070] W.B.: 121 in. Frt/Rear Tread: 56-1/2 in./59-3/8 in. Tires: 5.50 x 18. [Series 1060] W.B.: 116 in. Frt/Rear Tread: 56-1/2 in./60 in. Tires: 5.25. x 18.

TECHNICAL: Selective sliding gear transmission. Speeds: 3F/1R. Floor shift controls. Single dry plate clutch. Worm drive [1080,1090]. Spiral bevel drive [all others]. Semi-floating rear axle. Overall ratio: 4.50:1 [990], 1909]; 4.46:1 [980]; 4.43:1 [1080]; 4.73:1 [970, 960]; 4.44:1 [1070]; 4.70:1 [1060]. Mechanical brakes on four wheels. Artillery or wire wheels. Wheel size: 19 in. [990, 970, 960]; 18 in. [980, 1090, 1070, 1060]; 17 in. [1080]. Drivetrain Options: Free-wheeling.

OPTIONS: Single sidemount. Dual sidemount. Sidemount cover(s).

HISTORICAL: Introduced: June 1, 1931 [first series: 990 et al], March 1, 1932 [second series 1090 et al]. Innovations: Larger engines in all second series cars. Nash's first 4-door convertible sedans [1090 and 1080 series]. Worm drive [1080, 1090 series]. Calendar year registrations: 20,233 [both series]. Calendar year production: 17,696 [both series]. The president of Nash was E.H. McCarty. First time Nash offered two series in one model year. A dismal year for sales, thanks to the depression, but Nash made money in 1932 — the only auto manufacturer apart from General Motors to do so! (Profit for the fiscal year came to $1,029,552.) Nash held 1.85% of industry registrations for the year.

1932
Series 960, 6-cyl.

	FP	5	4	3	2	1
5P Tr	895	3650	7350	12,250	17,150	24,500
2P Cpe	795	825	1600	3950	5500	7900
4P Cpe	825	850	1650	4200	5850	8400
2 dr Sed	795	725	1400	3200	4850	6900
4 dr Sed	845	775	1500	3700	5200	7400

Series 970, 8-cyl., 116.5" wb

	FP	5	4	3	2	1
2P Cpe	945	975	2300	4950	6900	9900
4P Cpe	975	1025	2600	5200	7200	10,400
Conv Sed	1075	4900	9750	16,250	22,750	32,500
2 dr Sed	995	900	1800	4450	6250	8900
Spec Sed	955	950	2100	4700	6600	9400

Series 980 (Twin-Ign. 8-cyl.), 121" wb

	FP	5	4	3	2	1
2P Cpe	1245	1025	2600	5200	7200	10,400
4P Cpe	1285	1075	2900	5450	7600	10,900
Conv Sed	1325	5300	10,650	17,750	24,850	35,500
Sed	1295	1100	3400	5700	8000	11,400
Twn Sed	1375	1200	3700	6200	8700	12,400

Series 990 (Twin-Ign. 8-cyl.), 124"-133" wb

	FP	5	4	3	2	1
7P Tr	1595	4100	8250	13,750	19,250	27,500
2P Cpe	1695	1075	2900	5450	7600	10,900
4P Cpe	1745	1075	3100	5550	7750	11,100
Cabr	1695	5600	11,250	18,750	26,250	37,500
Vic	1765	2500	5500	9200	12,900	18,400
2 dr Sed	1565	1200	3700	6200	8700	12,400
Spec Sed	1825	1225	3800	6350	8850	12,700
Amb Sed	1825	1300	4050	6700	9400	13,400
7P Sed	1925	1350	4100	6850	9600	13,700
Limo	2025	1400	4150	6950	9750	13,900

1933

1933 Nash, convertible sedan, OCW

NASH — AMBASSADOR "EIGHT" — SERIES 1190 — EIGHT: Identical in apperance to 1090 seriess of 1932, except for a medallion with the number "8" mounted on headlamp tie bar. Models 1194-1199 were on the 142" chassis.

NASH — ADVANCED "EIGHT" — SERIES 1180 — EIGHT: Similar in appearance to 1190 series, but smaller; less brightwork on radiator shell than 1190.

NASH — SPECIAL "EIGHT" — SERIES 1170 — EIGHT: Identical in appearance to series 1070 standard "Eight" of 1932.

NASH — STANDARD "EIGHT" — SERIES 1130 — EIGHT: Identical in appearance to 1932 series 1060 "Big Six".

NASH — "BIG SIX" — SERIES 1120 — SIX: Identical in appearance to 1932 series 1060 "Big Six."

I.D. DATA: [Series 1190] Serial numbers on frame, opposite starting motor. Starting: 521191. Ending: 521800. Engine numbers on crankcase bell housing. Starting. 404491. Ending: 404992. [Series 1180] Serial numbers on frame, opposite starting motor. Starting: B70021. Ending: B70800. Engine numbers on crankcase bell housing. Starting: B82671. Ending: B83420. [Series 1170] Serial numbers on frame, right side. Starting: X25387. Ending: X26099. Engine numbers on left side near generator. Starting: XE25413. Ending: XE28189. [Series 1130] Serial numbers on frame, right side. Starting: X26100. Ending: X28203. Engine numbers on right side below valve cover. Starting: XE26000. Ending: XE28001. [Series 1120] Serial numbers on frame, right side. Starting: R274300. Ending: R278900. Engine numbers on right side below valve cover. Starting: E25700. Ending: E30211.

Model No.	Body Type & Seating	Price	Weight	Start. Ser. No.
1190	4-dr. Sed.-5P	1575	4350	521191
1191	2-dr. Conv. Rds.-2/4P	1645	4270	521191
1192R	2-dr. Cpe.-2/4P	1545	4300	521191
1193	4-dr. Conv. Sed.-5P	1875	4470	521191
1194	4-dr. Sed.-7P	1955	4600	521191
1195	4-dr. Limo.-7P	2055	4650	521191
1196	4-dr. LWB Sed.-5P	1855	4510	521191
1197	4-dr. Brgm.-5P	1820	4470	521191
1199	2-dr. Vic.-5P	1785	4300	521191
1180	4-dr. Sed.-5P	1320	4000	B70021
1181	2-dr. Conv. Rds.-2/4P	1395	3750	B70021
1182	2-dr. Cpe.-2P	1255	3710	B70021
1182R	2-dr. Cpe.-2/4P	1275	3800	B70021
1183	4-dr. Conv. Sed.-5P	1575	3870	B70021
1189	2-dr. Vic.-5P	1395	3840	B70021
1170	4-dr. Sed.-5P	1015	3400	X25387
1171	2-dr. Conv. Rds.-2/4P	1055	3270	X25387
1172	2-dr. Cpe.-2P	965	3250	X25387
1172R	2-dr. Cpe.-2/4P	1015	3300	X25387
1173	2-dr. Conv. Sed.-5P	1095	3275	X25387
1177	4-dr. Twn. Sed.-5P	975	3400	X25387
1130	4-dr. Sed.-5P	845	3200	X26100
1131	2-dr. Conv. Rds.-2/4P	900	3050	X26100
1132	2-dr. Cpe.-2P	830	3050	X26100
1132R	2-dr. Cpe.-2/4P	845	3100	X26100
1133	2-dr. Conv. Sed.-5P	945	3150	X26100
1137	4-dr. Twn. Sed.-5P	830	3175	X26100
1120	4-dr. Sed.-5P	745	3125	R274300
1121	2-dr. Conv. Rds.-2/4P	810	3000	R274300
1122	2-dr. Cpe.-2P	725	3000	R274300
1122R	2-dr. Cpe.-2/4P	745	3050	R274300
1123	2-dr. Conv. Sed.-5P	845	3100	R274300
1127	4-dr. Twn. Sed.-5P	695	3125	R274300

1933 Nash, model 1181, convertible roadster, AB

ENGINE: [Series 1190] OHV Straight. Eight. Cast iron block. B & S: 3-3/8 in. x 4-1/2 in. Disp.: 322.0 cu. in. C.R.: 5.2:1. Brake H.P.: 125 @ 3600 R.P.M. Taxable H.P.: 36.4. Main bearings: Nine. Valve lifters: Solid. Carb.: Stromberg UUR-2. [Series 1180] OHV Straight. Eight. Cast iron block. B & S: 3-1/8 in. x 4-1/4 in. Disp.: 260.8 cu. in. C.R.: 5.2:1. Brake H.P.: 100 @ 3200 R.P.M. Taxable H.P.: 31.2. Main bearings: Nine. Valve lifters: Solid. Carb.: Stromberg UUR-2. [Series 1170] L-head Straight. Eight. Cast iron block. B & S: 3-3/8 in. Disp.: 247.4 cu. in. C.R.: 5.1:1. Brake H.P.: 85 @ 3200 R.P.M. Taxable H.P.: 28.8. Main bearings: Seven. Valve lifters: Solid. Carb.: 1-7/16 in. Stromberg. [Series 1130] L-head Straight. Eight. Cast iron block. B & S: 3 in. x 4-3/8 in. Disp.: 247.4 cu. in. C.R.: 5.1:1. Brake H.P.: 80 @ 3200 R.P.M. Taxable H.P.: 28.8. Main bearings: Nine. Valve lifters: Solid. Carb.: Stromberg EX-2. Torque: 92 lbs.-ft. @ 1600 R.P.M. [Series 1120] L-head. Inline. Six. Cast iron block. B & S: 3 in. x 4-3/8 in. Disp.: 217.8 cu. in. C.R.: 5.3:1. Brake H.P.: 75 @ 3200 R.P.M. Taxable H.P.: 25.3. Main bearings: Seven. Valve lifters: Solid. Carb.: Stromberg EX-2.

CHASSIS: [Series 1190] W.B.: 133 in. & 142 in. Tires: 7.00 x 18. [Series 1180] W.B.: 128 in. Tires: 6.50 x 17. [Series 1170] W.B.: 121 in. Tires: 5.50 x 18. [Series 1130] W.B.: 116 in. Tires: 5.50 x 17. [Series 1120] W.B.: 116 in. Tires: 5.50 x 17.

TECHNICAL: Selective sliding gear transmission. Speeds: 3F/1R. Floor shift controls. Single dry plate clutch. Worm drive (1190, 1180), Spiral bevel (all others). Semi-floating rear axle. Overall ratio: 4.5:1 (1190), 4.71:1 (1180), 4.44:1 (1170, 1130), 4.70:1 (1120). Mechanical brakes on four wheels. Wire wheels. Wheel size: 18 in. (1190, 1170), 17 in. (all others).

OPTIONS: Single sidemount. Dual Sidemount. Sidemount cover(s).

HISTORICAL: Introduced Dec. 1, 1932. Innovations: "Big Six" engine bored, horsepower raised from 70 to 75. Calendar year registrations: 11,353. Calendar year production: 14,973. The president of Nash was E.H. McCarty. Some "Badge Engineering," and a new "8" on the "Big Six" chassis. Otherwise the 1933 line was carried over from the 1932 second series. Nash production lowest since 1918, and for the first time in its history, the company lost money. (The loss came to $1,188,863.) Share of new car registrations: 0.76%.

1933
Standard Series
(Deduct 20 percent on value; $100 on factory prices for 6-cyl.)

	FP	5	4	3	2	1
Rds	900	1650	4600	7700	10,800	15,400
2P Cpe	830	775	1500	3700	5200	7400
4P Cpe	845	825	1600	3950	5500	7900
4 dr Sed	845	800	1550	3850	5400	7700
Twn Sed	830	850	1650	4100	5700	8200
Special Series, 8-cyl.						
Rds	1055	1800	4900	8200	11,500	16,400
2P Cpe	965	875	1700	4350	6050	8700
4P Cpe	1015	900	1900	4500	6300	9000
4 dr Sed	1015	900	1800	4450	6250	8900
Conv Sed	1095	3100	6150	10,250	14,350	20,500
Twn Sed	975	950	2100	4700	6600	9400
Advanced Series, 8-cyl.						
Cabr	1395	2100	5250	8700	12,200	17,400
2P Cpe	1255	900	1800	4450	6250	8900
4P Cpe	1275	950	2100	4700	6600	9400
4 dr Sed	1320	900	1900	4500	6300	9000
Conv Sed	1575	3350	6750	11,250	15,750	22,500
Vic	1395	975	2300	4950	6900	9900
Ambassador Series, 8-cyl.						
Cabr	1695	3200	6450	10,750	15,050	21,500
Cpe	1545	950	2100	4700	6600	9400
4 dr Sed	1955	900	1800	4450	6250	8900
Conv Sed	1545	3650	7350	12,250	17,150	24,500
Vic	1855	1450	4300	7200	10,100	14,400
142" Brgm	1855	1200	3700	6200	8700	12,400
142" Sed	1855	1225	3850	6450	9000	12,900
142" Limo	2055	1300	4050	6700	9400	13,400

1934

1934 Nash Ambassador with C.W. Nash (left), Chairman & E.H. McCarty President of Nash Motors, AB

NASH — AMBASSADOR "EIGHT" — SERIES 1290 — EIGHT: High-styled body, designed by Count Alexis De Sakhnoffsky, featuring deep-skirted fenders; ribs running length of hood; horizontal door ventilators on hood sides; chromed, bullet-shaped headlamps; full beavertail rear section.

NASH — ADVANCED "EIGHT" — SERIES 1280 — EIGHT: Identical in appearance to Ambassador models (1290 series), but shorter.

NASH — "BIG SIX" — SERIES 1220 — SIX: Identical in appearance to 1280 series, but shorter hood and front fenders.

LA FAYETTE — SERIES 110 — SIX: Similar in design to Nash models, but smoother, less elaborate. (No embossing on hood and fenders, for instance.) Painted headlamp shells on standard models, chromed on others.

I.D. DATA: [Series 1290] Serial numbers on right side frame, under hood. Starting: 521801. Ending: 523253. Engine numbers on right side engine block. Starting: 405819. Ending: 406555. [Series 1280] Serial numbers on right side frame, under hood. Starting: B70801. Ending: B75001. Engine numbers on right side engine block. Starting: B85513. Ending: B87709. [Series 1220] Serial numbers on right side frame, under hood. Starting:

R278901. Ending: R294724. Engine numbers on right side engine block. Starting: E35651. Ending: E46124. LaFayette serial numbers on right frame, under hood. Starting: L1001. Ending: L13700. Engine numbers on right front of engine block, just below valve cover. Starting: LE501. Ending: LE13200.

Model No.	Body Type & Seating	Price	Weight	Start. Ser. No.
1290	4-dr. Sed.-5P	1575	4330	521801
1293	4-dr. Brgm.-5P	1625	4360	521801
1294	4-dr. Sed.-7P	1955	4590	521801
1295	4-dr. Limo.-7P	2055	4640	521801
1296	4-dr. Lwb. Sed.-5P	1955	4500	521801
1297	4-dr. Lwb. Brgm.-5P	1820	4460	521801
1280	4-dr. Sed.-5P	1065	3540	B70801
1282	2-dr. Cpe.-2P	1045	3460	B70801
1282R	2-dr. Cpe.-2/4P	1065	3510	B70801
1283	4-dr. Brgm.-5P	1085	3570	B70801
1287	4-dr. Twn. Sed.-5P	1035	3540	B70801
1288	4-dr. Brgm. Sed.-5P	1145	3570	B70801
1220	4-dr. Sed.-5P	785	3370	R278901
1222	2-dr. Cpe.-2P	765	3290	R278901
1222R	2-dr. Cpe.-2/4P	785	3340	R278901
1223	4-dr. Brgm.-5P	795	3400	R278901
1227	4-dr. Twn. Sed.-5P	745	3370	R278901
1228	4-dr. Brgm. Sed.-5P	865	3400	R278901
110	4-dr. Sed.-5P	695	3030	L1001
112	2-dr. Cpe.-2P	635	2925	L1001
112R	2-dr. Cpe.-2/4P	675	2970	L1001
113	4-dr. Brgm.-5P	745	3050	L10131
115	2-dr. Tr. Sed.-5P	685	3030	L1001
116	2-dr. Std. Sed.-5P	595	2970	L1001
117	4-dr. Std. Sed.-5P	645	3000	L4026
118	4-dr. Std. Brgm.-5P	695	3050	L10133

ENGINE: [Series 1290] OHV. Straight. Eight. Cast iron block. B & S: 3-3/8 in. x 4-1/2 in. Disp.: 322.0 cu. in. C.R.: 5.25:1. Brake H.P.: 125 @ 3600 R.P.M. Taxable H.P.: 36.4. Main bearings: Nine. Valve lifters: Solid. Carb.: Stromberg UUR-2. Torque: 115 lbs.-ft. at 400 R.P.M. [Series 1280] OHV. Straight. Eight. Cast iron block. B & S: 3-1/8 in. x 4-1/4 in. Disp.: 260.8 cu. in. C.R.: 5.25:1. Brake H.P.: 100 @ 3400 R.P.M. Taxable H.P.: 31.2. Main bearings: Nine. Valve lifters: Solid. Carb.: Stromberg EE-22. Torque: 110 lbs.-ft at 350 R.P.M. [Series 1220] OHV. Inline. Six. Cast iron block. B & S: 3-3/8 in. x 4-3/8 in. Disp.: 234.8 cu. in. C.R.: 5.25:1. Brake H.P.: 88 @ 3200 R.P.M. Taxable H.P.: 27.3. Main bearings: Seven. Valve lifters: Solid. Carb.: Stromberg EX-32. Torque: 100 lbs.-ft. at 350 R.P.M. [LaFayette] L-head. Inline. Six. Cast iron block. B & S: 3-1/4 in. x 4-3/8 in. Disp.: 217.8 cu. in. C.R.: 5.3:1. Brake H.P.: 75 @ 3200 R.P.M. Taxable H.P.: 25.3. Main bearings: Seven. Valve lifters: Solid. Carb.: Marvel "B".

CHASSIS: [Series 1290] W.B.: 133 in. & 142 in. O.L.: 214-1/4 in. Frt/Rear Tread: 57-1/4 in./60-1/4 in. Tires: 7.00 x 17. [Series 1280] W.B.: 121 in. O.L.: 198-3/16 in. Frt/Rear Tread: 57-7/8 in./60 in. Tires: 6.50 x 16. [Series 1220] W.B.: 116 in. O.L.: 194-1/2 in. Frt/Rear Tread: 57-7/8 in./60 in. Tires: 5.50 x 17 (6.25 x 16 opt.). [Series LaFayette (110)] W.B.: 113 in. Frt/Rear Tread: 56-1/2 in./59-11/16 in. Tires: 5.50 x 17 (6.25 x 16 optional).

TECHNICAL: Selective sliding gear transmission. Speeds: 3F/1R. Floor shift controls. Single dry plate clutch. Worm drive [Series 1290], Spiral bevel drive [all others]. Semi-floating rear axle. Overall ratio: 4.72:1 [1290], 4.10:1 [1280], 4.44:1 [1220], 4.70:1 [LaFayette]. Mechanical brakes on four wheels. Steel artillery wheels. Wheel size: 17 in. [Series 1280-16 in.] Baker axleflex indep. front suspension.

OPTIONS: Single sidemount. Dual sidemount. Sidemount cover(s). Fender skirts. Radio. Heater. Clock. Cigar lighter. Radio antenna. Trunk. Trunk rack.

HISTORICAL: Introduced: Oct. 1, 1933 (Nash), Jan. 10, 1934 (LaFayette). Innovations: First year for low-priced LaFayette. All Nash cars now using OHV engines. (L-head engine of previous "Big Six" now used in La Fayette). Draft-free ventilation system (all models). Calendar year registrations: 14,315 (Nash), 9,301 (LaFayette). Calendar year production: 28,664 (Nash and LaFayette). The president of Nash was E.H. McCarty. Millionth Nash car — a 1227 Town Sedan — was produced on April 27, 1934. A contest was held, to find the oldest Nash automobile still in use by its original owner. Nash #1,000,000 was the prize. It went to Dr. E. O. Nash (no relation) of Pueblo, Colorado. His car, the 517th Nash to have been built, had traveled 215,580 miles. Loss for the fiscal year came to $1,625,078. Share of industry registrations: 1.25% (Nash and La Fayette combined.) Styled by Count Alexis De Sakhnoffsky.

1934
Big Six, 6-cyl.

	FP	5	4	3	2	1
Bus Cpe	795	775	1500	3700	5200	7400
Cpe	815	875	1700	4300	6000	8600
Brgm	825	825	1600	3950	5500	7900
2 dr Sed	815	725	1400	3200	4850	6900
Twn Sed	775	750	1450	3500	5050	7200
Tr Sed	865	750	1450	3400	5000	7100

Advanced, 8-cyl.

	FP	5	4	3	2	1
Bus Cpe	1065	825	1600	3950	5500	7900
Cpe	1085	850	1650	4200	5850	8400
Brgm	1115	900	1800	4450	6250	8900
2 dr Sed	1095	750	1450	3400	5000	7100
Twn Sed	1065	850	1650	4200	5850	8400
Tr Sed	1145	800	1550	3800	5300	7600

Ambassador, 8-cyl.

	FP	5	4	3	2	1
Brgm	1820	850	1650	4200	5850	8400
2 dr Sed	1575	825	1600	3950	5500	7900
Tr Sed	1625	825	1600	4050	5650	8100
7P Sed	1955	875	1700	4300	6000	8600
Limo	2055	925	1900	4550	6350	9100

Lafayette, 6-cyl.

	FP	5	4	3	2	1
2 dr Sed	585	675	1300	2500	4350	6200
Twn Sed	635	700	1350	2700	4500	6400
Brgm	665	675	1300	2600	4400	6300
Spec Cpe	625	825	1600	3950	5500	7900
Spec 4P Cpe	665	825	1600	4050	5650	8100
Spec Tr Sed	675	675	1300	2600	4400	6300
Spec Sed	680	725	1400	3200	4850	6900
Brgm	715	750	1450	3400	5000	7100

1935

1935 Nash, sedan, JAC

NASH — AMBASSADOR & ADVANCED "EIGHTS" — SERIES 3580 — EIGHT: Fastback "Aeroform" styling; streamlined fenders; sharply sloping pressed steel grille; recessed spare tire, behind flush door; teardrop headlamps. Ambassador name applied to top trim line.

NASH — ADVANCED "SIX" — SERIES 3520 — SIX: Identical in appearance to series 3580, except for shorter hood and front fenders.

LAFAYETTE — SERIES 3510 — SIX: Styling similar to 1934 LaFayette, with the following changes: horizontal louvres replaced vent doors in hood sides; extremely convex headlamp lenses.

I.D. DATA: [Series 3580] Serial numbers on right side frame, under hood. Starting: B75010. Ending: B77324. Engine numbers on right side engine block. Starting: B87710. Ending: B90024. [Series 3520] Serial numbers on right side frame, under hood. Starting: R294725. Ending: R303300. Engine numbers on right side engine block. Starting: E46125. Ending: E54700. LaFayette serial numbers on right frame, under hood. Starting: L13701. Ending: L23100. Engine numbers on right front of engine block, just below valve cover. Starting: LE13201. Ending: LE22600.

Model No.	Body Type & Seating	Price	Weight	Start. Ser. No.
3580	4-dr. Sed.-6P	1165	3750	B75010
3585	2-dr. Vic.-6P	1115	3660	B75010
3588	4-dr. Amb. Sed.-6P	1290	3750	B75010
3589	2-dr. Amb. Vic.-6P	1240	3660	B75010
3520	4-dr. Sed.-6P	945	3630	R294725
3525	2-dr. Vic.-6P	895	3540	R294725
3510	4-dr. Std. Sed.-6P	670	3000	L13701
3512	2-dr Std. Cpe.-2P	585	2925	L13701
3512R	2-dr. Sp. Cpe.-2/4P	700	2970	L13701
3513	4-dr. Std. Brgm.-5P	700	3050	L13701
3515	2-dr. Std. Tr. Sed.-5P	650	3030	L13701
3516	2-dr. Std. Sed.-5P	620	2970	L13701
3517	4-dr. Sp. Sed.-5P	720	3030	L13701
3518	4-dr. Sp. Brgm.-5P	750	3050	L13701

ENGINE: [Series 3580] OHV Straight. Eight. Cast iron block. B & S: 3-1/8 in. x 4-1/4 in. Disp.: 260.8 cu. in. C.R.: 5.25:1. Brake H.P.: 100 @ 3400 R.P.M. Taxable H.P.: 31.25. Main bearings: Nine. Valve lifters: Solid. Carb.: Stromberg EE22. Torque: 110 lbs.-ft. @ 350 R.P.M. [Series 3520] OHV. Inline. Six. Cast iron block. B & S: 3-3/8 in. x 4-3/8 in. Disp.: 234.8 cu. in. C.R.: 5.25:1. Brake H.P.: 88 @ 3200 R.P.M. Taxable H.P.: 27.3. Main bearings: Seven. Valve lifters: Solid. Carb.: Stromberg EX32. Torque: 100 lbs.-ft. @ 350 R.P.M. [LaFayette] L-head. Inline. Six. Cast iron block. B & S: 3-1/4 in. x 4-3/8 in. Disp.: 217.7 cu. in. C.R.: 5.54:1. Brake H.P.: 80 @ 3200 R.P.M. Taxable H.P.: 25.3. Main bearings: Seven. Valve lifters: Solid. Carb.: Marvel "B".

CHASSIS: [Series 3580] W.B.: 125 in. O.L.: 207 in. Frt/Rear Tread: 57-7/8 in./60 in. Tires: 6.50 x 16. [Series 3520] W.B.: 120 in. O.L.: 202 in. Frt/Rear Tread: 57-7/8 in./60 in. Tires: 6.25 x 16. [Series 3510 (LaFayette)] W.B.: 113 in. O.L.: 189-1/2 in. Frt/Rear Tread: 56-1/2 / 59-11/16. Tires: (5.50 x 17 (Std.). (6.00 x 16 (Spec.).

TECHNICAL: Selective sliding gear transmission. Speeds: 3F/1R. Floor shift controls. Single dry plate clutch. Spiral bevel drive. Semi-floating rear axle. Overall ratio: 4.1:1 (3580), 4.4:1 (3520), 4.7:1 (LaFayette). Hydraulic brakes (Nash), Mechanical brakes (LaFayette) on four wheels. Steel artillery wheels. Wheel size: 16 in. (LaFayette Std. models 17 in.) Overdrive (Nash models only).

OPTIONS: Single sidemount. Dual Sidemount (LaFayette only). Sidemount cover(s). Fender skirts. Radio. Heater. Clock. Cigar Lighter. Radio Antenna.

1935 Nash LaFayette, coupe, OCW

HISTORICAL: Introduced Jan. 1, 1935. Innovations: Big, 322 C.I.D. "90" series gone from lineup. Number of body styles sharply reduced. First use of hydraulic brakes (Nash only; LaFayette still used mechanicals.) First year for all-steel body (Nash only). Calendar year registrations: 17,739 Nash, 17,445 LaFayette. Calendar year production: 44,637 (Nash and LaFayette). The president of Nash was E.H. McCarty. Loss for the year came to $610,227. Share of industry registrations: 1.29%.

1935
Lafayette, 6-cyl.

	FP	5	4	3	2	1
Bus Cpe	580	700	1350	2700	4500	6400
2 dr Sed	590	675	1300	2500	4350	6200
Brgm	670	700	1350	2800	4550	6500
Tr Sed	620	675	1300	2600	4400	6300
Twn Sed	640	700	1350	2700	4500	6400
Spec Cpe	650	825	1600	3950	5500	7900
Spec 6W Sed	680	725	1400	3200	4850	6900
6W Brgm	710	750	1450	3400	5000	7100
Advanced, 6-cyl.						
Vic	825	775	1500	3700	5200	7400
6W Sed	875	700	1350	2700	4500	6400
Advanced, 8-cyl.						
Vic	1040	800	1550	3800	5300	7600
6W Sed	1090	725	1400	3000	4700	6700
Ambassador, 8-cyl.						
Vic	1170	825	1600	3950	5500	7900
6W Sed	1220	725	1400	3200	4850	6900

1936

1936 Nash, 400, OCW

NASH — AMBASSADOR SUPER "EIGHT" — SERIES 3680 — EIGHT: Similar to 1935 model, but with steel top; die-cast chromed waterfall grille extending to top of hood; chromed, zeppelin-shaped die-cast vent grilles on hood sides; extruded trunk lid.

NASH — AMBASSADOR "SIX" — SERIES 3620 — SIX: Identical in appearance to series 3680 Ambassador Super "Eight".

NASH "400" — SERIES 3640 — SIX: Sharply sloping "alligator" hood with pressed steel grille; embossed steel disc wheels; fastback styling with no outside opening to luggage/spare tire compartment (sedan, victoria); extruded trunk lid (touring sedan & victoria); seamless steep top. The 400 was introduced May 20th, 1935 with a 3540 series number indicating a 1935 model car. Following the Lafayette introduction on June 15th, however, Nash began advertising the 400 as a 1936 model.

NASH "400" DELUXE — SERIES 3640A — SIX: Similar to series 3640 with the following exceptions: chromed, die-cast waterfall grille extending to top of hood. Side-opening hood. Chromed, zeppelin-shaped die-cast vent grilles on hood sides. Steel artillery wheels.

LAFAYETTE — SERIES 3610 — SIX: First series: pressed steel grille, embossed disc wheels. Second series: die-cast, chromed waterfall grille, steel artillery wheels. Both series: styling similar to 3640 and 3640A series, except for different front end treatment, side-opening hood.

I.D. DATA: [Series 3680] Serial numbers on right side frame, under hood. Starting: B77325. Ending: B80026. Engine numbers on right side engine block. Starting: B90025. Ending: B92726. [Series 3620] Serial numbers on right side frame, under hood. Starting: R303301. Ending: R309300. Engine numbers on right side engine block. Starting: E54701. Ending: E60700. [Series 3640] Serial numbers on right side frame, under hood. Starting: C1001. Ending: C9500. Engine numbers on right side engine block. Starting: CE501. Ending: CE9000. [Series 3640A] Serial numbers on right side frame, under hood. Starting: C9501. Ending: C23000. Engine numbers on right side engine block. Starting: CE9001. Ending: CE22500. [LaFayette] Serial numbers on right frame, under hood. Starting: L23101. Ending: L50780. Engine numbers on right front of engine block, just below valve cover. Starting: LE22601. Ending: LE50277.

Model No.	Body Type & Seating	Price	Weight	Start. Ser. No.
3680	4-dr. Sed.-6P	995	3820	B177325
3685*	2-dr. Vic.-6P*	945	3730	B177325

* Questionable whether this model was actually produced.

Model No.	Body Type & Seating	Price	Weight	Start Ser. No.
3620	4-dr. Sed.-6P	885	3710	R303301
3625	2-dr. Vic.-6P	835	3620	R303301
3640	4-dr. Sed.-6P	765	2970	C1001
3642	2-dr. Cpe.-3P	675	2900	C1001
3642R	2-dr. Cpe.-3/5P	725	2960	C1001
3643	2-dr. Tr. Vic.-6P	745	2970	C1001
3645	2-dr. Vic.-6P	715	2950	C1001
3648	4-dr. Tr. Sed.-6P	790	3000	C1001
3640A	4-dr. Sed.-6P	765	3020	C9501
3641A	2-dr. Cabr.-3/5P	800	3000	C9501
3642A	2-dr. Cpe.-3P	675	2950	C9501
3642AR	2-dr. Cpe.-3/5P	725	3010	C9501
3643A	2-dr. Tr. Vic.-6P	745	3020	C9501
3645A	2-dr. Vic.-6P	715	3000	C9501
3648A	4-dr. Tr. Sed.-6P	790	3050	C9501
3610	4-dr. Sed.-6P	675	2950	L23101
3611	2-dr. Cabr.-3/5P	740	2930	L23101
3612	2-dr. Cpe.-3P, 3W	595	2880	L23101
3612R	2-dr. Cpe.-3/5P, 3W	650	2930	L23101
W3612	2-dr. Cpe.-3P, 5W	610	2880	L23101
W3612R	2-dr. Cpe.-3/5P, 5W	665	2930	L23101
3613	2-dr. Tr. Vic.-6P	655	2950	L23101
3615	2-dr. Vic.-6P	625	2930	L23101
3618	4-dr. Tr. Sed.-6P	700	2980	L23101

1936 Nash, Lafayette, sport cabriolet, HAC

ENGINE: [Series 3680] OHV. Straight. Eight. Cast iron block. B & S: 3-1/8 in. x 4-1/4 in. Disp.: 260.8 cu. in. C.R.: 5.25:1. Brake H.P.: 102 @ 3400 R.P.M. Taxable H.P.: 31.25. Main bearings: Nine. Valve lifters: Solid. Carb.: Stromberg EE-1. Torque: 110 lbs.-ft. at 350 R.P.M. [Series 3620] OHV. Inline. Six. Cast iron block. B & S: 3-3/8 in. x 4-3/8 in. Disp.: 234.8 cu. in. C.R.: 5.70:1. Brake H.P.: 93 @ 3400 R.P.M. Taxable H.P.: 27.3. Main bearings: Seven. Valve lifters: Solid. Carb.: Stromberg Ex-2 or AX-2. Torque: 125 lbs.-ft. at 350 R.P.M. [Series 3640] L-head. Inline. Six. Cast iron block. B & S: 3-3/8 in. x 4-3/8 in. Disp.: 234.8 cu. in. C.R.: 5.61:1. Brake H.P.: 90 @ 3400 R.P.M. Taxable H.P.: 27.3. Main bearings: Seven. Valve lifters: Solid. Carb.: Stromberg EX-22. Torque: 125 lbs.-ft at 350 R.P.M. [Series 3640A] (Mechanically identical to Series 3640.) [LaFayette] L-head. Inline. Six. Cast iron block. B & S: 3-3/8 in. x 4-3/8 in. Disp.: 217.7 cu. in. C.R.: 5.61:1. Brake H.P.: 83 @ 3200 R.P.M. Taxable H.P.: 25.3. Main bearings: Seven. Valve lifters: Solid. Carb.: Marvel B2 (1st series), Stromberg AX2 (sec. series).

CHASSIS: [Series 3680] W.B.: 125 in. O.L.: 207-1/8 in. Frt/Rear Tread: 58 in./60 in. Tires: 6.50 x 16. [Series 3620] W.B.: 125 in. O.L.: 207-1/8 in. Frt/Rear Tread: 58 in./60 in. Tires: 6.25 x 16. [Series 3640, 3640A] W.B.: 117 in. O.L.: 191-1/8 in. Frt/Rear Tread: 58 in./60-1/4 in. Tires: 6.00 x 16. [Series 3610] W.B.: 113 in. Frt/Rear Tread: 58 in./60-1/4 in. Tires: 6.00 x 16.

TECHNICAL: Selective sliding gear transmission. Speeds: 3F/1R. Floor shift controls. Single dry plate clutch. Spiral bevel drive. Semi-floating rear axle. Overall ratio: 4.44 (Amb. Super 8), 4.11:1 all others. Hydraulic brakes on four wheels. Steel artillery wheels (steel disc, series 3640 and first series LaFayette). Wheel size: 16 in.

OPTIONS: Fender skirts. Radio. Heater. Clock. Cigar lighter. Radio antenna.

HISTORICAL: Introduced: Nov. 15, 1935 [Ambassadors, 3680 & 3610]; May 20, 1935 [(3640); June 15, 1935 [(LaFayette); Oct. 15, 1935 [3640A and second series LaFayette]. Innovations: 3640 ''400'' series; first to cast intake manifolds in engine block. ''Double Bed'' conversion offered in ''400'' and LaFayette sedans and victorias. Nash 400 first of its breed with one-piece steel top. Calendar year registrations: 43,070. Calendar year production: 53,038. The president of Nash was E.H. McCarty. Nash bought the remaining half interest in the Seaman Body Corp. during 1936. A profit of $1,020,708 was posted for the year. Share of industry registrations: 1.27%.

1936
Lafayette, 6-cyl.

	FP	5	4	3	2	1
Bus Cpe	595	650	1250	2400	4150	5900
Cpe	650	700	1350	2700	4500	6400
Cabr	740	1300	4050	6700	9400	13,400
Sed	675	650	1250	2400	4150	5900
Vic	625	675	1300	2500	4300	6100
Tr Sed	655	550	1150	2100	3700	5300

400 Series, 6-cyl.

	FP	5	4	3	2	1
Bus Cpe	665	550	1150	2100	3800	5400
Cpe	715	650	1250	2400	4150	5900
Vic	690	700	1350	2700	4500	6400
Tr Vic	720	675	1300	2500	4350	6200
Sed	740	675	1300	2500	4300	6100
Tr Sed	765	650	1250	2400	4150	5900
Spec Bus Cpe	675	650	1250	2400	4200	6000
Spec Cpe	725	650	1300	2500	4300	6100
Spec Spt Cabr	800	1300	4050	6700	9400	13,400
Spec Vic	715	700	1350	2700	4500	6400
Spec Tr Vic	745	700	1350	2700	4500	6400
Spec Sed	765	675	1300	2500	4300	6100
Spec Tr Sed	790	650	1250	2400	4200	6000

Ambassador Series, 6-cyl.

	FP	5	4	3	2	1
Vic	835	725	1400	3200	4850	6900
Tr Sed	885	650	1250	2400	4150	5900

Ambassador Series, 8-cyl.

	FP	5	4	3	2	1
Tr Sed	995	725	1400	3200	4850	6900

1937

1937 Nash, model 3788, sedan, JAC

NASH — AMBASSADOR "EIGHT" — SERIES 3780 — EIGHT: Vee'd Die-cast grille, vertical bars. Highly ornate radiator ornament. Chrome spear on hood sides. Integral trunk, sedans and victorias. Split windshield.

NASH — AMBASSADOR "SIX" — SERIES 3720 — SIX: Identical to series 3780 except with less elaborate radiator ornament consisting of stylized wing; shorter hood and front fenders.

LAFAYETTE — SERIES 3710 — SIX: Identical in styling to senior Nashes with the following exceptions: radiator ornament with circular theme; horizontal bars in grille; chevrons on hood sides; shorter hood and front fenders than Ambassador series.

I.D. DATA: [Series 3780] Serial numbers on right side frame, under hood. Starting: B80031. Ending: B86030. Engine numbers on right side engine block. Starting: B92731. Ending: B98730. [Series 3720] Serial numbers on right side frame, under hood. Starting: R309311. Ending: R324310. Engine numbers on right side engine block. Starting: E60711. Ending: E75710. [LaFayette] Serial numbers on right side frame under hood. Starting: L50781 or H1001. Ending: L106280 or H10500. NOTE: Prefix ''H'' indicates car was assembled in Kenosha. ''L'' indicates assembled in Racine. Engine numbers right side engine block. Starting: LE50281 or H1001 or HE501. Ending: LE105780 or H10500 or HE10000.

Model No.	Body Type & Seating	Price	Weight	Start. Ser. No.
3781	2-dr. Cabr.-3/5P	960	3640	B80031
3782	2-dr. Cpe.-3P	855	3590	B80031
3782R	2-dr. Cpe.-3/5P	895	3640	B80031
3782A	2-dr. A-P Cpe.3/5P	910	3610	B80031
3783	2-dr. Vic.-6P	895	3690	B80031
3788	4-dr. Sed.-6P	945	3720	B80031
3721	2-dr. Cabr.-3/5P	860	3320	R309311

Model No.	Body Type & Seating	Price	Weight	Prod. Total
3722	2-dr. Cpe.-3P	755	3290	R309311
3722R	2-dr. Cpe.-3/5P	795	3320	R309311
3722A	2-dr. A.P. Cpe.-3/5P	810	3310	R309311
3723	2-dr. Vic.-6P	795	3380	R309311
3728	4-dr. Sed.-6P	845	3400	R309311
3711	2-dr. Cabr.-3/5P	740	3180	L50781
3712	2-dr. Cpe.-3P	595	3140	L50781
3712R	2-dr. Cpe.-3/5P	650	3190	L50781
3712A	2-dr. A-P Cpe.-3/5P	660	3160	L50781
3713	2-dr. Vic.-6P	650	3200	Note 1
3718	4-dr. Sed.-6P	700	3240	Note 1

Note 1: L50781 or H1001.
Note 2: The ''All-Purpose'' coupes (3712A, 3722A and 3782A) replaced the rumble-seat coupes (3712R et. al.) on April 1st, 1937.

ENGINE: [Series 3780] OHV. Straight. Eight. Cast iron block. B & S: 3-1/8 in. x 4-1/4 in. Disp.: 260.8 cu. in. C.R.: 5.64:1. Brake H.P.: 105 @ 3400 R.P.M. Taxable H.P.: 31.25. Main bearings: Nine. Valve lifters: Solid. Carb.: Stromberg EE-1. Torque: 196 lbs.-ft. @ 1800 R.P.M. [Series 3720] OHV. Inline. Six. Cast iron block. B & S: 3-3/8 in. x 4-3/8 in. Disp.: 234.8 cu. in. C.R.: 5.67:1. Brake H.P.: 93 @ 3400 R.P.M. Taxable H.P.: 27.3. Main bearings: Seven. Valve lifters: Solid. Carb.: Stromberg EX-32. Torque: 174 lbs.-ft. @ 1600 R.P.M. [LaFayette] L-head. Inline. Six. Cast iron block. B & S: 3-3/8 in. x 4-3/8 in. Disp.: 234.8 cu. in. C.R.: 5.6:1. Brake H.P.: 90 @ 3400 R.P.M. Taxable H.P.: 27.3. Main bearings: Seven. Valve lifters: Solid. Carb.: Stromberg AX-2. Torque: 171 lbs.-ft. @ 1200 R.P.M.

CHASSIS: [Series 3780] W.B.: 125 in. O.L.: 204-7/16 in. Frt/Rear Tread: 58 in./60 in. Tires: 7.00 x 16. [Series 3720] W.B.: 121 in. O.L.: 200-7/16 in. Frt/Rear Tread: 58 in./60-1/4 in. Tires: 6.25 x 16. [Series 3710] W.B.: 117 in. O.L.: 196-7/16 in. Frt/Rear Tread: 58 in./60-1/4 in. Tires: 6.00 x 16.

1937 Nash Ambassador Six, cabriolet, AB

TECHNICAL: Selective sliding gear transmission. Speeds: 3F/1R. Floor shift controls. Single dry plate clutch. Spiral bevel drive. Semi-floating rear axle. Overall ratio: 4.11:1. Hydraulic brakes on four wheels. Steel artillery wheels. Wheel size: 16 in. Overdrive.

OPTIONS: Fender skirts. Radio. Heater. Clock. Cigar Lighter. Radio Antenna. Bed Conversion.

HISTORICAL: Introduced: Oct. 1, 1936. Calendar year registrations: 70,571. Calendar year production: 85,949. The president of Nash was George Mason. Merger of Nash Motors with Kelvinator Corp. to form Nash-Kelvinator Corp. effected this year. Nash ''400'' and LaFayette combined into a single series known (for 1937 only) as the ''Nash-LaFayette 400.'' Profit for the year came to $3,640,747. Share of industry registrations: 2.03%.

1937
Lafayette 400, 6-cyl.

	FP	5	4	3	2	1
Bus Cpe	740	500	1100	1850	3350	4900
Cpe	795	500	1100	1950	3600	5100
A-P Cpe	805	500	1100	1900	3500	5000
Cabr	885	1200	3700	6200	8700	12,400
Vic Sed	800	500	1100	1900	3500	5000
Tr Sed	845	500	1100	1950	3600	5100

Ambassador, 6-cyl.

	FP	5	4	3	2	1
Bus Cpe	935	650	1250	2400	4150	5900
Cpe	975	675	1300	2500	4350	6200
A-P Cpe	990	600	1200	2200	3900	5600
Cabr	1040	1300	4050	6700	9400	13,400
Vic Sed	975	550	1150	2100	3800	5400
Tr Sed	1025	650	1250	2400	4150	5900

Ambassador, 8-cyl.

	FP	5	4	3	2	1
Bus Cpe	1075	675	1300	2500	4350	6200
Cpe	1115	700	1350	2700	4500	6400
A-P Cpe	1130	650	1250	2400	4150	5900
Cabr	1180	1650	4600	7700	10,800	15,400
Vic Sed	1115	650	1250	2400	4150	5900
Tr Sed	1165	725	1400	3200	4850	6900

1938

1938 Nash, sedan, JAC

NASH — AMBASSADOR "EIGHT" — SERIES 3880 — EIGHT: Body styling similar to 1937 model, but with painted, bright-trimmed grille with horizontal bars. Series name on side of hood, wedge-shaped headlamps mounted on radiator sides. "Nash" in vertical letters at top of radiator grille.

NASH — AMBASSADOR "SIX" — SERIES 3820 — SIX: Identical in appearance to series 3880, except for shorter hood and front fenders.

NASH — LAFAYETTE — SERIES 3810 — SIX: Identical in appearance to senior Nashes, except for bullet-shaped headlamps and shorter hood/front fenders.

I.D. DATA: [Series 3880] Serial numbers on right front frame member. Starting: B86031. Ending: B88999. Engine numbers on right front side, engine block. Starting: B98731. Ending: B101699. [Series 3820] Serial numbers on right front frame member. Starting: R324311. Ending: R331399. Engine numbers on engine block, right front. Starting: E75711. Ending: E82799. [LaFayette] Serial numbers on right front frame member. Starting: L106281 or H10501. Ending: L128294 or H19449. Note: "L" indicates car assembled in Racine; "H" indicates assembly in Kenosha. Engine numbers on engine block, right front. Starting: LE105781 or HE10001. Ending: LE128424 or HE18949.

Model No.	Body Type & Seating	Price	Weight	Start. Ser. No.
3881	2-dr. Cabr.-3/5P	1240	3620	B86031
3882	2-dr. A.P. Cpe.-3/5P	1165	3640	B86031
3883	2-dr. Vic.-6P	1150	3780	B86031
3885	2-dr. Cpe.-3P	1120	3580	B86031
3888	4-dr. Sed.-6P	1200	3790	B86031
3821	2-dr. Cabr.-3/5P	1090	3340	R324311
3822	2-dr. A.P. Cpe.-3/5P	1015	3360	R324311
3823	2-dr. Vic.-6P	1000	3450	R324311
3825	2-dr. Cpe.-3P	970	3300	R324311
3828	4-dr. Sed.-6P	1050	3460	R324311
3811	2-dr. Del. Cabr.-3/5P	940	3240	Note 1
3812	2-dr. Del. A-PCP-3/5P	860	3230	Note 1
3813	2-dr. Del Vic.-6P	855	3290	Note 1
3814	2-dr. Del. Cp.-3P	820	3160	Note 1
3815	2-dr. Cpe.-3P	770	3120	Note 1
3816	2-dr. Sed.-6P	805	3190	Note 1
3817	4-dr. Sed.-6P	850	3200	Note 1
3818	4-dr. Del. Sed.-6P	900	3300	Note 1

Note 1: L106281 or H10501.

1938 Nash LaFayette, coupe, OCW

ENGINE: [Series 3880] OHV. Straight. Eight. Cast iron block. B & S: 3-1/8 in. x 4-1/4 in. Disp.: 260.8 cu. in. C.R.: 6.00:1. Brake H.P.: 115 @ 3400 R.P.M. Taxable H.P.: 31.2. Main bearings: Nine. Valve lifters: Solid. Carb.: Stromberg EE7. Torque: 200 lbs.-ft. at 1200 R.P.M. [Series 3820] OHV. Inline. Six. Cast iron block. B & S: 3-3/8 in. x 4-3/8 in. Disp.: 234.8 cu. in. C.R.: 6.00:1. Brake H.P.: 105 @ 3400 R.P.M. Taxable H.P.: 27.3. Main bearings: Seven. Valve lifters: Solid. Carb.: Stromberg EX32. Torque: 190 lbs.-ft at 1050 R.P.M. [LaFayette] L-head. Inline. Six. Cast iron block. B & S: 3-3/8 in. x 4-3/8 in. Disp.: 234.8 cu. in. C.R.: 5.83:1. Brake H.P.: 95 @ 3400 R.P.M. Taxable H.P.: 27.3. Main bearings: Seven. Valve lifters: Solid. Carb.: Stromberg EX22 or AX2. Torque: 175 lbs.-ft. at 1000 R.P.M.

CHASSIS: [Series 3880] W.B.: 125 in. O.L.: 204-11/16 in. Frt/Rear Tread: 58 in./61-3/8 in. Tires: 7.00 x 16. [Series 3820] W.B.: 121 in. O.L.: 200-11/16 in. Frt/Rear Tread: 58 in./60-1/4 in. Tires: 6.25 x 16. [Series 3810] W.B.: 117 in. O.L.: 196-11/16 in. Frt/Rear Tread: 58 in./60-1/4 in. Tires: 6.00 x 16.

TECHNICAL: Selective sliding gear transmission. Speeds: 3F/1R. Floor shift controls. Single dry plate clutch. Spiral bevel drive. Semi-floating rear axle. Overall ratio: 4.11:1. Hydraulic brakes on four wheels. Steel disc wheels. Wheel size: 16 in. Drivetrain Options: Hill-holder (10.00). Overdrive (50.00). Dash-mounted, vacuum-operated shift (30.00).

OPTIONS: Fender skirts (13.00). Radio (49.00). Heater (30.00). Clock. Cigar lighter. Radio antenna. White sidewall tires (3810) (20.00). White sidewall tires (3820) (22.50). White sidewall tires (3880) (27.50). Banjo steering wheel w/horn ring (11.00). Bed conversion.

HISTORICAL: Introduced Oct. 15, 1937. Innovations: Optional dash-mounted, vacuum-controlled gearshift. Calendar year registrations: 31,814. Calendar year production: 32,017. The president of Nash was George Mason. Share of industry registrations: 1.68%. "400" designation dropped from LaFayette name. Essentially, the LaFayette had become the base Nash series; the radiator badge read simply "Nash".

1938 Lafayette

Master, 6-cyl.	FP	5	4	3	2	1
Bus Cpe	770	400	1000	1600	3100	4400
Vic	805	450	1050	1700	3200	4600
Tr Sed	855	400	1000	1650	3150	4500
DeLuxe, 6-cyl.						
Bus Cpe	820	500	1100	1850	3350	4900
A-P Cpe	860	500	1100	1900	3500	5000
Cabr	940	1100	3400	5700	8000	11,400
Vic	855	500	1100	1900	3500	5000
Tr Sed	900	500	1100	1950	3600	5100
Ambassador, 6-cyl.						
Bus Cpe	970	650	1250	2400	4150	5900
A-P Cpe	1015	650	1250	2400	4200	6000
Cabr	1090	1300	4050	6700	9400	13,400
Vic	1000	550	1150	2100	3800	5400
Tr Sed	1050	650	1250	2400	4150	5900
Ambassador, 8-cyl.						
Bus Cpe	1120	675	1300	2500	4350	6200
A-P Cpe	1165	675	1300	2600	4400	6300
Cabr	1240	1650	4600	7700	10,800	15,400
Vic	1150	650	1200	2300	4100	5800
Tr Sed	1200	700	1350	2700	4500	6400

1939

NASH — AMBASSADOR "EIGHT" — SERIES 3980 — EIGHT: Tall, narrow grille with wide-spaced horizontal bars, suggesting that Nash styling this year may have been inspired by the LaSalle. Rectangular headlamps inset in fenders. Vertical Nash emblem at center of trunk lid. Nash script on hubcaps.

NASH — AMBASSADOR "SIX" — SERIES 3920 — SIX: Identical in appearance to Series 3980 except for shorter hood and front fenders.

NASH — LAFAYETTE — SERIES 3910 — SIX: Identical in appearance to senior Nashes except for shorter hood and front fenders. Small LaFayette body plate behind front fender, just above running board.

I.D. DATA: [Series 3980] Serial numbers on right front frame member. Starting: R89000. Ending: R106299. Engine numbers on engine block, right front. Starting: B101700. Ending: B105551. [Series 3920] Serial numbers on right front frame member. Starting: R331400. Ending: R339999. Engine numbers on engine block, right front. Starting: E82800. Ending: E339399. [Series LaFayette] Serial numbers on right front frame member. Starting: H19450. Ending: H56999. Engine numbers on upper left front, engine block. Starting: HE18950. Ending: HE56499.

1939 Nash Ambassador Six, sedan, JAC

Model No.	Body Type & Seating	Price	Weight	Start. Ser. No.
3980	4-dr. Tr. Sed.-6P	1235	3800	B89000
3981	2-dr. Cabr.-3/5P	1295	3740	B89000
3982	2-dr. A-P. Cpe.-3/tP	1210	3710	B89000
3983	2-dr. Vic.-6P	1205	3770	B89000
3985	2-dr. Cpe.-3P	1175	3720	B89000
3988	4-dr. Sed.-6P	1235	3800	B89000
3920	4-dr. Tr. Sed.-6P	985	3470	R331400
3921	2-dr. Cabr.-3/5P	1050	3430	R331400
3922	2-dr. A-P. Cpe.-3/5P	960	3360	R331400
3923	2-dr. Vic.-6P	955	3420	R331400
3925	2-dr. Cpe.-3P	925	3370	R331400
3928	4-dr. Sed.-6P	985	3450	R331400
3910	4-dr. Del. Sed.-6P	885	3350	H19450
3911	2-dr. Del. Cabr.-3/5P	950	3340	H19450
3912	2-dr. Del. A-P. Cpe.-3/5P	860	3260	H19450
3913	2-dr. Del. Vic.-6P	855	3320	H19450
3914	2-dr. Del. Cpe.-3P	825	3270	H19450
3915	2-dr. Cpe.-3P	770	3200	H19450
3916	2-dr. Sed.-6P	810	3250	H19450
3917	4-dr. Sed.-6P	840	3290	H19450
3918	4-dr. Del. Tr. Sed.-6P	885	3350	H19450
3919	4-dr. Tr. Sed.-6P	840	3285	H19450

ENGINE: [Series 3980] OHV. Straight. Eight. Cast iron block. B & S: 3-1/8 in. x 4-1/4 in. Disp.: 260.8 cu. in. C.R.: 6.00:1. Brake H.P.: 115 @ 3400 R.P.M. Taxable H.P.: 31.2. Main bearings: Nine. Valve lifters: Solid. Carb.: Carter 436S. Torque: 200 lbs.-ft. at 1200 R.P.M. [Series 3920] OHV. Inline. Six. Cast iron block. B & S: 3-3/8 in. x 4-3/8 in. Disp.: 234.8 cu. in. C.R.: 6.00:1. Brake H.P.: 105 @ 3400 R.P.M. Taxable H.P.: 27.3. Main bearings: Seven. Valve lifters: Solid. Carb.: Carter 435S. Torque: 190 lbs.-ft. @ 1050 R.P.M. [Series LaFayette] L-head. Inline. Six. Cast iron block. B & S: 3-3/8 in. x 4-3/8 in. Disp.: 234.8 cu. in. C.R.: 6.30:1. Brake H.P.: 99 @ 3400 R.P.M. Taxable H.P.: 27.3. Main bearings: Seven. Valve lifters: Solid. Carb.: Stromberg EE-1. Torque: 179 lbs.-ft. @ 1200 R.P.M.

1939 Nash Ambassador Eight, convertible coupe, HAC

CHASSIS: [Series 3980] W.B.: 125 in. O.L.: 208-1/4 in. Frt/Rear Tread: 55-3/8 in./61-3/8 in. Tires: 7.00 x 16. [Series 3920] W.B.: 121 in. O.L.: 204-1/4 in. Frt/Rear Tread: 58 in./60-1/4 in. Tires: 6.25 x 16. [Series 3910] W.B.: 117 in. O.L.: 200-1/4 in. Frt/Rear Tread: 58 in./60-1/4 in. Tires: 6.00 x 16.

TECHNICAL: Selective sliding gear transmission. 3F/1R. Steering column controls. Single dry plate clutch. Hypoid drive. Semi-floating rear axle. Overall Ratio: 4.10:1. Hydraulic brakes on four wheels. Steel disc wheels. Wheel size: 16 in. Drivetrain Options: Hill-Holder. Overdrive.

OPTIONS: Fender skirts. Radio. Heater. Clock. Cigar lighter. Radio Antenna. Fog lamps. Deluxe steering wheel. Bed conversion.

HISTORICAL: Introduced Oct. 15, 1938. Calendar year registrations: 54,050. Calendar year production: 65,662. The president of Nash was George Mason. Share of industry registrations: 2.86%. Styled by George W. Walker.

1939
Lafayette, 6-cyl.
(Add 10 percent for DeLuxe)

	FP	5	4	3	2	1
Bus Cpe	770	500	1100	1850	3350	4900
2 dr Sed	810	400	1000	1650	3150	4500
4 dr Sed	840	450	1050	1800	3300	4800
Tr Sed	940	450	1050	1700	3200	4600
A-P Cpe	860	350	950	1450	3000	4200
A-P Cabr	950	1200	3700	6200	8700	12,400
Tr Sed	885	450	1050	1700	3200	4600
Ambassador, 6-cyl.						
Bus Cpe	925	675	1300	2500	4300	6100
A-P Cpe	960	700	1350	2700	4500	6400
A-P Cabr	1050	1400	4150	6950	9750	13,900
2 dr Sed	955	550	1150	2000	3600	5200
4 dr Sed	985	550	1150	2100	3700	5300
Tr Sed	985	550	1150	2100	3800	5400
Ambassador, 8-cyl.						
Bus Cpe	1175	700	1350	2700	4500	6400
A-P Cpe	1210	700	1350	2900	4600	6600
A-P Cabr	1295	1550	4450	7450	10,400	14,900
2 dr Sed	1205	650	1250	2400	4150	5900
4 dr Sed	1235	650	1250	2400	4200	6000
Tr Sed	1235	650	1250	2400	4200	6000

1940 Nash, cabriolet, AB

NASH — AMBASSADOR "8" — SERIES 4080 — EIGHT: Tall, narrow grille, similar to 1939 Model except with thin, closely-spaced horizontal bars. Sealed beam headlamps. "Nash" script, lower right corner of trunk lid, and on hood sides just behind grille.

NASH — AMBASSADOR "SIX" — SERIES 4020 — SIX: Identical in appearance to 4080 Series except for shorter hood and front fenders.

NASH — LAFAYETTE — SERIES 4010 — SIX: Identical in appearance to Senior Nash Series except for shorter hood and front fenders. LaFayette body plate just above running board, behind front fender.

I.D. DATA: [Series 4080] Serial numbers on right front frame member. Starting: B106300. Ending: B110000. Engine numbers on engine block, right front. Starting: B105800. Ending: B109049. [Series 4020] Serial numbers on right front frame member. Starting: R340000. Ending: R353000. Engine numbers on engine block, right front. Starting: E339500. Ending: E352017. [Series LaFayette] Serial numbers on right front frame member. Starting: H57000. Ending: H76055. Engine numbers on upper left front, engine block. Starting: HE56500. Ending: H102862.

Model No.	Body Type & Seating	Price	Weight	Start. Ser. No.
4080	4-dr. Tr. Sed.-6P	1195	3710	B106300
4081	2-dr. Cabr.-3/5P	1295	3640	B106300
4082	2-dr. A-P. Cpe.-3/5P	1170	3575	B106300
4083	2-dr. Sed.-6P	1165	3620	B106300
4085	2-dr. Cpe.-3P	1135	3555	B106300
4088	4-dr. Sed.-6P	1195	3705	B106300
4020	4-dr. Tr. Sed.-6P	985	3385	R340000
4021	2-dr. Cabr.-3/5P	1085	3410	R340000
4022	2-dr. A-P. Cpe.-3/5P	960	3295	R340000
4023	2-dr. Sed.-6P	955	3350	R340000
4025	2-dr. Cpe.-3P	925	3290	R340000
4028	4-dr. Sed.-6P	985	3380	R340000
4010	4-dr. Tr. Sed.-6P	875	3280	H57000
4011	2-dr. Cabr.-3/5P	975	3310	H57000
4012	2-dr. A-P. Cpe.-3/5P	850	3190	H57000
4013	2-dr. Sed.-6P	845	3235	H57000
4015	2-dr. Cpe.-3P	795	3190	H57000
4018	4-dr. Sed.-6P	875	3275	H57000

1940 Nash Ambassador Eight, de Sakhnoffsky-modified cabriolet, AB

ENGINE: [Series 4080] OHV. Straight. Eight. Cast iron block. B & S: 3-1/8 in. x 4-1/4 in. Disp.: 260.8 cu. in. C.R.: 6.0:1. Brake H.P.: 115 @ 3400 R.P.M. Taxable H.P.: 31.2. Main bearings: Nine. Valve lifters: Solid. Carb.: Carter WDO-4655. Torque: 200 lbs.-ft. @ 1200 R.P.M. [Series 4020] OHV.

Inline. Six. Cast iron block. B & S: 3-3/8 in. x 4-3/8 in. Disp.: 234.8 cu. in. C.R.: 6.00:1. Brake H.P.: 105 @ 3400 R.P.M. Taxable H.P.: 27.3. Main bearings: Seven. Valve lifters: Solid. Carb.: Carter 435S. Torque: 190 lbs.-ft. @ 1050 R.P.M. [Series LaFayette] L-head. Inline. Six. Cast iron block. B & S: 3-3/8 in. x 4-3/8 in. Disp.: 234.8 cu. in. C.R.: 6.30:1. Brake H.P.: 99 @ 3400 R.P.M. Taxable H.P.: 27.3. Main bearings: Seven. Valve lifters: Solid. Carb.: Carter 458S. Torque: 179 lbs.-ft. @ 1200 R.P.M.

CHASSIS: [Series 4080] W.B.: 125 in. O.L.: 207-3/16 in. Frt/Rear Tread: 57-11/16 in./61-3/8 in. Tires: 7.00 x 15. [Series 4020] W.B.: 121 in. O.L.: 203-3/16 in. Frt/Rear Tread: 56-7/8 in./60-1/4 in. Tires: 6.25 x 16. [Series 4010] W.B.: 117 in. O.L.: 199-3/16 in. Frt/Rear Tread: 56-7/8 in./60-1/4 in. Tires: 6.00 x 16.

TECHNICAL: Selective sliding gear transmission. Speeds: 3F/1R. Steering column controls. Single dry plate clutch. Hypoid drive. Semi-floating rear axle. Overall Ratio: 4.10:1. Hydraulic brakes on four wheels. Steel disc wheels. Wheel size: 4080: 15 in., 4020 & 4010: 16 in. Drivetrain options: Hill-Holder. Overdrive (55.00).

OPTIONS: Fender skirts. Radio. Heater. Clock. Cigar lighter. Radio antenna. Bed conversion.

HISTORICAL: Introduced Sept. 15, 1939. Calendar year registrations: 52,853. Calendar year production: 63,617. The president of Nash was George Mason. Share of industry registrations: 1.5%. A profitable year, but a disappointing one in terms of sales.

1940 Nash LaFayette, coupe, AB

1940
DeLuxe Lafayette, 6-cyl.

	FP	5	4	3	2	1
Bus Cpe	795	650	1250	2400	4150	5900
A-P Cpe	850	675	1300	2500	4300	6100
A-P Cabr	975	1200	3700	6200	8700	12,400
2 dr FsBk	845	600	1200	2300	4000	5700
4 dr FsBk	875	650	1250	2400	4150	5900
Trk Sed	875	650	1200	2300	4100	5800

Ambassador, 6-cyl.

Bus Cpe	925	675	1300	2500	4300	6100
A-P Cpe	960	675	1300	2600	4400	6300
A-P Cabr	1085	1450	4300	7200	10,100	14,400
2 dr FsBk	955	675	1300	2500	4300	6100
4 dr FsBk	985	675	1300	2500	4350	6200
Trk Sed	985	675	1300	2600	4400	6300

Ambassador, 8-cyl.

Bus Cpe	1135	725	1400	3200	4850	6900
A-P Cpe	1170	750	1450	3300	4900	7000
A-P Cabr	1295	1650	4600	7700	10,800	15,400
2 dr FsBk	1165	700	1350	2700	4500	6400
4 dr FsBk	1195	700	1350	2800	4550	6500
Trk Sed	1195	700	1350	2900	4600	6600

1941

1941 Nash, sedan, OCW

NASH — AMBASSADOR "EIGHT" — SERIES 4180 — EIGHT: Pointed prow; split die-cast grilles on either side, featuring thin vertical ribs. Script on trunk reading "Nash 8".

NASH — AMBASSADOR "SIX" — SERIES 4160 — SIX: Identical to series 4180 except script on trunk reads "Nash 6".

NASH — AMBASSADOR "600" — SERIES 4140 — SIX: Identical to series 4180 except hood is substantially shorter; script on trunk reads "Nash 600"; shrouded rear fenders.

I.D. DATA: [Series 4180] Serial numbers on right front frame member. Starting: B110001. Ending: B113500. Engine numbers on engine block, right front. Starting: B110001. Ending: B113500. [Series 4160] Serial numbers on right front frame member. Starting: R353001. Ending: R383400. Engine numbers on engine block, right front. Starting: R353001. Ending: R383400. [Series 4140] Serial numbers on right frame member just ahead of dash. Starting: K5001. Ending: K55100. Engine numbers on right side of crankcase toward front. Starting: K5001. Ending: K55100.

Model No.	Body Type & Seating	Price	Weight	Start. Ser. No.
4180	4-dr. Tr. Sed.-6P	1151	3475	B110001
4181	2-dr. Cabr.-3/5P	1215	3580	B110001
4183	2-dr. Brgm.-5P	1081	3400	B110001
4187	4-dr. Sp. Sed.-6P	1051	3450	B110001
4188	4-dr. Sed.-6P	1101	3455	B110001
4160	4-dr. Tr. Sed.-6P	1030	3300	R353001
4161	2-dr. Cabr.-3/5P	1095	3430	R353001
4162	2-dr. Cpe.-3P	905	3310	R353001
4163	2-dr. Brgm.-5P	974	3235	R353001
4165	2-dr. Sp. Cpe.-3P	855	3180	R353001
4167	4-dr. Sp. Sed.-6P	930	3300	R353001
4168	4-dr. Sed.-6P	985	3300	R353001
4169	2-dr. Sp. Sed.-6P	898	3320	R353001
4140	4-dr. Tr. Sed.-6P	860	2655	K5001
4142	2-dr. Cpe.-3P	783	2500	K5001
4143	2-dr. Brgm.-5P	810	2575	K5001
4145	2-dr. Sp. Cpe.-3P	731	2490	K5001
4146	2-dr. Sp. Sed.-6P	745	2630	K5001
4147	4-dr. Sp. Sed.-6P	780	2615	K5001
4148	4-dr. Sed.-6P	810	2630	K5001
4149	2-dr. Sed.-6P	777	2640	K5001

1941 Nash Ambassador Eight, convertible coupe, HAC

ENGINE: [Series 4180] OHV. Straight. Eight. Cast iron block. B & S: 3-1/8 in. x 4-1/4 in. Disp.: 260.8 cu. in. C.R.: 6.30:1. Brake H.P.: 115 @ 3400 R.P.M. Taxable H.P.: 31.2. Main bearings: Nine. Valve lifters: Solid. Carb.: Carter 511S. Torque: 200 lbs.-ft. at 1600 R.P.M. [Series 4160] OHV. Inline. Six. Cast iron block. B & S: 3-3/8 in. x 4-3/8 in. Disp.: 234.8 cu. in. C.R.: 6.30:1. Brake H.P.: 105 @ 3400 R.P.M. Taxable H.P.: 27.3. Main bearings: Seven. Valve lifters: Solid. Carb.: Carter 435S. Torque: 195 lbs.-ft. at 1600 R.P.M. [Series 4140] L-head. Inline. Six. Cast iron block. B & S: 3-1/8 in. x 3-3/4 in. Disp.: 172.6 cu. in. C.R.: 6.87:1. Brake H.P.: 75 @ 3600 R.P.M. Taxable H.P.: 23.4. Main bearings: Four. Valve lifters: Solid. Carb.: Carter 513S. Torque: 136 lbs.-ft. at 1200 R.P.M.

CHASSIS: [Series 4180] W.B.: 121 in. O.L.: 200-3/4 in. Frt/Rear Tread: 57 in./61-1/4 in. Tires: 6.50 x 16. [Series 4160] W.B.: 121 in. O.L.: 200-3/4 in. Frt/Rear Tread: 57-1/2 in./60-1/2 in. Tires: 6.25 x 16. [Series 4140] W.B.: 112 in. O.L.: 194 in. Frt/Rear Tread: 56 in./59-3/4 in. Tires: 5.50 x 16.

TECHNICAL: Selective sliding gear transmission. Speeds: 3F/1R. Steering column controls. Single dry plate clutch. Hypoid drive. Semi-floating rear axle. Overall ratio: 4.10:1. Hydraulic brakes on four wheels. Steel disc wheels. Wheel size: 16 in. Drivetrain Options: Hill-holder (13.00). Overdrive (50.00 — 4140) (55.00 — 4160, 4180).

OPTIONS: Fender skirts (except 4140). Radio (Deluxe 45.00) (Custom 65.00). Heater (Weather eye) (35.00). Clock. Cigar lighter. Radio antenna. Bed equipment, standard (17.50). Bed equipment, deluxe (24.50). Two-tone paint (10.50). Deluxe steering wheel (15.00).

HISTORICAL: Introduced Oct. 1, 1940. Innovations: Ambassador "600" (4140) series pioneered unitized body/frame construction; first low-priced car with coil springs all around; sliding pillar type I.F.S., similar to Lancia; up to 30 mpg claimed (hence the name: 20 gal. fuel tank x 30 mpg – 600 mi. per tankful. Conventional construction and suspension used on 4160, 4180 series. Last year for "twin ignition". Calendar year registrations: 77,824. Calendar year production: 80,428. The president of Nash was George Mason. Share of industry registrations: 2.09%. Ambassador "600" marked Nash's re-entry into the low-priced field. Sales sharply up.

Ambassador 600, 6-cyl.

	FP	5	4	3	2	1
Bus Cpe	730	550	1150	2100	3800	5400
2 dr FsBk	765	500	1100	1950	3600	5100
4 dr FsBk	805	550	1150	2000	3600	5200
DeL Bus Cpe	775	600	1200	2200	3900	5600
DeL Brgm	835	650	1250	2400	4150	5900
DeL 2 dr FsBk	797	600	1200	2200	3850	5500
DeL 4 dr FsBk	837	550	1150	2100	3800	5400
Tr Sed	880	600	1200	2200	3900	5600

Ambassador, 6-cyl.

	FP	5	4	3	2	1
Bus Cpe	940	675	1300	2500	4300	6100
Spec Bus Cpe	890	650	1250	2400	4150	5900
A-P Cab	1130	1400	4150	6950	9750	13,900
Brgm	1009	675	1300	2600	4400	6300
Spec Sed	933	650	1250	2400	4150	5900
Spec FsBk	970	650	1250	2400	4200	6000
DeL FsBk	1020	675	1300	2500	4300	6100
Tr Sed	1065	700	1350	2700	4500	6400

Ambassador, 8-cyl.

	FP	5	4	3	2	1
A-P Cabr	1250	2000	5050	8450	11,800	16,900
DeL Brgm	1116	700	1350	2900	4600	6600
Spec FsBk	1091	700	1350	2700	4500	6400
DeL FsBk	1141	700	1350	2800	4550	6500
Tr Sed	1186	725	1400	3200	4850	6900

1942

1942 Nash Ambassador, sedan, OCW

NASH — AMBASSADOR "EIGHT" — SERIES 4280 — EIGHT: Similar to 1941 model, but with stainless steel grille at center, featuring short, horizontal blades. Parking lamps in fenders, above headlamps, chromed fender crowns and fender trim to match grille, deluxe-equipped cars only. Script on trunk reads "Nash 8."

NASH — AMBASSADOR "SIX" — SERIES 4260 — SIX: Identical in appearance to series 4280, except script on trunk reads "Nash 6."

NASH — AMBASSADOR "600" — SERIES 4240 — SIX: Identical in appearance to series 4280, except hood and front fenders are several inches shorter; script on trunk reads "Nash 600"; rear fenders shrouded.

I.D. DATA: [Series 4280] Serial numbers on right front frame member. Starting: B114001. Ending: B115000. Engine numbers on engine block, right front. Starting: B114001. Ending: B115000. [Series 4260] Serial numbers on right front frame member. Starting: R384001. Ending: R393090. Engine numbers on engine block, right front. Starting: R384001. Ending: R393090. [Series 4240] Serial numbers on right front frame member just ahead of dash. Starting: K56001. Ending: K77660. Engine numbers on right side of crankcase toward front. Starting: K56001. Ending: K77660.

Model No.	Body Type & Seating	Price	Weight	Start. Ser. No.
4280	4-dr. Tr. Sed.-6P	1209	3465	B114001
4282	2-dr. Cpe.-3P	1134	3350	B114001
4283	2-dr. Brgm.-5P	1174	3385	B114001
4288	4-dr. Sed.-6P	1184	3465	B114001
4289	2-dr. Sed.-6P	1164	3485	B114001
4260	4-dr. Tr. Sed.-6P	1159	3335	R384001
4262	2-dr. Cpe.-3P	1084	3200	R384001
4263	2-dr. Brgm.-5P	1124	3230	R384001
4268	4-dr. Sed.-6P	1134	3335	R384001
4269	2-dr. Sed.-6P	1114	3265	R384001
4240	4-dr. Tr. Sed.-6P	993	2655	K56001
4242	2-dr. Cpe.3P	918	2540	K56001
4243	2-dr. Brgm.-5P	958	2580	K56001
4248	4-dr. Sed.-6P	968	2655	K56001
4249	2-dr. Sed.-6P	948	2605	K56001

ENGINE: [Series 4280] OHV. Straight. Eight. Cast iron block. B & S: 3-1/8 in. x 4-1/4 in. Disp.: 260.8 cu. in. Compression ratio: 6.60:1. Brake H.P.: 115 @ 3400 R.P.M. Taxable H.P.: 31.2. Main bearings: Nine. Valve lifters: Solid. Carb.: Carter WDO-538S. Torque: 200 lbs.-ft. @ 1600 R.P.M. [Series 4260] OHV. Inline. Six. Cast iron block. B & S: 3-3/8 in. x 4-3/8 in. Disp.: 234.8 cu. in. C.R.: 6.50:1. Brake H.P.: 105 @ 3400 R.P.M. Taxable H.P.:

27.3. Main bearings: Seven. Valve lifters: Solid. Carb.: Carter WA1-462S. Torque: 203 lbs.-ft. @ 1600 R.P.M. [Series 4240] L-head. Inline. Six. Cast iron block. B & S: 3-1/8 in. x 3-3/4 in. Disp.: 172.6 cu. in. C.R.: 6.87:1.

Brake H.P.: 75 @ 3600 R.P.M. Taxable H.P.: 23.4. Main bearings: Four. Valve lifters: Solid. Carb.: Carter WDO-513S. Torque: 138 lbs.-ft. @ 1200 R.P.M.

CHASSIS: [Series 4280] W.B.: 121 in. O.L.: 205-1/2 in. Frt/Rear Tread: 57 in./60-1/4 in. Tires: 6.50 x 16. [Series 4260] W.B.: 121 in. O.L.: 205-1/2 in. Frt/Rear Tread: 57-1/2 in./60-1/2 in. Tires: 6.25 x 16. [Series 4240] W.B.: 112 in. O.L.: 196-1/2 in. Frt/Rear Tread: 56 in./59-3/4 in. Tires: 5.50 x 16.

TECHNICAL: Selective sliding gear transmission. Speeds: 3F/1R. Steering column controls. Single dry plate clutch. Hypoid drive. Semi-floating rear axle. Overall ratio: 4.11:1. Hydraulic brakes on four wheels. Steel disc wheels. Wheel size: 16 in. Hill-Holder. Overdrive.

OPTIONS: Bumper Front (Std.). Rear Bumper (Std.). Single sidemount (N/A). Dual Sidemount (N/A). Sidemount cover(s) (N/A). Fender skirts (except 4240). Bumper Guards (Std.). Radio (65.00). Heater (35.00). Clock (10.50). Cigar Lighter (2.10). Radio Antenna (incl. with radio). Seat Covers. Spotlight (17.75). Cowl lamps (N/A). Bulb Horn (N/A). Bed Equipment (21.00). Oil filter (9.00). Outside mirror (right or left) (2.45). Fog lights (12.00).

HISTORICAL: Introduced Oct. 1, 1941. Calendar year production: 5,428. The 1942 "4280" series was Nash's last straight-eight. The president of Nash was George Mason. Very short production year, due to U.S. entry into World War II. (Production ceased Feb. 1, 1942).

1942

Ambassador 600, 6-cyl.

	FP	5	4	3	2	1
Bus Cpe	843	600	1200	2300	4000	5700
Brgm	883	675	1300	2500	4300	6100
2 dr SS	873	650	1250	2400	4150	5900
4 dr SS	893	675	1300	2500	4350	6200
Tr Sed	918	650	1250	2400	4200	6000

Ambassador, 6-cyl.

	FP	5	4	3	2	1
Bus Cpe	994	650	1250	2400	4200	6000
Brgm	1034	675	1300	2600	4400	6300
2 dr SS	1024	675	1300	2500	4300	6100
4 dr SS	1044	675	1300	2500	4350	6200
Tr Sed	1069	675	1300	2600	4400	6300

Ambassador, 8-cyl.

	FP	5	4	3	2	1
Bus Cpe	1044	700	1350	2700	4500	6400
Brgm	1084	700	1350	2800	4550	6500
2 dr SS	1074	675	1300	2600	4400	6300
4 dr SS	1094	700	1350	2700	4500	6400
Tr Sed	1119	700	1350	2800	4550	6500

NATION — Oklahoma City, Oklahoma — (1912) — W.E. Nation bragged a lot, first that he was the proprietor of the largest retail harness and vehicle business between Kansas City and the Gulf of Mexico, second that he had come up with "a new development that works for efficiency and economy" and "which ultimately, doubtless, will revolutionize the automobile manufacturing business of the world." What he did come up with apparently was a single prototype of a gasoline automobile especially designed for the "mixed prairie formation of Oklahoma" although he didn't come up with the wherewithal to put it into production. As for his revolutionary new development, as *The Motor World* reported in June 1912, he planned to keep that "secret locked in his chest . . . until he holds in his hands the official patent both for its manufacture and the manufacture of the machinery by which it is made." Alas, we may never know.

NATIONAL — The word National as a prefix was a designation favored by numerous automotive hopefuls during the early years of the industry. The following companies called National are not believed to have proceeded into manufacture, however, or elected to call their car something else.

The National Association of Automobile Owners of Newark, New Jersey, organized early in 1909 with a capital stock of $125,000 "to manufacture motor cars, wagons and carriages." Incorporators were T.H. Ramsdell, J.F. Switzer and F.M.P. Pearse.

The National Association of Automobile Owners organized in Dover, Delaware during the fall of 1910 with a capital stock of $100,000 "to manufacture, repair, rebuild and take over automobiles, motor vehicles and trucks, and to establish and maintain garages, agencies and sub-agencies throughout the United States, Canada and the Republic of Mexico." Incorporators were Joseph E. Rice, Henry C. Long, Robert L. Van Duzen and Francis H. Hoffecker.

The National Auto-Cab Company of New York City, organized late in 1907 with a capital stock of $25,000 to "engage in the manufacture of self-propelled vehicles, motors, engines, carriages and wagons." Incorporators were W.R. Vouse and W. Mabry.

The National Automobile Company of St. Louis, Missouri, listed as an automobile manufacturer in the Hiscox book *Horseless Vehicles, Automobiles, Motor Cycles* published in 1900.

The National Automobile Company, organized in Philadelphia, Pennsylvania during the summer of 1900 with a $1.5 million capital stock and the plan to manufacture cars in Martinsburg, West Virginia. Incorporators were C. McGill, H. Wells, E. Sampson, J. Fisher, F. Turner and W.C. Leonard, all of Martinsburg.

The National Automobile Company, organized in Augusta, Maine late in 1902 with a $500,000 capital stock for the manufacture of automobiles. F.L. Fairbanks was president, J. Berry was treasurer.

The National Automobile Company of Providence, Rhode Island which was listed in *Cycle and Automobile Trade Journal* in January 1904 as the producers of both steam and electric vehicles.

The National Automobile Company of Jersey City, New Jersey, organized late in 1904 with a capital stock of $250,000 to manufacture and sell automobiles. Incorporators were Louis B. Dailey, H.C. Coughlan and B. Stafford Mantz.

The National Automobile & Motor Company of Portland, Maine, organized during the spring of 1901 with a capital stock of $350,000 for the "making and selling of autos and motors." H.B. Clark of Everett, Massachusetts was president, S.C. Allen of Portland was treasurer.

The National Bicycle and Motor Company of Bridgeport, Connecticut, listed as an automobile manufacturer in the Hiscox book *Horseless Vehicles, Automobiles, Motor Cycles* published in 1900.

The National Brick Company of Chicago, Illinois, indicated on various rosters as having built a car called the Bartlett in 1921.

The National and Commercial Manufacturing Company of Hammond, Indiana, organized late in 1906 with a capital stock of $12,000 to manufacture motor cars. Incorporators were Clarence Kistlen, L.F. Jones and E.J. Hathaway.

The National Elevator & Machine Company of Honesdale, Pennsylvania, indicated in *The Horseless Age* during the summer of 1903 as "preparing to engage in the manufacture of automobiles."

The National Manufacturing and Metal Company of Providence, Rhode Island, organized early in 1909 with a capital stock of $25,000 to "manufacture, buy, sell and repair automobiles." Incorporators were John B. Hartnett, David Rosenberg and John Mueller.

The National Motor Company of Jersey City, New Jersey, organized with a capital stock of $2000 during the summer of 1909 to manufacture engines and automobiles. Incorporators were John R. Turner, L.H. Gunther and B. Stafford Mantz. This seems to have been a successor incorporation to the National Motor Car Company organized with the same capital stock earlier in 1909 by H.C. Coughlan, Arthur W. Britton and B. Stafford Mantz. Coughlan and Mantz had previously been among the incorporators of the National Automobile Company in Jersey City in 1904.

The National Motor Carriage Company of Stamford, Connecticut which produced a car at the turn of the century most often referred to as a Klock. Refer to Klock.

The National Motor Device Company of Chicago, Illinois, organized during the spring of 1911 with a capital stock of $60,000 "to manufacture automobiles and accessories." Incorporators were C.O. Garmire, J.H. Hoglund and E.A. Biggs, all of Chicago.

The National Motor Transit Company of Buffalo, New York, listed as an automobile manufacturer in the Hiscox book *Horseless Vehicles, Automobiles, Motor Cycles* published in 1900.

The National Screw & Tack Company of Cleveland, Ohio the chief engineer of which built a car in 1908-1910. Refer to Hines.

The National Service Corporation organized in Wilmington, Delaware early in 1915 to "manufacture, sell and deal in motor cars and appliances." Incorporators were C.J. Jacobs, C.H. Bishop and H.W. Davis.

The National Spoke & Nipple Company organized in Dover, Delaware early in 1914 with a capital stock of $25,000 to "manufacture, sell and deal in motor cars." Incorporators were J.M. Satterfield, Walter P. Carrow and M.M. Hirons.

The National Transportation Company of Boston, Massachusetts, indicated on various rosters to have built a steam car from 1899-1900.

The National Transportation Company of Pen Argyl, Pennsylvania, organized late in 1912 with a capital stock of $100,000 to "manufacture, purchase and acquire patent rights on all kinds of motor vehicles." Incorporators included W.M. Whitney and L.H. Mounten of Pen Argyl.

NATIONAL — New York, New York — (1898) — The National Motor Carriage Company was grandly incorporated with a capital stock of a half-million dollars and opened offices at 1 Madison Avenue during the late fall of 1898. Behind this venture were Ernest E. Lorillard as president, General O.O. Howard as vice-president, David Allen Reed as treasure, and Arthur S. Winslow as secretary. Winslow indicated that the company was in the process of building 25 runabouts and 25 physicians' carriages, both to sell for a thousand dollars. One of the physicians' carriages was then on exhibition to New York City, and there had been plans to enter a National in the upcoming Boston motor carriage competition but what Winslow called "important negotiations pending" prevented that. What those negotiations were remains unclear. Conceivably, they may have been talks with Percy L. Klock who would organize as well as the National Motor Carriage Company the following year. This cannot be documented, however, and the Klock automobile went on to become an independent venture. Meanwhile, the National Motor Carriage Company organized by Ernest Lorillard and associates faded from the scene prior to the turn of the century. Among the last bits of news reported about the company arrived in October of 1899 when it was revealed that a judgment of $820 had been awarded in favor of C.A. Tower and George L. Weiss of Cleveland who had made prepayments on cars that were never delivered. This was the same George Weiss who worked so closely with James Ward Packard on the development of the early Packards.

NATIONAL — St. Louis, Missouri — (1899-1900) — A beer wagon coursing the streets of St. Louis was the impetus that moved the National Motor Company into the automotive field in April 1899. It was powered by an 8 hp engine invented by H.H. Hennegin, a marine engine producer of local repute, and it never failed to deliver the goods. Local capitalists were impressed enough to join H.H. and his brother Peter Hennegin, the Allard brothers (L. and M.E.) and John A. Robinson in a $100,000 capitalization for factory enlargement. By August National was completing five gasoline traps to meet local orders, and making even grander plans. Three sizes of two-cylinder engines — 2-1/2, 5 and 8 hp — were ready to power the forthcoming National machines. Capital stock was increased that month to $2 million. Something went awry. By March of 1900 National Motor Company was in receivership and its assets were disposed of by the bank trustees. The Missouri Motor Company superseded National and secured the services of inventor Hennegin, but the only products he would be designing now were engines. No further automobiles appeared.

NATIONAL STEAM — Wilmington, Delaware — (1900) — In 1900 John H. Parsons of Wilmington built a steam car. Its boiler was placed under the back seat, with water tank and condenser under the front seat, and the steam engine hung amidst the running gear somewhat treacherously low to the ground. Still, the vehicle was tested with satisfaction, at speeds of up to a claimed 40 mph, with the 7-gallon fuel tank and 33-gallon water tank allowing for a 10-hour run without replenishment. "It runs as quietly

1900 National Steamer, surrey, NAHC

as a bicycle," said John Parsons who, after fifteen years as a locomotive engineer for the Pennsylvania Railroad, believed himself now ready for the automotive field. M.B. Faulkner agreed, and he organized the National Automobile Company of Wilmington for the manufacture of Parsons' steam car. The McLear & Kendall Company, a Wilmington carriage manufacturer since 1866, was purchased to serve as the factory. Parsons would head its mechanical department, McLear would remain to take care of the coachwork. Formal announcement of this new automobile company was made on July 6th, 1900 by M.B. Faulkner. There were no further announcements. If any production ensued, it was minimal. By 1901 possibly John Parsons had returned to working on the railroad.

1901 National Electric, runabout, MVMA

NATIONAL — Indianapolis, Indiana — (1900-1924) — "Our electric vehicles are manufactured for those persons who find no pleasure in mechanical labor, persons for whom the solution of intricate problems has no fascination," read the National Automobile & Electric Company catalogue in 1901. The firm was founded by L.S. Dow and Philip Goetz, formerly of the Waverley branch of the American Bicycle Company, who had built their first experimental electric in 1900. National's electric, which was also occasionally called an Electrobile, was a simple little tiller-steered car offered in a proliferation of body styles. Initially, horsedrawn carriages were also built, but in September of 1902 that branch of the business was sold to Gates-Osborne Carriage Company, with the now newly reorganized National Vehicle Company to concentrate on the electric field exclusively. National's claim later that month that one of its vehicles ran 118 miles on one charge on asphalt streets was promptly disputed by the Waverley Electric people, who said it was impossible. Nonetheless, National introduced a new model for 1903 called the "Long Distance" and sporting a brass hood to resemble a gasoline car. By 1904, yet again reorganized as the National Motor Vehicle Company, the firm had introduced a gasoline car itself. Late in 1905, in a letter to potential customers, the company advised that "one great mistake some Automobilists make, is attempting to cover their requirements with a Gasoline Touring car and a number have found it to their decided advantage to also invest in a National Electric runabout for short quick trips." Nonetheless, although a commercial electric vehicle was continued awhile, the National electric passenger car was phased out in 1906. Most probably responsible for the growing National preference for gasoline cars was Arthur C. Newby, initially a director, subsequently the company president. An enthusiastic cyclist, and founder of the six-day bicycle races, Newby would also be among the founders of the Indianapolis Motor Speedway. The National gasoline car was introduced as a light twin and a four in 1903; by 1905 it had grown into a more powerful four (Rutenber engine), with shaft drive, three-speed selective transmission, and a round radiator which would remain a distin-

1902 National Electric, model 50, runabout, NAHC

guishing characteristic of the National until 1908 when a shield-like design was substituted. In 1905 a National won a 100-mile endurance contest at the Indiana Fairgrounds, and in a 24-hour marathon completed over 1094 miles for a record-breaking average of 51.9 mph. In 1906, with the discontinuation of the electric car, National introduced a six-cylinder gasoline model, one of the first sixes to be put on regular sale in America. Like the four, its cylinders were separately cast initially, though by 1908 a new range of National fours and sixes with cylinders cast in pairs arrived. With the opening of the Indianapolis Motor Speedway in 1909, not surprisingly, National went racing there and placed well in a number of events on the dirt track. When Indy was paved with bricks and the first 500 was inaugurated in 1911, National showed up with a three-car team, one of the cars finishing seventh. In 1912 Joe Dawson drove a National to a winning average of 78.22 mph in the 500. Other competition victories included the road races at Elgin (Illinois) and Santa Monica (California), and the Cactus Derby from Los Angeles to Phoenix, in 1911. After 1912 motor sport was eliminated from the National agenda, the company focusing on production of a variety of fine fours and sixes ranging in price from $2500 to nearly $5000. In May of 1915, at the same time that Packard introduced its Twin Six, National came forth with its Highway Twelve, an engine of National's own design which used blade and fork connecting rods. Interestingly, the twelve-cylinder National at $2000 was less expensive than the venerable National six, which was continued as the Newport at $2500. But another smaller six (Continental engine) was added to the range and at $1690 was the lowest priced National since the twin of 1903. In 1916, during a bout of ill health, Arthur Newby had retired from the company, relinquishing its presidency to his general manager, G.M. Dickinson. The twelve was discontinued after 1919, National moving into the Twenties with six-cylinder cars only, and moving into a merger in 1922 with the Dixie Flyer and the Jackson as Associated Motor Industries. Clarence A. Earl, who had recently resigned from Earl Motors, took over as president of this new combine. Both the Dixie Flyer and the Jackson names were discontinued thereafter, the cars themselves becoming the National models 4-H and 6-51. Introduced too was a brand-new National, a small six which at $795 was the cheapest car ever proposed by the company. Show and pilot models were built, but it never moved into manufacture. In May of 1923 National was sued on eight claims for failure to pay bills accrued in the preparation of catalogues and new models for the automobile shows. In January 1924 the company moved into receivership. "Five years of grace in which to put the business on a sound footing" was requested by Clarence Earl. The banks pretty much laughed. With that, Earl and his associates resigned, and the National died.

1903 National Electric, model 110, Park trap, HAC

1901 NATIONAL
Electric Cars

	FP	5	4	3	2	1
Style A Runabout	900	2000	3000	4200	6500	14,000
Style D Break	1600	2300	3300	4600	7500	16,000
Style F Stanhope	1750	2500	3500	5000	8500	18,000
Style G Road Wagon	—	2600	3600	5200	8700	18,500
Style H Surrey Top Road Wagon		2700	3600	5300	8800	19,000
Style C Park Trap	1200	2200	3200	4400	7000	15,000
Style E New York Trap	1650	2250	3300	4500	7300	15,500
Style B Brake/Delivery	1500	1800	2800	4000	6200	13,000

1902 NATIONAL
Electric Cars

	FP	5	4	3	2	1
Model 50 Runabout	850	2000	3000	4200	6500	14,000
Model 55 Piano Box	900	2200	3200	4400	7000	15,000
Model 60 Straight-Dash Rbt.	850	2200	3200	4400	7000	15,000
Model 65 Victoria	900	2300	3300	4600	7500	16,000
Model 70 Runabout	850	2000	3000	4200	6500	14,000
Model 75 Runabout	850	2000	3000	4200	6500	14,000
Model 85 Canopy Runabout	900	2300	3300	4600	7500	16,000
Model 90 Dos-a-Dos	1100	2400	3400	4800	8000	17,000

1903 National Electric, Long Distance, runabout, NAHC

1903 NATIONAL
Electric Cars

	FP	5	4	3	2	1
Model 50 Runabout	1000	2000	3000	4200	6500	14,000
Model 65 Straight-Dash Rbt.	1000	2200	3200	4400	7000	15,000
Model 110 Park Trap	1250	2200	3200	4400	7000	15,000
Model 75 Piano Box	1000	2200	3200	4400	7000	15,000
Model 85 Stanhope	1500	2300	3300	4600	7500	16,000
Model 100 Runabout	1200	2000	3000	4200	6500	14,000
Long Distance Electric	—	2400	3400	4800	8000	17,000

Gasoline Car — 4-cyl., 16 hp, 86" wb

	FP	5	4	3	2	1
Touring-5P	2500	2300	3300	4600	7500	16,000

Gasoline Car — 2-cyl., 8 hp, 72" wb

	FP	5	4	3	2	1
Light Touring-5P	1450	2000	3000	4200	6500	14,000

1904 National, model A, gasoline touring, HAC

1904 NATIONAL
Electric Cars

	FP	5	4	3	2	1
Model 50 Runabout	950	2000	3000	4200	6500	14,000
Model 65 Runabout	1000	2200	3200	4400	7000	15,000
Model 75 Runabout	1000	2200	3200	4400	7000	15,000
Model 85 Stanhope	1500	2300	3300	4600	7500	16,000
Model 100 Runabout	1200	2250	3300	4500	7300	15,500
Model 110 Park Trap	1250	2300	3300	4600	7500	16,000
Model 135 Runabout	2000	2400	3400	4800	8000	17,000

Gasoline Model A — 4-cyl., 40 hp, 96" wb

	FP	5	4	3	2	1
Touring-5P	3000	2700	3600	5300	8800	19,000

Gasoline Model B — 4-cyl., 20 hp, 96" wb

	FP	5	4	3	2	1
Touring-5P	2000	2500	3500	5000	8500	18,000

1905 NATIONAL
Electric Cars

	FP	5	4	3	2	1
Model 65 Road Wagon	1000	2000	3000	4200	6500	14,000
Model 135 Runabout	2000	2300	3300	4600	7500	16,000
Model 85 Stanhope	1500	2200	3200	4400	7000	15,000
Model 75 Runabout	1000	1800	2800	4000	6200	13,000
Model 110 Dos-a-Dos	1250	2000	3000	4200	6500	14,000
Model 100 Piano Box Runabout	1200	2000	3000	4200	6500	14,000
Model 50 Piano Box Runabout	950	2000	3000	4200	6500	14,000

Gasoline Model C — 4-cyl., 23/30 hp

	FP	5	4	3	2	1
Touring-5P	2500	2400	3400	4800	8000	17,000

991

1905 National, model C, touring, HAC

1906 National, model E, touring, HAC

1906 NATIONAL
Electric Cars

	FP	5	4	3	2	1
Model 100 Runabout	1200	1800	2800	4000	6200	13,000
Model 65 Runabout	1000	1600	2700	3800	5800	12,000
Model 50 Runabout	950	1500	2500	3600	5500	11,000
Gasoline Model D — 4-cyl., 35/40 hp, 104" wb						
Tonneau-5P	3000	3800	7650	12,750	17,850	25,500
Gasoline Model E — 6-cyl., 50/60 hp, 121" wb						
Tonneau-7P	4000	4000	7950	13,250	18,550	26,500

1907 National, model L, touring, HAC

1907 NATIONAL
Model F — 4-cyl., 40 hp, 104" wb

	FP	5	4	3	2	1
Touring-5P	3000	2300	3300	4600	7500	16,000
Runabout-3P	3000	2200	3200	4400	7000	15,000
Model H — 4-cyl., 50 hp, 112" wb						
Touring-5P	3500	3900	4800	7700	14,300	27,000
Runabout-3P	3500	3700	4700	7300	13,700	26,000
Model L — 6-cyl., 75 hp, 127" wb						
Touring-7P	5000	4000	5000	8000	15,000	28,000
Limousine-7P	6500	3100	4200	6300	10,500	22,000

1908 National, model N, limousine, OCW

1908 NATIONAL
Model K — 4-cyl., 40 hp, 112" wb

	FP	5	4	3	2	1
Touring-7P	3500	2700	3600	5300	8800	19,000
Roadster	3500	2500	3500	5000	8500	18,000
Runabout	3500	2200	3200	4400	7000	15,000
Limousine	4500	2300	3300	4600	7500	16,000
Model N — 4-cyl., 50 hp, 112" wb						
Touring-7P	3700	2900	3700	5600	9100	20,000
Roadster	3700	2700	3600	5300	8800	19,000
Runabout	3700	2500	3500	5000	8500	18,000
Limousine	4800	2400	3400	4800	8000	17,000
Model R — 6-cyl., 50 hp, 116" wb						
Touring-5P	4200	3100	4200	6300	10,500	22,000
Roadster	4200	3000	4000	6000	9500	21,000
Runabout	4200	2900	3700	5600	9100	20,000
Limousine	5500	2500	3500	5000	8500	18,000
Model T — 6-cyl., 75 hp, 127" wb						
Touring-7P	5000	3200	4300	6500	11,000	23,000
Limousine	6500	2700	3600	5300	8800	19,000

1909 National, model 9-40, limousine, HAC

1909 NATIONAL
Model 9-35 — 4-cyl., 35 hp, 117" wb

	FP	5	4	3	2	1
Touring-5P	2750	3300	4400	6700	12,000	24,000
Toy Tonneau-4P	2750	3200	4300	6500	11,000	23,000
Roadster-2P	2750	3200	4300	6500	11,000	23,000
Model 9-40 — 4-cyl., 40 hp, 125" wb						
Touring-7P	3700	3700	4700	7300	13,700	26,000
Toy Tonneau-4P	3700	3500	4500	7000	13,000	25,000
Roadster-2P	3700	3500	4500	7000	13,000	25,000
Model 9-50 — 6-cyl., 50 hp, 130" wb						
Touring-7P	4200	4200	5200	8400	15,700	29,000
Toy Tonneau-4P	4200	4000	5000	8000	15,000	28,000
Roadster-2P	4200	4000	5000	8000	15,000	28,000

1910 National, model 60, touring, HAC

1910 NATIONAL
Model 40 — 4-cyl., 40 hp, 124" wb

	FP	5	4	3	2	1
Touring-5P	2500	3700	4700	7300	13,700	26,000
Model 50 — 4-cyl., 50 hp, 130" wb						
Touring-7P	4200	4000	5000	8000	15,000	28,000
Model 60 — 6-cyl., 60 hp, 137" wb						
Touring-7P	5000	4300	5400	8700	16,500	30,000

1911 National, model 40, speedway roadster, HAC

1911 NATIONAL
Model 40 — 4-cyl., 40 hp, 124" wb

	FP	5	4	3	2	1
Speedway Roadster	2500	4000	5000	8000	15,000	28,000
Open Touring	2500	3900	4800	7700	14,300	27,000
Fore-Door Touring	2600	4000	5000	8000	15,000	28,000
Toy Tonneau	2600	3900	4800	7700	14,300	27,000
Limousine	3750	2700	3600	5300	8800	19,000
Fore-Door Limousine	4000	3000	4000	6000	9500	21,000
Fore-Door Touring-7P	3000	4200	5200	8400	15,700	29,000

1912 National, model 40, touring, HAC

1912 NATIONAL
Model 38 — 4-cyl., 38 hp, 128" wb

	FP	5	4	3	2	1
Touring-5P	2900	3900	4800	7700	14,300	27,000
Toy Tonneau-4P	2900	3700	4700	7300	13,700	26,000
Speedway Rds. (120" wb)	2750	4000	5000	8000	15,000	28,000
Touring-7P	3000	4200	5200	8400	15,700	29,000

Model 40 — 4-cyl., 40 hp, 124" wb

	FP	5	4	3	2	1
Roadster	2500	4200	5200	8400	15,700	29,000
Touring-5P	2600	4000	5000	8000	15,000	28,000
Touring-7P	3000	4200	5200	8400	15,700	29,000

1913 National, series V, toy tonneau, HAC

1913 National, series V, touring, JAC

1913 NATIONAL
Series V — 4-cyl., 40 hp, 128" wb

	FP	5	4	3	2	1
Touring-5P	3300	4000	5000	8000	15,000	28,000
Semi-Racing Roadster	2750	4400	5600	9200	17,300	31,000
Speedway Roadster	3150	4500	5800	9500	18,000	32,000
Toy Tonneau-4P	3300	4200	5200	8400	15,700	29,000
Touring-7P	3400	4300	5400	8700	16,500	30,000
Coupe	3500	2700	3600	5300	8800	19,000
Sedan	4600	2200	3200	4400	7000	15,000
Limousine	4800	3100	4200	6300	10,500	22,000

1914 National, series V, semi-racing roadster, HAC

1914 NATIONAL
Six — 34 hp, 132" wb

	FP	5	4	3	2	1
Touring-5P	2375	3700	4700	7300	13,700	26,000
Torpedo	2375	3900	4800	7700	14,300	27,000
Coupe	2850	2500	3500	5000	8500	18,000

Series V — 4-cyl., 40 hp, 128" wb

	FP	5	4	3	2	1
Touring-5P	3300	4000	5000	8000	15,000	28,000
Semi-Racing Roadster	2750	4200	5200	8400	15,700	29,000
Speedway Roadster	3150	4400	5600	9200	17,300	31,000
Toy Tonneau-4P	3300	4300	5400	8700	16,500	30,000
Touring-7P	3400	4400	5600	9200	17,300	31,000
Coupe	3500	2700	3600	5300	8800	19,000
Sedan	4600	2300	3300	4600	7500	16,000
Limousine	4800	2900	3700	5600	9100	20,000

1915 National, series AA, parlor car, JAC

1915 NATIONAL
Six, Series AA — 34 hp, 132" wb

	FP	5	4	3	2	1
Touring-6P	2500	3900	4800	7700	14,300	27,000
Roadster-2P	2375	3700	4700	7300	13,700	26,000
Toy Tonneau-4P	2375	4000	5000	8000	15,000	28,000
Touring-5P	2375	3700	4700	7300	13,700	26,000
Coupe-4P	2850	2500	3500	5000	8500	18,000
Cabriolet-3P	2700	3100	4200	6300	10,500	22,000
Parlor Car-4P	2700	3000	4000	6000	9500	21,000

1916 National Newport Six, roadster, HAC

1916 NATIONAL
Highway Six — 6-cyl., 29.4 hp, 128" wb

	FP	5	4	3	2	1
Touring-4P	1690	3500	4500	7000	13,000	25,000
Touring-6P	1720	3700	4700	7300	13,700	26,000
Roadster-3P	1690	3700	4700	7300	13,700	26,000
Coupe-4P	2350	2700	3600	5300	8800	19,000
Sedan-5P	2900	2000	3000	4200	6500	14,000

Highway Twelve — 12-cyl., 36.3 hp, 128" wb

	FP	5	4	3	2	1
Touring-3P	1990	3500	4500	7000	13,000	25,000
Touring-4P	1990	3700	4700	7300	13,700	26,000
Touring-6P	2020	4000	5000	8000	15,000	28,000
Roadster-3P	1990	3900	4800	7700	14,300	27,000
Coupe-4P	2650	2900	3700	5600	9100	20,000
Sedan-5P	3200	2200	3200	4400	7000	15,000

Newport Six — 6-cyl., 33.75 hp, 134" wb

	FP	5	4	3	2	1
Touring-6P	2500	3900	4800	7700	14,300	27,000
Toy Tonneau-4P	2375	4000	5000	8000	15,000	28,000
Touring-5P	2375	4000	5000	8000	15,000	28,000
Touring-7P	2400	4400	5600	9200	17,300	31,000
Roadster-3P	2375	4000	5000	8000	15,000	28,000
Coupe-4P	2850	3000	4000	6000	9500	21,000
Sedan-5P	3400	2300	3300	4600	7500	16,000

1917 National Highway Six, sport phaeton, HAC

1917 NATIONAL
Highway Six — 6-cyl., 29.4 hp, 128" wb

Roadster-4P	1750	3700	4700	7300	13,700	26,000
Touring-7P	1750	3900	4800	7700	14,300	27,000
Sport Phaeton-4P	1750	4000	5000	8000	15,000	28,000
Coupe-4P	2400	2500	3500	5000	8500	18,000
Touring Sedan-5P	2350	2000	3000	4200	6500	14,000

Highway Twelve — 12-cyl., 39.68 hp, 128" wb

Touring-7P	2150	4200	5200	8400	15,700	29,000
Roadster-4P	2150	4000	5000	8000	15,000	28,000
Sport Phaeton-4P	2150	4200	5200	8400	15,700	29,000
Coupe-4P	2800	2700	3600	5300	8800	19,000
Touring Sedan-5P	2750	2200	3200	4400	7000	15,000

1918 National Highway Six, sedan, HAC

1918 NATIONAL
Highway Six — 6-cyl., 29.4 hp, 128" wb

Roadster-4P	1995	3700	4700	7300	13,700	26,000
Touring-7P	1995	3900	4800	7700	14,300	27,000
Sport Phaeton-4P	1995	4000	5000	8000	15,000	28,000
Touring Sedan-7P	2820	2000	3000	4200	6500	14,000

Highway Twelve — 12-cyl., 39.68 hp, 128" wb

Touring-7P	2595	4200	5200	8400	15,700	29,000
Roadster-4P	2595	4000	5000	8000	15,000	28,000
Sport Phaeton-4P	2595	4200	5200	8400	15,700	29,000
Touring Sedan-7P	3420	2200	3200	4400	7000	15,000
Speedster-2P	2850	4500	5800	9500	18,000	32,000

1919 National Highway Twelve, roadster, HAC

1919 NATIONAL
Highway Six — 6-cyl., 29.4 hp, 128" wb

Roadster-4P	2450	3900	4800	7700	14,300	27,000
Touring-7P	2450	4000	5000	8000	15,000	28,000
Phaeton-4P	2450	4000	5000	8000	15,000	28,000
Touring Sedan-7P	3120	2000	3000	4200	6500	14,000

Highway Twelve — 12-cyl., 39.68 hp, 128" wb

	FP	5	4	3	2	1
Touring-7P	3050	4400	5600	9200	17,300	31,000
Roadster-4P	3050	4300	5400	8700	16,500	30,000
Phaeton-4P	3050	4400	5600	9200	17,300	31,000
Touring Sedan-7P	3720	2200	3200	4400	7000	15,000
Speedster-2P	3150	4700	6100	9900	19,000	33,000

1920 National Sextet, phaeton, JAC

1920 NATIONAL
Sextet — 6-cyl., 71 hp, 130" wb

Touring-7P	3500	3500	4500	7000	13,000	25,000
Phaeton-4P	3500	3500	4500	7000	13,000	25,000
Roadster-2P	3500	3300	4400	6700	12,000	24,000
Sedan-5P	4500	2000	3000	4200	6500	14,000
Coupe-4P	4650	2300	3300	4600	7500	16,000

1921 NATIONAL
Sextet — 6-cyl., 71 hp, 130" wb

Touring-7P	3750	3700	4700	7300	13,700	26,000
Phaeton-4P	3750	3700	4700	7300	13,700	26,000
Roadster-2P	3750	3500	4500	7000	13,000	25,000
Sedan-7P	4950	2200	3200	4400	7000	15,000
Coupe-4P	4900	2400	3400	4800	8000	17,000

1922 National, Sextet, phaeton, JAC

1922 NATIONAL
Sextet — 6-cyl., 71 bhp, 130" wb

Touring-7P	2990	3700	4700	7300	13,700	26,000
Phaeton-4P	2990	3700	4700	7300	13,700	26,000
Roadster-2P	2990	3500	4500	7000	13,000	25,000
Coupe-4P	4140	2400	3400	4800	8000	17,000
Sedan-7P	4240	2200	3200	4400	7000	15,000
Newport-4P	3500	3000	4000	6000	9500	21,000

1923 National, model 4-H, coupe, HAC

1923-1924 NATIONAL
Model 6-31 — 6-cyl., 31 hp, 112" wb

	FP	5	4	3	2	1
Phaeton-5P	795	2500	3500	5000	8500	18,000
Sedan-5P	1095	1600	2700	3800	5800	12,000

Model 4-H — 4-cyl., 35 hp, 112" wb

Roadster-2P	975	2700	3600	5300	8800	19,000
Touring-5P	975	2700	3600	5300	8800	19,000
Coupe-3P	1175	2200	3200	4400	7000	15,000
Sedan-5P	1175	1800	2800	4000	6200	13,000

1924 National, model 6-51, phaeton, HAC

Model 6-51 — 6-cyl., 51 hp, 121" wb

	FP	5	4	3	2	1
Phaeton-5P	1485	3100	4200	6300	10,500	22,000
Business Coupe	1785	2300	3300	4600	7500	16,000
Sedan-5P	1885	2000	3000	4200	6500	14,000

Model 6-71 — 6-cyl., 71 hp, 130" wb

Phaeton-4P	2485	3300	4400	6700	12,000	24,000
Phaeton-7P	2485	3700	4700	7300	13,700	26,000
Close-Coupled Sedan-5P	3285	2300	3300	4600	7500	16,000
Sedan-7P	3285	2200	3200	4400	7000	15,000

Note: The Model 4-H was the former Dixie Flyer, the Model 6-51 the former Jackson. Model 6-31 was built in show and pilot models only.

NATIONAL — Oshkosh & Milwaukee, Wisconsin — (1902-1903) — H.H. Muggley and Charles Jameson were the proprietors of the National Automobile Company at 18 Light Street in Oshkosh, but an engineer from Fort Wayne (Indiana) named Marion Black designed their first car. It was a four-passenger tourer with a Renault-type hood that was completed in August 1902 and which the partners planned to sell for $1500. Unfortunately, Muggley and Jameson couldn't sell the town of Oshkosh on the idea of assisting them in manufacture. Thus, they left their machine shop there and moved to Milwaukee "because of the better facilities," so they said. The National Automobile and Motor Company was established there in February 1903 in a huge store at 181-183 Second Street. National would take over the upper floor, while the lower and the basement would be occupied by Orlando Weber, whose Weber Cycle Company was the Wisconsin agent for the new General car from Cleveland. Weber would now represent the new National as well. "Several Eastern men are interested," said H.H. Muggley. Apparently not interested enough, however, because in September of 1903 the National Automobile and Motor Company was petitioned into bankruptcy by three of its largest creditors. Assets were estimated at $3000, liabilities at $9000. "The concern assembled automobiles and attempted to manufacture motors and carburetors," *The Horseless Age* noted rather derisively in its obituary. The National assets were sold at auction on October 12th. Orlando Weber remained in the old National building, and continued to sell the General from Cleveland until the Ohio company went under later during 1903. In 1905 he tried to market his own automobile, but the Weber from Milwaukee never made it off the ground.

NATIONAL — Oakland, California — (1908) — The National Marine Water Autodrumbile Company was organized in Oakland early in 1908 by a group of businessmen from San Francisco. "Whether the Swedish government is interested in the venture or not is not stated," noted one reporter wryly, "but it is certain some of Scandinavia has put up its hard earned coin, as evidenced in the names of the following incorporators: Charles F. Hilden, Axel Gundersen, John Swensen, Herman Hansen, Victor Thoren and Hans Johansen." Autodrumbile was the designation chosen by this sextet to describe the vehicle they planned to produce: an automobile "equipped to navigate through streams of water as well as through muddy roads." Whether a prototype was successfully demonstrated has not been determined with certainty. But certainly the project proceeded no further than that. The last word of the venture was that of its $500,000 capital stock, only $4800 had been subscribed.

NATIONAL CYCLECAR — In 1914 the National United Service Company of Detroit produced two cyclecars called the Arrow and the United, and served as the marketing agency for the Beisel manufactured in Monroe (Michigan) and the Arrow manufactured in Dayton (Ohio). Refer to Arrow and United.

NATIONAL JUVENILE — Toledo, Ohio — (1913-1917) — As its name suggests, the National Juvenile Auto Company of Toledo produced a small gasoline car for children. In 1917 the firm set its sights somewhat higher and announced the impending production of a cyclecar. "Low upkeep and operating costs are to be the feature of the new machine," reported *The Automobile and Automotive Industries,* "and it is expected that a mileage of from 80 to 90 mpg may be obtained." Whether manufacture followed has not been documented. The National Juvenile officers were Dr. H.C. Kuebler as president, K.C. Merrill as vice-president, J.G. Hickok as treasurer, Robert L. Hinds as secretary and Charles F. Hamel as general manager.

NATIONAL ROAD CAR — This was an alternative name to Eldredge used by the National Sewing Machine Company of Belvidere, Illinois for its small runabout produced from 1903 to 1906. Refer to Eldredge.

NAVARRE — Springfield, Massachusetts — (1921) — One car, a five-passenger sedan, was built at the Package Machinery Company in Springfield and was exhibited at the Hotel Astor during New York Automobile Show week in January 1921. It was designed by A.C. Schultz, whose previous credits included stints in the engineering departments of Locomobile and Mercer. The Navarre was powered by an overhead valve six-cylinder engine of Schultz's design featuring a full-pressure lubrication system. The sedan, which was to sell for $6000, was on a 131-inch wheelbase, a dimension it was to share with the $4500-$5000 open touring cars to follow. Associated with Schultz in this venture was A.T. Murray, president of the American-Bosch Magneto Company in Springfield. But the Navarre never was. The project died aborning.

NEAL — The Neal, Clark and Neal Company was organized in Buffalo, New York late in 1910 with a capital stock of $75,000 "to manufacture and sell bicycles, motor cars and accessories." Incorporators were O.L. Neal, H.B. Clark and R.E. Neal. Manufacture of an automobile is doubted.

NEBRASKA — The Nebraska Cyclecar Company has been indicated on various rosters as producing an automobile in Omaha in 1914. There is no evidence this firm was anything more than a hopeful.

1903 Neftel, gas-electric touring, NAHC

NEFTEL — Brooklyn, New York — (1902-1903) — The Neftel Automobile Company of Brooklyn was a one-man operation, and the first name of the one man appears lost to history. Neftel did design an electric with an 8½ hp Telecom motor and dynamo that he entered in the New York to Buffalo Endurance Run of 1902. Subsequently, he revised his design into a gas-electric touring car in 1903. This car was built for him by the Vehicle Equipment Company of Long Island City (makers of the V.E. electric) and was marketed for him by the Rainier company of New York City. Neftel seems to have given up on the automobile field by the end of 1903. He never did formally incorporate his company.

NEIL — Tyrone, Pennsylvania — (1902) — Late in 1902 S.S. Neil of Tyrone completed his automobile, which was an impressive effort for an amateur-built car. Its engine was a single-cylinder two-stroke developing 8 hp, its frame was wood lined with steel and inside which was a subframe of angle iron supporting the motor and chain-and-sprocket transmission gear. The wheelbase was 94 inches, the tread 62, the front wheels measured 26 inches, the rears 40. Except for the tires, wheels, dynamo and differential (which was a Brown & Lipe), Neil built every part of the car himself in his small backyard shop which measured twelve by sixteen feet.

NEILSON — The Neilson from Detroit was an occasional typographical error in trade journals of 1906 and 1907. Refer to Nielson.

NELDNER — The Neldner Hub Motor Company was organized in Milwaukee, Wisconsin late in 1915 with a capital stock of $25,000 to "manufacture motor cars, machinery devices and appliances." Incorporators were S.W. Neldner, J.J. McJeskey and J.S. Stover. Manufacture of an automobile is doubted.

NELSON — The Nelson Manufacturing Company was organized in Willmar, Minnesota during the fall of 1907 with a capital stock of $600,000 to "manufacture automobiles, gasoline engines and agricultural and other machinery." Incorporators were J. Emil Nelson, Charles B. Carlson, Andrew Nordloef, Nels H. Nelson and Walter De La Hunt. Manufacture of a car is doubted.

The Nelson Wheel Company was organized in Chicago, Illinois during the fall of 1907 with a capital stock of $200,000 "to manufacture motors, vehicles and parts of same." Incorporators were N.A. Nelson, E.A. Nelson and R.R. Longenecker. Manufacture of an automobile is doubted.

NELSON ELECTRIC — Redfield, Iowa — Precisely when he built his full-sized electric car is not known, but Henry D. Nelson of Redfield, Iowa is believed to have completed a working model of it prior to the Civil War. A confirmed eccentric, Nelson liked to boast to Redfield residents that he was a forger and that the coins in his pocket were so freshly minted that they were still hot. His electric inventions included a dynamo and an "arthritis machine." According to a story in an 1898 issue of the Chicago

Sunday *Tribune*, his full-sized 300-pound two-seater electric had been exhibited for a number of years previous before being pushed off a steamer into the Illinois River by angry viewers who believed it was a wind-up fraud. The working model of the Nelson electric, which remains extant, indicates that it had the possibility of being viable, however. Purportedly, Nelson's inventions during the California gold rush years included an electric panning device.

1905 Nelson, runabout, NAHC

NELSON — New Britain, Connecticut — (1905) — This car from New Britain had three different powerplants: first, a motorcycle engine, second a stationary gasoline engine, third a 2-1/2 hp air-cooled single-cylinder designed by Nels J. Nelson and cast for him by a machine shop in town. All other parts of the car, including its shaft drive and two-speed transmission, were built by Nelson, who was assisted by his friend Ernest Powell. The boys were teenagers.

1905 Nelson, touring, WLB

NELSON — Harlan, Iowa — (1905) — T.K. Nelson began manufacturing gasoline engines in Harlan in 1896, and he established the first automobile repair shop in Shelby County. In 1905, for a short while, his Nelson Gas Engine Company became the Nelson Gas Engine & Automobile Company. The first car he built had a three-cylinder four-stroke air-cooled engine of his own design, and T.K. Nelson also built its frame, friction drive mechanism, differential and brakes. He handled the upholstery and made the fenders. Possibly he farmed out the body to another shop. His thoughts of proceeding into manufacture were quickly turned aside, because of his belief that the automobile would remain a plaything for the rich. Nelson thereafter rebuilt automobiles, but never tried again himself. He remained in the industry, however. Among his later inventions were motor stands, burning-in stands, a crankshaft truing device and other pieces of equipment for the burgeoning garage field.

1917 Nelson, sedan, NAHC

996

NELSON — Detroit, Michigan — (1917-1921) — Because his resume included engineering work with Packard and Oldsmobile as well as the design of the popular Hupmobile models 20 and 32, Emil A. Nelson's venture into automobile manufacture was greeted with enormous enthusiasm in the trade press. "The Car with the Aeroplane Motor" was an overhead camshaft four-cylinder with unit transmission and a total weight in touring form of but 2200 pounds. From 25 to 30 mpg was claimed, and the car was officially timed accelerating from 5 to 35 mph in 13.5 seconds, which was exemplary for that era. The only problem the car had was the timing of its introduction. Although he had the moral assistance of several fellow Hupmobile employees, Emil Nelson was the E.A. Nelson Motor Car Company all by himself; he financed the entire enterprise, built his own factory in Detroit, and set up a production capacity of ten cars a day. But then he confronted the postwar depression. A plan to consolidate with the engine-building Gray Company of Detroit fell through in 1919, he suffered his first bankruptcy in March of 1920, in September of 1920 he reorganized as the E.A. Nelson Automobile Company. Final bankruptcy arrived exactly one year later. Liabilities were $122,207. Assets were nominally $501,013, but $432,000 was credited to patents, copyrights, trademarks and development work. Cash on hand was $25.00. Approximately 500 Nelsons had been built. At least one is known to survive.

1919 Nelson, roadster, MVMA

1917-1919 NELSON
Four — 29 hp, 104" wb

	FP	5	4	3	2	1
Touring	1500	2500	3500	5000	8500	18,000
Roadster	1200	2400	3400	4800	8000	17,000
Sedan	2200	1800	2800	4000	6200	13,000

1920 Nelson, model D, touring, HAC

1920 NELSON
Model D — 4-cyl., 29 hp, 104" wb

Touring	1700	2500	3500	5000	8500	18,000
Roadster	1700	2400	3400	4800	8000	17,000

1921 Nelson, model E, touring, JAC

1921 NELSON
Model E — 4-cyl., 30 hp, 104" wb

Touring	1900	2500	3500	5000	8500	18,000
Roadster	1900	2400	3400	4800	8000	17,000

NELSON — Hartford, Connecticut — (1919) — This Nelson was built by an erstwhile aviator named Nels Nelson who in 1919 was working for the Oldsmobile dealership in Hartford. Its engine was an air-cooled four, its wheelbase 86 inches, its tread 34 inches, and it was shod with 20-by-4-inch airplane tires. Designed and built by Nelson chiefly as an advertising gimmick for the Olds dealership, brief consideration was given to manufacturing the vehicle in quantity. The single car built remained the only one, however. And it was fast, 50 mph or better. Aaron G. Cohen, who headed the Hartford Olds dealership, took the Nelson car out for a spin on one occasion and reportedly "his speed was such as to cause the state motorcycle policemen to give him a little attention."

1922 Ner-A-Car, runabout, WLB

NER-A-CAR — Syracuse, New York — (1921-1924) — The Ner-A-Car wasn't really very near to being a car. Designed by Carl Neracher of Syracuse, who organized the Ner-A-Car Corporation for its manufacture, the Ner-A-Car was powered by a single-cylinder, two-stroke, air-cooled 13-1/2 hp engine. It weighed 165 pounds and was priced at $225. A two-wheeler on a 55-inch wheelbase, it was handle-bar steered though the bars were not part of the fork as standard motorcycle practice. The vehicle could be partially enclosed; there was provision for only a driver though a single passenger seat was an option. In 1922 Cannon Ball Baker drove a Ner-A-Car from New York City to Los Angeles, averaging 20 mph and over 84 mpg. Production of the Ner-A-Car ended in Syracuse in 1924.

NESKOV-MUMPEROW — The Neskov-Mumperow Motor Car Company of St. Louis, Missouri was an agency for Anderson, Dort and Gardner automobiles. From 1921 to 1923, the firm attempted to enter the field as a manufacturer of a car called the St. Louis. Refer to St. Louis.

NESOM — Nesom Motors Company was organized in Indianapolis, Indiana during the spring of 1912 with a capital stock of $200,000 for the manufacture of motor vehicles. Incorporators were C.T. Nesom, F.B. Brown, Louis Sagalowsky and J.A. Moriarity. Manufacture of a car is doubted.

1903 Neustadt-Perry, gasoline runabout, NAHC

NEUSTADT — St. Louis, Missouri — (1901-1907, 1915) — J.H. Neustadt was, with A.L. Dyke, among the earliest manufacturers in America of automobile parts and accessories. Indeed, in a laudatory article about him appearing in the February 11th, 1905 edition of *Automobile Review*, Neustadt was described as "one of the very few, if not the only one, in the United States, of whom anyone desiring special vehicles can get every requisite part from the body to the leather trimmings, or the gasoline to propel the motor." Components for the making of cars were frequently put together into kits, and given catchy names like Bluff Climber, Genevieve, Traveler, Berkeley and Princess, among others. Neustadt used his own initials, J.H.N., for one kit. The Neustadt business had initially been a partnership, the Neustadt-Perry Company, but it appears that Neustadt had bought out Perry in 1904 to become the Neustadt Automobile & Supply Company. Kits were available for steam cars (from 1901 through 1903) and as gasoline cars through 1907. Engines were either singles, twins or fours, with choice of air or water cooling, and both planetary and friction transmissions could be had, as well as final drive by single or double chain. A few cars may have been sold assembled at the factory, but the vast preponderance of the Neustadt business was in kits. Indeed, the company offered to provide all parts necessary to build a customer's design of his own; all the customer had to do was provide the specs. Although the Neustadt passenger car department closed down in 1907, commercial vehicles in kit form were available thereafter — and in 1911 J.H. Neustadt even had a go at complete manufacture of a Neustadt

1903 Neustadt-Perry, J.H.N. touring, HAC

truck, which was built into 1914. In 1915 he built three special four-wheel drive cars for a customer named H.M. Boyd. After the First World War, J.H. Neustadt retired to California and became a car dealer.

NEVADA FLYER — This was an alternative designation for the car projected to be produced by the Nevada Motor Car Company of Reno in 1908. Refer to Desert Flyer.

NEVELS — The Nevels Manufacturing Company was organized in Hartford, Connecticut during the spring of 1908 with a capital stock of $100,000 for the manufacture of automobiles. Anthony L. Nevels, Frank J. Knox and I.G. Cranton were behind this venture. Manufacture is doubted.

NEVILLE — Oshkosh, Wisconsin — (1908-1914) — Thomas Neville was a carriagemaker at 21 Church Street in Oshkosh who, beginning around 1908, began advertising his T. Neville & Company as "manufacturers and dealers in automobiles," a declaration he continued into at least 1914. The rebuilding and repairing of automobiles undoubtedly was his main activity, together with the fabricating of limousine and roadster bodies which he declared a specialty in later years. But for anyone in Oshkosh desiring a complete car, Thomas Neville was more than willing. Like many small shops in the Midwest during this period, Neville's automobile manufacture was on a per-order basis.

NEW — The New Garage & Electric Company was organized in Newark, Delaware late in 1911 with a capital stock of $5000 to manufacture and deal in automobiles. Incorporators were G. Fader, E.G. Fader and A.F. Fader. Manufacture is doubted.

The New Manufacturing Company was organized in Detroit, Michigan during the summer of 1913 with a capital stock of $150,000 for the manufacture of automobiles. Incorporators were C.W. Jackson and B.W. Denison. Manufacture is doubted.

The New Taxicab & Auto Company was organized in New York City early in 1910 with a capital stock of $25,000 to manufacture, deal in and repair motor vehicles. Incorporators were G.H. Reaney, F.J. Manning and M.W. Cooper. Manufacture is doubted.

NEW BEDFORD — New Bedford, Massachusetts — (1902) — Dr. J.C. Thuot, George W. Cary, U.E. Collette and J.B. Gregoire were the people behind the New Bedford Manufacturing Company which was organized in May of 1902 to produce automobiles and motorcycles. A factory at 105 Bowditch Street had been secured, the company said, and the firm had just completed two automobiles. Probably not many more followed before New Bedford was out of business by year's end.

NEW CASTLE — During the fall of 1907 the New Castle Automobile Company was organized with plans to erect a factory in New Castle, Pennsylvania and "have a six-cylinder car on the market in season for the 1908 demand." Daniel Morgan of Pittsburgh was reported as the man behind this venture who had "enlisted the local capital" for the cause. That manufacture ever began is doubted.

NEW COLUMBUS — New Columbus was the name given to the electric cars produced in 1915 in Columbus, Ohio which had been built since 1903 by the Columbus Buggy Company. Refer to Columbus Electric.

NEW CONCORD — The New Concord Automobile Company was organized during the summer of 1902 in Columbus, Ohio with a capital stock of $50,000 for the manufacture of automobiles in New Concord. Behind this venture were H.L. Warner of Dayton, J.M. Ickes of Newark, D.S. Burt of Byesville, and L.C. Taylor and John S. Black of Cambridge. "The contract for the erection of the plant has been let to Burt & Bodine of Cambridge," *The Motor Age* reported in August, "and the grounds have been laid off preparatory to beginning work at once." This venture seems to have stalled before manufacture began.

NEW DEPARTURE — The New Departure Manufacturing Company of Bristol, Connecticut was producer of the Houpt (1909) and Houpt-Rockwell (1910) cars. The automobiles were never marketed under the New Departure name. Refer to Houpt/Houpt-Rockwell.

NEW ENGLAND — The New England Automobile Equipment Company was organized in Boston, Massachusetts late in 1906 with a capital stock of $10,000 for the manufacture of motor cars, power boats and accessories. Incorporators were Henry M. Wing and John B. Sullivan, Jr. Manufacture of an automobile is doubted.

The New England Automobile Manufacturing Company was organized in Massachusetts during the spring of 1906 with plans to locate in Woodville. "A disused factory building" had been purchased there, according to *The Motor World*, for the manufacture of gasoline pleasure and commercial vehicles, with the expected output to be 2000 cars per year. The unexpected appears to have followed, however, and manufacture never began.

The New England Cycle Company of Keene, New Hampshire was owned by Harry T. Kingsbury, who built a car in 1900. Refer to Kingsbury.

The New England Motor Cycle Company of Boston, Massachusetts was indicated as an automobile manufacturer in the Hiscox book *Horseless Vehicles, Automobiles, Motor Cycles* published in 1900. Further documentation is lacking. A company of that name is not listed in turn-of-the-century Boston city directories.

1899 New England, runabout, NAHC

NEW ENGLAND STEAM — **Boston & Waltham, Massachusetts** — **(1898-1899)** — The New England Motor Carriage Company was incorporated in February of 1898 by Alfred N. Goodhue, W.P. Burnell, Charles A. Skerry, William A. Ingham and Francis M. Young. Offices were leased at 31 State Street in Boston. Elsewhere in the city the first prototype steam carriage was built, and the firm was said to be engaged in completing an electric. Capital stock in the venture was a cool million dollars. What production followed was of the steam car only, a 600-pound runabout powered by two small high-pressure engines. Gasoline was used for fuel, with the gasoline tank placed about three feet ahead of the boiler. The car was lever steered. In May of 1899 the company moved into permanent manufacturing quarters in Waltham. In September the manufacture of Comet bicycles was launched, and the automobile department was sold off to Stanton. This progression was quite the reverse of most manufacturers of the day.

NEW ENGLAND ELECTRIC — **Boston, Massachusetts** — **(1899-1901)** / **Camden, New Jersey** — **(1899-1901)** — The New England Electric Vehicle Company at 541 Tremont Street in Boston and the New England Electric Vehicle Transportation Company in Camden were offshoots of the Electric Vehicle Company of Hartford, Connecticut. Some of New England's cars were produced in Hartford, the larger delivery versions mostly, the New England factories in Boston and Camden concentrating upon smaller passenger automobiles, including the three-wheeler designed by Charles Barrows from whom manufacturing rights were obtained. Initially, the New England product was offered on a lease basis only. In May of 1901 the Boston Company began "offering to sell at private sale its electric vehicles, and solicits an examination of them." The Camden Company followed suit a few months later, disposing of about ninety cabs, broughams and delivery wagons, its entire stock of vehicles. By 1902 both the Boston and Camden factories had been shut down.

NEW ERA — New Era was to be the name of the automobile produced by the Charles A. Balton Engineering Corporation of Buffalo, New York in 1919. Refer to Balton.

The New Era Automobile Company was a $300,000 Maine incorporation from the spring of 1900 organized by W.P. Burrell, A. Pennington, J.R. McLean, A.J. Diamond, H.L. Cramm, W.H. Abbott and O.B. French. Manufacture is doubted.

The New Era Motor Company of Boston, Massachusetts was indicated as an automobile manufacturer in the Hiscox book *Horseless Vehicles, Automobiles, Motor Cycles* published in 1900. Further documentation is lacking. The only firm listed in turn-of-the-century Boston city directories with a similar name was the New Era Carbonator Company.

The New Era Motor and Manufacturing Company was organized in Lansing, Michigan late in 1911 with a capital stock of $50,000 for the manufacture of automobiles. Incorporators were William R. Smith, George Gilmore and John Scheidegger. Manufacture is doubted. George Gilmore had previously built automobiles in Detroit. Refer to Gilmore.

998

1902 New Era, runabout, NAHC

NEW ERA — **Camden, New Jersey** — **(1901-1902)** — Shortly after the turn of the century, the Automobile & Marine Power Company decided to advance out of the manufacture of engines and into the production of automobiles. The automobile produced was called New Era, but it scarcely epitomized that. The car was a runabout with a 7 hp motor under the seat, a buggy-type dash, center tiller steering, side crank, chain drive, and wooden wheels. It weighed 950 pounds and was priced at $700, quickly raised to $850. The New Era was over by the end of 1902.

1916 New Era, Simplicity, touring, WLB

NEW ERA — **Joliet, Illinois** — **(1916)** — The New Era Engineering Company of Joliet was organized in mid-1915 by Forrest J. Alvin, with assistance from James P. Buckley, Winthrop Burdick and W.J. Burdick. Alvin, formerly a United States court reporter and more recently a salesman with the American Ever-Ready Company, was New Era's president and he talked W.O. Dayton into resigning his engineering post with the Crusader Motor Car Company in town to join him. This couldn't have required much persuasion, since Crusader was well on its way out of business by now anyway. The car Dayton designed for New Era was a small 16 hp four on a 104-inch wheelbase. It had thermo-syphon cooling, multiple disc clutch, Allis-Chalmers starting and lighting, Atwater-Kent ignition — and was not very much unlike the Crusader. It survived just about as long. In July of 1916 the assets and the factory of the New Era Engineering Company were purchased by the Elgin Motor Car Corporation. Where Dayton proceeded next is not known, but Alvin immediately took himself up north to Harvey, where he tried again with a new car called the Geneva.

1916 NEW ERA
Four — 16 hp. 104" wb

	FP	5	4	3	2	1
Simplicity Tour.-5P	650	2500	3500	5000	8500	18,000
Simplicity Rdstr.-2P	600	2400	3400	4800	8000	17,000

1934 New Era, sedan, MVMA

NEW ERA — New York, New York — (1933-1934) — With chassis by Ford, body by LeBaron, the New Era was an $850 taxi, $975 sedan and $1040 limousine produced by New Era Motors Corporation of 1775 Broadway in New York City. The taxi was the largest seller — advertised in *Ford Dealer & Service Field* as the antithesis of the "expensive, over-weight, 'gas eating' cabs" of the past which had been rendered obsolete by "the economic upheaval of 1929." Among new owners of the New Era seven-passenger sedan was Mrs. Eddie Cantor. Most New Era sales were probably in the Metropolitan New York area. This New Era venture should not be confused with the company of the same name organized a few years earlier by Archie Andrews which was the sponsoring organization for production of the front-wheel-drive Ruxton.

1933-1934 NEW ERA

	FP	5	4	3	2	1
Taxicab	850	2500	3500	5000	8500	18,000
Sedan	975	1800	2800	4000	6200	13,000
Limousine	1040	3000	4000	6000	9500	21,000

NEW HAVEN — The New Haven Carriage Company of the Connecticut city of that name received the most lucrative contract in the industry at the turn of the century: one-half of an order for 4200 electric automobile bodies. "No such contract as this was ever made before," *The Automobile* reported in the fall of 1899. "It indicates that the business is getting on to a substantial basis, and it ought to be sufficient to convince those who have long been talking about Automobilism as being a fad, that it has long since passed that stage of experience." The other half of the contract was awarded by the Electric Vehicle Company to its automobile-building subsidiary, the Columbia Automobile Company, of Hartford. A two-year period was allowed for fulfillment of the contract. Although indicated on various rosters as an automobile builder, New Haven produced only coachwork and continued in business until the mid-Twenties. It was a major supplier to Rolls-Royce of America during its early years. New Haven designer Collis O. Beck subsequently left to head the American Rolls-Royce body department and then continued with Brewster following its absorption by Rolls-Royce of America.

NEW HOME — New Home was the designation under which the Grout Brothers marketed their steam car in Orange, Massachusetts from 1899 through 1901. Thereafter the cars were called simply Grout, and they were produced to 1912. Refer to Grout.

NEW JERSEY — Four companies carrying the name New Jersey were organized with the expressed intention of building automobiles but these ventures appear to have died before the building of a single car.
The New Jersey Automobile Company of Irvington, organized with a capital stock of $50,000 early in 1907. Incorporators were Alexander M. Brummer, William F. Underwood and Frederick W. Tidey.
The New Jersey Automobile and Supply Company of Camden, organized with a capital stock of $125,000 during the fall of 1911. Incorporators were H. Morgan Hatch, J.R. Mick and Wilfred B. Wolcott.
The New Jersey Motor Company of Rutherford, organized during the spring of 1908 with a capital stock of $10,000. Incorporators were H.W. Kuhl, W.E. Walter and J.P. Walter.
The New Jersey Touring Car Company of Atlantic City, organized with a capital stock of $60,000 late in 1905.

NEW LONDON — In 1895 the New London Specialty Company of New London, Ohio was a prosperous manufacturer of wood carving instruments and probably should have stuck with what it knew. In that year, however, the firm announced that it had "perfected a petroleum bicycle" which it would market for the 1896 trade. Why New London has appeared as an automobile maker on so many lists is something of a mystery, because the only automotive vehicle built was a motorcycle — and the cost of getting it to market practically broke the company. In 1898 it was reported that the Ward-Stilson Company had rented the Specialty shops to make typewriter ribbons.

NEW MADISON — The New Madison Garage Company was organized in Chicago, Illinois during the spring of 1916 with a capital stock of $2500 "to manufacture, sell and deal in motor cars." Incorporators were W.E. Stevens, W.S. Lewis, A.J. Ratty and J.O. Harvey. Manufacture is doubted.

NEW MONARCH — New Monarch was the designation in 1904 for the car which had been sold as the Monarch in 1903 by the Milwaukee Motor Manufacturing Company. Refer to Monarch.

NEW ORLEANS — The product of the New Orleans Cyclecar Company, Ltd., which was organized early in 1914 in Louisiana, was marketed as the Mino. Refer to Mino.

NEW ORLEANS — New Orleans, Louisiana — (1906) — T.W. Castleman of New Orleans was the organizer and W.L. Judson of Chicago was described as the "practical man" of the New Orleans Autocar and Boat Company which was incorporated in Louisiana in February 1906 with a capital stock of $250,000 for the manufacture of automobiles and launches and gasoline engines for launches. Dixie Motor and Boat Company was another designation under which this venture was organized. The firm's specialty was to be a car designed specifically for the muddy roads of that part of the country, its special feature the fact that final drive would not be by chain but by a wire cable enclosed in flax. The company is known to have raised about $60,000 of its capitalization, enough possibly for the building of a prototype. But then the New Orleans Autocar and Boat Company sank.

NEW PARRY — The New Parry was the 1911 successor to the car which had sold in Indianapolis, Indiana in 1910 as the Parry. The car seems to have been "new" only in its higher price tag. Refer to Parry.

NEW PITTSBURGH — Although New Pittsburgh has appeared on occasional rosters as the name of the car produced in 1915 by The Motors Company of Pittsburgh, Pennsylvania, the automobile in actuality was the Pennsy. Refer to Pennsy.

NEW POWER — Trenton, New Jersey — (1897-1898) — Lewis B. White was the mechanical engineer for the New Power Company. The "new power" was carbonic acid, and White had invented a motor utilizing it. "The liquid gas is to be stored in the tubular frame of the vehicle," *The Horseless Age* explained in August 1897, "and maintained at a standard temperature of 90 degrees by means of a flame generated from 'sestalit,' a well-known patent fuel, a small quantity of which will last for twenty-four hours." The motor, which weighed just seventy pounds and was said to generate 15 hp at a very high (for the period) 2000 rpm, was placed on the frame of a wagon and connected with the rear axle by means of a telescopic rod. One lever was used for steering and regulating speed, another for reversing the motor. New Power's experimental vehicle was already on the road, and the company was planning to build forty more and to establish a taxicab plant in New York City which would supply the liquid gas at a central station. "The acid will be drawn off from the storage tanks like water," the company said. The people behind the New Power Company, in addition of course to Lewis White, included Leon Abbett as president, John Briggs as secretary and treasurer, and William L. Howard of the Howard Cycle Company in Trenton who would serve as superintendent of wagon construction. Whether the forty cabs were built is not known, but probably they were not. The October 1898 edition of *The Horseless Age* reported that Lewis B. White's invention had now been taken over by the Industrial Investment and Development Company of 1123 Broadway in New York City, and this firm was now planning the same forty-cab program New Power had announced the year before. In April 1899, Lewis White himself was organizing yet another firm, the White Motor Wagon Company with offices across the street at 1128 Broadway, and a capital stock of a cool $10 million. White and his carbonic acid carriage disappeared from public print after that. Meanwhile William L. Howard had returned to his own endeavors, which included building a car under his own name in Trenton.

NEW ROCHELLE — New Rochelle, New York — (1903) — In April of 1903 Clifford Bonneville filed the papers which officially designated his New Rochelle Motor Company as a corporation for the manufacture of automobiles and power boats. Shortly thereafter he moved the company into its newly erected three-story building at 55 Boston Road. Less than three months later — on July 28th — fire broke out. It started near a dynamo in the basement, with the flames leaping so high they were seen as far away as Larchmont where the local fire chief gathered a dozen Larchmont volunteers and hurried to the scene to assist the New Rochelle Fire Department. The factory was wood framed and tar roofed, and didn't last long. Two scorched automobiles were pulled from the burning building. Fourteen automobiles and two steam launches inside, as well as ultimately the building itself, were reduced to ashes. Fifty thousand dollars had gone up in smoke that night, Clifford Bonneville estimating the overall loss to the company at about $225,000. He was insured for only $14,000. Details regarding the cars that had been built in the factory are lacking. Though Bonneville stated at the time that he would build anew, and a brick factory this time, he did not do so, leaving New Rochelle the year following instead. Subsequently, in 1909, there was a New Rochelle Motor Car Company which came to town, but Bonneville was not involved and that venture operated as a dealership only.

NEW SOUTH — During the summer of 1910, the New South Automobile Company was organized to manufacture cars in Augusta, Georgia. Its capital stock was $1,000,000 of which very little must have been paid in. Whether pipe dream or stock scheme, this venture died aborning, probably before the completion of a single prototype. The *Augusta Chronicle* mentions the New South Automobile Company not at all, nor does it appear in the city directory or local histories of the period.

NEW WAY — Lansing, Michigan — (1905-1907) — William H. Newbrough and Charles H. Way were the two principals behind the New Way Motor Company which was reorganized from the Clarkmobile Company of Lansing on January 23rd, 1905. Of the $100,000 at which the new venture was capitalized, almost half was paid up, there having been $44,800 in patents and other property that Clarkmobile turned over to New Way. Newbrough would serve as treasurer and manager of the company, Way as mechanical engineer and the designer of an air-cooled engine which essentially was the *raison d'etre* for this venture. One A.C. Stebbins, who probably put up a good deal of the money, was installed as New Way's president. Although some automobiles were produced by the New Way Motor Company, it would appear that these were simply the old Clarkmobile chassis into which the New Way air-cooled engine was fitted. Motor manufacture was the company's predominant production. New Way automobiles were built into 1907. New Way engines until late 1908. The company apparently faltered thereafter. Charles H. Way joined Motor Wheel Corporation in 1909 and remained with that firm for over two decades.

NEW WILLAR — Lebanon, Pennsylvania — (1909) — In July of 1909 G.W. Hall of Lebanon announced that he was about to undertake manufacture of an automobile known as the New Willar. The factory at Twelfth and Warner streets which had previously been the home of the Acme Motor Company was then being considered as the new home for the New Willar. There is no indication the car moved into that factory, or any other. Probably only a prototype was built.

NEW YORK — The New York Auto Car Company was organized with a capital stock of $30,000 during the spring of 1903 for the manufacture of vehicles. Incorporators were Bernard Uhren, John Lurie and James J. Head, all of Manhattan. Manufacture of a car is doubted.

The New York Auto Sales Company was organized in New York City early in 1907 with a capital stock of $1000 "to manufacture vehicles and parts thereof." Incorporators were E.P. Billin and I.L. Bowder. Manufacture of a car is doubted.

The New York Automobile Company was organized in Westfield, New Jersey during the spring of 1900 with a capital stock of $200,000. Incorporators were Charles G. Bliss, Frank R. Slade, Edward Rode, M.J. Hester and Henry B. Shute. Manufacture of an automobile is doubted.

The New York Automobile Devices Company, Inc. was organized in New York City early in 1914 with a capital stock of $250,000 for the manufacture and sale of automobiles and supplies. Incorporators were W. Boyd, W.I.N. Lofland and W.F.P. Lofland. Manufacture of a car is doubted.

The New York Carriage Company of East Orange, New Jersey was organized during the fall of 1903 with a capital stock of $50,000 for the manufacture of automobiles. Incorporators were James B. Richardson, Walter H. Bond and Gardner W. Kimball. Manufacture of a car is doubted.

The New York Electric Vehicle Transportation Company of New York City was indicated as a manufacture of automobiles in the Hiscox book *Horseless Vehicles, Automobiles, Motor Cycles* published in 1900. Further documentation is lacking. The firm was listed in the 1899 New York City directory at 1634 Broadway, with further locations opened the year following at 541 Fifth Avenue and 820 Eighth Avenue. The likelihood is that this company functioned as an automobile leasing organization and did not itself manufacture automobiles.

The New York Garage Company was organized in East Orange, New Jersey during the fall of 1903 with a capital stock of $50,000 "to build and deal in motor vehicles and engines." Incorporators were James B. Richardson, Walter H. Bond and Gardner W. Kimball. Manufacture of an automobile is doubted.

The New York Kerosene Oil Engine Company of 31 Burling Slip in New York City was indicated as an automobile manufacturer in the Hiscox book *Horseless Vehicles, Automobiles, Motor Cycles* published in 1900. Further documentation is lacking. The firm had been incorporated purportedly for the manufacture of automobiles, and it is known to have owned the engine patents of one Feodor C. Hirsch. Although the firm evolved into the New York Kerosene Automobile Company, it is believed engines only resulted from this venture which was out of business by 1906.

The New York Motor Car Company was organized in New York City early in 1905 with a capital stock of $25,000 for the manufacture of automobiles. Incorporators were A.S. McMurtry, H.W. Pratt and G. Lamberty. Manufacture is doubted. Alden S. McMurtry was well known in New York City at the turn of the century as the agent for the Packard automobile built in Warren, Ohio.

The New York Motor Vehicle Company was organized in Brooklyn during the summer of 1900, but did not proceed into vehicle manufacture until 1902. The car produced was a steamer called the Volomobile. Refer to Volomobile.

The New York Motor Works was organized in New York City late in 1911 with a capital stock of $70,000 for the manufacture of automobiles and engines. Incorporators were M.L. Rogers and S.E. Roberson. Manufacture of a car is doubted.

The New York & Ohio Company was the sponsoring organization which produced the first Packard automobiles from 1899 to September 10th, 1900 when the firm's name changed to Ohio Automobile Company and subsequently in October of 1902 to Packard Motor Car Company, which it remained until its demise in the late Fifties. Refer to Packard.

The New York Wagon Company, Inc. was organized during the summer of 1899 with a capital stock of $25,000 and the plan "to include motor vehicles among its manufactures." Behind this venture were Isaac A. Remsen (described as a "prominent carriage dealer of Brooklyn") and Everett A. Cooper and Frank Carlough. Manufacture of a car is doubted.

NEW YORK — New York & Syracuse, New York — (1900-1901) — The New York Automobile Company evolved from the partnership of John Wilkinson, Fred D. and Ernest I. White, and Arthur R. Peck. The firm was organized in New York City, and some experimental work was conducted there, but operations moved up to Syracuse within months where the prototype was completed. According to *The Motor Review* of July 25th, 1901, the first vehicle was then being tested on Syracuse streets. "It is reported that the company will get to work in a short time, and put its machine on the market," the magazine said. Not quite. Two air-cooled cars to Wilkinson's designs were completed, but Wilkinson was not paid for his work. Understandably nettled at this, he began looking elsewhere and joined forces with another Syracuse native named H.H. Franklin, who thought an air-cooled car was a good idea too. The New York Automobile Company was subsequently absorbed by H.H. Franklin, but not without a fight. The firm sued Franklin for patent infringement and the hiring of Wilkinson, but lost the case, as well as the two appeals that followed.

NEW YORK — Kingston, New York — (1907) — The New York Car & Truck Company was organized with a capital stock of $2.5 million by J.H. Turner, H.S. Rossell and T.S. Strong, Jr. during the spring of 1906 for the manufacture of "railway and street cars, carriages, automobiles, omnibuses and other vehicles." A factory for all this was secured in Kingston. The company's automobile arrived for 1907, a high-class, high-powered four-cylinder tourabout designed by Walter C. Allen, the foreign car importer at 3 West 44th Street in New York City. The new New York, the company said, was "fully equal in mechanical construction, finish and luxury of appointments to any European built machine, [and] could be sold for about half the price of the foreign productions simply because of the 45 percent import duty on automobiles." Early in 1908 the New York Car and Truck Company collapsed, probably under the weight of its own ambition. Walter C. Allen, whose import emporium was independent of the New York venture, took over the Kingston factory and continued the car in production as the Allen-Kingston.

NEW YORK ROADSTER — Canastota, New York — (1910) — The New York Roadster was the idea of J.E. Roantree and Cleon E. Clark of Canastota, and they proceeded as far as a prototype of their air-cooled two-cylinder two-stroke 12 hp car. Though they announced their intention to enter "the market shortly" in March 1910, apparently they never secured the capital to do so.

1928 New York Six, sedan, KM

NEW YORK SIX — Illinois, Indiana & Maryland — (1927-1928) — Actually, it was a pretty good idea. The invention of Villor P. Williams was called the Parkmobile, a set of small wheels mounted under a car which would hydraulically raise it and allow it to roll sideways into a parking space and thus avoid the usual maneuvering necessary to get into a parallel spot. That it operated "through the regular gearshift lever in conjunction with an extra lever operated from the transmission" was the only explanation offered as to its *modus operandi*, and although ease of parking was its only widely touted feature, and had a comic aspect, the device could have proved useful for changing tires, putting on or removing chains, or simply keeping the car off the ground if laid up for an extended period. But all this was not to be. Initially, Villor Williams organized New York Motors in Moline, Illinois for manufacture of the device, first fitting it to a Velie, that car being a Moline product. But a few months later the self-parking device turned up in Baltimore, Maryland as the product of the Parkmobile Corporation, but it didn't remain there long either. By now, another company, Automotive Corporation of America had taken over New York Motors. Thus far, Villor Williams had organized three companies, and only had one Parkmobile-equipped car (the Velie) to show for it. Next, plans he had for manufacture in the Moller factory in Hagerstown, Maryland fell through. Then, finally, in February 1928, Williams purchased the foundering George W. Davis Motor Car Company of Richmond, Indiana. At last he had a car for his Parkmobile. The New York Six name was to be retained for the former Davis Six. And a Davis Eight was also to be Parkmobile-equipped. A few cars were built with the device, but obviously the Parkmobile proved to be a gimmick and not a breakthrough.

NEWARK — The Newark Motor Car Company was organized in New Jersey early in 1906 with a capital stock of $100,000 for the manufacture of "automobiles, locomotive and other motor vehicles." Incorporators were Peter Broderson of Newark, James F. Kelly of Orange and George F. Walters of East Orange. Manufacture of a car is doubted.

The Newark Motor Car Company was organized in New Jersey early in 1910 with a capital stock of $50,000 for the manufacture of automobiles and motorcycles. Incorporators were J.M. Schwerin, F. Dudley and A.A. Russell. Manufacture of a car is doubted.

The Newark Motor Vehicle Company was organized in New Jersey during the summer of 1901 with a capital stock of $100,000 for the manufacture of automobiles. Incorporators were F.K. Irving, H.C. Hess and L.D.H. Gilmore. Manufacture of a car is doubted.

NEWARK — Newark, New Jersey — (1924) — "Newark...Cradle of the First Steam Locomotive...now the Birthplace of the First Practical Steam Auto." No false modesty here, just horrific overstatement. The Newark Steam Auto Corporation was located at 20 Clinton Street in Newark and promised all sorts of things. To wit — a new suction-type burner mixing fuel and air and incapable of carbonizing; a flash-type boiler with coiled steel tubing that insured instantaneous steaming and promised no welds and a "non-explosive" guarantee; the flexibility of using fuel oil, kerosene, gasoline or alcohol; a two-cylinder double-acting slide-valve engine which, at 900 rpm, provided 60 miles an hour without vibration. None of the faults of previous steamers would be present in the Newark Steamer. It started from spark and required no pilot light. Sedan models to sell at popular prices were promised for early 1925. "We sell cars not stock," the company boasted. "Representatives wanted all over the Country." How many potential dealers fell for the hype is unknown. So is the number of Newark Steamers built. Doubtless this venture ended at the prototype stage.

NEWCOMB STEAM — New York, New York — (1903 et seqq.) — E.C. Newcomb was a Bostonian who moved to New York City in 1903, settled into offices at 49 Wall Street, and began to search for backing to get into manufacture of a steam car he had invented. It was a neat-looking machine with an absence of the extensive piping so often seen on steam-

1903 Newcomb Steamer, runabout, NAHC

1904 Niagara, runabout, NAHC

ers of the period. A number of its features Newcomb patented. He took the greatest pride in the car's simplicity of operation; "absolutely no hand regulation is required aside from manipulating the throttle," he said. The engine was a single-acting three-cylinder 6 hp unit; the boiler was of coil type without water gauge, "so the necessity of watching this device is avoided." The vehicle weighed 1100 pounds; its water tank was good for a 40-mile range. There seem to have been two companies organized to produce the car: the Newcomb Motor Company in Long Island City in 1905 and the Newcomb Engine Company in Harrison (Westchester County) in 1909. Both ventures were capitalized at $400,000. If automobile manufacture followed either of these organizations, it was minimal. It would appear that Newcomb sold more of his steam engines than ever he did his cars. During his Boston days, he had been associated with Holtzer-Cabot. Among his subsequent inventions was a carburetor used by Simplex among others.

NEWPORT — Newport Motors, Inc. has been indicated on various rosters as the manufacturer of an automobile in New York City in 1920. Documentation is lacking. New York City directories of the period do not include a listing for the Newport company.

NEWPORT — Newport, Rhode Island — (1903) — A. Livington Mason moved to Newport in 1894 and with his son, Earl P. Mason, established the Newport Engineering Works which at the turn of the century advertised itself as "consulting and contracting engineers, machinists and boiler makers, builders and repairers of steam and gas engines, launches and automobiles." The company was located at 359-367 Thames Street on the Harbor Front, and marine engines and motor launches were its specialty. During 1903, however, the Masons did build a few 4 hp gasoline automobiles, "combining French and American designs," they said, and mostly to custom order. Thereafter they returned to their yacht and steamboat work.

NEWTON — T.P. Newton was a machinist in Butte, Montana who during the fall of 1899 was reported by *The Horseless Age* as "the inventor of a gasoline carriage." Further details are lacking.

The J.E. Newton Company was organized in Fall River, Massachusetts late in 1913 with a capital stock of $50,000 to "manufacture and repair bicycles, motorcycles and motor cars." Incorporators were James E. Newton, Newton R. Gifford and Fred Crossley. Manufacture of a car is doubted.

The Newton Garage & Automobile Company was a $10,000 Maine incorporation of late 1906 for the manufacture and sale of automobiles. President was N. Clifford, secretary-treasurer was E.C. Verrill.

NIAGARA — The Niagara Motor Car Corporation produced a juvenile car from 1912 to 1914 in Niagara Falls, New York which was marketed as the Lad's Car. Refer to Lad's Car.

NIAGARA — Niagara Falls, New York — (1900-1902) — "Niagara Falls has a new industry. It is an automobile manufacturing plant, and its proprietors are McQuain and Pysher, two practical machinists who have gone in the venture to win." Thus reported the *Niagara Falls Gazette* on September 22nd, 1900. The *Gazette* had jumped the gun a little bit. Two days later, the rival *Daily Cataract-Journal* noted that Thomas McQuain and H.N. Pysher had indeed built an automobile, the first in Niagara Falls, and it had been successfully tested, but the partners, although "jubilant over the success they have attained," hadn't quite made it to the manufacturing stage. Their car was a 4 hp gasoline runabout with accommodation for four passengers. The partners took pains to emphasize their vehicle's advantages over a steamer with its danger of explosion and an electric with its short running range. Still, it was March 29th, 1901 before McQuain (who appears to have left Pysher behind by now) found the financing necessary to establish the Niagara Automobile Company. There had been another firm incorporated under that name in Niagara Falls in 1899 but that one had produced no cars at all. McQuain did proceed into manufacture of his automobile, but its life was short. By early fall of 1902, the Niagara Automobile Company was bankrupt.

NIAGARA — Wilson, New York — (1903-1905) — The Wilson Automobile Manufacturing Company produced a typical small two-passenger runabout. "The truss frame that sustains the motor is pivoted on the front axle, which gives a very flexible running gear," *Cycle and Automobile Trade Journal* noted in January 1904. "Any of the wheels can be removed by merely taking off the dust cap and end nut. The axles are of great strength, the rear axle being of one piece. The arrangement of operating levers is very convenient, and the steering wheel tilts." The car was started from the driver's seat, and there was an auxiliary seat folding down from the dash. Although occasionally referred to in the trade press by the company name, Wilson itself preferred to call its car the Niagara. Its single-cylinder engine developed 5 hp from 1903-1904, upped to 8 hp for 1905, the final year of production. In the spring of 1905 the LaSalle-Niagara Automobile Company took over the assets and equipment of the Wilson firm and proceeded to build its own car called the LaSalle-Niagara.

1903-1904 NIAGARA

	FP	5	4	3	2	1
Rbt. (1-cyl., 5 hp)	850	1600	2700	3800	5800	12,000
1905 NIAGARA						
Rbt. (1-cyl., 8 hp, 78" wb)	900	1700	2800	3900	6000	12,500

NIAGARA — Buffalo & Dunkirk, New York — (1913) — This Niagara is a puzzlement. The Niagara Motors Manufacturing Company was organized in early 1913 in Buffalo, but by March had moved to Dunkirk. Its first car was completed that month and was shipped to a customer in New Orleans. According to the December 3rd, 1913 edition of *The Automobile*, the Dunkirk plant had by that time been shut down. "The local board of trade is said to have promised to arrange for stock subscriptions," *The Automobile* advised, "but as the latter were not paid for, according to the company, the plant had to cease operations despite projects of success." Possibly the projects of success referred to was the one sale to New Orleans.

1902 Niagara Electric, runabout, NAHC

NIAGARA ELECTRIC — Buffalo, New York — (1902) — In December of 1901 Charles Lindstrom left the Hewitt-Lindstrom company in Chicago and traveled east to build another electric. It fared no better than had his Hewitt-Lindstrom. The Niagara Electric was a light car offered as runabout, road wagon and delivery. The prototype had been completed in a Buffalo machine shop in January 1902, and the Niagara Motor Vehicle Company had been organized shortly thereafter for its manufacture. Minimal production followed, and early that autumn the firm was voluntarily dissolved. Its property and parts were sold at public auction on February 25th, 1904. Meanwhile Charles Lindstrom had taken himself to Towanda, Pennsylvania to build the Towanda Electric.

1916 Niagara Four, 5-pass. touring car, WLB

NIAGARA FOUR — **Buffalo, New York** — **(1915-1916)** — At least three different companies in the Buffalo area were involved in this Niagara automotive venture, but not one of them built the car. Instead, the Niagara Four was manufactured in Elkhart, Indiana by the Crow company, which made it a practice to provide budding entrepreneurs a quick and easy entrance into the automotive field. The Niagara Four was a $740 20 hp open car on a 112-inch wheelbase not unlike the Crow four save for nomenclature and radiator badge. Its sponsor in Buffalo was the Mutual Motor Car Company. Mutual in turn invited the Poppenberg Motor Company, a local dealership, to assist in the marketing — and these two forces were soon irresistibly drawn together as the Niagara Automobile Company. The Wilson company in nearby Wilson, which had built a car of its own a decade earlier, and now was a dealership, apparently considered joining in but then thought better of it. In two years a total of about 500 Niagara Fours were sold.

1915-1916 NIAGARA FOURS
Model C-16 — 4-cyl., 20 hp, 112" wb

	FP	5	4	3	2	1
Tour.-5P	740	2700	3600	5300	8800	19,000
Rdst.-2P	740	2500	3500	5000	8500	18,000

NICHOLS — The A.B. Nichols Company was organized in New York City during the fall of 1906 with a capital stock of $25,000 for the manufacture of motor cars. Joining Nichols in the venture were J.W. Richter and J.F. Taylor. Manufacture of an automobile is doubted.

NICHOLS — **Boston, Massachusetts** — **(1908)** — The car built by D.P. Nichols & Company of 116-122 West Brookline Street in Boston was a convertible with a difference. A vehicle which doubled as a light delivery/touring car was a commonplace during this period; the Nichols, however, did duo duty as an ambulance and limousine. When in the latter mode, it was provided with a cot, pneumatic mattress and assorted medical paraphernalia; with those accoutrements removed, it became a spacious eight-passenger canopied tourer. "This car is intended for hospital and private service, where patrons wish to avoid the conspicuousness of an ordinary ambulance," explained *The Automobile*. Possibly too, being sick with style had a certain appeal, or so the Nichols company hoped. One of these cars, built to the order of J.M. Duggan, is known to have been built. Possibly a few more were as well.

1925 Nichols, roadster, FR

NICHOLS — **Waltham, Massachusetts** — **(1925)** — Arthur Nichols, his father and a number of machinists of the W.H. Nichols Company of Waltham built this front-wheel-drive roadster in 1925. In essence, it was a college assignment. A student at M.I.T., Arthur Nichols had chosen front-wheel-drive mechanisms as his thesis topic, building one for testing purposes being an integral part of it. A Model T Ford was thusly converted. Actually, two cars were built, the second for Arthur's brother who lent it to a friend, the friend smashing it into a pole which ended that car's life. The first car remains extant and is owned by Arthur Nichols' son.

NICHOLS & SHEPARD — **Battle Creek, Michigan** — **(1910-1911)** — The Nichols & Shepard Company of Battle Creek had been in the farm implement business since shortly after the Civil War. The firm was early to mechanize, using a portable steam engine designed along the lines of "Macomber's Marvel" (the steam powerplant invented by Richard Merritt and Dan Kellogg of Battle Creek) which had first been successfully tested in 1873. Seeing a Nichols & Shepard steam thresher in 1876 left an indelible impression on one young boy; a photograph of the machine hung in the office of Henry Ford for years, a reminder of the vehicle which had first interested him in the idea of mechanized transport. In addition to threshers and other farm implements, the Nichols & Shepard Company built a gasoline automobile from 1910 to 1911. This was strictly a sideline activity, and production was minimal. State motor vehicle department records for the period indicate at least one Nichols & Shepard registered in Michigan.

NICHOL-WINCKELHOFER — The Nichol-Winckelhofer Company was organized in Newark, New Jersey during the fall of 1910 with a capital stock of $25,000 to manufacture and deal in motor cars and supplies. The partners involved were James Douglas Nichol and August A. Winckelhofer. Manufacture of an automobile is doubted.

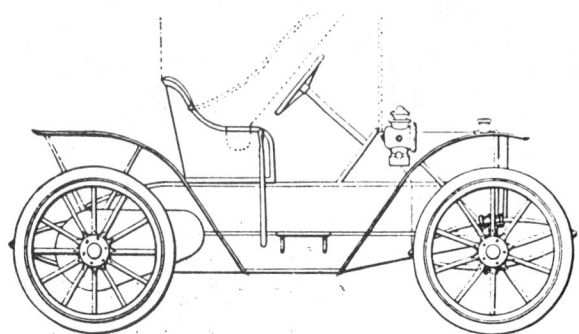

1907 Nielson, model 7, runabout, NAHC

NIELSON — **Detroit, Michigan** — **(1906-1907)** — Although occasional references indicate the spelling to be Neilson, the vast preponderance of trade press articles in 1906 and 1907 refer to the Nielson Motor Car Company. The firm was incorporated early in 1906 to produce a single-cylinder air-cooled 12 hp runabout on an 84-inch wheelbase with friction transmission and double chain drive. A prototype truck was also built by June of '06, but it did not go into production. The number of Nielsons produced may only have been one as well. A January 1908 reference in *The Horseless Age* noted that the car's designer, E.A. Nielson, had recently driven his runabout to New York City and had exhibited it in the Selzer garage. Earlier references indicate Nielson's former work with the Packard company. An Emil A. Nelson had worked for Packard, as well as Olds Motor Works. If this was the same man, immediately after the failure of his runabout, Nielson/Nelson joined the new Hupp Motor Car Corporation in Detroit, and was subsequently responsible for the design of the Hupmobile 20 and 32 and in 1917 for another car of his own called the Nelson.

1906-1907 NIELSON
Model No. 7 — 1-cyl., 12 hp, 84" wb

	FP	5	4	3	2	1
Rbt.	800	1600	2700	3800	5800	12,000

NIKE — The Nike was one of two models produced by the Detroit-Dearborn Motor Car Company in 1910. Refer to Detroit-Dearborn. Nike was also among the models of the American Napier produced from 1904-1910. Refer to American Napier.

NILES — The Niles Automobile and Gas Engine Company was organized in Niles, Michigan during the spring of 1903 with a capital stock of $25,000. "The company expects to employ 100 skilled mechanics, and will build automobiles under contract," *The Motor Age* reported in May. Documentation of actual manufacture has not been discovered.

The Niles Auto & Machine Company was organized in Niles, Ohio late in 1913 "to repair and build motor cars." Incorporators were H.A. Wilson and R.G. Adams. Manufacture of an automobile is doubted.

"The Niles Automobile Company are to erect a factory in Evansville, Indiana," *The Horseless Age* reported in November 1904. Further word was not heard.

NISWENDER — **Trotwood, Ohio** — **(1903)** — "Roman Niswender of Trotwood has built an automobile said to have several superior points and he is now looking for a manufacturer to handle it" was the total report provided by *The Motor Age* in May 1903 regarding this Ohioan's hope for automotive glory which appears to have ended soon after the announcement.

NOBLE — **Cleveland, Ohio** — **(1902)** — The story was datelined September 28th, 1902, and it indicated that the Noble Automobile Manufacturing Company of Cleveland would "shortly enter the field of active manufacturers." The company's factory was at 1174 Hamilton Street, and experimentation had been ongoing for some months. Although larger cars were promised for the future, production initially was to be confined to a single-cylinder 6½ hp runabout to sell for $800. One of the Noble chassis had already been custom-built for a scissors grinder in Washington, D.C. who planned to adapt it into a portable workshop with "the paraphernalia of his trade and the grindstones...operated by belts from the extended engine shaft." The man behind the Noble company was elsewhere reported to be

J.C. Meader, and he saw a bright future for himself in the commercial field if the scissors grinder in the District of Columbia made a viable working vehicle of the Noble chassis. Apparently a few runabouts were produced, and perhaps an example or two of a 10 hp two-cylinder touring car. But this Noble venture ended almost as quickly as it was begun. Later in October the company was attached for back wages, and that was the last heard of it.

NOBLE — Detroit, Michigan — (1914 et seq.) — Although no manufactured automobile bore his name, Warren Noble was responsible for a number of prototypes built under contract for various manufacturers. A native of Great Britain, he had been a gynecologist in Dublin prior to emigrating to the United States to become an automotive engineer. Among his clients during his years in Detroit as a member of the consulting engineering firm of Noble & Harris were Walter E. Flanders, John N. Willys and Henry Ford. During the Thirties he served as Supreme Director of Industrialization for the Union of Socialist Soviet Republics and later as consultant to Rumanian automakers. Prior to World War II his experiments included the design and development of a detachable power unit for automobiles. He died in Amityville, New York in 1950 at the age of sixty-five.

NOEL DUPLEX — Jersey City, New Jersey — (1923) — The Noel Duplex promised to be quite a car. Among its numerous features were these: air-cooled valveless engine operating on compressed air and gasoline, four-wheel drive and steering with the latter controlled by both the exhaust and compressed air, air cylinders replacing the usual spring suspension system, air-pressure lever substituting for foot pedal and steering wheel, sliding doors and disappearing steps, parlor car comfort in circassian walnut or mahogany with velour upholstery, speeds of up to 150 mph, fuel economy of 50 miles per gallon. The Noel Duplex was the idea of the J.C.N. Noel Motor Car Company of Jersey City, which was capitalized in 1923 at $10 million. Reporting on its stock-selling efforts, the National Vigilance Committee in its *Truth-in-Advertising Bulletin* commented that the car "appears well on paper" but "no mention is made of the price to be asked or is any assurance of production given." The Noel Duplex undoubtedly never left the paper upon which its incredible specifications were printed.

1919 Noma, roadster, WLB

NOMA — New York, New York — (1919-1923) — Noma Motors Corporation had its factory at 155 Avenue D on the Lower East Side of New York City and the pilot model of its car ready for the New York Automobile Show in January 1919. The Noma was the only new marque on display at the show, and was occasionally misspelled as the Norma. It was an assembled car (Continental or Beaver six-cylinder engines would be fitted) distinguished by its handsome and low-slung coachwork. In essence, Noma was a subsidiary of the Walton Body Company, the founders of the former being officials of the latter. During the war Walton had turned its entire factory facilities over to the production of airplane wings for the government, and as a result of this experience, lightness with strength became the company's aim for the Noma. Its body frame was laminated wood covered with aluminum. The car's wheelbase of 128 inches was exceptionally long for a car powered by a 55 hp engine, but road performance was good, and the rakish appearance even better. Individual step-plates took the place of running boards, Houk wire wheels were standard, and the car's radiator was distinctive. Probably 300 Nomas were built during the marque's half decade of production.

1920 NOMA
Model 1 — 6-cyl., 55 hp, 128" wb

	FP	5	4	3	2	1
Speedster-2P	2600	4300	5400	8700	16,500	30,000
Foursome	2900	3900	4800	7700	14,300	27,000

1921 NOMA
Model C — 6-cyl., 55 hp, 128" wb

Speedster-2P	3000	4300	5400	8700	16,500	30,000
Foursome	3200	3900	4800	7700	14,300	27,000

1922 NOMA
Model C — 6-cyl., 55 bhp, 128" wb

Speedster-2P	2000	4300	5400	8700	16,500	30,000
Foursome	2100	3900	4800	7700	14,300	27,000
Touring-6P	2200	4000	5000	8000	15,000	28,000
Sedan-5P	3200	2200	3200	4400	7000	15,000

1923 NOMA
Model C — 6-cyl., 55 bhp, 128" wb

Speedster-2P	2500	4300	5400	8700	16,500	30,000
Sport-4P	2500	4200	5200	8400	15,700	29,000
Touring-6P	2600	4300	5300	8600	16,100	29,500
Sedan-5P	3500	2200	3200	4400	7000	15,000

NORCROSS — Boston, Massachusetts — (1865) — Among the pioneer steam car inventors in the United States was Captain Alvin C. Norcross who was a native of Bradford, Vermont and who built his vehicle in Boston, Massachusetts in 1865. The car was operated successfully but purportedly "scared Boston traffic so much" that eventually Norcross gave up its use. He died June 1912 of neuralgia of the heart in Boston at age sixty-nine. This car should not be confused with the gasoline car promoted four decades later in Norcross, Georgia which is correctly spelled Nor-X.

NORDYKE — Despite roster appearances, there never was a Nordyke car. The Nordyke & Marmon Company, subsequently the Marmon Motor Car Company, did however produce the esteemed Marmon motorcar from shortly after the turn of the century into the early Thirties. Refer to Marmon.

NORMAN LIONEL — Norman Lionel of 40 State Street in Boston, Massachusetts was listed as the producer of an automobile sleigh in the "Buyers' Guide" section of the *Cycle and Automobile Trade Journal* in 1905. Further documentation is lacking. Secondary references have indicated a Norman Motor Sleigh Company exhibiting at the New York Automobile show in 1905. This is in error. There was an American Motor Sleigh Company which did exhibit at the show, however. This firm was based in Boston, but whether Norman Lionel was involved has not been substantiated.

NORRIS — The Norris Motor Car Company was organized in Cambridge, Massachusetts late in 1908 with a capital stock of $50,000 to manufacture and deal in automobiles and accessories. Wesley S. Young was president. Manufacture of a car is doubted.

NORTH AMERICAN — The North American Motor Corporation was organized in New York City during the summer of 1909 to manufacture "motors, vehicles, boats and motorcycles" in the Stapleton section of Staten Island. Capital stock was $10,000. Among the people behind this venture were Chauncey Cleveland and H. Bernard Layman. Manufacture of an automobile is doubted.

NORTHERN — The Northern Motor Car Company was organized in Albany, New York during the summer of 1912 with a capital stock of $25,000 for the manufacture of automobiles. Arthur P. James and R. Dudley Cannon were the incorporators. Manufacture is doubted.

1904 Northern, touring, HAC

NORTHERN — Detroit & Port Huron, Michigan — (1902-1908) — The Northern Manufacturing Company was organized during the summer of 1902 by Charles B. King and Jonathan D. Maxwell, both alumni of Olds Motors Works. King had built the first successful gasoline automobile in Detroit in 1896, and Maxwell was a whiz of a mechanic who had designed the single-cylinder 5 hp engine that would power the first Northern. Not surprisingly, the car resembled an Olds runabout. Early versions were called Silent Northern; 300 were sold in 1903. A twin followed in 1904, and a four in 1906. "Utility is the Basis of Beauty," read one Northern slogan, "Built for Business" another. The partners were practical men, but they weren't partners for long, Jonathan Maxwell finding Benjamin Briscoe and going off to build his own car in 1904. All engineering thereafter was Charles King's doing. Shaft drive and left-hand steering were progressive features of the early Northern. Air-operated brakes and clutch were featured on the 1906 four, and for 1908 King incorporated all operating controls on the steering column of the limousine model. In 1906 the firm changed its name to Northern Motor Car Company, and in 1907 another plant was opened in Port Huron to manufacture the Northern two-cylinder cars, with the Detroit factory to confine its efforts to the fours. In June of 1908, Northern merged with the Wayne Automobile Company, and soon thereafter E-M-F took over the entire plants and equipment of both Northern and Wayne. Although initial reports indicated that the Northern would be continued in manufacture, it was dropped by December. Charles King had left earlier in the year, with plans to manufacture a car under his own name.

1902-1903 NORTHERN
Single — 5 hp, 68" wb

	FP	5	4	3	2	1
Runabout	800	1800	2800	4000	6200	13,000

1904 NORTHERN
Single — 6-1/2 hp, 67" wb

Runabout-2P	750	1800	2800	4000	6200	13,000

Twin — 15 hp, 88" wb

Touring-5P	1500	2200	3200	4400	7000	15,000

1905 Northern, roadster, WLB

1905 NORTHERN
Single — 7 hp, 70" wb

Runabout-2P	650	2000	3000	4200	6500	14,000

Twin — 18 hp, 88" wb

Touring-2P	1500	2200	3200	4400	7000	15,000

Twin — 17 hp, 100" wb

Touring-5P	1700	2300	3300	4600	7500	16,000
Limo.-5) (102" wb)	2500	2400	3400	4800	8000	17,000

1906 NORTHERN
Single — 7 hp, 70" wb

Runabout	650	2000	3000	4200	6500	14,000

Type C — 2-cyl., 20 hp, 106" wb

Touring-5P	1800	2500	3500	5000	8500	18,000
Limousine-4/5P	2800	2400	3400	4800	8000	17,000
Runabout-2P (88" wb)	1650	2300	3300	4600	7500	16,000

Type K — 4-cyl., 30 hp, 112" wb

Touring-5P	3000	2700	3600	5300	8800	19,000

1907 NORTHERN
Type B — 1-cyl., 7 hp, 70" wb

Runabout-2P	650	2000	3000	4200	6500	14,000

Type C — 2-cyl., 20 hp

Runabout-2P (88" wb)	1600	2200	3200	4400	7000	15,000
Touring-5P (100" wb)	1700	2300	3300	4600	7500	16,000
Touring-5P (106" wb)	1700	2350	3400	4700	7800	16,500
Limousine-5P (106" wb)	3000	2500	3500	5000	8500	18,000

Type L — 4-cyl., 50 hp, 119" wb

Touring-6P	3500	3700	4700	7300	13,700	26,000
Runabout-2P	3500	3500	4500	7000	13,000	25,000
Limousine-6P	4500	4000	5000	8000	15,000	28,000

1908 NORTHERN
Model B — 1-cyl., 7 hp, 90" wb

Runabout	650	2000	3000	4200	6500	14,000

Model C — 2-cyl., 24 hp, 106" wb

Tonneau	1600	2700	3600	5300	8800	19,000
Roadster (100" wb)	1600	2500	3500	5000	8500	18,000
Limousine	2800	2900	3700	5600	9100	20,000

Model L — 4-cyl., 40 hp, 119" wb

Tonneau	3500	3100	4200	6300	10,500	22,000
Roadster	3500	3000	4000	6000	9500	21,000

NORTH JERSEY — The North Jersey Garage was organized in Morristown during the spring of 1909 with a capital stock of $25,000 for the manufacture of automobiles. Incorporators were R.H. Nevins, R.S. Foster, Joseph Van Dyke and Harvey Archer. Manufacture is doubted.

NORTH SHORE — The North Shore Garage Company was organized early in 1909 with a capital stock of $1500 to ''manufacture, repair and lease cars, carriages, wagons and boats'' in Richmond Hill (Queens), New York. Involved in this venture were Philip J. Freund of Tompkinsville, Henry M. Schloss of West New Brighton and Henry Decker of Manhattan. Manufacture of an automobile is doubted.

The North Shore Transfer Company was organized in Boston, Massachusetts during the summer of 1906 with a capital stock of $10,000 to ''manufacture and lease automobiles, carriages and other vehicles.'' Incorporators were C.W. Pierce and William G. Brown, both of Gloucester. Manufacture is doubted.

NORTH STAR — Stillwater, Minnesota — (1909-1910) — The capitalization was $100,000, and the incorporators were Alexander J. Perron, George Johnson, C.E., Mosier, James O'Neal and Roscoe Johnson. It was during the summer of 1909 that the North Star Automobile Company was formed, reportedly in Stillwater, Oklahoma although that seems to have been an editorial error for Minnesota. The company's product was to be a four-cylinder 60 hp touring car with a $2500 price tag, and a companion $1700 runabout. Early in 1910 the North Star Company was heard from again, announcing that ''shop room'' had been secured in the plant of the Northwest Thresher Company in Stillwater. Possibly a prototype was built there, but the North Star never appeared on the market.

1921 Northway, coupe, WLB

NORTHWAY — Natick, Massachusetts — (1921-1922) — Ralph E. Northway arrived in Natick via Detroit (where his engine-producing Northway Company had been taken over by General Motors) and Carthage, Ohio (where he had built the Crescent). Prominent Boston capitalists were behind his new Northway Motors Corporation, which was organized in January 1918 for the manufacture of cars and trucks. A Northway truck was an early arrival in the marketplace, the first Northway car followed in January 1921. Introduced at the Hotel Astor in New York City, it was a 303-cubic-inch 61 hp six on a 128-inch wheelbase and featured a Rolls-Royce-type radiator grille. The price range was $2800-$4950. Assisting Ralph Northway in the car's design was A.J. Romer. The Northway was built into early 1922; the earliest reference to its discontinuation is the May 18th issue that year of *The Automobile*. That article also indicates the reason for the dropping of the Northway: a rather critical need of cash. A cash subscription was to be requested of stockholders, and unfinished trucks were to be completed in the meantime. ''Stockholders Wrangle Over Fate of Northway Motors'' was a 1923 headline. They were still wrangling in 1925 when the company went into irrevocable receivership. Meantime Ralph Northway had left in 1922 to build Maxim fire engines, and A.J. Romer had departed even earlier with plans to produce a car under his own name. The Northway factory was subsequently taken over by the State Quartermaster.

1921-1922 NORTHWAY
Six — 61 hp, 128" wb

	FP	5	4	3	2	1
Touring-6P	3800	5000	6500	11,000	22,000	35,000
Sport-2P	3800	4900	6300	10,300	21,000	34,000
Coupe-4P	4900	2500	3500	5000	8500	18,000
Sed. Lim.-7P	4950	3000	4000	6000	9500	21,000

NORTHWEST — The Northwest Motor Company was organized in Oklahoma City, Oklahoma during the fall of 1910 with a capital stock of $100,000 to manufacture and deal in automobiles and engines. Incorporators were L.R. Weiss, Charles E. Sockler, Charles P. Wickmiller and Earl Worl. Manufacture of a car is doubted.

NORTHWESTERN — The Northwestern Automobile Manufacturing Company of Seattle, Washington has been indicated as the producer of a car in 1914. Documentation is lacking.

The Northwestern Cyclecar Works of Chicago, Illinois produced an automobile in 1914 which was marketed under the name of Logan. Refer to Logan.

The Northwestern Furniture Company of Milwaukee, Wisconsin added an automobile to its product line in 1902. The car was named after the company's president. Refer to Haase.

NORTON — F.G. Norton of Waukegan, Illinois was among the hopefuls who announced the entry of an automobile of his own design in the Chicago Times-Herald Contest of 1895. He did not make it to the starting line, however, and that he ever completed the building of his automobile has not been documented.

1902 Norton, runabout, NAHC

NORTON — Lowell, Massachusetts — (1901-1902) — James J. Norton had been a dealer and repairer of bicycles in Lowell since 1898. In 1901 he devised a single-cylinder 3-1/2 hp four-stroke air-cooled engine which he attached to the front axle of a tiller-steered carriage runabout. Speeds of 6 to 20 mph were claimed. The Norton's total weight was 365 pounds and its price tag $500. Production was minimal; James Norton did not organize a company for manufacture. Subsequently he formed the Auto Tire Vulcanizing Company in Lowell.

1902 Norton Steamer, surrey, NAHC

NORTON STEAM — Torrington, Connecticut — (1902) — According to the April 12th, 1892 edition of the *Torrington Register*, W.P. Norton was "an inventor, skilled draughtsman and practical machinist." Among his recent inventions at the time was a screw-cutting lathe which cut screw threads of different sizes without change of adjustment. In 1892 he joined the Henday Machine Company in Torrington as general superintendant. A decade later he built his steam car, after experiencing problems with the Locomobile he had earlier purchased. The Norton steamer mounted its horizontal two-cylinder engine direct to the differential at the center of the rear axle. That he wasn't particularly happy with this vehicle either is indicated by the fact that he sold it a year or two later, accepting a horse and buggy as part payment. W.P. Norton remained in the machine tool business for the remainer of his career. And he quickly became an automobilist again when he discovered that the horse which had been part of the Norton steamer deal had a habit of rearing up at inopportune moments. W.P. Norton continued to drive automobiles until his death in the 1950's.

1911 Norwalk, model 35, touring, HAC

NORWALK — Norwalk, Ohio — (1910-1911) / Martinsburg, West Virginia — (1912-1922) — The Norwalk Motor Car Company was an outgrowth of the Auto Bug Company, and was organized by Arthur E. Skadden early in 1910 because he recognized the waning marketing potential of his Auto Bug highwheeler. His new company was in trouble almost immediately. That summer rumors were afloat that Skadden was desperately trying "to raise more capital," which obviously he didn't because Norwalk was bankrupt precisely one year later. The company machinery and equipment, including three completed cars and a demonstrator, were acquired by Norwalk's largest creditor, the Model Gas Engine Company of Peru, Indiana. This left Skadden with nothing but his idea for the car, and he took that to Martinsburg, West Virginia where a new set of entrepreneurs took over. Gilbert W. McKown was president, James M. Rothwell vice-president, Charles F. Glaser secretary, Thomas W. Martin treasurer. Skadden ran the new plant. The 251-cubic-inch four that had powered the Norwalks in Norwalk was continued in manufacture, but a six was added to the line immediately — and Norwalks became sixes exclusively in 1913. In 1912 the feature for which Norwalk became most famous — its underslung frame — was introduced. The new 525-cubic-inch 50/70 hp models for 1913 were incredibly potent machines, low and long on 144-inch wheelbases and with four-speed Vulcan electric transmissions (direct in third) which provided for sporting performance. An electric emergency brake was adopted in 1914. "The Car of Absolute Exclusiveness" was a Norwalk slogan; prices were $2750-$3750. But now this company was in trouble too. Norwalk went into receivership in Martinsburg in the fall of 1914; its factory was ordered closed in February 1915 and was sold on April 24th. Though the Martinsburg entrepreneurs departed, the Norwalk Motor Car Company remained, with Skadden taking its helm, assisted by A.E. Clohan and T.G. Coppersmith. They set up shop in a more modest facility down the street from the original factory and occupied themselves "overhauling and paint-

ing," according to the 1915 Martinsburg City Directory. Manufacture of the Norwalk automobile did not resume until 1918, and the new Norwalk was utterly unakin its predecessor. No longer underslung, it was a quite common Lycoming-engined assembled car in the $1000 price range. Norwalk also badge-engineered its automobile to be sold, among others, as the Marshall in Chicago and the Stork-Kar in New York City. Arthur Skadden died in 1919. When the Norwalk Motor Car Company faded into oblivion in October 1922, his widow, Clara Skadden, was its president. Norwalk's last days were filled with intrigue. The company had been making parts for John H.Bush (Bush) and W.A. Taylor (Piedmont). The Bush/Piedmont group, with inside help in Norwalk, began maneuvering a takeover of the Martinsburg Company. Because Bush and Taylor were registered socialist party members, and the Skadden clan were staunch Republicans, Clara would have none of it. She simply dissolved the Norwalk Corporation.

1910 NORWALK
Model 35 — 4-cyl., 35 hp, 117" wb

	FP	5	4	3	2	1
Touring-5P	1700	3100	4200	6300	10,500	22,000
Runabout-2P	1600	3000	4000	6000	9500	21,000

1911 NORWALK
Model 35 — 4-cyl., 35 hp, 117" wb

Touring-4P	1700	3100	4200	6300	10,500	22,000
Torpedo Roadster-2P	1700	3200	4300	6500	11,000	23,000
Touring-5P	1600	3000	4000	6000	9500	21,000
Fore-Door Touring-5P	1700	3100	4200	6300	10,500	22,000

Model 40 — 4-cyl., 40 hp, 117" wb

Torpedo Roadster-2P	1850	3300	4400	6700	12,000	24,000
Torpedo-4P	1850	3300	4400	6700	12,000	24,000
Fore-Door Touring-5P	1850	3300	4400	6700	12,000	24,000

Model 45 — 4-cyl., 45 hp, 117" wb

Torpedo-4P	2150	3500	4500	7000	13,000	25,000
Fore-Door Touring-5P	2150	3500	4500	7000	13,000	25,000
Torpedo Roadster-2P	2150	3500	4500	7000	13,000	25,000

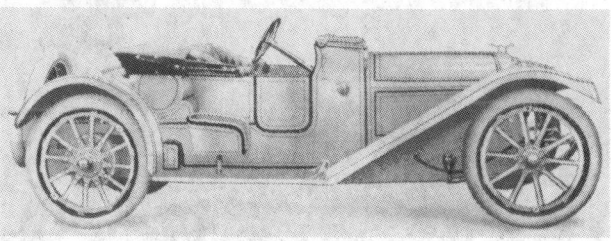

1912 Norwalk Underslung Six, roadster, HAC

1912 NORWALK
Model 45 — 4-cyl., 45 hp, 124" wb

Touring-6P	2150	3900	4800	7700	14,300	27,000
Speedster-2P	—	4200	5200	8400	15,700	29,000

Six — 6-cyl., 38 hp, 136" wb

Touring-6P	2950	4500	5800	9500	18,000	32,000

1913 Norwalk, touring, WLB

1913 NORWALK
Model A — 6-cyl., 40/60 hp, 127" wb

Roadster-2P	2750	4000	5000	8000	15,000	28,000
Touring-5P	2750	4200	5200	8400	15,700	29,000

Model A — 6-cyl., 40/60 hp, 136" wb

Special Roadster-2P	2900	4400	5600	9200	17,300	31,000
Special Tourer-6P	3100	4700	6100	9900	19,000	33,000

Model B — 6-cyl., 50/70 hp, 144" wb

Roadster-2P	3650	5000	6500	11,000	22,000	35,000
Touring-6P	3750	5200	6800	11,300	23,000	36,000

1914 Norwalk, model A, touring, HAC

1914-1915 NORWALK
Model A — 6-cyl., 40/50 hp, 131" wb

	FP	5	4	3	2	1
Touring-5P	2750	4200	5200	8400	15,700	29,000
Roadster-2P	2750	4000	5000	8000	15,000	28,000
Model B — 6-cyl., 40/60 hp, 136" wb						
Enclosed Tourer-4P	3750	4400	5600	9200	17,300	31,000
Enclosed Roadster-4P	3750	4300	5400	8700	16,500	30,000

NOTE: Manufacturing ceased February 1915 and did not resume in 1916 or 1917.

1918 Norwalk, model 4-18, touring, HAC

1918 NORWALK
Model 4-18 — 4-cyl., 35 hp, 116" wb

Touring-5P	875	2900	3700	5600	9100	20,000
Model 6-18 — 6-cyl., 116" wb						
Touring-5P	975	3000	4000	6000	9500	21,000
1919 NORWALK						
Model 4-19 — 4-cyl., 35 hp, 116" wb						
Touring-5P	1065	2900	3700	5600	9100	20,000
1920 NORWALK						
Model 4-30 — 4-cyl., 35 hp, 116" wb						
Touring-5P	—	2900	3700	5600	9100	20,000
1921 NORWALK						
Model 4-30-KS — 4-cyl., 35 hp, 116" wb						
Touring-5P	1035	2900	3700	5600	9100	20,000
1922 NORWALK						
Model 4-40 — 4-cyl., 40 hp, 116" wb						
Touring-5P	1035	3000	4000	6000	9500	21,000

NORWOOD — The Norwood Automobile Company was organized in Cincinnati, Ohio during the late summer of 1905 to manufacture, repair and sell automobiles in Norwood. Behind this $25,000 venture were J.H. Schneider, W.S. Tredway, R.J. Sander, Edward P. Moulinier and William H. Albers. Manufacture is doubted, but the firm is known to have subsequently opened a dealership at 4141 Main Avenue for the Wayne automobile.

NOR-X — Norcross, Georgia — (1907) — At first glance it might seem that the man behind the Nor-X from Norcross — reportedly an erstwhile New Yorker named Ed Buchanan — was trying to be clever in naming his car. Perhaps, however, he was merely trying to be accurate. The car was marketed by the United Electrical Manufacturing Company only in the Norcross area, at price tags of $800-$850 for roadster or touring, and a local advertisement with illustration, indicated it to be a lookalike for the 1907 Knox. Possibly the Nor-X *was* a Knox, bought used or as leftovers at season's end in Massachusetts, and sold in the South with the only change from Knox specifications, aside from spiffing up, being a Nor-X radiator badge, which of course would have made it considerably more marketable in Norcross, Georgia.

NOVARA — Bristol, Rhode Island — (1917) — The Novara was, the brochure said, "the perfect embodiment of two aims — lightweight and exceptional acceleration." The car weighed only 1500 pounds and guaranteed over 50 mph in second gear, over 70 in top. Its engine was an overhead valve Sterling racing four with drilled rods and pistons. The rakish two-seater body had a cedar frame with mahogany outer skin "protected

1917 Novara, roadster, GR

by many coats of the finest spar finish" and copper-riveted a la boat style. The wheelbase was 110 inches, Houk wire wheels were fitted, and the spare tire was placed almost horizontally at the rear to serve as a bumper. The nautical dash of the Novara was not unexpected given its designer, Sidney DeWolf Herreshoff. The prototype was completed in the fall of 1916 in the plant of the family's yacht-building Herreshoff Manufacturing Company in Bristol, Rhode Island. Plans called for the car to be introduced for the 1917 model year, with its marketing to be handled by Gorham N. Thurber's Isotta Fraschini Motors Company in New York City. Had the car been built when the Twenties were roaring instead of in the midst of World War I, it might very well have enjoyed considerable success. But the Novara was a sporting car, and at a projected $2750 price tag a rather expensive one. With America's entrance into the war, it was rather wisely decided that most potential buyers of the Novara would be sent overseas — and the project was halted for the duration. Gorham Thurber's death in an automobile accident was probably the principal reason it was not resumed. At least three Novaras had been built.

NUGENT — The Nugent Automobile Works has been indicated on various rosters as the producer of an automobile in New York City during 1909-1910. Documentation is lacking. No such firm is listed in the New York City directory for this period.

NUSE — The Nuse Wagon & Automobile Company was organized in Newark, New Jersey early in 1912 with a capital stock of $50,000 for the manufacture of automobiles. The Nuses involved were G.W.; F., Sr.; F., Jr.; and L. Manufacture is doubted.

NYBERG — Chicago, Illinois — (1903-1904) — Henry Nyberg graduated from technical school in his native Malmo, Sweden and emigrated to the United States shortly thereafter. Settling in Chicago, he built his first automobile, a two-cylinder runabout on a 78-inch wheelbase in 1903. Curiously, he followed the building of his twin with a single-cylinder runabout. Then he began looking for someone to finance the Nyberg's manufacture. He found a fellow named Waller. The Nyberg-Waller Automobile Company was thusly organized in late 1903. In March 1904 this budding venture moved out of Nyberg's small machine shop and into a new building at 30th Street and Michigan Avenue where, Nyberg and Waller explained, their "facilities for turning out new cars and for repair work will be much greater than formerly." It would seem repair work largely occupied the firm; the Nyberg runabout was built for only a while. By 1907 Nyberg had shed himself of Waller and found another financial angel named H.E. Jennings. When the new Nyberg Automobile Works was organized in 1907, its stated purpose was to "reconstruct and sell second-hand cars." Subsequently, in 1908, the company announced that manufacture of new cars would be forthcoming, but it never was. Henry Nyberg didn't get into proper manufacture until 1911 when he moved to Anderson, Indiana.

1913 Nyberg Six, 5-pass. touring, WLB

NYBERG — Anderson, Indiana — (1911-1913) — Finally, after trying for years in Chicago, Henry Nyberg made it into production in Anderson, Indiana. In February of 1911 he bought the old Rider-Lewis plant, moved in and was in manufacture of the Nyberg four by the end of the year. A six joined the lineup in 1912, employment in Anderson stood at seventy workers, and Nyberg opened another plant in Chattanooga, Tennessee. It was full speed ahead until September of 1913, when the gross undercapitalization of his Nyberg Automobile Works finally caught up with him. Nyberg's factory was ordered closed, his company moved in receivership. Henry Nyberg blamed most of his troubles on the severe losses caused by the spring floods in Anderson, but that was more excuse than reason. In February of 1914, the Nyberg organization was bought out by A.C. Barley, the manufacturer of the Halliday car in Streator, Illinois. Barley indicated that he planned to resume manufacture of the Nyberg and retain Henry as plant manager. But Barley preferred to sow his oats elsewhere and soon gave up on the Nyberg altogether. When the old Nyberg factory finally reopened in March of 1915, a new car was built there. It was called the Madison, and Henry Nyberg was the man behind it. After Barley's departure, he had found another financial backer, Cecil Gibson who had formerly been connected with the Empire Company of Indianapolis.

1911 NYBERG
Model 35 — 4-cyl., 35/40 hp, 116" wb

	FP	5	4	3	2	1
Touring-5P	1250	3900	4800	7700	14,300	27,000

1912 NYBERG
Model 35 — 4-cyl., 35/40 hp, 116" wb

Touring-5P	1250	3500	4500	7000	13,000	25,000

Model 42 — 4-cyl., 35/40 hp, 126" wb

Touring-7P	1650	4000	5000	8000	15,000	28,000

Sixty — 6-cyl., 60 hp, 136" wb

Touring-5P	2100	4200	5200	8400	15,700	29,000
Touring-7P	2100	4400	5600	9200	17,300	31,000
Roadster	2100	4300	5400	8700	16,500	30,000

1913 NYBERG
Model 4-37 — 4-cyl., 37 hp, 118" wb

	FP	5	4	3	2	1
Roadster-2P	1285	3300	4400	6700	12,000	24,000
Touring-5P	1295	3500	4500	7000	13,000	25,000

Model 4-40 — 4-cyl., 40 hp, 118" wb

Roadster-2P	1650	3500	4500	7000	13,000	25,000
Touring-5P	1650	3700	4700	7300	13,700	26,000

Model 4-42 — 4-cyl., 40 hp, 128" wb

Tourabout-4P	1750	3900	4800	7700	14,300	27,000

Six-45 — 45 hp, 126" wb

Roadster-2P	1950	3700	4700	7300	13,700	26,000
Tourabout-4P	2000	3900	4800	7700	14,300	27,000
Touring-5P	2000	3900	4800	7700	14,300	27,000
Touring-7P (136" wb)	2100	4500	5800	9500	18,000	32,000
Landaulet-7P (136" wb)	3000	3100	4200	6300	10,500	22,000

Six-60 — 60 hp, 128" wb

Roadster-2P	2200	3900	4800	7700	14,300	27,000
Tourabout-4P	2500	4000	5000	8000	15,000	28,000
Touring-5P	2500	3900	4800	7700	14,300	27,000
Touring-7P (138" wb)	2550	4700	6100	9900	19,000	33,000
Limousine-7P (138" wb)	3250	3200	4300	6500	11,000	23,000

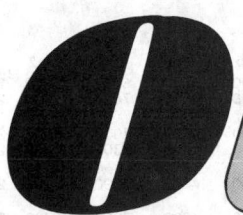

OAKLAND — The Oakland Iron Works was listed as an automobile manufacturer in Oakland, California in the Hiscox book *Horseless Vehicles, Automobiles, Motor Cycles* published in 1900. The firm was located at Second and Jefferson streets and indicated its activity in the Oakland city directory as "manufacturers of Tutthill water wheels, marine and stationary engines, boilers, ice and refrigeration machinery; also sheet, wrought and cast iron work of every description." Certainly the shop had the capability of producing an automobile, although that it did cannot be confirmed. One James C. Baker was employed as salesman by the Oakland Iron Works. His name is also included in the Hiscox book as an automobile builder. Quite possibly, the Baker and Oakland, if built, could be the same vehicle.

1908 Oakland, model A, touring, HAC

OAKLAND — Pontiac, Michigan — (1907-1931) — The Oakland was the idea of two men: Edward M. Murphy, who was anxious to move his Pontiac Buggy Company into the automotive age, and Alanson P. Brush, who had been responsible for the design of the early Cadillacs. They met around 1906, by which time Brush had set himself up in business as an engineering consultant in Detroit, and Brush showed Murphy his design for a small two-cylinder car which Cadillac had rejected. Its vertical engine rotated counterclockwise, and its planetary transmission was unusual for a lack of braking bands, clutches running in oil being the substitute. Murphy bought this automotive idea, which he decided should carry the name Oakland (as did his horsedrawn vehicles) — and during the summer of 1907 organized the Oakland Motor Car Company. The Oakland car was ready by automobile show time in January 1908, though Brush was no longer in Pontiac; having found Frank Briscoe available with funds, he was back in Detroit building his single-cylinder Brush Runabout. Lackluster sales of less than 300 Oaklands in 1908 must have convinced Murphy that Cadillac had been right in rejecting the Brush-designed twin because for 1909 a line of 40 hp fours with sliding gear transmissions were introduced. Tragically, at the age of forty-four, Edward M. Murphy died suddenly in September that year. Five months earlier he had met with another former buggy man named William C. Durant, and Oakland had become part of Durant's General Motors empire. Oakland became a four exclusively in 1910, and sales of 3000 to 5000 cars a year became the norm. "The Car with a Conscience" was an Oakland slogan, and the marque acquitted itself admirably in motor sport, particularly reliability runs and hill climbs, winning no less than 25 of the latter, including Giant's Despair and Dead Horse Hill. Oakland's first six — a big 334-cubic-inch 60 hp car on a 130-inch wheelbase — arrived in 1913, together with self-starter and electric lights, and an eye-catching rounded-vee radiator, for all Oaklands. Almost 9000 cars were sold that year. Production increased to nearly 12,000 in 1915, and more than doubled the year following, when the Oakland range included fours, sixes and a new V-8. Wartime exigencies resulted in the V-8's discontinuation for 1918, with company efforts focused on its six which would be produced without noticeable change into the Twenties. It was during this period that Billy Durant was undergoing his second-and-irrevocable departure from General Motors. In its wake, and with the arrival of Alfred P. Sloan, Jr., all divisions of the corporation were given a fresh look. The peering into Oakland affairs revealed a haphazard production schedule (maybe 50 cars built one day, only 10 the next) and a loss of quality (some cars had to be repaired even before leaving the factory). Fred W. Warner, a Durant man, resigned as Oakland's general manager in 1921, and was succeeded by George W. Hannum, who had begun his career at Autocar in 1907 and who had worked in various GM-related companies before arriving in Pontiac. The official statement from General Motors indicated that Oakland would continue its present line "with gradual improvements." The big news for Oakland arrived in 1924: a new L-head engine, four-wheel brakes, centralized controls, automatic spark advance — and Duco. Oakland's choice of color in pioneering the new nitro-cellulose lacquer was a shade of blue which allowed the company promotion of the car as the "True Blue Oakland Six." And it could be had

for as low as $995. Unfortunately, insofar as being "true blue" as a GM man, George Hannum wasn't. The GM-decreed slot for the Oakland among the corporation cars was between the top-of-the-line Chevrolet and the bread-and-butter Buick. Among other flagrancies, the Oakland was too heavy for its slot, which was not entirely Hannum's fault since the car's chassis was eight years old. He was guilty of occasionally not considering sales demand when shipping Oaklands to dealers, but Chevrolet was guilty of that too. Nonetheless, and in spite of a healthy annual production of over 35,000 cars in both 1923 and 1924, Hannum was eased out of Oakland. By early 1925 his place had been taken by Alfred R. Glancy, a likeable Irishman who had joined Oakland the year previous as assistant general manager. Although the concept of the car had first been bruited in the early Twenties by George Hannum, it was Al Glancy who would introduce the Pontiac, a quality six to sell at a four's price, in 1926. It was a runaway success, and undoubtedly an impetus to the later marketing of the Marquette by Buick and the Viking by Oldsmobile. (Cadillac's LaSalle was on the boards, but not on the market at this time.) The Pontiac was unique in GM history in being the only offspring ever to kill its parent. After its smashing debut, the demise of the Oakland became only a matter of time. The cars for 1927 were called the Greater Oakland Sixes, with All-American Six becoming a designation for the Oakland senior models that summer, and the cars were restyled for 1929. But most of the attention at the Oakland company was diverted to the Pontiac. In 1930 there was an 85 hp V-8 under the hood of the Oakland, but calendar year production was just 24,443 cars. There were over 188,000 Pontiacs built in that same period. In October of 1930 Irving J. Reuter moved into Al Glancy's job at Oakland. Oaklands for '31 featured a new synchromesh with silent second. Fewer than 9000 cars were produced that year. With the effects of the Great Depression now weighing heavy everywhere, Pontiac sales plummeted too. But, still, there were nearly seven times more of them built in '31 than the Oakland. At year's end, Irving Reuter announced the demise of the Oakland name. Its V-8 series would be revamped into a Pontiac model. During 1932 the name of the Oakland Motor Car Company was changed to Pontiac Motor Company.

1907
Model A, 4-cyl., 96" wb - 100" wb

	FP	5	4	3	2	1
All Body Styles	1600	4950	9900	16,500	23,100	33,000

1909 Oakland, model 40, touring, OCW

1909
Model 20, 2-cyl., 112" wb

All Body Styles	1600	4500	9000	15,000	21,000	30,000

Model 40, 4-cyl., 112" wb

All Body Styles	1700	4200	8400	14,000	19,600	28,000

1910 Oakland, model 24, touring, HAC

1910-1911

Model 24, 4-cyl., 96" wb

	FP	5	4	3	2	1
Rds	1700	3300	6600	11,000	15,400	22,000
Model 25, 4-cyl., 100" wb						
Tr	1700	3000	6000	10,000	14,000	20,000
Model 33, 4-cyl., 106" wb						
Tr	1700	3600	7200	12,000	16,800	24,000
Model K, 4-cyl., 102" wb						
Tr	1700	3900	7800	13,000	18,200	26,000
Model M, 4-cyl., 112" wb						
Rds	1700	4050	8100	13,500	18,900	27,000

NOTE: Model 33 1911 only.

1911 Oakland, model 33, touring, HAC

1912 Oakland, model 40, sociable roadster, HAC

1912

Model 30, 4-cyl., 106" wb

5P Tr	1250	1400	4200	7000	9800	14,000
Rbt	1260	1500	4350	7250	10,150	14,500
Model 40, 4-cyl., 112" wb						
5P Tr	1450	1500	4350	7250	10,150	14,500
Cpe	1900	1025	2500	5150	7150	10,300
Rds	1450	1650	4650	7750	10,850	15,500
Model 45, 4-cyl., 120" wb						
7P Tr	2100	2950	5900	9800	13,700	19,600
4P Tr	2250	3150	6300	10,500	14,700	21,000
Limo	3000	2950	5900	9800	13,700	19,600

1913 Oakland, model 42, sociable roadster, HAC

1913

Greyhound 6-60, 6-cyl., 130" wb

4P Tr	2500	2950	5900	9800	13,700	19,600
7P Tr	2550	3400	6900	11,500	16,100	23,000
Rbt	2400	2600	5550	9300	13,000	18,600
Model 42, 4-cyl., 116" wb						
5P Tr	1800	1250	3900	6500	9100	13,000
3P Rds	1600	1225	3850	6450	9000	12,900
4P Cpe	2500	1000	2400	5000	7000	10,000
Model 35, 4-cyl., 112" wb						
5P Tr	1200	1250	3900	6500	9100	13,000
3P Rds	1000	1150	3550	5950	8300	11,900
Model 40, 4-cyl., 114" wb						
5P Tr	1450	1400	4200	7000	9800	14,000
Model 45, 4-cyl., 120" wb						
7P Limo	3000	1500	4350	7250	10,150	14,500

1914 Oakland, model 36, touring, HAC

1914

Model 6-60, 6-cyl., 130" wb

	FP	5	4	3	2	1
Rbt	2450	1400	4200	7000	9800	14,000
Rds	2450	1400	4200	7050	9850	14,100
Cl Cpl	2450	1650	4650	7750	10,850	15,500
Tr	2450	3400	6900	11,500	16,100	23,000
Model 6-48, 6-cyl., 130" wb						
Spt	1785	1150	3550	5950	8300	11,900
Rds	1785	1150	3550	5950	8300	11,900
Tr	1785	1300	4050	6750	9450	13,500
Model 43, 4-cyl., 116" wb						
5P Tr	2700	1025	2500	5150	7150	10,300
Cpe	2500	900	1800	4400	6150	8800
Sed	2600	875	1700	4250	5900	8500
Model 36, 4-cyl., 112" wb						
5P Tr	1200	1000	2400	5000	7000	10,000
Cabr	1585	1150	3550	5950	8300	11,900
Model 35, 4-cyl., 112" wb						
Rds	1150	1000	2400	5000	7000	10,000
5P Tr	1200	1025	2600	5250	7300	10,500

1915 Oakland, model 37, touring, HAC

1915-1916

Model 37-Model 38, 4-cyl., 112" wb

Tr	1050	1000	2400	5000	7000	10,000
Rds	1050	1000	2400	5000	7000	10,000
Spd	1050	900	1800	4400	6150	8800
Model 49-Model 32, 6-cyl., 110"-123.5" wb						
Tr	795	1200	3750	6250	8750	12,500
Rds	795	1225	3850	6450	9000	12,900
Model 50, 8-cyl., 127" wb						
7P Tr	1585	1800	4950	8250	11,550	16,500

NOTE: Model 37 and model 49 are 1915 models.

1917 Oakland, model 34, roadster, HAC

1917
Model 34, 6-cyl., 112" wb

	FP	5	4	3	2	1
Rds	945	900	1900	4500	6300	9000
5P Tr	945	1025	2500	5150	7150	10,300
Cpe	995	900	1800	4400	6150	8800
Sed	1020	875	1700	4250	5900	8500

Model 50, 8-cyl., 127" wb

	FP	5	4	3	2	1
7P Tr	1600	1250	3900	6500	9100	13,000

1918 Oakland, model 34-B, roadster, OCW

1918
Model 34-B, 6-cyl., 112" wb

	FP	5	4	3	2	1
5P Tr	1050	1075	3000	5500	7700	11,000
Rds	1050	1025	2600	5250	7300	10,500
Rds Cpe	1210	900	1900	4500	6300	9000
Tr Sed	1250	900	1900	4500	6300	9000
4P Cpe	1550	825	1600	4000	5600	8000
Sed	1550	750	1450	3300	4900	7000

1919 Oakland Sensible Six, sedan, HAC

1919
Model 34-B, 6-cyl., 112" wb

	FP	5	4	3	2	1
5P Tr	1075	1075	3000	5500	7700	11,000
Rds	1075	1025	2600	5250	7300	10,500
Rds Cpe	1210	900	1900	4500	6300	9000
Cpe	1650	775	1500	3750	5250	7500
Sed	1650	750	1450	3300	4900	7000

1920 Oakland Sensible Six, touring, HAC

1920
Model 34-C, 6-cyl., 112" wb

	FP	5	4	3	2	1
Tr	1235	1075	3000	5500	7700	11,000
Rds	1235	1025	2600	5250	7300	10,500
Sed	1885	750	1450	3300	4900	7000
Cpe	1885	800	1550	3800	5300	7600

1922 Oakland, model 34-C, sedan, HAC

1921-22
Model 34-C, 6-cyl., 115" wb

	FP	5	4	3	2	1
Tr	1395	1150	3600	6000	8400	12,000
Rds	1395	1200	3750	6250	8750	12,500
Sed	2065	750	1450	3500	5050	7200
Cpe	2065	800	1550	3900	5450	7800

1923 Oakland, model 6-54, 5-pass. sedan, AA

1923
Model 6-44, 6-cyl., 115" wb

Rds	975	1075	3000	5500	7700	11,000
Tr	995	1150	3600	6000	8400	12,000
Spt Rds	1145	1025	2600	5250	7300	10,500
Spt Tr	1165	1200	3750	6250	8750	12,500
2P Cpe	1185	725	1400	3000	4700	6700
4P Cpe	1495	750	1450	3300	4900	7000
Sed	1545	600	1200	2300	4000	5700

1924 Oakland, model 6-54, touring, OCW

1925 Oakland, model 6-54, landau sedan, AA

1924-25
Model 6-54, 6-cyl., 113" wb

	FP	5	4	3	2	1
5P Tr	1095	1400	4200	7000	9800	14,000
Spl Tr	1195	1550	4500	7500	10,500	15,000
Rds	1095	1300	4050	6750	9450	13,500
Spl Rds	1195	1300	4050	6750	9450	13,500
4P Cpe	1495	750	1450	3300	4900	7000
Lan Cpe	1295	775	1500	3600	5100	7300
Sed	1545	600	1200	2300	4000	5700
Lan Sed	1645	650	1250	2400	4200	6000
2 dr Sed	1215	500	1100	1900	3500	5000
2 dr Lan Sed	1295	600	1200	2300	4000	5700

1926 Oakland, Greater Six, roadster, OCW

1927 Oakland, Greater Six, sport phaeton, AA

1926-27
Greater Six, 6-cyl., 113" wb

		5	4	3	2	1
Tr	1025	1300	4050	6750	9450	13,500
Spt Phae	1095	1500	4350	7250	10,150	14,500
Spt Rds	1175	1400	4200	7000	9800	14,000
2 dr Sed	1095	650	1250	2400	4200	6000
Lan Cpe	1125	675	1300	2500	4350	6200
Sed	1195	600	1200	2200	3850	5500
Lan Sed	1295	600	1200	2300	4000	5700
Rds	975	1250	3900	6500	9100	13,000

1928 Oakland, All-American, 4-dr. sedan, AA

1928
Model 212, All-American, 6-cyl., 117" wb

		5	4	3	2	1
Spt Rds	1075	1550	4500	7500	10,500	15,000
Phae	1075	1650	4650	7750	10,850	15,500
Lan Cpe	1045	1000	2400	5000	7000	10,000
Cabr	1145	1500	4350	7250	10,150	14,500
2 dr Sed	1045	650	1250	2400	4200	6000
Sed	1145	700	1350	2800	4550	6500
Lan Sed	1265	775	1500	3750	5250	7500

1929 Oakland, All-American, roadster, OCW

1929
Model 212, All American — 6-cyl., 117" wb

	FP	5	4	3	2	1
Spt Rds	1145	3000	6000	10,000	14,000	20,000
Spt Phae	1145	3150	6300	10,500	14,700	21,000
Cpe	1145	1000	2400	5000	7000	10,000
Conv	1265	1750	4800	8000	11,200	16,000
2 dr Sed	1145	600	1200	2200	3850	5500
Brgm	1195	750	1450	3300	4900	7000
Sed	1245	700	1350	2800	4550	6500
Spl Sed	1320	725	1400	3000	4700	6700
Lan Sed	1375	725	1400	3100	4800	6800

1930 Oakland Eight, model 101, roadster, JAC

1930
Model 101, V-8, 117" wb

		5	4	3	2	1
Spt Rds	895	3600	7200	12,000	16,800	24,000
Phae	945	3750	7500	12,500	17,500	25,000
Cpe	895	1250	3900	6500	9100	13,000
Spt Cpe	965	1400	4200	7000	9800	14,000
2 dr Sed	895	775	1500	3750	5250	7500
Sed	995	800	1550	3800	5300	7600
Cus Sed	1045	800	1550	3850	5400	7700

1931 Oakland Eight, model 301, sedan, JAC

1931
Model 301, V-8, 117" Wb

		5	4	3	2	1
Cpe	895	1400	4200	7000	9800	14,000
Spt Cpe	975	1550	4500	7500	10,500	15,000
Conv	995	3000	6000	10,000	14,000	20,000
2 dr Sed	895	800	1550	3800	5300	7600
Sed	995	800	1550	3850	5400	7700
Cus Sed	1055	825	1600	4000	5600	8000

1011

OAKMAN — At the turn of the century, in Greenfield, Massachusetts, the Oakman Motor Vehicle Company produced a gasoline runabout which was marketed under the name of its designer. Refer to Hertel.

OAK PARK — The Oak Park Taxi Company was organized in Oak Park, Illinois early in 1915 with a capital stock of $2500 to manufacture and deal in automobiles. Incorporators were C.J. Bassler, G.D. Rose and N.F. Bippus. Manufacture is doubted.

OAK SIX — **Chicago, Illinois** — **(1917)** — The Oak Six was the idea of S.O. D'Orlow of Chicago. It had a rotary sleeve-valve engine of the Argyll type produced in Scotland, as revised by D'Orlow presumably out of harm's way of possible patent infringement. It also had a hydraulic transmission that was said to be automatic and was D'Orlow's own doing completely. The price of the Oak Six was slated to be in the $1500 range. Though an Oak Manufacturing Company was casually organized for manufacture, the car never proceeded beyond the prototype stage.

OBERLIN — **McKeesport, Pennsylvania** — **(1902-1903)** — In November of 1902 *The Automobile and Motor Review* reported that Oliver S. Oberlin of McKeesport was preparing to erect a $25,000 factory for the manufacture of automobiles. This ambitious project was not realized though Oberlin may have produced a few cars for area residents in the McKeesport shop where he made sewing machines and bicycles.

O'BRIEN — The Joseph F. O'Brien Manufacturing Company was organized in New York City during the spring of 1911 with a capital stock of $20,000 for the manufacture of automobiles. Joining Joseph O'Brien in the venture were Daniel O'Brien and Maurice V. Theall. Manufacture is doubted.

O'BRIEN ELECTRIC — **San Francisco, California** — **(1900)** — At least five electrics — two stanhopes, two dos-a-dos and a road wagon — were built by O'Brien & Sons, carriage builders of San Francisco. Conceivably, there was a small further production. The O'Brien's electric running gear and batteries were designed by William H. Hanscom, who was chief electrician of the Union Iron Works. "If Mr. Hanscom's inventions prove to be what he claims for them," commented *The Motor Vehicle Review* in August 1900, "he should have no trouble in successfully competing with the electric vehicles of Eastern manufacture." Apparently they were not, because he did not.

1916 O'Connor, model D, 5-pass. touring, WLB

O'CONNOR — **Chicago, Illinois** — **(1916)** — Although the O'Connor Corporation of Chicago announced an impressive lineup of four- and six-cylinder models for the 1916 season, the only thing it produced in quantity was stock certificates. The scam was uncovered by March of that year. H.U. Broenstrup and A.E. Patchin were the principals involved, and they had floated the O'Connor Aeroplane Company first, followed by the O'Connor Hydroplane Company, followed by the O'Connor Motor Car Company, followed by the O'Connor Corporation. What they might have followed the last named with is anyone's guess, but they were caught. "Post office inspectors questioned Broenstrup, who 'explained' matters," reported *Automobile Topics*. "The questioning and explanation seems to have resulted in the hurried departure of the accused for other fields of endeavor." Pictures of the O'Connor car which had been submitted to the trade press reveal a crude-looking machine that was either hastily built or perhaps simply revised from a photograph of an already existing car made by someone else. Patchin was reported to have been a disbarred lawyer. Broenstrup's credentials are not known.

OCTOAUTO — The Octoauto, as its name suggests, was an eight-wheeled car built on an Overland chassis in 1911 by Milton O. Reeves of Columbus, Indiana. Refer to Reeves.

ODELOT — **Toledo, Ohio** — **(1915)** — The Odelot was Toledo spelled backwards, and it was built in that Ohio city by the Lawrence Stamping Company. A two-passenger bucket-seat raceabout on a 96-inch chassis was the only model, its hood and fenders finished in black, with a choice of red, green or yellow for cowl and seats. A four-cylinder 20 hp engine was fitted, with motor, clutch and change gear combined in unit and supported on the frame at three points. Wire wheels were a natty touch, and the whole package was priced at $450. Lawrence Stamping announced its new raceabout in May of 1915 and promised a touring variation by the following January. The company didn't remain in the automobile business long enough to deliver on its promise.

1915 Odelot Raceabout, NAHC

ODENBRETT — **Milwaukee, Wisconsin** — **(1899)** — In 1899 George Odenbrett built a gasoline-powered automobile which he later admitted was "rude" and which he never could get to run right. He discarded it after purchasing a Winton later that year. The Odenbrett name as the builder of an automobile on various rosters is the result of an editorial error. In the October 4th, 1899 issue of *The Horseless Age*, mention was made that the Wisconsin man had exhibited a gasoline car of his own manufacture at a local fair. Odenbrett immediately wrote the editors to correct the error, which was subsequently noted in the October 25th issue. The vehicle in question was the Winton, which Odenbrett said was the first gasoline car in Milwaukee. Subsequently, Odenbrett revised the car to his liking, so much so in fact that he wrote *The Motor Review* in 1901 that it would not be recognized even by Alexander Winton. "It is the fastest machine in Milwaukee today, and it can go about forty miles an hour," he stated. "I took off the old dashboard and put on a new one, put in a new sprocket wheel and a new igniter. These changes have made the machine conform with my ideas." But it was not Odenbrett's idea to become an automobile manufacturer. Instead he became a race car driver and a junior partner in the Bates Odenbrett Automobile Company of Milwaukee which served as a dealership for both Winton and Buick. In 1909 George Odenbrett was killed by the explosion of an acetylene tank in the depot of the Gas Tank Recharging Company in Milwaukee.

OESON — The Oeson Automobile Company was organized in New York City during the summer of 1909 with a capital stock of $10,000 to manufacture automobiles, parts and accessories. Incorporators were H.M. Kilborn, W.E. Matterson and Richard Sutro. Manufacture of a car is doubted.

1901 Ofeldt, motor carriage, WLB

OFELDT STEAM — **Brooklyn, New York** — **(1899-1900) / Newark, New Jersey** — **(1901-1902)** — The firm of F.W. Ofeldt & Sons at the foot of Twenty-Fifth Street in south Brooklyn was well known as one of New York's principal builders of marine launches. In 1899 Ernest F. Ofeldt fitted one of the Ofeldt steam engines into a carriage. The powerplant consisted of two compound engines with cylinders and crankshafts set at a 90° angle. It was among the earliest vee-type steam engines in America. The water tank carried fifteen gallons, the fuel tank five, and the vehicle could travel twenty miles between replenishments. It was crudely built. "It is not a thing of beauty," reported *The Horseless Age*, "but was constructed merely to demonstrate the practicability of the power." The second car was a surrey with fringe on top. As Ernest Ofeldt explained in later years, "We wanted to have the car look as much like a horsedrawn vehicle so that it wouldn't scare horses." Just the two cars were built in Brooklyn. In 1901 the company secured another factory on Ferry Street in Newark, and there at least one further steam car and one large express wagon were produced. But automobile manufacture was not embarked upon, although the company was producing components for steam cars as late as 1905. For a good many years Ofeldt remained prominent in the field of marine launches. In 1905, in collaboration with Charles L. Seabury, the Ofeldt company produced a gasoline car called the Speedway.

OGDEN — **Columbus, Indiana** — **(1902)** — One of the earliest juvenile vehicles in America was built by Dore Ogden, the manager of the Western Union telegraph office in Columbus, Indiana. It was 38 inches long, bicycle-wheeled, tiller-steered, and was powered by a small motor with jump spark ignition, Dyke carburetor and a gravity oil and gasoline feed. The

1902 Ogden, NAHC

body was smartly finished in black with red stripes and was upholstered in leather. The car's owner was Hubert S. Ogden, three years old, and probably America's youngest driver at the time. Young Hubert frequently motored from his home to his father's office, a distance of a mile, and reportedly was a skillful driver. Dore Ogden always accompanied his son on a bicycle. Whether he owned an automobile himself is not known, but he was rather famous in the area for "thinking up weird ideas and new inventions which made good (newspaper) copy but seldom reached perfection." Among these was a white cream which removed hair without a razor, but also several layers of skin — and a device for installation in offices which would signal the approach of a streetcar from a block away.

OGDEN — Ogden, Utah — (1906-1907) — The Ogden Automobile Company was incorporated in Salt Lake City in October of 1906 by Albert Scowcroft, John S. Corlow and G.W. McCune. "The company will engage in a general motor car manufacturing business, repair shop and garage," reported *The Motor Age*, "also in the manufacture, repairing, buying, selling of vehicles and machinery of every kind the directors may desire." Probably Ogden did put together a few cars for area residents, but this Utah company undoubtedly operated principally as a garage.

OGONTZ — Sandusky, Ohio — (1916) — The Ogontz Motor Car Company was a classic example of good money following bad. It was incorporated for $25,000 in March of 1916 to take over the Wolverine which had just gone bust in Michigan. George M. Muehlhauser was the proprietor of the Ogontz Garage at Market and Decatur in Sandusky, and he thought reviving a dead car might be an easy way to get into the automobile manufacturing business. It wasn't. Very soon the Ogontz Motor Car Company was simply the Ogontz Garage again.

1921 Ogren, Six, 4-dr. sedan, WLB

OGREN — Chicago & Waukegan, Illinois — (1915-1917) / Milwaukee, Wisconsin — (1920-1923) — In the fall of 1914, Hugo W. Ogren who had most recently designed the Colby in Mason City (Iowa), arrived in Chicago and organized the Ogren Motor Car Company. Although one-off race cars, sold under Ogren's initials H.W.O., were this new venture's principal output initially, a six-cylinder touring car was offered in 1915. In 1916 the company was reorganized as Ogren Motor Works, Inc., with capital stock increased from $25,000 to $1,000,000, and Ogren moved to a large new factory in nearby Waukegan. A full line of sixes was offered that year and continued into the next. A healthy increase in capital stock was meaningless, however, without cash on hand — and Hugo Ogren didn't have that. His company went to the auction block on November 22nd, 1917. The All-

American truck moved into the old Ogren plant in Waukegan in 1918. By 1919 the Ogren had been resurrected. In September the new Ogren Motor Car Company was organized with a capital stock of $500,000 in Milwaukee, with the former Elite ice skating rink to be remodeled into a factory. Production was planned to begin in October, but the rink renovation took longer than expected, and the first new Ogren didn't appear until July of 1920. Five cars were built that month, with a 25-car-per-month schedule planned for the rest of the year. The new Ogren was snazzier looking, heftier (65 hp Beaver six engine vis-a-vis the former 34 hp unit) and more expensive ($3750+ vis-a-vis $2500+) than its predecessor. And for 1922 it was heftier yet, with a 70 hp Continental engine replacing the former Beaver. In November there were further changes made. The Ogren company announced an impending reorganization, with Fred G. Smith, one of the original Milwaukee Ogren stockholders taking over as president and general manager because Hugo Ogren had left the premises to join another group of automotive hopefuls in a new car called the Commander. By now production had ceased, though leftover Ogrens continued to be sold into the summer of 1923. Receivership followed that November. By January of 1924 the Huffman people in Elkhart (Indiana) had bought most of the Ogren tools and equipment, and the rest of what was saleable from the company was sold by late spring. Tax claims took every cent that was received; neither Ogren stockholders nor Ogren creditors were left with a thing. Total Ogren production in both its lives was probably less than 200 cars.

1915 OGREN
Model P — 6-cyl., 34 hp, 133" wb

	FP	5	4	3	2	1
Touring-7P	2500	3900	4800	7700	14,300	27,000

1916-1917 OGREN
Model P — 6-cyl., 34 hp, 133" wb

	FP	5	4	3	2	1
Touring-7P	2500	3900	4800	7700	14,300	27,000
Roadster-2P	2500	3700	4700	7300	13,700	26,000
Limousine-7P	3750	2700	3600	5300	8800	19,000
Berline-7P	3750	2700	3600	5300	8800	19,000
Toy Tonneau-5P	2500	3900	4800	7700	14,300	27,000

1920 OGREN
Six — 65 hp, 132" wb

	FP	5	4	3	2	1
Touring-7P	3750	4000	5000	8000	15,000	28,000
Sport-4P	3750	4200	5200	8400	15,700	29,000

1921 OGREN
Six — 65 hp, 134" wb

	FP	5	4	3	2	1
Touring-7P	3900	4200	5200	8400	15,700	29,000
Sport-4P	3900	4300	5400	8700	16,500	30,000

1922 Ogren, Six, touring, OCW

1922-1923 OGREN
Six — 70 hp, 134" wb

	FP	5	4	3	2	1
Sport-5P	4250	4400	5600	9200	17,300	31,000
Roadster-4P	4350	4200	5200	8400	15,700	29,000
Touring-7P	4375	4300	5400	8700	16,500	30,000
Coupe-4P	5200	2700	3600	5300	8800	19,000
Sedan-7P	5500	2200	3200	4400	7000	15,000

OHIO — The Ohio Automobile Company was the sponsoring organization from September of 1900 to October of 1902 which built the Packard automobile in Warren, Ohio. The firm evolved into the Packard Motor Car Company on October 13th, and one year later moved to Detroit where it remained for the next five decades. Refer to Packard.

The Ohio Garage and Repair Company was organized in Cleveland late in 1905 with a capital stock of $10,000 to manufacture, deal in, rent, store and repair automobiles and to handle accessories. Incorporators were George W. Hale, E.F. Gibbons, H.D Messick and I.D. Hogg. Manufacture of a car is doubted.

The Ohio Motor Vehicle Company of Cleveland built a car called the Ferris from 1920-1922. Refer to Ferris.

The Ohio Universal Truck Company was organized in Warren during the summer of 1911 with a capital stock of $200,000 to "manufacture and deal in commercial and pleasure vehicles." Incorporators were George T. Fillius, Z.F. Craver, O.R. Grimmesey, P.W. Balcom and W.H. Hostetter. Manufacture of a car is doubted.

OHIO — Carthage, Ohio — (1909-1912) — "Built on Integrity, Guaranteed for Life" was the slogan for this marque which was occasionally written OhiO and which was headquartered in Cincinnati, with factory in Carthage. The Ohio had a tripartite existence in the same factory. First, in 1909, it was the product of the Jewell Carriage Company, that firm falling into financial difficulties in 1910 and lifting itself out of receivership in mid-1912 by reorganizing as the Ohio Motor Car Company with Jewell president C.F. Pratt remaining onboard. This was a case of baby becoming mother, since Ohio Motor Car had previously been the sales organization for the parent Jewell Company. But the move was obviously a palliative

1910 Ohio, model 40-A, touring, NAHC

because the new organization was in trouble immediately with internal dissension and creditors beating at the door. A few short months later, in December 1912, Ralph E. Northway arrived from Detroit, having just sold his engine-manufacturing Northway Company to General Motors, and with enough money to buy out the entire operation. He reorganized as the Crescent Motor Car Company, retaining the Ohio name only as a model of the new Crescent. The car survived as such only through 1914. The Ohio's problem was a simple one. It was just a thoroughly ordinary four-cylinder motorcar set on a 115-inch wheelbase. Most of the ingenuity in the company appears to have been in the promotion department, where it was decided in 1912 that each of the models should be named as well as designated. The Ohio that was sent on a transcontinental trek in 1911 was nicknamed the "Mud Hen." The production models for 1912 carried evocative names too. But that was not enough to sell the car.

1910 OHIO
Forty — 4-cyl., 35/40 hp, 115" wb

	FP	5	4	3	2	1
Model 40-A Tour.-5P	1850	2500	3500	5000	8500	18,000
Model 40-D Toy Tonneau-5P	1850	2500	3500	5000	8500	18,000
Model 40-C Sub.-4P	1850	2700	3600	5300	8800	19,000
Model 40-E Rdstr.-4P	1750	2500	3500	5000	8500	18,000
Model 40-F Rdstr.-3P	1750	2500	3500	5000	8500	18,000
Model 40-G Rdstr.-2P	1750	2500	3500	5000	8500	18,000

1911 Ohio Four, roadster, HAC

1911 OHIO
Four — 28 hp, 115" wb

Roadster-3P	2150	2400	3400	4800	8000	17,000

Forty — 4-cyl., 40 hp, 115" wb

Model 40-C Tour.-5P	2150	2500	3500	5000	8500	18,000
Model 40-D Cl. C.-5P	2150	2700	3600	5300	8800	19,000
Model 40-G Torpedo-2P	2450	2900	3700	5600	9100	20,000
Model 40-H Cpe.-3P	2750	2300	3300	4600	7500	16,000
Model 40-M Four-Door Tour.-5P	2250	2600	3600	5200	8700	18,500
Model 40-N Four-Door Cl.C.-4P	2250	2800	3700	5500	9000	19,500
Model 40-F Rbt.-2P	2150	2300	3300	4600	7500	16,000
Model 40-J Lim.-7P	3350	2500	3500	5000	8500	18,000

1912 OHIO
Forty — 4-cyl., 40 hp, 115" wb

Clifton Tour.-5P	2500	2700	3600	5300	8800	19,000
Euclid Torpedo-5P	2500	2700	3600	5300	8800	19,000
Grand Prix Bullet Rdstr.-2P	2500	2500	3500	5000	8500	18,000
Brighton Beach Spdst.-2P (105" wb)	2250	2900	3700	5600	9100	20,000
Avondale Tour.-5P	2250	2700	3600	5300	8800	19,000
Grandin Tonneau-4P	2250	2700	3600	5300	8800	19,000
Ohio Service Car Delivery	2150	2300	3300	4600	7500	16,000

1912 Ohio "Grand Prix", bullet roadster, HAC

1910 Ohio Electric, coupe, HAC

OHIO ELECTRIC — Toledo, Ohio — (1910-1918) — The Ohio Electric Car Company of Toledo provided for the emancipation of women a decade before the U.S. Constitution. Although the electric vehicle was frequently advertised with the feminine driver in mind, no manufacturer of electrics did so with more vigor than Ohio. Nor did any consider so profoundly the conveniences thought necessary for fashionable distaff motoring during that era. It was Ohio, for example, which popularized tiller steering from both front and rear seat, so that a woman could drive "with a clear view ahead and in privacy at all times...(not) in the front seat like a chauffeur uncomfortably conspicuous." And Ohio was in the forefront of motoring convenience with its magnetic control rendering the governing of every operation of the car from a small disc, with brakes applied by the press of a button. Both double drive and magnetic control were patented by the company, and were among the reasons the Ohio Electric was touted as "The Only Car for the Woman of Refinement Today." The company, of course, was run entirely by men. The Ohio Electric Car Compay was incorporated with $75,000 capital stock in September of 1909 by Henry P. Dodge, Rathbun Fuller, Henry E. Marvin, James Brown Bell and Robert E. Lee. Initially, the firm shared the offices and factory of the Milburn Wagon Company, but in 1911 moved into its own plant. Twelve cars were built during its maiden 1910 season; production was 300 cars in 1915, over 650 in 1916. In 1915 the Ohio Electric leadership changed, with M.V. Barbour now as president, C.M. Foster vice-president and general manager, Herman H. Brand as secretary-treasurer. By 1917, when George W. Shaw took over as president, half of the Ohio Electric activity was devoted to the making of bodies for other manufacturers, half to building electrics in that now-waning market. The company was dissolved in 1918, its machinery and equipment sold at public auction in June.

1911 Ohio Electric, model D, coupe, HAC

1014

1910 OHIO ELECTRIC

	FP	5	4	3	2	1
Shaft Drive Cpe.	2600	1900	2900	4100	6400	13,500

1911 OHIO ELECTRIC

	FP	5	4	3	2	1
Model D Cpe.(80'' wb)	2600	2000	3000	4200	6500	14,000
Model F Vict. (80'' wb)	2300	1800	2800	4000	6200	13,000
Model G Large Cpe. (80'' wb)	—	2100	3100	4300	6800	14,500

1912 Ohio Electric, model F, victoria

1912 OHIO ELECTRIC

	FP	5	4	3	2	1
Model F Vict. (90'' wb)	2300	1800	2800	4000	6200	13,000
Model Q Vict. (90'' wb)	2300	1800	2800	4000	6200	13,000
Model D Cpe. (80'' wb)	2600	2000	3000	4200	6500	14,000
Model G Cpe. (90'' wb)	2700	2100	3100	4300	6800	14,500
Model K Cpe. (90'' wb)	2900	2100	3100	4300	6800	14,500
Model X DeL. Cpe. (102'' wb)	4000	2200	3200	4400	7000	15,000

1913 Ohio Electric, model O, Dresden brougham, HAC

1913 OHIO ELECTRIC

	FP	5	4	3	2	1
Model L Colonial Brgm. (106'' wb)	3200	2200	3200	4400	7000	15,000
Model M Straight-Line Brgm. (106'' wb)	3200	2200	3200	4400	7000	15,000
Model O Dresden Brgm. (106'' wb)	2900	2000	3000	4200	6500	14,000
Model Y Brgm. (106'' wb)	3500	1900	2900	4100	6400	13,500
Model Q Vict. (90'' wb)	3500	1800	2800	4000	6200	13,000
Model F Stnhpe.	2300	1600	2700	3800	5800	12,000

1914 Ohio Electric, model 50, coupe, HAC

1914 OHIO ELECTRIC

	FP	5	4	3	2	1
Model 50 Cpe. (98'' wb)	3200	2000	3000	4200	6500	14,000
Model 40 Dresden Design-4P (98'' wb)	2900	1800	2800	4000	6200	13,000
Model 60 Viennese Design-5P (98'' wb)	3500	2200	3200	4400	7000	15,000

1915 Ohio Electric, model 61, double-drive coupe, HAC

1915 OHIO ELECTRIC

	FP	5	4	3	2	1
Model 41 Brgm. (98-1/2'' wb)	2900	2200	3200	4400	7000	15,000
Model 21 Rdstr. (98-1/2'' wb)	2650	2200	3200	4400	7000	15,000
Model 51 Double-Drive Brgm. (98-1/2'' wb)	3000	2300	3300	4600	7500	16,000
Model 11 Single-Drive Cpe. (98-1/2'' wb)	2400	2250	3300	4500	7300	15,500
Model 61 Double-Drive Cpe. (98-1/2'' wb)	3250	2000	3000	4200	6500	14,000
Rdstr.-2P (98-1/2'' wb)	2650	1800	2800	4000	6200	13,000
Single-Drive Brgm.-4P (98-1/2'' wb)	2600	2200	3200	4400	7000	15,000
Single-Drive Brgm.-5P (98-1/2'' wb)	2900	2200	3200	4400	7000	15,000
Double-Drive Brgm.-5P (98-1/2'' wb)	3000	2200	3200	4400	7000	15,000

1916 Ohio Electric, model 62, brougham, HAC

1917 Ohio Electric, model 12, coupe, HAC

1916 OHIO ELECTRIC

	FP	5	4	3	2	1
Model 62 Brgm.-5P (103" wb)	3250	2300	3300	4600	7500	16,000
Model 42 Single-Drive Brgm. (103" wb)	2900	2200	3200	4400	7000	15,000
Model 12 Brgm.-4P (94" wb)	2400	2000	3000	4200	6500	14,000
Single-Drive Cpe. (103" wb)	2400	1800	2800	4000	6200	13,000
Roadster (103" wb)	2650	1600	2700	3800	5800	12,000

1917 OHIO ELECTRIC

Model 63 Brgm. (103" wb)	3250	2300	3300	4600	7500	16,000
Model 43 Brgm. (103" wb)	2900	2200	3200	4400	7000	15,000
Model 12 Cpe. (103" wb)	2400	2000	3000	4200	6500	14,000
Single-Drive Rdstr. (103" wb)	2650	1800	2800	4000	6200	13,000
Coach (103" wb)	3250	2250	3300	4500	7300	15,500

1918 Ohio Electric, model 63, coupe, HAC

1918 OHIO ELECTRIC

Coach (103" wb)	2680	2250	3300	4500	7300	15,500
Brougham (103" wb)	3250	2300	3300	4600	7500	16,000

OHIO FALLS — The car produced in New Albany, Indiana from 1913-1914 by the Ohio Falls Motor Car Company was marketed as the Pilgrim. Refer to Pilgrim.

OHL — Percy C. Ohl of Plainfield, New Jersey was indicated as the manufacturer of an automobile in the Hiscox book *Horseless Vehicles, Automobiles, Motor Cycles* published in 1900. Further documentation is lacking.

O.K. — Although the O.K. Machine Works of Buffalo, New York introduced its new touring car under its own name in January 1904, the company quickly decided to call it a Red Jacket instead. Refer to Red Jacket.

1906 Okey, runabout, NAHC

OKEY — Columbus, Ohio — (1896-1907) — Perry Okey had a machine shop of his own at age sixteen. It was in the back of the Columbus Electric Light and Power Company where he worked as an apprentice electrician, and it was there that he built his first car, a tricycle, in 1896, which he fitted first with a four-stroke single-cylinder water-cooled engine of his own design, then a four-stroke air-cooled engine. All his work was experimental and conducted evenings and Sundays. In 1900 Perry Okey became a one-man automobile company. His next engine was another water-cooled one-lunger that generated an estimable 14 hp at 1000 rpm and could propel the chain drive runabout into which it was fitted at a brisk 35 mph clip. It was sold in 1901. Another car followed that was purchased for $750 by a local physician in 1902. By 1904 Okey was building his fifth car, and he had switched his pleasure to two cylinders and two-stroke engines. Four runabouts with this new engine and bevel gear drive (and the same planetary transmission as the predecessor cars) were built and sold by the end of 1905. Hugh Dolnar took a ride in one of these cars in the early summer of 1906 and reported enthusiastically in *Cycle and Automobile Trade Journal:* "The little motor performed to admiration. Perfect combustion, no odor whatever, and a musical exhaust in perfect rhythm when the muffler was open, and perfect silence on the high gear with muffler closed. The motor started constantly on the spark, and except the low-power hill climbing the action of the Okey Runabout was simply ideal." Perry Okey, now in his early thirties, was still a one-man operation, and Dolnar was obviously championing his cause. Believing him to be capable of producing "better and lower cost light cars than any other man can make," he subtly pleaded for someone to finance the young man's manufacturing endeavors. Some minimal financing did follow and the Okey Motor Car Company was organized in Columbus in January 1907. His new production car was a three-cylinder two-stroke 20 hp runabout with shaft drive, a 92-inch wheelbase and a $1400 price tag. It was altogether admirable. But the money ran out by November. In December the Okey receiver was authorized to borrow $2000 to continue the business until all orders on hand were completed. It is tantalizing to consider what Perry Okey might have done in the industry if he had been more substantially backed with capital.

OKLAHOMA SIX — Oklahoma City, Oklahoma — (1917) — The Midland Motor Car & Truck Company was a million-dollar incorporation backed entirely by Oklahoma men. Heading the group was James Aydelotte, described as an "oil expert and chairman of the state board of affairs." George L. Cooke, who was cashier of the State National Bank, was treasurer of the venture. W. Phelan of Norman, A.T. Alison of Tulsa, E.C. Million of McAlester and W.C. Greenings of Oklahoma City were involved as well. That the company's new car was to be called the Oklahoma Six represents the total of what has been discovered about it. Possibly the Oklahoma Six never reached the prototype stage. Certainly it never passed it. There may have been some trucks built, but by the end of 1918 the Midland Motor Car & Truck Company was no more.

OLDFIELD — Minneapolis, Minnesota — (1914) — Whether the fact that he shared a last name with America's most flamboyant race driver enhanced or hindered Lee Oldfield's competition career is open to conjecture, but in 1912 this Oldfield hung up his driving gloves after a modest motor sports success. Initially establishing a garage and Marmon dealership in Wichita, Kansas in October that year, Oldfield subsequently decided that Minneapolis might be a greener pasture for his automotive ambitions. There, late in 1913, he designed a cyclecar his plans for manufacture of which he announced a few months later. By March of 1914 he had changed his mind, however, informing the trade press that he would retain the "one car for experimenting and devote the present year to bringing this car to perfection." That perfection was realized is doubtful, that the car was never produced is certain. By early spring Oldfield had taken over the presidency of the Shapiro-Michaelson Motor Car Company the proposed product of which was the Michaelson cyclecar.

1924 Oldfield, coupe, (Barney at wheel), KM

OLDFIELD — Los Angeles, California — (1924) — With a name like Barney's, how could the Oldfield miss? Doubtless this was the reason for the $10 million incorporation of Oldfield Motors Corporation in Los Angeles in January 1917. Arthur Fisk, a politician and former postmaster of San Francisco, James J. Jeffries and W.L. Wilson joined Barney Oldfield in this venture, which followed the announcement of his retirement from racing. This company went nowhere, and did it before the building of even a prototype. Thereupon, in the tradition of sports figures which has come down to this day, Barney Oldfield joined Harvey Firestone's promotion department. "'Firestone Tires are my only life insurance,' says Barney Oldfield, world's greatest driver," the ads read; the Oldfield tire became Firestone's racing division. Barney sold out his Firestone interests in 1924, and tried the automobile industry again. The new Oldfield Motors Corporation (and the principals behind this one remain a mystery) was announced early in 1924 — and this time a prototype was built. A six-cylinder 75 hp Wisconsin-engined coupe on a 130-inch wheelbase, the car was put together in the Long Beach branch plant of the Kimball Truck Company. It featured balloon tires, four-wheel brakes, a mahogany dashboard curved to fit the cowl and a dash-mounted gasoline gauge. In May Barney Oldfield announced that he was driving the car to Indianapolis for the 500, not to race it there, of course, but to promote it. By now he had decided on $3550 for the Oldfield's price, but whether he took any orders at Indy is not known. Returning to Los Angeles, a showroom was opened, and the Oldfield prototype became an eight (possibly a Miller engine). And that's where the project ended. Barney Oldfield had fallen in love, and took off for Europe on his honeymoon. By the time he returned, interest in the project had dissipated. Five years later, the Wall Street crash wiped him out. He never ventured into the automobile industry again. He wrote his memoirs and was featured in a movie about himself. Prior to his death in 1946, he was an employee at a California country club.

OLDS — Crookston, Minnesota — (1900) — Ransom Eli wasn't the only Olds to build an automobile. In 1900 in Crookston a man by the name of W.H. Olds built a gasoline runabout too, which he reported to *The Motor Vehicle Review* was "giving satisfaction." That December he was also at work on several other gasoline vehicles and declared himself in the market for good motor vehicle supplies. He never did, however, proceed into manufacture.

OLDSMOBILE

1897 Oldsmobile, gasoline experimental, JAC

1901 Oldsmobile, with Roy Chaplin at the tiller, JAC

OLDSMOBILE — Detroit & Lansing, Michigan — (1897-1942 et. seq.) — The Olds Motor Vehicle Company was organized in Lansing, Michigan on August 21st, 1897, and Oldsmobile remains today America's oldest manufacturer of automobiles. The selection of 1897 as the official Olds beginning in the automotive field is somewhat arbitrary, because Ransom Eli Olds had already been experimenting for a decade by that time. Indeed, he tested his first car in 1887, a cumbersome three-wheeled steamer which ran but not very well; in 1891 he followed with another steamer which ran better and even made the pages of *Scientific American*. His first gasoline car arrived in 1896, a dos-a-dos four-seater perched high on its chassis, and powered by a single-cylinder 5 hp engine. Several others resulted, which in turn resulted in Ransom Olds organizing the Olds Motor Vehicle Company that August in '97 because the family business of P.F. Olds & Son (renamed Olds Gasoline Engine Works in November) was too busy being one of the biggest manufacturers of gasoline engines in central Michigan to get into the automobile business. By the middle of 1898, Olds had managed to produce only a half-dozen cars at best. This lamentable situation was resolved on May 8th, 1899 when Olds Motor Works was organized with a capital stock of a half-million dollars, acquiring the previous Olds businesses, and finally getting things moving. Ransom Old's personal investment was $400; $199,600 was provided by lumber millionaire Samuel L. Smith, whose sons Frederick and Angus had just graduated from college and needed gainful employment. With so much money now to hand, Ransom Olds returned to experimentation. From 1899 to 1900 about eleven different automobiles were built (some of them electrics) in the new Olds factory in Detroit, and plans were made to put a number of them on the market in 1901. But it didn't happen that way. Although there is no evidence that anyone at Olds Motor Works started it, the fire at the plant on March 9th, 1901 was later referred to by Fred Smith as "the best move ever made by the management." Rescued from the blaze was a single gasoline runabout upon which all company hopes now of necessity had to be focused. It was the curved dash Oldsmobile, as delectable a little car as ever was built. Powered by a single-cylinder four-stroke engine developing 7 hp at 500 rpm and good for "one chug per telegraph pole," the Olds featured an all-spur geared two-speed transmission, center chain drive, two longitudinal springs running fore and aft which served as side frame members, a total weight of 700 pounds and an asking price of $650. Many people asked for it. From 425 cars in 1901, Olds production rose to 2500 in 1902, 4000 in 1903 and 5508 in 1904. The curved dash Oldsmobile was America's first quantity-produced car. No doubt its success encouraged others of mechanical mind to enter the automotive field, and persuaded those with the money to invest that the automobile was not a passing fad but a potentially viable business. This is not to discredit the pioneering of Alexander Winton, with whom Random Olds diced, incidentally, at Ormond-Daytona in 1902, pitting his single-cylinder racing Olds Pirate against Winton's four-cylinder Bullet I. (Neither claimed victory, both said they put up 57 mph.) But Winton, the first in America to set up

orderly production of a gasoline automobile, was building relatively expensive cars in relatively small numbers in Cleveland. In Detroit (and from 1904 back home in Lansing), Ransom Olds was building cars that more people could afford — and he was building many more of them. Certainly, too, Olds Motor Works proved to be probably the best apprentice training school in America. Many subsequent key figures in the industry got their start putting together the curved dash Oldsmobile. The factors contributing to the car's success included an all-out promotion campaign (extensive advertising, and performances at fairs throughout the Midwest), young Roy Chapin's epic drive to New York City during the fall of 1901 for the automobile show, the cross-country trek of L.L. Whitman and Eugene Hammond in 1903, followed by the transcontinental of two curved dashes nicknamed Old Steady and Old Scout in 1905. Despite popular assumption, the curved dash Oldsmobile was not the only model offered by Olds Motor Works during these years, nor was it discontinued in 1905 when production reached 6500 cars, and Gus Edwards and Vincent Bryan wrote "In My Merry Oldsmobile." The demise of the curved dash had been a foregone conclusion the year before, however, when Ransom Olds and the Smiths quarreled regarding the car's future — and Olds lost. By now the Smiths were anxious to move on to bigger and more luxurious cars and because Olds wasn't he left the company in January 1904 and very soon thereafter began manufacture of the Reo. Meanwhile, the Smiths continued the curved dash in production through 1907, though relegating it further and further back in the company catalogue as rather grander Oldsmobiles began to take its place, the grandest a 36 hp four on a 106-inch wheelbase (fully sixty inches longer than the curved dash) and priced at $2750 as the "Palace Touring" and "Flying Roadster" in 1907. Whether it was that America was not yet ready to accept a big Oldsmobile, or that the Smiths couldn't manage as well without Olds, or simply that one generally cannot sell more $2750 cars than $650 ones anyway, the result was a nosedive in the marketplace. In 1906, 1600 Oldsmobiles were produced, in 1907 just 1200, in 1908 down further to 1055. But by December of 1908 William C. Durant had bought Olds Motor Works for his new General Motors company. The Smiths received $17,279 in cash and a little over $3 million in GM stock. Billy Durant received a company in financial distress. "That's a hell of a price to pay for a bunch of road signs," he commented regarding the nationwide network of Olds billboards which seemed to be one of the company's chief tangible assets. But Durant was aware as well that the Olds name and history were intangible assets worth far, far more. Durant made many foolish purchases for General Motors; Olds Motor Works wasn't one of them. By now there was a $4500 six-cylinder Oldsmobile (introduced for 1908) which was continued with the $2750 four for 1909, together with a new smaller $1250 four called the Model 20 that was makeshifted from the Buick Model 10 — and which accounted for 5325 of the 6575 Oldsmobiles sold that year. No doubt the Olds 20, built just that one season, was produced to bring some fast cash into the company's treasury because in 1910 and for the years following, Oldsmobiles were all-out luxury cars: the four-cylinder Special followed by the Autocrat and Defender, and the Limited, with six cylinders, 707 cubic inches, a wheelbase which stretched 138 inches in 1911 over wheels a colossal 42 inches in diameter. It was the Limited which inspired the famous William Harnden Foster painting, "Setting the Pace." The Limited's pace was a wicked 70 mph. By 1913, when the Defender was reduced in price and a less formidable six replaced the Limited, the future course of Oldsmobile as a builder of quality cars of medium price was set — this policy cemented with introduction of a smaller $1285 four (the "baby Olds") in 1914, and two years later by a very attractively priced V-8 announced at $1295 and continued in production through 1923. Production of 10,507 cars in 1916 doubled to 22,613 in 1917. By this time, having been ousted from General Motors once, Billy Durant was back at the helm again, though his GM tenure would irrevocably end in November 1920. Oldsmobile seems not to have suffered in that turmoil, though GM asked Olds president Edward Ver Linden to leave shortly thereafter (purportedly for lending himself money from the Olds treasury without GM knowledge), and A.B.C. Hardy, longtime Durant associate, took over the Olds managership. It was Hardy who made all Oldsmobiles sixes in 1924, and Cannon Ball Baker who proved their stamina by taking a new Model 30 six (which was introduced at only $750) cross-country that year in twelve-and-a-half days. Olds production in '24 was 44,854 cars, double that of 1922. In 1928 — now with Irving Reuter in charge — production doubled again, to

86,593. The reason this time was the new F-28, a 197-7-cubic-inch 55 hp (up from 40) six, with the four-wheel brakes introduced on Oldsmobiles the year previous. During the year the stock market crashed, Oldsmobile topped the 100,000 mark for the first time. The Viking V-8, an Olds companion car introduced for 1929, didn't long survive, however, and for a while it appeared Oldsmobile might not either, as production dropped to 17,502 cars in 1932. Synchromesh in '31 and a new 82 hp straight-eight for '32 had not helped Oldsmobile fortunes during the Depression's early years, but there was an upswing in 1933 to 36,072 cars when Oldsmobiles received fresh new styling highlighted by what journalists of the day referred to as "beaver-tail rears" — and a terrific surge to 82,150 cars in 1934 when Oldsmobile offered independent front suspension. Heading Oldsmobile now was former engineer C.L. McCuen. With the economy recovering, what Oldsmobile represented — good, solid transportation in a wide line of sixes and eights at good prices — brought good fortune to the company: 183,752 cars in '35, 187,638 in '36, 212,767 in '37. For the 1938 model year the company introduced its "Safety Automatic Transmission," admitting that "a certain amount of manipulation of the gear selector" was necessary for full performance. But for 1940, Hydra-Matic arrived as a fully automatic four-speed transmission available as a $57 option on all Oldsmobiles. The company called it "the most important engineering advancement since the self-starter." In 1941, Oldsmobile had its best year thus far: 230,703 cars. On January 1st, 1942, the venerable name Olds Motor Works gave way to Oldsmobile Division, General Motors. The month following, Sherrod E. Skinner (who had replaced McCuen in 1940) turned all efforts to war production. Ammunition would be the Oldsmobile specialty until peace came.

Oldsmobile Data Compilation
by Dennis Casteele

Curved Dash Olds Data Compilation
by Gary Hoonsbeen

1901-1902-1903

1901 Oldsmobile, curved dash, runabout, OCW

OLDSMOBILE — MODEL R (CDO): The Model "R" was the first of three models to be known as the Curved Dash Oldsmobile and the first car produced by the Olds Motor Works to bear the name Oldsmobile.

Its early design was conceived in late 1900 and a dozen or so prototypes were built before the Detroit factory was destroyed by fire in March of 1901. Production cars first reached the public market in late summer of 1901 and it is generally accepted that about 425 cars were built that year.

The Model "R" CDO was a two-passenger car which could be fitted with an optional dos-a-dos (French for back to back) seat to carry one additional adult or two small children. The body was fabricated from wood and the design was very distinctive with its toboggan-like front. The body was painted black with trim in a cherry color. The frame and body were decorated with a gold pin striping.

The engine crankshaft was designed to hold the flywheel, planetary transmission and high speed clutch assembly. A third outboard bearing, mounted on the frame, supported this additional weight and load. The transmission contains a reverse, brake and low speed drum. A chain drive sprocket is located between the reverse and brake drum. The outside surface of the low speed drum also serves as the high speed clutch plate. A shifting lever at the right side of the operator controls the low speed and reverse transmission bands along with the mechanism which engages the high speed clutch pads.

A brake pedal on the floor operates the transmission brake band. Next to the brake pedal is a foot throttle which connects to the carburetor via a thin iron wire.

All Curved Dash Oldsmobiles are right hand drive and steered by means of a tiller. A crank handle is permanently fixed to the engine and extends out the side of the body such that the operator can start it while sitting in the seat.

The Model "R" CDO was changed during the years it was sold and major changes did not coincide with the calendar year. The earliest Model "R" cars were first modified during 1902 by adding truss rods under the front and rear axles, providing an emergency brake system in the rear differential housing, the carburetor was changed from a crude mixer requiring a fuel pump to a simple floatless design which was gravity fed from the fuel tank and relocating the water tank to allow more water capacity.

Another round of major changes was introduced again in mid-1903 which included redesigning the differential housing to a more conventional bolt-together style from ones that screwed together, changing the cylinder head block so a separate water jacket sleeve was no longer needed along with adding some cooling fins, replacing the #4 block chain with a #46 roller chain and improving the water cooling by replacing the smooth tubed radiator and centrifugal pump with a finned radiator and a positive flow gear pump.

The early Model "R" Oldsmobiles were equipped with tubeless 28 by 2-1/2 inch tires on wire wheels. During the life of the Model "R" as many as seven other variations of wheels were offered. These include 12 and 14 spoke wooden artillery wheels, a metal-spoked wheel and a staggered-spoked design. All these were offered for both tubeless and 28 by 3 clincher tires.

There is some evidence that the production of the Model "R" Oldsmobile continued well into 1904 with rear hub brakes being added primarily for the foreign market.

Early Model "R" Oldsmobiles were supplied with a 3 inch bicycle bell mounted on the tiller which was replaced by a bulb horn in 1903. Lights were offered as an option and were supplied by "Neverout". A buggy top was also an option and supplied either in leather or rubber cloth. If the top was ordered a special bag was installed under the inside of the curved dash to hold the side curtains.

I.D. DATA: Serial numbers were found on compression release pedal, patent plate & cylinder head casting. Starting: (1901) 6000. (1902) 6451. (1903) 10000. Ending: (1901) 6450 (est.). (1902) 9999. (1903) 19999. Note: Above is a range of serial numbers but it appears blocks within these ranges were not used.

Model No.	Body Type & Seating	Price	Weight	Prod. Total
R	2-Pass.	650	650	—

ENGINE: Horizontal cylinder. One. Cast iron block. B & S: 4-1/2 x 6 in. Brake H.P. 4-1/2 @ 600 R.P.M. Main bearings: Two. Valve lifters: Mechanical. Carb.: mixer.

CHASSIS: [Series R] W.B.: 66 in. Frt/Rear Tread: 5 in. Tires: 28 x 3.

TECHNICAL: Planetary transmission. Speeds: 2F/1R. Controls located on right side of driver-hand control. Clutch: fingers (4). Chain drive. Semi-floating rear axle. Overall ratio: 3.1666:1. Mechanical brakes on rear differential & transmission. Tubeless/clincher-wooden artillery wheels.

OPTIONS: Top. Fenders.

HISTORICAL: Calendar year production: (1901) 425. (1902) 2500 (est.). (1903) 3924.

1903 Oldsmobile, curved dash runabout, OCW

1901
Curved dash 1 cyl.

	FP	5	4	3	2	1
Rbt	650	3750	7500	12,500	17,500	25,000

1902
Curved Dash, 1-cyl.

Rbt	650	3600	7200	12,000	16,800	24,000

1903
Curved Dash, 1-cyl.

Rbt	650	3600	7200	12,000	16,800	24,000

1904

1904 Oldsmobile, curved dash runabout, OCW

OLDSMOBILE — MODEL "6C" (CDO): The Model "6C" Curved Dash Oldsmobile was first introduced to the public in April of 1904 and looked almost identical to its predecessor the Model "R". It remained in production until the end of calendar 1904. Although the Models "R" and "6C" appeared to be the same they were in fact totally different cars. The body on the "6C" was slightly larger and contained more reinforcing, the running gear was heavier and stronger, the transmission contained only a low speed and reverse drum and hub brakes were added to the rear wheels while retaining the brake in the rear axle differential housing.

A new Holley carburetor was used which contained a conventional cork float. The wheels remained 28 by 3 inch and 12 spoke artillery wheels were standard. Early Model "6C" cars used ball bearings in the front wheels but after a few hundred cars these were replaced with roller bearings. The rear wheel hub brakes were first supplied with external bands but this was later changed to internal expanding brake shoes.

The body was all wood, painted black with a bright red trim. There is some evidence that dark green cars were also offered. Controls for operating the "6C" were almost identical to those offered on the earlier model "R".

I.D. DATA: Serial numbers were located on patent plate & brass plug on cylinder head. Starting: 20000. Ending: 25000 (est.).

Model No.	Body Type & Seating	Price	Weight	Prod. Total
6C	Std. Rbt.-2P	650	800	2500

ENGINE: Horizontal. One. Cast iron block. B & S: 5 x 6 in. Brake H.P. 7 @ 600 R.P.M. Main bearings: Two. Valve lifters: Mechanical. Carb.: Holley.4

OLDSMOBILE — TOURING RUNABOUT — ONE-CYLINDER: The Oldsmobile Touring Runabout was a larger car than the Model "6C" Curved Dash Oldsmobile. It is popularly known as the "French Front" model. The wheelbase was 10 inches longer than that of the Curved Dash. The Touring Runabout had a conventional hood with louvers on the side, twin bucket seats to accommodate two passengers and a sloping rear deck. The fenders were larger than those used on the Curved Dash and a steering wheel was featured. The horizontal engine was mounted under the "body", which was little more than a pedestal held in place with just four bolts. Standard equipment included pressure feed lubrication, jump spark ignition, single chain drive, angle steel frame, tires and tools. A 1904 Oldsmobile advertisement claimed, "For business or pleasure, in rain or sunshine, the pioneer runabout has no equal. It is always ready. It represents the latest and best in automobile construction — the product of the largest automobile plant in the world." Colors for the Touring Runabout were dark red or dark green. Oil brass side lamps were included.

I.D. DATA: Serial number information not available.

Model No.	Body Type & Seating	Price	Weight	Prod. Total
TR	Tr. Rbt.-2P	750	NA	Note 1

Note 1: Production of the Touring Runabout and Light Tonneau combined is believed to be 2500 units.

ENGINE: Horizontal. One. Cast iron block. B & S: 5 x 6 in. Brake H.P.: 7 @ 600 R.P.M. Main bearings: Two. Valve lifters: Mechanical. Carb.: Holley model 4.

OLDSMOBILE — LIGHT TONNEAU — ONE-CYLINDER: Another new model for 1904 was the Oldsmobile Light Tonneau Touring Car. It was a four-passenger model with a detachable tonneau body. With the tonneau removed, it looked like a larger version of the Touring Runabout. It was built on a chassis with an eight inch longer wheelbase than the Touring Runabout. The hood on both models did not cover an engine, but instead housed the gas and water tanks and battery. The list of standard equipment and body finish colors was the same for both models. The tonneau incorporated rear entrance provisions with a door in the center of the rear. This year the car could be ordered with or without a rear seat. Oil brass side lamps were included.

I.D. DATA: Serial number information not available.

1904 Oldsmobile, curved dash runabout, HAC

Model No.	Body Type & Seating	Price	Weight	Prod. Total
LT	Lt. Tonn. w/o rear seat-2P	850	NA	Note 1
LT	Lt. Tonn. w/rear seat-4P	950	NA	Note 1

Note 1: Production of the Touring Runabout and Light Tonneau combined believed to be 2500 units.

ENGINE: Horizontal. One. Cast iron block. B & S: 5-1/2 x 6 in. Brake H.P.: 10 @ 600 R.P.M. Main bearings: Two. Valve lifters: Mechanical. Carb.: Holley.

CHASSIS: [Series "6C"] W.B.: 66 in. Frt./Rear Tread: 56 in. Tires: 28 x 3. [Touring Runabout] W.B.: 76 in. Frt./Rear Tread: 56 in. Tires: 28 x 3. [Light Tonneau] W.B.: 83 in. Frt./Rear Tread: 56 in. Tires: 30 x 3-1/2.

TECHNICAL: [All Models] Planetary transmission. Speeds: 2F/1R. Controls located outboard of right-hand driver's position. Disk type clutch. Semi-floating rear axle. Overall ratio: 3.44:1. Mechanical two-wheel brakes. Clincher type wood artillery wheels.

OPTIONS: Top of leather. Bulb type horn. Rear seat in Light Tonneau (100.00).

HISTORICAL: Introduced: April, 1904. Production: *The Production Figure Book For U.S. Cars* shows total production of 5,508 cars and commercial vehicles combined. Other sources say that 2,234 Curved Dash models were assembled in 1904.

Innovations: New models introduced. Steering wheels used on new models. Holley carburetor introduced. Curved Dash engine had larger bore size, larger cooling system, improved main bearing design and rear drum brakes.

R.E. Olds left Oldsmobile and formed Reo Motor Car Co. By the end of the year Olds employment rose to an all-time high of 500 workers. Two slogans used in 1904 were "You see them wherever you go; They go wherever you see them," and "All roads alike to the Oldsmobile." Oldsmobile was America's top auto-maker in 1904. One advertisement offered, "A captivating and beautifully illustrated automobile story 'Golden Gate to Hell Gate,'" which would be sent to interested parties upon receipt of a two-cent stamp. Oldsmobile also claimed "Record breaking sales" and "a host of satisfied customers."

1904
Curved Dash, 1-cyl.

	FP	5	4	3	2	1
Rbt	675	3600	7200	12,000	16,800	24,000
French Front, 1-cyl., 7 hp						
Rbt	750	3300	6600	11,000	15,400	22,000
Light Tonneau, 1-cyl., 10 hp						
Ton	1050	3150	6300	10.500	14,700	21,000

1905

OLDSMOBILE — MODEL B (CDO): The Model "B" Curved Dash Oldsmobile was introduced around the beginning of 1905 and remained in production until late 1906. It looked very much like its predecessors the Model "R" and "6C" but was an entirely new car in design.

The engine design was similar to the Model "6C" but contained more reinforcing. The connecting rod was changed to a marine type, with a separate cap, while the models "R" and "6C" had a hinged bearing cap. The water jacket inlets and outlets were also improved over the Model "6C" to

1905 Oldsmobile, touring runabout, OCW

eliminate hot spots in the cylinder head. The flywheel on the Models "R" and "6C" had spokes whereas the Model "B" flywheel was cast with a few holes between the hub and the rim.

All the spring leaves on the Model "B" run from the front to rear axles. On the earlier models only the bottom spring leaf is continuous with the upper leaves terminating at the frame leaving a long gap which is filled in with a wooden block.

The front axle on the Model "B" does not contain a truss rod and there are 2 truss rods on the rear. The Model "B" did not use a brake drum in the rear differential housing but a brake drum was added to the transmission. Two brake pedals were used, one for the rear hub brakes and one for the transmission brake.

I.D. DATA: Serial numbers located on patent plate and brass plug on cylinder head. Starting: 50000. Ending: 52000 (est.).

Model No.	Body Type & Seating	Price	Weight	Prod. Total
B	Std. Rbt.-2P	650	NA	NA

ENGINE: Horizontal. One. Cast iron block. B & S: 5 x 6 in. Brake H.P. 7 @ 600 R.P.M. Main bearings: Two. Valve lifters: Mechanical. Carb.: float type.

1905 Oldsmobile, touring runabout (Howard Coffin at wheel), JAC

OLDSMOBILE — TOURING RUNABOUT — ONE-CYLINDER: The Touring Runabout was carried over as a 1905 model with no major changes. The two-passenger model again had a louvered hood, with top access door, containing fuel, water and battery. The radiator was again of honeycomb design. Standard equipment included a steering wheel on a brass column, brass plated side lamps, horizontal seven horsepower one-cylinder engine under the body, two-speed and reverse planetary transmission, pressure feed lubrication, jump spark ignition, single chain drive, angle steel frame, 76-inch wheelbase, 28 x 3-inch tires and tools. Colors were once again dark green and red.

I.D. DATA: Serial number information not available.

Model No.	Body Type & Seating	Price	Weight	Prod. Total
TR	Tr. Rbt.-2P	750	NA	NA

ENGINE: Horizontal. One. Cast iron block. B & S: 5 x 6 in. Brake H.P.: 7 @ 600 R.P.M. Main bearings: Two. Valve lifters: Mechanical. Carb.: Holley.

OLDSMOBILE — LIGHT TONNEAU — ONE-CYLINDER: The Light Tonneau or rear-entrance Tonneau Touring car was carried over for 1905 with no changes to speak of. Standard equipment included a four-passenger detachable tonneau body, single cylinder horizontal engine under body, two-speed reverse and planetary transmission, pressure feed lubrication, jump spark ignition, single chain drive, angle steel frame, 83-inch wheelbase, 3-1/2 x 30-inch tires and tools. There is no indication, in 1905

1020

advertisements, of continued availability without a rear seat. There was now a Light Delivery Car — actually a van — built on this chassis. It sold for $1,000, but fits technically into the commercial vehicle field. The Light Tonneau again had brass side lamps and came in colors of dark green and red.

I.D. DATA: Serial number information not available.

Model No.	Body Type & Seating	Price	Weight	Prod. Total
LT	Lt. Tonn.-4P	950	NA	NA

ENGINE: Horizontal. One. Cast iron block. B & S: 5-1/2 x 6 in. Brake H.P.: 10 @ 600 R.P.M. Main bearings: Two. Valve lifters: Mechanical. Carb.: Holley.

1905 Oldsmobile, side entrance touring, JAC

OLDSMOBILE — SIDE ENTRANCE TOURING — TWO-CYLINDER: *Cycle and Automobile Trade Journal* said that the new two-cylinder Oldsmobile Touring Car was "quite a departure for this concern." It was of side entrance design. Essentially, the body sections sat on two pedestals. The front one carried twin bucket seats and featured open sides for passenger access. The rear pedestal carried a wide tonneau with a solid back. Passengers entered the rear tonneau by means of hinged doors which shielded the area between the two pedestals and the tonneau and the bucket seatbacks. The body was constructed of wood and finished in dark blue. Running gear was painted yellow, making for an attractive combination. Standard equipment included the two-cylinder horizontally-opposed engine mounted amid ships, two-speed and reverse planetary transmission, mechanical lubrication, jump spark ignition, single chain drive, angle steel frame, 30 x 4-inch tires in rear, 30 x 3-1/2-inch tires in front, tools and brass oil lamps. The factory claimed a top speed of 40 mph. The two-cylinder car had a conventional hood and honeycomb brass radiator up front.

I.D. DATA: Serial number information not available.

Model No.	Body Type & Seating	Price	Weight	Prod. Total
TR	2-dr. Side Ent. Tonn. Tr.-5P	1400	2350	NA

ENGINE: Horizontal-opposed. Two. Cast iron block. B & S: 5-1/4 x 6 in. Brake H.P.: 20 @ 600 R.P.M. Main bearings: Four. Valve lifters: Mechanical. Carb.: Holley.

CHASSIS: [Series "B"] W.B.: 66 in. Frt./Rear Tread: 56 in. Tires: 28 x 3. [Touring Runabout] W.B.: 76 in. Frt./Rear Tread: 56 in. Tires: 28 x 3. [Light Tonneau] W.B.: 83 in. Frt./Rear Tread: 56 in. Tires: 30 x 3-1/2. [Two-Cylinder Touring] W.B.: 90 in. Frt./Rear Tread: 55 in. Tires: (front) 30 x 3-1/2; (rear) 30 x 4.

TECHNICAL: [All Models] Planetary transmission. Speeds: 2F/1R. Right-hand (outboard) mounted gearshift. Disk type clutch. Semi-floating rear axle. Overall ratio: 3.44:1. Two-wheel mechanical brakes. (Two-cylinder touring also has third brake acting on transmission). Wood-spoke artillery wheels.

OPTIONS: Bulb horn (w/c). Leather top (CDO). Brass dashboard "grab" rail.

HISTORICAL: Calendar year production: 6500 [All Models] Innovations: New two-cylinder model. Marine type connecting rods in CDO engine. Improved CDO engine waterjacketing. Improved springs on Curved Dash models.

This was the last year that Oldsmobile ranked as America's number one auto-maker. A new high of 612 employees turned out 36 cars per day. Percy Megargel and Dwight Huss made a cross-country trip in a Curved Dash Oldsmobile, nicknamed "Old Scout," which is still owned by the company. Oldsmobile was a member of the Association of Licensed Automobile Manufacturers. One ad slogan used in 1905 read, "The Best Line of Light Cars ever placed on the market."

1905

Curved Dash, 1-cyl.

	FP	5	4	3	2	1
Rbt	675	3600	7200	12,000	16,800	24,000
French Front, 1-cyl., 7 hp						
Rbt	750	3300	6600	11,000	15,400	22,000
Touring Car, 2-cyl.						
Tr	1400	3150	6300	10,500	14,700	21,000

1906

1906 Oldsmobile, straight-dash runabout, OCW

OLDSMOBILE — CURVED DASH MODEL "B" — ONE-CYLINDER: The Model "B" Curved Dash Oldsmobile was carried over. The primary change was the addition of several accessories as standard equipment to perk-up sagging popularity of this model. A top and storm front with celluloid windows was now included at regular price by the time of the New York Automobile Show at the old Madison Square Garden, Oldsmobile was not even showing the Curved Dash in much of its 1906 advertising.

I.D. DATA: Serial number information not available.

Model No.	Body Type & Seating	Price	Weight	Prod. Total
B	Std. Rbt.-2P	650	NA	Note 1

Note 1: Oldsmobile built 100 one-cylinder cars in 1906. Only some of these had Curved Dash styling. The others were Straight Dash types.

ENGINE: Horizontal. One. Cast iron block. B & S: 5 x 6 in. Brake H.P.: 7 @ 600 R.P.M. Main bearings: Two. Valve lifters: Mechanical. Carb.: Holley model 4.

OLDSMOBILE — STRAIGHT DASH MODEL "B" — ONE-CYLINDER: In 1906, Oldsmobile offered a "Straight" or "piano box" front for the Model "B", in addition to the Curved Dash. The running gear was essentially the same for both models. The body was of wood, as in previous models, painted black or green with red trim. Controls for operating the Model "B" remained the same as earlier models with the exception of an extra brake pedal (see 1905).

I.D. DATA: Serial number information not available.

Model No.	Body Type & Seating	Price	Weight	Prod. Total
B	Std. Rbt.-2P	650	NA	Note 1

Note 1: Total production of the Model "B" was 100 units including both Curved Dash and Straight Dash styles.

OLDSMOBILE — MODEL "L" — TWO-CYLINDER: New for 1906 from Oldsmobile was the two-cycle Model "L" which was an updated and upgraded two-cylinder automobile. One advertisement described it as "the sensation of the season." It was available as a 4-5 passenger touring car with a rear tonneau attached. It also came as a runabout, with twin bucket seats and no tonneau attachment. The tonneau used was of side entrance design. The car also had low-cut front doors, making it what was known as a "fore-door" model. The hood and radiator were much higher than in the past and the fenders much fuller. Standard equipment included brass headlamps and side lights, a pressed steel frame, selective sliding gear transmission, bevel gear drive and a 24 horsepower engine that was claimed to have "only three working parts in the motor itself." Oldsmobile said that this rare machine was "The only novelty in automobiles in five years." It had no gears, valves or guides in the motor. Tools and batteries were located in a box on the right-hand runningboard. Taillights and a horn were included.

I.D. DATA: Serial number information not available.

Model No.	Body Type & Seating	Price	Weight	Prod. Tota.
L	2-dr. Rbt.-2P	1150	1800	Note 1
L	4-dr. Tr.-4/5P	1250	2000	Note 1

Note 1: Total production was 100 units with no breakout available as to body style.

ENGINE: "Double-Action" (Two-Cycle). Two. Cast iron block. B & S: 5 x 5 in. Brake H.P.: 24. Carb.: one-barrel.

OLDSMOBILE — MODEL "S" — FOUR: Oldsmobile's new Model "S" line was promoted as "the best thing on wheels." The large car was said to be of European style and came as a Gentleman's Roadster or Palace Touring Car. Both had a new four-cylinder engine below the hood and featured clamshell front fenders, runningboards, straight-back rear fenders and a high hood/radiator line. The roadster could be ordered with a mother-in-law seat on the rear deck. The front axle was well forward, under the radiator, giving an extra-long wheelbase. Standard features included a pressed steel frame (channel section) with a sub-frame supporting the motor and radiator, sliding gear transmission, bevel gear drive, two acetylene lamps, two oil lamps, a horn and a full set of tools. Runningboards and fenders were designed for easy removal. An accessory cape type folding top was available for the Palace Touring Car. Other features included mechanical valves, forged steel connecting rods, a two-section aluminum crankcase, gravity feed, 15-gallon gas tank, jump spark ignition with four unit dash coils, pump cooling, and a clutch which could be activated by either a foot pedal or the emergency brake lever.

I.D. DATA: Serial number information not available.

Model No.	Body Type & Seating	Price	Weight	Prod. Total
L	Gentleman's Rds.-2P	2250	2100	Note 1
L	Gentleman's Rds.-3P	2250	2200	Note 1
L	4-dr. Palace Tr.-5/6P	2250	2300	Note 1

Note: Total series production was 1400 units.

ENGINE: Vertical. L-head. Cast en bloc. Four. Cast iron block. B & S: 4-1/4 x 4-3/4 in. Brake H.P.: 26-28. Valve lifters: Mechanical. Carb.: Holley.

CHASSIS: [Model "B"] W.B.: 66 in. Frt./Rear Tread: 56 in. Tires: 28 x 3. [Model "L"] W.B.: 102 in. Frt./Rear Tread: 56 in. Tires: (Frt.) 30 x 3-1/2; (Rear) 30 x 4. [Model "S"] W.B.: 106 in. Frt./Rear Tread: 56 in. Tires: (Frt.) 32 x 3-1/2; (Rear) 32 x 4.

Note: Larger wheels and tires on Model "S" Gentleman's Roadster.

1906 Oldsmobile, model L, touring, JAC

TECHNICAL: [Model "B"] Planetary; [Models "S" & "L"]: Selective sliding gear. Speeds: [Model "B"] 2F/1R; [Models "S" & "L"] 3F/1R. Right-hand outboard mounted gearshift. Disk type clutch. Semi-floating rear axle. Two-wheel brakes w/transmission brake. Wood spoke artillery wheels.

OPTIONS: Mother-in-law seat. Folding top. Runningboard luggage rack. Speedometer. Side curtains. Taillights. Adjustable side lamps.

HISTORICAL: Introduced: [Models "S" & "L"] Dec.-Jan., 1905/1906. Calendar year production: [Model "B"]: 100, [Model "S"]: 1400, [Model "L"]: 100. Total: 1600.

Innovations: New straight dash option for Model "B". Two-cycle vertical two-cylinder engine with three working parts for Model "L". Regulation outfit, sliding gear transmission, pressed steel frame, bevel gear drive on Models "L" & "S". Engines below hood on Models "L" & "S". New European type styling.

Oldsmobile dropped to sixth rank among U.S. auto-makers. Corporate headquarters and production facilities were centralized in Lansing, Mich. A 1906 Oldsmobile piloted by Ernest Keeler and Harry Miller competed in Vanderbilt Cup Race. Oldsmobile's 1906 advertisements included coupons to send for catalogs on each model; to order a large Art Calendar designed by George Gibbs (10-cents) and to request a 25-cent one-year subscription to "Motor Talk" magazine. "Motor Talk" was devoted to automobiling.

1906

		FP	5	4	3	2	1
Straight Dash B, 1-cyl.							
Rbt		650	2000	5100	8500	11,900	17,000
Curved Dash B, 1-cyl.							
Rbt		650	3150	6300	10,500	14,700	21,000
Model L, 2-cyl.							
Tr		1250	2800	5700	9500	13,300	19,000
Model S, 4-cyl.							
Tr		2250	3300	6600	11,000	15,400	22,000

1907

1907 Oldsmobile, model H, flying roadster, HAC

OLDSMOBILE — MODEL F — ONE-CYLINDER: The one-cylinder Oldsmobile runabout was offered for the last time this year. Designated the Model "F", it was available in both Curved Dash and Straight Dash Styles. Prices and specifications were the same as in the previous year. Consult the 1906 listings for details.

OLDSMOBILE — MODEL H FLYING ROADSTER — FOUR: The Model H was a single model series. The Oldsmobile catalog for 1907 called it a "pacemaker" and "a car which is distinctive and sportsmanlike, and has plenty of reserve power and speed."

1907 Oldsmobile, model A, touring, HJE

OLDSMOBILE — MODEL A — FOUR: The two-model Model A series was the basic Olds for 1907. Olds claimed this design was at least partially due to Olds performance in the 1906 Glidden Tour. 1907 was the final year the old Curved Dash (or straight dash) model was to be found and it would go on to bigger and more expensive cars for the next few model years.

I.D. DATA: Location of serial numbers is not available. Starting: 60000. Ending: 61200. Engine number location is not available. Starting: 54500. Ending: 55999.

Model No.	Body Type & Seating	Price	Weight	Prod. Total
H	Rds.-3P	2750	2200	Note 1
A	4-dr. Tr.-5P	2750	2600	Note 1
A	2-dr. Limo.-5P	3800	2900	Note 1

Note 1: Oldsmobile model year total was 1,200.

ENGINE: (Both Model A & H used identical engines.) Straight four. Cast gray iron block. B & S: 4-1/2 x 4-3/4 in. Disp.: 302 cu. in. Brake H.P.: 35/40. Main bearings: Three.

CHASSIS: [Model H] W.B.: 106-1/2 in. Frt/Rear tread: both 55 inches. Tires: front 34 x 3-1/2, rear 34 x 4. [Model A] W.B.: 106 in. Frt/Rear tread: both 55 inches. Tires: front 34 x 3-1/2, rear 34 x 4.

TECHNICAL: Sliding gear transmission. Speeds: 3F/1R. Right side control lever. Steel propeller shaft drive. Overall ratio: aprox. 3:1. Pedal operated brakes on shaft, lever operated on rear hubs. Wood artillery wheels.

OPTIONS: Standard equipment on Model H Roadster and Model A Palace Touring included: A full set of tools, two acetylene headlights, two oil tail lamps, a large horn and luggage carrier. Standard equipment on Model A Limousine included: speaking tube, full toilet set, perfumery bottles, ash tray and silk trim. Model H Roadster colors: Red or French Gray. Limousine usual colors: Dark green and black. Model A Palace touring colors: Gray, Brewster Green or Red.

HISTORICAL: Innovations: introduced nickel plating. Model year sales: 1,200. Model year production: 1,200. Company president of Oldsmobile was F.L. Smith (General Manager).

1907

		FP	5	4	3	2	1
Straight Dash F, 2-cyl.							
Rbt		1200	2000	5100	8500	11,900	17,000
Model H, 4-cyl.							
Fly Rds		2750	3150	6300	10,500	14,700	21,000
Model A, 4-cyl.							
Pal Tr		2750	3600	7200	12,000	16,800	24,000
Limo		2750	3400	6900	11,500	16,100	23,000

1908

1908 Oldsmobile, model M, touring, HJE

OLDSMOBILE — SERIES M/MR — FOUR: This was a continuation of the four cylinder Oldsmobile with a slight increase in displacement over the previous year. The M designation was applied to the touring car and M/R applied to the roadster.

OLDSMOBILE — SERIES Z — SIX: The all new six cylinder series for 1908. Olds began experimental work with this power plant back in 1905.

1908 Oldsmobile, model X, touring, JAC

OLDSMOBILE — SERIES X — FOUR: The X was a second four cylinder car and was very similar to cars built by Olds in 1907. The model carried a very different looking angled front fender design.

I.D. DATA: [Series M, MR & X] Location of serial number is not available. Starting: 61500. Ending: 62500. Engine number location is not available. Starting: 57000. Ending: 58000. [Series Model Z] Location of serial number is not available. Starting: 65000. Ending: 65055. Engine number location is not available. Starting: 60001. Ending: 60055.

Model No.	Body Type & Seating	Price	Weight	Prod. Total
MR	Rds.-2P	2750	2200	Note 1
M	4-dr. Tr.-5P	2750	2600	Note 1
X	4-dr. Tr.-4P	1900	2100	Note 1
Z	4-dr. Tr.-5P	4200	3000	55

Note 1: Oldsmobile model year total for MR, M & X Series was 1,000.

ENGINE: [Series M & MR] Inline four. Cast iron block. B & S: 4-3/4 x 4-3/4 in. Disp.: 336 cu. in. Brake H.P.: 36. Main bearings: Three. [Series X] Inline four. Cast iron block. B & S: 4-1/2 x 4-3/4 in. Disp.: 336 cu. in. Brake H.P.: 32. Main bearings: Three. [Series Z] Inline six. Cast iron block. B & S: 4-1/2 x 4-3/4 in. Disp.: 453 cu. in. Brake H.P.: 48.

CHASSIS: [Series M] W.B.: 112 in. Frt/Rear Tread: 55 in. Tires: front 34 x 3-1/2, rear 34 x 4. [Series MR] W.B.: 106 in. Frt/Rear Tread: 55 in. Tires: front 34 x 3-1/2, rear 34 x 4. [Series X] W.B.: 106 in. Frt/Rear Tread: 55 in. Tires: front 34 x 3-1/2, rear 34 x 4. [Series Z] W.B.: 130 in. Frt/Rear Tread: 56-1/2 in. Tires: Front 36 x 4-1/2, rear 36 x 5.

TECHNICAL: Sliding gear transmission. Speeds: 3F/1R. Right side control lever. Shaft drive. Overall ratio: approx. 3:1. Pedal operated brakes on shaft, lever operated on rear hubs. Wood artillery wheels.

OPTIONS: Standard equipment on Model M, MR & X included: Full tool set, two acetylene headlights, two oil tail lamps, horn and luggage carrier. Standard equipment on Model Z: Tool set, tire irons, muffler cut-out, 9-inch headlamps, Prest-O-Lite tank and oil side and tail lamps.

HISTORICAL: Innovations: Won the Glidden Reliability tour. Calendar year sales: 1,055. Calendar year production: 1,055. Company president of Oldsmobile was W.J. Mead, general manager.
 In late 1908 Oldsmobile became a cornerstone division of General Motors. Introduction of the new six cylinder Model Z's came at Madison Square Garden.

1908
Model X, 4-cyl.

	FP	5	4	3	2	1
Tr	1900	3150	6300	10,500	14,700	21,000
Model M-MR, 4-cyl.						
Rds	2750	3300	6600	11,000	15,400	22,000
Tr	2750	3150	6300	10,500	14,700	21,000
Model Z, 6-cyl.						
Tr	4200	4650	9300	15,500	21,700	31,000

1909

1909 Oldsmobile, model DR, roadster, OCW

OLDSMOBILE — SERIES D/DR — FOUR: The D & DR models were the main line four cylinder cars of this model year. The D model designation was applied to the larger touring cars in this series while the DR was the tag used on the roadster and rare coupe models.

OLDSMOBILE — SERIES X — FOUR: The X series was a carryover from 1908 and offered a slightly smaller four cylinder motor than the D series.

OLDSMOBILE — SERIES Z — SIX: Introduced late in 1908, production continued on this six cylinder series in 1909. This series was the most expensive and rarest Oldsmobile built this year and was the fore runner to the fabled Limited Series offered the next three model years.

OLDSMOBILE — SERIES 20 — FOUR: The most interesting car in the 1909 lineup was the Model 20. A direct result of Oldsmobile's new position in Durant's General Motors, little appears on this model in any factory literature of the day. Most accounts of this car have it as a thinly disguised Buick.

I.D. DATA: [Model D, DR & X] Location of serial number is not available. Starting: 62500. Ending: 63600. Engine number location is not available. Starting: 58000. Ending: 59100. [Model Z] Location of serial number is not available. Starting: 65100. Ending: 65250. Engine number location is not available. Starting: 60501. Ending: 60650. [Model 20] Location of serial number, starting and ending serial numbers and engine number location are not available. Staring engine no.: 4050. Ending: 9375.

1909 Oldsmobile, model D, touring, HJE

Model No.	Body Type & Seating	Price	Weight	Prod. Total
D	4-dr. Tr.-5P	2750	2600	Note 1
D	4-dr. Limo.-5P	3800	2900	Note 1
D	4-dr. Land.-5P	4000	2900	Note 1
DR	2-dr. Rds.-2P	2750	2400	Note 1
DR	2-dr. Cpe.-2P	3500	2600	Note 1
X	2-dr. Spec. Rds.-2P	2000	2300	Note 1
20	4-dr. Tr.-4P	1200	2100	5325
Z	4-dr. Tr.-7P	4000	3000	Note 2
Z	2-dr. Rds.-2P	4000	2800	Note 2

Note 1: Oldsmobile model year total for D & DR Series was 1,100.
Note 2: Oldsmobile model year total for Z Series was 150.

ENGINE: [Model D & DR] Inline four. Cast iron block. B & S: 4-3/4 x 4-3/4 in. Disp.: 336 cu. in. Brake H.P.: 40. Main bearings: Three. Valve lifters: Mechanical. [Model X] Inline four. Cast iron block. B & S: 4-1/2 x 4-3/4 in. Disp.: 302 cu. in. Brake H.P.: 32. Main bearings: Three. Valve lifters: Mechanical. [Model 20] Inline four. Cast iron block. B & S: 3-3/4 x 3-3/4 in. Disp.: 165 cu. in. Brake H.P.: 22. Main bearings: Three. Valve lifters: Mechanical. [Model Z] Inline six. Cast iron block. B & S: 4-3/4 x 4-3/4 in. Disp.: 505 cu. in. Brake H.P.: 60. Valve lifters: Mechanical.

CHASSIS: [Series D & DR] W.B.: 112 in. Frt/Rear Tread: 56-1/2 in. Tires: front 34 x 3-1/2, rear 34 x 4. [Series X] W.B.: 106 in. Frt/Rear Tread: 55 in. Tires: front 32 x 3-1/2, rear 32 x 4. [Model 20] W.B.: 91 in. Frt Tread: 54 in. Tires: front 30 x 3-1/2, rear 30 x 4. [Model Z] W.B.: 130 in. Frt/Rear Tread: 56-1/2 in. Tires: front 36 x 4-1/2, rear 36 x 5.

TECHNICAL: Sliding gear transmission. Speeds: 3F/1R. Side controls. Leather faced cone clutch. Shaft drive. Overall ratio: approx. 3:1. Foot lever external brakes on two wheels. Artillery wheels.

OPTIONS: Model D, DR & X standard equipment: 8-inch headlights, acetylene generator, oil side and tail lamps, full tool set, coat rail, foot rest, trunk rack and horn. Model Z standard equipment: 9-inch headlamps, Prest-O-Lite tank, oil side and tail lamps, full set of tools and tool box, coat rail, foot rest, horn, tire iron and muffler cut-out.

HISTORICAL: Calendar year sales: 6575. Calendar year production: 6575. Company president of Oldsmobile was W.J. Mead, general manager.
 Highest production ouput thus far by Olds. General Motors influence gradually takes over. More closed car production this year.

1909
Model D, 4-cyl.

	FP	5	4	3	2	1
Tr	2750	3150	6300	10,500	14,700	21,000
Limo	3800	3300	6600	11,000	15,400	22,000
Lan	4000	3150	6300	10,500	14,700	21,000
Model DR, 4-cyl.						
Rds	2750	3400	6900	11,500	16,100	23,000
Cpe	3500	3300	6600	11,000	15,400	22,000
Model X, 4-cyl.						
Rbt	2000	3150	6300	10,500	14,700	21,000
Model Z, 6-cyl.						
Rbt	4000	4350	8700	14,500	20,300	29,000
Tr	4000	4500	9000	15,000	21,000	30,000

1910

OLDSMOBILE — SPECIAL — SERIES 22-25 — FOUR: The Special series was a continuation of several years of four cylinder production by Olds. The motor was slightly modified this year and a four speed transmission was fitted. Larger wheelbase, larger tires and an improved suspension system came on 1910 Oldsmobile four cylinders and the new Special nameplate was first applied.

OLDSMOBILE — LIMITED — SERIES 23-24 — SIX: The factory catalog from 1910 says: "The Oldsmobile Limited has created a new standard of luxury in motoring." This model drew heavily from Z series cars of the past two years, but the Limited series Oldsmobile was the largest and most powerful Olds ever built. The Limited nameplate came from the following catalog statement: "While the output (for 1910) has been increased, such a car cannot be produced rapidly, therefore a limited quantity can be built."

1909 Oldsmobile, Limited, touring, OCW

I.D. DATA: [Special] Location of serial numbers is not available. Starting: 67000. Ending: 68525. Engine number location is not available. Starting: 62000. Ending: 63350. [Limited] Location of serial number is not available. Starting: 65500. Ending: 65825. Engine number location is not available. Starting: 60650. Ending: 60950.

Model No.	Body Type & Seating	Price	Weight	Prod. Total
Special Series				
22	4-dr. Tr.-5P	3000	NA	Note 1
25	2-dr. Rds.-2P	3000	NA	Note 1
NA	4-dr. Limo.-5P	4200	NA	Note 1
Limited Series				
23	4-dr. Tr.-7P	4600	NA	Note 2
24	2-dr. Rds.-2P	4600	NA	Note 2
NA	4-dr. C.C. Tr.-5P	4600	NA	Note 2
NA	4-dr. Limo.-5P	5800	NA	Note 2

Note 1: Oldsmobile model year total for Special Series was 1,525.
Note 2: Oldsmobile model year total for Limited Series was 325.

1910 Oldsmobile, Special, roadster, JAC

ENGINE: [Special Series] Inline, cast in pairs. Four. Cast iron block. B & S: 4-3/4 x 4-3/4 in. Disp.: 336 cu. in. Brake H.P.: 40. Main bearings: Three. Valve lifters: Mechanical. Carb.: Oldsmobile. [Limited Series] Inline, cast in pairs. Six. Cast iron block. Disp.: 505 cu. in. Brake H.P.: 60. Valve lifters: Mechanical. Carb.: Oldsmobile.

CHASSIS: [Special Series] W.B.: 118 in. O.L.: 14-1/2 ft. Frt/Rear Tread: 56 in./56 in. Tires: 36 x 4. [Limited Series] W.B.: 130 in. O.L.: 15-1/2 ft. Frt/Rear Tread: 56 in./56 in. Tires: 42 x 4-1/2.

TECHNICAL: Sliding gear, selective transmission. Speeds: 4F/1R. Side lever controls. Leather faced cone clutch. Full floating rear axle. Shaft drive. Overall ratio: approx. 3:1. Internal & external brakes on two wheels. Artillery wheels.

OPTIONS: Mohair top (125.00). Pantasote top (100.00). Glass front. Speedometer. Clock. Extra tires. Special signaling apparatus. Colors other than standard (Green, Blue, Black, Red) (50.00 extra).

HISTORICAL: Calendar year sales: 1,850. Calendar year production: 1,850. Model year sales & production: 1,850. Company president of Oldsmobile was W.J. Mead, general manager.

1910 Oldsmobile, Special, touring, HJE

Oldsmobile continued to offer some of the most powerful and expensive models built by General Motors. Employment dropped to 850 this year. In the introduction year for the "Limited" the famous William Harnden Foster painting "Setting the Pace" was created. Prints would be used several times as Olds advertising pieces.

1910

Special, 4-cyl.	FP	5	4	3	2	1
Rbt	3000	3150	6300	10,500	14,700	21,000
Tr	3000	3400	6900	11,500	16,100	23,000
Limo	4200	3750	7500	12,500	17,500	25,000
Limited, 6-cyl.						
Rbt	4600	9000	18,000	30,000	42,000	60,000
Tr	4600	12,900	25,800	48,200	66,000	86,000
Limo	5800	7800	15,600	26,000	36,400	52,000

1911

1911 Oldsmobile, Limited, limousine, OCW

OLDSMOBILE — SPECIAL — SERIES 26 — FOUR: The Special series was a basic carryover from the previous model year. Little change was made from 1910. This was the least expensive series offered by Olds and this was the last season for the Special series. With its low volume production Olds had little need for two four cylinder powered series and the Autocrat would be carried on to the next model year.

OLDSMOBILE — AUTOCRAT — SERIES 28 — FOUR: New for 1911, the Autocrat offered the most powerful four cylinder engine ever seen in an Oldsmobile. A physically larger car than the Special, the Autocrat would be carried over to the next model year. The Autocrat shared many mechanical features with the larger Limited series Oldsmobiles.

OLDSMOBILE — LIMITED — SERIES 27 — FOUR: The Limited remained one of the largest and most powerful American cars built this season. The 1911 catalog stated: "In the Limited we offer a car which leaves nothing to be desired in design, construction, finish, power or equipment. It stands in the front rank of high grade cars; the greatest of a line universally recognized and ranked among leaders. The motor is the companion to the Autocrat, having the same bore and stroke and incorporating the same mechanical features."

I.D. DATA: [Special series & Autocrat series] Location of serial numbers is not available. Starting: 70000. Ending: 71000. Engine number location is not available. Starting: 65001. Ending: 65999. [Limited series] Location of serial numbers is not available. Starting: 75000. Ending: 75250. Engine number location is not available. Starting: 64000. Ending: 64200.

1911 Oldsmobile, Autocrat, touring, HAC

Model No.	Body Type & Seating	Price	Weight	Prod. Total
Special Series				
NA	2-dr. Rbt.-2P	3000	NA	Note 1
NA	4-dr. Tr.-7P	3000	NA	Note 1
NA	4-dr. Limo.-7P	4200	NA	Note 1
Autocrat Series				
NA	2-dr. Rbt.-2P	3500	NA	Note 1
NA	4-dr. Tr.-7P	3500	NA	Note 1
NA	4-dr. Trbt.-4P	3500	NA	Note 1
NA	4-dr. Limo.-7P	5000	NA	Note 1
Limited Series				
NA	2-dr. Rbt.-2P	5000	NA	Note 2
NA	4-dr. Tr.-7P	5000	NA	Note 2
NA	4-dr. Trbt.-4P	5000	NA	Note 2
NA	4-dr. Limo.-7P	7000	NA	Note 2

Note 1: Oldsmobile model year total for Special Series was 1,000.
Note 2: Oldsmobile model year total for Limited Series was 250.

ENGINE: [Special Series] Inline, cast in pairs. Four. Cast iron block. B & S: 4-3/4 x 4-3/4 in. Disp.: 336 cu. in. Brake H.P.: 36. Main bearings: Three. Valve lifters: Mechanical. Carb.: Oldsmobile. [Autocrat Series] Inline, T-head, cast in pairs. Four. Cast iron block. B & S: 5 x 6 in. Disp.: 471 cu. in. Brake H.P.: 40. Main bearings: Three. Valve lifters: Mechanical. Carb.: Oldsmobile design, constant level float. [Limited Series] Inline, six, T-head, cast in pairs. Six. Cast iron block. B & S: 5 x 6 in. Disp.: 706 cu. in. Brake H.P.: 60. Valve lifters: Mechanical. Carb.: Oldsmobile design, constant level float.

CHASSIS: [Special Series] W.B.: 118 in. O.L.: 13 ft., 10 in. Frt/Rear Tread: 56 in. Tires: 36 x 4. [Autocrat Series] W.B.: 124 in. O.L.: 14 ft., 9 in. Frt/Rear Tread: 56 in. Tires: 38 x 4-1/2, Bailey tread. [Limited Series] W.B.: 138 in. O.L.: 16 ft., 6 in. Frt/Rear Tread: 56 in. Tires: 42 x 4-1/2, Bailey tread.

TECHNICAL: Sliding gear transmission. Speeds: 4F/1R. Outside lever controls. Cone clutch, springs under facing. (Special & Autocrat: leather faced cone clutch). Shaft drive, enclosed in torsion tube. Full floating rear axle. Overall ratio: approx. 3:1. Expanding and contracting brakes on rear wheels, service foot pedal, emergency hand lever. Artillery wheels made of second growth hickory.

OPTIONS: Standard equipment on all series: headlights, side and tail lamps, Prest-O-Lite tank, tire irons, Trauffault-Hartford shock absorbers, Dragon horn, baggage rack, robe rail, floor mat, set of tools and removable seats on some models.

HISTORICAL: Innovations: First time for air type self starter by Oldsmobile. Calendar year sales & production: 1,250. Model year sales & production: 1,250. Company president was W.J. Mead, general manager.

1911
Special, 4-cyl.

	FP	5	4	3	2	1
Rbt	3000	3150	6300	10,500	14,700	21,000
Tr	3000	3400	6900	11,500	16,100	23,000
Limo	4200	3300	6600	11,000	15,400	22,000
Autocrat, 4-cyl.						
Rbt	3500	3300	6600	11,000	15,400	22,000
Tr	3500	3400	6900	11,500	16,100	23,000
Limo	5000	3400	6900	11,500	16,100	23,000
Limited, 6-cyl.						
Rbt	5000	9000	18,000	30,000	42,000	60,000
Tr	5000	12,900	25,800	48,200	66,000	86,000
Limo	7000	7500	15,000	25,000	35,000	50,000

1912

OLDSMOBILE — DEFENDER — SERIES 40 — FOUR: New to the model lineup in 1912 was the Defender series. The smaller of the two four cylinders offered this year, the Defender was a predictor of things to come. After starting out with the small nimble Curved Dash models, Olds offerings grew to the massive Limited; in the years to come the Oldsmobiles would get a bit smaller.

OLDSMOBILE — AUTOCRAT — SERIES 32 — FOUR: A carryover model in 1912 was the Autocrat series. This series was a large four cylinder model sharing many items with the fabled Limited series. This was the final year for the Oldsmobile Autocrat.

1912 Oldsmobile, Autocrat, roadster, HAC

OLDSMOBILE — LIMITED — SERIES 33 — SIX: In its final year of a three-year run, the mighty Limited would leave an imprint on Oldsmobile history. Its huge size and awesome powerplant made it one of the most talked about cars of the era. Although production was well under 1,000 for the three year run, several fine examples of this collector car remain today including a Limited the Olds factory has owned since the 1930's.

I.D. DATA: [Defender Series] Location of serial number is not available. Starting: 80000. Ending: 80325. Engine number location is not available. Starting: 70000. Ending: 70330. [Autocrat Series] Serial number was on brass tag under left front seat. Starting: 71100. Ending: 71600. Engine number location is not available. Starting: 66000. Ending: 66560. [Limited Series] Serial number was on brass tag under left front seat. Starting: 76000. Ending: 76250. Engine number location is not available. Starting: 64500. Ending: 64750.

1912 Oldsmobile, Limited, tourabout, HJE

Model No.	Body Type & Seating	Price	Weight	Prod. Total
Defender Series				
NA	4-dr. Trbt.-4P	3000	NA	Note 1
NA	4-dr. Tr.-5P	3000	NA	Note 1
NA	2-dr. Rdst.-2P	3000	NA	Note 1
NA	2-dr. Cpe.-2P	3600	NA	Note 1
NA	2-dr. Cpe.-5P	3900	NA	Note 1
Autocrat Series				
NA	2-dr. Rdst.-2P	3500	NA	Note 2
NA	4-dr. Tr.-7P	3500	NA	Note 2
NA	4-dr. Trbt.-4P	3500	NA	Note 2
NA	4-dr. Limo.-7P	4700	NA	Note 2
Limited Series				
NA	2-dr. Rdst.-2P	5000	NA	Note 3
NA	4-dr. Trbt.-4P	5000	NA	Note 3
NA	4-dr. Tr.-7P	5000	NA	Note 3
NA	4-dr. Limo.-7P	6300	NA	Note 3

Note 1: Oldsmobile model year total for Defender Series was 325.
Note 2: Oldsmobile model year total for Autocrat Series was 500.
Note 3: Oldsmobile model year total for Limited Series was 250.

ENGINE: [Defender Series] Inline, T-head, cast in pairs. Four. Cast iron block. B & S: 4 x 5-15/16 in. Disp.: 267 cu. in. Brake H.P.: 35. Main bearings: Three. Valve lifters: Mechanical. Carb.: Rayfield Model D. [Autocrat Series] Inline, T-head, cast in pairs. Four. Cast iron block. B & S: 5 x 6 in. Disp.: 471 cu. in. Main bearings: Three. Valve lifters: Mechanical. Carb.: Rayfield Model D. [Limited Series] Inline, T-head, cast in pairs. Six. Cast iron block. B & S: 5 x 6 in. Disp.: 707 cu. in. Brake H.P.: 60. Valve lifters: Mechanical. Carb.: Rayfield Model D.

CHASSIS: [Defender Series] W.B.: 116 in. O.L.: 12 ft., 5 in. Frt/Rear Tread: 60 in. Tires: 36 x 4. [Autocrat Series] W.B.: 126 in. O.L.: 14 ft., 11 in. Frt/Rear Tread: 60 in. Tires: 38 x 4-1/2. [Limited Series] W.B.: 140 in. O.L.: 16 ft., 8 in. Frt/Rear Tread: 60 in. Tires: 42 x 4-1/2.

TECHNICAL: Selective, sliding gear transmission. Speeds: 4F/1R. Side lever controls. (Limited — outside lever controls). Cone clutch, springs under facing. Shaft drive enclosed in torsion tube. Full floating rear axle, pressen steel housing. Overall ratio: approx. 3:1. Internal expanding brakes; external contracting on rear wheels; sevice by foot pedal; emergency by hand lever. Artillery wheels of second growth hickory.

OPTIONS: Nickel trim. Gas headlamps. Side lamps. Tail lamps. Prest-O-Lite tank. Pantasote top. Windshield. Luggage rack. Robe rail. Shock absorbers. Dragon horn. Jones speedometer with light. Tire irons. Tool kit.

HISTORICAL: Innovations: An addition to the main assembly plant was made. Calendar year sales & production: 1,075. Model year sales & production: 1,075. Company president was O.C. Hutchinson, general manager.

1912
Autocrat, 4-cyl., 40 hp

	FP	5	4	3	2	1
Rds	3500	3000	600C	10,000	14,000	20,000
Tr	3500	3150	6300	10,500	14,700	21,000
Limo	4700	3300	6600	11,000	15,400	22,000
Despatch, 4-cyl., 26 hp						
Rds	3000	2800	5700	9500	13,300	19,000
Tr	3000	3000	6000	10,000	14,000	20,000
Cpe	3600	2800	5700	9500	13,300	19,000
Defender, 4-cyl., 35 hp						
2P Tr	3000	3000	6000	10,000	14,000	20,000
4P Tr	3000	3000	6000	10,000	14,000	20,000
2P Rds	3000	2800	5700	9500	13,300	19,000
3P Cpe	3600	3000	6000	10,000	14,000	20,000
5P Cpe	3800	2800	5700	9500	13,300	19,000
Limited, 6-cyl.						
Rds	5000	8250	16,500	27,500	38,500	55,000
Tr	5000	12,900	25,800	48,200	66,000	86,000
Limo	6300	6750	13,500	22,500	31,500	45,000

1913

1913 Oldsmobile, model 53, touring, JAC

OLDSMOBILE — DEFENDER — SERIES 40 — FOUR: Essentially a carryover from the 1912 model year, the Defender series made its final appearance this year. There were some special bodied Defenders in 1913 and most of the production came in this series.

OLDSMOBILE SIX — SERIES 53 — SIX: This was Oldsmobile's new offering for 1913. The least expensive six cylinder offered by Olds, this series would be continued for several years. While the Limited was a well known and recognized machine, its sales levels were less than sustaining. Olds officials hoped this new, lighter six would sell better. The Olds catalog for the Model 53 said, "Without sacrificing any of the rugged strength and dependability for which the Oldsmobile is famous, the entire chassis of the new car has been refined, standardized and lightened."

I.D. DATA: [Defender Series] Serial number on brass tag under left front seat. Starting: 80325. Ending: 80999. Engine number location not available. Starting: 70330. Ending: 70499. [Model 53] Serial number on brass tag under left front seat. Starting: 81000. Ending: 81500. Engine number location not available. Starting: 614180. Ending: 614700.

Model No.	Body Type & Seating	Price	Weight	Prod. Total
DEFENDER				
	4-dr. Tr.-7P	2500	NA	1,000 total
MODEL 53				
	4-dr. Tr.-5P	3200	4625	Note 1
	4-dr. Tr.-7P	3350	4700	Note 1
	4-dr. Trbt.-4P	3200	4635	Note 1

Note 1: Oldsmobile model year total was 500.

ENGINE: [Defender] Cast in pairs, inline, T-head. Four. Cast iron block. B & S: 4 x 5-5/16. Disp.: 267 cu. in. Brake H.P.: 35. Main bearings: Three. Valve lifters: Mechanical. Carb.: Rayfield, Model D. [Model 53] Inline, cast in pairs. Six. Cast iron block. B & S: 4-1/8 x 4-3/4. Disp.: 380 cu. in. Brake H.P.: 50. Valve lifters: Mechanical. Carb.: 1-1/4 float feed.

CHASSIS: [Defender] W.B.: 116 in. O.L.: 12 ft., 5 in. Frt/Rear Tread: 60 in. Tires: 36 x 4. [Model 53] W.B.: 135 in. Tires: front 36 x 4-1/2, rear 36 x 5.

TECHNICAL: Selective, sliding gear transmission. Speeds: [Defender] 4F/1R; [Model 53] 3R/1R. Outside lever controls. [Defender] Cone clutch, springs under facing. [Model 53] Cone clutch, leather faced. Shaft drive. Floating rear axle. Overall ratio: approx. 3:1. Internal expanding brakes; external contracting; service by foot pedal; emergency by hand lever. Artillery wheels made of second growth hickory.

OPTIONS: [Defender] 9-1/2 inch gas headlights, oil/electric side and tail lamps, Prest-O-Lite tank, Pantasote top with cover, windshield, robe rail, shock absorbers, Dragon horn, Jones speedometer with light, floor carpet, tire irons, tool kit and black enamel and white nickel trimmings. [Model 53] Delco self starting ignition, lighting system, 10-1/4 inch electric headlamps, storage battery, power tire pump, top with boot, windshield, robe rail, foot rest, Truffault-Hartford shock absorbers, Klaxon horn, Warner speedometer, Waltham 8-day clock, tire irons, jack and complete tool outfit.

HISTORICAL: Innovations: offered the Delco light/starting system for the first time. Calendar year sales & production: 1,175. Model year sales & production: 1,175. Company president was Charles Nash, general manager. Olds on a campaign to downsize and simplify its model offerings.

1913
Light Six, 6-cyl.

	FP	5	4	3	2	1
4P Tr	3200	3150	6300	10,500	14,700	21,000
Phae	3200	3300	6600	11,000	15,400	22,000
7P Tr	3350	2300	5400	9000	12,600	18,000
Limo	5000	3000	6000	10,000	14,000	20,000
6-cyl., 60 hp						
Tr	5000	3400	6900	11,500	16,100	23,000
4-cyl., 35 hp						
Tr	2500	2000	5100	8500	11,900	17,000

1914

1914 Oldsmobile, model 54, touring, HJE

OLDSMOBILE — BABY OLDS SERIES — MODEL 42 — FOUR: This was an attempt by Oldsmobile to move back into the lighter car market. A late introduction in this model year this was the physically smallest Oldsmobile available in the past few model years. This type of four cylinder car would remain a staple of the Olds lineup for the next few years.

OLDSMOBILE — SIXTH SERIES — MODEL 54 — SIX: The Model 54, a relatively modest update of last year's Model 53, was the mainstay of the 1914 Oldsmobile lineup. The catalog for this year said of the Model 54: "While standards are the outgrowth of development, there is one standard which has made Oldsmobile development possible, and that is the desire and the ability to build each year a car just a little better than anything else on wheels — not only from an engineering standard but from an artistic viewpoint as well."

1914 Oldsmobile, model 47, 7-pass. touring, HJE

I.D. DATA: Model 42. Serial numbers located on brass tag under right front seat cushion. Starting: 84001. Ending: 84399. Starting engine no.: 723700. Model 54. Serial numbers located on brass tag under left front seat. Starting: 83000. Ending: 83999. Starting engine no.: 646653. Ending: N/A.

Model No.	Body Type & Seating	Price	Weight	Prod. Total
42	4-dr. Tr.-5P	1350	2700	400
54	4-dr. Tr.-5P	2975	4300	1000
54	4-dr. Tr.-7P	3150	4350	1000
54	4-dr. Limo.-7P	4300	4530	1000

ENGINE: [Model 42] Inline four. Cast iron block. B & S: 3-1/2 x 5. Disp.: 192 c.i. Brake H.P.: 20. Main bearings: Three. Valve lifters: Mechanical. [Model 54] Inline six. B & S: 4-1/4 x 5-1/4 in. Disp.: 611 c.i. Brake H.P.: 50. Valve lifters: Mechanical. Carb.: Float-feed.

CHASSIS: [Model 42] W.B.: 112 in. Tires: 33 x 4, non-skid in rear. [Model 54] W.B.: 132 inches, all but 7-passenger touring-139 inches. Tires: 36 x 5 either Fisk or Goodyear.

TECHNICAL: [Model 42] Manual transmission. Speeds: 3F/1R. Floor shift. Clutch: cone. Shaft drive, enclosed within torsion tube. Three-quarter floating axle. Brakes: two-wheel rear service, foot control pedal. No drivetrain options. [Model 54] Manual transmission. Speeds: 3F/1R. Controls located right side of driver. Cone clutch. Shaft drive. Floating rear axle. Foot and hand brakes for two wheels. Wooden wheels. Wire wheels.

OPTIONS: $50 extra for any color other than green, blue or gray. Trunks: (50.00 for single trunk, 80.00 for pair of trunks). Other options included special covers and special make tires.

TECHNICAL: The Model 42 or Baby Olds marked the return of Olds to the smaller car market. Model year & calendar year sales: total 1400. President and general manager was C.W. Nash.

1914
Model 54, 6-cyl.

	FP	5	4	3	2	1
Phae	2975	3300	6600	11,000	15,400	22,000
5P Tr	2975	3000	6000	10,000	14,000	20,000
7P Tr	3150	3750	7500	12,500	17,500	25,000
Limo	4300	3000	6000	10,000	14,000	20,000
Model 42, 4-cyl.						
5P Tr	1350	2000	5100	8500	11,900	17,000

1915

1915 Oldsmobile, model 42, roadster, HAC

OLDSMOBILE — BABY OLDS SERIES — MODEL 42 — FOUR: Oldsmobile continued the model 42 basically unchanged for the second model year in 1915. Later in the year this smaller four would be replaced by the larger Model 43 Four. This was the first car which brought Olds back into the popular market place.

OLDSMOBILE — FOURTH SERIES — MODEL 43 — FOUR: Gradually during 1915 Oldsmobile's bread and butter car became the slightly larger Model 43 four. This car would carry over largely unchanged to the next model year. Wheelbase was up eight inches over the Model 42. A Delco Electric system was fitted for starting, lighting and ignition. Power came from valve-in-head motor of less than 200 cubic inches.

OLDSMOBILE — SIXTH SERIES — MODEL 55 — SIX: Oldsmobile had been in the big car business for several years and that front was covered in 1915 with the carryover Model 55. A large six cylinder car, the Model 55 was a limited sales success. Easily traceable back through the 1914 Model 54 to the 1913 Model 53, the most obvious change on the six cylinder was a left hand drive for this season.

I.D. DATA: Model 42. Serial numbers are found on the nameplate under the right front seat cushion. Starting: 84500 for touring. 91500 for roadster. Ending: 91499 for touring; 92499 for roadster. Starting engine no.: 725006. Ending: N/A. Model 43. Serial numbers located on brass tag under right front seat cushion. Starting: 93000. Ending: N/A. Starting engine no.: 738822. Ending: N/A. Model 55. Serial numbers located on brass tag under right front seat cushion. Starting: 92500. Ending: N/A. Starting engine no: 736531. Ending: N/A.

Model No.	Body Type & Seating	Price	Weight	Prod. Total
42-T	4-dr. Tr.-5P	1285	2495	1319
42-R	2-dr. Rds.-2P	1285	2495	1319
43-T	4-dr. Tr.-5P	1095	2620	5921
43-R	2-dr. Rds.-2P	1095	2620	5921
55-T	4-dr. Tr.-7P	2975	4186	114

ENGINE: [Series 42] Inline four. Cast-iron block. B & S: 3-1/2 x 5 in. Disp.: 194.2 c.i. H.P.: 30. Main bearings: Three. Valve lifters: Overhead. Carb.: float-feed. [Series 43] Inline four, valve in head. Cast iron block. B & S: 3-1/2 x 5 in. Disp.: 192 c.i. H.P.: 30. Main bearings: Three. Valve lifters: Overhead. Carb.: float-feed. [Series 55] Inline six, L-head. Cast-iron block. B & S: 4-1/4 x 5-1/4 in. Disp.: 446 c.i. H.P.: 50. Valve lifters: Mechanical. Carb.: float-feed.

1915 Oldsmobile, model 55, 7-pass. touring, HAC

CHASSIS: [Series 42] W.B.: 112 in. Tires: 33 x 4. [Series 43] W.B.: 120 in. Frt/Rear Tread: 56 in. Tires: 33 x 4. [Series 55] W.B.: 139 in. Tires: 36 x 5. Non-skid tread on rear.

TECHNICAL: [Series 42] Manual transmission. Speeds: 3F/1R. Center, floor shift. Cone clutch. Shaft drive, enclosed within torsion tube. Three-quarter floating rear axle. Service brakes on two wheels with foot pedal control. Wooden, hickory wheels. [Series 43] Manual transmission. Speeds: 3F/1R. Center, floor shift. Leather faced cone clutch. Shaft drive with two universal joints. Three-quarter floating rear axle. Service brakes on two wheels with foot pedal control. Wheels: wooden, hickory, natural finish. [Series 55] Manual transmission. Speeds: 3F/1R. Center, floor shift. Cone clutch. Shaft drive with two universal joints. Full floating rear axle. Service brakes on two wheels, foot pedal operated. Wheels: wooden, hickory, natural finish.

OPTIONS: $50 extra for any color other than green, blue or gray. Single or dual trunks offered. 8-day clock. Tool set.

HISTORICAL: Calendar year and model year sales & production: 7,696. President and general manager was C.W. Nash. Oldsmobile employed 2,000 employees in 1915.

1915
Model 42, 4-cyl.

	FP	5	4	3	2	1
Rds	1285	1075	3000	5500	7700	11,000
Tr	1285	1150	3600	6000	8400	12,000
Model 55, 6-cyl.						
Tr	2975	3150	6300	10,500	14,700	21,000

1916

1916 Oldsmobile, touring, OCW

OLDSMOBILE — FOURTH SERIES — MODEL 43 — FOUR: A carryover from 1915 was the nimble four cylinder Model 43 with its valve in head motor. This year the roadster in this series could be rumble seat fitted. This was the final four cylinder Olds offering for awhile and the model 42 and 43's proved to be reliable motorcars and good sellers for Oldsmobile.

1027

OLDSMOBILE — LIGHT EIGHT SERIES — MODEL 44 — EIGHT: Actually Oldsmobile began production of this model in August of 1915. The biggest of the Olds lineup now rolled on a wheelbase of 120 inches. The all new Olds offered expanded closed models coupled with a pair of open air models. The motoring public gave the Model 44 a warm reception with almost 8,000 sales.

I.D. DATA: Series 43. Serial numbers found on brass tag under right front seat cushion. Starting: 93000. Ending: N/A. Starting Engine No.: 738822. Ending: N/A. Series 44. Serial numbers found on brass tag under right front seat cushion. Starting: 109500. Ending: N/A. Starting Engine No.: 50000. Ending: N/A.

Model No.	Body Type & Seating	Price	Weight	Prod. Total
43-T	4-dr. Tour.-5P	1095	2260	2189
43-T	2-dr. Rds.-2P	1095	2260	2189
44-T	4-dr. Tour.-5P	1195	2750	8000
44-R	2-dr. Rds.-2P	1195	2750	8000
44-S	4-dr. Sed.-5P	1850	3160	8000
44-C	2-dr. Cabr.-2P	1775	2832	8000

1916 Oldsmobile, model 43, roadster, HAC

ENGINE: [Series 43] Valve-in-head, inline four. Cast iron block. B & S: 3-1/2 x 5 in. Disp.: 192 c.i. H.P.: 30. Main bearings: Three. Valve lifters: Overhead. Carb.: float-feed. [Series 44 V-type] Eight. Cast iron block. B & S: 2-7/8 x 4-3/4 in. Disp.: 246 c.i. H.P.: 40 @ 2000 rpm. Valve lifters: Mechanical. Carb.: float-feed.

CHASSIS: [Series 43] W.B.: 120 in. Frt/Rear Tread: 56 in. Tires: 33 x4, non skid on rears. [Series 44] W.B.: 120 in. Frt/Rear Tread: 56 in. Tires: 33 x 4, non-skid on rears.

TECHNICAL: [Series 43] Manual transmission. Speeds: 3F/1R. Floor mounted, center shift. Leather faced cone clutch. Shaft drive, with two universal joints. Three quarter floating rear axle. Service brakes on two wheels operated by foot pedal. Wheels: wooden, hickory, natural finish. [Series 44] Manual transmission. Speeds: 3F/1R. Floor mounted, center shift. Leather faced cone clutch. Shaft drive with two universal joints. Floating rear axle. Service brakes on two wheels operated by pedal. Wheels: wooden, hickory, natural finish.

HISTORICAL: Introduced August 15, 1915. Calendar year and model year sales & prod.: 10,507. Company president and general manager was C.W. Nash.

Miss Amada Preuss drove a Model 44 V-8 roadster from San Francisco to New York via the Lincoln Highway in 11 days, five hours and 45 minutes to establish a new woman's transcontinental driving record. Production of closed cars increased.

1916
Model 43, 4-cyl.

	FP	5	4	3	2	1
Rds	1095	950	2100	4750	6650	9500
5P Tr	1095	1000	2400	5000	7000	10,000
Model 44, V-8						
Rds	1195	1550	4500	7500	10,500	15,000
Tr	1195	1650	4650	7750	10,850	15,500
Sed	1850	875	1700	4250	5900	8500
Cabr	1775	1550	4500	7500	10,500	15,000

1917

1917 Oldsmobile, model 45, touring, HAC

1028

OLDSMOBILE — SIXTH SERIES — MODEL 37 — SIX: After a year out of the market Oldsmobile came back with an all new six cylinder line in 1917 with the model 37. Dealing heavily with the closed models this was the less popular of the two series offered this year. Olds went back to slightly smaller cars with the Model 37 and was trying to appeal to a more popular price market than just a few years ago.

OLDSMOBILE — LIGHT EIGHT SERIES — MODEL 45 — EIGHT: This model year saw a few Model 44 Light V-8's built, but the majority of the eight cylinders produced this year were the new Model 45's. The light continued to be a sales winner for Olds. These two models gave Oldsmobile its strongest lineup in years and sales doubled over 1916.

I.D. DATA: Model 37. Serial numbers located on brass plate under right front seat cushion. Starting: 150000. Ending: N/A. Engine No. Location: sme as serial number. Starting: D-101-50000. Ending: N/A. Model 45. Serial numbers located on brass plate under right front seat cushion. Starting: 119000. Ending: N/A. Engine: N/A.

Model No.	Body Type & Seating	Price	Weight	Prod. Total
37-T	4-dr. Tr.-5P	1295	2390	8045
37-R	2-dr. Rds.-2P	1467	2380	8045
37-C	2-dr. Cabr.-3P	1775	2580	8045
37-S	4-dr. Sed.-5P	1850	2616	8045
Model 45				
45-T	4-dr. Tr.-5P	1185	3066	13,440
45-T	4-dr. Tr.-7P	1185	3066	13,440
45-R	2-dr. Tr.-2P	1185	2860	13,440
45-S	4-dr. Sed.-5P	1595	3150	13,440

ENGINE: [Model 37] Inline six. Cast iron block. B & S: 2-13/16 x 4-3/4 in. Disp.: 177 c.i. H.P.: 44. Valve lifters: Overhead. Carb.: full-float. [Model 45] Cylinder Layout V-Eight. Cast iron block. B & S: 2-7/8 x 4-3/4 in. Disp.: 246 c.i. H.P.: 58. Main bearings: Two. Valve lifters: Mechanical. Carb.: full-float.

CHASSIS: [Model 37] W.B.: 112 in. Frt/Rear Tread: 56 in. Tires: 32 x 4, non skid on rear. [Model 45] W.B.: 120 in. Frt/Rear Tread: 56 in. Tires: 34 x 4.

TECHNICAL: [Model 37] Manual transmission. Speeds: 3F/1R. Center, floor mounted shift. Leather faced cone cluth. Shaft drive. Floating rear axle. Service brakes on two wheels, pedal operated. Wheels: wooden, hickory, natural finish. [Model 45] Manual transmission. Speeds: 3F/1R. Center, floor mounted shift. Leather faced cone clutch. Shaft drive with universal joints. Full floating rear axle. Overall ratio: 4-1/12 to 1. Service brakes on two wheels, pedal operated. Artillery wheels, 12-spoke, naturally finished wood.

HISTORICAL: Calendar year sales & production: 10,507. Model year sales & production: 9,279. Company president was Edward Ver Linden.

Oldsmobile began some war production which included building kitchen trailers for Army use and building Liberty aircraft engines. Aluminum pistons were used for the first time in an Olds motor. Employment stood at 4,000 — an all time Olds high.

1917 Oldsmobile, model 45, cabriolet, HAC

1917
Model 37, 6-cyl.

	FP	5	4	3	2	1
Tr	1295	1400	4200	7000	9800	14,000
Rds	1467	1250	3900	6500	9100	13,000
Cabr	1775	1300	4050	6750	9450	13,500
Sed	1850	900	1900	4500	6300	9000
Model 45, V-8						
5P Tr	1185	1750	4800	8000	11,200	16,000
7P Tr	1185	2000	5100	8500	11,900	17,000
Conv Sed	1595	2000	5100	8500	11,900	17,000
Rds	1185	1550	4500	7500	10,500	15,000
Model 44-B, V-8						
Rds	1295	1750	4800	8000	11,200	16,000
Tr	1295	1550	4500	7500	10,500	15,000

1918

OLDSMOBILE — SIXTH SERIES — MODEL 37 — SIX: Oldsmobile stood pat with a carryover lineup from the 1917 model year. The six cylinders continued to be slightly more popular with Olds buyers. This series continued to emphasize the closed automobile with several versions offered.

1918 Oldsmobile, model 45-A, touring, HAC

OLDSMOBILE — MODEL 45-A — EIGHT: The light eight cylinder Oldsmobile designation became 45-A for this season. Two versions of the touring car - a five and seven passenger - could be ordered in this series and closed cars were offered as well. Olds rose to eighth place in the sales race for 1918 and the good sales of the 45-A partially accounted for this triumph.

I.D. DATA: Model 37. Serial numbers were located on brass plate under the right hand seat cushion. Starting: touring cars: 150000; other 190000. Engine no. location: same as serial number. Starting: D101-50000. Ending: N/A. Model 45-A. Serial numbers were located on brass plate under the right hand set cushion. Starting: 145000. Ending: N/A. Engine no. location: same as serial number. Starting: X85000. Ending: N/A.

Model No.	Body Type & Seating	Price	Weight	Prod. Total
37-R	2-dr. Rds.-2P	1195	2380	11,033
37-T	4-dr. Tr.-5P	1195	2390	11,033
37-Ca	2-dr. Cabr.-3P	1595	2527	11,033
37-Co	2-dr. Cpe.2P	1595	2632	11,033
37-S	4-dr. Sed.-5P	1695	2682	11,033
45A-T	4-dr. Tr.-5P	1295	3065	8132
45A-T	4-dr. Tr.-7P	1295	3095	8132
45A-R	2-dr. Rds.-2P	1550	3040	8132
45A-S Sptr.	4-dr. Tr.-5P	1550	3065	8132
45A-C	2-dr. Cabr.-3P	1775	3085	8132
45A-S	4-dr. Sed.-5P	1850	3190	8132

ENGINE: [Model 37] Inline, valve-in-head. Six. Cast iron block. B & S: 2-13/16 x 4-3/4 in. Disp.: 177 cu. in. H.P.: 44. Valve lifters: Overhead. Carb.: automatic compensating. [Model 45-A] Cylinder Layout V-type. Eight. Cast iron block. B & S: 2-7/8 x 4-3/4 in. Disp.: 246 c.i. H.P.: 58. Main bearings: Two. Valve lifters: Mechanical. Carb. Automatic compensating, Ball & Ball.

CHASSIS: [Model 37] W.B.: 112 in. Front/Rear Tread: 56 in. Tires: 32 x 4. [Model 45-A] W.B.: 120 in. Front/Rear Tread: 56 in. Tires: 34 x 4.

TECHNICAL: [Model 37] Sliding gear, selective transmission. Speeds: 3F/1R. Center floor mounted controls. Leather cone clutch. Shaft drive. Spiral bevel, full floating rear axle. Service brakes on two wheels, external contracting. Wooden wheels, hickory, natural finish. [Model 45-A] Selective gear transmission. Speeds: 3F/1R. Center, floor mounted controls. Leather cone clutch. Shaft drive. Spiral bevel, full floating rear axle. Service brakes on two wheels, external contracting. Artillery wheels, wood, natural finish.

HISTORICAL: Calendar year sales and production: 19,169. Model year sales and production: 19,165. Company president and general manager was Edward Ver Linden.
  A new motor plant was completed this year. The first of several special models - the sportster touring - was marketed in 1918.

1918
Model 37, 6-cyl.

	FP	5	4	3	2	1
Rds	1195	1250	3900	6500	9100	13,000
Tr	1195	1300	4050	6750	9450	13,500
Cabr	1595	1300	4050	6750	9450	13,500
Cpe	1595	1075	3000	5500	7700	11,000
Sed	1695	1000	2400	5000	7000	10,000

Model 45-A, V-8

	FP	5	4	3	2	1
5P Tr	1295	1750	4800	8000	11,200	16,000
7P Tr	1550	1750	4800	8000	11,200	16,000
Rds	1550	1550	4500	7500	10,500	15,000
Spt	1550	1400	4200	7000	9800	14,000
Cabr	1775	1550	4500	7500	10,500	15,000
Sed	1850	1000	2400	5000	7000	10,000

1919

OLDSMOBILE — SIXTH SERIES — MODEL 37-A — SIX: Once again the most popular Olds offering was the six cylinder series, this year tagged the 37-A. Wheelbase on this series continued at 112 inches and there continued to be good availability of closed models.

OLDSMOBILE — PACEMAKER SERIES — MODEL 45-A — EIGHT: One of two light eights offered in 1919, this was essentially a carryover from

1919 Oldsmobile, touring, FSA

1918. Sales were just about equally divided between the two eight cylinder offerings, but together they did not equal six cylinder output.

OLDSMOBILE — PACEMAKER SERIES — MODEL 45-B — EIGHT: Wheelbase and overall size was increased slightly on the Model 45-B's. Mechanically the two cars were nearly identical. Closed cars were becoming more common in the Oldsmobile light 8 models.

I.D. DATA: Model 37-A. Serial numbers located on brass plate under hood on the right side of dash. Starting: 37A-2780. Ending: N/A. Engine no. location: same as serial number. Starting: ED-1001. Ending: N/A. Model 45-A. Serial number located on brass plate under right seat cushion. Starting: 145000. Ending: N/A. Engine no. locaton: same as serial number. Starting: X850000. Ending: N/A. Model 45-B. Serial numbers located on brass plate under right seat cushion. Starting: 45B-599. Ending: N/A. Engine no. location: same as serial number. Starting: 45B1-11444. Ending: N/A.

Model No.	Body Type & Seating	Price	Weight	Prod. Total
37-R	2-dr. Rds.-2P	1395	2380	21,968
37-T	4-dr. Tour.-5P	1395	2390	21,968
37-S	4-dr. Sed.-5P	1895	2632	21,968
37-C	2-dr. Cpe.-3P	1895	2490	21,968
45-AR	2-dr. Rds.-2P	1700	3065	5631
45-AT	4-dr. Tour.-5P	1700	3085	5631
45-BT	4-dr. Tour.-5P	1895	3175	5826
45-BT	4-dr. Tour.-7P	1895	3185	5862

ENGINE: [Model 37-A] Inline. Six. Cast iron block. B & S: 2-13/16 x 4-3/4 in. Disp.: 177 c.i. H.P.: 44. Main bearings: Three. Valve lifters: Overhead. Carb.: Automatic compensating. [Model 45-A] V-type. Eight. Cast iron block. B & S: 2-7/8 x 4-3/4 in. Disp.: 246 c.i. H.P.: 58. Main bearings: Two. Valve lifters: Mechanical. Carb.: Two stage, Ball & Ball. [Model 45-B] V-type. Eight cyl. Cast iron block. B & S: 2-7/8 x 4-3/4 in. Disp.: 246 c.i. H.P.: 58. Main bearings: Two. Valve lifters: Mechanical. Carb.: Two stage, Ball & Ball.

CHASSIS: [Model 37-A] W.B.: 112 in. Frt/Rear Tread: 56 in. Tire: 32 x 4. [Model 45-A] W.B.: 120 in. Front/Rear Tread: 56 in. Tires: 34 x 4. [Model 45-B] W.B.: 122 in. Frt/Rear Tread: 56 in. Tires: 34 x 4-1/2, non-skid on rear.

TECHNICAL: [Model 37-A] Selective, manual transmission. Speeds: 3F/1R. Floor mounted, center controls. Leather faced cone clutch. Shaft drive. Full floating, spiral bevel rear axle. Service brakes on two wheels, external contracting & emergency internal expanding. Hickory wheels, natural finish. [Model 45-A] Selective, manual transmission. Speeds: 3F/1R. Center, floor mounted controls. Leather cone clutch. Shaft drive. Spiral bevel; full floating rear axle. Service brakes on two wheels, external contracting. Artillery wheels, wood, natural. [Model 45-B] Selective, sliding gear manual transmission. Speeds: 3F/1R. Center, floor mounted controls. Leather faced cone clutch. Shaft drive. Full floating, spiral bevel rear axle. Foot brake external contracting; hand brake internal expanding. Artillery, wood wheels.

OPTIONS: Klaxon horn (4.80). Heater (25.00). Clock (Sessions) (7.10). Gas tank gauge (1.55).

HISTORICAL: Calendar year sales and production: 33,425, does not include truck production. Model year sales and production: same as above. Company president of Oldsmobile was Edward Ver Linden.
  Oldsmobile's manufacturing fortunes were on the way up. As a result the company began an aggressive expansion plan for its facilities in Lansing, Michigan.

1919
Model 37-A, 6-cyl.

	FP	5	4	3	2	1
Rds	1395	1250	3900	6500	9100	13,000
Tr	1395	1400	4200	7000	9800	14,000
Sed	1895	1000	2400	5000	7000	10,000
Cpe	1895	1000	2500	5100	7100	10,200

Model 45-A, V-8

	FP	5	4	3	2	1
Rds	1700	1200	3750	6250	8750	12,500
Tr	1700	1250	3900	6500	9100	13,000

Model 45-B, V-8

	FP	5	4	3	2	1
4P Tr	1895	1300	4050	6750	9450	13,500
7P Tr	1895	1500	4350	7250	10,150	14,500

1920

1920 Oldsmobile, model 37-A, touring, HAC

OLDSMOBILE — SIXTH SERIES — MODEL 37A & B — SIX: For this model year Oldsmobile designated its open cars of six cylinder design as 37-A's, while the closed cars were 37-B's. The cars shared mechanical and chassis components. The six cylinder models continued as the most popular Oldsmobiles in 1920. The series 37 cars were essentially carryover models from 1919.

OLDSMOBILE — THOROBRED SERIES — MODEL 45-B — V-8: This would be the final year that the designation 45 would be used on the Olds V-8. Largely unchanged from 1919, the powerplant remained a 246 cubic inch unit. Detachable heads were fitted and horsepower levels remained at 58. Both closed and open cars were available in this series for 1920.

I.D. DATA: Models 37-A & 37-B. Serial numbers located on a brass plate underhood on the right side of dashboard. Starting: 37-28140. Ending: N/A. Engine no. location: same as serial number. Starting: D101-50000. Ending: N/A. Model 45-B. Serial numbers located on brass plate underhood on the right sdie of dashboard. Starting: 45-599. Ending: N/A. Engine no. location: same as serial number. Starting: 45B1-11444. Ending: N/A/

Model No.	Body Type & Seating	Price	Weight	Prod. Total
Series 37-A				
37-AR	2-dr. Rds.-2P	1450	2380	14,073
37-AT	4-dr. Tr.-5P	1450	2390	14,073
Series 37-B				
37-BC	2-dr. Cpe.-3P	2145	2527	3,871
37-BS	4-dr. Sed.-5P	2145	2632	3871
Series 45B				
45-BP	4-dr. Tr.-4P	2100	3160	7215
45-BT	4-dr. Tr.-5P	2100	3180	7215
45-BS	4-dr. Sed.-5P	3300	3695	7215

ENGINE: [Models 37-A & B] Cylinder layout. Inline. Six. Cast iron block. B & S: 2-13/16 x 4-3/4. Disp. 177 c.i. H.P.: 44. Main bearings: Three. Valve lifters: valve in head, mechanical. Carb.: Automatic compensating. [Model 45-B] Cylinder layout V-type. Eight. Cast iron block. B & S: 2-7/8 x 4-3/4 in. Disp. 246 c.i. H.P.: 58. Main bearings: Two. Valve lifters: Mechanical. Carb.: Two stage.

CHASSIS: [Series 37-A & B] W.B.: 112 in. Frt/Rear Tread: 56 in. Tires: 32 x 4. [Series 45-B] W.B.: 122 in. Frt/Rear Tread: 56 in. Tires: 33 x 4-1/2 non-skid on rear.

TECHNICAL: [Model 37-A & B] Sliding gear transmission. Speeds: 3F/1R. Center, floor mounted controls. Leather faced cone clutch. Shaft drive. Spiral bevel, full floating rear axle. External contracting service brakes on two wheels, internal expanding emergency brake. Selected hickory, natural finish wheels. [Model 45-B] Sliding gear transmission. Speeds: 3F/1R. Center, floor mounted controls. Leather faced cone clutch. Shaft drive. Spiral bevel, full floating rear axle. External contracting service brakes on two wheels, internal expanding. Selected hickory, natural finish wheels.

OPTIONS: Trojan horn (4.80). Klaxon horn (4.80). Sessions clock (7.10). Keyless clock. Sedan heater (25.65). Hand tire pump (1.50)

HISTORICAL: Calendar year sales & production: 26,291. Model year sales & production: 25,159. Company president of Oldsmobile was Edward Ver Linden.

A major plant expansion program was completed including updated facilities for building axles, sheetmetal and enameling. Oldsmobile today retains a 1920 Model 37B sedan in its divisional collection.

1920

		FP	5	4	3	2	1
Model 37-A, 6-cyl.							
Rds		1450	1250	3900	6500	9100	13,000
Tr		1450	1400	4200	7000	9800	14,000
Model 37-B, 6-cyl.							
Cpe		2145	1000	2400	5000	7000	10,000
Sed		2145	1000	2400	5000	7000	10,000
Model 45-B, V-8							
4P Tr		2100	1500	4350	7250	10,150	14,500
5P Tr		2100	1400	4200	7000	9800	14,000
7P Sed		3300	825	1600	4000	5600	8000

1921

1921 Oldsmobile, model 43-A, touring, HAC

OLDSMOBILE — MODEL 37 — SIX: The Model 37's built this year were direct carryovers from the previous model year. Power came from the tried and true in line six displacing 177 cubic inches and producing 44 horsepower.

OLDSMOBILE — MODEL 46 — EIGHT: Another direct carryover from 1920 was the Model 46 eight cylinder series. This machine rode on a 122-inch wheelbase and was powered by a 247 cubic inch motor developing 58 horsepower.

OLDSMOBILE — MODEL 43-A — FOUR: Back in the four cylinder auto production business after a few years, the Model 43-A was a welcome addition in 1921. Oldsmobile launched this new lineup with an extensive ad camping which included the Saturday Evening Post. Both open and closed Model 43-A's were available with the open cars cheaper to buy and more popular in the marketplace. The model 43-A's were built on a wheelbase of 115 inches. Engines developed 43 hp.

OLDSMOBILE — MODEL 47 — EIGHT: Another new offering in this transition year for Oldsmobile was the Model 47 8 cylinder. This was a physically smaller and less powerful model than Model 46. Both open and closed cars came in this series. A 234 cubic inch motor put out 53 horsepower.

I.D. DATA: Model 37 serial numbers on brass plate under hood on right side of dash. Starting: 37A — 2780. Ending: N/A. Engine numbers were in same location as serial numbers. Starting: D-101. Ending: N/A. Model 46 serial numbers in same location. Starting: 46T-1. Ending: N/A. Engine numbers in same location. Starting: 46-1. Ending: N/A. Model 43 serial numbers in same location. Starting: 43A-1. Ending: N/A. Engine numbers in same location. Starting: A-1. Ending: N/A Model 47 serial numbers in same location. Starting: 46-1. Ending: N/A. Engine numbers in same location. Starting: 47-1. Ending: N/A.

Model No.	Body Type & Seating	Price	Weight	Prod. Total
37-R	2-dr. Rds.-2P	1450	2380	Note 1
37-T	4-dr. Tr.-5P	1450	2390	Note 1
37-C	2-dr. Cpe.-3P	2145	2527	Note 1
37-S	4-dr. Sed.-5P	2145	2632	Note 1
46-P	4-dr. Tr.-4P	1735	3160	Note 2
46-T	4-dr. Tr.-5P	1735	3183	Note 2
46-S	4-dr. Sed.-5P	2635	3695	Note 2
43-R	2-dr. Rds.-2P	1325	2742	Note 3
43-T	4-dr. Tr.-5P	1345	2767	Note 3
43-C	2-dr. Cpe.-3P	1895	2917	Note 3
47-T	4-dr. Tr.-5P	1825	2854	Note 4
47-C	2-dr. Cpe.-3P	2145	3082	Note 4
47-S	4-dr. Sed.-5P	2295	3146	Note 4

Note 1: Total production for Model 37 was 948.
Note 2: Total production for Model 46 was 745.
Note 3: Total production for Model 43 was 13,867.
Note 4: Total production for Model 47 was 3,085.

ENGINE: [Model 37] Inline. Six. Cast iron block. B & S: 2-13/16 x 4-3/4. Disp.: 177 c.i. H.P.: 44. Main bearings: Three. Valve lifters: Mechanical. Automatic compensating carb. [Model 46] V-type. Eight. Cast iron block. B & S: 2-7/8 x 4-3/4. Disp.: 246 c.i. H.P.: 58. Main bearings: Two. Valve lifters: Mechanical. Two-stage carb. [Model 43] Inline. Cast iron block. B & S: 3-11/16 x 5-1/4. Disp.: 224 c.i. H.P.: 44. Main bearings: Three. Valve lifters: Mechanical. Fuel nozzle type carb. [Model 47] V-type. Eight. Cast iron block. B & S: 2-7/8 x 4-1/2. Disp.: 233 c.i. H.P.: 60. Main bearings: Three. Valve lifters: Mechanical. Special adapted Johnson carb.

CHASSIS: [Model 37] W.B.: 112 in. Frt/Rear Tread: standard. Tires: 34 x 4, non-skid on rear. [Model 46] W.B.: 122 in. Frt/rear tread: standard. Tires: 34 x 4-1/2, non-skid on rear. [Model 43] W.B.: 115 in. Frt/rear tread: standard. Tires: 32 x 4 cords, non-skid on rear. [Model 47] W.B.: 115 in. Frt/rear tread: standard. Tires: 32 x 4 cord, non-skid on rear.

TECHNICAL: [Model 37] Selective, center control. Selective sliding gear. Speeds: 3F/1R. Center floor shift. Leather faced cone clutch. [Model 46] Large, leather faced cone clutch. [Model 43] Single plate, dry disk clutch. [Model 47] Borg & Beck 10 in. disc clutch. [Model 47] Torque tube, shaft drive. Shaft drive. Spiral bevel, full floating rear axle. [Model 47] Overall Ratio: 4-2/3:1. External contracting brakes on two wheels. [Model 37] National finish hickory wheels. [Model 46] Wooden, natural finish, artillery wheels. [Model 43] Wooden or disc wheels. [Model 47] Hickory, artillery wheels.

1921 Oldsmobile, model 43-A, sedan, HJE

OPTIONS: Tuarc disc wheels. Wire wheels. California top. Extra spare tire. Motometer.

HISTORICAL: Calendar & Model year sales & production: 19,157. President of Oldsmobile was ABC Hardy. Employment at 2,500 for this year.

1921
Model 37, 6-cyl.

	FP	5	4	3	2	1
Rds	1450	1150	3600	6000	8400	12,000
Tr	1450	1200	3750	6250	8750	12,500
Cpe	2145	825	1600	4000	5600	8000
Sed	2145	875	1700	4250	5900	8500

Model 43-A, 4-cyl.

Rds	1325	1075	3000	5500	7700	11,000
Tr	1345	1000	2400	5000	7000	10,000
Cpe	1895	750	1450	3300	4900	7000

Model 46, V-8

4P Tr	1735	1500	4350	7250	10,150	14,500
Tr	1735	1400	4200	7000	9800	14,000
7P Sed	2635	825	1600	4000	5600	8000

Model 47, V-8

Spt Tr	1825	1550	4500	7500	10,500	15,000
4P Cpe	2145	750	1450	3300	4900	7000
5P Sed	2295	1000	2400	5000	7000	10,000

1922

1922 Oldsmobile, touring, FSA

OLDSMOBILE — MODEL 43-A — FOUR: The Model 43-A's continued as one of the most successful Olds series ever offered. This was a quality line of four cylinder motorcars featuring both open and closed models. A special factory installed California top was available and a special sport touring offered leather side rails, Tuarc disc wheels and special red paint. Prices were brought down on this series for 1922.

OLDSMOBILE — MODEL 47 — EIGHT: This model year saw a great deal of overlap with two eight cylinder models for a manufacturer which probably should have fielded just one. Several sporty models were offered in this series also.

OLDSMOBILE — MODEL 46 — EIGHT: Carried over largely unchanged from 1920 was the Model 46. Both open and closed models were offered in limited numbers from this V-8 powered series.

1922 Oldsmobile, roadster, HJE

I.D. DATA: Model 43-A serial numbers on tag under hood on right hand front side of dash. Starting: 787. Ending: N/A. Engine numbers in same location as serial numbers. Starting: A-26395. Ending: N/A. Model 46 serial numbers in same location. Starting: 218. Ending: N/A. Engine numbers in same location. Starting: 1721. Ending: N/A. Model 47 serial numbers in same location. Starting: 1. Ending: N/A. Engine numbers in same location. Starting: 2823. Ending: N/A.

Model No.	Body Type & Seating	Price	Weight	Prod. Total
43-AR	2-dr. Rds.-2P	1095	2742	Note 1
43-AT	4-dr. Tour.-5P	1095	2767	Note 1
43-AC	2-dr. Cpe.-3P	1595	2917	Note 1
43-AS	4-dr. Sed.-5P	1745	3027	Note 1
46-ST	4-dr. Tour.-4P	1735	3115	Note 2
46-T	4-dr. Tour.-4P	1735	3125	Note 2
46-T	4-dr. Tour.-7P	1735	3130	Note 2
46-S	4-dr. Sed.-5P	2635	3695	Note 2
47-R	2-dr. Rds.-3P	1495	2910	Note 3
47-R	4-dr. Tour.-5P	1495	3175	Note 3
47-ST	4-dr. Tour.-4P	1825	3190	Note 3
47-C	2-dr. Cpe.-3P	2145	3345	Note 3
47-S	4-dr. Sed.-5P	2295	3387	Note 3

Note 1: Total production for Model 43-A was 14,839.
Note 2: Total production for Model 46 was 2,733.
Note 3: Total production for Model 47 was 2,723.

ENGINE: [Model 43] Inline. Four. Cast iron block. B & S: 3-11/16 x 5-1/4. Disp.: 224 c.i. H.P.: 40. Main bearings: Three. Valve lifters: Mechanical. Two stage carb. [Model 46] V-type. Eight. Cast iron block. B & S: 2-7/8 x 4-3/4. Disp.: 246 c.i. H.P.: 58. Main bearings: Two. Valve lifters: Mechanical. Two stage carb. [Model 47] V-type. Eight. Cast iron block. B & S: 2-7/8 x 4-1/2. Disp.: 233 c.i. H.P.: 63. Main bearings: Two. Valve lifters: Mechanical. Special Johnson carb.

1922 Oldsmobile, coupe, HJE

CHASSIS: [Model 43-A] W.B.: 115 in. Frt/Rear Tread: standard. Tires: 32 x 4 cords, non-skid. [Model 46] W.B.: 122 in. Frt/Rear Tread: standard. Tires: 33 x 4-1/2 cord, non-skids on rear. [Model 47] W.B.: 115 in. Frt/Rear Tread: standard. Tires: 32 x4 cords, non-skid on rear.

TECHNICAL: Selective sliding gear transmission. Speeds: 3F/1R. Center floor shift. Model 43-A. Single plate, dry disc clutch. Model 46. Leather faced cone clutch. Model 47. Borg & Beck 10 in. disc clutch. Shaft drive. Spiral bevel, floating rear axle. [Model 43-A] Overall ratio: 4-2/3:1. [Model 47] 5-1/10:1. External contracting; internal expanding brakes on two wheels. Hickory, artillery wheels.

OPTIONS: Tuarc disc wheels. Wire wheels. Motormeter. Trojan horn. Klaxon horn. Sessions clock. Keyless clock. Sedan heater. Tire pump.

HISTORICAL: Model and Calendar year sales and production 21,499. General manager of Oldsmobile was ABC Hardy. A special Olds racer set a speed record of 67 miles per hour for 15 hours.

1922
Model 46, V-8

	FP	5	4	3	2	1
Spt Tr	1735	1750	4800	8000	11,200	16,000
4P Tr	1735	1550	4500	7500	10,500	15,000
7P Tr	1735	1550	4500	7500	10,500	15,000
7P Sed	2635	1000	2400	5000	7000	10,000
Model 47, V-8						
Rds	1495	1550	4500	7500	10,500	15,000
Tr	1495	1750	4800	8000	11,200	16,000
4P Spt	1825	1500	4350	7250	10,150	14,500
4P Cpe	2145	1000	2400	5000	7000	10,000
5P Sed	2295	825	1600	4000	5600	8000

1923

1923 Oldsmobile, model 43-A, 4-dr., sedan, OCW

OLDSMOBILE — MODEL 30-A — SIX: Moving back into the six cylinder market, Oldsmobile picked 1923 to introduce its long running Model 30 series. Production and sales of this all new model began in July and quickly picked up pace for the balance of the year. The new six cylinder models became the lowest priced Oldsmobiles for many years with touring car prices starting as low as $850. Both closed and open cars were offered in the series and Fisher bodies were featured. The powerplant or the new series was a 42 horsepower job with 170 cubic inches.

OLDSMOBILE — MODEL 43-A — FOUR: This model year marked the end of the line for some time on four cylinder Olsmobiles in general and specifically the Model 43-A. Prices came down again slightly on this series in 1923 and production dropped after the new six cylinders hit the dealer showrooms. Overall the 43-A was one of the best selling series ever offered by Oldsmobile.

OLDSMOBILE — MODEL 47 — EIGHT: Also in its final year was the V-8 powered 47 series. It would be almost a decade before Olds would again offer an eight, and then it would be the straight eight version (although the companion Viking was built in 1929 & 30). Prices were lowered in this series as well and by mid-summer the Model 47 assembly line was forever silenced.

I.D. DATA: [Model 30-A] Serial number was stamped on brass plate on right front door pillar. Starting: 30-1. Ending: NA. Engine number location same as serial number. Starting: A-1. Ending: NA. [Model 43-A] Serial number was on brass plate located underhood. Starting: 43A-1. Ending: NA. Engine number location same as serial number. Starting: B-18501. Ending: B-27734. [Model 47] Serial number was on brass plate located underhood. Starting: 47-1. Ending: NA. Engine number location same as serial number. Starting: 47-4601. Ending: NA.

Model No.	Body Type & Seating	Price	Weight	Prod. Total
Model 30-A				
30-AR	2-dr. Rds.-2P	850	2220	Note 1
30-AT	4-dr. Tr.-5P	850	2305	Note 1
30-AC	2-dr. Cpe.-3P	1250	2460	Note 1
30-AS	4-dr. Sed.-5P	1250	2570	Note 1
30-AST	4-dr. Tr.-4P	1000	2330	Note 1
Model 43-A				
43-AR	2-dr. Rds.-2P	1325	2870	Note 2
43-AT	4-dr. Tr.-5P	1345	2900	Note 2
43-AC	2-dr. Cpe.-3P	1895	3075	Note 2
43-AB	2-dr. Brgm.-4P	1795	2925	Note 2
43-AS	4-dr. Sed.-5P	1695	3140	Note 2
Model 47				
47T	4-dr. Tr.-4P	1495	3110	Note 3
47TB	4-dr. Tr.-5P	1495	3120	Note 3
47R	2-dr. Rds.-2P	1495	3085	Note 3
47S	4-dr. Sed.-5P	2295	3220	Note 3
47C	2-dr. Cpe.-3P	2145	3175	Note 3
47ST	4-dr. Tr.-4P	1825	3115	Note 3

Note 1: Oldsmobile total production for Model 30-A was 12,264.
Note 2: Oldsmobile total production for Model 43-A was 19,017.
Note 3: Oldsmobile total production for Model 47 was 2,148.

ENGINE: [Model 30-A] Inline. Six. Cast iron block. B & S: 2-3/4 x 4-3/4 in. Disp.: 169 cu. in. Brake H.P.: 42. Main bearings: Three. Valve lifters: Mechanical. Carb.: Zenith. [Model 43-A] Inline. Four. Cast iron block. B &

S: 3-11/16 x 5-1/4 in. Disp.: 224 cu. in. Brake H.P.: 40. Main bearings: Three. Valve lifters: Mechanical. Carb.: two stage. [Model 47] V-type. Eight. Cast iron block. B & S: 2-7/8 x 4-1/2 in. Disp.: 233 cu. in. Brake H.P.: 54. Main bearings: Two. Valve lifters: Mechanical. Carb.: Special Johnson model.

1923 Oldsmobile, model 47, sport roadster, HAC

CHASSIS: [Model 30-A] W.B.: 110 in. Frt/Rear Tread: standard. Tires: 31 x 4 cord, non-skid on rear. [Model 43-A] W.B.: 115 in. Frt/Rear Tread: standard. Tires: 32 x 4 cord, non-skid on rear. [Model 47] W.B.: 115 in. Frt/Rear Tread: standard. Tires: 32 x 4 cords, non-skid on rear.

TECHNICAL: Selective sliding gear transmission. Speeds: 3F/1R. Center, floor controls. [Model 30-A] Borg & Beck, single plate clutch. [Model 43-A] Single plate dry disc clutch. [Model 47] Borg & Beck disc clutch. Shaft drive. [Model 30-A] Spiral bevel, semi-floating rear axle. [Model 43-A & 47] Spiral bevel, floating axle. [Model 43-A & 47] Overall ratio: 4-2/3:1. Service brakes on rear wheels. [Model 30-A] Artillery wood wheels or Tuarc steel. [Model 43-A & 47] Artillery, hickory wheels.

OPTIONS: Klaxon horn. Motometer. California top. Tuarc disc wheels. Wire wheels.

HISTORICAL: Calendar and model year sales and production: 34,811. Company general manager: ABC Hardy.
New plant areas — including a new Fisher Body building plant — were completed this model year. For the first time since the Curved Dash era Olds tooled up for a single series powered with just one motor. "Cannonball" Baker completed a transcontinental run from New York to Los Angeles in 12-1/2 days with a Model 30-A touring car locked in high gear.

1923
Model M30-A, 6-cyl.

	FP	5	4	3	2	1
Rds	850	1400	4200	7000	9800	14,000
Tr	850	1550	4500	7500	10,500	15,000
Cpe	1250	775	1500	3750	5250	7500
Sed	1250	700	1350	2800	4550	6500
Spt Tr	1000	1400	4200	7000	9800	14,000
Model 43-A, 4-cyl.						
Rds	1325	1250	3900	6500	9100	13,000
Tr	1345	1400	4200	7000	9800	14,000
Cpe	1895	750	1450	3300	4900	7000
Sed	—	650	1250	2400	4200	6000
Brgm	—	700	1350	2800	4550	6500
Cal Tp Sed	—	775	1500	3750	5250	7500
Model 47, V-8						
4P Tr	1495	1750	4800	8000	11,200	16,000
5P Tr	1495	1750	4800	8000	11,200	16,000
Rds	1495	2000	5100	8500	11,900	17,000
Sed	2295	750	1450	3300	4900	7000
Cpe	2145	775	1500	3750	5250	7500
Spt Tr	1825	2200	5250	8750	12,250	17,500

1924

1924 Oldsmobile, model 30-B, sedan, HJE

OLDSMOBILE — MODEL 30-B — SIX: Oldsmobile took a big step toward simplification this year as just a 30 series model — the 30-B — was offered. This would be the trend for the next few years — a single Olds series with just one powerplant offered. Sales improved dramatically with this single series format. Closed cars became more popular this year and Fisher was the body supplier.

I.D. DATA: Serial number on plate located on right side of toe board. Starting: 30B-1. Ending: NA. Engine location: same as serial number. Starting: B-1. Ending: NA.

Model No.	Body Type & Seating	Price	Weight	Prod. Total
30-BR	2-dr. Rds.-2P	880	2145	1800
30-BT	4-dr. Tr.-5P	880	2170	10,586
30-BCB	2-dr. Cpe.-2P	1175	2295	2169
30-BST	4-dr. Tr.-5P	1005	2320	8847
30-BBR	2-dr. Brgm.-4P	1365	2410	8839
30-BS	4-dr. Sed.-5P	1280	2570	3225

ENGINE: Inline. Six. Cast iron block. B & S: 2-3/4 x 4-3/4 in. Disp.: 169 cu. in. Brake H.P.: 42. Main bearings: Three. Valve lifters: Mechanical. Carb.: Zenith.

CHASSIS: W.B.: 110 in. Frt/Rear tread: standard. Tires: 31 x 4 cords, non-skids on rear.

1924 Oldsmobile, model 30-B, touring, HAC

TECHNICAL: Selective sliding gear transmission. Speeds: 3F/1R. Center, floor mounted shift. Borg & Beck, single plate dry disc clutch. Shaft drive. Spiral bevel, semi-floating rear axle. Service brakes on rear wheels. Artillery wheels.

OPTIONS: Klaxon horn. Motometer. Tuarc disc wheels. Wire wheels.

HISTORICAL: Calendar and Model year sales and production: 44,854. General Manager: ABC Hardy. This year Oldsmobile switched to lacquer for its products.

1924
Model 30-B, 6-cyl.

	FP	5	4	3	2	1
Rds	880	1550	4500	7500	10,500	15,000
Tr	880	1750	4800	8000	11,200	16,000
Spt Rds	975	1750	4800	8000	11,200	16,000
Spt Tr	1005	2000	5100	8500	11,900	17,000
Cpe	1175	825	1600	4000	5600	8000
Sed	1280	750	1450	3300	4900	7000
2 dr Sed	1365	700	1350	2800	4550	6500
DeL Sed	1005	750	1450	3300	4900	7000

1925

1925 Oldsmobile, model 30-C, 4-dr. sedan, AA

OLDSMOBILE — MODEL 30-C — SIX: Olds continued to offer its six cylinder models and added both deluxe roadsters and sedans this year. A new and distinctive style radiator shell was featured this year and in midyear chrome replaced nickel plating. A new instrument panel was fitted and prices rose slightly over 1924 levels. Both model C's and D's were offered this year, with the 30-C being the primary model.

I.D. DATA: Serial number on plate on right end of front seat. Starting: 1. Ending: NA. Engine number location: same as serial number. Starting: C-1. Ending: NA.

1925 Oldsmobile, model 30-C, coupe, HJE

Model No.	Body Type & Seating	Price	Weight	Prod. Total
30-CR	2-dr. Rds.-2P	890	2145	2090
30-CSR	2-dr. Dl. Rds.-2P	985	2270	1765
30-CC	2-dr. Cpe.-4P	1175	2460	2338
30-CS	4-dr. Sed.-5P	1285	2570	5820
30-CDS	4-dr. Dl. Sed.-5P	1375	2740	7075
30-CST	4-dr. Spt. Tr.-5P	1015	2360	4569
30-CT	4-dr. Tr.-5P	890	2200	7328
30-CD2S	2-dr. Sed.-4P	985	2440	9896

ENGINE: Inline. Six. Cast iron block. B & S: 2-3/4 x 4-3/4 in. Disp.: 169 cu. in. Brake H.P.: 40. Main bearings: Three. Valve lifters: Mechanical. Carb.: Zenith.

CHASSIS: W.B.: 110-1/2 in. Frt/Rear tread: standard. Tires: 30 x 4.95 cords, non-skid on rear.

TECHNICAL: Selective sliding gear transmission. Speeds: 3F/1R. Borg & Beck, single plate clutch. Spiral bevel, semi-floating rear axle. Overall ratio: 5.1:1. Service brakes on two wheels. Twelve spoke, artillery wheels.

OPTIONS: Ballon tires & disc wheels (50.00). Deluxe equipment package: Tuarc disc wheels, nickeled double bumpers, windshield wings, spotlight, aluminum step plates and enameled trunk on special platform.

1925 Oldsmobile, model 30-C, roadster, HJE

HISTORICAL: Speed records: Floyd Clymer drove a 30 touring car to records climbing Lookout Mountain and Pike's Peak. Model year sales & production: 19,506. Calendar year sales & production: 43,386. General manager: ABC Hardy. Other highlights: A Duco finishing process was introduced. Employment rose to a record 4,250 this model year.

1925
Series 30-C, 6-cyl.

	FP	5	4	3	2	1
Rds	890	1550	4500	7500	10,500	15,000
Tr	890	1750	4800	8000	11,200	16,000
Spt Rds	985	1750	4800	8000	11,200	16,000
Spt Tr	1015	2000	5100	8500	11,900	17,000
Cpe	1175	750	1450	3300	4900	7000
Sed	1285	700	1350	2800	4550	6500
DeL Sed	1375	725	1400	3100	4800	6800
DeL 2 dr	1075	650	1250	2400	4200	6000

1926

1926 Oldsmobile, model 30-D, 4-dr. sedan, AA

OLDSMOBILE — MODEL 30-D — SIX: Olds remained with its single power-plant selection. As with most cars of this era, closed models continued to gain in popularity. The Fisher Body nameplate had been a fixture for several years at Olds. Standard and deluxe versions of most series cars were offered this year. A slightly different body line was offered in 1926 and two-tone paint schemes were available. Upholstery was a cord material on closed cars & leather on open models.

I.D. DATA: Serial number on plate under front seat. Starting: D-1 & up. Ending: NA. Engine number location same as serial number. Starting: D-1 & up. Ending: NA.

Model No.	Body Type & Seating	Price	Weight	Prod. Total
30-DDR	2-dr. Rds.-2P	975	2317	1249
30-DT	4-dr. Tr.-5P	875	2225	1124
30-DDT	4-dr. Dbl. Tr.-5P	980	2380	774
30-DC	2-dr. Cpe.-2P	925	2347	1528
30-DDC	2-dr. Dbl. Cpe.-2P	990	2470	3296
30-D2S	2-dr. Sed.-4P	1025	2450	6388
30-DD2S	2-dr. Dbl. Sed.-4P	1040	2620	13,906
30-D4S	4-dr. Sed.-5P	1025	2690	3404
30-DD4S	4-dr. Dbl. Sed.-5P	1115	2700	15,302
30-DLS	4-dr. Lan. Sed.-5P	1190	2705	1205

ENGINE: Inline. Six. Cast iron block. B & S: 2-3/4 x 4-3/4 in. Disp.: 169 cu. in. Brake H.P.: 41. Main bearings: Three. Valve lifters: Mechanical. Carb.: Zenith.

CHASSIS: W.B.: 110-1/2 in. Frt/Rear Tread: standard. Tires: 30 x 4.95, balloon cord.

1926 Oldsmobile, model 30-D, touring, HJE

TECHNICAL: Selective, sliding gear transmission. Speeds: 3F/1R. Center mounted, floor shift controls. Single plate, dry disc clutch. Shaft drive. Semi-floating rear axle. Overall ratio: 5.1:1. Service brakes on two wheels. Artillery, wire or steel disc wheels.

OPTIONS: Front bumper (8.00). Rear bumper (13.45). Heater. Clock. Spotlight. K-S gas telegauge. Wire wheels. Spare tire cover. Trunk platform (15.00). Trunk (47.00). Road Commander aerlectric horn (12.50).

HISTORICAL: Speed records: 301-mile run Chicago/Detroit less than 6 hrs by Floyd Clymer. Calendar year sales and production: 57,878. Model year sales and production: 53,015. The general manager was I.J. Reuter. Manufacturing plant expansion announced.

1926
Model 30-D, 6-cyl.

	FP	5	4	3	2	1
DeL Rds	975	2300	5400	9000	12,600	18,000
Tr	875	2000	5100	8500	11,900	17,000
DeL Tr	980	2200	5250	8750	12,250	17,500
Cpe	925	825	1600	4000	5600	8000
DeL Cpe	990	875	1700	4250	5900	8500
2 dr Sed	1025	600	1200	2200	3850	5500
DeL 2 dr Sed	1040	650	1250	2400	4200	6000
Sed	1025	650	1250	2400	4200	6000
DeL Sed	1115	700	1350	2800	4550	6500
Lan Sed	1065	1250	3900	6500	9100	13,000

1927

1927 Oldsmobile, model 30-E, touring, HJE

OLDSMOBILE — MODEL 30-E — SIX: The 30 Series six cylinder was again the lone Oldsmobile offering this year. Over the life of the series — which began in late 1923 — the E models realized the most changes. Biggest of these alterations was Oldsmobile's first four wheel brake system. Prices held steady and both closed and open models were sold in both standard and deluxe form. The deluxe package consisted of front and rear bumpers, locking motometer and steel disc or wooden wheels. This model year would mark the final time the 30 designation would be used.

I.D. DATA: Serial number was on tag under front seat. Starting: E-1. Ending: NA. Engine number location same as serial number. Starting: E-1. Ending: NA.

Model No.	Body Type & Seating	Price	Weight	Prod. Total
30-EDR	2-dr. Del. Rds.-2P	975	2317	2342
30-ET	4-dr. Tr.-5P	875	2335	99
30-EDT	4-dr. Del. Tr.-5P	895	2490	204
30-EC	2-dr. Cpe.-3P	875	2450	3258
30-EDC	2-dr. Del. Cpe.-3P	930	2540	5359
30-ESC	2-dr. Spt. Cpe.-3P	932	2560	3996
30-E2S	2-dr. Sed.-4P	950	2570	12,422
30-ED2S	2-dr. Del. Sed.-4P	1050	2720	11,308
30-ES	4-dr. Sed.-5P	975	2625	6945
30-EDS	4-dr. Del. Sed.-5P	1055	2780	11,298
30-EL	4-dr. Lan. Sed.-5P	1075	2785	16,792

ENGINE: Inline. Six. Cast iron block. B & S: 2-7/8 x 4-3/4 in. Disp.: 185 cu. in. Brake H.P.: 47. Main bearings: Three. Valve lifters: Mechanical. Carb.: Zenith.

CHASSIS: W.B.: 110-1/2 in. Frt/Rear Tread: standard. Tires: 30 x 5.25 balloon.

TECHNICAL: Selective, sliding gear transmission. Speeds: 3F/1R. Center, floor mounted shift. Dry disc clutch. Shaft drive. Semi-floating rear axle. Overall ratio: 5.1:1. External contracting service brakes on all wheels. Disc, wooden artillery or wire wheels.

OPTIONS: Front bumper (8.50). Rear bumper (13.45). Heater. Cigar lighter. Spotlight. Trunk (50.00). Trunk platform (15.00). Wire wheels. Spare tire cover.

HISTORICAL: Calendar year sales and production: 54,234. Model year sales and production: 82,955. Company president and general manager was I.J. Reuter.
Plant expansion completed. It included an enlarged motor plant, a new 2-story shipping dock, a new engineering lab and new heat treating area. In Canada for 1927 a similar "Jubilee Series" of Oldsmobiles was marketed.

1927 Oldsmobile, model 30-E, landau sedan, DC

1927
Series 30-E, 6-cyl.

	FP	5	4	3	2	1
DeL Rds	892	1400	4200	7000	9800	14,000
Tr	875	1250	3900	6500	9100	13,000
DeL Tr	895	1400	4200	7000	9800	14,000
Cpe	875	825	1600	4000	5600	8000
DeL Cpe	930	875	1700	4250	5900	8500
Spt Cpe	932	900	1900	4500	6300	9000
2 dr Sed	975	700	1350	2800	4550	6500
DeL 2 dr Sed	955	750	1450	3300	4900	7000
Sed	975	750	1450	3300	4900	7000
DeL Sed	1055	775	1500	3750	5250	7500
Lan	1075	1075	3000	5500	7700	11,000

1928

1928 Oldsmobile, model F-28, touring, HJE

OLDSMOBILE — MODEL F-28 — SIX: The previous model year marked the end of the 30 series designation. For 1928 the designation F was coupled with the model year to create the F-28. The F designation would carry on for many years with the six cylinders — even after eights were added. There was a new, larger and more powerful six cylinder engine underhood. A physically larger chassis was used. Both deluxe and standard versions were offered in a variety of body styles. The deluxe package included sidemounts, trunk platform, chrome plated headlamp shells, leather boots on springs and special paint work.

I.D. DATA: Serial number on right hand body sill under front mat. Starting: 1. Ending: NA. Engine number location same as serial number. Starting: F1. Ending: NA.

Model No.	Body Type & Seating	Price	Weight	Prod. Total
F-28R	2-dr. Rds.-2P	995	2695	2791
F-28DR	2-dr. Del. Rds.-2P	1145	2845	200
F-28T	4-dr. Tr.-5P	995	2915	804
F-28ST	4-dr. Spt. Tr.-5P	1145	3065	2933
F-28C	2-dr. Cpe.-3P	925	2705	9164
F-28SC	2-dr. Spt. Cpe.-3P	995	2760	5079
F-28DSC	2-dr. Del. Spt. Cpe.-3P	1145	2910	1038
F-282S	2-dr. Sed.-4P	925	2790	23,572
F-28S	4-dr. Sed.-5P	1025	2890	27,849
F-28DS	4-dr. Del. Sed.-5P	1175	3040	2221
F-28L	4-dr. Lan.-5P	1085	2805	10,485
F-28DL	4-dr. Del. Lan.-5P	1235	3050	1576

ENGINE: Inline. Six. Cast iron block. B & S: 3-3/16 x 4-1/8 in. Disp.: 197 cu. in. Brake H.P.: 55 @ 3,000 R.P.M. Main bearings: Four. Valve lifters: Mechanical. Carb.: Schebler.

CHASSIS: W.B.: 113-1/2 in. Frt./Rear Tread: standard. Tires: 28 x 5.25.

TECHNICAL: Sliding gear, selective transmission. Speeds: 3F/1R. Center, floor shift controls. Dry disc clutch. Shaft drive. Semi floating rear axle. Overall ratio: 4.41:1. External expanding service brakes on all wheels. Wood, wire or disc wheels.

1928 Oldsmobile, model F-28, sedan, HJE

OPTIONS: Front bumper. Rear bumper. Dual sidemount. Sidemount cover(s). Heater. Clock. Cigar lighter. Spotlight.

HISTORICAL: Introduced January 12, 1928. Calendar year sales and production: 86,593. Model year sales and production: 84,635. General manager was I.J. Reuter.

In 1928 Olds reached a new high employment peak of 6,234. Additional production capacity made.

1928
Model F-28, 6-cyl.

	FP	5	4	3	2	1
Rds	995	1250	3900	6500	9100	13,000
DeL Rds	1145	1400	4200	7000	9800	14,000
Tr	995	1400	4200	7000	9800	14,000
DeL Tr	1145	1550	4500	7500	10,500	15,000
Cpe	925	775	1500	3750	5250	7500
Spec Cpe	995	825	1600	4000	5600	8000
Spt Cpe	995	875	1700	4250	5900	8500
DeL Spt Cpe	1145	900	1900	4500	6300	9000
2 dr Sed	925	650	1250	2400	4200	6000
Sed	1025	750	1450	3300	4900	7000
DeL Sed	1175	750	1450	3500	5050	7200
Lan	1085	1000	2400	5000	7000	10,000
DeL Lan	1235	1075	3000	5500	7700	11,000

1929

1929 Oldsmobile, model F-29, 4-dr. landau sedan, AA

OLDSMOBILE — MODEL F-29 — SIX: Minor changes were made to the successful six cylinder Olds series in 1929. Power was up slightly to 62 horsepower this year. The model lineup was simplified this year. In addition to the standard models; special and deluxe packages were available. Special equipment included: twin sidemounts, trunk rack and front and rear bumpers. Deluxe equipment included sidemounted wire wheels, trunk rack, front and rear bumpers and chrome plated headlight shells.

1929 Oldsmobile, model F-29, Deluxe roadster, HJE

I.D. DATA: Serial number on right hand body sill under front mat. Starting: D-1. Ending: NA. Engine number location same as serial number. Starting: F-100,001. Ending: F-196,900.

Model No.	Body Type & Seating	Price	Weight	Prod. Total
F-29R	2-dr. Rds.-2P	945	2716	st.-947
F-29R	2-dr. Rds.-2P	945	2716	spl.-335
F-29R	2-dr. Rds.-2P	945	2716	del.-1013
F-29T	4-dr. Tr.-5P	945	2734	st.-18
F-29T	4-dr. Tr.-5P	945	2734	spl.-9
F-29T	4-dr. Tr.-5P	945	2734	del.-51
F-29C	2-dr. Cpe.-3P	875	2830	st.-8135
F-29C	2-dr. Cpe.-3P	875	2830	spl.-2011
F-29C	2-dr. Cpe.-3P	875	2830	del.-646
F-292S	2-dr. Sed.-4P	875	3075	st.-21,266
F-292S	2-dr. Sed.-4P	875	3075	spl.-4284
F-292S	2-dr. Sed.-4P	875	3075	del.-1544
F-29S	4-dr. Sed.-5P	975	3128	st.-25,433
F-29S	4-dr. Sed.-5P	975	3128	spl.-3138
F-29S	4-dr. Sed.-5P	975	3128	del.-7197
F-29L	4-dr. Lan.-5P	1035	3140	st.-2459
F-29L	4-dr. Lan.-5P	1035	3140	spl.-601
F-29L	4-dr. Lan.-5P	1035	3140	de.-1774

1929 Oldsmobile, model F-29, 2-dr. sedan, HJE

ENGINE: Inline. Six. Cast iron block. B & S: 3-3/16 x 4-1/8 in. Disp.: 197 cu. in. Brake H.P.: 61 @ 2600 R.P.M. Main bearings: Four. Valve lifters: Mechanical, mushroom type. Carb.: Schebler.

CHASSIS: W.B.: 113-1/2 in. Frt/Rear Tread: standard. Tires: 28 x 5.25 non-skid.

TECHNICAL: Selective, sliding gear transmission. Speeds: 3F/1R. Center, floor mounted shift controls. Single plate disc type clutch. Shaft drive. Semi floating rear axle. Overall ratio: 4.41:1. Front Bendix 3-shoe brakes, rear external contracting brakes. Wood, wire or disc wheels. Wheel size: 18 in.

OPTIONS: Front bumper. Rear bumper. Heater. Clock. Cigar lighter. Cowl lamps. Special Package — twin sidemounted spares, trunk rack and front & rear bumpers (75.00). Deluxe Package — twin sidemounted wire wheels, trunk rack, front & rear bumpers and chrome headlight shells (130.00).

HISTORICAL: Calendar year sales and production: 97,395. Model year sales and production: 97,395. General manager was I.J. Reuter.
   Highest General Motors employment ever in Lansing, Oldsmobile and Fisher body, 7,213. Three city blocks of additional land acquired for expansion. Work begun on new administration complex.

1929
Model F-29, 6-cyl.

	FP	5	4	3	2	1
Rds	945	2800	5700	9500	13,300	19,000
Conv	1075	2600	5500	9250	12,950	18,500
Tr	945	3000	6000	10,000	14,000	20,000
Cpe	875	900	1900	4500	6300	9000
2 dr Sed	875	675	1300	2600	4400	6300
Sed	975	675	1300	2600	4400	6300
Spt Cpe	945	950	2100	4750	6650	9500
Lan	1035	775	1500	3750	5250	7500

1929
Viking, V-8

Conv Cpe	1695	3750	7500	12,500	17,500	25,000
Sed	1695	3000	6000	10,000	14,000	20,000
CC Sed	1695	1400	4200	7000	9800	14,000

1930

OLDSMOBILE — MODEL F-30 — SIX: Olds stood with its traditional six cylinder models from a single series in 1930. Mohair upholstery was used in most closed Oldsmobiles, while leather was found on open cars. Three versions of most 1930 Oldsmobiles were available. The standard model was fitted with basic equipment. The special models had sidemounted spare tires, front and rear bumpers and a folding trunk rack. The deluxe package included sidemounted wire wheels, both bumpers, folding trunk rack and chrome plated headlight shells.

1930 Oldsmobile, model F-30, 4-dr. sedan, DC

I.D. DATA: Serial number on right hand body sill under front mat. Starting: 1. Ending: NA. Engine number location same as serial number. Starting: F-200001. Ending: F-252106.

Model No.	Body Type & Seating	Price	Weight	Prod. Total
30-FR	2-dr. Rds.-2P	995	2832	2979
30-FT	4-dr. Tr.-5P	965	2965	103
30-FC	2-dr. Cpe.-3P	895	2775	5008
30-FSC	2-dr. Spt. Cpe.-3P	965	2810	4870
30-F2S	2-dr. Sed.-4P	895	2840	13,165
30-FS	4-dr. Sed.-5P	995	2940	19,087
30-FPS	4-dr. Pat. Sed.-5P	1190	2950	4269

1930 Oldsmobile, model F-30, 2-dr. sedan, JAC

1930 Oldsmobile, model F-30, touring, HJE

ENGINE: Inline. Six. Cast iron block. B & S: 3-3/16 x 4-1/8 in. Disp.: 197 cu. in. Brake H.P.: 62 @ 3000 R.P.M. Main bearings: Four. Valve lifters: Mechanical, mushroom. Carb.: Model H.

CHASSIS: W.B.: 113-1/2 in. Frt/Rear Tread: standard. Tires: 28 x 5.25.

TECHNICAL: Selective, sliding gear transmission. Speeds: 3F/1R. Floor mounted, center shift controls. Dry disc clutch. Shaft drive. Semi-floating rear axle. Overall ratio: 4.54:1. Bendix 3-shoe front brakes; rear external contracting brakes. Wood, wire wheels.

OPTIONS: Front bumper. Rear bumper. Heater. Clock. Cigar lighter. Spotlight. Special: Sidemounts (twin), both bumpers & folding trunk rack (35.00). Deluxe Package — Sidemounts (twin wire), both bumpers, folding trunk rack and chrome plated headlamp shells (75.00).

HISTORICAL: Calendar year sales and production: 49,994. Model year sales and production: 49,994. General manager was D.S. Eddins.
   Work continued on additions to the manufacturing area within Lansing.

1930 Oldsmobile, model F-30, roadster, JAC

1930
Model F-30, 6-cyl.

	FP	5	4	3	2	1
Conv	995	3000	6000	10,000	14,000	20,000
Tr	965	3300	6600	11,000	15,400	22,000
Cpe	895	1000	2400	5000	7000	10,000
Spt Cpe	965	1000	2400	5000	7000	10,000
2 dr Sed	895	825	1600	4000	5600	8000
Sed	995	875	1700	4250	5900	8500
Pat Sed	1060	900	1900	4500	6300	9000

1930
Viking, V-8

	FP	5	4	3	2	1
Conv Cpe	1695	3900	7800	13,000	18,200	26,000
Sed	1695	1150	3600	6000	8400	12,000
CC Sed	1695	1250	3900	6500	9100	13,000

1931

1931 Oldsmobile, model F-31, convertible roadster, AA

OLDSMOBILE — MODEL F-31 — SIX: Olds continued to offer just a single series of cars this year, powered by the tried and true six cylinder powerplant. A synchromesh transmission was added this year. Standard and deluxe equipment packages were offered in a variety of open and closed body styles. The deluxe models came with twin sidemounts, both bumpers and a trunk platform.

I.D. DATA: Serial numbers were located on pillar of bodywork. Starting no.: 1-. Ending: NA. Engine no. located same as serial number. Starting engine no.: F-253001. Ending: F301655.

Model No.	Body Type & Seating	Price	Weight	Prod. Total
31-FCR	2-dr. Rds.-2P	995	2965	3500
31-FC	2-dr. Cpe.-3P	910	3040	3700
31-FSC	2-dr. Spt. Cpe.-3P	960	3115	4900
31-FK	2-dr. Sed.-4P	910	3155	10,555
31-FS	4-dr. Sed.-5P	960	3260	17,812
31-FP*	4-dr. Ptr. Sed.-5P	1025	3275	4415

* Deluxe models in any body style carried the letter prefix D.

1931 Oldsmobile, model F-31, Deluxe 4-dr. sedan, JAC

ENGINE: Inline. Six. Cast iron block. B & S: 3-3/16 in. x 4-1/8 in. Disp.: 197 cubic in. C.R.: 5.06 to 1. Brake H.P.: 65 @ 3350 R.P.M. N.A.C.C. H.P.: 24.4. Main bearings: Four. Valve lifters: Mechanical. Carb.: Downdraft, Stromberg.

CHASSIS: [Series 31-F] W.B.: 112-1/2 in. O.L.: 173 in. Height: 69-1/4 in. Frt/Rear Tread: Standard. Tires: 28 x 5.25 inches, non-skid balloon cords.

TECHNICAL: Synchromesh transmission. Center, floor controls. Single, dry disc clutch. Tubular, shaft drive. Semi-floating rear axle. Overall ratio: 4.56 to 1. Internal expanding, two-shoe. Self energizing brakes. Four wooden wheels.

1931 Oldsmobile, model F-31, business coupe, HJE

OPTIONS: Both bumpers (20.00). Rear metal tire cover (11.00). Olds/Waltham Clock (15.00). Cigar lighter (1.35). Spotlight (16.50). Ornamental radiator cap (5.00). Road light (22.50). Spring covers (7.50). Seat covers (17.50). Backup light (3.50). Wheel lock (2.50). Trunk (30.00). Fender light (6.00 pair).
Accessory Groups
#1 (bumpers, wheel lock, spare tire) (37.50)
#2 (#1 items plus ornamental radiator cap, spring covers, fender lights & backup light) (65.00)
#3 (Items from #2 plus metal tire cover, spotlight & clock) (103.00)
#4 (radiator cap, spring covers, fender lights, backup light) (27.50)
#5 (items from #4 plus metal tire covers, spotlight, clock) (77.00)
#6 (items from #5 plus trunk) (107.00)

HISTORICAL: Introduced January 1, 1931. First time Olds had offered a synchromesh transmission. Calendar year sales and production: 48,777. Model year sales and production: 47,316. D.S. Eddins was general manager.
  The 1931 Oldsmobile re-created the transcontinental 1905 curved dash run from New York to Portland, Oregon. Car building and shipping capacity stood at 800 per day by 1931.

1931
Model F-31, 6-cyl.

	FP	5	4	3	2	1
Conv	1000	3750	7500	12,500	17,500	25,000
Cpe	910	1200	3750	6250	8750	12,500
Spt Cpe	960	1000	2400	5000	7000	10,000
2 dr Sed	910	1000	2400	5000	7000	10,000
Sed	960	1000	2400	5000	7000	10,000
Pat Sed	1025	1025	2600	5250	7300	10,500

1932

1932 Oldsmobile, Eight, Sport coupe, DC

OLDSMOBILE — SERIES F — SIX: Olds retained its basic six cylinder models again this year. Six models were used. Despite the addition of a new series this year, sales dropped dramatically over 1931 totals. A slightly more powerful six cylinder engine was fitted this year and horsepower climbed to 74. A free wheeling system was found on both series 1932 models.

OLDSMOBILE — SERIES L — EIGHT:
Olds came back with a two series lineup for 1932 adding the straight-eight powered L series. Ironically, Olds had used V-8 motors several times before — as early as 1916 — but this was the first venture with a straight eight motor. This two-series combination would last through 1948. The chassis on both series was similar.

1932 Oldsmobile, Six, 2-dr. sedan, HJE

I.D. DATA: Serial numbers were located on pillar of bodywork. Starting no.: 1-. Ending: NA. Engine no. location same as serial number. Starting engine no.: [Six] 302001, [Eight] L-1001. Ending: [Six] 316568, [Eight] L-6557.

Six Cylinders [F Series]

Model No.	Body Type & Seating	Price	Weight	Prod. Total
32-FCR	2-dr. Rds.-3P	1000	2870	723
32-FC	2-dr. Cpe.-3P	920	2845	1083
32-FSC	2-dr. Spt. Cpe.-3P	970	2925	1173
32-FK	2-dr. Sed.-5P	920	2960	2804
32-FS	4-dr. Sed.-5P	1000	3035	5900
32-FP	4-dr. Sed.-5P	1035	3040	2114

Eight Cylinder [L Series]

Model No.	Body Type & Seating	Price	Weight	Prod. Total
32-LCR	2-dr. Rds.-3P	1055	2995	394
32-LC	2-dr. Cpe.-3P	975	2970	216
32-LSC	2-dr. Spt. Cpe.-3P	1025	3045	476
32-LK	2-dr. Sed.-5P	975	3080	271
32-LS	4-dr. Sed.-5P	1055	3165	1710
32-LP	4-dr. Sed.-5P	1090	3175	2262

Note 1: Deluxe models in any body style carried the prefix letter D in model number.

ENGINE: [Series F] Inline. Six. Cast iron block. B & S: 3-5/16 in. x 4-1/8 in. Disp.: 213 cubic in. C.R.: 5.59 to 1. Brake H.P.: 74 @ 3200 R.P.M. Main bearings: Four. Valve lifters: Mushroom type. Carb.: Downdraft. [Series L] Inline. Eight. Cast iron block. B & S: 3 in. x 4-1/4 in. Disp.: 240 cubic in. C.R.: 5.74 to 1. Brake H.P.: 87 @ 3350 R.P.M. Main bearings: Five. Valve lifters: Mushroom type. Carb.: Duplex downdraft w/automatic choke.

1932 Oldsmobile, Eight, Deluxe convertible roadster, JAC

CHASSIS: [Series F & L] W.B.: 116-1/2 in. O.L.: 178-3/4 in. Height: 67-7/8 in. Frt/Rear Tread: Standard. Tires: 17 x 6.00 inches, non-skid balloon cords.

TECHNICAL: Synchromesh transmission. Speeds: 3F/1R. Center, floor controls. Single, dry disc clutch. Shaft drive. Semi-floating rear axle. Overall ratio: 4.56 to 1. Internal expanding, two-shoe, duo servo. Four wooden wheels. Rear axle: 4.77 to 1.

OPTIONS: Both bumpers (33.00). Sidemount cover(s) (11.00). Electric Clock (9.85). Spotlight (18.75). Tire mirror (7.50 pair). Rt. hd. sunvisor (3.75). Trunk (30.00). Tire gauge (2.75). Luggage set (17.50).

HISTORICAL: Freewheeling. Calendar year sales and production: 17,502. Model year sales and production: 19,239. D.S. Eddins was general manager.

1932
Model F-32, 6-cyl.

	FP	5	4	3	2	1
Conv	1000	4200	8400	14,000	19,600	28,000
Cpe	920	1250	3900	6500	9100	13,000
Spt Cpe	970	1400	4200	7000	9800	14,000
2 dr Sed	920	1000	2400	5000	7000	10,000
Sed	1000	1075	3000	5500	7700	11,000
Pat Sed	1035	1125	3450	5750	8050	11,500

Model L-32, 8-cyl.

	FP	5	4	3	2	1
Conv	1055	4650	9300	15,500	21,700	31,000
Cpe	975	1400	4200	7000	9800	14,000
Spt Cpe	1025	1550	4500	7500	10,500	15,000
2 dr Sed	975	1075	3000	5500	7700	11,000
Sed	1055	1125	3450	5750	8050	11,500
Pat Sed	1090	1150	3600	6000	8400	12,000

1933

1933 Oldsmobile, Six, 2-dr. sedan, JAC

OLDSMOBILE — F-SERIES — SIX: A modernized and completely re-styled group of Oldsmobiles came to the market place in 1933. Once again the six cylinder models were the most popular offerings. The six cylinders now utilized a slightly smaller chassis. Olds called its models this year "style leaders."

OLDSMOBILE — L-SERIES — EIGHT: With a totally new styling package on the outside, the L or eight cylinder running gear remained largely unchanged this year. This model was physically larger than its six cylinder counterpart and a most distinctive grille was fitted.

I.D. DATA: Serial numbers were located on body pillar. Starting: Six-24001, Eight-7001. Ending: Six-50075, Eight-17600. Location of engine numbers was the same as serial no. Starting engine number: NA. Ending: NA.

Model No.	Body Type & Seating	Price	Weight	Prod. Total
Six Cylinder (F Series)				
33407	2-dr. Cpe.-3P	745	3045	1547
33428	2-dr. Spt. Cpe.-3P	780	3105	1738
33418	2-dr. Conv.-3P	825	3155	317
33401	2-dr. Sed.-5P	775	3195	3978
33431	2-dr. Tr. Sed.-5P	825	3205	5464
33409	4-dr. Sed.-5P	825	3215	7194
33419	4-dr. Tr. Sed.-5P	855	3255	5720
Eight Cylinder (L-Series)				
33418	2-dr. Conv.-3P	925	3305	267
33407	2-dr. Cpe.-3P	845	3295	396
33428	2-dr. Spt. Cpe.-3P	880	3305	827
33401	2-dr. Sed.-5P	875	3320	203
33431	2-dr. Tr. Sed.-5P	895	3360	1901
33409	4-dr. Sed.-5P	925	3440	2639
33419	4-dr. Tr. Sed.-5P	955	3445	4357

1933 Oldsmobile, Eight, convertible coupe, JAC

ENGINE: [Six] Inline L-head. Six. Cast iron block. B & S: 3-3/8 in. x 4-1/8 in. Disp.: 221 cu. in. C.R.: 5.3 to 1. Brake H.P.: 80. Main bearings: Four. Valve lifters: Mushroom. Carb.: Downdraft, Stromberg EC-22. Torque:

154. [Eight] Inline L-head. Eight. Cast iron block. B & S: 3 in. x 4-1/4 in. Disp.: 240 cu. in. C.R.: 5.5 to 1. Brake H.P.: 90. Main bearings: Five. Valve lifters: Mushroom. Carb.: Downdraft, Stromberg EE-22. Torque: 168.

CHASSIS: [F-Six] W.B.: 115 in. Height: 68-3/4 in. Frt/Rear Tread: 58-1/2 in./60-1/2 in. Tires: 17x5.50-4 ply. [L-Eight] W.B.: 119 in. Height: 68-3/4 in. Frt/Rear Tread: 58-1/2 in./60-1/2 in. Tires: 17x6.00-4 ply.

TECHNICAL: Manual/sliding gear transmission. Speeds: 3F/1R. Center, floor mounted controls. Dry-plate, single disc clutch. Shaft drive. 10-spline, semi-floating rear axle. Overall Ratio: 4.56-standard. Bendix duo-servo brakes. Four steel or wire wheels. Drivetrain Options: 4.78 mountain gear ratio.

OPTIONS: Sidemount cover(s) (14.00 pr). Bumper guards (3.50). Radio (Air Mate) (45.00). Heater (Deluxe) (14.95). Mirror clock (3.95). Cigar lighter (1.95). Seat covers (7.00). Spotlight (14.95). Gas tank lock (2.25). Deluxe gear shift ball (50 cents). Luggage (42.75).

1933 Oldsmobile, Six, 4-dr. sedan, HJE

HISTORICAL: Served as an "official car," not official pace car, at Indy. Calendar year sales & production: 36,072. Model year sales & production: 36,673. The general manager was I.J. Reuter.

1933
Model F-33, 6-cyl.

	FP	5	4	3	2	1
Conv	825	3300	6600	11,000	15,400	22,000
Bus Cpe	745	950	2100	4750	6650	9500
Spt Cpe	780	1000	2400	5000	7000	10,000
5P Cpe	745	1000	2400	5000	7000	10,000
Tr Cpe	775	950	2100	4750	6650	9500
Sed	825	925	2000	4600	6400	9200
Trk Sed	855	950	2100	4750	6650	9500

Model L-33, 8-cyl.

	FP	5	4	3	2	1
Conv	925	3600	7200	12,000	16,800	24,000
Bus Cpe	845	1000	2400	5000	7000	10,000
Spt Cpe	880	1025	2600	5250	7300	10,500
5P Cpe	875	1000	2400	5000	7000	10,000
Sed	925	950	2100	4750	6650	9500
Trk Sed	955	1000	2400	5000	7000	10,000

1934

1934 Oldsmobile, Eight, 4-dr. sedan, AA

OLDSMOBILE — SERIES F — SIX: Once again the basic Oldsmobile series was the six cylinder of F-series. Sales were on the rebound this year in general and Olds made a surge into sixth place in sales standings. Horsepower was upped slightly on the six and styling was mildly updated this year. GM officials seriously considered combining or doing away with either Olds, Buick or Pontiac, but by 1934 this notion had passed.

OLDSMOBILE — SERIES L — EIGHT: Despite the fact the six cylinder models were far more popular and the engines were almost as powerful and even more dependable, Oldsmobile continued to offer the straight-eight powered L-series in 1934. The L-series continued to be a physically larger car than the F-series.

I.D. DATA: Serial numbers were on frame left side rail under hood. Starting: Six-51001; Eight-18001. Ending: Six-102103; Eight-43079. Engine numbers were on upper left corner of cylinder block. Starting: NA. Ending: NA.

1934 Oldsmobile, Six, 4-dr. sedan, HJE

Model No.	Body Type & Seating	Price	Weight	Prod. Total
Series F, Six-cyl.				
34457	2-dr. Bs. Cpe.-3P	650	2980	3728
	*206 additional sidemounted			
34478	2-dr. Spt. Cpe.-3P	695	3040	2135
	*236 add'l sidemounted			
34451	2-dr. Sed.-5P	695	3055	4632
	*47 add'l sidemounted			
34472	2-dr. Tr. Sed.-5P	725	3135	11,734
	*570 add'l sidemounted			
34459	4-dr. Sed.-5P	755	3130	6492
	*w add'l 522 sidemounted			
34469	4-dr. Tr. Sed.-5P	785	3210	19,099
	*1682 add'l sidemounted			
Series L, Eight-cyl.				
34418	2-dr. Conv.-3P	975	3350	537
	w add'l 378 sidemounted			
34407	2-dr. Bs. Cpe.-3P	885	3425	770
	* add'l 128 sidemounted			
34428	2-dr. Spt. Cpe.-3P	920	3395	1024
	w add'l 253 sidemounted			
34401	2-dr. Sed.-5P	895	3405	621
	* w add'l 28 sidemounted			
34422	2-dr. Tr. Sed.-5P	925	3485	3816
	* w add'l 475 sidemounted			
34409	4-dr. Sed.-5P	965	3490	3593
	* w add'l 594 sidemounted			
34419	4-dr. Tr. Sed.-5P	995	3570	8857
	w add'l 3445 sidemounted			

1934 Oldsmobile, Six, sport coupe, JAC

ENGINE: Inline. L-head. Six. Cast iron block. B & S: 3-5/16 x 4-1/8 in. Disp.: 213 cu. in. C.R.: 5.7:1. Brake H.P.: 84. Main bearings: Four. Valve lifters: Cylindrical. Carb.: Downdraft single Stromberg EX 22. Inline, L-head. Eight. Cast iron block. B & S: 3 x 4-1/4 in. Disp.: 240 cu. in. C.R.: 5.7:1. Brake H.P.: 90. Main bearings: Five. Valve lifters: Mushroom. Carb.: Downdraft duplex Stromberg EE1. Torque: 168.

1934 Oldsmobile, Eight, convertible coupe, HJE

CHASSIS: [Series F-Six] W.B.: 114 in. O.L.: 189-1/2 in. H.: 67-1/8 in. Frt/Rear Tread: 58 inches both. Tires: 5.50 x 17. [Series L-Eight] W.B.: 119 in. O.L.: 197-3/4 in. H.: 66-3/8 in. Frt/Rear Tread: 59/60-1/2 in. Tires: 16 x 7.00 - 4-ply.

TECHNICAL: Synchronizing/helical transmission. Speeds: 3F/1R. Floor mounted, center controls. Dry-plate clutch. Shaft drive. Semi-floating rear axle, 10-spline. Overall ratio: [Series F] 4.56; [Series L] 4.78. Bendix hydraulic brakes on four wheels. Demountable steel spoke wheels.

OPTIONS: Bumper guards (3.50). Radio (airmate 47.95; air chief 62.50). Heater (14.95). Clock (mirror watch (30-hour) 3.95). Cigar lighter (1.50). Seat covers (standard 9.95; deluxe 11.95). Spotlight (14.95). Locking gas cap (2.25). Deluxe gear shift ball (.50). License plate frames (2.45). Luggage (43.75). Safety glass all windows (18.00). Group A (bumpers, spare tire covers, wheel locks and spring covers) (36.00). Group B (double windshield wiper, dual trumpet horns and automatic choke) (12.50). Group C (oversize tires, wheel trim moldings and spare tire cover) (32.00). Dealer installed Group X (right hand inside sun visor, cigar lighter, gear shift ball, bumper guards) (7.50). Dealer Installed Group Y (cigar lighter, gear shift ball, bumper guards, license plate frames, clock and wheel trim moldings) (23.95).

HISTORICAL: Calendar year sales & production: 82,150. Model year sales & production: 79,814. The general manager of Oldsmobile was C.L. McCuen.

Late in 1934 Olds began a major expansion effort. A total of 2-1/2 million dollars was budgeted for equipment and major assembly line improvements. Shipping facilities also underwent renovation.

1934
Model F-34, 6-cyl.

	FP	5	4	3	2	1
Bus Cpe	650	950	2100	4750	6650	9500
Spt Cpe	695	1000	2400	5000	7000	10,000
5P Cpe	695	875	1700	4250	5900	8500
SB Sed	755	825	1600	4000	5600	8000
Trk Sed	785	850	1650	4150	5800	8300

Model L-34, 8-cyl.

Conv	975	4050	8100	13,500	18,900	27,000
Bus Cpe	885	1025	2500	5150	7150	10,300
Spt Cpe	920	1050	2800	5400	7500	10,800
5P Cpe	895	1000	2400	5000	7000	10,000
Tr Cpe	925	1000	2400	5000	7000	10,000
Sed	965	1000	2400	5000	7000	10,000
Trk Sed	995	1025	2500	5150	7150	10,300

1935

1935 Oldsmobile, Six, 4-dr. touring sedan, DC

OLDSMOBILE — SERIES F — SIX: A complete restyle came on the outside for 1935, but the mechanical nature of things stayed about the same. The F-series remained the better seller of the two models offered. A re-designed cylinder head boosted the six cylinder output to 90 hp. Although smaller than the eight cylinder, the main distinguishing feature of the six was its distinctive front grille.

1935 Oldsmobile, Eight, 2-dr. sedan, DC

OLDSMOBILE — SERIES L — EIGHT: The straight eight L-series continued to offer a full line of body styles in 1935. As in the six cylinder model a re-designed cylinder head boosted horsepower taking the eight to the even 100 mark. Olds offered major suspension changes the previous year and the so-called "knee action" system was further fine tuned this model year.

I.D. DATA: Serial numbers were located on frame left side rail under hood. Starting: 103001-Six; 44001-Eight. Ending: 193468-Six; 73977-Eight. Engine numbers were on upper left corner of cylinder block. Starting: NA. Ending: NA

Model No.	Body Type & Seating	Price	Weight	Prod. Total
Series F, Six-cyl.				
353867	2-dr. Conv.-3P	800	3155	1598
353607C	2-dr. Clb. Cpe.-3P	725	3115	200
353607	2-dr. Bus. Cpe.-3P	675	3110	8468
353657	2-dr. Spt. Cpe.-3P	725	3150	2885
353601	2-dr. Sed.-5P	755	3225	14,785
353611	2-dr. Tr. Sed.-5P	765	3235	19,821
353609	4-dr. Sed.-5P	790	3285	13,009
353619	4-dr. Tr. Sed.-5P	820	3295	34,647

* This is some indication Olds built a handful of six cylinder station wagons this year but no production records exist on these cars.

Model No.	Body Type & Seating	Price	Weight	Prod. Total
Series L, Eight-cyl.				
353867	2-dr. Conv.-3P	950	3390	910
353807C	2-dr. Clb. Cpe.-3P	870	3340	74
353807	2-dr. Bs. Cpe.-3P	860	3335	1226
353857	2-dr. Spt. Cpe.-3P	895	3380	959
353801	2-dr. Sed.-5P	895	3480	870
353811	2-dr. Tr. Sed.-5P	900	3485	4862
353809	4-dr. Sed.-5P	940	3530	2976
353819	4-dr. Tr. Sed.-5P	970	3545	18,058

1935 Oldsmobile, Six, station wagon, HJE

ENGINE: Inline. Six. L-head. Cast iron block. B & S: 3-5/16 x 4-1/8 in. Disp.: 213 cu. in. C.R.: 6 to 1. Brake H.P.: 90 @ 3400 R.P.M. Main bearings: Four thin-wall. Valve lifters: Cylindrical. Carb.: Single, downdraft Stromberg EX-22. Torque: 165 lbs.-ft. @ 2000 R.P.M. Inline. L-head. Eight. Cast iron block. B & S: 3 x 4-1/4 in. Disp.: 240 cu. in. C.R.: 6.2 to 1. Brake H.P.: 100 @ 3400 R.P.M. Main bearings: Five. Valve lifters: Mushroom. Carb.: Duplex downdraft, Stromberg EE1. Torque: 182 lbs.-ft. @ 1800 R.P.M.

CHASSIS: [Series F] W.B.: 115 in. O.L.: 188-11/32 in. H.: 67 in. Frt/Rear Tread: 58/59 in. Tires: 6.25 x 16 - 4 ply. [Series L] W.B.: 121 in. O.L.: 193-23/32 in. H.: 67-7/16 in. Frt/Rear Tread: 58/59 in. Tires: 7.00 x 16.

TECHNICAL: Manual, sliding gear transmission. Speeds: 3F/1R. Center, floor mounted controls. Dry-plate clutch. Shaft drive. 10-spline, semi-floating rear axle. Overall ratio: 4.44 to 1. Bendix-hydraulic brakes on four wheels. Demountable, steel spoke wheels.

OPTIONS: Fender skirts (11.50, lacquered & installed). Radio (standard w antenna 51.70; deluxe w antenna 66.25). Heater (standard 13.90; deluxe 18.65). Clock (electric 11.50). Cigar lighter (1.50). Spotlight (17.95). Right tail lamp for six (5.50). Luggage compartment light (2.00). License plate frames (2.95). Defroster (3.25). Home battery charger (7.95). Fender markers (1.25). Mirror watch (4.00). Insect screen (1.50). Luggage compartment floor mat (1.75). Safety glass all windows (10.00). Group A - factory inst (bumpers, guards, spare tire & spring covers) (45.00). Group B - factory inst (dual horns, double windshield wiper and automatic choke) 6 cyl only (12.50). Group C - factory inst (oversize tires & tubes) (30.00). Group X - dlr instl (cigar lighter, gear shift ball, right hand sunvisor, mirror clock) (8.00).

HISTORICAL: Oldsmobile added its "turret top" this model year. Calendar year sales & production: 183,152. Model year sales & production: 126,768.

Oldsmobile purchased the modern Durant Lansing, Michigan plant and this became the new home of Lansing's Fisher Body operations. Olds then took over former Fisher Body floor space within the main Oldsmobile assembly plant.

1935
F-35, 6-cyl.

	FP	5	4	3	2	1
Conv	800	3500	7050	11,750	16,450	23,500
Clb Cpe	725	875	1700	4350	6050	8700
Bus Cpe	675	850	1650	4200	5850	8400
Spt Cpe	725	900	1800	4450	6250	8900
Tr Cpe	755	850	1650	4150	5800	8300
Sed	790	750	1450	3400	5000	7100
Trk Sed	820	750	1450	3500	5050	7200

L-35, 8-cyl.

	FP	5	4	3	2	1
Conv	950	3800	7650	12,750	17,850	25,500
Clb Cpe	870	900	1800	4450	6250	8900
Bus Cpe	860	875	1700	4300	6000	8600
Spt Cpe	895	950	2100	4700	6600	9400
2 dr Sed	895	750	1450	3500	5050	7200
2 dr Trk Sed	900	775	1500	3700	5200	7400
Sed	755	775	1500	3700	5200	7400
Trk Sed	785	800	1550	3800	5300	7600

1936

1936 Oldsmobile, Six, 2-dr. sedan, AA

OLDSMOBILE — SERIES F — SIX: A very mild re-style greeted Olds buyers this model year. Door handles were located from the front of the doors to the rear this year giving an easy distinguishing point from 1935 models. Headlights rose higher on the front end sheet metal this year. The six cylinder continued as the most popular Oldsmobile. Little changed on this series mechanically.

OLDSMOBILE — SERIES L — EIGHT: The L-series remained physically larger automobiles than their six cylinder counterparts - but styling was very similar. The quickest way to distinguish the two models was in the differing grille design. Attractive fender mounted parking lamps came as standard equipment on L-series cars in 1936. Chassis-wise and mechanically, few changes were made in this group of cars over 1935 models.

I.D. DATA: Serial numbers were located on frame left side rail under hood. Starting: Six (F) - 200001; Eight (L) - 100001. Ending: Six (F) - 352356; Eight (L) - 139925. Engine numbers were on upper left corner of cylinder block. Starting: Six (F) - 506001; Eight (L) - 202001. Ending: Six (F) - 670000; Eight (L) - 250000.

Model No.	Body Type & Seating	Price	Weight	Prod. Total
Series F				
363667	2-dr. Conv.-3P	805	3109	2073
363607	2-dr. Bs. Cpe.-3P	665	3019	20,346
363657	2-dr. Spt. Cpe.-3P	730	3054	2831
363601	2-dr. Sed.-5P	735	3144	13,143
363611	2-dr. Tr. Sed.-5P	755	3155	46,373
363609	4-dr. Sed.-5P	795	3179	4082
363619	4-dr. Tr. Sed.-5P	820	3194	69,443
Series L				
363857	2-dr. Conv.-3P	935	3321	914
363807	2-dr. Bs. Cpe.-3P	810	3231	2181
363857	2-dr. Spt. Cpe.-3P	845	3261	959
363801	2-dr. Sed.-5P	850	3376	237
363811	2-dr. Tr. Sed.-5P	870	3385	6626
363809	4-dr. Sed.-5P	910	3401	406
363819	4-dr. Tr. Sed.-5P	935	3421	29,373

1936 Oldsmobile, Eight, sport coupe, HJE

ENGINE: Inline, L-head. Six. Cast iron block. B & S: 3-5/16 x 4-1/8 in. Disp.: 213 cu. in. C.R.: 6 to 1. Brake H.P.: 90 @ 3400 R.P.M. Main bearings: Four. Valve lifters: Cylindrical. Carb.: Single downdraft. Inline, L-head. Eight. Cast iron block. B & S: 3 x 4-1/4 in. Disp.: 240 cu. in. C.R.: 6.2 to 1. Brake H.P.: 100 @ 3400 R.P.M. Main bearings: Five. Valve lifters: Mushroom. Carb.: Duplex, downdraft.

CHASSIS: [Series F] W.B.: 115 in. O.L.: 188-13/16 in. H.: 67 in. Frt/Rear Tread: 58/59 in. Tires: 16 x 6.50. [Series L] W.B.: 121 in. O.L.: 194-3/16 in. H.: 67 in. Frt/Rear Tread: 58/59 in. Tires: 16 x 7.00.

OPTIONS: Fender skirts (10.00 pair). Bumper guards (2.25 pair). Radio (deluxe 67.50; standard 54.50). Heater (deluxe 16.75; standard 11.95). Clock (electric dash 11.50; mirror 4.75). Seat covers (9.80). Spotlight (15.95). Rt hand tail lamp (for F-series) (4.50). Wheel trim rings (13.55). Defrosting fan (5.25). Luggage compartment light (1.75). Luggage carrier (10.00). Visor vanity mirror (1.00). Jack (3.00). Exhaust deflector (1.00). Matching gear shift ball/cigar lighter (1.50). Grille insect shields (1.50). Home battery charger (7.95). Fender markers (2.50 pr). Luggage compartment mat (1.75). License plate frames (2.45).

HISTORICAL: Calendar year sales & production: 187,638. Model year sales & production: 200,546. C.L. McCuen was general manager of Oldsmobile.
In 1936 Olds began a vast $6 million expansion effort in Lansing.

1936
F-36, 6-cyl.

	FP	5	4	3	2	1
Conv	805	3650	7350	12,250	17,150	24,500
Bus Cpe	665	900	1800	4450	6250	8900
Spt Cpe	730	975	2300	4950	6900	9900
2 dr Sed	735	775	1500	3600	5100	7300
2 dr Trk Sed	755	775	1500	3750	5250	7500
Sed	795	800	1550	3800	5300	7600
Trk Sed	820	800	1550	3850	5400	7700

L-36, 8-cyl.

	FP	5	4	3	2	1
Conv	935	4000	7950	13,250	18,550	26,500
Bus Cpe	810	925	2000	4650	6500	9300
Spt Cpe	845	1025	2600	5200	7200	10,400
2 dr Sed	850	800	1550	3850	5400	7700
2 dr Trk Sed	870	825	1600	4000	5600	8000
Sed	910	850	1650	4100	5700	8200
Trk Sed	935	850	1650	4200	5850	8400

1937

1937 Oldsmobile, Six, 2-dr., sedan, DC

OLDSMOBILE — SERIES F — SIX: A complete restyle welcomed buyers of Oldsmobile in 1937. Once again the F-series, or six cylinder models, were responsible for most of the sales. Less wood could be found on this new series of Fisher bodies this year. The six cylinder had eight less inches of wheelbase. Displacement was upped slightly on the tried and true flathead six cylinder and horsepower was increased by 5 to 95 overall.

OLDSMOBILE — SERIES L — EIGHT: A distinctive new front styling package made the Olds straight eight series one of the most noticed cars on the road. Rolling on a wheelbase of 124 inches, cubic inches on the L-series went up to 257. Horsepower went to 110.

1937 Oldsmobile, Eight, business coupe, HJE

1041

I.D. DATA: Serial numbers were on frame left side rail under hood. Starting: [Eight] California-CL-140001; Linden, N.J.-LL-195001; Lansing, MI.-L-146001. Ending: [Eight] California-CL-143240; Linden, N.J.-LL-196512; Lansing, L-MI-186544. Starting: [Sixes] California built cars-CF35001; Linden, N.J. built-LF-195001; Lansing built-F-372001. Ending: [Sixes] California-CF-364520; Linden, N.J.-LF-544720; Lansing, MI-F-503300. Engine numbers were on upper left corner of cylinder block. Starting: [Six] 670001; [Eight] 296001. Ending: [Six] 818948; [Eight] 295824.

Model No.	Body Type & Seating	Price	Weight	Prod. Total
Series F, Six-cyl.				
373667	2-dr. Conv.-3P	965	3295	1619
373627B	2-dr. Bs. Cpe.-3P	810	3220	13,908
373627	2-dr. Clb. Cpe.-3P	870	3225	7426
373601	2-dr. Sed.-5P	870	3275	9664
373611	2-dr. Tr. Sed.-5P	895	3285	38,043
373609	4-dr. Sed.-5P	920	3310	4020
373619	4-dr. Tr. Sed.-5P	945	3395	62,933
Series L, Eight-cyl.				
373867	2-dr. Conv.-3P	1080	3450	728
373827	2-dr. Clb. Cpe.-3P	985	3405	2302
373827B	2-dr. Bs. Cpe.-3P	925	3395	2150
373811	2-dr. Sed.-5P	985	3480	5818
373801	2-dr. Tr. Sed.-5P	1010	3480	398
373809	4-dr. Sed.-5P	1035	3510	457
373819	4-dr. Tr. Sed.-5P	1060	3525	30,465

ENGINE: Inline, L-head. Six. Cast iron block. B & S: 3-7/16 x 4-1/8 in. Disp.: 230 cu. in. C.R.: 6.1 to 1. Brake H.P.: 95 @ 3400 R.P.M. Main bearings: Four. Valve lifters: Mushroom. Carb.: Single downdraft with automatic choke. Inline, L-head. Eight. Cast iron block. B & S: 3-1/4 x 3-7/8. Disp.: 257 cu. in. C.R.: 6.2 to 1. Brake H.P.: 110 @ 3600 R.P.M. Main bearings: Five. Valve lifters: Mushroom. Carb.: Duplex downdraft with automatic choke.

1937 Oldsmobile, Eight, 4-dr. touring sedan w/trunk, DC

CHASSIS: [Series F] W.B.: 117 in. O.L.: 192-13/16 in. Frt/Rear Tread: 58/59 in. Tires: 16 x 6.50. [Series L] W.B.: 124 in. O.L.: 199-9/16 in. Frt/Rear Tread: 58/59 in. Tires: 16 x 7.00.

TECHNICAL: Manual, sliding gear transmission. Speeds: 3F/1R. Center, floor mounted controls. Single plate clutch. Shaft drive. Spiral bevel, semi-floating rear axle. Overall ratio: 4.375 to 1. Triple sealed hydraulic brakes on four wheels. Steel wheels.

OPTIONS: Single sidemount (50.00). Bumper guards (3.00 pair). Radio (standard 53.00; deluxe with twin speakers 66.50). Heater (standard 13.95; deluxe 18.75). Clock (header board clock 4.25; electric clock 12.25). Cigar lighter (1.75). Seat covers (11.80). Spotlight (17.95). Dual windshield defroster (8.25). Fan defroster (6.25). Wheel trim rings (10.75). Wheel discs (12.75). Deluxe steering wheel (12.75). Luggage compartment mat (1.75). Luggage compartment light (1.25). Fender markers (1.25). Fog lamps (6.25). Insect window screens (2.00). Winter grille cover (1.25). Winter radiator shutter controlled from instrument panel (11.35).

HISTORICAL: The safety automatic transmission was an innovation introduced late in the 1937 model year by Oldsmobile. Initially it was offered on L-series cars. It was the first column shifter offered by Olds. Calendar year sales & production: 212,767. Model year sales & production: 200,546. C.L. McCuen was the general manager of Oldsmobile.
Olds began work on a new customer drive away center at its main plant in Lansing.

1937

F-37, 6-cyl.	FP	5	4	3	2	1
Conv	965	4300	8550	14,250	19,950	28,500
Bus Cpe	810	900	1800	4450	6250	8900
Clb Cpe	870	950	2100	4750	6650	9500
2 dr Sed	870	850	1650	4200	5850	8400
2 dr Trk Sed	895	875	1700	4300	6000	8600
Sed	920	850	1650	4200	5850	8400
Trk Sed	945	875	1700	4350	6050	8700
L-37, 8-cyl.						
Conv	1080	4700	9450	15,750	22,050	31,500
Clb Cpe	985	975	2200	4850	6800	9700
Bus Cpe	925	950	2100	4700	6600	9400
2 dr Sed	985	875	1700	4350	6050	8700
2 dr Trk Sed	1010	900	1800	4400	6150	8800
Sed	1035	875	1700	4350	6050	8700
Trk Sed	1060	900	1800	4450	6250	8900

1938 Oldsmobile, Six, 4-dr. sedan, AA

OLDSMOBILE — SERIES F — SIX: Oldsmobile continued its two series format in 1938 with the F, or six cylinder, continuing to be the division sales leader. This would mark the final year for the two series format. New front end treatments were found on both series and the F-models offered a slightly cleaner front end package. Mechanically things stayed almost exactly the same; the six powerplant developed 95 horsepower.

OLDSMOBILE — SERIES L — EIGHT: The straight eight, an Olds fixture since 1932, continued in 1938. Sales were down this year in general and Olds was in the industry's seventh sales slot. Both the six and eight cylinder models offered an unusual and attractive dash layout this year.

I.D. DATA: Serial numbers were located on frame left side rail under hood. Starting: [Series F] California built-CF-504001; Linden, N.J. built-LF-545001; Lansing, MI built-F600001. Starting: [Series L] California built-CL-187001; Linden, N.J. built-LL-197001; Lansing, MI built-L-212001. Ending: [Series F] California built-CF-510598; Linden, N.J. built-LF-551236; Lansing, MI built-F-662212. Ending: [Series L] California built-CL-188760; Linden, N.J. built-LL-198759 and Lansing, MI built-L-228126. Engine numbers were on upper left corner of cylinder block. Starting: F-series: 828001; L-series: 296001. Ending: F-series: 905000; L-series: 298859. On engine codes any engine with C-prefix first letter was California built. F, L or G letter prefix indicates Lansing production. LF, LG or LL numbers indicate Linden, NJ built engine.

Model No.	Body Type & Seating	Price	Weight	Prod. Total
Series F, Six-cyl.				
383667	2-dr. Conv.-3P	1046	3360	1184
383627B	2-dr. Bs. Cpe.-3P	873	3205	8538
383627	2-dr. Clb. Cpe.-3P	929	3215	5632
383601	2-dr. Sed.-5P	919	3275	3975
383611	2-dr. Tr. Sed.-5P	944	3285	22,390
383609	4-dr. Sed.-5P	970	3290	1477
383619	4-dr. Tr. Sed.-5P	995	3305	36,484
Series L, Eight-cyl.				
383867	2-dr. Conv.-3P	1163	3530	475
383827B	2-dr. Bs. Cpe.-3P	989	3400	1098
383827	2-dr. Clb. Cpe.-3P	1035	3410	1136
383801	2-dr. Sed.-5P	1030	3275	143
383811	2-dr. Tr. Sed.-5P	1056	3287	1948
383809	4-dr. Sed.-5P	1081	3290	200
383819	4-dr. Tr. Sed.-5P	1107	3295	14,987

ENGINE: Inline, L-head. Six. Cast iron block. B & S: 3-7/16 x 4-1/8 in. Disp.: 230 cu. in. C.R.: 6.1 to 1. Brake H.P.: 95 @ 3400 R.P.M. Main bearings: Four. Valve lifters: Mushroom. Carb.: Single downdraft, automatic choke. Inline, L-head. Eight. Cast iron block. B & S: 3-1/4 x 3-7/8 in. Disp.: 257 cu. in. C.R.: 6.2 to 1. Brake H.P.: 110 @ 3600 R.P.M. Main bearings: Five. Valve lifters: Mushroom. Carb.: Duplex downdraft with automatic choke.

1938 Oldsmobile, Eight, 4-dr. sedan, AA

CHASSIS: [Series L] W.B.: 124 in. O.L.: 197-7/8 in. Frt/Rear Tread: 58/59 in. Tires: 16 x 7.00. [Series F] W.B.: 117 in. O.L.: 190-7/16 in. Frt/Rear Tread: 58/59 in. Tires: 16 x 6.50.

TECHNICAL: Sliding gear synchro-mesh transmission. Speeds: 3F/1R. Floor mounted center gear shift, column mounted on optional semi-automatic. Single plate clutch. Shaft drive. Spiral bevel, semi-floating rear axle. Overall ratio: Standard: 4.375 to 1; semi-automatic: 3.55 to 1. Cast iron drum, hydraulic brakes on four wheels. Pressed steel wheels. Wheel size: 16 x 4.50. Drivetrain Options: Safety automatic transmission (100.00).

OPTIONS: Dual sidemount (65.00). Bumper guards (2.00 each). Radio (standard radio 53.00; deluxe radio 66.50). Heater (standard hot water heater 14.45; deluxe hot water heater 19.95). Clock (header board clock 12.25; electric clock 15.00). Cigar lighter (1.75). Radio antenna (turret top antenna 7.00). Seat covers (standard 12.95; deluxe 16.95). Dual windshield defroster (8.25). Defroster fan (4.40). Gear shift ball (.50). Wheel chrome mouldings (10.75). Exhaust deflector (1.00). License plate frames (2.75). Luggage compartment mat (1.75). Luggage compartment light (1.25). Fender markers (3.25). Fog lamps (6.25). Winter grille covers (1.00). Locking gas cap (1.50).

HISTORICAL: An air cooled battery introduced this model year. Safety-Automatic Transmission (shared with Buick) continued this model year. Calendar year sales & production: 93,706. Model year sales & production: 99,951. C.L. McCuen was the general manager for Oldsmobile.

Manufacturing efforts for cars and engines strengthened in California and New Jersey, though most Oldsmobiles continued to be built in Lansing, Michigan.

**1938
F-38, 6-cyl.**

	FP	5	4	3	2	1
Conv	1046	4400	8850	14,750	20,650	29,500
Bus Cpe	873	950	2100	4700	6600	9400
Clb Cpe	929	950	2100	4700	6600	9400
2 dr Sed	919	875	1700	4250	5900	8500
2 dr Tr Sed	944	900	1800	4450	6250	8900
Sed	970	850	1650	4200	5850	8400
Tr Sed	995	900	1800	4450	6250	8900

L-38, 8-cyl.

	FP	5	4	3	2	1
Conv	1163	4900	9750	16,250	22,750	32,500
Bus Cpe	989	950	2100	4700	6600	9400
Clb Cpe	1035	975	2200	4850	6800	9700
2 dr Sed	1030	900	1800	4450	6250	8900
2 dr Tr Sed	1056	950	2100	4700	6600	9400
Sed	1081	900	1800	4450	6250	8900
Tr Sed	1107	950	2100	4700	6600	9400

1939

1939 Oldsmobile, Six, club coupe, JAC

OLDSMOBILE — SERIES 60 — SIX: The F-series remained the bottom line Oldsmobile for the model year and as all 1939's it was completely restyled. The F-series lineup was restricted to just four body styles. A pair of coupes, a two door and four door were offered with no open cars in the series. The wheelbase of the F-series came down to 115 inches and a smaller displacement six cylinder motor was fitted.

OLDSMOBILE — G-SERIES 70 — SIX: The new Oldsmobile for 1939, was actually a combination of two previous Olds offerings. Essentially the G-series cars were the larger (previously L-series) chassis fitted with the smaller (F-series) powerplant. For 1939, this automotive group was fitted with a slightly larger six cylinder motor than F-series cars. Body styles were shared with L-series cars and a convertible could be found in both groups.

OLDSMOBILE — L-SERIES 80 — EIGHT: The top line Olds was again the straight eight powered L-series. This was the lone year Olds would use the 80 series designation. Despite a complete external styling change, mechanics remained largely unchanged on L-series cars. Interior space was increased and all 1939 models once again the semi-automatic ("Safety Automatic") transmission was offered. A column-mounted shifter was added for standard shift cars this year.

1939 Oldsmobile, Eight, convertible coupe, JAC

I.D. DATA: Serial numbers were on frame left side rail under hood. Starting: [Series F (60)] California-built cars-CF-511001; Linden, N.J. built-FL-551301; Lansing, MI-built-F-663001. Starting: [Series G-(70)] California built-CG-10001; Linden, N.J. built-LG-10001; Lansing, MI-built-G-300001. Starting: [Series L (80)] California-built cars-CL-189001; Linden, N.J. built-LL-199001; Lansing, MI built-L-228201. Ending: [Series F (60)] California built-CF-514115; Linden, N.J. built-LF-555385; Lansing, MI-built-F-702588. Ending: [Series G (70)] California built-CG-15325; Linden, N.J. built-LG-107782; Lansing, MI built-G-354522. Ending: [Series L (80)] California built-CL-190358; Linden, N.J. built-LL-201119; Lansing, MI built-L-241850. Engine numbers were on upper left corner of cylinder block. Starting: [Series F (60)] 905001; [Series G (70)] 10001; [Series L (80)] 316001. Ending: [Series F (60)] 952701; [Series G (70)] 78471; [Series L (80)] 333127. Engines with first prefix letter C-California built. Engine with first prefix letter L-Linden, N.J. Engines with just single prefix letter built in Lansing, MI.

Model No.	Body Type & Seating	Price	Weight	Prod. Total
Series F (60)				
393527B	2-dr. Bs. Cpe.-3P	777	2870	5565
393527	2-dr. Clb. Cpe.-3P	833	2915	2273
393511	2-dr. Sed.-5P	838	2965	16,910
393519	4-dr. Sed.-5P	889	3000	15,948
Series G (70)				
393667	2-dr. Conv.-3P	1045	3230	1714
393627B	2-dr. Bs. Cpe.-3P	840	3040	5211
393627	2-dr. Clb. Cpe.-3P	891	3080	4795
393611	2-dr. Sed.-5P	901	3140	19,427
	*add'l 17 built w sunroof			
393619	4-dr. Sed.-5P	952	3180	38,145
	add'l 79 built w sunroof			
Series L (80)				
393887	2-dr. Conv.-3P	1119	3390	472
393827B	2-dr. Bs. Cpe.-3P	920	3190	738
393827	2-dr. Clb. Cpe.-3P	971	3230	1149
393811	2-dr. Sed.-5P	992	3290	1564
	*add'l 2 built w sunroof			
393819	4-dr. Sed.-5P	1043	3340	12,242
	*add'l 84 built w sunroof			

1939 Oldsmobile, Six, 2-dr. sedan, AA

ENGINE: [Series F (60)] Inline, L-head. Six. Cast iron block. B & S: 3-7/16 x 3-7/8 in. Disp.: 215 cu. in. C.R.: 6.2 to 1. Brake H.P.: 90 @ 3400 R.P.M. Main bearings: Four. Valve lifters: Steel spherical mushroom. Carb.: 1-1/4 single downdraft with automatic choke. Torque: 170. [Series F (70)] Inline, L-head. Six. Cast iron block. B & S: 3-7/16 x 4-1/8 in. Disp.: 230 cu. in. C.R.: 6.1 to 1. Brake H.P.: 95 @ 3400 R.P.M. Main bearings: Four. Valve lifters: Steel spherical mushroom. Carb.: 1-1/4 single downdraft with automatic choke. Torque: 180. [Series L (80)] Inline, L-head. Eight. Cast iron block. B & S: 3-1/4 x 3-7/8 in. Disp.: 257 cu. in. C.R.: 6.1 to 1. Brake H.P.: 110 @ 3400 R.P.M. Main bearings: Five. Valve lifters: Mushroom. Carb.: 1-1/4 dual downdraft with automatic choke. Torque: 200.

CHASSIS: [Series F (60)] W.B.: 115 in. O.L.: 189 in. H.: 66 in. Frt/Rear Tread: 58/59 in. Tires: 6.00 x 16. [Series G (70)] W.B.: 120 in. O.L.: 197 in. H.: 65-3/4 in. Frt/Rear Tread: 58/59 in. Tires: 6.00 x 16. [Series L (80)] W.B.: 120 in. O.L.: 197 in. H.: 65-3/4 in. Frt/Rear Tread: 58/59 in. Tires: 6.50 x 16.

TECHNICAL: Selective, sliding gear transmission. Speeds: 3F/1R. Steering column controls. Single dry plate clutch. Shaft drive. Semi-floating rear axle. Overall ratio: 4.55 to 1. Hydraulic internal expanding brakes on four wheels. Steel wheels. Drivetrain Options: Safety automatic transmission (75.00).

1939 Oldsmobile, Six, 4-dr. sedan, OCW

OPTIONS: Fender skirts (streamline fender panels 15.00). Bumper guards (2.50 pair). Radio (standard 46.00; deluxe 55.00; super deluxe pushbutton 61.00). Heater (standard hot water 13.95; deluxe hot water 18.45). Clock (glove box (30-hour wind) 4.25; electric 11.25. Cigar lighter (2.00). Radio antenna (cowl antenna 2.00). Seat covers (San Toy seat covers 11.95). Spotlight (14.50). Rear seat heater (19.95). Dual defroster (8.00). Defroster fan (4.25). Visor vanity mirror (1.00). Deluxe wheel discs (12.00). Wheel trim rings (8.50). Exhaust deflector (1.00). License plate frames (2.75). Luggage compartment light (1.25). Panel and glove box light (1.75). Fog lamps (10.50). Winter grille cover (1.00). Locking gas cap (1.50). Backup lights (6.00). Deluxe driving lights (10.95). Fender marker lights (6.00). Windshield washer (4.75). Sunshine Turret Top (37.50). Whitewall tires (16.25). Oversize tires (20.00). Deluxe steering wheel (12.50). Oil filter (5.00).

HISTORICAL: Olds shared an innovative but rare factory sunroof with several other divisions. Running boards were a no charge delete option for the first time this year. Calendar year sales & production: 158,560. Model year sales & production: 137,249. The general manager of Oldsmobile was C.L. McCuen.

1939
F-39 "60" Series, 6-cyl.

	FP	5	4	3	2	1
Bus Cpe	777	850	1650	4150	5800	8300
Clb Cpe	833	850	1650	4200	5850	8400
2 dr Sed	838	850	1650	4100	5700	8200
Sed	889	850	1650	4200	5850	8400

G-39 "70" Series, 6-cyl.

Conv	1045	4100	8250	13,750	19,250	27,500
Bus Cpe	840	875	1700	4250	5900	8500
Clb Cpe	891	875	1700	4300	6000	8600
2 dr Sed	901	850	1650	4200	5850	8400
2 dr SR Sed	951	875	1700	4300	6000	8600
Sed	952	875	1700	4250	5900	8500
SR Sed	1002	875	1700	4300	6000	8600

L-39, 8-cyl.

Conv	1119	4700	9450	15,750	22,050	31,500
Bus Cpe	920	925	1900	4550	6350	9100
Clb Cpe	971	950	2100	4700	6600	9400
2 dr Sed	992	875	1700	4300	6000	8600
2 dr SR Sed	1042	900	1800	4400	6150	8800
Sed	1043	875	1700	4300	6000	8600
SR Sed	1093	900	1800	4400	6150	8800

1940

1940 Oldsmobile, 70, coupe, DC

OLDSMOBILE — SPECIAL — SERIES 60 — SIX: The 60 series Oldsmobile was again the bottom line in a three series lineup. Sales reached an all-time high in 1940. The 60 series grew 9 inches over its counterpart in 1939. A convertible was added to the model lineup for 1940 and for the first time an official station wagon was added to factory literature of the day.
Description: This model year the 70 series did not share a wheelbase with the top of the line 90 series - but instead rolled on a 120 wheelbase of its own. This year the 95 horsepower six cylinder motor was shared with 60 series models. Five basic body styles were to be found here: a pair of coupes, two door and four door sedans and a convertible.

1940 Oldsmobile, 60, station wagon, JAC

OLDSMOBILE — CUSTOM CRUISER — SERIES 90 — EIGHT: Oldsmobile again got serious in the luxury sales race in 1940 with its 90 series models. The numerical designation was raised from the previous year's 80 tag. A buy here was the only way to obtain an eight cylinder Oldsmobile. An exclusive 124 inch wheelbase was used. Just four 90 series models were offered. Two open cars were offered including the two door convertible and the super rare phaeton. Also available were a club coupe and four door sedan.

I.D. DATA: Serial numbers were on frame left side rail under hood. Starting: [Series 60] California built-CF515001; Linden, N.J. built-LF-556001; Lansing, MI built-F703001. [Series 70] California built-CG-16001; Linden, N.J. built-LG-108001; Lansing, Michigan built-G35501. [Series 90] California built-CL-190501; Linden, N.J. built-LL-202001; Lansing, MI built-L-242001. Ending: [Series 60] California built-CF-519651; Linden, N.J. built LF-563473; Lansing, MI built-F-758579. [Series 70] California built-CG-21070; Linden, N.J. built LG-117596; Lansing, MI built-G-417928. [Series 90] California built-CL-192700; Linden, NJ built-LL-205267; Lansing, MI built-L-281191. Engine numbers were on upper left corner of cylinder block. Starting: [Series 60] 79001; [Series 70] 79001; [Series 90] 334001. Ending: [Series 60] 224652; [Series 70] 224652; [Series 90] 378661. Engine number with the first prefix letter C were California built. Engine numbers with the first prefix letter L were Linden, NJ built. Engine numbers with just a single prefix letter were Lansing, MI built.

1940 Oldsmobile, 90, 4-dr. sedan, TVB

Model No.	Body Type & Seating	Price	Weight	Prod. Total
403567	2-dr. Conv.-3P	1021	3150	1347
403527B	2-dr. Bs. Cpe.-3P	807	2950	2752
403527	2-dr. Clb. Cpe.-3P	848	2995	11,583
403511	2-dr. Sed.-5P	853	3045	29,220
403519	4-dr. Sed.-5P	899	3060	24,422
403565	4-dr. St. Wgn.-6P	1042	3542	633
G-Series (Dynamic)-70				
403667	2-dr. Conv.-3P	1045	3290	1070
403627B	2-dr. Bs. Cpe.-3P	865	3090	4337
403627	2-dr. Clb. Cpe.-3P	901	3130	8505
403611	2-dr. Sed.-5P	912	3190	22,486
403619	4-dr. Sed.-5P	963	3230	42,467
L-Series (Custom Cruiser)-90				
403967	2-dr. Conv.-3P	1222	3440	290
403929	2-dr. Phae.-5P	1570	3670	50
403927C	2-dr. Clb. Cpe.-3P	1069	3280	10,243
403919	4-dr. Sed.-5P	1131	3390	33,075

ENGINE: [Series 60 & 70] Inline, L-head. Six. Cast iron block. B & S: 3-7/16 x 4-1/8 in. Disp.: 230 cu. in. C.R.: 6.1 to 1. Brake H.P.: 95 @ 3200 R.P.M. Main bearings: Four. Valve lifters: Mushroom. Carb.: Single downdraft w. automatic choke. [Series 90] Inline, L-head. Six. Cast iron block. B & S: 3-1/4 x 3-7/8 in. Disp.: 257 cu. in. C.R.: 6.2 to 1. Brake H.P.: 110 @ 3200 R.P.M. Main bearings: Five. Valve lifters: Mushroom. Carb.: Dual downdraft with automatic choke.

CHASSIS: [Series 60-F] W.B.: 116 in. O.L.: 197-3/4 in. H.: 65 in. Frt/Rear Tread: 58/59 in. Tires: 16 x 6.00. [Series 70-G] W.B.: 120 in. O.L.: 199-3/4 in. H.: 65 in. Frt/Rear Tread: 58/59 in. Tires: 16 x 6.50. [Series 90-L] W.B.: 124 in. O.L.: 210-3/4 in. H.: 65 in. Frt/Rear Tread: 58/59 in. Tires: 15 x 7.00.

TECHNICAL: Manual, synchromesh sliding gear transmission. Speeds: 3F/1R. Column shifted. Single plate clutch. Shaft drive. Semi-floating, hypoid rear axle. Overall Ratio: [Series 60] 4.1 to 1; [Series 70 & 90] 4.3 to 1. Hydraulic brakes with cast iron drums on four wheels. Pressed steel wheels. Drivetrain Options: Automatic transmission HydraMatic (100.00).

OPTIONS: Fender skirts (15.00). Bumper guards (2.00 pair). Radio (standard-45.00; deluxe-56.60). Heater (dash-13.45; defroster-8.25; underseat-19.75; defroster-10.75). Clock (30-hour hand wind-5.50; electric w. automatic glove box light-12.90). Cigar lighter (2.00). Seat covers (12.85). Deluxe steering wheel (12.50). Vanity visor mirror (1.00). Wheel trim rings (8.00). Directional signals (9.85). Fog lamp (5.45 each). Backup lights (6.00 pair). License frames (2.75 pair). Exhaust deflector (1.00). Trunk light (1.25). Winter grille cover (1.00). Locking gas cap (1.50).

1940 Oldsmobile, 90, convertible coupe, JAC

HISTORICAL: A combined effort between Olds and GM engineers produced the first HydraMatic equipped cars this model year. Although certainly not the first automatic transmission, probably the best unit to this date. Calendar year sales & production: 215,028. Model year sales & production: 192,692. The general manager of Oldsmobile was S.E. Skinner.

1940
Series 60, 6-cyl.

	FP	5	4	3	2	1
Conv	1021	3800	7650	12,750	17,850	25,500
Bus Cpe	807	850	1650	4200	5850	8400
Clb Cpe	848	900	1800	4450	6250	8900
Sta Wag	1042	1650	4600	7700	10,800	15,400
2 dr Sed	853	800	1550	3850	5400	7700
2 dr SR Sed	903	825	1600	3950	5500	7900
Sed	899	800	1550	3900	5450	7800
SR Sed	949	825	1600	4050	5650	8100
Series 70, 6-cyl.						
Conv	1045	4100	8250	13,750	19,250	27,500
Bus Cpe	865	900	1800	4450	6250	8900
Clb Cpe	901	950	2100	4700	6600	9400
2 dr Sed	912	850	1650	4200	5850	8400
Sed	963	875	1700	4300	6000	8600
Series 90, 8-cyl.						
Phae	1570	4900	9750	16,250	22,750	32,500
Conv	1222	4700	9450	15,750	22,050	31,500
Clb Cpe	1069	1100	3400	5700	8000	11,400
Tr Sed	1131	1025	2600	5200	7200	10,400

1941

OLDSMOBILE — SPECIAL — SERIES 60 — SIX OR EIGHT: Olds moved up to sixth place this model year with its three series format. The major change this year found a six cylinder or eight cylinder version of each series offered. The special series was a price leader that offered a pair of coupes, two and four door sedans, the rare station wagon and a convertible coupe. A deluxe equipment package was also offered in this long running series.

OLDSMOBILE — SERIES 90 — SIX OR EIGHT: Just a pair of fastback sedan body styles were offered in this series for 1941. A wheelbase of 125 inches was shared with the 90 series. A deluxe equipment package was offered here. The top of the line Oldsmobile in 1941 came in four body styles. Rarest of these cars was the phaeton which was offered by Oldsmobile only in 1940 and 1941. Joining the four door open car was a convertible coupe, club coupe and four door sedan. This was the only year in Olds history that a model 96 - a ninety series car with a six cylinder engine was available. Few were sold. HydraMatic was a popular option on 90 series cars this year.

1941 Oldsmobile, 66, station wagon, AA

I.D. DATA: Serial numbers were on frame left side rail under hood. Starting: [Series Sixty] California built-66C or 68C-1001; Linden, NJ built-66L or 68L-1001; Lansing, MI built-66 or 68-1001. [Series Seventy] California built-76C or 78C-1001; Linden, NJ built-76L or 78L-1001; Lansing, MI built-76 or 78-1001. [Series Ninety] California built-96C or 98C-1001; Linden, NJ built 96L or 98L-1001; Lansing, MI built-96 or 98-1001. Ending: [Series Sixty] California built-66C or 68C-8827; Linden, NJ built-66L or 68L-8622; Lansing, MI built-66 or 68-8817. [Series Seventy] California built-76C or 78C-6843; Linden, NJ built-76L or 78L-10426; Lansing, MI built-76 or 78-47617. [Series Ninety] California built-96C or 98C-3352; Linden, NJ built-13195; Lansing, MI built-96 or 98-24679. Engine numbers were on upper left corner of cylinder block. Starting: [Six cylinder] 225001; [Eight] 37901. Ending: [Six cylinder] 42209; [Eight] 449095. Engines with one letter prefix (F, L or G) Lansing, MI. Engine with two letters prefix with first letter C built in California, with first letter L built in Linden, NJ.

1941 Oldsmobile, 98, coupe, OCW

Model No.	Body Type & Seating	Price	Weight	Prod. Total
413567	2-dr. Conv.-3P	1048	3355	2833
413527B	2-dr. Bs. Cpe.-3P	852	3145	6433
413527	2-dr. Clb. Cpe.-3P	893	3185	23,796
413511	2-dr. Sed.-5P	898	3190	32,475
413519	4-dr. Sed.-5P	945	3230	37,820
4135SW	4-dr. SW.-6P	1176	NA	NA
68 Models				
413567	2-dr. Conv.-3P	1089	3445	776
413527B	2-dr. Bs. Cpe.-3P	893	3260	188
413527	2-dr. Clb. Cpe.-3P	935	3330	2684
413511	2-dr. Sed.-5P	940	3335	3878
413519	4-dr. Sed.-5P	987	3390	6009
4135SW	4-dr. SW.-6P	1217	NA	NA
76 Models				
413627B	2-dr. Cpe.-3P	908	3315	353
413627	2-dr. Clb. Sed.-5P	954	3320	std. 41,938
				dlx. 6947
413609	4-dr. Sed.-5P	1010	3390	std. 31,074
				dlx. 9645
78 Models				
413627B	2-dr. Cpe.-3P	1029	3403	51
413627	2-dr. Clb. Sed.-5P	1074	3420	std. 8260
				dlx. 5338
413609	4-dr. Sed.-5P	1130	3500	std. 8046
				dlx. 7534
96 Models				
413967	2-dr. Conv.-3P	1191	3525	325
413927	2-dr. Cpe.-3P	1043	3320	2176
413919	4-dr. Sed.-5P	1099	3410	4176
98 Models				
413967	2-dr. Conv.-3P	1227	3600	1263
413967	4-dr. Phae.-6P	1575	3790	119
413927	2-dr. Cpe.-3P	1059	3430	1263
413919	4-dr. Sed.-5P	1135	3500	22,081

ENGINE: Six cylinder, same on all series. Inline, L-head. Six. Cast iron block. B & S: 3-1/2 x 4-1/8 in. Disp.: 238 cu. in. C.R.: 6.1 to 1. Brake H.P.: 100 @ 3200 R.P.M. Main bearings: Four. Valve lifters: Mushroom. Carb.: Single downdraft w. automatic choke. Eight. Cast iron block. B & S: 3-1/2 x 4-1/8 in. Disp.: 257 cu. in. C.R.: 6.3 to 1. Brake H.P.: 110 2 3400 R.P.M. Main bearings: Five. Valve lifters: Mushroom. Carb.: Dual downdraft w automatic choke.

1941 Oldsmobile, 98, convertible sedan, TVB

CHASSIS: [Series Sixty (six or eight)] W.B.: 119 in. O.L.: 204 in. Frt/Rear Tread: 58/61-1/2 in. Tires: 16 x 6.00. [Series Seventy (six or eight)] W.B.: 125 in. O.L.: 211 in. Frt/Rear Tread: 58/61-1/2 in. Tires: 16 x 7.50. [Series Ninety (six or eight)] W.B.: 125 in. O.L.: 213 in. Frt/Rear Tread: 58/61-1/2 in. Tires: 15 x 7.00.

TECHNICAL: Sliding gear, synchromesh manual transmission. Speeds: 3F/1R. Steering column controls. Single plate dry disc clutch. Shaft drive. Semi-floating hypoid rear axle. Overall Ratio: [Series 60] 4.1 to 1; [Series 70 & 90] 4.3 to 1. Sealed hydraulic, cast iron drum brakes on four wheels. Pressed steel wheels. Drivetrain Options: Automatic transmission (100.00).

OPTIONS: Fender skirts (14.00). Bumper guards (3.75 ea.). Radio (deluxe 62.50; standard 52.50). Heater (condition-air htr 30.50; deluxe 22.00; underseat 19.75). Clock (30-wind 5.50; electric 12.25). Cigar lighter (2.00). Seat covers (13.75). Glovebox light ($.90). Deluxe steering wheel (12.50). Visor vanity mirror (1.00). Rear seat foot rests (1.85). Wheel trim rings (8.00). Directional signals (10.95). Fog lamps (10.90 pair). Backup light (4.45). License plate frames (2.75 per pair). Exhaust deflector (1.25).

HISTORICAL: Introduced: Sept. 23, 1940. Calendar year sales & production: 230,703. Model year sales & production: 270,040. The general manager of Oldsmobile was S.E. Skinner. The 2-millionth Olds built this model year. Increasing amounts of manufacturing efforts were turned to war supplies. Olds was building a number of different government munitions this year.

1941 Oldsmobile, 70, 4-dr. sedan, HJE

1941
Series 66, 6-cyl.

	FP	5	4	3	2	1
Conv	1048	3650	7350	12,250	17,150	24,500
Bus Cpe	852	900	1800	4400	6150	8800
Clb Cpe	893	925	2000	4600	6400	9200
2 dr Sed	898	850	1650	4200	5850	8400
Sed	945	875	1700	4300	6000	8600
Twn Sed	945	875	1700	4350	6050	8700
Sta Wag	1176	1650	4600	7700	10,800	15,400
Series 68, 8-cyl.						
Conv	1089	4000	7950	13,250	18,550	26,500
Bus Cpe	893	900	1900	4500	6300	9000
Clb Cpe	935	950	2100	4750	6650	9500
2 dr Sed	940	875	1700	4300	6000	8600
Sed	987	900	1800	4400	6150	8800
Twn Sed	987	900	1800	4450	6250	8900
Sta Wag	1217	1650	4600	7700	10,800	15,400
Series 76, 6-cyl.						
Bus Cpe	908	925	1900	4550	6350	9100
Clb Sed	954	925	2000	4600	6400	9200
Sed	1010	900	1800	4450	6250	8900
Series 78, 8-cyl.						
Bus Sed	1029	925	1900	4550	6350	9100
Clb Sed	1074	950	2100	4700	6600	9400
Sed	1130	950	2100	4750	6650	9500
Series 96, 6-cyl.						
Conv	1191	4600	9150	15,250	21,350	30,500
Clb Cpe	1043	1075	2900	5450	7600	10,900
Sed	1099	1025	2600	5200	7200	10,400
Series 98, 8-cyl.						
Conv	1227	5000	10,050	16,750	23,450	33,500
Phae	1575	5200	10,350	17,250	24,150	34,500
Clb Cpe	1079	1100	3400	5700	8000	11,400
Sed	1135	1075	2900	5450	7600	10,900

1046

1942 Oldsmobile, 66, 2-dr. sedan, CX

OLDSMOBILE — SPECIAL — SERIES 66 OR 68 — SIX OR EIGHT: Olds stayed with its special series on the bottom of a three series format. As with all auto makers production was halted early in year due to the war. Both a six or eight cylinder motor could be ordered. Extremely rare - both a convertible and station wagon was available.
Description: The Olds "fastback series was down to just two body styles this year. A 125-inch wheelbase was exclusive to the series and either a six or eight.

OLDSMOBILE — CUSTOM CRUISER — SERIES 98 — EIGHT: Description: Once again the Custom Cruiser was the Olds entrant in the luxury market. Gone was the single year offering of the 96. All cars in this series were powered by the straight eight engine. Also gone for this shortened model year was the ultra rare phaeton. An exclusive 127-inch wheelbase was used in this series.

I.D. DATA: Serial numbers were located on upper left front face of dash. Starting: [Series Sixty] California built-66C or 68C-3001; Linden, N.J. built-66L or 68L-3001; Lansing, MI built-66 or 68-9001. [Series Seventy] California built-76C or 78C-4001; Linden, N.J. built-76L or 78L-4001 Lansing, MI built-76 or 78-26001. [Series Ninety] California built-98C-4001; Linden, N.J. built-98L-6001; Lansing, MI built-98-25001. Ending: NA. Engine numbers were on upper left corner of cylinder block. Starting: [Six G] 424001; [Eight L] 45001. Ending: [Six G] 472869; [Eight L] 468773. Engines with single letter prefix were Lansing, MI built. Engines with two letter prefix and first letter C - California built; first letter L - Linden, N.J. built.

Model No.	Body Type & Seating	Price	Weight	Prod. Total
Series 60				
423527B	2-dr. Bs. Cpe.-3P	992	3230	1166
423527	2-dr. Clb. Cpe.-3P	1035	3205	4173
423507	2-dr. Clb. Sed.-5P	1050	3270	10,766
423511	2-dr. Sed.-5P	1040	3275	3688
423519	4-dr. Sed.-5P	1088	3320	8053
423569	4-dr. Twn. Sed.-5P	1088	3315	3888
423567	2-dr. Conv.-3P	1277	3400	848
4235SW	4-dr. SW.-6P	1376	3515	NA
Series 70				
423607	2-dr. Clb. Sed.-5P	1095	3485	14,701
423609	4-dr. Sed.-5P	1153	3510	12,566
Series 90				
423967	2-dr. Conv.-4P	1561	3740	216
423907	2-dr. Clb. Sed.-5P	1319	3620	1771
423969	4-dr. Sed.-5P	1376	3780	4672

1942 Oldsmobile, 98, 4-dr. sedan, AA

ENGINE: [Six cyl.] Inline, L-head. Six. Cast iron block. B & S: 3-1/2 x 4-1/8 in. Disp.: 238 cu. in. C.R.: 6.5 to 1. Brake H.P.: 100 @ 3200 R.P.M. Main bearings: Four. Valve lifters: Mushroom. Carb.: Single downdraft with automatic choke. Torque: 190. [Eight cyl.] Inline, L-head. Eight. Cast iron block. B & S: 3-1/4 x 3-7/8 in. Disp.: 257 cu. in. C.R.: 6.5 to 1. Brake H.P.: 110 @ 3400 R.P.M. Main bearings: Five. Valve lifters: Mushroom. Carb.: Dual downdraft with automatic choke. Torque: 200.

CHASSIS: [Series 60-Special] W.B.: 119 in. O.L.: 204 in. Frt/Rear Tread: 58/61-1/2 in. Tires: 6.00 x 16. [Series 70-Dynamic Cruiser] W.B.: 125 in. O.L.: 212 in. Frt/Rear Tread: 58/61-1/2 in. Tires: 6.50 x 15. [Series 90-Custom Cruiser] W.B.: 127 in. O.L.: 216 in. Frt/Rear Tread: 58/61-1/2 in. Tires: 7.00 x 15.

TECHNICAL: Manual, synchromesh transmission. Speeds 3F/1R. Steering column controls. Single plate dry disc clutch. Tubular dry shaft. Hypoid, semi floating rear axle. Overall Ratio: [Series 60] 4.1 to 1; [Others] 4.3 to 1. Sealed hydraulic, cast iron drum brakes on four wheels. Pressed steel wheels. Drivetrain Options: Automatic transmission: HydraMatic (95.00). Heavy duty air cleaner (3.75). Solenoid starter (7.50). Oil filter (5.25).

OPTIONS: Fender skirts (14.00 pair). Bumper guards (4.50). Radio (master 68.50; standard 58.00; universal 29.45). Heater (condition-air 39.95; dual-flow 23.50; underseat 22.00; universal 14.45). Clock (electric 12.95; 30 hr. wind 6.00). Seat covers (satin-rayon 29.50). Spotlight (14.50). Glove box light (1.00). Plastic steering wheel (14.00). Visor utility kit (2.95). Visor vanity mirror (1.35). Wheel trim rings (8.00). Fog lamps (11.50). Direction signals (11.40). Backup light (4.75). Outside rear view mirror (2.50). Underhood light (1.25). Gas tank cover lock (1.25). ''In-A-Car'' bed (19.50).

HISTORICAL: Heavy-duty front bumper system. Calendar year sales & production: 12,230. Model year sales & production: 67,999. The general manager of Oldsmobile was S.E. Skinner. Auto production halted on Feb. 5, 1942 for war production. Main war effort rocket and mortar shells, cannon and aircraft propellers and engines.

1942 Oldsmobile, 98, convertible, OCW

1942
Special Series 66 & 68

	FP	5	4	3	2	1
Conv	1225	3300	6600	11,000	15,400	22,000
Bus Cpe	955	775	1500	3750	5250	7500
Clb Cpe	995	825	1600	4000	5600	8000
Clb Sed	1010	800	1550	3800	5300	7600
2 dr Sed	1000	775	1500	3600	5100	7300
Sed	1045	775	1500	3750	5250	7500
Twn Sed	1045	800	1550	3850	5400	7700
Sta Wag	1320	1450	4250	7150	10,000	14,300

Dynamic Series 76-78

	FP	5	4	3	2	1
Clb Sed	1050	825	1600	3950	5500	7900
Sed	1105	800	1550	3850	5400	7700

Custom Series 98, 8-cyl.

	FP	5	4	3	2	1
Conv	1450	3650	7350	12,250	17,150	24,500
Clb Sed	1220	850	1650	4150	5800	8300
Sed	1275	825	1600	4050	5650	8100

OLIVE — The Harry L. Olive Company was organized in Spokane, Washington early in 1913 with a heady capital stock of $2 million for the manufacture of motor cars. Joining Olive in this venture was Arthur J. West. Manufacture is doubted.

OLIVE STEAM — Syracuse, New York — (1901) — What stopped this automotive venture in its tracks is not known for sure. Experimentation for steam car manufacture had been ongoing at the Olive Wheel Company in Syracuse for some time, but company president F.W. Gridley elected not to make note of it until manufacture was assured. And on July 21st, 1901 he was so assured, announcing that production would begin September 1st. Until now, the Olive Wheel Company had dealt exclusively in the building of bicycles, and its factory in Syracuse was to be enlarged by two or three stories. Gridley was described in the press as ''president of the Salt Springs National Bank, and a man of unlimited means to carry out his plans.'' Among the reasons the Olive steam car did not proceed into man-

ufacture may have been the sudden death of company manager Don B. Smith. The company did, however, fulfill its contract to produce a run of motor bicycles for the Holley Motor Company of Bradford, Pennsylvania.

OLIVER — South Bend, Indiana — (1905) — The Oliver was a standard $1500 five-passenger tonneau powered by a two-cylinder 12 hp front-mounted horizontal engine, with wheel steering and double chain drive. The Oliver idea was something else again. Apparently Frederick William Oliver was unconvinced that a standard automobile was the way he should go. After exhibiting the ordinary Oliver at the Chicago Automobile Show in 1905, he organized the Oliver Trackless Car Company in South Bend for the purpose of manufacturing ''pleasure automobiles and traction cars powered with either gasoline or steam engines and driving through a single traction drum called a 'fifth wheel'.'' Save for that drum-like fifth wheel, mounted under the center of the vehicle and running in bearings on two hinged arms, this Oliver resembled the first, though commercial and agricultural applications were also planned for it. Trackless trolleys would have been the obvious next step, which never came — and even the ordinary Oliver was gone by year's end.

OLIVER ELECTRIC — Following his selling out of DeMars Electrical Vehicle Company of Cleveland in February 1906, William O. DeMars joined the newly established Oliver Electric Vehicle Company, also in Cleveland, as general manager. Its business was predominantly service and repair. Refer to DeMars Electric.

OLSEN & HUNT — This typographical error is a frequent one in car rosters. The firm was correctly designated Osen & Hunt, though the names of its partners were reversed for the automobile built in San Jose, California in 1900. Refer to Hunt & Osen.

OLSESE — The Olsese Motor Car Company was organized in Chicago, Illinois during the summer of 1915 with a capital stock of $2500 to manufacture and deal in automobiles, parts and accessories. Involved in the venture were C.W. Olsese, W.D. Belton and A.R. Bales. Manufacture of a car is doubted.

OLSON — Pittsboro, Indiana — (1908) — An automobile was built in the shops of the C.J. Olson Buggy & Carriage Manufacturing Company of Pittsboro in 1908. Apparently the car was produced for the use of the Olson family; manufacture was not contemplated.

OLSSON — Chicago, Illinois — (1900-1905) — Although his shop at 364 Wells Street in Chicago was a small one and his output was never very large, Ivan W. Olsson remained in the car-building business for a half decade. A repairer and maker of gasoline and steam engines for over ten years previous to building his first car at the turn of the century, Olsson built to customer order exclusively until the end of 1902. Although he offered to supply electric power for those desiring it, his stock designs were an $850 steam runabout, $1100 steam stanhope, $900 and $1400 gasoline runabouts, and two large gasoline tonneaus, a 10 hp at $1700 and a 24 hp at $2800. For the 1903 season, Olsson announced that he planned to place his cars on the general market, but he never advertised extensively and probably continued manufacturing only as the orders came in.

OLYMPIA — The Olympia Manufacturing & Service Company was organized in Jersey City, New Jersey during the spring of 1911 with a capital stock of $100,000 for the manufacture of automobiles. Incorporators were R. Segelken, H. Schmidt and R. Segelken, Jr., all of Jersey City. Manufacture is doubted.

1917 Olympian, 5-pass. touring, WLB

OLYMPIAN — Pontiac, Michigan — (1917-1920) — Whether R.A. Palmer was aware of the availability of the old Cartercar plant in Pontiac before or after he organized the Olympian Motors Company is not known. But when General Motors decided to dispose of the property early in 1917, Palmer bought immediately. As general manager of the plant from 1905 to 1912 when Cartercars were built there, he was aware of what a fine facility it was. In 1915 Palmer had begun the Pontiac Chassis Company, and now he would produce a new car in the under-$1000 price class, the four-cylinder Olympian. A panoply of color choices — wine, green, blue, red and gray distinguished the car from most of its low-priced competitors. Production stood at ten cars a day by early 1918, and although war work interrupted the schedule that year, the factory returned to normal production and a fifteen-car-per-day schedule by early 1919. But something went amok. Early in 1920, amid charges of mismanagement, Olympian Motors Company was sold to Otis Friend of Friend Motors Corporation. The Friend followed the Olympian on the same assembly line which had previously seen the building of the Cartercar.

1917 OLYMPIAN
Model 37 — 4-cyl., 23 hp, 112" wb

	FP	5	4	3	2	1
Touring-5P	795	2300	3300	4600	7500	16,000
Roadster-4P	825	2200	3200	4400	7000	15,000
Roadster-2P	850	2250	3300	4500	7300	15,500

1918-1919 OLYMPIAN
Model 37 — 4-cyl., 23 hp, 112" wb

Roadster-2P	965	2400	3400	4800	8000	17,000
Sedan-5P	1565	1600	2700	3800	5800	12,000

1920 OLYMPIAN
Model 37 — 4-cyl., 23 hp, 112" wb

Touring-5P	1240	2400	3400	4800	8000	17,000
Roadster-2P	1240	2300	3300	4600	7500	16,000

OLYMPIC — The Olympic of 1909 was a model of the Gearless from Rochester, New York which had a conventional transmission as opposed to the friction transmission used in other Gearless cars. Refer to Gearless.

OLYMPIC — Syracuse, New York — (1936) — The Olympic Motor Car Company, Inc. was an attempt to return automobile manufacture to the H.H. Franklin factory in Syracuse which had been idle for over a year by September of 1936 when Olympic moved in. This venture to build a line of small low-priced cars was headed by two very respected men of the industry: Alfred Glancy, the former general manager of Pontiac who during the early years of the Depression had served as assistant NRA Administrator for Code Compliance, and Arthur Brandt, who had been Glancy's works manager at Pontiac. Though their Olympic venture ended probably before the completion of a single prototype car, the attempt had been a bona fide one. When it ended, Brandt went on to serve as a trustee for Reo, Glancy to work for the War Department, ultimately retiring after World War II with the rank of brigadier general.

OMAHA — The Omaha Motor Car Company was organized in Nebraska during the summer of 1910 with a capital stock of $200,000 for the manufacture and sale of automobiles. Incorporators were G.H. Downs, W.S. Stryker, H.M. Rigley, W.G. Wallace and R.M. Homan. Manufacture is doubted.
The Omaha Motor Car Company of early 1912 was a $1 million Maine incorporation for the manufacture and sale of automobiles. Incorporators were R.S. Buzzell, L.J. Coleman and E.J. Pike. Manufacture is doubted.
There appears to be no connection between either of these ventures and David W. Henry's Omaha Motor Car Company which saw a minimal production in Omaha, Nebraska in 1912-1913.

OMAHA — Omaha, Nebraska — (1899) — Henry C. Akin, H.K. Clover, Dalton Risley, Dr. F.E. Coulter and O.E. Gugler were the principals behind the 1899 incorporation of the Omaha Gas Engine & Motor Company. Capital stock was $150,000, and the company's purpose was the manufacture of gasoline engines and motor vehicles. Clover, a lieutenant in the United States Navy, designed the engine; Gugler, who was superintendent at the Union Pacific shops, was in charge of vehicle construction. The Omaha engine was a two-cylinder horizontal with an rpm range of 200 to 1000. It weighed 300 pounds and developed 8 hp. "The exhaust is deodorized by passing through a preparation of magnesia, lime and charcoal," reported *The Horseless Age* in August 1899. "The vaporizer is claimed as a special feature of this motor. A portion of the exhaust is used to dry the gas, and no air is taken in through the vaporizer, the air being mixed with the gasoline vapor just before entering the cylinder." A special attachment was provided the motor for those occasions when kerosene would be used as fuel. And a special "pneumatic tire in five sections and resembling a Norwegian snowshoe" would be available for mud and snow motoring. How many Omaha engines and automobiles were built is not known, but by the turn of the century the company had faded from sight. Dalton Risley resurfaced in Omaha in 1901, however, in a new venture with the Badeker Gas Engine Company.

1912 Omaha, touring, NAHC

1048

OMAHA — Omaha, Nebraska — (1912-1913) — From Mason City, Iowa, where he had just been fired as chief engineer of the Colby Motor Car Company, David W. Henry traveled to Omaha where he persuaded local capitalists to finance a new car he had designed. It was a 233-cubic-inch four with shaft drive and an underslung frame that he proposed to sell at $1250. Early in 1912 the Omaha Motor Car Company was incorporated, with $500,000 capital stock, and production was begun in April at the Stroud Machine Company at Ames and 20th Streets pending completion of the Omaha factory next door. First deliveries were made in May. Most probably the new Omaha plant never saw production. In late September of 1913 the Omaha Motor Car Company requested a voluntary petition in bankruptcy. Its assets were $10,140, its liabilities $46,908.

1912-1913 OMAHA
Model 30 — 4-cyl., 30 hp

	FP	5	4	3	2	1
Touring-5P	1250	2500	3500	5000	8500	18,000

OMAR — Omar was an anagram of Mora, and the two companies were really one and the same. The Mora Motor Car Company produced a full-sized car called the Mora. The Omar Motor Car Company produced a juvenile roadster called the Browniekar. It was in production in Newark, New York from 1908 to 1911. Refer to Browniekar.

O'NEIL — Lawrence, Massachusetts — (1903) — That it had three cylinders and generated twenty horsepower are the confirmed facts regarding the experimental car built by J.E. O'Neil of Lawrence in 1903. O'Neil never proceeded into manufacture.

O'NEILL-OLLIER — The O'Neill-Ollier Company of Chicago, Illinois was organized during the summer of 1906 with a capital stock of $1000 for the manufacture of automobiles. Charles C. O'Neill and L.J. Ollier were joined in this venture by S.E. Gillard. Manufacture is doubted.

1910 Only, racetype torpedo, HAC

ONLY — Port Jefferson, New York — (1909-1913) — The engine only had one cylinder, with a five-inch bore and ten-inch stroke, displacing 201 cubic inches. Its ball-bearing-mounted crankshaft had a flywheel at each end. This imposing powerplant was designed by Francois Richard and was placed under the long hood of a two-seat roadster. Sixty miles an hour and thirty miles a gallon were claimed — and all for the price of $700. Fred W. Edwards, Fred Seymour and Henry N. Dickinson thought Richard was really on to something, and they incorporated the Only Motor Car Company to build his car in 1909. A few Onlys followed, including at least one four-passenger version in 1911, but mostly the firm's Port Jefferson factory lay idle...until 1912 when Francois Richard worked up another idea. It was a four-cylinder engine — again following the long-stroke principle (4-1/2 by 7-7/8) — which was fitted to a runabout and touring marketed at price tags of $1000 and $1250 respectively. Apparently the Only backers thought the Only name somewhat of a liability, however, because shortly after introducing the car the decision was made to build only the raceabout version and to call it the Metropol. Conceivably the awareness of impending bankruptcy prompted this move. Bankruptcy did arrive during the spring of 1913, with Only liabilities revealed to be $148,405.96, twice the assets. The Only factory was sold in July to the Maxim Tri-Car Company. The Metropol, which was built elsewhere in Port Jefferson, survived a year longer. When both cars were dead, Francois Richard went to Cleveland to build another one under his own name and equally as outrageous.

1909-1910 ONLY
Model A — 1-cyl., 12 hp, 104" wb

	FP	5	4	3	2	1
Racytype Torpedo	700	2350	3400	4700	7800	16,500

1911 ONLY
Model A — 1-cyl., 12 hp, 104" wb

Racytype Torpedo	800	2350	3400	4700	7800	16,500

Model F — 1-cyl., 12 hp, 104" wb

Four-Passenger Torpedo	1050	2500	3500	5000	8500	18,000

1912-1913 ONLY
Four — 30 hp, 112" wb

Model A Raceabout	1000	2400	3400	4800	8000	17,000
Model B Tour.	1250	2500	3500	5000	8500	18,000

ONONDAGA — The Onondaga Taxicab Company was organized in Syracuse, New York late in 1910 with a capital stock of $25,000 to "manufacture and sell automobiles, motor trucks and other power vehicles." Incorporators were J.J. McCarthy, J.H. Coolican and R.P. Byrne, all of Syracuse. Manufacture of a car is doubted.

ONONDAGA — Syracuse, New York — (1906) — G.L. Gridley, G.E. DeLong and J.S. Palmer organized the Onondaga Automobile Company of Syracuse during the spring of 1903 with a $150,000 capital stock. For the two years following, the firm operated as a dealership, but during the fall of 1906 decided to market a car of its own. Though the producing organization was termed the Cronin Automobile Company — most probably because a fellow named Cronin provided needed financing — the car was to be called an Onondaga. It was a four-cylinder 30 hp touring — and the evidence suggests it did not pass the prototype stage.

ONTARIO — Although the experimental model was announced by the Ontario Industrial Company during the late summer of 1909, the venture for which it was built was the Pell Motor Car Company of Oswego, New York. Refer to Pell.

OPHIR STEAM — Syracuse, New York — (1901) — The Ophir was a small steam runabout which was sent overseas by the Century Motor Vehicle Company of Syracuse, New York to be sold in London by the British and Colonial Motor Car Company, Limited. Its feature of shaft drive was quite unusual for a steamer of this period on either side of the Atlantic. So far as is known, the Ophir was offered only in 1901. The Century steamer was continued in Syracuse until the end of 1902.

OPTENBERG — Sheboygan, Wisconsin — (1878) — No doubt the lure of the $10,000 prize by the Wisconsin state legislature was sufficient inducement for him to have tried, but John Henry Optenberg's claim in later years that he succeeded is patently false. "Pioneer Steamer Inventor Retires" was the headline in 1913 announcing his leavetaking from the Optenberg Iron Works which had manufactured steam powerplant equipment and accessories in Sheboygan since 1884. Optenberg stated at the time that parts of the steam car he had built in 1878 were still on exhibit at his plant, which may have been true, but true too was the fact that the car had not been in the historic 1878 Wisconsin race. Only the Green Bay and the Oshkosh were, and there is no evidence that Optenberg was involved in the building of either of those machines.

ORCUTT — In 1899 Edward L. Orcutt of Somerville, Massachusetts built his first steam car, and the year following interested local businessmen in its manufacture. The Pilgrim Motor Vehicle Company was organized early in 1900. Refer to Pilgrim.

OREGON — Although the Oregon has been noted as a car produced by the Beaver State Motor Company in 1916, that firm had long since given up the automobile idea. Two Beaver prototypes were built in 1912. Refer to Beaver.

ORIENT — Waltham, Massachusetts — (1899-1907) — In 1893 Charles Herman Metz organized the Waltham Manufacturing Company for the production of Orient bicycles. The first car to carry the Orient name was an electric introduced at the New York Cycle & Automobile Show at Madison Square Garden in February 1899. It was built by two Waltham employees, George M. Tinker and John W. Piper. A four-wheeled carriage on an 60-inch wheelbase, the Orient was powered by a General Electric motor. C.H. Metz didn't like it much; neither apparently did Piper and Tinker, because when they left the company the following year to enter the automobile business themselves, it was to build a steamer called the Waltham. The only reason the Orient Electric had been built was to satisfy the request of Charles A. Coffin, who had provided Metz some needed capital, and who also was the president of General Electric. The car was not put into production and Metz proceeded to devote all energy to gasoline-powered automobiles. By the spring of 1899 he had contracted with De Dion-Bouton et Cie. in France to sell its quadricycles and tricycles in the United States. He also began importing the French Aster engine, and by 1900 was offering his own quads and trikes — as the Autogo — with a choice of 3 hp Aster or 5 hp De Dion powerplants. Waltham began building its own engines in 1902, and the first really proper Orient car arrived that year, a single-cylinder 8 hp runabout with $875 price tag. Approximately fifty were sold in 1902. By that time, however, Metz, irritated by the continuing interference of stockholder Charles Coffin, and M.P. Clough who had also invested heavily in the firm, left Waltham to accept the technical editorship of *Cycle and Automobile Trade Journal*. Coffin and Clough immediately hired Leonard B. Gaylor, who had been building Tribune bicycles in Pennsylvania and who now designed the famous Orient Buckboard. "The Cheapest Automobile in the World," the Waltham ads ballyhooed. "Everybody Should Have One." The car had a 4 hp engine, weighed 400 pounds and provided speeds of 4 to 30 mph. A tiller provided the steering, and the wooden platform the suspension; there were no springs. The price was $375. In 1904 John Robbins, who had been with Metz from the beginning, left the company, and the new Waltham superintendent was the formidable bearded Russian, Leo Melanowski. Four-cylinder touring models followed, as did de-emphasis of the Orient name for non-Buckboard versions. Indeed, for a while, the company appears to have interchangeably used both Waltham and Orient to designate its cars. By 1908 all cars from the company were called Waltham (occasionally Waltham-Orient). The Buckboard was continued through 1907, but Orient appeared only as its model name. Meantime, Leo Melanowski had left for Philadelphia to design the Dragon.

1900-1901 ORIENT

	FP	5	4	3	2	1
Orient Autogo Quadricycle	600	1100	2200	3200	4900	9000
Orient Autogo Tricycle	450	1000	2000	3000	4600	8000

1902 ORIENT

	FP	5	4	3	2	1
Orient Rbt. (1-cyl., 8hp, 80" wb)	875	1500	2500	3600	5500	11,000

1903 Orient Buckboard, HAC

1903 ORIENT
Model No. 9 — 1-cyl., 8 hp, 80" wb

	FP	5	4	3	2	1
Orient Rbt.	950	1500	2500	3600	5500	11,000
Buckboard — 1-cyl., 4 hp, 80" wb						
Orient Buckboard	375	1200	2300	3300	5100	9500

1904 ORIENT
Buckboard — 1-cyl., 4 hp, 80" wb

	FP	5	4	3	2	1
Orient Buckboard-2P	425	1200	2300	3300	5100	9500
Orient Buckboard-3P	450	1400	2400	3500	5300	10,000
Orient Buckboard Delivery	443	1200	2300	3300	5100	9500

1905 Orient, touring, HAC

1905-1907 ORIENT
Buckboard — 1-cyl., 4 hp, 80" wb

	FP	5	4	3	2	1
Orient Buckboard	375	1000	2100	3100	4800	8500
Orient Buckboard Surrey	450	1100	2200	3200	4900	9000
Orient Buckboard Rbt.	475	1200	2300	3300	5100	9500
Orient Buckboard Tonneau	525	1200	2300	3300	5100	9500
Four — 16 hp, 82" wb						
Orient Light Tour.	1650	1500	2500	3600	5500	11,000
Four — 20 hp, 110" wb						
Orient Deluxe Touring	3200	1600	2700	3800	5800	12,000

ORIENTAL-DETROIT — The Oriental-Detroit Motor Car Company was organized in Birmingham, Michigan early in 1910 with a capital stock of $100,000 for the manufacture of automobiles. Incorporators were George E. Daines, Guy L. Watkins, Ellsworth Randall, G. William Crary, Frank Ford, Edgar A. Parks and T.B. Smith. Manufacture is doubted.

ORIGINATOR — The Originator Manufacturing Company was organized in Jersey City, New Jersey during the spring of 1909 with a capital stock of $125,000 for the manufacture of automobiles. Incorporators were Vernon J. Mills, John C. Inwright and Barret L. Inwright. Manufacture is doubted.

ORIOLE — Fond du Lac, Wisconsin — (1910) — The Oriole was a four-cylinder 45 hp touring car that was set into a 126-inch wheelbase chassis with big 40-inch wheels and four-inch tires. It was designed by Harry W. Cleveland of Fond du Lac, and he announced the completion of the prototype in May of 1910, with production to commence immediately by the Giddings and Lewis Manufacturing Company. Giddings and Lewis was a big machinery concern in Fond du Lac, and its president was Harry's father, C.E. Cleveland. How many further Orioles were built is not known, but they were not built for long.

ORLO — Jackson, Michigan — (1904) — The Orlo was a companion car to the Jackson which was introduced, as the Jackson Automobile Company stated rather cumbersomely, "to get something that is convenient for riders to get in and out of, and at the same time distribute the weight of

1904 Orlo, touring, HAC

the engine and the passenger load that it might not be too heavy on either front or rear tires and at the same time be able to use a double opposed motor placed forward and aft of the machine, so that the vibrations of the motor, if any, would not be crossways of the vehicle so as to have a tendency to roll the tires, as this is the case more or less with all motors placed crossways." But it was the getting in and out of that impressed automotive writers. Most medium-priced touring cars of the day sported a rear entrance tonneau, the Orlo's was at the side, making it more likely that passengers could enter the vehicle without stepping in the mud. *Automobile Review* quoted Mayor Tom Johnson of Cleveland as remarking when he was trying to squeeze himself into the rear door of an automobile that he didn't know of but two other types of vehicle with doors at the back, one being a dump cart and the other a hearse, and neither of which he was inclined to enter at the present. (Peerless and Reliance were also side entrance for 1904 as well.) The Orlo was announced as a two-cylinder 16 hp touring car at $1125. Although a runabout with half the cylinders and half the horsepower, as well as a panel delivery, were later to be made available, it is doubted that they ever reached the production line. At the end of the 1904 season, the Orlo was discontinued, its features incorporated into the regular Jackson line.

ORMOND — The Ormond Automobile Company was organized in Brooklyn, New York during the summer of 1903 with a capital stock of $7500 for the manufacture of automobiles. H.A. Lyons, Wilfred Burr and R.W. Hoff, all of Brooklyn, backed this venture. Manufacture is doubted.

The Ormond Motor Car Company was organized in Brooklyn, New York late in 1911 with a capital stock of $100,000 for the manufacture of automobiles. Incorporators were G.H. Howell, R. McKeller and T. Downs. Manufacture is doubted.

1905 Ormond Steamer, MVMA

ORMOND STEAMER — Boston, Massachusetts — (1904-1905) — "Built — Not Manufactured" was the very effective slogan of the United Motor & Vehicle Company of Boston. Its $3000 Ormond Steamer was offered as a larger tourer with canopy top and elaborately flared front fenders. A four-cylinder 25 hp single-acting engine powered the car. The burner was kerosene, the boiler flash-type. A nicety was the swinging and self-locking steering wheel. United Motor & Vehicle Company exhibited at the New York Automobile Show in January 1905 and located a temporary office at 150 Nassau Street in the Financial District in order to promote sales in the Greater New York area. Unfortunately, they didn't ensue; neither did many sales in the Greater Boston area. The company was out of business before the end of 1905.

ORR — The Orr Motor Car Company was organized during the summer of 1907 with a capital stock of $25,000 for the manufacture of automobiles in Kenosha, Wisconsin. Manufacture does not seem to have followed. Whether the Orr involved in this venture was the C.D. Orr who subsequently ventured to Yazoo City, Mississippi is not known.

ORR — Yazoo City, Mississippi — (1915) — The Orr Modern Motor Car Company was a two-million-dollar incorporation and was organized at Yazoo City by G.A. Wilson and C.D. Orr. Its purpose was the manufacture of a dual gear, multi-speed, gear-driving mechanism invented by Orr. "The

basic principle of the invention is the worm drive," Orr explained. "Power is applied directly to the rear wheels in a straight line, doing away with all but one universal joint and many small parts." A single prototype automobile was assembled to demonstrate the efficacy of the Orr invention. The company was not in business long.

1911 Orson, touring, HAC

ORSON — Springfield, Massachusetts — (1910-1911) — It was dubbed the "Banker's Car" and the "Millionaire's Car" — and it was promoted "with great dignity," so the press said, by Horace M. Kilborn, the vice-president of the National City Bank of New York. Named for Kilborn's son Orson, who had the idea, the automobile itself was nothing extraordinary, just a large four-cylinder 40 hp touring car on a 130-inch wheelbase. But the Orson was to be built by a cooperative — 100 of Wall Street's most prominent bankers who would share the cost of building 100 cars. Once they were supplied, so the plan went, the Orson was to be placed on the market. Actual manufacture took place in Springfield, Massachusetts — chassis by Brightwood Manufacturing Company, coachwork by Springfield Metal Body Company. The bankers' cars were finished by 1911, and for a while it appeared that marketing of the Orson would follow. Orson Automobile Manufacturing Company was organized in 1912, and the year following began negotiations to combine Brightwood and Springfield Metal Body, in addition to the Atlas and Knox companies which were already on their last legs in Springfield. But the merger and the Orson plan fell apart very quickly. When journalists dug into the story in 1914, they discovered that a total of 80 cars had been built at a cost of $560,000. In 1915 the National Surety Company sued one of the Orson owners, Daniel M. Brady, to collect an additional $2500 due on the automobile for which he had already paid $3900. Brady, who said that he had spent an additional $1000 in repairs before his Orson "blew up," was sometimes known as "Brass Dan," to distinguish him from his brother "Diamond Jim."

ORUKTER AMPHIBOLOS — This pioneering automotive effort of 1805 is more appropriately referred to by the name of its inventor, Oliver Evans. Refer to Evans Steam Amphibian.

O-S — Chicago, Illinois — (1914-1915) — The initials stood for John L. Owen and George Schoeneck who in March of 1914 organized the Owen-Schoeneck Company in Chicago for the manufacture of a car designed by Schoeneck. It was a four with a Herschell-Spillman engine which was sold as a $2350 touring car direct to the consumer. Schoeneck's previous work in the automotive field had included engineering stints with Renault in France and Palmer & Singer in New York. Owen's resume was not published, but by the end of 1915 he had left anyway. Apparently the O-S adventure had been a shoestring operation. The company was looking to "open a plant in one of the tri-cities," but this was not done before Owen's departure. Thereon Schoeneck allied himself with F.J. Alvin, former head of New Era, and together they established themselves in a factory in nearby Harvey. The six-cylinder car that Schoeneck had designed to be the 1916 O-S, and which some trade press references referred to as an Owen-Schoeneck, did not arrive on the market under either of those names. Instead it was called a Geneva, which probably was Alvin's idea.

OSBORN — Clarksburg, West Virginia — (1899) — In 1899 A.C. Osborn of the Pioneer Iron Works in Clarksburg built an experimental automobile which burned naptha and was started by electric spark. There is no indication that Osborn built more than one car, or that the Pioneer company subsequently entered the automotive field.

OSBORN — New York, New York — (1906) — The Osborn was a three-wheeler in which the single front wheel both drove and steered the vehicle. Alden E. Osborn patented his car in 1903 — and at that time *The Automobile* wondered editorially how sufficient weight for traction could be put on the front wheel without impairing stability. Osborn replied that the vehicle was intended only as a low-speed runabout and that the position of the motor just back of the front wheel "favors the stability." Osborn did not build his car until 1906 — and was not heard from again until 1914 and the onset of the cyclecar rage. At that time he reported that he had been driving the car for the seven years past with complete satisfaction, and that he was now considering manufacture. When he brought his three-wheeler to market, he called it the Auto-Tricar.

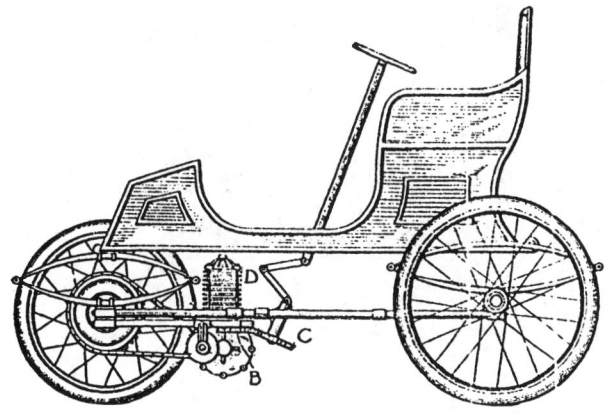

1906 Osborn, three-wheeler, NAHC

OSBOURNE — The D.M. Osbourne Company manufactured agricultural implements in Auburn, New York and during the spring of 1908 was reported by *The Horseless Age* to have begun "the manufacture of automobiles in a factory in Ohio." Documentation is lacking.

OSCAR LEAR — From 1904-1909 the Oscar Lear Automobile Company of Columbus, Ohio produced a car called the Frayer-Miller. Refer to Frayer-Miller.

OSGOOD — The Osgood Motor Car Company was organized in Brooklyn, New York during the fall of 1911 with a capital stock of $10,000 for the manufacture and sale of automobiles and supplies. Samuel H. Miskind was behind this venture. Manufacture of a car is doubted.

OSHKOSH STEAM — **Oshkosh, Wisconsin** — **(1878)** — The Oshkosh was one of the two steam cars — the Green Bay was the other — which competed in the 200-mile trial sponsored by the State of Wisconsin in July of 1878 to determine the winner of the $10,000 prize being offered by the legislature to any citizen of Wisconsin who invented "a cheap and practical substitute for use of horses and other animals on the highway and farm." The Oshkosh was named after the town in which it had been built by Frank A. Shomer, Hans Farrand, A. Gallinger and O.F. Morse. The vehicle produced by this quartet had a two-cylinder engine, one speed forward and one reverse, and weighed just under 10,000 pounds, a third less than the Green Bay. Although acknowledged to be a slower machine than the Green Bay, the Oshkosh could run ten miles before needing to be replenished with fuel and water. Like the Green Bay, the Oshkosh carried its replenishment in its own trailered wagon, there being no gas stations along the way, of course. Had not the Green Bay driven into a culvert early on, necessitating repairs on the road, the race that followed might have been a closer one. As it happened, the Oshkosh won handily, covering 201 miles in 33 hours and 27 minutes, which calculates to a little more than 6 mph. This met the speed requirement of the contest, and thus, ostensibly, the prize belonged to the Oshkosh. But the Wisconsin legislature argued — and with some justification — that what the inventive quartet from Oshkosh had come up with was not "cheap and practical." According to an August 1878 issue of the *Fond du Lac Commonwealth*, the inventors stood ready to sue the State for their money. Perhaps this might not have been necessary. After some filibustering, another report indicates, the legislature decided to award half the prize instead.

OSTERBERG & SUTTON — **New York, New York** — **(1900)** — Fred Osterberg and Frank Sutton were consulting engineers with offices at 11 Broadway in Manhattan. In 1900 they built an electric car, probably as a prototype for an industry hopeful although this cannot be documented with certainty. Osterberg and Sutton did not attempt the industry themselves, however. Indeed, within a year, Max Osterberg was the engineer at the partners' former 11 Broadway offices, Fred Osterberg had left town, and Frank Sutton was advertising himself as a mechanical engineer at 49 Wall Street.

OSTLER & ZANES — The Ostler & Zanes Company of Newark, New Jersey was organized during the summer of 1906 with a capital stock of $100,000 for the manufacture of motor vehicles. Joining Alexander Ostler and Delancy Zanes in this venture was W. Eugene Turton. Manufacture of a car is doubted.

OSWALD — The Oswald of 1911 was one of numerous cars produced in kit form by the Auto Parts Company of Chicago, Illinois. Refer to Auto Parts.

The Oswald Motor Company was organized in Goshen, Indiana during the spring of 1907 with Elmer Newell as president, J.W. Miller as vice-president, O.M. Curtiss as treasurer and manager, Charles Shoup as secretary and W.T. Oswald as superintendent. "They will engage in the manufacture of gasoline cars and marine engines," *The Motor Age* reported in May, "and will place on the market single and double cylinder types, as well as a 40-horsepower motor." Manufacture of a car is doubted.

The Oswald Motor Car & Supply Company was organized early in 1911 in Grand Rapids, Michigan with a capital stock of $12,000 for the manufac-

ture and sale of automobiles and supplies. Behind this venture were Charles J. Oswald, Frank P. Oswald and Edward G. Winchester. Manufacture is doubted but the firm is known to have become agents for the Kisselkar and the Baker electric.

OSWALD — **Kalamazoo, Michigan** — **(1900)** — W.E. Oswald was the foreman of the Kalamazoo Wagon Company and in 1900 built a canopy-top surrey in his company's shops. Its engine was a 4-1/2 hp four-cylinder Buffalo, and the car featured Oswald's own version of four-wheel drive. "He believes that an automobile driven by all four wheels is better adapted to the rough roads of Michigan than any other," reported *The Hub* that April. Manufacture of the car was not contemplated.

OSWALD — **Bay City, Michigan** — **(1910)** — The Oswald Automobile Company of Bay City, which announced its existence to the trade press in late spring of 1910, was one of a number of companies launched by Peter J. Oswald. The Farmer's Auto & Machinery Company was another. Among Oswald's inventions was a "perpetual motion device," but he seems to have been more adept at selling stock than anything else, as Bay City residents recall to this day. Whether Oswald ever built an Oswald is very much open to question. He most certainly never built more than one. For a while, he was the local Studebaker agent. During the 1930's he was killed in an automobile accident while returning to Bay City from Frankenmuth, where he had conducted an ox roast.

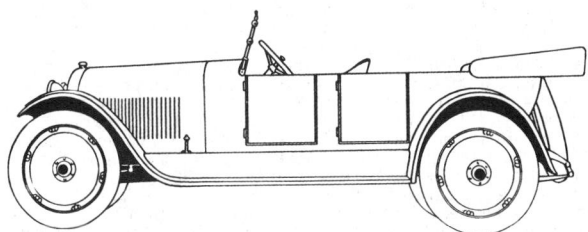

1918 Oswald, 5-pass. touring, WLB

OSWALD — **Grand Haven, Michigan** — **(1918)** — The Oswald from Grand Haven was the Hamilton resurrected — or that was the plan anyway. The H.A. Oswald Engineering Company had served as consulting engineers to Guy Hamilton's automotive venture and when Hamilton decided to focus attention on the commercial field, H.A. Oswald took the car over himself. The specs for the Hamilton and the Oswald were the same — 28 hp L-head four, 112-inch wheelbase, five-passenger touring body. A rather curious new emblem — the word "Oswald" superimposed on a starfish design with the legend "Monstrani astra viam" underneath — was concocted. And, as with the Hamilton, a six was promised but never delivered. The number of Oswalds delivered was minimal at best. Subsequently, H.A. Oswald became chief engineer and works manager for Hamilton Motors Company which produced the Panhard truck during the World War I years and the Apex from 1919 to 1922. Early in 1921, from Grand Haven, Oswald announced his intention to assay the automobile field once again. According to *Motor West*, he had designed "and will build in the near future a sample model of a 116-inch wheelbase car which will have many new features. The car will also incorporate a spring base of 130 inches, and will have a steering post made up of two pieces, which will permit the driver to place the hand wheel in any position desired. There will be brakes on all four wheels." That Oswald ever completed the building of this prototype has not been documented; certainly manufacture did not follow.

O.T. SIX — Advertisements following its appearance at the 1909 Chicago Automobile Show indicate that the name O.T. Six was planned for the automobile designed by W. Owen Thomas and to be produced in Janesville, Wisconsin. Subsequent references indicate the name Owen Thomas. Refer to Owen Thomas.

OTHO — Otho was the middle name of the man responsible for this car's building. Ralph Otho Hood of Danvers, Massachusetts produced a number of cars from 1899 to 1910. The Otho, which was begun in 1908 and completed in 1910, was his last. Refer to Hood Steamer.

OTIS — The Otis Motor Car Company was organized in South Bend, Indiana during the summer of 1912 with a capital stock of $10,000 for the manufacture of automobiles. Involved in this venture were N.L. Otis, J.B. Beattie and Gilbert Squires. Manufacture is doubted.

OTTAWA — The Ottawa Garage Company was organized early in 1911 with a capital stock of $20,000 to manufacture and deal in automobiles in Ottawa, Illinois. Walter E. Ners, John O. Langman and Jesse E. Rasmussen were the backers of this venture. Manufacture is doubted.

OTTO — The Otto Motor Car Company was organized in New York City late in 1910 with a capital stock of $50,000 for the manufacture of "engines, motor vehicles, motors, machinery, etc." Incorporators were J.J. McDonald, J.M. Lang and H.A. Bedell. Manufacture of an automobile is doubted.

1911 Otto, touring, HAC

OTTO — Philadelphia, Pennsylvania — (1910-1911)/**OTTOMOBILE** — (1912) — The Otto Gas Engine Works of Philadelphia was among the biggest names in its field when it became an automobile manufacturer in 1910. "The Largest and Oldest Builders of Gas and Gasoline Engines in the World," the brochures said, paying voluminous homage to Nicholas August Otto who invented his gas engine in 1867, though not mentioning that he invented it in Germany. The outcome of the Selden Patent case would be a promotional plus too, the company quoting extensively Judge Noyes' written decision that "had he (Selden) appreciated the superiority of the Otto engine and adapted that type (instead of the Brayton) for his combination, his patent would cover the modern automobile." The first Otto cars used the company's 241-cubic-inch 30/35 hp four fitted into a 123-inch wheelbase chassis that was offered in three body styles in 1910, eight in 1911. These were handsome cars, long and low, and sturdily built. The Philadelphia firm's principal problem seemed to be marketing. The Otto Motor Car Company in New York City initially handled sales, but went broke in April of 1911. The Ottomobile Company of Mt. Holly, New Jersey took over, but it went into receivership during the summer of 1912. Although Otto in Philadelphia was quick to disclaim any corporate connection with these selling concerns, there had to be a certain amount of confidence lost. The cars for 1912 carried Otto's 286- and 318-cubic-inch fours, and were called Ottomobiles. Otto president Murrell Dobbins announced that henceforth his company would both manufacture and sell the Ottomobile direct to dealers. Plans were made as well to establish a plant in Mt. Holly, and one reference indicates that production began there in late summer of 1912. By 1913, however, Otto was out of the automobile manufacturing business.

1910 OTTO
Four — 30/35 hp, 123" wb

	FP	5	4	3	2	1
Roadster-2/3/4P	1950	2400	3400	4800	8000	17,000
Demi-Tonneau-4P	2000	2500	3500	5000	8500	18,000
Touring-5P	2000	2700	3600	5300	8800	19,000

1911 OTTO
Four — 35 hp, 123" wb

Touring-5P	2000	2500	3500	5000	8500	18,000
Four-Door Tour.-5P	2150	2700	3600	5300	8800	19,000
Roadster-2/3/4P	1950	2400	3400	4800	8000	17,000
Victoria	2250	2300	3300	4600	7500	16,000
Coupe	2800	2200	3200	4400	7000	15,000
Limousine	3250	2700	3600	5300	8800	19,000
Landaulet	3250	2800	3700	5500	9000	19,500
Sportsman's Rdstr.	2150	3000	4000	6000	9500	21,000

1912 Ottomobile, model KK, parlor car, NAHC

1912 OTTOMOBILE
Model 2 — 4-cyl., 38.9 hp, 123" wb

Type A Demi Tonneau-5P	1850	2700	3600	5300	8800	19,000
Type B Rdstr.-3P	1850	2500	3500	5000	8500	18,000
Type D Demi Tonneau-4P	2000	2700	3600	5300	8800	19,000
Type L Rdstr.-2P	1900	2500	3500	5000	8500	18,000
Type E Rdstr.-2P	2000	2500	3500	5000	8500	18,000
Type F Colonial Limo.-7P	3250	3000	4000	6000	9500	21,000
Type H Colonial Cpe.-4P	2850	2500	3500	5000	8500	18,000
Type G Colonial Ottoette	3250	2700	3600	5300	8800	19,000
Type I Vict.-5P	2250	2400	3400	4800	8000	17,000
Type J Colonial Limo.-7P	3250	3000	4000	6000	9500	21,000

Model 3 — 4-cyl., 32.4 hp, 123" wb

Type KK Parlor Car-5/7P	2300	2400	3400	4800	8000	17,000

OTTOKAR — Cleveland, Ohio — (1902-1904) — In late September of 1902 Otto Konigslow of Cleveland advertised his availability as an automobile manufacturer in the trade press, explaining that he had built no fewer than 10,000 OK bicycles and had been experimenting with gasoline cars since 1898. His experimental work had been done in secret; his first car for public view rolled out the door of his Otto Konigslow Machine Company during the summer of '02. In 1903 Konigslow raced his OttoKar at Glen-

1903 OttoKar, runabout, NAHC

ville Track in Cleveland, finishing second in two events, behind an Olds in the first, a Stearns in the second. He sold fifteen cars that year. His 1902 car had a Renault-type hood; for 1903 it was given a boxier configuration. Two models, a single and a twin, were available in 1903, and his production was approximately fifty cars. For 1904 he offered only a one-lunger. His prices were modest, but so alas were his sales. He sold no more than ten cars in 1904. In June that year his plant and his business were bought by the Globe Machine & Stamping Company of Cleveland, Konigslow being made a stockholder, director and superintendent of operations. The Otto-Kar was discontinued. Otto Konigslow remained in the steel stamping business until his death in 1932.

1903 OTTOKAR
Single — 6 hp, 78" wb

	FP	5	4	3	2	1
Runabout-2P	750	2000	3000	4200	6500	14,000
Twin — 14 hp						
Tonneau-4P	850	2200	3200	4400	7000	15,000

1904 OttoKar, runabout, NAHC

1904 OTTOKAR
Single — 6 hp, 78" wb

Runabout-2P	650	1800	2800	4000	6200	13,000

OTTO-MOBILE — Omaha, Nebraska — (1899) — In 1899 Otto Bayersdorfer, a bicycle repairer from Omaha, built a light gasoline carriage which he sometimes referred to as his Otto-Mobile. This car, which was never manufactured, should not be confused with the more famous Otto/Ottomobile from Philadelphia.

OUGH & WALTENBAUGH — This car built in San Francisco at the turn of the century by J.M. Ough and George Waltenbaugh is more properly referred to as a Eureka. Refer to Eureka.

OUTING — The Outing Motor Company was organized in Lansing, Michigan during the fall of 1909 with a capital stock of $100,000 for the manufacture of automobiles in Detroit. The evidence is lacking that manufacture ever began.

OVENDEN — West Boylston, Massachusetts — (1898) — William Charles Ovenden was a native of England who arrived in Worcester, Massachusetts as a teenager and who, following his marriage to a girl in West Boylston, settled down in that town in 1890 to open a machine shop. Early in 1898 Henry Minter, a prominent retired businessman from Worcester, commissioned him to build a steam carriage. Ovenden spent most of the year working on it. The engine was a double tandem compound with piston valves and link motors, the boiler was a high pressure water-tube type of the sort that Ovenden had previously been building for house heating and portable farm engines. Gasoline was the fuel used, final drive was by sprocket and chain, and the vehicle was tiller steered. "The machine is substantially built and is capable of standing the racket of New England country roads,'' the Worcester *Telegram* reported on December 3rd, 1898. Except for painting and the fitting of rubber tires to its wooden wheels, the Ovenden steamer was completed by that date. It was delivered soon after to its new owner. Although Ovenden never built another car, he remained in the automobile business as a mechanic until his death in 1921.

OVERBAUGH-MARTIN — The Overbaugh-Martin Motor Car Company was organized in New York City early in 1909 with a capital stock of $50,000 for the manufacture of automobiles. The partners involved were D.C. Overbaugh, A.L. Martin and R.H. Overbaugh. Manufacture is doubted.

OVERFIELD — The Overfield Auto Company was organized in Brooklyn, New York late in 1914 with a capital stock of $1000 to manufacture "automobiles, dynamos and electric machinery.'' Behind this venture were F.A. and Eda Overfield, G.S. Hice and G.H. Boyce. Manufacture of a car is doubted.

OVERHOLT — During 1909, its maiden year in production, the automobile produced by the Overholt Company of Galesburg, Illinois was referred to by the company name. By the end of the year, however, Ed Overholt decided to call his car an Illinois instead. Refer to Illinois.

1903 Overland, runabout, JAC

OVERLAND — Terre Haute, Indiana — (1903-1905) / Indianapolis, Indiana — (1905-1909) / Toledo, Ohio — (1909-1926, 1939) — The name for the car was decided over a coffeebreak one day during the fall of 1902 by Charles Minshall, president of the Standard Wheel Company of Terre Haute, and Claude E. Cox, who had just graduated from the Ross Polytechnic Institute in town. The sum total of both these men's experience in the automobile field was Cox's senior thesis project for which he had devised a four-wheeler out of a motorized tricycle. This, Minshall believed, was sufficient acquaintanceship with motor matters for Cox to design an automobile and head Standard Wheel's new automobile department. With some trepidation, the young man proceeded and came up with an Overland that was a quite advanced little car for its day. Its water-cooled 5 hp single-cylinder engine was mounted up front under a hood, a two-speed planetary transmission controlled by a foot pedal was fitted, together with jump spark ignition and a two-way switch plug for changeover between the two dry batteries, the plug being removable for "carrying in the pocket when the machine is left standing on the street to prevent any unauthorized person from starting it.'' The prototype of the Overland was tested in Terre Haute on February 12th, 1903 with about twelve more built that year. Production doubled in 1904, when a two-cylinder model was added, and Cox was already at work on a revised twin and new four, both incorporating a steering wheel and shaft drive, for 1905. By January that year, the facilities in Terre Haute being cramped, Cox moved the Overland automobile department into an abandoned Standard Wheel plant in Indianapolis. Scarcely had he got down to business there when Minshall had a change of heart; thus far his automotive venture had made no profit, a situation he concluded was not likely to improve, so he decided to forget the whole thing. Fortunately for Claude Cox, a buggy manufacturer in Indianapolis who was a Standard Wheel customer and who earlier had tried to build an automobile himself was fascinated by the two new Overland models and offered to back Cox in their production. For fifty-one percent of the stock, David M. Parry put up all the money necessary to organize the Overland Auto Company on March 31st, 1906 and hastily built a few additions to his Parry Manufacturing Company factory. Production began, and the Panic of '07 arrived. So did John North Willys. An automobile dealer from Elmira (New York), Willys had contracted for the Overland company's entire output (47 cars) for 1906, and had sent in a hefty order for 500 cars, with a $10,000 deposit, for 1907. When no cars were deli-

vered and correspondence from the factory ceased, Willys entrained for Indianapolis to find out what was going on. There he discovered Parry had lost everything including his house in the Panic (a few years later he would recoup sufficiently to build the Parry automobile), and that parts were on hand for less than three automobiles. Willys took over. For the year following, until he could secure factory facilities, he built the Overlands in a circus tent, some 465 cars in 1908, all of them 20/24 hp fours. In January 1909, aghast at the feverish pace Willys was setting, Claude Cox left the company in anger. Willys' production of Overlands that year was an incredible 4907 cars, some of them a new 45 hp six. Also in 1909, Willys bought a controlling interest in the Marion Motor Car Company in Marion, Ohio; purchased the huge and idle factory in Toledo which had formerly seen production of the Pope-Toledo and into which he would now move his Overland; and brought together all his varied interests in a new organization called the Willys-Overland Company. Production in 1910 tripled to 15,598 cars. Fours only were produced, in a confusing and staggering array of models, from 1910 through 1914, some varieties fitted with sliding gear transmissions by 1912. In 1915 left-hand drive was introduced, and a six was returned to the line. But the biggest news from Willys-Overland arrived in October 1917, when the company announced an Overland four to challenge the Model T Ford head-on with a price tag of less than $500 to include self-starter and electric lights. John North Willys was riding high. From 1912 through the World War I years, only Henry Ford outproduced him. From a 1912 output of 28,572 cars, Willys-Overland production soared to 140,111 by 1916, mostly Overlands though a healthy percentage of Willys' new Willys-Knight car introduced in 1914 was included. From a net Overland profit of $1 million in 1908, the Willys-Overland coffers were augmented by a $10 million profit in 1915. Meanwhile, John North Willys had taken to buying things: companies like Moline Plow (makers of the Stephens Salient Six in Illinois) and factories like the gargantuan Duesenberg facility in Elizabeth (New Jersey), these purchases made in 1918 and 1919 respectively. In 1917 a merger with Curtiss had put Willys in the presidency of that East Coast aviation company. By now Willys had removed himself from Toledo to New York City from whence he managed the affairs of Willys Corporation, his new holding company. Back in Ohio he installed Clarence A. Earl, a former hardware manufacturing executive, to see to continuing fortuitous production, which alas Earl did not do. A disastrous strike in Toledo, in addition to wartime exigencies, delayed introduction of the Overland competitor to the Model T until October of 1919, and when finally it was introduced its price tag was $845 and the Ford in the meantime had been provided a self-starter, which made the new Overland really no competitor at all. A new line of Willys-Knight fours was moving well in the marketplace, and an interesting Willys six was being developed in the former Duesenberg plant, but none of this forestalled the financial disaster toward which Willys Corporation was plummeting when the postwar recession hit. In order to survive, Willys needed the help of a bank, and Chase in Manhattan offered same with the condition that former Buick president Walter Percy Chrysler be brought in to manage things. Chrysler agreed for a flat million-dollar-a-year salary; his first two acts on the job were to cut John North Willys' salary in half (to $75,000, which was clearly a power play) and to fire Clarence Earl (which he probably had coming, though he immediately found fresh employment with Benjamin Briscoe). Enamoured neither of the low-priced field nor the sleeve-valve engine, Chrysler wasn't impressed with the Overland or the Willys-Knight, though he was intrigued by the Willys six being developed in the Duesenberg plant. After two years of instituting cost-cutting measures for Willys, Chrysler left to take on a similar salvage job for Maxwell-Chalmers. Through a clever maneuvering of Willys Corporation into receivership and himself back into the driver's seat at Willys-Overland, John North Willys had his company back. The Willys interest in Curtiss was disposed of. The former Duesenberg plant in Elizabeth was sold off to Billy Durant, and through a curious set of circumstances, the Willys six which had been developed there would ultimately evolve into the first Chrysler. Meanwhile, John North Willys was back on the job in Toledo and doing phenomenally well in revitalizing his company via the two cars which Chrysler had pooh-poohed: the Willys-Knight and the Overland. Realizing by now that a head-on competitor to the Model T was not a viable idea, Willys revised the Overland four into a slightly larger and more powerful — and prettier — car to which he attached appealing model designations like Blue Bird and Red Bird, and equally attractive price tags in the $700 range. Willys-Overland sales soared: from 48,016 cars in 1921 to 215,000 in 1925. During that same period, the Willys-Overland treasury improved from a deficit of $20 million to a profit nearly approaching that figure. In 1925 an Overland six was added to the line, to be continued together with the Overland fours the following year. But these would be the last cars from the company to bear the Overland name for over a decade. In 1927

1903 Overland, runabout, JAC

the Whippet arrived, superseding the Overland. The Whippet would be discontinued in 1931, all succeeding cars carrying the Willys name as the country plunged into the Great Depression and Willys-Overland into receivership again. The Overland name returned briefly in 1939 for a line of low-priced fours which evolved into the Willys Americar by 1941. But by that time the man who had saved the Overland from oblivion in 1907 was no longer there. John North Willys died in August 1935.

1903 OVERLAND
Model 13 — 1-cyl.

	FP	5	4	3	2	1
Rbt.	595	2500	3500	5000	8500	18,000

1904 Overland, model 15, runabout, JAC

1904 OVERLAND
Model 13 — 1-cyl.

Rbt.	2400	2400	3400	4800	8000	17,000

Model 15 — 2-cyl., 6½ hp, 72″ wb

Rbt.	600	2500	3500	5000	8500	18,000

1905 Overland, model 17, runabout, JAC

1905 OVERLAND
Model 15 — 2-cyl., 7 hp, 72″ wb

Rbt.	600	2400	3400	4800	8000	17,000

Model 17 — 2-cyl., 9 hp, 78″ wb

Rbt.	750	2500	3500	5000	8500	18,000

Model 18 — 4-cyl., 16 hp, 90″ wb

Side Ent. Tonn.	1500	3000	4000	6000	9500	21,000

1906 OVERLAND
Model 16 — 2-cyl., 9 hp, 78″ wb

Rbt.	1250	2500	3500	5000	8500	18,000

Model 18 — 4-cyl., 16 hp, 90″ wb

Tonn.-4P	1250	3000	4000	6000	9500	21,000

1906 Overland, model 18, tonneau, JAC

1907 Overland, model 22, special runabout, JAC

1907 OVERLAND
Model 22 — 4-cyl., 16/18 hp, 86″ wb

	FP	5	4	3	2	1
Spl. Rbt.	1250	2900	3700	5600	9100	20,000
Tr.-5P	1250	3000	4000	6000	9500	21,000

1908 OVERLAND
Model 24 — 4-cyl., 20/22 hp, 96″ wb

Rbt.	1250	3000	4000	6000	9500	21,000
Tr.-5P	1250	3100	4200	6300	10,500	22,000

1909 Overland, model 30, roadster, JAC

1909 OVERLAND
Model 30 — 4-cyl., 30 hp, 108″ wb

Rds.-4P	1300	3000	4000	6000	9500	21,000
Cpe.-2P	1650	2500	5000	5000	8500	18,000
Tonn.-5P	1400	3100	4200	6300	10,500	22,000

Model 31 — 4-cyl., 30 hp, 110″ wb

Tourist	1400	3100	4200	6300	10,500	22,000
Toy Tonn.	1400	3100	4200	6300	10,500	22,000
Taxi	1400	2700	3600	5300	8800	19,000

Model 32 — 4-cyl., 30 hp, 110″ wb, 3-spd. transmission

Tr.-5P	1500	3100	4200	6300	10,500	22,000
Rds.-3P	1500	3100	4200	6300	10,600	22,000
Rds.-4P	1500	3100	4200	6300	10,500	22,000

Model 34 — 6-cyl., 35 hp, 116″ wb

Rds.-4P	2000	3200	4300	6500	11,000	23,000

1910 Overland, model 41, touring, JAC

1910 OVERLAND
Model 38 — 4-cyl., 25 hp, 102" wb

	FP	5	4	3	2	1
Rds.-2P	1000	3000	4000	6000	9500	21,000
Rds.-3P	1000	3000	4000	6000	9500	21,000
Rds.-4P	1000	3000	4000	6000	9500	21,000
Toy Tonn.	1000	3100	—	—	—	22,000
Model 40 — 4-cyl., 35 hp, 112" wb						
Rds.-3P	1250	3100	4200	6300	10,500	22,000
Rds.-4P	1450	3100	4200	6300	10,500	22,000
Model 41 — 4-cyl., 35 hp, 112" wb						
Tr.-5P	1450	3100	4200	6300	10,500	22,000
C.C. Tr.-4P	1500	3100	4200	6300	10,500	22,000
Model 42 — 4-cyl., 35 hp, 112" wb						
Tr.-5P	1500	3200	4300	6500	11,000	23,000
C.C. Tr.-4P	1850	3200	4300	6500	11,000	23,000

1911 Overland, touring, HAC

1911 OVERLAND
4-cyl., 20 hp, 96" wb

	FP	5	4	3	2	1
Mod. 45 Rds.-2P	775	2900	3700	5600	9100	20,000
Mod. 46 Torp. Rds.-2P	850	3000	4000	6000	9500	21,000
Mod. 47 Tr.-5P	850	3000	4000	6000	9500	21,000
Cpe.-3P (102" wb)	1250	2500	3500	5000	8500	18,000
4-cyl., 25 hp, 102" wb						
Mod. 49 Tr.-5P	1095	3100	4200	6300	10,500	22,000
4-cyl., 30 hp, 110" wb						
Mod. 50 Torp. Rds.-2P	1250	3100	4200	6300	10,500	22,000
Mod. 51 Fore-Door Tr.-5P	1250	3100	4200	6300	10,500	22,000
4-cyl., 40 hp, 118" wb						
Mod. 53 Torp. Rds.-2P	1600	3200	4300	6500	11,000	23,000
Mod. 54 Torp. Rds.-4P	1675	3200	4300	6500	11,000	23,000
Mod. 55 Fore-Door Tr.-5P	1300	3200	4300	6500	11,000	23,000
Mod. 52 Limo.-7P	2750	2700	3600	5300	8800	19,000
Mod. 56 Tr.-7P	1350	3300	4400	6700	12,000	24,000

1912 Overland, model 60-F, touring, HAC

1912 OVERLAND
Model 58 — 4-cyl., 25 hp, 96" wb

	FP	5	4	3	2	1
Rds.	850	2900	3700	5600	9100	20,000
Model 59 — 4-cyl., 30 hp, 106" wb						
Rds.	900	3000	4000	6000	9500	21,000
Tr.	900	3000	4000	6000	9500	21,000
Dly.	900	2300	3300	4000	7500	16,000
Cpe.	1250	2500	3500	5000	8500	18,000
Model 60 — 4-cyl., 35 hp, 114" wb						
Tr.-4P	1200	3000	4000	6000	9500	21,000
Tr.-5P	1200	3000	4000	6000	9500	21,000
Model 61 — 4-cyl., 45 hp, 118" wb						
Rds.	1500	3100	4200	6300	10,500	22,000
Tr.-4P	1500	3100	4200	6300	10,500	22,000
Tr.-5P	1500	3100	4200	6300	10,500	22,000
Cpe.	2000	2700	3600	5300	8800	19,000

1913 Overland, model 69-C, coupe, HAC

1913 OVERLAND
Model 69 — 4-cyl., 25.6 hp, 110" wb

	FP	5	4	3	2	1
Tr.-5P	985	3000	4000	6000	9500	21,000
Rds.-2P	985	3000	4000	6000	9500	21,000
Tr.-4P	1010	3000	4000	6000	9500	21,000
Cpe.-3P	1500	2500	3500	5000	8500	18,000
Model 71 — 4-cyl., 30.6 hp, 114" wb						
Tr.-5P	1475	3100	4200	6300	10,500	22,000
Rds.-2P	1475	3100	4200	6300	10,500	22,000
Tr.-4P	1475	3100	4200	6300	10,500	22,000

1914 Overland, model 79-R, roadster, HAC

1914 OVERLAND
Model 79 — 4-cyl., 35 hp, 114" wb

	FP	5	4	3	2	1
Rds.-2P	950	3100	4200	6300	10,500	22,000
Tr.-5P	950	3100	4200	6300	10,500	22,000
Cpe.-4P	1550	2500	3500	5000	8500	18,000
Model 46 — 4-cyl., 35 hp						
Tr.-5P	1075	3200	4300	6500	11,000	23,000

1915 Overland, model 80-C, coupe, HAC

1915 OVERLAND

Model 81 — 4-cyl., 30 hp, 106" wb

	FP	5	4	3	2	1
Tr.-5P	850	3100	4200	6300	10,500	22,000
Rds.-2P	795	3100	4200	6300	10,500	22,000
Pan. Dly.	895	2300	3300	4600	7500	16,000
Ex. Dly.	850	2200	3200	4400	7000	15,000

Model 80 — 4-cyl., 35 hp, 114" wb

Tr.-5P	1075	3200	4300	6500	11,000	23,000
Rds.-2P	1050	3200	4300	6500	11,000	23,000
Cpe.-4P	1600	2700	3600	5300	8800	19,000

Model 82 — 6-cyl., 45/50 hp, 125" wb

Tr.-7P	1475	3700	4700	7300	13,700	26,000

1916 Overland, model 83, limousine, HAC

1916 OVERLAND

Model 75 — 4-cyl., 20/25 hp, 104" wb

Tr.-5P	615	3100	4200	6300	10,500	22,000
Rds.-2P	595	3100	4200	6300	10,500	22,000

Model 83 — 4-cyl., 35 hp, 106" wb

Tr.-5P	750	3200	4300	6500	11,000	23,000
Win. Top Tr.-5P	950	3300	4400	6700	12,000	24,000
Rds.	725	3200	4300	6500	11,000	23,000
Win. Top Rds.	875	3300	4400	6700	12,000	24,000
Pan. Dly.	750	2300	3300	4600	7500	16,000
Open Dly.	725	2400	3400	4800	8000	17,000
Limo.	950	2700	3600	5300	8800	19,000
Cpe.	875	2500	3500	5000	8500	18,000

Model 84 — 4-cyl., 40 hp, 114" wb

Rds.	1095	3500	4500	7000	13,000	25,000
Tr.	1125	3500	4500	7000	13,000	25,000
Cpe.	1500	2700	3600	5300	8800	19,000
Limo.	1750	3000	4000	6000	9500	21,000

Model 86 — 6-cyl., 45/50 hp, 125" wb

Tr.-7P	1145	3900	4800	7700	14,300	27,000

1917 Overland, Light Four 90, country club roadster, JAC

1917 OVERLAND

Light Four 90 — 4-cyl., 32 hp, 106" wb

Tr.-5P	665	3000	4000	6000	9500	21,000
Rds.-2P	650	3000	4000	6000	9500	21,000
Cty. Clb. Rds.	750	3100	4200	6300	10,500	22,000
Sed.-5P	1340	2400	3400	4800	8000	17,000

Big Four 85 — 4-cyl., 35 hp, 112" wb

Rds.-3P	795	3100	4200	6300	10,500	22,000
Tr.-5P	795	3100	4200	6300	10,500	22,000
Tr. Cpe.	1045	2700	3600	5300	8800	19,000
Tr. Sed.-5P	1195	2500	3500	5000	8500	18,000

Light Six 85 — 6-cyl., 35/40 hp, 116" wb

Rds.-3P	970	3200	4300	6500	11,000	23,000
Tr.-5P	985	3200	4300	6500	11,000	23,000
Tr. Cpe.-3P	1385	2900	3700	5600	9100	20,000
Tr. Sed.-5P	1585	2700	3600	5300	8800	19,000

1056

1918 Overland, Light Six 85, touring sedan, JAC

1918 OVERLAND

Light Four 90 — 4-cyl., 32 hp, 106" wb

	FP	5	4	3	2	1
Tr.-5P	795	3000	4000	6000	9500	21,000
Rds.-2P	780	3000	4000	6000	9500	21,000
Cty. Clb. Rds.	840	3100	4200	6300	10,500	22,000
Sed.-5P	1240	1600	2700	3800	5800	12,000

Big Four 85 — 4-cyl., 35 hp, 112" wb

Tr.-5P	930	3100	4200	6300	10,500	22,000
Rds.-3P	915	3100	4200	6300	10,500	22,000

Light Six 85 — 6-cyl., 35/40 hp, 116" wb

Rds.-3P	1115	3300	4400	6700	12,000	24,000
Tr.-5P	1130	3300	4400	6700	12,000	24,000
Tr. Sed.-5P	1620	1800	2800	4000	6200	13,000
Tr. Cpe.-3P	1420	2200	3200	4400	7000	15,000

1919 Overland, Light Four 90, sedan, JAC

1919 OVERLAND

Light Four 90 — 4-cyl., 32 hp, 106" wb

Tr.-5P	985	3200	4300	6500	11,000	23,000
Rds.-3P	985	3200	4300	6500	11,000	23,000
Sed.-5P	1495	1800	2800	4000	6200	13,000

1920 Overland, model 4, touring, JAC

1920 OVERLAND
Model 4 — 4-cyl., 27 hp, 100" wb

	FP	5	4	3	2	1
Tr.-5P	945	3200	4300	6500	11,000	23,000
Rds.-2P	945	3200	4300	6500	11,000	23,000
Cpe.-4P	1525	2200	3200	4400	7000	15,000
Sed.-4P	1575	1800	2800	4000	6200	13,000

1921 Overland, model 4, touring, JAC

1921 OVERLAND
Model 4 — 4-cyl., 27 hp, 100" wb

Tr.-5P	985	3000	4000	6000	9500	21,000
Rds.-2P	985	3000	4000	6000	9500	21,000
Cpe.-4P	1525	2200	3200	4400	7000	15,000
Sed.-4P	1575	1600	2700	3800	5800	12,000

1922 Overland, model 4, touring, HAC

1922 OVERLAND
Model 4 — 4-cyl., 27 hp, 100" wb

Tr.	595	3000	4000	6000	9500	21,000
Rds.-3P	595	3000	4000	6000	9500	21,000
Cpe.-3P	850	2200	3200	4400	7000	15,000
Sed.-5P	895	1600	2700	3800	5800	12,000

1923 Overland, model 91, coupe, JAC

1923 OVERLAND
Model 91 — 4-cyl., 27 hp, 100" wb

Tr.-5P	525	3000	4000	6000	9500	21,000
Rds.-2P	525	3000	4000	6000	9500	21,000
Cpe.-4P	795	2200	3200	4400	7000	15,000
Sed.-5P	875	1600	2700	3800	5800	12,000

Model 92 — 4-cyl., 30 hp, 106" wb

Redbird	750	3200	4300	6500	11,000	23,000

1924 Overland, model 91, touring, HAC

1924 Overland, model 91, coupe, JAC

1924 OVERLAND
Model 91 — 4-cyl., 27 hp, 100" wb

	FP	5	4	3	2	1
Tr.-5P	495	3000	4000	6000	9500	21,000
Rds.-2P	495	3000	4000	6000	9500	21,000
Champ. Sed.-5P	695	1600	2700	3800	4800	12,000
Sed.-5P	795	1500	2500	3600	5500	11,000

Model 92 — 4-cyl., 30 hp, 106" wb

Redbird	—	3200	4300	6500	11,000	23,000
Blackbird	—	3200	4300	6500	11,000	23,000
Bluebird	—	3200	4300	6500	11,000	23,000

1925 Overland, model 91, sedan, JAC

1925 OVERLAND
Model 91 — 4-cyl., 27 hp, 100" wb

Tr.-5P	530	3100	4200	6300	10,500	22,000
Rds.-2P	530	3100	4200	6300	10,500	22,000
Cpe.-2P	695	2200	3200	4400	7000	15,000
Sed.-5P	850	1800	2800	4000	6200	13,000
Tr.-5P	725	3500	4500	7000	13,000	25,000

Model 92 — 4-cyl., 30 hp, 106" wb

Bluebird	495	3700	4700	7300	13,700	26,000

Model 93 — 6-cyl., 38 hp, 113" wb

Sed.-5P	825	2000	3000	4200	6500	14,000
Del. Sed.-5P	—	2200	3200	4400	7000	15,000

1926 Overland Six, touring, JAC

1926 OVERLAND
Model 91 — 4-cyl., 27 hp, 100" wh

	FP	5	4	3	2	1
Tr.-5P	495	3100	4200	6300	10,500	22,000
Cpe.-2P	625	2200	3200	4400	7000	15,000
Sed.-5P	595	1800	2800	4000	6200	13,000
Del. Sed.-5P	895	2000	3000	4200	6500	14,000

Model 92 — 4-cyl., 30 hp, 106" wb

	FP	5	4	3	2	1
Tr.-5P	—	3500	4500	7000	13,000	25,000

Model 93 — 6-cyl., 38 hp, 113" wb

	FP	5	4	3	2	1
Tr.-5P	825	3700	4700	7300	13,700	26,000
Sed.-5P	895	2200	3200	4400	7000	15,000
Del. Sed.-5P	1095	2300	3300	4600	7500	16,000
Cpe.-2P	—	2500	3500	5000	8500	18,000

1939 Overland, sedan, JAC

1898 Overman, runabout, NAHC

OVERMAN — Chicopee Falls, Massachusetts — (1895-1898) — For three years the Overman Wheel Company of Chicopee Falls experimented with a gasoline automobile. The first was built in 1895 and had four wheels and three small 2 hp air-cooled motors. Another car followed in 1896-1897, yet another in 1898. The man most responsible for these cars was Harry A. Knox. When his boss, A.H. Overman, finally decided to get into commercial manufacture in 1899, it was with a steam car, however, which would be marketed under the tradename of Victor. With Overman's decision for steam, Harry Knox immediately left the company for Springfield where he produced a gasoline car under his own name. The Victor steam car was manufactured until early 1903. The Knox was built until 1915.

OWATONNA — Owatonna, Minnesota — (1895-1896) — There were several cars produced before the turn of the century in Owatonna, though two of them were more often referred to as Ames: one a gasoline car built by D.J. Ames of Owatonna, another a steam car built by an Owatonna

mechanic for A.C. Ames of Chicago. Both of these vehicles were built in 1895. An electric car designed by D.J. Ames and called the Owatonna Motocycle followed in 1896, but like the predecessor vehicles was made in a single example only. During this same period another local mechanic was at work on his car as well: L.S. Nichols, who had talked the Owatonna Manufacturing Company into producing it. (D.J. Ames was the president of that company.) Nichols' invention was a rotary gasoline engine which initially had been planned to be completed in 1895 but was found to require more time than anticipated. Nichols and Owatonna were still experimenting with the car in February of 1896 when *The Horseless Age* received a letter from Nichlos with an update: "They will not be satisfied," the magazine reported, "until they have produced a vehicle that a woman can handle with ease. He reports progress." Sufficient progress did not follow, however, for this project to exceed the building of a single car.

OWATONNA — Owatonna, Minnesota — (1901-1903) — The first automobile to be built in Owatonna in units of more than one arrived in 1901 when three of the town's citizens — D.E. Virtue, C.L. Pound and E.T. Winship — built three gasoline automobiles and began an automobile factory. What subsequent production the plant saw, however, seems to have been confined to engine manufacture predominantly, with the automobiles produced being used principally to demonstrate the efficiency of the partners' 10 hp motor. The cars were priced at $1250 and were not formally placed on the market until early 1903. Winship soon departed, and the firm of Virtue & Pound continued in business up to the First World War manufacturing engines for farm and shop use.

1914 O-We-Go Cyclecar, NAHC

O-WE-GO — Owego, New York — (1914) — The rather cute hyphenation of the New York town in which it was manufactured, and the fact that the firm planned to build its own two-cylinder air-cooled engine instead of ordering out from Spacke or Deluxe, were marks of distinction for the O-We-Go Car Company. The O-We-Go cyclecar was, however, a typical tandem two-seater with friction transmission and belt drive. The company building it was incorporated with a capital stock of $150,000 on February 4th, 1914, and it seemed to be a more solidly based effort than most of the new cyclecar manufacturers in the field. President George Ramsey was a prominent New York banker, vice-president W.I. Payne had Standard Oil connections. Designer of the O-We-Go was Charles B. Hatfield, Jr., who formerly had been general manager of the Hatfield Auto Truck Company in Elmira and who earlier had built the Hatfield highwheeler in Miamisburg, Ohio. In April of 1914 he announced that the prototype O-We-Go had finished an extensive testing period of three months during which it had shown a top speed of 58 mph. Hatfield also commented that he personally had driven the car from New York City to Yonkers and return "through some very hilly country without a change of gear." Production began that month. Apparently among the early decisions made by the company was not to build its own engine after all, but to use an Ives motorcycle unit. Production continued for a short while after October 30th when the company went into trusteeship. In January 1915 O-We-Go proceeded into voluntary bankruptcy, listing liabilities of $43,642, assets of $25,078, and $672 cash in the bank.

1914 O-WE-GO
Cyclecar — 2-cyl., 12 hp, 104" wb

	FP	5	4	3	2	1
Tandem Rdstr.-2P	385	1800	2800	4000	6200	13,000
Open Body Delivery	395	1600	2700	3800	5800	12,000
Closed Body Delivery	405	1700	2800	3900	6000	12,500

OWEN — The Owen Motor Car Company has been indicated on various rosters as the producer of an automobile in Toledo, Ohio in 1914. City directory references indicate no such company in town, and the likelihood is that this Owen has been confused with the automotive ventures of the Owen brothers of Cleveland.

The Percy Owen Company, Inc. was organized in New York City during the spring of 1907 with a capital stock of $75,000 for the manufacture of motor vehicles. Joining Percy Owen in this venture was H.C. Smith. Percy Owen was well known as a Winton driver (having raced in the 1903 Gordon-Bennett) and perhaps believed that he could parlay his fine sporting reputation into a profitable career as an automobile manufacturer. There is no evidence that manufacture followed, however, though Owen did enjoy success as an automobile dealer.

OWEN — Cleveland, Ohio — (1899-1901) — The Owen Brothers — Raymond M. and Ralph R. — were the proprietors of the R.M. Owen Carpet Cleaning and Rug Manufacturing Company of Cleveland. In 1899 they fitted an 8 hp gasoline engine of their own design into a motor wagon for the delivery of their goods. So pleased were they with the results that they made others for sale as dual-purpose vehicles: a delivery wagon which "by removing lettered signboards and replacing them with an extra seat"

1899 Owen Gasoline Carriage, NAHC

could be converted into a passenger car in minutes. A few vehicles with single purpose — both delivery wagons and passenger cars — were built as well. This was strictly a low-key operation. In February of 1900 the brothers organized as the Phoenix Motor Vehicle & Engine Company, though by that summer they decided to call themselves the Owen Motor Carriage Company. Vehicles were sold under both the Owen and Phoenix names. Very soon thereafter, however, they elected to give up their Owen-Phoenix business and become Oldsmobile dealers instead. Ransom Eli Olds obviously impressed them a good deal. In 1901 Raymond Owen left for New York City to set up R.M. Owen & Company as the New York distributorship for Oldsmobiles, and Ralph Owen subsequently went to Lansing to serve as factory manager of Olds Motor Works. Ransom Olds made his celebrated exit from Olds in 1904 to establish his new Reo company; Raymond M. Owen immediately switched allegiance and became distributor for Reo in New York. In 1910 brother Ralph allied himself with several former Olds Motor Works people to build a new Owen car in Detroit.

1911 Owen, 50, touring, WLB

OWEN — Detroit, Michigan — (1910-1911) — In January of 1910 the Owen Motor Car Company was organized, with a capital stock of $500,000, by Ralph R. Owen, Angus Smith and Frank E. Robson. The new Owen was a 425-cubic-inch 50 hp four on a 120-inch wheelbase offered in open body styles at $3200 and as a berline limousine at $4800. The car's centrally-mounted gearshift was progressive for the period, though its big 42-inch wheels, while providing admirable ground clearance, made for an overbearing appearance. The new company soon discovered that building an automobile and selling it presented two separate problems, and to allay the latter Ralph Owen contacted his brother Raymond M. whose R.M. Owen & Company was serving as distributor for the Reo automobiles built by Ransom Olds. By October the entire Owen organization had been sold to Reo in exchange for which Owen, Smith and Robson received Reo stock. There was a nice irony in this, since those three men were former Olds Motor Works people, and it was from that company that Ransom Olds had angrily left in 1904 to found Reo. The new Owen-Reo arrangement called for Reo's completing the Owens for which parts were on hand, which Reo did, finishing 35 cars of which 31 were sold through the Reo sales organization. That experience indicated to Reo that further production of the Owen was not "commercially practicable" which of course did not please the Owen people. Reo discontinued the Owen in 1911, and Ralph Owen marketed some of the last cars himself as the R.O. Whether he meant this as a sly dig at Ransom E. Olds is not known, though Reo of course translated to Olds' initials. There was some ill feeling between Owen and Reo during this period, and a lawsuit was threatened. Any friction this might have caused between the two brothers (Raymond M. Owen was then a solid Reo man) soon disappeared, however, and the Owens subsequently became partners again to build the Owen Magnetic. Meanwhile the Owen factory was taken over by the Krit Motor Car Company, with former Owen factory manager Alwin A. Gloetzner remaining on as the new Krit factory manager.

1910-1911 OWEN
Four — 50 hp, 120" wb

	FP	5	4	3	2	1
Touring	3200	4000	5000	8000	15,000	28,000
Close-Coupled	3200	3700	4700	7300	13,700	26,000
Runabout	3200	3500	4500	7000	13,000	25,000
Ber. Limo.	4800	3000	4000	6000	9500	21,000

1915 Owen Magnetic, model IV, victoria touring, HAC

OWEN MAGNETIC — New York, New York — (1915)/Cleveland, Ohio — (1916-1919)/Wilkes Barre, Pennsylvania — (1920-1921) — Although Justus B. Entz had introduced his Entz Six at the New York Automobile Show in January 1914, had demonstrated it at a meeting of the Society of Automobile Engineers that summer, indicating that manufacture would follow, the Entz did not become a production car. Instead, the Entz electric transmission was acquired and fitted to the new Owen Magnetic which was introduced at the New York Automobile Show in January 1915. The car was sponsored by R.M. Owen & Company. Both Raymond M. Owen, and his brother Ralph R., had been working on Entz principle refinements in New York since 1912, the same year that Walter C. Baker in Cleveland (the Owens' hometown) had bought the Entz patents. The first Owen Magnetics were produced in a factory that the Owens secured at 142nd Street and Fifth Avenue in New York and were built under license from Baker. Production in New York totaled 250 cars. In December of 1915 the Owen Magnetic moved to Cleveland. By now Walter C. Baker and the Rauch & Lang people who had been building electric cars independently in Cleveland joined forces as the new Baker R & L Company, Inc. Recognizing the waning marketability of electric vehicles, they decided to focus manufacturing attention on the Owen Magnetic. R.M. Owen & Company joined this consolidation in December. The Baker factory would produce the Owen Magnetic engines and chassis, the R & L plant the coachwork, and Raymond M. Owen would direct the car's sales. The Owen Magnetic line was greatly expanded in 1916, and in mid-year was joined by a striking sport tourer with Holbrook body that was priced at $6000. The standard line ranged from $3000+ to $5000+. Owen Magnetics were large luxury cars which attracted a celebrity following. Both Enrico Caruso and John McCormack were owners, as were several other noted musicians, which may have encouraged the Baker R & L promotion department to come up with its evocative "Driving a Melody" advertising campaign in 1917. A Biddle from Bryn Mawr also owned an Owen Magnetic, as did Arthur Brisbane in New York. Larger and brand-new models were introduced at the New York Automobile Show in January 1918. Prices now ranged up to $6500, making the Owen Magnetic one of the most expensive cars in America. Few cars were produced in 1918, as Baker R & L turned to war work. When the company decided to discontinue production in mid-1919, Raymond Owen took the car to Wilkes Barre. There he allied himself with Frank Matheson and resumed Owen Magnetic production in the former Matheson plant which had most recently been used for the manufacture of munitions. The most success enjoyed by the new Owen Magnetic Motor Car Corporation of Wilkes Barre was an order received early in 1920 from the English firm Crown Limited. The order was for 500 units, with specified delivery over a period of several years, these cars being exported under the name Crown Magnetic. By the fall of 1920 Owen Magnetic was in receivership. The company receivers authorized the borrowing of $100,000 to complete twenty-five Owen Magnetics already under construction, but when these were finished so was the car. In November of 1921, Frank Matheson bought back his old factory and turned it into an automobile distributorship. Probably the Owen Magnetic would not have survived the postwar depression in any case, but by now its complicated and expensive electric transmission had proven impracticable to both manufacture and market.

1915 OWEN MAGNETIC
Six — 34 hp, 136" wb

Touring-7P	3700	5500	7500	12,000	26,000	39,000
Roadster-2P	3700	5400	7300	11,800	25,000	38,000

1916-1917 OWEN MAGNETIC
Model M-25 — 6-cyl., 29 hp, 125" wb

Touring-5P	3150	4200	5200	8400	15,700	29,000
Limousine	4200	3100	4200	6300	10,500	22,000
Coupe	3500	2700	3600	5300	8800	19,000
Town Car	4200	3200	4300	6500	11,000	23,000
Landaulet	4400	3500	4500	7000	13,000	25,000

Model O-36 — 6-cyl., 34 hp, 136" wb

Touring-4P	3750	5400	7300	11,800	25,000	38,000
Cloverleaf Rdstr.-3P	3750	5200	6800	11,300	23,000	36,000
Limousine	4800	3500	4500	7000	13,000	25,000
Landaulet	5000	3900	4800	7700	14,300	27,000
Touring-7P	3950	5500	7500	12,000	26,000	39,000
Holbrook Spt. Tour.	6000	6000	8500	13,000	30,000	42,000

1059

1916 Owen Magnetic, roadster, HAC

1917 Owen Magnetic, roadster, HAC

1917 Owen Magnetic, Holbrook sport touring, HAC

1918 Owen Magnetic, touring, OCW

1918-1919 OWEN MAGNETIC
Six — 40 hp, 142" wb

	FP	5	4	3	2	1
	—	5400	7300	11,800	25,000	38,000
Model O — 6-cyl., 34 hp, 136" wb						
	—	5200	6800	11,300	23,000	36,000
Six — 43.2 hp, 128" wb						
	—	5200	6800	11,300	23,000	36,000

1919 Owen Magnetic, touring, OCW

1920 Owen Magnetic, touring, WLB

1921 Owen Magnetic, touring, HAC

1920-1921 OWEN MAGNETIC
Six — 70 hp, 142" wb

	FP	5	4	3	2	1
Touring-4P	5800	5400	7300	11,800	25,000	38,000
Touring-7P	5300	5800	8000	12,500	28,000	40,000
Coupe-4P	5800	3000	4000	6000	9500	21,000
Sedan-7P	6300	2400	3400	4800	8000	17,000
Limousine-7P	6300	4200	5200	8400	15,700	29,000

OWEN-SCHOENECK — Although John L. Owen and George Schoeneck called their venture the Owen-Schoeneck Company, they named their car the O-S. It was built in Chicago from 1914-1915. Refer to O-S.

1909 Owens-Thomas, roadster, NAHC

OWEN-THOMAS — Janesville, Wisconsin — (1908-1910) — W. Owen Thomas was a Chicago engineer of considerable ingenuity. In January 1907 he organized the Owen Thomas Motor Car Company and secured sufficient capital for development work on the prototype of his new six-cylinder car. By early 1908 it was being tested at the Knight & Kilbourne shops in Chicago under the auspices of the prestigious Armour Institute. Then Owen Thomas began shopping up north in Wisconsin for a manufacturing site. In July 1908 he was negotiating with the Chicago & North Western Railroad for lease of its former machine shop in Janesville, now obsolete since the railroad's new roundhouse had been completed. By early fall it appeared the negotiations were proceeding nicely; by November the C & NW decided it might tear down the building instead. Frustrations like these seemed to confront Owen Thomas at every turn with his car. The Chicago Automobile Show in February 1909 was his highpoint. The Owen Thomas — then called the O.T. Six — was viewed with fascination as the one car there, and at any of the major shows for that matter, which represented a radical departure from the norm. "This machine has no starting crank, no water jackets or cooling flanges, no carburetor and no electrical distributor," *The Horseless Age* reported. "The six cylinder, four cycle engine is fitted with rotary valves in the head; the compression used is 120 pounds and all the spark plugs operate continuously." A half-horsepower generator built into the forward part of the crankcase and geared directly to the engine shaft supplied current for ignition and for charging the storage battery. A fuel injection system, based on aviation practice, was fitted. The engine was air cooled, and built in unit with the transmission. Imported D.W.F. bearings were used throughout the engine, transmission and running gear. The four ball bearings in the crankshaft were nine inches in diameter. The Owen Thomas was a big car, its six-cylinder engine developing 60 hp, its wheelbase 136 inches. The projected price tag was $3000. After the euphoria engendered by the response to the car at the Chicago show ebbed, Owen Thomas found himself confronted with reality once again. He had by now moved into the Janesville machine shop which the C & NW had decided not to tear down after all. Two more cars were built and tested, and Thomas began setting up a welding plant because he had decided he didn't want a single rivet to appear in his car's body or frame. But he was not into production yet, and his money ran out. Salvation arrived, or seemed to, that September when the Wisconsin Engine Company in Corliss took an interest in Owen Thomas and his car. Manufacture on a large scale was promised, and the Corliss Motor Company was organized with $1,000,000 capital stock. In January of 1910 fourteen carloads of steel arrived from Pittsburgh to begin the construction of the new factory for the Owen Thomas. (The Wisconsin Engine Company was controlled by Pennsylvania steel mill tycoons.) The future looked bright, but everything quickly turned dark. In September it was announced that the Corliss Motor Company had abandoned the idea of manufacturing the Owen Thomas car. The official reason given was the inability of its backers to secure a Selden license, which probably was a factor though, ironically, the court decision in the Selden case would render the patent unenforceable four months later. Most likely, Corliss backed out on the Owen Thomas principally because it would have been too expensive to build profitably as designed by W. Owen Thomas — and that's a pity. Corliss subsequently entered the commercial vehicle field with a truck produced from 1917-1918.

OWENS STEAM — Springfield, Ohio — (1900) — H.E. Owens was the superintendent of the Thomas Manufacturing Company of Springfield and in 1900 he completed the building of a steam carriage in the firm's shops. Mechanical details are lacking, but *The Motor Vehicle Review* noted that the Owens car was "a very neat piece of work." Its construction was a private venture by Owens, and the Thomas Manufacturing Company never envisioned production.

1922 Owens, NAHC

OWENS — St. Paul, Minnesota — (1922) — Owens Motor Sales' answer to the "you gotta have a gimmick" approach to promotion was this locomotive car which was used in its road service work. "The engineer's cab carries five passengers, so the unfortunate motorists who have to be picked up will travel in comfort out of the dust," reported *Motor Age* in 1922. This vehicle, of which the St. Paul firm was inordinately proud, was built on a Ford one-ton truck chassis and was a steamer, its boiler courtesy of Berg Brothers Manufacturing Company of Minneapolis. To heighten the resemblance to a locomotive, the Owens exhaust exited through the smoke stack.

OWENSBORO — Owensboro, Kentucky — (1903) — That the car was designed by A.J. Kemper of Danville, that Dr. J.H. Hickman of Owensboro was spearheading the movement to get it into manufacture and that he had the support of the Owensboro Wagon Company are the facts known regarding this car-building venture of 1903. A prototype seems to have been built, but production seems not to have followed. Subsequently there was an automobile which did get into manufacture in Owensboro; it was called the Ames and was another venture entirely.

OWNERS — The Owner's Automobile Company was organized in St. Louis, Missouri early in 1904 with a capital stock of $2000 to manufacture and deal in automobiles and bicycles. Incorporators were Horace A. Davis, William C. Woods and George L. Moselle. Manufacture is doubted.

OWOSSO — Owosso, Michigan — (1902, 1910) — There were two companies in Owosso which attempted the automobile field, neither of them with enduring success. The first was the Owosso Carriage Company which completed its car during the late summer of 1902 and continued experimenting with it for the ten months following. In June of 1903 the car — a two-stroke 12 hp four-passenger touring designed by C.P. Malcolm, an engine manufacturer from Oxford who had built a few cars on his own in 1900 — was publicly tested for the first time, the company announcing that if it "proves the success anticipated, the making of carriages and cutters will be discontinued within a few months." The Owosso Carriage Company continued in the horsedrawn trade, however, and any automobile manufacture which might have followed was minimal. Whether any of the Owosso Carriage people were involved in the subsequent organization in December of 1909 of the Owosso Motor (later Motor Car) Company is not known. J.I. Page of Owosso had built an experimental automobile that year which may have been considered for possible production. But by early 1910 the Owosso company announced its intention to enter the commercial field only, with C.V. Richardson and E.M. Clarke (formerly with the Reliance Motor Truck Company) to oversee the technical department. Of that venture, *The Horseless Age* reported late in 1911 that after "manufacturing motor trucks, under certain handicaps, the Owosso Motor Car Company has decided to wind up its affairs."

OXFORD — The Oxford Motor Car Company of Pittsburgh, Pennsylvania was a $500,000 Delaware incorporation from early 1905 for the manufacture and sale of "motor cars and vehicles of all types." Incorporators were D.G. Neagley, J.K. Neagley and L.E. McLain. Manufacture of an automobile is doubted.

1900 Oxford Autocycle, trike, RD

OXFORD — Oxford, Pennsylvania — (1900) — In 1900 the Carroll Manufacturing Company of Philadelphia got together with the Smith Motor Company of Newark, New Jersey to form the Oxford Manufacturing Company. Fifty thousand dollars was the capitalization and manufacture of bicycles, motors, motorcycles, tricycles and automobiles was the aim. The town of Oxford, in Chester County, had invited the new venture to locate there, hence the company name. Carroll had previously been a bicycle builder exclusively, Smith was manufacturer of the single-cylinder 3 hp motor of that name. The closest the new venture came to an automobile during its borning year was the Oxford Autocycle, which carried a price tag of $400 and was available as either a three- or four-wheeler with accommodations for two. Production was minimal. Thereafter Oxford concentrated on bikes, motorcycles and Parkin gasoline motors. The Parkin family was the moving spirit behind this enterprise and in subsequent years produced a variety of race cars and prototypes under the Parkin name.

OXFORD — Everett, Massachusetts — (1900) — In May of 1900 a group of Bostonians who had organized in Maine as the Oxford Automobile Company acquired the total assets of Milne and Killam, makers of the Everett Steamer in Everett, and moved to town to build their own steam car. Among the men involved were G.F. Killane, C.W. Jones and C.M. Randall. Their Oxford was available as a two-seater runabout at $850, a victoria stanhope at $1000, and a four-passenger family carriage at $1200. "The steam is so condensed within the vehicle that none is visible without," *The Automobile* commented. "The method of starting, or firing-up, is very simple. A little gasoline is allowed to escape, so as to fill a projection below the admission valve; the pilot light is lighted; the burner soon begins to act, and steam rapidly rises. The time required is four or five minutes from the first touch until you are on the road." The Oxford's boiler was the typical tubular arrangement; its storage tanks held twenty-four gallons of water and five of gasoline. "It is said to be a thoroughly serviceable automobile, and it gives in comfort and speed all that is ordinarily required," concluded *The Automobile*. Nonetheless, Oxford was out of business in Everett within the year.

1900 OXFORD

	FP	5	4	3	2	1
Oxford Steam Runabout	850	2200	3200	4400	7000	15,000
Oxford Family Carriage	1200	2400	3400	4800	8000	17,000
Oxford Victoria Stanhope	1000	2300	3300	4600	7500	16,000

OXFORD — Boston, Massachusetts — (1901) — The tenure of the Oxford Manufacturing Company of Boston in the automobile field was quite abbreviated. "A young lawyer named Stevens owns the concern," reported *The Motor Age* in 1901. "He built two carriages and endeavored to form a stock company, but failed to interest capitalists, and now says he has had all the experience he requires."

1905 Oxford, touring, NAHC

1905 Oxford, touring, WLB

OXFORD — Oxford, Michigan — (1905) — William H. Radford graduated from the University of Michigan in June 1903 with a degree in mechanical engineering, hiring on immediately as a draftsman with Olds Motor Works. During off-hours, with assistance from a colleague named Clyde J. Smith, he invented a carburetor and worked up a design for a two-cylinder 16 hp touring car set in a 90-inch wheelbase chassis. Shopping around for potential backers brought the pair in contact with Clarence H. Crawford who headed the Oxford Carriage Company in Oxford and who would happily lend his facilities for production. Further investment capital was secured and on January 30th, 1905 the Detroit-Oxford Manufacturing Company was organized for production of the S and R Automatic Carburetor and the new touring car. Radford and Smith immediately quit their Detroit jobs, Clarence Crawford took the company's presidential chair, and the offices of the firm were filled by people from Oxford and Pigeon, and by a dentist from Detroit named Dumas. Although the new car was occasionally referred to as a Detroit-Oxford, it was more usually called simply the Oxford. "The most pronounced machine design feature of this Oxford car," *Cycle and Automobile Trade Journal* said quite ponderously, "is the

amplitude of the dimensions of the details, which are all so large as to secure against breakage, and have bearings with surface enough to assure long life." Friction transmission, shaft drive and right-hand steering were featured. By the time the prototype was built — August 1905 — the company had spent $15,000, with a few debts as yet unpaid, and no money to pay them. An anguished letter from Dr. Dumas dated November 5th, 1905 urged borrowing from a bank to erase the indebtedness and pleaded that "no one needs to lose money" in the company. Apparently, bailing out was adjudged to be the wiser course. Detroit-Oxford advertised that it would sell off its machinery and assets "at considerably less than inventory figures" and what resulted in January 1906 might be regarded as America's first big garage sale. Numerous manufacturers in the area, C.H. Blomstrom among them, were reported to have attended the event. Thereafter the Detroit-Oxford people divided the proceeds, and William Radford took the one thing he had left, the Oxford prototype, and moved to Fostoria (Ohio) where he interested townspeople there in his manufacturing idea. The Fostoria Motor Car Company was organized — and, ergo, the Oxford became the Fostoria. The car was produced for slightly more than a year.

OYLER — The Oyler from Minneapolis, Minnesota has frequently appeared on rosters as an automobile built in 1900. There are trade press references from that year which indicate the $50,000 incorporation of the Oyler Manufacturing Company for the purpose of building cars. John T. Oyler and Charles H. Speck of Minneapolis, and William F. Fuller of Warren, Minnesota, were the people involved. However, the Oyler name does not appear in any Minneapolis city directory from the years 1899 through 1903. If an Oyler was built in Minneapolis in 1900, its makers apparently did not want anyone in town to know about it. More likely, this was one of the countless automotive ventures which never proceeded from idea to reality.

PACIFIC — The founders of the Portland Cyclecar Company of Portland, Oregon in 1914 couldn't make up their minds whether to call their product a Pacific or a Portland. They announced both names. Refer to Portland.

The Pacific Motor & Automobile Company of Redondo, California promoted a car called the Coyote Special in1908-1909. Refer to Coyote Special.

The Pacific Traction Company was a $3 million Maine incorporation from the summer of 1907 for the manufacture of motor cars and appliances. J. Berry and L.A. Burleigh, both of Augusta, were the incorporators. Manufacture of an automobile is doubted.

PACIFIC — Los Angeles, California — (1900-1901) — The Pacific Automobile Company was organized in Los Angeles during the summer of 1900. Capitalization was a cool million dollars, little of which probably was paid in. No fewer than eight people were involved in the venture; Arthur L. Hawes ws president, Lee Chamberlain secretary. Chamberlain's son Henry recalled the original firm name as Pacific Automobile Stables, which served as an automobile showroom and maintenance shop. Grand manufacturing plans now called for the production of electric runabouts, stanhopes "and a big four-seater affair known as a brake." The venture quickly failed, however, and what was left was divided up between Chamberlain and Hawes. This consisted of two runabouts which the firm apparently had been renting out. According to Lee Chamberlain's recollection, the cars "would only run a few miles at a time." The L.A. address of this Pacific venture had been 331 South Main Street.

1900 Pacific, runabout, (Oakland, California) NAHC

PACIFIC — Oakland, California — (1900-1904) — Hiram T. Bradley of Oakland was described as "a mechanical engineer well and favorably known on the Pacific Coast." The gasoline carriage he completed during the summer of 1900 was a neat machine and appeared more substantially built than most of that era. It was powered by a two-cylinder 5-1/2 hp engine, with transmission of power direct from motor shaft through a variable speed device and via chain and sprocket to the rear axle. The body was so fitted to the frame to be removable in fifteen minutes for maintenance work. The total weight of the carriage, including sufficient water and gasoline for an eighty-mile run, was 960 pounds. In September of 1900 the Pacific Motor Vehicle Company was organized, with a capital stock of $100,000, to manufacture Bradley's car. Incorporators included his father John T. Bradley, and L. Luther Doble, a real estate man. J.L. Doble, J.B. McChesney and J.F. Smith. In 1903 plans were made to erect a new factory to cost $120,000 and include a "reception room for ladies; grill-room; carriage building and upholstering departments; machine and blacksmith shop; supply room and a club-room and library." This magnificent edifice seems never to have been completed, though the Pacific appears to have been built to custom order in Oakland in 1904. J. Luther Doble remained involved until early 1903 when he was sent to prison for burglarizing a Seventh Day Adventist church in town. Interestingly, following incorporation, the *Oakland Tribune* reported that plans were for production of "vehicles propelled by electricity, gasoline, compressed air and petroleum." Most probably, only gasoline cars followed, however.

PACIFIC — Renton, Washington — (1913) — This Pacific was to be a six built in two models and assembled from such standard parts available in the industry as Wisconsin engines, Hess axles, Warner gears and Gemmer steering systems. "Plans for turning out Pacific cars in the plant of the Seattle Car and Foundry Company, Renton, are rapidly assuming concrete shape," *The Horseless Age* reported in March of 1913. "Buildings have been set aside for the assembling shops and work is to begin at once on a testing track." That the work was completed and production begun has not been documented. In any case, the Seattle Company had quick second thoughts and returned to its business of building railroad cars by 1914.

PACIFIC — Seattle, Washington — (1914) — The Pacific Cyclecar Company was organized in Seattle early in 1914 with a capital stock of $40,000 by F.W Bishop, T.F. Murphine and Tom Anderson. That the firm was at that time in the process of building a prototype and that one of the company's representatives was touring Chicago and Detroit in search of the ideal motor for it is known. But this venture most likely never passed the prototype stage.

PACIFIC SPECIAL — Fruitvale, California — (1911-1913) — Fruitvale is a suburb of Oakland and in 1911 a factory there was leased by the California Motor Car Company as the home for its new Pacific Special. Earlier in the year the firm had planned to call its automobile the California, but made aware that a Los Angeles company had already preempted the name quickly came up with another one. The Pacific Special was a four-cylinder Continental-engined touring car (A.O. Smith frame) with a price tag of ₰1750. Its designer was Andrew J. Schram, erstwhile Midwest automotive engineer and now vice-president and general manager of the California Motor Car Company. Walter G. Sachs was president. "All of our body work is to be handled within our own shops," Schram said. "We are to have facilities for the construction of special types of bodies whenever such are ordered." The Pacific Special prototype was on the road for testing in late 1911; the first dozen cars were ready for delivery the following summer. Little was heard of this venture thereafter until 1913 by which time Schram had departed for the state of Washington to try again with a car named for himself and Frederick W. Cole took his place. The former Cole automobile dealer for San Francisco, Frederick Cole obviously provided needed cash to Walter Sachs who remained president of the firm which was now renamed the Cole California Car Company. Announcements later that fall revealed imminent production of a lower-priced four-cylinder or higher-priced six-cylinder Pacific Special, or possibly both. Cole and Sachs never had to make up their minds about that, however, because by early 1914 the *Oakland Tribune* carried a legal notice that the Cole California Company had defaulted on factory lease payments and a public sale would be held on April 21st. The number of Pacific Specials produced is not known; California registrations indicate a touring car with serial number 111 and a roadster with serial number 160. The car's emblem was a setting sun. Appropriately.

1895 Packard (Lucius B.), runabout, NAHC

PACKARD — Salem, Massachusetts — (1895-1898) — Lucius B. Packard had been an enthusiast of wheel transport since the late 1860's when he built the first velocipede in Peabody (Massachusetts) and the late 1870's when he built the first bicycle in Salem. In the 1890's he was a wheelwright

1898 Packard (Lucius B.), electric runabout, NAHC

and cabinetmaker in Salem, and he built three cars. The first, which he completed in 1895, was a four-wheeled runabout powered by a 2 hp American engine. "Speed is regulated by a lever at the right hand of the operator," he explained. "When the lever is erect the power is off, though the engine is still running. Moving the lever forward increases the speed, and pushing it backward decreases the speed. A small lever in the rear of the seat is for the purpose of backing the carriage." Even before he finished it, Lucius Packard had sold his car. He indicated in 1896 he built another car, this one an electric four-wheeled carriage, and he built another electric, a three-wheeler this time, in 1898. This seems to represent the total of Lucius Packard's production. He continued working out of his shop at Liberty and Derby Streets in Salem until June 25th, 1914 when the building burned to the ground. On October 14th, 1914 he died.

PACKARD

1899 Packard, runabout, OCW

PACKARD — Warren, Ohio — (1899-1903) / Detroit, Michigan — (1903-1942 et. seq.) — "Mr. Winton...replied...to the effect that the Winton waggon as it stood was the ripened and perfected product of many years of lofty thought, aided by mechanical skill of the highest grade, and could not be improved in any detail, and that if Mr. Packard wanted any of his own cats and dogs worked into a waggon, he had better build it himself, as he, Winton, would not stultify himself by any departure whatever from his own incontestably superior productions." Thus did automotive journalist Hugh Dolnar write in 1901 of the conversational exchange which had occurred two years previous and which led inexorably to the building of the first Packard. That James Ward Packard had encountered numerous problems with the Winton he had purchased in 1898 is documented in his and his brother William Doud's diaries, that he thought he could do better is very much evident, and that incontestably he did is a fact that Packard people today will not even deign to argue. Two men from Winton's camp, George Weiss and William A. Hatcher, defected to help him — and on November 6th, 1899 the first Packard was completed in the shops of the brothers' New York and Ohio Company, a successful manufacturer of incandescent lamps and transformers in Warren, Ohio. Detail refinements followed in the four further Model A's built in 1899 and the Model B which followed in 1900, of which 49 were produced. The 7 hp single-cylinder four-stroke engine which powered these early Packards was conventional, as was the car's two-speed planetary transmission and center chain drive. Most

unusual, however, and only years later to become standard automobile practice, were the Packard's automatic spark advance and "H" gear slot. On September 10th, 1900 the Ohio Automobile Company was officially organized for the manufacture of the Packard automobile, with the Packard Brothers, Weiss, Hatcher and James P. Gilbert (from the Packards' electric business) as stockholders. "Ask the Man Who Owns One" became the company's slogan in the fall of 1901. Among Packard owners already were William D. Rockefeller, who previously had favored Wintons but who purchased his first two (of many subsequent) Packards at the New York Automobile Show in November 1900. Exhibited there was the new 1901 12 hp Model C, with wheel steering, which would be followed in 1902 by the Model F in which a three-speed sliding gear transmission replaced the former planetary. Purchasing a Model F (his second Packard) was a wealthy Detroit businessman named Henry B. Joy, who also began purchasing quantities of stock in the Ohio Automobile Company. The stage was being set. On October 13th, 1902, the Ohio Automobile Company became the Packard Motor Car Company, with 2500 additional shares of stock authorized for sale, all of them bought by Henry Joy and his associates. One year later — on October 10th, 1903 — the Packard Motor Car Company moved to Detroit. The decision to relocate there had been made in January 1903, with construction begun that spring on a huge and modern reinforced concrete factory designed by Albert Kahn. Meanwhile, in Warren, the Model K, Packard's first four, was in production, replacing Packard's first twin, the Model G introduced during the summer of '02. Still, it was the venerable single-cylinder Model F which provided the most news for Packard during the summer of 1903 with the epic 61-day drive from San Francisco to New York made by Tom Fetch in the car nicknamed Old Pacific, which beat the Winton's record set the month previous by two days. Fetch's companion on the trip had been Marius Krarup, editor of *The Automobile;* the press coverage, needless to say, was lavish. By early fall the Packard making news was a racing Model K called Gray Wolf driven by the man who had designed it and the production Model K: former Mors engineer Charles Schmidt. Schmidt tended to crash the car on occasion but his straightaway mile record of 77.6 mph at Daytona (subsequently broken by Henry Ford's 999) in January 1904, and his fourth place in the inaugural Vanderbilt Cup that October, were fine efforts. (Schmidt, who had been hired by Joy, would leave Packard for Peerless in January of 1905, being replaced as chief engineer by Russell Huff, who had joined the company at the turn of the century.) By the time of the Vanderbilt, Packard had been in Detroit a year, where production of the new Model L (introduced in November of '03) was ongoing. And by now too, the future course of Packard was being indelibly writ. Neither Weiss nor Hatcher had made the move to Detroit, and the Packards themselves would soon be out of the Packard picture. Further, the Model L introduced the radiator configuration which would become a Packard hallmark for decades to follow. The L and the subsequent N were L-head fours, the first T-head Packard arrived with the S in 1906, superseded by the famous Model Thirty which began its five-year run in model year 1907, accompanied by the smaller companion Model Eighteen for 1909. Packard was solidly established with these cars: Total company production through the Model S had been 1691 cars, there would be 11,818 Models Thirty and Eighteen built. Among the very fine cars being produced in America, there were three P's now: Packard, Pierce-Arrow and Peerless. Packard's first six, a four-main-bearing T-head introduced in April 1911 at 74 bhp, was up to 82 bhp in 1912, when a smaller seven-main-bearing L-head 60 hp six — with electric starter and lights, and left hand drive — joined the line in December that year. Spiral bevel gears were introduced on the larger six in April 1914. By now Packard had the services of two men who would be inextricably linked with the marque for decades thereafter: In 1911 Henry Joy had hired Alvan Macauley, general manager of the Burroughs Adding Machine Company, as Packard's general manager; and Macauley (who would succeed to Packard's presidency in 1916) in turn hired a Burroughs colleague, Jesse G. Vincent, to head Packard engineering in 1912. The Twin Six arrived for 1916. The first twelve-cylinder car put into series production anywhere in the world, and attractively priced as low as $2600 at introduction in 1915, the Twin Six would be built until 1923, by which time more than 35,000 (four times that of the preceding sixes) had been sold. An L-head 60° vee, the engine was refined in subsequent years, detachable cylinder heads arriving for 1917 and the Fuelizer added for 1920. The Twin Six years were heady ones for Packard, though not heady enough for Henry Joy, whose expansionist tendencies had brought Packard to eminence but who left the Packard chairmanship in 1917 purportedly because his further ideas for broadening Packard's place in the industry included merger, and few members of the board then believed it would benefit Packard to merge with anyone. The World War I years saw Packard's eminence enhanced even further via the company's role in development of the Liberty, the finest airplane engine produced up to that time (according to Orville Wright), which, installed in a special Packard racer, broke all existing track records at Sheepshead Bay in 1917, and powered hundreds of aircraft sent Over There prior to the Armistice. By 1920 the Packard Motor Car Company stood ready to roar with the Twenties. Introduced that year was the L-head Single Six joining the Twin Six, the latter car replaced by the L-head Single Eight for 1924, during which year four-wheel brakes were introduced. Packard production for calendar year 1925 was 32,027, twice that of '24. By now Packard was being flattered by imitation, its classic radiator shape adapted by Buick and Dagmar among others, though when Dagmar also adopted red hexagonal hubcaps, Packard's legal department was not so flattered to avoid mentioning that the Packard hubs were a registered trademark. "Original Creations by Master Designers" was the phrase Packard used in 1926 to announce its inauguration of series custom cars designed by custom coachbuilders. Bijur chassis lubrication had been introduced in 1925; hypoid gears followed in 1927. In 1928, in memory of James Ward Packard who died that year, the Packard family crest became the official Packard emblem. In 1929 all Packards had eight cylinders. Aware of Cadillac's forthcoming V-16, Packard had built an experimental Monobloc Twelve in 1929, but for production in 1930 countered Cadillac's multi-cylinders with the eight-cylinder 734 Speedster series which could be had with a high compression head for 145 bhp at 3400 rpm. But in 1932 the Twin Six arrived with 160 hp, as Packard went twelve again. (Twin Six would be the car's designation only in '32, incidentally; it became simply the Twelve for the remainder of its production run through 1939.) Interestingly, this car was initially planned for front wheel drive, but the prototype (designed by Cornelius Van Ranst, who had been part of the L-29 Cord team) was as far as that project proceeded. Front wheel drive had been considered because it would have made feasible a multi-cylinder automobile at an attractive price, but with the reversion to a standard chassis (featuring synchromesh and vacuum-boosted four wheel brakes), Packard's twelve-cylinder car was brought to market with price tags from $3650 to $7950. Joining it in '32 was a popularly-priced Packard, the 110 hp Light Eight introduced at $1750 and surviving one year only. From a calendar year production in 1928 which just missed the 50,000 mark, Packard plunged precipitously to 9010 in 1932, 9893 in 1933, 6265 in 1934, ironically these years producing what many people today believe to be the most beautiful Packards ever. In 1935 the One-Twenty arrived with 110 hp L-head eight-cylinder engine, independent front suspension, hydraulic brakes and a price range of $980-$1095 — vis-a-vis the Eight/Super Eight range that year of $2385-$5815 and the Twelves at $3820-$6435. Packard had moved into the lower-priced range. An even less expensive ($795-$1295 at introduction) L-head 100 hp six was added for 1937. Calendar year production soared: 52,045 cars in 1935, 80,987 in 1936, 109,518 in 1937. That the Junior Packards (as these lesser-priced cars became known, the more expensive cars of course becoming the Seniors) resulted in a loss of prestige to the Packard luxury car image from which the company never recovered has since been vigorously debated. But undoubtedly the Packard company could not have survived the Depression without this product line. From 1935 to 1942, a total of 479,500 Junior Packards were produced, about 42,000 of the Senior cars. Whether Packard should have called its cheaper car something else is really the only factor worthy of argument — and could be debated both ways; Marmon did very poorly with its cheaper Roosevelt, Cadillac did well with its LaSalle though not in numbers approaching the output of the Junior Packards. By the late Thirties, the Senior Packards were being produced in rapidly diminishing numbers. The Twelve was discontinued after 1939; 1940 saw 7500 Senior eights built, 1941 not quite 4500. Custom coachwork was still available on these cars, the most memorable perhaps the Packards designed by Howard "Dutch" Darrin, who also plied his art on Junior Packard chassis. The Weather-Conditioner — an air conditioning unit only partially effective — was introduced as an option for 1940, amd 1941 brought the Clipper, a strikingly good-looking car whose design is credited chiefly to Darrin, though others kibitzed. Priced midway between the top-rung Junior and bottom-rung Senior Packard, the Clipper was designed to give a shot in the arm to company sales which had languished since the 1938 recession year, principally because Packard styling had not kept pace with the industry. That it succeeded is indicated by 1941 calendar year figures when more Clippers (16,600) were sold than any other model in the Packard line. Overall, in 1941, Packard outproduced Cadillac Division. During World War II the Packard Motor Car Company sold the dies for both the Junior and Senior Packards to the U.S.S.R., where the Packard reappeared as the Russian Z.I.S. in 1945. In 1946 all Packards of necessity had to be the Clipper, which given its prewar welcome could not be regarded as unfortunate. Unfortunate, however, were the problems which befell the company postwar — and the tragic mistakes made — which ultimately resulted in the proud name of Packard being forever stilled in the industry in the late Fifties.

Packard Data Compilation
by Dr. William Bell

1899

1899 Packard, model A, runabout, JAC

PACKARD — MODEL A — ONE: The first test run of the first Packard was November 6th, 1899, the *Warren* (Ohio) *Tribune* reporting, "the successful completion of the machine will probably mean a factory for automobiles in this city." Five Model A Packards were built, with construction on all of them having begun by the end of 1899. Ostensibly all of these cars might be regarded as prototypes for production, since there were differences in each and continuing refinements. The famous Packard H-gate shift lever was installed on the first car soon after the test run. The fifth and final Model A was the first Packard sold, to George D. Kirkham, a Warren businessman.

ENGINE: Horizontal. One, 4-cycle. Cast iron block. B & S: 5-1/2 in. x 6 in. Disp.: 142.6 cu. in. Brake H.P.: 9 @ 800 R.P.M. Valve lifters: Mechanical exhaust, intake suction. Carb.: float-feed.

CHASSIS: W.B.: 71-1/2 in. Tires: 34 x 3.

TECHNICAL: Planetary transmission. Speeds: 2F/1R. Chain drive. Bicycle-type wheels.

1899
Model A, 1-cyl.

		FP	5	4	3	2	1
Rds		—		value not estimable			

1900

1900 Packard, model B, runabout, HAC

PACKARD — MODEL B — ONE: The first production Packard was the Model B, introduced during the spring of 1900, with 49 built by the end of the year. Engineering features included an automatic spark advance with rotating governor and a foot pedal to control engine speed. Only one body style, a single-seat roadster, was available at $1200, though dos-a-dos seating was available as an option. Steering was by spade handle lever, upon which a bulb horn was fitted. A foot chime was also provided. A single solar light was mounted in front. The Model B was displayed at the New York Automobile Show in November 1900, and it continued to be listed in the 1901 Packard catalog as a "lower horsepower" companion to the new Model C.

ENGINE: Horizontal. One, 4-cycle. Cast iron block. B & S: 5-1/2 in. x 6 in. Disp.: 142.6 cu. in. Brake H.P.: 9 @ 800 R.P.M. Valve lifters: Mechanical exhaust, intake suction. Carb.: float-feed.

CHASSIS: W.B.: 76 in. Tires: 34 x 3.

TECHNICAL: Planetary transmission. Speeds: 2F/1R. Chain drive. Wire spoke wheels.

OPTIONS: Dos-a-Dos seat (50.00). Tops (50.00-75.00).

1900
Model B, 1-cyl.

		FP	5	4	3	2	1
Rds		—		value not estimable			

1901

1901 Packard, model C, runabout, OCW

PACKARD — MODEL C — ONE: The Model C was the first Packard to feature a steering wheel which, with its spoke-mounted bulb horn, was mounted on the right side of the car. The foot chime was continued as standard. A pair of Dietz oil lamps replaced the single solar lamp provided in the Model B. Horsepower was now up to 12. The dos-a-dos body style was standard, with a forward-facing rear seat also available, in addition to a surrey. Prices for these three body styles was a uniform $1500. Three factory and two private Packards were entered in the New York to Buffalo race of 1901, four of them receiving first-class certificates. Top speed of the Model C was 25 mph, though Packard offered a third gear ''for up to 30 miles per hour . . . if desired.'' A total of 81 of these cars was built.

I.D. DATA: Engine No. Starting: 29. Ending: 140.

Model No.	Body Type & Seating	Price	Weight	Prod. Total
C	Rds.-single seat	1500	—	—
C	Rds.-dos-a-dos seat	1500	—	—
C	Surrey-4P	1500	—	—
C	Rds.-w/rear seat	1500	—	—

ENGINE: Horizontal. One, 4-cycle. Cast iron block. B & S: 6 in. x 6-1/2 in. Disp.: 183.8 cu. in. Brake H.P.: 12 @ 850 R.P.M. Net H.P.: 12. Main bearings: Two. Valve lifters: Mechanical exhaust, intake suction. Carb.: float-feed.

CHASSIS: W.B. 76 in. Tires: 34 x 4.

TECHNICAL: Planetary. Speeds: 2F/1R. Chain drive. Wire spoke wheels.

OPTIONS: Top grade leather seat cover. Tops (50.00-75.00).

HISTORICAL: Introduced November, 1900. Model year production: 81.

1901
Model C, 1-cyl.

	FP	5	4	3	2	1
Rds	—				value not estimable	

1902

1902 Packard, model F, Special for J.W. Packard, OCW

PACKARD — MODEL F — ONE: Though retaining the same engine as the Model C, the Model F was a vastly changed car and marked the beginning of Packard's evolution from buggy-type to automobile. Wheelbase was 84 inches, a rear tonneau was available, wooden artillery wheels were used, and the transmission was now a three-speed selective. Two acetylene headlights were added, the side oil lamps being retained. In an economy contest, a Model F averaged 27-1/2 mpg. At $2500 for the tonneau, this was the most expensive Packard to date. The Model F was continued into the 1903 model year, with detail refinements (including a four-inch increase in wheelbase) and lower prices ($2300 for tonneau). It was a Model F named Old Pacific that made the celebrated run from San Francisco to New York during the summer of 1903, Tom Fetch driving, Marius Krarup assisting.

I.D. DATA: Engine No. Starting: 141. Ending: 241.

Model No.	Body Type & Seating	Price	Weight	Prod. Total
F	Rds.-2P	2250	—	—
F	Rear Tonneau-5P	2500	—	—

Note: Prices reduced to $2000 and $2300 for 1903 model year.

ENGINE: Horizontal. One, 4-cycle. Cast iron block. B & S: 6 in. x 6-1/2 in. Disp.: 183.8 cu. in. Brake H.P.: 12 @ 850 R.P.M. Net H.P.: 12. Main bearings: Two. Valve lifters: Intake suction. Carb.: float-feed.

CHASSIS: W.B.: 84 in., increased to 88 in. for 1903 model year. Tires: 34 x 4.

1902 Packard, model F, tonneau, HAC

TECHNICAL: Sliding gear transmission. Speeds: 3F/1R. Clutch: Chain drive with spur differential. Hand and foot brakes, on rear wheels only. Wood artillery wheels.

OPTIONS: Tonneau seating (250.00). Top grain leather seat covers.

HISTORICAL: Introduced November, 1901. Model year (1902-1903) sales: 179.

PACKARD — MODEL G — TWO: The Model G was Packard's first and only two-cylinder car, though it was essentially arrived at by simply joining together two singles, each with its own carburetor. Large bulbous hubs extended out from the artillery wheels, and the cars were very weighty at about 4000 pounds. Only four were built.

Model No.	Body Type & Seating	Price	Weight	Prod. Total
G	Rear Tonneau-8P	—	—	—
G	Surrey-4P	—	—	—

ENGINE: Horizontal, opposed. Two. Cast iron block. Brake H.P.: 24. Net H.P.: 24. Valve lifters: Suction intake. Carb.: float-feed.

CHASSIS: W.B.: 91 in. Tires: 36 x 4-1/2.

TECHNICAL: Sliding gear transmission. Speeds: 3F/1R. Mechanical brakes on two wheels. Artillery wheels.

OPTIONS: Front instruments. Speedometer. Sight oil & gas gauges. Ignition switch.

HISTORICAL: Introduced late summer 1902. Model year production: 4.

1903

1903 Packard, model F, ''Old Pacific'', HFM

PACKARD — MODEL F — ONE: The Model F was continued with detail refinements as a 1903 model. Included among the changes was a more sloping Renault-type hood and a longer (88-in.) wheelbase. See 1902 for further description.

PACKARD — MODEK K — FOUR: At more than $7000, the Model K was one of the most expensive cars in America in 1903. No regular production Packard would ever again be priced that high. The first Packard with its engine located in front, and the first four-cylinder Packard as well, the K also featured the company's first use of a four-speed transmission. Thoroughly disliked by Henry Joy, production totaled just 34 units. Packard engineer Charles Schmidt did enjoy some success racing the Model K Gray Wolf, however, including a run at Ormond-Daytona Beach where he put up a 77.6 mph mile.

Model No.	Body Type & Seating	Price	Weight	Prod. Total
K	Rear Tonneau	7300	—	—
K	King of Belgium Tonneau	7300	—	—

ENGINE: Inline. Four. Cast iron block. B & S: 4 in. x 5 in. Brake H.P.: 24 @ 1000 R.P.M. Net H.P.: 24. Valve lifters: Automatic inlet. Carb.: float-feed.

CHASSIS: W.B.: 92 in. Tires: 36 x 4.

TECHNICAL: Sliding gear transmission. Speeds: 4F/1R. Shaft drive. Bevel gear differential. Mechanical brakes, on two rear wheels. Artillery wheels.

HISTORICAL: Introduced November, 1902. Model year production: 34.

1902-03
Model F, 4-cyl.

	FP	5	4	3	2	1
Tr	4850	9000	18,000	30,000	42,000	60,000

1904

1904 Packard, model L, runabout, HFM

PACKARD — MODEL L — FOUR: The distinctive Packard radiator outline and flat-hood configuration arrived with the Model L. A combination transmission-differential was located over the rear axle. The body was aluminum over wood, with aluminum also used for the crankcase. Top speed of the car was 40 mph, though widely touted was the "1000 Miles at 33-1/2 Miles Per Hour" that had been achieved in a company test. The standard paint combination for the Model L was Richelieu blue body with black molding and cream yellow striping, the running gear cream yellow with black and blue striping. Standard equipment included two side oil lamps, one rear oil lamp, bulb horn and tube, front and rear storm aprons, and a tool kit.

I.D. DATA: Engine No. Starting: 501. Ending: 705.

Model No.	Body Type & Seating	Price	Weight	Prod. Total
L	Tonneau	3000	1900	—
L	Surrey	3000	1900	—
L	Runabout	3000	1900	—

ENGINE: L-head. Four. Cast iron block. B & S: 3-7/8 in. x 5-1/8 in. Disp.: 241.7 cu. in. Brake H.P.: 22 @ 900 R.P.M. Net H.P.: 22. Main bearings: Three. Carb.: float-feed.

CHASSIS: W.B.: 94 in. Tires: 34 x 4.

TECHNICAL: Sliding gear transmission on rear axle. Speeds: 3F/1R. Bevel gear differential. Mechanical brakes on two rear wheels. Artillery wheels.

OPTIONS: Wicker side baskets. Head lamps, sight feed oil gauge.

HISTORICAL: Introduced November, 1903. Model year production: 207.

1904
Model L, 4-cyl.

	FP	5	4	3	2	1
Tr	3500	7500	15,000	25,000	35,000	50,000

Model M, 4-cyl.

	FP	5	4	3	2	1
Tr	3500	7500	15,000	25,000	35,000	50,000

1905

1905 Packard, model N, limousine, OCW

PACKARD — MODEL N — FOUR: The Model N marked the beginning of Packard's expansion of body styles, five being offered this year ranging from runabout to limousine in a price range from $3400 to $4600. The wheelbase was extended a foot, and the four-cylinder engine had six more horses than the previous Model L. A single-jet carburetor with auxiliary automatic inlet and warm water jacket was a new feature. In addition, tonneaus were now double-side-entrance instead of the previous rear-entrance. Standard equipment included two side oil lamps, one rear oil lamp, brackets for head lights, complete tool kit, tire repair kit, front and rear storm aprons.

I.D. DATA: Engine Nos. Starting: 1002. Ending: 1405.

Model No.	Body Type & Seating	Price	Weight	Prod. Total
N	Brgm.	4100	—	—
N	Tr.	3600	—	—
N	Rbt.	3400	—	—
N	Limo.	4600	—	—
N	Tonneau	3675	—	—

ENGINE: L-head. Four. Cast iron block. B & S: 4-1/16 in. x 5-1/8 in. Disp.: 265.7 cu. in. Brake H.P.: 28 @ 900 R.P.M. Net H.P.: 28. Main bearings: Three. Valve lifters: Mechanical. Carb.: float-feed.

CHASSIS: W.B.: 106 in. Tires: 34 x 4.

TECHNICAL: Sliding gear transmission on rear axle. Speeds: 3F/1R. Expanding flywheel clutch. Shaft drive. Bevel gear differential. External clamping & internal expanding brakes on two rear wheels. Wood artillery wheels.

OPTIONS: Cowl lamps. Head lamps. Wicker side baskets.

HISTORICAL: Introduced November, 1904. Model year production: 403.

1905
Model N, 4-cyl.

	FP	5	4	3	2	1
Tr	3500	6000	12,000	20,000	28,000	40,000

1906

PACKARD — MODEL S or 24 — FOUR: The Model S was also known as the 24, indicating horsepower ostensibly although tests showed as much as 40-50 hp being developed by the S's four-cylinder engine. First of the Packard T-heads, this engine also marked the first use of magneto jump spark ignition. A hydraulic governor was fitted to the engine. Wheelbases were stretched to 119 inches (except for the runabout) and made for considerably more commodious tonneaus. Introduced this year was the soon-to-be-famous Packard hexagon-shaped hubcap; their centers were painted black on the Model S and ensuing models, until 1913 when the black was changed to red and remained so for the next 40 years.

I.D. DATA: Engine No. Starting: 2003. Ending: 2739.

Model No.	Body Type & Seating	Price	Weight	Prod. Total
24	Tr.	4000	—	—
24	Rbt.	4000	—	—
24	Limo.	5200	—	—
24	Land.	5225	—	—
24	Victoria	4189	—	—

ENGINE: T-head. Four. Cast iron block. B & S: 4-1/2 in. x 5-1/2 in. Disp.: 349.9 cu. in. Brake H.P.: 24 @ 650 R.P.M. Net H.P.: 24. Main bearings: Three. Valve lifters: Solid. Carb.: float-feed with water jacket.

CHASSIS: W.B.: 119 in. (Rbt. 108 in.) Tires: 34 x 4 front, 34 x 4-1/2 rear.

1906 Packard, model S, runabout, OCW

TECHNICAL: Sliding gear transmission on rear axle. Speeds: 3F/1R. Expanding flywheel clutch. Shaft drive. Bevel gear differential. Mechanical brakes on two rear wheels. Wood artillery wheels.

OPTIONS: Single sidemount.

HISTORICAL: Introduced September, 1905. Model year sales: 728.

1906
Model S, 4-cyl., 24 hp

	FP	5	4	3	2	1
Tr	4200	6000	12,000	20,000	28,000	40,000

1907

1907 Packard, model Thirty, runabout, HAC

PACKARD — MODEL THIRTY (U) — FOUR: The new Thirty was basically a refinement over the previous S. Cylinder tops and valve chambers now had a flat top instead of the previous dome, and valves were larger. Front wheels now ran on ball instead of roller bearings. The wheelbase was slightly longer, most of the added length in the hood. Added to the usual standard equipment were headlights, irons for an extension cape cart top, and the tire repair kit now included jack and pump, and irons for carrying extra tires.

I.D. DATA: Engine No. Starting: 3003. Ending: 4134.

Model No.	Body Type & Seating	Price	Weight	Prod. Total
30 (U)	Rbt.	4200	—	—
30 (U)	Tr.	4200	—	—
30 (U)	Limo.	5500	—	—
30 (U)	Land.	5600	—	—

ENGINE: T-head. Four. Cast iron block. B & S: 5 in. x 5-1/2 in. Disp.: 431.9 cu. in. Brake H.P.: 30 @ 650 R.P.M. Net H.P.: 30. Main bearings: Three. Valve lifters: Solid. Carb.: float-feed, warm water jacket.

CHASSIS: W.B.: 122 in. Tires: 34 x 4 front, 34 x 4-1/2 rear. Runabout W.B.: 108 in. Tires: 34 x 3-1/2 front, 34 x 4 rear.

TECHNICAL: Sliding gear transmission on rear axle. Speeds: 3F/1R. Expanding flywheel clutch. Shaft drive. Bevel gear differential. Mechanical brakes on rear wheels only. Wood, artillery wheels.

HISTORICAL: Introduced August, 1906. Model year sales: 1,128.

1907
Model U, 4-cyl., 30 hp

	FP	5	4	3	2	1
Tr	4200	6750	13,500	22,500	31,500	45,000

1908

1908 Packard, model Thirty, runabout, OCW

PACKARD — MODEL THIRTY (UA) — FOUR: A longer wheelbase and larger wheels were among the few changes in the UA model of 1908. The frame was slightly lowered. A bayonet-type locking radiator cap (also seen on some of the final 1907 cars) became standard, replacing the former screw cap. One new body style was introduced, a close-coupled touring with one-person rumble seat.

I.D. DATA: Engine No. Starting: 5006. Ending: 6311.

Model No.	Body Type & Seating	Price	Weight	Prod. Total
30 (UA)	Rbt.	4200	—	—
30 (UA)	Tr.	4200	—	—
30 (UA)	Limo.	5500	—	—
30 (UA)	Limo.	5600	—	—
30 (UA)	Close-coupled Tr.	—	—	—

ENGINE: T-head. Four. Cast iron block. B & S: 5 in. x 5-1/2 in. Disp.: 431.9 cu. in. Brake H.P.: 30 @ 650 R.P.M. Net H.P.: 30. Main bearings: Three. Valve lifters: Solid. Carb.: float-feed, warm water jacket.

CHASSIS: W.B.: 123-1/2 in. Tires: 36 x 4 front, 36 x 4-1/2 rear. Runabout W.B.: 108 in. Tires: 36 x 3-1/2 front, 36 x 4 rear.

TECHNICAL: Sliding gear transmission on rear axle. Speeds: 3F/1R. Expanding ring clutch. Shaft drive & bevel gear differential. Mechanical brakes on rear wheels. Wood artillery wheels.

OPTIONS: Victoria top (325.00). Glass-back canopy top (470.00). Adjustable glass windshield (70.00). Special colors, body and gear (50.00).

HISTORICAL: Introduced May, 1907. Model year production: 1303.

1908
Model UA, 4-cyl., 30 hp

	FP	5	4	3	2	1
Tr	4200	7500	15,000	25,000	35,000	50,000
Rds	4200	6600	13,200	22,000	30,800	44,000

1909

PACKARD — MODEL EIGHTEEN (NA) — FOUR: The Model Eighteen was the first attempt to down-size a Packard. It was built with the same "quality at all costs" that typified the Model Thirty. The car featured a smaller engine and shorter wheelbase — and price tags about $1000 less. It was not as successful as the company had hoped, being outsold by the Model Thirty by about two to one this year, even more in succeeding years. Initially offered in runabout, limousine, landaulet and touring body styles, a demi-limousine was added to the line in December of 1909.

I.D. DATA: Engine No. Starting: 9001. Ending: 9801.

Model No.	Body Type & Seating	Price	Weight	Prod. Total
18 (NA)	Rbt.	3200	—	—
18 (NA)	Limo.	4300	—	—
18 (NA)	Land.	2900	—	—
18 (NA)	Tr.	3200	—	—
18 (NA)	Demi. Limo.	—		

ENGINE: T-head. Four. Cast iron block. B & S: 4-1/16 in. x 5-1/8 in. Disp.: 265.7 cu. in Brake H.P.: 18 @ 650 R.P.M. Net H.P.: 18. Main bearings: Three. Valve lifters: Solid. Carb.: float-feed, warm water jacket.

CHASSIS: W.B. 112 in. Tires: 34 x 4. Runabout W.B.: 102 in. Tires: 34 x 3-1/2 front, 34 x 4 rear.

TECHNICAL: Sliding gear transmission on rear axle. Speeds: 3F/1R. Expanding flywheel clutch. Shaft drive & bevel gear differential. Mechanical brakes on two rear wheels. Wood artillery wheels.

OPTIONS: Cape cart top (135.00). Victoria top (150.00). Material seat covers (67.50 touring, 32.50 runabout). Special colors, body and gear (50.00).

HISTORICAL: Introduced summer 1908. Model year production: 802.

1909 Packard, model Thirty, demi-limousine, OCW

PACKARD — MODEL THIRTY (UB, UBS) — FOUR: Changes were few in the Thirty for 1909. The radiator was revised to a cellular type, and a four-gallon gasoline reserve tank was added. A redesigned linkage eliminated the necessity for the separate reverse lever which had been present on all Packards since 1904. The front fenders were hooded, with a mudguard placed between frame and runningboards. UB was the designation for all body styles (including the new demi-limousine introduced in December), except for the short wheelbase runabout which was designated UBS.

I.D. DATA: Engine No. Starting: 6481 & 7501. Ending: 7086 & 8999.

Model No.	Body Type & Seating	Price	Weight	Prod. Total
30 UBS	Rbt.	4200	—	—
30 UB	Tour.	4200	—	—
30 UB	Limo.	5500	—	—
30 UB	Land.	5600	—	—
30 UB	Close-Coupled Tour.	—	—	—
30 UB	Demi-Limo.	—	—	—

ENGINE: T-head. Four. Cast iron block. B & S: 5 in. x 5-1/2 in. Disp.: 431.9 cu. in. Brake H.P.: 30 @ 650 R.P.M. Net H.P.: 30. Main bearings: Three. Valve lifters: Mechanical. Carb.: float-feed, warm water jacket.

CHASSIS: [Thirty UB] W.B.: 123-1/2 in. Tires: 36 x 4 front, 36 x 4-1/2 rear. [Thirty UBS] W.B.: 108 in. [Runabout] Tires: 36 x 3-1/2 front, 36 x 4-1/2 rear.

TECHNICAL: Sliding gear transmission on rear axle. Speeds: 3F/1R. Expanding flywheel clutch. Shaft drive & bevel gear differential. Mechanical brakes on rear wheels only. Wood, artillery wheels.

HISTORICAL: Introduced summer 1908. Model year production: 1,501.

1909
Model UB UBS, 4-cyl., 30 hp

	FP	5	4	3	2	1
Tr	4200	8250	16,500	27,500	38,500	55,000
Rbt	4200	6450	12,900	21,500	30,100	43,000
Model NA, 4-cyl., 18 hp						
Tr	3200	6000	12.000	20.000	28.000	40.000

1910

PACKARD — MODEL EIGHTEEN (NB) — FOUR: The Model Eighteen for 1910 shared the same refinements as the Model Thirty. The new phaeton body style which was provided on the Thirty was not made available on the Eighteen, however, nor was the demi-limousine continued as a catalogued Eighteen model. Model Eighteen body styles now numbered just four. This year the Model Thirty outsold the Eighteen by more than three to one.

I.D. DATA: Engine No. Starting: 120001. Ending: 12837.

Model No.	Body Type & Seating	Price	Weight	Prod. Total
18 (NB)	Rbt.	3200	—	—
18 (NB)	Tr.	3200	—	—
18 (NB)	Limo.	4400	—	—
18 (NB)	Land.	4500	—	—

ENGINE: T-head. Four. Cast iron block. B & S: 4-1/16 in. x 5-1/8 in. Disp.: 267.5 cu. in. Brake H.P.: 18 @ 650 R.P.M. Net H.P.: 18. Main bearings: Three. Valve lifters: Solid. Carb.: float-feed, warm water jacket.

CHASSIS: W.B.: 112 in. Tires: 34 x 4. [Runabout] W.B.: 102 in. Tires: 34 x 3-1/2 front, 34 x 4 rear.

TECHNICAL: Sliding gear transmission. Speeds: 3F/1R. Dry plate clutch. Bevel gear differential. Mechanical brakes on two rear wheels. Wood artillery wheels.

HISTORICAL: Introduced summer 1909. Model year production: 766.

1910 Packard, model Thirty, runabout, OCW

PACKARD — MODEL THIRTY (UC, UCS) — FOUR: Engineering changes for the Thirty UC included replacement of the expanding ring clutch (which had been fitted for a half decade) with a dry plate type, and the addition of shock absorbers as standard equipment to smooth out the suspension. The front fenders were more massive, the mudguard between them and the body deeper. Also enlarged was the steering wheel, its wood rim now extending to the wheel's periphery and to part of the spokes. A phaeton was a new body style.

I.D. DATA: Engine No. Starting: (UC) 10000, (UCS) 13001. Ending: (UC) 11999, (UCS) 13518.

Model No.	Body Type & Seating	Price	Weight	Prod. Total
30 (UCS)	Rbt.	4200	—	—
30 (UC)	Tr.	4200	—	—
30 (UC)	Limo.	5500	—	—
30 (UC)	Land.	5600	—	—
30 (UC)	CC. Twn. Car	NA	NA	NA
30 (UC)	Demi-Limo.	NA	NA	NA
30 (UC)	Phae.	NA	NA	NA

ENGINE: T-head. Four. Cast iron block. B & S: 5 in. x 5-1/2 in. Disp.: 431.9 cu. in. Brake H.P.: 30 @ 650 R.P.M. Net H.P.: 30. Main bearings: Three. Valve lifters: Mechanical.

CHASSIS: [Model 30 UC] W.B.: 123-1/2 in. Tires: 36 x 4 front, 36 x 4-1/2 rear. [Model 30 UCS] W.B.: 108 in. Tires: 36 x 3-1/2 front. 36 x 4-1/2 rear.

TECHNICAL: Sliding gear transmission. Speeds: 3F/1R. Dry plate clutch. Bevel gear differential. Mechanical brakes on two rear wheels. Wood artillery wheels.

HISTORICAL: Introduced summer, 1909. Model year production: 2,493.

1911

1911 Packard, model Eighteen, close coupled touring, OCW

PACKARD — MODEL EIGHTEEN (NC) — FOUR: The Eighteen NC shared the changes made to the Thirty UD. Although the smaller Packard did not share the variety of body styles available for the Thirty, it did receive a new close-coupled touring and coupe this year. Sales of fewer than 400 cars were disappointing, however, vis-a-vis the Thirty's more than 1800.

I.D. DATA: Engine No. Starting: 180001. Ending: 19176.

Model No.	Body Type & Seating	Price	Weight	Prod. Total
18 (NC)	Rbt.	3200	—	—
18 (NC)	Tr.	3200	—	—
18 (NC)	Limo.	4400	—	—
18 (NC)	Land.	4500	—	—
18 (NC)	Close-Coupled	3200	—	—
18 (NC)	Coupe	3900	—	—

ENGINE: T-head. Four. Cast iron block. B & S: 4-1/16 in. x 5-1/8 in. Disp.: 267.5 cu. in. Brake H.P.: 18 @ 650 R.P.M. Net H.P.: 18. Main bearings: Three. Valve lifters: Solid. Carb.: float-feed, warm water jacket.

CHASSIS: W.B.: 112 in. Tires: 34 x 4. [Runabout] W.B.: 102 in. Tires: 34 x 3-1/2 front, 34 x 4 rear.

TECHNICAL: Sliding gear transmission. Speeds: 3F/1R. Dry plate clutch. Bevel gear differential. Mechanical brakes on two rear wheels. Wood artillery wheels.

OPTIONS: Fore-doors for limousine and landaulet (200.00). Seat covers (30.00 to 60.00). Storm-tilt windshield (60.00).

HISTORICAL: Introduced summer 1910. Model year production: 360.

PACKARD — MODEL THIRTY (UD, UDS) — FOUR: The big news from Packard this year was a new standard paint scheme, Packard blue with gray striping for bodies; moldings, frame, hood, radiator, fenders, battery and tool boxes in black. For open cars, the wheels, axles and below-frame running gear were gray with black striping; the reverse was used on closed cars. Fore doors were available optionally. Open cars were upholstered in tufted straight-grain leather; enclosed bodies had untufted straight-grain leather in front; in the rear, tufted blue goatskin was used below the belt, with untufted blue broadcloth for roof and quarters. Engineering changes were minimal, the rear semi-elliptic suspension being beefed up with the addition of three short leaves. New options included combination oil and electric side and rear lights, and the second battery necessary for them. Two new body styles were a coupe and a brougham, for the latter of which all metal parts were nickel-plated and the interior outfitted in gray checked broadcloth.

I.D. DATA: UD engine starting: 15001. UD engine ending: 15999. UDS engine starting: 16000. UDS engine ending: 16884.

Model No.	Body Type & Seating	Price	Weight	Prod. Total
30 (UDS)	Rbt.	4200	—	—
30 (UD)	Tr.	4200	—	—
30 (UD)	Limo.	5450	—	—
30 (UD)	Close-Coupled Twn. Car	4200	—	—
30 (UD)	Brgm.	4200	—	—
30 (UD)	Phae.	5550	—	—
30 (UD)	Cpe.	4900	—	—
30 (UD)	Brgm.	—	—	—

ENGINE: T-head. Four. Cast iron block. B & S: 5 in. x 5-1/2 in. Disp.: 431.9 cu. in. Brake H.P.: 30 @ 650 R.P.M. Net H.P.: 30. Main bearings: Three. Valve lifters: Mechanical. Carb.: float feed, warm water jacket.

CHASSIS: [Thirty UD] W.B.: 123 in. Tires: 36 x 4-1/2. [Thirty UDS] W.B.: 108 in. Tires: 36 x 4-1/2.

TECHNICAL: Sliding gear transmission over rear axle. Speeds: 3F/1R. Dry plate clutch. Mechanical brakes on two wheels. Wood artillery wheels.

OPTIONS: Fore-doors for limousine and landaulet (200.00), seat covers (30.00 to 60.00); storm-tilt windshield (60.00).

HISTORICAL: Introduced summer, 1910. Model year production: 1,865.

1910-11
Model UC UCS, 4-cyl., 30 hp

	FP	5	4	3	2	1
Tr	4200	8250	16,500	27,500	38,500	55,000
Rbt	4200	6450	12,900	21,500	30,100	43,000
Model NB, 4-cyl., 18 hp						
Tr	3200	6000	12,000	20,000	28,000	40,000

1912

PACKARD — MODEL EIGHTEEN (NE) — FOUR: The re-engineered clutch design of the Thirty UE was incorporated in the Eighteen NE. (The ND designation was skipped for conformity's sake in this the last model year of the Thirty and Eighteen.) The oil and electric side and rear light combination was standard; headlights were gas. There was a reshuffling of body styles, and the runabout was given a six-inch-longer wheelbase than previously.

I.D. DATA: Engine No. Starting: 26001. Ending: 27000.

Model No.	Body Type & Seating	Price	Weight	Prod. Total
NE	Tr.	3200	—	—
NE	Rbt.	3200	—	—
NE	Limo.	4400	—	—
NE	Land.	4500	—	—
NE	Imp. Limo.	4600	—	—
NE	Cpe.	3900	—	—

ENGINE: T-head. Four. Cast iron block. B & S: 4-1/16 in. x 5-1/8 in. Disp.: 267.5 cu. in. Brake H.P.: 18 @ 650 R.P.M. Net H.P.: 18. Main bearings: Three. Valve lifters: Solid. Carb.: float-feed, warm water jacket.

1912 Packard, model Thirty, runabout, OCW

CHASSIS: W.B.: 112 in. Tires: 34 x 4. [Runabout] W.B.: 108 in. Tires: 34 x 3-1/2 front, 34 x 4 rear.

TECHNICAL: Sliding gear transmission. Speeds: 3F/1R. Dry plate clutch. Bevel gear differential. Mechanical brakes on two rear wheels. Wood artillery wheels.

HISTORICAL: Introduced summer 1911. Model year production: 350.

1912 Packard, model Thirty, touring, HAC

PACKARD — MODEL THIRTY (UE) — FOUR: The most important engineering change in the Thirty UE was the remounting of the dry disc clutch directly behind the engine, the clutch and flywheel now a rigid extension of the crankcase. Using the "S" sub-designation for the runabout was discontinued; the standard wheelbase was now 123-1/2 inches, the runabout's was six inches longer at 114, and the limousine and landaulet were now on a 129-1/2-inch wheelbase all their own. A brougham was a new body style. The combination oil and electric side and rear lights which were available optionally in 1911 were now fitted as standard equipment; headlights were gas.

I.D. DATA: Engine No. Starting: 200001. Ending: 23000.

Model No.	Body Type & Seating	Price	Weight	Prod. Total
UE	Phae.	4200	—	—
UE	Cape Cart Tr.	4200	—	—
UE	Tr.	4200	—	—
UE	Rbt.	4200	—	—
UE	Limo.	5450	—	—
UE	Land.	5550	—	—
UE	Imp. Limo.	5650	—	—
UE	Imp. Land.	5750	—	—
UE	Brgm.	5500	—	—
UE	Cpe.	4900	—	—

ENGINE: T-head. Four. Cast iron block. B & S: 5 in. x 5-1/2 in. Disp.: 431.9 cu. in. Brake H.P.: 30 @ 650 R.P.M. Net H.P.: 30. Main bearings: Three. Valve lifters: Mechanical. Carb.: float-feed, warm water, jacketed.

CHASSIS: [Thirty UE] W.B.: 123-1/2 in. Tires: 36 x 4-1/2 front, 37 x 5 rear. [Thirty Runabout] W.B.: 114 in. Tires: 36 x 4-1/2 front, 37 x 5 rear. [Limousine/Landaulet] W.B.: 129-1/2 in. Tires: 36 x 4-1/2 front, 37 x 5 rear.

TECHNICAL: Sliding gear transmission on rear axle. Speeds: 3F/1R. Dry plate clutch. Bevel gear differential. Mechanical brakes on two rear wheels. Wood artillery wheels.

HISTORICAL: Introduced summer 1911. Model year production: 1,250.

PACKARD — SERIES 1-48 — SIX: This new car was introduced simply as the Packard Six, receiving its 1-48 series designation in retrospect with the arrival of succeeding models. Cast in three blocks of two, the T-head six developed 74 brake horsepower. In road testing, a top speed of about 80 mph was recorded, with 0-60 acceleration time at 30 seconds. Three differential ratios were available. Main and reserve gas tanks were mounted under the front seat. Combination oil and electric side and tail-lamps, and gas headlamps, were fitted. The number of body styles available numbered thirteen, and in addition to the standard Packard paint scheme, a customer could have virtually his heart's desire optionally.

I.D. DATA: Engine No. Starting: 23,001. Ending: 26,000.

Model No.	Body Type & Seating	Price	Weight	Prod. Total
1-48	Tr.-7P	5000	3900	—
1-48	Phae.-5P	5000	3800	—
1-48	Rbt.-2P	5000	3300	—
1-48	Close-Coupled-5P	5000	4175	—
1-48	Victoria Tr.-7P	5250	3900	—
1-48	Victoria Phae.-5P	5215	3800	—
1-48	Canopy Tr.-7P	5445	4000	—
1-48	Limo.-7P	6250	4100	—
1-48	Land.-7P	6350	4395	—
1-48	Imp. Limo.-7P	6450	4200	—
1-48	Imp. Land.-7P	6550	4495	—
1-48	Brgm.-4P	6300	4100	—
1-48	Cpe.	5700	3700	—

ENGINE: T-head. Six. Cast iron block. B & S: 4-1/2 in. x 5-1/2 in. Disp.: 525 cu. in. Brake H.P.: 74 @ 1720 R.P.M. Net H.P.: 48. Main bearings: Four. Valve lifters: Mechanical. Carb.: Packard combined float-feed and automatic mixture regulation.

CHASSIS: W.B.: 133 in. O.L.: 183-1/2 in. Tires: 36 x 4-1/2 front, 37 x 5 rear. [Phaeton & Brougham] W.B.: 139 in. O.L.: 189-1/2 in. Tires: 36 x 4-1/2 front, 37 x 5 rear. [Coupe & Runabout] W.B.: 121-1/2 in. O.L.: 172-1/2 in. Tires: 36 x 4-1/2 front, 37 x 5 rear.

TECHNICAL: Rear mounted, sliding gear transmission. Speeds: 3F/1R. Packard multi-disc clutch. Overall ratio: 3.27. Opt.: 3.05 & 3.52. Internal expanding and external contracting brakes on two rear wheels. Wood artillery wheels.

HISTORICAL: Introduced April, 1911. Model year production: 1329.

1912
Model NE, 4-cyl., 18 hp

	FP	5	4	3	2	1
Tr	3200	6000	12,000	20,000	28,000	40,000
Rbt	3200	6150	12,300	20,500	28,700	41,000
Cpe	3900	3750	7500	12,500	17,500	25,000
Limo	4400	4800	9600	16,000	22,400	32,000
Imp Limo	4600	5250	10,500	17,500	24,500	35,000

1911-12
Model UE, 4-cyl., 30 hp

	FP	5	4	3	2	1
Tr	4200	9000	18,000	30,000	42,000	60,000
Phae	4200	9300	18,600	31,000	43,400	62,000
Rbt	4200	9600	19,200	32,000	44,800	64,000
Cpe	4900	4350	8700	14,500	20,300	29,000
Brgm	5500	4050	8100	13,500	18,900	27,000
Limo	5450	4500	9000	15,000	21,000	30,000
Imp Limo	5650	5100	10,200	17,000	23,800	34,000

1912
Model 12-48, 6-cyl., 36 hp

	FP	5	4	3	2	1
Tr	5000	11,400	22,800	38,000	56,000	76,000
Phae	5000	10,500	21,000	35,000	49,000	70,000
Rbt	5000	9900	19,800	33,000	46,200	66,000
Cpe	5700	5250	10,500	17,500	24,500	35,000
Brgm	6300	4800	9600	16,000	22,400	32,000
Limo	6250	5700	11,400	19,000	26,600	38,000
Imp Limo	6450	6000	12,000	20,000	28,000	40,000

1913

PACKARD — SERIES 1-38 — SIX: Introduced as the "38" (the Series 1-38 designation arriving later), this Packard was an L-head six cast in three blocks of two. Unlike the preceding "48," its valves were located on the right and enclosed by aluminum covers. The Series 1-38 was noteworthy as the first Packard to use an electric starter and the first to have left-hand drive. Introduced in December of 1912, it was succeeded in February of 1913 by the "1438" which was essentially a continuation of the previous car.

I.D. DATA: Engine No. Starting: 38,000. Ending: 42,000.

Model No.	Body Type & Seating	Price	Weight	Prod. Total
1-38	Tr.-5P	4150	—	—
1-38	Phae.-5P	4150	—	—
1-38	Imp. Limo.-5P	5400	4510	—
1-38	Imp. Land.-5P	—	—	—
1-38	Limo.-5P	5200	—	—
1-38	Land.-5P	5300	—	—
1-38	Phae.-4P	—	—	—
1-38	Brgm.-4P	5200	—	—
1-38	Imp. Cpe.-4P	4900	—	—
1-38	Rbt.-2P	4050	3820	—
1-38	Cpe.-2P	4500	—	—

ENGINE: L-head. Six. Cast iron block. B & S: 4 in. x 5-1/2 in. Disp.: 415 cu. in. Brake H.P.: 60 @ 1720 R.P.M. Net H.P.: 38. Main bearings: Seven. Valve lifters: Mechanical. Carb.: Packard, float-feed, acetylene primer.

CHASSIS: W.B.: 134 in. O.L.: 175-1/2 in. Tires: 36 x 4-1/2 front, 37 x 5 rear. Phaeton & brougham series W.B.: 138 in. O.L.: 179-1.4 in. Tires: 36 x 4-1/2 front, 37 x 5 rear. Runabout series W.B.: 115-1/2 in. O.L. 156-3.4 in. Tires: 34 x 4-1/2 front, 37 x 5 rear.

TECHNICAL: Rear mounted, sliding gear transmission. Speeds: 3F/1R. Dry, multi-disc clutch. Overall ratio: 3.8. Mechanical brakes on two rear wheels. Wood artillery wheels.

HISTORICAL: Introduced December, 1912. Model year production: 1,618. (includes the 1914 '1438' model which was merely the continuation of the Model 1-38, introduced in February 1913.)

1913 Packard, Series 2-48, runabout, OCW

PACKARD — SERIES 2-48 (1348) — SIX: Although an electric generator (no starter) was incorporated on the 2-48 (which also bore the designation "1348"), the car retained right-hand drive. Retained too were the combination oil and electric side and rear lights, but the handles on the former were now located on the side rather than on top of the lamp bodies. Electric headlights replaced the previous gas units. Engineering changes included direct lubrication of pison pin bearings. Motor support was now three point instead of four; the water pump and dual magneto moved to the rear. The fuel tank was removed from under the seat to the back of the car; the battery and toolbox moved from the runningboard to under the driver's seat. Horsepower of the T-head six was up to 82. The touring car now joined the phaeton and brougham on the 139-inch wheelbase; the runabout and coupe remained on the 121-1/2-inch chassis; the 133-inch chassis was retained for all other body styles.

I.D. DATA: Engine No. Starting: 35,026. Ending: 37,999.

Model No.	Body Type & Seating	Price	Weight	Prod. Total
2-48 (1348)	Brgm.-5P	5800	—	—
2-48 (1348)	Cpe.-3P	5100	—	—
2-48 (1348)	Tr.-7P	4850	4560	—
2-48 (1348)	Imp. Limo.-7P	6050	—	—
2-48 (1348)	Land.-7P	5950	—	—
2-48 (1348)	Phae.-5P	4750	4450	—
2-48 (1348)	Rbt.-5P	4650	4010	—
2-48 (1348)	Limo.	5850	—	—

ENGINE: T-head. Six. Cast iron block. Brake H.P.: 82 @ 1720 R.P.M. Net H.P.: 48. Main bearings: Four. Valve lifters: Mechanical. Carb.: float-feed, mixture regulation, acetylene primer added.

CHASSIS: W.B.: 121-1/2 - 139 in. O.L.: 172-1/2 - 189-1/2 in. Tires: 36 x 4-1/2 front, 37 x 4 rear.

TECHNICAL: Rear mounted, sliding gear transmission. Speeds: 3F/1R. Multi-disc clutch. Bevel gear rear axle. Overall ratio: 3.27. Mechanical brakes on two rear wheels. Wood artillery wheels.

HISTORICAL: Introduced June, 1912. Model year production: 1,000.

1913
Model 1-38, 6-cyl., 38 hp

Tr	4150	8250	16,500	27,500	38,500	55,000
Phae	4150	8400	16,800	28,000	39,200	56,000
4P Phae	4150	8550	17,100	28,500	39,900	57,000
Rbt	4050	6750	13,500	22,500	31,500	45,000
Cpe	4500	4800	9600	16,000	22,400	32,000
Imp Cpe	4900	4950	9900	16,500	23,100	33,000
Lan'let	5300	4800	9600	16,000	22,400	32,000
Imp Lan'let	5500	4950	9900	16,500	23,100	33,000
Limo	5200	5250	10,500	17,500	24,500	35,000
Imp Limo	5400	5550	11,100	18,500	25,900	37,000

1913
Model 13-48, 6-cyl.

Tr	4850	8250	16,500	27,500	38,500	55,000

1914

PACKARD — SERIES 1-38 — SIX: This Packard, introduced in February 1913 ostensibly as a 1914 model, was simply a continuation of the L-head 1-38 of the previous season. Company owners manuals for 1914 used the same description for this car as for the 1913 1-38. Little further data is available. One reference indicates a total of 678 cars produced.

1914 Packard, touring, OCW

1914 Packard, Series 3-48 (1448), landaulet, HAC

PACKARD — SERIES 2-38 — SIX: A new L-head engine cast in two blocks of three was the big news for the 2-38, together with the adoption of spiral bevel gears. Further engineering refinements included a hot water jacketed intake manifold, mud webs cast integrally with the crankcase, pressure-fed lubrication to 35 points, brake drums increased to 17 inches, and dual exahusts. Spare tires were now carried at the rear. The gas pedal was repositioned to the right of the brake pedal. Headlights were complete with dimmer switch. All body styles were now placed on a single 140-inch wheelbase chassis.

I.D. DATA: Engine No. Starting: 53026. Ending: 56000.

Model No.	Body Type & Seating	Price	Weight	Prod. Total
2-38	Tr.-7P	3850	—	—
2-38	Spec. Tr.-6P	3350	—	—
2-38	Salon Tr.-6P	3850	—	—
2-38	Phae.-4/5P	3750	—	—
2-38	Rbt.-2P	3750	—	—
2-38	Limo.-6P	4900	—	—
2-38	Limo.-7P	4950	—	—
2-38	Cab Sides Limo.-6P	4950	—	—
2-38	Cab Sides Limo.-7P	5000	—	—
2-38	Land.-6P	4900	—	—
2-38	Land.-7P	4950	—	—
2-38	Cab Sides Land.-7P	5000	—	—
2-38	All-Weather Conv.-7P	4525	—	—
2-38	Imp. Limo.-6P	5100	—	—
2-38	Imp. Limo.-7P	5150	—	—
2-38	Salon Limo.-7P	5100	—	—
2-38	Brgm.-6P	5000	—	—
2-38	Salon Brgm.-6P	4950	—	—
2-38	Coupe-3P	4450	—	—

ENGINE: L-head. Six. Cast iron block. B & S: 4 in. x 5-1/2 in.. Disp.: 415 cu. in. Brake H.P.: 60 @ 1720 R.P.M. Net H.P.: 38. Main bearings: Seven. Valve lifters: Mechnical. Carburetor: float-feed, acetylene primer.

CHASSIS: W.B.: 140 in. O.L.: 198 in. (201 in.-touring). Tires: 37 x 4-1/2 front, 37 x 5 rear.

TECHNICAL: Rear mounted, sliding gear transmission. Speeds: 3F/1R. Dry disc clutch. Spiral bevel gears. Overall ratio: 3.9. Optional: 3.53. Mechanical brakes on two rear wheels. Wood artillery wheels.

HISTORICAL: Introduced December, 1913. Model year production: 1501.

PACKARD — SERIES 3-48 (1448) — SIX: The 3-48 went left-hand drive, necessitating a 180° remounting of the T-head six-cylinder engine. The exhaust now vented on the right with the carburetion complex on the left. A combination self-starter and generator was fitted. Driver controls were mounted on the steering column. Spiral bevel gears were incorporated with the rear axle. A 139-inch wheelbase carried all bodies except the runabout, which was 121-1/2 in. Bodies were wider, body styles more numerous, and 42 exterior color combinations were available.

I.D. DATA: Engine No. Starting: 50026. Ending: 52000.

Model No.	Body Type & Seating	Price	Weight	Prod. Total
3-48 (1448)	Tr.-7P	4850	—	—
3-48 (1448)	Phae.-5P	4750	—	—
3-48 (1448)	Phae. Rbt.-2P	4700	—	—
3-48 (1448)	Rbt.-2P (+ rumble)	4650	—	—
3-48 (1448)	Limo.-7P	5900	—	—
3-48 (1448)	Imp. Limo.-7P	6100	—	—
3-48 (1448)	Salon Limo.-7P	6050	—	—
3-48 (1448)	Land.-7P	5900	—	—
3-48 (1448)	Cabette-4P	5800	—	—
3-48 (1448)	Brgm.-4P	5900	—	—
3-48 (1448)	Salon Brgm.-4P	5850	—	—
3-48 (1448)	Cpe.-2P	5400	—	—
3-48 (1448)	Imp. Cpe.-4P	5600	—	—
3-48 (1448)	Vic. Tr.-7P	5065	—	—

ENGINE: T-head. Six. Cast iron block. B & S: 4-1/2 in. x 5-1/2 in. Disp.: 525 cu. in. Brake H.P.: 82 @ 1720 R.P.M. Main bearings: Four. Valve lifters: Solid. Carb.: float-feed and automatic mixture regulation with primer.

CHASSIS: W.B.: 139 to 121-1/2 in. O.L.: 202 to 180 in.

TECHNICAL: Rear mounted, sliding gear transmission. Speeds: 3F/1R. Disc clutch. Shaft drive with spiral bevel gears. Mechanical brakes on two rear wheels. Wood artillery wheels.

OPTIONS: Clock. Speedometer, Trunk rack. Klaxon horn. Tire covers. Hat box. Trunk with 3 leather cases. Power tire pump. Seat covers for open cars. Ammeter. Speaking tubes. Sterling silver trim (inside).

HISTORICAL: Introduced April, 1913. Model year production: 1499.

PACKARD — SERIES 4-48 — SIX: From a four-main bearing T-head, the 48 was now a seven-main-bearing L-head. The intake manifold was water jacketed. Seventeen-inch brake drums replaced the former fifteens. The 2-38's lubrication system was adopted. Dual exhausts were fitted. All body styles (including runabout) were carried on a huge 144-inch wheelbase. A Warner speedometer, Klaxon horn and Waltham clock were fitted as standard, and the spare tires were now rear-mounted. Seventy-two man hours were required to assemble each engine. Each car was road tested prior to delivery. Prices ranged from $4750 to $6510. Total 4-48 production was 441 cars.

I.D. DATA: Engine No. Starting: 63026. Ending: 66000.

Model No.	Body Type & Seating	Price	Weight	Prod. Total
4-48	Cab sides Limo.-7P	—	—	—
4-48	Cab sides Land.-7P	—	—	—
4-48	Stand. Limo.-6P	—	—	—
4-48	Cab sides Limo.-6P	—	—	—
4-48	Land.-6P	—	—	—
4-48	Imp. Limo.-6P	—	—	—
4-48	Brgm.-6P	—	—	—
4-48	Phae.-4P	—	—	—
4-48	Imp. Cpe.-4P	—	—	—
4-48	Cpe.-2P	—	—	—

ENGINE: L-head. Six. Cast iron block. B & S: 4-1/2 in. x 5-1/2 in. Disp.: 525 cu. in. Brake H.P.: 60 @ 1200 R.P.M. Main bearings: Seven. Valve lifters: Mechanical.

CHASSIS: W.B.: 144 in. O.L.: 204-3/4 in. Tires: 37 x 5.

TECHNICAL: Rear mounted sliding gear transmission. Speeds: 3F/1R. Rear mounted, disc clutch. Overall ratio: 3.53. Optional: 3.28. Mechanical brakes on two rear wheels. Wood artillery wheels.

HISTORICAL: Introduced Feb. 1914. Model year production: 441.

1914
Model 2-38, 6-cyl.

	FP	5	4	3	2	1
Tr	3850	7050	14,100	23,500	32,900	47,000
Sal Tr	3850	7050	14,100	23,500	32,900	47,000
Spec Tr	3350	6750	13,500	22,500	31,500	45,000
Phae	3750	7050	14,100	23,500	32,900	47,000
4P Phae	3750	7800	15,600	26,000	36,400	52,000
Cpe	4450	6000	12,000	20,000	28,000	40,000
Brgm	5000	5250	10,500	17,500	24,500	35,000
4P Brgm	4950	5250	10,500	17,500	24,500	35,000
2-38						
Lan'let	4900	5400	10,800	18,000	25,200	36,000
Cabr Lan'let	5000	6000	12,000	20,000	28,000	40,000
Limo	4900	5250	10,500	17,500	24,500	35,000
Cabr Limo	5000	5850	11,700	19,500	27,300	39,000
Imp Limo	5150	6000	12,000	20,000	28,000	40,000
Sal Limo	5100	6000	12,000	20,000	28,000	40,000
Model 14-48, 6-cyl.						
Tr	4850	6750	13,500	22,500	31,500	45,000
1914						
Model 4-48, 6-cyl., 48 hp						
Tr	4850	5850	11,700	19,500	27,300	39,000
Sal Tr	4850	5850	11,700	19,500	27,300	39,000
Phae	4750	6450	12,900	21,500	30,100	43,000
4P Phae	4750	6600	13,200	22,000	30,800	44,000
Cpe	5450	5100	10,200	17,000	23,800	34,000
Brgm	6000	4950	9900	16,500	23,100	33,000
Sal Brgm	5950	4950	9900	16,500	23,100	33,000
Lan'let	5900	5100	10,200	17,000	23,800	34,000
Cabr Lan'let	6000	5550	11,100	18,500	25,900	37,000
Limo	5950	5250	10,500	17,500	24,500	35,000
Imp Limo	6150	5400	10,800	18,000	25,200	36,000
Sal Limo	6100	5400	10,800	18,000	25,200	36,000

1915

1915 Packard, Series 3-38, touring, OCW

PACKARD — SERIES 3-38 — SIX: An increase of five horsepower (to 65) was the most significant engineering difference of the 3-38 over its 2-38 predecessor. Lighting was now completely electric, with headlights incorporating a mini auxiliary light within the overall design. A "combination rear lamp and license tag illuminator" was new and located on the left. A limousine with cab sides was a new body style.

I.D. DATA: Engine No. Starting: 75,026. Ending: 76,999.

Model No.	Body Type & Seating	Price	Weight	Prod. Total
3-38	Phae.-5P	3750	—	—
3-38	Phae.-4P	3750	—	—
3-38	Rbt.-2P	3750	—	—
3-38	Brgm.-6P	5000	—	—
3-38	Salon Brgm.-4P	4950	—	—
3-38	Cpe.-3P	4450	—	—
3-38	Cab sides Limo.-6P	—	—	—
3-38	Tour.-7P	—	—	—
3-38	Imp. Limo.-7P	—	—	—
3-38	Salon Limo.-7P	—	—	—
3-38	All W. Conv.-7P	—	—	—
3-38	Stand. Limo.-7P	—	—	—
3-38	Cab sides Limo.-7P	—	—	—
3-38	Stan. Land.-7P	—	—	—
3-38	Cab sides Land.-7P	—	—	—
3-38	Salon Tour.-6P	—	—	—
3-38	Spec. Tour.-6P	—	—	—
3-38	Stan. Limo.-6P	—	—	—
3-38	Cab sides Limo.-6P	—	—	—
3-38	Land.-6P	—	—	—
3-38	Imp. Limo.-5P	—	—	—
3-38	Limo.-5P	—	—	—
3-38	Land.-5P	—	—	—
3-38	Imp. Cpe.-4P	—	—	—

ENGINE: L-head. Six. Cast iron block. B & S: 4 in. x 5-1/2 in. Disp.: 415 cu. in. Brake H.P.: 65 @ 1720 R.P.M. Net H.P.: 38. Main bearings: Seven. Valve lifters: Mechanical. Carb.: float-feed, acetylene primer.

CHASSIS: W.B.: 140 in. O.L.: 198-1/2 in. (Touring-201 in.). Tires: 37 x 4-1/2 front, 37 x 5 rear.

TECHNICAL: Rear mounted sliding gear transmission. Speeds: 3F/1R. Dry disc clutch. Spiral bevel gears. Overall ratio: 3.9. Mechanical brakes on two rear wheels, 17 in. drum. Wood, artillery wheels.

1915 Packard, Series 5-48, limousine, HAC

PACKARD — SERIES 5-48 — SIX: The 5-48 was little changed from the 4-48. All-electric lighting was featured, the main headlight incorporating a smaller auxiliary in the front, the tail-license plate light moved to the left at the rear. The wheelbase remained a gargantuan 144 inches, with some Packards stretching out overall to a length of almost 17 feet, and the heaviest weighing in at over two-and-a-half tons. A high-speed rear axle ratio (3.11:1) was available optionally.

I.D. DATA: Engine No. Starting: 78026. Ending: 78586.

Model No.	Body Type & Seating	Price	Weight	Prod. Total
5-48	Tr.-7P	4850	—	—
5-48	Salon Tr.-7P	4850	—	—
5-48	Phae.-5P	4750	—	—
5-48	Phae.-4P	4750	—	—
5-48	Rbt.-2P	4750	—	—
5-48	Limo.-7P	6000	—	—
5-48	Land.-7P	6000	—	—
5-48	Limo.-6P	5950	—	—
5-48	Land.-6P	5950	—	—
5-48	Imp. Limo.-6P	6100	—	—
5-48	Imp. Limo.-7P	6150	—	—
5-48	Salon Limo.-7P	6100	—	—
5-48	Brgm.-6P	6000	—	—
5-48	Salon Brgm.-4P	5950	—	—
5-48	Cpe.-3P	5450	—	—

ENGINE: L-head. Six. Cast iron block. B & S: 4-1/2 in. x 5-1/2 in. Disp.: 525 cu. in. Brake H.P.: 60 @ 1200 R.P.M.

CHASSIS: W.B.: 144 in. O.L.: 202-1/4 in. (Touring — 204-3/4 in.)

TECHNICAL: Rear mounted sliding gear transmission. Speeds: 3F/1R. Disc clutch. Overall ratio: 3.28. Optional: 3.11. Mechanical brakes on two rear wheels. Wood, artillery wheels.

HISTORICAL: Introduced October, 1914. Model year production: 360.

1915
Model 3-38, 6-cyl.

	FP	5	4	3	2	1
Tr	3850	5700	11,400	19,000	26,600	38,000
Sal Tr	3850	5700	11,400	19,000	26,600	38,000
Spec Tr	3350	5400	10,800	18,000	25,200	36,000
Phae	3750	5550	11,100	18,500	25,900	37,000
4P Phae	3750	5850	11,700	19,500	27,300	39,000
3-38 (38 hp)						
Brgm	5000	4350	8700	14,500	20,300	29,000
4P Brgm	4950	4200	8400	14,000	19,600	28,000
Cpe	4450	4500	9000	15,000	21,000	30,000
Lan'let	4900	4800	9600	16,000	22,400	32,000
Cabr Lan'let	5000	5400	10,800	18,000	25,200	36,000
Limo	4900	5250	10,500	17,500	24,500	35,000
Limo Cabr	5000	5700	11,400	19,000	26,600	38,000
Imp Limo	5150	5400	10,800	18,000	25,200	36,000
Sal Limo	5100	5400	10,800	18,000	25,200	36,000
Model 5-48, 6-cyl., 48 hp						
Tr	4850	5850	11,700	19,500	27,300	39,000
Sal Tr	4850	5850	11,700	19,500	27,300	39,000
Phae	4750	6000	12,000	20,000	28,000	40,000
4P Phae	4750	6150	12,300	20,500	28,700	41,000
Rbt	4750	6750	13,500	22,500	31,500	45,000
Cpe	5450	4050	8100	13,500	18,900	27,000
Brgm	6000	3600	7200	12,000	16,800	24,000
Sal Brgm	5950	3600	7200	12,000	16,800	24,000
Lan'let	5900	6900	13,800	23,000	32,200	46,000
Cabr Lan'let	6000	7200	14,400	24,000	33,600	48,000
Limo	5950	6750	13,500	22,500	31,500	45,000
Cabr Limo	6000	7350	14,700	24,500	34,300	49,000
Imp Limo	6150	7500	15,000	25,000	35,000	50,000

1916

1916 Packard, Twin Six, touring, HAC

PACKARD — TWIN-SIX (1-25, 1-35) — TWELVE: This was the first year of the famous Twin Six, the model designations corresponding to the two wheelbase lengths of 125 and 135 inches. With this car, Packard relocated its gearbox from the rear axle to a position behind the clutch housing (although the shift lever was still to the left of the driver). Top speed was 70 miles an hour, this model being noted for its smooth acceleration in high from a sedate 4 mph. The Twin Six standard paint scheme for open cars was Packard blue striped with cream yellow for body and door panels; underbody, body front, hood, radiator, frame, fenders, splashers, moldings and all running gear parts were black with no striping; wheels were cream yellow striped with black. For closed cars, the standard was Packard blue striped with black for body and door panels, with exterior hardware in black. Exterior hardware on open bodies was furnished in nickel only. Standard equipment included a one-man top, side curtains, windshield, Sparton horn, complete tool kit, Warner speedometer, Waltham clock, tire carrier, power tire pump.

1916 Packard, Twin Six, cab-sides limousine, Kimball, AA

I.D.DATA: Engine No. Starting: 80000. Ending: 87787.

Model No.	Body Type & Seating	Price	Weight	Prod. Total
1-35	Tr.-7P	2950	—	—
1-35	Salon Tr.-7P	2950	—	—
1-35	Phae.-5P	2950	—	—
1-35	Salon Phae.-5P	2950	—	—
1-35	Limo.-7P	4440	—	—
1-35	Cab Sides Limo.-7P	4450	—	—
1-35	Imp. Limo.-7P	4600	—	—
1-35	Limo.-6P	4350	—	—
1-35	Land.-6P	4350	—	—
1-35	Brgm.-4P	4400	—	—
1-25	Tr.-7P	2600	—	—
1-25	Salon Tr.-7P	2600	—	—
1-25	Phae.-5P	2600	—	—
1-25	Salon Phae.-5P	2600	—	—
1-25	Rbt.-2P	2600	—	—
1-25	Limo.-6P	4000	—	—
1-25	Land.-6P	4000	—	—
1-25	Cpe.-3P	3550	—	—
1-25	Brgm.-4P	4050	—	—

ENGINE: L-head, 60° V-12. Two cast iron blocks of 6. B & S: 3 in. x 5 in. Disp.: 424.1 cu. in. Brake H.P.: 88 @ 2600 R.P.M. Net H.P.: 43.2. Main bearings: Three. Valve lifters: Mechanical, solid. Carb.: Packard pressure-feed.

CHASSIS: W.B.: 125 in. Tires: 36 x 4-1/2 front, 37 x 5 rear. W.B.: 135 in. Tires: 36 x 4-1/2 front, 37 x 5 rear.

TECHNICAL: Sliding gear transmission. Speeds: 3F/1R. Multi-disc clutch. Mechanical brakes only on rear wheels. Artillery wheels.

HISTORICAL: Introduced May, 1915. Model year production: 3606.

1916
Twin Six, 12-cyl., 125" wb

	FP	5	4	3	2	1
Tr	3050	6150	12,300	20,500	28,700	41,000
Sal Tr	3050	6150	12,300	20,500	28,700	41,000
Phae	3050	6450	12,900	21,500	30,100	43,000
Sal Phae	3050	6600	13,200	22,000	30,800	44,000
Rbt	3050	6300	12,600	21,000	29,400	42,000
Brgm	4500	4350	8700	14,500	20,300	29,000
Cpe	4150	4650	9300	15,500	21,700	31,000
Lan'let	4500	4950	9900	16,500	23,100	33,000
Limo	4450	5100	10,200	17,000	23,800	34,000

Twin Six, 12-cyl., 135" wb

	FP	5	4	3	2	1
Tr	3500	6300	12,600	21,000	29,400	42,000
Sal Tr	3500	6300	12,600	21,000	29,400	42,000
Phae	3500	6600	13,200	22,000	30,800	44,000
Sal Phae	3500	6750	13,500	22,500	31,500	45,000
Brgm	4950	4500	9000	15,000	21,000	30,000
Lan'let	4950	5100	10,200	17,000	23,800	34,000
Sal Lan'let	5000	5250	10,500	17,500	24,500	35,000
Cabr Lan'let	5050	5550	11,100	18,500	25,900	37,000
Limo	4950	5250	10,500	17,500	24,500	35,000
Cabr Limo	5000	5700	11,400	19,000	26,600	38,000
Imp Limo	5150	5850	11,700	19,500	27,300	39,000

1917

PACKARD — TWIN SIX (2-25, 2-35) — TWELVE: Engineering refinements to the second series of the Twin Six included detachable cylinder heads and removal of the thermostat from the block to the upper tank of the radiator. With smaller (35 x 5) wheels used all around, these new cars appeared considerably lower than their predecessors. The 2-25's wheelbase was increased an inch-and-a-half, and a four-passenger runabout was a new body style. As in the previous year, no runabout was offered in the longer-wheelbase 2-35 line.

I.D. DATA: Engine No. Starting: 125051. Ending: 150000.

Model No.	Body Type & Seating	Price	Weight	Prod. Total
2-35	Tr.-7P	3265	—	—
2-35	Salon Tr.-7P	3265	—	—
2-35	Phae.-5P	3265	—	—
2-35	Salon Phae.-5P	3265	—	—

Model No.	Body Type & Seating	Price	Weight	Prod. Total
2-35	Limo.-7P	4715	—	—
2-35	Cab Sides Limo.-7P	4765	—	—
2-35	Imp. Limo.-7P	4915	—	—
2-35	Land.-7P	4765	—	—
2-35	Cab Sides Land.-7P	4815	—	—
2-35	Limo.-6P	4665	—	—
2-35	Land.-6P	4715	—	—
2-35	Brgm.-4P	4715	—	—
2-25	Tr.-7P	2865	—	—
2-25	Phae.-5P	2865	—	—
2-25	Salon Phae.-5P	2865	—	—
2-25	Rbt.-2P	2865	—	—
2-25	Rbt.-4P	2965	—	—
2-25	Limo.-6P	4265	—	—
2-25	Land.-6P	4315	—	—
2-25	Brgm.-4P	4315	—	—
2-25	Cpe.-3P	3965	—	—

1917 Packard, Twin Six, limousine, HAC

ENGINE: L-head, 60° V-12. Two cast iron blocks of 6. B & S: 3 in. x 5 in. Disp.: 424.1 cu. in. Brake H.P.: 88 @ 2600 R.P.M. Net H.P.: 43.2. Main bearings: Three. Valve lifters: Mechanical. Carb.: Packard pressure-feed.

CHASSIS: W.B.: 126-1/2 in. [2-35, 135 in.] Tires: 35 x 5.

TECHNICAL: Sliding gear transmission. Speeds: 3F/1R. Multi-disc clutch. Spiral bevel gear. Mechanical brakes on rear wheels. Artillery wheels.

HISTORICAL: Introduced August, 1916. Model year production: [2-25] 4950 units. [2-35] 4049 units.

1917 Series II
Twin Six, 12-cyl., 126" wb

	FP	5	4	3	2	1
Tr	3950	6150	12,300	20,500	28,700	41,000
Phae	3950	6300	12,600	21,000	29,400	42,000
Sal Phae	3950	6450	12,900	21,500	30,100	43,000
2P Rbt	3950	6000	12,000	20,000	28,000	40,000
4P Rbt	3950	6150	12,300	20,500	28,700	41,000
Brgm	5650	3600	7200	12,000	16,800	24,000
Cpe	5300	3900	7800	13,000	18,200	26,000
Lan'let	5550	4950	9900	16,500	23,100	33,000
Limo	5500	5100	10,200	17,000	23,800	34,000

Twin Six, 12-cyl., 135" wb

	FP	5	4	3	2	1
Tr	4100	6300	12,600	21,000	29,400	42,000
Sal Tr	4100	6450	12,900	21,500	30,100	43,000
Phae	4100	6600	13,200	22,000	30,800	44,000
Sal Phae	4100	6750	13,500	22,500	31,500	45,000
Brgm	4950	3750	7500	12,500	17,500	25,000
Lan'let	4950	5100	10,200	17,000	23,800	34,000
Cabr Lan'let	5050	5550	11,100	18,500	25,900	37,000
Limo	4950	5400	10,800	18,000	25,200	36,000
Cabr Limo	5000	5550	11,100	18,500	25,900	37,000
Imp Limo	5150	5700	11,400	19,000	26,600	38,000

1918-1919

1918 Packard, Twin Six, Imperial limousine, OCW

PACKARD — TWIN SIX (3-25, 3-35) TWELVE: The third series Twin Six was an evolution of the second series. Improved head design of the twelve-cylinder engine provided better breathing and a modest horsepower increase. The gearshift lever was relocated from the driver's left to the center of the floor. The speedometer cable drive was moved from the front wheel to the rear of the transmission. Wheelbases of both the 3-25 and 3-35 were lengthened slightly. Interestingly, there were more 3-25 body styles offered than 3-35 body styles, a reverse of the previous seasons. The third series Twin Six was introduced June 1st, 1917 for the 1918 model year, and was continued through 1919. Production for the period totaled 4180 units of the 3-25, 5406 units of the 3-35.

I.D. DATA: Engine No. Starting: 150051.

Model No.	Body Type & Seating	Price	Weight	Prod. Total
3-25	Tr.-7P	3450	—	—
3-25	Salon Tr.-7P	3450	—	—
3-25	Phae.-5P	3450	—	—
3-25	Salon Phae.-5P	3450	—	—
3-25	Rbt.-4P	3450	—	—
3-25	Cpe.-4P	4800	—	—
3-25	Limo.-7P	5000	—	—
3-25	Land.-7P	5050	—	—
3-25	Imp. Limo.-7P	5200	—	—
3-25	Brgm.-6P	5050	—	—
3-25	Brgm.-7P	5150	—	—
3-35	Tr.-7P	3850	—	—
3-35	Salon Tr.-7P	3850	—	--
3-35	Limo.-7P	5400	—	—
3-35	Land.-7P	5450	—	—
3-35	Imp. Limo.-7P	5600	—	—
3-35	Brgm.-7P	5500	—	—

1919 Packard, Twin Six, limousine, Kimball, OCW

ENGINE: L-head, 60° V-12. Two cast iron blocks of 6. B & S: 3 in. x 5 in. Disp.: 424.1 cu. in. Brake H.P.: 90 @ 2600 R.P.M. Net H.P.: 43.2. Main bearings: Three. Valve lifters: Mechanical, solid. Carb.: Packard pressure-feed.

CHASSIS: W.B.: [3-35] 136 in. [3-25] 128 in.

1919 Packard, Twin Six, coupe, OCW

TECHNICAL: Sliding gear transmission. Speeds: 3F/1R. Multi-disc clutch. Spiral bevel gear. Mechanical brakes on rear wheels. Artillery wheels.

HISTORICAL: Introduced June, 1917. Model 3-25 production: 1788 cars (1917), 1518 (1918), 874 (1919). Model 3-35 production: 1470 cars (1917), 1221 (1918, 2715 (1919).

1918-1919-1920
Twin Six, 12-cyl., 128" wb

	FP	5	4	3	2	1
Tr	4300	5850	11,700	19,500	27,300	39,000
Sal Tr	4300	6000	12,000	20,000	28,000	40,000
Phae	4300	6300	12,600	21,000	29,400	42,000
Sal Phae	4300	6600	13,200	22,000	30,800	44,000
Rbt	4300	6450	12,900	21,500	30,100	43,000
2 dr Brgm	6000	3900	7800	13,000	18,200	26,000
Cpe	5650	4200	8400	14,000	19,600	28,000
Lan'let	5900	5550	11,100	18,500	25,900	37,000
Limo	5850	5850	11,700	19,500	27,300	39,000
Twin Six, 12-cyl., 136" wb						
Tr	4650	6150	12,300	20,500	28,700	41,000
Sal Tr	4650	6300	12,600	21,000	29,400	42,000
Brgm	6350	4200	8400	14,000	19,600	28,000
Lan'let	6250	5850	11,700	19,500	27,300	39,000
Limo	6400	6000	12,000	20,000	28,000	40,000
Imp Limo	6200	6300	12,600	21,000	29,400	42,000

1920-1923

1920 Packard, Twin Six, sedan, OCW

PACKARD — TWIN SIX (3-35) — TWELVE: Following the end of the First World War, the 3-25 was phased out in 1919, one final car being built in 1920. The 3-35 continued to be built through 1923, with prices progressively reduced in the wake of the postwar recession. The Packard company came to the conclusion that the Twin Six was simply too expensive to build. New to the 3-35 in 1920 was the "Fuelizer" incorporating a spark plug in the intake manifold to help vaporize the gasoline, with "Fuelizer" kits provided for the earlier models. In 1921 Warren G. Harding became the first U.S. President to travel to his inaugural in an automobile. The automobile was a Packard Twin Six. A total of 8750 Twin Sixes were built from 1920 until discontinuation in 1923.

I.D. DATA: Engine No. Starting: 21000.

Model No.	Body Type & Seating	Price	Weight	Prod. Total
1920				
3-35	Tr.-7P	5500	—	—
3-35	Phae.-5P	5500	—	—
3-35	Rbt.-4P	5500	—	—
3-35	Cpe.-5P	7750	—	—
3-35	Duplex Cpe.-5P	7750	—	—
3-35	Sed.-7P	NA	—	—
3-35	Duplex Sed.-7P	8000	—	—
3-35	Limo.-7P	7900	—	—
1921				
3-35	Tr.-7P	4850	—	—
3-35	Phae.-5P	4850	—	—
3-35	Rbt.-4P	4850	—	—
3-35	Cpe.-5P	6600	—	—
3-35	Duplex Cpe.-5P	6600	—	—
3-35	Sed.-7P	6600	—	—
3-35	Duplex Sed.-7P	6600	—	—
3-35	Limo.-7P	6650	—	—
1922-1923				
3-35	Tr.-7P	3850	—	—
3-35	Phae.-5P	3850	—	—
3-35	Rbt.-4P	3850	—	—
3-35	Cpe.-5P	5250	—	—
3-35	Duplex Cpe.-5P	5250	—	—
3-35	Sed.-7P	5400	—	—
3-35	Duplex Sed.-7P	5400	—	—
3-35	Limo.-7P	5275	—	—

ENGINE: L-head, 60° V-12. Two cast iron blocks of six. B & S: 3 in. x 5 in. Disp.: 424.1 cu. in. Brake H.P.: 90 @ 2600 R.P.M. Net H.P.: 43.2. Main bearings: Three. Valve lifters: Solid. Carb.: Packard downdraft with Fuelizer.

CHASSIS: W.B.: 136 in. Tires: 33 x 5.

TECHNICAL: Selective sliding gear transmission. Speeds: 3F/1R. Multiple disc clutch. Spiral bevel gears. Overall ratio: 4.36:1. Mechanical brakes on rear wheels. Artillery wheels on detachable rims.

1921-1922

1921 Packard, Single Six, sedan, HAC

PACKARD — SINGLE SIX (116) — SIX: The Single Six was introduced to provide a more economical alternative to the Twin Six, both for Packard to build and customers to buy. Benefiting from the company's Liberty aero engine development during World War I, its L-head 241.5-cubic-inch straight six developed 52 hp, nearly as much power as a prewar six at twice the displacement and twice the weight. Both cast aluminum crankcase and oil pan were bolted to the cast iron cylinder block, the oil pan easily removable. The Fuelizer introduced on the Twin Six was retained. The hand brake was placed on the driver's left. Closed bodies used whipcord with leather for the front seat and doors; open cars were completely leather upholstered. Unfortunately, the Single Six's development had been costly, with the result that the car was introduced with price tags dangerously close to the Twin Six's. Still, price was not the Single Six's principal problem, as successive price reductions during the model year proved. The principal problem was that this new Packard didn't seem to be a Packard at all. Its wheelbase was a short 116 inches which made for a boxy look; its body styles were only four none of which seated more than five passengers. The standard paint scheme was Packard blue for body, black for fenders and running gear, no striping. The Single Six was introduced in September 1920, with 1,042 cars built in the remainder of that year; only 6,374 cars were sold for the whole of the 1921 calendar year. In February of 1922, rumors spread that a new version of the Single Six was imminent. The official announcement arrived in April. Only 1,384 Single Six 116's were built in calendar year 1922 — for a total production for the model of just 8,800 units.

I.D. DATA: Engine No. Starting: 26. Ending: 8850.

Body No.	Body Type & Seating	Price	Weight	Prod. Total
190	Tr.-5P	3640	—	—
191	Rbt.-2P	3640	—	—
192	Sed.-5P	4940	—	—
193	Cpe.-4P	4835	—	—

Note: Single Six prices were reduced several times, and by October, 1921 the cars were selling for $2350 (touring and runabout), $3350 (sedan), $3125 (coupe).

ENGINE: L-head, straight six. Cast en bloc. B & S: 3-3/8 in. x 4-1/2 in. Disp.: 241.5 cu. in. Brake H.P.: 52 @ 2400 R.P.M. Net H.P.: 27.3. Main bearings: Seven. Carb.: Packard-updraft with Fuelizer.

CHASSIS: W.B.: 116 in. Tires: 33 x 4-1/2.

TECHNICAL: Selective transmission. Speeds: 3F/1R. Seven plate, eight inch clutch. Bevel gears. Overall ratio: 4.31:1. Mechanical brakes on rear wheels. Wood spoke wheels.

1922 Packard, Single Six, roadster, OCW

1921-1922
Single Six (1st Series), 116" wb

	FP	5	4	3	2	1
5P Tr	3975	4350	8700	14,500	20,300	29,000
Rbt	2975	4200	8400	14,000	19,600	28,000
7P Tr	2975	4500	9000	15,000	21,000	30,000
Cpe	3975	3600	7200	12,000	16,800	24,000
Sed	3975	3300	6600	11,000	15,400	22,000
Single Six, 6-cyl., 126" wb						
Rbt	2485	4650	9300	15,500	21,700	31,000
Rds	3165	4950	9900	16,500	23,100	33,000
Tr	3225	4800	9600	16,000	22,400	32,000
Cpe	3300	3750	7500	12,500	17,500	25,000
5P Cpe	3360	3600	7200	12,000	16,800	24,000
Sed	3455	3400	6900	11,500	16,100	23,000
Limo Sed	3525	3900	7800	13,000	18,200	26,000
Single Six, 6-cyl., 133" wb						
Tr	2685	5250	10,500	17,500	24,500	35,000
Sed	3525	3750	7500	12,500	17,500	25,000
Limo	3575	4200	8400	14,000	19,600	28,000
Single Eight, 8-cyl., 136" wb						
Rbt	3850	5250	10,500	17,500	24,500	37,000
Spt Rds	3800	5550	11,100	18,500	25,900	37,000
Cpe	4550	4050	8100	13,500	18,900	27,000
5P Cpe	4725	3900	7800	13,000	18,200	26,000
Sed	4650	3600	7200	12,000	16,800	24,000
Sed Limo	4700	4050	8100	13,500	18,900	27,000
Single Eight, 8-cyl., 143" wb						
Tr	3850	5100	10,200	17,000	23,800	34,000
Sed	4900	3750	7500	12,500	17,500	25,000
Sed Limo	4950	4200	8400	14,000	19,600	28,000
Rds	3800	5550	11,100	18,500	25,900	37,000

1922-1923

1923 Packard, Single Six, touring, HAC

PACKARD — SINGLE SIX (126, 133) — SIX: Although this new Single Six incorporated such engineering revisions as a somewhat complicated nine-plate clutch, a slight increase in stroke for 54 hp and the removal of the water pump to the front of the engine, the really big news was wheelbase and body styling, and the number of body styles available. There were five now on a 126-inch chassis, including a debonair four-passenger Sport Model that was two inches lower and rode on disc wheels as standard. Three seven-passenger body styles were also added, on a 133-inch chassis. A new belt molding ran the entire length of open car bodies, a feature other manufacturers would soon imitate. The standard paint scheme was Packard Blue striped with gold, fenders and running gear in black enamel. Closed cars were black above the belt. To the original eight body styles introduced in April, 1922, a Coupe and Sedan-Limousine for five passengers were added in October of that year, a five-passenger Touring Sedan following in June of 1923. Total Single Six 126-133 production was 26,560 cars, a healthy increase over the 116 which preceded it.

I.D. DATA: Engine No. Starting: 9,000. Ending: 35,942.

Body No.	Body Type & Seating	Price	Weight	Prod. Total
220	Tr.-5P	2485	—	—
223	Rbt.-2P	2485	—	—
224	Spt. Mod.-4P	2650	—	—
222	Cpe.-4P	3175	—	—
221	Sed.-5P	3275	—	—
225	Tr.-7P	2685	—	—
229	Sed. Limo.-7P	3575	—	—
228	Sed.-7P	3525	—	—
NA	Cpe.-5P	3550	—	—
NA	Sed. Limo.-5P	3325	—	—
NA	Tr. Sed.-5P	2750	—	—

ENGINE: L-head. Straight Six. Cast en bloc. B & S: 3-3/8 in. x 5 in. Disp.: 268.4 cu. in. C.R.: 4.8:1. Brake H.P.: 54 @ 2700 R.P.M. Main bearings: Seven. Carb.: Packard-updraft with Fuelizer.

CHASSIS: W.B.: 126 in. & 133 in. Tires: 33 x 4-1/2.

TECHNICAL: Selective transmission. Speeds: 3F/1R. Nine plate, eight inch clutch. Bevel gear, spiral type rear axle. Overall ratio: [126] 4.3, [133] 4.66. Mechanical brakes on rear wheels. Wood & disc wheels.

OPTIONS: Disc wheels (35.00) — standard on only the Sport Model.

1924

1924 Packard, Single Eight, sedan, HAC

PACKARD — SINGLE EIGHT (136, 143) — EIGHT: Eight cylinders and four-wheel brakes were introduced to Packard with this model. Like the Single Six, its 136 and 143 model designations reflected the two wheelbase lengths, which were ten inches longer than the six, with all of that length put up front in the hood. Again, seven-passenger models were on the longer wheelbase. Packard's new nine-bearing straight-eight developed 85 bhp. The Fuelizer was retained, and a Lanchester vibration damper fitted on the front end of the crankshaft. There was four-point mounting of the engine. An air tire pump ran off the transmission; the service brake activated rear stoplights. Watson stabilizers were installed front and rear. Front and rear bumpers were standard, as were a Motometer and disc wheels. The Winterfront, standard initially, was discontinued as such in December, available thereafter only as an option. A divided windshield with built-in hand-operated windshield wiper was fitted, as was a center-mounted rear-view mirror inside. Single Eight bodies were essentially the same as the Single Six, but interior trim and upholstery was more luxurious and appointments more elegant. Black remained the standard for fenders and running gear, and above the belt for closed cars. Closed bodies were Packard Blue striped with red until December, the striping thereafter Azure Blue. Open cars were a vermillion-striped Dust Proof Gray, with upholstery in hand crushed brown Spanish leather. Particularly rakish was the runabout with rumble seat and golf-bag compartment.

I.D. DATA: Engine No. Starting: 200001. Ending: 208428.

Body No.	Body Type & Seating	Price	Weight	Prod. Total
244	Tr.-5P	3650	—	—
234	Rbt.-2/4P	3850	—	—
246	Spt. Mod.-4P	3800	—	—
239	Cpe.-4P	4550	—	—
242	Cpe.-5P	4725	—	—
237	Sed.-5P	4650	—	—
243	Sed. Limo.-5P	4700	—	—
245	Tr.-7P	3850	—	—
240	Sed.-7P	4900	—	—
241	Sed. Limo.-7P	4950	—	—

1924 Packard, Single Eight, touring, HAC

ENGINE: L-head. Straight eight. Cast en bloc. B & S: 3-3/8 in. x 5 in. Disp.: 357.8 cu. in. C.R.: 4.51:1. Brake H.P.: 85 @ 3000 R.P.M. Net H.P.: 36.4. Main bearings: Nine. Valve lifters: Mechanical. Carb.: Packard updraft with Fuelizer.

CHASSIS: W.B.: 136 & 143 in. Tires: 35 x 5.

TECHNICAL: Selective transmission. Speeds: 3F/1R. Nine plate clutch. Shaft drive to spiral bevel gears. Overall ratio: 4.7 (4.8 on roadster and sport models). Mechanical brakes on all wheels. Disc wheels.

HISTORICAL: Introduced June 14, 1923. Model year sales: (136) 3,507. (143) 4,894.

PACKARD — SINGLE SIX (226, 233) — SIX: Introduced in December of 1923, six months after the Single Eight, the new Packard Single Six incorporated many of the larger car's features: four-wheel brakes, service-brake-activated stoplight, rear-view mirror and divided windshield with windshield wiper among them. A battery box was fitted into the right front fender. The general $100 increase in prices was to accommodate the addition of the four-wheel braking system. Operating economy of the new Single Six was stressed, as much as 20 mpg and 20,000 miles on a set of tires being advertised. Open cars featured a tonneau light, and long grain black leather upholstery. Though not as elegantly appointed, closed car interiors did include vanity cases and smoking sets. Body styles on the longer 133-inch wheelbase remained the same three seven-passenger cars as the year previous. Four new body styles were added on the 126-inch wheelbase, though the touring sedan would be discontinued before the end of the model run. The former two-passenger runabout had been replaced with a rumble-seat version with golf-bag compartment.

I.D. DATA: Engine No. Starting: 37,000. Ending: 48,917.

Body No.	Body Type & Seating	Price	Weight	Prod. Total
220	Tour.-5P	2585	—	—
223	Rbt.-2/4P	2785	—	—
230	Cpe.-5P	3450	—	—
232	Tour. Sed.-5P	2850	—	—
222	Cpe.-4P	3275	—	—
221	Sed.-5P	3375	—	—
231	Sed. Limo.-5P	3425	—	—
224	Spt. Model-4P	2750	—	—
225	Tour. Sed.-7P	2785	3432	—
229	Sed. Limo.-7P	3675	3817	—
228	Sed.-7P	3625	3715	—

ENGINE: L-head. Straight six. Cast iron block. B & S: 3-3/8 in. x 5 in. Disp.: 268.4 cu. in. C.R.: 4.8:1. Brake H.P.: 54 @ 2700 R.P.M. Net H.P.: 27.34. Main bearings: Seven. Valve lifters: Mechanical. Carb.: Packard updraft with Fuelizer.

CHASSIS: W.B.: 126 in. & 133 in. Tires: 33 x 5.

TECHNICAL: Selective transmission. Speeds: 3F/1R. Nine plate, eight in. clutch. Bevel gear, spiral type rear axle. Overall ratio: 4.36:1. Mechanical brakes on four wheels. Wood wheels.

HISTORICAL: Introduced December 27, 1923. Model year production: [226] 8,094. [233] 3,131.

1923-24
Single Six, 6-cyl., 126" wb

	FP	5	4	3	2	1
Rbt	2785	4800	9600	16,000	22,400	32,000
Spt Rds	2750	5100	10,200	17,000	23,800	34,000
Tr	2585	4950	9900	16,500	23,100	33,000
Sed	2585	3600	7200	12,000	16,800	24,000
Tr Sed	3850	3750	7500	12,500	17,500	25,000
Limo Sed	2785	4200	8400	14,000	19,600	28,000

Single Six, 6-cyl., 133" wb

	FP	5	4	3	2	1
Tr	2785	5250	10,500	17,500	24,500	35,000
Sed	2785	3750	7500	12,500	17,500	25,000
Sed Limo	2885	4350	8700	14,500	20,300	29,000

Single Eight, 8-cyl., 136" wb

	FP	5	4	3	2	1
Tr	3750	6000	12,000	20,000	28,000	40,000
Rbt	3950	6300	12,600	21,000	29,400	42,000
Spt Rds	3900	6750	13,500	22,500	31,500	45,000
Cpe	4650	4200	8400	14,000	19,600	28,000
5P Cpe	4850	4050	8100	13,500	18,900	27,000
Sed	4750	3900	7800	13,000	18,200	26,000
Sed Limo	4850	4500	9000	15,000	21,000	30,000

Single Eight, 8-cyl., 143" wb

	FP	5	4	3	2	1
Tr	3950	6300	12,600	21,000	29,400	42,000
Sed	5000	4050	8100	13,500	18,900	27,000
Clb Sed	4890	4200	8400	14,000	19,600	28,000
Sed Limo	5100	4650	9300	15,500	21,700	31,000

1925-1926

1925 Packard, model 236, roadster, OCW

PACKARD — SECOND SERIES (236, 243) — EIGHT: The Single Eight designation was dropped, the cars being simply called the Eight now. Bijur chassis lubrication was a fine and progressive new addition, the Skinner Oil

Rectifier was not. Disc wheels and balloon tires were standard. Hotchkiss drive was adopted during the spring of 1926. Though weighing in at an average of 4000 pounds, these cars could do as much as 80 mph. The cars had been introduced in February, 1925 in the usual Packard paint schemes, but by that summer, with the availability of pyroxylin lacquers, the colors available were broadened. Mid-model run, too, saw revision to a simplified Bendix braking system and the replacement of the former divided windshield with a one-piece. A Club Sedan was the first five-passenger car to be catalogued on the longer 143-inch wheelbase. A Holbrook Coupe was the first custom car to be catalogued on the 133-inch chassis. But available from the spring of 1926 too was a variety of custom cars, advertised as "Original Creations by Master Designers," on the 143-inch wheelbase. These were presented in a special custom catalogue and included a four-passenger Sedan Cabriolet by Judkins (Style No. 6413), a five-passenger Stationary Town Cabriolet by Derham (Style No. 3509), a five-passenger Stationary Town Cabriolet by Fleetwood (Style No. 1509), a seven-passenger Inside Drive Limousine Sedan by Holbrook (Style No. 2711), and the following designs by Dietrich: five-passenger Stationary Town Cabriolet (Style No. 1177), two-passenger Convertible Coupe (Style No. 1222), four-passenger Sedan (Style No. 1176).

1926 Packard, model 236, touring, OCW

I.D. DATA: Engine No. Starting: 208,997. Ending: 219,002.

Body No.	Body Type & Seating	Price	Weight	Prod. Total
236	Cpe.-4P	4550	—	—
242	Cpe.-5P	4725	—	—
281	Holbrook-2P	5775	—	—
234	Rbt.-4P	3850	—	—
253	Sed.-5P	4650	—	—
257	Sed. Limo.-5P	4700	—	—
246	Spt.-4P	3800	—	—
244	Tr.-5P	3650	—	—
254	Sed.-7P	4900	—	—
255	Club Sed.-5P	4890	—	—
256	Sed. Limo.-7P	4950	—	—
245	Tr.-7P	3850	—	—

ENGINE: L-head. Straight eight. Cast iron block. B & S: 3-3/8 in. x 5 in. Disp.: 357.8 cu. in. C.R.: 4.51:1. Brake H.P.: 85 @ 3000 R.P.M. Net H.P.: 36.4. Main bearings: Nine. Valve lifters: Mechanical. Carb.: Packard updraft with Fuelizer.

CHASSIS: W.B.: 136 & 143 in. Tires: 33 x 6.75.

TECHNICAL: Selective transmission. Speeds: 3F/1R. Multi-disc clutch. Shaft drive & bevel gear rear axle. Overall ratio: 4.66 (4.08 for roadster and sport models). Mechanical brakes on all wheels. Disc wheels.

HISTORICAL: Introduced February 2, 1925. Model year production: (236)-2,794. (243)-5,118.

PACKARD — THIRD SERIES (326, 333) — SIX: The Single Six became simply the Six this year, its engine bored out to 3-1/2 inches for an increase in horsepower to 60. Disc wheels were standard. The Six enjoyed the Eight's engineering changes, including Bijur and Skinner Oil Rectifier — and the wider color availability with lacquer. Phaeton was a new body style for the 126-inch wheelbase, as was a four-passenger Coupe with separate trunk though it was discontinued by the end of 1925. The Club Sedan was a new addition on the longer 133-inch wheelbase. The introduction of the custom catalogue during the spring of 1926 saw these body styles available also on the Six's 133-inch wheelbase, and the Holbrook coupe became available at that time on the 126-inch chassis as well.

I.D. DATA: Engine No. Starting: 49501. Ending: 90463.

Body No.	Body Type & Seating	Price	Weight	Prod. Total
222	Cpe.-4P	3275	—	—
230	Cpe.-5P	3450	—	—
226	Phae.-5P	—	—	—
223	Rbt.-4P	2785	—	—
221	Sed.-5P	3375	—	—
231	Sed. Limo.-5P	3425	—	—
224	Spt. Model-5P	2750	—	—
220	Tr.-5P	2585	—	—
265	Club Sed.-5P	2725	—	—
266	Sed.-7P	2785	—	—
267	Sed. Limo.-7P	3675	—	—
225	Tr.-7P	2785	—	—

ENGINE: L-head. Straight six. Cast en bloc. B & S: 3-1/2 in. x 5 in. Disp.: 288.6 cu. in. C.R.: 4.8:1. Brake H.P.: 60 @ 3200 R.P.M. Net H.P.: 29.4. Main bearings: Seven. Valve lifters: Mechanical. Carburetor: Packard updraft with Fuelizer.

CHASSIS: W.B.: 126 in. O.L.: 16 ft. Tires: 33 x 5.7. W.B.: 133 in. Tires: 33 x 5.7.

TECHNICAL: Selective transmission. Speeds: 3F/1R. Nine plate, eight in. clutch. Hotchkiss rear axle. Overall ratio: 4.31:1. Mechanical brakes on four wheels. Disc wheels.

HISTORICAL: Introduced February 2, 1925. Model year production: (326) 24,668. (333) 15,690.

1925-26
Single Six (3rd Series), 6-cyl., 126" wb

	FP	5	4	3	2	1
Rbt	2785	5100	10,200	17,000	23,800	34,000
Spt Rds	2750	5550	11,100	18,500	25,900	37,000
Phae	2585	5700	11,400	19,000	26,600	38,000
2P Cpe	2660	3900	7800	13,000	18,200	26,000
Cpe	2585	3750	7500	12,500	17,500	25,000
5P Cpe	2685	3600	7200	12,000	16,800	24,000
Sed	2585	3300	6600	11,000	15,400	22,000
Sed Limo	2785	4050	8100	13,500	18,900	27,000

Single Six (3rd Series), 6-cyl., 133" wb

	FP	5	4	3	2	1
Tr	2785	4800	9600	16,000	22,400	32,000
Sed	2785	3400	6900	11,500	16,100	23,000
Clb Sed	2725	3600	7200	12,000	16,800	24,000
Sed Limo	2885	4200	8400	14,000	19,600	28,000

1927

1927 Packard, model 336, runabout, Derham, AA

PACKARD — THIRD SERIES (336, 343) — EIGHT: Massive engineering changes to Packard's straight-eight — including aluminum pistons, turbohead combustion chamber, revised manifolding, a boring out to 3-1/2 inches — resulted in a considerable increase of horsepower to 109. The Fuelizer was dropped at introduction in August, 1926, with the Skinner Oil Rectifier discontinued during the model run. The two-plate clutch and hypoid differential were new. The Phaeton replaced the Sport Model, and all cars featured full crown one-piece fenders. The Holbrook Coupe was transferred to the custom department. Body styles on the 136-inch wheelbase were reduced to three: Phaeton, Runabout, Sedan. A four-passenger Coupe joined the previous offerings on the 143-inch chassis.

I.D. DATA: Engine No. Starting: 220000. Ending: 224999.

Body No.	Body Type & Seating	Price	Weight	Prod. Total
291	Phae.-5P	3750	—	—
292	Rbt.-2/4P	3850	—	—
293	Sed.-5P	4750	—	—
294	Sed.-7P	5000	—	—
295	Sed. Limo.-7P	5100	—	—
296	Club Sed.-5P	4890	—	—
297	Cpe.-4P	4750	—	—
290	Tr.-7P	3950	—	—

ENGINE: L-head. Straight eight. Cast en bloc. B & S: 3-1/2 in. x 5 in. Disp.: 384.8 cu. in. Brake H.P.: 109 @ 3200 R.P.M. Net H.P.: 39.2. Main bearings: Nine. Valve lifters: Mechanical. Carb.: Packard updraft.

CHASSIS: W.B.: 136 & 143 in. Tires: 33 x 6.75.

TECHNICAL: Selective transmission. Speeds: 3F/1R. Two plate clutch. Shaft drive & hypoid differential. Overall ratio: 4.33 (4.66 and 4.1 optional). Mechanical brakes. Disc wheels.

HISTORICAL: Introduced August 1926. Model year production: (336)-1,245. (343)-3,241.

PACKARD — FOURTH SERIES (426, 433) — SIX: The same engineering changes that made a phenomenally better performer of the Packard Eight accomplished the same thing on the Six: though bore/stroke measurements and displacement remained the same, horsepower was now up to 81. The Fuelizer was dropped immediately, the Skinner Oil Rectifier later in the year. The two-plate clutch and hypoid differential were new. A reorganization of body styles eliminated many on the 126-inch wheelbase, with a Five-Passenger Sedan the only closed car available on that chassis. All other closed cars — the new four-passenger Coupe included — were on the 133-inch wheelbase.

I.D. DATA: Engine No. Starting: 950007. Ending: 120407.

Model No.	Body Type & Seating	Price	Weight	Prod. Total
301	Phae.-5P	2585	—	—
302	Rbt.-4P	2685	—	—
303	Sed.-5P	2585	—	—
300	Tr.-7P	2785	—	—
304	Sed.-7P	2785	—	—
305	Sed. Limo.-7P	2885	—	—
306	Club Sed.-5P	2725	—	—
307	Cpe.-4P	2685	—	—

ENGINE: L-head. Eight. Cast en bloc. B & S: 3-1/2 in. x 5 in. Disp.: 288.6 cu. in. Brake H.P.: 81 @ 3200 R.P.M. Net H.P.: 29.4. Main bearings: Seven. Valve lifters: Mechanical. Carb.: Packard updraft.

CHASSIS: W.B.: 126 & 133 in. Tires: 33 x 5.70.

TECHNICAL: Selective transmission. Speeds: 3F/1R. Two plate clutch. Shaft drive & hypoid differential. Overall ratio: 4.66 (5.1 and 4.33 optional). Mechanical brakes on all wheels. Disc wheels.

HISTORICAL: Introduced August, 1926. Model year production: (426) 14,401. (433) 10,934.

1927
Single Six (4th Series), 6-cyl.. 126" wb

	FP	5	4	3	2	1
Rds	2685	5400	10,800	18,000	25,200	36,000
Phae	2585	5550	11,100	18,500	25,900	37,000
Sed	2585	3600	7200	12,000	16,800	24,000
Single Six (4th Series), 6-cyl., 133" wb						
Tr	2785	5550	11,100	18,500	25,900	37,000
Cpe	2685	3900	7800	13,000	18,200	26,000
Sed	2785	3750	7500	12,500	17,500	25,000
Clb Sed	2725	3900	7800	13,000	18,200	26,000
Sed Limo	2885	4350	8700	14,500	20,300	29,000
Single Eight (3rd Series), 8-cyl., 136" wb						
Rbt	3850	6600	13,200	22,000	30,800	44,000
Phae	3750	6450	12,900	21,500	30,100	43,000
Sed	4750	3600	7200	12,000	16,800	24,000
Single Eight (3rd Series), 8-cyl., 143" wb						
Tr	3950	6900	13,800	23,000	32,200	46,000
Cpe	4750	4200	8400	14,000	19,600	28,000
Sed	5000	3750	7500	12,500	17,500	25,000
Clb Sed	4850	3900	7800	13,000	18,200	26,000
Sed Limo	5100	4350	8700	14,500	20,300	29,000

1928

1928 Packard, Custom Eight 443, sedan, Dietrich, AA

PACKARD — FOURTH SERIES, CUSTOM AND STANDARD MODEL (443) — EIGHT: A single wheelbase, 143 inches in length, carried all eight-cylinder Packards in the Fourth Series. The Custom Eight was introduced in July, 1927, and was really a misnomer since the real custom cars were in Packard's custom coachwork catalogue: twenty designs from eight coachbuilders (Rollston, Holbrook, Dietrich, LeBaron, Judkins, Derham, Murphy and Fleetwood). The nine production styles available in the Custom Eight 443 were repeated in the Standard Model which was introduced seven months later, on March 1st, 1928. The Standard Model 443 was essentially the Custom 443 in a less luxurious and significantly less pricier car. Side-mounted spares and a full range of color options were offered in the Custom 443; rear-mounted spares and fewer color options were offered on the Standard Model 443. The Packard straight-eight engine now had dual coils and an oil spray cylinder lubrication device. An oil filter and rubber engine mounts were new this year too. The wisdom of introducing a less expensive eight-cylinder Packard was reflected in the production totals: only 4,486 Packard eights had been built during the 1927 model year; the figure for 1928 would be 7,800 cars.

I.D. DATA: Engine No. Starting: 225013. Ending: 232815.

Body No.	Body Type & Seating	Price	Weight	Prod. Total
311	Phae.-5P	3975	—	—
312	Rbt.-2/4P	3975	—	—
318	Cpe.-2/4P	4150	—	—
317	Cpe.-4P	4950	—	—
319	Conv. Cpe.-2/4P	4250	—	—
316	Club Cpe.-5P	4950	—	—
314	Sed.-7P	5150	—	—
315	Sed. Limo.-7P	5250	—	—
310	Tr.-7P	4040	—	—
381	Phae.-5P	3650	—	—
382	Rbt.-2/4P	3650	—	—
388	Cpe.-2/4P	3550	—	—
387	Cpe.-4P	3750	—	—
389	Conv. Cpe.-2/4P	3650	—	—
386	Club Sed.-5P	3750	—	—
384	Sed.-7P	3750	—	—
385	Sed. Limo.-7P	3850	—	—
380	Tr.-7P	3550	—	—

ENGINE: L-head. Straight eight. Cast en bloc. B & S: 3-1/2 in. x 5 in. Disp.: 384.8 cu. in. Brake H.P.: 109 @ 3200 R.P.M. Net H.P.: 39.2. Main bearings: Nine. Valve lifters: Mechanical. Carb.: Packard updraft.

CHASSIS: W.B.: 143 in. Tires: 32 x 6.75.

TECHNICAL: Selective transmission. Speeds: 3F/1R. Two-plate clutch. Hypoid differential. Overall ratio: 4.33 (closed cars), 4.07 (open cars). Mechanical brakes on all wheels. Disc wheels.

HISTORICAL: Introduced July, 1927. Model year production: 7,800 units.

PACKARD — FIFTH SERIES (526, 533) — SIX: These would be the last six-cylinder Packards until 1937. New cylinder lubrication (choke operated), an oil filter and four-point engine mounting (instead of the former three) were featured. Although few were ordered, the coachbuilt body styles in Packard's custom car catalogue were available on the longer 133-inch Six wheelbase. A Phaeton and two-passenger Runabout were new production bodies on that chassis; a Coupe and Convertible Coupe were added on the 126-inch Six wheelbase.

I.D. DATA: Engine No. Starting: 125013. Ending: 166770.

Body No.	Body Type & Seating	Price	Weight	Prod. Total
331	Phae.-5P	2275	—	—
332	Rbt.-4P	2275	—	—
323	Sed.-5P	2285	—	—
328	Cpe.-2/4P	2350	—	—
329	Conv. Cpe.-2/4P	2425	—	—
320	Tr.-7P	2485	—	—
324	Sed.-7P	2685	—	—
325	Sed. Limo.-7P	2785	—	—
327	Cpe.-4P	2685	—	—
321	Phae.-5P	2385	—	—
322	Rbt.-4P	2385	—	—

ENGINE: L-head. Straight six. Cast en bloc. B & S: 3-1/2 in. x 5 in. Brake H.P.: 81 @ 3200 R.P.M. Net H.P.: 29.4. Main bearings: Seven. Valve lifters: Mechanical. Carb.: Packard updraft.

CHASSIS: [Model 526] W.B.: 126 in. Tires: 32 x 6. [Model 533] W.B.: 133 in. Tires: 32 x 6.75.

TECHNICAL: Selective transmission. Speeds: 3F/1R. Two-plate clutch. Hypoid differential. Overall ratio: 4.33. Mechanical brakes on all wheels. Disc wheels.

OPTIONS: Single sidemount. Cowl lights (45.00).

HISTORICAL: Introduced July 1, 1927. Model year production: (526)-28,336. (533)-13,414.

1928
Single Six (5th Series), 6-cyl., 126" wb

	FP	5	4	3	2	1
Phae	1975	6750	13,500	22,500	31,500	45,000
Rbt	1975	6600	13,200	22,000	30,800	44,000
Conv	2125	6000	12,000	20,000	28,000	40,000
RS Cpe	2050	4350	8700	14,500	20,300	29,000
Sed	1985	4050	8100	13,500	18,900	27,000
Single Six (5th Series), 6-cyl., 133" wb						
Phae	2085	7500	15,000	25,000	35,000	50,000
7P Tr	2185	7800	15,600	26,000	36,400	52,000
Rbt	2085	7350	14,700	24,500	34,300	49,000
Sed	2385	4200	8400	14,000	19,600	28,000
Clb Sed	2385	4350	8700	14,500	20,300	29,000
Sed Limo	2485	4500	9000	15,000	21,000	30,000
Standard, Single Eight (4th Series), 8-cyl., 143" wb						
Rds	3875	8250	16,500	27,500	38,500	55,000
Phae	3875	8550	17,100	28,500	39,900	57,000
Conv	4250	7350	14,700	24,500	34,300	49,000
7P Tr	3975	8400	16,800	28,000	39,200	56,000
4P Cpe	4450	4200	8400	14,000	19,600	28,000
4P Cpe	4150	4350	8700	14,500	20,300	29,000
5P Cpe	4450	4500	9000	15,000	21,000	30,000
Sed	4450	4050	8100	13,500	18,900	27,000
Clb Sed	4450	4200	8400	14,000	19,600	28,000
Sed Limo	4550	4500	9000	15,000	21,000	30,000
Custom, Single Eight (4th Series), 8-cyl., 143" wb						
7P Tr	3975	8550	17,100	28,500	39,900	57,000
Phae	3875	9900	19,800	33,000	46,200	66,000
Rbt	3875	9000	18,000	30,000	42,000	60,000
Conv Cpe	4250	8250	16,500	27,500	38,500	55,000
RS Cpe	4450	4500	9000	15,000	21,000	30,000
7P Sed	4150	4350	8700	14,500	20,300	29,000
Sed	4450	4200	8400	14,000	19,600	28,000
Sed Limo	4550	4650	9300	15,500	21,700	31,000

1929

1929 Packard, Standard Eight 633, coupe, HAC

PACKARD — SIXTH SERIES, STANDARD EIGHT (626, 633) — EIGHT: Packard went straight-eight across the board in 1929. The new Standard Eight replaced the former Six, retaining its two chassis lengths though with a half-inch increment to 126-1/2 and 133-1/2 inches. Packard-designed shock absorbers replaced the Watson Stabilizers. The new 319.2-cubic-inch engine was basically a smaller brother to the 348.8-cubic-inch Custom and DeLuxe Eight, sharing the same stroke but with a slightly smaller bore. Many parts were interchangeable. The Motometer was gone, replaced by a temperature gauge on the dash. Parabolic headlamps replaced the former drum types. All brightwork on the car was now chrome-plated, rather than painted as previously. Disc wheels remained standard. The Standard Eight Model 626 offered a sedan, coupe and convertible coupe. All other body styles were on the longer Standard Eight Model 633.

I.D. DATA: Engine No. Starting: 233017. Ending: 276166.

Body No.	Body Type & Seating	Price	Weight	Prod. Total
333	Sed.-5P	2285	4185	—
338	Cpe.-2/4P	2350	4100	—
339	Conv. Cpe.-2/4P	2425	4020	—
351	Phae.-5P	2385	3905	—
352	Rbt.-2/4P	2385	3805	—
330	Tr.-7P	2485	3950	—
334	Sed.-7P	2685	4440	—
335	Sed. Limo.-7P	2785	4473	—
336	Club Sed.-5P	2685	4340	—
337	Cpe.-4P		4225	—

ENGINE: L-head. Straight eight. Cast en bloc. B & S: 3-3/16 in. x 5 in. Disp.: 319.2. Brake H.P.: 90 @ 3200 R.P.M. Main bearings: Nine. Vibration damper. Carb.: Packard updraft.

CHASSIS: W.B.: 126-1/2 in. (626); 133-1/2 in. (633) Tires: 32 x 6.00. [626], 32 x 7.00 [633].

TECHNICAL: Selective transmission. Speeds 3F/1R. Single-plate clutch. Shaft drive and hypoid differential. Overall ratio: 4.38 (4.69 and 5.08 optional). Disc wheels.

HISTORICAL: Introduced August, 1928. Model year production: 26,070 [626], 17,060 [633].

1929 Packard, Standard Eight 626, 4-dr. sedan, HAC

PACKARD — SIXTH SERIES, SPEEDSTER (626) — EIGHT: This was the hot Packard for 1929. Ostensibly it was the big eight engine in the small eight chassis, but it was much more than that. A high-lift camshaft, high compression head, metric plugs and a high-speed vacuum pump, amid other fine tuning, provided for 130 bhp and a 100 mph top speed. Even a muffler cutout was provided. Production was limited to just 70 cars of which only one has been confirmed as extant today.

I.D. DATA: Engine No. Starting: 166942. Ending: 167012.

Body No.	Body Type & Seating	Price	Weight	Prod. Total
626	Phae.-4P	5000	4065	—
626	Rds.	5000	4165	—
626	Sed.	—	—	—

ENGINE: L-head. Straight eight. Cast en bloc. B & S: 3-1/2 in. x 5 in. Disp.: 384.4. Brake H.P.: 130 @ 3200 R.P.M. Main bearings: Nine. Valve lifters: Solid. Carb.: Packard.

CHASSIS: W.B.: 126-1/2 in. Tires: 32 x 6.00.

TECHNICAL: Selective transmission. Speeds 3F/1R. Two-plate clutch. Shaft drive and hypoid differential. Overall ratio: 3.31.1. Mechanical brakes on all wheels. Disc wheels.

HISTORICAL: Introduced 1929. Model year production: 70.

1929 Packard, DeLuxe Eight 645, sport phaeton, AA

PACKARD — SIXTH SERIES, CUSTOM EIGHT (640), DELUXE EIGHT (645) — EIGHT: Packard's big straight-eight was offered in the 140-1/2-inch-wheelbase Custom Eight 640 and 145-1/2-inch-wheelbase DeLuxe Eight 645. Body styles proliferated, with most available on either chassis, though the Sport Phaeton was strictly for the 645, the Convertible Coupe strictly for the 640. In addition, the "Individual Custom Line" featured thirteen body designs from Dietrich, LeBaron and Rollston on the 645 chassis, three Dietrich designs on the 640 chassis. As with the Standard Eight, the Motometer had given way to a temperature gauge on the dash, parabolic headlamps replaced the former drum types and all brightwork was chrome-plated. Disc wheels remained standard, however.

I.D. DATA: Engine No. Starting: 167001. Ending: 178879.

Body No.	Body Type & Seating	Price	Weight	Prod. Total
342	Rbt.-2/4P	3175	4285	—
341	Phae.-5P	3175	4370	—
348	Cpe.-2/4P	3250	4560	—
340	Tour.-7P	3275	4390	—
349	Conv. Cpe.-2/4P	3350	4475	—
347	Cpe.-4P	3750	4535	—
346	Club Sed.-5P	3750	4655	—
344	Sed.-7P	3750	4835	—
345	Sed. Limo.-7P	3850	4910	—
372	Rbt.-2/4P	4585	4785	—
371	Phae.-5P	4585	4870	—
378	Cpe.-2/4P	5385	5060	—
373	Spt. Phae.-5P	4935	4890	—
370	Tour.-7P	4585	4890	—
377	Cpe.-5P	5735	5125	—
376	Club Sed.	5785	5155	—
374	Sed.-7P	5785	5335	—
375	Sed. Limo.-7P	5985	5410	—

ENGINE: L-head. Straight eight. Cast iron, cast en bloc. B & S: 3-1/2 in. x 5 in. Disp.: 384.8 cu. in. Brake H.P.: 105 @ 3200 R.P.M. Net H.P.: 39.2. Main bearings: Nine. Valve lifters: Mechanical. Carb.: Packard.

CHASSIS: [Custom] W.B.: 140-1/2 in. Tires: 32 x 7. [DeLuxe] W.B.: 145-1/2 in. Tires: 32 x 7.

TECHNICAL: Selective transmission. Speeds 3F/1R. Two-plate clutch. Shaft drive & hypoid differential. Overall ratio: 4.07 open cars, 4.38 closed. Mechanical brakes on all wheels. Disc wheels.

OPTIONS: Dual Sidemount (240.00). Sidemount cover(s). Wire wheels (80.00). Wood spoke (102.00).

HISTORICAL: Introduced August 1, 1928 [Custom]. September 1, 1928 [Deluxe]. Model year production: [640]-9,801. [645]-2,061.

1929
Model 626, Standard Eight (6th Series). 8-cyl.

	FP	5	4	3	2	1
Conv	2135	8250	16,500	27,500	38,500	55,000
Cpe	2060	5250	10,500	17,500	24,500	35,000
Sed	1985	4500	9000	15,000	21,000	30,000
Model 633, Standard Eight (6th Series), 8-cyl.						
Phae	2085	11,400	22,800	38,000	56,000	76,000
Rbt	2085	12,000	24,000	40,000	60,000	80,000
7P Tr	2185	9900	19,800	33,000	46,200	66,000
Cpe	2285	6750	13,500	22,500	31,500	45,000
Sed	2285	4800	9600	16,000	22,400	32,000
Clb Sed	2285	4950	9900	16,500	23,100	33,000
Limo Sed	2385	5850	11,700	19,500	27,300	39,000
Model 634, Speedster Eight (6th Series), 8-cyl.						
Phae	5000	38,000	67,000	105,000	133,000	190,000
Rds	5000	40,000	70,000	110,000	140,000	200,000

1929

Model 640, Custom Eight (6th Series), 8-cyl.

	FP	5	4	3	2	1
DC Phae	3175	27,900	51,000	79,000	106,000	136,000
7P Tr	3275	24,100	42,000	68,000	98,000	126,000
Rds	3175	25,500	45,000	73,000	100,000	130,000
Conv	3350	12,000	24,000	40,000	60,000	80,000
RS Cpe	3250	8250	16,500	27,500	38,500	55,000
4P Cpe	3750	7500	15,000	25,000	35,000	50,000
Sed	3750	5100	10,200	17,000	23,800	34,000
Clb Sed	3750	5250	10,500	17,500	24,500	35,000
Limo	3850	5700	11,400	19,000	26,600	38,000

Model 645, DeLuxe Eight (6th Series), 8-cyl.

Phae	4585	30,300	57,000	86,000	112,000	145,000
Spt Phae	4935	31,100	58,000	88,000	114,000	150,000
7P Tr	4585	25,500	45,000	73,000	100,000	130,000
Rds	4585	29,500	55,000	84,000	110,000	140,000
RS Cpe	5385	8250	16,500	27,500	38,500	55,000
5P Cpe	5735	7500	15,000	25,000	35,000	50,000
Sed	5785	6000	12,000	20,000	28,000	40,000
Clb Sed	5785	6300	12,600	21,000	29,400	42,000
Limo	5985	6900	13,800	23,000	32,200	46,000

1930

1930 Packard, Standard Eight, 733, convertible coupe, OCW

PACKARD — SEVENTH SERIES, STANDARD EIGHT (726, 733) — EIGHT: Wheelbases for the Standard Eight were increased an inch this year to accommodate the redesigned water pump, now with dual fan belts. The motor thermostat was eliminated, thermostatically controlled radiator shutters taking over temperature control completely. Horsepower was up to 90, the new carburetor was an updraft Detroit Lubricator, and the transmission now a four-speed with the addition of an extra low gear. Hoods of the Standard Eight featured louvered vents as previously, though an accessory hood with three louver doors was available to provide the Standard Packards more of the look of their four-door-louvered big brothers. A single body style was offered in the 127-1/2-inch-wheelbase Model 726, and it was the five-passenger sedan. All other body styles were on the longer 134-1/2-inch-wheelbase Model 733.

I.D. DATA: Engine No. Starting: 277013. Ending: 305283.

Body No.	Body Type & Seating	Price	Weight	Prod. Total
403	Sed.-5P	2375	4265	—
402	Rds.-2/4P	2425	3945	—
401	Phae.-4P	2425	3935	—
431	Spt. Phae.-4P	2725	4130	—
400	Tr.-7P	2525	4055	—
408	Cpe.-2/4P	2525	4180	—
409	Conv. Cpe.-2/4P	2550	4100	—
407	Cpe.-5P	2675	4255	—
406	Clb. Sed.-5P	2675	4325	—
404	Sed.-7P	2675	4500	—
405	Sed. Limo.-7P	2775	4555	—

ENGINE: L-head, straight eight. Cast en bloc. B & S: 3-3/16 in. x 5 in. Disp.: 319.2 cu in. Brake H.P.: 90 @ 3200 R.P.M. Net H.P.: 32.5. Main bearings: Nine. Valve lifters: Solid. Carb.: Detroit Lubricators updraft.

CHASSIS: [Model 726] W.B.: 127-1/2 in. Tires: 20 x 6.00. [Model 733] W.B.: 134-1/2 in. Tires: 20 x 6.50.

TECHNICAL: Selective transmission. Speeds: 4F/1R. Single-plate clutch. Shaft drive & hypoid differential. Overall ratio: 4.38:1, 4.69:1, 5.08:1. Mechanical brakes on all wheels. Disc wheels.

OPTIONS: Three louver-door hood. Dual sidemount. Trunk rack. Fender parking lights (20.00)

HISTORICAL: Introduced August, 1929. Model year production: [726]-15,731. [733]-12,531.

PACKARD — SEVENTH SERIES, SPEEDSTER (734) — EIGHT: The 734 Speedster was Packard's answer to Cadillac's new V-16. Basically, it was a highly modified Standard Eight chassis of 134-1/2 inches into which was stuffed an equally modified DeLuxe eight engine. Different gear ratios and cylinder heads were provided, the choice up to the customer and at no extra cost. The hottest combination, the 8.0 head and the 3.3 differential, made for a Packard capable of better than 100 mph. A dual updraft carburetor was unique to the Speedster Series. Most Speedsters came complete with a tachometer. Their bodies were lower and narrower than the

Packard norm, and catalogued body styles numbered four: Speedster Runabout (the two-passenger boattailed version and the most famous), Phaeton, Victoria and Sedan. A runabout version with rumble seat was made available later, as was the 734 chassis to outside coachbuilders. Quite obviously, the 734 Speedster Series had its parentage in the 626 Speedster, the limited production model of the year previous. For reasons unknown, Packard chose not to promote its new 734 Speedster, and its production was limited as well. Only 113 of these cars were built.

I.D. DATA: Engine No. Starting: 184003. Ending: 184120.

Body No.	Body Type & Seating	Price	Weight	Prod. Total
422	Speedster Rbt.-2P	5200	4210	—
452	Rbt.-4P	5200	4295	—
445	Phae.-4P	5200	4300	—
447	Vic.-4P	6000	4525	—
443	Sed.-4P	6000	4580	—

ENGINE: L-head, straight eight. Cast en bloc. B & S: 3-1/2 in. x 5 in. Disp.: 384.8 cu. in. C.R.: 4.85:1 standard, 6.00:1 high comp. head. Brake H.P.: 125 @ 3400 with standard compression; with high compression head 145 @ 3400 R.P.M. Main bearings: Nine. Carb.: dual updraft Detroit Lubricator.

CHASSIS: W.B.: 134-1/2 in. Tires: 19 x 6.50.

TECHNICAL: Selective transmission. Speeds: 4F/1R. Shaft drive, hypoid differential. Overall ratio: 3.33:1 & 4.66:1. Mechanical brakes on all wheels. Wire or disc wheels.

HISTORICAL: Introduced January, 1930. Model year production: 113.

1930 Packard, Custom Eight 740, sedan, HAC

PACKARD — SEVENTH SERIES, CUSTOM EIGHT (740), DELUXE EIGHT (745) — EIGHT: Wheelbases remained the same for the big Packards this year, but the four-speed transmission was new and a 4.69 rear axle ratio was added. The carburetor was a Detroit updraft, and dual fan belts were fitted. A vacuum booster pump was added mid-year. Non-shatter laminated glass was in all windows, there was a glove compartment on each side of the dashboard, and both driver's seat and steering wheel were adjustable. Parking lamps were now fendermounted, and headlamps exchanged their former parabolic look for one resembling half a cantalope. Dual mounted spares were standard on the 745, an option on the 740. Fifteen designs were offered in the Individual Custom line: six from LeBaron, five from Brewster, and two each from Rollston and Dietrich.

I.D. DATA: Engine No. Starting: 179001 & 184501. Ending: 184000 & 187508.

Body No.	Body Type & Seating	Price	Weight	Prod. Total
418	Cpe.-2/4P	3295	4500	—
417	Cpe.-5P	3650	4555	—
419	Conv. Cpe.-2/4P	3350	4425	—
411	Phae.-4P	3190	4250	—
441	Spt. Phae.-4P	3490	4450	—
412	Rds.-2/4P	3190	4245	—
410	Tr.-7P	3325	4345	—
413	Sed.-5P	3585	4560	—
416	Club Sed.-5P	3750	4580	—
414	Sed.-7P	3785	4765	—
415	Sed. Limo.-7P	3885	4810	—
422	Rds.-2/4P	4585	4695	—
421	Phae.-4P	4585	4695	—
451	Spt. Phae.-4P	4885	4845	—
420	Tr.-7P	4585	4745	—
428	Cpe.-2/4P	4785	4875	—
429	Conv. Cpe.-2/4P	4885	4745	—
427	Cpe.-5P	5100	4995	—
423	Sed.-5P	4985	4805	—
426	Clb. Sed.-5P	5150	5000	—
424	Sed.-7P	5185	5095	—
425	Sed. Limo.-7P	5350	5140	—

Note: The first eleven body numbers are Model 740, the final eleven Model 745.

ENGINE: L-head, straight eight. Cast en bloc. B & S: 3-1/2 in. x 5 in. Disp.: 384.8 cu. in. Brake H.P.: 106 @ 3200 R.P.M. Net H.P.: 39.2. Main bearings: Nine. Valve lifters: Mechanical. Carb.: Detroit Lubricator updraft.

CHASSIS: [Model 740] W.B.: 140-1/2. Tires: 19 x 7.00. [Model 745] W.B.: 145-1/2 in. Tires: 19 x 7.00.

1930 Packard, DeLuxe Eight 745, roadster, OCW

TECHNICAL: Sliding gear transmission. Speeds: 4F/1R. Two-plate clutch. Shaft drive, hypoid differential. Overall ratio: 4.07, 4.38, 4.69:1. Mechanical brakes on all wheels. Disc wheels.

OPTIONS: Spotlight. Wire wheels (90.00). Spoke wheels (110.00)

HISTORICAL: Introduced August, 1929. Model year production: [740]-6,200. [745]-1,789.

1930
Model 726, Standard 8 (7th Series), 8-cyl.

	FP	5	4	3	2	1
Sed	2485	5250	10,500	17,500	24,500	35,000

Model 733, Standard 8 (7th Series), 8-cyl., 134" wb

	FP	5	4	3	2	1
Phae	2425	24,800	44,000	70,000	99,000	128,000
Spt Phae	2725	25,500	45,000	73,000	100,000	130,000
Rds	2425	25,500	45,000	73,000	100,000	130,000
7P Tr	2525	24,100	42,000	68,000	98,000	126,000
RS Cpe	2525	9000	18,000	30,000	42,000	60,000
4P Cpe	2675	6000	12,000	20,000	28,000	40,000
Conv	2550	15,000	30,000	50,000	80,000	100,000
Sed	2675	6300	12,600	21,000	29,400	42,000
Clb Sed	2675	6600	13,200	22,000	30,800	44,000
Limo Sed	2775	7200	14,400	24,000	33,600	48,000

Model 734, Speedster Eight (7th Series), 8-cyl.

	FP	5	4	3	2	1
Boat	5210	40,000	70,000	110,000	140,000	200,000
RS Rds	5200	38,000	67,000	105,000	133,000	190,000
Phae	5200	39,000	69,000	108,000	137,000	195,000
Vic	6000	14,400	28,800	48,000	76,000	96,000
Sed	6000	11,400	22,800	38,000	56,000	76,000

Model 740, Custom Eight (7th Series), 8-cyl.

	FP	5	4	3	2	1
Phae	3190	29,500	55,000	84,000	110,000	140,000
Spt Phae	3490	30,300	57,000	86,000	112,000	145,000
7P Tr	3325	28,700	53,000	81,000	108,000	138,000
Rds	3190	32,700	60,000	92,000	118,000	160,000
Conv	3350	15,000	30,000	50,000	80,000	100,000
RS Cpe	3295	9000	18,000	30,000	42,000	60,000
5P Cpe	3650	6750	13,500	22,500	31,500	45,000
Sed	3585	6450	12,900	21,500	30,100	43,000
7P Sed	3785	6600	13,200	22,000	30,800	44,000
Clb Sed	3750	6750	13,500	22,500	31,500	45,000
Limo	3885	7350	14,700	24,500	34,300	49,000

Model 745, DeLuxe Eight (7th Series)

	FP	5	4	3	2	1
Phae	4585	40,000	70,000	110,000	140,000	200,000
Spt Phae	4885	41,000	72,000	113,000	144,000	205,000
Rds	4585	39,000	69,000	108,000	137,000	195,000
Conv	4885	24,100	42,000	68,000	98,000	126,000
7P Tr	4585	25,500	45,000	73,000	100,000	130,000
RS Cpe	4785	9000	18,000	30,000	42,000	60,000
5P Cpe	5100	8250	16,500	27,500	38,500	55,000
Sed	4985	6750	13,500	22,500	31,500	45,000
7P Sed	5185	7050	14,100	23,500	32,900	47,000
Clb Sed	5150	7200	14,400	24,000	33,600	48,000
Limo	5350	7800	15,600	26,000	36,400	52,000

1931

PACKARD — EIGHTH SERIES, STANDARD EIGHT (826, 833), INDIVIDUAL CUSTOM EIGHT (833) — EIGHT: With the adoption of valves and manifolding from the 734 Speedster, horsepower of the Standard Eight engine was up to 100. A 4.07 rear axle ratio was added to the former 4.38, 4.69 and 5.08. A Stewart Warner fuel pump replaced the former vacuum tank. The Bijur lubrication went automatic (vacuum-operated). Hubcaps were larger, tires smaller, disc wheels still standard though with wire or wood optional. Steering wheels dropped the number of spokes to three. The Model 826, again, was a single body style on a 127-1/2-inch wheelbase: the $2385 price-leading sedan. All Standard Eight 833's were on the 134-1/2 inch wheelbase, with eleven body styles offered. There were nine body styles in the Individual Custom 833, the same as offered for the big Packard eight and an attempt to stimulate custom sales during this Great Depression year.

I.D. DATA: Engine No. Starting: 320001. Ending: 332111.

Body No.	Body Type & Seating	Price	Weight	Prod. Total
463	Sed.-5P	2385	4479	—
462	Rds.-2/4P	2425	4140	—
461	Phae.-4P	2425	4185	—
481	Spt. Phae.-4P	2725	4285	—
460	Tr.-7P	2525	4256	—
468	Cpe.-2/4P	2525	4360	—
469	Conv. Cpe.-2/4P	2550	4290	—

Body No.	Body Type & Seating	Price	Weight	Prod. Total
467	Cpe.-5P	2675	4308	—
466	Club Sed.-5P	2675	4488	—
464	Sed.-7P	2785	4732	—
465	Sed. Limo.-7P	2885	4638	—
483	Conv. Sed.-5P	3445	—	—
1879	Conv. Vict.	4275	—	—
1881	Conv. Sed.	4375	—	—
3000	All W. Cab.	4850	—	—
3001	All W. Land.	5050	—	—
3002	All W. Twn. Car	4975	—	—
3003	All W. Twn. Car Land.	—	5175	—
3004	Cab. Sed. Limo.	4490	—	—
3008	All W. Spt. Cab.	4850	—	—
3009	All W. Spt. Land.	5050	—	—

Note: The Individual Custom styles have the four-digit numbers.

ENGINE: L-head, straight eight. Cast iron block. B & S: 3-3/16 in. x 5 in. Disp.: 319.2 cu. in. Brake H.P.: 100 @ 3200 R.P.M. Net H.P.: 32.5. Main bearings: Nine. Carb.: Detroit.

CHASSIS: [Standard Eight (826)] W.B.: 127-1/2 in. Tires: 19 x 6.50. [Standard Eight (833)] W.B.: 134-1/2 in. Tires: 19 x 6.50. [Individual Custom Eight (833)] W.B.: 134-1/2 in. Tires: 19 x 6.50.

TECHNICAL: Selective transmission. Speeds: 4F/1R. Single plate clutch. Shaft drive & hypoid differential. Overall ratio: 4.38:1, 4.69:1, 5.08:1 & 4.07:1. Mechanical brakes on all wheels. Disc wheels.

OPTIONS: Dual Sidemount. Sidemount cover(s). Bumper Guards. Spotlight.

HISTORICAL: Introduced August 1930. Model year production: Standard 826-6,009. Standard 833-6,096.

1931 Packard, DeLuxe Eight 840, roadster, OCW

PACKARD — EIGHTH SERIES, DELUXE EIGHT (840, 845), INDIVIDUAL CUSTOM EIGHT (840) — EIGHT: Engineering refinements for the Standard Eight were adopted on the larger eights, its horsepower now up to 120. The former "Custom" designation was dropped, both 840 and 845 now being called DeLuxe. Wheelbase lengths remained the same, but the longer 145-1/2-inch 845 now offered only two seven-passenger body styles: Sedan and Sedan-Limousine. All other DeLuxe body styles were carried on the shorter 140-1/2-inch chassis. The Individual Custom line was on the shorter wheelbase as well, and offered two Dietrich designs (Convertible Victoria and Convertible Sedan) and seven "Custom Made by Packard" styles. This represented the finalization of the Packard company's long-desired resolve to make the Individual Custom line an in-house operation.

I.D. DATA: Engine No. Starting: 188,001. Ending: 191,345.

Body No.	Body Type & Seating	Price	Weight	Prod. Total
472	Rds.-2/4P	3490	4383	—
471	Phae.-4P	3490	4439	—
491	Spt. Phae.-4P	3790	4535	—
470	Tr.-7P	3595	4507	—
478	Cpe.-2/4P	3545	4592	—
479	Conv. Cpe.-2/4P	3595	4523	—
473	Cpe.-5P	3850	4673	—
476	Sed.-5P	3795	4955	—
474	Club Sed.-5P	3950	4720	—
475	Sed.-7P	4150	5010	—
1879	Sed. Limo.-7P	4285	5080	—
1881	Conv. Vict.	5175	—	—
3000	Conv. Sed.	5275	—	—
3001	All w. Cabr.	5750	—	—
3002	All w. Land.	5950	—	—
3003	All w. Twn. Car	5875	—	—
3004	All w. Twn. Car land.	6075	—	—
3008	Cabr. Sed. Limo.	5390	—	—
3009	All w. Sport cab.	5750	—	—
840	All w. Sport land.	5950	—	—

Note: Only two body styles were included in the Model 845, the seven-passenger sedan and sedan-limousine. The Individual Custom 840's are represented by the four-digit numbers.

ENGINE: L-head, straight eight. Cast en bloc. B & S: 3-1/2 in. x 5 in. Disp.: 384.8 cu. in. Brake H.P.: 120 @ 3200 R.P.M. Net H.P.: 39.2. Main bearings: Nine. Valve lifters: Mechanical. Carb.: Detroit.

CHASSIS: [Deluxe Eight (840) & Individual Custom Eight] W.B.: 140-1/2 in. Tires: 19 x 7.00. [Deluxe Eight (845)] W.B.: 145-1/2 in. Tires: 19 x 7.00.

TECHNICAL: Selective transmission. Speeds: 4F/1R. Single plate clutch. Shaft drive, hypoid differential. Overall ratio: 4.38:1, 4.69:1, 5.08:1 & 4.97:1. Mechanical brakes on all wheels. Disc wheels.

OPTIONS: Dual sidemount (148.00). Luggage rack. Wire wheels (60.00). Stone guard (27.50). Deluxe emblem (10.00). Windwings (25.00). Trunk (125.00).

HISTORICAL: Introduced September 9, 1930. Model year production: [840]-2,035. [845]-1,310.

1931
Model 826, Standard Eight (8th Series)

	FP	5	4	3	2	1
Sed	2485	5250	10,500	17,500	24,500	35,000

Model 833, Standard Eight (8th Series)

	FP	5	4	3	2	1
Phae	2425	25,500	45,000	73,000	100,000	130,000
Spt Phae	2395	26,300	47,000	75,000	102,000	132,000
7P Tr	2525	24,100	42,000	68,000	98,000	126,000
Conv Sed	3445	27,900	51,000	79,000	106,000	136,000
Rds	2425	25,500	45,000	73,000	100,000	130,000
Conv	2550	17,100	31,800	53,000	85,000	106,000
RS Cpe	2525	9300	18,600	31,000	43,400	62,000
5P Cpe	2675	8700	17,400	29,000	40,600	58,000
7P Sed	2785	6750	13,500	22,500	31,500	45,000
Clb Sed	2675	6900	13,800	23,000	32,200	46,000

NOTE: Add 20 percent for 845 models.

Model 840, Custom

	FP	5	4	3	2	1
A-W Cabr	4850	31,100	58,000	88,000	114,000	150,000
A-W Spt Cabr	4850	31,900	59,000	90,000	116,000	155,000
A-W Lan'let	5050	32,700	60,000	92,000	118,000	160,000
A-W Spt Lan'let	5050	33,500	61,000	94,000	120,000	165,000
Dtrch Cv Sed	4490	35,100	63,000	98,000	124,000	175,000
Limo Cabr	4490	35,100	63,000	98,000	124,000	175,000
A-W Twn Car	4975	34,300	62,000	96,000	122,000	170,000
Dtrch Cv Vic	4275	38,000	67,000	105,000	133,000	190,000
Conv	4275	39,000	69,000	108,000	137,000	195,000
Spt Phae	4375	45,000	79,000	124,000	158,000	225,000
Phae	4375	44,000	77,000	121,000	154,000	220,000
Rds	2425	43,000	76,000	119,000	151,000	215,000
Tr	2525	39,000	69,000	108,000	137,000	195,000
Rs Cpe	2525	9900	19,800	33,000	46,200	66,000
5P Cpe	2675	7500	15,000	25,000	35,000	50,000
Sed	2785	6750	13,500	22,500	31,500	45,000
Clb Sed	2675	7200	14,400	24,000	33,600	48,000

Model 840, Individual Custom

	FP	5	4	3	2	1
A-W Cabr	5750	46,000	81,000	127,000	161,000	230,000
A-W Spt Cabr	5750	47,000	83,000	130,000	165,000	235,000
A-W Lan'let	5950	39,000	69,000	108,000	137,000	195,000
A-W Spt Lan'let	5950	40,000	70,000	110,000	140,000	200,000
Dtrch Conv Sed	5275	46,000	81,000	127,000	161,000	230,000
Cabr Sed Limo	5390	40,000	70,000	110,000	140,000	200,000
A-W Twn Car	5875	45,000	79,000	124,000	158,000	225,000
Lan'let Twn Car	6075	37,000	65,000	102,000	130,000	185,000
Conv Vic	5175	47,000	83,000	130,000	165,000	235,000
Sed	4150	7500	15,000	25,000	35,000	50,000
Sed Limo	4285	8250	16.500	27.500	38.500	55,000

1932

1932 Packard Light Eight 900, sedan, JAC

PACKARD — NINTH SERIES, LIGHT EIGHT (900) — EIGHT: The Light Eight was Packard's first attempt to truly counter the Depression with a lower-priced model. The car failed to do this, through no fault of its own, and was produced for less than a year. The Light Eight's problem was that it was too expensive to build and not significantly enough lower-priced to introduce an all-new clientele for the company. But it was nonetheless a remarkable car. Its engine featured a block thermostat with no shutters and a warm-air heater for the carburetor intake. Bijur lubrication was absent, only grease fittings being needed and used. The chassis featured ride control, angleset differential, automatic clutch and vacuum-powered brakes. Horsepower was 110, top speed was 72 mph. The Light Eight was perhaps most memorable for its sweeping modern lines and its distinctive "shovel nose."

I.D. DATA: Starting: 360009. Ending: 366794.

Body No.	Body Type & Seating	Price	Weight	Prod. Total
569	Cpe.-Rds.-2/4P	1795	3930	—
568	Cpe.-2/4P	1795	3990	—
553	Sed.-5P	1750	4115	—
563	Cpe. Sed.-5P	1795	4060	—

Note: The sedan was raised to $1895, the other body styles to $1940 during the model year.

ENGINE: L-head. Straight eight. Cast en bloc. B & S: 3-3/16 in. x 5 in. Disp.: 319.2 cu. in. C.R.: 6:1. Brake H.P.: 110. Net H.P.: 32.5. Main bearings: Nine. Valve lifters: Solid. Carb.: Packard.

CHASSIS: W.B.: 127-3/4 in. Tires: 17 x 6.50.

TECHNICAL: Selective synchromesh. Speeds: 3F/1R. Floor shift controls. Single plate clutch. Shaft drive & angleset hypoid differential. Mechanical brakes on all wheels. Steel disc wheels. Free-wheeling. Vacuum clutch.

OPTIONS: Dual Sidemount. Sidemount cover(s). Cigar Lighter. Righthand taillight. Dual rear mounted spares. Luggage rack, sidemount spares, full rear bumper & fender park lights (65.00).

TECHNICAL: Introduced January, 1932. Model year production: 6,750 units.

1932 Packard, Standard Eight 901, sedan, JAC

PACKARD — NINTH SERIES, STANDARD EIGHT (901, 902) — EIGHT: The Standard Eight had new numerical designations with no reference to wheelbase, and two new wheelbases this year that were two inches longer at 129-1/2 inches for Model 901 (the $2485 five-passenger sedan) and 136-1/2 inches for the Model 902 which was offered in twelve body styles. Individual Customs were unavailable for the Standard Eight this year. But engineering refinements were many. The standard compression ratio was raised to 6.0 (with lower or higher ratios available optionally); horsepower was boosted to 110. The frame was a new double-drop design with X-bracing. Ride control was standard, and the harmonic stabilizer front-bumper an option. The cars were introduced with the four-speed transmission, but late in the model run a three-speed with synchromesh and vacuum clutch was fitted.

I.D. DATA: Engine No. Starting: 340057. Ending: 347720.

Body No.	Body Type & Seating	Price	Weight	Prod. Total
503	Sed.-5P	2485	4570	—
508	Cpe.-2/4P	2675	4420	—
507	Cpe.-5P	2795	4505	—
509	Cpe. Rds.-2/4P	2650	4420	—
501	Phae.-4P	2650	4300	—
521	Sport Phae.-4P	2950	4400	—
543	Sed.-5P	2685	4590	—
504	Sed.-5/7P	2885	4735	—
506	Club Sed.-5P	2775	4555	—
523	Conv. Sed.-5P	3445	4573	—
505	Sed. Limo.-5/7P	2985	4770	—
500	Tr.-5/7P	2775	4345	—
527	Conv. Vic.-5P	3395	4317	—

ENGINE: L-head, straight eight. Cast en bloc. B & S: 3-3/16 in. x 5 in. Disp.: 319.2 cu. in. C.R.: 6:1. Brake H.P.: 110 @ 3200 R.P.M. Net H.P.: 32.5. Main bearings: Nine. Valve lifters: Solid. Carb.: Detroit Lubricator updraft.

CHASSIS: [Standard Eight (901)] W.B.: 129-1.2 in. Tires: 17 x 7.00. [Standard Eight (902)] W.B.: 136-1/2 in. Tires: 17 x 7.00.

TECHNICAL: Selective (synchromesh with three-speed). Speeds: 4F/1R, later 3F, 1R. Floor shift controls. Single plate clutch. One piece driveshaft to hypoid differential. Overall ratio: 4.41:1, 4.69:1 & 5.07:1 opt. on 4 spd. Mechanical brakes on all wheels. Disc wheels.

OPTIONS: Harmonic stabilizer front bumper. Dual sidemount. Sidemount cover(s). Cigar lighter. Spotlight. Fender lights & trunk rack (97.00). Trunk (45.00). Wire wheels (50.00). Special paint (110.00). Front stone guard (35.00). Whitewall tires (10.00).

TECHNICAL: Introduced June 1931. Model year production: (901)-3,922. (902)-3,737.

PACKARD — NINTH SERIES, DELUXE EIGHT (903, 904), INDIVIDUAL CUSTOM EIGHT (904) — EIGHT: Horsepower was up to 135, and wheelbases now measured 142-1/2 for the 903 and 147-1/2 for the 904. The frame was a new double-drop design with X-bracing. Ride control and the harmonic stabilizer front bumper were standard. Also standard were fender lamps and dual trumpet horns mounted under the headlights. The four-speed transmission was fitted to the cars at introduction, but late in the model year was replaced with a three-speed with synchromesh and vacuum clutch. Top speed was 85 mph, with 0 to 60 in 18.8 seconds. With radios becoming popular, the company tested various types in this series. The Dietrich-designed Convertible Sedan and Convertible Victoria which the year previous had been in the Individual Custom line were moved to the DeLuxe Eight 903 line this year, joining nine other body styles. The long-wheelbase DeLuxe Eight 904 carried only the 5/7-passenger sedan and sedan-limousine. The Individual Custom 904 offered five Dietrich designs (stationary coupe, convertible coupe, sport phaeton, convertible sedan and convertible victoria), together with ten "Custom Made by Packard" body styles.

I.D. DATA: Engine No. Starting: 193051. Ending: 194708.

Model No.	Body Type & Seating	Price	Weight	Prod. Total
518	Cpe.-2/4P	3725	4890	—
517	Cpe.-5P	3850	4985	—
519	Cpe. Rds.-2/4P	3750	4890	—
511	Phae.-4P	3690	4715	—
531	Sport Phae.-4P	3990	4795	—
513	Sed.-5P	3845	5045	—
516	Club Sed.-5P	3890	5000	—
533	Conv. Sed.-5P	4550	4983	—
510	Tr.-5/7P	3795	4760	—
537	Conv. Vic.-5P	4495	4727	—
514	Sed.-5/7P	4150	5195	—
515	Sed. Limo.-5/6P	4285	5240	—
2068	Sta. Cpe.-2/4P	5900	—	—
2071	Conv. Cpe.-2/4P	6050	—	—
2069	Spt. Phae.-4P	5800	—	—
2070	Conv. Sed.-5P	6250	—	—
2072	Conv. Vic.-4P	6150	—	—
4000	All W. Cab.-5/7P	6850	—	—
4001	All W. Land.-5/7P	7250	—	—
4002	All W. Town Car-5/7P	6850	—	—
4003	All W. Town Car Land.-5/7P	7250	—	—
4004	Sed. Cab. Limo.-6P	6850	—	—
4005	Spt. Sed.-5P	6850	—	—
4006	All W. Brgm.-5/7P	6850	—	—
4007	Limo. Sed.-6P	6850	—	—
4008	All W. Cab. Sport Cab.-5/7P	6850	—	—
4009	All W. Land.-5/7P	7250	—	—

Note: Body numbers 514 and 515 were the two DeLuxe Eight 904 cars offered. The four digit numbers represent the Individual Custom 904 cars, the "2000" digits being the Dietrich designs, the "4000" digits the "Custom Made by Packard."

ENGINE: L-head, straight eight. Cast en bloc. B & S: 3-1/2 in. x 5 in. Disp.: 384.8 cu. in. C.R.: 6:1. Brake H.P.: 135 @ 3200 R.P.M. Main bearings: Nine. Valve lifters: Solid. Carb.: Detroit Lubricator updraft.

CHASSIS: [Deluxe Eight (903).] W.B.: 142-1/2 in. Tires: 19 x 7.00. [Deluxe Eight (904) & Individual Custom Eight (904).] W.B.: 147-1/2 in. Tires: 19 x 7.00.

TECHNICAL: Selective. Speeds: 4F/1R, later changed to 3F/1R. Two-plate clutch. Split drive shaft to hypoid differential. Overall ratio: 4.06:1, 4.41:1. 4.69:1 & 5.07:1 opt. with 4 speed. Mechanical brakes on all wheels. Disc wheels. Free-wheeling. Vacuum clutch.

OPTIONS: Front bumper. Rear bumper. Dual sidemount. Sidemount cover(s). Clock. Cigar lighter.

HISTORICAL: Introduced June, 1931. Model year production: [903]-955, [904]-700, Ind. Cust. Eight-N/A.

1932 Packard, Twin Six 906, Dietrich convertible sedan, OCW

PACKARD — NINTH SERIES, TWIN SIX (905,906) — TWELVE: Introduced together with the Light Eight at New York Automobile Show time in January 1932, the Twin Six was Packard's entry in the multi-cylinder race, its designation a nostalgic remembering of the World-War-I-era Twin Sixes, and used this first year only. The wheelbases were 142-1/2 inches for the 905, 147-1/2 inches for the 906 which included the Individual Custom cars. Prices began at $3650 and rose from there to $7950, but they bought a lot of car. Horsepower was 160, and though a Twin Six five-passenger sedan was clocked at 101 mph, Packard brochures understated the car's performance and claimed a speed only in excess of 85. Interior appointments were lavish. Ten body styles were offered on the 905 chassis; the eleven body styles on the 906 chassis included a 5/7-passenger sedan and sedan-limousine, the remainder of the line being the Individual Custom cars.

I.D. DATA: Serial numbers located on a rectangular plate mounted on the firewall. Starting: 900001. Ending: 901000. The vehicle number was the body type followed by the production number of that particular car.

Body No.	Body Type & Seating	Price	Weight	Prod. Total
570	Tr.-5/7P	3895	5315	*
571	Phae.-5P	3790	5275	—
581	Spt. Phae.-5P	4090	5375	—
573	Sed.-5P	3745	5635	—
583	Conv. Sed.-5P	4395	5255	—
576	Clb. Sed.-5P	3895	5585	—
577	Cpe.-5P	3850	5485	—
587	Conv. Vict.-5P	4325	5180	—
578	Cpe.-2/4P	3650	5425	—
579	Cpe. Rds.-2/4P	3750	5350	—
574	Sed.-5/7P	3995	5765	*
575	Sed. Limo.-5/7P	4195	5830	—
4000	All w. Cabr.-5/7P	7550	5430	—
4001	All w. Land'let.-5/7P	7950	5430	—
4002	All w. twn. Car.-5/7P	7550	5490	—
4003	All w. Twn. Car Lan.-5/7P	7950	5490	—
2068	Stat. Cpe. Dietrich-2/4P	6600	5180	—
2069	Spt. Phae. Dietrich-4P	6500	4980	—
2070	Conv. Sed. Dietrich-5P	6950	5280	—
2071	Conv. Rds. Dietrich-2/4P	6750	5145	—
2072	Conv. Vict. Dietrich-4P	6850	4995	—
2069	Spt. Phae. Dietrich-4P	6500	4980	—

Note: The first ten body numbers represent Model 904; the following two the standard production 905, with the four digit numbers comprising the Individual Custom 905.

ENGINE: 67° V-block. Modified L. Twelve. Cast iron monobloc. Aluminum alloy pistons, 4 ring. B & S: 3-7/16 in. x 4 in. Disp.: 445.5 cu. in. C.R.: 6.0. Brake H.P.: 160 @ 3200 R.P.M. Net H.P.: 56.7. Main bearings: Four. Zero lash automatic valve silencers. Carburetor: Stromberg-Duplex.

CHASSIS: [905 Series] W.B.: 142-1/8 in. Tires: 7.50 x 18. [906 Series] W.B.: 147-1/8 in. Tires: 7.50 x 18.

TECHNICAL: Selective synchromesh. Speeds: 3F/1R. Outer floor-cane controls. Double plate clutch. Overall ratio: open cars; 4.41:1, closed; 4.69:1, opt. 4.06 or 5.07. Mechanical brakes on four wheels. Wire or wood spoke wheels. Free-wheeling finger control on steering column.

HISTORICAL: Introduced January, 1932. Model year production: 311 (905), 238 (906).

1932
Model 900, Light Eight (9th Series)

	FP	5	4	3	2	1
Rds	1940	9900	19,800	33,000	46,200	66,000
Cpe	1940	5400	10,800	18,000	25,200	36,000
Cpe Sed	1940	5100	10,200	17,000	23,800	34,000
Sed	1895	4950	9900	16,500	23,100	33,000

1932
Model 901 Standard Eight (9th Series) 129" wb

Sed	2485	4800	9600	16,000	22,400	32,000

Model 902 Standard Eight (9th Series) 136" wb

Rds	2850	20,600	34,800	58,000	91,000	116,000
Phae	2850	27,100	49,000	77,000	104,000	134,000
Spt Phae	3150	27,900	51,000	79,000	106,000	136,000
RS Cpe	2795	8250	16,500	27,500	38,500	55,000
5P Cpe	2945	7500	15,000	25,000	35,000	50,000
Sed	2885	5400	10,800	18,000	25,200	36,000
7P Sed	3035	5550	11,100	18,500	25,900	37,000
Clb Sed	2975	5700	11,400	19,000	26,600	38,000
Limo	3185	6000	12,000	20,000	28,000	40,000
Tr	2700	26,300	47,000	75,000	102,000	132,000
Conv Sed	3450	28,700	53,000	81,000	108,000	138,000
Conv Vic	3395	29,500	55,000	84,000	110,000	140,000

Model 903, DeLuxe Eight, 142" wb

Conv	3750	25,500	45,000	73,000	100,000	130,000
Phae	3690	27,100	49,000	77,000	104,000	134,000
Spt Phae	3990	27,900	51,000	79,000	106,000	136,000
Conv Sed	4550	29,500	55,000	84,000	110,000	140,000
Conv Vic	4495	30,300	57,000	86,000	112,000	145,000
7P Tr	3795	18,500	33,000	55,000	88,000	110,000
RS Cpe	3725	9000	18,000	30,000	42,000	60,000
5P Cpe	3850	8250	16,500	27,500	38,500	55,000
Sed	3845	5550	11,100	18,500	25,900	37,000
Clb Sed	3890	5850	11,700	19,500	27,300	39,000

Model 904, DeLuxe Eight, 147" wb

Sed	4150	8250	16,500	27,500	38,500	55,000
Limo	4285	9900	19,800	33,000	46,200	66,000

Model 904, Individual Custom, 147" wb

Dtrch Conv Cpe	5900	48,000	84,000	132,000	168,000	240,000
Dtrch Cpe	6050	34,300	62,000	96,000	122,000	170,000
Cabr	6850	47,000	83,000	130,000	165,000	235,000
Spt Cabr	6850	48,000	84,000	132,000	168,000	240,000
A-W Brgm	6850	49,000	86,000	135,000	172,000	245,000
Dtrch Spt Phae	5800	52,000	91,000	143,000	182,000	260,000
Dtrch Conv Sed	6850	52,000	91,000	143,000	182,000	260,000
Spt Sed	6850	31,900	59,000	90,000	116,000	155,000
Limo Cabr	6850	53,000	93,000	146,000	186,000	265,000
Dtrch Limo	6850	35,100	63,000	98,000	124,000	175,000
A-W Twn Car	6850	55,000	97,000	152,000	193,000	275,000
Dtrch Conv Vic	6150	58,000	102,000	160,000	203,000	290,000
Lan'let	7250	35,900	64,000	100,000	126,000	180,000
Spt Lan	7250	37,000	65,000	102,000	130,000	185,000
Twn Car Lan'let	7250	38,000	67,000	105,000	133,000	190,000

Model 905, Twin Six, (9th Series) 142" wb

Conv	3750	56,000	98,000	154,000	196,000	280,000
Phae	3790	53,000	93,000	146,000	186,000	265,000
Spt Phae	4090	54,000	95,000	149,000	189,000	270,000
7P Tr	3895	50,000	88,000	138,000	175,000	250,000
Conv Sed	4395	54,000	95,000	149,000	189,000	270,000
Conv Vic	4325	55,000	97,000	152,000	193,000	275,000
RS Cpe	3650	9900	19,800	33,000	46,200	66,000
5P Cpe	3850	8250	16,500	27,500	38,500	55,000
Sed	3745	6300	12,600	21,000	29,400	42,000
Clb Sed	3895	6750	13,500	22,500	31,500	45,000

1932
Model 906, Twin Six, 147" wb

	FP	5	4	3	2	1
7P Sed	4495	9900	19,800	33,000	46,200	66,000
Limo	4695	12,900	25,800	48,200	66,000	86,000

Model 906, Individual Custom, Twin Six, 147" wb

Conv	6550	value not estimable
Cabr	7350	value not estimable
Dtrch Spt Phae	6300	value not estimable
Dtrch Conv Vic	6650	value not estimable
Dtrch Sed	6750	value not estimable
Dtrch Cpe	5900	value not estimable
Lan'let	7750	value not estimable
Twn Car Lan'let	7750	value not estimable
A-W Twn Car	7350	value not estimable

1933

1933 Packard, Super Eight, 1004, club sedan, OCW

PACKARD — TENTH SERIES, EIGHT (1001, 1002) — EIGHT: The Standard Eight became simply the Eight this year, with horsepower now up to 120 courtesy of such engine refinements as a new dual downdraft Stromberg carburetor, revised manifolding, an automatic choke and smaller flywheel. Three-point motor suspension was adopted. The Bendix-BK vacuum booster brakes of the Twin Six were fitted. Wire wheels were now standard, with disc and wood optional. The angleset hypoid differential introduced on the Light Eight was incorporated. The former vacuum-plate clutch was replaced by a single-plate, with automatic clutch control available optionally. The fender-mounted battery and tool boxes were gone, and the new pivoted pane window ventilation would be offered this one model year only on all eights and twelves. Whereas the 127-1/2-inch wheelbase had previously carried only a five-passenger sedan, now in the Eight Model 1001 it carried the four body styles offered the previous year in the Light Eight. The Eight Model 1002's wheelbase was 136 inches, and it carried 13 body styles.

I.D. DATA: Starting: 370001. Ending: 373010.

Body No.	Body Type & Seating	Price	Weight	Prod. Total
603	Sed.-5P	2150	4335	—
602	Cpe. Sed.-5P	2190	4245	—
608	Cpe.-2/4P	2160	4200	—
609	Cpe. Rds.-2/4P	2250	4150	—
618	Cpe. Rds.-2/4P	2350	4450	—
617	Cpe.-5P	2440	4500	—
619	Cpe. Rds.-2/4P	2380	—	—
611	Phae.-5P	2370	4270	—
621	Sport Phae.-5P			—
613	Sed.-5P	2385	4590	—
614	Sed.-5/7P	2455	—	—
616	Club Sed.-5P	2390	4545	—
623	Conv. Sed.-5P	2890	4515	—
627	Conv. Vic.-5P	2780	4540	—
610	Tr.-5/7P	2390	4275	—
615	Sed. Limo.-5/7P	2550	4725	—
5613	Formal Sed.-5/7P	3085	4900	—

Note: The first four body numbers were the 1001 cars, the remainder were Model 1002.

ENGINE: L-head. Straight eight. Cast en bloc. B & S: 3-3/16 in. x 5 in. Disp.: 319.2 cu. in. C.R.: 6.0 standard, 6.38 & 5.0 opt. Brake H.P.: 120 @ 3200 R.P.M. Net H.P.: 32.5. Main bearings: Nine. Valve lifters: Solid. Carburetor: Stromberg.

CHASSIS: [Tenth Series (1001)] W.B.: 127-1/2 in. Tires: 17 x 7.00. [Tenth Series (1002)] W.B.: 136 in. Tires: 17 x 7.00

TECHNICAL: Selective synchromesh. Speeds: 3F/1R. Single plate clutch. Shaft drive & angleset hypoid differential. Overall ratio: 4.36 standard, 4.69 & 4.07 opt. Mechanical brakes on all wheels. Wire wheels.

OPTIONS: Dual sidemount. Sidemount cover(s). Spotlight.

HISTORICAL: Introduced Jan., 1933. Model year production: (100)-1,881. (1002)-1,099.

PACKARD — TENTH SERIES, SUPER EIGHT (1003, 1004) — EIGHT: The former DeLuxe Eight was now the Super Eight. It featured the same engineering refinements given the Tenth Series Eight. Wheelbases were revised to 135 inches for Model 1003, which remained in a single five-passenger sedan body style. Thirteen body styles were available in Model 1004, which now was on a 142-inch wheelbase. The former 147-1/2-inch wheelbase was dropped, with the result that all custom cars now were offered only on a twelve-cylinder chassis.

I.D. DATA: Starting: 750000. Ending: 751327.

Body No.	Body Type & Seating	Price	Weight	Prod. Total
653	Sed.-5P	2750	4815	—
658	Cpe.-2/4P	2780	4670	—
657	Cpe.-5P	2980	4780	—
659	Cpe. Rds.-2/4P	2870	4625	—
651	Phae.-5P	2890	4490	—
661	Spt. Phae.-5P	3150	4690	—
673	Sed.-5P	—	—	—
654	Sed.-5/7P	3090	4965	—
656	Club Sed.-5P	2975	4830	—
663	Conv. Sed.-5P	3590	4840	—
627	Conv. Vic.-5P	3440	4795	—
610	Tr.-5/7P	2890	4610	—
615	Sed. Limo.-5/7P	3280	5025	—
5613	Formal Sed.-5/7P	3600	5155	—

ENGINE: L-head. Straight eight. Cast en bloc. B & S: 3-1/2 in. x 5 in. Disp.: 384.8 cu. in. C.R.: 6.0 standard, 6.38 & 5.0 opt. Brake H.P.: 145 @ 3200 R.P.M. Net H.P.: 39.2. Main bearings: Nine. Carb.: Stromberg.

CHASSIS: [Super Eight (1003)] W.B.: 135 in. Tires: 17 x 7.00. [Super Eight (1004)] W.B.: 142 in. Tires: 17 x 7.00.

TECHNICAL: Selective synchromesh. Speeds: 3F/1R. Single plate clutch. Shaft drive, angleset hypoid differential. Overall ratio: 4.36 standard, 4.69 & 4.07 optional. Mechanical brakes on all wheels. Wire wheels.

HISTORICAL: Introduced January, 1933. Model year production: (1003)-512, (1004)-788.

1933 Packard, Twelve, 1006, Dietrich sport phaeton, JAC

PACKARD — TENTH SERIES, TWELVE (1005, 1006) — TWELVE: The double-drop frame of the Twin Six became a tapered frame in the Twelve, which was the new designation for Packard's multi-cylindered car. Refinements included a single dry-plate clutch replacing the former two-plate, with vacuum control free wheeling an option. The Stromberg carburetor was given an automatic choke with fast idle. The Model 1005 was on a 142-inch wheelbase offering touring, phaeton, sport phaeton, sedan, convertible sedan, formal sedan, club sedan, convertible victoria, coupe-roadster and five-passenger as well as 2/4-passenger coupe body styles. The Model 1006 on a 147-inch wheelbase included a 5/7-passenger sedan and sedan-limousine together with the custom cars. The designation "Individual Custom" was no longer used, and the dropping of the long wheelbase chassis for the Super Eight meant that anyone desiring a custom Packard this year had to go for twelve cylinders.

I.D. DATA: Serial number located on a rectangular plate mounted on the firewall. Starting: 901001. Ending: 901600.

Body No.	Body Type & Seating	Price	Weight	Prod. Total
630	Tr.-5/7P	—	—	—
631	Phae.-5P	3790	5095	—
641	Spt. Phae.-5P	4090	5175	—
633	Sed.-5P	3860	5385	—
643	Conv. Sed.-5P	4650	5405	—
5633	Formal Sed.-5P	4560	5690	—
636	Clb. Sed.-5P	3960	5400	—
637	Cpe.-5P	3890	5300	—
647	Conv. Vict.-5P	4490	5225	—
638	Cpe.-2/4P	3720	5255	—
639	Cpe. Rds.-2/4P	3850	5160	—
634	Sed.-5/7P	4085	5600	—
635	Sed. Limo.-5/7P	4285	5650	—
4000	All W. Cabr.-5/7P	6030	5650	—
D-758	All W. Cabr. LeB.-5/7P	7000	5610	—
4001	All W. Land'let.-5/7P	6250	5650	—
4002	All W. Twn. Car-5/7P	6080	5610	—
D-759	All W. Twn. Car LeB.-5/7P	7000	5670	—
4003	All W. Twn. Car-Lan.-5/7P	6250	5610	—
4004	Cab. Sed. Limo.-6P	6000	5650	—

Body No.	Body Type & Seating	Price	Weight	Prod. Total
4005	Spt. Sed.-5P	6000	5330	—
4007	Sed. Limo.-5/7P	6045	5650	—
3068	Stat. Cpe. Dietrich-2/4P	6000	5360	—
3069	Spt. Phae. Dietrich-4P	5875	5160	—
3070	Conv. Sed. Dietrich-5P	6570	5460	—
3071	Conv. Rbt. Dietrich-2/4P	6080	5325	—
3072	Conv. Vict. Dietrich-4P	6070	5175	—
3182	Spt. Sed. Dietrich-5/7P	7000	5735	—

Note: It was a Dietrich Sport Sedan (3182) which became the basis for the famous ''Car of the Dome'' exhibited at the Century of Progress Exposition in Chicago.

ENGINE: 67° V-block. Modified L. Twelve. Cast iron monobloc. B & S: 3-7/16 in. x 4 in. Disp.: 445.5 cu. in., 7.5 liters. C.R.: 6.0:1. Brake H.P.: 160 @ 3200 R.P.M. Net H.P.: 56.7. Main bearings: Four. Valve lifters: Zero lash. Carb.: Stromberg.

CHASSIS: [1005 Series] W.B.: 142 in. Tires: 7.50 x 17. [1006] W.B.: 147 in. Tires: 7.50 x 17.

TECHNICAL: Selective transmission. Speeds: 3F/1R. Floor shift controls. Single dry plate clutch. Shaft drive. Overall ratio: open cars: 4.41, closed: 4.69, opt.: 4.06 or 5.07. Mechanical brakes on four wheels. Wire or wood spoke wheels.

OPTIONS: Front bumper w/vibration dampers. Rear bumper. Dual sidemount. Sidemount cover(s). Heater. Spotlight (inc. on open cars, opt. on others).

HISTORICAL: Introduced January, 1933. Model year production: 520.

1933
10th Series

Model 1001, Eight, 127" wb

	FP	5	4	3	2	1
Conv	2250	13,500	27,000	45,000	70,000	90,000
RS Cpe	2160	6000	12,000	20,000	28,000	40,000
Cpe Sed	2190	5700	11,400	19,000	26,600	38,000
Sed	2150	5400	10,800	18,000	25,200	36,000

Model 1002, Eight, 136" wb

Phae	2370	32,700	60,000	92,000	118,000	160,000
Conv Sed	2890	33,500	61,000	94,000	120,000	165,000
Conv Vic	2780	34,300	62,000	96,000	122,000	170,000
7P Tr	2390	30,300	57,000	86,000	112,000	145,000
RS Cpe	2350	6750	13,500	22,500	31,500	45,000
5P Cpe	2440	6300	12,600	21,000	29,400	42,000
Sed	2385	6000	12,000	20,000	28,000	40,000
7P Sed	2455	6150	12,300	20,500	28,700	41,000
Clb Sed	2390	6300	12,600	21,000	29,400	42,000
Limo	3085	6750	13,500	22,500	31,500	45,000

Model 1003, Super Eight, 135" wb

Sed	2750	6750	13,500	22,500	31,500	45,000

Model 1004, Super Eight, 142" wb

Conv	2870	38,000	67,000	105,000	133,000	190,000
Phae	2890	39,000	69,000	108,000	137,000	195,000
Spt Phae	3150	42,000	74,000	116,000	147,000	210,000
Conv Vic	3440	44,000	77,000	121,000	154,000	220,000
Conv Sed	3590	42,000	74,000	116,000	147,000	210,000
7P Tr	2980	40,000	70,000	110,000	140,000	200,000
RS Cpe	2780	9000	18,000	30,000	42,000	60,000
5P Cpe	2980	8250	16,500	27,500	38,500	55,000
Sed	3090	6000	12,000	20,000	28,000	40,000
Clb Sed	2975	6300	12,600	21,000	29,400	42,000
Limo	3280	7350	14,700	24,500	34,300	49,000
Fml Sed	3600	7800	15,600	26,000	36,400	52,000

Model 1005, Twelve, 142" wb

Conv	3850	51,000	90,000	141,000	179,000	255,000
Spt Phae	4090	52,000	91,000	143,000	182,000	260,000
Conv Sed	4650	52,000	91,000	143,000	182,000	260,000
Conv Vic	4490	53,000	93,000	146,000	186,000	265,000
RS Cpe	3720	9900	19,800	33,000	46,200	66,000
5P Cpe	3890	8550	17,100	28,500	39,900	57,000
Sed	3860	6750	13,500	22,500	31,500	45,000
Fml Sed	4560	7200	14,400	24,000	33,600	48,000
Clb Sed	3880	7350	14,700	24,500	34,300	49,000

Model 1006, Standard, 147" wb

7P Sed	4085	9000	18,000	30,000	42,000	60,000
Limo	4285	11,400	22,800	38,000	56,000	76,000

Model 1006, Custom Twelve, 147" wb, Dietrich

Conv	6085	55,000	93,000	146,000	186,000	265,000
Conv Vic	6070	55,000	97,000	152,000	193,000	275,000
Spt Phae	5875	54,000	95,000	149,000	189,000	270,000
Conv Sed	6570	55,000	97,000	152,000	193,000	275,000
Cpe	6000	9900	19,800	33,000	46,200	66,000
Fml Sed	7000	10,500	21,000	35,000	49,000	70,000

Model 1006, LeBaron Custom, Twelve, 147" wb

A-W Cabr	7000	value not estimable
A-W Twn Car	7000	value not estimable

Model 1006, Packard Custom, Twelve, 147" wb

A-W Cabr	6030	value not estimable
A-W Lan'let	6250	value not estimable
Spt Sed	6000	value not estimable
A-W Twn Car	6250	value not estimable
Twn Car Lan'let	6250	value not estimable
Limo	6045	value not estimable
Lan'let Limo	6000	value not estimable
A-W Cabr	6030	value not estimable
A-W Twn Car	6080	value not estimable

1934

PACKARD — ELEVENTH SERIES, EIGHT (1100, 1101, 1102) — EIGHT: Many detail changes highlighted the Eleventh Series. An oil temperature regulator was added, and the gas tank filler was built into the left rear taillight assembly. The new bumpers were slotted, simulating a double-bar look. The car was re-engineered for radio, necessitating a larger, heavy duty generator, with a vacuum-tube radio becoming an option. The pivot window treatment of the year previous gave way to an angle vent wing. The three model numbers for the Eleventh Series Packard Eight reflected three new wheelbase lengths. Model 1100 was 129-1/2 inches, and once again was provided with only a single five-passenger sedan. Model 1102 was 141-1/4 inches and offered a sedan and sedan-limousine for seven passengers. Model 1101 was 136-1/4 inches, with ten body styles offered.

I.D. DATA: Starting: 374001. Ending: 379149.

1934 Packard, Eight, 1100, sedan, JAC

Body No.	Body Type & Seating	Price	Weight	Prod. Total
703	Sed.-5P	2350	4640	—
719	Cpe. Rds.-2/4P	2580	4430	—
711	Phae.-4P	2570	4350	—
710	Tr.-7P	2590	4400	—
718	Cpe.-2/4P	2550	4500	—
717	Cpe.-5P	2640	4580	—
716	Clb. Sed.-5P	2670	4730	—
713	Sed.-5P	2585	4660	—
723	Conv. Sed.-5P	3090	4680	—
712	Formal Sed.-5P	3285	4760	—
727	Conv. Vict.-5P	2980	4710	—
714	Sed.-7P	2655	4945	—
715	Sed. Limo.-7P	2790	5000	—

ENGINE: L-head. Straight eight. Cast en bloc. B & S: 3-3/16 in. x 5 in. Disp.: 319.2 cu. in. Brake H.P.: 120 @ 3200 R.P.M. Net H.P.: 32.5. Main bearings: Nine. Valve lifters: Solid. Carb.: Stromberg.

CHASSIS: [Eleventh Series (1100)] W.B.: 129-1/2. Tires: 17 x 7.00. [Eleventh Series (1101)] W.B.: 136-1/4. Tires: 17 x 7.00. [Eleventh Series (1102)] W.B.: 141-1/2. Tires: 17 x 7.00.

TECHNICAL: Selective synchromesh. Speeds: 3F/1R. Single plate clutch. Shaft drive, angleset hypoid differential. Overall ratio: 4.35 standard, 4.69 & 4.07 opt. Mechanical brakes on all wheels. Wire wheels. Drivetrain options: Free-wheeling.

OPTIONS: Dual sidemount. Sidemount cover(s). Radio (79.50). Cigar lighter. Chrome plate wheel covers (10.00 ea). Deluxe radiator ornament (10.00). Pelican radiator ornament (20.00). Six disc wheels (25.00). Six wood wheels (78.00). Six chrome wire wheels (192.00). Six chrome disc wheels (85.00). Six chrome wheel trimming (12.00). Side mirrors (16.00 pr.).

HISTORICAL: Introduced August, 1933. Model year production: 5,120.

1934 Packard, Super Eight, 5-pass. sedan, OCW

PACKARD — ELEVENTH SERIES, SUPER EIGHT (1103, 1104, 1105) — EIGHT: Though the same refinements made to the Eight were incorporated in the Super Eight as well, the big news this year was the return of custom cars to the Super Eight line. The Model 1103 remained the bread-and-butter sedan, at a new low price of $2350. The Model 1104 offered eleven body styles, the same lineup as the previous year with the exception of the seven-passenger sedan and sedan-limousine. These now moved to the 147-inch wheelbase which was newly reinstated for the Super Eight Model 1105, which also carried all the custom bodies provided the Twelve except for the LeBaron Sport Runabout and Sport Coupe by Packard.

PACKARD — ELEVENTH SERIES, SUPER EIGHT (1103, 1104, 1105) —

EIGHT: Though the same refinements made to the Eight were incorporated in the Super eight as well, the big news this year was the return of custom cars to the Super Eight line. The Model 1103 remained the bread-and-butter sedan, at a new low price of $2350. The Model 1104 offered eleven body styles, the same lineup as the previous year with the exception of the seven-passenger sedan and sedan-limousine. These were moved to the 147-inch wheelbase which was newly reinstated for the Super Eight Model 1105, which also carried all the custom bodies provided the Twelve except for the LeBaron Sport Runabout and Sport Coupe by Packard.

I.D. DATA: Starting: 752001. Ending: 753946.

Body No.	Body Type & Seating	Price	Weight	Prod. Total
753	Sed.-5P	2950	4890	—
759	Cpe. Rds.-2/4P	3070	4680	—
751	Phae.-5P	3090	4645	—
761	Spt. Phae.-4P	3350	4740	—
750	Tr.-7P	3180	4720	—
758	Cpe.-2/4P	2980	4800	—
757	Cpe.-5P	3180	4885	—
756	Club Sed.-5P	3255	4985	—
763	Conv. Sed.-5P	3790	4390	—
752	Formal Sed.-5P	3800	5010	—
767	Conv. Vict.-5P	3640	4875	—
754	Sed.-7P	3290	5245	—
755	Limo.-7P	3480	5275	—

The following are Custom cars which were returned to the Eleventh Series Model 1105 Super Eight line:

Body No.	Body Type & Seating	Price	Weight	Prod. Total
4068	Stat. Cpe. by Dietrich-2/4P		5445	—
4071	Conv. Rbt. by Dietrich-2/4P		5363	—
4070	Conv. Sed. by Dietrich-5P		5800	—
4072	Conv. Vict. by Dietrich-5P		5345	—
4182	Spt. Sed. by Dietrich-5P		6295	—
858	All W. Cabr. by LeBaron-5/7P		5450	—
859	All W. Twn. Car by LeBaron-5/7P		5450	—
280	Spt. Phae. by LeBaron-5P		7065	—

ENGINE: L-head. Straight eight. Cast en bloc. B & S: 3-1/2 in. x 5 in. Disp.: 384.8 cu. in. C.R.: 6.0 standard, 6.38 & 5.0 opt. Brake H.P.: 145 @ 3200 R.P.M. Net H.P.: 39.2. Main bearings: Nine. Carb.: Stromberg.

CHASSIS: [Super Eight (1103)] W.B.: 134-7/8 in. Tires: 17 x 7.00. [Super Eight (1104)] W.B. 141-7/8 in. Tires: 17 x 7.00. [Super Eight (1105)]W.B.: 146-7/8 in. Tires: 17 x 7.00.

TECHNICAL: Selective synchromesh. Speeds: 3F/1R. Single plate clutch. Shaft drive, angleset hypoid differential. Overall ratio: 4.36 standard, 4.69 & 4.07 opt. Mechanical brakes on all wheels. Wire wheels. Drivetrain options: vacuum clutch.

OPTIONS: Dual sidemount. Sidemount cover(s). Deluxe radio (79.50). Clock. Cigar lighter. Spotlight. Mirrors. Luggage rack (144.00). Rumble seat windshield (175.00). V-lensed headlight & parking lights.

HISTORICAL: Introduced August 1933. Model year production: 1,920.

1934 Packard, Twelve, 1108, Dietrich convertible victoria, AA

PACKARD — ELEVENTH SERIES, TWELVE (1106, 1107, 1108) —

TWELVE: Three wheelbases carried the Packard Twelve this year. The Model 1106 was a Twelve on the Super Eight's 135-inch wheelbase chassis and offered in two memorable models: the LeBaron Runabout Speedster and the Sport Coupe by Packard. Model 1107 was the 142-inch wheelbase and carried eleven production body styles. Model 1108 was the long 147-inch wheelbase and offered the seven-passenger production sedan and sedan-limousine, as well as a variety of LeBaron and Dietrich custom cars. There were engineering refinements throughout the Twelve model lines. In the interior the instrument panel was redesigned, and radio was a popular new option. Though weighing well over 5000 pounds, these Packard Twelves were fine performing cars, with 0 to 60 in 20.4. seconds.

I.D. DATA: Serial numbers located on a rectangular plate mounted on the firewall. Starting: 901601. Ending: 903000.

Body No.	Body Type & Seating	Price	Weight	Prod. Total
NA	Spt. Cpe. by Packard-4P	NA	NA	—
275	Rbt. Spd. LeB.-2P	7746	5400	—
730	Tr.-5/7P	3980	5415	—
731	Phae.-5P	3890	5325	—
741	Spt. Phae.-5P	4190	5400	—
733	Sed.-5P	3960	5530	—
743	Conv. Sed.-5P	4750	5470	—
732	Fml. Sed.-5P	4660	5630	—
736	Clb. Sed.-5P	4060	5660	—
737	Cpe.-5P	3990	5530	—
747	Conv. Vict.	4590	5440	—
738	Cpe.-2/4P	3820	5585	—
739	Cpe. Rds.-2/4P	3850	5330	—
734	Sed.-5/7P	4185	5700	—
735	Sed. limo.-5/7P	4385	5750	—
858	All W. Cabr. LeB.-5/7P	6155	5655	—
4002	All W. Twn. Car Dietrich	5695	5715	—
859	All W. Twn. Car LeB.	6155	5655	—
4068	State. Cpe. Dietrich-2/4P	6185	5405	—
4069	Spt. Phae. Dietrich-4P	5180	5400	—
4070	Conv. Sed. Dietrich-5P	6555	5505	—
4071	Conv. Rbt. Dietrich-2/4P	6100	5370	—
4072	Conv. Vict. Dietrich-4P	6080	5220	—
4182	Spt. Sed. Dietrich-5P	7060	5130	—
280	Spt. Phae. LeB.-4P	7065	5130	—

ENGINE: 67° V-block. Modified L. Twelve. Cast iron monobloc. B & S: 3-7/16 in. x 4 in. Disp.: 445.5 cu. in., 7.5 liters. C.R.: 6.0 with cast heads, 6.0 & 6.8 with aluminum heads. Brake H.P.: 160 @ 3200 R.P.M. Net H.P.: 56.7. Main bearings: Four. Valve lifters: Mechanical Zero lash. Carb.: Stromberg.

CHASSIS: [1106 Series] W.B.: 134-7/8 in. Tires: 7.00 x 17. [1107 Series] W.B.: 141-7/8 in. Tires: 7.50 x 17. [1108 Series] W.B.: 146-7/8 in. tires: 7.50 x 17.

TECHNICAL: Selective synchromesh. Speeds: 3F/1R. Floor shift controls. Single dry plate clutch with vacuum assist. Shaft drive. Overall ratio: 4.41 open cars, 4.69 closed, 4.06 or 5.07 opt. Mechanical, vacuum assisted brakes on four wheels. Wire or wood spoke wheels.

OPTIONS: Sidemount cover(s). Radio (79.50). Heater. Radio Antenna. Spotlight.

HISTORICAL: Introduced August, 1933. Model year production: 960.

1934
11th Series

Model 1100, Eight, 129" wb

	FP	5	4	3	2	1
Sed	2350	6750	13,500	22,500	31,500	45,000

Model 1101, Eight, 141" wb

Conv	2580	22,000	36,000	60,000	93,000	120,000
Phae	2570	24,100	42,000	68,000	98,000	126,000
Conv Vic	2980	24,800	44,000	70,000	99,000	128,000
Conv Sed	3090	25,500	45,000	73,000	100,000	130,000
RS Cpe	2550	7500	15,000	25,000	35,000	50,000
5P Cpe	2640	7050	14,100	23,500	32,900	47,000
Sed	2585	6750	13,500	22,500	31,500	45,000
Clb Sed	2670	6900	13,800	23,000	32,200	46,000
Fml Sed	3285	7050	14,100	23,500	32,900	47,000

Model 1102, Eight, 141" wb

7P Sed	2655	7200	14,400	24,000	33,600	48,000
Limo	2790	7500	15,000	25,000	35,000	50,000

Model 1103, Super Eight, 135" wb

Sed	2950	7350	14,700	24,500	34,300	49,000

Model 1104, Super Eight, 142" wb

Conv	3070	24,100	42,000	68,000	98,000	126,000
Phae	3090	25,500	45,000	73,000	100,000	130,000
Spt Phae	3350	27,900	51,000	79,000	106,000	136,000
Conv Vic	3640	29,500	55,000	84,000	110,000	140,000
Conv Sed	3790	30,300	57,000	86,000	112,000	145,000
RS Cpe	2980	9000	18,000	30,000	42,000	60,000
5P Cpe	3180	7500	15,000	25,000	35,000	50,000
Clb Sed	3255	7200	14,400	24,000	33,600	48,000
Fml Sed	3800	7500	15,000	25,000	35,000	50,000

Model 1105, Super Eight, Standard, 147" wb

7P Sed	5245	8250	16,500	27,500	38,500	55,000
Limo	5275	9000	18,000	30,000	42,000	60,000

Model 1105, Dietrich, Super Eight, 147" wb

Conv	5365	22,000	36,000	60,000	93,000	120,000
Conv Vic	5345	31,100	58,000	88,000	114,000	150,000
Conv Sed	5800	30,300	57,000	86,000	112,000	145,000
Cpe	5445	9900	19,800	33,000	46,200	66,000
Spt Sed	6295	9900	19,800	33,000	46,200	66,000

Model 1105, LeBaron, Super Eight, 147" wb
Model 1106, Twelve, LeBaron, 135" wb

Spds	7260			value not estimable		
Spt Phae	7065			value not estimable		

Model 1107, Twelve, 142" wb

Conv	3850			value not estimable		
Phae	3890			value not estimable		
Spt Phae	4190			value not estimable		
Conv Vic	4590			value not estimable		
Conv Sed	4750			value not estimable		
7P Tr	3980			value not estimable		
RS Cpe	3820			value not estimable		
5P Cpe	3990			value not estimable		
Sed	3960			value not estimable		
Clb Sed	4060			value not estimable		
Fml Sed	4660			value not estimable		

1934
Model 1108, Twelve, Standard, 147" wb

	FP	5	4	3	2	1
7P Sed	4185	8550	17,100	28,500	39,900	57,000
Limo	4385	9300	18,600	31,000	43,400	62,000

Model 1108, Twelve, Dietrich, 147" wb

	FP	
Conv	6100	value not estimable
Spt Phae	5180	value not estimable
Conv Sed	6555	value not estimable
Vic Conv	6080	value not estimable
Cpe	6185	value not estimable
Spt Sed	7060	value not estimable

Model 1108, Twelve, LeBaron, 147" wb

	FP	
Cabr	6150	value not estimable
Spt Phae	7820	value not estimable
A-W Twn Car	6150	value not estimable

1935

1935 Packard, One Twenty, 4-dr. sedan, AA

PACKARD — TWELFTH SERIES, ONE TWENTY — EIGHT: With this car, Packard indelibly entered the medium-priced field. Its engine was typically Packard, an L-head straight eight delivering 110 horsepower. The wheelbase was 120 inches, hence the new model's designation. Nearly 25,000 were sold in 1935, during which year not quite 7,000 of all the other cars Packard was producing found buyers. The One Twenty was a smash hit in the marketplace, and it was a medium-priced car of total Packard integrity. Independent front suspension and hydraulic brakes were two of the One Twenty's features which would not be adopted on the larger cars for several years.

I.D. DATA: Serial number located on a metal firewall plate. The plate also showed the body type number and the production number of that particular car, starting with a 200 base number. Starting: body type number plus 201. Engine numbers located on boss on upper left corner of cylinder block. Starting: X-1501. Ending: X-27499.

Body No.	Body Type & Seating	Price	Weight	Prod. Total
898	Bus. Cpe.-2P	980	3400	—
899	Conv. Cpe.-2/4P	1070	3385	—
895	Spt. Cpe.-2/4P	1020	3435	—
894	Tr. Cpe.-5P	1025	3455	—
893	Sed.-5P	1060	3510	—
896	Clb. Sed.-5P	1085	3515	—
892	Tr. Sed.-5P	1095	3550	—

ENGINE: L-head. Straight eight. Cast iron. B & S: 3-1/4 in. x 3-7/8 in. Disp.: 256.16 cu. in. C.R.: 6.5 standard, 7.0 opt. Brake H.P.: 110 @ 3850 R.P.M. Net H.P.: 33.8. Main bearings: Five. Valve lifters: Mechanical. Carb.: Stromberg.

CHASSIS: [120 Series] W.B.: 120 in. Tires: 7.00 x 16. [Commercial] W.B.: 158 in. Tires: 7.00 x 16.

TECHNICAL: Selective synchromesh. Speeds: 3F/1R. Floor shift controls. Dry plate clutch. Shaft drive. Overall ratio: 4.36 or 4.54 (depending on body style). Hydraulic brakes on four wheels. Disc wheels.

OPTIONS: Dual sidemount. Sidemount cover(s). Bumper guards. Radio. Heater. Clock. Radio antenna. Spotlight.

HISTORICAL: Introduced Jan., 1935. Model year production: 24,995.

PACKARD — TWELFTH SERIES, EIGHT (1200, 1201, 1202) — EIGHT: Aluminum cylinder heads were standard, the compression ratio was changed to 6.5, and horsepower was up to 130 with the Twelfth Series Eight. Top speed was over 90 mph. In the chassis, the X-member was extended to form boxed side rails, eliminating the traditional tubular front cross member. On the outside, there was a new look to the car beginning up front with a five-degree slant to the radiator and carrying the pontoon fenders in the rear. Chrome side louvers were a distinguishing feature. Side mounts could be ordered, but if they were not, the spare tire was concealed in the sloping rear panel. The 127-inch-wheelbase Model 1200 remained the five-passenger sedan. Body styles on the 134-inch-wheel-

1935 Packard, Eight, 1201, sedan, JAC

base Model 1201 were ten in number and included a LeBaron Cabriolet. On Model 1202's 139-inch wheelbase were seven body styles, including a new "Business" sedan and limousine and just one custom, the LeBaron Town Car.

I.D. DATA: Serial number located on metal rectangular plate on the firewall. The plate also showed body type number plus the production number for that particular car starting with a base number of 200. Starting: body type number plus 201. Engine numbers located on base on upper left corner of cylinder block. Starting: 385001. Ending: 390499.

Body No.	Body Type & Seating	Price	Weight	Prod. Total
803	Sed.-5P	2385	4780	—
818	Cpe.-2/4P	2470	4475	—
817	Cpe.-5P	2560	4760	—
819	Cpe. Rds.-2/4P	2580	4725	—
811	Phae.-5P	2870	4690	—
811	Spt. Phae.-5P	NA	NA	—
813	Sed.-5P	2585	4815	—
816	Clb. Sed.-5P	2580	4820	—
812	Formal Sed.-5/7P	3285	5035	—
807	Conv. Vict.-5P	3200	4835	—
195	Cabr. LeB.-5/7P	5240	5185	—
814	Sed.-5/7P	2755	4955	—
814	Bus. Sed.-5/8P	2630	4985	—
815	Limo.-5/7P	2890	5045	—
815	Bus. Limo.-5/8P	2765	5150	—
863	Conv. Sed.-5P	3300	5140	—
810	Tr.-5/7P	3170	4400	—
194	Tr. Car LeB.-5/7P	5385	5225	—

ENGINE: L-head. Straight eight. B & S: 3-3/16 in. x 5 in. Disp.: 320 cu. in. C.R.: 6.5 standard, 6.0 optional. Brake H.P.: 130 @ 3200 R.P.M. Net H.P.: 32.5. Main bearings: Nine. Valve lifters: Roller cam. Carb.: Stromberg-Duplex.

CHASSIS: [1200] W.B.: 127 in. Tires: 7.00 x 17 low pressure. [1201] W.B.: 134 in. Tires: 7.00 x 17 low pressure.]1202[W.B.: 139 in. (comm. vehicles — 160 in.) Tires: 7.00 x 17 low pressure.

TECHNICAL: Selective synchromesh. Speeds: 3F/1R. Floor shift controls. Single disc clutch. Shaft drive. Overall ratio: 4.69 standard, 4.36 & 4.07 opt. Mechanical brakes on four wheels. Welded spoke wheels.

OPTIONS: Dual sidemount. Sidemount cover(s). Bumper guards. Radio. Heater. Clock. Radio antenna. Spotlight. Disc and wood wheels.

HISTORICAL: Introduced August, 1934. Model year production: 4,781.

1935 Packard, Super Eight, 1204, phaeton, AA

PACKARD — TWELETH SERIES, SUPER EIGHT (1203, 1204, 1205) — EIGHT: With the same engineering refinements as the Eight, the Super Eight for 1935 enjoyed a horsepower increase to 150. The new body styling theme of the Eight was followed on the Super Eight; the only sedan with a trunk bulge was the Club Sedan. The hand brake was relocated under the cowl, which was a good idea; the front doors were hinged at the rear, which arguably was not — both these features in the Eight as well. Like the Eight, the Super Eight was offered in three wheelbases. The 132-inch Model 1203 was the five-passenger sedan. The 139-inch Model 1204 was offered in ten body styles, including the LeBaron Cabriolet. The 144-inch Model 1205 was offered in seven body styles, including a new "Business" sedan and limousine, and the LeBaron Town Car.

Serial number located on metal rectangular plate on the firewall. The plate also showed body type number plus the production number of that particular car starting with a base number of 200. Starting: body type number plus 201. Engine numbers located on upper half of crankcase, left side, front end. Upper cylinder left side front on 12 only. Starting: 755001. Ending: 756999.

Body No.	Body Type & Seating	Price	Weight	Prod. Total
843	Sed.-5P	2990	5030	—
858	Cpe.-2/4P	2880	4935	—
857	Cpe.-5P	3080	5015	—
859	Cpe. Rds.-2/4P	3070	5045	—
851	Phae.-5P	3390	5120	—
841	Spt. Phae.-5P	3650	5350	—
856	Clb. Sed.-5P	3170	5150	—
852	Fml. Sed.-5/7P	3800	5250	—
847	Conv. Vict.-5P	3860	5095	—
853	Sed.-5P	NA	NA	—
195	Cabr. LeB.-5/7P	5670	5300	—
854	Sed.-5/7P	3390	5300	—
854	Bus. Sed.-5/8P	3265	5320	—
855	Limo.-5/7P	3580	5350	—
855	Bus. Limo-5/8P	3455	5380	—
883	Conv. Sed.-5P	4010	5050	—
850	Tr.-5/7P	3690	4729	—
194	Twn. Car LeB.-5/7P	5815	5525	—

ENGINE: L-head. Straight eight. Cast en block. B & S: 3-1/2 in. x 5 in. Disp.: 384.4 cu. in. C.R.: 6.3 standard, 6.9 opt. Brake H.P.: 150 @ 3200 R.P.M. Net H.P.: 39.2. Main bearings: Nine. Valve lifters: Roller cam. Carb.: Stromberg-Duplex.

CHASSIS: [1203 Series] W.B.: 132 in. Tires: 7.00 x 17. [1204 Series] W.B.: 139 in. Tires: 7.00 x 17. [1205 Series] W.B.: 144 In. (comm. vehicles -165 in.) Tires: 7.00 x 17.

TECHNICAL: Selective synchromesh. Speeds: 3F/1R. Floor shift controls. Single disc clutch. Shaft drive. Overall ratio: 4.41:1. Mechanical brakes on four wheels. Welded spoke wheels.

OPTIONS: Front bumper (stabilizer). Dual sidemount. Sidemount cover(s). Bumper guards. Radio. Heater. Spotlight.

HISTORICAL: Introduced August, 1934. Model year production: 1,392.

1935 Packard, Twelve, 1208, 7-pass. sedan, JAC

PACKARD — TWELVETH SERIES, TWELVE (1206, 1207, 1208) — TWELVE: Aluminum heads and an increase in stroke to 4-1/4 inches were among the refinements resulting in a horsepower increase to 175 for the Twelve. With the optional high compression head, 180 bhp was on tap. Three-point rubber suspension of the engine was adopted. Chassis and body styling changes followed the Eight and Super Eight theme. Presumably, Model 1206 was a short-wheelbase sedan, though surviving Packard records did not include it in production rosters. Model 1207 was on the 139-1/4-inch wheelbase and featured ten body styles, a LeBaron All-Weather Cabriolet the only custom. Model 1208 was on the 144-1/4-inch chassis, and offered five body styles with a LeBaron All-Weather Town Car the only custom.

I.D. DATA: Serial number located on a rectangular plate mounted on the firewall. Starting: 903001. Ending: 903587. There was also a body type number and the production number of that particular car, starting with a base number of 200. Starting: body number plus 201.

Body No.	Body Type & Seating	Price	Weight	Prod. Total
NA	Short 5P Sed.			
831	Phae.-5P	4190	5475	—
821	Spt. Phae.-5P	4490	5830	—
833	Sed.-5P	3960	5700	—
832	Formal Sed.-5P	4660	5695	—
836	Clb. Sed.-5P	4060	5640	—
837	Cpe.-5P	3990	5545	—
827	Conv. Vict.-5P	4890	5605	—
838	Cpe.-2/4P	3820	5535	—
839	Cpe. Rds.-2/4P	3850	5480	—
195	All W. Cabr. LeB.-5/7P	6290	5930	—
830	Tr.-7P	4490	5415	—
873	Conv. Sed.-5P	5050	5990	—
834	Sed.-7P	4285	5790	—
835	Limo.-7P	4485	5840	—
194	All W. Twn. Car Leb.-7P	6435	5950	—

ENGINE: 67° V-block. Modified L. Twelve. Cast iron monobloc. B & S: 3-7/16 in. x 4-1/4 in. Disp.: 473.3 cu. in. C.R.: 6.0, 6.25, 7.0. Brake H.P.: 175 @ 3200 R.P.M. Net H.P.: 56.7. Main bearings: Four. Valve lifters: Mechanical with zero lash take-up mechanisms. Carb.: Stromberg-Duplex.

CHASSIS: [1206] W.B.: 132-1/2 in. [1207] W.B.: 139-1/4 in. Tires: 7.50 x 17. [1208] W.B.: 144-1/4 in. Tires: 7.50 x 17.

TECHNICAL: Selective synchromesh. Speeds: 3F/1R. Floor shift control. Single plate clutch with vacuum assist. Shaft drive. Overall ratio: 4.41 standard, 4.06, 4.69, 5.07 opt. Mechanical vacuum assist brakes on four wheels. Wire or wood spoke wheels. Vacuum clutch.

OPTIONS: Dual sidemount (65.00). Sidemount cover(s). Bumper Guards. Radio. Heater. Spotlight.

HISTORICAL: Introduced August, 1934. Model year production: 788.

1935
120-A, 8 cyl., 120" wb

	FP	5	4	3	2	1
Conv	1095	7500	15,000	25,000	35,000	50,000
Bus Cpe	980	4200	8400	14,000	19,600	28,000
Spt Cpe	1020	4500	9000	15,000	21,000	30,000
Tr Cpe	1025	4500	9000	15,000	21,000	30,000
Sed	1060	3750	7500	12,500	17,500	25,000
Clb Sed	1085	3900	7800	13,000	18,200	26,000
Tr Sed	1095	3900	7800	13,000	18,200	26,000

Series 1200, 8 cyl., 127" wb

	FP	5	4	3	2	1
Sed	2385	4500	9000	15,000	21,000	30,000

Series 1201, 8 cyl., 134" wb

	FP	5	4	3	2	1
Cpe Rds	2580	8250	16,500	27,500	38,500	55,000
Phae	2670	8550	17,100	28,500	39,900	57,000
Conv Vic	3100	8550	17,100	28,500	39,900	57,000
LeB A-W Cabr	5240	9900	19,800	33,000	46,200	66,000
RS Cpe	2470	6450	12,900	21,500	30,100	43,000
5P Cpe	2560	6300	12,600	21,000	29,400	42,000
Sed	2585	5250	10,500	17,500	24,500	35,000
Fml Sed	3285	5100	10,200	17,000	23,800	34,000
Clb Sed	3200	5400	10,800	18,000	25,200	36,000

Series 1202, 8 cyl., 139" wb

	FP	5	4	3	2	1
7P Sed	2755	6000	12,000	20,000	28,000	40,000
Limo	2890	6750	13,500	22,500	31,500	45,000
Conv Sed	3200	21,000	35,000	49,000	70,000	
LeB A-W Twn Car	5385	11,400	22,800	38,000	56,000	76,000

Series 1203, Super 8, 132" wb

	FP	5	4	3	2	1
5P Sed	2990	6750	13,500	22,500	31,500	45,000

Series 1204, Super 8, 139" wb

	FP	5	4	3	2	1
Rds	3070	9900	19,800	33,000	46,200	66,000
Phae	3190	10,200	20,400	34,000	47,600	68,000
Spt Phae	3450	10,500	21,000	35,000	49,000	70,000
Conv Vic	3760	10,500	21,000	35,000	49,000	70,000
RS Cpe	2880	8250	16,500	27,500	38,500	55,000
5P Cpe	3080	7200	14,400	24,000	33,600	48,000
Clb Sed	3170	6600	13,200	22,000	30,800	44,000
Fml Sed	3800	6450	12,900	21,500	30,100	43,000
LeB A-W Cabr	5670	10,500	21,000	35,000	49,000	70,000

Series 1205, Super 8, 144" wb

	FP	5	4	3	2	1
Tr Sed	3690	9900	19,800	33,000	46,200	66,000
Conv Sed	4010	18,500	33,000	55,000	88,000	110,000
7P Sed	3390	7500	15,000	25,000	35,000	50,000
Limo	3580	8250	16,500	27,500	38,500	55,000
LeB A-W Twn Car	5815	14,400	28,800	48,000	76,000	96,000

Series 1207, V-12, 139" wb

	FP	5	4	3	2	1
Rds	3990	30,300	57,000	86,000	112,000	145,000
Phae	3990	31,100	58,000	88,000	114,000	150,000
Spt Phae	4290	31,100	58,000	88,000	114,000	150,000
RS Cpe	3820	9900	19,800	33,000	46,200	66,000
5P Cpe	3990	7500	15,000	25,000	35,000	50,000
Clb Cpe	4060	7800	15,600	26,000	36,400	52,000
Sed	3960	6750	13,500	22,500	31,500	45,000
Fml Sed	4660	7050	14,100	23,500	32,900	47,000
Conv Vic	4790	30,300	57,000	86,000	112,000	145,000
LeB A-W Cabr	6290	31,100	58,000	88,000	114,000	150,000

Series 1208, V-12, 144" wb

	FP	5	4	3	2	1
Conv Sed	5050	38,000	67,000	105,000	133,000	190,000
7P Sed	4285	7500	15,000	25,000	35,000	50,000
Limo	4485	8250	16,500	27,500	38,500	55,000
LeB A-W Twn Car	6435	35,100	63,000	98,000	124,000	175,000

1936

1936 Packard, One Twenty, 120-B, 4-dr. sedan, AA

PACKARD — FOURTEENTH SERIES, ONE TWENTY (120-B) — EIGHT: Engineering refinements including an increase in stroke to 4-1/2 inches made for 120 hp — and the rather neat fact that now both horsepower and wheelbase matched the One Twenty's designation. The cars were capable of a genuine 85 mph, and 0 to 60 in 19.9 seconds. The suicide doors were gone, and the 120-B's sales of 55,000 cars more than doubled the previous year's figure. The Convertible Sedan was a new body style.

I.D. DATA: Serial numbers located on a metal firewall plate. The plate also showed the body type number and the production number of that particular car, starting with a base number of 200. Starting: body type number plus 201. Engine numbers located on boss on upper left corner of cylinder block. Starting: X-27500. Ending: 99999.

Body No.	Body Type & Seating	Price	Weight	Prod. Total
998	Bus. Cpe.-2P	990	3380	—
999	Conv. Cpe.-2/4P	1110	3525	—
995	Spt. Cpe.-2/4P	1030	3455	—
994	Tr. Cpe.-5P	1040	3475	—
993	Sed.-5P	1075	3505	—
996	Clb. Sed.-5P	1090	3495	—
992	Tr. Sed.-5P	1115	3560	—
997	Conv. Sed.-5P	1395	3660	—

ENGINE: L-head. Straight eight. Cast iron. B & S: 3-1/4 in. x 4-1/2 in. Disp.: 282 cu. in. C.R.: 6.5 standard, 7.0 opt. Brake H.P.: 120 @ 3800 R.P.M. Net H.P.: 33.8. Main bearings: Five. Valve lifters: Mechanical. Carb.: Stromberg.

CHASSIS: W.B. 120 in. Tires: 7.00 x 16.

TECHNICAL: Selective synchromesh. Speeds: 3F/1R. Floorshift control. Clutch: 10 in. plate. Shaft drive. Overall ratio: 4.09 standard, 4.54 & 4.7 opt. Hydraulic brakes on four wheels. Disc or steel artillery wheels.

OPTIONS: Single sidemount. Sidemount cover(s). Radio. Heater. Clock. Radio antenna.

HISTORICAL: Introduced August, 1935. Model year production: 55,042.

1936 Packard, Eight, 1401, 5-pass. coupe, JAC

PACKARD — FOURTEENTH SERIES, EIGHT (1400, 1401, 1402) — EIGHT: Except for numerical designation, the Fourteenth Series Eights were essentially a reprise of the Twelfth Series. (Superstition had resulted in there being no Thirteenth Series.) Chrome strip ribs were added to the headlights, the radiator was sloped another five degrees and the front fenders modified accordingly — but that was about it. Engineering changes included Delco-Remy ignition with octane selector and clutch bearings that were now permanently lubricated. Body styles remained the same, on the same three wheelbase lengths.

I.D. DATA: Serial number located on a metal rectangular plate on the firewall. The plate also showed body type number plus the production number of that particular car, starting with a base number of 200. Starting: body type number plus 201. Engine numbers located on boss on upper left corner of cylinder block. Starting: 390500. Ending: 395499.

Body No.	Body Type & Seating	Price	Weight	Prod. Total
903	Sed.-5P	2385	4815	—
918	Cpe.-2/4P	2470	4735	—
917	Cpe.-5P	2560	4745	—
919	Cpe. Rds.-2/4P	2730	4740	—
911	Phae.-5P	3020	4990	—
901	Spt. Phae.-5P	NA	NA	—
913	Sed.-5P	2585	4978	—
916	Clb. Sed.-5P	2580	4815	—
912	Formal Sed.-5/7P	3285	4958	—
907	Conv. Vict.-5P	3200	4810	—
294	Cabr. LeB.-5/7P	5240	5185	—
914	Sed-5/7P	2755	4950	—
914	Bus. Sed.-5/8P	2630	5020	—
915	Limo.-5/7P	2890	5035	—
915	Bus. Limo.-5/8P	2765	5068	—
963	Conv. Sed.-5P	3400	5103	—
910	Tr.-5/7P	3270	5060	—
295	Twn. Car LeB.-5/7P	5385	5517	—

ENGINE: L-head. Straight eight. Cast en bloc. B & S: 3-3/16 in. x 5 in. Disp.: 320 cu. in. C.R.: 6.5 standard, 6.0 opt. Brake H.P.: 130 @ 3200 R.P.M. Net H.P.: 32.5. Main bearings: Nine. Valve lifters: Roller cam. Carb.: Stromberg-Duplex.

CHASSIS: [1400 Series] W.B.: 127 in. Tires: 7.00 x 17. [1401 Series] W.B.: 134 in. Tires: 7.00 x 17. [1402 Series] W.B.: 139 in. (comm. vehicles — 160 in.) Tires: 7.00 x 17.

TECHNICAL: Selective synchromesh. Speeds: 3F/1R. Floor shift control. Clutch: Single disc. Shaft drive rear axle. Overall ratio: 4.69 standard, 4.36 & 4.07 opt. Mechanical brakes on four wheels. Welded spoke wheels.

OPTIONS: Dual sidemount. Sidemount cover(s). Bumper guards. Radio. Heater. Spotlight.

HISTORICAL: Introduced August, 1935. Model year production: 3,973.

1936 Packard, Super Eight, 1404, coupe roadster, AA

PACKARD — FOURTEENTH SERIES, SUPER EIGHT (1403, 1404, 1405) — EIGHT: The few changes accorded the Eight were also accorded the Super Eight. Body styles and wheelbases remained the same. The Fourteenth Series was memorable as Packard's last for Bijur lubrication, ride control, semi-elliptic suspension, mechanical brakes — and the big 384-cubic-inch engine.

I.D. DATA: Serial number located on a metal rectangular plate on the firewall. The plate also showed body type number plus the production number of that particular car, starting with a base number of 200. Starting: body type number plus 201. Engine numbers located on upper half of crankcase, left side, front end. Starting: 757000. Ending: 758499.

Model No.	Body Type & Seating	Price	Weight	Prod. Total
943	Sed.-5P	2990	5080	—
958	Cpe.-2/4P	2880	4933	—
957	Cpe.-5P	3080	5010	—
959	Cpe. Rds.-2/4P	3070	4993	—
951	Phae.-5P	3390	5080	—
941	Spt. Phae.-5P	3650	5200	—
956	Clb. Sed.-5P	3170	5178	—
952	Formal Sed.-5/7P	3800	5245	—
947	Conv. Vict.-5P	3860	5122	—
294	Cabr. LeB.-5/7P	5670	5300	—
954	Sed.-5/7P	3390	5280	—
954	Bus. Sed.-5/8P	3265	5380	—
955	Limo.-5/7P	3580	5328	—
955	Bus. Limo.-5/8P	3455	5380	—
983	Conv. Sed.-5P	4010	5430	—
950	Tr.-5/7P	3690	5200	—
295	Town Car LeB.-5/7P	5815	5525	—

ENGINE: L-head. Straight eight. Cast en bloc. B & S: 3-1/2 in. x 5 in. Disp.: 384.4 cu. in. C.R.: 6.3 standard, 6.0 opt. Brake H.P.: 150 @ 3200 R.P.M. Net H.P.: 39.2. Main bearings: Nine. Valve lifters: Roller cam. Carb.: Stromberg-Duplex.

CHASSIS: [1403] W.B.: 132 in. Tires: 7 x 17. [1404] W.B.: 139 in. Tires: 7 x 17. [1405] W.B.: 144 in. Tires: 7 x 17.

TECHNICAL: Selective synchromesh. Speeds: 3F/1R. Floor shift control. Single disc clutch. Shaft drive. Overall ratio: 4.41:1. Mechanical brakes on 4 wheels. Welded spoke wheels.

OPTIONS: Dual sidemount. Sidemount cover(s). Bumper guards. Radio. Heater. Spotlight.

HISTORICAL: Introduced August, 1935. Model year production: 1,330.

1936 Packard, Twelve, 1407, convertible sedan, JAC

PACKARD — FOURTEENTH SERIES, TWELVE (1406, 1407, 1408) — TWELVE: The Twelve's engine now had a conventionally designed oil temperature regulator, but further engineering changes were virtually nil. Styling changes for the Eight and Super Eight were also accorded the Twelve. Body styles and wheelbases remained the same. LeBaron's All Weather Cabriolet and All Weather Town Car continued to be the priciest Twelves in the line, at more than $6000.

I.D. DATA: The body type code plus the production number (vehicle number) was used on the rectangular plate mounted on the firewall. In 1936 the body type and production numbers started with a 200 base. Body type number plus 201. Motor Serial Numbers Starting: 904000. Ending: 905499.

Body No.	Body Type & Seating	Price	Weight	Prod. Total
931	Phae.-5P	4190	5480	—
921	Spt. Phae.-5P	4490	5785	—
933	Sed.-5P	3960	5695	—
932	Fml. Sed.-6P	4660	5880	—
936	Clb. Sed.-5P	4060	5760	—
937	Cpe.-5P	3990	5495	—
927	Conv. Vict.-5P	4890	5585	—
938	Cpe.-2/4P	3820	5495	—
939	Cpe. Rds.-2/4P	3850	5495	—
294	All W. Cabr. LeB.-5/7P	6290	5900	—
930	Tr.-7P	4490	5460	—
973	Conv. Sed.-5P	5050	5945	—
934	Sed.-7P	4285	5790	—
935	Sed. Limo.-7P	4485	5890	—
295	All W. Twn. Car LeB.-7P	6435	5950	—

ENGINE: 67° V-block. Modified L. Twelve. B & S: 3-7/16 in. x 4-1/2 in. Disp.: 473.3 cu. in. C.R.: 6.0, 6.25, 7.0. Brake H.P.: 175 @ 3200 R.P.M. (180 @ 3200 with high comp. heads). Net H.P.: 56.7. Main bearings: Four. Valve lifters: Mechanical with zero lash. Carb.: Stromberg-Duplex.

CHASSIS: [1407] W.B.: 139-1/4 in. Tires: 7.50 x 17. [1408] W.B.: 144-1/2 in. Tires: 7.50 x 17.

TECHNICAL: Selective synchromesh. Speeds: 3F/1R. Floor shift control. Single plate clutch. Shaft drive. Overall ratio: 4.41 standard, 4.06, 4.69 & 5.07 opt. Mechanical-vacuum assist brakes on four wheels. Wire spoke wheels.

OPTIONS: Dual sidemount. Sidemount cover(s). Bumper guards. Radio. Heater. Spotlight.

HISTORICAL: Introduced Aug. 1935. Model year production: 682.

1936 14th Series
Series 120-B, 8 cyl., 120" wb

	FP	5	4	3	2	1
Conv	1110	8550	17,100	28,500	39,900	57,000
Conv Sed	1395	9000	18,000	30,000	42,000	60,000
Bus Cpe	990	4500	9000	15,000	21,000	30,000
Spt Cpe	1030	4650	9300	15,500	21,700	31,000
Tr Cpe	1040	4500	9000	15,000	21,000	30,000
2 dr Sed	1075	3150	6300	10,500	14,700	21,000
Sed	1075	3300	6600	11,000	15,400	22,000
Clb Sed	1090	3400	6900	11,500	16,100	23,000
Tr Sed	1115	3300	6600	11,000	15,400	22,000
Series 1400, 8 cyl., 127" wb						
Sed	2385	4050	8100	13,500	18,900	27,000
Series 1401, 8 cyl., 134" wb						
Rds	2730	12,000	24,000	40,000	60,000	80,000
Phae	3020	12,300	24,600	41,000	62,000	82,000
Conv Vic	3200	13,200	26,400	44,000	68,000	88,000
LeB A-W Cabr	5240	13,500	27,000	45,000	70,000	90,000
RS Cpe	2470	6000	12,000	20,000	28,000	40,000
5P Cpe	2560	5400	10,800	18,000	25,200	36,000
Clb Sed	2580	5400	10,800	18,000	25,200	36,000
Sed	2585	4650	9300	15,500	21,700	31,000
Fml Sed	3285	4950	9900	16,500	23,100	33,000
Series 1402, 8 cyl., 139" wb						
Conv Sed	3400	13,500	27,000	45,000	70,000	90,000
7P Tr	3270	13,200	26,400	44,000	68,000	88,000
7P Sed	2755	5250	10,500	17,500	24,500	35,000
Bus Sed	2630	5250	10,500	17,500	24,500	35,000
Limo	2890	6000	12,000	20,000	28,000	40,000
Bus Limo	2765	5700	11,400	19,000	26,600	38,000
LeB Twn Car	5385	9000	18,000	30,000	42,000	60,000
Series 1403, Super 8, 132" wb						
Sed	2990	4500	9000	15,000	21,000	30,000
Series 1404, Super 8, 139" wb						
Cpe Rds	3070	12,900	25,800	48,200	66,000	86,000
Phae	3390	13,200	26,400	44,000	68,000	88,000
Spt Phae	3650	13,500	27,000	45,000	70,000	90,000
Conv Vic	3860	13,500	27,000	45,000	70,000	90,000
LeB A-W Cabr	5670	15,000	30,000	50,000	80,000	100,000
RS Cpe	2880	6750	13,500	22,500	31,500	45,000
5P Cpe	3080	6300	12,600	21,000	29,400	42,000
Clb Sed	3170	6150	12,300	20,500	28,700	41,000
Fml Sed	3800	6000	12,000	20,000	28,000	40,000
Series 1405, Super 8, 144" wb						
7P Tr	3690	15,000	30,000	50,000	80,000	100,000
Conv Sed	4010	18,500	33,000	55,000	88,000	110,000
Series 1407, V-12, 139" wb						
Cpe Rds	3850	31,900	59,000	90,000	116,000	155,000
Phae	4190	32,700	60,000	92,000	118,000	160,000
Spt Phae	4490	32,700	60,000	92,000	118,000	160,000
LeB A-W Cabr	6290	33,500	61,000	94,000	120,000	165,000
RS Cpe	3820	9900	19,800	33,000	46,200	66,000
5P Cpe	3990	9000	18,000	30,000	42,000	60,000
Clb Sed	4060	7500	15,000	25,000	35,000	50,000
Sed	3960	7050	14,100	23,500	32,900	47,000
Fml Sed	4660	7200	14,400	24,000	33,600	48,000
Series 1408, V-12, 144" wb						
7P Tr	4490	32,700	60,000	92,000	118,000	160,000
Conv Sed	5050	34,300	62,000	96,000	122,000	170,000
7P Sed	4285	7500	15,000	25,000	35,000	50,000
Limo	4485	9900	19,800	33,000	46,200	66,000
LeB A-W Twn Car	6435	33,500	61,000	94,000	120,000	165,000

1937

1937 Packard, Six, 115-C, station wagon, OCW

PACKARD — FIFTEENTH SERIES, SIX (115-C) — SIX: Packard's first six-cylinder car since the Fifth Series in 1927 was introduced as a lower-priced companion to the wildly successful One Twenty. Its engine was basically the One Twenty's minus two cylinders, a 237-cubic-inch L-head six good for 100 mph. Its wheelbase was five inches shorter at 115 inches. From the cowl back, the two Junior Packards looked quite alike, distinguishing differences appearing in the shorter hood and front fenders of the new Six, in addition to trim variations (the ornamental hood louvers on the One Twenty were chrome plated, whereas on the Six they were sheet metal stampings). Interiors were less expensively appointed, with no chrome trim on the dashboard. Sidemounts were not available. But the price was right — at $795 to $1295. And the range of body styles included both a convertible coupe and a station wagon, the latter introduced mid-model year.

I.D. DATA: Serial number located on metal firewall plate. The plate also showed body type number plus the actual production number of that body type, starting with a base number of 200. Starting: body type number plus 201. Engine numbers located on boss on upper left corner of cylinder block. Starting: T-1500. Ending: 99999.

Body No.	Body Type & Seating	Price	Weight	Prod. Total
1088	Bus. Cpe.-2P	795	3140	—
1089	Conv. Cpe.-2/4P	910	3285	—
1085	Spt. Cpe.-2/4P	840	3215	—
1084	Tr. Cpe.-5P	860	3235	—
1083	Sed.-5P	895	3265	—
1086	Clb. Sed.-5P	900	3275	—
1082	Tr. Sed.-5P	910	3310	—
NA	Sta. Wag.	1295	NA	—

ENGINE: L-head. Inline six. Cast iron block. B & S: 3-7/16 in. x 4-1/4 in. Disp.: 237 cu. in. C.R.: 6.3 standard, 7.0 opt. Brake H.P.: 100 @ 3600 R.P.M. Net H.P.: 29.4. Main bearings: Four. Valve lifters: Mechanical. Carb.: Chandler-Grove.

CHASSIS: [115C] W.B.: 115 in. Tires 16 x 6.50.

TECHNICAL: Selective synchromesh. Speeds: 3F/1R. Floor shift control. Single disc clutch. Shaft drive. Overall ratio: 4.36 standard, 4.54 opt. Hydraulic brakes on four wheels. Disc or opt. steel artillery wheels.

OPTIONS: Clock (11.50). Windshield defroster (6.75). Fender lights (13.50). Radiator screen (1.75). Vanity mirror (.95). Radio (59.50). Cigar lighter (2.50). Deluxe emblem (6.00).

HISTORICAL: Introduced September, 1936. Model year production: 30,050.

1937 Packard, One Twenty, 120-C, convertible sedan, OCW

PACKARD — FIFTEENTH SERIES, ONE TWENTY (120-C, 120-CD, 138-CD) — EIGHT: A station wagon was a One Twenty addition for 1937, but so also were three body styles (touring coupe, club sedan, touring sedan) designated 120-CD, the "d" translating to "deluxe" and providing such luxuries as a clock, deluxe radiator ornament, prettier trim, white wall tires, full Marshall springs in the seats, a banjo spoke steering wheel, sponge-backed carpets and automatic radiator shutters. Then, late in the model year, two more versions of the One Twenty joined the model line, these on a 138-inch wheelbase, seven-passenger touring sedan and limousine in the $2000 range. Despite competition from its new six-cylinder companion Junior Packard, One Twenty sales for the model year were above the 50,000 mark.

I.D. DATA: Serial number located on a metal firewall plate. The plate also showed the body type number and the actual production number of that body type, starting with a base number of 200. Starting: body type numbers plus 201. Engine numbers located on boss on upper left corner of cyliner block. Starting: X-100000. Ending: 199999.

Body No.	Body Type & Seating	Price	Weight	Prod. Total
1098	Bus. Cpe.-2P	1130	3340	—
1095	Spt. Cpe.-2/4P	1175	3415	—
1094	Tr. Cpe.-5P	1200	3435	—
1903	Sed.-5P	1235	3465	—
1096	Clb. Sed.-5P	1240	3455	—
1099	Conv. Cpe.-2/4P	1250	3485	—
1092	Tr. Sed.-5P	1250	3520	—
1097	Conv. Sed.-5P	1550	3630	—
NA	Sta. Wag.-8P	NA	NA	—
1094CD	Tr. Cpe.-5P	1415	3465	—
1096CD	Clb. Sed.-5P	1455	3485	—
1092CD	Tr. Sed.-5P	1465	3550	—
CD1091	Tr. Sed.-7P	1900	3835	—
CD1090	Tr. Limo.-7P	2050	3900	—

ENGINE: L-head. Straight eight. Cast iron. B & S: 3-1/4 in. x 4-1/2 in. Disp.: 282 cu. in. C.R.: 6.5 standard, 7.0 opt. Brake H.P.: 120 @ 3800 R.P.M. Net H.P.: 33.8. Main bearings: Five. Valve lifters: Mechanical. Carb.: Stromberg or Carter.

CHASSIS: [120C Series] W.B.: 120 in. Tires: 7.00 x 16. [120CD Series.] W.B.: 120 in. Tires: 7.00 x 16. [138CD] W.B.: 138 in. Tires: 7.00 x 16.

TECHNICAL: Selective synchromesh. Speeds: 3F/1R. Floor shift control. Shaft drive rear axle. Overall ratio: 4.09 standard, 4.54 & 4.7 opt. Hydraulic brakes on four wheels. Disc. & opt. steel artillery wheels.

OPTIONS: Rear bumper. Single sidemount. Sidemount cover(s). Bumper guards. Radio. Heater. Clock (opt. 120C, standard-120CD & 138CD). Cigar lighter. Radio antenna. Spotlight.

HISTORICAL: Introduced September, 1936. Model year production: 50,100.

1937 Packard, Super Eight, 1502, touring sedan, JAC

PACKARD — FIFTEENTH SERIES, SUPER EIGHT (1500, 1501, 1502) — EIGHT: The Super Eight received the Fourteenth Series Eight's 320-cubic-inch engine, and what had been the Eight in the Fourteenth Series was now called a Super Eight too. These were among many changes. Bijur lubrication was no more. But independent front suspension arrived, as did hydraulic brakes with centrifuse drums. And the rear-hinged doors were gone. Bumpers were new front and rear, and the radiator was given a thirty degree slant. The 127-inch-wheelbase Model 1500 Super Eight was the bread-and-butter five-passenger sedan priced at $2335. The 134-inch-wheelbase Model 1501 included eight body styles ranging in price from $2420 to $4850 for the LeBaron Cabriolet. The 139-inch-wheelbase Model 1502 offered six body styles ranging from a $2705 Touring Sedan to the $4990 LeBaron Town Car.

I.D. DATA: Serial number located on a metal rectangular plate on the firewall. The plate also showed body type number plus the production number of that particular car, starting with a base number of 200. Starting: body type number plus 201. Engine numbers located on left side of crankcase near starter. Starting: 395500. Ending: 449999.

Body No.	Body Type & Seating	Price	Weight	Prod. Total
1003	Tr. Sed.-5P	2335	4530	—
1018	Cpe.-2/4P	2420	4585	—
1017	Cpe.-5P	2510	4595	—
1019	Cpe. Rds.-2/4P	2680	4580	—
1016	Clb. Sed.-5P	2530	4600	—
1012	Formal Sed.-5P	3235	4795	—
1017	Conv. Vict.-5P	3150	4650	—
1013	Tr. Sed.-5P	2535	4670	—
L-394	Cabr. LeB.-5/7P	4850	4965	—
1014	Tr. Sed.-5P	2705	4700	—
1014B	Bus. Sed.-5/8P	2580	4755	—
1015	Limo.-5/7P	2840	4815	—
1015B	Bus. Sed.-5/8P	2715	4925	—
1063	Conv. Sed.-5P	3350	4945	—
L-395	Twn. Car. LeB.-5/7P	4990	5360	—

ENGINE: L-head. Straight eight. Cast en bloc. B & S: 3-3/16 in. x 5 in. Disp.: 320 cu. in. C.R.: 6.5 standard, 7.0 opt. Brake H.P.: 135 @ 3200 R.P.M. Net H.P.: 32.5. Main bearings: Nine. Valve lifters: Roller cam. Carb.: Stromberg.

CHASSIS: [1500] W.B.: 127 in. Tires: 7.50 x 16. [1501] W.B.: 134 in. Tires: 7.50 x 16. [1502] W.B.: 139 in. (comm. vehicles — 165 in.) Tires: 7.50 x 16.

TECHNICAL: Selective synchromesh. Speeds: 3F/1R. Floor shift control. Single disc clutch. Shaft drive. Overall ratio: 4.69:1. Hydraulic brakes on four wheels. Disc wheels.

OPTIONS: Dual sidemount. Sidemount cover(s). Bumper guards. Radio. Heater & defroster. Spotlight.

HISTORICAL: Introduced September, 1936. Model year production: 5,793.

1937 Packard, Twelve, 1507, coupe, JAC

PACKARD — FIFTEENTH SERIES, TWELVE (1506, 1507, 1508) — TWELVE: Generally, the Twelve received the same changes as the Super Eight: independent front suspension and hydraulic brakes were fitted; Bijur lubrication was gone, as were the rear-hinged doors. Wheelbases were 132-1/4 inches for the five-passenger sedan in Model 1506. The 139-1/4-inch-wheelbase Model 1507 had eight body styles ranging from $3560 to $5700 for the LeBaron All-Weather Cabriolet. The four body styles in the 144-1/4-inch-wheelbase Model 1508 were Convertible Sedan, Touring Sedan, Touring Limousine and LeBaron All Weather Town Car. Since the longest wheelbase available in a Fifteenth Series Super Eight was 139 inches, anybody wanting a longer Packard had to take a twelve-cylinder engine with it. The Packard Twelve enjoyed its best sales year in 1937: 1,300 cars.

I.D. DATA: Serial number located on a rectangular plate mounted on the firewall. They used the body type number and production number for that body type. These started with a 200 base. Starting: body number plus 201. Engine numbers located on left side of block below distributor. Starting: 905500. Ending: 919999.

Model No.	Body Type & Seating	Price	Weight	Prod. Total
1023	Tr. Sed.-5P	3490	5395	—
1033	Tr. Sed.-5P	3560	5525	—
1032	Formal Sed.-6P	4260	5520	—
1036	Clb. Sed.-5P	3660	5520	—
1037	Cpe.-5P	3590	5415	—
1027	Conv. Vict.-5P	4490	5345	—
1039	Cpe.-2/4P	3420	5255	—
1039	Cpe. Rds.-2/4P	3450	5255	—
L-394	All W. Cabr. LeB.-5/7P	5700	5740	—
1073	Conv. Sed.-5P	4650	5680	—
1034	Tr. Sed.-7P	3885	5600	—
1035	Tr. Limo.-7P	4085	5660	—
L-395	All W. Twn. Car LeB.-5/7P	5900	5790	—

Note: Touring, Phaeton and Sport Phaeton were available on special order only.

ENGINE: 67° V-block. Modified L. Twelve. Cast iron monobloc. B & S: 3-7/16 in. x 4-1/4 in. Disp.: 473.3 cu. in. C.R.: 6.0 standard, 6.4 & 7.0 opt. Brake H.P.: 175 @ 3200 R.P.M. (180 @ 3200 with high compression heads). Net H.P.: 56.7. Main bearings: Four. Valve lifters: Mechanical with zero lash take up mechanism. Carb.: Stromberg.

CHASSIS: [1506] W.B.: 132-1/4 in. Tires: 8.25 x 16. [1507] W.B.: 139-1/4 in. Tires: 8.25 x 16. [1508] W.B.: 144-1/4 in. Tires: 8.25 x 16.

TECHNICAL: Selective synchromesh. Speeds: 3F/1R. Floor shift control. Single plate vacuum assist clutch. Shaft drive. Overall ratio: 4.41 standard, 4.06, 4.69 & 5.07 opt. Hydraulic brakes with vacuum booster, hand brake mechanical to rear drums. Steel disc wheels.

OPTIONS: Dual sidemount w/covers & luggage rack (240.00). Bumper guards. Radio. Heater. Spotlight.

HISTORICAL: Introduced September, 1936. Model year production: 1,300.

1937 15th Series
Model 115-C, 6 cyl., 115" wb

	FP	5	4	3	2	1
Conv	1075	6750	13,500	22,500	31,500	45,000
Bus Cpe	960	3750	7500	12,500	17,500	25,000
Spt Cpe	1005	4050	8100	13,500	18,900	27,000
2 dr Sed	1025	3000	6000	10,000	14,000	20,000
Sed	1060	3000	6000	10,000	14,000	20,000
Clb Sed	1065	3300	6600	11,000	15,400	22,000
Tr Sed	1075	3150	6300	10,500	14,700	21,000
Sta Wag	1295	6750	13,500	22,500	31,500	45,000

Model 120-C, 8 cyl., 120" wb

	FP	5	4	3	2	1
Conv	1250	7500	15,000	25,000	35,000	50,000
Conv Sed	1550	7800	15,600	26,000	36,400	52,000
Bus Cpe	1130	4050	8100	13,500	18,900	27,000
Spt Cpe	1175	4200	8400	14,000	19,600	28,000
2 dr Sed	1200	3300	6600	11,000	15,400	22,000
Sed	1235	3400	6900	11,500	16,100	23,000
Clb Sed	1240	3600	7200	12,000	16,800	24,000
Tr Sed	1250	3300	6600	11,000	15,400	22,000
Sta Wag	1485	7050	14,100	23,500	32,900	47,000

Model 120-CD, 8 cyl., 120" wb

	FP	5	4	3	2	1
2 dr Sed	1415	3750	7500	12,500	17,500	25,000
Clb Sed	1455	3900	7800	13,000	18,200	26,000
Tr Sed	1465	3750	7500	12,500	17,500	25,000

Model 138-CD, 8 cyl., 138" wb

	FP	5	4	3	2	1
Tr Sed	1835	4050	8100	13,500	18,900	27,000
Tr Limo	1985	4500	9000	15,000	21,000	30,000

Model 1500, Super 8, 127" wb

	FP	5	4	3	2	1
Sed	2630	4800	9600	16,000	22,400	32,000

Model 1501, Super 8, 134" wb

	FP	5	4	3	2	1
Conv	2980	13,200	26,400	44,000	68,000	88,000
LeB A-W Cabr	5050	13,500	27,000	45,000	70,000	90,000
RS Cpe	2715	8250	16,500	27,500	38,500	55,000
5P Cpe	2810	7500	15,000	25,000	35,000	50,000
Clb Sed	2830	5250	10,500	17,500	24,500	35,000
Tr Sed	2835	4800	9600	16,000	22,400	32,000
Fml Sed	3550	4950	9900	16,500	23,100	33,000
Vic	3460	11,400	22,800	38,000	56,000	76,000

Model 1502, Super 8, 139" wb

	FP	5	4	3	2	1
Conv Sed	3665	15,000	30,000	50,000	80,000	100,000
Bus Sed	2880	5250	10,500	17,500	24,500	35,000
Tr Sed	3010	5400	10,800	18,000	25,200	36,000
Tr Limo	3145	6000	12,000	20,000	28,000	40,000
Bus Limo	3020	5850	11,700	19,500	27,300	39,000
LeB A-W Twn Car	5190	12,000	24,000	40,000	60,000	80,000

Model 1506, V-12, 132" wb

	FP	5	4	3	2	1
Tr Sed	3870	6750	13,500	22,500	31,500	45,000

Model 1507, V-12, 139" wb

	FP	5	4	3	2	1
Conv	3450	32,700	60,000	92,000	118,000	160,000
LeB A-W Cabr	5925	33,500	61,000	94,000	120,000	165,000
RS Cpe	3420	9900	19,800	33,000	46,200	66,000
5P Cpe	3590	9000	18,000	30,000	42,000	60,000
Clb Sed	4045	6750	13,500	22,500	31,500	45,000
Fml Sed	4655	6600	13,200	22,000	30,800	44,000
Tr Sed	3940	6450	12,900	21,500	30,100	43,000
Conv Vic	4490	33,500	61,000	94,000	120,000	165,000

Model 1508, V-12, 144" wb

	FP	5	4	3	2	1
Conv Sed	4650	54,000	95,000	149,000	189,000	270,000
Tr Sed	4270	12,000	24,000	40,000	60,000	80,000
Tr Limo	4475	12,900	25,800	48,200	66,000	86,000
LeB A-W Twn Car	6130	42,000	74,000	116,000	147,000	210,000

1938

1938 Packard, Eight, 1602, touring limousine, AA

PACKARD — SIXTEENTH SERIES, SIX (1600) — SIX: The Six's engine was bored out to 3-1/2 inches which increased displacement to 245 cubic inches; though horsepower remained 100, low speed torque was improved. A Six could now accelerate from 9 to 50 in 15.8 seconds, and 78 mph was top. A heavier water pump, redesigned fan and increased radiator capacity were among the other engineering changes. The wheelbase was increased to 122 inches, and the all-steel bodies were all-new. There weren't as many of them, however; though a two-door touring sedan and club coupe were added to the line, five body styles were dropped, including the station wagon. The most distinctive aspect of the new body styling was the chrome strip which ran the length of the hood, up the windshield and into the roof of the car.

I.D. DATA: Serial number located on decal, which also indicated the body type number plus production number starting with a base number of 2000. Starting: body type number plus 2001. Engine numbers located on boss on upper left corner of cylinder block. Starting: B-1501. Ending: 99999.

Model No.	Body Type & Seating	Price	Weight	Prod. Total
1188	Bus. Cpe.-2P	975	3450	—
1185	Clb. Cpe.-2/4P	1020	3425	—
1189	Conv. Cpe.-2/4P	1135	3500	—
1184	2-dr. Tr. Sed.-5P	1040	3475	—
1182	4-dr. Tr. Sed.-5P	1070	3525	—

ENGINE: L-head. Inline six. Cast iron. B & S: 3-1/2 in. x 4-1/4 in. Disp.: 245 cu. in. C.R.: 6.52 standard, 7.05 opt. Brake H.P.: 100 @ 3600 R.P.M. Net H.P.: 29.4. Main bearings: Four. Valve lifters: Pressure lubricated. Carb.: Chandler-Grove.

CHASSIS: W.B.: 122 in. Tires: 16 x 6.50.

TECHNICAL: Selective synchromesh. Speeds: 3F/1R. Floor shift control. Single plate clutch. Shaft drive rear axle. Overall ratio: 4.54. Hydraulic brakes on four wheels. Disc wheels.

OPTIONS: Radio. Heater. Clock. Spotlight.

HISTORICAL: Introduced September, 1937. Model year production: 30,050.

1938 Packard, Eight, 1601, 5-pass. sedan, JAC

PACKARD — SIXTEENTH SERIES, EIGHT (1601, 1601D, 1602) — EIGHT: The One Twenty became the Eight this year. Like the Six, its wheelbase was increased seven inches (to 127, the same length as the shortest Senior Packard) for the 1601 cars, with a 148-inch chassis arriving for Model 1602. Compression ratio was changed to 6.6, with a 7.05 aluminum option available. Only the four-door touring sedan was available as a DeLuxe model, though any of the body styles could be "deluxed" via the extensive accessory catalogue. Though the station wagon was dropped, the Eight did not lose as many body styles as the Six — and among the new ones were three elegant custom creations from Rollston. These were $5000-range cars, the most expensive Junior Packards ever. The long-wheelbase Model 1602 limousine and sedan remained in the $2000 range. Cars in the 1601 line could be purchased for $1225 to $1650.

I.D. DATA: Serial number located on a decal vehicle plate. It contained the body type number plus the production number, starting with a base number of 2000. Starting: body type number plus 2001. Engine numbers located on boss on upper left corner of cylinder block. Starting: A-300001. Ending: 399999.

Body No.	Body Type & Seating	Price	Weight	Prod. Total
1198	Bus. Cpe.-2P	1225	3570	—
1195	Clb. Cpe.-2/4P	1270	3550	—
1199	Conv. Cpe.-2/4P	1365	3625	—
1197	Conv. Sed.-5P	1650	3775	—
1194	2-dr. Tr. Sed.-5P	1295	3600	—
1192	4-dr. Tr. Sed.-5P	1325	3650	—
1172	4-dr. Tr. Sed. Deluxe-5P	1540	3685	—
1665	All W. Cabr. Roll.-5/7P	4810	NA	—
1669	All W. Twn. Car Roll.-5/7P	4885	NA	—
1668	All W. Brgm. Roll.-4P	5100	NA	—
1190	Tr. Limo.-5/7P	2110	4245	—
1191	Tr. Sed.-5/7P	1955	4195	—

ENGINE: L-head. Straight eight. Cast iron. B & S: 3-1/4 in. x 4-1/2 in. Disp.: 282 cu. in. C.R.: 6.6 standard, 7.05 opt. Brake H.P.: 120 @ 3800 R.P.M. Net H.P.: 33.8. Main bearings: Five. Valve lifters: Pressure lubricated. Carb.: Stromberg.

CHASSIS: [1601 Series] W.B.: 127 in. Tires: 7.00 x 16. [1602] W.B.: 148 in.

TECHNICAL: Selective synchromesh. Speeds: 3F/1R. Floor shift control. Shaft drive rear axle. Overall ratio: 4.36 standard. Hydraulic brakes on four wheels. Disc wheels.

OPTIONS: DeLuxe steering wheel (12.50). Gearshift ball (.50). Radiator emblem (6.75). Electric clock (11.75). Chrome wheel discs (20.00). Custom radio (65.75). Heater (19.85). Luggage (29.50).

HISTORICAL: Introduced September, 1937. Model year production: 22,624.

1938 Packard, Super Eight, 1605, touring sedan, JAC

PACKARD — SIXTEENTH SERIES, TWELVE (1607, 1608) — TWELVE: Not only did the Twelve share the same changes as the Super Eight, but it also joined the latter car on the same chassis. Gone were the Twelve's 132-, 139- and 144-inch wheelbases. Presumably there was a Twelve five-passenger sedan offered on the Super Eight's 127-inch wheelbase as Model 1606 (which would have been logical given the company's new numbering code), but that car failed to show up in Packard brochures. On the 134-inch-wheelbase Model 1607 were seven production body styles and the Rollston All-Weather Cabriolet. On the 139-inch Model 1608 were three production and three custom cars. Just 566 Twelves were produced during the model year.

I.D. DATA: Serial number was on a vehicle decal which was located on the cowl. The number was the body type number and the production number for that particular car, starting with a base number of 2000. Starting: body number plus 2000. Engine numbers located on left side of block below distributor. Starting: A-600001. Ending: 620,999.
Note: The decal had the unfortunate tendency to chip away and become illegible. This was the only year Packard used the decal in lieu of an engraved plate.

Body No.	Body Type & Seating	Price	Weight	Prod. Total
1132	Formal Sed.-5P	4865	5550	—
1133	Tr. Sed.-5P	4155	5525	—
1136	Clb. Sed.-5P	4255	5520	—
1137	Cpe.-5P	4185	5415	—
1138	Cpe.-2/4P	4135	5255	—
1139	Conv. Cpe.-2/4P	4370	5255	—
1127	Conv. Vict.-5P	5320	5345	—
494	All W. Cabr. Roll.-5/7P	6730	5740	—
1134	Tour. Sed.-7P	4485	5600	—
1135	Sed. Limo. Tr.-7P	4690	5660	—
1153	Conv. Sed.-5P	5390	5680	—
495	All W. Twn. Car Roll.-5/7P	6880	5735	—
4087	All W. Cabr. Brunn-5/7P	8510	5730	—
4086	Tr. Cabr. Brunn-5/7P	8510	5725	—

ENGINE: 67° V-block. Modified L. Twelve. Cast iron monobloc. B & S: 3-7/16 in. x 4-1/4 in. Disp.: 473.3 cu. in. C.R.: 6.0 standard, 6.4 & 7.0 opt. Brake H.P.: 175 @ 3200 R.P.M. Main bearings: Four. Valve lifters: Mechanical with zero lash take up mechanisms. Carb.: Stromberg.

CHASSIS: [1607 Series] W.B.: 134-3/8 in. Tires: 8.25 x 16. [1608 Series] W.B.: 139-3/8 in. Tires: 8.25 x 16.

TECHNICAL: Selective synchromesh. Speeds: 3F/1R. Floor shift control. 12-in. — single-plate vacuum clutch-vacuum assisted. Shaft drive. Overall ratio: 4.41. Hydraulic brakes with vacuum booster, hand brake mechanical to rear drums.

HISTORICAL: Introduced September, 1938. Model year production: 566.

PACKARD — SIXTEENTH SERIES, SUPER EIGHT (1603, 1604, 1605) — EIGHT: Engineering changes were minimal. Appearance changes were prominent, many of them (split vee windshield with chrome center strip, for example) introduced also as on the Junior Packards. Fenders were pontoon, enveloping the sidemount on those cars carrying same. The radiator cap was pressurized, its filler moved under the hood. Super Eight standard equipment continued to include such niceties as an electric clock and cigar lighter, and package purchases of the "Custom Accessory Group" or "DeLuxe Accessory Group" added further amenities. Whitewall tires were $17.50 for a set of five, $23.50 for six — and the extensive accessory catalogue offered a new item this year: a "Guest Speaker" to be mounted in the center of the driver's seat back which insured "perfect radio reception for rear seat passengers." Wheelbases remained the same, though model numbers were 1603 (the former 1500), 1604 (the former 1501) and 1605 (for former 1502) now that the Junior Packards had been brought into the company numbering code. A Rollston All-Weather Cabriolet was a new entry for Model 1604. A Rollston Town Car and two Brunn customs were added to the Model 1605 line.

I.D. DATA: Serial number located on a decal vehicle plate that was placed on the firewall. (The decal tended to disintegrate over the years.) The decal showed the body type number plus the production number for that particular car starting with a base number of 2000. Starting: body type number plus 2001. Engine numbers located on left side of crankcase near starter. Starting: A-500001. Ending: 599999.

Body No.	Body Type & Seating	Price	Weight	Prod. Total
1103	Tr. Sed.-5P	2790	4530	—
1118	Cpe.-2/4P	2925	4585	—
1117	Cpe.-5P	2965	4595	—
1119	Conv. Cpe.-2/4P	3210	4580	—
1116	Clb. Sed.-5P	2990	4600	—
1112	Fml. Sed.-5P	3710	4795	—
1107	Conv. Vict.-5P	3670	4650	—
1113	Tr. Sed.-5P	2995	4670	—
494	All W. Cabr. Roll.	5790	NA	—
1114	Tour. Sed.-5/7P	3165	4700	—
1114	Bus. Sed.-5/8P	3165	4815	—
1115	Limo.-5/7P	3305	4815	—
1115	Bus. Limo.-5/8P	3305	4815	—
1143	Conv. Sed.-5P	3970	4945	—
3087	All W. Cabr. Brunn-5/7P	7475	NA	—
3086	Tour. Cabr. Brunn-5/6P	7475	NA	—
495	Twn. Car Roll.-5/7P	5890	NA	—

1938 Packard, Twelve, 1608, all-weather town car, Rollston, JAC

ENGINE: L-head. Straight eight. Cast en bloc. B & S: 3-3/16 in. x 5. Disp.: 320 cu. in. C.R.: 6.5 standard, 7.0 opt. Brake H.P.: 130 @ 3200 R.P.M. Net H.P.: 32.5. Main bearings: Nine. Valve lifters: Roller cam. Carb.: Stromberg.

CHASSIS: [1603] W.B.: 127 in. Tires: 7.50 x 16. [1604] W.B.: 134 in. Tires: 7.50 x 16. [1605] W.B.: 139 in. Tires: 7.50 x 16.

TECHNICAL: Selective synchromesh. Speeds: 3F/1R. Floor shift control. Single plate clutch. Semi-floating rear axle. Overall ratio: 4.69:1. Hydraulic brakes on four wheels. Disc wheels.

OPTIONS: Spotlight (18.50). Chrome wheel discs (20.00). Fog lights (6.95). Bumper guards (2.95). Windshield defroster (7.95). DeLuxe heater (19.85). DeLuxe radio (78.50). DeLuxe emblem (6.75). Pelican (10.00).

HISTORICAL: Introduced September, 1937. Model year production: 2,478.

1938 16th Series

Model 1600, 6 cyl., 122" wb	FP	5	4	3	2	1
Conv	1235	6000	12,000	20,000	28,000	40,000
Bus Cpe	1075	3150	6300	10,500	14,700	21,000
Clb Cpe	1120	3000	6000	10,000	14,000	20,000
2 dr Sed	1145	1150	3600	6000	8400	12,000
Sed	1175	1150	3600	6000	8400	12,000
Model 1601, 8 cyl., 127" wb						
Conv	1365	6300	12,600	21,000	29,400	42,000
Conv Sed	1650	6750	13,500	22,500	31,500	45,000
Bus Cpe	1225	1400	4200	7000	9800	14,000
Clb Cpe	1270	1750	4800	8000	11,200	16,000
2 dr Sed	1295	1075	3000	5500	7700	11,000
Sed	1325	1150	3600	6000	8400	12,000
Model 1601-D, 8 cyl., 127" wb						
Tr Sed	1540	1400	4200	7000	9800	14,000
Model 1601, 8 cyl., 139" wb						
Roll A-W Cabr	4810	22,000	36,000	60,000	93,000	120,000
Roll A-W Twn Car	4885	15,000	30,000	50,000	80,000	100,000
Roll Brgm	5100	14,400	28,800	48,000	76,000	96,000
Model 1602, 8 cyl., 148" wb						
Tr Sed	2110	5250	10,500	17,500	24,500	35,000
Tr Limo	1955	6000	12,000	20,000	28,000	40,000
Model 1603, Super 8, 127" wb						
Tr Sed	2790	5400	10,800	18,000	25,200	36,000
Model 1604, Super 8, 134" wb						
Conv	3210	12,000	24,000	40,000	60,000	80,000
RS Cpe	2925	6750	13,500	22,500	31,500	45,000
5P Cpe	2965	6000	12,000	20,000	28,000	40,000
Clb Sed	2990	4800	9600	16,000	22,400	32,000
Tr Sed	2995	4500	9000	15,000	21,000	30,000
Fml Sed	3710	4650	9300	15,500	21,700	31,000
Vic	3670	11,400	22,800	38,000	56,000	76,000
Model 1605, Super 8, 139" wb						
Bus Sed	3165	6000	12,000	20,000	28,000	40,000
Conv Sed	3970	15,000	30,000	50,000	80,000	100,000
Bus Limo	3305	7500	15,000	25,000	35,000	50,000
Model 1605, Super 8, Customs						
Brn A-W Cabr	7475			value not estimable		
Brn Tr Cabr	7475			value not estimable		
Roll A-W Cabr	5790			value not estimable		
Roll A-W Twn Car	5890			value not estimable		

1938

Model 1607, V-12, 134" wb

	FP	5	4	3	2	1
Conv Cpe	4370	34,300	62,000	96,000	122,000	170,000
2-4P Cpe	4135	9300	18,600	31,000	43,400	62,000
5P Cpe	4185	9000	18,000	30,000	42,000	60,000
Clb Sed	4255	8250	16,500	27,500	38,500	55,000
Vic	5230	9600	19,200	32,000	44,800	64,000
Tr Sed	4155	6000	12,000	20,000	28,000	40,000
Fml Sed	4865	6750	13,500	22,500	31,500	45,000

Model 1608, V-12, 139" wb

	FP	5	4	3	2	1
Conv Sed	5390	35,100	63,000	98,000	124,000	175,000
Tr Sed	4485	9900	19,800	33,000	46,200	66,000
Tr Limo	4690	10,500	21,000	35,000	49,000	70,000

Model 1607-8, V-12, 139" wb

	FP					
Brn A-W Cabr	8510				value not estimable	
Brn Tr Cabr	8510				value not estimable	
Roll A-W Cabr	6730				value not estimable	
Roll A-W Twn Car	6880				value not estimable	

1939

1939 Packard, Six, 1700, 5-pass. sedan, JAC

PACKARD — SEVENTEENTH SERIES, SIX (1700) — SIX: Outside the look was substantially the same, but inside the Six for 1939 the gearshift was column mounted (called Handishift) and a new option was overdrive (called Econo-Drive). Another option was called No-Rol, a device to aid in starting and holding the car on an incline. The rear-leaf springs introduced in '38 were given a ''fifth'' leaf in '39. The body styles offered previously were brought back, but brought back too was the station wagon which had been missing in '38.

I.D. DATA: Serial number located on metal plate on firewall. This also included body type number plus the production number of that particular car, starting with a base number of 2000. Starting: body type number plus 2001. Engine number located on boss on upper left corner of cylinder block. Starting B-1501. Ending: 99999.

Model No.	Body Type & Seating	Price	Weight	Prod. Total
1288	Bus. Cpe.-2P	888	3295	—
1285	Clb. Cpe.-2/4P	944	3365	—
1289	Conv. Cpe.-2/4P	1092	3385	—
1284	2-dr. Tr. Sed.-5P	964	3390	—
1282	4-dr. Tr. Sed.-5P	995	3400	—
NA	Sta. Wag.-7P	1404	NA	—

ENGINE: L-head. Inline six. Cast iron block. B & S: 3-1/2 in. x 4-1/4 in. Disp.: 245 cu. in. C.R.: 6.52 standard, 7.05 opt. Brake H.P.: 100 @ 3200 R.P.M. Net H.P.: 29.4. Main bearings: Four. Valve lifters: Pressure lubricated. Carb.: Chandler-Grove.

CHASSIS: [1700] W.B.: 122 in. Tires: 6.50 x 16.

TECHNICAL: Selective synchromesh. Speeds: 3F/1R. Column-mounted gearshift control. Single plate clutch. Shaft drive. Overall ratio: 4.54 standard. Hydraulic brakes on four wheels. Disc wheels.

OPTIONS: Radio. Heater. Clock. Spotlight. No-Rol. Tachometer.

HISTORICAL: Introduced September, 1938. Model year production: 24,350.

1939 Packard, One Twenty, 1701, 4-dr. sedan, AA

PACKARD — SEVENTEENTH SERIES, ONE TWENTY (1701, 1702) — EIGHT: The One Twenty name was back for the eight-cylinder Packard. The car shared the same new features as the Six: Handishift standard, and Econo-Drive, No-Rol and tachometer optional. Compression ratios were revised to 6.40 standard, with 6.85 optional and the former aluminum cylinder head replaced by cast iron. The station wagon returned to the line, and the long-wheelbase sedan and limousine were retained.

I.D. DATA: Serial number located on metal plate on firewall. This also included the body type number plus production number of that particular model, the last number having a starting base of 2000. Starting: body type number plus 2001. Engine numbers located on boss on upper left corner of cylinder block. Starting: B-300001. Ending: 39999.

Model No.	Body Type & Seating	Price	Weight	Prod. Total
1298	Bus. Cpe.-2P	1099	3490	—
1295	Clb. Cpe.-2/4P	1145	3535	—
1299	Conv. Cpe.-2/4P	1288	3545	—
1297	Conv. Sed.-5P	1600	3780	—
1294	2-dr. Tr. Sed.-5P	1166	3595	—
1292	4-dr. Tr. Sed.	1196	3605	—
NA	Sta. Wag.-7P	1636	NA	—
1290	Tr. Limo.-7P	1856	4185	—
1291	Tr. Sed.-7P	1702	4100	—

ENGINE: L-head. Straight eight. Cast iron. B & S: 3-1/4 in. x 4-1/2 in. Disp.: 282 cu. in. C.R.: 6.41 standard, 6.85 opt. Brake H.P.: 120 @ 3800 r.p.m. Net H.P.: 33.8. Main bearings: Five. Valve lifters: Pressure lubricated. Carb.: Duplex or Stromberg.

CHASSIS: [1701 Series] W.B.: 127 in. Tires: 7.00 x 16. [1702 Series] W.B.: 148 in. Tires: 7.00 x 16.

TECHNICAL: Selective synchromesh. Speeds: 3F/1R. Column shift control. Single plate clutch. Regular differential. Overall ratio: 4.36 standard 4.09, 4.54, 4.7 and 4.9 opt; 4.54 standard with overdrive. Hydraulic brakes on four wheels. Disc wheels.

OPTIONS: Dual sidemount. Sidemount cover(s). Radio. Clock. Spotlight. Econo-Drive (overdrive). No-Rol. Tachometer.

HISTORICAL: Introduced September, 1938. Model year production: 17,647.

1939 Packard, Super Eight, 1703, convertible coupe, JAC

PACKARD — SEVENTEENTH SERIES, SUPER EIGHT (1703, 1705) — EIGHT: There was a drastic reduction in Super Eight body styles this year; from fifteen in '38, there were now just six (four on the 127-inch wheelbase, two on the 148-inch wheelbase) and custom cars were gone. Like the Junior Packards, the Super Eight had a column-mounted gearshift — and offered overdrive, the hill-holding device and a tachometer among many options. Cylinder heads were now all cast iron, and both compression ratios and rear axle ratios were revised. By now the Super Eight was very close to being simply a Junior Packard with more elaborate appointments and ten extra horsepower. This would be the final year for the Super Eight's venerable 130 hp engine.

I.D. DATA: Serial number located on a metal rectangular plate on the firewall. The plate also showed the body type number plus the production number of that particular car, starting with a base number of 2000. Starting: body type number plus 2001. Engine numbers located on upper half of crankcase, left side, front end. Starting: B-500001. Ending: 599999.

Model No.	Body Type & Seating	Price	Weight	Prod. Total
1275	Clb. Cpe.-2/4P	1650	3860	—
1279	Conv. Cpe.-2/4P	1875	3870	—
1272	Tr. Sed.-5P	1732	3930	—
1277	Conv. Sed.-5P	2130	4005	—
1270	Tr. Limo.-5/8P	2294	4510	—
1271	Tr. Sed.-5/8P	2156	4425	—

ENGINE: L-head. Straight. Eight. Cast en bloc. B & S: 3-3/16 in. x 5 in. Disp.: 320 cu. in. C.R.: 6.45:1 standard, 6.85 opt. Brake H.P.: 130 @ 3200 R.P.M. Net H.P.: 32.5. Main bearings: Nine. Valve lifters: Roller cam. Carb.: Stromberg.

CHASSIS: [1703] W.B.: 127 in. Tires: 16 x 7.00 [1705] W.B.: 148 in. Tires: 16 x 7.00

TECHNICAL: Selective synchromesh. Speeds: 3F/1R. Column-mounted gearshift control. Single plate clutch. Floating rear axle. Overall ratio: 4.36 (1703), 4.54 (1705). Hydraulic brakes on 4 wheels. Steel disc wheels. Drivetrain options: hill-holder.

HISTORICAL: Introduced September, 1938. Model year production: 3,962.

1939 Packard, Twelve, 1707, convertible victoria, AA

PACKARD — SEVENTEENTH SERIES, TWELVE (1707, 1708) — TWELVE: Fewer than 500 cars would be built in this the last year of the Packard Twelve. Wheelbases and body styles remained the same, including the custom cars. The only customs this year in the entire Packard lineup were Twelves. The column-mounted gearshift was an option on the Twelve, together with a host of others including a burled walnut instrument panel and a pushbutton radio.

I.D. DATA: Serial number located on rectangular plate on the firewall. In 1939 this plate showed the body type code plus the production number for that body type starting with a 2000. Starting: body type number plus 2001. Engine numbers located on left side of block below distributor. Starting: B-600001. Ending: 620999.

Model No.	Body Type & Seating	Price	Weight	Prod. Total
1232	Formal sed.-5P	4865	5745	—
1233	Tr. Sed.-5P	4155	5670	—
1236	Clb. Sed.-5P	4255	5590	—
1237	Cpe.-5P	4185	5425	—
1238	Cpe.-2/4P	4140	5400	—
1239	Conv. Cpe.-2/4P	4375	5540	—
1227	Conv. Vict.-5P	5230	5570	—
594	All W. Cabr. Roll.-5/7P	6730	4950	—
1234	Tr. Sed.-7P	4485	5750	—
1235	Sed. Limo. Tr.-7P	4690	5825	—
1253	Conv. Sed.-5P	5395	5890	—
595	All W. Twn. Car Roll.-5/7P	6880	5075	—
4087	All W. Cabr. Brunn-5/7P	8355	5845	—
4086	Tr. Cabr. Brunn-5/7P	8355	5845	—

ENGINE: 67° V-block. Modified L head. Twelve. Cast iron monobloc. B & S: 3-7/16 in. x 4-1/4. Disp.: 473.3 cu. in. C.R.: 6.0 standard, 6.4 & 7.0 opt. Brake H.P.: 175 @ 3200 R.P.M. Net H.P.: 56.7. Main bearings: Four. Valve lifters: Mechanical with zero lash take up mechanisms. Carb.: Stromberg.

CHASSIS: [1707 Series] W.B.: 134-3/8 in. Tires: 8.25 x 16. [1708 Series] W.B.: 139-3/8 in. Tires: 8.25 x 16.

TECHNICAL: Selective synchromesh. Speeds: 3F/1R (with optional column shift), floor-mounted gearshift control. Vacuum assist-12 in. clutch. Shaft drive. Overall ratio: 4.41. Hydraulic brakes with vacuum booster.

OPTIONS: Dual sidemount mirrors (20.00). Sidemount cover(s). Radio. Heater and defroster (40.00). Clock. Cigarette lighter. Radio antenna. Spotlight. Luggage rack (240.00). Auxiliary front bumper guard (40.00). Deluxe steering wheel (20.00). Optional column shift (240.00).

HISTORICAL: Introduced September, 1938. Model year production: 446.

1939 17th Series
Model 1700, 6 cyl., 122" wb

	FP	5	4	3	2	1
Conv	1195	4800	9600	16,000	22,400	32,000
Bus Cpe	1000	1400	4200	7000	9800	14,000
Clb Cpe	1045	1550	4500	7500	10,500	15,000
2 dr Sed	1065	900	1900	4500	6300	9000
Tr Sed	1095	925	2000	4600	6400	9200
Sta Wag	1404	6000	12,000	20,000	28,000	40,000

Model 1701, 8 cyl., 127" wb

	FP	5	4	3	2	1
Conv	1390	6750	13,500	22,500	31,500	45,000
Conv Sed	1700	7050	14,100	23,500	32,900	47,000
Clb Cpe	1245	2300	5400	9000	12,600	18,000
Bus Cpe	1200	1750	4800	8000	11,200	16,000
2 dr Sed	1265	1150	3600	6000	8400	12,000
Sed	1295	1150	3600	6000	8400	12,000
Sta Wag	1636	6750	13,500	22,500	31,500	45,000

1939
Model 1702, 8-cyl., 148" wb

Tr Sed	4100	4050	8100	13,500	18,900	27,000
Tr Limo	4185	4500	9000	15,000	21,000	30,000

Model 1703, Super 8, 127" wb

Tr Sed	2035	3900	7800	13,000	18,200	26,000
Conv	2180	22,000	36,000	60,000	84,000	120,000
Conv Sed	2130	24,100	42,000	68,000	98,000	126,000
Clb Cpe	1955	4500	9000	15,000	21,000	30,000

Model 1705, Super 8, 148" wb

Tr Sed	2460	4500	9000	15,000	21,000	30,000
Tr Limo	2600	5250	10,500	17,500	24,500	35,000

Model 1707, V-12, 134" wb

Conv Cpe	4375	33,500	61,000	94,000	120,000	165,000
Conv Vic	5230	33,500	61,000	94,000	120,000	165,000
Roll A-W Cabr	6730	18,500	33,000	55,000	88,000	110,000
2-4P Cpe	4185	9900	19,800	33,000	46,200	66,000
5P Cpe	4185	9000	18,000	30,000	42,000	60,000
Sed	4155	5250	10,500	17,500	24,500	35,000
Clb Sed	4255	5400	10,800	18,000	25,200	36,000
Fml Sed	4865	5550	11,100	18,500	25,900	37,000

Model 1708, V-12, 139" wb

Conv Sed	5395			value not estimable		
Brn Tr Cabr	8355			value not estimable		
Brn A-W Cabr	8355			value not estimable		
Tr Sed	4485	9900	19,800	33,000	46,200	66,000
Tr Limo	4690	11,400	22,800	38,000	56,000	76,000
Roll A-W Twn Car	6880			value not estimable		

1940

1940 Packard, One-Ten, 1800, station wagon, AA

PACKARD — EIGHTEENTH SERIES, ONE-TEN (1800) — SIX: The One-Ten designation was new, and so was this Junior Packard's look this year, with the tall Packard radiator grille flanked by two vertical side grilles, and the side hood louvers being given a step design. Sealed beam headlights were fitted directly on the fenders, with parking lights mounted on the fender crowns. Engineering changes were few, with revisions to compression ratios and rear axle ratios among them. The overdrive was now a Warner Gear. Standard equipment included bumpers and bumper guards front and rear, assist cords in both sedans, and a robe rail in the four-door version.

I.D. DATA: Serial number located on a metal plate on the firewall. Also included on the plate is the body type number plus the production number of that particular car, using a base number of 2000. Starting: body type number plus 2001. Engine numbers located on a boss on left side of cylinder block between No. 2 and No. 3 cyl. Starting: C-1501. Ending: 64111.

Model No.	Body Type & Seating	Price	Weight	Prod. Total
1388	Bus. Cpe.-2P	867	3120	—
1385	Clb. Cpe.-2/4P	940	3165	—
1389	Conv. Cpe.-2/4P	1104	3200	—
1384	2-dr Tr. Sed.-5P	964	3190	—
1382	4-dr Tr. Sed.-5P	996	3200	—
1383	Sta. Wag.-8P	1200	3380	—

ENGINE: L-head. Inline. Six. Cast iron block. B & S: 3-1/2 in. x 4-1/4 in. Disp.: 245 cu. in. C.R.: 6.39 standard, 6.71 opt. Brake H.P.: 100 @ 3200 R.P.M. Net H.P.: 29.4. Main bearings: Four. Valve lifters: Adjustable tappet. Carb.: Stromberg model BXOV-26.

CHASSIS: [1800] W.B.: 122 in. Tires: 6.25 x 16.

TECHNICAL: Selective synchromesh. Speeds: 3F/1R. Column-mounted gearshift controls. Single plate clutch. Shaft drive. Overall ratio: 4.3 standard. Hydraulic brakes on four wheels. Disc wheels.

OPTIONS: Radio. Heater. Clock. Cigar lighter. Spotlight.

HISTORICAL: Introduced August, 1939. Model year production: 62,300.

PACKARD — EIGHTEENTH SERIES, ONE-TWENTY (1801) — EIGHT: The One-Twenty designation was hyphenated this year, and the car enjoyed the same engineering and styling changes as the new One-Ten. Cylinder heads were redesigned for better intake gas flow. The greater length of the hood allowed for easier mounting of spare wheels for those ordering them. Window moldings were described as a ''stunningly grained'' luxury feature, and there were more options than ever, including a rear-seat center armrest. The long-wheelbase model was discontinued. But Dutch Darrin, who had begun customizing the One-Twenty in California in 1938, came aboard officially with a convertible victoria.

I.D. DATA: Serial number located on metal plate on firewall. The plate also included the body type number plus the production number of that particular car, starting with a base number of 2000. Starting: body type number plus 2001. Engine numbers located on boss on upper left corner of cylinder block. Starting: C-300001. Ending: 328320.

1940 Packard, One-Twenty, 1801, club sedan, JAC

Body No.	Body Type & Seating	Price	Weight	Prod. Total
1398	Bus. Cpe.-2P	1038	3340	—
1395	Clb. Cpe.-2/4P	1111	3450	—
1399	Conv. Cpe.-2/4P	1277	3540	—
1396	4-dr. Clb. Sed.-5P	1239	3520	—
1397	Conv. Sed.-5P	1573	3710	—
1394	2-dr. Tr. Sed.-5P	1135	3510	—
1393	Sta. Wag.-8P	1404	3590	—
1392	4-dr. Tr. Sed.-5P	1166	3520	—
700	Conv. Vict. Darrin-5P	3819	3826	—
Deluxe Series				
1395D	Clb. Cpe.-2/4P	1161	3400	—
1399D	Conv. Cpe.-2/4P	1318	3470	—
1396D	Clb. Sed.-5P	1314	3480	—
1392D	Tr. Sed.-5P	1246	3495	—

ENGINE: L-head. Inline. Eight. Cast iron. B & S: 3-1/4 in. x 4-1/2 in. Disp.: 282 cu. in. C.R.: 6.41 standard, 6.85 opt. Brake H.P.: 120 @ 3600 R.P.M. Net H.P.: 33.8. Main bearings: Five. Valve lifters: Pressure lubricated.

CHASSIS: [1801 Series] W.B.: 127 in. Tires: 6.50 x 16.

TECHNICAL: Selective synchromesh. Speeds: 3F/1R. Column shift control. Single plate clutch. Shaft drive. Overall ratio: 4.09 standard. Hydraulic brakes on four wheels. Disc wheels.

OPTIONS: Dual sidemount. Radio. Spotlight.

HISTORICAL: Introduced August, 1939. Model year production: 28,138.

1940 Packard, Super-8 One-Sixty, 1803, convertible sedan, JAC

PACKARD — EIGHTEENTH SERIES, SUPER-8 ONE-SIXTY (1803, 1804, 1805) — EIGHT: One-Sixty designated the horsepower of the new engine powering all Senior Packards this year. Styling generally followed Junior Packard themes, with differences between the One-Sixty and the One-Eighty being in hood louvers, hubcaps and the mascot in front (the One-Sixty had the goddess, the One-Eighty the pelican). The One-Sixty was provided three wheelbases; the 127-inch Model 1803 carrying most of the body styles, the 138-inch Model 1804 offering just a five-passenger sedan, and the 148-inch Model 1805 providing a touring limousine and a sedan with accommodations for up to eight passengers. Air conditioning — "Cooled by Mechanical Refrigeration," as Packard said — was an option, which did not work too well.

I.D. DATA: Serial number located on a rectangular plate on the firewall. The plate also showed the body type number plus the production number of that particular car, starting with a base number of 2000. Starting: body type number plus 2001. Engine numbers located on upper left side of cylinder block between no. 3 and no. 4 cyl. Starting: 500001. Ending: 507697.

Body No.	Body Type & Seating	Price	Weight	Prod. Total
1378	Bus. Cpe.-2P	1524	3665	—
1375	Clb. Cpe.-2/4P	1595	3735	—
1379	Conv. Cpe.-4P	1775	3795	—
1376	Clb. Sed.-5P	1717	3780	—
1377	Conv. Sed.-5P	2050	3990	—
1372	Tr. Sed.-5P	1632	3825	—
1362	Tr. Sed.-5P	1895	4070	—
1370	Tr. Limo.-5/8P	2154	4460	—
1371	Tr. Sed-5/8P	2026	4350	—

ENGINE: L-head. Straight eight. Cast iron. B & S: 3-1/2 in. x 4-5/8 in. Disp.: 356 cu. in. C.R.: 6.45:1 standard, 6.85 opt. Brake H.P.: 160 @ 3200 R.P.M. Net H.P.: 39.2. Main bearings: Nine. Valve lifters: Silent, hydraulic. Aluminum pistons.

CHASSIS: [1803 Series] W.B.: 127 in. Tires: 7.00 x 16. [1804 Series] W.B.: 138 in. Tires: 7.00 x 16. [1805 Series] W.B.: 148 in. Tires: 7.00 x 16.

TECHNICAL: Selective synchromesh. Speeds: 3F/1R. Column-mounted gearshift control. Single plate clutch. Shaft drive rear axle. Overall ratio: 3.92 standard (1803), 4.09 (1804), 4.36 (1805). Hydraulic brakes, on four wheels. Disc wheels.

OPTIONS: Dual sidemount. Bumper guards. Radio. Heater. Spotlight. Steel spoke wheels.

HISTORICAL: Introduced August, 1939. Model year production: 5,662.

1940 Packard, Custom Super-8 One-Eighty, 1806 Darrin convertible victoria, AA

PACKARD — EIGHTEENTH SERIES, CUSTOM SUPER-8 ONE-EIGHTY — EIGHT: The One-Eighty's engine was the same as the One-Sixty, as were the three chassis on which all body styles were carried. As successor to the Twelve, however, the One-Eighty was considerably more lavish in trim and appointments, and it was the model which carried the custom cars in the Senior Packard line. The Rollson offerings were updated variations of the cars previously available on the Twelve; the Darrins were all-new and the most widely promoted. "Glamour Car of the Year!" was the company's advertising headline. The Darrin Convertible Victoria was on the 127-inch Model 1806 chassis, joining a Club Sedan, the Darrin Convertible Sedan was on the 138-inch Model 1807 chassis, together with the Rollson All-Weather Cabriolet and touring and formal sedans. The long 148-inch-wheelbase Model 1808 carried a limousine and sedan in addition to the Rollson All-Weather Town Car.

I.D. DATA: Serial number located on metal rectangular plate on the firewall. The plate also showed the body type number plus the production number of that particular car, starting with a base number of 2000. Starting: body type number plus 2001. Engine numbers located on upper left side of cylinder block between No. 3 and No. 4 cyl. Starting: CC-500001. Ending: 507697.

Body No.	Body Type & Seating	Price	Weight	Prod. Total
1356	Clb. Sed.-5P	2243	3900	—
700	Conv. Vict. Darrin-5P	4570	4121	—
1342	Tr. Sed.-5P	2410	4175	—
1332	Formal Sed.-5P	2840	4210	—
694	All W. Cabr. Roll.-5/7P	4450	4050	—
710	Conv. Sed. Darrin	6300	4050	—
720	Spt. Sed. Darrin-5P	6100	4215	—
1350	Tr. Limo.-5/8P	2669	4585	—
1351	Tr. Sed.-5/8P	2541	4510	—
695	All W. Twn. Car Roll.	4574	4175	—

ENGINE: L-head. Straight eight. Cast en bloc. B & S: 3-1/2 in. x 4-5/8 in. Disp.: 356 cu. in. C.R.: 6.45:1. Brake H.P.: 160 @ 3500 R.P.M. Net H.P.: 39.2. Main bearings: Nine. Valve lifters: Silent, hydraulic.

CHASSIS: [1806] W.B.: 127 in. Tires: 7.00 x 16. [1807] W.B.: 138 in. Tires: 7.00 x 16. [1808] W.B.: 148 in. Tires: 7.00 x 16.

TECHNICAL: Selective synchromesh. Speeds: 3F/1R. Column-mounted gearshift control. Single plate clutch. Shaft drive. Overall ratio: 3.92:1 (1806), 4.90:1 (1807), 4.36:1 (1808). Hydraulic brakes on four wheels. Disc wheels.

OPTIONS: Single sidemount. Bumper guards. Radio. Heater. Spotlight.

HISTORICAL: Introduced August, 1939. Model year production: 1,900.

1940 18th Series
Model 1800, 6 cyl., 122" wb, (110)

	FP	5	4	3	2	1
Conv	1104	5250	10,500	17,500	24,500	35,000
Bus Cpe	867	1650	4650	7750	10,850	15,500
Clb Cpe	940	1750	4800	8000	11,200	16,000
2 dr Sed	964	1000	2400	5000	7000	10,000
Sed	996	1000	2400	5000	7000	10,000
Sta Wag	1200	3400	6900	11,500	16,100	23,000

Model 1801, Std., 8 cyl., 127" wb, (120)

	FP	5	4	3	2	1
Conv	1277	6000	12,000	20,000	28,000	40,000
Conv Sed	1573	6300	12,600	21,000	29,400	42,000
Bus Cpe	1038	2000	5100	8500	11,900	17,000
Clb Cpe	1111	2300	5400	9000	12,600	18,000
2 dr Sed	1135	1150	3600	6000	8400	12,000
Clb Sed	1239	1250	3900	6500	9100	13,000
Sed	1166	1150	3600	6000	8400	12,000
Darr Vic	3800	10,500	21,000	35,000	49,000	70,000
Sta Wag	1404	7050	14,100	23,500	32,900	47,000

Model 1801, DeLuxe, 8-cyl., 127" wb, (120)

	FP	5	4	3	2	1
Conv	1277	6750	13,500	22,500	31,500	45,000
Clb Cpe	1111	1400	4200	7000	9800	14,000
Clb Sed	1239	1250	3900	6500	9100	13,000
Tr Sed	1135	1150	3600	6000	8400	12,000

Model 1803, Super 8, 127" wb, (160)

	FP	5	4	3	2	1
Conv	1797	11,400	22,800	38,000	56,000	76,000
Conv Sed	2075	12,000	24,000	40,000	60,000	80,000
Bus Cpe	1524	3000	6000	10,000	14,000	20,000
Clb Cpe	1614	3300	6600	11,000	15,400	22,000
Clb Sed	1740	3150	6300	10,500	14,700	21,000
Sed	1655	2900	5850	9750	13,650	19,500

Model 1804, Super 8, 138" wb, (160)

	FP	5	4	3	2	1
Sed	1919	3300	6600	11,000	15,400	22,000

Model 1805, Super 8, 148" wb, (160)

	FP	5	4	3	2	1
Tr Sed	2051	3350	6750	11,250	15,750	22,500
Tr Limo	2179	3600	7200	12,000	16,800	24,000

Model 1806, Custom, Super 8, 127" wb, (180)

	FP	5	4	3	2	1
Clb Sed	2243	3400	6900	11,500	16,100	23,000
Darr Conv Vic	4570	13,500	27,000	45,000	70,000	90,000

Model 1807, Custom, Super 8, 138" wb, (180)

	FP	5	4	3	2	1
Darr Conv Sed	6300	14,400	28,800	48,000	76,000	96,000
Roll A-W Cabr	4450	13,200	26,400	44,000	68,000	88,000
Darr Spt Sed	6100	12,000	24,000	40,000	60,000	80,000
Fml Sed	2855	4800	9600	16,000	22,400	32,000
Tr Sed	2422	4200	8400	14,000	19,600	28,000

Model 1808, Custom, Super 8, 148" wb, (180)

	FP	5	4	3	2	1
Roll A-W Twn Car	4575	13,500	27,000	45,000	70,000	90,000
Tr Sed	2554	5250	10,500	17,500	24,500	35,000
Tr Limo	2683	6000	12,000	20,000	28,000	40,000

1941

1941 Packard, One-Ten, 1900, convertible coupe, OCW

PACKARD — NINETEENTH SERIES, ONE-TEN (1900) — SIX: Because of blockbuster sales in 1940, the most junior of the Junior Packards was offered in a wide variety of body styles for '41, with DeLuxe versions available for every One-Ten except the Business Coupe. A new 133-inch six-cylinder chassis was added as well, with Packard now entering the taxicab business in earnest. ''Electromatic'' was Packard's name for the new semi-automatic clutch, and overdrive was now called Aero-Drive. Two-tone paint schemes were new, and the runningboards were off (though still remaining available optionally). The shortened hood louvers also served as hood releases.

I.D. DATA: Serial number located on metal plate on firewall. Also included on the plate was the body type number plus the production number of that particular car, starting with a base number of 2000. Starting: body type number plus 2001. Engine numbers located on a boss on left side of cylinder block between No. 2 and No. 3 cyl. Starting: D-1501. Ending: 36327.

Body No.	Body Type & Seating	Price	Weight	Prod. Total
1488	Bus. Cpe.-2P	927	3150	—
1485	Clb. Cpe.-2/4P	1020	3200	—
1489	Conv. Cpe.-2/4P	1195	3310	—
1484	2-dr. Tr. Sed.-5P	1010	3245	—
1482	4-dr. Tr. Sed.-5P	1076	3250	—
1483	Sta. Wag.-8P	1251	3460	—
NA	Taxicab-5P	NA	NA	—
Deluxe				
1485DE	Clb. Cpe.-2/4P	1058	3205	—
1489DE	Conv. Cpe.-2/4P	1229	3315	—
1484DE	2-dr. Tr. Sed.-5P	1070	3270	—
1482DE	4-dr. Tr. Sed.-5P	1136	3270	—
1463	Sta. Wag.-8P	1326	3470	—

ENGINE: L-head. Inline. Six. Cast iron. B & S: 3-1/2 in. x 4-1/4 in. Disp.: 245 cu. in. C.R.: 6.39 standard, 6.71 opt. Brake H.P.: 100 @ 3200 R.P.M. Net H.P.: 29.4. Main bearings: Four. Valve lifters: Adjustable tappet. Carb.: Stromberg. Model BXOV-26.

1941 Packard, One-Ten, 1900, station wagon, OCW

CHASSIS: [1900 Series] W.B.: 122 in. Tires: 6.50 x 15. [Taxi-Cab] W.B.: 133 in. Tires: 6.50 x 15.

TECHNICAL: Selective synchromesh. Speeds: 3F/1R. Column shift control. Disc clutch. Shaft drive rear axle. Overall ratio: 4.3 standard. Hydraulic brakes on four wheels. Disc wheels.

OPTIONS: Radio. Heater. Spotlight. Air conditioning.

HISTORICAL: Introduced September, 1940. Model year production: 34,700.

1941 Packard, One-Twenty, 1901, coupe, JAC

PACKARD — NINETEENTH SERIES, ONE-TWENTY (1901) — EIGHT: What was given to the One-Ten was taken away from the One-Twenty in '41. Body styles were reduced to eight. Styling changes were common to the two cars. Headlights now settled completely into the fenders, and the one-piece sidemounts (when ordered) were sunk even deeper therein. The former divided rear window was now a one-piece.

I.D. DATA: Serial number located on metal plate on firewall. Also included was the body type number plus the production number of that particular car, starting with a base number of 2000. Starting: body type number plus 2001. Engine numbers located on a boss upper left side of cylinder block-boss is painted white. Starting: D-300001. Ending: 317238.

Body No.	Body Type & Seating	Price	Weight	Prod. Total
1498	Bus. Cpe.-2P	1142	3385	—
1495	Clb. Cpe.-2/4P	1235	3430	—
1499	Conv. Cpe.-2/4P	1407	3585	—
1497	Conv. Sed.-5P	1753	3725	—
1494	2-dr. Tr. Sed.-5P	1260	3504	—
1492	4-dr. Tr. Sed.-5P	1291	3510	—
1493	Sta. Wag.-8P	1466	3720	—
1473	Sta. Wag. DeL.-8P	1541	3730	—

ENGINE: L-head. Straight eight. Cast iron. B & S: 3-1/4 in. x 4-1/2 in. Disp.: 282 cu. in. C.R.: 6.41 standard, 6.85 optional. Brake H.P.: 120 @ 3600 R.P.M. Net H.P.: 33.8. Main bearings: Five. Valve lifters: Pressure lubricated. Carb.: Carter model WA1.

CHASSIS: [1901 Series] W.B.: 127 in. Tires: 7.00 x 15.

TECHNICAL: Selective synchromesh. Speeds: 3F/1R. Column shift control. Conventional clutch. Shaft drive. Overall ratio: 4.09 standard. Hydraulic brakes on four wheels. Disc wheels.

OPTIONS: Dual sidemount. Radio. Heater. Spotlight. Turn signals. Air conditioning (275.00).

HISTORICAL: Introduced September, 1940. Model year production: 17,100.

PACKARD — NINETEENTH SERIES, SUPER-8 ONE-SIXTY (1903, 1904, 1905) — EIGHT: Engineering changes were minimal, but the look was different this year throughout the Packard line. The Senior cars appeared longer (which they were by five inches), though the wheelbases remained the same. Radiators were pushed forward, and headlamps were now completely inset into the fenders, with the parking lamps mounted directly above them. Two-toning was in, if a customer wished; and runningboards were out, also at customer request. In their place a black rubber gravel shield was given the rear fender of One-Sixty closed cars (the shield was chrome on the convertibles). Models 1904 and 1905 offered the same body styles as the year previous; in Model 1903 the club sedan and the touring sedan were eliminated, but DeLuxe versions of both the convertible sedan and coupe were added.

I.D. DATA: Serial number located on a metal rectangular plate on the firewall. The plate also showed the body type number plus the production number of that particular car, starting with a base number of 2000. Starting: body type number plus 2001. Engine numbers located on a boss upper left side of cylinder block — boss is painted white. Starting: D-500001. Ending: 504550.

Body No.	Body Type & Seating	Price	Weight	Prod. Total
1478	Bus. Cpe.-2P	1594	3875	—
1475	Clb. Cpe.-4P	1709	3800	—
1479	Conv. Cpe.-4P	1892	3965	—
1479DE	Conv. Cpe. DeL.-4P	2067	3985	—
1477	Conv. Sed.-5P	2180	4140	—
1477DE	Conv. Sed. DeL.-5P	2405	4160	—
1462	Tr. Sed.-5P	2009	4305	—
1471	Tr. Sed.-7P	2161	4495	—
1470	Tr. Limo.-7P	2289	4570	—

ENGINE: L-head. Straight eight. Cast iron block. B & S: 3-1/2 in. x 4-5/8 in. Disp.: 356 cu. in. C.R.: 6.45:1 standard, 6.85:1 opt. Brake H.P.: 160 @ 3500 R.P.M. Net H.P.: 39.2. Main bearings: Nine. Valve lifters: Silent hydraulic.

CHASSIS: [1903] W.B.: 127 in. Tires: 7.00 x 16. [1905] W.B.: 138 in. Tires: 7.00 x 16. [1905] W.B.: 148 in. Tires: 7.00 x 16.

TECHNICAL: Selective synchromesh. Speeds: 3F/1R. Column-mounted gearshift control. Single plate clutch. Shaft drive. Overall ratio: 3.92:1. Hydraulic brakes on four wheels. Disc wheels.

OPTIONS: Dual sidemount. Fender skirts. Radio (63.50). Heater and defroster. Spotlight. Air conditioning (275.00). Electromagnetic clutch (37.50). Aero-Drive.

HISTORICAL: Introduced September, 1940. Model year production: 3,525.

1941 Packard, Super-8 One-Eighty, 1906, Darrin convertible victoria, OCW

PACKARD — NINETEENTH SERIES, SUPER-8 ONE-EIGHTY (1906, 1907, 1908) — EIGHT: Though the One-Sixty and the One-Eighty were essentially the same cars save for trim and appointments, the Packard company this year strove to make the most of the difference. Catalogues specified that all One-Eighty models were custom cars available on special order. Independent coachbuilders accounted for six of the eleven body styles available, Packard providing the rest. Windows were larger in the One-Eighty, and hydraulically-operated in the closed cars. In the closed cars too, wood replaced the wood-grained metal moldings of the year previous. And all One-Eighty cars were provided chrome gravel shields when runningboards weren't ordered. Wheelbases remained the same, though body styles available were revised. In the Model 1906 the club sedan was dropped, leaving only the Darrin Convertible Victoria. In the Model 1907 the Darrin Convertible Sedan was replaced by a LeBaron Sport Brougham. The Model 1908 line was augmented with a new touring sedan and touring limousine by LeBaron.

I.D. DATA: Serial number located on metal rectangular plate on the firewall. The plate also showed the body type number plus the production number of that particular car, starting with a base number of 2000. Starting: body type number plus 2001. Engine numbers located on a boss upper left side of cylinder block-boss is painted white. Starting: CD-500001. Ending: 504550.

Body No.	Body Type & Seating	Price	Weight	Prod. Total
1429	Conv. Vict. Darrin-5P	4595	4040	—
1452	Spt. Brgm. LeB.-5P	3545	4450	—
1422	Spt. Sed. Darrin-5P	4795	4490	—
794	All W. Cabr. Roll.-7P	4695	4075	—
1432	Formal Sed.-6P	3095	4380	—
1442	Tr. Sed.-5P	2632	4350	—
1451	Tr. Sed.-7P	2769	4590	—
1450	Tr. Limo.-7P	2913	4650	—
1421	Tr. Sed. LeB.-7P	5345	4740	—
1420	Tr. Limo. LeB.-7P	5595	4850	—
795	All W. Twn. Car Roll.-7P	4820	4200	—

ENGINE: L-head. Straight eight. Cast en bloc. B & S: 3-1/2 in. x 4-5/8 in. Disp.: 356 cu. in. C.R.: 6.45:1 standard, 6.85:1 opt. Brake H.P.: 160 @ 3500 R.P.M. Net H.P.: 39.2. Main bearings: Nine. Valve lifters: Silent hydraulic.

CHASSIS: [1905 Series] W.B.: 127 in. Tires: 7.00 x 16. [1906 Series] W.B.: 138 in. Tires: 7.00 x 16. [1907 Series] W.B.: 148 in. Tires: 7.00 x 16.

TECHNICAL: Selective synchromesh. Speeds: 3F/1R. Column shift control. Single plate clutch. Shaft drive rear axle. Overall ratio: 3.92:1. Hydraulic brakes on four wheels. Disc wheels.

OPTIONS: Dual sidemount. Sidemount cover(s). Fender skirts. Radio (63.50). Heater and defroster. Spotlight. Electromagnetic clutch. Aero-Drive. Air conditioning.

HISTORICAL: Introduced September, 1940. Model year production: 930.

PACKARD — NINETEENTH SERIES, CLIPPER (1951) — EIGHT: The Clipper borrowed the One-Twenty's engine, though a new compression ratio provided five more horsepower. The Clipper's wheelbase was 127 inches as was the One-Twenty and the smallest Super-8, though the chassis was thoroughly redesigned. What the Clipper didn't borrow from any other Packard, of course, was its unique new look. Only one body style was available in Model 1951 (a four-door sedan), and it was priced at $1420 (midway between the One-Twenty and One-Sixty). The Clipper was lower than any other Packard on the market, and wider than virtually any other car in the industry. Its pacesetting styling would be carried in many Junior and Senior Packards for the Twentieth Series.

I.D. DATA: Serial number located on metal plate on firewall. Also included on the plate was the body type number and the production number for that particular car, starting with a base number of 2000. Starting: body type number plus 2001. Engine numbers located on a boss upper left side of cylinder block — boss is painted white. Starting: D-400001. Ending: 499999.

Body No.	Body Type & Seating	Price	Weight	Prod. Total
1401	Tr. Sed.-5P	1420	3725	—

ENGINE: L-head. Straight eight. Cast iron block. B & S: 3-1/4 in. x 4-1/2 in. Disp.: 282 cu. in. C.R.: 6.85:1. Brake H.P.: 125 @ 3600 R.P.M. Net H.P.: 33.8. Main bearings: Five. Valve lifters: Adjustable. Carb.: Carter model WDO-512-S.

CHASSIS: [1951] W.B.: 127 in. Tires: 7.00 x 15.

TECHNICAL: Selective synchronized. Speeds: 3F/1R. Column-mounted gearshift control. Disc clutch. Shaft drive. Packard-Hypoid Angleset differential. Overall ratio: 4.09 standard, 4.36 opt. Hydraulic brakes on four wheels. Disc wheels.

OPTIONS: Fender skirts. Bumper guards. Radio. Spotlight. Air conditioning. Electromatic clutch. Aero-Drive.

HISTORICAL: Introduced April, 1941. Model year production: 16,600.

1941 19th Series
Model 1900, Std., 6 cyl., 122" wb, (110)

	FP	5	4	3	2	1
Conv	1175	4800	9600	16,000	22,400	32,000
Bus Cpe	907	1150	3600	6000	8400	12,000
Clb Cpe	1000	1250	3900	6500	9100	13,000
2 dr Sed	1024	900	1900	4500	6300	9000
Tr Sed	1056	925	2000	4600	6400	9200
Sta Wag	1231	6300	12,600	21,000	29,400	42,000

Model 1900, Dlx., 6-cyl., 122" wb, (110)

	FP	5	4	3	2	1
Conv	1229	4950	9900	16,500	23,100	33,000
Clb Cpe	1058	1250	3900	6500	9100	13,000
2 dr Sed	1020	1025	2600	5250	7300	10,500
Sed	1136	950	2100	4750	6650	9500
Sta Wag	1326	6750	13,500	22,500	31,500	45,000

Model 1901, 8-cyl., 127" wb, (120)

	FP	5	4	3	2	1
Conv	1407	5400	10,800	18,000	25,200	36,000
Conv Sed	1753	5700	11,400	19,000	26,600	38,000
Bus Cpe	1142	1400	4200	7000	9800	14,000
Clb Cpe	1235	1550	4500	7500	10,500	15,000
2 dr Sed	1260	1000	2400	5000	7000	10,000
Sed	1291	1000	2500	5100	7100	10,200
Sta Wag	1466	7050	14,100	23,500	32,900	47,000
DeL Sta Wag	1541	7200	14,400	24,000	33,600	48,000

Model 1903, Super 8, 127" wb, (160)

	FP	5	4	3	2	1
Conv	1937	10,800	21,600	36,000	50,500	72,000
DeL Conv	2112	11,100	22,200	37,000	52,000	74,000
Conv Sed	2225	11,400	22,800	38,000	56,000	76,000
DeL Conv Sed	2450	11,700	23,400	39,000	58,000	78,000
Clb Cpe	1754	3000	6000	10,000	14,000	20,000
Bus Cpe	1639	2800	5700	9500	13,300	19,000
Sed	1795	2700	5600	9350	13,100	18,700

Model 1904, Super 8, 138" wb, (160)

	FP	5	4	3	2	1
Sed	2054	3350	6750	11,250	15,750	22,500

Model 1905, Super 8, 148" wb, (160)

	FP	5	4	3	2	1
Tr Sed	2206	3300	6600	11,000	15,400	22,000
Tr Limo	2334	3750	7500	12,500	17,500	25,000

Model 1906, Custom, Super 8, 127" wb, (180)

	FP	5	4	3	2	1
Darr Conv Vic	4595	12,900	25,800	48,200	66,000	86,000

Model 1907, Custom, Super 8, 138" wb, (180)

	FP	5	4	3	2	1
Leb Spt Brgm	3545	9900	19,800	33,000	46,200	66,000
Roll A-W Cabr	4695	14,400	28,800	48,000	76,000	96,000
Darr Spt Sed	4795	9000	18,000	30,000	42,000	60,000
Tr Sed	2632	4350	8700	14,500	20,300	29,000
Fml Sed	3090	4500	9000	15,000	21,000	30,000

Model 1908, Custom, Super 8, 148" wb, (180)

	FP	5	4	3	2	1
Roll A-W Twn Car	4820	12,900	25,800	48,200	66,000	86,000
Tr Sed	2769	4800	9600	16,000	22,400	32,000
LeB Tr Sed	5345	6750	13,500	22,500	31,500	45,000
Tr Limo	2913	4500	9000	15,000	21,000	30,000
LeB Tr Limo	5595	7500	15,000	25,000	35,000	50,000

Series 1951, Clipper, 8 cyl., 127" wb

	FP	5	4	3	2	1
Sed	1420	1075	3000	5500	7700	11,000

1942

1942 Packard, Six Special, 2020, convertible coupe, JAC

PACKARD — TWENTIETH SERIES, SIX (2000, 2010, 2020, 2030) — SIX:
The former One-Ten was once again renamed the Six, with the Clipper engine in all cars and Clipper styling in most. The station wagon and the convertible sedan offered the previous year were dropped; the convertible coupe (2020) and taxi (2030) were the only cars to retain the traditional One-Ten look. All bodies in the Special (2000) and Custom (2010) featured Clipper styling. Dish-shaped wheelcovers without the Packard name were fitted this year. And wheelbases were three: 120 inches for Models 2000 and 2010, 122 inches for Model 2020, 133 inches for Model 2030.

I.D. DATA: Serial number located on metal plate on firewall. Also included was the body type number plus the production number of that particular car, starting with a base of 2000. Starting: body type number plus 2001. Engine numbers located on a boss upper left side of cylinder block — boss is painted white. Starting: E-1501. Ending: 12906.

Body No.	Body Type & Seating	Price	Weight	Prod. Total
Special Series 2000				
1588	Bus. Cpe.-3P	1248	3365	—
1585	Clb. Sed.-6P	1283	3415	—
1582	Tr. Sed.-6P	1318	3435	—
Custom Series 2010				
1505	Clb. Sed.-6P	1353	3440	—
1502	Tr. Sed.-6P	1388	3460	—
Series 2020				
1589	Conv. Cpe.-5P	1468	3315	—
Series 2030				
1584	Taxi Cab-6P	NA	3980	—

ENGINE: L-head. Inline six. Cast iron block. B & S: 3-1/4 in. x 4-1/4 in. Disp.: 245 cu. in. C.R.: 6.39 standard, 6.71 opt. Brake H.P.: 105 @ 3600 R.P.M. Net H.P.: 29.4. Main bearings: Four. Valve lifters: Adjustable. Carb.: Carter model WAI-530-S.

CHASSIS: [2000, 2010] W.B.: 120 in. Tires: 6.50 x 15. [2020] W.B.: 122 in. Tires: 6.50 x 15. [2030] W.B.: 133 in. Tires: 6.50 x 15.

TECHNICAL: Selective synchromesh. Speeds: 3F/1R. Column-mounted gearshift control. Disc clutch. Shaft drive. Overall ratio: 4.3 standard, 4.55 opt. Hydraulic brakes on four wheels. Disc wheels.

OPTIONS: Radio. Vacuum radio antenna. Electromatic. Turn signals (standard on the Custom).

HISTORICAL: Introduced August, 1941. Model year production: 11,325.

PACKARD — TWENTIETH SERIES, EIGHT (2001, 2011, 2021) — EIGHT:
This series, formerly the One-Twenty, was as "Clipperized" as the One-Ten. Again, only a single production car — the Model 2021 Convertible Coupe — retained the One-Twenty styling, and on the traditional 127-inch wheelbase. All other cars rode on a 120-inch wheelbase and carried Clipper styling, these designated the Special (2001) and the Custom (2011). Turn signals, automatic courtesy lights, electric clock and automatic cigar lighter were among the amenities supplied as standard equipment on the Eight Custom, available optionally on the Eight Special.

I.D. DATA: Serial number located on metal plate on firewall. The body type number plus the production number for that particular car was also included on the plate, starting with a base number of 2000. Starting: body type number plus 2001. Engine numbers located on a boss upper left side of cylinder block — boss is painted white. Starting: E-300001. Ending: 319350.

Body No.	Body Type & Seating	Price	Weight	Prod. Total
Special Series 2001				
1598	Bus. Cpe.-3P	1303	3490	—
1595	Clb. Sed.-6P	1338	3540	—
1592	Tr. Sed.-6P	1373	3560	—
Custom Series 2011				
1515	Clb. Sed.-6P	1408	3565	—
1512	Tr. Sed.-6P	1443	3585	—
Series 2021				
1599	Conv. Cpe.-6P	1578	3585	—

ENGINE: L-head. Straight eight. Cast iron block. B & S: 3-1/4 in. x 4-1/2 in. Disp.: 282 cu. in. C.R.: 6.85:1. Brake H.P.: 125 @ 3600 R.P.M. Net H.P.: 33.8. Main bearings: Five. Valve lifters: Adjustable.

CHASSIS: [2001, 2011] W.B.: 120 in. Tires: 6.50 x 15. [2021] W.B.: 127 in. Tires: 6.50 x 15.

TECHNICAL: Selective synchromesh. Speeds: 3F/1R. Column-mounted gearshift control. Disc clutch. Shaft drive. Overall ratio: 4.1 standard. Hydraulic brakes on four wheels. Disc wheels.

OPTIONS: Radio. Heater. Vacuum radio antenna. Electromatic. Air conditioning. Turn signals.

HISTORICAL: Introduced August, 1941. Model year production: 19,199.

1942 Packard Clipper, Custom One-Sixty, 2003, club sedan, JAC

PACKARD — TWENTIETH SERIES, SUPER-8 ONE-SIXTY (2003, 2004, 2005, 2023, 2055) — EIGHT: Turn indicators and dish-shaped hubcaps that didn't say Packard were common to both Junior and Senior Packards for '42. There was news unique to the Seniors, however; the cars' straight-eight engine now generated 165 hp, though that fact was not publicized during a year when the big Packard word was "Clipper." Clipper styling came to the One-Sixty in a club sedan and touring sedan on the 127-inch wheelbase, the convertible coupe being the only traditionally-styled One-Sixty now on that chassis. The traditional One-Sixty look remained on the 138-inch and 148-inch cars, the latter chassis now including a new business sedan and limousine. There was a nod to the Clipper even in these models, however, with the change from vertical to horizontal in the grilles flanking the radiator (all non-Clippers featured this). Electric windshield wipers and an accelerator pedal starter were also new to the One-Sixty this year.

I.D. DATA: Serial number located on a metal rectangular plate on the firewall. The plate also showed the body type number plus the production number of that particular car, starting with a base number of 2000. Starting: body type number plus 2001. Engine numbers on a boss upper left side of cylinder block-boss is painted white. Starting: F5000000. Ending: E504000.

Body No.	Body Type & Seating	Price	Weight	Prod. Total
Model 2003 Clipper (127" wb)				
1575	Clb. Sed.-6P	1635	—	—
1572	Tr. Sed.-6P	1695	—	—
Model 2023 (127" wb)				
1579	Conv. Cpe.-5P	1795	—	—
Model 2004 (138" wb)				
1562	Tr. Sed.-6P	1905	—	—
Model 2005 (148" wb)				
1571	Tr. Sed.-5/7P	2050	—	—
1570	Tr. Limo.-5/7P	2175	—	—
Model 2055 (148" wb)				
1591	Bus. Sed.-5/7P	1900	—	—
1590	Bus. Limo.-5/7P	2025	—	—

ENGINE: L-head. Straight eight. Cast en bloc. B & S: 3-1/2 in. x 4-5/8 in. Disp.: 356 cu. in. C.R.: 6.85:1. Brake H.P.: 165 @ 3600 R.P.M. Net H.P.: 39.2. Main bearings: Nine. Valve lifters: Hydraulic.

CHASSIS: [2003] W.B.: 127 in. Tires: 7.00 x 16. [2023] W.B.: 127 in. Tires: 7.00 x 16. [2004] W.B.: 138 in. Tires: 7.00 x 16. [2005, 2055] W.B.: 148 in. Tires: 7.00 x 16.

TECHNICAL: Selective synchromesh. Speeds: 3F/1R. Column-mounted gearshift control. Single plate clutch. Shaft drive. Overall ratio: 3.92:1. Hydraulic brakes on four wheels. Disc wheels.

HISTORICAL: Introduced August 25, 1941. Model year production: 2,580.

PACKARD — TWENTIETH SERIES, SUPER-8 ONE-EIGHTY (2006, 2007, 2008) — EIGHT: The One-Eighty was provided the same changes as the One-Sixty — and the same neglect in the wake of the attention-getting Clipper. As with the One-Sixty, Clipper styling arrived in two body styles on the 127-inch wheelbase, the Darrin Convertible Victoria the sole non-Clipper now on that chassis. Though the Darrin Sport Sedan and LeBaron Sport Brougham were dropped, LeBaron remained represented with two custom bodies, as did Rollson. This was, of course, the last year for the Super-8.

I.D. DATA: Serial number located on a metal rectangular plate on the firewall. The plate also showed the body type number plus the production number of that particular car, starting with base number of 2000. Starting: body type number plus 2001. Engine numbers located on a boss upper left side of cylinder block — boss is painted white. Starting: CE-500001. Ending: 503371.

Body No.	Body Type & Seating	Price	Weight	Prod. Total
Model 2006 Clipper (127" wb)				
1525	Clb. Sed.-6P	2115	4010	—
1522	Tr. Sed.-6P	2215	4030	—

Body No.	Body Type & Seating	Price	Weight	Prod. Total
Model 2006 Special (127" wb)				
1529	Darrin Conv. Vic.-5P	4595	3920	—
Model 2007 (138" wb)				
1532	Formal Sed.-6P	3050	4390	—
1542	Tr. Sed.-6P	2465	4280	—
894	All W. Cabr. Roll.-7P	4875	4525	—
Model 2008 (148" wb)				
1551	Tr. Sed.-7P	2550	4525	—
1550	Tr. Limo.-7P	2675	4540	—
1521	Tr. Sed. LeB.-7P	5545	4740	—
1520	Tr. Limo. LeB.-7P	5795	4850	—
895	All W. Twn. Car Roll.-7P	4975	4200	—

ENGINE: L-head. Straight eight. Cast en bloc. B & S: 3-1/2 in. x 4-5/8 in. Disp.: 356 cu. in. C.R.: 6.85:1. Brake H.P.: 165 @ 3600 R.P.M. Net H.P.: 39.2. Main bearings: Nine. Valve lifters: Hydraulic.

CHASSIS: [2006] W.B.: 127 in. Tires: 7.00 x 16. [2007] W.B.: 138 in. Tires: 7.00 x 16. [2008] W.B.: 148 in. Tires: 7.00 x 16.

TECHNICAL: Selective synchromesh. Speeds: 3F/1R. Column-mounted gearshift control. Single plate clutch. Shaft drive. Overall ratio: 3.92:1. Hydraulic brakes on four wheels. Disc wheels.

OPTIONS: Dual sidemount. Fender skirts. Radio (57.50). Heater with defroster (40.00). Clock. Radio. Spotlight. Turn indicators (9.75). Overdrive (60.00).

HISTORICAL: Introduced August, 25, 1941. Model year production: 672.

1942 20th Series
Clipper Series -- (6 cyl.)
Series 2000, Special, 120" wb

	FP	5	4	3	2	1
Bus Cpe	1248	1250	3900	6500	9100	13,000
Clb Sed	1283	1400	4200	7000	9800	14,000
Tr Sed	1318	1250	3900	6500	9100	13,000
Series 2010, Custom, 120" wb						
Clb Sed	1353	1550	4500	7500	10,500	15,000
Tr Sed	1388	1400	4200	7000	9800	14,000
Series 2020, Custom, 122" wb						
Conv	1468	5400	10,800	18,000	25,200	36,000
Clipper Series -- (8 cyl.)						
Series 2001, Special, 120" wb						
Bus Cpe	1303	1550	4500	7500	10,500	15,000
Clb Sed	1338	1550	4500	7500	10,500	15,000
Tr Sed	1373	1500	4350	7250	10,150	14,500
Series 2011, Custom, 120" wb						
Clb Sed	1408	1400	4200	7000	9800	14,000
Tr Sed	1443	1500	4350	7250	10,150	14,500
Series 2021, Custom, 127" wb						
Conv	1578	5700	11,400	19,000	26,600	38,000
Super 8, 160 Series, Clipper, 127" wb, 2003						
Clb Sed	1753	1750	4800	8000	11,200	16,000
Tr Sed	1814	1800	4950	8250	11,550	16,500
Super 8, 160, 127" wb, 2023						
Conv	1917	7050	14,100	23,500	32,900	47,000
Super 8, 160, 138" wb, 2004						
Tr Sed	2029	3300	6600	11,000	15,400	22,000
Super 8, 160, 148" wb, 2005						
7P Sed	2178	3150	6300	10,500	14,700	21,000
Limo	2306	3750	7500	12,500	17,500	25,000
Super 8, 160, 148" wb, 2055						
Bus Sed	2024	3000	6000	10,000	14,000	20,000
Bus Limo	2152	3600	7200	12,000	16,800	24,000
Super 8, 180, Clipper, 127" wb, 2006						
Clb Sed	2244	1550	4500	7500	10,500	15,000
Tr Sed	2346	1750	4800	8000	11,200	16,000
Super 8, 180, Special, 127" wb, 2006						
Darr Conv Vic	4783	11,400	22,800	38,000	56,000	76,000
Super 8, 180, 138" wb, 2007						
Tr Sed	2602	2800	5700	9500	13,300	19,000
Fml Sed	3201	3000	6000	10,000	14,000	20,000
Roll A-W Cabr	5070	6000	12,000	20,000	28,000	40,000
Super 8, 180, 148" wb, 2008						
Tr Sed	2689	3750	7500	12,500	17,500	25,000
Limo	2817	4350	8700	14,500	20,300	29,000
LeB Sed	5756	4050	8100	13,500	18,900	27,000
LeB Limo	6012	5250	10,500	17,500	24,500	35,000
Roll A-W Twn Car	5172	6750	13,500	22,500	31,500	45,000

PACKET — Packet was the designation given by James Scripps-Booth to the delivery version of the cyclecar he produced in Detroit in 1914. Refer to Scripps-Booth.

The Packet cyclecar which purportedly was produced in Seattle, Washington in 1914 was merely a misspelling of the Pacific. Refer to Pacific.

PACKET — Minneapolis, Minnesota — (1916-1917) — The Packet Motor Car Manufacturing Company was successor to the Brasie Motor Car Company. Previously Packet had been a model designation of the Brasie, originally for just the light delivery version. Now it identified all cars produced by this Minneapolis company. Four-cylinder 18 hp Prugh engines were featured. Roadster price was $325, but it would appear that most Packet production centered on the commercial version.

PACO — Chicago, Illinois — (1908-1909) — The Pietsch Automobile Company was incorporated with a capital stock of $30,000 in the fall of 1906 in Chicago by Laurence J. Pietsch, Edward A. Becker and Carlos J. Ward for the manufacture of automobiles to be called Paco. Although a small run of a delivery wagon may have begun earlier, a Paco automobile did not arrive until 1908, by which time Pietsch Auto & Marine Company was the company's designation. The Paco was a two-cylinder highwheeled buggy that was available as a $400 runabout, a $500 surrey and a $500 panel delivery. Although the engines were mounted under the seats,

1908 Paco, runabout, NAHC

there was an attempt at modernity in the Paco with its false hood in front and its wheel for steering. The company advertised in *Popular Mechanics* and elsewhere during 1908, and production appears to have continued into 1909. During August of that year Laurence Pietsch announced his plans to raise capitalization from $30,000 to $100,000, to relocate in Kalamazoo, Michigan, and to carry on there with the manufacture of "delivery vehicles in large quantities." Negotiations in Kalamazoo apparently fell through. The Paco was no longer heard from following 1910.

1908-1909 PACO

	FP	5	4	3	2	1
Runabout (2-cyl., 10 hp)	400	1600	2700	3800	5800	12,000
Surrey (2-cyl., 10 hp)	500	1800	2800	4000	6200	13,000
Light Delivery (2-cyl., 12 hp)	500	1500	2500	3600	5500	11,000

PAGE — J.I. Page of Owosso, Michigan built an experimental car in 1909 which may have been considered for possible manufacture. Refer to Owosso.

The Page-Toledo has been indicated on rosters as an automobile produced by the Toledo Motor Company in Toledo, Ohio from 1910-1911. Though documentation is lacking, it is believed that this car was planned as a continuation of the Page from Adrian, Michigan. Conceivably, entrepreneurs in Toledo may have acquired rights to the Adrian-built experimental Pages, but any manufacture would have been minimal. Most certainly, the Page-Toledo was not the successor to the Pope-Toledo as has been suggested through the years. When John North Willys bought the Pope-Toledo plant in 1909, he initially organized as the Toledo Motor Car Company but that designation was changed within months to the Willys-Overland Company.

1906 Page, runabout, NAHC

PAGE — Providence, Rhode Island — (1906-1908) — The Page Motor Vehicle Company was organized during the summer of 1905 with a capital stock of $50,000 and the backing of a number of prominent Providence businessmen. The Page was designed by J.H. McHardy, but was named for two other men in the organization: A.A. Page who would serve as sales manager, and Victor W. Page who would take charge of mechanical construction. The car was fitted with a two-cylinder 10 hp engine which was air cooled and featured overhead valves. The engine was under the hood, and the chassis had an 84-inch wheelbase. A $750 runabout with right-hand steering wheel was the only model offered. In February of 1906 the company announced the completion of three runabouts and, curiously, that it was about to organize — again. In the fall of 1907, a four-cylinder 20 hp runabout on a 100-inch wheelbase chassis was added, but that appeared to be the end of the line for this Page. After the First World War, Victor Page was back with another car, this one carrying his full name.

PAGE — Adrian, Michigan — (1907-1909) — The Church Manufacturing Company had produced both wire fences and automobiles in the Adrian factory into which the Page Woven Wire Fence Company moved in late 1906 with the intention to do precisely the same. The company promised a light runabout and a touring car, and hinted that a truck would follow.

Promotion of this new venture was lavish. The vehicles produced were only prototypes. The firm did subsequently manufacture a number of air-cooled, two-stroke motors as the newly styled Page Gas Engine Company after 1907, but the only automobiles which followed were, again, experimental. In 1909 J. Wallace Page bought patent rights to the ''gyroscopic'' engine owned by the Blomstrom Manufacturing Company, but once more plans proceeded no further than a prototype. Some of the Page people thereafter joined the Lion people across town in their new automotive venture. Other of the Page people mended their fences.

PAGENKOPF — That a William Pagenkopf of Goldfield, Nevada built an automobile in 1906 has been indicated on various car rosters. Documentation for this is lacking.

PAIGE — Batavia, New York — (1900) — Edison W. Paige was a paperhanger from Batavia and the builder of the first automobile in town. It was completed and had its maiden run to Rochester on August 9th, 1900. ''That was really something,'' he recalled to a Batavia reporter decades later. ''All the people of Batavia lined the streets to see me take off about 10 o'clock in the morning. It was a gray runabout with white stripes, an elevated rear section and the front seat rounded toward the dash . . . a one-cylinder buggy without top or fenders. It made the trip to Rochester at the rate of 22 miles an hour.'' The car had been built in the kitchen of his home. Paige later sold it for $355 to Fred Remsen, the ticket agent at the New York Central railway station in Pembroke. He never built another car, although subsequently he operated two garages, and ran a repair and taxi service. In 1915 he built a workshop at the rear of his home and spent the rest of his life as a master tool maker and sharpener. He died in 1949.

1909 Paige-Detroit, model no.1, roadster, HAC

PAIGE-DETROIT — Detroit, Michigan — (1909-1910)/**PAIGE** — (1911-1928) — In 1895 Harry M. Jewett shipped into Michigan the first West Virginia coal ever sold in the state, and in the twelve years following he made a fortune in the mining industry. Concluding he could do the same in the automobile field, he began looking around for a likely car with which to do it and during the summer of 1909 took a test ride in a two-stroke three-cylinder 25 hp roadster designed by Andrew Bachle which was being promoted by Fred O. Paige. Since Jewett didn't know much about cars, since the car ran well in the test drive, and since Paige had been president of the Reliance Motor Car Company prior to its takeover by General Motors, Jewett thought he was on to a good thing. That fall, with $100,000 in cash (some of it his own, the rest from business friends), he organized the Paige-Detroit Motor Car Company and installed Fred Paige in the presidency. Production began, and Harry Jewett began to learn a little more about cars. His quoted assessment from the spring of 1910 regarding the Paige-Detroit was: ''It's rotten. A piece of junk.'' Jewett eased Paige out of the company, installed himself as president, shut down the assembly line, and cleaned house in the engineering department. The new Paige for 1911 — interestingly, Jewett dropped ''Detroit'' but didn't change the car's name — was a conventional four-stroke 25 hp four. In 1912 Jewett attached voguish designations (Kenilworth, LaMarquise, Brunswick, et al.) to the various Paige models which now included several open sporting cars. By now he had also worked himself into the presidency of Lozier in Detroit, though not for long. His Paige, however, was progressing nicely: 4631 cars in 1914, 7749 in 1915, 12,456 in 1916. The first six-cylinder Paige arrived in 1915; only sixes were produced from 1916. In addition to the preponderance of sporting models in the Paige lineup, the marque also became well-known for its chic and graceful styling, though the slogan ''The Most Beautiful Car in America'' was perhaps overdoing it. The Paige sporting prowess was effectively demonstrated, however, in 1921 when Ralph Mulford drove a stripped 6-66 roadster to a one-mile straightaway speed record of 102.83 mph at Daytona Beach. Paige followed this success in 1922 with a semi-production version called the Daytona, a dashing three-passenger roadster with seats inside for two and a pull-out drawer on the right side aft of the running board for anyone brave enough to sit in it. Also in 1922 the company introduced a smaller companion car called the Jewett, which was produced through 1926, then absorbed into the Paige lineup in 1927 as the Model 6-45. Although the company built all its own engines through the World War I years, the higher-powered Paiges of the Twenties carried Continentals, and the straight-eight introduced for 1927 was a Lycoming. The Paige-Detroit Motor Car Company had felt the effects of the postwar depression, but the firm had survived easily. Production for these years was: 15,766 cars in 1919, 16,090 in 1920, 8698 in 1921, 9323 in 1922. In 1923, with the Jewett to help, sales soared to 43,556 cars. In early 1925 the company moved into 10th place in the

1911 Paige, model B, roadster, WLB

industry, celebrating this fortuitous turn of events with a brochure entitled ''43 Ghosts'' — the number of car companies which had succumbed in the past two years — and advising that ''Paige-Jewett has men, money and machinery to build good automobiles and to keep building them.'' Unfortunately, the company fortunes flagged later that year, with sales of not quite 40,000 cars by December. In 1926 the company shipped even fewer cars — 37,222 — and lost money. Harry Jewett decided he had enough of the automobile industry. As his losses mounted toward $2.5 million for 1927, he sold out to the Graham brothers that June, who reorganized as Graham-Paige Motors Corporation. Graham-Paige continued the Paige as a 1928 model (beginning in August 1927), but this doubtless was to deplete inventory on hand at the time of the takeover.

1909-1910 PAIGE-DETROIT
Model No. 1 — 3-cyl., 25 hp, 90'' wb

	FP	5	4	3	2	1
Roadster-2P	800	2300	3300	4600	7500	16,000

1911 PAIGE
Model B — 4-cyl., 25 hp, 90'' wb

Roadster-2P	800	2300	3300	4600	7500	16,000

Model C — 4-cyl., 25 hp, 104'' wb

Coupe	1250	2200	3200	4400	7000	15,000
Surrey	975	2400	3400	4800	8000	17,000
Touring	975	2400	3400	4800	8000	17,000

1912 Paige Four, Brooklands racer, HAC

1912 PAIGE
Four — 25 hp, 104'' wb

Beverly Touring-5P	975	2500	3500	5000	8500	18,000
Kenilworth Roadster-3P	975	2400	3400	4800	8000	17,000
Brooklands Racer-2P	975	3700	4700	7300	13,700	26,000
LaMarquise Coupe-4P	1600	2300	3300	4600	7500	16,000
Rockland Runabout-2P	925	2400	3400	4800	8000	17,000
Brunswick Touring-5P	1000	2500	3500	5000	8500	18,000
Pinehurst Surrey-5P	900	2450	3500	4900	8300	17,500

1913 Paige, model 36, touring, OWC

1913 PAIGE
Model 25 — 4-cyl., 22.5 hp, 110" wb

	FP	5	4	3	2	1
Brunswick Touring-5P	950	2500	3500	5000	8500	18,000
Kenilworth Roadster	950	2400	3400	4800	8000	17,000
Speedster	950	3300	4400	6700	12,000	24,000

Model 36 — 4-cyl., 25.6 hp, 116" wb

	FP	5	4	3	2	1
Glenwood Touring-5P	1275	3000	4000	6000	9500	21,000
Glenwood Roadster	1275	2900	3700	5600	9100	20,000
Speedster	1275	3700	4700	7300	13,700	26,000
Sultan Sedan-5P	1950	2000	3000	4200	6500	14,000
La Marquise Coupe-3P	1850	2300	3300	4600	7500	16,000

1914 Paige, model 36, Westbrook runabout, HAC

1914 PAIGE
Model 25 — 4-cyl., 22.5 hp, 110" wb

	FP	5	4	3	2	1
Brunswick Touring-5P	975	2500	3500	5000	8500	18,000
Kenilworth Runabout	975	2400	3400	4800	8000	17,000

Model 36 — 4-cyl., 25.6 hp, 116" wb

	FP	5	4	3	2	1
Glenwood Touring-5P	1275	3000	4000	6000	9500	21,000
Westbrook Runabout	1275	2900	3700	5600	9100	20,000
Montrose Coupe	1850	2500	3500	5000	8500	18,000
Speedway Raceabout	1275	3900	4800	7700	14,300	27,000

1915 Paige, model 36, Glenwood touring, HAC

1915 PAIGE
Model 36 — 4-cyl., 25.6 hp, 116" wb

	FP	5	4	3	2	1
Glenwood Touring-5P	1075	3000	4000	6000	9500	21,000
Westbrook Runabout	1075	2900	3700	5600	9100	20,000
Montrose Coupe	1600	2500	3500	5000	8500	18,000
Speedway Raceabout	1275	3900	4800	7700	14,300	27,000

Six — 29.4 hp, 123 1/2" wb

	FP	5	4	3	2	1
Fairfield Touring-5/7P	1395	4400	5600	9200	17,300	31,000
Meadowbrook Runabout	1395	4300	5400	8700	16,500	30,000
Dartmore Raceabout	1420	5000	6500	11,000	22,000	35,000

1916 Paige, model 6-46, coupe, HAC

1916 PAIGE
Model 6-36 — 6-cyl., 22 hp, 112" wb

	FP	5	4	3	2	1
Touring-5P	1095	3100	4200	6300	10,500	22,000

Model 6-46 — 6-cyl., 29 hp, 123" wb

	FP	5	4	3	2	1
Touring-7P	1295	4400	5600	9200	17,300	31,000
Winter Top Touring-7P	1545	4500	5800	9500	18,000	32,000
Roadster-3P	1295	4300	5400	8700	16,500	30,000
Coupe-3P	1700	2500	3500	5000	8500	18,000
Sedan-7P	1900	2200	3200	4400	7000	15,000
Town Car-7P	2250	2700	3600	5300	8800	19,000
Cabriolet-3P	1600	3200	4300	6500	11,000	23,000

1917 Paige, model 6-45, boattail roadster, AA

1917 PAIGE
Model 6-45 — 6-cyl., 23.44 hp, 117" wb

	FP	5	4	3	2	1
Linwood Touring-5P	1175	3100	4200	6300	10,500	22,000
Roadster-2/3P	1175	3000	4000	6000	9500	21,000
Convertible Sedan-5P	1775	2900	3700	5600	9100	20,000

Model 6-51 — 6-cyl., 29.4 hp, 127" wb

	FP	5	4	3	2	1
Stratford Touring-7P	1495	4000	5000	8000	15,000	28,000
Sedan-7P	2300	2200	3200	4400	7000	15,000
Limousine-7P	2750	2700	3600	5300	8800	19,000
Town Car-7P	2750	3000	4000	6000	9500	21,000
Coupe-3/4P	2100	2400	3400	4800	8000	17,000
Convertible Roadster-4P	1695	3300	4400	6700	12,000	24,000

1918 Paige, model 6-55, Essex touring, HAC

1918 PAIGE
Model 6-40 — 6-cyl., 23.44 hp, 117" wb

	FP	5	4	3	2	1
Linwood Touring-5P	1330	3100	4200	6300	10,500	22,000
Roadster-2/3P	1330	3000	4000	6000	9500	21,000
Glendale Cloverleaf Rdst.	1330	3000	4000	6000	9500	21,000

Model 6-55 — 6-cyl., 29.4 hp, 127" wb

	FP	5	4	3	2	1
Essex Touring-7P	1775	4200	5200	8400	15,700	29,000
Sedan-7P	2850	2300	3300	4600	7500	16,000
Town Car-7P	3230	3100	4200	6300	10,500	22,000
Limousine-7P	3230	2900	3700	5600	9100	20,000
Coupe-3/4P	2850	2500	3500	5000	8500	18,000

1919 PAIGE
Model 6-40 — 6-cyl., 23.44 hp, 117" wb

	FP	5	4	3	2	1
Linwood Touring-5P	1555	3200	4300	6500	11,000	23,000
Cabriolet-3P	1885	2900	3700	5600	9100	20,000
Roadster-2P	1555	3100	4200	6300	10,500	22,000
Roadster-3P	1555	3100	4200	6300	10,500	22,000

Model 6-55 — 6-cyl., 29.4 hp, 127" wb

	FP	5	4	3	2	1
Essex Touring-7P	2060	4000	5000	8000	15,000	28,000
Sport-4P	2165	4200	5200	8400	15,700	29,000
Coupe-3P	2950	2700	3600	5300	8800	19,000
Coupe-4P	2950	2700	3600	5300	8800	19,000
Sedan-7P	2950	2000	3000	4200	6500	14,000
Limousine-7P	3330	2900	3700	5600	9100	20,000
Town Car-7P	3330	3100	4200	6300	10,500	22,000
Larchmont-4P	2165	4200	5200	8400	15,700	29,000

1920 Paige, model 6-55, coupe, AA

1920 PAIGE

Model 6-42 — 6-cyl., 23.44 hp, 119" wb

	FP	5	4	3	2	1
Glenbrook Touring	1670	3200	4300	6500	11,000	23,000
Sedan	2395	2000	3000	4200	6500	14,000
Coupe	2295	2300	3300	4600	7500	16,000
Roadster	1670	3100	4200	6300	10,500	22,000

Model 6-55 — 6-cyl., 29.4 hp, 127" wb

	FP	5	4	3	2	1
Larchmont Touring	2165	4000	5000	8000	15,000	28,000
Touring-7P	2060	4200	5200	8400	15,700	29,000
Coupe-4P	2950	2700	3600	5300	8800	19,000
Sedan-7P	2950	2000	3000	4200	6500	14,000
Limousine-7P	3330	2900	3700	5600	9100	20,000
Town Car-7P	3330	3100	4200	6300	10,500	22,000

1921 Paige, model 6-42, touring, AA

1921 PAIGE

Model 6-42 — 6-cyl., 43 hp, 119" wb

	FP	5	4	3	2	1
Glenbrook Touring-5P	1770	3900	4800	7700	14,300	27,000
Lenox Roadster-3P	1770	3700	4700	7300	13,700	26,000
Ardmore Sport-4P	1990	4000	5000	8000	15,000	28,000
Coupe-4P	2525	2700	3600	5300	8800	19,000
Sedan-5P	2645	2200	3200	4400	7000	15,000

Model 6-66 — 6-cyl., 70 hp, 131" wb

	FP	5	4	3	2	1
Touring-7P	2795	4900	6300	10,300	21,000	34,000
Roadster-4P	2895	4700	6100	9900	19,000	33,000
Coupe-5P	3675	3200	4300	6500	11,000	23,000
Sedan-7P	3750	2900	3700	5600	9100	20,000

1922 Paige, model 6-66, Daytona roadster, HFM

1922 Paige, model 6-44, roadster, AA

1922 PAIGE

Model 6-44 — 6-cyl., 45 hp, 119" wb

	FP	5	4	3	2	1
Touring-5P	1635	3900	4800	7700	14,300	27,000
Ardmore Sport-4P	1925	4000	5000	8000	15,700	28,000
Roadster-3P	1635	3700	4700	7300	13,700	26,000
Coupe-3P	2450	2700	3600	5300	8800	19,000
Sedan-5P	2570	2200	3200	4400	7000	15,000

Model 6-66 — 6-cyl., 70 hp, 131" wb

	FP	5	4	3	2	1
Touring-7P	2875	4900	6300	10,300	21,000	34,000
Coupe-5P	2755	3200	4300	6500	11,000	23,000
Sedan-7P	3830	2900	3700	5600	9100	20,000
Sunflower Sedan-7P	4030	3000	4000	6000	9500	21,000
Daytona Roadster-3P	—	4700	6100	9900	19,000	33,000
Sport-4P		4500	5800	9500	18,000	32,000
Limousine-5P		3700	4700	7300	13,700	26,000

1923 Paige, model 6-70, touring, HAC

1923 PAIGE

Model 6-70 — 6-cyl., 70 hp, 131" wb

	FP	5	4	3	2	1
Touring-7P	2195	4700	6100	9900	19,000	33,000
Sport-4P	2245	4900	6300	10,300	21,000	34,000
Daytona Roadster-3P	—	4500	5800	9500	18,000	32,000
Speedster-2P	2495	5000	6500	11,000	22,000	35,000
Coupe-5P	3100	3100	4200	6300	10,500	22,000
Sedan-7P	3155	2900	3700	5600	9100	20,000
Limousine-7P	3350	3500	4500	7000	13,000	25,000

1924 Paige, model 6-70, landau brougham, AA

1924 PAIGE

Model 6-70 — 6-cyl., 75 hp, 131" wb

	FP	5	4	3	2	1
Touring-7P	—	4700	6100	9900	19,000	33,000
Phaeton-4P	—	4500	5800	9500	18,000	32,000
Brougham-5P	—	3300	4400	6700	12,000	24,000
Sedan-7P	—	3200	4300	6500	11,000	23,000
Limousine-7P	—	3500	4500	7000	13,000	25,000
Touring-5P	—	4500	5800	9500	18,000	32,000

1925 Paige, model 6-70, deluxe sedan, AA

1925 PAIGE
Model 6-70 — 6-cyl., 73 hp, 131" wb

	FP	5	4	3	2	1
Phaeton-7P	2165	4500	5800	9500	18,000	32,000
Phaeton-4P	2165	4400	5600	9200	17,300	31,000
Brougham-4P	2395	3300	4400	6700	12,000	24,000
Sedan-7P	2770	3200	4300	6500	11,000	23,000
Limousine-7P	2965	3500	4500	7000	13,000	25,000

1926 Paige, model 24/26, deluxe sedan, HAC

1926 PAIGE
Model 24/26 — 6-cyl., 63 hp, 115 & 125" wb

Touring-7P	—	3700	4700	7300	13,700	26,000
Sedan-5P	1495	2000	3000	4200	6500	14,000
DeLuxe Sedan-5P	1670	2100	3100	4300	6800	14,500
Sedan-7P	1995	2100	3100	4300	6800	14,500
Limousine-7P	—	2500	3500	5000	8500	18,000
Cabriolet-2P	—	3200	4300	6500	11,000	23,000
Phaeton-4P	—	3500	4500	7000	13,000	25,000

1927 Paige, model 6-65, 5-pass. sedan, AA

1927 Paige, model 6-45, coupe, AA

1927 PAIGE
Model 6-45 — 6-cyl., 43 hp, 109" wb

Sedan-5P	1295	1800	2800	4000	6200	13,000
Brougham-5P	1195	2300	3300	4600	7500	16,000
Touring-5P	1150	4000	5000	8000	15,000	28,000
Cabriolet Roadster-4P	1360	3900	4800	7700	14,300	27,000
Coupe-2P	1165	2400	3400	4800	8000	17,000

Model 6-65 — 6-cyl., 64 hp, 115" wb

Landaulet Brougham-5P	1395	2700	3600	5300	8800	19,000
Brougham-5P	1395	2500	3500	5000	8500	18,000
Sedan-5P	1540	2000	3000	4200	6500	14,000
Roadster-4P	1540	3500	4500	7000	13,000	25,000

Model 6-75 — 6-cyl., 68 hp, 125" wb

Phaeton-5P	1655	4000	5000	8000	15,000	28,000
Sedan-5P	1695	2200	3200	4400	7000	15,000
Sedan-7P	1995	2250	3300	4500	7300	15,500
Cabriolet Roadster-4P	1995	3700	4700	7300	13,700	26,000
Coupe-4P	1995	2500	3500	5000	8500	18,000
Limousine-7P	2245	2700	3600	5300	8800	19,000

Model 8-85 — 8-cyl., 80 hp, 130 1/2" wb

Sedan-5P	2885	2700	3600	5300	8800	19,000

PAINE — Westerville, Ohio — (1914) — In February of 1914, H.S. Paine of the Westerville Garage completed the prototype of his cyclecar. Powered by a four-cylinder engine, it featured a friction-type transmission, a wheelbase of 100 inches and a tread of 44. During the first week of March, Paine took the car to Columbus to show it and secure financial backing for manufacture. Alas, he found no takers and returned to Westerville. There, later that month, John A. Scharf briefly considered producing the Paine car. His Scharf Gearless Motor Car Company was an automobile dealership which he had organized in Westerville in 1912. That he elected to remain a dealer despite the cyclecar craze was doubtless a wise decision.

PALACE — The Palace Automobile and Machine Company was organized in New York City during the summer of 1905 with a capital stock of $30,000 for the manufacture and sale of automobiles. Incorporators were Hamilton Farnham, Charles H. Darmstadt and Louis F. Darmstadt. Manufacture is doubted.

The Palace Motor Car Company was organized in San Francisco, California during the spring of 1903 with a capital stock of $25,000 for the manufacture of automobiles. Involved in this venture were A.B. Costigan, G.R. Baker and H.R. Larzelere of San Francisco, and R.P. Green of Sausalito. Manufacture is doubted.

The Palace Motor Car Company of early 1912 was a venture backed by Pittsburgh capital for the manufacture of automobiles in nearby Rochester, Pennsylvania. The car planned was to carry a four-cylinder 40 hp engine in a 118-inch wheelbase chassis and to be known as the Palace 40. Manufacture is doubted.

PALMER — The Palmer-Herring Motor Company was organized in Brooklyn, New York during the summer of 1910 with a capital stock of $20,000 for the manufacture of automobiles, engines and motor boats. H.W. Palmer, C.N. Herring and F.P. Twyford were the indicated incorporators. Manufacture of a car is doubted. Conceivably H.W. Palmer was a misspelling of Henry U. Palmer of the Palmer & Singer Manufacturing Company which was then producing the Palmer-Singer automobile.

The Palmer-Meyer Motor Company was organized in St. Louis, Missouri during the summer of 1913 with a capital stock of $100,000 to "manufacture motor cars and accessories and equip a repair shop." Incorporators were Charles W. Palmer, Frederick C. Meyer and Ferdinand A. Meier. Manufacture of an automobile is doubted.

The Palmer-Paine Motors Company was a $500,000 Delaware incorporation from late 1915 for the manufacture of motor vehicles. J.H. Nixon, C.J. Jacobs and H.W. Davis were the incorporators. Manufacture of a car is doubted.

1899 Palmer, NAHC

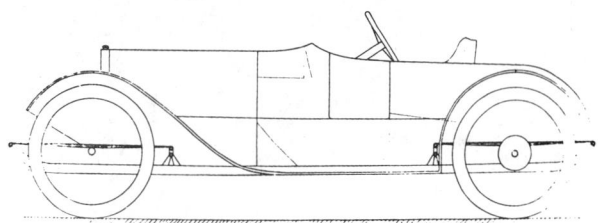

1915 Palmer Light Car, HAC

PALMER — Mianus, Connecticut — (1899) / **PALMER LIGHT CAR** — Cos Cob, Connecticut — (1914-1915) — Frank and Ray Palmer are generally credited with having built the first two-stroke marine engine on the East Coast in 1894. The brothers went into production in 1895, and soon were manufacturing three or four marine engines a week. In 1899 they built an experimental car to test one of their new two-cylinder two-stroke motors, but at that time had no thought of entering the automobile field. Shortly after the turn of the century, having outgrown their Mianus facilities, the Palmers moved into a new factory in Cos Cob where, in 1914, they decided to give the automotive industry a fling. The Palmers built a most commendable cyclecar. It featured a four-cylinder water-cooled engine placed in a 100-inch wheelbase chassis with 42-inch tread and side-by-side seating for two passengers. Available in two models, the Stream-Line Roadster at $350 and the Bear-Cat Type Roadster at $325, the Palmer guaranteed 40 mph and 35 mpg. Electric lighting was standard. But a cyclecar even if called a light car was a cyclecar still — and, though an admirable one, the Palmer could not escape the fate suffered by all vehicles of that genre. Manufacture of the Palmer was discontinued in 1915. By that time the Palmer Brothers were offering no fewer than thirty models of marine engines from 2 to 75 hp, and their company prospered for decades thereafter. Frank Palmer died in 1944, his brother followed in 1953. The company was carried on by associates until the early Seventies.

1906 Palmer, runabout, WLB

PALMER — Cleveland & Astabula, Ohio — (1906) — Herbert R. Palmer was a man with a couple of ideas in 1906. The first was an engine fueled by crude oil and with a combustion chamber so designed and insulated as to make cooling unnecessary. He soon forgot about that one. His second idea was a single-cylinder 8 hp engine with no valves, the admittance and expulsion of gases taking place as the piston passed over ports in the cylinder walls. This, he believed, had possibilities — and the Palmer Automobile Manufacturing Company was incorporated in Ashtabula in January 1906. Its $50,000 capitalization was to take care of getting the Palmer highwheeler with his valveless engine into production. Priced at $400, the Palmer was aimed at that vast market of "inexperienced persons" who wished to become automobilists cheaply. A two-passenger runabout was the only model available; it was on a 60-inch wheelbase, with four-speed planetary transmission, and final drive by wire cable and rope belt. Provided an "inexperienced person" could properly train his foot, the Palmer was a breeze to drive. The same pedal provided for engaging the clutch (ball of foot necessary) and obtaining reverse gear (heel of foot necessary). A wheel was provided for steering. Interestingly, although Ashtabula remained the head office, manufacture seems to have begun in a factory in Cleveland about March. Production of 300 cars that year was the cheerful estimate. In August the company was reported to have found larger facilities in Ashtabula, and possibly manufacture did commence there before the Palmer was out of business by year's end. At that point, Herbert Palmer moved back to Cleveland to build another car called the Euclid.

1913 Palmer, runabout, NAHC

PALMER — Detroit, Michigan — (1912-1913) — In November of 1912 Randall A. Palmer resigned as vice-president of the Cartercar Company to take over the defunct Suburban Motor Car Company. He immediately organized the Palmer Motor Car Company. Six months later, in June of 1913, he joined forces with the Partin Manufacturing Company of Chicago. All cars to be produced would henceforth carry the name Partin-Palmer. Prototype models with the Palmer emblem had been produced, but no cars had been manufactured under that name.

PALMER-SINGER — Long Island City, New York — (1908-1914) — Henry U. Palmer was a member of one of the oldest families in the Williamsburg section of Brooklyn and a successful barrel maker; and Charles A. Singer was a scion of the Singer sewing machine family and lived in swank Westchester County. In 1907 the two men joined forces to serve as dealers for the Simplex, Matheson and Isotta-Fraschini automobiles, with showrooms at 1620-24 Broadway in New York City — and in 1908 their Palmer &

1908 Palmer-Singer Skimabout, roadster, JAC

Singer Manufacturing Company became an automobile producer too. Initially the cars were referred to both as the P & S and the Palmer-Singer, but by 1909 only the latter name was used. Initially, too, the cars were manufactured in the Matheson plant in Pennsylvania, but this was only an interim measure pending completion of the firm's new factory in Long Island City. A short-wheelbase four called the Skimabout was the company's first offering, followed soon by a long-wheelbase six. All Palmer-Singers were shaft drive from the beginning, an interesting feature since few large cars of that period (including the Simplex and the Matheson) were. "The Best in Motor Cars" was a company slogan. In 1911 — the year in which Henry U. Palmer died at the age of forty-eight — a Palmer-Singer won the 182-mile Long Island Motor Derby at Riverhead in 179 minutes, and its performance in a twenty-four-hour race at Brighton Beach (thirty miles in thirty minutes at night) prompted the naming of a subsequent model as the Brighton. In May of 1913 arrangements were made with the Maritime Motor Company of St. Johns, New Brunswick for the assembly in Canada of the Maritime-Singer Six which was built from components supplied by the Long Island City factory. In January 1914 a new Palmer-Singer model was announced in New York; it was called the Magic Six and featured the slide-valve engine invented by Swiss engineer Martin Fischer. This same engine was also promoted that year by the Aristos Company in a car called the Mondex Magic. It did not work at all well. When the Palmer & Singer Manufacturing Company went bankrupt in March of 1914, "costly experiments" were cited as one of the reasons. In May the company property was sold to William Wooster, described as a "New York supplyman," who proposed to build a car with a price tag of less than $500 under the Palmer-Singer name. This would have been the antithesis of the big, powerful and finely built Palmer-Singers which had preceded it, and Wooster almost immediately thought better of the idea. Instead, in June, he resold the Palmer & Singer assets to Charles A. Singer, who scrapped the Magic engine, substituted a Herschell-Spillman, and introduced the result as the Singer that summer.

1908 PALMER-SINGER
Skimabout — 4-cyl., 28 hp, 106" wb

	FP	5	4	3	2	1
Roadster-2P	1950	4700	6100	9900	19,000	33,000
Model 6-60 — 6-cyl., 60 hp, 126" wb						
Runabout-3P	3100	8900	17,500	24,500	49,500	71,000
Toy Tonneau Runabout-4P	3300	9000	18,000	25,000	50,000	72,000
Toy Tonneau-4P	3500	9200	18,300	25,500	51,300	73,000

1909 Palmer-Singer, model 6-60, touring, WLB

1909 PALMER-SINGER
Model 4-40 — 4-cyl., 40 hp, 107" wb

Runabout-2P	2250	7800	13,000	20,000	43,500	58,000
Single Rumble Runabout-3P	2250	7800	13,000	20,000	43,500	58,000
Landaulet-6P	3500	7300	11,800	18,400	40,400	52,000
Limousine-6P	3650	7200	11,300	17,700	38,700	50,000
Touring-7P (126" wb)	4000	7600	12,500	19,400	42,400	55,000
Model 6-60 — 6-cyl., 60 hp, 126" wb						
Runabout-3P	3100	9000	18,000	25,000	50,000	72,000
Toy Tonneau Runabout-4P	3300	9200	18,300	25,500	51,300	73,000
Toy Tonneau-4P	3500	9300	18,500	26,000	52,500	74,000

1910 Palmer-Singer, model 4-30, town car landaulet, HAC

1910 PALMER-SINGER
Model 4-30 — 4-cyl., 30 hp, 115" wb

	FP	5	4	3	2	1
Roadster-2P	2150	7800	13,000	20,000	43,500	58,000
Toy Tonneau-4P	2500	7800	13,200	20,200	43,800	59,000
Town Car-6P	2500	7300	11,800	18,400	40,400	52,000
Town Car Landaulet (120" wb)	3500	7500	12,300	19,100	41,700	54,000

Model 6-40 — 6-cyl., 40 hp, 124" wb

	FP	5	4	3	2	1
Toy Tonneau-5/7P	3500	7800	13,300	20,300	44,000	60,000
Gunboat Roadster-5P	3900	7900	13,700	20,700	44,500	62,000

Model 4-50 — 4-cyl., 50 hp, 127" wb

	FP	5	4	3	2	1
Touring-7P	3900	8200	14,500	21,500	45,800	65,000

Model 6-60 — 6-cyl., 60 hp, 132" wb

	FP	5	4	3	2	1
Touring-5/7P	4100	10,500	20,500	31,000	62,000	82,000

1911 Palmer-Singer, model 6-60, Gunboat roadster, HAC

1911 Palmer-Singer, model 4-50, seven passenger touring, HAC

1911 PALMER-SINGER
Model 6-40 — 6-cyl., 40 hp, 125" wb

	FP	5	4	3	2	1
Touring-5P	3300	8200	14,500	21,500	45,800	65,000
Runabout-2P	3300	8000	14,000	21,000	45,000	64,000

Model 4-30 — 4-cyl., 30 hp, 120" wb

	FP	5	4	3	2	1
Town Car	3650	6800	10,300	16,000	35,500	48,000
Landaulet	3750	7200	11,300	17,700	38,700	50,000
Limousine	3650	6800	10,300	16,000	35,500	48,000

Model 4-50 — 4-cyl., 50 hp, 129" wb

	FP	5	4	3	2	1
Runabout-2P	3500	8500	16,000	23,000	48,000	68,000
Milord Touring-5P	3500	8700	16,500	23,500	48,500	69,000
Touring-7P	3900	8800	17,000	24,000	49,000	70,000
Gunboat Roadster-5P	3900	8700	16,500	23,500	48,500	69,000
Limousine	4900	7200	11,300	17,700	38,700	50,000
Landaulet	5000	7400	12,100	18,800	41,100	53,000

Model 6-60 — 6-cyl., 60 hp, 138" wb

	FP	5	4	3	2	1
Touring-7P	4200	10,000	20,000	30,000	60,000	80,000
Gunboat Roadster-5P	4200	9800	19,500	28,500	57,500	78,000
Touring-5P	4000	9400	18,800	26,500	53,800	75,000
Runabout-2P	4000	9400	18,800	26,500	53,800	75,000
Limousine	5200	7600	12,500	19,400	42,400	55,000
Landaulet	5300	7800	12,900	19,900	43,300	57,000

1912 Palmer-Singer, model 6-60, touring, HAC

1912 PALMER-SINGER
Model 46 — 6-cyl., 40 hp, 125" wb

	FP	5	4	3	2	1
Runabout	2500	7600	12,500	19,400	42,400	55,000
Toy Tonneau	2500	7700	12,700	19,700	43,000	56,000
Touring-5P	2500	7800	12,900	19,900	43,300	57,000
Touring-7P	2700	7800	13,000	20,000	43,500	58,000
Brighton Fore-Dr. (127" wb)	2000	7300	11,800	18,400	40,400	52,000

Model 6-60 — 6-cyl., 60 hp, 138" wb

	FP	5	4	3	2	1
Runabout	3000	8800	17,000	24,000	49,000	70,000
Touring-5P	3000	9000	18,000	25,000	50,000	72,000
Touring-7P	3200	9400	18,800	26,500	53,800	75,000
Limousine	4500	8700	16,500	23,500	48,500	69,000
Landaulet	4600	8900	17,500	24,500	49,500	71,000

1913 Palmer-Singer, Brighton model, touring, HAC

1913 PALMER-SINGER
Brighton — 6-cyl., 45 hp, 127" wb

	FP	5	4	3	2	1
Touring-5P	2295	7800	13,000	20,000	43,500	58,000
Runabout-2P	2000	7800	12,700	19,900	43,300	57,000

Model LXIV — 6-cyl., 60 hp, 138" wb

	FP	5	4	3	2	1
Runabout-2P	3325	8800	17,000	24,000	49,000	70,000
Touring-5P	3325	9200	18,300	25,500	51,300	73,000
Touring-7P	3200	9400	18,800	26,500	53,800	75,000

1914 Palmer-Singer, Brighton model, touring, HAC

1914 PALMER-SINGER
Model K — 6-cyl., 38 hp, 128" wb

	FP	5	4	3	2	1
Touring-5P	2295	7800	12,900	19,900	43,300	57,000
Roadster-2P	2295	7700	12,700	19,700	43,000	56,000

Brighton — 6-cyl., 45 hp, 127" wb

	FP	5	4	3	2	1
Touring-5P	2495	7800	13,300	20,300	44,000	60,000

Magic Six — 6-cyl., 60 hp, 140" wb

	FP	5	4	3	2	1
Touring-7P	3500	9000	18,000	25,000	50,000	72,000

1919 Pan, touring, JAC

PAN — St. Cloud, Minnesota — (1919-1921) — The Pan from St. Cloud was advertised as the "Queen of the Highway." The man behind it, Samuel Conner Pandolfo, could have advertised himself as the "King of the Conmen." An insurance agent from the Southwest, Pandolfo trekked to Minnesota to establish his Pan Motor Company in St. Cloud in January 1917. Forty-seven acres of land nearby were purchased in March, and construction of a factory began in June. Meantime, ten Pan cars were built in Indianapolis, in one of which Sam Pandolfo drove back to St. Cloud for a slambang Fourth of July barbecue on the new factory site which attracted some 70,000 people who got a look at the new Pan and a chance to buy some stock. The Pan was a quite ordinary touring car on a 108-inch wheelbase. Its price tag was $1000, raised to $1250 by the summer of 1918, though as yet no cars at all had been manufactured. Manufactured instead was a catalog/prospectus that was among the most lavish and expensive ever produced in the automobile industry, and in which Sam Pandolfo promised to build as many cars as Henry Ford was the Model T, with commensurate windfall profits to accrue for anyone wise enough to invest in this budding new empire. A good many people invested. A factory indeed was completed in St. Cloud, together with a pleasant residential community adjacent for its workers. It was ready in 1919, but by now the Federal Government was ready for Sam Pandolfo too. In February a Federal grand jury indicted him, in June complaint was brought against him by the Federal Trade Commission. Twelve other members of the Pan Motor Company were tried with Pandolfo; they were acquitted; in December Sam Pandolfo got ten years, and the extent of his operation was revealed. The Pan Motor Company had sold some $9,500,000 in stock to some 70,000 people. "One of the outstanding features of Pandolfo's flotation," *Automobile Topics* reported, was "his success in selling to persons who bore local reputations as hard-headed businessmen," He was also rather successful in selling himself to his board of directors. His agreement with the company was fifty percent of all cash taken in on stock sales; approximately $7,500,000 was collected, most of the remaining $2,000,000 was the other fifty percent, or the company's share. In December 1919, when the verdict was handed down, the Pan Motor Company owed about $250,000 and had $5000 cash on hand. While Sam Pandolfo appealed his conviction in what was termed then as "one of the most remarkable cases in the history of big advertising frauds," the eleven innocent officials of the Pan Motor Company attempted to pick up the pieces. Production of the Pan had begun in March 1919, with the cars built in Minnesota fitted with 50 hp F-head engines of in-house manufacture (the ten Indianapolis cars had sported Continentals). Thus far about 200 Pans had been built, with manufacture now continued on a two-car-per-day schedule in order to reduce overhead for the payment of outstanding debts. But the adverse publicity had already killed the Pan. In September of 1922 Sam Pandolfo lost his appeal. In October the Pan Motor Company was in receivership, its liabilities more than $500,000. In April 1923 Sam Pandolfo surrendered to the United States Marshal in Chicago and was transferred that night to Leavenworth. In August the Pan Motor Company went to the auction block in Minnesota. Pan production had ceased in late 1921. Though reportedly at the time, the total was 2500 cars, history since has revealed the Pans built to have been 737, possibly ten more. Sam Pandolfo served less than a year of his ten-year sentence. His pardon was vociferously protested by the National Advertising Convention. A good number of the former Pan officials subsequently got together to build the Masterbilt Six, but Sam Pandolfo was not among them.

1903 Panam, touring, NAHC

PANAM — Mamaroneck, New York — (1902-1903) — The board of directors read like a page out of the Social Register and a Who's Who of Wall Street: Winthrop E. Scarritt, George F. Chamberlin, Albert C. Bostwick, A.W.S. Cochrane, John H. Flagler, V. Everitt Macy, Sidney Dillon Ripley, J. Dunbar Wright. Why the Pan-American Motor Company failed to succeed is something of a mystery. Certainly availability of investment capital was not a problem, but probably the quick disillusionment of the investors was. Albert Bostwick was the moving spirit behind the venture; he chose James E. Woodbridge (formerly of Pratt & Whitney) as general manager, William M. Power as mechanical engineer. Early in 1902, the word Panam (no hyphen) was registered as the company's trademark, and by January of 1903 the former Gasmobile factory in Marion, New Jersey had been bought. John Flagler had been the Gasomobile president, and the purchase was simply for the equipment on hand, which was immediately dispatched to Mamaroneck where the plant of the Larchmont Electric Lighting Company had been leased pending the selection of a permanent factory site in New York or Connecticut. A permanent site was never found necessary. The first Panam, tested in late fall of 1902, was an experiment that failed, a car with a freakish motor which featured suction intake valves fitted inside the exhaust valves. The second Panam was a conventional car in which, its makers unabashedly admitted, the most successful features of European practice had been "freely adopted." It was introduced on the market early in 1903 as a four-cylinder touring car offered in a 15 hp Model C on an 84-inch wheelbase and a 25 hp Model B on a 96-inch wheelbase. Double chain drive, leather cone clutch, and a three-speed progressive transmission were featured. No more than twenty-five cars were built, however, before the Pan-American board of directors decided to forget the whole thing. By late spring of 1903, the Panam assets were disposed of to the Commercial Motor Company of Jersey City, New Jersey which proceeded to build a steam truck which lasted no longer than had the Panam.

PANAMA — The Panama Equipment Company was organized in St. Louis, Missouri during the spring of 1914 with a capital stock of $5000 to manufacture, sell and repair motor cars. Incorporators were H.F. Herfuth, John F. Schneider and Garfield G. Giese. Manufacture of a car is doubted.

1918 Pan-American, American Beauty touring, HAC

PAN-AMERICAN — Decatur, Illinois — (1917-1922) — Pan-American Motors Corporation was organized in Chicago in January of 1917 and tentatively referred to its car as the Chicago Light Six. In February the company announced that it was seeking a location downstate and would rename its product after the city that would be its new home. By December Pan-American was in Decatur, however, and reneged. All subsequent cars would carry the Pan-American name, and most would be designated as American Beauty models. In Decatur there was a quick change of management, and a July 13th, 1918 letter to stockholders from new president Edward Danner indicated that the new regime had been able to "smooth out the rugged places and correct the conditions that existed the first of the year." Two hundred cars had thus far been built, and production now stood at "three complete jobs a day." The Pan-American was an assembled car which used a variety of proprietary six-cylinder engines (Rutenber, Continental and Herschell-Spillman); a lower-priced four-cylinder companion car was available for the 1919 and 1920 model years, but very few were built. Commercial vehicles were also produced from 1917 to 1919, but passenger cars were the only product thereafter, and the company soon began to feel the effects of the postwar depression — in addition to continuing internal problems. In October of 1921 Edward Danner announced that auditors working on the books of his company had uncovered a $40,000 shortage. A few weeks earlier company secretary-treasurer W.A. Phares had disappeared. In late December of 1921 the Pan-American board of directors voted to liquidate while still solvent, with the phase-out of production beginning in January 1922. In May W.A. Phares was found and arrested in Columbus, Ohio; he was indicted for embezzlement, was tried in early June and sentenced to prison. In July the assets of the Pan-American Motors Corporation were sold at auction. The machinery, accessories and parts had been inventoried at $100,000; the auction brought $19,817. There were a lot of bargains procured by other small-time manufacturers that day. One firm bought sixty-six sets of fenders for $147; 330 fuel tanks were purchased by another for $443. Roadster bodies were picked up for $25 apiece, and 189 sets of wire wheels were sold for a dollar a set. Total Pan-American production in a half-decade had been about 4000 cars.

1917 PAN-AMERICAN
Chicago Light Six — 50 hp, 122" wb

	FP	5	4	3	2	1
Touring-5P	1285	4300	5400	8700	16,500	30,000

1918 PAN-AMERICAN
American Beauty — 6-cyl., 50 hp, 120" wb

	FP	5	4	3	2	1
Touring-5P	1500	4200	5200	8400	15,700	29,000

1919 Pan-American, touring, WLB

1919 PAN-AMERICAN
Model 250 — 4-cyl., 16.9 hp, 108" wb

	FP	5	4	3	2	1
Touring-5P	1250	3500	4500	7000	13,000	25,000
American Beauty — 6-cyl., 50 hp, 121" wb						
Touring-5P	2000	4300	5400	8700	16,500	30,000
Roadster-2P	2000	4200	5200	8400	15,700	29,000
1920 PAN-AMERICAN						
American Beauty — 6-cyl., 55 hp, 121" wb						
Touring-5P	2000	4500	5800	9500	18,000	32,000
Roadster-2P	2000	4400	5600	9200	17,300	31,000
Sedan-5P	3000	2000	3000	4200	6500	14,000
1921 PAN-AMERICAN						
Model 6-55 — 6-cyl., 57 hp, 121" wb						
Touring-5P	2450	4900	6300	10,300	21,000	34,000
Roadster-2P	2450	4700	6100	9900	19,000	33,000

1922 Pan-American, model 6-55, touring, HAC

1922 PAN-AMERICAN
Model 6-55 — 6-cyl., 57 hp, 121" wb

Touring-5P	2000	4700	6100	9900	19,000	33,000
Roadster-2P	2000	4500	5800	9500	18,000	32,000
Touring-7P	2100	5000	6500	11,000	22,000	35,000
Artcraft-5P	2500	4900	6300	10,300	21,000	34,000
Artcraft-7P	2600	5300	7000	11,500	24,000	37,000
Pan Model A — 4-cyl., 108" wb						
Touring-5P	1190	4000	5000	8000	15,000	28,000

PAN CHRONE — The Pan Chrone Press Manufacturing Company was organized during the spring of 1910 with a capital stock of $100,000 to manufacture automobiles and printing presses in Corinth, Illinois. Incorporators were H.C. Moore; M.A. Candler; George Cox, Sr.; H.O. Caffey; E.S. Candler, Jr., G.A. Hazard and L.C. Steele. Manufacture of a car is doubted.

1940 Pankotan, MVMA

PANKOTAN — Miami, Florida — (1940) — Paul Pankotan called it an auto-boat; he patented the vehicle and rather hoped someone would want to manufacture it. *Automobile Trade Journal* commented that "we've often wished for something like this for a combined touring-cruising vacation." Its gasoline engine produced 90 hp, good for 90 mph on land, about 35 mph on sea. The conversion from the former mode to the latter was easily seen to by the lifting of a lever which gently raised the wheels out of the way of the waves. Pankotan's hopes and *ATJ*'s wish notwithstanding, the Pankotan auto-boat was never manufactured.

1909 Panther, runabout, WLB

PANTHER — Boston, Massachusetts — (1909) — The Panther Car Company, Inc. of Boston exhibited one of the lightest cars at the Boston Automobile Show in early March of 1909. It weighed but 300 pounds and had the look of a toy car, though the single-cylinder 7 hp engine mounted up front under the hood was said to be "capable of driving it along at a pace not always equaled by the much larger cars." Twenty miles an hour on a fifteen percent grade was promised; on the flat, with a tailwind, performance doubled. The Panther had no transmission; drive was direct through a small multiple-disc clutch near the flywheel to the differential mounted on the rear axle. In April the Panther Car Company metamorphosed into the Panther Motor Car Company, and shortly thereafter the venture died. Any production would have been minimal.

1906 Paragon, runabout, WLB

PARAGON — Detroit, Michigan — (1906) — When J.P. La Vigne abruptly gave up on his La Petite, the Detroit Automobile Manufacturing Company which had been organized for its production found itself in a quandary which it immediately solved by offering another car called the Paragon. Except for a wheelbase lengthened to 68 inches, the specifications of the new Paragon were the same as the old La Petite. The small runabout weighed but 650 pounds and was powered by a single-cylinder two-stroke air cooled 5 hp engine, with planetary transmission and shaft drive featured. A maximum speed of 22 mph was promised, and the car's price tag remained at $375. Within the year the Detroit Automobile Manufacturing Company people realized that J.P. La Vigne had been right in the first place. They sold out to another group which moved into the factory to produce the Marvel the year following.

PARAGON — Connellsville, Pennsylvania — (1920-1921) / Cumberland, Maryland — (1921) — Announcement of the new Paragon Motor Car Company was made in Cleveland (Ohio) early in 1920, and its engineering department was headquartered there at 6545 Carnegie Avenue. Paul F. Hackenthal, who formerly had been assistant chief engineer for Mercer and Templar, was the man behind the Paragon. The engine he designed for it was a 60 hp four with overhead valves (two inlet valves and one exhaust per cylinder), and he fitted it into a low-slung chassis of 122-inch wheelbase. Both the weight and price were the same: 3000 pounds, 3000 dollars. A five-passenger touring, four-passenger sport car and two-passenger roadster were the proposed models. Hackenthal had the skill to design the car, what he did not have was the money to build it. When J. Fred Kurtz of Connellsville, Pennsylvania offered same, Hackenthal promptly offered him the presidency of the company. Four prototypes were built in Cleveland in 1920, manufacture was set to begin in Connellsville following the completion of a factory. The Paragon was introduced at the Cleveland Automobile Show in February 1921, and the prototypes

1921 Paragon, roadster, HAC

were taken to Connellsville shortly thereafter. They were good-looking cars with a radiator configuration that looked something like a Packard and a patented prismatic windshield that was all its own. Meanwhile, four more prototypes were under construction back in Cleveland. Then Connellsville backed out of the project. Less than a month later, Hackenthal found another financial angel, Philip M. Blake of Cumberland, Maryland. In April of 1921 he became president of the firm which was now renamed Paragon Motor Company with offices in the J.P. Wiesel building on Baltimore Street. Three further prototypes were built in Cumberland and displayed around town to interest the populace in investing in the venture. Mayor Thomas W. Koon was present on August 28th, 1921 when the cornerstone for the new Paragon factory on Mount Savage Road was laid. "We are conservatively optimistic," Philip Blake said that day, "and we feel that our twelve hundred stockholders will be augmented by many hundreds more who will all come to realize what Paragon means to them as an investment." As it happened, it meant a complete loss. The Cumberland Chamber of Commerce refused to back the venture after assaying the firm's financial status. The factory was never built. The car never moved beyond prototype. Although there have been suggestions that the Paragon was yet another in the myriad stock-selling scams of the period, it would appear that this was not the case. Paul Hackenthal's sincerity in designing and promoting the automobile was genuine. The Paragon was simply a car that didn't make it.

1924 Paramount, all-weather coupe, NAHC

PARAMOUNT — Azusa, California — (1923-1924) — No more than three of these Paramounts were made. Their engines were small air-cooled, motorcycle-type units, the 112-inch chassis used a suspension system rather like the Orient Buckboard's at the turn of the century, and the entire venture went bust very soon. But it had been an ambitious one, spearheaded by Fred S. Lack of Phoenix, Arizona who organized Paramount Motors Corporation early in 1923 in Los Angeles. Murray C. Tunison, an auto and aircraft engine designer, designed the product which was advertised as providing "Two Car Utility for the Price of One." The price was $750, which bought an "all weather" model "quickly convertible from open to closed car." In October of 1923 *Motor West* reported the "wave of excitement" which had hit the town of Azusa when Fred Lack announced his plans for the building of a million-dollar factory there. In July of 1924 Lack raised that figure to $7.5 million, indicating that the ground-breaking ceremony for the Paramount factory edifice had already taken place. A few Paramount prototypes were built. The factory never was. Tunison had come to this Paramount venture fresh from a try in Oakland with a car that carried his name. Subsequently his patents would range from parking garages to aircraft styling.

PARAMOUNT — Hagerstown, Maryland — (1927-1931) — "The Car Beautiful" was a slogan, and advertising prose grandiosely enthused that "in days of powdered wigs and courtly gestures, nobility rode in Sedan Chairs by right of birth . . . Today, New Yorkers, by preference, hail the new Paramount, their personal limousine, because it is the ultimate in smart, luxurious transportation." The small rear window also afforded a measure of privacy that no doubt was preferred by some New York taxi riders too. Produced by the Moller factory in Hagerstown, the Paramount was marketed by the Paramount Cab Manufacturing Company of New York City. A super luxury version was called, not surprisingly, the Super Paramount, and the Moller works built as well such taxis as the Aristocrat, the Astor, the Blue Light, the Five-Boro and the Twentieth Century.

1930 Paramount, taxicab, NAHC

1931 Paramount, taxicab, KM

PARAMOUNT — Hagerstown, Maryland — (1927-1931) — "The Car Beautiful" was a slogan, and advertising prose grandiosely enthused that "in days of powdered wigs and courtly gestures, nobility rode in Sedan Chairs by right of birth . . . Today, New Yorkers, by preference, hail the new Paramount, their personal limousine, because it is the ultimate in smart, luxurious transportation." The small rear window also afforded a measure of privacy that no doubt was preferred by some New York taxi riders too. Produced by the Moller factory in Hagerstown, the Paramount was marketed by the Paramount Cab Manufacturing Company of New York City. A super luxury version was called, not surprisingly, the Super Paramount, and the Moller works built as well such taxis as the Aristocrat, the Astor, the Blue Light, the Five-Boro and the Twentieth Century.

PARCEL POST — The Parcel Post Equipment Company of Grand Rapids, Michigan introduced its new car at the Boston Truck Show in 1914 under its own name. Later that year, having decided to offer the same vehicle as a roadster, the tradename Decatur was chosen. Refer to Decatur.

PARDESSUS — New London, Connecticut — (1905) — Only for a single year, 1905, did Rene M. Pardessus list himself as an automobile manufacturer (at 15 Moore Court) in the city directory of New London. Five years earlier, in November of 1900, he had informed *The Horseless Age* that he was then in the process of constructing an 18 hp gasoline truck. Details regarding the cars he was building in 1905 are unknown. He died shortly thereafter.

1921 Parenti, touring, WLB

PARENTI — Buffalo, New York — (1920-1922) — In December of 1919 announcement was made that Lieutenant Dion Parenti of the Parenti-Bissi Company of Italy was in Buffalo to help Joseph S. Parenti to get his car company going. Parenti Motors Corporation followed early in 1920, and so did the Parenti car, which had a number of intriguing ideas. First, it had no axles, Parenti Springs and Ten Point Suspension serving as substitute. (There were three transverse springs in the front, two in the rear.) Second, the car had considerably less metal than most, its unit-built body and frame being Haskelite plywood, the use of plywood extending even to the disc wheels. Third was the engine, an in-house design, what Parenti called its ''Direct Blast'' air-cooled V-8. Were not all of the foregoing enough to attract attention, some of the early models were painted in bright orange, purple and yellow to make sure they would not be missed in the show-room. Despite all this, or perhaps because of it, the Parenti did not enjoy an immediate following. It did enjoy the flattery of imitation, however, and in October of 1921 Parenti sued Adria for patent infringement of its sus-pension system, alleging that three former employees (Adria's president among them) had obtained secret possession of Parenti blueprints and patents while assisting him in experimental work. The former employees argued they had taught Parenti everything he knew. Meanwhile, the Parenti ''Direct Blast'' V-8 had been scrapped for an air-cooled Cameron six-cylinder engine, which in turn was replaced by a Falls six for 1922. By that time plywood had given way to a pressed steel frame and aluminum body. The suspension system was the only intriguing idea remaining in the car. Alas, Parenti discovered the ordinary didn't sell any better than the extraordinary. By the summer of '22 the firm had no cash in the bank. The Parenti plant and assets were sold to the Hanover Motor Car Company of Pennsylvania, though it would be six months before the purchase was fina-lized. A total of $225,000 was realized in the sale, less than half the amount of the claims filed against Parenti in Federal court. More than 11,000 people had invested $3,000,000 in Parenti Motors Corporation, and they would not receive a penny. A total of eighteen Parenti cars had been built.

1920-1921 PARENTI
Eight — 35 hp, 123" wb

	FP	5	4	3	2	1
Touring	2000	3900	4800	7700	14,300	27,000
Sedan	3000	1800	2800	4000	6200	13,000
Town Car	5000	2700	3600	5300	8800	19,000
Limousine	—	2500	3500	5000	8500	18,000

Note: The air-cooled Cameron six was announced as the new Parenti engine in August of 1920. Doubtless very few cars following incorporated the ''Direct Blast'' V-8.

1922 Parenti, roadster, HAC

1922 PARENTI
Six — 46 hp, 121" wb

Touring	2000	3500	4500	7000	13,000	25,000
Roadster	2000	3300	4400	6700	12,000	24,000

PARISH-FERRELL — The Parish-Ferrell Manufacturing Company was organized in Harrisburg, Illinois during the summer of 1913 with a capital stock of $50,000 for the manufacture of automobiles and motor trucks. Incorporators were Fred C. Ferrell, C.L. Parish and John J. Parish. Manu-facture is doubted.

PARK — ''A.E. Park of Brattleboro, Vermont is at work on a motor vehicle which he expects to have in running order before long,'' reported *The Motor Vehicle Review* in April of 1900. That the Park car was to be gasoline powered represented the only details given.

The Park Automobile Company was organized in Chicago, Illinois during the spring of 1904 with a capital stock of $2500 ''to manufacture automo-biles and operate bowling alleys and billiard rooms.'' Incorporators were F.H.T. Potter, M.J. Merki and O.T. Cody. Manufacture of a car is doubted.

The Park Automobile Company of Johnstown, Pennsylvania was an early 1910 incorporation to manufacture, buy, sell, lease, repair and deal in motor cars. F.J. Irwin, E.L. Irwin and Bruce H. Campbell were the promot-ers. Manufacture of an automobile is doubted.

The Park Motors Company was organized in Columbus, Ohio during the fall of 1910 by Scott Van Etten, who formerly had headed the repair department of the Columbus Buggy Company. Refer to Van Etten.

The Park Avenue Garage was organized in New York City late in 1908 with a capital stock of $125,000 for the manufacture and sale of automo-biles. W.H. Barnard and W.H. MacIlroy were the incorporators. Manufac-ture is doubted.

The Park Avenue Livery Company was organized in New York City during the spring of 1908 to ''deal in horses, manufacture motor cars, carriages, etc. and to operate a general livery business.'' Incorporators were Thomas Daly, J.L. Walsh and Sterling Pierson. Manufacture of a car is doubted.

The Park Circle Garage was organized in Brooklyn, New York early in 1907 with a capital stock of $10,000 ''to manufacture, operate and store vehicles.'' J.A. Anderson and F.D. Skeal of Manhattan were joined in this venture by F.L. Hagerty of Brooklyn. Manufacture of a car is doubted.

The Park City Motor Car Company was organized in Hartford, Connecti-cut early in 1911 with a capital stock of $50,000 to manufacture and deal in automobiles. F.H. Macfarlane, P.S. Chapman and S.A. Foulds were the incorporators. Manufacture is doubted.

PARK — Henderson, Kentucky — (1909) — During the summer of 1909, John J. and A.G. Delker, whose Park Carriage Company was located on Green Street in Henderson, completed their first 18 hp four-passenger automobile. ''It is planned to make 100 this season,'' they announced, ''after which the production will be increased.'' There is no evidence this happened; probably the first batch of Parks, if completed, was also the last.

PARKER — The E.R. Parker Company was organized in Boston, Massa-chusetts during the fall of 1910 with a capital stock of $125,000 for the manufacture of motorcars. Incorporators were Frank Kock, Willard C. Fisk and Clinton E. Fisk. Manufacture is doubted.

The F.R. Parker Company was organized in Boston, Massachusetts dur-ing the fall of 1910 with a capital stock of $50,000 to manufacture and deal in automobiles. Frank R. Parker, Clarence C. Colby and James A. Murphy were the incorporators. Manufacture is doubted.

The Jerome P. Parker Company was organized in Memphis, Tennessee early in 1910 with a capital stock of $100,000 to manufacture motorcars, bicycles and carriages. Joining Parker in this venture were M.P. Patterson and J.E. Squire. Manufacture of an automobile is doubted.

The Parker Motor Company of Hartford, Connecticut was organized during the fall of 1909 with a capital stock of $50,000 for the manufacture of ''motors, automobiles, automobile parts and all kinds of machinery.'' Lucius F. Robinson, Francis W. Cole and Albion B. Wilson were the incor-porators. Lewis D. Parker was president. Manufacture of an automobile is doubted, but the firm did proceed into production of four-cylinder auto-mobile engines, most of which were destined for the McCue Company of Hartford. In 1911 the Parker Motor Company went into receivership.

The Parker Motor Wagon Company was organized in New York City late in 1912 with a capital stock of $10,000 for the manufacture and sale of motor vehicles. Henry C. Cottfried of St. Louis, Missouri; Drew McKenna of Brooklyn and Charles E. Wood of Manhattan were the principals involved. Manufacture of a car is doubted.

The Parker Motor Car Company of Seattle, Washington produced an automobile from 1914-1915 which the Parker brothers marketed under the tradename of Ajax. Refer to Ajax.

PARKER STEAM — Edgar County, Illinois — (1825) — In 1825 T.W. Parker of Edgar County built a working model of a light steam carriage powered by a double-cylinder engine. It was a three-wheeler, the two rear wheels of which were eight feet in diameter.

1936 Parker, 2-dr. sedan, WLB

PARKER — Ellsworth, Maine — (1936) — The parts of seventeen differ-ent cars went into the Parker's internal makeup, so its inventor said, but most of them came from a 1933 Terraplane Six. Harry S. Parker of Ells-worth worked eight hours a day for a year and five months to complete his vehicle. Its wheelbase was 128 inches. The body frame was steel, sheathed with oak and over which were laid metal panels of 24-gauge black iron. The engine was in the rear, and the streamlining effects Parker sought were at least partially realized. The car's top speed was 85 mph, with a 23 mph fuel economy. The car sat four, and slept two. ''Now that it's done I cannot enjoy it,'' Harry Parker lamented to *MoToR* magazine in 1936, ''because so many people flock around it as soon as I stop.'' There is no indication he built another car.

PARKIN — Oxford & Philadelphia, Pennsylvania — (1903-1908) — The Parkins of Pennsylvania believed in living in the fast lane. The father was a racer of high-wheeled, sprint and six-man bicycles — and he persuaded his sons Joe, Jr. and George into the field of racing. Since this was at the advent of the automotive age, logically, the horseless vehicle became among the modes raced. At the turn of the century, at the invitation of businessmen of Oxford, Pennsylvania, the family located there and estab-lished the Oxford Manufacturing Company, which evolved out of two other firms (Carroll Manufacturing and Smith Motor). Approximately eight Oxford motorcycles and several Oxford Autocycles were produced, as well as Parkin gasoline motors of 1 1/2 to 10 hp, together with several auto-mobile prototypes, all of them featuring chain drive, tiller steering and a gearchange with two speeds forward but no reverse. The motorcycles were raced, the cars were short-lived — and the Parkins departed Oxford thereafter for Philadelphia and more concerted racing. Joe Parkin, Jr. car-ried the family honor as race driver, with his father often his riding mechanic and brother George as substitute. The special Parkin race cars were 60 hp sixes that cost $3000 apiece to build. They finished in the money at Trenton, Point Breeze and other racing locales. Trade press references from 1908 indicate some intention on the part of the Parkins to seriously market their car, but this did not follow. Instead the family confined manufacturing efforts to the components field. They had also served as Philadelphia agents for the Clement-Bayard and the Mitchell.

PARKISON — Brook, Indiana — (1909) — W.H. Parkison's transmission-producing Parkison Gear Company was in Rensselaer but he chose Brook as the home for the automobile he was planning to manufacture. The car was to be a four to sell for $1250 and to incorporate the Parkison transmission, naturally. During the mid-summer of 1909, Parkison announced his plans to begin its production as soon as factory space could be obtained in Brook. But then something went wrong. Possibly it was the presence in town of another automobile entrepreneur who had already enlisted the support of local businessmen with his plans. That car (which would have been called the Brook or Ade) didn't arrive either. Very soon, Parkison returned to his gear business in Rensselaer.

PARKMOBILE — The Parkmobile was a device to make parallel parking easier and was attempted to be marketed during the late Twenties. Among the cars to which it was fitted was the New York Six. Refer to New York Six.

PARKS-OSGOOD — The Parks-Osgood Company was organized in Malden, Massachusetts during the fall of 1915 with a capital stock of $25,000 for the manufacture of automobiles. Involved in the venture were Howard Osgood, George A. Parks and Paul M. Foss. Manufacture is doubted.

PARKWAY — The Parkway Company was organized in Atlantic City, New Jersey during the fall of 1913 with a capital stock of $100,000 to manufacture and deal in automobiles. Incorporators were William Lewis, Robert L. Beyer and James H. Hayes, Jr. Manufacture is doubted.

The Parkway Garage Company was organized in New York early in 1907 with a capital stock of $4000 to manufacture and store automobiles in Bay Shore, Long Island. Incorporators were Charles H. Covell, C. Herbert Covell and Richard H. Fenker. Manufacture is doubted.

PARNESSUS — This car-that-never-was is simply a typographical error appearing on many rosters. Refer to Pardessus.

PARRETT — Parrett Motors Corporation was organized in Richmond, Virginia late in 1911 with a $2 million capital stock to manufacture and deal in "tractors, trucks and automobiles." Incorporators were Dent Parrett and W.R. Crump. Manufacture of a car is doubted.

PARRISH — Richmond, Indiana — (1915) — Whether William N. Parrish and his son Russel ever completed its building is not known, but the Parrish idea was an "aero-automobile" to carry seven-passengers, resemble a touring car and be able to fly. "The first model will be completed as soon as patent applications have been filed," the elder Parrish revealed in mid-December 1915. "When operated over the roads, the planes [doubtless he meant wings] will be folded into the body." Likely as not, the Parrish project never got off the ground.

1910 Parry, touring, WLB

PARRY — Indianapolis, Indiana — (1910) / NEW PARRY — (1911-1912) — The Parry Manufacturing Company of Indianapolis was among the largest carriage factories in the world during the 1890's when David M. Parry first began experimentation with automobiles. His first vehicle, begun in 1892 and completed four years later, was an electric the pneumatic tires for which he fashioned from bits of garden hose. It was not produced because of opposition from his carriage-preferring brothers, and also because it wasn't much good. In 1906, however, David Parry did get into the automobile business through his controlling interest in the Overland Automobile Company in Indianapolis, which ultimately he relinquished to John North Willys. By now he was convinced he had the answer to success in the automobile field. He would not experiment but would base his car upon the proven past experience of others, he would build it in two models only and in sufficient quantity to offer it at a selling price that was sure to be a winner. On July 28th, 1909 the foundation of his Parry Auto Company was laid; in sixty-five days Parry was working 389 men, preparing for over 3000 employees, occupying seven large buildings leased from the Stan-

dard Wheel Company, and delivering his first cars to dealers. "Now," David Parry said, "if the Parry Auto Company can turn out 5000 cars for the year of 1910, it will have established a world's record for the first year of any such business." Because his car was renamed the New Parry the year following, and because basically it was "New" only in its higher price, one might have assumed then that he had not succeeded in his plans. One would have been sure of it the following year when another sign went up over the factory reading Motor Car Manufacturing Company, and there was another car on the assembly line called the Pathfinder. For a short while the New Parry was built alongside it. David Parry's problem had been a simple one: overenthusiasm and overextension. His company had been capitalized at $1,000,000, but only $150,000 had been paid in. Most of this was spent that first year in heavy advertising and outlays for equipment. The 900 cars sold in 1910 resulted in a heavy loss, and there was no working capital left. Parry was in receivership before Christmas that year. A few years later two of his brothers financed the building of the Comet cyclecar in Indianapolis. By then David Parry was dead, having contracted a fatal illness aboard ship during a tour abroad in 1915 as a member of the Foreign Trade Commission of the National Association of Manufacturers.

1910 PARRY
Parry — 4-cyl., 35 hp, 116" wb

	FP	5	4	3	2	1
Model 35 Runabout-4P	1285	3100	4200	6300	10,500	22,000

Parry — 4-cyl., 40 hp, 116" wb

	FP	5	4	3	2	1
Model 40 Touring-5P	1485	3300	4400	6700	12,000	24,000

1911 NEW PARRY
New Parry — 4-cyl., 35 hp, 116" wb

	FP	5	4	3	2	1
Model 42 Touring-5P	1350	3100	4200	6300	10,500	22,000
Model 39 Roadster-2P	1350	3000	4000	6000	9500	21,000
Model 37 Baby Tonneau-4P	1350	3100	4200	6300	10,500	22,000
Model 48 Tr.-5P (118" wb)	1750	3200	4300	6500	11,000	23,000

1912 NEW PARRY
New Parry — 4-cyl., 35 hp, 116" wb

	FP	5	4	3	2	1
Model 51 Roadster-2P	1350	3000	4000	6000	9500	21,000
Model 52 Touring-5P	1450	3200	4300	6500	11,000	23,000
Model 53 Phaeton-4P	1400	3100	4200	6300	10,500	22,000

PARSONS — In 1900 a locomotive engineer from Wilmington, Delaware named John H. Parsons built a steam car. Subsequently, the National Automobile Company was organized for its manufacture. Refer to National steam.

1914 Partin-Palmer, model 38, touring, HAC

PARSONS ELECTRIC — Cleveland, Ohio — (1905-1906) — Although John G. Parsons had indicated initially that he would have his new car ready for the automobile shows of 1905, he didn't hit the show circuit until January 1906. His Parsons Electric Motor Carriage Company was organized in December of 1905, and its first product was a $1500 electric panel delivery with a 500-pound capacity. The Parsons passenger car followed a month later, and it was a stanhope powered by an 8 hp Elwell-Parker motor and set into a 66-inch wheelbase chassis, four inches shorter than the panel delivery. Final drive was by double-chain to the rear wheels, a four-speed silent helical geared transmission was fitted, and the car's frame was a combined wood and steel springboard. The Parsons Electric stanhope was priced at $1600. Neither it nor the panel delivery was produced after 1906.

PARTIN — Chicago, Illinois — (1913) / PARTIN-PALMER — Chicago & Rochelle, Illinois — (1913-1917) — The Partin Manufacturing Company was a large automobile sales agency in Chicago which joined with the Palmer Motor Car Company of Detroit in June of 1913. The company's new product line was to include a cyclecar called the Pioneer, a model 45 to be known as the Partin, and a Model 38 to be called the Partin-Palmer. The cyclecar was dropped before year's end, as was the Partin model; all subsequent products would be called Partin-Palmers. Although a few cars may have been assembled in Detroit, all operations had been moved into the old Staver plant in Chicago by 1914. Only the Model 38 (Mason engine) was produced in 1914, but it was joined in 1915 by a small 20 hp roadster that sold for a low $495. Doubtless this latter car was to replace the erstwhile Pioneer, although an eight was added for 1916, it sold not at all well, though the company's new Lycoming-engined Model 32 fared better. By now both Randall A. Palmer and G.H. Partin appear to have left the organization. The company was in trouble. In April of 1915, C.C. Darnall (who had formerly been sales manager of the Partin Manufacturing Company) became president of Commonwealth Motors Corporation, which would henceforth serve as the sales agency for Partin-Palmer cars. Manufacture now moved from Chicago to Rochelle where the George D. Whitcomb Company (makers of gas engines and electrical mining machinery) would put the cars together. Partin-Palmer as a marque name continued through the summer of 1917. That fall the car's name was changed to Commonwealth. It was the forerunner of the famous Checker taxicab.

1913 PARTIN-PALMER
Model 38 — 4-cyl., 38 hp, 115'' wb

	FP	5	4	3	2	1
Touring-6P	975	4200	5200	8400	15,700	29,000

Model 45 — 4-cyl., 45 hp, 115'' wb

Touring-6P	1275	4300	5400	8700	16,500	30,000

1914 PARTIN-PALMER
Model 38 — 4-cyl., 38 hp, 115'' wb

Touring-6P	975	4200	5200	8400	15,700	29,000

1915 Partin-Palmer, model 20, roadster, HAC

1915 PARTIN-PALMER
Model 20 — 4-cyl., 20 hp, 96'' wb

Roadster-2P	495	3100	4200	6300	10,500	22,000

Model 38 — 4-cyl., 38 hp, 115'' wb

Touring-6P	1075	4000	5000	8000	15,000	28,000

Model "32"—$695.00

1917 Partin-Palmer, model 32, touring, WLB

1916 PARTIN-PALMER
Model 20 — 4-cyl., 20 hp, 96'' wb

Roadster-2P	495	3100	4200	6300	10,500	22,000

Model 32 — 4-cyl., 32 hp, 110'' wb

Touring-5P	675	3300	4400	6700	12,000	24,000

Model 8-45 — 8-cyl., 45 hp, 115'' wb

Touring-6P	1195	4200	5200	8400	15,700	29,000

1917 PARTIN-PALMER
Model 20 — 4-cyl., 20 hp, 96'' wb

Roadster-2P	545	3500	4500	7000	13,000	25,000

Model 32 — 4-cyl., 32 hp, 110'' wb

Touring-5P	695	3900	4800	7700	14,300	27,000

PARTRIDGE — The firm of Partridge, Clark and Kerrigan was organized in Albany, New York early in 1914 with a capital stock of $100,000 for the manufacture of motorcars. Incorporators were E.S. Partridge, B.A. Wordemann and S.J. Wagstaff. Manufacture is doubted.

PASSAIC — The Passaic Motor Car Company was organized during the summer of 1906 with a capital stock of $50,000 "to manufacture and store automobiles and do a general electrical engineering business" in Passaic, New Jersey. Incorporators were J.B. Ryall, Alice W. Ryall and George Ryall. Manufacture is doubted.

The Passaic Valley Transportation Company was organized during the summer of 1910 with a capital stock of $25,000 to "manufacture and construct cabs, vehicles, etc., also to conduct a transportation business" in New Providence, Rhode Island. Incorporators were W. Woodruff, P.G. Honeyman, J.H. Peck, A.A. Potter, W.D. Clark, W.M. Myers and J. Fraser. Manufacture of a car is doubted.

PATERSON — William Paterson of Chicago, Illinois was among those who announced entry in the Chicago Times-Herald Contest of 1895 and failed to produce a car at the starting line. Among the five William Patersons listed in the Chicago city directory of 1895 were three clerks, one broker and one baker. Which of these was the William Paterson with automotive ambitions is not known, nor whether the car planned was ever completed.

The Paterson Automobile Storage & Exchange Company was organized late in 1903 with a capital stock of $25,000 to manufacture automobiles and engines in Paterson, New Jersey. Incorporators were Levi E. Van Sickle, Frank L. Habben and Jacob Van Der Click. Manufacture of a car is doubted.

The Paterson Wagon Company of Paterson, New Jersey was the possessor of a steam automobile in 1900, though the firm did not build the vehicle itself. Instead the car was built by D.D. Mott of Passaic.

1910 Paterson, model 30, tourabout, HAC

PATERSON — Flint, Michigan — (1908-1923) — William A. Paterson was born in Canada in 1838 and arrived in Flint in 1869 to set up his carriage-making business. By the turn of the century the W.A. Patterson Company was a thriving concern, and although its founder was somewhat tardy in entering the automobile field, when he did so his commitment was total. In 1910, two years after building his first prototype automobile, he discontinued carriage manufacture altogether. The first Paterson was a typical motor buggy with two-cylinder air-cooled engine, planetary transmission, double chain drive and solid rubber tires. It was introduced late in 1908, and by the end of 1909 a total of sixty-four cars had been built. In 1910 the Paterson grew up into a standard car with four-cylinder 30 hp engines, selective transmission and shaft drive. Sales increased to 450 cars that year. In 1915 a six was introduced, and sales rose to 900 units. Fours were dropped after 1916, and sixes only (Continental engines) were produced for the remainder of the Paterson's life. There was never anything extraordinary about a Paterson, but it was a well built car. Its lines were as conservative as the company building it. In September of 1921, at the age of eighty-three, William A. Paterson died. Something of his company seems to have died with him. Though his son W.C. Paterson and associate W.R. Hubbard carried on, they couldn't manage the fight against the effects of the postwar depression. In July of 1923 they sold out to Dallas Winslow, the Dodge dealer in Flint, who announced that he would retain the services of E.C. Kollmorgen (the Paterson engineering and production manager for the nine years past) who would now be charged with revising the Paterson for continued production. Winslow quickly changed his mind, however, and the Paterson automobile died. Dallas Winslow's Dodge affiliation made him a fortune.

1908-1909 PATERSON
Model 14 — 2-cyl., 14 hp, 80'' wb

	FP	5	4	3	2	1
Motor Buggy		1600	2700	3800	5800	12,000

1910 PATERSON
Model 30 — 4-cyl., 30 hp, 104'' wb

Touring-5P	1400	3100	4200	6300	10,500	22,000
Demi-Tonneau-4P	1400	3100	4200	6300	10,500	22,000
Tourabout-4P	1400	3100	4200	6300	10,500	22,000

1911 Paterson, model F, roadster, HAC

1911 PATERSON
Model 30 — 4-cyl., 30 hp, 106'' wb

Model A Touring-5P	1300	3100	4200	6300	10,500	22,000
Model B Demi-Tonneau-4P	1175	3000	4000	6000	9500	21,000
Model C Tourabout-4P	1175	3000	4000	6000	9500	21,000
Model F Roadster-2P	1200	2900	3700	5600	9100	20,000
Model E Fore-Dr.-4P (110'' wb)	1425	1800	2800	4000	6200	13,000
Model I Fore-Dr.-5P (110'' wb)	1425	1900	2900	4100	6400	13,500

Model 38 — 4-cyl., 38 hp, 118'' wb

Model G Fore-Dr. Tour-5P	1500	3500	4500	7000	13,000	25,000

1912 Paterson, model 35, touring, HAC

1912 PATERSON
Model 35 — 4-cyl., 30 hp, 108" wb

	FP	5	4	3	2	1
Touring-5P	1250	3100	4200	6300	10,500	22,000

Model 45 — 4-cyl., 45 hp, 120" wb

Touring-5P	1800	2300	4400	6700	12,000	24,000
Touring-7P	1850	3500	4500	7000	13,000	25,000

1913 Paterson, model 43, touring, JAC

1913 PATERSON
Model 41 — 4-cyl., 40 hp, 116" wb

Touring-5P	1500	2300	4400	6700	12,000	24,000

Model 43 — 4-cyl., 40 hp, 116" wb

Touring-5P	1685	3500	4500	7000	13,000	25,000

Model 47 — 4-cyl., 45 hp, 122" wb

Touring-7P	1985	3700	4700	7300	13,700	26,000

1914 Paterson, model 33, touring, HAC

1914 PATERSON
Four — 32 hp, 112" wb

Model 32 Roadster-2P	1200	3000	4000	6000	9500	21,000
Model 33 Touring-5P	1235	3100	4200	6300	10,500	22,000

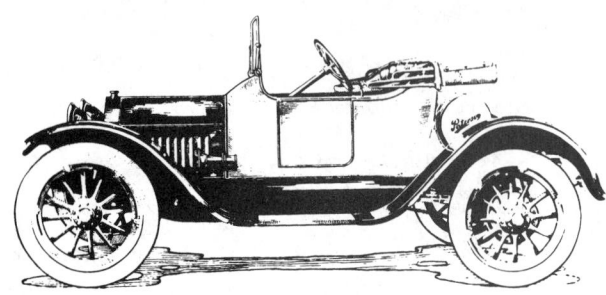

1915 Paterson, model 4-32, runabout, HAC

1114

1915 PATERSON
Model 4-32 — 4-cyl., 32 hp, 112" wb

	FP	5	4	3	2	1
Runabout/Touring	1095	3100	4200	6300	10,500	22,000

Model 6-48 — 6-cyl., 40 hp, 17" wb

Touring-5P	1485	3300	4400	6700	12,000	24,000

1916 Paterson, model 6-42, touring, HAC

1916 PATERSON
Model 4-32 — 4-cyl., 32 hp, 112" wb

Touring-5P	985	3100	4200	6300	10,500	22,000

Model 6-42 — 6-cyl., 40 hp

Touring-5P	985	3400	4500	6900	12,500	24,500
Touring-7P	1060	3600	4600	7200	13,400	25,500

1917 Paterson, model 6-45, touring, JAC

1917 PATERSON
Model 6-45 — 6-cyl., 40 hp, 117" wb

Touring-5P	1095	3700	4700	7300	13,700	26,000
Roadster-4P	1095	3300	4400	6700	12,000	24,000
Touring-7P	1120	3900	4800	7700	14,300	27,000

1918 Paterson, model 6-45, touring, HAC

1918 PATERSON
Model 6-45 — 6-cyl., 40 hp, 117" wb

Touring-5P	1265	3700	4700	7300	13,700	26,000
Touring-7P	1295	3900	4800	7700	14,300	27,000
Roadster-4P	1295	3300	4400	6700	12,000	24,000
Sedan-5P	1795	1800	2800	4000	6200	13,000

1919 PATERSON
Model 6-45 — 6-cyl., 40 hp, 120" wb

Touring-5P	1595	3700	4700	7300	13,700	26,000
Touring-7P	1625	3900	4800	7700	14,300	27,000
Roadster-4P	1595	3300	4400	6700	12,000	24,000
Sedan-5P	1895	1800	2800	4000	6200	13,000

1919 Paterson, model 6-45, touring, HAC

1920 Paterson, model 6-47, touring, HAC

1920 PATERSON
Model 6-47 — 6-cyl., 42 hp, 120" wb

	FP	5	4	3	2	1
Touring-5P	1695	3700	4700	7300	13,700	26,000
Touring-7P	1725	3900	4800	7700	14,300	27,000
Sedan-6P	2600	1800	2800	4000	6200	13,000
Sedan-7P	2600	1900	2900	4100	6400	13,500
Coupe-5P	2600	2200	3200	4400	7000	15,000

1921 Paterson, model 6-50, coupe, HAC

1921 PATERSON
Model 6-50 — 6-cyl., 55 hp, 120" wb

	FP	5	4	3	2	1
Touring-5P	1895	3300	4400	6700	12,000	24,000
Touring-7P	1925	3500	4500	7000	13,000	25,000
Coupe-5P	2895	2300	3300	4600	7500	16,000
Sedan-5P	2895	2000	3000	4200	6500	14,000

1922 Paterson, model 22, touring, JAC

1922 PATERSON
Model 22 — 6-cyl., 55 hp, 120" wb

	FP	5	4	3	2	1
Sedan-5P	2695	1800	2800	4000	6200	13,000
Coupe-5P	2695	2300	3300	4600	7500	16,000
Touring-5P	1395	3300	4400	6700	12,000	24,000
Touring-7P	1450	3400	4500	6900	12,500	24,500

1923 Paterson, model 22, sport, HAC

1923 PATERSON
Model 22 — 6-cyl., 55 hp. 120" wb

	FP	5	4	3	2	1
Touring-5P	1390	3300	4400	6700	12,000	24,000
Touring-7P	1425	3500	4500	7000	13,000	25,000
Sedan-5P	2395	2000	3000	4200	6500	14,000
Coupe-4P	2395	2300	3300	4600	7500	16,000
Sport-5P	1465	3600	4600	7200	13,400	25,500
Brougham-5P	2395	2200	3200	4400	7000	15,000

PATHFINDER — The Pathfinder Manufacturing Company of Chicago, Illinois has been indicated as the producer of an automobile in 1899. This has not been documented. The firm, listed in turn-of-the-century Chicago city directories at 74 West Lake Street, noted "bicycles" as its sole product. George Gormack was president, Harry L. Dodson was secretary.

1912 Pathfinder, model XII, roadster, WLB

PATHFINDER — Indianapolis, Indiana — (1912-1917) — When the Parry Auto Company moved into receivership in December of 1910, its creditors took over and reorganized as the Motor Car Manufacturing Company, using that designation simply because they did not know what they wished to name their new car. For the moment, the New Parry was continued in production; the new Pathfinder was not introduced until 1912. Officers of the Motor Car Manufacturing Company (its name would not be changed to the Pathfinder Company until 1916) included W.C. Teasdale (a former official of the Parry company) as president, G.O. Simons (formerly of the Dayton Motor Car Company) as vice-president, W.K. Bromley as secretary, and Fred C. Dorn (treasurer of the American Ball Bearing Company) and Frank H. Teagle (a director of Standard Oil) as board members. "This new company looks like a strong organization," *The Automobile* reported; it does not appear that David M. Parry was involved. His New Parry automobile was phased out as the Pathfinder was phased in. Although a Pathfinder slogan was "known for reliability," the car became more widely regarded for its looks. Body styling appears to have been a principal concern of the company, and Pathfinder's ingenuity and innovation in this regard included putting a boattail on a speedster, covering the spare wheel, concealing a roadster's top into a paneled recess, and designing a coach called the Martha Washington which would have been ceremonial enough for the Father of our Country to have motored in his inaugural in. Pathfinder also eschewed what it called the "drab days of color repression" with bright and captivating color schemes. That the Pathfinder was as good a car as it looked was demonstrated by the certificate of performance issued by the Royal Automobile Club of England following its participation in the London-Land's End-John O'Groats-Edinburgh-London trial of 1912. That year, too, one E.M. Pierce (described by the company as a "New York millionaire") and his chauffeur traveled 10,000 miles around the United States in a Pathfinder that "never was in distress." Beginning production with four-cylinder cars, Pathfinder proceeded into sixes with vee radiators, and in 1916 introduced a model powered by a Weidely twelve-cylinder engine that was called "Pathfinder the Great, King of Twelves." With the last named, Pathfinder advertising, which had always tended to the haughty, became positively snobbish. "The Family equipage is as true an index of culture and taste as the home itself," the catalog read. "When Pathfinder the Great rules the Garage the family is usually well worth knowing." In 1916 a Pathfinder twelve was driven cross-country by Walter Weidely (son of engine designer George Weidely) with an average fuel consumption of 10.2 mpg for 4921 miles. Shortage of materials during World War I severely handicapped the Pathfinder operation; there were rumors in January 1917 of a possible merger with Empire, but instead the company went under before year's end. The highest bid received for the Pathfinder assets during the first week of December 1917 was $59,000. The factory was bought by a company that moved in to make shoe polish.

1912 PATHFINDER
Series XII — 4-cyl., 40 hp, 118" wb

	FP	5	4	3	2	1
Model A Touring	1750	3300	4400	6700	12,000	24,000
Model B Phaeton	1750	3300	4400	6700	12,000	24,000
Model C Armored Roadster	1750	3200	4300	6500	11,000	23,000
Model D Martha Washington Coach	2250	2700	3600	5300	8800	19,000

1913 Pathfinder, model XIII-A, touring, HAC

1913 PATHFINDER
Series XIII — 4-cyl., 40 hp, 118" wb

	FP	5	4	3	2	1
Model A Touring	1875	3300	4400	6700	12,000	24,000
Model B Phaeton	1875	3300	4400	6700	12,000	24,000
Model C Armored Roadster	1875	3200	4300	6500	11,000	23,000
Model D Martha Washington Coach	2500	2700	3600	5300	8800	19,000
Model E Cruiser	2000	2300	3300	4600	7500	16,000
Delivery Wagon	2000	2000	3000	4200	6500	14,000

1914 Pathfinder, model XIV-A, touring, HAC

1914 PATHFINDER
Series XIV — 4-cyl., 40 hp, 120" wb

	FP	5	4	3	2	1
Model A Touring	2185	3500	4500	7000	13,000	25,000
Model C Armored Roadster	2160	3300	4400	6700	12,000	24,000
Model E Cruiser	2175	2400	3400	4800	8000	17,000
Model D Martha Washington Coach	2500	2700	3600	5300	8800	19,000

Six — 41 hp, 134" wb

	FP	5	4	3	2	1
Leather Stocking Tour.-6P	2750	3900	4800	7700	14,300	27,000

1915 Pathfinder, model VII, touring, HAC

1915 PATHFINDER
Series VII — 6-cyl., 34 hp, 124" wb

	FP	5	4	3	2	1
Model C Roadster	2222	3300	4400	6700	12,000	24,000
Model E Cruiser	2322	3300	4400	6700	12,000	24,000
Daniel Boone Touring-7P	2322	3500	4500	7000	13,000	25,000

Series VII — 6-cyl., 41 hp, 134" wb

	FP	5	4	3	2	1
Model B Limousine	2997	2900	3700	5600	9100	20,000
Leather Stocking Tour.-7P	2750	3900	4800	7700	14,300	27,000

1916 Pathfinder Twelve, LaSalle touring, HAC

1916 Pathfinder Twelve, LaSalle touring, HAC

1916 PATHFINDER
Six — 50 hp, 122" wb

	FP	5	4	3	2	1
Fremont Touring-7P	1695	4400	5600	9200	17,300	31,000
Fremont Touring-5P	1695	4000	5000	8000	15,000	28,000
Fremont Roadster-2P	1695	3900	4800	7700	14,300	27,000
Fremont Roadster-4P	1695	3900	4800	7700	14,300	27,000

Twelve — 60 hp, 130" wb

	FP	5	4	3	2	1
LaSalle Touring-7P	2750	5000	6500	11,000	22,000	35,000
Cloverleaf Roadster-4P	2900	4500	5800	9500	18,000	32,000
Berline Limousine-7P	4250	4000	5000	8000	15,000	28,000

1917 Pathfinder Twelve, Cloverleaf roadster, HAC

1917 PATHFINDER
Twelve — 60 hp, 130" wb

	FP	5	4	3	2	1
LaSalle Touring	2750	5000	6500	11,000	22,000	35,000
Cloverleaf Roadster-4P	2900	4500	5800	9500	18,000	32,000
Limousine	4250	4000	5000	8000	15,000	28,000

PATTERSON-GREENFIELD — Greenfield, Ohio — (1916-1919) — C.R. Patterson was born into slavery in 1833 and as a free man in 1865 moved from Virginia to settle in Greenfield, Ohio where he took up work as a blacksmith. His talent served him well. By the turn of the century he was a successful carriagemaker, and his company — C.R. Patterson & Sons — was thriving. The son most involved was Fred, who was educated at Ohio State University where reportedly he was the first black on the football team. He was also, like his father, a natural mechanic. Although the younger Patterson may have built his first car as early as 1902, it was not until 1916 that formal manufacture of an automobile was embarked upon. "If

1916 Patterson-Greenfield, roadster, NAHC

it's a Patterson it's a good one'' had been a slogan for the company's carriages, and that was equally true of the company's automobile. Its engine was a 30 hp four from Continental, and its component parts — cantilever springs, full floating rear axle, demountable rims — were well put together. "You are cordially invited to visit our factory. Glad to have you," advertising said. "Glad to show you how good we make this Patterson-Greenfield Automobile. It will pay you to come and look around." Patterson-Greenfields were offered as tourers and roadsters, and the price tag was about $850. Estimates of the total number built have ranged from 30 to 150 cars. At least one car is known to be extant. The reason manufacture was discontinued in 1919 was the move of the company into another area of the industry: the production of custom bodies for commercial vehicles. All of the design work for the hearses and buses, moving vans, ice, bakery and milk trucks to follow was seen to by Fred Patterson, Jr., the third-generation Patterson in the family business. The company continued in the body-building field until felled by the Depression in the mid-Thirties.

PATRIOT — Havelock, Nebraska — (1920) — The Patriot Motor Company was incorporated in 1920 as an outgrowth of the A.G. Hebb Quality Bodies factories of Lincoln, Nebraska. It moved into its new plant in Havelock (a suburb of Lincoln) later in 1920, and manufacture was embarked upon there. Although the Patriot has found its way into automobile rosters, surviving company records indicate that trucks only were the product. "Made in the West; Built for the World" was a slogan. Although a Patriot passenger car may have been assayed, it did not proceed beyond the prototype stage. Manufacture of Patriot trucks continued through 1926, when the marque name changed to Woods. The company, which had survived an early receivership in 1920, remained in business into 1931.

PAUL — Eureka, California — (1900) — That J.E. Paul of Eureka completed a gasoline carriage for a local doctor named Mohawk was announced in a September 1900 issue of *The Horseless Age*. That Paul ever built another car has not been confirmed.

PAWTUCKET ELECTRIC — Pawtucket, Rhode Island — (1897) — In 1897 the Pawtucket Motor Carriage Company was organized as a subsidiary to the Campbell Machine Company of Pawtucket, whose charter did not permit the manufacture of vehicles. The Pawtucket purpose was to build, on a royalty basis, the electric car designed by Harry E. Dey, which was being produced in New York City as the Dey-Griswold. A few cars were put together, but the Campbell people soon decided that their best interests were served by adhering to their company's charter.

1901 Pawtucket, Steam Carriage, NAHC

PAWTUCKET STEAM — Pawtucket, Rhode Island — (1901-1902) — The Pawtucket Steamboat Company was located at 54 East Avenue in Pawtucket and produced a sturdy and substantial steam carriage designed by James A. Moncrief and powered by a 7 hp double-acting engine with vertical tubular boiler. Lengthy motoring runs were possible in a Pawtucket because both its gasoline and water tanks were huge, 14 and 35 gallons respectively. A two-passenger 1700-pound runabout was the first model made available, followed by smaller 1100-pound and 800-pound cars. The Pawtucket Steamboat Company remained in the automobile business only through 1902.

1908 Payne-Modern, 5-pass. touring, NAHC

PAYNE-MODERN — Erie, Pennsylvania — (1907-1908) — The Modern Tool Company manufactured screw machine products at the corner of Fourth and State in Erie. Calvin N. Payne was its president, and he began experimenting with an automobile in 1904 with his son Frank. In 1906 Gilbert Loomis, who had earlier built his own car in Massachusetts, joined them in development, but soon moved on to help build the Speedwell in Ohio. The Payne-Modern was indeed modern. Offered as a four and a six, both engines were air-cooled overhead valve units built in 60° vee configuration. The transmission was patented and described as "four speeds forward and reverse, with gears loose on line shaft, until engaged by steel balls in slots, to engage individual gears." Suspension likewise was unusual; semi-elliptic springs placed at a 15-degree angle with the outboard ends above the frame, the inside ends below. There were no outside hand levers on the Payne-Modern at all; the gearshift lever was located on the steering wheel. Final drive was by shaft. In 1908 Hugh Dolnar of *Cycle and Automobile Trade Journal* was given a test ride in the Payne-Modern, and came away quite impressed: "The observer was not once tossed up clear from his seat, and after the first reassuring ten miles he ceased to 'ride the road' at all, simply sitting back and trusting all to the inclined car springs." What doomed the Payne-Modern most likely was its complication. Production was discontinued late in 1908.

1907-1908 PAYNE-MODERN
Four — 24 hp, 100" wb

	FP	5	4	3	2	1
Runabout	2200	2300	3300	4600	7500	16,000
Touring	2200	2400	3400	4800	8000	17,000
Six — 36 hp, 118" wb						
Runabout	4000	2500	3500	5000	8500	18,000
Touring	4000	2700	3600	5300	8800	19,000

PEARL — P.S. Pearl and Company was organized in 1907 with a capital stock of $5000 to manufacture and deal in motor cars in Passaic, New Jersey. The Pearls involved were Eugene, Julia and Philip S. Manufacture is doubted.

1898 Peck, gasoline carriage, NAHC

PECK — Detroit, Michigan — (1897-1899) — Barton Lee Peck was the son of a successful dry goods merchant in Detroit and this happy circumstance of birth certainly helped in assisting his automotive predilection. His father provided the funds and a shop in which to spend them building his first automobile in 1897. In 1898, while testing his vehicle on the streets of Detroit, Peck was arrested and received what was probably one of the first speeding tickets in America. The Peck carriage was a rather flamboyant victoria in which he fitted a four-cylinder vertical gasoline engine of his own design. During the fall of 1898 he indicated that he had established the Detroit Horseless Carriage Company for manufacture, although by February of 1899 he was able only to report that he was in work on a second carriage and that he was finding his system of direct belt transmission to the hub "somewhat deficient in hill climbing." By August he had come to the conclusion that the gasoline-engined automobile would not be a commercial success unless its odor, which he found "sickening," was eliminated. He abandoned his smelly contraption soon thereafter. Subsequently he involved himself with electrical furnace supplies, a hair-restoring product, aviation, and real estate in Florida. On September 6th, 1928 he was drowned while swimming at Daytona Beach.

PECKHAM — The Peckham Motor Car Company has been indicated as the manufacturer of an automobile in Toledo, Ohio during 1915. Documentation is lacking. Possibly this firm was confused with the Peckham Railway Car Truck Company of Kingston, New York the factory of which was purchased the year following for automobile production by the Emerson Motors Company. Peckham, of course, had manufactured cars only for railway use.

PEDALMOBILE — The Pedalmobile Manufacturing Company was organized in Indianapolis, Indiana late in 1911 with a capital stock of $2500 for the manufacture of automobiles. Incorporators were George Herff, J.F. Minthorne, A.T. Purcell and P.A. Porteous. Manufacture is doubted. In 1913 George Herff was among the Herff brothers involved, with H.H. Brooks, in the establishment of the Herff-Brooks Corporation in Indianapolis. The Herff-Brooks car followed from this venture.

1922 Pedersen, roadster, WLB

PEDERSEN — Chicago, Illinois — (1922) — The L.C. Pedersen Motor Car Company, Inc. was located at 6126 Broadway in Chicago, though the firm intended to sell fewer of its cars there than through mail order. The Pedersen was a small and light (70-inch wheelbase, 46-inch tread, 820 pounds) two-passenger roadster which boasted a two-cylinder air-cooled Deluxe engine, two-speed selective transmission, shaft drive, and a big bird as a hood ornament. Two headlamps, a taillight, top and windshield were also included in the incredibly low price of $295. How many Pedersens were built is not known. "The Car of the Future," brochures had said; the future for the company was over within a year.

PEDRO — Pedro was the name announced as the product of the Franco-American Automobile Company of Marion, New Jersey in 1902, but the car never arrived. Refer to Franco-American.

PEER — The Peer Automobile Company was organized in Chicago, Illinois early in 1905 with a capital stock of $2500 to manufacture and repair automobiles. Incorporators were Godfrey Johnson, Charles Stilwell and C.C. Bowersock. Manufacture is doubted.

PEERLESS — Peerless was an occasional designation for the car promoted at the turn of the century by the Liquid Air Power and Automobile Company of Boston and New York City. Refer to Liquid Air.

PEERLESS — Cleveland, Ohio — (1900-1931) — Pierce-Arrow began with birdcages in Buffalo; in Cleveland, Peerless began with clothes wringers. In addition to the humble origins shared by the marques which rose to preeminence as two of the famed Three P's (Packard the third), there were other remarkable similarities between these two companies. Like Pierce-Arrow in New York, Peerless in Ohio extended its product line to include bicycles before the turn of the century, and turned horseless thereafter initially by building single-cylinder buggies called Motorettes powered by De Dion engines. Louis P. Mooers was responsible for the first Peerless that was all Peerless. Mooers had built a car of his own on the East Coast in 1897, but never was able to find financial backing to get into production. Consequently, when Peerless advertised for a chief engineer, he hastened to the Midwest and got the job. His first prototype was a single-cylinder, completed in the summer of 1901, followed by two vertical twins twelve months later. And he had a four-cylinder ready for the New

1903 Peerless, runabout, OCW

York Automobile Show at Madison Square Garden in January 1904. All of these cars were strikingly modern for the era, with front-mounted engines a la Panhard, shaft drive and a bevel-geared fully floating live rear axle. The pressed steel channel frame of the four was unusual, and the forward-tilting steering wheel for ease of entrance and egress may have been a first. Pacesetting, too, was the coachwork which was more gracefully proportioned than the norm, and which included a side-entrance tonneau and a limousine model for 1904, these among the first in the industry. (Jackson's Orlo was also side entrance that year, as was the Reliance.) Ninety cars had been built in 1902, and in that year the Peerless Manufacturing Company became the Peerless Motor Car Company. By now Peerless had gone racing, often with Louis P. Mooers himself behind the wheel. Indeed, it was Mooers who took a Peerless to Ireland for the 1903 Gordon Bennett Cup — and though he crashed there, the effort was notable as being among the very few forays of an American manufacturer (Winton was another) into European racing of that era. At home the Peerless racing success was formidable. Mooers was firmly of the opinion that racing improved the breed (and advertised the product). In 1904 he designed a gargantuan 60 hp racer and hired a race driver already famous for his prowess with Henry Ford's 999 and Alexander Winton's Bullets to take its wheel. The combination of Barney Oldfield and Peerless Green Dragon resulted in a splurge of speed records and publicity that made the Peerless name famous from coast to coast. Oldfield's circus antics, however, were not considered respectable enough for a prestige automobile — and Peerless management soon sent Barney packing. About the same time Louis Mooers packed too, and left for Moon in St. Louis. Whether there was any connection between the two events is problematical. In any case, Peerless hired Charles B. Schmidt away from Packard in 1905 to take Mooers' place, and proceeded to phase out competition and phase in an all-out attack on the luxury market. In 1906 Peerless built 1176 cars, about five hundred less than Packard and Pierce-Arrow. "All That the Name Implies" would be the new Peerless slogan. Peerless was early to market with a six-cylinder car in 1907, and quickly followed Cadillac with a V-8 for 1916. From 1913 through the World War I years, Peerless endured a number of management changes, as huge blocks of its stock were traded and controlling interest changed with seemingly revolving-door frequency. The one constant during this period was Lewis H. Kittredge who had joined Peerless in 1897, had been president of the company from 1906 and remained on the board through all the early upheavals. But this was to change in 1921 when Peerless was sold to Richard H. Collins, the former president and general manager of Cadillac who brought a number of Cadillac engineers with him. (The Peerless chief engineer then was W.R. Strick-

1904 Peerless, tonneau, OCW

1905 Peerless, limousine, OCW

1906 Peerless, model 14, touring, HAC

land, and he promptly went over to Cadillac.) Peerless assets were nearly $14 million which certainly looked good — and production of 6000 cars for 1920, 3500 for 1921, 4240 for 1922 and 5700 for 1923 indicated the company was taking in stride the postwar recession that was playing havoc with the fortunes of so many other automobile manufacturers. But the management upheavals continued. By the end of 1923, Collins was out, and so were the former Cadillac engineers, whose next big assignment would be a new car called the Pontiac. A new Peerless management team was in, with former Oldsmobile president Edward Ver Linden taking the helm; the new chief engineer was Fred W. Slack who had apprenticed at Packard and joined Peerless in 1908. The ad headline of 1925 that declared ''Now There's a Peerless for Everyone'' signalled the entrance of the company into the popular priced field. The car was a six — with the engine from Continental — and it sold in the $1500 range. (It had borrowed liberally from the Collins Six prototype that R.H. Collins had brought with him from Detroit.) Upholding Peerless prestige was the V-8, priced in the $4000 range, now called the Equipoised Eight and featuring detachable cylinder heads and four-wheel brakes. The revolving management door at Peerless turned again in 1928 with Ver Linden leaving for Jordan and vice-president Leon R. German taking over, and revolved yet again the following year when James A. Bohannon (a former Marmon vice-president) became the top man at Peerless. The Peerless V-8 was phased out in 1928, its place taken by a straight-eight built by Continental. Though technically lackluster now, the Peerless line for 1930 was a styling tour de force because the brilliant young Russian emigre Alexis de Sakhnoffsky was hired to design it. The handsome new Peerless — the sleekest the company ever produced — was introduced as Wall Street crashed. A company as managerially unstable as Peerless had been during the boom years could not cope with the exigencies of a nation gone bust. On June 30th, 1931, the last Peerless to be delivered to a customer left the assembly line. But there was one more Peerless after that and, fittingly, it was the grandest Peerless of all. It was a V-16 of 464 cubic inches and 173 bhp. The sedan body was by Murphy. And the Peerless package was almost entirely aluminum, the result of collaborative experiments Peerless had begun with Alcoa (that company was also Cleveland-based) a number of years before. The car would be tested at over 100 mph at Muroc Dry Lake in 1932. But the wistful hope that this fabulous motorcar might restore Peerless to the eminence of its glory years had already been dashed that June day in 1931 when the last production car ever to be built in the city of Cleveland had left the Peerless assembly line. Cars remaining in inventory were marketed as 1932 models. Only the one V-16 prototype had been built. It is on display today at the Crawford Auto-Aviation Museum in Cleveland. The Peerless company remains in Cleveland as well although the Peerless name was dropped a number of years after the firm became the enormously successful brewers of ales and beers known as Carlings.

1900-1902 PEERLESS
Type B — 1-cyl., 2-3/4 hp

	FP	5	4	3	2	1
Motorette	—	1400	2400	3500	5300	10,000

Type C — 1-cyl., 3 1/2 hp

Motorette	—	1400	2400	3500	5300	10,000

1902-1903 PEERLESS
Type 4 — 2-cyl., 16 hp

Tonneau	—	2300	3300	4600	7500	16,000

1904 PEERLESS
Four-Cylinder — 16/22 hp, 86'' wb

Limousine-6/8P	5000	2700	3600	5300	8800	19,000

Type 8 — 4-cyl., 24 hp, 104'' wb

Touring-5P	4000	3100	4200	6300	10,500	22,000
Limousine-5P	5000	2500	3500	5000	8500	18,000

Type 7 — 4-cyl., 35 hp, 102'' wb

Touring-5P	6000	3500	4500	7000	13,000	25,000

1905 PEERLESS
Model 9 — 4-cyl., 24 hp, 102'' wb

King of Belgian Touring-5P	3200	3300	4400	6700	12,000	24,000
Limousine-5P	4000	3000	4000	6000	9500	21,000
Limousine-7P	4000	3100	4200	6400	10,000	22,000

Model 10 — 4-cyl., 30 hp, 104'' wb

Side Entrance Tonneau	3750	3900	4800	7700	14,300	27,000

Model 11 — 4-cyl., 35 hp, 104'' wb

Side Entrance Tonneau	4000	4200	5200	8400	15,700	29,000

Model 12 — 4-cyl., 60 hp, 107'' wb

Victoria Tonneau-5P	6250	4500	5800	9500	18,000	32,000

1906 PEERLESS
Model 14 — 4-cyl., 30 hp, 107'' wb

	FP	5	4	3	2	1
Touring-5P	3750	4000	5000	8000	15,000	28,000
Limousine-7P	4500	3100	4200	6400	10,000	22,000
Racing Runabout-2P	3750	4500	5800	9500	18,000	32,000

Model 15 — 4-cyl., 45 hp, 114'' wb

Touring-5P	5000	4500	5800	9500	18,000	32,000
Limousine-7P	6000	3000	4000	6000	9500	21,000

1907 Peerless, model 15, roadster, HAC

1907 PEERLESS
Model 16 — 4-cyl., 30 hp, 109'' wb

Touring-5P	4000	4000	5000	8000	15,000	28,000
Limousine-7P	5000	3000	4000	6000	9500	21,000

Model 15 — 4-cyl., 45 hp, 114'' wb

Roadster-3P	5000	4000	5000	8000	15,000	28,000
Touring-5P	5000	4200	5200	8400	15,700	29,000
Limousine-7P	6000	3100	4200	6400	10,000	22,000
Touring-7P	5000	4400	5600	9200	17,300	31,000

1908 Peerless, model 18, touring, HAC

1908 PEERLESS
Model 20 — 6-cyl., 50 hp, 132 1/2'' wb

Touring-7P	6000	4700	6100	9900	19,000	33,000
Roadster	6000	4300	5400	8700	16,500	30,000
Limousine	7000	3000	4000	6000	9500	21,000
Landaulette	5800	3100	4200	6300	10,500	22,000

Model 18 — 6-cyl., 50 hp, 118'' wb

Touring-7P	4300	3900	4800	7700	14,300	27,000
Landaulette	5800	3100	4200	6400	10,000	22,000
Roadster	4300	3700	4700	7300	13,700	26,000
Limousine-7P	5500	2900	3700	5600	9100	20,000

1909 Peerless, model 19, close-coupled touring, HAC

1909 PEERLESS
Model 19 — 4-cyl., 30 hp, 122" wb

	FP	5	4	3	2	1
Touring-7P	4300	3900	4800	7700	14,300	27,000
Cape Top Touring-7P	4475	4000	5000	8000	15,000	28,000
Close-Coupled Touring-5P	4300	3700	4700	7300	13,700	26,000
Cl.C. Cape Top Tr.-5P	4475	3900	4800	7700	14,300	27,000
Roadster-3P	4300	3700	4700	7300	13,700	26,000
Cape Top Roadster	4475	3900	4800	7700	14,300	27,000
Limousine-7P	5500	3000	4000	6000	9500	21,000
Landaulet-7P	5800	3100	4200	6400	10,000	22,000

Model 25 — 6-cyl., 50 hp, 136" wb

	FP	5	4	3	2	1
Touring-7P	6000	4700	6100	9900	19,000	33,000
Cape Top Touring-7P	6175	4900	6300	10,300	21,000	34,000
Limousine-7P	7000	3100	4200	6300	10,500	22,000
Landaulet-7P	7300	3200	4300	6500	11,000	23,000

1910 Peerless, model 27, limousine, HAC

1910 PEERLESS
Model 27 — 4-cyl., 30 hp, 118 1/2" wb

	FP	5	4	3	2	1
Roadster	4300	3700	4700	7300	13,700	26,000
Pony Tonneau	4300	3900	4800	7700	14,300	27,000

Model 27 — 4-cyl., 30 hp, 122" wb

	FP	5	4	3	2	1
Touring-7P	4300	4200	5200	8400	15,700	29,000
Close-Coupled Touring-5P	4300	4200	5200	8400	15,700	29,000
Limousine-7P	5500	3000	4000	6000	9500	21,000
Landaulet-7P	5800	3200	4400	6800	10,500	23,000
Demi-Limousine	4800	3100	4200	6400	10,000	22,000

Model 28 — 6-cyl., 50 hp, 136" wb

	FP	5	4	3	2	1
Touring-7P	6000	4700	6100	9900	19,000	33,000
Roadster	6000	4500	5800	9500	18,000	32,000
Pony Tonneau	6000	4700	6100	9900	19,000	33,000
Close-Coupled Touring	6000	4700	6100	9900	19,000	33,000
Limousine-7P	7000	3500	4500	7000	13,000	25,000
Landaulet-7P	7000	3700	4700	7300	13,700	26,000

1911 Peerless, model 32, demi-limousine, HAC

1911 PEERLESS
Model 29 — 4-cyl., 20 hp, 113" wb

	FP	5	4	3	2	1
Limousine-6P	4200	3000	4000	6000	9500	21,000
Landaulet-6P	4300	3100	4200	6400	10,000	22,000

Model 31 — 4-cyl., 30 hp, 123" wb

	FP	5	4	3	2	1
Touring-5P	4300	4200	5200	8400	15,700	29,000
Roadster	4300	4000	5000	8000	15,000	28,000
Phaeton	4300	4200	5200	8400	15,700	29,000
Pony Tonneau	4300	4200	5200	8400	15,700	29,000
Torpedo	4300	4000	5000	8000	15,000	28,000
Limousine	5400	2900	3700	5600	9100	20,000
Landaulet	5500	3000	4000	6000	9500	21,000
Demi-Limousine	4800	2900	3700	5600	9100	20,000

Model 32 — 6-cyl., 45 hp, 136" wb

	FP	5	4	3	2	1
Touring-7P	6000	4900	6300	10,300	21,000	34,000
Roadster	6000	4500	5800	9500	18,000	32,000
Close-Coupled Touring	6000	4700	6100	9900	19,000	33,000
Phaeton	6000	4700	6100	9900	19,000	33,000
Pony Tonneau	6000	4500	5800	9500	18,000	32,000
Torpedo	6000	4900	6300	10,300	21,000	34,000
Limousine	7000	3500	4500	7000	13,000	25,000
Landaulet	7000	3700	4700	7300	13,700	26,000
Demi-Limousine	6500	3500	4500	7000	13,000	25,000

1912 Peerless, model 48-Six, phaeton, HAC

1912 PEERLESS
Town Car — 4-cyl., 24 hp, 113" wb

	FP	5	4	3	2	1
Landaulet	4300	3200	4300	6500	11,000	23,000
Limousine	4200	3100	4200	6300	10,500	22,000

Model 38-Six — 6-cyl., 38 hp, 125" wb

	FP	5	4	3	2	1
Touring	4000	4400	5600	9200	17,300	31,000
Torpedo	4000	4400	5600	9200	17,300	31,000
Roadster	4000	4300	5400	8700	16,500	30,000
Coupe	4700	2900	3700	5600	9100	20,000
Limousine	5000	3300	4400	6700	12,000	24,000
Berlin Limousine	5200	3500	4500	7000	13,000	25,000
Landaulet	5100	3500	4500	7000	13,000	25,000

Model 48-Six — 6-cyl., 48 hp, 137" wb

	FP	5	4	3	2	1
Touring	5000	5000	6500	11,000	22,000	35,000
Torpedo	5000	5000	6500	11,000	22,000	35,000
Phaeton	5000	5000	6500	11,000	22,000	35,000
Limousine	6000	4000	4800	7700	14,300	27,000
Berlin Limousine	6200	4000	5000	8000	15,000	28,000
Landaulet	6100	4000	5000	8000	15,000	28,000

Model 60-Six — 6-cyl., 60 hp, 140" wb

	FP	5	4	3	2	1
Touring	6000	5400	7300	11,800	25,000	38,000
Torpedo	6000	5400	7300	11,800	25,000	38,000
Phaeton	6000	5400	7300	11,800	25,000	38,000
Limousine	7000	4000	5000	8000	15,000	28,000
Berlin Limousine	7200	4200	5200	8400	15,700	29,000
Landaulet	7100	4200	5200	8400	15,700	29,000

Model 40-Four — 4-cyl., 40 hp, 125" wb

	FP	5	4	3	2	1
Touring	4300	4700	6100	9900	19,000	33,000
Torpedo	4300	4700	6100	9900	19,000	33,000
Phaeton	4300	4700	6100	9900	19,000	33,000
Limousine	5300	3700	4700	7300	13,700	27,000
Berlin Limousine	5500	3900	4800	7700	14,300	27,000
Landaulet	5400	3900	4800	7700	14,300	27,000

1913 Peerless, model 38-Six, roadster, HAC

1913 PEERLESS
Model 24-Four — 4-cyl., 25.6 hp, 113" wb

	FP	5	4	3	2	1
Town Car-6P	4200	3100	4200	6300	10,500	22,000
Limousine-6P	4200	3000	4000	6000	9500	21,000
Landaulet-6P	4300	3200	4300	6500	11,000	23,000

1913 PEERLESS
Model 38-Six — 6-cyl., 38.4 hp, 125" wb

	FP	5	4	3	2	1
Roadster-3P	4300	4300	5400	8700	16,500	30,000
Torpedo-4P	4300	4400	5600	9200	17,300	31,000
Touring Car-5P	4300	4400	5600	9200	17,300	31,000
Coupe-3P	5000	2900	3700	5600	9100	20,000
Limousine-7P	5300	3200	4300	6500	11,000	23,000
Landaulet-7P	5400	3300	4400	6700	12,000	24,000
Berline Limousine	5500	3400	4500	7000	13,000	25,000

Model 40-Four — 4-cyl., 40 hp, 125" wb

	FP	5	4	3	2	1
Landaulet-7P	5400	3500	4500	7000	13,000	25,000
Touring-7P	4300	4900	6300	10,300	21,000	34,000
Torpedo-6P	4300	4700	6100	9900	19,000	33,000
Limousine-7P	5300	3300	4400	6700	12,000	24,000
Berline Limousine	5500	3500	4500	7000	13,000	25,000

Model 48-Six — 6-cyl., 48.6 hp, 137" wb

	FP	5	4	3	2	1
Torpedo-6P	5000	5000	6500	11,000	22,000	35,000
Touring-7P	5000	5200	6800	11,300	23,000	36,000
Limousine-7P	6000	3900	4800	7700	14,300	27,000
Landaulet-7P	6100	4000	5000	8000	15,000	28,000
Berline Limousine	6200	4000	5000	8000	15,000	28,000

Model 60-Six — 6-cyl., 60 hp, 140" wb

	FP	5	4	3	2	1
Touring-7P	6000	5500	7500	12,000	26,000	39,000
Torpedo-6P	6000	5400	7300	11,800	25,000	38,000
Limousine-7P	7000	4000	5000	8000	15,000	28,000
Landaulet-7P	7100	4200	5200	8400	15,700	29,000
Berline Limousine	7200	4200	5200	8400	15,700	29,000

1914 Peerless, touring, OCW

1914 PEERLESS
Model 38-Six — 6-cyl., 38.4 hp, 125" wb

	FP	5	4	3	2	1
Torpedo-4P	4300	4700	6100	9900	19,000	33,000
Touring-5P	4300	4700	6100	9900	19,000	33,000
Roadster	4300	4500	5800	9500	18,000	32,000
Coupe	5000	2900	3700	5600	9100	20,000
Limousine	5300	3100	4200	6300	10,500	22,000
Landaulette	5400	3200	4300	6500	11,000	23,000
Berline-Limousine	5500	3200	4300	6500	11,000	23,000

Model 48-Six — 6-cyl., 48.6 hp, 137" wb

	FP	5	4	3	2	1
Touring-7P	5000	5000	6500	11,000	22,000	35,000
Torpedo	5000	4900	6300	10,300	21,000	34,000
Limousine	6000	3300	4400	6700	12,000	24,000
Landaulette	6100	3500	4500	7000	13,000	25,000
Berline-Limousine	6200	3500	4500	7000	13,000	25,000

Model 60-Six — 6-cyl., 60 hp, 140" wb

	FP	5	4	3	2	1
Limousine-7P	7000	3700	4700	7300	13,700	26,000
Torpedo	6000	5400	7300	11,800	25,000	38,000
Touring-7P	6000	5500	7500	12,000	26,000	39,000
Landaulette	7100	3900	4800	7700	14,300	27,000
Berline-Limousine	7200	3900	4800	7700	14,300	27,000

1915 Peerless, model 55, touring, HAC

1915 PEERLESS
Model 54 — 4-cyl., 22.5 hp, 113" wb

	FP	5	4	3	2	1
Touring-5P	2000	4000	5000	8000	15,000	28,000
Roadster	2000	3900	4800	7700	14,300	27,000
Limousine	3100	3100	4200	6300	10,500	22,000
Cabriolet	2300	3500	4500	7000	13,000	25,000
Sedan-5P	3100	2500	3500	5000	8500	18,000

1915 PEERLESS
Model 55 — 6-cyl., 29.4 hp, 121" wb

	FP	5	4	3	2	1
Touring-5P	2250	4300	5400	8700	16,500	30,000
Roadster	2250	4200	5200	8400	15,700	29,000
Limousine	3350	3200	4300	6500	11,000	23,000
Cabriolet	2550	3900	4800	7700	14,300	27,000
Sedan	3350	2700	3600	5300	8800	19,000

Model 48 — 6-cyl., 48.6 hp, 137" wb

	FP	5	4	3	2	1
Touring-7P	5000	4900	6300	10,300	21,000	34,000
Limousine-7P	6000	3500	4500	7000	13,000	25,000
Roadster-3P	4900	4700	6100	9900	19,000	33,000
Berline-7P	6200	3900	4800	7700	14,300	27,000
Landaulet	6100	3900	4800	7700	14,300	27,000
Sedan	—	2900	3700	5600	9100	20,000

1916 Peerless, model 56, touring, HAC

1916 PEERLESS
Model 56 — 8-cyl., 33.8 hp, 125" wb

	FP	5	4	3	2	1
Touring-7P	1890	5000	6500	11,000	22,000	35,000
Roadster-3P	1890	4900	6300	10,300	21,000	34,000
Limousine-7P	3060	3300	4400	6700	12,000	24,000

1917 Peerless, model 56, touring, HAC

1917 PEERLESS
Model 56 — 8-cyl., 33.8 hp, 125" wb

	FP	5	4	3	2	1
Touring-7P	1980	5000	6500	11,000	22,000	35,000
Roadster	1980	4900	6300	10,300	21,000	34,000
Limousine	3350	3200	4300	6500	11,000	23,000
Sedan	2840	2000	3000	4200	6500	14,000
Coupe	2700	2300	3300	4600	7500	16,000

1918 Peerless, model 56, sedan, HAC

1918 PEERLESS
Model 56 — 8-cyl., 33.8 hp, 125" wb

	FP	5	4	3	2	1
Touring-7P	2340	5000	6500	11,000	22,000	35,000
Roadster-4P	2340	4900	6300	10,300	21,000	34,000
Spt. Rdstr.-2P	2490	5000	6500	11,000	22,000	35,000
Sedan-6P	2990	2000	3000	4200	6500	14,000
Coupe-4P	2850	2300	3300	4600	7500	16,000
Limousine-7P	3690	3200	4300	6500	11,000	23,000

1919 Peerless, model 56, sedan-limousine, HAC

1919 PEERLESS
Model 56 — 8-cyl., 33.8 hp, 125" wb

	FP	5	4	3	2	1
Touring-7P	2760	5200	6800	11,300	23,000	36,000
Roadster-4P	2760	5000	6500	11,000	22,000	35,000
Sedan-7P	3520	2000	3000	4200	6500	14,000
Coupe-4P	3320	2300	3300	4600	7500	16,000
Sed.-Lim.-7P	3720	3000	4000	6000	9500	21,000

1920 Peerless, model 56, 4-pass. roadster, AA

1921 Peerless, model 56, roadster, HAC

1921 Peerless, model 56, touring, HAC

1920 PEERLESS
Model 56 — 8-cyl., 80 hp, 125" wb

	FP	5	4	3	2	1
Touring-7P	2900	5300	7000	11,500	24,000	37,000
Roadster-4P	2900	5200	6800	11,300	23,000	36,000
Coupe-4P	3500	2400	3400	4800	8000	17,000
Sedan-7P	3700	2200	3200	4400	7000	15,000
Sed.-Lim.-7P	3900	3100	4200	6300	10,500	22,000

1921 PEERLESS
Model 56 — 8-cyl., 80 hp, 125" wb

	FP	5	4	3	2	1
Roadster-4P	3200	5200	6800	11,300	23,000	36,000
Touring-7P	3230	5300	7000	11,500	24,000	37,000
Coupe-4P	3920	2400	3400	4800	8000	17,000
Sedan-7P	4140	2200	3200	4400	7000	15,000
Limousine-7P	4400	3100	4200	6300	10,500	22,000

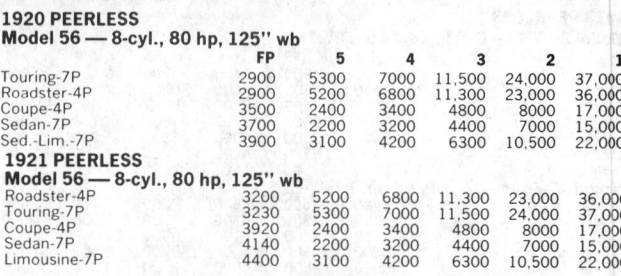

1922 Peerless, model 56-7, sedan, HAC

1922 PEERLESS
Model 56-7 — 8-cyl., 80 bhp, 125" wb

	FP	5	4	3	2	1
Roadster-4P	2880	5200	6800	11,300	23,000	36,000
Touring-7P	2880	5300	7000	11,500	24,000	37,000
Coupe-4P	3500	2400	3400	4800	8000	17,000
Sedan-5P	3650	2200	3200	4400	7000	15,000
Sedan-7P	3790	2300	3300	4600	7500	16,000
Limo. Sed.-7P	4060	3100	4200	6300	10,500	22,000

1923 Peerless, Budd bodied limousine, AA

1923 Peerless, model 66, 7-pass. touring, AA

1923 PEERLESS
Model 66 — 8-cyl., 70 hp, 128" wb

	FP	5	4	3	2	1
Touring-7P	2990	5300	7000	11,500	24,000	37,000
Phaeton-4P	2990	5300	7000	11,500	24,000	37,000
Coupe-2P	3300	2400	3400	4800	8000	17,000
Coupe-4P	3400	2450	3500	4900	8300	17,500
Sedan-5P	3900	2200	3200	4400	7000	15,000
Sedan-7P	4090	2300	3300	4600	7500	16,000

1924 Peerless, model 66, town brougham, AA

1924 PEERLESS
Model 66 — 8-cyl., 70 hp, 128'' wb

	FP	5	4	3	2	1
Touring-7P	2750	5300	7000	11,500	24,000	37,000
Phaeton-4P	2690	5300	7000	11,500	24,000	37,000
Coupe-2P	3300	2400	3400	4800	8000	17,000
Victoria-4P	3690	2500	3500	5000	8500	18,000
Sub. Sed.-7P	3840	2300	3300	4600	7500	16,000
Town Sed.-5P	—	2200	3200	4400	7000	15,000
Town Brgm.-5P	—	2300	3300	4600	7500	16,000
Sub. Sed.-5P	—	2500	3500	5000	8500	18,000
Ber. Lim.-7P	—	3100	4200	6300	10,500	22,000

1925 Peerless, roadster, HAC

1925 Peerless, 4-dr. touring, AA

1925 PEERLESS
Model 6-70 — 6-cyl., 70 hp, 126'' wb

	FP	5	4	3	2	1
Roadster-2P	2335	4500	5800	9500	18,000	32,000
Touring-5P	2285	4700	6100	9900	19,000	33,000
Coupe-4P	2950	2300	3300	4600	7500	16,000
Sedan-5P	2995	2000	3000	4200	6500	14,000

Model 6-70 — 8-cyl., 70 hp, 133'' wb

	FP	5	4	3	2	1
Touring-7P	2485	4700	6100	9900	19,000	33,000
Sedan-7P	3295	2200	3200	4400	7000	15,000
Limousine-7P	3470	2700	3600	5300	8800	19,000

Model 8-67 — 8-cyl., 70 hp, 128'' wb

	FP	5	4	3	2	1
Phaeton-4P	3285	5300	7000	11,500	24,000	37,000
Victoria-4P	3950	4500	5800	9500	18,000	32,000
Coupe-5P	4175	3000	4000	6000	9500	21,000
Town Sedan-5P	4250	2500	3500	5000	8500	18,000
Town Brgm.-5P	4250	2700	3600	5300	8800	19,000
Suburban-7P	4450	2900	3700	5600	9100	20,000
Ber. Limo.-7P	4725	3200	4300	6500	11,000	23,000

1926 Peerless, roadster, AA

1926 PEERLESS
Model 6-80 — 6-cyl., 63 hp, 116'' wb

	FP	5	4	3	2	1
Touring-5P		4300	5400	8700	16,500	30,000
Roadster		4200	5200	8400	15,700	29,000
Sedan-5P	1595	2000	3000	4200	6500	14,000
Close-Coupled Sedan-5P		2200	3200	4400	7000	15,000
Two-Door Sedan-5P		1800	2800	4000	6200	13,000
Coupe-2P		2300	3300	4600	7500	16,000

Model 6-70 — 6-cyl., 70 hp, 126'' wb

	FP	5	4	3	2	1
Phaeton-5P	1995	4500	5800	9500	18,000	32,000
Sedan-5P	2395	2200	3200	4400	7000	15,000
Coupe-5P	2295	2400	3400	4800	8000	17,000

Model 6-72 — 6-cyl., 70 hp, 133'' wb

	FP	5	4	3	2	1
Roadster-2/4P	2195	4700	6100	9900	19,000	33,000
Phaeton-7P	2195	4900	6300	10,300	21,000	34,000
Sedan-7P	2595	2200	3200	4400	7000	15,000
Limousine-7P	2695	3100	4200	6300	10,500	22,000

Model 8-69 — 8-cyl., 70 hp, 128'' wb

	FP	5	4	3	2	1
Brougham-5P	3495	2500	3500	5000	8500	18,000
Sedan-5P	3495	2300	3300	4600	7500	16,000
Phaeton-7P	2895	5400	7300	11,800	25,000	38,000
Victoria-4P	3245	2500	3500	5000	8500	18,000
Coupe-5P	3295	2500	3500	5000	8500	18,000
Suburban Sedan-7P	3595	2300	3300	4600	7500	16,000
Berline-7P	3795	4000	5000	8000	15,000	28,000

1927 Peerless, model 8-69, boattail roadster, OCW

1927 Peerless, model 8-69, sedan, HAC

1927 PEERLESS
Model 6-90 — 6-cyl., 70 hp, 120'' wb

	FP	5	4	3	2	1
Roadster-4P	1695	4700	6100	9900	19,000	33,000
Coupe-4P	1725	2700	3600	5300	8800	19,000
Close-Coupled Sedan-4P	1895	2500	3500	5000	8500	18,000
Sedan-5P	1895	2300	3300	4600	7500	16,000
Roadster Coupe	1725	4900	6300	10,300	21,000	34,000
Phaeton-5P	1695	5300	7000	11,500	24,000	37,000
Landaulet-5P	1995	3200	4300	6500	11,000	23,000

Model 6-72 — 6-cyl., 70 hp, 126½'' wb

	FP	5	4	3	2	1
Sedan-5P	2395	2400	3400	4800	8000	12,000
Roadster-4P	2195	4900	6300	10,300	21,000	34,000
Coupe-5P	1895	2900	3700	5600	9100	20,000

1927 Peerless, model 8-69, coupe, HAC

1929 Peerless, model 125, sedan, HAC

1927 PEERLESS
Model 6-72 — 6-cyl., 70 hp, 133½" wb

	FP	5	4	3	2	1
Sedan-7P	2595	2500	3500	5000	8500	18,000
Limousine-7P	2695	3100	4200	6300	10,500	22,000
Deluxe Sedan-5P	2795	2700	3600	5300	8800	19,000
Deluxe Sedan-7P	2995	2900	3700	5600	9100	20,000

Model 8-69 — 8-cyl., 70 hp, 126½" wb

Standard Sedan-5P	2995	2700	3600	5300	8800	19,000
Standard Coupe-5P	2795	3100	4200	6300	10,500	22,000
Standard Sedan-7P	3095	2900	3700	5600	9100	20,000

Model 8-69 — 8-cyl., 70 hp, 133" wb

Custom Roadster-4P	2995	5200	6800	11,300	23,000	36,000
Sedan-7P	3595	2500	3500	5000	8500	18,000
Custom Sedan-5P	3495	2700	3600	5300	8800	19,000
Sedan Limousine-5P	3795	3300	4400	6700	12,000	24,000

Model 6-80 — 6-cyl., 68 hp, 116" wb

Phaeton	1395	5400	7300	11,800	25,000	38,000
Roadster	1495	5300	7000	11,500	24,000	37,000
Two-Door Sedan	1395	2700	3600	5300	8800	19,000
Roadster Coupe	1565	5000	6500	11,000	22,000	36,000
Four-Door Sedan	1595	2900	3700	5600	9100	20,000

1929 PEERLESS
Model 6-61 — 6-cyl., 62 hp, 116" wb

	FP	5	4	3	2	1
Roadster-4P		6200	9500	15,000	34,000	47,000
Sedan-5P	3075	2700	3600	5300	8800	19,000
Deluxe Sedan-5P		2900	3700	5600	9100	20,000

Model 6-81 — 6-cyl., 66 hp, 116" wb

Phaeton-5P	1540	6800	10,300	16,000	35,500	48,000
Phaeton-7P	1595	7000	10,800	16,900	37,100	49,000
Coupe-4P	1595	3500	4500	7000	13,000	25,000
Victoria-4P	1595	3300	4400	6700	12,000	24,000
Deluxe Sedan		3100	4200	6300	10,500	22,000

Model 125 — 8-cyl., 114 hp, 130/138" wb

Coupe-4P		3900	4800	7700	14,300	27,000
Sedan-5P	2195	3500	4500	7000	13,000	25,000
Victoria-4P		3700	4700	7300	13,700	26,000
Sedan-7P		3700	4700	7300	13,700	26,000

1928 Peerless, model 6-60, sedan, HAC

1928 PEERLESS
Model 6-60 — 6-cyl., 62 hp, 116" wb

Roadster-4P	1295	5400	7300	11,800	25,000	38,000
Phaeton-5P	1295	5500	7500	12,000	26,000	39,000
Coupe-4P	1345	3200	4300	6500	11,000	23,000
Sedan-5P	1345	2300	3300	4600	7500	16,000

Model 6-80 — 6-cyl., 63 hp, 116" wb

Sedan-5P	1595	2400	3400	4800	8000	17,000
Cl.C. Spt. Sed.-5P	1595	2500	3500	5000	8500	18,000

Model 6-91 — 6-cyl., 70 hp, 120" wb

Cabriolet	1895	4500	5800	9500	18,000	32,000
Victoria	1895	4000	5000	8000	15,000	28,000
Sedan-5P	1895	2700	3600	5300	8800	19,000
Sedan-7P	1895	2900	3700	5600	9100	20,000

Model 8-69 — 8-cyl., 80 hp, 126-1/2" wb

Roadster-4P	2995	6400	9300	14,500	33,000	45,000
Coupe-5P	2795	4200	5200	8400	15,700	29,000
Custom Sedan-5P	2995	3100	4200	6300	10,500	22,000
Custom Sedan-7P	3095	3200	4300	6500	11,000	23,000
Custom Sedan Limo.7P	3295	3500	4500	7000	13,000	25,000

1930 Peerless, sedan, HAC

1930 PEERLESS
Standard 8 — 85 hp, 118" wb

Sedan	1495	3700	4700	7300	13,700	26,000
Coupe	1495	4000	5000	8000	15,000	28,000
Brougham	1545	3900	4800	7700	14,300	27,000
Club Sedan	1545	4000	5000	8000	15,000	28,000
Cabriolet	1595	5400	7300	11,800	25,000	38,000

Master 8 — 120 hp, 125" wb

Sedan	1995	3900	4800	7700	14,300	27,000
Coupe	1995	4200	5200	8400	15,700	29,000
Cabriolet	2095	5500	7500	12,000	26,000	39,000
Metropolitan Sedan-5P	—	4200	5200	8400	15,700	29,000
Metropolitan Sedan-7P	—	4300	5300	8600	16,100	29,500

Custom 8 — 120 hp, 138" wb

Sedan-5P	2945	4300	5400	8700	16,500	30,000
Coupe	2945	4700	6100	9900	19,000	33,000
Sedan-7P	3145	4400	5600	9200	17,300	31,000
Limousine	3345	4700	6100	9900	19,000	33,000
Metropolitan Sedan-5P	—	4900	6300	10,300	21,000	34,000
Metropolitan Sedan-7P	—	5000	6400	10,700	21,500	34,500

1929 Peerless, model 6-81, 2-4 pass. coupe, OCW

1931 Peerless Eight, limousine, Weymann, HAC

1931 Peerless, Master Eight Deluxe, 4-dr. sedan, AA

1931 PEERLESS

Standard 8 — 120 hp, 118" wb

	FP	5	4	3	2	1
Sedan	1495	3700	4700	7300	13,700	26,000
Coupe	1495	4200	5200	8400	15,700	29,000
Brougham	1545	3900	4800	7700	14,300	27,000
Club Sedan	1545	4000	5000	8000	15,000	28,000
Cabriolet	1595	5500	7500	12,000	26,000	39,000

Master 8 — 120 hp, 125" wb

Sedan	1995	3900	4800	7700	14,300	27,000
Coupe	1995	4300	5400	8700	16,500	30,000
Club Sedan	2045	4200	5200	8400	15,700	29,000
Brougham	2045	4000	5000	8000	15,000	28,000
Cabriolet	2095	5800	8000	12,500	28,000	40,000

Custom 8 — 120 hp, 138" wb

Coupe	2795	4500	5800	9500	18,000	32,000
Sedan-5P	2795	4200	5200	8400	15,700	29,000
Club Sedan	2845	4400	5600	9200	17,300	31,000
Brougham	2845	4300	5400	8700	16,500	30,000
Sedan-7P	2945	4300	5400	8700	16,500	30,000
Limousine	3145	4500	5800	9500	18,000	32,000

PEERLESS STEAM — Washington, D.C. — (1901) — C.H. Peck, a former bicycle man from Chicago, was the man behind the Peerless Long-Distance Steam Carriage Company which was located at 910 F Street in Washington, D.C. The firm's specialty was a kit for the conversion of any horsedrawn carriage into a steam vehicle. All necessary parts, plus a set of working drawings, were marketed, beginning in 1900, at a price of $450. The steam engine alone, which was a high-pressure compound of the marine type, was available for $350. This unit, which was fueled by kerosene, was claimed to develop 16 hp, and to provide speeds up to 39 mph. The water tanks furnished were said to be good for a 100-mile run. In February 1901 the Peerless Long-Distance Steam Carriage Company also announced its availability for the production of complete steam carriages to order. The Peerless steam car was built for one year only.

PEET — The Peet Motor Corporation of Hollis, New York has been indicated on various rosters as the manufacturer of an automobile. The firm did produce trucks on Long Island from 1923-1924 but the evidence is lacking that a Peet automobile was ever built.

PEET STEAM — Brooklyn, New York — (1901) — Dr. A.J. Peet of 1020 Avenue C in Brooklyn built himself a novel steam engine in 1900. It had four single-acting vertical cylinders with pistons similar to a gasoline motor. Four horsepower was developed, and gasoline was used as fuel. The flash boiler was of standard coiled tube design. By the summer of 1901 A.J. Peet had completed a two-seater carriage for his car, and it was successfully tested. Although Dr. Peet indicated at the time that, in association with Dr. William T. Jenkins, with whom he shared his office, plans were being made to market the vehicle, it appears the doctors remained partners only in their medical practice. The Peet steam car was not put into manufacture.

PEGASUS — Harvey, Illinois — (1902) — In January of 1902 the Pegasus Automobile Company was incorporated in Harvey with a capital stock of $10,000 for the purpose of manufacturing automobiles. The first board of directors meeting was held on Saturday, February 15th for the election of officers and the making of plans. That the company moved into a factory in Harvey (on the west side of Park Avenue between 152nd and 153rd streets) can be documented. On March 26th the Pegasus Automobile Company took out an insurance policy for one year with the National Assurance Company of Ireland. The premium was $11.29 and the insured valuation was $537.50 which included all machinery ($375.00), office furniture and fixtures ($37.50) and automobiles "manufactured, unmanufactured and in process of manufacture" ($125.00). Special permission was granted Pegasus to keep and use gasoline for testing purposes, provided it was in quantities of not more than five gallons at a time and that it was kept in "an approved metal safety can" thirty feet from the building. Most likely, Pegasus did build and test a prototype or prototypes of its car. The company did not proceed into manufacture, however, and its insurance policy was not renewed.

PEKIN — The Pekin Garage and Outing Company was organized in Peoria, Illinois late in 1910 with a capital stock of $5000 "to manufacture, rebuild, repair, buy, sell, rent and store motorcars and conduct a general garage." Incorporators were Herman Kaemmerling, Walter E. Green and William Kaemmerling. Manufacture is doubted.

PELL — Oswego, New York — (1909) — Several years before, Chauncey C. Place had left his job as superintendent of the Electric Vehicle Company of Hartford, Connecticut to set himself up in business in Oswego as the Oswego Tool Company. In the early fall of 1909 he talked several local businessmen — David W. Pell and Albert N. Radcliffe among them — into joining him in financing a company for the manufacture of low-priced four-cylinder automobiles. Subsequently, the Pell Motor Car Company was incorporated with $150,000 in capital stock. Construction of a factory on West Albany Street was immediately begun by the Ontario Industrial Company. When it was completed, however, someone else moved in. A pilot model of the Pell automobile had been built, but the venture never proceeded further. During this period, incidentally, Chauncey Place ran for mayor of Oswego — and lost.

PELLETIER — LeRoy Pelletier covered the Klondike gold rush for *The New York Times*, was Henry Ford's personal secretary, and the automobile industry's first great adman. Although he was involved with many automobiles, including the Duquesne built in Jamestown, New York from 1904-1906, he never produced a car bearing his name. Refer to Duquesne.

PEMBROKE — The Pembroke Manufacturing Company was organized in Rochester, New York during the spring of 1912 with a capital stock of $50,000 to manufacture automobiles and parts. Incorporators were Charles J. Pembroke, Winfield P. Pembroke and Walter J. Fellows. Manufacture of a car is doubted.

PENDERS — Joseph H. Penders, Inc. was organized late in 1912 in New York City for the manufacture of automobiles, taxicabs and motorcycles. John H. Penders of 218 East 49th Street was noted in *Automobile Topics* as "the moving spirit of the enterprise." Manufacture of a car is doubted.

PENDLETON — Culver City, California — (1914) — That the Pendleton Manufacturing Company of Culver City had begun the "active manufacture" of cyclecars was revealed in *The Carette and American Cyclecar* in August 1914. Details regarding the car itself are lacking.

1905 Pendleton, touring, GR

PENDLETON — Warren, Ohio — (1899-1905) — In the 1890's the Trumbull Manufacturing Company was the linear descendant of the Warren Machine Works which had been established in the city of Warren, Trumbull County, in 1850. William C. Pendleton, and Justin W. Spangenberg were the two partners in the Trumbull company, though the latter had divorced himself from the firm's activity to join Warren Packard in his new lumber planing mill. General foundry and machine work had by now been joined by production of steam engines and bicycle repair. And all of this was joined in 1899 by an automobile. It was one of Warren's first; another which also arrived in 1899 was built on the north end of town by James Ward Packard, son of Warren Packard. The Trumbull Manufacturing Company car of 1899 had a single-cylinder engine mounted under the seat, tiller steering, wire spoke wheels — "and on occasion it ran," according to Thorn Pendleton, grandson of the man who built it. A fire at the machine shop, and the subsequent time necessary for rebuilding, prevented another car being built in 1900. But in 1901 a steamer was produced, and it was followed in 1902 by a handsome gasoline car with nickel-plated radiator and leather upholstery. A canopy top touring car with folding steering wheel was a 1905 model, together with another 28/42 hp four with double side-entrance tonneau. Although a brochure was printed and occasional advertising taken in the trade press, the Trumbull Manufacturing Company viewed its automotive activity as a sideline; when such necessities as sending a mechanic all the way to Kansas to help a new owner get his car started began to nettle William Pendleton in 1905, he simply got out of the automobile business to get on with other things. Total production had been seven cars, and they were named Pendleton or Trumbull "somewhat capriciously," according to Thorn Pendleton. Three brass nameplates reading Pendleton are all that remains of the cars in the family archive. None of the cars are believed to exist. The Trumbull Manufacturing Company survives to this day as Warren Tool Corporation, Warren's oldest industrial concern.

PENINSULAR — In February of 1912 the Marquette Motor Car Company of Saginaw, Michigan was renamed the Peninsular Motor Company. The Marquette was built in 1912 only; some of the later cars may have borne a Peninsular emblem. Refer to Marquette.

PENN — "The Penn Auto Company of Philadelphia, capital stock $5000, is the first company incorporated in the Keystone State for the purpose of manufacturing automobiles," reported *The Horseless Age* during the summer of 1901. That did not happen to be true, but true certainly it is that this venture never got off the ground.

1908 Penn, MVMA

PENN — Washington, D.C. — (1908) — Dr. Shakespeare Penn was a poet and a preacher, and despite his first name he seemed more to resemble Walt Whitman than the Bard of Avon. He was not much of an automobile designer, though he did build a car for himself in 1908. It was a canopied single-seater with four flimsy wheels. Dr. Penn arranged to have himself photographed in his vehicle for the edification of the trade press. The photography site was not his home in Washington, D.C., however. It was the White House.

1911 Penn, Thirty, roadster, WLB

PENN — Pittsburgh and New Castle, Pennsylvania — (1911-1912) — The Penn Motor Car Company was organized in Pittsburgh in November of 1910 with a capital stock of $150,000 and a factory already leased at 7510 Thomas Boulevard. By early 1911 the new four-cylinder Penn Thirty was coming off the line. It was offered as a roadster and touring on a 105-inch wheelbase. "We have no apology to make for the Penn Thirty," the brochure said. "We honestly believe it is fully up to the high standard we have set for it, viz; the best not only at our price, but the best at any price." In 1912 a 45 hp four on a 115-inch wheelbase was added to the line. And Penn also announced its impending move to New Castle, where local financing was seeing to the construction of a new $90,000 factory. The plant was completed, but the Penn company moved in only to be abruptly moved out. According to a subsequent report in *Automobile*

Topics, the New Castle backers "lost courage" and petitioned the company into bankruptcy before a single car was built there. The sale date for the new factory was scheduled for January 21st, 1913, with two groups said to be interested, one which would move in to manufacture both passenger and commercial vehicles, the other which "would remodel the plant so as to make it suitable for other manufacturing purposes." The latter won out, and at a bargain $54,000. Elmore Gregg, Penn's former sales manager, had headed the former group and when his plans in New Castle went asunder, he returned to Pittsburgh where he went on to build the Pennsy a few years later. In addition to the cars produced in Pennsylvania, incidentally, the Penn also was the nucleus around which the McKay was built in Novia Scotia.

1911 PENN
Thirty — 4-cyl., 30 hp, 105" wb

	FP	5	4	3	2	1
Model R Roadster-2P	975	4400	5600	9200	17,300	31,000
Model T Touring-5P	1075	4500	5800	9500	18,000	32,000

1912 PENN
Thirty — 4-cyl., 30 hp, 105" wb

Model R-F Fore-Dr. Rbt.-2P	1000	4300	5400	8700	16,500	30,000
Model T-4 Fore-Dr. Tr.-5P	1100	4700	6100	9900	19,000	33,000
Comet Roadster	1200	4500	5800	9500	18,000	32,000

Forty-Five — 4-cyl., 45 hp, 115" wb

Model T-R Pirate Rbt.-2P	1350	4500	5800	9500	18,000	32,000
Model T-5 Aristocrat Tour.	1400	4900	6300	10,300	21,000	34,000
Comet Roadster	1600	4700	6100	9900	19,000	33,000

1924 Pennant, taxicab, NAHC

PENNANT — Kalamazoo, Michigan — (1924-1925) — The Pennant was the taxicab manufactured by the Barley Motor Car Company of Kalamazoo, makers of the Roamer and the Barley. Like most taxis of the period, it carried a Buda four-cylinder engine on a 115-inch wheelbase chassis. Its disc wheels and brown Spanish leather upholstery were distinctive — and a dome light and heater were included as standard equipment. The Pennant was introduced during the summer of 1923 and was continued in production through 1925.

PENNEY — "It is reported that J.W. Penney & Sons, Mechanic Falls, Maine, will organize a company to build motor carriages there," declared *The Horseless Age* in February 1899. Further declarations regarding the Penney enterprise were not forthcoming.

1901 Penney, steamer, NAHC

PENNEY STEAM — (1901) — Having "contracted a bad case of the automobile fever" in the summer of 1901, H.D. Penney built himself a steam runabout powered by a two-cylinder vertical engine. Initially trying a kerosene burner, he discovered that he had come up with a "highly efficient . . . means for creating excitement among the populace and exercise for the members of the fire department, who on several occasions chased me along the street with fire extinguishers." Nor was that Penney's only problem — from lighting the pilot light to working up sufficient steam to get underway usually required an hour and a half "when the pilot light was on its good behavior." It was back to the drawing board. Gasoline was used for fuel thereafter, and the carriage was virtually rebuilt, with a wheel substituted for the original lever which had been mightily unsteady. Numerous other problems evolved and were ultimately solved, "but only after a large amount of study and experiment, backed by a liberal amount of money, never mind how much." Had he to do it over again, H.D. Penney said, he wouldn't. Just about the only matter Penney didn't mention in his long, wonderfully hilarious story about his car, which appeared in *The Automobile* in 1905, was where he had built it.

1895 Pennington, (Kane-Pennington), victoria, NAHC

PENNINGTON — Ohio, New York, Wisconsin, et al. — (1894-1900) —
Had communication been more sophisticated in those days, the budding automobile industry might have seen Edward Joel Pennington coming. Even before the advent of the horseless age, he had proven himself remarkably adept as a confidence man, promoting gargantuan schemes and floating grandiose companies for the production or exploitation of such sundries as freight elevators, airships and monorails. His performance upon coming to town was of consummate artistry — a visit to the local bank or businessman's club, a fabulous display of wealth, a prodigious dropping of big names, a lavish exhibition of official parchment documents. He tended to travel around a lot. He was in Chicago in March of 1893 when he applied for his first automotive patent, which he assigned to his Motor Cycle Company of Cleveland. During the summer of 1894 he was in Cortland, New York talking C.B. Hitchcock into manufacturing a line of Pennington-designed motorcycles and victorias, but the one experimental model he produced couldn't travel a block without overheating and seizing up — so Pennington left town, and the Hitchcock Manufacturing Company, heretofore a prosperous wagon producer, went into receivership. That fall he was briefly back in Cleveland to apply for a patent on a two-wheeler with oversized pneumatic tires that Pennington called "impuncturable," though they were scarcely that, and then he took off for Wisconsin when a wealthy industrialist from Racine named Thomas Kane offered development money. Kane manufactured church and school furniture and stationary engines for dairies — and was anxious to break into the automobile industry. The Racine Motor Vehicle Company was organized for this purpose. Pennington provided a patent based on his "long-

1897 Pennington, three-wheeler, NAHC

1900 Pennington, runabout, NAHC

mingling spark ignition system" which did away with a carburetor and allowed an engine to be run on virtually any sort of fuel. Pennington was fond of using candle wax in model demonstrations. Both the engine and the victoria in which it was placed were referred to by the name of Kane-Pennington. A few of these cars were built, and none ran very far. They appeared to be made up of the frames of two girl's bicycles with a platform inbetween and two small engines coupled together and driven on a common shaft. Pennington said he was building four entries for the Chicago Times-Herald Contest of 1895, but they were not among the official starters, and on the day of the contest Pennington was on his way to England anyway, where he allied himself with Harry John Lawson who had plans to establish a monopoly in the British motor industry and thought Pennington could help. A few cars resulted from this but the plan did not work, whereupon Pennington returned to the United States to establish the Anglo-American Rapid Vehicle Company in New York in 1900, which purportedly was preparing to manufacture Pennington cars in the Barnes bicycle plant in Syracuse managed by E.C. Stearns, who later got into the automobile business himself legitimately. During this same period, Pennington established the Pennsylvania Steam Vehicle Company to promote the Tractobile, a forecarriage engine attachment to make a horsedrawn carriage horseless. Pennington was back in Racine briefly during 1902 because it is on record that he left town in October before paying his bill at the Hotel Racine. (The hotel got part of its money back by selling some of the clothing he left behind in what must have been a hasty departure.) Thereafter Pennington also jumped hotel bills in Cincinnati and Pittsburgh, and in the fall of 1903 was back in Cleveland. This time the new Pennington enterprise was called the Cleveland Motor Company, and the plan was to build low-priced delivery wagons and "touring cars of 160 horse power to cost from $20,000 to $30,000 apiece." One of these cars was reportedly being built for the general manager of the May Company, a prominent Cleveland department store. At the 1904 Cleveland Automobile Show, Pennington exhibited his new "Automobile Horse" (his old Tractobile), a motorized baby buggy and a motor boat — but no cars. He entertained lavishly from a luxurious suite of rooms in one of the best hotels in Cleveland, paid for by four checks, all of which bounced. His movements from then until 1906 are unknown, which suggests that someone somewhere may have caught up with him, and the room he was now occupying was courtesy of the state. In 1907 he was in Milwaukee promoting a 16 hp $300 car, which was never built. Then he disappeared again. Around 1910 he was in Massachusetts unsuccessfully trying to sue Hendee Manufacturing Company for infringement of his patents in the Indian motorcycle, and also promoting an aeronautical school in Springfield, which never opened. He died in that city the following year. Ironically, not all of Pennington's ideas were as outlandish as his schemes. The 1896 Penninton three-wheeler on display at the National Motor Museum in England — the only known surviving Pennington vehicle — features a form of fuel injection which though primitive was certainly a progressive idea before the turn of the century.

1917 Pennsy, 5-pass. touring, WLB

1127

PENNSY — Pittsburgh, Pennsylvania — (1916-1918) — Following the failure of the Penn in New Castle, Elmore Gregg returned to Pittsburgh to try again with the Pennsy. That he wasn't sure what he wanted to call this new venture initially is indicated by the fact that it was referred to only as The Motors Company while in the process of organization in 1915. A contest to name the firm — with the first car off the line to be the prize — was won by a man from Duquesne who suggested Pennsy. Early in 1916 Pennsy Motors Company was formally established with a capital stock of $500,000. The new firm absorbed the truck-building Kosmath Company of Detroit, and a good many Kosmath people trekked to Pittsburgh too. The Kosmath truck was to be continued in production alongside the new passenger car. The Pennsy, advertised as the "Pride of Pittsburgh," was a four-cylinder (Lycoming or GB&S engine) roadster or touring car, each carrying an $855 price tag. The car was designed by Edward T. Birdsall, and the pilot models were built in Detroit; superintendent of the Pennsy factory in Pittsburgh was Guy Sintz, son of Clark Sintz, the old engine man from Grand Rapids. Production began during the summer of 1916, haltingly. In January 1917 the Kosmath truck was discontinued; in March Edward Birdsall left to join the Pullman Motor Car Company in York, taking his chief draftsman with him. The month previous Pennsy Motors Company had been petitioned into receivership as charges of mismanagement and stock oversubscription were flung about. Later during 1917 Elmore Gregg and some of the other Pennsy people reorganized as the Pennsylvania Motor Car Company and for the 1918 model year offered the old Pennsy (occasionally referring to it as the new Pennsylvania) and adding a six-cylinder (Continental engine) companion car as well. But nobody was fooled. In January 1919, *Motor Age* reported that the company was "believed to be out of business," as it indeed was.

1916-1917 PENNSY
Model R — 4-cyl., 30/35 hp, 114" wb

	FP	5	4	3	2	1
Touring-5P	855	4000	5000	8000	15,000	28,000
Roadster-2P	855	3900	4800	7700	14,300	27,000

1918 PENNSY
Four — 35/40 hp, 115" wb

	FP	5	4	3	2	1
Roadster-2P	1185	4200	5200	8400	15,700	29,000
Touring-5P	1185	4300	5400	8700	16,500	30,000

Six — 48 hp, 119" wb

	FP	5	4	3	2	1
Roadster-4P	1685	4900	6300	10,300	21,000	34,000
Touring-5P	1685	5000	6500	11,000	22,000	35,000

PENNSYLVANIA — The Pennsylvania Automotive Corporation was a $50,000 Delaware incorporation from early 1920 for the manufacture and sale of automobiles. Incorporators were W.I.N. Lofland, Frank Jackson and Mark W. Cole. Manufacture is doubted.

The Pennsylvania Electric Vehicle Company was organized in 1899 with a $6 million capital stock to serve as the dealership in that state for the Columbia electrics built by the Electric Vehicle Company in Hartford, Connecticut, and also to operate a taxi service in Philadelphia. The firm did no manufacturing itself and was dissolved during the summer of 1906, though disgruntled stockholders kept the company alive for several years thereafter in the courts.

The Pennsylvania Electrical & Railway Supply Company of Pittsburgh produced the Rex Buckboard in 1903. Refer to Rex Buckboard.

The Pennsylvania Motor Car Company was organized in Philadelphia, Pennsylvania during the summer of 1910 with a capital stock of $200,000 to manufacture and deal in automobiles. Incorporators were C.L. Hearn, V. Atkinson and J.M. Frere. Manufacture is doubted.

The Pennsylvania Motor Car Company was organized in New York City during the fall of 1910 with a capital stock of $50,000 to "manufacture various kinds of motors, engines, motor cars, motorcycles, motor boats, aeroplanes, etc." Incorporators were D. Hamilton, A.A. Russell and B.H. Denny. Manufacture of a car is doubted.

The Pennsylvania Steam Vehicle Company of Carlisle was a turn-of-the-century venture promoted by Edward Joel Pennington. Its product was the Tractobile, a device for converting a horsedrawn carriage into a horseless one. Refer to Tractobile.

"It is stated that the Pennsylvania Railroad is to manufacture automobiles in its Altoona shops," reported *The Horseless Age* in August 1907," to be used in place of the cabs now in the terminal service of the road." It appears the Pennsylvania Railroad changed its mind.

PENNSYLVANIA — Washington, D.C. — (1900-1901) — The Pennsylvania Horseless Carriage Company was organized in Washington D.C. in 1900 for the manufacture of an automobile using coal oil for fuel. The claim that the prototype had traveled sixty miles on two gallons of coal oil was made that June, followed in July by manager Thomas C. Poe's revelation that the car would be sold for a phenomenally low $450. "A rush to buy them is confidently expected," reported *The Motor Vehicle Review.* No rush ensued. Meanwhile, the company also announced its intention to market an attachment for conversion of a horse-drawn carriage into a horseless one. "A new and different set of wheels and axles are required," it was explained, "but beyond that there is no change in the vehicle necessitated by its being converted into a motor vehicle." No rush ensued on that one either.

1907 Pennsylvania, model 7, touring, HAC

1128

PENNSYLVANIA — Bryn Mawr, Pennsylvania — (1907-1911) — The Pennsylvania Auto-Motor Company was organized in Bryn Mawr late in 1906 by Phineas Prouty, A.E. Kennedy, C.J. McIlvaine — and introduced its product at the Grand Central Palace show in New York City at year's end. The first Pennsylvania carried a four-cylinder 35 hp Rutenber engine, all subsequent cars were fitted with powerplants of the company's own design. These were fours and sixes which ranged from 29 to 75 hp. Price tags were equally wide ranging at $2100 to $4700. Pennsylvania advertising laid heavy emphasis on the fact that many of its bodies were made by Quinby, "recognized and accepted as America's best." The company was in financial trouble by the fall of 1910, but at that time a plan was evolved to settle with creditors and continue the business. In August of 1911 another creditor sued, however, and this one was J.M. Quinby & Company, alleging that Pennsylvania had reneged on its 1909 contract before the full delivery of bodies ordered. The end came quickly after that, further Pennsylvania creditors petitioning the company into involuntary bankruptcy by October 1911.

1907 PENNSYLVANIA
Model 7 — 4-cyl., 35 hp, 112" wb

	FP	5	4	3	2	1
Touring-5P	2800	4200	5200	8400	15,700	29,000

1908 Pennsylvania, type C, touring, HAC

1908 PENNSYLVANIA
Type C — 4-cyl., 50 hp, 114" wb

Touring	2800	6400	9300	14,500	33,000	45,000
Roadster	2800	6300	9000	14,000	32,000	44,000

1909 Pennsylvania, type C, touring, WLB

1909 Pennsylvania, type F-6, baby tonneau, HAC

1909 PENNSYLVANIA

Type D — 4-cyl., 29 hp, 110" wb

	FP	5	4	3	2	1
Touring-5P	2100	4200	5200	8400	15,700	29,000
Roadster-2P	2000	4000	5000	8000	15,000	28,000
Baby Tonneau-5P	2100	4200	5200	8400	15,700	29,000

Type C — 4-cyl., 50 hp, 114" wb

Touring-5P	3000	6400	9300	14,500	33,000	45,000
Touring-7P	3200	6500	9500	15,000	34,000	46,000

Type E — 4-cyl., 36 hp, 122" wb

Touring-7P	3800	4200	5200	8400	15,700	29,000

Type F6 — 6-cyl., 54 hp, 129" wb

Baby Tonneau-5P	4500	6400	9300	14,500	33,000	45,000

1910 Pennsylvania, model F-675, touring, HAC

1910 PENNSYLVANIA

Model D-25 — 4-cyl., 29 hp, 114" wb

	FP	5	4	3	2	1
Touring-4/5P	2500	—	—	—	—	32,000

Model C-50 — 4-cyl., 50 hp, 114" wb

Touring-4/5P	3000	6400	9300	14,500	33,000	45,000

Model B-50 — 4-cyl., 50 hp, 122" wb

Touring-7P	3500	7200	11,300	17,700	38,700	50,000

Model F-675 — 6-cyl., 75 hp, 129" wb

Touring-5/7P	4500	7600	12,500	19,400	42,400	55,000

1911 Pennsylvania, model C-50, touring, HAC

1911 PENNSYLVANIA

Model C-50 — 4-cyl., 50 hp, 117" wb

Toy Tonneau-4P	3000	5800	8000	12,500	28,000	40,000
Touring-5P	3000	6000	8500	13,000	30,000	42,000

Model B-50 — 4-cyl., 50 hp, 122" wb

Touring-7P	3500	6400	9300	14,500	33,000	45,000

Model F-6 — 6-cyl., 60 hp, 137" wb

Touring-7P	4500	7200	11,300	17,700	38,700	50,000
Toy Tonneau-4P	4500	7000	10,800	16,900	37,100	49,000

Model H-6 — 6-cyl., 60 hp, 137" wb

Touring-7P	4700	7600	12,500	19,400	42,400	55,000

PENNSYLVANIA — Chester, Pennsylvania — (1908) — During the summer of 1908 the Pennsylvania Taximeter Cab Company of Philadelphia announced the completion of thirty cars for its service, the vehicles having been built at the Hinckle-O'Brien-Lewis Company in Chester. John C. Hinckle was the president of both companies, and the cars were intended for taxi service and not for sale. They were also the largest taxicabs in Philadelphia, so Hinckle bragged, with accommodations for five persons besides the driver. The Pennsylvania company operated out of the Bellevue-Stratford garage. How long it continued to manufacture its own taxis in Chester is not known.

PENNSYLVANIA SIX — The Pennsylvania Six was built in Yonkers, New York in 1909 — and whether any cars were indeed marketed under that name is problematical. Within months the venture had moved to Du Bois, Pennsylvania and the name Keystone Six had been decided upon. Refer to Keystone Six.

PENOBSCOT — The Penobscot Motor Company was organized in Bangor, Maine late in 1910 with a capital stock of $100,000 to "manufacture and sell automobiles, motors, engines, motor boats, and aeroplanes." Incorporators were Fred D. Oliver and J.S. Howe, both of Bangor. Manufacture of a car is doubted.

PENTON — The Penton Motor Company was incorporated with a capital stock of $50,000 in 1927. E.W. Penton was president, H.S. Sherman vice-president and J.F. Potts secretary-treasurer of this Cleveland, Ohio company. The Penton plant was located at 1890 East 40th Street, and the firm indicated its products as "electric goods." That an automobile may have been among them was reported, but has not been documented with certainty.

PEOPLE'S — The People's Auto-Delivery Company was organized in Buffalo, New York during the spring of 1908 with a capital stock of $100,000 to "run a baggage and freight transfer business and manufacture motor cars, carriages, carts, motor vehicles, etc." Incorporators were D.S. Ferris and H.E. Barnett. Manufacture of a car is doubted.

The People's Taxicab Company was organized in New York City during the summer of 1910 with a capital stock of $20,000 to manufacture, deal in and operate taxicabs and motorcars. Incorporators were Joseph H. Wittemann, E.L. Merry and T.H. Wilson. Manufacture is doubted.

1900 People's, runabout, NAHC

PEOPLE'S — Cleveland, Ohio — (1900-1902) — The People's Automobile Company was organized in 1900 as the result of a prolonged street railway men's strike in Cleveland. It was capitalized at $50,000 and a local engineer named Paul Gaeth was put in charge. The plan was to operate motor omnibuses in lieu of the idle streetcars and to garner a nice profit doing it. Two factors contrived to upset this plan. First, the "rail-less streetcar," as it was called, was fully twenty-two feet long and was fitted with a single-cylinder 3 hp engine which could scarcely have been adequate to the task. The first prototype didn't operate at all, but Paul Gaeth finally got one running, and several examples were built. Then the second factor arrived; the striking rail workers wouldn't allow the vehicles on the streets. So much for that plan. Thereupon the engines were removed from the buses and fitted into small two-passenger runabouts — for which they were much better suited anyway — and were marketed as People's automobiles for $650. People's also offered its bus for sale ("seats 26 persons; will carry all who can get on") and built a kit car that it sold under the name Buckmobile. All this activity ended in January 1902 when People's went into receivership. Some months later, Paul Gaeth began his own automobile company. The Gaeth was an eminently more successful car.

PEORIA — The Peoria Automobile Company was organized during the summer of 1904 with a capital stock of $5000 for the manufacture of motor vehicles in Peoria, Illinois. Incorporators were S.K. Hatfield, Charles L. Gage and E.M. Giles. Manufacture of a car is doubted.

The Peoria Motor Vehicle Company was a $150,000 incorporation from early 1900 for the manufacture of automobiles in Peoria, Illinois. "The works will have the capacity of three vehicles per day," The Automobile Review noted in February. Manufacture, however, is doubted.

The Peoria Rubber & Manufacturing Company of Peoria, Illinois was listed as an automobile manufacturer in the Hiscox book Horseless Vehicles, Automobiles, Motor Cycles published in 1900. The only vehicle known to have been built at the factory was a "motor gun carriage" for a Major Davidson in 1899.

The Peoria Specialty Company was a $50,000 Delaware incorporation from late 1915 for the manufacture of motor cars, trucks and accessories. Incorporators were P.P. Cooley, R.S. Cooley and B.N. Cooley. Manufacture of a car is doubted.

PERFECT — A car called the Perfect has been indicated on various car rosters as being manufactured by the Saint Anne Kerosene Motor Company of Saint Anne, Illinois in 1906. This is in error. The firm was organized in March that year with a capital stock of $100,000 by B.H. Pomeroy, A. Sutton and W.A. Quertim, but manufacture was indicated from the beginning to be of engines only, which carried the Perfect tradename. Obviously the designation was not an apt one, because the Saint Anne Kerosene Motor Company was out of business by the spring of 1907, its machinery and equipment subsequently purchased by the Dolson Automobile Company of Charlotte, Michigan.

"The Perfect Automobile Manufacturing Company, 1446 Bedford Avenue, Brooklyn, expect to place a car upon the market soon," reported The Horseless Age during the summer of 1905. Expectations do not appear to have been fulfilled, however, there being no evidence that this New York City venture ever got off the ground.

1908 Perfection, 5-pass. touring, NAHC

PERFECTION — South Bend, Indiana — (1907-1908) — The Perfection Automobile Works provides a sterling example of everything going wrong quickly. The company was organized in Niles, Michigan but moved to South Bend in February in 1907 before a single car had been built. In South Bend the plan was to build the C-F car for Cornish-Friedberg of Chicago, but that company decided to build its own instead. The Perfection arrived a few months later as a 42 hp four and a 70 hp six. Sales were lackluster. In January of 1908 Newton C. Gauntt arrived from Yakima, Washington with an offer to buy Perfection out which was too attractive to resist. The deal was consummated, but what Gauntt received from it remains a mystery. Apparently the Perfection people had neglected to advise its creditors of this maneuver and a couple of others. In February the Perfection creditors filed a bankruptcy petition against the company, alleging that $10,000 worth of its cars had been transferred to American Trust Company as a delaying action. It would appear at that time the Gauntt deal was still under wraps. It probably remained there.

1907-1908 PERFECTION
Four — 42 hp, 116" wb

	FP	5	4	3	2	1
Touring-5P	1850	4500	5800	9500	18,000	32,000
Six — 70 hp, 124" wb						
Touring	2500	6700	9900	15,500	34,800	47,000

1913 Perfex, roadster, WLB

PERFEX — Los Angeles, California — (1912-1913) — The first Perfex was tested on the streets of Los Angeles on June 29th, 1912. It was designed by James R. Fouch who was described as the "moving spirit in the enterprise," although the money for its manufacture was supplied by several Los Angeles capitalists who put themselves into the company's executive chairs. James Fouch managed the factory. The Perfex was a four-cylinder 199-cubic-inch (G.B. & S engine) roadster with selective sliding gear transmission and a $1050 price tag. A dozen cars were built in 1912, and the Perfex roadster was continued in production into 1913. In July of 1913 a truck using the same T-head engine as the Perfex car was added to the line, and by year's end Perfex president Paul Brown, Jr. announced that commercial vehicles only would be produced in the future. Whether this decision was not to James Fouch's liking is unknown, but he immediately left the company and set himself up in a little machine shop elsewhere in Los Angeles to market a car under his own name. The Perfex truck continued in manufacture into the World War I years. The Perfex venture had risen from the ashes of the Moro — and was housed at the same 126 East Jefferson facility. Former Moro secretary Ora Hutchings had stayed on; J.B. Morrow had departed.

1912-1913 PERFEX
Four — 22.5 hp, 106" wb

Roadster-2P	1050	3100	4200	6300	10,500	22,000

PERKINS — This experimental car was produced in Springfield, Massachusetts in 1906 by Julian L. and James A. Perkins. It went into production the year following as the Bailey, named for Bertram Bailey, the man who had put up the money for manufacture. Refer to Bailey.

PERKINS — Detroit, Michigan — (1914-1915) — A car called the Perkins has been reported to have been built in 1914-1915 by the Massnick-Phipps Manufacturing Company of Detroit. Details regarding it are lacking, but it is known that the firm built the Robie for a Chicago cyclecar producer in 1914 and made the V-8 engine for the Remington of 1915. "Contracting machinists and auto parts" was the way Walter Phipps and Frederick C. Massnick described their work in Detroit city directories of the period. Their plant was located in 1091 Champlain, and their modesty was becoming. The Perkins four- and eight-cylinder engines they produced were well respected.

PERMAX — Los Angeles, California — (1914-1915) — The Permax was the second automobile from the Union Car Company of Los Angeles. Shortly after introducing its first, the Gage cyclecar, the company decided that it was too flimsy a machine for West Coast conditions. A Macomber 18/20 rotary engine was to power the new Permax, which was to be offered as a two-seater roadster on a 108-inch wheelbase, with standard tread and a selective sliding gear transmission. Fuel efficiency of 40-50 mpg was claimed, and a price tag of $385 was promised. "It is not our intention to operate east of the Rocky Mountains," the Union Car Company announced in December of 1914, "But to confine our efforts to the western part of the country and build a right car at a right price that will bring in purchasers in the right number." Something went wrong. Quite possibly the only production the Permax saw were the pilot models. L.J. Newberry was president of this venture, Thomas H.P. Purman the general manager.

1900 Perret Electric, MVMA

PERRET ELECTRIC — New York, New York — (1900) — In 1896, in association with his partner J.A. Barrett, A. Frank Perret built an electric car in New York City. Although it operated successfully, it was a five-passenger vehicle requiring heavy storage batteries and thus was quite cumbersome, which distressed Perret. The car was not marketed, and the Barrett-Perret partnership broke up soon thereafter. On his own now, Perret began experimentation in storage battery design. According to a February 1900 issue of *Electrical World and Engineer*, Perret believed by that time that he had come up with a battery combining "lightness in weight, high rate of charge and discharge, long life and freedom from buckling." It was a lead and sulfuric acid type, and he organized the Perret Storage Battery Company at 21 State Street in New York for its manufacture. By 1900 too he had built a small runabout to test the battery, and he indicated that he would build further cars to order though the main focus of his production would be storage batteries.

PERRINE — The Perrine Manufacturing Company was organized in Cleveland, Ohio during the fall of 1912 with a capital stock of $10,000 to manufacture and deal in automobiles. Incorporators were R.A. Wilbur, Charles S. Watner, H.H. Burton, Benjamin A. Gage and A.S. Dole. Manufacture is doubted.

PERRY — Boston, Massachusetts — (1896) — In 1896 O.H. Perry of 31 Milk Street in Boston reported that he was completing a motor carriage in which he was fitting a friction transmission invented by H.H. Cummings, who resided at 110 High Street. This car was never marketed. Two years later, however, Perry was marketing a vehicle he called the Boston-Haynes-Apperson. This was nothing more than the Haynes-Apperson from Kokomo, Indiana to which Perry fitted a few custom accessories. There is no indication that he sold this car in any year other than 1898.

PERRY LEWIS — St. Louis, Missouri — (1895) — J.D. Perry Lewis of 3014 Morgan Street in St. Louis built an electric car in 1895 which, *The Horseless Age* said, "he conducted around the streets of that city with considerable eclat." It was a two-seater highwheeler with a 30-cell chloride battery underneath. Its motor, which Lewis called a quadrupler, consisted of a large armature surrounded by four secondary coils; connected to this was a ratchet wheel which fit into a large cogged wheel built solid with the axle. Ten hours were required to charge the battery, whereafter the vehicle could be run for four hours at a speed of 12 mph. A street-car type controller regulated the speed; the car was steered by lever and braked by foot. Its inventor did not consider manufacture.

PERRYMOBILE — The Perrymobile Company of Los Angeles, California has been indicated on various rosters as the manufacturer of an automobile from 1942-1945. This is not the case. "The Power of Liquid & Air," Frank R. Perry advertised, "A Sensational New Type Power Plant using Non-Rationed Fuel." In lieu of gasoline, the Perry-designed engine functioned with "kerosene, stove oil, distillate or any low-grade fuel," and the Perrymobile Company was obviously an attempt to provide a wartime fuel-deprived public with an alternative to stay on the road. The Perrymobile engine was made available as a twenty-five-dollar set of plans; the purchaser had to build the engine himself, or have it built for him, the Perrymobile Company doing no manufacturing itself. Frank R. Perry installed one of his engines in a modified Ford, but that was as close as the Perrymobile ever came to being a car.

PESAGUS — This frequent typographical error from 1902 indicates that some trade press editors didn't know their mythology well. The company which built this car in Harvey, Illinois was called the Pegasus Automobile Company. Refer to Pegasus.

P.E.T. — Detroit, Michigan — (1913-1914) — In November of 1913 Philip E. Teats announced the forthcoming manufacture of his cyclecar, which he planned, probably wisely, to market under his initials rather than his name. A four-cylinder engine, a 42-inch tread, a 104-inch wheelbase and a $340 price tag represented the total information he provided regarding his P.E.T. A prototype definitely was built, but although Teats mentioned that he had secured capital for its production from Canadian capitalists across the river from Detroit, it does not appear that production followed. Most probably, Philip Teats then returned to his regular job, which was as assistant accountant for the city of Detroit.

PETELER — Although the Peteler Car Company of St. Paul, Minnesota has been indicated on various rosters as an automobile producer in 1912-1913, this appears unlikely. City directory listings for the firm indicate its product variously as "cars, wheels and narrow-gauge railways" and "dump cars, car wheels and castings." Any cars built by Peteler undoubtedly were destined for the rails and not the roads.

1900 Peteler, NOPL

PETELER — New Orleans, Louisiana — (1900) — "The first automobile built in this city, and the only carriage automobile here, is the product of the mechanical genius of Adolph Peteler, a young Westerner who settled here a few years ago as a bicycle repair man and who decided to build a gasoline automobile in his leisure moments." Thus reported the *Times-Democrat* of New Orleans on June 18th, 1900. Although the Gardner

Motor Company, Ltd. may have built an automobile using one of its engines earlier in New Orleans, that vehicle was strictly experimental and was not publicized. Adolph Peteler apparently wanted everyone in town to know about his car; he drove it repeatedly at the turn of the century. The design of the entire vehicle was his own, though he had the engine cast and the woodworking done outside. Peteler's engine was a two-cylinder unit developing 7 hp at 500 rpm. It was fitted under the body of the carriage, with final drive to the rear wheels by means of friction clutches operated by a single lever. Maximum speed was 20 mph. An automatic divided axle connection enabled the driving wheels to revolve at different speeds, and the front wheels were arranged to allow the outer wheel to traverse a circle of greater radius than the inner — all this to make turning easier. "Mechanics pronounce Mr. Peteler's automobile a very superior mechanism in every respect, and judges of automobiles say that it is a most graceful-appearing gas automobile," declared the *Times-Democrat*. "Four and a half gallons of gasoline will run the carriage ten hours at from 15 to 18 miles an hour, covering 150 to 180 miles at a cost of 67 1/2 cents." Admirable though the machine was, there is no indication that Adolph Peteler ever built another.

1914 Peter Pan, cyclecar, touring, WLB

PETER PAN — Quincy, Massachusetts — (1914-1915) — "A New Englander that shows class" was the assessment of *Light Car Age* regarding this cyclecar called the Peter Pan. It was produced by the Randall Company which shared its offices and factory with the Wollaston Foundry Company in Quincy. L.W. Newell was general manager of the firm. Unlike most cyclecars, the Peter Pan's engine was its own, an ohv water-cooled 24 hp four built by the Wollaston Foundry. Both a four-passenger touring car and a two-passenger roadster were offered on the same 106-inch chassis with 48-inch tread. A channel steel frame, suspension by semi-elliptics in front with full-floating cantilever springs in the rear, a three-speed selective transmission and final drive by shaft were especially progressive features for a cyclecar. The price range of $400-$450 was attractive, and the sharp vee of the Peter Pan's radiator distinctive. Nonetheless, like more than ninety percent of the cyclecars introduced in America in 1914, the Peter Pan did not survive 1915.

1914-1915 PETER PAN
Cyclecar — 4-cyl., 24 hp, 106" wb

	FP	5	4	3	2	1
Touring-4P	450	2300	3300	4600	7500	16,000
Roadster-2P	400	2200	3200	4400	7000	15,000

1921 Peters, roadster, WLB

PETERS — Pleasantville & Trenton, New Jersey — (1921) / Bethlehem, Pennsylvania — (1922) — Although Peters Motor Corporation had three different factories in three different cities in three short years, it would appear that little manufacturing was done in any of them. The Peters car was simply a Brook by another name, and probably the Spacke Machine & Tool Company of Indianapolis which manufactured the Brook put together most of the Peters cars as well, though Peters may have provided the nameplate and final detailing in its own plant. The plant of Peters Motor Corporation was in Pleasantville, New Jersey initially, although by August of 1920 president E. James Peters announced its removal to Trenton and the former Reeves-Cubberley engine factory there. Introduced as a 1921 model, the Peters was advertised as "Everybody's Car" with an operating expense of a cent a mile. It was powered by Spacke's two-cylinder 9/13 hp air-cooled engine and featured a two-speed planetary transmission and a dummy radiator which served to house, somewhat hazardously, the gasoline tank. The wheelbase was 90 inches, the tread 46. The price tag was $385, and it bought a two-seater roadster which could be easily converted

1131

to a light delivery. Because the Spacke company was operating under receivership in 1921, E. James Peters began searching that year for better quarters than Trenton provided, since the likelihood was that he would soon find it necessary to manufacture all of his car himself. In April of 1922 he began moving equipment from his Trenton factory to a building formerly occupied by the Bethlehem Paper Company in Bethlehem, Pennsylvania. At the same time, he commenced negotiations for fifteen acres adjacent for future expansion. His firm was now renamed Peters Autocar Company, but after Autocar sued, it was again renamed to Peters Motor Car Division of Romer Motor Corporation. Romer was a new manufacturer in Massachusetts, but whether any Peters cars were ever produced there is very much open to question. Specifications for the Peters as a Romer product were 10/14 hp engine, 100-inch wheelbase, 51-inch tread and $295 price tag.

1915 Peters-Walton, cyclecar three-wheeler, WLB

PETERS-WALTON — Philadelphia, Pennsylvania — (1915) / PETERS TRICAR — (1916) — The Peters-Walton was a cyclecar produced by the Ludlow Auto Engineering Company of Philadelphia. It was a three-wheeler with its two-cylinder 9 hp air-cooled engine mounted over the single front wheel. The wheelbase was 82 inches, with accommodations for two passengers seated tandem. The transmission was said to be hydraulic. The price was $390, and the vehicle was continued in production a short while in 1916 when it was marketed under the name Peters Tricar as a commercial light delivery. The Peters involved in this venture was Karl R., incidentally, and although he appears to have continued his efforts to produce the three-wheeler in quantity into the early Twenties, there is no evidence that he was involved with the four-wheeled Peters of that period.

1915-1916 PETERS-WALTON/PETERS TRICAR
Cyclecar — 2-cyl., 9 hp, 82" wb

	FP	5	4	3	2	1
Tandem Roadster-2P	390	1600	2700	3800	5800	12,000

PETERSON — Kenmare, North Dakota — (c.1914) — Precisely when Hilmer Peterson of Kenmare built his automobile is not known, but it was a 12 hp runabout that was licensed in 1914. Further details are lacking.

PETERSON-CULP — This was one of three varying designations given to the steam car to be produced by the Peterson-Culp Gearless Steam Automobile Company of Denver, Colorado in 1918-1919. Refer to Gearless.

1909 Petrel, roadster, HAC

PETREL — Kenosha, Wisconsin — (1909) / Milwaukee, Wisconsin — (1909-1912) — In November of 1908 the new Petrel Motor Car Company moved into the Kenosha factory of the defunct Earl Motor Car Company. The man who put it there was Samuel W. Watkins, whose Beaver Manufacturing Company of Milwaukee was well known in the engine-building field and who had been persuaded to enter the automotive arena by John and Harry Waite. The Waite brothers had already built several cars themselves in a small rented store on Milwaukee's south side. Now, with Watkins' backing, they were ready for the big time. Watkins was general manager of the new company, Harry Waite was chief engineer, John Waite plant superintendent. The name Petrel had been chosen for the new car because of its "unusual ability to make good speed over very rough roads." It veritably flew, advertising claimed. A friction transmission and double chain drive were featured. Although a six-cylinder Petrel was

offered in 1909, it was discontinued in 1910, and "The Aristocrat of Medium Priced Cars," as the Petrel was promoted, remained a four for the rest of its life. During the summer of 1909 Petrel left the former typewriter factory which had been the Earl's home in Kenosha and moved to new quarters in a plant on Virginia Street in Milwaukee owned by the furniture-manufacturing W.S. Seaman Company. It was for Petrel that Seaman built its first automobile bodies. Seaman later became prominent in the coachbuilding field, of course, and ultimately became part of the Nash empire. As for the Petrel, its reign was decidedly brief. On February 11th, 1910 involuntary bankruptcy proceedings were instituted against the company. By January of 1911 Samuel Watkins had found an expedient way out of his problems; he sold both Petrel and Beaver to Filer and Stowell, the builders of the Corliss steam engine in Milwaukee. Filer and Stowell moved the Petrel part and parcel into a brand-new factory just outside the city limits. There the Petrel was continued in production into the 1912 model year, and a new car called the F.S. was introduced. Both were gone by the end of 1912, however. Total Petrel and F.S. production was fewer than a thousand cars.

1909 PETREL
Four — 30 hp

	FP	5	4	3	2	1
Touring-5P (115" wb)	1500	3100	4200	6300	10,500	22,000
Roadster-2P (107" wb)	1350	3000	4000	6000	9500	21,000

Six — 50 hp

	FP	5	4	3	2	1
Touring-5P (122" wb)	2500	5000	6500	11,000	22,000	35,000
Roadster-2P (116" wb)	2500	4900	6300	10,300	21,000	34,000

1910 Petrel, model F, touring, HAC

1910 PETREL
Four — 30 hp

	FP	5	4	3	2	1
Model D Rds. (109" wb)	1350	4000	5000	8000	15,000	28,000
Model E Toy Tonn.-4P (115" wb)	1500	4200	5200	8400	15,700	29,000
Model F Tr.-5P (115" wb)	1500	4200	5200	8400	15,700	29,000

1911 Petrel, model 40, roadster, WLB

1912 Petrel, model 25, roadster, HAC

1911 PETREL

Four — 22 hp, 98" wb

	FP	5	4	3	2	1
Model 25 Torpedo-2P	850	4000	5000	8000	15,000	28,000
Model 25 Torpedo-4P	1000	4200	5200	8400	15,700	29,000

Four — 30 hp, 115" wb

	FP	5	4	3	2	1
Model 45 Toy Tonneau	1350	4400	5600	9200	17,300	31,000
Model 55 Touring	1350	4400	5600	9200	17,300	31,000
Model 40 Rds. (108" wb)	1350	4300	5400	8700	16,500	30,000

Four — 40 hp, 118" wb

	FP	5	4	3	2	1
Model 65 Fore-Door Tr.	1600	5000	6500	11,000	22,000	35,000
Model 65 Toy Tonneau	1600	5000	6500	11,000	22,000	35,000
Model 75 Torpedo	1600	5000	6500	11,000	22,000	35,000

1912 PETREL

Four — 25 hp, 100" wb

	FP	5	4	3	2	1
Model 25 Fore-Door Rds.	850	3100	4200	6300	10,500	22,000
Model 35 Fore-Door Tr.	1000	3200	4300	6500	11,000	23,000

Four — 35/40 hp, 108" wb

	FP	5	4	3	2	1
Model 40 Roadster	1350	4700	6100	9900	19,000	33,000
Model 45 Toy Tonneau	1500	4700	6100	9900	19,000	33,000
Model 55 Touring	1500	4900	6300	10,300	21,000	34,000

Four — 40/45 hp, 118" wb

	FP	5	4	3	2	1
Model 65 Fore-Door Toy Tonneau	1600	5800	8000	12,500	28,000	40,000
Model 75 Fore-Door Tr.	1600	5800	8000	12,500	28,000	40,000

PETROLEUM — The Petroleum Automobile Engine Company was organized in New York City during the summer of 1906 with a capital stock of $250,000. Behind this venture were Samuel B. Howard of Millbrook, J. Disbrow Baker of Yonkers and Arthur W. Britton of East Orange. That July *The Motor Way* reported the firm's intention to include automobiles in its manufacture, but it is doubted that Petroleum ever produced a car.

PETROMOBILE — The Petromobile was a gasoline car of 1900 which was planned to be produced by the Kidder Motor Vehicle Company of New Haven, Connecticut. It does not appear to have proceeded into manufacture, however. Kidder did produce a number of steam cars under its own name. Refer to Kidder.

PETROMOBILE — Brooklyn, New York — (1902) — The Petromobile Company of 114 Front Street in Brooklyn produced a gasoline wagon every part of which, save for transmission, wheels and tires, was of the firm's own manufacture. The engine, which developed 9 hp, was placed under the seat, with drive by single chain to the countershaft, and from there to the solid rear axle. A Champion speed clutch with two speeds forward and reverse was fitted, as were wooden wheels with solid tires. Steering was by side tiller, though a wheel could be had as an option. "There is not a brazed joint on the wagon," *The Automobile Review and Automobile News* reported in July 1902. "Every nut and bolt is standard and can be purchased at any hardware store." The Petromobile was produced for one year only.

PHANTOM CORSAIR — Pasadena, California — (1938) — Drawings of the car were first seen in *Esquire* magazine in 1937, where it was called a "conception of the car of tomorrow." When completed, it appeared on the cover of *Motor Age* in March 1938 and later that year was featured in the movie *The Young in Heart* where it was dubbed, now very flatteringly, as the "Flying Wombat." The Phantom Corsair had cost $24,000 to build, a hefty sum to most in 1938, though not for Rust Heinz, the twenty-three-year-old scion of the H.J. Heinz ('57 — at that time — Varieties) family. The car's chassis was a Cord 810, its Lycoming V-8 engine beefed up with a semi-racing camshaft designed by Andy Granatelli. Coachwork design was Rust Heinz's doing, built for him by Maurice Schwartz (Bohman & Schwartz) of Pasadena. A planned limited production of the Phantom Corsair, with a price tag in the $12,500 range, was circumvented by Rust Heinz's death during the summer of 1939. The car passed through the hands of many owners thereafter, the most famous being Herb Shriner. The Phantom Corsair remains extant, and is part of Harrah's Automobile Collection.

1904 Phelps, touring, NAHC

PHELPS — Stoneham, Massachusetts — (1903-1905) — In February of 1903 the Phelps Motor Vehicle Company succeeded the Phelps Motor Company and was reorganized with a capital stock of $300,000 in order to begin the manufacture of automobiles. L.J. Phelps was the man in charge, and the designer of both the Phelps engine and the new Phelps car. The engine was a three-cylinder vertical unit which developed 15 hp at 900 rpm. The chassis was remarkable, with the engine and transmission supported on the axles, eliminating the usual frame and substituting a large long tube through which the driving shaft attached to the motor casing in the front and the transmission case at the rear. Initially, the radiator was a finned coil mounted beneath a Renault-type hood; later models featured a standard honeycomb radiator. Each year L.J. Phelps made his car just a little bit bigger, and he seemed to relish competing with it in events on the East Coast. On August 25th, 1903 he established the first official record (1 hour 46 minutes) in a climb up Mt. Washington in New Hampshire. "Phelps Again" was the headline in the *Stoneham Independent* of December 5th, 1903 following his performance in the hill climb at West Orange, New Jersey where he was a minute and a half faster than the closest competitor in his class. In May 1904 he was the featured speaker at the meeting of the Town Improvement Association in Stoneham, and spoke enthusiastically about the future. "The Phelps Touring Car has now been before the public for two full seasons . . . ," the company brochure for 1905 stated. "It is not widely known. Few in the United States ever heard of it because it has not been advertised, almost the entire output having been sold from the factory before it was completed, without noise or bombast." Production plans for 1905 indicated 125 cars to be built and sold quietly. In September of 1905, L.J. Phelps announced that he was leaving his business and moving to California to retire. Without L.J. there really was no Phelps, although reportedly production was to continue under a new organization called the Courier Motor Company — and the $4000 four-cylinder Phelps which had been a custom-order only for 1905 would be a catalogued model for 1906. Instead there was neither a Phelps nor a Courier at all in 1906. In December of the year previous, the Shawmut Motor Company had moved into the Phelps factory to build the Shawmut.

1903 PHELPS

Three — 15 hp, 78" wb

	FP	5	4	3	2	1
Touring-5P	2000	2300	3300	4600	7500	16,000

1904 PHELPS

Three — 20 hp, 84" wb

	FP	5	4	3	2	1
Touring-5P	2500	2350	3400	4700	7800	16,500

1905 PHELPS

Three — 24 hp, 106" wb

	FP	5	4	3	2	1
Touring-5P	2500	2400	3400	4800	8000	17,000

1918 Phianna, town car, WLB

PHIANNA — Newark, New Jersey — (1917-1918) / Long Island City, New York — (1919-1922) — The name was derived from Phyllis and Anna, the twin daughters of one of the organizers of the Phianna Motors Company. Phianna was the venture which succeeded the S.G.V. Company, which had produced the S.G.V. car in Reading, Pennsylvania from 1911 to 1915. When S.G.V. went under, its factory and assets were purchased by a consortium of businessmen including R.J. Metzler, T.M. Pepperday and John A. Bell. They immediately moved operations to Newark, New Jersey where production of the Phianna began. Like the S.G.V., it was a small four-cylinder 25 hp car on a 115 1/2-inch wheelbase chassis, and its chassis price was $3600. Its oval-shaped radiator was patented. The people of Phianna soon discovered the harsh reality visited upon S.G.V. just a few years before: Small, well built and distinctively styled cars simply did not sell very well in this country. By the time of America's entrance into World War I, sales had slowed to a trickle, and the Phianna factory in Newark was taken over by Wright-Martin Aircraft Corporation. Fortunately, one of the previous purchasers of a Phianna had been a young automobile enthusiast named Miles Harold Carpenter. When informed that Phianna was interested in selling its drawings, dies, jigs, tools, et al., Carpenter immediately bought them and moved Phianna into a new factory in Long Island City. There, he retained the Phianna's four-cylinder engine, but lengthened the wheelbase to 125 inches. Fred Charavey, a designer of airplane propellers, styled a laminated walnut and ash fan for the Phianna which was mounted co-axially with the flywheel, and was a real beauty. Indeed, everything under the hood of a Phianna was designed with aesthetics in mind. The engine compartment verily glistened. Although the wheelbase of a Phianna remained short by contemporary luxury-car standards, the car's ride was the equal of larger automobiles by virtue of the sixty-inch cantilever rear suspension. This second-generation Phianna was introduced at the New York Automobile Show in October 1919. Coachwork on the Phianna was custom-built, with prices ranging from $6000 for a standard brougham, to $9500 for a special touring car, to $11,500 for a limousine. Obviously, the

Phianna was a prestige car for the few — and among the few who purchased it were royal personages in Europe and diplomats in the United States. The King of Spain had a Phianna, so did Bainbridge Colby, Secretary of State in the Wilson administration. During 1921 Miles Carpenter set forth plans to build a much larger six-cylinder Phianna on a 142-inch wheelbase, and he was also at that time producing a limited edition of the Curtiss car with OX-5 engine and Phianna chassis for his friend Glenn Curtiss. The postwar depression killed both those ventures — and the Phianna car itself. A few pilot models of the Phianna six were built, but it was never marketed. The last Phianna fours were assembled from parts on hand during 1922.

1919 Phianna, town car, AA

1919 Phianna, touring, FP

PHILADELPHIA — The Philadelphia Automobile Company was organized early in 1903 in Camden, New Jersey with a capital stock of $50,000 for the manufacture of automobiles. Included among the incorporators were Edward E. Ziegler, Edwin L. Hoffman, Thomas J. Mahoney and William Vees. Manufacture is doubted.

The Philadelphia Electric Company has been indicated on car rosters as the producer of an automobile in 1911. Documentation is lacking. The only firm of that name in Philadelphia during this period obviously produced only electricity.

The Philadelphia Motor Company was organized during the summer of 1911 as a $100,000 Delaware incorporation for the manufacture and sale of automobiles and engines. Incorporators were J.F. Greene of Philadelphia, and J.L. Wolcott and H.R. Martindale of Dover, Delaware. Manufacture is doubted.

The Philadelphia Motor Carriage Company was organized during the summer of 1899 with a capital stock of $1 million to manufacture and sell electric vehicles. Incorporators were C.P. King of Philadelphia, and J.T. McGraw, C.R. Durbin, F.H. Treat and Claude S. Jarvies, all of Grafton, West Virginia. Manufacture is doubted.

The Philadelphia Motor Vehicle Company produced a gasoline runabout at the turn of the century which was marketed under the tradename of Imperial. Refer to Imperial.

The Philadelphia Motor Wagon Company was indicated as an automobile manufacturer in the Hiscox book *Horseless Vehicles, Automobiles, Motor Cycles* published in 1900. This does not appear to be the case. The firm was organized with the intention of introducing electric cabs in Philadelphia, but not with the intention of manufacturing them. Instead the cars were built by the Electric Vehicle Company. By the spring of 1899 the Philadelphia firm's designation had been changed to Pennsylvania Electric Vehicle Company, at the request of the New York-based Electric Vehicle Company.

The Philadelphia Rapid Transit Company sponsored the building of a hybrid taxicab in 1929. Refer to Gas-Electric.

PHILBRICK — Hartford, Connecticut — (1900) — Intrigued by the new and lighter storage battery system invented by Frederick W. Barhoff, Halsey B. Philbrick, the secretary of the Hartford Accumulator Company, ordered a prototype car built featuring the Barhoff battery as well as some ideas of his own and a controller invented by Charles R. Reynolds. The Philbrick prototype, also referred to as a Barhoff in trade press articles,

1900 Philbrick, NAHC

was quite light for an electric of this period — just 1200 pounds — and was described as the "smoothest and stillest in locomotion" of any electric in town. Philbrick tested the car for over 2000 miles without a battery change, and proudly announced that on two occasions he had made runs of 35 miles on a single charge. Although the Hartford Accumulator Company planned production of the car initially, ultimately the firm manufactured only the battery instead. At least two prototypes were built, however.

PHILBRICK STEAMER — In 1887, in Beverly, Massachusetts, J. Elmer Woods and Andrew J. Philbrick collaborated on the building of a steam carriage. Refer to Woods & Philbrick.

PHILION — Akron, Ohio — (1892) — The Philion was a coal-burning steamer built by circus showman Achille Philion, who had met a lovely Akron girl named Bell Melvin while she was traveling in his native France and who arrived in America soon after their marriage. The car was begun in 1887 and was patented and made its first appearance on the streets of Akron in 1892. Philion was by now a featured performer in an Akron-based circus and was widely reputed to be one of the finest balancing artists of his time, his specialty walking a rubber ball (naturally, this was Akron, and B.F. Goodrich made the balls) up a spiral tower and then descending at great speed to a blaze of fireworks at the bottom. He had built the steamer to call attention to himself and his act, and used it in numerous parades which always preceded a circus coming to town. Philion even played the 1893 Chicago World's Fair. In the late 1890's, following a fall while performing in the East, Achille Philion retired from the circus world. He remained in Akron where he opened a movie theatre in 1904 and where, in 1907, the Philion steamer was exhibited at Akron's first automobile show. Following Philion's death, the car was acquired by a motion picture entrepreneur and appeared in such movies as *The Magnificent Ambersons* with Orson Welles and *Excuse My Dust* with Red Skelton. Later acquired by Harrah's Automobile Collection, the Philion steamer remains extant.

PHINNEY — Fred S. Phinney was a machinist at 100 Madison Street in Brooklyn who incorporated himself with a capital stock of $5000 during the summer of 1914 for the purpose of manufacturing automobiles and accessories. Joining him in this venture were A.N. Phinney and A.S. Phinney. Manufacture of a car is doubted.

PHIPPS — The Phipps Road Car Company was organized in Trenton, New Jersey during the spring of 1902 with a $1 million capital stock for the manufacture of machinery and vehicles of all kinds. Incorporators were E.H. Phipps, H.F. Parker and Frank A. Reynolds, all of Jersey City. Manufacture of a car is doubted.

1911 Phipps-Grinnell, coupe, NAHC

PHIPPS-GRINNELL — Detroit, Michigan — (1911) / PHIPPS ELECTRIC — (1912) — Ira and C.A. Grinnell were prosperous music dealers in Detroit, and Joel G. Phipps was a struggling young electric car designer. Their partnership resulted in the Phipps-Grinnell Automobile Company which produced two two-passenger cars and one delivery truck during 1911. Although no reason was given, the partnership was disbanded before year's end. The Grinnells bought out Phipps and went on to manufacture the Grinnell Electric. Phipps allied himself with one C.W. Whitson and refined his car into a longer-wheelbase Phipps Electric for 1912. Apparently Phipps' resources were considerably the lesser to the Grinnells'. The Phipps Electric Company was out of business by 1913. The Grinnell Electric continued to be produced until 1916.

1911 PHIPPS-GRINNELL
Phipps-Grinnell Electric

	FP	5	4	3	2	1
Model C Cpe. (78" wb)	2500	2000	3000	4200	6500	14,000
Model D Extension Cpe. (88½" wb)	2750	2100	3100	4300	6800	14,500

1912 PHIPPS ELECTRIC

	FP	5	4	3	2	1
Phipps Electric Brgm. (107" wb)	—	2250	3300	4500	7300	15,500

PHOENIX — The cars produced by the Owen brothers of Cleveland, Ohio at the turn of the century were alternately referred to under the names of Phoenix and Owen. Refer to Owen.

The Phoenix Motor Car & Truck Company was organized in Brooklyn, New York during the spring of 1911 with a $100,000 capital stock for the manufacture of "commercial motor vehicles and other automobiles." Incorporators were F.W. Heiman, H.A. Bedell and H.P. Heiman, all of Brooklyn. Manufacture of an automobile is doubted.

That Phoenix was to be the name of a new automobile to be produced by the Industrial Machine Company was reported by *The Motor Review* in January 1902. The magazine erred somewhat. Phoenix, New York was to be the location of the factory. Refer to De Long.

PHOENIX — Freeport, Illinois — (1905) — D.C. Stover of Freeport built the Phoenix bicycle and in 1905 decided to build an automobile using alcohol as fuel and to market it as the Phoenix as well. That summer he announced the impending formation of the Stover Automobile Company. It died aborning. Thereafter the Stover Manufacturing Company branched from bicycles into gasoline engine production — and in 1909 D.C. Stover again attempted to enter the automobile field with a car named after himself.

PHOENIX — Coldwater, Michigan — (1905) — Nettleton & Company was an automobile garage in Coldwater. In the fall of 1905 its proprietors announced that they were considering manufacture. They had recently purchased the burned wreck of a car belonging to Homer Dickenson and were now in the process of constructing a new one from its remains. Conceivably, this Phoenix may have risen from the ashes, but it never proceeded into manufacture. Nettleton & Company did display a rather wry sense of humor in naming their car, however.

1909 Pickard, touring, WLB

PICKARD — Brockton, Massachusetts — (1909-1912) — In 1896, Emil J., Benjamin J. and Alfred Pickard established a machine stop in Brockton which they called Pickard Brothers. Bicycle repairing was its first main order of business, followed by automobile repairing at the turn of the century. In 1903 the brothers built their first car, powered by a single-cylinder 5 hp engine, which they drove and tested for four years. All the while they were experimenting further, and in October of 1908 decided that at last they had an automobile ready for market. The production Pickard was powered by a four-cylinder air-cooled engine, and featured a sliding gear transmission and shaft drive. The car had a wooden frame with truss under each sill, and the bands of the brakes were lined with camel's hair. "A Lot of Car for the Money" was a Pickard slogan, and although occasional models were sold in the $1500 price range, most were offered for less than a thousand dollars. In 1910, declaring themselves "handicapped by lack of capital," the Pickard brothers announced their intention to leave Brockton "unless local support is forthcoming." It never was, nor apparently did support arrive from any other area. The Pickard died in Brockton during 1912.

1909 PICKARD
Four — 25 hp, 110" wb

	FP	5	4	3	2	1
Model A Rbt.-2P	1400	1500	2500	3600	5500	11,000
Model B Rdst.-3P	1400	1600	2700	3800	5800	12,000
Model C Tour.-4P	1450	1800	2800	4000	6200	13,000
Model D Tour.-5P	1500	2000	3000	4200	6500	14,000
Model E Rbt.	750	1400	2400	3500	5300	10,000
Model F Rbt.	800	1450	2450	3600	5400	10,500
Model G Surrey	825	1700	2800	3900	6000	12,500
Model H Tour.	850	1600	2700	3800	5800	12,000

1910 Pickard, touring, JAC

1910 PICKARD
Four — 25 hp, 100" wb

Model E Rbt.-2P	750	1500	2500	3600	5500	11,000
Model F Rdst.-3P	800	1600	2700	3800	5800	12,000
Model G Surrey	825	1700	2800	3900	6000	12,500
Model H Tour.-4P	850	1600	2700	3800	5800	12,000

MODEL E, $750

1911 Pickard, model E, runabout, HAC

1911 PICKARD
Four — 25 hp, 100" wb

Model E Rbt.-2P	750	1600	2700	3800	5800	12,000
Model F Rdst.-3P	800	1800	2800	4000	6200	13,000
Model G Tour. (30 hp)	825	1900	2900	4100	6400	13,500
Model H Tour.-4P	850	2000	3000	4200	6500	14,000

1912 Pickard, model H, touring, HAC

1135

1912 PICKARD
Four — 26 hp, 100" wb

	FP	5	4	3	2	1
Model E Rbt.	800	1600	2700	3800	5800	12,000
Model F Rdst.	850	1800	2800	4000	6200	13,000
Model G Surrey	925	2000	3000	4200	6500	14,000
Model H Tour.	950	2000	3000	4200	6500	14,000
Model J Tour. (104" wb)		2100	3100	4300	6800	14,500
Model K Tour. (104" wb)	1600	2100	3100	4300	6800	14,500

1905 Pickford, touring, GR

PICKFORD — Palmerton, Pennsylvania — (1905-1906) — A machinist and foreman with the New Jersey Zinc Company, Llewellyn Pickford began building his automobile in 1904 following his purchase of a six-cylinder 30 hp Trebert engine. The first chassis he ran up proved too insubstantial for the big engine, so he discarded it and built another. His son James used the original chassis to build his own two-cylinder car in 1906. Llewellyn Pickford's car was completed in 1905, and featured a three-speed sliding gear transmission, single chain drive, and a radiator the coils of which wrapped all the way 'round the hood. Although the Pickfords, father and son, later built several engines of their own, they never again built another automobile.

1906 Pickle, NAHC

PICKLE — Greenville, Michigan — (1906) — The Pickle was powered by a two-cylinder 3½ hp engine and used ordinary bicycle wheels. Fred Pickle of Greenville spent months building his idea of an automobile which he completed in 1906 and traveled in all over western Michigan thereafter.

PIEDMONT — The Piedmont Auto Manufacturing Company was organized in Fairburn, Georgia during the fall of 1911 with a capital stock of $100,000 for the manufacture of automobiles. Incorporators were Robert F. Butler, W.L. Moor and H. Knight. Manufacture is doubted.

PIEDMONT — Monroe, North Carolina — (1908) — During the summer of 1908 the Piedmont Buggy Company of Monroe announced that it had completed an 800-pound, solid-tired motor buggy powered by a 10 hp air-cooled engine. A very small production of these cars appears to have followed in 1908, but did not survive into 1909. W.C. Heath was the president of the Piedmont Buggy Company, O.W. Kochtitzky the secretary, and T.J. Paine the general manager.

PIEDMONT — Lynchburg, Virginia — (1917-1922) — "The Piedmont is not an assembled car," one brochure said. "It is manufactured at the company's own extensive factory." The factory was in Lynchburg, Virginia, the company was the Piedmont Motor Car Company — and, its claim to the contrary, the Piedmont was an assembled car. The only part of it produced in Lynchburg was the body and even that, one former employee admitted, was copied from the Hudson — and until 1918 was

1920 Piedmont, model 6-40, touring, HAC

purchased outside too, from the Norwalk Motor Car Company of Martinsburg, West Virginia. (Ironically, the last Norwalks were produced by Piedmont.) The Piedmont was not, one might say, bristling with innovation. An open tourer was the usual body style, available with either a four-cylinder Lycoming or six-cylinder Continental engine — and, except for radiator configuration both cars looked the same. The standard color was Piedmont Green, though the company did try for a little variety on one occasion by sending two special cars to the National Automobile Show in New York City. These were painted light blue, with nickel radiator shells instead of the usual black enamel. Production in Lynchburg averaged about 500 units a year, but not all of these were Piedmonts. The company also built cars for Lone Star in Texas and Bush in Chicago, among others. Generally, they varied little from the Piedmont in Virginia. The company seemed to focus more of its attention on sales of cars to other producers than deliveries of Piedmonts to its own dealers (who screamed a lot) or effective promotion of the car in its own hometown. Prior to 1920 Piedmont advertised virtually not at all locally, though in the December 19th edition of the *Lynchburg News* that year there did appear an advertisement practically

1921 Piedmont, model 6-40, touring, WLB

begging the citizenry to buy its cars: "We have set aside 20 of our latest model automobiles — 10 six cylinder touring cars and 10 four cylinder touring cars — to be sold between tomorrow and January 15th, 1921 only to residents of Lynchburg, Campbell, Bedford, Amherst and Appomattox at the following prices." The prices quoted were $500 less than the usual, a substantial savings, and the fact that Piedmont believed it necessary to hold the "sale" for a month indicates the lack of enthusiasm in Lynchburg for the car. Reportedly, sales manager George Hay went to great effort before finally persuading the local police department to use Piedmont cars because "it would look better" for the company. Piedmont's president from the beginning had been W.A. Taylor, though a physician named Norford who had formerly been on the faculty of the University of Virginia was called in during the final years to help turn things around. He found an unhealthy company he could not save. In anticipation of an ever-increasing flood of orders from outside producers Piedmont had overloaded its shelves. Receivership arrived in October of 1922. Inventorying the parts and equipment was a time-consuming task because there was so much of it, $225,000 worth of components alone. The Piedmont factory was sold at auction in November and was razed some years later. A bakery occupies the site today. A try to revive the company as Virginia Motors, Inc. in January 1923 never got off the ground.

1917-1919 PIEDMONT
Model 4-30 — 4-cyl., 30 hp, 116" wb

	FP	5	4	3	2	1
Tour.-5P	1095	3100	4200	6300	10,500	22,000
Model 6-40 — 6-cyl., 42 hp, 122" wb						
Tour.-5P	1945	3500	4500	7000	13,000	25,000
1920 PIEDMONT						
Model 4-30 — 4-cyl., 30 hp, 116" wb						
Tour.-5P	1395	3100	4200	6300	10,500	22,000
Model 6-40 — 6-cyl., 42 hp, 122" wb						
Tour.-5P	1865	3500	4500	7000	13,000	25,000

1922 Piedmont, model 4-30, touring, HAC

1921-1922 PIEDMONT
Model 4-30 — 4-cyl., 30 hp, 122" wb

	FP	5	4	3	2	1
Tour.-5P	1485	3100	4200	6300	10,500	22,000
Model 6-40 — 6-cyl., 42 hp, 122" wb						
Tour.-5P	1945	3500	4500	7000	13,000	25,000

Note: A club roadster was offered during the 1918 and 1920 model years.

PIERCE — "The C.A. Pierce Cycle Company, Johnstown, Pennsylvania, write us that they are preparing to build automobiles, but have not yet found a water-cooled gasoline motor to suit them, although they have been looking around for six months," *Cycle and Automobile Trade Journal* reported during the summer of 1900. Conceivably the Pierce people never did find an engine they liked since the evidence suggests the company never ventured into automobile manufacture.

The Pierce, Wells and Keedwell Company was organized in New York City early in 1912 with a capital stock of $10,000 to manufacture and deal in motors and motor cars. Incorporators were P. Kruider, Jr., A.C. Keedwell and A.D. Keedwell. Manufacture of a car is doubted.

The Pierce Supply Company was organized in Cleveland, Ohio late in 1915 with a capital stock of $5000 to manufacture and deal in motor cars. Incorporators were W.E. Crawford, James A. McKay, I. Rose, Max Painter and C. Fowler. Manufacture is doubted.

PIERCE & CROUCH — In 1895 the New Brighton, Pennsylvania machine shop of Pierce & Crouch built an experimental automobile. W. Lee Crouch built a number of subsequent cars into the turn of the century in both Pennsylvania and Maryland. Refer to Crouch.

1902 Pierce Electric, runabout, NAHC

PIERCE ELECTRIC — Newark & Bound Brook, New Jersey — (1900-1904) — Many physicians in America built their own cars at the turn of the century. Dr. Ray V. Pierce is one of the few who went into manufacture. Associated with him were Dr. V. Mott Pierce and Hugh C. Pierce. His first automotive vehicle was an electric powered wagon designed especially for newspaper delivery work and built in 1900 in his native Buffalo, New York. Later that year he organized the Dr. Pierce Auto Manufacturing Company in Newark, but remained there only a short time. By early 1901 he had moved to Bound Brook where he had extensive real estate holdings as well as a heavy interest in the American Engine Company, which supplied him the electric motors used in his vehicles. Now his firm was restyled the Pierce Electric Company, and its product range was expanded to include several varieties of passenger phaeton and light delivery vehicles. History does not record Pierce's competence in the medical field, but if it matched his talent as an automobile designer, he was a very good doctor. "Our vehicles are built as attractively as is possible without a sacrifice of strength to beauty, which would be dangerous to the stability of the vehi-

cle or perilous to the life of its occupants," the brochure said. "Our automobiles have not any of the sulky or spider effect, but are good, staunch-looking vehicles, ready for any test or ordeal." Pierce Electrics were built in Bound Brook into 1904; that spring the Pierce Motor Vehicle Company, as it had been redesignated, filed a certificate of dissolution.

1903 Pierce, motorette, HAC

PIERCE-ARROW — Buffalo, New York — (1901-1938) — Among the more delightful anomalies in the history of the American automobile is that the Pierce-Arrow, one of the most revered and prestigious motorcars ever to grace the highway, descended from a company engaged in the manufacture of birdcages. The company was Heintz, Pierce and Munschauer, founded in Buffalo in 1865, and it produced ice boxes and other varied household items as well. In 1872 the middle partner bought controlling interest in the firm, and it was reorganized as the George N. Pierce Company. By 1896 bicycles were an additional product, and there was a new addition to the company roster, Colonel Charles Clifton as treasurer. It was Clifton who first assayed the possibility of automobile manufacture, a steam car completed in the summer of 1900 being the company's first effort. It was a failure; following a trip to Europe, Clifton recommended the French De Dion motor, and it powered the first gasoline car completed that November. Early in 1901 David Fergusson, an English-born engineer then employed by the E.C. Stearns Company in nearby Syracuse, stopped by Buffalo to offer his services — and the Pierce company had its chief engineer for the next two decades. By May the first two examples of Fergusson's De Dion-engined design were completed, and the rest of the year was spent testing the cars and demonstrating them to Pierce bicycle agents throughout the country. Manufacture of the Motorette, as the single-cylinder models were called, was begun late in 1901, and 150 of them had been produced by the end of the year following. Two cylinders followed in 1903, the Arrow designation arrived for these cars in 1904, as well as the Great Arrow name for the four-cylinder cars also introduced that year. The first of the famed Glidden Tours was held in July 1905, and the Great Arrow driven by Percy Pierce (son of George N.) won it. The company from Buffalo captured the next four events too, for an unrivaled conquest of the Glidden Trophy. The first six-cylinder car made its debut in 1907, and two years later both the company and the marque name were changed to Pierce-Arrow. Although the company would pioneer in the extensive use of aluminum and in power braking, would introduce the first hydraulic tappets, as well, and featured such idiosyncrasies as a steering wheel gear lever (until 1908) and right hand drive (until 1920), the most famous of all Pierce-Arrow features arrived in 1913 — and this was the fender headlamp, designed in-house and patented by Herbert M. Dawley. Drum headlamps would remain an option through 1932, but most purchasers opted instead for the standard, and exclusive, fender treatment. By January 1915 Pierce-Arrow had built its 12,000th motorcar and was

1911 Pierce-Arrow, model 36T, touring, HAC

1917 Pierce-Arrow (President Wilson's limousine), HAC

1902 Pierce Motorette, HAC

1904 Pierce Great Arrow, touring, HAC

preeminent in the highest echelon of the luxury car market in terms of both prestige and output. The big sixes, of which the 66 was the mightiest and one of the largest stock cars ever built in the United States, found their way into the most elegant garages in America. The Dual Valve Six was introduced in October 1918 and, in addition to retaining the preference for the cars among Pierce-Arrow's usual clientele, also became a favorite among rum-runners because of the reliability and quiet of its engine. By now Cadillac had its V-8 and Packard its Twin-Six, but Pierce-Arrow continued to believe six cylinders remained the optimum number a motorcar should have. Following the First World War, the Pierce-Arrow management retired, and the New York banking firm of Seligman Company took over. Among the bankers' ideas for the company was development of a sleeve-valve engine; Fergusson was furious and abruptly resigned. Barney Roos was his successor, but resigned almost as abruptly, and succeeding him was Charles L. Sheppy. In 1921 The Pierce-Arrow Motor Car Company had a new president as well, Myron E. Forbes, who had joined the firm as treasurer in 1919. A smaller six, the L-Head Series 80, was introduced for 1924. Nineteen twenty-six brought four-wheel brakes incorporating the vacuum-powered booster developed by Victor Kliesrath and Caleb Bragg. But by now Pierce-Arrow was hurting, wounded in the marketplace by its clinging to the traditional both in styling and in paucity of cylinders, which still remained at only six. In 1928 Colonel Clifton died and Myron Forbes, believing that the day of the independent manufacturer was fast drawing to a close, got together with Albert R. Erskine and negotiated a merger between Studebaker and Pierce-Arrow. It would prove a happy marriage for neither party, though in the short run it did result in a doubling of Pierce-Arrow sales to 10,000 units in 1929. The new cars were straight-eights which had been in development in Buffalo for some time prior to the entrance of Studebaker upon the scene. Though Myron Forbes would resign in 1929, with Albert Erskine taking over the Pierce-Arrow presidency, Pierce-Arrow functioned as an independent operating entity. In the multi-cylinder race that followed the Wall Street crash, Pierce-Arrow's entry (a V-12 designed by new chief engineer Karl Wise) was introduced in November 1931. Although at Bonneville Ab Jenkins blithely broke fourteen official international records with the Pierce-Arrow twelve (including a twenty-four-hour mark following which Jenkins emerged from the car clean shaven, having wielded a safety razor during the final hour — at over 125 mph), the story in Buffalo was taking a tragic turn. In 1933 Studebaker was in receivership, and Albert Erskine committed suicide. The Pierce-Arrow company was acquired by a group of Buffalo bankers and businessmen and was an independent once again. Arthur J. Chanter, a former Studebaker man who held Pierce-Arrow's presidency for several months prior to Erskine's death, was retained in that position. Nineteen thirty-three brought hydraulic tappets, an industry first, and the startlingly streamlined Silver Arrow which was the smash hit of the New York Automobile Show and a precursor of styling trends to come. But Pierce-Arrow sales for 1933 totaled 2152 units, 500 less than the year previous and nearly a thousand less than the 3,000-unit break-even point. Only five Silver Arrows, priced at $10,000 each, were built. Their fastback styling and dual fender headlights were incorporated in Pierces of 1934 which were called Silver Arrow models, but they were more standard Pierce than revolutionary Silver Arrow cars. In 1935 pointed reference was made by Arthur Chanter to the fact that, alone among American manufacturers, Pierce-Arrow was devoted to luxury car production exclusively. Only 875 luxury Pierces were sold in 1935. The figure dwindled to 787 in 1936, and plummeted to 167 in 1937. In the spring of 1938 — the 13th of May, a Friday — the Pierce-Arrow company was sold at auction. The last Pierce-Arrow was built that summer for chief engineer Karl Wise from parts he had secured from the receivers.

1901	FP	5	4	3	2	1
1-cyl., 2-3/4 hp						
Motorette	—	4800	9600	16,000	22,400	32,000
1-cyl., 3-3/4 hp						
Motorette	—	5250	10,500	17,500	24,500	35,000
1902						
1-cyl., 3-1/2 hp, 58" wb						
Motorette	—	5250	10,500	17,500	24,500	35,000
1903						
1-cyl., 5 hp						
Rbt	950	5550	11,100	18,500	25,900	37,000
1-cyl., 6-1/2 hp						
Stanhope	1150	5850	11,700	19,500	27,300	39,000
2-cyl., 15 hp						
5P Tr	2500	6750	13,500	22,500	31,500	45,000

1904						
1-cyl., 8 hp, 70" wb						
	FP	5	4	3	2	1
Stanhope	1200	6000	12,000	20,000	28,000	40,000
Stanhope-2P	1200	5700	11,400	19,000	26,600	38,000
4 cyl., 24/28 hp, 93" wb						
Great Arrow 5P Tr	4000	11,400	22,800	38,000	56,000	76,000
2-cyl., 15 hp, 81" wb						
5P Tr	2500	6750	13,500	22,500	31,500	45,000
4-cyl., 24/28 hp 93" wb						
Great Arrow Tr	4000	10,200	20,400	34,000	47,600	68,000

1905 Pierce Great Arrow, opera coach, HAC

1905 Pierce Great Arrow (Glidden Tour car), HAC

1905

1-cyl., 8 hp, 70" wb

	FP	5	4	3	2	1
Stanhope	—	5700	11,400	19,000	26,600	38,000
Stanhope	1200	6000	12,000	20,000	28,000	40,000

Great Arrow- 4-cyl., 24/28 hp, 100" wb

5P Tonneau	3500	9900	19,800	33,000	46,200	66,000
5P Canopy Tonneau	3750	10,200	20,400	34,000	47,600	68,000
5P Vic	3650	9000	18,000	30,000	42,000	60,000
5P Cape Tonneau	3650	9300	18,600	31,000	43,400	62,000

Great Arrow- 4-cyl., 28/32 hp, 104" wb

5P Tonneau	4000	10,500	21,000	35,000	49,000	70,000
5P Canopy Tonneau	4250	10,200	20,400	34,000	47,600	68,000
5P Vic	4150	9900	19,800	33,000	46,200	66,000
5P Cape Tonneau	4150	10,200	20,400	34,000	47,600	68,000

Great Arrow- 4-cyl., 28/32 hp, 109" wb

7P Lan'let	5000	8250	16,500	27,500	38,500	55,000
7P Sub	5000	7500	15,000	25,000	35,000	50,000
8P Opera Coach	5000	8550	17,100	28,500	39,900	57,000

4-cyl., 24/28 hp, 100" wb

Great Arrow Tr	4000	10,200	20,400	34,000	47,600	68,000
Great Arrow Lan'let	—	9600	19,200	32,000	44,800	64,000
Great Arrow Sub	—	9000	18,000	30,000	42,000	60,000

4-cyl., 28/32 hp, 104" wb

Great Arrow Opera Coach	—	10,800	21,600	36,000	50,500	72,000

1906 Pierce Great Arrow, victoria tonneau, HAC

1906

Motorette - 1-cyl., 8 hp, 70" wb

Stanhope	900	5250	10,500	17,500	24,500	35,000

Great Arrow - 4-cyl., 28/32 hp, 107" wb

5P Tr	4000	10,500	21,000	35,000	49,000	70,000
5P Vic	4150	9000	18,000	30,000	42,000	60,000
8P Open Coach	5000	11,100	22,200	37,000	52,000	74,000
7P Sub	5000	10,800	21,600	36,000	50,500	72,000
7P Lan'let	5250	9900	19,800	33,000	46,200	66,000

Great Arrow - 4-cyl., 40/45 hp, 109" wb

7P Tr	5000	11,400	22,800	38,000	56,000	76,000
8P Open Coach	6000	11,700	23,400	39,000	58,000	78,000
7P Sub	6000	11,400	22,800	38,000	56,000	76,000
7P Lan'let	6250	10,500	21,000	35,000	49,000	70,000

1907 Pierce Great Arrow, touring, HAC

1907

Great Arrow - 4-cyl., 28/32 hp, 112" wb

	FP	5	4	3	2	1
5P Tr	4000	11,700	23,400	39,000	58,000	78,000
5P Limo	5000	10,500	21,000	35,000	49,000	70,000
7P Sub	5000	10,800	21,600	36,000	50,500	72,000

Great Arrow - 4-cyl., 40/45 hp, 124" wb

7P Tr	5000	12,000	24,000	40,000	60,000	80,000
7P Limo	6250	11,400	22,800	38,000	56,000	76,000
7P Sub	6250	11,700	23,400	39,000	58,000	78,000

Great Arrow - 6-cyl., 65 hp, 135" wb

7P Tr	6500	12,000	24,000	40,000	60,000	80,000

1908 Pierce Great Arrow, suburban, WLB

1908

Great Arrow - 4-cyl., 30 hp, 112" wb

Tr	4000	10,500	21,000	35,000	49,000	70,000

Great Arrow - 4-cyl., 40 hp, 124" wb

Tr	5000	12,000	24,000	40,000	60,000	80,000
Sub	6250	11,400	22,800	38,000	56,000	76,000

Great Arrow - 6-cyl., 40 hp, 130" wb

Tr	5500	12,900	25,800	48,200	66,000	86,000
Sub	—	12,000	24,000	40,000	60,000	80,000
Rdstr	—	12,600	25,200	42,000	64,000	84,000

Great Arrow - 6-cyl., 60 hp, 135" wb

Tr	6500	13,500	27,000	45,000	70,000	90,000
Sub	—	12,000	24,000	40,000	60,000	80,000
Rdstr	—	12,900	25,800	48,200	66,000	86,000

1909 Pierce-Arrow, model 40, suburban, HAC

1909

Model 24 - 4 cyl., 24 hp, 111-1/2" wb

3P Rbt	3100	5250	10,500	17,500	24,500	35,000
3P Vic Top Rbt	3300	5550	11,100	18,500	25,900	37,000
2P Rbt	3050	5100	10,200	17,000	23,800	34,000
4P Tr Car	3150	6000	12,000	20,000	28,000	40,000
5P Lan'let	3950	5700	11,400	19,000	26,600	38,000
5P Brgm	4050	5850	11,700	19,500	27,300	39,000

Model 36 - 6-cyl., 36 hp, 119" wb

5P Tr	4000	6600	13,200	22,000	30,800	44,000
5P Cape Top Tr	4175	6750	13,500	22,500	31,500	45,000
2P Rbt	3700	5850	11,700	19,500	27,300	39,000
3P Rbt	3750	5900	11,850	19,750	27,650	39,500
4P Tr	3800	6450	12,900	21,500	30,100	43,000
5P Brgm	4650	6000	12,000	20,000	28,000	40,000
5P Lan'let	4700	6300	12,600	21,000	29,400	42,000

Model 40 - 4-cyl., 40 hp, 124" wb

7P Sub	5400	8250	16,500	27,500	38,500	55,000
4P Tr Car	4100	8100	16,200	27,000	37,800	54,000
7P Tr	4300	8250	16,500	27,500	38,500	55,000
7P Lan	5500	7500	15,000	25,000	35,000	50,000

Model 48 - 6-cyl., 48 hp, 130" wb

4P Tr	4800	9300	18,600	31,000	43,400	62,000
4P Cape Top Tr	5000	9600	19,200	32,000	44,800	64,000
2P Tr	4700	9000	18,000	30,000	42,000	60,000
3P Tr	4750	9300	18,600	31,000	43,400	62,000
7P Tr	5000	9900	19,800	33,000	46,200	66,000
7P Lan	6200	9000	18,000	30,000	42,000	60,000
7P Sub	6100	9900	19,800	33,000	46,200	66,000

Model 60 - 6-cyl., 60 hp, 135" wb

7P Tr	6000	11,400	22,800	38,000	56,000	76,000
7P Cape Top Tr	6200	11,700	23,400	39,000	58,000	78,000
7P Sub	7100	11,700	23,400	39,000	58,000	78,000
7P Lan	7200	10,500	21,000	35,000	49,000	70,000

1910 Pierce-Arrow, model 36, runabout, HAC

1910
Model 36 - 6-cyl., 36 hp, 125" wb

	FP	5	4	3	2	1
5P Lan'let	5000	6600	13,200	22,000	30,800	44,000
4P Miniature Tonneau	4000	6300	12,600	21,000	29,400	42,000
5P Tr	4000	6600	13,200	22,000	30,800	44,000
5P Brgm	4900	6000	12,000	20,000	28,000	40,000
Rbt (119" wb)	3850	6000	12,000	20,000	28,000	40,000

Model 48 - 6-cyl., 48 hp, 134-1/2" wb
7P Lan'let	6200	7500	15,000	25,000	35,000	50,000
Miniature Tonneau	4850	7200	14,400	24,000	33,600	48,000
7P Tr	5000	8250	16,500	27,500	38,500	55,000
7P Sub	6100	8250	16,500	27,500	38,500	55,000
Rbt (128" wb)	4850	7500	15,000	25,000	35,000	50,000

Model 66 - 6-cyl., 66 hp, 140" wb
7P Tr	6000	11,400	22,800	38,000	56,000	76,000
4P Miniature Tonneau	5850	10,500	21,000	35,000	49,000	70,000
7P Sub	7100	11,400	22,800	38,000	56,000	76,000
7P Lan'let	7200	10,500	21,000	35,000	49,000	70,000
Rbt (133-1/2" wb)	5850	10,200	20,400	34,000	47,600	68,000

1911 Pierce-Arrow, runabout, OCW

1912 Pierce-Arrow, runabout, OCW

1911
Model 36T - 6-cyl., 38 hp, 125" wb

	FP	5	4	3	2	1
5P Tr	4000	10,800	21,600	36,000	50,500	72,000
3P Rbt	4000	10,200	20,400	34,000	47,600	68,000
4P Miniature Tonneau	4000	10,200	20,400	34,000	47,600	68,000
5P Brgm	4900	9300	18,600	31,000	43,400	62,000
5P Lan'let	5000	9900	19,800	33,000	46,200	66,000

Model 48T - 6-cyl., 48 hp, 134-1/2" wb
7P Tr	5000	11,700	23,400	39,000	58,000	78,000
Rbt	4950	10,500	21,000	35,000	49,000	70,000
Miniature Tonneau	4850	10,800	21,600	36,000	50,500	72,000
5P Close Coupled	5000	9000	18,000	30,000	42,000	60,000
5P Protected Tr	5000	10,500	21,000	35,000	49,000	70,000
Sub	6100	11,400	22,800	38,000	56,000	76,000
Lan	6200	11,400	22,800	38,000	56,000	76,000

Model 66T - 6-cyl., 66 hp, 140" wb
7P Tr	6000	12,300	24,600	41,000	62,000	82,000
Rbt	5050	11,400	22,800	38,000	56,000	76,000
Miniature Tonneau	5850	11,700	23,400	39,000	58,000	78,000
5P Protected Tr	6000	11,400	22,800	38,000	56,000	76,000
Close Coupled	6000	9900	19,800	33,000	46,200	66,000
Sub	7100	12,000	24,000	40,000	60,000	80,000
Lan	7200	12,000	24,000	40,000	60,000	80,000

1912
Model 36T - 6 cyl., 36 hp, 127-1/2" wb

4P Tr	4000	10,500	21,000	35,000	49,000	70,000
5P Tr	4000	10,500	21,000	35,000	49,000	70,000
Brgm	4900	9900	19,800	33,000	46,200	66,000
Lan'let	4900	9900	19,800	33,000	46,200	66,000
Rbt (119" wb)	4000	10,200	20,400	34,000	47,600	68,000

Model 48 - 6-cyl., 48 hp, 134-1/2" wb
4P Tr	4850	11,400	22,800	38,000	56,000	76,000
5P Tr	4850	11,400	22,800	38,000	56,000	76,000
7P Tr	5000	11,700	23,400	39,000	58,000	78,000
Brgm	5750	10,500	21,000	35,000	49,000	70,000
Lan'let	5750	10,500	21,000	35,000	49,000	70,000
Sub	6100	11,100	22,200	37,000	52,000	74,000
Lan	6100	11,100	22,200	37,000	52,000	74,000
Vestibule Sub	6450	11,100	22,200	37,000	52,000	74,000
Rbt (128" wb)	4850	10,800	21,600	36,000	50,500	72,000

Model 66 - 6-cyl., 66 hp, 140" wb
4P Tr	5850	12,000	24,000	40,000	60,000	80,000
5P Tr	5850	12,300	24,600	41,000	62,000	82,000
7P Tr	6000	12,600	25,200	42,000	64,000	84,000
Sub	7100	12,300	24,600	41,000	62,000	82,000
Lan	7100	12,000	24,000	40,000	60,000	80,000
Vestibule Sub	7450	12,000	24,000	40,000	60,000	80,000
Rbt (133-1/2" wb)	5850	12,000	24,000	40,000	60,000	80,000

1913 Pierce-Arrow, model 38-C, landaulet, HAC

1913
Model 38-C - 6-cyl., 38.4 hp, 119" wb

3P Rbt	4300	9000	18,000	30,000	42,000	60,000
4P Tr	4300	9300	18,600	31,000	43,400	62,000
5P Tr	4300	9600	19,200	32,000	44,800	64,000
6P Brgm	5200	8700	17,400	29,000	40,600	58,000
6P Lan'let	5200	8850	17,700	29,500	41,300	59,000

Model 48-B - 6-cyl., 48.6 hp, 134-1/2" wb
5P Tr	4850	11,400	22,800	38,000	56,000	76,000
Rbt	4850	11,100	22,200	37,000	52,000	74,000
4P Tr	4850	11,400	22,800	38,000	56,000	76,000
7P Tr	5000	11,700	23,400	39,000	58,000	78,000
Brgm	6100	9000	18,000	30,000	42,000	60,000
Lan'let	6100	9300	18,600	31,000	43,400	62,000
7P Sub	6100	9900	19,800	33,000	46,200	66,000
7P Lan	6100	9600	19,200	32,000	44,800	64,000
Vestibule Sub	6300	10,200	20,400	34,000	47,600	68,000
Vestibule Lan	6300	10,200	20,400	34,000	47,600	68,000

Model 66-A - 6-cyl., 60 hp, 147-1/2" wb
7P Tr	6000	13,200	26,400	44,000	68,000	88,000
Rbt	5850	12,000	24,000	40,000	60,000	80,000
4P Tr	5850	12,900	25,800	48,200	66,000	86,000
5P Tr	5850	12,900	25,800	48,200	66,000	86,000
Brgm	7100	10,500	21,000	35,000	49,000	70,000
Lan'let	7100	10,500	21,000	35,000	49,000	70,000
7P Sub	7100	11,400	22,800	38,000	56,000	76,000
7P Lan	7100	11,400	22,800	38,000	56,000	76,000
Vestibule Sub	7300	11,700	23,400	39,000	58,000	78,000
Vestibule Lan	7300	11,700	23,400	39,000	58,000	78,000

1914
Model 38-C - 6-cyl., 38.4 hp, 132" wb

5P Tr	4300	9600	19,200	32,000	44,800	64,000
4P Tr	4300	9300	18,600	31,000	43,400	62,000
7P Brgm	5200	8700	17,400	29,000	40,600	58,000
7P Lan'let	5200	8850	17,700	29,500	41,300	59,000
Vestibule Brgm	5400	9000	18,000	30,000	42,000	60,000
Vestibule Lan	5400	9000	18,000	30,000	42,000	60,000
3P Rbt (127-1/2" wb)	4300	9300	18,600	31,000	43,400	62,000

1914 Pierce-Arrow, model 48-B, touring, HAC

1914
Model 48-B - 6-cyl., 48.6 hp, 142" wb

	FP	5	4	3	2	1
4P Tr	4850	11,400	22,800	38,000	56,000	76,000
5P Tr	4850	11,700	23,400	39,000	58,000	78,000
7P Tr	5000	12,000	24,000	40,000	60,000	80,000
7P Sub	6100	11,700	23,400	39,000	58,000	78,000
7P Lan	6100	10,800	21,600	36,000	50,500	72,000
Vestibule Sub	6300	10,500	21,000	35,000	49,000	70,000
Vestibule Lan	6300	10,500	21,000	35,000	49,000	70,000
Brgm	5800	10,500	21,000	35,000	49,000	70,000
Lan	5800	10,800	21,600	36,000	50,500	72,000
Vestibule Brgm	6000	10,800	21,600	36,000	50,500	72,000
Vestibule Lan'let	6000	10,800	21,600	36,000	50,500	72,000
3P Rbt (134-1/2 "wb)	4850	11,100	22,200	37,000	52,000	74,000

Model 66-A - 6-cyl., 60 hp, 147-1/2" wb

	FP	5	4	3	2	1
4P Tr	5850	12,600	25,200	42,000	64,000	84,000
5P Tr	5850	12,900	25,800	48,200	66,000	86,000
7P Tr	5850	13,200	26,400	44,000	68,000	88,000
7P Sub	7100	12,600	25,200	42,000	64,000	84,000
7P Lan	7100	12,000	24,000	40,000	60,000	80,000
Vestibule Lan	7300	12,000	24,000	40,000	60,000	80,000
7P Brgm	6800	12,000	24,000	40,000	60,000	80,000
7P Lan	6800	12,000	24,000	40,000	60,000	80,000
Vestibule Brgm	7000	12,300	24,600	41,000	62,000	82,000
Vestibule Lan	7000	12,300	24,600	41,000	62,000	82,000
3P Rbt	5850	12,300	24,600	41,000	62,000	82,000

1915 Pierce-Arrow, suburban, OCW

1915
Model 38-C - 6-cyl., 38.4 hp, 134" wb

		5	4	3	2	1
5P Tr	4300	9300	18,600	31,000	43,400	62,000
4P Tr	4300	9000	18,000	30,000	42,000	60,000
2P Rbt	4300	8550	17,100	28,500	39,900	57,000
2P Cpe Rbt	4575	8250	16,500	27,500	38,500	55,000
7P Brgm	5200	8100	16,200	27,000	37,800	54,000
7P Lan'let	5200	8100	16,200	27,000	37,800	54,000
7P Sed	5200	7500	15,000	25,000	35,000	50,000
7P Brgm Lan'let	5200	8250	16,500	27,500	38,500	55,000
Vestibule Brgm	5350	8550	17,100	28,500	39,900	57,000
Vestibule Lan'let	5350	8550	17,100	28,500	39,900	57,000
Vestibule Brgm Lan'let	5350	8550	17,100	28,500	39,900	57,000

Model 48-B - 6-cyl., 48.6 hp, 142" wb

		5	4	3	2	1
5P Tr	4900	11,100	22,200	37,000	52,000	74,000
4P Tr	4900	11,100	22,200	37,000	52,000	74,000
7P Tr	5000	11,400	22,800	38,000	56,000	76,000
2P Rbt	4900	10,800	21,600	36,000	50,500	72,000
2P Cpe Rbt	5175	10,500	21,000	35,000	49,000	70,000
Cpe	5700	10,500	21,000	35,000	49,000	70,000
7P Sub	6000	10,500	21,000	35,000	49,000	70,000
7P Lan	6000	10,500	21,000	35,000	49,000	70,000
7P Brgm	5800	10,500	21,000	35,000	49,000	70,000
Sub Lan	6000	10,800	21,600	36,000	50,500	72,000
Vestibule Sub	6200	10,800	21,600	36,000	50,500	72,000
Vestibule Lan	6200	10,800	21,600	36,000	50,500	72,000
Vestibule Brgm	5950	10,500	21,000	35,000	49,000	70,000
Vestibule Sub Lan	6200	10,500	21,000	35,000	49,000	70,000

Model 66-A - 6-cyl., 60 hp, 147-1/2" wb

		5	4	3	2	1
7P Tr	6000	13,200	26,400	44,000	68,000	88,000
4P Tr	5900	12,600	25,200	42,000	64,000	84,000
5P Tr	5900	12,900	25,800	48,200	66,000	86,000
2P Rbt	5900	12,300	24,600	41,000	62,000	82,000
2P Cpe Rbt	5900	12,000	24,000	40,000	60,000	80,000
7P Sub	7000	12,600	25,200	42,000	64,000	84,000
7P Lan	7000	12,600	25,200	42,000	64,000	84,000
7P Brgm	6800	12,600	25,200	42,000	64,000	84,000
7P Sub Lan	7000	12,600	25,200	42,000	64,000	84,000
Vestibule Lan	7200	12,900	25,800	48,200	66,000	86,000
Vestibule Sub	7200	12,900	25,800	48,200	66,000	86,000
Vestibule Brgm	6950	12,600	25,200	42,000	64,000	84,000
Vestibule Sub Lan	7200	12,900	25,800	48,200	66,000	86,000

1916 Pierce-Arrow, suburban, OCW

1916
Model 38-C - 6-cyl., 38.4 hp, 134" wb

	FP	5	4	3	2	1
5P Tr	4300	10,200	20,400	34,000	47,600	68,000
4P Tr	4300	10,200	20,400	34,000	47,600	68,000
2P Rbt	4300	9900	19,800	33,000	46,200	66,000
3P Rbt	4300	9900	19,800	33,000	46,200	66,000
3P Cpe	5000	8250	16,500	27,500	38,500	55,000
2P Cpe	5000	8250	16,500	27,500	38,500	55,000
7P Brgm	5200	8100	16,200	27,000	37,800	54,000
7P Lan'let	5200	8100	16,200	27,000	37,800	54,000
7P Sed	5200	7800	15,600	26,000	36,400	52,000
Brgm Lan'let	5200	8250	16,500	27,500	38,500	55,000
Vestibule Brgm	5350	8550	17,100	28,500	39,900	57,000
Vestibule Lan'let	5350	8550	17,100	28,500	39,900	57,000
Vestibule Brgm Lan'let	5350	8550	17,100	28,500	39,900	57,000

Model 48-B - 6-cyl., 48.6 hp, 142" wb

		5	4	3	2	1
7P Tr	5000	11,700	23,400	39,000	58,000	78,000
4P Tr	4900	11,400	22,800	38,000	56,000	76,000
5P Tr	4900	11,700	23,400	39,000	58,000	78,000
2P Rbt	4900	11,400	22,800	38,000	56,000	76,000
3P Rbt	4900	11,400	22,800	38,000	56,000	76,000
2P Cpe	5700	9900	19,800	33,000	46,200	66,000
3P Cpe	5700	9900	19,800	33,000	46,200	66,000
7P Sub	6000	10,500	21,000	35,000	49,000	70,000
7P Lan	6000	10,500	21,000	35,000	49,000	70,000
7P Brgm	5800	10,200	20,400	34,000	47,600	68,000
Sub Lan	6000	10,500	21,000	35,000	49,000	70,000
Vestibule Sub	6200	10,500	21,000	35,000	49,000	70,000
Vestibule Lan	6200	10,500	21,000	35,000	49,000	70,000
Vestibule Brgm	5950	10,200	20,400	34,000	47,600	68,000
Vestibule Sub Lan	6200	10,500	21,000	35,000	49,000	70,000

Model 66-A - 6-cyl., 60 hp, 147-1/2" wb

		5	4	3	2	1
7P Tr	6000	12,900	25,800	48,200	66,000	86,000
4P Tr	5900	12,600	25,200	42,000	64,000	84,000
5P Tr	5900	12,600	25,200	42,000	64,000	84,000
2P Rbt	5900	12,300	24,600	41,000	62,000	82,000
3P Rbt	5900	12,600	25,200	42,000	64,000	84,000
2P Cpe	6700	11,400	22,800	38,000	56,000	76,000
3P Cpe	6700	11,400	22,800	38,000	56,000	76,000
7P Sub	7000	12,000	24,000	40,000	60,000	80,000
7P Lan	7000	11,700	23,400	39,000	58,000	78,000
7P Brgm	6800	11,700	23,400	39,000	58,000	78,000
Sub Lan	7000	11,700	23,400	39,000	58,000	78,000
Vestibule Lan	7200	11,700	23,400	39,000	58,000	78,000
Vestibule Sub	7200	11,700	23,400	39,000	58,000	78,000
Vestibule Brgm	6950	11,700	23,400	39,000	58,000	78,000
Vestibule Sub Lan	7200	11,700	23,400	39,000	58,000	78,000

1917
Model 38 - 6-cyl., 38.4 hp, 134" wb

		5	4	3	2	1
5P Tr	4800	9000	18,000	30,000	42,000	60,000
2P Rbt	4800	8700	17,400	29,000	40,600	58,000
3P Rbt	4800	8700	17,400	29,000	40,600	58,000
2P Cpe	5700	6750	13,500	22,500	31,500	45,000
3P Cpe	5700	6900	13,800	23,000	32,200	46,000
4P Tr	4800	8850	17,700	29,500	41,300	59,000
Brgm	5900	6600	13,200	22,000	30,800	44,000
Lan'let	5900	6600	13,200	22,000	30,800	44,000
Sed	5900	6150	12,300	20,500	28,700	41,000
Vestibule Brgm	6100	6750	13,500	22,500	31,500	45,000
Brgm Lan'let	5900	6750	13,500	22,500	31,500	45,000
Vestibule Brgm-Lan'let	6100	7050	14,100	23,500	32,900	47,000
Fr Brgm	5900	7050	14,100	23,500	32,900	47,000
Fr Brgm-Lan'let	5900	7050	14,100	23,500	32,900	47,000

Model 48 - 6-cyl., 48.6 hp, 142" wb

		5	4	3	2	1
7P Tr	5500	10,500	21,000	35,000	49,000	70,000
2P Rbt	5400	9900	19,800	33,000	46,200	66,000
3P Rbt	5400	10,200	20,400	34,000	47,600	68,000
2P Cpe	6400	8250	16,500	27,500	38,500	55,000
3P Cpe	6400	8250	16,500	27,500	38,500	55,000
5P Tr	5400	10,500	21,000	35,000	49,000	70,000
4P Tr	5400	10,200	20,400	34,000	47,600	68,000
Brgm	6600	8100	16,200	27,000	37,800	54,000
Sub	6800	8250	16,500	27,500	38,500	55,000
Lan	6800	8250	16,500	27,500	38,500	55,000
Sub-Lan	6800	8250	16,500	27,500	38,500	55,000
Vestibule Sub	7000	8550	17,100	28,500	39,900	57,000
Vestibule Lan	7000	8550	17,100	28,500	39,900	57,000
Vestibule Brgm	6800	8400	16,800	28,000	39,200	56,000
Vestibule Sub-Lan	7000	8550	17,100	28,500	39,900	57,000

1917 Pierce-Arrow, model 66, touring, AA

1918 Pierce-Arrow, model 48, roadster, HAC

1918
Model 66 - 6-cyl., 60 hp, 147-1/2" wb

	FP	5	4	3	2	1
2P Rbt	6400	12,000	24,000	40,000	60,000	80,000
3P Rbt	6400	12,000	24,000	40,000	60,000	80,000
2P Cpe	7400	11,400	22,800	38,000	56,000	76,000
3P Cpe	7400	11,400	22,800	38,000	56,000	76,000
2P Con Rds	7400	12,000	24,000	40,000	60,000	80,000
3P Con Rds	7400	12,300	24,600	41,000	62,000	82,000
4P Tr	6400	12,600	25,200	42,000	64,000	84,000
5P Tr	6400	12,600	25,200	42,000	64,000	84,000
7P Tr	6500	12,900	25,800	48,200	66,000	86,000
Brgm	7600	10,500	21,000	35,000	49,000	70,000
Sub	7800	10,800	21,600	36,000	50,500	72,000
Lan	7800	10,800	21,600	36,000	50,500	72,000
Sub-Lan	7800	10,800	21,600	36,000	50,500	72,000
Vestibule Lan	8000	11,400	22,800	38,000	56,000	76,000
Vestibule Brgm	7800	11,400	22,800	38,000	56,000	76,000
Vestibule Sub	8000	11,400	22,800	38,000	56,000	76,000
Vestibule Sub Lan	8000	11,400	22,800	38,000	56,000	76,000

1917 Pierce-Arrow, model 66, touring, HAC

1917
Model 66 - 6-cyl., 60 hp, 147-1/2" wb

	FP	5	4	3	2	1
7P Tr	6500	12,900	25,800	48,200	66,000	86,000
2P Rbt	6400	12,300	24,600	41,000	62,000	82,000
3P Rbt	6400	12,300	24,600	41,000	62,000	82,000
2P Cpe	7400	11,400	22,800	38,000	56,000	76,000
3P Cpe	7400	11,400	22,800	38,000	56,000	76,000
4P Tr	6400	12,600	25,200	42,000	64,000	84,000
5P Tr	6400	12,600	25,200	42,000	64,000	84,000
Brgm	7600	10,200	20,400	34,000	47,600	68,000
Sub	7800	10,500	21,000	35,000	49,000	70,000
Lan	7800	10,500	21,000	35,000	49,000	70,000
Sub-Lan	7800	10,500	21,000	35,000	49,000	70,000
Vestibule Sub	8000	10,500	21,000	35,000	49,000	70,000
Vestibule Lan	8000	10,500	21,000	35,000	49,000	70,000
Vestibule Brgm	7800	10,500	21,000	35,000	49,000	70,000
Vestibule Sub-Lan	8000	10.500	21.000	35.000	49.000	70.000

1918
Model 38 - 6-cyl., 38.4 hp, 134" wb

	FP	5	4	3	2	1
5P Tr	4800	10,500	21,000	35,000	49,000	70,000
2P Rbt	4800	10,200	20,400	34,000	47,600	68,000
3P Rbt	4800	10,200	20,400	34,000	47,600	68,000
2P Cpe	5700	8850	17,700	29,500	41,300	59,000
3P Cpe	5700	8850	17,700	29,500	41,300	59,000
2P Conv Rds	5700	10,200	20,400	34,000	47,600	68,000
3P Conv Rds	5700	10,200	20,400	34,000	47,600	68,000
4P Rds	4800	10,500	21,000	35,000	49,000	70,000
4P Tr	4800	10,200	20,400	34,000	47,600	68,000
Brgm	5900	9000	18,000	30,000	42,000	60,000
Lan'let	5900	9000	18,000	30,000	42,000	60,000
Sed	5900	8250	16,500	27,500	38,500	55,000
Vestibule Brgm	6100	8550	17,100	28,500	39,900	57,000
Brgm-Lan'let	5900	8400	16,800	28,000	39,200	56,000
Vestibule Lan'let	6100	8850	17,700	29,500	41,300	59,000
Vestibule Brgm-Lan'let	6100	8850	17,700	29,500	41,300	59,000
Fr Brgm	5900	8700	17,400	29,000	40,600	58,000
Fr Brgm-Lan'let	5900	8700	17,400	29,000	40,600	58,000
Twn Brgm	5900	8700	17,400	29,000	40,600	58,000

Model 48 - 6-cyl., 48.6 hp, 142" wb

	FP	5	4	3	2	1
2P Rbt	5400	10,500	21,000	35,000	49,000	70,000
4P Rbt	5400	10,500	21,000	35,000	49,000	70,000
3P Rbt	5400	10,500	21,000	35,000	49,000	70,000
2P Cpe	6400	9300	18,600	31,000	43,400	62,000
3P Cpe	6400	9300	18,600	31,000	43,400	62,000
2P Conv Rds	6400	10,500	21,000	35,000	49,000	70,000
3P Conv Rds	6400	10,800	21,600	36,000	50,500	72,000
4P Tr	5400	11,100	22,200	37,000	52,000	74,000
5P Tr	5400	11,100	22,200	37,000	52,000	74,000
Brgm	6600	9900	19,800	33,000	46,200	66,000
Sub	6800	9900	19,800	33,000	46,200	66,000
Lan	6800	9900	19,800	33,000	46,200	66,000
Sub Lan	6800	9900	19,800	33,000	46,200	66,000
Vestibule Sub	7000	9900	19,800	33,000	46,200	66,000
Vestibule Lan	7000	9900	19,800	33,000	46,200	66,000
Vestibule Brgm	6800	10,200	20,400	34,000	47,600	68,000
Vestibule Sub-Lan	7000	10,500	21,000	35,000	49,000	70,000
Fr Brgm	6600	9900	19,800	33,000	46,200	66,000
7P Tr	5500	11,400	22,800	38,000	56,000	76,000
7P Sub Lan	6800	10,500	21,000	35,000	49,000	70,000

1919 Pierce-Arrow, model 48-B-5, touring, HAC

1919
Model 48-B-5 - 6-cyl., 48.6 hp, 142" wb

	FP	5	4	3	2	1
7P Tr	6500	12,900	25,800	48,200	66,000	86,000
2P Rbt	6400	11,700	23,400	39,000	58,000	78,000
3P Rbt	6400	11,700	23,400	39,000	58,000	78,000
4P Tr	6400	12,000	24,000	40,000	60,000	80,000
4P Rds	6400	12,600	25,200	42,000	64,000	84,000
5P Tr	6400	12,900	25,800	48,200	66,000	86,000
2P Cpe	7500	10,500	21,000	35,000	49,000	70,000
3P Cpe	7500	10,500	21,000	35,000	49,000	70,000
2P Con Rds	7500	10,500	21,000	35,000	49,000	70,000
3P Con Rds	7500	11,400	22,800	38,000	56,000	76,000
Brgm	7800	10,500	21,000	35,000	49,000	70,000
Brgm Lan'let	7800	10,500	21,000	35,000	49,000	70,000
Fr Brgm	7800	10,500	21,000	35,000	49,000	70,000
Fr Brgm Lan'let	7800	10,500	21,000	35,000	49,000	70,000
Sub	8000	10,500	21,000	35,000	49,000	70,000
Sub Lan	8000	10,500	21,000	35,000	49,000	70,000
Vestibule Brgm	8000	10,500	21,000	35,000	49,000	70,000
Vestibule Brgm Lan	8000	10,500	21,000	35,000	49,000	70,000
Vestibule Sub	8200	10,800	21,600	36,000	50,500	72,000
Vestibule Lan	8200	10,800	21,600	36,000	50,500	72,000
Vestibule Sub Lan	8200	10,800	21,600	36,000	50,500	72,000

1920 Pierce-Arrow, model 38, roadster, AA

1920
Model 38 - 6 cyl., 38 hp, 134" wb

	FP	5	4	3	2	1
2P & 3P Rbt	7250	9900	19,800	33,000	46,200	66,000
4P Tr	7250	9900	19,800	33,000	46,200	66,000
4P Rds	7250	9900	19,800	33,000	46,200	66,000
5P Tr	7250	10,200	20,400	34,000	47,600	68,000
7P Tr	7250	10,500	21,000	35,000	49,000	70,000
2P & 3P Cpe	8250	8250	16,500	27,500	38,500	55,000
4P Sed	8550	6000	12,000	20,000	28,000	40,000
7P Sed	8750	6300	12,600	21,000	29,400	42,000
Brgm	8550	6750	13,500	22,500	31,500	45,000
Fr Brgm	8550	7050	14,100	23,500	32,900	47,000
Brgm Lan'let	8550	7050	14,100	23,500	32,900	47,000
Tourer Brgm	8550	7050	14,100	23,500	32,900	47,000
Vestibule Brgm	8750	7200	14,400	24,000	33,600	48,000

Model 48 - 6-cyl., 48 hp, 142" wb

	FP	5	4	3	2	1
2P & 4P Rbt	7650	10,200	20,400	34,000	47,600	68,000
4P Tr	7650	10,500	21,000	35,000	49,000	70,000
4P Rds	7650	10,500	21,000	35,000	49,000	70,000
5P Tr	7650	10,800	21,600	36,000	50,500	72,000
6P Tr	7750	11,400	22,800	38,000	56,000	76,000
2P & 3P Cpe	8750	9000	18,000	30,000	42,000	60,000
5P Brgm	9050	9600	19,200	32,000	44,800	64,000
7P Fr Brgm	9050	9600	19,200	32,000	44,800	64,000
7P Sub	9250	9900	19,800	33,000	46,200	66,000
7P Vestibule Sub	9450	10,200	20,400	34,000	47,600	68,000
7P Fr Sub	9250	9900	19,800	33,000	46,200	66,000

1921
Model 38 - 6-cyl., 38 hp, 138" wb

	FP	5	4	3	2	1
4P Tr	7500	9900	19,800	33,000	46,200	66,000
6P Tr	7500	9900	19,800	33,000	46,200	66,000
7P Tr	7500	10,200	20,400	34,000	47,600	68,000
3P Rds	8000	10,200	20,400	34,000	47,600	68,000
4P Cpe	8500	8250	16,500	27,500	38,500	55,000
7P Brgm	8500	7500	15,000	25,000	35,000	50,000
7P Limo	8750	7800	15,600	26,000	36,400	52,000
6P Sed	9000	7500	15,000	25,000	35,000	50,000
Vestibule 6P Sed	9000	7800	15,600	26,000	36,400	52,000
7P Lan	9000	8100	16,200	27,000	37,800	54,000

1922 Pierce-Arrow, model 33, touring, AA

1922 Pierce-Arrow, model 33, touring, HAC

1922 Pierce-Arrow, model 33, coupe, HAC

1922
Model 38 - 6-cyl., 38 hp, 138" wb

	FP	5	4	3	2	1
4P Tr	6500	9900	19,800	33,000	46,200	66,000
7P Tr	6500	10,200	20,400	34,000	47,600	68,000
3P Rds	7000	9900	19,800	33,000	46,200	66,000
7P Brgm	8000	7500	15,000	25,000	35,000	50,000
Cpe Sed	8000	7350	14,700	24,500	34,300	49,000
3P Cpe	8000	8250	16,500	27,500	38,500	55,000
4P Sed	8250	8400	16,800	28,000	39,200	56,000
Lan'let	8240	7350	14,700	24,500	34,300	49,000
Limo	8250	7500	15,000	25,000	35,000	50,000
Fml Limo	8250	7800	15,600	26,000	36,400	52,000
Vestibule Sed	8500	8100	16,200	27,000	37,800	54,000
Sed	8500	8250	16,500	27,500	38,500	55,000

1923 Pierce-Arrow, model 33, touring, HAC

1923
Model 38 - 6-cyl., 138" wb

	FP	5	4	3	2	1
7P Tr	5250	9000	18,000	30,000	42,000	60,000
4P Tr	5250	8700	17,400	29,000	40,600	58,000
2P Rbt	5250	8250	16,500	27,500	38,500	55,000
3P Cpe	6800	7200	14,400	24,000	33,600	48,000
4P Cpe Sed	6800	6900	13,800	23,000	32,200	46,000
6P Brgm	6800	6750	13,500	22,500	31,500	45,000
4P Sed	6900	6300	12,600	21,000	29,400	42,000
7P Sed	7000	6600	13,200	22,000	30,800	44,000
6P Lan'let	7000	7500	15,000	25,000	35,000	50,000
7P Limo	7000	7800	15,600	26,000	36,400	52,000
7P Encl Drive Limo	7000	8100	16,200	27,000	37,800	54,000
7P Fml Limo	7000	8250	16,500	27,500	38,500	55,000

1924 Pierce-Arrow, model 33, convertible coupe, OCW

1924
Model 33 - 6-cyl., 138" wb

	FP	5	4	3	2	1
7P Tr	5250	9000	18,000	30,000	42,000	60,000
6P Tr	5250	8700	17,400	29,000	40,600	58,000
4P Tr	5250	8400	16,800	28,000	39,200	56,000
Rbt	5250	7800	15,600	26,000	36,400	52,000
6P Brgm	6800	6750	13,500	22,500	31,500	45,000
3P Cpe	6800	7500	15,000	25,000	35,000	50,000
4P Cpe Sed	6900	7650	15,300	25,500	35,700	51,000
4P 4 dr Sed	6900	7200	14,400	24,000	33,600	48,000
7P Encl Drive Limo	7000	8550	17,100	28,500	39,900	57,000
7P Fml Limo	7000	8700	17,400	29,000	40,600	58,000
6P Lan'let	7000	8700	17,400	29,000	40,600	58,000
7P Limo	7000	8700	17,400	29,000	40,600	58,000
7P Sed	7000	8700	17,400	29,000	40,600	58,000
7P Fml Lan	7500	8850	17,700	29,500	41,300	59,000
7P Limo Lan	7500	8850	17,700	29,500	41,300	59,000
4P Sed Lan	7500	8850	17,700	29,500	41,300	59,000
3P Cpe Lan	8000	9000	18,000	30,000	42,000	60,000
7P Encl Drive Lan	8000	9000	18,000	30,000	42,000	60,000
7P Sed Lan	8000	9000	18,000	30,000	42,000	60,000

1925 Pierce-Arrow, model 80, runabout, HAC

1925
Model 80 - 6-cyl., 130" wb

	FP	5	4	3	2	1
7P Tr	2895	8250	16,500	27,500	38,500	55,000
4P Tr	—	8100	16,200	27,000	37,800	54,000
5P Sed	3895	6300	12,600	21,000	29,400	42,000
4P Cpe	—	7050	14,100	23,500	32,900	47,000
7P Sed	3995	6450	12,900	21,500	30,100	43,000
Encl Drive Limo	4045	7500	15,000	25,000	35,000	50,000
2P Rbt	2895	7800	15,600	26,000	36,400	52,000

Model 33 - 6-cyl., 138" wb

	FP	5	4	3	2	1
2P Rbt	5250	8550	17,100	28,500	39,900	57,000
4P Tr	5250	8700	17,400	29,000	40,600	58,000
6P Tr	5250	8850	17,700	29,500	41,300	59,000
7P Tr	5250	9000	18,000	30,000	42,000	60,000
Brgm	6800	7800	15,600	26,000	36,400	52,000
Cpe	6800	8250	16,500	27,500	38,500	55,000
4P Sed	6900	7500	15,000	25,000	35,000	50,000
Cpe Sed	6900	7500	15,000	25,000	35,000	50,000
Lan'let	7000	7800	15,600	26,000	36,400	52,000
7P Sed	7000	7650	15,300	25,500	35,700	51,000
Encl Drive Sed	7000	7800	15,600	26,000	36,400	52,000
Limo	7000	8250	16,500	27,500	38,500	55,000
Lan	7500	8250	16,500	27,500	38,500	55,000
Encl Drive Lan	8000	8400	16,800	28,000	39,200	56,000

1926
Model 33 - 6-cyl., 100 hp, 138" wb

	FP	5	4	3	2	1
4P Tr	5250	9000	18,000	30,000	42,000	60,000
2P Rbt	5250	8700	17,400	29,000	40,600	58,000
6P Tr	5250	9300	18,600	31,000	43,400	62,000
7P Tr	5250	9900	19,800	33,000	46,200	66,000
6P Brgm	6800	8250	16,500	27,500	38,500	55,000
3P Cpe	6800	7050	14,100	23,500	32,900	47,000
4P Sed	6900	6750	13,500	22,500	31,500	45,000
4P Cpe Sed	6900	6900	13,800	23,000	32,200	46,000
4P Encl Drive Limo	7000	8400	16,800	28,000	39,200	56,000
7P Sed	7000	7800	15,600	26,000	36,400	52,000
6P Lan'let	7000	8550	17,100	28,500	39,900	57,000
7P Fr Limo	7000	8550	17,100	28,500	39,900	57,000
7P Sed Lan'let	8000	8700	17,400	29,000	40,600	58,000
4P Sed Lan'let	7500	8550	17,100	28,500	39,900	57,000
3P Cpe Lan'let	8000	8550	17,100	28,500	39,900	57,000
7P Limo	7000	8550	17,100	28,500	39,900	57,000
7P Encl Drive Limo	7000	8400	16,800	28,000	39,200	56,000
7P Encl Drive Lan'let	8000	9000	18,000	30,000	42,000	60,000

1926 Pierce-Arrow, model 80, 4-dr. sedan, AA

1927 Pierce-Arrow, model 36, landau, AA

1926 Pierce-Arrow, model 80, roadster, HAC

1927 Pierce-Arrow, model 36, two-passenger coupe, Judkins, HAC

1927
Model 80 - 6-cyl., 70 hp, 130" wb

	FP	5	4	3	2	1
7P Tr	2895	8400	16,800	28,000	39,200	56,000
4P Tr	3095	8250	16,500	27,500	38,500	55,000
2P Rds	2895	8100	16,200	27,000	37,800	54,000
4P Cpe	3695	7200	14,400	24,000	33,600	48,000
7P Sed	3995	6300	12,600	21,000	29,400	42,000
7P Encl Drive Limo	4045	8250	16,500	27,500	38,500	55,000
5P Sed	3895	6150	12,300	20,500	28,700	41,000
5P 2 dr Coach	2995	6300	12,600	21,000	29,400	42,000
5P 4 dr Coach	3250	6750	13,500	22,500	31,500	45,000
4P Cpe	3695	7350	14,700	24,500	34,300	49,000
2P Cpe	3100	7050	14,100	23,500	32,900	47,000
7P 4 dr Coach	3350	7050	14,100	23,500	32,900	47,000
7P Limo Coach	3450	7800	15,600	26,000	36,400	52,000

Model 36 - 6-cyl., 100 hp, 138" wb

	FP	5	4	3	2	1
2P Rbt	5875	9300	18,600	31,000	43,400	62,000
4P Tr	5875	9600	19,200	32,000	44,800	64,000
7P Tr	5875	9900	19,800	33,000	46,200	66,000
3P Cpe	6375	8850	17,700	29,500	41,300	59,000
4P 4 dr Sed	6375	7500	15,000	25,000	35,000	50,000
4P Cpe Sed	6375	7800	15,600	26,000	36,400	52,000
4P Encl Drive Limo	6375	8700	17,400	29,000	40,600	58,000
7P Encl Drive Lan	6000	8550	17,100	28,500	39,900	57,000
7P Sed	5875	8250	16,500	27,500	38,500	55,000
7P Sed Lan	6000	8100	16,200	27,000	37,800	54,000
4P Sed Lan	6600	8250	16,500	27,500	38,500	55,000
7P Encl Drive Limo	5875	8400	16,800	28,000	39,200	56,000
7P Fr Limo	7500	8550	17,100	28,500	39,900	57,000
4P Encl Drive Limo	6600	8250	16,500	27,500	38,500	55,000

1926 Pierce-Arrow, model 80, sedan, HAC

1926
Model 80 - 6-cyl., 70 hp, 130" wb

	FP	5	4	3	2	1
7P Tr	2895	8250	16,500	27,500	38,500	55,000
4P Tr	3095	7800	15,600	26,000	36,400	52,000
2P Rds	2895	7950	15,900	26,500	37,100	53,000
4P Cpe	3695	7200	14,400	24,000	33,600	48,000
7P Sed	3995	6750	13,500	22,500	31,500	45,000
7P Encl Drive Limo	4045	7500	15,000	25,000	35,000	50,000
5P Sed	3895	6600	13,200	22,000	30,800	44,000
4P Cpe Lan	3820	6900	13,800	23,000	32,200	46,000
5P Coach	3150	6300	12,600	21,000	29,400	42,000

1928 Pierce-Arrow, model 81, sedan, HAC

1928
Model 81 - 6-cyl., 75 hp, 130" wb

	FP	5	4	3	2	1
4P Rbt	2900	9300	18,600	31,000	43,400	62,000
4P Tr	3100	9600	19,200	32,000	44,800	64,000
4P Rds	3450	9600	19,200	32,000	44,800	64,000
5P Brgm	3250	8100	16,200	27,000	37,800	54,000
2P Cpe	3250	8250	16,500	27,500	38,500	55,000
5P Clb Sed	3300	8250	16,500	27,500	38,500	55,000
4P Cpe	3350	8400	16,800	28,000	39,200	56,000
5P Sed	3350	7800	15,600	26,000	36,400	52,000
Spt Sed Lan	3350	7950	15,900	26,500	37,100	53,000
Clb Sed Lan	3400	8100	16,200	27,000	37,800	54,000
7P Sed	3450	8100	16,200	27,000	37,800	54,000
4P Cpe DeL	3450	8550	17,100	28,500	39,900	57,000
7P Encl Drive Limo	3550	8850	17,700	29,500	41,300	59,000

Model 36 - 6-cyl., 100 hp, 138" wb

4P Rbt	5875	11,400	22,800	38,000	56,000	76,000
4P Tr	5875	11,700	23,400	39,000	58,000	78,000
7P Tr	5875	12,000	24,000	40,000	60,000	80,000
Encl Drive Limo	5875	10,500	21,000	35,000	49,000	70,000
7P Sed	5875	9900	19,800	33,000	46,200	66,000
7P Encl Drive Lan'let	6000	10,500	21,000	35,000	49,000	70,000
7P Sed Lan	6000	10,200	20,400	34,000	47,600	68,000
3P Cpe	6375	10,200	20,400	34,000	47,600	68,000
4P Cpe Sed	6375	10,200	20,400	34,000	47,600	68,000
4P Encl Drive Sed	6375	9900	19,800	33,000	46,200	66,000
4P Sed	6375	9000	18,000	30,000	42,000	60,000
6P Encl Drive Limo	6375	10,500	21,000	35,000	49,000	70,000
4P C.C.Sed	6475	9300	18,600	31,000	43,400	62,000
4P Sed Lan	6600	9600	19,200	32,000	44,800	64,000
4P Encl Drive Lan	6600	9300	18,600	31,000	43,400	62,000
6P Fml Limo	7500	10,800	21,600	36,000	50,500	72,000
6P Fr Lan	8000	11,100	22,200	37,000	52,000	74,000

1929 Pierce-Arrow, model 125, 7-pass. sedan, AA

1929 Pierce-Arrow, model 126, 4-dr. sedan, AA

1929
Model 125 - 8-cyl., 125 hp, 133" wb

	FP	5	4	3	2	1
4P Rds	2875	12,300	24,600	41,000	62,000	82,000
4P Tr	2975	12,000	24,000	40,000	60,000	80,000
5P Brgm	2775	9000	18,000	30,000	42,000	60,000
4P Cpe	2875	9900	19,800	33,000	46,200	66,000
5P Sed	2975	9300	18,600	31,000	43,400	62,000
5P Twn Sed	3150	9600	19,200	32,000	44,800	64,000
7P Sed	3150	9600	19,200	32,000	44,800	64,000
7P Encl Drive Limo	3350	10,200	20,400	34,000	47,600	68,000

1929
Model 126 - 8-cyl., 125 hp, 143" wb

	FP	5	4	3	2	1
7P Tr	3750	12,900	25,800	48,200	66,000	86,000
4P Conv Cpe	3750	11,400	22,800	38,000	56,000	76,000
7P Sed	3975	10,200	20,400	34,000	47,600	68,000
7P Encl Drive Limo	3750	10,500	21,000	35,000	49,000	70,000
4P Sed	5750	9900	19,800	33,000	46,200	66,000

1930 Pierce-Arrow, model C, club brougham, Weymann, AA

1930
Model C - 8-cyl., 115 hp, 132" wb

Clb Brgm	2595	6750	13,500	22,500	31,500	45,000
Cpe	2750	7050	14,100	23,500	32,900	47,000
Sed	2750	6300	12,600	21,000	29,400	42,000

Model B - 8-cyl., 125 hp, 134" wb

Rds	2975	14,700	29,400	49,000	78,000	98,000
Tr	2975	14,400	28,800	48,000	76,000	96,000
Spt Phaeton	3275	15,000	30,000	50,000	80,000	100,000
Conv Cpe	3250	14,400	28,800	48,000	76,000	96,000

Model B- 8-cyl., 125 hp, 139" wb

5P Sed	3275	9900	19,800	33,000	46,200	66,000
Vic Cpe	3350	10,200	20,400	34,000	47,600	68,000
7P Sed	3475	9900	19,800	33,000	46,200	66,000
Clb Sed	3550	10,500	21,000	35,000	49,000	70,000
Encl Drive Limo	3675	11,400	22,800	38,000	56,000	76,000

Model A - 8-cyl., 132 hp, 144" wb

Tr	3975	18,500	33,000	55,000	88,000	110,000
Conv Cpe	3975	17,100	31,800	53,000	85,000	106,000
Sed	4275	11,400	22,800	38,000	56,000	76,000
Encl Drive Limo	4475	12,000	24,000	40,000	60,000	80,000
Twn Car	6250	12,300	24,600	41,000	62,000	82,000

1931 Pierce-Arrow, model 41, LeBaron custom club sedan, AA

1931 Pierce-Arrow, town car, Willoughby, HAC

1931
Model 43 - 8-cyl., 125 hp, 134" wb

Rds	2895	15,000	30,000	50,000	80,000	100,000
Tourer	2895	15,000	30,000	50,000	80,000	100,000
Cpe	2685	9900	19,800	33,000	46,200	66,000

Model 43 - 8-cyl., 125 hp, 137" wb

5P Sed	2685	6750	13,500	22,500	31,500	45,000
Clb Sed	2785	7050	14,100	23,500	32,900	47,000
7P Sed	2995	6900	13,800	23,000	32,200	46,000
Encl Drive Limo	3145	7500	15,000	25,000	35,000	50,000

1931
Model 42 - 8-cyl., 132 hp, 142" wb

	FP	5	4	3	2	1
Rds	3325	18,500	33,000	55,000	88,000	110,000
Tourer	3325	18,500	33,000	55,000	88,000	110,000
Spt Tourer	3625	20,600	34,800	58,000	91,000	116,000
Conv Cpe	3550	15,000	30,000	50,000	80,000	100,000
5P Sed	3695	7500	15,000	25,000	35,000	50,000
Clb Sed	3695	7950	15,900	26,500	37,100	53,000
7P Sed	3825	7800	15,600	26,000	36,400	52,000
Clb Berl	3895	8250	16,500	27,500	38,500	55,000
Encl Drive Limo	3995	9000	18,000	30,000	42,000	60,000

Model 41 - 8-cyl., 132 hp, 147" wb

	FP	5	4	3	2	1
Touring	4275	18,500	33,000	55,000	88,000	110,000
Conv Cpe	4275	17,100	31,800	53,000	85,000	106,000
Sed	4785	8100	16,200	27,000	37,800	54,000
Encl Drive Limo	4985	9300	18,600	31,000	43,400	62,000
Twn Car	6250	9600	19,200	32,000	44,800	64,000

1933 Pierce Silver Arrow, show car, AA

1932 Pierce-Arrow, model 54, convertible, HAC

1933 Pierce-Arrow, club brougham, OCW

1933
Model 836 - 8-cyl., 135 hp, 136" wb

	FP	5	4	3	2	1
5P Clb Brgm	2385	6150	12,300	20,500	28,700	41,000
5P Sed	2575	6300	12,600	21,000	29,400	42,000
5P Clb Sed	2695	6900	13,800	23,000	32,200	46,000
7P Sed	2850	6450	12,900	21,500	30,100	43,000
7P Encl Drive Limo	2976	7500	15,000	25,000	35,000	50,000

Model 1236 - 12-cyl., 160 hp, 136" wb

	FP	5	4	3	2	1
5P Clb Brgm	2785	6900	13,800	23,000	32,200	46,000
5P Sed	2975	7050	14,100	23,500	32,900	47,000
5P Clb Sed	3095	7650	15,300	25,500	35,700	51,000
7P Sed (139")	3250	7200	14,400	24,000	33,600	48,000
7P Encl Drive Limo	3375	8250	16,500	27,500	38,500	55,000

Model 1242 - 12-cyl., 175 hp, 137" wb

	FP	5	4	3	2	1
5P Tr	3950	13,500	27,000	45,000	70,000	90,000
5P Spt Phae	4150	14,400	28,800	48,000	76,000	96,000
7P Tourer (142")	4250	13,800	27,600	46,000	73,500	92,000
5P Clb Brgm	3650	7200	14,400	24,000	33,600	48,000
5P Sed	3785	7350	14,700	24,500	34,300	49,000
5P Clb Sed	3950	7950	15,900	26,500	37,100	53,000
5P Clb Berl	4150	8250	16,500	27,500	38,500	55,000
4P Cpe	3785	8550	17,100	28,500	39,900	57,000
4P Cust Rds	3900	14,700	29,400	49,000	78,000	98,000
5P Conv Sed	4250	13,500	27,000	45,000	70,000	90,000
7P Sed (142")	3985	7500	15,000	25,000	35,000	50,000
7P Encl Drive Limo	4250	9000	18,000	30,000	42,000	60,000

Model 1247 - 12-cyl., 175 hp, 142" wb

	FP	5	4	3	2	1
5P Sed	4295	9000	18,000	30,000	42,000	60,000
5P Clb Sed	4400	9300	18,600	31,000	43,400	62,000
7P Sed (147")	4535	9300	18,600	31,000	43,400	62,000
5P Clb Berl	4600	9300	18,600	31,000	43,400	62,000
7P Encl Drive Limo	4800	9900	19,800	33,000	46,200	66,000
5P Conv Sed	4250	13,500	27,000	45,000	70,000	90,000
4P Cpe (147")	5300	10,500	21,000	35,000	49,000	70,000
5P Conv Sed (147")	5700	20,600	34,800	58,000	91,000	116,000
5P Clb Sed (147")	5700	9900	19,800	33,000	46,200	66,000
5P Conv Sed (147")	6100	22,800	36,000	60,000	93,000	120,000
Encl Drive Limo (147")	6200	10,500	21,000	35,000	49,000	70,000
7P Twn Brgm (147")	6700	10,800	21,600	36,000	50,500	72,000
7P Twn Car (147")	6700	11,400	22,800	38,000	56,000	76,000
7P Twn Cabr (147")	7200	20,600	34,800	58,000	91,000	116,000
7P Encl Drive Brgm	7200	11,400	22,800	38,000	56,000	76,000

1932 Pierce-Arrow, model 53, convertible, AA

1932
Model 54 - 8-cyl., 125 hp, 137" wb

	FP	5	4	3	2	1
Conv Cpe Rds	2650	14,400	28,800	48,000	76,000	96,000
5P Tr	2750	14,100	28,200	47,000	74,000	94,000
Phae	3050	14,400	28,800	48,000	76,000	96,000
Brgm	3050	7350	14,700	24,500	34,300	49,000
Cpe	2485	8250	16,500	27,500	38,500	55,000
5P Sed	2485	7200	14,400	24,000	33,600	48,000
Clb Sed	2650	7350	14,700	24,500	34,300	49,000
Clb Berl	2850	7500	15,000	25,000	35,000	50,000
Con Sed	2950	14,400	28,800	48,000	76,000	96,000

Model 54 - 8-cyl., 125 hp, 142" wb

	FP	5	4	3	2	1
7P Tr	2850	15,000	30,000	50,000	80,000	100,000
7P Sed	2750	7500	15,000	25,000	35,000	50,000
Limo	2950	8250	16,500	27,500	38,500	55,000

Model 53 - 12-cyl., 140 hp, 137" wb

	FP	5	4	3	2	1
Conv Cpe Rds	3450	18,500	33,000	55,000	88,000	110,000
5P Tr	3550	20,600	34,800	58,000	91,000	116,000
Phae	3850	18,500	33,000	55,000	88,000	110,000
Clb Brgm	3185	8250	16,500	27,500	38,500	55,000
Cpe	3285	8550	17,100	28,500	39,900	57,000
5P Sed	3285	7800	15,600	26,000	36,400	52,000
Clb Sed	3450	8100	16,200	27,000	37,800	54,000
Clb Berl	3650	9000	18,000	30,000	42,000	60,000
Con Sed	3750	15,000	30,000	50,000	80,000	100,000

Model 53 - 12-cyl., 140 hp, 142" wb

	FP	5	4	3	2	1
7P Tr	3650	18,500	33,000	55,000	88,000	110,000
7P Sed	3550	9000	18,000	30,000	42,000	60,000
Limo	3750	9900	19,800	33,000	46,200	66,000

Model 51 - 12-cyl., 150 hp, 147" wb

	FP	5	4	3	2	1
Cpe	5550	9300	18,600	31,000	43,400	62,000
Conv Vic Cpe	5300	20,600	34,800	58,000	91,000	116,000
Clb Sed	5800	9300	18,600	31,000	43,400	62,000
Conv Sed	5800	18,500	33,000	55,000	88,000	110,000
Encl Drive Limo	6300	11,400	22,800	38,000	56,000	76,000
A.W. Twn Brgm	6800	13,500	27,000	45,000	70,000	90,000
A.W. Twn Cabr	7300	14,400	28,800	48,000	76,000	96,000
Encl Drive Brgm	—	12,900	25,800	48,200	66,000	86,000

1934 Pierce-Arrow, model 1240A, Rollston convertible sedan, AA

1934
Model 840A - 8-cyl., 139" wb

	FP	5	4	3	2	1
Rds	2995	9900	19,800	33,000	46,200	66,000
Brgm	2795	7050	14,100	23,500	32,900	47,000
Sed	2895	7200	14,400	24,000	33,600	48,000
Clb Sed	2995	7350	14,700	24,500	34,300	49,000
Cpe	2895	7800	15,600	26,000	36,400	52,000

Model 840A - 8-cyl., 144" wb

	FP	5	4	3	2	1
Silver Arrow	3495	18,500	33,000	55,000	88,000	110,000
Sed	3200	7500	15,000	25,000	35,000	50,000
Encl Drive Limo	3350	9000	18,000	30,000	42,000	60,000

Model 1240A - 12-cyl., 139" wb

	FP	5	4	3	2	1
Rds	3395	12,900	25,800	48,200	66,000	86,000
Brgm	3195	7500	15,000	25,000	35,000	50,000
Sed	3295	7650	15,300	25,500	35,700	51,000
Clb Sed	3395	7800	15,600	26,000	36,400	52,000
Cpe	3895	8250	16,500	27,500	38,500	55,000

Model 1250A - 12-cyl., 144" wb

	FP	5	4	3	2	1
Silver Arrow	3295	22,000	36,000	60,000	93,000	120,000
Sed	3600	8250	16,500	27,500	38,500	55,000
Encl Drive Limo	3750	9900	19,800	33,000	46,200	66,000

Model 1248A - 12-cyl., 147" wb

	FP	5	4	3	2	1
Sed	4295	9000	18,000	30,000	42,000	60,000
Encl Drive Limo	4495	10,500	21,000	35,000	49,000	70,000

1935 Pierce-Arrow, Brunn town car, AA

1935 Pierce-Arrow, model 845, sedan, HAC

1935
Model 845 - 8-cyl., 140 hp, 138" wb

	FP	5	4	3	2	1
Conv Rds	2995	9600	19,200	32,000	44,800	64,000
Clb Brgm	2795	6750	13,500	22,500	31,500	45,000
Cpe	2895	7350	14,700	24,500	34,300	49,000
5P Sed	2895	6900	13,800	23,000	32,200	46,000
Clb Sed	3200	7050	14,100	23,500	32,900	47,000

Model 845 - 8-cyl., 140 hp, 144" wb

	FP	5	4	3	2	1
7P Sed	3200	7200	14,400	24,000	33,600	48,000
Encl Drive Limo	3350	8250	16,500	27,500	38,500	55,000
Silver Arrow	3495	18,500	33,000	55,000	88,000	110,000

Model 1245 - 12-cyl., 175 hp, 138" wb

	FP	5	4	3	2	1
Conv Rds	3395	12,000	24,000	40,000	60,000	80,000
Clb Brgm	3195	7500	15,000	25,000	35,000	50,000
Cpe	3295	8250	16,500	27,500	38,500	55,000
5P Sed	3295	7650	15,300	25,500	35,700	51,000
Clb Sed	3395	7800	15,600	26,000	36,400	52,000

Model 1245 - 12-cyl., 175 hp, 144" wb

	FP	5	4	3	2	1
7P Sed	3600	8550	17,100	28,500	39,900	57,000
Encl Drive Limo	3750	9000	18,000	30,000	42,000	60,000
Silver Arrow	3895	22,000	36,000	60,000	93,000	120,000

Model 1255 - 12-cyl., 175 hp, 147" wb

	FP	5	4	3	2	1
7P Sed	4295	9000	18,000	30,000	42,000	60,000
Encl Drive Limo	4495	9900	19,800	33,000	46,200	66,000

1936 Pierce-Arrow, Salon Twelve, sedan, AA

1936 Pierce-Arrow, metropolitan town brougham, Brunn, HAC

1936
Deluxe 8 - 150 hp, 139" wb

	FP	5	4	3	2	1
Cpe	3195	6750	13,500	22,500	31,500	45,000
Ctry Club Rds	3295	9000	18,000	30,000	42,000	60,000
Clb Sed	3295	6000	12,000	20,000	28,000	40,000
5P Sed	3195	5850	11,700	19,500	27,300	39,000
Clb Berl	3445	6750	13,500	22,500	31,500	45,000

Deluxe 8 - 150 hp, 144" wb

	FP	5	4	3	2	1
7P Sed	3500	6300	12,600	21,000	29,400	42,000
Limo	3650	7500	15,000	25,000	35,000	50,000
Metropolitan Twn Car	5295	8250	16,500	27,500	38,500	55,000
Conv Sed	4100	9900	19,800	33,000	46,200	66,000

Salon Twelve - 185 hp, 139" wb

	FP	5	4	3	2	1
Cpe	3695	7500	15,000	25,000	35,000	50,000
Ctry Club Rds	3795	10,500	21,000	35,000	49,000	70,000
Clb Sed	3795	6600	13,200	22,000	30,800	44,000
5P Sed	3695	6450	12,900	21,500	30,100	43,000
Clb Berl	3795	7500	15,000	25,000	35,000	50,000

Salon Twelve - 185 hp, 144" wb

	FP	5	4	3	2	1
7P Sed	4000	7200	14,400	24,000	33,600	48,000
Limo	4150	8250	16,500	27,500	38,500	55,000
Metropolitan Twn Car	5795	9000	18,000	30,000	42,000	60,000
Conv Sed	4600	11,400	22,800	38,000	56,000	76,000
7P Sed (147")	4795	8250	16,500	27,500	38,500	55,000
7P Encl Drive Limo	4995	9300	18,600	31,000	43,400	62,000

1937 Pierce-Arrow, Salon Twelve, sedan, HAC

1937
Pierce-Arrow 8 - 150 hp, 138" wb

	FP	5	4	3	2	1
Cpe	3195	6600	13,200	22,000	30,800	44,000
5P Sed	3195	5700	11,400	19,000	26,600	38,000
Conv Rds	3295	9000	18,000	30,000	42,000	60,000
Clb Sed	3295	5850	11,700	19,500	27,300	39,000
Clb Berl	3495	6000	12,000	20,000	28,000	40,000
Fml Sed	3630	6900	13,800	23,000	32,200	46,000

Pierce-Arrow 8 - 150 hp, 144" wb

	FP	5	4	3	2	1
7P Fml Sed	3495	7500	15,000	25,000	35,000	50,000
7P Sed	3500	7050	14,100	23,500	32,900	47,000
Limo	3650	8250	16,500	27,500	38,500	55,000
Conv Sed	4100	10,500	21,000	35,000	49,000	70,000
Brunn Metro Twn Car	5295	9000	18,000	30,000	42,000	60,000
Twn Brgm	5520	8550	17,100	28,500	39,900	57,000
5P Encl Drive Limo (147")	4415	8400	16,800	28,000	39,200	56,000

Pierce-Arrow 12 - 185 hp, 139" wb

	FP	5	4	3	2	1
Cpe	3795	7200	14,400	24,000	33,600	48,000
5P Sed	3695	6300	12,600	21,000	29,400	42,000
Conv Rds	3695	10,500	21,000	35,000	49,000	70,000
Clb Sed	3795	6450	12,900	21,500	30,100	43,000
Clb Berl	3795	6600	13,200	22,000	30,800	44,000
5P Fml Sed	3945	7500	15,000	25,000	35,000	50,000

Pierce-Arrow 12 - 185 hp, 144" wb

	FP	5	4	3	2	1
7P Sed	4000	6750	13,500	22,500	31,500	45,000
Limo	4150	7500	15,000	25,000	35,000	50,000
Conv Sed	4650	12,900	25,800	48,200	66,000	86,000
Brunn Metro Twn Brgm	6040	10,500	21,000	35,000	49,000	70,000

Pierce-Arrow 12 - 185 hp, 147" wb

	FP	5	4	3	2	1
7P Sed	5220	8250	16,500	27,500	38,500	55,000
Encl Drive Limo	6760	9300	18,600	31,000	43,400	62,000
Metro Twn Car	7270	10,800	21,600	36,000	50,500	72,000

1938
Pierce-Arrow 8 - 150 hp, 139" wb

	FP	5	4	3	2	1
5P Sed	3375	5400	10,800	18,000	25,200	36,000
Clb Sed	3480	5700	11,400	19,000	26,600	38,000
Cpe	3375	6450	12,900	21,500	30,100	43,000
Conv Cpe	3460	9000	18,000	30,000	42,000	60,000
Clb Berl	3630	6300	12,600	21,000	29,400	42,000
Fml Sed	3630	5850	11,700	19,500	27,300	39,000

1938
Pierce-Arrow 8 - 150 hp, 144" wb

	FP	5	4	3	2	1
Brunn Metro Twn Brgm	5520	8400	16,800	28,000	39,200	56,000
7P Sed	3690	7200	14,400	24,000	33,600	48,000
Encl Drive Limo	3840	7800	15,600	26,000	36,400	52,000
Con Sed	4300	10,500	21,000	35,000	49,000	70,000
Spl Sed	3530	7050	14,100	23,500	32,900	47,000
Fml Sed	4350	7500	15,000	25,000	35,000	50,000

Pierce-Arrow 12 - 185 hp, 139" wb

	FP	5	4	3	2	1
5P Sed	3895	7500	15,000	25,000	35,000	50,000
Clb Sed	4000	7800	15,600	26,000	36,400	52,000
Cpe	3895	8700	17,400	29,000	40,600	58,000
Conv Cpe	4000	11,400	22,800	38,000	56,000	76,000
Clb Berl	4155	6750	13,500	22,500	31,500	45,000
Fml Sed	4155	6750	13,500	22,500	31,500	45,000

Pierce-Arrow 12 - 185 hp, 144" wb

	FP	5	4	3	2	1
Spl Sed	4045	8250	16,500	27,500	38,500	55,000
7P Sed	4210	8550	17,100	28,500	39,900	57,000
Encl Drive Limo	4360	9900	19,800	33,000	46,200	66,000
Conv Sed	5075	11,700	23,400	39,000	58,000	78,000
Brunn Metro Twn Brgm	6040	10,200	20,400	34,000	47,600	68,000

Pierce-Arrow 12 - 147" wb

	FP	5	4	3	2	1
7P Sed	5015	8850	17,700	29,500	41,300	59,000
Encl Drive Limo	5220	10,500	21,000	35,000	49,000	70,000

1904 Pierce-Racine, model A, runabout, HAC

PIERCE-RACINE — Racine, Wisconsin — (1904-1911) — In 1892 Andrew J. Pierce left his job as superintendent of the engine department at the Racine Hardware Company to establish the Pierce Engine Company. Marine engines and launches were the mainstay of his business. He built his first car, a single-cylinder surrey with fringe on top, in 1895; his second, a two-cylinder two-stroke carriage, followed in 1899; a third two years later. In 1903 Andrew Pierce built the first Mitchell cars marketed by the Western Wheel Works across town in Racine, and in 1904 Pierce hit the market himself with a car of his own. The first Pierce-Racine was a single-cylinder 8 hp water-cooled runabout with planetary transmission, chain drive and wheel steering. He sold 150 of them in 1904, and the same number in 1905 when a 16 hp twin was added to the line. A flurry of models, including two fours, followed for 1906, when sales fell to 90 units — and in 1907 Andrew Pierce decided to concentrate production on a single car, a much larger 40 hp four with selective transmission and shaft drive which was claimed capable of 60 mph. Sales climbed to 200 cars that year. For purposes of expansion, Andrew Pierce reorganized in 1909 as the Pierce Motor Company; a good deal of the additional financing came from Racine businessmen who were also prominent stockholders in the J.I. Case Threshing Machine Company in Racine. Charles L. McIntosh, who was treasurer of the Case company, now became president of Pierce. And the die was cast for the ultimate takeover. On April 6th, 1910 Charles McIntosh died at the age of sixty-three while vacationing in Naples, Italy. This did not, however, delay the inevitable. By August advertisements were published in the trade press announcing that the Pierce Motor Company had been acquired by Case, and the Pierce-Racine would be superseded by the Case. The last Pierce-Racine automobiles were assembled in early 1911 alongside the new Case. Andrew Pierce died in 1921.

1904 PIERCE-RACINE
Model A — 1-cyl., 8 hp, 76" wb

	FP	5	4	3	2	1
Rbt.	750	1500	2500	3600	5500	11,000

1905 PIERCE-RACINE
Series A — 1-cyl., 8 hp, 76" wb

	FP	5	4	3	2	1
A-1 Rbt.	750	1500	2500	3600	5500	11,000
A-2 Tonneau	850	1600	2700	3800	5800	12,000

Series B — 2-cyl., 16 hp, 90" wb

	FP	5	4	3	2	1
B-1 Rbt.	1100	1600	2700	3800	5800	12,000
B-2 Tonneau (side-entrance)	1250	1800	2800	4000	6200	13,000
B-2 Tonneau (rear-entrance)	1200	1800	2800	4000	6200	13,000

1906 PIERCE-RACINE
Model A-3 — 2-cyl., 12 hp, 85" wb

	FP	5	4	3	2	1
Rbt.-2P	750	1600	2700	3800	5800	12,000

Model A-4 — 2-cyl., 14 hp, 85" wb

	FP	5	4	3	2	1
Tour.-5P	850	1700	2800	3900	6000	12,500

Model B-2 — 2-cyl., 16 hp, 90" wb

	FP	5	4	3	2	1
Tonneau-5P	1150	1800	2800	4000	6200	13,000

Model C — 4-cyl., 24/28 hp, 100" wb

	FP	5	4	3	2	1
Tour.-5P	1750	2300	3300	4600	7500	16,000

Model D — 4-cyl., 18 hp, 94" wb

	FP	5	4	3	2	1
Tour.-5P	1250	2000	3000	4200	6500	14,000

1905 Pierce-Racine, model A-1, runabout, HAC

1906 Pierce-Racine, model A-3, runabout, HAC

1907 Pierce-Racine, model D, touring, HAC

1907 PIERCE-ARROW
Model D — 4-cyl., 40 hp, 106" wb

	FP	5	4	3	2	1
Tour.-5P	2600	4050	8100	13,500	18,900	27,000

1908 Pierce-Racine, model E, touring, HAC

1908 PIERCE-RACINE
Model D — 4-cyl., 40 hp, 106" wb

	FP	5	4	3	2	1
Tour.-5P	2500	4000	7950	13,250	18,550	26,500

Model E — 4-cyl., 30 hp, 104" wb

	FP	5	4	3	2	1
Tour.-5P	2000	3900	7800	13,000	18,200	26,000

1909 PIERCE-RACINE
Model G — 4-cyl., 40 hp, 106" wb

	FP	5	4	3	2	1
Tour.-5P	1500	4000	7950	13,250	18,550	26,500

Model H — 4-cyl., 45 hp, 112" wb

Tour.-5/7P	2000	4100	8250	13,750	19,250	27,500

1910 Pierce-Racine, model K, touring, WLB

1910-1911 PIERCE-RACINE
Model K — 4-cyl., 30 hp, 112" wb

Tour.-5P	1850	2400	3400	4800	8000	17,000
Sub.-4P	1850	2400	3400	4800	8000	17,000
Torpedo-4P	1950	2300	3300	4600	7500	16,000

PIERCE STEAMER — Sistersville, West Virginia — (1895) — A tricycle which, complete with boiler and 2 hp engine, weighed but 360 pounds was the invention of W.A. Pierce of Sistersville. One-inch iron pipe was used for the vehicle's frame, and its wheels were wood. Fifteen gallons of water could be carried in its galvanized iron tank, and the fuel used was crude oil, carried in a five-gallon tank. Pierce said he could raise 150 pounds of steam in four minutes. Although he intended to enter his vehicle in the Chicago Times-Herald Contest, he didn't complete it in time.

1898 Pierre, motor carriage, SDSHS

PIERRE — Pierre, South Dakota — (1898) — The first gasoline car built in Pierre, and possibly in all of South Dakota, was put together in a blacksmith shop by Frank Edson and Louis Greenough. Its engine was a two-cylinder Wolverine imported from Detroit; its enclosed body came from a wagon factory in Elkhart, Indiana. The engine was fitted under the rear seats with final drive by chain to the rear wheels. Six passengers and a driver could be accommodated in the vehicle and, unlike many early "limousines," the chauffeur of the Pierre was provided a permanent covering too. The car was said to run well "and without too much noise" on level prairie roads and city streets. So ably did it perform in fact that Frank Edson was hired by the local post office to ferry the mail between Pierre and Fort Sully. A plan to ferry passengers from Pierre to the Black Hills didn't work out, however, because the car was too underpowered for uphill climbs. Yet another plan, to sell rides in at country fares, was outlawed by local authorities who didn't wish to assume responsibility for any accidents which might occur. Still, the Pierre remained quite an attraction in town for some years thereafter.

PIERSON — The Pierson Motor Supply Company was organized in New York City late in 1908 with a capital stock of $20,000 to manufacture "motors, engines, machines, automobiles, cars, wagons and boats." Incorporators were F.W. Mills, H.M. Brown and E.J. Forhan. Manufacture of a car is doubted.

The Pierson-Harris Company was organized in Atlantic City, New Jersey during the fall of 1912 with a capital stock of $50,000 for the manufacture of automobiles. The partners involved were Gilbert Pierson and Edward G. Harris. Manufacture is doubted.

PIETSCH — The Pietsch Automobile Company of Chicago was organized during the late fall of 1906 for the manufacture of automobiles. Between announcement date and arrival date, the decision was made to call the Pietsch product a Paco. Refer to Paco.

1909 Piggins, Six, touring, NAHC

PIGGINS — Racine, Wisconsin — (1908-1910) — Charles R. Piggins and his brother Frederick H. were machinists in Racine who built a steam car in 1883, an electric in 1897 and their first gasoline car in 1902. All these vehicles were strictly for experimental purposes, though the experimentation resulted in the brothers concluding that the internal combustion engine was the most effective of powerplants and the one they would manufacture. Soon thereafter their machine shop at 1113 Sixth Street was producing automobile engines of two, four and six-cylinders, in addition to a special line of two-stroke marine engines. In 1908 the Piggins brothers declared that they had designed a gasoline motor that was smokeless and so noiseless that it could not be heard at a distance of six feet. Now they felt ready to tackle the automobile industry, and they did so with the biggest and most expensive car yet produced in Racine. It was a T-head six offered in two models: a 50 hp at $4700 and a 36 hp at $3500. "Piggins: The Name That Stands for Perfection in High Class Automobile Building," the ads said. In addition to its "luxurious beauty" and "splendid efficiency," the quiet of the Piggins motor was emphasized. With the engine running, the Piggins brothers claimed, a penny would stand on edge on the base of the car, and a nickel wouldn't fall over on the fender. During the summer of 1909 the firm of Piggins Brothers consolidated with the Racine Manufacturing Company. A few more cars may have been built into 1910, but by now the brothers were preparing for their next step. Early in 1912 a new organization arrived: the Piggins Motor Truck Company. Pleasure car manufacture was forever forgotten, and a truck called "The Practical Piggins" was produced until 1916, when it was superseded by the Reliance which was continued in manufacture in Racine and Appleton into the mid-Twenties.

1908-1910 PIGGINS
Six — 50 hp, 135" wb

	FP	5	4	3	2	1
Touring-7P	4700	4500	5800	9500	18,000	32,000

Six — 36 hp, 117" wb

Touring-5P	3500	3100	4200	6300	10,500	22,000

PILAIN — The Pilain has been indicated on various car rosters as an automobile produced from 1907-1908 in New York City by the De Barress Automobile Company. This is in error. The car referred to was the Roland-Pilain which was produced in France and imported by De Barress.

PILGRIM — The Pilgrim Motor Vehicle Company of Cambridge, Massachusetts was listed as an automobile manufacturer in the Hiscox book *Horseless Vehicles, Automobile, Motor Cycles* published in 1900. Documentation is lacking. A company of that same name was in operation in Somerville, Massachusetts during this period, however.

PILGRIM STEAM — Somerville, Massachusetts — (1899-1900) — In 1865, at the age of four, as his parents later said, Edward L. Orcutt was discovered examining a Boston & Maine steam engine in the shed of the family home. When he grew up he began inventing things, sometimes engaging in the candy business to finance his endeavors. Among the things he invented, in 1899, was a steam carriage in which he claimed to have completely eliminated the steam trail. He interested a group of Boston businessmen in his invention, and in early 1900 the Pilgrim Motor Vehicle Company was organized with offices at 12 School Street in Boston, and a small factory near Orcutt's home in Somerville. Elmer N. Hutchins was president of the company, B. Alden Prince treasurer, and William M. McDonald business manager. Edward Orcutt was to take charge of the factory. Precisely what happened next is not known, but for some reason this automotive manufacturing venture failed after the building of just a few pilot models. Edward Orcutt died in 1914, and his obituary in the *Somerville Journal* notes his invention of an electrically-controlled automatic railroad crossing signal prominently, but does not mention his steam car at all.

PILGRIM — New Albany, Indiana — (1913-1914) — Actually, Ferdinand Kahler believed he had no choice other than to produce an automobile. He was the proprietor of the New Albany woodworking and furniture company which had produced bodies for the Jonz automobile, and when the Jonz met its rather unsavory end, Kahler was stuck with a good many of them. Anxious to protect his investment, Kahler bought what assets of the Jonz remained and moved into its factory. He organized the Ohio Falls Motor Car Company, and selected the name of Pilgrim for his car. From Continental, he secured 44-50 hp four-cylinder engines, which he mounted in a 120-inch wheelbase chassis, which he cloaked with the Jonz-contracted bodies. "A $2250 car for $1800," he advertised. "Buy your automobile direct from our factory." Unfortunately, only about a dozen people did; Kahler might better have taken a loss on the bodies. The Ohio Falls Motor

1913 Pilgrim, touring, (New Albany, Indiana), NAHC

Car Company purportedly went through three receiverships in two years. Ultimately, Kahler wearied of it all and sold out to the Crown Motor Car Company of Louisville, Kentucky which arrived in town in mid-1914 and reorganized as Hercules.

1913-1914 PILGRIM
Pilgrim — 4-cyl., 44/50 hp, 120" wb

	FP	5	4	3	2	1
Touring-5P	1800	4000	5000	8000	15,000	28,000

1915 Pilgrim, touring, (Detroit, Michigan), NAHC

PILGRIM — Detroit, Michigan — (1915-1918) — Following his work in the engineering departments of Olds, Warren-Detroit and Hudson, and his attempts to build the Oxford and Fostoria, William Radford was back in the news again in 1914 with his latest effort. It was a light car with a 106-inch wheelbase and standard tread, and fitted with a standard three-speed selective transmission. Its engine was a water-cooled four of 17 hp, and it was to be offered in three models in a $685-$835 price range. To back him in manufacture, Radford selected — and not too wisely — one Clarence H. Leete who became president of the newly formed Pilgrim Motor Car Company. Temporary offices were taken in the Moffat Building in Detroit, and production was slated to begin in February of 1915. It did not. Instead, in May, Leete was arrested on a charge of fraud, the allegation being that he had "sold" jobs in the company to prospective employees, netting over $9000. Radford was not involved, but he may have been the person who had Leete arrested, and he left the company immediately. Only pilot models of the Radford car had thus far been built. By September of 1916 the car was still not in manufacture, but C.H. Leete, who had declared his innocence, remained in charge of the company and was now suing Radford for alleged damaging letters circulated by the latter. The history of the Pilgrim thus far had been murky, its subsequent history is simply confusing. R.C. Aland — who was building a car under his own name — was called in during 1916 to redesign the Pilgrim, which became a little bit bigger and a little bit more expensive. The company appears to have been reorganized that year with a new incorporation being filed in Portland, Maine (that state's lenient laws making such things very easy) — and at least a modicum of production did follow. Sometime during 1918, however, the Pilgrim just quietly faded from the scene.

1915 PILGRIM
Four — 17 hp, 106" wb

	FP	5	4	3	2	1
Touring-5P	685	2400	3400	4800	8000	17,000
Roadster-2P	685	2300	3300	4600	7500	16,000
Cabriolet-3P	835	2000	3000	4200	6500	14,000

1916-1917 PILGRIM
Model 37 — 4-cyl., 22.5 hp, 112" wb

	FP	5	4	3	2	1
Touring-5P	735	2500	3500	5000	8500	18,000

1918 PILGRIM
Model 37 — 4-cyl., 22.5 hp, 114" wb

	FP	5	4	3	2	1
Touring-5P	895	2500	3500	5000	8500	18,000

PILLINGS — The George T. Pillings Engine and Machine Company was organized in April of 1899 in Elgin, Illinois for the manufacture of steam engines. That fall *The Autobain* reported that the Pillings' "plans have been changed, and now the company will make [automobiles] under patents owned and controlled by Mr. Pillings." Manufacture of a car does not appear to have followed, however.

PILLINGS STEAMER — (1907) — Though C.T. Pillings completed his car in 1904, he wasn't finished with it. Among other refinements and changes made during the three years following was the revision from water tube to flash boiler. "This machine I have built in my spare time and evenings," Pillings wrote *The Horseless Age*. "With the experimenting that I have done it has cost me a good deal of money and time, but then I can cross the

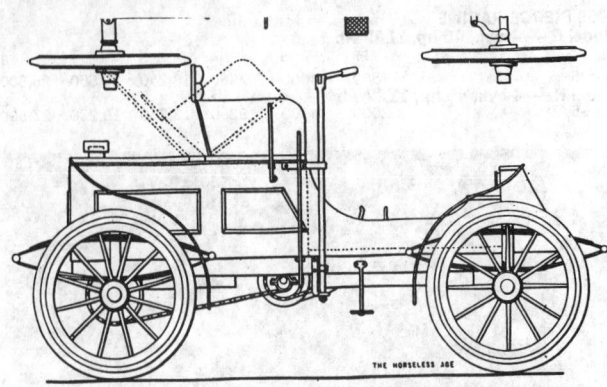
1907 Pillings Steamer, NAHC

continent with it and not carry over 160 pounds of steam. I have also spent a good deal of time experimenting with coal oil burners and while coal oil makes a good hot fire, you can depend on the gasoline much better. I have given this car the most severe test that any car can receive, and it is the easiest riding and lightest running car I ever sat in." Where he built it is not known.

1916 Pilliod, 5-pass. touring, WLB

PILLIOD — Toledo, Ohio — (1915-1916) — The Pilliod was introduced at the 1915 Toledo Automobile Show as the first eight-cylinder sleeve-valve-engined car in America. The cylinders were cast in two blocks of four at a 90° angle, with the sleeves located on the sides of the cylinders and cooling their length both inside and out. Force-feed lubrication and thermosyphon cooling were featured. The designer of the engine and the car was Charles J. Pilliod, who set up shop as the Pilliod Motor Company at 1212 Oakwood Avenue in Toledo. Between the automobile show in February and the onset of production later that year, however, the Pilliod became a four-cylinder car. Like the eight, it remained a sleeve valve made of aluminum. Among the first engines in America to extensively use the alloy the Pilliod unit weighed 390 pounds and developed 27 hp. A five-passenger touring car was the only model offered; advertisements from March of 1916 indicate its price as $1485. By June the Pilliod was no more, as the company was declared bankrupt with assets of $9559 and liabilities of $30,320. Although Charles Pilliod never built another car, he spent the remainder of his career in the mechanical engineering field.

1915-1916 PILLIOD
Model F — 4-cyl., 27 hp, 120" wb

	FP	5	4	3	2	1
Touring-5P	1485	2500	3500	5000	8500	18,000

PILOT — The Pilot Automobile Company was organized in Chicago, Illinois early in 1912 with a capital stock of $5400 to manufacture automobiles and accessories. Incorporators were W.A. Dugane, C.H. Rodenbach and A.E. Pattison. Manufacture of a car is doubted.

1911 Pilot, model 35, touring, HAC

PILOT — Richmond, Indiana — (1909-1924) — "The Car Ahead" was a slogan appropriate to its name if not the automobile itself. The Pilot car was not a leader by any definition. It was just a good, prosaic assembled car that sold at reasonable prices and in sufficient numbers for the Pilot Motor Car Company to remain in business for fifteen years. The firm was an outgrowth of the Seidel Buggy Company of Richmond, and George Seidel remained its president from beginning to end. The first cars were built in the buggy factory in 1909, while the Pilot's permanent home was being completed across town. Seidel had selected his car's name, incidentally, because he had always wanted to be a river boat pilot. "The prospects for a particularly bright business year for the Pilot Motor Company are exceedingly flattering," the *Richmond Palladium and Sun-Telegram* reported in March 1910 when construction was completed. The factory had a 500-car-a-year capacity. That George Seidel might have been thinking more grandly is indicated by his announcing a few months later that he might move his firm to Des Moines if sufficient inducement were offered. It was not, and Seidel contented himself with 500 cars a year in Richmond. He also prided himself on the fact that he was among the first in the industry to employ women, though he hired them only to sew curtains and finish upholstery. From 1909 to 1912 Pilots were fours exclusively, a six was introduced in 1913. and a V-8 had a one-year run in 1916. From 1917 to 1924 all Pilots were sixes. Engines for the Pilots were usually Teetors from Hagerstown, Indiana, though the higher-horsepower cars of the early Twenties were Herschell-Spillmans from Tonawanda, New York. The Sportster model introduced in June of 1922 had barrel-type headlights and no running-boards — and was the most dashing Pilot ever produced. Like many small independent producers, the Pilot Motor Car Company could not survive the effects of the postwar depression, despite a sideline activity of building cars called Lorraine. The company went into receivership in November of 1923. The last Pilot cars were assembled early in 1924. In April that year the factory was sold to a local junk dealer named Sam Jaffe for $28,500. During the 1940's George Seidel received a letter from a car dealer in South America, where a healthy number of cars had been exported, asking if any were still available and how much they were. The Pilot may not have been a very interesting automobile, but it was a good and durable one.

1909-1910 PILOT
Thirty-Five — 4-cyl., 30/36 hp, 118" wb

	FP	5	4	3	2	1
Roadster	1500	3000	4000	6000	9500	21,000

1911 PILOT
Thirty-Five — 4-cyl., 30/36 hp, 118" wb

Model D Touring	1500	3000	4000	6000	9500	21,000
Model D Roadster	1500	2900	3700	5600	9100	20,000

Fifty — 4-cyl., 45/50 hp, 118" wb

Model B Touring	1800	4500	5800	9500	18,000	32,000
Model B Roadster	1800	4400	5600	9200	17,300	31,000

1912 Pilot, model 35, touring, HAC

1912 PILOT
Thirty-Five — 4-cyl., 30/36 hp, 120" wb

Touring-5P	1800	3100	4200	6300	10,500	22,000
Roadster-2P	1750	3000	4000	6000	9500	21,000
Speedster-2P	1600	3100	4200	6300	10,500	22,000

1913 Pilot, model 50, touring, HAC

1913 PILOT
Model 40 — 4-cyl., 40 hp, 120" wb

Roadster-2P	2000	4000	5000	8000	15,000	28,000
Touring-5P	2000	4200	5200	8400	15,700	29,000

Model 50 — 4-cyl., 50 hp, 126" wb

Touring-5P	2250	4900	6300	10,300	21,000	34,000

Model 60 — 6-cyl., 60 hp, 132" wb

Touring-7P	2500	5400	7300	11,800	25,000	38,000

1914 Pilot, model 60, touring, HAC

1914 PILOT
Model 40 — 4-cyl., 40 hp, 120" wb

	FP	5	4	3	2	1
Touring-5P	2250	5000	8000	15,000	28,000	

Model 50 — 4-cyl., 50 hp, 126" wb

Touring-7P	2500	4900	6300	10,300	21,000	34,000

Model 60 — 6-cyl., 60 hp, 132" wb

Touring-5/7P	2785	5400	7300	11,800	25,000	38,000
Roadster-2/4P	2785	5300	7000	11,500	24,000	37,000

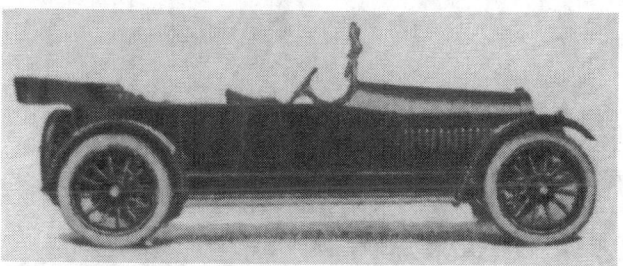

1915 Pilot, model 55, touring, HAC

1915 PILOT
Model 55 — 6-cyl., 55 hp, 126" wb

Touring-5P	1885	5400	7300	11,800	25,000	38,000

Model 75 — 6-cyl., 75 hp, 132" wb

Touring-7P	2885	6400	9300	14,500	33,000	45,000
Touring-5P	2885	6300	9000	14,000	32,000	44,000
Roadster-2P	2885	6200	8800	13,500	31,000	43,000

1916 Pilot, model 6-55, touring, HAC

1916 PILOT
Model 6-45 — 6-cyl., 45 hp, 119" wb

Touring-5P	1100	4000	5000	8000	15,000	28,000
Roadster-4P	1100	3900	4800	7700	14,300	27,000

Model 6-55 — 6-cyl., 55 hp, 126" wb

Touring-5P	1685	4500	5800	9500	18,000	32,000
Touring-7P	1735	4700	6100	9900	19,000	33,000
Roadster-2P	1685	4500	5800	9500	18,000	32,000

Model 8-55 — 8-cyl., 55 hp, 126" wb

Touring-5P	1785	5400	7300	11,800	25,000	38,000
Touring-7P	1785	5500	7500	12,000	26,000	39,000
Runabout-2P	1785	5000	6000	11,000	22,000	35,000

Model 6-75 — 6-cyl., 75 hp, 132" wb

Touring-7P	2485	6700	9900	15,500	34,800	47,000
Touring-5P	2400	6400	9300	14,500	33,000	45,000
Roadster-2P	2400	6200	8800	13,500	31,000	43,000

1917 Pilot, model 6-45, touring, HAC

1917 PILOT
Model 6-45 — 6-cyl., 43.5 hp, 119" wb

	FP	5	4	3	2	1
Chummy Roadster-4P	1150	3700	4700	7300	13,700	26,000
Touring-5P	1150	3900	4800	7700	14,300	27,000

1918 Pilot, model 6-45, sedan, JAC

1918 PILOT
Model 6-45 — 6-cyl., 43.5 hp, 120" wb

Roadster-4P	1295	3900	4800	7700	14,300	27,000

1919 Pilot, model 6-45, sedan, HAC

1919 PILOT
Model 6-45 — 6-cyl., 43.5 hp, 120" wb

Touring-5P	1495	3700	4700	7300	13,700	26,000
Roadster-4P	1545	3500	4500	7000	13,000	25,000
Sedan-5P	2145	1800	2800	4000	6200	13,000

1920 Pilot, model 6-45, touring, HAC

1920 PILOT
Model 6-45 — 6-cyl., 43.5 hp, 120" wb

Touring-5P	2890	3700	4700	7300	13,700	26,000
Roadster-4P	2830	3500	4500	7000	13,000	25,000
Sedan-5P	3425	1800	2800	4000	6200	13,000
Coupe-4P	3225	2200	3200	4400	7000	15,000

1921 PILOT
Model 6-50 — 6-cyl., 43.5 hp, 126" wb

Touring-5P	1895	3700	4700	7300	13,700	26,000
Military Roadster-2P	1950	3500	4500	7000	13,000	25,000
Coupe-4P	2850	2250	3300	4500	7300	15,500
Sedan-5P	2900	1900	2900	4100	6400	13,500

1922 PILOT
Model 6-56 — 6-cyl., 68 hp, 126" wb

Touring-5P	2285	4400	5600	9200	17,300	31,000
Roadster-3P	2285	4500	5800	9500	18,000	32,000
Touring-7P	2335	4700	6100	9900	19,000	33,000
Coupe-4P	3350	2300	3300	4600	7500	16,000
Sedan-5P	3400	2000	3000	4200	6500	14,000
Sportster-4P	—	5000	6500	11,000	22,000	35,000

1152

1921 Pilot, model 6-50, touring, HAC

1923 Pilot, model 6-56, touring, HAC

1923 PILOT
Model 6-56 — 6-cyl., 69 hp, 126" wb

	FP	5	4	3	2	1
Touring-5P	2000	4300	5400	8700	16,500	30,000
Sport-4P	2100	4900	6300	10,300	21,000	34,000
Touring-7P	2050	4700	6100	9900	19,000	33,000
Roadster-3P	2050	4300	5400	8700	16,500	30,000
Coupe-4P	2950	2200	3200	4400	7000	15,000
Sedan-5P	3000	1800	2800	4000	6200	13,000
Sedan-7P	3150	2000	3000	4200	6500	14,000

1924 Pilot, model 6-56, roadster, WLB

1924 PILOT
Model 6-56 — 6-cyl., 68 hp, 126" wb

Touring-5P	1695	4300	5400	8700	16,500	30,000
Speedster-2P	1745	4900	6300	10,300	21,000	34,000
Brougham-4P	2495	2300	3300	4600	7500	16,000
Sedan-5P	2495	1800	2800	4000	6200	13,000
Sportster-4P	1795	5000	6500	11,000	22,000	35,000
Touring-7P	1745	4900	6300	10,300	21,000	34,000
Coupe-4P	2445	2200	3200	4400	7000	15,000
Sedan-7P	2645	2000	3000	4200	6500	14,000

PIONEER — The Pioneer of 1912 from Grand Rapids, Michigan was planned as successor to the Van roadster produced in Grand Haven in 1911. Refer to Van.

The Pioneer Foundry in La Crosse, Wisconsin was the venue in which Alfred James built a car in 1904. Refer to James.

The Pioneer Iron Works in Clarksburg, Virginia was the shop in which A.C. Osborn built an automobile in 1899. Refer to Osborn.

The Pioneer Manhattan Automobile Exchange was organized in New York City during the spring of 1907 with a capital stock of $5000 to manufacture and deal in automobiles. Incorporators were Louis E. Spier, Sidney D. Lichtenstein and William Nolan, all of New York City. Manufacture is doubted.

The Pioneer Motor Company of Marquette, Michigan was incorporated during the spring of 1909 with a capital stock of $30,000. Manufacture of an automobile is doubted.

The Pioneer Motor Company of Muskogee, Oklahoma was organized with a capital stock of $5000 late in 1912 for the manufacture of automobiles. G.S. Waddell was the indicated incorporator. Manufacture is doubted.

The Pioneer Motor Car Company of Troy, New York produced the Harvard automobile during the World War I years. Refer to Harvard.

The Pioneer Motor Car Company was organized in Marietta, Ohio during the fall of 1911 with a capital stock of $18,000 to make and deal in automobiles. Incorporators were Tasker B. Bosworth, A.J. Watson, A.A. Crawford, T. McCune and H.L. Cosn. Manufacture is doubted.

1909 Pioneer, runabout, NAHC

PIONEER — El Reno, Oklahoma — (1907-1910) / Oklahoma City, Oklahoma — (1911-1912) — The Pioneer from El Reno was built by Edward Wright and W. Roy Roberts who organized their business in 1907 as the W.R.C. Auto Works. A highwheeler on a 91-inch wheelbase, the Pioneer was powered by a two-cylinder 20 hp engine and featured a planetary transmission and shaft drive. By the spring of 1909 the partners had sold twenty-two cars, renamed their venture the Pioneer Car Company and incorporated it with a fully paid up capital of $10,000. That year a Pioneer was the only car from the state to enter the Oklahoma City to Kansas City endurance run, and its progress in that event was enthusiastically reported in the *El Reno Daily American*. On the first seven days of the run, the Pioneer suffered only two broken fenders and one lost hubcap, and was lying second to a Mitchell on day eight when, alas, a connecting rod broke and the car was unable to finish. Nonetheless, the Pioneer showing was a splendid one, which advertised the product throughout Oklahoma and Kansas, and the company received more orders than it could handle. The Wichita (Kansas) Commercial Club beckoned with attractive offers to Pioneer to locate its factory there. With that, the *El Reno Daily American* began to champion the cause of keeping the Pioneer at home. ''An industry that is getting too big for its clothes . . . must have help to buy new ones,'' the newspaper editorialized. ''The Commercial Club can well afford to drop every other proposition which it has under consideration until it has placed the Pioneer Car Company on an adequate financial footing.'' Meanwhile, W. Roy Roberts arrived back from the Wichita Automobile Show and reported that he sold fifty cars there — and he was adding to the line for 1910 a bigger and better four-cylinder model. El Reno really wanted to keep Pioneer in town now. In December of 1909 the city council made what it thought was an attractive offer, but it was not attractive enough. By the end of 1910, El Reno lost the Pioneer Car Company to Oklahoma City, that metropolis offering $15,000 (five thousand more than El Reno) and a factory site. Conceivably, Wright and Roberts might have been better advised to remain in El Reno. They found the going rough in Oklahoma City and in February 1912 sold out to the Tulsa Auto & Manufacturing Company.

1907-1909 PIONEER						
Model A — 2-cyl., 20 hp, 91" wb						
	FP	5	4	3	2	1
Rdst.	750	2300	3300	4600	7500	16,000
1910 PIONEER						
Model A — 2-cyl., 20 hp, 91" wb						
Rdst.	750	2200	3200	4400	7000	15,000
Model B — 4-cyl., 30 hp, 105" wb						
Surrey	1050	2300	3300	4600	7500	16,000
1911-1912 PIONEER						
Model B — 4-cyl., 30 hp, 105" wb						
Fore-Door Tour.	—	2300	3300	4600	7500	16,000

1896 Pioneer, runabout, WLB

PIONEER — San Francisco, California — (1896-1899) — In 1893 a German-born machinist named J.A. Meyer began planning a gasoline car. It was a weekend basement-machine-shop project which required three years for completion, but in 1896 the car was finished and successfully tested. A two-passenger runabout with single-cylinder gasoline engine, the vehicle was dubbed the Pioneer by its inventor. Reportedly, Meyer was the first motorist to make a complete driving tour of the San Francisco Bay area. He built two more cars, the first of which he sold to Dr. J.W. Jesse of Santa Rosa who used it for house calls throughout Sonoma County, the second of which was delivered to George Colgate, publisher of the *Orland Register*. The whereabouts of those two cars is unknown, but the first car built by J.A. Meyer remains extant in the Oakland City Museum. His final two cars, incidentally, were probably built in the shops of the J.L. Hicks Gas Engine Company in San Francisco, Meyer having been employed there since 1894 and serving as foreman since 1897.

1898 Pioneer, runabout, WLB

PIONEER — Detroit, Michigan — (1898) — Patrick Sullivan of Detroit called his car the Pioneer, which it was for him though he had no intention of introducing the vehicle on the market. It had a small gasoline engine and high wheels which Sullivan claimed would follow nicely in street-car tracks when he locked the steering tiller. Purportedly, he drove this car for a decade following its completion in 1898.

1914 Pioneer, cyclecar, runabout, NAHC

PIONEER — Chicago, Illinois — (1914) — ''Although not definitely so announced, it is understood that real automobile men are interested in the American Manufacturing Company,'' declared *The Horseless Age* in one of its early 1914 issues. If that had been true, it would really have been news because the Pioneer built by the American Manufacturing Company of Chicago was a cyclecar — and ''real'' automobile manufacturers then were routinely announcing that they would ''have nothing to do'' with the genre. (History has proven that, generally they did not.) The Pioneer was a typical cyclecar with an air-cooled V-twin, friction transmission and belt drive. Though the seating was advertised as side by side, the passenger sat about a foot to the rear of the driver to allow for sufficient elbow room within the forty-inch-wide body. The company did survive long enough for the trade press to learn that the "real automobile men" behind the Pioneer were the folks who would enjoy a little more success marketing the Partin-Palmer car.

1914 PIONEER
Cyclecar — 2-cyl., 9 hp, 96" wb

	FP	5	4	3	2	1
Rdst.-2P	385	1600	2700	3800	5800	12,000

PIPER & TINKER — Waltham, Massachusetts — (1899-1900) — The number of cars that carried the names of John W. Piper and George M. Tinker is problemmatical. The men worked for Charles Herman Metz's Waltham Manufacturing Company, and because their boss allowed them to use a back room of the factory to build their first steam car, they respectfully named it after the company. The two vehicles which followed, however, although still built under Metz's roof, carried the Piper & Tinker name. The partners struck out on their own shortly after the turn of the century and, again, the first steamers they produced were called Piper & Tinker. But then the men had a new idea, which was really an old idea. They organized the Waltham Automobile Company and the steamers they produced now were called Walthams again.

PIQUA — The Piqua Motor Company was organized with a capital stock of $50,000 during the fall of 1911 to manufacture automobiles in Piqua, Ohio. Incorporators included L.H. Wessel, J.C. Fahnenstock, Rupert Fahnenstock and Edward K. Keifer. Manufacture is doubted.

PIRATE — The Pirate was a runabout model of the B.L.M. produced in Brooklyn, New York from 1906-1907. Refer to B.L.M.

1901 Piskorski, steam runabout, HAC

PISKORSKI STEAM — St. Louis, Missouri — (1901) — Daniel J. Piskorski built his car in the basement of his home at 1229 North Tenth Street in St. Louis. Upon completion it had to be taken apart and reassembled outside, since the vehicle was too large to get out as a whole. (A half decade earlier Henry Ford had solved a similar problem with his first car by taking an axe to the side of the shed in which he built it.) Piskorski's car was a steamer, powered by a two-cylinder engine and fire-tube boiler, and provided with a body allowing for two or four passengers (with two, the lid on the front part of the body could be used as a footrest; with four, it was raised to be a backrest). This 1901 effort was Piskorski's only automobile. In 1910 he built a bicycle aeroplane. Both were spare-time efforts. His vocation was that of a machinist; he owned the Union Machine Works at 1413 North Tenth in St. Louis.

PITCAIRN — Philadelphia, Pennsylvania — (1934) — Although better known for its prowess in the air than on the ground, the Pitcairn A-35 built in 1934 by the Autogiro Company of America could take to the highway with a folding of its wing blades. Powered by a 135 hp engine mounted in the rear and driven by a shaft between the two passenger seats to the propeller up front, the Pitcairn's cruising air speed was 120 mph, its highway speed considerably more modest.

PITTSBURGH — A car called the Pittsburgh was purported to have been built by the Chester Engineering Company of Chester, Pennsylvania in 1912. Documentation is lacking.

The Pittsburgh Autocar Company was attempted to be organized in the fall of 1903 by J.H. Hildebrand to take up the manufacture of the Loomis car then being built in Westfield, Massachusetts. Andrew Carnegie's disinterest in investing squelched the deal. Refer to Loomis.

The Pittsburgh Automobile Company was organized with a capital stock of $5000 during the late summer of 1905 for the manufacture of automobiles. Incorporators were James F. Burke, C.L. Roberts, E.T. Brockman, S.R. Ireland and H.C. Ward. Manufacture is doubted.

The Pittsburgh Cage & Supply Company was the progenitor of the Duquesne Motor Car Company which built the Duquesne in Pittsburgh from 1912-1913. Refer to Duquesne.

The Pittsburgh Motor Car Company was a $100,000 Delaware incorporation from the summer of 1914 to manufacture and deal in automobiles. Incorporators were J.M. Frere, H.L. Davis and G. Shearer. Manufacture is doubted.

NOTE: In the interest of historical accuracy, it should be mentioned that for the years from 1890 to 1911 the official spelling of the city of Pittsburgh, Pennsylvania was "Pittsburg." Pittsburgh had been founded in 1758 and had remained thus until the U.S. Board on Geographic Names decreed in 1890 that all cities and towns in the United States ending in "burgh" drop the "h" thereafter. People in Pittsburgh were none too happy with this, though generally compliance with the order was followed, until 1911 when Pittsburgh citizens banded together and descended upon the office of the U.S. Board on Geographic Names, and the Board was persuaded to restore the "h" to Pittsburg. Thus, although some of the cars and companies included here were spelled without the "h," for the sake of uniformity the spelling of Pittsburgh is retained throughout just as the citizens of the city had always desired it.

1898 Pittsburgh, phaeton, NAHC

PITTSBURGH — Pittsburgh, Pennsylvania — (1897-1899) — The Pittsburgh Motor Vehicle Company was incorporated in 1897 to build a gasoline powered tandem tricycle. It weighed but 120 pounds. In 1898 another wheel was added and another seat for another passenger. The four-wheeled Pittsburgh weighed 160 pounds — including 55-pound 2 hp engine — and was composed of a wicker seat in front for two and a bicycle seat in the rear for the driver. It looked rather like a motorized baby buggy. A 300 pound four-passenger light phaeton followed. In 1899 Pittsburgh Motor Vehicle Company announced a closeout sale of its tricycle parts because that model was being discontinued. Production of the four-wheelers continued a short while in the Pittsburgh factory at the corner of Third and Ferry streets, but the company really got going in 1900 when it moved to nearby Ardmore and began building the Autocar.

PITTSBURGH ELECTRIC — The Pittsburgh Motor Vehicle Company built the Pittsburgh Electric from 1905 to 1910, but the presence of the vehicle on automobile rosters is in error. Delivery wagons and other commercial vehicles were the sole products of the firm; no passenger cars were marketed. In 1910 the man behind the Pittsburgh company, Charles A. Ward, moved to the Bronx in New York City where he reorganized as the Ward Motor Vehicle Company. This venture did produce a passenger car. Refer to Ward Electric.

1909 Pittsburgh Six, roadster, WLB

1154

PITTSBURGH SIX — New Kensington, Pennsylvania — (1908-1910) / Pittsburgh, Pennsylvania — (1911) — Although it wasn't built for long, the Pittsburgh Six was a spectacular car with a certainly colorful history. All this was largely because of the man who designed it: B.G. von Rottweiler who emigrated from Germany in 1905 and who arrived in New Kensington the year following, saying he was an automobile engineer and a baron. He was most assuredly the former. His initial dream was to build the world's greatest race car, and he was persuasive enough to talk J.A. Sturtevant and William E. Ward, owners of a small machine shop in town, to help him. The result was a six-cylinder engine of mammoth proportion (seven-inch bore, nine-inch stroke) that was fully six feet long *sans* transmission and which developed a reported 200 hp on engine test. The racer was never completed, but it did give birth to the idea of scaling down the engine for a production automobile. More practical bore/stroke dimensions (4 ¾ by 5¼) and more manageable horsepower (72 bhp) followed. And following this, financial backing was secured when H.M. Schmitt of Pittsburgh was persuaded to sell out his insurance agency and become president of the Fort Pitt Motor Manufacturing Company which was organized late in 1907 in New Kensington for production of the Pittsburgh Six. (Occasional trade press references to the contrary, the car was never marketed as a Fort Pitt.) Sturtevant and Ward took the vice-presidential and secretarial chairs respectively in the new company, and Arthur J. Paige was enlisted as superintendent and general manager. A workforce of fifteen to eighteen men was also engaged. Although the engine of the Pittsburgh Six was completely machined and manufactured in New Kensington, the three-speed selective transmission of the car was from Warner, the clutch from Hele-Shaw, the rear axle from A.O. Smith — and the frames and aluminum bodies were made in Detroit. The car was incredibly expensive to build. In December of 1909 the Fort Pitt Motor Manufacturing Company was reorganized by the General Engineering Company of Pittsburgh. General Engineering couldn't make a go of it either. In April of 1910 the Pittsburgh Motor Car Company was organized in order to move the whole operation to Braddock, Pennsylvania — but that didn't pan out either. On July 1st, 1910 production ceased in New Kensington. In February 1911 the Pittsburgh Motor Car Company announced that it had secured the plant of the Pittsburgh Steel Pulley Company and would move there immediately. Quite possibly the last few cars were put together in Pittsburgh. A roadster and a touring car were shown at Grand Central Palace in New York City in January 1911, but the company and the car faded away very soon thereafter. Von Rottweiler, incidentally had left the firm early on to build another car called the Vanderbilt. He returned to his homeland thereafter, though he was back in Pennsylvania a few years later. During World War I, he was reportedly executed as a German spy in Erie.

1908 PITTSBURGH
Six — 72 hp, 121" wb

	FP	5	4	3	2	1
Rbt.	2000	5000	6500	11,000	22,000	35,000
Rumble-Seat Rbt.	2150	5200	6800	11,300	23,000	36,000
Rdst.	2200	5300	7000	11,500	24,000	37,000
Tour.	2500	5400	7300	11,800	25,000	38,000

1909 PITTSBURGH
Six — 72 hp, 121" wb

Model A Rbt.-2P	2750	5000	6500	11,000	22,000	35,000
Model B Rdst.-3P	2800	5200	6800	11,300	23,000	36,000
Model C Tourabout-4P	3000	5300	7000	11,500	24,000	37,000
Model D Tour.-7P (124" wb)	3250	5400	7300	11,800	25,000	38,000

1910 PITTSBURGH
Six — 60 hp

Model B Rbt.-3P (122" wb)	3000	4400	5600	9200	17,300	31,000
Model C Tour.-5P (124" wb)	3200	4700	6100	9900	19,000	33,000
Model D Tour.-7P (134" wb)	3500	5000	6500	11,000	22,000	35,000

1911 PITTSBURGH
Six — 60 hp

Rdst.-3P	3500	4300	5400	8700	16,500	30,000
Tour.-7P	4000	5000	6500	11,000	22,000	35,000

PITTSBURGH STEAMER — Allegheny, Pennsylvania — (1905-1908) — The automotive activity of the Pittsburgh Machine Tool Company of Allegheny was not reported upon much in the trade press, but the firm seems to have built steam cars from 1905 to 1908, those being the inclusive dates indicated in *MoToR's* "Historical Table of the Motor Car Industry" published in March 1909. The firm was regularly listed during those years under "Steam Automobiles" in the Buyers Guide sections of *Cycle and Automobile Trade Journal*. F.J. Curtis was secretary of the company, and its factory was located at 61 Darrah in Allegheny. Details regarding the cars built are lacking.

PITTSFIELD — In January 1907 the Pittsfield Motor Carriage Company announced its entry into the ranks of automobile builders. This Massachusetts venture did produce a car, but it was not called the Pittsfield. Instead, by March, the venture had been renamed for the man who supplied most of the money for manufacture. Refer to Stilson.

PIXLEY — Boston, Massachusetts — (1909) — The G.H. Pixley Company was organized in Boston late in 1908 with a capital stock of $50,000 and the plan to engage in a general motor car business. At the Boston Automobile Show in March 1909 a Pixley was indicated as among the automobiles on exhibit. George H. Pixley probably built the car for demonstration purposes, because manufacture of it did not follow. Instead, later that spring, the Pixley carburetor was placed on the market.

PLAINFIELD — The Plainfield Auto Garage was organized during the summer of 1904 with a capital stock of $25,000 to manufacture, deal in and repair automobiles in Plainfield, New Jersey. Incorporators were Andrew H. Wilson and Joseph B. Longhead. Manufacture is doubted.

The Plainfield Auto Sales Company was organized in Elizabeth, New Jersey during the spring of 1909 with a capital stock of $25,000 for the manufacture and sale of motor cars "of all kinds, as well as supplies and fixtures." Incorporators were C.C. Brown, C.C. Rocap and S.A. Aldrich. Manufacture of a car is doubted.

The Plainfield Motor Car Company was organized late in 1906 with a capital stock of $25,000 to manufacture and sell automobiles in Plainfield, New Jersey. Incorporators were Frank W. Runyon, Paul F. Gillette and Hiram O. Hence. Manufacture is doubted.

PLANCHE — Etienne Planche was the man who designed this car which was introduced for the 1909 model year in Trenton, New Jersey. The car, however, is more properly referred to as the Roebling-Planche. Refer to Roebling-Planche.

PLANET — Minneapolis, Minnesota — (1914) — The Planet Motor Works was located at 611 East 28th Street in Minneapolis and early in 1914 advised *Cyclecar and Motorette* that it was "building cyclecars" and would welcome information and prices from cyclecar parts makers. That appears to have been the first and last ever heard of this short-lived Minnesota venture.

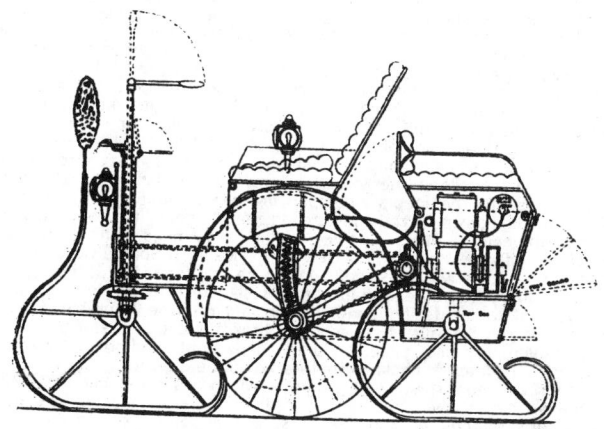

1895 Plass Motor Sleigh, NAHC

PLASS — Brooklyn, New York — (1895) / Pierre, South Dakota — (1900) — In 1895 Reuben H. Plass of Brooklyn designed a motor sleigh powered by a two-cylinder gasoline engine, with friction drive and single pivot steering. It was an ungainly machine which one cannot imagine very easily dashing through the snow. That Plass built more than one is doubtful. Most probably he simply returned to the usual activity of his machine shop. The turn of the century found him in Pierre, South Dakota where on January 7th, together with fellow Brooklynite J. S. Reynolds and one Charles S. DeLand of Pierre, he incorporated the three-million-dollar Plass Motor-Wagon Company for "the production, sale and rental of mail, express, merchandise and other self-propelling vehicles in the United States of America under Letters Patent granted to Reuben H. Plass of the Borough of Brooklyn, Greater New York and to others whose rights this Corporation may acquire." That corporation never left the paper it was drawn up upon. Reuben Plass returned to Brooklyn thereafter, where four years later he met with a reporter from *The Horseless Age* and told him all about the vehicle he had designed in 1870, which was powered by a four-cylinder water-cooled poppet-valve gasoline engine, and which he had driven on the streets of New York until the local authorities intervened. To say that Reuben Plass had a vivid imagination is putting it mildly. The facts in his story do not check out; if they did, Reuben Plass would hold today the position in the history of the automobile that has been accorded Gottlieb Daimler and Carl Benz. That cumbersome motor sleigh he built in 1895, however, may have been America's first snowmobile.

PLEASANTON — Pleasanton, California — (1903) — The Pleasanton Iron Works has frequently been cited as a producer of automobiles in 1903. There indeed was such a company in Pleasanton, California that year, operated by S.J. Tutthill who had just taken over the wagon-building establishment of J.A. Bilz. Tutthill's business card read "machine shop, blacksmithing and carriage manufacturing and repairing." It is possible that Tutthill's Pleasanton Works built an automobile that year, but an article about the company headlined "A Thriving Institution Which Does a High Class of Work" and appearing in the December 19th, 1903 edition of the *Pleasanton Times* mentions no activity other than that appearing on Tutthill's business card.

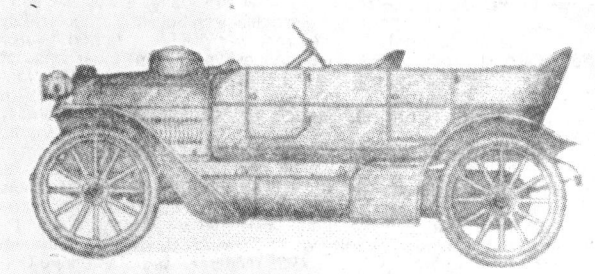

1910 Plymouth, touring, NAHC

1155

PLYMOUTH — Plymouth, Ohio — (1910) — The lone automobile built by the Plymouth Motor Truck Company of Plymouth, Ohio was as effective as a telegram in suggesting what the firm's usual product was. The Plymouth touring car was a massive affair, powered by a four-cylinder 40 hp Wisconsin engine and set in a 112-inch wheelbase chassis featuring chain drive and a double-disc truck transmission. The domed bulge on the hood housed a gravity-feed gasoline tank with a filler cap eight inches in diameter to allow the pouring of gasoline from an ordinary bucket. A price tag of $2500 was decided upon for the vehicle, and following its completion in 1910 it was sent on a test drive to New York City in July 1911. The car made it to Manhattan in fine fettle, but a cracked cylinder on the return trip forced its homecoming to be made in a railroad car. Thereafter the Plymouth Motor Truck Company elected to confine production to commercial vehicles only. Plymouth trucks were built from 1906 into 1914.

PLYMOUTH

PLYMOUTH — Detroit, Michigan — (1928-1942 et. seq.) — Because it typified "the endurance and strength, the rugged honesty, the enterprise, that determination of achievement and the freedom from old limitations of that Pilgrim band who were the first American colonists," the new car from Chrysler Corporation was to be called the Plymouth. Like the Chrysler, a perfect car for the Twenties, the stalwart little Plymouth was tailormade for the Thirties. Though Walter P. Chrysler did not foresee the stock market upheaval when he introduced the Plymouth, there can be little doubt that, without it, Chrysler Corporation would have found survival in the Great Depression difficult at the very least. In 1928 the Plymouth was intended, however, simply as a staid, inexpensive family car to take on America's best-sellers: Chevrolet and Ford. It debuted in July 1928, about six months after the hoopla accompanying the introduction of the Model A Ford had died down — and amid a good deal of hoopla itself, with dealers across the country dressed up like Pilgrims and Amelia Earhart sharing a platform with the Plymouth at New York's Madison Square Garden. The car, about which all the fuss had been made, was indeed new, though not revolutionary. It was evolutionary, redesigned from the four-cylinder Chrysler 52, which itself had metamorphosed from the venerable Maxwell four. Features like four-wheel hydraulic brakes, full pressure engine lubrication, aluminum alloy pistons and an independent hand brake, however, made for a complete package that would not be offered by Chevrolet or Ford for a decade. The new Plymouth — which was introduced as a 1929 model — did not overwhelm its opposition, of course. Maiden year deliveries of something over 50,000 cars paled in comparison to the more than a half-million Fords and nearly a million Chevrolets. But the inroads in the marketplace made by the car as the Depression deepened were impressive. In 1931 Plymouth production passed the 100,000 mark for the first time, and displaced Buick in the number three spot in the industry. In 1933 the comparative figures were: 218,419 Plymouths, 271,994 Fords and 438,888 Chevrolets. That Plymouth could accomplish this was due to factors in addition to the car itself. Walter Chrysler's purchase of Dodge was most significant in the estimable dealer organization it made available to sell the car. And Chrysler's gung-ho enthusiasm in seeing to a proper home for its assembly helped too. Shortly after the Plymouth's introduction, a new factory was completed in Detroit in only three months' time, two crews of workmen building in from each of the ends, two more crews building out from the middle. The "New Finer" Plymouth for 1932 was on a 112-inch wheelbase (longer by three inches than the Chevrolet, by five and a half than the Ford), and it had "Free Wheeling" and "Floating Power." When Plymouth went to a six in 1933, the initial offering on a 107-inch wheelbase met with disappointing sales results, a matter quickly set right with the addition of a 112-inch wheelbase Deluxe model which offered a cavalcade of color and gadget options — one windshield wiper or two, two spare wheels or one, a flurry of paint and upholstery choices, rather like the "have it your way" campaign Burger King launched in its asserted attack on McDonald's supremacy. By the end of 1933, one out of four cars in America was a Plymouth; and two out of three Plymouths built that year were the "have it your way" Deluxe model. Independent front suspension was given a one-year run in the Plymouth for '34; 85 hp arrived in '35; in '36 Plymouth built more than 500,000 cars. On its tenth anniversary in 1938, Plymouth could look back on a first decade of sales surpassing that of any other new automobile in American history. By the time World War II brought an end to automobile production in 1942, more than four million Plymouths had been built.

Plymouth Data Compilation by Jim Benjaminson

1928

CHRYSLER PLYMOUTH — MODEL Q — FOUR: Walter Chrysler's entry into the low priced field was introduced at Madison Square Garden on July 7, 1928. The first car entering the arena was driven by famed Aviatrix Amelia Earhart. Ironically, or shrewdly perhaps, the new car was not known solely as a Plymouth, but as the Chrysler Plymouth. The little four cylinder car was the only 4 cylindered car in the Chrysler lineup (it replaced the former Chrysler Model "52"), joining the six cylinder Chrysler "65" and "75" models. The new "Chrysler" Plymouth shared many mechanical and body parts with the newly introduced six cylinder DeSoto and for the first years the Plymouth and DeSoto would share the same production facilities. Priced as low as $670, the new car was sold exclusively by Chrysler dealers and found a ready market, with nearly 60,000 units sold during its first model year. The new Model Q Plymouth, although sold throughout the remainer of the year 1928 was actually considered by the Corporation to be a 1929 model but with no definite Corporate guidelines the Q and ensuing models through 1931 suffered from a lack of model year identity.

The Chrysler Plymouth styling closely matched that of its larger brethren and featured among other things, the Chrysler pioneered "thin-line" radiator shell in which most of the radiator chrome trim was concealed. Identifying features of the model Q included the wording "Chrysler Plymouth" on the radiator medallion, two piece front and rear bumpers that featured painted grooves on the flat surfaces, Depress Beam headlamps and hex headed hub caps bearing a stylized letter "P". All cars used the Fedco numbering system, which consisted of a series of letters and numbers stamped onto a multi-piece medallion on the instrument panel for identification rather than a normal serial number plate. This Fedco code could be converted to a numerical sequence by converting the letters to their proper number using the following system:
WPCHRYSLER
0123456789, but this repeated the letter "R" so the solution was the substitution of "O" for the last "R".

Thus, HL-950-P would convert to the Numeric Serial Number 379501.

Despite being a new make, Plymouth ended the sales year in 15th place.

I.D. DATA: Serial numbers on closed cars: medallion on center of upper dash rail. Open cars: Medallion on instrument panel. (Fedco numbering system) Detroit, Michigan Starting: HL-950-P Ending: HD-999-D. Detroit, Michigan Starting: RW-000-P Ending RH-977-H. Windsor, Ontario Starting GP-000-P Ending: GP-582-E. Engine numbers on left front corner of cylinder block. (All model Q Plymouths had an engine serial number prefixed by the letter Q). Starting: Q 175,000. Ending: Q242482.

Body No.	Body Type & Seating	Price	Weight	Prod. Total
NA	2-dr. Rds.-2P	670	2210	See Note 1
R	2-dr. R/S Rds.-2/4P	675	2210	—
328	2-dr. DeL. Cpe.-2/4P	720	2345	—
T	4-dr. Tr.-5P	695	2305	—
321	2-dr. Sed.-5P	690	2485	—
320	4-dr. Sed.-5P	725	2510	See Note 2
322	2-dr. Std. Cpe.-2P	670	NA	—

Note 1: Body style production figures are not available.
Note 2: Body code number 320 indicates Briggs body; body code number 88 indicates Hayes body on four-door sedans only.

ENGINE: Inline. Valve in block. Four. Cast iron block. B & S: 3-5/8 in. x 4-1/8 in. Disp.: 170.3 CID. C.R.: 4.6. Brake H.P.: 45 @ 2800 R.P.M. Taxable/A.L.A.M./N.A.C.C. H.P.: 21.03. Main bearings: Three. Valve lifters: Solid. Carb.: Carter RJHO8-112S (U.S.); DRJHO8-114S (L.H.D. export); DRJHO8-113S (R.H.D. export).

TECHNICAL: Sliding gear (spur gears) transmission. Speeds: 3F/1R. Floor shift controls. Single plate, dry clutch. Driveshaft, fabric universal discs. Semi floating rear axle. Overall Ratio: 4.3. Four wheel hydraulic brakes. Wood spoke standard wheels, wire wheel optional. Rim size: 4.75 x 20 in.

CHASSIS: [Series Q] W.B.: 109-3/4 in. O.L.: 169 in. Frt/Rear Tread: 56/56 in. Tires: 4.75 x 20.

OPTIONS: Front & rear bumpers, as a set (15.00). Heater floor type, hot air heat (30.00). Clock 8 day, header board mount, dial wind (12.50). Cigar lighter in combination w/utility light (12.00). Disc wheels, set of 5 (25.00). Wire wheels (set of 5) (35.00). Tire cover (1.50). Tire lock (Oakes stud type) (3.50). "Red Head" cylinder head (std. on roadster) (10.00). Spring covers (8.00). Trunk rack (only when side mount equipped) (12.00). Trunk (20.00). Top boot (10.00). Top bow rest (2.00). Windshield wings for open cars (std. on roadster) (10.00). Monograms, painted type, black letters only (10.00). Monograms, sterling silver, applied type, 3 letters maximum (10.00). Special colors, body only (35.00). Special colors on fenders, splash guards, frame horns, rear deck, & tire carrier (35.00). Leather upholstery (closed models) (25.00). Mohair upholstery (Coupe) (10.00). Broadcloth (2 & 4 door sedan) (35.00). Broadcloth (Coupe) (20.00). Sidemount fenders: When only one sidemount ordered, mounted in left fender. 1 fender with tire & tube (25.00). 2 fenders with tire & tube (50.00). 1 fender, tire & tube when equipped with 5 disc wheels (50.00). 2 fenders, tires & tubes when equipped with 6 disc wheels (75.00). 1 fender with tire & tube when equipped with 5 wire wheels (60.00). 2 fenders with tires, tubes when equipped with 6 wire wheels (90.00). Cowl lamps with chrome cowl mouldings, dealer installed (20.00).

HISTORICAL: Production began June 14, 1928, completed February 4, 1929. Model year production: 66,097. Plymouth shared the Chrysler/DeSoto production facilities at the Highland Park (Mich.) assembly plant until a new factory could be constructed. Each Plymouth engine was stamped with a serial number and a series of code letters to let garage owners and mechanics know that the engine installed in the car was fitted with certain undersize or oversize components. In addition, each engine had a code letter that corresponded to the model code of the car — that is, that a PE engine was fitted into a PE chassis. There are some exceptions to that rule that have been noted under the individual engine specification charts for each model.

The engine number in all cases is located on the left front corner of the cylinder block on a flat boss, usually directly above the generator.

A typical example is shown below:

A	P12	123456	A

The first symbol (A) is the production number.The second symbol (P12) is the model code number.
The next group of symbols (123456) is the sequential serial #.
The last symbol (A) is the letter size number (no letter = standard)

Letter Size Number Codes

A = .020 oversize cylinder bore
B = .010 undersize main and connecting rod bearings
C = .005 oversize rod bearings
AB = .020 oversize cylinders, .010 undersize main and connecting rod bearings
E = smaller carburetor (economy engine)
Export engines have the letter X following the model code number, indicating small bore engine (Example P12X)
Canadian engines have the letter C following the model code number, indicating the larger block engine (Example P12C)

1928
Model Q, 4-cyl.

	FP	5	4	3	2	1
Rds	670	3750	7500	12,500	17,500	25,000
Tr	695	3600	7200	12,000	16,800	24,000
Cpe	670	925	1900	4550	6350	9100
DeL Cpe	695	950	2100	4750	6650	9500
2 dr Sed	690	800	1550	3850	5400	7700
Sed	725	825	1600	4000	5600	8000
DeL Sed	750	825	1600	4050	5650	8100

1929

1929 Plymouth, model U, 2-dr. sedan, AA

PLYMOUTH — MODEL U — FOUR: An updated version of the Model Q, the 1929 Plymouth Model U went into production in early January. It was the first "Plymouth" model, the "Chrysler" prefix being dropped and was well derivative engine that had been used in the early 4 cylinder Chrysler's and the Model Q. Notable changes in this new engine included relocation of the distributor to a vertical position and the moving of the exhaust pipe to the forward side of the engine. Internally the engine was only slightly larger and despite an increase of 5 cubic inches horsepower remained at 45.

Stylewise the Model U took a sharp eye to discern from its Model Q ancestry. Notable changes included only the word Plymouth on the radiator medallion, two piece rounded bumpers, Twolite headlamps and mushroom shaped hubcaps.

The Model U continued in production into 1930 and was considered at various times by the factory as either a 1929 or 1930 model.

Body parts and most mechanical pieces with the exception of the engine, were interchangeable between the Model Q and Model U.

Plymouth ended the year in 10th place in the national sales picture.

I.D. DATA: Serial numbers on closed cars: Medallion on center of upper dash rail. Open cars: Medallion on instrument panel. (Fedco numbering system) Detroit, Michigan Starting: RR-120-P Ending RD-999-D. Detroit, Michigan Starting: Y-000-WP Ending: Y-403-EP. Windsor, Ontario Starting: GP-583-W Ending GC-499-L. Engine numbers on left front corner of cylinder block. Starting: U-999. Ending: U110.000.

Body No.	Body Type & Seating	Price	Weight	Prod. Total
322	2-dr. Bus. Cpe.-2P	655	N/A	See Note 1
328	2-dr. Del. R/S Cpe.-2/4P	695	N/A	—
321	2-dr. Sed.-5P	675	2485	—
320	4-dr. Sed.-5P	695	2510	See Note 2
320	4-dr. Del. Sed.-5P	745	2590	See Note 2
R	2-dr. R/S Rds.-2/4P	675	N/A	—
T	4-dr. Tr.-5P	695	N/A	—

Note 1: Body style production totals unavailable.
Note 2: Body code number 320 indicates Briggs body; body code number 88 indicates Hayes body on four-door sedans only. 3,999 U's were built with right-hand drive.

1929 Plymouth, model U, deluxe rumble-seat coupe, HAC

ENGINE: Inline. Valve in block. Four. Cast iron block. B & S: 3-5/8 in. x 4-1/4 in. Disp.: 175.4 CID. C.R.: 4.6. Brake H.P.: 45 @ 2800 R.P.M. Taxable/A.L.A.M./N.A.C.C. H.P.: 21.03. Main bearings: Three. Valve lifters: Solid. Carb.: Carter 103-S (U.S.); 131-S & 121-SA (U.S. built for export); 132-SA all R.H.D.

TECHNICAL: Sliding gear (spur gears) transmission. Speeds: 3F/1R.. Floor shift controls. Single plate, dry disc clutch. Driveshaft with fabric universal discs. Semi floating rear axle. Overall Ratio: 4.3. Hydraulic brakes on four wheels. Wood spoke wheels, wire optional. Rim size: 4.75 x 20 up to car #Y076LE, then 4.75 x 19.

CHASSIS: [Series U] W.B.: 109-3/4 in. O.L.: 169 in. Frt/Rear Tread: 56/56 in. Tires: 4.75 x 20/19.

OPTIONS: Front & rear bumper, as a set (15.00). Heater hot air, under floor type (30.00). Clock 8 day, header board mount, dial wind (12.50). Cigar lighter in combo with utility light (12.00). Upholstery: leather (all closed models) (25.00). Velour (coupe only) (10.00). Broadcloth (2 or 4 door sedan) (35.00). Broadcloth (coupe) (20.00). Disc wheels set of 5, (25.00) (rear mounted spare). Wire wheels, set of 5, rear mount only (35.00). Tire covers (1.50). Oaks stud type tire lock (3.50). Spring covers, set of 8 (8.00). Trunk rack, folding type available only with sidemounts (12.00). Trunk (20.00). Top boot (10.00). Top bow rests, set of 4 (2.00). Windshield wind wings (open cars only) (10.00). Monograms, painted, black letters only (10.00). Monograms, sterling silver, applied type, maximum of three (10.00). Special colors: Body only (35.00). Special paint on fenders, splash pans, frame horns, rear deck and metal tire carriers (35.00). Special paint, chassis & running gear (20.00). Fender with well (including tires, tire lock and keys). When only one unit is supplied, left side is furnished. 1 fender well, 1 tire & tube (25.00). 2 fenders w/well, 2 tires & tubes (50.00). 5 disc wheels, spare tire & tube (50.00). 6 disc wheels, 2 spare tires & tubes (75.00). 5 wire wheels, tire & tube (60.00). 6 wire wheels, tires & tubes (90.00).

HISTORICAL: Production began January 7, 1929, ended April 5, 1930. Model year production: 108,345. W.P. Chrysler was Corporate & Division head. A Model U broke the world's endurance record by being driven non-stop for 632 hours and 36 minutes before being voluntarily stopped. During the time the car had covered 11,419 miles and was serviced while "on the go". To meet demand for Plymouths a crash program to build a new factory on Lynch Rd., in Detroit, was undertaken. Workmen toiled through the dead of winter to complete the structure, while a steam locomotive parked on a spur track provided steam heat to the assembly line workers inside. They were busily building new cars while the building went up around them!

1930

1930 Plymouth, model 30U, 4-dr. sedan, OCW

PLYMOUTH — MODEL 30U — FOUR: An updated version of the Model U, the Model 30U went into production in April of 1930 and continued until early in 1931. Most notable of the changes in the 30U was a full width, chrome plated radiator shell which replaced the "thin-line" shell of the preceding Q and U models. In other external appearances the 30U looked like its brethren but in fact the fenders were of a heavier design and did not interchange with previous models. Also new was an external mounted horn, centered on the headlamp bar. Headlamps were now painted, rather than stainless as had been the previous models.

Mechanically the 30U had a larger engine with an increase of horsepower. Throughout the year many other drivetrain improvements were made in the 30U, including a change to helical cut gears in the transmission, replacement of the fabric universal discs with universal joints, addition of a water pump and a fuel pump to replace the vacuum tank system.

It was during the 30U production year that Walter Chrysler announced that the Plymouth would now be sold by all Corporate dealers, not just through Chrysler franchised dealers. It was this move that more than anything else can be credited with Plymouth's spectacular rises in the sales arena, the number of Plymouth dealers jumping from slightly over 3,000 to more than 10,000 dealers. Plymouth ended the year in 8th place but the stage was set for Plymouth's takeover of the number three sales position.

Many 30U sedans were fitted with an oval rear window as production continued, while most of the early models had been fitted with rectangular rear windows. New for the year was the introduction of a convertible coupe in addition to the roadster models, the convertible featuring a fixed windshield post, roll up side glass windows and a rumble seat. A commercial (sedan) delivery was offered but sales were poor and the model was dropped. The Fedco identification system was dropped and all cars were now assigned a numerical serial number. Beginning with car no. 1530245 the 30U was considered a 1931 model.

I.D. DATA: Serial numbers on right front door post. Detroit, Michigan Starting: 1500001 Ending: 1570188. Windsor, Ontario Starting: 9300001 Ending: 9305327. Engine numbers on left front corner of cylinder block. Starting: U200.001. Ending: U277.000.

Body No.	Body Type & Seating	Price	Weight	Prod. Total
R	2-dr. Spt. Rds.-2/4P	610	2280	2884
BR	2-dr. Bus. Rds.-2P	535	2245	169
383	2-dr. Bus. Cpe.-2P	590	2420	9189
382	2-dr. R/S Coupe-2/4P	625	2510	5850
T	4-dr. Spt. Phae.-5P	625	2340	632
384	2-dr. Conv.-2/4P	695	2450	1272
380	4-dr. Sedan-5P	625	2595	47,152
381	2-dr. Sedan-5P	565	2497	7980
NA	2-dr. Comm. Sedan-2P	750	N/A	80
NA	Chassis			302

Note: 1,627 Model 30U's were built with right-hand drive.

ENGINE: Inline. Valve in block. Four. Cast iron block. B & S: 3-5/8 in. x 4-3/4 in. Disp.: 196.1 CID. C.R.: 4.6. Brake H.P.: 48 @ 2800 R.P.M. Taxable/A.L.A.M./N.A.C.C. H.P.: 21.03. Main bearings: Three. Valve lifters: Solid. Carb.: Early production 30U: Carter 130S & 130SA; later production Carter 156-S; 158-S all export; 157-S all R.H.D. Torque (Compression) 120 lbs.-ft @ 1200 R.P.M.

TECHNICAL: Sliding gear (early production had spur gears; mid year change to helical type gears). Speeds: 3F/1R. Floor shift controls. Single disc. dry clutch. Driveshaft with fabric universal discs with a mid year change to regular u joints. Semi-floating rear axle. Overall Ratio: 4.3. Hydraulic brakes on four wheels. Wood spoke wheels, wire optional. Rim size: 4.75 x 19.

CHASSIS: [Series 30U] W.B.: 109-3/4'' in. O.L.: 169 in. Frt/Rear Tread: 56-1/4 / 56-1/8 in. Tires: 4.75 x 19.

1930 Plymouth, model 30U, sport roadster, JAC

OPTIONS: Front bumper. Rear bumper. Single sidemount. Dual sidemount. Clock (clock/mirror) also 8 day pull wind; 24 hr or electric. Cigar lighter. 6 bolt lug pattern wire wheels; 5 bolt lug pattern wire wheels; trunk; windwings; gearshift knobs in onyx, french biege or ivory; radiator cap safety chain; Kool Kushion; umbrella & case; windshield defroster; spring covers.

HISTORICAL: Production began April 8, 1930; ended June 8, 1931. Model year production: 76,950. W.P. Chrysler was Corporate head; F.L. Rockelman, Division head.

1929-30
Model U, 4-cyl.

	FP	5	4	3	2	1
Rds	670	3900	7800	13,000	18,200	26,000
Tr	695	3750	7500	12,500	17,500	25,000
Cpe	670	825	1600	4000	5600	8000
DeL Cpe	695	875	1700	4250	5900	8500
2 dr Sed	690	825	1600	4050	5650	8100
Sed	725	825	1600	4000	5600	8000
DeL Sed	750	875	1700	4250	5900	8500

NOTE: Factory prices reduced app. 40 percent for 1930 model year.

1931

PLYMOUTH — MODEL PA — FOUR: The Model PA signaled Plymouth's permanent takeover of the 3rd place in the national new car sales picture, and the coining of the term "The Big Three". The redesigned PA was the result of a 2-1/2 million dollar investment by Chrysler Corporation. If nothing else can be said of Walter Chrysler, it must be said that he showed no fear to the face of the Great Depression. Offering more car for less money, the PA took the showrooms by storm as people lined up to buy this new model. Drawing much attention was the new "Floating Power" engine mountings — a unique system of mounting the engine in rubber and suspending the engine along its own center of gravity. Although still of four cylinders, the engine rocked in the chassis but the rubber mountings absorbed any shock resulting in a smoother ride to the passengers. Battling Chevie's 6 cylinder engine and Ford's planned V8, the car was touted as having the "Smoothness of a Six and the Economy of a Four!". With the first really all new design since its inception, the new Plymouth was quite handsome in appearance with its gently rounded radiator shell, bowl shaped headlamps and oval rear windows. Offered with a full line of optional equipment the car found many ready buyers and with its heritage based on the DeSoto and Chrysler Sixes, many buyers who could not afford those models readily snapped up the new Plymouth.

1931 Plymouth, model PA, 4-dr. sedan, AA

The PA was the first Plymouth to have a built in radiator grill and each radiator cap was adorned with an attractive "short bodied" Flying Lady, and all '31 enclosed models were factory wired with a radio antennae. The PA was also the last model to have been designated during two separate models years as both a 1931 and 1932 model, with future models all taking on certain year designations regardless of when they were built.

I.D. DATA: Serial numbers on right front door post. Detroit, Michigan Starting: 1570301 Ending: 1667963. Windsor, Ontario Starting: 9305401 Ending 9307933. Detroit, Michigan Starting: 1668000 Ending 1668001 (1 car built PA Special Deluxe). Detroit, Michigan Starting: 1669001 Ending: 1669644 (PA Thrift). Detroit, Michigan Starting: 1670001 Ending: 1674250 (PA Thrift). Engine No. Location: Left front corner of cylinder block. Starting: PA-1001. Ending: PA-107093.

Body No.	Body Type & Seating	Price	Weight	Prod. Total
480	4-dr. Thrift Sed.-5P	575	2655	See Note
481	2-dr. Thrift Sed.-5P	495	2690	See Note
T	4-dr. Phae.-5P	595	2545	528
BR	2-dr. Bus. Rds.-2P	535	2440	200
R	2-dr. Spt. Rds.-2/4P	595	2470	2680
483	2-dr. Std. Cpe.-2P	565	2600	12,079
482	2-dr. R/S Cpe.-2/4P	610	2645	9696
484	2-dr. Conv.-2/4P	645	2615	2783
480	4-dr. Sed.-5P	635	2730	49,465
481	2-dr. Sed.-5P	575	2650	23,038
485	4-dr. Del. Sed.-5P	690	2795	4384
NA	4-dr. Taxi-5P	N/A	N/A	112
	Chassis	—	—	131

Note 1: PA Thrift models. Sources list 4,892 of both body types built but serial numbers asigned would indicate 4,894 built. 1,479 PA's and six PA Thrifts were built with right-hand drive.

1931 Plymouth, model PA, 2-dr. sedan, JAC

ENGINE: Inline. Valve in block. Four. Cast iron block. 3-5/8 in. x 4-3/4 in. Disp.: 196.1 CID. C.R.: 4.9. Brake H.P.: 56 @ 2800 R.P.M. Taxable/A.L.A.M./N.A.C.C. H.P.: 21.03. Main bearings: Three. Valve lifters: Solid. Carb.: Carter D-290S. Torque: 130 lbs.-ft. @ 1600 R.P.M. Small bore export engines had a bore of 3-1/8''. Only 85 PA and four PA Thrift cars were shipped with this engine.

TECHNICAL: Sliding gear transmission. Speeds: 3F/1R. Floor shift controls. Single disc, dry 8-7/8 in. clutch. Driveshaft. Semi floating; spiral bevel rear axle. Overall Ratio: 4.3 to 1. Hydraulic brakes on four wheels. Wire or wood spoke wheels. (PA Thrift 1st series had wood spoke, 2nd series wire). Rim size: 4.75 x 19.

CHASSIS: [Series PA] W.B.: 109 in. O.L.: 169-3/4 in. Frt/Rear Tread: 56-1/4 / 56-1/8 in. Tires: 4.75 x 19.

OPTIONS: Front & rear bumper, as set (15.00). Single sidemount w/5 wire wheels or 4 wood, spare rim & tire lock (10.00), w/6 wire wheels, 2 tire locks (30.00). Dual sidemount w/2 spare rims for wood wheels, 2 locks

(22.00). Radio Philco Transitone (99.80). Clock 8 day, header board mount (5.00). Cigar lighter in combination w/utility lamp (3.50). Cowl lamps including cowl moulding, all chrome $7.50 factory installed option only. Special body colors (30.00). Special color, fenders & sheet metal (10.00). Leather upholstery, sedan (18.50). Coupe (5.00). Trunk rack (sidemount cars) (10.00). Trunk (30.00). Top boot, roadster & phaeton (6.00). Convertible coupe (8.00). Tire covers (fabric) (1.50). Metal tire cover (10.50). Tire locks (3.50). Chrome headlamps & taillamp (5.00). Chrome radiator grill (5.00). Chrome radiator louvers (5.00). Spring covers (8.00). Windwings, open cars, non-shatterable glass (12.00). Plain glass (9.00). Flying lady radiator cap, safety glass, windshield only (5.00). All windows, sedan (30.00). All windows, coupe (20.00). On special order the running gear would be painted the fender color except for the engine. PA Thrift models: Only had three dash guages, painted radiator shell and headlamps. Early models were only equipped with wood wheels, later ones with wire wheels.

HISTORICAL: Production began May 1, 1931; end July 13, 1932 (See note 2). Model year production: 106,896. W.P. Chrysler, Corporate head; F.L. Rockelman, Division head. Overseas assembly plants were opened in England, Denmark and Sweden for final assembly of SKD or CKD (semi or completely knocked down) vehicles.

Note 2: PA Thrift production began Jan. 1, 1932 and ended Sept. 23, 1932 A 1931 PA 4 door sedan, which had been picked at random from the Detroit assembly line was shipped to San Francisco where it was fitted with an extra gas tank in the rear seat and a third spare tire in addition to twin fendermounted spares. Driven by 57 year old Louis B. Miller and co-driver Louis Pribek the car was driven from San Francisco to New York City and return in a time of five days, 12 hours and 9 minutes, breaking the previous round trip speed record by 9-1/2 hours. Covering 6,287 miles they averaged 47.52 miles an hour for the trip. They were to have been greeted in New York City by Walter Chrysler himself but they were so far ahead of schedule that after an hour and a quarter's time, spent servicing the car, they headed westward, without meeting Mr. Chrysler, to establish their record. They also bettered the time of "Cannonball" Baker, driving a Franklin, over the shorter Los Angeles to New York course.

**1931
PA, 4-cyl.**

	FP	5	4	3	2	1
Rds	535	4050	8100	13,500	18,900	27,000
Tr	625	3900	7800	13,000	18,200	26,000
Conv	695	1750	4800	8000	11,200	16,000
Cpe	565	950	2100	4750	6650	9500
2 dr Sed	565	750	1450	3400	5000	7100
Sed	625	800	1550	3850	5400	7700
DeL Sed	625	875	1700	4250	5900	8500

1932

1932 Plymouth, model PB, coupe, AA

PLYMOUTH NEW FINER — MODEL PB — FOUR: Although the model PB saw one of Plymouth's shortest production years, it was without doubt Plymouth's zenith of 4 cylinder car production and is the most "collectable" of all the 4 cylinder models today. The model PB also has the distinction of being the first Plymouth model to have been assigned a model year classification by the Corporation; the PB WAS a 1932 model.

Armed with a vast array of body styles including five open models (business roadster, sport roadster, convertible coupe, convertible sedan and phaeton) and beautifully proportioned styling, the PB looked much ritzier than any 4 cylinder automobile — and improvements in the engine, as well as an optional high compression cylinder head, gave the car sparkling performance.

Style wise, the PB featured Plymouth's first one piece front fenders, free standing, chrome plated headlamps and on many models, chrome external trumpet horns mounted beneath the lamps. The hood stretched from the radiator shell (which itself was chrome plated) over the cowl to the windshield giving the illusion of a much longer car. Breaking the expanse of the hood were twin cowl ventilators mounted on either side of the hood centerline. Wire wheels and standard (on some models) twin fender mounted spare tires added to the attractive looks of the new cars. An extended wheelbase also added much to the "big car" illusion of the PB and was, in fact, a move made to facilitate the installation of a 6 cylinder

engine in the chassis — a move which came late in 1932 with the succeeding model PC.

The PB was the first and only year for the two door convertible sedan body style and it was also the last year that Plymouth offered a roadster body style. Sensing the public's rejection of drafty, open cars, the PB was also the last year for a phaeton (touring car) body style as well. Those few that were built were all five-passenger models although extant photos show at least one prototype seven-passenger touring. The PB was Plymouth's last 4 cylinder automobile until 1971.

In addition to the PB line, leftover PA models were sold as the PA Thrift model. These cars, available only as two or four door sedans, were made from a hodge-podge of leftover parts and were discontinued as supplies were used up.

I.D. DATA: Serial numbers on right front door post. Detroit, Michigan Starting: 1680001 Ending: 1758001. Windsor, Ontario Starting 9307951 Ending: 9310965. Engine numbers on left front corner of cylinder block. Starting: PB1001. Ending: PB-82450.

Body No.	Body Type & Seating	Price	Weight	Prod. Total
BR	2-dr. Bus. Rds.-2P	495	2545	325
RS	2-dr. Spt. Rds.-2/4P	595	2595	2163
T	4-dr. Phae.-5P	595	2655	259
532	2-dr. R/S Cpe.-2/4P	610	2750	8159
533	2-dr. Bus. Cpe.-2P	565	2695	11,126
531	2-dr. Sed.-5P	575	2825	13,031
530	4-dr. Sed.-5P	635	2870	38,066
534	2-dr. Conv.-2/4P	645	2730	4853
536	2-dr. Conv. Sed.-5P	785	2920	690
537	4-dr. Sed.-7P	725	3075	2179
NA	Chassis	—	—	159

Note: 928 PB's were built with right-hand drive.

ENGINE: Inline. Valve in block. Four. Cast iron block. B & S: 3-5/8 in. x 4-3/4 in. Disp.: 196.1 CID. C.R.: 4.9. Brake H.P.: 65 @ 3400 R.P.M. Taxable/A.L.A.M./N.A.C.C. H.P.: 21.03. Main bearings: Three. Valve lifters: Solid. Carb.: Carter 4A2 or 4A3. Torque: 136 lbs.-ft. @ 1600 R.P.M. with optional high-compression cylinder head the compression ratio was 5.6:1. Small bore export engines had a bore of 3-7/64" but only 58 cars were shipped with this engine.

1932 Plymouth, model PB, 4-dr. sedan, JAC

TECHNICAL: Sliding gear transmission. 3F/1R. Floor shift. Single plate, dry disc clutch. Driveshaft. Semi floating, spiral bevel rear axle. Overall ratio: 4.3 to 1. Hydraulic brakes on four wheels. Wire spoke wheels. Rim size: 4.75 x 19. Free-Wheeling Standard.

CHASSIS: [Series PB] W.B.: 112" in. (121 in. 7 passenger) O.L.: 175-1/32 in. (7 Pass. 184-1/32 in.) Frt/Rear Tread: 57-5/16; 56-15/16 in. Tires: 5.25 x 18 in.

OPTIONS: Front & rear bumper as package (15.00). Single sidemount. Dual Sidemount. Radio Philco (69.50). Heater several type offered, hot water & exhaust type. Clock. Cigar lighter (3.50). Automatic clutch (8.00). Leather upholstery (coupes) (8.00); (sedans) (18.50). Trunk rack (only for cars with sidemounts) (11.00). Front opening trunks (sedans only) (40.00). Suitcase set (45.00). Top boot for roadster or phaeton (6.00). Top boot for convertible coupe or convertible sedan (8.00). Fabric tire cover (1.50). Metal tire cover (9.00). Tire lock for rear mount (1.50). Twin chrome taillamps (6.00). External trumpet horns (10.00). "Red Head" cylinder head & decarbonizer (5.00). RH windshield wiper (4.50). Chrome plated radiator louvers (5.00). Fabric spring covers (8.00). Windshield side wings for open cars, with safety glass (12.00 pair); same, with plate glass (9.00). Duplate Safety Glass for roadster (3.00). Phaeton (4.00). Closed cars (windshield only) (3.50). Closed cars (all windows) (17.50). Convertible sedan (14.50). Coupe (all windows) (9.50). 5.50 x 17" wire wheels (set of 5) (10.00). Clocks: 8 day, header board mount (8.00). Clock/mirror (10.00). Instrument panel mount (8.00). Instrument panel mount, electric (15.00).

HISTORICAL: Production began Feb. 4, 1932; ended Sept. 27, 1932. Public announcements date was April 3, 1932. Model year production: 83,910. W.P. Chrysler was corporate head. F.L. Rockelman, Division head who was replaced by B.E. Hutchinson during the year. For $40 extra, Plymouth offered the Collegiate Special Roadster. The only distinguishing feature of the car was that for the extra money, the buyer got a car painted in his school colors, regardless of what that combination may have been. It was not noted how many cars were sold as such.

1932 Plymouth, model PB, sport roadster, JAC

1932
Model PA, 4-cyl., 109" wb

	FP	5	4	3	2	1
Rds	535	3600	7200	12,000	16,800	24,000
Conv	645	3750	7500	12,500	17,500	25,000
Cpe	565	1000	2400	5000	7000	10,000
RS Cpe	610	1000	2400	5000	7000	10,000
2 dr Sed	575	875	1700	4250	5900	8500
Sed	635	875	1700	4250	5900	8500
Phae	595	3750	7500	12,500	17,500	25,000

Model PB, 4-cyl., 112" wb
NOTE: Add 5 percent for 6 cyl. models.

	FP	5	4	3	2	1
Rds	495	3400	6900	11,500	16,100	23,000
Conv	645	3600	7200	12,000	16,800	24,000
Conv Sed	785	3600	7200	12,000	16,800	24,000
RS Cpe	610	1000	2400	5000	7000	10,000
2 dr Sed	575	900	1900	4500	6300	9000
Sed	635	900	1900	4500	6300	9000
DeL Sed	725	925	2000	4600	6400	9200

1933

1933 Plymouth, model PD, convertible, OCW

PLYMOUTH — MODEL PC — SIX: After spending $9 million in research and development, Chrysler Corporation unveiled its first six cylinder Plymouth before the end of 1932. Considered a 1933 model the new model PC was completely redesigned but despite its low price (as low as $495, the same as the previous 4 cylinder PB model) and the addition of two extra cylinders, the car met with heavy dealer and customer sales resistance. With its short wheelbase, slanted, chrome plated radiator shell, and design of hood and louver slope that did not "synch" with the cut of the forward opening doors the car took on a decidedly awkward appearance. To many people, the new six cylinder car looked more like a four cylinder car than had the 4 cylinder PB of the previous year!

Realizing their predicament Plymouth engineers put a crash program into gear to market a restyled car before the spring selling season. The result was the Deluxe model PD Plymouth; the PC was dropped altogether from production. In its place was the model PCXX, a car restyled to look much like the new PD.

The PC was distinguished by its short wheelbase, (which was increased by one inch early in production to accommodate fender mounted spare tires), chromed radiator shell with bolted-in-place Flying Lady ornament and painted headlamp shells in the shape of a bowl. On the interior the instruments were placed in an engine turned panel in the center of the dash, but the car lacked a temperature gauge.

The new six cylinder engine, at 189 cubic inches was actually smaller internally than the 4 cylinder which it replaced but developed 5 more horsepower and an optional high compression cylinder head added another 6 horsepower. The basic six cylinder engine would remain in Plymouth production until the end of the 1959 model year — and into the 60's in Dodge trucks.

PLYMOUTH STANDARD — MODEL PCXX — SIX: Replacing the PC model in mid-year, the PCXX was styled to closely match it's PD big brother. The radiator shell now sat more upright, with a painted shell, removable external radiator cap (usually in the form of a Flying Lady) and large, painted,

bowl shaped headlamps. Various other differences between the PC and the PCXX were made, a fact that today can drive a '33 Plymouth restorer up the wall in attempting to obtain correct parts for his car.

The PCXX was offered in a full range of body styles with the exception of a convertible coupe which was relegated to the Deluxe line only. Prices of the PCXX were lowered (to $445 for the business coupe) and sales were about equal to that of the PC which it replaced.

PLYMOUTH DELUXE — MODEL PD — SIX: When it became apparent to Chrysler personnel that the new 6 cylinder PC was not being well received a crash program was put into effect to bring out a significantly restyled car before the spring selling season. To accomplish the task, Plymouth engineers took a Dodge Model DP frame, modified the wheelbase slightly and, maintaining the basic body structure, proceeded to design a new front end for the car. By juggling hood panels, front fenders, running boards and splash aprons the engineers could build a "new" car without excessive expense in redesigning a new body.

Built on a 112" WB, and with an additional 4" in overall length, the PD corrected all the "wrongs" of the original PC design. The painted radiator shell housed either a chrome plated or painted grill, while the hood stretched back over the cowling to the windshield. The trailing edge of the hood, along with the hood louvers, now slanted on the same angle as did the leading edge of the forward opening doors. Chrome plated, bullet shaped headlamps added much to the looks of the car. Wood or wire wheels and long, flowing fenders also helped to alleviate the "stubby" look of the PC. A free flowing, long body "Flying Lady" radiator cap accented the front end of the car and many were fitted with the optional chrome plated externally mounted trumpet horns beneath the headlamps.

The redesigned car remained mechanically the same as the previous PC and PCXX. With prices starting as low as $495, sales of the new car sky rocketed setting a new production record for Plymouth and placing the car solidly in 3rd place in national car sales.

I.D. DATA: [Model PC] Serial numbers on right front door post. Detroit, Michigan Starting: 1759001 Ending: 1817044. Los Angeles, California Starting: 3000001 ending 3000604. Windsor, Ontario Starting: 9311001 Ending 9313273. Windsor Starting 9315001 Ending 9315375. Engine No. Location: Left front corner of cylinder block. Starting: PC-1001. Ending: PC-60979. [Model PCXX] Serial numbers on right front door post. Detroit, Michigan Starting: 1817101 Ending: 1858419. Los Angeles, California Starting: 3000610 Ending: 3001395. Engine numbers in left front corner of cylinder block. Starting: PC75001. Ending: PC118731. Plymouth also used the single letter "X" in its engine code numbers to designate a small bore, export engine. This practice was continued throughout the years of production. [Model PD] Serial numbers on right front door post. Detroit, Michigan Starting: 2000001 Ending: 2186951. Los Angeles, California Starting: 3002501 Ending: 3007678. Windsor, Ontario Starting: 9320001 Ending: 9321902. Windsor Starting: 9395001 Ending: 9396071. Engine numbers on left front corner of cylinder block. Starting: PD-1001. Ending: PD-195997.

1933 Plymouth, model PD, convertible coupe, JAC

Body Code	Body Type & Seating	Price	Weight	Prod. Total
Plymouth PC				
BC	2-dr. Bus. Cpe.-2P	495	2418	10,853
TPC	2-dr. RS Cpe.-2/4P	545	2473	8894
585	2-dr. Sed.-5P	505	2498	4008
588	4-dr. Sed.-5P	575	2553	33,815
CC	2-dr. Conv. Cpe.-2/4P	595	2483	2034
NA	Chassis	—	—	396
Plymouth PCXX				
BC	2-dr. Bus. Cpe.-2P	445	2353	9200
TPC	2-dr. RS Cpe.-2/4P	485	2497	2497
588	4-dr. Sed.-5P	510	2523	13,661
585	2-dr. Sed.-5P	465	2443	17,736
NA	Chassis	—	—	309
Plymouth PD				
TPC	2-dr. RS Cpe.-2/4P	545	2545	20,821
BC	2-dr. Bus. Cpe.-2P	495	2485	30,728
588	4-dr. Sed.-5P	575	2645	88,404
585	2-dr. Sed.-5P	525	2560	49,826
CC	2-dr. Conv. Cpe.-2/4P	595	2530	4596
NA	Chassis	—	—	779

Note: 1,283 PC's, 625 PCXX's and 1,517 PD's were built with right-hand drive.

1933 Plymouth, model PC, 2-dr. sedan, JAC

	FP	5	4	3	2	1
Conv	565	3150	6300	10,500	14,700	21,000
Cpe	495	825	1600	4000	5600	8000
RS Cpe	525	875	1700	4250	5900	8500
2 dr Sed	505	750	1450	3500	5050	7200
Sed	545	750	1450	3300	4900	7000

PD, 6-cyl.
NOTE: Add 4 percent for PCXX models.

	FP	5	4	3	2	1
Conv	595	3300	6600	11,000	15,400	22,000
Cpe	495	900	1900	4500	6300	9000
RS Cpe	545	1000	2400	5000	7000	10,000
2 dr Sed	525	825	1600	4000	5600	8000
Sed	575	825	1600	4050	5650	8100

1934

1934 Plymouth, model PE, 4-dr. sedan, AA

ENGINE: Inline. Valve in block. Six. Cast iron block. B & S: 3-1/8 in. x 4-1/8 in. Disp.: 189.8 CID. C.R.: 5.5. Brake H.P.: 70 @ 3600 R.P.M. Taxable/A.L.A.M./N.A.C.C. H.P.: 23.44. Main bearings: Four. Valve lifters: Solid. Carb.: Carter C6A-C6A2-C6A3 or C6A4. Torque (Compression): 130 lbs.-ft. @ 1200 R.P.M. Optional "Redhead" high compression head; later replaced by high compression aluminum cylinder head. Small bore export engines had a bore of 2-7/8''; 437 PC, 21 PCXX and 193 PD's were shipped with this engine.

TECHNICAL: [Plymouth PC] Sliding gear transmission. Speeds: 3F/1R. Floor shift controls. Single plate, dry clutch. Driveshaft. Semi floating rear axle. Overall Ratio: 4.375. Hydraulic brakes on four wheels. Wire or wood spoke wheels. Rim size: 5.25 x 17. [Plymouth PCXX] Sliding gear transmission. Speeds: 3F/1R. Floor shift controls. Single disc, dry clutch. Driveshaft. Semi floating rear axle. Overall Ratio: 4.1. Hydraulic brakes on four wheels. Wire or wood spoke wheels. Rim size: 5.25 x 17. [Plymouth PD] Sliding gear transmission. Speeds: 3F/1R. Floor shift controls. Single disc, dry clutch. Driveshaft. Semi-floating rear axle. Overall Ratio: 4.375. Hydraulic brakes on four wheels. Wire wheels wood spoke optional. rim size: 6.00 x 16 / 5.25 x 17. Vacuum Clutch optional. Free-wheeling standard.

CHASSIS: [Series PC] (Includes PCXX) W.B.: 107/108 in. (Change early in production) O.L.: 174 in. Frt/Rear Tread: 56-1/4 / 56-1/4 in. Tires: 5.25 x 17. [Series PD] W.B.: 112 in. O.L.: 178-1/2 in. Frt/Rear Tread: 56 / 56-1/4 in. Tires: 5.25 x 17 / 6.00 x 16 in.

OPTIONS: Bumper optional as set (15.00). Radio Philco Transitone No. 5 (factory installed) (39.95). Radio Antenna. Special paint, body (30.00). Special paint, fenders & sheetmetal (10.00). Automatic clutch (PD only) (8.00). Flying lady radiator ornament (2.50). Rubber mat for rear compartment of business coupe (1.50). Spare Wheel lock (1.20). Thermostat (PC models) (1.50). Black enamel rear tire cover (1.00). Metal spare tire cover with emblem (5.00). Trunk rack (only for cars with sidemounts) (7.50). 16" wire "Airwheels", set of 5 with 4 tires & tubes (20.00) (PD Only); 16" wood ("Airwheels) with 5 wheels and 4 tires & tubes, PC or PD (20.00). Duplate safety glass. Dual rear mounted spare tires (12.00). Metal "form fit" trunk for sedans. 20" high clearance wheels. Accessory Group A for PD $15; Same for PC $17 included: dual horns, auxiliary windshield wiper, cigar lighter, dual taillamps on PD. Also included chrome headlamps and taillamp on PC. Antenna prices: All PC models without radio (5.00), with radio (1.00). For PD convertible coupe w/o radio (10.00). Antenna for convertible coupe, no charge. Single Sidemount (right fender only) available *only* on business coupe, either PC or PD: PC or PD with 5 17" wire wheels (7.00). PC with 5 17" painted wood wheels not available. PD with 5 17" painted wood wheels (7.00). PD with 5 16" wire "Airwheels" (27.00). PC with 5 16" wood "Airwheels" (27.00). PD with 5 16" wood "Airwheels" (27.00). Two Sidemount Fenders PC or PD with 6 17" wire wheels (15.00). PD with 6 17" painted demountable wood wheels (15.00). PC or PD with 6 16" wire "Airwheels" (35.00). PC or PD with 6 16" wood "Airwheels" (35.00). Note on Sidemount fenders: Early production PC models with the 107" wheelbase could not be fitted with sidemount fenders. Early in production the wheelbase on these cars was stretched to 108" to accommodate fender mount spare tires.

HISTORICAL: Plymouth PC Production began November 11, 1932; ended April 7, 1933. Model year production: 60,000. Plymouth PCXX production began April 14, 1933; ended December 5, 1933. Model year production: 43,403. Plymouth PD production began March 17, 1933; ended January 27, 1934. Model year production: 195,154. W.P. Chrysler, Corporate head; B.E. Hutchinson, Division head.
Miss Irma Brandt became the first woman to compete in the Monte Carlo Rally driving a 1933 PC Plymouth coach in the 1934 Rally. She won her division, driving the car from Norway to Monte Carlo. The car remained in Miss Brandt's possession at her farm near Oslo, Norway. During the German occupation of Norway in World War Two it was common practice for people to strip the wheels, tires or vital engine parts from their vehicles to keep the Nazi soldiers from confiscating the vehicle. Miss Brandt did likewise and the car has remained in her possession. The car was completely restored in 1984. Miss Brandt later drove a 1934 PE Plymouth to a second place finish in the 1935 running of the Monte Carlo Rally.

PLYMOUTH DELUXE — MODEL PE — SIX: The Deluxe Plymouth for 1934 perhaps reached an all time high for Plymouth in the looks and equipment department. With a larger engine than the previous year (now at 201 cubic inches and 77 horsepower) the Deluxe Plymouth featured independent coil spring front suspension, an industry first in the low price field. With a longer wheelbase, skirted fenders, a radiator cap located under the hood, and a special hood which featured not only rows of louvers but twin opening ventilating doors on either side, the PE Plymouth found itself in ready demand — so much so that before the year was over, the '34 had surpassed the production record set in 1933 and had also seen the one millionth Plymouth built in August, a car which was driven off the line by Walter Chrysler himself. It had taken Plymouth only six years to build its first million cars — it had taken Henry Ford twelve years to reach that mark and Chevrolet nine years!
First offered in this year was the first factory available wooden bodied station wagon (the bodies were built by U.S. Body & Forging at a plant in Tell City, Indiana) and a close-coupled Town Sedan which featured a built on metal trunk at the rear of the body. Although the official announcement date of the '34 models was January 13, the cars were shown one week early to take advantage of the New York Automobile Show which opened on January 6th. By the end of January production had reached 1,500 cars per day. Early PE's were equipped with a host of special equipment including free wheeling transmission and automatic vacuum controlled clutch, but this piece of equipment was made optional later in the model year.
Unique to the PE was a ventilating wind wing built into the front door window system. In normal operation the wind wing could be swung out via a crank handle and the side window rolled down in normal fashion. By closing both the windwing and the side window, then locking them in place by throwing a lever, the entire system could be rolled down as one unit into the door for a completely unobstructed opening. The plant these cars were built in, located on Detroit's Lynch Road, was the largest automobile factory under one roof in the world.

PLYMOUTH SIX — MODEL PF — SIX: Introduced at the same time as the Deluxe PE, the PF was a lower priced, shorter wheelbase (by 4") automobile. Closely resembling its bigger brother, the PF lacked the ventilating doors on the hood but retained the newly introduced independent front suspension system. Also missing was the combination vent window system and there was no provision for a glove compartment or ash receiver on the dash. In addition, the instrument gauges had white numerals on a black background rather than the gold type panel used on the Deluxe model.
The PF consisted of the entire range of body styles except for the convertible coupe, station wagon or the Town Sedan which was introduced in mid year.

PLYMOUTH SPECIAL SIX — MODEL PFXX — SIX: Introduced in May for the spring selling season, the PF Special Six (better known as a PFXX) was a slightly higher priced car than its predecessor PF. Fitted with such appointments as a glove compartment, ash receiver (which could be replaced by the remote control head for a radio) and Accessory Group C which included such items as a Valchrome grille, dual externally mounted trumpet horns and twin taillamps, the PFXX was priced within $5 of the Ford Deluxe V8. Whereas the original PF has been mostly equipped with wire wheels, the PFXX was fitted with the steel artillery wheels like the PE (wires were still optional if the purchaser desired them) with earlier cars carrying 17" wheels which were later changed to 16" like the Deluxe PE.

1934 Plymouth, model PE, coupe, JAC

Although not considered by the factory as a separate sales line, production of the series nearly equalled that of the PF line. With the mid year introduction of the Town Sedan, a model was offered on the PFXX chassis but only 574 were built.

Throughout the 1934 year, Plymouth juggled prices between its lines and at one point was forced by the government to reduce its prices after an announced price hike. PF prices did esculate after the introduction of the PG series which took over the PF original price slots.

PLYMOUTH STANDARD SIX — MODEL PG — SIX: Introduced in March, three months after the PE and PF showings, the PG became the Plymouth business line. Offered in only two body styles, a coupe and a tudor (a handful of four door sedans were built but were not cataloged) the PG had the same 108'' wheelbase as its PF sister, but had a drop forged I beam front axle rather than independent front suspension like the PE and PF models. As the price leader, the PG's austerity was evident in its lack of trim which included no glove compartment, ash receiver or mechanical equipment such as that found on the other '34 models. It was not possible to even order such equipment as free wheeling or automatic vacuum clutch even though they would have easily fit the car. As a cheap car for business people, the car was ideal and such options as a split front seat on the coupe allowed salesman to reach their samples in the trunk simply by folding the passenger seat forward. For those requiring extra road clearance oversize wheels and tires were offered. Despite its low cost, the PG line saw the least production of any models.

I.D. DATA: Plymouth PE Serial numbers on right front door post. Detroit, Michigan Starting: 2188001. Ending: 2397536. Los Angeles, California Starting: 3007701. Ending: 3019347. Windsor, Ontario Starting: 9321911. Ending: 9326544. Engine numbers on left front corner of cylinder block. Starting: PE-1001 all PE series engines began with prefix PE. Ending: PE 230836. Plymouth PF Serial numbers on right front door post. Detroit, Michigan Starting: 1859001. Ending: 1894740. Los Angeles, California Starting: 3100001. Ending: 3101358. Windsor, Ontario Starting: 9315376. Ending: 9316221. Engine numbers on left front corner of cylinder block. Starting: PF-1001 all PF series engines began with prefix PF. Ending: PF-7232. Plymouth PFXX Serial number on right front door post. Detroit, Michigan Starting: 1909001. Ending: 1941945. Los Angeles, California Starting: 3092001. Ending: 3094353. Engine numbers on left front corner of cylinder block. All began with prefix PF: Starting PF-41059. Ending: PF-96379. Plymouth PG Serial numbers on right front door post. Detroit, Michigan Starting: 10200001. Ending: 1039039. Los Angeles, California Starting: 3150001. Ending: 3151472. Engine numbers on left front corner of cyliner block. Starting: PF-7232 All PG series cars used PF series engines. Ending: PF 41049.

Body Code	Body Type & Seating	Price	Weight	Prod. Total
Plymouth PE				
BC	2-dr. Bus. Cpe.-2P	595	2668	28,433
TPC	2-dr. RS Cpe.-2/4P	630	2733	15,658
CC	2-dr. Conv. Cpe.-2/4P	685	2698	4,482
600	4-dr. Sed.-5P	660	2848	108,407
641	2-dr. Sed.-5P	610	2773	58,535
601	4-dr. Twn. Sed.-5P	695	2898	7,049
602	4-dr. Sed.-7P	1075	NA	891
NA	4-dr. Westchester Sub.-7/8P	820	NA	35
NA	Chassis	NA	NA	2,362

Note: Seven-passenger sedan price for 602 shown in 1934 Canadian dollars as most, if not all, of these were built in Canada.

Body Code	Body Type & Seating	Price	Weight	Prod. Total
Plymouth PF				
BC	2-dr. Bus. Cpe.-2P	540	2513	6,980
TPC	2-dr. RS Cpe.-2/4P	570	2573	2,061
NA	2-dr. Sed.-5P	560	2603	12,562
609	4-dr. Sed.-5P	600	2693	16,789
NA	Chassis	NA	NA	1,152
Plymouth PFXX				
BC	2-dr. Bus. Cpe.-2P	560	2563	3,721
TPC	2-dr. RS Cpe.-2/4P	590	2600	1,746
NA	2-dr. Sed.-5P	580	2658	12,497
604	4-dr. Sed.-5P	620	2708	16,760
NA	4-dr. Town Sed.-5P	655	2783	574
NA	Chassis	—	—	—
Plymouth PG				
BC	2-dr. Bus. Cpe.-2P	485	2438	7,844
644	2-dr. Sed.-5P	510	2538	12,603
NA	4-dr. Sed.-5P	NA	NA	62
NA	Chassis	NA	NA	3

Engine specifications same for all PF and PE series. 6,682 PE's and 3,422 PF's were built with right-hand drive; no PG's were so built.

ENGINE: Inline. Valve in block. Six. Cast iron block. B & S: 3-1/8 in. x 4-3/8 in. Disp.: 201.3 CID. C.R.: 5.8. Brake H.P.: 77 @ 3600 R.P.M. Taxable/A.L.A.M./N.A.C.C. H.P.: 23.44. Main bearings: Four. Valve lifters: Solid. Carb.: Carter B & B C6B. Torque (Compression) 140 lbs.-ft @ 1200 R.P.M. Optional aluminum high compression cylinder head. C.R.: 6.5. Brake H.P.: 82 @ 3600 R.P.M.
Note: Cars built for export were equipped with 170.4 CID engine, 2-7/8'' bore x 4-3/8'' stroke. Engines were identified by engine number code PEX of PFX. 1,196 PE and 333 PF's were equipped with this small-bore engine.

CHASSIS: [Series PE] 1934 W.B.: 114 in. (124'' seven-passenger) O.L.: 181-5/16 in. coupe & conv.; 187-3/8 in. sedans. Frt/Rear Tread: 56-1/2 / 56-1/4 in. Tires: 6.00 x 16. [Series PF & PFXX] 1934 W.B.: 108 in. O.L.: 181-7/16 in. sedan; 176 in. coupes. Frt/Rear Tread: 56-1/8 in. / 56-3/8 in. Tires: 5.25 x 17/6.00 x 16. [Series PG] 1934 W.B.: 108 in. O.L.: 181-7/16 in. sedan; 176 in. coupe. Frt/Rear Tread: 56-1/8; 56-3/8 in. Tires: 5/25 x 17.

TECHNICAL: Sliding gear transmission. Speeds: 3F/1R. Floor shift controls. Single disc, dry 9 in. clutch. Driveshaft. Semi floating rear axle. Overall ratio: 4.375 sedans; 4.11 coupes. Hydraulic brakes on four wheels. Wire spoke or steel artillery wheels. Rim size: 6.00 x 16 in. (4 in. rim) on PE & PFXX; 5.25 x 17 in. (3 in. rim) on PF & PG. Free-wheeling is standard on PE only.
Note: Although the vacuum clutch was an $8 option it was installed on all PE models produced through February production; from that point on the dealer had to specify its installation. It was not available on PF or PG models.

1934 Plymouth, model PG, coupe, AA

OPTIONS: Bumpers were still optional on all models in 1934. The complete bumper package which includes front and rear bumper face plates, spare tires & tube cost $22 on the PE series; $21 on PF & PG series. Single sidemount, all models 15.00 except town sedan (10.00); dual sidemounts PF-PG 40.00, PE 42.50; PE town sedan 37.50, PFXX town sedan 35.00. Sidemount cover(s). Fender skirts (9.00 pair). Bumper guards (3.00 for set of 4). Radio in dash mount Philco Transitione (PE & PFXX) (55.00 Deluxe) (42.50 Standard). Heater: Several choices offered, all hot water type. Clock: Elgin 8 day dash clock (7.50). Waltham 8 day headerboard (12.50). Clock mirror (12.50). Cigar lighter (1.25). Radio antenna PE & PFXX factory wired, utilizing "chicken wire" fabric roof support (1.00 optional on PF & PG models). Seat covers: Several types offered including driver only "Kool Kushion". External sun shade: spotlight (20.00). Form fit metal trunk for 2 & 4 door sedans (35.00). Fitted luggage (18.00). Hat box (6.50). Metal spare tire cover (std. on PE) (6.50). RH taillamp (3.50). Klaxon K-26-M external mount dual horns (9.00). RH windshield wiper (4.95). Wheel trim rings (6.75 for set of 5). License plate frames (2.50 pair). RH interior sunvisor (2.00). Locking gas cap (1.50). Automatic choke (5.25). Casco defroster (3.00). High compression aluminum cylinder head (5.00). Vacuum clutch (PE only) (8.00). Split front seat on coupe (for access to rear compartment without leaving vehicle) (5.00). "Mayflower" sailing ship ornament (3.50). Vent wings for PF or PG (7.50). Rear spring covers (3.50). Mohair upholstery (5.00). (Mohair was made optional at no extra cost later in the production year). 20'' high clearnace wheels. PE Accessory Group sold for $15 and included dual external horns, RH taillamp, RH windshield wiper and cigar lighter. PF Accessory Group sold for $20 and included dual external horns, RH taillamp, RH windshield wiper, cigar lighter, chrome headlamps and a chrome grill. Note on PE grilles: At the start of production grilles on PE series were chrome plated; around February the grilles were painted fender color; later in the year they received a treatment called Valchrome which gave a satiny "chrome" finish. During the painted grille period chrome grilles could be had for $17.50 extra, but this option was dropped when Valchrome use began.

HISTORICAL: Plymouth PE Production began December 19, 1933; Ended September 28, 1934. Public announcement date for PE and PF models was January 13, 1934. Model year production: 225,817.

The one millionth Plymouth was built in August and was driven off the Detroit assembly lin by Walter P. Chrysler himself. The car was thensold to Mrs. Ethel Miller of Turlock, California. Mrs. Miller had been the purchaser of the first Plymouth ever sold in 1928 and traded that car in on the one millionth Plymouth. The '28 was subsequently put on display at the Chicago World's Fair.

A PE Plymouth placed second in the large car division of the 1935 Monte Carlo Rallye, driven by two women. Miss Irma-Darre Brandt and Miss Lena Christinsen. Another '34 Plymouth won the 400 mile Durban to Johannesburg (South Africa) speed-endurance test, setting a new record over the course.

1934 Plymouth, model PF, 4-dr. sedan, JAC

1934
Standard PG, 6-cyl., 108" wb

	FP	5	4	3	2	1
Bus Cpe	485	775	1500	3750	5250	7500
2 dr Sed	510	750	1450	3300	4900	7000
Standard PF, 6-cyl., 108" wb						
Bus Cpe	560	825	1600	4000	5600	8000
RS Cpe	590	875	1700	4250	5900	8500
2 dr Sed	580	750	1450	3500	5050	7200
Sed	620	775	1500	3600	5100	7300
DeLuxe PE, 6-cyl., 114" wb						
Conv	685	3300	6600	11,000	15,400	22,000
Cpe	595	900	1900	4500	6300	9000
RS Cpe	630	1000	2400	5000	7000	10,000
2 dr Sed	610	825	1600	4000	5600	8000
Sed	660	825	1600	4050	5650	8100
Twn Sed	695	950	2100	4750	6650	9500

1935

1935 Plymouth, model PJ, station wagon, AA

PLYMOUTH DELUXE — MODEL PJ — SIX: The PJ was a completely new, from the frame up, automobile and marked Plymouth's styling change from "square" to "round". Starting with a heavier, X braced frame, the new body was bolted to the frame both vertically and horizontally at 46 different points! This was called Unit Frame & Body Construction, making the frame an integral part of the body structure and the body an equal integral part of the frame.

The entire body, from the front fenders, to the radiator shell, to the rear of the body, now featured a gentle, more rounded styling, taking on a semblance of aerodynamics, and influenced, no doubt, by the Corporation's Airflow DeSoto and Chryslers.

Mechanically, the engine received a great deal of attention, including the addition of extra water jacketing in addition to a directional water cooling tube inside the water jacket which "directed" cool water to hot spots inside the engine. Additional changes were made to ventilate the clutch plate along with changes in the transmission. Oddly enough, Plymouth abandoned independent front suspension and returned to semi-elliptic springs and a tube front axle with the PJ models. Changes in spring lengths were credited with achieving "Balanced Weight" and improved ride qualities.

A line of sedans called "Touring" models were now offered, which featured a built in "hump style" trunk on the rear of the body. These proved extremely popular despite a slightly higher price over the regular sedans. A line of long wheelbase 5 and 7 passenger sedans was also offered.

Deluxe models are easily identified by their bullet shaped, chrome plated headlamps and hood trim that consisted of five chrome circles beneath three horizontal chrome bars.

PLYMOUTH BUSINESS SIX — MODEL PJ — SIX: Mechanically the same as other PJ models with the exception of a choke type thermostat rather than a by-pass type, the Business Six was Plymouth's price leader, starting at a low of $510. Plymouth's wooden bodied station wagon, the Westchester Suburban, was built on this chassis and in a return to a body style first offered in 1930, a return was made to the Commercial Sedan. This vehicle was based on a two door sedan body style, with the addition of a single door at the rear of the body. Advertised as the perfect commercial vehicle

for the small businessman, the Commercial Sedan was easily converted into a regular passenger sedan by the addition of an optional rear seat. The rear quarter windows, when used in a commercial capacity, were filled with window blanks that could be easily removed. The Commercial Sedan met with limited success but was carried on into future years production. The Business Six was easily identified by its hood trim which consisted only of three horizontal chrome bars and painted headlamps.

PLYMOUTH — MODEL PJ — SIX: This was a limited series consisting of only two body styles. The series was mid-priced between the Business and Deluxe lines. It is identified by its Deluxe style hood chrome trim and painted headlamps. Most of these cars were built and sold in Canada.

I.D. DATA: [Plymouth PJ] Serial numbers on right front door post. Detroit, Michigan Starting: 1675001 Ending 1675032. Windsor, Ontario Starting: 9386551 Ending: 9387355. Starting: PJ-1001. Ending: PJ—359025. [Plymouth PJ Business Six] Serial numbers on right front door post. Detroit, Michigan Starting: 1039101 Ending 1111645. Los Angeles, California Starting: 3151501 Ending: 3157116. Windsor, Ontario Starting: 9396076 Ending 9397345. [Plymouth PJ Deluxe] Serial numbers on right front door post. Detroit, Michigan Starting: 2397601 Ending: 2641320. Los Angeles, California Starting: 3019401 Ending: 3040567. Windsor, Ontario Starting: 9326551 Ending 9332281. Engine numbers on left front corner of cylinder block. Starting: PJ-1001. Ending: PJ-359025.

1935 Plymouth, model PJ, 2-dr. sedan, JAC

Body Code	Body Type & Seating	Price	Weight	Prod. Total
Plymouth PJ Standard Six				
BC	2-dr. Bus. Cpe.-2P	565	2665	6664
651	2-dr. Sed.-5P	615	2670	7284
NA	Chassis	—	—	2680
Note 1: Chassis production is for all three PJ lines.				
Plymouth PJ Business Six				
BC	2-dr. Bus. Cpe.-2P	510	2635	16,691
651	2-dr. Sed.-5P	535	2680	29,942
650	4-dr. Sed.-5P	570	2720	15,761
651-B	2-dr. Comm. Sed.-1P	635	2735	1142
NA	4-dr. Westchester-7/8P	765	N/A	119
Plymouth PJ Deluxe				
BC	2-dr. Bus. Cpe.-2P	575	2685	29,190
TPC	2-dr. RS Cpe.-2/4P	630	2730	12,118
654	2-dr. Conv. Cpe.-2/4P	695	2810	2308
651	2-dr. Sed.-5P	625	2730	12,424
656	2-dr. Tr. Sed.-5P	650	2790	45,203
650	4-dr. Sed.-5P	660	2790	66,083
655	4-dr. Tr. Sed.-5P	685	2834	82,068
NA	4-dr. Sed.-7P	895	3130	350***
NA	4-dr. Travelers Sed.-5P	N/A		77***

Note 1: Touring sedan refers to those cars with built in "humpback" style trunks.
Note 2: *** 128" wheelbase.

General Note: 10,375 PJ Deluxe and 240 PJ Standards were built with right-hand drive.

ENGINE: Inline. Valve in block. Six. Cast iron block. B & S: 3-1/8 in. x 4-3/8 in. Disp.: 201.3 CID. C.R.: 6.7. Brake H.P.: 82 @ 3600 R.P.M. Taxable/A.L.A.M./N.A.C.C. H.P.: 23.44. Main bearings: Four. Valve lifters: Solid. Carb. Carter BB439S. Torque: 145 lbs.-ft. @ 1200 R.P.M. Small bore export engines had a bore of 2-7/8"; 748 PJ DeLuxe and six PJ Standards were shipped with this engine.

TECHNICAL: Sliding gear transmission. Speeds: 3F/1R. Floor shift controls. Single disc, dry 9-1/2" clutch. Driveshaft. Semi-floating rear axle. Overall Ratio: 4.125. Hydraulic brakes on four wheels. Steel spoke "artillery" wheels. 5.25 x 17 in. / 6.00 x 16 in.

CHASSIS: Series PJ (A11) W.B.: 113 in. (128 in. 5 pass. Traveler and 7 pass. sedan). O.L.: 187-7/8 sed.; 189-5/8 cpe. & cv. Frt/Rear Tread: 56-1/4 / 58 in. Tires: 5.25 x 17 / 6.00 x 16 in.

OPTIONS: Front and rear bumper, spare tire & tube plus tire cover covered in one package on all except Touring models; $26.50 on touring as spare was carried inside trunk. (33.00). Single sidemount (5.75). Dual sidemounts (39.50). Sidemount cover. Fender skirts (9.00 pair). Bumper guards. Radio Philco Transitone dash mount (39.95 std., 44.95 deluxe). Clock Electric in glove box door (11.75). Cigar lighter (1.00). Radio Antenna chicken wire supporting roof fabric served as radio antennae. Seat covers several sets offered. Spotlight (15.95). Automatic choke (3.00). Clock mirror (3.95). Footrest (3.50). Locking gas cap (2.25). Dual Air-Tone horns (externally mounted) (12.00). Kool Kushion (2.95). License

1935 Plymouth, model PJ, 4-dr. sedan, JAC

plate frames (2.45). Radiator grill cover (1.25). RH sun visor (1.75). Metal spring covers (6.00). RH taillamp (3.30). Metal spare tire cover (6.50). Fabric spare tire cover (2.00). Visor vanity mirror (1.00). Wheel trim rings (1.35 each). RH windshield wiper (4.95); Oil bath air cleaner (2.50). Duplate safety glass (7.50) coupes/$10 sedans. Trunk rack (16.50). "Mayflower" sailing ship radiator ornament (3.50). Economy engine package. Heater packages included Duo-Airstream (19.95). Deluxe hot water (15.95) and Standard hot water (12.95). 20" high clearance wheels. Accessory Package AD for the Deluxe PJ series consisted of dual chrome external horns, RH taillamp, RH windshield wiper and RH interior sun visor, cigar lighter for $18.50. The same accessory package was also offered on the PJ Business series but included chrome headlamps. Package sold for $23.00.

HISTORICAL: Plymouth PJ Six Production began November 17, 1934; ended August 15, 1935. Public announcement dates for the PJ models was January 5, 1935. Model year production: 13,948. Model year PJ Business Six production began ?; ended August 15, 1935. Model year production: 63,536. PJ Deluxe Production began November 6, 1934; ended August 15, 1935. Model year production: 249,940. K.T. Keller, corporate head; Dan S. Eddins, Division head. Endurance racer Bob MacKenzie set a new coast to coast record in a PJ business coupe, driving from Los Angeles to New York City and return in a time of 121 hours and 52 minutes, covering 6,492 miles and averaging 53.7 miles per hour. Jimmy Lynch and his "Devil Dodgers" used PJ Plymouths exclusively in their thrill shows. Ole Fahlin and Swen built an experimental airplane powered by a '35 Plymouth engine converted for aviation use to enter a government sponsored contest to come up with a practical design for a cheap "everyman's" airplane. The plane was ceritified and Fahlin was paid by Chrylser to bring the plane to Detroit for further examination. When the Fahlin-Swanson design (called the Plymocoupe or SF-2) failed to win the government contest and following the death of Swanson from pneumonia the plane was sold to a party who attempted to set an endurance record from Anchorage, Alaska to Mexico. Taking off in "marginal weather conditions" the plane was crashed somewhere in the wilds between Anchorage and Seattle. The pilot was rescued but the plane remains at the crash site to this day. In an effort to capitalize on its Plymouth heritage the plane also used the '35 hood trim on the cowling, a "saling ship" radiator ornament on the radiator shrouding and passenger car instruments converted to aeronautical uses on the planes instrument board. Walter P. Chrysler retired from active corporate duties, turning the company reins over to his longtime associate K.T. Keller. Overseas final assembly plants were opened in Ireland and New Zealand.

1935
PJ, 6-cyl., 113" wb

	FP	5	4	3	2	1
2P Cpe	565	725	1400	3100	4800	6800
2 dr Sed	615	675	1300	2600	4400	6300
Bus Cpe	510	725	1400	3200	4850	6900
2 dr Sed	535	675	1300	2600	4400	6300
Bus Sed	570	725	1400	3100	4800	6800

PJ DeLuxe, 6-cyl., 113" wb

Conv	695	3100	6150	10,250	14,350	20,500
Bus Cpe	575	800	1550	3900	5450	7800
RS Cpe	630	850	1650	4150	5800	8300
2 dr Sed	625	725	1400	3100	4800	6800
2 dr Tr Sed	650	750	1450	3300	4900	7000
Sed	660	775	1500	3600	5100	7300
Tr Sed	650	800	1550	3900	5450	7800
7P Sed	895	850	1650	4150	5800	8300
Trav Sed	895	900	1800	4400	6150	8800

1936

PLYMOUTH BUSINESS — MODEL P1 — SIX: The P1 Business line was Plymouth's price leader and differed in trim levels to achieve its low price. Most noticeable difference externally was the lack of the three chrome chevrons on the headlamp stanchions and a painted rather then chrome plated windshield frame. The station wagon was a part of this series as was a completely redesigned sedan delivery which was no longer built on a version of the two door sedan as had been done the year before. Two unique options for 1936 included a removable pickup box, complete with tailgate, for the business coupe models and an ambulance/hearse conversion of the four door sedans.

PLYMOUTH DELUXE — MODEL P2 — SIX: To many people the 1936 Plymouth was simply a rehashed version of the '35, which had been an all new car. It was an error on the part of many, as the '36 was also an all new

car. Improving on the basic design of the '35 frame, the '36 frame featured not only boxed side rail members, but a large X unit riveted to an oval center section. Again the body was bolted both vertically and horizontally to the frame, giving the car extra rigidity. Other improvements included a kick shackle on the left front semi-elliptic spring and improvements in the transmission.

Style wise, the car appeared much thinner than the '35 with a high, narrow radiator shell with a three piece grille insert, the center insert which was painted to match the body color. Also gone were the familiar chrome plated bullet shaped headlamps, replaced by free standing painted lamps in the fender catwalks. The fenders received beading over the wheelcutouts, which flowed into the line of the running boards. The hood height, lower window opening height and top of the deck lid were all on one plane to give a balanced look.

A complete line of models, including both trunkless and humpback style two and four door sedans were offered with the trunk style sedans outselling the trunkless models by a wide margin. 1936 was the last year for fender mounted spare tire carriers in the passenger line and few cars were so equipped making a car with those options today quite rare. Deluxe models are most easily identified by the three chevron like chrome strips located on the headlamp stands at the front of the car. Coupe models had the spare tire mounted behind the passenger's seat for the first time and the gas tank filler was now relocated to the left rear fender from its former perch on the body itself. Taillamps on all models except the touring sedans were located on the rear fenders. On the interior, all the instruments were relocated to one huge dial in the center of the instrument panel. A glove compartment on the right side (on LHD cars) was matched by a dummy panel on the left in a perfectly symmetrical dash layout. A special trim and option package was offered with a deluxe, chrome trimmed interior which included overstuffed seats and throw pillows. Plymouth production surpassed the half million unit per year mark with the 1936 models — a production record which would only stand until the next year.

1936 Plymouth, model PI, coupe, AA

I.D. DATA: Plymouth P1 Serial numbers on right front door post. Detroit Starting: 1111701 Ending: 1183569. Los Angeles Starting: 3157151 Ending: 3162365. Evansville, Indiana Starting: 9000101 Ending: 9012724. Windsor Starting: 9397351 Ending: 9400000. Windsor Starting: 9376551 Ending: 9376669. All P1 and P2 series of 1936 used engine numbers beginning with the prefix P2. Plymouth P2 Serial numbers on right front door post. Detroit, Michigan Starting: 2641401 Ending: 2987635. Los Angeles, California Starting: 3040601 Ending: 3077397. Evansville, Indiana Starting: 9025101 Ending: 9062168. Windsor, Ontario Starting: 9332286 Ending: 9339684. Engine numbers on left front corner of cylinder block. Starting: P2-1001. Ending: P2-532087.

Body Code	Body Type & Seating	Price	Weight	Prod. Total
Plymouth P1				
BC	2-dr. Bus. Cpe.-2P Cpe.-2P	510	2770	26,856
811	2-dr. Sed.-5P	545	2825	39,516
810	4-dr. Sed.-5P	590	2890	19,104
NA	2-dr. Comm. Sed.-1P	605	2880	3527
NA	Chassis	—	—	1211
806	2-dr. Tr. Sed.-5P	—	—	768
805	4-dr. Tr. Sed.-5P	—	—	1544
Plymouth P2				
BC	2-dr. Bus. Cpe.-2P	580	2800	54,601
TPC	2-dr. RS Cpe.-2/4P	620	2870	9663
804	2-dr. Conv. Cpe.-2/4P	725	2945	3297
811	2-dr. Sed.-5P	625	2785	6149
810	4-dr. Sed.-5P	660	2820	10,001
805	4-dr. Tr. Sed.-5P	680	2955	240,136
806	2-dr. Tr. Sed.-5P	645	2910	99,373
NA	4-dr. Sed.-7P	895	3265	1504
NA	4-dr. Westchester-7/8P	765	NA	309
NA	Chassis	—	—	2775

Note 1: Touring sedans have humpback styling.
Note 2: The 7-pass. sedan has a 125-in. wheelbase.
Note 3: The Westchester is the wood-bodied station wagon.

Engine specifications same for all 1936 models P1 & P2. 2,808 P1's and 11,102 P2's were built with right-hand drive.

ENGINE: Inline. Valve in block. Six. Cast iron block. 3-1/8 in. x 4-3/8 in. Disp.: 201.3 CID. C.R.: 6.7. Brake H.P.: 82 @ 3600 R.P.M. Taxable/A.L.A.M./N.A.C.C. H.P.: 23.44. Main bearings: Four. Valve lifters:

Solid. Carb.: Carter BB439S or Carter B6F1 or Carter C6E1-2. Torque (Compression) 145 lbs.-ft. @ 1200 R.P.M. Economy engine option has 1-in. carburetor, 65 bhp and 3.7 rear axle ratio.
Note: Cars built for export were equipped with 170.4 CID engine. 2-7/8'' bore x 4-3/8'' stroke. Engines were identified by engine code number P2X. 88 P1 and 573 P2 models were shipped with this export engine.

1936 Plymouth, model P2, 4-dr. sedan, JAC

TECHNICAL: Sliding gear transmission. Speeds: 3F/1R. Floor shift controls. Single disc, dry 9-1/4'' clutch. Driveshaft. Spiral bevel semi floating; Hotchkiss drive rear axle. Overall Ratio: 4.125 (3.88 P1 business coupe). Hydraulic brakes on four wheels. Artillery (steel) spoke wheels. Rim size: 5.25 x 17 on P1; 6.00 x 16 in. on P2.

CHASSIS: [Series P1 1936] W.B.: 113 in. O.L.: 191-3/8 4-dr Touring sedan. 184-13/32 all except/tudor sedan. Frt/Rear Tread: 55-7/8 / 58 in. Tires: 5.25 x 17. [Series P-2 1936] W.B.: 113 in. (128 in. 7 pass.) O.L.: same as listed for P1 models (7 p. 203-3/8). Frt/Rear Tread: 56-1/16 / 58-3/16. Tires: 6.00 x 16.

OPTIONS: Bumpers were still extra cost in 1936 and came in three packages depending on the body style or model of the car. Bumper Group A sold for $35 for trunkless Deluxe 4 door sedans, trunkless Deluxe 2 door sedans and the convertible. It included front and rear bumpers, bumper guards, spare tire & tube, metal rear spring covers, spare tire lock and metal spare tire cover. Bumper Group B sold for $25.50 for all Business (P1) models. It included front and rear bumpers, spare tire and tube. Bumper Group C sold for $28.50 for all other Deluxe models not covered in Group A and included front & rear bumpers, bumper guards, spare tire & tube and metal rear spring covers. Single sidemount RF fender (5.75). Dual sidemount (38.00 on P2 Deluxe; 30.00 on P1 Business). Fender skirts (9.00 pair). Sidemount cover(s). Fender skirts. Radio in dash mount (49.50). Heater several types optional, all hot water heat. Clock 30 hour clock mirror (3.95); 8 day clock mirror (11.00). Cigar lighter (1.60). Radio Antenna standard on all closed body styles, using the fabric roof "chicken wire" support. Seat covers several types offered. Spotlight (15.95). Heavy duty air cleaner (2.50). Special body colors (30.00). Fender & sheet metal color (5.00). Safety glass (coupe) (7.50). (Sedan) (10.00). Leather upholstery (coupe) (10.00). (Sedan) (16.00). Radiator ornament (3.50). Metal rear springs covers (Business series) (4.50). 16'' wheels (business series) (15.00). Deluxe steering wheel (5.00). 20'' high clearance wheels (15.00). Metal spare tire cover (6.50). Fabric rear tire cover (2.00). Trunk rack (15.00). Rear seat foot rests (3.50). Glove box lock (1.00). Locking gas cap (1.50). Dual external "Airtone" horns (12.00). RH taillamp (2.85). RH wiper (4.50). RH inside sun visor (1.50). Radiator grill cover (1.25). Hand brake extension lever (1.50). Exhaust extention (1.00). Chrome wheel discs (2.30 each). Pair license plate frame (2.45). Defroster (1.50). Electric defrost fan (6.50). Ambulance conversion (40.00). Hearse conversion (65.00). (Ambulance & hearse conversion available only on 4 door sedan models). Removable pickup box for coupe body style, approximately (16.00). **Accessory Group A:** $17.50 included dual external "Airtone" horns, RH taillamp, RH windshield wiper, RH interior sunvisor and cigar lighter. **Accessory Group B:** $5 included RH taillamp and RH windshield wiper. **Special Note On Paint:** Although a complete line of colors was offered for the body of the car, unless the customer paid extra, the fenders and sheet metal were painted black — regardless of the body color. Today we tend to think of this "two tone" as an option but on the 1936 models, if the customer wanted his car a solid color, he had to pay extra to get it!

HISTORICAL: Plymouth P1 Production began September 19, 1935; ended August 21, 1936. Model year production: 92,526. A Swedish woman, Greta Molander, drove a '36 Plymouth in both the 1936 and 1937 Monte Carlo Rally, winning the ladies division of the Rallye. Plymouth P2 production began September 6, 1935; ended August 21, 1936. Model year production: 427,499. K.T. Keller, Corporate head; Dan S. Eddins, Division head.

1936
P1 Business Line, 6-cyl., 113" wb

	FP	5	4	3	2	1
Bus Cpe	510	775	1500	3600	5100	7300
2 dr Bus Sed	545	725	1400	3100	4800	6800
Bus Sed	590	725	1400	3200	4850	6900
Sta Wag	765	1025	2500	5150	7150	10,300
P2 DeLuxe, 6-cyl., 113"-125" wb						
Conv	725	3500	7050	11,750	16,450	23,500
Cpe	580	850	1650	4150	5800	8300
RS Cpe	620	900	1800	4400	6150	8800
2 dr Sed	625	775	1500	3600	5100	7300
2 dr Tr Sed	645	800	1550	3900	5450	7800
Sed	660	775	1500	3600	5100	7300
Tr Sed	680	800	1550	3900	5450	7800
7P Sed	895	900	1800	4400	6150	8800

1937

1937 Plymouth, model P4, coupe, AA

PLYMOUTH BUSINESS — MODEL P3 — SIX: With Plymouth's introduction in 1937 of a truck chassis commercial car line which included a pickup, cab & chassis, station wagon and a sedan delivery, the Business line consisted only of passenger type vehicles although the removable pickup box was offered for the business coupe. Distinguishing features of the business line included the lack of vent windows on front doors, less chrome trim and painted, rather than wood grain dashboards. All business models now rode on 16'' wheels, with smaller tires fitted than those used on the DeLuxe lines. Fenders and sheet metal were painted black on all Business models regardless of the body color unless the customer paid extra to have the car one solid color.

PLYMOUTH DELUXE — MODEL P4 — SIX: Despite a one inch shorter wheelbase, the 1937 models grew in overall length and in general terms of styling, was "fattened" considerably over the "narrow" styling of the '36 models. Despite a crippling labor strike, the '37 set an overall production record, with the second year in a row of over half a million units produced — a record which would stand until 1951.
New was an all steel roof stamping which replaced the cloth insert found on previous models. Mechanically the car remained much the same as the previous year with the major mechanical change being in the fitting of a hypoid, rather than spiral bevel gear, differential. All cars were now also fitted with airplane type shock absorbers for better handling. Wind wings in the front doors were also fitted to all DeLuxe models after an absence since the 1934 DeLuxe PE's complicated system.
On the interior new "Safety Styling" was emphasized which included the removal of all protruding knobs from the instrument panel and placing them under the panel where they would be out of reach of passengers' knees in the event of an accident. Front seat backs were heavily padded to prevent injury to back seat passengers. The instrument gauges were now relocated in two dials directly in front of the driver. 1937 was to be the last year for opening windshields for ventilation.

PLYMOUTH COMMERCIAL CAR — MODEL PT50 — SIX: Plymouth entered the commercial car field in 1937 as the result of dealers' demands to have a commercial vehicle to sell when the dealer was not dualed with a Dodge dealership. Plymouth's entry into the field allowed Chrysler-Plymouth and DeSoto-Plymouth dealers extra opportunity for vehicle sales. Based on passenger car styling, in reality, no pieces interchanged between the passenger car line and the commercial line. Entering the market with a full range of vehicles, including the wooden bodied Westchester station wagon and a sedan delivery, these models were short lived on the truck chassis and reverted back to the passenger car chassis in ensuing years.
1937 was the best year as far as sales were concerned for the Plymouth commercial line but the lines similarity to the Dodge commercial eventually spelled its doom. The Plymouth commercial was only a minor facelift of the basic Dodge commercial vehicle. In Canada, a similiar companion line called the Fargo was also introduced as no Plymouth commercials were ever built or sold in the Dominion. After the demise of Plymouth, the Fargo name was carried on as a companion make in Canada and the name was still used in various parts of the world until the late 1970s.

I.D. DATA: [Plymouth P3] Serial numbers on right front door post. Detroit, Michigan Starting: 1184001 Ending: 1237460. Los Angeles, California

Starting: 3101401 Ending: 3105159. Evansville, Indiana Starting: 9085551 Ending: 9097493. Windsor, Ontario Starting: 9376676 Ending: 9381157. All 1937 models P3 & P4 used engines with serial number prefix P4. [Plymouth P4] Serial numbers on right front door post. Detroit, Michigan Starting: 10101001 Ending: 10468044. Los Angeles, California Starting: 3162501 Ending: 3205879. Evansville, Indiana Starting: 9950001 Ending: 9999021. Evansville, Indiana Starting: 9190000 Ending: 9199074. Windsor, Ontario Starting: 9339691 Ending: 9349561. Engine numbers on left front corner of cylinder block. Starting: P4-1001. Ending: P4-571569. [Plymouth PT50] The vehicle serial number appears on the plate showing model code, which is mounted on the engine side of the cowl over the steering column, or on the right front door front pillar post. Detroit, Michigan Starting: 8850101 Ending: 8861664. Los Angeles, California Starting: 9206601 Ending: 9208113. Evansville, Indiana Starting: 9182701 Ending: 9185187. Engine numbers on left front corner of cylinder block. Starting: T50-1001.

1937 Plymouth, model P4, 4-dr. sedan, OCW

Body Code	Body Type & Seating	Price	Weight	Prod. Total
Plymouth P3				
911	2-dr. Sed.-5P	550	2770	28,685
BC	2-dr. Bus. Cpe.-2P	510	2700	18,202
910	4-dr. Sed.-5P	595	2770	16,000
915	4-dr. Tr. Sed.-5P	—	—	7,842
	2-dr. Tr. Sed.-5P	—	—	1,350
TPC	RS Cpe.-2/4P	—	—	540
—	Chassis	—	—	1,025

Note: The RS Coupe and most 4-dr. touring sedans were built for export.

Plymouth P4				
905	4-dr. Tr. Sed.-5P	680	2840	269,062
906	2-dr. Tr. Sed.-5P	650	2840	111,099
BC	2-dr. Bus. Cpe.-2P	575	2765	67,144
900	4-dr. Sed.-5P	670	2840	9,000
901	2-dr. Sed.-5P	640	2825	7,926
TPC	RS Cpe.-2/4P	625	2810	6,877
904	2-dr. Conv. Cpe.-2/4P	745	2920	3,110
—	4-dr. Sed.-7P	915	3255	1,840
—	4-dr. Taxi-7P	—	—	500
—	4-dr. Limo. Sed.-7P	—	—	63
—	Chassis	—	—	1,729

Plymouth PT50				
K-8-2-LR	Pickup	525	—	10,709
NA	Cab & Chassis	495	—	158
NA	Sed. Del.	655	—	3256
NA	Sta. Wag.	740	—	602

7,114 P3's and 9,586 P4's were built with right-hand drive.

ENGINE: Specifications same for all 1937 models P3 & P4. Inline. Valve in block. Six. Cast iron block. B & S: 3-1/8 in. x 4-3/8 in. Disp.: 201.3 CID. C.R.: 6.7. Brake H.P.: 82 @ 3600 R.P.M. Taxable/A.L.A.M./N.A.C.C. H.P.: 23.44. Main bearings: Four. Valve lifters: Solid. Carb.: Carter BB439S or Carter C6H1 of Carter B6G1 or C6F1-5. Torque (compression): 145 lbs.-ft. @ 1200 R.P.M. Plymouth also offered an "economy" engine package which developed 65 h.p. at 3,500 rpm. Equipment included a 1" carberator and 3.73 rear axle ratio. [Plymouth PT50] Inline. Six. Cast iron block. B & S: 3-1/8 in. x 4-3/8 in. Disp.: 201 CID. C.R.: 6.7. Brake H.P.: 70 @ 3,000 R.P.M. Taxable/A.L.A.M./N.A.C.C. H.P.: 23.44. Main bearings: Four. Valve lifters: Solid. Carb.: Chandler Groves A2. Torque (compression): 145 lbs.-ft. @ 1,200 R.P.M.

NOTE: Cars built for export were equipped with 170.4 CID engine, 2-7/8" bore x 4-3/8" stroke. Engines were identified by engine numbers coded P4X. 132 P3's and 525 P4's were shipped with this export engine.

CHASSIS: [Series P3] W.B.: 112 in. O.L.: 193-5/16 in. Frt/Rear Tread: 56/60 in. Tires: 5.50 x 16. [Series P4] W.B.: 112 in. (132 in. 7 passenger). O.L.: 193-5/16 in. (214-3/16 7 passenger). Frt/Rear Tread: 56/60 in. Tires: 6.00 x 16. [Series PT50] W.B.: 116 in. Tires: 6.00 x 16.

TECHNICAL: [Plymouth P3 & P4] Sliding gear transmission. Speeds: 3F/1R. Floor shift controls. Single disc, dry 9-1/4" clutch. Driveshaft. Hypoid, semi floating; Hotchkiss drive. Overall Ratio: 4.1 (DeLuxe sedans); 4.3 (7 passenger); 3.9 [DeLuxe coupes & ALL business P3 models]. Hydraulic brakes on four wheels. Steel disc wheels. Rim size: 5.50 x 16 on P3; 6.00 x 16 on P4. [Plymouth PT50] Three speed standard transmission. Floor shift controls. Single disc, dry 10" diameter clutch. Driveshaft. Hypoid, semi floating rear axle. Hydraulic brakes on four wheels. Steel disc wheels. Rim size: 6.00 x 16.

1937 Plymouth, model P4, convertible coupe, JAC

OPTIONS: Philco Transitione radio, with antenna (53.95). Electric clock, in glove box door (10.00). Heavy duty air cleaner (2.50). Special body colors (30.00). Fender & sheet metal color other than black (5.00). Leather upholstery, coupes (10.00); sedans (16.00). Life guard tubes (35.00). Glove compartment lock (1.00). Radiator ornament (3.50). Metal spring cover (Business P3) (4.50). Deluxe steering wheel (5.00). 6.00 x 16 " wheels & tires (Business P3) (15.00); 20" wheels (15.00). Junior model heater (8.95). Defroster attachment (1.25). Standard heater (12.95). Tri-Airstream Heater (15.95). Super Tri-Airstream Heater (19.95). Defroster attachment for Airstream heaters (3.45). Electric defrost fan (5.95). Rear seat speaker (5.95). Roadway radio (under running board) antenna (4.45). Accessory Group A including dual airtone trumpet horns, right hand taillamp, RH windshield, RH sunvisor and cigar lighter (17.50). Accessory Group B including RH taillamp and RH windshield wiper (5.00). Bumper groups: For Deluxe P4 consisting of bumpers, bumper guards, spare tire, tube and metal spring covers (28.50). For Business P3 consisting of bumpers, bumper guards, spare tire and tube (25.50). For 7 passenger models consisting of bumpers, bumper guards, spare tires, tube and metal spring covers (32.50).

HISTORICAL: [Plymouth P3] Production began September 15, 1936; Ended August 30, 1937. Public announcement date for the 1937 models was November 7, 1936. Model year production: 73,644. [Plymouth P4] Production began September 10, 1936; Ended August 30, 1937. Model year production: 478,350.

The two Millionth Plymouth was built durin 1937. This car was sold to Mrs. Ethel Miller of Turlock, California. She had been the purchaser of the first Plymouth ever sold, as well as the purchaser of the one millionth Plymouth built in 1934.

Plymouth PT50 Production began December, 1936; Ended August 23, 1937. Model year production: 14,725. K.T. Keller, Corporate President, Dan Eddins, Division head. All corporate debt incurred when Chrysler purchased Dodge Bros. in 1928 was retired by the end of 1936.

An overseas assembly plant was opened in Norway for assembly of unfinished cars from the United States.

1937
Roadking, 6-cyl., 112" wb

	FP	5	4	3	2	1
Cpe	580	775	1500	3600	5100	7300
2 dr Sed	620	600	1200	2200	3900	5600
Sed	665	650	1200	2300	4100	5800
DeLuxe, 6-cyl., 112"-132" wb						
Conv	830	3500	7050	11,750	16,450	23,500
Cpe	650	800	1550	3900	5450	7800
RS Cpe	700	850	1650	4150	5800	8300
2 dr Sed	715	675	1300	2500	4350	6200
2 dr Tr Sed	725	700	1350	2700	4500	6400
Sed	745	675	1300	2600	4400	6300
Tr Sed	755	700	1350	2800	4550	6500
Limo	1095	850	1650	4150	5800	8300
Sub	995	1100	3300	5650	7900	11,300

1938

1938 Plymouth, model P5, 4-dr. sedan, AA

PLYMOUTH BUSINESS/ROADKING — MODEL P5 — SIX: Again the price leader, the "Business" series was renamed the "Roadking" mid way through production to appease those people who objected to buying the business model just because they bought the cheaper series. Distinguishing features of the Business/Roadking was the lack of vent windows on all models, painted rather than wood grain instrument panels and 17" wheels while the Deluxe rode on 16". For the first time, the windshield was permanently fixed on all models. Not only did the recession of '38 hinder sales, but the fact that dealers' lots were full of used cars from the record sales set the year previous hurt as well.

PLYMOUTH DELUXE — MODEL P6 — SIX: 1938 was not a good year for Plymouth. The recession of '38 saw Plymouth's sales fall by nearly 50% (as did the rest of the industry). A restyled version of the '37 models, the '38 was not well received by either the dealer network or the buying public. With a "fatter" look resulting from a short, stubby waterfall grill and headlamps mounted high on the side of the radiator shell the car took on an "ugly duckling" appearance. Dealer unrest was so bad that the factory relocated the headlamps mid-way through production, lowering them two inches and moving them rearward another 4", a move which did much to improve the looks of the car.

1938 was Plymouth's tenth anniversary year but the factory did little to exploit the occasion and no special models were offered. Some advertising did make mention of the "Jubilee Plymouth" however. 1938 would mark the first year that the Plymouth did not enjoy a gain in sales over the previous year since its introduction in 1928. "Safety Styling" continued on the interior with all protruding knobs again hidden to prevent injury in accidents and safety glass was standard on all models.

PLYMOUTH COMMERICAL CAR — MODEL PT57 — SIX: With only a minor facelifting to match that of its passenger car counterpart, Plymouth's commercial entry for 1938 saw a drastic drop in sales for the model year, to less than one half of its introductory year, caused not only by an increase in prices but by the Recession of 1938. This would be the last year that the pickup would bear passenger car styling but as in the year previous, no sheet metal or trim parts interchanged between the commercial and the passenger line. This would be the last year as well for the truck chassis sedan delivery as well as the final year for the spare tires to be fitted into the front fenders on the commercial car line.

1938 Plymouth, model P6, convertible coupe, JAC

I.D. DATA: [P5] Serial numbers on right front door post. Detroit, Michigan Starting: 1240001 Ending: 1296615. Los Angeles, California Starting: 3105301 Ending: 3109407. Evansville, Indiana Starting: 9097601 Ending: 9107725. Windsor, Ontario Starting: 9381161 Ending: 9385097. All P5 & P6 series used engines with P6 prefix. [P6] Serial numbers on right front door post. Detroit, Michigan Starting: 10470001 Ending: 10625650. Los Angeles, California Starting: 3206001 Ending: 3220997. Evansville, Indiana Starting: 20001001 Ending: 20025900. Windsor, Ontario Starting: 9349566 Ending 9358622. Engine numbers on left front corner of cylinder block. Starting: P6-1001. Ending: P6-286619. PT57 Serial number appears on the plate showing the model code, which is mounted on the engine side of the cowl over the steering column, or on the right front door front pillar post. Detroit, Michigan Starting: 8618701 Ending: 8624135. Los Angeles, California Starting: 9208201 Ending: 9208797. Evansville, Indiana Starting: 9185301 Ending: 9186416. Engine numbers on left front corner of cylinde block. Starting: T57-1001.

Body Code	Body Type & Seating	Price	Weight	Prod. Total
P5 Business "Road King" Line				
BC	2-dr. Bus. Cpe.-2P	645	2694	15,932
406	2-dr. Tr. Sed.-5P	701	2779	16,413
416	2-dr. Sed.-5P	685	2744	15,393
405	4-dr. Tr. Sed.-5P	746	2824	18,664
415	4-dr. Sed.-5P	730	2774	6459
TPC	2-dr. RS Cpe.-2/4P	—	—	338

Note 1: The P5 Rumbleseat Coupe was built for export only.

Body Code	Body Type & Seating	Price	Weight	Prod. Total
P6 Deluxe Line				
BC	2-dr. Bus. Cpe.-2P	730	2754	27,181
TPC	2-dr. RS Cpe.-2/4P	770	2799	2000
406	2-dr. Tr. Sed.-5P	785	2819	46,669
416	2-dr. Sed.-5P	773	2814	1222
405	4-dr. Tr. Sed.-5P	815	2844	119,669
415	4-dr. Sed.-5P	803	2834	1446
404	2-dr. Conv. Cpe.-2/4P	850	2964	1900
NA	4-dr. Limo.-7P	1095	3289	75
408	4-dr. Sed.-7P	1005	3239	1824
NA	4-dr. Westchester-7/8P	880	3039	555
NA	4-dr. Taxi-7P	—	—	35
NA	Chassis	—	—	2004
NA	Chassis-7P	—	—	23

Body Code	Body Type & Seating	Price	Weight	Prod. Total
PT57 Commercial Line				
K-8-2-LR	2-dr. Pickup-2P	585	—	4620
NA	2-dr. Cab & Chassis-2P	560	—	95
K-1-3	2-dr. Sed. Del.-2P	695	—	1601

Engine specifications are the same for all 1938 Models P5 & P6. 7,046 P5's and 7,345 P6's were built with right-hand drive.

ENGINE: [Std.] Inline. Valve in block. Six. Cast iron block. B & S: 3-1/8 in. x 4-3/8 in. Disp.: 201.3 CID. C.R.: 6.7. Brake H.P.: 82 @ 3600 R.P.M. Taxable/A.L.A.M./N.A.C.C. H.P.: 23.44. Main bearings: Four. Valve lifters: Solid. Carb.: Carter BB439S, B6H1, B6J1, C6J1 or C6K1. Torque (Compression) 145 lbs.-ft. @ 1200 R.P.M. [Opt. Engine] Inline. Valve in block. Six. Cast iron block. B & S: 3-1/8 in. x 4-3/8 in. Disp.: 201.3 CID. C.R.: 7.0. Brake H.P.: 86 @ 3600 R.P.M. Main bearings: Four. Valve lifters: Solid. Carb.: see above specs. Torque (Compression) 156 lbs.-ft. @ 1200 R.P.M. [Commercial Engine] Inline. Valve in block. Six. Cast iron block. B & S: 3-1/8 in. x 4-3/8 in. Disp.: 201. C.R.: 6.7. Brake H.P.: 70 @ 3000 R.P.M. Taxable/A.L.A.M./N.A.C.C. H.P.: 23.44. Main bearings: 4. Valve lifters: solid. Torque (Compression) 145 lbs.-ft. @ 1200 R.P.M.

Engine Note 1: Optional economy engine package with 1" carb developed 65 horsepower. All other specs the same.
Engine Note 2: Cars built for export were equipped with 170.4 CID engine. 2-7/8" bore x 4-3/8" stroke. Engines were identified by engine number coded P6X. 109 P5's and 224 P6's were shipped with this export engine.
Engine Note 3: Some 1938 Canadian cars may have been fitted with a different "long block" Canadian engine.

TECHNICAL: [P5 & P6] Sliding gear transmission. Speeds: 3F/1R. Floor shift controls. Single disc, dry 9-1/4" clutch. Driveshaft. Hypoid, semi floating; Hotchkiss drive rear axle. Overall Ratio: 4.1. Hydraulic brakes on four wheels. Steel disc wheels. Rim size: 5.50 x 16 on P5; 6.00 x 16 on P6. [PT57] Three speed standard with optional four speed w/power takeoff opening. Floor shift controls. Single disc, dry plate 10 in. diameter clutch. Hypoid gear, semi-floating rear axle. Overall Ratio: 4.1. Hydraulic brakes on four wheels. Steel disc wheels. Rim size: 6.00 x 16 in.

CHASSIS: [P5] W.B.: 112 in. O.L.: 194-3/16 in. Frt/Rear Tread: 56/60. Tires: 5.50 x 16. [P6] W.B.: 112 in. (132 in. 7-pass) O.L.: 194-3/16 7 pass. 214-3/16). Frt/Rear Tread: 56/60 in. Tires: 6.00 x 16. [PT57] W.B.: 116 in. Frt/Rear Tread: 56 in, 57-7/8 in. Tires: 6.00 x 16.

OPTIONS: Fender skirts (12.00). Radio in dash, pushbotton (56.70). Clock electric in glove box door (10.00). Cigar lighter. Spotlight. HD air cleaner (2.50). Ambulance conversion (57.50). Glove box lock (1.00). Oil filter (Roadking) (2.75). Rear seat speaker (5.95). Deluxe steering wheel (5.00). Metal rearspring covers (Roadking) (5.50). Chrome wheel rings (8.00 for set of 5). Wiper vacuum booster pump (3.50). Rear compartment heater attachment (8.50). Roadway (running board mount) antennae (5.95). Skyway (cowl mount) antenna (5.95). Heaters offered included Duo Airstream (18.95). Tri Airstream (21.95). Super Airstream (24.95). Defroster (4.50). Rubber bladed electric fan; trunk lamp; glareshield sunvisor (inside); foglamps; front & rear center superguard bumper guard; radiator grille cover; adjustable radiator shutters; radiator insect screen; exhaust entention; license plate frames; wheel trim rings; wheel discs; locking gas cap; 30 hour clock-mirror; 200 hour clock-mirror glove box lock. 20" high clearance wheels. Accessory Group A: RH taillamp, RH windshield wiper, RH interior sunvisor, cigar lighter, dual trumpet horns (underhood) (19.00) ***. Accessory Group B: RH taillamp, RH windshield wiper (6.00). *** Accessory Group A cost $13 on convertible as twin taillamps were std. on it. Accessory Group C: Included all items in Group A in addition to special "pillow-type" upholstery, special door upholstery, carpet strips on door panel bottoms, chrome trim on door panels, special front seat-back trim, light wood grain, contrasting color on instrument panel, colored escutcheons on all handles, color steering wheel, front armrests on L&R doors, chrome horn ring, special gearshift knob, front bumper grill guard, two chrome license plate frames, chrome windshield wipers, wheel trim rings, glove box lock and chrome trim on running boards. Package price $35.00. Economy Group 1: 1" diameter carberator & intake manifold. 3.73 rear axle ratio on Deluxe P6 models, 3.54 rear axle on Business/Roadking P5 models. 65 Horsepower at 3,000 RPM. Economy Group 2: included items in Group 1 in addition to manifold heat shields and throttle stop at 45 m.p.h.

1938 Plymouth PT57 Rear bumper chrome plated (8.50). Single sidemount standard, right side only. Dual sidemount included extra well, tire &

1938 Plymouth, model P6, business coupe, JAC

tube, tire lock (10.00). Bumper guards (1.50 pair). Chassis accessory Group included chrome radiator shell, chrome headlamps and double acting front & rear shocks (17.00). Dual horns (7.50). Coach lamps for commercial sedan (8.50). Long arm rearview mirror (1.50). Adjustable long arm rearview mirror (2.50). Sunvisors (2.00 each). Metal spare tire cover (6.50). Chrome windshield frame (3.00). Auxiliary taillamp (4.00). Economy engine package (Group 1) (2.50). Engine economy group two (3.00). Four speed transmission (25.00). Painted sheet metal (fenders, splash aprons, running boards) (5.00) (Note: Unless extra fees were paid these items remained black regardless of body color) . . Five 6.00 x 16" 6 ply tires (14.25). Five 20" wheels with 5.25 x 20" 4 ply tires and 4.78 rear axle (25.00). Six 20" wheels with 5x25 x 20" 4 ply tires and 4.78 rear axle (35.00). Oil bath air cleaner (3.75). Vortox air cleaner w/std. cap (17.50); with Vortox cap (19.50). Governor (5.00). Chrome headlamps (2.75). Oil filter (3.25). Chrome radiator shell (6.00). Auxiliary seat (commercial sedan) (10.00). Double acting shocks (4.75 front), (4.75 rear). Auxiliary windshield wiper (4.00).

HISTORICAL: [P5] Production began September 22, 1937; ended July 19, 1938. Public announcement date for the 1938 models was October 30, 1937. Model year production: 74,785. [P6] Production began Sept. 3, 1937; ended July 19, 1938. Model year production: 204,603. [PT57] Production began Sept. 16,1937; ended August 17, 1938. Model year production: 6316. K.T. Keller, Corporate had; Dan S. Eddins, Division head.

1938
Roadking, 6-cyl., 112" wb

	FP	5	4	3	2	1
Cpe	645	775	1500	3600	5100	7300
2 dr Sed	685	600	1200	2200	3900	5600
Sed	730	650	1200	2300	4100	5800
2 dr Tr Sed	701	650	1250	2400	4200	6000
Tr Sed	746	650	1250	2400	4150	5900

DeLuxe, 6-cyl., 112"-132" wb

	FP	5	4	3	2	1
Conv	850	3500	7050	11,750	16,450	23,500
Cpe	730	800	1550	3900	5450	7800
RS Cpe	770	850	1650	4150	5800	8300
2 dr Sed	773	675	1300	2500	4350	6200
2 dr Tr Sed	785	700	1350	2700	4500	640ʋ
Sed	803	675	1300	2600	4400	6300
Tr Sed	815	700	1350	2800	4550	6500
7P Sed	1005	800	1550	3900	5450	7800
Limo	1095	850	1650	4150	5800	8300
Sub	880	1100	3300	5650	7900	11,300

1939

1939 Plymouth, model P8, business coupe, AA

PLYMOUTH ROADKING — MODEL P7 — SIX: Once again Plymouth's price leader, the Roadking series enjoyed brisk sales as the effects of the '38 recession wore off. Easily identified by the belt line chrome trim that ends mid way down the length of the hood, the Roadking truly became Plymouth's "business" line with the introduction of a "Utility Sedan" model and the return of the sedan delivery to the passenger car chassis from its two year stint on the truck chassis. The utility sedan was simply a two door with no rear seat or passenger's seat (although one was optional). The utility could be fitted with a screen partition between driver and rear compartment and there was no partition between the passenger area and trunk. With a special body, the Sedan Delivery had two doors at the rear of the body. Causing much confusion was the fact that the spare tires on these models rode in fender mounts, which were not offered on the regular line of passenger cars. Because of their interchangeability these fenders have shown up in later years on other body styles although they are not aesthetically correct. Also offered in the Roadking line was the ambulance conversion (and on the Deluxe line as well) in addition to the optional removable pickup box with tailgate which could be fitted into the business coupe.

PLYMOUTH DELUXE — MODEL P8 — SIX: While the rest of the Corporation enjoyed new bodies, Plymouth was forced to make do with the old bodies in use since 1937. By clever facelifting most people then, as well as today, do not realize the relationship between the '37-38 and '39 models. A new cowling with a split, vee'd two piece windshield added considerable length to the old body, effectively hiding the car's origins while a new roof stamping on sedans added more length to the rear of the bodies. A completely new, prow shaped front end with headlamps mounted in the fenders completed the transformation. At the rear, tear drop shaped taillamps were fitted in to the fenders. Still retaining the old bulb/reflector type headlamps, 1939 would be the last year for cars with rumble seats and

saw the introduction of the first power operated convertible top in the entire automobile industry. Actuated by two vacuum cylinders located behind the front seat, the top moved up or down at the touch of a dash board mounted control switch.

New for the year was an extended wheelbase four door convertible sedan — the first and last such offering from Plymouth. In reality the body was the same as that which had been used on the '37 & '38 DeSoto and Chrysler convertible sedans. Oddly enough, Plymouth offered the only open cars in the entire Chrysler Corporation in 1939 (not even GM's Chevrolet offered a convertible!.) With its rectangular headlamps and multi-piece chrome grille the '39 model has proven to be highly collectable.

Deluxe models all featured remote control gear shifting while Roadking models retained floor shifting and instrument panels featured the "Safety Signal" speedometer that changed colors as the speed of the vehicle increased. In addition the '39 models returned to independent front suspension which Plymouth had introduced with the 1934 models but had abandoned in 1935.

1939 Plymouth, model P8, convertible sedan, JAC

PLYMOUTH COMMERCIAL CAR — MODEL PT81 — SIX: Plymouth's commercial chassis entry this year was an entirely new body with a decidedly "truck" look to it. Without much doubt the Plymouth pickup now looked almost identical to its Dodge counterpart. A new "three man cab" was touted to be the largest in the industry and a unique door latch located at the top of the door was designed to prevent the doors from popping open when the vehicle was used on rough terrain. The body now sat farther ahead on the chassis while the box was enlarged in size. The spare tire now rode in a carrier underneath the pickup box. As in years past, the tailgate on some models was plain, while others spelled out the word "Plymouth" — no reason has ever been given for these two tailgate types! Cab & chassis models came factory equipped with full length running boards and rear fenders. Prices were decreased slightly and sales increased by nearly 40%.

I.D. DATA: [Plymouth P7] Serial numbers on right front door post. Detroit, Michigan Starting: 1298001. Ending: 1377475. Los Angeles, California Starting: 3110001. Ending: 3114680. Evansville, Indiana Starting: 9150401. Ending: 9164593. Windsor, Ontario Starting: 9603586. Ending: 9607605. All 1938 P7 & P8 engines began with prefix P8. [Plymouth P8] Serial numbers on right front door post. Detroit, Michigan Starting: 10630001. Ending: 10879874. Los Angeles, California Starting: 3222001. Ending: 3242203. Evansville, Indiana Starting: 20027001. Ending: 20062199. Windsor, Ontario Starting: 9358626. Ending: 9368510. Engine numbers on left front corner of cylinder block. Starting: P8-1001. Ending: P8-411923. [Plymouth PT81] Serial number appears on the plate showing the model code, which is mounted on the engine side of the cowl over the steering column, or on the front door front pillar post. Detroit, Michigan Starting: 8624201. Ending: 8630418. Los Angeles, California Starting: 9208851. Ending: 9209340. Engine numbers on left front corner of cylinder block. Starting: T81-1001.

Body Code	Body Type & Seating	Price	Weight	Prod. Total
P7 Road King Line				
103	2-dr. Bus. Cpe.-3P	645	2274	22,537
116	2-dr. Sed.-5P	685	2824	7,499
106	2-dr. Tr. Sed.-5P	699	2824	42,186
115	4-dr. Sed.-5P	726	2839	2,553
105	4-dr. Tr. Sed.-5P	740	2829	23,047
NA	2-dr. Utility Sed.-1P	685	NA	341
723	2-dr. Panel D'ly.-1P	715	NA	2,270
NA	2-dr. RS Cpe.-2/4P	NA	NA	222
NA	4-dr. Sta. Wag.-7/8P	NA	NA	97
NA	Chassis	NA	NA	1,616

Note 1: The P7 Rumbleseat Coupe and Station Wagon were built for export only.

Body Code	Body Type & Seating	Price	Weight	Prod. Total
P8 Deluxe Line				
103	2-dr. Bus. Cpe.-3P	725	2789	41,924
NA	2-dr. RS Cpe.-2/4P	755	2874	1,332
116	2-dr. Sed.-5P	761	2889	2,666
106	2-dr. Tr. Sed.-5P	775	2894	80,981
115	4-dr. Sed.-5P	791	2909	2,279
105	4-dr. Tr. Sed.-5P	805	2919	175,054
CS	4-dr. Conv. Sed.-5P	1,150	NA	387
NA	4-dr. Sed.-7P	1,005	3374	1,837
NA	4-dr. Limo.-7P	1,095	3374	98
NA	4-dr. Sta. Wag.-7/8P	970**	3189	1,680
NA	2-dr. Utility Sed.-1P	NA	NA	13
NA	4-dr. Taxi-7P	NA	NA	12
NA	Chassis	NA	NA	900
NA	Chassis-7P	Chassis	NA	35

Note 2: Convertible Sedan has body by Murray.
Note 3: This wagon has glass in all windows; wagon with glass in windshield and front doors only was priced $930.

Plymouth PT81 Commericial

M-1-2	Pickup	575	2,800	6,181
NA	Cab & Chassis	545	2,600	140

Specifications same for all 1939 models P7 & P8. 5,627 P7's and 4,938 P8's were built with right-hand drive.

STD. ENGINE: Inline. Valve in block. Six. Cast iron block. B & S: 3-1/8 in. x 4-3/8 in. Disp.: 201.3 CID. C.R.: 6.7. Brake H.P.: 82 @ 3600 R.P.M. Taxable/A.L.A.M./N.A.C.C. H.P.: 23.44. Main bearings: Four. Valve lifters: Solid. Carb.: Carter B6K1, B6M1, DGA1-2 or D6C1-1. Torque (Compression) 145 lbs.-ft @ 1200 R.P.M.

OPT. ENGINE: Aluminum cylinder head. Inline. Valve in block. Six. Cast iron block. B & S: 3-1/8 in. x 4-3/8 in. Disp.: 201.3 CID. C.R.: 7.0. Brake H.P.: 86 @ 3600 R.P.M. Main bearings: Four. Valve lifters: Solid. Carb.: Carter B6K1, B6M1, DGA1-2 or D6C1-2. Torque (Compression) 156 lbs.-ft. @ 1200 R.P.M.

Note 1: Cars built for export were equipped with 170.4 CID engine, 2-7/8" bore x 4-3/8" stroke. Engines were identified by engine code numbers P8x. 71 P7's and 202 P8's were shipped with this small-bore engine.

Engine Note 2: In 1938, an engine foundry was built in Windsor, Ontario to produce engines solely for the Canadian built vehicles. Because of lower production demands it was deemed unneccesary to build two different engine blocks as was being done in the United States. In the U.S. the Plymouth and Dodge both shared the same 23" engine block, while Chrysler and DeSoto shared the larger 25" engine block. With less vehicles produced in the Canadian market it was decided that only the larger 25" block would be used in all Canadian built vehicles. With a bore of 3-3/8" and a stroke of 3-3/4" the engine displaced 201.3 cubic inches. (Note, despite the different bore and stroke size, the ultimate displacement remained the same as the smaller 23" U.S. built engine block.) This practice of using a larger block would continue through Plymouth production of the flat head six cylinder engine in Canada.

These engines are also identified by the code letter C in the engine code serial number - example P8C.

COMMERCIAL ENGINE: Inline. Six. Cast iron block. B & S: 3-1/8 in. x 4-3/8 in. Disp.: 201 CID. C.R.: 6.7. Brake H.P.: 70 @ 3,000 R.P.M. Taxable/A.L.A.M./N.A.C.C. H.P.: Four. Valve lifters: Solid. Torque (Compression) 145 lbs.-ft. @ 1,200 R.P.M.

1939 Plymouth, model P8, 4-dr. sedan, OCW

CHASSIS: [Series P7 1939] W.B.: 114 in. O.L.: 182-3/16 in. Frt/Rear Tread: 56-1/4 / 60 in. Tires: 5.50 x 16. [Series P8 1939] W.B.: 114 in. (134 in. 7 pass.) Frt/Rear Tread: 56-1/4 / 60 in. Tires: 6.00 x 16. [Series P8 1939] Convertible Sedan W.B.: 117 in. Frt/Rear Tread: 56-1/4 / 60 in. Tires: 6.00 x 16. [Series PT81] W.B.: 116 in. Frt/Rear Tread: 56 - 60. Tires: 6.00 x 16.

TECHNICAL: Sliding gear transmission. Speeds: 3F/1R. Floor shift on P7; column shift on P8 Deluxe. Single disc, dry 9-1/4" clutch. Driveshaft. Hyphoid, semi-floating axles; Hotchkiss drive rear axle. Overall ratio: 3.9. Hydraulic brakes on four wheels. Steel disc wheels. Rim size: 5.50 x 16 on P7; 6.00 x 16 on P8.

OPTIONS: Single sidemount available only on Sedan Delivery & Station Wagon although fenders would fit passenger cars and some were so fitted in the "aftermarket". Fender skirts (8.25). Bumper guards (4.50 per pair). Electric clock (glove box door) (10.00). Cigar lighter (2.00). Seat covers: several versions offered. Spotlight (14.50). Ambulance conversion (55.00). Chrome wheel discs (8.00). Economy Group 1 (2.50). Economy group 2 (3.00). Stone deflector (1.00). Whitewall tires (15.75 for 6.00 x 16). Whitewalls (13.75 for 5.50 x 16"). HD Air cleaner (2.00). Leather upholstery (Coupes) (13.50). Leather upholstery sedans (22.00). 20" high clearance wheels (18.00). Glove box lock ($.75). Oil filter (Roadking) (2.75). Rear seat speaker (5.95). Deluxe steering wheel (5.00). Rear spring covers (Roadking) (3.00). Power gear shift (9.50). Clock mirror (3.95). Dual trumpet horns (underhood mount) (8.25). Rear body gravel deflector (2.50). RH inside sun visor (1.75). License plate frames (pair) (1.75). Illuminated vanity mirror (1.95). Outside rear view mirror (1.95). Spare tire outside valve extention (1.00). Running board side mouldings (1.50). Glare shield (1.00). Exhaust extension (1.00). Locking

gas cap (1.50). Removeable pickup box with tailgate & extended taillamp for installation in trunk area of coupe (23.95). Heaters: Super airstream (24.45). Tri airstream (21.45). Deluxe (18.45). Duo airstream (15.45). Defroster (4.50). Fresh air attachment (7.00). Radio P8 (Deluxe) Pushbutton with Skyway antenna (51.00). Pushbutton with Roadway antenna (53.45). P7 (Roadking) Manual with Skyway antenna (41.50). Manual with Roadway antenna (43.95). Skyway antenna (cowl mounted external) (2.95). Roadway antenna (under running board mount) (6.25). (for dual antennas). Some accessories were also sold in package groups: Accessory Group A - included RH taillamp, RH wiper, RH sun visor, cigar lighter & dual trumpet horns for $19. Accessory Group B - included auxiliary taillamp and wiper for $6.

Plymouth 1939 PT81 Oil bath air cleaner (3.25). Auxiliary taillamp (4.00). Chrome headlamps (2.75). Dual horns (7.50). Colored sheet metal (5.00). Chrome radiator shell (6.00). Long arm stationary mirror (1.50). Long arm adjustable mirror (2.50). Sunvisor (2.00). Four speed transmission (17.50). Chrome windshield frame (3.00). RH windshield wiper (4.00). Express type rear bumper (6.00). Spare wheel lock (1.50).

HISTORICAL: [Plymouth P7] Production began August 18, 1938; Ended August 18, 1939. Public announcement date for the 1939 models was September 24, 1938. Model year production: 102,368. [Plymouth P8] Production began August 18, 1938; Ended August 18, 1939. Model year production: 315,161.

The three millionth Plymouth was built in 1939.

For its "Safety Signal" speedometer and other safety related items, the 1939 Plymouths were awarded the Eastern Safety Conference Award.

Plymouth PT81 Production began November 1, 1938; Ended August 31, 1939. Model year production: 6,321.

1939
P7 Roadking, 6-cyl., 114" wb

	FP	5	4	3	2	1
Cpe	645	800	1550	3900	5450	7800
2 dr Sed	685	650	1250	2400	4200	6000
2 dr Tr Sed	699	675	1300	2500	4300	6100
Sed	726	675	1300	2500	4350	6200
Tr Sed	740	675	1300	2600	4400	6300
Utl Sed	685	675	1300	2500	4350	6200

P8 DeLuxe, 6-cyl., 114"-134" wb

Conv	895	3650	7350	12,250	17,150	24,500
Conv Sed	1150	3800	7650	12,750	17,850	25,500
2P Cpe	750	850	1650	4150	5800	8300
RS Cpe	755	900	1800	4400	6150	8800
2 dr Sed	761	700	1350	2800	4550	6500
2 dr Tr Sed	775	700	1350	2900	4600	6600
Sed	791	700	1350	2800	4550	6500
Tr Sed	805	725	1400	3000	4700	6700
Sta Wag W/C	930	1175	3700	6150	8600	12,300
Sta Wag W/G	970	1300	4000	6650	9300	13,300
7P Ewb Sed	1005	700	1350	2700	4500	6400
Ewb Limo	1095	925	2000	4650	6500	9300

1940

1940 Plymouth, model P10, 2-dr. sedan, OCW

PLYMOUTH DELUXE — MODEL P10 — SIX: Advertised as the "Low Priced Beauty with the Luxury Ride" the 1940 Plymouth finally received the new body the rest of the Corporation had received a year earlier. With a 3" longer wheelbase, the engine moved forward 4" and the rear axle aft 7-1/2" the car took on over 10 cubic feet of additional interior space over the '39 models. Adding much to appearance of the car was a full length hood, and increased glass area (up 23% over 1939) and a one piece rear window. Although the 1940 design followed the general styling theme set down by the '39 models, the only interchangeable piece of sheetmetal or trim was the radiator ornament!

With the discontinuance of the rumble seat an auxiliary seat coupe was offered in its place — a model which would more commonly become known as the Club Coupe. In addition, a rear seat was added to the convertible coupe for additional passengers. Adding to the sleek appearance of these cars were the concealed front door hinges and concealed trunk lid hinges (on all models except the convertible and coupe). A stone deflector was now fitted between the rear of the body and the bumper face plate and runningboards were made a delete option. When not equipped with runningboards a chrome strip took their place on the body and a gravel pad was fitted to the leading edge of the rear fender. Sealed beam headlamps were fitted to all 1940 models replacing the old bulb/reflector lamps of previous years.

On the interior, the Safety Signal speedometer was continued and all models had column mounted gear shifting. An "All Weather Air Control System" provided a dual heater and defroster system for interior climate control. Full width rear doors and a new transmission which offered the passengers a completely flat floor along with suspension changes resulted in one of the best handling cars Plymouth had ever built. Early sales projections showed the new Plymouth would take over second place in sales from Ford, but a last minute blitz by Ford successfully thwarted this goal and Plymouth remained in third place.

PLYMOUTH COMMERCIAL CAR — MODEL PT105 — SIX: Only minor improvements were made for 1940, taking a sharp eye to discern the differences between this year and the previous year. Most obvious was the addition of sealed beam headlamps, replacing the old bulb/reflector units of the year past. With the addition of sealed beams, the parking lamps were now mounted in small pods on top of the headlamp shell. Also changed was the addition of three chromed grill bars to the otherwise steel stamped face of the grille. Despite a $10 price increase sales increased slightly over the PT81.

I.D. DATA: [P9] Serial numbers on right front door post. Detroit, Michigan Starting: 1378001 Ending: 1454303. Los Angeles, California Starting: 3114801 Ending: 3121385. Evansville, Indiana Starting: 9062201 Ending: 9081375. Windsor, Ontario Starting: 9368516 Ending: 9373193. Engine numbers on left front corner of cylinder lock. Starting: P9-1001. Ending: P9-415461. [P10] Serial numbers on right front door post. Detroit, Michigan Starting: 10883001 Ending: 11122538. Los Angeles, California Starting: 3242501 Ending: 3269066. Evansville, Indiana Starting: 20063001 Ending: 20104165. Windsor, Ontario Starting: 9607611 Ending: 9616760. Engine numbers on left front corner of cylinder block. Starting: P10-1001. Ending: P10-415462. [PT105] Serial number appears on the plate showing the model code, which is mounted on the engine side of the cowl over the steering column, or on the right front door front pillar post. Detroit, Michigan Starting: 8631001 Ending: 8637730. Los Angeles, California Starting: 9209351 Ending: 9210053. Engine numbers on left front corner of cylinder block. Starting: PT105-1001. Ending: PT105-34654.

1940 Plymouth, model P10, convertible coupe, JAC

Body Code	Body Type & Seating	Price	Weight	Prod. Total
P9 Road King				
TPC	2-dr. Bus. Cpe.-3P	645	2801	26,745
211	2-dr. Tr. Sed.-5P	699	2866	55,092
210	4-dr. Tr. Sed.-5P	740	2901	20,076
NA	2-dr. Utility Sed.-1P	699	2769	589
755	2-dr. Panel-1P	720	NA	2889
NA	2-dr. Clb. Cpe.-2P	—	—	360
NA	4-dr. Sta. Wag.-7/8P	—	—	80
NA	Chassis	—	—	907

Note 1: The P9 club coupe and station wagon were built for export only.

Body Code	Body Type & Seating	Price	Weight	Prod. Total
P10 Deluxe				
ASC	2-dr. Clb. Cpe.-5P	770	2881	32,244
TPC	2-dr. Bus. Cpe.-3P	725	2836	22,174
201	2-dr. Sed.-5P	775	2921	76,781
200	4-dr. Sed.-5P	805	2956	173,351
204	2-dr. Conv. Cpe.-5P	950	3081	6986
NA	4-dr. Sta. Wag.-7/8P	970	3144	3126
NA	4-dr. Sed.-7P	1005	3391	1179
NA	4-dr. Limo.-7P	1080	NA	68
NA	Chassis	—	—	18
NA	Chassis-7P	—	—	18
PT105 Commercial				
4012	Pickup	585	2800	6879
NA	Cab & Chassis	555	2600	174

Specifications same for all 1940 Models P9 & P10. 3,532 P9's and 3,377 P10's were built with right-hand drive.

STD. ENGINE: Inline. Valve in block. Six. Cast iron block. B & S: 3-1/8 in. x 4-1/8 in. Disp.: 201.3 CID. C.R.: 6.7. Brake H.P.: 84 @ 3600 R.P.M. Taxable/A.L.A.M./N.A.C.C. H.P.: 23.44. Main bearings: Four. Valve lifters: Solid. Carb.: Carter D6A1-2, D6C1-2, D6P1. Torque (Compression) 154 lbs.-ft. @ 1200 R.P.M. Cars built for export were equipped with 170.4 CID engine, 2-7/8" bore x 4-3/8" stroke. Rated at 70 horsepower. Engines were identified by engine code number P9X or P10X-6.07 compression ratio. Only one P9 and no P10 models are recorded as being shipped with this export engine, caused no doubt by the fact that most small bore engines were shipped to England for final assembly in the Kew plant; England was by this time at war with Germany and all car production had come to a halt.

OPT. ENGINE: Inline. Valve in block. Six. Cast iron block. B & S: 3-1/8 in. x 4-3/8 in. Disp.: 201.3 CID. Compression Ratio: 7.0. Brake H.P.: 87 @ 3600 R.P.M. Main bearings: Four. Valve lifters: Solid. Torque (Compression) 158 lbs.-ft. @ 1200 R.P.M.

ENGINE NOTE: Canadian built vehicles utilized the larger 25" block with 3-3/8" bore x 4-1/16" stroke, for a displacement of 218.6 cubic inches.

COMMERCIAL ENGINE: Inline. Six. Cast iron block. B & S: 3-1/8 in. x 4-3/8 in. Disp.: 210 CID. C.R.: 6.7. Brake H.P.: 79 @ 3000 R.P.M. Main bearings: Four. Valve lifters: Solid. Torque (Compression) 154 lbs.-ft. @ 1200 R.P.M.

TECHNICAL: [P9 & P10] Sliding gear transmission. Speeds: 3F/1R. Column shift controls (all models). Single disc. dry 9-1/4" clutch. Driveshaft. Hypoid, semi floating; Hotchkiss drive rear axle. Overall Ratio: 4.1 on Deluxe; 3.9 on Roadking P9. Hydraulic brakes on four wheels. Steel disc wheels. Rim size: 5.50 x 16 on P9 Roadking; 6.00 x 16 on P10 Deluxe. 4 in. width. [PT105] Three speed standard with option 4 speed w/power take-off opening. Floor shift controls. Single disc, dry plate 10 in diameter clutch. Driveshaft. Hypoid, semi-floating rear axle. Overall Ratio: 4.1 standard. Hydraulic brakes on four wheels. Steel disc wheels. Rim size: 6.00 x 16 standard see list for other options. Optional rear axle ratios 3.73; 4.3 or 4.78. Optional tire & wheel sizes included 5.25 x 20 4 ply; 5.25 x 20 6 ply; 6.00 x 16 6 ply; 6.00 x 18 6 ply; 6.25 x 16 6 ply; 6.50 x 16 4 ply or 6.50 x 16 6 ply.

CHASSIS: [P9] W.B.: 117 in. O.L.: 194-1/2 in. Frt/Rear Tread: 57 / 59-15/16 in. Tires: 5.50 x 16. [P10] W.B.: 117 in. (137 in. 7 passenger) O.L.: 194-1/2 in. (7 pass. 214-1/2). Frt/Rear Tread: 57 in. 59-15/16 in. Tires: 6.00 x 16. [PT105] W.B.: 116 in. Frt/Rear Tread: 56-60 in. Tires: 6.00 x 16.

1940 Plymouth, model P10, station wagon, OCW

OPTIONS: Radio pushbutton dash mount (47.50). Heater all weather heat system (45.50). Clock electric mounted in glovebox door (12.00). Radio antenna "Skyway" external cowl mount. Seat covers several varieties offered. Spotlight right or left side (14.50). Back up lamp (2.95). Exhaust extention (1.00). Fender grill guard (11.20). Fender protectors (6.25). Fog lamps (12.00). Locking gas cap (1.50). Grill guard (6.95). Rear seat heater (11.95). Dual trumpet horns (underhood mount) (8.50). License frames (1.50). Outside rear view mirror (1.95). Deluxe steering wheel (8.50). Bumper (center) "Superguard" (1.75). Rear bumper center "Superguard" (2.50). Wheel discs (1.50 each). Wheel trim rings (1.50 each). 20" high clearance wheels. PT105 oil bath air cleaner (2.50). Vortex air cleaner (17.50 w/standard cap or 19.50 with Vortex cap). Airfoam seat cushion & back (10.00). Auxiliary taillamp (2.50). Domelamp (3.50). Glove box lock (1.50). 32 amp generator for slow speed operation (14.00). Governor (5.00). Chrome headlamps (3.50). Grill guard (7.50). Dual horns (7.50). Heater & defroster (25.00). Deluxe Purolator oil filter (5.00). Colored sheet metal (5.00). Long arm stationary mirror (1.50). Same for right side (2.50). Long arm adjustable mirror LH (2.50). Same RH (3.00). Sunvisor (2.00). Inside rear view mirror (1.00). Four speed transmission (17.50). Chrome windshield frame (3.00). RH windshield wiper (vacuum) (4.00). Electric windshield wiper LH (6.00). Dual electric windshield wipers (13.00). Express type rear bumper (6.00). Spare wheel lock (1.50). Economy group 1 (2.50). Economy Group 2 (3.00). Wheel & tire equipment (in sets of 5) 5.25 x 20 4 ply (18.00). 5x25 x 20 6 ply (35.00). 6.00 x 16 6 ply (14.50). 6.00 x 18 6 ply (Not listed). 6.25 x 16 6 ply (23.50). 6.50 x 16 4 ply (13.50). 6.50 x 16 6 ply (28.25).

HISTORICAL: [P9] Production began August 15, 1939; ended July 12, 1940. Public announcement date for the 1940 models was Thursday, September 21, 1939. Model year production: 106,738. K.T. Keller, Corporated head; Dan S. Eddins, Division head. [P10] Production began August 15, 1939; ended July 12, 1940. Model year production: 316,417. For the second year in a row, Plymouth was awarded the Eastern Safety Conference Award. [PT105] Production beganSept. 26, 1939; ended August 20, 1940. Model year production: 7,053. Walter P. Chrysler died in August at the age of 65, after suffering a cerebral hemorrhage. He had been ill the last few years of his life.

1940
P9 Roadking, 6-cyl., 117" wb

	FP	5	4	3	2	1
Cpe	645	775	1500	3600	5100	7300
2 dr Tr Sed	699	650	1200	2300	4100	5800
4 dr Tr Sed	740	650	1250	2400	4200	6000
Utl Sed	699	650	1200	2300	4100	5800

P10 DeLuxe, 6-cyl., 137" wb

	FP	5	4	3	2	1
Conv	950	3500	7050	11,750	16,450	23,500
DeL Cpe	725	800	1550	3900	5450	7800
4P Cpe	770	825	1600	4000	5600	8000
2 dr Sed	775	600	1200	2200	3850	5500
Sed	805	650	1250	2400	4150	5900
Sta Wag	970	1300	4000	6650	9300	13,300
7P Sed	1005	775	1500	3600	5100	7300
Sed Limo	1080	925	2000	4650	6500	9300

1941

1941 Plymouth, model P12, convertible coupe, OCW

PLYMOUTH — MODEL P11 — SIX: The "no frills" line this year was the "Plymouth" line. Identified by its lack of vent windows on the front doors, little chrome, one windshield wiper and one inside sun visor on the drivers side, the model was the division's price leader. Also identified by its "Plymouth" name plate on the hood side panels, many options were not available for this line and when they were, they were not as "deluxe" as other models — the optional vent wing package came with painted, rather than chrome trim for example. Despite this the line sold slightly better than the upgraded P11D Deluxe series.

PLYMOUTH DELUXE — MODEL P11D — SIX: Considered by some to be merely a '40 Plymouth with a "chrome plated bib for a grille", the '41 Plymouth saw many refinements over the previous year. Most notable among the changes this year was the one piece, "alligator" opening hood, the battery mounted under the hood rather than under the drivers seat and spring loaded hinges on the trunk lid, replacing the cam-locking device of years past. At the rear, the stop lamp was fitted in the center of the deck lid, incorporated with the license plate holder. This lamp, situated slightly higher than the taillamps, eliminated the "tailgating" driver not seeing the brake lights. Delete runningboards continued as an option but the high clearance wheel option was reduced from 20" wheels to 18".

Although not considered by the factory as a separate line, the P11D featured better appointments than the P11 Deluxe but less than the Special Deluxe P12 series. Most noticeable among the P11D's features was chrome trim around the windshield and side windows and the word "Deluxe" on the hood side panels.

PLYMOUTH SPECIAL DELUXE — MODEL P12 — SIX: Two tone paints and upholstery were the most noted features of the 1941 Special Deluxe series. Carrying the two toning ever further, the wooden bodied Westchester station wagon could be had in two trim levels, with the woodwork finished in one solid shade, or with the flat panels stained a darker shade for contrast! Most Special Deluxes were fitted with the optional bumper end "wingtips" and a center "Superguard" — the rear guard of the folding type to prevent the guard from interfering with the opening of the deck lid. Sales were spectacular as more people became employed in industry catering to the war goods production for England and perhaps many saw the handwriting on the wall as this country edged closer to involvement in the conflict.

PLYMOUTH COMMERCIAL CAR — MODEL PT125 — SIX: 1941 would prove to be the last and final year for Plymouth's commercial car venture until the 1974 Trail Duster (which itself was based on a similar Dodge model). With minimal sales and Dodge needing the factory capacity to meet growing truck demands prior to our entry in World War II, the Plymouth Commercial cars production was discontinued at the end of the model run.

Still using the basic body introduced in 1939, the '41 model saw the most changes. The sealed beam headlamps were moved outward and mounted on the crowning vee of the fender, giving the vehicle a very bug-eyed look. The front grille piece now featured an overlay of chromed grille trim and the front bumper had a decided vee shape to it as well. In another change, the "Plymouth" name badge was moved from the radiator shell to a point midway on the side of the hood upper panels and the parking lamps were moved to the cowl just below the windshield. Prices were increased substantially, with production just below the level it had been the year before. With the introduction of the new body style in '39 truck production had taken place only in the Detroit and Los Angeles assembly plants.

I.D. DATA: [Plymouth P11 and P11D] Serial numbers on right front door post. Detroit Starting: 15000101. Ending: 15135030. Los Angeles Starting: 3121501. Ending: 3133962. Evansville Starting: 22001001. Ending: 22036667. Windsor Starting: 9821241. Ending: 9829853. Engine numbers on left front corner of cylinder block. Starting: P11 - 1001. Ending: P11 - 535085. [Plymouth P12] Serial numbers on right front door post. Detroit Starting: 11123001. Ending: 11399250. Los Angeles Starting: 3269301. Ending: 3296572. Evansville Starting: 20105101. Ending: 20147921. Windsor Starting: 9616761. Ending: 9624457. Engine numbers on left front corner of cylinder block. Starting: P12-1001. Ending: P12-535085. [Plymouth PT125] Serial number appears on the plate showing the model code, which is mounted on the engine side of the cowl over the steering column, or on the right front door front pillar post. Detroit, Michigan Starting: 81000101. Ending: 81006107. Los Angeles, California Starting: 9210101. Ending: 9210700. Engine numbers on left front corner of cylinder block. Starting: PT125-1001.

Body Code	Body Type & Seating	Price	Weight	Prod. Total
Plymouth P11 Deluxe				
303	2-dr. Bus. Cpe.-3P	685	2849	23,754
302	2-dr. Clb. Cpe.-4P	NA	NA	994
311	2-dr. Sed.-5P	739	2899	46,646
310	4-dr. Sed.-5P	780	2929	21,175
NA	2-dr. Utility Sed.-1P	739	2794	468
820	2-dr. Panel Del'y-1P	745	NA	3,200
NA	4-dr. Sta. Wag.-7/8P	NA	NA	217
NA	Chassis	NA	NA	676
P11D Deluxe				
311	2-dr Sed.-5P	779	2939	46,138
310	4-dr. Sed.-5P	820	2964	32,336
303	2-dr. Bus. Cpe.-3P	729	2879	15,862
302	2-dr. Clb. Cpe.-4P	NA	NA	204
NA	2-dr. Utility Sed.-1P	NA	NA	1
820	2-dr. Panel Del'y-1P	NA	NA	1
P12 Special Deluxe				
303	2-dr. Bus. Cpe.-3P	760	2899	23,851
302	2-dr. Clb. Cpe.-4P	805	2974	37,352
301	2-dr. Sed.-5P	810	2974	84,810
300	4-dr. Sed.-5P	840	2999	190,513
304	2-dr. Conv. Cpe.-4P	970	3206	10,545
NA	4-dr. Sed.-7P	1045	3379	1,127
NA	4-dr. Limo.-7P	1120	3379	24
NA	4-dr. Sta. Wag.-7/8P	995	3194	5,594
NA	2-dr. Utility Sed.-1P	NA	NA	2
NA	Chassis	NA	NA	323
PT125				
4112	2-dr. Pickup-3P	625	2,800	6,073
NA	Cab & Chassis-3P	590	2,600	196

Body production code numbers also indicate by a series of letters the type of coupe body fitted: ASC indicates auxiliary seat (club) coupe; letters TPC indicate two-passenger (business) coupe.

Specifications same for all 1941 models P11 & P12 (Including P11D). 1,387 P11's, 1,046 P11D's and 3,024 P12's were built with right-hand drive.

1941 Plymouth, model P12, station wagon, JAC

STD. ENGINE: Inline. Valve in block. Six. Cast iron block. B & S: 3-1/8 in. x 4-3/8 in. Disp.: 201.3 CID. C.R.: 6.7. Brake H.P.: 87 @ 3800 R.P.M. Taxable/A.L.A.M./N.A.C.C. H.P.: 23.44. Main bearings: Four. Valve lifters: Solid. Carb.: Carter D6A1-2, D6C1-2, B6P1. Torque (Compression) 160 lbs.-ft. @ 1200 R.P.M.

OPT. ENGINE: Aluminum cylinder head. Inline. Valve in block. Six. Cast iron block. B & S: 3-1/8 in. x 4-3/8 in. Disp.: 201.3 CID. C.R.: 7.25. Brake H.P.: 92 @ 3800 R.P.M. Main bearings: Four. Valve lifters: Solid. Carb.: Carter D6A1-2, D6C1-2, B6P1. Torque (Compression) 164 lbs.-ft. @ 1200 R.P.M. [Plymouth PT125] Inline. Six. Cast iron block. B & S: 3-1/8 in. x 4-3/8 in. Disp.: 201 CID. Brake H.P.: 82. Main bearings: Four. Valve lifters: Solid.

ENGINE NOTE: Canadian built vehicles utilized the larger 25" block with 3-3/8" bore x 4-1/16" stroke for 218.6 CID.

CHASSIS: [P11] W.B.: 117 in. O.L.: 194-3/4 in. Frt/Rear Tread: 57 in./59-15/16 in. Tires: 6.00 x 16 in. [P11D & P12] W.B.: 117 in. O.L.: 198-1/4 in. Frt/Rear Tread: 57 in./59-15/16 in. Tires: 6.00 x 16 in. 4 in. rim. [P12] W.B.: 137-1/2 in. O.L.: 220-13/16 in. Frt/Rear Tread: 57 in./60-9/32 in. Tires: 6.50 x 16 in. 4-1/2 in. rim. [PT125] W.B.: 116 in. Frt/Rear Tread: 55-15/16 in./60 in. Tires: 6.00 x 16 in.

TECHNICAL: [P11, P11D & P12] Sliding gear transmission. Speeds: 3F/1R. Column shift controls. Single disc, dry 9-1/4" clutch. Driveshaft. Hypoid, semi floating; Hotchkiss drive rear axle. Overall ratio: 4.1. [P11 and P11D, 4.3 P12] Four wheel hydraulic brakes. Steel disc wheels 6.00 x 16 in. (7 pass 6.50 x 16 in.). "Powermatic" vacuum shift opt. [PT125] Sliding gear transmission. Speeds: 3F/1R. 4 speed with power take off opening opt. Single disc, dry 10" clutch. Driveshaft, hypoid, semi floating Hotchkiss drive rear axle. Overall ratio: 4.1 std., optional 3.73, 4.3 or 4.78. Four wheel hydraulic brakes. Steel disc wheels. Rim size: 6.00 x 16 in.

OPTIONS: Accessory Group A (P11D & P12) including glove box lock with steel glove box, rear wheel shields, cigar lighter, stainless steel wheel trim rings, chrome wheel discs and chrome license plate frames (25.00). Accessory Group A for station wagon (does not include wheel shields) (16.00). Accessory Group B (P11D & P12) including cigar lighter, glove box lock with steel glove box, stainless steel wheel trim rings (10.00). Accessory Group C (P11 only) RH windshield wiper and RH sun visor (5.00). Bumper fender guards (P11 only) (8.00). Bumper center guards (P11 only) (3.00). Chrome wheel discs (set of 4) (6.00). Chrome wheel trim rings (set of 5) (7.50). Electric clock (P12 only) (10.00). Front door armrest (1.75 each). Front door vent wings (P11 only) (12.00). Glove box lock with steel glove box (1.00). Dual horns (P11D & P12) (2.00). Dual horns (P11) (5.00). Powermatic shifting (6.50). 8 tube pushbutton radio (46.75). 6 tube radio (35.15). Windshield antennae (ex. convertible) (6.20). Cowl mounted antennae (5.55). Rear wheel shields (9.00). Stainless steel window reveals (ex. 7 passenger) (7.50). Two tone paint (P12 only) (10.00). Lifeguard inner tubes set of 5, 6.00 x 16, (44.00) set of 5, 6.50 x 16, (49.00). Economy group 1, small bore carb, small bore intake manifold and 3.73 axle ratio (2.50). Economy group 2, same as group one except includes throttle stop and heat shields (3.50). Taxi Cab package 1 including heavy duty springs, shock absorbers and special crankcase ventilation, 11" clutch plate (8.75). Taxi Cab package 2, same equipment but 10" clutch plate (3.75). Back up signal, body side shields, emergency brake alarm, cigarette lighter, Kool Kushion, exhaust extension, fog lights, locking gas cap, heater (six different models), cowl mounted outside rear view mirrors, grill guard, insect screen, rear window venitian blind, seat covers, spotlights (LH or RH), spare tire air valve extension, vanity case. [PT125] Vortox air cleaner with standard cap (17.50), with Vortox cap (19.50). Airfoam seat cushion and back (10.00). Extra taillamp (2.50). Dome light in cab (2.50). Economy Group 1 (3.00). Economy Group 2 (5.00). Economy Group 3 (7.50). Glove box door lock (1.50). "Handy" Governor (5.00). 32 amp generator (slow speed operation) (8.00). Chrome windshield frame (3.00). Chrome headlamps & parking lamps (3.50). Radiator grille guard (3.00). Dual Airtone horns (5.00). Heater & defroster (25.00). Purolator heavy duty oil filter (6.00). Oil filter (3.25). Long arm rearview mirror, LH stationary (1.50), RH stationary (2.50), LH adjustable (2.50), RH adjustable (3.00). Extra inside rear view mirror (1.00). Sun visor (2.00). 4 speed transmission w/power takeoff opening (17.50). RH vacuum windshield wiper (4.00). Dual electric wipers (13.00). Express type rear bumber (1.00). Wheel & tire equipment 5.25 x 20, 4 ply, (18.00) 5.25 x 20, 6 ply, (35.00) 6.00 x 16, 6 ply, (14.50) 6.00 x 18, 6 ply, Not listed; 6.25 x 16, 6 ply, (23.50) 6.50 x 16, 6 ply, (28.25). P11 Panel Delivery & Utility Sedan options: Accessory Group C including RH windshield wiper, RH sun visor (5.00). Dual taillamps (3.00). Auxiliary seat for Panel Delivery (12.00). Screen partition for Utility sedan (25.00). Rear seat conversion package including rear seat cushion and seat back, seat riser and side armrests (price not listed).

HISTORICAL: Plymouth P11 & P11D Production began August 8, 1940; Ended July 16, 1941. Model year production: 97,130 P11 models; 94,542 P11D models. K. T. Keller, Corporate head; Dan S. Eddins, Division head.

On November 18, 1940, a specially prepared 1941 P11 4 door sedan left Detroit, Michigan in an attempt to be the first to drive from Detroit to the tip of South America via the proposed route of the Pan American Highway. The Richardson Pan American Highway Expedition consisted of three men, Sullivan C. Richardson, Arnold Whitaker and Kenneth C. Van Hee. Mapping out the proposed route of the Pan American Highway, it took the three men and their '41 Plymouth eight months to reach Magallanes, Chile via a route that included countless miles of swamp, mountain and desert terrrain through Mexico, Central and South America. Their eight month expedition covered 15,745 miles one way.

Plymouth P12 Production began August 8, 1940; Ended July 16, 1941. Model year production: 354,139.

The four millionth Plymouth was built in 1941, with young actor Mickey Rooney painting the symbolic numbers on a convertible at the Los Angeles assembly plant. Rooney was playing in the popular "Hardy Boys" series at the time.

Plymouth PT125 Production began September 18, 1940; End of production not known. Model year production: 6,269.

An overseas assembly plant was opened in South Africa. It would close in 1942 for the duration of the war, then reopen in 1946.

1941
P11 Standard, 6-cyl., 117" wb

	FP	5	4	3	2	1
Cpe	720	775	1500	3600	5100	7300
2 dr Sed	769	600	1200	2200	3900	5600
Sed	800	650	1200	2300	4100	5800
Utl Sed	760	600	1200	2300	4000	5700

P11 DeLuxe, 6-cyl., 117" wb

	FP	5	4	3	2	1
Cpe	760	775	1500	3750	5250	7500
2 dr Sed	809	600	1200	2300	4000	5700
Sed	545	650	1250	2400	4150	5900

P12 Special DeLuxe, 6 cyl., 117"-137" wb

	FP	5	4	3	2	1
Conv	1007	3800	7650	12,750	17,850	25,500
DeL Cpe	795	800	1550	3900	5450	7800
4P Cpe	842	825	1600	4000	5600	8000
2 dr Sed	845	650	1250	2400	4200	6000
Sed	877	750	1450	3400	5000	7100
Sta Wag	1031	1450	4250	7150	10,000	14,300
7P Sed	1078	775	1500	3600	5100	7300
Limo	1120	925	2000	4650	6500	9300

1172

1942 Plymouth, model P14C, Special Deluxe, town sedan, OCW

PLYMOUTH DELUXE — MODEL P14S — SIX: Easily identified by the lack of chrome trim around the windshield, the Deluxe line continued to be the Division's price leader. Available only in a limited amount of body styles the entire commercial lineup was eliminated from the sales picture. Gone were the sedan delivery and the ambulance conversion, but a small handful (less than 100) Utility Sedans were built. Also missing was the truck chassis commercial line as well for 1942. All models could be had with the normal list of options except for two tone paint on the coupes. As production wore on and more materials were being taken for the war effort, many cars were either fitted with shortened pieces of chrome (especially the front fender trim) or the chrome trim was painted over in what would become known as "black out" models. Some cars were even reported to have been delivered to the military bearing wooden bumpers!

1942 Plymouth, P14C, Special Deluxe, club coupe, AA

PLYMOUTH SPECIAL DELUXE — MODEL P14C — SIX: Despite the war shortened production year, Plymouth enjoyed brisk sales. Production began late in July and ended on January 31st, 1942. Many of the new cars not already in consumers hands were impounded by the government with the result that many of these vehicles saw military service. The '42 Plymouth was nearly an all new car. Gone was the old familiar X braced frame, replaced by a box perimeter frame. The new body sat lower on the chassis and for the first time the runningboards, or what remained of them, were concealed by the doors which flared out at their lower extremities to cover them. At the front a new, massive grille with the headlamps placed at the outer ends was featured, along with a sheet metal air scoop (inspired by race cars so the advertising claimed) to help cool air entering the engine compartment. Highly touted as an accessory was the vacuum controlled shifting mechanism which had been offered the previous year. The system was not sold in any great quantities and disappeared forever after production ceased. This accessory may have been offered to appease those customers for the low priced Plymouth line not having any form of automatic transmission as higher priced Chrysler Corporation cars had.

Gone from the sales line up was the 7 passenger sedan and the ambulance conversion. A one year offering was the Town Sedan which featured normal opening rear doors (rather than suicide style doors found on regular sedans). The Town Sedan also placed the rear quarter window into the door frame itself. Convertibles were standard equipped with fender shields and leather upholstery. The station wagon was still offered with two choices of wood trim and for this year only the wooden body was trimmed by full length belt mouldings of chrome trim, at least those models built in early production, prior to cut-backs caused by war related material shortages.

I.D. DATA: [Plymouth P14S] Serial numbers on right front door post. Detroit Starting: 15135501. Ending: 15153935. Los Angeles Starting: 3134501 Ending: 3136266. Evansville Starting: 22037001 Ending: 22041356. Windsor Starting: 9829856 Ending: 9836986. [P14C] Serial numbers on right front door post. Detroit Starting: 11399501 Ending: 11494048. Los Angeles Starting: 3297001 Ending: 3306756. Evansville Starting: 20148001 Ending: 20164436. Windsor Starting: 9829856 Ending 9836986. Engine numbers on left front corner of cylinder block. Starting: P14-1001. Ending: P14-149161.

Body Code	Body Type & Seating	Price	Weight	Prod. Total
P14S Deluxe				
TPC	2-dr. Bus. Cpe.-2/3P	812	2930	3783
412	2-dr. Clb. Cpe.-4P	885	2990	2458
400	4-dr. Sed.-5P	889	3025	11,973
411	2-dr. Sed.-5P	850	2985	9350
NA	2-dr. Utility Sed.-1P	842	2985	80
NA	Chassis	—	—	1
P14C Special Deluxe				
TPC	2-dr. Bus. Cpe.-2/3P	855	2955	7258
402	2-dr. Clb. Cpe.-4P	928	3035	14,685
401	2-dr. Sed.-5P	895	3020	24,142
400	4-dr. Sed.-5P	935	3060	68,924
405	4-dr. Twn. Sed.-5P	980	3085	5821
404	2-dr. Conv. Cpe.-4P	1078	3255	2806
NA	4-dr. Sta. Wag.-7/8P	1145	NA	1136
NA	Chassis	—	—	10

Specifications same for all 1942 models P14S & P14C. 942 P14's and 1,457 P14C's were built with right-hand drive.

ENGINE: Inline. Valve in block. Six. Cast iron block. B & S: 3-1/4 in. x 4-3/8 in. Disp.: 217.8 CID. C.R.: 6.8. Brake H.P.: 95 @ 3400 R.P.M. Taxable/A.L.A.M./N.A.C.C. H.P.: 25.35. Main bearings: Four. Valve lifters: Solid. Carb.: Carter B6P1, B6G1. Torque (Compression) 172 lbs.-ft. at 1600 R.P.M.
Note: Canadian built vehicles utilized the larger 25" block with 3-3/8" bore x 4-1/16" stroke for 218.6 CID. 88 hp @ 3,800 RPM. 27.34 H.P.

CHASSIS: [Series P14S] W.B.: 117 in. O.L.: 195-9/16 in. Frt/Rear Tread: 57 / 59-15/16 in. Tires: 6.00 x 16. [Series P14C] W.B.: 117 in. O.L.: 195-9/16 in. Frt/Rear Tread: 57-59-15/16 in. Tires: 6.00 x 16.

TECHNICAL: Sliding gear transmission. Speeds: 3F/1R. Column shift controls. Single disc, dry 9-1/4" clutch. Driveshaft. Hypoid, semi-floating, Hotchkiss drive rear axle. Overall Ratio: 3.9. Hydralic brakes on four wheels. Steel disc wheels. Rim size: 6.00 x 16 in. Other rear axle ratios: 3.73 with economy group package. 4.1 on Suburban (station wagon). 4.56 on Suburban with 18" wheel option. 4.78 on all export models.

OPTIONS: Fender skirts (std on convertible) (12.50). Radio 8 tube push-button (type 801) (54.85). Heater all weather heating system (49.20). Clock electric (std on convertible) (9.75). Cigar lighter (2.00). Radio antenna windshield header (5.50). Seat covers several types offered. Spotlight right or left side (15.80 each). Foglamps (12.40). License plate frames (2.20). Windshield washer (3.95). Hand brake alarm (2.50). Locking gas cap (1.80). Rear window wiper (9.50). Outside rear view mirror (2.35). Powermatic shift (7.85). Direction signals (10.00). Rear fender wingtip guards; Rear bumper center "Superguard"; spare tire airvalve extention (to fill spare tire from outside car without opening trunk!); rear window sunshade; exhaust extension; wheel trim discs; wheel trim rings; buzzer type hand brake alarm; flashing light type hand brake alarm; other radios offered were type "601" 6 tube pushbutton radio and a universal mount radio. Other radio antennaes offered included external "Skyway" cowl mounted; INTERNAL cowl mounted; crank operated "Cowl Concealed" and a power operated "Cowl Concealed" antennae. Delete option on the Deluxe series included no ventpanes in front door glass, no RH windshield wiper and no front bumper guards to keep price down. A major option offered in 1942 was two tone paint on all models except the business coupe. Standard upholstery in the convertible was red leather, but buyer could choose optional blue or tan leather if desired.

HISTORICAL: P14S Production began July 25, 1941; Ended January 31, 1942. Model year production: 27,645. Dan S. Eddins, Division head. P14C Production began July 25, 1941; ended January 31, 1942. Model year production: 124,782.

1942
P14S DeLuxe, 6-cyl., 117" wb

	FP	5	4	3	2	1
Cpe	812	725	1400	3100	4800	6800
2 dr Sed	850	550	1150	2100	3800	5400
Utl Sed	842	500	1100	1950	3600	5100
Clb Cpe	885	650	1250	2400	4200	6000
Sed	889	550	1150	2000	3600	5200
P14C Special DeLuxe, 6-cyl., 117" wb						
Conv	1078	3200	6450	10,750	15,050	21,500
Cpe	855	775	1500	3600	5100	7300
2 dr Sed	895	600	1200	2200	3850	5500
Sed	935	550	1150	2100	3800	5400
Twn Sed	980	600	1200	2200	3850	5500
Clb Cpe	928	775	1500	3750	5250	7500
Sta Wag	1145	1150	3500	5900	8250	11,800

P.M.C. — **New York, New York** — **(1908)** — Like the Boston High Wheel, the P.M.C. was a vehicle so unlikely to succeed that C.S. Peets might be regarded as one of the most cockeyed optimists ever to enter the motor industry. In 1908 he founded his C.S. Peets Manufacturing Company and proceeded to build a two-cylinder air-cooled 12 hp two-seater with right-hand wheel steering, planetary transmission, 38-inch wheels and solid rubber tires. The price was right at $550, but this bucolic conveyance must have looked a bit absurd on Broadway. C.S. Peets' company was located

1908 P.M.C., runabout, NAHC

at 60 West 43rd Street in the heart of New York City. Sales from the hinterlands were not sufficient to keep him in business for a year.

PNEU — The Pneu "L" Electric Company was organized in New York City during the summer of 1907 with a capital stock of $200,000 for the manufacture of "horseless vehicles, motors, engines, etc." Incorporators were W.C. Button and Francis Fitch. Manufacture of a car is doubted.

PNEUMATIC — The Pneumatic No-Puncture Wheel Company was organized in Philadelphia, Pennsylvania during the summer of 1906 with a $1 million capital stock to "manufacture, buy, sell and deal in automobiles and all other kinds of horseless vehicles." Incorporators were D.J. Simon, H.E. Hekler and J.J. Hirschfield. Manufacture of a car is doubted.

1898 Pneumatic, NAHC

PNEUMATIC — **New York, New York** — **(1896-1899)** — The Pneumatic Carriage Company was organized in 1895 with a capital stock of $500,000 and one A.H. Hoadley as president. Offices were taken at 253 Broadway in New York City, but all experimentation was conducted in the factory of the American Wheelock Engine Company in Worcester, Massachusetts. The first experimental Pneumatic automobile was completed in 1896 and was part of the parade on Flag Day (October 31st) in Worcester. It was a six-seater, and its motive power was compressed air. "The air is conducted to the motor by a pressure reducing valve of new design, which gives a constant pressure on the motor of 100 pounds to the square inch," *The Horseless Age* explained. "The motor, of the reciprocating type, weighs 400 pounds and operates at 350 revolutions, when the carriage is making 15 miles an hour." The carriage was also claimed capable of climbing a twenty percent grade. Wooden wheels of 30 inches (front) and 42 inches (rear) were fitted with pneumatic tires, and the car's total weight was 2700 pounds. Twenty miles "over ordinary good roads" was possible on one compressed air charge. To obtain heat and expansion, the air was surcharged with hot water carried in a separate tank before it entered the motor. Five pounds of water were required for each mile traversed. It would seem that automobile manufacture was not the firm's aim, but rather urban transit. In 1899 grand plans were laid for the establishment of a bus line on Fifth Avenue to compete with the trolley already in operation a few blocks over on Third. Had there been a metropolitan air pollution problem at the time — other than the leavings of horses, of course — the idea of compressed air transport might have been developed further. As it happened, the Pneumatic Carriage Company faded from the scene before the turn of the century.

1915 Pneumobile, model 6-30, 4-pass. touring, WLB

PNEUMOBILE — Chicago, Illinois — (1914-1915) — In the early fall of 1914, after nine years of development, so the company said, the Cowles-MacDowell Pneumobile Company of Chicago was at last ready to unveil its automotive offering. The most striking feature of the Pneumobile was its lack of mechanical springs; it may have been America's first car to use air suspension completely. "It involves a system of cylinders mounted on the frame and coacting with plungers rigidly supported by the axle," *Automobile Topics* explained. "There is no metallic connection between wheels and axles and the frame, so that minor vibrations should be successfully absorbed by the system. For sustaining and equalizing purposes, each unit, of which there are four — one adjacent to each wheel — is joined to a central piping system." Body styling of the Pneumobile was unusual as well, its hood rounding over the radiator for the appearance of a blunt-nosed bullet. The engine was a 58 hp Buda six, and the chassis was a long 132 inches between the axles. A Warner clutch and four-speed selective transmission were fitted. Irving Cowles and E.H. MacDowell, whose offices were in the McCormick Building in Chicago, planned to establish a factory in Anderson, Indiana. But it would appear that the few cars produced before their company went under were built for them by another manufacturer.

1914-1915 PNEUMOBILE
Model 6-30 — 6-cyl., 29 hp, 132" wb

	FP	5	4	3	2	1
Touring-4P	1975	3100	4200	6300	10,500	22,000
Touring-6P	2000	3200	4300	6500	11,000	23,000
Roadster-2P	1975	3100	4200	6300	10,500	22,000

PNUCAR — The Pnucar Company was organized in Washington, D.C. during the fall of 1912 with a capital stock of $500,000 to manufacture and deal in automobiles "and supplies for same." Incorporators were Louis A. Hill, Louis E. Bradford and Benjamin R. Shockley. Manufacture of a car is doubted.

POCOCK — Philadelphia, Pennsylvania — (1899) — In 1899 Francis A. Pocock of Philadelphia was granted a patent on an electric car, which he assigned to the Electric Power Development Company. Perhaps a prototype of this car was built, but this cannot be documented with certainty. It is known that Pocock contributed some of the design ideas for the Kennedy Electric that was built in Philadelphia from 1898 to 1903.

POKORNEY — From 1904-1906, H. Pokorney of Indianapolis and later Guthrie, Indiana produced a little gasoline-engined car which he marketed as the Tricolet. Refer to Tricolet.

POLAR — The Polar Motor Car Company was organized in New York City early in 1910 with a capital stock of $5000 for the manufacture of automobiles. Incorporators were F.M. York, C. Kenney and M. Jones. Manufacture is doubted.

POLHEMUS & THOMAS — New Brunswick, New Jersey — (1902) — In its June 1902 edition, *Cycle and Automobile Trade Journal* reported that Polhemus & Thomas of New Brunswick were building a steam carriage to sell for $850.00. If the vehicle was completed, it was probably the only one built. New Brunswick city directories of the period do not indicate any business partnership or company bearing the Polhemus & Thomas name. There was a Peter G. Polhemus in town, who was a real estate and insurance man. There were no fewer than twenty-two people in New Brunswick with the surname Thomas, with occupations varying from dressmaker to janitor. Among them too was an engineer named William Thomas, as well as two Robert L.'s, one of them giving his occupation as engineer, the other as bicycle repairer. Probably Peter G. Polhemus allied himself with one of these Thomases in this automotive venture which obviously never got off the ground.

POL-WEIR — Pol-Weir was to be the name of the car resulting from the partnership of Max N. Weir, a designing engineer, and Howard Foster of the Foster Engineering Company of Newark, New Jersey. In March 1907 *The Motor Way* reported rumors that "within a short time a large automobile plant will be in the course of construction" for manufacture of the Pol-Weir car. Further word of this venture was not heard.

POMEROY — Brooklyn, New York — (1902) — An advertisement from March of 1902 indicates that B.H. Pomeroy of the Pomeroy Manufacturing Company initially chose to refer to his new car as the Keromobile. By July, however, when he incorporated his Pomeroy Motor Vehicle Company for $120,000 (its address was the same, 249 Willoughby Street in Brooklyn), he decided his car should bear his name. The Pomeroy was powered by a two-cylinder two-stroke 8 hp engine that weighed 85 pounds and used kerosene for fuel. Starting the vehicle was accomplished by the raise of a handle on the floorboards. A thousand miles on ten gallons of

1902 Pomeroy, runabout, NAHC

kerosene was claimed. "Kerosene contains a much larger number of calories than gasoline," Pomeroy advertised. "consequently it develops more force, has a greater explosive power . . . It is obvious, then, that kerosene ought to be chosen in preference to gasoline, isn't it?" Obviously, it wasn't. B.H. Pomeroy's automobile did not survive 1902. Interestingly, the Pomeroy has frequently been cited as an electric automobile. B.H. Pomeroy did mention on one occasion that his running gear was adaptable to an electric, but it does not appear that he himself ever marketed one. All his Pomeroys used the kerosene engine.

1902 POMEROY

	FP	5	4	3	2	1
Pomeroy Runabout-2P	650	1800	2800	4000	6200	13,000
Pomeroy Surrey-6P	800	2000	3000	4200	6500	14,000
Pomeroy Covered Del. Wagon	800	2100	3100	4300	6800	14,500
Pomeroy Family Combination (runabout/surrey/delivery)	1000	2200	3200	4400	7000	15,000

1924 Pomeroy, 7-pass. sedan, JAC

POMEROY — Cleveland, Ohio — (1920-1922) — Buffalo, New York — (1923-1924) — The car was the idea of the Aluminum Company of America (later Alcoa), which set up the subsidiary Aluminum Manufacturers, Inc. for its development in 1919. The project was conducted in the utmost secrecy. The Pomeroy was named for its designer Lawrence H. Pomeroy, who was renowned in England as the man responsible for the Prince Henry Vauxhall and the Double-Six Daimler. He arrived in Cleveland in 1921 to supervise its building, where he was assisted by Forrest Cameron, designer of the Cameron. Several hundred thousand dollars was reportedly spent in experimental work, and six cars were built in Cleveland. The engines were fours, the wheelbase was 126 inches, the body style was a five-passenger touring — and approximately eighty-five percent of everything in the Pomeroy was, not surprisingly, aluminum. The cars were extensively tested, and were revealed to the public in April of 1922. Marketing did not follow, however. Instead the scene shifted the following year to Buffalo, New York and the factory of the Pierce-Arrow Motor Car Company. There a six-cylinder 75 hp aluminum engine (similar to the Pierce-Arrow 80) was developed and placed in a long 133-inch wheelbase chassis. Again, marketing did not follow. The Aluminum Company of America was not prepared for automobile manufacture, and it has been said that American automobile manufacturers were reluctant to produce an aluminum car simply because one company in the United States at the time had a practical monopoly on the alloy. Doubtless memories of the Selden Patent attempt at monopoly in the American automobile industry still remained fresh in mind.

POND — Worcester, Massachusetts — (1905) — In December of 1905, the L.W. Pond Machine & Foundry Company of Worcester announced to the trade press that its entire plant was to be turned over to the manufacture of commercial and passenger automobiles. A pilot model was scheduled to be completed in two months, and it may well have been — but thereafter the Pond company elected to become an automobile agency instead dealing in Ford, Premier and Reo cars. The obituary of M. Thomas O'Leary, who had joined the Pond company in 1894 and who thereafter rose through the ranks to become general manager and president noted that he was a pioneer in the automobile business in Worcester, but as a dealer only. He was also related by marriage to the manager of the Boston Red Sox, and regularly joined the team for its spring training sessions. O'Leary died in 1919 at the age of sixty-two.

PONDER — The Ponder of 1923 was successor to the Bour-Davis. A Continental-engined six on the same 126-inch wheelbase as the Bour-Davis, it was produced as a prototype only. Refer to Bour-Davis.

PONTIAC — Various automobile rosters have included a flurry of cars called Pontiac which were never built at all. They are the following:

The Pontiac Body Company of Pontiac, Michigan manufactured bodies only according to its annual report of 1905 and numerous advertisements in the trade press.

The Pontiac Buggy Company of Pontiac, Michigan announced its entry into automotive ranks in 1907. By the time its car arrived on the market, Pontiac Buggy had evolved into the Oakland Motor Car Company. The car carried the name Oakland as well, which had been the tradename for the company's carriages. Not until two decades later did Oakland — as a division of General Motors — introduce its first Pontiac.

The Pontiac Motor Car Company of Pontiac, Illinois was an agency for Ford, but never manufactured any automobile itself.

The Pontiac Motor Car Company was organized in Pontiac, Michigan during the fall of 1913 with a capital stock of $25,000 for the manufacture of automobiles and engines. Incorporators were F.J. Smith, W.H. Jenkins and H.E. Torrance. Manufacture did not follow.

The Pontiac Wheel Company of Pontiac, Michigan, according to its annual report of 1911, was engaged in "the manufacture and sale of wood vehicle wheels." There is no evidence of a car having been built.

PONTIAC — Pontiac, Michigan — (1906) — Martin Halfpenny was the man behind this Pontiac, and in late 1904 he incorporated his Pontiac Motor Company with a capital stock of $25,000 in Pontiac, Michigan. Nothing further was heard from him for the next year. In January 1906, however, by which time he had revised his company's designation to Pontiac Motor Car Company, Halfpenny announced that he had leased a cider mill in town and intended to begin building two-cylinder commercial cars and combination commercial/pleasure cars there. That May he completed the prototype of his car which, *The Motor Way* reported, was being "tested on the roads near the factory." Though Halfpenny declared "entire satisfaction" with the car's performance, there is no evidence that manufacture ever began.

1908 Pontiac, runabout, OCW

PONTIAC — Pontiac, Michigan — (1907-1908) — The Pontiac Spring and Wagon Works was incorporated in July of 1899 by Albert G. North and Harry G. Hamilton. By 1905 they had taken over manufacture of the Rapid truck which had been introduced by Max Grabowsky in Detroit two years earlier. And in 1907 they decided to produce an automobile too. The new Pontiac, which was introduced that fall, was a highwheeler weighing a thousand pounds and powered by a two-cylinder water-cooled 12 hp engine. The prototype was displayed in October at an exhibition sponsored by the Carriage Dealers' Association in New York City's Grand Central Palace. In December several of the new Pontiacs were exhibited at the Chicago Automobile Show. Well received by the press, the car featured final drive by double chain and a friction transmission. The wheelbase was 70 inches, front wheels 38, with 40's in the rear, and solid tires all-around. The first deliveries were probably made in early 1908, but after about thirty to forty units were dispatched to new owners, "The Car That's Built to Get There," as the slogan put it, went no further. By November of 1908 North and Hamilton sold out to the Motorcar Company of Detroit, which now moved to Pontiac to build the Cartercar. With the purchase arrange-

ment, the two partners received Cartercar stock. Selling out was probably a wise decision on their part, since the Cartercar proved considerably more successful than the Pontiac ever could have hoped to have been.

1908 PONTIAC
Pontiac — 2-cyl., 12 hp, 70" wb

	FP	5	4	3	2	1
High Wheel Runabout	600	1800	2800	4000	6200	13,000
Model D No. 8 Salesmen's Car	650	1900	2900	4100	6400	13,500

PONTIAC — Pontiac, Michigan — (1915) — This Pontiac was available only as a chassis of 106-inch wheelbase fitted with a three-speed selective transmission and powered by a four-cylinder 25 hp Perkins engine. The Pontiac Chassis Company was organized early in 1915 and soon thereafter acquired the former Flanders Manufacturing Company plant in Pontiac. Its founders were R.A. Palmer (the former general manager for Cartercar) and H.H. Brooks (the former sales manager for Marathon). By September of 1915, Brooks had disposed of his interest in the venture, however, to devote all energy to the Herff-Brooks car. About a year later, Palmer established Olympian Motors Company, absorbing Pontiac Chassis Company, for the production of a new automobile called the Olympian — which was made available with the body and tires that had never been provided the Pontiac. Manufacture of the Pontiac chassis was discontinued soon after that. Reportedly, Pontiac had built the chassis for Charles Duryea's GEM as well.

PONTIAC

PONTIAC — Pontiac, Michigan — (1926-1942 et. seq.) — In January 1926 the new car was given its official debut at the New York Automobile Show, followed by a sales meeting at the Commodore. The hotel was renamed the "Wigwam" for the day, the conference designated the "Pow Wow" and "Heap Big Eats" being served for lunch. The car named for an Indian chief, the salesmen of the Oakland Motor Car Company believed, was sure to bring plenty of "wampum" into their dealerships. The Pontiac had arrived. It would become a unique car in General Motors history: the only one ever to establish a maiden year sales record (bettering the Chrysler mark of 1924, though overtaken in 1927 by the new Graham-Paige), and it was the only companion car in the GM lineup ever to eclipse its parent. The Pontiac's genesis dated back to the early Twenties when George Hannum was Oakland's general manager and toyed with a low-priced idea car code named "Relot." Alfred P. Sloan liked the concept and set experimental engineers Ormond E. Hunt and Henry M. Crane onto it. Ultimately the idea — Chevrolet chassis with six-cylinder engine — was transferred to Chevrolet for final development. By the mid-Twenties, Hannum had been booted out of Oakland, but the car came back to be produced there in order to give a shot in the arm to flagging Oakland sales. Alfred Glancy, a congenially feisty Irishman who for about a dozen years had been what he called "a sort of business doctor for General Motors and the DuPonts," was Oakland's general manager now. As chief engineer, Glancy hired Ben Anibal, who brought with him Fenn Holden, Hermann Schwarze and Roy Milner. These "Four Horsemen," as they were known, had been together for fifteen years already, a decade with Cadillac, a shorter tenure at Peerless — and they readied the production Pontiac. Its name was a natural: the Pontiac Buggy Company had been genesis of the Oakland automobile, and naming this new car from Oakland after the Indian chief made selection of a mascot *fait accompli*. When the pilot model was completed, Glancy invited Oakland executives and area dealers to an official christening during which he broke what he called "the only bottle of champagne in Oakland County" — this was Prohibition, of course — over the Indian head hood ornament, and the Pontiac was on its way, first to New York for the automobile show, then to sales of 76,696 cars its first year. All of them were closed models, incidentally, this directive from Alfred Sloan himself, and probably because he had been embarrassed a few years earlier when Hudson scooped GM in introducing the low-priced Essex coach. There was nothing really remarkable about the new Pontiac; its chassis was completely conventional; its L-head six-cylinder engine had a biggish bore (3.25 inches), the shortest stroke (3.75) thus far in a standard American production car; its displacement was a quite large 185 cubic inches, with 40 hp developed at a rather lazy 2400 rpm. Only "moderate speed operation" was claimed for the Pontiac which, the Oakland company said, had been "designed specifically to dominate the field of low-priced sixes." And so it did, with a price of $825 for coach or coupe; only the Essex Six was cheaper, and that car at the time boasted only 145 cubic inches and was suffering reliability problems. A sprightly sport roadster and cabriolet were added to the Pontiac line for 1927, and the 100,000th car was produced in March that year. Four wheel brakes were a 1928 addition, replaced in '29 by a new and bigger L-head six-cylinder engine (200 cubic inches developing 57 hp at 3000 rpm), self-energizing brakes, Hotchkiss drive, and a brand-new styling look courtesy of W. Everett Miller, former designer for Murphy, which was a pleasing combination of Oakland, LaSalle and Oldsmobile. The 500,000th Pontiac was built in June 1929, the stock market crashed that October. Probably of all members of the GM family, it was the people behind the Pontiac who were the most overwhelmed by the Great Depression. From meteoric success, Pontiac fortunes plunged toward dispair. Glancy left in 1930 to serve the government in a number of Depression-created public positions, and former Olds president Irving J. Reuter took over the Oakland company. Although there was some corporate level discussion about discontinuing both the Oakland and the Pontiac, the decision was quickly made to kill only the more expensive car. There was no new Oakland at the automobile show in January 1932, and that summer official word came that the name was now Pontiac Motor Company. Joining the Pontiac line of sixes for '32 had been a new V-8 developed from the unit which had previously powered the Oakland. An expensive engine to produce, it was destined for only a single year's run by Pontiac. In January 1933 Pontiac went straight-eight across the board, offering 223.4 cubic inches, 77 hp, an actual 78 mph — and at price tags beginning at $635. "The Big Straight Eight in the Low Price Field," Pontiac advertised; "overbuilt to preserve traditional

1175

Pontiac stamina," *Automobile Topics* said; *Automobile Trade Journal* commented on the "striking new streamlined bodies," courtesy this time of another former Murphy designer, Frank Q. Hershey. In 1934 Pontiacs were provided Knee-Action, and the Pontiac company was given the services of Harry Klingler, the super salesman who had helped to make Chevrolet number one in the industry and who now took over as Pontiac's general manager. During 1935, from the nadir of 42,633 cars in '32, Pontiac production rose to more than 175,000. Reintroduced that year was a six, announced during automobile show week in a deluxe version only slightly less expensive than the eight, with a standard model following a month later which brought Pontiac closer to the lowest-priced field than ever it had been before. Now there were Pontiacs for just about anybody who could afford any car at all. No-draft ventilation and Turret Top bodies also arrived for '35, as did the Silver Streak styling motif (Frank Hershey's idea) which would distinguish Pontiacs from other cars on the road for years thereafter. Arguing with success seldom being a particularly good idea, Klingler didn't in '36, with Pontiacs merely refined in detail and sales rising above 178,000. But for '37 he decided to splurge with heftier engines (the six now 223 cubic inches for 85 hp, the eight 249 for an even 100) installed in chassis five inches longer (117 for the six, 122 for the eight). Pontiac had its best year thus far in '37: 235,322 cars. Together with the rest of the industry, company production ebbed appreciably during the 1938 recession year, but by 1940 had risen to a new high of 249,303. The Torpedo was introduced that year, followed in '41 by Harry Klingler's decision to go Torpedo all the way, with eleven different body styles (designed by Bob Lauer and Joe Schemansky under the direction of Vincent Kaptur) and including fastback Streamliners that caught the public fancy immediately. Nineteen forty-one brought another Pontiac production high — 282,087 cars — and fifth place in the industry. What Harry Klingler had accomplished at Pontiac was nothing short of phenomenal. But then Klingler was a phenomenon. During 1941 he began production in Pontiac of Oerlikon anti-aircraft cannon. One month after Pearl Harbor, the Pontiac Motor Car Company became the first in the industry to receive a Navy "E." Conversion to total war production followed on February 10th, 1942. For the six years preceding, Pontiac motorcars had been advertised as "built to last 100,000 miles." Many of them on the road in '42 would do far more than that during the car-starved war and early postwar years.

Pontiac Data Compilation
by John A. Gunnell

1926

1926 Pontiac, landau coupe, CP

PONTIAC — SERIES 6-27 — SIX: Fisher bodies with double beading, plate glass windows, V.V. windshield and automatic windshield wipers. Coupe has landau bars on roof and safety lock on right-hand door. Coach has foot rest, carpeting and dome lamp. Triple-steppe front fenders on both models. Drum style headlamps and wraparound type sunvisors. Honeycomb radiator with Indian head mascot. Cowl lamps standard. Coupe finished in light Sage Green with Faerie Red striping. Coach finished in Arizona Grey. Black fenders on both.

I.D. DATA: Car number stamped on brass plate on rear frame crossmember. Starting: P-1. Ending: 84262-27. Engine number on block above water pump. All cars built in Ponitac, Mich.

Model No.	Body Type & Seating	Price	Weight	Prod. Total
6650	2-dr. Coach-5P	825	2335	Note 1
6640	2-dr. Cpe.-2P	825	2270	Note 1

Note 1: Body style breakouts not available. About 42,000 early 1926 models believed built.
Note 2: 204,553 of these cars built between 12/28/25 and 10/31/27.

ENGINE: L-head. Inline. (split-head). Sixl. Cast iron block. B & S: 3-1/4 x 3-3/4 in. Disp: 186.5 cu. in. C.R.: 4.8:1. Brake H.P.: 40 @ 2400 R.P.M. NACC H.P. 25.35. Main bearings: Three. Valve lifters: Solid. Carb.: Carter 1V.

CHASSIS: W.B.: 110 in. O.L.: 151-1/4 in. Frt./Rear tread: 56/56 in. Tires: 29 x 4.75.

TECHNICAL: Manual transmission. Speeds: 3F/1R. Floor shift controls. Ventilated single dry disc clutch. Shaft drive. Semi-floating rear axle. Overall ratio: 4.18:1. Mechanical brakes on two (rear) wheels. Wood-spoke wheels. Rim size: 20 in.

OPTIONS: Front bumper. Rear fender guards. Heater. Special colors. Rear mount spare tire (spare rim standard).

HISTORICAL: Introduced 1/3/26. First Pontiac. Built by Oakland as a small "companion" car. First series 6-27 models were built 12/28/25 through 2/27. A total of 76,742 cars were sold in the nameplate's first 12 months.

1926 Pontiac, landau sedan, CG

1926
Model 6-26, 6-cyl.

	FP	5	4	3	2	1
Cpe	825	950	2100	4750	6650	9500
2 dr Sed	825	825	1600	4000	5600	8000

1926½

PONTIAC — SERIES 6-27 — SIX: The 1926-1/2 Pontiacs, built after Aug. 1926, were sold as early 1927 models. They had some small changes from the original 1926 models. A Landau Sedan was introduced at this time. It had a leather covered top with dummy landau bars. The coupe and coach could now be had in other colors and with different color striping. In Oct. 1926 a 3/4-ton Pontiac Deluxe Delivery truck was added. In Nov. 1926, Deluxe versions of the coupe and Landau Sedan were introduced. They had nickel plated bumpers and fender guards, mohair upholstery and a foot operated headlight dimmer switch. A new type of sun visor with exposed brackets was first seen on these Deluxe cars.

I.D. DATA: Car number stamped on brass plate on rear frame cross-member. Starting: 41716-25. Engine numbers on block above water pump. All cars built in Pontiac, Mich.

Model No.	Body Type & Seating	Price	Weight	Prod. Total
6650	2-dr. Coach-5P	825	2335	Note 1
6640	2-dr. Cpe.-2P	825	2270	Note 1
7160	4-dr. Lan. Sed.-5P	895	2455	Note 1
7160D	4-dr. Del. Lan. Sed.-5P	975	2565	Note 1
6640D	2-dr. Del. Cpe.-2/4P	895	2380	Note 1

Note 1: Body style breakouts are not available. Approximately 34,700 cars were built.

ENGINE: L-head. Inline. (split-head). Six. Cast iron block. B & S: 3-1/4 x 3-3/4 in. Disp.: 186.5 cu. in. C.R.: 4.8:1. Brake H.P.: 40 @ 2400 R.P.M. N.A.C.C. H.P.: 25.35. Main bearings: Three. Valve lifters: Solid. Carb.: Carter 1V.

CHASSIS: W.B.: 110 in. O.L.: 151-1/4 in. Frt./Rear Tread: 56/56 in. Tires: 29 x 4.75.

TECHNICAL: Manual transmission. Speeds: 3F/1R. Floor shift controls. Ventilated single dry disc clutch. Shaft drive. Semi-floating rear axle. Overall ratio: 4.18:1. Mechanical brakes on two (rear) wheels. Wood-spoke wheels. Rim size: 20 in.

OPTIONS: Front bumper (std. on Deluxe). Rear fender guards (std. on Deluxe). Heater. Rear mounted spare tire (spare rim standard).

HISTORICAL: Introduced Aug. 1926. New colors: coupe in blue with red stripe; coach in blue or grey with orange stripe; Landau Sedan in green with red stripe. Deluxe models finished in Peter Pan Blue with matching fenders. Company president is A.R. Glancy. For more information on Deluxe delivery truck see Krause Publications' *Complete Encyclopedia of Commercial Vehicles.*

1927

NEW-FINER — SERIES 6-27 — SIX: These were Pontiac's true 1927 models which were built and sold from Jan. 1927 to July 1927. Smooth, full-crown front fenders were introduced. Flat sun visors with exposed sides were used on all models. A Sport Roadster with a Stewart body was introduced. The Deluxe Coupe was replaced by a Sport Cabriolet (closed coupe) with rumbleseat.

1927 Pontiac, landau sedan, OCW

I.D. DATA: Car number stamped on a brass plate on rear frame cross-member. Starting numbers continued from 1926-1/2 series. Ending: 144999 (approximate). Engine number on block above water pump. All cars built in Pontiac, Mich.

Model No.	Body Type & Seating	Price	Weight	Prod. Total
Road	2-dr. Spt. Rds.-2/4P	775	2160	Note 1
7430	2-dr. Cpe.-2P	775	2270	Note 1
7460	2-dr. Spt. Cabr.-2/4P	835	2401	Note 1
7440	2-dr. Coach-5P	775	2335	Note 1
7450	2-dr. Lan. Sed.-5P	895	2455	Note 1
7450D	4-dr. Del. Lan. Sed.-5P	975	2565	Note 1

Note 1: Body style breakouts not available. Approximately 68,300 cars were built.

ENGINE: L-head. Inline (split-head) Six. Cast iron block. B & S: 3-1/4 x 3-3/4 in. Disp.: 186.5 cu. in. C.R.: 4.8:1. Brake H.P.: 40 @ 2400 R.P.M. N.A.C.C. H.P.: 25.35. Main bearings: Three. Valve lifters: Solid. Carb.: Carter 1V.

CHASSIS: W.B.: 110 in. O.L.: 151-1/4 in. Frt./Rear Tread: 56/ 56 in. Tires: 29 x 4.75.

TECHNICAL: Manual transmission. Speeds: 3F/1R. Floor shift controls. Improved type ventilated single dry disc clutch. Shaft drive. Semi-floating rear axle. Overall ratio: 4.18:1. Mechanical brakes on two (rear) wheels. Wood-spoked wheels. Rim size: 20 in.

OPTIONS: Front bumper (std. Deluxe). Rear fender guards (std. Deluxe). Single sidemount tires on Sport models only. Heater.

HISTORICAL: Introduced Jan. 1927. New body styles include first open Pontiac. Improved clutch. Larger cooling system capacity. Foot operated tilt-beam headlights standard. President of Pontiac is A.R. Glancy.

1927
Model 6-27, 6-cyl.

	FP	5	4	3	2	1
Spt Rds	775	1250	3900	6500	9100	13,000
Spt Cabr	835	1300	4050	6750	9450	13,500
Cpe	775	800	1550	3900	5450	7800
DeL Cpe	895	825	1600	4000	5600	8000
2 dr Sed	775	750	1450	3300	4900	7000
Lan Sed	975	900	1800	4400	6150	8800

1927½

PONTIAC — NEW-FINER — SERIES 6-27 — SIX: The 1927-1/2 Pontiacs were virtually identical to the true 1927 models, but were sold as 1928 models. The only changes in these cars was the use of a smaller (11-gallon) gas tank plus a few new exterior paint colors. They had lower prices and slight adjustments in shipping weight.

I.D. DATA: Serial numbers were on the right side of the rear frame cross-member or on the frame under the left front fender. Starting: 145000-27. Ending: 204000-27. Motor numbers were on the left side of the crankcase or near the left front corner of the block. Starting: P156250. Ending: P220000 (approximate). All cars built in Pontiac, Mich.

Model No.	Body Type & Seating	Price	Weight	Prod. Total
ROAD	2-dr. R/S Rds.-2/4P	745	2160	Note 1
7430	2-dr. Cpe.-2P	745	2275	Note 1
7460	2-dr. R/S Cabr.-2/4P	795	2345	Note 1
7440	2-dr. Sed.-5P	745	2275	Note 1
7450D	4-dr. Del. Sed.-5P	925	2510	Note 1
7450	4-dr. Lan. Sed.-5P	845	2460	Note 1

Note 1: Body style breakouts not available. Approximately 59,000 cars were built from July-Oct. 1927.

ENGINE: L-head. Inline (split-head) Six. Cast iron block. B & S: 3-1/4 x 3-3/4 in. Disp.: 186.5 cu. in. C.R.: 4.8:1. Brake H.P. 40 @ 2400 R.P.M. N.A.C.C. H.P. 25.35. Main bearings: Three. Valve lifters: Solid. Carb.: Carter 1V.

CHASSIS: W.B.: 110 in. O.L.: 151-1/4 inches. Frt./Rear Tread: 56/56 in. Tires: 29 x 4.75.

TECHNICAL: Manual transmission. Speeds: 3F/1R. Floor shift controls. Improved type ventilated dry disc clutch. Shaft drive. Semi-floating rear axle. Overall ratio: 4.18:1. Mechanical brakes on two (rear) wheels. Wood-spoked wheels. Rim size: 20 in.

OPTIONS: Front bumper (std. Deluxe). Rear fender guards (std. Deluxe). Single sidemounts on Sport models only. Heater.

HISTORICAL: Introduced July 1927. Interchangeable bronze backed bearings. Automatic spark control. Indirectly lighted dashboard. Last Pontiacs to use vacuum tank. A.R. Glancy was president of Oakland.

1928

1928 Pontiac, coupe, OCW

PONTIAC — NEW SERIES 6-28 — SIX: The true 1928 Pontiacs had a higher, deeper, narrower radiator shell and lower, more sweeping body lines. A cross-flow radiator was introduced. There was a new, raised panel along the top of the hood. Deep crowned front fenders with beaded edges were used. The Deluxe Landau Sedan was renamed the Sport Sedan. A 4-door Sport Phaeton with a Stewart body was introduced. Many technical changes were seen in the engine, drivetrain and running gear. The Indian chief on the hood became an Indian brave. New headlights were used. The Sport Cabriolet was now called Sport Coupe.

I.D. DATA: Serial numbers were on the right side of the rear frame cross-member or on the frame under the left front fender. Starting: 204001-28. Ending: 334005-28. Motor numbers were on the left side of the crank case or near the left front corner of the block. Starting: P220001. Ending: P376340 (approximate). All cars built in Pontiac, Mich.

Model No.	Body Type & Seating	Price	Weight	Prod. Total
Rds.	2-dr. R/S Rds.-2/4P	745	2270	Note 1
Phae.	4-dr. Spt. Phae.-5P	775	2390	Note 1
8250	2-dr. Cpe.-2P	745	2435	Note 1
8260	2-dr. Spt. Cpe.-4P	795	2455	Note 1
8240	2-dr. Sed.-5P	745	2520	Note 1
8820	4-dr. Sed.-5P	825	2595	Note 1
8230	4-dr. Spt. Sed.-5P	875	2640	Note 1

Note 1: Body style breakouts not available. Approximately 130,000 cars were built.

ENGINE: L-head. Inline. (GMR cylinder head) Six. Cast iron block. B & S: 3-1/4 x 3-3/4. Disp.: 186.5 cu. in. C.R.: 4.9:1. N.A.C.C. H.P.: 25.3. Main bearings: Three. Valve lifters: Solid. Carb.: Carter 1V.

CHASSIS: W.B.: 110 in. Tires: 29 x 5.00.

1928 Pontiac rumble-seat roadster, JAC

TECHNICAL: Manual transmission. Speeds: 3F/1R. Floor shift controls. New dry disc clutch. Shaft drive (torque tube). Semi-floating rear axle. Overall ratio: 4.18:1. Four-wheel mechanical brakes. 12-spoke wood artillery wheels.

OPTIONS: Front bumper (std. on Deluxe). Rear bumper (std. on Deluxe). Single sidemount. Heater. Disc wheels. Wind wings (open cars).

HISTORICAL: Introduced Jan. 1928. New Carter updraft carburetor. Larger intake manifold. New Oakland type muffler. Improved steering gear. New frame and front axle. Blossom coincidental ignition lock. New thermostat, steering wheel and dash-mounted gas gauge. New "Daylight" factory opens in Pontiac, Mich. Higher compression GMR cylinder head. Internal front wheel brakes. AC fuel filter and fuel pump. A.R. Glancy remained president of Oakland.

1928 Pontiac, 4-dr. sedan, CP

1928
Model 6-28, 6-cyl.

	FP	5	4	3	2	1
Rds	745	1750	4800	8000	11,200	16,000
Cabr	795	1550	4500	7500	10,500	15,000
Phae	825	1550	4500	7500	10,500	15,000
2 dr Sed	745	500	1100	1900	3500	5000
Sed	875	650	1250	2400	4200	6000
Trs	875	650	1250	2400	4200	6000
Cpe	745	750	1450	3300	4900	7000
Spt Cpe	795	825	1600	4000	5600	8000
Lan Sed	875	875	1700	4250	5900	8500

1928½

1928½ Pontiac, coupe, CP

PONTIAC — NEW SERIES 6-28 — SIX: New Series 6-28 Pontiacs built after June 1928 were sold as 1929 models. They were identical to the true 1928 models except for minor technical alterations. A Marvel carburetor, heavier 10-spoke Jaxon wood-spoke artillery wheels and a new rear axle ratio were the major changes. An increase in horsepower was noted on specifications sheets.

I.D. DATA: Serial numbers were on the rear frame cross-member or under the left front fender. Starting: 334006. Ending: 410100. Engine numbers were on left side of crankcase or near left front corner of block. Starting: P376341. Ending: P461000 (approx.) All cars built at Pontiac, Mich.

Model No.	Body Type & Seating	Price	Weight	Prod. Total
ROAD	2-dr. R/S Rds.-2/4P	745	2270	Note 1
PHAE	4-dr. Phae.-5P	775	2390	Note 1
8250	2-dr. Cpe.-2P	745	2435	Note 1
8260	2-dr. Spt Cpe.-2/4P	795	2455	Note 1
8240	2-dr. Sed.-5P	745	2520	Note 1
8820	4-dr. Sed.-5P	825	2595	Note 1
8230	4-dr. Spt Sed.-5P	875	2640	Note 1

Note 1: Body style breakouts not available. Approximately 80,000 series 6-28 Pontiacs were sold as 1929 models.

ENGINE: L-head. Inline. Six. Cast iron block. B & S: 3-1/4 x 3-3/4 in. Disp.: 186.5 cu. in. C.R.: 4.9:1. Brake H.P. 48 @ 2850 R.P.M. NACC H.P. 25.35. Main bearings: Three. Valve lifters: Solid. Carb. Marvel 1V.

CHASSIS: W.B.: 110 in. Tires: 29 x 5.00.

TECHNICAL: Manual transmission. Speeds: 3F/1R. Floor shift controls. Dry disc clutch. Shaft drive (Torque tube). Semi-floating rear axle. Overall ratio: 4.36:1. Four-wheel mechanical brakes. Jaxon 10-spoke wood artillery.

OPTIONS: Front bumper (std. Deluxe). Rear bumper (std. Deluxe). Single sidemount. Heater. Disc wheels. Wind wings (open cars).

HISTORICAL: Introduced June, 1928. First year with Marvel carburetor. New, heavier wheels. Instruments grouped in metal case in center. A.R. Glancy was president of Oakland.

1929

1929 Pontiac, sedan (with Richard Dix), JAC

PONTIAC — NEW-BIG SIX — SERIES 6-29 — SIX: The true 1929 Pontiacs had new styling derived from the British Vauxhall. The radiator grille had a vertical center divider. A corrugated apron covered the gas tank in the rear. Larger, bullet-shaped headlights were seen. Wider hood sills and more deeply crowned fenders were used. The bodies gained a handsome, concave belt molding. From January to April, a handsome hood with horizontal louvers was employed. Because of heat warpage problems, a vertically louvered hood was used thereafter. Interiors were upgraded. Closed cars had oval rear windows. The new Landaulet featured a collapsible rear roof section. A bigger, more powerful engine was one of many technical changes. Pontiac introduced its first Convertible Cabriolet this year. (Earlier models called Cabriolets were really Sports Coupes). Standard equipment on all models included an automatic windshield wiper, rear view mirror, dash gasoline gauge and combination transmission and ignition lock.

I.D. DATA: Serial numbers were on the right side of rear cross-member or under left front fender. Starting: 410101. Ending: 530874. Engine numbers were on the left side of crankcase or near left front corner of block. Starting: P376341. Ending: P461000 approximate. All cars built in Pontiac, Mich.

Model No.	Body Type & Seating	Price	Weight	Prod. Total
ROAD	2-dr. R/S Rds.-2/4P	775	2342	Note 1
PHAE	4-dr. Phae.-5P	825	2407	Note 1
8950	2-dr. Cpe.-2P	745	2532	Note 1
8960	2-dr. Cabr. Conv.-2/4P	845	2537	Note 1
8940	2-dr. Sed.-5P	745	2595	Note 1
8920	4-dr. Sed.-5P	845	2717	Note 1
8930	4-dr. Lan.'et-5P	895	2702	Note 1

Note 1: Body style breakouts are not available. Approximately 120,000 "New Big Sixes" were made as 1929 models.

ENGINE: L-head. Inline Six. Cast iron block. B & S: 3-5/16 x 3-7/8. Disp.: 200 cu. in. C.R.: 4.9:1. Brake H.P.: 60 @ 3000 R.P.M. NACC H.P.: 26.3. Main bearings: Three. Valve lifters: Solid. Carb.: Marvel 1V.

1929 Pontiac, coupe, CP

CHASSIS: Wheelbase: 110 in. O.L.: 169 in. Tires: 29 x 5.00.

TECHNICAL: Improved manual transmission. Speeds: 3F/1R. Floor shift controls. Dry disc clutch. Hotchkiss drive. Semi-floating axle. Four-wheel mechanical brakes. Wood-spoke wheels.

OPTIONS: Front bumper. Rear bumper. Single sidemounts. Dual sidemount. Leather sidemount cover(s). Heater. Spotlight. Pedestal mirrors. Windwings (open cars). Running lamps. Spare tire cover. Lovejoy shock absorbers.

HISTORICAL: Introduced Jan., 1929. Twenty percent more powerful engine. Counter-weighted crankshaft. Self-energizing brakes. Adjustable front seats. Improved transmission. Larger carburetor. Wider intake manifold. Larger valves with increased lift. First true Pontiac convertible. A.R. Glancy was president of the company.

1929 Pontiac, sedan, CP

1929
Model 6-29A, 6-cyl.

	FP	5	4	3	2	1
Rds	775	2800	5700	9500	13,300	19,000
Phae	825	2300	5400	9000	12,600	18,000
Conv	795	2300	5400	9000	12,600	18,000
Cpe	745	875	1700	4250	5900	8500
2 dr Sed	745	700	1350	2800	4550	6500
4 dr Sed	845	725	1400	3100	4800	6800
Spt Lan Sed	895	975	2300	4950	6900	9900

NOTE: Add 5 percent for horizontal louvers on early year cars.

1929½

PONTIAC — BIG SIX — 6-29A — SIX: This would be the last season for carrying over a mid-year series into the next model year. Pontiacs with serial numbers above 530875-29 were considered 1930 automobiles. There were no specifications changes in these cars, but several models were dropped. Cut from the line were the Convertible Cabriolet and Landaulette Sedan.

I.D. DATA: Serial numbers were on the right side of rear cross-member or under left front fender. Starting: 530875. Ending: 591500. Engine numbers were on the left side of crankcase or near left front corner of block. Starting: 608157. Ending: 673500. All cars built at Pontiac, Mich.

Model No.	Body Type & Seating	Price	Weight	Prod. Total
ROAD	2-dr. R/S Rds.-2/4P	775	2342	Note 1
PHAE	4-dr. Phae.-5P	825	2407	Note 1
8950	2-dr. Cpe.-2P	745	2532	Note 1
8940	2-dr. Sed.-5P	745	2595	Note 1
8920	4-dr. Sed.-5P	845	2717	Note 1

Note 1: Body style breakouts are not available. Approximately 60,625 cars were built in the 6-29A series (Aug. 1929-Oct. 31, 1929).

ENGINE: L-head. Inline. Six. Cast iron block. B & S: 3-5/16 x 3-7/8 in. Disp.: 200 cu. in. C.R.: 4.9:1. Brake H.P. 60 @ 3000 R.P.M. NACC H.P. 26.3. Main bearings: Three. Valve lifters: Solid. Marvel 1V.

CHASSIS: W.B.: 110 in. O.L.: 169 in. Tires: 29 x 5.00.

TECHNICAL: Improved manual transmission. Speeds: 3F/1R. Floor shift controls. Dry disc clutch. Hotchkiss drive. Semi-floating rear axle. Overall ratio: 4.42:1. Four-wheel mechanical brakes. Wood-spoke wheels.

OPTIONS: Front bumper. Rear bumper. Single sidemount. Leather sidemount cover(s). Heater. Spotlight. Pedestal mirrors. Wind wings (open cars). Running lamps. Spare tire cover. Lovejoy shock absorbers.

HISTORICAL: Introduced August 1929. A.R. Glancy continued as president of Oakland.

1930

PONTIAC — BIG SIX — 6-30B — SIX: A sloping windshield characterized the "real" 1930 Pontiac's new looks. Horizontal lines were emphasized by a half-oval belt molding which extended entirely around the car and over the hood to the radiator. The hood had 31 thin, vertical louvers. The vertical cowl feature line was straightened. A host of technical advances were led by improvements to the engine mounting and suspension systems. A

1930 Pontiac, four-door sedan, OCW

Custom Sedan and Sport Coupe were new body styles. Closed cars had oval rear windows again. Plated headlamp buckets were used on Sport and Custom models. Closed models had cadet style sun visors.

I.D. DATA: Serial numbers on right side of rear cross-member or under left front fender. Starting: 591501. Ending: 64900. Engine numbers on left side of crankcase or left front corner of block. Starting: 673501. Ending: 744000 (approx.). All cars built at Pontiac, Mich.

Model No.	Body Type & Seating	Price	Weight	Prod. Total
ROAD	2-dr. Spt. Rds.-2/4P	765	2345	Note 1
PHAE	4-dr. Phae.-5P	795	2410	Note 1
30307	2-dr. Cpe.-2P	745	2518	Note 1
30308	2-dr. Spt. Cpe.-2/4P	825	2590	Note 1
30301	2-dr. Sed.-5P	775	2630	Note 1
30302	4-dr. Sed.-5P	825	2680	Note 1
30309	4-dr. Cust. Sed.-5P	875	2720	Note 1

Note 1: Body style breakouts not available. Series production total was 62,888 cars in 1930 model year.

ENGINE: Inline. L-head. Six. Cast iron block. B & S: 3-5/16 x 3-7/8 in. Disp.: 200 cu. in. C.R.: 4.9:1. Brake H.P. 60 @ 3000 R.P.M. N.A.C.C. H.P. 26.3. Main bearings: Three. Valve lifters: Solid. Marvel 1V.

CHASSIS: W.B.: 110 in. O.L.: 167.63 in. Tires: 29 x 5.00.

1930 Pontiac, sport roadster, HAC

TECHNICAL: Manual transmission. Speeds: 3F/1R. Floor shift controls. Dry disc clutch. Hotchkiss drive. Overall ratio: 4.42:1. Four-wheel mechanical brakes. Wood-spoke wheels. Rim size: 19-inch.

OPTIONS: Front bumper. Rear bumper. Single sidemount. Dual sidemount. Sidemount cover(s). Radio. Heater. Spotlight. Wind wings (open cars). Wire-spoke wheels.

HISTORICAL: Introduced January 1930. Brake drums increased to 12 inches. Metric spark plugs. Four-point, rubber-cushioned engine mounting. Coil lock ignition. Manual gear starter. Ribbing added to base of engine block. Four-wheel hand-brake. Lovejoy shock absorbers standard. Model year production: 62,888. A.R. Glancy was company president.

1930
Model 6-30B, 6-cyl.

	FP	5	4	3	2	1
Spt Rds	765	2800	5700	9500	13,300	19,000
Phae	825	2600	5500	9250	12,950	18,500
Cpe	745	900	1800	4400	6150	8800
Spt Cpe	825	900	1900	4500	6300	9000
2 dr Sed	775	650	1200	2300	4100	5800
4 dr Sed	845	650	1250	2400	4200	6000
Cus Sed	875	825	1600	4000	5600	8000

1931

PONTIAC — FINE SIX — SERIES 401 — SIX: For 1931 Pontiac featured a longer wheelbase and new bodies. A V-shaped chrome plated radiator with a wire grille was used. Headlamps were chrome plated on all models and mounted on a curved tie bar. One-piece full crown fenders carried parking lights on top. Hoods were secured by a single handle lock on each side. The splash apron on the rear extended from fender to fender. Aluminum moldings decorated the molded running board mats. Single-bar bumpers, were considered "standard" at slight extra cost. Wire wheels became standard equipment in mid-year. Technical refinements to the engine and chassis and running gear changes were among technical improvements. A new convertible coupe replaced the roadster and phaeton.

1179

1931 Pontiac, coupe, AA

I.D. DATA: Serial numbers on right side of rear cross-member or under left front fender. Starting: 649001. Ending: 729000. Engine numbers on left side of crankcase or left front corner of block. Starting: 744001. Ending: 835000. All cars built at Pontiac, Mich.

Model No.	Body Type & Seating	Price	Weight	Prod. Total
31307	2-dr. Cpe.-2P	675	2558	Note 1
31308	2-dr. Spt. Cpe.-2/4P	715	2618	Note 1
31318	2-dr. Conv. Cpe.-2/4P	745	2598	Note 1
31301	2-dr. Sed.-5P	675	2653	Note 1
31309	4-dr. Sed.-5P	745	2733	Note 1
31319	4-dr. Cus. Sed.-5P	785	2743	Note 1

Note 1: Body style breakouts not available. Model year production total of Series 401 Pontiacs was 84,708 cars.

ENGINE: L-head. Inline. Six. Cast iron block. B & S: 3-5/16 x 3-7/8 in. Disp.: 200 cu. in. Brake H.P. 60 @ 3000 R.P.M. N.A.C.C. H.P.: 26.3. Main bearings: Three. Valve lifters: Solid. Marvel 1V.

CHASSIS: W.B.: 112 in. Tires: 29 x 5.00.

1931 Pontiac, 4-dr. sedan, JAC

TECHNICAL: Manual transmission. Speeds: 3F/1R. Floor shift controls. Dry disc clutch. Hotchkiss drive. Semi-floating rear axle. Overall ratio: 4.55:1. Four-wheel mechanical brakes. Wire-spoke wheels (Kelsey-Hayes). Rim size: 19 inches.

OPTIONS: Front bumper. Rear bumper. Dual sidemount. Sidemount cover(s). Radio. Heater. Clock. Spotlight. Pedestal mirrors. Trunk rack. Touring trunk. Wood-spoke wheels. Dual windshield wipers. Trippe lights.

HISTORICAL: Introduced January 1931. Steeldraulic brakes. Full-pressure lubrication. New AC intake silencer. Improved engine mounting. Heavier, sturdier frame. Inlox spring bushings. Stronger rear axle with Hyatt roller pinion bearings. Redesigned brake toggles. Last year for Oakland.

1931
Model 401, 6-cyl.

	FP	5	4	3	2	1
Conv	745	2800	5700	9500	13,300	19,000
2P Cpe	675	900	1800	4450	6250	8900
Spt Cpe	715	1000	2400	5000	7000	10,000
2 dr Sed	675	650	1250	2400	4200	6000
Sed	745	675	1300	2500	4350	6200
Cus Sed	785	750	1450	3300	4900	7000

1932

PONTIAC — SERIES 402 — SIX: The Oakland became the Pontiac V-8 in 1932. Pontiac also offered a separate six-cylinder line. The new sixes had a longer wheelbase and longer, roomier bodies. They featured a slanted windshield without an outside sun visor. A new V-shaped radiator with vertical grille bars was used. The sides of the hood had four ventilator doors. Dual horns and front fender lights were standard on Custom models. The six-cylinder hood ornament had an Indian head within a circle.

1932 Pontiac Six, 2-dr. sedan, CP

I.D. DATA: Serial numbers were on the right side of rear cross-member or under left front fender. Starting: 729001. Ending: 763983. Engine numbers on left side of crankcase or near left front corner of block. Starting: 835001. Ending: 879565 (approx.). All cars built in Pontiac, Mich.

Model No.	Body Type & Seating	Price	Weight	Prod. Total
32317	2-dr. Cpe.-2P	635	2689	Note 1
32308	2-dr. Spt. Cpe.-2/4P	715	2734	Note 1
32318	2-dr. Conv. Cpe.-2/4P	765	2694	Note 1
32301	2-dr. Sed.-5P	645	2794	Note 1
32309	4-dr. Sed.-5P	725	2884	Note 1
32319	4-dr. Cus. Sed.-5P	795	2889	Note 1

Note 1: Body style breakouts not available. Total series production was 35,059 units.

ENGINE: L-head. Inline. Six. Cast iron block. B & S: 3-5/16 x 3-7/8 in. Disp.: 200 cu. in. C.R.: 5.1:1. Brake H.P.: 65 @ 3200 R.P.M. N.A.C.C. H.P.: 26.3. Main bearings: Three. Valve lifters: Solid. Marvel 1V.

CHASSIS: W.B.: 114 in. Tires: 18 x 5.25.

TECHNICAL: Synchromesh transmission (Muncie). Speeds: 3F/1R. Floor shift controls. Dry disc clutch. Hotchkiss drive. Semi-floating rear axle. Overall ratio: 4.55:1. Four-wheel mechanical brakes. Kelsey-Hayes wire spoke wheels. Freewheeling standard.

1932 Pontiac, V-8, coupe, OCW

PONTIAC V-8 — SERIES 302 — EIGHT: The 1932 Pontiac V-8s were a continuation of the 1931 Oakland with a new name and updated styling. They used a V-type radiator shell with built-in grille. A slanting windshield was seen. Sun visors were moved from outside to inside. Door type hood ventilators appeared. All models had new radiator emblems, dual horns and front fender lights. A bird with raised wings was the V-8 hood ornament.

I.D. DATA: Serial numbers on right side of rear cross-member or under left front fender. Starting: 310001. Ending: 316282. Engine number on left side of crankcase or near left front corner of block. All cars built in Pontiac, Mich.

Model No.	Body Type & Seating	Price	Weight	Prod. Total
32367	2-dr. Cpe.-2P	845	3069	Note 1
32358	2-dr. Spt. Cpe.-2/4P	925	3129	Note 1
32368	2-dr. Conv. Cpe.-2/4P	945	3089	Note 1
32351	2-dr. Sed.-5P	845	3149	Note 1
32359	4-dr. Sed.-5P	945	3224	Note 1
32369	4-dr. Cus. Sed.-5P	1025	3259	Note 1

Note 1: Body style breakouts not available. Total series production was 6,281 units.

ENGINE: L-head. Vee-block. Eight. Cast iron block. B & S: 3-7/16 x 3-3/8 in. Disp.: 251 cu. in. C.R.: 5.2:1. Brake H.P.: 85 @ 3200 R.P.M. N.A.C.C. H.P.: 37.8. Main bearings: Three. Valve lifters: Solid. Marvel 1V.

CHASSIS: W.B.: 117 in. Tires: 17 x 6.00.

TECHNICAL: Synchromesh transmission (Muncie). Speeds: 3F/1R. Floor shift controls. Dry disc clutch. Hotchkiss drive. Semi-floating rear axle. Overall ratio: 4.22:1. Four-wheel mechanical brakes. Wire spoke wheels.

OPTIONS: Front bumper. Rear bumper. Dual sidemount. Sidemount cover(s) (fabric or metal). Radio. Heater. Clock. Cigar lighter. Radio antenna (under runningboard). Spotlight. Trippe lights. Tandem windshield wipers. Dual horns (std. on Custom). Dual taillights (std. on Custom). Pedestal mirrors. Trunk rack. Touring trunk. Rear view mirror.

1932 Pontiac, V-8, convertible rdstr., JAC

HISTORICAL: Production of six began 12/8/31. Production of V-8 began 12/22/31. Interchangeable steel-backed bearings. Floorboard mounted hand brake. Valve guides with tapered holes. First Pontiac eight and first V-8. Manually operated "Ride Control". Synchromesh transmission with silent second gear. Free wheeling. Smaller tires. Improved cooling. Calendar year registrations: 47,926 cars. Model year production: 41,340 cars.

Irving J. Reuter and F.O. Tanner shared general managership of Oakland Motor Co. In early 1932, Pontiac became part of General Motors Corps.' new B-O-P (Buick-Olds-Pontiac) division. The name Pontiac Motors was adopted around June 1932.

1932
Model 402, 6-cyl.

	FP	5	4	3	2	1
Conv	765	3300	6600	11,000	15,400	22,000
Cpe	635	1025	2600	5250	7300	10,500
RS Cpe	715	1075	3000	5500	7700	11,000
2 dr Sed	645	650	1250	2400	4200	6000
Cus Sed	795	700	1350	2900	4600	6600

Model 302, V-8

	FP	5	4	3	2	1
Conv	945	3750	7500	12,500	17,500	25,000
Cpe	845	1200	3750	6250	8750	12,500
Spt Cpe	925	1300	4050	6750	9450	13,500
2 dr Sed	845	950	2100	4750	6650	9500
4 dr Sed	945	1000	2400	5000	7000	10,000
Cus Sed	1025	1025	2600	5250	7300	10,500

1933

1933 Pontiac, roadster, OCW

PONTIAC — ECONOMY EIGHT — SERIES 601: The 1933 Pontiacs had a new straight eight plus many styling and technical changes. A new Fisher body with beaver tail rear styling was used. There was a slanting, V-type radiator with vertical bars. The hood had four wide, slanting louvers back towards the cowl. Valanced front fenders gave a streamlined look. There was an airplane type instrument panel on the left and glove compartment on the right of the dash. Pontiacs were made in five different assembly plants. The hood ornament was a brave's head in a circle with a round base.

I.D. DATA: Serial numbers were in the previous locations. Pontiac, Mich. numbers: 770001 to 838455. Oakland, Ca. numbers: C3001 to C5678. Atlanta, Ga. numbers: A1001 to A3195. Tarrytown, N.Y. numbers: T1001 to T10,600. St. Louis, Mo. numbers S1001 to S4996. Engine numbers were in the same location. Pontiac, Mich. numbers: 885001 to 987400. (Numbers for other factories not available.)

1933 Pontiac, 4-dr. sedan, JAC

Model No.	Body Type & Seating	Price	Weight	Prod. Total
ROAD	2-dr. Rds.-2/4P	585	2675	Note 1
33317	2-dr. Cpe.-2P	635	2865	Note 1
33328	2-dr. Spt. Cpe.-2/4P	670	2930	Note 1
33318	2-dr. Conv. Cpe.-2/4P	695	2905	Note 1
33301	2-dr. Sed.-5P	635	2945	Note 1
33331	2-dr. Tr. Sed-5P	675	2995	Note 1
33309	4-dr. Sed.-5P	695	3020	Note 1

Note 1: Body style breakouts not available. Series production total: 90,198 units.

ENGINE: Inline. L-head. Eight. Cast iron block. B & S: 3-3/16 x 3-1/2 in. Disp.: 223.4 cu. in. C.R.: 5.7:1. Brake H.P.: 77 @ 3600 R.P.M. N.A.C.C. H.P. 32.52. Main bearings: Five. Valve lifters: Solid. Carb. Carter 1V.

CHASSIS: W.B.: 115 in. O.L.: 181.5 in. Height: 67-3/4 in. Tires: 17 x 5.50.

1933 Pontiac, 2-dr. sedan, JAC

TECHNICAL: Muncie Synchromesh transmission. Speeds: 3F/1R. Floor shift. Single plate clutch. Torque tube drive. Semi-floating rear axle. Overall ratio: 4.44:1. Four-wheel mechanical brakes. K-H 40-spoke wire wheels. Rim Size: 17 x 3.62 in. Freewheeling standard.

OPTIONS: Front bumper. Rear bumper. Dual sidemounts. Sidemount cover(s). Bumper guards. Radio. Heater. Clock. Cigar lighter. Radio antenna (under runningboard). Spotlight. Disc wheels. Jumbo tires. Trunk rack. Touring trunk. Rear tire cover. Mud guards. Rear view mirror.

HISTORICAL: Entered production 12/7/32. Closed production 10/6/33. Individually controlled No-Draft ventilation system. Safety glass in windshield and vent windows. New, stronger frame. Twelve Flxible-Pontiac funeral cars built this year. Roadster reintroduced for one, final season. Model year production: 90,198 units. Late in the year the B-O-P program was dissolved and Harry J. Klinger was appointed Pontiac general manager.

1933
Model 601, 8-cyl.

	FP	5	4	3	2	1
Rds	585	3300	6600	11,000	15,400	22,000
Conv	695	3000	6000	10,000	14,000	20,000
Cpe	635	825	1600	4000	5600	8000
Spt Cpe	670	900	1900	4500	6300	9000
2 dr Sed	635	775	1500	3750	5250	7500
2 dr Tr Sed	675	750	1450	3300	4900	7000
Sed	695	800	1550	3850	5400	7700

NOTE: First year for Pontiac straight 8.
Add 5 percent for sidemount tires for all 1933-1938 Pontiac (rare option).

1934

1934 Pontiac, 4-dr. w/trunk, AA

PONTIAC — SERIES 603 — EIGHT: Larger Fisher bodies were used for 1934. Deep skirted fenders were seen. Longer, bullet-shaped headlamp buckets appeared. The cowl ventilator opened towards the rear. Horizontal grille type hood louvers were new. Hoods were seven inches longer. Cars with standard equipment had hood ornaments with a brave's head in a circle on a teardrop base. Cars with Deluxe equipment had an Indian maiden hood ornament.

I.D. DATA: Serial numbers were in the previous locations. Pontiac, Mich. numbers were 83850 and up. Engine numbers were in the previous locations. Numbers were 987401 and up.

Model No.	Body Type & Seating	Price	Weight	Prod. Total
34317	2-dr. Cpe.-2P	675	3185	Note 1
34328	2-dr. Spt. Cpe.-2/4P	725	3260	Note 1
34318	2-dr. Cabr.-2/4P	765	3225	Note 1
34301	2-dr. Sed.-5P	705	3280	Note 1
34331	2-dr. Tr. Sed.-5P	745	3300	Note 1
34309	4-dr. Sed.-5P	765	3350	Note 1
34319	4-dr. Tr. Sed.-5P	805	3405	Note 1

Note 1: Body style breakouts not available. Series production was 78,859 units.

1934 Pontiac, sport coupe, JAC

ENGINE: L-head. Inline. Eight. Cast iron block. B & S: 3-3/16 x 3-1/2 in. Disp.: 223.4 cu. in. C.R.: 6.2:1. Brake H.P. 84 @ 3800 R.P.M. N.A.C.C. H.P.: 32.51. Main bearings: Five. Valve lifters: Solid. Carb.: Carter 1V.

CHASSIS: W.B.: 117-1/4 in. O.L.: 187-1/4 in. Height: 68-7/16 in. Tires: 17 x 6.00.

TECHNICAL: Synchromesh transmission. Speeds: 3F/1R. Floor shift controls. Single plate clutch. Torque tube drive. Semi-floating rear axle. Overall ratio: 4.55:1. Four-wheel mechanical brakes. Wire-spoke wheels.

OPTIONS: Front bumper. Dual sidemount. Sidemount cover(s). Bumper guards. Radio (Air Chief). Heater. Clock. Cigar Lighter. Radio antenna. Seat covers. Spotlight. Touring trunk. Spare tire cover. Trunk rack. Stand-up sedan trunk. Tripple lights. Supertone horn. Right-hand sun visor. Ash receiver set. Right-hand taillamp. Luggage sets. Twin windshield wipers. License plate frame.

HISTORICAL: Production began Jan. 1, 1934. 1934 Pontiac convertible was Indy 500 "Official Speedway" car. Stock Pontiac hit 93 m.p.h. at Muroc Dry Lake speed trial. "Knee-Action" front suspension introduced. Multi-beam headlights. Roomier bodies. New G.M.R. high-compression head. Gaselector added to distributor. Harry J. Klingler general manager. Gas mileage (in tests): 19-24 m.p.g.

1934 Model 603, 8-cyl.

	FP	5	4	3	2	1
Conv	765	1550	4500	7500	10,500	15,000
Cpe	675	825	1600	4000	5600	8000
Spt Cpe	725	900	1900	4500	6300	9000
2 dr Sed	705	775	1500	3750	5250	7500
2 dr Tr Sed	745	750	1450	3300	4900	7000
Sed	765	800	1550	3850	5400	7700
Tr Sed	805	825	1600	4000	5600	8000

1935

1935 Pontiac, 2-dr. sedan, OCW

PONTIAC — STANDARD — SERIES 701-B — SIX: Pontiacs came in Standard and Deluxe six and Improved eight car-lines this year. The Standard six models had transmissions with non-Synchromesh first gears, solid I-beam front axles and headlamp beam indicators on the instrument dial. They did not have parking lamps on the front fenders. A single taillamp was standard and fenders only came with black finish. The year's new styling featured a waterfall grille and "Silver Streak" trim moldings on the hood. More rounded grille shells and fenders were seen. The hood ornament on sixes was a brave's head in a circle. The headlamps were mounted on pedestals between fenders and grilles.

I.D. DATA: Serial numbers on a plate or right side of frame center of right front wheel. Starting: P6AB-1001. Ending: P6AB-46752. Engine numbers in previous location. Starting Engine No.: 6-1001 and up.

Model No.	Body Type & Seating	Price	Weight	Prod. Total
2107AB	2-dr. Cpe.-2P	615	3065	Note 1
211AB	2-dr. Tr. Sed.-5P	695	3195	Note 1
2101AB	2-dr. Sed.-5P	665	3195	Note 1
2119AB	4-dr. Tr. Sed.-5P	745	3245	Note 1
2109AB	4-dr. Sed.-5P	715	3245	Note 1

Note 1: Body style breakouts not available. Series production: 49,302 units.

ENGINE: L-head. Inline. Six. Cast iron block. B & S: 3-3.8 x 3-7/8 in. Disp.: 208 cu. in. C.R.: Brake H.P. 80 @ 3600 R.P.M. N.A.C.C. H.P.: 27.34. Main bearings: Four. Valve lifters: Solid. Carb.: Carter 1V (manual choke).

CHASSIS: W.B.: 112 in. O.L.: 189 in. Tires: 16 x 6.00.

TECHNICAL: Manual transmission (non-Synchro. 1st) Speeds: 3F/1R. Floor-shift controls. Single plate clutch. Torque tube drive. Semi-floating rear axle. Overall ratio: 4.44:1. Hydraulic brakes. Steel spoke wheels.

1935 Pontiac, 4-dr. sedan, JAC

PONTIAC — DELUXE — SERIES 701-A — SIX: The Deluxe sixes had the same wheelbase and engine as standard models. They had "Knee-Action" front suspension and all-Synchromesh transmissions. Multi-beam headlights were used. Streamlined parking lights sat atop front fenders. Single taillamps were regular equipment but dual taillamps were a common option. Styling changes were the same as standard models had.

I.D. DATA: Serial and engine number locations were the same as on the Standard six models. Starting serial no.: 6AA-100. Ending serial no.: 6AA-32,187. Engine nos.: 6-1001 and up.

Model No.	Body Type & Seating	Price	Weight	Prod. Total
2107AA	2-dr. Cpe.-2P	675	3125	Note 1
2157AA	2-dr. Spt. Cpe.-2/4P	725	3150	Note 1
2167AA	2-dr. Cabr.-2/4P	775	3180	Note 1
2111AA	2-dr. Tr. Sed.-5P	745	3245	Note 1
2101AA	2-dr. Sed.-5P	715	3245	Note 1
2119AA	4-dr. Tr. Sed.-5P	795	3300	Note 1
2109AA	4-dr. Sed.-5P	765	3300	Note 1

Note 1: Body style breakouts not available. Series production: 36,032 units.

ENGINE: L-head. Inline. Six. Cast iron block. B & S: 3-3/8 x 3-7/8 in. Disp.: 208 cu. in. C.R.: 6.2:1. Brake H.P.: 80 @ 3600 R.P.M. N.A.C.C. H.P. 27.34. Main bearings: Four. Valve lifters: Solid. Carb. Carter 1V (manual choke).

CHASSIS: W.B.: 112 in. O.L.: 189 in. Tires: 16 x 6.00.

TECHNICAL: All-Synchromesh. Speeds: 3F/1R. Floor shift controls. Single plate clutch. Torque tubedrive. Semi floating rear axle. Overall ratio: 4.44:1. Hydraulic brakes. Wire-spoke wheels.

PONTIAC — IMPROVED — SERIES 605 — EIGHT: The eight-cylinder Pontiac chassis had a 4-5/8 in. longer wheelbase. While the main body was identical to that used by sixes, the front end sheet metal was longer. Styling changes were the same as on other car-lines. An Indian maiden hood ornament was used. Dual taillights were standard equipment, along with twin windshield wipers and fender safety lamps. "Pontiac Eight" grille badges were used. The rear windows on 4-door sedans and 2-door touring sedans featured ventipanes.

I.D. DATA: Serial and engine number locations were as on Standard Six. Starting serial no.: 8AA-1001. Ending serial no.: 8AA-42561. Engine nos.: 8-1001 and up.

Model No.	Body Type & Seating	Price	Weight	Prod. Total
2007	2-dr. Cpe.-2P	730	3260	Note 1
2057	2-dr. Spt. Cpe.-2/4P	780	3290	Note 1
2067	2-dr. Cabr.-2/4P	840	3305	Note 1
2011	2-dr. Tr. Sed.-5P	805	3400	Note 1
2001	2-dr. Sed.-5P	775	3400	Note 1
2019	4-dr. Tr. Sed.-5P	860	3450	Note 1
2009	4-dr. Sed.-5P	830	3450	Note 1

Note 1: Body style breakouts not available. Series production: 44,134 units.

ENGINE: L-head. Inline. Eight. Cast iron block. B & S: 3-3/16 x 3-1/2 in.. Disp.: 223.4 cu. in. C.R.: 6.2:1. Brake H.P. 84 @ 3800 R.P.M. N.A.C.C. H.P.: 32.51. Main bearings: Five. Valve lifters: Solid. Carb. Carter 1V.

CHASSIS: W.B.: 116-5/8 in. O.L.: 193-5/8 in. Tires: 16 x 6.50.

TECHNICAL: All-Synchromesh. Speeds: 3F/1R. Floor shift controls. Dry plate clutch. Torque tube drive. Semi-floating rear axle. Overall ratio: 4.55:1. Hydraulic brakes. Wire-spoke wheels.

OPTIONS: Anti-freeze (3.15). Right-hand taillamp (3.45). Dual horn kit (12.50). Triplex air cleaner (6.50). Wheel disc (2.30). Five wheel discs (11.25). Five wheel trim rings (8.50). Four bumper guards (3.95). Outdraft heater (7.50). Deluxe heater (12.25). Heater ports pkg. (4.00). Air Chief radio (62.50). Air Mate radio (47.95). Radio antenna pkg. (3.00). Glove box smoker set & watch (13.50). Dash watch (10.00). 30-hr mirror watch (3.95). Safety light (15.95). License frame (2.45). Luggage set (19.75). Rear mat (1.75). Visor vanity mirror (1.00). Right-hand inside visor (2.00). Dual sidemounts (not avail. on std. six).

HISTORICAL: Date of Introduction: Dec. 29, 1934. Innovations: "Suicide" front door hinging. Hydraulic brakes. Micro polished engine bearings. Improved double-drop "KY" frame. Model year production: 129,463 units. Company president: Harry J. Klinger.

1935
Master Series 701, 6-cyl.

	FP	5	4	3	2	1
Cpe	615	825	1600	3950	5500	7900
2 dr Sed	665	700	1350	2700	4500	6400
2 dr Tr Sed	805	700	1350	2800	4550	6500
Sed	715	725	1400	3200	4850	6900
Tr Sed	745	750	1450	3300	4900	7000

DeLuxe Series 701, 6-cyl.

	FP	5	4	3	2	1
Cpe	675	850	1650	4200	5850	8400
Spt Cpe	725	900	1800	4450	6250	8900
Cabr	775	1800	4900	8200	11,500	16,400
2 dr Sed	715	700	1350	2800	4550	6500
2 dr Tr Sed	745	700	1350	2900	4600	6600
Sed	765	725	1400	3000	4700	6700
Tr Sed	795	725	1400	3200	4850	6900

Series 605, 8-cyl.

	FP	5	4	3	2	1
Cpe	730	950	2100	4700	6600	9400
Spt Cpe	780	975	2300	4950	6900	9900
Cabr	840	2100	5250	8700	12,200	17,400
2 dr Sed	775	700	1350	2900	4600	6600
2 dr Tr Sed	805	725	1400	3200	4850	6900
Sed	830	725	1400	3100	4800	6800
Tr Sed	860	725	1400	3200	4850	6900

1936

MASTER — SERIES 6BB — SIX: The 1936 Pontiac had a new, waterfall grille with a thinner shell, fewer "silver streaks" and the outer sections finished in body color. The horizontal hood louvers came to a point at the front this year. Longer, slimmer headlamps were mounted on the sides of the hood. The fenders no longer had "speedlines" sculpted into them. The Master Six could most easily be identified by its solid front axle. It also had a non-locking glove box, taupe mohair or brown pattern broadcloth upholstery and black bakelite door handle and instrument panel hardware. Two door sedans at first came only with bucket front seats, with a bench seat option introduced at mid-year. Standard equipment included Delco-Remy ignition, hydraulic brakes, cross-flow cooling and foot-operated starter buttons. Flush mounted taillights were used on some Master Sixes built early in the model year.

1936 Pontiac, 4-dr. sedan, AA

DELUXE — SERIES 6BA — SIX: The Deluxe Six was virtually identical to the Master Six, except that it had "Knee Action" independent front suspension. Upholstery in closed cars was taupe mohair or modified tweed pattern taupe woolen cloth. Deluxe sixes also had translucent dash knobs and door handle knobs. Additional standard equipment in this series included a larger gas tank, higher capacity 6-volt battery and automatic choke.

DELUXE — SERIES 8BA — EIGHT: The Pontiac Deluxe Eight had the company's longest wheelbase. The extra length was taken up in the hood and runningboards. Fenders varied slightly in the manner in which they overlapped the cowl, but were actually the same with the attachment holes drilled differently. The words "Pontiac 8" appeared on the grille and the hood ornament was a distinctive, circular design instead of the oblong-loop style used on sixes. Standard sedan equipment included front and rear arm rests, twin assist straps, oriental grain interior moldings and a dash mounted clock. The eight had "Knee-Action" front suspension, a pressurized cooling system, automatic choke and a new type of clutch.

I.D. DATA: [Series 6BB] Serial numbers were located on top of frame just ahead of steering gear. Starting: 6BB-1001. Ending: 6BB-91362. Pacific Coast numbers were C-1001 to C-1400. Bench seat cars had an "AB" prefix instead of "BB". Engine numbers located on left side of crankcase and on front left corner of cylinder block. Starting: 6-84001. Ending: 6-219182. [Series 6BA] Serial numbers were in the same location. Starting: 6BA-1001. Ending: 6BA-41352. Pacific coast numbers were C-1001 to C-1300. Engine numbers were in the same location. Starting: 6-84001. Ending: 6-219182. [Series 8BA] Serial numbers were in the same location. Starting: 8BA-1001. Ending: 8BA-38371. Pacific Coast numbers were C-1001 to C-1260. Engine numbers were in the same locations. Starting: 8-44001. Ending: 8-82040.

1936 Pontiac, 2-dr. sedan, HAC

Model No.	Body Type & Seating	Price	Weight	Prod. Total
6BB	2-dr. Cpe.-2P	615	3085	Note 1
6BB	2-dr. Spt. Cpe.-2/4P	675	3120	Note 1
6BB	2-dr. Cabr.-2/4P	760	3125	Note 1
6BB	2-dr. Sed.-5P	675	3195	Note 1
6BB	2-dr. Tr. Sed.-5P	700	3195	Note 1
6BB	4-dr. Sed.-5P	720	3235	Note 1
6BB	4-dr. Tr. Sed.-5P	745	3245	Note 1

Note 1: Series production was 93,475.

Model No.	Body Type & Seating	Price	Weight	Prod. Total
6BA	2-dr. Cpe.-2P	665	3130	Note 1
6BA	2-dr. Spt. Cpe.-2/4P	720	3165	Note 1
6BA	2-dr. Cabr.-2/4P	810	3200	Note 1
6BA	2-dr. Sed.-5P	720	3265	Note 1
6BA	2-dr. Tr. Sed.-5P	745	3270	Note 1
6BA	4-dr. Sed.-5P	770	3300	Note 1
6BA	4-dr. Tr. Sed.-5P	795	3300	Note 1

Note 1: Total series production was 44,040.

Model No.	Body Type & Seating	Price	Weight	Prod. Total
8BA	2-dr. Cpe.-2P	730	3250	Note 1
8BA	2-dr. Spt. Cpe.-2/4P	785	3285	Note 1
8BA	2-dr. Cabr.-2/4P	855	3335	Note 1
8BA	2-dr. Sed.-5P	770	3390	Note 1
8BA	2-dr. Tr. Sed.-5P	795	3390	Note 1
8BA	4-dr. Sed.-5P	815	3415	Note 1
8BA	4-dr. Tr. Sed.-5P	840	3420	Note 1

Note 1: Total series production was 38,755.

ENGINE: [Series 6BB] Inline. L-head. Six. Cast iron block. B & S: 3-3/8 in. x 3-7/8 in. Disp.: 208 cu. in. C.R.: 6.2:1. Brake H.P.: 81 @ 3600 R.P.M. Net H.P.: 27.34. Main bearings: Four. Valve lifters: Solid. Carb.: Carter 1V model 340S. [Series 6BA] Inline. L-head. Six. Cast iron block. B & S: 3-3/8 in. x 3-7/8 in. Disp.: 208 cu. in. C.R.: 6.2:1. Brake H.P.: 81 @ 3600 R.P.M. Net H.P.: 27.34. Main bearings: Four. Valve lifters: Solid. Carb.: Carter 1V model 342S. [Series 8BA] Inline. L-head. Eight. Cast iron block. B & S: 3-1/4 in. x 3-1/2 in. Disp.: 232.3 cu. in. C.R.: 6.5:1. Brake H.P.: 87 @ 3800 R.P.M. Net H.P.: 33.8. Main bearings: Five. Valve lifters: Solid. Carb.: Carter 1V model 322S.

CHASSIS: [Series 6BB] W.B.: 112 in. O.L.: 189-3/4 in. H.: 67-9/16 in. Tires: 16 x 6.00. [Series 6AB] W.B.: 112 in. O.L.: 189-3/4 in. H.: 67-9/16 in. Tires: 16 x 6.00. [Series 8AB] W.B.: 116-5/8 in. O.L.: 194-5/16 in. H.: 67-9/16 in. Tires: 16 x 6.50.

TECHNICAL: Manual synchromesh transmission. Speeds: 3F/1R. Floor mounted controls. Ventilated dry disc clutch. Semi-floating rear axle. Overall Ratio: (std.) 4.55:1; (mountain) 4.85:1; (plains) 4.11:1. Four-wheel hydraulic brakes. Steel spoke wheels.

OPTIONS: Front bumper. Rear bumper. Dual sidemount. Sidemount cover(s). Fender skirts. Bumper guards (set of 4/$3.95). Air Chief Radio (62.50). Air Mate Radio (47.95). Outdraft heater (7.50). Deluxe heater (12.25). Clock (10.00). Cigar lighter (1.50). Radio antenna package (3.00). Seat covers (Santoy). Spotlight(s) (3.45). R.H. taillight. Dual horn kit (12.50). Triplex air cleaner (6.50). Set of 5 wire wheel discs (11.25). Set of 5 wheel trim rings (8.50). Glove compartment smoker set and clock (13.50). Pull-wind clock (3.95). Safety light (15.95). License frame set (2.45). Luggage set (19.75). R.H. inside visor (2.00).

HISTORICAL: Introduced: Sept. 25, 1935. Innovations: Larger bore eight. Improved clutch. Improved cooling system on eight. New front suspension with King pins mounted in floating bronze bearings. Automatic choke on deluxe models. Model year production: 176,270. The president of Pontiac was Harry Klingler. Pontiac held six rank in U.S. auto sales for 1936. The new models were called "The Most Beautiful Thing on Wheels."

1936
DeLuxe Series Silver Streak, 6-cyl.

	FP	5	4	3	2	1
Cpe	665	850	1650	4200	5850	8400
Spt Cpe	720	900	1800	4450	6250	8900
Cabr	810	1800	4900	8200	11,500	16,400
2 dr Sed	720	700	1350	2700	4500	6400
2 dr Tr Sed	745	700	1350	2900	4600	6600
4 dr Sed	770	725	1400	3000	4700	6700
4 dr Tr Sed	795	725	1400	3200	4850	6900

DeLuxe Series Silver Streak, 8-cyl.

	FP	5	4	3	2	1
Cpe	730	900	1800	4450	6250	8900
Spt Cpe	785	950	2100	4700	6600	9400
Cabr	855	2500	5500	9200	12,900	18,400
2 dr Sed	770	725	1400	3200	4850	6900
2 dr Tr Sed	795	750	1450	3400	5000	7100
4 dr Sed	875	725	1400	3200	4850	6900
4 dr Tr Sed	840	750	1450	3400	5000	7100

1937

PONTIAC — DELUXE — SERIES 26 — SIX: The 1937 Pontiacs had longer, one-piece solid bodies with Turret tops. The hoodline was higher and the radiator grille was narrower. Silver Streak moldings ran down the center of the hood and over the grille in waterfall fashion. The side grilles had chrome horizontal bars grouped into four lower segments and a narrower upper segment that continued down the sides of the hood. New, one-piece front fenders with a split-pear shape were used. Longer headlamp buckets were mounted on pedestals attached to the fender catwalks. A wider windshield with a rakish 39-degree slant gave a more modern appearance. The six-cylinder hood ornament was a flat, solid Indian head.

1937 Pontiac, convertible sedan, OCW

I.D. DATA: Serial numbers on top of frame ahead of steering gear (visible upon raising hood). Starting: 6CA-1001. Ending 6CA-154827 (Pontiac, Mich.) Cars built at Southgate, Calif. had serial number prefix "C". Cars built at Linden, N.J. had prefix "L". Engine numbers on front left corner of block. Starting: 6-220001. Ending: 6-399286.

Model No.	Body Type & Seating	Price	Weight	Prod. Total
2627B	2-dr. Cpe.-2P	781	3165	Note 1
2627	2-dr. Spt Cpe.2/4P	853	3165	Note 1
2667	2-dr. Cabr.-2/4P	945	3250	Note 1
2601	2-dr. Sed.-5P	830	3240	Note 1
2611	2-dr. Tr. Sed.-5P	855	3240	Note 1
2609	4-dr. Sed.-5P	881	3265	Note 1
2619	4-dr. Tr. Sed.-5P	906	3275	Note 1
2649	4-dr. Conv. Sed.-5P	1197	3375	Note 1
STAWAG	4-dr. Sta. Wag.-7P	992	3340	Note 1

Note 1: Body style breakouts not available. Series production total was 179,244 cars.

ENGINE: L-head. Inline. Six. Cast iron block. B & S: 3-7/16 x 4. Disp.: 222.7 cu. in. C.R.: 6.2:1. Brake H.P. 85 @ 3520 R.P.M. NACC H.P.: 28.3. Main bearings: Four. Valve lifters: Solid. Carb.: Carter 1V.

CHASSIS: W.B.: 117 in. O.L.: 193.06 in. Height: 67 in. Tires: 16 x 6.00.

TECHNICAL: Synchromesh transmission. Speeds: 3F/1R. Floor shift controls. Dry disc clutch. Hotchkiss drive. Semi-floating axle. Overall ratio: 4.37:1. Four-wheel hydraulic brakes. Steel disc wheels.

1937 Pontiac, 4-dr. sedan, HAC

PONTIAC — DELUXE — SERIES 28 — EIGHT: Pontiac Eights were longer cars. They had longer hoods and fenders. Styling was similar to the Pontiac Sixes. The winged nose badge and trunk emblem said Pontiac Eight. The hood ornament was a flat brave's head that projected above the hood moldings and served as a hood latch handle.

I.D. DATA: Serial numbers on top of frame ahead of steering gear. Starting: 8CA-1001. Ending: 8CA-49442. Calif. cars had a "C" prefix. New Jersey cars had an "L" prefix. Engine numbers on front left corner of block. Starting: 8-830001. Ending: 8-139968.

Model No.	Body Type & Seating	Price	Weight	Prod. Total
2827B	2-dr. Cpe.-2P	857	3305	Note 1
2827	2-dr. Spt. Cpe.-2/4P	913	3305	Note 1
2867	2-dr. Cabr.-2/4P	985	3360	Note 1
2801	2-dr. Sed.-5P	893	3385	Note 1
2811	2-dr. Tr. Sed.-5P	919	3380	Note 1
2809	4-dr. Sed.-5P	939	3410	Note 1
2819	4-dr. Tr. Sed.-5P	965	3400	Note 1
2849	4 dr. Conv. Sed.-5P	1235	3505	Note 1

Note 1: Body style breakouts not available. Series production total was 56,945 cars.

ENGINE: L-head. Inline. Eight. Cast iron block. B & S: 3-1/4 x 3-3/4. Disp.: 248.9 cu. in. C.R.: 6.2:1. Brake H.P. 100 @ 3800 R.P.M. N.A.C.C. H.P.: 33.8. Main bearings: Five. Valve lifters: Solid. Carb.: Carter 1-V.

CHASSIS: W.B.: 122 in. O.L. 198.06 in. Height: 67 in. Tires: 16 x 6.50.

TECHNICAL: Drivetrain: Same as Pontiac Six.

OPTIONS: Deluxe radio. Master radio. Deluxe heater. Master heater. Running board antennas (dual). Anti-freeze. Tenite shift ball. Commercial pickup box (coupes). Locking gas cap. Tour top luggage carrier. Santoy seat covers. Electric dash clock. Pull wind headboard clock. Battery charger. Wheel discs. Dual safety defroster. Electric fan defroster. Electric windshield defroster. Tailpipe extension. License frames. Master guard. License jewel unit. Fog lamp. R.H. taillamp. Safety light. Cigar lighter. Fender marker. Luggage mat. Wheel moldings. Rain deflector. Peep mirror. OSRV. Visor mirror. Fuel pump vacuum booster. Ash receiver. Rear luggage compartment strap. Insect screen. Frost shields. R.H. sun visor. Flexible steering wheel. Sidemount tires. Metal sidemount tire covers. Three-passenger gearshift lever. Oil bath air cleaner.

HISTORICAL: Introduced: Nov. 1936. All-steel bodies. First Pontiac station wagon. New 19:1 steering gear ratio. Larger GM-B bodies. Stronger X-member frames. Two-piece propellor shaft. Hotchkiss drive reintroduced. Calendar year production: 235,322. Model year production: 236,189. Company manager: Harry J. Klingler. Advertised as "America's finest low-priced car." Pontiac claimed its products cost only 15¢ more per day to own than low-priced models. Best sales year in Pontiac history to date.

DeLuxe Model 6CA, 6-cyl.

	FP	5	4	3	2	1
Conv	945	2900	5800	9700	13,600	19,400
Bus Cpe	781	825	1600	3950	5500	7900
Spt Cpe	853	850	1650	4200	5850	8400
2 dr Sed	830	650	1250	2400	4150	5900
2 dr Tr Sed	855	675	1300	2500	4300	6100
4 dr Sed	881	675	1300	2500	4300	6100
4 dr Tr Sed	906	700	1350	2700	4500	6400
Sta Wag	992	1300	4050	6750	9450	13,500

DeLuxe Model 8CA, 8-cyl.

	FP	5	4	3	2	1
Conv	985	3350	6750	11,250	15,750	22,500
Conv Sed	1235	3650	7350	12,250	17,150	24,500
Bus Cpe	857	850	1650	4200	5850	8400
Spt Cpe	913	900	1800	4450	6250	8900
2 dr Sed	893	700	1350	2700	4500	6400
2 dr Tr Sed	919	725	1400	3200	4850	6900
4 dr Sed	939	725	1400	3200	4850	6900
4 dr Tr Sed	965	775	1500	3700	5200	7400

1938

1938 Pontiac, Six, station wagon, AA

DELUXE — SERIES 26 — SIX: The 1938 Pontiac used the same body as previous models. Wide, horizontal bars characterized the new grille design. On sixes there was a "6" emblem at bottom center. Chrome ribs ran along the top of the hood and down the center of the radiator grille. There were vertical hood louvers with the Pontiac name between chrome bars near the radiator on the Six. The six-cylinder hood ornament was a long, low Indian head.

I.D. DATA: Serial numbers on top of frame ahead of steering gear (visible upon raising hood). Starting: 6DA-1616 or C-60A-1001. Ending: 6DA-60416 or C-6DA-1615 (Pontiac, Mich.) Cars built at Southgate, Calif. were numbered C6DA-2001 to C6DA-8155. Cars built at Linden, N.J. had an "L" prefix. Engine numbers on front left corner of block. Starting: 6-399501. Ending: 6-486022.

Model No.	Body Type & Seating	Price	Weight	Prod. Total
2627B	2-dr. Cpe.-2P	835	3190	Note 1
2627	2-dr. Spt. Cpe.-2/4P	891	3200	Note 1
2667	2-dr. Cabr.-2/4P	993	3285	Note 1
2601	2-dr. Sed.-5P	865	3265	Note 1
2611	2-dr. Tr. Sed.-5P	891	3265	Note 1
2609	4-dr. Sed.-5P	916	3295	Note 1
2619	4-dr. Tr. Sed.-5P	942	3280	Note 1
2649	4-dr. Conv. Sed.-5P	1310	3410	Note 1
STA WAG	4-dr. Sta. Wag.-7P	1110	3420	Note 1

Note 1: No body style breakouts. Series production total was 77,713 cars.

ENGINE: L-head. Inline. Six. Cast iron block. B & S: 3-7/16 x 4. Disp.: 222.7 cu. in. C.R.: 6.2:1. Brake H.P.: 85 @ 3520 R.P.M. NACC H.P.: 28.3. Main bearings: Four. Valve lifters: Solid. Carter 1V.

CHASSIS: W.B.: 117 in. O.L. 192 in. Height: 67 in. Tires: 16 x 6.00.

1938 Pontiac, Eight, 4-dr. sedan, JAC

TECHNICAL: Synchromesh transmission. Speeds: 3F/1R. Floor shift controls (standard). Dry disc clutch. Hotchkiss Drive. Semi-floating rear axle. Overall ratio: 4.37:1. Four wheel hydraulic brakes. Steel disc wheels. Column gearshift $10 extra.

PONTIAC — DELUXE — SERIES 28 — EIGHT: Pontiac Eight again had slightly longer front end sheet metal. Styling was similar to the Pontiac Six. Emblem at bottom center of grille bore "8" designation. Trunk emblem read Pontiac Eight. Louvers on the side of the hood had an extra chrome bar in middle and no Pontiac name. Eight-cylinder hood ornament was a short Indian head with fin-like feathers.

I.D. DATA: Serial numbers on top of frame ahead of steering gear. Starting: 8DA-1001. Ending: 8DA-15729. Calif. cars had a "C" prefix. New Jersey cars had an "L" prefix. Engine numbers on front left corner of block. Starting: 8-140001. Ending: 8-159441.

Model No.	Body Type & Seating	Price	Weight	Prod. Total
2827B	2-dr. Cpe.-2P	898	3320	Note 1
2827	2-dr. Spt. Cpe.-2/4P	955	3325	Note 1
2867	2-dr. Cabr.-2/4P	1057	3390	Note 1
2801	2-dr. Sed.-5P	934	3395	Note 1
2811	2-dr. Tr. Sed.-5P	960	3385	Note 1
2809	4-dr. Sed.-5P	980	3415	Note 1
2819	4-dr. Tr. Sed.-5P	1006	3410	Note 1
2849	4-dr. Conv. Sed.-5P	1353	3530	Note 1

Note 1: No body style breakouts. Total series production was 97,139 cars.

ENGINE: L-head. Inline. Eight. Cast iron block. B & S: 3-1/4 x 3-3/4. Disp.: 248.9 cu. in. C.R.: 6.2:1. Brake H.P. 100 @ 3700 R.P.M. NACC H.P. 33.8. Main bearings: Five. Valve lifters: Solid. Carb. Carter: 1V.

CHASSIS: W.B. 122 in. O.L. 196.63 in. Height: 67 in. Tires: 16 x 6.50.

TECHNICAL: Drivetrain: Same as Pontiac Six.

OPTIONS: Deluxe radio (58.25). Master radio (44.70). Dual runningboard antenna (5.25). Overhead antenna (5.25). Deluxe heater (17.95). Master heater (12.75). Defroster (7.90). Tenite shift ball (.50). Commercial pickup box (25.00). Seat covers (set): front (5.95); front & rear (10.95). Battery charger (8.50). Dash electric clock (11.65). Header board windup clock (4.00). Single wheel disc (2.30). Electric windshield defroster (3.00). Tailpipe extension (1.00). Pair, license frames (2.45). Front master guard (2.25). Rear master guard (3.90). Dual horns (10.95). Jewel license unit (4.68). Fog lamp (5.00). R.H. taillamp (4.95). Cigar lighter (2.25). Fender marker (1.25). Rear mats in sedan (2.25); in coupes (3.75). Peep mirror (1.50). Visor mirror (1.00). Rear view mirror (1.25). Wheel molding (1.58). Fuel pump vacuum booster (12.00). Ash receiver (1.25). Single sun visor (2.40). Flexible steering wheel (11.50). Sidemounts (price n.a.).

HISTORICAL: Introduced: Oct. 1937. Improved transmission synchronizers. Quieter gear shift yoke design. Toggle action helper springs added to clutch. Larger generator. Larger water pump with ball bearings. Battery moved under hood. Improved front suspension. Calendar year production: 95,128. Model year production: 97,139. The president of Pontiac was Harry J. Klingler. Advertised as a "better looking, better built, better buy." Factory delivery program.

DeLuxe Model 6DA, 6-cyl.

	FP	5	4	3	2	1
Conv	993	2900	5800	9700	13,600	19,400
Conv Sed	1310	3500	7050	11,750	16,450	23,500
Bus Cpe	835	775	1500	3700	5200	7400
Spt Cpe	891	825	1600	3950	5500	7900
2 dr Sed	865	700	1350	2700	4500	6400
4 dr Sed	916	725	1400	3200	4850	6900
4 dr Tr Sed	942	750	1450	3400	5000	7100
Sta Wag	1110	750	1450	3500	5050	7200

DeLuxe Model 8DA, 8-cyl.

	FP	5	4	3	2	1
Conv	1057	3350	6750	11,250	15,750	22,500
Conv Sed	1353	3650	7350	12,250	17,150	24,500
Bus Cpe	898	825	1600	3950	5500	7900
Spt Cpe	955	850	1650	4200	5850	8400
2 dr Sed	934	775	1500	3700	5200	7400
2 dr Tr Sed	960	800	1550	3800	5300	7600
4 dr Sed	980	775	1500	3750	5250	7500
4 dr Tr Sed	1006	800	1550	3850	5400	7700

1939

1939 Pontiac, Six, 4-dr. sedan, AA

PONTIAC — QUALITY 115 — SERIES 25 — SIX: The 1939 Pontiac Quality Six was a new type of economy class model. It employed the Chevrolet A-body shell with Pontiac front end sheet metal, making it a small car with a big car look. All 1939 Pontiacs had a new, streamlined appearance. The thin, rounded nose was brightened by Silver Streak moldings running to the bumper line. There were four groups of four horizontal, louver type grille bars on either side of the Silver Streaks. Each lower group of louvers were shorter. Separate, twin side grilles had multiple vertical bars over high front fender splash aprons. The headlights rested directly on the front fender cat-walks. Horizontal louvers were placed on the hood sides near the cowl. The Quality Six came only with conventional runningboards.

I.D. DATA: Serial numbers on front cross-member behind radiator. Starting: P6EA-1001. Ending: P6EA-43679 (Pontiac, Mich.) Cars built at Southgate, Calif. had a ''C'' prefix. Cars built in Linden, N.J. had an ''L'' prefix. Engine numbers on front left corner of block. Starting: 6-486201. Ending: 6-595763.

Model No.	Body Type & Seating	Price	Weight	Prod. Total
2527B	2-dr. Cpe.-3P	758	2875	Note 1
2527	2-dr. Spt. Cpe.-5P	809	2920	Note 1
2511	2-dr. Tr. Sed.-5P	820	2965	Note 1
2519	4-dr. Tr. Sed.-6P	866	3000	Note 1
STA WAG	4-dr. Sta. Wag.-8P	990	3175	Note 1

Note 1: No body style breakouts. Total series production was 55,736 cars.

ENGINE: L-head. Inline. Six. Cast iron block. B & S: 3-7/16 x 4. Disp.: 222.7 cu. in. C.R.: 6.2:1. Brake H.P.: 85 @ 3520 R.P.M. NACC H.P.: 28.3. Main bearings: Four. Valve lifers: Solid. Carb.: Carter 1V.

CHASSIS: W.B.: 115 in. O.L.: 190 in. Tires: 16 x 6.00.

TECHNICAL: Synchromesh transmission. Speeds: 3F/1R. Column gear shift controls. Dry disc clutch. Hotchkiss drive. Semi-floating rear axle. Overall ratio: 4.1:1. Four-wheel hydraulic brakes. Steel disc wheels.

PONTIAC — DELUXE 120 — SERIES 26 — SIX: The 1939 Pontiac Deluxe Six models used the larger GM A-body. They were longer and wider, but lower than Quality Six models. Front end styling changes were similar for both lines. The Deluxe bodies had larger windshields, wider back windows, V-shaped window openings and bright metal beltline trim. They could be ordered with conventional runningboards or streamlined ''body skirts.''

I.D. DATA: Serial numbers on front cross-member behind radiator. Starting: P6EB-1001. Ending: P6EB-41263 (Pontiac, Mich.) Calif. cars had a ''C'' prefix. New Jersey cars had an ''L'' prefix. Engine numbers on front left corner of block. Starting: 6-486201. Ending: 6-595763.

Model No.	Body Type & Seating	Price	Weight	Prod. Total
2627B	2-dr. Cpe.-3P	814	3020	Note 1
2627	2-dr. Spt. Cpe.-5P	865	3055	Note 1
2667	2-dr. Conv. Cpe.-5P	993	3155	Note 1
2611	2-dr. Tr. Sed.-6P	871	3115	Note 1
2619	4-dr. Tr. Sed.-6P	922	3165	Note 1

Note 1: No body style breakouts. Total series production was 53,830 cars.

ENGINE: Same as Quality Six engine.

CHASSIS: W.B.: 120 in. O.L.: 196.25 in. Tires: 16 x 6.00.

TECHNICAL: Drive train same as Quality Six except overall gear ratio is 4.3:1.

1939 Pontiac, Deluxe Eight, sport coupe, JAC

PONTIAC — SERIES 28 — EIGHT — The 1939 Pontiac Deluxe Eight models used the same body as the Deluxe ''120'' six models. The Indian head hood ornaments on eight-cylinder cars had a fin-like feather design, compared to the straight-back feather design used on six-cylinder models. A ''Pontiac Eight'' emblem was affixed to the cars' rear decks. There was also a fancier trim plate around the circular badge on the front bumper.

I.D. DATA: Serial numbers on front cross-member behind radiator. Starting: P8EA-1001. Ending: P8EA-27627 (Pontiac, Mich.). Calif. cars had a ''C'' prefix. New Jersey cars had an ''L'' prefix. Engine numbers on front left corner of block. Starting: 8-159601. Ending: 8-194380.

Model No.	Body Type & Seating	Price	Weight	Prod. Total
2827B	2-dr. Cpe.-3P	862	3115	Note 1
2827	2-dr. Spt. Cpe.-5P	912	3165	Note 1
2867	2-dr. Conv. Cpe.-5P	1046	3250	Note 1
2811	2-dr. Tr. Sed.-5P	919	3225	Note 1
2819	4-dr. Tr. Sed.-5P	970	3265	Note 1

Note 1: No body style breakouts. Total series production was 34,774 cars.

ENGINE: L-head. Inline. Eight. Cast iron block. B & S: 3-1/4 x 3-3/4. Disp.: 248.9 cu. in. C.R.: 6.2:1. Brake H.P.: 100 @ 3700 R.P.M. NACC H.P.: 33.8. Main bearings: Five. Valve lifters: Solid. Carb.: Carter 1V.

CHASSIS: W.B.: 120 in. O.L.: 196.25 in. Tires: 16 x 6.50.

TECHNICAL: Drive train same as Deluxe Six.

OPTIONS: Master radio (Quality Six only). Deluxe radio. Dual horns. R.H. taillight. Fender skirts. Bumper guards. Constant-action wiper pump. Deluxe heater. Electric clock. Wind-up clock. Cigar lighter. Master cowl antenna. Runningboard antenna. Seat covers. Whitewall tires. Spotlight. Exhaust deflector. License plate frame. Weather Chief heater and defroster. Special runningboard. Flexible steering wheel. Ash receiver. Wheel covers. Wheel trim moldings. Oil bath air cleaner. Oil filter. Fog lamps. Sunshine roof.

HISTORICAL: Introduced October, 1938. Redesigned clutch. Variable rate Duflex springs. Revised transmission. Improved long-life muffler. Column-mounted Safety Gearshift standardized. Three-passenger front seating. No-Rol device optional. Calendar year registrations: 212,403. Calendar year production: 170,726. Model year production: 144,340. The president of Pontiac was Harry J. Klingler. Advertised as ''America's Finest Low-Priced Car.'' A ''see-through'' 1939 Pontiac Deluxe Six 4-door Touring Sedan with plexiglass body panels was built for exhibition at the 1939 New York World's Fair.

1939
Special Series 25, 6-cyl.

	FP	5	4	3	2	1
Bus Cpe	758	850	1650	4200	5850	8400
Spt Cpe	809	900	1800	4450	6250	8900
2 dr Tr Sed	820	825	1600	3950	5500	7900
4 dr Tr Sed	866	825	1600	4000	5600	8000
Sta Wag	990	1100	3400	5700	8000	11,400
DeLuxe Series 26, 6-cyl.						
Conv	993	2900	5800	9700	13,600	19,400
Bus Cpe	814	875	1700	4300	6000	8600
Spt Cpe	865	925	2000	4600	6400	9200
2 dr Sed	871	825	1600	4050	5650	8100
4 dr Sed	922	850	1650	4100	5700	8200
DeLuxe Series 28, 8-cyl.						
Conv	1046	3100	6150	10,250	14,350	20,500
Bus Cpe	862	900	1800	4450	6250	8900
Spt Cpe	913	950	2100	4700	6600	9400
2 dr Sed	919	850	1650	4150	5800	8300
4 dr Tr Sed	970	850	1650	4200	5850	8400

1940

1940 Pontiac, 4-door touring sedan, OCW

PONTIAC — SPECIAL — SERIES 25 — SIX: Characteristics of 1940 Pontiacs included larger and more streamlined bodies; more massive front fenders with built in headlight fairings; lower floors and ''alligator'' type hoods trimmed with three sets of slanting louvers. The 1940 grilles had horizontal bars, arranged in top point formation. The grilles were placed on either side of the ''Silver Streak'' center rail which carried a Pontiac nameplate and chevron emblem below. The Special Six models employed the small GM A-body. Distinguishing styling characteristics of the series included six-window 4-door sedans; exposed lower front door hinges; Key hole type door handles and gas filler caps on the right rear fenders. They came only with conventional runningboards. The six-cylinder hood ornament was a chrome plated, solid Indian head which also served as a hood latch mechanism. The Special Six had a more rounded rear deck. The Special Six station wagon came standard with a single, side-mounted spare tire.

I.D. DATA: Serial numbers on front cross-member behind radiator. Starting: P6HA-1001. Ending: P6HA-84545 (Pontiac, Mich.) Cars built in Southgate, Calif. had a ''C'' prefix. Cars built in Linden, N.J. had an ''L'' prefix. Engine numbers on front left corner of block. Starting: 6-595801. Ending: 6-761162.

Model No.	Body Type & Seating	Price	Weight	Prod. Total
2527B	2-dr. Cpe.-3P	783	3060	Note 1
2527	2-dr. Spt. Cpe.-4P	819	3045	Note 1
2511	2-dr. Tr. Sed.-5P	830	3095	Note 1
2519	4-dr. Tr. Sed.-5P	876	3125	Note 1
STA WAG	4-dr. Sta. Wag.-8P	1015	3295	Note 1

Note 1: No body style breakouts. Total series production was 106,892 cars.

ENGINE: L-head. Inline. Six. Cast iron block. B & S: 3-7/16 x 4. Disp.: 22^7 cu. in. C.R.: 6.5:1. Brake H.P. 100 @ 3700 R.P.M. N.A.C.C. H.P.: 28.3. Main bearings: Four. Valve lifters: Solid. Carb.: Carter 1V.

CHASSIS: W.B.: 116.5 in. O.L.: 198.75 in. Height: 66.75 in. Frt. tread: 58 in. Rear tread: 59 in. Tires: 16 x 6.00.

ENGINE: Synchromesh transmission. Speeds: 3F/1R. Steering column gear shift. Inland single disc clutch. Hotchkiss drive. Semi-floating rear axle. Overall ratio: 4.3:1. Duo-servo hydraulic. Duo-servo four-wheel hydraulic brakes. Steel disc wheels. Rim size: 4.5 in. Drivetrain options: Hill-Holder.

1940 Pontiac, conv. cpe., JAC

PONTIAC — DELUXE — SERIES 26 — SIX: Deluxe Six models used the larger GM B-body. Front sheet metal styling was the same as for the Special Six models. Concealed hinges were used in all places except lower front doors. The door handles had weather sealed keyholes. Gas filler doors were on the left rear fenders. Buyers could order optional body skirts in place of conventional runningboards. The hood ornament was the same used on Special Six models. Deluxe Sixes had a squared-off rear deck.

I.D. DATA: Serial numbers on front cross-member behind radiator. Starting: P6HB-1001. Ending: P6HB-44296 (Pontiac, Mich.) California cars had a "C" prefix. New Jersey cars had an "L" prefix. Engine numbers on front left corner of block. Starting: 6-595801. Ending: 6-761162.

Model No.	Body Type & Seating	Price	Weight	Prod. Total
2627B	2-dr. Cpe.-3P	835	3115	Note 1
2627	2-dr. Spt. Cpe.-4P	876	3105	Note 1
2667	2-dr. Cabr.-4P	1003	3190	Note 1
2611	2-dr. Tr. Sed.-5P	881	3170	Note 1
2619	4-dr. Tr. Sed.-5P	932	3210	Note 1

Note 1: No body style breakouts. Total series production was 58,452 cars.

ENGINE: Same as Special Six engine.

CHASSIS: W.B.: 120.25 in. O.L.: 199.75 in. Height: 66 in. Frt. tread: 58 in. Rear tread: 59 in. Tires: 6.00 x 16.

TECHNICAL: Drivetrain same as Special Six.

PONTIAC — DELUXE — SERIES 28 — EIGHT: The Deluxe Eight models used the same bodies as Deluxe Six models. An "8" emblem was affixed to the front chevron-shaped trim plate. A Pontiac Eight nameplate was on the rear deck. The eight-cylinder hood ornament had a plastic Indian head mounted in a metal base.

I.D. DATA: Serial numbers on front cross-member behind radiator. Starting: P8HA-1001. Ending: P8HA-16817 (Pontiac, Mich.). California cars had a "C" prefix. New Jersey cars had an "L" prefix. Engine numbers on front left corner of block. Starting: 8-194401. Ending: 8-246073.

Model No.	Body Type & Seating	Price	Weight	Prod. Total
2827B	2-dr. Cpe.-3P	875	3180	Note 1
2827	2-dr. Spt. Cpe.-4P	913	3195	Note 1
2867	2-dr. Cabr.-4P	1046	3280	Note 1
2811	2-dr. Tr. Sed.-5P	919	3250	Note 1
2819	4-dr. Tr. Sed.-5P	970	3300	Note 1

Note 1: No body style breakouts. Total series production was 20,433 cars.

ENGINE: L-head. Inline. Eight. Cast iron block. B & S: 3-1/4 in. x 3-3/4 in. Disp.: 248.9 cu. in. C.R.: 6.5:1. Brake H.P. 100 @ 3700 R.P.M. N.A.C.C. H.P.: 33.8. Main bearings: Five. Valve lifters: Solid. Carb.: Carter 1V. Torque: 175 lbs.-ft. @ 1600 R.P.M.

CHASSIS: W.B.: 120.25 in. O.L.: 200 in. Height: 66-3/8 in. Frt. tread: 58 in. Rear tread: 59 in. Tires: 16 x 6.50.

TECHNICAL: Drivetrain same as Deluxe Six specifications.

1940 Pontiac Torpedo, 4-dr. sedan, AA

PONTIAC — TORPEDO — SERIES 29 — EIGHT: New this year was the Torpedo Eight using the extra-large GM C-body. These cars had larger windows, wider seats, front and rear ventipanes on 4-door sedans and long, gracefully streamlined rear decks. Concealed hinges were used on all doors. The doors were extra-wide. The hood ornament was the same as on Deluxe eights. Front end sheet metal looked like that on other Pontiacs. Eight-cylinder badges were used front and rear. The door locks had weather sealed keyholes. Gas filler tubes were enclosed under "flip-up" lids on the left rear fenders. The window openings were trimmed with bright metal moldings.

I.D. DATA: Serial numbers on front cross-member behind radiator. Starting: P8HB-1001. Ending: P8HB-24376. (Pontiac, Mich.). California cars had a "C" prefix. New Jersey cars had an "L" prefix. Engine numbers on front left corner of block. Starting: 8-194401. Ending: 8-246073.

Model No.	Body Type & Seating	Price	Weight	Prod. Total
2927C	2-dr. Spt. Cpe.-4P	1016	3390	Note 1
2919	4-dr. Tr. Sed.-5P	1072	3475	Note 1

Note 1: No body style breakouts. Total series production was 31,224 cars.

ENGINE: L-head. Inline. Eight. Cast iron block. B & S: 3-1/4 in. x 3-3/4 in. Disp.: 248.9 cu. in. C.R.: 6.5:1. Brake H.P. 103 @ 3700 R.P.M. N.A.C.C. H.P.: 33.8. Main bearings: Five. Valve lifters: Solid. Carb.: Carter 2V. Torque: 175 lbs.-ft. @ 1600 R.P.M.

CHASSIS: W.B.: 121-1/2 in. O.L.: 207-1/2 in. Height: 65 in. Frt. tread: 58 in. Rear tread: 59 in. Tires: 16 x 6.50.

TECHNICAL: Drivetrain same as Deluxe Six.

OPTIONS: Vacuum booster fuel pump. Cigar lighter. Electric clock. Deluxe 6-tube electric tuning radio. Automatic tuning 6-tube radio. Automatic tuning 5-tube radio. Portable radio. Master dash heater. Weather Chief dash heater. Auto furnace. Defroster. Fresh air intake. Deluxe steering wheel. White sidewall tire. Glove box light. Trunk light. Directional signals. Vacuum radio antenna. Master grille guards. Fender skirts. Body skirts (except Special Sixes). Wheel discs. Wheel trim rings. Rear view mirror. Cowl antenna.

HISTORICAL: Introduced: August, 1939. Center arm rest in Torpedo sedan. Sealed beam headlights. Safety roll front seat backs. New anti-skid tires. Improved Safety Shift gear control. Tilting and adjustable front seats. New, high-compression cylinder head. New gasoline filter. Calendar year production: 249,303. Calendar year registrations: 235,815. Model year production: 217,001. The president of Pontiac was H.J. Klingler. A plexiglass bodied "see through" Pontiac appeared at the N.Y. World's Fair again. This may have been a new show car, or the 1939 model with a new front end. The "see through" Pontiac survives today in the collection of an Indiana hobbyist.

1940
Special Series 25, 6-cyl., 117" wb

	FP	5	4	3	2	1
Bus Cpe	783	825	1600	3950	5500	7900
Spt Cpe	819	825	1600	4050	5650	8100
2 dr Sed	830	775	1500	3700	5200	7400
4 dr Sed	876	775	1500	3750	5250	7500
Sta Wag	1015	1300	4050	6700	9400	13,400
DeLuxe Series 26, 6-cyl., 120" wb						
Conv	1033	2900	5800	9700	13,600	19,400
Bus Cpe	835	825	1600	4050	5650	8100
Spt Cpe	876	850	1650	4200	5850	8400
2 dr Sed	881	800	1550	3800	5300	7600
4 dr Sed	932	800	1550	3850	5400	7700
DeLuxe Series 28, 8-cyl., 120" wb						
Conv	1046	3100	6150	10,250	14,350	20,500
Bus Cpe	875	850	1650	4200	5850	8400
Spt Cpe	913	875	1700	4300	6000	8600
2 dr Sed	919	800	1550	3850	5400	7700
4 dr Sed	970	800	1550	3900	5450	7800
Torpedo Series 29, 8-cyl., 122" wb						
Spt Cpe	1016	900	1800	4450	6250	8900
Sed	1072	850	1650	4200	5850	8400

1941

1941 Pontiac Torpedo, 4-dr. sedan, AA

PONTIAC — DELUXE TORPEDO — JA LINE — SIX/EIGHT: A wide grille with horizontal bars was used on 1941 Pontiacs. The parking lights were built into the grille. Headlamps were fully recessed into the new, wider fenders. Speed-line ribbing was molded into the sides of both front and rear fenders. DeLuxe Sixes were in Series 25. Deluxe Eights were in Series 27. The sixes had shorter hood ornaments, a "6" badge on the hood and Pontiac lettering on the side. The eights had larger hood ornaments, an "8" badge on the hood and Pontiac Eight lettering on the side. All 1941 Pontiacs were nick-named "Torpedos." Deluxe Torpedos used the small GM A-body shell with notchback styling. Streamlined body skirts replaced conventional runningboards on all models. The Metropolitan Sedan had four-window styling and was added to the line at mid-year.

I.D. DATA: Serial numbers on left side of dash. Starting: [Six] P6JA-1001/[Eight] P8JA-1001. Ending: [Six] P6JA-80460/[Eight] P8JA-27219. These codes apply to cars built at Pontiac, Mich. Cars built at Southgate, Calif. had a "C" prefix. Cars built at Linden, N.J. had an "L" prefix. Engine numbers on front left corner of block. Starting: [Six] 6-761501/[Eight] 8-246501. Ending: [Six] 6-971768/[Eight] 8-368240.

Model No.	Body Type & Seating	Price	Weight	Prod. Total
SERIES 25 (Deluxe Six)				
2527B	2-dr. Bus. Cpe.-3P	828	3145	Note 1
2527	2-dr. Sed. Cpe.-5P	864	3180	Note 1
2567	2-dr. Conv. Cpe.-5P	1023	3335	Note 1
2511	2-dr. Sed.-5P	874	3190	Note 1
2519	4-dr. Sed.-5P	921	3235	Note 1
2569	4-dr. Metro. Sed.-5P	921	3230	Note 1
SERIES 27 (Deluxe Eight)				
2727B	2-dr. Bus. Cpe.-3P	853	3220	Note 2
2727	2-dr. Sed. Cpe.-5P	889	3250	Note 2
2767	2-dr. Conv. Cpe.-5P	1048	3390	Note 2
2711	2-dr. Sed.-5P	899	3250	Note 2
2719	4-dr. Sed.-5P	946	3285	Note 2
2769	4-dr. Metro Sed.-5P	946	3295	Note 2

Note 1: No body style breakouts. Total series production was 117,976 cars.
Note 2: No body style breakouts. Total series production was 37,823 cars.

ENGINE:
[Six-cylinder] L-head. Inline. Six. Cast iron block. B & S: 3-9/16 in. x 4 in. Disp.: 239.2 cu. in. C.R.: 6.5:1. (7.2:1 optional). Brake H.P.: 90 @ 3200 R.P.M. NACC H.P.: 30.4. Main bearings: Four. Valve lifters: Solid. Carb.: Carter 1V. Torque: 175 lbs.-ft. @ 1400 R.P.M.

[Eight-cylinder] L-head. Inline. Eight. Cast iron block. B & S: 3-1/4 in. x 3-3/4 in. Disp.: 248.9 cu. in. C.R.: 6.5:1. (7.2:1 optional). Brake H.P.: 103 @ 3500 R.P.M. N.A.C.C. H.P.: 33.8. Main bearings: Five. Valve lifters: Solid. Carb.: Carter 2V. Torque: 190 lbs.-ft. @ 2200 R.P.M.

CHASSIS: W.B.: 191 in. O.L.: 201-1/2 in. Height: 66 in. Frt. tread: 58 cu. in. Rear tread: 61-1/2 in. Tires: 16 x 6.00.

ENGINE: Synchromesh transmission. Speeds: 3F/1R. Column shift control. Inland single disc clutch. Hotchkiss drive. Semi-floating rear axle. Overall ratio: 4.1:1. Duo servo hydraulic brakes on four wheels. Steel disc wheels. Rim size: 4-1/2 in. Drivetrain options: "No Rol" device to keep car from rolling backwards on hill.

PONTIAC — STREAMLINER TORPEDO — JB LINE — SIX/EIGHT: Sleek, fastback styling characterized Pontiac's 1941 Streamliner Torpedo models. Their rooflines swept from the windshield to the rear bumper in one, smooth curve. The front end sheet metal was of the same design used on Deluxe Torpedos and trim differences between Sixes and Eights were also the same. Beige corded wool cloth upholstery was featured. Streamliners utilized GM's larger B-body. There was also a Super Streamliner sub-series. Supers had the same body styling and trim, but featured two-tone worsted wool cloth upholstery with pin stripes. They also added sponge rubber seat cushions, electric clocks, deluxe flexible steering wheels and divan type seats with folding center arm rests. Streamliners (and Customs) had concealed interior steps.

I.D. DATA: Serial numbers on left side of dash. Starting: (six) P6JB-1001/(eight) P8JB-1001. These codes apply to cars built at Pontiac, Mich. California cars had a "C" prefix. New Jersey cars had an "L" prefix. Engine numbers on front left corner of block. Numbers were the same given for Deluxe Torpedo engines. Ending: (six) P6JB-62545/(eight) P8JB-52428.

Model No.	Body Type & Seating	Price	Weight	Prod. Total
SERIES 26 (Streamliner Six)				
2627	2-dr. Sed. Cpe.-5P	923	3305	Note 1
2609	4-dr. Sed.-5P	980	3365	Note 1
SERIES 26 (Super Streamliner Six)				
2627D	2-dr. Sed. cpe.-5P	969	3320	Note 1
2609D	4-dr. Sed.-5P	1026	3400	Note 1
SERIES 28 (Streamliner Eight)				
2827	2-dr. Sed. Cpe.-5P	948	3370	Note 2
2809	4-dr. Sed.-5P	1005	3425	Note 2
SERIES 28 (Super Streamliner Eight)				
2827D	2-dr. Sed. cpe.-5P	994	3385	Note 2
2809D	4-dr. Sed.-5P	1051	3460	Note 2

Note 1: No body style breakouts. Total production of Streamliner and Super Streamliner Sixes was 82,527 cars.
Note 2: No body style breakouts. Total production of Streamliner and Super Streamliner Eights was 66,287 cars.

ENGINE: The Streamliner Torpedo engines had the same specifications as Deluxe Torpedo engines.

CHASSIS: W.B.: 122 in. O.L.: 207-1/2 in. Height: 65-3/4 in. Frt. tread: 58 in. Rear tread: 61-1/2 in. Tires: 16 x 6.50.

TECHNICAL: Drivetrain same as Deluxe Torpedo drivetrain.

PONTIAC — CUSTOM TORPEDO — JC LINE — SIX/EIGHT: The extra-large GM C-body was used for 1941 Pontiac Custom Torpedos. This line included a notch back sedan and coupe, plus the standard and Deluxe wood-bodied station wagons. Annual styling changes were the same seen for other lines, as were trim variations between Sixes and Eights. Station wagon bodies were built by Hercules and Ionia. The Ionia bodies had a more rounded rear end treatment. Standard station wagons had imitation leather upholstery while Deluxe types had genuine leather cushions.

I.D. DATA: Serial numbers on left side of dash. Starting: (six) P6JC-1001/(eight) P8JC-1001. Ending: (six) P6JC-6345/(eight) P8JC-12576. These codes apply to cars built at Pontiac, Mich. California cars had a "C" prefix. New Jersey cars had an "L" prefix. Engine numbers on front left corner of block. Numbers were the same given for Deluxe Torpedo engines.

Model No.	Body Type & Seating	Price	Weight	Prod. Total
SERIES 24 (Custom Torpedo Six)				
2427	2-dr. Sed. cpe.-5P	995	3260	Note 1
2419	4-dr. Sed.-5P	1052	3355	Note 1
STA WAG	4-dr. Sta. Wag.-8P	1175	3650	Note 1
STA WAG	4-dr. Del. Sta. Wag.-8P	1225	3665	Note 1
SERIES 29 (Custom Torpedo Eight)				
2927	2-dr. Sed. cpe.-5P	1020	3325	Note 2
2919	4-dr. Sed.-5P	1077	3430	Note 2
STA WAG	4-dr. Sta. Wag.-8P	1200	3715	Note 2
STA WAG	4-dr. Del. Sta. Wag.-8P	1250	3730	Note 2

Note 1: No body style breakouts. Total series production (six) was 8,257 cars.
Note 2: No body style breakouts. Total series production (eight) was 17,191 cars.

ENGINE: The Custom Torpedo engines had the same specifications as Deluxe Torpedo engines.

CHASSIS: W.B.: 122 in. O.L.: 201 in. Height: 65 in. Frt. tread: 58 in. Rear tread: 61-1/2 in. Tires: 16 x 6.50.

TECHNICAL: Drivetrain same as Deluxe Torpedo drivetrain.

OPTIONS: Exhaust deflector. Wheel trim rings. Bumper wing tips. White sidewall tires. Fender skirts. Master grille guards. Deluxe 7-tube radio. Weather Chief heater. Electric clock (std. in Super and Custom). Cigar lighter. Mast radio antenna (std. with radio). Spotlight. Wide running boards (Custom Torpedo only). Vacuum radio antenna. Master 5-tube radio. Safety-flex steering wheel (std. in Super and Custom). Safe sight airight defroster control. Electric visor vanity mirror. Back window sun baffle. Non-glare rear view mirror. Directional signals. Constant action wiper pump. Glove box light. Luggage compartment light. Chrome foglamp. Deluxe safety light. Rear bumper hinge guard.

HISTORICAL: Introduced Sept. 1940. New clutch pedal booster. Adjustable sun visors. Power operated convertible top. New bridge type frames. Improved multi-seal brakes. New, built-in, permanent oil cleaner. Dual rear lamps had automatic stop signal feature. New semi-automatic safety shift. Calendar year registrations: 286,123. Calendar year production: 282,087. Model year production: 330,061. The president of Pontiac was H.J. Klingler. Pontiac became the best-selling car in the middle-price class in 1941.

1941
DeLuxe Torpedo, 8-cyl.

	FP	5	4	3	2	1
Bus Cpe	853	825	1600	3950	5500	7900
Spt Cpe	889	850	1650	4100	5700	8200
Conv	1048	3200	6450	10,750	15,050	21,500
2 dr Sed	899	775	1500	3700	5200	7400
4W Sed	946	800	1550	3800	5300	7600
6W Sed	946	775	1500	3750	5250	7500
Streamliner, 8-cyl.						
Cpe	948	850	1650	4200	5850	8400
4 dr Sed	1005	825	1600	3950	5500	7900
Super Streamliner, 8-cyl.						
Cpe	994	875	1700	4350	6050	8700
4 dr Sed	1051	850	1650	4200	5850	8400
Custom, 8-cyl.						
Cpe	1020	900	1800	4450	6250	8900
4W Sed	1077	875	1700	4300	6000	8600
6W Sed	1120	875	1700	4250	5900	8500
Sta Wag	1200	1300	4050	6700	9400	13,400
DeL Sta Wag	1250	1400	4150	6950	9750	13,900

NOTE: Deduct 10 percent for 6-cyl. models.

1942

1942 Pontiac, station wagon, AA

PONTIAC — TORPEDO — KA LINE — SIX/EIGHT: All 1942 Pontiacs looked lower, heavier and wider. Extension caps on the front doors lengthened the forward fender lines. The hood extended back to the front doors, eliminating the cowl. The grille, bumper and hood were widened and headlamps were farther apart. Long, horizontal parking lamps sat just above the verticle side grilles. The horseshoe shaped center grille had horizontal bars and a circular emblem in the middle of the upper main surround molding. Torpedos used the GM A-body and featured notch back styling. After Dec. 15, 1941 war time "blackout" trim was used. All parts previously chrome plated were finished in Duco Gun-Metal Grey. The word Pontiac appeared on the hood side molding of six-cylinder models, while the moldings on eight-cylinder cars said Pontiac Eight.

I.D. DATA: Serial numbers on left side of dash. Starting: (six) P6KA-1001/(eight) P8KA-1001. Ending: (six) P6KA-25802/(eight) P8KA-13146. Above numbers for cars built in Pontiac, Mich. Cars built in Southgate, Calif. had a "C" prefix. Cars built in Linden, N.J. had an "L" prefix. Engine numbers on front left corner of block. Starting: same as serial numbers. Ending: same as serial numbers.

Model No.	Body Type & Seating	Price	Weight	Prod. Total
SERIES 25 (Torpedo Six)				
2527B	2-dr. Cpe.-3P	895	3210	Note 1
2507	2-dr. Sed. Cpe.-5P	950	3255	Note 1
2527	2-dr. Spt. Cpe.-5P	935	3260	Note 1
2567	2-dr. Conv. Cpe.-5P	1165	3535	Note 1
2511	2-dr. Sed.-5P	940	3265	Note 1
2519	4-dr. Sed.-5P	985	3305	Note 1
2569	4-dr. Metro Sed.-5P	985	3295	Note 1
SERIES 27 (Torpedo Eight)				
2727B	2-dr. Cpe.-3P	920	3270	Note 2
2707	2-dr. Sed. Cpe.-5P	975	3320	Note 2
2727	2-dr. Spt. Cpe.-5P	960	3320	Note 2
2767	2-dr. Conv. Cpe.-5P	1190	3605	Note 2
2711	2-dr. Sed.-5P	965	3325	Note 2
2719	4-dr. Sed.-5P	1010	3360	Note 2
2569	4-dr. Metro Sed.-5P	1010	3355	Note 2

Note 1: No body style breakouts. Total series production (six) was 29,886 cars.
Note 2: No body style breakouts. Total series production (eight) was 14,421 cars.

ENGINES:
(Six) L-head. Inline. Six. Cast iron block. B & S: 3-9/16 in. x 4 in. Disp.: 239.2 cu. in. C.R.: 6.5:1. (7.5:1 optional). Brake H.P.: 90 @ 3200 R.P.M. N.A.C.C. H.P.: 30.4. Main bearings: Four. Valve lifters: Solid. Carb.: Carter 1V. Torque: 175 lbs.-ft. @ 1400 R.P.M.

(Eight) L-head. Inline. Eight. Cast iron block. B & S: 3-1/4 in. x 3-3/4 in. Disp.: 248.9 cu. in. C.R.: 6.5:1. (7.5:1 optional). Brake H.P.: 103 @ 3500 R.P.M. N.A.C.C. H.P.: 33.8. Main bearings: Five. Valve lifters: Solid. Carb.: Carter 2V. Torque: 190 lbs.-ft. @ 2200 R.P.M.

CHASSIS: W.B.: 119 in. O.L.: 204-1/2 in. Height: 66 in. Frt. tread: 58 in. Rear tread: 61-1/2 in. Tires: 16 x 6.00.

TECHNICAL: Synchromesh transmission. Speeds: 3F/1R. Column gear shift controls. Single disc clutch. Hotchkiss drive. Semi-floating rear axle. Overall ratio: 4.1:1. Duo-servo hydraulic brakes on four wheels. Steel disc wheels. Rim size: 4-1/2 in. Drivetrain options: No-Rol. Economy (3.9) or Mountain (4.55) axles.

PONTIAC — STREAMLINER — KB LINE — SIX/EIGHT: Streamliner styling changes were the same as Torpedo changes. Streamliners used the larger GM B-body and had fastback rooflines (except station wagons). The 1941 Super models with folding rear seat center arm rests were called Chieftains in 1942. The hood side moldings on Sixes and Eights carried different wording.

I.D. DATA: Serial numbers on left side of dash. Starting: (six) P6KB-1001/(eight) P8KB-1001. Ending: (six) P6KB-11115/(eight) P8KB-22928. (Pontiac, Mich.). California cars had a "C" prefix. New Jersey cars had an "L" prefix. Engine numbers on front left corner of block. Starting: same as serial numbers. Ending: same as serial numbers.

Model No.	Body Type & Seating	Price	Weight	Prod. Total
SERIES 26 (Streamliner Six)				
2607	2-dr. Sed. Cpe.-5P	980	3355	Note 1
2609	4-dr. Sed.-5P	1035	3415	Note 1
STA WAG	4-dr. Sta. Wag.-8P	1265	3810	Note 1
SERIES 26 (Chieftain Six)				
2607D	2-dr. Sed. cpe.-5P	1030	3400	Note 1
2609D	4-dr. Sed.-5P	1085	3460	Note 1
STA WAG	4-dr. Sta. Wag.-8P	1315	3785	Note 1
SERIES 28 (Streamliner Eight)				
2807	2-dr. Sed. Cpe.-5P	1005	3430	Note 2
2809	4-dr. Sed.-5P	1060	3485	Note 2
STA WAG	4-dr. Sta. Wag.-8P	1290	3885	Note 2
SERIES 28 (Chieftain Eight)				
2807D	2-dr. Sed. Cpe.-5P	1055	3460	Note 2
2809D	2-dr. Sed.-5P	1110	3515	Note 2
STA WAG	4-dr. Sta. Wag.-8P	1340	3865	Note 2

Note 1: No body style breakouts. Total series production (six) was 12,742 cars. (Includes 2,458 Chieftains).
Note 2: No body style breakouts. Total series production (eight) was 26,506 cars. (Includes 11,041 Chieftains).

ENGINE: Same specifications as Torpedo engines.

CHASSIS: W.B.: 122 in. O.L.: 210-1/4 in. Height: 65-1/4 in. Frt. tread: 58 in. Rear tread: 61-1/2 in. Tires: 16 x 6.50.

TECHNICAL: Drivetrain same specifications as Torpedos, except overall drive ratio is 4.3:1.

OPTIONS: Master grille guard. Bumper wing tip guards. Wheel trim rings. Oil bath air cleaner. Electric clock (std. in Chieftains). Safety-flex steering wheel (std. in Chieftains). Five-tube radio. Seven-tube radio. Mast antenna (std. with radio pkg.). Vacuum antenna. Rear view mirror. Weather chief header. Fender skirts. Seat covers.

1942 Pontiac, 4-dr. sedan, HAC

HISTORICAL: Introduced: Sept. 1941. Steering wheel with center horn button. Bigger front brakes. Oil cleaner redesigned and improved. Triple-sealed brakes. Duplex rear springs improved to eliminate squeaks. Rheostat dash panel lighting. Calendar year production: 15,404. Model year production: 85,555. Company president: H.J. Klingler. Production halted Feb. 10, 1942 because of U.S. entry into WWII. In Jan. 1942, Pontiac became first U.S. auto-maker to win U.S. Navy "E" pennant for production excellence.

1942
Torpedo, 8-cyl.

	FP	5	4	3	2	1
Conv	1190	3100	6150	10,250	14,350	20,500
Bus Cpe	920	675	1300	2600	4400	6300
Spt Cpe	960	700	1350	2800	4550	6500
5P Cpe	975	700	1350	2900	4600	6600
2 dr Sed	965	650	1200	2300	4100	5800
4 dr Sed	1010	650	1250	2400	4150	5900
Metro Sed	1010	675	1300	2600	4400	6300
Streamliner, 8-cyl.						
Cpe	1005	750	1450	3300	4900	7000
Sed	1060	675	1300	2600	4400	6300
Sta Wag	1290	1300	4000	6650	9300	13,300
Chieftain, 8-cyl.						
Cpe	1055	775	1500	3600	5100	7300
Sed	1110	700	1350	2800	4550	6500
Sta Wag	1340	1350	4150	6900	9700	13,800

NOTE: Deduct 10 percent for 6-cyl. models.

POPE-HARTFORD — Hartford, Connecticut — (1904-1914) — The Pope empire had its beginnings in Boston after the Civil War. In 1876 Colonel Albert A. Pope established his Pope Manufacturing Company for the production of small patented articles. The first Pope-designed bicycle followed in 1877 with manufacture consigned to the Weed Sewing Machine Company in Hartford, Connecticut. In 1880 Pope took over the Weed factory and moved into bicycle building in earnest. The American Bicycle Company, the "bicycle trust" which was a consolidation of some forty-five bicycle-producing firms, was a Pope creation in 1899 — and laid the basis for the empire to follow. The first Pope foray into the automotive field had arrived two years earlier; the car was called Columbia (the tradename of the original Pope bicycle) and was ultimately produced in collaboration with the Electric Vehicle Company. Shortly after the turn of the century, with the dying out of the "bicycle craze," Pope strode more emphatically into the automotive field. A flurry of further Pope automobiles arrived, these built solely under the Pope aegis. The Pope-Hartford was the longest-lived of these — and only one produced in the Pope Manufacturing Company's headquarters town of Hartford, Connecticut. The prototype of the single-cylinder Pope-Hartford was tested during the summer of

1904 Pope-Hartford, model B, tonneau, HAC

1903 and was introduced on the market for 1904. A twin followed for 1905, a four for 1906; a six-cylinder Pope-Hartford did not arrive until 1911. A 1910 Pope-Hartford Forty won the free-for-all race in November of 1909 celebrating the 300th anniversary of the discovery of San Francisco Bay by Don Gaspar de Portola, and for 1911 Pope-Hartford made available a chain-drive Fiat chassis fitted with a Pope engine and marketed as the Fiat-Portola. On August 10th, 1909 Colonel Albert A. Pope had died at the age of sixty-six, his place at the Pope empire's helm being taken by his brother George. But already that empire was beginning to crumble. The receivership into which the company was flung in 1913 was Pope's third. By now all of the other Pope automobiles had disappeared. Pope-Hartford production continued under receivership, what commercial success it enjoyed now being simply the result of its longtime reputation as a solidly built if quite conservative motorcar. Like the Pope empire itself, the Pope-Hartford was burdened by its own weight, in this case a welter of models far too numerous for a production that was never more than 700 cars annually. For 1914 the Pope-Hartford was offered in three body styles on a single chassis. But this retrenchment was far too late. Since its receivership in 1913, the Pope Manufacturing Company had gradually been selling off its property. During the first week of January 1915 the final sale was made, of its main plant in Hartford. It was bought for $300,000 by Pratt & Whitney. George Pope died on April 19th, 1918 at the age of seventy-five.

1904 POPE-HARTFORD
Single — 10 hp, 78" wb

	FP	5	4	3	2	1
Model A Runabout-2P	1050	2300	3300	4600	7500	16,000
Model B Tonneau-4P	1200	2400	3400	4800	8000	17,000

1905 Pope-Hartford, model D, tonneau, HAC

1905 POPE-HARTFORD
Single — 10 hp, 78" wb

Model B Tonneau	1000	2300	3300	4600	7500	16,000
Twin — 16 hp, 88" wb						
Model D Tonneau	1600	2400	3400	4800	8000	17,000

1906 POPE-HARTFORD
Model G — 2 cyl., 18 hp, 88" wb

Touring-5P	1600	2300	3300	4600	7500	16,000
Model F — 4 cyl., 20/25 hp, 98" wb						
Touring-5P	2500	2400	3400	4800	8000	17,000

1907 POPE-HARTFORD
Model G — 2 cyl., 18 hp, 88" wb

Touring-5P	1600	2400	3400	4800	8000	17,000
Model X — 2 cyl., 16/20 hp, 95" wb						
Runabout-2P	1750	2200	3200	4400	7000	15,000
Model L — 4 cyl., 25/30 hp, 102" wb						
Touring-5P	2750	2500	3500	5000	8500	18,000
Runabout-4P	2750	2400	3400	4800	8000	17,000
Limousine	3750	2200	3200	4400	7000	15,000

1906 Pope-Hartford, model F, touring, HAC

1907 Pope-Hartford, model L, runabout, WLB

1908 POPE-HARTFORD
Model R — 4 cyl., 25 hp, 102" wb

	FP	5	4	3	2	1
Runabout-2P	2500	2500	3500	5000	8500	18,000
Touring-5P	2500	2700	3600	5300	8800	19,000
Model M — 4 cyl., 30 hp, 112" wb						
Touring-5P	2750	2900	3700	5600	9100	20,000
Runabout-2P	2750	2700	3600	5300	8800	19,000
Limousine	2750	2400	3400	4800	8000	17,000

1909 Pope-Hartford, model S, pony tonneau, HAC

1909 POPE-HARTFORD
Model S — 4 cyl., 30 hp, 114" wb

Touring-5P	2750	2700	3600	5300	8800	19,000
Cape Top Touring-5P	2900	3000	4000	6000	9500	21,000
Touring-7P	3000	3100	4200	6300	10,500	22,000
Small Tonneau-4P	2750	2400	3400	4800	8000	17,000
Cape Top Small Tonneau-4P	2875	2500	3500	5000	8500	18,000
Roadster-5P	2750	2700	3600	5300	8800	19,000
Landaulet-7P	3750	2500	3500	5000	8500	18,000

1910 Pope-Hartford, model T, roadster, HAC

Model T — 4 cyl., 40 hp, 122" wb

	FP	5	4	3	2	1
Roadster-4P	2750	3100	4200	6300	10,500	22,000
Touring-5P	2750	3200	4300	6500	11,000	23,000
Limousine	3750	2500	3500	5000	8500	18,000
Landaulet	4750	2700	3600	5300	8800	19,000
Touring-7P	3000	3300	4400	6700	12,000	24,000
Pony Tonneau-4P	2750	3200	4300	6500	11,000	23,000

1911 Pope-Hartford, model W, touring, HAC

1911 POPE-HARTFORD
Model W — 4 cyl., 50 hp, 124" wb

	FP	5	4	3	2	1
Touring-5P	3000	4000	5000	8000	15,000	28,000
Pony Tonneau-4P	3000	3900	4800	7700	14,300	27,000
Roadster-4P	3000	3700	4700	7300	13,700	26,000
Limousine	4150	2900	3700	5600	9100	20,000
Landaulet	4150	3000	4000	6000	9500	21,000
Touring-7P	3250	4200	5200	8400	15,700	29,000

Model Y — 6 cyl., 50 hp, 134" wb

	FP	5	4	3	2	1
Touring-5P	4000	4900	6300	10,300	21,000	34,000
Roadster-4P	4000	4700	6100	9900	19,000	33,000
Limousine	5150	4400	5600	9200	17,300	31,000
Landaulet	5150	4500	5800	9500	18,000	32,000

1912 Pope-Hartford, model 28, touring, FR

1912 POPE-HARTFORD
Model 27 — 4 cyl., 50 hp, 124" wb

	FP	5	4	3	2	1
Touring-5P	3000	4700	6100	9900	19,000	33,000
Phaeton-5P	3000	4700	6100	9900	19,000	33,000
Pony Tonneau-4P	3000	4900	6300	10,300	21,000	34,000
Roadster-2P	3000	4500	5800	9500	18,000	32,000
Roadster-4P	3000	4700	6100	9900	19,000	33,000
Touring-7P	3250	5000	6500	11,000	22,000	35,000
Limousine	4150	3500	4500	7000	13,000	25,000
Landaulet	4150	3700	4700	7300	13,700	26,000
Berline	4400	3900	4800	7700	14,300	27,000

Model 28 — 6 cyl., 60 hp, 134" wb

	FP	5	4	3	2	1
Touring-7P	4000	5400	7300	11,800	25,000	38,000
Phaeton-5P	4000	5200	6800	11,300	23,000	36,000
Pony Tonneau-4P	4000	5300	7000	11,500	24,000	37,000
Roadster-2P	4000	5200	6800	11,300	23,000	36,000
Roadster-4P	4000	5300	6900	11,400	23,500	36,500
Limousine	5150	4200	5200	8400	15,700	29,000
Landaulet	5150	4300	5400	8700	16,500	30,000
Berline	5400	4400	5600	9200	17,300	31,000

1913 POPE-HARTFORD
Model 31 — 4 cyl., 40 hp, 118" wb

	FP	5	4	3	2	1
Touring-5P	2250	4200	5200	8400	15,700	29,000
Phaeton-4P	2250	4200	5200	8400	15,700	29,000
Roadster-2P	2250	4000	5000	8000	15,000	28,000
Limousine-5P	3250	2700	3600	5300	8800	19,000
Coupe-3P	2850	2200	3200	4400	7000	15,000

Model 33 — 4 cyl., 50 hp, 124" wb

	FP	5	4	3	2	1
Touring-5P	3250	4500	5800	9500	18,000	32,000
Touring-7P	3500	5000	6500	11,000	22,000	35,000
Phaeton-5P	3250	4900	6300	10,300	21,000	34,000
Roadster-2P	3250	4700	6100	9900	19,000	33,000
Limousine-7P	4300	3100	4200	6300	10,500	22,000
Landaulet-7P	4300	3200	4300	6500	11,000	23,000
Berline-7P	4550	3500	4500	7000	14,300	25,000

1913 Pope-Hartford, model 29, roadster, HAC

Model 29 — 6 cyl., 60 hp, 133" wb

	FP	5	4	3	2	1
Touring-7P	4250	5800	8000	12,500	28,000	40,000
Touring-5P	4250	5500	7500	12,000	26,000	39,000
Roadster-2P	4250	5400	7300	11,800	25,000	38,000
Limousine-7P	5300	3300	4400	6700	12,000	24,000
Landaulet-7P	5300	3500	4500	7000	13,000	25,000
Berline-7P	5550	3900	4800	7700	14,300	27,000

1914 Pope-Hartford, model 35, touring, HAC

1914 POPE-HARTFORD
Model 35 — 4 cyl., 40 hp, 118½" wb

	FP	5	4	3	2	1
Touring-5P	2250	4200	5200	8400	15,700	29,000
Roadster-2P	2250	4000	5000	8000	15,000	28,000
Coupe-3P	2850	2200	3200	4400	7000	15,000

1904 Pope-Robinson, touring, WLB

POPE-ROBINSON — Hyde Park, Massachusetts — (1903-1904) — Sometime during the summer of 1902 the Robinson Motor Vehicle Company which had been established in Hyde Park in May of 1901 was acquired by Colonel Albert A. Pope. John T. Robinson remained as president, but the Colonel dispatched his nephew Edward W. Pope to serve as secretary-treasurer of the new Pope-Robinson Company which was formally incorporated in September with an increase in capital stock from $100,000 to $200,000. Construction of a new factory in Hyde Park was immediately begun. For the remainder of the year, orders already on hand for the Robinson were filled; the new Pope-Robinson was introduced in January 1903. It was a bigger four than its predecessor and, at $6000, was twice as expensive. One of the first Pope-Robinsons was delivered to Mr. Smith of typewriter fame in Syracuse, New York, another was destined for the garage of Charles J. Glidden. A T-head engine of 24 hp, final drive by double chain, a maximum speed of 35 mph, and high quality construction throughout were among the distinguishing features of the Pope-Robinson. But its price was terribly high, and a slashing to $4500 for the 1904 model year was too late to be effective. The Pope-Robinson was discontinued later that year, as the Popes busied themselves with the other cars in their empire. Among other reasons for the Popes' abrupt dismissal of this car might have been John T. Robinson's illness, which led to his death in November 1904. The Pope-Robinson company was purchased by Buick at year's end as a convenient means by which the Flint company could acquire an A.L.A.M. license. The Selden Patent case was raging through the courts at the time.

1903 POPE-ROBINSON
Four — 24 hp, 81" wb

	FP	5	4	3	2	1
Touring-5/6P	6000	3100	4200	6300	10,500	22,000

1904 POPE-ROBINSON
Four — 24 hp, 95" wb

	FP	5	4	3	2	1
Touring-5/6P	4500	3100	4200	6300	10,500	22,000

1904 Pope-Toledo, twin touring, HAC

POPE-TOLEDO — Toledo, Ohio — (1904-1909) — The Pope Toledo was the star of the Pope empire. It was the successor to the Toledo built by the International Motor Car Company, that firm having also been part of the Pope empire. On May 27th, 1903 the announcement was made that the new Pope Motor Car Company would henceforth occupy the old International's factory, and that a new car called the Pope-Toledo would be introduced for the 1904 model year. On the West Coast, in November of 1903, a stock four-cylinder 24 hp model was entered in numerous events in both San Francisco and Los Angeles — and won most of them, sometimes defeating such formidable foreign competition as Mercedes and Mors. It was an impressive way to launch a new marque, and "The Mile-a-Minute Car" was the slogan for 1904. In addition to its $3500 24 hp four, Pope-Toledo offered a $2000 two-cylinder touring car during its maiden season. The twin was dropped for 1905, however, and all subsequent cars were big, expensive fours. In October 1904 a 24 hp Pope-Toledo driven by Herbert Lytle had finished third in the prestigious Vanderbilt Cup, lending further credence to the marque's performance image. Subsequent advertising played more heavily on the quality angle: "The Car That Meets Every Requirement" from 1907, "The All Ball Bearing — All Alloyed Steel Car" from 1908. A robustly built automobile, copper water jackets, suction intake valves, three-speed sliding gear transmissions and double chain drive were typical Pope-Toledo features. Nineteen eight was the marque's final full year. Beset with difficulties within the Pope empire, the Pope Motor Car Company was driven into bankruptcy early that year. The last cars — designated 1909 models — were produced under receivership. In January 1909, Richard D. Apperson (the vice-president of the American National Bank of Lynchburg, Virginia, and no relation to the Appersons of Kokomo, Indiana) announced that he would acquire the Pope-Toledo plant and continue the car in production as the Toledo. Apperson displayed one of the Pope-cum-Toledos at the Chicago Automobile Show in January 1909, but by April his negotiations with the Pope-Toledo receivers had fallen through. Instead, in April 1909 the Pope-Toledo plant was acquired by Overland — and the Pope-Toledo was no more.

1904 POPE-TOLEDO
Twin — 14 hp, 76" wb

Touring-5P	2000	2000	3000	4200	6500	14,000

Four — 24 hp, 94" wb

Touring-5P	3500	2300	3300	4600	7500	16,000

1905 Pope-Toledo, type IX, tonneau, HAC

1905 POPE-TOLEDO
Model X — 4 cyl., 20 hp, 88" wb

Side-Entrance Tonneau	2800	1800	2800	4000	6200	13,000

Model VII — 4 cyl., 30 hp, 96" wb

Front-Entrance Tonneau	3200	2000	3000	4200	6500	14,000

Model VIII — 4 cyl., 30 hp, 100" wb

Side-Entrance Tonneau	3500	2200	3200	4400	7000	15,000

Model IX — 4 cyl., 45 hp, 104" wb

Side-Entrance Tonneau	6000	4100	8250	13,750	19,250	27,500

1906 Pope-Toledo, type XII, touring, WLB

1906 POPE-TOLEDO
Type VII — 4 cyl., 30/35 hp, 96" wb

	FP	5	4	3	2	1
Victoria Tour. Rbt.-2P	2500	2400	3400	4800	8000	17,000

Type X — 4 cyl., 20/24-hp, 88" wb

Touring-5P	2800	2450	3500	4900	8300	17,500
Landaulette-5P	4000	2500	3500	5000	8500	18,000

Type XII — 4 cyl., 35/40 hp, 104" wb

Touring-5P	3500	4100	8250	13,750	19,250	27,500
Limousine-5P	5000	2900	3700	5600	9100	20,000

1907 Pope-Toledo, type XII, touring, HAC

1907 POPE-TOLEDO
Type XII — 4 cyl., 35/40 hp, 104" wb

Touring-7P	3500	3500	4500	7000	13,000	25,000
Limousine	5000	3000	4000	6000	9500	21,000

Type XV — 4 cyl., 50 hp, 115" wb

Touring-7P	4250	4000	5000	8000	15,000	28,000
Limousine	6000	3300	4400	6700	12,000	24,000

1908 Pope-Toledo, type 17, cape top landaulet touring, JAC

1908 Pope-Toledo, type XVIII, runabout, HAC

1908 POPE-TOLEDO
Type XII — 4 cyl., 35/40 hp, 104'' wb

	FP	5	4	3	2	1
Touring	3000	3700	4700	7300	13,700	26,000

Type XVII — 4 cyl., 50 hp, 126'' wb

Touring	4500	4000	5000	8000	15,000	28,000

Type XVIII — 4 cyl., 50 hp, 126'' wb

Runabout	4500	4000	5000	8000	15,000	28,000

Type XVI — 4 cyl., 50 hp, 115'' wb

Touring	4250	4300	5400	8700	16,500	30,000

1909 POPE-TOLEDO
Type XXI — 4 cyl., 50 hp, 115'' wb

Touring-4P	4250	3900	4800	7700	14,300	27,000
Cape Top Tour.-4P	4475	4000	5000	8000	15,000	28,000

Type XXIII — 4 cyl., 50 hp, 115'' wb

Limousine	—	3700	4700	7300	13,700	26,000

Type XXII — 4 cyl., 50 hp, 126'' wb

Touring-7P	4250	4000	5000	8000	15,000	28,000
Cape Top Tour.-7P	4475	4200	5200	8400	15,700	29,000

1904 Pope-Tribune, runabout, WLB

POPE-TRIBUNE — Hagerstown, Maryland — (1904-1908) — The smallest and the least expensive car in the Pope domain, the Pope-Tribune was built in Hagerstown, Maryland in the factory which formerly had been used for the manufacture of the Crawford bicycle. Harold Pope, son of Colonel Albert A. Pope, was in charge. Shaft drive from the beginning, the Pope-Tribune was introduced as a $650 one-cylinder runabout in 1904. A 12 hp twin was added to the line for 1905; it was made heftier for 1906 and was the only model that year. Thus far, no Pope-Tribune had exceeded the $1000 mark, but for 1907 a bigger four was the marque's offering, and the price tag zoomed to $1750. Prices were higher still in 1908; by that time the Pope-Tribune had effectively lost its market, and the Pope empire was rapidly proceeding into disarray. In November of 1908 the Hagerstown plant — which had never shown a profit — was sold at a loss to the Montrose Metal Casket Company.

1904 POPE-TRIBUNE

Rbt. (1-cyl., 6 hp, 65'' wb)	650	1800	2800	4000	6200	13,000

1905 Pope-Tribune, model IV, touring, HAC

1905 POPE-TRIBUNE
Model II — 1-cyl., 6 hp, 65'' wb

	FP	5	4	3	2	1
Runabout-2P	500	1800	2800	4000	6200	13,000

Model IV — 2-cyl., 12 hp, 82'' wb

Tonneau-4P	900	2200	3200	4400	7000	15,000

1906 Pope-Tribune, model VI, runabout, HAC

1906 POPE-TRIBUNE
Model V/VI — 2-cyl., 14 hp, 85'' wb

Runabout/Touring	900	2200	3200	4400	7000	15,000

1907 Pope-Tribune, model X, runabout, HAC

1907 POPE-TRIBUNE
Model X — 4-cyl., 16/20 hp, 95'' wb

Runabout/Touring-2/4P	1750	2700	3600	5300	8800	19,000

1908 Pope-Tribune, model X, touring, HAC

1908 POPE-TRIBUNE
Model X — 4-cyl., 16/20 hp, 95'' wb

Runabout/Touring-2/4P	1750	2700	3600	5300	8800	19,000

Model M — 4-cyl., 30 hp, 112'' wb

Touring-5P	2750	3100	4200	6300	10,500	22,000
Runabout-2P (108'' wb)	2750	3000	4000	6000	9500	21,000

1905 Pope-Waverley, Chelsea runabout, HAC

POPE-WAVERLEY ELECTRIC — Indianapolis, Indiana — (1904-1908) —

The only electric car produced by Colonel Albert A. Pope, the Pope-Waverley was initially called just the Waverley. It was introduced as such in 1898 following the consolidation of the American Electric Vehicle Company of Chicago and the Indiana Bicycle Company of Indianapolis. The latter firm was one of the nearly fifty in Colonel Pope's bicycle "trust" known as the American Bicycle Company. The Waverley became the Pope-Waverley for the 1904 model year and continued as same for the four years following, produced now by the Waverley Department of the Pope Motor Car Company of Indianapolis. This was merely a case of a new sign being put up over the factory door. As the Pope-Waverley, however, the line was considerably expanded into a flurry of different models, which most probably was a mistake. By 1907 the Pope-Waverley was being continued in production under receivership, as was the Pope-Tribune in Hagerstown, Maryland. But not for long. In September of 1908 — two months before unloading the Hagerstown plant — the Pope organization sold its Indianapolis factory to a local syndicate which moved in, reorganized and promptly renamed the product a Waverley again.

1906 Pope-Waverley, model 60B, surrey, HAC

1904 POPE-WAVERLEY

	FP	5	4	3	2	1
Model 21 Road Wagon (61" wb)	850	2200	3200	4400	7000	15,000
Model 29 Physician's Road Wagon (72" wb)	1050	2300	3300	4600	7500	16,000
Model 27 Stanhope (70" wb)	1400	2400	3400	4800	8000	17,000
Model 26 Chelsea (80" wb)	1100	2200	3200	4400	7000	15,000
Model 26C Coupe Top Chelsea (80" wb)	1200	2300	3300	4600	7500	16,000
Model 20 Surrey (77½" wb)	1500	2400	3400	4800	8000	17,000
Model 28 Special Edison Battery (87" wb)	2250	2500	3500	5000	8500	18,000
Model 30 Station Wagon (77½" wb)	1800	2300	3300	4600	7500	16,000
Model 23 Delivery Wagon (80" wb)	1400	2200	3200	4400	7000	15,000
Model 24 Service Wagon (80" wb)	1400	2200	3200	4400	7000	15,000

1905 POPE-WAVERLEY

	FP	5	4	3	2	1
Model 20 Surrey (77-1/2" wb)	1500	2400	3400	4800	8000	17,000
Model 27 Stanhope (70" wb)	1400	2300	3300	4600	7500	16,000
Model 36 Spd. Road Wagon (76" wb)	900	2000	3000	4200	6500	14,000
Model 26 Chelsea (80" wb)	1100	2300	3300	4600	7500	16,000

1905 POPE-WAVERLEY

	FP	5	4	3	2	1
Model 26 Cpe. Top Chelsea (80" wb)	1450	2400	3400	4800	8000	17,000
Model 28 Spe. Wagon (87" wb)	1800	2300	3300	4600	7500	16,000
Model 21 Road Wagon (61" wb)	850	1900	2900	4100	6400	13,500
Model 30 Sta. Wag. (77-1/2" wb)	2250	2200	3200	4400	7000	15,000
Model 29 Physician's Road Wagon (72" wb)	1100	2200	3200	4400	7000	15,000

1906 Pope-Waverley, Speed Road Wagon, runabout, OCW

1906 POPE-WAVERLEY

	FP	5	4	3	2	1
Model 21 Runabout (61" wb)	850	2000	3000	4200	6500	14,000
Model 36B Speed Road Wagon (72" wb)	950	2100	3100	4300	6800	14,500
Model 60B Surrey (90" wb)	1700	2400	3400	4800	8000	17,000
Model 65 Sthp. (70" wb)	1400	2300	3300	4600	7500	16,000
Model 30 Sta. Wag. (77-1/2" wb)	2250	2200	3200	4400	7000	15,000
Model 26C Chelsea Cpe. (80" wb)	1600	2300	3300	4600	7500	16,000
Model 29 Physician's Road Wagon (72" wb)	1150	2200	3200	4400	7000	15,000
Model 29C Canopy Top Road Wagon (72" wb)	1250	2000	3000	4200	6500	14,000

1907 Pope-Waverley, runabout, WLB

1907 POPE-WAVERLEY

	FP	5	4	3	2	1
Model 67 Runabout	1600	2200	3200	4400	7000	15,000
Model 53-A Victoria	2000	2400	3400	4800	8000	17,000
Model 53-B Coupe	2200	2500	3500	5000	8500	18,000
Model 60-B Surrey	1825	2400	3400	4800	8000	17,000
Model 65 Stanhope	1500	2300	3300	4600	7500	16,000

	FP	5	4	3	2	1
Model 30 Outside Drive	2250	2500	3500	5000	8500	18,000
Model 69B Runabout	1225	2000	3000	4200	6500	14,000
Model 26B Runabout	1475	2300	3300	4600	7500	16,000
Model 26C Chelsea Coupe	1700	2400	3400	4800	8000	17,000
Model 36 Road Wagon	900	2200	3200	4400	7000	15,000
Model 21 Runabout	850	2200	3200	4400	7000	15,000
Model 29 Physician's Wagon	1150	2300	3300	4600	7500	16,000
Model 29C Physician's Wagon	1200	2300	3300	4600	7500	16,000

1908 Pope-Waverley, model 60, surrey, HAC

1908 POPE-WAVERLEY

	FP	5	4	3	2	1
Model 70 Victoria Coupe	1900	2500	3500	5000	8500	18,000
Model 71 Runabout	1425	2000	3000	4200	6500	14,000
Model 65 Stanhope	1500	2300	3300	4600	7500	16,000
Model 60 Surrey	1750	2400	3400	4800	8000	17,000
Model 30 Station Wagon	2000	2200	3200	4400	7000	15,000
Model 67 Victoria Phaeton	1525	2400	3400	4800	8000	17,000
Model 26 Chelsea	1400	2300	3300	4600	7500	16,000
Model 26 Chelsea Leather Top	1475	2500	3500	5000	8500	18,000
Model 26 Chelsea Removable Coupe	1700	2700	3600	5300	8800	19,000
Model 69 Runabout	1150	2300	3300	4600	7500	16,000
Model 69 Runabout Leather Top	1225	2400	3400	4800	8000	17,000

POPPENBERG — The Poppenberg Motor Company was one of three firms involved in the production and marketing of the Niagara Four which was manufactured in Buffalo, New York from 1915-1916. Refer to Niagara Four.

POPPY — Los Angeles, California — (1917) — A decade after building his Compound on the East Coast, John W. Eisenhuth headed west to try again. After promoting a "noiseless engine" in San Francisco (an unhappy investor had him arrested), Eisenhuth showed up in Los Angeles with a new car to be called the Poppy, after the state flower of California. In late December of 1917, he organized the Eisenhuth Motor Company in Los Angeles, with a whopping capital stock of $10,000,000. Plans called for the construction of a factory in L.A.'s San Pedro district, and the manufacture of a $650 five-cylinder car on a 120-inch wheelbase destined to be a world-beater. "No transmission will be used, and a secret and exclusive system of reverse is to be featured," the press release said. "By use of a new gear invention the drive will be direct. Through various manipulations 1202 parts of the present standard car will be eliminated." Among the latter, the Poppy five-cylinder engine had just 79 parts "against the customary more than 200 in a four-cylinder type." The Poppy assuredly never made it into manufacture. History is left wondering what Eisenhuth planned instead of a transmission, and what his secret system of backing up might have been. His secret died with him on May 14th, 1918.

POPULAIRE — Although occasionally shortened to Populaire, the automobile built by the American Automobile and Power Company of Sanford, Maine from 1904-1905 was more usually designated the American Populaire. Refer to American Populaire.

PORTER STEAM — Allston, Massachusetts — (1900-1901) — Major D. Porter of New York was the inventor, and Dr. Abner T. Wells and Dalton Fallon put up the money. Together they established the Porter Motor Company, took offices in the Tremont Building in Boston, and secured a 100-by-36-foot factory in nearby Allston. Porter, who had been in the motor business since 1886, designed a two-cylinder single-acting steam engine which could use either kerosene or gasoline as fuel. The boiler was tubular, divided into three compartments and had been tested to 1000 pounds pressure "to insure against explosion." The two-passenger runabout body was unusual for the period in being made entirely of aluminum, with watertight compartments to carry the fuel and water supply. One supply of each was sufficient for fifty miles running, at about a half cent a mile. Interesting, too, was the Porter's safety device; whenever the hand was removed from the single controlling lever, the power shut off. The Porter, or Portermobile as it was alternately known, was priced in the $750-$1000 range and was in production for approximately two years.

1900 Porter, steamer, runabout, GR

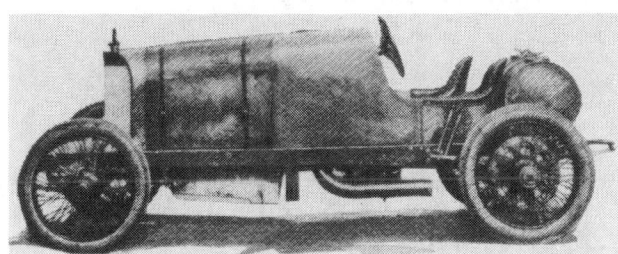

1915 Porter-Knight, racer, NAHC

PORTER — Bridgeport, Connecticut — (1919-1922) — The F.R.P. and the Porter were essentially the same cars with different names — and the name referred to in each case was Finley Robertson Porter, the man who became famous as the designer and engineer of the legendary T-head Mercer. Following his departure from the Trenton company in 1914, Porter built three Knight-engined race cars for the Indianapolis 500 but they failed with engine problems before making it to the starting line. But the production car that Porter built called the F.R.P. was a smashing success, a high-class automobile good for at least 80 mph and 12 mpg, both remarkable figures given the size of the car. What halted the F.R.P.'s production after only a few were built was World War I. With America's entrance into the conflict, the Port Jefferson, Long Island factory that was the home of the F.R.P. was taken over by the government. Following the Armistice, the decision was made to resume manufacture, but to leave the work of it to others. The second-generation cars, now to be called Porter, would be built by the American & British Manufacturing Corporation of Bridgeport (Connecticut) and they would be distributed by the Morton W. Smith Company of New York City. Although efficiency and economy were features stressed by Porter the man, Porter the car was anything but cheap. There was a Mercedes look to the car, and a Rolls-Royce aura as well, enhanced by the right-hand drive, certainly a curiosity on American roads by that date. The four-cylinder engine of the F.R.P. had been beefed up from 100 to 125 hp for the Porter, and while the former car had been built on several chassis varying in length from 110 to 140 inches, the latter had but one chassis which stretched an enormous 142 inches. All of the cars were custom built by the cream of the American coachmaker's crop:

1920 Porter, touring, WLB

1920 Porter, small enclosed drive limousine, HAC

Brewster, Fleetwood, Demarest, among them. Chassis price was $6750; with coachwork the Porter's price could range upwards of $10,000. Not surprisingly, the car was received spectacularly at automobile shows. Not surprisingly, too, it failed to survive the postwar recession. A total of thirty-six Porters were built.

PORTLAND — The Portland & Rockland Automobile Company was organized in Portland, Maine late in 1906 with a $10,000 capital stock to manufacture and sell automobiles. Heading this venture was J.A. Lester of South Thomaston. Manufacture is doubted.

1914 Portland cyclecar, 2-pass. tandem, WLB

PORTLAND — Portland, Oregon — (1914) — Whether to call the product a Portland or a Pacific seems to have been among the dilemmas confronting Lewis I. Thompson and C.J. McPherson. The product was a tandem two-seater cyclecar on a 96-inch wheelbase powered by a two-cylinder two-stroke vee engine. A planetary transmission and belt drive were featured — and the price was $395. In January of 1914 the Messrs. Thompson and McPherson organized their Portland Cyclecar Company and issued conflicting statements regarding what the car would be called. Whatever the final decision, the Portland/Pacific was not in manufacture long.

PORTO RICO — The Porto Rico Motors Company was organized in Greenwich, Connecticut during the spring of 1912 with a capital stock of $150,000 for the manufacture of automobiles. Incorporators were M.A. Mills, Jr., L.J. Whiteside and E.J. Ryan. Manufacture is doubted.

PORTSMOUTH — The Portsmouth Automobile & Machine Company was organized with a capital stock of $10,000 late in 1911 to manufacture and deal in automobiles in Portsmouth, Ohio. Behind this venture were Lincoln Poole, Walter O. Ruhlman, Ray A. Oakes, Filmore Musser and Edward C. Riegel. Manufacture is doubted.

POSITIVE TRACTION — That a front wheel drive car was built in 1926 by the Positive Traction Motors Corporation of Brookline, Massachusetts has been indicated on numerous rosters. The city directories for Brookline indicate no such company in town for the years from 1925 through 1927, and Boston directories for the same period reveal no Positive Traction either. The company is not included in the *Marvyn Scudder Manual of Extinct or Obsolete Companies*. But it appears that at one time such a company existed. After his car venture, Maurice G. Dusseau patented a universal joint, 95% of which he assigned to the Positive Traction Motors Corporation.

POSS — The Poss Motor Company was organized in Detroit, Michigan during the summer of 1911 with a capital stock of $250,000 to manufacture and deal in automobiles, motors and motor vehicles. Incorporators were Frank P. Poss, Robert R. McKinley, Joseph M. Ness and George W. Bailey. The firm did build commercial vehicles in Detroit the year following but is not believed to have manufactured an automobile.

POST — The Post Lock Register Company was organized in New York City early in 1910 with a capital stock of $150,000 for the manufacture of taxicabs "and lock registers for same." Incorporators were T.W. Post, G.W. Morse and C. Colgate. Manufacture of taxis is doubted.

POST — New London, Ohio — (1909) — In 1909 Charles Bushnell Post of New London built an automobile for himself powered by an air-cooled gasoline engine with friction transmission. It was a highwheeler seating four people and riding on rubber tires. There is no evidence that he built another car, though he did put together a motorcycle. He is known to have designed and built a tractor as well. He was an inveterate tinkerer, and whenever a local industrial plant needed some gadget or device to make production easier, Charles Bushnell Post could usually come up with it.

1907 Postal, model 2, runabout, NAHC

POSTAL — New Bedford, Indiana — (1906-1908) — Fred Postal of New Bedford had an idea and fortunately the Anderson Machine Company in town had just gone out of business so he had a place to see it through. Like the Anderson, the Postal was a highwheeler, with tiller steering, two-cylinder air-cooled engine and drive by steel cable. But the machine differed in that it was said to be "especially designed for rural mail service." Whether this was indeed the case, and whether the presence of fenders on the rear wheels only was the "especially designed" aspect is not known. More likely, the canny inventor of this very unsophisticated highwheeler thought his last name made for a great gimmick. How many Postals in fact carried the mail in Indiana is not known either. Toward the end of 1908 the Postal Automobile & Engineering Company was bought by the Buggy Car Company of Cincinnati and moved to Ohio.

1906-1908 POSTAL
Model 2 — 2-cyl., 12½ hp, 70" wb

	FP	5	4	3	2	1
Runabout	475	1600	2700	3800	5800	12,000

POSTE — Columbus, Ohio — (1899) — Beale E. Poste, John Hamilton Poste, Charles D. Hinman, Henry Gumble and Frank C. Smith were the men behind the $25,000 capitalization of the Poste Brothers Buggy Company in Columbus during the spring of 1899. The incorporation "empowered" the company to make and deal in motor vehicles. Having the power to do so, particularly in those early days, might not mean a company necessarily ever did. Poste is listed as a manufacturer in the Hiscox book *Horseless Vehicles, Automobiles, Motor Cycles* published in 1900. Possibly a few cars were built, but there is no evidence of sustained manufacture. Columbus city directory listings at the turn of the century revealed the Poste Brothers Buggy Company as manufacturers of buggies and carriages only.

POTOMIC — The Potomic Motor Company, Inc. was organized in Washington, D.C. early in 1920 with a capital stock of $75,000 for the manufacture and sale of automobiles and trucks. Elmer G. Hilgesen, Howard R. Stewart and Philip B. Key were the incorporators. Manufacture is doubted.

POTTS — The Potts Trolley Wheel Company was organized in Detroit, Michigan during the spring of 1902 with a capital stock of $30,000 for the manufacture of "trolley wheels, automobiles, gas and gasoline engines" in Wyandotte. Behind this venture were E.W. Potts, B.F. Pashby, A.R. McInnes, Collie McPherson and John D. McPherson. Manufacture of a car is doubted.

POWELL — Powell Special has been the incorrect designation occasionally seen for the car designed by Alvah A. Powell and built at the Elcar plant in Elkhart, Indiana in 1930. Its proper designation is Lever. Refer to Lever.
The Powell Engine Corporation was organized in Brooklyn, New York during the fall of 1910 with a $50,000 capital stock for the manufacture of "automobiles, machinery, motors and engines." Incorporators were L.P. Powell, R.W. Powell and C.I. McLaughlin. Manufacture of a car is doubted.

POWELL — Chicago, Illinois — (1918) — Bill Powell of 1730 West Erie Street in Chicago built this midget in 1918. Its engine was an 11 hp Harley-Davidson twin, its transmission a three-speed selective, its weight 400 pounds, its fuel consumption 600 mpg. Airplane tires were fitted. "Mr. Powell built the wheels," *Motor Age* advised. "The gas tanks are in the rear and the oil is in the radiator."

1918 Powell, MVMA

POWER

POWER — The Power Car Company was organized in Indianapolis, Indiana during the spring of 1914 with a capital stock of $15,000 for the manufacture of "self-propelled motor cars." Incorporators were F.M. Fauvre, E.H. Darrach and P.H. White. Manufacture is doubted.

POWER — Montclair, New Jersey — (1901) — In April of 1901, W.M. Power of Montclair announced the impending organization of a $100,000 company for the manufacture of a gasoline car he had invented. By June he had completed his prototype, with plans for production being finalized at his Power Manufacturing Company in nearby Bloomfield, that firm being "well known by reason of excellence of its cycle chains," according to *The Motor Age*. It does not appear that manufacture of the Power car ever followed, however.

1910 Powercar, Thirty, touring, WLB

POWERCAR — Cincinnati, Ohio — (1909-1911) — The name was a misnomer. A four-cylinder 30 hp engine scarcely made for a blazing performance, and during the Powercar's maiden season only a five-passenger touring was offered. Subsequently, the Powercar Automobile Company of Cincinnati provided sportier models, which like the touring featured shaft drive and selective three-speed transmission. But the company — which had been headed by A.H. Miller and Joseph Kroeger — was out of business by the end of 1911. In May of 1912 the Cincinnati Motors Manufacturing Company, headed by F. Alter, Harry T. Alter and J.B. Doan, moved into the defunct Powercar factory and the Alter truck was later built there.

1909 POWERCAR Four — 30 hp, 108" wb	FP	5	4	3	2	1
Touring-5P	1250	3100	4200	6300	10,500	22,000
1910 POWERCAR Four — 30 hp, 108" wb						
Touring-5P	1250	3100	4200	6300	10,500	22,000
Roadster-2P	1250	3000	4000	6000	9500	21,000
Tourabout-4P	1250	3100	4200	6300	10,500	22,000
1911 POWERCAR Four — 30 hp, 115" wb						
Touring-5P	1500	3200	4300	6500	11,000	23,000
Torpedo Roadster-2P	1250	3100	4200	6300	10,500	22,000

PRACTICAL — Although Dr. D.D. Culver of Aurora, Illinois organized the Practical Automobile Company in 1905 to manufacture the highwheeler he had invented, and occasionally he referred to the car by that name too, the one he preferred was his own. Refer to Culver.

PRADO — New York, New York — (1921-1922) — At 90 hp and $9000, the Prado was among the more powerful and expensive cars of the early Twenties. But it was among the least successful as well. Probably fewer than ten cars were produced in all, probably all of them custom-built to owner specification. Prado Motors Corporation was willing to build both open and closed body types, noting a three-passenger Deluxe Speedster as an especially appealing sporting car. A common wheelbase of 142 inches was used for all types. The powerplant was a revised Curtiss OX-5 aircraft engine, a unit which Glenn Curtiss himself had put into a sporting

1921 Prado, touring, KM

car of his own, the Wharton from Dallas also being OX-5 powered during these years. None of the cars survived long. The only change in Prado specifications from 1921 to 1922 seems to have been the replacement of steel with aluminum in many of the chassis parts. The 1921 Prado weighed 3900 pounds, the 1922 had slimmed down to 3175. Disteel wheels and individual fenders remained for both model years. The Prado simply faded away after that.

PRALL — Washington, D.C. — (1897) — W. Edgar Prall invented a rotary engine six inches in length and six inches in diameter which weighed fifty pounds and which he claimed was self-starting and developed four horsepower. The motor was exhibited at the Hotel Arno in Washington in late 1896, and in 1897 Prall built an automobile to demonstrate it. "Mr. Prall makes extraordinary claims for this motor, which he says runs without explosion or jar, and shows an efficiency greater than any other gas engine yet invented," *The Horseless Age* reported. Obviously W. Edgar Prall's extraordinary claims did not prove out any better than those of John E. Praul of Philadelphia two years before. Because the names were so similar, and both engines were a rotary, there is the delicious possibility that these two people were one — and simply trying to sell the same bad idea under another guise.

PRATT — Joliet, Illinois — (1912) — The Economy Motor Buggy Company produced a highwheeler from 1908 through 1911 without notable commercial success. Economy president William R. Everett had also run up during this period an experimental electric-powered roadster and light delivery car, which remained on hand when the personal property of the bankrupt Economy company was put up for sale in Joliet early in 1912. William E. Pratt of the Pratt Manufacturing Company in town bought the property and the Everett electric idea and immediately announced plans for the latter's production under his own name. "Owing to the unsettled matters regarding the plant the new managers will not make any definite statements," *Automobile Trade Journal* reported in April, "but it is known that the car will be priced at not over $1000." No definite statements followed regarding the extent of any production, but more than likely it was either minimal or nonexistent. By September of that year, Everett was in Valparaiso, Indiana attempting to talk the Commercial Club there into manufacturing his car. He had no luck.

1910 Pratt-Elkhart, model I, touring, HAC

PRATT-ELKHART/ Elkhart, Indiana — (1909-1911) / **PRATT** — (1911-1915) — The Elkhart Carriage & Harness Manufacturing Company was big business in Indiana at the turn of the century. The brothers Pratt (William B. serving as president and secretary, George B. as vice-president and treasurer) took the Sears, Roebuck catalog route and advertised themselves as "the Largest Manufacturers of Vehicles and Harness in the World selling to Consumers Exclusively." Probably they were right; their company was a phenomenal success. Unfortunately, applying the direct mail approach to the business of selling cars did not work out nearly as well. The Pratts had built their first car, a motorized buggy, in 1906 but were totally dissatisfied with it. Trial and error finally produced a fine four-cylinder touring car in 1909, and the realization very soon that their mailing list of carriage customers wasn't very useful since the Pratt-Elkhart car was too expensive for their old clientele. But the Pratts, always sticklers for quality, couldn't build it for less. So they rethought, started advertising for dealers, dropped "Elkhart" from their product's name when another company flew into town to build a car called the Crow-Elkhart, and came up with a flurry of new models that were even bigger and more highly priced. When that didn't work either, they retrenched to offering a single model only for 1914, though they added a six and an eight with proprietary engines when they changed the name of their firm to Pratt Motor Car Company in 1915. Just before Halloween that year, they changed their minds again, about everything this time. The company was reorganized as the Elkhart Carriage & Motor Car Company to manufacture an entirely

1911 Pratt-Elkhart, model F, touring, HAC

new car called the Elcar. Answering their country's call during World War I, the Pratts destroyed most of the horsedrawn side of their business to make way for the building of ambulance bodies. Carriage and harness production was never resumed. The Elcar was, in 1919. In 1921 the Pratts retired, leaving the subsequent checkered history of the Elcar to be made by the new business consortium that took charge, many of whose members had worked previously in a nearby town building the Auburn.

1909-1910 PRATT-ELKHART
Model 1 — 4-cyl., 30/35 hp, 117" wb

	FP	5	4	3	2	1
Touring-5P	1600	3700	4700	7300	13,700	26,000

1911 Pratt-Elkhart, model F, roadster, WLB

1911 PRATT-ELKHART
Model F — 4-cyl., 30/35 hp, 117" wb

Fore-Door Touring-5P	1800	3700	4700	7300	13,700	26,000
Open Touring-5P	1750	3500	4500	7000	13,000	25,000
Roadster-2P	1750	3300	4400	6700	12,000	24,000
Limousine-7P	2000	2900	3700	5600	9100	20,000

1912 Pratt, model H, touring, HFM

1912 PRATT
Forty — 4-cyl., 40 hp, 120" wb

Model L Demi-Tonneau-4P	2000	3700	4700	7300	13,700	26,000
Model H Touring-5P	2100	3900	4800	7700	14,300	27,000
Model M Touring-7P	2100	4000	5000	8000	15,000	28,000
Model N Runabout-2P	—	3500	4500	7000	13,000	25,000

1198

1913 Pratt Forty, model H, touring, HAC

1913 PRATT
Model R — 4-cyl., 30 hp, 114" wb

	FP	5	4	3	2	1
Roadster-2P	1400	3500	4500	7000	13,000	25,000
Touring-5P	1400	3700	4700	7300	13,700	26,000

Model H — 4- cyl., 40 hp, 120" wb

Roadster-2P	1850	3700	4700	7300	13,700	26,000
Touring-5P	1850	3900	4800	7700	14,300	27,000
Touring-7P	1950	4000	5000	8000	15,000	28,000

Model C — 4-cyl., 50 hp, 122" wb

Touring-4/5P	2150	4000	5000	8000	15,000	28,000
Touring-7P	2300	4200	5200	8400	15,700	29,000

1914 Pratt, model Fifty, touring, WLB

1914 PRATT
Fifty — 4-cyl., 32 hp, 122" wb

Touring-7P	2300	3200	4300	6500	11,000	23,000
Roadster-2P	2100	3100	4200	6300	10,500	22,000
Tourabout-4P	2150	3200	4300	6500	11,000	23,000
Touring-5P	2150	3200	4300	6500	11,000	23,000

1915 Pratt, model 6-50, touring, HAC

1915 PRATT
Model 4-40 — 4-cyl., 27 hp, 122" wb

Touring-5P	1950	3200	4300	6500	11,000	23,000
Roadster-2P	1950	3100	4200	6300	10,500	22,000

Model 6-50 — 6-cyl., 34 hp, 132" wb

Touring-7P	2250	4000	5000	8000	15,000	28,000
Touring-5P	2150	3900	4800	7700	14,300	27,000
Roadster-2P	2150	3700	4700	7300	13,700	26,000

PRATT SIX-WHEELER — Frankfort, New York — (1907) — Charles T. Pratt of the Pratt Chuck Works in Frankfort built himself quite a car. Its engine was 75 hp, but there was nothing sporting about the Pratt. Its wheelbase was 168 inches, and there were three rows of seats in the touring body. There were also three sets of wheels. The car was driven by the rear wheels only; both the front wheels and the center wheels steered, however, the intermediate set at a lesser angle than the two forward. There were two steering wheels inside to handle the maneuvering. Charles Pratt built this car for his own use only, never intending manufacture. Interestingly, the Pullman six-wheeler designed by Albert Broomell in 1903 in York, Pennsylvania was driven from its center wheels, with both front

1907 Pratt Six-Wheel, touring, NAHC

and rear wheels providing the steering. Only one of those was built as well. The most famous of the multi-wheeled cars in America, of course, was the Reeves from Indianapolis.

PRAUL — Philadelphia, Pennsylvania — (1895) — John E. Praul of 262 North Broad Street in Philadelphia originally envisioned his rotary engine for aviation use but quickly decided to stay on the ground. In 1895 his Praul Aero-motor Company was succeeded by his Praul Motocycle Company, which was capitalized at $100,000 — and Praul immediately began building an automobile to enter in the Chicago Times-Herald Contest, the perfect launching pad for his new product. The contest vehicle was a four-wheeled bicycle-like contrivance which, complete with fuel, weighed only about 100 pounds. Praul figured he could sell it for $250, and he had plans for a variety of further automobiles. The Praul engine was described by its inventor as a "differential piston rotary" — a separate cylinder was used to compress the charge and deliver it to the cylinder of the engine, with two working strokes for each revolution. No flywheel was required. Praul never made it to the starting line of the Chicago Times-Herald Contest, and his Praul Motocycle Company apparently never made it off the ground.

PREFERRED — Louisville, Kentucky — (1920) — The Preferred Motor Car Company was a $2 million Delaware incorporation the announced plan for which was the manufacture of $1200-$1400-range automobiles in Louisville. Ira Chase Koshne, Louis Lescuson and S.C. Bodner were the incorporators of this venture, and one F.W. Young was its president. Temporary offices were taken in Indianapolis, as the people from Preferred negotiated with officials of the Louisville Industrial Foundation regarding incentives for locating the factory there. Apparently, Louisville preferred not. This venture never left the prototype stage.

PREMIER — The Premier Motor Company was organized during the fall of 1911 with a capital stock of $25,000 under the laws of West Virginia to manufacture automobiles and maintain a garage near Pittsburgh, Pennsylvania. Behind this venture were W.R. Clifton and A.C. Osburn of Beaver Falls; H.A. Wilder, B.J. Ross, C.S. Forkum, P.M. Moore and L.H. Pyle of Woodlawn; and C.H. Martin of Pittsburgh. Manufacture is doubted.

1903 Premier, model A, runabout, HAC

PREMIER — Indianapolis, Indiana — (1902-1926) — The first car built by George B. Weidely was a water-cooled motor buggy which he sold in 1902, though his experience with it convinced him that air cooling was a better way to go. In 1903, together with Harold O. Smith, he organized the Premier Motor Manufacturing Company, with a capital stock of $50,000, for the production of air-cooled cars. The name Premier had been suggested the year previous by Sam Miles, publisher of *The Motor Age*, and the company would claim that the oak leaf on its radiator badge represented the first use of an emblem as an automobile trademark. The Premier was a very up-to-date car with overhead valves, sliding gear transmission and shaft drive. In December of 1905, *Cycle and Automobile Trade Journal* reporter Hugh Dolnar took a test ride in the 1906 Model L and was most impressed: "This car can hold a 50-mile clip steadily and take everything on high gear where it has a free road, while the springs are perfection, and show that full elliptics properly proportioned need no helps of any kind to make easy riding." Second thoughts about water cooling brought the availability of both water- and air-cooled models in 1907, with the irrevocable decision for water-cooled engines following a year later. By 1910 the Premier had completed three Glidden Tours with a perfect score, a marvelous record. Not so marvelous was the marque's competition record though the effort was a valiant one. A special air-cooled racer built in 1905 did a quarter-mile in ten seconds in a private trial, but could not qualify for

1904 Premier, model F, tonneau, HAC

the Vanderbilt Cup because it was sixty-five pounds overweight. In 1916, at the behest of the Indianapolis Motor Speedway which feared a dismal contest because the war in Europe had curtailed foreign entries, the Premier company built three racers for the 500. One finished seventh, the second crashed, the third went out with a broken oil line. That rather exemplified the further life of the Premier itself. On October 15th, 1914 the Premier company went into receivership, and the month following George Weidely and Harold Smith went off to found Weidely Motor Company for the manufacture of proprietary engines for the trade. In December of 1915, Premier was sold to a syndicate headed by F.W. Woodruff, a banker from Joliet, Illinois who paid off the company's indebtedness and reorganized as the Premier Motor Car Company. Premier had introduced its first six in 1908, and sixes only had been built from 1913. "The Aluminum Six with Magnetic Gear Shift" became the Premier slogan for 1918. The Premier's engine had been a one-piece aluminum casting with aluminum crankcase and pistons since the fall of 1916; new now was the Cutler-Hammer electric transmission operated by a steering-wheel-mounted lever. The Cutler-Hammer would be continued in 1920, though by that time control of the Premier company had changed hands again. At the helm now was L.S. Skelton, an erstwhile physician who had made a fortune in oil and who was also promoting another car called the Skelton in St. Louis, Missouri. In Indianapolis, Skelton paid off the latest Premier regime's indebtedness and reorganized as the Premier Motor Corporation. Unfortunately, Skelton died in January of 1921, which sent the company into turmoil again . . . and receivership, though a friendly one from which it emerged by the spring of 1923 when Frederick L. Barrows of Connersville, Indiana took over, paid up debts and reorganized as Premier Motors, Inc. Eyeing the company at the same time was Frank E. Strattan who had just purchased the defunct Monroe of Indianapolis, and who announced plans for a Strattan-Premier car as well, though obviously prematurely because within months it was Barrows who had bought Monroe from Strattan. The former Monroe four was continued as the Premier Model B of 1924. The Premier six-cylinder car, now up to 79 hp and still a highly regarded automobile, remained too — but only through November of 1924. Then everybody at Premier had a different idea altogether. Shortly after Barrows had taken over in 1923 the company received a contract for the building of 1000 Premier taxicabs, and now he announced that taxicabs only would be the firm's product. And so they were until October of 1926 when Premier Motors, Inc. sold out to the National Cab & Truck Company of Indianapolis, which very quickly moved into oblivion.

1903 PREMIER
Model A — 4-cyl., 16 hp, 82" wb

	FP	5	4	3	2	1
Runabout	1250	2500	3500	5000	8500	18,000

1904 PREMIER
Model F — 4-cyl., 16 hp, 82" wb

Tonneau	1400	2500	3500	5000	8500	18,000

Model A — 4-cyl., 16 hp, 82" wb

Runabout	1250	2400	3400	4800	8000	17,000

Two-Cylinder — 20 hp, 88" wb

Touring-5P	2500	2700	3600	5300	8800	19,000

1905 Premier, model F, rear entrance tonneau, HAC

1905 PREMIER
Model F — 4-cyl., 16 hp, 96" wb

Touring-5P	1500	2700	3600	5300	8800	19,000
Runabout-2P	1250	2500	3500	5000	8500	18,000

1906 Premier, Doctor's Special, HAC

1906 PREMIER
Model H — 2-cyl., 10 hp, 84" wb

	FP	5	4	3	2	1
Runabout-2P	1250	2400	3400	4800	8000	17,000

Doctor's Special — 4-cyl., 16 hp, 90" wb

Runabout-2P	1425	2500	3500	5000	8500	18,000

Model F — 4-cyl., 16 hp, 96" wb

Touring-5P	1500	2600	3600	5200	8700	18,500

Model L — 4-cyl., 20/24 hp, 104" wb

Touring-5P	2250	2700	3600	5300	8800	19,000

1907 Premier, model 24, runabout, HAC

1907 PREMIER
Model 24 — 4-cyl., 24 hp, 108-1/2" wb

Touring-5P	2250	2700	3600	5300	8800	19,000
Runabout-2/3P	2250	2400	3400	4800	8000	17,000
Landaulet-5P	3250	2500	3500	5000	8500	18,000
Limousine-5P	3250	2400	3400	4800	8000	17,000

1908 Premier, model 30, limousine, HAC

1908 PREMIER
Model 24 — 4-cyl., 24/28 hp, 108-1/2" wb

Touring	2250	2900	3700	5600	9100	20,000

Model 30 — 4-cyl., 30/35 hp, 108-1/2" wb

Touring-5P	2600	3300	4400	6700	12,000	24,000
Runabout	2600	3100	4200	6300	10,500	20,000
Limousine	—	2900	3700	5600	9100	20,000

Model 45 — 6-cyl., 45/55 hp, 124" wb

Touring-7P	3750	4500	5800	9500	18,000	32,000
Runabout	3500	4000	5000	8000	15,000	28,000

1909 Premier, model 30, roadster, HAC

1909 PREMIER
Model 30 — 4-cyl., 30/35 hp, 108-1/2" wb

	FP	5	4	3	2	1
Touring-5P	2600	4000	5000	8000	15,000	28,000
Roadster-3/4P	2500	3900	4800	7700	14,300	27,000
Limousine	3500	2900	3700	5600	9100	20,000
Landaulet	3600	3000	4000	6000	9500	21,000

Model 45 — 6-cyl., 45/55 hp, 124" wb

Touring-7P	3500	5000	6500	11,000	22,000	35,000
Roadster-3/4P	3500	4500	5800	9500	18,000	32,000
Limousine	4750	4000	5000	8000	15,000	28,000

1910 Premier, model 6-60, touring, HAC

1910 PREMIER
Model 4-40 — 4-cyl., 40 hp, 120" wb

Touring-5P	2500	4000	5000	8000	15,000	28,000
Roadster	2500	3900	4800	7700	14,300	27,000

Model 6-60 — 6-cyl., 60 hp, 140" wb

Touring-5P	3500	5000	6500	11,000	22,000	35,000
Touring-7P	3500	5200	6800	11,300	23,000	36,000

1911 Premier, model 4-40, clubman, HAC

1911 PREMIER
Model 4-40 — 4-cyl., 40 hp, 126" wb

Touring	3000	4200	5200	8400	15,700	29,000
Clubman	3000	4200	5200	8400	15,700	29,000
Roadster	2800	4000	5000	8000	15,000	28,000
Limousine	4200	3100	4200	6300	10,500	22,000

Model 6-60 — 6-cyl., 60 hp, 140" wb

Touring-7P	3500	5200	6800	11,300	23,000	36,000
Clubman	3500	5200	6800	11,300	23,000	36,000
Roadster	3500	5000	6500	11,000	22,000	35,000
Limousine	5000	4200	5200	8400	15,700	29,000

1912 PREMIER
Model 4-40 — 4-cyl., 40 hp, 126" wb

Touring-7P	3000	4500	5800	9500	18,000	32,000
Touring-5P	3000	4400	5600	9200	17,300	31,000
Clubman-5P	3000	4400	5600	9200	17,300	31,000
Roadster-2P	3000	4300	5400	8700	16,500	30,000
Limousine-7P	4200	3100	4200	6300	10,500	22,000
Berlin Limousine-7P	4700	3300	4400	6700	12,000	24,000

Model 6-60 — 6-cyl., 60 hp, 140" wb

Touring-7P	3750	5300	7000	11,500	24,000	37,000
Clubman-5P	3750	5200	6800	11,300	23,000	36,000
Roadster-2P	3750	5000	6500	11,000	22,000	35,000
Berlin Limousine-7P	5500	4400	5600	9200	17,300	31,000
Limousine-7P	5000	4200	5200	8400	15,700	29,000

1912 Premier, model 6-60, roadster, HAC

1913 Premier, model 6-60, limousine, HAC

1913 PREMIER
Model 6-40 — 6-cyl., 38.4 hp, 132" wb

	FP	5	4	3	2	1
Touring-5P	2735	4700	6100	9900	19,000	33,000
Limousine	4250	4000	5000	8000	15,000	28,000
Coupe	3750	3100	4200	6300	10,500	22,000
Clubman	2735	4700	6100	9900	19,000	33,000
Roadster	2735	4500	5800	9500	18,000	32,000

Model 6-60 — 6-cyl., 48.6 hp, 140" wb

	FP	5	4	3	2	1
Touring-7P	4000	5300	7000	11,500	24,000	37,000
Deluxe Touring	6000	5500	7500	12,000	26,000	39,000
Coupe	5000	4000	5000	8000	15,000	28,000
Limousine	5500	4200	5200	8400	15,700	29,000
Roadster	4000	5000	6500	11,000	22,000	35,000
Clubman	4000	5300	7000	11,500	24,000	37,000

1914 Premier, model 6-48, roadster, HAC

1915 Premier, model 6-50, touring, HAC

1914 PREMIER
Weidely Model — 6-cyl., 38.4 hp, 132" wb

	FP	5	4	3	2	1
Roadster	2700	4900	6300	10,300	21,000	34,000
Touring	2700	5000	6500	11,000	22,000	35,000

Model 6-48 — 6-cyl., 38.4 hp, 132" wb

	FP	5	4	3	2	1
Touring-7P	2835	5300	7000	11,500	24,000	37,000
Touring-5P	2785	5200	6800	11,300	23,000	36,000
Roadster-2P	2785	5000	6500	11,000	22,000	35,000

1915 PREMIER
Model 6-49 — 6-cyl., 31.6 hp, 132" wb

	FP	5	4	3	2	1
Roadster-2P	1985	4900	6300	10,300	21,000	34,000

Model 6-50 — 6-cyl., 38.4 hp, 132" wb

	FP	5	4	3	2	1
Touring-7P	2750	5400	7300	11,800	25,000	38,000
Roadster-2P	2700	5000	6500	11,000	22,000	35,000
Touring-5P	2700	5300	7000	11,500	24,000	37,000
Limousine-5P	4200	4300	5400	8700	16,500	30,000
Coupe	3350	4000	5000	8000	15,000	28,000

1916 Premier, model 6-56, roadster, JAC

1916 PREMIER
Model 6-56 — 6-cyl., 38.4 hp, 134" wb

	FP	5	4	3	2	1
Touring-7P	2300	5200	6800	11,300	23,000	36,000
Roadster-3P	2300	4900	6300	10,300	21,000	34,000
Cloverleaf Rdstr.-3P	2300	5000	6500	11,000	22,000	35,000
Yacht-4P	2300	4900	6300	10,300	21,000	34,000
Speedster-2P	2300	5400	7300	11,800	25,000	38,000
Coupelet-2P	2500	4300	5400	8700	16,500	30,000

1917 Premier, model 6-B, touring, OCW

1917 PREMIER
Model 6B — 6-cyl., 27.34 hp, 125-1/2" wb

	FP	5	4	3	2	1
Foursome Roadster	1895	4000	5000	8000	15,000	28,000
Touring-7P	1895	4300	5400	8700	16,500	30,000
Limousine	3150	3900	4800	7700	14,300	27,000
Town Car	3150	3900	4800	7700	14,300	27,000
Touring Sedan	2900	2300	3300	4600	7500	16,000

1918 Premier, model 6-C, foursome, HAC

1918 PREMIER
Model 6C — 6-cyl., 27.34 hp, 125-1/2" wb

	FP	5	4	3	2	1
Foursome Roadster	2285	4000	5000	8000	15,000	28,000
Touring-7P	2285	4300	5400	8700	16,500	30,000
Limousine-7P	3285	3700	4700	7300	13,700	26,000

1919 Premier, model 6-C, foursome, HAC

1919 PREMIER
Model 6C — 6-cyl., 27.34 hp, 125-1/2" wb

Foursome Roadster	2585	4000	5000	8000	15,000	28,000
Touring-7P	2585	4300	5400	8700	16,500	30,000
Limousine-7P	3585	3700	4700	7300	13,700	26,000

1920 Premier, model 6-D, touring, HAC

1920 PREMIER
Model 6-D — 6-cyl., 65 hp, 126-3/4" wb

Touring-7P	4300	4500	5800	9500	18,000	32,000
Sport-4P	4300	4700	6100	9900	19,000	33,000
Speedster-2P	4300	4900	6300	10,300	21,000	34,000
Sedan-4P	5700	2700	3600	5300	8800	19,000
Sedan 7P	5800	2900	3700	5600	9100	20,000

1921 Premier, model 6-D, roadster, HAC

1921 PREMIER
Model 6-D — 6-cyl., 60 hp, 126-3/4" wb

Touring-4P	4600	4200	5200	8400	15,700	29,000
Touring-7P	4600	4400	5600	9200	17,300	31,000
Roadster-2P	4600	4300	5400	8700	16,500	30,000
Coupe-4P	5600	2900	3700	5600	9100	20,000
Sedan-4P	6000	2500	3500	5000	8500	18,000
Limousine-7P	6100	3100	4200	6300	10,500	22,000

1922 PREMIER
Model 6-D — 6-cyl., 60 hp, 126-3/4" wb

Touring-4P	3690	4200	5200	8400	15,700	29,000
Touring-7P	3890	4400	5600	9200	17,300	31,000
Roadster-2P	3790	4300	5400	8700	16,500	30,000
Artcraft-4P	4090	2700	3600	5300	8800	19,000
Artcraft-7P	4290	2900	3700	5600	9100	20,000
Coupe-4P	5090	3000	4000	6000	9500	21,000
Sedan-7P	5190	2900	3700	5600	9100	20,000

1922 Premier, model 6-D, touring, HAC

1923 Premier, model 6-D, sedan, HAC

1923 PREMIER
Model 6-D — 6-cyl., 79 hp, 126-3/4" wb

	FP	5	4	3	2	1
Touring-4P	3100	4700	6100	9900	19,000	33,000
Roadster-2P	3150	4500	5800	9500	18,000	32,000
Touring-7P	3250	4900	6300	10,300	21,000	34,000
Tourster-4P	3300	5000	6500	11,000	22,000	35,000
Brougham-4P	4300	2700	3600	5300	8800	19,000
Sedan-4P	5000	2400	3400	4800	8000	17,000
Sedan-7P	5100	2500	3500	5000	8500	18,000
Berline-7P	5200	2900	3700	5600	9100	20,000

1924 Premier, roadster, JAC

1924 PREMIER
Model B — 4-cyl., 35 hp, 115" wb

Touring-5P	1000	4300	5400	8700	16,500	30,000
Roadster-2P	1000	4200	5200	8400	15,700	29,000
Sedan-5P	1500	2300	3300	4600	7500	16,000

Model 6-D — 6-cyl., 79 hp, 126-3/4" wb

Touring-5P	2535	4700	6100	9900	19,000	33,000
Roadster-2P	2535	4500	5800	9500	18,000	32,000
Touring-7P	2585	4900	6300	10,300	21,000	34,000
Brougham-5P	3385	2700	3600	5300	8800	19,000
Sedan-7P	3585	2500	3700	5600	9100	18,000

1925 Premier, roadster, AA

1925 PREMIER
6-cyl., 79 hp, 126 3/4'' wb

	FP	5	4	3	2	1
Touring-5P	2535	4700	6000	9900	19,000	33,000
Roadster-2P	2535	4500	5800	9500	18,000	32,000
Touring-7P	2585	4900	6300	10,300	21,000	34,000
Brougham-5P	3385	2700	3600	5300	8800	19,000
Sedan-7P	3385	2500	3700	5600	9100	18,000

4-cyl., 35 hp, 115'' wb

Touring-5P	1000	4300	5400	8700	16,500	30,000
Roadster	1000	4200	5200	8400	15,700	29,000
Sedan	1500	2300	3300	4600	7500	16,000

1926 Premier, taxicab, KM

1921 Premocar, touring, WLB

PREMOCAR — Birmingham, Alabama — (1920-1923) — The Preston Motor Car Company was organized during the spring of 1918 by Charles A. Dexter for the manufacture of a $1000 truck and a $600 passenger car designed by W.H. Tarpley of Newark, New Jersey. Parts for the first car, which was to be called a Preston, were being made at the time at the Sandusky Forging Company in Birmingham, and the former site of the Birmingham Boiler Works was selected for the factory. But the money very quickly ran out. Preston was heard from again in 1919, however, when the firm was reorganized as Preston Motors Corporation by Ross A. Skinner (president), Joeseph T. Driver (vice-president) and Preston Orr (secretary/treasurer). They scrapped Dexter's plans and Tarpley's designs — and came up with another truck and an entirely new car, both to be marketed under the name Premocar. A public reception to officially open the new factory at 18th Avenue and Vanderbilt Road in Birmingham was held during the late summer of 1920. The first cars arrived for the 1921 model year. Although a $2290 six with the Fischer Magic engine had been planned, it was not marketed. Instead the line for 1921 was composed of two models: a 40 hp Falls-engined six at $1295 and a 75 hp Rochester-Duesenberg four at $3865. The latter car was built in 1921 only, the Falls six surviving for two more seasons, together with some truck production. The high points in the Premocar history appear to have been the success several special-built Premocar racers achieved (Bob Robinson, Laurie Stone and Ralph Hankinson driving) in various racing events in the South, the extra special ivory tourer with ivory kid upholstery that was built in 1921 for President Warren G. Harding's visit to Birmingham (interestingly, this one had the Magic engine), and the shipment of one car that year to

1921 Premocar, roadster, KM

Yugoslavia which was seen as presaging a fine export business, which alas did not arrive. The low points in the Premocar history were its move into involuntary receivership in May of 1923, and the reported indictment of Skinner, Driver and Orr that October for alleged violation of the Alabama blue sky laws. The company's plant at 18th and Vanderbilt was sold in May of 1924.

1921 PREMOCAR
Model 6-40A — 6-cyl., 40 hp, 117'' wb

	FP	5	4	3	2	1
Touring/Roadster	1295	4200	5200	8400	15,700	29,000

Model 4-8: 4-cyl., 75 hp, 127'' wb

Touring-5P	6100	4700	610000	9900	19,000	33,000

1922-1923 PREMOCAR
Model 6-40A — 6-cyl., 40 hp, 117'' wb

Touring/Roadster	2250	4300	5400	8700	16,500	30,000

1901 Prescott, steam runabout, NAHC

PRESCOTT STEAM — Passaic, New Jersey — (1901-1905) — The Prescott Automobile Manufacturing Company had its offices in the Wall Street section of New York City, its plant across the Hudson in Passaic — and it produced an admirable steam car that sold in the $1000 range. Its two-cylinder compound engine generated 7½ hp, and its wheelbase was 68 inches. The brake shoes were brass, and included as standard equipment was a steam-operated air pump for inflating the tires. In addition to certificates won in the Long Island and Automobile Club of America 100-mile

1903 Prescott, steam runabout, NAHC

1905 Prescott, steam runabout, HAC

endurance tests, a Prescott was awarded a gold medal for its perfect score in the New York-Boston Reliability Run of 1903. "Going Touring?," advertisements asked, "Then . . . Get a Gold Medal Winner." But probably the Prescott's proudest moment came in the 1905 Eagle Rock Hill Climb where, as president A.L. Prescott told everyone, one of his $1200 cars was 10-2/5ths seconds faster than a $2500 White Steamer and only 2/5ths of a second slower than an $8000 French Decauville. But the downfall of the company also arrived in 1905, when A.L. Prescott handed a company representative a good deal of cash from the safe to take to Europe to set up the Prescott export business. The representative was never heard from again. A Prescott steam runabout remains extant, in the collection of the Prescott family.

1901-1902 PRESCOTT STEAM

	FP	5	4	3	2	1
Model No. 1 Runabout	1000	2000	3000	4200	6500	14,000

1903-1906 PRESCOTT STEAM

Two-Seater Runabout	1100	2000	3000	4200	6500	14,000
Four-Seater Runabout	1100	2200	3200	4400	7000	15,000
Open-Top Runabout	1200	1800	2800	4000	6200	13,000
Victoria-Top Runabout	1200	2200	3200	4400	7000	15,000

PRESTON — When initially organized during the spring of 1918, the Preston Motor Car Company of Birmingham, Alabama indicated its plans to call its product a Preston as well. But, by 1920, when actual production began, the name had been changed to Premocar. Refer to Premocar.

1936 Preston, roadster, MVMA

PRESTON — Wichita, Kansas — (1936) — Ben Preston was a Wichita mechanic and not a superstitious man. In 1936 he built a roadster composed of the salvageable and workable of twenty-five wrecked automobiles. Some of the cars had belonged to gangsters, Preston reported, but most had been involved in more ordinary but equally deadly automobile accidents.

1937 Pribil, MVMA

PRIBIL — Saginaw, Michigan — (1936-1937) — Alexius R. Pribil was president of the Saginaw Stamping & Tool Company, and among his employees was the winner of the first Indianapolis 500, Ray Harroun. The idea behind his car was mostly Pribil's, but Harroun assisted during its one-and-a-half-year development time. The Pribil Safety Aircar Company was organized to produce the vehicle, which followed the prevailing streamlined teardrop school of advanced body design. The car was powered by a four-cylinder 30 hp Continental engine, with a frame of vanadium steel tubing and a 126-inch wheelbase. The rear wheels were so close together — fourteen inches — as to obviate the necessity of a differential. Its total length was sixteen feet; and it was as high as it was wide, six-and-a-half feet in each direction. What was most significant about the Pribil, however, were its amenities. Its interior included sleeping accommodations for two on a davenport in the back, a folding dining table, refrig-

erator and sink with water tank. The vehicle was intended, Pribil said, "to render present camp trailers obsolete by combining car and trailer in one compact unit." The Pribil was about three decades ahead of its time. With the sudden death of Alexius Pribil in April 1938 at the age of fifty-seven, the Pribil project died too. Just the single prototype was built.

PRICE — The Price Auto Works was organized in Chicago, Illinois during the spring of 1911 with a capital stock of $20,000 to manufacture "automobile trucks, motor cars, machinery, implements, etc." Incorporators were Arthur C. Price, Lavina E. Price and George Walker. Manufacture of a car is doubted.

R.P. Price & Company of Chicago, Illinois promoted a car called the Benson in 1901. Refer to Benson.

1907 Price, runabout, NAHC

PRICE — Chicago, Illinois — (1907-1908) — W.C. Price of Chicago had his first car under test on the streets of Chicago on May 5th, 1907. It was a runabout on a 100-inch wheelbase, powered by a two-cylinder 12 hp Beaver engine. This was quite usual, what was unusual about the Price was its maker's construction of the vehicle. He placed the engine upfront lengthwise of the chassis frame with power transmitted by a belt to a countershaft with planetary gearchange and from there by sprocket and single chain to the rear axle. Driving speeds were varied by tightening or loosening the belt tension. Both runabout and surrey models were offered, the former selling for a little under $700, the latter a little over. The tiller steering of the prototype was replaced by a wheel in the production cars. In September 1907 Price organized his Price Belt Auto Company for manufacture, and he is believed to have built a few cars into 1908. References indicating that the Price car was produced as late as 1909 are in error.

PRIDEMORE — Northfield, Minnesota — (1914) — W.A. Pridemore of the Pridemore Machine Works designed this racy underslung cyclecar from Minnesota. It was powered by a two-cylinder air-cooled 12/14 engine; friction transmission and chain drive were featured. The wheelbase was 100 inches and the tread 40, with both a tandem and a side-by-side two-seater planned to be marketed in addition to a light delivery. The Pridemore was designed along "foreign lines," its maker said, and it did have a French Bedelia look about it. The prototype was completed and displayed at an automobile show in February 1914. Whether any manufacture followed is to be doubted.

PRIGG — The cyclecar produced in 1914 in Anderson, Indiana by H. Paul Prigg was marketed under the tradename of Real. Refer to Real.

1911 Primo, touring, WLB

PRIMO — Atlanta, Georgia — (1910-1912) — "A Southern automobile company, backed by men worth many millions, but capitalized at $200,000, as a starter, all of which will be paid in before the first car is on the streets; and a company that will make practically all of its parts, save bodies and wheels, has been launched in Atlanta." Thus reported *The Automobile* in May of 1910. The new venture was styled the Primo Motor Company, and the man behind it was E. Van Winkle of the Van Winkle Gin and Machine Company, which purportedly had a million-dollar plant in Atlanta and another one almost as large in Gulfport, Mississippi which "sends cotton gins 'round the world." The Primo was introduced as "The Southern Automobile" in a variety of models fitted with four-cylinder 25 hp engines. The company moved into bankruptcy by mid-1911, but its directors raised some cash and kept it going. By early 1912, however, the Primo Motor Company was irrevocably bankrupt. Later it was revealed that of the $200,000 capital stock, only $133,000 had been paid in. Most likely, the Primo board of directors lost interest when a quick profit was not made. Apparently a truck that was produced at the same time under the Van Winkle name was more successful immediately, because it was continued in manufacture for several more seasons.

1910-1912 PRIMO
Four — 25 hp, 110" wb

	FP	5	4	3	2	1
Model FP Touring-5P	1750	2700	3600	5300	8800	19,000
Model TT Toy Toneau-4P	1750	2700	3600	5300	8800	19,000
Model R Roadster-3P	1500	2500	3500	5000	8500	18,000
Model LR Rdstr.-2P (100" wb)	1250	2600	3600	5200	8700	18,500

PRINCE — The Prince Motor Car Company was organized in Warrensville, Ohio late in 1911 with a capital stock of $200,000 to manufacture and sell automobiles. Incorporators were W.F. Kehnes, Thomas J. Atkinson, John G. Schultz, E.B. Hecker and J.A. Hecker. Manufacture is doubted.

PRINCE HENRY — Prince Henry was the model designation provided the car built by Alfred J. Wildman in Morrisville, Pennsylvania in 1902. Refer to Wildman.

PRINCESS — From 1904-1905 the Royal Automobile Company of Chicago, Illinois produced both an electric and a gasoline car. Both carried the marque name of Royal, the gasoline car bearing the model designation of Princess. Refer to Royal Princess.
The Princess Runabout of 1904 was among several kit cars offered that year by the Neustadt-Perry Company of St. Louis, Missouri. Refer to Neustadt.

1917 Princess, 4-36, touring, WLB

PRINCESS — Detroit, Michigan — (1914-1918) — The first Princess was a cyclecar. It was designed by C.J. Thornewill, an Englishman who had worked for Wolseley-Siddeley before emigrating to America. Not surprisingly, there was an English look to the car. It was powered by a two-cylinder 12 hp Farmer engine and featured a gearless differential. Its wheelbase was 92 inches, the tread 44 inches. L.N. White headed the Princess Cyclecar Company which was organized in December of 1913 with a capital stock of $200,000. The car was placed on the market as the Little Princess. First deliveries began February 1st, 1914, and they ended soon after. Formal dissolution of the company was reported that September. Thereon a new group of investors (including some businessmen from Memphis, Tennessee) took over and reorganized as the Princess Motor Car Corporation. Capital stock was subsequently raised to a full million. Production of the former Little Princess was continued for 1915 but the car was now called simply the Princess. In May of 1915 a shipment of 65 cars was dispatched to Ireland. Most of the Princess sales, however, would seem to have been stateside. In September that year the company moved into larger quarters, the old Saxon plant at 1305 Bellevue. There the Princess grew up into a four-cylinder 24 hp (GB&S engine) car, and thus she remained for the balance of her career. In January of 1919, *Motor Age* reported that the Princess Motor Car Corporation was "permanently out of business."

1914 PRINCESS
Model B — 4-cyl., 12 hp, 92" wb

	FP	5	4	3	2	1
Little Princess Rdstr.-2P	445	2000	3000	4200	6500	14,000

1915 PRINCESS
Model C — 4-cyl., 12 hp, 92" wb

Princess Roadster-2P	495	2000	3000	4200	6500	14,000

1916 PRINCESS
Model 30 — 4-cyl., 23 hp, 104" wb

Touring-5P	695	2200	3200	4400	7000	15,000
Roadster-2P	495	2000	3000	4200	6500	14,000

1917 PRINCESS
Model 30-D — 4-cyl., 23 hp, 104" wb

Touring-5P	695	2300	3300	4600	7500	16,000
Roadster-3P	695	2200	3200	4400	7000	15,000
Speedster-2P	695	2500	3500	5000	8500	18,000

Model 4-36 — 4-cyl., 23 hp, 108" wb

Touring-5P	775	2400	3400	4800	8000	17,000
Roadster-3P	775	2300	3300	4600	7500	16,000

1918 PRINCESS
Model 30-D — 4-cyl., 23 hp, 104" wb

Touring-5P	695	2300	3300	4600	7500	16,000
Roadster-3P	695	2200	3200	4400	7000	15,000
Speedster-2P	695	2500	3500	5000	8500	18,000

Model 4-36-F — 4-cyl., 23 hp, 108" wb

	FP	5	4	3	2	1
Touring-5P	775	2400	3400	4800	8000	17,000
Roadster-3P	775	2300	3300	4600	7500	16,000

1923 Princeton, 4-pass. sport touring, WLB

PRINCETON — Muncie, Indiana — (1923-1924) — William C. Durant looked upon the Princeton as his second Cadillac. He had lost his first, of course, when he was forced out of General Motors — and now at work in creating his second empire, he needed a car to fill the market gap between the Flint which he had just introduced and the Locomobile which he had purchased a few years before. A prototype of the new Princeton was quickly run up for display at the New York Automobile Show in January 1923, where it was announced that the car would be put into production at Durant's Muncie, Indiana plant. An Ansted six-cylinder engine was to power all Princetons which were to be made available in six body types, with open cars on a 128-inch wheelbase and closed models on 132 inches. The projected price range was $2485-$3675. By the summer of 1923 a few test cars had been built in Muncie, but it was announced that manufacture, slated to begin the following spring, would be transferred to the Locomobile plant in Bridgeport, Connecticut. Somewhere between Muncie and Bridgeport, Billy Durant decided against the Princeton. The car was never put into manufacture. Instead, Durant's "second Cadillac" was subsequently introduced as simply a larger model of the Flint, with Continental engine replacing the Princeton's Ansted.

PRITCHARD-LYON — The Pritchard-Lyon Motor Company was organized in Rochester, New York during the summer of 1914 with a capital stock of $25,000 for the manufacture of automobiles. The partners involved were Curtis B. Lyon and Albert R. Pritchard. Manufacture is doubted.

1907 Proctor, runabout, HS

PROCTOR — Gloucester, Massachusetts — (1907) — Although he had been sketching cars in his diary since before the turn of the century, Albert Proctor of Gloucester didn't build a vehicle until 1907. It was a simple runabout with a flat water tank in front of the dash and its engine (originally a small one-lunger, later replaced with a 15 hp twin) under the seat. Albert Proctor built his car for his own use, and it remains extant in a collection in Rhode Island.

PRODAL — New York, New York — (1909-1911) — P.A. Proal and E.M. Dalley operated a garage in Manhattan called the Motor Car Repair Company which catered especially to the problems experienced by affluent New Yorkers with their foreign cars. In 1909 the partners, believing they could build a car as well as the Europeans, took a few letters from each of their surnames — and, ergo, the Prodal. It was powered by a four-cylinder 28 hp engine and, as its makers unabashedly admitted, followed "the lines of the Renault." The cars were all custom built, some with combination open/closed bodies. An interesting feature was the placement of a tool kit within the spare tires, which were running-board-mounted next to the driver. One Prodal owner was Lyman Rhodes, vice-president of the Chase National Bank; registration lists indicate that at least five other Prodals were built. Proal and Dalley continued to operate their garage in Manhattan for a number of years after discontinuing the Prodal.

PROGRESSIVE — The Progressive Motor Car Company was organized in Barker, New York late in 1912 with a capital stock of $30,000 to manufacture and deal in automobiles. Involved in the venture were Arthur H. Terleeson, John B. Smith and Harry S. Schuhr. Manufacture is doubted.

1902 Prospect, gas runabout, NAHC

PROSPECT — Prospect, Ohio — (1902, 1907-1908) — The Wottring family of carriage builders from Prospect built automobiles on two occasions. The first was 1902 when the business was called Wottring Brothers, and they decided upon the name Prospect for the car. The Prospect was a comely little runabout powered by a 6 hp engine and weighing 1050 pounds complete. The car was tiller steered, with the transmission providing two speeds forward, and the Prospect's maximum road going was claimed at 30 mph. Ostensibly a two-passenger car, a collapsible upholstered bench carried within the dash bought total seating to four if required. It would appear the Wottrings built the Prospect only during 1902. The family was back in the field in 1907, however, as Wottring & Son Automobile Works. These second-generation cars were built entirely to customer order, and some orders may have arrived into 1908.

PROSPECT HEIGHTS — The Prospect Heights Motor Company was organized in Brooklyn, New York late in 1908 with a capital stock of $25,000 to manufacture and deal in automobiles. Incorporators were R.L. Kelly, T.F. Reilly and L.C. Howard. Manufacture is doubted.

PROSPERITY — Elkhart, Indiana — (1933) — The Prosperity was a taxi produced by the Allied Cab Manufacturing Company for the New York City market and built in the former Elcar plant in Elkhart, Indiana. Its wheelbase was 123 inches, its engine a Continental Red Seal six. "The Cab of the Future," the brochure hailed. "Price $1950 Delivered. Down Payment $395." Both the attractive terms for purchase and the taxi's name paid cognizance to the Great Depression which was raging through the land. But, unfortunately, the Prosperity belied its designation. Only twelve were built in 1933. The Allied company struggled on a while longer producing taxis under its own name.

PROTECTIVE — The Protective Manufacturing and Sales Company was organized in New York City during the spring of 1910 with a capital stock of $15,000 to manufacture and deal in "motors, engines, motor cars, carriages and supplies for same." Incorporators were Charles E. Terrell, Charles A. Tilly and Hewlett Smith. Manufacture of a car is doubted.

1897 Prouty, NAHC

PROUTY — Chicago, Illinois — (1897) — Enoch Prouty of Chicago is believed to have built just one car, and this to demonstrate his gasoline engine and transmission device. The former was a single-cylinder vertical unit, and though his transmission principles were not out of the ordinary for this period, he was more articulate than most mechanics in explaining same, which was probably the reason his ideas received extensive coverage in the press.

P & S — Although occasionally referred to unofficially by its initials, the car built in Long Island City, New York from 1908-1914 by Henry Palmer and Charles A. Singer was always marketed under the hyphenated names of the partners. Refer to Palmer-Singer.

P.T. — New York, New York — (1901-1902) — The first P.T. engine was a one-lunger developing one horsepower, which could be operated on either gasoline or "illuminating gas" and which was marketed for bicycle use at $75.00 per unit in 1900. In the spring of that year, rights to the engine were sold to Crescent. It was not until late fall of 1901 that the men behind the P.T. — A.M. Hudson (president) and F.B. Widmayer (secretary-treasurer) — incorporated the P.T. Motor Company with a capital stock of $100,000. The firm's office was at 2312 Broadway in New York City, with its factory at Seventh Avenue and the corner of 28th Street, near the Garment Center. As the company's name suggests, its principal product continued to be engines, but now for automobile use. These were single-cylinder air-cooled units of 3, 4, 6 and 8 hp. In addition to building a motorcycle using the 3 hp unit, the P.T. Motor Company also produced a gasoline runabout (engine unspecified) which was marketed in the $500 range.

PUGH — Davenport, Iowa — (1901) — "I have been offered $500,000 for the invention, but I do not think that I will sell it. My plan is to have the invention patented in all the countries of the Old World, and these patents I will sell. But the United States will be kept under my control. I don't have to sell the thing anyway." William J. Pugh was speaking, early in 1901, of the gasoline automobile he had just built in Davenport. Later that year Pugh showed up in Chicago to buy machinery to take back to his Pugh & Bofinger machine shop in order to get into manufacture. "It is stated as the intention of Mssrs. Pugh & Bofinger to manufacture automobiles on a small scale for a year," *The Motor Age* reported in December. "They are of the opinion that after they manufacture a number of automobiles they will be in a position to solicit capital for the establishment of a large factory in Davenport." Unfortunately, the capitalists of Davenport were not of a similar opinion.

1906 Pullman Four, runabout, HAC

PULLMAN — York, Pennsylvania — (1905-1917) — Both Albert P. Broomell and Samuel E. Baily were important figures in the industrial community of York, Broomell in steam heating equipment manufacture, Baily in carriage building. Broomell was the first of the two to build a car, the six-wheeled monstrosity that he designed in 1903 and called a Pullman. He had subsequently torn that car apart and come up with another that he thought worthy of manufacture. Samuel E. Baily agreed. Early in 1905 they published a brochure to test the marketing possibilities of Broomell's new car, calling it a York to mitigate any lingering bad memories in the area of the six-wheeler. Response to the brochure was heartening. By mid-1905 James A. Kline, a young master mechanic from Harrisburg, was invited to town to assist in the formation of the York Motor Car Company and to refine the York car for production. That fall the first production test cars were displayed at the York County Fair, and by now the marque name had been changed back to Pullman. (Apparently, the pilot cars carried the York name, but the cars were never marketed as other than Pullmans.) Sam Baily served as president of the company; James Kline was general manager and the man responsible for the design of the subsequent cars. Broomell, now nearing retirement age, advised — but spent more of his time directing operations of his Broomell, Schmidt & Steacy Company. The first generation Pullmans were big, expensive cars with shaft drive and horsepower up to forty. They sold reasonably well, but in the Panic of '07 the company required assistance and this arrived via two financiers from New York City: Thomas O'Connor and Oscar Stephenson. Within a year Kline had been eased out of the firm, and Sam Baily followed him, to join hands in a new company which would result in the Kline Kar. In 1909 the New York financiers reorganized the York Motor Car Company into the

Pullman Motor Car Company. A Pullman won the famed Fairmount Park Road Race in Philadelphia in 1910, and in 1911 was awarded three gold medals at the Russian Exposition in Rost on Don, an unprecedented "victory" for an American automobile manufacturer. Sales continued high, and it was this success which was the company's undoing. In the rush to meet demand, quality was sacrificed — and the Pullman reputation for superb motorcars was tarnished. Bankruptcy seemed unavoidable, but a group of York businessmen headed by John C. Schmidt made a rescue attempt in October of 1915. E.T. Birdsall was imported from the White Motor Company in Cleveland to design a line of lower-priced cars to carry the designation Pullman Junior. But it was too late. After production of 15,000 cars in a little over a decade, Pullman declared bankruptcy in December of 1916. The final 1917 models were assembled in the sad months to follow. The company's assets were sold July 24th, 1917.

1905 PULLMAN
Four — 18/20 hp, 93" wb

	FP	5	4	3	2	1
Surrey	2000	2300	3300	4600	7500	16,000

1906 PULLMAN
Four — 24/28 hp, 96" wb

Model C Touring	2000	2300	3300	4600	7500	16,000
Model E Runabout	1850	2200	3200	4400	7000	15,000

Four — 30/35 hp

Model D Touring (103" wb)	2500	2500	3500	5000	8500	18,000
Model F Rbt. (100" wb)	2350	2400	3400	4800	8000	17,000

1907 Pullman, model G, touring, NAHC

1907 PULLMAN
Model E — 4-cyl., 20 hp, 92" wb

Touring	1850	2300	3300	4600	7500	16,000
Runabout	1800	2200	3200	4400	7000	15,000
Limousine	2500	2000	3000	4200	6500	14,000

Model F — 4-cyl., 40 hp, 110" wb

Touring-5P	3000	2900	3700	5600	9100	20,000

Model G — 4-cyl., 40 hp, 110" wb

Touring-7P	—	3000	3750	5700	9300	21,000

1908 Pullman, model 4-40, gentleman's roadster, HAC

1908 PULLMAN
Model H — 4-cyl., 20 hp, 100" wb

Detachable Tonneau	1875	2500	3500	5000	8500	18,000
Runabout	1825	2400	3400	4800	8000	17,000

Model 6-30 — 6-cyl., 30 hp, 104" wb

Speed Car	2750	2700	3600	5300	8800	19,000

Model 4-40 — 4-cyl., 40 hp, 108" wb

Gentleman's Roadster	3000	2900	3700	5600	9100	20,000

Model I — 4-cyl., 40 hp, 118" wb

Touring-5P	3250	3100	4200	6300	10,500	22,000

Model J — 4-cyl., 40 hp, 118" wb

Touring-7P	3500	3500	4500	7000	13,000	25,000

1909 Pullman, model 6-30, speed car, HAC

1909 PULLMAN
Model L — 4-cyl., 20 hp, 102" wb

	FP	5	4	3	2	1
Toy Tonneau	1600	2500	3500	5000	8500	18,000
Roadster	1500	2400	3400	4800	8000	17,000

Model K — 4-cyl., 30 hp, 107" wb

Touring	2000	2900	3700	5600	9100	20,000
Roadster	2000	2700	3600	5300	8800	19,000
Limousine	3000	2500	3500	5000	8500	18,000
Toy Tonneau	2000	2900	3700	5600	9100	20,000

Model 6-30 — 6-cyl., 30 hp, 104" wb

Speed Car	2500	3000	4000	6000	9500	21,000

Model 4-40 — 4-cyl., 40 hp, 110" wb

Gentleman's Roadster	3000	3100	4200	6300	10,500	22,000

Model M — 4-cyl., 40 hp, 120" wb

Touring	3500	2900	3700	5600	9100	20,000
Limousine	4500	2700	3600	5300	8800	19,000

1910 Pullman, touring, RP

1910 PULLMAN
Model O — 4-cyl., 30 hp, 108" wb

	FP	5	4	3	2	1
Toy Tonneau-4P	1650	2700	3600	5300	8800	19,000
Roadster	1650	2500	3500	5000	8500	18,000

Model K — 4-cyl., 35 hp, 112" wb

Touring-5P	2000	3300	4400	6700	12,000	24,000

Model 4-40 — 4-cyl., 40 hp, 112" wb

Runabout-3P	3000	3900	4800	7700	14,300	27,000

Model M — 4-cyl., 50 hp, 126" wb

Touring-7P	3500	4500	5800	9500	18,000	32,000

1911 Pullman, model O-11, toy tonneau, HAC

1911 PULLMAN
Model O — 4-cyl., 30 hp, 110" wb

Toy Tonneau-4P	1650	3000	4000	6000	9500	21,000
Vestibuled Touring-5P	1750	3300	4400	6700	12,000	24,000
Roadster-3P	1650	3200	4300	6500	11,000	23,000

Model K — 4-cyl., 35 hp, 115" wb

Toy Tonneau-4P	2000	3700	4700	7300	13,700	26,000
Touring-5P	2000	3900	4800	7700	14,300	27,000
Vestibuled Touring-5P	2100	4000	5000	8000	15,000	28,000
Roadster-3P	2000	3900	4800	7700	14,300	27,000

Model M — 4-cyl., 50 hp, 127" wb

Touring-7P	3500	5200	6800	11,300	23,000	36,000
Toy Tonneau-4P	3500	5000	6500	11,000	22,000	35,000
Roadster-3P	3500	4900	6300	10,300	21,000	34,000
Vestibuled Touring-7P	4000	5400	7300	11,800	25,000	38,000

1912 PULLMAN
Model 4-30 — 4-cyl., 30 hp, 118" wb

Touring-5P	1675	4200	5200	8400	15,700	29,000
Coupe	—	2700	3600	5300	8800	19,000
Landaulet	—	3100	4200	6300	10,500	22,000
Limousine	—	2900	3700	5600	9100	20,000
Toy Tonneau	—	4000	5000	8000	15,000	28,000
Roadster	—	3900	4800	7700	14,300	27,000
Taxicab (110" wb)	1500	2900	3700	5600	9100	20,000

1912 Pullman, model 6-60, speedster, HAC

Model 4-40 — 4-cyl., 40 hp, 122" wb

	FP	5	4	3	2	1
Touring-5P	2150	4500	5800	9500	18,000	32,000
Coupe	—	3000	4000	6000	9500	21,000
Landaulet	—	3500	4500	7000	13,000	25,000
Limousine	—	3200	4300	6500	11,000	23,000
Toy Tonneau	—	4400	5600	9200	17,300	31,000
Roadster	4300	5400	8700	16,500	30,000	

Model 4-50 — 4-cyl., 50 hp, 127" wb

Touring-7P	2700	5000	6500	11,000	16,500	35,000

Model 6-60 — 6-cyl., 60 hp, 138" wb

Touring-7P	2750	5300	7000	11,500	24,000	37,000
Coupe	—	3200	4300	6500	11,000	23,000
Landaulet	—	3700	4700	7300	13,700	26,000
Limousine	—	3300	4400	6700	12,000	24,000
Toy Tonneau	—	5200	6800	11,300	23,000	36,000
Roadster	—	5000	6500	11,000	22,000	35,000

1913 Pullman, model 4-44, vestibule touring, HAC

1913 PULLMAN

Model 4-36 — 4-cyl., 36 hp, 118" wb

Vestibuled Touring-5P	1675	4200	5200	8400	15,700	29,000
Speedster	1675	4500	5800	9500	18,000	32,000

Model 4-44 — 4-cyl., 44 hp, 122" wb

Vestibuled Touring	2150	4500	5800	9500	18,000	32,000

Model 4-50 — 4-cyl., 50 hp, 127" wb

Vestibuled Family Car	2400	4900	6300	10,300	21,000	34,000

Model 6-66 — 6-cyl., 66 hp, 138" wb

Touring-7P	2750	5300	7000	11,500	24,000	37,000

1914 PULLMAN

Model 4-36 — 4-cyl., 26 hp, 118" wb

Touring-5P	1575	4300	5400	8700	16,500	30,000

Model 4-44 — 4-cyl., 31 hp, 122" wb

Touring-5P	1975	4700	6100	9900	19,000	33,000

Model 6-46 — 6-cyl., 46 hp, 130" wb

Touring-5P	2400	5200	6800	11,300	23,000	36,000
Limousine	3500	4200	5200	8400	15,700	29,000
Landaulet	3350	4300	5400	8700	16,500	30,000
Coupe	3000	3900	4800	7700	14,300	27,000

Model 6-66 — 6-cyl., 66 hp, 138" wb

Touring-7P	2850	5400	7300	11,800	25,000	38,000

1915 Pullman, model 6-48, touring, HAC

1915 PULLMAN

Junior — 4-cyl., 22.5 hp, 110" wb

	FP	5	4	3	2	1
Touring-5P	740	3100	4200	6300	10,500	22,000
Roadster-2P	740	3000	4000	6000	9500	21,000
Winter-Top Tour. (114" wb)	875	3200	4300	6500	11,000	23,000

Model 6-48 — 6-cyl., 48 hp, 134" wb

Touring-5P	2500	4200	5200	8400	15,700	29,000
Touring-7P	2550	4300	5400	8700	16,500	30,000
Limousine	3500	2900	3700	5600	9100	20,000
Landaulet	3500	3000	4000	6000	9500	21,000
Sedan	3200	2300	3300	4600	7500	16,000
Cabriolet	2800	3500	4500	7000	13,000	25,000

1916 Pullman Junior, coupe sedan, HAC

1916 PULLMAN

Junior — 4-cyl., 22.5 hp, 114" wb

Touring-5P	740	3200	4300	6500	11,000	23,000
Winter-Top Touring	875	3300	4400	6700	12,000	24,000
Roadster-2P	740	3100	4200	6300	10,500	22,000
Roadster-3P	740	3200	4300	6400	10,800	22,500
Cpe. (32 hp, Cutler-Hammer)	990	2200	3200	4400	7000	15,000

Model 6-48 — 6-cyl., 48 hp, 134" wb

Touring-5P	1850	4000	5000	8000	15,000	28,000
Touring-7P	1900	4200	5200	8400	15,700	29,000
Roadster-2P	1850	3900	4800	7700	14,300	27,000

1917 Pullman, model 424, club roadster, HAC

1917 PULLMAN

Model 424-32 — 4-cyl., 22.5 hp, 114" wb

Touring-5P	825	3200	4300	6500	11,000	23,000
Club Roadster-4P	825	3100	4200	6300	10,500	22,000
Roadster-2P	825	3000	4000	6000	9500	21,000
Open Express Delivery	750	2300	3300	4600	7500	16,000
Full Panel Delivery	775	2400	3400	4800	8000	17,000

PULLMAN FLYER — Chicago, Illinois — (1907-1908) — Although the Pullman Motor Car Company at 131-133 LaSalle Street in Chicago had been operating as a dealership since 1904, it was not until 1907 that the firm decided to venture into the automotive field as a producer. The Pullman Motor Vehicle Company, as this new enterprise was named, did no manufacturing, however. The cars were made for Pullman by Model in Peru. According to the company, "the meritorious features of fifty of the world's best cars" were combined in the Pullman Flyer. It was offered as a 45/50 hp four on a 120-inch wheelbase in touring, limousine and "speed car" models; a six was also available as a touring and "speed car." The price range was $3800 to $5000. A selective transmission provided four forward speeds with direct drive on third, and the chassis was provided a total of five brakes, one of them an air-cooled transmission brake operated by an emergency pedal. The Pullman Flyer was available for two seasons only.

1903 Pullman, six-wheeler, KM

PULLMAN SIX-WHEELER — York, Pennsylvania — (1903) — The first car to carry the Pullman name in York was a two-cylinder six-wheeled behemoth in which the power was supplied to the middle pair of wheels with the front and rear wheels providing the steering (they turned in opposite directions during cornering). The name was selected by the car's inventor, Albert P. Broomell, because he thought association with the comfortable ride of the railway sleeping car invented by George Mortimer Pullman would be a boon. Unfortunately, its name was the most meritorious feature of this Pullman. The vehicle itself, which was completed in 1903 in the shops of the Hardinge Company in York, was a disaster. Broomell tore the car apart, added two cylinders to the engine, took two wheels off the chassis and concluded that now he was on to something. He was. The next Pullman from York was produced for more than a decade.

PULLMAN TAXI — The Pullman Taxicab Company was a $100,000 Delaware incorporation from early 1913 with a capital stock of $100,000 to "manufacture, sell and deal in motor vehicles of all kinds" in New York City. Incorporators were E.C. Boyd, P.L. Garrett and W.A. Joslyn. Manufacture is doubted.

1905 Pungs-Finch, model D, touring, HAC

PUNGS-FINCH — Detroit, Michigan — (1904-1910) — W.A. was the Pungs and the father; E.B. was the Finch and the son-in-law. In this partnership which resulted in the Pungs-Finch automobile, however, Pungs provided only his money and the use of a surname which made for one of the most whimsical hyphenates in American motorcar history. E.B. Finch was the brains of the duo, an engineer who had studied at the University of Michigan and who had built his first automobile in 1902. In late 1904 father and son-in-law organized the Pungs-Finch Auto and Gas Engine Company, bought out Clark Sintz's Sintz Gas Engine Company and put up a factory at Pungs' boat-building works in Detroit. The very first Pungs-Finches — which were built at the Sintz works — featured shaft drive and sliding gear transmissions, which was certainly out of the ordinary for that era. But for the 1906 season, E.B. went positively avant-garde with a car that would be called the Finch Limited. Its engine was a huge four (each cylinder displacing 132 cubic inches) with hemispherical combustion chambers and inclined overhead valves operated by a single overhead camshaft. Fifty horsepower and 55 mph were guaranteed. Reportedly, Henry Ford told Pungs it was the finest car he had ever seen. The words between Pungs and Finch, however, were not nearly so pleasant. The two argued incessantly and, after one memorable altercation, Finch walked out to ply his technical expertise at Packard and Chalmers initially, deciding finally to forgo engineering altogether and become the Chalmers dealer in Cleveland in 1910. Pungs, who had tried to carry on without Finch and even introduced a very ordinary 50 hp four that he hoped would replace the Limited, gave up automobile manufacture that year too. At the most, several hundred Pungs-Finches may have been produced. Only one is known to exist today — and, fortuitously, it is the Limited. It was rescued by Henry Austin Clark, Jr., and is on display today at the San Antonio Museum of Transportation in Texas.

1904 PUNGS-FINCH
Twin — 14 hp, 76" wb

	FP	5	4	3	2	1
Runabout-2P	1450	2500	3500	5000	8500	18,000
Twin — 20 hp, 92" wb						
Canopy Top Tonneau	2550	2700	3600	5300	8800	19,000
1905 PUNGS-FINCH						
Model D — 4-cyl., 20 hp, 80" wb						
Rear Entrance Tonneau	1700	2700	3600	5300	8800	19,000
Model F — 4-cyl., 24 hp, 97" wb						
Side Entrance Toneau	1850	2700	3600	5300	8800	19,000

1906 Pungs-Finch, Finch Limited, roadster, OCW

1906 PUNGS-FINCH
Model F — 4-cyl., 22 hp, 98" wb

Touring-5P	1850	2700	3600	5300	8800	19,000
Model H — 4-cyl., 28/32 hp, 106" wb						
Touring-5P	2200	2900	3700	5600	9100	20,000
Finch Limited — 4-cyl., 50/60 hp, 111" wb						
Touring-7P	3500	4700	6100	9900	19,000	33,000
Roadster-2P	3000	4500	5800	9500	18,000	32,000

1907 Pungs-Finch, model H, victoria touring, HAC

1907 PUNGS-FINCH
Model F — 4-cyl., 22 hp, 98" wb

Touring-5P	2000	3000	4000	6000	9500	21,000
Runabout-2P	2000	2900	3700	5600	9100	20,000
Model 35 — 4-cyl., 40 hp, 106" wb						
Runabout-3P	2500	3200	4300	6500	11,000	23,000
Model H — 4-cyl., 40 hp, 110" wb						
Touring-5P	2500	3700	4700	7300	13,700	26,000

1908 Pungs-Finch, model 50, touring, WLB

1209

1908 PUNGS-FINCH
Four — 22 hp, 98" wb

	FP	5	4	3	2	1
Model F Touring-5P	2000	3200	4300	6500	11,000	23,000
Model F Runabout-2P	2000	3100	4200	6300	10,500	22,000
Four — 40 hp, 106" wb						
Model H Touring-5P	2500	4000	5000	8000	15,000	28,000
Model 35 Runabout-3P	2500	3900	4800	7700	14,300	27,000
Four — 50 hp, 116" wb						
Model 50 Touring	3500	5000	6500	11,000	22,000	35,000

1909 Pungs-Finch, model 35, runabout, HAC

1909 PUNGS-FINCH
Four — 22 hp, 98" wb

Model F Touring-5P	2000	3300	4400	6700	12,000	24,000
Model F Runabout-2P	2000	3200	4300	6500	11,000	23,000
Four — 38/40 hp, 106" wb						
Model H Touring-5P	2500	4800	5200	8400	15,700	9000
Model 35 Runabout-3P	2500	4000	5000	8000	15,000	28,000

1910 Pungs-Finch, model H, touring, HAC

1910 PUNGS-FINCH
Model F — 4-cyl., 22 hp, 100" wb

Touring-5P	1450	3300	4400	6700	12,000	24,000
Runabout-2P	1400	3200	4300	6500	11,000	23,000
Model H — 4-cyl., 40 hp, 106" wb						
Touring-5P	1700	4200	5200	8400	15,700	29,000
Runabout-3P	1650	4000	5000	8000	15,000	28,000

PURITAN — The Puritan Motor Company was organized in Boston, Massachusetts early in 1907 with a capital stock of $25,000 for the manufacture of automobiles and engines. E.O. Hoges of Cambridge was the man behind this venture. Manufacture of a car is doubted.

1903 Puritan Steamer, runabout, NAHC

PURITAN STEAM — Salem, Massachusetts — (1902-1905) — The Locke Regulator Company was a manufacturer of engines, axles and change speed gears in Salem, and in June of 1902 Albert N. Locke built his first steam car which was successfully tested. Later that month he organized the Puritan Motor Car Company with a capital stock of $135,000 to handle its marketing and also to act as a dealership for other makes of cars, Charles C. Smith served as president, Joseph B. Dow as treasurer. The Puritan would be built in his Locke Regulator factory. It was an attractive little runabout on 72-inch wheelbase, powered by a two-cylinder 6 hp vertical engine. Progressive features for the period included a foot throttle and a steering wheel which was hinged center-shaft to provide ease of entrance and egress. In 1904 A.N. Locke gave thought to building a gasoline car, but dismissed the idea after printing a few brochures. Instead, the British Waddington car was imported that year. The Locke Regulator Company left the automobile manufacturing field sometime in 1905.

1914 Puritan Cyclecar

PURITAN — Chicago, Illinois — (1913-1914) — The Puritan Motor Company was organized by F.P. Choate, formerly president of the Kissel Motor Car Company, with the help of four Chicago businessmen. A $150,000 corporation, Puritan had all the earmarks of success, except for the product it was about to manufacture. The Puritan cyclecar was designed by Choate, and was a neat looking little machine. Powered by a two-cylinder 10 hp DeLuxe engine placed in a 108-inch chassis, with 42-inch tread, side-by-side seating for two passengers was provided. Belt drive was typical for a cyclecar, but the Puritan's two-speed planetary transmission was unusual. The prototype was painted cherry red with white striping, but a variety of colors would be available in production. Three hundred fifty dollars was the price tag. The car was tested extensively late in 1913, and in November that year, F.P. Choate took the prototype abroad to exhibit at the cyclecar show in London, followed by Paris. Export was planned, but only as a sideline. "The field abroad is big, but I think it will develop into a bigger field here," commented F.P. Choate. "The Puritan, in my estimation — but of course I'm the designer and may be overzealous — is a cyclecar that will be best adapted to American conditions. . . .Next year cyclecars will be sold by the thousands in this country." Choate was right about the numbers but undoubtedly didn't anticipate how quickly the cyclecar would die. Subsequent vehicle registration figures for various states in the Midwest indicate that probably more Puritan cyclecars were sold than many of the myriad others which blossomed into production in 1914.

PURITAN — Framingham, Massachusetts — (1917) — This Puritan was introduced at the Grand Central Palace during automobile show week in New York City, January 1917. It was the product of Puritan Motors Company of Framingham, an assembled car with Buda four-cylinder engine, Warner clutch, American Ball Bearing axle, Eisemann magneto, Gray & Davis electrics. The show car sported what was described at the time as "a particularly comfortable and good-appearing four-passenger body made by the Farman-Nelson company." Its price tag was $2775. Further production of the Puritan has not been documented. Possibly this venture ended with the show car; certainly it ended the same year it began.

PURMAX — This Los Angeles car of 1914-1915 is simply a frequent typographical error appearing on car rosters. Refer to Permax.

PUTNAM — Mendon, Michigan — (1901) — According to an August 1901 issue of *The Motor Age*, one R.S. Putnam of Mendon built an automobile that year. Details are lacking.

1876 Pyott Steamer, LC

PYOTT STEAM — Philadelphia, Pennsylvania — (1876) — The Pyott was a steamer designed by L.T. Pyott and built in association with F.A. Morse and William Devine in 1876. The three partners were at the time employed as foremen at the Baldwin Locomotive Works in Philadelphia, and the vehicle was completed at the Baldwin shops. Purportedly, it was inspected that year by Dom Pedro, the Emperor of Brazil, on a visit to the Baldwin shops. It was also displayed at the Centennial Exposition in Philadelphia. The Pyott had cost $2200 to build, not including Pyott's time. A seven-passenger wagon with its boiler mounted at the rear, the steamer was fueled by anthracite coal and was steered awkwardly. As later described by *The Motor World*, "the steering device was of peculiar construction, the front axle being held in position by radial arms centering 48 inches from arm of dials. Seated on top of front springs was a radial rachet, on which rolled a flanged gear, which caused the main frame to traverse from right to left, thus each axle assumed a radial line to the curve being made and the wheels traced in line." The Pyott was successfully driven.

PYRAMID — The Pyramid Motor Car Company was organized during the spring of 1907 for the manufacture of cars in Danbury, Connecticut. What may have emanated thereafter from the Pyramid shops is unknown, but all activity stopped during the fall of 1910. "The shops and garage of the concern, which started with a small capital some months ago (sic), have been closed," reported *The Horseless Age* that September. A creditor's petition in bankruptcy against Pyramid had been filed that week in the U.S. District Court in Hartford.

PYRO-PNEUMATIC — Chicago, Illinois — (1895) — Pyro-Pneumatic was the designation given by P.E. McDonnell and W.A. Brennan of Chicago, Illinois to the simple gasoline-powered buggy they built that year. Details are lacking, but manufacture did not follow.

1895 Pyro-Pneumatic, auto-buggy, HAC

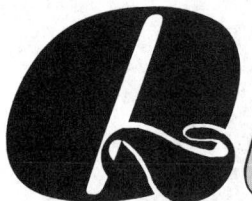
QUAKER CITY — The Quaker City Automobile Company was established in Philadelphia, Pennsylvania at the turn of the century, purchasing the business and location of Maurice Loeb at 306 North Broad Street in 1901 and establishing an agency for the Duryea there. By 1903 the firm had moved to 138-140 Broad Street, and its lines were Oldsmobile, Pope-Toledo, Franklin and White. Although the Quaker City Automobile Company has been indicated on various rosters as an automobile manufacturer, it operated as a dealership only, and was the largest in Philadelphia during this period. Certainly the company may have customized cars at client request but it did not produce them. In 1904 the various cars for which Quaker City held agency were separated into their own selling organizations, and the Quaker City Automobile Company itself henceforth devoted its full attention to the storage and repair of vehicles.

QUAKERTOWN — Quakertown, Pennsylvania — (1902-1904) — J.S. Nicholas was the proprietor of the Quakertown Buggy Works and in early 1902 he completed his first gasoline car. That summer *Cycle and Automobile Trade Journal* reported Nicholas' desire "to interest a partner with capital to go into the manufacture of automobiles." Apparently a partner was found because early in 1903 the name of the Quakertown Buggy Works was changed to Quakertown Automobile Manufacturing Company. A modest production is believed to have followed.

1904 Queen, runabout, OCW

QUEEN — Detroit, Michigan — (1904-1906) — "Big Power and Few Parts" was the slogan for the first Queen, and there was truth in it. The car was a simple little runabout with one cylinder of commanding 5½-by-6-inch bore-stroke dimensions developing 8 hp, which was high for a one-lunger. A double-opposed engine was also available which, the company said, took no more space than the single. A four was added for 1905, and the one-lunger was dropped. The Queen was built by the C.H. Blomstrom Motor Company of Detroit. During the summer of 1906 the firm was in trouble with the authorities, charged with having been "defectively incorporated." Blomstrom's dilemma was nicely resolved that October when the promoters of the Car De Luxe negotiated a merger with his firm which sent the C.H. Blomstrom Motor Company into blessed oblivion and provided Blomstrom himself with cash and Car De Luxe stock. He moved across town in Detroit, organized the Blomstrom Manufacturing Company, and introduced a new car called the Blomstrom in 1907. Total production of his Queen has been estimated as 1500 units.

1904 Queen, runabout, HAC

1904 QUEEN

	FP	5	4	3	2	1
Runabout (1- cyl.)	650	2400	3400	4800	8000	17,000
Rbt. w/Tonneau (1- cyl.)	750	2450	3500	4900	8300	17,500
Runabout (2- cyl.)	850	2500	3500	5000	8500	18,000
Rbt. w/Tonneau (2- cyl.)	950	2600	3600	5200	8700	18,500

1905 Queen, touring, OCW

1905 QUEEN
Model B — 2-cyl., 12 hp, 73" wb

	FP	5	4	3	2	1
Runabout	775	2500	3500	5000	8500	18,000
Detachable Tonneau	875	2600	3600	5200	8700	18,500
Model C — 2-cyl., 16 hp, 80" wb						
Detachable Tonneau	950	2700	3600	5300	8800	19,000
Model E — 2-cyl., 16 hp, 84" wb						
Side Entrance Tonneau	1000	2700	3600	5300	8800	19,000
Model D — 4-cyl., 24 hp, 96" wb						
Side Entrance Tonneau	2000	3100	4200	6300	10,500	22,000

1906 Queen, model K, touring, HAC

1906 QUEEN
Model F — 2-cyl., 12/16 hp, 76" wb

	FP	5	4	3	2	1
Runabout-2P	800	2500	3500	5000	8500	18,000
Model E — 2-cyl., 16/20 hp, 84" wb						
Touring-5P	1100	2700	3600	5300	8800	19,999
Model K — 4-cyl., 26/28 hp, 100" wb						
Touring-5P	2000	2900	3700	5600	9100	20,000

QUEEN CITY — Buffalo, New York — (1911) — In Buffalo, during the early fall of 1911, the Queen City Electric Automobile Company was organized with a capital stock of $50,000 for the manufacture of automobiles. A.C. Towne, C.S. Chamberlain and Moses T. Day were the principals involved. Manufacture did not follow.

1900 Quick, runabout, GR

QUICK — Paterson, New Jersey — (1899-1900) / Newark, New Jersey — (1900) — The only thing fast about the Quick was its run to obscurity. It was powered by a two-cylinder water-cooled engine which developed 4 hp at 700 rpm. A two-seater buggy with tiller steering and single chain drive was the only model offered, and it appears the Quick Manufacturing Company had a good deal of difficulty even coming up with that. In its December 26th, 1899 issue, *The Motor Vehicle Review* described the "many trials and disappointments during the past two years" suffered by the company before finally announcing that production at the rate of one car per day had begun. H.M. Quick was the man behind the car, and he was joined by E.M. Rodrock and R.E. Horton in establishing the Quick business which also manufactured the Quick gasoline motor and a Quick-patented steering device, in addition to the Quick bicycle which had been its inventor's first endeavor. The Quick motor had not been his doing, however, the 4 hp twin having been the invention of one F.A. Phelps, Jr. The Quick factory was first located at 96 Broadway in Paterson, with a move made to 52 Washington Street in Paterson early in 1900, followed by a move to 3-5-7 Oliver Street in Newark by May of 1900. The Quick became the dead that fall. Burdened by debts, the company sold out to Remington of Ilion, New York in October — in a deal that was later declared fraudulent.

QUINBY — Newark, New Jersey — (1899-1900) — "It is an unfailing sign of the times," *The Horseless Age* reported with delight in March 1899, "when one of the oldest carriage-building firms in the country, noted for more than half a century for the excellence of their product, embarks in the manufacture of electric carriages." J.M. Quinby & Company had been established in Newark in 1834. Its foray into automobile building was a short one, however. Electric carriages were built to custom order only, though the firm provided a variety of adaptable styles. Most of the vehicles appear to have been exported. Shortly after the turn of the century, when the Quinby electric car was discontinued, the firm turned to coachbuilding for the automotive industry. In 1916 there was a brief flurry of excitement as trade journals rumored that "from its position as one of the leading makers of custom bodies in the East," Quinby was planning to "expand into larger existence as a car maker." Among the principals behind this effort was William O. Houck, former vice-president and sales manager for Keeton, and the plan was reorganization of the company to increase capital stock from $200,000 to $2.1 million. This did not happen. In March 1917 Quinby announced its retirement from business, "after eighty years' activity." The Quinby factory in Newark was put up for sale at $400,000.

QUINCY — Quincy, Illinois — (1906) — In 1900 John W. Cassidy, the president of the Egg-O-See Cereal Company of Quincy, ordered a White Steamer from the Quincy Automobile Company, a dealership in town which by 1904 was dealing as well in the Pope-Toledo, Dumont, Cadillac and Oldsmobile. Soon thereafter, Cassidy acquired the Quincy dealership, and in 1906 had a large touring car custom built for himself. This car was strictly a one-off, however, and the Quincy company thereafter confined its efforts to selling the automobiles of other manufacturers.

QUINLAN — Brookline, Massachusetts — (1904) — That a Quinlan automobile was built in Brookline in 1904 cannot be documented with certainty. Michael W. Quinlan had been manufacturing carriages and harnesses since before the turn of the century in his factory at the corner of Boylston, Walnut and High streets. With the coming of the automobile age, he expanded his business into automobile repairing and painting, in addition to body building. Certainly he possessed the facility and the expertise to produce a car in 1904, and he may well have either for his own use or on behalf of a local client. Automobile manufacture was never embarked upon, however. The Quinlan automobile business remained in operation at the same location into the 1920's.

1904 Quinsler, runabout, NAHC

QUINSLER — Boston, Massachusetts — (1904) — In November of 1899, Quinsler & Company, a carriage-building firm on Cambria Street in Boston, announced its completion of twenty hansom cab bodies built for the Electric Vehicle Company, producers of the Columbia. Quinsler also announced that it was "prepared to execute any kind of automobile body work." In 1904, and for that season only, Quinsler marketed an automobile itself. It was a rumble-seat runabout powered by a single-cylinder 7 hp De Dion engine fitted upfront under a hood. A nicely finished little vehicle, it carried a $950 price tag. By 1905 George W. McNear was one of the partners in the company. Quinsler's advertisement in the 1906 Boston Automobile Show program included a photo of a handsome long-wheelbase Packard limousine. By 1911 the firm was advertising as "George W. McNear, successor to Quinsler & Company." Coachbuilding remained its trade. Numerous bodies were produced for individuals and dealers in the area, including at least ten Rolls-Royces and a couple of Model A Duesenbergs. At some point the firm also became a Nash dealership and, following World War II, quarters were shared with the local Rolls-Royce outlet, into which organization the McNear company merged. During the 1960's Foreign Motors Inc. became the firm's new title; today it is Foreign Motors West in Natick.

RABER-LANG — South Bend, Indiana — (1909) — In December of 1909, Charles McLaughlin, the superintendent of the Raber-Lang Company of South Bend, announced completion of the firm's first two cars, both with twin-cylinder engines, one of sixteen horsepower, the other of twenty. Presumably these models were a presage of forthcoming quantity manufacture, but not many cars were built and not for long.

R.A.C. — South Bend, Indiana — (1910-1911) — R.A.C. represented the initials of the Ricketts Automobile Company and was used from 1910-1911 for the car which had been produced as the Ricketts the year previously. "New in name, and practically a new vehicle" was the phrase Ricketts used, though that was largely advertising-ese. A lengthening of wheelbases was the only discernible change in specifications, with a new seven-passenger touring model on an even longer 142-inch wheelbase announced but apparently never produced. That J.W. Ricketts' company was in trouble during this period is indicated by the fact that he also referred to some of his last cars as Diamonds, with his firm's name being thusly changed also. Receivership followed in May of 1911.

1910-1911 R.A.C.
Model H — 4-cyl., 35 hp, 121" wb

	FP	5	4	3	2	1
Touring-5P	1550	3100	4200	6300	10,500	22,000
Baby Tonneau-4P	1550	3000	4000	6000	9500	21,000
Roadster-4P	1550	3000	4000	6000	9500	21,000

Model G-6 — 6-cyl., 50 hp, 133" wb

Touring-7P	2200	3300	4400	6700	12,000	24,000

RACINE — The town of Racine, Wisconsin saw a number of automobile-building ventures begun or contemplated during the early years of the industry:

The Racine Motor Vehicle Company produced a few automobiles in 1895-1896. The firm was organized, however, more for promotion than production. The notorious Edward Joel Pennington was the man behind it. Refer to Pennington.

In January of 1902 the Racine Wagon and Carriage Company announced plans to enlarge its plant and add the manufacture of automobiles. The Racine city directory that year indicates H.E. Miles as president and superintendent, Theo Starks as vice president, J.C. Lund as secretary-treasurer. The extent of any automobile manufacture has not been determined.

Also in 1902, the Racine Boat Manufacturing Company announced its plans to enter automobile manufacturing, although in 1903 when its factory burned down, only boats were indicated as having been destroyed.

In 1911 the Racine Automobile & Motor Works was incorporated with a capital stock of $5000 to manufacture and deal in automobiles and parts. Soren Peterson, Jans Mikhelsen and George Gammelgaard were the principals involved. Most probably, this venture operated as a dealership only.

RACINE — Detroit, Michigan — (1909-1911) — In November of 1908 the Racine Boat Manufacturing Company of 182 Jefferson Avenue in Detroit announced its impending production of a four-cylinder, four-stroke 22-1/2 hp automobile with sliding gear transmission and shaft drive. Apparently a small production ensued, and possibly for two years following. By 1911 the firm, now titled Racine Boat and Auto Company, was located at 253-255 Jefferson Avenue. W. Sidney Sumner was the manager. Further production has not been documented.

RACINE-SATTLEY — Racine, Wisconsin — (1910-1911) — The Racine-Sattley Company was a carriage-building establishment located at Junction Avenue Southwest on the corner of 16th in Racine. It had evolved from the partnership of Hans Sattley of Sheboygan, who had built an experimental gasoline car soon after the turn of the century, and H.E. Miles of Racine. Both of these gentlemen had retired by late 1909, however, when the company decided to enter the automotive field. The new Racine-Sattley president was George H. Yule (a heavy stockholder in the Badger Brass Manufacturing Company), with Logan Hay as vice-president, George B. Lourie as secretary and T.M. Kearney as treasurer. P.H. Connolly, an automobile engineer from Pontiac, Michigan, was hired to superintend the automobile department. Early in 1910 the firm announced completion of its first automobile which was exhibited at the Chicago Automobile Show, but so quietly as to go unnoticed. The company did have a modest production of cars thereafter, their four-cylinder engines provided by the Holbrook-Armstrong Iron Company across the street in Racine. Some years later the Racine-Sattley Company consolidated its manufacturing in Springfield, Illinois, though by that time automobiles were not among its products.

RADELL — The Radell Company was organized in Syracuse, New York during the spring of 1910 with a capital stock of $1000 to manufacture and deal in "motor cars and mechanical devices." Incorporators were Emma L. Radell, William A. O'Brien and Arthur J. O'Connor. Manufacture of a car is doubted.

RADFORD — Oshkosh, Wisconsin — (1895) — W.J. Radford of 58 Union Street in Oshkosh was among the dozens of inventors urged on to automotive effort by the announcement of the Chicago Times-Herald Contest in 1895. Although he did not make it to the starting line, there is evidence that he did complete and successfully test his car. In 1945 his sister, Mrs. George Finch, was interviewed by the *Oshkosh Daily Northwestern* and although she did not recall the vehicle she believed it "entirely probable" to have been built. Her brother was always "tinkering and puttering" around machinery, she remembered, and "he always said the day would come when people would ride by power instead of the horse." Though he was correct in his prediction, Radford did not enter the automobile industry himself. In 1895, when he built his car, W.J. Radford was engaged, with his brothers, in the manufacture of lumber, sash, doors, blinds and other wood products.

1903 Radford, tonneau, GR

RADFORD — Boston, Massachusetts — (1903) — A.L. Radford of 43 Columbus Avenue in Boston built at least two cars on custom order for a Boston financier. The first was a 35 hp four, the second a 45 hp. Both vehicles were touring cars, the higher-powered version on a 102-inch wheelbase with an overall length of 156 inches, a fringed canopy top, and accommodations for eight passengers. With the exception of an Upton transmission, the tires and muffler, the cars were entirely of Radford's construction.

RADFORD LIGHT CAR — This light car of 1915-1916 was designed by William Radford and was slated to be produced by the Pilgrim Motor Car Company of Detroit. Refer to Pilgrim.

1902 Rae Electric, NAHC

RAE ELECTRIC — Chicago, Illinois — (1898, 1902) / Springfield, Vermont — (1909) — Despite three attempts at manufacture, it seems likely that the Rae Electric was never built as other than a prototype. The first arrived in 1898. In April that year the Rae Motocycle Company was organized in Chicago for manufacture of a vehicle powered by an electric motor designed by F.B. Rae, with the Porter storage battery to be used, and the Sterling Cycle Company to build the running gear. By October the finishing touches were being put on the prototype, an electric cab with driver's seat in front. Nothing further was heard from the Rae Motocycle Company. In 1902 F.B. Rae resurfaced as the Rae Motor Cycle Company in Chicago, but went under again before year's end. His most ambitious effort followed in 1909 when he turned up in Springfield, Vermont all set to organize his new Rae Electric Vehicle Company with a proposed $600,000 capital stock. According to the Springfield *Reporter*, plans called for a full-line production of victoria, coupe, gentleman's runabout, taxicab, four-passenger victoria and delivery wagon. A two-building factory was begun at Bates Meadow near Muckross Park, but the Rae Electric never moved in. Prior to completion of the plant, F.B. Rae's final automotive effort was rendered asunder. Undercapitalization had been his problem, precipitated by — as a local historian put it — "Vermonters' well-known reluctance to open their pocketbooks carelessly."

RAGAN — The Ragan, Brown & Lange Company was organized in Napoleon, Ohio late in 1910 with a capital stock of $40,000 for the manufacture of "motors and all kinds of vehicles, including motor cars." The partners involved were James P. Ragan, Jacob F. Brown and Henry Lange. Manufacture of an automobile is doubted.

RAGO — The Rago Motor Company was organized in New York City early in 1912 with a capital stock of $20,000 for the manufacture of automobiles. Incorporators were George C. Andrews of 1 Madison Avenue, E.C. Gorham of 220 West 49th Street, and Thomas H. Farrell of Jersey City, New Jersey. Manufacture is doubted.

RAILSBACH — Saginaw, Michigan — (1914) — Working as a draftsman for the Valley Boat & Engine Company of Saginaw, L.M. Railsbach followed the development of that firm's Saginaw Cyclecar — and apparently believed he could do as well on his own. Although he classified his Railsbach as a light car, its 36-inch tread placed it definitively in cyclecar ranks. The car was powered by a four-cylinder 92.5-cubic-inch water-cooled engine, and a friction transmission was employed. No factory location was ever cited for the Railsbach, nor did Railsbach organize a company for manufacture. One car is known to have been built; whether Railsbach built any others is not.

1905 Rainier, model A, double-side-entrance tonneau, HAC

RAINIER — Flushing, New York — (1905-1907) / Saginaw, Michigan — (1907-1911) — Prior to building the car which bore his name, John T. Rainier was among the organizers of the Vehicle Equipment Company of Long Island City and in 1902 established the Rainier Company of Manhattan to serve as sales agency for the V.E. car. In 1905 he struck out on his own as the Rainier Motor Car Company, retaining his Manhattan dealership as the firm's headquarters and locating its factory in Flushing, Queens. Final assembly only was seen to in Flushing, however, the Rainier chassis being built by Garford in Elyria. The first Rainier was a 22/28 hp four which distinguished itself as a formidable hill climber and fine performance car in competition events at Bretton Woods, in the Adirondacks and along the Jersey Coast. The "Pullman of Motor Cars," which was the marque's slogan in 1905, remained for 1906, as did the Rainier "guarantee of a year's use without repair expenses." As year passed year, Rainiers became bigger and more powerful. In mid-1907 — when Studebaker's involvement with Garford meant that firm would no longer supply chassis the company moved to Saginaw, Michigan where production of the 1908 models was begun in a new factory at 6th and Washington. Moving with the company was James G. Heaslet, who had designed the original Rainier and would continue to design the Saginaw-built cars. Three hundred Rainiers were produced in 1908. In November that year the company was petitioned into involuntary bankruptcy. "It is simply a case of not having enough cash to get through the product we had planned for 1909," Rainier general manager Paul Lineberger told the press. "Our assets are far in excess of our liabilities, but during the financial stringency [the Panic of '07] we have been unable to raise the cash to meet our material bills and our large payrolls." On January 25th, 1909 the Rainier factory was sold at auction for $20,000; its purchaser was George C. Comstock, an attorney representing John T. Rainier, who was desperately trying to save his business. But he simply could not come up with the money. In May the Rainier factory was acquired by General Motors, and the Marquette Motor Company was organized to operate it. Marquette itself was under direct management of the Buick Motor Company. The Rainier was continued in production through 1911; by 1912 it had been superseded by the Marquette automobile.

1905 RAINIER
Model A — 4-cyl., 22/28 hp, 98" wb

	FP	5	4	3	2	1
Touring-5P	3500	2400	3400	4800	8000	17,000

1906 RAINIER
Model A — 4-cyl., 22/28 hp, 98" wb

	FP	5	4	3	2	1
Touring-5P	3500	2400	3400	4800	8000	17,000

Model B — 4-cyl., 30/35 hp, 104" wb

	FP	5	4	3	2	1
Town Car-7P	4000	2000	3300	4600	7500	16,000

1907 Rainier, model C, touring, HAC

1907 RAINIER
Model C — 4-cyl., 30/35 hp, 104" wb

	FP	5	4	3	2	1
Touring-5P	4250	2400	3400	4800	8000	17,000
Landaulet-7P	4250	2200	3200	4400	7000	15,000

1908 Rainier, model D, touring, JAC

1908-1909 RAINIER
Model D — 4-cyl., 40/50 hp, 114" wb

	FP	5	4	3	2	1
Touring-5P	4500	3200	4300	6500	11,000	23,000
Limousine-7P	5500	2500	3500	5000	8500	18,000

1910 Rainier, model F, touring, HAC

1911 Rainier, model F, roadster, WLB

1910 RAINIER
Model F — 4-cyl., 50 hp, 119" wb

	FP	5	4	3	2	1
Enclosed Touring-7P	4500	3700	4700	7300	13,700	26,000
Touring-7P	4500	3900	4800	7700	14,300	27,000
Baby Tonneau-5P	4500	3700	4700	7300	13,700	26,000
Close-Coupled Touring-5P	4500	3700	4700	7300	13,700	26,000
Limousine-7P	5750	2500	3500	5000	8500	18,000
Landaulet-7P	5850	2700	3600	5300	8800	19,000

1911 RAINIER
Model F — 4-cyl., 50 hp, 120" wb

Regulation Touring-7P	4250	3900	4800	7700	14,300	27,000
Special Touring-7P	4250	3900	4800	7700	14,300	27,000
Landaulet-7P	4600	2700	3600	5300	8800	19,000
Limousine-7P	4600	2500	3500	5000	8500	18,000
Roadster-2P	4250	3500	4500	7000	13,000	25,000
Close-Coupled Touring-4P	4250	3700	4700	7300	13,700	26,000

Raleigh Special Touring Car

1921 Raleigh, Special, touring, WLB

RALEIGH — Bridgeton, New Jersey — (1921) / Reading, Pennsylvania — (1921-1922) — Raleigh Motors Corporation was organized in Bridgeton early in 1921 by J.R. Sutterlee, Leroy Sutterlee and George Quimby. A Model 6-60 at $2750 and a Model 4-40 at $2050 represented the company's projected production, but it appears only the six-cylinder car made it to the assembly line. The Raleigh's engine was from Herschell-Spillman, and the remainder of its components arrived from divers sources: axles from Spacke, electrics from Westinghouse, carburetor from Stromberg, steering gear from Gemmer, vacuum system from Stewart. The touring car was also called the Princess Pat, after the famous Canadian regiment and the Victor Herbert operetta. Scarcely had production begun in Bridgeton when the Raleigh people decided to move to Reading. By year's end 1921, Raleigh Motors, Inc. (as the firm had been redesignated) was in its new Reading factory at 426 North Second Street, where it remained for approximately six months. A further relocation to Buffalo, New York was planned but never consummated. By the summer of '22, Raleigh was out of business. Total production has been estimated at approximately two dozen cars.

1921-1922 RALEIGH
Model A-6-60 — 6-cyl., 57 hp, 122' wb

Touring-5P	2750	4000	5000	8000	15,000	28,000

RAMAPAUGH STEAMER — Middletown, Ohio — (1901-1902) — The Miami Cycle and Manufacturing Company was one of the biggest industries in Middletown at the turn of the century. It employed twenty-seven traveling salesmen and in 1900 sold 19,000 Racycles (a bicycle designed by Colonel Frank F. Ray, who was described as a vice-president of the Continental Tobacco Company) of which 2000 were exported to Japan. Flushed with commercial success, Miami president A.H. decided to enter the automobile field the following year with a steam car. Although *The Automobile and Motor Review* indicated in 1902 that its designer was Colonel Ray, he seems to have served largely as kibitzer. The man most responsible for the car was Charles A. Ball, a locomotive designer. He named the car Ramapaugh (after the Indian tribe) and saw to the details of its construction. It was gargantuan, a big eight-passenger tourer with wheel steering, wood wheels, solid rubber tires, and its fire-tube boiler mounted up front under the hood. It weighed two tons, carried twenty-four gallons of gasoline and sixty-eight of water, developed a claimed 60 hp and could travel at speeds up to forty miles an hour between fill-ups. The Ramapaugh's public debut was February 26th, 1902, when it was displayed in front of the U.S. Hotel in town. It took to the streets of Middletown thereafter, invariably with Ball driving, until April 12th, when tragedy struck. The car collided with a boy on a bicycle, and the youngster was killed. It was the first automobile fatality in the city. Middletown was outraged. Almost immediately, Charles Ball left for the East Coast, taking the Ramapaugh Steamer with him. He is known to have designed two more steam cars. The Miami Cycle and Manufacturing Company did not build another self-propelled vehicle until 1911 when the company undertook production of Joseph Merkel's "Flying Merkel" motorcycle.

RAMBLER — From 1903 to 1904, in Rockaway, New Jersey, the Rockaway Automobile Company built a car which has occasionally been referred to as the Rambler. Refer to Rockaway.

RAMBLER — Chicago, Illinois — (1897-1900) / Kenosha, Wisconsin — (1902-1913) — Rambler was the name of the bicycle produced in Chicago prior to the turn of the century by Thomas B. Jeffery and R. Philip Gormully, who operated the second largest bicycle factory in the United States, Colonel Albert Pope on the East Coast being first. The partners manufactured tires as well, as the G & J Tire Company, which ultimately became part of United States Rubber. Of the two men, it was Thomas Jeffery who was the most ardent about entering the automotive age, his young son Charles T. Jeffery enthusiastically urging him on. In 1897 Tom Jeffery built his first single-cylinder gasoline car; in 1898 Charles Jeffery

1897 Rambler, runabout, JAC

built two more considerably more sophisticated machines. Aside from brief mentions in the press that Jeffery, along with E.C. Stearns and George N. Pierce were "among the bicycle manufacturers who are experimenting with the motor vehicle," little attention was initially paid to these vehicles. In 1900, however, the cars were displayed at the automobile shows in Chicago in September and in New York City in November — and reporters recognized a good story when they saw it. The Jeffery-designed car was alternately referred to in the press as the G & J or the Rambler; it carried no plaque, so the confusion was understandable, though both Thomas and Charles Jeffery preferred the latter designation. However called, its features of a front-mounted engine and left-hand drive were very advanced for an American car of the period, and press reaction was enthusiastic, though *The Motor Age* wondered about the marketability of the notion of steering from the left side of a car: "Whether this will become popular remains to be seen," the magazine commented. "It has many points in its favor, however." By now Thomas and Charles Jeffery had made two important decisions. The first was to sell out their bicycle business — following the sudden death of Philip Gormully — to the American Bicycle Company, the conglomerate engineered by Colonel Pope which was an attempt to monopolize bicycle manufacture in this country. The second was to buy a huge factory in Kenosha, Wisconsin from which to launch themselves wholeheartedly into the automobile business. They retained rights to the Rambler name; the car left behind in their Chicago factory was produced for a while in 1901 by the American Bicycle people as the Hydro-Car. No doubt it was a variation of the earliest Thomas Jeffery car; the car taken to Kenosha was the son's more advanced design, which Charles advanced further by replacing the tiller with a steering wheel. Suddenly Thomas Jeffery had second thoughts, however, about the public acceptance of an automobile with front-mounted engine, left-hand drive and wheel steering. This delayed the onset of production, and when the new Rambler was introduced in February 1902 it had its engine mounted under the seat and was steered by tiller from the right side. Still, it was a honey of a car. "Its low price, $750, almost warrants some one in expecting something infinitely inferior . . . ," *The Motor World* reported. "The vehicle is plainly a high class one . . . rare value for the money." Plainly, too, Tom Jeffery's conservatism paid off; a total of 1500 cars was produced in 1902, a figure exceeded only by Ransom Olds with his curved dash runabout. Unlike Ransom Olds, Thomas Jeffery did not long remain content with a one-lunger. In 1904 Jeffery built 2342 cars, some of them higher-powered two-cylinder versions with front-mounted engines — and all Ramblers had steering wheels now. The year following the company made an even more drastic change, discontinuing the single-cylinder midyear and focusing all effort on three larger two-cylinder cars priced from $1200 to $3000. Sales in 1905 increased to 3807 cars. A Rambler four was introduced in 1906, and so was a certain savoir faire to Rambler advertising. From "The Right Car at the Right Price," Rambler promotion

1901 Rambler, runabout, WLB

1902 Rambler, model C, runabout, OCW

burst forth with "June Time Is Rambler Time" and other evocative phrases, all courtesy of new employee Edward S. Jordan, who would rise to become Jeffery's secretary and general manager before leaving to give the world the Jordan car and "Somewhere West of Laramie." By now the Jeffery company was an industry leader, and the Kenosha factory in which it turned out its Rambler cars was not only the largest in the country but was also widely reputed to be the best equipped. Thomas Jeffery was sitting on top of the world. Mass production, however, never interested him. Actually, the fortune he was making in the manufacture of medium-priced high-quality cars was a splendid one anyway. But on April 2nd, 1910, while vacationing in Italy, Thomas Jeffery died of a heart attack. His will stipulated that his business, which had previously traded under the name of Thomas B. Jeffery & Company, would now be incorporated as the Thomas B. Jeffery Company, though ownership remained entirely with the Jeffery family. His son Charles took over as president, and some changes followed, including the raising of production by about 500 cars a year from the 3000-more-or-less that his father had preferred, and the attaching of such designations as Country Club, Knickerbocker and Valkyrie (Ned Jordan's idea, naturally) to various of the Rambler models. Not changed, however, was the Rambler's right-hand drive. The biggest change came in 1914. It was a new car altogether. The decision was a gutsy one, Rambler being among the oldest and most respected names in the industry. But now it was no more. The new car from the big Kenosha factory would be called the Jeffery.

1902 Rambler, model C, runabout, OCW

1902
One cylinder, 4 hp

	FP	5	4	3	2	1
2P Rbt	750	3300	6600	11,000	15,400	22,000

1903
One cylinder, 6 hp

	FP	5	4	3	2	1
2/4P Lt Tr	750	3150	6300	10,500	14,700	21,000

1904 Rambler, rear entrance tonneau, OCW

1904

	FP	5	4	3	2	1
Model E, 1-cyl., 7 hp, 78" wb						
Rbt	650	2000	5100	8500	11,900	17,000
Model G, 1-cyl., 7 hp, 81" wb						
Rbt	750	2200	5250	8750	12,250	17,500
Model H, 1-cyl., 7 hp, 81" wb						
Tonneau	850	2200	5250	8750	12,250	17,500
Model J, 2-cyl., 16 hp, 84" wb						
Rbt	1100	2300	5400	9000	12,600	18,000
Model K, 2-cyl., 16 hp, 84" wb						
Tonneau	1200	2300	5400	9000	12,600	18,000
Model L, 2-cyl., 16 hp, 84" wb						
Canopy Ton	1350	2600	5500	9250	12,950	18,500

1905 Rambler type I, surrey, JAC

1905

	FP	5	4	3	2	1
Model G, 1-cyl., 8 hp, 81" wb						
Rbt	750	2000	5100	8500	11,900	17,000
Model H, 1-cyl., 8 hp, 81" wb						
Tr	850	2000	5100	8500	11,900	17,000
Type One, 2-cyl., 18 hp, 90" wb						
Tr	1200	2300	5400	9000	12,600	18,000
Type Two, 2-cyl., 20 hp, 100" wb						
Surrey	1650	2800	5700	9500	13,300	19,000
Limo	3000	3300	6600	11,000	15,400	22,000

1906 Rambler, type I, surrey, OCW

1217

1906
Model 17, 2-cyl., 10/12 hp, 88" wb

	FP	5	4	3	2	1
2P Rbt	800	1750	4800	8000	11,200	16,000
Type One, 2-cyl., 18/20 hp, 90" wb						
5P Surrey	1200	2000	5100	8500	11,900	17,000
Type Two, 2-cyl., 20 hp, 100" wb						
5P Surrey	1650	2200	5250	8750	12,250	17,500
Type Three, 2-cyl., 18/20 hp, 96" wb						
5P Surrey	1350	2300	5400	9000	12,600	18,000
Model 14, 4-cyl., 25 hp, 106" wb						
5P Tr	1750	2600	5500	9250	12,950	18,500
Model 15, 4-cyl., 35/40 hp, 112" wb						
5P Tr	2500	2800	5700	9500	13,300	19,000
Model 16, 4-cyl., 35/40 hp, 112" wb						
5P Limo	3000	2900	5850	9750	13,650	19,500

1907 Rambler, model 21, roadster, JAC

1907
Model 27, 2-cyl., 14/16 hp, 90" wb

	FP	5	4	3	2	1
2P Rbt	950	1750	4800	8000	11,200	16,000
Model 22, 2-cyl., 20/22 hp, 100" wb						
2P Rbt	1250	1800	4950	8250	11,550	16,500
Model 21, 2-cyl., 20/22 hp, 100" wb						
5P Tr	1350	2000	5100	8500	11,900	17,000
Model 24, 4-cyl., 25/30 hp, 108" wb						
5P Tr	2000	2200	5250	8750	12,250	17,500
Model 25, 4-cyl., 35/40 hp, 112" wb						
5P Tr	2500	2300	5400	9000	12,600	18,000

1908 Rambler, limousine, OCW

1909 Rambler, touring, JAC

1908
Model 31, 2-cyl., 22 hp, 106" wb

	FP	5	4	3	2	1
Det Tonneau	1400	2300	5400	9000	12,600	18,000
Model 34, 4-cyl., 32 hp, 112" wb						
3P Rds	2250	2600	5500	9250	12,950	18,500
5P Tr	2250	2800	5700	9500	13,300	19,000

1909
Model 47, 2-cyl., 22 hp, 106" wb

	FP	5	4	3	2	1
2P Rbt	1150	2300	5400	9000	12,600	18,000
Model 41, 2-cyl., 22 hp, 106" wb						
5P Tr	1350	2800	5700	9500	13,300	19,000
Model 44, 4-cyl., 34 hp, 112" wb						
5P Tr	2250	3000	6000	10,000	14,000	20,000
4P C.C. Tr	2250	3000	6000	10,000	14,000	20,000
Model 45, 4-cyl., 45 hp, 123" wb						
7P Tr	2500	3900	7800	13,000	18,200	26,000
4P C.C. Tr	2500	3900	7800	13,000	18,200	26,000
3P Rds	2500	3750	7500	12,500	17,500	25,000

1910 Rambler, roadster, OCW

1910
Model 53, 4-cyl., 34 hp, 109" wb

	FP	5	4	3	2	1
Tr	1800	3600	7200	12,000	16,800	24,000
Model 54, 4-cyl., 45 hp, 117" wb						
Tr	2250	3900	7800	13,000	18,200	26,000
Model 55, 4-cyl., 45 hp, 123" wb						
Tr	2500	4200	8400	14,000	19,600	28,000
Limo	3350	2800	5700	9500	13,300	19,000

1911 Rambler, touring, JAC

1912 Rambler, Cross Country touring, JAC

1902 Randall, steam runabout, NAHC

1911
Model 63, 4-cyl., 34 hp, 112" wb

	FP	5	4	3	2	1
Tr	2175	3750	7500	12,500	17,500	25,000
Rds	2105	3600	7200	12,000	16,800	24,000
Cpe	2605	1750	4800	8000	11,200	16,000
Twn Car	2800	2300	5400	9000	12,600	18,000

Model 64, 4-cyl., 34 hp, 120" wb

Tr	2775	4050	8100	13,500	18,900	27,000
Toy Ton	2775	4050	8100	13,500	18,900	27,000
Lan'let	3650	2800	5700	9500	13,300	19,000

Model 65, 4-cyl., 34 hp, 128" wb

Tr	3050	4200	8400	14,000	19,600	28,000
Toy Ton	3050	4200	8400	14,000	19,600	28,000
Limo	4150	3000	6000	10,000	14,000	20,000

1912
Four, 38 hp, 120" wb

5P CrCtry Tr	1650	4200	8400	14,000	19,600	28,000
4P Sub Ctry Club	1650	4200	8400	14,000	19,600	28,000
2P Rds	1600	4050	8100	13,500	18,900	27,000
4P Sed	2500	1750	4800	8000	11,200	16,000
7P Gotham Limo	2750	2800	5700	9500	13,300	19,000

Four, 50 hp, 120" wb

Ctry Club	2250	4800	9600	16,000	22,400	32,000
Valkyrie	2250	4800	9600	16,000	22,400	32,000

Four, 50 hp, 128" wb

Morraine Tr	2500	5250	10,500	17,500	24,500	35,000
Metropolitan	2850	5400	10,800	18,000	25,200	36,000
Greyhound	2850	5400	10,800	18,000	25,200	36,000
Knickerbocker	4200	5850	11,700	19,500	27,300	39,000

1905 Randall, gasoline runabout, NAHC

1913 Rambler, touring

1913
Four, 42 hp, 120" wb

2/3P CrCtry Rds	1650	4500	9000	15,000	21,000	30,000
4/5P CrCtry Tr	1700	4650	9300	15,500	21,700	31,000
4P Inside Drive Cpe	2500	2800	5700	9500	13,300	19,000
7P Gotham Limo	2750	3300	6600	11,000	15,400	22,000

RAND & HARVEY STEAM — Lewiston, Maine — (1899) — In 1899 Clarence Rand, together with a man named Harvey (whose first name appears lost to history), built the first automobile in Lewiston. The vehicle was propelled by steam, and its maiden trip was to the Maine State Fairgrounds and back. Although some rosters have indicated that production of this car followed into the turn of the century, there is no evidence that more than the one vehicle was ever built. Subsequently, Rand & Harvey became a dealership for the Stanley. Rand's experience with the Rand & Harvey experimental car did, however, lead to the development of one of his more important inventions: a gasoline burner for steam automobiles which was subsequently sold to a prominent steam car manufacturer. Attachments for shoe machinery were among his other inventions. Clarence Rand died in August of 1932. The lead sentence in his obituary mentioned his building of Lewiston's first automobile.

RANDALL — The Randall Company of Quincy, Massachusetts built a cyclecar called the Peter Pan in 1914. Refer to Peter Pan.

The Randall Motor Car Company was organized in Fort Wayne, Indiana during the spring of 1904 with a capital stock of $10,000 for the manufacture of automobiles. A.L. Randall and Louis Ohnhaus were the principals involved. Manufacture is doubted.

RANDALL STEAM — Meadville, Pennsylvania — (1902-1903) — George N. Randall was a trolley-car conductor from Meadville who rather hoped he could become an automobile manufacturer instead. In 1902 he designed and built a 6 hp steam engine; then he ordered an Oswego Boiler, a Kelly Generator, a Locke "Beats-All" Regulator, an Eastman metal body and Diamond tires. He put all these various components together into a two-passenger runabout that he listed for sale at $750. Possibly he may have built a few more into 1903, but since his business address was also his home address, one might assume that George Randall never did become a serious automobile manufacturer.

RANDALL — San Jose, California — (1905) — In 1905 Charles V. Randall of San Jose built a 365-pound runabout powered by a 2-1/4 hp De Dion motor which was mounted up front. The wheelbase was 54 inches, the tread 36 inches — and the car was geared to operate on the highway at about 18 mph. Wheel steering and wire wheels were featured and, as a homemade car, it was a surprisingly good-looking machine. "I use leather instead of wood to finish the appearance of the body," Charles Randall wrote *Motor Field*. "That eliminates the rumbling sound, and gives it the sewing machine sound." Randall built the car for his own pleasure, never intending manufacture. There is evidence that he built at least one other car for himself as well. This probably was because his first effort had pleased him so much. "The machine taken as a whole exceeds my expectations by about 40 percent," he had commented.

1903 Randall, 3-wheel runabout, WLB

RANDALL THREE-WHEELER — Newtown, Pennsylvania — (1903-1905) — At the turn of the century, James Vansant Randall was one of the best-known and largest carriage manufacturers in Bucks County. Since 1895, when he brought his nephew Clarence Randall into the firm, the business had been operating under the name J.V. & C. Randall. In addition to its large carriage trade, the Randall company also offered an automobile from 1903 through 1905. It was undoubtedly one of the most stylish and substantial three-wheeled cars of the period. The single wheel was in front, with two-thirds of the vehicle's weight being carried by the back wheels. "The front wheel easily takes the horse path in centre," *Cycle and Automobile Trade Journal* reported in February of 1903, "and great ease of control as well as smooth and comfortable riding, is claimed as a result of this construction." The car sat four comfortably under a fringed canopy. A long tiller reached from the front wheel into the driving compartment for steering — and power was provided by a two-cylinder engine that was increased from 8 to 12 hp in the 1905 model. That year, too, also saw the substitution of a three-speed selective sliding gear for the original friction transmission — though the price of the Randall remained at $800. The Randall company continued in the carriage business for some years following the cessation of its automotive three-wheeler at the end of 1905.

RANDOLPH — The Randolph Motor Car Company was organized in Chicago, Illinois late in 1908 with a capital stock of $300,000 for the manufacture of automobiles and accessories. Incorporators were E.C. Gage, N.W. Burgstresser and S. Hyrowitz. Manufacture of a car is doubted.

1906 Rands, touring, GR

RANDS — Detroit, Michigan — (1906-1907) — The Rands Manufacturing Company of Detroit made only one foray into automobile manufacture, and that would seem to have been more to satisfy a whim of W.H. Rands than a concerted entrance into the market. The Rands car was a 30 hp air-cooled four with sliding gear transmission and 106-inch wheelbase. Rands built one for his own pleasure in his company's shops, with a small production run following into 1907. So far as is known, no further automobiles were built by Rands. In 1913 the company purchased the plant and equipment of the defunct Warren Motor Car Company in Detroit at auction for $14,600, but without any intention of continuing the Warren-Detroit car.

1910 Ranger, runabout, WLB

RANGER — Chicago, Illinois — (1907-1910) — This Chicago manufacturer began in 1907 as the Ranger Motor Works with a buggy-type runabout sporting 40-inch wheels in front and 44-inch in the rear. Right-hand lever steering and double chain drive were featured, and the car was delivered with fenders and a top, comparatively more "fully equipped" than most highwheelers and something of a bargain at $395. During the late summer of 1909, Oscar F. Schmidt reorganized the firm as the Ranger Automobile Company, dropped the highwheeler, substituted a standard-tired small runabout at the same price, and lingered in business a while

longer. During the early summer of 1910, Ranger announced its move from 1224 East 46th Street to a three-story building at the rear of 931-935 East 43rd, where double the floor space was available. In November the company was in receivership.

1907-1909 RANGER

	FP	5	4	3	2	1
High-Wheeled Runabout	395	2000	3000	4200	6500	14,000
1910 RANGER						
Model D — 2-cyl., 12 hp, 70" wb						
Runabout	395	2000	3000	4200	6500	14,000
Model C — 2-cyl., 12 hp, 74" wb						
Runabout	395	2200	3200	4400	7000	15,000

1921 Ranger, touring, WLB

RANGER — Houston, Texas — (1920-1922) — The Southern Motors Manufacturing Association, Ltd. was the lofty designation given this enterprise which was established in Houston in 1920 for the manufacture of trucks, tractors, trailers and an automobile to be known as the Ranger. Involved in this undertaking were Jacques E. Blevins, E.F. Reid and C.E. Shively. The first Ranger was announced in the September 26th, 1920 edition of *The Houston Post*. Its four-cylinder L-head 31 hp Southern-built engine was especially designed for Texas climatic conditions. It was a sprightly looking car on a 116-inch wheelbase, available in either "Ranger maroon" or "Blevins blue" with black chassis and fenders. Already the Ranger had been subjected to a 35,000 mile road test, during which consistent speeds of 50 mph were held. The touring car was priced at $1850. The $1595 roadster was especially rakish, with rivets along the hood edges, cycle fenders and aluminum step-plates. A new six-cylinder 57 hp model on a longer 123-inch wheelbase was announced during the summer of 1921, along with such appealing sporty designations for it as Commodore, Newport, Blue Bonnet and Pal o'Mine. The subsequent history of Southern Motors is murky. Receivership ensued in late 1922, followed by a widely publicized merger with the conglomerate National Motors Corporation. Following that, in 1924, was scandal. Fourteen people who had been associated with Southern and National were indicted for fraud. One of them was a woman, which was considered shocking at the time. Six million dollars was the figure cited in the indictment as having been collected from the public. Government charges alleged that the Ranger Six had not been built at all and that manufacture of the Ranger Four had been in small numbers "largely for stock selling purposes and many times at a loss." The same group of cars reportedly was shuffled back and forth between the company's lavish showrooms in downtown Houston and the factory which was an elaborate stage set on the outskirts of town. Prospective investors were entertained in both locations. A few cars had been sold, mostly to stockholders. The Ranger's shadowy demise was rather a pity, because all indications are that it was a very fine car that just might have succeeded on its own merits.

1900 Ranlet, NAHC

RANLET — St. Johnsbury, Vermont — (1900) — According to the *St. Johnsbury Caledonian* of June 27th, 1900, Charles T. Ranlet had "made a close study of the subject of horseless vehicles and during the past year . . . visited every cycle and automobile show and nearly every factory in the East and Middlewest." Following this extensive reconnaissance trip, he built his first automobile, designing it especially for the hilly terrain of Vermont. The Ranlet was a four-cylinder car (most unusual for this early period) developing 6 hp. Final drive was by chain, and the vehicle was tiller steered, with a lever at the driver's left for changing speed from high to low. Charles Ranlet upholstered his prototype in whipcord, but offered to change this at customer desire. The car was a four-seater; the rear seat folded down when not in use and also could be reversed if a dos-a-dos ride was preferred. Side panels were Brewster green with black trim, the running gear maroon striped in black. Charles Ranlet's car appeared to be an altogether admirable machine, but he was unable to secure the necessary financing for production. His Ranlet Automobile Company died aborning. Possibly only the prototype was built. Subsequently, Charles Ranlet became a dealer for several established manufacturers — and by 1904 he was conducting a thriving printing establishment in St. Johnsbury.

RANTZ — The Rantz Motor Company was organized in Bridgeport, Connecticut early in 1910 with a capital stock of $25,000 for the manufacture of automobiles and parts. F.A. Rantz was president, G. Langdon vice-president and A. Wood secretary-treasurer. Manufacture of a car is doubted.

1903 Rapid, touring, NAHC

RAPID — Grand Rapids, Michigan — (1903) — The Rapid Motor Car Company of Grand Rapids introduced its car early in 1903. It featured a two-cylinder 15 hp engine, an 84-inch wheelbase, three-speed selective transmission, double-chain drive, semi-elliptic springs, and a $2000 price tag. The car was described in the March 1903 issue of *Cycle and Automobile Trade Journal*. In the June issue it was revealed that the Rapids Motor Car Company had been bought out by M.B. Martin. The reason for Martin's purchase of the firm remains unclear, but it was not to continue the Rapid.

1906 Rauch & Lang, stanhope, HAC

RAUCH & LANG ELECTRIC — Cleveland, Ohio— (1905-1920) / Chicopee Falls, Massachusetts — (1920-1928) — The Rauch & Lang Carriage Company was incorporated in 1884, the result of the partnership of Jacob Rauch, a German immigrant who had set himself up in business in Cleveland as a blacksmith and wagon repairer in 1853 and who had later expanded into wagon-building, and Charles E.J. Lang, a Cleveland real

estate magnate. By the turn of the century, Rauch & Lang carriages were among the best known and most expensive in the area. The company tip-toed into the automotive age in 1903 by taking on the Cleveland agency for the Buffalo Electric, and in 1905 waded in stalwartly with an electric of its own. An open stanhope was the firm's first effort, 18 of these being completed by June of 1905, with 32 more cars, including coupes and depot wagons, being built by year's end. In 1907 Rauch & Lang bought out the Hertner Electric Company, supplier of the Rauch & Lang motors and controllers; John H. Hertner was installed as chief engineer of the Rauch & Lang automobile department, and thereafter the company made all parts of its car under one roof. In 1908 the firm couldn't make enough of them; production had risen to 500 cars that year, but Rauch & Lang could have sold 300 more. Worm drive was introduced on some Rauch & Lang models in 1912; bevel gear transmission was provided on other models in 1914. In 1911 Rauch & Lang had endured the unpleasantry of being sued by the Baker Motor Vehicle Company for infringement of patent relating to the mounting of rear springs, but any lingering animosity had dissipated by 1915 when, in the face of declining electric car sales nationwide, the two firms elected to merge. The Baker R. & L. Company, incorporated at $2.5 million, was the official result, though the firm became more popularly known as Baker-Raulang, as did the cars, though in neither case was this an official designation. The Baker name continued only through 1916; only Rauch & Langs were produced thereafter. By now the cars were available in a variety of body styles, including some with four doors (unusual for an electric) and others with a choice of front- or back-seat steering. The Owen Magnetic was produced in the Baker R & L Company plants as well from 1916 to 1919. During the latter year, a total of 700 Rauch & Lang electrics were built, and the company entered the coachbuilding field as Raulang Body Division of the Baker R & L Company. There was a further division of the company later that year, with another department set up to produce electric industrial trucks. In January 1920, Ray S. Deering, the president of the Stevens-Duryea Company of Chicopee Falls, Massachusetts announced that he had bought out the electric passenger car business of Baker, R & L which he reorganized as Rauch & Lang, Inc. and moved into a new factory built next to the Stevens-Duryea plant in Chicopee Falls. There, in 1922, Rauch & Lang, Inc. entered the taxicab field, with production of both electric and gasoline versions marketed under the initials of R & L. Three hundred gasoline taxis were built in 1923, and it appears this car was the mainstay of the Rauch & Lang production effort through the Twenties. The electric taxi did not sell nearly as well, and the electric passenger cars were produced only in handfuls. In 1924 Rauch & Lang, Inc. was in financial trouble, with the Chicopee Falls plant slated to be offered for sale to satisfy tax claims. An extension of time was granted, however, and the firm struggled on for a while longer. Late in 1928 half of the Rauch & Lang factory was leased to Moth Aircraft Corporation, and passenger car production ceased later that year. Shortly before the Wall Street crash, an experimental 60 hp gas-electric (the gasoline engine being a 35 hp sleeve valve six) was built at Rauch & Lang in collaboration with General Electric Company engineers. It was sold to Colonel E.H.R. Green, son of multi-millionaire Hetty Green. The stock market debacle later that fall precluded any possible plans of production.

1905-1906 RAUCH & LANG ELECTRIC

	FP	5	4	3	2	1
Stanhope — (67" wb)	1800	2300	3300	4600	7500	16,000
Coupe — (68" wb)	2000	2000	3000	4200	6500	14,000
Depot Wagon — (87" wb)	3000	2200	3200	4400	7000	15,000

1907 Rauch & Lang, depot wagon, HAC

1908 Rauch & Lang, victoria, HAC

1907 RAUCH & LANG ELECTRIC

	FP	5	4	3	2	1
Stanhope — (67" wb)	1850	2300	3300	4600	7500	16,000
Coupe — (68" wb)	2100	2000	3000	4200	6500	14,000
Depot Wagon — (87" wb)	3200	2200	3200	4400	7000	15,000
Surrey — (91" wb)	2800	2300	3300	4600	7500	16,000

1909 Rauch & Lang, extension top surrey, HAC

1908-1909 RAUCH & LANG ELECTRIC

	FP	5	4	3	2	1
Stanhope — (74" wb)	1850	2400	3200	4400	7000	15,000
Coupe — (67" wb)	2100	2200	3200	4200	7000	15,000
Extension Cpe. — (74" wb)	2400	2250	3300	4500	7300	15,500
Surrey — (103" wb)	3000	2400	3400	4800	8000	17,000
Victoria — (85" wb)	3200	2300	3300	4600	7500	16,000
Brougham — (85" wb)	4000	2400	3400	4800	8000	17,000

1910 Rauch & Lang, runabout, HAC

1911 Rauch & Lang, runabout, WLB

1910-1911 RAUCH & LANG ELECTRIC

	FP	5	4	3	2	1
Runabout — (85" wb)	2100	2400	3400	4800	8000	17,000
Stanhope — (77" wb)	1900	2300	3300	4600	7500	16,000
Stanhope — (85" wb)	2250	2400	3400	4800	8000	17,000
Victoria — (85" wb)	2200	2500	3500	5000	8500	18,000
Extension Cpe. — (85" wb)	2700	2300	3300	4600	7500	16,000
Coupe — (85" wb)	2200	2250	3300	4500	7300	15,500

1912 Rauch & Lang, roadster, HAC

1912 RAUCH & LANG ELECTRIC
Stanhope Model — 83-1/2" wb

	FP	5	4	3	2	1
Coupe	2400	2200	3200	4400	7000	15,000
Coupe	2550	2200	3200	4400	7000	15,000
Coupe	2650	2200	3200	4400	7000	15,000
Stanhope	2100	2300	3300	4600	7500	16,000
Stanhope	2250	2300	3300	4600	7500	16,000
Stanhope	2350	2300	3300	4600	7500	16,000
Brougham Model — 91" wb						
Landaulet	3000	2400	3400	4800	8000	17,000
Landaulet	3100	2400	3400	4800	8000	17,000
Brougham	2800	2300	3300	4600	7500	16,000
Brougham	2900	2300	3300	4600	7500	16,000
Victoria	2450	2300	3300	4500	7300	15,500
Victoria	2550	2300	3300	4500	7300	15,500
Roadster — (91" wb)	2600	2400	3400	4800	8000	17,000
Demi-Brgm. Model — (83-1/2" wb)	2700	2350	3400	4700	7800	16,500
Club Roadster Model — (91" wb)	2800	2450	3500	4900	8300	17,500
Coach Model — (109" wb)	3800	2300	3300	4600	7500	16,000

1913 Rauch & Lang, model J, coach, JAC

1913 Rauch & Lang, model TC, town car, HAC

1913 RAUCH & LANG ELECTRIC

	FP	5	4	3	2	1
Model B — 92" wb						
Brougham-4P	2900	2400	3400	4800	8000	17,000
Model XT Colonial — 92" wb						
Brougham-4P	2900	2400	3400	4800	8000	17,000
Model T — 92" wb						
Brougham-5P	3000	2400	3400	4800	8000	17,000
Model J — 105" wb						
Coach-4P	3100	2300	3300	4600	7500	16,000
Model TC — 105" wb						
Town Car-5P	3800	2500	3500	5000	8500	18,000
Model DB — 86" wb						
Demi-Brougham-4P	2800	2300	3300	4600	7500	16,000
Model R — 92" wb						
Roadster-2P	2600	2400	3400	4800	8000	17,000
Model CR — 92" wb						
Club Roadster	2800	2450	3500	4900	8300	17,500

1914 Rauch & Lang, model R, roadster, OCW

1914 RAUCH & LANG ELECTRIC

Model J4 Coach — 100" wb						
Double Control	3200	2700	3600	5300	8800	19,000
Front Control	3100	2500	3500	5000	8500	18,000
Wheel Steer	3150	2400	3400	4800	8000	17,000
Rear Control	3100	2500	3500	5000	8500	18,000
Model CR — 92" wb						
Coupe-2P	2800	2300	3300	4600	7500	16,000
Model B4 — 96" wb						
Brougham	2950	2200	3200	4400	7000	15,000
Model R — 92" wb						
Roadster	2600	2300	3300	4600	7500	16,000

1915 Rauch & Lang, model J5, coach, HAC

1915 RAUCH & LANG ELECTRIC

Model J5 Coach — 102" wb						
Double Control	3200	2700	3600	5300	8800	19,000
Front Control	3100	2500	3500	5000	8500	18,000
Rear Control	3100	2400	3400	4800	8000	17,000
Model R5 — 92" wb						
Roadster	2600	2300	3300	4600	7500	16,000
Model B5 — 96" wb						
Brougham	2950	2200	3200	4400	7000	15,000
Model BX5 — 92" wb						
Brougham	2950	2200	3200	4400	7000	15,000
Model CR5 — 92" wb						
Club Roadster	2800	2350	3400	4700	7800	16,500
Model L-5 — 100" wb						
Limousine	4000	2450	3500	4900	8300	17,500
Model TC-5 — 109" wb						
Town Car	4000	2500	3500	5000	8500	18,000

1916 Rauch & Lang, model J6, coach, HAC

1916 RAUCH & LANG ELECTRIC

Model J6 Double Control — 100" wb	FP	5	4	3	2	1
Coach	3000	2000	3000	4200	6500	14,000
Model TXC6 — 100" wb						
Town Car	4000	2500	3500	5000	8500	18,000
Model B6 — 96" wb						
Brougham	2800	2300	3300	4600	7500	16,000
Model R6 — 92" wb						
Roadster	2600	2400	3400	4800	8000	17,000
Model TC6 — 109" wb						
Town Car	4500	2500	3500	5000	8500	18,000
Model CR6 — 92" wb						
Club Roadster	2800	2350	3400	4700	7800	16,500
Model BX6 — 92" wb						
Brougham	2800	2400	3400	4800	8000	17,000

1918 Rauch & Lang, model BX-7, brougham, HAC

1917-1918 RAUCH & LANG ELECTRIC

Model RX-7 — 92" wb						
Roadster-2P	2600	2500	3500	5000	8500	18,000
Model JX-7 — 100" wb						
Brougham-5P	3000	2700	3600	5000	8800	19,000
Town Car-5P	4000	2900	3700	5600	9100	20,000
Model BX-7 — 92" wb						
Brougham-5P	2800	2400	3400	4800	8000	17,000
Roadster-2P	2600	2500	3500	5000	8500	18,000
Model TC-7 — 109" wb						
Town Car-5P	4000	2700	3600	5000	8800	19,000

1919 Rauch & Lang, model C-35, double drive coach, HAC

1919 RAUCH & LANG ELECTRIC
Coach — 102" wb

	FP	5	4	3	2	1
Double Drive	3600	2700	3600	5000	8800	19,000
Rear Drive	3500	2400	3400	4800	8000	17,000
Front Drive	3500	2500	3500	5000	8500	18,000
Single Rear Drive — 92" wb						
Brougham	3350	2500	3500	5000	8500	18,000

1920 Rauch & Lang, model C-45, double drive coach, HAC

1920 RAUCH & LANG ELECTRIC

Model B-36 Brgm.	3700	2300	3300	4600	7500	16,000
Model C-45 C'ch Single Con.	4000	2500	3500	5000	8500	18,000
Model C-45 C'ch Dual Con.	4000	2700	3600	5000	8800	19,000

1921 RAUCH & LANG ELECTRIC

Model C-55 Dbl. Drive C'ch	—	2700	3600	5000	8800	19,000
Model B-46 Single Drive Brgm.	—	2500	3500	5000	8500	18,000

1922 Rauch & Lang, taxi, NAHC

1922 Rauch & Lang, model C-505, coach, JAC

1922-1923 RAUCH & LANG ELECTRIC
Model C-505 Rear Drive

C'ch	4250	2700	3600	5000	8800	19,000
Taxicab (gasoline)	2350	2700	3600	5000	8800	19,000
Taxicab (electric)	2750	2500	3500	5000	8500	18,000

1924 Rauch & Lang, model B-68, brougham, HAC

1924 RAUCH & LANG ELECTRIC

	FP	5	4	3	2	1
Model B-68 Brgm.	4250	2700	3600	5300	8800	19,000
Taxicab (gasoline)	2350	2700	3600	5300	8800	19,000
Taxicab (electric)	2750	2500	3500	5000	8500	18,000

1925 Rauch & Lang, model T-68, taxicab, HAC

1925 RAUCH & LANG ELECTRIC

Model B-68 Brgm.	4250	2700	3600	5300	8800	19,000
Model S-68 Four-Door Sed.	4250	2400	3400	4800	8000	17,000
Taxicab (gasoline)	2350	2700	3600	5300	8800	19,000
Taxicab (electric)	2750	2500	3500	5000	8500	18,000

1926-1928 RAUCH & LANG ELECTRIC

Model S-68 Four-Door Sed.	5000	2400	3400	4800	8000	17,000
Taxicab (gasoline)	2350	2700	3600	5300	8800	19,000
Taxicab (electric)	2750	2500	3500	5000	8500	18,000

1906 Rawnsley, runabout, LC

RAWNSLEY — Sanford, Maine — (1906) — Hollon Rawnsley was a superintendent for the Goodall Worsted machine shop in Sanford. Since his job occupied his working day, he worked on his automobile only during spare hours. Three years were required for its building. Its engine was a two-cylinder opposed; Rawnsley made all of his own forgings and gears. Following its completion in 1906, Hollon Rawnsley drove his car for several years. Its top speed was 12 mph. The car remains in the Rawnsley family to this day.

RAY — F.L. Ray of Castile in Wyoming County (near Batavia), New York was indicated in a trade directory of 1903 as a builder of automobiles. Documentation is lacking.

Frank S. Ray of 1231 Fulton Street in Brooklyn, New York was a general mechanic "whose experience with all classes of automobiles is of the highest order," reported *The Motor World* in May 1902, and who "has gone into the business of designing and building hydro-carbon business and pleasure automobiles to order." Further details are lacking.

The Ray Motor Company was organized in Connersville, Indiana late in 1906 with a capital stock of $100,000 for the manufacture of automobiles. Bowen Ray, J.J. Maloney, J.F. Geary, W.S. Calder and Lewis B. McFall were the principals involved. Manufacture is doubted.

1911 Rayfield Jr., model A, runabout, NAHC

RAYFIELD — Springfield, Illinois — (1911-1912) / Chrisman, Illinois — (1912-1915) — The Rayfield name appeared on carburetors, engines, big touring cars and little cyclecars. The carburetor had been invented by Charles Rayfield, the cars were the work of sons Bill and John. Basis for their automotive venture was the purchase of the faltering Springfield Motor Car Company in 1910. Initially they organized their Rayfield Motor Car Company in Springfield in late summer of 1910, but they moved to Chrisman during the summer of 1912 following the building of a factory there. In Springfield, a Junior roadster four had been part of the Rayfield production, but with the relocation, manufacture was concentrated on sixes. A special-built Rayfield entered in the Indianapolis 500 of 1914 was to be driven by Hughie Hughes; it reached 95 mph during time trials, but mechanical problems eliminated it from the race itself. (Hughes drove relief for Mercer in the 500 that year.) Rayfield sixes were water-cooled cars, with their radiators mounted to the rear of the engine, and with sloping Renault-type hoods. In 1914 the Rayfields added a cyclecar to their line, which they should not have designated as such because it really was not a cyclecar. It featured a standard 56-inch tread, a four-cylinder water-cooled engine, selective sliding gear transmission, rack-and-pinion steering and a sturdy pressed sheet steel body. For the 1915 model year the Rayfields contracted with the Great Western people of Peru (Indiana) to build their cars for them. It was a deal they should not have made. Great Western was in receivership, and ultimately could not fulfill its contract. Rayfield sued, but couldn't collect. The company was finished. The Rayfield assets were sold at public auction in February 1916 for $14,000.

1911 RAYFIELD
Four — 14/16 hp, 116" wb

	FP	5	4	3	2	1
Junior Roadster	1500	2900	3700	5600	9100	20,000
Six — 22/25 hp, 116" wb						
Roadster-6P	1850	3100	4200	6300	10,500	22,000
Toy Tonneau-4P	2000	3200	4300	6500	11,000	23,000

1912 Rayfield Six, 5-pass. touring, JAC

1912 RAYFIELD
Model 6 — 6-cyl., 30 hp, 117" wb

	FP	5	4	3	2	1
Roadster-2P	2500	3100	4200	6300	10,500	22,000
Touring-5P	2500	3200	4300	6500	11,000	23,000
1913 RAYFIELD						
Model 6 — 6-cyl., 30 hp, 117" wb						
Touring-5P	2500	3100	4200	6300	10,500	22,000

1914 Rayfield, cyclecar, roadster, WLB

1914 RAYFIELD
Cyclecar — 4-cyl., 14 hp, 96" wb

	FP	5	4	3	2	1
Roadster-2P	375	2300	3300	4600	7500	16,000
Model 14 — 6-cyl., 38 hp, 130" wb						
Touring-5P	2600	3100	4200	6300	10,500	22,000
1915 RAYFIELD						
Cyclecar — 4-cyl., 14 hp, 96" wb						
Roadster-2P	375	2300	3300	4600	7500	16,000

RAYMOND — Hillsdale, Michigan — (1905, 1908) — Two men named Raymond built cars in Hillsdale, Michigan. The first was William Raymond who built his in 1905 for his own use. The second was John Raymond whose efforts produced just one vehicle as well, though he had certainly hoped for more, having been involved in the organization of two different companies — the Hillsdale Motor Company and the Mercury Motor Car Company — in 1908, both of which failed before production ever began.

RAYMOND — Hudson, Massachusetts — (1912-1913) — Early in 1912, Arthur B. Raymond moved his new Raymond Engineering Company into the former laundry building at Lincoln Park in Hudson. It was a fine two-story brick edifice large enough for a twenty-car-a-day production capacity, though Raymond declared his intention not to "crowd things" and said he would build no more than a thousand cars his first year. A graduate of Cornell University, he had previously headed the calculating department at the Cramp shipyard and engine works in Philadelphia, and thereafter had developed an engine called the R-V which had been in production for several years. His new Raymond car was to be a 22 hp four on a 100-inch wheelbase to sell at the startlingly low figure of $445. This attractive price tag was possible, Raymond told a reporter from the local Hudson paper, because of the drive system he had invented which "allows a full range of speed, both forward and reverse, without using a clutch, change speed gear or differential, three of the most expensive parts of the average car." What the Raymond used as a substitute appears lost to history. More than likely, the car did not advance beyond the prototype stage.

RAZOUX — In July 1914 *The Automobile* published a roster of "abandoned automobile manufacturing enterprises." Included on the list was a Razoux in Boston, Massachusetts. Turn-of-the-century Boston city directories include a Charles L. Razoux who, in partnership with William B. Handy, had operated a bicycle emporium at 444 Tremont Street in 1894-1895. Thereafter Charles Razoux operated the shop himself, until 1910 when he moved to New York. Like many bicycle builders of that period, Razoux could have produced an automobile, but definitive documentation of this is lacking.

1912 R.C.H., roadster, HAC

R.C.H. — Detroit, Michigan — (1912-1915) — In August of 1911 a new car called the R.C.H. was introduced as the product of the new Hupp Corporation. The car duly arrived for the 1912 model year as a small 22 hp four widely touted as the first under-$1000 automobile in the country to provide self starting (gas initially, then electric). Hupp Corporation duly departed. The man behind both was Robert C. Hupp, who had left his Hupp Motor Car Company because, he said, its board of directors had insisted he build more expensive Hupmobiles and also that he declare stock dividends instead of plowing profits back into the business. It was, needless to say, an acrimonious leavetaking, and now the people building the Hupmobile demanded that Robert C. Hupp's new venture not be named Hupp because it would be injurious to their business — and the courts agreed. Thus by February of 1912, the firm's designation became R.C.H. Corporation. "R.C. Hupp, Manufacturer," early brochures read. "Distinct From and Having No Connection Whatever with the Hupp Motor Car Company." Nomenclature was the least of R.C. Hupp's problems, however. The first that he had with his new R.C.H. was its phenomenal initial success. Seven thousand cars were sold in 1912, and orders on the books for the 1913 models totaled more than 15,000. Hupp lacked the working capital to cope with this large business. In January 1913 he handed over the presidency of his company to J.F. Hartz, who was well-known in Detroit for his business acumen. Hupp stepped down to vice-president; and the former vice-president, Charles P. Seider, moved over to secretary. The company remained troubled, however, and on July 25th, 1913 moved into receivership in what was called "a friendly suit to readjust finances." The final readjustment put former vice-president/secretary Charles Seider into the driver's seat, and Robert C. Hupp — whose other cars during this period were the Hupp-Yeats and the Monarch — out of the company. Seider led a group which purchased the bulk of the R.C.H. Corporation assets in February 1914 following the receiver's sale. Seider's previous business experience had been as an awning manufacturer; he elected to change neither the name of the company nor the character of the product. R.C.H. production resumed sometime later in 1914 and was discontinued sometime during 1915. By now the second problem of the R.C.H. had arisen, which was directly related to the first. In the rush to meet the initial demand, quality in construction had been sacrificed. A good many cars in users' hands were falling apart. Because the reputation of the car had been severely damaged, Seider decided to quit production and move into smaller quarters in Detroit to concentrate on the manufacture of repair parts. As a business decision, it was probably the wisest one.

1912 R.C.H.
Four — 22 hp, 86" wb

	FP	5	4	3	2	1
Runabout-2P	700	2000	3000	4200	6500	14,000
Roadster-4P	750	2200	3200	4400	7000	15,000
Coupe-3P	1050	1800	2800	4000	6200	13,000
Touring Roadster-2P	800	2300	3300	4600	7500	16,000
Touring-5P (110" wb)	850	2350	3400	4700	7800	16,500

Note 1: Prest-O-Lite starting added $50 to the price tags.)

1913 R.C.H., touring, WLB

1913 R.C.H.
Four — 25 hp, 110" wb

Touring-5P	900	2350	3400	4700	7800	16,500
Roadster-2P	900	2250	3300	4500	7300	15,500
Coupe-3P	1300	2000	3000	4200	6500	14,000

1915 R.C.H., model K, touring, HAC

1914-1915 R.C.H.
Four — 25 hp, 110" wb

Model K Touring-5P	900	2350	3400	4700	7800	16,500

R.E. — The R.E. Manufacturing Company was organized in New York City during the spring of 1910 with a capital stock of $5000 to manufacture and deal in motor cars, motor boats and bicycle accessories. Incorporators were Barnett Epstein, Morris Epstein and Samuel Greenberg. Manufacture of a car is doubted.

REA — Rushville, Indiana — (1901-1902) — The Rea Machine Company of Rushville announced its intention to enter the automobile field in 1901. Specifications regarding the gasoline car produced are lacking but it is known that a Rea was driven from the factory to Indianapolis for the automobile show there in February of 1902. Production of the car was modest, however, and short-lived.

READ — Danvers, Massachusetts — (1791) — A graduate of Harvard College, class of 1781, Nathan Read lived in Danvers and was proprietor of an apothecary in Salem in 1788 when he first began studying steam propulsion. He built a steamboat which plied the Danvers River in 1789 and — though sources conflict — is believed to have completed a model of a steam road vehicle soon thereafter. The design of the latter — which showed an ingenuous though interesting form of power steering — was patented in 1791, the year the U.S. Patent Office opened. Though Read espoused his steam ideas before the U.S. Congress, the legislative body wasn't interested. As he later wrote, "I was too early with my steam projects, and the country was then too poor and I have derived neither honor nor profit from the time and money expended." Nathan Read subsequently became a U.S. congressman himself, and later served as a justice in the state courts of Massachusetts and Maine.

1913 Read, touring, WLB

READ — Detroit, Michigan — (1913-1914) — The Read Motor Company of Detroit was incorporated in mid-1913 by Ray J. Read, Joseph Beatty and Roy Herald for the manufacture of a four-cylinder 20 hp touring car on a 115-inch wheelbase. Its designation as the "Model X" was the most intriguing thing about it; the Read was otherwise a pedestrian car with a $850 price tag. Company offices and showrooms were at 541 Woodward Avenue, with the factory at 68 Champlain Street. In December of 1913 a creditor named Albert Schneider sued Read, alleging that the firm was insolvent and that he had been swindled out of a thousand dollars. Schneider was perhaps overstating his case a bit. But the Read Motor Car Company was finished in the business.

READING — The Reading Chassis & Motor Corporation was organized late in 1917 with a capital stock of $100,000 for the manufacture of motors, cyclecars and automobiles in Reading, Pennsylvania. Incorporators were S.S. Shears, C.W. Bliss and E. Cahn. Manufacture of a car is doubted.

1910-11 Reading, model 40, roadster, JAC

READING — Reading, Pennsylvania — (1910-1913) — A product of the Middleby Automobile Company of Reading, the Reading was an up-market companion car to the Middleby. It had a slightly larger four-cylinder engine, was a foot longer in wheelbase, and was priced several hundred dollars more. Scant attention was paid it by the company, and indeed it would appear the reason may have been its name, Charles M. Middleby deciding that his top-of-the-line car might better carry his own as well — which it did beginning in 1911 when a bigger and pricier Middleby was introduced. This rendered the Reading nonessential, but it remained in production until both marques died in 1913.

1910-1911 READING
Forty — 4-cyl., 40 hp, 120" wb

	FP	5	4	3	2	1
Touring	1250	3200	4300	6500	11,000	23,000
Roadster	1250	3100	4200	6300	10,500	22,000

1912-1913 READING
Forty — 4-cyl., 40 hp, 122' wb

	FP	5	4	3	2	1
Touring	1725	3200	4300	6500	11,000	23,000
Roadster	1650	3100	4200	6300	10,500	22,000
Fore-Door Touring	1750	3300	4400	6600	11,500	23,500

1901 Reading Steamer, runabout, WLB

READING STEAMER — Reading, Pennsylvania — (1901-1902) — With the highest of hopes, Irvin D. Lengel incorporated the Steam Vehicle Company of America in the fall of 1901. The previous year he had conducted test drives of his steam car prototype at speeds of 8 mph on city streets and in a 14-hour trip to New York City. "Runs indefinitely without attention," Lengel would advertise. The Reading Steamer was unusual in being available with a four-cylinder engine at a time when the steamer norm was two cylinders. It was not unusual in being short-lived. Barely a year into production, the creditors moved in, followed by the Meteor Engineering Company whose incorporators — including Lengel — purchased the moribund company's assets and proceeded to build another steam car called the Meteor. It lasted about a year too. Twelve years later Irvin Lengel joined forces with Fred K. Dick to build a gasoline car called the Dile.

1901 READING STEAMER

	FP	5	4	3	2	1
Steam Stanhope	850	2400	3400	4800	8000	17,000
Steam Delivery	1000	2300	3300	4600	7500	16,000

1902 Reading Steamer, runabout, HAC

1902 READING STEAMER

Style E Steam Stanhope	800	2400	3400	4800	8000	17,000
Style F Steam Dos-a-Dos	850	2500	3500	5000	8500	18,000
Style G Steam Surrey	1400	2700	3600	5300	8800	19,000
Style J Steam Light Delivery	1200	2300	3300	4600	7500	16,000
Style K Steam Delivery	1000	2200	3200	4400	7000	15,000
Style L Steam Tr. Dos-a-Dos	1200	2600	3600	5200	8700	18,500
Style H Steam Tr. Carriage	1100	2800	3700	5500	9000	19,500

REAL CYCLECAR — Anderson, Indiana — (1914) / **REAL LIGHT CAR** — Converse, Indiana — (1914-1915) — H. Paul Prigg of Anderson produced a cyclecar that was rather different than most. Its two-cylinder air-cooled Wizard engine was placed in the extreme rear of a 100-inch wheelbase frame that was made of spruce and overslung to provide a ground clearance of fifteen inches. The car was available with a 36-inch or standard 56-inch tread. Gasoline consumption was claimed as 40 mpg, with a maximum speed of 50 mph. The steel body could be removed by loosening two bolts. There was a front seat for the driver and a 35-inch rear seat which could "if necessary, accommodate two." The price was $290. "One of the

simplest and unquestionably the cheapest...," the press said upon the Real's introduction. But still it was a cyclecar. During the winter of 1914, H. Paul Prigg changed the name of his company from Real Cyclecar Company to Real Light Car Company and moved his factory from Anderson to Converse — and tried again. But the Real Light Car was basically the Real cyclecar, offered in standard tread only, and it quickly shared the fate of its predecessor. Bankruptcy was declared in December 1915. Some years later, H. Paul Prigg moved to Miami, Florida to build boats.

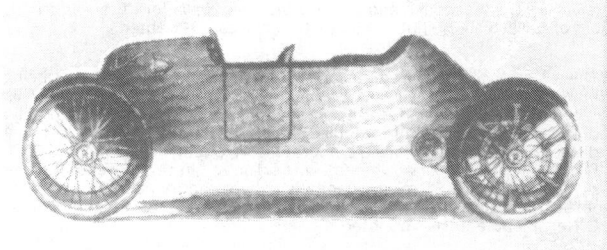

1914 Real, tandem cyclecar, WLB

1914 REAL CYCLECAR
Cyclecar — 2-cyl., 9 hp, 102" wb

	FP	5	4	3	2	1
Tandem Roadster-3P	290	2000	3000	4200	6500	14,000
Light Delivery	375	1800	2800	4000	6200	13,000

1915 Real Light Car, runabout, WLB

1915 REAL CYCLECAR
Light Twin — 13 hp, 100" wb

	FP	5	4	3	2	1
Tandem Roadster-3P	290	2000	3000	4200	6500	14,000
Light Delivery	375	1800	2800	4000	6200	13,000

Light Four — 12 hp, 100" wb

	FP	5	4	3	2	1
Roadster-2P	375	2000	3000	4200	6500	14,000

1903 Reber, touring, NAHC

REBER — Reading, Pennsylvania — (1902-1903) — James C. Reber had been building the Stormer bicycle in his Acme Manufacturing Company factory since 1892. His firm became one of the American Bicycle Company affiliates at the turn of the century, and his plant was shut down during the waning days of the "bicycle craze." Now Reber was ready for the automobile business. He had built a car of his own in 1900, but was aware that maiden effort wasn't worthy of production. So he hired James Heaslet out of Autocar in Ardmore to design him a car of the "French type." The result was a two-cylinder 12 hp five-seater rear-entrance tonneau priced at $1800 that was put on the market in 1902 as the Reber. By mid-1903, however, James Reber had changed his mind on both his product and its name, importing Victor Jakob from Daimler in Germany to engineer a new car that Reber would subsequently market as the Acme.

RECH — Philadelphia, Pennsylvania — (1900) / **RECH-MARBAKER** — (1906) — The firm of Jacob Rech & Sons was a long time Philadelphia carriagebuilder which first entered the automotive age with a steam runabout in 1900. The automatic boiler and the single-cylinder engine were mounted under the front seat, with the water tank to the rear. The gasoline tank was stored under the footboard, and the firm was patenting a device for burning gasoline with an absolutely blue flame. According to Edward Rech, trial tests of the car had proved most satisfactory, but still only a minimal production followed that year. The firm did not again build a car until 1906 by which time a merger had made it the Rech-Marbaker Company. The vehicle this time was an electric, and possibly only a prototype was built. Rech-Marbaker remained in the automotive field, however, as builders of components, including the Sendelbach Resilient Wheel which saw considerable duty on armoured gun carriers and other automotive military vehicles during World War I.

RECOMETER — The Recometer Company of America was organized in Hasbrouck Heights, New Jersey late in 1907 with a capital stock of $300,000 for the manufacture of automobiles and accessories. Incorporators were F.H. Waggoner and F.E. Carstarp of New York City, and D.M. Miers of Hasbrouck Heights. Manufacture of a car is doubted.

RED — A car called the Red has appeared on numerous rosters as being built in 1905 by J.W. Linscott & Company of Boston, Massachusetts. This is in error. The Linscott Motor Company functioned as a dealership only, and at the 1905 Boston Automobile Show exhibited the Corbin, National and Reo. Plainly, the Red was a typographical blooper.

The Red Arrow Motors Company was organized in South Bend, Indiana early in 1920 with a $1 million capital stock for the manufacture of automobiles. Incorporators were Irving L. Stoney, Albert B. Bowman and Louis E. O'Neil. Manufacture is doubted.

RED ARROW — Orange, Massachusetts — (1914) — In August of 1914 the factory in Orange which had formerly been used for manufacture of the Grout was leased by the Red Arrow Automobile Company, an enterprise organized by Arthur F. Kirkpatrick and Warren P. Shumway for the manufacture of a cyclecar. A prototype was built, but the car never saw serious production. By 1915 Kirkpatrick and Shumway had operated a service and storage station in the old Grout plant — and became Oldsmobile dealers.

1924 Red Bug Flyer, HAC

RED BUG — North Bergen, New Jersey — (1924-1930) — Red Bug was one of several names for the same little buckboard which had been put into quantity production in late 1916 by the A.O. Smith Company in Milwaukee. It was called the Smith Flyer then, provided by the Smith Motor Wheel. In 1919 Briggs & Stratton (another Milwaukee firm) bought manufacturing rights to the Smith Motor Wheel and the Smith Flyer, renamed both Briggs & Stratton — and in 1924 sold these same rights to Automotive Electric Service Corporation in North Bergen. The New Jersey company decided to call the vehicle a Red Bug, and occasionally the Auto Red Bug as well. (Ads generally used the former, serial number plates the latter.) Although the Briggs Motor Wheel powered some Red Bugs, others were propelled by a 12-volt Northeast electric motor, the same one used to start Dodge Brothers cars of the period. Among further outlets, the Red Bug was sold through Abercrombie & Fitch and F.A.O. Schwartz in New York City. References are inconclusive, but it would appear that the Red Bug continued in production at least until 1928. During that year, Automotive Standards, Inc. (as the New Jersey firm had been renamed some time previous) established a subsidiary company for development of the vehicle for amusement park use. In March 1930 a news report indicated that the Indian Motorcycle Company in Springfield, Masschusetts had been contracted by Automotive Standards to manufacture the Red Bug on a cost-plus basis. But in May Indian was acquired by Paul du Pont, and though some of the last du Pont automobiles were built in the Indian plant, it would appear that no Red Bugs were.

1924-1928 RED BUG

	FP	5	4	3	2	1
Red Bug Flyer 1-cyl., 5 hp, 62" wb	150	1400	2400	3500	5300	10,000
Red Bug Electric Roadster 62" wb	150	1100	2200	3200	4900	9,000

RED DIAMOND — The first announcement of Red Diamond Motors of Atlanta came during the summer of 1920. The Georgia company had been organized with a capital stock of $5,000,000 by W.H. Seabrooker, P.E. Hicks and Henry Short. Plans had been drawn up by the H.D. Best Company for the construction of a $250,000 plant, with three additional units including machine shop and foundry to be built alongside. Machinery had been ordered, and the manufacture of automobiles was expected to begin later that year. In March of 1921, Red Diamond Motors was reported to be in bankruptcy. If a prototype car had been built, the trade press was not made aware of it.

1904 Red Jacket, touring, NAHC

RED JACKET — Buffalo, New York — (1904-1905) — The O.K. Machine Works of Buffalo manufactured transmission gears and diverse auto supplies and for the 1904-1905 seasons produced a touring car called the Red Jacket. It had a single headlight and lots of brass. A two-cylinder 10 hp water-cooled engine was mounted under the hood, the transmission was a three-speed selective, and final drive was by double chain. The wheelbase was 87 inches, and the price $1500. Following the discontinuation of the Red Jacket, O.K. Machine Works continued in the automotive supply field. A certificate of involuntary bankruptcy was filed against the company in early February of 1908.

RED ROVER — New York, New York — (1901) — The Red Rover was a special-built touring car produced by the Automobile Company of America, makers of the Gasmobile, for the Automobile Touring Company of New York City. Powered by a 10 hp three-cylinder gasoline engine, the Red Rover was capable of speeds up to 18 mph and was put into service making daily trips from the Waldorf-Astoria Hotel in New York City to Westchester County and Long Island.

RED SHIELD — Detroit, Michigan — (1911) — Although frequently cited as the producer of an automobile in 1911, the Red Shield Hustler Power Company did not manufacture a car, though perhaps a single example may have been run up on the company's two-cylinder 20 hp, 86-inch-wheelbase truck chassis. The principal product of this short-lived Detroit company was a high-wheeled chain-drive delivery wagon.

RED WING — Red Wing, Minnesota — (1909) — In December of 1909 the Red Wing Boat Manufacturing Company announced an increase in its capital stock from $50,000 to $250,000 and the change of its name to Red Wing Motor Company. The reason for all this was the decision by the firm to enter the automobile field. A modification of its motor boat engine was to be used in a new car to be marketed as the Red Wing. This vehicle did not pass the prototype stage, although at least one prototype was built.

REDDEN — The Redden Motor Sales Corporation was organized in New York City during the summer of 1917 with a capital stock of $50,000 for the manufacture of automobiles and trucks. Incorporators were R.L. Delisser, S.E.A. Stern and H.C. Moses. Manufacture is doubted.

REED — In 1909 the W.S. Reed Company of Massillon, Ohio produced a six-cylinder gasoline car which was marketed under the name of Massillon. Refer to Massillon.

REED STEAM — New York, New York — (1859 et seq.) — John A. Reed was a New York engineer who designed and built three steam road wagons under contract from Joseph Renshaw Brown of St. Paul, Minnesota. The vehicles were completed in 1859, 1862 and 1870. The final vehicle was tested, though it never left the Reed shops. The other two made it to Minnesota.

REEK — Hillsdale, Michigan — (1907) — "Hillsdale Proud of Its Firstborn" read the trade press headline announcing the birth of a single-cylinder 15 hp runabout delivered by the Hillsdale machine shop of Reek Brothers in October 1907. The car had been tested and "showed up well" — and the Reek Brothers noted an intention to market it at $450. This was the plan, certainly, though it was not the Reeks who contemplated the marketing. Instead, a venture styled as the Hillsdale Motor Company was organized in January 1908 for that purpose. As a production car, the Hillsdale appears to have been a stillborn.

REES — The Rees Company was organized in New York City early in 1907 with a capital stock of $120,000 for the manufacture of automobiles. Incorporators were John J. Karniol, Royal E. Fox, Jr. and Albert B. Foose, all of Manhattan. Manufacture is doubted.

REES — Attica, Ohio — (1921) — John Howard Rees was an engineer who had worked for Hudson, and in June of 1920 he announced his plans to build a light four-cylinder car to sell for $1450. Six years of experimentation had preceded this announcement, he said. Interestingly, there was no subsequent announcement in 1920 of the incorporation of a company to do it. But, in May of 1921, Rees revealed that the Rees Motor Company had been "reincorporated" with a capital stock of $300,000 and that the firm's officers were Rees as president and general manager, J.L. Stanton as vice-president, S.W. Moiselle as secretary and M.R. Slayback as treasurer. They were now looking for a plant to set up their assembly line. Further particulars about the new Rees were revealed. Its engine was described as a two-liter four designed by Rees, the wheelbase was 112 inches, and a spring suspension system was featured. In June the Rees people found and purchased a plant, the factory at Attica formerly used by Halladay Motors Corporation, and now nicely vacant since Halladay had moved to Newark. Townspeople who resided in Attica during the early 1920's have certified that from two to five complete Rees cars were built before the company failed. John Howard Rees returned in 1928 to try again with the Howard in Detroit.

1899 Reese, three-wheeled runabout, LC

REESE — Plymouth, Pennsylvania — (1887-1904) — Raised in Plymouth from the age of four, Sephaniah Reese went to work for the Delaware & Lackawanna Railroad at age sixteen, and at age twenty-two incorporated his machine shop which did a brisk business with the local coal mines. In the window of that shop, from the turn of the century until 1970, a three-wheeled automobile was displayed, a placard attached to it dating the car as 1884. That no doubt was when Seph Reese began its building, subsequent correspondence indicating a completion date of 1887-1888. At the behest of Seph Reese's sons in October 1959, several longtime residents of Plymouth notarized statements that they had seen the car successfully operated on Shawnee Avenue in Plymouth during that period. Little is known about the engine it carried initially save that its crankcase was purportedly machined from bauxite (Seph Reese is believed to have traded an expensive bicycle for the imported metal) and that the engine was cast at the oldest steel foundry in America, located in the Palisades area of New Jersey. Seph Reese was the first manufacturer of bicycles in the Wilkes Barre area. Prior to his placing the car in the window, he made a number of revisions, including the substitution of a single-cylinder De Dion-type engine which may have been built by the Lowell Motor Company of Massachusetts, and a number of parts which were probably purchased from the Charles Miller catalog. The Reese car was tiller steered, with final drive direct on the rear axle. Its tubular steel frame was welded, and its front wheel forks were fashioned from Civil War bayonet scabbards manufactured by the Ames Sword Company. The wheels were hand-made and bicycle type. Although not known for certain, the updating of the Reese car was probably for a single reason: service as a prototype for production. In 1899 the prototype went into the machine shop window, and Seph Reese began making cars for sale, in which activity he remained until 1904. The S. Reese Machine Tool Works in Plymouth was unquestionably a busy place then, with the additional manufacture of racing and other quality bicycles marketed under the tradenames of Reese and Shawnee; gasoline, electric and steam engines; bicycle and automobile running gear and other component parts. Seph Reese also operated the first service station in the area, and was an early automobile dealer as well, holding the local agency for Cadillac, Regal and Lambert among others. During World War I and World War II, the Reese shop was involved in military production. Seph Reese died near the close of the Second World War, his sons carrying on his business until 1970 when the shop was closed. How many cars Seph Reese built during his half-decade of production is not known, but the three-wheeler that was in the window for seventy years remains extant, owned by a collector in New Jersey who in addition to acquiring the car acquired also the original torches that Seph Reese had used to braze it. As legend has it, he hooked up to the town pipe line to purloin the gas to do the torching.

REESE AERO-CAR — Huron, South Dakota — (1921) — Everything about this car was small, including the price. It was a 150-pound two-seater roadster with a wheelbase of sixty inches, a track of thirty, and a price tag of $160. Its inventor was Sheldon F. Reese. He announced his new invention as the Aero-Car, which was apt since the vehicle was driven by an air-screw propeller through a two-cylinder two-stroke air-cooled 6 hp engine. It was the only valveless, springless, chainless, beltless and gearless motor in the world, its inventor said. "The circular device at the rear is not to carry a 'spare'," *Motor West* commented with tongue subtly in cheek, "but is a guard to spare all concerned, including the 36x8 inch seasoned walnut propeller it encloses, from inconvenient collision." Reese described his car as a "joy wagon...which provides a successful combination of the thrills of an aeroplane, the safety of an automobile, and the economy of a bicycle." Economical it was, since tests indicated sixty miles

1922 Reese Aero-Car, runabout, WLB

on only a gallon-and-a-half of gasoline. Top speed was 40 mph. For sections of the country with winter seasons, a pair of runners would be made available to turn the Reese into an ice boat. With the ice equipment, the car could reach 60 mph. The Sheldon F. Reese Company, Inc. was organized in Huron to promote its manufacture, and in September of 1921 Reese made a tour of the West Coast to stir up investor interest, but he did not find enough of it to proceed into manufacture.

REEVE — The Frank A. Reeve Company was organized in Montclair, New Jersey during the fall of 1911 with a capital stock of $50,000 for the manufacture of motorcars. Joining Reeve in this venture were J.A. Butler of Montclair and D.H. Slayback of Verona. Manufacture is doubted.

1896 Reeves, runabout, OCW

REEVES — Columbus, Indiana — (1896-1898, 1905-1912) — Had Milton O. Reeves not been so often diverted by the main business of his Reeves Pulley Company, no doubt his total production of automobiles would have been considerably greater. Still, though spasmodic, his several forays into building cars were certainly interesting. His first effort, which he called a Motocycle, was built in 1896 to demonstrate the variable speed transmission (VST) which he was planning for his pulley company to manufacture for industrial use. A four-wheeler powered by a Sintz engine, it was tested in the early fall of 1896 and so frightened horses and enraged neighbors that Reeves made two separate attempts to literally quiet things down: first, he installed a muffler on the engine (and certainly he was one of the earliest, if not the first, to do so) and second, he bought a papier-mache horse which had previously graced the entrance to a local blacksmith's shop, cut off the head and stuck it on the front of the car. The muffler stayed, the horse's head did not. Ultimately, Reeves installed a fine polished ebony body, his Motocycle received rave reviews in the automobile press, and he began to receive orders. No fewer than five motor vehicles were built in the year which followed, all fitted with the VST and double chain drive, some powered by Sintz engines, others by an air-cooled unit of Reeves' own design, and one a huge motor bus with axles seven feet long and rear wheels almost six feet tall. In the early spring of 1898, however, the Reeves Pulley Company announced its intention to discontinue manufacture of complete cars to focus on the manufacture of the VST and motors only. By the turn of the century, improvements in automobile transmissions had rendered the VST principle impractical for automotive use, but the four-cylinder air-cooled motors Reeves had designed found a ready acceptance. In late 1905 Alexander Y. Malcomson contracted for the entire Reeves output for a year — a total of 500 engines — for use in the new automobile he was planning to build in Detroit. Unfortunately, Malcomson's Aerocar venture was short-lived, which left Reeves stuck with a good many engines, a situation he solved by building complete cars himself. These included both fours and sixes, with chain drive fitted on the larger models, shaft drive on the smaller. In 1907 he added a highwheeler called the Go-Buggy, powered by a two-cylinder air-cooled motor, fitted with double chain drive, and usually offered at $450 *sans* coachwork, though Reeves was willing to supply a body (a task he farmed out to a local carriagemaker) if a purchaser desired. The Go-Buggy proved immensely popular with Indiana farmers. Meanwhile, the main business of the Reeves Pulley Company — the VST industrial pulley systems — was booming, and in 1910 the decision was made to concentrate on that specialized field. Automobile manufacture was discontinued. Still, Milton O. Reeves had one more automotive theory to prove, and he set about it

1229

immediately. Believing that an equation existed between the riding comfort of a car and the number of wheels it possessed, he built one of the former with eight of the latter. His Octoauto was redesigned from a 1910 Overland chassis and was completed in time for the first Indianapolis 500 in 1911. Milton Reeves attended the event only as a spectator, of course, but his huge eight-wheeler did manage to attract almost as much attention as Ray Harroun's bright yellow Marmon Wasp, which won the race. Reeves actually believed his Octoauto had marketing possibilities: "The eight wheeled idea is applicable to any kind of vehicle and privilege to use same may be had," he advertised. "Therefore, if interested, write your automobile manufacturer or myself." Whether Milton Reeves received any letters at all is not known, but obviously the concept of a car with a 180-inch wheelbase and 248-inch overall length didn't appeal to many. In 1912 he decided to think a little bit smaller, believing — as he said — that he could "get as good results with six wheels as with eight." At least two Sextoautos were built: the first simply an Octoauto with a standard front axle, the second revised from a Stutz chassis. Interestingly, he had quoted a price of $3200 for his Octoauto; his Sextoauto was up to $5000. It attracted no buyers either, and Milton O. Reeves thereafter returned forever to his other industry pursuits.

1906 Reeves, touring, WLB

1911 Reeves Octoauto, touring, HAC

1912 Reeves Sextoauto, touring, WLB

1905-1912 REEVES

	FP	5	4	3	2	1
Reeves	—	—	—	—	—	—
Go-Buggy	—	—	—	—	—	—
Octoauto	—	—	—	—	—	—
Sextoauto	—	—	—	—	—	—

REGAL — The Regal Gasoline Engine Company was organized in Coldwater, Michigan during the early fall of 1901 and indicated at that time its intention of "making an automobile in connection with the engine business." Manufacture is doubted.

The Regal Motor Car Company was organized in New York City during the spring of 1908 with a capital stock of $50,000 for the manufacture of engines, cars and boats. Incorporators were Henry Amerman, F.P. Rawle and J.C. Austin. Manufacture of an automobile is doubted.

1910 Regal, model E, touring, JAC

REGAL — Detroit, Michigan — (1908-1918) — The Regal was the result of a partnership among the Lambert Brothers — Charles R., J.E., and Bert — and Fred W. Haines. Haines was a prominent Detroit engineer and, though Regal brochures indicated the Lamberts' previous activity as the manufacture of "brass goods," it would appear that was a euphemism for plumbing supplies. Early in the fall of 1907, they incorporated their Regal Motor Car Company with a capital stock of $100,000, and hired Paul Arthur to design their car. The Regal was a conventional, medium-sized, medium-priced car, but it was widely advertised and quite successful. Particularly effective promotion followed the trek of the Regal "Plugger" — a stock 30 hp model — which traveled from New York to San Francisco in the summer of 1909, and then crossed the country five more times before finally returning home to Detroit during the summer of 1910 after 22,000 miles. "The greatest endurance car in the world," Regal said, and with "plenty of life left." Regal's famous underslung model was introduced later that year. Production figures chart the company's continuing progress: 1907, 175 cars; 1908, 250; 1909, 2,000; 1910, 3,500; 1911, 4,500; 1912, 5,800; 1913, 7,500. In 1913 the Regal Motor Car Company increased its capitalization to $3 million. Management remained the same. By now Regal was among the leading exporters in the industry, enjoying a particularly brisk trade in England. Export models were referred to sometimes as the Seabrook-R.M.C. Through 1914 Regal cars were powered by four-cylinder engines of the company's own manufacture. For 1915 a V-8 and a light four were introduced, both of which were designed by S.G. Jenks and supplied by the Port Huron Construction Company. Regal never produced a six. The company's financial problems seem to have arrived with the shortage of materials concomitant to World War I. Receivership followed in February of 1918. Company assets were $1.5 million, while its liabilities were only $600,000, though this was said to be "exclusive of contingent liabilities." Whatever they were, they did the company in. At a creditors meeting to decide whether to liquidate or continue, the decision was made for the former. By the summer of 1918 Maurice Rothschild (presumably no relation to the famous family) had purchased the Regal property and kept the factory open awhile making spare parts and operating a service business.

1908 REGAL
Twenty-Five — 4-cyl., 25 hp, 100" wb

	FP	5	4	3	2	1
Touring-5P	1250	2400	3400	4800	8000	17,000
Runabout-3P	1250	2300	3300	4600	7500	16,000

1909 Regal Thirty, touring, HAC

1909 REGAL
Thirty — 4-cyl., 30 hp, 105" wb

	FP	5	4	3	2	1
Touring-5P	1250	2400	3400	4800	8000	17,000
Runabout-3P	1250	2300	3300	4600	7500	16,000
Baby Tonneau-4P	1250	2400	3400	4800	8000	17,000

1910 REGAL
Thirty — 4-cyl., 30 hp, 107" wb

	FP	5	4	3	2	1
Touring-5P	1250	2450	3500	4900	8300	17,500
Runabout-3P	1250	2350	3400	4700	7800	16,500
Coupe-3P	1750	2000	3000	4200	6500	14,000
Limousine-7P	2050	2300	3300	4600	7500	16,000

Forty — 4-cyl., 40 hp, 123" wb

	FP	5	4	3	2	1
Touring-5P	1750	2700	3600	5300	8800	19,000

1911 Regal Twenty, roadster, HAC

1911 REGAL
Twenty — 4-cyl., 20 hp, 100" wb

	FP	5	4	3	2	1
Model N Runabout	900	2300	3300	4600	7500	16,000

Thirty — 4-cyl., 30 hp, 110" wb

Model L Touring-5P	1000	2500	3500	5000	8500	18,000
Model LF Fore-Dr. Tr.-5P	1050	2600	3600	5200	8700	18,500

Forty — 4-cyl., 40 hp, 123" wb

Model S Touring-7P	1600	3100	4200	6300	10,500	22,000
Model SF Fore-Dr. Tr.-7P	1650	3200	4300	6500	11,000	23,000

1912 Regal, model SF, touring, HAC

1912 REGAL
Twenty-Five — 4-cyl., 25 hp, 100" wb

Model N Runabout	900	2500	3500	5000	8500	18,000
Model NC Colonial Coupe	1250	2300	3300	4600	7500	16,000

Thirty — 4-cyl., 30 hp, 110" wb

Model L Touring	1000	2700	3600	5300	8800	19,000
Model LF Fore-Door Touring	1050	2800	3700	5500	9000	19,500
Model LO Torpedo	1050	2800	3700	5500	9000	19,500

Thirty-Five — 4-cyl., 35 hp, 118" wb

Model H Touring	1400	2900	3700	5600	9100	20,000

Forty — 4-cyl., 40 hp, 123" wb

Model S Touring	1600	3100	4200	6300	10,500	22,000
Model SF Fore-Door Touring	1650	3200	4300	6400	10,800	22,500

1913 Regal, model H, underslung touring, HAC

1913 REGAL
Twenty-Five — 4-cyl., 25 hp, 108" wb

Model T Touring-4P	950	2700	3600	5300	8800	19,000
Model N Roadster-2P	900	2500	3500	5000	8500	18,000
Model NC Coupe-3P	1250	2300	3300	4600	7500	16,000

Thirty — 4-cyl., 30 hp, 116" wb

Model C Touring-5P	1250	2900	3700	5600	9100	20,000

Thirty-Five — 4-cyl., 35 hp, 118" wb

Model H Touring-5P	1400	3100	4200	6300	10,500	22,000

1914 REGAL
Twenty-Five — 4-cyl., 25 hp, 108" wb

Model T Touring-5P	1125	2900	3700	5600	9100	20,000
Model N Roadster-2P	1125	2700	3600	5300	8800	19,000
Model NC Coupe-3P	1600	2300	3300	4600	7500	16,000

Thirty-Five — 4-cyl., 35 hp, 116" wb

Model C Touring-5P	1350	3100	4200	6300	10,500	22,000

1914 Regal, model NC, colonial coupe, HAC

1915 Regal, model D, touring, HAC

1915 REGAL
Light Four — 20 hp, 106" wb

	FP	5	4	3	2	1
Roadster-2P	650	2400	3400	4800	8000	17,000
Touring-5P	650	2500	3500	5000	8500	18,000

Four — 39 hp, 110" wb

Model D Touring-5P	1085	2700	3600	5300	8800	19,000
Model R Roadster-2P	1085	2500	3500	5000	8500	18,000

Eight — 40 hp, 112" wb

Roadster-2P	1250	2700	3600	5300	8800	19,000
Touring-5P	1250	2900	3700	5600	9100	20,000

1916 Regal, model E, light four roadser, HAC

1916 REGAL
Model E — 4-cyl., 27 hp, 106" wb

Touring-5P	650	2400	3400	4800	8000	17,000
Roadster-2P	650	2300	3300	4600	7500	16,000

Model D — 4-cyl., 39 hp, 115" wb

Roadster-2P	950	2700	3600	5300	8800	19,000
Touring-5P	950	2900	3700	5600	9100	20,000

Model F — 8-cyl., 44 hp, 115" wb

Touring-5P	1200	3100	4200	6300	10,500	22,000
Roadster-2P	1200	3000	4000	6000	9500	21,000

1917 Regal, model J, touring, HAC

1917 REGAL
Model J — 4-cyl., 20 hp, 108" wb

	FP	5	4	3	2	1
Touring-5P	695	2700	3600	5300	8800	19,000

Model F — 8-cyl., 29 hp, 15" wb

	FP	5	4	3	2	1
Touring-5P	1200	3100	4200	6300	10,500	22,000
Roadster-2P	1200	3000	4000	6000	9500	21,000
Touring Sedan-5P	1385	2000	3000	4200	6500	14,000

1918 REGAL
Model J — 4-cyl., 20 hp, 108" wb

	FP	5	4	3	2	1
High Power Four Tr.-5P	795	3000	4000	6000	9500	21,000

1904 Regas, model B, runabout, NAHC

REGAS — Rochester, New York — (1903-1905) — Frederick Sager spelled his name backwards, and thus was born Regas. It began as the Regas Vehicle Company at the turn of the century in Rochester, and its product line then included spring frames for bicycles and a few bicycles fitted with motors. During the summer of 1903, Sager retired his Regas Vehicle Company and reorganized as the Regas Automobile Company. Capital stock was stated as $100,000. The first Regas automobile was a small single-cylinder 7 hp runabout on a 72-inch wheelbase which was sold for $750 in 1903. For 1904 the Regas grew up into a 12 hp vee-twin on an 81-inch wheelbase available as a tourer and runabout for $1500; a 20 hp V-4 on an 86-inch wheelbase was also made available. The Regas featured a Marble-Swift friction transmission, a "bunsen tube" type cooling system rather like the Knox but of Sager's own design, and shaft drive. Although he exhibited five cars at the National Automobile Show in New York City in January 1904, Frederick Sager apparently found himself in financial trouble soon thereafter. That summer he sold out to D.D. Dunn, who was already famous as the inventor of Sen-Sen, and who hired William H. Birdsall to design a new Regas for 1905. It was a four on a 100-inch wheelbase with a three-speed sliding gear transmission. Dunn soon decided he didn't enjoy the automobile business. The official certificate of dissolution for the Regas Automobile Company was filed during the summer of 1906.

REGENT — The Regent Automobile and Machine Company was organized in Brooklyn, New York during the spring of 1902 with a capital stock of $50,000 for manufacture of gasoline automobiles and the Mezger jump spark plug. Incorporators were Charles A. Mezger and George W. Barthol. Manufacture of a car is doubted.

REGESTER — Rock Island, Illinois — (1900) — Formerly factory foreman for the Rock Island Plow Company, T.L. Regester built an automobile in 1900 powered by a horizontal two-cylinder four-stroke engine fitted under the forward seat of a two-seater carriage. The engine weighed 205 pounds, the complete vehicle 850 pounds. Final drive by single chain, and speeds up to 20 mph were claimed. Regester is not known to have built another car.

1895 Reid Electric, MVMA

REID ELECTRIC — Chicago, Illinois — (1895) — "Those interested in electric motors and many others say the coming motor vehicle will win on electric lines," commented *The Carriage Monthly* in November 1895 in its report of the two electric vehicles built by Charles G. Reid of Chicago. One was a four-passenger carriage powered by fifteen storage batteries, the other a two-passenger runabout powered by seven storage batteries. The vehicles were publicly presented and demonstrated in Chicago on November 1st, 1895. Although participation in the Chicago Times-Herald Contest was also planned, it did not follow — and Charles Reid did not proceed into manufacture.

1903 Reilly, steam surrey, NAHC

REILLY STEAM — New York, New York — (1902-1903) — The total automobile production of the James Reilly Repair and Supply Company of New York City may have been several vehicles, or conceivably just one, the experience with which forever cooled Reilly's enthusiasm for the automotive field. The one car documented to have been produced was a handsome four-passenger steam surrey which was built to custom order and completed in the late fall of 1902. Alas, it would appear that the customer for whom the automobile had been built reneged on the deal. James Reilly began advertising the car for sale in November 1902 issues of automobile magazines and presumably had unloaded it by the spring of 1903 because Reilly cancelled the ad thereafter.

1902 Reinertson, runabout, NAHC

REINERTSON — Milwaukee, Wisconsin — (1901) — In 1901, in his machine shop in Milwaukee, Rex Reinertson built a gasoline automobile. "I made the body, motor, transmission, frame, patterns necessary for castings, and also did all machine work and fitting necessary to complete the vehicle," he wrote *The Horseless Age.* A runabout weighing 900 pounds, the Reinertson had a 70-inch wheelbase with 50-inch tread and was powered by a single-cylinder four-stroke engine. After driving the car for a short while in Milwaukee, Reinertson accepted a machinist's job in Buffalo, New York, shipped his car there, and put another 1000 miles on it. Sometime late in 1902, he moved again, to Pittsburgh where he accepted a position as shop superintendent of the Pennsylvania Electric & Supply Company. During 1903 he built a small Orient-Buckboard-like car which he marketed that year in Pittsburgh as the Rex Buckboard.

REIVE-THOMPSON — The Reive-Thompson Motor Company of Columbus, Ohio was indicated as a manufacturer in the Hiscox book *Horseless Vehicles, Automobiles, Motor Cycles* published in 1900. Documentation is lacking. A company of that name was not listed in turn-of-the-century Columbus city directories.

RELAY — Reading, Pennsylvania — (1903-1904) — At the turn of the century, the Reading Automobile Company evolved from the Relay Manufacturing Company and proceeded to engage itself in the production of

1904 Relay, touring, WLB

1908 Reliable Dayton, model E, special coupe, HAC

automobile parts. On February 3rd, 1903, when the decision was made to enter the automobile manufacturing field, the company was reorganized as the Relay Motor Car Company. Most probably, the return to its original name was made because there was already another Reading automobile being made in town. The new Relay was powered by a three-cylinder 24 hp overhead valve Wyoma engine. Brass water jackets and an aluminum crankcase were featured. The transmission was a three-speed sliding gear, and final drive was by shaft. Two thousand dollars was the price tag, and it bought a King of Belgium-type tourer with two individual front seats and a removable tonneau for three passengers. The body and hood were available in either Brewster Green or Blue, with running gear and wood wheels in carmine red. All bright parts were brass plated. The Relay was displayed at the New York Automobile Show in January 1904, and the company announced its plans at the time to build twenty-five cars that year. The car had been discontinued by 1905.

1908 RELIABLE DAYTON
Model F — 2-cyl., 15 hp, 103" wb

	FP	5	4	3	2	1
Surrey	925	2300	3300	4600	7500	16,000
Model E — 2-cyl., 15 hp, 84" wb						
Runabout	780	2200	3200	4400	7000	15,000
Coupe	1200	2000	3000	4200	6500	14,000

1909 Improved (Reliable) Dayton, model B, runabout, NAHC

1909 RELIABLE DAYTON
Reliable Dayton — 2-cyl., 15 hp

	FP	5	4	3	2	1
Model E Runabout (84" wb)	800	2300	3300	4600	7500	16,000
Model F Surrey (103" wb)	925	2400	3400	4800	8000	17,000
Improved Dayton — 2-cyl., 18/20 hp						
Model B Runabout (84" wb)	600	2500	3500	5000	8500	18,000

1906 Reliable Dayton, model C, coupe, NAHC

RELIABLE DAYTON — Chicago, Illinois — (1906-1909) — The Reliable Dayton Motor Car Company of Chicago was perhaps the only high-wheelers producer in America whose catalog resembled a Kentucky Derby program. The frontispiece illustration was not of any of the varying vehicles the company produced, but was a portrait of a horse to which, Reliable Dayton said, it was the "first real successor." The first Reliable Daytons appeared during the spring of 1906, although William O. Dayton did not organize his company, with a capital stock of $25,000, until late fall. Rope drive and solid rubber tires were featured on the Reliable Dayton, and the earliest cars had a fin-tube radiator over the front axle. Later models sported a Renault-type hood in front, but the engine remained beneath the seat, the hood housing the gasoline and water tanks. Changes from the traditional at Reliable Dayton were apparently entered into only reluctantly. When the company abandoned its two-stroke for a four-cycle engine, it was — a trade periodical of the day noted — "to meet the demand of the buying public rather than on account of their own convictions." All engines for the Reliable Dayton were built at the Dayton & Mashey Automobile Works in Chicago. During 1909 the Reliable Dayton factory was taken over by the Fal Motor Company for production of the F.A.L. automobile. William O. Dayton's immediate movements thereafter are not known, but in 1912 he showed up in Joliet, Illinois to attempt the automobile industry again with the Matrix, the Dayton, the Crusader and the New Era.

RELIANCE — The Reliance Automobile Company was organized with a capital stock of $250,000 during the fall of 1903 for the manufacture of motorcars in Pierre, South Dakota. Manufacture is doubted.

The Reliance Buggy Company was organized in St. Louis, Missouri late in 1913 with a capital stock of $200,000 to manufacture and deal in buggies, automobiles and trucks. Incorporators were Frank W. Edlin, Alpha T. Stevens and P.E. Ebreng. Manufacture of a car is doubted.

"The Reliance Motorcycle Company, Owego, New York, has commenced the manufacture of automobiles as well," The Motor World reported during the fall of 1909. "At present they are buying nearly all the parts, but a project is on foot for local capital to build a more complete motor car factory." There is no evidence the plan was realized.

1906-1907 RELIABLE DAYTON
Model C — 2-cyl., 15 hp, 84" wb

	FP	5	4	3	2	1
Motor Buggy	600	2200	3200	4400	7000	15,000
Model I — 2-cyl., 15 hp, 98" wb						
Surrey	700	2300	3300	4600	7500	16,000

1905 Reliance, touring, HAC

RELIANCE — Detroit, Michigan — (1904-1906) — The Reliance Automobile Manufacturing Company was organized in Detroit in late 1903, with its first cars coming off the assembly line several months later. Subsequent Reliance brochures would predate the car's first model year to 1903 because the Reliance's body style was a side-entrance tonneau and the company wished to advertise being the first in the United States to introduce it. (The Orlo and the Peerless for 1904 had also featured side entrance.) The firm's juggling of truth-in-advertising notwithstanding, the Reliance was a good two-cylinder car with selective transmission and shaft drive, designed by E.O. Abbott and W.K. Ackerman, both formerly of Cadillac. Undercapitalization of the venture resulted in a reorganization in 1904 to Reliance Motor Car Company, with J.M. Mulky taking charge, followed shortly thereafter by Fred O. Paige. Overkill in sloganeering seemed to be a Reliance penchant: If one motto was good, a half-dozen might be even better. The brochure for 1905 had a different one on virtually every page — "The Car Too Good for the Price," "The Light-Heavyweight Touring Car," "Reliance — All Made Under One Roof." In 1906 a commercial vehicle was added to the line, and in February 1907 the company announced that it would henceforth build trucks only. Reliance sold its passenger car later that year to a group of entrepreneurs in Detroit who planned to continue production under the name Crescent. Reliance, in turn, was sold in 1909 to General Motors — and the Reliance truck subsequently evolved into the GMC. Fred Paige went on to build the Paige-Detroit car.

1904 RELIANCE
Two — 15 hp, 86" wb

	FP	5	4	3	2	1
Canopy Touring-5P	1250	2500	3500	5000	8500	18,000

1905 RELIANCE
Two — 18/22 hp, 92" wb

	FP	5	4	3	2	1
King of Belgium Tonneau-5P	1250	2700	3600	5300	8800	19,000

1906 Reliance, touring, HAC

1907 Reliance, runabout, NAHC

1906 RELIANCE
Model C-D — 2-cyl., 22 hp, 92" wb

	FP	5	4	3	2	1
Touring-5P	1250	2700	3600	5300	8800	19,000

Model E — 2-cyl., 28 hp, 109" wb

	FP	5	4	3	2	1
Touring-5P	2500	3000	4000	6000	9500	21,000

REMAL-VINCENT STEAM — Oakland, California — (1923) — The Remal-Vincent Steam Car Company of Oakland appropriated the chassis of a well-known (but unidentified) gasoline car and turned it into a steamer. A four-cylinder vee engine and tubular boiler were fitted, together with an auxiliary engine for generating electricity and pumping the water feed. No pilot light was necessary since ignition was by a patented spark plug. The object of this exercise was to interest California capitalists in investing in steam car manufacture in their state. The Remal-Vincent was exhibited in Oakland during the summer of 1923, but Californians weren't interested. Reportedly two vehicles — each a five-passenger sedan — were built before the project was abandoned. The Vincent half of the Remal-Vincent partnership was an Oakland machinist named Ernest H. Vincent. Remal's identity remains unknown. In 1922 Vincent had patented a condenser and steam boiler and was president of the Steam Automotive Corporation of Oakland which purported to be the manufacturers of steam trucks, with offices in the Pacific Building on Jefferson Street and a factory at 369 Third Street. By 1924 the firm had moved to 942 23rd Avenue in Oakland. During this same period a Steam Car Corporation of California, based in San Francisco, was selling stock in Remal-Vincent's "Vincent Steam Generator" which was slated to sell at $1500. There seems to have been more companies involved in this venture than automobiles built.

1902 Remington, NAHC

REMINGTON — Utica, New York — (1895) / Ilion, New York — (1900-1901) / Utica, New York — (1901-1904) — The Remington name, already famous at the turn of the century for firearms and typewriters, was used on a number of automobiles before the First World War, though without nearly the success. In 1895 the Remington Arms Company of Utica reported its experimentation with a kerosene motor and its intention to apply it to bicycles and trikes. This venture remained ever at the experimental stage, and was the only official one by the company in the automobile field. Though Remington was not involved in any subsequent automotive activity, a Remington was — Philo E., grandson of the man who had founded the dynasty and who managed to smoothtalk Remington directors into implying an affiliation that really was not there. This, Philo obviously thought, would be good for business, and also couldn't hurt in selling stock. At the turn of the century, in Ilion, and in association with Peter A. Stubblebein, Remington established the Remington Automobile & Motor Company. The Remington engine — an unusual four-cylinder unit which used acetylene or hydrogen gas for ignition — was designed by William A. Schmidt, who had formerly worked on Remington typewriters. Either four- or six-horsepower models were available, with accommodations for two or four passengers. Prices were $750 to $1500. The former plant of a novelty works in Ilion was purchased for manufacture, as well as the machinery and equipment of the defunct Quick automobile company of Newark, New Jersey. The first Remingtons were placed on sale October 30th, 1900; the following year the car was occasionally referred to as a Remington Standard, that being the designation under which the famous typewriter was sold. In 1901, too, during the early spring, the Remington Automobile & Motor Company moved to Utica. Moving with it was James S. Holmes, who had been prominent in the bicycle business in Ilion and whom Philo Remington had hired as his general manager. Only seven cars thus far had been built. In Utica, two local firms later to become famous in the automobile industry were enlisted to assist in Remington production: Weston Mott, which provided the wheels for the cars; Willoughby, which provided the bodies. C.S. Mott became both a Remington owner and stockholder. By now the four-cylinder Remington engine had been replaced by a more conventional one-lunger of 4/6 hp. A 10 hp twin arrived early in 1902. That November the company reported that it was "financially embarrassed"; involuntary bankruptcy proceedings followed a few weeks later. This irked Philo Remington mightily. Still, on February 11th, 1903, his Remington factory was sold at public auction. The purchasers were John B. Wild, who was well-known in the textile business, and A.J. Baechle, a prominent real estate man. They reorganized as the Remington Motor Vehicle Company, and in June declared that ten cars were under construction. The new Remington was quite like the old, a 10 hp twin offered as an $850 runabout on a 76-inch wheelbase and a $1350 tonneau on an 84-inch wheelbase. In July of 1904 John Wild sold the Remington plant to the Black Diamond Automobile Company of Geneva. Black Diamond discontinued the Remington immediately, though it produced the Buckmobile (another Utica product) in the old Remington factory for a short while. In the March 2nd, 1913 edition of the *Utica Sunday Tribune*, in an article summarizing the city's industrial progress, a local automobile dealer was asked what had been wrong with the Remington. "Pretty much everything," he replied. ". . . ignition troubles were many. Carburetors were imperfect and motors lacked the refinement of design that marks the gasoline engine of today. The manufacturers were exerting every effort to make cars that would run and giving little attention to comfort or beauty . . ." The Remington Motor Vehicle Company had left the scene quietly. The predecessor Remington Automobile & Motor Company remained in litigation as late as 1911, with Philo Remington suing old stockholders who had subscribed but never paid for their stock. One of them was ordered by the court to pay seventy-five cents on the dollar to meet his pledge.

REMINGTON — Charleston, West Virginia — (1910-1913) — Following the failure of his Remington of Utica and Ilion, and while he was still suing his former stockholders, Philo E. Remington tried again in 1910 in Charleston, West Virginia. There, together with Eliphalet Remington, he organized the Remington Standard Motor Company and set up headquarters in the former Baldwin Steel works. The initial announced intention of this venture was to manufacture automobiles and aeroplanes. Possibly a prototype of an automobile followed in Charleston, though this has not been documented with certainty. Definitely built was the prototype of a truck, which the Remington Standard Motor Company assembled in Farmingdale, Long

Island, New York, and which used the patented Manly hydraulic transmission. In January 1912, Charles M. Manly secured a writ of attachment against Philo Remington's company, his claim being for labor, material, one transmission and royalties due him. The Remington Standard Motor Company proceeded into involuntary bankruptcy in January of 1913.

REMINGTON — Rahway, New Jersey — (1914-1915) / Kingston, New York — (1915-1916) — Following his Charleston adventure, Philo E. Remington returned north to try the automotive field again, and the result was his finest effort. The Remington Motor Company was launched during the summer of 1914 with headquarters at 2 Columbus Circle in New York City and its factory across the Hudson in Rahway, New Jersey. The new Remington was one of the most sophisticated cyclecars of its day. It was powered by a four-cylinder 12 hp water-cooled engine set into a 100-inch wheelbase chassis (42-inch tread) of pressed steel with an I-beam front axle and a three-quarter floating rear axle. Suspension was via chrome vanadium semi-elliptic springs in front, three-quarter elliptics in the rear. Clarence P. Hollister was the company's chief engineer, and the inventor of the pre-selective Hollister automatic transmission which was featured in the car. The final drive was shaft. The side-by-side two seater roadster — which *Light Car Age* called "fetching" — was upholstered in tufted leather, and standard equipment included top, windshield, speedometer, and electric starter, lights (with dimmer) and horn. The price for this admirable little machine was just $495. In 1915 the roadster was joined by a larger four offered as the Narragansett Touring for $695 and a V-8 (Massnick-Phipps engine) offered as the Greyhound in two-, four- and six-passenger versions with a common $1495 price tag. In November that year the company moved into the former Vaughan Car Company plant in Kingston. For 1916 both the cyclecar roadster and the Greyhound V-8 were dropped, and production was concentrated on the Narragansett model. Among the reasons for the failure of this automotive venture were its cyclecar beginnings and the materials shortages as the war in Europe pressed on. After Philo Remington gave up, there was talk awhile that a new organization styled as Remington Motors, Inc. might take up the cause again, but it came to nothing. In 1917 Philo Remington was rumored to be heading up another company for the manufacture of a rotary valve engine, but nothing apparently came of that either.

1914 Remington, model R, roadster, NAHC

1914 REMINGTON
Model R — 4-cyl., 12 hp, 100" wb

	FP	5	4	3	2	1
Roadster-2P	495	3300	4400	6700	12,000	24,000

1915 REMINGTON
Model R — 4-cyl., 12 hp, 100" wb

Roadster-2P	495	3300	4400	6700	12,000	24,000

Model E — 4-cyl., 25 hp, 106" wb

Narragansett Touring-4P	695	3500	4500	7000	13,000	25,000

Greyhound — 8-cyl., 45 hp, 116" wb

Touring-2/4/6P	1495	4700	6100	9900	19,000	33,000

1916 Remington, model E, 5-pass. touring, WLB

1916 REMINGTON
Narragansett — 4-cyl., 29 hp, 110" wb

Touring-5P	795	4000	5000	8000	15,000	28,000

REMINGTON DART — Philadelphia, Pennsylvania — (1909-1910) — The Remington Dart was a two-cylinder 500-pound runabout produced and marketed by the Remington Automobile Company of 1351-53 Ridge Avenue in Philadelphia. The total production run was less than a year.

RENNO-LESLIE — The Renno-Leslie Motor Company was organized in Philadelphia, Pennsylvania during the spring of 1917 with a capital stock of $750,000 for the manufacture of automobiles and farm tractors. Incorporators were J.W. Hills, Jr., C.H. Reed and W.L Connor. Manufacture of a car is doubted.

RENAULT — The Renault Taxi-Service was organized in New York City early in 1909 with a capital stock of $10,000 to "manufacture and operate vehicles of all kinds." Incorporators included H.U. Kibbe, H.F. Sewell and J.P. Murray. Manufacture is doubted. Whether this firm was in any way allied with the Renault company in France is unknown. The French Renault was imported into this country, but never built here.

RENO FLYER — This was an alternative designation for the car projected to be produced by the Nevada Motor Car Company of Reno in 1908. Refer to Desert Flyer.

RENVILLE — Minneapolis, Minnesota — (1911) — The Renville was a larger companion car to the M.B. produced by the Motor Buggy Manufacturing Company of Minneapolis. A four-cylinder 45 hp five-passenger touring, it was introduced for 1911 and produced that year only. "The car for the farmer," the company advertised. "More value for the money than ever before offered."

1905 Reo, touring, HAC

REO — Lansing, Michigan — (1905-1936) — "For certain reasons" was the public relations explanation given in January 1904 when Ransom Eli Olds left the company he had founded, though insiders in the industry knew it was principally because the Smiths, who held controlling interest in Olds Motor Works, wanted to phase out his beloved curved dash Oldsmobile and build more luxurious models instead. Ransom Olds was livid. Rumors of his retirement from the automobile industry were short-lived, however, because by that summer he had started another firm, the R.E. Olds Company — and now it was Olds Motor Works' turn to be livid. The use of the name Olds, the Smiths cried, was an infringement of the rights Ransom Olds had sold to them when he left the company. But he had not sold them his initials. Thus was the Reo Motor Car Company born. The first Reo motor car was completed October 15th, 1904 and was tested for 2000 miles, mostly with Ransom Olds behind the wheel. It was introduced at the New York Automobile Show in Madison Square Garden in January 1905 and was a smash hit. A 16 hp two-cylinder five-passenger tonneau priced at $1250, the first Reo was soon joined by a 7-1/2 hp single-cylinder runabout described by Ransom Olds as "chip of (sic) the old block" — less than subtle reference to his curved dash which the Smiths could do nothing about. Interestingly, though the one-lunger would be offered through 1910, it was the larger two-cylinder Reo which was the more promoted. A $2500 24 hp four was offered in 1906, although by the time it was on the assembly line Ransom Olds decided it was a price echelon away from what he thought a Reo should be, and so he didn't even bother to advertise it. More in the old Olds tradition was his sending of a Reo cross country twice in 1905, the first double transcontinental ever, in addition to highly successful Glidden Tour and other endurance competition. In 1907, having begun his company only with his reputation three years before, Ransom Olds moved into the number three spot (behind Ford and Buick) in the industry. It was the introduction of Henry Ford's Model T late the following year which convinced Olds that despite the sales success of his chain-drive two-cylinder cars, he really needed a four as well. It was a honey — a 226-cubic-inch F-head developing 35 hp — which was introduced in August 1909 at $1250. Olds pretended that the earlier $2500 four had never existed, and the press went along with him. The new Reo four featured shaft drive, a multiple disc clutch, left-hand steering and a worm-and-sector type steering gear which presaged the "self-steering" idea soon to become universal. By now Ransom Olds had been in the automobile industry nearly a quarter of a century, and he was plainly becoming tired. It showed in 1912, with his introduction of Reo the Fifth. "The Car That Marks My Limit," the famous signed advertisement said. "I have only to say that, after 25 years...here's the best I know. I call it My Farewell Car." Basically a refinement of the previous four, Reo the Fifth introduced center gearshift control, eliminating the cumbersome

1906 Reo, roadster, JAC

side lever of yore. Thereafter, having done his best, Ransom Olds turned his attention to other business interests and his Reo to other managers. He remained in charge sufficiently, however, to say no, which he frequently did to plaints of his dealers. Ransom Olds was unusual in the industry in often not building as many cars as he could sell — he had no desire to emulate Ford — and sometimes in being just plain stubborn. It was only two years after Chalmers and others introduced a popularly priced six, for example, that Reo dealers had one, in 1916, a fine 45 hp car with modish "Sheer-Line" body. Despite the Reo Company's low-production policy, profits remained excellent through the World War I years, during which the firm enjoyed lucrative government truck-building contracts. (Reo had entered the commercial field in 1908, and would begin building taxis after the war.) For 1919 Reo's only automotive offering was a four. In 1920 the Reo T-6 made its debut. A 50 hp F-head, it again was a refinement of previous Reos, featuring the Hotchkiss drive which had replaced torque tube in 1918 and Reo's pet feature of the interconnecting clutch-brake with no hand lever. Both clutch pedal (operating on the transmission brake) and brake pedal were equipped with ratchets for parking on hills. The brake was released by rocking the pedal plate. Not until 1926 would an emergency hand brake be fitted. In 1927 the Reo Flying Cloud followed. An L-head six with seven-bearing crankshaft, it developed 73 hp, though a mod-

1907 Reo, four-seat runabout, HAC

est 65 was reported. The Flying Cloud was the first car to utilize Lockheed's new internal-expanding hydraulic brakes, and its body styling (by Fabio Segardi) was fresh and new. Like many manufacturers during this period, the Reo Motor Car Company introduced a cheaper companion car called the Wolverine. Like many too, it was short-lived, superseded in 1929 by a smaller version of the Flying Cloud. Two years later, in the desolation of the Depression and with the Reo Motor Car Company now losing money, the most fabulous Reo of all arrived: the Royale. A 125 hp straight eight with nine-bearing crankshaft, it featured one-shot lubrication, thermostatically controlled radiator shutters, and gorgeous coachwork courtesy of Amos Northup, chief body designer for Murray. Wheelbases were a generous 135 and 131 inches, though a special custom version was available in '32 on a whopping 152-inch wheelbase. The Self-Shifter — Reo's automatic transmission mounted in unit with the engine — arrived in 1933. By now Reo was in deep financial trouble, and in late 1934, following stockholder committee squabbles, Ransom Olds gave up effective control of his company. Merger rumors — with E.L. Cord's empire, with Hupp, Graham-Paige, Franklin, among others — floated about for a while. But the ultimate Reo reality came during the summer of 1936 when the announcement was made that Reo cars would no longer be built, that Reo henceforth would concentrate exclusively in the commercial vehicle field. Ransom Olds was over seventy now, and the decision could not have pleased him, he never liked trucks much. In January 1937 he severed his last tie with his company in resigning the board chairmanship. He died in 1950.

1905
Two Cyl., 16 hp, 88" wb

	FP	5	4	3	2	1
Detachable Ton-5P	1250	1550	4500	7500	10,500	15,000
One Cyl., 7-1/2 hp, 76" wb						
Rbt	650	1400	4200	7000	9800	14,000

1236

1906
One Cyl., 8 hp, 76" wb

	FP	5	4	3	2	1
Bus Rbt - 2P	685	1400	4200	7000	9800	14,000
One Cyl., 8 hp, 78" wb						
Rbt-4P	650	1500	4350	7250	10,150	14,500
Two Cyl., 16 hp, 90" wb						
Physician's Vehicle-2P	1190	1550	4500	7500	10,500	15,000
Cpe/Depot Wag-4P	1800	1750	4800	8000	11,200	16,000
Tr-5P	1250	1550	4500	7500	10,500	15,000
Four - 24 hp, 100" wb						
Tr-5P	2500	1750	4800	8000	11,200	16,000
1907						
Two Cyl., 16/20 hp, 94" wb						
Tr - 5P	1250	1750	4800	8000	11,200	16,000
Limo-7P	2500	2000	5100	8500	11,900	17,000
One Cyl., 8 hp, 78" wb						
Rbt-2/4P	675	1400	4200	7000	9800	14,000
Rbt-2P	650	1300	4050	6750	9450	13,500

1908 Reo, gentleman's roadster, HAC

1908
One Cyl., 8/10 hp, 78" wb

	FP	5	4	3	2	1
Rbt	650	1400	4200	7000	9800	14,000
Two Cyl., 18/20 hp, 94" wb						
Tr	1250	1550	4500	7500	10,500	15,000
Rds	1000	1500	4350	7250	10,150	14,500

1909 Reo, touring, HAC

1910 Reo, runabout, HAC

1909
One Cyl., 10/12 hp, 78" wb

	FP	5	4	3	2	1
Rbt	500	1400	4200	7000	9800	14,000
Two Cyl., 20/22 hp, 96" wb						
Tr	1000	1550	4500	7500	10,500	15,000
Semi-Racer	1000	1550	4500	7500	10,500	15,000

1910
One Cyl., 10/12 hp, 78" wb

	FP	5	4	3	2	1
Rbt	500	1400	4200	7000	9800	14,000
Two Cyl., 20 hp, 96" wb						
Tr	1000	1550	4500	7500	10,500	15,000
Four, 35 hp, 108" wb						
Tr-5P	1250	1750	4800	8000	11,200	16,000
Demi-Ton-4P	1250	1650	4650	7750	10,850	15,500

1911 Reo, touring, OCW

1911
Twenty-Five, 4-cyl., 22.5 hp, 98" wb

Rbt	850	1750	4800	8000	11,200	16,000
Thirty, 4-cyl., 30 hp, 108" wb						
Torp Rds-2P	1050	2200	5250	8750	12,250	17,500
Tr-5P	1250	2300	5400	9000	12,600	18,000
Rds-4P	1250	2000	5100	8500	11,900	17,000
Thirty-Five, 4-cyl., 35 hp, 108" wb						
Tr-5P	1250	2900	5850	9750	13,650	19,500
Demi-Ton-4P	1250	2800	5700	9500	13,300	19,000

1912 Reo the Fifth, roadster, HAC

1913 Reo the Fifth, town car, HAC

1912
The Fifth, 4-cyl., 30/35 hp, 112" wb

Tr-5P	1055	2300	5400	9000	12,600	18,000
Rds-4P	—	2000	5100	8500	11,900	17,000
Rbt-2P	1000	1750	4800	8000	11,200	16,000

1913
The Fifth, 4-cyl., 30/35 hp, 112" wb

	FP	5	4	3	2	1
Rds-2P	1095	1750	4800	8000	11,900	16,000
Tr-5P	1095	2000	5100	8500	11.900	17.000

1914 Reo the Fifth, runabout, HAC

1914
The Fifth, 4-cyl., 30/35 hp, 112" wb

Tr-5P	1175	2000	5100	8500	11,900	17,000
Rbt-2P	1175	1750	4800	8000	11,200	16,000

1915 Reo the Fifth, coupe, HAC

1915
The Fifth, 4-cyl., 30/35 hp, 115" wb

Tr-5P	1050	2000	5100	8500	11,900	17,000
Rds-2P	1000	1750	4800	8000	11,200	16,000
Cpe-3P	1575	1400	4200	7000	9800	14,000

1916 Reo the Fifth, touring, HAC

1916
The Fifth, 4-cyl., 30/35 hp, 115" wb

Tr-5P	875	2000	5100	8500	11,900	17,000
Rbt-3P	875	1750	4800	8000	11,200	16,000
Model M, 6-cyl., 45 hp, 126" wb						
Tr-7P	1250	2800	5700	9500	13,300	19,000

1917
The Fifth, 4-cyl., 30/35 hp, 115" wb

Tr-5P	875	2000	5100	8500	11,900	17,000
Rds-3P	875	1750	4800	8000	11,200	16,000
Model M, 6-cyl., 45 hp, 126" wb						
Tr-7P	1225	2800	5700	9500	13,300	19,000
Rds-4P	1150	2300	5400	9000	12,600	18,000
Sed-7P	1750	1400	4200	7000	9800	14,000

1918
The Fifth, 4-cyl., 30/35 hp, 120" wb

Tr-5P	1225	2000	5100	8500	11,900	17,000
Rds-3P	1225	1750	4800	8000	11,200	16,000
Model M, 6-cyl., 45 hp, 126" wb						
Tr-7P	1550	2800	5700	9500	13,300	19,000
Rds-4P	1550	2300	5400	9000	12,600	18,000

1918 Reo, model M, enclosed roadster, HAC

	FP	5	4	3	2	1
Encl Rds-4P	1750	2600	5500	9250	12,950	18,500
Sed-7P	1950	1400	4200	7000	9800	14,000

1919 Reo, the Fifth, touring, HAC

1919
The Fifth, 4-cyl., 30/35 hp, 120" wb

	FP	5	4	3	2	1
Tr-5P	1395	2300	5400	9000	12,600	18,000
Rds-3P	1395	1750	4800	8000	11,200	16,000
Cpe-4P	2175	1550	4500	7500	10,500	15,000
Sed-5P	2175	1250	3900	6500	9100	13,000

1920
Model T-6, 6-cyl., 50 hp, 120" wb

	FP	5	4	3	2	1
Tr-5P	1650	2800	5700	9500	13,300	19,000
Rds-3P	1650	2300	5400	9000	12,600	18,000
Sed-5P	2400	1150	3600	6000	8400	12,000
Cpe-4P	2300	1550	4500	7500	10,500	15,000

1921 Reo, model T-6, touring, HAC

1921
Model T-6, 6-cyl., 50 hp, 120" wb

	FP	5	4	3	2	1
Tr-5P	1850	2800	5700	9500	13,300	19,000
Rds-3P	1850	2300	5400	9000	12,600	18,000
Cpe-4P	2700	1550	4500	7500	10,500	15,000
Sed-5P	2750	1150	3600	6000	8400	12,000

1922
Model T-6, 6-cyl., 50 hp, 120" wb

	FP	5	4	3	2	1
Tr-7P	1685	2800	5700	9500	13,300	19,000
Rds-3P	1650	2300	5400	9000	12,600	18,000
Bus Cpe-3P	2150	1400	4200	7000	9800	14,000
Cpe-4P	2700	1550	4500	7500	10,500	15,000
Sed-5P	2750	1150	3600	6000	8400	12,000

1923
Model T-6, 6-cyl., 50 hp, 120" wb

	FP	5	4	3	2	1
Tr-7P	1485	2800	5700	9500	13,300	19,000
Phae-5P	1645	2300	5400	9000	12,600	18,000
Cpe-4P	1855	1550	4500	7500	10,500	15,000
Sed-5P	1885	1150	3600	6000	8400	12,000
Cpe-4P	2355	1400	4200	7000	9800	14,000
Sed-5P	2435	1250	3900	6500	9100	13,000

1238

1922 Reo, model T-6, touring, OCW

1923 Reo, model T-6, all-steel paneled sedan, HAC

1924
Model T-6, 6-cyl., 50 hp, 120" wb

	FP	5	4	3	2	1
Tr-5P	1335	3000	6000	10,000	14,000	20,000
Phae-5P	1545	3150	6300	10,500	14,700	21,000
Cpe-4P	1875	1550	4500	7500	10,500	15,000
Sed-5P	1985	1250	3900	6500	9100	13,000
Brgm-5P	2235	1400	4200	7000	9800	14,000

1925 Reo, model T-6, taxicab, HAC

1925
Model T-6, 6-cyl., 50 hp, 120" wb

	FP	5	4	3	2	1
Tr-5P	1595	3150	6300	10,500	14,700	21,000
Sed-5P	1595	1400	4200	7000	9800	14,000
Cpe-4P	1975	1750	4800	8000	11,200	16,000
Sed-5P	2085	1550	4500	7500	10,500	15,000
Brgm-5P	2235	1750	4800	8000	11,200	16,000

1926
Model T-6, 6-cyl., 50 hp, 120" wb

	FP	5	4	3	2	1
Rds-4P	1765	3000	6000	10,000	14,000	20,000
Cpe-2P	1495	1400	4200	7000	9800	14,000
Sed-5P	1565	1250	3900	6500	9100	13,000
Tr-5P	1395	3150	6300	10,500	14,700	21,000

1927
Flying Cloud, 6-cyl., 65 hp, 121" wb

	FP	5	4	3	2	1
Spt Rds-4P	—	3300	6600	11,000	15,400	22,000

1926 Reo, model T-6, coupe, HAC

1927 Reo, Flying Cloud, roadster, OCW

	FP	5	4	3	2	1
Cpe-4P	—	1750	4800	8000	11,200	16,000
DeL Cpe-4P	—	2000	5100	8500	11,900	17,000
2 dr Brgm-5P	—	1750	4800	8000	11,200	16,000
DeL Sed-5P	—	1550	4500	7500	10,500	15,000

1928 Reo, Flying Cloud, sedan, HAC

1928
Flying Cloud, 6-cyl., 65 hp, 121" wb

	FP	5	4	3	2	1
Spt Rds-4P	—	3300	6600	11,000	15,400	22,000
Cpe-4P	—	1750	4800	8000	11,200	16,000
DeL Cpe-4P	—	2000	5100	8500	11,900	17,000
2 dr Brgm-5P	—	1550	4500	7500	10,500	15,000
DeL Sed-5P	—	1400	4200	7000	9800	14,000

1929
Flying Cloud Mate, 6-cyl., 65 hp, 115" wb

	FP	5	4	3	2	1
Sed-5P	1395	1250	3900	6500	9100	13,000
Cpe-4P	1375	1400	4200	7000	9800	14,000

Flying Cloud Master, 6-cyl., 80 hp, 121" wb

	FP	5	4	3	2	1
Rds-4P	1685	4350	8700	14,500	20,300	29,000
Cpe-4P	1625	1750	4800	8000	11,200	16,000
Brgm-5P	1685	1550	4500	7500	10,500	15,000
Sed-5P	1895	1400	4200	7000	9800	14,000
Vic-4P	1895	1550	4500	7500	10,500	15,000

1930
Flying Cloud, Model 15, 6-cyl., 60 hp, 115" wb

	FP	5	4	3	2	1
Sed-5P	1195	1400	4200	7000	9800	14,000
Cpe-2P	—	1750	4800	8000	11,200	16,000
Cpe-4P	—	2000	5100	8500	11,900	17,000

Flying Cloud, Model 20, 6-cyl., 80 hp, 120" wb

	FP	5	4	3	2	1
Sed-5P	1595	1550	4500	7500	10,500	15,000
Cpe-2P	—	2000	5100	8500	11,900	17,000
Cpe-4P	—	2300	5400	9000	12,600	18,000

Flying Cloud, Model 25, 6-cyl., 80 hp, 124" wb

	FP	5	4	3	2	1
Sed-7P	1845	1750	4800	8000	11,200	16,000

1929 Reo, Flying Cloud, 4-dr. sedan, OCW

1930 Reo, Flying Cloud, 4-dr. sedan, AA

1931 Reo, Flying Cloud Eight, coupe, JAC

1931
Flying Cloud, Model 15, 6-cyl., 60 hp, 116" wb

	FP	5	4	3	2	1
Phae-5P	920	4200	8400	14,000	19,600	28,000
Sed-5P	1095	1750	4800	8000	11,200	16,000
Cpe-2P	900	2300	5400	9000	12,600	18,000
Cpe-4P	970	2800	5700	9500	13,300	19,000

Flying Cloud, Model 20, 6-cyl., 85 hp, 120" wb

	FP	5	4	3	2	1
Sed-5P	1295	2000	5100	8500	11,900	17,000
Spt Cpe	1405	2800	5700	9500	13,300	19,000
Spt Sed	1405	2300	5400	9000	12,600	18,000
Cpe-4P	1295	2300	5400	9000	12,600	18,000

Flying Cloud, Model 25, 6-cyl., 85 hp, 125" wb

	FP	5	4	3	2	1
Sed	1695	2000	5100	8500	11,900	17,000
Vic	1695	2300	5400	9000	12,600	18,000
Cpe-4P	1695	2600	5500	9250	12,950	18,500
Spt Sed	1780	2600	5500	9250	12,950	18,500
Spt Vic	1780	2500	5500	9500	13,300	19,000
Spt Cpe	1780	2800	5700	9500	13,300	19,000

Flying Cloud, Model 30, 8-cyl., 125 hp, 130" wb

	FP	5	4	3	2	1
Sed	1995	3150	6300	10,500	14,700	21,000
Vic	1995	3400	6900	11,500	16,100	23,000
Cpe-4P	1995	3400	6900	11,500	16,100	23,000
Spt Sed	2080	3300	6600	11,000	15,400	22,000

	FP	5	4	3	2	1
Spt Vic	2080	3600	7200	12,000	16,800	24,000
Spt Cpe	2080	3600	7200	12,000	16,800	24,000
Royale, Model 35, 8-cyl., 125 hp, 135" wb						
Sed	2485	3400	6900	11,500	16,100	23,000
Vic	2485	3600	7200	12,000	16,800	24,000
Cpe-4P	2485	3600	7200	12,000	16,800	24,000

1932 Reo, Royale, 4-dr. sedan, AA

1932

Flying Cloud, Model 6-21, 6-cyl., 85 hp, 121" wb						
Sed	995	3400	6900	11,500	16,100	23,000
Spt Sed	1110	3600	7200	12,000	16,800	24,000
Flying Cloud, Model 8-21, 8-cyl., 90 hp, 121" wb						
Sed	1195	3600	7200	12,000	16,800	24,000
Spt Sed	1310	3750	7500	12,500	17,500	25,000
Flying Cloud, Model 6-25						
Vic	1565	4200	8400	14,000	19,600	28,000
Sed	1565	3900	7800	13,000	18,200	26,000
Cpe	1565	4050	8100	13,500	18,900	27,000
Flying Cloud, Model 8-25, 8-cyl., 90 hp, 125" wb						
Sed	1565	3750	7500	12,500	17,500	25,000
Vic	1565	4050	8100	13,500	18,900	27,000
Cpe	1565	4050	8100	13,500	18,900	27,000
Spt Sed	1650	3900	7800	13,000	18,200	26,000
Spt Vic	1650	4200	8400	14,000	19,600	28,000
Spt Cpe	1650	4200	8400	14,000	19,600	28,000
Royale, Model 8-31, 8-cyl., 125 hp, 131" wb						
Sed	1985	3900	7800	13,000	18,200	26,000
Vic	1985	4200	8400	14,000	19,600	28,000
Cpe	1985	4200	8400	14,000	19,600	28,000
Spt Sed	2070	4050	8100	13,500	18,900	27,000
Spt Vic	2070	4350	8700	14,500	20,300	29,000
Spt Cpe	2070	4350	8700	14,500	20,300	29,000
Royale, Model 8-35, 8-cyl., 125 hp, 135" wb						
Sed	2445	4050	8100	13,500	18,900	27,000
Vic	2445	4350	8700	14,500	20,300	29,000
Cpe	2445	4350	8700	14,500	20,300	29,000
Conv Cpe	2995	6300	12,600	21,000	29,400	42,000
Flying Cloud, Model S						
Std Cpe	995	3150	6300	10,500	14,700	21,000
Std Conv Cpe	1045	4350	8700	14,500	20,300	29,000
Std Sed	995	2300	5400	9000	12,600	18,000
Spt Cpe	1070	3300	6600	11,000	15,400	22,000
Spt Conv Cpe	1120	4500	9000	15,000	21,000	30,000
Spt Sed	1070	2800	5700	9500	13,300	19,000
Del Cpe	1155	3300	6600	11,000	15,400	22,000
Del Conv Cpe	1205	4650	9300	15,500	21,700	31,000
Del Sed	1155	3000	6000	10,000	14,000	20,000

NOTE: Model 8-31 had been introduced April 1931; Model 8-21 May 1931.

1933 Reo, sedan, OCW

1933

Flying Cloud, 6-cyl., 85 hp, 117-1/2" wb						
Sed-5P	1785	3400	6900	11,500	16,100	23,000
Cpe-4P	1785	3900	7800	13,000	18,200	26,000
Vic	1785	3750	7500	12,500	17,500	25,000
Royale, 8-cyl., 125 hp, 131" wb						
Sed-5P	2445	3600	7200	12,000	16,800	24,000
Vic-5P	2445	4050	8100	13,500	18,900	27,000
Cpe-4P	2995	3900	7800	13,000	18,200	26,000
Conv Cpe	—	6000	12,000	20,000	28,000	40,000

1934

Flying Cloud, 6-cyl., 95 hp, 118" wb						
Cpe	795	3600	7200	12,000	16,800	24,000
Sed-5P	795	3400	6900	11,500	16,100	23,000

1240

1934 Reo, coupe, OCW

	FP	5	4	3	2	1
Cpe	845	3750	7500	12,500	17,500	25,000
Sed-5P	845	3600	7200	12,000	16,800	24,000
Elite Sed	920	3750	7500	12,500	17,500	25,000
Elite Sed	920	3900	7800	13,000	18,200	26,000
Royale, 8-cyl., 95 hp, 131" wb						
Sed-5P	1745	3750	7500	12,500	17,500	25,000
Vic	1745	4050	8100	13,500	18,900	27,000
Elite Sed	1845	3900	7800	13,000	18,200	26,000
Elite Vic	1845	4200	8400	14,000	19,600	28,000
Elite Cpe	1845	4350	8700	14,500	20,300	29,000
Royale, 8-cyl., 95 hp, 135" wb						
Cus Sed	2445	4050	8100	13,500	18,900	27,000
Cus Vic	2445	4350	8700	14,500	20,300	29,000
Cus Cpe	2445	4500	9000	15,000	21,000	30,000
1935						
Flying Cloud, 6-cyl., 85 hp, 115" wb						
Cpe	795	3400	6900	11,500	16,100	23,000
Sed	895	3000	6000	10,000	14,000	20,000
Flying Cloud, 6-cyl., 85 hp, 118" wb						
Sed	945	3150	6300	10,500	14,700	21,000
Conv Cpe	975	4800	9600	16,000	22,400	32,000
Cpe-2P	895	3600	7200	12,000	16,800	24,000
Cpe-4P	945	3750	7500	12,500	17,500	25,000

1936 Reo Flying Cloud, sedan, HAC

1936

Flying Cloud, 6-cyl., 85 hp, 115" wb						
Coach	795	3150	6300	10,500	14,700	21,000
Sed	845	3300	6600	11,000	15,400	22,000
DeL Brgm	845	3600	7200	12,000	16,800	24,000
DeL Sed	895	3400	6900	11,500	16,100	23,000

REPUBLIC — The Republic Motor Company was organized in Stillwater, Minnesota during the fall of 1912 with a capital stock of $10,000 for the manufacture of automobiles. Incorporators included G.H. Sullivan, L.L. Manvering and Paul H. Guilford. Manufacture is doubted.

The Republic Motors Company was organized in Brooklyn, New York during the spring of 1912 with a capital stock of $2000 for the manufacture of automobiles and engines. Incorporators included S.G. Frere, E.J. Ellenwood and W.J. Maloney. Manufacture of a car is doubted.

REPUBLIC — Hamilton, Ohio — (1910-1916) — This venture was initially organized as the Imperial Motor Car Company in July of 1909, but by January of 1910 the name had been changed to Republic Motor Car Company, probably because its backers were made aware that there was already another Imperial being made in Jackson, Michigan. That they hadn't known this before is not surprising, because the people behind the Imperial-cum-Republic did not come from the automobile field. But they were a formidable lot. Chief backer of the company George Adam Rentschler was a prominent Hamilton industrialist who already owned a couple of other companies in town (a machine foundry and an ice delivery firm) in addition to board directorships in several others. C.U. Carpenter was president of the Herring-Hall-Marvin Safe Company. George H. Helvey

1911 Republic Four, touring, NAHC

had superintended the affairs of a successful Hamilton company building steam engines, and George Stanley Helvey had previously been associated with Allis-Chalmers in Milwaukee. During the summer of '09 this consortium purchased the old Snider paper mill property on Middletown Pike opposite the Fairgrounds, as well as the existing plant formerly used by the Pioneer Knitting Mills Company — and by early 1910 they were in business. ''Classiest of All'' was perhaps overdoing it for a slogan, but the Republic was a handsome car and well put together. Early models carried 40 hp T-head four-cylinder engines with offset crankshafts and featured selective transmissions and shaft drive. The Republic became a six in 1914 and continued in production for two more seasons. Manufacture ceased in January 1917 principally because of materials shortages due to the First World War. Its backers certainly had enough other interests to occupy them in Hamilton in any case. Although the Republic has almost invariably been cited as having been produced during its final years in Tarrytown, New York, that assuredly was not true. The Republic never left Hamilton. Undoubtedly the error occurred (and has been perpetuated) because in 1913 William C. Durant chose the name Republic when he set up a holding company to buy the old Maxwell-Briscoe plant in Tarrytown and to absorb the Little Motor Car Company of Flint. Durant's new firm was called Republic Motor Company, but he never produced a car by that name, either in Tarrytown or anywhere else.

1910-1911 REPUBLIC
Model 101 — 4-cyl., 35/40 hp, 116'' wb

	FP	5	4	3	2	1
Fore-Door Touring-5P	2200	4200	5200	8400	15,700	29,000
Fore-Door Torpedo Rds.-2P	2200	4000	5000	8000	15,000	28,000

1912 Republic Four, touring, HAC

1912 REPUBLIC
Four — 35/40 hp, 120'' wb

Model 111 Touring-5P	2250	4400	5600	9200	17,300	31,000
Model 112 Roadster-2P	2250	4300	5400	8700	16,500	30,000
Model 113 Toy Tonneau-4P	2250	4400	5600	9200	17,300	31,000

1913 Republic Six, touring, HAC

1913 REPUBLIC
Series D — 4-cyl., 28.9 hp, 120'' wb

	FP	5	4	3	2	1
Touring-5P	2350	3700	4700	7300	13,700	26,000
Tonneau-4P	2350	3500	4500	7000	13,000	25,000
Roadster-2P	2350	3500	4500	7000	13,000	25,000

Series E — 6-cyl., 43.3 hp, 132'' wb

Touring-5P	2950	4700	6100	9900	19,000	33,000
Tonneau-4P	2950	4700	6100	9900	19,000	33,000
Roadster-2P	2950	4500	5800	9500	18,000	32,000
Touring-7P	3100	5000	6500	11,000	22,000	35,000

1914 REPUBLIC
Model E — 6-cyl., 43 hp, 133'' wb

Touring-5/7P	2950	5200	6800	11,300	23,000	36,000

1915 REPUBLIC
Model E — 6-cyl., 43 hp, 133'' wb

Touring-7P	2950	5200	6800	11,300	23,000	36,000
Touring-4P	2950	4900	6300	10,300	21,000	34,000

1916 REPUBLIC
Model C-16 — 6-cyl., 43 hp, 133'' wb

Touring-7P	2950	5200	6800	11,300	23,000	36,000
Touring-4P	2950	4900	6300	10,300	21,000	34,000

REPUBLIC ELECTRIC — Minneapolis, Minnesota — (1902) — J. Fallis Linton was the manager of the Republic Motor Vehicle Company located at 322 Third Avenue South in Minneapolis. The firm operated principally as a dealership though it had a short and ill-starred foray into manufacture. In 1901 Republic was given a contract to produce five electric cars for delivery of mail in Minneapolis, a project that was probably launched for test purposes. Alas, in January of 1902, Linton found it necessary to make arrangements with the street railway company to carry the mails since the parts he had ordered for the five electrics hadn't arrived yet. No doubt ultimately they did, and he finished the job. But that apparently was the last of the Republic Electric.

REPUBLICAN — The Republican Motor Company of Massachusetts was organized in Boston during the summer of 1912 with a capital stock of $1000 to manufacture automobiles. Incorporators included Norman J. MacGaffin and E.M. Churchill. Manufacture is doubted.

REQUA — The Requa European Motor Company was organized in New York City early in 1912 with a capital stock of $10,000 for the manufacture of engines and automobiles. Incorporators were L.F. Requa, F. Charavy and E.S. Roach. Manufacture is doubted.

RESERVE — The Reserve Automobile Company was organized in Camden, New Jersey in late 1902 with a capital stock of $50,000 for the manufacture of ''all kinds of automobiles.'' Manufacture is doubted.

REUTER — ''The Reuter Manufacturing Company has acquired an old doll factory in Pleasantville, New Jersey, where it will begin the building of automobiles and motors as soon as the necessary alterations have been made,'' The Automobile reported in February 1906. ''A quantity of new machinery will be installed during the present week and twenty-five hands will be employed.'' Whether manufacture ever began has not been documented.

REUTER STEAM — Davenport, Iowa — (1900-1901) — J.C. Reuter of Davenport built and patented a steam automobile in 1900 and spent nearly two years promoting its manufacture. There is no evidence he ever succeeded. In April 1900 there was a ''temporary organization'' of the Reuter Automobile Company in Davenport which obviously never became permanent, because by the early fall of 1901, Reuter was in Peoria Heights, Illinois negotiating for the old Rouse-Hazard building. That November the Rouse-Hazard facility was finally bought by the Cereal Refining Company of St. Louis, though Reuter was still reported to be in Peoria Heights looking for capital and ''meeting with considerable success,'' or so he said. Either truth wasn't his greatest virtue, or ''considerable success'' meant that some people would at least talk to him. No one apparently gave him the money for a factory, however.

REUTER ELECTRIC — San Antonio, Texas — (1920) — Odds and ends from a Ford and a Pierce-Arrow were put together in this children's car built by Fritz Reuter in 1920. Reuter, who operated an automobile machine shop in San Antonio, used a small electric motor and storage battery to power the machine.

1919 ReVere, model A, four-passenger touring, HAC

REVERE — Logansport, Indiana — (1918-1926) — The preliminary announcement was surprisingly subdued. In May of 1917 the ReVere

Motor Car Corporation was reported to be in the process of organization in Logansport for the manufacture of a car using the four-cylinder Duesenberg engine. Not until early 1918 were the men behind the new ReVere revealed, at least some of them — and they were Gil Anderson and Tom Mooney, noted drivers for the racing teams of Stutz and Premier respectively, and Adolph Monsen, who had built a car under his own name in Chicago a decade previous. That trio had collaborated on the design of a high-powered, high-performance car to be marketed under the name of the celebrated Revolutionary War hero. (Though a representation of Paul Revere would grace the car's emblem, the name was most often spelled ReVere.) Monsen modified the engine somewhat; Gil Anderson did much of the chassis work, including devising the out-board semi-elliptic rear springs and the designed-in provision (unusual at the time) for shock absorbers; Mooney apparently kibitzed a lot. "America's Incomparable Car" was the slogan, "the last word in classy design built by people who know, for people who want the classiest . . ." The car's price tag was as high as its performance potential, and in the racy speedster to follow that would be saying something. Although closed cars would be offered, ReVere became most famous for its sporty open models. During 1918 pilot cars were built, and one of the tourers was driven 16,234.5 promotional miles around the country by Cannon Ball Baker. The ReVere was introduced at big city automobile shows that year, and by early 1919 the production line was humming. Among early customers was Alfonso XIII, King of Spain, who ordered the first of the new victoria models. Meanwhile, a good deal of stock in the company was being sold. The men behind the design of the ReVere were not also the men behind the company, who were engaged in designing of a different sort. The ReVere officers were Newton Van Zandt as president; A.A. Seagraves as vice-president; C.H. Wilson as treasurer; E.R. Mattingly as secretary. A stock prospectus claimed the ReVere output for the next five years had been contracted for by an Eastern syndicate, the total figure represented being $45,000,000, which allowed for a $500 profit on each car sold — a terrific deal, prospective stockholders thought. A muddle followed. In late December of 1920 three Chicago creditors petitioned ReVere into bankruptcy, and the case moved into court early in 1921. In August a stockholder from Buffalo (New York) brought suit against Van Zandt for grand larceny, alleging that the Eastern syndicate contract did not exist. It did not, but Van Zandt was subsequently absolved of any wrongdoing in the company's affairs. As a search for the real wrongdoers was ongoing, the ReVere company went under. In November of 1922 its factory was sold for $52,000, and in February of 1923 a new group took over, reorganizing as ReVere Motor Company. Only Adolph Monsen of the original ReVere contingent remained, as vice-president and general manager. ReVere's new president was Charles E. Barnes, secretary was Fred J. Steffens, treasurer was Henry A. Kraut. Monsen revised the Rochester-Duesenberg engine into an in-house, though still very similar, design — and for the 1925 model year a Continental-engined six was added to the line. Among the interesting features of the last ReVeres was a dual steering wheel which offered a sort of primitive power steering. But the damage wreaked to the ReVere reputation and name could not be undone, and the car quietly faded from view after 1926.

1920 ReVere, model A, touring, JAC

1919-1920 REVERE
Model A — 4-cyl., 100 hp, 131" wb

	FP	5	4	3	2	1
Touring-5P	3850	5500	7500	12,000	26,000	39,000
Roadster-2P	3850	5400	7300	11,800	25,000	38,000
Victoria-4P	3850	4500	5800	9500	18,000	32,000

1921 ReVere, model C, roadster, JAC

1921 REVERE
Model C — 4-cyl., 100 hp, 131" wb

	FP	5	4	3	2	1
Touring-4P	4650	5500	7500	12,000	26,000	39,000
Roadster-4P	4650	5400	7300	11,800	55,000	38,000
Speedster-2P	4850	6400	9300	14,500	33,000	45,000
Sedan-5P	6500	3100	4200	6300	10,500	22,000

1923 ReVere, model D, touring, WLB

1922-1923 REVERE
Model D — 4-cyl., 100 hp, 131" wb

	FP	5	4	3	2	1
Touring-5P	3850	5500	7500	12,000	26,000	39,000
Roadster-4P	3850	5400	7300	11,800	25,000	38,000
Coupe-3P	4250	3300	4400	6700	12,000	24,000
Sedan-5P	4500	3000	4000	6000	9500	21,000

1924 ReVere, model M, touring, JAC

1924 REVERE
Model M — 4-cyl., 100 hp, 131" wb

	FP	5	4	3	2	1
Touring-5P	3200	5500	7500	12,000	26,000	39,000
Roadster-4P	3200	5400	7300	11,800	25,000	38,000
Sedan-5P	4500	3000	4000	6000	9500	21,000

1926 ReVere, model 25, roadster, KM

1925-1926 REVERE
Model M — 4-cyl., 100 hp, 131" wb

	FP	5	4	3	2	1
Touring-5P	3200	5800	8000	12,500	28,000	40,000
Roadster-4P	3200	5500	7500	12,000	26,000	39,000
Sedan-5P	4500	3100	4200	6300	10,500	22,000

Model 25 — 6-cyl., 70 hp, 131" wb

	FP	5	4	3	2	1
Touring-5P	2750	5800	8000	12,500	28,000	40,000

REX — "The Rex Automobile Company of Cleveland is a new enterprise in the industrial field," *The Automobile* reported in July of 1903. "Its first gasoline machine, still in the experimental stage is being built on the single-cylinder plan." Further details regarding this Ohio automotive venture are lacking.

The Rex Machine Works was located at 90-92 Eldert Street in Brooklyn,

New York and built a cyclecar in 1914, according to trade directories of the period. Details are lacking.

The Rex Motor Car Company of Indianapolis, Indiana (occasionally referred to as the Rex Automobile Car Company) apparently built a high-wheeled solid-tired motor buggy beginning in 1908. In February 1909 *The Horseless Age* revealed that the Rex company was contemplating "moving its factory from Indianapolis to Greencastle, Indiana where the Commercial Club has offered a free site." There is no evidence the company ever did this.

That a car called the Rexroad was built in Hutchinson, Kansas in 1917 has been indicated on various car rosters. This is in error. The Rexroad Engineering Company was organized in Hutchinson in 1916 but commercial vehicles only was its focus, and it does not appear this venture reached the manufacturing stage in any case.

REX — New Orleans, Louisiana — (1919-1920) — Among the cadre of organizers of the Rex Motor Car Manufacturing Company of New Orleans, the two most important were Robert Booth, who would serve as president, and A.C. Sinclair, who was a board director. Booth was an Englishman and the inventor of the Booth sectional export body. Sinclair hailed from New Orleans and was the inventor of the six-cylinder 65 hp engine that was to power the Rex and which, *The Automotive Manufacturer* reported, "has had the approval of the professors of engineering of Tulane University." The initial announcement of the company and its car — which was to sell for $985 — arrived in September 1919. In October it was revealed that a subsidiary organization was being set up to manufacture motor work-boats propelled by a marine-type Sinclair engine. A few weeks later the news was that a Rex truck was coming too. In late November further word revealed that capital stock in the company was being increased from $250,000 to $1,000,000 in order to construct the larger plant that was now necessary because of the augmented Rex activity. Robert Booth was then on an extended tour of the major automobile manufacturing plants of the U.S. to get ideas for the new Rex factory in New Orleans. Perhaps he was still out there getting ideas when the money ran out in early 1920.

1914 Rex, 2-pass. roadster, WLB

REX — Detroit, Michigan — (1914) — Whether the car itself or the man behind it represent the greater historic significance is a debatable point. But the Rex was yet another adventure of the inimitable C.H. Blomstrom whose previous automotive efforts had included the Queen, the Blomstrom and the Gyroscope, and who had been involved as well with the Car De Luxe and the Lion. The Rex was Blomstrom's only cyclecar. Its front wheel drive was most unusual for a vehicle of its type, the power taken by cardan shaft to the front left wheel only which eliminated the need for a differential. The friction transmission had its discs at the front of the engine instead of the rear. The water-cooled four-cylinder 14½/18 hp engine of the Rex was designed by Blomstrom. The car was on a 100-inch wheelbase, with 48-inch tread, though a standard 56-inch tread was to be made available. A side-by-side two-seater, the Rex weighed 580 pounds and was priced at $395. "We have attained a speed of over 45 miles per hour with the Rex, and have accomplished over 30 miles to the gallon of fuel," C.H. Blomstrom reported enthusiastically. Backing him in the formation of the Rex Motor Company were W.J. Frasier, Frank Lemerise, Alfred Robinson and C.H. Riopelle. In March of 1914 the company was reported to be erecting a factory in Ford City for large scale manufacture, but most likely the Rex cyclecar never left the small quarters in Detroit in which it had been born. Following the demise of the Rex, C.H. Blomstrom showed up next in New Jersey where his new car this time was the Frontmobile.

1914 REX
Cyclecar — 4-cyl., 14½/18 hp, 100" wb

	FP	5	4	3	2	1
Side-by-Side Roadster-2P	395	2400	3400	4800	8000	17,000

REX BUCKBOARD — Pittsburgh, Pennsylvania — (1903) — In 1901, in his native Milwaukee, a machinist named Rex Reinertson built his first automobile, a 900-pound gasoline runabout which he drove awhile in Wisconsin and subsequently in New York State when he moved there in 1902. Nineteen three found Reinertson in Pittsburgh where he became shop superintendent of the Pennsylvania Electrical & Railway Supply Company. During off-hours he designed a small 600-pound Orient-Buckboard-like car powered by a 4-1/2 hp single-cylinder gasoline engine which he called the Rex Buckboard. A small run of these cars was produced in his company's shops during 1903. Marketed locally, the cars were priced at $550 and were claimed good for 30 mph.

REXROAD — Although there was no Rexroad car, Guy C. Rexroad of Hutchinson, Kansas did build a few Sellers cars after acquiring the factory in 1912. Refer to Sellers.

REYA — Napoleon, Ohio — (1917) — During the summer of 1917 the Reya Motor Company was organized as the truck-building auxiliary of the Napoleon Motor Company. Malcolm Hall Ayer was general manager of the Napoleon venture — and the Reya was his last name spelled backwards. Though trucks were the Reya specialty, a few passenger cars were built in 1917 carrying that designation as well, one of which is known to remain extant. Reya trucks were produced into 1918, Napoleon cars into 1919.

REYNOLDS — In January of 1901 Alfred Reynolds of Joplin, Missouri announced that he had purchased property at the corner of Third Street and Kentucky Avenue, adjoining the Kansas City Southern Railroad tracks, where he planned to build a two-story brick building of 50 by 100 feet for the manufacture of automobiles. At this time, Reynolds was a wagon and carriage producer at 507 Virginia Avenue. Associated with Reynolds in his automotive venture was George Graves, who was described as a "well known mechanic and former railroad engineer." Whether Reynolds and Graves did indeed proceed into automobile building has not been documented.

REYNOLDS — Oil City, Pennsylvania — (1899-1901) — In October of 1899, W.E. Reynolds declared himself "hard at work on a motor vehicle in which he hopes to have points of superiority over any of these machines yet built," as *The Motor Vehicle Review* put it. Reynolds had formerly been with the South Penn Oil Company, and more recently the general manager of the Parkersburg-Marietta Traction Company, before settling down in Oil City to become an automobile manufacturer. When the Reynolds arrived, it was a prosaic runabout with no discernible superiority though the purchaser was given a choice of either a steam or a gasoline engine. Reynolds produced his car at least through 1901, the vehicle being featured in the automobile catalog of the E.H. Hall Company that year.

RHODE ISLAND — The Rhode Island Auto Carriage Company of Olneyville, Rhode Island produced steam cars at the turn of the century which are more correctly referred to by their builders' names. Refer to Hughes & Atkin.

The Rhode Island Electro Mobile Company was organized in Augusta, Maine during the fall of 1903 with a capital stock of $200,000 to "make and sell electro storage batteries" in Providence. Among the directors of this venture were I.L. Fairbanks, L.A. Burleigh, W.B. Snow, L.W. Horton and W.H. Horton. Despite trade directory references listing this company as an automobile manufacturer, the evidence suggests a car was never built.

The Rhode Island Machine Company was organized in Providence during the spring of 1906 with a capital stock of $20,000 to manufacture automobiles and parts. John W. Bishop, Clayton Harris, Edwin G. Pinkham, Robert D. McLeod and Walter M. Jordan were the officers of the firm, with Jordan (whose previous experience included several years in the gear-cutting department at Brown & Sharpe) as manager. "While it is the intention of the concern to ultimately build automobiles complete," *Automobile Topics* reported, "at present attention will be directed to manufacturing gears and constructing automobile engines." Automobile manufacture seems never to have been embarked upon.

RIALTO — The Rialto Automobile Exchange was organized in New York City early in 1907 with a capital stock of $2000 to "manufacture, store and rent automobiles, and also to instruct chauffeurs." Directors of the firm were Harold J. Siegel, Tracey L. Freeman and Lamuel Leibovitz, all of New York City. Manufacture is doubted.

RICE — The C.B. Rice Company was organized in New York City early in 1907 with a capital stock of $75,000 for the manufacture of automobiles. Incorporators included E.M. Jones and Ludwig Zeisler of New York City, and A.B. Foster Beach of West Orange, New Jersey. Manufacture is doubted.

The firm of John V. Rice, Jr. & Company was organized in Bordentown, New Jersey during the fall of 1904 to manufacture and deal in motors, motor boats and automobiles. Manufacture of a car is doubted.

RICE STEAM — Hallowell, Maine — (1858) — The first automobile in Maine was a steamer built in 1858 by Richard D. Rice, a judge in the state Supreme Court, and Frank and George McClench, machinists of Hallowell. The judge did the designing, the McClenches did the work. A stone cart was procured, and the front wheels removed and replaced with a single wheel with tiller attached for steering. The engine and milkcan-like boiler made for a claimed 10 hp, with final drive by chain and sprocket. The vehicle was successfully tested, with Judge Rice cutting a dashing figure behind the tiller in his tall stovepipe hat, and George McClench at the rear shoveling wood to an ever hungry boiler. Finding a chain equal to the strain of the two-ton steamer was the Rice's principal problem, and after several breakages, the vehicle was abandoned.

1915 RiChard, touring, HAC

RICHARD — Cleveland, Ohio — (1914-1919) — Fresh from his long-stroke experience with the Only and the Metropol on the East Coast, engineer Francois Richard turned west to Ohio and really outdid himself. The four-cylinder car that would be produced by the Richard Automobile Manufacturing Company of Cleveland had a stroke of 7-7/8ths inches initially, a full nine inches by 1917 for a displacement of 352 cubic inches. Rated at 25 horsepower, Richard claimed 96 was developed. The hood of the seven- or nine-passenger touring car in which it was placed was rather long, naturally. The roadster was something else. Richard introduced the car at the Cleveland Automobile Show in 1914 and noted at the time that he would sell it for $1850. By the time the Richard reached the market, however, it was considerably more highly priced. From 1916 on, he began spelling both his and his car's name as "RiChard," apparently hoping that in this way the proper "ree-shar" pronunciation might be persuaded upon the populace. For 1918, he planned a RiChard Magnetic (not unsimilar the Owen Magnetic), but this model never reached the marketplace. Instead, a V-8 (3-3/4-inch bore, a 6-3/4-inch stroke, nearly 600 cubic inches) of Richard's design was fitted into a nine-passenger boattailed touring car that was priced at $8000. "Chemineau" was the word Richard used for its streamlined form. Francois Richard must have been a man with enormous Gallic charm. Production of his Richard was minimal, and by 1919 he realized it was a failure. That same year he found further financial backing, and proceeded to build an altogether different car (the $1485 LaMarne) in the same factory.

1916 RiChard, touring, WLB

1915-1916 RICHARD
Four — 25 hp, 137" wb

	FP	5	4	3	2	1
Touring-7P	3500	3900	4800	7700	14,300	27,000
Touring-9P	3500	4000	5000	8000	15,000	28,000
Roadster-2P	3500	3700	4700	7300	13,700	26,000
Limousine-7P	4800	3100	4200	6300	10,500	22,000

1917 RICHARD
Four — 25 hp, 137" wb

	FP	5	4	3	2	1
Touring-9P	7500	4000	5000	8000	15,000	28,000

1918-1919 RICHARD
Eight — 45 hp, 137" wb

	FP	5	4	3	2	1
Boattail Touring-9P	8000	5400	7300	11,800	25,000	38,000

RICHARDS — Trenton, New Jersey — (1896-1903) — Walter Richards was a Trenton mechanic who built three single-cylinder gasoline cars in his machine shop on Jackson Street in 1896. Two years later he built a four-cylinder touring car for a local doctor. At the turn of the century he moved to Warren Street, establishing Trenton's first garage for the storage of automobiles there. He also continued to assemble automobiles for local residents who requested them. There could not have been more than a handful. On one occasion he drove General William F. Sadler in one of his cars to Hightstown and back. He covered the distance of fourteen miles in forty-five minutes going, but returning he slowed his pace because General Sadler threatened to get out and walk if the excessive speed was maintained. In 1901, now calling himself the Richards Automobile Company and switching his product to steam, Walter Richards declared himself "running day and night" to produce his new steamer, which was available as a $900 runabout, $1000 phaeton and $1350 delivery. Most likely, Richards built his last car in 1903. The following year he relocated to State Street and took on the Trenton agency for the Franklin automobile. In 1905 he opened what was referred to as the first "modern" repair garage in the city. He continued in this business for some years. His dealership/garage was located on the site where the Trenton City Hall now stands.

RICHARDS — Aurora, Illinois — (1902) — "As it was necessary for me to earn the money required for the building of the carriage, I was forced to divide my working time between blacking stoves and automobile building," wrote Mark Richards in the late fall of 1902. The car he built was powered by a single-cylinder water-cooled engine of his own design, and its running gear was made of gas pipe with malleable iron pipe fittings. "While building the machine, many of my friends made fun of it," Richards commented, "but I stuck to the job and am gratified with the result." The car required two years to complete.

RICHARDS — Manitowoc, Wisconsin — (1910) — "The Richards Iron Works is experimenting in the manufacture of motors for commercial and pleasure vehicles," The Automobile reported in January 1910, "and on the success of the experiment depends the matter of the establishment of a large plant for the construction of complete cars and trucks." Neither passenger car nor motor vehicle production was subsequently launched, though prototypes may have been built. No doubt the appearance of a Richards on automobile rosters has resulted from that preliminary announcement of experimentation. Henry C. Richard's company, however, remained prosperous for a number of years in the general machining field, and by the early 1920's was advertising the only complete stock of power transmissions north of Milwaukee. The company was in business from approximately 1884 until 1928.

1902 Richards, (Aurora, Illinois), MVMA

RICHARDSON — B.W. Richardson of Lake Street and Prospect Avenue in Peoria, Illinois was reported by The Horseless Age in May 1903 to be "building a gasoline machine" with the expectation of organizing a company for manufacture. The expectation does not appear to have been realized.

The W.H. Richardson Company was organized in Paterson, New Jersey early in 1915 with a capital stock of $50,000 to manufacture motor vehicles. Incorporators were W.H. Richardson, C.H. Richardson and B.J. Burke. Manufacture of an automobile is doubted.

RICHARDSON — Athol, Massachusetts — (1899) — C. Fred Richardson was a native of Athol who followed into the family's general machine jobbing business shortly after the Civil War and added the manufacture of carpenter's levels and transits. With the advent of the bicycle age, the firm switched emphasis to the repair and sale of two-wheelers. And in 1899 C.F. Richardson & Son (the latter Fred R. who had by now joined his father in business) built an automobile. Very little is known about it, but Richardson did contemplate manufacture. Both the Athol Transcript and the Athol Chronicle reported his plans in early January issues of 1899. According to the Chronicle, the Richardson experiments were being conducted "with a view to manufacturing a motor carriage which can be sold at a low price, doing away with any unnecessary construction, and still having speed and durability." Apparently Richardson was never satisfied with his results. In 1900 he was reported to be quite content driving his Stanley steamer. In 1901 C.F. Richardson & Son became the local agents for the Locomobile steam car.

1922 Richelieu, touring, WLB

RICHELIEU — Asbury Park, New Jersey — (1922-1923) — The Richelieu was named for the 17th Century French statesman and cardinal whose visage appeared along with the car in company advertisements. No one involved with the Richelieu, however, seems to have been remotely French. Most of its backers were veterans of Duesenberg Motors Corporation, including president N.G. Rost (former sales manager) and vice-president William Beekman (former assistant to Fred Duesenberg). Further officers in the new Richelieu Motor Car Corporation included bank presidents and varied other high-powered businessmen. The initial announcement of the venture arrived in October of 1921, and the car made its debut at the Automobile Salon in New York City during late November and early December. The Richelieu was a high-powered, high-priced performance car carrying the 85 hp Duesenberg four-cylinder engine. "The new Richelieu deliberately sets out to be America's most desirable car," advertising said — and for the sporting driver, it was desirable indeed, a snazzy-looking four-passenger tourer with two step-plates on each side replacing the usual running boards. Fleetwood was responsible for the bodies, which for the 1923 model year would include a roadster and a sedan as well. But the Richelieu's short life was just about over by then. Interestingly, Newton Van Zandt, who earlier had been president of ReVere, appears to have been involved in the Richelieu venture. Precisely how cannot be documented precisely. He was not among the principals indicated in Richelieu brochures and press releases as company officers or board directors, but he was among the principal creditors listed in February of 1923 when Richelieu Motor Car Corporation filed a statement in court noting its liabilities as $46,851 and its assets as $2,723. Needless to say, that rather dismal accounting spelled the end for Richelieu. In the fall the Richelieu company was succeeded by a new organization named Advanced Motors which revealed its plans to build a four-cylinder car called the Barbarino. The Barbarino was named for Salvatore Barbarino, who made cement blocks in Brooklyn. It shared a fate similar to the Richelieu's.

1923 Richelieu, touring, JAC

1922 RICHELIEU
Model T-85 — 4-cyl., 85 hp, 131" wb

	FP	5	4	3	2	1
Touring	3950	4000	5000	8000	15,000	28,000

1923 RICHELIEU
Model T-85 — 4-cyl., 85 hp, 131" wb

Touring-4P	4200	4000	5000	8000	15,000	28,000
Roadster-2P	4200	3900	4800	7700	14,300	27,000
Sedan-7P	6000	3000	4000	6000	9500	21,000

RICHLAND — Mansfield, Ohio — (1899) — That the Richland Buggy Company of Mansfield was building a motor carriage was affirmed in an August 1899 issue of *The Horseless Age*. Manufacture does not appear to have followed.

RICHMOBILE — That the Richmobile Company of Boston, Massachusetts produced an automobile in 1912 has been indicated on various car rosters. This has not been documented. No company of that name was listed in Boston city directories of the period.

RICHMOND — The Richmond Auto and Supply Company was organized in Staten Island, New York during the spring of 1909 with a capital stock of $15,000 for the manufacture of automobiles and "other vehicles." Incorporators were E.K. Forhan, H.M. Browne and J.J. Harper. Manufacture of a car is doubted.

The Richmond Automobile Company was organized in New York City early in 1904 with a capital stock of $10,000 for the manufacture of engines and automobiles. Incorporators were K.K. McGonegal, C.J. Campbell and J.H. Kellum. Manufacture of a car is doubted.

The Richmond Automobile Company was organized in Martinez, California during the spring of 1914 with a capital stock of $500,000 for the manufacture of motor cars and parts. Incorporators were W.R. Gilmore and J.H. Reemers of Richmond, and A.S. Houston of Oakland. This was a latter-day attempt of the A Automobile Company to relocate its Blue & Gold venture to Richmond, California. Refer to Blue & Gold.

The Richmond Iron Works produced a car called the Virginian in Richmond, Virginia from 1911-1912. Refer to Virginian.

"The Richmond Manufacturing Company of Richmond, Indiana has built two automobiles equipped with a new design of gasoline engine and is now testing them out," *The Horseless Age* reported early in 1909. "If the tests prove satisfactory, the company will manufacture them for the market." Apparently the tests weren't satisfactory.

The Richmond Motor Company of Custer, Michigan has been indicated on various car rosters as the producer of an automobile in 1916. Documentation is lacking.

Th Richmond Taximeter Company was organized in Stapleton (Staten Island), New York during the spring of 1909 with a capital stock of $5000

to manufacture and operate "cars, carriages, cabs and trucks." Incorporators were Maurice Carr, Julia V. Simons and Frederick Spencer. Manufacture is doubted.

1905 Richmond Amphibian, MVMA

RICHMOND — Jessup, Iowa — (1905) — This automotive curiosity, powered by a three-cylinder gasoline engine, was built by T. Richmond of Jessup in 1905. The road was but one of three venues available to the Richmond. "In the water a set of hinged paddles, which can be attached to the wheels, automatically open and close as the wheels revolve," it was explained. "For an ice boat spikes are fastened to the driving wheels and a runner placed under the forward wheel; two runners are also placed beneath the craft inside the driving wheels." Presumably conversion of the craft for water, land or frozen H2O use required only a few mintues.

1903 Richmond, steamer, NAHC

RICHMOND STEAM — Richmond, Indiana — (1902-1903) — "This engine is the simplest on earth," R.L. Sackett of the Richmond Automobile Company claimed. "It is the most compact steam vehicle engine on the market." Compact it was, with two cylinders of 2½-by-3½-inch bore/stroke, weighing just 46 pounds, and developing 6 hp at 960 rpm. Richmond began manufacturing the engine in 1901, and in 1902 introduced the Richmond car, a chain-drive dos-a-dos four-seater. Although automobile production ceased in 1903, the Richmond Automobile Company is believed to have continued in engine production for a while longer. The engine manufactured by Richmond most probably was designed by Isham Sedgwick, who had built a car of his own in Richmond in 1899.

RICHMOND — Richmond, Indiana — (1904-1917) — The Wayne Works in Richmond had been manufacturers of farm implements since the 1870's. Exactly when the firm built its first automobile is not known, but local legend places the date around the turn of the century. One day in 1901, so the story goes, Wayne president Walter W. Schultz walked into the tool room and asked his chief engineer Jack St. John to build an automobile because "everyone else is." St. John ran up a two-cylinder air-cooled touring car, which the company subsequently sold to a local carriage painter named Harry Landis. Another car like it was sold the following year, but it was not until 1904 that the company went into manufacture in earnest. Although occasional trade press references from 1904-1905 refer to the car as a Wayne, as did some townspeople at the time, it appears the company called its car the Richmond from the beginning. It began its production life as a four-cylinder automobile, and fours were

1907 Richmond, model F, family car, HAC

continued to be built until the end. The Richmond was a quite conventional car, though it enjoyed a local reputation for its reliability and hill climbing. The most radical change in the Richmond during its history was the substitution of water for air cooling in 1910. The biggest news thereafter was the addition of a six-cylinder model in 1914. After 1917 the automobile department of Wayne Works was closed down, and the Richmond was no more. That the company lacked the "push" necessary to make it in the highly competitive automobile industry was the reason usually given for the marque's discontinuation. Wayne Works continued in the agricultural implement field for a number of years thereafter.

1904-1906 RICHMOND
Four — 20 hp, 90" wb

	FP	5	4	3	2	1
Side Entrance Tonneau	1750	2500	3500	5000	8500	18,000

1907 RICHMOND
Four — 20 hp, 90" wb

Model E Runabout	1350	2600	3600	5200	8700	18,500
Model F Touring	1450	2700	3600	5300	8800	19,000

1908 Richmond, model J, runabout, OCW

1908 RICHMOND
Model J — 4-cyl., 22 hp, 88" wb

Runabout-2P	1000	2300	3300	4600	7500	16,000
Model H — 4-cyl., 26 hp, 91" wb						
Touring-4P	1200	2900	3700	5600	9100	20,000
Model I — 4-cyl., 30 hp, 108" wb						
Touring-5P	2000	3100	4200	6300	10,500	22,000

1909 Richmond, model J-3, touring, HAC

1909 RICHMOND
Model J-1 — 4-cyl., 22.5 hp, 88" wb

Runabout-2P	900	2300	3300	4600	7500	16,000
Model J-2 — 4-cyl., 22.5 hp, 96" wb						
Runabout-3P	950	2350	3400	4700	7800	16,500
Model J-3 — 4-cyl., 25.6 hp, 102" wb						
Light Touring-4P	1150	2500	3500	5000	8500	18,000

1910 Richmond, model K-3, touring, NAHC

1910 RICHMOND
Model J-1 — 4-cyl., 22.5 hp, 100" wb

	FP	5	4	3	2	1
Roadster-2P	950	2500	3500	5000	8500	18,000
Model K-1 — 4-cyl., 25 hp, 100" wb						
Roadster-2P	1000	2700	3600	5300	8800	19,000
Model J-3 — 4-cyl., 25 hp, 106"						
Touring-5P	1225	2900	3700	5600	9100	20,000
Model K-3 — 4-cyl., 25 hp, 106" wb						
Touring-5P	1275	3000	4000	6000	9500	21,000

1911 RICHMOND
Model L-1 — 4-cyl., 35 hp, 100" wb

Roadster-2P	1000	2700	3600	5300	8800	19,000
Model L-2 — 4-cyl., 35 hp, 106" wb						
Surrey-4P	1100	2800	3700	5500	9000	19,500
Model L-3 — 4-cyl., 40 hp, 112" wb						
Touring-5P	1350	3200	4300	6500	11,000	23,000

1912 RICHMOND
Model N — 4-cyl., 30 hp, 106" wb

Roadster-2P	950	2400	3400	4800	8000	17,000
Touring-5P	1025	2500	3500	5000	8500	18,000
Model M — 4-cyl., 40 hp, 112" wb						
Roadster-2P	1250	2500	3500	5000	8500	18,000
Touring-5P	1400	3200	4300	6500	11,000	23,000

1913 Richmond, model P, touring, HAC

1913 RICHMOND
Model O — 4-cyl., 30 hp, 112" wb

Roadster-2P	1100	2400	3400	4800	8000	17,000
Touring-5P	1100	2500	3500	5000	8500	18,000
Model P — 4-cyl., 40 hp, 116" wb						
Touring-5P	1800	3200	4300	6500	11,000	23,000

1914 Richmond, model T, touring, HAC

1914 RICHMOND
Model R — 4-cyl., 30 hp, 114" wb

Touring-5P	1250	2500	3500	5000	8500	18,000
Roadster-2P	1150	2400	3400	4800	8000	17,000
Model S — 4-cyl., 40 hp, 117" wb						
Touring-5P	1350	2700	3600	5300	8800	19,000
Model T — 6-cyl., 45 hp, 123" wb						
Touring-5P	1500	3100	4200	6300	10,500	22,000

1915 RICHMOND
Model 4-35 — 4-cyl., 35 hp, 110" wb

	FP	5	4	3	2	1
Roadster-2P	1100	2700	3600	5300	8800	19,000
Touring-5P	1100	2900	3700	5600	9100	20,000

Model 6-48 — 6-cyl., 48 hp, 120" wb

Roadster-2P	1375	3100	4200	6300	10,500	22,000
Touring-5P	1375	3200	4300	6500	11,000	23,000

1916 RICHMOND
Model 4-35 — 4-cyl., 35 hp, 110" wb

Touring-5P	885	3000	4000	6000	9500	21,000
Roadster-2P	885	2900	3700	5600	9100	20,000

Model H-6-50 — 6-cyl., 50 hp, 120" wb

Touring-5P	1095	4000	5000	8000	15,000	28,000
Roadster-2P	1095	3900	4800	7700	14,300	27,000

1917 RICHMOND
Model 4-35 — 4-cyl., 35 hp, 110" wb

Touring-5P	750	3300	4400	6700	12,000	24,000

RICHTER — Brazil, Indiana — (1902) — In 1902 in Brazil a bicycle repairman named Henry Richter built an automobile. He is not known to have proceeded into manufacture.

RICK — F.F. Rick & Company was organized in Buffalo, New York early in 1907 with a capital stock of $10,000 for the manufacture of motor vehicles. The Ricks involved were Frederick F., Otto R. and Thomas A. Manufacture of a car is doubted.

1922 Rickenbacker, coupe, HAC

RICKENBACKER — Detroit, Michigan — (1922-1927) — The car carried the name of America's ace of aces, Captain Eddie Rickenbacker, former racing driver and hero of World War I. He lent his name, his prestige and his advice, but the real driving force of the Rickenbacker Motor Company of Detroit was the triumvirate which earlier had created the E-M-F: Barney Everitt, William Metzger and Walter Flanders. Touring, sedan and coupe models made their debut at the New York Automobile Show in January 1922. The engine was a three-main-bearing six of 218 cubic inches developing 58 hp and guaranteeing a speed of 60 mph. Novel — and guaranteeing a complete lack of vibration, the company said — were the two flywheels at either end of the crankshaft. Also at the show was an experimental chassis with four wheel brakes, but no one paid it much attention. Considerable attention was paid, however, on June 27th, 1923 when Rickenbacker announced that its cars would henceforth feature four-wheel brakes. Probably Packard's similar announcement sixteen days earlier spurred the company to offer what it had already had for a year. Rickenbacker was the first medium-priced American car with four-wheel brakes. Duesenberg had pioneered the idea in America, together with Kenworthy, Heine-Velox and Leon Rubay, but these last companies were already dead. Buick, Oakland, Cadillac, Marmon, Chalmers, Elgin, Paige and Locomobile followed Rickenbacker on the four-wheel-brake bandwagon soon thereafter. Companies not offering four-wheel brakes began a promotion campaign suggesting they were unsafe, which probably hurt the new Rickenbacker company's sales promotion. Certainly the death of Walter Flanders in an automobile accident about this time slowed momentum as well. Rickenbacker never really got off the ground. Offerings for 1925 included the 80 hp Vertical 8 Super-fine (an L-head with nine-bearing crank displacing 268 cubic inches), plus a new seven-bearing 236-cubic-inch six developing 68 hp. Also introduced was a coach-brougham body style which would account for sixty percent of subsequent production. The Super Sport boattail model introduced at the 1926 New York Show was touted as America's fastest stock car, capable of 90 mph. Sale of Rickenbacker stock was suspended in January 1926; in September Eddie Rickenbacker resigned from the company. Barney Everitt struggled on in receivership, and on December 1st announced the new '27 models and plans to build 500 cars immediately. Total production for the marque was probably somewhat less than 34,500 cars, depending upon how many 1927 models were produced before Barney Everitt gave up in February of that year. Documented production figures are 3,709 cars for 1922; 8,539 for 1923; 7,187 for 1924; 9,214 for 1925. Nineteen twenty-six production is estimated at 5,400 cars.

1922 RICKENBACKER
Six — 58 hp, 117" wb

	FP	5	4	3	2	1
Touring-5P	1485	4200	5200	8400	15,700	29,000
Coupe-4P	1885	2700	3600	5300	8800	19,000
Sedan-5P	1985	2000	3000	4200	6500	14,000

1923 RICKENBACKER
Model B — 6-cyl., 58 hp, 117" wb

Phaeton-5P	1485	4200	5200	8400	15,700	29,000

1923 Rickenbacker, coupe, JAC

	FP	5	4	3	2	1
Coupe-4P	1885	2700	3600	5300	8800	19,000
Sedan-5P	1985	2000	3000	4200	6500	14,000

1924 Rickenbacker, coupe, HAC

1924 RICKENBACKER
Model C — 6-cyl., 58 hp, 117" wb

	FP	5	4	3	2	1
Sport Phaeton-5P	1645	4300	5400	8700	16,500	30,000
Sport Roadster-2P	1595	4200	5200	8400	15,700	29,000
Coupe-4P	2035	2700	3600	5300	8800	19,000
Sedan-5P	2135	2000	3000	4200	6500	14,000

1925 Rickenbacker, custom coupe, JAC

1925 Rickenbacker Eight, coupe, HAC

1925 RICKENBACKER
Model C — 6-cyl., 58 hp, 117" wb

	FP	5	4	3	2	1
Sport Phaeton-5P	1395	4700	6100	9900	19,000	33,000
Sport Roadster-2P	1595	4500	5800	9500	18,000	32,000
Coupe-4P	1895	2900	3700	5600	9100	20,000

<table>
</table>

	FP	5	4	3	2	1
Sedan-5P	1995	2200	3200	4400	7000	15,000
Coach Brougham-5P	1595	2300	3300	4600	7500	16,000
Eight — 80 hp, 121½" wb						
Sport Phaeton-5P	2195	6000	8500	13,000	30,000	42,000
Coupe-4P	2695	3200	4300	6500	11,000	23,000
Sedan-5P	2795	2500	3500	5000	8500	18,000
Coach Brougham-5P	2395	2700	3600	5300	8800	19,000

1926 Rickenbacker Eight, brougham, HAC

1926 RICKENBACKER
Six — 60 hp, 117" wb

Sedan-5P	2095	2300	3300	4600	7500	16,000
Coach Brougham-5P	1895	2200	3200	4400	7000	15,000
Coupe Roadster-4P	1920	4900	5200	8400	15,700	29,000
Coupe Sedan-5P	1695	3000	4000	6000	9500	21,000
Touring-5P	1750	4200	5200	8400	15,700	29,000
Touring-7P	1795	4300	5400	8700	16,500	30,000
Roadster-4P	1795	4000	5000	8000	15,000	28,000
Sedan-7P	2195	2400	3400	4800	8000	17,000
Deluxe Coupe-4P	1995	3100	4200	6300	10,500	22,000

Eight — 80 hp, 121½" wb

Sedan-5P	2495	2500	3500	5000	8500	18,000
Coach Brougham-5P	2295	2400	3400	4800	8000	17,000
Coupe Roadster-2P	2320	4900	6300	10,300	21,000	34,000
Coupe Sedan-5P	2095	3300	4400	6700	12,000	24,000
Brougham-5P	2120	3400	4400	6900	12,500	24,500
Touring-5P	2150	4700	6100	9900	19,000	32,000
Touring-7P	2150	4900	6300	10,300	21,000	34,000
Roadster-4P	2595	4500	5800	9500	18,000	32,000
Sedan-7P	2595	2700	3600	5300	8800	19,000
Deluxe Coupe-4P	2395	3500	4500	7000	13,000	25,000

1927 Rickenbacker, model 8-90, sedan, HAC

1927 RICKENBACKER
Model 6-70 — 6-cyl., 70 hp, 118½" wb

Sedan-5P	1920	2300	3300	4600	7500	16,000
Brougham Victoria-5P	1720	2400	3400	4800	7700	17,000
Coupe Roadster-4P	1920	4900	6300	10,300	21,000	34,000
Coupe Sedan-5P	1695	3200	4300	6500	11,000	23,000
Phaeton-5P	1750	5200	6800	11,300	23,000	36,000
Roadster-4P	1595	4700	6100	9900	19,000	33,000
Sedan-7P	2095	2400	3400	4800	8000	17,000

Model 8-80 — 8-cyl., 80 hp, 121½" wb

Sedan-5P	1795	2500	3500	5000	8500	18,000
Brougham Victoria-5P	1795	2700	3600	5300	8800	19,000
Sedan-5P	2320	2700	3600	5300	8800	19,000
Sedan-7P	2495	2900	3700	5600	9100	20,000
Coupe Roadster-2P	2320	5400	7300	11,800	25,000	38,000
Coupe Sedan-5P	2095	3500	4500	7000	13,000	25,000
Brougham-5P	2295	3100	4200	6300	10,500	22,000
Phaeton-5P	2150	5800	8000	12,500	28,000	40,000
Roadster-4P	2195	5500	7500	12,000	26,000	39,000

Model 8-90 — 8-cyl., 95 hp, 136" wb

Sedan-5P	2595	2700	3600	5300	8800	19,000
Brougham-Victoria	2695	2900	3700	5600	9100	20,000

RICKETTS — South Bend, Indiana — (1909-1911) — The early history of the Ricketts Automobile Company is difficult to document. The family was British, one Richard Ricketts having purportedly built a steam car in England in 1858 and two more in 1860. Just when the Ricketts family arrived in the United States is not known, but by 1909 in South Bend the Ricketts Automobile Company had been born. Some rosters indicate the company having commenced automobile production in 1905, but this has not been substantively documented. The first Ricketts cars of which the trade press was made aware were introduced for the 1909 model year, and there were two models, a four and a six. Thomas Ricketts, who headed the company, died in May that year; Joseph W. Ricketts carried on

1910 Ricketts, model G6, touring, NAHC

in his stead. Sales were dismal. Conceivably, Joseph Ricketts may have concluded that the reason for this was the pejorative connotation his last name engendered, because in January of 1910 he announced that the firm's name had been changed to Diamond Automobile Company; in February he let it be known that the car would now be called the R.A.C., which represented the initials of his old company. But sometimes he called the car a Diamond too. It remained much the same whatever it was called, a quite conventional automobile with sliding gear transmission, multiple disc clutch and shaft drive. Lengthening the wheelbase seems to have been the one major change. In October of 1910 a paint shop fire destroyed thirty-two partially finished cars, and pretty much finished the company. The firm's financial difficulties were reported in December, and six months later — in May of 1911 — the Diamond Automobile Company was in receivership. That fall Joseph Ricketts was in Michigan City, Indiana attempting to begin another automobile company for the manufacture of a $450 runabout, but that venture went up in smoke even without a factory fire.

1909 RICKETTS
Model F — 4-cyl., 30/35 hp, 115" wb

	FP	5	4	3	2	1
Touring-5P	1325	3700	4700	7300	13,700	26,000
Rdst./Business Wagon-5P	1325	3500	4500	7000	13,000	25,000
Model D — 6-cyl., 50 hp, 121" wb						
Touring-7P	2250	4000	5000	8000	15,000	28,000

1910-1911 RICKETTS
Model H — 4-cyl., 35 hp, 121" wb

Touring-5P	1550	3700	4700	7300	13,700	26,000
Baby Tonneau-4P	1550	3500	4500	7000	13,000	25,000
Roadster-4P	1550	3300	4400	6700	12,000	24,000
Model G-6 — 6-cyl., 50 hp, 133" wb						
Touring-7P	2200	4000	5000	8000	15,000	28,000

RIDDELL — San Francisco, California — (1900) — According to a 1900 San Francisco census, William Riddell was an automobile manufacturer. Nothing is known about the cars he was building, but in March of 1901 he did patent a friction drive mechanism that he had invented. Riddell had come to San Francisco in 1874 and at the turn of the century was living with his wife at a boarding house on Harrison Street. His name does not appear in San Francisco city directories following the earthquake.

1921 Riddle, 4-dr. sedan, WLB

RIDDLE — Ravenna, Ohio — (1916-1926) — The Riddle family had been building horsedrawn funeral carriages in Ravenna for decades before building a complete car. At least two American presidents (William McKinley in 1901 and Warren Harding in 1923) made their final drive down Constitution Avenue in Washington in a Riddle-designed carriage. The company began building complete cars about 1916 and continued for a decade thereafter. Hearses and ambulances were the mainstay of production, though a few examples of what Riddle called its "Double Side Door Convertible Seven Passenger Sedan" were also built. This vehicle had no center pillar on the right-hand side of the car to allow easy entry and egress of a wheelchair. Limousines for eight and nine passengers were also produced, the Riddle catalogue noting their useful application for "public and private service of the funeral director, his family or patrons." Riddle cars carried 55 hp six-cylinder Continental engines, and the usual price range was $4850 to $5500. Most of them sold within the funeral directors' trade. The few that were purchased by private clients were no doubt on custom order. Unlike other stalwarts in the professional car field — i.e., Cun-

1909 Rider-Lewis, type IX, roadster, NAHC

RIDER-LEWIS — Muncie & Anderson, Indiana — (1908-1911) — Ralph Lewis designed the car, and George D. Rider put up most of the money for its manufacture, which doubtless was the reason for his top billing in the marque name. The car's slogan was "Excellent Six" — and the engine was an ohv overhead cam unit of 40/45 hp and quite advanced for the period. The Rider-Lewis Motor Car Company introduced its new automobile at the Indianapolis show in late March of 1908. Production began in Muncie soon thereafter in the former plant of the Anchor Silver Plate Company which had been hurriedly converted into an automobile factory, though not very effectively because by December the decision had been made to move to more amenable facilities in Anderson. For 1910 the "Excellent Six" was joined by a lesser-powered four which was not provided a slogan. In September that year the company was in receivership, though production continued while a plan for reorganization was formulated, Rider-Lewis creditors being said to favor this action. Within a month they had changed their minds, however. In October the Rider-Lewis property in Anderson was attached by court order when those to whom the company owed money concluded that Rider-Lewis was preparing to move out of state in order to escape them. In December it was revealed that a total of 250 cars had been built, with the company operating at a loss from the beginning. Apparently a few more fours were built into early 1911, but by March the Rider-Lewis plant had been sold to another group of entrepreneurs who moved in to build the Nyberg there. Ultimately, the Rider-Lewis creditors received seven percent on their claims.

1908 RIDER-LEWIS
Six — 40/45 hp, 122" wb

	FP	5	4	3	2	1
Type VIII Touring-5/7P	2500	4400	5600	9200	17,300	31,000
Type IX Roadster-2/3P	2500	4300	5400	8700	16,500	30,000

1909 RIDER-LEWIS
Six — 40/45 hp, 122" wb

Type VIII Touring-5/7P	2500	4400	5600	9200	17,300	31,000
Type IX Roadster-2/3P	2500	4300	5400	8700	16,500	30,000
Type X Tonneauette-4P	2500	4300	5400	8700	16,500	30,000

1910 Rider-Lewis Six, tonneautte, HAC

1910 RIDER-LEWIS
Four — 30/32 hp, 104" wb

Type IV Touring-5P	1050	4200	5200	8400	15,700	29,000
Type V Roadster-2P	1050	4000	5000	8000	15,000	28,000
Six — 40/45 hp, 123" wb						
Type VIII Touring-7P	2500	4700	6100	9900	19,000	33,000
Type X Tonneauette	2500	4500	5800	9500	18,000	32,000
Type IX Roadster	2500	4500	5800	9500	18,000	32,000

1911 RIDER-LEWIS
Four — 30 hp, 110" wb

Model G Fore-Dr. Tr.-5P	1300	4200	5200	8400	15,700	29,000
Model F Touring-5P	1250	4000	5000	8000	15,000	28,000
Model H Roadster-2P	1250	4000	5000	8000	15,000	28,000

RIDLEY — In March of 1909, Dr. F.M. Ridley, Jr. announced the forthcoming manufacture of automobiles in La Grange, Georgia. Ridley, together with W.W. Wisdom, were in the process of gathering together a number of Atlanta businessmen with money to invest in the venture. "A feature of the car to be built is a double steering gear invented by an Atlanta inventor," *The Horseless Age* reported. That was the last heard of this venture.

1911 Rider-Lewis, model H, roadster, HAC

RIESS ROYAL — York, Pennsylvania — (1921) — In June of 1921 Charles E. Riess announced that he was taking over the bankrupt Bell Motor Car Company of York which he would reorganize into Riess Motors, Inc. for production of the Riess Royal. This new car was to carry a 57 hp Herschell-Spillman six-cylinder engine on the former Bell's 114-inch wheelbase chassis. Its price was slated to be $1495, a hundred dollars more than the four-cylinder Bell. Riess' plans went awry almost immediately, however, and the transaction to take over Bell was never formally completed. Possibly some of the last Bell cars assembled bore a Riess Royal emblem, but by October of 1921 the Bell property was again on the market and was sold at a private sale for $26,000 to William Stoffel, who had no car plans at all. Prior to his adventure with the Riess Royal, Charles Riess had been the New York City distributor for the Hupmobile.

RIGA — The J.G. Riga & Sons Company was organized in Springfield, Massachusetts early in 1914 with a capital stock of $25,000 for the manufacture of motorcars. The Riga sons involved were J.C. and H.M. Manufacture is doubted.

RIGS THAT RUN — This was the slogan of the St. Louis Motor Carriage Company for the cars it produced at the turn of the century in St. Louis, Missouri. So extensively did the company advertise the slogan that many people at that time, and since, have considered it the name of the car. Refer to St. Louis.

1897 Riker, victoria, JAC

RIKER — Brooklyn, New York — (1897-1899) / Elizabethport, New Jersey — (1899-1902) — Andrew Lawrence Riker believed in planning ahead. Although the electric three-wheeler he designed in 1884 never left the paper on which he sketched it, and the vehicle he did build in 1887 was merely an English Coventry tricycle to which he added electric power, he founded the Riker Electric Motor Company in Brooklyn in 1888. Experimentation continued to absorb him. In 1894 he put together his first complete car, though it was essentially a pair of Remington bicycles to which electric power was added. That year he also began building an electric racer which won handsomely over the gasoline-car competition at the 1896 Narragansett Park race in Rhode Island — and at the turn of the century, in a special low-slung electric torpedo, he did a mile in an unofficial but widely reported 63 seconds on the roads of Long Island. He also won Long Island's first road race (from Springfield to Babylon and return) in 1900. His penchant for derring-do left him scant time to carefully consider the vagaries of manufacture, though he did produce a number of

1899 Riker, victoria, HAC

1900 Riker, cabriolet, HAC

1901 Riker Electric, surrey, HAC

two-seater runabouts, four-seater dos-a-dos, hansom cabs and heavy trucks. His first four-wheeled electric passenger car had been built in 1895; his first commercial sale of a vehicle was in 1897. For a while in 1899 he became quite serious about the automobile business, incorporated as the Riker Electric Vehicle Company that June, and moved out of his small Brooklyn shop in July and into the old Lewis & Fowler factory in Elizabethport, New Jersey. At the time he said he planned to step up production to five cars a day there, but he soon became enamoured of

racing again. In December of 1900 he sold his business to the Electric Vehicle Company, producers of the Columbia. As late as 1902, Riker electrics were carried under that name in the E.V.C. catalogues. Andrew Riker had long since become bored with them. Indeed, the reason he had been so willing to sell his electric business was because he decided the gasoline car was more challenging. Already he had designed one gasoline model, which he sold to the Electric Vehicle Company. Thereupon he continued development on his own in Elizabethport as the Riker Motor Vehicle Company. Both a two-cylinder 8 hp car and a 16 hp four were built. They were not marketed, however. Instead Andrew Riker formed an alliance with an automobile company in Bridgeport, Connecticut and designed the first gasoline car to carry the name Locomobile. Andrew Riker was the first president of the Society of Automotive Engineers. He died on June 1st, 1930.

RILEY — During the summer of 1902 the Riley Engine Company of Paterson, New Jersey was incorporated for the purpose of manufacturing motor vehicles and engines. Manufacture of a car is doubted.

RILEY & COWLEY — Brooklyn, New York — (1902) — This was a steam car built to the order of B.M. Whitlock at the shops of Riley & Cowley in Brooklyn. It was a large car weighing 4000 pounds, with a 102-inch wheelbase and 56-inch tread. An aluminum hood shrouded the fire-tube boiler which was mounted up front. The engine was a vertical compound developing 12 bhp. An Upton two-speed transmission was fitted. "Flames from the burner cannot reach inflammable material," its makers claimed. Final drive was by chain, and semi-elliptic springs were used. All machinery, including differential, was secured to the vehicle's frame, which was built up of two steel channels joined together in the middle at front and rear. There was a large sixteen-inch steering wheel mounted on an inclined column.

RIOTTE — New York, New York — (1895, 1899) — The Riotte & Hadden Manufacturing Company of 462 East 136th Street in New York City built an experimental kerosene-powered motor carriage in 1895. Nothing further was heard of it, but C.C. Riotte was heard from again in 1899. By that time he was on his own as a manufacturer of gasoline engines at 132nd Street and Park Avenue, and was in the process of completing another automobile. Apparently he made the mistake of talking a bit too much about it because the man backing him — a Wall Street broker named Bernard Lande — notified the press that Riotte had "no authority to make contracts . . . for the sale of motor vehicles." That seems to have squelched that deal. The year following, in 1900, Riotte hired on as designer of the new U.S. Long Distance Automobile Company, and the first cars turned out by that firm were occasionally referred to by their designer's name in the trade press. Probably this was because C.C. Riotte was talking too much again. The U.S. Long Distance Automobile Company called the car a Long Distance.

1903 Ripper, runabout, GR

RIPPER — Buffalo, New York — (1903) — At the Buffalo Automobile Show in March of 1903, the Ripper Motor Carriage Company exhibited a light runabout on a 64-inch wheelbase which featured a 5 hp engine, chain drive and right-hand lever steering. The price tag quoted was $575. The car was advertised through that summer, but then seemed to disappear by year's end. By autumn of the year following, the man behind the Ripper also disappeared. He was Victor E. Ripper. His Ripper Motor Carriage Company had been headquartered at 616 Main Street in Buffalo, and he was the proprietor of three other stores which sold bicycles and automobiles of other manufacturers. Victor Ripper's disappearance was said to have been the result of certain illegalities in the conduct of his various businesses. Forging promissory notes was among them. Ripper's list of creditors included two Buffalo banks, many local businesses and several prominent businessmen. His total liabilities exceeded $50,000. It was presumed he had taken his assets with him.

RISLEY — In 1901 Dalton Risley was experimenting with an automobile in Omaha, Nebraska for the manufacture of which the Badeker Gas Engine Company was organized. Refer to Badeker.

RITCHIE — Hamilton, Ohio — (1899) — William Ritchie was the president of the Advance Manufacturing Company located at the southwest corner of Vine and Lowell streets in Hamilton. Oscar N. Ritchie served as secretary/treasurer of this family-operated business. In 1899 William Ritchie announced that he had completed a gasoline carriage, but this appears to have been the only vehicle he built. Subsequently, his Advance Manufacturing Company enjoyed a number of years of success in the gasoline engine producing field, though by 1940 the firm had switched its product line to tobacco packing equipment and special contract machine work.

RITTER — Milton, Pennsylvania — (1896-1901) — Edward E. Ritter was born in Milton in 1863, died in 1924 — and for a few years around the turn of the century built automobiles. This was a low-key venture which emanated first from Ritter's bicycle shop on North Front Street. Subsequently it moved to the corner of Second and Arch streets. No company was ever incorporated. The total number of cars built is not known, but one of them was a steamer and another employed a "friction engine" of Ritter's own design. A blacksmith in town built the frames for the cars. Surviving descendants of Edward Ritter recall that he subsequently became a dealer for the Jackson automobile.

RITTER — Madison, Wisconsin — (1912) — The Ritter was built by a former Detroit wholesale liquor dealer who had tried first with the DeMot or DeMotCar. When that venture failed in Michigan, C.H. Ritter reacquired control of the Demotcar Company and moved to Wisconsin. Traveling with him were R.A. Skinner (who previously had been in the printing business) and A.W. Voege (one of the trustees of the defunct Demotocar Company). Newly organized with $25,000 capital stock as the Ritter Automobile Company in Madison, this triumvirate produced a car with four cylinders (two more than the DeMotCar) and 15 hp (five more horses) that was available only as a runabout on a 90-inch wheelbase (ten inches more lengthy) for $685 ($135 more expensive). The Ritter was even more shortlived than its predecessor.

1914 Ritz Cyclecar, HAC

RITZ — New York, New York — (1914-1915) — Carl. D. Ritzwoller, Solomon Satzauer and A. Russell Smith were the men behind this venture which was headquartered at 246 West 65th Street in Manhattan. Though the product was advertised as "The Miniature Car for Everyone," the Ritz Cyclecar Company gave itself away with its name. The Ritz, however, which had been designed by Smith, was considerably more substantial than most cyclecars. Vanadium steel was used throughout, and the front axle was a tubular drop forged I-beam. Shaft drive was used. "One of the features of our planetary transmission," Smith boasted, "and one which I have never seen employed in any other motorcar, is the selective type of gearset which we use. We can change speeds instantly with a lever-thrust without the aid of a clutch, the selective gear set doing the work effectively." The Ritz began life as an air-cooled vee-twin, but became a water-cooled four for 1915. A side-by-side roadster (44-inch tread) was the only model offered. As a cyclecar, the Ritz would have found the going rough in any case, but matters were further complicated by the fact that the cars were built for the company by Driggs-Seabury in Sharon, Pennsylvania. Early in 1915 Ritz sued Driggs for $50,000 in damages for failure to deliver cars contracted for; Driggs countered that Ritz had failed to pay for work done. The U.S. District Court ultimately decided in favor of Ritz, but that was not until late November of 1916 — and the company had been long dead by then. A total of 205 Ritz cyclecars had been built. Interestingly, a reference from *The American Cyclecar* in 1914 indicates that a Charles W. Bury was purchasing agent for the Ritz company. No doubt this was the same Charles W. Bury who attempted to market a small car patterned after the Austin Seven under his own name in New York in 1927.

1915 Ritz, roadster, WLB

1914 RITZ
Cyclecar — 2-cyl., 10/12 hp, 98" wb

	FP	5	4	3	2	1
Side-by-Side Roadster	395	1800	2800	4000	6200	13,000

1915 RITZ
Cyclecar — 4-cyl., 15 hp, 100" wb

Side-by-Side Roadster	425	2000	3000	4200	6500	14,000

R.I.V. — The R.I.V. Company was organized in New York City during the summer of 1908 with a capital stock of $10,000 for the manufacture of motor cars and parts. Incorporators were H.M. Wise, H.M. Ashley, Jr. and R.W. Ashley. Manufacture is doubted, the firm apparently moving into the importation field (principally ball bearings) thereafter.

RIVAL — The cyclecar from Texas announced by Theodore F. Lane as the Rival was introduced as the Wichita Falls in 1914 and was succeeded by the Lane in 1915. Refer to Wichita Falls.

RIVERSIDE — The Riverside Automobile Company was organized in New York City during the spring of 1908 with a capital stock of $10,000 for the manufacture of motorcars. Incorporators were J.D. Baker and S.B. Howard. Manufacture is doubted.

RIVERVIEW — The Riverview Bronze and Manufacturing Company was organized with a capital stock of $50,000 during the fall of 1909 for the manufacture of "vehicles, engines, machines, cars, carriages, wagons and trucks." Incorporators were P.F. Woods, R.L. Dearnorf and W.R. Mample. Manufacture of an automobile is doubted.

1912 Rivett Special, runabout, HAC

RIVETT SPECIAL — Syracuse, New York — (1912) — A blacksmith from Scriba Corners fashioned this three-wheeler for himself in 1912. Claude Rivett used odds and ends: iron-rimmed wheels on the front, a rubber tire on the rear, a chain for final drive big enough for a truck, an old packing box for the body and chicken wire over the hood. Its engine was a water-cooled twin, and Rivett insisted he put the whole thing together with a hammer, a monkey wrench, a screw driver and a saw. "It looks it," commented *The Automobile*. Nonetheless, Claude Rivett was sufficiently proud of his creation to exhibit it at the 1912 Oswego Automobile Show.

1907 Riviera, NAHC

RIVIERA — Lebanon, Pennsylvania — (1907) — Milton H. Schnader introduced his Riviera at the New York Automobile Show in January 1907. To provide his car a little instant history, he designated it the Model B, and subsequently said in advertisements that it had created a sensation at the show because it was the only five-passenger touring car on hand with three-point spring suspension and cushion tires. The Riviera was powered by a two-cylinder 20 hp water-cooled engine. The wheelbase was 106 inches, and featured shaft drive and a two-speed planetary transmission. Schnader's price for the car was $1850. The Riviera was built at the Lebanon Motor Works, which produced the Upton, and in which venture Schnader was also involved. The Riviera was an entirely different car, however, and was probably his pet project. His pet died, however, by the spring of 1907 when the Lebanon company went out of business. Certainly very few Rivieras were built.

1907 RIVIERA
Model B — 2-cyl., 20 hp, 106" wb

	FP	5	4	3	2	1
Touring-5P	1850	2700	3600	5300	8800	19,000

R & L — Chicopee Falls, Massachusetts — (1922-1928) — The R & L was the taxicab produced by Rauch & Lang, Inc. and was introduced in both electric and gasoline versions during the summer of 1922. The electric was smaller (102-inch wheelbase) and pricier ($2750). The gasoline car used a four-cylinder Buda engine in a 112-inch wheelbase chassis and was available as a $2350 limousine and $2475 limousine-landaulet. Three hundred of the gasoline versions were built in 1923, outselling the electric handsomely. Indeed, it appears the R & L gasoline taxicab was the mainstay of production during this venerable electric manufacturer's twilight years in the industry. Both the initials and the full name were used to designate the taxi, incidentally. Refer to Rauch & Lang.

R.L. MORGAN — In 1897 in Worcester, Massachusetts, Ralph L. Morgan built a steam car. Refer to Morgan.

R.M.C. — Although occasionally the company initials were used unofficially, the car produced from 1907 through 1918 in Detroit by the Regal Motor Car Company was always marketed under the name of Regal. An export version did carry the name Seabrook-R.M.C., however. Refer to Regal.

R-O — From 1910-1911 the Owen Motor Car Company produced a four-cylinder car in Detroit. Most of these cars bore the name Owen, though a few of the final cars in 1911 were marketed as the R-O. Refer to Owen.

ROACH — Philadelphia, Pennsylvania — (1899) — W.E. Roach completed his first car in Philadelphia in 1899. It had a two-cylinder gasoline engine, a two-passenger runabout body, and wire wheels. Although manufacture was contemplated, it was not realized. A subsequent electric sometimes credited to Roach and which he occasionally advertised under his own name was not a Roach at all, but a Waverley.

ROACH & ALBANUS — Ft. Wayne, Indiana — (1899-1900) — Roach & Albanus were carriagemakers in Ft. Wayne who announced late in 1899 their intention to manufacture an automobile powered by an engine invented by Henry R. Hart, also of Ft. Wayne. "It is claimed there will be no jerking motion to the carriage owing to the explosions of the engine," *The Motor Vehicle Review* stated. "This has been overcome by a clever arrangement." The arrangement was otherwise unexplained, though Henry Hart stated that his unit was "as near perfection as any vehicle motor now before the public." Probably not; the Roach & Albanus with Henry Hart's engine was produced in very small numbers for less than a year.

ROADAPLANE — Roadaplane was the name given to all models of the Apperson for 1917. The car was advertised extensively in the late spring of 1916 in a teaser campaign which did not reveal the manufacturer's name. In mid-June, however, an official press release datelined Kokomo, Indiana revealed that the Apperson brothers were behind the car, and it was officially introduced that month for the 1917 model year. Refer to Apperson.

1911 Roader, runabout, HAC

ROADER — Brockton, Massachusetts — (1911-1912) — Roader was a term used during this period to describe a horse swift of gait. How fast the Roader car was does not appear to have been recorded, but it was offered only as a roadster with dropped frame, sliding gear transmission and round gasoline tank on the rear deck. The Roader Car Company of Brockton — organized in Maine with a million-dollar capital stock — introduced its car late in 1910 for the 1911 model season, offering it in two four-cylinder models of 20 and 30 hp respectively. Although the company subsequently announced that the Model 20 would be dropped and the 30 only continued, there was a change of mind on this — and the only model offered for 1912 was the Model 20 on a longer wheelbase. Roader failed later that year.

1911 ROADER
Model 20 — 4-cyl., 20 hp, 93" wb

	FP	5	4	3	2	1
Runabout-2P	650	3300	4400	6700	12,000	24,000

1252

Model 30 — 4-cyl., 30 hp, 104" wb

	FP	5	4	3	2	1
Roadster-2P	750	3700	4700	7300	13,700	26,000

1912 ROADER
Model 20 — 4-cyl., 20 hp, 105" wb

	FP	5	4	3	2	1
Runabout-2P	700	3100	4200	6300	10,500	22,000
Fore-Door Runabout-2P	700	3200	4300	6500	11,000	23,000

ROAD KING — Road King was the advertised designation of the Monarch built in 1908 by the Monarch Machine Company of Des Moines, Iowa. Refer to Monarch.

ROADRUNNER — Los Angeles, California — (1904) — The Roadrunner Automobile & Power Company was organized in Los Angeles early in 1904 by S.P. Smoot, C.W. Raymond, R.E. Shaw, John Albright and F.A. Stephenson. Its capital stock was $50,000 of which $20,503 had been subscribed. The name of the company derived from the bicycle which Smoot had been building in Los Angeles for several years past. Now it was to be applied to a line of gasoline runabouts and production cars. How many Roadrunners were built before the money ran out is not known.

ROAMER — The H.J. Roamer Company of Taunton, Massachusetts has been indicated on various car rosters as the manufacturer of a cyclecar in 1914. This represents both typographical and geographical errors. A.J. Romer was the man involved, and he was located elsewhere in Massachusetts. Refer to Romer.

1916 Roamer, touring, JAC

ROAMER — Streator, Illinois — (1916-1917) / Kalamazoo, Michigan — (1917-1929) — The Roamer resulted when Cloyd Y. Kenworthy, the New York distributor for the Rauch & Lang, began looking for a good gasoline car to sell because electrics were ebbing in popularity — and decided he couldn't find one. In association with Karl H. Martin (who was later to design the Wasp) and Albert C. Barley (who was then building the Halladay), the Roamer was consequently born. Its name, suggested by Kenworthy's chauffeur, was that of a famous race horse of the day — and it was an apt one since the car was planned to have racy lines and sporting potential. An assembled automobile, the Roamer had a radiator that was an unabashed copy of the Rolls-Royce from birth to demise and was available with a Duesenberg engine from 1918 through 1924. (Continental sixes and Lycoming eights powered other Roamer models.) "America's Smartest Car" was a company slogan; brochures quoted Oscar Wilde and used tony phrases like "a certain insouciance" to describe the product. The Roamer was a fine car, and was introduced during the fall of 1916. By spring of the following year, Albert Barley had divested himself of the Halladay in Streator, Illinois and moved his reorganized Barley Motor Car Company to Kalamazoo, Michigan (the old Michigan Buggy plant) for production of the Roamer. Wartime contingencies held production down to the 1500-unit range annually at first, but the Armistice and plant expansion meant the Roamer could roar with the Twenties, though without either Kenworthy or Martin, who had left by now to build their own cars, the Kenworthy and Wasp respectively. In 1921 a stock Roamer with four-cylinder Rochester-Duesenberg engine was driven by company chief engineer L.F. Goodspeed to an unofficial world's stock chassis record of 105.08 mph at Daytona Beach. Double cantilever suspension was adopted that year. In 1922 the Roamer was joined by a smaller companion car called the Barley and a taxicab called the Pennant followed in 1924. Neither survived long. And the car that had been named for a race horse was now on its last legs too. In 1924 Albert Barley had sold his company and retired to a board directorship. In the reorganization that followed the firm's name was changed to Roamer Motor Car Company, with George P. Wigginton as president. Now Canadian interests were largely in control, though the factory remained in Kalamazoo. Most probably, the Roamer's difficulty was that although it was a relatively expensive car (some models in the $4000 range), it was also an assembled car. True, it was to an extent "custom-built" as the ads said — in 1916 the Roamer was offered in any paint scheme desired by the owner, with the factory providing "a lengthy list of color combinations" as a guide — but there remained an onus in a large part of the public sector regarding assembled cars. Mary Pickford and Buster Keaton bought Roamers, but there were not enough other purchasers to allow the car to survive. It faded away shortly before the Wall Street crash. Models for 1930 were introduced, but built only briefly.

1916 ROAMER
Six — 23 hp, 124" wb

	FP	5	4	3	2	1
Touring-5P	1800	3100	4200	6300	10,500	22,000

1917 Roamer, touring, JAC

1917 ROAMER
Six — 23 hp, 124" wb

	FP	5	4	3	2	1
Touring-5P	1850	3100	4200	6300	10,500	22,000
Sedan	2350	2000	3000	4200	6500	14,000
Town Car	2850	2300	3300	4600	7500	16,000
Six — 38 hp, 135" wb						
Touring	2950	3700	4700	7300	13,700	26,000

1918 Roamer, touring, HAC

1919 Roamer, touring, JAC

1918-1919 ROAMER
Model C-6-54 — 6-cyl., 54 hp, 128" wb

Touring-7P	2750	4900	6300	10,300	21,000	34,000
Touring-4P	2575	4700	6100	9900	19,000	33,000
Sport-4P	—	4900	6300	10,300	21,000	34,000
Roadster-2/4P	—	4500	5800	9500	18,000	32,000
Cabriolet	—	4300	5400	8700	16,500	30,000
Town Car	—	3900	4800	7700	14,300	27,000
Touring Sedan	—	2300	3300	4600	7500	16,000
Standard Sedan	—	2200	3200	4400	7000	15,000
Model D-4-75 — 4-cyl., 75 hp, 128" wb						
Touring-4P	2950	5300	7000	11,500	24,000	37,000
Touring-7P	2950	5400	7300	11,800	25,000	38,000

1920 ROAMER
Model C-6-54 — 6-cyl., 54 hp, 128 1/4" wb

Tourer-4P	2750	4700	6100	9900	19,000	33,000
Sport-4P	2875	4900	6300	10,300	21,000	34,000
Roadster-2/4P	2875	4500	5800	9500	18,000	32,000
Roadster-2P	2850	4400	5600	9200	17,300	31,000
Touring-7P	2950	5000	6500	11,000	22,000	35,000
Cabriolet-3P	3550	4300	5400	8700	16,500	30,000

1920 Roamer, model C-6-54, sedan, HAC

	FP	5	4	3	2	1
Coupe-4P	3750	3300	4400	6700	12,000	24,000
Sedan-5P	3950	3000	4000	6000	9500	21,000
Sedan-7P	3950	3100	4200	6300	10,500	22,000
Town Car-7P	3950	3500	4500	7000	13,000	25,000

1921 Roamer, touring, JAC

1921 ROAMER
Model C-6-54 — 6-cyl., 54 hp, 130" wb

Touring-4P	3250	4900	6300	10,300	21,000	34,000
Roadster-4P	3375	4700	6100	9900	19,000	33,000
Sport-4P	3375	5000	6500	11,000	22,000	35,000
Touring-7P	3450	5200	6800	11,300	23,000	36,000
Speedster-2P	3450	6000	8500	13,000	30,000	42,000
Coupe-4P	4250	3300	4400	6700	12,000	24,000
Sedan-5P	4400	3000	4000	6000	9500	21,000
Town Car-5P	4500	3500	4500	7000	13,000	25,000
Suburban Sedan-7P	4500	3500	4500	7000	13,000	25,000
Model D-4-75 — 4-cyl., 80 hp, 130" wb						
Roadster-4P	4375	5300	7000	11,500	24,000	37,000
Sport-4P	4375	5400	7300	11,800	25,000	38,000
Touring-7P	4475	5800	8000	12,500	28,000	40,000
Speedster-2P	4475	6300	9000	14,000	32,000	44,000

1922 Roamer, sport sedan, JAC

1922 ROAMER
Model 6-45-E — 6-cyl., 54 hp, 128" wb

Touring-5P	2485	4900	6300	10,300	21,000	34,000
Touring-7P	2750	5000	6500	11,000	22,000	35,000
Cabriolet-3P	3650	4300	5400	8700	16,500	30,000
Coupe-5P	3850	3100	4200	6300	10,500	22,000
Sport-4P	2650	5200	6800	11,300	23,000	36,000
Sedan-5P	3950	2300	3300	4600	7500	16,000
Sedan-7P	4250	2400	3400	4800	8000	17,000

Model 4-75-E — 4-cyl., 75 hp, 128" wb

	FP	5	4	3	2	1
Touring-4P	3650	5000	6500	11,000	22,000	35,000
Sport-4P	3785	5300	7000	11,500	24,000	37,000
Roadster-4P	3850	4900	6300	10,300	21,000	34,000
Speedster-2P	3985	5800	8000	12,500	28,000	40,000
Sedan-4P	4750	2300	3300	4600	7500	16,000

1923 Roamer, sedan, JAC

1923 ROAMER
Model 6-54 — 6-cyl., 54 hp, 128" & 138" wb

	FP	5	4	3	2	1
Touring-4P	2275	4700	6100	9900	19,000	33,000
Standard Touring-4P	2485	4500	5800	9500	18,000	32,000
Roadster-2/4P	2685	4400	5600	9200	17,300	31,000
Sport-4P	2750	4900	6300	10,300	21,000	34,000
Cabriolet-3P	3285	4300	5400	8700	16,500	30,000
Coupe-5P	3585	3100	4200	6300	10,500	22,000
Sedan-5P	3585	2900	3700	5600	9100	20,000
Sedan-7P	3950	3000	4000	6000	9500	21,000

1924 Roamer, model 6-54, sport tourer, HAC

1924 ROAMER
Model 6-54 — 6-cyl., 54 hp, 128" wb

Touring-4P	2485	4300	5400	8700	16,500	30,000
Touring-7P	2685	4400	5600	9200	17,300	31,000
Roadster-2/4P	2685	4300	5400	8700	16,500	30,000
Sport-4P	2750	4500	5800	9500	18,000	32,000
Cabriolet-3P	3250	4200	5200	8400	15,700	29,000
Sedan-5P	3585	2000	3000	4200	6500	14,000

Note: Model 4-75 continued as year previous.

1925 ROAMER
Model 8-88 — 8-cyl., 88 hp, 134" wb

Touring-5P	2485	4400	5600	9200	17,300	31,000
Sport-4P	2750	4700	6100	9900	19,000	33,000
Touring-7P	2685	4500	5800	9500	18,000	32,000
Roadster-2/4P	2685	4400	5600	9200	17,300	31,000
Cabriolet-3P	3250	4300	5400	8700	16,500	30,000
Sedan-5P	3485	2200	3200	4400	7000	15,000
Special Sport Sedan-5P	3985	2300	3300	4600	7500	16,000

1926 Roamer, model 8-88, sedan, HAC

1926 Roamer, model 8-88, sport touring, HAC

1926 ROAMER
Model 8-88 — 8-cyl., 80 hp, 132" wb

	FP	5	4	3	2	1
Tourer-5P	2495	4400	5600	9200	17,300	31,000
Sport-5P	2750	4500	5800	9500	18,000	32,000
Tourer-7P	2585	4700	6100	9900	19,000	33,000
Roadster-2/4P	2750	4500	5800	9500	18,000	32,000
Cabriolet-3P	2950	4300	5400	8700	16,500	30,000
Special Sedan-5P	3785	2000	3000	4200	6500	14,000
Regular Sedan-5P	2785	1800	2800	4000	6200	13,000
Speedster-2P	2985	5300	7000	11,500	24,000	37,000
Brougham-5P	2985	2300	3300	4600	7500	16,000

Model 6-50 — 6-cyl., 50 hp, 115" wb

Touring-5P	1295	3700	4700	7300	13,700	26,000

1927 Roamer, model 8-80, club sedan, HAC

1927 ROAMER
Model 8-80 — 8-cyl., 80 hp, 126" wb

Sedan-5P	1985	2000	3000	4200	6500	14,000
Coupe-2P	1985	2300	3300	4600	7500	16,000
Roadster-2P	1895	4300	5400	8700	16,500	30,000
Brougham-4P	1985	2300	3300	4600	7500	16,000

Model 8-88 — 8-cyl., 88 hp, 132" wb

Tourer-5P	2495	4500	5800	9500	18,000	32,000
Sport Tourer-5P	2750	4900	6300	10,300	21,000	34,000
Roadster-3P	2750	4500	5800	9500	18,000	32,000
Tourer-7P	2585	4700	6100	9900	19,000	33,000
Cabriolet-3P	2950	4300	5400	8700	16,500	30,000
Special Sedan-5P	3485	2300	3300	4600	7500	16,000
Speedster-2P	2985	5300	7000	11,500	24,000	37,000
Sedan-7P	3285	2200	3200	4400	7000	15,000
Brougham-5P	2895	2300	3300	4600	7500	16,000
Sedan-5P	2985	2000	3000	4200	6500	14,000

1928 Roamer, model 8-88, sedan, HAC

1928 ROAMER
Model 8-88 — 8-cyl., 88 hp, 136" wb

Sedan-5P	2985	2000	3000	4200	6500	14,000

	FP	5	4	3	2	1
Sedan-7P	3285	2200	3200	4400	7000	15,000
Speedster-2P	2985	5300	7000	11,500	24,000	37,000
Tourer-5P	2495	4500	5800	9500	18,000	32,000
Sport Tourer-5P	2750	4900	6300	10,300	21,000	34,000
Roadster-2/4P	2985	4500	5800	9500	18,000	32,000

1929 Roamer, model 8-88, special sport, HAC

1929-1930 ROAMER
Model 8-88 — 8-cyl., 88 hp, 136" wb

	FP	5	4	3	2	1
Sedan-5P	2985	2200	3200	4400	7000	15,000
Sedan-7P	3285	2300	3300	4600	7500	16,000
Speedster-2P	2985	5400	7300	11,800	25,000	38,000
Tourer-5P	2495	4700	6100	9900	19,000	33,000
Sport Tourer-5P	2750	5000	6500	11,000	22,000	35,000
Roadster-2/4P	2985	4700	6100	9900	19,000	33,000

ROBB — St. Louis, Missouri — (1901) — Dr. Malcolm Robb built an automobile in St. Louis in 1901 which had the interesting feature of a front axle made entirely of wood, including the steering knuckles with their bronze sockets. A single-cylinder De Dion gasoline engine powered the car, and final drive was by double chain. The chains had a habit of jumping off their sprockets, unfortunately, which was no doubt the reason that, after a couple years of use, Dr. Robb sold the car. He is not known to have built another. The Robb had cost him $700 to build.

1914 Robe, cyclecar, WLB

ROBE — Portsmouth, Ohio — (1914-1915) — W.B. Robe's first venture into the automotive industry was a cyclecar which he announced to the automotive press late in 1913. Having experimented for the three years past and having built a total of three prototypes thus far, he was now ready for the market. He organized as W.B. Robe & Company. The Robe was powered by a four-cylinder 70.8-cubic-inch water-cooled engine which was set in a 100-inch wheelbase chassis with shaft drive and two-speed sliding gear transmission. The car's tread was 46 inches, though a 56-inch standard tread was offered as an option. The price was $325 for the two-passenger side-by-side roadster, with a deluxe model (which included electric starting) at $375. Full crown fenders were fitted, as was a long running board. Fuel economy was said to be 50 to 70 mpg, which was undoubtedly an exaggeration, but the Robe was otherwise a commendable car, though it failed quickly as all cyclecars did. W.B. Robe returned to the automobile industry with another car bearing his name less than a decade later.

1914-1915 ROBE
Cyclecar — 4-cyl., 100" wb

	FP	5	4	3	2	1
Stnd. Rdstr.	325	2000	3000	4200	6500	14,000
Four-Door Torpedo Rdstr.	375	2200	3200	4400	7000	15,000

ROBE — Nansemond, Virginia — (1923) — The financing for W.B. Robe's second automotive venture was provided by J.D. Stone, president of a Virginia real estate firm, and a factory for its manufacture was secured in Nansemond between Norfolk and Suffolk. Although the car was announced to the press as a light six to be sold for $895, it appears that the handful of cars which resulted were all fours. Stock in the company was sold, and the Robe prototype was taken to a corn field near Portsmouth for a demonstration of its riding qualities in rough terrain. The Robe's suspension consisted of a single long leaf spring on each side of the car to which the axles were attached, a throwback to the turn-of-the-century designs of small runabouts like the curved dash Oldsmobile. Model T

1923 Robe, 5-pass. touring, WLB

Ford valves were used in the Robe's aluminum four-cylinder engine, and the rear axle of the prototype was also purloined from Model T. Three more Robe cars may have been built, but manufacture was never begun. The Robe Motor Corporation died aborning.

ROBERTS STEAM — Providence, Rhode Island — (1884) — J.H. Roberts, who was described as a well-known manufacturer in Providence, built a steam automobile in 1884. "During its career, Mr. Roberts' steam wagon proved that mechanical traction was feasible," reported *The Motor Vehicle Review* in 1900, "but at that time the public was not interested in the use of steam power on highways and for that reason the inventor did not perfect his vehicle."

ROBERTS — Columbus, Ohio — (1904) — The tenure of O.G. Roberts as a manufacturer was brief and, although he may have built an automobile in 1904, only a gasoline truck has been documented with certainty. Roberts remained in the automobile business after 1904, building a fine cement garage on Gay Street in Columbus, establishing a local agency for Ford, Overland and Stoddard-Dayton, and formally incorporating his O.G. Roberts Company in 1916.

ROBERTS — Sandusky, Ohio — (1915) — The Roberts Motor Manufacturing Company was organized in Clyde, Ohio in 1905 and moved to Sandusky in 1908, locating its new factory at the corner of Columbus Avenue and the B. & O. Railroad. The company was among the early manufacturers of aviation engines, but marine and automotive powerplants ranging from 3 hp to 60 hp accounted for most of its business. In 1915 Roberts president William H. Burke announced the Roberts automobile, powered by the company's six-cylinder 60 hp engine. The car survived one season only. Roberts remained in the engine-building field for a number of years thereafter.

1897 Roberts Electric, runabout, GR

ROBERTS ELECTRIC — Chicago, Illinois — (1897) — The Roberts Electric was a handsome stanhope built by C.E. Roberts, later president of the Chicago Steel Screw Company, in 1897. Power was generated by two 60-volt motors, each driving one rear wheel. Using both motors provided three speeds forward, the left motor only provided three speeds in reverse. The car's cruising speed was 20 mph, its cruising range 40 miles between charges. Though C.E. Roberts may have built other electrics prior to the turn of the century, only one is known to exist. In 1960 it was referred to as "the oldest operating electric automobile in the United States."

ROBERTSON — G.W. Robertson of Mt. Vernon, Indiana was among the hopefuls who entered the Chicago Times-Herald Contest of 1895 with an automobile of his own design. He was also among the many who did not make it to the starting line. Whether he ever completed his car is not known.

Lew Robertson of Ames, Iowa built a steam runabout for his own use in 1909. Kerosene was used as fuel, and the engine was secured directly to the rear axle. The car's weight was 1400 pounds.

ROBERTSON — **San Antonio, Texas** — **(1921)** — Capitalists from both Mexico and Texas were said to be behind the financing of the Robertson Company of San Antonio, but they weren't behind it for long. The Robertson car was announced during the summer of 1921 as having been "especially worked out for pulling on mountains, sand, rock and mud roads." It carried a four-cylinder 192.4-cubic-inch Herschell-Spillman engine rated at 35.5 hp and fitted into a 115-inch wheelbase chassis. Prototypes were built, but conclusive evidence of subsequent manufacture is wanting.

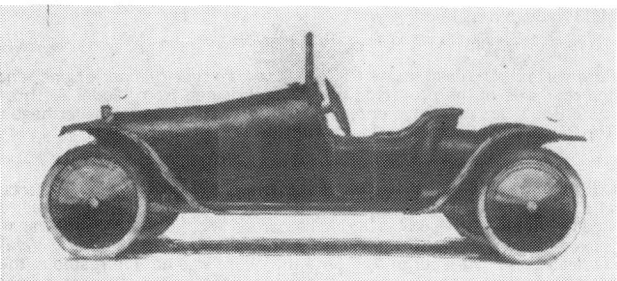

1914 Robie, 2-pass. staggered seat roadster, WLB

ROBIE — **Chicago, Illinois** — **(1914)** — Fred G. Robie was a Chicagoan who designed one of the raciest cyclecars on the market. It had swoopy fenders and disc wheels, and a frontal aspect that looked mean and race-car-like. Actually, there were two Robies. The first was introduced in January of 1914 and was fitted with a two-cylinder air-cooled engine. Its wheelbase was 108 inches, its tread 36 inches, and its seating a two-passenger tandem. It was built for the Robie Motor Car Company by Massnick-Phipps Manufacturing Company in Detroit. Fred Robie wasn't satisfied with the car, however, and that summer came up with another. Its engine was a water-cooled four, its wheelbase 102 inches, its tread 44 inches, and its seating two-passenger staggered. The swoopy fenders and disc wheels remained, as did the $450 price tag and the promise of 45 mph and 45 mpg. Robie planned to have his second generation cyclecar built for him by Pullman in York, Pennsylvania, but the negotiations fell through — and then his money ran out. For the decade previous to his cyclecar adventure, Robie had been in the automobile accessory business in Chicago and it was probably to that field that he returned.

ROBINSON — The Robinson Motor Car Company of Galesburg, Illinois has been indicated on car rosters as an automobile producer in 1910. Documentation is lacking.

The Robinson Motor Car Construction Company was organized in Detroit, Michigan during the spring of 1919 with a capital stock of $20,000 for the manufacture of automobiles, parts and accessories. Incorporators were M.M. Robinson, C.C. Currie and William Elsey. Manufacture of a car is doubted.

1900 Robinson, style A, runabout, HAC

ROBINSON — **Hyde Park Massachusetts** — **(1900-1902)** — The Bramwell-Robinson automotive partnership broke up during 1900, and in May that year John T. Robinson set up shop himself in Hyde Park as the Robinson Motor Vehicle Company. Initially, his new Robinson cars were Bramwell-Robinson like, but within a year he had come up with a 16 hp four sporting Upton two-speed transmission, double chain drive, a steering

1901 Robinson, four cylinder tonneau, HAC

1902 Robinson, touring, NAHC

wheel and a sprightly look. *The Automobile* commented that this new Robinson was "a far cry from the antiquated and ponderous vehicle exhibited last year." In the New York-Buffalo Endurance Run it secured a first-class certificate, carrying four passengers and 175 pounds of luggage at an average speed of 13.63 mph. This four-cylinder car was priced at $3500, though Robinson also continued the predecessor two-cylinder car at $1500 for victoria stanhope and $1400 for open stanhope. But none of these cars was marketed for long. By the spring of 1902 John Robinson had found another partner, Edward W. Pope, nephew to Colonel Albert A. Pope, who added Robinson's automobile to the burgeoning Pope empire.

ROBINSON — **Los Angeles, California** — **(1914)** — Chalis Robinson was a Los Angeles high school student who built a cyclecar which, *The American Cyclecar* noted approvingly, embodied "several unique ideas found in the larger machines." A three-wheeler, it was steered from the single rear wheel, with the power transmitted by direct drive to one front wheel only. Robinson claimed a top speed of 35 mph.

1909 Robson, runabout, NAHC

ROBSON — **Galesburg, Illinois** — **(1909)** — From 1905 through 1907 the Western Tool Works in Galesburg manufactured the Gale automobile. The exact reason for the financial failure of the company is not known, though there are two versions. The official one was the Panic of '07. Unofficially, according to D.W. Cook who had designed the Gale car, "a couple of the big boys in the Western Tool Works company had a little trouble keeping their money separated from the company's, and one day awoke to the fact that they were not only broke, but deep in debt, with not much chance of getting well." (This version was provided in an interview with Cook published in the February 19th, 1949 edition of *The Daily Register* of Galesburg.) Whatever the reason, Percy Robson of Western Tool, who had been the man responsible for bringing the Gale to Galesburg, reorganized the following year as the E.P. Robson Manufacturing Company, and brought back the Gale as the Robson, including a four-cylinder model which had been in the experimental stages when Gale production had been halted. Although the car was announced to the trade press as the Robson, no Robson brochures ever were published. The car was simply made up of Gale parts on hand, and conceivably not even a new radiator badge was fitted. When the parts were used up, the Gale-cum-Robson was finished. Subsequent city directories indicate the Robson Manufacturing Company as a machine shop specializing in the manufacture of spring starters and Robson emery grinders.

1909 ROBSON
1-cyl., 8/10 hp, 73" wb

	FP	5	4	3	2	1
Model C Runabout-2P	600	1800	2800	4000	6200	13,000
2-cyl., 30/32 hp, 95" wb						
Model K-09 Touring-5P	1250	2200	3200	4400	7000	15,000
Model G-S Runabout-2P	1000	2000	3000	4200	6500	14,000
4-cyl., 40/45 hp, 112" wb						
Model R Touring-5P	2250	4000	5000	8000	15,000	28,000

ROBY — That George L. Roby of Albion, Michigan built an automobile in 1899 has been indicated on various car rosters. Documentation is lacking.

1925 Roche, touring, WJL

ROCHE — Los Angeles, California — (1924-1925) — Front wheel drive and engine design were Clifton Roche's preoccupations, and he held a number of patents in both areas by the mid-Thirties. His first patent was issued in November 1924, at which time Roche was in Detroit. Arriving in Los Angeles in 1925 he vainly attempted to promote manufacture of the car prototype he had built. In addition to front wheel drive, the Roche car featured a two-stroke V-8 engine, for which he filed for patent in February of 1925, the patent being granted in 1929. By that time, Clifton Roche had given up on the idea of manufacturing. The mid-Twenties in Los Angeles was hardly the propitious time and place to promote a new venture. In addition to a wide variety of bunko artists operating in the area, California was also enduring the most formidable Ku Klux Klan uprisings in history, a vigorous crackdown on illegal liquor traffic and the worst ever epidemic of hoof and mouth disease. No one was interested in Clifton Roche's interesting automobile ideas.

ROCHELLE — The Rochelle Motor Company was organized during the spring of 1906 with a capital stock of $150,000 for the manufacture of automobiles in New Rochelle, New York. Incorporators were E.T. Birdsall, E.S. Winslow, G.W. Vaughn, George Moore and Edgar K. Bourne. Within a month this venture was being referred to as the Birdsall Automobile Company the product of which was to be a six-cylinder touring car. Manufacture is doubted.

ROCHESTER — The Rochester Electric Motor Company of Rochester, New York was indicated as an automobile manufacturer in the Hiscox book *Horseless Vehicles, Automobiles, Motor Cycles* published in 1900. Documentation is lacking.

The Rochester Motors Company promoted the Service cyclecar in Rochester, New York in 1914. Refer to Service.

The Rochester Steam Motor Works was incorporated in Rochester, New York during the spring of 1901 with a capital stock of $100,000 for the manufacture of automobile. Directors were F.W. Zimmer, W.T. Fox and G.B. Watkins, all of Rochester. Manufacture is doubted.

The Rochester Timer Company was organized in Rochester, New York during the spring of 1908 with a capital stock of $20,000 for the manufacture of motorcars. Incorporators were Emil Broeker, C.W. Hall and F.W. Hodgkinson. Manufacture is doubted.

ROCHESTER — Rochester, New York — (1901-1902) — The Rochester Gasoline Carriage & Motor Company opened for business in leased quarters at 55 South Avenue in Rochester early in 1901, announcing a forthcoming production of both steam and gasoline cars and guaranteeing delivery within five days of receiving an order. H.E. De Loura was Rochester's manager, and he tended to brag a lot. The gasoline engine used in the Rochester was of De Loura's design, "non-vibrating . . . one of the specialties of the firm," its inventor said. Whether De Loura also designed Rochester's steam engine is not known, but the Wagner Manufacturing Company (which also supplied the Foster) is documented to have served De Loura his running gear. The Rochester steamer was a simple runabout with a two-cylinder engine which was priced at $600 with fourteen-inch

1902 Rochester steam runabout, (Rochester Gasoline), NAHC

boiler and spindle seat, $700 with sixteen-inch boiler and full back seat. Several Rochesters were built for a company operating a taxi transportation service between Buffalo and Niagara Falls, but when *The Motor Age* advised during the summer of 1901 that the company "seems to be doing a fair business," it must have been only because H.E. De Loura said so. In 1902 he closed up shop in Rochester — which now was 157 State Street and headed west to try again in Iowa under his own name.

1901 Rochester, steam runabout, (Rochester Cycle), NAHC

ROCHESTER STEAM — Rochester, New York — (1901) — The Rochester Cycle Manufacturing Company launched itself into the steam car business early in 1901 with a light runabout priced at $750 and fitted with a vertical two-cylinder engine. A thousand-dollar surrey was added to the line that summer and was described as one of the handsomest vehicles in the city. Single chain drive and tiller steering were featured in both models, though the latter was revised into a steering handle later that year which, it was said at the time, "eliminates entirely the vibration attendant upon the [former] device." Driving comfort was a principal Rochester requisite. Full elliptic springs were provided at the rear, with a single transverse elliptic up front. It was claimed that either of the front wheels could take a fifteen-inch vertical movement without jarring the passenger compartment appreciably. The Rochester Cycle Manufacturing Company, which was located at 108 Exchange Street, does not seem to have survived in the automobile business into 1902.

ROCHESTER SPECIAL — Rochester, New York — (1910) — The Rochester Special was a large car (75 hp Herschell-Spillman six-cylinder engine, 40-inch wheels) which was built locally and exhibited at the February 1910 Rochester Automobile Show by C.P. Smith & Company, Rochester automotive dealers. It was the only Rochester-built car on display that year, and C.P. Smith was reported to have been "considering the building of a very large number of these cars this year." More than likely, only a few cars were built — and the Rochester Special was not continued into 1911.

ROCKAWAY — Rockaway, New York — (1902-1903) — Alexander Mohler was a native of Mechanicsburg, Pennsylvania who went to Mexico City to build a car in 1896. Precisely why he chose Mexico is not known, but he did find a partner there named W.A. DeGress. Doubtless theirs was one of the first automobiles built south of the border, though Mohler and DeGress did not remain in Mexico long. Around the turn of the century, after building two further automobiles there, they headed north, settling in the Astoria section of Queens in New York City. They brought one of the Mexican-built cars with them, but there is no evidence that any subse-

1257

1902 Rockaway, runabout, NAHC

quent vehicles were marketed under the name of Mohler & DeGress. The principal activity of the partners initially was engine building. In 1902, however, they began manufacture of a light runabout. Its name derived from the beach town of Rockaway on Long Island where the partners set themselves up for car production. The Rockaway car was powered by a single or double-cylinder water-cooled engine, with shaft drive and wheel steering, and was available in several styles. It was marketed for the partners by Charles D. Shain in New York City, who sometimes arbitrarily gave his own name to the car, and who even more arbitrarily raised its price from $650 to $1500 in 1903. Mohler and DeGress discontinued the car's manufacture by the end of that year, and in 1904 commenced production of automotive parts and accessories. Late in 1905 they sold their business to F.A. Seitz.

1902 ROCKAWAY

	FP	5	4	3	2	1
Style A Rbt. (1-cyl., 5 hp, 66″ wb)	650	1600	2700	3800	5800	12,000
Style B Rbt. (1-cyl., 8 hp, 72″ wb)	—	1700	2800	3900	6000	12,500
Style B-1 Vic. (1-cyl., 8 hp, 72″ wb)	—	1800	2800	4000	6200	13,000
Style C Rbt. (2-cyl., 16 hp, 72″ wb)	—	2000	3000	4200	6500	14,000
Style C-1 Detachable Tonneau (2-cyl., 16 hp, 72″ wb)	—	2100	3100	4300	6800	14,500

1903 Rockaway, runabout, NAHC

1903 ROCKAWAY

One-cylinder Runabout-2P	1500	1800	2800	4000	6200	13,000
Two-cylinder Runabout-4P	1500	2000	3000	4200	6500	14,000

ROCKAWAY — Rockaway, New Jersey — (1903-1904) — The Rockaway from New Jersey was built by the Rockaway Automobile Company in that city. Although occasional references indicate it having been built at the turn of the century, it would appear that the few cars produced were put together beginning in early 1903 when the company was incorporated. They were quite primeval vehicles, powered by single-cylinder four-stroke marine engines and with final drive by single chain. "Simplicity, Durability, Reliability, Accessibility," the ads said. "Why Walk?" The cars were priced at $650 in 1903 and $700 in 1904. In later years, Russell T. Westbrook, who owned one of the cars, and C.W. Kelsey, who was a car manufacturer himself, recalled that these Rockaways were called Ramblers. Although references contemporary to the 1903-1904 period do not confirm this, it is possible that the cars might have been nicknamed or unofficially called Ramblers simply to distinguish them from the Rockaways being built in

1903 Rockaway, runabout, MVMA

New York. Any confusion was short-lived, however. Later in 1904 the Rockaway Automobile Company switched its focus to the manufacture of starting devises for gasoline automobiles. One of these was an undescribed electric starter, which doubtless didn't work well. The other was a spring starter, which was described as being "thrown into operation by a small pedal, and after starting the engines is automatically rewound by the end, and when fully wound is automatically disengaged." One cannot imagine it working well either.

ROCK CREEK — Washington, D.C. — (1907-1908) — Early in 1907 the Rock Creek Auto & Wagon Works at 2613 Pennsylvania Avenue in Washington announced its intention to build a number of "strong runabout cars" using two-cylinder 18/20 hp engines. A limited production followed. When receivership was declared in August 1908, Rock Creek's assets were indicated as $26,000, its liabilities as $16,000.

ROCKET — Rocket was the designation given by James Scripps-Booth to the tandem two-seater cyclecar he produced in Detroit in 1914. Refer to Scripps-Booth.

ROCKET — Los Angeles, California — (1903) — The Rocket was a four-cylinder four-stroke 24 hp touring car built in 1903 and planned to be produced by Samuel D. Sturgis and his brother William. Though this venture seems to have ended at the prototype stage, the Sturgis brothers, in association with James Philip Erie, do have the distinction of building one of California's early pioneer cars, the Erie & Sturgis of 1895.

1919 Rock Falls, 142, 4-dr. sedan, NAHC

ROCK FALLS — Sterling, Illinois — (1919-1925) — The Rock Falls Manufacturing Company of Sterling had been in the business of building custom bodies since 1878. Most of these bodies were of the large enclosed type, and what they enclosed most frequently was a coffin. Rock Falls was a big name in the funeral industry. Motorized hearses were built beginning in 1909. A decade later Rock Falls president E.G. Brookfield decided to make available an automobile for live passengers, and chief engineer W.H. Thomas ran one up for him. It was introduced that spring at $3650. An assembled car on a 135-inch wheelbase, the Rock Falls used standard components throughout (including 52 hp Buda six-cylinder engine) and boasted one unusual feature. Its gasoline tank was mounted at the side of the chassis under the left frame rail, with filler cap and gas gauge protruding through the floorboard under the driver's feet. This feature does not appear to have survived into the Twenties. Subsequent Rock Falls were produced largely for the funeral industry, though a few of the approximately fifty units manufactured annually were offered as large limousines or sedans. Prices now were in the $4800-$5000 range, the wheelbase was 136 inches and the engine was a Continental 9A 73 hp six. Prices decreased to $4600 later during the Twenties, with a concomitant decrease in wheelbase to 132 inches and the fitting of a 6T Continental 70 hp six. The company failed during 1925.

ROCKFORD — Rockford, Illinois — (1901) — In 1901 a group of Rockford businessmen were approached by two Chicagoans, R.K. Swift and

M.H. Detrick, and were persuaded to back them in the $100,000 incorporation of the Rockford Automobile Company. Swift and Detrick had built at least one experimental car in the Windy City, but it does not appear any manufacture followed in Rockford. This 1901 effort is not to be confused, incidentally, with the prototype built in 1903 by J.J. Cole and his son which they planned to introduce under the Rockford name. That car didn't go into production either, though the Coles remained in Rockford as automobile dealers. Swift and Detrick probably returned to Chicago.

ROCKFORD — Rockford, Illinois — (1908) — The Rockford of 1908 had been the Federal of 1907 and would be a Federal again in 1909. A typical high-wheeled motor buggy, its new name followed the move of the Federal Automobile Company of Chicago to Rockford where it was reincorporated as the Rockford Automobile & Engine Company. By 1909 the Rockford was in financial trouble in Rockford, and the entire venture moved again, to Elkhart, Indiana, where the car enjoyed its last days as a Federal.

ROCKLIFF — Brooklyn, New York — (1901) — In 1901 Charles Rockliff of Brooklyn built a gasoline-powered surrey and invited several members of the Long Island Automobile Club to accompany him on a Sunday outing from Rockville Center to Long Beach. The idea of the excursion was, according to *The Motor Vehicle Review*, "to show local residents . . . that he has a motor vehicle suited to the needs of those who are planning to operate stage lines." Then he had another idea: building trucks. This he began in 1902 and continued through 1906. Among his clients were New York City department stores and the Brooklyn Rapid Transit Company which bought a trolley repair wagon. He did not, however, enter into manufacture of pleasure vehicles under his own name, although the Long Island Motor Company which he managed at 32 Hanson Place in Brooklyn did produce a few Long Island automobiles. The Rockliff trucks emanated from 446 Hudson Avenue in Brooklyn.

ROCK HILL — Rock Hill, South Carolina — (1910) — The Rock Hill was John Gary Anderson's first attempt as an automobile manufacturer, and it did not survive the prototype stage. The prototype itself was a four-cylinder 35 hp Norwalk built by the company of that same name in the city of that same name in Ohio. As Arthur E. Skadden, president of the Norwalk Motor Company, explained, "we make most of the car and you finish it, then badge and sell it under whatever name suits you." The name that suited Anderson was the same as that of his successful Rock Hill Buggy Company. Anderson planned to sell his Norwalk-cum-Rock Hill for $1600, as a toy tonneau only with the option of either a 56- or 60-inch tread. (Many manufacturers of that era offered cars with choice of tread, the wider of the two being favored in rural areas where farm tractor and hay wagon ruts were sixty or more inches apart.) In addition to all Rock Hill specs matching the Norwalk, so did the catalog printer's cut on the single piece of promotion Anderson produced for his automotive venture. Very quickly he decided that the automobile was not for him, and returned to carriage work exclusively. In 1913, however, Anderson established the Rock Hill Body Company to manufacture coachwork for commercial automotive vehicles. And in 1916 he tried the automotive industry once again, and considerably more successfully, with the Anderson car.

ROCKNE — Detroit, Michigan — (1932-1933) — In late March of 1931 Albert Erskine announced that his longtime friend Knute Rockne had been appointed sales promotion manager of Studebaker Corporation though it was emphasized that his new position would not interfere with his duties on the football field at Notre Dame. On the last day of that month Knute Rockne was killed in a plane crash. Clearly, the plan had been for the football coach to lend little more than his name and occasional presence to the product which would be built and marketed by Rockne Motors Corporation in Detroit. Now the Rockne automobile would serve as a memorial to him. Its practical purpose was to provide Studebaker its second attempt (the first was the Erskine) to crack the low-priced field. The Rockne engine was an L-head Studebaker-built six offered in two sizes initially (190 and 205 cubic inches, delivering 66 and 72 bhp at 3200 rpm) as well as two wheelbase lengths. Unlike the overpriced Erskine, the Rockne was tagged more competitively in the $600 range. But like the Erskine, it collided with a new car from Ford which outperformed and undersold it, and had two more cylinders besides. The Rockne was introduced in February of 1932, and on Easter weekend of 1933 the Rockne plant in Detroit was closed down. What could be used in South Bend was transferred there, including the Rockne engine which was continued in the Studebaker Dictator for the years following. Total Rockne production was 23,201 units.

1932 Rockne, model 65, 5-pass. coach, AA

1932 ROCKNE
Model 65 — 6-cyl., 66 hp, 110" wb

	FP	5	4	3	2	1
Coupe-2P	585	1100	2200	3200	4900	9000
Sedan-5P	635	1000	2000	3000	4600	8000
Sedan-2 dr.	595	1000	1900	2900	4400	7500
Convertible Sedan-5P	695	3300	4400	6700	12,000	24,000
Roadster	695	4200	5200	88400	15,700	29,000

1932 Rockne, model 75, convertible sedan, AA

Model 75 — 6-cyl., 72 hp, 114" wb

Coupe-2P	685	1200	2300	3300	5100	9500
Coupe-4P	720	1300	2350	3400	5200	9700
Sedan-5P	735	1000	2100	3100	4800	8500
Deluxe Coupe-2P	730	1300	2350	3400	5200	9700
Deluxe Coupe-4P	765	1350	2400	3450	5250	9900
Deluxe Sedan-5P	780	1050	2150	3150	4850	8700
Roadster	775	4400	5600	9200	17,300	31,000
Convertible Sedan	795	4300	5400	8700	16,500	30,000

1933 Rockne, Deluxe, convertible roadster, AA

1933 ROCKNE
Six — 70 hp, 110" wb

Convertible-4P	675	3100	4200	6300	10,500	22,000
Deluxe Conv. Rdstr.-4P	720	3300	4400	6700	12,000	24,000
Coupe-2P	585	1400	2400	3500	5300	10,000
Coach-5P	595	1000	1900	2900	4400	7500
Coupe-4P	620	1450	2450	3600	5400	10,500
Deluxe Coupe-2P	630	1500	2500	3600	5500	11,000
Sedan-5P	635	1000	2000	3000	4600	8000
Deluxe Coach-5P	640	1000	2000	3000	4600	8000
Deluxe Coupe-4P	665	1550	2600	3700	5700	11,500
Deluxe Sedan-5P	680	1000	2100	3100	4800	8500
Conv. Sed.-5P	695	3300	4400	6700	12,000	24,000
Deluxe Conv. Sed.-5P	740	3900	4800	7700	14,300	27,000

ROCKNEY — Portland, North Dakota — (1911) — In 1911 Bennette E. Rockney of Portland built himself a 30 hp runabout. So far as is known, this is the only vehicle he built.

ROCK RIVER — The Rock River Manufacturing Company was organized in Dixon, Illinois early in 1904 with a capital stock of $50,000 to "manufacture automobiles and automobile wheels and do a general foundry business." Manufacture of a car is doubted.

ROCKWELL — Bristol, Connecticut — (1910-1911) — The Rockwell was a taxi named for Albert F. Rockwell who, in association with Ernest R. Burwell, Charles T. Treadway, Ira Newcomb and T.H. Holdsworth, organized the Connecticut Cab Company early in 1910 for its manufacture. The car itself was designed by the Bristol Engineering Company, was built by the New Departure Manufacturing Company, and was generally regarded during the period as among the finest taxicabs in America. Fred Moskovics, of later Stutz fame, was a member of the Bristol Engineering team. New Departure, called "one of the foremost industrial enterprises of the Nutmeg State" by *Cycle and Automobile Trade Journal*, also manufactured the Houpt-Rockwell and Allen-Kingston cars. The handsome Rockwell landaulet taxicab was priced at $3000 and was powered by a four-cylinder four-stroke water-cooled 18/20 hp engine fitted into a 106-inch wheelbase chassis which featured a selective transmission and shaft drive. Two hundred of these Rockwell landaulets were in taxi service in New York City by late 1910, and the cars were successfully offered for general sale as well. Production continued into 1911, the Rockwell surviving about six months longer than the Houpt-Rockwell. In 1910 Albert Rockwell had been ousted from his position of power in both New Departure and Bristol. In 1914 he tried again with another taxi called the Mason-Seaman.

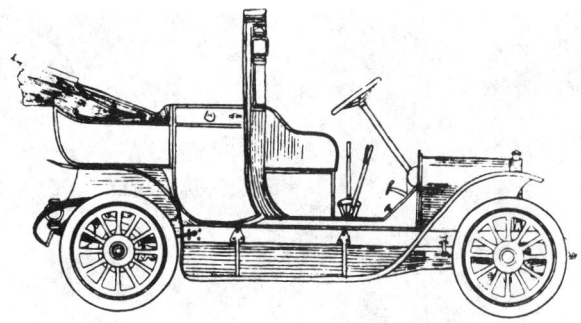

1909 Rockwell, landaulette, WLB

1909-1911 ROCKWELL
Four — 18/20 hp, 106" wb

	FP	5	4	3	2	1
Landaulet Taxi	3000	3300	4400	6700	12,000	24,000

ROCOIT — The Rocoit was a car that Carl Lipman of Beloit, Wisconsin planned to build in 1909. Refer to Lipman.

RODEFELD — **Richmond, Indiana** — **(1909-1917)** — Production was a total of about twenty-five, and it included cars and trucks. The Rodefeld was built by A.H. Rodefeld who had begun as a blacksmith in Richmond and who shortly after the turn of the century established one of the earliest automobile repair shops in eastern Indiana. Beginning in 1909 and with the assistance of his sons Gus and Bill, Rodefeld commenced the production of four-cylinder air-cooled touring cars and one-ton trucks. Chain drive was featured in both passenger and commercial vehicles. The Rodefelds produced the engines, transmissions and all other mechanical parts themselves, purchasing bodies, wheels, magnetos and spark plugs outside. All vehicles were built strictly to customer order. A family member later recalled one touring car in which the engine was installed sideways with the crank at the side. Most Rodefelds cranked in the front. Among the commercial vehicles produced was a panel truck with seats for about a dozen passengers that was ordered by the Wayne County Highway Department to transport county jail prisoners to their work on the chain gang. Vehicle production was discontinued around 1917, whereon the Rodefelds began manufacture of water pumps for Model T Fords, and in the mid-Twenties established a parts jobbing business which evolved into the Rodefeld Company, Inc., wholesale distributors of automotive parts and home appliances.

RODGERS — The cars built in 1903-1904 by Rodgers & Company of Columbus, Ohio were occasionally referred to as the Rodgers or the Columbus in the trade press. The company itself had selected the designation Imperial. Refer to Imperial.

RODGERS — **New York, New York** — **(1921)** — Little is known about the Scientific Automotive Corporation which produced the Rodgers save for the fact that it was organized and chartered in New York City in August of 1920 for $3 million. Likely as not, there was a man named Rodgers behind it. Rodgers the car was a 36 hp four on a 112-inch wheelbase which had a price of $1295 in touring car form. Given the New York City location of this venture, it seems probable that the Rodgers was intended principally for the export market. Although as late as March of 1923 *The Automobile Journal* was publishing the Rodgers specs in its roster of current passenger cars, there is no further documentation that the car was built that long.

RODIN — **San Francisco, California** — **(1910)** — This was not a vehicle built from the ground up, but rather a Mitchell rebuilt by C.F. Rodin in order to demonstrate the feasibility of his rather unique approach to rear suspension. He pronounced the result a sterling success. "The light wear on tires was a great surprise to everyone. It has run 1,500 miles since I rebuilt it, and the tires show scarcely any wear," he wrote the editors of *The Motor Age* in 1910. "The heavy upthrow, so annoying in the regular car, is entirely prevented in the tonneau of the car, with the four rear wheels. The skidding propensities have disappeared." This Rodin is the only one thought to have been built by this tinkerer from San Francisco.

ROEBLING-PLANCHE — **Trenton, New Jersey** — **(1909)** — The Roebling-Planche was the transition car between the Walter and the Mercer. Around 1906 Etienne Planche, a French automobile engineer who was a veteran of Peugeot, joined the Walter Automobile Company, and when that firm relocated from New York City to Trenton later that year, he moved with it. About this same time the monied Roebling family became interested in the automobile business and the Walter venture. By 1908 Planche was general manager of the Walter organization, and was moonlighting a lot. A small air-cooled four-cylinder motorcycle engine he designed was built by the Motor Car Specialty Company of Trenton beginning in the early fall of that

1909 Roebling Planche, touring, NAHC

year, and that October Washington A. Roebling announced his intention to produce ten examples of a four-cylinder car developing a whopping 140 hp which had been designed by Planche. Only one is known to have been built, however, and Roebling raced it at Spring Lake, New Jersey the following year. Also in 1908 it was announced that the Sharp Arrow car designed by William H. Sharp of Trenton would be built in the Walter factory too, and twenty-five cars ultimately were. By early 1909 the financial difficulties of William Walter resulted in his exit from the Walter Company, with the Roeblings taking over totally. The four-cylinder 50 hp car which had initially been announced as a Walter was renamed the Roebling-Planche. Trade press references indicate the brief existence of a Roebling-Planche Company, but it was never incorporated. Instead, in May of 1909, the Walter Automobile Company evolved into the Mercer Automobile Company. A few Roebling-Planches were subsequently built, including a smaller 20 hp landaulet, but that car was soon superseded by the new Mercer. Etienne Planche did not remain with Mercer long; by 1911 he had joined Louis Chevrolet (who also had briefly worked for Walter) to help him design the first Chevrolet car in Detroit, and in 1915 he became chief engineer of the Dort Motor Car Company. Meanwhile, back in Trenton, the Mercer became fabulously famous.

1909 ROEBLING-PLANCHE
Model P — 4-cyl., 20 hp, 104" wb

	FP	5	4	3	2	1
Landaulet-6P	3500	3300	4400	6700	12,000	24,000

Model M — 4-cyl., 50 hp, 122" wb

	FP	5	4	3	2	1
Touring-7P	5000	5000	6500	11,000	22,000	35,000
Cape Top Tour.-7P	5175	5200	6800	11,300	23,000	36,000
Runabout-4P	4500	4500	5800	9500	18,000	32,000

ROEBUCK — The Roebuck Automobile Company was organized in Brooklyn, New York late in 1903 with a capital stock of $5000 for the manufacture of automobiles. Incorporators were George E. Roebuck, S.H. Roebuck and William N. Payne, all of Brooklyn. Manufacture is doubted.

1895 Roger-Benz Petroleum Carriage, NAHC

ROGER-AMERICAN — **New York, New York** — **(1895-1896)** — In 1895 Emile Roger, who held the French agency for the German Benz, arrived in this country with three of his cars which he subsequently sold to Macy's, Gimbel's and Wanamaker's department stores. Macy's entered its vehicle in the Chicago Times-Herald Contest, where it performed admirably prior to colliding with a horsedrawn hack. Meanwhile, Emile Roger remained in New York trying to sell the idea of Benz production in the United States. The Roger American Mechanical Carriage Company was organized with offices at 80 Broadway in Manhattan, and W.P. Williams, an American engineer, was hired to revise the Benz to withstand the pounding of U.S. roads of the day. Single- and two-seated carriages, surreys, wagonettes, coupes and delivery wagons were the envisioned products, but only prototypes resulted. One of these was entered in the Cosmopolitan Race of 1896. In 1897 Emile Roger died, and his plans died with him.

ROGERS — H.A. Rogers of Oak Park, Illinois was indicated as the builder of a cyclecar in the March 1914 issue of *Motor Print*. Details are lacking.

The Rogers Automobile Company of Springfield, Massachusetts made trade press news only upon leaving the industry. In 1906 *The Motor World* announced a "petition for dissolution" of the company had been filed in Superior Court. There were no outstanding debts or liabilities. "The company set out to build cars," the magazine reported, "but failed to produce any."

The Rogers Locomotive Works was organized in Paterson, New Jersey late in 1900 with one Joseph Leiter purportedly at the helm and the promise to employ 5000 men in the construction of automobiles. As *The Motor Age* reported in early January, "The thought that strikes the observing person is that the company, whatever it is, has engaged an ingenious press agent." Manufacture is doubted.

The Rogers-Sargent Motor Company was organized in Philadelphia, Pennsylvania during the spring of 1916 with a capital stock of $25,000 for the manufacture of motor cars. Incorporators were Herbert E. Latter, Norman P. Coffin and Clement M. Egner. Manufacture is doubted.

1900 Rogers, runabout, NAHC

ROGERS — Boston, Massachusetts — (1899-1900) — W.S. Rogers was the manager of the Ball Bearing Company of Boston and an energetic member of the American Society of Mechanical Engineers. In 1899 he built a 3 hp gasoline runabout and produced a 23-page brochure extolling its virtues. The latter represented what was doubtless the only instance in American advertising in which a baby in a baby buggy was the only illustration on the front cover of an automobile catalog. The baby was Rogers' infant daughter Ruth, and her name appeared on the side of the car. The construction of the Rogers car was standard for the period, except for its crank-lever control which Rogers patented. This allowed the vehicle to be started with one turn of the crank, followed by a push of the operating handle to engage the transmission, with subsequent nudges increasing the car's speed to its maximum of 16 mph. The first Rogers was completed during July of 1899, but its inventor did not begin his promotional push until the following summer. At that time he boasted that his special driving mechanism rendered the Rogers out of harm's way of the Selden patent and he promised "nothing but profits to the investors and pleasure to the purchasers of these carriages." He also announced plans to form a company for their manufacture, but it does not appear he was ever able to do this. References to the building of the Rogers car in Beloit, Wisconsin as late as 1904 seem to be in error, or wishful thinking. Available documentation indicates that W.S. Rogers never left the East Coast. In 1901 he was in Keene, New Hampshire where his new car was the Steamobile.

1911 Rogers, model B-2, runabout, NAHC

ROGERS — Omaha, Nebraska — (1911-1912) — Ralph F. Rogers of Chicago didn't get around to designing a highwheeler until 1909. Later that year, with fellow Chicagoan C.A. Overholt, he organized the Rogers Motor Car Company with a capital stock of $25,000 to produce it. The firm was headquartered in Omaha, Nebraska, with factory in nearby Ralston. Lack of ready cash prevented the onset of manufacture of the air-cooled, friction-transmission, chain-drive Rogers buggy until the beginning of the 1911 model season. This provides Rogers the distinction of introducing

the last new make of highwheeler in America. The Rogers exited the automotive scene with the last of the highwheelers little more than a year later. Less than 500 cars had been built. Ralph Rogers subsequently returned to Chicago where he organized the Rogers Manufacturing Company during the summer of 1914 to manufacture and deal in "motor vehicles, motorcycles, accessories and parts." Only a dealership followed.

1911 ROGERS
Series B — 2-cyl., 18 hp, 90" wb

	FP	5	4	3	2	1
Model B-2 Runabout-2P	700	2300	3300	4600	7500	16,000
Model B-3 Roadster-3P	725	2400	3400	4800	8000	17,000
Model B-4 Surrey-4P	750	2700	3600	5300	8800	19,000

1912 ROGERS
Series C — 2-cyl., 18 hp, 90" wb

	FP	5	4	3	2	1
Model C-2 Runabout-2P	700	2300	3300	4600	7500	16,000
Model C-4 Surrey-4P	750	2700	3600	5300	8800	19,000

1902 Rogers & Hanford, surrey, NAHC

ROGERS & HANFORD — Cleveland, Ohio — (1899-1902) — George Hanford was the president of his freshman class at Case School of Applied Science in the 1890's and following his academic days he joined with Frank Rogers, also of Cleveland, to build the Rogers & Hanford car in 1899. It is believed to be the first four-cylinder rotary-engined car ever built. (The Adams Company of Dubuque produced a rotary in 1898, but it was a three-cylinder.) Subsequently the partners organized as the Rogers & Hanford Company, and in 1901 introduced their car to the market. Its engine was claimed to be "self-starting, reversible and perfectly balanced." The car featured semi-elliptic springs, single chain drive, and high wagon wheels shod with pneumatic tires. A small 700-pound runabout was offered, as well as a 1400-pound four-seater. Production was minimal, and manufacture was discontinued by the end of 1902.

1903 Rogers & Thacher, runabout, GR

ROGERS & THACHER — Cleveland, Ohio — (1903) — In February of 1903, George D. Rogers and A.Q. Thacher announced the organization of their Rogers & Thacher Automobile Company. Its capital stock was $150,000, and the partners hoped to have the prototype of their new car completed for the Cleveland Automobile Show later that month. They did make it to the show on time, but not with a complete car. Instead only the chassis was exhibited, placed over a large mirror to show off its construction. Its engine was a 35 hp four mounted under the floorboard with gasoline and water tanks carried under the hood up front. Toggle shaft drive was featured, and a two-speed bevel gear transmission. The Rogers & Thacher was planned as a triple-threat car: with tonneau mounted, it carried four; with tonneau removed, it became a two-passenger roadster; with one of the front bucket seats taken away, it became a racer for one. Manufacture was slated to begin by mid-1903, but it never did. Several years later, George Rogers was among the founders of the Continental Motor Manufacturing Company.

ROLAND — The Roland Gas-Electric Vehicle Corporation has been indicated on various car rosters as the producer of an automobile in 1915. The smallest vehicle known to have been produced by Roland was a one-ton truck, the largest a seven-ton bus.

1925 Rollin, model G, sedan, OCW

ROLLIN — Cleveland, Ohio — (1924-1925) —

In 1914, principally because he wanted to build a tractor, Rollin Henry White left his long-time job as chief engineer of the White Company of Cleveland. Part of his subsequent R&D, and a little R&R, was conducted at his older brother's pineapple plantation in Hawaii. Upon his return to Cleveland, he finished his designs, and in January 1916 set into motion the organization of the company which was to produce the famous Cletrac tractor. By the early Twenties, however, he had become enthused once again with the idea of building an automobile. Cleveland industrialist E.E. Allyne offered to help, and a former Studebaker engineer named Fred M. Zeder offered the high compression engine he had designed. In the spring of 1922 the automobile trade press gave considerable space to this new enterprise. The new car was alternately said to be the Zeder or the Allyne-Zeder, and White's Cleveland Tractor Company was to be merged into a new parent organization which would manufacture both the car and the Cletrac. These plans had fallen apart by fall, however. Zeder went off to join engineering colleagues Owen Skelton and Carl Breer — and to design the new Chrysler. And Rollin White pressed on without him. There is some evidence that the first prototypes built wore Cletrac emblems, but well before production began the decision was made for the first name of the man whose idea the car was. In May of 1923 the Rollin Motors Company was organized with a $2 million capital stock. Rollin White placed himself as chairman of the board, filling the executive chairs with a good many Studebaker veterans, including James G. Heaslet as president. The Rollin automobile arrived on the market in the fall of 1923 as one of the earliest in America to feature four-wheel brakes. The touring car was priced at an attractively low $895; the deluxe touring at $975, the coupe-roadster at $1775 and the sedan at $1275 featured disc wheels and balloon tires. The Rollin's engine was a high compression 41 hp four with four main bearings and aluminum connecting rods and pistons. All models were on a 112-inch wheelbase. The coachwork was stylish. The trade press was enthusiastic. "The Thoroughbred of the Thoroughfare" was the Rollin slogan, and the car was widely regarded as the "only fine small car" built in America. And that was its problem. Though the quality was high and the price was low, the Rollin was small and Americans liked big. Larger cars with more cylinders were widely available on the U.S. market, especially in 1925 when the Rollin prices increased a couple of hundred dollars. Output in 1924 was a little over 6100 cars; about 2400 Rollins were built in 1925 before the assembly line was shut down in November and bankruptcy declared in December. Rollin assets were listed as $741,280, with liabilities $958,035. Rollin White returned to his tractor business, from which he retired in 1944. He died in 1962 at age ninety.

1924 ROLLIN
Model G — 4-cyl., 41 hp, 112" wb

	FP	5	4	3	2	1
Touring-5P	895	3900	4800	7700	14,300	27,000
DeLuxe Touring-5P	975	4000	5000	8000	15,000	28,000
Coupe-Roadster-3P	1175	3900	4800	7700	14,300	27,000
Sedan-5P	1275	2300	3300	4600	7500	16,000

1925 Rollin, model G, deluxe coupe, OCW

1925 ROLLIN
Model G — 4-cyl., 41 hp, 112" wb

Phaeton-5P	1155	3900	4800	7700	14,300	27,000
Coupe-Roadster-3P	1325	3900	4800	7700	14,300	27,000
Sedan-5P	1455	2300	3300	4600	7500	16,000
Brougham-5P	1325	2200	3200	4400	7000	15,000

1924 Rolls-Royce, Silver Ghost, Piccadilly roadster, OCW

ROLLS-ROYCE — Springfield, Massachusetts — (1921-1935) —

On October 4th, 1919 the first Rolls-Royce to reach the United States since the Armistice ending World War I arrived from England. Two months later announcement was made in New York that the Rolls-Royce would now be built in the United States as well by a newly-formed $7 million company called Rolls-Royce of America, Inc., which purchased the plant of the American Wire Wheel Company in Springfield in early December. The two-to-three-year backlog of orders in England following the war was the reason the British company decided to build American, though emphasis was made in advertisements during the summer of 1920 that the cars would be produced by "British mechanics under British supervision." The first American Rolls-Royce arrived on January 17th, 1921, the venerable Silver Ghost with six-cylinder engine and 143 1/2-inch wheelbase. Its chassis price was $11,750, somewhat cheaper than the British version. The 100th Springfield Rolls rolled off the assembly line that August. Total 1921 production was 135 cars; 1922, 230; 1924 saw a rise to 320 units. Unlike the British Rolls, the American version was offered, beginning in the fall of 1922, in both chassis form and as a complete car, the company cataloging eleven different body designs. In December 1925 Rolls-Royce of America, Inc. acquired the Brewster coachbuilding house, William Brewster remaining as president of the Brewster organization and becoming a vice-president of Rolls-Royce. Although the car remained as British as crumpets and tea for awhile, it was inevitable that certain American vestiges would creep in. In 1923 the company frankly admitted that American mechanics were helping to build it (and were doing fine), and two years later the car became a left-hand drive (the company building 50 right-hand cars in 1925 before switching over and building another 300 with left-hand drive). In 1926 the ohv six-cylinder New Phantom (retrospectively designated Phantom I) arrived in two chassis sizes (143 1/2 and 146 1/2 inches) priced a couple of thousand dollars more than the former Silver Ghost chassis. Thereafter, Rolls-Royce prices became "available upon application." In late September of 1929, Rolls-Royce of America, Inc. proudly announced that it was enjoying its best year since organization, with New Phantom production at the rate of twelve units a week. The month following Wall Street crashed. "Register one more ten-yard loss against the

1924 Rolls-Royce, Silver Ghost, Pall Mall phaeton, HAC

calamity carriers," *Automobile Topics* reported in November. "Rolls-Royce of America has had just one cancellation since the break in the stock market." By the end of 1931 — during which year J.S. Inskip took over the company presidency — a total of 2944 American Rolls-Royces (1703 Silver Ghosts and 1241 New Phantoms) had been made in the decade of Rolls-Royce manufacture in America. Production would continue, though haphazardly as the effect of the Great Depression took hold. The introduction of the Phantom II in England in 1929 rocked Rolls-Royce of America; the company simply couldn't afford to tool up for production of this new car. Considerable parts for P-I's remained in Springfield fortunately, and thus the company continued to put these cars together and sell them as new for the next several years, though at prices considerably reduced from pre-Depression levels. It is known that in 1932 — when the Phantom II in England was entering its third year and the Phantom I only a faintly remembered anachronism there — approximately 100 new P-I's were built and delivered from Springfield. Some 125 P-II chassis equipped with left-hand drive were imported into this country between 1931 and 1934 as well, and were sent to Springfield to be made appropriate for "American road conditions." In 1934 Brewster began building special coachbuilt cars too on Ford chassis. Rolls-Royce in England objected vociferously to that, and so Rolls-Royce of America, Inc. changed its name to Springfield Manufacturing Corporation — and renegotiated its contract with the British firm for further importation of Rolls-Royce cars in this country. In 1935 the Springfield company went into bankruptcy, and was purchased the year following by Dallas E. Winslow. In 1937 the Brewster assets were sold. Meanwhile, John S. Inskip incorporated a new company of his own to handle authorized sales and service of Rolls-Royce cars in the United States. The precise date the last American-built Rolls-Royce was produced in this country is a mystery, though the cars were being sold as new as late as the summer of 1935.

1921 ROLLS ROYCE
Silver Ghost, 6-cyl., 40/50 hp, 143.5" wb

	FP	5	4	3	2	1
Chassis	11,750	—	—	—	—	—

1922 ROLLS ROYCE
Silver Ghost, 6-cyl., 40/50 hp, 143.5" wb

Chassis	NA	—	—	—	—	—

Note 1: All cars custom-built.

1923 ROLLS ROYCE
Silver Ghost, 6-cyl., 40/50 hp, 143.5" wb

Chassis	NA	—	—	—	—	—

1924 ROLLS ROYCE
Silver Ghost, 6-cyl., 40/50 hp, 143.5" wb
Value Inestimatible

Chassis	11,385	—	—	—	—	—
Chassis w/fenders	11,895	—	—	—	—	—
Pall Mall Tr.-5P	12,930	—	—	—	—	—
Piccadilly Rds.-2P	13,450	—	—	—	—	—
Pickwick Sed.-6P	14,970	—	—	—	—	—
Salamanca Twn. Car-5P	15,560	—	—	—	—	—

Note 2: These were the catalogued models available; the Silver Ghost was also available in chassis form for special custom coachwork of owner preference.

1925 Rolls-Royce, Silver Ghost, Tilbury sedan, FR

1925 ROLLS ROYCE
Silver Ghost, 6-cyl., 40/50 hp, 143.5" wb

Chassis	12,900	—	—	—	—	—

1926 ROLLS ROYCE
Silver Ghost, 6-cyl., 40/50 hp, 143.5" wb

Chassis	12,800	—	—	—	—	—

1927 Rolls-Royce Phantom I, coupe, Brewster, HAC

1927 ROLLS ROYCE
Silver Ghost, 6-cyl., 48.60 hp (80 bhp), 143.5" wb

Chassis	12,335	—	—	—	—	—

Phantom (I), 6-cyl., 43.35 hp, 143.5/146.5" wb

Chassis	13,835	—	—	—	—	—

1928 Rolls-Royce Phantom I, limousine, Brewster, JAC

1928 ROLLS ROYCE
Phantom (I), 6-cyl., 43.35 hp, 143.5/146.5" wb

Chassis	13,325	—	—	—	—	—

1929 Rolls-Royce Phantom I, convertible coupe, Brewster, HAC

1929 Rolls-Royce Phantom I, Ascot tourer, FR

1929 ROLLS ROYCE
Phantom (I) "40-65", 6-cyl., 43.35 hp, 143.5/146.5" wb

	FP	5	4	3	2	1
Derby Tr.-4P	17,840				Value Inestimatible	
York Rds.-2/4P	17,840				Value Inestimatible	
Avon Sed.	17,860				Value Inestimatible	
Huntington Limo.-7/8P	18,885				Value Inestimatible	
Newmarket Conv. Sed.-4P	18,885				Value Inestimatible	
Hibb. & Darr. Conv. Sed.	19,665				Value Inestimatible	
Trouville Twn. Car	19,965				Value Inestimatible	
Chassis	13,335				Value Inestimatible	
Chassis w/fenders	13,865				Value Inestimatible	

1930 Rolls-Royce Phantom I, limousine, Brewster, JAC

1930-1931 ROLLS ROYCE
Phantom I "40-65," 6-cyl., 43.35 hp, 143.5/146.5 wb

Chassis	13,325	—	—	—	—	—

1932 ROLLS ROYCE
Phantom II, 6-cyl., 43.30 hp, 144.8" wb

Chassis	13,325	—	—	—	—	—

1933 ROLLS ROYCE
Phantom II, 6-cyl., 43.30 hp, 144.8" wb

Chassis	12,939	—	—	—	—	—

1909 Roman, touring, GR

ROMAN — Rome, New York — **(1909)** — The Rome Motor Vehicle Company was organized early in 1909 with a capital stock of $5000 for the manufacture of automobiles in Rome, New York. Incorporators were W.H. McIntyre and Christian S. and L.M. Fitch. Roman was to be the name of the company's product. A prototype was built. Manufacture is doubted.

ROMER — New York, New York — (1915) — The designation was RomeR, as the Adams & Montant Company explained, "the two large R's being somewhat similar to the effect secured by the Rolls-Royce, which the projected car is expected to somewhat resemble." The RomeR was planned to be sold in the $1800 range, together with a smaller companion car to be called the Lampo. Adams & Montant was a long-time New York City dealership specializing in European imports; these two new cars were to be built in the United States, saving import duties, which were ever on the increase. In the late summer of 1915, the chassis of the new RomeR was completed and was dispatched to a New York City coachbuilding house for completion. The RomeR venture ended there. Neither it nor the Lampo proceeded into manufacture.

1921 Romer, touring, KM

ROMER — Danvers, Massachusetts — (1921) — Albert J. Romer began his career as a mechanical engineer with the U.S. Motor Company, subsequently moving up to work for Otis Elevator, and later designing a cyclecar in 1914 which was never produced. Subsequent employment found him assisting in the design of the Northway automobile and serving as an engineer for the Murray Motor Car Company. In 1921 he believed himself ready to take on the automobile industry with a car of his own. The Romer Motors Corporation was organized in March with offices in Boston and a factory in Danvers. J. Ellis Nightingale and James L. Roope were the chief financial backers. A Continental 7R six-cylinder engine powered the Romer, and standard components were used throughout. Automobile production was discontinued late in 1921. The plan now was manufacture of a 1-1/2-ton truck. In 1922 the Romer factory was relocated in Taunton, and Albert Romer bought out the Peters Autocar Company of Bethlehem, Pennsylvania. By mid-1922 Romer manufacture had ceased altogether.

1921 ROMER
Six — 52 hp, 120" wb

	FP	5	4	3	2	1
Touring-5P	1975	3900	4800	7700	14,300	27,000
Roadster-2P	1975	3700	4700	7300	13,700	26,000
Touring-7P	2050	4000	5000	8000	15,000	28,000
Coupe-4P	2400	2700	3600	5300	8800	19,000
Sedan-5P	2700	2300	3300	4600	7500	16,000

ROMMEL — The Rommel Motor Car Company was organized in Louisville, Kentucky during the fall of 1912 with a capital stock of $15,000 to manufacture and sell automobiles. Incorporators were John Rommel, Henry E. Rommel and Joseph H. Kaltenbach. Manufacture is doubted.

ROOS — The Roos Automobile Company was organized in Chicago, Illinois early in 1909 with a capital stock of $5000 for the manufacture and sale of automobiles and accessories. Incorporators were H.D. Roos, F.E. Matthews and H.C. Bangs. Manufacture of a car is doubted.

ROOSEVELT — The Roosevelt Auto Company was organized in Rahway, New Jersey early in 1907 with a capital stock of $50,000 for the manufacture of motor vehicles. Incorporators were R.E. Bracher, H.L. Pendleton and W.A. Reason. Manufacture is doubted.

1929 Roosevelt Eight, sedan, JAC

ROOSEVELT — Indianapolis, Indiana — (1929-1930) — "Smart Transportation for the Thrifty" was an advertising catchline for the Roosevelt, which was the first straight-eight in America to be priced at less than $1000 and the lowest priced car built by the Marmon Motor Car Company. Named for the Rough Rider and former U.S. President (whose image frequently appeared in ads), the Roosevelt was announced in December of 1928 and arrived on the market in March of 1929. Although it was presented that year as a separate make, it was offered in 1930 as the Roosevelt model of Marmon. The name disappeared for 1931, though the car itself was refined into the new Model 70 Marmon.

1929 Roosevelt Eight, sedan, HAC

1929-1930 ROOSEVELT
Eight — 72 hp, 113" wb

	FP	5	4	3	2	1
Sedan	995	1600	2700	3800	5800	12,000
Coupe	995	2400	3400	4800	8000	17,000
Victoria Coupe	1065	2500	3500	5000	8500	18,000
Collegiate Coupe	1905	2900	3700	5600	9100	20,000

1865 Roper, steam carriage, HFM

ROPER STEAM — Roxbury, Massachusetts — (1860-1896) — Stephen Roper was a manufacturer of marine steam engines who built a total of ten steam vehicles in approximately a quarter of a century. Although he began experimentation in 1859, Roper and his work did not come to national prominence until 1863 when *Scientific American* published an article describing his latest effort, a two-passenger four-wheeler with a two-horsepower steam engine and a 2-to-25 mph speed range. Coal, carried under the seat, was used as fuel, and the cost to operate per mile was claimed to be a penny. Many of Roper's vehicles were two-wheelers during this era of the Velocipede. Among the four-wheelers was one that Roper sold to W.W. Austen, a carnival man who toured fairs and race tracks throughout the East Coast promoting demonstrations of "the greatest wonder of the world," though frequently without giving credit for the invention to Roper. Roper's last four-wheeler was built and sold to a Boston brick manufacturer in 1894. Two years later, while testing his latest two-wheeler at Charles River Track in Boston, Stephen Roper crashed. Reports differ as to whether Roper died as a direct result of the accident or the heart attack he suffered because of it. He was seventy-three years old. A four-wheeled Roper steam carriage is on display at the Henry Ford Museum in Greenfield Village.

ROSE CITY — The Rose City Auto Company was organized in New Castle, Indiana late in 1912 with a capital stock of $10,000 for the manufacture of automobiles. Incorporators included Frank E. Smith, Charles W. Mouch, William F. Byrket, Howard M. Van Matre, Gordon Cameron, Lawrence W. Bailey and Albert D. Ogborn. Manufacture is doubted.

ROSENBAUER — **Milwaukee, Wisconsin** — **(1900-1901)** — George A. Rosenbauer was half of the Sanger & Rosenbauer Plating Company of Milwaukee, which became the Sanger Handle Bar Company when he left in 1900. In November that year Rosenbauer announced his invention of a compressed air motor for automobiles for which he planned to organize a manufacturing company, but apparently changed his mind. Instead he built a gasoline-powered automobile later that year, and in January 1901 organized the Rosenbauer Automobile & Power Company at 3202 Vliet Street in Milwaukee for its manufacture. In addition to the car, which was to be offered as a runabout and stanhope, Rosenbauer also planned to produce gasoline engines, running gear, axles and steering levers, all of his own design. The one thing he had not considered, perhaps, was the money necessary to do all this, and when he found it his backers insisted on a name change to Milwaukee Automobile and Brass Specialty Company. Some production of his car as the Milwaukee did follow.

ROSENBERGER — In 1907 Ernest Rosenberger of Mankato, Minnesota announced his forthcoming incorporation of a $50,000 company for the manufacture of automobiles. His subsequent cars were variously referred to as Kato, Mankato and Four Traction. Refer to Kato.

ROSEVILLE — The Roseville Motor Company was organized in Newark, New Jersey late in 1905 with a capital stock of $25,000 to manufacture and deal in automobiles and engines. Ernest H. Mott, Henry Tetlow and George M. Barnes were the incorporators. Manufacture of a car is doubted.

ROSS — The Ross Automobile Company was organized in Auburn, New York during the spring of 1913 with a capital stock of $10,000 for the manufacture of motorcars and engines. Incorporators were Edward A. Ross, Maurice E. Tuller and Harry A. Barr, all of Auburn. Manufacture of an automobile is doubted.

The Ross Machine Company was organized in Lafayette, Indiana during the fall of 1911 with a capital stock of $15,000 to manufacture and sell automobiles. William Ross headed the venture. Manufacture is doubted.

1918 Ross, Six, 2-pass. roadster, WLB

ROSS — **Detroit, Michigan** — **(1915-1918)** — In January of 1915 John L. Ross announced that his Ross & Young Machine Company, which had long been prominent in the parts and machining business in Detroit, would enter the automotive field. The Ross Automobile Company was formally incorporated that summer with a capital stock of $300,000. The firm's first car was a V-8 (Herschell-Spillman engine) offered as a $1350 touring on a 115-inch wheelbase. A longer 130-inch wheelbase $1850 model followed in 1916, as did an expansion of the body-style range. In October that year a Ross Eight climbed the Fillmore Street hill in high gear, the first Detroit-built car to do it, so the company said. But the company was in an uphill struggle by now too. Late in 1916 New York capitalists arrived with money and a reorganization plan. The result was chaos. The Ross body style lineup remained the same (touring, coupe, sedan, roadster, suburban and town car) but what engine was under the hood of the last Ross cars built remains an enigma. In August of 1917 the new regime announced that the V-8 had been dropped and that the Ross was now a six (Continental Red Seal engine). In November further announcement revealed that the six was to be discontinued and the V-8 reinstated. The New York capitalists returned to the East Coast. By February of 1918 the Ross company plant had been sold to Shipman Iron & Metal Company for $180,000 which, with other monies collected in the winding down of its affairs, meant that all Ross creditors would be paid in full, a rarity in those days.

ROSS & KRAMER — The Ross & Kramer Automobile Company has been indicated on various car rosters as an automobile manufacturer in Chicago, Illinois in 1904. Documentation is lacking. The firm, which was located at 5607 Halsted Street, was busy in the accesories business during this period, however, offering products as varied as gear and rotary circulating pumps, engine mufflers and (beginning in 1908) glass windshields.

ROSS STEAMER — **Newtonville, Massachusetts** — **(1906-1909)** — Louis S. Ross was born in Newtonville in 1877. He first came to national prominence racing Stanley steam cars shortly after the turn of the century, and at Ormond-Daytona Beach in 1904 the "Wogglebug" he designed (which looked like an upside down canoe) beat all comers. Ross was one of the first American drivers ever to turn a mile under a minute, and he was a genuine sports hero. By 1906, however, he had decided to hang up his racing gloves and get down to serious business as an automobile manufacturer. He introduced his new car at the Boston Automobile Show that year, although he did not then, or subsequently, formally incorporate a company. The Ross Steamer was fitted with a two-cylinder double-acting engine — and was widely touted as the first steam car to locate all its

1906 Ross Steamer, touring, NAHC

mechanism (engine, boiler and tanks) up front under the hood. The five-passenger wooden-bodied touring car weighed 2800 pounds and was priced at 2800 dollars. A runabout joined the line in 1907. Like the touring, it was shaft drive. The first automobile ever used by the Boston Fire Department was built in the Ross shops. The Ross Steamer was discontinued in 1909 simply because Louis Ross became interested in inventing other things. His last invention killed him in 1927. It was a signal torpedo for use by railroads which he believed would not explode except when crushed by an onrushing locomotive. Taking a box of these new torpedoes to a field near his Central Railway Signal Company factory in Waltham, he fired at them with a revolver. It was his last experiment.

1906 ROSS STEAMER
Two — 25 hp, 108" wb

	FP	5	4	3	2	1
Touring	2800	2700	3600	5300	8800	19,000
1907-1908 ROSS STEAMER						
Two — 25 hp						
Touring (108" wb)	2800	2700	3600	5300	8800	19,000
Runabout (100" wb)	2250	2500	3500	5000	8500	18,000
1909 ROSS STEAMER						
Two — 25 hp, 108" wb						
Touring	2800	2700	3600	5300	8800	19,000
Runabout	2250	2500	3500	5000	8500	18,000

ROSSEL — The Rossel Motor Car Company was organized in Toledo, Ohio late in 1910 with a capital stock of $120,000 to manufacture and deal in automobiles. E.C. Rossel was behind this venture. Manufacture is doubted.

ROSSLER — **Buffalo, New York** — **(1906-1907)** — The C. Rossler Manufacturing Company was incorporated in Buffalo in 1903 with a capital stock of $60,000. For three years following, Rossler sanguinely plied its business as a wagon builder until William A. de Schaum arrived in town and talked the company into building a car. De Schaum finished the prototype of the Rossler high-wheeled runabout in March of 1906. It was powered by a single-cylinder 10/12 hp water-cooled engine. Single chain drive and solid rubber tires were featured. Though production was embarked upon, de Schaum was unsatisfied with its laggardly pace and left to build his own car under his own name. There is some evidence that Rossler high-wheelers may have been built into early 1908, by which time the de Schaum highwheeler was coming out the door in another plant across town in Buffalo.

1904 Rotary, touring, LC

ROTARY — **Boston, Massachusetts** — **(1903-1905)** — The Rotary Motor Vehicle Company was an outgrowth of the American Rotary Engine Company. It was incorporated in December of 1899 with a capital stock of $400,000 by E.R. Porter and W.R. Whiting of Boston and N.S.H. Sanders of nearby Danvers. A factory was secured at 43 Columbus Avenue in Boston. "The company believes firmly in the principle that 'carriages on the street' are the best evidences of progress and prosperity and is bending all its energies to turning out motors and practical carriages," *The Motor Age* reported in January 1900. "As the company is not in need of money, is having a reasonable measure of success and the first carriage is promised within a few weeks." It was fortuitous that financing was not a problem for the Rotary Motor Vehicle Company because its car did not make it to market until the 1903 model year. The Rotary's engine was curious, an 8 hp single cylinder with two connecting rods on the one piston rotating two shafts in opposite direction. This configuration presumably rendered the unit vibrationless. Shaft drive was featured, and the car was available as a $1250 wire-wheeled runabout and $1500 wooden-wheeled tonneau. Advertisements indicate that Rotary liked to call its car the "Intrepid," though it did not live up to that name. After three years in the making, Rotary's "Intrepid" was but two years in manufacture.

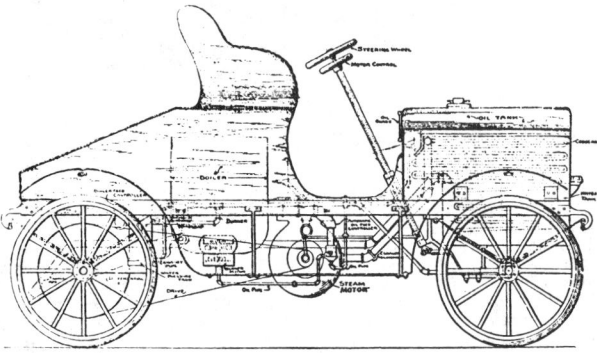

1906 Rotary, runabout, NAHC

ROTARY — New York, New York — (1906) — This Rotary was unusual in being a steamer, its system comprising a rotary steam engine, non-rotary flash boiler and rotary burner. The invention of Edward C. Warren, it was promoted by the Rotary Motor Car Company of America, which was incorporated with a capital stock of $100,000 in New York during the summer of 1906. Great things were expected. "As evidence of the fact that the Warren rotary engine is not of the Sunday newspaper variety," *The Motor World* commented, "it may be stated that Louis Duncan, the man who planned and carried out the electrification of the Third Avenue surface road in New York City in 1892, and who has twice served as president of the American Institute of Electrical Engineers, C.E. Wilson, president of the Keystone Telegraph and Telephone Company of Philadelphia, and Lamar Lyndon, a consulting engineer of note, who once served the Pope interests, have investigated the merits of the invention and given it their support." The heavyweight support notwithstanding, this Rotary never made it into manufacture.

1922 Rotary, touring, NAHC

ROTARY — Hoboken, New Jersey — (1921-1923) — The pilot models, including the demonstrator that was given a transcontinental test run during the fall of 1921, were called Rotarian but by the time the car hit the market later that year, its name had been changed to Rotary. The man behind the Rotary was Eugene Bournonville, a Belgian who had been in this country for a number of years and who was described as one of the pioneers in the development of oxy-acetylene welding. In 1914 he developed and patented a rotary valve engine which featured an adjustable sleeve and shoe which acted as a seal and replaced the solid sleeve that had been the norm in previous sleeve-valve engine design. He was unable to interest any automobile manufacturers in his engine, and with the outbreak of World War I he revised the unit for aircraft use hoping to interest the U.S. Government. He fared no better there either. Finally he decided that if any conveyance with his engine were to be built, he had best build it himself. Bournonville Motors Company of Hoboken introduced its new car at the New York Automobile Show in November of 1921. Aside from its engine, a six developing 60 hp, the new Rotary was built of standard components (Parish & Bingham frame, Brown-Lipe transmission, Columbia axles, Borg & Beck clutch). But the car was very well put together and veritably oozed quality. A seven-passenger touring car on a 130-inch wheelbase was the only vehicle shown, and its price tag was $6000. But Bournonville's automotive venture was grossly undercapitalized, and the Rotary didn't stand a chance. In 1923 Bournonville slashed his price to $3800, and discontinued building the car later that year. Thereon Bournonville returned to his native Belgium where at last he found a manufac-

turer interested in his engine design: Minerva, which perfected and later marketed a sleeve valve engine based on his ideas. In America, in late October of 1924, the Bournonville Rotary Valve Motor Car Company was organized to manufacture cars under Eugene Bournonville's patents, but that venture died aborning. Bournonville's luck in the United States hadn't changed at all.

ROTHSCHILD — Rothschild & Company was organized in New York City during the spring of 1906 with a capital stock of $30,000 for the manufacture of automobiles. The Rothschilds involved were variously indicated to be H.J. and Maurice M.; their relationship to the famed House of Rothschild was probably tenuous. Also invoved were W.H. Mendel and Nathaniel D. Reich. Manufacture is doubted.

ROUNDS — Plymouth, Massachusetts — (1901) — The Rounds was a steam car built in two variations by George E. Rounds of 32 Vernon Street in Plymouth. A two-passenger runabout with 8 hp engine and a four-passenger with 15 hp engine were offered. A tubular boiler was fitted to both, as well as a patented device of Rounds for the "disposing of the exhaust steam." Production does not seem to have survived 1901.

ROVAN — Columbus, Ohio — (1912-1913) — Initially, the Rovan was simply a front-wheel-drive conversion kit for commercial vehicles. A Rovan truck was put on the market in 1911, however, and several cars were built thereafter. Among these was a Rovan Special Front Drive racer in which Harry C. Knight unfortunately met his death in a 200-mile event at Columbus in 1913, and a special touring car for Ralph H. Rosenberg which he had personally driven for more than 8000 miles by that summer. Rosenberg was the inventor of the special universal joint used in the Rovan front-drive unit, and the car probably was built as a demonstrator. The Kinnear Manufacturing Company of Columbus produced both the Rovan cars and trucks.

ROVENA — Little is known about the Rovena Motor Company which purportedly built an automobile in 1926 in Kansas City, Missouri except that it was a Delaware incorporation and was officially dissolved in 1930. Unconfirmed references suggest that Ben Gregory, who was experimenting with front-wheel-drive cars in Kansas City during this period may have been involved, but the documentation is lacking that a Rovena car was ever produced.

ROWE — Martinsville, Illinois — (1906) — "A.M. Rowe of Martinsville...has begun the manufacture of cars" reported *The Horseless Age* in April of 1906. Details are lacking, but the venture almost surely was a short one.

ROWE — Waynesboro, Pennsylvania — (1908, 1910) — Samuel D. Rowe founded the Rowe Motor Company in Waynesboro in 1908 and during that year built an experimental automobile with a five-cylinder air-cooled engine. The vehicle was never marketed, and Rowe contented himself with the manufacture of motors thereafter. In 1910 he again attempted to get his car into production, but he failed once more, His luck changed in 1911, however, when his company moved to Coatesville and he decided to confine his automotive ambitions to a truck instead. Rowe trucks were subsequently produced in Coatesville through 1913, in Downington through 1918, and in Lancaster through 1925. "Rowe Runs Right" was a company slogan.

ROWELL — Auburn, Maine — (1902) — Captain A.E. Rowell of Auburn was a master at repairing steam engines and for decades, whenever a steamboat on the Rangeley Lakes needed fixing, Captain Rowell was the man who fixed it. He was employed for fifty-three years by the local Brown Company. In 1902 he constructed a steam automobile which he used for his personal transport. It was a runabout with a fringed umbrella overhead. He built most of its mechanical parts at the shop of Rand & Harvey in Lewiston. (That firm had built a steam vehicle of its own in 1899.) The body was built for him by Wade & Dunton. The brass hubcaps on the wooden wheels carried the initial "R." The Rowell's boiler was made of copper, and had been imported from Scotland. A kerosene burner was fitted. Although the water tank held twenty-five gallons, there were occasions upon which the vehicle found itself short of H2O during a pleasure trip. As Captain Rowell's son George later remembered, "That was when Father would ingeniously suck up the needed water from handy mud puddles, by using a hose that was always carried in the steamer."

ROWERDINK — The W.H. Rowerdink & Son Company was organized in Rochester, New York early in 1910 with a capital stock of $100,000 for the manufacture of motorcars. The son was H.J. Rowerdink. Manufacture is doubted.

ROYAL — Royal was the designation provided the six-cylinder car built in Carthage, Ohio from 1913-1914 by the Crescent Motor Company. The Crescent four was called an Ohio. Refer to Crescent.

Royal Amston was the name given to a proposed luxury car to be produced by the Amston Motor Car Company of Amston, Connecticut. Refer to AMS-Sterling.

The Royal Automobile Company was organized in Trenton, New Jersey during the summer of 1903 with a capital stock of $250,000 for the manufacture of automobiles. Louis B. Dailey, Warren N. Akers and K.K. McLaren were the incorporators. Manufacture is doubted.

The Royal Motor Car Company was organized in Detroit, Michigan late in 1907 with a capital stock of $100,000 to manufacture "motor-driven vehicles." Paul Arthur and Robert M. Webster were behind this venture. Manufacture of an automobile is doubted.

The Royal Motor Works of Worcester, Massachusetts is a curiosity. The company was first organized during the fall of 1901 as a $10,000 Maine incorporation to ''develop, manufacture and sell vehicles of all kinds and appliances for propelling same.'' It was reorganized as a $100,000 Delaware incorporation late in 1906 for the manufacture of ''carriages, motor cars and other vehicles.'' The people behind this venture were never indicated. Manufacture is doubted.

The Royal Taxicab Company was organized in Youngstown, Ohio during the summer of 1913 with a $25,000 capital stock to manufacture taxicabs and motor trucks. Incorporators were Charles Gaither, H.A. Husted, T.J. Raftican, Dr. W.H. Buechner and I.M. Hartzell. Manufacture is doubted.

1913 Royal, model 45, 5-pass. touring, NAHC

ROYAL — Elkhart, Indiana — (1913) — The Royal Motor Company was in business in Elkhart for one season only. Two models were produced: the $895 Royal ''35'' and the $1095 Royal ''45.'' Both were five-passenger touring cars powered by four-cylinder T-head engines. The cars were shaft drive with selective three-speed sliding gear transmissions. Semi-elliptic springs were featured front and rear. The car seems to have been well built, but the company was obviously underfinanced.

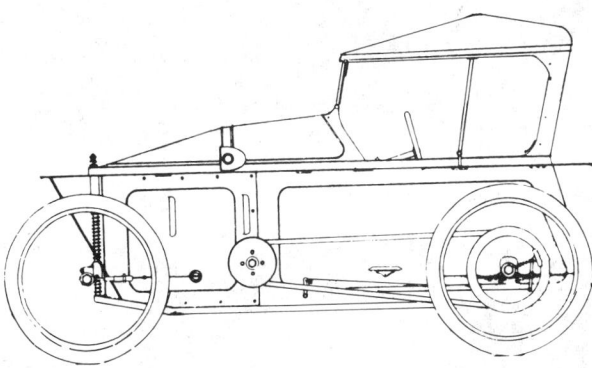

1915 Royal, cyclecar, HAC

ROYAL — Bridgeport, Connecticut — (1915) — By 1915 most cyclecar manufacturers were passing off their products as light cars, but the Royal Cyclecar Company entered the field that year unabashedly extolling its version as ''a true Cyclecar in weight, tread and economic operation with all of the strength and reliability of the larger Automobile, carrying one passenger and his or her baggage with comfort and safety.'' The Royal's weight was 400 pounds, its tread was 36 inches and its economic operation was ''40 miles plus per gallon.'' Whether it was strong and reliable remains doubtful. The car was powered by a single-cylinder 5/7 hp air-cooled engine. Its wheelbase was a short 75 inches, but since the seating accommodation was only for one, the vehicle was probably comfortable enough. The car featured a friction transmission with final drive by ''imported oil tanned belt to rear pulleys.'' The price was $250. Probably the Royal Cyclecar Company envisioned its principal market to be the traveling salesman. But among the stories traveling salesmen were telling in 1915 were horror tales of what traveling by cyclecar had been like in 1914 — and the company didn't survive the year.

1905 Royal Electric, victoria, NAHC

ROYAL ELECTRIC — Chicago, Illinois — (1904-1905) / ROYAL PRINCESS — (1904-1905) — Although the Royal Automobile Company was incorporated in the state of New Jersey, its founders (Louis B. Dailey, Warren N. Akers and K.K. McLaren) took themselves to Chicago for manufacture. There a factory was secured at 144 Green Street, and production of both electric and gasoline cars commenced. The Royal Electric was offered in a variety of body styles on a 60-inch wheelbase, and 75 miles on a single charge was guaranteed. The gasoline car was called the Royal Princess, and it was a 16 hp twin on an 82-inch wheelbase offered as a double side entrance tonneau only. A two-speed planetary transmission and single chain drive were featured. The manufacture of both these cars came to an abrupt end in November 1905 when the Royal Automobile Company found itself petitioned into involuntary bankruptcy.

1904 ROYAL ELECTRIC / ROYAL PRINCESS

	FP	5	4	3	2	1
Royal Electric Runabout	600	1600	2700	3800	5800	12,000
Royal Electric Phaeton	1200	2000	3000	4200	6500	14,000
Royal Electric Stanhope	1800	2200	3200	4400	7000	15,000
Royal Princess Tonneau	1500	2100	3100	4300	6800	14,500

1905 ROYAL ELECTRIC / ROYAL PRINCESS

	FP	5	4	3	2	1
Royal Electric Runabout	650	1600	2700	3800	5800	12,000
Royal Electric Phaeton	1800	2000	3000	4200	6500	14,000
Royal Electric Stanhope	1900	2200	3200	4400	7000	15,000
Royal Electric Queen Victoria	1800	2300	3300	4600	7500	16,000
Royal Princess Tonneau	1500	2100	3100	4300	6800	14,500

ROYAL MARTEL — Elkhart, Indiana — (1925-1927) — The Royal Martel Taxi Corporation was the idea of Jules Martin. The taxi itself was built by one of the taxi-producing offshoots of the Elcar company of Elkhart. Its engine was a Lycoming, and most of the cars built were destined for service in New York City. Introduced in May of 1925, Royal Martel indicated at that time a projected hefty production of 5000 cars a year. The total actually produced in two-and-a-half years, however, is believed to be closer to 200, and included the Martel taxis as well. What made a Martel ''Royal'' seems to have been the addition of bumpers and shock absorbers.

ROYALMOBILE — Salt Lake City, Utah — (1901) — H.K. Clover of Salt Lake City claimed he had over 200 patents to his credit and an idea for a steam car with a compound engine and chainless driving mechanism that would make millions. He called his car the Royalmobile, though whether he ever successfully built and tested one is open to conjecture. Certainly he promoted his car with vigor, and almost succeeded. Ashland, Ohio seemed receptive. ''The city is to furnish, in trust, a four-acre lot and $15,000 bonus,'' The Motor Review reported in March 1901, ''in return for which Mr. Clover agrees to build a factory employing not less than 100 men and operate the same for a period of four years. If the provisions are carried out for a period of two years the real estate and bonus are to revert to the company.'' But the Royalmobile never made it to Ashland. Perhaps the city, unlike so many others in that era, got wise quickly. As The Motor Age remarked about Clover that year, ''His double may be found in every town where there are people willing to invest in the automobile industry, or where there is a bonus to be secured.''

1904 Royal, model K, touring, HAC

ROYAL TOURIST — Cleveland, Ohio — (1904-1911) — Late in 1903 Edward Schurmer acquired control of the Hoffman Automobile and Manufacturing Company which he reorganized as the Royal Motor Car Company for the production of a new car called the Royal Tourist. As his chief engineer, he hired Robert Jardine, a Frenchman with extensive European experience who most recently had been involved in the design of the Berg automobile built in Cleveland. The two-cylinder Royal Tourist made its debut in the New York Automobile Show in January 1904, with the four-cylinder version following within a few weeks. Both models featured selective sliding gear transmissions and shaft drive, quite advanced for the period. The Royal Tourist received a rousing reception, and over 100 cars were built and sold in 1904. Though it did not participate in the race itself, the Royal Tourist made a fine showing in the Vanderbilt Cup qualification events in September 1905. ''Duplicate of the Royal Tourist that we want to sell to you finished third in elimination trials for Vanderbilt Cup Race,'' brochures subsequently headlined. These were big and luxurious cars and if ''The Pink of Perfection'' was a slogan perhaps a bit too precious, the Royal Tourist itself was a paragon of glamorous sophistication. And it was a marvelous looking car, the roundness of radiator, hood and cowl which graced 1905 models remaining a distinguishing keynote of the Royal Tourist to the end. Sales continued to be encouraging. In November of 1906 the firm was reorganized as the Royal Motor Car and Manufacturing Company, with capital stock increased from $200,000 to $500,000. In September of 1907 the Royal company moved into a spacious new factory with a workforce of 400 men. A new six-cylinder model was prepared for introduction in 1908. The Panic of '07 prevented that. Royal survived a receivership, and reorganized as the Royal Tourist Car Company in October 1908. There was no Royal Tourist six in 1909 either, but there was a decided novelty on the Royal Tourist four. Its horn was under the hood, with only the bulb for sounding it at the steering wheel hub. This was considered revolutionary, and was claimed as the first. But financial problems continued to plague the company. Ultimately, in March of 1911, Royal Tourist merged with Croxton of Cleveland and the Acme Body & Veneer Company of Rahway, New Jersey to form the Consolidated Motor Car Company. Herbert Croxton was made president, Edward Schurmer was made treasurer. Robert Jardine left immediately to join the engineering department of Jeffery in Kenosha, Wisconsin. Within months the merger fell apart, and so did any lingering hope of saving the Royal Tourist.

1904 ROYAL TOURIST
Model O — 2-cyl., 18/20 hp, 90" wb

	FP	5	4	3	2	1
Touring	2300	2700	3600	5300	8800	19,000

Model K — 4-cyl., 32/35 hp, 90" wb

	FP	5	4	3	2	1
Touring	3000	3300	4400	6700	12,000	24,000

1905 Royal Tourist, model F, touring, HAC

1905 ROYAL TOURIST
Model F — 4-cyl., 32/38 hp, 108" wb

	FP	5	4	3	2	1
Touring	3000	3500	4500	7000	13,000	25,000
Limousine	4000	3100	4200	6300	10,500	22,000

1906 Royal Tourist, model F, touring, HAC

1906 ROYAL TOURIST
Model F — 4-cyl., 40 hp, 110" wb

	FP	5	4	3	2	1
Touring-5P	3500	3900	4800	7700	14,300	27,000
Limousine-7P	4750	3100	4200	6300	10,500	22,000
Limousine-7P	5000	3200	4300	6500	11,000	23,000
Runabout-2P	3500	3500	4500	7000	13,000	25,000
Demi-Limousine	4000	2900	3700	5600	9100	20,000

1907 ROYAL TOURIST
Series G — 4-cyl., 45 hp, 114" wb

	FP	5	4	3	2	1
Runabout-2P	3500	3700	4700	7300	13,700	26,000
Touring-7P	4000	4000	5000	8000	15,000	28,000
Special Touring-7P	4000	4200	5200	8400	15,700	29,000
Limousine-7P	5000	3200	4300	6500	11,000	23,000

1908 ROYAL TOURIST
Series G — 4-cyl., 45 hp, 114" wb

	FP	5	4	3	2	1
Touring-7P	4000	3700	4700	7300	13,700	26,000
Limousine-7P	5000	3200	4300	6500	11,000	23,000

1909 ROYAL TOURIST
Model X — 4-cyl., 42 hp, 114" wb

	FP	5	4	3	2	1
Touring-7P	3500	3500	4500	7000	13,000	25,000
Cape Cod Touring-7P	3650	3700	4700	7300	13,700	26,000

Model Y — 4-cyl., 42 hp, 118" wb

	FP	5	4	3	2	1
Close-Coupled Touring-4P	3500	3700	4700	7300	13,700	26,000
Cape Cod Touring-4P	3650	3900	4800	7700	14,300	27,000

Model M — 4-cyl., 48 hp, 126" wb

	FP	5	4	3	2	1
Touring-7P	4500	3900	4800	7700	14,300	27,000
Cape Cod Touring-7P	4675	4000	5000	8000	15,000	28,000
Limousine-7P	5700	3100	4200	6300	10,500	22,000

1910 ROYAL TOURIST
Model M — 4-cyl., 48.4 hp, 126" wb

	FP	5	4	3	2	1
Touring-7P	4500	4200	5200	8400	15,700	29,000
Limousine-7P	57C0	3300	4400	6700	12,000	24,000

1908 Royal Tourist, touring, WLB

1909 Royal Tourist, touring, HAC

1911 Royal Tourist, touring, HAC

1911 ROYAL TOURIST
Model M-3 — 4-cyl., 48 hp, 126" wb

	FP	5	4	3	2	1
Touring-7P	4500	4200	5200	8400	15,700	29,000
Touring-5P	4500	4000	5000	8000	15,000	28,000
Limousine-7P	5700	3300	4400	6700	12,000	24,000

R.R.R. — The R.R.R. Company was chartered in Delaware during the summer of 1921 as a $3 million venture for the manufacture of automobiles and accessories. The incorporators were stated to be residents of Hartford, Connecticut. "The company . . . has designed a four-cylinder car with air-cooled engine and with air compression shock absorbers connecting the frame and axles to take the place of springs," *Motor Age* reported that June. "The company has also designed a large water-cooled engine to use a mixture of gasoline and crude oil." The evidence is lacking, however, that R.R.R. ever manufactured anything.

RUBAY — Leon Rubay was a Frenchman who arrived in this country shortly after the turn of the century. He became famous as a coachbuilder early on, and from 1922 to 1923 produced a line of motorcars bearing his name. Although his company carried only his last name, his coachwork and his cars were always referred to by his full name. Refer to Leon Rubay.

RUBBER BILL — The Rubber Bill Company was organized in La Porte, Indiana during the spring of 1919 with a capital stock of $25,000 to manufacture and sell automobiles. Incorporators were Axel E. Lindgren, William E. Pelz, Bernard L. Pelz, Gerald O. Dawson and Joseph N. Nelson. Manufacture is doubted.

RUBEL — R.O. Rubel, Jr. & Company has been indicated on various rosters as the producer of an automobile in Louisville, Kentucky during 1911. The firm was building aeroplanes that year at its plant on Fourth Avenue, with advertisements in *Cycle and Automobile Trade Journal* offering a "44-page illustrated Catalogue of 37 models of Motors and Aeronautical Supplies for 10 cents in stamps." But a Rubel automobile was not among the firm's products.

RUDD — The Rudd Taxi Company was organized in Brooklyn, New York late in 1909 with a capital stock of $5000 for the manufacture of "cars, cabs, vehicles, etc." Incorporators were B.R. Shears, B.W. Rudd and W.V. Burke. Manufacture is doubted.

RUDOLPH — **Philadelphia, Pennsylvania** — **(1901)** — Whether William F. Rudolph ever got into production with an automobile remains doubtful, but he did exhibit a gasoline-driven carriage of his own design at the 1901 Philadelphia Automobile Show. Although otherwise a typical motor buggy of the period, the Rudolph was distinguished by water mufflers. By 1903 William Rudolph was an automobile dealer in Philadelphia, representing the Long Distance, Packard and American automobiles.

RUGGLES — **Ware, Massachusetts** — **(1905)** — The friction-drive gasoline vehicle built by Frank W. Ruggles in 1905 in his native Ware, Massachusetts was more properly a truck than an automobile, though the Ruggles has appeared on numerous automotive rosters through the years. Ruggles himself described it as a light delivery wagon and informed the press that he was endeavoring to establish a company for manufacture. He never was able to do this in Ware, but in 1921 Frank Ruggles was in Saginaw, Michigan where he organized the Ruggles Motor Truck Company which continued in the commercial vehicle field into 1928.

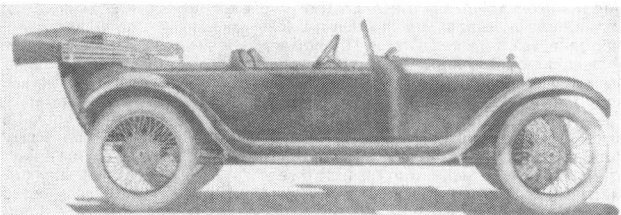

1917 Ruler, touring, WLB

RULER — **Aurora, Illinois** — **(1917)** — The Ruler did away with the usual chassis frame via a three-point arrangement with the rear wheels acting as two points and stretching to a ball-and-socket joint in the center of the front cross member as the third point. Within the triangle resulting, the clutch, transmission and differential were cradled. The body of the car therefore acted as the frame, and it could be readily removed by unfastening the ball on the front end of the cradle and disconnecting the rear springs and brakes. This frameless principle of dubious merit was patented. The Ruler's four-cylinder 17 hp overhead valve engine had a roller-type camshaft and an enclosed flywheel in front which also served as a lubricating pump. The wheelbase of the Ruler was 120 inches, and both a touring and a roadster were offered at a common $595 price. The car was introduced late in 1916 as a 1917 model, but the Ruler Motor Car Company of Aurora was out of business before the season ended.

RUNDLETT & REYNOLDS — Rundlett & Reynolds, Inc. was organized in Pelham Manor, New York during the summer of 1908 with a capital stock of $10,000 to manufacture and deal in "motor cars, motorcycles, accessories and supplies." Incorporators were G.O. Reynolds, C.W. Rundlett and George O. Reynolds. Manufacture of an automobile is doubted.

RUPP — **Kendallville, Indiana** — **(1910)** — The Rupps were carriage-makers in Kendallville who announced in July of 1910 the "satisfactory in every respect" completion of their first automobile. A four-cylinder 30 hp Waukesha engine had been used. "The management of the factory has been drafing and working on this car for some time," *Automobile Topics* reported, "and its aim has been to make it simple and durable." The extent of any production has not been documented.

RUSH — The Rush Motor Truck Company was organized in Philadelphia, Pennsylvania during the summer of 1916 with a capital stock of $500,000 for the manufacture of commercial and pleasure cars. Incorporators were Charles L. Guerin, J.D. Morelli and Emanuel Nageli, Jr. Manufacture followed, but of commercial vehicles only. Rush trucks were built into 1918.

RUSHMOBILE — Rushmobile was the designation given the steam car produced by the Brecht Automobile Company of St. Louis, Missouri from 1901-1903. Brecht also manufactured an electric. Refer to Brecht.

RUSSEL — **Detroit, Michigan** — **(1921)** — During the early Twenties, the Russel Wheel & Foundry Company of Detroit advertised its services as "car manufacturing, iron and semi-steel casting, machine and structural steel work, auto body forming and die casting." Such "manufacturing" of automobiles as the company did was undoubtedly limited to prototypes for other manufacturers or budding entrepreneurs. Among the prototypes known to have been built was a small touring model for the export market in 1921. Most probably the company built others prior to and after this date. Russel Wheel & Foundry, which was located at 8130 Joseph Campau

1921 Russel, touring, HAC

Avenue and the Belt Line Railroad, had entered the automobile industry in 1909 with the establishment of a separate department for the manufacture of axles and bevel gears. The company was a family-operated business with the Russels involved in 1921 including Walter S., C.W., Sydney R., and Albert W.

RUSSELL — "Messrs. Russell & Company [of Massillon, Ohio] are about to commence the manufacture of automobiles under the patents of Mr. C.O. Heggan, superintendent of the firm," reported *The Automobile Review* in April 1900. Manufacture is doubted, however.

The Russell Motor Vehicle was organized under Arizona laws during the fall of 1902 with a $1 million capital stock. E.L. Russell, C.E. Thompson and P.L. Russell were behind this venture. "A new hydrocarbon gas will be exploited," reported *The Horseles Age*. Manufacture is doubted.

1903 Russell, gas runabout, NAHC

RUSSELL — **Cleveland, Ohio** — **(1903-1904)** — Two levers controlled the Russell from Cleveland. A forward movement of the small one on the left side of the seat started the engine, with a further movement engaging low gear, another forward thrust kicking the car into high. A backward thrust provided reverse. A wheel provided the steering and all intermediate speeds — and that was that. Shaft drive was also featured. This quite advanced gasoline runabout was the idea of a young mechanical engineer from Cleveland named E.L. Russell, and he interested several prominent local businessmen — C.E. Thompson and F.L. Langer among them — in his automotive idea. In November of 1902 the Russell Motor Vehicle Company was organized with a capital stock of a cool million dollars, and young Russell was given the go-ahead to translate his concept into a prototype. The first car was completed during the summer of 1903. It had four cylinders and developed 6 hp. The neat two-passenger stanhope body enclosed the water and fuel tanks. The price tag was $800. From the specifications, it appeared that Russell had a world-beater. Early in 1904 the company announced its purchase of a large woolen mill which would be converted into a factory. But then the Russell faded from sight. Conceivably, young Russell's advanced ideas did not work well in production reality.

RUSSELL-DEIBLER — **Ripon, Wisconsin** — **(1908-1909)** — Frank Russell was the owner of the Frank Russell Moccasin Company in Ripon, and Ed Deibler seems to have been remembered by area residents chiefly because he always carried a live parrot on his shoulders. Both were automobile enthusiasts, and built several cars together. The first was completed during the summer of 1908, and the second (a tourer on a 116-inch wheelbase and powered by a four-cylinder 40 hp Rutenber engine) was finished that December. The latter was sold to Charles Kulnick, the mayor of Ripon. A serious foray into automobile manufacture was not considered by either Russell or Deibler, though Frank Russell told a reporter from the *Berlin Evening Journal* in 1909 that he was selling his 40 hp Pope-Toledo because he preferred his own cars. At that time he was at work on a six. His sideline automotive activity came to an abrupt halt, however, in 1910 when he invited fellow Ripon auto enthusiast William Schaefer (who had also built a car of his own) over to help with a carburetion problem. A broken light bulb and an oil-soaked floor resulted in the biggest fire in local history — and Frank Russell had to devote all his energies thereafter to rebuilding his moccasin factory.

1903 Russell-Springfield, runabout, NAHC

1929 Ruxton, 4-dr. sedan, OCW

RUSSELL-SPRINGFIELD — Springfield, Ohio — (1903) — At the turn of the century the Brennings of Springfield built at least one example of an electric car patented by Dr. C.W. Russell, also of Springfield. Dr. Russell's next car was gasoline powered which he introduced late in 1902 as a 1903 model and which he decided to market on his own as the Russell-Springfield. It was powered by a single-cylinder 9 hp water-cooled engine mounted under the seat of the two-passenger runabout body, featured a three-speed selective transmission, chain drive, force-feed lubrication and right-hand wheel steering. The price for all this was $1250, which was rather exhorbitant and doubtless the reason Dr. Russell never formally organized a company for manufacture, and presumably returned to his doctoring instead.

RUTAN — The Rutan Auto Company was organized in Port Jervis, New York early in 1911 with a capital stock of $45,000 for the manufacture and sale of motorcars and engines. The Rutans involved were P.C., J.S. and J.A. Manufacture is doubted.

RUTENBER — Logansport, Indiana — (1902) — During the summer of 1902, shortly following the move of the Rutenber Manufacturing Company from Chicago to Logansport, the firm commenced the production of ten automobiles. One of these is known to have been destined for C.W. Swift of the famous Chicago meat packing house. So far as is known, this series of cars was Rutenber's first and last. The company subsequently became famous, of course, as an engine builder.

1907 Ruth, runabout, LC

RUTH — North Webster, Indiana — (1907) — The Ruth Automobile Company of North Webster was a small car-building venture organized by Mack Mock, Charlie Daniels and Henry Outcelt. Since each of them had a daughter named Ruth, they decided to call their car that too. The Ruth was a highwheeler with chain drive, flexible spring suspension, a right-hand steering wheel, oil-burning lamps and substantial running boards which extended to the front to become fenders. Sales were modest, and to area residents only, including one to the town doctor who used his Ruth in making house calls. Charlie Daniels supplied the barn in which the vehicles were built. Mack Mock was known locally as "Tinker" because it was said he could make parts to fix everything from a watch to a threshing machine. Later he was associated with Henry Outcelt in the Rapid Rim Company, which produced an early variation of the demountable wheel rim.

RUXTON — St. Louis, Missouri & Hartford, Wisconsin — (1929-1930) — During the summer of 1929 C.W. Burst was president of the Moon Motor Car Company, having succeeded Stewart McDonald the year previous. His product line was composed of the Windsor automobile and a cottonpicker built under contract from the American Cottonpicker Corporation. During the summer of 1930, William Muller was president of Moon, and the com-

pany was also producing the Ruxton, the new front-wheel-drive automobile of Muller's design. What happened in between has as much intrigue as most espionage dramas. During the late Twenties, while working as an experimental engineer at the Edward G. Budd Manufacturing Company (producer of automobile bodies in Philadelphia), Muller persuaded management to allow him to develop a front-wheel-drive prototype. The idea was to sell the design to some manufacturer, with bodies by Budd, of course. Muller completed his prototype — its body designed by Joseph Ledwinka — during the fall of 1928; the engine was a Studebaker six, the wheelbase was 130 inches, and the car was just a tad over 63 inches high. (Most automobiles on the road then were about ten inches higher.) Instead of a manufacturer, however, a free-wheeling promoter and financier became interested: Archie M. Andrews, whose several board director-ships included Budd and the Hupp Motor Car Corporation. When he could not convince Hupp to produce the car, Andrews decided to do it himself and in April 1929 organized New Era Motors, Inc. with headquarters at 17 East 45th Street in New York City — but no factory. Where that would be became the next order of business following Muller's completion of a production prototype (with 100 hp Continental straight-eight engine) soon after. Andrews struck out in his first three tries — Peerless, Gardner and Marmon — following the Hupp turn-down, but though his inning seemed over, it was not. In November 1929 announcement came from St. Louis that Moon would build the Ruxton. No doubt the Moon people viewed the car as the perfect vehicle to lift their company out of the sales doldrums it had been in for the past few years. No doubt they didn't reckon on losing their company in the process. And that's precisely what happened, Andrews managing a deft controlling percentage of the Moon stock in exchange for the Ruxton design and patent rights. With Alamo-like determination, C.W. Burst and his officers barricaded themselves in Moon's St. Louis plant. Andrews and his gang — including Muller, whom he appointed

1929 Ruxton, multi-colored sedan, JAC

to the Moon presidency — were equally determined, and broke in . . . court order in hand. The entire matter of Moon control went to court thereafter, with suits followed by countersuits, but by June of 1930 the Ruxton had joined the Windsor on the assembly line in St. Louis, Missouri — about the same time that it joined the Kissel on its assembly line in Hartford, Wisconsin. Archie Andrews had maneuvered a deal with the Kissel brothers too. They didn't bother to sue; instead, in mid-September, rather than allow their company to fall into Andrews' hands, George and Will Kissel requested receivership. Since part of the Kissel contract had been for production in Hartford of transmissions and final drive assemblies for all Ruxtons, the operation in St. Louis was stymied. The Ruxton venture had depleted the Moon treasury in any case, and that factory's doors were closed on November 10th, followed by receivership on November 15th. Both Moon and Kissel were out of the automobile business, though Kissel was reorganized as Kissel Industries for other work, and Moon's tangled affairs were not irrevocably wound up until 1965. (The company's plant and assets had been sold in 1935, but payment of a claim awarded the firm in the Pennsylvania courts ten years earlier was pursued relentlessly by a Philadelphia law firm, until finally in the mid-Sixties 355 Moon creditors of record divvied up $26,000.) Archie Andrews, meanwhile, jumped from Ruxton, Moon and his now-bankrupt New Era Motors to Hupp Motor Car Corporation where he assumed the chairmanship of the board, until

1930 Ruxton, roadster, OCW

the courts and angry stockholders took it away from him. Andrews died in 1938 at age fifty-nine. The Ruxton had died eight years earlier, though some of the approximately 500 cars built were not sold until 1932. Most of the production had occurred at Moon, with only about twenty-five cars assembled at Kissel, including two special phaetons for the Kissel brothers. There were other occasional custom-built cars, but the majority of Ruxtons were roadster or sedans (the open bodies by Raulang, the closed by Budd). They were good cars, and strikingly handsome, with looks as dramatic as the life of the Ruxton itself, especially the sedans provided those wild multi-colored striped paint schemes. There were no running boards on any Ruxton, and many of them sported cat's-eye Woodlites. On the radiator, tire covers and large hubcaps was a beautifully stylized rendering of a griffin, the half-eagle, half-lion monster of classic mythology. Though the machinations of Archie Andrews in attempting to bring the Ruxton to life were often monstrous, it seems evident he was genuinely interested in the Ruxton as a car, which tends to make its story just a little bit sad. The car's name, incidentally, was borrowed from William V.C. Ruxton, who was a major figure in the New York Stock Exchange at the time and a minor acquaintance of Andrews' — and whom the latter hoped to interest in investing in New Era Motors. Ruxton never did invest, though he had to take Archie Andrews to court to prove it.

1930 Ruxton, custom leather-top, brougham, HAC

1929-1930 RUXTON
Eight — 100 hp, 130" wb

	FP	5	4	3	2	1
Roadster	3195	31,000	58,000	88,000	114,000	150,000
Sedan	3195	13,500	27,000	45,000	70,000	90,000
Phaeton				Value Inestimatible		
Town Car	—	25,500	45,000	73,000	100,000	130,000

1920 R&V Knight, model J, sedan, JAC

R&V KNIGHT — East Moline, Illinois — (1920-1924) — The initials of this sleeve-valve-engined car referred to Orlando J. Root and W.H. Vandervoort whose partnership dated back to 1899 and the establishment of the Root & Vandervoort Engineering Company for the production of gasoline engines in East Moline. In 1904 the partners organized the Moline Automobile Company and from that year through 1919 manufactured the Moline and subsequently the Moline-Knight under its auspices. The new R&V Knight of 1920 was simply a continuation of the Moline-Knight, marketed by the Root & Vandervoort Engineering Company. Production for 1920 totaled 767 cars, the first half of 1921 saw 450 R&V's built. Two factors conspired to undermine the success of this longtime automotive firm. The first was the death in 1921 of W.H. Vandervoort. The second took longer to arrive, but its seeds had been planted during World War I when the company undertook a major expansion following the awarding of lucrative government contracts. The debts incurred had not been repaid when the postwar depression set in, and the economic downturn forced the company out of existence late in 1924. Its assets save for rights to the R&V four-cylinder engine sold the year previous to Yellow — were assigned to Moline Body Corporation, one of R&V's largest creditors. Orlando J. Root died in 1928 from a self-inflicted bullet wound.

1920 R&V KNIGHT
Model R — 4-cyl., 43 hp, 115" wb

	FP	5	4	3	2	1
Touring-5P	2150	3900	4800	7700	14,300	27,000
Sedan-5P	2700	2000	3000	4200	6500	14,000

Model J — 6-cyl., 60 hp, 127" wb

	FP	5	4	3	2	1
Touring-7P	3050	4500	5800	9500	18,000	32,000
Sport-4P	3050	4700	6100	9900	19,000	33,000
Roadster-2P	3050	4500	5800	9500	18,000	32,000
Sedan-7P	3800	2500	3500	5000	8500	18,000
Coupe-4P	3700	2900	3700	5600	9100	20,000

1921 R&V Knight, model J, roadster, WLB

1921 R&V KNIGHT
Model R — 4-cyl., 44 hp, 115" wb

	FP	5	4	3	2	1
Touring-5P	2150	3900	4800	7700	14,300	27,000

Model J — 6-cyl., 54 hp, 127" wb

	FP	5	4	3	2	1
Touring-7P	3350	4500	5800	9500	18,000	32,000
Roadster-2P	3350	4500	5800	9500	18,000	32,000
Sport-5P	3350	4700	6100	9900	19,000	33,000
Coupe-4P	4000	2900	3700	5600	9100	20,000
Sedan-7P	4200	2500	3500	5000	8500	18,000

1922 R&V Knight, model J, sedan, HAC

1922 R&V KNIGHT
Model R — 4-cyl., 44 bhp, 116" wb

	FP	5	4	3	2	1
Coupe-4P	2650	2300	3300	4600	7500	16,000
Sedan-5P	2750	2000	3000	4200	6500	14,000
Touring-5P	1850	3700	4700	7300	13,700	26,000

Model J — 6-cyl., 54 bhp, 127" wb

	FP	5	4	3	2	1
Coupe-4P	4000	2500	3500	5000	8500	18,000
Sedan-7P	4200	2300	3300	4600	7500	16,000
Touring-7P	3350	4400	5600	9200	17,300	31,000
Sport-4P	3350	4500	5800	9500	18,000	32,000
Roadster-2P	3350	4400	5600	9200	17,300	31,000

1923 R&V KNIGHT
Model R — 4-cyl., 44 hp, 116" wb

	FP	5	4	3	2	1
Touring-5P	1665	3700	4700	7300	13,700	26,000
Coupe-4P	2385	2300	3300	4600	7500	16,000
Sedan-5P	2475	2000	3000	4200	6500	14,000

1923 R&V Knight, model H, touring, HAC

Model H — 6-cyl., 56 hp, 124" wb

	FP	5	4	3	2	1
Touring-5P	2850	4300	5400	8700	16,500	30,000
Sport-4P	2850	4500	5800	9500	18,000	32,000
Touring-7P	2900	4400	5600	9200	17,300	31,000
Club Sedan-5P	3500	2400	3400	4800	8000	17,000
Sedan-7P	3700	2300	3300	4600	7500	16,000

1924 R&V Knight, model H, sedan, OCW

1924 R&V KNIGHT
Model H — 6-cyl., 56 hp, 124" wb

	5	4	3	2	1
Touring-5P	2495	4300	5400	8700	16,500	30,000
Touring-7P	2575	4400	5600	9200	17,300	31,000
Coupe-5P	3225	2500	3500	5000	8500	18,000
Club Sedan-5P	3275	2300	3300	4600	7500	16,000
Sedan-7P	3495	2200	3200	4400	7000	15,000
Sport-4P	2595	2000	3000	4200	6500	14,000

RYDER — San Francisco, California — (1900) — Bainbridge L. Ryder first came to public notice in the vehicle field when he attempted to build a gasoline-powered street car in 1896-1897. His Ryder Electro Motor Company was located in the Mills Building on Bush Street in San Francisco, and compressed air apparently was planned to augment internal combustion in the trolley he was endeavoring to produce. On October 4th, 1897 the *Berkeley Gazette* reported that the owners of the horse car line had decided to give up on Ryder, however, having become "weary of promises" after numerous false starts and failures. The budding inventor had better luck with his automobile. This Ryder was a small air-cooled two-cylinder gasoline runabout which B.L. attempted to market under his own name in 1900. The necessary capital failing him, Ryder joined the California Automobile Company later that year, and became superintendent of its factory. Among the cars produced there was the air-cooled Ryder runabout, now renamed California.

RYDER — San Francisco, California — (1900) — B.L. Ryder of San Francisco built a small air-cooled two-cylinder gasoline runabout in 1900 which he attempted to market under his own name. The necessary capital failing him, he joined the California Automobile Company later that year, and became superintendent of its factory. Among the cars produced there was the air-cooled Ryder runabout, now renamed California.

RYLANDER — The Rylander Manufacturing Company was organized in Biddeford, Maine early in 1914 with a capital stock of $400,000 for the manufacture and sale of motor vehicles of all kinds. Incorporators were J.A. Snow of Scarborough and F.B. Ross of Biddeford. Manufacture of a car is doubted.

SAFETY — Although the Safety Buggy Company of Lancaster, Pennsylvania was cited as the producer of an automobile in 1902 by *Cycle and Automobile Trade Journal*, it did not build a car. Instead, the firm manufactured wooden bodies for other car producers (the Autocar and Imperial of Pennsylvania among them), with production of these beginning in 1901 and continuing until 1907 when the firm failed because it lacked the money to outfit its plant for manufacture of wood-framed metal coachwork. Late in the year previous B.G. Dodge, L.G. Dodge and A.B. Dodge had grandly incorporated the Safety Buggy Company with a capital stock of $250,000 but obviously had been unable to interest investment capital.

The Safety Electric Operating Company was organized in Jersey City, New Jersey during the summer of 1908 with a capital stock of $500,000 to "manufacture, operate, buy and sell motor vehicles." Incorporators were H.W. Andrews, G.E. Osborne and Charles D. Montague. Manufacture is doubted.

The Safety Shredder Company of New Castle, Indiana produced a car called the Lawter in 1909. Refer to Lawter.

The Safety Steering Gear Company was organized in Gloucester, Massachusetts late in 1914 with a capital stock of $50,000 for the manufacture of motor cars. Incorporators were F.H. Tarr and H.C. Tufts. Manufacture is doubted.

The Safety Three Wheel Vehicle Company was indicated as an automobile manufacturer in New York City in the Hiscox book *Horseless Vehicles, Automobiles, Motor Cycles* published in 1900. Documentation is lacking. The firm was in existence at the turn of the century, however, at 306 West 53rd Street and was one of three automotive enterprises (International Motor Wheel and G. Edgar Allen the other two) on that block.

1901 Safety Steamer, MVMA

SAFETY STEAM — **Ipswich, Massachusetts** — **(1901-1902)** — The Safety Steam Automobile Company located its headquarters in Boston and its factory near Depot Square in Ipswich. Its product was a small runabout which, the company said, profited by retaining the good and getting rid of the bad features of earlier steam vehicles on the market. The Safety featured a single-cylinder engine, tubular boiler, seven-gallon gasoline and thirty-gallon water tanks, elliptical springs and tiller steering. The Safety Company boasted that all the nuts and bolts it used were standard and could be duplicated anywhere. While this was not exactly standardization of parts, it was a noble effort. A large toolbox was mounted up front and a smaller one under the seat for emergency purposes. In addition to the runabout, the company offered a four-passenger brake and a light delivery wagon. Production was discontinued sometime during 1902.

SAFETY FIRST — **Kalamazoo, Michigan** — **(1914-1915)** — The Safety-First Motor Car Company was organized in Kalamazoo in August of 1914 with a capital stock of $10,000 and a plan to manufacture four-wheel-drive automobiles and trucks according to a patent secured by Frank Dentler. F.A. Young was president of the company, W.P. Haines vice-president and George J. Haines secretary-treasurer. Offices were taken in Kalamazoo, and announcement was made that the factory would be located in Plainwell. Safety-First went under before moving into the plant, however. At least one truck, and possibly a car, were built at the Reed Manufacturing Company prior to Safety-First giving up on the automotive idea. Interestingly, a car called the Safety-First was given a good deal of publicity that year during a coast-to-coast trek, but that vehicle was not this Safety-First. It was the nickname given to a 1915 Jeffery Four touring the country in the cause of highway safety.

SAF-T-CAB — **Cleveland, Ohio** — **(1926-1928)** — The Saf-T-Cab Corporation of Cleveland was the taxi-building arm of the Auburn Automobile Company of Auburn, Indiana. The taxis were built in the Auburn factory, though it was carefully emphasized that they were not simply converted Auburns. Instead, the Saf-T-Cab carried a special Lycoming six-cylinder bus-type engine, and its chassis featured heavy-duty chassis frames, axles, transmission, clutch and other components.

1914 Saginaw, cyclecar, NAHC

SAGINAW — **Saginaw, Michigan** — **(1914)** — Flamboyant was the word for the Saginaw cyclecar. Its fenders, which were built in unit with the body, flowed in an extravagant curve from the rear all the way up to the front, where the headlights peeked out a la Pierce-Arrow. The car, which originally was to be called the Faultless, was the product of the Valley Boat & Engine Company and was powered by the firm's own four-stroke 9/12 hp vee-twin. Its frame was wood and steel braced by truss rods, with quarter-elliptic cantilever springs front and rear. Friction transmission was used, and final drive was by vee belt. The price was $395, which included top, curtains, Stewart-Warner speedometer, tools, a tire repair kit, and an "electric horn of the vibrator type." Fifty miles an hour was promised, as was fifty miles to a gallon of fuel. Early in 1914 Valley company president Newell Barnard announced that the prototype car had been driven for several test months and had successfully negotiated snow drifts which had forced horsedrawn vehicles back to the barn. The Saginaw cyclecar's road clearance was eight-and-a-half inches, this "liberal" dimension being provided, as the Valley company said, "in order that it could travel through the sandy roads of summer or the snow-clad highways of winter." Production of the Saginaw cyclecar was discontinued late in 1914. Valley remained in the boat business until approximately 1920.

1914 SAGINAW
Cyclecar — 2-cyl., 9/12 hp, 100½" wb

	FP	5	4	3	2	1
Side-by-Side Roadster	395	1800	2800	4000	6200	13,000

SAGINAW EIGHT — **Saginaw, Michigan** — **(1916)** — Residents of Saginaw were informed of the news in their local paper on January 15th, 1916. A new automobile venture known as the Lehr Motor Company was coming to town, and the Saginaw Chamber of Commerce was enthusiastic and optimistic. "We have investigated Mr. MacKaye and the plans," a spokesman told a reporter from the *Saginaw Daily News*, "and found through competent sources that everything is all right." Apparently it wasn't. Harry MacKaye was an engineer from Cleveland who had designed the eight-cylinder car which was planned to be sold at an attractive $1050. He would be Lehr's general manager. The company's officers were William M. Guider as president, Alfred F. Myer as vice-president and Cury M. Schwahn as secretary-treasurer — all of these men residents of Saginaw. The Lehr Motor Company was incorporated under the lenient laws of Maine with a capital stock of $400,000. A factory was secured somewhere on River Street. Calling the product a Saginaw was good public relations. It would appear that a few Saginaw Eights were built, and possibly a couple of examples of a four-cylinder version — but the Lehr Motor Company was out of business by year's end, its notice of dissolution being filed October 24th, 1916. Interestingly, Lehr's most significant coup — other than selling stock in the venture — was no doubt its success in preventing another automotive enterprise which came to town that year from calling its product a Saginaw too. Thus, the new Saginaw Motor Car Company was forced to rename its product the Yale. It was a considerably more successful car.

SAGINAW SPEEDSTER — The Saginaw Speedster of 1914 began life in Detroit as the Detroit Cyclecar. The name change followed its promoter's move to Saginaw; the car remained the same. Refer to Detroit.

ST. CLAIR — The St. Clair Motor Company was organized in Detroit, Michigan during the spring of 1906 with a capital stock of $35,000 for the manufacture of engines, automobiles and power boats. Incorporators were Harry D. Baird, Earl Roscoe Ryno and Ulrich A. Abrahams. Manufacture of a car is doubted.

ST. CHARLES — The St. Charles Motor Truck Company was organized in St. Charles, Missouri during the summer of 1914 with a capital stock of $150,000 for the manufacture of motor cars and trucks. Incorporators were William F. Breedlove and C.E. Tillman. Manufacture is doubted.

The St. Charles Specialty Company was organized in St. Charles, Illinois during the spring of 1912 with a capital stock of $10,000 to manufacture and repair automobiles. Incorporators were H.G. Hempstead, Lawrence H. Jensen and Mary M. Andrews. Manufacture is doubted.

ST. JOE — **Elkhart, Indiana** — **(1908)** — The total number of cars built bearing the St. Joe emblem is not known, but there could not have been many, since the car was in essence a transition between the Shoemaker and the Sellers. The St. Joe Motor Car Company was organized in the late spring of 1908 to take over the assets of the defunct Shoemaker company. Harry C. Shoemaker was part of the organization team, and it would seem a shoestring represented its operating funds. Late that fall a group of businessmen from Hutchinson, Kansas arrived in Elkhart with the promise to subscribe sufficient capital for a plant to be located there — and Harry Shoemaker jumped at the chance. Trade press references from December indicate that the move to Hutchinson would be followed by a change of the firm's name to Sunflower Motor Car Company. But when St. Joe arrived in Kansas in February of 1909, its name became instead the Sellers Motor Car Company. O.G. Sellers had been a stockholder and officer of the Shoemaker company since its early days in Freeport, Illinois.

1908 St. Joe, touring, WLB

1909 ST. JOE
Model D — 4-cyl., 35/40 hp, 120" wb

	FP	5	4	3	2	1
Touring-5P	2500	3700	4700	7300	13,700	26,000

1903 St. John, runabout, GR

ST. JOHN — **Canon City, Colorado** — **(1903)** — Only one of these cars was built by S.H. St. John & Son of 620 Main Street in Canon City, and its purpose was to encourage investor interest in its manufacture. The St. John featured a single-cylinder engine and single chain drive. Its unusual, and patented, feature was the presence of two flywheels operating in opposite directions. This construction made it possible to reverse the vehicle quickly, "and as the flywheel continues to revolve for a full minute, the automobile is ready to go forward again instantly." Only the loose flywheel was used for starting, and this again was for ease of operation or, as St. John put it, "the braking effect of compression in the cylinder is thus avoided, (and) a lady can start the engine with ease and from the seat." St. John & Son declared itself anxious to talk to anyone interested in securing rights to its patent. Whether anyone was is not known.

ST. LOUIS — In addition to the St. Louis cars which are documented to have been built in Missouri, there were a number of ventures named St. Louis which were organized for the purpose of automobile manufacture but which seem never to have reached the building stage.

The St. Louis Automobile Car Company organized during the spring of 1908 with a capital stock of $20,000 by L.A. Hopkins and W.S. Metas.

The St. Louis Automobile & Truck Company organized late in 1903 with a capital stock of $20,000 by E. Reubel, C.J. Briner and Ferdinand C. Schwidtman.

The St. Louis Motor Car Company organized late in 1904 with a capital stock of $100,000 by Marshall A. Sattley, Marquis Eaton and M.M. Keiner.

The St. Louis Woodwork Manufacturing Company organized early in 1918 with a capital stock of $100,000 by John S. Hunt, Samuel G. Hunsaker, Fred W. Fegel, John T. White, Fred W. Bensing, Larry J. Murphy and Albert F. Diederich.

ST. LOUIS — **St. Louis, Missouri** — **(1899)** — In November of 1898 the St. Louis Gasolene Motor Company was incorporated with a capital stock of $50,000. Involved in this venture were L.H. Daman, O.L. Anderson, J.D. Fishback and Louis Langan. Langan had already built at least two automobiles himself and doubtless was the designer of the new St. Louis car. Its engine was a 2 hp four-stroke one-lunger which, it was said, could be "run for one day with one filling of water and oil and costs but one-half cent per hour." What the employees were paid who were putting together the St. Louis is not known but by January of 1900 five of them had attached the company for back wages. The officers of the firm were said at the time to be "out of the city." By now Louis Langan had ventured east to join the Buffalo Gasoline Motor Company in Upstate New York. And this St. Louis from St. Louis was no more.

1899 St. Louis, runabout, JAC

ST. LOUIS — **St. Louis, Missouri** — **(1899-1905)/Peoria, Illinois** — **(1905-1907)** — The St. Louis Motor Carriage Company was organized by two men from Nashville, Tennessee: George Dorris, who built his first experimental car back home in 1895, and John L. French, who left home that year for St. Louis to join his father's Jesse French Piano and Organ Company. In 1898 French and Dorris got together in Missouri to begin their automobile company. John French brought in his entire family; the only officers other than Dorris noted in the $30,000 incorporation of the St. Louis Motor Carriage Company were Joseph French, Callie French, H.E. French and Jesse French, Jr. The factory built on North Vandewater Avenue in St. Louis in 1899 was described at the time as "one of the few buildings in the United States erected specially for the manufacture of gasoline vehicles." The St. Louis Carriage Company was the first successful automobile business west of the Mississippi. From 1899 to 1900 the firm produced 130 cars; production totals for 1902-1903 were 250 cars, with 230 cars built in 1904, 300 in 1905. Single- and two-cylinder engines powered the tiller-steered chain-drive dos-a-dos runabouts which St. Louis produced into the turn of the century. Wheel steering followed in 1902, together with a four-cylinder model. The chief asset of the St. Louis company was its chief engineer, George Dorris. An example of his progressive engineering was the very early use by St. Louis of a unit-type powerplant — sliding gear transmission in the crankcase and submerged in oil — though the transmission-operated single wooden brake shoe which was continued on all cars into 1904 was retrograde. During these early years the cars were advertised by the effective slogan, "Rigs That Run," with the company proving it in numerous endurance contests of the period. When an article appearing in *The Horseless Age* reported that a St. Louis had to be towed in one event, John L. French wrote a nicely indignant letter to the editor, which the magazine reprinted under the headline, "The St. Louis, as Everybody Knows, Is a Good Hill Climber." Perhaps it was the company's success which was its undoing. John French decided to expand and to relocate. Late in 1905 the firm reorganized as the St. Louis Motor Car Company and moved to Peoria, Illinois and a large new three-story factory on ten acres of land. George Dorris preferred to remain in St. Louis and build a new car to carry his own name. His old company fared not at all well without him. All Peoria-built St. Louis cars were shaft-drive fours. In

July 1907, Jesse French, Jr. admitted that his family enterprise was "financially embarrassed," in August the firm was petitioned into receivership by creditors. Fifty-one cars were in the process of construction then. They were completed, and the Peoria plant was sold in December for $10,000.

1900 St. Louis, runabout, JAC

1901 St. Louis, runabout, JAC

1903 St. Louis, Boston Carriage, NAHC

1904 St. Louis, tonneau, MVMA

1905 St. Louis, side entrance tonneau, HAC

1901 ST. LOUIS
Single-Cylinder

	FP	5	4	3	2	1
Runabout (7 hp)	1000	2300	3300	4600	7500	16,000
Trap (9 hp)	1250	2350	3400	4900	7800	16,500
Delivery (10 hp)	1250	2200	3200	4400	7000	15,000
Two-Cylinder						
Delivery (15 hp)	—	2300	3300	4600	7500	16,000
Bus (25 hp)	—	2300	3300	4600	7500	16,000

1902 ST. LOUIS
Boston Carriage — 1-cyl., 8 hp

	FP	5	4	3	2	1
Touring	—	2200	3200	4400	7000	15,000
Four Cylinder — 35 hp						
Touring	—	2400	3400	4800	8000	17,000

1903 ST. LOUIS
Boston Carriage — 1-cyl., 8 hp

	FP	5	4	3	2	1
Touring	1200	2300	3300	4600	7500	16,000
Light Tonneau — 1-cyl., 9 hp						
Touring	1500	2300	3300	4600	7500	16,000
Two Cylinder — 16 hp						
Victoria	5000	2400	3400	4800	8000	17,000

1904 ST. LOUIS
Single Cylinder — 9 hp, 75'' wb

	FP	5	4	3	2	1
Runabout	1200	2300	3300	4600	7500	16,000
Single Cylinder — 10-1/2 hp, 80'' wb						
Tonneau	1500	2400	3400	4800	8000	17,000
Three Cylinder — 24 hp, 90'' wb						
Tonneau	2500	2500	3500	5000	8500	18,000

1905 ST. LOUIS
Single Cylinder — 12 hp, 86'' wb

	FP	5	4	3	2	1
Side Entrance Tonneau	1400	2400	3400	4800	8000	17,000
Two Cylinder — 16 hp, 86'' wb						
Side Entrance Tonneau	1600	2500	3500	5000	8500	18,000
Three Cylinder — 20/24 hp, 86'' wb						
Side Entrance Tonneau	2100	2700	3600	5300	8800	19,000

1906 ST. LOUIS
Type XV — 4-cyl., 30/34 hp, 104'' wb

	FP	5	4	3	2	1
Touring-5P	2200	3300	4400	6700	12,000	24,000
Type XVI — 4-cyl., 32/36 hp, 108'' wb						
Touring-5P	2500	3700	4700	7300	13,700	26,000

1907 ST. LOUIS
Type XVIII — 4-cyl., 35 hp, 108'' wb

	FP	5	4	3	2	1
Touring-5P	2500	3300	4400	6700	12,000	24,000
Type XVII — 4-cyl., 35 hp, 108'' wb						
Runabout-2P	2250	3200	4300	6500	11,000	23,000
Type XIX — 4-cyl., 45/50 hp, 112'' wb						
Touring-5/7P	3000	4300	5400	8700	16,500	30,000

1906 St. Louis, touring, OCW

1907 St. Louis, touring, HAC

ST. LOUIS — St. Louis, Missouri — (1905) — In 1905 the St. Louis Car Company, which had long been in the business of building railroad cars in Missouri, made its first attempt in the automobile field. The light two-cylinder runabout designed by company superintendent Theodore P. Meinhard and announced as the St. Louis was not a success, however, and few were built. The year following the St. Louis Car Company returned to the automobile field with a new car called the Kobusch, named for company president George J. Kobusch.

ST. LOUIS — St. Louis, Missouri — (1911) — In 1911 a Philadelphia engineer by the name of W.D. Williams was in St. Louis scouting for money and a factory site in order to manufacture automobiles using a rotary steam engine of his invention. He found the money — with the St. Louis Automobile and Engine Company being organized with a capital stock of $50,000 — and there was at least one prototype built, but the flow of venture capital came to an abrupt halt, and no factory site ever was necessary.

ST. LOUIS — St. Louis, Missouri — (1921-1923) — The Neskov-Mumperow Motor Car Company was a distributor for the Anderson car and a dealer for the Dort and Gardner. Neskov was John M.; Mumperow's first name seems lost to history, but it would appear that he had retired from the business by 1921 in any case. The new car to be built by the company wasn't initially given a name but it was, in John Neskov's words, to be a "tailored automobile, outfitted to suit the taste of the purchaser with color scheme to match." Two cars, designed by John A. Schroeder, were nearing completion for exhibit at the Automobile Exposition to be held in the General Motors plant in St. Louis in mid-October 1921. One was a four-passenger sporting car, the other a speedster for three passengers. The wheelbase was 125 inches, and the price was calculated in the $2600 range. Both four-cylinder Weidely and Rochester-Duesenberg engines

would be available. By the time the cars arrived at the Exposition, a name had been decided upon. It was St. Louis. In 1922 John Neskov organized the St. Louis Automotive Company for manufacture. And the car subsequently appeared at both the 1922 and 1923 St. Louis Automobile Shows. But plans for manufacture were dashed. In August of 1923 John Neskov requested receivership, lamenting that all of his assets had been eaten up in salaries and the building of a total of five St. Louis cars which were now in storage and against which there were mortgages. He had debts of several thousand dollars, and $2.85 cash in the bank. The St. Louis venture was decidely over.

ST. LOUIS ELECTRIC — At the turn of the century in St. Louis, Missouri, Andrew Lee Dyke established the first automobile supply business in America and became a pioneer in the kit car business too. In 1899 he organized the St. Louis Electric Automobile Company and produced an assembled stanhope and runabout variously called a Dyke or St. Louis. These were the first electric vehicles manufactured west of the Mississippi. Refer to Dyke.

1895 Salisbury, gasoline carriage, NAHC

SALISBURY — Chicago, Illinois — (1895) — The inventor of this pioneer gasoline car was either Walter S. Salisbury (according to *The Carriage Monthly*) or Wilbur I. Salisbury (*The Horseless Age*). Conceivably, he may have had a dreadful handwriting. He had a curious notion of what an automobile might be, too. The Salisbury was powered by a single-cylinder 5 hp engine and it was a three-wheeler with the driving wheel in the center at the rear and geared direct by shaft to the engine up front. Each of the three wheels were forty-eight inches in diameter, and Salisbury noted that he could easily revise the vehicle into a four-wheeler if desired. Already he had organized his Horseless Carriage Company and encouraged inquiries to 1616 Masonic Temple in Chicago. His company never got off the ground.

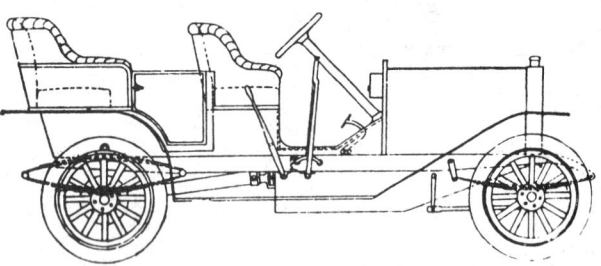

1910 Salter, model A, touring, NAHC

SALTER — Kansas City, Missouri — (1909-1915) — The W.A. Salter Motor Company was organized in Kansas City in September of 1909 and moved into its new factory at 1516 Oakland Street later that year. The Salter automobile was a 30 hp four on a 110-inch wheelbase which was offered as a roadster for $1700 and a tourer for $1750. The car was conventional save for one feature of William Salter's own design. The transmission was a planetary with two speeds forward, but reverse was not combined with the change-speed gears but instead was fitted with the driving gears on the rear axle. Salter patented this idea and apparently produced his car in small numbers for six years. Thereafter, however, he converted his factory into a general machine shop.

SALVADOR — Boston, Massachusetts — (1914)/S-J-R — (1915-1916) — The man behind the Salvador and the S-J-R was Salvador J. Richards who located his offices in the Farragut Building at 126 Massachusetts Avenue

1914 Salvador, 2-pass. cyclecar, WLB

and his factory at 28 Scotia Street in Boston. His first automotive effort was a cyclecar powered by a four-cylinder 12 hp water-cooled engine built in unit with a three-speed selective transmission, most unusual for a cyclecar. Shaft drive and worm-and-sector steering were featured in the Salvador, which had a wheelbase of 100 inches and a price tag of $485 — and in May of 1914 Richards announced that he had three cars "in active running on Massachusetts roads" and that his Salvador Motor Company would be ready to make "a limited number of deliveries" in June. Limited would be the total production of the Salvador, however, because the car was discontinued by year's end. But by February of 1915, Richards was back again announcing his new S.J.R. Motor Company which he initially said would manufacture both a narrow-tread and a standard-tread car. Reflecting upon the cyclecar debacle of the season previous, he ultimately decided to produce just the latter. Like the Salvador, the new S-J-R was a three-passenger roadster which resembled its predecessor, though the standard tread made it more comfortable and its designation as a "Boulevard-Roadster" made it more chic. "The beautiful dull-gray finished body, with its clean, racy, snappy lines, calls compellingly to red-blooded men and women," brochures said. The S-J-R was powered by a four-cylinder 25/30 hp water-cooled engine again built in unit with a three-speed selective transmission, and shaft drive was featured in its 108-inch wheelbase chassis. But there was a hefty premium for the extra power and the extra room. The S-J-R was priced at $855. Though production was indicated to have continued into mid-1916, total output was minimal.

1916 S.J.R., boulevard roadster, WLB

SALZMAN — Boston, Massachusetts — (1897, 1910) — George S. Salzman built an experimental gasoline car in Boston in 1897. It was not put into manufacture. Subsequently, Salzman — who claimed to hold degrees from both Princeton and M.I.T. — became production manager for the E.R. Thomas Company in Buffalo, New York. By 1910 he had relocated to the Pacific Northwest where he showed up in a number of local road races, and designed another car which the Patent Holding and Manufacturing Company of Spokane, Washington indicated it would manufacture. Again, however, manufacture did not follow. Instead Salzman returned east where he worked awhile for the American Simplex company in Mishawaka, Indiana. In 1913 he designed the Grant that was produced in Detroit.

1911 Sampson, 35, touring, NAHC

SAMPSON — Detroit, Michigan — (1911) — In 1911 the Alden Sampson Manufacturing Company of Pittsfield, Massachusetts was sold for a reported $200,000 to the United States Motor Company, the ill-fated conglomerate that Benjamin Briscoe was attempting to put together along General Motors lines. In 1904 a car called the Alden Sampson had been produced in Pittsfield, although company focus thereafter was confined to the manufacture of Sampson trucks. With the removal now of the Alden

Sampson factory to Detroit, United States Motor decided that the firm should once again produce a passenger car. This time it was marketed as a Sampson. A 35 hp four on a 114-inch wheelbase, the new car featured shaft drive and right-hand steering. The price tag was $1325, approximately one-third the price of the previous Alden Sampson. Though the Sampson's exterior finish was said to have seventeen coats of paint, this second-generation car did not approximate the upper-class quality of the first. Both the Sampson car and the Sampson truck died with the collapse of United States Motor in 1912.

1919 Samson Whole Family Car, GMI

SAMSON — Janesville, Wisconsin — (1919) — Projected production for 1919 was 2250 units; for 1920, 5000 units. Instead, just one was built. Powered by the Chevrolet FB engine and set into a 118-inch wheelbase chassis, the Samson was introduced in 1919 as the "first and only farm-designed car," seating nine, with the rear seat and jumpseats removable to allow quick conversion to pick-up truck use. Dubbed the "Whole Family Car," it was built by the Samson Tractor Company of Janesville, which was part of General Motors and an attempt by William C. Durant to emulate the success of Henry Ford in the field of farm mechanization. The Samson tractor proved no competition for Ford, though the Samson truck was produced with some success through 1923. The Samson Whole Family Car was not produced at all, but remains significant in General Motors history as the only automobile publicly advertised by the company that was never marketed.

1899 Samuels Electric, MVMA

SAMUELS ELECTRIC — Moline, Illinois — (1899) — Arnold A. Samuels lived at 1120 Eleventh Street in Moline and in 1899 built a 670-pound electric runabout fitted with a 2 1/2 hp motor and a dry cell battery weighing 184 pounds. During the late fall of that year, he notified the automotive press of his achievement, but it does not appear that he proceeded into manufacture.

SAN ANTONIO — In 1910 the Commercial Motor Car Company of San Antonio, Texas announced its forthcoming manufacture of a car to be called the San Antonio. The announcement was obviously premature because the San Antonio never arrived on the market. Conceivably, this firm may have moved to Houston the year following to try again, because a Commercial Motor Car Company in that city announced a new car called the Brandon in 1911. It never arrived either.

SANDUSKY — Sandusky, Ohio — (1902-1904) — The Sandusky automotive idea began not in Sandusky but in two other Ohio towns and by two divergent organizations. In 1899, in Akron, Francis X. Frantz of the Frantz Body Manufacturing Company announced that he was pursuing the notion

1904 Sandusky, runabout, WLB

of entering the automobile industry. The following year, in Bucyrus, the assets of the Ohio Gas Engine Company were purchased by a consortium which included F.M. Underwood and which announced its intention to transfer operations to Sandusky and to begin automobile manufacture. This group did make it to Sandusky, styling itself as the Sandusky Automobile Manufacturing Company, but dissension immediately broke out, and Underwood resigned during the spring of 1900. The Sandusky project seems to have remained dormant thereafter, until 1902 when F.X. Frantz came to town, having been unable to get his automotive venture going in Akron. He interested local businessmen in investing, and in July the first Sandusky car was turned out, followed by several more, both gasoline and electrics. But dissension arrived again, and by year's end another group took over, reorganizing as the Sandusky Automobile Company which was capitalized at $150,000 and which purchased forty-three acres of land just outside town where a three-story brick factory and homes for workmen would be built. By now James J. Hinde had become the moving spirit of the venture. Early in 1903 the new company announced that ten cars were in the process of construction, and that two to three Sandusky runabouts would be the scheduled output in temporary quarters pending completion of the new factory. The Sandusky was a typical light runabout of the day. Its engine was a 5 hp one-lunger, its wheelbase was 65 inches, its transmission was planetary, its final drive by single chain. The price was $700. Seating accommodations were for two only because, as the company said, "no additional seat is provided, the intention being not to overload the vehicle." The Sandusky weighed 600 pounds. For the 1904 model year a slightly larger car called the Courier was added to the line. The Sandusky Automobile Company was petitioned into bankruptcy in October of 1904, with assets of $25,000 and liabilities of $55,000. Reorganized once again in April of 1905, with James Hinde remaining in charge, the firm struggled on for a few months more, though its final production was of the larger Courier only.

SANDUSKY — Sandusky, Ohio — (1911-1914) — The Sandusky Auto Parts & Motor Truck Company began building commercial vehicles in Ohio in 1911 and was out of business by 1914. Two sizes of trucks were produced and, in addition, the company contemplated manufacture of passenger cars as well. Two or three pilot model automobiles were built, but their manufacture never began.

SANGAMON — The Sangamon Auto Garage Company was organized in Springfield, Illinois during the fall of 1906 with a capital stock of $6000 for the manufacture, repair and storing of automobiles. Incorporators were W.B. Chittenden, W.K. Zewadaki and E.E. Barclay. Manufacture is doubted.

1904 Santos Dumont, touring, WLB

SANTOS DUMONT — Columbus, Ohio — (1902-1904) — "This One Flies But Never Falters" was the slogan. Named for the famed French balloonist, and possibly without his permission, the Santos Dumont was the idea of Charles W. Groff and J. Frank Runkle who originally organized their venture under their own names but changed within months to the Columbus

Motor Vehicle Company. Experimentation had begun as early as 1899, but the first prototype was not tested until late 1901, and the Santos Dumont car did not arrive until late the year following. Its two-cylinder 12 hp water-cooled engine was mounted under the seat, and its tonneau body accommodated four passengers. Final drive was by chain, and the price was $1500. A single-cylinder 9 hp runabout for $1250 was added to the line for 1903. By March that year, however, Groff and Runkle found themselves in financial trouble; the company was reorganized, with its capital stock doubled from $50,000 to $100,000 and William Frisbe took over as president. The Santos Dumont became another car altogether for 1904. Its four-cylinder 20 hp engine was mounted up front under a hood, and it was air cooled. Five passengers were accommodated in a large roomy tonneau. The price was $2000. William Frisbe announced his intention to change the name of the car to Dumont. Advertisements from 1904 show Dumont being used sometimes, Santos Dumont others. No final decision on nomenclature was ever necessary, unfortunately, because Frisbe soon found himself in the same financial trouble as had beset Groff and Runkle. The Columbus Motor Vehicle Company was petitioned into bankruptcy during the fall of 1904, with announcement made in October that the firm had "compromised 95 percent of the claims against them, and that court proceedings will, therefore, be dropped." There was a promise of reorganization as well, but it was never realized.

SARATOGA TOURIST — Saratoga Tourist was the designation given to the gasoline car produced alongside the Elite steam cars manufactured in Utica, New York by D.B. Smith & Company from 1901-1902. Refer to Elite.

SARONI STEAM — St. Paul, Minnesota — (1880) — This pioneer steam wagon from St. Paul was designed by Herman Saroni and built in Henry Bonn's coppersmith shop on Cedar Street in 1880. The vehicle was successfully tested on the streets of the city, and is believed to have been the first automobile in Minnesota.

SAUER — Frank Sauer of 19 Broadway in Cleveland, Ohio was reported to be experimenting with an automobile in a February 1902 issue of *Automobile & Motor Review*. Details are lacking.

SAUL & VAN WAGONER — Charles F. Saul and William Van Wagoner joined together in Syracuse, New York at the turn of the century in two automotive ventures. Refer to Van Wagoner and Century.

SAVAGE — Although a few of the cars may have borne the Savage name, most of the vehicles marketed by the M.W. Savage Factories Company of Minneapolis, Minnesota from 1910-1911 were named after a famous race horse. Refer to Dan Patch.

SAVOY — The Savoy Auto and Taximeter Cab Company was organized late in 1908 with a capital stock of $30,000 to manufacture and operate motor cars and taxicabs in Far Rockaway, New York. Manufacture is doubted.

1914 Savage, 4-pass. touring, WLB

SAVAGE — Detroit, Michigan — (1914) — The Savage Motor Car Company was the idea of Delbert H. Cummings, Edwin E. Taylor and Robert W. Fishback. "The Car the World Has Waited For," as the Savage 20 was advertised, was a $595 four-cylinder light car that wasn't. This attempt to get rich quick fell asunder just months after promotion began. When the authorities moved in on the Savage offices in Detroit in August of 1914, they discovered one electric headlight and reams of advertising material. The photograph of the Savage factory in an elaborately embossed booklet was said by postal authorities to be that of the Speedwell Motor Car Company in Dayton, Ohio. Speedwell was reported to be "disagreeably surprised." Cummings, Taylor and Fishback were immediately arrested. The trio had collected a total of $50,000 thus far, mostly from prospective dealers, of which $32,000 remained in the bank. Their plan to use this money for bail was thwarted when the Savage Motor Car Company was petitioned into involuntary bankruptcy. Ultimately, the people who had invested in the company received a good part of their money back. They were luckier than most. Actually, so were the men behind the Savage. Fishback, whom the Savage literature proclaimed was a "world-famous engineer, whose name in Europe stands for solidarity," was unknown on the Continent, though he was a small-time Detroit engine builder. Cummings was a former typewriter salesman, and Taylor was an advertising man. When tried in Cincinnati (the town from which all three originated), the judge directed the petit jury to return a not guilty verdict. "It is a general practice in the automobile business for auto concerns to very much exaggerate their plants when it comes to publishing pictures of them," the judge said, and "exaggeration or 'puffing' in advertising" was scarcely a new thing either, so he believed the defendants should be given "the benefit of any doubt as to their intent to defraud." A grand jury in Detroit thought otherwise, however, and the trio was re-arrested, though the evidence suggests none of them ever went to jail. Apparently Fishback hadn't his first time around either, when he promoted the Fishback Motor Company in Waterloo, Iowa in 1912.

SAWYER — The Sawyer Gear & Manufacturing Company was organized in late 1916 with a capital stock of $15,000 for the manufacture of automobile parts in Cleveland, Ohio. Incorporators were H.W. Kilpatrick, D.H. Wilder, O.W. Johnson and E. Miller France. Whether any automobiles were manufactured has not been documented. A six-cylinder Sawyer car was indicated in an *American Automobile Digest* roster as having been built in 1920 (Rutenber engine) and 1921 (Continental engine) — and the Sawyer Six was among the cars for which the McCord Manufacturing Company of Detroit advertised in 1920 that it could provide gaskets. The Sawyer, however, remains a mystery.

1914 Saxon, roadster, OCW

SAXON — Detroit, Michigan — (1913-1922)/Ypsilanti, Michigan — (1922) — "A high-grade, well-designed, carefully built, two-passenger automobile with four-cylinder motor, standard tread and other standard features, produced by an experienced organization, soundly financed and well managed." Ninety percent of the foregoing advertising phrase which introduced the product of the Saxon Motor Company of Detroit was quite accurate; it was the ten percent which wasn't which ultimately did the Saxon in. The car was sold at a cyclecar price ($395) but offered such big car features as a four-cylinder water-cooled engine (Ferro), shaft drive, selective transmission (two-speed, later three-speed, rear axle mounted) and electric lights (optional initially, standard beginning in 1915). The Saxon was the idea of Hugh Chalmers whose Chalmers car was among the most popular medium-priced automobiles in the country. As Saxon president, he installed his former Chalmers advertising manager, Harry W. Ford, who got down to business initially in the former Demotcar factory in Detroit, beginning in December of 1913, with 3000 cars produced in the next three months. In 1914 a Saxon roadster was driven 135 miles a day for 30 days, a total of 4050 miles with an average of 30 mpg, and in the course of its transcontinental trek, it was among the cars to christen the new Lincoln Highway. Sales skyrocketed. In early 1915, the Demotcar plant being hopelessly inadequate, the company moved into the former Abbott factory, and in late 1915 Harry W. Ford bought out Hugh Chalmers' interest and reorganized as the Saxon Motor Car Corporation. Sales in 1915 totaled nearly 12,000 cars, a figure that would double the year following. In 1916 a $785 six-cylinder (Continental engine) touring car joined the four-cylinder roadster in production. Saxon now ranked eighth in the industry, and industry observers commented that Harry Ford was coming on big, like that other Ford nearby named Henry. Peak production arrived in 1917, with nearly 28,000 Saxons built, but already the company had made a serious mistake. In order to greatly expand production, a huge inventory of materials was ordered, and construction begun on an equally huge new factory in Detroit. Suddenly the company found itself strapped for operating cash. Moreover, Harry Ford was sick. He resigned for reasons of health in December of 1917 (and died the following year). Benjamin Gotfredson took over. With wartime materials shortages, only 3426 Saxons were built in 1919 — and meanwhile the brand-new Saxon factory, which the company couldn't pay for, was sold to General Motors. Only the six-cylinder Saxon had been produced in 1918 and 1919, but for 1920 it was joined by a new overhead valve four (R & V or Gray engine) called the Saxon Duplex. The six was dropped for 1921. Continued, however, was the turmoil of the company; Gotfredson resigned the presidency in 1919; now at the Saxon helm was C.A. Pfeffer, an old Chalmers man. Reorganization was painfully slow because, as *MoToR* revealed, stock in Saxon was held in small amounts by a large number of people who "seemed indifferent as to what happened." What happened in April 1921 was the sale of the Saxon

parts business for former models (not including the Duplex), though of the $550,000 realized, $485,000 had to be used to pay off accrued loans and claims. That didn't leave Saxon much to even retrench with. Early in 1922 quarters were leased in the Ace factory in Ypsilanti in order to continue production of the Duplex, but the company proceeded no further than the setting up of a pilot line there. That summer C.A. Pfeffer resigned. There was no new Saxon president. The company was bankrupt by year's end.

1915 Saxon, roadster, HFM

1913-1915 SAXON
Model A — 4-cyl., 12.1 hp, 96" wb

	FP	5	4	3	2	1
Roadster-2P	395	2000	3000	4200	6500	14,000

1916 Saxon, roadster, GR

1916 SAXON
Model 14 — 4-cyl., 12.1 hp, 96" wb

Roadster-2P	395	2000	3000	4200	6500	14,000
Winter Top Roadster-2P	455	2200	3200	4400	7000	15,000

Model S-2 — 6-cyl., 19.84 hp, 112" wb

Touring-5P	785	2200	3200	4400	7000	15,000
Winter Top Touring-5P	935	2300	3300	4600	7500	16,000
Roadster-3P	785	2200	3200	4400	7000	15,000

1917 Saxon Six, touring, HAC

1917 SAXON
Model B5R — 4-cyl., 12.1 hp, 96" wb

Roadster-2P	495	2000	3000	4200	6500	14,000

Model S4T — 6-cyl., 20 hp, 112" wb

Chummy Roadster-4P	865	2200	3200	4400	7000	15,000
Sedan-5P	1250	1600	2700	3800	5800	12,000

1918 SAXON
Model Y-18-T — 6-cyl., 20 hp, 112" wb

	FP	5	4	3	2	1
Touring-5P	935	2300	3300	4600	7500	16,000
Chummy Roadster-4P	935	2200	3200	4400	7000	15,000
Sedan-5P	1395	1600	2700	3800	5800	12,000

1919 Saxon Y-18-T, touring, HAC

1919 SAXON
Model Y-18-T — 6-cyl., 20 hp, 112" wb

Touring-5P	1195	2300	3300	4600	7500	16,000
Roadster-4P	1195	2200	3200	4400	7000	15,000

1920 SAXON
Model Y-18-T — 6-cyl., 20 hp, 112" wb

Touring-5P	1295	2400	3400	4800	8000	17,000
Roadster-4P	1295	2300	3300	4600	7500	16,000

Duplex 125 — 4-cyl., 45 hp, 112" wb

Touring-5P	1785	2500	3500	5000	8500	18,000
Sedan-5P	2685	1800	2800	4000	6200	13,000

1921 Saxon Duplex, touring, JAC

1921 SAXON
Duplex 125 — 4-cyl., 45 hp, 112" wb

Touring-5P	1675	2500	3500	5000	8500	18,000
Sedan-5P	2475	1800	2800	4000	6200	13,000
Foursome Coupe-4P	2475	2200	3200	4400	7000	15,000
Blackstone Touring-5P	—	2700	3600	5300	8800	19,000

1922 Saxon Duplex, coupe, HAC

1922 SAXON
Duplex 125 — 4-cyl., 45 hp, 112" wb

Touring-5P	1295	2500	3500	5000	8500	18,000
Roadster-2P	1295	2400	3400	4800	8000	17,000
Roadster-3P	1345	2450	3500	4900	8300	17,500
Blackstone Touring-5P	1495	2700	3700	5500	9000	19,000
Coupe-3P	1995	2200	3200	4400	7000	15,000
Sedan-5P	1995	1800	2800	4000	6200	13,000

Note: 1923 models were announced, but they were merely carryovers of the 1922 line, with very few built.

1919 Sayers Six, touring, HAC

SAYERS — Cincinnati, Ohio — (1917-1924) — William A. Sayers opened his carriage shop in Cincinnati in 1876 and admitted A.K. Scovill to partnership the year following, with the firm's name changing to Sayers & Scovill Company, which it remained for the whole of its existence. Although horsedrawn hearses were a Sayers & Scovill speciality, and an experimental automobile was built in 1906, the company's first production automotive vehicle was a two-ton truck introduced in 1907. It was produced through 1912, with hearse and ambulance prototypes being built during that period. Production of hearses and ambulances was begun in 1913, and three years later the company decided to provide a model line of cars for the presumably healthy as well. H.K. Reinoehl, formerly of the Allen Motor Company, was the engineer of the new Sayers passenger car, and John A. Campbell was its designer. Mechanically, the Sayers was an undistinguished assembled car of the period, powered by the same Continental six-cylinder engine used in the hearses and ambulances. The quality of its coachwork was exemplary, however, and was much lauded during this era. The Sayers' wheelbase was 118 inches, the original $1295 price tag crept inexorably upward into the $2000-plus range thereafter, and the cars do not seem to have changed much otherwise in the seven succeeding years, though they began carrying appealing model names like Avondale, Glendale and Derby in the early Twenties. Production in 1917 had been approximately 100 cars; it is doubted that the annual output surpassed 200 units in any single year following. In May of 1924 the Sayers & Scovill Company announced that it had disposed of all of the Sayers sixes remaining in stock, and henceforth would confine production to hearses, ambulances and funeral limousines. This was obviously a hasty decision, because a few months later the firm was back with another car called the S & S. Unlike the Sayers, however, the S & S was designed almost exclusively as a bearers' car, with passenger car use being predominantly for Sunday and holiday excursions of funeral directors.

1917 SAYERS
Sayers — 6-cyl., 55 hp, 118" wb

	FP	5	4	3	2	1
Touring-5P	1295	3300	4400	6700	12,000	24,000

1918 SAYERS
Sayers — 6-cyl., 55 hp, 118" wb

Touring-5P	1395	3300	4400	6700	12,000	24,000
Roadster-4P	1395	3200	4300	6500	11,000	23,000

1919 SAYERS
Sayers — 6-cyl., 55 hp, 118" wb

Touring-5P	1695	3500	4500	7000	13,000	25,000
Roadster-4P	1695	3300	4400	6700	12,000	24,000

1920 Sayers, Six, touring, WLB

1920 SAYERS
Sayers — 6-cyl., 55 hp, 118" wb

Touring-5P	1765	3500	4500	7000	13,000	25,000
Sedan-5P	2795	1800	2800	4000	6200	13,000
Roadster-2/3P	1765	3300	4400	6700	12,000	24,000
Limousine-5P	2795	2900	3700	5600	9100	20,000

1921 SAYERS
Sayers — 6-cyl., 55 hp, 118" wb

Avondale Touring-5P	2195	3500	4500	7000	13,000	25,000
Derby Roadster-3P	2595	3300	4400	6700	12,000	24,000
Glendale Sedan-5P	3295	2200	3200	4400	7000	15,000

1921 Sayers Six Avondale, touring, JAC

1922 SAYERS
Sayers — 6-cyl., 55 hp, 118" wb

	FP	5	4	3	2	1
Avondale Touring-5P	1795	3500	4500	7000	13,000	25,000
Derby Roadster-3P	2095	3300	4400	6700	12,000	24,000
Glendale Sedan-5P	2995	2200	3200	4400	7000	15,000

1923-1924 SAYERS
Sayers — 6-cyl., 55 hp, 118" wb

	FP	5	4	3	2	1
Avondale Touring-5P	1645	3500	4500	7000	13,000	25,000
Derby Roadster-2/3P	1645	3300	4400	6700	12,000	24,000
Brighton Sedan-5P	2645	1800	2800	4000	6200	13,000
Linwood Coupe-5P	2645	2200	3200	4400	7000	15,000

1901 S.B.M., runabout, NAHC

**S.B.M. STEAM — Lockport, New York — (1901) / SHAEFFER-BUNCE —
(1902)** — Shaeffer, Bunce & Marvin of Lockport produced automobile
accessories, compound and duplex steam engines and complete running
gear for steam automobiles. The company's marketing of the S.B.M.
steam car in 1901 might have lasted longer except for the fact that there
was a falling out among the partners and Marvin left. Conceivably he was
the engineer of the triumvirate and took his engines with him, because the
subsequent Shaeffer-Bunce car produced by Shaeffer, Bunce & Company
was marketed without a powerplant.

1936 Scarab, sedan, JAC

SCARAB — Detroit, Michigan — (1932-1936) — In 1913, while working
as an editor for *Motor Age*, William B. Stout designed a cyclecar for which
he was unable to secure the capital necessary for manufacture. The year
following, however, he secured a job as general sales manager for the W.H.
McIntyre Company of Auburn (Indiana), and while there designed the Imp
cyclecar. In 1915 he was chief engineer for Scripps-Booth, and in 1916
joined Packard in its aircraft division. The field of aviation engaged his talents for many years thereafter. Just after the First World War, Stout developed the first internally-braced cantilever-winged aircraft in America; he
has frequently been referred to as the father of the modern airplane. The
automobile engaged his interest once again in 1932, when he set up the
Stout Engineering Laboratories in Detroit. There he built his first experimental Scarab. Like the Sterkenburg designed earlier by John Tjaarda, the
Scarab was rear-engined and aerodynamic. Its V-8 Ford engine was
mounted in unit with a three-speed transmission modified by Stout into a
differential/transaxle. Inside, all seats except the driver's were movable
within the cabin, and the lounge-type atmosphere was enhanced by a fold-
down table that could be set up for card-playing or dining. Visibility on
three sides was observation-car-like, but to the rear was minimal. Stout
refined this car in the two years which followed, and came up with a production prototype in 1935. Again, unit construction was employed, but the
vehicle's body this time was steel instead of duraluminum. And the suspension was a new design: coil springs at all four wheels, with each axle
being independent. Early in 1936 William Stout announced that his car was
now being sold "by invitation to a selected list"; who was on his list, he
didn't specify, but of the handful of Scarabs built — probably no more
than five in all — a couple went to Hollywood personalities. In concept, the
Scarab was decades ahead of its time. It was also unrelievedly ugly. A
third, and infinitely more attractive, Scarab followed after the war, in
1946.

1900 Schaap, gasoline tricycle, MVMA

SCHAAP — Brooklyn, New York — (1900) — The Schaap Cycle Company
of 1693 Fulton Street in Brooklyn produced a tricycle powered by a small
two-cylinder engine coupled directly to the single driven wheel in the rear.
The gasoline tank was good for a 25-mile run, and an auxiliary tank was
furnished which could be fitted in the triangle of the frame. The car, which
was designated the Schaap Automote, was priced at $450 and was built to
custom order in the Schaap shop in 1900. Thereafter A.K. Schaap confined his activity to automobile repair, relocating his business to 1740 Fulton Street and in 1903 assisting J.B. MacDuff of Brooklyn in the building of
his "automobile air sled."

1910 Schacht, high wheel buggy, OCW

SCHACHT — Cincinnati, Ohio — (1904-1913) — The Schacht Manufacturing Company of Cincinnati was an old-time buggy builder which began a sideline business of producing automotive components soon after the turn of the century. Schacht's first automobile was a two-cylinder 10 hp runabout in 1904. In 1905 a larger four was added to the line, but it was discontinued in 1907, and Schacht produced only high-wheelers for the next few years. They made the company famous. The Schacht Auto-Runabout was, according to Gustav A. Schacht, "the simplest, most practical, efficient and economical car made." It also had one of the prettiest and brassiest radiators of any highwheeler built. The "Invincible Schacht" became the company's slogan, and the "Three Purpose Car" (a runabout convertible to family car and delivery wagon) was a popular body style. All Schachts were water cooled and wheel steered. Later cars again had four-cylinder engines, outgrew their buggy appearance and were offered with either pneumatic or solid rubber tires. The firm was renamed Schacht Motor Car Company in 1909. Although not as sophisticated as "Somewhere West of Laramie," there was a Jordanesque quality to Schacht advertising: "It is just you and the one you care to take with you out on the open road, drinking in all of Nature's delights and taking your choice of those only which appeal to you." Following the discontinuation of the Schacht car after about 8000 were built, this reportedly because of a "lack of good business system in all departments," Gustav Schacht and his brother William reorganized as the Schacht Motor Truck Company in June 1913 and apparently inaugurated a better business system since the Schacht truck continued in manufacture into the late Thirties.

1904 SCHACHT
Twin — 10 hp, 65'' wb

	FP	5	4	3	2	1
Runabout	650	1600	2700	3800	5800	12,000

1905 Schacht, touring, GR

1905 SCHACHT
Twin — 10 hp, 65'' wb

Runabout	650	1600	2700	3800	5800	12,000

Four — 30 hp, 102'' wb

Touring	—	2700	3600	5300	8800	19,000

1906 SCHACHT
Twin — 10 hp, 65'' wb

Runabout	650	1600	2700	3800	5800	12,000

Four — 40 hp, 102'' wb

Model F Touring	2850	3500	4500	7000	13,000	25,000
Model G Touring	3000	3600	4600	7200	13,400	25,500

1907 Schacht, high wheel buggy, HAC

1907 SCHACHT
Model H — 2-cyl., 10/12 hp, 66'' wb

High Wheel Runabout	640	1800	2800	4000	6200	13,000

Model B — 4-cyl., 40 hp, 110'' wb

Touring	3200	3900	4800	7700	14,300	27,000

1908 SCHACHT
Model K — 2-cyl., 12 hp, 65'' wb

High Wheel Buggy	680	1800	2800	4000	6200	13,000

1282

1908 Schacht, high wheel buggy, JAC

1909 Schacht, model K, runabout, HAC

1909 SCHACHT

Model K — 2-cyl., 18/20 hp, 74'' wb	FP	5	4	3	2	1
	680	2200	3200	4400	7000	15,000

1910 Schacht, four-passenger family car, HAC

1910 SCHACHT
Model B — 2-cyl., 24 hp, 104'' wb

High Wheel Surrey	850	1800	2800	4000	6200	13,000

Model R — 2-cyl., 24 hp, 90'' wb

High Wheel Runabout	730	1600	2700	3800	5800	12,000

1911 SCHACHT
Twin — 24 hp, 103'' wb

Model B Surrey	850	2000	3000	4200	6500	14,000
Model D Delivery	975	1600	2700	3800	5800	12,000

Four — 40 hp, 120'' wb

Model AA Touring-5P	1385	3500	4500	7000	13,000	25,000
Model AA Touring-7P	1385	3700	4700	7300	13,700	26,000

1911 Schacht, model AA, touring, JAC

1912 Schacht, model GF, touring, HAC

1912 SCHACHT
Model FL — 4-cyl., 40 hp, 110" wb

	FP	5	4	3	2	1
Fore-Door Roadster-2P	1600	3200	4300	6500	11,000	23,000
Model GF — 4-cyl., 40 hp, 120" wb						
Open Touring-7P	1750	3300	4400	6700	12,000	24,000
Fore-Door Touring-7P	1750	3500	4500	7000	13,000	25,000
Model JM — 4-cyl., 45/50 hp, 120" wb						
Fore-Door Touring-7P	1900	3900	4800	7700	14,300	27,000

1913 Schacht, model N.S., touring, JAC

1913 SCHACHT
Four — 45/50 hp, 120" wb

Model N.S. Touring-5P	1850	3700	4700	7300	13,700	26,000
Model K.L. Roadster-2P	1750	3500	4500	7000	13,000	25,000
Model P.P. Touring-8P						
(138" wb)	2500	4000	5000	8000	15,000	28,000

SCHAEFER — **Berlin, Wisconsin** — **(1909)** — The W.E. Schaefer Manufacturing Company is frequently indicated on rosters to have built an automobile in Ripon, Wisconsin in 1901. This undoubtedly was the result of William Schaefer's announcement to the press that year of his incorporation of the company with a capital stock of $40,000 for the purpose of manufacturing automobiles, launches and bicycles. Schaefer had operated a machine shop and foundry in Ripon since 1884 and, while it is possible he did build an experimental vehicle that year, documentation of it is lacking. His principal work during this period was with industrial engines. In 1908 he moved to Berlin, however, and the two vehicles he built there were documented the year following in the *Berlin Evening Journal*. The first, completed in October, was a two-cylinder 24 hp "locomotive" produced for use at the quarry in Redgranite. The second was a delivery wagon which was finished and successfully tested in December. His plans for truck manufacture were thwarted, though, by his inability to secure financial backing. So William Schaefer became a Buick dealer instead. In 1910, while helping Frank Russell with a carburetion problem on the car Russell

had built in his moccasin factory in Berlin, Schaefer accidentally broke a light bulb which set fire to the oil-soaked floor — and burned the place down. In 1913 William Schaefer returned to Ripon where he reopened his foundry, continued as a Buick agent, and opened an automobile garage.

SCHANKEN — The Schanken Brothers Manufacturing Company was organized in Baltimore, Maryland early in 1911 with a capital stock of $300,000 for the manufacture and sale of motor vehicles. The brothers involved were William Schanken of 2400 Wilkins Avenue and Emil A. Schanken of 2402 Wilkens. Manufacture is doubted.

SCHARF GEARLESS — In March of 1914 the Scharf Gearless Motor Car Company announced its plans to produce the cyclecar designed by H.S. Paine of Westerville, Ohio. Refer to Paine.

1900 Schaum, runabout, NAHC

SCHAUM — **Baltimore, Maryland** — **(1900-1903)** — The Schaum Automobile & Motor Manufacturing Company was organized in Baltimore in March of 1900 with a capital stock of $50,000. Company president was William A. Schaum. The company's products were a spark plug among other automotive accessories, and a gasoline runabout for two, four or six, passengers. The car was powered by a single-cylinder 4 to 7 hp engine, was fitted with side chain drive, and was given no brakes. Schaum insisted his car would stop on any hill at any speed, though he didn't mention how. The car had a top speed of 20 mph, with fuel and water tanks good for a fifty-mile run. In addition to building his own car, Schaum also produced ten vehicles for the Autocarette Company of Washington, D.C. These proved to be a disaster, with Autocarette and Schaum exchanging nasty words as to whether the balance due on the $40,000 purchase price had to be paid. Most probably, Schaum ended the conversation by leaving town. When next heard from, he was in Buffalo, New York with a new car bearing his name. But his name now was William A. de Schaum.

1908 Schebler, 12-cyl., roadster, WLB

SCHEBLER — **Indianapolis, Indiana** — **(1908-1909)** — This car was the idea of George Schebler and it was built in the shops of the Wheeler & Schebler Carburetor Company during the winter of 1908-1909. A very early example of multi-cylinder engine construction, the Schebler was powered by a V-12 built by Philip Schmoll, a member of the company's engineering staff. A Marion chassis was used, and the car's engine had two carburetors, Scheblers naturally. Production of the vehicle was not considered, its building, it would appear, was mostly to satisfy a whim of George Schebler's. The car could be operated as either a six or a twelve, one bank of cylinders being easily cut out. "Mr. Schebler employs six cylinders when the roads are good and no difficulties are met with," reported *Motor Age*, "and twelve when a sand pit is encountered or the car is required to pull through deep mud." By 1915 George Schebler had put 30,000 miles on the car, and it was still going strong.

SCHEEL — St. Louis, Missouri — (1923) — Herbert Scheel was the president of the Scheel Motors Company of St. Louis and the designer of a four-cylinder rotary valve engine claimed to develop in excess of eighty horsepower. Its application was intended for automobiles, trucks, airplanes and boats. In 1923, in collaboration with Louis Chevrolet, Herbert Scheel planned to take on the Indy 500. Four Scheel-Frontenac race cars were to be fielded; one is documented to have been completed, though it did not race in the event. That same year an automobile with five-passenger touring body and disc wheels was built at the Scheel factory at 3922 West Pine Boulevard. And in late December it appeared that Scheel's automobile venture might really take off. A syndicate of Eastern investors headed by Arthur Sinclair announced that a new $10 million company was being organized to manufacture the Sinclair car using the Scheel engine, with Indianapolis selected as the factory site. The contract Herbert Scheel signed with the Sinclair group called for an advance royalty payment of $100,000 to the Scheel company, payable in four quarterly installments. How much of that Scheel actually received is not known. But the Sinclair automobile never arrived. Total production of Scheel-engined cars was probably the one race car and the one tourer.

SCHICK — The Herman L. Schick Company was organized in Elizabeth, New Jersey early in 1911 with a capital stock of $25,000 for the manufacture of carriages, wagons and automobiles. Incorporators were P.J. and F.G. Olde of Elizabeth and J.H. Olde of Roselle, New Jersey. Manufacture is doubted.

SCHILLING — San Francisco, California — (1893) — In its November 1895 issue, *The Horseless Age* dated the Schilling as having been built "about a year and a half ago." It was a gasoline-powered tricycle produced for a resident of Santa Maria, and most likely the only car ever produced by A. Schilling & Sons of San Francisco. Schilling was the manufacturer of the Golden Gate gasoline engine, and one of the company's 2 hp units was naturally used, "placed in front of the seat in full view," *The Automobile* said. The trike was a two-passenger vehicle for which a speed of 10 to 12 mph was claimed. The name Golden Gate was also used for the vehicle.

SCHILLO — The Schillo Motor Sales Company was organized in Chicago, Illinois during the fall of 1912 with a capital stock of $15,000 to manufacture and deal in automobiles. Incorporators were Albert G. Schillo, E.W. Schillo and Leonard Lorimer. In 1917 there was a subsequent reorganization of this firm as both a $300,000 Maine and Delaware incorporation. Manufacture is doubted.

SCHINDLER — A.J. Schindler of Chicago, Illinois was among the many hopefuls who entered the Chicago Times-Herald Contest of 1895 with an automobile of his own design. The car did not make it to the starting line, however, and whether Schindler ever completed it is not known.

SCHLIG — Evanston, Illinois — (1904-1905) — Early in 1904, at 1725 Maple Avenue in Evanston, the Schlig Automobile Works was organized as a storage and charging station, with quarters taken in the Park Building near Davis Street for the assembly of automobiles. John Schlig was the promoter of this venture, and he allied himself with Mark W. Shaw of the Roth-McMahon Machine Works and John Green who had formerly worked at the Locomobile dealership in Chicago. "The company buys parts and assembles them into complete vehicles," *The Automobile* said. Two cars are documented to have been built that spring, with probably a further small production following. By 1906, however, the Schlig Automobile Works was functioning as a garage only.

1892 Schloemer, runabout, GR

SCHLOEMER — Milwaukee, Wisconsin — (1892) — According to someone who was there at the time, this pioneer vehicle was conceived "over a bucket of beer" and hours of talking and sketching. The discussions were between Gottfried Schloemer, proprietor of a cooperage shop in Milwau-

kee, and his friend Frank Toepfer, who was a locksmith. The Sintz Machinery Company of Grand Rapids (Michigan) provided the design for the two-stroke gasoline engine, which was ignited by two points of steel striking together, with current supplied by wet batteries. A differential was featured, and the carburetor (which was patented by Schloemer) included wicks extending into the fuel tank and so constructed as to make flooding impossible. The Shadbolt and Boyd Iron Company of Milwaukee provided the wheels for the project, with various sizes used during the development stages. The two-seater car was completed and tested in 1892. It remains in existence today, on display at the Milwaukee Public Museum. So far as is known, this was the only automobile ever built by either Schloemer or Toepfer, although Schloemer did subsequently devise a tractor with plows at both ends to obviate the necessity of turning the vehicle while working the fields.

SCHLOSSER — New York, New York — (1910, 1912) — The W.H. Schlosser Manufacturing Company was organized in New York City in late 1906 by Conrad, Phillip and J.B. Schlosser for the production of engines for automobiles, trucks and boats. In 1910 the firm built a four-cylinder 32 hp touring car on a 120-inch wheelbase which it intended to market but apparently never did. Two years later, however, Schlosser did follow through on its announcement of manufacture. The car this time was powered by one of the firm's four-cylinder 471-cubic-inch 40 hp T-head engines, fitted into a 126-inch wheelbase chassis and offered in three models: a runabout for $4200, a touring for $4500 and a limousine for $5400. By 1913 Schlosser had discontinued automobile building and discounted the few touring cars left in stock to $2370. The Schlosser factory was at 151 East 126th Street in Manhattan.

SCHMICK — That C.S. Schmick of Catawissa, Pennsylvania was building a steam carriage was reported in the February 14th, 1900 issue of *The Horseless Age*. Details are lacking.

SCHMIDT — J.A. Schmidt of 286 Becker Avenue in Cleveland, Ohio was reported to be experimenting with an automobile in a February 1902 issue of *Automobile & Motor Review*. Details are lacking.

The Schmidt Motor Company was a $30,000 incorporation from early 1912 for the manufacture and sale of automobiles in Shreveport, Louisiana. Manufacture is doubted.

SCHNADER — From 1906-1907, in Reading, Pennsylvania, Milton H. Schnader built an automobile which he usually marketed under the name Riviera. Refer to Riviera.

SCHNEIDER — J.P. Schneider of Detroit, Michigan has been indicated on various rosters as the manufacturer of an automobile from 1902-1904. This has not been documented. John P. Schneider is known to have served as the agent for Peerless, Autocar and Columbia during this period. In 1908 he was handling the Franklin and was described in the press as "one of Detroit's pioneer dealers" when he secured quarters at the southwest corner of Woodward and Bagg in Detroit for the erection of "one of the finest modern garages in the city."

The Schneider Manufacturing Company was organized in Jersey City, New Jersey early in 1907 with a capital stock of $300,000 for the manufacture of automobiles. Behind this venture were G.C. Murray, D.E. Wing and T.H. Hopkirk, all of New York City. Manufacture is doubted.

SCHOENECK — George Schoeneck was chief engineer for the O-S car built in Chicago from 1914-1915 and the Geneva built in Harvey, Illinois from 1916-1917. Refer to O-S and Geneva.

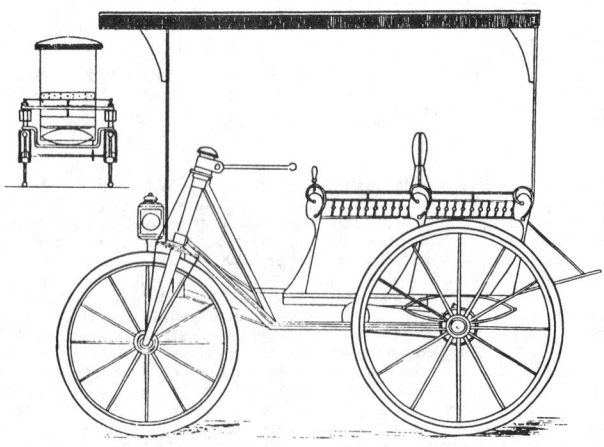

1895 Schoening, kerosene carriage, NAHC

SCHOENING — Oak Park, Illinois — (1895) — "The drawing power is a double cylinder kerosene engine of decidely peculiar construction, yet remarkable power, both piston rods operating on one crank in a horizontal plane," reported *The Horseless Age*. "The valve mechanism, oil pump and water circulator are operated by one rod and one movement." This curious pioneer automobile was built by C.J. and J.W. Schoening. That they ever built another has not been documented. Among the features of which the Schoenings were most proud was the vehicle's safety. Accidental fire to clothing was deemed impossible, and the Schoenings pointed out that an eight-year-old child had brought the car to a stop from a speed of 15 mph in approximately forty feet.

SCHOLZE — Pawtucket, Rhode Island — (1901-1903) — In 1901 the Scholze Gas Engine Company was organized by Edward F. Scholze with a capital stock of $20,000. His first engine was a vertical twin, which he may or may not have fitted into an operable carriage. Subsequently, he designed an air-cooled four-cylinder four-stroke engine (two twin-cylinder motors on one crankshaft) which attracted the attention of the United States Auto-Motor Company in Attleboro, Massachusetts. (Scholze had provided the gasoline engine used in the Bliss Chainless from Attleboro.) This time a car definitely was built by Scholze, begun in his Pawtucket shop and probably completed in Attleboro. The vehicle was successfully tested, but the United States Auto-Motor Company ultimately decided that its electric car was a more viable proposition. The Scholze was subsequently traded to a jewelry buyer for thirty pieces of cut glass; the jewelry buyer in turn traded the car in on a large quantity of collar buttons.

SCHRAM — Seattle, Washington — (1913-1914) — The Schram Motor Car Company was organized during the spring of 1913 with a capital stock of $500,000. The company and the car were named for Andrew J. Schram, who previously had been vice-president of the California Motor Car Company, manufacturers of the Pacific Special. F.J. Carver, W.R. McClelland and F.A. Mitchell were also involved in this new venture which established itself in Seattle. Initial announcement indicated the production of two models and an output of 500 cars during the first year. The first model arrived during the late fall of 1913, and it was a 38 hp six on a 130-inch wheelbase offered as a five-passenger tourer with a price tag of $2300. Nothing further was heard from the company for almost a year. During the early fall of 1914, however, further announcement revealed that Schram was now preparing to build 1000 light cars powered by a four-cylinder 20 hp engine and carrying a $600 price tag. Undoubtedly, the Schram Motor Car Company did more announcing than producing. The firm faded from sight shortly thereafter.

SCHUEL — Fred E. Schuel & Brother manufactured carriages and wagons at 100-10 Detroit Street in Milwaukee and in late 1909 announced that a $30,000 addition to the Schuel factory would be made for the purpose of automobile manufacture. That any automobiles followed has not been documented.

1924 Schuler, roadster, NAHC

SCHULER — Milwaukee, Wisconsin — (1924) — The Schuler was introduced at the Wisconsin State Automobile Show in Milwaukee in January 1924. The man behind it was Harry E. Schuler, secretary of the Mar-Tan Motor Car Manufacturing Company, who organized the Schuler Motor Car Company for automobile production. A water-cooled 15 hp V-twin Mar-Tan engine was used in the Schuler, which was a tiny little car set on a 78-inch wheelbase and weighing but 800 pounds. Two models were offered: roadster at $295 and coupe at $495. A speed of 45 mph and fuel economy of 50 mpg was guaranteed. In May of 1924, Schuler announced that he had purchased a plant in Slinger, Wisconsin where production would begin. There had been an earlier report that Mar-Tan was moving from Milwaukee to Peoria, Illinois because of "unreasonable tax burdens." Few Schulers were built, and whether they were put together in Milwaukee, Peoria or Slinger has not been documented with certainty. The car had faded from sight by year's end in any case.

SCHULER-MORRIS-JONES — "Heavily laded with name," as *The Motor World* coyly put it, the Schuler-Morris-Jones Motor Car and Electric Company announced during the summer of 1908 its intention to "manufacture a line of cars from standard parts." Rebuilding and repair work would also be a Schuler-Morris-Jones specialty. The company was located in Pontiac, Michigan. Further documentation is lacking. Possibly the Schuler of this venture was Harry E., who turned up in Milwaukee, Wisconsin during the 1920's with another automotive venture.

SCHULTZ — That a John L. Schultz manufactured automobiles in New York City from 1901-1903 has been indicated on various car rosters. There was a machinist named John Schultz at 625 East 156th Street in the Bronx during this period, but documentation of automobile manufacture is lacking.

The G.J. Schultz Company was organized in New York City during the spring of 1907 with a capital stock of $10,000 for the manufacture of automobiles. Incorporators were C.H. Clems, G.J. Schultz and J.C. Schultz. Manufacture is doubted.

SCHUYLER — Oceanside, California — (1898) — Whether Wilton S. Schuyler of Oceanside ever completed and successfully tested an automobile cannot be authoritatively ascertained. But he assuredly had the facilities to do so. In 1898 the *Oceanside Blade* described his machine shop as "one of the best fitted and arranged...in Southern California" and he is known to have been granted seventeen claims for patents on a motor carriage that year. Mentions in the turn of the century automotive trade press indicate only that he was building a car. Co-owner with two brothers in the Schuyler Hardware Company, Wilton S. Schuyler seems to have built a number of engines for varying applications, including a water-powered motor for washing machines in areas with no electricity. Most of his inventions revolved around engines or machine parts.

SCHUYLER — Edward Schuyler of 1126 East Fayette Street in Syracuse, New York announced during the spring of 1902 that he had finished the design and patterns of a new gasoline runabout which would be "simple, neat and strong" and, as *The Motor Age* reported, he "wants to make arrangements with someone to manufacture in quantities." The evidence suggests he never found anyone willing to.

SCHWARZ — Philadelphia, Pennsylvania — (1899-1900) — The Schwarz Automobile & Carriage Company was organized with a capital stock of $200,000 during the fall of 1899 by Charles F. Matz, Charles L. Schwarz and Francis M. John. Although incorporation took place in Trenton, New Jersey, the firm located at 317 North Broad Street and Callowhill in Philadelphia. That automobiles were expected to be among the Schwarz products is certain, though the production seen had to have been minimal at best. The 1900 city directory for Philadelphia lists the company under "carriages" but not under "automobiles."

SCHWINN — Chicago, Illinois — (1896-1902) — Arnold, Schwinn & Company was a prosperous cycle manufacturer at 240-254 West Lake Street in Chicago in the mid-1890's, its World bicycles well-known throughout the United States. Adolph Arnold and Ignaz Schwinn were the partners involved. The automotive activity of the firm was schizophrenic, undoubtedly because Arnold was a horse lover with no admiration at all for horseless vehicles. Schwinn purportedly built an electric car in 1896, and in 1902 the firm was listed as a gasoline car manufacturer in the "Buyer's Guide Index" of *Cycle and Automobile Trade Journal*, with some references indicating the name World being applied to the cars. But the fact was that Arnold, Schwinn & Company was never really an automobile manufacturer. Only about a half-dozen cars were built in a half-dozen years, and these were strictly for Schwinn's own use. Ultimately, Schwinn bought out Arnold and continued in business on his own, adding the Excelsior motorcycle to the Schwinn product line.

SCHWORM STEAM — Massillon, Ohio — (1888) — In 1888, in Massillon, Melville F. Schworm completed his steam automobile which reportedly had cost him $198 to build. Its engine was a single-cylinder, and its wheels were solid wood. When one of the latter cracked during a day's outing, the Schworm suffered an automobile accident from which it never recovered. Melville Schworm never built another automobile himself, but in 1909 allied himself with W.S. Reed in the short-lived venture which was the Massillon car.

SCIENTIFIC — The Scientific Auto Tube Company was organized in Chicago, Illinois during the summer of 1912 with a capital stock of $200,000 for the manufacture of automobiles and machinery. Incorporators were Ralph E. Cruzen, Howard C. Lewis and H.V. Shepard. Manufacture of a car is doubted.

The Scientific Automotive Corporation built a car called the Rodgers in New York City during 1921. Refer to Rodgers.

The Scientific Research Company was organized in New York City early in 1909 with a capital stock of $100,000 for the manufacture of motor cars, motor boats and machinery. Incorporators were A.E. Ranney, A.M. Day and A.J. Robinson. Manufacture of a car is doubted.

SCIOTO — Although the firm was called the Scioto Car Company in 1911, the venture was renamed the ArBenz Car Company in 1912. ArBenz cars were manufactured in Chillicothe, Ohio until late 1917. Refer to ArBenz.

SCOTT — R.S. Scott of Flint, Michigan has been indicated as the builder of an automobile in 1896 on several car rosters. Documentation is lacking.

W.H. Scott of 4511 Lincoln Avenue in Chicago, Illinois was reported to be building a steam cyclecar in 1914 although, as *The American Cyclecar* explained that January, he was "not ready to make his plans known." Further revelations were not forthcoming.

The Scott & Clark Corporation has been indicated on various car rosters as the producers of an automobile during 1912-1913 in Norwich, Connecticut. This is in error. John H. Scott and William L. Clark were the partners involved; city directory advertisements for their business indicate their manufacture to be of carriages and wagons only, together with general repairing, automobile trimming and horseshoeing. Scott & Clark also served as the local agents for the Rambler and dealt in auto trucks as well.

SCOTT STEAM — Cadiz, Ohio — (1897) — During the summer of 1897, R.P. Scott of Cadiz put the finishing touches on a steam carriage he had built which weighed 275 pounds and which was capable, he said, of a mile in two minutes on a smooth boulevard. *The Hub* reported in July that Scott planned a trip to Baltimore and had already incorporated some defensive features in his vehicle. "If vicious dogs run at the carriage," the magazine explained, "by a hose attachment a quart of boiling water can be turned on them."

1901 Scott Electric, runabout, GR

SCOTT — St. Louis, Missouri — (1900-1901, 1903) — Together with his brother Semple, Ashley Scott had begun experimenting with automobiles in 1898, building an eight-passenger electric bus that year, followed by an electric runabout in 1899. The brothers hadn't the finances to consider manufacture, but in 1900 Ashley Scott found someone in town who did. He was Todd K. Cooper. Thus was the Scott & Cooper Manufacturing Company born, with a capital stock of $20,000, in September of 1900. The new partners proceeded to build three electric automobiles, two stanhopes and a panel delivery. Meanwhile, Ashley's brother Semple had found an even more worthy financial backer, or so it seemed. He was Charles Drummond, the result of their partnership being the Scott Automobile Company incorporated at $30,000 later in 1900. This new venture almost immediately absorbed the Scott & Cooper company, which reunited the brothers, and sent Todd Cooper off to work for other local automobile companies like St. Louis and Moon. Very few of the subsequent Scott-produced vehicles were Scott-designed. Early in 1901 the company bought out the electric car business of auto supply magnate A.L. Dyke and simply continued building the cars previously known as the Dyke or the St. Louis under the Scott name. In addition, a steam car prototype was assembled. During the summer of 1901, Ashley Scott fell down an elevator shaft in the factory, which was unfortunate though his injuries were not calamitous, and Charles Drummond lost faith in the business, which was disastrous. That fall Drummond announced liquidation of the Scott Automobile Company, its assets standing at $25,000, its liabilities $19,000. "The trouble seems to have been that too much of the capital was put into plant and materials," *The Motor World* reported. "No one was disposed to put in more capital, so it was agreed to quit the business." Thereupon the Scotts joined Todd Cooper in continuing their automotive activity in the employ of other St. Louis companies, though Semple Scott tried again with a new idea in 1903: a small wicker-bodied electric for transporting visitors at the forthcoming World's Fair. Only a prototype was built. Semple Scott just couldn't find anybody to back him in its manufacture.

SCOTT — St. Louis, Missouri — (1902-1903) — In the early fall of 1902 the J.A. Scott Motor Works in St. Louis reported that its factory was operating twenty-two hours per day to meet the demand for its 8 hp horizontal-type gasoline engines. Automobiles to special order were also being built whenever there was the time. "Increased facilities are being added to cope with the popularity of these goods," *The Automobile Review* noted. Apparently, J.A. Scott began looking outside St. Louis. Early in 1903 it was reported that the Scott cars would be manufactured by the C.F. Sparks Machine Company in Alton, Illinois. There is no evidence they ever were, however, nor that Scott continued in the building of automobiles in St. Louis.

SCOTT — Baltimore, Maryland — (1901-1904) — Though never a bonafide manufacturer of automobiles, the Scott Iron Works of Baltimore did build a number of cars to custom order beginning about 1901. The most formidable of these arrived in 1904, a massive touring car on a 126-inch wheelbase chassis ordered by Harlan W. Whipple (president of the American Automobile Association) and designed by R.B. Wasson. Its engine was a four-cylinder of 6-by-6-inch bore/stroke dimensions generating some 80 hp. A four-speed sliding gear transmission was fitted. The car was first shown to the automotive press in chassis form with a metal cover over the engine and rough board seats. "In its present shape it is rather more

impressive than pretty," reported *The Motor Age*, but "it is planned to fit it with a side entrance tonneau body of gorgeous design and big enough to seat half of the population of Greater New York." Actually, the body which was subsequently fitted sat only seven, and was built by Quinby.

SCOTT — Denver, Colorado — (1908) — Charles A. Scott operated a machine shop at 1569 Emerson Street in Denver which *Motor Field* said was "equipped with every conceivable device for the expeditious handling of general automobile construction and repair work." Scott built automobiles to order for area residents, an activity about which he wrote engagingly. "I am an automobile tailor," he said. ". . . For example, a man comes to me and says that he wants a machine with a big body to carry the whole family. However, he is not particular about having a very powerful engine. He wants an economical engine not too big. That man might have a hard time trying to find what he wants from the dealers as stock cars probably would not meet his needs, so we get his measurements and turn him out exactly what he is looking for in the way of a custom-made car." The number of such cars he built, and how long he remained in the activity, are not known.

1920 Scott-Newcomb, touring, NAHC

SCOTT-NEWCOMB STEAM — St. Louis, Missouri — (1920-1921) — L.L. Scott and E.C. Newcomb were the men behind this latterday steam car venture. The car purportedly had been under developement for three years, and a full head of steam within sixty seconds was one of its touted features. Its engine was a horizontal twin-cylinder which burned kerosene. References conflict as to whether the vehicle was marketed as the Scott-Newcomb or as the Standard Steam Car. An occasional reference even called the car an S.N. Whatever its name, the prototype was built by the Standard Engineering Company of St. Louis, the car's birth announcement having been published during 1920. During the spring of 1921 further word revealed that the Standard Steam Corporation would be organized for manufacture, and that the Fifth Avenue Coach Company had sent an observer to the St. Louis factory to investigate the possibility of a steam bus contract. References from October of 1921 indicate that by then the venture had been renamed the Scott-Newcomb Motor Car Company. St. Louis remained its address. The only vehicles produced by Standard/Scott-Newcomb were five-passenger touring cars. The bus contract fell through, and this venture disappeared by 1922.

1914 Scout, cyclecar, NAHC

SCOUT — Muskogee, Oklahoma — (1914) — The Scout cyclecar was powered by a four-cylinder air-cooled engine fitted into a 100-inch wheelbase chassis with 36-inch tread. A tandem two-seater, the car featured a selective transmission and precariously long vee-belt drive. Though a selling price of $375 was announced, the evidence suggests the Scout Cyclecar Company of Muskogee never reached the selling stage. The Scout cyclecar probably died as a prototype.

SCOUTOMOBILE — Scoutomobile, and occasionally Scootomobile or Scootmobile, were among the various projected tradenames for the three-wheeler which Charles H. Martin planned to build in Springfield, Massachusetts in 1921-1922. Refer to Martin.

SCRANTON — The Scranton Automobile Company was organized during the late summer of 1914 with a capital stock of $100,000 for the manufacture of motor cars in Scranton, Pennsylvania. H.R. Shaw, T. Prevost and L.G. Stark, all of Scranton, were the partners involved. Manufacture is doubted.

1914 Scripps-Booth Rocket, tandem roadster, HAC

SCRIPPS-BOOTH — Detroit, Michigan — (1912-1922) — A fascinating variety and an appealing eccentricity marked the cars of James Scripps-Booth. The scion of the newspaper publishing family could not be termed a formidable success in the automobile industry, but the cars he produced certainly make automobile history more interesting. His most extraordinary exercise was his first, completed in 1912. "Detroit Man Designs Strange Vehicle," *The Automobile* said of the Bi-Autogo, a three-seater that was a cross between motorcar and motorcycle; below 20 mph two auxiliary wheels (rather like the bicycle training type) assisted in stability, a lever in the cockpit raising them above that speed whereupon the Bi-Autogo could sail up to 75 mph, or so James Scripps-Booth claimed. Probably the claim was correct. Powering the Bi-Autogo was a 45 hp L-head V-8 engine, the first ever built in Detroit, predating the Cadillac V-8 by three years. A compressed air self-starter, four-speed transmission and fully-enclosed chain drive were fitted; the body was enhanced and engine cooling effected by 450 feet of copper tubing which ran alongside and up over the hood like playfully twisted pipes of an organ. The prototype cost $25,000 to build, probably the reason production was not considered once it was completed. James Scripps-Booth's next exercise was put into manufacture, however. This was the tandem-seat cyclecar he called Rocket (there was a pointed rocket-like protuberance at the front which actually was the fuel tank); the delivery version was called Packet. Power was provided this time by an air-cooled Spacke vee-twin, the wheelbase was 100 inches, the tread 36, with two-speed planetary transmission and belt drive fitted. Though the prototype was driven from the rear seat, the production version moved the steering wheel to the front, where it tilted for ease of entrance and egress. The price for Rocket was $385, for Packet $395. "This firm has no worries as to capital," the reporter for *The Automobile* remarked in January 1914, and indeed the Scripps-Booth Cyclecar Company's three-story factory at Lincoln Avenue and Michigan Central Railroad in Detroit was lavishly outfitted and equipped. Had the cyclecar fad endured for more than a year, undoubtedly the Scripps-Booth version would have as well; it was among the more admirable and durable cyclecars built, and one of the faster as its performance in various light car events demonstrated. But, following the production of about 400 of these cars, production was discontinued. By that time James Scripps-Booth had another idea anyway, what he called a "luxurious light car." With a fresh infusion of capital from his uncle Will Scripps, he organized the Scripps-Booth Company late in 1914, and hired William B. Stout (designer of the Imp cyclecar) to help him. Production had begun by early 1915. A staggered three-seat roadster, the Scripps-Booth Model C was fitted with a four-cylinder ohv Sterling engine, shaft drive and boasted such innovations as a step-down frame and a steering-wheel horn button. Its pointed German silver radiator shell, Houk wire wheels and torpedo rear deck made for a sprightly looking package and, though its price was but $775, the car was soon found in some very elegant garages, including those of Mrs. Jay Gould and Reggie Vanderbilt in America, and the Queen of Holland and King of Spain in Europe. Winston Churchill bought one in England. Next, James Scripps-Booth planned a sporting variation to compete with the Mercer and Stutz and called the Vitesse, with power by the Alanson Brush-designed Ferro V-8 engine and a top speed of 75 mph. A prototype was exhibited at the 1916 automobile shows and generated a good deal of interest, but company directors vetoed its production, deciding to use the engine in a larger four-seater instead: the Model D, priced in cloverleaf roadster form at $1175, and also available with a removable hardtop (another Scripps-Booth innovation). A few town cars also would be built,

including a custom version for wealthy athletic star Eleonora Sears. By the fall of 1916, when the Model D followed the Cadillac as America's second production V-8, Scripps-Booth production stood at 6000 cars. But already the seeds of the marque's demise were being sown. With the purchase of the Sterling Motor Company of Detroit in November 1916, the Scripps-Booth venture had gone public, a reality James Scripps-Booth didn't like any better than the earlier turn-down of his Vitesse. By now the four-cylinder Model C had demonstrated reliability problems in extended owner use — "Scraps-Bolts" and "Slips-Loose" were frequently heard epithets — and the Sterling engine had been replaced by a Chevrolet 490 in the Model G, a solution James Scripps-Booth didn't like either, believing the company should design and build its own unit. Turned down again, he resigned from the company. By the end of 1917, Chevrolet absorbed the Scripps-Booth company, Billy Durant installing his friend and former Buick manager A.H. Sarver as president. Within months Durant had regained control of General Motors, and the Scripps-Booth became simply another GM car: Oakland chassis, Northway six-cylinder engine. In 1921, with the final exit of Durant from GM and the arrival of Alfred P. Sloan, Jr., the death knell for the Scripps-Booth sounded. By now the Scripps-Booth had even lost its distinctive vee-radiator. Sloan could find no justification for its existence in the GM lineup. A total of 60,000 Scripps-Booths had been built, the last cars put together from parts on hand in 1922. By that time, on the West Coast, James Scripps-Booth had come up with a brand-new automotive idea called the Da Vinci, which included among its specification an underslung worm drive, Argyll sleeve-valve engine, fully-adjustable hanging pedals, a parking brake on the transmission and hood latches cable-operated from inside the car. During 1923 he tried to sell the idea to a variety of manufacturers in the Midwest including Stutz, but no one bought. In 1925 he did have a prototype built at a personal cost of about $100,000, but still could find no takers. Ironically, about the time James Scripps-Booth had approached Stutz, so had Fred Moskovics with his own car design incorporating an underslung worm drive. When the Moskovics-designed Stutz arrived on the market in January 1926, James Scripps-Booth sued the company for breach of confidence. During the long involved court case which followed, he developed a tandem two-seater cyclecar variation of his Da Vinci called the Pup. That one cost him $30,000. Its body-frame was aluminum, its powerplant a Henderson motorcycle unit (later replaced by a Van Blerck marine engine), its drive by steel-core belt. Completed in 1930, the Pup was good for a remarkable 90 mph. Again, only the prototype was built. In 1935, finally, the Stutz lawsuit was settled, in James Scripps-Booth's favor, but the Stutz company was by now approaching bankruptcy; the $40,000 the Da Vinci inventor received in damages equalled the figure he had spent in contesting the case. James-Scripps Booth left the automotive field forever. He died in 1955 at age sixty-six.

1914 SCRIPPS-BOOTH
Rocket — 2-cyl., 10 hp, 100" wb

	FP	5	4	3	2	1
Tandem Roadster-2P	385	2400	3400	4800	8000	17,000
Packet — 2-cyl., 10 hp, 100" wb						
Light Delivery	395	2200	3200	4400	7000	15,000

1915 SCRIPPS-BOOTH
Model C — 4-cyl., 18 hp, 110" wb

Roadster-3P	775	2500	3500	5000	8500	18,000
Coupe-3P	1450	1600	2700	3800	5800	12,000

1916 Scripps-Booth, model D, town car, FR

1915 Scripps-Booth, coupe, JAC

1916 Scripps-Booth Vitesse, roadster, HAC

1916 SCRIPPS-BOOTH
Model C — 4-cyl., 20 hp, 110" wb

	FP	5	4	3	2	1
Roadster-3P	775	2600	3600	5200	8700	18,500
Coupe-3P	1450	1700	2800	3900	6000	12,500

Model D — 8-cyl., 35 hp, 120" wb

Roadster-3P	1175	2800	3700	5500	9000	19,500
Coupe-3P	1450	2000	3000	4200	6500	14,000
Town Car	—	2300	3300	4600	7500	16,000

1917 Scripps-Booth, model D, Cloverleaf roadster, HAC

1917 SCRIPPS-BOOTH
Model G — 4-cyl., 21 hp, 110" wb

Roadster-3P	935	2200	3200	4400	7000	15,000

Model D — 8-cyl., 35 hp, 120" wb

Roadster-3P	1175	2400	3400	4800	8000	17,000

1918 Scripps-Booth, roadster, HFM

1919 Scripps-Booth, Six-39, touring, HAC

1918-1919 SCRIPPS-BOOTH
Model G — 4-cyl., 22.5 hp, 110" wb

Roadster-3P	1065	2400	3400	4800	8000	17,000

Model Six-39 — 6-cyl., 40 hp, 112" wb

Touring-5P	1295	3300	4400	6700	12,000	24,000
Roadster-3P	1295	3200	4300	6500	11,000	23,000
Coupe-4P	1985	2300	3300	4600	7500	16,000
Sedan-5P	1985	2000	3000	4200	6500	14,000

1920 SCRIPPS-BOOTH
Series B — 6-cyl., 44 hp, 115" wb

Roadster-3P	1425	3100	4200	6300	10,500	22,000
Touring-5P	1425	3300	4400	6700	12,000	24,000
Sedan-5P	2175	1600	2700	3800	5800	12,000
Coupe-4P	2095	2200	3200	4400	7000	15,000
Sportster-4P	1425	3000	4000	6000	9500	21,000

1921 SCRIPPS-BOOTH
Series B — 6-cyl., 44 hp, 115" wb

Touring-5P	1545	3100	4200	6300	10,500	22,000
Roadster-3P	1545	3000	4000	6000	9500	21,000
Coupe-4P	2215	2200	3200	4400	7000	15,000
Sedan-5P	2295	1600	2700	3800	5800	12,000

1288

1920 Scripps-Booth B-42, coupe, HAC

1921 Scripps-Booth B-39, touring, HAC

1922 Scripps-Booth F-45, sedan, HAC

1922 SCRIPPS-BOOTH
Series B — 6-cyl., 44 hp, 115" wb

	FP	5	4	3	2	1
Touring-5P	1295	3200	4300	6500	11,000	23,000
Roadster-3P	1275	3100	4200	6300	10,500	22,000
Coupe-4P	1950	2300	3300	4600	7500	16,000
Sedan-5P	2100	1800	2800	4000	6200	13,000

Series F — 6-cyl., 50 hp, 115" wb

Touring-5P	1490	3700	4700	7300	13,700	26,000
Roadster-3P	1470	3500	4500	7000	13,000	25,000
Coupe-4P	2350	2700	3600	5300	8800	19,000
Sedan-5P	2375	2200	3200	4400	7000	15,000

S.D. — The S.D. Manufacturing Company was organized in Brooklyn, New York during the summer of 1911 with a capital stock of $30,000 to manufacture and deal in automobiles, motorcycles and accessories. J.R. and H.B. Spangler, and Otto C. DeWald, were the partners involved. Manufacture of a car is doubted.

The S & D Motor Vehicle Company was organized in Oakland, California during the fall of 1911 with a capital stock of $500,000 to manufacture and deal in automobiles and trucks. Charles Schmidt and B.E. Duckworth were allied in this venture. Manufacture did not follow, but a prototype of a truck is believed to have been built.

SEABROOK-R.M.C. — The Seabrook-R.M.C. was the export model of the Regal which was produced in Detroit from 1907 to 1918. Refer to Regal.

SEABURY — Morris Heights, New York — (1904-1905) — The Seabury was simply the largest model of the Howard which was facelifted and continued in production in November of 1904 following the purchase by Charles L. Seabury of the automobile business of William S. Howard. Its engine remained a 24 hp four, its body style a five-passenger tonneau on a 105-inch wheelbase chassis. The few changes requested by Seabury were seen to by Budd D. Gray, a mechanical engineer from the LaFrance Fire

Engine Company. Gray also designed the Speedway automobile for Seabury, which entered production about the same time. The Seabury car was discontinued early in 1905; the Speedway survived a few months longer.

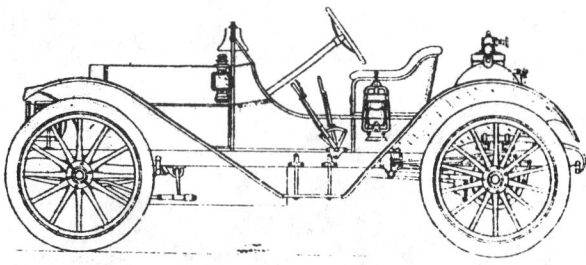

1914 Seagrave Chief's Auto

SEAGRAVE — Columbus, Ohio — (1914) — A Chief's Auto with passenger accommodations for two and a chemical tank, or seats for five and no tank, was built by the Seagrave Company of Columbus in 1914. A shaft-drive car, it was fitted with one of two engines: a 28/30 hp four or a 40/45 hp six. Thought production apparently was planned, and some prototypes followed, Seagrave ultimately decided to confine its efforts to the fire apparatus for which it was already well known.

1901 Searchmont, wagonette, HAC

SEARCHMONT — Philadelphia, Pennsylvania — (1900-1903) — In November of 1900 a group of high-powered businessmen — including Theodore C. Search, the head of the Stetson Hat Company, and Spencer Trask, the redoubtable capitalist — bought out the Keystone Motor Company of Philadelphia. Edward B. Gallaher, the man behind the Keystone, remained on duty as plant manager. Among the vehicles he had been producing was a tiller-steered, two-seater buggy with rear-mounted engine called the Wagonette, which the new Searchmont Motor Company produced through 1902. But Searchmont was thinking considerably more grandly than that. The famous French racing driver Henri Fournier, who had recently won back-to-back victories in the epic Paris-Bordeaux and Paris-Berlin races with a Mors, happened to be wintering in America — and Spencer Trask latched on to him. Indeed, his celebrity value was such that the company was renamed Fournier-Searchmont in 1902, though Henri himself returned to France to race the Paris-Vienna later that year and never returned. How many Fournier ideas found their way into the new Searchmont is unknown, though its force-feed lubrication (a first for America) may have been one of them. Gallaher was responsible for part of the car's design, but most of it was the work of a gifted American engineer named Lee Sherman Chadwick. Using as many Wagonette parts as possible, he designed a two-cylinder front-engined touring car with double chain drive, which Searchmont overpriced in the $2000-$2500 range. Chadwick also came up with a 32 hp four, parts for it were ordered and preliminary work began. But Wall Street became a little shaky and, as Lee Chadwick later reminisced, "Spencer Trask got pinched in the stock market . . . and the rest of the gang just quit." About a hundred of the two-cylinder models remained in stock; they had cost over $1100 apiece to build. The John Wanamaker Department Store in Philadelphia bought the entire lot at $750 apiece, put $1200 price tags on them (a good fifty percent savings over the original price) and sold them easily. Lee Chadwick bought a wagonload of parts for the four-cylinder car, took them to a small foundry and proceeded to develop the famous Chadwick car.

1900-1901 SEARCHMONT
Wagonette — 1-cyl., 52" wb

	FP	5	4	3	2	1
Runabout (5 hp)	750	1600	2700	3800	5800	12,000
Runabout (10 hp)	850	1800	2800	4000	6200	13,000

1902 Searchmont (Fournier), NAHC

1902 SEARCHMONT
Wagonette — 1-cyl., 5 hp, 52" wb

	FP	5	4	3	2	1
Runabout	750	1800	2800	4000	6200	13,000

Type IV — 1-cyl., 6 hp, 70" wb

Runabout	1200	2000	3000	4200	6500	14,000

Type III — 2-cyl., 12 hp, 66" wb

Runabout	2000	2200	3200	4400	7000	15,000

Type V — 2-cyl., 12 hp, 78" wb

Touring-4P	2250	2300	3300	4600	7500	16,000

1903 Searchmont, touring, HAC

1903 SEARCHMONT
Type VII — 2-cyl., 10 hp, 81" wb

Touring	2500	2300	3300	4600	7500	16,000

Type VI — 2-cyl., 8 hp, 78" wb

Touring	2000	2200	3200	4400	7000	15,000

SEARS — The Sears-Cross Company was organized in New York City during the summer of 1910 with a capital stock of $30,000 to manufacture and deal in motor vehicles, speedometers and other appliances. Incorporators were P. Muller of Brooklyn, E.S. Gellatly of Manhattan and W.F. Kendall of West Haverstraw. Manufacture of a car is doubted.

The Sears-Nattinger Company was organized in Des Moines, Iowa during the fall of 1906 with a capital stock of $10,000 to manufacture and deal in automobiles, engines, parts and sundries. W.W. Sears and O.R. Nattinger were the partners involved. Manufacture of a car is doubted.

SEARS STEAM — Indianapolis, Indiana — (1901) — Charles W. Sears, together with his brothers, had been in the bicycle business for years at 803-805 Massachusetts Avenue in Indianapolis when, in 1901, the firm built its first steam automobile. The Sears brothers produced the car's engine themselves, the running gear was purchased from Deibel-Eppler of Philadelphia. "I am under the impression that the vehicle just completed will be too heavy and unless we can improve upon it, we will not go into the business," Charles Sears said frankly in February. "The vehicle weighs almost 1000 pounds. It can attain a speed of about fifteen miles an hour which, in my estimation, is not enough." Apparently sufficient improvements were not realized, because the Sears was not put into manufacture.

1908 Sears, runabout, HFM

SEARS — Chicago, Illinois — (1908-1912)

Its catalogue number was 21R333, and for a half-decade it appeared in the book which in many American homes occupied a position of importance second only to the Bible. If any single year in American automobile history might be pointed to as more significant than any other in putting this country irrevocably on wheels, it was 1908. The Model T Ford was introduced. And Sears, Roebuck and Company put itself into the automobile business. The venerable Chicago mail order house has never been known for its sense of the avant-garde; when the automobile made the pages of the Sears catalogue, one had to know it was here to stay. The Sears was a delectable little high-wheeler, the perfect car for the company's clientele. It was powered by a two-cylinder 10 hp (up to 14 hp by 1910) gasoline engine, and it featured friction transmission and double chain drive. The Sears was designed by Alvaro S. Krotz, who had built an electric car under his own name in his native Ohio from 1903-1904. How Krotz happened to acquire this assignment is not known, but apparently he was not the person who convinced Sears president Robert E. Wood to get into manufacture. Wood had been persuaded instead by his personal friend Colonel William H. McCurdy of Evansville, Indiana. Indeed, it was in McCurdy's buggy-producing Hercules factory in Evansville that the initial run of Sears motor buggies was produced. By late 1909, however, the Sears Motor Car Works factory at Harrison and Loomis in Chicago was ready, and operations commenced there. By then Alvaro Krotz was gone, however, having in the meantime come up with an idea for a gas-electric car which was too sophisticated for Sears' tastes, so he returned to Ohio to build it himself. The new Sears had made its first appearance in the Fall 1908 Catalogue No. 118. It was offered only as a $395 solid-tired runabout through 1909. In 1910 there arrived a bunch of new catalogue numbers as the line was expanded to five models plus a light delivery. All of these cars were variations on the same Sears theme. Model G provided only the basics; with Model H one received fenders and top; Model J had fenders, top and runningboards; Model K had everything that J had, but with cushion tires; Model L was the K with pneumatics. A "cozy coupe top" was provided in the 1911 Model M. The price of the basic Model G was $370 in 1910, $325 in 1911. The variations could set a Sears customer back as much as $485. The Sears was a well-built little machine, and some 3500 customers ordered one between 1908 and 1912. Many of them wrote glowing testimonials to Chicago, as Harry Dobbins of Sharpsburg, Ohio: "It beats a horse bad, as it don't eat when I ain't working it and it stands without hitching, and, best of all, it don't get scared at automobiles." There was a delicious logic to that. The principal reason the Sears was discontinued in 1912 was simply that, although the car was a wonderful buy for its customers, the car was a loss for Sears. Someone in accounting eventually computed that the product was costing Sears more to build than its catalogue price. Sears finished up its vehicles on hand, turning over much of its machinery to the Lincoln Motor Car Works, and got out of the automobile business. It returned for a short period in the early Fifties, of course, with the Allstate.

1910 Sears, model G, runabout, WLB

1290

1908-1909 SEARS
Two-Cylinder — 10 hp, 72" wb

	FP	5	4	3	2	1
Runabout	395	2200	3200	4400	7000	15,000

1910 SEARS
Two-Cylinder — 14 hp, 72" wb

	FP	5	4	3	2	1
Model G Runabout	370	2200	3200	4400	7000	15,000
Model H Runabout	395	2200	3200	4400	7000	15,000
Model J Runabout	410	2200	3200	4400	7000	15,000
Model K Runabout	475	2200	3200	4400	7000	15,000
Model L Runabout	495	2200	3200	4400	7000	15,000

1911 Sears, model H, runabout, HAC

1911-1912 SEARS
Two-Cylinder — 14 hp, 72" wb

	FP	5	4	3	2	1
Model G Runabout	325	2200	3200	4400	7000	15,000
Model H Runabout	365	2200	3200	4400	7000	15,000
Model J Runabout	400	2200	3200	4400	7000	15,000
Model K Runabout	475	2200	3200	4400	7000	15,000
Model L Runabout	475	2200	3200	4400	7000	15,000
Model M Coupe	485	2400	3400	4800	8000	17,000
Model P Business/Pleasure Car (87" wb)	445	—	—	—	—	—

SEATTLE

The Seattle Car and Foundry Company built a car called the Pacific in Renton, Washington during 1913. Refer to Pacific.

Although the trade press referred to the company as the Seattle Cyclecar Company in 1914, this Seattle, Washington venture in actuality was the Pacific Cyclecar Company. Refer to Pacific.

The Seattle Loxauto Manufacturing Company was organized in Cleveland, Ohio during the fall of 1915 with a capital stock of $50,000 for the manufacture of motor cars. Incorporators were R.W. Dearmorn, H.J. Dearmorn and E.M. Cox. Manufacture is doubted.

1910 Sebring, Six, touring, NAHC

SEBRING — Sebring, Ohio — (1910-1912)

Sixes exclusively were the product of the Sebring Motor Car Company which was organized late in 1909 by the brothers O.H. and B.H. Sebring for the manufacture of a car designed by James Gwin and Robert Allen. The prototype was completed in January 1910 and was given a test run from Sebring to East Liverpool and back, the entire trip being made on high gear. There was a sporting flair to "The Thoroughbred Car," as the Sebring was dubbed; if desired, the roadster was available with a monocle windshield. The Sebring was given its public debut at the Cleveland Automobile Show in March 1910. Production began immediately after in the Old Forge Works building in Sebring. Production was discontinued early in 1912 following the manufacture of approximately 25 cars.

1910-1911 SEBRING
Six — 35/40 hp, 122" wb

Torpedo-5P	2750	3700	4700	7300	13,700	26,000
Baby Tonneau-5P	2750	3900	4800	7700	14,300	27,000
Cross Country Roadster-5P	2750	4000	5000	8000	15,000	28,000

1912 SEBRING
Six — 35/40 hp, 122" wb

Torpedo-5P	2750	3700	4700	7300	13,700	26,000

SECURO — The Securo Manufacturing Company was organized in New York City during the spring of 1908 with a capital stock of $25,000 for the manufacture of automobiles and engines. Incorporators were R. Magee, C.B. Young and H.S. Reynolds. Manufacture of a car is doubted.

SEDGWICK STEAM — Richmond, Indiana — (1899-1901) — In early April of 1899, *The Horseless Age* reported that Isham Sedgwick of Richmond had built a pair of steam rotary engines for use in a twelve-passenger touring wagon he had designed. The magazine corrected itself several weeks later by publishing a letter from the Railway Cycle Manufacturing Company of Hagerstown, Indiana which indicated that the engines in question had been built there and were the invention of Zachariah and Charles N. Teeter. The automobile, however, was Sedgwick's design, "its steering and propelling apparatus being wholly unique." By 1900 the inventor was busy trying to sell his automotive idea in Anderson. "Sedgwick was formerly in the wire fence manufacturing business at Richmond and was rich," reported *The Motor Vehicle Review* that August. "He lost everything and hopes to recuperate (sic) his fortune with his new invention." In 1901 he completed another automobile to demonstrate his ideas, and he built a steam truck later that year. Financial backing for his endeavors remained wanting, however, though a steam engine he designed during this period was used in the Richmond car of 1902-1903. In 1913 the Sedgwick Manufacturing Company was organized in Richmond for the production of the Sedgwick automobile jack. The Sedgwicks involved were Richard and J.R., possibly the sons of Isham.

1904 Seeliger, gasoline carriage, MVMA

SEELIGER — Lockhart, Texas — (1904) — At the turn of the century, Emil Seeliger was a blacksmith in Lockhart. In 1902 he began building an automobile to his own design, which he completed in 1904. It had a single-cylinder gasoline engine, a two-speed transmission, chain-and-sprocket drive, and a top speed of 16 mph. The vehicle cost him $200 to build and created quite a sensation in Lockhart. Although he did not build another car, Emil Seeliger subsequently opened an automobile garage in town.

SEELY — Pittsburgh, Pennsylvania — (1901-1902) — D.N. Seely got into the automobile business by fortuitous accident. In 1899 he was engaged in the manufacture of X-ray machines in a small shop on Beatty Street in Pittsburgh when an automobile belonging to a traveling circus troupe was brought to him for an emergency repair. That task proving easier than making X-ray machines, Seely decided to change his line of work. By 1901 his small automobile repair shop had blossomed into the Seely Manufacturing Company, a $100,000 incorporation, in which venture he associated himself with W.N. Murray. The title of the firm was somewhat misleading, because manufacturing was strictly a sideline activity. Seely did build a gasoline-powered wagon for himself in 1901, as well as a 8 hp four-passenger steam surrey for Thomas Hartley of Pittsburgh later that year, and an occasional further vehicle to customer order. But most of the company's subsequent prosperity was due to its repair business and flourishing trade as a dealership. Among other cars, Seely held agencies for Locomobile, Winton, Columbia, Oldsmobile and Long Distance — and in 1902 his partner Murray went abroad and brought back a number of French cars, including Panhard-Levassor, Gardner-Serpollet and Darracq. "One New 12 H.P. Darracq," a Seely ad that year read, "First check for $2,600 takes it." Emblazoned atop the Seely building at Baum and Beatty streets in Pittsburgh were the words "The Automobile Theatre," and the grand roccoco structure did have a movie palace aura to it. During the summer of 1903, Seely retired, selling out his interest in the company for $100,000 to his partner Murray, who reorganized as the Standard Automobile Company.

SEELY STEAM — Princeton, New Jersey — (1905) — F.L. Seely of Princeton built himself a steam car in 1905 with a fail-safe system. It had a double powerplant so arranged that if one engine was disabled, the car could proceed with facility on the other. Two Tonkin boilers were used, fired by kerosene burners, with the engines being driven to each rear wheel *sans* differential gearing. The Seely was built in touring configura-

1905 Seely Steamer, NAHC

tion, and was large and comfortable, with its fenders designed to divert road splash away from passengers. Seely claimed that he could drive the car with only one engine in use and the passengers none the wiser. "The machine has never been towed home, nor anywhere else, for that matter," he wrote the editor of *The Automobile* in August 1905. "I have, however, towed others who have got into trouble, and one man was good enough to tell me after I had pulled him nine miles, that he really had gotten home quicker than he would have done if he had not broken down."

SEENEY — In February of 1914 *The American Cyclecar* announced the impending production of an automobile by the Seeney Manufacturing Company of Muncie, Indiana — and the Seeney has since appeared on numerous rosters to this day. There never was a Seeney, however. It was merely a typo for the Feeny.

SEERY — The Seery Steam Carriage Company of Hartford, Connecticut was indicated as an automobile manufacturer in the Hiscox book *Horseless Vehicles, Automobiles, Motor Cycles* published in 1900. Documentation is lacking.

SEFRIN — Brooklyn, New York — (1904-1905) — The Sefrin was successor to the Graham Motorette and was produced in the same Brooklyn factory following the takeover of the Graham Automobile Company by Charles Sefrin, who reorganized as the Charles Sefrin Motor Carriage Company early in 1904 and gave his own name to the small single-cylinder runabout which had been produced as the Graham Motorette since 1902. Added to the model line soon was a touring car which at 9 hp was three times more powerful than the runabout. Early in 1905 Sefrin announced its testing of two new models — a touring car and delivery wagon — equipped with two-cylinder air-cooled engines. "The cylinders are cooled by means of spiral metal springs inserted into annular grooves and metallically connected to the cylinders by electro deposition," the company explained. A three-speed planetary transmission and bevel gear drive were featured in these prototypes, which do not seem to have been put into production. Sefrin was out of the automobile manufacturing business by the end of 1905.

SEIDEL — Richmond, Indiana — (1908-1909) — The Seidel was a high-wheeled motor buggy produced by the Seidel Buggy Company of Richmond. When it was introduced during the fall of 1908, it became the sixteenth car of its type to be built in the state. "Indications are that within the next year every carriage manufacturing concern in Indiana will be manfacturing motor buggies," *The Motor Age* commented.

SEITZ — The F.A. Seitz Company was organized in Newark, New Jersey late in 1906 with a capital stock of $125,000 for the manufacture of engines, motor boats, motor vehicles and motorcycles. Joining F.A. Seitz in this venture were Albert Seitz and George Wood. Manufacture of a car is doubted.

Edward G. Seitz of 745 Bowen Avenue in Chicago, Illinois was listed in 1908 trade directories as the manufacturer of an automobile. Documentation is lacking.

1923 Sekine, touring, NAHC

1291

SEKINE — New York, New York — (1923) — Austin M. Wolf designed this unusual car for the import/export house of I. Sekine & Company of New York City. Outwardly just another pedestrian five-passenger touring car, the Sekine bristled with novelties underneath. Its four-cylinder engine was placed diagonally (17°) in the 108-inch wheelbase chassis with a diagonal driveshaft carrying power to the left rear wheel hub. The right rear wheel saw to the only braking the car enjoyed. Double transverse springs replaced conventional axles front and rear. There was no differential. During the summer of 1923, the company announced that although export to Japan had originally been the sole plan, the Sekine would now be marketed in the United States as well. The Sekine automobile had disappeared by year's end. Possibly only the prototype was ever built. According to the New York City directory of 1925, I. Sekine & Company was engaged in the importation of toilet brushes into the United States.

1877 Selden Patent Car, HAC

SELDEN — Rochester, New York — (1907-1914) — George Baldwin Selden of Rochester was the man behind the famous patent which wreaked havoc in the American automobile industry prior to the First World War. In 1877 he designed an automotive vehicle to be powered by an internal combustion engine; he applied for a patent on it two years later, which ultimately was granted in 1895, and was acquired by the Electric Vehicle Company at the turn of the century. The Electric Vehicle Company produced Columbia electric, and later gasoline, cars in Hartford, Connecticut. Armed with the Selden patent, Electric Vehicle also attempted to gain a stranglehold on American gasoline car manufacturers, and did succeed in so doing for a number of years while the case dragged through the courts. Selden had not built a vehicle at the time he had applied for his patent, though as the court battle raged, two cars were built, one in Rochester by Selden himself, the other in Hartford by the Electric Vehicle Company. (Both these vehicles remain extant, the Rochester Selden at the Henry Ford Museum, the Hartford Selden at the Connecticut State Library in Hartford.) Just about the time the Selden Patent vehicle was undergoing a public test, George B. Selden became an automobile manufacturer. He did not design his production car, however, this was done for him by the ubiquitous E.T. Birdsall. The Selden Motor Vehicle Company was incorporated in Rochester in the fall of 1906 absorbing the Buffalo Gasoline Motor Company. The first of the new Seldens was on the road in June of 1907. A four-cylinder car in the $2000-$2500 price range for the whole of its life, the Selden lost its peculiar hood styling early on, and grew from a 109-inch-wheelbase car to a 125-inch. Nineteen eleven was a bad year for George Selden. His patent was declared unenforceable in the industry, and his factory had a fire that summer, though insurance covered the damages and production continued. That fall the company was reorganized internally, with Frederick A. Law (who had previously designed the Columbia gasoline car) coming aboard as designer and plant superintendent. The last Selden passenger cars were built in 1914. The year previous the Selden Motor Vehicle Company had entered the commercial field. Selden trucks were continued in manufacture into 1932. George B. Selden died in 1923.

1908 Selden, model 28, touring, HAC

1292

1907-1908 SELDEN
Model 28 — 4-cyl., 30 hp, 109" wb

	FP	5	4	3	2	1
Touring	2000	3700	4700	7300	13,700	26,000
Runabout	2000	3500	4500	7000	13,000	25,000
Limousine	2000	2900	3700	5600	9100	20,000

1909 Selden, model 29, roadster, HAC

1909 SELDEN
Model 29 — 4-cyl., 30 hp, 114" wb

Touring-5P	2000	3700	4700	7300	13,700	26,000
Limousine-6P	3000	2900	3700	5600	9100	20,000
Roadster-3/4P	2000	3500	4500	7000	13,000	25,000
Toy Tonneau-4/5P	2000	3500	4500	7000	13,000	25,000

1910 Selden, model 35, touring, WLB

1910 SELDEN
Model 35 — 4-cyl., 40 hp, 116-1/2" wb

Touring-5P	2000	4000	5000	8000	15,000	28,000
Torpedo Tonneau	2250	3900	4800	7700	14,300	27,000
Roadster-3/4P	2000	3700	4700	7300	13,700	26,000

Model 35-S — 4-cyl., 40 hp, 122-1/2" wb

Touring-7P	2500	4200	5200	8400	15,700	29,000

Model 35-L — 4-cyl., 28 hp, 114" wb

Limousine-6P	3000	3200	4300	6500	11,000	23,000

1911 Selden, model 40-R, varsity roadster, HAC

1911 SELDEN
Model 44 — 4-cyl., 40 hp, 124" wb

Torpedo-4P	2500	3700	4700	7300	13,700	26,000

Model 40-R — 4-cyl., 40 hp, 125" wb

Roadster-3P	2500	3500	4500	7000	13,000	25,000

Model 46 — 4-cyl., 40 hp, 125" wb

Torpedo-6P	2600	3800	4800	7500	14,000	26,500

Model 40-S — 4-cyl., 40 hp, 122" wb

Touring-5P	2500	3500	4500	7000	13,000	25,000

Model 40-T — 4-cyl., 40 hp, 116" wb

Touring-5P	2250	3300	4400	6700	12,000	24,000

Model 45 — 4-cyl., 40 hp, 125" wb

Torpedo-5P	2600	3700	4700	7300	13,700	26,000

1912 Selden, model 47, touring, HAC

1912 SELDEN
Model 47 — 4-cyl., 40 hp, 125" wb

	FP	5	4	3	2	1
Touring-5P	2500	3700	4700	7300	13,700	26,000
Torpedo-4P	2500	3700	4700	7300	13,700	26,000
Roadster-2P	2500	3500	4500	7000	13,000	25,000
Touring-7P	2600	3900	4800	7700	14,300	27,000
Limousine-7P	3750	3100	4200	6300	10,500	22,000

1913 Selden, model 48, touring, HAC

1913 SELDEN
Model 48 — 4-cyl., 40 hp, 125" wb

Touring-5P	2500	3700	4700	7300	13,700	26,000
Touring-7P	2750	3900	4800	7700	14,300	27,000
Torpedo-4P	2500	3700	4700	7300	13,700	26,000
Roadster-2P	2500	3500	4500	7000	13,000	25,000
Limousine-7P	3750	3100	4200	6300	10,500	22,000

1914 SELDEN
Model 48 — 4-cyl., 40 hp, 125" wb

Touring-5P	2500	3700	4700	7300	13,700	26,000
Touring-7P	2600	3900	4800	7700	14,300	27,000
Torpedo-4P	2500	3700	4700	7300	13,700	26,000
Roadster-2P	2500	3500	4500	7000	13,000	25,000
Limousine-7P	3750	3100	4200	6300	10,500	22,000

1908 Selden (Arthur), runabout, RD

SELDEN — Rochester, New York — (1908) — Arthur R. Selden was George's brother. No controversy surrounded him, nor did he manufacture an automobile. But he did build one, beginning in 1903 and completing it in 1908. Front wheel drive through a chain transmission connected to a jackshaft was an unusual feature, as was its one-seater "sport" bodystyle. The engine was an air-cooled two-cylinder Brennan. Arthur Selden was a mechanical engineer; all other parts of his car were designed and built by him.

SELF-CONTAINED — In 1896 the Self-Contained Equipment Motor Vehicle Company of Dorchester, Massachusetts entered two vehicles, an electric and a gasoline-powered, in the Cosmopolitan Race. They are more properly referred to by the name of their designer, L.E. Walkins. Refer to Walkins.

1910 Sellers, touring, LC

SELLERS — Hutchinson, Kansas — (1909-1912) — The Sellers was the linear descendant to Shoemaker and St. Joe of Freeport, Illinois and Elkhart, Indiana, though the only men involved with the two previous organizations who followed the new venture to Kansas were O.G. Sellers and Harry Shoemaker. Hutchinson money and Hutchinson businessmen were responsible for the organization of the Sellers Motor Car Company. Harry Shoemaker designed the Sellers car and served as superintendent of the factory. The Sellers was a 35 hp four on a 112-inch wheelbase chassis which featured shaft drive, a four-speed selective transmission and a full-floating type axle. Like the Shoemaker, it was robustly built: "No waiting for repairs when you own a Sellers" was a company slogan. Of the two cars entered in the Kansas-Colorado Endurance Run of 1909, one finished with a perfect score, the other made the fastest time of the event. Krupp steel was imported from Germany for the Sellers transmission, and the durability of that transmission was routinely demonstrated to prospective customers by throwing the car into reverse while it was being driven forward at speed during test runs. A five-passenger touring car was the only model offered, and it sold for $1700. The pilot model of the Sellers had been completed in late May of 1909, with the first production car shipped to its new owner in Oklahoma City that July. Though out-of-state sales were frequent, the Sellers was aimed particularly at the Kansas market. Three cars a week was the usual Sellers output, but ultimately this proved insufficient to support the high manufacturing costs, and there was not enough fresh capital available in town to expand. "Several Hutchinson men had invested their all in the plant," a resident remembered later. "They emerged broke." By June of 1912 Sellers was succeeded by the Central States Engineering Company which began the manufacture of automotive clutches. The old Sellers factory was purchased by Guy C. Rexroad who sold the remaining Sellers cars on hand, completed a few more for which parts remained on hand, and operated a service and repair station thereafter.

SELMA — The Selma Automobile Company was organized during the summer of 1900 with a capital stock of $250,000 for the manufacture of motor vehicles in Selma, Fresno County, California. Behind this venture were Joe Brownstone, N.W. Stewart, A.B. Wasgatt, E.L. Shortridge and E.E. Shepard. Manufacture of a car is doubted.

SELNIK-KLINGER — The Selnik-Klinger Company was organized in New York City during the spring of 1910 with a capital stock of $5000 to manufacture and deal in automobiles and parts. Henry Selnik and Louis Klinger were the partners involved. Manufacture of a car is doubted.

S.E.M. — Although its initials were the announced designation for the cyclecar produced in 1914 in Detroit by the Sharp Engineering & Manufacturing Company, by the time the vehicle appeared on the market, its name had been changed to Sharp. Refer to Sharp Cyclecar.

SENACA — The Senaca Auto Supply Company was organized in Springfield, Illinois during the summer of 1907 with a capital stock of $10,000 to manufacture automobiles and accessories. Incorporators were Charles W. Eagan, Andrew J. Scram and Walter S. Holden. Manufacture of a car is doubted.

SENATE — The Senate Motor Car Company was organized in New York City during the spring of 1908 with a capital stock of $100,000 to manufacture and deal in automobiles. Incorporators were A.M. Meisel, F.O. Fuller and C.B. Craske. Manufacture is doubted.

1910 Senator, touring, NAHC

SENATOR — Ridgefield, Indiana — (1907-1910) — In November of 1906 the Victor Automobile Company was organized in Ridgefield to manufacture a car called the Senator using the air-cooled Carrico motor. Initially, only a 20/24 hp four in the $2000 price range was offered, but a smaller 14/16 twin at $650 was added to the line in 1909. It was manufactured that one season only. Senator production ceased altogether by the end of 1910. The partners behind the Victor Automobile Company were Joseph and S.C. Lay. Their factory was at Portland and 4th in Ridgefield.

1907-1908 SENATOR
Four — 20/24 hp, 106" wb

	FP	5	4	3	2	1
Touring	2000	2500	3500	5000	8500	18,000
Roadster	2000	2400	3400	4800	8000	17,000

1909 SENATOR
Two — 14/16 hp, 100" wb

Runabout	650	2200	3200	4400	7000	15,000

Four — 20/24 hp, 106" wb

Touring	2000	2500	3500	5000	8500	18,000
Roadster	2000	2400	3400	4800	8000	17,000

1910 SENATOR
Four — 22/24 hp, 107" wb

Roadster	2000	2400	3400	4800	8000	17,000
Baby Tonneau	2000	2500	3500	5000	8500	18,000
Touring	2000	2500	3500	5000	8500	18,000

SENATOR — Pittsburgh, Pennsylvania — (1912) — This Senator was offered as 40 hp $1250 roadster and $1800 touring car. The roadster, on a 116-inch wheelbase, was the most heavily promoted. "It will have a straight line drive, low center of gravity, thus distributing the vibration between the axles," the company said in introducing it. "A feature of the car will be the straight pulls on the brakes." The Senator Motor Car Company expected to build a thousand of them in 1912; though undoubtedly that figure was not even approached, there does seem to have been some production, and of the touring car as well, though the commercial vehicles which were also promised apparently were stillborn. This venture was organized with a capital stock of $200,000 during the summer of 1911 by a group of Pennsylvania businessmen. Heading the Senator company was C.E. Vance of the Consolidated Manufacturing Company and the Anchor Packing Company of Philadelphia. P.T. Coburn, former advertising manager of the Westinghouse Electric & Manufacturing Company of Pittsburgh, was treasurer. Dr. E.R. Walters, head of the Department of Health in Pittsburgh, was on the board of directors. The Senator offices were in the Jenkins Arcade Building on Liberty Avenue, with its factory on Pennsylvania Avenue. Presiding there as manager was A.F. Schmidt, whose previous automotive experience had been with the Penn Motor Car Company of Pittsburgh.

1921 Seneca, roadster, WLB

SENECA — Fostoria, Ohio — (1917-1924) — The Seneca was the Fostoria renamed, because the latter had suffered a very bad year. Ira Cadwallader, one of the original Fostoria stockholders, took over as president of the new Seneca Motor Car Company, and put his son Lester in charge of managing the factory. The Seneca was a typical assembled car of the period and was a four for the whole of its life, LeRoi engines used through 1921 and Lycomings thereafter. Only open cars — tourers and roadsters — were built. Seneca enjoyed a modest success, with an annual output of several hundred cars, about half of them exported, the other half sold in the immediate area. Increasing competition in the industry ultimately saw to the shutdown of the Seneca assembly line in 1924. There was no bankruptcy nor sale of assets. The Seneca company continued to make replacement parts available for years afterwards.

1294

1917-1918 SENECA
Four — 27 hp, 108" wb

	FP	5	4	3	2	1
Touring-5P	735	2700	3600	5300	8800	19,000
Roadster-2P	735	2500	3500	5000	8500	18,000

1919 SENECA
Four — 27 hp, 108" wb

Touring-5P	990	2700	3600	5300	8800	19,000
Roadster-2P	990	2500	3500	5000	8500	18,000

1920 SENECA
Model L — 4-cyl., 27 hp, 108" wb

Touring-5P	1185	2700	3600	5300	8800	19,000
Roadster-2P	1185	2500	3500	5000	8500	18,000

1921 SENECA
Model R-21 — 4-cyl., 27 hp, 108" wb

Touring-5P	1185	2700	3600	5300	8800	19,000
Roadster-2P	1185	2500	3500	5000	8500	18,000

1922 SENECA
Model 50 — 4-cyl., 27 hp, 112" wb

Touring-5P	945	2700	3600	5300	8800	19,000
Roadster-2P	945	2500	3500	5000	8500	18,000

1923 SENECA
Model 50 — 4-cyl., 40 hp, 112" wb

Touring-5P	985	3700	4700	7300	13,700	26,000
Roadster-2P	935	3500	4500	7000	13,000	25,000

Model L2 — 4-cyl., 35 hp, 108" wb

Touring/Roadster	—	3100	4200	6300	10,500	22,000

1924 SENECA
Model 50 — 4-cyl., 40 hp, 112" wb

Touring-5P	875	3700	4700	7300	13,700	26,000
Roadster-2P	875	3500	4500	7000	13,000	25,000

1901 Senseeney, runabout, NAHC

SENSEENEY — St. Louis, Missouri — (1898-1901) — Dr. E.M. Senseeney of St. Louis built his own cars simply because he could find no others on the market which satisfied him. His first was a two-passenger buckboard which he completed in the basement of his residence at 2829 Washington Avenue during 1898. It was only marginally satisfactory. With that experience behind him, he built another car at the turn of the century. This one was a small 500-pound runabout with 60-inch wheelbase and 41-inch tread, powered by a 3½ hp water-cooled single-cylinder Dyke engine. Dr. Senseeney drove it frequently with no problems encountered. The vehicle's success prompted A.L. Dyke of St. Louis to offer the Senseeney in his auto supply catalog as "Dyke Automorette No. 0" — available complete or in kit form — in 1901.

SEQUOIA — San Leandro, California — (1914) — The Sequoia Motor Car Company had offices at 58 Sutter Street in San Francisco and grand plans for San Leandro. On April 4th, 1914 the company purchased the factory owned by the Holt Manufacturing Company there. At the turn of the century that factory had seen production of several Best automobiles; in 1908 the Best family had sold the facility to Holt. Headquartered in Stockton, Holt used the San Leandro building to manufacture electric trucks under the banner of the Holt Motor Company — until thinking better of the idea. Sequoia took over both the idea and the factory. By the fall of 1914 the new company had begun manufacture of electric trucks and development of an electric car to add to the line. By early 1915 the whole Sequoia venture went asunder. In March Holt repossessed the factory.

1926 Sequoia, roadster, SIA

SEQUOIA — Glendale, California — (1926) — Sequoia was the name given to the two roadsters that Gilbert E. Porter of Glendale built in 1926 and which he sold for $3000 apiece. He had hoped to sell a lot more but, as he later reminisced, "we got involved in suing a subcontractor, so I was forced out of business." Porter's principal livelihood was as a builder of bodies for trucks and buses, though he did some custom designing of cars as a sideline. The Sequoia was his idea of what a small sporting car should be: short in wheelbase (98 inches) and with a boattail rear deck. A proprietary six-cylinder engine provided the power; Porter's ingenuity was evident in the car's three-piece curved windshield which was integrated with a sunvisor. Gilber Porter's Sequoia, incidentally, was the second California car reputed to have carried the name. The first, an electric from San Leandro in 1916, appears never to have been built, however, since there was no mention of it in local newspapers for the entire year of 1916.

SERRIFILE — Hollis, New York — (1921-1922) — Although indisputable proof is lacking, it appears the Serrifile Motor Company was successor to Mercury Cars, Inc. which had been in production in Hollis with the Mercury from 1918 into 1920. If the same people were not involved, the Serrifile certainly moved into the same Long Island factory. Unlike the Mercury, which had been a four offered in a variety of body styles with a $2750-$3900 price range, the Serrifile was a try at producing just a single high-priced model. Available only as a five-passenger sedan carrying a six-cylinder 70 hp Continental engine, the car's price tag was $5000. Its life was even shorter than the Mercury's.

1915 Serpentina, roadster, LC

SERPENTINA — New York, New York — (1915) — Serpentina was the name given to the unusual automobile built by Claudius Mezzacasa of New York City in 1915. Its wheels were placed as in a baseball diamond, a configuration which enjoyed some vogue in the British Sunbeam-Mabley but was seldom considered on this side of the Atlantic. Nimble negotiation in congested city traffic was the idea. In the Serpentina, the steering arm was arranged to turn the front and rear wheels in opposite directions. "As a result the car practically spins around on its center wheels, the front and rear wheels standing at right angles of the chassis," reported *Scientific American* in April 1915. "Traffic policeman stationed at important points, such as Columbus Circle, did not trust their eyes when the car showed up for the first time. The driver swung the steering wheel around just as the car reached the policeman, and it performed a pirouette of the most amazing swiftness. Before the surpised policeman could open his mouth it had darted off in a right-angled direction — after having described an arc of 450 degrees." The Serpentina was not put into manufacture.

SERVICE — Kankakee, Illinois — (1911) — The Service Motor Car Company was headquartered in Chicago with its factory downstate in Kankakee. The firm began building trucks in 1911 and during its maiden season built a utility car as well: a four on a 98-inch wheelbase which featured a friction transmission and double chain drive. The car was discontinued in 1912, by which time the Service company had relocated in Wabash, Indiana where it remained in truck manufacture through 1926. Service trucks were subsequently built from 1927 into 1932 by Relay Motors Corporation in Lima, Ohio.

SERVICE — Rochester, New York — (1914) — A two-cylinder cyclecar with the choice of friction transmission or a selective sliding gearchange was the idea of the Rochester Motors Company of Rochester. The car was to be called the Service, but it does not appear it saw any. This cyclecar didn't survive the prototype stage.

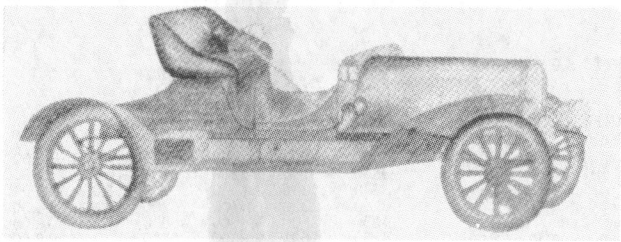

1907 Servitor, model B, runabout, NAHC

SERVITOR — Sandusky, Ohio — (1907) — "The Servitor is all the name implies," the Barnes Manufacturing Company of Sandusky advertised. "A Car for Service." A 20 hp four on a 90-inch wheelbase with shaft drive and a patented two-speed planetary transmission which purportedly eliminated the danger of stripping gears, the Servitor was offered only as a two-seater roadster and sold for $1250. It was built in 1907 only. Barnes was also building a similar car called the Barnes at the time and, despite the implication of the Servitor name, the company decided to use only its own thereafter.

1904 Sessions, steam runabout, NAHC

SESSIONS — Waynesville, Illinois — (1904, 1914) — Shortly after the turn of the century, Claude Sessions of Waynesville, then aged fourteen, built himself a steam car. He described the vehicle delightfully in a 1945 issue of *Antique Automobile:* "A small model steam engine and boiler was purchased. The flues leaked badly, so a hot water tank was substituted. Of course it didn't have any flues but that made little difference. Three burners from an old gasoline stove, three bicycle wheels, two-by-fours for the frame, some bicycle chain and sprockets, a box for the seat, and there were the essentials. The job was completed one Saturday night, a lantern hung on front, steam was up, so we headed for the courthouse square. Everything went fine, but we had failed to anticipate the crowd which followed for several blocks and hampered our progress but allowed us to keep up steam which later we found would last for about 8 to 10 blocks; then a stop of several minutes to generate more. Anyhow I had built an auto and it would run!" Around 1914 Claude Sessions put together a four-cylinder air-cooled cyclecar. Those were the only two automobiles he built.

SEVEN LITTLE BUFFALOES — Buffalo, New York — (1909) — The Seven Little Buffaloes of 1909 was the same car which had been marketed in 1908 as the De Schaum. A friction-drive highwheeler, it was powered by a two-cylinder 10 hp air-cooled engine, was priced at $500, and didn't sell any better than the year before.

1921 Severin, Six, 5-pass. touring, WLB

SEVERIN — Kansas City, Missouri — (1920-1921) — Homer T. Severin had been in the automobile business as a dealer since 1906. In 1920 he became a manufacturer of a six-cylinder assembled car using a Continental engine. Joining him in his new Severin Motor Car Company was J.F. Platt as vice-president. Production began in July of 1920, with about a car per week built through year's end. Output increased early in 1921, but trouble arrived by late summer. At that time Severin announced his plans to move operations from his native Kansas City to the West Coast. A site in Oakland was decided upon, and Severin began selling company stock in California. Unfortunately, he forgot to pay the necessary permit deposit to do so, which put him in a bit of difficulty with the authorities. He quickly decided to forget the automobile business altogether, remained in California, and went into real estate. Meanwhile, back in Kansas City, the Severin operation had been succeeded by Mohawk Motor Company which was bankrupt within a month and was taken over in turn by Metropolitan Motors Corporation. Metropolitan announced that it would continue manufacture only until the parts on hand — enough for about 300 cars — were disposed of. The last Severins were probably put together early in 1922.

<table>
<tr><td colspan="7">1920 SEVERIN
Model H — 6-cyl., 65 hp, 122-1/2" wb</td></tr>
<tr><td></td><td>FP</td><td>5</td><td>4</td><td>3</td><td>2</td><td>1</td></tr>
<tr><td>Touring-5P</td><td>2400</td><td>4700</td><td>6100</td><td>9900</td><td>19,000</td><td>33,000</td></tr>
<tr><td colspan="7">1921 SEVERIN
Model H — 6-cyl., 65 hp, 122-1/2" wb</td></tr>
<tr><td>Touring-5P</td><td>2550</td><td>4700</td><td>6100</td><td>9900</td><td>19,000</td><td>33,000</td></tr>
</table>

SEXTOAUTO — The Sextoauto was, as its name suggests, a six-wheeled car built in 1912 by Milton O. Reeves of Columbus, Indiana. Refer to Reeves.

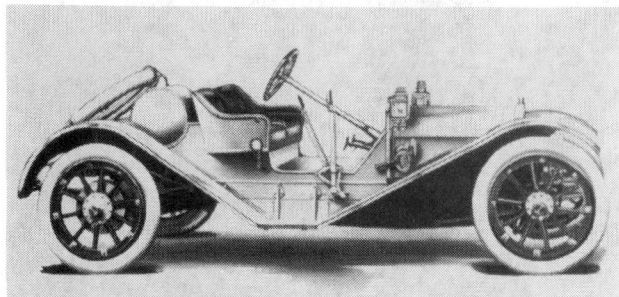

1911 S.G.V., model B, runabout, HAC

S.G.V. — Reading, Pennsylvania — (1911-1915) — The initials translated to Herbert M. Sternbergh, Robert E. Graham and Fred Van Tine, whose idea the venture was. The S.G.V. Company of Reading was the successor to the Acme and inherited its penchant for problems in the front office. This was a pity, for back in the shop engineer Van Tine had come up with a fine four-cylinder, shaft-drive car inspired by the Italian Lancia. Boasting such advanced features as force-feed lubrication to engine bearings/pistons and a hot-water-jacketed intake manifold, the S.G.V. was a luxury product with Circassian walnut dashboards, and a flurry of standard models priced from $2500 to $4250. Custom coachwork from Quinby and Fleetwood was also available, which could put the bill up to $12,000. The Hol-Tan Company, which handled the Lancia in New York City, was a distributor for the S.G.V., as was the Gotham Motor Car Company. Popular with the "aristocracy" in America (the Drexels, Vanderbilts, Astors and Biddles were all owners), the S.G.V. also found its way into such royal garages abroad as the King's in England, the Kaiser's in Germany and the Czar's in Russia. Then S.G.V. decided to try the Vulcan. The Vulcan four-speed electric gearshift (mounted in the steering wheel spoke and push-button actuated) resulted in one of the industry's very early recalls (an entire shipment of S.G.V. cars) and created disastrous publicity that the already shaky company administration could not counter. During the good years, as many as 35 to 40 S.G.V. motorcars were being produced monthly. The good times ended during the summer of 1915 when the entire S.G.V. plant went to the auction block. According to press reports, the inventory included "thirty-two complete chassis of the latest model 1915, 100 assorted up-to-date Quinby and Fleetwood bodies, a large quantity of radiators, etc." One R.J. Metzler bought the factory and said he planned to continue the S.G.V. in manufacture. But he did not. Instead he joined with a consortium of several other businessmen who went on to produce the Phianna.

<table>
<tr><td colspan="7">1911 S.G.V.
Model A — 4-cyl., 25 hp, 115 1/2" wb</td></tr>
<tr><td>Touring</td><td>2500</td><td>3700</td><td>4700</td><td>7300</td><td>13,700</td><td>26,000</td></tr>
<tr><td>Close-Coupled</td><td>2500</td><td>3100</td><td>4200</td><td>6300</td><td>10,500</td><td>22,000</td></tr>
<tr><td>Landaulet</td><td>3500</td><td>3300</td><td>4400</td><td>6700</td><td>12,000</td><td>24,000</td></tr>
<tr><td>Limousine</td><td>3500</td><td>3200</td><td>4300</td><td>6500</td><td>11,000</td><td>23,000</td></tr>
<tr><td colspan="7">Model B — 4-cyl., 25 hp, 115 1/2" wb</td></tr>
<tr><td>Runabout</td><td>2500</td><td>3100</td><td>4200</td><td>6300</td><td>10,500</td><td>22,000</td></tr>
</table>

1912 S.G.V., landau touring, WLB

<table>
<tr><td colspan="7">1912 S.G.V.
Model A — 4-cyl., 25 hp, 115-3/4" wb</td></tr>
<tr><td>Touring</td><td>2500</td><td>3700</td><td>4700</td><td>7300</td><td>13,700</td><td>26,000</td></tr>
<tr><td>Limousine</td><td>3500</td><td>3100</td><td>4200</td><td>6300</td><td>10,500</td><td>22,000</td></tr>
</table>

<table>
<tr><td colspan="7">Model B — 4-cyl., 25 hp, 115-3/4" wb</td></tr>
<tr><td></td><td>FP</td><td>5</td><td>4</td><td>3</td><td>2</td><td>1</td></tr>
<tr><td>Runabout</td><td>2500</td><td>3500</td><td>4500</td><td>7000</td><td>13,000</td><td>25,000</td></tr>
<tr><td colspan="7">Model D — 4-cyl., 35 hp, 118" wb</td></tr>
<tr><td>Touring</td><td>3250</td><td>3900</td><td>4800</td><td>7700</td><td>14,300</td><td>27,000</td></tr>
<tr><td>Coupe-Landaulet</td><td>4000</td><td>3100</td><td>4200</td><td>6300</td><td>10,500</td><td>22,000</td></tr>
<tr><td colspan="7">Model E — 4-cyl., 35 hp, 115-3/4" wb</td></tr>
<tr><td>Runabout</td><td>3000</td><td>3700</td><td>4700</td><td>7300</td><td>13,700</td><td>26,000</td></tr>
</table>

1913 S.G.V., limousine brougham, HAC

<table>
<tr><td colspan="7">1913 S.G.V.
Model A — 4-cyl., 25 hp, 116" wb</td></tr>
<tr><td>Touring-5P</td><td>2500</td><td>3300</td><td>4400</td><td>6700</td><td>12,000</td><td>24,000</td></tr>
<tr><td>Touring-4P</td><td>2500</td><td>3200</td><td>4300</td><td>6500</td><td>11,000</td><td>23,000</td></tr>
<tr><td>Runabout</td><td>2500</td><td>3100</td><td>4200</td><td>6300</td><td>10,500</td><td>22,000</td></tr>
<tr><td>Limousine Brougham</td><td>3500</td><td>2700</td><td>3600</td><td>5300</td><td>8800</td><td>19,000</td></tr>
<tr><td>Landau Brougham</td><td>3500</td><td>2900</td><td>3700</td><td>5600</td><td>9100</td><td>20,000</td></tr>
<tr><td>Limousine</td><td>3500</td><td>2500</td><td>3500</td><td>5000</td><td>8500</td><td>18,000</td></tr>
<tr><td>Landaulet</td><td>3500</td><td>2700</td><td>3600</td><td>5300</td><td>8800</td><td>19,000</td></tr>
<tr><td>Dipped Roof Model</td><td>3750</td><td>2800</td><td>3700</td><td>5500</td><td>9000</td><td>19,500</td></tr>
<tr><td colspan="7">Model D — 4-cyl., 35 hp, 118" wb</td></tr>
<tr><td>Touring-5P</td><td>3250</td><td>3700</td><td>4700</td><td>7300</td><td>13,700</td><td>26,000</td></tr>
<tr><td>Runabout</td><td>3000</td><td>3500</td><td>4500</td><td>7000</td><td>13,000</td><td>25,000</td></tr>
<tr><td>Landaulet</td><td>4250</td><td>2900</td><td>3700</td><td>5600</td><td>9100</td><td>20,000</td></tr>
<tr><td>Landau Brougham</td><td>4000</td><td>2700</td><td>3600</td><td>5300</td><td>8800</td><td>19,000</td></tr>
<tr><td>Limousine Brougham</td><td>4000</td><td>2700</td><td>3600</td><td>5300</td><td>8800</td><td>19,000</td></tr>
<tr><td>Limousine</td><td>4000</td><td>2500</td><td>3500</td><td>5000</td><td>8500</td><td>18,000</td></tr>
<tr><td>Landaulet</td><td>4000</td><td>2600</td><td>3600</td><td>5200</td><td>8700</td><td>18,500</td></tr>
</table>

1914 S.G.V., custom touring, Fleetwood, JAC

1914 S.G.V., coupe, HAC

<table>
<tr><td colspan="7">1914 S.G.V.
Model F — 4-cyl., 36 hp, 120" wb</td></tr>
<tr><td>Landaulet</td><td>4250</td><td>2700</td><td>3600</td><td>5300</td><td>8800</td><td>19,000</td></tr>
<tr><td>Runabout</td><td>3500</td><td>3100</td><td>4200</td><td>6300</td><td>10,500</td><td>22,000</td></tr>
<tr><td>Touring-4P</td><td>3500</td><td>3200</td><td>4300</td><td>6500</td><td>11,000</td><td>23,000</td></tr>
<tr><td>Touring-5P</td><td>3500</td><td>3300</td><td>4400</td><td>6700</td><td>12,000</td><td>24,000</td></tr>
<tr><td>Limousine-7P</td><td>4250</td><td>2500</td><td>3500</td><td>5000</td><td>8500</td><td>18,000</td></tr>
<tr><td>Limousine Brougham-7P</td><td>4250</td><td>2600</td><td>3600</td><td>5200</td><td>8700</td><td>18,500</td></tr>
<tr><td>Landaulet Brougham-7P</td><td>4250</td><td>2600</td><td>3600</td><td>5200</td><td>8700</td><td>18,500</td></tr>
<tr><td>Coupe-3P</td><td>4250</td><td>2400</td><td>3400</td><td>4800</td><td>8000</td><td>17,000</td></tr>
</table>

1914 S.G.V., landaulet brougham, HAC

1915 S.G.V., model J, limousine brougham, HAC

1915 S.G.V.
Model J — 4-cyl., 25 hp, 118" wb

	FP	5	4	3	2	1
Brougham-5P	3200	2900	3700	5600	9100	20,000
Touring-4P	3200	3200	4300	6500	11,000	23,000
Roadster-2P	3200	3100	4200	6300	10,500	22,000
Runabout-2P	3300	3200	4300	6500	11,000	23,000
Sedan-5P	4000	2300	3300	4600	7500	16,000
Coupe-3P	4000	2500	3500	5000	8500	18,000
Limousine-7P	4000	2700	3600	5300	8800	19,000
Berline-7P	4000	2700	3600	5300	8800	19,000
Toy Tonneau-4P	3300	3100	4200	6300	10,500	22,000

Model F — 4-cyl., 36 hp, 120" wb

	FP	5	4	3	2	1
Touring-4P	3500	3100	4200	6300	10,500	22,000
Touring-7P	3500	3300	4400	6700	12,000	24,000
Roadster-2P	3500	3200	4300	6500	11,000	23,000
Runabout-2P	3500	3100	4200	6300	10,500	22,000
Limousine-7P	4250	2700	3600	5300	8800	19,000
Berline-7P	4500	2800	3700	5500	9000	19,500
Toy Tonneau-4P	3500	3100	4200	6300	10,500	22,000

SHAD-WYCK — Frankfort, Indiana — (1917-1918) — Although probably so named to evoke association with the famed Chadwick, there was at least a semblance of legitimacy to the Shadburne brothers referring to their car as a Shad-Wyck. There, apparently, the legitimacy ends. Wade H. Shadburne had been in the automobile business in Chicago since 1908 selling Brushes, Oaklands and Velies, and in 1915 joining with his brother Leonard to set up the distributorship for Moon. In 1917 the Shadburnes announced their purchase of the foundering Dixie Flyer (Louisville, Kentucky) and Bour-Davis (Detroit) — as well as a factory in Frankfort, Indiana in which to produce both those cars, and the new Shad-Wyck. That announcement proved correct in only two particulars: the factory indeed was purchased and the Bour-Davis would be built there for a short while. Obviously the Shadburne brothers had jumped the gun on the Dixie purchase, however, since two weeks later the sale of the company was consummated, but the new Dixie owner was the Kentucky Wagon Works of Louisville. The Kentucky Wagon people had been the former Dixie owners and had simply bought the company back. Perhaps they suspected something. As for the Shad-Wyck, the brothers, believing time of the essence in promotion and having no car yet to promote, used a photograph of a Roamer in their July 1917 advertisement "announcing the Shad-Wyck 6 DeLuxe." They didn't even bother to retouch it. About twenty-five people were employed in the Shadburne Brothers Company factory in Frankfort, and they built an approximately equal number of Bour-Davises before this venture fell apart. According to factory employees there at the time, the closest the Shad-Wyck came to reality was a wood model about three feet long constructed by chief engineer Sam Hunsiker. In February 1918 the Shadburne brothers, in desperate need of cash, got into the last Bour-Davis built in Frankfort and, in the midst of the worst blizzard of the year, set out for Indianapolis. They never made it. Managing to get themselves stuck in a snowbank, they were ultimately towed back to the factory, the doors of which were forever closed the next day. Subsequently, the Bour-Davis receivers in Detroit resold that company to a new group of entrepreneurs in Louisiana, who continued the Bour-Davis in production into the early Twenties. By that time, the Shadburne brothers had returned to Chi-

cago where they set themselves up in business as loan brokers. Interestingly, the Shadburnes hadn't completely given up their Shad-Wyck idea, and routinely told the trade press of their intention to manufacture a Rochester-Duesenberg-engined tourer to sell for $4000. That pipe dream continued as late as 1923.

SHAEFFER-BUNCE — The Shaeffer-Bunce built in Lockport, New York in 1902 was the successor to the S.B.M. built in 1901. Refer to S.B.M.

SHAFER-DECKER — The Shafer-Decker Company was organized in Rochester, New York during the summer of 1912 with a capital stock of $50,000 for the manufacture of motor vehicles. Incorporators were Charles B. Shafer, Frederick J. Decker and C.P. Hugo Schoellkop. Manufacture is doubted, though a prototype of a truck is believed to have been built in 1916. Various car rosters have indicated a C.B. Shafer as the manufacturer of an automobile in Detroit, Michigan in 1915. No documentation has been found to support this at all.

SHAFFER — The Shaffer Boiler & Engine Manufacturing Company was indicated in trade directory listings of 1903 and 1904 as the producer of a steam automobile in Baltimore, Maryland. That Shaffer built complete cars, however, has not been documented. The firm, which originated in Baltimore as Shaffer Machine & Manufacturing at the turn of the century, did produce boilers, engines and burners, however.

The Shaffer Motor Company was organized in New York City during the fall of 1910 with a capital stock of $100,000 to manufacture and deal in automobiles and engines. Incorporators were C.W. Shaffer, Earle W. Webb, John L. Lyttle. Manufacture of a car is doubted, but the firm is known to have held the New York agency for the R.C.H. in 1912.

SHAIN — Although Charles B. Shain had a penchant for naming the cars he sold under his own name, he did not build them. In reality, he was merely the New York City dealer for the automobiles built by Mohler and Degress in Rockaway from 1902-1903. Refer to Rockaway.

1906 Shamrock, Jr., runabout, WLB

SHAMROCK JUNIOR — Seattle, Washington — (1906) — A total of two hundred dollars built the Shamrock Junior, a neat little two-seater runabout on a 52-inch wheelbase powered by a 2 1/4 hp Holley motorcycle engine. The gasoline tank held three gallons, which was good for a 75-mile run or better, at speeds of up to 13 mph. This homemade car was built by Henry J. Casey, who lived at 1417 Twenty-Third Avenue in Seattle, and who was a copyboy for the Seattle *Times*.

SHANNON — The Shannon Automobile Company has been indicated on various car rosters as the producer of a car in Owosso, Michigan from 1902-1903. There was no mention of this company in the local paper during this period, however, although a car called the Owosso was built in town in 1902.

1915 Sharon Cyclecar, runabout, WLB

1297

SHARON — Sharon, Pennsylvania — (1915) — Sharon was the new name given to the cyclecar that the Driggs-Seabury Ordnance Corporation had manufactured earlier that year under its own name. The specifications of the tandem two-seater Sharon with its underslung frame, friction transmission and four-cylinder water-cooled engine were an echo of the Driggs-Seabury cyclecar specs. Even the $395 price tag was the same.

1901 Sharp, steam carriage, NAHC

SHARP STEAM — Omaha, Nebraska — (1901) — *The Motor Age* described the steam carriage built by Harry Sharp as "high" and "stately." It was high. Sharp built the vehicle for his own use at his home at 1314 Howard Street in Omaha. It was fitted with a double-cylinder vertical marine engine and used a heat flue boiler with automatic water feed. "The steam passes into a coil of pipe in the water tank," Harry Sharp said, "and after the vehicle has been run a short while the water will be warmed and the vapor discharged at the final outlet will be hardly noticeable."

1914 Sharp, 2-pass. staggered seat roadster, WLB

SHARP — Detroit, Michigan — (1914) — The Sharp cyclecar was produced by the Sharp Engineering & Manufacturing Company of Detroit. Although the car was announced using the company's initials S.E.M., the vehicle had been renamed by the time it was introduced. At $295, the Sharp was among the cheapest cyclecars on the market. It was powered by a two-cylinder 7 hp air-cooled engine mounted in a 90-inch wheelbase chassis which featured a two-speed transmission and shaft drive. A staggered two-seater roadster was the only model. Production didn't survive the year. In October 1914 the Sharp company indicated its intention to build a standard-sized car (six-cylinder, 120-inch wheelbase) to sell for $1000, but that plan had died by year's end as well.

1909 Sharp Arrow, speedabout, NAHC

SHARP ARROW — Trenton, New Jersey — (1908-1910) — William H. Sharp was a photographer, car dealer and race driver. His photography studio was at the corner of South Clinton Avenue and Beatty Street in Trenton, with a shop next door where he operated an authorized agency for Mitchell cars, and where in 1908 he built a formidable racing machine which he entered in a number of East Coast events, including the Long Island Sweepstakes that fall, where he handily won his class. "This car went along at a 60-mile rate with apparent ease until Mr. Sharp found out that he was distancing his field and took it easy," a Brooklyn paper reported. For a car with such speed, the name Sharp Arrow was a natural, and with the publicity garnered racing, proceeding into manufacture was a natural too. In December of 1908 the Sharp Arrow Automobile Company was organized. Joining William Sharp in this venture was his brother Fred, who had been his race mechanic, together with local businessmen A.N. Yetter, F.W. Bennett and J.R. Farlee. Already the Sharp brothers had found a factory; John A. Roebling agreed to produce the car for them in the Trenton plant where the Walter was being built and where the new Mercer soon would be. "Speed King of American Stock Cars" was the Sharp Arrow's slogan. It was offered as runabout, speedabout, toy tonneau and touring. A handsome brochure was printed, and production began in the Trenton factory. By January 1910 word of the car had reached receptive ears in Stroudsburg, Pennsylvania where the president of the International Boiler Company decided he wanted to be involved with the Sharp Arrow too. The negotiations which followed concluded with a contract whereby the International Boiler Company acquired the patent rights to the Sharp Arrow car with both William and Fred Sharp to join the firm as managing partners. Production, which was approaching a total of twenty-five cars in the Trenton factory, was to be greatly stepped up upon move of the entire venture to Stroudsburg. Unfortunately, the Sharp Arrow never made it there. Ever anxious to prove his car in competition, William Sharp tweaked its four-cylinder 40 hp engine sufficiently to raise top speed from 80 to 90 mph — and he took the car to the Grand Prize race in Savannah, Georgia in November 1910. He was killed during practice. This tragedy was followed shortly thereafter by the death of the president of the International Boiler Company. And the Sharp Arrow died too.

1908-1909 SHARP ARROW
Four — 40 hp, 106" wb

	FP	5	4	3	2	1
Speedabout-2P	2750	4500	5800	9500	18,000	32,000
Runabout-3P	2800	3900	4800	7700	14,300	27,000
Four — 40 hp, 116" wb						
Toy Tonneau-4P	2850	4000	5000	8000	15,000	28,000
Touring-5P	2850	4200	5200	8400	15,700	29,000
1910 SHARP ARROW						
Four — 40 hp, 106" wb						
Speedabout-2P	3000	4500	5800	9500	18,000	32,000
Runabout-3P	3000	3900	4800	7700	14,300	27,000
Four — 40 hp, 120" wb						
Toy Tonneau-4P	3050	4000	5000	8000	15,000	28,000
Touring-5P	3050	4200	5200	8400	15,700	29,000

SHARP & RUSH — The Sharp & Rush Brothers Company was organized as a $75,000 Delaware incorporation in late 1914 for the manufacture of motor cars and wagons. Incorporators were F.R. Hansell of Philadelphia, G.H.B. Martin and S.C. Seymour of Camden, New Jersey. Manufacture is doubted.

1901 Shatswell, steam runabout, NAHC

SHATSWELL STEAM — Dedham, Massachusetts — (1901-1903) — H.K. Shatswell built a steam runabout in 1901. It featured a four-cylinder single-acting motor fueled by gasoline, with a flash boiler and combined feed water heater and muffler. Water and gasoline tank capacities were thirty and eight gallons respectively. During the late spring of 1901, Shatswell offered this vehicle for sale at $750, and announced the availability of larger models for $1200 to $1500. H.K. Shatswell & Company did market a few complete steam cars thereafter, but this Dedham firm preferred the components business and most of its trade was devoted to steam car parts and accessories, with a complete kit offered for the making of a steam car by the do-it-yourselfer.

SHAUM — There was no Shaum car or company in Baltimore, Maryland. This was an occasional typographical error in trade journals. Refer to Schaum.

1895 Shaver Steamer, NAHC

SHAVER STEAM — Milwaukee, Wisconsin — (1895) — Joseph Shaver was a marble and granite dealer from Milwaukee who sent in his entry to the Chicago Times-Herald Contest but couldn't get his vehicle to the starting line on time. Subsequently, he did complete and successfully test the car in December 1895. The Shaver was a steamer and a rather handsome one. Its gasoline-fueled engine was placed up front, with vertical boiler to the rear, and the total weight of both just eighty pounds. Three cents an hour was the vehicle's operating cost, and Shaver alternately claimed 30 mph and 40 mph as its top speed. The change-speed gear was operated by a double-acting friction pulley, and the car could be run backwards or forwards, "and as fast one way as the other," according to its inventor. Shaver went back to his marble and granite business after completing his steam car. But four years later, in 1899, he wrote *The Horseless Age* that his next new project would be a gasoline car. Conceivably, he may have built several vehicles, but he never considered manufacture.

SHAW — The Shaw-Brown Motor Company was organized in New York City during the summer of 1906 with a capital stock of $15,000 for the manufacture of automobiles and motor boats. Incorporators were William Heddick, Charles E. Shaw and Garnet C. Brown. Manufacture of a car is doubted.

The Shaw Merillat Company was organized during the summer of 1910 in Chicago, Illinois with a capital stock of $10,000 for the manufacture of motor vehicles and accessories. Incorporators were Howard I. Shaw, Lloyd Merillat and E. Raymond Bliss, Jr. Manufacture of a car is doubted.

The Shaw Motor Car Company was organized in Newark, New Jersey during the spring of 1917 with a capital stock of $45,000 to manufacture and repair automobiles. Incorporators were Melvin E. Shaw and Theodore G. Betzler of Newark and William H. Raab of East Orange. Manufacture is doubted.

SHAW STEAM — Lowell, Massachusetts — (1902) — J.E. Shaw & Company of Lowell built several steam automobiles in 1902, according to a report in *The Motor World* that June. No further reference has been found to these vehicles.

SHAW — Boston, Massachusetts — (1902) — In Boston in early 1902, Quincy A. Shaw, Jr. completed an automobile of his own design, according to a report in *The Horseless Age*. Details are lacking.

SHAW STEAM — Boston, Massachusetts — (1900) — In January of 1900, the newly organized Shaw Motor Vehicle Company of Boston announced that the prototype of its steam carriage was nearing completion. Behind this automotive venture were C.M. Martin as president, Henry F. Shaw as vice-president, W.G. Nixon as treasurer and C.L. Marston as clerk. Henry Shaw was described as the "inventor and mechanical expert" and, according to *The Motor Vehicle Review*, he claimed to have completely eliminated "the vibration bogie." Some of Shaw's steam ideas were patented, but his car was never put into production.

SHAW — Chicago, Illinois — (1920-1921) — In 1908 the Walden W. Shaw Livery Company was launched into the automobile business with a line of Reo, Premier and American Berliet cars. Walden Shaw chose unwisely by a third, the American Berliet being discontinued within months of his contracting for the cars. That he realized himself not a completely astute businessman may be indicated by the fact that by the close of 1908 he had taken himself a partner, a gentleman by the name of John Hertz who had joined Shaw as a salesman three years before. Hertz was given a one-third

1921 Shaw, touring, JAC

interest in the Shaw business in exchange for a modest investment and a promise to get things moving. Move Hertz did, and quickly, initially purchasing secondhand automobiles to sell until Shaw's bank balance was healthy enough to afford the addition of nine new cars from the E.R. Thomas Company in Buffalo (New York). Several years later the company was making its own taxi chassis, and in 1915 the Yellow Cab Manufacturing Company of Chicago was incorporated to handle the taxicab operation, with the Walden W. Shaw Livery Corporation set up as the holding company. It was not until after the First World War that the Shaw company decided to expand its line to include production automobiles. Though ostensibly this long gestation period should have resulted in a smooth transition to the marketplace, it seemed apparent from the beginning that the company had not prepared well. First, the new car, introduced at the Hotel Congress during Chicago Automobile Show week in February 1920, was initially called a Shaw. But there were immediate second thoughts about using a designation prominently known in the taxicab field, and so another was chosen: Colonial. This was probably no improvement, because there had already been a number of cars built by other manufacturers which were called the same thing. Then Shaw changed its mind about the engine which would power its new production car. Initially it was a four-cylinder Rochester-Duesenberg. By July of 1920, however, that unit was abandoned, its place taken by a Weidely twelve. The decision for the Weidely was probably made for the same reason as the decision for the Colonial name: to lend the cachet of multi cylinders to the product, to ameliorate lingering confusion between it and the Shaw taxicab — and, concomitantly, to boost sales that were lamentably dismal. It didn't work either. By the time the Chicago Automobile Show of 1921 rolled around, there had been another change. By now John Hertz was in complete charge of the company, and he reintroduced the same car with a new engine and a new name: Ambassador.

1920-1921 SHAW
Shaw/Colonial — 4-cyl., 136" wb

	FP	5	4	3	2	1
Touring-2/4/7P	5000	5300	7000	11,500	24,000	37,000

Shaw/Colonial — 12-cyl., 136" wb

	FP	5	4	3	2	1
Touring-2/4/7P	5000	6000	8500	13,000	30,000	42,000

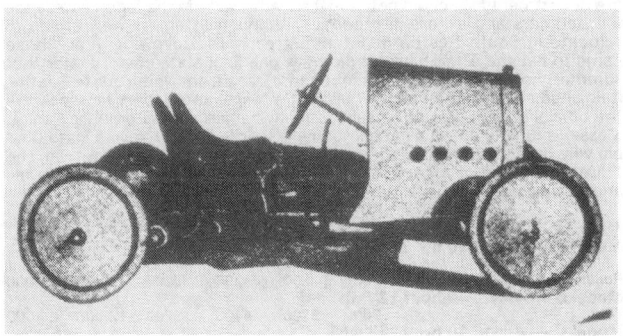

1926 Shaw, runabout, LC

SHAW — Galesburg, Kansas — (1920-1930) — "Anyone who can use a hammer, screw driver and other ordinary tools can build the Shaw Speedster," the company said. For anyone who could not, or didn't care to, the Shaw Manufacturing Company of Galesburg offered the car complete, in a price range of $125-$165. Although Stanley Shaw insisted that his speedster was not a toy but a real automobile, its specifications indicate that children would have been most comfortable in the Shaw buckboard. Its wheelbase was 70 inches, its tread 36, its engine a 2½ hp variously of Shaw or Briggs & Stratton manufacture. The transmission was a single-speed; final drive initially was by chain or belt, though a shaft-drive model became available in 1926. Stanley Shaw had begun his Kansas manufacturing company in 1903 by motorizing bicycles. For a few year prior to the First World War, he built motorcycles as well. No doubt the success of the buckboard which had begun life as the Smith Flyer in Milwaukee (and later was built as the Briggs & Stratton and the Red Bug) was the impetus which persuaded Stanley Shaw into manufacture of his buckboard speedster. He guaranteed up to 25 mph and 90 mph. For a number of years after he ceased manufacture of the Shaw speedster in 1930, he continued to offer it on a do-it-yourself basis. By now his factory was busiest producing the Shaw Du-All mowers and garden tractors, in which activity Stanley Shaw remained until his retirement in 1962 when he sold his firm to the manufacture of the Brush Hog, a rotary mower which is still produced in the Galesburg factory.

SHAW BROTHERS — Detroit, Michigan — (1921) — The brothers were William and Roy G. Shaw, the former a Buick salesman, the latter a plant manager at Ford. The car they planned to produce after leaving their respective jobs was a four in the $700-$800 price range which had been designed for them by E.R. De Duiz, erstwhile engineer from Ford. For their sales manager, the Shaws selected a veteran Buick man, E.P. Telotte, who had established the successful Telotte Buick Sales Company in Detroit in 1917 and who had retired from that business four months earlier to develop his real estate interests in California and Florida. Commenting upon his quick return to the automobile industry, Telotte said that he could not resist the opportunity "to affiliate myself with a young concern that gives promise of being a really big success." That was in the early fall of 1921, when the announcement of the formation of the Shaw Brothers Motor Car Company, capitalized at $3 million, was made. "The car will be known as the Shaw Brothers, or Shaw, the name not being fully determined," *Motor World* reported. That determination never proved necessary, because this venture very quickly foundered. Prototype models are known to have been built.

1907 Shawmut, touring, WLB

SHAWMUT — Stoneham, Massachusetts — (1906-1908) — In December 1905 the Shawmut Motor Company moved into the Stoneham factory which had previously seen the manufacture of the Phelps. The Phelps had been marketed as a three-cylinder car in the $2500 range, though in 1905 a $4000 four had been made available on custom order. It was this latter car which was produced beginning in 1906 as the Shawmut. A 40 hp automobile with shaft drive and four-speed selective transmission, the Shawmut was offered in four body styles priced from $4750 to $6500. Disaster struck in November that year. "The fire was discovered by the night watchman," the press reported afterward, "but so rapidly did the flames spread over the oil-soaked floors that the combined efforts of (all) local fire departments . . . could not stop its headway . . . In the factory were ten finished cars and others in process." Although attempts were made to relocate in South Boston or Fitchburg early the following year, these came to naught. The Shawmut did have one final blaze of glory later that summer, however. In the transcontinental race from New York to Seattle, it finished second to a Ford. T. Arthur Pettengill and Robert Messer were the official drivers. Pettengill subsequently became an automobile dealer, Messer a funeral director. Accompanying them on the trek was Earle Chapin who described the race decades later as a "fight for survival" with the "direction sense of a carrier pigeon" necessary for the wild and wooly, and uncharted, West.

1906-1908 SHAWMUT
Model A — 4-cyl., 40 hp, 118" wb

	FP	5	4	3	2	1
Roadster	4750	3200	4300	6500	11,000	23,000
Model B — 4-cyl., 40 hp, 112" wb						
Touring	5000	3300	4400	6700	12,000	24,000
Model C — 4-cyl., 40 hp, 126" wb						
Limousine	5750	2900	3700	5600	9100	20,000
Model D — 4-cyl., 40 hp, 126" wb						
Landaulet	6500	3000	4000	6000	9500	21,000

SHEETS — The F.M. Sheets Motor Company was organized in Wheeling, West Virginia during the spring of 1918 with a capital stock of $25,000 for the manufacturing of automobiles. Joining F.M. Sheets in this venture were E.C. Prince, Guy D. Sheets, L.M. Kline and E.C. Sheets. Manufacture is doubted.

SHELBY — The Shelby Stove & Manufacturing Company was organized in the fall of 1901 in Shelby, Ohio with a capital stock of $70,000 to "manufacture stoves and engines and automobiles and deal in the same." The presence of Thomas B. Jeffery among the incorporators of this venture indicates that it was an outgrowth of the Shelby bicycle works in town which had been established before the turn of the century by Jeffery together with his partner Philip Gormully. Automobile manufacture does not seem to have followed. This Shelby enterprise is not to be confused with the company organized by Beardsley and Hubbs in 1902, although Thomas B. Jeffery did purchase the machinery of that firm when it failed in 1903.

SHELBY — Shelby, Ohio — (1903) — In September of 1901, Volmer Beardsley and Charles Hubbs moved their Beardsley & Hubbs Manufacturing Company from Mansfield to Shelby, Ohio where they installed themselves in a factory which had formerly seen production of umbrella ribs.

1903 Shelby, touring, WLB

There, in 1902, they continued building the Darling car, and then had a better idea. By early summer the partners were in negotiation with the Shelby Board of Industry, explaining their wish to increase capitalization from $82,000 to $125,000. Forty men were then building three Darlings a week. The goal was a workforce of 100 men and a weekly output of six cars. The town of Shelby came through for Beardsley and Hubbs, and on November 11th they incorporated the Shelby Motor Car Company for manufacture of a new automobile called the Shelby to be offered in two models: a 20 hp twin with touring body and a single-cylinder 10 hp runabout with front seat folding into the dash. Prices were $2500 and $1200 respectively. The Shelby was introduced at the New York Automobile Show in January 1903, and that spring Volmer Beardsley drove one of the cars all the way to California with "scarcely a break worth mentioning." Production which had begun in January ended abruptly that summer with bankruptcy. At the auction held December 10th, the high bidder for the Shelby machinery was Thomas B. Jeffery, who shipped the equipment to Kenosha, Wisconsin to assist in the building of his Rambler. Obviously Volmer Beardsley must have enjoyed his sojourn on the West Coast with his Shelby. Subsequently, he moved to California where he built the Beardsley Electric.

1903 SHELBY
No. 5 — 2-cyl., 20 hp, 91" wb

	FP	5	4	3	2	1
Touring-5P	2500	2300	3300	4600	7500	16,000
No. 3 — 1-cyl., 10 hp, 78" wb						
Runabout-2/4P	1200	2000	3000	4200	6500	14,000

SHELDON — Skagway, Alaska — (1905) — The Sheldon family left Seattle, Washington and headed north in 1899 during the Klondike gold rush. In 1905 Robert E. Sheldon, then aged seventeen, built Alaska's first automobile, a gasoline buggy he designed himself using a magazine article as a guide and a Gray marine engine for power. Although Robert Sheldon never built another car, he remained, in his own words, "an automobile man" ever after. In 1913 his was the first Model T Ford in Fairbanks; he established an auto stage line between Fairbanks and various coastal cities a few years later, and ultimately extended the route all the way from Fairbanks to Seattle, cutting that trip to ten days from the thirty previously required by river boat. During the Twenties he served in Alaska's Territorial Legislature, during the Thirties he was Fairbanks' postmaster, and two decades later, following the granting of statehood to Alaska, he served in the House of Representatives, First State Legislature. Robert Sheldon died in 1983 at the age of ninety-nine. The car he built in 1905 is on exhibit today at the Museum of the University of Alaska in Fairbanks.

SHELDON — Wilkes Barre, Pennsylvania — (1909) — In 1909 the Sheldon Axle Company of Wilkes Barre announced its intention to enter into the manufacture of both motorcars and commercial vehicles. Conceivably prototypes may have followed, but manufacture did not. Instead the firm moved into the components field exclusively, with Sheldon axles, springs and chassis (without motor or radiator and largely for commercial use) being produced in the decade following. In 1922, by which time its name was Sheldon Axle & Spring Company, the firm collaborated on the venture which resulted in the Frankford car. In 1926 Sheldon sold out to Timken-Detroit.

SHELDON — Redmond, Oregon — (1941) — Roy Sheldon was a mechanic for the Redmond Motor Company and in 1941 came up with an idea that virtually everyone else had forgotten about since shortly after the turn of the century. His "automobile" was horse-drawn. The horse was a merry-go-round-type fake mounted on four wheels and fitted with a gasoline engine. A wagon was hitched behind, with reins for the driver — and the gearshift and brakes, of course. The horse was said to have "knee action," galloping up and down as it pulled the wagon, its head turning with the wagon wheels. A gallon of gasoline lasted all day, and 15 mph was the top speed. Sheldon built his "horse car" from cream separators, a washing machine, a lawn mower and assorted Ford parts. He obviously had a great sense of humor.

SHEPARD — The Shepard Cycle Company of 53 Clinton Street in Chicago, Illinois was reported by *The Horseless Age* during the summer of 1903 to be building an electric carriage. Details are lacking.

The Walter E. Shepard Company was organized in Melrose, Massachusetts during the fall of 1906 with a capital stock of $10,000 to manufacture motor vehicles. Incorporators were Walter L. and Chester B. Shepard, both of Melrose Heights. Manufacture is doubted.

SHEPHERD — William G. Shepherd was a mechanical engineer from Seneca Falls, New York who announced his impending establishment of an automobile factory in that town during the fall of 1901. There is no evidence he followed through on this.

The Shepherd Engineering & Automobile Company was organized in Camden, New Jersey during the spring of 1901 with a capital stock of $600,000 for the manufacture of motor vehicles. Incorporators were F.R. Hansell, Max Phillips and P.W. Miller. Manufacture is doubted.

SHEPMOBILE — Los Angeles, California — (1903-1905) — Robert C. Shepherd was a Los Angeles machinist who built boat engines for several years prior to joining with Russell J. Waters and Ross R. Foster in the formation of the Shepherd Auto-Engine Company shortly after the turn of the century. The firm's factory was at 877 Stephenson Avenue, and in December 1903 an automobile called the Shepmobile was added to the product line. It was a single-cylinder 7 hp runabout with a detachable tonneau and a sloping French-type brass hood. The Shepmobile was discontinued in April of 1904, the company announcing that hereafter it would "only build gasoline delivery wagons, not having time to turn out runabouts." Apparently a lucrative contract for fifty such wagons had been received. In 1905 both Shepherd and Waters left the company, and John R. Newberry became its president. Reportedly, he built a few cars that year, but was out of business by 1906.

1921 Sheridan, roadster, NAHC

SHERIDAN — Muncie, Indiana — (1920-1921) — Though it wasn't his idea initially, the Sheridan became one of the last projects spearheaded by William C. Durant during his second tenure as chief of General Motors. One of his old Buick men, D.A. Burke, the branch manager of Buick's Chicago operation, had come to him early in 1920 with designs for a four-cylinder moderately-priced ($1700 range) car which would slip nicely into the slot between the Chevrolet and Oakland. Burke envisioned an eight as well, at twice the price of the four, which would slot just below the Cadillac. Durant said go ahead. The result was the Sheridan Motor Car Company, a wholly-owned subsidiary of General Motors, and the former Inter-State factory in Muncie was purchased for manufacture. GM Northway engines were to be used in both the Sheridan cars, a 35 hp four and an 80 hp eight, with wheelbases of 116 and 132 inches respectively. Only pilot models of the eight ensued, and a small production of the four. Billy Durant left General Motors for the final time shortly thereafter. During the summer of 1921, General Motors sold both the Sheridan Company and the Muncie plant to him. Sheridan production continued under GM auspices until August 1st, 1921, when formal transfer to Durant took place. Durant quickly scuttled the Sheridan, but used its factory as one of several bases from which to launch his new empire. The Durant six was subsequently built there.

1921 SHERIDAN
Four — 35 hp, 116" wb

	FP	5	4	3	2	1
Roadster	1685	3300	4400	6700	12,000	24,000
Touring	1685	3500	4500	7000	13,000	25,000
Coupe	2060	2500	3500	5000	8500	18,000
Sedan	2360	2000	3000	4200	6500	14,000

SHERMAN — Rollin Sherman of 133 South Clinton Street in Chicago, Illinois was indicated as the producer of an electric automobile in a 1904 "Buyer's Guide" issue of *Cycle and Automobile Trade Journal*. Documentation is lacking.

SHERRILL & SMITH — Tullahoma, Tennessee — (1911) — "Tullahoma to Have Factory" headlined *The Horseless Age* in announcing that the local carriage-building firm of Sherrill & Smith had secured the machinery and were about to commence in the manufacture of high-wheeled buggies and roadsters. How long the company continued in this activity is not known.

SHILLITO — Cincinnati, Ohio — (1901) — That a steam car called the Shillito was built in Cincinnati in 1901 is indicated on numerous automobile rosters. There was a John Shillito Company in Cincinnati during this period, its products being dry goods and carpets, and its steam car having been built for the firm, most probably for delivery purposes. Certainly in 1901 then-president Stewart Shillito had no intention of manufacture. Neither did succeeding presidents of the company. As Shillito-Rikes today, the firm is the largest department store in Cincinnati.

SHIMER — Anderson, Indiana — (1901) — Shimer & Company, a machine shop in Anderson, announced the impending completion of its first automobile in the early spring of 1901. "The work on the machine is progressing rapidly and [it] will be ready to run on the streets by the middle of next week," said the company enthusiastically. "Additional buildings will be built at once. The present building has sprung up almost as if by magic. Six weeks ago ground was not broken for the plant." The Shimer enthusiasm was short-lived, however, as was the tenure of this company in the automobile-manufacturing field.

1908 Shoemaker, touring, GR

SHOEMAKER — Freeport, Illinois — (1906-1907)/Elkhart, Indiana — (1907-1908) — Although Freeport city directory references indicate that Charles Clinton Shoemaker may have begun building automobiles as early as 1903, it was not until late 1906 that he incorporated the Shoemaker Automobile Company and moved into formal manufacture. The Shoemaker was a robustly-built four-cylinder touring car which boasted such progressive features as a tubular front axle, three-speed sliding gear transmission and shaft drive. Shoemaker designed the car together with his son Harry C., and it was the latter who entered the 1500-mile mud-plugging tour sponsored by the AAA during the summer of 1907. "Though (he) traveled in the worst kind of hard luck throughout," reported *The Automobile*, "he pluckily stuck at it, getting through in excellent shape." In October 1907, after twenty-five cars had been built in Freeport, Shoemaker manufacture was relocated to a new factory in Elkhart, Indiana. Harry Shoemaker moved with the company; his father remained in Freeport to carry on the manufacture of incubators which had been built alongside the Shoemaker automobile. Less than a month following relocation, the Shoemaker Automobile Company announced its financial failure, noting that the cars already in the course of construction would be completed. The factory was closed down early in 1908, as Harry Shoemaker scurried about town trying to secure capital to begin again. By late spring he had found it, as a new organization called the St. Joe Motor Car Company was organized to take over the Shoemaker assets and build a new car called the St. Joe.

1907 SHOEMAKER
Model 6 — 4-cyl., 30/35 hp, 102" wb

	FP	5	4	3	2	1
Touring-5P	2200	3700	4700	7300	13,700	26,000

1908 SHOEMAKER
Model B — 4-cyl., 28 hp, 102" wb

	FP	5	4	3	2	1
Touring-5P	2000	3500	4500	7000	13,000	25,000

Model C — 4-cyl., 40 hp, 102" wb

	FP	5	4	3	2	1
Touring-5P	2500	3900	4800	7700	14,300	27,000

SHORT — O.E. Short and Company, Inc. was organized in New York City during the spring of 1912 with a capital stock of $25,000 for the manufacture and sale of engines and automobiles. Joining Orville E. Short in this venture were Harlan W. Short and H.L. Starr. Manufacture is doubted.

Short & Wright, Inc. was organized in New York City during the spring of 1910 with a capital stock of $1000 to manufacture and deal in motor vehicles. The partners involved were Orville E. Short and Fred. W. Wright. Manufacture is doubted.

SHORT — Penn Yan, New York — (1914) — Henry M. Short built his cyclecar at the plant of his employer, the Flexible Conduit Company of Penn Yan. Powered by a water-cooled 10/16 hp engine, its wheelbase was 107 inches, its tread 42 inches, its weight 700 pounds, its two-passenger roadster body providing side-by-side seating. Though Short indicated his intention to place the car on the market, there is no evidence he proceeded into manufacture.

SHOWMEE-DACHSHUND — St. Louis, Missouri — (1912) — It was so named because Missouri was the "show-me" state, and the car's lines were long and low. Indeed, a dachshund was the radiator emblem. The people behind this St. Louis venture are not known, but further details of the automobile are. Its engine was a Continental, its wheelbase 120 inches; a full-floating rear axle and multiple disc clutch were featured. An $1800 price tag was contemplated. In July of 1912, road testing of the first prototype was announced. "If it works right with a tryout the machine will be immediately put on the market," *The Automobile* said. Perhaps the car was a dog. There is no evidence the Showmee-Dachshund was ever manufactured.

SHROYER — Miltondale, Kansas — (1908) — The inclusive years of automobile manufacture by W.H. Shroyer of Miltondale cannot be stated with certainty. It is known that he purchased all component parts in the East, assembled them and added the body and upholstery himself in Miltondale. In 1908 Shroyer wrote *The Horseless Age* regarding his operation. "The automobile is actually supplanting the horse in his state," the magazine revealed. Added Shroyer: "The motor car is especially practical in Kansas, where there are long stretches of level prairie roads and great distances between points."

SHUGERS — Coldwater, Michigan — (1899) — The Shugers brothers of Coldwater ran a cycle shop at 24 East Chicago Street in Coldwater where in 1899 they built their first gasoline-powered motor carriage. Possibly, it was also their last. The brothers remained in the automobile field, however, as engine producers. By 1901 the Shugers Gasoline Engine Works was advertising 4 hp units for light cars and 1-1/2 hp motors for bicycles and trikes. During the spring of 1903 the Shugers brothers sold out to the partnership of Allen & Rogers.

SHUNK — Bucyrus, Ohio — (1908) — In 1908 the Shunk Plow Company of Bucyrus had a short fling as an automobile manufacturer. Its car was a typical highwheeler of the period, equipped with a two-stroke 12 hp engine, Ross steering gear and a two-speed planetary transmission which was fitted with the differential at the center of the rear axle.

1911 Sibley, 2-pass. roadster, NAHC

SIBLEY — Detroit, Michigan — (1910-1911) — F.M. Sibley, a Michigan lumber dealer, was the principal financial backer of the Sibley Motor Car Company and probably among his motivations for getting into the automobile business was to provide his son Eugene with something interesting to do. Others involved in the venture were J.G. Utz, formerly chief engineer for Chalmers, and C.P. Warner, who served as Sibley's president. Company offices were taken at 870 Woodward Avenue and the former plant of the Detroit Valve & Fitting Company was leased for the factory. Manufacture began during the spring of 1910. The Sibley was sold in a single model: a two-passenger roadster on a 106-inch wheelbase. Its engine was a 30 hp four, its transmission a three-speed selective, and its price tag $900. The Sibley was short-lived. In January 1911 Detroit Valve and Fittings sued the company for recovery of its plant, charging default on the lease agreement. Later that year Eugene Sibley showed up in Connecticut with an idea for another car called the Sibley-Curtiss.

1912 Sibley-Curtiss, touring, NAHC

SIBLEY-CURTISS — Simsbury, Connecticut — (1911-1912) — In the early fall of 1911, the organization of the Sibley-Curtiss Motor Company was announced from Simsbury. Joseph J. Curtiss was a local automobile dealer whose showroom stock included Velie, Hupmobile and Cartercar. Eugene Sibley was from Detroit, and had been involved with the Sibley car there the year previous. Although the stated purpose of the new company was the manufacture of automobiles, a Simsbury resident who was there at the time recalls that the real plan was to purchase the previous year's models of another Connecticut manufacturer and market them under the Sibley-Curtiss name. Only two Sibley-Curtiss cars were sold during the winter of 1911-1912: one to Arthur Humphrey, the other to Robert Welch.

SIEFKER — Seymour, Indiana — (1880) — In 1880 a German immigrant named William Siefker who lived in Seymour built a steam automobile. It had two separate engines, one for each set of wheels, and a fourteen-inch fire-tube boiler. The Siefker used coal for fuel, and purportedly attained a speed of 10-12 mph. William Siefker is not known to have built another car.

SIEG — Kenosha, Wisconsin — (1899) — That the C.H. Sieg Manufacturing Company of Kenosha intended to enter the automobile field has been documented, that it ever indeed did so has not. An initial reference to this Wisconsin bicycle manufacturer's automotive plans came in July of 1899, followed that October by the announcement that C.H. Sieg, in collaboration with John Kehler of Kenosha and F.B. Magaw of Chicago, had capitalized the venture at $20,000 and had taken over the Morgan & Wright property in town. Further news was not forthcoming.

SIEGMUND-BAYLIES — The Siegmund-Baylies Company was organized in Chicago, Illinois during the summer of 1909 with a capital stock of $40,000 to manufacture and deal in automobiles. Incorporators were O.S. Baylies, E.H. Arnold and A.C. Noble. Manufacture is doubted.

SIEMENS-HALSKE — The Siemens-Halske Electric Company is indicated as a manufacturer of automobiles in the Hiscox volume, *Horseless Vehicles, Automobiles, Motor Cycles* published in 1900. The firm did build a car during this period but it was marketed as the Illinois Electric. Refer to Illinois Electric.

SIEVER — Oneida, New York — (1903) — The Siever Carriage Company of Oneida announced the building of an experimental gasoline touring car during the summer of 1903. Its transmission was designed by company president H.M. Reynolds, with construction of the vehicle supervised by secretary-treasurer M.R. Siever. The Siever Carriage Company did not, however, proceed from experiment into manufacture.

SIGMA — A cyclecar called the Sigma has been indicated on various car rosters as having been produced in Boston, Massachusetts in 1914. The car did appear there in October that year as a participant in the racing program held at Combination Park in Medford. But the Sigma was not manufactured in this country. Instead it was built by the Societe des Automobiles Sigma of Paris and was imported from France by Robert P. Breeze of New York City.

SIGNET — Signet was a name considered and announced to the trade press by the Fenton Cyclecar Company of Fenton, Michigan. When the car arrived on the market during the fall of 1913, however, it was called the Fenton, which was later succeeded by the Koppin. Refer to Fenton.

SIGNOR — Elkhart, Indiana — (1901) — That A.J. Signor of Elkhart was building an automobile was announced in the March 13th, 1901 edition of *The Motor Age*. "Here is the town's chance to find a successor to the late lamented Soudan Manufacturing Company," the magazine said. Manufacture of the Signor car did not follow, however.

SILENT — The Silent Motor Car Company was organized in New Kensington, Pennsylvania early in 1910 with a capital stock of $300,000 for the manufacture of automobiles. Incorporators were Julius Sturtevant, J.W. Walsch, C.C. Conkle and J.W. Dorsey. Manufacture is doubted.

The Silent Motor Car & Engineering Company of Los Angeles, California was organized during the spring of 1914 with a capital stock of $1 million by J.H. Grube, E.T. Houston, S.T. Allen and F.M. Casey. By February 1915 the firm, which has since been renamed the American Silent Motors Company, announced from its L.A. offices at 253 South Broadway that a parcel of land had been purchased nearby on which would be erected a factory for the manufacture of $500 touring, roadster and light truck to be called the Silent. This venture seems to have died aborning.

1907 Silent-Knight, touring, WLB

SILENT KNIGHT — Chicago, Illinois — (1905-1907) — Charles Yale Knight was a Hoosier by birth and a printer and publisher by profession. The turn of the century found him in Chicago printing and publishing *Dairy Produce*, a magazine he had founded. It also found him driving an air-cooled Knox, the noisy valve gear of which annoyed him. His desire for a valve action that was quiet led, in 1904, to his invention of a sleeve-valve engine. He called it the Silent Knight, and the following year he formed a partnership with L.B. Kilbourne in Chicago. The building of a number of his engines immediately followed, as did a few examples of a 35/40 hp Silent Knight touring car. These cars featured shaft drive, a selective sliding gear transmission and a $3500 price tag — but the idea was not so much for Knight and Kilbourne to get into the manufacturing business themselves as to demonstrate the viability of the sleeve-valve engine and to grant licenses for its manufacture to a plethora of American automobile manufacturers. Their plan did not work at all well initially. Firstly, the few Silent Knights they built were crudely put together and not much of an advertisement for the product. Secondly, the car that Charles Knight entered in the 1906 Glidden Tour dropped out on the first day and resulted in bad publicity. Consequently, in 1907 Knight took one of his cars to Europe. In England, the Daimler Motor Company saw possibilities in a refined version of the Knight engine and secured a license. As did Mercedes in Germany, Minerva in Belgium, and Panhard et Levassor in France. With success in Europe, Charles Knight returned to America to a more pleasant reception among U.S. manufacturers. His first American license was taken by the F.B. Stearns Company in Cleveland, followed by Stoddard-Dayton, Columbia (Hartford, Connecticut) and Atlas (Indianapolis). Among the other cars built with the sleeve-valve engine ultimately were the Edwards-Knight, the Moline-Knight, the Sterling-Knight, the Falcon-Knight and — in the most numbers — the Willys-Knight.

1905-1907 SILENT KNIGHT
Four — 30/40 hp, 112" wb

	FP	5	4	3	2	1
Touring-5P	3500	3900	4800	7700	14,300	27,000

SILENT NORTHERN — This was the designation given in 1902 and 1903 to the car produced by the Northern Manufacturing Company of Detroit, later Port Huron, Michigan. Northerns were built from 1902-1908. Refer to Northern.

SILENT SIOUX — A total of five of these cars were built, alternately designated the Silent Sioux or the Fawick Flyer. The venture was the idea of Thomas L. Fawick of Sioux Falls, South Dakota. Refer to Fawick Flyer.

1915 Silver-Knight (Willys-Knight), roadster, HAC

SILVER — New York, New York — (1914-1919) — Conover Thomas Silver was a slender, shy and quiet man who was born in Little Silver, New Jersey and who made his fame and fortune as a car dealer in New York City. Baptized in the trade selling Buicks in Brooklyn, by 1913 Silver was the Greater New York distributor for Willys-Overland and Peerless, and in January 1914 he bought the grandiose $1.8 million Peerless marble palace on Broadway and 56th Street as the home for his C.T. Silver Motor Company. He also became a car designer that year. His style was marked by swoopy lines, semi-cut-down doors, curvaceous convertible tops that folded like a saddle, rear decks shaped like a turtle or bumblebee, and smart bullet-shaped headlights. Willys was the first to build one of his cars, a turtle-deck Willys-Knight runabout in the fall of 1914. The Silver-Knight, as it was called, was followed by a Silver-Peerless and a six-passenger $2200 Overland roadster with body design by Silver. But his most famous cars were yet to come. In August of 1916, C.T. Silver switched allegiance to Chalmers; no Silver specials are believed to have resulted from that alliance. But in 1917 Silver became New York distributor for Apperson and Kissel, and his special designs on those chassis became the stars of the New York Automobile Show. The Silver-Apperson was called that only in 1918, though the Silver styling touches were retained in the regular Apperson line into the Twenties. Silver-Kissels or Kissel Silver Specials

1915 Silver-Knight (Willys-Knight), roadster, HAC

seem to have been so called for two years. The hubcaps on some cars bore the legend, "C.T. Silver, Inc., New York." Conover T. Silver's design career seems to have ended in 1919, when he gave up his distributorship. Rumors in 1920 that he was about to announce a new popularly-priced car came to naught.

1918 Silver Special (Kissel), speedster, HAC

SILVER ARROW — The streamlined Silver Arrow show car was the smash hit of the New York Automobile Show in 1933, and subsequently the Pierce-Arrow Motor Car Company of Buffalo used the name as a model designation beginning in 1934. Refer to Pierce-Arrow.

SILVESTER — St. Louis, Missouri — (1897) — Compressed air supplied the power for the horseless carriage built in 1897 by Henry Silvester, a carriagemaker and real estate dealer residing at 5523 Virginia Avenue in St. Louis. "By a system of mechanism underneath the vehicle, compressed air is supplied to a receiving chamber, and from there flows out into valves so arranged as to turn the wheels and propel the vehicle on about the same principle that a steam engine is operated by steam," the St. Louis *Republican* reported that year. "The advantage of Mr. Silvester's invention lies in the fact that the upward and downward motion of the bed of the vehicle upon its springs supplies the force which moves it forward. When it is considered that the weight bearing down upon the chambers where the air is compressed is nearly ten times greater than the force required to propel the vehicle, it is readily apparent that the power created would be adequate for the purpose." Undoubtedly, Henry Silvester's automotive idea did not work out nearly so well as he had anticipated.

SIMKIN — The Simkin Manufacturing Company was organized in Chicago, Illinois late in 1911 with a $2000 capital stock to manufacture and deal in motor cars and accessories. Incorporators were A.J. Elliott, H. Prather Elliott and John T. Evans. Manufacture of a car is doubted.

SIMMONS — The Simmons Automobile Company was organized in New York City late in 1910 with a capital stock of $10,000 for the manufacture and sale of automobiles and engines. Incorporators were John G. Simmons, George L. Lewis and Daniel E. Wing. Manufacture of a car is doubted.

1920 Simms, touring, RBB

SIMMS — Atlanta, Georgia — (1920) — Jackson H. Simms had been plant manager at the Chevrolet factory in Atlanta for a decade when, shortly after the First World War, he resigned his position to begin his own automobile company. His chief financial backer was Thomas H. Mars, who took the presidency of the new Simms Motor Car Corporation, which was incorporated with a capital stock of $2.5 million in April of 1920. Simms was vice-president and general manager, E.W. van Duzen (formerly of Pullman, Columbia, Mitchell-Lewis and Reo) was chief engineer, with Henry L. Innes production manager. The Simms was a light four, with a 36 hp valve-in-head engine of the company's own design. The wheelbase was 114 inches, and the projected price tag was $1200. Disc wheels were to be standard. Three prototypes had been built by early October when the Simms company was petitioned into involuntary bankruptcy. Thereafter Henry L. Innes took the Simms automobile idea to Jacksonville, Florida where he revived it under his own name.

SIMON — The E.C Simon Cyclecar Company of Detroit, Michigan was indicated as building an automobile in the March 1914 issue of *Motor Print*. Documentation is lacking.

"Simon Brothers, Webster City, Iowa, have invented a new motor carriage, and a stock company with a capital stock of $150,000 has been organized to establish a factory," reported *The Motor Vehicle Review* during the fall of 1899. That any manufacture followed has not been documented.

1893 Simonds Steam Carriage, NAHC

SIMONDS STEAM — **Lynn, Massachusetts** — **(1893)** — Clarence L. Simonds was an engineer employed with the Lynn Gas & Electric Company in 1893 during which year he built a steam car. It was fitted with a two-cylinder vertical engine, using naptha as fuel, and featured a porcupine-type boiler. "There are two pumps, one to feed the boiler, the other to blow the air blast through the naptha," reported *The Horseless Age*. "The exhaust steam passes through a feed water heater and is then delivered to the naphtha flame, where its presence stifles the noise." A good head of steam was claimed within five minutes, as was a speed of 10 mph. Originally Simonds had built the vehicle for his own use in getting from home to office and had obtained permission from Lynn authorities to use it on the road between certain hours. Some local promoters learned of the vehicle, however, and Simonds sold it to them for what he described as "a round sum" for exhibition purposes. Subsequently, Simonds is known to have been friendly with the Stanley brothers and exchanged steam-car talk with them, but he is not believed to have built another car.

SIMPLEX — Simplex Steamer was one of the three names used by Ralph Otho Hood for the steam cars he produced in Danvers, Massachusetts from 1899 to 1901. Hood organized the Simplex Motor Vehicle Company as a $500,000 Maine incorporation during the spring of 1900. Refer to Hood Steamer.

The Simplex Auto Cranker Company was organized in Chicago, Illinois during the fall of 1911 with a capital stock of $100,000 to manufacture and deal in automobiles and machinery. Incorporators were Edwin A. Garner, Ignatius F. Holton and Willard Patrick. Manufacture of a car is doubted.

The Simplex Manufacturing Company was organized in Cleveland, Ohio in 1908 by Earl Sherbondy for the production of a car called Derain. Refer to Derain.

1909 Simplex, 50 hp, speed car, HAC

1304

SIMPLEX — **New York, New York (1907-1913)/New Brunswick, New Jersey** — **(1913-1919)** — The Simplex Automobile Company produced one of the most renowned cars in America during the pre-World War I period. In 1907 textile importer Herman Broesel, Sr. bought out the assets of the New York firm which manufactured the S & M Simplex, including its 614 East 83rd Street factory and the services of chief engineer Edward Franquist. At the time of purchase, Franquist had just completed final work on a new and more powerful four-cylinder model with short-stroke (bore/stroke dimensions were 5-3/4 inches square) T-head 50 hp engine, and this car was introduced as the Simplex. Though other models with horsepower up to 90 would follow, it was the Simplex 50 which was the most popular; about 250 of them were sold in the next half decade. With their robust construction, four-speed selective transmissions and double chain drive, these cars were formidable sporting machines and enjoyed a fine success in motor competition, a Simplex finishing sixth in the first Indianapolis 500. With coachwork by Quinby, Demarest, Holbrook, Brewster and Healey, they were also massive, luxury cars which enjoyed an elite clientele. Prices were in the $5000 range. In 1911 a smaller shaft-drive Model 38 was added to the line, and 1912 saw introduction of a Model 75 with choice of shaft or chain drive. During the fall of 1912, Herman Broesel died, and in September of the year following his sons sold out to the New York firm of Goodrich, Lockhart and Smith. (C.C. and David Goodrich were sons of the tire-making B.F.) Though the Broesels and Franquist remained on to manage operations, the factory itself was moved from Manhattan to New Brunswick, New Jersey. In 1914 the short-stroke Simplex 50 gave way to the long-stroke (5-3/8 by 6½). In the fall of that year, the new Simplex management purchased the Crane Motor Car Company which had been building a super-expensive ($8000 for chassis alone) six-cylinder shaft-drive car in small numbers in Bayonne, New Jersey. The talents of Henry Crane were part of the purchase price — Crane would become a second vice-president of Simplex — and his factory equipment was moved from Bayonne to New Brunswick early in 1915. Although the gutsy and venerable four-cylinder chain-drive Simplex was made available for a while longer alongside the shaft-drive Crane-designed six, it was the latter which became the principal production of the Simplex Automobile Company. The car remained an expensive one. Though introduced in the Simplex price range rather than the heretofore rarefied realm of the Crane, the price of the chassis increased yearly, from $5000 in 1915 to $7000 in 1917. The official name of the car was Simplex, Crane Model 5, though it became popularly known as the Crane-Simplex. Its clientele included many members of America's gentry; the Rockefeller garage in Pocantico Hills housed two touring cars, painted in the "house colors" of maroon with red striping. In 1916 the Simplex Automobile Company was acquired by Wright-Martin Aircraft Corporation, and following America's entrance into World War I, the New Brunswick factory was used to produce Hispano-Suiza aircraft engines. At the end of October 1917, Wright-Martin announced the cessation of Simplex production for "the period of the war." At least 467 Crane-designed Simplexes had been built. After the Armistice, Wright-Martin management decided to discontinue automobile production. Available stock meant some cars were put together in 1918 and 1919, however. The definitive end for the Simplex Automobile Company began on February 27th, 1920, the day former Packard vice-president Emlen S. Hare launched his ill-fated Hare's Motors, an operating company which bought Simplex, together with Mercer and Locomobile, three of America's most distinguished marques. Hare's empire was destined for a quick oblivion. In late 1922 Henry Crane purchased the Simplex assets from the Hare group with the hope of reviving the car he had designed under the name of Crane-Simplex, but that hope was quickly dashed.

1907-1908 SIMPLEX
Model 50 — 4-cyl., 50 hp, 124" wb

	FP	5	4	3	2	1
Toy Tonneau-4P	5500	9400	18,800	26,500	53,800	75,000

1909 Simplex, 50 hp, touring, OCW

1909 SIMPLEX
Model 50 — 4-cyl., 50 hp, 124" wb

Speed Car-2P	5500	10,000	20,000	30,000	60,000	80,000
Toy Tonneau-4P	5750	9400	18,800	26,500	53,800	75,000
Model 50 — 4-cyl., 50 hp, 127" wb						
Laudaulet-7P	6750	7800	13,300	20,300	44,000	60,000
Limousine-7P	6750	7800	13,300	20,300	44,000	60,000
Model 50 — 4-cyl., 50 hp, 129" wb						
Touring-7P	5750	11,300	21,300	32,500	65,000	85,000

1910 SIMPLEX
Model 50 — 4-cyl., 50 hp, 124" wb

Runabout	4450	9400	18,800	26,500	53,800	75,000
Model 50 — 4-cyl., 50 hp, 129" wb						
Touring	4450	10,000	20,000	30,000	60,000	80,000
Model 90 — 4-cyl., 90 hp, 124" wb						
Touring-5/7P	5250	13,000	23,000	36,000	72,000	92,000

1910 Simplex, 50 hp, toy tonneau, HAC

1911 Simplex, 50 hp, runabout, OCW

1911 SIMPLEX
Model 38 — 4-cyl., 38 hp, 127" wb

	FP	5	4	3	2	1
Touring-7P	4850	11,800	21,800	33,500	67,000	87,000
Model 50 — 4-cyl., 50 hp, 124 & 129" wb						
Chassis	4500					
Model 90 — 4-cyl., 90 hp, 124" wb						
Chassis	5350	—	—	—	—	—
Touring-5P	6250	13,000	23,000	36,000	72,000	92,000

1912 Simplex, 38 hp, coach-landaulet, HAC

1913 Simplex, limousine, JAC

1912-1913 SIMPLEX
Model 38 — 4-cyl., 38 hp, 127" wb

Touring-4P	4850	8800	17,000	24,000	49,000	70,000
Touring-5P	4850	9000	18,000	25,000	50,000	72,000

Model 38 — 4-cyl., 38 hp, 137" wb

	FP	5	4	3	2	1
Touring-7P	4850	9400	18,800	26,500	53,800	75,000
Landaulet-7P	5800	8200	14,500	21,500	45,800	65,000
Limousine-7P	5800	8000	14,000	21,000	45,000	64,000
Model 50 — 4-cyl., 50 hp, 124" wb						
Touring-4P	5400	10,000	20,000	30,000	60,000	80,000
Model 50 — 4-cyl., 50 hp, 129" wb						
Touring-7P	5700	10,500	20,500	31,000	62,000	82,000
Model 50 — 4-cyl., 50 hp, 137" wb						
Touring-7P	5700	11,300	21,300	32,500	65,000	85,000
Landaulet-7P	6400	9400	18,800	26,500	53,800	75,000
Limousine-7P	6400	9300	18,500	26,000	52,500	74,000
Model 90 — 4-cyl., 90 hp, 124" wb						
Touring-4P	6250	11,500	21,500	33,000	66,000	86,000
Touring-5P	6450	11,800	21,800	33,500	67,000	87,000
Model 75 — 4-cyl., 90 hp, 124" wb						
Touring-4P	6950	12,500	22,500	35,000	70,000	90,000
Touring-7P	7050	13,800	23,800	37,500	75,000	95,000
Runabout-2P	5350	11,300	21,300	32,500	65,000	85,000
Limousine	7850	10,000	20,000	30,000	60,000	80,000
Landaulet	7850	10,500	20,500	31,000	62,000	82,000

1914 Simplex, 50 hp, limousine, HAC

1914 SIMPLEX
Model 38 — 4-cyl., 38 hp, 137" wb

Tourabout-4P	5500	9500	19,000	27,000	55,000	76,000
Coach-7P	6500	7600	12,500	19,400	42,400	55,000
Chassis	4000	—	—	—	—	—
Model 50 — 4-cyl., 50 hp, 137" wb						
Tourabout-4P	6000	10,000	20,000	30,000	60,000	80,000
Chassis	4500	—	—	—	—	—
Model 75 — 4-cyl., 75 hp, 124" wb						
Chassis	5350					

1915 Simplex, 50 hp, touring, HAC

1915 SIMPLEX
Model 38 — 4-cyl., 38 hp, 137" wb

Limousine-7P	6500	8200	14,500	21,500	45,800	65,000
Chassis	4000	—	—	—	—	—
Model 50 — 4-cyl., 50 hp, 137" wb						
Touring-5P	6100	11,300	21,300	32,500	65,000	85,000
Chassis	4500	—	—	—	—	—
Model 75 — 4-cyl., 75 hp, 124" wb						
Chassis	5350	—	—	—	—	—
Crane, Model 5 — 6-cyl., 46 hp, 144" wb						
Chassis	5000	—	—	—	—	—
Touring-7P	6500	10,000	20,000	30,000	60,000	80,000

1916 Simplex, Crane model 5, touring, HAC

1916 SIMPLEX
Model 50 — 4-cyl., 50 hp, 137" wb

Chassis	4600					
Touring-5P	6200	13,800	23,800	37,500	75,000	95,000
Crane, Model 5 — 6-cyl., 46 hp, 144" wb						
Chassis	6000					
Touring-7P	7500	11,800	21,800	33,500	67,000	87,000

1917 Simplex, Crane model 5, town car, GR

1918 Simplex, Crane model 5, touring, HAC

1919 Simplex, Crane model 5, limousine, HAC

1917-1919 SIMPLEX
Crane, Model 5 — 6-cyl., 46 hp, 144" wb

	FP	5	4	3	2	1
Chassis	7000	—	—	—	—	—

SIMPLICIA — New Orleans, Louisiana — (1910) — During the early fall of 1910, Charles Levy, who described himself as a member of the New Orleans Banking and Cotton Exchange, announced his plans for the manufacture of a "newly patented" car he called the Simplicia. The idea for this "car without a chassis" had presumably originated in France, its distinguishing feature described in the *New England Automobile Journal* as "the front of the engine being attached to the front axle in a novel manner, while engine, transmission and rear axle form a unit." Levy planned for the Simplicia to be produced in a medium-priced range of delivery wagons, taxicabs and touring cars. The Simplicia Automobile Company was incorporated with a $2 million capital stock in Brooklyn, New York, and with Stuart L. Jaffray of New York City, James McBrian of New Brighton (New York) and Simon J. Schlenker of New Orleans listed as the incorporators. About this time the Adams Business Men's Association of Adams, Massachusetts announced its interest in having the Simplicia factory located there. Whether it ever was cannot be documented, but the Simplicia apparently did see some production somewhere. Connecticut registration lists for 1914-1915 indicate two cars of that name.

SIMPLICITIES — Middletown, Connecticut — (1905) — There was one Simplicities car built in 1905 in Middletown, Connecticut. It was a four-cylinder 24 hp touring. The Simplicities Automobile Company was one of several stock promotion swindles perpetrated by W.H. Kitto, whose efforts are best recounted under his own name. Refer to Kitto.

SIMPLICITY — Greensburg, Indiana — (1902) — The Simplicity was a one-cylinder gasoline runabout built in Greensburg in 1902 by Ira J. Hollensbee. The car, which was apparently the only one built by Hollensbee, was extant in the mid-Fifties, though its whereabouts today have not been confirmed. Dates of 1904 and 1911 have also been given for this car, the 1902 year having been attested to in 1956 by Hollensbee's grandson.

1908 Simplicity, model C, roadster, HAC

SIMPLICITY — Evansville, Indiana — (1907-1911) — By the time he built his Simplicity, Willis Copeland already had an extensive career as an automobile man, having produced the Zentmobile, the Single Center, the Windsor and the Worth in his Single Center Buggy Company of Evansville. For this new car, he formed a new enterprise, the Evansville Automobile Company, for which he successfully sold stock to a number of friends in town, including the mayor. He also set up a proper assembly line for the first time. The Simplicity was a four-cylinder water-cooled car offered in a variety of body styles. Its most distinctive feature was its friction gear transmission which did away with the clanking chains Copeland had disliked in the previous cars, but which created a certain problem. The Simplicity performed admirably in fair weather, but whenever it rained, it stalled. The engine started, but the car wouldn't move. When finally Copeland discovered the reason for this was moisture in the friction gears, he also discovered that it could be solved by enclosing same. This he did. Recognizing now that some damage had been done to the Simplicity reputation by its performance in foul weather, he formed the Traveler Automobile Company late in 1909 which built a car called the Traveler. The Traveler was merely the Simplicity under another name and, curiously, he also continued the Simplicity, which he now overpriced outrageously. Both cars featured enclosed friction drive. Copeland's money, and perhaps his patience, ran out as an automobile manufacturer ran out in late 1911. By 1912 he had decided to confine his efforts to producing replacement parts for existing marques, and to becoming Evansville's first Chevrolet dealer. The early Chevrolet had transmission problems too. Later he was a dealer for the Flint.

1907-1908 SIMPLICITY
Model C — 4-cyl., 35/40 hp, 105" wb

	FP	5	4	3	2	1
Touring-5P	3000	5000	6500	11,000	22,000	35,000
Roadster-2/4P	2500	4500	5800	9500	18,000	32,000
Limousine-5/7P	4500	3500	4500	7000	13,000	25,000

1909 SIMPLICITY
Model 4-20 — 4-cyl., 20 hp, 96" wb

Runabout-2P	650	2500	3500	5000	8500	18,000
Single Rumble Rbt.-3P	675	2900	3700	5600	9100	20,000
Double Rumble Rbt.-4P	700	3100	4200	6300	10,500	22,000
Toy Tonneau-4P	700	3300	4400	6700	12,000	24,000

Model 4-30 — 4-cyl., 30 hp, 105" wb

Double Rumble Rdstr.	1000	3700	4700	7300	13,700	26,000
Victoria	1200	3500	4500	7000	13,000	25,000

1910 Simplicity, model C, touring, HAC

1910 SIMPLICITY
Model C — 4-cyl., 40 hp, 105" wb

Touring	3000	4300	5400	8700	16,500	30,000
Tulip Touring	3000	4300	5400	8700	16,500	30,000
Victoria	3000	3900	4800	7700	14,300	27,000
Canopy Touring	3150	4200	5200	8400	15,700	29,000
Runabout	2500	4000	5000	8000	15,000	28,000

1911 SIMPLICITY
Model C — 4-cyl., 40 hp, 105" wb

Touring	2000	4300	5400	8700	16,500	30,000
Victoria	2000	4200	5200	8400	15,700	29,000
Roadster	1500	4000	5000	8000	15,000	28,000

1920 Simplicity Six, touring, WLB

SIMPLICITY SIX — Seattle, Washington — (1920) — This Seattle car was the idea of H.L. Deputy who designed it and who served as president of the Simplicity Motors Company. The firm's offices were at 307 Boston Block in Seattle. The Simplicity was powered by a six-cylinder 60 hp Beaver engine set into a 134-inch wheelbase chassis with cantilever plus full-elliptic springs. The frame was laminated spruce, following airplane practice — and the car's selective transmission was an unusual design, being controlled by clutch pedal and a lever on the steering post. Both the service and the emergency brake operated from one pedal. With prices in the $4500 range, the Simplicity was planned for the luxury car market. In July of 1920, Deputy reported that he was taking the prototype on a test trip to include the cities of Portland, Walla Walla, Spokane and Lewiston (Idaho). Within three months he planned to be turning out at least eight cars a day. His venture died before production began, but it is known that at least five pilot models were built. An interesting marketing idea for the Simplicity Six, as indicated in the company's brochure, was the order-by-number approach among the variations planned in chassis and body styles. Had the car been put into manufacture, a customer could have ordered, for example, a No. 1 chassis with a No. 4 body, rather like the Column-A-Column-B offerings on a Chinese menu.

1909 Simplo, model L, runabout, NAHC

SIMPLO — St. Louis, Missouri — (1908-1909) — The product of the Cook Motor Vehicle Company of St. Louis was advertised as the biggest automobile value in America. It was certainly not that, although as a high-wheeler the Simplo was offered in more variations than most vehicles of that genre. Both air- and water-cooled engines were available, and both solid- and pneumatic-tired models. The pneumatics added fifty dollars to the price tag. All Simplos featured a friction transmission, double chain drive and right-hand wheel steering. After a year of trying, the Cook Motor Vehicle Company gave up on the Simplo. The firm had been a carriage maker prior to its Simplo venture; it continued in business as a multi-marque automobile dealership.

1909 Simplo, model S, surrey, JAC

1908-1909 SIMPLO
Model C — 2-cyl., 14/16 hp, 86" wb

	FP	5	4	3	2	1
Runabout-2P	600	2300	3300	4600	7500	16,000
Model L — 2-cyl., 14/16 hp, 86" wb						
Roadster-3P	650	2400	3400	4800	8000	17,000
Model S — 2-cyl., 16/18 hp, 86" wb						
Surrey-4P	675	2500	3500	5000	8500	18,000

SIMPSON — Detroit, Michigan — (1906) — William G. Simpson was a consulting engineer from Detroit who decided to produce a gasoline motor of such constant torque that a geared transmission would be unnecessary. He designed and patented the result which he called a "steeple" engine. "There will be eight four-cycle cylinders altogether, and each pair of cylinders will work through a single crank and will produce an explosion every revolution," explained *The Automobile*. "Thus the crankshaft will receive a power impulse every quarter of a revolution, giving the same turning effect as two double-acting steam cylinders." Simpson stated his intention to place a steeple-engined car on the market in 1907. Work on a prototype was begun — the car's features including an air-controlled gearless transmission as well as air brakes and air clutch — but whether it was ever completed is not known. Simpson's steeple-engined car certainly never made it to the market in 1907.

SINCLAIR — The car produced in Baltimore, Maryland by the Sinclair-Scott Company was marketed as the Maryland. Maryland cars were built from 1907-1910. Refer to Maryland.

In 1923, from St. Louis, Missouri, came word that a new car called the Sinclair was to be produced using the Scheel rotary valve engine. Refer to Scheel.

1915 Singer, touring, HAC

SINGER — New York, New York — (1914-1918)/Mount Vernon, New York — (1919-1920) — Charles A. Singer always went first class. Scion of the Singer sewing machine family, he began his automotive career in association with Henry U. Palmer, the partners initially serving as New York City dealers for the Simplex, Matheson and Isotta-Fraschini — and ultimately producing their own high-quality Palmer-Singer car from 1908 through 1914. The Singer was its linear descendant. A high-priced automobile from the beginning, distinguished by the deep vee of its radiator shell and the guarantee of at least 72 mph on the road, the Singer was available in a variety of catalogued models, and with special custom coachwork from America's finest purveyors of the art which could raise price tags to the $9000 range. A 50 hp Herschell-Spillman six-cylinder engine powered the Singer from 1914 to the end, with a Weidely V-12 added to the line in 1920. The first Singer was on the road in mid-June of 1914, shortly following the incorporation of the Singer Motor Company, Inc. in New York. First deliveries commenced July 15th. Initially, the Singer was built entirely in New York City, at plants on West 47th Street near West End Avenue in Manhattan and at the former Alco service facility in Long Island City, Queens. Output was about 200 cars a year. In 1919 the company established its offices in Mount Vernon and moved into a new factory there. Assembly, road testing and all experimental development emanated from Mount Vernon thereafter, with body and trim work only being seen to in the West 47th Street plant in Manhattan. Doubtless the introduction of the V-12 Singer for 1920 was a last-gasp effort of the firm to revive flagging luxury sales. It didn't work. The Singer Motor Company, Inc. was in receivership that October and was declared bankrupt in November. Automotive trade publications continued to list the Singer in 1921, but the cars sold that year were simply 1920 models purveyed in the final winding down of the company affairs. Charles A. Singer died in August 1922.

1916 Singer, runabout, HAC

1914-1915 SINGER
Six — 50 hp, 138" wb

	FP	5	4	3	2	1
Touring-5P	2350	7600	12,500	19,400	42,400	55,000

1916 SINGER
Six — 50 hp, 138" wb

Touring-7P	3200	7600	12,500	19,400	42,400	55,000
Touring-4P	3200	7400	12,100	18,800	41,100	53,000
Runabout-2/3P	3200	7300	11,800	18,400	40,400	52,000
Limousine-7P	4200	5000	6500	11,000	22,000	35,000
Landaulet-7P	4350	5200	6800	11,300	23,000	36,000

1917 Singer, victoria touring, HAC

1917-1919 SINGER
Six — 50 hp, 138" wb

Touring-7P	3800	7600	12,500	19,400	42,400	55,000
Touring-4P	3800	7400	12,100	18,800	41,100	53,000
Roadster-2P	3800	7300	11,800	18,400	40,400	52,000
Runabout-4P	4000	7200	11,300	17,700	38,700	50,000
Limousine-7P	4750	5000	6500	11,000	22,000	35,000
Sedan-5P	4800	4200	5200	8400	15,700	29,000
Landaulet-7P	4850	5200	6800	11,300	23,000	36,000
Brougham-6P	5350	5400	7300	11,800	25,000	38,000

1920 SINGER
Six — 50 hp, 138" wb

Roadster-2P	5250	7400	12,100	18,800	41,100	53,000
Touring-4P	5250	7500	12,300	19,100	41,700	54,000
Touring-7P	5250	7700	12,700	19,700	43,000	56,000
Limousine-7P	7200	5200	6800	11,300	23,000	36,000
Sedan-6P	7200	4300	5400	8700	16,500	30,000
Brougham-6P	7300	5400	7300	11,800	25,000	38,000

Twelve — 90 hp, 138" wb

Roadster-2P	6500	7800	13,300	20,300	44,000	60,000
Touring-4P	6500	7900	13,700	20,700	44,500	62,000
Touring-7P	6500	8200	14,500	21,500	45,800	65,000
Victoria-7P	6750	8200	14,500	21,500	45,800	65,000
Limousine-7P	8600	5500	7500	12,000	26,000	39,000
Brougham-5P	8800	6000	8500	13,000	30,000	42,000

1908 Single Center, auto-buggy, NAHC

SINGLE CENTER — Evansville, Indiana — (1906-1908) — The Single Center Spring Company was established in Evansville in 1886. It was the idea of Willis Copeland, a traveling salesman who had arrived in town five years earlier to sell vehicle parts and who eventually persuaded Thomas B. Jones and J.O. St. John to join him in parts manufacture. Originally, Single Center produced only springs, but gears quickly followed and then entire buggies. Just when the company produced its first motorized buggy is not known, but apparently Copeland stood ready to build one for anyone in town who asked. Jones and St. John were violently opposed, and departed. All this happened sometime around the turn of the century. In 1903 Copeland built the Zentmobile for Schuyler Zent, and in 1906 the Windsor for J.A. Windsor. These involvements aside, he continued to build his own motorized buggies which were not given a proper name until 1906. During that year Copeland also involved himself with W.O. Worth, builder of the Worth car and designer for Copeland of a bigger chain-drive motorized buggy that was offered for the 1906 model year as the Single Center. By now Copeland was anxious to become a bit more serious about his automotive efforts, and though he continued to offer his Single Center motorized buggies, he began selling stock in town for a new enterprise called the Evansville Automobile Company. For this venture a proper assembly line was set up, and it was soon producing a new car called the Simplicity.

1906-1908 SINGLE CENTER
Auto Buggy — (2-cyl., 12 hp, 84" wb)

	FP	5	4	3	2	1
Auto Buggy	675	2500	3500	5000	8500	18,000

Roadster — (2-cyl., 15/17 hp, 86" wb)

Roadster	800	2700	3600	5300	8800	19,000

1897 Sintz, gasoline motor carriage, NAHC

SINTZ — Grand Rapids, Michigan — (1902-1904) — Clark Sintz of Grand Rapids began building his first car in 1895 in order to compete in the Chicago Times-Herald Contest in November that year. He didn't make it; in fact, he didn't complete the car until 1897. Meantime he had begun manufacturing gasoline engines as the Wolverine Motor Works, and in this field he made a fine name for himself. In 1902 he put together another car, on an 84-inch-wheelbase chassis, using one of his two-cylinder 15 hp engines, and he talked awhile with the Matheson brothers of Grand Rapids about the possibility of getting into manufacture. These negotiations went nowhere, however, and the Mathesons went to Holyoke, Massachusetts to talk with Charles Greuter, the Matheson car being the result. Meanwhile Clark Sintz had sold his Wolverine engine business in order to finance his automotive ambition. In this venture he was allied with his two sons, Claude and Guy. Two companies were organized: Claude Sintz, Inc. for the building of automobiles and the Sintz Gas Engine Company for production of marine, stationary and automobile motors. By January 1904, both these ventures were kaput. Only six Sintz automobiles had been built; the engine business was sold that month to W.A. Pungs and his son-in-law E.B. Finch who went on to build the Pungs-Finch. Clark Sintz was killed in an automobile accident a few years later. His sons continued in the field as engineers for a number of car manufacturing companies including Pennsy, Pullman and Bell.

SIOUX CITY — "The Sioux City Automobile & Manufacturing Company of Sioux City, Iowa expects to have its first vehicle completed April 1st," reported The Motor Age in March of 1901. "This trial machine is being constructed in a local factory and upon its success depends the decision of the company to build a factory at Sioux City." Apparently the tests were unsuccessful.

SIPE & SIGLER ELECTRIC — Cleveland, Ohio — (1900) — The Sipe & Sigler Company of Cleveland built an electric stanhope in 1900 powered by a 2 hp Elwell-Parker motor and Willard storage battery. The vehicle had a range of 40 miles between charges, three forward speeds of 3, 5 1/2 and 12 mph, was built to demonstrate his battery, which Sipe & Sigler manufactured. Willard would subsequently attempt automobile manufacture himself, but Sipe & Sigler — according to an April 1900 issue of Electrical World and Engineer — had no intention of doing so. In 1901 the Sipe & Sigler Company announced that it was planning to move its factory to Niagara Falls because power was about nine times cheaper there than in Cleveland.

SISSON — The Sisson Company was organized in Pittsfield, Massachusetts during the spring of 1911 with a capital stock of $100,000 to manufacture and deal in automobiles. H.D. Sisson was the man behind this venture. Manufacture is doubted.

SIX & VANCE — Logansport, Indiana — (1914) — Various parts of motorcycles and light cars went into the makeup of the car built in 1914 by Don Six and Claire Vance of Logansport. They called it a windwagon. Its motor was a single-cylinder air-cooled Racycle connected by roller chain to a 44-inch airplane-type propeller. The boys declared their machine capable of 30 mph with "plenty of reserve power to climb hills."

1914 Six & Vance, wind wagon, LC

SIXTH CITY — The Sixth City Machine Company was organized in Cleveland, Ohio late in 1913 with a capital stock of $10,000 to manufacture and deal in motor cars. Incorporators were Ray C. Skeel, Charles M. Ringle, C.F. Bruggemeier, E.M. Becker and A.F. Goldenbogen. Manufacture is doubted.

SIZER — **Buffalo, New York** — **(1908)** — That the Sizer Forge Company of Buffalo was "working on the plans of a high-powered runabout with a view of engaging in its manufacture" was reported in August of 1908 by *The Motor World*, the magazine also announcing that Sizer was "in the market for a number of the necessary components." Most probably, a prototype was completed, but despite subsequent references to impending manufacture by Sizer, the weight of evidence indicates that it never happened.

S-J-R — The S-J-R produced in Boston, Massachusetts from 1915-1916 was the lineal successor to the Salvador of 1914. Both cars were the idea of Salvador J. Richards. Refer to Salvador.

1920 Skelton, model 35, touring, WLB

SKELTON — **St. Louis, Missouri** — **(1920-1922)** — Although E.B. Meissner was the president of the Skelton Motor Corporation and W.A. Chapman (formerly of Dort) was its general manager, the money that made this automotive venture possible belonged to Dr. L.S. Skelton. A practicing physician in Indiana until 1893 when he moved to Oklahoma for his health, Skelton had begun dabbling in oil refineries, gas companies, cement, glass and brick factories and other enterprises in the Southwest. He had made several fortunes by the time he became interested in the automobile industry following the First World War. In addition to promoting the car that would bear his name, Skelton also aquired a controlling interest in Premier of Indianapolis at the same time. The Skelton was built at the St. Louis Car Company (of which Meissner was president) in buildings formerly utilized for munitions and other war work. The St. Louis firm, long famous as a railway car producer, had twice before engaged in the automobile industry (building the American Mors and Standard Six cars before World War I), and Meissner doubtless had found Skelton's offer irresistible, since it would both return St. Louis to the automobile field and make profitable use of facilities which had laid vacant since the Armistice. The Skelton was an assembled car (Lycoming engine, Westinghouse electrics, Borg & Beck clutch, Muncie transmission and Carter carburetor) with body styling resembling the Cole of Indianapolis. Its price range was attractive, and

it doubtless would have survived longer than it did, except for the fact that Dr. Skelton died in January of 1921. Sputtering attempts at reorganization followed — including a try by W.F. Traves of the Talbott Reel Manufacturing and American Knockdown Bottle Case companies of Kansas City — but the postwar recession combined with the confusion to render the Skelton asunder in 1922.

1920 SKELTON
Model 35 — 4-cyl., 37 hp, 112" wb

	FP	5	4	3	2	1
Touring-5P	1295	4400	5600	9200	17,300	31,000
Roadster-2P	1295	4300	5400	8700	16,500	30,000

1921 Skelton Seasonette, model 35CT, JAC

1921 SKELTON
Model 35 — 4-cyl., 37 hp, 112" wb

Touring-5P	1295	4400	5600	9200	17,300	31,000
Roadster-2P	1295	4300	5400	8700	16,500	30,000
Sedan-5P	2350	2200	3200	4400	7000	15,000

1922 SKELTON
Model 35 — 4-cyl., 37 hp, 112" wb

Touring-5P	995	4500	5800	9500	18,000	32,000
Roadster-2P	995	4400	5600	9200	17,300	31,000

1901 Skene Steam Carriage, WLB

SKENE STEAM — **Lewiston, Maine** — **(1900-1901)** — Early in 1900 the J.W. Skene Cycle Company of Lewiston announced completion of its first steam carriage, with two more in the construction stage, but obviously James W. Skene didn't have the wherewithal to proceed much further on his own because his automotive venture went nowhere until December. Then, R.H.B. Warburton of Springfield, Massachusetts entered the scene and helped Skene organize, with a capital stock of $500,000, the Skene American Automobile Company. Company headquarters were in Springfield, the factory remained in Maine. The Skene was among the simplest steam buggies of the period. It was powered by a 5 hp double-acting two-cylinder engine and had a boiler with a working pressure of 160 pounds. The gasoline tank carried five gallons, and the tank for water was sufficient for a 25-mile run. Speeds up to 30 mph were promised. All parts of the Skene were built in the Lewiston plant, a fact in which the Skene company took particular pride. By January of 1901, Skene was busy in Lewiston on a production run of twenty cars, and Warburton decided that a lavish display at the Philadelphia Automobile Show that month was just what the company needed to get its business really going. This didn't work out precisely as planned. As *The Motor Age* put it, "a miscalculation on the part of the railroad officials tied up four Skene machines somewhere between Springfield and Philadelphia, and a space big enough to comfortably exhibit half a dozen vehicles looked bare with but one." Warburton was usually out on the track demonstrating the other car. Subsequently, he reported "excellent results" for his week's work in Philadelphia, but unfortunately the partners' money ran out. Sometime that spring the Skene American Automobile Company was attached for $5000 by creditors. Skene subsequently became a Rambler dealer, and spent the rest of his life in the automobile business in Maine. He was killed in 1936 in an accident in the garage he then owned in Augusta. Warburton's subsequent ventures are not known.

1901 SKENE STEAM

	FP	5	4	3	2	1
Model 1 Steam Stanhope	750	3100	4200	6300	10,500	22,000
Model 2 Steam Victoria	850	3200	4300	6500	11,000	23,000
Model 4 Steam Surrey	1200	3300	4400	6700	12,000	24,000
Model 5 Canopy Steam Surrey	1300	3500	4500	7000	13,000	25,000

SKIDDOODLER — Columbus, Ohio — (1909) — This cute name was chosen for the car of J. Shrum of Columbus simply because he had to come up with one. "Inasmuch as he had constructed it himself of material gathered or made by him," *The Automobile* explained in 1909, "he could not name it by any of those applied by the manufacturers of autos." Instead of choosing his own name, as many did, Shrum opted for Skiddoodler. Its number was one, and so far as is known was the only. In 1910 Shrum built a motorized sleigh, however, from an ordinary sled which was equipped with a third runner for steering and with a circular saw which combined with a small motor to supply the motive power.

SKIMABOUT — The Skimabout was the first roadster produced by the Palmer & Singer Manufacturing Company of Long Island City, New York. It was offered for the 1908 model year only. All other cars of the company carried the Palmer-Singer name. The firm remained in production until 1914. Refer to Palmer-Singer.

SKINNER — During the fall of 1913, F.W. Skinner reported his plans to manufacture a cyclecar in Davenport, Iowa. When the car arrived on the market, however, its tradename was Zip. Refer to Zip.

The Skinner & Skinner Company was organized in Chicago, Illinois early in 1909 with a capital stock of $2500 for the manufacture of automobiles and accessories. Incorporators were Stephen G. Skinner, Ada B. Skinner and Franklin J. Mayo. Manufacture is doubted.

1905 Sklarek, runabout, WLB

SKLAREK — Canton, Illinois — (1905) — Clifford Sklarek built his car as a teenager with his allowance money and further funds he earned installing electric doorbells in Canton homes. Its engine was a vertical water-cooled one-lunger he designed himself. Its radiator was purloined from a turn of the century French car, its muffler was copied from the Oldsmobile, and its carburetor was made from a plumber's Lunkenheimer brass check valve. The rest of the car was put together from divers bits and pieces. Only when he ran out of money to buy tires did he inform his parents of what he had been doing. The car was completed, and young Sklarek drove it for a year. Then his father bought him a new Buick, and the Sklarek was abandoned. Though Clifford Sklarek never built another car, he remained an enthusiast of the automobile for the rest of his life. From 1918 to 1932, he designed and manufactured Lorraine spotlights. A member of the Society of Automotive Engineers since 1929, he was an early member of the Automotive Old Timers as well as all the early collector car clubs. He spent his retirement years researching and writing about automobile history, most especially for *Antique Motor News*.

SLAMA STEAM — Humboldt, Nebraska — (1901) — Lewis Slama was a jeweler in Humboldt who built a steam car for himself in 1901. "I worked at it just at times when I wasn't busy at my jeweler's bench," he said. Its running gear was purchased second-hand and rebuilt, the remainder of

the carriage was of Slama's own devising. By the fall of 1901 he had put over 100 miles on the car. "It is quite a curiosity here, as it is the only automobile in this county, and very few people here have ever seen one," Lewis Slama reported. "In fact, I had never seen one myself until lately one went through here."

1889 Slattery Electric, tricycle, LC

SLATTERY ELECTRIC — Ft. Wayne, Indiana — (1889) — This pioneer electric was a tricycle built by M.M.M. Slattery in Ft. Wayne in 1889. Its engine was a small half-horsepower which was shunt-wound, and its storage battery was composed of 13 cells and weighed 143 pounds. Although Slattery is not known to have built another car, he did subsequently design alternating current motors and generators for the Jenny Electric Light Company of Ft. Wayne.

SLOAN — Bridgeport, Connecticut — (1900) — Ernest V. Sloan was chief engineer of the American Graphophone Company in Bridgeport and during odd hours at the plant in 1900 he built a gasoline motor carriage. Technical details are lacking, but Sloan claimed that "in point of simplicity of construction and operation, combined with the comparatively small cost of its mechanism," his car was superior to "many of the self-propelling vehicles upon the market today." It was never manufactured, however.

SLOAN & OLDS — The firm of Sloan & Olds has been indicated on various car rosters as an automobile manufacturer in Chicago, Illinois during 1905. This has not been documented. No firm of such name was listed in Chicago city directories for this period.

SLY STEAM — Norwalk, Ohio — (1902) — The first automobile in Norwalk was a steam car built in 1902 by Ethan E. Sly, who was employed at the time in the shops of the Wheeling and Lake Erie Railway. The boiler and 6-1/2 hp engine Sly built himself, the chassis he farmed out to a local machine shop. Firing up the Sly required five minutes, on the road its water consumption was seven gallons every eighteen miles. Ethan Sly drove the car for years thereafter. When he died in 1915, he was heading the Sly Gas Saver Company which manufactured a fuel-saving device he had invented.

1914 S & M, model 48, touring, WLB

S & M — Detroit, Michigan — (1913) — The S & M was built in Detroit by two New Yorkers who arrived in town in May of 1912. They were Edward E. Stroebel, who had made furniture on Long Island, and Walter C. Martin, who had sold Cadillacs in Manhattan. To design their car, they called in R.C. Aland of Detroit. The S & M was a big six (Continental engine) on a 130-inch wheelbase, with standard components used throughout. It was announced as being produced for "the market in New York" in September of 1912, but it does not appear that any assembly took place in the new S & M factory at 1900 Mt. Elliott Avenue in Detroit until late 1913. By January of 1914 the S & M Motor Company was petitioned into bankruptcy, with its assets acquired later that month by George Benham who put a new emblem on the car and called it a Benham. R.C. Aland subsequently went on to build a car under his own name in Detroit. Stroebel and Martin probably returned to New York. A total of about 40 S & M's had been built.

1913 S & M
Model 48 — 6-cyl., 48 hp, 130" wb

	FP	5	4	3	2	1
Touring-5P	2485	4300	5400	8700	16,500	30,000
Roadster-2/4P	2485	4200	5200	8400	15,700	29,000
Touring-7P	2535	4500	5800	9500	18,000	32,000
Limousine-7P	3500	3500	4500	7000	13,000	25,000

1906 S & M Simplex, touring, WLB

S & M SIMPLEX — New York, New York — (1904-1907) — A.D. Proctor Smith and Carlton R. Mabley were the importers in New York City of some of the finest cars produced in Europe — Renault, Panhard, Fiat and Mercedes among them. Another Smith & Mabley import was the French C.G.V., and from 1902 to 1903 the partners produced a few of those cars in this country as the American C.G.V. With that experience behind them, and seeking to avoid hefty customs duties (imported components also being taxed), they elected to build an all-American car of a quality comparable to the best of the Europeans, one European particularly, the Mercedes Simplex. The S & M Simplex was the result, and it was built in a five-story factory purchased at 614 East 83rd Street in Manhattan. Smith and Mabley established a showroom at 513 Seventh Avenue and 38th Street, and brought in Edward Franquist to design their car. It carried a four-cylinder 30/35 hp T-head engine mounted vertically behind a cellular radiator. A four-speed selective transmission and double chain drive were featured. King of Belgium tonneau coachwork, with body of Quinby, was fitted — and the price was steep, $6750. Forty of these cars were built in 1904. A smaller and lesser priced 18 hp model was also offered that year, but it had disappeared quietly by 1905. The exit of another S & M Simplex that year was rather more spectacular; it was the 70 hp racer ordered by Frank M. Croker for participation in the Vanderbilt Cup during the fall of 1904. In order to meet the weight limit, the chassis was drilled full of holes; mid-race it collapsed, with Croker finishing the contest in low gear dragging his transmission underneath him. Sadly, with the frame fixed, Croker was killed in the races at Ormond Beach (Florida) in January 1905. In 1906 Smith and Mabley moved their showroom to 1765 Broadway near 56th Street, the area that would come to be known as Automobile Row. The year following they expanded their model line, and also met with the Panic of '07. Unable to continue their business, Smith and Mabley sold out to a friend and customer, textile importer Herman Broesel, Sr. His car would carry a single name. It was the famous Simplex.

1904 S & M SIMPLEX
Four — 30/35 hp, 105" wb

	FP	5	4	3	2	1
Touring-5P	6750	4500	5800	9500	18,000	32,000
Four — 18 hp, 90-3/4" wb						
Runabout-2P	5250	3100	4200	6300	10,500	22,000
Tonneau-5P	5750	3200	4300	6500	11,000	23,000
1905 S & M SIMPLEX						
Four — 30/35 hp, 106" wb						
Brougham	7000	4000	5000	8000	15,000	28,000
1906 S & M SIMPLEX						
Four — 30 hp, 106" wb						
Touring-5P	6300	4300	5400	8700	16,500	30,000
Four — 30 hp, 113" wb						
Touring-7P	6500	4700	6100	9900	19,000	33,000
1907 S & M SIMPLEX						
Four — 30/35 hp, 106" wb						
Runabout-3P	4950	3900	4800	7700	14,300	27,000
Touring-5P	4950	4300	5400	8700	16,500	30,000
Four — 30/35 hp, 111" wb						
Touring-5P	5600	4500	5800	9500	18,000	32,000
Four — 30/35 hp, 114" wb						
Touring-7P	5600	4900	6300	10,300	21,000	34,000
Four — 50/70 hp, 124" wb						
Limousine-5/7P	6400	4500	5800	9500	18,000	32,000

SMALL — The Small Motor Car Company built an automobile called the Cavac in Detroit, Michigan from 1910-1911. A company of that same name has been listed on various car rosters as producing a car called the Small in 1915. This seems unlikely, there being no Small Motor Car Company indicated as being in business in Detroit by that late date. Probably it has been confused with the earlier Small venture.

SMART — The Smart Auto & Manufacturing Company was organized in Indianapolis, Indiana early in 1912 with a capital stock of $50,000 for the manufacture of automobiles, parts and accessories. Company directors were O.S. Srader, D.W. Reed, F.W. McCredie, O.E. Cummings, Brinay Smart, I.H. Shelton, L.B. Willis, Thomas Singleton and W.A. Virtue. Manufacture of a car is doubted.

SMELSER — Akron, Ohio — (1904) — In the Akron city directory for 1904, Luther W. Smelser indicated his occupation simply as "automobiles." He built them only to order, among the orders he is known to have received that year being a 30 hp touring car that C.C. Goodrich (assistant superintendent of the B.F. Goodrich Company in town) had designed for his own use. Although Smelser referred to himself as the "Smelser Automobile Company" when writing to automobile trade journals, he never formally organized any such firm.

1900 Smisor, NAHC

SMISOR — Webster City, Iowa — (1900) — The Smisor brothers — there were four of them — moved to Webster City in the late 1890's to open a bicycle and tire shop, and to begin manufacture of a bicycle handlebar they had invented. In 1899 they built a 500-pound two-seater buggy powered by a single-cylinder gasoline engine. It was the first automobile in Webster City. Initially the car had a top speed of 10 mph, but the brothers revised the gearing and doubled the speed. Although *The Motor Age* reported in October of 1899 that the Smisors were completely satisfied with the vehicle, the reality was quite to the contrary. During the summer of 1900, they wrote a long, anguished letter to that magazine relating the innumerable problems they had encountered with the gasoline engines purchased from outside sources. In desperation the Smisors built their own, and completed a successful gasoline carriage which was described in the October 1900 issue of *Cycle and Automobile Trade Journal*. Although the brothers may have proceeded into engine manufacture, they did not move into production of a Smisor automobile.

SMITH — D.B. Smith produced automobiles at the turn of the century in Utica, New York which were sold under the tradenames of Elite and Saratoga Tourist. Refer to Elite.

Frederick A. Smith, Inc. was organized in New York City early in 1911 with a capital stock of $25,000 to manufacture and deal in automobiles and supplies. Joining Smith in this venture were Albert Rosen and Moses Wolf. Manufacture of a car is doubted.

H. Smith & Sons Company was organized in Manteno, Illinois during the summer of 1911 with a capital stock of $20,000 to manufacture and deal in motor vehicles. The Smiths who incorporated this venture were Samuel J., Joseph O., Raoul E., Edward E., Napoleon and Armand E. Manufacture of a car is doubted.

Herbert E. Smith of Park Place in Batavia, New York was reported in *The Motor Age* in August of 1901 to have built an automobile. Details are lacking.

I.D. Smith of Pittsburgh, Pennsylvania was among the hopefuls who entered the Chicago Times-Herald Contest of 1895 with a car of his own design. He did not make it to the starting line, however, and whether he completed his car has not been documented.

L. Porter Smith, in association with his brothers, produced a runabout called the Cyclop in Indianapolis in 1910. Refer to Cyclop.

Uriah Smith of Battle Creek, Michigan had a rather interesting automotive idea in 1899. Refer to Horsey Horseless.

The Smith Auto Service Company, Inc. was organized in Brooklyn, New York during the spring of 1918 with a capital stock of $1000 for the manufacture of automobiles and accessories. Incorporators were Ada Smith, William C. Clendenen and William C. Conlon. Manufacture of a car is doubted.

The Smith Bicycle, Automobile & Light Machinery Company of Massillon, Ohio was indicated in a trade directory of 1902 as the producer of an automobile. Documentation is lacking.

The Smith-Eggers Company of 6th and Sycamore streets in Cincinnati, Ohio was indicated as the manufacturer of an automobile in the Hiscox book *Horseless Vehicles, Automobiles, Motor Cycles* published in 1900. This has not been documented. The firm, which was headed by Herman Eggers, George F. Smith and Albert G. Eggers, indicated its activity only as carriage building in turn of the century Cincinnati city directories.

The Smith Motor Company at 54 Morris & Essex Railroad Avenue in

Newark, New Jersey was indicated as the producer of an automobile in the Hiscox book *Horseless Vehicles, Automobiles, Motor Cycles* published in 1900. Documentation is lacking.

The Smith Motor Car Company was organized in Birmingham, Alabama during the fall of 1910 with a capital stock of $12,500 to manufacture, buy, sell, and repair automobiles. Incorporators were C.S. Silby, S.L. Smith and J.B. Garber. Manufacture is doubted.

Smith, Norem & Company was organized in New York City during the spring of 1915 with a capital stock of $15,000 for the manufacture of automobiles. Incorporators were R.U. Kraus, W.M. Smith and H.P. Norem, all of 1790 Broadway. Manufacture is doubted.

The Smith-Rolfe Company was a $25,000 Maine incorporation from August of 1909 for the manufacture and sale of automobiles and engines. J.H. Pierce was president, J.H. Ridge was treasurer. Manufacture is doubted.

The W.B. Smith Manufacturing Company was organized in Terre Haute, Indiana during the spring of 1910 with a capital stock of $20,000 to manufacture automobiles, automobile parts and engines. Manufacture is doubted.

The Wilson S. Smith Company was organized in San Diego, California during the spring of 1909 for the manufacture of automobiles. Smith himself subscribed $8320 to the firm's capital stock, with W.B. Connery and N. Cotten contributing $3340 each and the partners establishing themselves at Sixth Street near I. Manufacture is doubted.

SMITH STEAM — Smithville, New Jersey — (1885) — Hezekiah Bradley Smith was born in Vermont where he learned the cabinetmaker's trade and moved to Massachusetts where he began manufacture of woodworking machinery, until 1865 when he decided to settle in New Jersey. There he purchased the entire village of Shreveville, with its 2000 acres of land, and renamed the town for himself. The Smith Machine Company prospered in its new location manufacturing over 150 different products, including the high-wheeled Star bicycle. It was the Star bicycle which Lucius Copeland used for the building of one of his steam vehicles in the early 1880's, and it was doubtless Copeland's experience which prompted H.B. Smith to build a steam vehicle of his own. The Smith tricycle was begun in 1884 and completed in 1885. Its engine was a small single-cylinder; its tubular boiler was of copper and heated by fuel oil carried in the hollow frame and sprayed through a burner. There were two large wheels in the rear, a single one in front — and the entire machine rather resembled the Copeland. The Smith vehicle was patented, one among over forty patents H.B. Smith was awarded during his lifetime. At the time he built his steam tricycle, H.B. Smith was also a Senator for the state of New Jersey.

SMITH — Hartford, Connecticut — (1895) — Whether the automobile built by Otis E. Smith of Hartford was ever successfully tested is not known, but it would have been a delight to witness. It was powered by compressed spiral springs acting directly upon the rear axle. These springs in turn were operated by another heavy coil spring which, the inventor explained, "is wound up and in unwinding sets in motion mechanism that causes the spiral springs to push and pull on a crank, thus causing the rotary motion." A dozen turns would wind up the Smith, and Smith hoped for a distance of fifteen miles on one winding. Doubtless that would not have been uphill.

SMITH — Springfield, Massachusetts — (1896-1899) — Hinsdale Smith was the manager of the Springfield Cornice Works and built his first experimental gasoline car in 1896. It was fitted with an American motor, a transmission of Smith's own design, and a body built by the New Haven Carriage Company. A few further cars were produced into the turn of the century and were sometimes referred to as the Smith Spring Motor. Serious manufacture was not contemplated until 1900, however, and when it was embarked upon, the name of the car was changed to Meteor.

SMITH STEAM — Aurora, Illinois — (1901) — In 1901 Dr. Courtney L. Smith of Aurora built himself a steam car. Apparently, he was not entirely satisfied with the results, because soon after he purchased a curved dash Oldsmobile. Another physician in Aurora would prove much more tenacious in the automobile-building field, Dr. James Selkirk being involved in both the Aurora and Kirksel companies in town.

c.1900 Smith, runabout, OCW

SMITH — Los Angeles, California — (1900-1907) — The Smith Automobile and Machine Company at 649 Sante Fe Avenue in Los Angeles purportedly built its first car in 1900. Its engine was an air-cooled opposed two-cylinder unit built by Alonzo F. and R. Stanley Smith; its carburetor was a Tillotson. The little runabout was tiller steered and driven by two flat belts from engine to rear axle. The car remains extant, though the 1900 date is questionable. City directory references do not indicate the Sante Fe Avenue shop prior to 1905. The extent of the Smiths' subsequent automotive activity is a mystery, though the brothers continued to advertise themselves as manufacturers of automobiles and trucks as late as 1907, and as a truck producer in 1908. By now their address had changed to 653 Santa Fe Avenue, and there in 1909 they continued in business as a dealership and garage. The company ceased to exist in 1911.

1901 Smith, touring, NAHC

SMITH — Bridgeton, New Jersey — (1901) — When he built the car in 1901 he didn't bother publicizing the fact, but a decade later Fred F. Smith came forth with the claim that his was the first four-cylinder car in America. In 1898 he had begun construction of a two-cylinder automobile in his machine shop in Bridgeton but following a trip to France and a visit to the Paris Exposition, he decided on a four and ordered an engine with that number of cylinders from Buffalo. The car's body was built for him by the Columbus Buggy Company in Ohio to his own design, and it looked French save for the extra fuel tank in front which was his own idea because of the scarcity of refueling stations in America at that time. Following its completion, Smith took the car on a 1000-mile tour and he was driving it still in 1912 when he put forth his claim that it was America's first four. The publicity he received in *The Motor World* evoked an immediate response from Charles B. King of Detroit, who said that not only had he built a four-cylinder car himself before the turn of the century but that he had sold the patterns and drawings for its engine to a party in Buffalo, so the car built by Smith in 1901 doubtless used a four-cylinder engine of his design too. Fred Smith was not heard from again.

1906 Smith, surrey, JAC

SMITH — Topeka, Kansas — (1898-1907) / GREAT SMITH — (1907-1911) — The Smith family was well-known in Topeka for the manufacture of artificial limbs and trusses and probably wouldn't have entered the automobile industry at all except that Dr. Clement Smith became fascinated in 1898 by the horseless carriage being built by a Topeka mechanic named Terry Stafford. Later that year Dr. Smith and his brother Anton formed a partnership with Stafford to build automobiles. The venture was very low-key in the beginning, a few more gasoline cars were built at the turn of the century, and two steamers in 1902, all of these vehicles put together in Stafford's machine shop. Manufacture in earnest did not begin until 1903 when a small factory at 10th and Jefferson was built for that purpose; the venture moved into high gear the year following with the incorporation of the Smith Automobile Company, with a capital stock of $100,000. The early cars were marketed under the tradename of Veracity: ''It makes no matter if your Automobile is made in France or Topeka,'' the brochure said. These cars were simple two-cylinder buggy types with planetary transmissions and chain drive. With the arrival of a four-cylinder car and shaft drive in 1906, the marque became known simply as the Smith. Although a poorly designed intake manifold hurt sales that year, production was up to 100 cars in 1907, which seemed to satisfy the Smiths, but not Terry Stafford who left to build another car under his own name. The Great Smith introduced in 1907 was simply the Smith gone chic. It was, the firm admitted, the ''well tried out machinery'' of the old Smith but its new raiment (solid mahogany dash, paneled mahogany seat fronts, and a finish overall ''of the best grade of pianos'') had verily cried out for a name not quite as common as Smith. A six-cylinder Great Smith was offered in 1907, but only ten were sold and the model was discontinued the year following. By now the Smith family had begun to lose interest in its automotive adventure. Clement Smith sold out his holdings in 1908, followed shortly thereafter by Anton Smith. By late 1909 the Smith Automobile Company had come under the control of a consortium of seventeen businessmen from Grand Rapids, Michigan who planned to move the company to that city. The Association of Licensed Automobile Manufacturers refused to grant them a license if they did, however. The A.L.A.M. (whose power was the Selden patent) wanted geographic distribution of automobile manufacture in the United States; Michigan had numerous automobile plants already, Kansas had few. Thwarted in their relocation plans, the Grand Rapids men lost interest in the Smith Automobile Company after that, and it pretty much died because of neglect. Receivership arrived late in 1910, and the plant was sold the following year to Charles and George Southwick who assembled the remaining Great Smith cars on hand and announced plans to use the factory as well for the manufacture of a new car to be called the Westerner. By 1912, however, the Great Smith plant was sold to a Kansas City company which manufactured silos.

1904 Smith, Veracity observation car, LC

1903-1905 SMITH
Veracity — 2-cyl.

	FP	5	4	3	2	1
Observation Car	1600	3000	4000	6000	9500	21,000
Traveler's Car	1250	2900	3700	5600	9100	20,000

1906 SMITH
Smith — 4-cyl., 98'' wb

Side Door Tonneau (24 hp)	2500	3500	4500	7000	13,000	25,000
Surrey (20 hp)	2300	3700	4700	7300	13,700	26,000

1907 Great Smith, touring, NAHC

1907 GREAT SMITH
Great Smith — 4-cyl., 24 hp, 107''wb

Model Q Roadster-2P	2500	3900	4800	7700	14,300	27,000
Model R Touring-5P	2500	4000	5000	8000	15,000	28,000

Great Smith — 6-cyl., 50/60 hp, 131-1/2'' wb

Touring-7P		5000	6500	11,000	22,000	35,000

1908 GREAT SMITH
Great Smith — 4-cyl., 24 hp, 110'' wb

Type S Baby Tonneau	2750	4000	5000	8000	15,000	28,000
Type T Roadster	2650	3900	4800	7700	14,300	27,000

1909 GREAT SMITH
Great Smith — 4-cyl., 45 hp, 110'' wb

Series XX Touring	2650	4300	5400	8700	16,500	30,000
Series XX Gentlemen's Rds.	2650	4200	5200	8400	15,700	29,000
Series XX Baby Tonneau	2650	4200	5200	8400	15,700	29,000

1910 GREAT SMITH
Great Smith — 4-cyl., 45 hp. 110'' wb

	FP	5	4	3	2	1
Model XXI Touring-5P	2650	4300	5400	8700	16,500	30,000
Model XXII Toy Tonneau-4P	2650	4200	5200	8400	15,700	29,000

1911 GREAT SMITH
Great Smith — 4-cyl., 45 hp. 114'' wb

Model E Touring-5P	2650	4300	5400	8700	16,500	30,000
Model EB Baby Tonneau-4P	2500	4200	5200	8400	15,700	29,000

Great Smith — 4-cyl., 45 hp, 115'' wb

Model EC Enclosed Cruiser	2500	4000	5000	8000	15,000	28,000

Great Smith — 4-cyl., 45 hp, 110'' wb

Model ET Touring-5P	2250	4200	5200	8400	15,700	29,000

SMITH & BIGGS — St. Paul, Minnesota — (1900) — The collaboration of A.D. Smith and George T. Biggs of St. Paul seems to have produced but a single automobile. Smith was a bicycle dealer and Biggs was a bicycle repairer, and that they contemplated entering the ranks of automobile builders was scarcely unusual during this period. The first and last heard of this venture, however, was a report in the August 1900 issue of *The Autobain* announcing that with several other ''local men'' they had formed ''a company and are now building a trial carriage.''

SMITH & DIENHART — Lafayette, Indiana — (1901) — In 1901 in Lafayette, Edgar F. Smith and Frank Dienhart built an automobile. That the car was tested with success was reported that June in *The Motor Age*. Despite subsequent trade directory listings indicating these partners as automobile producers, there is no evidence they ever proceeded into manufacture.

1917 Smith Flyer, buckboard, WLB

SMITH FLYER — Milwaukee, Wisconsin — (1916-1919) — The Smith Flyer was a light but sturdy little buckboard with a wheelbase of 70 inches, a tread of 30 inches, a weight of 135 pounds, and a speed capability of 20-25 mph whether running on wheels or the interchangeable sled runners that were available for wintry driving. This delightful automotive plaything — for adults or children — was produced by the A.O. Smith Corporation and was priced at $125 f.o.b. Milwaukee. Although the bicycle-building Smith company had produced several automobiles shortly after the turn of the century, these cars were strictly for experimental purposes and had never been marketed. By 1903, having purchased the Federal stamping plant in Milwaukee, Smith was on its way to success and prosperity as the manufacturer of pressed steel frames and rear axle housings for the automotive trade. Probably the firm wouldn't have considered building a complete vehicle of any kind, but this one practically fell into its lap. In 1914 A.O. Smith acquired U.S. manufacturing rights to the Wall Auto Wheel from England. A wire-spoked wheel with 1 hp air-cooled engine attached and chain driven off a two-lobe camshaft, the Wall had become immensely popular across the Atlantic as an inexpensive way to motorize a bicycle. Smith improved upon the design, changing the wire wheel to a disc and driving the wheel directly from the camshaft — and found itself with a very lucrative sideline business. The Smith Motor Wheel was priced at $60 apiece, and by the fall of 1915 fully $500,000 worth of them had been sold to bicycle manufacturers and dealers in the United States. Among other purchasers was the American Motor Vehicle Company, producers of the juvenile car called the American Junior in Lafayette (Indiana), which designed a buckboard around the Smith Motor Wheel that was announced as the Red Bug. Almost immediately, thinking perhaps ''why didn't we think of that?,'' the A.O. Smith people acquired rights to the design, changed its name to Smith Flyer, and placed it on the market in November 1916, the same month the A.O. Smith Company went public, becoming the A.O. Smith Corporation with an offering of $3 million on the New York Stock Exchange. Among numerous purchasers of the Smith Flyer were Mr. and Mrs. Eddie Foy who bought two for the Seven Little Foys. In 1919 Smith sold the rights to its Motor Wheel and Flyer to the Briggs & Stratton Company of Milwaukee, which continued manufacture of both under its own name.

SMITH F.W.D. BUGGY — Lexington Junction, Missouri — (1906) — The car built by D.G.W. Smith in 1906 in Lexington Junction was powered by a single-cylinder 3 hp engine, was fitted with a planetary transmission and was otherwise unextraordinary except for its feature of four-wheel-drive. The chain driving shaft extended from front to rear axle, driving direct to the rear differential and via a short vertical shaft with two pinions to the front. "It is claimed by the inventor that the front axle enables the car to ride easily and successfully over obstructions which tend to raise one wheel only, the pinion engagement making this possible," reported *The Horseless Age.* Though the car was patented, Smith did not proceed into manufacture.

SMITH & MABLEY — The car produced from 1904-1907 in New York City by A.D. Proctor Smith and Carlton R. Mabley was called the S & M Simplex. Refer to S & M Simplex.

SMITH-PREMIER — Syracuse, New York — (1905) — That the Smith Premier Typewriter Company was planning to manufacture an automobile in 1905 was strictly a rumor, though one widely bruited in the trade press that summer. For more than a year, the firm had been experimenting with a gasoline automobile, but that remained as far as the project ever carried. By November of 1905 the company announced officially that manufacture would not be embarked upon. The Smith-Premier typewriter had been the idea of Alexander T. Brown, who was involved in many businesses in Upstate New York during this period, some of them automotive related. With W.C. Lipe, he was the producer of the Brown-Lipe transmission, and he was largely responsible for persuading H.H. Franklin to enter the automobile field. His son Julian built the radial-engined Julian in Syracuse in the mid-Twenties.

SMITH STEAMER — Only two of these cars were built by 1902, and they were the only steamers ever produced by the firm. Gasoline cars were the prime focus of manufacture for the Smith Automobile Company, which produced the Smith until 1907, followed by the Great Smith until 1911. Refer to Smith.

SMYSER — New York, New York — (1902) — The number of cars produced by L.B. Smyser & Company of 11 Broadway in Manhattan is not known, but certainly all of them were to custom order and probably all were gasoline cars. A huge touring car is known to have been built in 1902 for Henry B. Wick of Youngstown, Ohio who briefly harbored the notion of proceeding into manufacture with it back home. (Refer to Wick.) During that year as well the Smyser Company was negotiating for the purchase of the Dunlop tire factory on the Passaic River near Newark, New Jersey, though that deal appears to have fallen through, with Smyser remaining in Manhattan.

S.N. — The initials translate to Scott-Newcomb, and this 1920-1921 car was a steamer built in St. Louis, Missouri which was occasionally referred to as a Standard as well. Refer to Scott-Newcomb.

1900 Snell, runabout, WLB

SNELL — Waterville, New York — (1900) — "Frank Snell, Waterville, N.Y., is putting the finishing touches on a gasoline carriage," *The Horseless Age* reported in mid-March 1900. Finishing probably took a little more time than Snell had envisioned because it was not until early November that the car was first tried out. "It ran nicely," the *Waterville Times* noted on November 9th, "but was rather too fast for everyday use on our roads." Frank Snell was a mechanic and a blacksmith, and apparently as talented in those endeavors as he was in building an automobile. The engine he fashioned had two cylinders with four pistons, and Snell fitted two flywheels too. A pipe forging with two glass windows served for the carburetor. Perhaps to keep his neighbors happy, he installed a large eighteen-inch muffler. Snell used a two-speed (with reverse) planetary transmission, with different knobs for each speed so they could be identified

without taking one's eyes from the road. To reduce the speed propensity of the Snell, which had shown itself during that late test, the inventor fitted a ball governor from a steam engine onto the camshaft. About 25 mph was its top speed thereafter. Though he did not produce another car, Frank Snell drove the one he did build frequently and for about a dozen years. His car remains extant today.

SNELL — Though the Snell Motor Car & Truck Company of Toledo is frequently cited as the producer of an automobile from 1904-1905, the evidence suggests that the company's only product was a commercial vehicle. The first Snell truck was completed in November of 1904; in December Samuel Snell severed his connection with the firm, and its name was changed to American Motor Truck Company.

SNOBURNER — A car called the Snoburner has been indicated on various car rosters as having been built by the Pittmans & Dean Company of Detroit, Michigan in 1914. This has not been documented. The firm, which was located at 8-10 Adams Avenue West, advertised its activity as "jobbers and retailers of coal and ice." Undoubtedly, the Snoburner was a demonstration vehicle built for the company and probably for promotional purposes.

SNODEAL — Baltimore, Maryland — (1902) — George R. Snodeal operated a livery at 2552 Madison Avenue in Baltimore which also served as a supply and repair depot, and a place for electric cars to come in for a charge. During 1902 he renamed his operation the Snodeal Manufacturing Company and produced a few gasoline and electric cars as well. Although that venture was short-lived, Snodeal remained in the automobile end of things for years afterwards. The 1913 Baltimore city directory indicated that he was then the president and manager of the Palace Garage at North and Mount Royal avenues.

SNYDER — That George Snyder of Hartford, Wisconsin — in collaboration with James Faror — built a gasoline automobile late in 1902 was reported by *The Horseless Age* early the following year. Details are lacking.

Snyder & Company of Newark, New Jersey was organized during the fall of 1906 with a capital stock of $25,000 for the manufacture of automobiles. Incorporators were Harry H. Picking, Charles O. Geyer and A.W. Condit. Manufacture is doubted.

SNYDER STEAM — Little Falls, New York — (1900) — More than likely, H.P. Snyder & Company thought better of the idea. The bicycle manufactory in Little Falls announced its engagement in the steam carriage business in October of 1900. At least one car was built, but then Snyder & Company returned to bicycles exclusively before year's end.

1909 Snyder, runabout, NAHC

SNYDER — Danville, Illinois — (1908-1909) — Although the carriage and buggy building firm of D.D. Snyder & Company of Danville may have produced an occasional car previously, it was not until 1908 that proper manufacture was embarked upon. The Snyder was a simple motor buggy which featured a two-cylinder 10/12 hp air-cooled engine, two-speed planetary transmission, double chain drive and right-hand wheel steering. The price was $450. David D. Snyder produced the car at his 236-246 West Main Street factory for two seasons only, then returned to his horse-drawn business, remaining in the automobile field only as a painter and trimmer of car bodies.

SNYDER — Cleveland, Ohio — (1914) — The Snyder was large for a cyclecar. Its wheelbase was 100 inches, its tread was 50 inches. Shaft drive and a two-speed planetary transmission were features of this product of the Snyder Motor & Manufacturing Company of Cleveland, and three models were available. The biggest was a four-passenger touring car with a four-cylinder 12 hp engine; its price tag was $450. A two-passenger roadster with the same engine sold for $425, and that same body style was offered with a 9 hp two-cylinder engine for $390. The electric generator was combined in the radiator fan in all these models. Like the preponderance of cyclecars on the market in 1914, the Snyder did not survive the year. The men behind the cyclecar — G.J. Snyder and R.E. Blackwell — were also the producers of the Snyder motorcycle.

MODEL D TONNEAU

1905 Sommer, model D, touring, HAC

SOMMER — Detroit, Michigan — (1904-1905) — In the spring of 1904 the Hammer-Sommer became the Sommer because the partners building the former car couldn't see eye-to-eye. Henry F. Hammer was now building his Hammer, a car with twice the cylinders, horsepower and price of the Hammer-Sommer. And Herman A. and William J. Sommer continued building the old Hammer-Sommer as simply the Sommer. In May of 1904 they also incorporated the Sommer Motor Company with a capital stock of $40,000 for its production. Manufacture continued into 1905, but whether the Sommer lasted any longer than the Hammer is not known. Both were dead by the fall of 1905, however. Thereon the Sommers' superintendent of production, Harry Tarkington, moved on to Marysville (Ohio) to attempt the manufacture of another car called the Marysville. It wasn't built at all. Hammer and the Sommers apparently never tried the automobile field again. A Sommer brother — L.A. — who had been involved with the partners did, however. L.A. Sommer was subsequently involved with the Allen brothers and their automotive venture in Ohio.

1904-1905 SOMMER
Model D — 2-cyl., 15 hp, 80" wb

	FP	5	4	3	2	1
Touring-5P	1250	3000	4000	6000	9500	21,000

SOMMER — Bucyrus, Ohio — (1910-1911) — The Sommer Motor Company of Bucyrus was a venture independent of the Detroit Sommer operation. Among the people behind the Ohio car were L.A. Sommer, L.M. Smith, F.C. Hopley, S.S. White and D.F. Flohn. In November of 1910 they announced the organization of their company, with a capital stock of $125,000. Apparently the Sommer company had been building engines previously in Aurora, Illinois; with the move to Bucyrus, the manufacture of automobiles commenced. It ceased quickly. In November of 1910 the Sommer company noted that it had been building cars on a small scale "for several months." Conclusive references indicate manufacture into early 1911 only, although cars may have been built on a per-order basis for a few years thereafter. By 1914, however, the Sommer Motor Company announced that its sole product now was engines.

SOONER — The Sooner Manufacturing Company was the designation decided upon by J.B. Worthington and Arthur Fishbeck of Manitowoc, Wisconsin when they journeyed to Oklahoma City in 1909 with the idea of convincing the local citizenry to support their plan for the manufacture of automobiles in Oklahoma. The car they envisioned building was described as a "combination road vehicle and portable power plant for the operation of saw mills, feed mills and other machinery." That even a prototype was completed has not been documented.

SORTER-CONWAY — The Sorter-Conway Company was organized in Chicago, Illinois late in 1910 with a capital stock of $5000 for the manufacture of automobiles, aeroplanes and machinery. Incorporators were P. Steele, P.F. O'Malley and Abe Lapine. Manufacture is doubted.

SOUDAN — Elkhart, Indiana — (1900-1901) — That the Soudan Manufacturing Company of Elkhart, Indiana produced at least a few automobiles at the turn of the century is indicated. The firm was defunct by the spring of 1901, however, most of its stock being purchased by the Acme Cycle Company of Elkhart. About that same time it was revealed that one A.J. Signor was building an automobile in town. "Here is the town's chance to find a successor to the late lamented Soudan Manufacturing Company," reported *The Motor Age*. Signor did not proceed into manufacture, however.

SOULE-SMITH — The Soule-Smith Company was a $10,000 Maine incorporation from the fall of 1912 for the manufacture and sale of motor vehicles. The partners involved were W.E. Soule and A.T. Smith. Manufacture is doubted.

SOUTH BEND — The South Bend Automobile and Garage Company was organized in South Bend, Indiana during the spring of 1900 with a capital stock of $5000 to manufacture cars and do a general garage business. Incorporators were Harry D. Johnson, Nelson J. Riley, George M. Studebaker, E.L. Kuhns and C.A. Carlisle. Manufacture of a car is doubted.

The South Bend Machine Manufacturing Company was organized in South Bend, Indiana during the summer of 1905 with a capital stock of $50,000 to manufacture and sell machinery, tools and vehicles of all kinds. Directors of the firm were David McHenry, George Brown, Henry M. Huston, Elmer J. Martin, William F. Koeller, Stuart MacKibbin and Shirley Reynolds. Manufacture of a car is doubted.

The South Bend Motor Vehicle Company was organized in South Bend, Indiana during the summer of 1903 for the manufacture of automobiles. Officers of the company were Parker H. Sercombe of Chicago, and Jacob Woolverton and J.B. Birdsell of South Bend. Initial plans called for the purchase of the Miller-Knoblock Electric Manufacturing Company plant in town, but this venture seems to have died aborning.

SOUTH BEND — South Bend, Indiana — (1913-1914) — The South Bend Motor Car Works was organized in 1912 and secured a small factory in town in which production began in 1913. The company specialized in trucks and fire apparatus, but in 1913-1914 also produced a line of long-wheelbase six-cylinder shaft-drive cars in the $2250-$2450 range. The firm remained in business until 1916. John D.J. Farneman, Alfred G. Mechlenburg and Hilton Hammond were the promoters of this venture.

1913-1914 SOUTH BEND
Model 55 — 6-cyl., 38 hp, 128" wb

	FP	5	4	3	2	1
Roadster-2P	2250	3900	4800	7700	14,300	27,000
Touring-5P	2250	4000	5000	8000	15,000	28,000

Model 55 — 6-cyl., 38 hp, 136" wb

	FP	5	4	3	2	1
Touring-7P	2450	4200	5200	8400	15,700	29,000

SOUTH CAROLINA — The South Carolina Automobile Company has been indicated on various rosters as the producer of a car in Columbia, South Carolina in 1901. Documentation is lacking. A company by that name was not listed in Columbia city directories of the period.

SOUTHEASTERN — The Southeastern Automobile and Machine Company was organized in Hattiesburg, Mississippi late in 1911 with a capital stock of $50,000 for the manufacture of automobiles. R.R. Boykin headed this venture. Manufacture is doubted.

SOUTHERN — The Southern Auto & Machinery Company was organized in St. Louis, Missouri during the fall of 1910 with a capital stock of $7500 to manufacture and deal in automobiles. Incorporators were Emil Hitz, Herman Miller and William Wehrenbrecht. Manufacture is doubted.

The Southern Automobile Company was organized in Columbia, Georgia during the summer of 1908 with a capital stock of $1000 to manufacture, buy, sell and rent automobiles and bicycles. J.J. Albright and G.B. Phillips were behind this venture. Manufacture is doubted.

The Southern Automobile Company was organized in Nashville, Tennessee during the spring of 1906 for the manufacture of automobiles under the direction of J.H. Lawrence, a mechanical engineer from Vanderbilt University. A factory was described as being "fitted up . . . in the old Broad Street amusement hall on Broadway," and commercial cars were to be the firm's specialty. Manufacture is doubted.

The Southern Cyclecar Manufacturing Company of New Orleans, Louisiana was organized during the spring of 1914 with a capital stock of $10,000. Officers were David Fisher (president), Paul Heckler (vice-president), George W. Hunter (secretary) and Granville Pollock (treasurer). This venture was subsequently reorganized that summer as the Southern Automobile & Supply Company and recapitalized at a cool million dollars. Plans now called for the "construction of seven buildings to cover five acres and the installation of machinery to manufacture every part of an automobile." Purportedly, ten acres of land in St. Bernard Parish was subsequently purchased but the evidence suggests no factory was ever built there nor was manufacture of a car begun anywhere else.

The Southern Machine Manufacturing Company was organized in Manchester, Virginia during the summer of 1903 with a capital stock of $25,000 for the manufacture of light machinery and automobiles. Incorporators were A.C. Goode, F.A. Warren, W.D. Leake, W.A. Bicker and F.B. Hobson. Manufacture of a car is doubted.

The Southern Motor Company was organized in Jackson, Tennessee during the spring of 1908 with a capital stock of $50,000 for the manufacture of automobiles and engines in a building opposite the Southern Boiler Works on Royal Street. "Many of the most prominent businessmen in Jackson" were reported behind this venture, which seems to have gone nowhere.

In 1908 the Southern Motor Car Company was incorporated in Houston, Texas for the manufacture of automobiles designed by E.M. Pavey. The cars produced for the three years following were marketed under the tradename of Dixie. Refer to Dixie.

The Southern Motor Sales Company of Houston, Texas was the venue in which Glenn D. Gearhart produced a few special-built automobiles in 1911-1912. Refer to Gearhart.

The Southern Motor Works was organized in Jackson, Tennessee in 1908. The cars it produced there were alternatively known as Southerns or Marathons. Following the company's move to Nashville in 1910, however, both the firm's name and the car's name were irrevocably changed to Marathon. Refer to Marathon.

The Southern Motors Manufacturing Association, Ltd. produced a car called the Ranger in Houston, Texas from 1920-1922. Refer to Ranger.

The Southern Tire & Supply Company was organized in Jacksonville, Florida during the summer of 1913 to "manufacture and sell, import and export, motor vehicles, supplies and accessories." Incorporators were H.E. Perryman, Sam Dunlap and C.E. Brown. Manufacture is doubted.

SOUTHERN — Jacksonville, Florida — (1906-1908) — In April of 1906 the Southern Automobile Manufacturing Company was organized in Jacksonville by John B. McDonald, H.C. Stone and Hugh Partridge for the manufacture of a highwheeler. Its two-cylinder engine was mounted under the seat and, like many cars of its genre, the vehicle had the look of a buggy that had lost its horse. With an air-cooled 12 hp engine, the car sold for $500; with a 20 hp water-cooled unit, the price was $650. "The car is provided with a back lock safety steering gear, a foot brake and a chime signal operated from the exhaust," McDonald explained, and its wheels, which were a McDonald invention, were described as "sort of double dished, there being two sets of spokes, inclined in opposite directions to the plane of the wheel and forming a single circle at the rim." Although the Southern does not seem to have survived into 1909, it was the first concerted attempt at automobile manufacture in the state of Florida.

SOUTHERN SIX — The Southern Motors Manufacturing Association, Ltd. was established in Houston, Texas in 1920 for the manufacture of a four-cylinder car to be known as the Ranger. During the summer of 1921, a six was announced as an addition to the line which was occasionally referred to as the Southern Six, but more often as the Ranger Six. Refer to Ranger.

SOUTHERN SIX — Memphis, Tennessee — (1920) — According to its founders, the Southern Automobile Manufacturing Company of Memphis was "A Million Dollar Organization Composed of Southern People." The Southern people involved were W.A. King, L.P. Miller, W.A. Schibley and W.N. Frazee, and they proposed to build cars, trucks, tractors and tire equipment. The car was called the Southern Six, a five-passenger touring with 57 hp Continental engine, 127-inch wheelbase and $2395 price tag. Residents of Memphis who were there at the time remember it as a very smartly styled automobile. Two examples may have been built. The first was mounted on a float and paraded down Main Street, and later came to an unseemly end in a local garage during a shootout between a bootlegger and the police. The second was owned for some years by the brother-in-law of W.A. Schibley and was later traded in on a tractor. Conceivably, car number two may have been car number one with its bullet-riddled body repaired. The similarity between the Southern Six and the Drake produced the year following in Knoxville was doubtless less coincidence than the probability that both were designed by the same man: W.F. Drake.

1920 SOUTHERN SIX
Six-60 — 6-cyl., 57 hp, 127" wb

	FP	5	4	3	2	1
Touring-5P	2395	4400	5600	9200	17,300	31,000

SOUTHLAND — Owensboro, Kentucky — (1910) — Little is known about the Southland Motor Car Company of Owensboro, though it can be surmised that the "Advance Announcement" brochure that the firm published regarding the car being introduced for the 1910 season was the first and last. The Southland was a 30 hp water-cooled four on a 108-inch wheelbase chassis carrying a $1500 price tag. "The body is perhaps the most conspicuous part of the automobile and it gives us a great deal of pleasure to state that we manufacture our own . . .," the company noted. "It is of the convex design and . . . will be used extensively in the East on cars selling at three to four thousand dollars, during 1910. It is equipped with a secret tool box in the floor which is a great convenience."

SOUTH SIDE — The South Side Automobile Station was organized in Chicago, Illinois early in 1904 with a capital stock of $2500 for the purpose of "manufacturing, repairing and housing automobiles." Incorporators were Frank Johnson, Jr., George M. Haynes and E.E. Ellington. Manufacture is doubted.

SOVEREIGN — Camden, New Jersey — (1906-1907) — In 1906 the Matthews Motor Company was organized in Camden, and by 1907 had bought out the defunct Jones-Corbin Automobile Company of Philadelphia. Although the car produced was occasionally referred to as the Matthews, it was officially called the Sovereign. A 40 hp (water-cooled) four on a 120-inch wheelbase chassis, it featured a four-speed selective transmission, dual ignition and double chain drive. Its large aluminum touring body sat eight. "The Car That Lasts" was the company's slogan, but the Sovereign didn't. The Matthews Motor Company was out of business by the end of 1907.

S & P — The S & P Manufacturing Company was organized in New York City during the spring of 1919 with a capital stock of $5000 for the manufacture of automobiles. Incorporators were F.A. Stroh, B.P. Ryan and A.E. Gutgsell. Manufacture is doubted.

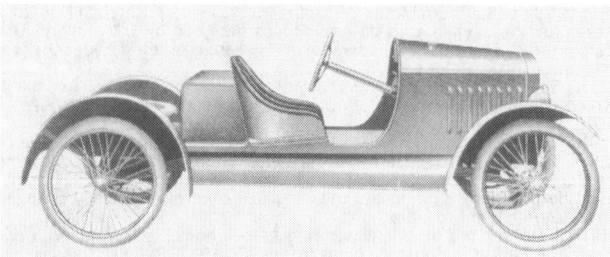
1919 Spacke, runabout, WLB

SPACKE — Indianapolis, Indiana — (1919) — Fred W. Spacke was among the founders of the Indianapolis company which produced the Reeves and in 1905 in the same city established his F.W. Spacke Machine Company for the manufacture of automobile engines and components. His business prospered; a good many of the cyclecars of the 1914-1915 era were fitted with Spacke engines. In January of the latter year, Fred Spacke died. Two years later his sons sold out the family business to a consortium headed

by Daniel S. Brooks (of Peru Auto Parts), and the firm was reorganized as Spacke Machine & Tool Company. In 1919 this new regime announced its entry into the automobile manufacturing field with a product called a light car but the specifications for which read like the myriad cyclecars that had been powered by Spacke engines a half decade previously. The new Spacke was fitted with one of the company's two-cylinder air-cooled 9/13 hp units; transmission was a two-speed planetary, there was no differential, and the car was driven by the right rear wheel only. The wheelbase was 90 inches, the tread 46, and the only body style offered was a $295 roadster with two bucket seats and a square-ish gasoline tank on the rear deck. For the 1920 model year the car was redesignated the Brook. The only significant design change was the removal of the rear-deck fuel tank. What looked to be the radiator up front now enclosed the gasoline tank, certainly a dubious engineering revision.

1895 Spahr, runabout, OCW

SPAHR — Millersburg, Ohio — (1895) — Otto Spahr built his car in Millersburg in 1895. It was powered by a water-cooled gasoline engine of his own design and featured a friction transmission and a differential to drive both rear wheels — a most advanced feature for this early date. The modesty of his resources was the reason he didn't proceed further than the building of the one car. Like his father before him, and his sons after, Otto Spahr remained a machinist for the whole of his life. His skill and ingenuity in custom repairing and fabrication of parts for everything from firearms to gasoline engines was widely known in the area.

SPANGLER — Lewistown, Pennsylvania — (1903) — Though E.E. Spangler of Lewistown built his car in 1903, it was not until 1905 that he discovered how really useful it could be. "Recently he took it to a blacksmith and constructed a rough frame on which he attached a circular saw to the hub of one of the rear wheels," reported *Motor Age* that winter. "The gearing and motor were arranged so that power could be furnished to the saw. When the machine was taken on the ice it worked perfectly, and it is claimed that it does the work of more than twenty men."

SPARKS — San Francisco, California — (1899-1903) — The Sparks Automobile Company was organized in San Francisco in the early fall of 1899 by Charles H. Taylor, W.J. Barnett, T.J. Sparks, John Curtin and S. Goodenough. The firm was incorporated for $1,000,000 to sell stock and to build two-cylinder 4 hp gasoline carriages, the smallest of which would be placed on the market for $700. Belt drive and what was described as a "compensating, equalizing spring" were among the Sparks' special features. Undoubtedly more stock was sold than gasoline carriages built. "The picture which adorns the front page of the company's prospectus," noted *The Horseless Age* wryly in November 1899, "bears a striking resemblance to the electric phaeton of the Woods Motor Vehicle Company." The Sparks venture continued into the turn of the century but was extinguished by 1904.

1910 Spartan, touring, KM

SPARTAN — Hartford, Connecticut — (1910) — The sketches for this car had been drawn up in the Tarrytown (New York) home of Carl Kelsey, who was at the time general sales manager for the Maxwell-Briscoe Motor Company. It was to be rather like any other Maxwell touring car, except for its feature of full front doors; it was to be built in Maxwell's Rhode Island factory and called the Pilgrim of Pawtucket. Production costs were deemed too high, however, and the project was abandoned at the paper stage. Later in 1910, when Kelsey left the company following a disagreement with Benjamin Briscoe, he took up the idea again on his own, and called it the Spartan: "This name in itself has value, suggesting as it does, strength, durability, honor and distinction." The most distinctive aspect of the Spartan remained the full front doors; it was otherwise a moderately-powered four, with three-speed selective transmission and shaft drive on a 104-inch wheelbase chassis. The Spartan had a Maxwell look overall but with a Pierce-Arrow-like radiator shell. Its price was $1000, and its total production was one, the prototype which Carl Kelsey was roadtesting that September, shortly after he organized the C.W. Kelsey Manufacturing Company in Hartford. Kelsey's decision not to produce the Spartan was based on two factors: first, although the fore-door idea in touring cars wouldn't become the norm in the industry until 1912, some other manufacturers had already adopted it, which effectively eliminated the one novelty of the Spartan; and second, Henry Ford had slashed a couple of hundred dollars off his Model T, which was the price class at which the Spartan was aimed, and Kelsey was aware he could no longer produce the car as a T competitor. So, if he could not compete with Ford on a par, Kelsey reasoned, he would come up with a car to undersell him. For this certain cost-cutting measures in manufacture were necessary, and Kelsey decided he could meet them by eliminating a wheel. His new car was the three-wheeled Motorette.

SPAULDING — In 1898 A.G. Spaulding & Brothers, the well-known sporting goods house, contracted with the Lamb Manufacturing Company of Chicopee Falls, Massachusetts for the building of a gasoline car for possible Spaulding distribution. Refer to Lamb.

1902 Spaulding, runabout, NAHC

SPAULDING — Buffalo, New York — (1902-1903) — In January of 1902, Henry F. Spaulding and his brother C.M. incorporated the Spaulding Automobile & Motor Company in Buffalo. (The previous family business had been the Spaulding Machine Screw Company.) The immediate start-up of production was delayed by a lawsuit brought by the Olds Motor Works regarding infringement of its motor patents. Spaulding got around that by redesigning its single-cylinder engine, and manufacture of a run of 100 runabouts began thereafter. The spring suspension of the new Spaudling was very much like the curved-dash Oldsmobile as well, and again Olds sued. The runabout sold for $650 in 1902, which was raised to $700 by January 1903, by which time a larger two-cylinder touring car was added to the line. The tourer had wheel steering and a three-speed sliding gear transmission. The runabout steered by tiller and featured a planetary transmission. By February of 1903 the company was in financial trouble, no doubt because of the money spent for lawyers, and in March was sold at a receiver's sale to J.F. Morlock who proceeded to build a Spaulding lookalike under his own name. That Henry F. Spaulding considered his company's bankruptcy merely an inconvenience to his continuing in the automobile business is indicated by the fact that in August that year he was testing a new experimental car on the tow path of the Erie Canal. Unfortunately, he drove the car into the canal and was drowned.

1902 SPAULDING
Single Cylinder — 4 hp

	FP	5	4	3	2	1
Runabout	650	1800	2800	4000	6200	13,000

1903 SPAULDING
Single Cylinder — 6 hp

Runabout	700	2000	3000	4200	6500	14,000
Double Cylinder — 25 hp						
Touring	—	2300	3300	4600	7500	16,000

1903 Spaulding, touring, NAHC

SPAULDING — Grinnell, Iowa — (1910-1916) — Henry W. Spaulding was born in Vermont in 1846 and arrived in Iowa in 1876 where he set up shop as a blacksmith and carriage manufacturer in Grinnell. At the turn of the century the Spaulding Manufacturing Company was the oldest and largest producer of vehicles west of the Mississippi. By now Spaulding's sons, Frederick E. and Ernest H., had joined their father in the family business. The Spauldings went automotive in 1910 with a pair of four-cylinder 30 hp cars: Model C with three-speed sliding gear transmission and Model D with a two-speed planetary. The wheelbase was 112 inches, and the price $1500. These cars were sold through the Spaulding carriage agents. In 1911 the Model D became a larger (122-inch wheelbase) and more expensive ($2500) 40 hp car, which the Spauldings attempted to market through established automobile dealers. This did not work well, apparently, for in 1912 Spaulding returned to using its carriage outlets almost exclusively. In 1913 the Spaulding was revised into a 40 hp four on a 120-inch wheelbase, and remained thus for the rest of its life. An interesting model for 1915 was called the "Sleeping Car," which provided overnight accommodations. Difficulty in getting parts transported to Grinnell and underfinancing of the venture spelled the end for the Spaulding car in 1916. Thereafter the firm survived building truck bodies, and by the early Twenties the Spaulding Manufacturing Company was producing road machinery. Henry W. Spaulding died in 1937 at the age of ninety-one. In addition to building the only automobile in Grinnell, he was also for a time mayor of the town and president of the Citizens National Bank.

1910 SPAULDING
Model C — 4-cyl., 30 hp, 112" wb

	FP	5	4	3	2	1
Touring-5P	1500	3000	4000	6000	9500	21,000
Pony Tonneau-4P	1500	3000	4000	6000	9500	21,000
Roadster-3P	1500	2900	3700	5600	9100	20,000
Model D — 4-cyl., 30 hp, 112" wb						
Touring-5P	1500	3000	4000	6000	9500	21,000
Pony Tonneau-4P	1500	3000	4000	6000	9500	21,000
Roadster-3P	1500	2900	3700	5600	9100	20,000

1911 Spaulding, model D, touring, HAC

1911 SPAULDING
Model C — 4-cyl., 30 hp, 112" wb

Roadster-3P	1400	3000	4000	6000	9500	21,000
Touring-5P	1550	3100	4200	6300	10,500	22,000
Pony Tonneau-4P	1550	3100	4200	6300	10,500	22,000
Fore-Door Touring-5P	1600	3200	4300	6500	11,000	23,000
Roadster-2P	1450	3100	4200	6300	10,500	22,000
Model D — 4-cyl., 40 hp, 122" wb						
Touring-5P	2500	3500	4500	7000	13,000	25,000
Pony Tonneau-4P	2500	3500	4500	7000	13,000	25,000
Fore-Door Touring-5P	2550	3700	4700	7300	13,700	26,000
Roadster-2P	2400	3200	4300	6500	11,000	23,000

1912 Spaulding, model C, 5-pass. touring, WLB

1912 SPAULDING
Model C — 4-cyl., 30 hp, 112" wb

	FP	5	4	3	2	1
Touring-5P	1550	3000	4000	6000	9500	21,000
Pony Tonneau-4P	1550	3000	4000	6000	9500	21,000
Roadster-3P	1350	2900	3700	5600	9100	20,000
Model E — 4-cyl., 35/40 hp, 117" wb						
Touring-5P	1750	3300	4400	6700	12,000	24,000

1913 Spaulding, model G, touring, HAC

1913 SPAULDING
Model G — 4-cyl., 40 hp, 120" wb

Roadster-3P	1750	3200	4300	6500	11,000	23,000
Touring-5P	1800	3300	4400	6700	12,000	24,000
Model H — 4-cyl., 40 hp, 120" wb						
Roadster-2P	1600	3100	4200	6300	10,500	22,000

1914 SPAULDING
Model H — 4-cyl., 40 hp, 120" wb

Touring-5P	1875	3500	4500	7000	13,000	25,000

1915 Spaulding, model H, touring, HAC

1915 SPAULDING
Model H — 4-cyl., 40 hp, 120" wb

Touring-5P	1680	3500	4500	7000	13,000	25,000
Sleeping Car	1730	3100	4200	6300	10,500	22,000

1916 SPAULDING
Model H — 4-cyl., 40 hp, 120" wb

Touring-5P	1250	3500	4500	7000	13,000	25,000
Roadster-3P	1250	3300	4400	6700	12,000	24,000

SPEAR — William A. Spear of 212 Garfield Building in Cleveland, Ohio was reported to be experimenting with automobiles in the February 28th, 1902 edition of *Automobile & Motor Review*. Details are lacking.

SPECIAL — The Special built in Milwaukee, Wisconsin from 1908-1910 was one of several models produced by the Johnson Service Company. Refer to Johnson.

SPECIAL — Cincinnati, Ohio — (1904) — Acting as a local agency for the Ford was the mainstay of business for the Special Motor Vehicle Company of Cleveland, but the firm was anxious to expand. "They also do a line of repairing," *Automobile Review* reported in May 1904, "and are building a car with 9 hp motor transmission without internal gears and shaft drive, made of three flat pieces of steel, forming a square fitting into square socket." The Special car was built to customer order only, and it appears not too many orders were received.

SPECIALTY ELECTRIC — Cincinnati, Ohio — (1898) — "Horseless carriages are an assured fact," the company advertisement said in June of 1898 although, probably wisely, it concluded by adding, "We also make all kinds of horse vehicles." This electric car was called a Specialty only by the people who built it at the Specialty Carriage Company in Cincinnati. Specialty did not market the automobiles itself but instead built them under contract from the Electric Vehicle Company of New York City. A total of fifty broughams and fifty hansoms were completed and shipped east for use in taxi and livery service in Manhattan. Subsequently, the Electric Vehicle Company built its own cars under the name Columbia. And Specialty returned to its horsedrawn trade.

1898 Specialty Electric, NAHC

1905 Speedway, NAHC

SPEEDWAY — Morris Heights, New York — (1904-1905) — Speedway traditionally defined the road along a river bank reserved for fast horsemen. This Speedway was built on the west bank of the Harlem River in New York City, overlooking the Bronx. It was produced by the Gas Engine & Power Company, the well-known launch and automotive engine building concern founded by F.W. Ofeldt, in collaboration with Charles L. Seabury & Company, also of New York City. Seabury had originally been a partner of Ofeldt's, but had left to form his own steam-yacht manufacturing company. He was also already on the market with a car of his own called the Seabury. The Speedway, which was designed by Budd D. Gray, was an attractive side-entrance tonneau that seated five passengers, was powered by a 28 hp four-cylinder engine and featured shaft drive on a 108-inch wheelbase. Its $4700 price tag tended toward the exorbitant, however. The Speedway was discontinued during the summer of 1905, just about the time W.S. Howard (whose Howard car had used running gear supplied by Gas Engine & Power) joined the company as chief engineer. The Gas Engine & Power Company evolved into the Consolidated Shipbuilding Company in 1919.

SPEEDWAY SPECIAL — Speedway Special was the model designation for the sporting car that was promoted by the Wolverine Motor Car Company of Kalamazoo, Michigan in 1917. Refer to Wolverine.

1903 Speedwell, runabout, NAHC

SPEEDWELL — Milwaukee, Wisconsin — (1903-1904) — Speedwell was the name used in 1903 to 1904 for the cars which had been sold as the Kunz in 1902 and would be so called again in 1905. A single-cylinder 8 hp runabout on a 68-inch wheelbase with a $1000 price tag, the Speedwell was fitted with a two-speed planetary transmission. John L. Kunz was the man behind the Speedwell Automobile Company, and in 1905 he changed both his company's name and his car's back to his own.

1903-1904 SPEEDWELL
One Cylinder — 8 hp, 68" wb

	FP	5	4	3	2	1
Runabout	1000	1800	2800	4000	6200	13,000

SPEED-WELL — Reading & Oakland, Pennsylvania — (1904-1909) — Although never on a large scale, A.H. Yocum and his father George Y. Yocum built gasoline runabouts in addition to gasoline engines for a half-decade in Reading. Their small establishment was called A.H. Yocum Company, Inc. (following its formal incorporation in 1907), they employed about twenty men, and they called their car the Speed-Well. Probably extended ambition was their undoing. In the early fall of 1909, Yocum announced forthcoming removal to a new factory in Oakland where two-, three- and four-cylinder "valveless" cars of 10 to 40 hp would be built. The venture failed soon after.

1908 Speedwell, model C, roadster, HAC

SPEEDWELL — Dayton, Ohio — (1907-1914) — It was common practice during the early days for automobiles to be named after their founder. Pierce D. Schenck of Dayton apparently thought better of that idea and, after talking four fellow Daytonians out of the $50,000 he needed to start his automotive enterprise, established the Speedwell Motor Car Company instead. For his chief engineer, he selected the multi-experienced Gilbert J. Loomis, who had been building cars that he did name for himself in Massachusetts at the turn of the century. At first, the production philosophy of Speedwell was the more the merrier, with Rutenber four- and six-cylinder engines offered on two wheelbases of 116 and 132 inches. In the wake of the Panic of '07, however, the decision was made to confine efforts to one chassis of 120 inches and one four-cylinder engine which Speedwell would make itself. This was obviously a good idea since production for the 1909 model year quadrupled from the 25 cars produced in '07. Schenck began expanding his factory facilities with a vengeance, until there were nine buildings in all — an embarrassment of riches initially because he leased out one of them to Orville and Wilbur Wright to build their new flying machines until their own factory was completed. The Speedwell's base price was $2500. "It would be folly to pay more," the company neatly said. "It would be unwise to pay less." The Speedwell was a well thought out car and well built, with an admirable dedication to detail. Gearbox leakage, a common malady of the era, never happened on a Speedwell because a "stuffing box" on both ends of the driveshaft prevented the escape of grease or oil. Speedwell was among the earliest companies to market a torpedo and the only one to use concealed door hinges and place the horn under the hood. And the one-chassis policy was obviously not limiting, since the number of Speedwell body styles increased as year passed year. For 1911-1912, a showroom attention-getter called the Cruiser was also offered. And Speedwell was by now manufacturing a variety of light and heavy duty delivery trucks as well. Of the 4000 Speedwells built during the lifetime of the marque, most arrived during the salad days of 1909 to mid-1912. This was a most respectable production, and augured well for the future. Unfortunately, Pierce Schenck apparently tired of his automotive venture and turned his interest instead to malleable iron, Gilbert Loomis left Dayton, and some people who were enamoured of the rotary valve engine designed by Cyrus E. Mead bought into the company. It was a disaster. Ensuing contretemps among the board of directors resulted in the Mead people pushing through a rotary-valve car for production, while the Speedwell people insisted that a standard car be offered as well. This did provide the company the fillip of being the first in the industry to offer both poppet and non-poppet valve cars. But then Cyrus Mead had the misfortune to be killed in an automobile accident, which meant that further refinements to the engine would no longer be afforded the expertise of its inventor — and a vicious flood hit Dayton, which meant that not even the standard cars could be produced as the company bailed out its plant. The distribution network for Speedwell was among the healthiest in the industry, but dealers deserted in droves when their deliveries didn't arrive. Bankruptcy was declared early in 1915. The Speedwell factory was leased awhile to the Recording and Computing Machines Company and was ultimately sold to the W.M. Pattison Supply Company. The repair parts and business of Speedwell was quickly acquired by the Puritan Machine Company, headed by A.O. Dunk who made a practice of carefully watching the trade papers and buying up automobile companies immediately after their obituaries were written. Speedwell was his sixty-first such purchase.

1907-1908 SPEEDWELL
Four — 40 hp, 116" wb

	FP	5	4	3	2	1
Model C Rdstr.	2500	4400	5600	9200	17,300	31,000
Model D Tour.	2500	4500	5800	9500	18,000	32,000
Model E Lim.	3500	3500	4500	7000	13,000	29,000

Six — 60 hp, 132" wb

| Model B Tour. | 4250 | 6400 | 9300 | 14,500 | 33,000 | 45,000 |
| Model A Rdstr. | 4250 | 6200 | 8700 | 13,500 | 31,000 | 43,000 |

1909 Speedwell, model 9-C, touring, HAC

1909 SPEEDWELL
Series 9 — 4-cyl., 40 hp, 120" wb

	FP	5	4	3	2	1
Surrey Seat Rdstr.-4P	2500	5000	6500	11,000	22,000	35,000
Double Rumble Rdstr.-4P	2500	5000	6500	11,000	22,000	35,000
Single Rumble Rdstr.-3P	2500	4900	6300	10,300	21,000	34,000
Baby Tonneau-4P	2500	5200	6800	11,300	23,000	36,000
Touring-5/7P	2500	5300	7000	11,500	24,000	37,000
Limousine-7P	3500	4300	5400	8700	16,500	30,000

1910 Speedwell, model 10-C, tonneau, HAC

1910 SPEEDWELL
Series 10 — 4-cyl., 50 hp, 121" wb

	FP	5	4	3	2	1
Model C Toy Tonneau-4P	2500	5300	7000	11,500	24,000	37,000
Model D Tour.-5P	2500	5300	7000	11,500	24,000	37,000
Model H Semi-Racer	2500	5800	8000	12,500	28,000	40,000
Model K Close-Coupled-5P	2650	4900	6300	10,300	21,000	34,000
Model G Torpedo-7P	2650	5200	6800	11,300	23,000	36,000
Model F Tour.-7P	2650	5200	6800	11,300	23,000	36,000
Model E Lim.-7P	3850	4300	5400	8700	16,500	30,000

1911 Speedwell, model 11-H, special roadster, HAC

1911 SPEEDWELL
Series 11 — 4-cyl., 50 hp, 121" wb

	FP	5	4	3	2	1
Model H Spec. Rdstr.	2500	5400	7300	11,800	25,000	38,000
Model H Spec. Smi-Racing Rds.	2500	6000	8500	13,000	30,000	42,000
Model C Toy Tonneau	2625	5500	7500	12,000	26,000	39,000
Model D Touring	2650	5800	8000	12,500	28,000	40,000
Model K Close-Coupled-5P	2650	5200	6800	11,300	23,000	36,000
Model G Torpedo	2700	5300	7000	11,500	24,000	37,000
Model D Four-Door Tour.	2750	5400	7300	11,800	25,000	38,000

	FP	5	4	3	2	1
Model F Tour.-7P	2800	5500	7500	12,000	26,000	39,000
Model E Lim.-7P	2850	4300	5400	8700	16,500	30,000
Model E Duck Boat	2750	4700	6100	9900	19,000	33,000
Series 11 — 4-cyl., 50 hp, 132" wb						
Model A Cruiser	3500	5800	8000	12,500	28,000	40,000
Model F Sp. Four-Door Tr.-7P	2900	5800	8000	12,500	28,000	40,000

1912 Speedwell, model 12-G, torpedo, HAC

1912 SPEEDWELL
Series 12 — 4-cyl., 50 hp, 123" wb

	FP	5	4	3	2	1
Model H Rdstr.	2500	5400	7300	11,800	25,000	38,000
Model C Toy Tonneau	2625	5500	7500	12,000	26,000	39,000
Model K Tour.	2650	5500	7500	12,000	26,000	39,000
Model G Torpedo	2700	5400	7300	11,800	25,000	38,000
Model H Speed Car 2P	2700	5800	8000	12,500	28,000	40,000
Model J Cl. C. Tour.-4P	2700	5800	8000	12,500	28,000	40,000
Model D Spec. Tour.-5P	2900	5900	8300	12,800	29,000	41,000
Model F Spec. Tour.-7P	2900	6000	8500	13,000	30,000	42,000
Model E Cruiser	2850	5800	8000	12,500	28,000	40,000

1913 Speedwell, series G, model B, touring, HAC

1913 SPEEDWELL
Series G — 6-cyl., 60 hp, 135" wb

	FP	5	4	3	2	1
Model B Tour.-4/5P	2850	6200	8500	13,000	30,000	43,000
Model B Tour.-7P	2950	6400	9300	14,500	33,000	45,000

1914 Speedwell, series 1, rotary touring, HAC

1914 SPEEDWELL
Series H — 6-cyl., 41 hp, 135" wb

	FP	5	4	3	2	1
Model HB Tour.-5P	2850	4000	5000	8000	15,000	28,000
Model MC Tour.-7P	2950	4200	5200	8400	15,700	29,000
Model HA Tour.-4P	2850	3900	4800	7700	14,300	27,000

1915 SPEEDWELL
Series I — 6-cyl., 41 hp, 135" wb

	FP	5	4	3	2	1
Touring-7P	2950	4300	5400	8700	16,500	30,000
Touring-5P	2850	4200	5200	8400	15,700	29,000
Roadster-2P	2850	4000	5000	8000	15,000	28,000
Touring-4P	2850	4000	5000	8000	15,000	28,000
Touring-6P	2950	4200	5200	8400	15,700	29,000

SPEIRS — Worcester, Massachusetts — (1895, 1898) — The Speirs Manufacturing Company of Worcester produced both the Speirs and Lovell Diamond bicycles. In 1895 company draftsman and mechanic Charles Fletcher designed a two-passenger electric runabout which he built that year strictly for his own pleasure. Three years later, his boss, John C. Speirs built a car for himself as well, this vehicle being a steamer. The Speirs company never envisioned automobile manufacture, although it did enter the automobile industry at the turn of the century, if only by the back door. In February that year Amzi Lorenzo Barber leased the entire Speirs factory for the production of engines for his new Locomobile steamer. The entire workforce of Speirs Manufacturing was retained for this new venture.

SPENCER — The Spencer Manufacturing Company was organized in Spencer, Ohio during the fall of 1914 with a capital stock of $50,000 to manufacture and sell automobiles of all kinds. Incorporators were C.R. Aldrich, J.J. Christy, J.H. Firestone, P.J. White and G.W. Hartman. Manufacture is doubted.

The Spencer Motor Company of Rahway, New Jersey was incorporated with a capital stock of $125,000 during the fall of 1909 by A. Gibbey Spencer. Irving Street was the firm's location. "The company manufactures the Spencer four-cycle internal combustion motor, and also makes motor vehicles of all kinds," reported *The Motor Age*. Manufacture of an automobile is doubted.

1902 Spencer Steam Carriage, WLB

SPENCER STEAM — Manchester, Connecticut — (1862) / Windsor & Hartford, Connecticut — (1901-1902) — In 1862 Christopher Miner Spencer of Manchester built a steam wagon which he used to ferry himself between his home and his job at Colt's Armory in Hartford until the town fathers requested that he keep the vehicle off the road because it frightened horses. A more successful invention of Spencer's during this period was a repeating rifle, which was personally tested by President Lincoln, with 200,000 ultimately manufactured for the Army of the North. Of this rifle, a Confederate officer commented, "the Yankees loaded on Sunday for the rest of the week." Following the Civil War, Christopher Spencer perfected the principles of the firearm, and in 1883 the Spencer Arms Company was organized for its manufacture. Thereafter, Christopher Spencer turned his inventive attention to improvement of screw machines and founded the Spencer Automatic Screw Machine Company in Hartford. He also returned to his horseless carriage idea, building another experimental steam carriage in 1899. From 1901 to 1902 he built nine more (seven in Windsor and two in Hartford) which were sold. These vehicles were powered by four single-acting cylinders fitted under the body and fueled by kerosene, with the boiler hung in back. A chain took power from the engine to jackshaft and differential. One of these vehicles was a light wagon which was delivered under its own power from Hartford to R.H. Macy & Company on 34th Street in New York City. Other inventions occupied the time of Christopher Spencer thereafter, though he did assist Raymond Goodrich in building a steam tonneau in 1903. He died in February 1922.

SPENCER — Hartford, Connecticut — (1914) — This cyclecar was built by P.H. Spencer, whose father was Christopher Spencer, whose brother was the local Kisselkar dealer, and who was at the time a freshman in the Hartford Public High School. His was, he proudly stated, the first cyclecar in town. Young Spencer used two single-cylinder Thrall marine motors coupled together which he said produced 6 hp and propelled the vehicle at a 35 mph clip. The transmission was friction (purloined from an old Metz), the final drive by leather belt. The wheelbase was 100 inches, the track 40. "The owner states he will build another car for his own amusement to be equipped with a four-cylinder, water-cooled motor," *The Automobile* reported in March 1914. Whether he did was not subsequently recorded.

SPENCER — Dayton, Ohio — (1921-1922) — In November of 1920 the Research Engineering Company of Dayton increased its capitalization to $200,000 in order to promote the manufacture of a light four-cylinder car designed by O.H. Spencer, who also happened to be president of the Research Engineering Company. The car's overhead-valve air-cooled 42 hp engine was of Spencer's own design. The vehicle was placed on a 103-inch wheelbase, and weighed but 1500 pounds. Temporary quarters were taken in Dayton. A permanent factory site on the outskirts of town was to be selected by mid-1921, and the building of trucks was to be added later. Probably neither of these plans came to fruition. Very few Spencers were built; a five-passenger touring was the only model offered. In 1921 the car had a price tag of $1200. For 1922 it was slashed to $850. The Spencer disappeared later that year.

SPENCER — Los Angeles, California — (1923) — Considerable mystery surrounds the Spencer car from Los Angeles, but at least one example is known to have been built. Designed by Earl B. Spencer and Victor J. Wagoner of Glendale, the car was introduced to the press as the product of the Tokyo Auto Manufacturing Company of Los Angeles, and the prototype of a new export car to be fabricated in L.A. and then shipped to Japan for final assembly. The Spencer was a small automobile with wheelbase of 90 inches and tread of 48. The car that was shown to the press was later taken to Japan by a K. Mitsuso, but whether the Tokyo Auto Manufacturing Company ever moved into viable operation in Los Angeles is not known. The year previous Earl Spencer had been involved with another partner, George B. Morrow, in another proposed export car called the Fujioka.

SPENNY — Tucson, Arizona — (1913) / Holland, Michigan — (1914) — In 1913 Charles A. Spenny built three six-cylinder cars in Tucson. This was a good beginning, he thought, but he didn't believe Arizona was the place to make his fortune as an automobile manufacturer. So he headed for the mecca of motordom later that summer, and began talking to chambers of commerce throughout Michigan. Holland seemed interested. The Spenny Motor Car Company was organized there in October with a capital stock of $500,000. The former plant of the Dearborn Engraving Company was leased, pending the selection of a site and the construction of a factory in 1914. Newspaper reports in the *Holland City News* for this period reflect an on-again/off-again enthusiasm in town for the Spenny venture. Finally, enthusiasm was off forever. Apparently a few Spenny cars had been put together in the temporary quarters, however, because references indicate that a Spenny 6-60 touring car at $3750, as well as a 4-30 at $1075, were being sold in Chicago in January 1915.

1922 Sperling, 4dr. sedan, WLB

SPERLING — New York, New York — (1921-1923) — Yet another export car was the Sperling. It was designed by Oscar Sperling, who had been vice-president of the Rotary Scraper Company of New York and who relinquished that position to begin his Associated Motors Corporation, with offices at 1926 Broadway. Manufacture of the Sperling was handled in Elkhart, Indiana by the Crow company. The Sperling was built as a right-hand drive car only, and sold for about a thousand dollars. Its engine was a four-cylinder 34 hp unit from Supreme, and the remainder of components set into its 114-inch wheelbase chassis were the standard assembled-car pieces of the era. The car was sold complete — in either touring or sedan guise — or as a chassis, either assembled or unassembled. Oscar Sperling may have continued in his export auto business into 1923, but directory listings indicate that he became a civil engineer for the city of New York thereafter.

1898 Sperry Electric, HAC

1900 Sperry Electric, NAHC

1901 Sperry Electric, runabout, NAHC

SPERRY ELECTRIC — Cleveland, Ohio — (1899-1901) — Prior to the turn of the century, the name Elmer A. Sperry was already well known in the field of electric power. Electric arc lamps and electrically driven mining equipment had been among his inventions when he arrived in Cleveland during the early 1890's to assist in the establishment of an electric street railway company in the city. With the organization of his Sperry Engineering Company, Sperry began experimenting with electric motors for passenger car use. His first electric carriage was completed in October 1898. During the summer of 1899 Sperry contracted with A.L. Moore, the president of the Cleveland Machine Screw Company, to build his automobile for the market. It was powered by a 3-1/2 hp motor and was offered in eight body styles. The price range was $1800 to $2200. Speeds up to 18 mph were promised, and the cars sported electric lamps controlled by push buttons, and a gong that rang electrically. Most significant was the vehicle's single lever for control (side movements for direction, a push down to increase speed, a pull up to turn off current and apply the brakes) which subsequently became the norm for electric automobiles. The early cars were called Cleveland, Sperry System; the final cars carried just the name Sperry. The Sperry won a gold medal at the Paris Exposition in 1900, and manufacturing rights were sold in France. At least 100 Sperry electrics were exported to France as well by the Cleveland Machine Screw Company, which was controlled by a consortium of French businessmen. In January 1901 the Cleveland company sold the Sperry cars on hand, together with the patents for them, to the American Bicycle Company. A good many Sperry innovations subsequently found their way into the Waverley electric. The Cleveland Machine Screw Company subsequently built a gasoline car called the Cleveland from 1902 to 1904. Meanwhile, Elmer Sperry had turned his ingenuity to other fields, and soon became famous as the inventor of the Sperry Gyroscope. His Sperry Gyroscope Company ultimately evolved into the Sperry Rand Corporation. He died in 1930.

SPHINX — the Sphinx Motor Company was a $600,000 Delaware incorporation from the spring of 1911 to manufacture and deal in automobiles and engines in New York City. G. Faster and W.H. Turner were behind this venture, both of New York City. Manufacture is doubted.

SPHINX — York, Pennsylvania — (1914-1916) — In April of 1914, H.R. Averill, who had been the sales manager for the Pullman Company in New York for the seven years past, decided to strike out on his own. What America needed, he concluded, was a good $700 touring car. He spent the next few months persuading people with money in York, Reading, Lancaster and nearby Baltimore (Maryland) to invest in the project — and also to having the pilot model run up in Detroit. In September the Sphinx Motor

1915 Sphinx, touring, WLB

Car Company was formally established, and the Hart-Kraft Motor Car Company plant in York was acquired for its home. The first Sphinx cars were 1915 models, introduced before year's end. Designed by E.T. Gilliard and powered by a Lycoming four, the Sphinx was mounted on a 112-inch wheelbase, sported a cone clutch, three-speed transmission, cantilever springs all around — and became the DuPont later in 1915. Or did it? In July that year an announcement was made that the Sphinx venture was being reorganized as the DuPont Motor Car Company. The specs for the new DuPont were exactly the same as for the Sphinx — except for the price tag which, at $595, was a hundred dollars lower. Whether any cars were marketed as the DuPont, or whether the du Ponts of Delaware objected — as well they might have — to the flagrant purloining of their prominent family name is not known. By October, however, when announcement was made of the 1916 model line, the cars were again called Sphinx. They survived one year longer. The Sphinx Company also built a few cars for Bush of Chicago that year. In October of 1916 H.R Averill gave up the automobile business, disposing of part of his plant to his old employer, Pullman, for the building of automobile bodies, selling the rest to a new group of entrepreneurs for the building of another car called the Bell. The du Ponts of Delaware, of course, later proceeded in automobile manufacture as well.

1915 SPHINX
Model A-15 — 4-cyl., 18 hp, 112" wb

	FP	5	4	3	2	1
Touring-5P	695	3000	4000	6000	9500	21,000
Roadster-2P	695	2900	3700	5600	9100	20,000

1916 SPHINX
Model B-16 — 4-cyl., 18 hp, 112" wb

	FP	5	4	3	2	1
Touring-5P	640	3000	4000	6000	9500	21,000
Roadster-2P	640	2900	3700	5600	9100	20,000

1902 Spicer, runabout, GR

SPICER — Plainfield, New Jersey — (1902) — In 1902, while a student at Cornell University, Clarence W. Spicer built an experimental automobile to test an idea he had. He never built another car, but he did pursue the idea: it was a propeller shaft with a universal joint at each end, which he patented. With six men in a small shop on Second Street in Plainfield, he began producing his universal joint. Eventually the Spicer Manufacturing Company expanded into huge plants in South Plainfield; Pottstown, Pennsylvania and Toledo, Ohio — and Spicer became one of the mainstays of the automobile component industry. Clarence Spicer died in Miami on November 21st, 1939 at the age of sixty-three.

SPIDER — Detroit, Michigan — (1914) — The Detroit Body Company was indicated as the builder of a cyclecar called the Spider in the March 1914 issue of *Motor Print*. Undoubtedly, the car was produced as a prototype and probably for an outside client. The Detroit Body Company, which had been organized in 1911, was headed by H.W. Paton, William A. Kirby, Hermann C. Maise and P.O. Pennington and was located at the corner of Clay and St. Aubin Streets in Detroit. "Expert designers and builders of automobile bodies" was the way the company advertised itself. There seems to be no connection, incidentally, between this Spider cyclecar and that which Theodore Millington was planning to build either under the Spider name or under his own during this period.

SPILLMAN — From 1901 to 1904, in North Tonawanda, New York, Herschell-Spillman, Inc. built four automobiles as an adjunct to its successful motor-building business. Refer to Herschell-Spillman.

SPIRAL — The Spiral Spring and Auto Company of New York City was organized during the fall of 1907 with a capital stock of $10,000 to manufacture and deal in automobiles and supplies and conduct a garage. Incorporators were A.J. Cahill, W. Neiss and L.S. Abberley. Manufacture of a car is doubted.

SPLITT — Milwaukee, Wisconsin — (1909) — Probably the first motor buggy he built was also the last, but early in 1909 Louis Splitt of Milwaukee had grand plans for its future. That he had "definitely decided to establish a small motor car factory at Manitowoc" was reported in *The Horseless Age* in January; that he figured on subsequently purchasing the Manitowoc Beach Hotel and converting it into a big factory was reported in *Motor Age* the following month. A colleague of Splitt's, one Charles R. Davis, did appear in Manitowoc to investigate the prospects. But there is no evidence the Splitt motor buggy ever arrived there.

1910 Spoerer, model B, touring, NAHC

SPOERER — Baltimore, Maryland — (1908-1914) — Following the retirement of their father from active engagement in the family carriage business, Charles and Jacob Spoerer decided to enter the automotive field. Their first car was completed in 1907 and was subsequently introduced at the Baltimore Automobile Show but full-scale production and promotion of the product did not arrive until the fall of 1909. In September that year a Spoerer entered the 1282-mile reliability run from Washington, D.C. to Boston and return sponsored by publishing magnate Frank A. Munsey. Amongst a field of forty-odd entrants, the Baltimore car finished seventh. "One of the surprises of the run was the excellent work of the home-made Spoerer...," commented the *Baltimore News*. "This car was comparatively unknown, except to Baltimoreans, and it made 'outsiders' sit up and take notice by its fine showing." This performance also prompted the Carl Spoerer's Sons Company to regard the Spoerer as a national rather than a purely regional product, and beginning with the 1910 model year the firm began promoting and advertising its product in the automotive trade press. Prior to the summer of 1909, only a handful of cars had been built; by the time of the Munsey Reliability Run, ten cars were in the process of construction. The Spoerer was a big car, patterned after the Mercedes, and offered as a 40 hp four only initially, with a smaller 25 hp companion model introduced for 1911. The 40 hp engine was a Herschell-Spillman, the 25 hp an Excelsior. A three-speed selective sliding gear transmission and shaft drive were featured in both models. Commercial vehicles were added to the line in 1912, and Carl Spoerer's Sons was instrumental in converting the Baltimore police and fire departments to motorized equipment. Financial problems closed the company sometime during 1914.

1910 SPOERER
Four — 40 hp, 118" wb

	FP	5	4	3	2	1
Model A Tour.-5P	3000	4200	5200	8400	15,000	29,000
Model B Tour.-4P	3000	4000	5000	8000	15,000	28,000
Model C-10 Tour.-7P	3250	4500	5800	9500	18,000	32,000
Model D-10 Rbt.-2P	2850	4300	5400	8700	16,500	30,000

1911 SPOERER
Model DA — 4-cyl., 25 hp, 120" wb

	FP	5	4	3	2	1
Touring-5P	2000	4200	5200	8400	15,700	29,000
Roadster-2/3P	1900	4000	5000	8000	15,000	28,000

Model C — 4-cyl., 40 hp, 120" wb

	FP	5	4	3	2	1
Touring-7P	3250	4400	5600	9200	17,300	31,000
Roadster-2/3P	2750	4300	5400	8700	16,500	30,000

1912-1913 SPOERER
Model 25 A — 4-cyl., 27 hp, 120" wb

	FP	5	4	3	2	1
Roadster	2000	4200	5200	8400	15,700	29,000
Toy Tonneau	2000	4300	5400	8700	16,500	30,000
Touring-5P	2000	4300	5400	8700	16,500	30,000
Town Car	2500	3900	4800	7700	14,300	27,000

Model 40 C — 4-cyl., 40 hp, 120" wb

	FP	5	4	3	2	1
Roadster	2950	4300	5400	8700	16,500	30,000
Touring-5P	3000	4400	5600	9200	17,300	31,000
Toy Tonneau-4P	3000	4400	5600	9200	17,300	31,000
Touring-7P	3250	4700	6100	9900	19,000	33,000
Limousine	4000	4000	5000	8000	15,000	28,000
Landaulette	4150	4200	5200	8400	15,700	29,000

1912 Spoerer, model 25-A, roadster, HAC

1914 Spoerer, model 40C, touring, HAC

1914 SPOERER
Model 25 A — 4-cyl., 27 hp, 120" wb

	FP	5	4	3	2	1
Roadster	2000	4300	5400	8700	16,500	30,000
Toy Tonneau	2000	4400	5600	9200	17,300	31,000
Touring-5P	2000	4400	5600	9200	17,300	31,000
Town Car	2500	4000	5000	8000	15,000	28,000

Model 40 C — 4-cyl., 40 hp, 120" wb

Touring-5P	3000	4900	6300	10,300	21,000	34,000
Roadster-2P	2950	4700	6100	9900	19,000	33,000
Toy Tonneau-4P	3000	4900	6300	10,300	21,000	34,000
Touring-7P	3250	5000	6500	11,000	22,000	35,000
Limousine	4000	4200	5200	8400	15,700	29,000
Landaulette	4150	4300	5400	8700	16,500	30,000

SPOKANE — The Spokane Taxicab Company was headed by G.E. Riegel and operated a taxicab service in Spokane, Washington in 1914. That year Riegel announced that the firm's taxicabs would now be manufactured as well in its own new factory. Documentation that manufacture ever began has not been discovered.

SPOKANE STEAM — **Spokane, Washington** — **(1904-1905)** — The Spokane Motor Company was incorporated in November of 1904 with a capital stock of $50,000 by B.W. Wolverton, A.W. Gallagher and Levi Rhodes of Spokane. Their new car was to be a steamer which, they said, would "revolutionize the automobile industry." The reason for this was the burner developed for the Spokane, which used crude petroleum for fuel. Gallagher claimed that the vehicle could travel fifteen miles to a single gallon of crude "and that the cost will amount to only 8 cents a gallon." The Spokane did not make it beyond the prototype stage, though as late as March of 1906 Levi Rhodes was announcing that construction of a factory was ongoing. By 1907 the Spokane Motor Company apparently had given up because organized early that year by many of the same principals was the Acme Engine Company, also in Spokane, which rather more promptly went nowhere as well.

SPRAGUE — **Fowlerville, Michigan** — **(1895-1896)** — In the fall of 1895, H.A. Sprague of Fowlerville announced his intention to build automotive vehicles of both two and four wheels "in which the most approved methods will be used to secure lightness, strength and the reduction of friction in both motor and vehicle." Gasoline engines of the Otto type were to be utilized. In the two-wheeler, speed would be regulated by the engine only, with the motor connected directly to the main wheel. A change-speed transmission would be provided the four-wheeler, with alternate gears of rawhide to reduce noise. Whether Sprague successfully tested his vehicles is not known; the *Fowlerville Review* for 1896 contains neither an advertisement nor an article regarding any production or marketing of the Sprague.

SPRINGER — **New York, New York** — **(1903-1905)** — In April of 1903, John H. Springer purchased the Kidder Motor Vehicle Company of New Haven, Connecticut with the intention of continuing manufacture of that firm's steam car. He changed his mind, however, after only a few steamers were built and after talking to Frank T. Clark, the Knox agent in New

1904 Springer, touring, WLB

1905 Springer, touring, NAHC

Haven, who had designed a gasoline car. By that summer the Springer Motor Vehicle Company had moved out of New Haven and into a factory at 242-244 West 41st Street in New York City to produce the Clark-designed car. Frank Clark was superintendent of manufacture. Initially, a 12 hp two-cylinder roadster on an 84-inch wheelbase was the company's only offering, but it was soon followed by a four-cylinder touring car. Both these models were water-cooled. For 1905 the twin was enlarged to a 92-inch wheelbase chassis, while the four (indicated as a 40 hp the year previous, a 30 hp now) retained its 105-inch wheelbase. Prices were $2500 and $3500 respectively. The larger car had a very high one-piece windshield and a long hood which did not, however, house the engine. Instead the powerplant was under the body, comprised of two separate engines of two cylinders each which could be disconnected so that one could be run alone. Production was discontinued sometime during 1905.

SPRINGFIELD — The car produced by the Springfield Cornice Works of Springfield, Massachusetts from 1900-1901 was marketed as the Meteor. Refer to Meteor.

The Springfield-Hampden Motor Vehicle Company was organized in Springfield, Massachusetts during the summer of 1905 with a capital stock of $24,000 for the manufacture of automobiles. Silas B. Abbey and Horatio G. Hawkins were the partners involved. Manufacture is doubted.

The Springfield Machine & Tool Company of Springfield, Ohio announced during the summer of 1904 that it was at work on the building of an automobile designed by P.E.Montanus, the head of the company. "If the machine is successful the regular manufacture will be undertaken," *The Horseless Age* reported. Manufacture is doubted.

SPRINGFIELD — **Springfield, Ohio** — **(1899/1903)** — During the spring of 1899, the Springfield Automobile & Industrial Company of Springfield, Ohio announced that it was exhibiting its 555-pound gasoline carriage "in the principal cities of Maine." Nothing productive seems to have come of this venture. In 1903, however, W.C. Bramwell and his son C.C. — who had been building the Bramwell-Robinson in Hyde Park, Massachusetts — arrived in town and talked the firm, now renamed Springfield Automobile Company, into manufacture of their small runabout. About three cars a week were being produced by that summer. The Springfield was powered by a single-cylinder two-stroke water cooled 8 hp engine, its chassis had a 72-inch wheelbase and featured planetary transmission and single chain drive. Though the Bramwells began simply as managers of the Springfield company, by year's end they had bought out the owners, and continued their car in production as the Bramwell in 1904-1905.

SPRINGFIELD STEAM — Springfield, Massachusetts — (1900-1901) — In 1900 ten Springfield businessmen put up the money for the building of an experimental motor vehicle designed by S.H. Barrett and R. Hale Smith and constructed in the machine shop of M.J. Dunn & Company in Springfield. A light delivery wagon powered by a 4 hp steam engine, the vehicle was neat and a success in operation. "The engine condenses the steam, using the water over and over," reported *The Motor Vehicle Review*. "This feature also allows the machine to run 200 miles or more without taking a second supply of water." The prototype was purchased by Charles A. Royce, one of the ten backers and owner of the Royce Laundry Company at 104 Worthington Street who planned to use it in the collection and delivery of laundry bundles. It was the first motor vehicle in Springfield designed for a mercantile purpose. In October 1900 the Springfield Motor Vehicle Company was organized with a capital stock of $50,000, Royce taking the presidential chair and others of the original ten backers filling various executive posts. Though pleasure cars were planned, the firm's emphasis was stated to be the manufacture of delivery vans. The reason for the quick demise of this venture, despite its promising beginning, is not known.

1907 Springfield, model A, touring, NAHC

SPRINGFIELD — Springfield, Massachusetts — (1907-1908)/Springfield, Illinois — (1909-1910) — In February of 1907, Harry C. Medcraft and George C. Bowersox combined their talents and the first syllables of their last names into the Med-Bow Automobile Company of Springfield, Massachusetts for the manufacture of a four-cylinder 35 hp (Rutenber engine) touring car on a 107-inch wheelbase. Its price was $2500. Although the car was occasionally referred to as the Med-Bow, surviving brochures indicate that it was never marketed under any name other than Springfield. By the fall of 1907 the firm was renamed the H.C. Medcraft Automobile Company, which probably means George Bowersox was no longer around. For the 1908 model year the touring car, which promised 50 mph, was joined by a roadster, which promised 65 mph and was priced at $2750. Coincidentally, and fortuitously, the board of directors of the company was composed of people living in both Springfield, Massachusetts and Springfield, Illinois — and thus, when the company decided

1910 Springfield, five-passenger phaeton, JAC

to move headquarters to the Midwest early in 1909, there was no need for a change in name for the company product. Indeed, the firm's name was changed to Springfield Motor Car Company too upon arrival in the state capital of Illinois. Not making the move with the firm was George Readio, who had designed the Massachusetts Springfield and stayed at home now to produce another car under his own name. The first Illinois Springfield was off the assembly line later in 1909. Its engine remained the same, but the Springfield now was a much bigger car on a 128-inch wheelbase and marketed as a five- and seven-passenger touring and a four-passenger torpedo, all carrying a price tag of $2500. Probably the highlight of the company's history was the Springfield's use as the parade car when President William Howard Taft came to town to visit the Abraham Lincoln home and tomb in 1910. John Hobbs, who chauffeured the President that day, later recalled that Taft's weight "was sufficient to hold down the rear of the car." How many Springfields were built is a matter of dispute. "The 'Made-to-Order' Car for 300 Exacting People" was the slogan in the advertisement announcing the company's planned 1910 production. Production in Massachusetts seems to have been forty-six cars. A later reference indicates that 200 cars were built in Illinois, another that the figure was only eleven. More than likely, the latter was closer to actuality. Before the firm went completely under, it was purchased by the Rayfields who used it as a basis for their new automotive venture.

SPRINGFIELD ELECTRIC — Springfield, Illinois — (1908) — A prototype of an electric car was built in 1908 in the Springfield shops of the R. Haas Electric Manufacturing Company. Although manufacture was decided against, R. Haas himself kept at least a toe in the automotive business. A brochure for the 1907 Springfield manufactured in Springfield, Massachusetts included him as among recent satisfied owners of that year's model, and in 1909 when the New England Company elected to relocate in Springfield, Illinois, it moved into the third floor of the R. Haas Electric Manufacturing Company factory.

1914 Sprite, 2-pass. roadster, WLB

SPRITE — Aurora, Illinois — (1914) — "The lines of this Car are beautiful, The construction the best, The price only $425.00...," advertised W.S. Frazier & Company, which also alluded to itself as "one of the best known light vehicle builders in the country," without mentioning that its previous products had been road carts and racing sulkies whose power was provided by horses. The horsepower of Frazier's new Sprite was provided by a four-cylinder water-cooled Farmer engine. (A prototype, which had been announced under the Frazier name, had a 9 hp two-cylinder engine, but it was not marketed.) The Sprite was a cyclecar on a 94-inch wheelbase chassis fitted with a friction transmission, belt drive and a minimal little body allowing two-abreast seating. Like most vehicles of that genre, Walter S. Frazier's cyclecar survived one season only. His company remained in the business of building road carts and racing sulkies into the 1920's.

SPROEHLE — The Sproehle Manufacturing Company was the producer of automobile parts in Philadelphia in 1910 when the firm announced its recapitalization at $2 million and its impending move to a large new factory in Frackville, Pennsylvania where the manufacture of complete cars would be undertaken. There is no evidence that this followed.

1900 Spurr, runabout, MVMA

SPURR — New York, New York — (1900-1901) — This short-lived automobile was announced by the Spurr family of East Orange, New Jersey during the summer of 1900, though the Spurr Automobile Company did not commence production until December, giving its address as 116 Nassau Street in New York City at that time. Most of the Spurrs in East Orange were in the hat and dressmaking business, the one with the automotive yen was Charles W., Jr., who allied himself with Cyrus O. Baker, Jr. and Fred W. Barker. The Spurr automobile was a simple dos-a-dos buggy fitted with a two-cylinder water-cooled engine started from the seat. A two-speed transmission provided a range of 8 to 24 mph. The most advanced feature of the Spurr was its wheel for steering. Production does not seem to have survived 1901.

SQUARE DEAL — The 1910 Square Deal was a two-cylinder 14 hp high-wheeler on an 82-inch wheelbase with a price tag of $385. It was one of a number of cars marketed by the Automobile Parts & Equipment Company of Chicago. Refer to Auto Parts.

SQUIER STEAM — **Virginia City, Nevada** — **(1899)** — In 1899, in collaboration with A.J. Root, W.E. Squier built what was probably the first automobile in the state of Nevada. It was a steam car fitted with a pair of single-cylinder engines (one for each driving wheel) which used gasoline for fuel. The boiler was said to be "made of mercury flasks." This was apparently the only car built. A few years later Squier bought a second-hand Locomobile steamer in San Francisco which he drove thereafter.

SQUIRES — In May of 1919, John Squires, formerly chief engineer for the Signal Motor Truck Company, announced his organization of the Squires Engineering Company in Detroit, Michigan. In his new laboratory in Detroit, Squires already had built a new steam engine which, he said, produced its heat "from a distillate fuel." He also revealed plans to have his new engine, which was patented, "in operation in an experimental car by early fall." So far as is known, Squires never proceeded further than that.

S.R. — The S.R. Manufacturing Company was organized in Schenectady, New York during the fall of 1911 with a capital stock of $50,000 for the manufacture of engines and automobiles. Incorporators were C. Steenstrup and K.M. Rossi. Manufacture of a car is doubted.

1915 S.R.K., roadster, WLB

S.R.K. — **Detroit, Michigan** — **(1915)** — Initially this car was introduced as the Strouse, named for Dr. Clarence B. Strouse, the professor of engineering who designed it. Soon thereafter, however, the product came to be called the S.R.K., the initials of Strouse, Frederick T. Ranney (a real estate dealer) and Thomas D. Knight (a Detroit lawyer). In February of 1915 this trio organized the S.R.K. Motor Company in Detroit for the manufacture of the Strouse-designed car. The S.R.K. was a johnny-come-lately cyclecar sporting a four-cylinder water-cooled Hermann engine, friction transmission and single chain drive. Its price was slated to be $300 for a two-passenger roadster on a 100-inch wheelbase with 42-inch tread, a standard-tread version being available for an extra $25. According to *Light Car Age*, the prototype had been tested for 2000 miles over Michigan country roads during which it put up 40 miles to a gallon of gasoline and 800 miles to a gallon of oil. There is no evidence the S.R.K. ever made it into production, however.

1924 S&S Brighton, sedan, HAC

S & S — **Cincinnati, Ohio** — **(1924-1929)** — The S & S was the second passenger car produced by the Sayers & Scovill Company of Cincinnati. Unlike the predecessor Sayers which was a standard production automobile, however, the S & S was merely a conversion from the firm's professional car line. Indeed, the S & S name was the same designation which had been used for the company's hearses and ambulances since their introduction in 1913. Following the May 1924 decision to abandon manufacture of the Sayers, though, Sayers & Scovill elected a few months later to at least tiptoe back into the production car field. The same 55 hp engine as had been fitted in the Sayers was placed in a 132-inch wheelbase hearse chassis (the Sayers had been 118 inches) and was named the S & S Brighton. It must have been woefully underpowered, because in 1925 a 66 hp Continental was substituted, the wheelbase lengthened to 136 inches, and the car was renamed the S & S Elmwood. It remained thus through 1926, and was renamed the Gotham in 1927 when the wheelbase was extended to 140 inches, four-wheel brakes were introduced, and a purchaser was given the option of wooden artillery or aluminum disc wheels. In 1928 the Gotham received an 85 hp Continental eight-cylinder engine, and yet another increase of an inch to its wheelbase. The year following the horsepower was up to 114 (a Continental 15K eight) and the wheelbase to 143 inches, and the car carried the designation Lakewood. That was the last passenger car S & S offered to the public. Since all of these cars had been eight-passenger limousines virtually no different from the bearers' cars sold to funeral directors, most probably few of them had found ready sale as private automobiles. The Sayers & Scovill Company remained in the hearse and automobile business exclusively thereafter, and in 1942 was reorganized as Hess and Eisenhardt.

1924 S & S
S & S — 6-cyl., 55 hp, 132" wb

	FP	5	4	3	2	1
Brighton Sed.-8P	—	4200	5200	8400	15,700	29,000

1925-26 S&S Elmwood, sedan, HAC

1925-1926 S & S
S & S — 6-cyl., 66 hp, 136" wb

Elmwood Sed.-8P		4300	5400	8700	16,500	30,000

1927 S&S Gotham, sedan, HAC

1929 S&S Lakewood, sedan, KM

1927 S & S
S & S — 6-cyl., 66 hp, 140" wb

	FP	5	4	3	2	1
Gotham Sed.-8P	—	4400	5600	9200	17,300	31,000

1928 S & S
S & S — 8-cyl., 85 hp, 141" wb

	FP	5	4	3	2	1
Gotham Sed.-8P	—	4500	5800	9500	18,000	32,000

1929 S & S
S & S — 8-cyl., 114 hp, 143" wb

	FP	5	4	3	2	1
Lakewood Sed.-8P	4275	4700	6100	9900	19,000	33,000

5755 S.S.E.

1917 S.S.E., runabout, LC

S.S.E. — Philadelphia, Pennsylvania — (1916-1917) — Whether this venture proceeded beyond ballyhoo is open to question, but the ballyhoo was wonderful — and not all of it came from S.S.E. people themselves. "This is truly a big piece of news for Philadelphia," the *Philadelphia Chamber of Commerce Journal* enthused in June 1916 when the S.S.E. folks came to town. "They selected this city as the place best adapted to the manufacture of the motorcar which is to be a rich man's toy...The new car will be on the market in the fall...then the company will go ahead in an effort to produce and market the first year five million dollars worth of these speedy marvels which are said to be equal to 115 miles an hour." No wonder Philadelphia was excited. The people behind the S.S.E. were Elmer E. Smathers (a New York oil capitalist), Charles B. Schaeffer (head of the Schaeffer-Smathers Oil Company in Chicago), and Victor L. Emerson (an engineer whose previous efforts included automotive and marine engines, and the Emerson and Military cars, failures both). Smathers and Schaeffer were described in the *Journal* as "nationally known for their wealth and business sagacity." Certainly they were rich. In May of 1916 this new venture was incorporated, with a capital stock of a heady $10 million, as the Emerson Motor Car Manufacturing Company — though by September its name had been changed to the S.S.E. Company. "A car built by Engineers with the afterthoughts left out" was a slogan for the S.S.E., which was announced as a six-cylinder 30 hp car on a 124-inch wheelbase to sell for $5000 in chassis form and, with coachwork added, at price tags from $6700 (for touring, runabout and roadster) to $8000 (for limousine and berline). A total of nine body styles represented the projected model lineup. In January 1917 the company announced its completion of a factory at B Street and Erie Avenue in Philadelphia. April brought the news that S.S.E. was in the process of building an addition to that plant. In May, Victor Emerson was quoted in *The Automobile* as saying that "although nothing will be turned out for several months, the plant is sold ahead for one year." Whether anything ever was turned out in the S.S.E. plant has not been documented. When the ballyhoo died down, the S.S.E. Company faded from sight.

1911 Stafford, touring, NAHC

STAFFORD — Topeka & Kansas City, Kansas — (1908-1914) — Terry Stafford was a Topeka mechanic who built his first car in 1898. This vehicle attracted the attention of Dr. Clement Smith and his brother Anton who formed a partnership with Stafford which resulted in the Smith Automobile Company. Terry Stafford was superintendent of the Smith factory. In mid-1908, about the time the Smiths were engaged in selling out their holdings to a group of Michigan businessmen, Terry Stafford left to become an automobile manufacturer on his own. Although initially headquartering his new Stafford Motor Car Company in Topeka, Terry Stafford moved operations to Kansas City in 1910 when fresh capital became available there. The Stafford was a 30 hp four-cylinder touring car on a 112-inch wheelbase which sold for $2350, with a companion roadster model usually being offered for about $1900. The ohc water-cooled engine was designed by Terry Stafford, and his car featured a selective sliding gear transmission and shaft drive. Increased competition in the industry forced the discontinuation of the Stafford during 1914, though Terry Stafford continued in the parts-making business for a while, and remained in general garage work thereafter. A total of 315 Stafford cars had been built. One of the 1913 touring models was the first car owned by a young man in Missouri named Harry S. Truman. "I had it remodeled into a hot sport roadster and took it to Camp Doniphan with me in 1917, where it was used by Battery 'F' as a kind of transportation truck for ice and whatever else was necessary to be hauled around the Battery," President Truman wrote Floyd Clymer in 1953. "I sold it to a Sergeant at Fort Sill in March 1918 just before I left for overseas....It was an excellent car and would take an awful beating. You can be sure of that if one lasted me as long as three years, which that one did." Give-'em-hell Harry must have been something of a scorcher.

STAMM — Los Angeles, California — (1901/1905) — Probably three Stamms were built, the first in 1901 by Frederick B. Stamm. Powered by a single-cylinder 4 hp engine built in unit with a two-speed planetary transmission, its two-passenger roadster body was initially fitted to the chassis in a double-three-point mounting though problems with control linkage flex ultimately forced Stamm to return to the conventional. The unconventional was tried again in 1905 in the second Stamm car, built by George T. Stamm. (Around 1902 a trio of Stamms — Frederick B., George T. and Godfrey T. had opened a Ford dealership in Los Angeles.) This Stamm took L.A. by storm, or "about two thousand words of laudation" in the local press, as *The Motor World* reported. Powering the 1905 effort was a four-cylinder, two-stroke, air-cooled engine that Stamm said generated 40 hp. The combination of a two-stroke and air cooling was an innovation that as, *Motor World* tut-tutted, "apparently has either been regarded as impracticable or simply was never thought worthwhile by anybody in the past." George Stamm also provided his engine with two carburetors, one for the forward two cylinders, the other for the rear, this because Stamm believed the engine of sufficient power to run on only half its available cylinders when not under heavy load. Either gasoline, kerosene or alcohol could be used in the car. In September of 1905 George Stamm announced that he was now at work on a second car to serve as the prototype for production. Production, however, did not follow.

1901 Stammobile, steam carriage, NAHC

STAMMOBILE — Stamford, Connecticut — (1900-1901) — The product of the Stammobile Manufacturing Company of Stamford was a steam car with accommodations for four passengers. It was powered by a double-cylinder engine fueled by gasoline, with its boiler fifteen inches in diameter. The gasoline tank held seven gallons, the water tank twenty-six. The body was mounted on a tubular frame, and was available with either panel or spindle seats, leather or whipcord upholstery, and wood or wire wheels. Production ended in 1901. Roster references indicating manufacture of the Stamford-built Stammobile continuing into 1905 are in error, the result of confusion with the Los Angeles automobile built by George T. Stamm, which occasionally was called a Stammobile as well.

STANDARD — The number of early automobile ventures apparently believing that use of the name Standard represented the first step toward success in the industry was positively astonishing. The companies following are not believed to have manufactured an automobile despite declaration of an intent to do so.

The Standard Company of Torrington, Connecticut which announced its forthcoming manufacture of automobiles during the summer of 1908. This firm, which had evolved from the Standard Spoke & Nipple Company of

Torrington in 1905, produced bicycle and automobile accessories.

The Standard Auto Company of Rockford, Illinois, organized late in 1908 with a capital stock of $10,000 by S.O. Widell, John Wester and S. Loan.

The Standard Auto Rolling Chair Company of New York City, organized during the fall of 1907 with a capital stock of $500,000 for the manufacture of motor rolling chairs and automobiles. Incorporators were J.H. Kahrs, L. Albert and L.J. Gregory, all of New York City.

The Standard Auto Specialties Company of Philadelphia, Pennsylvania, organized during the spring of 1914 with a capital stock of $50,000 for the manufacture of automobiles and wagons. Incorporators were L.H. Ryon of Philadelphia, W.C. Arnold of Landsdowne and J.M. Satterfield of Dover, New Jersey.

The Standard Auto Supply & Manufacturing Company of New York City, organized with a capital stock of $10,000 during the spring of 1907 by Octavius Knight, Octavius Knight, Jr. and Harry A. Knight, all of New York City.

The Standard Automobile Company of Camden, New Jersey, which announced its lease of property along the river front from 33rd to 37th streets during the spring of 1908 where a factory was to be erected for the manufacture of "motor cars, motor cycles and motor boats."

The Standard Automobile Company of Cleveland, Ohio, organized with a capital stock of $100,000 during the fall of 1905 to "manufacture, purchase, sell and store automobiles." Incorporators were F.B. Williams, T.H. Hoggsett, M.G. McAleenan, George H. Smith and George H. Kelly. This firm became agents in Northern Ohio for the Packard, Cadillac and Autocar.

The Standard Automobile Company of Indianapolis, Indiana, organized during the fall of 1902 with a capital stock of $1 million by William W. Spenser, John W. Holtzman and James H. Witty.

The Standard Automobile Company of Macon, Georgia, organized early in 1911 with a capital stock of $20,000 by J.W. Saunders, Ben C. Smith, R.C. Houser, W.E. Cookerly.

The Standard Automobile Company of New York City, organized during the fall of 1905 by Edward Stetson Gripping of New Rochelle, and George A. Burkhard and John G. Craig of Manhattan. This firm reportedly located a "large piece of land" in Long Island City upon which a factory was to be erected at once which would employ 500 to 700 people.

The Standard Automobile Company of San Francisco, California which established itself at 1236 Market Street during the spring of 1901 and was reportedly working on "an automobile motor of new design."

The Standard Car Construction Company of Philadelphia, Pennsylvania, organized during the spring of 1916 with a $1 million capital stock by F.R. Hansell, G.H.B. Martin and S.G. Seymour.

The Standard Engine and Automobile Company of Greenwood, Indiana which reported early in 1905 having reached an agreement with the citizens of that town for the construction of an automobile factory there.

The Standard Garage Company of Buffalo, New York, organized with a capital stock of $10,000 early in 1906 by Louis F. Gertsch, William C. Schultze, John G.W. Knoll, Grosvenor R. Trowbridge and Harry M. Kraft.

The Standard Limousine Company of Chicago, Illinois, organized early in 1910 with a capital stock of $5000 by B. and C.A. Carlson and C.B. Parsons.

The Standard Machinery Company of Mystic, Connecticut which reportedly was negotiating with New York people to manufacture motor cars under contract in 1909. "The first order offered is for 100 cars," *The Motor World* reported that September, "and if satisfactory arrangements are concluded, the company will adapt its equipment to this line of production."

The Standard Manufacturing Company of Kokomo, Indiana which had a brief fling with a car called the Goabout in 1901-1902, then evolved into the Standard Motor Company for the manufacture of engines only.

The Standard Metalwork Company of Thompsonville, Connecticut which produced automobile parts and announced in 1910 its intention to manufacture complete cars.

The Standard Motive Power Company of Canal Dover, Ohio, which was organized with a capital stock of $10,000,000 late in 1902 for the manufacture of locomotives and automobiles. Howard McNutt was president, Andrew Weis vice-president, W.H. Hoar secretary and Thornton Chase treasurer.

The Standard Motor Company of Mason City, Iowa, organized during the fall of 1913 by C.H. McNidder, F.E. Konasten and M.J. Scanlon.

The Standard Motor Company of New York City, organized as a $31 million Delaware incorporation early in 1913 to "manufacture, construct, maintain and operate automobiles, wagon trucks, motorcycles and flying machines." Incorporators were Donald Muhleman, William J. Maloney and Herbert E. Latter.

The Standard Motor Company of Warren, Ohio, which did build motor trucks from 1913-1915 but never an automobile.

The Standard Motor Car Company of Chicago, Illinois, organized early in 1914 with a $10,000 capital stock by Eric Kullberger, David Gordon and B. Christiansen.

The Standard Motor Car Company of Wheeling, West Virginia, organized late in 1909 with a capital stock of $25,000 by Thomas W. Norton, J.F. Ranson, Frank O'Brien, E.E. Shaffer and George A. Blackford.

The Standard Motor Carriage Company of Braintree, Massachusetts, listed as an automobile manufacturer in the Hiscox book *Horseless Vehicles, Automobiles, Motor Cycles* published in 1900.

The Standard Motor Parts Company of Detroit, Michigan, organized early in 1915 with a capital stock of $300,000 to manufacture and sell automobiles, repairs and accessories. Incorporators were E.J. Dayton, Oscar Cumbinsky and W.S. Grant.

The Standard Motor Sales Company of Passaic, New Jersey, organized with a capital stock of $30,000 early in 1920 by Maurice Finkelman, I.E. Bodner and S. Finkelman.

The Standard Motor Vehicle Company of Philadelphia, Pennsylvania, organized with a capital stock of $25,000 during the fall of 1900 by William H. Cole, A.L. Hull and Frank C. Egan. The company leased a factory at 110-112 Erie Street in Camden, New Jersey.

The Standard Motor Vehicle Company of Pierre, South Dakota, organized during the fall of 1901 with a capital stock of $500,000 by R.M. Wiles, J.C. Edgecombe and T.P. Estes.

The Standard Novelty Company of Port Huron, Michigan, which was reported "about to manufacture gasoline carriages" in *The Horseless Age*

issue of July 19th, 1899.

The Standard Pneumatic Tool Company of Aurora, New York which announced its impending consolidation with the Standard plant in Cleveland, Ohio during the spring of 1903, the manufacture of automobiles "in the near future" being the plan.

The Standard Pneumatic Wheel Company of East Orange, New Jersey, organized with a capital stock of $200,000 early in 1907 to manufacture automobiles, engines and machinery. Incorporators were C.O.T. Geyer, F.C. Ferguson and E.M. Smith.

The Standard Vehicle Company of 26-38 Broadway in Cleveland, Ohio which was reportedly experimenting with an automobile, according to *Automobile & Motor Review* in February 1902.

The Standard Vehicle Company, which was $5 million Maine incorporation from the summer of 1910 by Clarence E. Eaton and T.L. Croteau.

The Standard Wheel Company of Terre Haute, Indiana which had been making wooden wheels for the Electric Vehicle Company, the Winton Motor Carriage Company and the Chicago Motor Vehicle Company among others when, in 1899, the firm announced that it was "considering the manufacture of automobiles." Manufacture did follow in this case, but the car was called the Overland. Refer to Overland.

STANDARD — Chicago, Illinois — (1900-1901) — The Standard Automobile Company was organized in Chicago in December of 1899 with a capital stock of $1 million to manufacture and deal in automobiles. Involved in this venture were M.C. Alford of Lexington, Kentucky; T.C.H. Vance and J. Huppaker of Louisville, Kentucky; and H.W. White and J.M. Wier of Chicago. In the fall of 1900 *The Motor Vehicle Review* reported that the company "which has built only sample vehicles, is now in the market to locate a factory." Louisville, Kentucky seemed the most promising locale, and it was subsequently reported that a $100,000 plant would be built there. The venture failed before leaving Chicago, however.

STANDARD — Philadelphia, Pennsylvania — (1900) / Camden, New Jersey — (1901) — The Standard Motor Vehicle Company was organized in Philadelphia in 1900 and almost immediately moved to Camden, New Jersey. Its product was a small 550-pound 4 1/2 hp runabout priced at $500. In January 1901 the Standard was returned to Philadelphia for two weeks of exhibition at each of the two automobile shows that were competing against each other in town at the time. "The Standard has sprung into popularity at a bound," *The Motor Age* reported in February. "Speeds of from four to twenty miles an hour are obtainable with but little odor and a minimum of noise even at the highest speed." The Standard sprang out of popularity almost as quickly. The evidence indicates the company was out of business by the end of 1901.

STANDARD — Oakland, California — (1901-1902) — The Standard Motor Vehicle Company was organized early in 1901 in San Francisco with a capital stock of $30,000 by Solomon D. Rogers, Henry A. Brown, A.E. Brooke-Ridley, Wilson H. Sigourney and Henry C. Barrow. Of that group, Henry Brown was an Oakland machinist and would serve as superintendent of the factory on Twelfth Avenue in Oakland. "The new company will take an ordinary stage coach, express wagon, buggy or any other vehicle and convert it into an automobile at a nominal expense," the *Berkeley Gazette* reported in February. What that expense was is not known, nor is how many vehicles may have been converted. The Standard Motor Vehicle Company did offer a variety of engines for the purpose, however, ranging from a small 90-pound unit for buggies up to a 1500-pound engine for heavy wagons. After 1902 this venture seems to have been kaput. Henry Brown showed up in 1903 at the Stearns Brothers Spraying Machine Company plant in Oakland, where another automotive venture was aborning.

STANDARD — Columbus, Ohio — (1902) — The Standard Automobile Company of Columbus was organized during the spring of 1902 with a capital stock of $5000 for the purpose of manufacturing "automobiles, speed gears, sparking outfits, carburetors and other supplies for automobiles." Involved in this venture were Thomas P. Carboy, Charles McCarthy and W.V. Moler. "It has sold no machines yet, but is putting up a delivery wagon run by a 5 hp steam engine," *The Automobile and Motor Review* reported that summer. "The company buys the parts and assembles them, but is making outright a two-passenger runabout. The bodies are to be made by the Columbus Body and Seat Company. Plans for a regular factory are being made." Those plans seem not to have been fulfilled.

STANDARD STEAM — Philadelphia, Pennsylvania — (1902) — During the fall of 1902 the Standard Automobile Supply Company of 1112 Betz Building in Philadelphia perfected a device called a "vacuum smoke chimney and draft regulator" that was designed to suppress the backfiring on steam automobiles. Apparently, a single automobile was built to demonstrate the device. So assured was the Standard company of its new product's success that it offered to ship its chimney to any automobile owner to be paid for on delivery and returned for a complete refund if it did not prove "a perfect panacea." The company also announced its next new "better mousetrap" would be a non-destructible burner.

STANDARD — Pittsburgh, Pennsylvania — (1902-1903) — The Standard Automobile Company succeeded the Seely Manufacturing Company in the summer of 1902 following the retirement of D.N. Seely, who sold out his interest to his partner W.N. Murray. The firm's facilities were grandiose, including a large sales emporium called "The Automobile Theatre," an extensive repair and machine shop, and a huge storage building. The new Standard Automobile Company took over the former Seely agencies for such diverse automobiles as the Locomobile, Winton, Columbia, Oldsmobile and Long Distance. Like Seely, Standard would build an occasional car to custom order for clients requesting a "special," but the firm's principal business remained dealing in the cars of other manufacturers.

1902 Standard, steam carriage, MVMA

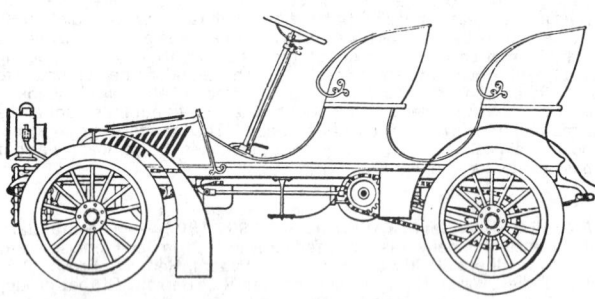

1903 Standard, NAHC

STANDARD — Chicago, Illinois — (1903) — The Standard Motor Vehicle Company was established in January 1903 by Willis Grant Murray who had previously built a car under his own name in Adrian, Michigan and by Bert M. Young, formerly of the Friedman company of Chicago. At the Chicago Automobile Show that year, they had a chassis ready which attracted considerable attention. Its four-cylinder 25 hp engine was carried longitudinally under the body of the car, as described by *Automobile Review*, with "but two connecting rods for the four cylinders, and each pair of opposing cylinders exactly opposite each other." The wheelbase was 90 inches, and the vehicle featured a three-speed sliding gear transmission and double chain drive. A honeycomb radiator was fitted, and steering was by wheel. At the show, an unfinished surrey body was shown alongside the chassis, and Murray and Young revealed at that time that they planned not "to push the manufacture and sale of pleasure automobiles so much as commercial vehicles." It does not appear they proceeded to do either very extensively.

1904 Standard, touring, NAHC

STANDARD — Jersey City, New Jersey — (1904-1905) — This Standard was the successor to the Long Distance of 1901 to 1903 and was built in the same 307 Whiton Street factory in Jersey City by the newly incorporated Standard Motor Construction Company. The new Standard was a bigger car than the former Long Distance, and was offered only as a four

on a single wheelbase chassis. (The Long Distance had been available with one-, two- or three-cylinder engines.) Probably for the sake of continuity, the car was referred to in 1904 as the Standard Tourist U.S. Long Distance, which was quite a mouthful. In 1905 it was called simply the Standard. In that year the wheelbase was increased from 95 to 109 inches, with a corresponding increase in price from $3000 to $3500. A $3900 Landaulet was added as well. All other specs — chain drive, three-speed sliding gear transmission, honeycomb radiator — remained the same. Apparently, adequate profitability was a problem for the company because during the summer of 1905, the Standard Motor Construction Company elected to retire from business. The firm sold its Selden Patent license to Edward Ringwood Hewitt, who proceeded into manufacture of the Hewitt in New York City.

1904 STANDARD
Four — 25 hp, 95" wb

	FP	5	4	3	2	1
Tourist	3000	3000	4000	6000	9500	21,000

1905 STANDARD
Four — 25 hp, 109" wb

| Touring | 3500 | 3200 | 4300 | 6500 | 11,000 | 23,000 |
| Landaulet | 3900 | 2700 | 3600 | 5300 | 8800 | 19,000 |

1916 Standard, victoria touring, HAC

STANDARD — Butler, Pennsylvania — (1914-1923) — Railway cars were the principal product of the Standard Steel Car Company of Butler during the summer of 1913 when the firm acknowledged that its new two-million-dollar factory nearing completion was for a brand-new Standard product: an automobile. The first Standard was a six which arrived early in 1914, and was joined by an eight in 1915. "Monarch of the Mountains" became a company slogan the year following, and from 1917 onward, only eights were produced. All cars were given a twenty-five-mile road test in the Butler area before distribution. Standard's biggest year was 1917 when about 2500 cars were built. Sales flagged thereafter. In January of 1921 the Standard Steel Car Company joined with a group of New York bankers with the avowed purpose of "popularizing the Standard product." Don C. McCord, whose career had begun with the American Mercedes and thereafter carried him through the Flanders Manufacturing Company, Willys-Overland and finally managership of the Bankers Commercial Security Company in New York, headed a reorganization called the Standard Motor Car Company. In 1923 the Standard Steel Car Company divested itself of any interest in the Standard automobile. Although Don McCord immediately announced continuing production of the Standard eight and a new lower-priced four-cylinder model, the four never arrived and the eight was no more by year's end. The factory in which the Standard cars had been built was sold a half decade later, and a new car called the American Austin moved in.

1914 STANDARD
Six — 38 hp, 126" wb

Touring	2100	3300	4400	6700	12,000	24,000

1915-1916 STANDARD
Eight — 29 hp, 121" wb

| Touring-7P | 1735 | 3100 | 4200 | 6300 | 10,500 | 22,000 |
| Roadster-3P | 1735 | 3000 | 4000 | 6000 | 9500 | 21,000 |

Six — 38 hp, 126" wb

Touring-5P	2100	3300	4400	6700	12,000	24,000
Runabout-3P	2100	3200	4300	6500	11,000	23,000
Limousine-7P	3600	2900	3700	5600	9100	20,000

1917 Standard, model F, eight limousine, HAC

1917 STANDARD
Model E — 8-cyl., 29.3 hp, 121" wb

Touring-5P	1900	3100	4200	6300	10,500	22,000
Roadster-4P	1850	3000	4000	6000	9500	21,000

Model F — 8-cyl., 33.8 hp, 127" wb

	FP	5	4	3	2	1
Touring-7P	2000	3700	4700	7300	13,700	26,000
Open Sedan-7P	2500	3300	4400	6700	12,000	24,000
Limousine-7P	3500	2900	3700	5600	9100	20,000
Roadster-2P	1950	3200	4300	6500	11,000	23,000

1918 Standard, model G, eight touring, HAC

1918 STANDARD
Model G — 8-cyl., 33.8 hp, 127" wb

	FP	5	4	3	2	1
Touring-7P	2450	3700	4700	7300	13,700	26,000
Limousine-7P	4000	2900	3700	5600	9100	20,000
Sedan-7P	3500	2300	3300	4600	7500	16,000
Roadster-4P	2450	3200	4300	6500	11,000	23,000
Roadster-2P	2450	3300	4400	6700	12,000	24,000
Coupe-3P	3500	2500	3500	5000	8500	18,000

1919 Standard, model G, touring, HAC

1919 STANDARD
Model G — 8-cyl., 33.8 hp, 127" wb

	FP	5	4	3	2	1
Touring-7P	2750	3900	4800	7700	14,300	27,000
Roadster-4P	2750	3300	4400	6700	12,000	24,000
Roadster-2P	2750	3500	4500	7000	13,000	25,000
Coupe-4P	3800	2700	3600	5300	8800	19,000
Sedan-7P	3800	2400	3400	4800	8000	17,000
Limousine-7P	4000	3100	4200	6300	10,500	22,000

1920 Standard, model I, touring, HAC

1920 STANDARD
Model I — 8-cyl., 70 hp, 127" wb

	FP	5	4	3	2	1
Roadster-2P	3000	4700	6100	9900	19,000	33,000
Roadster-4P	3000	4500	5800	9500	18,000	32,000
Touring-7P	3000	5000	6500	11,000	22,000	35,000
Sedan-7P	4100	2900	3700	5600	9100	20,000
Coupe-4P	4200	3100	4200	6300	10,500	22,000
Limousine-7P	4300	3500	4500	7000	13,000	25,000

1921 STANDARD
Model I — 8-cyl., 70 hp, 127" wb

	FP	5	4	3	2	1
Roadster-2P	—	4700	6100	9900	19,000	33,000
Speedster-4P	—	5000	6500	11,000	22,000	35,000
Touring-7P	—	4900	6300	10,300	21,000	34,000
Sedan-7P	—	2900	3700	5600	9100	20,000
Coupe-4P	—	3100	4200	6300	10,500	22,000
Limousine-7P	—	3500	4500	7000	13,000	25,000

1921 Standard, model I, vestibule sedan, HAC

1922 Standard, model II, touring, HAC

1922-1923 STANDARD
Model II — 8-cyl., 70 hp, 127" wb

	FP	5	4	3	2	1
Touring-7P	3400	5000	6500	11,000	22,000	35,000
Sport-4P	3400	5200	6800	11,300	23,000	36,000
Roadster-2P	3400	4900	6300	10,300	21,000	34,000
Coupe-4P	4500	3100	4200	6300	10,500	22,000
Sedanette-4P	4500	2900	3700	5600	9100	20,000
Sedan-7P	4800	3000	4000	6000	9500	21,000
Vestibule Sedan-7P	5000	3300	4400	6700	12,000	24,000

1914 Standard, cyclecar roadster, WLB

STANDARD — Chicago, Illinois — (1914) — "The Peer of Them All," the Standard Engineering Company said. "Simple — No Freak Construction — Powerful." In January of 1914 the Standard Cyclecar was powered by a 9/13 hp vee twin and its price was $375. In April of 1914 the car was powered by a 10/16 hp four and its price had risen to $425. Otherwise the Standard Cyclecar remained the same for the whole of its short life. The wheelbase was 100 inches, the tread 36, and seating in the two-passenger roadster was side-by-side. Both the frame and the body were steel; friction transmission was featured as was single chain ("under the car where it cannot be seen") drive to the rear axle. Self-starter and electric lights were standard, which was commendable, but the Standard was no more after 1914. Otto G. Knecht, Harry Hammill and Ernest Saunders had been the men behind its building.

STANDARD ELECTRIC — Jackson, Michigan — (1911-1915) — Although the firm's name was the Standard Electric Car Company, the firm's product was occasionally spelled "Electrique," strictly for its snob value. The Standard Electric was built in Jackson in the former factory of the Lewis Spring and Axle Company, and it was produced under the direction of Clem F. Krueger, who had previously toiled for seven years with the Studebaker Brothers in South Bend. The Standard Electric Car Company was well named, since advertising and promotion placed heavy emphasis upon the fact that there was nothing unusual at all about the car. Strict adher-

1912 Standard Electric, coupe, WLB

ence to prevailing electric vehicle practice was religiously followed. The most popular Standard Electric was a coupe, although a runabout was occasionally offered. One hundred ten miles between charges was a widely advertised Standard Electric feature; the car's top speed of 20 mph was not. The vehicle was steered by a tiller on the left side. In November 1913, a fresh infusion of capital resulted in reorganization to the Standard Car Manufacturing Company. A group of disgruntled stockholders attempted to petition the firm into receivership following this, but the Standard Company countered that its financial health was fine and that the suit had been brought to "get back at officials." The receivership petition was denied. What these same stockholders said two years later, in November of 1915, when the Standard Car Manufacturing Company discontinued its product and sold its factory to Benjamin Briscoe (who moved in to build the Argo cyclecar) was not recorded.

1911-1912 STANDARD ELECTRIC
Model M Coupe-4P (91" wb)

	FP	5	4	3	2	1
Model M Coupe-4P	1850	1600	2700	3800	5800	12,000
1913 STANDARD ELECTRIC						
Model M Coupe-4P (96" wb)						
Model M Coupe-4P	1885	1800	2800	4000	6200	13,000
Model M Runabout-2P (91" wb)						
Model M Rbt.-2P	1785	2000	3000	4200	6500	14,000
Model L Coupe-2P (90" wb)						
Model L Coupe-2P	1685	1600	2700	3800	5800	12,000
1914-1915 STANDARD ELECTRIC						
Model M Roadster-2P (96" wb)						
Model M Rdstr.-2P	1785	1800	2800	4000	6200	13,000
Model M Coupe-3P (96" wb)						
Model M Coupe-3P	1900	1600	2700	3800	5800	12,000

1910 Standard, G.E., touring, WLB

STANDARD G.E. — Philadelphia, Pennsylvania — (1909-1910) — The Standard Gas Electric Power Company was incorporated in Philadelphia in September of 1909 for manufacture of both a gas-electric car and truck. Samuel S. Eveland, president of the Standard Roller Bearing Company, spearheaded this venture. Powered by a four-cylinder 28 hp engine, the Standard G.E. was offered as both a touring ($1700) and a limousine ($1750) on a 114-inch wheelbase chassis. Shaft drive was featured, but the car's most interesting aspects were its use of an electric starter, predating Cadillac by two seasons, and its three-speed sliding gear transmission, the changes for which were effected by push buttons instead of a lever, an idea whose time would not come again for a half century. Despite these advanced features, or perhaps because they did not work well in practice, this Standard was quickly stalled in the marketplace.

STANDARD SIX — St. Louis, Missouri — (1910)/Wabash, Indiana — (1910-1911) — In August of 1909 the St. Louis Car Company announced its forthcoming manufacture of a six-cylinder automobile of entirely American design. For the three years past, the famed railway-car firm had been building the French Mors car under license as the American Mors. The American Mors had been preceded in turn by the Kobush, and George J. Kobusch who had been in charge of American Mors activity remained in charge of the factory producing the new Standard Six. It was a 50 hp car on a 124-inch wheelbase chassis which featured a three-speed selective sliding gear transmission and shaft drive. A uniform $3000 price bought a touring car, miniature tonneau and roadster; the limousine model was a thousand dollars more. In February of 1910 manufacture of the Standard

1330

1911 Standard Six, touring, NAHC

Six was transferred from St. Louis to the company's subsidiary plant in Wabash, Indiana. The sponsoring organization became known as the Standard Automobile Company of America at that time. Some financial difficulties were encountered in Indiana, and production was discontinued later in 1910. In February 1911 George Kobusch was booted out, and John I. Beggs arrived from Missouri to take over. Production was reinstated, but for a short time only. A decade later the St. Louis Car Company had another short sojourn in the automobile industry with the Skelton, and meanwhile John Beggs had returned to his native Kansas City to ultimately talk his wagon-building family into the automobile industry too.

STANDARD STEAM — The first few cars produced in 1900 by the Boston Automobile Company of Bar Harbor, Maine were referred to as Standards. Ultimately, Bar Harbor was chosen as the name for the company's product. Refer to Bar Harbor.

Both Standard Steam and Scott-Newcomb were among the designations announced for the steam car built in St. Louis, Missouri in 1920-1921. Refer to Scott-Newcomb.

The Standard Auto-Vehicle Company of Winchester, Massachusetts has been indicated on various car rosters as the producer of a steam car at the turn of the century. The firm is known to have been incorporated in the state of New Jersey with a capital stock of $250,000 during the fall of 1900, but manufacture is doubted.

The Standard Steam Automobile Company was organized in Boston, Massachusetts during the summer of 1906 with a capital stock of $40,000 for the manufacture of motor carriages. Incorporators were George Watson, H.H. Fuller and L.M. Campbell. Manufacture is doubted.

STANDARD TOURIST — This was the designation for 1904 only of the Standard built in Jersey City, New Jersey by the Standard Motor Construction Company. Refer to Standard.

1925 Standish, sedan, KM

STANDISH — Framingham, Massachusetts — (1924-1925) — The Standish was built by the Luxor Cab Manufacturing Company, which was among the varied enterprises of M.P. Moller, builder of the Crawford and Dagmar cars in Hagerstown, Maryland. The discovery of King Tut's tomb in Egypt had led to the naming of the taxi; for its standard passenger car Luxor went Puritan, selecting the name of the man who had told John Alden to speak for himself in Colonial America. Like the Luxor, the Standish was a luxury vehicle, with brass substituting for nickel trim. While the Luxor was powered by a Buda four, the Standish's engine was a Continental six. Prices were slated to begin at $2595 for closed models, $2100 for open. Although the first few Luxors were manufactured in Moller's factory in Hagerstown, no Standish was built until after operations moved to the plant of the R.H. Long Motor Car Company (makers of the Bay State) in Framingham, Massachusetts during the summer of 1924. A Standish sedan is known to have been completed, and possibly one open car, but that was the extent of production. The pointed radiator of the Standish was used for a new truck called the Elysee, yet another Moller enterprise, which was introduced in 1926.

STANFORD — Palo Alto, California — (1908) — In February 1908 ten men were at work in a garage at 511 Alma Street in Palo Alto putting together pilot models of a two-cylinder touring car which was to be put into production by the Stanford Automobile and Manufacturing Company, a new venture organized with a capital stock of $75,000 by H.W. Hooper, J.E. Sloan, Frank Sloan and F.S. Hutchins. Hooper and Hutchins were the designers of the car, some features of which they had patented. Apparently, this venture fizzled before any sustained manufacture ever got underway.

STANLEY — The Stanley Motor Company was organized in Liberty, Indiana during the fall of 1913 with a capital stock of $5000 to manufacture and sell automobiles. Incorporators were R.C. Connor, W.F. Stanley and C.C. Connor. Manufacture is doubted.

The Stanley Power Wagon Company was organized in Detroit, Michigan during the summer of 1910 with a capital stock of $10,000 to manufacture and deal in automobiles and accessories. Incorporators were John C. Shaw, H.A. Douglas, F.R. Hathaway, G.G. Scranton and Joseph G. Hamblen. Manufacture is doubted.

1897 Stanley runabout (with Stanley brothers aboard), HAC

STANLEY STEAM — **Watertown, Massachusetts** — **(1897-1899) / Lawrence, Massachusetts** — **(1899-1901) / Newton, Massachusetts** — **(1901-1927)** — Francis E. and Freeland O. Stanley were identical twins who looked rather like the Smith brothers on the cough drop box. They produced the most famous steam car in the world. Their first effort was completed in 1897, though they had tried and failed in a steam car project a decade earlier in Lewiston, Maine. In 1888 for business reasons they moved their Stanley Dry Plate Company (which produced photographic equipment) to the Boston area, settling in Newton and establishing their factory in nearby Watertown. A demonstration of the Field steam car had been the impetus behind their 1887 try at building a steamer in Lewiston. In 1896 in Boston the brothers saw the steam carriage built by George Whitney, and decided to try again, believing they could do better. By the spring of 1898 they had completed three light steam carriages, one of which was sold to a man from Boston for $600. That fall another of the cars was taken to Charles River Park, where it put up a speed of 27.4 mph in a short sprint, and placed third behind a De Dion tricycle and the Whitney steamer in a two-mile demonstration run. But most impressive was the Stanley's performance in the 80-foot incline contest, the final event of the day. All previous competitors had failed to make it to the top of the specially-constructed ramp, the Whitney having chuffed furiously to 76 feet 8 inches, the best performance thus far. The Stanley was the last to try. Not only did F.E. Stanley breeze to the top, for a precarious moment it appeared his car might teeter over it. There was amazement all around, and within two weeks the Stanleys had orders for over 200 cars. In a building next to their dry plate plant in Watertown, they set themselves up in business, procuring parts for an initial batch of 100 steamers. With production ongoing, the Stanley factory was visited early in 1899 by publisher John Brisben Walker, an automobile enthusiast who was anxious to get into the business. He offered to buy the Stanleys out. The brothers had been having some production problems, though were reluctant to give up, deciding finally to ask for a figure so high that Walker probably wouldn't

1906 Stanley, model EX, runabout, HAC

accept it. But Walker did; the Stanleys' figure was $250,000; their investment in the venture thus far had been $20,000. To come up with the purchase price, Walker allied himself with Amzi Lorenzo Barber, with whom he soon quarreled, the partners going their separate ways to produce the Stanley-designed steamer as the Locomobile and the Mobile respectively. Meanwhile, the Stanley brothers having put themselves out of the steam car business decided they wanted back in. Continuing experimentation, they developed a new design — with non-condensing engine driving directly on the rear axle and boiler mounted up front — and began production again in the spring of 1901 in a new factory in Newton, formally organizing as the Stanley Motor Carriage Company early in 1902. In addition to the usual difficulties attending any new business, the Stanleys initially had to contend with a lawsuit instigated by George Whitney for patent infringement and some contractural problems with Barber and Walker, but these were worked out. Whitney had been out of production since the turn of the century, the Mobile was discontinued in 1903, and Locomobile converted over to gasoline car manufacture that year. The Stanley steamed on. By 1906 its familiar coffin-like nose (concealing the boiler) had evolved, and wheel steering replaced the former tiller. At Daytona Beach that year, Fred Marriott, who headed the company repair department, drove the streamlined Stanley Woggle-Bug racer at 127.66 mph for the flying measure mile — and a world's land speed record. In an attempt to break his own record the year following, Marriott crashed at over 150 mph; he survived, but the Woggle-Bug was destroyed. Production Stanleys were raced as well, by Marriott, Louis Ross, F.E. Stanley himself and others, most particularly the Gentleman's Speedy Roadster (produced from 1906-1908) which following its 68.1 mph performance in a 15-mile handicap race at Ormond was advertised as the "Fastest Stock Car in the World." Motor sport participation was phased out in 1909. The final chapter for the Stanley began to be written in 1912, with the introduction by Cadillac of the self-starter, the signal event which irrevocably tipped the scales in the gasoline car's favor. Although faster in acceleration, a steamer was slower to start, and the warm-up period from cold became a detrimental marketing factor once a gasoline car could be started without the inconvenience of cranking. By now the White Company, Stanley's principal rival in the steam car field, had converted over to gasoline car production exclusively. Interestingly, though the Stanley was by far the more famous, the White steamer outsold it; 9122 cars by 1911 vis-a-vis the Stanley's 5200 for the same period. The White was extensively promoted, however; the Stanley brothers didn't believe in advertising. Conservatism was a Stanley byword — for years the cars had neither a flash boiler (which made for even slower starts than other steam cars) nor a condenser (which made for frequent water replenishment). In the wake of the self-starter, however, Stanleys became more modern. Cars for 1913 were introduced with electric lights, 1915 brought steel frames replacing the former wood. Commercial vehicle production, which had begun in 1909, ended in 1916. By 1917, with sales declining, a modest advertising campaign was launched, which the Stanley brothers probably abhorred, but they were in their late sixties by now and retired from active management of the company later that year. (F.E. Stanley died in an automobile accident in 1918.) The Stanley's rounded front end evolved into a slight vee by 1915, a sharp vee in 1918; by 1920 Stanleys had a flat radiator and from the outside resembled a gasoline car completely, even to radiator fill cap. But underneath the boiler was still up front, and the engine still driving direct on the rear axle. By 1923 Stanley was in receivership, its plant and assets sold early the following year for $572,204 to the Steam Vehicle Corporation of America, which continued Stanley production in Newton and announced grand plans for steam commercial vehicle production elsewhere. For 1925 Stanleys were made smaller, priced lower and offered with balloon tires and hydraulic four-wheel brakes. The car simply faded away after that. A liquidation sale was held in 1929. In the mid-Thirties there was an attempt to reorganize the firm as Stanley Steam Motor Corporation, with headquarters in Chicago, for the manufacture of a rear-engined steam bus. That effort died aborning. During this same period, in Massachusetts, the Stanley lived on awhile in the American Steam Car.

1901 STANLEY
Model A — 2-cyl., 6 1/2 hp, 78″ wb

	FP	5	4	3	2	1
Runabout	—	3000	4000	6000	9500	21,000

1902 STANLEY
Model B — 2-cyl., 6 1/2 hp, 78″ wb

Runabout	—	3000	4000	6000	9500	21,000

1903 Stanley, model C, stick-seat runabout, HAC

1903 STANLEY
Model C — 2-cyl., 6 1/2 hp, 78″ wb

Runabout	—	3000	4000	6000	9500	21,000

1904 STANLEY
Model C — 2-cyl., 6 1/2 hp, 78″ wb

Runabout. Panel Seat	—	3000	4000	6000	9500	21,000

Model BX — 2-cyl., 8 hp, 78" wb

	FP	5	4	3	2	1
Runabout, Spindle Seat	—	3000	4000	6000	9500	21,000
Model CX — 2-cyl., 8 hp, 78" wb						
Runabout, Panel Seat	—	3000	4000	6000	9500	21,000

1905 Stanley, model BX, runabout, HAC

1905 STANLEY

	FP	5	4	3	2	1
Model BX — 2-cyl., 8 hp, 78" wb						
Runabout, Spindle Seat	700	3000	4000	6000	9500	21,000
Model CX — 2-cyl., 8 hp, 78" wb						
Runabout, Panel Seat	725	3000	4000	6000	9500	21,000
Model DX — 2-cyl., 10 hp, 84" wb						
Surrey	1000	3100	4200	6300	10,500	22,000
Model E — 2-cyl., 10 hp, 84" wb						
Runabout	850	3100	4200	6300	10,500	22,000
Model F — 2-cyl., 20 hp, 98" wb						
Touring, Side Entrance	—	3300	4400	6700	12,000	24,000
Model G — 2-cyl., 10 hp, 78" wb						
Speedster	700	4000	5000	8000	15,000	28,000

1906 STANLEY

	FP	5	4	3	2	1
Model DX — 2-cyl., 10 hp, 90" wb						
Surrey	1000	3300	4400	6700	12,000	24,000
Model EX — 2-cyl., 10 hp, 90" wb						
Runabout	850	3500	4500	7000	13,000	25,000
Model F — 2-cyl., 20 hp, 100" wb						
Touring	1500	3900	4800	7700	14,300	27,000
Model H — 2-cyl., 20 hp, 100" wb						
Gentleman's Speedy Rds.	1000	4000	5000	8000	15,000	28,000

1907 Stanley, model H, gentleman's speedy roadster, HAC

1907 STANLEY

	FP	5	4	3	2	1
Model EX — 2-cyl., 10 hp, 90" wb						
Roadster-2/4P	850	3100	4200	6300	10,500	22,000
Model F — 2-cyl., 20 hp, 100" wb						
Touring-5P	1500	3300	4400	6700	12,000	24,000
Model H 4/5 — 2-cyl., 100" wb						
Gentleman's Speedy Rds.	1350	4000	5000	8000	15,000	28,000
Model K — 2-cyl., 25 hp, 100" wb						
Semi-Racer	1800	4300	5400	8700	16,500	30,000
Model J — 2-cyl., 20 hp, 100" wb						
Limousine	2500	3700	4700	7300	13,700	26,000
Model H — 2-cyl., 20 hp, 100" wb						
Fishtail Runabout-2P	1200	3900	4800	7700	14,300	27,000
Model CX — 2-cyl., 10 hp, 78" wb						
Doctor's Runabout-2/4P	800	3000	4000	6000	9500	21,000

1908 STANLEY

	FP	5	4	3	2	1
Model EX — 2-cyl., 10 hp, 90" wb						
Runabout-2/4P	850	3700	4700	7300	13,700	26,000
Model H 4/5 — 2-cyl., 20 hp, 100" wb						
Gentleman's Speedy Rds.	1350	4400	5600	9200	17,300	31,000
Model F — 2-cyl., 20 hp, 100" wb						
Touring	1500	4200	5200	8400	15,700	29,000
Model J — 2-cyl., 20 hp, 100" wb						
Limousine	2500	4000	5000	8000	15,000	28,000
Model K — 2-cyl., 25 hp, 100" wb						
Semi-Racer	1800	4700	6100	9900	19,000	33,000
Model M — 2-cyl., 30 hp, 114" wb						
Touring	2000	4500	5800	9500	18,000	32,000

1908 Stanley, model K, semi-racer, HAC

1909 Stanley, model Z, mountain wagon, HAC

1909 STANLEY
Model E2 — 2-cyl., 10 hp, 110" wb

	FP	5	4	3	2	1
Runabout-2/4P	850	3700	4700	7300	13,700	26,000
Model R — 2-cyl., 20 hp, 112" wb						
Roadster	—	4000	5000	8000	15,000	28,000
Model M — 2-cyl., 30 hp, 114" wb						
Touring	2000	4400	5600	9200	17,300	31,000
Model Z — 2-cyl., 30 hp, 118" wb						
Mountain Wagon-5P	2000	4300	5400	8700	16,500	30,000

1910 Stanley, model 60, runabout, HAC

1910 STANLEY

	FP	5	4	3	2	1
Model 60 — 2-cyl., 10 hp, 104" wb						
Runabout	850	4000	5000	8000	15,000	28,000
Toy Tonneau	1150	4300	5400	8700	16,500	30,000
Model U — 2-cyl., 20 hp, 112" wb						
Touring	1500	4500	5800	9500	18,000	32,000
Model 72 — 2-cyl., 20 hp, 115" wb						
Roadster	—	4400	5600	9200	17,300	31,000
Model 61 — 2-cyl., 10 hp, 104" wb						
Runabout	—	4200	5200	8400	15,700	29,000

1911 Stanley Steamer, model 62, runabout, OCW

1911 STANLEY
Model 62 — 2-cyl., 10 hp, 104" wb

	FP	5	4	3	2	1
Runabout	1000	4200	5200	8400	15,700	29,000
Model 63 — 2-cyl., 10 hp, 104" wb						
Toy Tonneau	1125	4300	5400	8700	16,500	30,000
Model 70 — 2-cyl., 20 hp, 115" wb						
Touring	1500	4700	6100	9900	19,000	33,000
Model 71 — 2-cyl., 20 hp, 115" wb						
Toy Tonneau	1400	4500	5800	9500	18,000	32,000
Model 72 — 2-cyl., 20 hp, 115" wb						
Roadster	—	4400	5600	9200	17,300	31,000
Model 86 — 2-cyl., 30 hp, 120" wb						
Mountain Wagon-9P	—	4300	5400	8700	16,500	30,000

1912 Stanley, model 62, rumble seat runabout, HAC

1912 STANLEY
Model 62 — 2-cyl., 10 hp, 104" wb

	FP	5	4	3	2	1
Runabout-2P	1000	4700	6100	9900	19,000	33,000
Model 63 — 2-cyl., 10 hp, 104" wb						
Toy Tonneau-4P	1175	4900	6300	10,300	21,000	34,000
Model 73 — 2-cyl., 20 hp, 120" wb						
Touring-5P	1660	5000	6500	11,000	22,000	35,000
Model 74 — 2-cyl., 20 hp, 120" wb						
Touring-4P	1600	4900	6300	10,300	21,000	34,000
Model 75 — 2-cyl., 20 hp, 115" wb						
Roadster	1600	4700	6100	9900	19,000	33,000
Model 87 — 2-cyl., 30 hp, 134" wb						
Touring-7P	2500	5200	6800	11,300	23,000	36,000
Model 88 — 2-cyl., 30 hp, 136" wb						
Mountain Wagon-12P	2500	4300	5400	8700	16,500	30,000

1913 Stanley, model 78, roadster, HAC

1913 STANLEY
Model 64 — 2-cyl., 10 hp, 112" wb

	FP	5	4	3	2	1
Roadster	1200	4700	6100	19,000	33,000	
Model 65 — 2-cyl., 10 hp, 112" wb						
Runabout-4P	1300	4900	6300	10,300	21,000	34,000
Model 76 — 2-cyl., 20 hp, 120" wb						
Touring-5P	1700	5000	6500	11,000	22,000	35,000
Model 77 — 2-cyl., 20 hp, 120" wb						
Touring-4P	1700	4900	6300	10,300	21,000	34,000
Model 78 — 2-cyl., 20 hp, 120" wb						
Roadster-4P	1650	5000	6500	11,000	22,000	35,000
Model 809 — 2-cyl., 30 hp, 134" wb						
Touring	2500	5300	7000	11,500	24,000	37,000
Model 810 — 2-cyl., 30 hp, 136" wb						
Mountain Wagon-12P	2300	5200	6800	11,300	23,000	36,000

1914 Stanley, model 712, roadster, HAC

1914 STANLEY
Model 606 — 2-cyl., 10 hp, 112" wb

	FP	5	4	3	2	1
Runabout-2P	1200	4700	6100	9900	19,000	33,000
Model 607 — 2-cyl., 10 hp, 112" wb						
Touring-4P	1300	5000	6500	11,000	22,000	35,000
Model 710 — 2-cyl., 20 hp, 120" wb						
Touring-5P	1700	5200	6800	11,300	23,000	36,000
Model 712 — 2-cyl., 20 hp, 115" wb						
Roadster-2P	1650	5300	7000	11,500	24,000	37,000
Model 811 — 2-cyl., 30 hp, 134" wb						
Touring-7P	2500	5400	7300	11,800	25,000	38,000
Model 812 — 2-cyl., 30 hp, 136" wb						
Mountain Wagon-12P	2300	5200	6800	11,300	23,000	36,000

1915 Stanley, model 720, touring, HAC

1915 STANLEY
Model 720 — 2-cyl., 20 hp, 120" wb

	FP	5	4	3	2	1
Touring-5P	1700	4900	6300	10,300	21,000	34,000
Model 722 — 2-cyl., 20 hp, 120" wb						
Roadster-2P	1650	4700	6100	9900	19,000	33,000
Model 723 — 2-cyl., 20 hp, 120" wb						
Touring-5P	1975	5000	6500	11,000	22,000	35,000

1916 Stanley, model 726, roadster, HAC

1333

1916 STANLEY
Model 725 — 2-cyl., 20 hp, 130" wb

	FP	5	4	3	2	1
Touring-5P	1975	4900	6300	10,300	21,000	34,000
Model 726 — 2-cyl., 20 hp, 130" wb						
Roadster-3P	1925	4700	6100	9900	19,000	33,000
Model 825 — 2-cyl., 30 hp, 136" wb						
Mountain Wagon-12P	—	5000	6500	11,000	22,000	35,000

1917 Stanley, model 728, touring, HAC

1917 STANLEY
Model 728 — 2-cyl., 20 hp, 130" wb

Touring-5P	1975	5000	6500	11,000	22,000	35,000
Model 729 — 2-cyl., 20 hp, 130" wb						
Touring-3P	—	4700	6100	9900	19,000	33,000
Model 730 — 2-cyl., 20 hp, 130" wb						
Roadster-3P	1925	4900	6300	10,300	21,000	34,000
Model 731 — 2-cyl., 20 hp, 130" wb						
Touring-7P	2075	5300	7000	11,500	24,000	37,000
Sedan-5P	—	3700	4700	7300	13,700	26,000

1918 STANLEY
Model 735 — 2-cyl., 20 hp, 130" wb

Touring-4P	2200	4700	6100	9900	19,000	33,000
Model 736 — 2-cyl., 20 hp, 130" wb						
Touring-7P	2300	5300	7000	11,500	24,000	37,000
Model 730 — 2-cyl., 20 hp, 130" wb						
Sedan-5P	—	3700	4700	7300	13,700	26,000

1919 Stanley, model 735B, touring, HAC

1919 STANLEY
Model 735A — 2-cyl., 20 hp, 130" wb

Touring-4P	3425	4900	6300	10,300	21,000	34,000
Model 735B — 2-cyl., 20 hp, 130" wb						
Touring-7P	3450	5400	7300	11,800	25,000	38,000
Model 735D — 2-cyl., 20 hp, 130" wb						
Sedan-5P	5100	4200	5200	8400	15,700	29,000
Coupe-4P	5100	4400	5600	9200	17,300	31,000

1920 Stanley, model 735D, sedan, HAC

1920 STANLEY
Model 735A — 2-cyl., 20 hp. 130" wb

	FP	5	4	3	2	1
Touring-5P	4275	5200	6800	11,300	23,000	36,000
Model 735B — 2-cyl., 20 hp, 130" wb						
Touring-7P	4275	5400	7300	11,800	25,000	38,000
Model 735C — 2-cyl., 20 hp, 130" wb						
Coupe-4P	5925	4400	5600	9200	17,300	31,000
Model 735D — 2-cyl., 20 hp, 130" wb						
Sedan-7P	6100	4200	5200	8400	15,700	29,000

1921 Stanley Steamer, opera coupe, OCW

1921 STANLEY
Model 735A — 2-cyl., 20 hp, 130" wb

Touring-4P	3950	4900	6300	10,300	21,000	34,000
Model 735B — 2-cyl., 20 hp, 130" wb						
Touring-7P	—	5400	7300	11,800	25,000	38,000
Model 735C — 2-cyl., 20 hp, 130" wb						
Coupe-4P	—	4400	5600	9200	17,300	31,000
Model 735D — 2-cyl., 20 hp, 130" wb						
Sedan-7P	—	4200	5200	8400	15,700	29,000

1922 Stanley, model 740, touring, HAC

1922 STANLEY
Series 735 — 2-cyl., 20 hp, 130" wb

Touring-4P	2750	5000	6500	11,000	22,000	35,000
Touring-7P	—	5500	7500	12,000	26,000	39,000
Coupe-4P	—	4500	5800	9500	18,000	32,000
Sedan-7P	—	4300	5400	8700	16,500	30,000
Roadster-2P	—	5200	6800	11,300	23,000	36,000
Series 740 — 2-cyl., 20 hp, 130" wb						
Touring-7P	—	5800	8000	12,500	28,000	40,000
Sedan-7P	—	4400	5600	9200	17,300	31,000
Roadster-2P	—	5300	7000	11,500	24,000	37,000
Brougham-4P	—	4200	5200	8400	15,700	29,000

1923 Stanley, model 740, sedan, HAC

1923 STANLEY
Series 740 — 2-cyl., 20 hp, 130" wb

	FP	5	4	3	2	1
Touring-5P	2750	5200	6800	11,300	23,000	36,000
Touring-7P	2750	5900	8300	12,800	29,000	41,000
Roadster-2P	2750	5300	7000	11,500	24,000	37,000
Brougham-4P	3950	4300	5400	8700	16,500	30,000
Sedan-7P	3985	4400	5600	9200	17,300	31,000
Utility Sedan-5P	—	4200	5200	8400	15,700	29,000

1924 Stanley, model 740, sedan, HAC

1924 STANLEY
Series 740 — 2-cyl., 20 hp, 130" wb

	FP	5	4	3	2	1
Touring-4/5P	2750	5200	6800	11,300	23,000	36,000
Roadster	—	5300	7000	11,500	24,000	37,000
Touring-7P	—	5900	8300	12,800	29,000	41,000
Sedan-7P	—	4400	5600	9200	17,300	31,000
Utility Sedan-5P	—	4300	5400	8700	16,500	30,000

1925 STANLEY
Model 252-V — 2-cyl., 20 hp, 122" wb

	FP	5	4	3	2	1
Touring-5P	2500	5500	7500	12,000	26,000	39,000
Sedan-5P	—	4300	5400	8700	16,500	30,000

1926 STANLEY
Model 262 — 2-cyl., 20 hp, 122" wb

	FP	5	4	3	2	1
Touring-5P	2500	5500	7500	12,000	26,000	39,000

1927 STANLEY
Model 770 — 2-cyl., 20 hp, 122" wb

	FP	5	4	3	2	1
Touring-5P	2960	5800	8000	12,500	28,000	40,000

1906 Stanley Steam Car, touring, HS

STANLEY STEAM CAR — Lynn, Massachusetts — (1906) — At the turn of the century, Arthur M. Stanley was employed in the Lynn plant of General Electric as foreman in charge of the experimental steam cars built there. Not surprisingly, a few years later he decided to build a steamer of his own. It was completed by the early summer of 1906, and Stanley was soon driving it along Revere Beach Boulevard at speeds up to 70 mph, he said, and for the first of the over 160,000 miles he would eventually put on the car. Its engine developed approximately 40 hp, the boiler was a flash type, and the car was apparently more fuel and water efficient than the White or the other Stanley being manufactured elsewhere in Massachusetts. Puportedly, Stanley had wanted to add such accessories to his car as a plate-glass windshield, front doors and a generator/battery for electric lights, but his associates at GE talked him out of it.

STANLEY — Mooreland, Indiana — (1907-1908)/Troy, Ohio — (1909-1910) — During the fall of 1905, several years before Henry Ford began talking widely about his car for the common man, James Stanley of Mooreland publicly announced his intention to manufacture a car for the unfortunate. *The Motor World* regarded his announcement with sarcastic suspicion: "Quite unselfish in his ambitions, Mr. Stanley is endeavoring to form a stock company to supply the poorer people with automobiles at $350 per — or less. No doubt the most worthy of the poor will be allowed to purchase a block of the stock." Unlike many dubious automotive ventures of that era, however, the Stanley Automobile Company did indeed produce a car, although it was 1907 before it arrived and its price tag by that time had risen to $575. The Stanley was powered by a two-cylinder water-cooled 20 hp engine fitted into an 87-inch wheelbase chassis which featured a planetary transmission and chain drive. (A shaft drive car was promised, but that one never arrived.) In the late fall of 1908, Stanley announced that he had joined forces with the Troy Buggy Company of Troy, Ohio and that he was moving his operation there to continue as the Troy Auto & Buggy Company. Apparently some production did follow in Troy beginning in January 1909, though the car's name remained the Stanley — and it wasn't produced for long. By February of 1910 the company's assets had been bought by an Anderson (Indiana) firm which manufactured wire fences and was considering getting into the automobile business. The Anderson company thought better of it before producing a single car. The number of Stanleys produced in both Mooreland and Troy was minimal.

STANLEY — Detroit, Michigan — (1910-1911) — The Stanley Motor Car Company of Detroit was headed by G.S. Murdock (president), A.A. Savois (secretary-treasurer) and F.E. Gibbard (general manager). This trio occupied temporary quarters at 318 Howard Street, and in November of 1910 announced forthcoming production of the Stanley "30" and Stanley "40" to sell for $1450 and $2000 respectively. A prototype of each of these cars had been built already, and a manufacturing schedule of a car a day had been set. Whether that schedule was ever put into effect is not known. The Stanley Motor Car Company disappeared soon thereafter. What production had followed was minimal.

STANLEY-WHITNEY — For a short time in 1899, the steam car built in Lawrence, Massachusetts by Frank J. Stanley under Whitney patent was known as the Stanley-Whitney. Later that year the car's name was changed to McKay. Refer to McKay.

STANTON — The Stanton Manufacturing Company was organized in Rochelle Park, New Jersey during the summer of 1905 with a capital stock of $100,000 for the manufacture of automobiles and parts. Incorporators were A.C. Stanton, Maxwell K. Willoughby and Frank Southmayd. Manufacture of a car is doubted.

1901 Stanton, steam runabout, HAC

STANTON STEAM — Waltham, Massachusetts — (1900-1901) — The Stanton Manufacturing Company of Waltham put itself into the steam car producing business with a minimum of fuss by simply buying out the automobile department of the New England Motor Carriage Company. The New England firm had recently taken up manufacture of the Comet bicycle and had elected to concentrate its energies on two-wheelers. The New England steam runabout was revised into the Stanton, with the strengthening of the running gear being the principal improvement. A surrey model was added as well. The new Stanton was built alongside the Comet bicycle in the New England factory in Waltham. It does not appear to have been produced beyond 1901.

1920 Stanwood, Six, touring, WLB

STANWOOD — St. Louis, Missouri — (1920-1922) — Fred H. Berger was the chief engineer of the Stanwood Motor Car Company, and he had an easy job coming up with the product. The Stanwood was an assembled car powered by a Continental six-cylinder engine and using standard components throughout (Grant-Lees transmission, Borg & Beck clutch, et cetera). Other members of Stanwood officialdom included N.D. Thompson, Jr. as president, L.W. Cranshaw as secretary, Leslie H. Thompson as treasurer, John D. Lazar as production manager, Norman Daut as advertising manager. If there was a Stanwood involved in Stanwood, he appears to have been a silent partner. The Stanwood company was out of business sometime during 1922. Its factory building remains as a warehouse.

1920 STANWOOD
Model A-20 — 6-cyl., 55 hp, 118" wb

	FP	5	4	3	2	1
Touring-5P	2050	4200	5200	8400	15,700	29,000

1921 STANWOOD
Model A-21 — 6-cyl., 55 hp, 118" wb

	FP	5	4	3	2	1
Touring-5P	2050	4200	5200	8400	15,700	29,000

1922 STANWOOD
Model A-22 — 6-cyl., 55 hp, 118" wb

	FP	5	4	3	2	1
Touring-5P	1765	4300	5400	8700	16,500	30,000
Roadster-3P	1765	4200	5200	8400	15,700	29,000
Sedan-4P	2750	3000	4000	6000	9500	21,000

STAPLES — Maryville, Missouri — (1899-1900) — By the fall of 1899, Willis Jay Staples of 105 West Main Street in Maryville had put a full 500 miles on the car he had completed earlier in the year. It was a gasoline-powered buggy which used a belt for the transmission of power from the single-cylinder 4 hp engine to the countershaft, with a chain running thence to the differential. Wooden wheels — 36 inches in the rear, 32 inches in front — were shod with 1-1/4 inch solid rubber tires. The maximum speed of the Staples was 12 mph. Willis Staples seems to have built a few more of these cars for sale into the turn of the century, though he never embarked upon serious manufacture. Later, he established the Staples Auto Company, a dealership which sold Chalmers and Hudson cars.

STAR — The Star Automobile company was organized in Buffalo, New York during the spring of 1904 with a capital stock of $10,000 for the manufacture of automobiles. Incorporators were Daniel B. Driscoll, Elmer E. Chambers and Daniel Burgmaster. Manufacture is doubted.

The Star Cyclecar Company was organized in Los Angeles, California during the early 1914 with a capital stock of $25,000. Directors of the firm were David L. Whitford (formerly of the Hydraulic Auto Truck Corporation), L. Robinson and William G. Crosby. The Star Cyclecar Company settled into headquarters at 235 East Washington Boulevard in L.A. Manufacture has not been documented.

1903 Star, runabout, NAHC

STAR — Cleveland, Ohio — (1902-1904) — When Gilbert R. Albaugh arrived to design the new product of the Star Automobile Company of Cleveland in late 1902, his automotive engineering credits already included stints with Rambler, Olds and Peerless. The men behind the organization of the Star company had equally impressive resumes: president H.H. Hodell was also president of the Cleveland Galvanizing Works; vice-president J.A. Mathews was from the Guardian Trust Company; secretary/treasurer W.A. Dutton was a partner of the Van Dorn & Dutton Company which had been supplying gears to the nascent automobile industry for a couple of years already. Taking charge of the managership of the Star factory was H.C. Robinson who had been in the chocolate-making business previously but who decided, as The Automobile so nicely punned, that "the progressive automobile industry (was) more to his taste." From this formidable team came the Star, its prototype completed in April of 1903, with ten machines sold by mid-summer. The Star was priced at $1250, which bought a single-cylinder four-stroke 8-1/2 hp runabout with detachable tonneau for a few extra passengers. A planetary transmission and chain drive were featured in the 76-inch wheelbase chassis. The Star's engine was mounted in the center of the car under the floorboard, with a coil radiator up front, and a squarish hood to shroud the gasoline and fuel tanks. The car was steered by a right-hand wheel with bulb horn mounted on top. A fine factory for the Star was outfitted at 6302 Kinsman Avenue S.E., but rather quickly the people behind the Star became disenchanted. "The stockholders of the Star Automobile Company have decided that the automobile business is not the bonanza that they believed it to be, and they will sell their remaining stock and withdraw from the business . . .," reported The Automobile in October 1903. "The company built about twenty cars and nearly all of these have been disposed of at fair prices, so that the company comes out about even." Taking over the Star assets and

factory was Harry S. Moore, a garage owner in town, who revised the Star's hood into an oval, increased its horsepower to nine, decreased its wheelbase to seventy-four inches, and lowered its price tag to $950. This new Star was introduced at the Cleveland Automobile Show in March 1904, but eclipsed soon thereafter. Moore subsequently became a dealer for Orient Buckboard, Queen and Stoddard-Dayton automobiles and in 1906 had a custom job made especially for himself called the Auburn-Moore. Gilbert Albaugh meanwhile had left to design the Wolverine in Michigan and later the Aldo in Chicago.

1907 Star, runabout, GR

STAR — Chicago, Illinois — (1907-1908) — The Star Automobile Company was incorporated in Chicago in January 1907 and immediately revealed itself to be "looking about for a favorable location for its factory." Marion, Indiana seemed promising, but Star never got there. Instead, the few cars that were built that year and into early 1908 were put together in the Windy City. The Star was a single-cylinder two-stroke 10 hp runabout which sold in three models for $500, $600 and $700. Its most distinctive feature was its friction transmission the disc of which was shifted by a hand wheel located below the steering wheel. The effect of this was the look of a double steering wheel.

1908 Star, model 12, touring, NAHC

STAR — Peru, Indiana — (1908-1909) — The Star was the Model renamed, and it was renamed because its manufacturer, E.A. Myers, also produced components for the building of automobiles under the Model name and thought this might represent something of a conflict of interest, or at least that his customers might think so. The Star, which had been built as a Model since 1902, was continued in production under the aegis of Myers' Model Automobile Company. In 1909 Myers changed the name of the firm as well, to Great Western Automobile Company. The Star became the Great Western then too.

1908 STAR
Model 12 — 2-cyl., 24 hp, 100" wb

	FP	5	4	3	2	1
Touring	1250	3300	4400	6700	12,000	24,000

Model 14 — 2-cyl., 24 hp, 104" wb

	FP	5	4	3	2	1
Touring	1350	3500	4500	7000	13,000	25,000
Roadster	1350	3300	4400	6700	12,000	24,000

Model 18 — 4-cyl., 35 hp, 108" wb

	FP	5	4	3	2	1
Touring	2500	4200	5200	8400	15,700	29,000

Model 16 — 4-cyl., 50 hp, 122" wb

	FP	5	4	3	2	1
Touring-7P	4000	5400	7300	11,800	25,000	38,000
Runabout	4000	5200	6800	11,300	23,000	36,000

1909 STAR
Model 24 — 2-cyl., 24 hp, 100" wb

	FP	5	4	3	2	1
Touring-5P	1600	3300	4400	6700	12,000	24,000

Model 30 — 4-cyl., 30 hp, 107" wb

	FP	5	4	3	2	1
Runabout-3/4P	1600	3300	4400	6700	12,000	24,000

Model 40 — 4-cyl., 40 hp, 114" wb

	FP	5	4	3	2	1
Touring-5P	3000	4200	5200	8400	15,700	29,000

Model 50 — 4-cyl., 50 hp, 122" wb

	FP	5	4	3	2	1
Touring-7P	4000	5400	7300	11,800	25,000	38,000

STAR — Indianapolis, Indiana — (1909-1911) — In November of 1909 the Star Motor Car Company was organized by Guy G. Shaw (president), J.W. Berauer (vice-president), S.J. Summer (secretary) and W.A. Rowland (treasurer). Although a number of different vehicles were to be produced, production was to be focused on a five-passenger touring car to sell for $1000. Capital stock in the company was $100,000, and the Star venture was reported to be the eleventh automobile manufacturing concern to be established in Indianapolis. In November of 1911 a stockholder named Theodore M. Weiss petitioned the Star Motor Car Company into involuntary bankruptcy. His claim that the firm was insolvent was upheld in court when it was revealed that in two years the Star company had built but one car.

STAR — Cincinnati, Ohio — (1916) — The Star Motor Car Company was organized in Cincinnati during the fall of 1916 with a capital stock of $200,000 for the manufacture of automobiles and trucks. Behind this venture were Louis Tyroler, David W. Rudisell, J.A. Finn, W. Cayce and William Fischer. "A demonstrating car is due to appear in ten days," *Automobile Topics* reported in September. "A site for a plant is still being sought." The demonstrator car was finished by early November, according to an article in *Motor Age* that month. Presumably the factory site was still being sought when this venture went under.

1922 Star, sedan, HAC

STAR — Elizabeth, New Jersey — (1922-1928) — Fresh from his final leavetaking of General Motors in 1920, William Crapo Durant launched his next empire, introduced a new medium-priced car named for himself, and followed this with plans for a low-priced car to compete with Henry Ford's Model T head-on. This was the Star, introduced by Durant Motors, Inc. in the early spring of 1922 and adjudged by the press as "a great deal of car for the money." A 35 hp four on a 102-inch wheelbase, the Star was announced as a $348 touring car, without self-starter or demountable rims, those extras adding about $100 to the price tag. Subsequently, the car was provided same, with a slight price increase. To move into quantity production quickly, Durant outbid Walter Chrysler for the huge factory in Elizabeth, New Jersey which the Willys Corporation sent to the auction block during receivership in 1922. Though the first Star cars were produced in Durant's Long Island City plant, and subsequently the cars would also be manufactured in other Durant factories (Lansing, Michigan; Oakland, California and Toronto among them), the big Elizabeth facility remained its principal home. Durant's Star was in the ascendant immediately; tens of thousands of people flocked to see it during its introductory showings, and on July 24th, 1923, less than a year after the first Star rolled off the assembly line, the 100,000th car was produced. Durant could have sold more of them had he had the initial capacity to do so. It was the Durant magic that sold the Star. Though a certainly admirable automobile, the car was completely conventional save for its three-speed transmission which was not unit-built. Moreover, the Star was an assembled car: Continental engine, Spicer universal and Timken axles initially, Adams axles after Durant bought that company in mid-1923. The Star was the first major American car to offer station wagon styling from the factory. In 1926 a 40 hp six joined the Star four as a companion model, and four-wheel brakes (Bendix) arrived in 1927. For awhile the Star enjoyed export success as the Rugby, but the car's fortunes overall were obviously tied to the health of the Durant empire. In 1928 Billy Durant celebrated his 25th anniversary in the automobile industry, though this was not a festive time for him. In the midst of a struggle to save his business, the phase-out of the Star had begun. The six-cylinder model became the Durant Model 55 in 1928; the four-cylinder Star was discontinued at the end of that year and became the Durant 4-40. It was an unfortunate demise for a car that had been so popular in America for more than a half-decade.

1922
Four, 35 hp, 102" wb

	FP	5	4	3	2	1
5P Tr	348	1075	3000	5500	7700	11,000
2P Rbt	319	900	1900	4500	6300	9000
4P Cpe	580	650	1250	2400	4200	6000
5P Sed	875	600	1200	2200	3850	5500

1923 Star, touring, OCW

1923
Four, 35 hp, 102" wb

	FP	5	4	3	2	1
5P Tr	443	1075	3000	5500	7700	11,000
2P Rds	414	900	1900	4500	6300	9000
4P Cpe	580	650	1250	2400	4200	6000
5P Sed	875	600	1200	2200	3850	5500

1924 Star, station wagon, HAC

1924
Model F, 4-cyl., 35 hp, 102" wb

	FP	5	4	3	2	1
5P Tr	490	1075	3000	5500	7700	11,000
2P Rds	490	1000	2400	5000	7000	10,000
2P Cpe	640	650	1250	2400	4200	6000
5P Spl Tr	640	1150	3600	6000	8400	12,000
5P Sed	785	600	1200	2200	3900	5600
5P Spl Sed	935	600	1200	2300	4000	5700

1925 Star, sedan, JAC

1925
Model F-25, 4-cyl., 35 hp, 102" wb

	FP	5	4	3	2	1
2P Rds	540	1000	2400	5000	7000	10,000
5P Tr	540	875	1700	4250	5900	8500
2P Cpe	750	650	1250	2400	4200	6000
5P Sed	820	600	1200	2300	4000	5700

1926 Star, landau sedan, JAC

1926
Four. 30 hp, 102" wb

	FP	5	4	3	2	1
2P Rds	525	1075	3000	5500	7700	11,000
5P Tr	525	1125	3450	5750	8050	11,500
2P Coupster	610	700	1350	2800	4550	6500
5P Coach	695	600	1200	2200	3900	5600
5P Sed	805	600	1200	2300	4000	5700
Six, 40 hp, 107" wb						
2P Coupster	745	725	1400	3100	4800	6800
2P Cpe	820	750	1450	3300	4900	7000
5P Coach	880	600	1200	2300	4000	5700
5P Tr	695	1150	3600	6000	8400	12,000

1927 Star Six, sport coupe, HAC

1927
Four, 30 hp, 102" wb

5P Tr	525	1150	3600	6000	8400	12,000
2P Rds	525	1125	3450	5750	8050	11,500
2P Cpe	675	875	1700	4250	5900	8500
5P Coach	695	650	1250	2400	4200	6000
5P Sed	795	700	1350	2800	4550	6500
Six (M-2), 40 hp, 107" wb						
5P Tr	725	1250	3900	6500	9100	13,000
4P Spt Rds	910	1200	3750	6250	8750	12,500
2P Cpe	820	900	1900	4500	6300	9000
4P Spt Cpe	975	950	2100	4750	6650	9500
4P Coach	880	700	1350	2800	4550	6500
5P Sed	975	750	1450	3300	4900	7000
5P Lan Sed	995	750	1450	3500	5050	7200

1928 Star, roadster, JG

1928
Four, 30 hp, 102" wb

2P Rds	550	1250	3900	6500	9100	13,000
2P Bus Cpe	650	875	1700	4250	5900	8500
5P 2 dr Sed	675	775	1500	3600	5100	7300
5P 4 dr Sed	765	775	1500	3750	5250	7500

1928 STAR
Four — 30 hp, 102" wb

	FP	5	4	3	2	1
Roadster-2P	550	1800	2800	4000	6200	13,000
Business Coupe-2P	650	1000	2100	3100	4800	8500
Two-Door Sedan-5P	675	1000	1800	2800	4200	7000
Four-Door Sedan-5P	765	1000	1900	2900	4400	7500

STARBUCK — Starbuck was one of the proposed names for the automobile projected to be built in 1919-1920 by the New York Air Brake Company. The venture was the idea of William P. Deppe. Refer to Deppe.

1903 Starin, runabout, NAHC

STARIN — North Tonawanda, New York — (1903-1904) — The Starin Company of North Tonawanda produced a single-cylinder runabout on a 72-inch wheelbase chassis fitted with a two-speed planetary transmission and single chain drive — and offered it in two models, a 6 hp at $800 and an 8 hp at $1000. Production began in 1903 — during which year Starin claimed five years' experience in automobile building, without mention of what had been built. Production ended in 1904. Thereafter the Starin Company became a used car dealership. "The Acme of Automobile Perfection" had been the Starin's grandiose slogan.

STARK — The Stark Auto Company was organized in Ridge, New Jersey during the fall of 1911 with a capital stock of $100,000 to manufacture and deal in motor cars. Incorporators were J.H. Stark, H.S. Stark, R.A. Sibbald and F.O. Mittage. Manufacture is doubted.

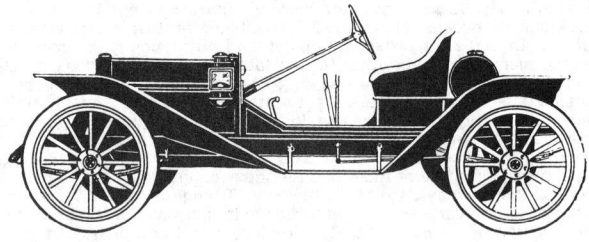

1910 Starr, runabout, WLB

STARR — Minneapolis, Minnesota — (1909-1910) — "The Wise Men of the East Followed the Star," the brochure said, "The Wise Men of the West Ride in the Starr." A roadster on a 100-inch wheelbase chassis, the Starr was offered with two engines, a four-cylinder 24 hp and a six-cylinder 36 hp (Brownell), with prices of $1000 and $1500 respectively. The men behind it were Fred W. Starr, who had previously worked for White in Cleveland, and Al S. Johnson, a former Hupmobile agent. They managed things in the factory, while S.H. Ponthan, V.H. Moffatt and B.J. Ferris handled administrative matters in the office. Both office and factory were at 522-524 South Tenth Street in Minneapolis. The initial announcement of this venture arrived during the fall of 1909. In July of 1910 Fred Starr followed up with the news that, although he would retain his selling organization in Minneapolis, he would locate his factory in Downing, Wisconsin which had "highly elated" the townspeople there. A surviving photograph shows Fred Starr and his Starr on the main street in Downing, with townspeople standing around — but the factory never moved there. Subsequent Starr advertisements in the trade press indicate the Minneapolis address. Minnesota vehicle registrations for this period reveal ten "Star" cars in the state: the likelihood is that most of these were the double-r

Starr. Production seems to have ended about the time the year 1910 did. In 1911 Fred Starr was working as a salesman for the Auto Inner Casing Company in Minneapolis. In 1912 he was reported to have moved to Dubuque, Iowa, though by November he was in Cleveland working as a mechanic and demonstrating an airplane he had built incorporating a safety device of his own invention. It was a crescent-shaped gas bag attached to the top of the plane which would be filled in flight by exhaust from the engine. "Starr asserts that in the event of an accident to the aeroplane proper," the *Cleveland Plain Dealer* reported, "the bag could float the plane for twenty miles, if necessary, to a safe landing."

STATES — The States Auto Supply Company was organized in Oskaloosa, Iowa during the fall of 1911 with a capital stock of $50,000 to manufacture and deal in automobiles. Incorporators were D.P. McClure, C.W. Payne and A.O. Watland. Manufacture is doubted.

1915 States, cyclecar, WLB

STATES — Detroit, Michigan — (1914-1915) — The States Cyclecar Company was organized in Detroit with a capital stock of $150,000 in July of 1914. Behind the venture were George W. Meredith, Samuel E. Jones and Victor W. Valade. Their car was a four-cylinder, two-passenger side-by-side two-seater cyclecar with a price tag of $365. The States was introduced at the Detroit Automobile Show in January 1915, and died very soon thereafter.

1914-1915 STATES
Cyclecar — 4-cyl., 90" wb

	FP	5	4	3	2	1
Side-by-Side Roadster-2P	365				—	12,000

1918 States, touring, WLB

STATES — Kalamazoo, Michigan — (1916-1918) — The States Motor Car Manufacturing Company evolved out of the States Motor Car Company which previously had built the Greyhound cycle- and light cars in the old Michigan Buggy Company plant in Kalamazoo. The new car of States was a four as had been the Greyhound, though it was slightly bigger, and its advertising was decidedly more flamboyant. Whereas the Greyhound had simply been called an "aristocrat," the design of the new States was vaingloriously referred to as "Breeze-Line . . . emulating the soft summery zephyrs." E.J. Cook was the designer of the car, and possibly the foregoing prose. The people behind the affairs of States were John A. Pyl as president, James H. Johnson and B.R. Barber as vice-presidents. In 1916, anyway. In 1917 the presidency belonged to G.B. Pulfer and the vice-presidency to V.G. Denmon. A six-cylinder companion car was added for 1918. But that was the end for the States. The company was reported to be "permanently out of business" in the January 23rd, 1919 issue of *Motor Age*. G.B. Pulfer immediately got himself another job as the manager of a corset company in town.

1916-1917 STATES
Model 4-32 — 4-cyl., 32 hp, 112" wb

	FP	5	4	3	2	1
Touring-5P	895	3100	4200	6300	10,500	22,000

1918 STATES
Model 4-32 — 4-cyl., 32 hp, 112" wb

	FP	5	4	3	2	1
Touring-5P	895	3100	4200	6300	10,500	22,000

Model 6-37 — 6-cyl., 37 hp, 112" wb

	FP	5	4	3	2	1
Touring-5P	1195	3500	4500	7000	13,000	25,000
Roadster-2P	995	3300	4400	6700	12,000	24,000

STATIC — The name of the car was Static Super Cooled Six, and the organization planning to produce it was the Static Motor Company of Philadelphia, Pennsylvania. The year was 1923. There is no evidence of this automobile ever having been put into manufacture.

STAVER — Chicago, Illinois — (1907-1914) — The Staver Carriage Company of Chicago was responsible for one of the biggest and most expensive highwheelers on the market. It had a two-cylinder engine, planetary transmission and a top speed of 30 mph, quite rapid for a highwheeler. It was tiller steered, chain driven and sported price tags in the $1000 range. In 1910 Harry B. Staver turned his company's manufacture over to four-cylinder conventional cars with selective transmission, shaft drive and higher price tags. Although the firm was renamed the Staver Motor Company in 1911, it remained in the horsedrawn vehicle industry throughout this period. In 1912 the company bought out the entire wagon business of Mitchell-Lewis of Racine, Wisconsin, which doubtless was not a good idea. Mitchell continued as a force in the automobile industry for a decade thereafter. The Staver Motor Company went under in 1914, and its factory was sold later that year for manufacture of the Partin-Palmer car. The Staver emblem had been a buck's head with an arrow through its neck.

1908 Staver, stanhope buggy, NAHC

1907-1908 STAVER
Model D — 2-cyl., 18/20 hp, 78" wb

	FP	5	4	3	2	1
Stanhope Buggy-2P	1000	1600	2700	3800	5800	12,000

1909 STAVER
Model 20 — 2-cyl., 24 hp, 86" wb

	FP	5	4	3	2	1
Runabout-2P	950	1800	2800	4000	6200	13,000

1910 Staver, model H, touring, HAC

1910 STAVER
Four — 30 hp, 112" wb

	FP	5	4	3	2	1
Model H Touring-5P	1600	2300	3300	4600	7500	16,000
Model J Surrey-4P	1600	2400	3400	4800	8000	17,000
Model K Baby Tonneau-4P	1600	2300	3300	4600	7500	16,000
Model I Torpedo-2P	1850	2400	3400	4800	8000	17,000

Four — 45 hp, 117" wb

	FP	5	4	3	2	1
Model L Runabout	2250	3900	4800	7700	14,300	27,000
Model M Touring	2250	4000	5000	8000	15,000	28,000

1339

1911 Staver, model 35, roadster, HAC

1911 STAVER

Four — 30 hp, 112" wb

	FP	5	4	3	2	1
Model T Touring-5P	1450	3700	4700	7300	13,700	26,000
Model B Baby Tonneau-4P	1450	3700	4700	7300	13,700	26,000
Model R Torpedo Rds.-5P	1450	3500	4500	7000	13,000	25,000
Model RR Racing Rds.-2P	1450	3900	4800	7700	14,300	27,000
Model F Fore-Door Tr.-5P	1500	3900	4800	7700	14,300	27,000

Four — 35 hp, 117" wb

	FP	5	4	3	2	1
Model I Touring-5P	1650	4200	5200	8400	15,700	29,000
Model I Fore-Door Tr.-5P	1850	4200	5200	8400	15,700	29,000
Model I Roadster (112" wb)	1650	4000	5000	8000	15,000	28,000

Four — 40 hp, 124" wb

	FP	5	4	3	2	1
Model R Touring-7P	1850	4400	5600	9200	17,300	31,000
Model R Fore-Door Tr.-7P	2000	4500	5800	9500	18,000	32,000
Model R Coupe	2500	3000	4000	6000	9500	21,000
Model R Limousine	3250	3500	4500	7000	13,000	25,000

1912 Staver, model 40, touring, HAC

1912 STAVER

Four — 35 hp, 112" wb

Model B Fore-Door Tr.-5P	1650	3900	4800	7700	14,300	27,000
Model BT Baby Tonneau-4P	1650	3700	4700	7300	13,700	26,000
Model R Torpedo Rds.-5P	1650	3900	4800	7700	14,300	27,000
Model RR Racing Rds.-2P	1650	4200	5200	8400	15,700	29,000
Model F Fore-Dr. Tr. (120" wb)	1850	4000	5000	8000	15,000	28,000
Model F Special (120" wb)	2250	4200	5200	8400	15,700	29,000
Model C Coupe	2500	3000	4000	6000	9500	21,000
Model D Limousine	2500	3500	4500	7000	13,000	25,000

Four — 40 hp, 124" wb

Model RR Racing Rds.-2P	2000	4200	5200	8400	15,700	29,000
Model L Limousine	3500	3700	4700	7300	13,700	26,000
Model F Fore-Door Touring	2000	4400	5600	9200	17,300	31,000
Model T Touring-5P	1850	4300	5400	8700	16,500	30,000
Model T Touring-7P	1900	4400	5600	9200	17,300	31,000

1913 Staver, model 35, roadster, HAC

1913 STAVER

Four — 30 hp, 120" wb

Algonquin Speed Roadster	1750	5300	7000	11,500	24,000	37,000

Four — 35 hp, 124" wb

Englewood Touring-5P	2250	3700	4700	7300	13,700	26,000

	FP	5	4	3	2	1
Englewood Limited Tr.-5P	2500	3900	4800	7700	14,300	27,000
Edgewater Touring-5P	2000	3500	4500	7000	13,000	25,000
Newport Touring-7P	2500	4000	5000	8000	15,000	28,000
Greyhound Spd. Rds.ter-4P	2250	5400	7300	11,800	25,000	38,000
Beverly Touring-5P	1750	3500	4500	7000	13,000	25,000
Berkley Tonneau-4P	1750	3300	4400	6700	12,000	24,000
Lakeport Roadster	1750	3200	4300	6500	11,000	23,000
South Shore Colonial Coupe	2750	2700	3600	5300	8800	19,000
North Shore Limousine	3500	3100	4200	6300	10,500	22,000

Four — 40 hp, 124" wb

	FP	5	4	3	2	1
Dictator Touring-5P	1885	4400	5600	9200	17,300	31,000

1914 Staver, model 65, touring, HAC

1914 STAVER

Model 45 — 4 cyl., 45 hp, 118" wb

Touring-5P	1875	4900	6300	10,300	21,000	34,000
Roadster-2P	1875	4700	6100	9900	19,000	33,000

Model 55 — 4-cyl., 55 hp, 120" wb

Touring-5P	2250	5000	6500	11,000	22,000	35,000
Speedster-2P	2250	5400	7300	11,800	25,000	38,000

Model 65 — 6-cyl., 70 hp, 138" wb

Touring-5P	2750	5400	7300	11,800	25,000	38,000
Touring-7P	2750	5500	7500	12,000	26,000	39,000

(Note: The 1914 models were introduced early in calendar year 1913)

STEALEY — San Francisco, California — (1899) — In 1898 A.D. Stealey of 450 Main Street in San Francisco began extensively advertising his engines for automotive use: a 2 hp unit for $150, a 3 hp for $180 and a 4 hp for $225. When he introduced his new 5 hp twin-cylinder later that year, the automotive press reported on his progress and noted that he was the only builder of gasoline vehicle engines on the West Coast. In 1899 Stealey built his most formidable effort yet: a two-cylinder which he claimed developed 47 bhp at 40 rpm. "The valves are exceedingly large," he said, "while the exhaust is remarkably quiet and cool as compared with that of most motors." In April he was building a bicycle powered by one of his smaller engines for a San Francisco client, and later that year he fitted another of his engines into an experimental four-wheeled carriage. Although he continued producing gasoline engines into the turn of the century, he did not become an automobile manufacturer.

STEAM — The Steam Moto Company was organized in New York City during the fall of 1900 with a capital stock of $250,000 for the manufacture of automobiles and carriages. All the people behind this venture were from Brooklyn, and included J.F. Davy, C. Otto, D.C. Demeritt, F. Grant and G.H. Roberts. Manufacture is doubted.

The Steam Vehicle Company of America located at 253 Broadway in New York City has appeared on various car rosters as the producer of a car called the Model in 1902. This firm, however, was the New York selling agency for the Steam Vehicle Company of Reading, Pennsylvania — and the "model" it sold was the Reading Steamer. "We Progress, Others Stand Still" was a company slogan. Refer to Reading Steamer.

1901 Steamobile, runabout, NAHC

STEAMOBILE — Keene, New Hampshire — (1901-1902) — In February of 1901 the Steamobile Company of America superseded the Trinity Cycle Manufacturing Company which had been producing a steam car under the name of Keene Steamobile since 1900. Keene was immediately dropped from the car's name. Production does not seem to have been halted during the transition, as W.S. Rogers (who had built a gasoline car under his own name two years earlier in Boston) took over as superintendent from Trinity man Reynold Janney. Three Steamobiles were exhibited at the Greenfield (Massachusetts) Fair that September, all of these the $850 two-seater runabout that had been the only model thus far produced. Twenty-five had been sold. The month following a dos-a-dos seat was provided the Steamobile in a second $900 model, and early in 1902 the $1000 Transit ensued, which featured a tonneau mounted in front of the driver's seat for the carrying of two extra passengers, or a parcel box which converted the vehicle into a light delivery. "The company has a considerable number of carriages to dispose of," the local Keene newspaper reported in June of 1902, "but it is not probable that it will manufacture any more new work." The Steamobile Company of America was perhaps the U.S. industry's first victim of overproduction. Soon thereafter the Steamobile assets — including forty unsold cars — were sold to the Standard Roller Bearing Company of Philadelphia.

1902 Steamobile, Transit, NAHC

1901-1902 STEAMOBILE

	FP	5	4	3	2	1
Runabout	850	2000	3000	4000	6500	14,000
Dos-a-Dos	900	2100	3100	4300	6800	14,500
Transit Tonneau	1000	2200	3200	4400	7000	15,000

STEARN — The Stearn Automobile Repair Company was organized in New York City during the summer of 1910 to "manufacture, buy and deal in automobiles." Incorporators were George Martensen, William T. Nicolai and Francis Fitch. Manufacture is doubted.

Dr. Stearn's Invalid Auto Company was organized in New York City during the summer of 1910 with a capital stock of $50,000 for the manufacture of vehicles and conveyances for invalids. Behind this venture were H.H. Stearn, M.T. Shier and C.H. Sanborn. Manufacture has not been documented.

1928 Stearns-Knight, show car, HAC

STEARNS — Cleveland, Ohio — (1901-1911) / **STEARNS-KNIGHT** — (1912-1929) — The first car he ever built was also the first car he ever drove, and the fact that he was able to build it in 1896, at age seventeen, was largely due to the indulgence of his father who equipped a fine machine shop for him in the basement of the family's elegant Euclid Avenue home in Cleveland. F.M. Stearns had made a sizeable fortune in the stone-quarry industry, and young Frank Ballou Stearns grew up in wealth and comfort. Not surprisingly, the Stearns cars reflected this background. For years they were widely regarded as among the finest automobiles in America, built with the affluent sporting motorist in mind. Frank Stearns began with a motor buggy, however, like virtually ever other budding automobile builder before the turn of the century. This was in 1898 when F.B. Stearns & Company was organized, the "& Company" referring to the Owen brothers of Cleveland who would leave early on for their own automotive ventures; in 1902 the ampersand was dropped from the firm's title, Frank B. Stearns taking the company executive positions of president, general manager and treasurer, his father becoming vice-president and secretary. Up to 1901, approximately 50 Stearns cars were produced; the 1901 model remained a single-cylinder but was now a whopping one, 6 1/4 by 7 1/2 inches for 11 bhp, and probably the largest one-lunger in America at the time. A two-cylinder 20 hp touring car was added in 1902. Twenty-five cars were built that year, fifty the year following. Always in the forefront with progressive features, the Stearns sported a steering wheel in 1901, a sliding gear transmission in 1902, a magneto in 1904, and a four-speed gearchange in 1905. Curiously, in 1902, left-hand drive was introduced to Stearns cars, but was dropped soon thereafter, not to return until the 1914 model year. "Runs like a Deer" was a Stearns slogan for 1904, and in 1905 the Stearns ran even faster, with a 40 hp, L-head four featuring paired cylinders and mechanically operated side valves. Priding itself on never building a special race car, the Stearns company competed in stock events with fine success in both track races and hill climbs. Guy Vaughan was often behind the wheel, though it was Al Poole with Cyrus Patschke who would put up the record-breaking 1253 miles in 24 hours at Brighton Beach in 1910. Another record, a mile in 41-2/5ths seconds, was also frequently touted. The two most impressive Stearns cars of this era arrived in the famous 30/60 hp four introduced in 1907, and the 45/90 hp six which came the following year. The latter figure in each case designated not only developed horsepower but top speed. Prices of Stearns fours hovered on both sides of the $5000 mark; the six was $6250-$7500. A 15/30 hp four, popularly known as the Baby Stearns, and priced as low as $3200, followed for 1909. It was Stearns' first shaft-drive car; the 30/60 was now thusly offered as an option though probably most sporting Stearns drivers opted for the double chain. Stearns production was ever on the increase: 243 cars in 1908, nearly 500 in 1909, 1000 in 1910, 1500 in 1911. During the summer of 1909 the Stearns company applied for a patent to protect its most distinctive identifying feature, the "white line radiator." In 1911 Stearns became a distinctive car of another kind, when the company acquired the first American license to the Knight engine. All Stearns cars were sleeve valves henceforth, the first introduced in June 1911; Stearns bought the factory of the defunct Royal Tourist shortly thereafter for Knight engine production. Only four-cylinder Stearns-Knights were offered through mid-year 1913, when a six was added. The line for 1914 included the first Stearns sedan and coupe, and a restyling along European lines. Nineteen fifteen brought the Model L-4 or Light Four, the first popularly priced ($1750) Stearns, which the company said it was building for "Mr. Substantial Citizen." A V-8 replaced the six in 1916, and 4000 fours and eights were built that year. During the fall of the year following, citing ill health, Frank B. Stearns retired from his company at age thirty-seven; George W. Booker of the St. Louis agency came in as president. There was no noticeable change in the company's direction. Fours only became the firm's product in 1920 and remained so until a six was reintroduced in 1923. Throughout, the Stearns-Knight had retained its position as a high-priced prestige car, and it continued the same after December 1925, when John North Willys bought the company. Willys made it clear immediately that he had no intention of integrating the Stearns into his Willys-Overland empire. As the new Stearns president, he imported H.J. Leonard who had previously been manager of production for the Stephens, a car from a Freeport (Illinois) company formerly controlled by Willys; and a short while later he named J.F. Trumble (formerly of Stephens also) as Stearns' new chief engineer. An in-line eight was a new Stearns-Knight addition for 1927; it boasted a 100 hp engine, 75 mph performance and price tags about $1000 more than the $3250-$3750 sixes. Both sixes and eights were produced thereafter, some of the latter on wheelbases that stretched 145 inches, with prices that stretched to $5800. It was all over late in 1929. What John North Willys had been unaware of at the time of purchase was that he had bought an ailing com-

1901 Stearns, gasoline runabout, HAC

pany. Indeed, 1925 proved to be its last profitable year. Having the Stearns-Knight to boast as his ultra-luxury prestige car lost its logic after the stock market crash. Production ceased on December 20th, 1929 when the Stearns shares which Willys had bought at $10 each less than five years before now stood at 12-1/2¢ a share. Stockholders voted for dissolution of the F.B. Stearns Company ten days later. Ironically, the month previous, Frank B. Stearns announced his development of a two-stroke overhead cam diesel engine, which he later sold to the United States Navy. Frank Stearns had come full circle. His career had begun in a machine shop in the basement of his father's home; once again he was operating out of a home laboratory. Organic farming became a later pursuit, before death claimed Frank Stearns in 1955.

1902 STEARNS
One-Cylinder — 11 hp

	FP	5	4	3	2	1
Suburban	—	2300	3300	4600	7500	16,000
Two-Cylinder — 20 hp						
Touring-5P	3000	2400	3400	4800	8000	17,000

1903 STEARNS
One-Cylinder — 11 hp

Suburban	—	2300	3300	4600	7500	16,000
Two-Cylinder — 24 hp, 78" wb						
Touring-5P	3000	2400	3400	4800	8000	17,000

1904 Stearns, 24 hp, touring, HAC

1904 STEARNS
Two-Cylinder — 24 hp, 96" wb

Touring-5P	3000	3500	7050	11,750	16,450	23,500
Four-Cylinder — 36 hp, 111" wb						
Touring-7P	4150	3600	7200	12,000	16,800	24,000

1905 Stearns, 40 hp, victoria touring, HAC

1905 STEARNS
Four — 32/40 hp, 118" wb

Touring-7P	4150	3750	7500	12,500	17,500	25,000

1906 Stearns, 40 hp, touring, HAC

1906 STEARNS
Four — 40/45 hp, 118" wb

Touring-5P		4250	4500	5800	9500	18,000	32,000

1342

1907 Stearns, 30/60 hp, touring, HAC

1907 STEARNS
Four — 30/60 hp, 120" wb

	FP	5	4	3	2	1
Touring-5/7P	4500	5000	6500	11,000	22,000	35,000
Pullman-7P	4759	5200	6800	11,300	23,000	36,000

1908 Stearns, limousine, HAC

1908 STEARNS
Four — 30/60 hp, 120" wb

Pullman Touring	4750	5300	7000	11,500	24,000	37,000
Touring Roadster	4600	5200	6800	11,300	23,000	36,000
Standard Touring	4600	5000	6500	11,000	22,000	35,000
Limousine	5750	4200	5200	8400	15,700	29,000
Landaulette	5750	4300	5400	8700	16,500	30,000
Six — 45/90 hp						
Pullman Touring	6400	6400	9300	14,500	33,000	45,000
Touring Roadster	6250	6200	8800	13,500	31,000	43,000
Standard Touring	6250	6300	9000	14,000	32,000	44,000
Limousine	7500	4500	5800	9500	18,000	32,000
Landaulette	7500	4700	6100	9900	19,000	33,000

1909 Stearns, toy tonneau, OCW

1909 STEARNS
Model 15-30 — 4-cyl., 32 hp, 116" wb

Landaulet-5/7P	3800	4400	5600	9200	17,300	31,000
Limousine-5/7P	3800	4200	5200	8400	15,700	29,000
Standard Touring-5P	3200	5200	6800	11,300	23,000	36,000
Model 30-60 — 4-cyl., 60 hp, 121" wb						
Toy Tonneau-4P	4600	5500	7500	12,000	26,000	39,000
Standard Touring-5/7P	4600	5500	7500	12,000	26,000	39,000
Pullman-7P	4750	5800	8000	12,500	28,000	40,000

	FP	5	4	3	2	1
Limousine-5P	5750	4300	5400	8700	16,500	30,000
Model 45-90 — 6-cyl., 90 hp						
Pullman Touring	6400	5900	8300	12,800	29,000	41,000
Touring Roadster	6250	5800	8000	12,500	28,000	40,000
Standard Touring	6250	6000	8500	13,000	30,000	42,000
Limousine	7500	4400	5600	9200	17,300	31,000
Landaulette	7500	5000	6500	11,000	22,000	35,000

1910 Stearns, 15/30 hp, touring, HAC

1910 STEARNS

Model 15-30 — 4-cyl., 32 hp, 116" wb	FP	5	4	3	2	1
Touring	3200	4200	5200	8400	15,700	29,000
Landaulet	4600	3700	4700	7300	13,700	26,000
Toy Tonneau	3200	4000	5000	8000	15,000	28,000
Limousine	4000	3500	4500	7000	13,000	25,000
Model 30-60 — 4-cyl., 60 hp, 121" wb						
Toy Tonneau	4600	4500	5800	9500	18,000	32,000
Model 30-60 — 4-cyl., 60 hp, 124" wb						
Touring	4600	5000	6500	11,000	22,000	35,000
Limousine	5750	3700	4700	7300	13,700	26,000
Landaulet	5850	3900	4800	7700	14,300	27,000
Model 45-90 — 6-cyl., 90 hp						
Pullman Touring	6400	5800	8000	12,500	28,000	40,000
Standard Touring	6250	5500	7500	12,000	26,000	39,000
Touring Roadster	6250	5400	7300	11,800	25,000	38,000
Limousine	7500	4200	5200	8400	15,700	29,000
Landaulette	7500		5400	8700	16,500	30,000

1911 Stearns, 15/30 hp, toy tonneau runabout, HAC

1911 STEARNS

Model 15-30 — 4-cyl., 32 hp, 116" wb	FP	5	4	3	2	1
Touring-5P	3200	4000	5000	8000	15,000	28,000
Toy Tonneau	3200	3900	4800	7700	14,300	27,000
Limousine	3200	3100	4200	6300	10,500	22,000
Landaulet	3200	3200	4300	6500	11,000	23,000
Model 30-60 — 4-cyl., 46 hp, 116" wb						
Touring	4600	4300	5400	8700	16,500	30,000
Toy Tonneau	4600	4200	5200	8400	15,700	29,000
Runabout	4600	4000	5000	8000	15,000	28,000
Landaulet	4600	3300	4400	6700	12,000	24,000
Limousine	4600	3200	4300	6500	11,000	23,000
Knight — 4-cyl., 28 hp, 116" wb						
Toy Tonneau Runabout	3500	4200	5200	8400	15,700	29,000
Roadster	3500	4000	5000	8000	15,000	28,000
Knight — 4-cyl., 28 hp, 121" wb						
Touring	3500	4500	5800	9500	18,000	32,000
Limousine	4800	2900	3700	5600	9100	20,000
Landaulet	4900	3000	4000	6000	9500	21,000

1912 STEARNS-KNIGHT

Knight — 4-cyl., 28 hp, 116" wb	FP	5	4	3	2	1
Toy Tonneau Runabout	3590	4400	5600	9200	17,300	31,000
Roadster	3500	4300	5400	8700	16,500	30,000
Knight — 4-cyl., 28 hp, 121" wb						
Touring	3500	4500	5800	9500	18,000	32,000
Limousine	4800	4000	5000	8000	15,000	28,000
Landaulet	4900	4200	5200	8400	15,700	29,000

1913 STEARNS-KNIGHT

Four — 28.9 hp, 121" wb	FP	5	4	3	2	1
Touring-5P	3750	4300	5400	8700	16,500	30,000
Touring-4P	3750	4200	5200	8400	15,700	29,000
Four — 28.9 hp, 116" wb						
Roadster-3P	3750	4300	5400	8700	16,500	30,000

1912 Stearns-Knight, landaulet, HAC

1913 Stearns-Knight, landaulet, HAC

Four — 28.9 hp, 127" wb	FP	5	4	3	2	1
Touring-7P	3900	4700	6100	9900	19,000	33,000
Limousine-7P	5000	3100	4200	6300	10,500	22,000
Landaulet-7P	5100	3300	4400	6700	12,000	24,000
Six — 43.8 hp, 134" wb						
Touring-5P	4850	5300	7000	11,500	24,000	37,000
Touring-4P	4850	5200	6800	11,300	23,000	36,000
Roadster-3P	4850	5000	6500	11,000	22,000	35,000
Six — 43.8 hp, 140" wb						
Touring-7P	5000	5400	7300	11,800	25,000	38,000
Limousine-7P	6100	3700	4700	7300	13,700	26,000
Landaulet-7P	6200	4000	5000	8000	15,000	28,000

1914 Stearns-Knight, touring, HAC

1914 STEARNS-KNIGHT

Model SK4 — 4-cyl., 29 hp, 121" wb	FP	5	4	3	2	1
Touring-5P	3750	4000	5000	8000	15,000	28,000
Coupe	4450	3100	4200	6300	10,500	22,000
Sedan	5000	2900	3700	5600	9100	20,000
Model SK4 — 4-cyl., 29 hp, 127" wb						
Touring-7P	3900	4200	5200	8400	15,700	29,000
Limousine-7P	5000	3300	4400	6700	12,000	24,000
Landaulet-7P	5000	3700	4700	7300	13,700	26,000
Model SK6 — 6-cyl., 43.3 hp, 140" wb						
Touring-5P	5000	4500	5800	9500	18,000	32,000
Light Touring-4P	4850	4400	5600	9200	17,300	31,000
Roadster-3P	4850	4500	5800	9500	18,000	32,000
Coupe-4P	5550	3300	4400	6700	12,000	24,000
Sedan-5P	6100	3100	4200	6300	10,500	22,000
Touring-6P	5000	4700	6100	9900	19,000	33,000
Touring-7P	5000	5200	6800	11,300	23,000	36,000
Limousine-7P	6100	4200	5200	8400	15,700	29,000
Landaulet-7P	6200	4300	5400	8700	16,500	30,000

1915 STEARNS-KNIGHT

Light Four — 22.5 hp, 119" wb	FP	5	4	3	2	1
Touring-5P	1750	3700	4700	7300	13,700	26,000
Roadster-3P	1750	3500	4500	7000	13,000	25,000
Cabriolet-3P	2250	3300	4400	6700	12,000	24,000
Limousine-7P	2850	3100	4200	6300	10,500	22,000

1915 Stearns-Knight, Six, touring, HAC

Big Four — 29 hp, 121" wb

	FP	5	4	3	2	1
Touring-5P	3750	3900	4800	7700	14,300	27,000
Touring-4P	3750	3700	4700	7300	13,700	26,000
Touring-6P	3900	4000	5000	8000	15,000	28,000
Touring-7P	3900	4200	5200	8400	15,700	29,000
Runabout-3P	3750	4000	5000	8000	15,000	28,000
Limousine-7P	5000	3200	4300	6500	11,000	23,000
Landaulet-7P	5100	3300	4400	6700	12,000	24,000

Six — 43.3 hp, 140" wb

Touring-7P	5000	4500	5800	9500	18,000	32,000
Touring-6P	5000	4400	5600	9200	17,300	31,000
Touring-5P	4850	4300	5400	8700	16,500	30,000
Light Touring-4P	4850	4200	5200	8400	15,700	29,000
Roadster-3P	4850	4400	5600	9200	17,300	31,000
Limousine-7P	6100	3300	4400	6700	12,000	24,000
Landaulet-7P	6200	3500	4500	7000	13,000	25,000

1916 Stearns-Knight, Seaman bodied sedan, OCW

1916 STEARNS-KNIGHT
Model SKL4 — 4-cyl., 23 hp, 119" wb

Touring-5P	1395	4000	5000	8000	15,000	28,000
Roadster-3P	1395	3900	4800	7700	14,300	27,000
Limousine-7P	2500	3100	4200	6300	10,500	22,000
Coupe-4P	1900	2900	3700	5600	9100	20,000
Cabriolet-3P	1900	3700	4700	7300	13,700	26,000

Model SK6 — 6-cyl., 43 hp, 134" wb

Touring-7P	1750	4200	5200	8400	15,700	29,000

Model SK8 — 8-cyl., 33.8 hp, 123" wb

Touring-7P	2050	4500	5800	9500	18,000	32,000
Roadster-3P	2050	4400	5600	9200	17,300	31,000
Limousine-7P	3350	3200	4300	6500	11,000	23,000
Brougham-7P	3300	3100	4200	6300	10,500	22,000
Coupe-4P	2650	3000	4000	6000	9500	21,000
Coupe Landaulet-4P	2650	3100	4200	6300	10,500	22,000
Landaulet-7P	3450	3300	4400	6700	12,000	24,000
Landau Brougham-7P	3400	3200	4300	6500	11,000	23,000

1917 Stearns-Knight, Eight, touring, HAC

1917 STEARNS-KNIGHT
Eight — 34 hp, 123" wb

Touring-7P	2150	4300	5400	8700	16,500	30,000
Roadster-4P	2150	4200	5200	8400	15,700	29,000
Runabout-4P	2150	4000	5000	8000	15,000	28,000
Limousine-7P	3500	3200	4300	6500	11,000	23,000

	FP	5	4	3	2	1
Limousine Brougham-7P	3500	3300	4400	6700	12,000	24,000
Coupe Landaulet-7P	2900	3200	4300	6500	11,000	23,000
Coupe-4P	2900	3100	4200	6300	10,500	22,000
Landaulet-7P	3600	3500	4500	7000	13,000	25,000
Landaulet Brougham-7P	3600	3700	4700	7300	13,700	26,000

Four — 23 hp, 119" wb

Touring-5P	1450	4000	5000	8000	15,000	28,000
Roadster-4P	1450	3900	4800	7700	14,300	27,000
Runabout-3P	1450	3700	4700	7300	13,700	26,000
Limousine-7P	2900	3000	4000	6000	9500	21,000
Coupe-4P	2050	2900	3700	5600	9100	20,000
Limousine Brougham-7P	3000	3100	4200	6300	10,500	23,000
Landaulet-7P	3000	3200	4300	6500	11,000	23,000
Landaulet Brougham-7P	3100	3400	4400	6700	12,000	24,000
Touring Sedan-7P	2050	4300	5400	8700	16,500	30,000

1918 Stearns-Knight, Four, coupe, HAC

1918 STEARNS-KNIGHT
Model SKL-4 — 4-cyl., 22.5 hp, 119" wb

Touring-5P	1785	4000	5000	8000	15,000	28,000
Cloverleaf Roadster	1785	3900	4800	7700	14,300	27,000
Coupe	2400	3100	4200	6300	10,500	22,000
Limousine	3350	3300	4400	6700	12,000	24,000
Limousine Brougham	3400	3500	4500	7000	13,000	25,000
Landaulet	3300	3700	4700	7300	13,700	26,000
Landaulet Brougham	3350	3900	4800	7700	14,300	27,000
Convertible Sedan	2535	4200	5200	8400	15,700	29,000
Touring-7P	2175	4500	5800	9500	18,000	32,000

Model SK-8 — 8-cyl., 33.8 hp, 125" wb

Touring-7P	2575	5000	6500	11,000	22,000	35,000
Cloverleaf Roadster	2575	4900	6300	10,300	21,000	34,000
Coupe	3200	4000	5000	8000	15,000	28,000
Coupe Landaulet	3200	4200	5200	8400	15,700	29,000
Limousine	3875	3700	4700	7300	13,700	26,000
Limousine Brougham	3875	3900	4800	7700	14,300	27,000
Landaulet	3985	4000	5000	8000	15,000	28,000
Landaulet Brougham	3985	4200	5200	8400	15,700	29,000

1919 Stearns-Knight, touring, HAC

1919 STEARNS-KNIGHT
Model SKL-4 — 4-cyl., 22.5 hp, 125" wb

Touring-5P	2100	3700	4700	7300	13,700	26,000
Touring-7P	2465	4000	5000	8000	15,000	28,000
Chummy Roadster	2100	3500	4500	7000	13,000	25,000

1920 Stearns-Knight, sedan, HAC

1920 STEARNS-KNIGHT
Model SKL-4 — 4-cyl., 23 hp, 125" wb

	FP	5	4	3	2	1
Roadster-3P	2350	3700	4700	7300	13,700	26,000
Militaire-4P	2375	3500	4500	7000	13,000	25,000
Touring-5P	2350	3900	4800	7700	14,300	27,000
Touring-7P	2575	4200	5200	8400	15,700	29,000
Coupe-4P	3150	3000	4000	6000	9500	21,000
Sedan-7P	3450	2400	3400	4800	8000	17,000
Limousine-7P	4000	3300	4400	6700	12,000	24,000
Town Car-7P	4150	3500	4500	7000	13,000	25,000

1921 Stearns-Knight, touring, HAC

1921 STEARNS/STEARNS-KNIGHT
Model SKL-4 — 4-cyl., 57 hp, 125" wb

	FP	5	4	3	2	1
Touring-5P	2450	4200	5200	8400	15,700	29,000
Touring-4P	2475	4000	5000	8000	15,000	28,000
Roadster	2550	3900	4800	7700	14,300	27,000
Touring-7P	2675	4400	5600	9200	17,300	31,000
Coupe-4P	3400	2900	3700	5600	9100	20,000
Sedan-7P	3700	2300	3300	4600	7500	16,000

1922 Stearns-Knight, brougham, HAC

1922 STEARNS-KNIGHT
Model SKL-4 — 4-cyl., 57 hp, 125" wb

	FP	5	4	3	2	1
Touring-5P	2450	4200	5200	8400	15,700	29,000
Roadster-3P	2450	4000	5000	8000	15,000	28,000
Touring-7P	2675	4400	5600	9200	17,300	31,000
Coupe-4P	3400	2900	3700	5600	9100	20,000
Brougham-5P	3600	3100	4200	6300	10,500	22,000
Sedan-7P	3700	2500	3500	5000	8500	18,000

1923 Stearns-Knight, 4-dr. sedan, HFM

1923 STEARNS-KNIGHT
Model SKL4 — 4-cyl., 63 hp, 125" wb

	FP	5	4	3	2	1
Touring-5P	2250	4200	5200	8400	15,700	29,000
Roadster	2250	4000	5000	8000	15,000	28,000
Militaire	2275	4200	5200	8400	15,700	29,000
Touring-7P	2450	4300	5400	8700	16,500	30,000
Coupe	3150	2700	3600	5300	8800	19,000
Coupe-Brougham	3250	2900	3700	5600	9100	20,000
Sedan	3450	2300	3300	4600	7500	16,000

Model SK6 — 6-cyl., 63 hp, 130" wb

	FP	5	4	3	2	1
Touring-5P	2700	4400	5600	9200	17,300	31,000
Roadster	2700	4300	5400	8700	16,500	30,000
Militaire	2700	4400	5600	9200	17,300	31,000
Touring-7P	2850	4500	5800	9500	18,000	32,000
Coupe	3350	2900	3700	5600	9100	20,000
Coupe-Brougham	3500	3000	4000	6000	9500	21,000
Sedan	3700	2400	3400	4800	8000	17,000

1924 Stearns-Knight, sport sedan, HAC

1924 STEARNS-KNIGHT
Four — 4-cyl., 64 hp, 119" wb

	FP	5	4	3	2	1
Touring-4/5P	1750	4000	5000	8000	15,000	28,000
Sport Coupe-2P	1750	2700	3600	5300	8800	19,000
Brougham-5P	2195	2800	3700	5500	9000	19,500
Sedan-5P	2350	2200	3200	4400	7000	15,000
Sport Sedan-5P	2450	2250	3300	4500	7300	15,500

Six — 6-cyl., 70 hp, 130" wb

	FP	5	4	3	2	1
Touring-4/5P	2395	4200	5200	8400	15,700	29,000
Sport Coupe-2P	3150	2900	3700	5600	9100	20,000
Brougham-5P	3295	3000	4000	6000	9500	21,000
Sedan-7P	3395	2250	3300	4500	7300	15,500
Sport Sedan-5P	3395	2300	3300	4600	7500	16,000

1925 Stearns-Knight, model 6-C, brougham, HAC

1925 STEARNS-KNIGHT
Model 4 — 4-cyl., 119" wb

	FP	5	4	3	2	1
Touring-4P	—	4200	5200	8400	15,700	29,000
Touring-5P	—	4300	5400	8700	16,500	30,000
Coupe Roadster-2P	—	4300	5400	8700	16,500	30,000
Coupe Brougham-4P	—	2300	3300	4600	7500	16,000
Sedan-5P	—	2000	3000	4200	6500	14,000
Brougham-5P	—	2200	3200	4400	7000	15,000

Model 6-C — 6-cyl., 130" wb

	FP	5	4	3	2	1
Sport Touring-4P	1875	4500	5800	9500	18,000	32,000
Touring-5P	1875	4400	5600	9200	17,300	31,000
Sport Coupe-2P	2185	2400	3400	4800	8000	17,000
Brougham-5P	—	2300	3300	4600	7500	16,000
Coupe Brougham-4P	2285	2450	3500	4900	8300	17,500
Sedan-5P	2475	2200	3200	4400	7000	15,000

Model 6-S — 6-cyl., 130" wb

	FP	5	4	3	2	1
Militaire-4P	2395	4500	5800	9500	18,000	32,000
Touring-5P	2395	4500	5800	9500	18,000	32,000
Touring-7P	2495	4700	6100	9900	19,000	33,000
Sport Coupe-3P	3150	2500	3500	5000	8500	18,000
Four-Door Sedan-5P	3000	2300	3300	4600	7500	16,000
Brougham-5P	3295	2400	3400	4800	8000	17,000
Sedan-7P	3395	2350	3400	4700	7800	16,500

1926 STEARNS-KNIGHT
6-C — 6-cyl., 55 hp, 121" wb

	FP	5	4	3	2	1
Roadster	—	4500	5800	9500	18,000	32,000
Touring-4P	1875	4700	6100	9900	19,000	33,000
Touring-5P	1875	4900	6300	10,300	21,000	34,000
Coupe-5P	2350	2700	3600	5300	8800	19,000

	FP	5	4	3	2	1
Sedan-5P	2475	2200	3200	4400	7000	15,000
Brougham-5P	2285	2300	3300	4600	7500	16,000
Coupe Roadster-3P	2185	4600	6000	9700	18,500	32,500
Model 6-S — 6-cyl., 65 hp, 130" wb						
Roadster	2395	4700	6100	9900	19,000	33,000
Touring-5P	2395	4900	6300	10,300	21,000	34,000
Touring-4P	2395	4700	6100	9900	19,000	33,000
Touring-7P	2495	5000	6500	11,000	22,000	35,000
Coupe-4P	3150	2900	3700	5600	9100	20,000
Sedan-5P	3000	2300	3300	4600	7500	16,000
Sport Sedan-5P	3250	2400	3400	4800	8000	17,000
Brougham-5P	3295	2500	3500	5000	8500	18,000
Sedan-7P	3395	2350	3400	4700	7800	16,500
Coupe Roadster-3P	3150	4800	6200	10,100	20,000	33,500

1926 Stearns-Knight, sport sedan, HAC

1927 Stearns-Knight, standard sedan, HAC

1927 STEARNS-KNIGHT

Model D-6-85 — 6-cyl., 81 hp, 107" wb	FP	5	4	3	2	1
Roadster-2P	3250	4500	5800	9500	18,000	32,000
Touring-4P	3250	4700	6100	9900	19,000	33,000
Coupe-2P	3350	2900	3700	5600	9100	20,000
Standard Sedan-5P	3350	2200	3200	4400	7000	15,000
Custom Sedan-5P	3350	2300	3300	4600	7500	16,000
Sedan-7P	3550	2250	3300	4500	7300	15,500
Limousine-7P	3750	2500	3500	5000	8500	18,000
Custom Sedan Limo.-5P	3550	2700	3600	5300	8800	19,000
Standard Sedan Limo.-5P	3550	2600	3600	5200	8700	18,500
Cabriolet-2/4P	3550	4300	5400	8700	16,500	30,000
Model G-8 — 8-cyl., 102 hp, 137 1/2" wb						
Roadster-2P	—	4900	6300	10,300	21,000	34,000
Touring-4P	—	5000	6500	11,000	22,000	35,000
Coupe-5P	—	3000	4000	6000	9500	21,000
Standard Sedan-5P	—	2300	3300	4600	7500	16,000
Sedan-7P	—	2350	3400	4700	7800	16,500
Limousine-7P	—	2700	3600	5300	8800	19,000
Standard Sedan Limousine	—	2800	3700	5500	9000	19,500
Cabriolet	—	4500	5800	9500	18,000	32,000

1928 Stearns-Knight, Eight, coupe, HAC

1928 STEARNS-KNIGHT

Model F6-85 — 6-cyl., 82 hp, 137" wb	FP	5	4	3	2	1
Roadster-6P	3250	4900	6300	10,300	21,000	34,000
Touring-4P	3250	5000	6500	11,000	22,000	35,000
Custom Sedan-5P	3350	2400	3400	4800	8000	17,000
Coupe-4P	3450	2700	3600	5300	8800	19,000
Standard Sedan-4P	3450	2300	3300	4600	7500	16,000
Cabriolet Roadster-4P	3550	4400	5600	9200	17,300	31,000

	FP	5	4	3	2	1
Sedan Limousine-5P	3700	3000	4000	6000	9500	21,000
Custom Sedan Limo.-5P	3700	3200	4300	6500	11,000	23,000
Sedan-7P	3750	2400	3400	4800	8000	17,000
Sedan Limousine-7P	3950	2500	3500	5000	8500	18,000
Model H — 8-cyl., 112 hp, 137 1/4" wb						
Roadster-4P	5500	5300	7000	11,500	24,000	37,000
Coupe-4P	5500	—	—	—	—	21,000
Victoria-5P	5500	—	—	—	—	22,000
Sedan-5P	5600	—	—	—	—	18,000
Model J — 8-cyl., 112 hp, 145" wb						
Touring-7P	5500	5800	8000	12,500	28,000	40,000
Sedan-7P	5500	—	—	—	—	19,000
Limousine-7P	5800	—	—	—	—	21,000
Town Car	—	—	—	—	—	23,000

1929 Stearns-Knight, coupe, JAC

1929 Stearns-Knight, 4-dr. sedan, OCW

1929 STEARNS-KNIGHT

Model M6-80 — 6-cyl., 70 hp, 126" wb	FP	5	4	3	2	1
Cabriolet-4P	2495	5000	6500	11,000	22,000	35,000
Close Coupled Sedan-5P	2495	4200	5200	8400	15,700	29,000
Sedan-5P	2495	4000	4900	7900	14,700	27,500
Model N6-80 — 6-cyl., 70 hp, 134" wb						
Coupe-5P	2645	4300	5400	8700	16,500	30,000
Sedan-7P	2845	4100	5100	8200	15,400	28,500
Limousine-7P	2945	4700	6100	9900	19,000	32,000
Model H8-90 — 8-cyl., 120 hp, 137" wb						
Roadster-4P	5500	5500	7500	12,000	26,000	39,000
Cabriolet-4P	5500	5200	6800	11,300	23,000	36,000
Coupe-4P	5500	4400	5600	9200	17,300	31,000
Coupe-5P	5500	4500	5800	9500	18,000	32,000
Sedan-5P	5500	4300	5300	8600	16,100	29,500
Model J8-90 — 8-cyl., 120 hp, 145" wb						
Touring-7P	5500	6200	8800	13,500	31,000	43,000
Sedan-7P	5600	4400	5600	9200	17,300	31,000
Limousine-7P	5800	4700	6100	9900	19,000	33,000

1930 STEARNS-KNIGHT

Model H8-90 — 8-cyl., 127 hp, 137" wb	FP	5	4	3	2	1
Roadster	5500	5800	8000	12,500	28,000	40,000
Cabriolet Roadster	5500	5400	7300	11,800	25,000	38,000
Coupe-2P	5500	3000	4000	6000	9500	21,000
Coupe-5P	5500	3100	4200	6300	10,500	22,000
Sedan	5500	2400	3400	4800	8000	17,000
Model J8-90 — 8-cyl., 127 hp, 145" wb						
Touring-7P	5500	6300	9000	14,000	32,000	44,000
Sedan	5600	4500	5800	9500	18,000	32,000
Limousine	5800	4900	6300	10,300	21,000	34,000

STEARNS — Oakland, California — (1905) — Since 1903 the Stearns Brothers Spraying Machine Company of Los Angeles had operated a branch plant in Oakland at 315 Eighth Street. In 1905 the firm decided to add the manufacture of automobiles to its traditional product line. Involved in this endeavor were Nels J. Herby, an Oakland machinist who had been in the automobile business in 1903, and Henry A. Brown who had been associated with the Standard Motor Vehicle Company in town. According to a 1905 list of Oakland car registrations, an experimental Stearns automobile appears to have been built. But minds were quickly changed. By 1906 Stearns had closed its Oakland plant.

1901 Stearns Steamers, GR

STEARNS ELECTRIC — Syracuse, New York — (1899-1900) / STEARNS STEAM — (1901-1903)

E.C. Stearns & Company began in Syracuse as a hardware store and evolved into a bicycle manufactory. In 1899 the company built its first experimental electric car. It was a cumbersome carriage fitted with a 2 1/2 hp motor and a battery weighing 900 pounds. The complete vehicle weighed 2200 pounds, and its spur gear drive provided three speeds: 5, 8 and 12 mph. The Stearns Electric was sold in small quantities through the fall of 1900, but then the company decided to place its fortunes on steam. The Stearns Steam Carriage Company was incorporated with a capital sock of $750,000; its backers included George M. Barnes, H.E. Maslin, Charles M. Warner, William Nottingham and Henry Trebert. Unlike the electric which had been designed by Stearns, the steamer was the work of George M. Barnes, a vehicle he had built in 1899 as the Barnes Steam Trap. It proved a much more successful product. A simple car of conventional design, it was powered by a twin-cylinder 8 hp engine, featured chain drive and tiller steering, and was offered in a wide variety of body styles including a station wagon (with three bench seats for six passengers and roll-down canvas sides) which was probably the first production vehicle of that genre in the world. By November of 1901, the Stearns Steam Carriage Company had produced over 100 cars. The future must have looked bright. But, alas, Edward C. Stearns had in the meantime allied himself with arch promoter and charlatan Edward Joel Pennington. He was vice-president of Pennington's Anglo-American Rapid Vehicle Company, to which a new million-dollar incorporation called the Stearns Automobile Company became a subsidiary. It was all over soon after that. During the summer of 1903 the property of the Stearns Automobile Company was sold at a receiver's sale for $595 to one Thomas Hooker; ultimately the plant was used by the LeFevre Arms Company for the manufacture of transmission gears. E.C. Stearns & Company remained a hardware store and subsequently became an automobile dealership in Syracuse.

1902 STEARNS ELECTRIC/STEARNS STEAM
Model A Runabout	900	1800	2800	4000	6200	13,000
Model A-A Semi-Touring	1000	2000	3000	4200	6500	14,000
Model B Dos-a-Dos	1200	2200	3200	4400	7000	15,000
Model C Delivery	1400	2000	3000	4200	6500	14,000
Model D Buggy Top Rbt.	900	1800	2800	4000	6200	13,000
Model E Victoria Top Rbt.	1050	2000	3000	4200	6500	14,000
Model F Surrey	1600	2200	3200	4400	7000	15,000
Model G Touring	1400	2000	3000	4200	6500	14,000
Model H Station Wagon	1600	2100	3100	4300	6800	14,500

1903 STEARNS ELECTRIC/STEARNS STEAM
Model D Buggy Top Rbt.	600	1800	2800	4000	6200	13,000
Model A-A Semi-Touring	650	2000	3000	4200	6500	14,000
Model F Surrey	1200	2200	3200	4400	7000	15,000
Model B Dos-a-Dos	800	2200	3200	4400	7000	15,000
Model G Touring	1050	2200	3200	4400	7000	15,000
Model H Station Wagon	1200	2100	3100	4300	6800	14,500
Model E Victoria Top Rbt.	750	1800	2800	4000	6200	13,000
Model C Delivery	1400	2000	3000	4200	6500	14,000

STEBER STEAM — Utica, New York — (c. 1860)

Antoine Steber was a mechanic who worked in the machine shops of Philo C. Curtis and who, with a man named Fischer, built a steam automobile during the Civil War period. The vehicle was successfully tested, but was too large and cumbersome to be practicable. Fischer subsequently traveled to France to check out automotive development there, and upon his return joined with Steber in trying to make the vehicle an efficient proposition. They were never able to do this, and the machine was later abandoned.

1914 Steco, cyclecar, WLB

STECO — Chicago, Illinois — (1914)

The Stevens Company of 7329 Bond Boulevard in Chicago was an engineering firm which believed its patented method of construction made the cyclecar idea viable. "The frame of the Steco is make of ash, side members built up with cross members and through bolts," the company said. "The formed steel body of the car is attached solidly to this frame, thus making a box girder form of construction, supported from three points by . . . equalizing transverse spring suspension in front, and two Lancaster type cantilever springs in the rear. Chrome vanadium steel is used." Otherwise the Steco specifications were typical of the cyclecar genre. Its engine was an air-cooled 9 hp twin; its wheelbase was 102 inches, its tread 36. Friction transmission and belt drive were featured, and the Steco sat two in tandem. Its price was $450. The Stevens Company provided the automotive press a description and photographs of its car during the summer of 1914, though experimentation remained ongoing. "We are still working at the problem of developing a genuine cyclecar," the company reported to *Carette* that December, "notwithstanding the fact that the many others who fell over themselves getting into the cyclecar game early, now are refusing to acknowledge their relationship to some of the productions they were so over-enthusiastic about." Stevens was now convinced its Steco was state of the art for the cyclecar. It may have been, but it was too late. The era of the cyclecar was drawing to a rapid close.

STEEL BALL STEAM — Chicago, Illinois — (1900-1901)

The Steel Ball Company of 840 Austin Avenue in Chicago completed its first automobile during the fall of 1900. It was a standard steam runabout of the period, distinguished only by the concerted effort to produce it as cheaply as possible. The car used bicycle tubing for the frame, for instance. "It was designed to meet the desires of that large class of people who want motor vehicles but who are not doing business on unlimited bank accounts," Steel Ball manager Tilden told *The Motor Vehicle Review*. An automobile department was set up in the Steel Ball Company factory, but the production which followed was minimal and short-lived.

1908 Steel Swallow, RFD car, WLB

STEEL SWALLOW — Jackson, Michigan — (1907-1908)

The Steel Swallow Automobile Company was organized in Jackson in August of 1906 to manufacture, assemble, buy, sell and repair automobiles, which seemed to cover all bases. The cars manufactured were to be under patents of David Dearing. Dearing was joined in this venture by J.C. Richardson, Louis F. Boos, William F. Bellows and Lee Alderdyce. Capital stock was $100,000 of which $60,000 was paid in. The first Steel Swallow was a two-cylinder air-cooled 8 hp friction-drive runabout on an 84-inch wheelbase which sold for $700. It was marketed through the 1907 model year, followed in March of 1908 by a light delivery. The last Steel Swallow model of record arrived that September, a "Special R.F.D." car designed for rural postal delivery. The company disappeared by year's end, though it was included in insurance books into 1909.

STEELE

Briefly, during the cyclecar craze of 1914, the William Steele Company which produced trucks in Worcester, Massachusetts considered a fling as a cyclecar manufacturer. Refer to Morgan.

STEEL-MOBILE

The Steel-Mobile Company was organized in New Concord, Ohio during the summer of 1902 with a capital stock of $40,000 for the manufacture of gasoline automobiles. The incorporators, all Ohioans, included H.L. Warner of Dayton, J.M. Ickes of Newark, D.S. Burt of Byesville, and L.C. Taylor and John S. Black of Cambridge. Plans to have a factory in operation by October 1st were announced. Manufacture is doubted, however.

STEELY — Detroit, Michigan — (1910)

The Steely Auto Engine Company of Detroit was organized during the summer of 1910 with a capital stock of $150,000 by W.J. McWain, M.G. Delaney, E.D. Snowden and J.J. Marks. "The goods they will manufacture cover a wide range," *Cycle and Automobile Trade Journal* reported, "and include two-cycle engines, steering gear of a new design, pneumatic tires of leather and canvas, and convertible type motor cars." The Steely car had a four-cylinder 35 hp engine and was the tourabout type which could be easily revised into a

1000-pound delivery car — and of course wore the Steely canvas-and-leather pneumatics. This automotive venture appears to have been very short-lived.

STEFFLES — The Peter Steffles Launch & Automobile Company was organized in Winona, Minnesota late in 1906 with a capital stock of $10,000 to manufacture and repair motor cars and launches. Joining Peter Steffles in this venture were John J. Glubka and Henry C. Miller. Manufacture is doubted.

STEFFY — The Steffy Manufacturing Company at 1313 Fourth Street in San Diego, California was indicated as an automobile producer in the Hiscox book *Horseless Vehicles, Automobiles, Motor Cycles* published in 1900. The reference was incorrect on two counts. By late 1899 the firm had moved from California to Philadelphia, Pennsylvania. And its product was a one-cylinder engine intended for motorcycles. Among purchasers was E. Paul duPont, age thirteen, who bought one to power his M&M bicycle. Steffy built a few complete motorcycles prior to his death in 1903.

STEGMAIER — The Stegmaier Brothers of Cumberland, Maryland have been indicated on various car rosters as the producers of an automobile in 1906-1907. Documentation is lacking. The only Stegmaiers noted in the automotive press of the period brewed beer in Wilkes Barre, Pennsylvania and bought a VE electric truck in 1903.

STEINBOCK — Westchester County, New York — (1912) — Probably only a single touring-car prototype resulted from this venture which was born as the ill-fated United States Motor Company was dying in 1911. Recognizing the handwriting on the wall, H.E. Steinbock and F.D. Dorman decided to strike out on their own. Dorman who had been in the automobile business since 1903 when he was among the organizers of the Cleveland Motor Carriage Company would serve as president of the new Steinbock Engineering Company. Steinbock was the engineer, having been in charge of the technical department at Maxwell-Briscoe since 1904, then with the organization of the United States Motor empire being transferred to the Brush Runabout Company in Detroit. None too happy there, he returned to Tarrytown, New York (home of Maxwell-Briscoe) where he found an equally unhappy employee in F.D. Dorman. Their plan was to build a new moderately-priced vehicle to be offered as a passenger car and light delivery wagon. A "number of moneyed men in Westchester County" were said to be financially backing the enterprise, but possibly the fiasco of United States Motor ultimately dissuaded them. No Steinbock automobile or truck was ever put into manufacture.

STEINHART-JENSEN — The Steinhart-Jensen Automobile Company was indicated on various 1908 trade directories as the producer of a car in Joliet, Illinois. Documentation is lacking. The Joliet city directory for 1908-1909 notes the company at 100 Cass, with E.W. Steinhart as president and C.F. Jensen as secretary, but provides no indication of whether the firm was a manufacturer or a dealer.

1922 Steinmetz, WLB

STEINMETZ ELECTRIC — Baltimore, Maryland — (1922-1923) — A good deal of hoopla followed announcement of this new car because the man behind it was Charles Steinmetz, whose repute in the electrical field was rivaled only by that of Thomas Edison. The Steinmetz Electric Motor Car Corporation was organized in Baltimore, though the four pilot models of the new Steinmetz electric car were built at the Thorne Machine Tool Company in Syracuse, New York. Interestingly, during the war years when he was assisting Harry E. Dey in his electric venture, Steinmetz had often voiced his dream of a $500 electric. Dey's car couldn't be produced for less than a thousand dollars, and now the projected price tag for Steinmetz's electric was twice that. In December of 1922, Steinmetz himself was testing the prototype of the new car. Its top speed was 40 mph, with a cruising radius of 200 miles on a single battery charge. It was a closed sedan with the look of a gasoline car. Testing continued through August of 1923, when announcement was made that commercial vehicle production

would commence immediately in the Baltimore factory, with the car to follow shortly. It never did. The Steinmetz company was in financial trouble quickly. Receivership was averted during the spring of 1924 by a refinancing, and a few more Steinmetz electric trucks trickled out of the factory before the venture was irrevocably abandoned in 1926. The only Steinmetz electric cars ever built, however, were the four prototypes.

STEPHENS — Chicago, Illinois — (1914) — The Stephens Engineering Company at 560 Monadnock Building in Chicago, served as consultants in the general engineering field. Edmund Egan was president, Anthony C. Stephens was vice-president and Edwin Ahlskog was secretary. In 1914 the firm built a prototype of a cyclecar for an undisclosed client, which may have been the Mitchell Automobile Company.

1917 Stephens Salient Six, roadster, HAC

STEPHENS — Freeport, Illinois — (1917-1924) — The Moline Plow Company was organized in 1870 in Moline, gradually enveloped smaller wagon and buggy producers in the area through the years, and was a thriving institution up to the First World War. The company was remarkably frank about the reasons for its entry into the automotive field, noting that it had been "forced to embark in this line, due to the decline in the demand for farm vehicles and buggies." Moline's new car would be called the Stephens, after G.A. Stephens, whose father had founded the company he now headed. And for the first half-decade of its life it would carry the captivating model designation of Salient Six. The prototype was designed by E.T. Birdsall (earlier the designer of the Selden, amongst many others), and it was on the road in the spring of 1916. Production followed for the 1917 model year. Initially, Continental engines were used in the Stephens, but in 1918 overhead valve units from the Root & Vandervoort Engineering Company of East Moline were substituted. In 1919 John North Willys acquired a controlling interest in the Moline Plow Company, though it remained an entity separate from his Willys-Overland empire. Many of the same directors stayed onboard. In 1920 the Moline company bought out Root & Vandervoort, which made good sense since Moline had previously purchased about eighty percent of the R & V output. Because a crisis in its farm implement business brought devastating losses to the firm in the early Twenties, the Stephens motor department was taken out of the parent organization in mid-1922 and reorganized as the Stephens Motor Car Company. Again, the same directors remained onboard. In 1923, for the first time in its history, the Stephens was offered in two model lines on two separate chassis. The cars were also extensively restyled, and were considerably more attractive than the dependable, if somewhat dowdy, models which had preceded. Disc or wire wheels were provided the Sport (or Foursome), which was undoubtedly the most rakish Stephens ever produced. Production ended in the summer of 1924, however, the parent company announcing that henceforth manufacture would be concentrated in the farm implement field. Interestingly, the year previous had been Stephens' second best ever in sales, with 4400 cars marketed. Its best year had been 1920, with 6956; total Stephens production in seven years was approximately 25,000 cars.

1917 STEPHENS
Salient Six — 25.35 hp, 115" wb

	FP	5	4	3	2	1
Touring-5P	1150	2500	3500	5000	8500	18,000
Roadster-3P	1150	2400	3400	4800	8000	17,000

1918 Stephens Salient Six, touring, HAC

1918 STEPHENS
Salient Six — 25.35. hp, 118" wb

	FP	5	4	3	2	1
Roadster-3P	1485	2900	3700	5600	9100	20,000
Touring-5P	1485	3000	4000	6000	9500	21,000
Sedan-5P	1985	2000	3000	4200	6500	14,000
Touring-4P	1550	3100	4200	6300	10,500	22,000

1919 Stephens Salient Six, touring, HAC

1919 STEPHENS
Salient Six — 25.35 hp, 118" wb

	FP	5	4	3	2	1
Touring-6P	1850	3100	4200	6300	10,500	22,000
Touring-4P	1775	2900	3700	5600	9100	20,000
Touring-5P	1675	3000	4000	6000	9500	21,000
Victoria-4P	1975	2300	3300	4600	7500	16,000

1920 Stephens Salient Six, touring, HAC

1920 STEPHENS
Salient Six — 57 hp, 122" wb

	FP	5	4	3	2	1
Roadster-2P	1975	3200	4300	6500	11,000	23,000
Roadster-4P	1975	3300	4400	6700	12,000	24,000
Touring-6P	2050	3500	4500	7000	13,000	25,000
Coupe-3P	3050	2700	3600	5300	8800	19,000
Sedan-5P	3050	2000	3000	4200	6500	14,000

1921 Stephens Salient Six, touring, HAC

1921 STEPHENS
Salient Six — 57 hp, 122" wb

	FP	5	4	3	2	1
Touring-6P	2400	3300	4400	6700	12,000	24,000
Touring-4P	2400	3200	4300	6500	11,000	23,000
Roadster-2P	2400	3200	4300	6500	11,000	23,000
Sedan-6P	3400	2000	3000	4200	6500	14,000

1922 STEPHENS
Salient Six — 57 hp, 122" wb

	FP	5	4	3	2	1
Roadster-2P	1800	3500	4500	7000	13,000	25,000
Touring-4P	1850	3700	4700	7300	13,700	26,000
Touring Victoria-4P	1850	3700	4700	7300	13,700	26,000

	FP	5	4	3	2	1
Roadster-2P	1900	3700	4700	7300	13,700	26,000
Touring-6P	1850	3900	4800	7700	14,300	27,000
Victoria-4P	1950	3900	4800	7700	14,300	27,000
Special Touring-6P	1950	4000	4900	7900	14,700	27,500
Sedanette-4P	2850	2200	3200	4400	7000	15,000
Sedan-7P	2850	2100	3100	4300	6800	14,500

1923 Stephens, model 10, touring, GR

1923 STEPHENS
Model 10 — 6-cyl., 59 hp, 117" wb

	FP	5	4	3	2	1
Touring-5P	1295	3300	4400	6700	12,000	24,000
Roadster-3P	1345	3100	4200	6300	10,500	22,000
Touring Sedan-5P	1595	3500	4500	7000	13,000	25,000
Sedan-5P	1895	2000	3000	4200	6500	14,000

Model 20 — 6-cyl., 57 hp, 124" wb

	FP	5	4	3	2	1
Touring-7P	1685	4000	5000	8000	15,000	28,000
Sport-4P	1985	4200	5200	8400	15,700	29,000
Sedan-7P	2385	2300	3300	4600	7500	16,000

1924 Stephens, model 6-20, sedan, HAC

1924 STEPHENS
Model 6-20 — 6-cyl., 59 hp, 124" wb

	FP	5	4	3	2	1
Touring-7P	1595	4000	5000	8000	15,000	28,000
Sport-5P	1750	4200	5200	8400	15,700	29,000
Sedan-7P	2250	2300	3300	4600	7500	16,000

STERKENBURG — Sterkenburg was the designation given by John Tjaarda to the series of rear-engined and progressively more streamlined automobiles he began designing in 1926 and which he spent the next five years refining and attempting to find the financing to build. In 1932 he joined the Briggs Manufacturing Company. Refer to Briggs.

STERLING — Clarence Sterling has been indicated on various rosters as the producer of an automobile in Bridgeport, Connecticut from 1897-1899. Documentation is lacking.

A car called the Sterling has been noted on various rosters as having been produced by the Howell & Meehan Company of Boston, Massachusetts. This is in error. The Howell & Meehan Company was a dealership and served as agency for the Springfield Cornice Works of Springfield, Massachusetts. Springfield sold its own car as the Meteor; Howell & Meehan called the same car the Sterling.

The Sterling Automobile & Manufacturing Company was organized in Sterling, Illinois early in 1902 with a capital stock of $15,000 for the manufacture of a steam car designed by Myron Detrick. Manufacture is doubted.

The Sterling Motor Company was organized in Flint, Michigan during the fall of 1912 by William C. Durant and J. Dallas Dort with a capital stock of $300,000 for the purpose of manufacturing engines to be used in the Little six-cylinder cars and "additional motors for the open market." The Sterling plant was moved to Detroit during the summer of 1913 and, Durant's announcements to the contrary, manufacture of a Sterling automobile never followed.

The Sterling Motor Car Company was a $10,000 Delaware incorporation from late 1914 for the manufacture and sale of automobiles. Incorporators were H.E. Latter, W.J. Maloney and O.J. Reichard. Manufacture is doubted.

The Sterling Motor Car Company of Binghamton, New York was organized during the fall of 1903 with a capital stock of $25,000 for the manufacture of automobiles. O.S. Heller, Fred H. Matthews and Arthur L. Brown were the incorporators, all residents of Binghamton. Manufacture is doubted, the company probably serving only as a dealership. When Sterling folded in 1909 its assets were sold "in bulk" for $310.

The Sterling Power Vehicle Company of Hoboken, New Jersey was organized during the fall of 1902 with a $1 million capital stock to "manufacture and deal in automobiles and other vehicles, and electric and other motors." Incorporators were Richard H. Dana, John F. Jewell and George Herbert Taylor. Manufacture is doubted.

The Sterling Transport & Auto Company was organized in St. Louis, Missouri during the spring of 1915 with a capital stock of $2000 to manufacture, repair and deal in automobiles. Incorporators were Gustave Koerner and Jacob Hagelstein. Manufacture is doubted.

The Sterling Vehicle Company was organized in Jersey City, New Jersey during the spring of 1908 with a capital stock of $300,000 for the manufacture of automobiles and motor boats. Incorporators were H.O. Coughlin, B.S. Mantz and L.H. Gunther. Manufacture of a car is doubted.

STERLING — Sterling, Illinois — (1909) — The Sterling Machine Works built its first motor buggy in early 1909. It was powered by a single-cylinder air-cooled engine which the company claimed developed 20 hp. This seems doubtful. That summer Sterling announced to the trade press that two automobiles had been completed, these the first "of a line which will be marketed in the near future." Some production appears to have followed, but not much and not for long.

1909 Sterling, touring, NAHC

STERLING — Elkhart, Indiana — (1909-1911) — The first car built late in 1907 in the factory of the Sterling-Hudson Whip Company in Elkhart was a prototype of the Menges, but the idea for its manufacture was dismissed early on. Departing too were Dr. E.C. Crow and his son Martin E., who had joined Willard W. Sterling and F.O. Hudson in the incorporation of the Elkhart Motor Car Company in April of 1908; they went off within a year to build a car of their own. This left Sterling and Hudson to soldier on together in their whip factory with production of an automobile they decided to call the Sterling. The firm's name remained Elkhart Motor Car Company, however. The new Sterling was a four produced in two models in the medium-price range. "Sterling Cars are Sterling Value," the ads said. The Elkhart company spent the next year and a half almost routinely increasing its capital stock. By March of 1910 it was up to a million dollars, and grand expansion plans were laid. Initial sales had been promising, it is true, but scarcely sufficient to warrant dreams of grandeur. In January 1911 the Model Gas Engine Company of nearby Peru sued Elkhart claiming the firm had reneged on an order for 1000 Model engines. Elkhart agreed that it had cancelled the contract after accepting only 118 units, but counterclaimed that the engines had been defective. The court didn't buy that. In May of 1911, Sterling and Hudson took the easy way out, selling their company's plant and assets to a consortium of former Haynes officials. This group moved into the Sterling factory with plans to build a new six called the Lohr initially, then the Elmer. For reasons of its own, the Elkhart Motor Car Company had taken to referring to some of its cars as the Komet in addition to the Sterling during its last model year. There apparently was no difference between them.

1909 STERLING
Model K — 4-cyl., 30 hp, 115"

	FP	5	4	3	2	1
Runabout	1500	4000	5000	8000	15,000	28,000
Surrey	1550	4200	5200	8400	15,700	29,000
Touring	1550	4300	5400	8700	16,500	30,000

Model C — 4-cyl., 40 hp, 118" wb

Touring	2750	4500	5800	9500	18,000	32,000

1910 STERLING
Model O — 4-cyl., 30 hp, 115" wb

Runabout	1700	4000	5000	8000	15,000	28,000
Touring	1750	4200	5200	8400	15,700	29,000
Torpedo	2000	4300	5400	8700	16,500	30,000

Model C — 4-cyl., 40 hp, 118" wb

Touring	2250	4700	6100	9900	19,000	33,000

1911 STERLING
Model R — 4-cyl., 30/40 hp, 125" wb

Speedster-2P	1850	4900	6300	10,300	21,000	34,000
Fore-Door Roadster-4P	2000	4700	6100	9900	19,000	33,000
Close-Coupled Touring-4P	2250	4500	5800	9500	18,000	32,000
Fore-Door Touring-6P	2500	4900	6300	10,300	21,000	34,000

1914 Sterling, MVMA

STERLING — White Plains, New York — (1914) — A Mr. Cronk was the proprietor of the Sterling Garage in White Plains and in 1914 built this little car for his two sons. "It has already demonstrated its value as a motor educator," he told *MoToR* magazine that April.

STERLING — Brockton, Massachusetts — (1915-1916) — Following the failure of his Vulcan in Ohio, Alonzo R. Marsh returned to his native Massachusetts where he joined his brothers in a new automotive venture. In December of 1914 the Sterling Motor Car Company was announced as the linear successor to the American Motor Company which had manufactured Marsh motorcycles as well as a runabout called the Marsh from 1905-1906. The new Sterling was a 13 hp four on a 102-inch wheelbase offered as a roadster for $550 and a touring at $650. The first prototype was on the road in June of 1915, and production began immediately thereafter. Production ended in May of the following year when the Sterling factory was acquired by the Consolidated Ordnance Company. Consolidated was another Marsh enterprise, begun for the manufacture of shrapnel adapters and other munitions for the war effort. Following the Armistice, the Marsh brothers ventured to Cleveland to build yet another car bearing their own name.

1920 Sterling, touring, KM

STERLING — Middlefield, Connecticut — (1920) — In October of 1919 the brothers Lazaro (Albert E. and Bert E.), together with Frank J. Kenney, organized the Consolidated Motor Car Company with a capital stock of $750,000. Headquarters for this venture was variously indicated to be New London, New Britain and Middlefield, Connecticut, only the last named appearing in advertisements. Bradford was indicated in the trade press as the hometown of the Consolidated partners, but no Connecticut town bears that name — the closest being Branford, which lies thirty miles from Amston. Whether this Sterling was the final metamorphosis of the car which had begun life as the Sterling-New York (built in Paterson, New Jersey in 1916) and continued it as the AMS-Sterling (built in Amston, Connecticut in 1917) is not known. The engine was the same (28 hp Le Roi four), but the new car did not outwardly resemble either predecessor. Two- and five-passenger models were offered "fully equipped" on a 100-inch-wheelbase chassis. The price for each was $1185. Concurrently, a sporting car called the B.E.L. (Bert Lazaro's initials) was offered as well at a bargain-basement price of $495. Sales were doubtlessly slim. Neither Sterling nor B.E.L. was advertised beyond 1920. Curiously, the 1922 *New England Directory* lists a "Sterling Motor Car Company" as Consolidated's dealer for Middlefield, Connecticut that year. This may have been simply an instance of disposing of cars already produced. The Sterling Motor Car Company also served as Eastern distributor for the Seneca during this period.

1916 Sterling-New York, roadster, KM

STERLING-NEW YORK — Paterson, New Jersey — (1916) — A lawyer, two automobile dealers and a furrier — respectively Charles Chambers, William and Edward Adelson, and Henry Hyman — were behind this venture. Incorporating their Sterling Automobile Manufacturing Company in New York City in 1913, the partners established headquarters at 1790 Broadway and leased a factory in Paterson, New Jersey, declaring they had "orders that will require several months to fill" and that they were negotiating with "several nations at war in Europe." Adoption of the British £ symbol in advertisements was a clever idea, and certainly more clever than the car. The Sterling-New York was touted as being "as mechanically perfect as the development of the industry will permit" — words carefully chosen because virtually all components and ideas were either purchased or borrowed from somebody else in the industry. Omnipresent New York engineer Joseph Anglada put them all together. The Sterling-New York's engine was a 28 hp Le Roi four with overhead valves. The radiator was "genuine honey comb with German Silver Shell polished." The inappropriately-named "One Man Jiffy Curtains" were stored in the top, and featured also was a two-piece windshield — in vogue at the time because it allowed vision in the rain, although it also let the rain in, which tended to impair vision. Prices were $595 for touring, $595 for roadster. Sales of the Sterling-New York (or Sterling, as it was occasionally listed) were minimal, and rather quickly the lawyer, two automobile dealers and furrier elected to seek their fortune elsewhere. By September of 1916 the Sterling Automobile Manufacturing Company was sold to Charles W. Ams, who moved operations to Amston, Connecticut and introduced a new car called the AMS-Sterling.

1916 STERLING-NEW YORK
Four — 28 hp, 102" wb

	FP	5	4	3	2	1
Touring	595	2400	3400	4800	8000	17,000
Roadster	590	2300	3300	4600	7500	16,000

1925 Sterling Knight, touring, WLB

STERLING-KNIGHT — Cleveland, Ohio — (1920-1922) / Warren Ohio, (1923-1926) — The Sterling-Knight was the idea of James G. "Pete" Sterling, longtime chief engineer of the F.B. Stearns Company who resigned from that firm in 1920 to build a luxury car using the Knight sleeve valve engine. Financed by a group of Cleveland businessmen who organized as the Sterling-Knight Syndicate, Pete Sterling carried on development work in a machine shop in Cleveland. Three test cars were completed within the year, and the Sterling-Knight was introduced at the Chicago Salon in December 1920 and at the Cleveland Automobile Show in January 1921. In April the syndicate was superseded by the million-dollar incorporation of the Sterling-Knight Motor Company. Among its directors was Alva Bradley, later owner of the Cleveland Indians baseball team, and Philip H. Withinton, earlier one of the founding officers of the Jordan Motor Car Company. Pete Sterling continued development of the car through 1921, and in April of 1922 the company announced its acquisition (for a reported million dollars) of the former Cleveland factory of the Accurate Machine Company at Colt Avenue and 134th Street. Production plans at the time were stated to be "frankly in the early stages." They remained ever thus in Cleveland. Only a half-dozen cars were built there before the postwar economic slump resulted in most of the Cleveland financial backers pulling out. Money for manufacture was ultimately secured in Warren, however, and in May of 1923 a new Sterling-Knight Company was capitalized at $1.5 million with the former Supreme Motor Company factory in Warren purchased for production. First deliveries from the new Sterling-Knight

assembly line began during mid-summer of 1923. The car from Warren remained much like the car from Cleveland, except for the curtailment of its wheelbase from 134 to 125 inches. Four body styles were offered initially in a $1985-$2800 price range, with a $3200 four-passenger offset coupe added to the line during the fall of 1924. All coachwork for the Sterling-Knight was provided by the Phillips Custom Body Company of Warren. Most components were purchased outside; the Sterling-Knight company manufactured only the engine in its entirety, the sleeve valves for which were cast by the Warren Foundry. By the end of 1924, approximately 450 Sterling-Knights had been built. During 1925 money problems suffered by the bank financing the Sterling-Knight venture meant the company had to operate on a cash basis henceforward. Production continued on a limited basis as debts mounted. Bankruptcy finally arrived for the Sterling-Knight in December of 1926.

1923-1926 STERLING-KNIGHT
Six — 78 hp, 125" wb

	FP	5	4	3	2	1
Phaeton-5P	1985	4000	5000	8000	15,000	28,000
Sporting Type-4P	2200	4200	5200	8400	15,700	29,000
Brougham-4P	2750	3100	4200	6300	10,500	22,000
Sedan-5P	2800	2400	3400	4800	8000	17,000
Offset Coupe-4P	3200	2700	3600	5300	8800	19,000

Note: The Offset Coupe was introduced during the fall of 1924 as a 1925 model.

STERLING STEAMER — The Sterling Steamer of 1901-1902 was merely the Empire Steamer of 1899-1900 built by a different sponsoring company in Sterling, Illinois. Refer to Empire Steamer.

STERN — The Stern Motor Company was organized in New York City late in 1910 with a capital stock of $100,000 for the manufacture of automobiles and engines. F.M. Randall, P.K. Stern and L. Rosenberg were the incorporators. Manufacture of a car is doubted.

1917 Sternad, locomotive automobile, NAHC

STERNAD — Chicago, Illinois — (1917) — A.F. Sternad, designing engineer of the Chicago Solder Company, set out to build himself a locomotive automobile, and certainly he succeeded. "Every locomotive feature has a part to play in its operation," Sternad said. "The cylinder and connecting rods on the sides that correspond to the driving parts of a steam locomotive are actual pumps that compress air up to 125 lb. pressure in the tank behind the cab. This compressed air is used to inflate tires and blow the whistle. The 'steam dome' in front of the cab affords access to the gasoline tank. The 'sand dome' provides an opening for ventilating the motor. The 'smoke stack' is the opening to the radiator. What looks like 'clean out doors' forward of and just below the cab, are handy ventilators for the cab; the 'air brake cylinders' above these doors are an auxiliary air supply for the whistle." The Sternad's engine was a 40 hp four and its top speed was 60 mph. The car first startled passersby when it appeared on the streets of Chicago in 1917. By 1924 Sternad had made several trips between Chicago and New York in the vehicle, and was about to toot his whistle and start on a trek to Southern California.

STERRETT — The Sterrett Automobile Company was organized in Denver, Colorado during the summer of 1908 for the purpose of manufacturing an electric car. L.G. Sterrett and Alva E. Brunson were the partners involved. "Both have practical experience in the electric car business, having conducted an exclusive electric garage for some time in Denver, and also having connection with construction works," *Motor Age* reported. "They expect to have their first Denver electric on the streets within a few months." Manufacture has not been documented.

STETSON — In December of 1916, the Stetson Motor Car Company was incorporated with a capital stock of $1 million in the state of Delaware. Although this venture never left the paper it was written upon, it remains interesting historically as an early automotive effort of Cornelius W. Van Ranst, the renowned engineer. In addition to Van Ranst, the people behind the ill-fated Stetson were P.A. Ziselman and W. Hanford. The Stetson that never was, incidentally, has frequently been given an extended longevity in automobile rosters. This was the result of a typographical error somewhere along the line which confused the Stetson and the Stilson.

STEUTERMAN — St. Louis, Missouri — (1899) — At his home in St. Louis in 1899, Frank Steuterman built a single-cylinder gasoline motor buggy which had one speed forward and no reverse, and a leather dash in front. It was the only automobile he ever built

STEVENS — The E.W. Stevens Company was organized in Somerville, New Jersey during the spring of 1908 with a capital stock of $200,000 for the manufacture of vehicles and engines of all kinds. Incorporators were E.D. Cronin, F. Knowlton and R.H. Osgoodby. Manufacture of a car is doubted.

The Stevens Company of Chicago, Illinois built a cyclecar called the Steco in 1914. Refer to Steco.

STEVENS — Peoria, Illinois — (1899) — Frederick Stevens of Peoria designed and built an automobile in 1899 which apparently was not very good. Nonetheless, he sold the patents for the car and the one example produced to a J.C. Birket for $3300. "Mr. Birket's faith in the ponderous machine is unshaken, notwithstanding the failures that have so far attended all attempts to make it practicable," reported *The Motor Age* that November. "He is at present engaged in the formation of a company for the manufacture of the cars, and will soon commence the repair and perfection of the wagon." There is no evidence manufacture followed.

1903 Stevens-Duryea, runabout, HAC

STEVENS-DURYEA — Chicopee Falls, Massachusetts — (1901-1927) — At the turn of the century, in Springfield, Massachusetts, J. Frank Duryea organized the Hampden Automobile & Launch Company. The car he built as a Hampden prototype became the Stevens-Duryea in 1901. His work having come to the attention of the J. Stevens Arms & Tool Company of Chicopee Falls, a deal was done which resulted in the entire Hampden operation moving into the top floor of the Overman factory which the armaments firm had earlier purchased. There the Stevens-Duryea was put into production late that year. A $1200 wire-wheeled runabout, it was powered by a two-cylinder 5 hp horizontal engine that was started from the seat and steered by a tiller. A three-speed sliding gear transmission was featured. Three-point motor suspension arrived in 1904, followed in 1905 by Stevens-Duryea's first four, a 20 hp $2500 touring car. In 1906 a huge 50 hp shaft-drive six was introduced at $5000, and the character of the Stevens-Duryea as a high-quality and high-priced car was irrevocably fixed. Prestigious conservatism was a mark of the Stevens-Duryea. Though "Twentieth Century Hustler" was used as a nickname in 1906, the company's product was more often identified with sedate slogans like "There is No Better Motor Car." An occasional roadster was offered, but the mainstay of the Stevens-Duryea production, which averaged about 100 cars a year, was composed of larger touring cars and limousines, the rear seats of which were adjustable several inches up and down, and fore and aft, on some models by 1912. Until 1906 the Stevens-Duryea had been built under the aegis of the J. Stevens Arms & Tool Company; in May that year the Stevens-Duryea Company was organized as an independent venture with a capital stock of $300,000. By January 1915 a total of 14,000 Stevens-Duryeas were on the road, but the company closed down its assembly line that month. Although free of debt, the firm lacked working capital; New York banking interests were willing to supply financial help, but certain conditions were specified, purportedly including the manufacture of a cheaper range of cars, to which J. Frank Duryea would not agree. For a short while he continued making and selling repair parts for his cars, but by June of 1915 the Stevens-Duryea factory (as well as the J. Stevens armaments plant) were sold for a million dollars apiece to Westinghouse, which needed the facilities for war work. Following the Armistice, in July 1919, Ray S. Deering, in association with Thomas L. Cowles (who would serve as chief engineer) and several former Stevens-Duryea people, purchased the name, goodwill and rights to the Stevens-Duryea, as well as its factory from Westinghouse. Reorganizing as Stevens-Duryea, Inc., Deering updated and revived the venerable Stevens-Duryea six, its horsepower now up to 80, though inflation spiralled its price tags to figures approaching $10,000. In January 1920 Deering also bought out the electric passenger car business of Baker, R & L, and began building the Rauch & Lang taxicab in a new plant in Chicopee Falls next to the Stevens-Duryea factory. In January 1921, John G. Perrin (well known in the field as the man behind the Lozier) joined the company staff as a consulting engineer. By the spring of 1922, however, what *Automobile Topics* called "a chain of misadventures" (including an unchecked inventory which had run wild,

and a bank failure) resulted in Stevens-Duryea, Inc. moving into receivership. The receivership endured fourteen months, during which the company built and sold 116 new cars and disposed of 92 reconditioned models. Thereafter a syndicate headed by Ray M. Owen (whose previous efforts had included the Owen Magnetic) purchased the company and announced plans to continue manufacture at the rate of 200 cars a year. Production under the Owen regime began in January 1924. Although designated the Model G, this Stevens-Duryea was essentially the same car which Deering had introduced as the Model E in 1920. During the fall of 1925, Stevens-Duryea, Inc. announced that production remained ongoing, with the cars being built as orders were received. The orders stopped sometime in 1927, and the Stevens-Duryea was gone forever.

1901-1902 STEVENS-DURYEA
Two-Cylinder — 5 hp, 69" wb

	FP	5	4	3	2	1
Runabout-2P	1200	2300	3300	4600	7500	16,000

1903 STEVENS-DURYEA
Two-Cylinder — 5 hp, 69" wb

Runabout-2P	1300	2300	3300	4600	7500	16,000

1904 Stevens-Duryea, runabout, HAC

1904 STEVENS-DURYEA
Model L — 2-cyl., 7 hp, 69" wb

Runabout-2/4P	1250	2400	3400	4800	8000	17,000

1905 Stevens-Duryea, touring, HAC

1905 STEVENS-DURYEA
Model L — 2-cyl., 7 hp, 69" wb

Runabout-2/4P	1250	2400	3400	4800	8000	17,000

Model R — 4-cyl., 20 hp, 90" wb

Touring-5P	2500	3750	7500	12,500	17,500	25,000

1906 STEVENS-DURYEA
Model L — 2-cyl., 7 hp, 69" wb

Runabout	1300	2400	3400	4800	8000	17,000

Model R — 4-cyl., 20 hp, 90" wb

Touring-5P	2500	3750	7500	12,500	17,500	25,000
Limousine	3000	3000	6000	10,000	14,000	20,000

Model S — 6-cyl., 50 hp, 122" wb

Big Six Touring-7P	5000	5000	6500	11,000	22,000	35,000

1906 Stevens-Duryea, Big Six, touring, OCW

1907 Stevens-Duryea, Little Six, touring, HAC

1907 STEVENS-DURYEA
Model R — 4-cyl., 20 hp, 90" wb

	FP	5	4	3	2	1
Runabout-2P	2400	3000	4000	6000	9500	21,000
Touring-5P	2500	3100	4200	6300	10,500	22,000
Limousine-5P	3300	2900	3700	5600	9100	20,000

Model U — 6-cyl., 30/35 hp, 114" wb

Little Six Touring-5P	3500	4000	5000	8000	15,000	28,000

Model S — 6-cyl., 50 hp, 122" wb

Big Six Touring-7P	6000	5000	6500	11,000	22,000	35,000

1908 Stevens-Duryea, model U, touring, HAC

1908 STEVENS-DURYEA
Model R — 4-cyl., 20 hp, 90" wb

Touring-5P	2500	3200	4300	6500	11,000	23,000
Limousine-5P	3300	3000	4000	6000	9500	21,000

Model U — 6-cyl., 35 hp, 114" wb

Touring-5P	3500	3700	4700	7300	13,700	26,000
Limousine-5P	4500	3300	4400	6700	12,000	24,000

Model S — 6-cyl., 50 hp, 122" wb

Touring-7P	6000	5200	6800	11,300	23,000	36,000

1909 STEVENS-DURYEA
Model XXX — 4-cyl., 24 hp, 109" wb

Runabout-3P	2850	3300	4400	6700	12,000	24,000

Model R — 4-cyl., 20 hp, 90" wb

Touring-5P	3300	3700	4700	7300	13,700	26,000

1909 Stevens-Duryea, model XXX, runabout, OCW

Model U — 6-cyl., 35 hp, 114" wb

	FP	5	4	3	2	1
Light Six Touring-5P	3500	4500	5800	9500	18,000	32,000
Light Six Limousine	4500	3300	4400	6700	12,000	24,000

Model S — 6-cyl., 50 hp, 122" wb

Big Six Touring-7P	6000	5200	6800	11,300	23,000	36,000

Model X — 4-cyl., 24 hp, 124" wb

Touring-5P	2750	3900	4800	7700	14,300	27,000
Limousine-7P	3850	3100	4200	6300	10,500	22,000

Model Y — 6-cyl., 40 hp, 142" wb

Touring-7P	4000	4900	6300	10,300	21,000	34,000

1910 Stevens-Duryea, model X, limousine, HAC

1910 STEVENS-DURYEA
Model XXX — 4-cyl., 36.1 hp, 109" wb

Runabout-3P	2850	3300	4400	6700	12,000	24,000
Baby Tonneau-4P	2850	3500	4500	7000	13,000	25,000

Model X — 4-cyl., 36.1 hp, 124" wb

Touring-5P	2850	3900	4800	7700	14,300	27,000
Touring-4P	2850	3700	4700	7300	13,700	26,000
Limousine	3750	3100	4200	6300	10,500	22,000

Model AA — 6-cyl., 43 hp, 128" wb

Touring-5P	3300	4500	5800	9500	18,000	32,000
Touring-4P	3300	4400	5600	9200	17,300	31,000

Model Y — 6-cyl., 54.1 hp, 142" wb

Touring-7P	4000	5000	6500	11,000	22,000	35,000
Limousine	5000	3900	4800	7700	14,300	27,000

1911 Stevens-Duryea, model AA, roadster, HAC

1911 STEVENS-DURYEA
Model X — 4-cyl., 36.1 hp, 124" wb

Limousine-7P	4000	3500	4500	7000	13,000	25,000
Touring	2850	4300	5400	8700	16,500	30,000
Roadster	2850	4200	5200	8400	15,700	29,000
Fore-Door Touring	3000	4500	5700	9400	17,700	31,500

Model AA — 6-cyl., 43.8 hp, 128" wb

Torpedo-5P	3600	4500	5800	9500	18,000	32,000
Touring	3500	4400	5600	9200	17,300	31,000
Roadster	3500	4300	5400	8700	16,500	30,000
Limousine	4600	3900	4800	7700	14,300	27,000
Landaulet	4800	4000	5000	8000	15,000	28,000

Model Y — 6-cyl., 54.1 hp, 143" wb

Touring-7P	4000	5200	6800	11,300	23,000	36,000
Fore-Door Touring	4150	5000	6500	11,000	22,000	35,000
Limousine	5150	4000	5000	8000	15,000	28,000

1353

1912 Stevens-Duryea, model AA, torpedo, HAC

1912 STEVENS-DURYEA
Model AA — 6-cyl., 43.8 hp, 128" wb

	FP	5	4	3	2	1
Touring-5P	3750	4400	5600	9200	17,300	31,000
Torpedo-5P	3850	4500	5800	9500	18,000	32,000
Touring-7P	3900	4700	6100	9900	19,000	33,000
Limousine-7P	4750	3100	4200	6300	10,500	22,000
Landaulet-7P	4950	3200	4300	6500	11,000	23,000
Berline-7P	5000	3300	4400	6700	12,000	24,000
Roadster-4P	3750	4400	5600	9200	17,300	31,000
Runabout-2P	3750	4300	5400	8700	16,500	30,000

Model X — 4-cyl., 36.1 hp, 142" wb

Touring-5P	2850	4700	6100	9900	19,000	33,000
Limousine-7P	4000	3000	4000	6000	9500	21,000

Model Y — 6-cyl., 54.1 hp, 142" wb

Touring-7P	4000	5200	6800	11,300	23,000	36,000
Limousine-7P	5150	3500	4500	7000	13,000	25,000

1913 Stevens-Duryea, model C-Six, touring, HAC

1913 Stevens-Duryea C-Six, couplet, HAC

1913 STEVENS-DURYEA
Model C-Six — 6-cyl., 44.6 hp, 131" wb

Touring-5P	4500	4500	5800	9500	18,000	32,000
Roadster	4500	4400	5600	9200	17,300	31,000
Coupelet-2P	5000	2700	3600	5300	8800	19,000
Convertible Phaeton-5P	5000	4300	5400	8700	16,500	30,000
Demi-Berline-5P	5550	3000	4000	6000	9500	21,000
Limousine-7P	5500	2900	3700	5600	9100	20,000
Berline-7P	5700	3100	4200	6300	10,500	22,000

Model C-Six — 6-cyl., 44.6 hp, 138" wb

Touring-7P	4750	5000	6500	11,000	22,000	35,000
Convertible Phaeton-7P	5250	4500	5800	9500	18,000	32,000
Limousine-7P	5750	3100	4200	6300	10,500	22,000
Berline-7P	5950	3300	4400	6700	12,000	24,000

1914 STEVENS-DURYEA
Model C-Six — 6-cyl., 44.8 hp, 131" wb

Limousine-7P	5800	3100	4200	6300	10,500	22,000
Roadster-2P	4550	4500	5800	9500	18,000	32,000
Coupelet-3P	5000	2700	3600	5300	8800	19,000
Touring-5P	4550	4700	6100	9900	19,000	33,000
Landau Phaeton-5P	5200	4900	6300	10,300	21,000	34,000
Demi-Berline-5P	5750	3300	4400	6700	12,000	24,000

1914 Stevens-Duryea, model C-Six, demi-berline, HAC

1915 Stevens-Duryea, limousine, JAC

1915 STEVENS-DURYEA
Model D-Six — 6-cyl., 46 hp, 131" wb

	FP	5	4	3	2	1
Limousine-7P	5800	3100	4200	6300	10,500	22,000
Touring-5P	4550	4500	5800	9500	18,000	32,000
Roadster-3P	4550	4400	5600	9200	17,300	31,000
Landau-Phaeton-5P	5400	4700	6100	9900	19,000	33,000
Demi-Berline	5750	3100	4200	6300	10,500	22,000

Model DD-Six — 6-cyl., 47.2 hp, 138" wb

Touring-7P	4800	5000	6500	11,000	22,000	35,000
Landau Phaeton-7P	5600	5200	6800	11,300	23,000	36,000
Limousine-7P	6100	3200	4300	6500	11,000	23,000
Berlin-7P	6200	3300	4400	6700	12,000	24,000
Landaulet-7P	6300	3500	4500	7000	13,000	25,000

Note: Production discontinued from January 1915 through 1919.

1920-1921 STEVENS-DURYEA
Model E — 6-cyl., 80 hp, 138" wb

Touring-7P	8000	6000	8500	13,000	30,000	42,000
Vestibule Limousine-7P	9500	4200	5200	8400	15,700	29,000
Sedan-4P	9500	3100	4200	6300	10,500	22,000
Close-Coupled Sport Tr.	8000	6200	8800	13,500	31,000	43,000

1922 Stevens-Duryea, model E, touring, HAC

1923 Stevens-Duryea, model E, close-coupled sport, HAC

1922-1923 STEVENS-DURYEA
Model E — 6-cyl., 80 hp, 138" wb

	FP	5	4	3	2	1
Touring-7P	6800	6400	9300	14,500	33,000	45,000
Touring-4P	6900	6000	8500	13,000	30,000	42,000
Vestibule Limousine-7P	8900	3100	4200	6300	10,500	22,000
Three-Quarter Limo.-7P	8900	3100	4200	6300	10,500	22,000
Sedan-4P	8900	2500	3500	5000	8500	18,000
Close-Coupled Sport Tr.	6900	6500	9500	15,000	34,000	46,000
Cabriolet	8900	6000	8500	13,000	30,000	42,000
Town Brougham	8900	3000	4000	6000	9500	21,000
Roadster	7250	5800	8000	12,500	28,000	40,000
Coupe	8500	2900	3700	5600	9100	20,000

1924 Stevens-Duryea, model G, vestibule limousine, HAC

1924-1927 STEVENS-DURYEA
Model G — 6-cyl., 80 hp, 138" wb

	FP	5	4	3	2	1
Touring-7P	7500	6400	9300	14,500	33,000	45,000
Sport Touring-4P	7750	6500	9500	15,000	34,000	46,000
Roadster-2P	8150	6000	8500	13,000	30,000	42,000
Coupe-4P	9000	2900	3700	5600	9100	20,000
Sedan-6P	9675	2500	3500	5000	8500	18,000
Vestibule Limousine-6P	9675	3100	4200	6300	10,500	22,000
Sedan-4P	10,000	2400	3400	4800	8000	17,000
Open Drive Limousine	10,175	3500	4500	7000	13,000	25,000
Vestibule Limousine-7P	10,175	3200	4300	6500	11,000	23,000
Town Brougham	10,175	3000	4000	6000	9500	21,000
Cabriolet	10,175	5800	8000	12,500	28,000	40,000

STEVENSON — The Stevenson-Switz Company was organized during the summer of 1907 with a capital stock of $10,000 for the manufacture and sale of automobiles in Schenectady, New York. Incorporators included C.D. Stevenson, H.D. Switz and P.C. Stevenson. Manufacture is doubted.

The William Stevenson Garage Company was organized in Morristown, New Jersey during the spring of 1909 with a capital stock of $50,000 to manufacture and repair automobiles. Incorporators included William Stevenson and W.W. Crane. Manufacture is doubted.

STEWART — "William C. Stewart, Lynn, Massachusetts, inventor of a patented boiler, is at work on a complete vehicle to demonstrate his ideas," reported *The Horseless Age* in October 1902. Details are lacking.

The Stewart Automobile Company was organized in New York City early in 1909 with a capital stock of $50,000 "to instruct in the use of automobiles, motor boats, flying machines and other vehicles, and to manufacture such vehicles." Incorporators were Arthur V. Lyall, F.S. Ferguson, Jr. and William H. Stewart, Jr. Manufacture is doubted.

1895 Stewart, gasoline wagon, LC

STEWART — Pocantico Hills, New York — (1895) — In 1895 Richard F. Stewart built a gasoline motor wagon in Pocantico Hills in order to demonstrate his ideas regarding the application of power in horseless carriages. The Stewart was fitted with a 2 hp Daimler engine which engaged and revolved a shaft extending lengthwise in the vehicle, this shaft brought into and out of engagement with the engine by means of a friction clutch. Richard Stewart did not build another car, but a year later began promoting his Stewart Automatic Clutch: "The only thing ever invented that will regulate the wheels on a solid axle when turning corners and work backwards as well as forwards." Advertisements from the turn of the century indicate that the device was being produced by the Stewart Clutch Company in Milwaukee, Wisconsin. Richard F. Stewart died in Tarrytown, New York in 1939 at the age of seventy-seven.

1904 Stewart-Garbutt, runabout, JHV

STEWART-GARBUTT — Los Angeles, California — (1904) — Alfred C. Stewart was the proprietor of Stewart's Automobile Machine Works at 1008 South Santee Street in Los Angeles. In 1904 he offered "special machines built to order," and one of his customers was Frank A. Garbutt, president of the Loma Oil Company, who ordered a 40 hp racer. The number of further custom cars Stewart may have built is not known. By 1907 he was a Dorris dealer and a marine engine manufacturer.

1915 Stewart, 7-pass. touring, WLB

STEWART — Buffalo, New York — (1915-1916) — The Stewart Motor Corporation was a prominent manufacturer of commercial vehicles in Buffalo from 1912 until just before the Second World War. For two seasons, 1915-1916, the company also offered a passenger car which, *Automobile Topics* adjudged, was "of more than ordinary pretentions, which are more than reasonably bought at its list price of $1950." Both a seven-passenger touring car and a three-passenger roadster were available at that price. A six-cylinder 29 hp Continental engine powered the Stewart, and its wheelbase was 127 inches. Like the Stewart truck, the Stewart car was distinguished by its sloping Renault-type hood. The vehicle's radiator was mounted just ahead of the dash. "Practical results have demonstrated that this design is free from liability to injury from external sources," the company said, "and that it cools well under a wide variety of conditions."

STEWART — Bowling Green, Ohio — (1921) / **STEWART-COATS** — (1922) — The Stewart Motor Car Company was organized in Bowling Green in March of 1920 with a capital stock of $500,000. Involved in the venture were Y. Frank Stewart, Charles H. Gifford, Irene Barringer, Willis Garner and C.S. Hatfield. The firm spent most of 1921 announcing all the various models of four- and six-cylinder cars it was planning to build. Total Stewart production, however, was a single gasoline touring car prototype. In 1922 George A. Coats contracted with the company for manufacture of his steam car which was occasionally referred to as a Stewart-Coats, this most likely by the Stewart people, Coats preferring only his own name. Again, only a prototype was built.

STICKNEY STEAM — Portland, Maine — (1901-1902) — Henry R. Stickney had a small machine shop in Portland in which he built small two-stroke gasoline and single-cylinder steam engines. A few of these he installed in buggies for a local clientele, but this was strictly a sideline activity to his engine building and his machining business.

STICKNEY — St. Paul, Minnesota — (1914) — In 1894, while a teenager, Charles A. Stickney built a three-wheeled steam automobile which, among other purloined components, was fitted with a chair from his mother's kitchen, two wheels from his father's spring wagon, and a third wheel from a

1914 Stickney Motorette, 2-pass. tandem, WLB

sister's pony cart. It was ordered dismantled soon after being discovered during its second test run. An apprentice machinist in the shops of the Great Western Railway (which his father had founded), Charles Stickney subsequently established the Charles A. Stickney Company in St. Paul for the manufacture of stationary gasoline engines. And in 1914 he introduced one of the niftier cyclecars on the market. The Stickney was a tandem two-seater steered by a wheel in the rear seat. Its body lines were crisp and rakish, its low, lithe look enhanced by a long wheelbase of 120 inches. The tread was 40 inches. A four-cylinder water-cooled 12/15 hp engine powered the Stickney, with friction transmission and double chain drive featured. In addition to the tandem roadster, a light delivery was available at the same $395 price. For $410 a combination roadster/light delivery could be had. Charles Stickney chose to call his car a "motorette . . . to distinguish it from the motor car on one hand and the motorcycle and cyclecar on the other." But it suffered the same fate as most cyclecars. During the summer of 1914 Charles Stickney announced that he had "given up the idea altogether." Thereafter, Stickney's engine business seemed to slide too. He left St. Paul awhile, to return in 1920 and open a pencil factory.

STILL — The Still Motor Company, listed at 707 Chamber of Commerce Building in Detroit, Michigan, was indicated as an automobile manufacturer in the Hiscox book *Horseless Vehicles, Automobiles, Motor Cycles* published in 1900. Documentation is lacking.

1908 Stilson, 50-60 hp touring, NAHC

STILSON — Pittsfield, Massachusetts — (1907-1909) — The January 1907 announcement of this new car from Massachusetts indicated that it was to be built by the Pittsfield Motor Carriage Company, but by March the firm's name had been changed to Stilson Motor Car Company. Herbert M. Stilson was the local jeweler and watchmaker who put up most of the money for manufacture; the Stilson was designed by Clarence P. Hollister, who had been one of the founders of the company producing the Berkshire in Pittsfield. Indeed, Stilson would share the same 92 Rennie Avenue address as the Berkshire. Whereas the Berkshire was a four, the Stilson was a six (Herschell-Spillman engine), and priced at about a thousand dollars more. It was not a very successful car, a trait it also shared with the Berkshire. Area residents recalled that the Stilson's engine was so powerful "that the least slip of the clutch would strip the gears like butter." This was perhaps less the result of the engine, however, than the special transmission patented by Hollister and used also in the Berkshire. It featured a type of fluid clutch using oil pumped by three planetary gears — and did not work very well. Nineteen eight seems to have been the only year that it was featured; in 1907 and 1909 a standard four-speed selective with direct drive in third was fitted. Although the Stilson Motor Car Company remained in existence during 1910, production is not believed to have continued beyond 1909. In December of 1910 the company was petitioned into bankruptcy. It was revealed at the time that of its original $100,000 capitalization, only $33,700 had been paid in. The Stilson assets were now less than $3000. Harry Stilson subsequently left for New York City where he set up a new jewelry business in Manhattan's Diamond District.

1907 STILSON
Six — 50/60 hp, 120" wb

	FP	5	4	3	2	1
Touring-7P	4500	6000	8500	13,000	30,000	42,000

1908 STILSON
Six — 50/60 hp, 123" wb

	FP	5	4	3	2	1
Type C Touring-7P	4500	6000	8500	13,000	30,000	42,000
Type C Limousine-7P	5500	4200	5200	8400	15,700	29,000

1909 STILSON
Six — 50/60 hp

	FP	5	4	3	2	1
Model H Tr.-7P (133" wb)	4500	6000	8500	13,000	30,000	42,000
Model J Rbt.-4P (122" wb)	4250	5800	8000	12,500	28,000	40,000

STIRLING — Newark, New Jersey — (1920-1921) — In late October of 1920, Stirling Motors, Inc. of Newark announced its entry into the automobile field. The first six cars were then being completed, and production was intended to be started within a month. The Stirling was an assembled car of standard components and offered as a roadster and touring. The price tag in October was stated to be $2350. By March of 1921, this had been slashed to $1185. And soon after that the Stirling was no more.

STOCKWELL — Grand Rapids, Michigan — (1905) — That M.E. Stockwell of Grand Rapids was engaged in the "manufacture of an automobile" was reported in a July 1905 issue of *The Horseless Age*. No details were forthcoming regarding what the car was.

1905 Stoddard-Dayton, touring, HAC

STODDARD-DAYTON — Dayton, Ohio — (1904-1913) — John W. Stoddard and his younger brother Charles G. gave up everything to build the Stoddard-Dayton. The family business had begun with the manufacture of hay rakes for horses in 1875 and had branched into a variety of other farm implements by 1884 when the Stoddard Manufacturing Company was formally incorporated. During a trip abroad in the mid-1890's, Charles Stoddard had become fascinated with the automobile and began experimenting. The work turned serious soon after the turn of the century when a young English engineer named H.J. Edwards was hired to help. In April of 1904 the Stoddard Manufacturing Company announced that a pilot model would soon be on the road. It arrived that summer, a Rutenber-engined four with its gearshift mounted on the steering column. Production began thereafter; in December the Dayton Motor Car Company succeeded the Stoddard Manufacturing Company, and hay rakes and baling forks were forever forgotten. "As Good as It Looks" was a company slogan in 1905, and that said it all. The Stoddard-Dayton was one of the really splendid automobiles of its era. Large, luxurious and sturdily built, the cars immediately found favor. There were 125 Stoddard-Daytons built in 1905, 385 in 1906; production zoomed to 2000 in 1907. By now, an overhead-valve engine of the company's own manufacture powered the car, and a six-cylinder model joined the four for a one-year run in 1908. During the summer of 1909, the Stoddards announced creation of the Courier Car Company for the manufacture of a less expensive car. Though the new Courier was designed by Stoddard-Dayton chief engineer H.J. Edwards, it was built in another factory purchased in Dayton. Company promotion was careful to separate the two marques. In 1910 the Stoddards made a fatal mistake by electing to join the conglomerate Benjamin Briscoe was forming. During the summer of 1911, the Stoddard-Dayton Division of the United States Motor Company became the second American manufacturer (after Stearns) to acquire a Knight license. A Knight-engined six joined the Stoddard-Dayton line of fours for 1912. Then Briscoe's U.S. Motor empire fell apart, and with it the Stoddard-Dayton. The only company among the flurry of firms in the conglomerate that was saved was Maxwell. In February of 1913, announcement was made that the Stoddard-Dayton would continue to be produced "for the time being" under Maxwell management. The time being was over within months.

1904-1905 STODDARD-DAYTON
Four — 26 hp, 96" wb

Side Entrance Touring	2000	2500	3500	5000	8500	18,000

1906 STODDARD-DAYTON
Model E — 4-cyl., 18 hp, 88" wb

Runabout	1250	2400	3400	4800	8000	17,000

Model D — 4-cyl., 35 hp, 103" wb

Touring	2250	3100	4200	6300	10,500	22,000
Limousine	3250	2500	3500	5000	8500	18,000

As good as it looks

1906 Stoddard-Dayton, model D, touring, HAC

1907 Stoddard-Dayton, model H, runabout, HAC

1907 Stoddard-Dayton, model K, runabout, NAHC

1907 STODDARD-DAYTON

Model H — 4-cyl., 15/18 hp, 88" wb

Runabout-2P	1750	2400	3400	4800	8000	17,000

Model F — 4-cyl., 30/35 hp, 105" wb

Touring-5P	2500	3100	4200	6300	10,500	22,000
Limousine-7P	3500	2500	3500	5000	8500	18,000

Model K — 4-cyl., 30/35 hp, 105" wb

Runabout-3P	2500	3000	4000	6000	9500	21,000

1908 Stoddard-Dayton, model 8-F, touring, HAC

1908 STODDARD-DAYTON

Model 8-H — 4-cyl., 18 hp, 92" wb

Runabout	1750	3100	4200	6300	10,500	22,000
Coupe	2150	2400	3400	4800	8000	17,000

Model 8-N — 4-cyl., 18 hp, 92" wb

	FP	5	4	3	2	1
Landaulet	2300	3200	4300	6500	11,000	23,000

Model 8-F — 4-cyl., 40/45 hp, 113 1/2" wb

Touring	2500	4500	5800	9500	18,000	32,000
Limousine	3500	3300	4400	6700	12,000	24,000

Model 8-K — 4-cyl., 40/45 hp, 113 1/2" wb

Roadster	2550	5000	6500	11,000	22,000	35,000

Model 8-G — 6-cyl., 50/60 hp, 128" wb

Touring	4500	5700	11,400	19,000	26,600	38,000
Roadster	—	5400	10,800	18,000	25,200	36,000
Limousine	—	4200	5200	8400	15,700	29,000

1909 Stoddard-Dayton, model 9-H, tonneau, HAC

1909 STODDARD-DAYTON

Model 9-C — 4-cyl., 35 hp, 105" wb

Roadster-2/3/4P	2000	3200	4300	6500	11,000	23,000

Model 9-H — 4-cyl., 25 hp, 103" wb

Runabout-2P	2000	3300	4400	6700	12,000	24,000
Touring-4/5/6P	3500	3700	4700	7300	13,700	26,000

Model 9-A — 4-cyl., 35 hp, 105" wb

Brougham	3500	3500	4500	7000	13,000	25,000
Victoria	2500	3100	4200	6300	10,500	22,000
Touring-5P	2000	4300	5400	8700	16,500	30,000

Model 9-K — 4-cyl., 45 hp, 113 1/2" wb

Roadster-2/3/4P	2500	3500	4500	7000	13,000	25,000

Model 9-F — 4-cyl., 45 hp, 113 1/2" wb

Touring-5/7P	2500	4400	5600	9200	17,300	31,000
Limousine-5/7P	3500	3700	4700	7300	13,700	26,000

1910 Stoddard-Dayton, model 10-C, baby tonneau, HAC

1911 Stoddard-Dayton, model 11-A, toy tonneau, IMS

1910 STODDARD-DAYTON

Model 10-B — 4-cyl., 30 hp, 108" wb

	FP	5	4	3	2	1
Touring-5P	1600	4300	5400	8700	16,500	30,000

Model 10-C — 4-cyl., 40 hp, 116" wb

	FP	5	4	3	2	1
Baby Tonneau-4P	2100	4400	5600	9200	17,300	31,000
Roadster-3P	2000	4400	5600	9200	17,300	30,000

Model 10-A — 4-cyl., 40 hp, 116" wb

	FP	5	4	3	2	1
Touring-5P	2100	4500	5800	9500	18,000	32,000

Model 10-K — 4-cyl., 50 hp, 120" wb

	FP	5	4	3	2	1
Roadster-3P	2650	5200	6800	11,300	23,000	36,000
Baby Tonneau-4P	2750	5400	7300	11,800	25,000	38,000
Baby Tonneau-5P	2750	5400	7300	11,800	25,000	38,000

Model 10-K — 4-cyl., 50 hp, 128" wb

	FP	5	4	3	2	1
Torpedo-4P	2800	5500	7500	12,000	26,000	39,000

Model 10-F — 4-cyl., 50 hp, 128" wb

	FP	5	4	3	2	1
Landaulet-7P	3800	4400	5600	9200	17,300	31,000
Limousine-7P	3800	4400	5200	8400	15,700	29,000
Touring-7P	2800	6000	8500	13,000	30,000	42,000

Model 10-H — 4-cyl., 30 hp, 108" wb

	FP	5	4	3	2	1
Roadster-2P	1500	3900	4800	7700	14,300	27,000
Coupe-4P	2100	2900	3700	5600	9100	20,000

Model 10-T — 4-cyl., 30 hp, 108" wb

	FP	5	4	3	2	1
Town Car	2800	3200	4300	6500	11,000	23,000
Limousine	2800	3100	4200	6300	10,500	22,000
Landaulet	2800	3200	4300	6500	11,000	23,000

1911 STODDARD-DAYTON

Model 11-H — 4-cyl., 30 hp, 114" wb

	FP	5	4	3	2	1
Roadster-2P	1550	4400	5600	9200	17,300	31,000
Limousine	2700	2900	3700	5600	9100	20,000
Landaulet	2700	3000	4000	6000	9500	21,000
Coupe	2250	2700	3600	5300	8800	19,000
Open Door Touring	1700	4300	5400	8700	16,500	30,000
Fore Door Touring	1750	4300	5400	8700	16,500	30,000
Semi-Torpedo	1625	4200	5200	8400	15,700	29,000

Model 11-A — 4-cyl., 40 hp, 120" wb

	FP	5	4	3	2	1
Touring-5P	2400	4700	6100	9900	19,000	33,000
Toy Tonneau-5P	2300	4500	5800	9500	18,000	32,000
Toy Tonneau-4P	2300	4500	5800	9500	18,000	32,000
Semi-Torpedo	2275	4400	5600	9200	17,300	31,000
Torpedo	2350	4500	5800	9500	18,000	32,000

Model 11 — 4-cyl., 50 hp, 106" wb

	FP	5	4	3	2	1
Racer	2800	6400	9300	14,500	33,000	45,000

Model 11-K — 4-cyl., 50 hp, 130" wb

	FP	5	4	3	2	1
Torpedo-5P	3000	5400	7300	11,800	25,000	38,000
Roadster	2850	5300	7000	11,500	24,000	37,000
Baby Tonneau	2900	5500	7500	12,000	26,000	38,000
Semi-Torpedo	2925	5700	7800	12,300	27,000	39,500

Model 11-F — 4-cyl., 50 hp, 130" wb

	FP	5	4	3	2	1
Limousine	4200	4000	5000	8000	15,000	28,000
Landaulet	4000	4200	5200	8400	15,700	29,000

1912 Stoddard-Dayton, Saybrook, semi-torpedo, HAC

1912 Stoddard-Dayton, Knight, touring, HAC

1912 STODDARD-DAYTON

Savoy — 4-cyl., 28 hp, 112" wb

	FP	5	4	3	2	1
Touring-5P	1450	4000	5000	8000	15,000	28,000
Roadster-2P	1450	3900	4800	7700	14,300	27,000
Torpedo Roadster-4P	1350	3700	4700	7300	13,700	26,000

Stratford — 4-cyl., 38 hp, 114" wb

	FP	5	4	3	2	1
Limousine-7P	2700	3500	4500	7000	13,000	25,000
Landaulet-7P	2750	3700	4700	7300	13,700	26,000
Coupe-4P	2350	2700	3600	5300	8800	19,000
Touring-5P	1850	4200	5200	8400	15,700	29,000
Torpedo Roadster-2P	1750	4000	5000	8000	15,000	28,000

Saybrook — 4-cyl., 48 hp, 122 1/2" wb

	FP	5	4	3	2	1
Limousine-7P	3900	3700	4700	7300	13,700	26,000
Touring-7P	2800	5200	6800	11,300	23,000	36,000
Torpedo-4P	2700	5000	6500	11,000	22,000	35,000
Semi-Torpedo-2P	2700	5000	6500	11,000	22,000	35,000

Special — 4-cyl., 58 hp, 122 1/2" & 130" wb

	FP	5	4	3	2	1
Torpedo	3300	6200	8800	13,500	31,000	43,000
Speedster	3300	6800	10,300	16,000	35,500	48,000
Torpedo-6P	3500	6000	8500	13,000	30,000	42,000
Touring-6P	3500	6000	8500	13,000	30,000	42,000
Limousine	4600	4000	5000	8000	15,000	28,000

Knight — 6-cyl., 70 hp, 133" wb

	FP	5	4	3	2	1
Touring-7P	5000	7200	11,300	17,700	38,700	50,000
Limousine-7P	6250	4500	5800	9500	18,000	32,000
Torpedo-4P	4900	7000	10,800	16,900	37,100	49,000
Roadster-2P	4900	6800	10,300	16,000	35,500	48,000

1913 Stoddard-Dayton, model 48, touring, HAC

1913 STODDARD-DAYTON

Model 30 — 4-cyl., 30 hp, 112" wb

	FP	5	4	3	2	1
Touring-5P	1450	4200	5200	8400	15,700	29,000
Roadster	1350	4000	5000	8000	15,000	28,000

Model 38 — 4-cyl., 38 hp, 114" wb

	FP	5	4	3	2	1
Touring-7P	1850	4400	5600	9200	17,300	31,000
Roadster	1750	4300	5400	8700	16,500	30,000
Landaulet	2750	3500	4500	7000	13,000	25,000
Coupe	2350	2900	3700	5600	9100	20,000

Model 48 — 4-cyl., 48 hp, 123" wb

	FP	5	4	3	2	1
Touring-7P	2800	5000	6500	11,000	22,000	35,000
Roadster	2700	4900	6300	10,300	21,000	34,000
Limousine	3900	3700	4700	7300	13,700	26,000

Knight — 6-cyl., 70 hp, 139" wb

	FP	5	4	3	2	1
Touring-7P	5000	6200	8800	13,500	31,000	43,000
Roadster	4900	6000	8500	13,000	30,000	42,000
Limousine	6250	4200	5200	8400	15,700	29,000

STOKESBARY — In February of 1923 the Steam Automotive Works of Denver, Colorado announced a reorganization to Stokesbary Steam Motors Company and a relocation to Los Angeles, California "where plans call for the erection of a factory in the near future." That was the last heard of this venture, which was headed by J.H. Stokesbary. Most probably not even a prototype was completed.

STOLTENBURG & REIMERS — The Stoltenburg & Reimers Company was organized in Davenport, Iowa during the fall of 1903 with a capital stock of $5000 to manufacture, repair and sell automobiles. The partners involved were Henry Stoltenburg and John Reimers. Manufacture is doubted.

STOLZ — Brooklyn, New York — (1900-1902) — The Stolz Cycle Company of Brooklyn evolved into the Stolz Automobile Company at the turn of the century. Added to bicycles now were gasoline engines, and W.G. Stolz offered to build complete gasoline cars to order. He could not have built very many. The probability is that neither the cars nor the Stolz engine was very good. By the summer of 1902 Stolz turned rights to his engine over to the Conger Manufacturing Company of Groton. (Stolz had designed a car for the Crandell Machine Company in that town.) The first word from the Conger people was that they had "perfected" the Stolz engine and were all set to introduce the Conger car.

STOMMEL — Plainfield, New Jersey — (1897-1899) — Hugh Stommel wasn't quite ready with his car but he was so anxious to test it before the winter set in that he rolled it out of his shop in Plainfield in late November 1897. Probably this was just as well. "The mud was thick in the streets and somewhat impeded the progress of the strange-looking vehicle, but it managed to go after a fashion . . ., reported the *Plainfield Press*. "The carriage weighed 600 pounds, considerably more than its inventor had expected, and the two horse power gasoline engine was only strong enough to move it but a short distance at a time. The carriage was tried on Park Avenue between Fifth Street and North Avenue and was found to be comparatively noiseless." A 4 hp engine would take care of the Stommel's lethargy problem, which the car's inventor saw to immediately that winter, and then spent most of 1898 perfecting his new friction transmission. This consisted of a twenty-inch disc together with two friction rollers four inches in diameter and driven by two spur gears, one of which was made of rawhide. His new transmission was geared to provide speeds of one to ten miles an hour, he said, and by 1899 Stommel had built a second automobile to demonstrate it. That summer he joined with Eli Teeker and De Forest P. Lozier in organizing the United States Standard Motor Vehicle Company with a capital stock of $25,000, upped that fall to a grand $1.5 million. Incorporation seems to have been as far as this New Jersey venture proceeded; manufacture did not follow.

STONE & MAYNARD — The Stone & Maynard Company of Avonia, Pennsylvania was among the hopefuls which entered the Chicago Times-Herald Contest of 1895 with an automobile of its own design. The company didn't make it to the starting line, however, and whether its vehicle was ever successfully completed has not been documented.

STOOPS — Although this cyclecar was announced under the name of its designer, Harry J. Stoops of the American Cyclecar Company of Detroit, the vehicle saw production in Bridgeport, Connecticut as the Trumbull. Refer to Trumbull.

1902 Storck Steamer, NAHC

STORCK STEAM — Red Bank, New Jersey — (1901-1902) — Frank C. Storck was the proprietor of a bicycle emporium in Red Bank and in 1898 was described in the town's business directory as "a hustler and . . . always the first to present novelties." In 1901 he began building the first — and ultimately only — automobile ever produced in Red Bank. The Storcks were steamers fitted with two-cylinder vertical double-acting engines fueled by gasoline. The boiler was water tube; cold water to steam was promised in two-and-a-half minutes. Runabouts were priced at $725 (wood body) and $800 (steel body), and a dos-a-dos available at $950. Frank Storck also was willing to build to order, though reluctantly. "If you want a steam wagon, and have ideas of your own which you desire embodied in your wagon, investigate the merits of the Storck Steam Carriages and then change your specifications to suit yourself," he advertised. "I build wagons for Jobbers, Dealers and Customers to order if desired, but my variety of models suits experienced critics." Frank C. Storck was a hustler. Nonetheless, it seems his steam car activity ended in 1902.

STORK-KAR — New York, New York — (1919-1921) — The Stork-Kar Sales Company was located in New York City. The Stork-Kar was built in Martinsburg, West Virginia by the Norwalk Motor Car Company. It was one of two badge-engineered automobiles (the other the Marshall of Chicago) that were merely Norwalks trading under another name. Powered by a Lycoming 35 hp four-cylinder engine, the car was offered as a five-passenger touring on a 116-inch wheelbase. Probably the last Stork-Kars were built in Lynchburg. Virginia at the Piedmont factory, since the last Norwalks were also built there.

STORM — The Storm Motor Car Company was organized in New York City early in 1912 with a capital stock of $10,000 to manufacture and sell automobiles. J.P. Storm and C.M. Storm were the partners involved. Manufacture is doubted.

1915 Storms Electric, roadster, NAHC

STORMS ELECTRIC — Detroit, Michigan — (1915) — The Storms was built in the Detroit factory at 807 Scotten in which the Mercury cyclecar had been born and died during 1914. The Storms was a cyclecar too, but it was unique in being an electric. The car was the idea of William E. Storms, who had formerly been associated with the Colonial Electric Car Company

and the Anderson Electric Car Company and who wanted to be the first in America to introduce a really cheap electric. Joining him in the organization of the Storms Electric Car Company were Ferdinand H. Zilisch, a Milwaukee businessman, and F.T. King of Detroit. Three models were offered on a single chassis (90-inch wheelbase, 44-inch tread), its frame of pressed steel, suspended in front by semi-elliptic and in the rear by three-quarter elliptic springs. Control was by lever, steering by wheel. Forty to fifty miles on a single battery charge was guaranteed, with 18 mph the top speed. Prices were $950 for coupe, $750 for roadster and $650 for light delivery. Unfortunately, an electric cyclecar appeared to be the answer to a question few people had asked, and the Storms Electric Car Company was out of business by the end of 1915. During the summer of 1916, William E. Storms showed up in Jonesville, Michigan where his new electric was the American Beauty.

STOUT — The automotive career of William B. Stout was estimable. Although the cyclecar he designed in 1913 while working as an editor for *Motor Age* was never produced, his next job (for the W.H. McIntyre Company) resulted in the Imp cyclecar. Subsequently he worked for both Scripps-Booth and Packard — and in the 1930's Stout created a number of streamlined cars called Scarab. Refer to Scarab.

STOVER — The Stover Motor Car Company was organized in Cincinnati, Ohio during the fall of 1910 with a capital stock of $25,000 to manufacture and sell automobiles and other vehicles. Incorporators were L.K. Emerson, George W. Platt, R.L. Dallings, Stanley M. Adams, Parker K. Gale and Alexander L. Parker. Manufacture is doubted.

STOVER — Freeport, Illinois — (1909) — After failing to make it to market with his Phoenix automobile in 1905, D.C. Stover tried again in 1909. He established a Stover Motor Car Company as adjunct to his gasoline-engine-producing Stover Manufacturing Company. Its total production was a few automobiles and a single railway motor inspection car in 1909. In December that year he sold the assets of his automobile venture to Buda, the engine-building manufacturer from Harvey, Illinois. Buda indicated its plans to establish an "automobile department," but ultimately decided against moving into car production. Meanwhile, in Freeport, the factory built for the Stover car was turned over to manufacture of Stover engines.

STOYLE-VOGEL — The Stoyle-Vogel Auto Company was organized in Camden, New Jersey early in 1909 with a capital stock of $100,000 to manufacture "automobiles, motor cars, carriages, coaches, cabs, etc." Behind this venture were Wilson H. Stoyle, Lewis G. Vogel and Frank A. Kuntz. Manufacture is doubted, but the firm is known to have become agents in Philadelphia for the American, Midland and Babcock Electric.

STRANAHAN-ELDRIDGE — The Stranahan-Eldridge Company was organized in Boston, Massachusetts during the fall of 1906 with a capital stock of $50,000 for the manufacture of motor cars and engines. F.D. Stranahan of Brookline and W.E. Eldridge of Boston were the partners involved. Manufacture is doubted, but the firm is believed to have operated as a dealership.

STRANG — "C.G. Strang of Colorado Springs, Colorado has nearly completed a 20 horsepower gasoline vehicle for C.E. Palmer of the same place," reported *The Horseless Age* in August 1902. Details are lacking.

The Strang Electric-Gasoline Car Company was organized in Kansas City, Missouri during the fall of 1905 with a capital stock of $100,000 for the manufacture of automobiles. "The company has patented a combination electric-gasoline motor power that can be employed in the moving of any class of vehicle designed to carry freight or passengers," reported *The Motor Age* that November. Behind this venture were Albert F. Hurt, Jr. of New York City, and Stephen J. Hyde, Frederick O'Flaherty and Hilda B. Holmgren of Kansas City. Manufacture of a car is doubted.

1901 Strathmore, runabout, WLB

STRATHMORE — Boston, Massachusetts — (1899-1901) — In July of 1899 the recently organized International Automobile Company of Boston announced the change of its name to Strathmore Automobile Company "to distinguish it from the numerous other motor vehicle concerns employing the word international in their titles." The vehicles built by Strathmore were powered by either steam or gasoline engines, and 6 hp was claimed for both. The cars were tiller steered and chain driven, and featured full elliptic springs both front and rear. Runabouts, coaches and panel delivery vans were offered, with the preponderance of Strathmore production being built to order for liveries or commercial enterprises in the Boston area.

1909 Stratton, tonneau, MVMA

1923 Strattan, touring, NAHC

STRATTAN — Indianapolis, Indiana — (1923) — Frank E. Strattan had big plans. In March of 1923 he acquired the Monroe assets from the Fletcher American National Bank in Indianapolis, and organized Strattan Motors Corporation to continue production of the Monroe and to introduce a lower-priced four called the Strattan to sell in the $695-$995 price range. The president of the Indianapolis-based Premier Motor Corporation, Frederick Barrows, was serving as vice-president and comptroller of Strattan Motors Corporation, and there was talk that Strattan was planning to purchase the Premier Company. These plans quickly went awry, however, and the shoe shifted to the other foot. In June the Monroe assets were bought by Barrows from Strattan, and the Monroe car was continued in manufacture as the Premier Model B. Strattan had announced his sale of Monroe to Premier as a logistical move in order to "concentrate on the production of only one car — the Strattan" for which he planned an output of fifty cars a day. Strattan Motors Corporation quickly fell apart. Only experimental models of the Strattan were produced, and by year's end Frank Strattan, who had had two cars in March, now had none at all.

STRATTON — New York, New York — (1901) — In the late fall of 1901 Edmond F. Stratton took over the plant of the defunct Manhattan Automobile Company at 502 West 38th Street in Manhattan. There, he announced, he would begin producing a compact gasoline runabout to retail for about $400. He is known to have completed at least one for display purposes. But the Stratton Motor Company which he evolved out of his former Stratton Motor Cycle Company was doomed to an even quicker death than the Manhattan had suffered. Allied with him in the ill-fated venture had been David Wood of New York City and G.H. Murray, Jr. of Hollis, Long Island.

STRATTON — Fitchburg, Massachusetts — (1907) — The Stratton Rotary Engine Company was organized early in 1907 with a $2 million capital stock by R.E. Erdman, Franklin Stratton and S.W. Beers. *The New England Automobile Journal* reported that January that Stratton held patent rights for a "rotary machine that has four separate engines combined" and that the company's plan was to build a "convertible runabout/touring car." At a board meeting in the company's Fitchburg headquarters that summer, models of the Stratton rotary for both automotive and marine use were demonstrated. The firm was listed as an automobile manufacturer in the January 1908 edition of *Cycle and Automobile Trade Journal*, but this appears to have been undue optimism on the Stratton company's part. The evidence suggests that the prototype stage was probably as far as this venture proceeded.

STRATTON — Muncie, Indiana — (1909) — Charles H. Stratton of Muncie was a buggy manufacturer who began supplying local Indiana horseless carriage builders with automobile bodies and tops and other accoutrements soon after the turn of the century. Though the Stratton Carriage Company venture into manufacture itself was short-lived, the highwheeler it produced was a very admirable one, with two-cylinder 14 hp engine under a hood in front, two-speed planetary transmission, double chain drive, and right-hand steering by wheel. The Stratton's wheelbase was a long 90 inches, and the car's ride on 36-inch wheels in front, 38-inch in rear was said to be quite comfortable. The first Stratton highwheeler was on the road in February 1909. Production ended later that year simply because of the company's inability to secure adequate financing for serious manufacture. The Stratton Carriage Company remained in the body-building field, however. Among Charles Stratton's new ideas in that line was a four-seater with an inflatable rubber cushion in the back which he believed perfect for physicians, since their house-call car could be converted into an ambulance on a moment's notice. Another was a runabout with a hidden rear seat which could be easily raised at the owner's convenience and

discretion. According to the *Muncie Press* in 1910, this neatly solved a problem common during that period, "the nuisance of hauling friends about on their business when the owner of the car has urgent business of his own to transact." Charles Stratton died in 1913, and his company with him.

1922 Stratton-Bliss, brougham, MVMA

STRATTON-BLISS — New York, New York — (1922) — The Stratton-Bliss Company was established as an automobile dealership in 1909 and came to prominence in the post-World War I era in New York as the agency for Dodge. In 1922 the firm marketed a custom automobile of its own, this probably being the idea of company president H.L. Stratton. A Dodge chassis was used, and the body style was a luxurious brougham with leather landau, square sidelamps, disc wheels, individual step-plates, separate fenders, even a telephone.

STRAUSS — The firm of Joseph Strauss & Son was organized in Buffalo, New York late in 1908 with a capital stock of $100,000 to manufacture and deal in bicycles and automobiles. Joseph Strauss and George C. Strauss were the partners involved. Manufacture of a car is doubted.

STREAMLINE — Indianapolis, Indiana — (1913) — The Streamline was to be a 40 hp roadster on a 110-inch wheelbase sporting wire wheels, left-hand steering, a torpedo body, electric lights and a $1300 price tag. This Indianapolis venture was initially announced in December of 1912 as being promoted "by a party of automobile men and capitalists whose names will not be disclosed for the present." History never did find out who they were, though a Streamline Motor Car Company was indicated for 1913 in trade directories. Certainly sustained manufacture of the Streamline car never ensued, however.

STREATOR — In 1902 L.P. Halladay established the Streator Automobile & Manufacturing Company in Streator, Illinois. His car was called the Halladay. Refer to Halladay.

STREUT — In 1935 in Hollywood, California one Allen F. Streut collaborated with Allen M. Hoppe on the design of a streamlined rear-engined car. Refer to Hoppe & Streut.

STRINGER — Marion, Ohio — (1899-1902) — In 1899 John W. Stringer, superintendent of the Marion Manufacturing Company, quit his job because he wanted to build automobiles. Just what kind of automobiles he wasn't sure, since he ran up both an experimental electric carriage and a gasoline car by year's end. In February of 1900 he secured financial backing from Horatio Chisholm of Marion and James H. Leonard of nearby

1902 Stringer, steam carriage, NAHC

LaRue, and the Stringer Automobile Company was organized with a capital stock of $20,000 and a factory secured on the west side of South High Street between Center and the railroad tracks. Although gasoline cars were stated to be the company's forthcoming product, the first Stringer to arrive later that summer was a steamer which was fitted with a four-cylinder engine and featured an "enclosed chainless drive." A gasoline car did not arrive until that December. Production of both these vehicles continued into 1902, but when the Stringer Automobile Company's money was depleted later that year, manufacture was discontinued.

STRONG — "Harry B. Strong, an 18-year-old genius of Scranton, Pennsylvania has constructed a gasoline carriage," reported *The Horseless Age* in August 1899. Details are lacking.

The Strong Motor Company at 32 Broadway in New York City was indicated as an automobile manufacturer in the Hiscox book *Horseless Vehicles, Automobiles, Motor Cycles* published in 1900. Documentation is lacking. New York City directories reveal the existence of this company at the turn of the century, however.

STRONG — Minneapolis, Minnesota — (1904) — Albert W. Strong was the president of the Strong and Northway Manufacturing Company which made flour milling machinery at 251-253 Third Avenue South in Minneapolis. In 1904 Strong leased the building next door and announced to the trade press a new enterprise called the Strong Automobile Manufacturing Company. Conceivably, a prototype of the car he was intending to produce may have been built, but it was never put into manufacture. By 1905 Albert Strong had returned to his flour milling machinery exclusively.

STRONG & GIBBONS — Chicago, Illinois — (1895) — Two Chicago engineers named Henry T. Strong and Alexander Gibbons began building an eight-passenger motor carriage at their shop at 181 West Madison Street early in 1895. Although the vehicle was entered in the Chicago Times-Herald Contest to be held that November, it was not completed in time. Subsequently, the Strong & Gibbons was described thusly in *The Horseless Age:* "The motor has many cylinders, the pistons working together on one common crankshaft. These cylinders are so arranged that when all are not needed some are allowed to rest and take up work again as required. An electric spark produces the explosion and one lever controls all movements of the vehicle, the weight of which is said to be about 800 pounds."

STRONG & ROGERS ELECTRIC — Cleveland, Ohio — (1900-1901) — Lewis H. Rogers, a wholesale druggist, and Edwin L. Strong, a Cleveland businessman, collaborated to produce the Strong & Rogers which was introduced in September 1900 at the Chicago Inter-Ocean Tournament. An electric stanhope, the vehicle was equipped with a forty-cell Willard battery which charged in 45 minutes and was good for a 30-40 mile run at up to 16 mph. The Strong & Rogers' motor was a 2 1/2 hp, mounted at and with direct drive to the right rear wheel, and the vehicle was provided six speeds forward and four in reverse. But most impressive in the Strong & Rogers was its body styling. The pretty pair of scrolls in front were both decorative and functional, being fastened to both the frame and the body to assure a smooth ride. In November of 1900 the Strong & Rogers was taken to New York City for the first annual automobile show held in Madison Square Garden. The standard model was offered at $1200, but available as well was a special deluxe version for $2000 with hand-carved decorative artwork gracing the wooden body, goatskin covering the seat and tiller bar, and the steering handle made of pearl inlaid with silver. In March of 1901 Lewis Rogers was forced to leave the venture for reasons of ill health. Edward Strong announced that he would carry on alone, but he did not do so for long. The Strong & Rogers was discontinued by the end of 1901.

1900 Strong & Rogers, electric runabout, NAHC

1919 Stroud, touring, WLB

STROUD — San Antonio, Texas — (1919) — "Would You Invest $500 to Make $50,000?," the 1919 prospectus asked enticingly, and followed that with a listing of cars that had make good, like the Saxon, Chalmers, Grant, Paige-Detroit, Hup (sic) and Chandler. "Statistics show there are fewer failures in the Automobile Manufacturing Business than in the Banking Business," it went on. The trademark of the Stroud Motor Manufacturing Association, Ltd. was a horseshoe, pointed down, perhaps significantly; a horseshoe should always be hung pointed up, so superstition has it, otherwise the luck will run out. One suspects the luck ran out rather quickly for Sam W. Stroud, Judge C.K. McDowell, F.W. Lemburg, D.L. Spero and the other Stroud people, at least insofar as their automobile-building venture was concerned. There was a drawing of the Stroud car in the prospectus, showing a standard five-passenger touring distinguished only by the horseshoe on the radiator. Indicated specifications were a Continental engine, Hotchkiss drive, Stromberg carburetor, Atwater Kent ignition, 114-inch wheelbase. The price fully equipped and delivered at San Antonio was $1050. A similar car built up East and shipped down South, it was carefully noted, would cost $1485. "Reliable authorities estimate that there is an immediate demand in Texas for 100,000 automobiles and about 150,000 tractors and trucks," Stroud said. "It is our aim to keep this Texas money in Texas for Texans." Whether a single Stroud car was built has not been confirmed; the Stroud truck seems to have died an equally quick death, though as late as 1922 the Stroud Motor Manufacturing Association was noting the imminent start-up of production on its tractor.

STROUSE — Although announced as the Strouse, this 1915 cyclecar from Detroit was quickly renamed the S.R.K. after Clarence B. Strouse happened upon Frederick T. Ranney and Thomas D. Knight, who provided him with the funds for manufacture. Refer to S.R.K.

STROUT — Peabody, Massachusetts — (1907) — From 1905 to 1906, the Corwin Manufacturing Company in Peabody produced the Gas-au-lec automobile and the Coulthard steam truck. In 1907 the firm leased its factory to the Machine Sales Company. Prior to going out of business in 1909, the Machine Sales Company built a kerosene engine and ten trucks for the Hewitt Motor Company of New York City. These were huge ten-tonners built chiefly for coal delivery and were the largest capacity American trucks of that period. A less formidable vehicle also built by Machine

Sales Company was a one-off automobile designed by Robert Strout who worked for the firm. Little is known about this vehicle, except that it was an air-cooled two-cylinder car mounted on a tubular frame through which the exhaust gases passed.

1897 Struss, four-cylinder runabout, HAC

STRUSS — New York, New York — (1897) — Henry W. Struss lived in New York City on 42nd Street where, in 1897, he built what he said was the first four-cylinder automobile in America. Perhaps he thought so, being unaware of Charles Brady King's four-cylinder car which had been tested on the streets of Detroit in May 1896. Certainly the Struss car was the first four in Manhattan. Its engine developed only one horsepower per cylinder and was mounted in the rear of a two-seater carriage which was built for him by Burr & Company. Wet liners and mechanically operated valves were avant-garde engineering features of the Struss, and all of its main bearings were roller type. Late in 1898 Henry Struss told reporters that he was planning to go into manufacture, but it would appear this never transpired. He was granted patents on his vehicle, however, in 1899.

STUDEBAKER

1907 Studebaker, Electric, model 22A, runabout, OCW

STUDEBAKER — South Bend, Indiana — (1902-1942 et. seq.) — The wagon-building Studebaker brothers of South Bend called themselves "The Largest Vehicle Builders in the World" in 1872 and launched themselves into the automobile business a half century later. There is some evidence they did this a little reluctantly. Having made a fortune supplying the army of the North in the Civil War, and British military forces in the Boer War, the Studebaker Brothers Manufacturing Company seemed content to reap profits in the horse-drawn field and experiment at its leisure in the burgeoning automotive arena. Though a horseless vehicle was developed as early as 1897, and the company built bodies for several electric-car manufacturers, it was not until 1902 that John M. Studebaker's son-in-law Fred Fish persuaded the family to produce a car of its own. It was an electric designed by Thomas Alva Edison, twenty were built that year, and production continued in small numbers until 1912. In 1904, following the purchase of the assets of the defunct General (Cleveland), Fred Fish persuaded Studebaker to build gasoline cars, despite John M.'s opinion that "they stink to high heaven." The chassis were supplied by Garford in Elyria (Ohio), initially a two-cylinder 16 hp chain-drive model, followed by a 20 hp shaft-drive four in 1905. Until 1908 this collaboration with the Garford organization was retained. That year Studebaker began its association with the Everett-Metzger-Flanders Company which resulted in Studebaker's marketing of the E-M-F car, and subsequently the Flanders 20, and ultimately in 1911 the takeover of E-M-F by Studebaker and the formation of the Studebaker Corporation. The E-M-F and Flanders 20 were continued by Studebaker for 1912, but thereafter the brothers' name was affixed to all cars to come from the corporation. For 1913 the new Studebaker cars were sold in six models of four or six cylinders, the latter distinguished by their monoblock engine castings, Studebaker and Premier pioneering in this construction, and Studebaker claiming its six for less than $2000 to be an American first. Though that fact could be mooted, the success of the Studebaker marketing strategy could not. Sales rose handsomely as year passed year. With the retirement from the Studebaker presidency of Fred Fish — his automotive enthusiasm had obviously paid off well personally too — vice-president Albert Russel Erskine took over in July of 1915. Studebaker was a supplier first to Europe and then the U.S. government during the First World War. During this period the engineering department was in the charge of Fred M. Zeder, Owen R. Skelton and Carl Breer: they prepared the first postwar Studebakers, then left the company to set themselves up as consultants, and later to bring to reality the motorcar vision of Walter P. Chrysler. In 1920 all Studebakers were sixes, the Light, the Special and the Big Six. Robust vehicles that were difficult to break, these were the cars, in Erskine's words, which "made Studebaker famous." When Packard and Rickenbacker, among others, introduced four-wheel brakes in 1923, Studebaker was one of the most vociferous opponents, declaring them unsafe in full-page advertisements, but by 1926 four-wheel braking became standard on Studebaker products. It was in 1926, too, that Albert Erskine noticed something had been missing from South Bend — and that was style and class. This was a problem he attacked on several fronts. First, he hired the Rose Room of the Plaza Hotel in New York City during new car introduction time that summer and exhibited "special creations" by noted custom coachbuilders on various six-cylinder Studebaker chassis. Then in October he introduced a new motorcar called the Erskine which had a European flair and was designed to carry the company fashionably into the lower-priced class. That venture didn't prove successful, but his third idea did — and this was an assault on the prestige segment of the marketplace. Eight cylinders was what he wanted, and when engineers Max Wollering and Guy Henry (who had taken over from the Zeder-Skelton-Breer triumvirate) objected, believing their sturdy and practical sixes quite sufficient, Erskine simply eased them out of the organization and brought in engineer Delmar G. "Barney" Roos who was happy to comply. The result was the Studebaker President, with a straight-eight engine initially delivering 100 bhp (raised to 132 by 1933 with the Speedway President line), styling upon which Ray Dietrich had consulted beautifully, and a price tag of $1985-$2485, a fine bargain in 1928. The new President was a smash. Lest the Studebaker six-cylinder line be forgotten, Erskine saw to it that those cars made news too by sending Commanders and Dictators to the races. Nineteen twenty-seven ended with Studebaker holding more stock car records than even the company could count, including 25,000 miles in less than 25,000 minutes by three Commanders. In 1928 a President sedan was sent to the board track at Atlantic City to take any records not broken by the Commanders, and a Dictator broke its own previous year's record (5000 miles in less than 4800 minutes) for good measure. "Builder of Champions," the ads said. The Commander and Dictator were given smaller eight-cylinder engines for 1929, and the big President eight took on the Indianapolis 500 in 1930 in two privately-entered specials which performed so admirably that the company fielded its own factory-sponsored team in 1932 (most rare for a giant American manufacturer), with Cliff Bergere finishing a fine third. But the following year was a tragic one for Studebaker. Its purchase of the Pierce-Arrow company in 1928 had since been proven to be a financial mistake, the new car called the Rockne which had been introduced in 1932 was faring badly, and now Erskine was in the midst of the nightmare resulting from his ill-advised attempt to buy the White Motor Company. In March of 1933 Studebaker went into receivership; in July Albert Erskine committed suicide. Picking up the pieces of the organization were Harold Vance and Paul Hoffman. Studebaker's Pierce-Arrow stock was sold for a million dollars, and $100,000 was spent on an ambitious "Studebaker Carries On" advertising campaign. Retrenchment meant the end for the big 337-cubic-inch Studebaker President, and for '34 the line consisted of the Dictator six, the Commander eight and the President eight carrying the Commander engine upgraded from 221 cubic inches to 250 for 110 bhp. By March of 1935 Studebaker was out of receivership; Hoffman became the corporation's president, Vance chairman of the board. Synchromesh, freewheeling and X-braced frames had been introduced in 1934, followed by planar independent front suspension and hydraulic brakes in '35, and Hill Holder in 1936. For 1937 an optional fully automatic overdrive followed the semi-automatic offered in '35, and a new hypoid rear axle became standard. The innovation of windshield washers followed in '38 models. But the best news from Studebaker arrived in 1939, and it was called the Champion. To prove it worthy of the name, this new six from Studebaker put up 15,000 miles at Indianapolis in under 15,000 minutes. More than 200,000 Champions were built prior to Pearl Harbor. By now Raymond Loewy had begun his collaboration with Studebaker, and it was his design studio which would be responsible for the first all-new car to arrive from any major American company after the Second World War. Jokes were cracked about the Studebaker that was "going both ways," but everyone watched it do it. The company looked in fine shape in 1946. But less than two decades later the proud name of Studebaker would be forever stilled in the American automobile industry.

Studebaker Data Compilation
by John A. Gunnell

1902-1912

1902 Studebaker Electric, runabout, JAC

STUDEBAKER — ELECTRIC: Studebaker Bros. Mfg. Co built a complete line of electric-powered cars and trucks from 1902-1912. The first models evolved from the firm's horse-drawn buggies while later models were more sophisticated. The 2-passenger runabout was a single seat, buggy-type vehicle with leather fenders, bar-lever steering, chain drive and a leather dashboard. The Victoria was basically the same vehicle with a "French" front hood, coach lights and an optional folding top. The Stanhope featured a curved tonneau type body with a single seat. It had coach lights, runningboards and an optional, canopy type folding top.

Early models of 1902-1903 used wire spoke bicycle wheels, which were later replaced with wooden artillery spoke wheels. Single-seat models had one electric motor. The 4-passenger Surrey, a two-seat model of under-slung design, had two motors, as did commercial vehicles. Commercials came as a light-duty Electric Delivery with a doorless, enclosed van-type body or in truck form with a variety of large wagon-type bodies having weight-carrying capacities of 1000, 2500 or 7500 pounds. A five-ton rated stake body truck was available after 1906. In addition, commercial body building to customer specifications was provided on special order jobs.

Four-passenger Electric coupes were added to the line at a later date. According to Floyd Clymer, these were available after 1906, although other sources place the introduction year as 1910. The coupes had what is called "phone booth" or "china closet" styling, with tall, 5-window bodies, a flat windshield/dash panel, small hood, deck and fenders. Coach lamps were mounted at the front, on the beltline.

1903 Studebaker Electric, runabout, HAC

All models had similar tiller controls, full-elliptic rear springs and semi-elliptic front springs. Solid rubber tires were used on the Surrey, other models having pneumatic tires on clincher type detachable wheels. Two separate brakes were provided on all models. One worked on the rear axle drums, except on the Surrey where it worked directly on the wheel hubs. The second brake worked on the countershaft(s) of the motor(s). Both were foot operated.

On Runabouts and Stanhopes the running gear frames were of tubular steel and independent of the body. On the Victoria and the Surrey, which were underslung, the running gear frames were integral with the framework of the body, which was reinforced with steel rocker plates for extra rigidity.

Controllers on all Studebaker Electrics gave four speeds in either direction. Drive on most cars (if not all) was by chain. The motor was mounted so that it could be swung back and forth to allow chain adjustments. Photos suggest that some late models may have featured some type of enclosed drive system without chains.

For 1904, the Stanhope came finished in rich shades of maroon or black in combination with dark green. The Victoria was available in dark shades of green or maroon with matching cloth upholstery. The Surrey was finished in Royal green with green leather upholstery and an optional canopy top was available.

Complete year-by-year data covering Studebaker Electrics was not available at the time this catalog went to press. We have included representative model listings, prices and technical specifications. It must be understood that these may have changed slightly from one year to the next.

1911 Studebaker Electric, model 17, victoria phaeton, HAC

I.D. DATA: Serial number and engine number information for Studebaker Electrics is not currently available.

Model No.	Body Type & Seating	Price	Weight	Prod. Total
Selected 1904-1910 Model Specifications				
NA	Rbt.-2P	NA	1350	Note 1
NA	Surrey w/o Top-4P	1800	NA	Note 1
NA	Surrey w/Top-4P	1850	NA	Note 1
1363	Stanhope w/o Top-2P	1100	1500	Note 1
1363	Stanhope w/Top-2P	1150	1525	Note 1
1396	Vic. w/o Top (Exide)-2P	1550	1575	Note 1
1396	Vic. w/Top (Exide)-2P	1600	1600	Note 1
1396	Vic. w/o Top (Edison)-2P	1725	1575	Note 1
1396	Vic. w/Top (Edison)-2P	1775	1600	Note 1
2019A	Delivery Wag.-2P	NA	NA	Note 1
17B	Cpe.-2P	2200	2450	Note 1
17D	Phae.-4P	NA	NA	Note 1
22F	Stanhope w/Top	NA	NA	Note 1
2012A	5-Ton Truck	NA	9700	Note 1

Note 1: A total of 1,841 Studebaker Electric vehicles were built between 1902 and 1912.
Note 2: The above chart gives representative models, prices and weights for Studebaker Electrics of various years and is not intended as a complete listing of all models available.

ENGINE: Runabout (1902): A single Westinghouse standard vehicle motor was used. It was rated 40-volts and 24-amperes. This was equivalent to approximately 1.7 NACC horsepower. The battery consisted of 24 cells with a total capacity of 96 amp./hrs. Top speed: 13 mph. Driving range: 40 miles per charge. **Victoria (1904):** The Victoria and other single-seat, two-passenger models used one electric motor rated 50-volts and 30-amperes. The standard battery consisted of 24 Exide cells. The Victoria was available with an optional 36-cell Edison battery. Top speed: 14 mph. Driving range: 40 miles per charge. **Surrey (1904):** The 4-passenger Surrey was equipped with two motors each rated at 80-volts and 12-amperes. Top speed: 14 mph. Driving range: NA. **Coupe (1906-1910):** The 4-passenger Model 17-B Electric Coupe used one Westinghouse electric motor rated at 48-volts and 26-amperes. Batteries (weighing 970 pounds) were carried in separate front and rear trays. Top speed: 15 mph. Driving range: 35 miles per charge. **Commercial Vehicles:** Commercial vehicles of 1000 pounds or over capacity had two electric motors rated 80-volts and 20-amperes. This was equivalent to approximately 4.3 NACC hp. The batteries consisted of 40 cells. They were divided into four separate trays containing 10 cells each. This allowed replacement of individual trays for recharging, without tying up all the remaining cells.

CHASSIS: Stanhope (1904): W.B.: 62 in. Tread: 54 in. Tires: 30 x 3 in. (detachable tires). Victoria (1904): W.B.: 69 in. Tread: 54 in. Tires: 30 x 3 in. (detachable tires). Surrey (1904): Tires: 36 x 3 in. (solid tires). Runabout (1902-1903): W.B.: 61 in. O.L.: 73 in. Tread: 53 in. Tires: 30 x 3 in. (detachabel tires).

TECHNICAL: Extra-heavy roller chain transmission. Speeds: 4F/4R. Electric speed control device on seat at driver's left, plus reversing switch and removable "Key" switch. Chain-drive. Differential gear mounted on rear axle. Two separate braking systems. Wire spoke or wood artillery wheels; Archibald type wheels with solid rubber tires corresponding to load capacity on commercial vehicles.

OPTIONS: Folding canopy top (50.00). Victoria with Edison battery (175.00 extra). Coach lights. Leather fenders. Headlight. Electric horn. Note: Some of these accessories were standard equipment on most models.

HISTORICAL: Introduction January, 1902. Innovations: First automobiles built by Studebaker Bros. Mfg. Co.; later became Studebaker Corp. Production: A total of 1,841 Studebaker Electrics were made in 10 years of production.

Company Patriarch J.M. Studebaker was said to favor the electrics over gas-powered Studebaker automobiles. The first Studebaker Electric was sold to F.W. Blees of Macon, Mo. on Feb. 12, 1902. It is believed that the second car made was purchased by Thomas Alva Edison. Studebaker advertised that its electrics "Can Be Run Any Day In The Year By Any Member Of The Family." The electrics were marketed concurrently with Studebaker-Garford gasoline automobiles from 1903-1911.

1903

STUDEBAKER-GARFORD — MODEL A — TWO: This seems to be a car that the Studebaker history books overlooked. According to a 1904 edition of *Cycle and Automobile Trade Journal*, it was brought out in late 1903 and carried over into the following season with some changes. The journal described it as "a remarkably satisfactory little touring car." The only details given about the model are sketchy ones. It was noted that the car used an eight horsepower, double-opposed horizontal engine and incorporated a mechanical lubrication system with a chain-driven pump. Otherwise, it was said to be "similar to the (1904) Model C in many other respects." The body had provisions for a detachable tonneau and could be quickly transformed into a Runabout. Finish was in maroon or royal green with upholstery in dark green leather. No other details about this model are readily available.

I.D. DATA: Serial number and engine number information is not available.

Model No.	Body Type & Seating	Price	Weight	Prod. Total
A	Tonneau Tr.-5P	NA	NA	NA

ENGINE: The only information available about the Model A engine is that it was a two-cylinder, horizontally-opposed power plant developing eight N.A.C.C. horsepower.

CHASSIS: The Model A was described as being "similar to the Model C (of 1904) in many other respects." Additional chassis data is not available.

DRIVETRAIN: The Model A was similar to the 1904 Model C in drivetrain layout.

OPTIONS: Information not available.

HISTORICAL: Introduced late 1903. First gasoline powered automobiles to bear the Studebaker nameplate. They had chassis built by the Garford Co. of Elyria, Ohio. The chassis were then shipped to the Studebaker factory, in South Bend, Ind., where bodies were installed. *The Studebaker Century* by Asa E. Hall and Richard M. Lanaworth says that the first gas powered Studebakers were built in 1904 and does not mention the Model A. *Studebaker: The Complete Story* by William A. Cannon and Fred K. Fox also does not mention the Model A and specifically dates the sale of the first gas powered Studebaker-Garford to July 22, 1904. In fact, the only mention of the 1903 Model A is in the 1904 edition of *Cycle and Automobile Trade Journal* from which the above information was taken.

1903
Model A, 8 hp

	FP	5	4	3	2	1
Tonn Tr	NA				Value inestimable	

1904

STUDEBAKER-GARFORD — MODELS A/B — TWO: According to *Cycle and Automobile Trade Journal* the mysterious Studebaker-Garford Model A gasoline powered touring car was again available with "numerous 1904 improvements and refinements." No additional details are known, except that body and chassis specifications were the same as in 1903.

The new Model B is also a somewhat mysterious vehicle that Studebaker historians have overlooked. It was a gasoline powered delivery wagon that used the same chassis as the Model A. *Cycle and Automobile Trade Journal* noted that "a very elegant little delivery wagon body" was used in place of the tonneau body. It had a carrying capacity of 500 pounds. The Model B was finished in maroon with black pinstriping. It weighed 1550 pounds and sold for $1100. No other details or specifications are available.

1904 Studebaker, model C, tonneau, HAC

STUDEBAKER-GARFORD — MODEL C — TWO: The new Model C is the car generally recognized as being the "first" gasoline powered Studebaker. It was a medium-sized touring car for five persons featuring a body with a detachable rear tonneau. The frame was of armoured wood. The short hood had vertical louvers. The steering wheel was on the right-hand side with brake and gear selector levers outside the body. The body was finished in dark maroons or dark blue or in Royal green striped with yellow. Upholstery was in dark, matching shades of leather. Headlights, cowl lamps, fenders and a 10-gallon gas tank were among standard equipment features. A canopy top added $150 to the basic price.

I.D. DATA: [Models A/B] Serial number and engine number information is not available. [Model C] Serial number and engine number information not available.

Model No.	Body Type & Seating	Price	Weight	Prod. Total
Model A				
A	Tonneau Tr.-5P	NA	NA	NA
Model B				
B	Delivery Wagon-2P	1100	1550	NA
Model C				
C	Tonneau Tr.-5P	1600	1800	NA

Note 1: Add $175 for canopy top.

ENGINE: [Models A/B] Two. Horizontally-opposed. Eight N.A.C.C. H.P. [Model C] Horizontal-opposed; under center type. Two. B & S: 5 in. x 5-1/2 in. Disp.: 215.9 cu. in. N.A.C.C. H.P.: 16. Valve lifters: Solid. Carb.: 1V.

CHASSIS: [Models A/B] Data not available. [Model C] W.B.: 82 in. Frt/Rear Tread: 56/56 in. Tires: 30 x 3-1/2 in.

TECHNICAL: [Models A/B] Layout similar to 1904 Model C. [Model C] Planetary transmission. Speeds: 2F/1R. Right-hand, outboard gear lever. Chain-drive. Spur differential on rear axle. Brakes: Two sets on rear hubs and differential. Artillery spoke wheels.

OPTIONS: Gas headlights. Kerosene side lamps. Canopy top (175.00). Windshield. Horn.

HISTORICAL: Introduced January, 1904. Innovations: New Model C touring car introduced. Officially claimed to be Studebaker's "first" gasoline automobile. The 1904 Studebaker-Garford models should not be confused with the later 1908 Garford Models A and B or 1909 Garford Model C which were 4-cylinder cars marketed under the Garford nameplate only. Studebaker officially credited Mr. H.D. Johnson, of South Bend, with the purchase of the "first" gas powered Studebaker on July 22, 1904 — a date which conflicts with the existence of the 1903 Model A Studebaker. The Studebaker-Garfords were actually marketed under only the Studebaker name in accordance with the contract between the two firms. However, the hyphenated name is preferred by Studebaker enthusiasts and historians today.

1904

Model A	FP	5	4	3	2	1
Tonn Tr	NA	2000	5100	8500	11,900	17,000
Model B						
Dely Wagon	1100	1550	4500	7500	10,500	15,000
Model C						
Tonn Tr	1600	2300	5400	9000	12,600	18,000

1905

STUDEBAKER-GARFORD — SERIES 15 HP — TWO: The Model C was carried over as the Model no. 9502 five-passenger touring car with detachable tonneau. It was now called a rear entrance touring car. There were virtually no changes in styling, finish or specifications although the price was lowered considerably. It was joined by a new Model no. 9502 five-passenger side entrance touring car. This model had a high, horizontal platform at the rear with a seat mounted on top of it. A door was used between the front and rear seat platforms. The new model came in either dark green or dark blue finish. Specifications of the two cars were otherwise identical.

1905 Studebaker, No. 9503, touring, HAC

STUDEBAKER-GARFORD — SERIES 20 HP — FOUR: New from Studebaker was a larger, four-cylinder touring car with a side entrance tonneau body and seating for five. Cataloged as Model 9503, this car had curved entranceways with doors at the rear. High-back, armchair style seats were of individual bucket type in the front and three-passenger ''bench'' type in the rear. Sweeping front fenders and higher rear fenders were used. This model came in either dark blue or dark green finish. A higher, rounder pressed steel dash, said to be of ''pleasing design,'' was seen.

I.D. DATA: [Model 9502] Serial number and engine number information not available. [Model 9503] Serial number and engine number information not available.

Model No.	Body Type & Seating	Price	Weight	Prod. Total
9502	Rear Entrance Tr.-5P	1250	1950	NA
9502	Side Entrance Tr.-5P	1350	1950	NA
9503	Side Entrance Tr.-5P	3000	2100	NA

Note 1: A folding top of desired style was extra-cost equipment.

ENGINE: [Model 9502] Engine specifications were the same as those of the 1904 Model C, except that the advertised horsepower rating was lowered to 15 hp. [Model 9503] Vertical. Cast en block. Four. Cast iron block. B & S: 3-7/8 in. x 4-1/2 in. Disp.: 212.3 cu. in. N.A.C.C. H.P.: 20. Valve lifters: Mechanical. Carb.: Float feed; constant level type.

CHASSIS: [Model 9502] W.B.: 82 in. Frt/Rear Tread: 56-1/2/56-1/2 in. Tires: 30 x 3-1/2 in. [Model 9503] W.B.: 96 in. Frt/Rear Tread: 54/54 in. Tires: 32 x 4 in.

TECHNICAL: [9502] Planetary transmission. Speeds: 2F/1R. Right-hand, outboard, gear selector. Chain-drive. Rear wheel brakes. Artillery spoke wheels. [9503] Selecting sliding transmission. Speeds: 3F/1R. Right-hand, outboard, gear selector. Cone clutch. Bevel gear drive. Rear wheel brakes. Artillery spoke wheels.

OPTIONS: Folding top (of desired style). Gas headlights. Kerosene side-lamps. Windshield. Horn.

HISTORICAL: Introduced January, 1905. Innovations: First four-cylinder Studebaker model released. Pressed steel frame construction on Model 9503. Selective sliding three-speed manual transmission in Model 9503. Garford continued to build Studebaker chassis in Ohio and ship them to South Bend for final assembly.

1905
Model 9502, 2-cyl.

	FP	5	4	3	2	1
Rear Ent Tr	1250	2800	5700	9500	13,300	19,000
Side Ent Tr	1350	3000	6000	10,000	14,000	20,000
Model 9503, 4-cyl.						
Side Ent Tr	3000	3300	6600	11,000	15,400	22,000

1906

1906 Studebaker, model E-20, touring, HAC

STUDEBAKER-GARFORD — SERIES E — FOUR: The Model no. 9503 was carried over, with lower prices, as the 1906 Series E touring car. It was again of side entrance design and the main styling changes were a two inch longer wheelbase, the addition of runningboards and new colors. Finish was now available in maroon or pearl gray, as well as the dark blue and dark green used in 1905. A new model available in the same line was a Town Car of huge proportions with an open-sided driver's compartment. There was a glass center partition and the passenger compartment had five-windows along with paneled doors and rear. Finish colors on the Town Car were to owner specifications.

STUDEBAKER-GARFORD — SERIES F — FOUR: The new Series F Studebaker was a large, heavy five-passenger touring car with a wider rear tonneau and more massive doors. Finish was available in dark blue, maroon, dark green or pearl gray. A cape style folding top was a popular extra-cost option.

STUDEBAKER-GARFORD — SERIES G — FOUR: The Series G five-passenger touring car was essentially a more powerful version of the Series F model. It had slightly fancier upholstery and sportier-looking front fenders, plus a higher, squarer dashboard. A landau style canopy top that covered only the rear compartment was available at extra cost. The foot brake on this model operated on the propeller shaft rather than the rear wheels and make-and-break magneto ignition was standard.

I.D. DATA: Serial number and engine number information not available.

Model No.	Body Type & Seating	Price	Weight	Prod. Total
Series E				
E-20	Side Entrance Tr.-5P	2600	2400	NA
E-20	Town Car-5P	4000	2750	NA
Note 1: Folding top optional on Side-Entrance Touring.				
Series F				
F-28	Side Entrance Tr.-5P	3000	2700	NA
Note 2: A cape style folding top was available.				
Series G				
G-30	Side Entrance Tr.-5P	3700	2700	NA
Note 3: A folding canopy top was optional.				

ENGINE: [Series E] Engine specifications were the same as on the 1905 Model 9503 except that the advertised horsepower rating was listed as 20 hp. [Series F] Vertical type. Cylinder cast en block. Four. Cast iron block. B & S: 4-3/8 in. x 4-3/4 in. Disp.: 285.6 cu. in. N.A.C.C. H.P.: 28. Jump spark ignition. Water-cooled via gear-driven pump, radiator and fan. Valve lifters: Mechanical. Float feed; constant level type carburetor. [Series G] Vertical type. Cylinders cast in blocks of two. Four. Cast iron block. B & S: 4-1/8 in. x 5-1/4 in. Disp.: 280.6 cu. in. N.A.C.C. H.P.: 30. Make-and-break ignition with magneto. Water-cooled via gear driven pump, radiator and fan. Valve lifters: Mechanical. Float feed, constant level type carburetor.

CHASSIS: [Series E] W.B.: 98 in. Frt/Rear Tread: 54/54 in. Tires: (Touring) 32 x 4; (Town Car) 32 x 4-1/2 in. [Series F] W.B.: 104 in. Frt/Rear Tread: 54/54 in. Tires: 34 x 4 in. [Series G] W.B.: 104 in. Frt/Rear Tread: 56/56 in. Tires: 34 x 4 in.

TECHNICAL: [All series] Sliding gear; direct on high transmission. Speeds: 3F/1R. Right-hand outboard gear selector controls. Cone clutch. Bevel gear drive. Floating rear axle. Rear wheel mechanical brakes. Wood artillery spoke wheels.

OPTIONS: Folding top. Gas headlights. Kerosene side lamps. Horn. Windshield. Side curtains.

HISTORICAL: Introduced January, 1906. Innovations: More powerful engines. First Studebaker Town Car. Longer wheelbases on new models. Make-and-break ignition with electric magneto introduced on G-30. The Model G-30 became the Garford Model A in 1908 when Studebaker took control of E-M-F and no longer needed Garford as its main chassis builder. However, some production of Studebaker-Garford cars continued through 1911. Garford was never able to build as many chassis as Studebaker could sell. Because of this, Studebaker formed associations with companies like E-M-F, of Detroit and Tincher Motor Car Co., of South Bend in hopes of achieving mergers that would provide additional production facilities.

1906
Model E, 20 N.A.C.C.H.P.

	FP	5	4	3	2	1
Side Ent Tr	2600	2300	5400	9000	12,600	18,000
Twn Car	4000	2000	5100	8500	11,900	17,000
Model F, 28 N.A.C.C.H.P.						
Side Ent Tr	3000	3000	6000	10,000	14,000	20,000
Model G, 30 N.A.C.C.H.P.						
Side Ent Tr	3700	3400	6900	11,500	16,100	23,000

1907-11

STUDEBAKER-GARFORD — 1907-1911 SERIES — FOURS: Year-by-year styling, finish and technical changes for the 1907-1911 Studebaker-Garford models are not available. The 1907 models were carried over from 1906, but had new alphabetical model designations. The first 40 horsepower Model B (Garford 40) was introduced in 1908. It had a T-head engine with cylinders cast in blocks of two. Bore and stroke was 4-3/4 x 5-1/4 inches giving a total displacement of 372.1 cu. in. A new 114 inch wheelbase was also used. The Model A of the same year was an improved version of the Model G of 1906-1907 with the same 30 hp, 280.6 cu. in. engine and 104 inch wheelbase. A Model H, with the same engine and wheelbase as the Model G, was also available in both 1907 and 1908.

1908 Studebaker, model H, runabout, HAC

1909 Studebaker-Garford, model D, touring, HAC

For 1909, the Model A and Model B series were carried over with minimal change. The Model H was refined and renamed Model C. All-new was the 40 horsepower Model D. It had the 372.1 cu. in. engine, but a longer 117-1/2 inch wheelbase. In 1910, the Model H returned and was joined by a new Model M. The latter was merely an improved version of the Model L, which was last cataloged back in 1907. It revived the 285.6 cu. in./28 horsepower four-cylinder engine. Also available was the G-7, an improved variant of the Model D.

During 1911, the last year of Studebaker-Garford production, the G-7 was carried over as the G-8 with slightly higher prices. Also for 1911, there was a new G-10. It had a distinctive 116 in. wheelbase and a four-cylinder. 30 horsepower powerplant of 297.8 cu. in. (4-1/4 x 5-1/4 bore and stroke).

Interestingly, the 1908 Models A and B were also marketed under the Garford name. Studebaker soon halted this practive by enforcing its contract provisions. However, the contract terminated during calendar 1910 and, for 1911, the G-7 was available as a Studebaker or a Garford. (See Garford section). The same is true of the 1911 G-8, which was sold under the Garford badge in 1912. The all-new G-10, however, appears to have been a Studebaker exclusive.

Even as the relationship between the two firms continued to deteriorate, Studebaker was expanding its own control over E-M-F, which it took over completely in 1910. E-M-F was merged into the new Studebaker Corporation on Jan. 1, 1911, about the same time Garford brokeout on its own. The non-Studebaker Garford automobiles were marketed until 1913, when Garford was absorbed into Willys-Overland. Studebaker, of course, survived very well without Garford for the next 55 years or so.

1910 Studebaker, Garford G-7, limousine, HAC

1366

1907
Model L, 4-cyl., 28 hp, 104" wb

	FP	5	4	3	2	1
5P Rear Ent Tr		3750	7500	12,500	17,500	25,000
Model G, 4-cyl., 30 hp, 104" wb						
5P Rear Ent Tr		3900	7800	13,000	18,200	26,000
Model H, 4-cyl., 30 hp, 104" wb						
5P Rear Ent Tr		3900	7800	13,000	18,200	26,000
1908						
Model H, 4-cyl., 30 hp, 104" wb						
5P Rear Ent Tr	3500	3900	7800	13,000	18,200	26,000
Model A, 4-cyl., 30 hp, 104" wb						
5P Tr	3500	3900	7800	13,000	18,200	26,000
5P Town Car	4200	3750	7500	12,500	17,500	25,000
2P Rbt		3600	7200	12,000	16,800	24,000
5P Lan'let		3900	7800	13,000	18,200	26,000
Model B, 4-cyl., 40 hp, 114" wb						
5P Tr	4000	4200	8400	14,000	19,600	28,000
2P Rbt		3900	7800	13,000	18,200	26,000
7P Limo		4050	8100	13,500	18,900	27,000
5P Lan'let		4200	8400	14,000	19,600	28,000
4P Trabt		4350	8700	14,500	20,300	29,000
3P Speed Car		4000	7950	13,250	18,550	26,500
1909						
Model A, 4-cyl., 30 hp, 104" wb						
5P Tr		3900	7800	13,000	18,200	26,000
5P Twn Car		3750	7500	12,500	17,500	25,000
Rbt		3600	7200	12,000	16,800	24,000
5P Lan'let		3900	7800	13,000	18,200	26,000
Model B, 4-cyl., 40 hp, 114" wb						
5P Tr		4200	8400	14,000	19,600	28,000
7P Limo		4050	8100	13,500	18,900	27,000
5P Lan'let		4200	8400	14,000	19,600	28,000
Model C, 4-cyl., 30 hp, 104" wb						
5P Tr		3900	7800	13,000	18,200	26,000
Model D, 4-cyl., 40 hp, 117.5" wb						
5P Tr		4350	8700	14,500	20,300	29,000
1910						
Model H, 4-cyl., 30 hp, 104" wb						
5P Tr		3900	7800	13,000	18,200	26,000
Model M, 4-cyl., 28 hp, 104" wb						
5P Tr		3750	7500	12,500	17,500	25,000
Model G-7, 4-cyl., 40 hp, 117.5" wb						
4/5P Tr	3500	4200	8400	14,000	19,600	28,000
7P Tr	3500	4350	8700	14,500	20,300	29,000
Limo (123" wb)	4750	3900	7800	13,000	18,200	26,000
1911						
Model G-8, 4-cyl., 40 hp, 117.5" wb						
7P Limo	4800	4050	8100	13,500	18,900	27,000
5P Lan'let	4900	4200	8400	14,000	19,600	28,000
4/6/7P Tr	3750	4350	8700	14,500	20,300	29,000
2P Rdst	3750	4500	9000	15,000	21,000	30,000
Model G-10, 4-cyl., 30 hp, 116" wb						
5P Tr		4200	8400	14,000	19,600	28,000

NOTE: Studebaker-Garford association was discontinued after 1911 model year.

1913

1913 Studebaker, model SA, touring, HAC

STUDEBAKER — SA25 — FOUR: The 1913 Studebaker 25 came in two body styles, roadster and touring. They were the company's small 4-cylinder models. Identifying features included a plain side hood and rear doors with wedge-shaped lower rear corners on the touring car. Cars in this line were the only Studebakers not equipped with electrical starting and lighting. Full-elliptical rear springs were featured. There were rear axle braces extending from the axle shaft housing to propeller shaft housing.

STUDEBAKER — AA35 — FOUR: The Studebaker 35 was the company's larger 4-cylinder line. It offered three body styles, touring, coupe and sedan. The doors had rounded corners doors. The coupe featured leather upholstery and plate glass windows with Japanese leather dashboard trim and nickle plated controls. The sedan had blue English broadcloth upholstery. Three-quarter elliptical rear springs were used. Radius rods extended from the rear axle to frame cross members.

STUDEBAKER — E — SIX: The 1913 Studebaker E-6 came in two body styles, touring and limousine. They were Studebaker's biggest cars. Under the extra-long hood was a long, six-cylinder engine with three blocks on a common crankcase. Each had two cylinders. Historians credit these as being the first mass production cars to have a six cast en bloc. Other features were three-quarter elliptical rear springs and radius rods bracing the axle to the frame. The coupe was equipped and trimmed similarly to the Model 35 coupe. The limousine offered broadcloth and Bedford cord upholstery with Turkish leather trims for the driver's compartment. None of these cars are known to survive today.

I.D. DATA: Series SA25 serial numbers were starting: 301501; ending: 315611. Engine numbers were starting: 25A-1; ending: 25A-15031. Series AA35 serial numbers were starting: 101501; ending: 110614. Engine numbers were starting: 35A-1; ending: 35A-10031. Series E serial numbers were starting: 600001 to 602800 and 602953 to 603002. Engine numbers: 6A-1 to 6A-3004.

Model No.	Body Type & Seating	Price	Weight	Prod. Total
25A	2-dr. Rds.-2P	875	NA	Note 1
25A	4-dr. Tr.-4P	885	NA	Note 1
Note 1: Total production was 15,000.				
35A	4-dr. Tr.-6P	1290	NA	Note 1
35A	2-dr. Cpe.-3P	1850	NA	Note 1
35A	4-dr. Sed.-4P	2050	NA	Note 1
Note 1: Total production was 10,000.				
E-6	4-dr. Tr.-6P	1550	NA	Note 1
E-6	4-dr. Limo.-6P	2500	NA	Note 1
Note 1: Total production was 3,000.				

ENGINE: [Model 25] L-head. Inline. Four. (cast en bloc). Gray cast iron. B & S: 3-1/2 in. x 5 in. Disp.: 192.4 cu. in. Brake H.P.: 25. Net H.P.: 20 N.A.C.C. Valve lifters: Solid. Carburetor: Holley 1V (sidedraft). [Model 35] L-head. Inline. Four. (cast en bloc). Gray cast iron. B & S: 4-1/8 in. x 5 in. Brake H.P.: 35. Net H.P.: 27 N.A.C.C. Valve lifters: Solid. Carburetor: Holley 1V sidedraft. [Model E] L-head. Inline. Six. (cast en bloc). Gray cast iron. B & S: 3-1/2 in. x 5 in. Disp.: 288.6 cu. in. Brake H.P.: 40. Net H.P.: 29 N.A.C.C. Valve lifters: Solid. Carburetor: Holley 1V sidedraft.

CHASSIS: [Series 25] W.B.: 102 in. Frt/Rear Tread: 56/56 in. [Series 35] W.B.: 115 in. Frt/Rear Tread: 56/56 in.

TECHNICAL: Selective sliding transmission (in unit with rear axle). Speeds: 3F/1R. Floor mounted gearshift controls. Clutch: Leather faced cone type. External contracting rear wheel brakes. 12-spoke wood artillery wheels.

OPTIONS: Spare tire(s). OSRV mirror.

HISTORICAL: Introduced [25 & 35] December, 1912; (E-6) Jan. 1913. Innovations: First six cast en bloc. First exclusively Studebaker models. Calendar year production: 35,410. Model year production: 25,000. The president of Studebaker was Frederick Fish. Studebaker was 4th largest American auto maker.

1913
Model SA-25, 4-cyl., 101" wb

	FP	5	4	3	2	1
Rds	875	1150	3600	6000	8400	12,000
Tr	885	1250	3900	6500	9100	13,000
Model AA-35, 4-cyl., 115.5" wb						
Tr	1290	1300	4050	6750	9450	13,500
Cpe	1850	1400	4200	7000	9800	14,000
Sed	2050	1500	4350	7250	10,150	14,500
Model E, 6-cyl., 121" wb						
Tr	1550	1500	4350	7250	10,150	14,500
Limo	2500	1550	4500	7500	10,500	15,000

1914

1914 Studebaker, model EB, 7-pass. touring, OCW

STUDEBAKER SC — SERIES 14 — FOUR: The cowl on 1914 Studebakers was redesigned to house the gas tank which was moved from its former location under the front seat. A bead molding was added to the upper hood panel. The front fenders now had a beveled edge. Steering wheels were changed to the left side of the car, with transmission and emergency brake levers at the center.

STUDEBAKER EB — SERIES 14 — SIX: Changes on the Studebaker Six were similar to those on the fours. The Sixes had a longer wheelbase and longer hoods. The six-cylinder touring was a seven passenger model with auxiliary folding seats in the rear passenger compartment. A distinctive model in this line was the five passenger sedan. It was equipped with heavy plate glass windows, coachlights on the side and double body beltline moldings.

I.D. DATA: [Series SC] The serial numbers for 1914 four-cylinder domestic SC models were 403001 to 420515. Cars built for export had serial numbers 400001 to 400407. Engine numbers were 4B-1 to 4B-18050. [Series EB] Serial numbers for 1914 sixes were 605001 to 612450. Engine numbers were 6B-4001 to 6B-11620. No export versions of the Studebaker six were built this year.

Model No.	Body Type & Seating	Price	Weight	Prod. Total
SC-4	4-dr. Tr.-5P	1050	NA	Note 1
SC-4	2-dr. Lan. Rds.-2P	1200	NA	Note 1
Note 1: Total production was 17,976.				
EB-6	4-dr. Tr.-7P	1575	NA	Note 1
EB-6	2-dr. Lan. Rds.-3P	1800	NA	Note 1
EB-6	2-dr. Sed.-5P	2250	NA	Note 1
Note 1: Total production was 7,625.				

ENGINE: [Series SC] L-head. Inline. Four. (cast en bloc). Gray cast iron. B & S: 3-1/2 in. x 5 in. Disp.: 192.4. Brake H.P.: 25. N.A.C.C. H.P.: 20. Valve lifters: Solid. Carb.: Holley 1V (sidedraft). [Series EB] L-head. Inline. Six. (cast en bloc). Gray cast iron. B & S: 3-1/2 in. x 5 in. Disp.: 288.6. Brake H.P.: 40. N.A.C.C. H.P.: 29. Valve lifters: Solid. Carb.: Holley 1V.

CHASSIS: [Model SC-4] W.B.: 108.3 in. Frt/Rear Tread: 56/56 in. [Model EB-6] W.B.: 121.3 in. Frt/Rear Tread: 56/56 in.

TECHNICAL: Selective sliding transmission. Speeds: 3F/1R. Floor-mounted gearshift controls. Clutch: Leather faced cone type full-floating. External contracting rear wheel brakes. Wood spoke artillery wheels.

OPTIONS: Spare tire(s). OSRV mirror.

HISTORICAL: Introduced [SC] Oct. 1913-June 1914; [EB] Oct. 1913-Mar. 1915. Calendar year production: 35,000. Model year production: 25,601. Innovations: Improved carburetor feed system. Wagner two-unit starter/generator with 6-volt battery. Centralized controls. Improved transmission.
Note: This was Frederick Fish's last year as president of Studebaker Corporation.

1914
Series 14, Model 1 SC, 4-cyl., 108.3" wb

	FP	5	4	3	2	1
Tr	1050	1300	4050	6750	9450	13,500
Lan Rds	1200	1350	4150	6900	9700	13,800
Series 14, Model EB, 6-cyl., 121.3" wb						
Tr	1575	1500	4350	7250	10,150	14,500
Lan Rds	1800	1550	4400	7400	10,400	14,800
2 dr Sed	2250	1550	4450	7450	10,400	14,900

1915

1915 Studebaker, model SD-4, roadster, HAC

STUDEBAKER — MODEL SD — SERIES 15 — FOUR: The 1915 Studebaker four looked much the same as the 1914 model. One obvious change was the relocation of the gas filler cap from the cowl to the right side of the instrument panel. Cowl lights were no longer used because the headlights had dimmer bulbs incorporated. Available models were a roadster and a touring car.

STUDEBAKER — MODEL EC — SERIES 15 — SIX: The 1915 Studebaker six looked much the same as the 1914 model. An obvious change was the relocation of the gas filler cap from the cowl to the right side of the instrument panel. Cowl lights were no longer used because the headlights had dimmer bulbs. Closed cars were not marketed.

I.D. DATA: [Model SD] The serial numbers for 1915 four-cylinder domestic SD models were 423001 to 447419. Cars built for export had serial numbers 449001 to 449443. Engine numbers were 4C-20001 to 4C-44931. [Model EC] Serial numbers for 1915 six-cylinder domestic EC models were 500001 to 504483 and 613001 to 617155. Export car serial numbers were 603001 to 603183. Engine numbers were 6C-12001 to 6C-20787.

Model No.	Body Type & Seating	Price	Weight	Prod. Total
SD-4	2-dr. Rds.-2P	985	NA	Note 1
SD-4	4-dr. Tr.-4P	985	NA	Note 1
Note 1: Total production was 24,849.				
EC-6	4-dr. Tr.-5P	1389	NA	Note 1
EC-6	4-dr. Tr.-7P	1450	NA	Note 1
Note 1: Total production was 8,751.				

ENGINE: [Model SD] L-head. Inline. Four. (cast en bloc). Gray cast iron. B & S: 3-1/2 in. x 5 in. Disp.: 192.4 cu. in. Brake H.P.: 30. N.A.C.C. H.P.: 20. Valve lifters: Solid. Carb.: Holley 1V. [Model EC] L-head. Inline. Six. (cast en bloc). Gray cast iron. B & S: 3-1/2 in. x 5 in. Disp.: 288.6 cu. in. Brake H.P.: 40. N.A.C.C. H.P.: 29. Valve lifters: Solid. Carb.: Holley 1V.

CHASSIS: [Model SD-4] W.B.: 108.3 in. Frt/Rear Tread: 56/56 in. Tires: 33 x 4. [Model EC-6] W.B.: 121.3 in. Frt/Rear Tread: 56/56 in.

TECHNICAL: Selective sliding transmission. Speeds: 3F/1R. Floor mounted gearshift controls. Leather faced cone clutch. Full-floating rear axle. External contracting rear wheel brakes. Wood spoke artillery wheels.

OPTIONS: Front bumper. Spare tire(s). OSRV mirror. "Fat Man" steering wheel.

HISTORICAL: Introduced [Model EC] July, 1914-June, 1915; [Model SD] June, 1914-June, 1915. Model year sales: 33,600. Innovations: Improved braking and steering systems. Gas tank stiffened and strengthened. Larger tires on SD four.
Note: Albert Erskine became president of Studebaker Corporation in 1915. Corporate profits exceeded $9 million. Frederick Fisher became Chairman of the Board. John M. Studebaker was named honorary president.

1915
Series 15, Model SD, 4-cyl., 108.3" wb

	FP	5	4	3	2	1
Rds	985	1300	4050	6700	9400	13,400
Tr	985	1300	4050	6750	9450	13,500

Series 15, Model EC, 6-cyl., 121.3" wb

	FP	5	4	3	2	1
5P Tr	1389	1400	4200	7000	9800	14,000
7P Tr	1450	1500	4350	7250	10,150	14,500

1916

1916 Studebaker, touring, OCW

STUDEBAKER — MODEL SF FOUR-FORTY — SERIES 16 & 17 — FOUR: New appearance features for 1916 Studebakers included smoother body lines and wider rear tonneaus for touring cars. The jump seats inside seven passenger open cars folded into the floor instead of the back of the front seat. The Landau Roadster, with a blind quarter top with top irons made a reappearance. It had oval shaped "opera" windows on each side. Colors for the year were dark Studebaker blue with white striping. The fenders, hood and runningboards were black. The wheels were finished in blue with black trim. Wheelbase increased to 112 inches.
Several changes occurred in the middle of the production run. A splash apron was added below the radiator. The fuel tank was moved to the rear of the chassis. A divided front seat replaced the contoured bench in touring cars. Vehicles having these changes were in Series 17 and were sold as first series 1917 models.

STUDEBAKER — MODEL ED-6 — SERIES 16 & 17 — SIX: The six-cylinder Studebaker for 1916 had the same appearance changes as seen on the fours. The sixes continued to feature a larger wheelbase and longer front end sheet metal. The wheel base increased to 122 inches. Body styles were the same as for model SF, plus a four passenger coupe, seven passenger limousine and a sedan.
Cars produced late in the production run had the same running modifications as described for four-cylinder cars. These cars were sold as 1917 models. An All-Weather Car was one new model.

SERIAL NUMBER DATA:
Model SF Series 16 (domestic): 460001 to 474180.
Model SF Series 16 (export): 450001 to 453228.
Model SF Series 17 (domestic): 474181 to 500369. Also: 100000 to 109500.
ENGINE NUMBERS:
Model SF Series 16: 50001 to 67100.
Model SF Series 17: 67151 to 96000 and 1000 to 9579.
SERIAL NUMBER DATA:
Model ED Series 16 (domestic): 630001 to 637260.
Model ED Series 16 (export): 624001 to 624865.
Model ED Series 17 (domestic): 637261 to 655270. Also: 200000 to 207500.

Model ED Series 17 (export) 624866 to 626023. Also: 200000 to 207500.
ENGINE NUMBERS:
Model ED Series 16: 25001 to 33153.
Model ED Series 17: 33270 to 51279 and 1000 to 7248.

Model No.	Body Type & Seating	Price	Weight	Prod. Total
SF	2-dr. Rds.-3P	850	NA	Note 1
SF	4-dr. Tr.-7P	885	NA	Note 1
SF	2-dr. Lan. Rds.-3P	1150	NA	Note 1
(1917 ONLY MODEL)				
SF	4-dr. A/W Sed.-7P	1565	NA	Note 1

Note 1: Total Model SF production was 80,842 cars between June 1915 and April 1918.
Note 2: Prices for the 1917 series were as follows: 2-dr. rds. ($850); 4-dr tr. ($875) and Lan. Rds. ($1150).

ED	2-dr. Rds.-3P	1000	—	Note 1
ED	2-dr. Lan. Rds.-3P	1350	—	Note 1
ED	4-dr. Tr.-7P	1050	—	Note 1
ED	2-dr. Cpe.-4P	1550	—	Note 1
ED	2-dr. Sed.-5P	1675	—	Note 1
ED	3-dr. Limo.-7P	2250	—	Note 1
(1917 ONLY MODEL)				
ED	4-dr. A/W Sed.-7P	1675	—	Note 1

Note 1: Total Model ED production was 60,712 cars between June 1915 and Jan. 1918.
Note 2: Prices for the 1917 Series were as follows: 2 dr. rds. ($1060); 2-dr. Lan. Rds. ($1350); 4-dr. tr. ($1085); 2-dr. cpe. ($1600); 2-dr. sed. ($1675) and 3-dr. Limo. ($2500).

ENGINE: [Model SF] L-head. Inline. Four. Gray cast iron. B & S: 3-7/8 in. x 5 in. Disp.: 235.6 cu. in. Brake H.P.: 44. N.A.C.C. H.P.: 24. Valve lifters: Solid. Carb.: Holley 1V. [Model ED] L-head. Inline. Six. Gray cast iron. B & S: 3-7/8 in. x 5 in. Disp.: 353.8 cu. in. Brake H.P.: 54. N.A.C.C. H.P.: 36. Valve lifters: Solid. Carb.: Holley 1V.

CHASSIS: [Model SF] W.B.: 112 in. Frt/Rear Tread: 56/56. Tires: 34 x 4. [Model ED] W.B.: 122. Frt/Rear Tread: 56/56. Tires: 34 x 4.

TECHNICAL: Selective sliding transmission. Speeds: 3F/1R. Floor-mounted gearshift controls. Leather faced cone-type clutch. Full-floating rear axle. External contracting rear wheel brakes. Wood spoke artillery wheels.

OPTIONS: Front bumper. Spare tire(s). OSRV mirror. "Fat Man" steering wheel.

HISTORICAL: Introduced June, 1915. Model production: 141,554. Innovations: (Series 16) Cylinder bore size increased. Carburetion improved and relocated. Improved water and oil pump drive systems. Improved clutch. Stronger propeller shaft. Larger brakes with equalizer. Sturdier rear axle. (Series 17) Fuel tank in rear. Vacuum tank replaces gravity feed. All-weather car added to line.
Note: Albert Erskine continued as Studebaker's president. About 25,000 cars were built in the 16th series.

1916
Model SF, 4-cyl., 112" wb

	FP	5	4	3	2	1
Rds	850	1300	4050	6750	9450	13,500
Lan Rds	885	1400	4200	7000	9800	14,000
7P Tr	1150	1250	3950	6600	9200	13,200
A/W Sed	1565	1300	4050	6700	9400	13,400

Series 16 & 17, Model ED, 6-cyl., 121.8" wb

	FP	5	4	3	2	1
Rds	1000	1400	4200	7000	9800	14,000
Lan Rds	1350	1550	4400	7400	10,400	14,800
7P Tr	1050	1400	4200	7000	9800	14,000
Cpe	1550	1025	2600	5250	7300	10,500
Sed	1675	1075	3000	5500	7700	11,000
Limo	2250	1150	3600	6000	8400	12,000
A/W Sed	1675	1400	4350	7250	10,150	14,500

NOTE: The All Weather sedan was available only in the Series 17.

1917

1917 Studebaker, model ED, touring, HAC

STUDEBAKER — MODEL SF — SERIES 18 — FOUR: The Model SF continued to be sold in the second part of the 1917 model year and the early part of the 1918 model year. Production continued until April 1918. Cars in the 18th Series had some changes in body styles and seating arrangements. One characteristic change was that the front passenger seat in the touring car could be reversed to face towards the rear. The jump seats now folded and slid under the contoured bench seat at the rear of the tonneau. Roadsters and touring cars could now be ordered in Gun metal gray.

STUDEBAKER — MODEL ED — SERIES 18 — SIX: The limousine had a handsome new body of elegant design and furnishings. Changes in other models were about the same as on fours, which used virtually the same bodies. The sixes had the longer chassis and front end sheet metal again.

SERIAL NUMBER DATA:
Model SF Series 18 (domestic): 109501 to 133051.
Model SF Series 18 (export): 10001 to 12906.
ENGINE NUMBERS:
Model SF Series 18: 7249 to 34600.
SERIAL NUMBER DATA
Model ED Series 18 (domestic): 207501 to 233495.
Model ED Series 18 (export): 20001 to 21334.
ENGINE NUMBERS:
Model ED Series 18: 9580 to 35966.

Model No.	Body Type & Seating	Price	Weight	Prod. Total
SF	2-dr. Rds.-3P	1025	NA	Note 1
SF	4-dr. Tr.-7P	1050	NA	Note 1
SF	2-dr. Lan. Rds.-3P	NA	NA	Note 1
SF	4-dr. A/W Sed.-7P	1250	NA	Note 1

Note 1: See 1916 production total.

ED	2-dr. Rds.-3P	1335	NA	Note 1
ED	2-dr. Lan. Rds.-3P	1550	NA	Note 1
ED	4-dr. Tr.-7P	1385	NA	Note 1
ED	2-dr. Cpe.-4P	1850	NA	Note 1
ED	2-dr. Sed.-5P	1850	NA	Note 1
ED	3-dr. Limo.-7P	2750	NA	Note 1
ED	4-dr. A/W Sed.-7P	1565	NA	Note 1

Note 1: See 1916 Production total.

ENGINE: [Model SF] L-head. Inline. Four. Gray cast iron. B & S: 3-7/8 in. x 5 in. Disp.: 235.6 cu. in. Brake H.P.: 44. Net H.P.: 24. Valve lifters: Solid. Carb.: Holley IV. [Model ED] L-head. Inline. Six. Gray cast iron. B & S: 3-7/8 in. x 5 in. Disp.: 353.8 cu. in. Brake H.P.: 54. Net H.P.: 36. Valve lifters: Solid. Carb.: Holley IV.

CHASSIS: [Model SF] W.B.: 112 in. Frt/Rear Tread: 56/56 in. Tires: 34 x 4. [Model ED] W.B.: 122 in. Frt/Rear Tread: 56/56 in. Tires: 34 x 4.

TECHNICAL: Selective sliding transmission. Speeds: 3F/1R. Floor-mounted gearshift controls. Leather faced cone type clutch. Full-floating rear axle. External contracting rear wheel brakes. Wood spoke artillery wheels.

OPTIONS: Front bumper. Spare tire(s). OSRV mirror. "Fat Man" steering wheel. Runningboard luggage gates.

HISTORICAL: See 1916 notes.

1917 (Series 18)
Series 18, Model SF, 4-cyl., 112" wb

	FP	5	4	3	2	1
Rds	—	1300	4050	6750	9450	13,500
Lan Rds	1050	1400	4200	7000	9800	14,000
7P Tr	NA	1300	4050	6750	9450	13,500
A/W Sed	1250	1300	4050	6700	9400	13,400

Series 18, Model ED, 6-cyl., 121.8" wb

Rds	1335	1400	4200	7000	9800	14,000
Lan Rds	1550	1550	4400	7400	10,400	14,800
7P Tr	1385	1450	4250	7100	9900	14,200
Cpe	1850	1025	2600	5250	7300	10,500
Sed	1850	1075	3000	5500	7700	11,000
Limo	2750	1175	3650	6100	8500	12,200
A/W Sed	1565	1500	4350	7250	10,150	14,500

1918-19

1918 Studebaker, touring, OCW

STUDEBAKER — "LIGHT FOUR" MODEL SH — SERIES 19 — FOUR: The Light Four of 1918 is a rare Studebaker model. It was built on a 112 inch wheelbase and came as a touring car, sedan and roadster. Appearance changes included smoother, more gently rounded body lines and a low-slung look to the entire car. The rear edge of the rear doors slanted diagonally upwards near the rear fender contours.

STUDEBAKER — "LIGHT SIX" MODEL EH — SERIES 19 — SIX: This car was introduced as a "Light Six" and later called the "Special Six." Low-slung bodies with smoothly rounded hood and cowl feature lines made these handsome automobiles. The roadster had a rounded rear deck and a new model was the four-passenger "Chummy" roadster on which the rear of the body swooped downward in a sharp curve. It had individual front bucket seats. Standard body colors were maroon or dark blue.

STUDEBAKER — "BIG SIX" MODEL EG — SERIES 19 — SIX: The Model EG Big Six came only as a touring car. The top panel of the hood and the cowl curved across the car. The main body feature line began at the radiator and ran in a straight line across the length of the hood sides and fully along the body belt line. The hood side panels were higher than on previous Studebakers. There were 14 very tall ventilating louvers on the rear half of the hood side panels. The headlight buckets had a curved rectangular shape housing circular lenses.

SERIAL NUMBER DATA: [Model SH] Serial numbers were stamped on a plate attached to the left frame member under the front fender. U.S. serial numbers were 133101 to 141975. Canadian serial numbers were 12951 and up. Engine numbers were 4001 to 4999; 41001 to 45000 and A.F. 1001 to A.F. 7950. [Model EH] Serial numbers were in the same location as on the "Light Four." Starting: 233501 to 257464. Canadian numbers were 21351 to 23256. Engine numbers were stamped on the starter motor support. Engine numbers were 6001 to 6999; 61001 to 70000 and BF 1001 to 18000. [Model EG] Serial numbers were in the same locations as on other 1918-19 models. U.S. numbers were 290001 to 301050. Canadian numbers were 29001 to 30138. Engine numbers were in the same location as on other 1918-19 models. Engine numbers were 7001 to 7999; 71001 to 73600 and CF 1001 to CF 31253.

Model No.	Body Type & Seating	Price	Weight	Prod. Total
SH	2-dr. Rds.-2P	1050	NA	Note 1
SH	4-dr. Tr.-5P	995	NA	Note 1
SH	4-dr. Sed.-5P	1525	NA	Note 1

6Note 1: Total production was 12,500 according to one source; 8,900 according to a second source.

EH	4-dr. Tr.-5P	1395	NA	Note 1
EH	4-dr. Clb. Rds.-4P	1395	NA	Note 1
EH	2-dr. Rds.-2P	1450	NA	Note 1
EH	4-dr. Sed.-5P	1950	NA	Note 1
EH	2-dr. Cpe.-4P	1950	NA	Note 1

Note 1: Total production was 25,801.
Note 2: The 4-passenger "Chummy" roadster was also called a Club Roadster as listed above.

EG	4-dr. Tr.-7P	1795	NA	11,757

ENGINE: [Model SH] L-head. Inline. Four. Cast iron block. B & S: 3-1/2 in. x 5 in. Disp.: 192.4 cu. in. Brake H.P.: 40 @ 2000 R.P.M. N.A.C.C. H.P.: 19.6. Valve lifters: Solid. Carb.: Stromberg 1V (plain tube). [Model EH] L-head. Inline. Six. Cast iron block. B & S: 3-1/2 in. x 5 in. Disp.: 288.6 cu. in. Brake h.P. 50 @ 2000 R.P.M. N.A.C.C. H.P.: 29.4. Valve lifters: Solid. Carb.: Ball & Ball 1V. [Model EG] L-head. Inline. Six. Cast iron block. B & S: 3-7/8 in. x 5 in. Disp.: 353.8 cu. in. C.R.: 4.1:1. Brake H.P.: 60 @ 2000 R.P.M. N.A.C.C. H.P.: 36. Main bearings: Four. Valve lifters: Solid. Carb.: Ball & Ball 1V.

CHASSIS: [Model SH] W.B.: 112 in. Frt/Rear Tread: 56/56 in. Tires: 32 x 3.5. [Model EH] W.B.: 119 in. Frt/Rear Tread: 56/56 in. Tires: 32 x 4. [Model EG] W.B.: 120 in. Frt/Rear Tread: 56/56 in.

TECHNICAL: Selective sliding transmission. Speeds: 3F/1R. Floor-mounted gearshift controls. Aluminum cone clutch with leather facing. Semi-floating rear axle. External contracting rear wheel brakes. Wood spoke artillery wheels.
Note: The rear axle transmission (transaxle) used on 1913-17 Studebakers was dropped this year on all models. Hotchkiss drive was adopted.

OPTIONS: Front bumper. Runningboard tool box. Motometer. Spare tire(s). Spotlight(s). OSRV mirror. Runningboard luggage gate. Wire spoke wheels.

HISTORICAL: Introduced February, 1918. Model year sales: 50,058. Model year production: (1918) 18,419; (1919) 35,051. Innovations: Transaxle eliminated. Aluminum cone clutch replaces pressed steel type. Redesigned frame narrowing at front. Hotchkiss drive. Underslung springs with bronze bushings. Detachable cylinder head on Big Six. Clutch brake. Note: This year's models marked a complete break from Studebaker's EMF origins as all three lines of cars were completely new. Albert Erskine continued as president of the corporation. Production was held down by effects of WWI.

1919 Studebaker, Six, touring, HAC

1918-1919

Series 19, Model SH, 4-cyl., 112" wb

	FP	5	4	3	2	1
Rds	1050	1150	3500	5900	8250	11,800
Tr	995	1150	3600	6000	8400	12,000
Sed	1525	825	1600	4050	5650	8100

Series 19, Model EH, 6-cyl., 119" wb

	FP	5	4	3	2	1
Tr	1395	1250	3900	6500	9100	13,000
Clb Rds	1395	1550	4500	7500	10,500	15,000
Rds	1450	1200	3750	6250	8750	12,500
Sed	1950	850	1650	4100	5700	8200
Cpe	1950	825	1600	4050	5650	8100

Series 19, Model EG, 6-cyl., 126" wb

	FP	5	4	3	2	1
7P Tr	1795	1400	4200	7000	9800	14,000

1920-21

1920 Studebaker Big Six, touring, JAC

STUDEBAKER LIGHT SIX — MODEL EJ — SERIES 20-21 — SIX: The Studebaker Light Six, Model EJ, was an all-new automobile. While the general size and appearance was somewhat similar to the earlier Light Six, detail changes created a more modern looking car. The radiator shell was flatter and had a square opening for the radiator core. It was finished in body color and decorated with a circular Studebaker badge. The hood was shorter and had vertical louvers along the length of the side panels. The new cowl panel had a gentle, upward sweep. Larger doors were seen. All cars in the EJ line were normally finished in black, which was the standard factory color. The main difference between 1920 (Series 20) and 1921 (Series 21) models was in body styles and factory prices.

STUDEBAKER SPECIAL SIX — MODEL EH — SERIES 20-21 — SIX: The Special Six, Model EH had only a few changes from 1919 models. Torpedo-shaped cowl lights and exterior door handles on open cars were among the changes. The rear fender design was slightly different than on the earlier cars in this line. Standard body colors continued to be maroon or dark blue.

STUDEBAKER BIG SIX — MODEL EG — SERIES 20-21 — SIX: The appearance of the Model EG Big Six was refined for 1920 and slightly updated for 1921. In 1920, cowl lights were added and the windshield frame was redesigned. It now had a straighter bottom section and slanted vertical uprights with one-piece glass. For 1921, a reverse curve was added to the back edge of the rear fenders.

I.D. DATA: [Model EJ] Serial numbers were located on the left side of frame over front axle. Starting: 1000001. Ending: 1035002. Engine numbers were located on a brass plate on the right rear motor support. Engine numbers are not available. [Model EH] Serial numbers were located on the left side of frame over front axle. Starting: 257465. Ending: 290000. Also: 504501 to 535876. Engine numbers were located on a brass plate on right rear motor support. Starting: BG 17001. Ending: BG 19537. Also: BG 49243 to BG 85644. [Model EG] Serial numbers were stamped on a plate attached to the left frame member under the front fender. Starting: 315701. Ending: 335069. Engine numbers were stamped on the starter motor support. Starting: CG 10001. Ending: CG 31253. Body serial numbers were stamped on the body frame just inside the right front door or stamped on a small aluminum plate attached to the body sill or embossed on a plate attached to engine side of firewall.

Model No.	Body Type & Seating	Price	Weight	Prod. Total
(1920)				
6EJ	4-dr. Tr.-5P	1485	2550	Note 1
6EJ	2-dr. Lan. Rds.-2P	1650	2670	Note 1
6EJ	4-dr. Sed.-5P	2150	2900	Note 1
(1921)				
6EJ	4-dr. Tr.-5P	1485	2550	Note 2
6EJ	2-dr. Rds.-2P	NA	2480	Note 2
6EJ	2-dr. Cpe. Rds.-2P	1650	2690	Note 2
6EJ	4-dr. Sed.-5P	2150	2900	Note 2

Note 1: About 7,000 Light Sixes were built in the (1920) Series 20.
Note 2: About 28,000 Light Sixes were built in the (1921) Series 21.

Model No.	Body Type & Seating	Price	Weight	Prod. Total
(1920)				
6EH	4-dr. Tr.-5P	NA	2995	Note 1
6EH	2-dr. Rds.-2P	NA	2895	Note 1
6EH	4-dr. Rds.-4P	NA	2940	Note 1
6EH	2-dr. Cpe.-4P	NA	3100	Note 1
6EH	4-dr. Sed.-5P	NA	3310	Note 1
(1921)				
6EH	4-dr. Tr.-5P	NA	3035	Note 2
6EH	4-dr. Rds.-4P	NA	3035	Note 2

1370

Model No.	Body Type & Seating	Price	Weight	Prod. Total
6EH	2-dr. Rds.-2P	NA	2895	Note 2
6EH	2-dr. Cpe.-4P	NA	3255	Note 2
6EH	4-dr. Sed.-5P	NA	3290	Note 2

Note 1: Total production for Series 20 was 45,096 cars built between Oct. 1919 and May 1921.
Note 2: Total production for Series 21 was 23,520 cars built between April 1921 and Dec. 1921.

Model No.	Body Type & Seating	Price	Weight	Prod. Total
(1920)				
6EG	4-dr. Tr.-7P	NA	3175	14,970
(1921)				
6EG	4-dr. Tr.-7P	NA	3230	Note 1
6EG	2-dr. Cpe.-4P	NA	3451	Note 1
6EG	4-dr. Sed.-7P	NA	3665	Note 1

Note 1: Total production for Series 21 (1921) was 6,277.
Note 2: The 1920 Big Sixes were built between Nov. 1919 and April 1921. The 1921 Big Sixes were built between April 1921 and Dec. 1921.

ENGINE: [Model EJ] L-head. Inline. Six. (Cast en bloc). Cast iron block (Aluminum cylinder head). B & S: 3-1/8 in. x 4-1/2 in. Disp.: 207.1 cu. in. C.R.: 4.1:1. Brake H.P.: 40 @ 2000 R.P.M. N.A.C.C. H.P.: 23.44. Valve lifters: Solid. Carb.: Stromberg 1V. [Model EH] L-head. Inline. Six. (Detachable cylinder head). Cast iron block. B & S: 3-1/2 in. x 5 in. Disp.: 288.6 cu. in. C.R.: 4.1:1. Brake H.P.: 50 @ 2000 R.P.M. N.A.C.C. H.P.: 29.04. Main bearings: Four. Valve lifters: Solid. Carb.: Stromberg 1V. [Model EG] L-head. Inline. Six. Cast iron block. B & S: 3-7/8 in. x 5 in. Disp.: 353.8 cu. in. C.R.: 4.1:1. Brake H.P.: 60 @ 2000 R.P.M. N.A.C.C. H.P.: 36.04. Main bearings: Four. Valve lifters: Solid. Carb.: Ball & Ball 1V.

CHASSIS: [Model EJ] W.B.: 112 in. Frt/Rear Tread: 56/56 in. Tires: 32 x 4. [Model EH] W.B.: 119 in. Frt/Rear Tread: 56/56 in. Tires: 32 x 4. [Model EG] W.B.: 126 in. Frt/Rear Tread: 56/56 in. Tires: 33 x 4.5.

TECHNICAL: Selective sliding transmission. Speeds: 3F/1R. Floor mounted gearshift controls. Clutch: (Light Six) Single-Disc; (others) cone type. Shaft drive. Semi-floating rear axle. Overall ratio: [Model EJ] 4.55:1; [Model EH] 4.33:1 and [Model EG] 3.71:1. External contracting rear wheel brakes. Wood spoke artillery wheels.

OPTIONS: Front bumper. Buddwire spoke wheels. Spare tire(s). OSRV mirror. Motometer. Luggage rack. Tool box (runningboard type). Spotlight(s). Windwings.

HISTORICAL: Introduced [EJ] April 1920; [EH] Oct. 1919; [EG] Nov. 1919. Innovations: [EJ] Improved valves. Single-disc clutch. Transmission lock. Aluminum head. Optional feed oiling. Optional rear end ratios of 4.08:1 or 5.0:1; [EH] Detachable cylinder head. Alemite lubrication; [EG] Body refinements. Alemite lubrication. Calendar year sales: (1920): 47,981; (1921) 69,863. Calendar year production: (1921) 65,000. Model year sales: (1920) 51,474; (1921) 66,423. Model year production: (1920) 67,066; (1921) 36,797 approximate.

Albert Erskine continued as president of Studebaker. A new plant was opened for manufacture of Light Sixes. The first car was turned out on April 30, 1920. Studebaker ended production of horse-drawn vehicles this year. The company was America's fourth-ranked automaker in 1921.

1920-21

Model EJ, 6-cyl., 112" wb

	FP	5	4	3	2	1
Tr	1485	1200	3750	6250	8750	12,500
Lan Rds *	1650	1250	3900	6500	9100	13,000
Rds	2150	1150	3600	6000	8400	12,000
Cpe Rds **	1485	1250	3950	6600	9200	13,200
Sed	—	825	1600	4000	5600	8000

Model EH, 6-cyl., 119" wb

	FP	5	4	3	2	1
Tr	1650	1300	4000	6650	9300	13,300
Rds	2150	1300	4050	6750	9450	13,500
4 dr Rds	—	1400	4200	7000	9800	14,000
Cpe	—	900	1800	4400	6150	8800
Sed	—	825	1600	4000	5600	8000

Model EG, Big Six

	FP	5	4	3	2	1
7P Tr	—	1500	4350	7250	10,150	14,500
Cpe **	—	950	2100	4750	6650	9500
7P Sed	—	875	1700	4250	5900	8500

* 1920 Model only.
** 1921 Model only.

1922

1922 Studebaker, Big Six, 4-pass. coupe, OCW

STUDEBAKER LIGHT SIX — MODEL EJ — SERIES 22 — SIX: The Light Six, Model EJ, continued into 1922 with only minor change. Cowl lamps that resembled miniature coach lights were added. Also new was an air ventilator on the top of the cowl. Reverse curve style rear fenders were also adopted. A crank case breather tube was a technical improvement.

STUDEBAKER SPECIAL SIX — MODEL EL — SERIES 22 — SIX: The 1922 Special Six had styling more like that of last year's Big Six, which was considered more modern. Obvious appearance changes included a more massive windshield frame with circular cowl lamps at the bottom corners. Touring cars had a one-piece windshield. Roadsters had a two-piece version with torpedo-shaped cowl lamps. Closed models had rectangular cowl lamps. A cowl ventilator was new for all body styles.

STUDEBAKER BIG SIX — MODEL EK — SERIES 22 — SIX: Several refinements were seen on the 1922 Studebaker Big Six Model EK. A one-piece windshield was used. New headlights were seen. A courtesy light was added to the left side of the cars for nighttime illumination.

I.D. DATA: [Model EJ] Serial numbers were located on the left side of the frame over front axle. Serial numbers were 1035003 and up. Engine numbers were located on a brass plate on the right rear motor support. Engine numbers are not available. [Model EL] Serial numbers were located on the left side of frame over front axle. Starting: 3000001. Ending: 3039122. Engine numbers were located on a brass plate on the right rear motor support. Engine numbers EL-1 and up were used. [Model EK] Serial numbers were stamped on a plate attached to left frame member under front fender. Starting: 2000001. Ending: 2017139. Engine numbers were stamped on the starter motor support. Engine numbers were EK-1 and up. The body serial numbering system was the same as 1920-21.

Model No.	Body Type & Seating	Price	Weight	Prod. Total
6EJ	Chassis	NA	1195	Note 1
6EJ	2-dr. Rds.-3P	NA	2480	Note 1
6EJ	4-dr. Tr.-5P	1045	2550	Note 1
6EJ	2-dr. Cpe. Rds.-2P	NA	2690	Note 1
6EJ	4-dr. Sed.-5P	NA	2900	Note 1

Note 1: Total production was approximately 49,000 Light Sixes built in the (1922) Series 22.
Note 2: Prices on all models was gradually lowered. For example, the touring car dropped from $1485 in 1921 to $1045 in 1922.

6EL	Chassis	NA	2500	Note 1
6EL	2-dr. Rds.-2P	NA	2920	Note 1
6EL	4-dr. Tr.-5P	NA	3155	Note 1
6EL	4-dr. Rds.-4P	NA	3085	Note 1
6EL	2-dr. Cpe.-4P	NA	3355	Note 1
6EL	4-dr. Sed.-5P	NA	3545	Note 1

Note 1: The Model EL Special Six was produced from Nov. 1921 to July 1924 as a 1922-1923-1924 model. A total of 111,443 were built for the three years combined.

6EK	Std. Chassis	NA	2543	Note 1
6EK	4-dr. Tr.-7P	NA	3310	Note 1
6EK	2-dr. Cpe.-4P	NA	3445	Note 1
6EK	4-dr. Sed.-7P	NA	3670	Note 1
6EK	Spl. Chassis	NA	NA	Note 1
6EK	4-dr. Spds.-5P	NA	3620	Note 1

Note 1: The Model EK Big Six was produced from Nov. 1921 to July 1924 as a 1922-1923-1924 model. A total of 48,892 were built for the three years combined.

ENGINE: See 1921 engine data. There were no major specifications changes for 1922. Light Sixes after engine number 35,810 had four ring pistons.

CHASSIS: [Model EJ] W.B.: 112 in. Frt/Rear Tread: 56/56 in. Tires: 32 x 4. [Model EL] W.B.: 119 in. Frt/Rear Tread: 56/56 in. Tires: 32 x 4. [Model EK] W.B.: 126 in. Frt/Rear Tread: 56/56 in. Tires: 33 x 4.5.

TECHNICAL: Selective sliding transmission. Speeds: 3F/1R. Floor mounted gearshift controls. Clutch: Single plate dry-disc type. Shaft drive. Semi-floating rear axle. Overall ratio: [EJ] 4.55:1. [EH] 4.33:1. [EK] 3.71:1. External contracting rear wheel brakes. Wood spoke artillery wheels.

OPTIONS: Bumper(s). Budd wire spoke wheels. Spare tire(s). OSRV mirror. Motometer. Luggage rack. Tool box (runningboard type). Spotlight(s). Wind wings.

HISTORICAL: Introduced [EJ] April, 1920; [EL] Nov., 1921; [EK] Nov., 1921. Innovations: [EJ] Oil filler in distributor housing support. Four ring pistons. Fuse location moved from cowl box to lighting switch. [EL] New disc clutch. [EK] New disc clutch. Body refinements. Calendar year sales: approximately 98,000. Model year sales: 110,269. Model year production: 107,378.
Total sales this year amounted to $133 million. Albert Erskine continued as company president.

1922
Model EJ, Light Six, 6-cyl., 112" wb

	FP	5	4	3	2	1
Rds	—	1250	3900	6500	9100	13,000
4 dr Tr	1045	1200	3750	6250	8750	12,500
Cpe Rds	—	1300	4050	6750	9450	13,500
Sed	—	825	1600	4000	5600	8000

Model EL, Special Six, 6-cyl., 119" wb

		5	4	3	2	1
Rds	—	1300	4050	6750	9450	13,500
Tr	—	1250	3900	6500	9100	13,000
4 dr Rds	—	1400	4200	7000	9800	14,000
Cpe	—	900	1800	4400	6150	8800
Sed	—	825	1600	4000	5600	8000

Model EK, Big Six, 6-cyl., 126" wb

		5	4	3	2	1
Tr	—	1400	4200	7000	9800	14,000
Cpe	—	950	2100	4750	6650	9500
Sed	—	875	1700	4250	5900	8500
4 dr Spds	—	1550	4500	7500	10,500	15,000

1923

1923 Studebaker, roadster, OCW

STUDEBAKER LIGHT SIX — MODEL EM — SERIES 23 — SIX: The new EM had nearly the same chassis as previous Studebaker Light Sixes. A new feature was an all-steel body. On open cars the cowl lamps were now set into the bottom corners of the windshield frame.

STUDEBAKER SPECIAL SIX — MODEL EL — SERIES 23 — SIX: All 1923 Special Sixes had one-piece windshields. Open styles had cowl lamps set into the lower corners with built-in visors at the top. Closed cars had glare-proof visors. Automatic wipers and taillights were now standard equipment. Step plates and aluminum kick plates were added to the running boards. Standard color was Studebaker blue for the main body. The hood was black and wheels were blue. Gold pinstriping was used on the wheels and hood louvers. An all-walnut steering wheel with updated spark/throttle controls was also new.

STUDEBAKER BIG SIX — MODEL EK — SERIES 23 — SIX: There were big changes in the appearance of the 1923 Big Six. Nickel plated radiator shells were used. Standard equipment included automatic wipers; stoplights; nickel-plated bumpers; motometer and disc wheels. A new model was the five passenger speedster. It carried dual side mounted spare tires, a rear mounted touring trunk and extra plated-parts included bright metal grab handles and runningboard kick plates.

I.D. DATA: [Model EM] Serial numbers were located on the left side of frame over front axle. Starting: 1084001. Ending: 1131849. An overlap in 1923-1924 Light Six serial numbers stems from the fact that each body style had a different starting number as follows: (Touring) - 1131728; (Roadster) - 1131727; (Sedan) - 1128270 and (Coupe Roadster) - 1131850. Engine numbers were located on a brass plate on the right rear motor support. Engine numbers are not available. [Model EL] Serial numbers were located on the left side of frame over front axle. Starting: 3039123. Ending: 3075316. Engine numbers were located on a brass plate on the right rear motor support. Engine numbers EL-1 and up were used. [Model EK] Serial numbers were stamped on a plate attached to the left frame member under front fender. Starting: 2027500. Ending: 2060000. Engine numbers were stamped on the starter motor support. Engine numbers were EK-1 and up. The body serial numbering system was the same as 1920-21.

Model No.	Body Type & Seating	Price	Weight	Prod. Total
6EM	Chassis	NA	1945	Note 1
6EM	2-dr. Rds.-2P	NA	2510	Note 1
6EM	4-dr. Tr.-5P	NA	2650	Note 1
6EM	2-dr. Cpe.-2P	NA	2730	Note 1
6EM	4-dr. Sed.-5P	NA	3030	Note 1

Note 1: The Model EM light six was produced from Dec. 1922 to July 1924 as a 1923-1924 model. A total of 118,022 were built for the two years combined.

6EL	Chassis	NA	2510	Note 1
6EL	4-dr. Tr.-5P	NA	3200	Note 1
6EL	2-dr. Cpe.-4P	NA	3405	Note 1
6EL	2-dr. Rds.-2P	NA	3015	Note 1
6EL	2-dr. Cpe.-5P	NA	3600	Note 1
6EL	4-dr. Sed.-5P	NA	3605	Note 1

Note 1: The Model EL Special Six was produced from Nov. 1921 to July 1924 as a 1922-1923-1924 model. A total of 111,443 were built for the three years combined.

6EK	Chassis	NA	2543	Note 1
6EK	4-dr. Tr.-7P	NA	3625	Note 1
6EK	4-dr. Spds.-5P	NA	3725	Note 1
6EK	2-dr. Cpe.-5P	NA	3750	Note 1
6EK	2-dr. Cpe.-4P	NA	3730	Note 1
6EK	4-dr. Sed.-7P	NA	4090	Note 1

Note 1: The Model EK Big Six was produced from Nov. 1921 to July 1924 as a 1922-1923-1924 model. A total of 48,892 were built for the three years combined.

ENGINE: See 1921 engine data for Light Six, Special Six and Big Six respectively.

1371

1923 Studebaker, Special Six, coupe, HAC

CHASSIS: [Model EM] W.B.: 112 in. Frt/Rear Tread: 56/56 in. Tires: 31 x 4. [Model EL] W.B.: 119 in. Frt/Rear Tread: 56/56 in. Tires: 32 x 4. [Model EK] W.B.: 126 in. Frt/Rear Tread: 56/56 in. Tires: 33 x 4.5.

TECHNICAL: See 1922 drive train data. The Light Six Model EM had the same chassis features as the Light Six Model EJ.

OPTIONS: Bumper(s). Budd wire spoke wheels. Disc wheels. Spare tire(s). OSRV mirror. Motometer. Luggage rack (rear mounted). Touring trunk. Spotlight(s). Wind wings.

HISTORICAL: Introduced [EM] Dec., 1922; [EL] Nov., 1921; [EK] Nov., 1921. Innovations: [EM] Cast iron cylinder head. New engine block. New intake system. [EL] New windshield design. New sunvisors. New controls. Stoplights. [EK] Nickel radiator. New speedster style. Disc wheels. Calendar year registrations: 94,023. Model year sales: 145,167. Model year production: 89,418. Studebaker Corporation's 1923 income was $18,342,223; the highest in its history.

1923
Model EM, Light Six

	FP	5	4	3	2	1
Rds	—	1250	3900	6500	9100	13,000
Tr	—	1200	3750	6250	8750	12,500
Cpe	—	850	1650	4100	5700	8200
Sed	—	825	1600	4000	5600	8000

Model EL, Special Six

	FP	5	4	3	2	1
Tr	—	1250	3900	6500	9100	13,000
4P Cpe	—	850	1650	4100	5700	8200
Rds	—	1350	4100	6800	9500	13,600
5P Cpe	—	900	1800	4450	6250	8900
Sed	—	825	1600	4000	5600	8000

Model EK, Big Six

	FP	5	4	3	2	1
Tr	—	1500	4350	7250	10,150	14,500
Spds	—	2000	5100	8500	11,900	17,000
5P Cpe	—	975	2300	4900	6850	9800
4P Cpe	—	975	2200	4850	6800	9700
Sed	—	900	1800	4450	6250	8900

1924

1924 Studebaker, touring, OCW

STUDEBAKER LIGHT SIX — MODEL EM — SERIES 24 — SIX: The 1924 Light Six got fancier. Standard equipment now included bumpers, balloon tires and nickle-plated radiator shells.

STUDEBAKER SPECIAL SIX — MODEL EL — SERIES 24 — SIX: A sharp crease line was added on the hood of 1924 Special Six models. A new nickel-plated radiator shell was also seen. The cowl housed a new type of

inspection lamp and closed cars had courtesy lamps on the lower lefthand side of the cowl, above the running board. The touring car was fitted with plated passenger grab handles and another new feature was running board kick plates. Standard body colors changed to Studebaker blue or Princess Louise Lake maroon. Wood spoke wheels were standard equipment.

STUDEBAKER BIG SIX — MODEL EK — SERIES 24 — SIX: The 1924 Big Six was nearly identical to the all new 1923 model. No major changes were make until the 1925 model production started in mid-1924.

I.D. DATA: [Model EM] Serial numbers were on left side of frame over front axle. Starting: 1128270. Ending: 1202000. An overlap of 1923-1924 Serial numbers stems from the fact that each body style had different starting numbers. (See 1923 serial number data). Engine number on brass plate on right rear motor support. Engine numbers not available. [Model EV] Serial numbers were on left side of frame over front axle. Starting: 3075317. Ending: 3120000. Engine numbers on brass plate on right rear motor support. Engine numbers were EL-1 and up. [Model EK] Serial numbers were on left side of frame over front axle. Starting: 2027500. Ending: 2060000. Engine numbers on brass plate on right rear motor support. Engine numers were EK-1 and up.

Model No.	Body Type & Seating	Price	Weight	Prod. Total
6EM	4-dr. Tr.-5P	1045	2650	Note 1
6EM	2-dr. Rds.-3P	1025	2510	Note 1
6EM	2-dr. Cpe. Rds.-2P	1395	2730	Note 1
6EM	4-dr. Cus. Tr.-5P	NA	2830	Note 1
6EM	4-dr. Sed.-5P	1485	3030	Note 1
6EM	2-dr. Cpe.-5P	1195	2955	Note 1

Note 1: The Model EM Light Six was produced from Dec. 1922 to July 1924 as a 1923-1924 model. A total of 118,022 were built for the two years combined.

6EL	4-dr. Tr.-5P	1425	3305	Note 1
6EL	2-dr. Rds.-2P	1400	3065	Note 1
6EL	2-dr. Cpe.-5P	1395	3600	Note 1
6EL	4-dr. Sed.-5P	1485	3650	Note 1

Note 1: The Model EL Special Six was produced from Nov. 1921 to July 1924 as a 1922-1923-1924 model. A total of 111,443 were built for the three years combined.

6EK	4-dr. Tr.-7P	1750	3630	Note 1
6EK	4-dr. Spds.-5P	1835	3745	Note 1
6EK	2-dr. Cpe.-5P	2495	3770	Note 1
6EK	4-dr. Sed.-7P	2685	4130	Note 1

Note 1: The Model EK Big Six was produced from Nov. 1921 to July 1924 as a 1922-1923-1924 model. A total of 48,892 were built for the three years combined.

1924 Studebaker, Big Six, touring, HAC

ENGINE: [Model EM] L-head. Inline. Six. Cast iron block. B & S: 3-1/8 in. x 4-1/2 in. Disp.: 207.1 cu. in. C.R.: 4.38:1. Brake H.P.: 40 @ 2000 R.P.M. N.A.C.C. H.P.: 23.44. Main bearings: Four. Valve lifters: Solid. Carb.: Stromberg 1V. [Model EL] L-head. Inline. Six. Cast iron block. B & S: 3-1/2 in. x 5 in. Disp.: 288.6 cu. in. C.R.: 4.1:1. Brake H.P.: 50-55 @ 2000 R.P.M. N.A.C.C. H.P.: 29.39. Main bearings: Four. Valve lifters: Solid. Carb.: Stromberg 1V. [Model EK] L-head. Inline. Six. Cast iron block. B & S: 3-7/8 in. x 5 in. Disp.: 353.8 cu. in. C.R.: 4.1:1. Brake H.P.: 60-65 @ 2000 R.P.M. N.A.C.C. H.P.: 36.04. Main bearings: Four. Valve lifters: Solid. Carb.: Ball & Ball.

CHASSIS: [Model EM] W.B.: 112 in. Frt/Rear Tread: 56/56. Tires: 31 x 4. [Model EL] W.B.: 119 in. Frt/Rear Tread: 56/56. Tires: 32 x 4. [Model EK] W.B.: 126 in. Frt/Rear Tread: 56/56. Tires: 33 x 4.5.

1924 Studebaker, Special Six, roadster, HAC

TECHNICAL: Selective sliding transmission. Speeds: 3F/1R. Floor mounted gearshift controls. Clutch: single plate dry-disc. Shaft-drive. Semi-floating rear axle. Overall ratio: (EM) 4.55:1; (EL) 4.33:1; (EK) 3.71:1. External contracting rear wheel brakes. Wood spoke artillery wheels.

OPTIONS: Front bumper. Rear bumper. Dual Sidemount (Big Six Speedster). Sidemount cover(s). Motometer. Spare tire(s). Whitewall tires. Runningboard kick plates. Luggage rack. Touring trunk. OSRV mirror. Budd wire spoke wheels. Disc wheels. Spotlight. Wind wings. Balloon tires.
Note: Some accessories were standard equipment on specific models.

HISTORICAL: Introduced [EM] Dec. 1922; [EL] Nov. 1921; [EK] Nov. 1921. Calendar year registrations: 94,700. Model year production: 159,782. Cast iron head on all 1924 models. [EM] Stromberg OE-1 Carburetor. More stylish trim. [EL] New styling. Nickle radiator shell. Balloon tires optional.
Notes: Production of 1924 models was halted in July 1924 for changeover to 1925 specifications. At the 1924 New York Automobile Show, Studebaker displayed a 1918 Big Six that had traveled over 500,000 miles in 5-1/2 years. Studebaker announced it had 225 acres of plant space in 1924 and employed 23,000 workers.

1924

Model EM, Light Six, 6-cyl., 112" wb

	FP	5	4	3	2	1
Tr	1045	1150	3600	6000	8400	12,000
Rds	1025	1150	3600	6000	8400	12,000
Cpe Rds	1395	1250	3900	6500	9100	13,000
Cus Tr	—	1250	3900	6500	9100	13,000
Sed	1485	700	1350	2800	4550	6500
Cpe	1195	750	1450	3500	5050	7200

Model EL, Special Six, 6-cyl., 119" wb

Tr	1425	1250	3900	6500	9100	13,000
Rds	1400	1300	4050	6750	9450	13,500
Cpe	1395	900	1900	4500	6300	9000
Sed	1485	875	1700	4250	5900	8500

Model EK, Big Six, 6-cyl., 126" wb

7P Tr	1750	1800	4950	8250	11,550	16,500
Spds	1835	2000	5100	8500	11,900	17,000
Cpe	2495	950	2100	4750	6650	9500
Sed	2685	900	1900	4500	6300	9000

1925-26

1925 Studebaker, Special Six, duplex phaeton, AA

STUDEBAKER STANDARD SIX — MODEL ER — SERIES 25-26 — SIX: The Model ER Standard Six replaced the Light Six in August 1924 and was sold as a 1925-1926 model. It was a completely restyled line of cars. Appearance changes included a higher, shorter, more rounded hood with a trim band at its rear edge. The multiple vertical louvers on the hood sides were contained within a raised rectangular panel with rounded corners. The front fenders had heavier beading. The rear fenders curved outward at both the front and rear edges. Windshields on open cars were nearly vertical and had heavier frames. Drum type headlamps were used. A new radiator shell was thicker and rounder and nickle plated. The Duplex models were open body cars with rigid, steel-reinforced tops and pull-down side curtains. Standard equipment included balloon tires, shock absorbers and heaters on all closed cars except the Coupe-Roadster. Upholstery was of fine quality Spanish leather in open cars and Angora mohair and wool in closed models. All closed cars also had robe rails, wool carpets and silk curtains. Lacquer finish was used on 1925 closed cars. Available colors were light Navaho gray or darker seminole gray. Open cars for 1925 were finished in black enamel with ivory pinstriping. There were numerous running production changes that restorers of today find confusing. Many new colors were added to the 1926 series.

STUDEBAKER SPECIAL SIX — MODEL EQ — SERIES 25-26 — SIX: The 1925 Special Six continued to feature a distinctive, fluted radiator shell. New models included a Duplex Phaeton and Duplex Roadster with rigid, steel-reinforced tops and pull-down side curtains. Drum style headlamps and heavier beaded front fenders were added. The hood side louver design was similar to that of the Standard Six, but the hood top panel was fluted to meet the radiator contours and had a crease along each upper edge. Other new models included a 4-passenger Victoria, 5-passenger Berline (small limousine), Brougham sedan, Country Club Coupe and 5-passenger coach. A special model, intended for police departments, was the Sheriff. It was essentially a Special Six touring car chassis with the Big Six engine installed.

STUDEBAKER BIG SIX — MODEL EP — SERIES 25-26 — SIX: The Big Six had the same basic styling changes as the Standard Six including the new radiator, hood line, hood side panels, front and rear fenders, more vertical windshields and heavier windshield frames. It was, of course, a larger, heavier, more powerful car. Duplex open bodies were available along with a special Sport Phaeton and new closed styles like the Brougham sedan and Berline. Standard equipment included: extra balloon tire, tube and tire cover; bumpers front and rear; motometer with lock and winged radiator cap; lights controlled from switch on steering wheel; automatic ignition system; one-piece windshield; glare-proof visor; automatic windshield cleaner; rear-view mirror; cowl and dome lights; extension lamp; stop and taillight; clock; speedometer; gas gauge; oil pressure indicator; ammeter; step pads and runningboard kick plates. As on other 1925 Studebakers, four-wheel hydraulic brakes were a new extra-cost option.

I.D. DATA: [Model ER] Serial numbers were on left side of frame over front axle. Starting: (1925) 1202001; (1926) 1284001. Ending: (1925) 1284000; (1926) 1346100. Engine numbers on brass plate on right rear motor support. Starting: ER-202,501. Ending: ER-350,001. [Model EQ] Serial numbers were on left side of frame over front axle. Starting: (1925) 3120001; (1926) 3161002. Ending: (1925) 3161001; (1926) 3172932. Engine numbers on brass plate on right rear motor support. Engine numbers were EQ-1 and up. [Model EP] Serial numbers were on left side of frame over front axle. Starting: (1925) 2060001; (1926) 2073001. Ending: (1925) 2073000; (1926) 2102299. Engine numbers on brass plate on right rear motor support. Engine numbers were EP-1 and up.

1926 Studebaker, Big Six, phaeton, AA

Model No.	Body Type & Seating	Price	Weight	Prod. Total
ER/T	4-dr. Dplx. Phae.-5P	1145	2870	Note 1
ER/R	2-dr. Dplx. Rds.-3P	1125	2760	Note 1
ER/F	2-dr. Coach-5P	1195	2980	Note 1
ER/Q	2-dr. Cty. Clb. Cpe.-3P	1395	2945	Note 1
ER/J	2-dr. Spt. Rds.-3P	1235	2820	Note 1
ER/L	4-dr. Spt. Phae.-5P	NA	2930	Note 1
ER/S	4-dr. Sed.-5P	1595	3260	Note 1
ER/Q	2-dr. Cpe. Rds.-3P	1395	NA	Note 1
ER/B	4-dr. w/Sed.-5P	1600	3260	Note 1
ER/K	2-dr. Cpe.-5P	1495	3110	Note 1
ER/W	4-dr. Ber.-5P	1650	3280	Note 1

Note 1: Total production between Aug. 1924 and Aug. 1926 was 147,099.
Note 2: Add 200 pounds for 4-wheel brakes.

EQ	2-dr. Dplx. Phae.-3P	1445	3475	Note 1
EQ	2-dr. Dplx. Rds.-3P	1395	3360	Note 1
EQ	2-dr. Vic.-4P	1750	3665	Note 1
EQ	4-dr. Sed.-5P	1895	3855	Note 1
EQ	4-dr. Ber.-5P	NA	3890	Note 1
EQ	4-dr. Brgm.-5P	2120	3785	Note 1
EQ	4-dr. Spt. Rds.-4P	1395	3480	Note 1
EQ	2-dr. Coach-5P	1445	3520	Note 1

Note 1: Total production between Aug. 1924 and July 1926 was 53,780.
Note 2: Add 200 pounds for 4-wheel brakes.

EP	4-dr. Dplx. Phae.-7P	1795	3785	Note 1
EP	2-dr. Cpe.-5P	1645	4030	Note 1
EP	4-dr. Brgm.-5P	2325	4095	Note 1
EP	4-dr. Sed.-7P	2245	4150	Note 1
EP	4-dr. Ber.-5P	2045	4200	Note 1
EP	4-dr. Sed.-5P	2245	3785	Note 1
EP	4-dr. Spt. Phae.-5P	1795	3505	Note 1
EP	2-dr. Clb. Cpe.-5P	2045	3570	Note 1

Note 1: Total production between Aug. 1924 and Aug. 1926 was 40,216.
Note 2: Add 200 pounds for 4-wheel brakes.

ENGINE: [Model ER] Inline. L-head. Six. Cast iron block. B & S: 3-3/8 in. x 4-1/2 in. Disp.: 241.6 cu. in. C.R.: 4.5:1. Brake H.P.: 50 @ 2200 R.P.M. N.A.C.C. H.P.: 27.34. Main bearings: Four. Valve lifters: Solid. Carb.: Stromberg 1V Model T1 or Model OE-1. [Model EQ] L-head. Inline. Six. Cast iron block. B & S: 3-1/2 in. x 5 in. Disp.: 288.6 cu. in. C.R.: 4.45:1. Brake H.P.: 65 @ 2400 R.P.M. N.A.C.C. H.P.: 29.40. Main bearings: Four. Valve lifters: Solid. Carb.: Stromberg 1V. [Model EP] L-head. Inline. Six. Cast iron block. B & S: 3-7/8 in. x 5 in. Disp.: 353.8 cu. in. C.R.: 4.45:1. Brake H.P.: 75 @ 2400 R.P.M. N.A.C.C. H.P.: 36.04. Main bearings: Four. Valve lifters: Solid. Carb.: Ball & Ball 1V.

CHASSIS: [Model ER] W.B.: 113 in. Tires: 31 x 5.25 (early); 30 x 5.25 (late). [Model EQ] W.B.: 120 in. Tires: 32 x 6.20. [Model EP] W.B.: 120-127 in. Tires: 34 x 7.30.

TECHNICAL: Manual transmission (unit type). Speeds: 3F/1R. Floor mounted gear shift controls. Clutch: single-plate dry disc. Shaft drive. Semi-floating rear axle. Overall ratio: (ER) 4.18:1, (EQ) 4.36:1; (EP) 4.36:1. Two-wheel mechanical brakes. Wood spoke artillery wheels.

OPTIONS: Front bumper. Rear bumper. Sparetire(s). Dual sidemount. Sidemount cover(s). Motometer. Winged radiator cap. Runningboard kick plates. Heater. Clock. Cigar lighter. OSRV mirror. Touring trunk. Trunk rack. Spotlight. Cowl lamps. Balloon tires. Four-wheel hydraulic brakes (75.00). Painted artillery wheels. Disc wheels. Special paint. Wind wings. Note: Some accessories were standard equipment on specific models.

HISTORICAL: Introduced [All Series] August, 1924. Calendar year registrations: (1925) 107,732; (1926) 93,475. Model year production: (1925) 80,365; (1926) 158,463. Innovations: [ER] Full-pressure lubrication. Unit powerplant/transmission. New motor mounts. Improved emergency brake. Alemite lubrication. Optional 4-wheel hydraulic brakes. [EQ] Full-pressure lubrication. Unit powerplant/transmission. Higher compression ratio. Improved crankshaft. Larger wheelbase.
Optional 4-wheel hydraulic brakes. [EP] Full-pressure lubrication. Unit powertrain. Improved crankshaft. Optional 4-wheel hydraulic brakes.
Notes: Ab Jenkins made many record setting runs in Studebaker models. Company paid largest dividend in history during 1925. Paul G. Hoffman named vice-president in charge of sales in 1925. Harold S. Vance named vice-president in charge of engineering and production in 1926. Barney Roos joins company in 1926 as chief engineer.

1925-1926
Model ER, Standard Six, 6-cyl., 113" wb

	FP	5	4	3	2	1
Dplx Phae	1145	1550	4500	7500	10,500	15,000
Dplx Rds	1125	1550	4500	7500	10,500	15,000
Coach	1195	650	1200	2300	4100	5800
Cty Clb Cpe	1395	1075	3000	5500	7700	11,000
Spt Rds	1235	1250	3900	6500	9100	13,000
Spt Phae	—	1250	3950	6600	9200	13,200
Sed	1495	650	1250	2400	4200	6000
Cpe Rds	1395	1750	4800	8000	11,200	16,000
w/Sed	1600	675	1300	2500	4300	6100
Sed	1495	650	1250	2400	4200	6000
Cpe	1495	700	1350	2800	4550	6500
Ber	1650	950	2100	4750	6650	9500

Model EQ, Special Six 6-cyl., 120" - 127" wb

Dplx Phae	1445	2300	5400	9000	12,600	18,000
Dplx Rds	1395	2800	5700	9500	13,300	19,000
Vic	1750	800	1550	3900	5450	7800
Sed	1895	775	1500	3750	5250	7500
Ber	—	1025	2600	5250	7300	10,500
Brgm	2120	825	1600	4000	5600	8000
Spt Rds	1395	2800	5700	9500	13,300	19,000
Coach	1445	750	1450	3300	4900	7000

Model EP, Big Six, 6-cyl., 120" wb

Dplx Phae	1795	2800	5700	9500	13,300	19,000
Cpe	1645	675	1300	2500	4350	6200
Brgm	2325	700	1350	2800	4550	6500
7P Sed	2245	700	1350	2700	4400	6400
Ber	2045	1075	3000	5500	7700	11,000
Sed	2245	675	1300	2500	4350	6200
Spt Phae	1795	2800	5700	9500	13,300	19,000
Clb Cpe	2045	675	1300	2500	4350	6200
Shff	—	1750	4800	8000	11,200	16,000
Dplx Shff	—	2000	5100	8500	11,900	17,000

NOTE: Add 10 percent for 4 wheel brake option.

1927

1927 Studebaker, Standard Six, custom sedan, AA

STUDEBAKER — STANDARD/DICTATOR — MODEL EU — SERIES 27 — SIX: Early in 1927, cars in this line were called Standard Sixes. In the middle of the summer, they were renamed Dictator Sixes. Appearance changes included new bullet shaped headlights, double bar bumpers with a fluted design and nickle plating, disc wheels and a new *Atlanta* hood ornament. Closed cars had French style roof visors. Double bead moldings set off the belt line. The lower molding continued across the upper side of the hood to the radiator shell. Attractive two-tone paint schemes were available. Late production cars had chrome plated bright metal parts. Sport models now included a two passenger rumble seat.

STUDEBAKER — SPECIAL SIX — MODEL EQ — SERIES 26-27 — SIX: Production of the Special Six ended in July 1926 and many sources do not show this car as a 1927 model. However, the Jan. 1927 *MoToR Annual Show Number* does list the car as being available as a 1927 model. Also,

NADA's Official Used Car Guide gives a range of serial numbers for 1927 Special Sixes. It can therefore be deduced that the model was marketed in early 1927 as a carryover series with few changes from 1926 specifications. Apparently, only four models were still offered. The Special Sixes were the only models still equipped with wood spoke artillery wheels. While other Studebakers had four wheel mechanical brakes, the Special Sixes had two wheel mechanical brakes with four wheel hydraulic brakes as a $75 option.

1927 Studebaker, Big Six, victoria, AA

STUDEBAKER — COMMANDER BIG SIX — MODEL EW — SERIES 27 — SIX: The Commander was Studebaker's slightly cheaper version of the former Big Six. The car was introduced in Jan. 1927, but was not named Commander until about April. The Commander had a 120 in. wheelbase. Styling features included bullet shaped headlights, double bar bumpers, French type visors, disc wheels and double bead body molding with the lower bead extending across the hoods. An *Atlanta* style hood mascot was added. Sport models had rumble seats.

1927 Studebaker, President Six, limousine, AA

STUDEBAKER — PRESIDENT BIG SIX — MODEL ES — SERIES 27 — SIX: Extensive styling changes marked the new model ES Big Six "President," a custom designed Studebaker sedan. They included lower bodies, more rounded roofs and body panels, two-tone paint (in lacquer), double bead belt moldings with scallops front and rear, disc wheels, large acorn headlights, French style visors, double-bar bumpers and luxury interior trim. Only a seven passenger sedan was sold at first. It was painted Croatan green with an ebony belt line and Ivory striping, or Ebony black with Thistle green belt line and yellow striping. The former had mohair upholstery, the latter was trimmed with broadcloth. Models added later included a seven passenger touring and a division window limousine with the driving compartment trimmed in leather. The *Atlanta* type hood mascot was used on all Presidents. Two wheelbases — 120 in. and 127 in. — were available for mounting of these bodies. Standard equipment included nickle plated bumpers; no-draft ventilating windshield; Watson stabilizers; engine thermometer; clock; hydrostatic gas gauge; coincidental lock; oil filter; Alemite chassis lubrication; automatic wiper; double rear vision mirror; vanity case; smoking set; arm rests; toggle grips; auto. dome light; rear signal light; emergency lamp on extension cord; 4-wheel mechanical brakes; disc wheels; balloon tires; cowl lights and twin beam acorn headlights. The limousine also had glass enclosure, leather upholstered driving compartment and auto-phone.

I.D. DATA: [Model EU] Serial numbers were located on left side of frame over front axle. Starting: 1346001. Ending: 1410000.
Note: Cars with serial numbers above 1385940 were sold as first series 1928 models. In this book the 1927 specifications apply to all EU Models, since all cars were built as 1927 models.
Motor numbers were located on the right side of block. Starting: EU-1. Ending: EU-65800. [Model EQ] Serial numbers were located on left side of frame over front axle. Starting: 3173001. Ending: 3200000. Engine numbers were on the starter motor support. The 1927 engine numbers are not available. [Model EW] Serial numbers were on the left side of frame over front axle or on left door hinge pillar. Starting: 4000001. Ending: 4039800. Engine numbers were stamped on right side of crankcase opposite no.1 cylinder. Starting: EW-1. Ending: EW-40700. Body symbols/numbers were embossed on plate on engine side of firewall. [Model ES] Serial numbers

were on a plate on left frame member under front fender. Starting: 2102301. Ending: 2114902. Engine numbers were on starter motor support. Engine numbers were ES-43301 and up. Body numbers were in the same locations as previous Big Six models.

Model No.	Body Type & Seating	Price	Weight	Prod. Total
EU	2-dr. Spt. Rds.-2/4P	1245	3000	Note 1
EU	4-dr. Tr.-5P	1165	3080	Note 1
EU	4-dr. Dplx. Tr.-5P	1195	3105	Note 1
EU	4-dr. Tr.-7P	1245	3090	Note 1
EU	2-dr. Bus. Cpe.-2P	1195	3120	Note 1
EU	2-dr. Spt. Cpe.-2/4P	1295	3165	Note 1
EU	2-dr. Vic.-4P	1295	3165	Note 1
EU	4-dr. Sed.(P)-5P	1195	3230	Note 1
EU	4-dr. Sed.(M)-5P	1295	3235	Note 1

Note 1: Total production between June 1926 and Sept. 1927 was 65,333.
Note 2: The (P) sedan has plush upholstery; the (M) sedan has mohair upholstery.

EQ	4-dr. Dplx. Phae.-5P	1480	3475	Note 1
EQ	2-dr. Coach-5P	1480	3520	Note 1
EQ	4-dr. Brgm.-5P	1830	3785	Note 1
EQ	4-dr. Spt. Rds.-5P	1630	3480	Note 1

Note 1: Total production between Aug. 1924 and July 1926 was 53,780.
Note 2: The above cars were the only models listed in the 1927 *MoToR Annual Show Number*. The above weights are per 1925-1926 specifications.

EW	2-dr. Spt. Rds.-2/4P	1595	3485	Note 1
EW	2-dr. Bus. Cpe.-2P	1545	NA	Note 1
EW	2-dr. Spt. Cpe.-2/4P	1645	3510	Note 1
EW	4-dr. Sed.-5P	1585	3570	Note 1
EW	2-dr. Cus. Vic.-5P	1575	3705	Note 1
EW	2-dr. Dplx. Rds.-3P	1530	3445	Note 1
EW	4-dr. Spt. Phae.-4P	1610	3580	Note 1
EW	4-dr. Cus. Brgm.-5P	1785	3835	Note 1

Note 1: Total production between Dec. 1926 and October 1927 was 40,668.

ES	4-dr. Cus. Sed.-7P	2245	4050	Note 1
ES	4-dr. Limo.-7P	2495	NA	Note 1
ES	4-dr. Dplx. Phae.-7P	1810	3720	Note 1

Note 1: Total production between June 1926 and Sept. 1927 was broken out by wheelbase. The figures were 7,949 cars on the 120 in. wheelbase and 9,405 cars on the 127 in wheelbase.

EU ENGINE: Inline. L-head. Six. Cast iron block. B & S: 3-3/8 in. x 4-1/2 in. Disp.: 242 cu. in. C.R.: 4.5:1. Brake H.P.: 50 @ 2200 R.P.M. N.A.C.C. H.P.: 27.3. Main bearings: Four. Valve lifters: Solid. Carb.: Stromberg 1V Model OE-1.

EQ ENGINE: Inline. L-head. Six. Cast iron block. B & S: 3-1/2 in. x 5 in. Disp.: 289 cu. in. C.R.: 4.45:1. Brake H.P.: 65 @ 2400 R.P.M. N.A.C.C. H.P.: 29.4. Main bearings: Four. Valve lifters: Solid. Carb.: Stromberg 1V Model LS-2.

EW/ES ENGINE: Inline. L-head. Six. Cast iron block. B & S: 3-7/8 in. x 5 in. Disp.: 354 cu. in. C.R.: 4.45:1. Brake H.P.: 75 @ 2400 R.P.M. N.A.C.C. H.P.: 36. Main bearings: Four. Valve lifters: Solid. Carb.: Ball & Ball 1V Model SV33.

CHASSIS: [Series EU] W.B.: 113 in. Tires: 31 x 5.25. [Series EQ] W.B.: 120 in. Tires: 32 x 6.00. [Series EW] W.B.: 120 in. Tires: 32 x 6.00. [Series ES] W.B.: 120 or 127 in. Tires: 32 x 6.75.

TECHNICAL: Manual transmission (unit type). Speeds: 3F/1R. Floor shift controls. Clutch: Multiple dry disc. Shaft drive. Semi-floating rear axle. Overall ratio: (EU) 4.6/4.18; (EQ) 4.08/4.36; (EW) 3.69/4.08; (ES) 4.36. External contracting brakes. Four wheel brakes standard on all models except Special Six. Disc wheels. Wheel Rim Size: (EU/EQ) 21 x 4.5; (EW/ES) 21 x 5.

OPTIONS: Front bumper (opt. on 3 models). Rear bumper (opt. on 3). Dual sidemount. Sidemount cover(s). Hyd. 4-wheel brakes (on Spec.). Wind wings (std. on Spt. Rds.). Heater. Clock (std. in Pres.). Cigar lighter. Trunk rack (std. on 2). Touring trunk. Wire wheels. Spotlight(s). Whitewalls. Spl. Paint. Engine thermo. (opt. on some Spec.). Smoking set (std. on 7). Vanity case (std. on Pres.). Backing light. Shock absorbers (std. on 8). Spring covers. Spare tire (std. on 3). Spare tire cover. Power tire pump.

HISTORICAL: Introduced (See notes in charts above). Calendar year registrations: 94,700. Model year production: 123,474. Innovations: New styling. Nickle plated trim. Kelsey-Hayes disc wheels. No-draft ventilation on President. New radiator caps designed by Carl Mose.

1927 was Studebaker's "Diamond Jubilee" celebration year. Engineering staff moved to new facilities in South Bend, Ind. Several famous record speed runs and endurance trials were undertaken by drivers of 1927 Studebaker Commanders.

1927
Dictator, Model EU Standard, 6-cyl., 113" wb

	FP	5	4	3	2	1
Spt Rds	1245	3150	6300	10,500	14,700	21,000
Tr	1165	2800	5700	9500	13,300	19,000
Dplx Tr	1195	3000	6000	10,000	14,000	20,000
7P Tr	1245	2300	5400	9000	12,600	18,000
Bus Cpe	1195	700	1350	2800	4550	6500
Spt Cpe	1295	775	1500	3750	5250	7500
Vic	1295	700	1350	2800	4550	6500
(P) Sed	1195	650	1250	2400	4200	6000
(M) Sed	1295	775	1500	3750	5250	7500

Special, Model EQ

	FP	5	4	3	2	1
Dplx Phae	1480	3400	6900	11,500	16,100	23,000
Coach	1480	750	1450	3300	4900	7000
Brgm	1830	825	1600	4000	5600	8000
Spt Rds	1630	3600	7200	12,000	16,800	24,000

Commander, Model EW

	FP	5	4	3	2	1
Spt Rds	1595	3400	6900	11,500	16,100	23,000
Bus Cpe	1545	900	1900	4500	6300	9000
Spt Cpe	1645	1000	2400	5000	7000	10,000
Sed	1585	775	1500	3750	5250	7500
Cus Vic	1575	875	1700	4250	5900	8500
Dplx Rds	1530	3600	7200	12,000	16,800	24,000
Spt Phae	1610	3600	7200	12,000	16,800	24,000
Cus Brgm	1785	800	1550	3850	5400	7700

President, Model ES

	FP	5	4	3	2	1
Cus Sed	2245	950	2100	4750	6650	9500
Limo	2495	2300	5400	9000	12,600	18,000
Dplx Phae	1810	3400	6900	11,500	16,100	23,000

1928

1928 Studebaker, Dictator Six, sport roadster, AA

STUDEBAKER — DICTATOR — SERIES GE — SIX: The Model EU Dictator Six (see 1927 specifications) was sold as a 1928 Studebaker from July 1927 until the fall when new cars were introduced. The all-new series introduced the Dictator GE line which featured all-steel bodies, integral style sun visors, narrower front pillars, cowl lamps mounted on surcingles, unit group instrumentation and a new radiator design. Other appearance highlights were crowned fenders, new bumpers and beltline trim like that on last year's President. Kelsey-Hayes steel disc wheels were standard again. Other standard equipment included a tire lock; speedometer; hydro static gas gauge; engine thermometer; rearview mirror; stop light; windshield cleaner; front bumper, rear fender guards, and shock absorbers. Open models and coupes came with leather upholstery. The sedan had plush velvet seats and the Sport Coupe was trimmed in mohair. A spare rim was standard.

1928 Studebaker, Commander Regal, victoria, AA

STUDEBAKER — COMMANDER — SERIES GB — SIX: The Commander GB was the new mid-sized, mid-priced line for the 1928 "Second Series" of Studebaker models introduced in the fall of 1927. Styling traits included all-steel bodies, integral sun visors and narrower front door pillars. Also seen was a flatter roof line, lower feature lines and distinctive belt line paneling on closed cars. Double bar bumpers of a more modern, non-fluted design were added. Budd steel disc wheels were standard fare. Other standard features were: a Stewart-Warner speedometer; hydrostatic gas gauge; coincidental lock; rearview mirror; stop light; automatic wiper; front bumper; rear fender guards; Gabriel shock absorbers; one spare disc wheel and a tire lock. Regal trim models also had: engine thermometers; cigar lighters; and a vanity case in the coupe. Roadsters and coupes were trimmed in leather. Other styles had mohair seats.

STUDEBAKER — PRESIDENT — SERIES ES — SIX: The President Six, Model ES, was carried over as a "First Series" 1928 Studebaker line until late fall. It was basically unchanged from the late 1927 offering. Features again included a no draft ventilating windshield, gas gauge on instrument panel, oil filter, disc wheels and 4-wheel mechanical brakes. Consult 1927 specifications for additional information.

1375

1928 Studebaker, President Eight, state cabriolet, AA

STUDEBAKER — PRESIDENT — SERIES FA — EIGHT: Studebaker's big 1928 news was a big straight eight series. The President Eight was a large, powerful, spacious car with outstanding acceleration and high maximum speed. Bodies on this model were full-visioned with extremely wide 28 in. doors. Interior furnishings included heavy 28-oz. broadcloth in two-tones on backs and cushions; single color headliners; deep tufted, form-fitting seats; double-deck, pillow type seat springs; heavily upholstered arm rests; two-tone walnut dash and garnish moldings; etched silver door medallions; Wilton velvet carpets and flap design door pockets. Standard equipment included chrome plated, twin-beam headlights, opal irredescent dome and rear corner lights; combination tail/stop light; rearview mirror; auto. wiper; coincidental ignition lock; no-draft ventilating windwhield; speedometer; 8-day clock; electric gas gauge and dash thermometer. Styling innovations included an integral "cadet" style sun visor, all-steel body, full crown fenders and narrower radiator. A double-bar bumper was of more modern design. There was an "8" emblem on the headlight tie bar.

I.D. DATA: [Series GE] Serial numbers were on the left side of frame over front axle. Starting: 1410001. Ending: 1437600. Engine numbers were on right side of motor block. Starting: GE-1. Ending: GE-49700. [Series GB] Serial numbers in same location. Starting: 4039801. Ending: 4062100. Engine numbers in same location. Starting: GB-1. Ending: GB-8450. Body numbers embossed on firewall plate. [Series ES] Serial numbers and engine numbers were the same as 1927. [Series FB] Serial numbers were in the same location. Starting: 6000001. Ending: 6008600. Engine numbers on front of motor block. Starting: FB-1. Ending: FB-17775.

Model No.	Body Type & Seating	Price	Weight	Prod. Total
GE	2-dr. Roy. Rds.-2/4P	1245	3000	Note 1
GE	4-dr. Roy. Tr.-5P	1195	3030	Note 1
GE	4-dr. Dplx. Tr.-5P	1195	3085	Note 1
GE	4-dr. Roy. Tr.-7P	1295	3050	Note 1
GE	2-dr. Bus. Cpe.-2P	1195	3095	Note 1
GE	2-dr. Roy. Cpe.-2/4P	1295	3140	Note 1
GE	2-dr. Roy. Vic.-4P	1295	3150	Note 1
GE	2-dr. Clb. Sed.-5P	1195	3190	Note 1
GE	4-dr. Sed.-5P	1265	3280	Note 1
GE	4-dr. Roy. Sed.-5P	1395	3420	Note 1

Note 1: Total production between Sept. 1927 and Oct. 1928 was 48,339 units. This includes 1929 (Third) Series Model GE Dictators.
Note 2: Roy. means "Royal."

GB	2-dr. Reg. Rds.-2/4P	1595	3340	Note 1
GB	2-dr. Cpe.-2P	1495	3395	Note 1
GB	2-dr. Reg. Cpe.-2/4P	1625	3455	Note 1
GB	2-dr. Reg. Cabr.-2/4P	1625	3425	Note 1
GB	2-dr. Vic.-4P	1495	3500	Note 1
GB	2-dr. Reg. Vic.-4P	1625	3560	Note 1
GB	4-dr. Sed.-5P	1495	3560	Note 1
GB	4-dr. Clb. Sed.-5P	1435	3530	Note 1
GB	4-dr. Reg. Sed.-5P	1625	3825	Note 1

Note 1: Total production Oct. 1927 to June 1928 was 22,848.
Note 2: Reg. means "Regal."

ES	4-dr. Cus. Sed.-7P	1985	4032	Note 1
ES	4-dr. Limo.-7P	2250	4080	Note 1
ES	4-dr. Cus. Tr.-7P	1795	3805	Note 1

Note 1: See 1927 production total.

FA	4-dr. Tr.-7P	2285	3920	Note 1
FA	2-dr. Sta. Cabr.-4P	2195	3980	Note 1
FA	4-dr. Sed.-5P	1985	4000	Note 1
FA	4-dr. Sta. Sed.-5P	2250	4185	Note 1
FA	4-dr. Sed.-7P	2085	4040	Note 1
FA	4-dr. Sta. Sed.-7P	2350	4225	Note 1
FA	4-dr. Limo.-7P	2450	4320	Note 1
FA	4-dr. Sta. Ber.-7P	2350	4320	Note 1

Note 1: Total production Dec. 1927 to Oct. 1928 was 13,186.
Note 2: Sta. means "State."

ENGINE: [Series GE] L-head. Inline. Six. Cast iron block. B & S: 3-3/8 in. x 4-1/2 in. Disp.: 242 cu. in. C.R.: 4.5:1. Brake H.P.: 50 @ 2200 R.P.M. N.A.C.C. H.P.: 27.34. Main bearings: Four. Valve lifters: Solid. Carb.: Stromberg 1V Model T1. [Series GB/ES] L-head. Inline. Six. Cast iron block. B & S: 3-7/8 in. x 5 in. Disp.: 354 cu. in. C.R.: 4.25:1. Brake H.P.: 75 @ 2400 R.P.M. N.A.C.C. H.P.: 36.04. Main bearings: Four. Valve lifters: Solid. Carb.: Stromberg 1V Model TX2. [Series FA] L-head. Inline. Eight. Cast iron block. B & S: 3-3/8 in. x 4-3/8 in. Disp.: 312.5 cu. in. C.R.: 4.7:1. Brake H.P.: 100 @ 2600 R.P.M. N.A.C.C. H.P.: 36.45. Main bearings: Five. Valve lifters: Solid. Carb.: Schebler 1V Model 1-1/2 in.

CHASSIS: [Series GE] W.B.: 113. Tires: 30 x 5.50. [Series GB] W.B.: 120. Tires: 30 x 5.50. [Series ES] W.B.: 127. Tires: 32 x 6.75. [Series FA] W.B.: 131. Tires: 31 x 6.20.

TECHNICAL: Manual (unit type) transmission. Speeds: 3F/1R. Floor shift controls. Multiple dry disc clutch. Shaft drive. Semi-floating rear axle. Overall ratio: (GE) 4.60:1; (GB) 3.31:1; (FA) 4.30:1. Four wheel brakes (except Special). President State has wire wheels; others have disc wheels. (Kelsey Hayes on Dictator.) (Budd on Commander.)

OPTIONS: Backing light. Wind wings. Disc wheels (opt. on Pres.). Dual Sidemounts. Sidemount covers. Smoking set (optional in 16 models). Vanity case (std. in Victorias). Wire wheels (Std. Pres. State models). Heater. Clock (std. Comm. and Pres.). Cigar lighter (opt. on 4). Trunk. Trunk rack. Whitewalls. Spotlight. Spring covers. Spare tire(s). Tire cover(s). Power tire pump.

HISTORICAL: Introduced See chart notes. Calendar year registrations: 107,234. Model year production: 105,968. Innovations: First Studebaker Eight. Four wheel Bendix self-energizing mechanical brakes standard on all Studebakers. Vibration dampener on new President Eight engine. Higher compression head on new Eight. AC fuel pump replaces vacuum feed system on all models. Torsion dampener type clutch. New 20 in. wheel rims on commanders. Dictator equipped with ball bearing spring shackles.

Commander Club Sedan offers lowest price ever for a Big Six. Studebaker gained controling interest in Pierce-Arrow Company with 1928 purchase of $2 million in stock.

1928
Dictator, Model GE

	FP	5	4	3	2	1
Roy Rds	1245	4500	9000	15,000	21,000	30,000
Tr	1195	4200	8400	14,000	19,600	28,000
Dplx Tr	1195	4350	8700	14,500	20,300	29,000
7P Roy Tr	1295	4400	8850	14,750	20,650	29,500
Bus Cpe	1195	750	1450	3300	4900	7000
Roy Cpe	1295	900	1900	4500	6300	9000
Roy Vic	1295	775	1500	3750	5250	7500
Clb Sed	1195	725	1400	3000	4700	6700
Sed	1265	675	1300	2500	4350	6200
Roy Sed	1395	700	1350	2800	4550	6500

Commander, Model GB

Reg Rds	1595	4650	9300	15,500	21,700	31,000
Cpe	1495	1000	2400	5000	7000	10,000
Reg Cpe	1625	1075	3000	5500	7700	11,000
Reg Cabr	1625	3750	7500	12,500	17,500	25,000
Vic	1495	875	1700	4250	5900	8500
Reg Vic	1625	900	1900	4500	6300	9000
Sed	1495	775	1500	3750	5250	7500
Clb Sed	1435	775	1500	3750	5250	7500
Reg Sed	1625	900	1900	4500	6300	9000

President Six, Model ES

Cus Sed	1985	950	2100	4750	6650	9500
Limo	2250	1750	4800	8000	11,200	16,000
Cus Tr	1795	3400	6900	11,500	16,100	23,000

President Eight, Model FA

7P Tr	2285	3750	7500	12,500	17,500	25,000
Sta Cabr	2195	3900	7800	13,000	18,200	26,000
Sed	1985	925	2000	4600	6400	9200
Sta Sed	2250	950	2100	4750	6650	9500
7P Sed	2085	950	2100	4750	6650	9500
7P Sta Sed	2350	1000	2400	5000	7000	10,000
Limo	2450	1750	4800	8000	11,200	16,000
Sta Ber	2350	2200	5250	8750	12,250	17,500

1928-1/2

STUDEBAKER — DICTATOR — SERIES GE — SIX: Like other automakers, Studebaker held summer and winter new model introductions this year. Following standard practice, the "new" summer line offered little more than slightly re-worked 1928 cars which were sold as 1929 automobiles. Cars in the six-cylinder Dictator GE lineup had the following styling changes: higher radiators, new lower crown fenders, cadet style sun visors, adjustable steering wheels and larger hub caps. The new radiator had a deeper, more squared-off design and an "s" emblem was placed in front of it on the headlight tie-bar.

STUDEBAKER — COMMANDER — SERIES GH — SIX: That Commander GH was a new 1928-1/2 Series composed of three models introduced in July 1928. These were the last Studebakers with the old 353.8 cu. in. Big Eight. New features included a higher radiator, redesigned crown fenders and lower bodies. The frontal appearance of these cars had a "military" look with the addition of cadet style sun visors in place of the former overhanging type. The headlight tie-bar supported a globe-shaped emblem in the center of Commander models. It had the inscription "World's Champion" written on it.

STUDEBAKER — PRESIDENT — SERIES FB/FA — EIGHT: The Model FA President Eight was carried over into the early 1929 selling season with several changes. They included wider crown fenders, ball bearing spring shackles and an adjustable steering wheel. New body styles were added. They included a State Cabriolet, tourer and State Tourer. (Note: State models had six-wheel equipment with wire spoke rims). Other 1928-1/2 styling changes were the addition of cadet style visors, a new flat radiator cap and redesigned headlamps and cowl lights. These features closely resemble 1929 features, but the 1928-1/2 FAs have a distinctive 131-inch wheelbase. The FBs were a new line of 121-inch wheelbase President Eights also introduced in mid-1928 for the early 1929 sales year. Styling was much the same as for the FA. These cars came in colors of Autumn brown; Deauville Sand; Duskblu burgundy; Suede gray; Damson Plum maroon; Spirea green and Port Wine red. Beltline moldings were done in contrasting tones of Ivory, Deauville Sand or red. Both models had a larger displacement "FB" straight eight engine. The headlight tie-bar emblem for Dictator models was an "8".

I.D. DATA:

[Series GE] Serial numbers were in the same location. Starting: 1437601. Ending: 1460000. Engine numbers were on the right side of block. See 1928 engine numbers. [Series GH] Serial numbers were in the same location. Starting: 4062101. Ending: 4070500. Engine numbers were on the right side of the block. Engine numbers were GH-1 and up. [Series FB/FA] Serial numbers were in the same location. Starting: [FB] 7000001; [FA] 6008601. Ending: [FB] 7013500; [FA] 6013000. Engine numbers on front of block. Both models used the same engine number prefix. Starting: FB-1. Ending: FB-17775.

Model No.	Body Type & Seating	Price	Weight	Prod. Total
GE	4-dr. Tr.-5P	1265	3050	Note 1
GE	4-dr. Tr.-7P	1325	3090	Note 1
GE	2-dr. Bus. Cpe.-2P	1265	3125	Note 1
GE	2-dr. Roy. Cabr.-4P	1395	3430	Note 1
GE	2-dr. Roy. Vic.-4P	1345	3210	Note 1
GE	2-dr. Clb. Sed.-5P	1185	3190	Note 1
GE	4-dr. Sed.-5P	1265	3280	Note 1
GE	4-dr. Roy. Sed.-5P	1395	3420	Note 1

Note 1: For total production Sept. 1927 to Oct. 1928 see 1928 specifications. Cars built after June 1928 were sold as 1929 models.

GH	4-dr. Reg. Vic.-5P	1625	3570	Note 1
GH	4-dr. Sed.-5P	1495	3670	Note 1
GH	4-dr. Reg. Sed.-5P	1665	3800	Note 1

Note 1: Total production between June 1928 and October 1928 was 8,428.

President FB

FB	2-dr. Sta. Rds.-4P	1850	3535	Note 1
FB	2-dr. Sta. Cabr.-4P	1850	3715	Note 1
FB	2-dr. Sta. Vic.-4P	1850	3820	Note 1
FB	4-dr. Sed.-5P	1685	3760	Note 1
FB	4-dr. Sta. Sed.-5P	1850	3900	Note 1

President FA (1928-1/2)

FA	4-dr. Tr.-7P	2285	3920	Note 2
FA	4-dr. Sta. Tr.-7P	2485	4125	Note 2
FA	2-dr. Sta. Cabr.-4P	2195	3980	Note 2
FA	4-dr. Sta. Sed.-5P	2250	4185	Note 2
FA	4-dr. Sed.-5P	2085	4040	Note 2
FA	4-dr. Sta. Sed.-7P	2350	4225	Note 2
FA	4-dr. Limo.-7P	2450	4320	Note 2

Note 1: Total production June 1928 to Oct. 1928 was 13,186.

Note 2: For total production Dec. 1927 to Oct. 1928 see 1928 specifications. Cars built after June 1928 were sold as 1929 models.

GE ENGINE: L-head. Inline. Six. Cast iron block. B & S: 3-3/8 in. x 4-1/2 in. Disp.: 242 cu. in. C.R.: 4.41:1. Brake H.P.: 67 @ 2800 R.P.M. N.A.C.C. H.P.: 27.3. Main bearings: Four. Valve lifters: Solid. Carb.: Stromberg 1V Model UX2.

GH ENGINE: L-head. Inline. Six. Cast iron block. B & S: 3-7/8 in. x 5 in. Disp.: 354 cu. in. C.R.: 4.6:1 (4.7:1 on roadster). Brake H.P.: 85 @ 2800 R.P.M. N.A.C.C. H.P.: 36. Main bearings: Four. Valve lifters: Solid. Carb.: Ball & Ball 1V.

FB ENGINE: L-head. Inline. Eight. Cast iron block. B & S: 3-1/2 in. x 4-3/8 in. Disp.: 337 cu. in. C.R.: 4.9:1. Brake H.P.: 109 @ 3200 R.P.M. N.A.C.C. H.P.: 39.2. Main bearings: Five. Valve lifters: Solid. Carb.: Schebler 1V. Note: The new "FB" engine was used in both FB and FA models produced after June 1928.

CHASSIS: [Series GE] W.B.: 113 in. Tires: 20 x 5.50. [Series GH] W.B.: 121 in. Tires: 30 x 5.50. [Series FB] W.B.: 121 in. Tires: 30 x 5.50. [Series FA] W.B.: 131 in. Tires: 31 x 6.20.

TECHNICAL: Unit type manual transmission. Speeds: 3F/1R. Floor shift controls. Multiple disc clutch. Shaft drive. Semi-floating rear axle. Overall ratio: [GE] 4.6:1; [GH] 3.31:1; [FB/FA] 4.1:1. Four wheel mechanical brakes on all series. Wood spoke artillery wheels or wire spoke wheels std. depending on series.

OPTIONS: Front bumper. Rear guards. Whitewall tires. Dual sidemount. Sidemount cover(s). OSRV mirror. Trunk rack. Touring rack. Heater. Clock. Cigar lighter. Spare tire. Wire spoke wheels. Pedestal sidemount mirrors. Spotlight(s). Special paint. Power tire pump. Disc wheels. Wind wings. Smoking set. Vanity case. Spring covers. Rear axle ratios.

HISTORICAL: Introduced See specification notes. Calendar year registrations: (1929) 82,839. Model year production: (1929) 57,790. Innovations: Larger displacement straight eight. New fuel pump. New Fafnir spring shackles. Model identification on headlight tie bar had "8" for Presidents; "World's Champion" globe for Commanders and "S" for Dictators. Dictator parking brake relocated to floor board.

Notes: In July 1928 four FB President models were taken to the Atlantic City, N.J. Speedway for an endurance run that broke all existing stock car speed and distance records. In Nov., 1928 two more Presidents returned to Atlantic City for even more record-breaking runs. By the end of the year, these cars held 116 total stock car records in their size and displacement class. Studebakers achieved an all-time record for pre-war sales in 1928 by selling $157 million worth of cars.

1928-1/2
Dictator, Model GE

	FP	5	4	3	2	1
Tr	1265	3600	7200	12,000	16,800	24,000
7P Tr	1325	3650	7350	12,250	17,150	24,500
Bus Cpe	1265	750	1450	3300	4900	7000
Roy Cabr	1395	3750	7500	12,500	17,500	25,000
Roy Vic	1345	775	1500	3750	5250	7500
Clb Sed	1185	725	1400	3000	4700	6700
Sed	1265	700	1350	2700	4500	6400
Roy Sed	1395	750	1450	3300	4900	7000

Commander, Model GH

	FP	5	4	3	2	1
Reg Vic	1625	875	1700	4350	6050	8700
Sed	1495	850	1650	4100	5700	8200
Reg Sed	1665	850	1650	4200	5850	8400

President, Model FB

	FP	5	4	3	2	1
Sta Rds	1850	3750	7500	12,500	17,500	25,000
Sta Cabr	1850	3600	7200	12,000	16,800	24,000
Sta Vic	1850	900	1800	4400	6150	8800
Sed	1685	850	1650	4200	5850	8400
Sta Sed	1850	875	1700	4300	6000	8600

President, Model FA

	FP	5	4	3	2	1
Tr	2285	3900	7800	13,000	18,200	26,000
Sta Tr	2485	3900	7800	13,000	18,200	26,000
Sta Cabr	2195	4050	8100	13,500	18,900	27,000
Sta Sed	2250	950	2200	4800	6700	9600
Sed	2085	925	2000	4600	6400	9200
7P Sta Sed	2350	975	2300	4950	6900	9900
Limo	2450	2300	5400	9000	12,600	18,000

1929

1929 Studebaker, Dictator Six, 4-pass. coupe, AA

STUDEBAKER — DICTATOR — SERIES GE — SIX: Production of the model GE Dictator had already ended by the time the "real" 1929 Studebakers were introduced in Jan. 1929. Following standard practice, the cars built to 1928-1/2 specifications continued to be sold as long as the inventory lasted. There were probably a few running production changes. According to the Jan. 1929 edition of *MoToR* there were only four models: sedan, cabriolet, Royal Sedan and Victoria Sedan. Standard equipment included a Stewart-Warner speedometer; gasoline gauge; engine thermometer; coincidental lock; rearview mirror; Trico vacuum windshield wiper; stop and tail light; Lovejoy shock absorbers and tire lock. The standard sedan had wood spoke wheels and a spare rim as optional equipment. The Cabriolet and Royal Sedan had six wheel equipment standard. The Victoria had wood spoke wheels and one spare rim as its standard equipment.

STUDEBAKER — COMMANDER — SERIES GJ — SIX: New Commander bodies were longer, lower and roomier. A double drop frame design permitted the extremely low lines. New features included safety glass windshields and adjustable driver's seats. Both the window reveals and belt panels were set off by new raised moldings. Chrome plated trim highlighted the bodies. Deluxe models carried six wire wheels (five on roadster). A new Brougham and convertible Cabriolet had nickle-plated windshield frames. Standard equipment included a Stewart-Warner speedometer; gasoline gauge; engine thermometer; coincidental lock; New Haven clock; cigar lighter; rearview mirror; windshield wiper; trunk on the Victoria, cabriolet and Regal sedan; tail and stop light; Lovejoy shock absorbers; wire wheels on roadsters, cabriolets and Regal sedan; wood spoke wheels on other models and spare tire lock. Double bar front bumpers and rear guards were optional at slight extra cost. The cadet sun visors were eliminated this year. Instead of a visor, the front window pillars on closed cars had a slight reverse curve that extended across the roof giving a slight visor-like effect. This was called a "French" windshield design.

STUDEBAKER — COMMANDER — SERIES FD — EIGHT: Appearance-wise, the all-new Commander Eight was identical to the Commander Six. The headlight tie-bar emblem was used for differentation. The Eight, of course, had the number "8" incorporated. Deluxe (Regal) models all carried six wire wheels except the roadster, which was fitted with five wire wheels. A clock was standard on all Commander Eights except the Regal roadster, sedan and victoria. A cigar lighter was optional on the same three models and standard on other Commander Eights. A trunk was standard on the Convertible cabriolet, Regal sedan and Brougham, optional on other models. Standard on all models was a speedometer; gas gauge; engine thermometer; tail and stop light; coincidental lock; rearview mirror; automatic wiper; lovejoy shock absorbers and a tire lock.

STUDEBAKER — PRESIDENT — SERIES FH/FE — EIGHT: The new double drop frame was also used on 1929 Presidents, allowing lower and slightly wider bodies. Safety glass windshields were new. The doors were also wider. The new handling of window reveals and belt panels — with raised moldings — was also seen on Presidents. The FH Cabriolet and FE Brougham had nickle plated windshield/window frames. Deluxe (State) models had six wire wheel equipment. The wheelbase was 125 inches on FHs and 135 inches on FEs. Cars in both lines used a new "FE" straight eight engine with improved carburetion and slightly higher compression. Standard equipment on all Presidents included a speedometer; gas gauge; engine thermometer; coincidental lock; clock; cigar lighter; Trico vacuum wiper; tail and stop lamp; Houdaille twin type hydraulic shock absorbers; spring covers; and tire lock. Kelsey-Hayes wood wheels and a single spare

1929 Studebaker, President Eight, sport roadster, AA

rim were standard on the sedans. Budd wire wheels with dual sidemounts were standard on Victorias, Cabriolets, Broughams, Limousines and all State sedans.

I.D. DATA: [Series GE] Serial and engine number same as 1928-1/2. [Series GJ] Serial numbers in same location. Starting: 4070501. Ending: 4081000. Engine numbers on right side of block. Starting: GJ-1 and up. [Series FD] Serial numbers in same location. Starting: 8000001. Ending: 8011000. Engine numbers were stamped on left side of block. Starting: FD-1 and up. [Series FE/FH] Serial numbers in same location. Starting: [FH] 7013501; [FE] 6013001. Ending: [FH] 7021000; [FE] 6016001. Engine numbers on right side of block. Starting: FE-1 and up.

Model No.	Body Type & Seating	Price	Weight	Prod. Total
GE	4-dr. Sed.-5P	1265	3280	Note 1
GE	2-dr. Cabr.-4P	1395	3280	Note 1
GE	4-dr. Roy. Sed.-5P	1395	3415	Note 1
GE	2-dr. Vic. Sed.-5P	1345	3210	Note 1

Note 1: For total production Sept. 1927 to Oct. 1928 see 1928 specifications. Cars sold after Jan. 1929 were considered 1929 "second series" models.

GJ	2-dr. Rds.-2/4P	1375	2970	Note 1
GJ	2-dr. Reg. Rds.-2/4P	1450	3000	Note 1
GJ	4-dr. Tr.-5P	1350	3070	Note 1
GJ	4-dr. Reg. Tr.-5P	1450	3200	Note 1
GJ	4-dr. Tr.-7P	1410	3125	Note 1
GJ	4-dr. Reg. Tr.-7P	1510	3275	Note 1
GJ	2-dr. Cpe.-2P	1350	3105	Note 1
GJ	2-dr. Spt. Cpe.-2/4P	1425	3160	Note 1
GJ	2-dr. Cabr.-2/4P	1495	3215	Note 1
GJ	2-dr. Vic.-4P	1375	3130	Note 1
GJ	4-dr. Sed.-5P	1375	3235	Note 1
GJ	4-dr. Reg. Sed.-5P	1495	3335	Note 1
GJ	4-dr. Reg. Brgm.-5P	1525	3415	Note 1

Note 1: Total production Dec. 1928 to April 1930 was 16,019.

FD	2-dr. Reg. Rds.-4P	1595	3040	Note 1
FD	4-dr. Reg. Tr.-5P	1495	3100	Note 1
FD	4-dr. Tr.-5P	1595	3250	Note 1
FD	4-dr. Tr.-7P	1545	3125	Note 1
FD	4-dr. Reg. Tr.-7P	1645	3275	Note 1
FD	2-dr. Bus. Cpe.-2P	1495	3140	Note 1
FD	2-dr. Spt. Cpe.-2/4P	1550	3195	Note 1
FD	2-dr. Reg. Conv.-2/4P	1645	3240	Note 1
FD	2-dr. Vic.-4P	1525	3170	Note 1
FD	4-dr. Reg. Brgm.-5P	1675	3440	Note 1
FD	4-dr. Sed.-5P	1525	3255	Note 1
FD	4-dr. Reg. Sed.-5P	1645	3385	Note 1

Note 1: Total production Dec. 1928 to June 1930 was 17,527.

Series FH, 125 in. W.B.

FH	2-dr. Rds.-4P	1735	3770	Note 1
FH	2-dr. Cabr.-4P	1875	3970	Note 1
FH	2-dr. Sta. Vic.-4P	1875	4015	Note 1
FH	4-dr. Sed.-5P	1735	4045	Note 1
FH	4-dr. Sta. Sed.-5P	1875	4160	Note 1

Series FE, 135 in W.B.

FE	4-dr. Tr.-7P	1785	4065	Note 2
FE	4-dr. Sta. Tr.-7P	2085	4210	Note 2
FE	4-dr. Brgm.-5P	2350	4360	Note 2
FE	4-dr. Sed.-7P	2175	4235	Note 2
FE	4-dr.Sta. Sed.-7P	2350	4370	Note 2
FE	4-dr. Limo.-7P	2575	4385	Note 2

Note 1: Total production Dec. 1928 to June 1930 was 17,527.
Note 2: Total production Dec. 1928 to June 1930 was 8,740.

SERIES GE ENGINE: L-head. Inline. Six. Cast iron block. B & S: 3-3/8 in. x 4-1/2 in. Disp.: 242 cu. in. C.R.: 4.41:1. Brake H.P.: 67 @ 2800 R.P.M. N.A.C.C. H.P.: 27.3. Main bearings: Four. Valve lifters: Solid. Carb.: Stromberg 1V Model UX2.

SERIES GJ ENGINE: L-head. Inline. Six. Cast iron block. B & S: 3-3/8 in. x 4-5/8 in. Disp.: 248.3 cu. in. C.R.: 4.95:1. Brake H.P.: 74 @ 3000 R.P.M. N.A.C.C. H.P.: 27.3. Main bearings: Four. Valve lifters: Solid. Carb.: Stromberg 1V Model UX2.

SERIES FD ENGINE: L-head. Inline. Eight. Cast iron block. B & S: 3-1/16 in. x 4-1/4 in. Disp.: 250.4 cu. in. C.R.: 5.05:1. Brake H.P.: 80 @ 3600 R.P.M. N.A.C.C. H.P.: 30.0. Main bearings: Nine. Valve lifters: Solid. Carb.: Stromberg 1V Model UX2.
Note: Top speed of the FD motor was 72 mph.

SERIES FH/FE ENGINE: L-head. Inline. Eight. Cast iron block. B & S: 3-1/2 in. x 4-3/8 in. Disp.: 337 cu. in. C.R.: (std.) 5.0:1; (opt.) 5.50:1 and 6.0:1. Brake H.P.: 114 @ 3200 R.P.M. N.A.C.C. H.P.: 39.2. Main bearings: Five. Valve lifters: Solid. Carb.: Stromberg 2V (duplex) Model UU2.

CHASSIS: [Series GE] W.B.: 113 in. Tread: 57/57 in. Tires: 20 x 5.50. [Series GJ] W.B.: 120 in. H: 69-5/16 in. Tread: 58/58 in. Tires: 19 x 5.50. [Series FD] W.B.: 120 in. H: 69-5/16 in. Tread: 58/58 in. Tires: 19 x 5.50. [Series FH] W.B.: 125 in. H: 71-5/16 in. Tread: 59/59 in. Tires: 20 x 6.00 six-ply balloon. [Series FE] W.B.: 135 in. H: 71-5/16 in. Tread: 59/59 in. Tires: 19 x 6.50 six-ply balloon.

TECHNICAL: Unit type manual transmission. Speeds: 3F/1R. Floor shift controls. Multiple-plate dry-disc clutch. (3 plates on Pres.; 2 on others). Shaft drive. Semi-floating rear axle. Overall ratio: [GE] 4.6:1; [GJ] 3.91:1; [FD] 4.36:1 or 3.91:1; [FE] 4.64:1; [FE] 4.78:1. Four wheel mechanical brakes. Kelsey-Hayes wood spoke artillery wheels or Budd wire wheels.

OPTIONS: Front bumper. Rear guards. Whitewall tires. Dual sidemount. Sidemount cover(s). Wind wings. Trunk rack. Touring trunk. Heater. Clock. Cigar lighter. Wire spoke wheels. Wood spoke wheels (on models with wire wheels std.). OSRV mirror. Spotlight(s). Smoking set. Vanity case. Backing lights. Stop light. Spring covers (std. on Pres.). Power tire pump. Tire cover. Pedestal type sidemount mirrors. Special paint. High-compression heads (President). Rear axle ratios.

HISTORICAL: Introduced See notes above. Calendar year registrations: (1929) 82,839. Model year production: (1929) 57,790. Innovations: Double drop frame. Duplex carburetion on President. Improved intake manifolding. Automatic choke. Larger brakes. Safer hand-brake system. Improved rear axles. Houdaille shocks on President. Nine bearings in new Commander eight.
Notes: Studebaker claimed to be the world's predominant manufacturer of eight-cylinder automobiles this year. President Eights were used as "Official Cars" at the Indianapolis 500. Actress Mae West drove one of them.

1929

Dictator GE, 6-cyl., 113" wb

	FP	5	4	3	2	1
5P Tr	1265	3600	7200	12,000	16,800	24,000
7P Tr	1325	3600	7200	12,000	16,800	24,000
Bus Cpe	1265	875	1700	4250	5900	8500
Cabr	1395	3600	7200	12,000	16,800	24,000
Vic Ryl	1345	900	1900	4500	6300	9000

Commander Six, Model GJ

Rds	1375	4650	9300	15,500	21,700	31,000
Reg Rds	1450	4800	9600	16,000	22,400	32,000
Tr	1350	4200	8400	14,000	19,600	28,000
Reg Tr	1450	4350	8700	14,500	20,300	29,000
7P Tr	1410	4200	8400	14,000	19,600	28,000
7P Reg Tr	1510	4350	8700	14,500	20,300	29,000
Cpe	1350	800	1550	3850	5400	7700
Spt Cpe	1425	900	1900	4500	6300	9000
Cabr	1495	4050	8100	13,500	18,900	27,000
Vic	1375	875	1700	4250	5900	8500
Sed	1375	825	1600	4000	5600	8000
Reg Sed	1495	900	1900	4500	6300	9000
Reg Brgm	1525	950	2100	4750	6650	9500

Commander Eight, Model FD

Reg Rds	1595	4950	9900	16,500	23,100	33,000
Tr	1495	4350	8700	14,500	20,300	29,000
Reg Tr	1595	4500	9000	15,000	21,000	30,000
7P Tr	1545	4350	8700	14,500	20,300	29,000
7P Reg Tr	1645	4500	9000	15,000	21,000	30,000
Bus Cpe	1495	875	1700	4250	5900	8500
Spt Cpe	1550	1000	2400	5000	7000	10,000
Reg Conv	1645	4200	8400	14,000	19,600	28,000
Vic	1525	950	2100	4750	6650	9500
Reg Brgm	1675	975	2300	4900	6850	9800
Sed	1525	875	1700	4250	5900	8500
Reg Sed	1645	925	2000	4650	6500	9300

President Eight, Model FH, 125" wb

Rds	1735	5550	11,100	18,500	25,900	37,000
Cabr	1875	4950	9900	16,500	23,100	33,000
Sta Vic	1875	1075	3000	5500	7700	11,000
Sed	1735	1000	2400	5000	7000	10,000
Sta Sed	1875	1075	3000	5500	7700	11,000

President Eight, Model FE, 135" wb

7P Tr	1785	5100	10,200	17,000	23,800	34,000
7P Sta Tr	2085	5100	10,200	17,000	23,800	34,000
Brgm	2350	1125	3500	5850	8200	11,700
7P Sed	2175	1075	3000	5500	7700	11,000
7P Sta Sed	2350	1125	3450	5750	8050	11,500
7P Limo	2575	1550	4500	7500	10,500	15,000

1930

1930 Studebaker, Dictator Six, 4-pass. roadster, AA

STUDEBAKER — DICTATOR — SERIES GL — SIX: The 1930 Dictator had a longer 115 inch wheelbase. A new double drop frame gave lower body lines. Hood louvers were grouped in a distinctive pattern of seven groupings, each with three vertical openings. A convex belt line panel was seen. The headlight tie-bar emblem was entirely eliminated on sixes. Standard equipment included a Stewart-Warner speedometer; gas gauge; thermometer; coincidental lock; shatterproof windshield; Trico wiper; tail and stop lamp; Kelsey-Hayes wood spoke wheels (except six wire wheels on Regal Tourer and Regal Sedan) and Lovejoy shock absorbers. Front and rear bumpers were said to be "standard," but were not included in list prices.

STUDEBAKER — DICTATOR — SERIES FC — EIGHT: The first eight-cylinder Dictator used the same body described above. Cars with serial numbers above 2,122,868 had a headlight tie-bar emblem with an "8" to identify the larger engine. Equipment features were the same as on the six-cylinder cars.

STUDEBAKER — COMMANDER — SERIES GJ — SIX: The Depression caused the Commander GJ to be carried over as a 1930 model. Specifications were unchanged. There were a few body style deletions and/or name changes. The standard roadster was dropped, the rumbleseat coupe was no longer called a Sport Coupe, the cabriolet was now a Convertible Cabriolet and the Regal Brougham was downgraded to a standard brougham.

1930 Studebaker, Commander Eight Regal, brougham, AA

STUDEBAKER — COMMANDER — SERIES FD — EIGHT: A second carryover series was the Commander FD eight-cylinder line. Specifications were the same as in 1929. The seven passenger standard and Regal touring cars were dropped, the Business Coupe was now called simply a coupe, the cabriolet became a Convertible Cabriolet and the Regal Brougham was downgraded to a standard brougham. Two new models were both seven passenger sedans — one standard and one with Regal equipment.

1930 Studeber, President Eight, state victoria, AA

STUDEBAKER — PRESIDENT — SERIES FH/FE — EIGHT: In keeping with Studebaker's policy of no all-new 1930 models, the 125- and 135-inch wheelbase Presidents were carried over from 1929. There was, however, one change in the appearance of closed models; the visorless "French" style windshield design was used. The FH cabriolet was now a Convertible Cabriolet and the long-wheelbase FE line got two new body styles, a seven passenger State Limousine and a five passenger State Victoria. The latter car was introduced at the New York Automobile show in January, 1930.

STUDEBAKER — SERIES 53 — SIX: In 1927, Studebaker had introduced a small "companion" car called the Erskine. It was still available in 1930, but after May of that year the Erskine 53 was renamed the Studebaker 53. Features of the car included vertical hood louvers in groups of three, chrome plated bright metal parts, a 114 inch wheelbase and a cadet style sun visor. The main changes in the new Studebaker were "S" logo hub caps and a Studebaker radiator nameplate. A kit was available from dealers to allow owners to retrofit their 1930 Erskines with these Studebaker parts. Cars with serial numbers higher than 5,083,248 were considered Studebakers according to National Automobile Dealer Association records.

I.D. DATA: [Series GL] Serial numbers were in the same location. Starting: 1460001. Ending: 1477293. Engine numbers were on the right side of block. Starting: GL-1. Ending: GL-18200. [Series FC] Serial numbers in same location. Starting: 2120001. Ending: 2134000. Motor numbers on left side of block. Motor numbers were FC-1 and up. [Series GJ] Serial numbers were in the same location. Starting: 4081001. Ending: 4086041. Engine numbers located on the right side of block. Engine numbers were GJ-1 and up. [Series FD] Serial numbers were in the same location. Starting: 8011001. Ending: 8025000. Engine numbers on left side of block. Engine numbers were FD-1 and up. [Series FH/FE] Serial numbers in same location. Starting: (FH) 7021001; [FE] 6016001. Ending: [FH] 7031000; [FE] 6022000. Engine numbers were on front of motor block. Engine numbers were FE-1 and up. [Series 53] Serial numbers in same location. Starting: 5083248. Ending: 5085000. Engine numbers on right side of block. Engine numbers were E-001 and up.

Model No.	Body Type & Seating	Price	Weight	Prod. Total
GL	4-dr. Tr.-5P	1145	2955	Note 1
GL	4-dr. Reg. Tr.-5P	1265	3075	Note 1
GL	2-dr. Cpe.-2P	1135	2915	Note 1
GL	2-dr. Spt. Cpe.-2/4P	1195	2980	Note 1
GL	4-dr. Brgm.-5P	1295	3250	Note 1
GL	2-dr. Clb. Sed.-5P	1095	2970	Note 1
GL	4-dr. Sed.-5P	1195	3080	Note 1
GL	4-dr. Reg. Sed.-5P	1295	3200	Note 1

Note 1: Total production June 1929 to May 1930 was 17,561.

Model No.	Body Type & Seating	Price	Weight	Prod. Total
FC	4-dr. Tr.-5P	1285	2980	Note 1
FC	4-dr. Reg. Tr.-5P	1385	3100	Note 1
FC	2-dr. Cpe.-2P	1255	2950	Note 1
FC	2-dr. Cpe.-2/4P	1315	3010	Note 1
FC	4-dr. Brgm.-5P	1415	3275	Note 1
FC	2-dr. Clb. Sed.-5P	1195	2990	Note 1
FC	4-dr. Sed.-5P	1295	3095	Note 1
FC	4-dr. Reg. Sed.-5P	1415	3230	Note 1

Note 1: Total production May 1929 to Aug. 1930 was 16,359.

Model No.	Body Type & Seating	Price	Weight	Prod. Total
GJ	2-dr. Reg. Rds.-2/4P	1495	3000	Note 1
GJ	4-dr. Tr.-5P	1395	3070	Note 1
GJ	4-dr. Reg. Tr.-5P	1495	3200	Note 1
GJ	4-dr. Tr.-7P	1360	3095	Note 1
GJ	4-dr. Reg. Tr.-7P	1460	3225	Note 1
GJ	2-dr. Cpe.-2P	1345	3105	Note 1
GJ	2-dr. Spt. Cpe.-2/4P	1425	3160	Note 1
GJ	2-dr. Conv. Cabr.-2/4P	1545	3215	Note 1
GJ	2-dr. Vic.-4P	1425	3130	Note 1
GJ	4-dr. Brgm.-5P	1575	3415	Note 1
GJ	4-dr. Sed.-5P	1525	3235	Note 1
GJ	4-dr. Reg. Sed.-5P	1545	3335	Note 1

Note 1: Total production Dec. 1928 to April 1930 was 16,019.

Model No.	Body Type & Seating	Price	Weight	Prod. Total
FD	2-dr. Reg. Rds.-2/4P	1595	3040	Note 1
FD	4-dr. Tr.-5P	1395	3100	Note 1
FD	4-dr. Reg. Tr.-5P	1595	3250	Note 1
FD	2-dr. Cpe.-2P	1495	3150	Note 1
FD	2-dr. Spt. Cpe.-2/4P	1545	3235	Note 1
FD	2-dr. Conv. Cabr.-2/4P	1695	3345	Note 1
FD	2-dr. Vic.-4P	1515	3200	Note 1
FD	4-dr. Brgm.-5P	1695	3540	Note 1
FD	4-dr. Sed.-5P	1515	3310	Note 1
FD	4-dr. Reg. Sed.-5P	1695	3435	Note 1
FD	4-dr. Sed.-7P	1695	3355	Note 1
FD	4-dr. Reg. Sed.-7P	1845	3470	Note 1

Note 1: Total production Dec. 1928 to June 1930 was 24,639.

Series FH, 125 in. W.B.

Model No.	Body Type & Seating	Price	Weight	Prod. Total
FH	2-dr. Rds.-2/4P	1795	3770	Note 1
FH	2-dr. Conv. Cabr.-2/4P	1975	3970	Note 1
FH	2-dr. Sta. Vic.-4P	1975	4015	Note 1
FH	4-dr. Sta. Sed.-5P	1795	4045	Note 1
FH	4-dr. Sta. Sed.-5P	1995	4160	Note 1

Series FE, 135 in. W.B.

Model No.	Body Type & Seating	Price	Weight	Prod. Total
FE	4-dr. Tr.-7P	1845	4020	Note 2
FE	4-dr. Sta. Tr.-7P	2145	4175	Note 2
FE	2-dr. Sta. Vic.-4P	2295	4230	Note 2
FE	4-dr. Brgm.-5P	2395	4440	Note 2
FE	4-dr. Sed.-7P	2095	4305	Note 2
FE	4-dr. Sta. Sed.-7P	2295	4435	Note 2
FE	4-dr. Limo.-7P	2595	4445	Note 2
FE	4-dr. Sta. Limo.-7P	2795	4445	Note 2

Note 1: Total production Dec. 1928 to June 1930 was 17,527.
Note 2: Total production Dec. 1928 to June 1930 was 8,740.

Model No.	Body Type & Seating	Price	Weight	Prod. Total
53	4-dr. Tr.-5P	965	2840	Note 1
53	4-dr. Reg. Tr.-5P	1065	2990	Note 1
53	2-dr. Bus. Cpe.-2P	895	2835	Note 1
53	2-dr. Reg. Cpe.-2/4P	985	2890	Note 1
53	2-dr. Clb. Sed.-5P	935	2875	Note 1
53	4-dr. Sed.-5P	985	2950	Note 1
53	4-dr. Reg. Sed.-5P	1085	3100	Note 1
53	4-dr. Lan. Sed.-5P	1125	3100	Note 1

Note 1: Total production Nov. 1929 to Nov. 1930 was 22,371.

SERIES GL ENGINE: L-head. Inline. Six. Cast iron block. B & S: 3-3/8 in. x 4-1/8 in. Disp.: 221 cu. in. C.R.: 4.8:1. Brake H.P.: 68 @ 3200 R.P.M. N.A.C.C. H.P.: 27.34. Main bearings: Four. Valve lifters: Solid. Carb.: Stromberg 1V Model UX2.

SERIES FC ENGINE: L-head. Inline. Eight. Cast iron block. B & S: 3-1/16 in. x 3-3/4 in. Disp.: 221 cu. in. C.R.: 5.0:1; (optional: 5.5:1). Brake H.P.: 70 @ 3200 R.P.M. N.A.C.C. H.P.: 30. Main bearings: Nine. Valve lifters: Solid. Carb.: Stromberg 1V Model UX2.

SERIES GJ ENGINE: L-head. Inline. Six. Cast iron block. B & S: 3-3/8 in. x 4-5/8 in. Disp.: 248.3 cu. in. C.R.: 4.8:1. Brake H.P.: 75 @ 3000 R.P.M. N.A.C.C. H.P.: 27.3. Main bearings: Four. Valve lifters: Solid. Carb.: Strombert 1V Model UX2.

SERIES FD ENGINE: L-head. Inline. Eight. Cast iron block. B & S: 3-1/6 in. x 4-1/4 in. Disp.: 250.4 cu. in. C.R.: 5.10:1. Brake H.P.: 80 @ 3200 R.P.M. N.A.C.C. H.P.: 30.04. Main bearings: Nine. Valve lifters: Solid. Carb.: Stromberg 1V Model UX2.

SERIES FE ENGINE: L-head. Inline. Eight. Cast iron block. B & S: 3-1/2 in. x 4-3/8 in. Disp.: 337 cu. in. C.R.: 5.05:1. Brake H.P.: 115 @ 3200 R.P.M. N.A.C.C. H.P.: 39.2. Main bearings: Five. Valve lifters: Solid. Carb.: Stromberg 2V Model UU2.

SERIES "53" ENGINE: L-head. Inline. Six. Cast iron block. B & S: 3-1/4 in. x 4-1/8 in. Disp.: 205.3 cu. in. C.R.: 5.20:1. Brake H.P.: 70 @ 3200 R.P.M. N.A.C.C. H.P.: 25.4. Main bearings: Four. Valve lifters: Solid. Carb.: Schebler 1V Model S.

CHASSIS: [Series GL] W.B.: 115 in. H: 69-7/16. Frt/Rear Tread: 58/58 in. Tires: 19 x 5.50. [Series FC] W.B.: 115 in. H: 69-7/16. Frt/Rear Tread: 58/58 in. Tires: 19 x 5.50. [Series GJ] W.B.: 120 in. H: 71-3/16. Frt/Rear Tread: 58/58 in. Tires: 19 x 5.50. [Series FD] W.B.: 120 in. H: 71-3/16. Frt/Rear Tread: 58/58 in. Tires: 19 x 5.50. [Series FH] W.B.: 125 in. H: 71-5/16. Frt/Rear Tread: 58/58 in. Tires: 20 x 6.00. [Series FE] W.B.: 135 in. H: 71-7/8. Frt/Rear Tread: 59/59 in. Tires: 19 x 6.50. [Series "53"] W.B.: 114 in. H: 69-1/4. Frt/Rear Tread: 58/58 in. Tires: 19 x 5.25.

TECHNICAL: Manual unit type transmission. Speeds: 3F/1R. Floor-mounted gearshift controls. Multiple dry disc clutch. Semi-floating rear axle. Overall ratio: (GL) 4.78:1; (FC) 4.78:1; (GJ) 3.91:1; (FD) 4.36:1 or 3.91:1; (FH) 4.31:1; (FE) 4.64:1; (53) 4.78:1. External contracting four wheel brakes. Wood spoke or wire wheels.

OPTIONS: Front bumper. Rear guards. Whitewalls. Dual sidemounts. Sidemount cover(s). Wind wings. Trunk rack. Trunk. Heater. Clock. Cigar lighter. Spare tire. Power tire pump. Stop lights. Spotlight(s). OSRV mirror. Wire wheels. Wood spoke wheels. Backing lights. Spring covers. Pedestal mirrors. Special paint. High compression head. Rear axle ratios. Smoking set. Vanity case.

HISTORICAL: Introduced See notes above. Calendar year registrations: 56,526. Model year production: 76,781. Innovations: Dictator Eight introduced. New Burgess power conserving mufflers. Automatic radiator shutters on Presidents. Valve spring dampeners on Presidents. Longer stroke Commander Six. Restyled Dictators with double drop frames. Improved Dictator emergency brake.
Notes: Studebaker's profits dropped to $1.5 million in 1930, but the company still paid $8 million out in dividends.

1930

Studebaker 53 Model, 6-cyl., 114" wb

	FP	5	4	3	2	1
Tr	1285	5400	10,800	18,000	25,200	36,000
Tr	965	4200	8400	14,000	19,600	28,000
Reg Tr	1065	4200	8400	14,000	19,600	28,000
Bus Cpe	895	900	1900	4500	6300	9000
Reg Cpe	985	950	2100	4750	6650	9500
Clb Sed	935	900	1900	4500	6300	9000
Sed	985	825	1600	4000	5600	8000
Reg Sed	1085	875	1700	4250	5900	8500
Lan Sed	1125	875	1700	4350	6050	8700

Dictator, 6 & 8 cyl., 115" wb

	FP	5	4	3	2	1
Tr	1285	4350	8700	14,500	20,300	29,000
Reg Tr	1385	4350	8700	14,500	20,300	29,000
Cpe	1255	950	2100	4750	6650	9500
Spt Cpe	1315	1025	2600	5250	7300	10,500
Brgm	1415	950	2100	4750	6650	9500
Clb Sed	1195	900	1900	4500	6300	9000
Sed	1295	900	1900	4500	6300	9000
Reg Sed	1415	950	2100	4750	6650	9500

NOTE: Add $200 for Dictator 8-cyl.

Commander 6 & 8 cyl., 120" wb
Commander FD

	FP	5	4	3	2	1
Reg Rds	1595	5250	10,500	17,500	24,500	35,000
Tr	1395	4950	9900	16,500	23,100	33,000
Reg Tr	1595	5100	10,200	17,000	23,800	34,000
7P Tr	1495	4950	9900	16,500	23,100	33,000
7P Reg Tr	1545	5100	10,200	17,000	23,800	34,000
Cpe	1695	900	1900	4500	6300	9000
Spt Cpe	1515	950	2100	4750	6650	9500
Conv Cabr	1695	4950	9900	16,500	23,100	33,000
Vic	1515	1000	2400	5000	7000	10,000
Brgm	1695	1025	2600	5250	7300	10,500
Sed	1695	900	1900	4500	6300	9000
Reg Sed	1845	950	2100	4750	6650	9500

NOTE: Add $200 for Commander 8-cyl.

President FH Model

	FP	5	4	3	2	1
Rds	1795	7200	14,400	24,000	33,600	48,000
Conv Cabr	1975	6300	12,600	21,000	29,400	42,000
Sta Vic	1975	1400	4200	7000	9800	14,000
Sed	1795	1000	2400	5000	7000	10,000
Sta Sed	1995	1125	3450	5750	8050	11,500

President FE Model

	FP	5	4	3	2	1
Tr	1845	6750	13,500	22,500	31,500	45,000
Sta Tr	2145	6900	13,800	23,000	32,200	46,000
Sta Vic	2295	4200	8400	14,000	19,600	28,000
Brgm	2395	1125	3500	5850	8200	11,700
Sed	2095	1075	3000	5500	7700	11,000
Sta Sed	2295	1125	3450	5750	8050	11,500
Limo	2595	2300	5400	9000	12,600	18,000
Sta Limo	2795	2800	5700	9500	13,300	19,000

1931

STUDEBAKER — SERIES 53/54 — SIX: The Series 53 Studebaker Six, which began life as an Erskine, was carried over into the first part of the 1931 selling season. Specifications were basically the same as before. The 1931 cars were those built from July 1930 to the end of series production in Nov. 1930.

The Series 54 made its debut in January 1931 as the "new" Studebaker Six. Changes included a larger radiator cap and a V-shaped radiator. Body styling was altered to make the six look more like other 1931 Studebakers, but cars in Series 54 had round headlights. A distinctive dual bar bumper was also seen. Standard equipment included a speedometer; gas gauge; thermometer; ignition lock; windshield wiper; tail and stop light and Lovejoy shock absorbers. Twenty-nine inch wire spoke wheels were standard on the Regal tourer, Regal Landau and Regal sedan; other models had 29 inch wood spoke wheels. New technical features included a fuel pump and four-point motor suspension.

1931 Studebaker, Dictator Eight, 2-pass. coupe, AA

STUDEBAKER — DICTATOR — SERIES FC/61 — EIGHT: The FC series Dictator Eight was carried over for the early part of the 1931 sales season. There were no basic changes from 1930 specifications. Cars built from July 1930 to Aug. 1930 were sold as 1931 models.

The new 1931 Dictator Series 61 entered production in Sept. 1930. It was also an eight-cylinder line. Wheelbase was reduced one inch. The body was restyled to look more like bigger Studebakers. The radiator shell was of a more rounded design with a thin molding run vertically down the center of the grille. This molding carried a Studebaker badge near its top. Slimmer headlight buckets were used and the headlights were slightly oval shaped. The hood sides no longer carried seven groups of three louvers inside a rectangular panel. Instead, there was thirty-two tall vertical louvers. Other new features included wider crown fenders with clearance lights on top of them, larger hub caps and single bar bumpers. Cowl lights were eliminated. Standard equipment included a speedometer; gas gauge; thermometer; ignition lock; windshield wiper; tail and stop lamp; Lovejoy shock absorbers and 29 inch Kelsey-Hayes wheels. Wood spoke wheels were standard on all models, except the Regal Sedan, which came with wire wheels.

There was no Dictator Six in 1931.

STUDEBAKER — COMMANDER — SERIES 70 — EIGHT: Production of the all-new, 1931 Commander Series 70 line began in July 1930 and continued to Sept. 1931. New styling features included a V-shaped radiator, larger, oval shaped headlights and parking lights atop the front fenders. The new single bar bumper, of sturdier construction, had a V-shaped dip in its center. The Commander wheelbase grew to 124 inches. Standard equipment included a speedometer, gasoline gauge, thermometer, ignition lock, non-shatterable glass (optional on Studebaker Six and Dictator), vacuum wiper, tail and stop light and Lovejoy shock absorbers. Free wheeling was also standard. The Commander had Bendix four-wheel mechanical brakes, an adjustable steering wheel, carburetor intake silencer and starter controls on the instrument panel. Kelsey-Hayes 31 inch wood spoke wheels were standard on standard models. Wire spoke wheels were included on Commander Regals.

1931 Studebaker, President Eight, state roadster, AA

STUDEBAKER — PRESIDENT — SERIES 80/90 — EIGHT: The President Eight came in "short" (130 in.) and long (136 in.) wheelbase versions. New design features included a V-shaped radiator, larger radiator cap, "Veed" single bar bumper, parking lamps on front fenders and large, oval shaped headlights. Standard equipment included free wheeling, ball bearing spring shackles, carburetor intake silencer, speedometer, gas gauge, thermometer, ignition lock, clock, cigar lighter, non-shatterable glass, windshield wiper, tail and stop light, Houdaille shock absorbers and spring covers. Kelsey-Hayes 31 inch wood spoke wheels were used on standard models. Kelsey-Hayes 31 inch wire spoke wheels were used on State models. An attractive new body style was the model 80 four-seasons convertible roadster.

I.D. DATA: [Series 53/54] Serial number in same location. Starting: (53) 5085001; (54) 5096001. Ending: (53) 5095787; (54) 5120000. Engine number on front of block on Model 53; on left side of block on model 54. Engine numbers were S-23001 and up. [Series FC/61] Serial number in same location. Starting: (FC) 2134001; (61) 9000001. Ending: (FC) 2136227; (61) 9015000. Engine number on left side of block. Engine numbers were (FC) FC-1 and up; (61) A-101 and up. [Series 70] Serial number in same location. Starting: 8025001. Ending: 8036000. Engine number on left side of block. Starting: C-101. Ending: C-12000. [Series 80/90] Serial number in same location. Starting: (80) 7031001; (90) 6022001. Ending: (80) 7037335; (90) 6025000. Engine number on front of block. Engine numbers were P-101 and up.

Series 53

Model No.	Body Type & Seating	Price	Weight	Prod. Total
53	2-dr. Rds.-2P	895	2700	Note 1
53	4-dr. Tr.-5P	895	2840	Note 1
53	4-dr. Reg. Tr.-5P	995	2990	Note 1
53	2-dr. Bus. Cpe.-2P	845	2790	Note 1
53	2-dr. Spt. Cpe.-2/4P	895	2840	Note 1
53	2-dr. Clb. Sed.-5P	845	2830	Note 1
53	4-dr. Sed.-5P	895	2930	Note 1
53	4-dr. Reg. Sed.-5P	995	3075	Note 1
53	4-dr. Lan. Sed.-5P	995	3110	Note 1

Series 54

Model No.	Body Type & Seating	Price	Weight	Prod. Total
54	2-dr. Rds.-2/4P	895	2700	Note 2
54	4-dr. Tr.-5P	895	2805	Note 2
54	4-dr. Reg. Tr.-5P	970	2960	Note 2
54	2-dr. Bus. Cpe.-2P	845	2790	Note 2
54	2-dr. Spt. Cpe.-2/4P	895	2840	Note 2
54	4-dr. Sed.-5P	895	2930	Note 2
54	4-dr. Reg. Sed.-5P	970	3075	Note 2

Note 1: Total production Nov. 1929 to Nov. 1930 was 22,371.
Note 2: Total production Dec. 1930 to Sept. 1931 was 23,917.

Dictator FC Series

Model No.	Body Type & Seating	Price	Weight	Prod. Total
FC	4-dr. Tr.-5P	1285	2980	Note 1
FC	4-dr. Reg. Tr.-5P	1385	3100	Note 1
FC	2-dr. Cpe.-2P	1255	2950	Note 1
FC	2-dr. Spt. Cpe.-2/4P	1315	3010	Note 1
FC	2-dr. Reg. Brgm.-5P	1415	3275	Note 1
FC	2-dr. Clb. Sed.-5P	1195	2990	Note 1
FC	4-dr. Sed.-5P	1295	3095	Note 1
FC	4-dr. Reg. Sed.-5P	1415	3230	Note 1

Dictator 61 Series

Model No.	Body Type & Seating	Price	Weight	Prod. Total
61	2-dr. Cpe.-2P	1095	2905	Note 2
61	2-dr. Spt. Cpe.-2/4P	1150	2955	Note 2
61	4-dr. Sed.-5P	1150	3055	Note 2
61	4-dr. Reg. Sed.-5P	1225	3195	Note 2

Note 1: Total production May 1929 to Aug. 1930 was 16,359.
Note 2: Total production Aug. 1930 to Sept. 1931 was 14,141.

Model No.	Body Type & Seating	Price	Weight	Prod. Total
70	2-dr. Cpe.-2/4P	1585	3400	Note 1
70	2-dr. Vic.-4P	1585	3390	Note 1
70	2-dr. Reg. Brgm.-5P	1685	3660	Note 1
70	4-dr. Sed.-5P	1585	3520	Note 1
70	4-dr. Reg. Sed.-5P	1685	3660	Note 1

Note 1: Total production June 1930 to Sept. 1931 was 10,823.

President Series 80

Model No.	Body Type & Seating	Price	Weight	Prod. Total
80	2-dr. Sta. Rds.-2/4P	1900	4130	Note 1
80	2-dr. Cpe.-2P	1850	3995	Note 1
80	2-dr. Sta. Cpe.-2/4P	1950	4200	Note 1
80	4-dr. Sed.-5P	1850	4230	Note 1
80	4-dr. Sta. Sed.-5P	1950	4385	Note 1

President Series 90

Model No.	Body Type & Seating	Price	Weight	Prod. Total
90	4-dr. Tr.-7P	1850	4125	Note 2
90	4-dr. Sta. Tr.-7P	2050	4265	Note 2
90	2-dr. Sta. Vic.-4P	2250	4275	Note 2
90	2-dr. Sta. Brgm.-5P	2250	4460	Note 2
90	4-dr. Sed.-7P	2150	4360	Note 2
90	4-dr. Sta. Sed.-7P	2250	4520	Note 2
90	4-dr. Sta. Limo.-7P	2550	4580	Note 2

Note 1: Total production June 1930 to Sept. 1931 was 6,340.
Note 2: Total production June 1930 to Sept. 1931 was 2,762.

1931 Studebaker, Commander Eight, 4-pass. coupe, AA

ENGINE: [Standard Six] L-head. Inline. Six. Cast iron block. B & S: 3-1/4 in. x 4-1/8 in. Disp.: 205.2 cu. in. C.R.: 5.2:1. Brake H.P.: 70 @ 3200 R.P.M. N.A.C.C. H.P.: 25.4. Main bearings: Four. Valve lifters: Solid. Carb.: Schebler 1V Model TX5. Torque (Compression) 104 lbs.-ft. at 1200 R.P.M. [Dictator Eight] L-head. Inline. Eight. Cast iron block. B & S: 3-1/16 in. x 3-3/4 in. Disp.: 221 cu. in. C.R.: (FC) 4.8:1; (61) 5.00:1, (opt. 61) 5.50:1. Brake H.P.: (FC) 70; (61) 81 @ 3200 R.P.M. N.A.C.C. H.P.: 30.4. Main bearings: Nine. Valve lifters: Solid. Carb.: Stromberg 2V Model UU2. Torque (Compression) 104 lbs.-ft. at 1200 R.P.M. [Commander Eight] L-head. Inline. Eight. Cast iron block. B & S: 3-1/16 in. x 4-1/4 in. Disp.: 250.4 cu. in. C.R.: 5.20:1; (opt.) 5.50:1 or 6.00:1. Brake H.P.: 101 @ 3200 R.P.M. N.A.C.C. H.P.: 30.04. Main bearings: Nine. Valve lifters: Solid. Carb.: Stromberg 2V Model UU2. Torque (Compression) 104 lbs.-ft. at 1200 R.P.M. [President Eight] L-head. Inline. Eight. Cast iron block. B & S: 3-1/2 in. x 4-3/8 in. Disp.: 337 cu. in. C.R.: 5.10:1; (opt.) 5.50:1 or 6.00:1. Brake H.P.: 122 @ 3200 R.P.M. N.A.C.C. H.P.: 39.2. Main bearings: Nine. Valve lifters: Solid. Carb.: Stromberg 2V Model UU2. Torque (Compression) 104 lbs.-ft. at 1200 R.P.M.

CHASSIS: [Series 53] W.B.: 114 in. H: 69-1/4 in. Frt/Rear Tread: 56.5/58 in. Tires: 19 x 5.25. [Series 54] W.B.: 114 in. H: 69-1/4 in. Frt/Rear Tread: 56.5/58 in. Tires: 19 x 5.25. [Series FC] W.B.: 115 in. H: 69-1/4 in. Frt/Rear Tread: 56.5/58 in. Tires: 19 x 5.50. [Series 61] W.B.: 114 in. H: 69-1/4 in. Tires: 19 x 5.25. [Series 70] W.B.: 124 in. H: 70-5/16 in. Frt/Rear Tread: 56.5/58 in. Tires: 19 x 6.00. [Series 80] W.B.: 122 in. H: 71-5/8 in. Frt/Rear Tread: 56-5/8 / 59 in. Tires: 19 x 6.50. [Series 90] W.B.: 136 in. H: 71-5/8 in. Frt/Rear Tread: 56-5/8 / 59 in. Tires: 19 x 6.50.

TECHNICAL: Manual transmission. Speeds: 3F/1R. Floor-mounted gearshift controls. Clutch: Multiple dry disc. Semi-floating rear axle. Overall ratio: (53) 4.78:1; (54) 4.72:1; (FC, 61 and 70) 4.73:1. (80 and 90) 4.31:1. Bendix external expanding four wheel mechanical brakes. Kelsey-Hayes wheels; wood spoke on standard models and wire spoke on Regal and State models. Drivetrain option: Free-wheeling.

OPTIONS: Front bumper. Rear guards. Whitewall tires. Dual sidemount. Sidemount cover(s). Backing light. Spring covers. Power tire pump. Heater. Clock (std. in Pres.). Cigar lighter (std. in Pres.). Wind wings. OSRV mirror. Pedestal mirrors. Spotlight. Trunk rack. Trunk. Wheel trim rings. Trippe lights. Special paint.

HISTORICAL: Introduced: See notes above. Calendar year registrations: 46,535. Model year production: 44,218. Innovations: Free wheeling. Improved steering gear. Improved brakes with cable control introduced at mid-year. Improved manifolding and carburetion on Commander/President. Silent gear transmission. Higher lift camshafts.

On Nov. 3, 1931 a President Model 80 set numerous stock car speed records at Muroc dry lake in California. In September, 1931 Studebaker introduced its low-priced Rockne line.

1931
Studebaker Six, Model 53, 114" wb

	FP	5	4	3	2	1
Rds	895	5400	10,800	18,000	25,200	36,000
Tr	895	4800	9600	16,000	22,400	32,000
Reg Tr	995	4950	9900	16,500	23,100	33,000
Bus Cpe	845	900	1900	4500	6300	9000
Spt Cpe	895	1000	2400	5000	7000	10,000
Clb Sed	845	825	1600	4000	5600	8000
Sed	895	750	1450	3300	4900	7000

Model 61 Dictator, 8-cyl., 115" wb

	FP	5	4	3	2	1
Reg Sed	995	775	1500	3700	5200	7400
Lan Sed	995	775	1500	3750	5250	7500

Series 54

	FP	5	4	3	2	1
Rds	895	6000	12,000	20,000	28,000	40,000
Tr	895	5700	11,400	19,000	26,600	38,000
Rea Tr	970	5850	11,700	19,500	27,300	39,000
Bus Cpe	845	875	1700	4250	5900	8500
Spt Cpe	895	900	1900	4500	6300	9000
Sed	895	750	1450	3300	4900	7000
Reg Sed	970	775	1500	3700	5200	7400

Dictator Eight, Model FC

	FP	5	4	3	2	1
Tr	1285	5850	11,700	19,500	27,300	39,000
Reg Tr	1385	6000	12,000	20,000	28,000	40,000
Cpe	1255	825	1600	4000	5600	8000
Spt Cpe	1315	950	2100	4750	6650	9500
Reg Brgm	1415	875	1700	4250	5900	8500
Clb Sed	1195	750	1450	3300	4900	7000
Sed	1295	775	1500	3750	5250	7500
Reg Sed	1415	800	1550	3850	5400	7700

Model 61

	FP	5	4	3	2	1
Cpe	1095	950	2100	4750	6650	9500
Spt Cpe	1150	1075	3000	5500	7700	11,000
Sed	1150	825	1600	4000	5600	8000
Reg Sed	1225	1000	2400	5000	7000	10,000

Commander Eight, Model 70

	FP	5	4	3	2	1
Cpe	1585	1000	2400	5000	7000	10,000
Vic	1585	1075	3000	5500	7700	11,000
Reg Brgm	1685	1125	3450	5750	8050	11,500
Sed	1585	1025	2600	5250	7300	10,500
Reg Sed	1685	1150	3600	6000	8400	12,000

President Eight, Model 80

	FP	5	4	3	2	1
Sta Rds	1900	8250	16,500	27,500	38,500	55,000
Cpe	1850	3300	6600	11,000	15,400	22,000
Sta Cpe	1950	3750	7500	12,500	17,500	25,000
Sed	1850	1550	4500	7500	10,500	15,000
Sta Sed	1950	1750	4800	8000	11,200	16,000

Model 90

	FP	5	4	3	2	1
Tr	1850	7200	14,400	24,000	33,600	48,000
Sta Tr	2050	7500	15,000	25,000	35,000	50,000
Sta Vic	2250	3150	6300	10,500	14,700	21,000
Sta Brgm	2250	3200	6450	10,750	15,050	21,500
Sed	2150	2800	5700	9500	13,300	19,000
Sta Sed	2250	3000	6000	10,000	14,000	20,000
Sta Limo	2550	3150	6300	10,500	14,700	21,000

1932

STUDEBAKER — SERIES 55 — SIX: Studebaker claimed that it had added 1-1/2 to 3 m.p.h. to the top speed of all its 1932 models by slanting the windshield and rounding the front body corners. Safety glass was now standard on all cars. A longer, 117 inch wheelbase was used for the cars in the six-cylinder series 55 line up. Visors over the windshield were eliminated. Also new was a single bar front bumper. A new, airplane type instrument panel with circular gauges inside an oval panel was seen. A key operated automatic starter, free wheeling and startix device were standard on all models. New models included the St. Regis Brougham, Regal St. Regis Brougham, convertible sedan and Regal Convertible Sedan. A 15 gallon fuel tank was used on sixes and Dictator Eights.

1932 Studebaker, Dictator Eight, roadster, AA

STUDEBAKER — DICTATOR — SERIES 62 — EIGHT: The 1932 Dictator Eights had a longer, 117 inch wheelbase. Styling features included a slanting windshield, V-shaped radiator, oval headlights, single bar bumpers and one piece crowned fenders. Standard equipment included a Stromberg carburetor, Delco Remy ignition, mechanical Bendix brakes, safety glass, free wheeling, startix device, Synchromesh transmission and vacuum advance distributor. All Studebaker Eights carried standard front fender parking lights.

STUDEBAKER — COMMANDER — SERIES 71 — EIGHT: For 1932, the Commander had basically the same styling features as the less expensive models on a longer 125 inch wheelbase. Appearance features included a more streamlined all-steel body, V-shaped radiator, sloping windshield with safety glass, wide one piece fenders with parking lights and a new airplane type instrument panel. Standard equipment included a synchromesh transmission, Houdaille automatic-ride shock absorbers, free wheeling, Startix automatic starting system, Stromberg carburetor, Delco Remy ignition, rubber mounted four point engine suspension and ball bearing spring shackles. A 17 gallon fuel tank was employed.

1932 Studebaker, President Eight, limousine, AA

STUDEBAKER — PRESIDENT — SERIES 91 — EIGHT: The 1932 President came on only a single, 135 inch wheelbase. The roofline was streamlined by eliminating the visor and adding a sloped windshield. The radiator grille had more of a wedge shaped look. It sloped sharply at its bottom. Steel artillery wheels were standard. Presidents had a clock and pass-around cigar lighter with dual ash receivers in Broughams and sedans. Standard equipment included a Stromberg carburetor; Delco-Remy ignition; mechanical Bendix brakes; Synchromesh transmission; free wheeling; Startix device; inside sun visor; Ride Control; vacuum distributor; hydraulic shock absorbers; airplane type instrument panel and metal spring covers.

I.D. DATA: [Series 55] Serial numbers were in the same location on the left side of frame over front axle. Starting: 5120001. Ending: 5133400. Engine numbers were on left side of block. Starting: S49001. Ending: S62821 (approx.). [Series 62] Serial numbers were in the same location. Starting: 9015001. Ending: 9020970. Engine numbers on left side of block. Starting: A15002. Ending: A21150 (approx.). [Series 71] Serial numbers were in the same locations. Starting: 8036001. Ending: 8040000. Engine numbers were on the left side of block. Starting: C12001. Ending C15745 (approx.). [Series 91] Serial numbers were in the same location. Starting: 6025001. Ending: 6027400. Engine numbers were on the front of the block. Starting: P10001. Ending: P12440 (approx.).

Model No.	Body Type & Seating	Price	Weight	Prod. Total
55	2-dr. Conv. Rds.-2/4P	915	3035	Note 1
55	2-dr. Reg. Conv. Rds.-2/4P	1020	3145	Note 1
55	2-dr. Cpe.-2P	840	3025	Note 1
55	2-dr. Reg. Cpe.-2P	945	3115	Note 1
55	2-dr. Spt. Cpe.-2/4P	890	3080	Note 1
55	2-dr. Reg. Spt. Cpe.-2/4P	995	3175	Note 1
55	2-dr. St. R. Brgm.-5P	915	3130	Note 1
55	2-dr. Reg. St. R. Brgm.-5P	1020	3190	Note 1
55	4-dr. Conv. Sed.-5P	985	3210	Note 1
55	4-dr. Reg. Conv. Sed.-5P	1000	3270	Note 1
55	4-dr. Sed.-5P	915	3170	Note 1
55	4-dr. Reg. Sed.-5P	1020	3270	Note 1

Note 1: Total production Nov. 1931 to Nov. 1932 was 13,647.

Model No.	Body Type & Seating	Price	Weight	Prod. Total
62	2-dr. Rds. Conv.-2/4P	1050	3115	Note 1
62	2-dr. Reg. Rds. Conv.-2/4P	1155	3190	Note 1
62	2-dr. Cpe.-2P	980	3085	Note 1
62	2-dr. Reg. Cpe.-2P	1085	3190	Note 1
62	2-dr. Spt. Cpe.-2/4P	1030	3160	Note 1
62	2-dr. Reg. Spt. Cpt.-2P	1135	3265	Note 1
62	2-dr. St. R. Brgm.-5P	1050	3225	Note 1
62	2-dr. St. R. Reg. Brgm.-5P	1155	3280	Note 1
62	4-dr. Conv. Sed.-5P	1125	3285	Note 1
62	4-dr. Reg. Conv. Sed.-5P	1230	3345	Note 1
62	4-dr. Sed.-5P	1050	3240	Note 1
62	4-dr. Reg. Sed.-5P	1155	3345	Note 1

Note 1: Total production Nov. 1931 to Nov. 1932 was 6,021.

Model No.	Body Type & Seating	Price	Weight	Prod. Total
71	2-dr. Rds. Conv.-2/4P	1445	3480	Note 1
71	2-dr. Reg. Rds. Conv.-2/4P	1550	3485	Note 1
71	2-dr. Spt. Cpe.-2/4P	1350	3415	Note 1
71	2-dr. Reg. Spt. Cpe.-2/4P	1455	3520	Note 1
71	2-dr. St. R. Brgm.-5P	1445	3465	Note 1
71	2-dr. Reg. St. R. Brgm.-5P	1550	3570	Note 1
71	4-dr. Conv. Sed.-5P	1560	3675	Note 1
71	4-dr. Reg. Conv. Sed.-5P	1665	3680	Note 1
71	4-dr. Sed.-5P	1445	3545	Note 1
71	4-dr. Reg. Sed.-5P	1550	3645	Note 1

Note 1: Total production Nov. 1931 to Nov. 1932 was 3,551.

Model No.	Body Type & Seating	Price	Weight	Prod. Total
91	2-dr. Rds. Conv.-2/4P	1750	4220	Note 1
91	2-dr. Sta. Rds. Conv.-2/4P	1855	4200	Note 1
91	2-dr. Cpe.-2P	1595	NA	Note 1
91	2-dr. Sta. Cpe.-2P	1700	NA	Note 1
91	2-dr. Spt. Cpe.-2/4P	1690	4255	Note 1
91	2-dr. Sta. Spt. Cpe.-2/4P	1795	4235	Note 1
91	2-dr. St. R. Brgm.-5P	1750	4300	Note 1
91	2-dr. Sta. St. R. Brgm.-5P	1855	4280	Note 1
91	4-dr. Conv. Sed.-5P	1880	4445	Note 1
91	4-dr. Sta. Conv. Sed.-5P	1985	4425	Note 1
91	4-dr. Sed.-5P	1750	4260	Note 1
91	4-dr. Sta. Sed.-5P	1855	4370	Note 1
91	4-dr. Sed.-7P	1890	4365	Note 1
91	4-dr. Sta. Sed.-7P	1995	4475	Note 1
91	4-dr. Limo.-7P	1990	4525	Note 1
91	4-dr. Sta. Limo.-7P	2095	4525	Note 1

Note 1: Total production Nov. 1931 to Dec. 1932 was 2,399.

ENGINE: [Six Engine] L-head. Inline. Six. Cast iron block. B & S: 3-1/4 in. x 4-5/8 in. Disp.: 230 cu. in. C.R.: 5.0:1. Brake H.P.: 80 @ 3200 R.P.M. N.A.C.C. H.P.: 25.4. Main bearings: Four. Valve lifters: Solid. Carb.: Stromberg model UUR-2 1V. [Dictator Engine] L-head. Inline. Eight. Cast iron block. B & S: 3-1/16 in. x 3-3/4 in. Disp.: 221 cu. in. C.R.: 5.0:1. Brake H.P.: 85 @ 3200 R.P.M. N.A.C.C. H.P.: 30.04. Main bearings: Nine. Valve lifters: Solid. Carb.: Stromberg model UUR-2 1V. [Commander Engine] L-head. Inline. Eight. Cast iron block. B & S: 3-1/16 in. x 4-1/4 in. Disp.: 250.4 cu. in. C.R.: 5.15:1. Brake H.P.: 101 @ 3200 R.P.M. N.A.C.C. H.P.: 30.04. Main bearings: Nine. Valve lifters: Solid. Carb.: Stromberg model UU-R 1V. [President Engine] L-head. Inline. Eight. Cast iron block. B & S: 3-1/2 in. x 4-3/8 in. Disp.: 337 cu. in. C.R.: 5.1:1. Brake H.P.: 122 @ 3200 R.P.M. N.A.C.C. H.P.: 39.2. Main bearings: Nine. Valve lifters: Solid. Carb.: Stromberg EE-22 2V.

CHASSIS: [Series 55] W.B.: 117 in. Tires: 18 x 5.50. [Series 62] W.B.: 117 in. Tires: 18 x 5.50. [Series 71] W.B.: 125 in. Tires: 18 x 6.00. [Series 91] W.B.: 135 in. Tires: 18 x 6.50.

TECHNICAL: Synchromesh transmission. Speeds 3F/1R. Floor mounted gearshift controls. Clutch: Single plate dry disc. Semi-floating rear axle. Overall ratio: (55) 4.27:1. (62) 4.73:1. (71) 4.73:1 and (91) 4.31:1. Bendix mechanical four wheel brakes. Steel artillery spoke wheels. Drivetrain Options: Free-wheeling. Startix device. Silent second gear.

OPTIONS: Front bumper. Rear bumper. OSRV mirror. Dual sidemount(s). Sidemount cover(s). Wire wheels. Pedestal mirrors. Radio. Heater. Clock. Cigar Lighter. Radio antenna. Seat Covers. Trippe lights. Spotlight(s). Parking lights (six). Trumpet horns. Trunk rack. Trunk. Whitewall tires. Chrome plated spoke wheels. Power tire pump. Special paint.

TECHNICAL: Introduced November, 1931. Calendar year registrations: 41,968 (incl. Rockne). Calendar year sales: 44,325 (incl. Rockne). Model year production: 47,950 (incl. Rockne). Innovations: Synchromesh transmission. Startix automatic starting system. Vacuum distributor. Higher, wider seats. Counterweighted crankshafts. Improved vibration dampening. Improved brakes. Drop center rims.
Note: Studebaker nearly merged with the White Motor Co. in Oct. 1932. Failure to achieve the merger put Studebaker on the brink of bankruptcy.

1932

Model 55, 6-cyl., 117" wb

	FP	5	4	3	2	1
Conv Rds	915	4950	9900	16,500	23,100	33,000
Reg Conv Rds	1020	5100	10,200	17,000	23,800	34,000
Cpe	840	775	1500	3750	5250	7500
Reg Cpe	945	800	1550	3850	5400	7700
Spt Cpe	890	875	1700	4250	5900	8500
Reg Spt Cpe	995	900	1900	4500	6300	9000
St R Brgm	915	950	2100	4750	6650	9500
Reg St R Brgm	1020	975	2300	4850	6800	9800
Conv Sed	985	4950	9900	16,500	23,100	33,000
Reg Conv Sed	1000	5100	10,200	17,000	23,800	34,000
Sed	915	900	1900	4500	6300	9000
Reg Sed	1020	925	2000	4600	6400	9200

Model 62 Dictator, 8-cyl., 117" wb

Conv Rds	1050	6000	12,000	20,000	28,000	40,000
Reg Conv Rds	1155	6150	12,300	20,500	28,700	41,000
Cpe	980	1550	4500	7500	10,500	15,000
Reg Cpe	1085	1750	4800	8000	11,200	16,000
Spt Cpe	1030	3300	6600	11,000	15,400	22,000
Reg Spt Cpe	1135	3350	6750	11,250	15,750	22,500
St R Brgm	1050	3600	7200	12,000	16,800	24,000
Reg St R Brgm	1155	3650	7350	12,250	17,150	24,500
Conv Sed	1125	5550	11,100	18,500	25,900	37,000
Reg Conv Sed	1230	5700	11,400	19,000	26,600	38,000
Sed	1050	3000	6000	10,000	14,000	20,000
Reg Sed	1155	3100	6150	10,250	14,350	20,500

Model 65 Rockne, 6-cyl., 110" wb

2P Cpe	585	875	1700	4250	5900	8500
5P Sed	635	900	1900	4500	6300	9000
2 dr Sed	595	875	1700	4250	5900	8500
5P Conv Sed	695	4350	8700	14,500	20,300	29,000
Rds	695	4950	9900	16,500	23,100	33,000

Model 71 Commander, 8-cyl.

Rds Conv	1445	6000	12,000	20,000	28,000	40,000
Reg Rds Conv	1550	6150	12,300	20,500	28,700	41,000
Spt Cpe	1350	3600	7200	12,000	16,800	24,000
Reg Spt Cpe	1455	3650	7350	12,250	17,150	24,500
St R Brgm	1445	3900	7800	13,000	18,200	26,000
Reg St R Brgm	1550	4000	7950	13,250	18,550	26,500
Conv Sed	1560	5850	11,700	19,500	27,300	39,000
Reg Conv Sed	1665	6000	12,000	20,000	28,000	40,000
Sed	1445	3000	6000	10,000	14,000	20,000
Reg Sed	1550	3100	6150	10,250	14,350	20,500

Model 75 Rockne, 6-cyl., 114" wb

2P Cpe	685	900	1900	4500	6300	9000
4P Cpe	720	975	2200	4850	6800	9700
5P Sed	735	1000	2400	5000	7000	10,000
2P DeL Cpe	730	975	2200	4850	6800	9700
4P DeL Sed	765	975	2300	4950	6900	9900
5P DeL Sed	780	1025	2600	5250	7300	10,500
Rds	775	5250	10,500	17,500	24,500	35,000
Conv Sed	795	5100	10,200	17,000	23,800	34,000

Model 91 President, 8-cyl.

Rds Conv	1750	8250	16,500	27,500	38,500	55,000
Sta Rds Conv	1855	8400	16,800	28,000	39,200	56,000
Cpe	1595	3750	7500	12,500	17,500	25,000
Sta Cpe	1700	3800	7650	12,750	17,850	25,500
Spt Cpe	1690	3800	7650	12,750	17,850	25,500
Sta Spt Cpe	1795	3800	7650	12,750	17,850	25,500
St R Brgm	1750	4050	8100	13,500	18,900	27,000
Sta St R Brgm	1855	4100	8250	13,750	19,250	27,500
Conv Sed	1880	8100	16,200	27,000	37,800	54,000
Sta Conv Sed	1985	8250	16,500	27,500	38,500	55,000
Sed	1750	3150	6300	10,500	14,700	21,000
Sta Sed	1855	3200	6450	10,750	15,050	21,500
Limo	1890	3300	6600	11,000	15,400	22,000
Sta Limo	1995	3350	6750	11,250	15,750	22,500
7P Sed	1990	3000	6000	10,000	14,000	20,000
7P Sta Sed	2095	3100	6150	10,250	14,350	20,500

1933

1933 Studebaker, Dictator Deluxe, roadster, OCW

STUDEBAKER — SERIES 56 — SIX: For 1933, the vertical grille bars on all Studebakers were extended further downward and came to a rounded "V" at the bottom. Front fenders were of a new, skirted design and the bottom of the leading edge of the rear fenders was given a more rounded contour. Oval-shaped headlights remained a Studebaker styling touch. The Six had larger sized tires and five more horsepower. The rear end styling was of a more streamlined "Beaver tail" design. Standard equipment on Series 56 models included a Stromberg carburetor, Delco Remy ignition, mechanical brakes, ball bearing spring shackles, automatic choke, automatic starter, automatic heat control and automatic ride control. With the company in receivership, sales were very low. The company's financial plight led to temporary discontinuance of the Dictator series.

1933 Studebaker, Commander Regal, convertible sedan, OCW

STUDEBAKER — COMMANDER — SERIES 73 — EIGHT: Like other 1933 models, the Commander-Eights had more streamlined looks with a radically sloped grille, skirted fenders, more sweeping rooflines and Beaver tail rear end styling. New standard included a Stromberg downdraft carburetor, automatic choke and fully automatic spark advance. Other features highlighted in advertising were mechanical brakes, Delco Remy ignition, ball bearing spring shackles, automatic ride control, automatic starter, safety glass and double inside sun visors. Ads also stressed that lubrication points were reduced to four fittings that required greasing at extended 2,500 mile intervals. Like the Studebaker Six, the Commander carried a 14 gallon fuel tank.

STUDEBAKER — PRESIDENT — SERIES 82 — EIGHT: Two President Eight series were offered in 1933. The 82 models were the smaller and less powerful of the two lines; virtually identical in size, performance and features to the 1932 Commander. Styling features included the more radical slant "V" type radiator, skirted fenders, double inside sun visors and Beaver tail rear styling. Standard equipment included a Stromberg carburetor, Delco Remy ignition, Bendix vacuum-boosted power brakes, automatic choke, automatic starter, automatic manifold heat control, downdraft carburetion, ball bearing spring shackles, free wheeling and a 17-1/2 gallon fuel tank.

STUDEBAKER — PRESIDENT SPEEDWAY — SERIES 92 — EIGHT: The most expensive Studebaker line for 1933 was called the Speedway President series. These cars also had new slanting "V" radiators, skirted fenders and Beaver tail rear ends. Double inside sun visors were featured. Gas filler caps were in the left rear fender. Standard equipment included a Stromberg carburetor, Delco Remy ignition, mechanical power brakes, automatic starter, free wheeling, automatic ride control, ball bearing spring shackles and 20-1/2 gallon fuel tanks.

I.D. DATA: [Series 56] Serial numbers were in the same location on the left side of frame over front axle. Starting: 5133401. Ending: 5140262. Engine numbers were on the left side of engine block. Engine numbers were S63001 and up. [Series 73] Serial numbers were in the same location. Starting: 8040001. Ending: 8043781. Engine numbers were on the left side of the block. Engine numbers were C16101 and up. [Series 82] Serial numbers were in the same location. Starting: 7040001. Ending: 7041169. Engine numbers were on the side of the block. Engine numbers were B101 and up. [Series 92] Serial numbers were in the same location. Starting: 6027401. Ending: 6028017. Engine numbers were on the front of the block. Engine numbers were P12501 and up.

Model No.	Body Type & Seating	Price	Weight	Prod. Total
56	2-dr. Conv.-2/4P	915	3165	Note 1
56	2-dr. Reg. Conv.-2/4P	1020	3260	Note 1
56	2-dr. Cpe.-2P	840	3160	Note 1
56	2-dr. Reg. Cpe.-2P	945	3245	Note 1
56	2-dr. Spt. Cpe.-2/4P	890	3210	Note 1
56	2-dr. Reg. Spt. Cpe.-2/4P	995	3300	Note 1
56	2-dr. St. R. Brgm.-5P	915	3300	Note 1
56	2-dr. Reg. St. R. Brgm.-5P	1020	3375	Note 1
56	4-dr. Conv. Sed.-5P	1015	3380	Note 1
56	4-dr. Reg. Conv. Sed.-5P	1120	3460	Note 1
56	4-dr. Sed.-5P	915	3310	Note 1
56	4-dr. Reg. Sed.-5P	1020	3435	Note 1

Note 1: Total production Nov. 1932 to July 1933 was 6,861.

73	2-dr. Rds. Conv.-2/4P	1095	3245	Note 1
73	2-dr. Reg. Rds. Conv.-2/4P	1200	3335	Note 1

Model No.	Body Type & Seating	Price	Weight	Prod. Total
73	2-dr. Cpe.-2P	1000	3220	Note 1
73	2-dr. Reg. Cpe.-2P	1105	3345	Note 1
73	2-dr. Spt. Cpe.-2/4P	1050	3275	Note 1
73	2-dr. Reg. Spt. Cpe.-2/4P	1155	3405	Note 1
73	2-dr. St. R. Brgm.-5P	1075	3375	Note 1
73	2-dr. Reg. St. R. Brgm.-5P	1180	3475	Note 1
73	4-dr. Conv. Sed.-5P	1195	3475	Note 1
73	4-dr. Reg. Conv. Sed.-5P	1300	3545	Note 1
73	4-dr. Sed.-5P	1075	3385	Note 1
73	4-dr. Reg. Sed.-5P	1180	3500	Note 1

Note 1: Total production Nov. 1932 to July 1933 was 3,841.

Model No.	Body Type & Seating	Price	Weight	Prod. Total
82	2-dr. Sta. Rds. Conv.-2/4P	1490	3560	Note 1
82	2-dr. Cpe.-2/4P	1325	3520	Note 1
82	2-dr. Sta. Cpe.-2/4P	1430	3600	Note 1
82	2-dr. St. R. Brgm.-5P	1385	3605	Note 1
82	2-dr. Sta. St. R. Brgm.-5P	1490	3670	Note 1
82	4-dr. Sta. Conv. Sed.-5P	1650	3745	Note 1
82	4-dr. Sed.-5P	1385	3640	Note 1
82	4-dr. Sta. Sed.-5P	1490	3720	Note 1

Note 1: Total production Nov. 1932 to July 1933 was 1,194.

Model No.	Body Type & Seating	Price	Weight	Prod. Total
92	2-dr. Sta. Rds. Conv.-2/4P	1790	4285	Note 1
92	2-dr. Sta. Cpe.-2/4P	1730	4335	Note 1
92	2-dr. Sta. St. Reg. Brgm.-5P	1790	4400	Note 1
92	2-dr. Sta. Conv.-5P	1960	4470	Note 1
92	4-dr. Sta. Sed.-5P	1685	4380	Note 1
92	4-dr. Sta. Sed.-5P	1790	4465	Note 1
92	4-dr. Sed.-7P	1835	4470	Note 1
92	4-dr. Sta. Sed.-7P	1940	4565	Note 1
92	4-dr. Sta. Limo.-7P	2040	4605	Note 1

Note 1: Total production Nov. 1932 to July 1933 was 635.

1933 Studebaker, President Eight Speedway, limousine, AA

ENGINE: [Series 56] L-head. Inline. Six. Cast iron block. B & S: 3-1/4 in. x 4-5/8 in. Disp.: 230 cu. in. C.R.: 5.5:1. Brake H.P.: 85 @ 3200 R.P.M. N.A.C.C. H.P.: 25.4. Main bearings: Four. Valve lifters: Solid. Carb.: Stromberg 2V model EE-22. [Series 73] L-head. Inline. Eight. Cast iron block. B & S: 3-1/16 in. x 4 in. Disp.: 235 cu. in. C.R.: 5.5:1. Brake H.P.: 100 @ 3800 R.P.M. N.A.C.C. H.P.: 30. Main bearings: Nine. Valve lifters: Solid. Carb.: Stromberg V model EX-22. [Series 82] L-head. Inline. Eight. Cast iron block. B & S: 3-1/16 in. x 4-1/4 in. Disp.: 250 cu. in. C.R.: 5.0:1. Brake H.P.: 110 @ 3600 R.P.M. N.A.C.C. H.P.: 30. Main bearings: Nine. Valve lifters: Solid. Carb.: Stromberg 2V model EE-22. [Series 92] L-head. Inline. Eight. Cast iron block. B & S 3-1/2 in. x 4-3/8 in. Disp.: 337 cu. in. C.R.: 5.5:1. Brake H.P.: 132 @ 3400 R.P.M. N.A.C.C. H.P.: 39.2. Main bearings: Nine. Valve lifters: Solid. Carb.: Stromberg 2V model EE-22.

CHASSIS: [Series 56] W.B.: 117 in. Tires: 17 x 5.50. [Series 73] W.B.: 117 in. Tires: 17 x 6.00. [Series 82] W.B.: 125 in. Tires: 17 x 6.50. [Series 92] W.B.: 135 in. Tires: 17 x 7.00.

TECHNICAL: Synchromesh manual transmission. Speeds: 3F/1R Floor mounted gearshift controls. Clutch: single dry disc. Semi-floating rear axle. Overall ratio: (56 and 73) 4.36:1. (82) 4.73:1 and (92) 4.31:1. Vacuum boosted power mechanical brakes. Steel spoke artillery wheels. Drivetrain Option: Free-wheeling.

OPTIONS: Front bumper. Rear bumper. Spare tire. Dual sidemounts. Sidemount cover(s). OSRV mirror. Pedestal mirrors. Radio. Heater. Clock. Cigar lighter. Radio antenna. Chrome plated wheels. Wire spoke wheels. Spotlight(s). Fog lamps. Trippe lights. Trunk rack. Trunk. White pencil stripe tires. Special paint. Dual trumpet horns. Wind wings.

HISTORICAL: Introduced Nov. 1932. Innovations: Downdraft carburetion. Power mechanical brakes. Improved chassis lubrication. Calendar year registrations: 36,242 (incl. Rockne). Model year sales: 43,024 (incl. Rockne). Model year production: 45,074 (incl. Rockne).
Studebaker went into receivership on March 18, 1933. Two weeks later, Rockne sales activities were merged with those of the parent firm and Rockne production was transferred to South Bend. Officers of White Motor Co. were appointed receivers of the corporation.

1933
Model 10 Rockne, 6-cyl., 110" wb

	FP	5	4	3	2	1
4P Conv	675	4200	8400	14,000	19,600	28,000
4P DeL Conv Rds	720	4350	8700	14,500	20,300	29,000
2P Cpe	585	950	2100	4750	6650	9500
5P Coach	595	900	1900	4500	6300	9000
4P Cpe	620	950	2100	4750	6650	9500
2P DeL Cpe	630	900	1900	4500	6300	9000
5P Sed	635	900	1900	4500	6300	9000
5P DeL Coach	640	950	2100	4750	6650	9500
4P DeL Cpe	665	1000	2400	5000	7000	10,000
5P DeL Sed	680	900	1900	4500	6300	9000
5P Conv Sed	695	4050	8100	13,500	18,900	27,000
5P DeL Conv Sed	740	4200	8400	14,000	19,600	28,000

Model 56 Studebaker, 6-cyl., 117" wb

	FP	5	4	3	2	1
Conv	915	4350	8700	14,500	20,300	29,000
Reg Conv	1020	4500	9000	15,000	21,000	30,000
Cpe	840	1150	3500	5900	8250	11,800
Reg Cpe	945	1125	3450	5750	8050	11,500
Spt Cpe	895	1125	3450	5800	8100	11,600
Reg Spt Cpe	995	1150	3550	5950	8300	11,900
St R Brgm	915	1400	4200	7000	9800	14,000
Reg St R Brgm	1020	1450	4250	7150	10,000	14,300
Conv Sed	1015	4200	8400	14,000	19,600	28,000
Reg Conv Sed	1120	4350	8700	14,500	20,300	29,000
Sed	915	1150	3600	6000	8400	12,000
Reg Sed	1020	1200	3750	6250	8750	12,500

Model 73 Commander, 8-cyl.

	FP	5	4	3	2	1
Rds Conv	1095	4500	9000	15,000	21,000	30,000
Reg Rds Conv	1200	4650	9300	15,500	21,700	31,000
Cpe	1000	1150	3600	6000	8400	12,000
Reg Cpe	1105	1200	3700	6200	8700	12,400
Spt Cpe	1050	1175	3650	6100	8500	12,200
Reg Spt Cpe	1155	1200	3800	6300	8800	12,600
St R Brgm	1075	1550	4500	7500	10,500	15,000
Reg St R Brgm	1180	1600	4600	7650	10,700	15,300
Conv Sed	1195	4500	9000	15,000	21,000	30,000
Reg Conv Sed	1300	4650	9300	15,500	21,700	31,000
Sed	1075	1550	4500	7500	10,500	15,000
Reg Sed	1180	1650	4600	7700	10,800	15,400

Model 82 President, 8-cyl.

	FP	5	4	3	2	1
Sta Rds Conv	1490	4950	9900	16,500	23,100	33,000
Cpe	1325	1400	4200	7000	9800	14,000
Sta Cpe	1430	1450	4300	7200	10,100	14,400
St R Brgm	1385	1550	4500	7500	10,500	15,000
Sta St R Brgm	1490	1650	4650	7750	10,850	15,500
Sta Conv Sed	1650	4950	9900	16,500	23,100	33,000
Sed	1385	1075	3000	5500	7700	11,000
Sta Sed	1490	1125	3450	5750	8050	11,500

Model 92 President Speedway, 8-cyl.

	FP	5	4	3	2	1
Sta Rds Conv	1790	5250	10,500	17,500	24,500	35,000
Sta Cpe	1730	1550	4500	7500	10,500	15,000
Sta St R Brgm	1790	2200	5250	8750	12,250	17,500
Sta Conv Sed	1960	5250	10,500	17,500	24,500	35,000
Sed	1685	1000	2400	5000	7000	10,000
Sta Sed	1790	1025	2600	5250	7300	10,500
7P Sed	1835	1100	3200	5600	7800	11,200
7P Sta Sed	1940	1125	3450	5750	8050	11,500
7P Sta Limo	2040	1750	4800	8000	11,200	16,000

1934

1934 Studebaker, Dictator, 5-pass. sedan, AA

STUDEBAKER — DICTATOR — SERIES A — SIX: For 1934, the Dictator returned to the Studebaker lineup as a six-cylinder series. Styling features included a newly designed "V" type slanting radiator, aero-dynamic streamlined bodies, more deeply skirted fenders, slanting hood louvers, single bar V-shaped bumpers and a body belt molding that ran across the hood side and over the body, dropping sharply at the rear. There was a new instrument panel and front windows with integral wind wings. Closed models had streamlined trunks. Regal trim models featured six-wheel equipment. Standard equipment included a Stromberg carburetor, Autolite ignition, steel draulic brakes, safety glass, free wheeling and automatic starter.

STUDEBAKER — DICTATOR — SERIES SPECIAL A — SIX: In Jan. 1934, Studebaker announced a new "Year Ahead" series. The basic features were the same as those found on cars in the Dictator A series. However, there were five additional body styles including an aerodynamic sedan that looked like the famous Pierce Silver Arrow. These cars also had vacuum operated power brakes — previously limited to use on more expensive Studebakers. Safety glass was used in the windshield only to keep selling prices low.

STUDEBAKER — COMMANDER — SERIES B — EIGHT: The 1934 Commanders had more aerodynamic body contours, round headlights with bullet shaped buckets, slanting vertical hood louvers (except horizontal louvers on Custom Land Cruiser sedan), "V" type slanting radiators, more deeply skirted fenders, single bar V-shaped bumpers, front windows with integral wind wings and a body belt molding that sloped sharply at the rear. Regal equipment included two welled fenders and sidemounts. Regal and Custom models had streamlined trunks. Standard features included a Stromberg carburetor, Delco Remy ignition, duo-power mechanical brakes, new instrumental panel and x-frame. The Custom Land Cruiser came with fender skirts.

STUDEBAKER — PRESIDENT — SERIES C — EIGHT: More pronounced streamlining was also seen on 1934 Presidents. They featured recessed trunks, more rounded V-shaped grilles, a wide "V" bumper, built-in taillights, streamlined round headlights and all features found on Commanders. These cars were smaller and lighter than previous Presidents. They had a much smaller, less powerful straight eight under their hoods.

I.D. DATA: [Series A] Serial numbers were in the same location on the left side of frame above front axle. Starting: 5145001 and up. Engine numbers were on the right side of motor block. Engine numbers were D101 and up. [Series Special A] Serial numbers were in the same location. Serial numbers were 5158151 and up. Engine numbers were on the right side of block. Engine numbers were DS101 and up. [Series B] Serial numbers were in the same location. Serial numbers were 8045001 and up. Engine numbers were on the right side of block. Engine numbers were 20001 and up. [Series C] Serial numbers were in the same location and began at 7045001 and up. Engine numbers were on the front of the block and began at B1401 and up.

Model No.	Body Type & Seating	Price	Weight	Prod. Total
A	2-dr. Reg. Cpe.-4P	875	2960	Note 1
A	2-dr. St. R. Sed.-5P	815	2850	Note 1
A	2-dr. Cus. St. R. Sed.-5P	865	2945	Note 1
A	4-dr. Sed.-5P	845	2920	Note 1
A	4-dr. Reg. Sed.-5P	895	3015	Note 1

Note 1: Total production Sept. 1933 to Oct. 1934 was 45,851.

Spl A	2-dr. Cpe.-2P	720	2790	Note 1
Spl A	2-dr. Reg. Cpe.-2P	755	2855	Note 1
Spl A	2-dr. Cpe.-4P	775	2860	Note 1
Spl A	2-dr. Reg. Cpe.-4P	805	2945	Note 1
Spl A	2-dr. St. R. Sed.-5P	745	2835	Note 1
Spl A	2-dr. Reg. St. R. Sed.-5P	795	2930	Note 1
Spl A	4-dr. Sed.-5P	775	2905	Note 1
Spl A	4-dr. Reg. Sed.-5P	825	3000	Note 1
Spl A	2-dr. St. R. Cus. Sed.-5P	795	2885	Note 1
Spl A	4-dr. Cus. Sed.-5P	825	2945	Note 1

Note 1: See Dictator A series total production above.

B	2-dr. Rds. Conv.-4P	1025	3265	Note 1
B	2-dr. Reg. Rds. Conv.-4P	1055	3345	Note 1
B	2-dr. Cpe.-2P	975	3215	Note 1
B	2-dr. Reg. Cpe.-2P	1005	3300	Note 1
B	2-dr. Cpe.-4P	1025	3290	Note 1
B	2-dr. Reg. Cpe.-4P	1055	3360	Note 1
B	2-dr. St. R. Sed.-5P	995	3245	Note 1
B	2-dr. Cus. St. Reg. Sed.-5P	1045	3365	Note 1
B	4-dr. Sed.-5P	1025	3320	Note 1
B	4-dr. Reg. Sed.-5P	1075	3445	Note 1
B	4-dr. Cus. Sed.-5P	1075	3370	Note 1
B	4-dr. Land Cruiser-5P	1220	NA	Note 1

Note 1: Total production Sept. 1933 to Oct. 1934 was 10,315.

C	2-dr. Rds. Conv.-2/4P	1285	3445	Note 1
C	2-dr. Reg. Rds. Conv.-2/4P	1315	3520	Note 1
C	2-dr. Cpe.-2P	1235	3380	Note 1
C	2-dr. Reg. Cpe.-2P	1265	3480	Note 1
C	2-dr. Cpe.-4P	1285	3420	Note 1
C	2-dr. Reg. Cpe.-4P	1315	3520	Note 1
C	4-dr. Sed.-5P	1285	3500	Note 1
C	4-dr. Reg. Sed.-5P	1335	3630	Note 1
C	4-dr. Cus. Sed.-5P	1335	3560	Note 1
C	4-dr. Cus. Berl.-5P	1485	3610	Note 1
C	4-dr. Reg. Berl.-5P	1485	3680	Note 1
C	4-dr. Ld. Cruiser Sed.-5P	1510	NA	Note 1

Note 1: Total production Sept. 1933 to Oct. 1934 was 3,698.

ENGINE: [Dictator Engine] L-head. Inline. Six. Cast iron block. (Aluminum cylinder head.) B & S: 3-1/4 in. x 4-1/8 in. Disp.: 205.3 cu. in. C.R.: 6.3:1. Brake H.P.: 88 @ 3600 R.P.M. N.A.C.C. H.P.: 25.35. Main bearings: Four. Valve lifters: Solid. Carb.: Stromberg 1V model UR21. [Commander Engine] L-head. Inline. Eight. Cast iron block. (aluminum cylinder head.) B & S: 3-1/16 in. x 3-3/4 in. Disp.: 221 cu. in. C.R.: 6.3:1. Brake H.P. 103 @ 3800 R.P.M. N.A.C.C. H.P.: 30. Main bearings: Nine. Valve lifters: Solid. Carb.: Stromberg 1V model E-33. [President Engine] L-head. Inline. Eight. Cast iron block. (Aluminum cylinder head). B & S: 3-1/16 in. x 4-1/4 in. Disp.: 250.4 cu. in. C.R.: 6.3:1. Brake H.P.: 110 @ 3600 R.P.M. N.A.C.C. H.P.: 30. Main bearings: Nine. Valve lifters: Solid. Carb.: Stromberg 2V model EE-22.

CHASSIS: [Series A & SPL.A] W.B.: 113 in. Tires: 17 x 5.50. [Series B] W.B.: 119 in. Tires: 17 x 6.00. [Series C] W.B.: 123 in. Tires: 17 x 6.50.

TECHNICAL: Synchromesh manual transmission. Speeds: 3F/1R. Floor mounted gearshift controls. Clutch: Single plate dry disc type. Semi-floating rear axle. Overall ratio: (Series A) 4.55:1; (Series B) 4.82:1 and (Series C) 4.70:1. Four wheel steeldraulic brakes. Steel artillery spoke wheels. Drivetrain Options: Free-wheeling. Vacuum clutch. Overdrive.

OPTIONS: Front bumper. Rear bumper. Pin stripe Whitewall tires. Dual sidemount(s). Sidemount cover(s). Fender skirts. Bumper guards. Radio. Heater. Clock. Cigar lighter. Radio antenna. Seat covers. Two-tone finish. Spotlight(s). External trumpet horns. Wind wings.

HISTORICAL: Introduced October 1933. Innovations: Steeldraulic brakes on Commander and President. High-compression aluminum cylinder heads. X-type frame. Clock faced speedometer. Triple beam headlights. Improved body construction. Calendar year sales: 46,103. Calendar year registrations: 41,560. Model year production: 51,773.
Studebaker was America's ninth ranked auto-maker in 1934. Paul G. Hoffman became Studebaker's president and lauched a brilliant $10 million advertising campaign that put the company back on its feet. The Studebaker Rockne was no longer manufactured.

1934
Model Special A, Dictator

	FP	5	4	3	2	1
Cpe	720	750	1450	3300	4900	7000
Reg Cpe	755	775	1500	3600	5100	7300
4P Cpe	775	775	1500	3700	5200	7400
4P Reg Cpe	805	800	1550	3850	5400	7700
St R Sed	745	775	1500	3750	5250	7500
Reg St R Sed	795	800	1550	3850	5400	7700
Sed	775	775	1500	3750	5250	7500
Reg Sed	825	800	1550	3900	5450	7800
Cus Reg St R	795	825	1600	4000	5600	8000
Cus Sed	825	825	1600	4050	5650	8100

Model A, Dictator

	FP	5	4	3	2	1
Rdst	800	3600	7200	12,000	16,800	24,000
Rdst Regal	830	3750	7500	12,500	17,500	25,000
Reg Cpe	875	775	1500	3600	5100	7300
St R Sed	815	775	1500	3750	5250	7500
Cus St R Sed	865	800	1550	3850	5400	7700
Sed	845	775	1500	3750	5250	7500
Reg Sed	895	800	1550	3900	5450	7800

Model B, Commander

	FP	5	4	3	2	1
Rds Conv	1025	3750	7500	12,500	17,500	25,000
Reg Rds Conv	1055	3900	7800	13,000	18,200	26,000
Cpe	975	775	1500	3750	5250	7500
Reg Cpe	1005	800	1550	3900	5450	7800
4P Cpe	1025	900	1900	4500	6300	9000
4P Reg Cpe	1055	925	2000	4650	6500	9300
St R Sed	995	800	1550	3900	5450	7800
Cus St R Sed	1045	825	1600	4050	5650	8100
Sed	1025	800	1550	3900	5450	7800
Reg Sed	1075	825	1600	4050	5650	8100
Cus Sed	1075	850	1650	4200	5850	8400
L Cruise	1220	900	1900	4500	6300	9000

Model C, President

	FP	5	4	3	2	1
Rds Conv	1285	4200	8400	14,000	19,600	28,000
Reg Rds Conv	1315	4350	8700	14,500	20,300	29,000
Cpe	1235	900	1800	4400	6150	8800
Reg Cpe	1265	925	1900	4550	6350	9100
4P Cpe	1285	950	2100	4750	6650	9500
4P Reg Cpe	1315	975	2300	4900	6850	9800
Sed	1285	950	2100	4700	6600	9400
Reg Sed	1335	975	2200	4850	6800	9700
Cus Sed	1335	1000	2400	5000	7000	10,000
Cus Berl	1485	1025	2500	5150	7150	10,300
L Cruise	1510	950	2200	4800	6700	9600

1935

1934 Studebaker, President, custom sedan, AA

1935 Studebaker, Dictator, 3-pass. coupe, AA

STUDEBAKER — DICTATOR — SERIES 1A/2A — SIX: A longer, narrower grille with a rakish slant was used on 1935 Dictators. It was topped with a bird-in-flight hood ornament. Long, horizontal louvers graced the hood side panels. Longer, bullet-shaped headlight buckets were seen. The front bumper was no longer V-shaped. It ran straight across the car, with a slight bow at its center. The Series 1A and 2A models were identical except for front axle design. The 1A models had a solid front axle. The 2A models had the new Independent Planar Wheel Suspension and cost $25 more on the coupe and $35 more on other standard body styles. On Dictator Regals the weight was 15 pounds higher and standard equipment included free wheeling, startix, dual windshield wipers, dual sun visors, dual tail-lamps, robe rail and ash receivers. Front opening "Suicide doors" were used on 1935 Studebakers. All 1935 Studebaker Roadsters had roll-up windows and were really true convertibles.

STUDEBAKER — COMMANDER — SERIES 1B — EIGHT: Styling changes for 1935 Commanders were basically the same as those seen on Dictators. The Commander wheelbase was six inches longer. External trumpet horns were mounted below the front headlights on Commander models. Planar front wheel suspension was standard equipment. A cast iron cylinder head was standard, while the high-compression aluminum head was optional.

1935 Studebaker, President Custom, 4-dr. sedan, OCW

STUDEBAKER — PRESIDENT — SERIES 1C — EIGHT: The 1935 President was virtually identical to the Commander in terms of its basic styling. The wheelbase was four inches longer. Presidents had a 17-1/2 gallon fuel tank, compared to 14-1/2 gallons on Dictators and Commanders. Although the two eight-cylinder lines used the same inline engine, the President had more horsepower due to its higher compression aluminum cylinder head. (Note: This feature was optional on Commanders.) Warner Gear automatic overdrive was standard equipment in Presidents. The cars in this series had a Flying Godess type hood mascot.

I.D. DATA: [Series 1A/2A] Serial numbers were stamped on a plate riveted to side member of frame under left front fender or to the left or right front door hinge pillar. Starting: 5500001. Ending: 5512000. Engine numbers were stamped on the left center of engine block above distributor. Starting: D-27501. Ending: D-62850. [Series 1B] Serial numbers were in the same location. Starting: 8103001. Ending: 8109000. Engine numbers were located on the left corner of engine above the water jacket cover. Starting: C-30501. Ending: C-36650. [Series 1C] Serial numbers were in the same location. Starting: 7101001. Ending: 7104000. Engine numbers were stamped on the left corner of block above water jacket cover. Starting: B-5501. Ending: B-7900.

Model No.	Body Type & Seating	Price	Weight	Prod. Total
1A/2A	2-dr. Rds.-3/5P	745	2985	Note 1
1A/2A	2-dr. Reg. Rds.-3/5P	775	3070	Note 1
1A/2A	2-dr. Cpe.-3P	695	2895	Note 1
1A/2A	2-dr. Reg. Cpe.-3P	725	3005	Note 1
1A/2A	2-dr. Cpe.-3/5P	745	2995	Note 1
1A/2A	2-dr. Reg. Cpe.-3/5P	775	3070	Note 1
1A/2A	2-dr. St. R. Sed.-5P	715	2965	Note 1
1A/2A	2-dr. Reg. St. Sed.-5P	755	3085	Note 1
1A/2A	2-dr. Cus. St. R. Sed.-5P	740	3035	Note 1
1A/2A	4-dr. Sed.-6P	745	3030	Note 1
1A/2A	4-dr. Reg. Sed.-6P	785	3160	Note 1
1A/2A	4-dr. Cus. Sed.-6P	770	3085	Note 1
1A/2A	4-dr. L. Cr. Sed.-5P	880	3100	Note 1
1A/2A	4-dr. Reg. L. Cr. Sed.-5P	895	3220	Note 1

Note 1: The Series 1A Dictator was built Dec. 1934 to Sept. 1935; total production was 11,742. The Series 2A Dictator was built Nov. 1934 to Sept. 1935; total production was 23,550.

Note 2: Series 2A Dictators had serial numbers 5,212,001 to 5,235,000 and engine numbers D-27501 to D-62850. The 3-passenger 2A coupe was $25 extra; the other standard 2A Dictators were $35 extra. Series 2A Regals were $40 extra.

Model No.	Body Type & Seating	Price	Weight	Prod. Total
1B	2-dr. Rds.-3/5P	980	3510	Note 1
1B	2-dr. Reg. Rds.-3/5P	1010	3570	Note 1
1B	2-dr. Cpe.-3P	925	3420	Note 1
1B	2-dr. Reg. Cpe.-3P	960	3510	Note 1
1B	2-dr. R/S Cpe.-3/5P	980	3520	Note 1
1B	2-dr. Reg. R/S Cpe.-3/5P	1010	3570	Note 1
1B	2-dr. Reg. St. R. Sed.-5P	1000	3620	Note 1
1B	2-dr. Cus. St. R. Sed.-5P	985	3550	Note 1
1B	4-dr. Reg. Sed.-6P	1030	3685	Note 1
1B	4-dr. Cus. Sed.-6P	1015	3600	Note 1

Model No.	Body Type & Seating	Price	Weight	Prod. Total
1B	4-dr. L. Cr. Sed.-5P	1115	3625	Note 1
1B	4-dr. Reg. L. Cr. Sed.-5P	1130	3720	Note 1

Note 1: Total production Nov. 1934 to Sept. 1935 was 6,085.

Model No.	Body Type & Seating	Price	Weight	Prod. Total
1C	2-dr. Rds.-3/5P	1295	3645	Note 1
1C	2-dr. Reg. Rds.-3/5P	1325	3740	Note 1
1C	2-dr. Cpe.-3P	1245	3600	Note 1
1C	2-dr. Reg. Cpe.-3P	1275	3685	Note 1
1C	2-dr. R/S Cpe.-3/5P	1295	3660	Note 1
1C	2-dr. Reg. R/S Cpe.-3/5P	1325	3740	Note 1
1C	4-dr. Reg. Sed.-6P	1345	3900	Note 1
1C	4-dr. Cus. Sed.-6P	1330	3790	Note 1
1C	4-dr. L. Cr.-5P	1430	3820	Note 1
1C	4-dr. Reg. L. Cr.-5P	1445	3900	Note 1
1C	4-dr. Cus. Berl.-5P	1430	3900	Note 1
1C	4-dr. Reg. Berl.-5P	1445	3970	Note 1

Note 1: Total production Nov. 1934 to Sept. 1935 was 2,305.

ENGINE: [Six-cylinder Engine] L-head. Inline. Six. Cast iron block. B & S: 3-1/4 in. x 4-1/8 in. Disp.: 205.3 cu. in. C.R.: 6.3:1. Brake H.P.: 88 @ 3600 R.P.M. N.A.C.C. H.P.: 25.35. Main bearings: Four. Valve lifters: Solid. Carb.: Stromberg 1V model EX22. [Eight-cylinder Engine] L-head. Inline. Eight. Cast iron blcok. B & S: 3-1/16 in. x 4-1/2 in. Disp.: 250 cu. in. C.R.: (1B) 6.0:1; (1C) 6.5:1. Brake H.P.: (1B) 107 at 3800 R.P.M.: (1C) 110 at 3600 R.P.M. N.A.C.C. H.P.: (both) 30.01. Main bearings: Nine. Valve lifters: Solid. Carb.: (1B) Stromberg EE-1; (1C) same.

CHASSIS: [Series 1A/2A] W.B.: 114 in. Tires: 16 x 6.00 or 17 x 5.50. [Series 1B] W.B.: 120 in. Tires: 16 x 6.50. [Series 1C] W.B.: 124 in. Tires: 16 x 7.00.

TECHNICAL: Synchromesh transmission. Speeds: 3F/1R. Floor shift controls. Single plate dry disc clutch. Shaft drive. Semi-floating rear axle. Overall ratios: (1A) 4.11:1; (1B) 4.09:1; (1C) 4.09:1. Four-wheel hydraulic brakes. Steel artillery spoke wheels. Drivetrain Options: Free-Wheeling. Overdrive was standard equipment on 1935 Presidents.

OPTIONS: Front bumper. Rear bumper. Whitewall tires. Dual sidemount(s). Sidemount cover(s). Fender skirts. Bumper guards. Radio. Heater. Clock. Cigar lighter. Radio antenna. Seat covers. OSRV mirror. Spotlight(s). Pedestal sidemount mirrors. Wheel trim rings. Two-tone paint. Planar suspension on Dictators ($25-40).

HISTORICAL: Introduced December 28, 1934. Innovations: Planar Front Wheel Suspension. Automatic overdrive. Hydraulic brakes. Champion name for advertising and promotional purposes. Provision for radio mounting in all cars. Calendar year registrations: 39,573. Calendar year sales: 49,062. Model year production: 36,504.

A 1935 Studebaker sedan, riding on the ties of the longest electric railway bridge in the world — near Berrien Springs, Mich., traveled 60 m.p.h. in a promotion designed to highlight the advantages of Planar front wheel suspension. Studebaker was America's 11th ranked auto-maker this season.

1935
Model 1A, Dictator Six

	FP	5	4	3	2	1
Rds	745	3300	6600	11,000	15,400	22,000
Reg Rds	775	3400	6900	11,500	16,100	23,000
Cpe	695	700	1350	2700	4500	6400
Reg Cpe	725	725	1400	3000	4700	6700
R/S Cpe	745	725	1400	3200	4850	6900
Reg R/S Cpe	775	750	1450	3500	5050	7200
St Reg	715	675	1300	2500	4350	6200
Reg St Reg	755	700	1350	2800	4550	6500
Cus St Reg	740	725	1400	3100	4800	6800
Sed	745	650	1250	2400	4200	6000
Reg Sed	785	675	1300	2600	4400	6300
Cus Sed	770	700	1350	2900	4600	6600
L Cr	880	700	1350	2900	4600	6600
Reg L Cr	895	725	1400	3200	4850	6900

Model 1B, Commander Eight

	FP	5	4	3	2	1
Rds	980	3750	7500	12,500	17,500	25,000
Reg Rds	1010	3900	7800	13,000	18,200	26,000
Cpe	925	800	1550	3800	5300	7600
Reg Cpe	960	825	1600	4000	5600	8000
R/S Cpe	980	900	1900	4500	6300	9000
Reg R/S Cpe	1010	950	2100	4750	6650	9500
Reg St R	1000	775	1500	3700	5200	7400
Cus St R	985	800	1550	3850	5400	7700
Reg Sed	1030	775	1500	3750	5250	7500
Cus Sed	1015	800	1550	3900	5450	7800
L Cr	1115	875	1700	4250	5900	8500
Reg L Cr	1130	900	1800	4400	6150	8800

Model 1C, President Eight

	FP	5	4	3	2	1
Rds	1295	3900	7800	13,000	18,200	26,000
Reg Rds	1325	4050	8100	13,500	18,900	27,000
Cpe	1245	875	1700	4350	6050	8700
Reg Cpe	1275	900	1900	4500	6300	9000
R/S Cpe	1295	950	2100	4700	6600	9400
Reg R/S Cpe	1325	975	2200	4850	6800	9700
Reg Sed	1345	950	2200	4800	6700	9600
Cus Sed	1330	975	2300	4950	6900	9900
L Cr	1430	1025	2600	5250	7300	10,500
Reg L Cr	1445	1050	2800	5400	7500	10,800
Cus Berl	1430	1250	3900	6500	9100	13,000
Reg Berl	1445	1300	4000	6650	9300	13,300

NOTE: Add 10 percent for 2A Dictator models.

1936

1936 Studebaker, Dictator, 3-pass. coupe, AA

STUDEBAKER — DICTATOR — SERIES 3A/4A — SIX: There was no Commander series in 1936. The Dictators were on a new 116 inch wheelbase. Styling was much more conventional, but still attractive. Features included a die-cast grille, divided windshield, even longer bullet shaped headlamps and hood trim with four, slim groupings of horizontal louvers with chrome spears on each end. New, free-standing, bullet-shaped taillights were seen. Studebaker returned to conventional front doors that were hinged at the A-pillar and opened from the rear. Planar front suspension was, again, a low cost option.

STUDEBAKER — PRESIDENT — SERIES 2C — EIGHT: President styling changes were basically the same ones that Dictators had. The President wheelbase was nine inches longer. A distinctive hood ornament that was raised above the nose was used for Presidents. The hood side louvers, while of generally similar design, were full-lengh moldings. Planar front wheel suspension was standard equipment. Designer interior appointments were featured.

I.D. DATA: [Series 3A/4A] Serial numbers were in the same location on a plate riveted to side member of frame under left front fender or on left or right front hinge pillar. Starting: 5,512,001; (West Coast) 5,850,001. Ending: 5536000; (West Coast) 5852800. Series 4A models, with independent suspension, had serial numbers 5235001 to 5255000 for South Bend production and serial numbers 5800001 to 5802500 for west coast production. Engine numbers were stamped on the left center of block above distributor. Starting: D-63001. Ending: D-112600. [Series 2C] Serial numbers were in the same location. Starting: 7104001; (West Coast) 7800001. Ending: 7111000; (West Coast) 7800800. Engine numbers were stamped on the left corner of block above water jacket cover. Starting: B-7901. Ending: B-15500.

Model No.	Body Type & Seating	Price	Weight	Prod. Total
3A/4A	2-dr. Bus. Cpe.-3P	665	2910	Note 1
3A/4A	2-dr. Cus. Cpe.-3P	695	2965	Note 1
3A/4A	2-dr. Cus. Cpe.-5P	720	3020	Note 1
3A/4A	2-dr. Cus. St. Reg.-5P	725	3075	Note 1
3A/4A	2-dr. Cr. St. Reg.-5P	745	3080	Note 1
3A/4A	4-dr. Cus. Sed.-6P	755	3110	Note 1
3A/4A	4-dr. Cr. Sed.-6P	775	3120	Note 1

Note 1: Total production Oct. 1935 to June 1936 included 26,634 Dictator 3As with conventional front axles and 22,029 Dictator 4As with independent front suspension.
Note 2: The "cruising" models (Cr. St. Reg. and Cr. Sed.) had built in trunks. The "custom" sedans were slant-back models.

2C	2-dr. Cus. Cpe.-3P	965	3460	Note 1
2C	2-dr. Cus. Cpe.-5P	995	3515	Note 1
2C	2-dr. St. Reg. Cus.-5P	1015	3560	Note 1
2C	2-dr. St. R. Cr.-5P	1035	3570	Note 1
2C	4-dr. Cus. Sed.-6P	1045	3600	Note 1
2C	4-dr. Cus. Cr. Sed.-6P	1065	3615	Note 1

Note 1: Total production Oct. 1935 to June 1936 was 7,297.

1936 Studebaker, President, 3-pass. coupe, AA

ENGINE: [Dictator Engine] L-head. Inline. Six. Cast iron block. B & S: 3-1/4 in. x 4-3/8 in. Disp.: 217.8 cu. in. C.R.: 6.3:1. Brake H.P.: 90 @ 3400 R.P.M. N.A.C.C. H.P.: 25.35. Main bearings: Four. Valve lifters: Solid. Carb.: Stromberg model EX23-1V. [President Engine] L-head. Inline. Eight. Cast iron block. B & S: 3-1/16 in. x 4-1/6 in. Disp.: 250.4 cu. in. C.R.: 6.5:1. Brake H.P.: 115 @ 3600 R.P.M. N.A.C.C. H.P.: 30.01. Main bearings: Nine. Valve lifters: Solid. Carb.: Stromberg 2V model EE-22.

CHASSIS: [Dictator Series 3A/4A] W.B.: 116 in. Tires: 16 x 6.00. [President Series 2C] W.B.: 125 in. Tires: 16 x 6.50.

TECHNICAL: Synchromesh manual transmission. Speeds: 3F/1R. Floor shift controls. Single plate dry disc clutch. Shaft drive. Semi-floating rear axle. Overall ratio: (all) 4.55:1. Four wheel hydraulic brakes. Steel artillery spoke wheels. Drivetrain Options: Vacuum clutch. Hill holder. Free wheeling.

OPTIONS: Front bumper. Rear bumper. Whitewall tires. Dual sidemount(s). Sidemount cover(s). Fender skirts. Bumper guards. Radio. Heater. Clock. Cigar lighter. Radio antenna. Seat covers. Dual taillights. Spotlight(s). Dual sun visors. OSRV mirror. Pedestal sidemount mirrors. Full wheel covers. Wheel trim ring(s). Independent front suspension, Dictator ($20).

HISTORICAL: Introduced November 2, 1935. Innovations: Hill-holder. Increased leg room. All-steel top construction. 18-gallon fuel tank on all Studebakers. Roomier bodies. Designer interiors by Miss Helen Dryden. Improved engine mountings. Dictator engine moved forward by four inches. Calendar year registrations: 67,835. Calendar year sales: 85,026. Model year production: 63,664.

A Dictator Six placed first in its class in California's National Gas Economy Classic by averaging 24.27 m.p.g. A President Eight was also first in its class with 20.34 m.p.g. Studebaker was America's ninth ranked manufacturer in 1936.

1936
Model 3A/4A, Dictator Six

	FP	5	4	3	2	1
Bus Cpe	665	650	1250	2400	4150	5900
Cus Cpe	695	675	1300	2500	4350	6200
5P Cus Cpe	720	725	1400	3000	4700	6700
Cus St R	725	600	1200	2300	4000	5700
Cr St R	745	650	1250	2400	4200	6000
Cus Sed	755	650	1250	2400	4200	6000
Cr Sed	775	675	1300	2600	4400	6300

Model 2C, President Eight

Cus Cpe	965	875	1700	4350	6050	8700
5P Cus Cpe	995	975	2200	4850	6800	9700
Cus St R	1015	875	1700	4350	6050	8700
Cr St R	1035	900	1900	4500	6300	9000
Cus Sed	1045	925	2000	4600	6400	9200
Cr Sed	1065	950	2100	4750	6650	9500

NOTE: Add 10 percent for Model 4A Dictator Six.

1937

1937 Studebaker, Dictator, 5-pass. coupe, AA

STUDEBAKER — DICTATOR — SERIES 5A/6A — SIX: All 1937 Studebakers had new front end styling. Hoods were of one piece construction. They were hinged at the cowl and raised from the front. The slanting, rounded radiator shell had horizontal grille bars. The top portion of the grille bars extended along the sides of the hood, forming ventilating louvers. A new feature, dual built-in warm air windshield defrosters, was available. A new flat type, 18 gallon gas tank, provided increased space in the trunk. A new safety feature was rotary door latches with safety catches. Standard equipment included a gas gauge, engine thermometer, Autolite ignition lock, Geo. W. Borg clock, Casco cigar lighter, safety glass, one sun visor, dual windshield wipers, bumper, Houde shock absorbers, spring covers and Budd steel disc wheels. Planar front wheel suspension was used on the Series 6A models, which cost $20 more than similar body styles having a straight front axle. The 2-door St. Regis Cruising Sedan and 4-door Cruising Sedan were trunk-back body styles.

STUDEBAKER — PRESIDENT — SERIES 3C — EIGHT: Styling for Presidents was virtually identical to that used for Dictators. The President chassis had a 125 inch wheelbase. The Presidents had a Delco Remy ignition system, instead of the Autolite system used in Dictators. Dual sun visors were standard, in addition to all other features included on Dictators. The "State" models, with deluxe equipment features, were $30 higher in price.

I.D. DATA: [Series 5A/6A] Serial numbers were in the same location, stamped on a plate riveted to frame side member under left front fender. Starting: 5536001; (W. Coast) 5852801. Ending: 5581500; (W. Coast) 5857400. Engine numbers were on the right center of block just below cylinder head. Starting: D-112601. Ending: D-201637. [Series 3C] Serial numbers were in the same location. Starting: 7111001; (W. Coast) 7800801. Ending: 7119150; (W. Coast) 7801750. Engine numbers were on the front of block between fan bracket and cylinder head. Starting: B-15501. Ending: B-24504.

Model No.	Body Type & Seating	Price	Weight	Prod. Total
5A/6A	2-dr. Bus. Cpe.-3P	765	2695	Note 1
5A/6A	2-dr. Cus. Cpe.-3P	820	3005	Note 1
5A/6A	2-dr. Cus. Cpe.-5P	845	3045	Note 1
5A/6A	2-dr. Cus. St. R.-5P	850	3100	Note 1
5A/6A	2-dr. St. R. Cr.-6P	870	3100	Note 1
5A/6A	4-dr. Cus. Sed.-6P	880	3130	Note 1
5A/6A	4-dr. Cr. Sed.-6P	900	3140	Note 1

Note 1: Total production of Series 5A Dictators from Aug. 1936 to July 1937 was 50,001. Total production of Series 6A Dictators from Aug. 1936 to July 1937 was 39,001.

Model No.	Body Type & Seating	Price	Weight	Prod. Total
3C	2-dr. Cus. Cpe.-3P	1085	3510	Note 1
3C	2-dr. Cus. Cpe.-5P	1115	3540	Note 1
3C	2-dr. Cus. St. R.-5P	1135	3600	Note 1
3C	2-dr. St. R. Cr.-5P	1155	3610	Note 1
3C	4-dr. Cus. Sed.-6P	1165	3620	Note 1
3C	4-dr. Cr. Sed.-6P	1185	3635	Note 1

Note 1: Total production Aug. 1936 to July 1937 was 9,001.
Note 2: Add $30 to list price for cars with State equipment.

ENGINE: [Dictator Engine] L-head. Inline. Six. Cast iron block. B & S: 3-1/4 in. x 4-3/8 in. Disp.: 217.8 cu. in. C.R.: 6.0:1. Brake H.P.: 90 @ 3400 R.P.M. N.A.C.C. H.P.: 25.4. Main bearings: Four. Valve lifters: Solid. Carb.: Stromberg. 1V model EX23. [President Engine] L-head. Inline. Eight. Cast iron block. B & S: 3-1/16 in. x 4-1/4 in. Disp.: 250.4 cu. in. C.R.: 6.5:1. Brake H.P.: 115 @ 3600 R.P.M. N.A.C.C. H.P.: 30.01. Main bearings: Nine. Valve lifters: Solid. Carb.: Stromberg 2V model EE-1.

CHASSIS: [Series 5A/6A] W.B.: 116 in. Tires: 16 x 6.00. [Series 3C] W.B.: 125 in. Tires 16 x 6.50.

TECHNICAL: Synchromesh manual transmission. Speeds: 3 F/1R. Floor-mounted gearshift controls. Clutch: Borg & Beck single dry disc clutch. Hypoid rear axle. Overall ratio: (all) 4.55:1. Four-wheel hydraulic brakes. Steel disc wheels. Drivetrain Options: Manual overdrive. Positive control automatic overdrive. Automatic Hill-Holder.

OPTIONS: Whitewall tires. Full wheel discs. Wheel trim rings. Dual sidemount(s). Sidemount cover(s). Fender skirts. Bumper guards. Radio. Heater. Clock. Cigar lighter. Radio antenna. Seat covers. Parking lights. Spotlight(s). Sun roof. License plate frames. Special paint. State president equipment (30.00). Dictator 6A planar front wheel suspension (20.00). OSRV mirror. Dual defroster system.

HISTORICAL: Introduced September 4, 1936. Innovations: Parking brake relocated. Built-in defroster system. Rotary door latches. Hypoid rear axles. Direct action front shock absorbers on 6A and 3C models. New automatic overdrive option. Calendar year registratons: 70,048. Model year sales: 80,993. Model year production: 82,627.

Some station wagons were built on the Dictator chassis by specialty body building firms. Studebaker made a small profit for the second year in a row. The company was America's 11th ranked auto-maker.

1937
Model 5A/6A, Dictator Six

	FP	5	4	3	2	1
Cpe Express	820	825	1600	4000	5600	8000
Bus Cpe	765	650	1250	2400	4150	5900
Cus Cpe	820	675	1300	2500	4350	6200
5P Cus Cpe	845	725	1400	3000	4700	6700
Cus St R	850	650	1250	2400	4200	6000
St R Cr	870	650	1250	2400	4150	5900
Cus Sed	880	650	1250	2400	4150	5900
Cr Sed	900	675	1300	2500	4350	6200

Model 3C, President Eight

Cus Cpe	1085	900	1900	4500	6300	9000
5P Cus Cpe	1115	925	2000	4650	6500	9300
Cus St R	1135	875	1700	4350	6050	8700
St R Cr	1155	875	1700	4300	6000	8600
Cus Sed	1165	875	1700	4300	6000	8600
Cr Sed	1185	900	1800	4450	6250	8900

NOTE: Add 10 percent for Dictator 6A models.

1938

STUDEBAKER — COMMANDER — SERIES 7A — SIX: All 1938 Studebakers had much smoother styling lines. The bodies were lower and six inches wider. Louvers were eliminated from the hood side panels. A chrome bead molding stretched from the grille to the rear deck. Seats were moved forward 5-1/2 inches and engines were moved forward 3-1/2 inches. The Dictator series was discontinued. Replacing it was the Studebaker/Commander Six. These cars had conventional, bullet shaped headlight buckets on the front fender catwalks. A new instrument panel had square guage clusters. In the center was a square-faced clock set into an ornate, rectangular trim panel decorated with horizontal moldings. A lower front tunnel was created by turning the transmission sideways. Planar suspension, safety glass, dual tallights, dual wipers and divided windshields were standard equipment. A single sun visor was featured. Also included at regular price was a speedometer, engine thermometer, Autolight ignition, Borg clock, Casco cigar lighter, two-way Houde shock absorbers, spring covers and Budd steel disc wheels. A new type of steer-

1938 Studebaker, Commander, cruising sedan, AA

STUDEBAKER — STATE COMMANDER — SERIES 8A — SIX: The State Commander was basically the same car as the base Commander, except that President type headlamps were added. They were oblong shaped and tapered to a rounded back which was faired into the fenders. Standard equipment for this line included everything used on the low-priced Commander plus a deluxe steering wheel, twin horns and Hill-Holder.

1938 Studebaker, President, convertible sedan, AA

STUDEBAKER — STATE PRESIDENT — SERIES 4C — EIGHT: The difference in wheelbase between Presidents and Commanders was down to 5-1/2 inches this year. Styling changes for these models were similar to those used for State Commanders including the oblong-tapered headlamp fairings. Standard equipment included everything found on State Commanders plus/except Delco Remy ignition, twin sun visors, larger tires and a different carburetor.

I.D. DATA: [Series 7A] Serial numbers were in the same location, stamped on a plate riveted to frame side member under left front fender. Starting: 5582001; (W. Coast) 5857501. Ending: 5599146; (W. Coast) 5859614. Engine numbers were on the right center of block just below cylinder head. Starting: H-101. Ending: H-42253. [Series 8A] Serial numbers were in the same location. Starting: 4090001; (W. Coast) 4800001. Ending: 4109817; (W. Coast) 4802235. Engine numbers were in the same location. Starting: H-101. Ending: H-42253. [Series 4C] Serial numbers were in the same location. Starting: 7120101; (W. Coast) 7801801. Ending: 7125062; (W. Coast) 7802311. Engine numbers were on the front of block between fan bracket and cylinder head. Starting: B-24601. Ending: B-30090.

Model No.	Body Type & Seating	Price	Weight	Prod. Total
7A	2-dr. Bus. Cpe.-3P	875	3045	Note 1
7A	2-dr. Cus. Cpe.-3P	900	3060	Note 1
7A	2-dr. Clb. Sed.-6P	955	3140	Note 1
7A	4-dr. Cr. Sed.-6P	965	3190	Note 1
7A	4-dr. Conv. Sed.-6P	1315	3390	Note 1

Note 1: Total production Sept. 1937 to July 1938 was 19,260.

8A	2-dr. Cus. Cpe.-3P	965	3095	Note 1
8A	2-dr. Clb. Sed.-6P	1030	3160	Note 1

Model No.	Body Type & Seating	Price	Weight	Prod. Total
8A	4-dr. Cr. Sed.-6P	1040	3215	Note 1
8A	4-dr. Conv. Sed.-6P	1365	3400	Note 1

Note 1: Total production Aug. 1937 to July 1938 was 22,053.

President Eight

4C	2-dr. Cpe-3P	1120	3315	Note 1
4C	2-dr. Clb. Sed.-6P	1185	3400	Note 1
4C	4-dr. Cr. Sed.-6P	1195	3455	Note 1

State President Eight

4C	2-dr. Cpe.-3P	1130	3315	Note 1
4C	2-dr. Clb. Sed.-6P	1195	3400	Note 1
4C	4-dr. Cr. Sed.-6P	1205	3455	Note 1
4C	4-dr. Conv. Sed.-6P	1555	3640	Note 1

Note 1: Total production Sept. 1937 to July 1938 was 5,474.

ENGINE: [Six-Cylinder Engine] L-head. Inline. Six. Cast iron block. B & S: 3-5/16 in. x 4-3/8 in. Disp.: 226.0 cu. in. C.R.: 6.0:1. Brake H.P.: 90 @ 3400 R.P.M. N.A.C.C. H.P.: 26.35. Main bearings: Four. Valve lifters: Solid. Carb.: Stromberg 1V model BX026. Compression: 105 lbs.-ft. at 150 R.P.M. [Eight-Cylinder] L-head. Inline. Eight. Cast iron block. B & S: 3-1/16 in. x 4-1/4 in. Disp.: 250.4 cu. in. C.R.: 6.0:1. Brake H.P.: 110 @ 3600 R.P.M. N.A.C.C. H.P.: 30.00. Main bearings: Nine. Valve lifters: Solid. Carb.: Stromberg 2V model AA0161. Compression: 105 lbs.-ft. at 150 R.P.M.

CHASSIS: [Series 7A] W.B.: 116-1/2 in. O.L.: 193-3/4 in. Frt/Rear Tread: 59.5/59.5 in. Tires: 6.00 x 16. [Series 8A] W.B.: 116-1/2 in. O.L.: 193-1/4 in. Frt/Rear Tread: 59.5/59.5 in. Tires: 6.00 x 16. [Series 4C] W.B.: 122 in. O.L.: 199-1/4 in. Frt/Rear Tread: 59.5/59.5 in. Tires: 6.50 x 16.

TECHNICAL: Synchromesh manual transmission. Speeds: 3F/1R. Floor-mounted gearshift controls. Single-disc dry plate clutch. Hypoid semi-floating rear axle. Overall ratio: (all) 4.55:1. Four wheel hydraulic brakes. Budd steel disc wheels. Drivetrain Options: Vacuum clutch. Hill-holder. Dash mounted transmission controls. Automatic overdrive.

OPTIONS: Whitewall tires. Full wheel discs. Wheel trim rings. Dual sidemount(s). Sidemount cover(s). Fender skirts. Bumper guards. Radio. Heater. Clock. Cigar lighter. Radio antenna. Seat covers. Special paint. Spotlight(s). Deluxe steering wheel (in base Six). Dual horns (on base Six). "Miracle" shift lever. OSRV mirror. Dual sun visors (Commanders). Defroster. Front fender parking lights.

HISTORICAL: Introduced September, 1937. Innovations: Optional dash mounted Miracle shift vacuum transmission control. Triple tie rod steering. Increased bore on six-cylinder engine. Five inch wider front seat cushions. Low profile transmission mounting. Wider brake linings. Calendar year registrations: 41,504. Calendar year production: 92,200. Model year sales: 46,207. Model year production: 46,787.

Studebaker was back in red ink this season despite moving to 10th position in domestic automobile sales. The reason for changing the Dictator name was negative associations with German dictator Adolf Hitler.

1938
Model 7A, Commander Six

	FP	5	4	3	2	1
Cpe Express	900	825	1600	4000	5600	8000
Bus Cpe	875	750	1450	3300	4900	7000
Cus Cpe	900	775	1500	3600	5100	7300
Clb Sed	955	750	1450	3400	5000	7100
Cr Sed	965	775	1500	3600	5100	7300
Conv Sed	1315	3750	7500	12,500	17,500	25,000

Model 8A, State Commander Six

Cus Cpe	965	775	1500	3600	5100	7300
Clb Sed	1030	750	1450	3400	5000	7100
Cr Sed	1040	775	1500	3600	5100	7300
Conv Sed	1365	3900	7800	13,000	18,200	26,000

Model 4C, President Eight

Cpe	1120	975	2300	4900	6850	9800
Clb Sed	1185	950	2100	4750	6650	9500
Cr Sed	1195	1000	2400	5000	7000	10,000

Model 4C, State President Eight

Cpe	1130	1000	2400	5050	7050	10,100
Clb Sed	1195	975	2300	4900	6850	9800
Cr Sed	1205	1025	2600	5250	7300	10,500
Conv Sed	1555	4350	8700	14,500	20,300	29,000

1939

1939 Studebaker, Champion, 5-pass. sedan, AA

STUDEBAKER — CHAMPION — SERIES G — SIX: The Champion was a new series for mid-1939. It featured horizontal radiator grille bars with vertical bars on each side. The side of the car was decorated with a long bead molding that ran from the rear quarter to the nose and two additional moldings below it on the hood side panels. Another chrome strip ran down the center of the hood and dropped to the grille. The front bumper was plain. Standard equipment on custom Champions included Planar front wheel suspension, steering column gear shift lever, variable ratio steering, speedometer, gas gauge, engine thermometer, Auto Lite ignition, Trico windshield wiper, bumpers, two-way Houde shock absorbers, spring covers, Budd steel disc wheels, single taillight, single sun visor and single horn. Custom models were the economy line and came without chrome inside door trim and with dashboards painted body color. Deluxe Champions also had front door arm rests, dual wipers, dual sun visors, dual taillamps, rear seat ash trays, ventilating quarter windows, broadcloth upholstery and chrome door sill panels.

1939 Studebaker, Commander, station wagon, OCW

STUDEBAKER — COMMANDER — SERIES 9A — SIX: The new Studebakers had a massive, but graceful hood that tapered to a prow-like front decorated with a verticle chrome strip. Flanking the hood were grilles with vertical chrome bars located in the front splash aprons. Headlamps and taillamps were flush with the fenders. The Studebaker name appeared in script on the center of the bumper and an attractive "S" emblem was placed just below the nose of the alligator style hood. A long chrome molding ran from the rear quarters to the nose, on the upper beltline. The hood side panels were decorated with two additional chrome strips running from the seam at the cowl, forward. They were about three-quarters of the length of the hood. Above these moldings, a Commander nameplate was positioned near the cowl. Standard equipment included: speedometer; gas gauge; engine thermometer; Auto Lite ignition; Borg clock; Casco cigar lighter; bumpers; guards; two-way Houde shock absorbers; spring covers; Budd disc wheels; twin taillights; dual inside sun visors; a single horn and dual windshield wipers; column mounted gearshift; Planar front wheel suspension and automatic Hill-Holder.

1939 Studebaker, President, 4-dr. sedan, AA

STUDEBAKER — STATE PRESIDENT — SERIES 5C — EIGHT: The State Presidents were larger and heavier than the Commanders, but looked about the same. The name President was on the hood sides, near the cowl seam (above the lower trim moldings.) The bumper identification also read, "Studebaker President." Standard equipment included everything listed for Commanders plus/or except Delco Remy ignition and dual horns. Also, the Houdaille shock absorbers, on cars in this line, were built into the independent front springing system.

I.D. DATA: [Series G] Serial numbers were in the same location on left front of frame. Starting: G-001; (W. Coast) 800001. Ending: G-30400; (W. Coast) 803600. Motor numbers were stamped on the left rear of engine near top of block or left front upper side of block. Starting: 001. Ending: 34100. [Series 9A] Serial numbers were in the same location. Starting: 4110001; (W. Coast) 4802301. Ending: 4148500; (W. Coast) 4807600. Engine numbers were in the same location. Starting: H-42501. Ending: H-87550. [Series 5C] Serial numbers were in the same location. Starting: 7125501; (W. Coast) 7802501. Ending: 7133050; (W. Coast) 7803250. Engine numbers were stamped on the left front corner of block above water jacket. Starting: B-30201. Ending: B-38500.

Custom Champion Six

Model No.	Body Type & Seating	Price	Weight	Prod. Total
G	2-dr. Cpe.-3P	660	2260	Note 1
G	2-dr. Clb. Sed.-6P	700	2330	Note 1
G	4-dr. Cr. Sed.-6P	740	2360	Note 1

Deluxe Champion Six

Model No.	Body Type & Seating	Price	Weight	Prod. Total
G	2-dr. Cpe.-3P	720	2275	Note 1
G	2-dr. Clb. Sed.-6P	760	2345	Note 1
G	4-dr. Cr. Sed.-6P	800	2375	Note 1

Note 1: Total production Jan. 1939 to July 1939 was 33,905.

Model No.	Body Type & Seating	Price	Weight	Prod. Total
9A	2-dr. Bus. Cpe.-3P	875	3045	Note 1
9A	2-dr. Cus. Cpe.-3P	900	3080	Note 1
9A	2-dr. Clb. Sed.-6P	955	3160	Note 1
9A	4-dr. Cr. Sed.-6P	965	3200	Note 1
9A	4-dr. Conv. Sed.-6P	1290	3400	Note 1

Note 1: Total production Aug. 1938 to Aug. 1939 was 43,724.

Model No.	Body Type & Seating	Price	Weight	Prod. Total
5C	2-dr. Cus. Cpe.-3P	1035	3300	Note 1
5C	2-dr. Clb. Sed.-6P	1100	3390	Note 1
5C	4-dr. Cr. Sed.-6P	1110	3440	Note 1
5C	4-dr. Conv. Sed.-6P	1460	3640	Note 1

Note 1: Total production Sept. 1938 to Aug. 1939 was 8,205.

ENGINE: [Champion Six Engine] L-head. Inline. Six. Cast iron block. B & S: 3 in. x 3-7/8 in. Disp.: 164.3 cu. in. C.R.: 6.5:1. Brake H.P.: 78 @ 4000 R.P.M. N.A.C.C. H.P.: 21.60. Main bearings: Four. Valve lifters: Solid. Carb.: Carter 1V model WO. Torque: 128 lbs.-ft. at 1600 R.P.M. [Commander Six Engine] L-head. Inline. Six. Cast iron block. B & S: 3-5/16 in. x 4-3/8 in. Disp.: 226 cu. in. C.R.: 6.0:1. Brake H.P.: 90 @ 3400 R.P.M. N.A.C.C. H.P.: 26.35. Main bearings: Four. Valve lifters: Solid. Carb.: Stromberg 1V model BX026. Torque: 174 lbs.-ft. at 1200 R.P.M. [President Eight Engine] L-head. Inline. Eight. Cast iron block. B & S: 3-1/16 in. x 4-1/4 in. Disp.: 250.4 cu. in. C.R.: 6.0:1. Brake H.P.: 110 @ 3600 R.P.M. N.A.C.C. H.P.: 30.01. Main bearings: Nine. Valve lifters: Solid. Carb.: Stromberg 2V model AAO161. Torque: 195 lbs.-ft. at 2000 R.P.M.

CHASSIS: [Series G] W.B.: 110 in. L: 188-3/4 in. H: 64-5/8 in. Frt/Rear Tread: 56-1/4 / 57 in. Tires: 16 x 5.50. [Series 9A] W.B.: 116.5 in. L: 197.5 in. H: 66-1/8 in. Frt/Rear Tread: 59-7/8 / 59-1/2 in. Tires: 16 x 6.00. [Series 5C] W.B.: 122 in. L: 203 in. H: 66-5/8 in. Frt/Rear Tread: 59-5/8 / 59-7/16 in. Tires: 16 x 6.50.

TECHNICAL: Synchromesh manual transmission. Speeds: 3F/1R. Steering column-mounted gearshift controls. Clutch: single disc dry plate type. Hypoid semi-floating rear axle. Overall ratio: (G) 4.56:1; (others) 4.55:1. Four wheel hydraulic brakes. Budd steel disc wheels. Drivetrain Options: Vacuum clutch. Hill-holder. Overdrive.

OPTIONS: Whitewall tires. Bumper guards. Wheel trim rings. Dual sidemounts. Sidemount cover(s). Fender skirts. Bumper guards. Radio. Heater. Clock. Cigar lighter. Radio antenna. Seat covers. External sun shade. Spotlight(s). Fog lamps. Dual horns. Full wheel discs. Special paint. OSRV mirror. Climatizer central fresh air ventilating and heating system.

HISTORICAL: Introduced August 11, 1938 (except Champion). Champion Introduced: Mar. 1939. Innovations: Column mount gearshift. New controlled overdrive. Climatizer ventilation system. Calendar year registrations: 84,660. Calendar year sales: 106,470. Calendar year production: 92,200. Model year production: 85,834.

Studebaker placed a stong 8th in the 1939 U.S. auto sales race. A Studebaker Champion set an AAA record of 27.25 miles per gallon in a 6,144 mile economy run from the San Francisco Golden Gate Exposition to the New York World's Fair.

1939

Model G, Custom Champion Six

	FP	5	4	3	2	1
Cpe	660	650	1250	2400	4200	6000
Clb Sed	700	675	1300	2500	4350	6200
Cr Sed	740	675	1300	2600	4400	6300

Model G, Deluxe Champion Six

	FP	5	4	3	2	1
Cpe	720	675	1300	2500	4350	6200
Clb Sed	760	700	1350	2700	4500	6400
Cr Sed	800	700	1350	2800	4550	6500

Model 9A, Commander Six

	FP	5	4	3	2	1
Cpe Express	900	900	1900	4500	6300	9000
Bus Cpe	875	825	1600	4000	5600	8000
Cus Cpe	900	850	1650	4100	5700	8200
Clb Sed	955	825	1600	4050	5650	8100
Cr Sed	965	850	1650	4100	5700	8200
Conv Sed	1290	4500	9000	15,000	21,000	30,000

Model 5C, State President Eight

	FP	5	4	3	2	1
Cus Cpe	1035	900	1900	4500	6300	9000
Clb Sed	1100	925	2000	4600	6400	9200
Cr Sed	1100	1000	2400	5000	7000	10,000
Conv Sed	1460	4650	9300	15,500	21,700	31,000

1940

STUDEBAKER — CHAMPION — SERIES 2-G — SIX: The 1940 Champion had slight changes to front end styling. The center grille had more horizontal bars added. The bars were of a thinner design. Only two horizontal trim moldings were used on the hood, instead of three. Another new feature was the use of sealed beam headlights. Standard equipment on the low-priced Custom models included a speedometer, gasoline gauge, engine thermometer, windshield wipers, bumpers, Houde shock absorbers, spring covers, steel disc wheels, one taillight, one sunvisor, one windshield wiper and single horn. Custom Deluxe models had twin wipers, taillights and horns, front door arm rests, a Phantom steering wheel, horn ring, stainless steel lower body finishing strips and four bumper guards. Deluxe and DeLux-Tone models also had assist cords, rear seat ash trays, robe rails, carpeted lower door panels and ventilating rear quarter windows (on Cruising Sedans). They also featured a two-tone interior. The Custom Champion had solid exterior and interior and the DeLux-Tone Champion had delux-tone exterior and interior.

1940 Studebaker, Champion, coupe, AA

STUDEBAKER — COMMANDER — SERIES 100-A — SIX: The 1940 Studebakers had more massive fenders and a greater degree of streamlining. The new Commander grille was of a large, lattice-bar design with low, chrome-plated ventilating grilles on both sides of the radiator. The model name appeared on the upper rear corner of the hood. Standard equipment included all found on Custom Champions, plus bumper guards, dual taillights, twin sun visors and two horns. A new, larger windshield was featured. Other new styling touches included sliding rear quarter windows, concealed gas filler caps and a hood lock operated via a lever on the steering column. Sedans in the new DeLux-Tone series had deluxe-tone exteriors and interiors. Coupes had solid exteriors and deluxe-tone interiors.

1940 Studebaker, President, club sedan, AA

STUDEBAKER — PRESIDENT — SERIES 6-C — EIGHT: The President, for 1940, had styling similar to that of Commanders. The model name appeared on the upper rear corner of the hood. Standard equipment included all found on Commanders plus a clock, cigar lighter and dual horns. Presidents had a 122 inch wheelbase and larger 6.50 x 16 tires.

I.D. DATA: [Champion] Serial numbers were in the same locations on a plate riveted to the side member of the frame under the left front fender or on the right left front door hinge pillar. Starting: G-30501; (W. Coast) G-803701. Ending: G-90069; (W. Coast) G-811191. Engine numbers were stamped on the left rear of engine near top of block or left front upper side of block. Starting: 34101. Ending: 101169. [Commander] Serial numbers were in the same location. Starting: 4148501; (W. Coast) 4807601. Ending: 4178797; (W. Coast) 4811895. Engine numbers were in the same location. Starting: H-87601. Ending: H-122190. [President] Serial numbers were in the same location. Starting: 5582001; (W. Coast) 5857501. Ending: 5599146; (W. Coast) 5859614. Motor numbers were in the same location. Starting: H-101. Ending: H-42253.

Model No.	Body Type & Seating	Price	Weight	Prod. Total
Champion Custom Line				
2-G	2-dr. Cpe.-3P	660	2290	Note 1
2-G	2-dr. OS Cpe.-5P	695	2335	Note 1
2-G	2-dr. Clb. Sed.-5P	700	2360	Note 1
2-G	4-dr. Cr. Sed.-5P	740	2390	Note 1
Custom Deluxe Line				
2-G	2-dr. Cpe.-3P	690	2300	Note 1
2-G	2-dr. OS Cpe.-5P	725	2345	Note 1
2-G	2-dr. Clb. Sed.-5P	730	2370	Note 1
2-G	4-dr. Cr. Sed.-5P	770	2400	Note 1
Deluxe Line				
2-G	2-dr. Cpe.-3P	705	2315	Note 1
2-G	2-dr. OS Cpe.-5P	740	2360	Note 1
2-G	2-dr. Clb. Sed.-5P	745	2385	Note 1
2-G	4-dr. Cr. Sed.-5P	785	2415	Note 1
Delux-Tone Line				
2-G	2-dr. Cpe.-3P	720	2315	Note 1
2-G	2-dr. OS Cpe.-5P	755	2360	Note 1

Model No.	Body Type & Seating	Price	Weight	Prod. Total
2-G	2-dr. Clb. Sed.-5P	760	2385	Note 1
2-G	2-dr. Cr. Sed.-5P	800	2415	Note 1

Note 1: Total production Aug. 1939 to June 1940 was 66,264.

Commander Line

10-A	2-dr. Cus. Cpe.-3P	895	3055	Note 1
10-A	2-dr. Clb. Sed.-6P	925	3135	Note 1
10-A	4-dr. Cr. Sed.-6P	965	3180	Note 1

Delux-Tone Commander

10-A	2-dr. Cus. Cpe.-3P	935	3060	Note 1
10-A	2-dr. Clb. Sed.-6P	965	3140	Note 1
10-A	4-dr. Cr. Sed.-6P	1005	3185	Note 1

Note 1: Total production Sept. 1939 to June 1940 was 34,477.

State President Line

6-C	2-dr. Cpe.-3P	1025	3280	Note 1
6-C	2-dr. Clb. Sed.-6P	1055	3370	Note 1
6-C	4-dr. Cr. Sed.-6P	1095	3420	Note 1

Delux-Tone Line

6-C	2-dr. Cpe.-3P	1065	3285	Note 1
6-C	2-dr. Clb. Sed.-6P	1095	3375	Note 1
6-C	4-dr. Cr. Sed.-6P	1135	3425	Note 1

Note 1: Total production Sept. 1939 to June 1940 was 6,444.

ENGINE: [Champion] L-head. Inline. Six. Cast iron block. B & S: 3 in. x 3-7/8 in. Disp.: 164.3 cu. in. C.R.: 6.50:1. Brake H.P.: 78 @ 4000 R.P.M. N.A.C.C. H.P.: 21.6. Main bearings: Four. Valve lifters: Solid. Carb.: Carter 1V Model WO. Torque 128 lbs.-ft. @ 1600 R.P.M. [Commander] L-head. Inline. Six. Cast iron block. B & S: 3-5/16 in. x 4-3/8 in. Disp.: 226 cu. in. C.R.: 6.0:1. Brake H.P.: 90 @ 3400 R.P.M. N.A.C.C. H.P.: 26.35. Main bearings: Four. Valve lifters: Solid. Carb.: Stromberg 1V Model BX026. Torque 174 lbs.-ft. @ 1200 R.P.M. [President] L-head. Inline. Eight. Cast iron block. B & S: 3-1/16 in. x 4-1/4 in. Disp.: 250.4 cu. in. C.R.: 6.0:1. Brake H.P.: 110 @ 3600 R.P.M. N.A.C.C. H.P.: 30.00. Main bearings: Nine. Valve lifters: Solid. Carb.: Stromberg 2V Model AA0161. Torque 110 lbs.-ft. @ 3600 R.P.M.

CHASSIS: [Series 2-G] W.B.: 110 in. O.L.: 188.75 in. H: 64-5/8 in. Frt/Rear Tread: 56.25 in./57 in. Tires: 16 x 5.50. [Series 10-A] W.B.: 116.5 in. O.L.: 197.5 in. H: 66-1/8 in. Frt/Rear Tread: 59-7/8 x 61 in. Tires: 16 x 6.00. [Series 6-C] W.B.: 122 in. O.L.: 203 in. H: 66-5/8 in. Frt/Rear Tread: 59.75 x 61 in. Tires: 16 x 6.50.

TECHNICAL: Manual transmission. Speeds: 3F/1R. Column mounted gearshift controls. Clutch: (Pres.) Molded; (others) Molded and woven. Shaft drive. Semi-floating rear axle. Overall ratio: (Champ.) 4.56:1; (others) 4.55:1. Four wheel hydraulic brakes. Buddsteel disc wheels. Drivetrain options: Vacuum clutch. Hill-holder. Overdrive.

OPTIONS: Whitewall tires. Wheel trim rings. OSRV mirror. Parking lamps. Fender skirts. Bumper guards. Radio. Heater. Clock. Cigar lighter. Radio antenna. Seat covers. Spotlight(s). Two-tone paint. Special paint. Bumper wing guards. Master grille guard.

HISTORICAL: Introduced Aug./Sept. 1939. Innovations: Pure air climatizer. Streamlined door handles. Sliding rear quarter windows on some models. Steering column hood lock. Improved door hinges. Delux-Tone two-tone models. Calendar year registrations: 102,281. Calendar year production: 117,091. Model year production: 120,543. Other notes: Studebaker was America's 8th ranked auto-maker in 1940. A Champion model won first place in its class in the Gilmore Exonomy Run averaging 27-1/4 m.p.g. during a cross-country trip at an average speed of 40 mph.

1940 Studebaker, Commander, cruising, sedan, AA

1940

Champion Custom

	FP	5	4	3	2	1
Cpe	660	650	1250	2400	4200	6000
OS Cpe	695	675	1300	2600	4400	6300
Clb Sed	700	675	1300	2500	4350	6200
Cr Sed	740	675	1300	2600	4400	6300

Champion Custom Deluxe

	FP	5	4	3	2	1
Cpe	690	675	1300	2500	4300	6100
OS Cpe	725	700	1350	2700	4400	6400
Clb Sed	730	675	1300	2600	4400	6300
Cr Sed	770	700	1350	2700	4500	6400

Champion Deluxe

	FP	5	4	3	2	1
Cpe	705	675	1300	2500	4350	6200
OS Cpe	740	700	1350	2800	4500	6500
Clb Sed	745	700	1350	2700	4500	6400
Cr Sed	785	700	1350	2800	4550	6500

Champion Deluxe-Tone

	FP	5	4	3	2	1
Cpe	720	675	1300	2500	4350	6200
OS Cpe	755	700	1350	2800	4550	6500
Clb Sed	760	700	1350	2700	4500	6400
Cr Sed	800	700	1350	2800	4550	6500

Commander

	FP	5	4	3	2	1
Cus Cpe	895	825	1600	4000	5600	8000
Clb Sed	925	825	1600	4050	5650	8100
Cr Sed	965	850	1650	4100	5700	8200

Commander Deluxe-Tone

	FP	5	4	3	2	1
Cus Cpe	935	825	1600	4000	5600	8000
Clb Sed	965	825	1600	4050	5650	8100
Cr Sed	1005	850	1650	4100	5700	8200

State President

	FP	5	4	3	2	1
Cpe	1025	900	1900	4500	6300	9000
Clb Sed	1055	925	2000	4600	6400	9200
Cr Sed	1095	1000	2400	5000	7000	10,000

President Deluxe-Tone

	FP	5	4	3	2	1
Cpe	1065	900	1900	4500	6300	9000
Clb Sed	1095	925	2000	4600	6400	9200
Cr Sed	1135	1000	2400	5000	7000	10,000

1941

1941 Studebaker, Champion, coupe, OCW

STUDEBAKER — CHAMPION — SERIES 3G — SIX — More streamlined bodies, designed by Raymond Lowey, were used on Champions this year. The cars were lower and longer, with a more massive front end appearance. Center grilles were eliminated. Low, die-cast grilles with multiple vertical bars were mounted in the front fender aprons on each side of the car. The nose was decorated with a large chrome emblem bearing the Studebaker "S" insignia. Twin chrome moldings ran from the hood peak to the upper rear quarters, tapering together as they moved back along the body. On DeLuxe-Tone models the area between the moldings were done in contrasting colors. Wider seats (54-1/4 inches front and 48 inches rear) were used in Champions. Standard equipment was the same as 1940, plus dual taillights. Custom Deluxe models also had dual wipers, sun visors and horns, front door arm rests and chrome instrument board moldings. They had solid exterior finish and two-tone interiors. Deluxe-Tone cars also had chrome door trim rings, ashtrays in the rear of Club and Cruising sedans and two-tone interiors and exteriors.

COMMANDER — SERIES 11A — SIX — The Commander had a longer wheelbase, wider doors, lower floors and reduction in overall height. Running boards were eliminated. A new model was the Land Cruiser, a sedan with rear quarter windows eliminated and reverse opening rear doors. A new grille and molding treatment was similar to that seen on Champions except that Commanders had a hood ornament. Customs were equipped the same as last year. Deluxe-tone cars also had chrome instrument board moldings and two-tone exteriors and interiors. Skyway models had chrome bands around all windows, chrome fender lights, two-tone instrument panels, two-tone exterior finish and bolster type pleated upholstery.

1941 Studebaker, President Skyway, coupe, OCW

PRESIDENT — SERIES 7C — EIGHT — Studebaker's fanciest series also had new Raymond Lowey styling with low, die-cast side grilles, increased glass area, air vents in the side of the cowl and longer, lower and wider lines. A mid-year model was a Sedan-Coupe with an innovative one-piece curved windshield. Custom models were quite plain. They had front fender lamps, but no other extraneous trim. DeLuxe-Tone cars had chrome instrument panel moldings and two-tone interiors and exteriors. Skyway models had wide chrome bands around all windows, chrome fender lights, two-tone instrument panels, two-tone exteriors (with tapering contrast band) and bolster type pleated upholstery.

I.D. DATA: [Series 3G] Serial numbers were in the same locations, on a plate riveted to side member of frame under left front fender or to left or right front door hinge pillars. Starting: G-90101; (W. Coast) G-811201. Ending: G-165400; (W. Coast) G-820902. Engine numbers were stamped on left rear of engine near top of block or left upper side of block near front. Starting: 101201. Ending: 186259. [Series 11A] Serial numbers were in the same locations. Starting: 4178801; (W. Coast) 4811901. Ending: 4216180; (W. Coast) 4816518. Engine numbers were in the same location. Starting: H-122201. Ending: H-164222. [Series 7C] Serial numbers were in the same locations. Starting: 7139101; (W. Coast) 7803901. Ending: 7145407; (W. Coast) 7804592. Engine numbers were located on the left corner of the block above water jacket cover. Starting: B-45001. Ending: B-52012.

Model No.	Body Type & Seating	Price	Weight	Prod. Total
Custom Line				
3-G	2-dr. Cpe.-3P	710	2370	Note 1
3-G	2-dr. Dbl. Date Cpe.-5P	750	2400	Note 1
3-G	2-dr. OS Cpe.-5P	750	2410	Note 1
3-G	2-dr. Clb. Sed.-5P	755	2450	Note 1
3-G	4-dr. Cr. Sed.-5P	795	2480	Note 1
Custom Deluxe Line				
3-G	2-dr. Cpe.-3P	745	2395	Note 1
3-G	2-dr. Dbl. Date Cpe.-5P	780	2435	Note 1
3-G	2-dr. OS Cpe.-5P	780	2425	Note 1
3-G	2-dr. Clb. Cpe.-5P	785	2470	Note 1
3-G	4-dr. Cr. Sed.-5P	825	2500	Note 1
Deluxe-Tone Line				
3-G	2-dr. Cpe.-3P	780	2400	Note 1
3-G	2-dr. Dbl. Date Cpe.-5P	815	2440	Note 1
3-G	2-dr. OS Cpe.-5P	815	2430	Note 1
3-G	2-dr. Clb. Sed.-5P	820	2470	Note 1
3-G	4-dr. Cr. Sed.-5P	860	2500	Note 1

Note 1: Total production Aug., 1940 to July 1941 was 84,910.

Model No.	Body Type & Seating	Price	Weight	Prod. Total
Custom Line				
11A	2-dr. Sed. Cpe.-6P	990	3160	Note 1
11A	4-dr. Cr. Sed.-6P	1010	3210	Note 1
11A	4-dr. L. Cruiser-6P	1055	3230	Note 1
DeLuxe-Tone Line				
11A	4-dr. Cr. Sed.-6P	1075	3225	Note 1
11A	4-dr. L. Cruiser-6P	1120	3245	Note 1
Skyway Line				
11A	2-dr. Sed. Cpe.-6P	1080	3200	Note 1
11A	4-dr. Cr. Sed.-6P	1100	3240	Note 1
11A	4-dr. L. Cruiser-6P	1130	3260	Note 1

Note 1: Total production Aug., 1940 to July 1941 was 41,996.

Model No.	Body Type & Seating	Price	Weight	Prod. Total
Custom Line				
7C	4-dr. Cr. Sed.-6P	1140	3450	Note 1
7C	4-dr. L. Cruiser-6P	1185	3475	Note 1
DeLuxe-Tone Line				
7C	4-dr. Cr. Sed.-6P	1205	3475	Note 1
7C	4-dr. L. Cruiser-6P	1250	3500	Note 1
Skyway Line				
7C	4-dr. Cr. Sed.-6P	1230	3500	Note 1
7C	4-dr. L. Cruiser-6P	1260	3520	Note 1
7C	2-dr. Sed. Cpe.-6P	1210	3440	Note 1

Note 1: Total production Aug., 1940 to July, 1941 was 6,994.

ENGINE: [Champion] L-head. Inline. Six. Cast iron block. B & S: 3 in. x 4 in. Disp.: 170 cu. in. C.R.: 6.5:1. Brake H.P.: 80 @ 4000 R.P.M. N.A.C.C. H.P.: 21.6. Main bearings: Four. Valve lifters: Solid. Carb.: Carter 1V Model WA1-4965. [Commander] L-head. Inline. Six. Cast iron block. B & S: 3-5/16 in. x 4-3/8 in. Disp.: 226.2 cu. in. C.R.: 6.5:1. Brake H.P.: 94 @ 3600 R.P.M. N.A.C.C. H.P.: 26.35. Main bearings: Four. Valve lifters: Solid. Carb.: Stromberg 1V Model BXOV-26. [President] L-head. Inline. Eight. Cast iron block. B & S: 3-1/16 in. x 4-1/4 in. Disp.: 250.4 cu. in. C.R.: 6.5:1. Brake H.P.: 117 @ 4000 R.P.M. N.A.C.C. H.P.: 30.00. Main bearings: Nine. Valve lifters: Solid. Carb.: Stromberg 2V Model AAV-26.

CHASSIS: [Champion] W.B.: 110 in. Tires: 16 x 5.50. [Commander Series] W.B.: 119 in. Tires: 16 x 6.25 [President] W.B.: 124.5 in. Tires: 16 x 7.00.

TECHNICAL: Manual transmission. Speeds: 3F/1R. Column mounted gearshift controls. Clutch: (Pres.) molded; (others) molded and woven. Shaft drive. Semi-floating rear axle. Overall ratio: (Champ) 4.56:1; (others) 4.55:1. Four-wheel hydraulic brakes. Budd Steel disc wheels. Drivetrain Options: Vacuum clutch. Hill-holder. Overdrive.

OPTIONS: Whitewall tires. Wheel trim rings. OSRV mirror. Parking lamps. Master grille guards. Fender skirts. Bumper guards. Radio. Heater. Clock. Cigar lighter. Radio antenna. Seat covers. External sun shade. Spotlight(s). Fender lamps. Full wheel discs. Front fender moldings. Front and rear fender wind split trim moldings. Two-tone paint. Fender skirt moldings. Bumper wing guards.

1941 Studebaker, Commander, sedan, HAC

HISTORICAL: Introduced August, 1940. Innovations: One-piece windshield on President Sedan-Coupe. Engine and body mountings moved forward. Wider seats. Running boards eliminated. Lower height with same headroom. Increased glass area. Improved manifolding and carburetion. Calendar year registrations: 114,331. Calendar year production: 119,325. Model year production: 133,900. Studebaker was 9th in U.S. auto sales this season. Sales climbed to over $100 million for the first time since 1929. The 1941 Champion had the largest production single model year in company history.

1941

Champion Custom	FP	5	4	3	2	1
Cpe	710	700	1350	2900	4600	6600
D D Cpe	750	700	1350	2900	4600	6600
OS Cpe	750	725	1400	3100	4800	6800
Clb Sed	755	725	1400	3000	4700	6700
Cr Sed	795	725	1400	3100	4800	6800
Champion Custom Deluxe						
Cpe	745	725	1400	3000	4700	6700
D D Cpe	780	725	1400	3000	4700	6700
OS Cpe	780	725	1400	3200	4850	6900
Clb Sed	785	725	1400	3100	4800	6800
Cr Sed	825	725	1400	3200	4850	6900
Champion Deluxe-Tone						
Cpe	780	725	1400	3000	4700	6700
D D Cpe	815	725	1400	3000	4700	6700
OS Cpe	815	725	1400	3200	4850	6900
Clb Sed	820	725	1400	3100	4800	6800
Cr Sed	860	725	1400	3200	4850	6900
Commander Custom						
Sed Cpe	990	875	1700	4250	5900	8500
Cr Cpe	1010	900	1800	4400	6150	8800
L Cruise	1055	900	1900	4500	6300	9000
Commander Deluxe-Tone						
Cr Sed	1075	925	2000	4650	6500	9300
L Cruise	1120	950	2100·	4750	6650	9500
Commander Skyway						
Sed Cpe	1080	975	2300	4900	6850	9800
Cr Sed	1100	1000	2400	5000	7000	10,000
L Cruise	1130	1025	2500	5150	7150	10,300
President Custom						
Cr Sed	1140	1100	3300	5650	7900	11,300
L Cruise	1185	1175	3700	6150	8600	12,300
President Deluxe-Tone						
Cr Sed	1205	1175	3700	6150	8600	12,300
L Cruise	1250	1300	4000	6650	9300	13,300
President Skyway						
Sed Cpe	1210	1300	4000	6650	9300	13,300
Cr Sed	1230	1450	4250	7150	10,000	14,300
L Cruise	1260	1600	4600	7650	10,700	15,300

1942

STUDEBAKER — CHAMPION — SERIES 4-G — SIX: The 1942 Champions had extensive body styling changes. There were wider, more massive bumpers up front, with a built in license plate assembly. The grille stretched completely across the front of the cars with large, round parking lamp assemblies at either side. Cross-hatching horizontal and vertical bars filled the grille on either side of a vertical center member. There was a large Studebaker emblem on the nose and a chrome hood ornament and molding along the center of the hood. Standard equipment included a speedometer, gas gauge, thermometer, ignition lock, wiper, spring covers, dual taillamps, one sun visor, a horn, double-acting shock absorbers and Budd steel disc wheels. Champion Deluxstyle equipment included dual wipers, dual sun visors, dual Airtone horns, front door arm rests, front seat back garnish trim panel and ashtray, two courtesy lights, chrome sill moldings and solid exterior and interior colors and trim.

STUDEBAKER — COMMANDER — SERIES 12-A — SIX: The Commander also had the new, wide grille with narrow horizontal ribs supported by less obvious vertical members. Fog lamps in the grille were optional equipment. Parking lamps were on top of the front fenders. New, dual rear lamps included a flashing indicator as well as tail and stop lamps, mounted in a large, chrome plated housing with ribbed side panels. The heavier, wraparound bumpers had a built-in license plate assembly in the center. Commander identification was stamped into the front of the bright metal

1942 Studebaker, Commander Custom, cruising sedan, AA

hood molding. Standard equipment was the same as on Champions plus dual sun visors, horns and wipers. AutoLite ignition was used for the Commander. Deluxstyle Commanders also had a front seat back garnish trim panel and ashtray, two automatic courtesy lights, stainless steel window reveal moldings, three chrome moldings on inside door panels and two-tone exterior and interior colors and trim. Skyway models also had bolster type pleated upholstery, chrome bands around all side windows, white painted wheel discs and Lucite door hardware panels.

STUDEBAKER — PRESIDENT — SERIES 8-C — EIGHT: The President for 1942 had the same general styling characteristics as other Studebakers. Standard equipment for Custom models was the same as on Commanders. Deluxstyle models had the same upgraded trim features as Deluxstyle Commanders and Skyway upgrading was also similar to that of Skyway Commanders. On the President the starter, instead of being operated by a button on the dash, was brought into operation by the clutch pedal. President model identification was found at the front of the hood trim molding on Custom and Deluxstyle models. Skyway editions had a President nameplate at the rear of the hood near the cowl. A unique 1942 Studebaker feature was a steering column mounted radio station selector lever on cars equipped with factory radios.

I.D. DATA: [Champion] Serial numbers were in the same locations, stamped on a plate riveted to the frame side member under left front fender or on the left or right front hinge pillars. Starting: G-165501; (W. Coast) G-821001. Ending: G-192583; (W. Coast) G-823645. Engine numbers were stamped on the left rear of engine near top of block or left front upper side of block. Starting: 186301. Ending: 216050. [Commander] Serial numbers were in the same locations. Starting: 4216501; (W. Coast) 4816601. Ending: 4232290; (W. Coast) 4818305. Engine numbers were in the same locations. Starting: H-164301. Ending: H-181812. [President] Serial numbers were in the same locations. Starting: 7145501; (W. Coast) 7804601. Ending: 7148659; (W. Coast) 7804943. Engine numbers were stamped on the left corner of the block above water jacket. Starting: B-52101. Ending: B-55608.

1942 Studebaker, President, cruising sedan, HAC

Model No.	Body Type & Seating	Price	Weight	Prod. Total
Champion				
Custom				
4G	2-dr. Cpe.-3P	744	2415	Note 1
4G	2-dr. Dbl. Date. Cpe.-5P	769	2455	Note 1
4G	2-dr. Clb. Sed.-5P	774	2495	Note 1
4G	4-dr. Cr. Sed.-6P	804	2520	Note 1
Deluxstyle				
4G	2-dr. Cpe.-3P	779	2435	Note 1
4G	2-dr. Dbl. Date. Cpe.-5P	804	2470	Note 1
4G	2-dr. Clb. Sed.-5P	809	2520	Note 1
4G	4-dr. Cr. Sed.-6P	839	2545	Note 1

Note 1: Total production Aug. 1941 to Jan. 1942 was 29,678.
Note 2: Production halted around Jan. 1942 due to outbreak of WW II.

Model No.	Body Type & Seating	Price	Weight	Prod. Total
Commander				
Custom				
12A	2-dr. Sed. Cpe.-6P	1025	3195	Note 1
12A	4-dr. Cr. Sed.-6P	1045	3265	Note 1
12A	4-dr. L. Cr.-6P	1080	3290	Note 1
Deluxstyle				
12A	2-dr. Sed. Cpe.-6P	1070	3210	Note 1
12A	4-dr. Cr. Sed.-6P	1090	3280	Note 1
12A	4-dr. L. Cr.-6P	1125	3305	Note 1
Skyway				
12A	2-dr. Sed. Cpe.-6P	1105	3240	Note 1
12A	4-dr. Cr. Sed.-6P	1125	3300	Note 1
12A	4-dr. L. Cr.-6P	1160	3315	Note 1

Note 1: Total production Aug. 1941 to Jan. 1942 was 17,500.
Note 2: Production halted around Jan. 1942 due to outbreak of WW II.

Model No.	Body Type & Seating	Price	Weight	Prod. Total
President				
Custom				
8C	2-dr. Sed. Cpe.-6P	1141	3440	Note 1
8C	4-dr. Cr. Sed.-6P	1161	3485	Note 1
8C	4-dr. L. Cr.-6P	1196	3510	Note 1
Deluxstyle				
8C	2-dr. Sed. Cpe.-6P	1186	3455	Note 1
8C	4-dr. Cr. Sed.-6P	1206	3500	Note 1
8C	4-dr. L. Cr.-6P	1241	3515	Note 1
Skyway				
8C	2-dr. Sed. Cpe.-6P	1221	3470	Note 1
8C	4-dr. Cr. Sed.-6P	1241	3540	Note 1
8C	4-dr. L. Cr.-6P	1276	3540	Note 1

Note 1: Total production Aug. 1941 to Jan. 1942 was 3,500.
Note 2: Production halted around Jan. 1942 due to outbreak of WW II.

ENGINE: [Champion] L-head. Inline. Six. Cast iron block. B & S: 3 in. x 4 in. Disp.: 170 cu. in. C.R.: 6.5:1; (opt.) 7.0:1. Brake H.P.: 80 @ 4000 R.P.M. Taxable H.P.: 21.60. Main bearings: Four. Valve lifters: Solid. Carb.: Carter 1V Model 496S. Torque: 134 lbs.-ft. @ 2000 R.P.M. [Commander] L-head. Inline. Six. Cast iron block. B & S: 3-5/16 in. x 4-3/8 in. Disp.: 226.2 cu. in. C.R.: 6.50:1; (opt.) 7.0:1. Brake H.P.: 94 @ 3600 R.P.M. Taxable H.P.: 26.35. Main bearings: Four. Valve lifters: Solid. Carb.: Stromberg 1V Model BXOV26. Torque: 176 lbs.-ft. @ 1600 R.P.M. [President] L-head. Inline. Eight. Cast iron block. B & S: 3-1/16 in. x 4-1/4 in. Disp.: 250.4 cu. in. C.R.: 6.5:1; (opt.) 7.0:1. Brake H.P.: 117 @ 3800 R.P.M. Taxable H.P.: 30.0. Main bearings: Nine. Valve lifters: Solid. Carb.: Stromberg 2V Model AAV26. Torque: 200 lbs.-ft. @ 2400 R.P.M.

CHASSIS: [Series 4G] W.B.: 110 in. O.L.: 193 in. Frt/Rear Tread: 56.25 /57 in. Tires: 16 x 5.50. [Series 12A] W.B.: 119.5 in. O.L.: 210.25 in. Frt/Rear Tread: 58.25/60-5/16 in. Tires: 16 x 6.25. [Series 8C] W.B.: 124.5 in. O.L.: 215.75 in. Frt/Rear Tread: 58-1/8/60-5/16 in. Tires: 15 x 7.00.

TECHNICAL: Warner Gear synchromesh transmission. Speeds: 3F/1R. Column mounted controls. (Pres.) Inland woven and molded clutch; (others) Borg & Beck molded clutch. Shaft drive. Semi-floating rear axle. Overall ratio: (Champ.) 4.1:1; (Comm.) 4.09:1; (Pres.) 4.09:1. Four wheel Bendix hydraulic brakes. Budd steel disc wheels. Drivetrain Options: Turbo-matic drive. Overdrive.
Note: Turbo-matic drive (avail. on Commander and President) consisted of a fluid coupling, an automatic vacuum-operated clutch and a conventional 3-speed transmission with kick-down overdrive. It eliminated the clutch pedal and reduced gear shifting to a minimum. Gearshift lever positions were conventional, but second was called Traffic range and high was called Cruising range.

OPTIONS: Whitewall tires. Wheel trim rings. Full wheel discs. Front fender parking lights. Bumper wing tips. Fender skirts. Bumper guards. Radio. Heater. Clock. Cigar lighter. Radio antenna. Seat covers. External sun shade. Spotlight(s). Fog lamps. Climatizer. Turbo-matic drive.

HISTORICAL: Introduced Sept. 1941. Innovations: Turbo-matic transmission. Dash controlled hood lock. Iron alloy pistons with Parco Lubrized surfaces. Larger clutch facing and vibration dampner on Champions. Clutch pedal starting. Calendar year registrations: 58,051. Calendar year sales: 9,285. Model year production: 47,678.
Studebaker was America's 8th ranked auto-maker. Like other U.S. manufacturers, Studebaker became heavily involved in the war production effort after Jan. 1942. The company built trucks, aircraft engines and "Weasals". The weasal was a lightweight, tracked vehicle designed for troop transport and built in Arctic and amphibious models for special purpose applications.

1942

Champion Custom Series	FP	5	4	3	2	1
Cpe	744	675	1300	2600	4400	6300
D D Cpe	769	700	1350	2700	4500	6400
Clb Sed	774	700	1350	2800	4550	6500
Cr Sed	804	700	1350	2900	4600	6600
Champion Deluxstyle Series						
Cpe	779	700	1350	2700	4500	6400
D D Cpe	804	700	1350	2700	4500	6400
Clb Sed	809	700	1350	2900	4600	6600
Cr Sed	839	725	1400	3000	4700	6700
Commander Custom Series						
2 dr Sed Cpe	1025	825	1600	4050	5650	8100
Cr Sed	1045	850	1650	4100	5700	8200
L Cr	1080	850	1650	4150	5800	8300
Commander Deluxstyle Series						
2 dr Sed Cpe	1070	850	1650	4150	5800	8300
Cr Sed	1090	900	1800	4400	6150	8800
L Cr	1125	925	2000	4650	6500	9300
Commander Skyway Series						
2 dr Sed Cpe	1105	925	2000	4650	6500	9300
Cr Sed	1125	1025	2500	5150	7150	10,300
L Cr	1160	1100	3300	5650	7900	11,300
President Custom Series						
2 dr Sed Cpe	1141	925	2000	4650	6500	9300
Cr Sed	1161	1025	2500	5150	7150	10,300
L Cr	1196	1100	3300	5650	7900	11,300

President Deluxstyle Series

	FP	5	4	3	2	1
2 dr Sed Cpe	1186	1025	2500	5150	7150	10,300
Cr Sed	1206	1100	3300	5650	7900	11,300
L Cr	1241	1175	3700	6150	8600	12,300

President Skyway Series

	FP	5	4	3	2	1
2 dr Sed Cpe	1221	1100	3300	5650	7900	11,300
Cr Sed	1241	1175	3700	6150	8600	12,300
L Cr	1276	1300	4000	6650	9300	13,300

STURGES ELECTRIC — Although Harold Sturges entered this pioneer electric vehicle in the Chicago Times Herald Contest of 1895, it is more appropriately referred to by the name of its designer: William Morrison of Des Moines, Iowa. Refer to Morrison Electric.

STURGIS — There were two partners involved in this 1897 electric car built in Los Angeles: John Philip Erie and Samuel D. Sturgis. The partnership was a short-lived one; Sturgis may have built a few gasoline vehicles after the turn of the century. Refer to Erie & Sturgis.

1905 Sturtevant, tonneau, NAHC

STURTEVANT — Boston, Massachusetts — (1905-1907) — The Sturtevant Mill Company, which was located at Park and Clayton streets in the Dorchester section of Boston, built its first experimental car in 1902. A second car, a four, arrived in 1904, again experimental. A six followed in 1905, and was the first car to be advertised. In May of that year it was revealed that a separate company was about to be organized to produce Sturtevant cars under the patents of T.J. Sturtevant. A separate company never followed, however, and it is likely that the cars built were more for the purpose of demonstrating the Sturtevant ideas to established manufacturers with the view of garnering profitable licensing fees or components orders. Among the patented Sturtevant ideas was its transmission: a three-speed consisting of a series of disc clutches operated by centrifugal force for the forward speeds, with a sliding gear fitted for reverse. Automatic Sturtevant was an occasional designation used for the car. Two distinct models were offered in 1906-1907, both of them fours: a 40/50 hp Automatic Touring on a 120-inch wheelbase at $5000, and a 30/35 hp Flying Roadster on a 98-inch wheelbase at $3500. Only a handful of Sturtevant cars were made, the last of them in 1907. The Sturtevant Mill Company remains in operation building industrial machinery to this day. This firm is not to be confused, incidentally, with the B.F. Sturtevant Company (located in the Hyde Park section of Boston) which built aircraft engines and possibly entire planes during the First World War. Although B.F. Sturtevant has occasionally been cited as building an automobile, that company never did.

1905 STURTEVANT
Six — 40/45 hp, 108" wb

Side Entrance Tonneau	5000	2400	3400	4800	8000	17,000

1907 Sturtevant, touring, NAHC

1906-1907 STURTEVANT
Flying Roadster — 4-cyl., 30/35 hp, 98" wb

Roadster-2/3P	3500	4000	5000	8000	15,000	28,000

Automatic — 4-cyl., 40/50 hp, 120" wb

Touring-7P	5000	4400	5600	9200	17,300	31,000

STUTZ — Dayton, Ohio — (1902) — Like most first efforts of impecunious farm lads who had deserted the agrarian life for the challenge of the mechanical age, Harry C. Stutz's maiden automobile of 1898 was cobbled up of abandoned agricultural parts, including a stationary gasoline engine and a binder chain which served for final drive. He called the car Old Hick-

ory, and he built another in 1900. Both these cars were entirely experimental. In 1899 Stutz had opened a small machine shop in Dayton, which he later grandly titled the Stutz Manufacturing Company. Its sole product initially was a small single-cylinder gasoline engine of Stutz's own design. In March of 1902 Stutz announced that he was building "a few runabouts" which sported a steering wheel in place of the tiller used on his experimental cars. Undoubtedly, these were simply for local people; proper manufacture was not embarked upon. By the fall of 1902 Stutz had sold the rights to his engine to the Lindsay Automobile Parts Company of Indianapolis, and he moved to that city to superintend its manufacture. His tenure at Lindsay was woefully short, however; by the spring of 1903 he was involved in the organization of the Central Motor Car Company, again briefly. Nineteen four found him with the G&J Tire Company, then the Schebler Carburetor Company. Subsequent to that he was employed as an engineer for American, Marion and Empire. Though he bounced around a lot, he never left Indianapolis. And it was there, in 1911, that he introduced "The Car That Made Good in a Day" — and the Stutz name was on its way to becoming among the most famous in automobile history.

1912 Stutz, series A, roadster, OCW

STUTZ — Indianapolis, Indiana — (1911-1935) — Mention the word Stutz and the Pavlovian-like response invariably is Bearcat. Seldom has a car become so indelibly etched in memory via a single model. The first Stutz built, however, was not a Bearcat. It was the widely-advertised "Car That Made Good in a Day" — and the day was the Indianapolis 500 in May 1911. Having made several primeval efforts at building an automobile in his native Ohio, Harry C. Stutz had arrived in Indianapolis in 1903, where he seems never to have lacked for a job in the automobile field though he did leapfrog from one to another. He also came up with the design for a rear-axle-mounted transmission, and by 1910 he had his own firm, the Stutz Auto Parts Company, for its manufacture. The year following, in just five weeks' time, he built the car that was taken immediately to the Indy track for the inaugural running of the 500. There the Stutz was driven by Gil Anderson to an eleventh-place finish, which was not good for any prize money but was good for the slogan which was used for several years thereafter. Though eleventh might not seem much to crow about, the Stutz had averaged 68.25 mph, every car ahead of it had considerably more cubic inches than its 389 — and, had not so many pit stops been necessary for tire changes, the car undoubtedly would have finished even higher. It had been a good day for Stutz. Several weeks later it was announced that the Ideal Motor Car Company had been organized for manufacture of the car which had done so well at Indy. And indeed it was a duplicate: T-head 50 hp Wisconsin four-cylinder engine (only in 1917 did Stutz begin to manufacture its own powerplants), trans/axle setup (a feature which would endure into 1921), and right-hand steering wheel (not until 1922 would the company go over to left-hand drive and initially only on closed models). The new Stutz was offered as a roadster, toy tonneau and touring, each priced at $2000. In 1912 a 60 hp six-cylinder line was added to the fours, and in both the famous Bearcat model was offered. In 1912, too, the Stutz was entered in thirty different racing contests and won twenty-five of them. Invariably the car was a stock (or nearly stock) Bearcat. A true sports car in the scant-body/scant-comfort idiom, the Bearcat was a hairy, masculine machine, though the story that Harry Stutz purposely designed his clutches with springs so stiff that a woman couldn't operate them is probably apocryphal. Not until 1915 were special Stutz race cars (with Wisconsin-built sohc 16-valve engines) campaigned, and they did extraordinarily well also. The "White Squadron," as the Stutz team was known, was the chief rival to the Mercer. In 1915, too, Cannon Ball Baker drove a four-cylinder Bearcat from San Diego to New York in a transcontinental-record-breaking 11 days 7 hours 15 minutes; and the Stutz Motor Car Company (as the firm had been renamed in May 1913 in a merger of Ideal and Stutz Auto Parts) augmented its line that year with a light 23 hp roadster called the H.C.S. model and priced at $1475, for those who couldn't afford a Bearcat. Stutz was acquitting itself nicely in the marketplace: 266 cars in 1912, 759 in 1913, 649 in 1914, 1079 in 1915, 1535 in 1916, 2207 in 1917. But already trouble was brewing. Because increased sales had necessitated increased facilities, and because further expansion was needed for the manufacture of its own engines (the 16-valve T-head four which would be the mainstay of production from model year 1917 through 1923), Stutz made the decision to go public. By 1916 a Wall Street stock speculator named Alan A. Ryan had bought controlling interest in Stutz; by 1919 Harry C. Stutz had left the company to build a new car called the H.C.S.; by 1921 Ryan had engineered the infamous corner on Stutz stock; by 1922 he was broke. Taking over control of Stutz now was Bethlehem Steel magnate Charles M.

Schwab. A new ohv 70 hp six joined the Stutz line for 1923, but soon there would be no Bearcat. Nor would there be for a number of years following, because in 1925 Frederick E. Moskovics strode into the Stutz presidency intent upon revising the marque's image from hairy beast into sophisticated beauty. He succeeded. The new Stutz Vertical Eight, Safety Chassis arrived for the 1926 model year. Its engine was a nine-main-bearing sohc dual-ignition eight developing 92 (late 115) bhp at 3200 rpm. Its centrally lubricated chassis featured an underslung worm drive which allowed for low and intoxicatingly sensuous bodies. Many of these Weymann fabric bodies, Stutz contracting to take Charles Weymann's entire American output during the spring of 1928. Because much about the new Stutz was more European than prevailing American practice, many of the new body styles were given chic European designations, Monte Carlo, Biarritz, Versailles. And this new beauty was fast too, a sedan capturing the Stevens Trophy Cup in 1927 after averaging 68.44 mph for twenty-four hours at Indy, the Black Hawk speedsters winning everything in sight to become the 1927 AAA Stock Car Champion. Early in 1928, following a two-way average of 106.53 mph at Daytona, the Black Hawk was America's fastest production car. True, a Black Hawk did lose the curious match race against a Hispano-Suiza at Indy that April, but the Hispano's sponsor, Charles Weymann, used a Stutz to enter Le Mans that year and in 1929. By that time the Stutz factory had quit racing itself, following the tragic death of Frank Lockhart in a land speed record attempt at Daytona with the Stutz Black Hawk Special the week after the Hispano match race. Though the Vertical Eight had been sensationally received, with more than $3 million in orders during the week of its introduction, matters were not easy within the company itself. The Stutz legal department was busy with lawsuits instigated by Weidely for breach of contract (apparently some of the last pre-Moskovics era engines were to have been built by Weidely, and the company alleged its subsequent receivership resulted when Stutz reneged), and by James Scripps-Booth for breach of confidence (Booth had approached Stutz with an underslung worm drive design and had been turned down prior to Moskovics' appearance on the scene with his own idea of the same concept). Despite the glory of the new Stutz, these were troubled years. In January 1929, shortly after the introduction of a new and cheaper six-cylinder car by Stutz called the Blackhawk (absorbed into the Stutz line in 1931), Moskovics resigned from the company. Fortunately Edgar S. Gorrell, a Moskovics man, was chosen to succeed him. And Gorrell retained Charles ''Pop'' Greuter in the engineering post which he had served so well since joining the company in 1925. The company, wisely, elected not to enter the multi-cylinder race. Instead, introduced for 1932 was a development of the Vertical Eight (now renamed SV-16): the new car was the fabulous DV-32 (dual overhead camshaft, four valves per cylinder) with a commanding 156 bhp. And it was for this model that the legendary Bearcat name was revived in a speedster that was guaranteed to exceed 100 mph. Even faster was the Super Bearcat, the same car on a truncated wheelbase (116 inches versus the Bearcat's 134-1/2). But the Depression was now in full swing. The company really tried, slashing prices and introducing some cost-cutting measures (viz., the substitution of a three-speed gearbox for the Warner four-speed used since '29). Ironically, the production figure for 1922 of 4200 cars, which had so alarmed Charles Schwab upon his takeover of Stutz, turned out to be the best ever for the marque except for the Vertical Eight's introductory year of 1926 when some 5000 cars were built. The figures for the late Twenties were: 2900 in 1927, 2600 in 1928, 2320 in 1929. During the Thirties fewer than 1500 cars were produced. In 1934 just six Stutzes left the factory. In January 1935 the company announced that ''it is not a part of the present program to continue manufacture and sale of the Stutz car.'' The present program was production instead of the Pak-Age-Car, a light delivery van. Stutzes continued to be bodied and marketed in England through 1935, and, astoundingly, in the United States a 1936 model was announced, which probably means there might have been some parts on hand with which to put together a new Stutz should anyone have asked. On April 3rd, 1937 the Stutz Motor Car Company admitted its insolvency in court. In 1939 the firm was liquidated.

1912
Series A, 4-cyl., 50 hp, 120" wb

	FP	5	4	3	2	1
2P Rds	2000	10,800	21,600	36,000	50,500	72,000
4P Toy Ton	2000	10,500	21,000	35,000	49,000	70,000
5P Tr	2000	10,500	21,000	35,000	49,000	70,000
2P Bearcat	2000	29,500	55,000	84,000	110,000	140,000
4P Cpe	2500	7500	15,000	25,000	35,000	50,000

Series A, 6-cyl., 60 hp, 124" wb
Touring - 6P (130" wb)

	FP	5	4	3	2	1
6P Tr	2250	9900	19,800	33,000	46,200	66,000
4P Toy Ton	2250	9600	19,200	32,000	44,800	64,000
2P Bearcat	2125	31,100	58,000	88,000	114,000	150,000

1913 Stutz, model 6-B, touring, HAC

1913
Series B, 4-cyl., 50 hp, 120" wb

2P Rds	2000	10,800	21,600	36,000	50,500	72,000
4P Toy Ton	2000	10,500	21,000	35,000	49,000	70,000
4P Tr (124" wb)	2000	10,500	21,000	35,000	49,000	70,000

	FP	5	4	3	2	1
2P Bearcat	2000	29,500	55,000	84,000	110,000	140,000
6P Tr (124" wb)	2050	11,100	22,200	37,000	52,000	74,000
Series B, 6-cyl., 60 hp, 124" wb						
2P Bearcat	2125	31,100	58,000	88,000	114,000	150,000
4P Toy Ton	2250	10,500	21,000	35,000	49,000	70,000
6P Tr (130" wb)	2300	11,400	22,800	37,000	56,000	76,000

1914 Stutz, model 6-E, touring, HAC

1914
Model 4E, 4-cyl., 50 hp, 120" wb

2P Rds	2000	10,500	21,000	35,000	49,000	70,000
Bearcat	2000	30,300	57,000	86,000	112,000	145,000
5P Tr	2150	10,500	21,000	35,000	49,000	70,000

Model 6E, 6-cyl., 55 hp, 130" wb

2P Rds	2250	11,400	22,800	38,000	56,000	76,000
6P Tr	2400	11,400	22,800	38,000	56,000	76,000

1915 Stutz, model 6-F, touring, JAC

1915
Model H.C.S., 4-cyl., 23 hp, 108" wb

2P Rds	1475	7500	15,000	25,000	35,000	50,000

Model 4F, 4-cyl., 36.1 hp, 120" wb

2P Rds	2000	9000	18,000	30,000	42,000	60,000
Bearcat	2000	27,900	51,000	79,000	106,000	136,000
Cpe	2600	4800	9600	16,000	22,400	32,000
Bulldog	2250	8700	17,400	29,000	40,600	58,000
5P Tr	2275	9300	18,600	31,000	43,400	62,000
5P Sed	3675	4350	8700	14,500	20,300	29,000

Model 6F, 6-cyl., 38.4 hp, 130" wb

2P Rds	2250	9600	19,200	32,000	44,800	64,000
Bearcat	2250	29,500	55,000	84,000	110,000	140,000
Cpe	2850	5250	10,500	17,500	24,500	35,000
5P Tr	2275	9900	19,800	33,000	46,200	66,000
6P Tr	2400	9900	19,800	33,000	46,200	66,000
5P Sed	3800	4500	9000	15,000	21,000	30,000

1916 Stutz, model C, Bearcat, HAC

1916
Model C, 4-cyl., 36.1 hp, 120" wb

	FP	5	4	3	2	1
2P Rds	2100	9000	18,000	30,000	42,200	60,000
Bearcat	2000	25,500	45,000	73,000	100,000	130,000
Bulldog	2250	9900	19,800	33,000	46,200	66,000
Sed	3695	4350	8700	14,500	20,300	29,000

Bulldog Special, 4-cyl., 36.1 hp, 130" wb

4P Tr	2250	9900	19,800	33,000	46,200	66,000
5P Tr	2300	10,200	20,400	34,000	47,600	68,000

1917 Stutz, series R, roadster, OCW

1917
Series R, 4-cyl., 80 hp, 130" wb

2P Rds	2375	10,500	21,000	35,000	49,000	70,000
4P Bulldog Spec	2550	9900	19,800	33,000	46,200	66,000
6P Bulldog Spec	2550	10,200	20,400	34,000	47,600	68,000
Bearcat (120" wb)	2300	27,900	51,000	79,000	106,000	136,000

1918 Stutz, series S, roadster, HAC

1918
Series S, 4-cyl., 80 hp, 130" wb

2P Rds	2550	10,500	21,000	35,000	49,000	70,000
4P Bulldog Spec	2650	9900	19,800	33,000	46,200	66,000
6P Bulldog Spec	2750	10,200	20,400	34,000	47,600	68,000
Bearcat (120" wb)	2550	27,900	51,000	79,000	106,000	136,000

1919 Stutz, series G, Bearcat, HAC

1919
Series G, 4-cyl., 80 hp, 130" wb

6P Tr	2850	10,800	21,600	36,000	50,500	72,000
2P Rds	2750	9900	19,800	33,000	46,200	66,000
4P C.C. Tr	2850	10,800	21,600	36,000	50,500	72,000
Bearcat (120" wb)	2750	27,900	51,000	79,000	106,000	136,000

1920 Stutz, series H, roadster, AA

1920
Series H, 4-cyl., 80 hp, 130" wb

	FP	5	4	3	2	1
2P Bearcat (120" wb)	3250	27,900	51,000	79,000	106,000	136,000
2P Rds	3250	10,500	21,000	35,000	49,000	70,000
4P/5P Tr	3350	10,800	21,600	36,000	50,500	72,000
6P/7P Tr	3350	11,100	22,200	37,000	52,000	74,000

1921 Stutz, series K, close-coupled touring, HAC

1921
Series K, 4-cyl., 80 hp, 130" wb

2P Bearcat (120" wb)	3900	27,900	51,000	79,000	106,000	136,000
2P Rds	3900	13,500	27,000	45,000	70,000	90,000
4P Tr	4000	10,800	21,600	36,000	50,500	72,000
6P Tr	4000	10,800	21,600	36,000	50,500	72,000
4P Cpe	5500	6000	12,000	20,000	28,000	40,000

1922
Series K, 4-cyl., 80 hp, 130" wb

3P Cpe	4800	6000	12,000	20,000	28,000	40,000
2P Rds	3250	10,500	21,000	35,000	49,000	70,000
Bearcat (120" wb)	3250	27,900	51,000	79,000	106,000	136,000
6P Tr	3350	10,800	21,600	36,000	50,500	72,000
4P Spt	3350	11,400	22,800	38,000	56,000	76,000

1923 Stutz, Speedway Four, coupe, JAC

1923
Special Six, 70 hp, 120" wb

5P Sed	—	5250	10,500	17,500	24,500	35,000
5P Tr	—	10,800	21,600	36,000	50,500	72,000
Rds	—	10,800	21,600	36,000	50,500	72,000

Speedway Four, 88 hp, 130" wb

6P Tr	2640	11,400	22,800	38,000	56,000	76,000
Sportster	2790	12,000	24,000	40,000	60,000	80,000
4P Cpe	3490	6000	12,000	20,000	28,000	40,000
Sportsedan	4450	5550	11,100	18,500	25,900	37,000
Rds	—	10,500	21,000	35,000	49,000	70,000
Bearcat	—	29,500	55,000	84,000	110,000	140,000
Calif Tr	—	11,700	23,400	39,000	58,000	78,000
Calif Sptstr	—	11,700	23,400	39,000	58,000	78,000

1924 Stutz, Special Six, sedan, JAC

1924
Special Six, 70 hp, 120" wb

	FP	5	4	3	2	1
5P Phae	1995	10,200	20,400	34,000	47,600	68,000
Tourabout	1995	10,200	20,400	34,000	47,600	68,000
2P Rds	1995	10,500	21,000	35,000	49,000	70,000
Palanquin	—	10,200	20,400	34,000	47,600	68,000
5P Sed	2550	4800	9600	16,000	22,400	32,000

Speedway Four, 4-cyl., 88 hp, 130" wb
2P Rds	2450	10,500	21,000	35,000	49,000	70,000
2P Bearcat	—	27,900	51,000	79,000	106,000	136,000
6P Tr	2640	10,800	21,600	36,000	50,500	72,000
4P Cpe	3490	6000	12,000	20,000	28,000	40,000

1925 Stutz, series 695, suburban, HAC

1925
Models 693-694, 6-cyl., 70 hp, 120" wb
5P Phae	2880	9900	19,800	33,000	46,200	66,000
5P Tourabout	3000	10,200	20,400	34,000	47,600	68,000
2P Rds	2880	9900	19,800	33,000	46,200	66,000
4P Cpe	—	5700	11,400	19,000	26,600	38,000
5P Sed	3580	4800	9600	16,000	22,400	32,000

Model 695, 6-cyl., 80 hp, 130" wb
7P Tourster	3570	10,200	20,400	34,000	47,600	68,000
5P Sportster	3535	10,200	20,400	34,000	47,600	68,000
7P Sub	4535	6750	13,500	22,500	31,500	45,000
Sportbrohm	4435	6600	13,200	22,000	30,800	44,000
7P Berline	4785	6900	13,800	23,000	32,200	46,000

1926 Stutz, Vertical Eight, 5-pass. speedster, OCW

1926
Vertical Eight, AA, 92 hp, 131" wb
4P Spds	2995	27,900	51,000	79,000	106,000	136,000
5P Spds	2995	27,900	51,000	79,000	106,000	136,000
4P Vic Cpe	2995	8250	16,500	27,500	38,500	55,000
5P Brgm	2995	7350	14,700	24,500	34,300	49,000
5P Sed	2995	6000	12,000	20,000	28,000	40,000

1927 Stutz, Vertical Eight, custom berline, LeBaron, OCW

1927
Vertical Eight, AA, 92 hp, 131" wb

	FP	5	4	3	2	1
4P Spds	3150	27,900	51,000	79,000	106,000	136,000
5P Spds	3160	27,900	51,000	79,000	106,000	136,000
2P Cpe	3165	7500	15,000	25,000	35,000	50,000
4P Cpe	3175	7500	15,000	25,000	35,000	50,000
5P Brgm	3195	7350	14,700	24,500	34,300	49,000
5P Sed	3195	6000	12,000	20,000	28,000	40,000
7P Berline	3785	7350	14,700	24,500	34,300	49,000
7P Sed	3685	6300	12,600	21,000	29,400	42,000

1928 Stutz, series BB, sedan, HAC

1928
Series BB, 8-cyl., 115 hp, 131 & 135" wb
2P Spds	3495	27,900	51,000	79,000	106,000	136,000
4P Spds	3595	27,900	51,000	79,000	106,000	136,000
5P Spds	3845	29,500	55,000	84,000	110,000	140,000
7P Spds	3895	28,700	53,000	81,000	108,000	138,000
2P Black Hawk Spds	4895	30,300	57,000	86,000	112,000	145,000
4P Black Hawk Spds	4945	30,300	57,000	86,000	112,000	145,000
4P Vic Cpe	3495	8250	16,500	27,500	38,500	55,000
2P Cpe	3495	7800	15,600	26,000	36,400	52,000
5P Sed	3570	6000	12,000	20,000	28,000	40,000
5P Brgm	3570	6150	12,300	20,500	28,700	41,000
2P Cabr Cpe	3695	13,500	27,000	45,000	70,000	90,000
7P Sed	3895	6300	12,600	21,000	29,400	42,000
7P Sed Limo	3995	7500	15,000	25,000	35,000	50,000
4P Deauville	4120	7800	15,600	26,000	36,400	52,000
5P Chantilly Sed	4120	7800	15,600	26,000	36,400	52,000
4P Monaco Cpe	4120	8400	16,800	28,000	39,200	56,000
5P Riv Sed	4420	8250	16,500	27,500	38,500	55,000
7P Biarritz Sed	4495	8250	16,500	27,500	38,500	55,000
5P Chamonix Sed	4545	8550	17,100	28,500	39,900	57,000
7P Fontainbleau	4745	8550	17,100	28,500	39,900	57,000
5P Aix Les Bains	4995	8550	17,100	28,500	39,900	57,000
7P Versailles	5295	9000	18,000	30,000	42,000	60,000
5P Prince of Wales	6345	9000	18,000	30,000	42,000	60,000
8P Prince of Wales	6345	9300	18,600	31,000	43,400	62,000
Transformable Twn Car	6895	11,400	22,800	38,000	56,000	76,000

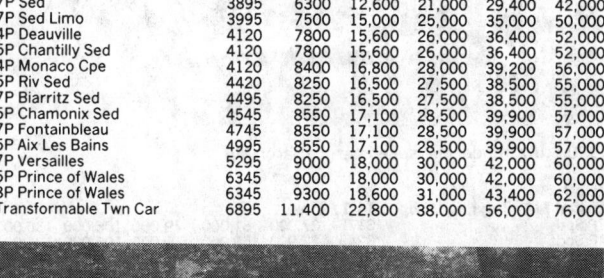

1929 Stutz, model M, town car, LeBaron, HAC

1929
Model M, 8-cyl., 115 hp, 134-1/2" wb
4P Spds	3535	27,900	51,000	79,000	106,000	136,000
4P Spds	3635	27,900	51,000	79,000	106,000	136,000

	FP	5	4	3	2	1
4P Spds	3745	27,900	51,000	79,000	106,000	136,000
4P Spds	3885	27,900	51,000	79,000	106,000	136,000
7P Spds	3895	28,700	53,000	81,000	108,000	138,000
4P Spds	3995	29,500	55,000	84,000	110,000	140,000
2P Speed Car	4735	29,500	55,000	84,000	110,000	140,000
5P Cpe	3395	7800	15,600	26,000	36,400	52,000
4P Cpe	3595	7800	15,600	26,000	36,400	52,000
2P Cabr	3595	13,500	27,000	45,000	70,000	90,000
5P Sed	3695	6300	12,600	21,000	29,400	42,000
5P Sed	3855	6300	12,600	21,000	29,400	42,000
7P Sed	3895	6450	12,900	21,500	30,100	43,000
5P Chantilly Sed	3895	7800	15,600	26,000	36,400	52,000
5P Monaco Cpe	3955	8400	16,800	28,000	39,200	56,000
5P Deauville	3955	7800	15,600	26,000	36,400	52,000
7P Limo	3995	7800	15,600	26,000	36,400	52,000
5P Sed	3995	6000	12,000	20,000	28,000	40,000
2P Cabr	3995	13,800	27,600	46,000	73,500	92,000
5P Biarritz	4115	8250	16,500	27,500	38,500	55,000
7P Fontainbleau	4145	8550	17,100	28,500	39,900	57,000
7P Aix Les Baines	4245	8550	17,100	28,500	39,900	57,000
5P Sed	4595	6750	13,500	22,500	31,500	45,000
5P Limo	4795	8250	16,500	27,500	38,500	55,000
6P Brgm	4795	8250	16,500	27,500	38,500	55,000
Brgm Limo	4995	8550	17,100	28,500	39,900	57,000
6P Sed	4995	6600	13,200	22,000	30,800	44,000
6P Sed Limo	4995	8700	17,400	29,000	40,600	58,000
7P Sed Limo	4995	8700	17,400	29,000	40,600	58,000
5P Transformable Cabr	5410	11,400	22,800	38,000	56,000	76,000
7P Trans Twn Car	5500	11,400	22,800	38,000	56,000	76,000
5P Trans Twn Car	6895	11,400	22,800	38,000	56,000	76,000

1929 Stutz, model M, town car, LeBaron, HAC

1930 Stutz, model MA, speedster, LeBaron, AA

1930
Model MA, 8-cyl., 115 hp, 134-1/2" wb
	FP	5	4	3	2	1
2P Spds	3175	27,900	51,000	79,000	106,000	136,000
4P Spds	3245	27,900	51,000	79,000	106,000	136,000
4P Spds	3745	27,900	51,000	79,000	106,000	136,000
2P Cpe	2995	8250	16,500	27,500	38,500	55,000
5P Cpe	2775	8250	16,500	27,500	38,500	55,000
Sed	2995	6000	12,000	20,000	28,000	40,000
Cabr	3350	13,500	27,000	45,000	70,000	90,000
Longchamps	3945	9900	19,800	33,000	46,200	66,000
Versailles	3945	9900	19,800	33,000	46,200	66,000
Torpedo	4735	10,500	21,000	35,000	49,000	70,000

Model MB, 8-cyl., 115 hp, 145" wb
	FP	5	4	3	2	1
4P Spds	3745	29,500	55,000	84,000	110,000	140,000
7P Spds	3895	29,500	55,000	84,000	110,000	140,000
4P Spds	3995	29,500	55,000	84,000	110,000	140,000
5P Sed	3855	6450	12,900	21,500	30,100	43,000
7P Sed	3895	6600	13,200	22,000	30,800	44,000
7P Limo	3995	7500	15,000	25,000	35,000	50,000
5P Sed	3995	6900	13,800	23,000	32,200	46,000
Cabr	3995	13,800	27,600	46,000	73,500	92,000
Chaumont	4345	9000	18,000	30,000	42,000	60,000
Monte Carlo	4495	9000	18,000	30,000	42,000	60,000
5P Sed	4595	7200	14,400	24,000	33,600	48,000
5P Limo	4795	7800	15,600	26,000	36,400	52,000
Brgm	4795	7500	15,000	25,000	35,000	50,000
Brgm Limo	4995	8250	16,500	27,500	38,500	55,000
6P Sed	4795	7350	14,700	24,500	34,300	49,000
6P Sed Limo	4995	8250	16,500	27,500	38,500	55,000
7P Sed Limo	4995	8550	17,100	28,500	39,900	57,000
Transformable Cabr	5410	11,400	22,800	38,000	56,000	76,000
Transformable Twn Car	5500	11,400	22,800	38,000	56,000	76,000
Transformable Tr Cabr	6985	11,400	22,800	38,000	56,000	76,000

1931 Stutz, model MA, victoria, Rollston, HAC

1931
Model LA, 6-cyl., 85 hp, 127-1/2" wb
	FP	5	4	3	2	1
4P Spds	2585	24,100	42,000	68,000	98,000	126,000
4P Spds	2785	24,100	42,000	68,000	98,000	126,000
5P Cpe	1995	6750	13,500	22,500	31,500	45,000
Sed	2245	5700	11,400	19,000	26,600	38,000
4P Cpe	2245	6900	13,800	23,000	32,200	46,000
Cabr Cpe	2445	11,400	22,800	38,000	56,000	76,000

Model MA, 8-cyl., 115 hp, 134-1/2" wb
	FP	5	4	3	2	1
4P Spds	3495	25,500	45,000	73,000	100,000	130,000
Torp	3595	13,800	27,600	46,000	73,500	92,000
4P Spds	3795	27,900	51,000	79,000	106,000	136,000
5P Cpe	3445	7500	15,000	25,000	35,000	50,000
4P Cpe	3495	7650	15,300	25,500	35,700	51,000
Cabr Cpe	3595	12,000	24,000	40,000	60,000	80,000
Sed	3695	6300	12,600	21,000	29,400	42,000
Longchamps	4145	6600	13,200	22,000	30,800	44,000
Versailles	4145	6600	13,200	22,000	30,800	44,000

Model MB, 8-cyl., 115 hp, 145" wb
	FP	5	4	3	2	1
7P Spds	3595	27,900	51,000	79,000	106,000	136,000
5P Sed	3855	6600	13,200	22,000	30,800	44,000
7P Sed	3895	7050	14,100	23,500	32,900	47,000
Limo	3995	7500	15,000	25,000	35,000	50,000
Cabr Cpe	3995	12,900	25,800	48,200	66,000	86,000
Conv Sed	4395	24,100	42,000	68,000	98,000	126,000
Chaumont	4545	12,900	25,800	48,200	66,000	86,000
Monte Carlo	4695	12,900	25,800	48,200	66,000	86,000
5P Sed	4795	7500	15,000	25,000	35,000	50,000
Brgm	4995	7800	15,600	26,000	36,400	52,000
7P Sed	4995	8250	16,500	27,500	38,500	55,000
Brgm Limo	5195	8550	17,100	28,500	39,900	57,000
6/7P Sed Limo	5195	9000	18,000	30,000	42,000	60,000
Transformable Cabr	5610	11,400	22,800	38,000	56,000	76,000
Transformable Twn Car	5700	11,400	22,800	38,000	56,000	76,000
Transformable Twn Car	7495	11,400	22,800	38,000	56,000	76,000

1932 Stutz, model LAA, sedan, AA

1932
Model LAA, 6-cyl., 85 hp, 127-1/2" wb
	FP	5	4	3	2	1
Sed	1620	6000	12,000	20,000	28,000	40,000
5P Cpe	1620	8250	16,500	27,500	38,500	55,000
4P Cpe	1620	8250	16,500	27,500	38,500	55,000
Club Sed	1620	6750	13,500	22,500	31,500	45,000

Model SV-16, 8-cyl., 115 hp, 134-1/2" wb
	FP	5	4	3	2	1
4P Spds	3495	24,100	42,000	68,000	98,000	126,000
Torp	3595	12,900	25,800	48,200	66,000	86,000
4P Spds	3795	25,500	45,000	73,000	100,000	130,000
5P Cpe	2695	7500	15,000	25,000	35,000	50,000
5P Sed	2995	6750	13,500	22,500	31,500	45,000
4P Cpe	2995	8250	16,500	27,500	38,500	55,000
Club Sed	3095	7050	14,100	23,500	32,900	47,000
Cabr Cpe	3345	11,400	22,800	38,000	56,000	76,000
Longchamps	4345	6750	13,500	22,500	31,500	45,000
Versailles	4395	6750	13,500	22,500	31,500	45,000
6P Sed	4795	6300	12,600	21,000	29,400	42,000
Cont Cpe	5775	8550	17,100	28,500	39,900	57,000

Model SV-16, 8 cyl., 115 hp, 145" wb
	FP	5	4	3	2	1
7P Spds	3895	30,300	57,000	86,000	112,000	145,000
7P Sed	3895	12,000	24,000	40,000	60,000	80,000
5P Sed	3895	11,400	22,800	38,000	56,000	76,000
Limo	3995	12,900	25,800	48,200	66,000	86,000

	FP	5	4	3	2	1
Conv Sed	4395	24,100	42,000	68,000	98,000	126,000
6P Sed	4395	12,300	24,600	41,000	62,000	82,000
Chaumont	4745	14,400	28,800	48,000	76,000	96,000
Brgm	4745	12,900	25,800	48,200	66,000	86,000
Monte Carlo	4895	13,200	26,400	44,000	68,000	88,000
Brgm Limo	4995	13,500	27,000	45,000	70,000	90,000
7P Sed Limo	4995	13,500	27,000	45,000	70,000	90,000
6P Sed Limo	4995	13,500	27,000	45,000	70,000	90,000
Transformable Cabr	5495	14,400	28,800	48,000	76,000	96,000
Monte Carlo	5895	14,700	29,400	49,000	78,000	98,000
Prince of Wales	6245	14,700	29,400	49,000	78,000	98,000
Conv Vic	6400	18,500	33,000	55,000	88,000	110,000
Spt Sed	7095	12,900	25,800	48,200	66,000	86,000
Tuxedo Cabr	7095	20,600	34,800	58,000	91,000	116,000
Patrician Cpe	7095	13,500	27,000	45,000	70,000	90,000
Transformable Twn Car	7495	15,000	30,000	50,000	80,000	100,000

Model DV-32, 8-cyl., 156 hp, 134-1/2" wb

	FP	5	4	3	2	1
Bearcat	5895	35,100	63,000	98,000	124,000	175,000

NOTE: All other models same as SV-16, with prices $1000 more than SV-16.

Model DV-32, 8-cyl., 156 hp, 145" wb

NOTE: All models same as SV-16, with prices $1000 more than SV-16.

Model DV-32, 8-cyl., 156 hp, 116" wb

	FP	5	4	3	2	1
Super Bearcat	5895	35,900	64,000	100,000	126,000	180,000

1933 Stutz, model DV-32, Bearcat roadster, AA

1933 Stutz, model SV-16, victoria, LeBaron, AA

1933
Model LAA, 6-cyl., 85 hp, 127-1/2" wb

	FP	5	4	3	2	1
5P Sed	1895	6300	12,600	21,000	29,400	42,000
5P Cpe	1895	7500	15,000	25,000	35,000	50,000
4P Cpe	1895	7650	15,300	25,500	35,700	51,000
5P Club Sed	1895	6750	13,500	22,500	31,500	45,000
4P Cabr Cpe	2185	11,400	22,800	38,000	56,000	76,000

Model SV-16, 8-cyl., 115 hp, 134-1/2" wb

	FP	5	4	3	2	1
4P Spds	3095	18,500	33,000	55,000	88,000	110,000
2P Torp	3195	12,000	24,000	40,000	60,000	80,000
4P Spds	3795	22,000	36,000	60,000	93,000	120,000
5P Cpe	2695	8550	17,100	28,500	39,900	57,000
5P Sed	2995	6750	13,500	22,500	31,500	45,000
4P Cpe	2995	8700	17,400	29,000	40,600	58,000
5P Club Sed	3095	7050	14,100	23,500	32,900	47,000
4P Cabr Cpe	3195	12,000	24,000	40,000	60,000	80,000
5P Versailles	4395	9900	19,800	33,000	46,200	66,000

Model SV-16, 8-cyl., 115 hp, 145" wb

	FP	5	4	3	2	1
4P Spds	3895	27,900	51,000	79,000	106,000	136,000
5P Sed	3410	8250	16,500	27,500	38,500	55,000
7P Sed	3460	8550	17,100	28,500	39,900	57,000
7P Limo	3660	9900	19,800	33,000	46,200	66,000
4P Cabr Cpe	3660	14,400	28,800	48,000	76,000	96,000
5P Conv Sed	3710	22,000	36,000	60,000	93,000	120,000
6P Sed	4745	8700	17,400	29,000	40,600	58,000
5P Chaumont	4745	9000	18,000	30,000	42,000	60,000
6P Brgm	4795	9000	18,000	30,000	42,000	60,000
6P Sed	4795	8700	17,400	29,000	40,600	58,000
5P Monte Carlo	4895	9300	18,600	31,000	43,400	62,000
6P Brgm Limo	4995	11,400	22,800	38,000	56,000	76,000
6P Sed Limo	4995	10,500	21,000	35,000	49,000	70,000
7P Twn Car	5495	12,000	24,000	40,000	60,000	80,000
5P Monte Carlo	5895	12,000	24,000	40,000	60,000	80,000

Series DV-32, 8-cyl., 156" wb

NOTE: Same models as the SV-16 on the two chassis, with prices $700 more. Bearcat and Super Bearcat continued from 1932.

1934 Stutz, model DV-32, sedan, LeBaron, AA

1934
Model SV-16, 8-cyl., 115 hp, 134-1/2" wb

	FP	5	4	3	2	1
Spds	3095	22,000	36,000	60,000	93,000	120,000
Spds	3195	22,000	36,000	60,000	93,000	120,000
Torp	3795	18,500	33,000	55,000	88,000	110,000
4P Cpe	—	7500	15,000	25,000	35,000	50,000
Conv Cpe	—	12,900	25,800	48,200	66,000	86,000
Club Sed	3195	9000	18,000	30,000	42,000	60,000
5P Sed	2995	8250	16,500	27,500	38,500	55,000
5P Cpe	3095	9000	18,000	30,000	42,000	60,000
Versailles		9000	18,000	30,000	42,000	60,000

Model SV-16, 8-cyl., 115 hp, 145" wb

	FP	5	4	3	2	1
Conv Cpe	3710	13,500	27,000	45,000	70,000	90,000
7P Sed	3660	8850	17,700	29,500	41,300	59,000
Limo	3660	9300	18,600	31,000	43,400	62,000
Chaumont	4745	9300	18,600	31,000	43,400	62,000
Monte Carlo	4895	9600	19,200	32,000	44,800	64,000

Model DV-32, 8-cyl., 156 hp, 134-1/2" wb

	FP	5	4	3	2	1
Spds	3165	25,500	45,000	73,000	100,000	130,000
Spds	3265	26,300	47,000	75,000	102,000	132,000
Torp	3865	24,800	44,000	70,000	99,000	128,000
4P Cpe	—	9000	18,000	30,000	42,000	60,000
Conv Cpe	—	24,100	42,000	68,000	98,000	126,000
Club Sed	3265	8850	17,700	29,500	41,300	59,000
5P Sed	3065	8700	17,400	29,000	40,600	58,000
5P Cpe	3165	9300	18,600	31,000	43,400	62,000
Versailles		9900	19,800	33,000	46,200	66,000

Model DV-32, 8-cyl., 156 hp, 145" wb

	FP	5	4	3	2	1
Conv Cpe	3780	22,000	36,000	60,000	93,000	120,000
7P Sed	3730	9000	18,000	30,000	42,000	60,000
Limo	3730	10,500	21,000	35,000	49,000	70,000
Chaumont	4815	10,500	21,000	35,000	49,000	70,000
Monte Carlo	4965	10,800	21,600	36,000	50,500	72,000

1935
Model SV-16, 8-cyl., 134 & 145" wb

	FP	5	4	3	2	1
2P Spds	3195	13,200	26,400	44,000	68,000	88,000
2P Cpe	3095	7800	15,600	26,000	36,400	52,000
5P Sed	3095	6300	12,600	21,000	29,400	42,000
7P Sed	3560	7200	14,400	24,000	33,600	48,000

Model DV-32, 8-cyl., 134 & 145" wb

	FP	5	4	3	2	1
2P Spds	3895	13,500	27,000	45,000	70,000	90,000
2/4P Cpe	3795	8250	16,500	27,500	38,500	55,000
5P Sed	3795	6300	12,600	21,000	29,400	42,000
7P Limo	4260	8250	16,500	27,500	38,500	55,000

STUTZMAN — Williamsport, Pennsylvania — (1899) — Frank Stutzman of the bicycle-manufacturing Elliot & Stutzman Company of Williamsport completed his first experimental automobile during the summer of 1899. It was powered by a gasoline engine and fitted with a friction transmission. The Williamsport *Gazette and Bulletin* reported the car's first test run on July 25th, which went well save for the vehicle's collision at the corner of West Fourth and Pine with a man on a bicycle. The man was uninjured, but the bicycle was a wreck. Frank Stutzman drove his car frequently thereafter, and in July of 1900 the Williamsport *Sun* revealed that manufacture was a possibility: "The gentlemen who are interested in the matter have acquainted themselves with the many good points of the Williamsport automobile, and are ready and willing to invest their capital in the concern." They must have reneged, however, because the evidence suggests Frank Stutzman's car was never put into manufacture.

1911 Stuyvesant, touring, NAHC

STUYVESANT — Cleveland, Ohio — (1911-1912) — The Stuyvesant began as the Stiverson. Frank E. Stiverson was a nuts and bolts manufacturer from Cleveland who had also served as a sales manager for White. In November of 1909 he organized the Stiverson Motor Car Company and one year later announced the completion of development of a six-cylinder automobile. About the same time he decided to change both his car and his company's name to Stuyvesant. The Stuyvesant was claimed to be the first en bloc six-cylinder car in the United States. Possibly it might have been, though this cannot be documented. In any case, it became apparent that Stiverson did not wish to place all his hopes on this one automobile. In November of 1910 the Stuyvesant Motor Car Company acquired the assets of the Gaeth Automobile Company in Cleveland and announced its continuing production of the Gaeth as the Stuyvesant Four. Plans called for an output of 200 fours and 100 sixes for 1911. Many fewer than that were produced when Stiverson found himself in financial hot water. In November that year the Stuyvesant assets were purchased by the Grant-Lees Machine Company of Cleveland. Because Grant-Lees was already producing the Grant Six designed by Harry Elmer, that company eschewed production of the Stuyvesant Six. Stuyvesant production for 1912 was a Gaeth-derived four-cylinder car only. The Stuyvesant Six was given a dubious encore, however. By 1913 Grant-Lees had disposed of its Stuyvesant assets to the newly organized Benton Motor Car Company of Benton, Illinois. Lavish promotion pieces were produced by Benton using Stuyvesant Six photographs, and a Stuyvesant Six touring car was grandly paraded through the streets of town as a "Made in Benton" automobile. Shortly thereafter, as the *Benton Evening News* put it, "the promoter and his car drove off in the sunset, never to be seen again." Meanwhile, back in Cleveland, Frank Stiverson, who by now had renamed himself Stuyvesant too, was back in business producing automobile accessories as the Hudson-Stuyvesant Motor Company.

1911 STUYVESANT
Model 6-60 — 6-cyl., 60 hp, 128" wb

	FP	5	4	3	2	1
Touring-7P	4200	5500	7500	12,000	26,000	39,000

Four — 40/45 hp, 120" wb

Touring-5P	3000	4400	5600	9200	17,300	31,000

1912 STUYVESANT
Model 50 — 4-cyl., 50 hp, 126" wb

Touring-7P	3500	5200	6800	11,300	23,000	36,000
Toy Tonneau-4P	3500	5000	6500	11,000	22,000	35,000

SUBURBAN — The Suburban Automobile Company was organized in Portland, Maine early in 1902 with a capital stock of $75,000 for the manufacture of "automobiles and all kinds of tools." Incorporators were C.E. Todd of Boston, G.H. Allan of Portland and F.H. Swan of Westbrook, Massachusetts. Manufacture of a car is doubted.

1911 Suburban, roadster, WLB

SUBURBAN — Detroit & Ecorse, Michigan — (1911-1912) — The Suburban was William A. de Schaum's low-water mark. Although the De Schaum highwheeler he built in Buffalo, New York from 1908-1910 may have been more promotion than production, the Suburban was even more so. It was, however, a nice car and a nice idea. Racy two-seater roadsters were to be the only offerings, available as a 20 hp Suburban four and a 28 hp Suburban Limited six, each carrying a $1200 price tag. In the early fall of 1910, de Schaum arrived in Detroit to organize the De Schaum Motor Car Company, and a prototype Suburban was being tested soon thereafter. In September 1911 the firm was reorganized as the Suburban Motor Car Company when de Schaum's plans grew to mammoth proportions. He had talked the mayor of Bad Axe into becoming president of his venture, and he was looking at 350 acres of land in nearby Ecorse upon which to build a factory and a model village for the employees. Scandal followed. Purportedly, at one point de Schaum put up a check for $150,000, which was later returned to him. Rumor said he didn't have $150 to his name. de Schaum withdrew from the company under fire in November 1912, and was succeeded by R.A. Palmer. A grand total of ten cars had thus far been built. Although Suburban production was initially planned to be continued, it was not, though fifteen further cars were completed before quits were called. Palmer reorganized as the Palmer Motor Car Company which in June of 1913 joined with the Partin Manufacturing Company of Chicago to produce the Partin and the Partin-Palmer in the Windy City. William A. de Schaum meantime was elsewhere in Detroit. His next effort was a cyclecar called the Tiger.

1911-1912 SUBURBAN
Series A — 4-cyl., 20 hp, 106" wb

Roadster	1200	2500	3500	5000	8500	18,000

Limited — 6-cyl., 28 hp, 108" wb

Roadster	1200	2700	3600	5300	8800	19,000

SUBURBAN STEAM — Although advertised independently under its own name, this Suburban was simply one of four steam car models produced by Edward S. Clark of Boston, Massachusetts in 1904. The other cars in

the line were known as Clarks. The Suburban model carried a two-cylinder engine and sixteen-inch boiler. It was the only Clark steam car offered on a 72-inch wheelbase that year, and it was not reoffered in 1905.

1908 Success, auto buggy, WLB

SUCCESS — St. Louis, Missouri — (1906-1909) — The Success Auto-Buggy Manufacturing Company of St. Louis produced one of the cheapest (as low as $250) and most economical (100 mpg was claimed) high-wheelers on the market. The first model had a short 62-inch wheelbase, its single-cylinder air-cooled engine mounted on the right side of the body next to the seat, with power transmitted via a two-speed planetary gear to a sprocket on the right wheel only. Steel wheels were standard, rubber was $25 extra. The last models were somewhat more sophisticated, with either two- or four-cylinder engines and a choice of water or air cooling. The Success remained a motor buggy for the whole of its life, however. Just what it was about the car that warranted compensation is not known, but some features of the car were patented, and the company demanded royalties from other highwheeler manufacturers. Economy of Ft. Wayne and Kiblinger of Auburn, Indiana were two of the firms Success took to court on the matter. The Success Company failed — after the building of over 600 cars — while the litigation was pending. Interestingly, the man behind the Success Company was John C. Higdon, who built his first car under his own name in 1896. At that time, he said he had no plans to build another and that anyone anywhere could feel free to copy it. When he subsequently began to press his claims in court some journalists took to referring to him as the Selden of the highwheeler world.

1906 SUCCESS
Model A — 1-cyl., 2/3 hp, 62" wb

	FP	5	4	3	2	1
Runabout	250	2200	3200	4400	7000	15,000

1907 SUCCESS
Model B — 1-cyl., 4 hp, 62" wb

Runabout	275	2300	3300	4600	7500	16,000

Model C — 2-cyl., 10 hp, 72" wb

Runabout	400	2400	3300	4800	8000	17,000

1908 SUCCESS
Model B — 1-cyl., 4 hp, 62" wb

Runabout	250	2300	3300	4600	7500	16,000

Model C — 2-cyl., 12 hp, 72" wb

Runabout	400	2400	3400	4800	8000	17,000
Surrey	500	2500	3500	5000	8500	18,000
Delivery Wagon	500	2200	3200	4400	7000	15,000

1909 SUCCESS
Model C — 2-cyl., 12 hp, 72" wb

Runabout	400	2400	3400	4800	8000	17,000

Model E — 2-cyl., 16 hp, 96" wb

Conv. Rbt.	425	2500	3500	5000	8500	18,000

Model D — 2-cyl., 18 hp, 80" wb

Surrey	450	2500	3500	5000	8500	18,000

Model F — 4-cyl., 24 hp, 84" wb

Runabout	800	2700	3600	5300	8800	19,000

SUFFOLK — The Suffolk Motor Company was organized in Boston, Massachusetts during the fall of 1906 with a capital stock of $55,000 for the manufacture of motor cars, motor boats and engines. James J. O'Brien and Robert M. Currier were behind this venture. Manufacture of a car is doubted.

SUITZ — In November of 1902 the Suitz Motor Carriage Company of Grand Rapids, Michigan announced its plans to exhibit a 16 hp two-cylinder two-stroke tonneau with shaft drive at the New York Automobile Show at Madison Square Garden the following month. The car didn't make it to the show, however, and Suitz does not appear to have moved into manufacture.

SULLIVAN — The A.H. Sullivan Manufacturing Company was organized in St. Louis, Missouri early in 1914 with a capital stock of $30,000 to manufacture and deal in automobiles, tools and machinery. Joining Sullivan in this venture were Arthur F. Barnes and David H. Leitch. Manufacture of an automobile is doubted, though it appears Sullivan briefly considered entering the ranks of cyclecar producers.

Roger J. Sullivan & Company has been indicated on various rosters as the manufacturer of an automobile in Detroit, Michigan in 1904. This seems highly unlikely. The firm was included among the list of exhibitors at the Chicago Automobile Show that year, but with no indication of the product exhibited. Because the Detroit city directory for 1904 notes the Sullivan Company as makers of "furniture, carpets, stoves, desks, matting and oil cloths," it seems probable that Sullivan was exhibiting in the accessories section.

1908 Sultan, 5-pass. touring, WLB

SULTAN — Springfield, Massachusetts — (1908-1912) — The Sultan Motor Company was organized in New York City in 1904 by Henri de Buren to promote the licensed manufacture in America of the Sultane produced in Paris by Lethimonnier et Cie. Initially, only taxicabs and a commercial vehicle were built here, their assembly being assigned to the Elektron Manufacturing Company in Springfield, Massachusetts. Sultan was not entirely pleased with the Elektron performance, however, because when the company decided to offer its cars on the general market in 1908, the building of the prototype and the first production cars was entrusted to the Otis Elevator Company in Springfield and not to Elektron. Ultimately, it would appear Sultan found its own factory in Springfield, into which chief engineer Nelson Bliss immediately moved. The Sultan was a four-cylinder car (a six was announced but never produced) fitted with a three-speed selective transmission and shaft drive. The Sultan passenger-market cars were largely similar to the Sultans sold for livery service, though the feature of a demountable power unit in the latter was not available on the former. Sultan manufacture ceased sometime during 1912. Among the car's problems had been its use of many parts imported from France; they were metric measure, with the result that U.S. tools couldn't fit them. American mechanics didn't like the Sultan at all.

1908-1909 SULTAN
Four — 12/15 hp, 98-1/2" wb

	FP	5	4	3	2	1
Touring/Landaulet	3000	3900	4800	7700	14,300	27,000

Note: The car was introduced at $4000 but its price was decreased to $3000 within months.

1910 Sultan, landaulet, MVMA

1910 SULTAN
Four — 12/15 hp, 98" wb

Landaulet	3000	3900	4800	7700	14,300	27,000
Limousine	3000	3700	4700	7300	13,700	26,000
Runabout	2800	3700	4700	7300	13,700	26,000

1911 SULTAN
Four — 12/15 hp, 98" wb

Town Car	2850	3900	4800	7700	14,300	27,000
Runabout	2250	3700	4700	7300	13,700	27,000

1912 SULTAN
Four — 12/15 hp, 98" wb

Limousine	2550	3700	4700	7300	13,700	27,000
Landaulet	2400	4000	5000	8000	15,000	28,000

SUMMIT — The Summit Automobile Company was organized in Akron, Ohio early in 1913 with a capital stock of $10,000 to manufacture and deal "in pleasure and commercial motor vehicles." Incorporators were E.J. Elben, J.M. Saunder and F.L. Metz. Manufacture of a car is doubted.

The Summit Garage Company was organized in Summit, New Jersey during the fall of 1905 to manufacture and rent automobiles and motor vehicles. Capital stock was $25,000; behind this venture were Walter C. Sampson, W.C. Johnson, Charles A. Grant, William J. Lamson, Charles S.

Hardy, Edward Benedict and B.C. Wilson. Manufacture is doubted, but the firm subsequently operated one of the most successful garages in Summit.

The Summit Motor Car Company was organized in Summit, New Jersey early in 1909 with a capital stock of $5000 for the manufacture of automobiles, bicycles and supplies. Howard I. Day and Harry Baldwin were among the principals involved. Manufacture of a car is doubted.

1907 Summitt "Carriage-Mobile", auto-buggy, NAHC

SUMMIT — Waterloo, Iowa — (1907-1909) — The Summit Carriage-Mobile Company of Waterloo produced a highwheeler quite unlike any other. Its motive force was a hollow piston with mechanically operated valves placed in a stationary head running in guides like the crosshead of a steam engine, the piston movement assisting in the cooling. Summit called all this its "Caldwell cylinderless self-cooling engine" and was convinced it was the revolutionary powerplant of the future. The Caldwell engine was built with one, two, three and four pistons, developing 8 to 40 hp. The Summit chassis dispensed with steering knuckles as well as a differential, the entire front axle turning on a king-bolt, this a throwback to horsedrawn carriage days. Apparently this marriage of the traditional and the unconventional was not a happy one. During 1907 Summit advertised its highwheeler as the Farmer-Mobile. From 1908 through 1909, it carried only the Summit name.

SUMNER — Cincinnati, Ohio — (1901-1902) — Operating out of his Cincinnati machine shop, Harry Sumner built a number of gasoline automobiles to custom order at the turn of the century. Details regarding their construction are lacking, but it is known that among his first orders in 1902 was a six-seater touring car for E.V. Wilbern of Cincinnati who planned to tour the world in it. Most probably that ambition would not be realized, but Wilbern indicated that he had recently made the run from Cincinnati to Hamilton (30 miles in 55 minutes) in another car that Sumner had built for him.

1916 Sun, touring, WLB

SUN — Elkhart, Indiana — (1916-1917) — "The Sun Outshines Them All," the company said, none too cleverly. It was a light six designed by Roscoe C. Hoffman that was rated at 23 hp though the Sun Motor Car Company insisted that it developed at least 50 bhp. That was doubtful. A single 116-inch wheelbase featuring shaft drive and a three-speed selective sliding gear transmission was used for a model line of four body styles priced in the $1000 range. President of the Sun venture was R. Crawford, like Hoffman a veteran of the Haynes Automobile Company of Kokomo, Indiana. Initially, Sun was organized in Buffalo, New York where headquarters were established in an old silk mill but prior to the onset of production the company moved to Elkhart, Indiana and into the two factory buildings formerly occupied by the defunct Sterling and Elmer. In December of 1915, Sun ordered 3500 of its engines to be built under contract by the Beaver Manufacturing Company of Milwaukee. This was wildly optimistic. The Sun car did enjoy a mild initial success, but receivership arrived in September 1917. At the receiver's sale, the Sun assets were purchased by the Automotive Corporation of Toledo which came up with a Sun of its own in 1921.

1916-1917 SUN
Six — 23 hp, 116" wb

	FP	5	4	3	2	1
Sedan-5P	1295	2200	3200	4400	7000	15,000
Touring-5P	1095	3100	4200	6300	10,500	22,000
Touring-7P	1145	3500	4500	7000	13,000	25,000
Roadster-4P	1145	3300	4400	6700	12,000	24,000

1922 Sun, roadster, NAHC

SUN — Toledo, Ohio — (1921-1922) — Said the brochure, "The new Sun is not a toy — not a freak — not a racer — not an inventor's dream but a real honest-to-goodness automobile with large possibilities." It was a small two-passenger roadster powered by a small air-cooled four-cylinder 10/20 hp engine designed by Everett Cameron. Its wheelbase was 91 inches, and its disc wheels were cute. Both 50 mph and 50 mpg were claimed. "America's Greatest Little Car" was produced by the Automotive Corporation which had been building tractors in Toledo since shortly before the end of the First World War. At that same time, the firm had purchased the assets of the defunct Sun Motor Car Company of Elkhart, Indiana, supplying parts and providing service to former Sun owners thereafter and probably getting some useful pointers about motorcar manufacture in the process. When Automotive Corporation gave birth to its own Sun, however, it was a different car altogether, the only asset of the Elkhart Sun retained being its logo. The Toledo Sun was introduced in 1921 at $375. That figure was crossed out in brochures the following year, with $475 rubber-stamped in. Automotive Corporation was obviously chintzy in the graphics and promotion department, though probably the firm couldn't afford to be otherwise. Despite an impressive lineup of open and closed models — with bigger engines, longer wheelbases and higher prices — that was announced for 1923, there was no new Sun that year.

SUNDERLIN — "Boone, Iowa has a new automobile company which is to make cars designed by F.B. Sunderlin, formerly of Des Moines," reported *The Motor World* in December 1908. Backing Sunderlin in this venture were J.L. Stevens and Dr. C.W. Payne. Manufacture is doubted.

1901 Sunset, steam runabout, NAHC

SUNSET — San Francisco, California — (1900-1906) — San Jose, California — (1906-1913) — At the turn of the century, at 1336 Mission Street in San Francisco, the Sunset Automobile Company began building a small $900 steam runabout. It used a Mason engine, a Dyke chassis, was a Locomobile look-alike — and was produced principally to raise the money necessary for company manager Dorville Libby, Jr. to continue development of the gasoline car which everyone at Sunset thought was a sure winner. Shortly thereafter Sunset headquarters relocated to 1814 Market

Street, and part of that facility was profitably leased to the Holle Automobile and Manufacturing Company. By the fall of 1904 the new gasoline car was ready, and finis was spelled for the little Sunset steamer. The new Sunset featured a 10 hp two-cylinder two-stroke engine mounted up front under a hood with drive through planetary transmission and propeller shaft to a divided rear axle. It was offered as an 84-inch-wheelbase runabout only through 1905, with surrey and touring versions joining the line for 1906, as well as a 20 hp four-cylinder car. Assisting in the development of these later Sunsets was Frank H. Holmes, an erstwhile farmer who had built a car of his own in San Jose at the turn of the century. Matters were well in hand for Sunset until April 18, 1906 when its factory was destroyed in the San Francisco earthquake. Previously, Harry Knox from Springfield, Massachusetts had inquired about building the Sunset two-stroke car on the East Coast as the Atlas runabout, and now the Sunset people gladly took him up on the offer, the money from the Knox agreement being desperately needed if they were to stay in business. Rescue was also offered by Bert Knapp, a San Jose automobilist who suggested partnership. At this point, Dorville Libby chose to remain in San Francisco where he opened a repair shop. The Victory Motor Car Company was the nicely designated name given to the consolidation of the Sunset Automobile Company and the Knapp Manufacturing Company. Frank Holmes was president, Bert Knapp vice-president. A new factory was built at 896 South First Street in San Jose, and while it was under construction Sunset bodies were produced in the Knapp shops on South Third. The new plant was completed in August of 1906. For 1907 three Sunset versions were offered: a two-cylinder $950 Model A runabout, a three-cylinder $1250 Model B runabout and a three-cylinder $1400 Model C touring. Wheelbase was 84 inches, horsepower 15. The Sunset people were particularly proud that theirs was a "manufactured" car with most of its parts built in their own factory. By the end of 1908 the factory was turning out eight cars a month; more than 230 Sunsets were in use in San Jose alone. A new roadster model had been introduced that year, and a specially-prepared version was sent racing in the area. Its best showing was victory in three of five races entered in Fresno in September of 1908. By 1909 the Sunset was advertised as "guaranteed to make a mile a minute." This was the new Model 30 with Continental engine offered as a $1450 roadster and $1500 touring on a 110-inch-wheelbase chassis. The two-stroke cars continued in production. Both Frank Holmes and Bert Knapp left the company around 1910. Holmes opened an automobile dealership in town, but Knapp seems to have left the area. The new man in charge of the Sunset venture was Herbert S. Swanton. He had something of a personnel problem. In 1911 one of his salesmen was arrested for stealing batteries and gasoline from a Sunset car undergoing repairs in the paint shop. The man explained that he had "appropriated the accessories under the impression that anything found in a Sunset shop could be taken without question by a Sunset agent." Unfortunately, the car from which he had appropriated the accessories belonged to the local district attorney. Swanton bowed out of the firm by the end of 1912. A report from 1913 indicated that the Sunset car was then being built under the aegis of the California Motor Car Company. This was short-lived. That September the Sunset factory was sold, and the Sunset was no more.

1906 Sunset, touring, NAHC

SUPER — Super Allied was the name under which the 1935 version of the taxi produced in 1932-1934 as the Allied was promoted. These cars were assembled in the former Elcar factory in Elkhart, Indiana. Refer to Allied.

The Super Paramount was merely a super-luxury version of the Paramount, itself a luxury-type taxicab that was produced by the Moller organization in Hagerstown, Maryland and marketed in New York City by the Paramount Cab Manufacturing Company from 1927-1931. Refer to Paramount.

SUPERIOR — Apparently these Superior automobile ventures weren't. Despite an announced intention to build automobiles, documentation has not been discovered proving that any of these companies did.

The Superior Automobile Company of Chicago, Illinois, organized early in 1905 with a capital stock of $2500 by Richard H. Mather, Willis H. Hutson and Benson Wright.

The Superior Chicopee Motor Company of St. Louis, Missouri, organized during the summer of 1912 with a capital stock of $15,000 by T.H. Burns, George C. Ward and Harry C. Carr.

The Superior Motor and Machine Works of Duluth, Minnesota, organized during the summer of 1909 with a capital stock of $15,000 by Solon L. Perrin, Dr. H.J. O'Brien and H.C. Lavery.

The Superior Motor Sales Company of St. Louis, Missouri, organized with a capital stock of $75,000 during the fall of 1910 by Oliver L. Garrison and Oliver L. Garrison, Jr. of St. Louis, and Murray M. Baker of Peoria, Illinois.

The Superior Motor Vehicle Company of Buffalo, New York, organized early in 1910 with a capital stock of $200,000 by H.A. Hamman, J. Lansing and I.T. Gleason.

SUPERIOR — West Superior, Wisconsin — (1900) — During the summer of 1900, M.R. Martin, who was the manager of the Superior Cycle Company, announced his intention of adding an automobile department in his factory. "He has already purchased considerable machinery for the purpose of making these machines," *The Autobain* reported, "and is now working on his first vehicle." That any sustained manufacture followed has not been documented.

SUPERIOR — Cleveland, Ohio — (1902) — I.H. Lewis was a bicycle man from Cleveland and in 1902 he established a small factory on Clara Street which he called the Superior Automobile Company. He built a few single-cylinder runabouts there later in 1902, but his automotive venture does not seem to have survived into 1903.

1908 Superior (Briggs & Stratton), touring, JAC

SUPERIOR — Milwaukee, Wisconsin — (1908) — The Briggs & Stratton Company of Milwaukee manufactured automobile accessories, and in 1907 decided to give the automobile a whirl. Superior was the name chosen for the car, which was something of a misnomer. A total of three Superiors — two tourings, one roadster — resulted from this effort. The cars carried four-cylinder Continental engines. Their fate was succinctly recorded in the Briggs & Stratton company history: "One caught fire and was destroyed, another allegedly was pushed off Milwaukee's 14th Street viaduct by an irate owner and the remaining vehicle simply disappeared." Thereafter the company returned to the manufacture of accessories solely, until after the First World War when Briggs & Stratton commenced to build a piquant little buckboard that was quite successful.

SUPERIOR — Superior, Wisconsin — (1909) — This Superior was built by the firemen of the Superior Fire Department for a local man named Dell See, who had lost both legs in an accident several years previously. The car was designed by fire department engineer Al Hunter. Three feet long, eighteen inches high and shod with solid eight-inch rubber tires, the vehicle was powered by a 3/4-hp engine and was capable of 15 mph. "The seat holds one person and is on a pivot," *The Motor Age* reported. "The car is a curiosity."

SUPERIOR — St. Louis, Missouri — (1914) — The Crescent Motor Car Company was organized in April of 1914 by George A. Root, Albert G. Nelson, Jr., William H. Foster and Edward L. Beebe. A four-cylinder car in the $1000 price range was announced to be the firm's product, with a roadster and touring to be offered on a 116-inch wheelbase, both sporting right-hand drive. Within a week after organization, Crescent moved into a leased building at the corner of Main and St. George streets in St. Louis to build its car. The first Crescent rolled out in May. Only two more were produced by July, at which time the Crescent Motor Car Company announced that the cars thus far built and all future cars would carry the name Superior. The company was out of business before its directors had a chance to decide or announce whether the firm's name would be changed too.

SUPER-STEAMER — Denver, Colorado — (1918-1919) — The Peterson-Culp Gearless Steam Automobile Company was the mouthful of a name for this venture which was organized in 1918 in Denver. Super-Steamer was to be the name of the car, and it was touted as "America's Latest Creation in Motive Power." Its engine was a four-cylinder, and its boiler a fire-tube. "The engine is so connected with the rear axle," noted *Motor Record*, "that each rear wheel has its own independent power, which is claimed to keep the car from skidding and avoid stalling on bad roads." Only a single prototype was built. The Peterson-Culp venture originated at 1637 Court Place in Denver, moved to 727 Symes Building in 1919, and stalled forever soon thereafter.

1919 Super-Steamer, touring, MVMA

SUPREME — Cleveland, Astabula & Warren, Ohio — (1917-1922) — Supreme Motors Corporation was organized during the summer of 1917 for the manufacture of four-, six- and twelve-cylinder engines. The men behind the company were all veterans of the industry: C.J. Jamison (Saxon and Elgin), B.J. Cline (Pierce-Arrow, Thomas and Chandler), C.N. Mitchell (Lozier and Chandler), and Charles H. Davids and C.E. Manning, whose previous experience had been in engines only, not motorcars. The few automobiles built by the Supreme company were solely for demonstration purposes and were not marketed. From Cleveland, the firm moved to Ashtabula in 1918, and subsequently to Warren, and never did establish a solid footing. During the summer of 1922 there were rumors the firm would merge with Colonial Motors Company (also of Warren) and consolidate with the Apperson organization in Kokomo, Indiana. Instead, that fall Supreme Motors went into bankruptcy with liabilities of $1,067,099 and assets of $238,653. Of the latter, $101 was in cash, $1870 in the bank, and the rest in real estate and machinery subsequently acquired by Sterling-Knight.

SUTCLIFFE — William Sutcliffe first announced his automotive ambitions from Paterson, New Jersey during the fall of 1901 when he reported his plans to manufacture cars there in association with Charles E. Abert. Apparently those plans quickly fell through because a couple of years later he was in Louisville, Kentucky as Sutcliffe & Company. He fared no better. By early 1904, with liabilities of $119,104.24 and assets of $55,826, his business was in receivership. Whether he had ever managed to manufacture a car has not been documented.

SWAN — The Swan Motor Car Company was organized in Indianapolis, Indiana during the summer of 1915 with a capital stock of $50,000 for the manufacture and sale of automobiles. Harry J. Herff, L. Porter Smith and H. Ralph Smith were the principals involved. Manufacture is doubted. In 1910 L. Porter Smith had built the Cyclop car in Indianapolis. Whether Harry J. Herff was related to the three other Herffs of Indianapolis then producing the Herff-Brooks car is not known, but seems likely.

The Swan Motor Corporation was organized in Rockford, Illinois during the spring of 1918 with a capital stock of $5000 for the manufacture of automobiles. Incorporators were F.E. Teachout, Gordon West, Fred Swan and Thomas Kelly. Both fours and sixes were slated to be produced, but the only promotional material known to have been issued was an office blotter indicating the company office as the Trust Building and the company phone number as Forest 21. A drawing of a touring car also appeared on the blotter, but manufacture is doubted.

SWAN — Middletown, Connecticut — (1903-1904) — In 1903 a Middletown electrician named William J. Swan built a single-cylinder air-cooled 5 hp gasoline runabout with wheel steering, wooden wheels and shaft drive which he believed he could profitably market at the attractive price of $450. Searching for the financial backing necessary, he found most of it in Hartford where the Swan Manufacturing Company was organized in the early spring of 1904 with a capital stock of $50,000. Joining Swan in the venture were Frank H. Harriman of Hartford and Z.E. Dowd of Meriden, and the plan was to manufacture both the Swan gasoline car and a variety of other products including engines, machinery, electric apparatus and divers automobile supplies. How much manufacturing ensued in the allied areas is not known, but the Swan car was produced in only small quantities, if that, and for a short period.

SWANSON — During the spring of 1903, J.M. Swanson announced that he was organizing a $10,000 company in Marathon, Iowa for manufacture of the four-wheel-drive automobile he had invented. Further news of this venture was not forthcoming, and manufacture is doubted.

The Swanson Motor Car Company was organized in Chicago early in 1912 with a capital stock of $50,000 for the manufacture of automobiles and accessories. Backing this venture were C.E. Swanson, E.E. Challenger and M.E. Callion. Manufacture of a car is doubted.

SWANSON — Stromsburg, Nebraska — (1910) — This delightful miniature automobile was built in 1910 by the Swanson Brothers who operated a garage in Stromsburg. The brothers designed the vehicle completely themselves, though they sent the patterns to Lincoln for casting. The small two-cylinder gasoline engine had bore/stroke dimensions of 1-1/2

1910 Swanson, juvenile car, LC

inches and generated about half a horsepower. The carburetor was float-feed, the ignition by battery, the lubrication a splash system. A cone clutch and two-speed sliding gear transmission were featured, as was shaft drive. The car complete weighed 156 pounds.

SWEANY — The Sweany steam car of 1895 is a frequent entry on car rosters, this resulting from its being captioned as such in the November 1895 issue of *The Horseless Age*. In the subsequent issue, however, the magazine corrected itself. The car had not been designed by Sweany, but instead was the conception of the Charles F. Caffrey Company. Refer to Caffrey.

SWEDLAND — Atwater, Minnesota — (c.1902) — E.J. Swedland was an Atwater jeweler who built two cars, the first around 1902. Its engine he purchased from a mail order house, and he placed it in the front of a small carriage fitted with a transmission of his own design, which he patented. He used that same engine in the second car he built, but placed it in the rear this time of a larger chassis.

SWEENEY — The Sweeney Automobile Company was organized in Camden, New Jersey during the spring of 1910 with a $10,000 capital stock for the manufacture of automobiles and motorcycles. Incorporators were F.R. Hansell, John A. MacPeak and William F. Eidell. Manufacture of a car is doubted.

SWENEY — Marion, Ohio — (1901) — In 1901 Busby P. Sweney of Marion built himself a friction-drive gasoline runabout which, he reported to *The Motor Age* modestly, "has been tested to 20 miles per hour and is working tolerably satisfactorily." Certainly that was true, given the vehicle's performance after Busby ran it into a ditch while on a touring excursion with a friend. "On examination we did not find anything broken or disarranged in the automobile," he wrote, "and as soon as we got the dirt off ourselves we started the machine and rode home on it." Sweney seems to have purchased all his subsequent automobiles.

SWIFT — Swift & Company of St. Joseph, Missouri has been indicated on various car rosters as the producer of an automobile from 1899-1900. This is unlikely. The Swift packing house began operations in St. Joseph around the turn of the century, and undoubtedly any automobiles or trucks that it used were built for the firm.
   "Swift & Detrick of Rock Falls, Illinois have built a vehicle which has been tested and pronounced satisfactory," *The Motor Age* announced in June of 1901. "The firm will now make arrangements to manufacture a large number. The plant is to be enlarged." It would appear, however, that this never happened. Early in 1902 the Sterling Automobile & Manufacturing Company was organized in Sterling, Illinois for manufacture of Myron Detrick's steam car. Manufacture does not appear to have followed in that case either.

SWIFT — Wayne, Michigan — (1910) — "The village of Wayne, which has lain dormant for many years, is awakening," a local newspaper reported in July of 1910, "and the progressive element of the pretty little residence town believes that within a twelve-month the town will have a population of 4000, and that within five years it will rank with Ypsilanti, Ann Arbor and other neighboring cities." The reason was that the Swift Automobile Company was coming to town. This automotive venture was headed by William A. Armstrong of Detroit, who enlisted support from E.W. Potts, George Stellwagen and Dr. E.L. Lee of Wayne. The Wayne car was to be offered in two four-cylinder models: a 20 hp roadster, and a 40 hp touring, roadster, demi-tonneau and light delivery. Two prototypes were built, as well as a

fine two-story brick factory. Stock was sold, and an office staff of three traveled daily from Detroit (in a car of another manufacturer) to take care of administrative matters. Then the venture fell apart. In October of 1910 stockholder E.W. Potts asked for receivership before manufacture had yet to begin, charging that "such mismanagement has characterized the conduct of the young company that the court's assistance is necessary to insure its future." Ultimately, it was decided the company had no future at all. The fine new factory built for the Swift did see automobile manufacture a decade later, however, when the Detroit Air Cooled Automobile Car Company moved in to build the D.A.C.

SWOPE — Early in 1911 the Swope Garage and Machine Company was organized in Washington Court House, Ohio with a capital stock of $10,000 to manufacture and deal in automobiles, parts and accessories. Incorporators were George B. Swope, Elmer Junk, P.F. Ortman, C.V. Lanum and J.E. McLean. Manufacture is doubted.

1905 Synnestvedt, electric stanhope, NAHC

SYNNESTVEDT ELECTRIC — Pittsburgh, Pennsylvania — (1904-1905) — Paul Synnestvedt was a Chicago attorney who moved his office to Pittsburgh at the turn of the century and specialized thereafter in securing patent protection for inventors and their inventions. Undoubtedly some of these patents were utilized by Synnestvedt himself when he entered the automobile field. Recognizing the immense possibilities of the horseless age as early as 1893, he began designing an electric vehicle that year, though it was a decade — June 1903 — before the first Synnestvedt was publicly tested. The Synnestvedt Machine Company moved into a new factory at 4117 Liberty Avenue in Pittsburgh later that year, and manufacture began. Most Synnestvedts were delivery wagons and public buses, but in the fall of 1904 a small solid-tired electric stanhope was marketed as well. It listed for $1500, and provided a 20 mph top speed and 50 miles between charges. Said *Cycle and Automobile Trade Journal* of the car: "In practical tests over the hilly drives and boulevards about Pittsburgh — anyone who has been there knows what they are — the Stanhope has shown remarkable traveling qualities." Reportedly, the Synnestvedt could climb hills a gasoline car could not, remarkable for an electric. Paul Synnestvedt remained convinced, however, that his fame and fortune was in the commercial field, and the stanhope was discontinued after 1905. Synnestvedt electric trucks and buses were manufactured through 1907.

1921 Sypher, juvenile car, LC

SYPHER — Toledo, Ohio — (1921-1922) — The Sypher was a juvenile car that was produced by the Sypher Manufacturing Company of Toledo. "Oh Boy! Build This Car" was an advertising headline. The vehicle was gasoline driven and capable of speeds up to 25 mph. The Sypher's cost was not advertised, but thirty cents bought the building plans and a price list of the parts available.

SYRACUSE — The Syracuse Auto Supply Company, Inc. was organized in Syracuse, New York early in 1912 with a capital stock of $25,000 for the manufacture of motor vehicles and parts. Incorporators were B.R. Newhall, C. Arthur Benjamin and M.C. Klock. Manufacture of a car is doubted. At the turn of the century, Benjamin had been president of the Syracuse Automobile Company which did produce cars.

The Syracuse Automobile & Motor Company was among the ventures promoted by George Erwin De Long in his attempts to get his automobile into manufacture in Phoenix or Syracuse, New York in 1902-1903. Refer to De Long.

SYRACUSE — **Syracuse, New York** — **(1899-1903)** — The Syracuse Automobile Company was established in 1899 at 336 South Warren Street for the manufacture of a gasoline car. C. Arthur Benjamin, formerly manager of the Olive Wheel Company, was president. Among the other incorporators were William D. Andrews and Henry Trebert; the salesman for the company was William H. Birdsall. Details regarding the automobile produced are lacking, though the principal person behind its design must have been Birdsall, since he subsequently went on to build such other automobiles as the Buckmobile, the Regas and the Mora. A Syracuse newspaper reference from 1901 indicates that Benjamin and Birdsall drove from Buffalo, curiously, to New York City in one of the cars that year. The total number of automobiles built is not known, but Syracuse city directories list the company at its South Warren Street location through 1903. Henry Trebert left this venture early on, first to join Stearns in Syracuse, then to build gasoline engines under his own name in Rochester. This Syracuse venture, incidentally, should not be confused with the automobile-building partnership of Charles F. Saul and William Van Wagoner, which also operated in Syracuse but produced cars correctly designated as the Van Wagoner and the Century.

1923 Tarkington, phaeton, WLB

1901 Taft, steam runabout, LC

TAFT STEAM — Worcester & Westborough, Massachusetts — (1901-1902) — William E. Taft of Boston was the inventor of a steam carriage which featured a cross-compound engine designed by Gustaf A. Hoist, a water-tube boiler and a hydrocarbon burner. He completed the car early in 1901 and spent the next year endeavoring to find the financing and factory necessary to produce it. Meanwhile he grandly organized as the United States Mobile & Power Company in Worcester. September 1901 found Taft receiving a very favorable review of his car in *The Automobile Magazine:* "The boiler is of the water tube type, and presents a square appearance, the tubes being expanded into steel heads at each end. These heads are square in outline and the sheets are about two inches apart. They are very solidly built up and should give no trouble from leakage." By this time Taft was producing his car in small quantities in what he called "small quarters" in Worcester and was planning to "work men night and day" until the many orders he had received were fulfilled. October 1901 found him, according to *The Horseless Age*, touring the State of Massachusetts in his car, "disposing of stock in the concern at 50 cents a share." Apparently he sold enough of it to purchase the plant of the Arriston Bicycle Company in Westborough where he moved in January of 1902. By February, unfortunately, William Taft's property there was in the hands of the mortgagee. And by May what remained of value back in Worcester was sold at public auction.

TALLMAN — The Tallman Motor Car Company was organized in New York City during the spring of 1905 with a capital stock of $30,000 for the manufacture of automobiles and engines. Incorporators were John A. Tallman, Leonard M. Fessler and Walter F. Sherwood. Manufacture of a car is doubted.

TAMPSEN — "A Mr. Tampsen is building a few automobiles at Hamburg, Pennsylvania," reported *The Motor Age* in May 1901. "The mayor and city engineer of Reading were formerly connected with Mr. Tampsen." Details are lacking.

TANNER-HOWER — The Tanner-Hower Manufacturing Company was organized in Akron, Ohio during the fall of 1913 with a capital stock of $50,000 to manufacture and sell automobiles and parts. Involved in the venture were Perry B. Tanner, M. Otis Hower, William T. Helfer, John Claude Stafford and John Johnsen. Manufacture of a car is doubted.

TARKINGTON — In May of 1906 *The Horseless Age* reported that one H. Tarkington of Marysville, Ohio had built a 20 hp car and was "trying to interest capital to manufacture it." Harry Tarkington planned to market the car under the name of the town in which it was to be built. Refer to Marysville.

TARKINGTON — Rockford, Illinois — (1922-1923) — The Tarkington represents one of the more poignant failures in the history of the American automobile. The car was a long time in coming, and it was a pity it did not succeed. The idea for the Tarkington began in 1918 during a conversation between William C. Durant and Pehr August Peterson. At that time Durant was once again back in the driver's seat at General Motors, and Peterson was president of the Mechanics Machine Company of Rockford, which supplied transmissions and universal joints for Chevrolets and Oak-lands. Durant happened to comment that Rockford's location was ideal for an automobile factory, which set Peterson to thinking. His company was also producing heavy transmissions for military vehicles built by the Kissel Motor Car Company and on a business trip to Hartford (Wisconsin), Peterson met Kissel plant manager, J. Arthur Tarkington. Had the Tarkington succeeded, that meeting would have become the stuff of legend. Peterson knew nothing about automobile engineering, nor much about the automobile really, but he saw an automobile company as a fine new industry for Rockford, and a profitable new outlet for his Mechanics Machine products. Tarkington knew a great deal about automobiles, having worked for Haynes-Apperson, Rutenber and Dayton (builders of the Stoddard) before joining Kissel, and had spent occasional spare hours sketching his "ideal" motorcar. Peterson's offer was irresistible. Late in 1919 Tarkington moved with his family to Rockford, where he became chief engineer and plant manager of the new Tarkington Motor Car Company. The firm was incorporated with a capital stock of $500,000 in January 1920, with construction of a new factory begun that summer adjacent to the Mechanics Machine Company. Not until the early spring of 1921 was the trade press made aware of the Tarkington venture. Not until the late fall of 1922 was the pilot model completed. The problems which caused the delay are not known. Carl E. Swenson, inventor of the universal joint produced by Mechanics Machine Company, assisted Tarkington in the car's design, and did not allude to the prototype's difficulties in an interview in the early Sixties. (He did note, however, that J. Arthur Tarkington was not a brother of Booth Tarkington, as has been supposed, though he was related in some distant way to the celebrated Indiana novelist.) The Tarkington was given its official debut during automobile show week in Chicago in early 1923. The car was also advertised at that time in the major trade publications. Its emblem was a T set under a chevron, with "Tarkington" and "Rockford" set in sans serif type below, a very modern design for the period. And so was the Tarkington car. Its engine was an overhead valve 260-cubic-inch 54 hp six with detachable cylinder head and aluminum crankcase. Its 126-inch wheelbase chassis bristled with ingenuity: underslung rear springs mounted inboard of the frame, a drop-forged front axle with a built-in oil reservoir, polished steel ball joints on the tie rod in lieu of the usual yoked ends. The automotive trade press greeted the Tarkington enthusiastically. But enthusiasm quickly waned among the men who had put up the money for the company. Six cars in all were built. "They operated quite successfully," Carl E. Swenson later remembered, "but the difficulty in raising the huge capital necessary for large scale production caused the venture to be abandoned before any cars were marketed." The Tarkington Motor Car Company was dissolved on June 1st, 1923. J. Arthur Tarkington was devastated. After failing to secure another position in the automobile industry, and after refusing a job at the Rockford Drilling Machine Company, he left his home in Rockford one day, and was never seen again. All six of his Tarkington automobiles were ultimately scrapped.

TATE — The Tate Gas-Electric Motor Vehicle Company was organized in Jersey City, New Jersey during the fall of 1909 with a capital stock of $100,000 for the manufacture of "automobiles, motor boats and aerial machines." The Tates behind this venture were J.L., C.E. and J.L., Jr. Manufacture of a car is doubted.

TAUNTON — Taunton, Massachusetts — (1901-1903) — The Taunton Automobile Company evolved out of the Taunton Steam Engine Company during the early fall of 1901. The men behind it were D.L. Brownell, who served as president, and Everett S. Cameron, who was manager. The partners moved into a factory at 28 Court Street which had been previously used to manufacture tacks, and got down to business. The Taunton steam car, like the Eclipse which Cameron had previously designed, featured a three-cylinder engine connected directly to the rear axle and a water-tube boiler. Full elliptic springs were used front and rear, and both a runabout and touring were offered. The price tag for each was $1000. Approximately twenty-five cars were built and sold — some of them under Cameron's name — before January of 1903 when the Taunton Automobile Company went bankrupt. At the sheriff's sale the following month, the stock on hand and the machinery were sold for $785. Meanwhile Everett

1902 Taunton, steam runabout, NAHC

S. Cameron, by this time skeptical of the future of steam, had proceeded to Pawtucket, Rhode Island to build an air-cooled gasoline car under his own name. And someone else moved into the old tack factory to build a gasoline car also called Taunton.

TAUNTON — Taunton, Massachusetts — (1904-1905) — Although its 28 Court Street address was the same, there does not appear to have been any connection between the Taunton Motor Carriage Company which manufactured a gasoline car there in 1904 and the Taunton Automobile Company which had preceded it with a steam car in 1901-1903. The new Taunton of 1904 was powered by a single-cylinder 7 hp engine and was offered as an $850 runabout on a 68-inch wheelbase with an auxiliary seat folding down from the dash for two more passengers. In 1905 the Taunton Motor Carriage Company moved to new quarters at 31 Tremont. Its gasoline car was discontinued later that year, and the company reorganized as the Taunton Motor Manufacturing Company and relocated yet again (24 Merchants Lane) where its product line consisted of motors only for bicycles, boats and automobiles.

TAXI — Although the following companies prefixed Taxi indicated an intention to both manufacture and operate taxicabs, the likelihood seems that these ventures merely operated a taxi service, with the cars supplied by other manufacturers.

The Taxi Cab Service Company of New York City, organized early in 1909 with a capital stock of $2000 by H.M. Browne, D.M. Barrett and E.J. Forbes.

The Taxi Service Company of Baltimore, Maryland, organized early in 1910 with a capital stock of $50,000 by F.C. McKinney, J.R. Mapleton and R.E. Taylor.

The Taxicab Association, Inc. of New York City, organized during the fall of 1913 with a capital stock of $50,000 by L.H. Bigelow, Jr. of Brooklyn, and A.L. Loomis and A. Wichfield of Manhattan.

The Taxicab Company of America, organized in Detroit, Michigan early in 1910 by J.J. O'Connor, Thomas N. Navin and Michael P. Bourke.

The Taximeter Auto Company of Paterson, New Jersey, organized early in 1908 with a capital stock of $125,000 by W.F. Harding, A.A. Fischer and J.F. Blauvet.

The Taximeter and Cab Company of America, organized in New York City during the spring of 1907 with a capital stock of $1,250,000 by J.W. Ockford, C.A. Sparks and D.R. Faulkner.

The Taxi-Motor Car Company of Philadelphia, organized in Trenton, New Jersey during the spring of 1908 with a capital stock of $300,000 by Cornelius A. Cole, Richard F. Tully and Franklin Vreeland.

The Taximotor Cab Company of Boston, Massachusetts, organized during the summer of 1908 with a capital stock of $500,000 by Cornelius A. Cole, Richard F. Tully and Franklin Vreeland.

TAYLOR — Henry Seth Taylor built a steam car in 1867 in Stanstead, Quebec. *The Automobile* in 1915 in a retrospective article on pre-Twentieth Century automobile history indicated Taylor's machine as having been built in Derby Line, Vermont which is the reason the Taylor steamer has so frequently appeared on rosters of U.S.-built cars. But this automobile was undeniably of Canadian origin, and undoubtedly was the Dominion's first.

"Will Taylor, Niles, Ohio has invented a motor carriage," reported *The Horseless Age* in August of 1899. Details are lacking.

The Taylor Motors Corporation was organized in New York City during the fall of 1917 with a capital stock of $100,000 for the manufacture of automobiles and engines. Incorporators were A.E. Moore, G.F. Jerbett and A.F. McCabe. Manufacture of a car is doubted.

TAYLOR — Long Beach, California — (1899) — In 1899 George W. Taylor of Long Beach built a gasoline automobile. Details regarding the car are lacking, but it is known to have been a three-wheeler with accommodations for two passengers.

TAYLOR — Fitchburg, Massachusetts — (1895) — Elwood E. Taylor was a civil and mechanical engineer in Fitchburg, as well as a dealer in supplies for engineers, architects and draftsmen. In 1895 he entered the Chicago Times-Herald Contest, but he never made it to the starting line. The car he was building was a steamer, and he seems to have kept it a secret. *The Fitchburg Sentinel* published a souvenir edition that year, and Taylor's steam car was not mentioned. Had the car been a smashing success, no doubt it would have been.

T.C.M. — The T.C.M. Manufacturing Company was organized in Newark, New Jersey during the spring of 1910 with a capital stock of $100,000 for the manufacture of automobiles and parts. The initials translated to A. Morris Thompson, Allan Coats and William McKay. Manufacture of a car is doubted.

TEABOLDT — C.R. Teaboldt & Company was organized in New York City during the fall of 1910 with a capital stock of $50,000 to manufacture and deal in vehicles. Joining Teaboldt in this venture were Emerson Brooks and George F. Aitken. Manufacture is doubted; Teaboldt, who formerly had been in charge of the E.R. Thomas branch in New York, subsequently secured the agencies for the Owen and Bergdoll automobiles.

TEEL — Medford, Massachusetts — (1912-1914) — The Teel Manufacturing Company of Medford produced a truck called the Teel-Medford from 1912-1914. That the firm also manufactured an automobile was indicated in the *Chilton Automobile Directory* of July 1921 in its listings of "Piston Ring Sizes, Passenger Automobiles." The Chilton reference noted that the car had been "discontinued." Such manufacture as it saw must have been minimal. Trade press publications of the 1912-1914 period do not reveal mentions of the Teel automobile.

TEETOR-HARTLEY — Hagerstown, Indiana — (1916) — The Teetor-Hartley Motor Company was organized in Hagerstown during the fall of 1913 with a capital stock of $10,000 to "conduct a general motor vehicle business." The Teetors involved in this venture were Joseph, J.H. and C.N. Purportedly, they built an experimental automobile in 1916 which undoubtedly was for the purpose of testing out one of their new engines. Engine building remained the Teetor-Hartley focus thereafter.

TEG — The Teg Motor Company was organized in Chicago, Illinois during the summer of 1907 with a capital stock of $2500 for the manufacture of automobiles and parts. Incorporators were Ohren C. Smith, Fred H. Smith and William J. Sneal. Manufacture of a car is doubted.

TEMPCO — The Tempco Manufacturing Company was organized in Chicago, Illinois during the summer of 1915 with a capital stock of $25,000 for the manufacture and sale of automobiles and accessories. Involved in this venture were Frank Templeman and Carl J. Sharp. Manufacture of a car is doubted.

1919 Templar, touring roadster, HAC

TEMPLAR — Cleveland, Ohio — (1917-1924) — The "Super-Fine Small Car" was precisely that. Though its name derived from the crusades of the Middle Ages, and its emblem was the Maltese cross, the Templar was stylish, sporting and thoroughly modern. Its engine was an overhead valve four with valves enclosed in an aluminum case ("Vitalic Top-Valve," the ads said) which displaced 197 cubic inches and developed 43 horsepower. Save for the engine, the Templar was an assembled car, though extremely well designed, with semi-elliptic springs, semi-floating rear axle and Hotchkiss drive. The engineers who designed it were A.M. Dean (formerly of Pope-Hartford and Matheson), assisted by P.F. Hackethal (from Mercer), Allen Bartlett (from Stearns) and M.E. Morningstart (from Chalmers). The man behind Templar Motors Corporation was M.F. Bramley, the president of the Cleveland Trinidad Paving Company, who served Templar's presidency too. Stock in the company was initially offered in February of 1917, and the first Templar car was completed that July. Few more were delivered prior to the Armistice, however, as the company's factory in the Cleveland suburb of Lakewood was turned over for munitions production. By the end of 1919 some 1800 Templars had been built, in July that year the car being given a tremendous publicity boost when Cannon Ball Baker blazed from New York to Chicago in 26 hours 50 minutes for a new driving record which beat the old one by more than six hours. The Templar surely seemed a car for the Twenties. Among other delights for that frivolous decade, some models came equipped with a Kodak camera and a compass. But the Templar company had problems aplenty. In addition to the usual material shortages and the economic downturn in the wake of World War I, a disgruntled stockholder petitioned for receivership in 1920. Templar indicated its financial condition to be assets of $8 million against liabilities of about $600,000, and the court judge in dismissing the case commented that "the severest discipline should be applied to any attorney who would lend himself to groundless charges of this kind," a run on a bank being deemed the moral equivalent to what the disenchanted stockholder had tried to do. Nonetheless, Templar was heading straight for more trouble. Production for 1920 totaled 1850 cars, but sales from September that year until March the year following were but 128 Templars. Sales picked up though, and by December stood at 732 cars. Then, on December 13th, most of the Templar factory burned down. Production resumed, though erratically, within the week in the portion which remained standing. Receivership again was petitioned in 1922, this time by a supplier, and this time it was accepted. One of Bramley's assistants,

T.L. Hausmann, was named receiver. In the fall of 1923, Hausmann became president of the reorganized Templar Motor Car Company. A line of sixes with four-wheel brakes was added for '24, Templar's last year in manufacture. In the fall of 1924, after production of approximately 6000 cars, the Templar company was taken over by a Cleveland bank for default on a loan. Insult to injury was added early in 1925 when a group of Templar stock salesmen were indicted for violations of the Ohio blue sky laws. The Templar deserved a better fate.

1917-1918 TEMPLAR
Four — 43 hp, 118" wb

	FP	5	4	3	2	1
Touring-5P	1250	3700	4700	7300	13,700	26,000
Touring-4P	1250	3300	4400	6700	12,000	24,000
Roadster-2P	1250	3300	4400	6700	12,000	24,000
Sedan-5P	1850	2000	3000	4200	6500	14,000

1919 TEMPLAR
Model 4-45 — 43 hp, 118" wb

Victoria Elite-4P	2285	3000	4000	6000	9500	21,000
Touring-5P	2185	3300	4400	6700	12,000	24,000
Touring Roadster-2P	2385	3200	4300	6500	11,000	23,000
Sportette-4P	2185	3300	4400	6700	12,000	24,000
Sedan-5P	3295	2000	3000	4200	6500	14,000

1920 Templar, roadster, HAC

1920 TEMPLAR
Model 4-45 — 43 hp, 118" wb

Touring-5P	2685	3500	4500	7000	13,000	25,000
Sportette-2P	2685	3500	4500	7000	13,000	25,000
Roadster-2P	2685	3300	4400	6700	12,000	24,000
Sedan-5P	3585	2000	3000	4200	6500	14,000
Coupe-4P	3585	2300	3300	4600	7500	16,000

1921 Templar, touring, JAC

1921 TEMPLAR
Model 4-45 — 43 hp, 118" wb

Touring-5P	2885	3500	4500	7000	13,000	25,000
Roadster-2P	2885	3300	4400	6700	12,000	24,000
Sportette-2P	2885	3500	4500	7000	13,000	25,000
Coupe-4P	3785	2300	3300	4600	7500	16,000
Sedan-5P	3785	2000	3000	4200	6500	14,000

1922 Templar, roadster, OCW

1922 Templar, Deluxe, touring, WLB

1922 TEMPLAR
Model 4-45 — 43 hp, 118" wb

	FP	5	4	3	2	1
Touring-5P	1985	3500	4500	7000	13,000	25,000
Sportette-4P	1985	3500	4500	7000	13,000	25,000
Roadster-2P	1985	3300	4400	6700	12,000	24,000
Sedan-5P	2985	2000	3000	4200	6500	14,000
Coupe-3P	2985	2300	3300	4600	7500	16,000

1923 Templar, touring, HAC

1923 TEMPLAR
Model 4-45 — 43 hp, 118" wb

Touring-5P	2125	3500	4500	7000	13,000	25,000
Roadster-2P	2025	3300	4400	6700	12,000	24,000
Sport-4P	2175	3500	4500	7000	13,000	25,000
Coupe-4P	2650	2300	3300	4600	7500	16,000
Sedan-5P	2785	2000	3000	4200	6500	14,000

1924 Templar, brougham, HAC

1924 TEMPLAR
Model 4-45 — 43 hp, 118" wb

Touring-5P	1895	3700	4700	7300	13,700	26,000
Roadster-2P	1795	3500	4500	7000	13,000	25,000
Sport-4P	—	3700	4700	7300	13,700	26,000
Coupe-4P	—	2400	3400	4800	8000	17,000
Sedan-5P	—	2200	3200	4400	7000	15,000

Six — 27.34 hp, 122" wb

Phaeton-5P	1950	3500	4500	7000	13,000	25,000
Sport-4P	1995	3500	4500	7000	13,000	25,000
Brougham-4P	2495	2400	3400	4800	8000	17,000
Sedan-5P	2595	2200	3200	4400	7000	15,000

TEMPLE — Denver, Colorado — (1899) — Among the pioneer automobiles of Colorado was the gasoline car designed and built in 1899 by Robert Temple. The vehicle was described, with appealing ingenuousness, in the July 21st, 1899 edition of the *Denver Evening Post:* "The wagon is as handsome as it is possible to make a vehicle of that nature. Silver leaf, gold, dark red and maroon on the body contrast with the yellow and brown

1899 Temple, gasoline wagon, LC

of the solid-tired wheels. The gasoline engine is of a 10 to 12 horse power. The motor is what is technically known as a hydro-carbon motor, with double cylinder, two separate engines coupled together in order that if one gets broken the operator can rely on the other. Each of the rear wheels, on which fall 90 per cent of the total weight of 2,000 pounds, is driven independently by the agency of a heavy steel chain, the principle being the same as that on a bicycle, with special lubricators. Safety and emergency brakes, so the wagon can be stopped in almost the twinkling of an eye, are features, with acetylene lamps for use at night. The operator does not have to move from his seat in guiding the wagon." The car was apparently produced to the order of a doctor from Cripple Creek. A Mr. and Mrs. E.J. Cabler were purportedly planning to drive the Temple from Denver up the steep, mountainous trails to Victor, near Cripple Creek. One cannot imagine a car of that period being equal to the Rockies. It did successfully negotiate the streets of Denver, however.

TEMPLE — McPherson, Kansas — (1902-1903) — That T.W. Temple of McPherson "makes a specialty of building automobiles to order" was reported in *The Horseless Age* in January 1903. How long he may have been doing that is not known. Since 1897 Temple had been a partner in the McPherson Cycle Company, and in January 1903 he took over the entire bicycle and automobile business of the firm.

TEMPLE-MARVEL — Chicago, Illinois — (1907) — Ralph Temple was an automobile dealer in Chicago who handled, among other cars, the Marvel built by the Marvel Motor Car Company in Detroit. The Temple-Marvel was his idea of what the Marvel should be. Its two-cylinder 14/16 hp engine was the same, and it was a shaft-drive roadster as well, but rather spiffier, with turtle decks or rumble seats in the rear. At $850, the Temple-Marvel was fifty dollars more than the mere Marvel. It was built for Ralph Temple by Marvel in Detroit, and sold only by him in Chicago. Needless to say, when Marvel went out of business in Detroit later in 1907, Temple-Marvels ceased to arrive in the Windy City.

TEMPLE-WESTCOTT — Framingham, Massachusetts — (1921-1922) — The Temple-Westcott is a conundrum. Apparently the car, which was a six, was built in the shops of the Bela Body Company in Framingham. A total production of both ten and twenty Temple-Westcotts has been reported, but for whom were the cars built? That remains a mystery. The possibility that the vehicles were produced on special order for a Temple Westcott dealership in the area seemed likely, but alas there were no dealerships during the early Twenties in Boston, Framingham or Amesbury that carried the name of either Temple or Westcott. And there was no relationship between this car and the Westcott then being built in Ohio. When the Bela Body Company subsequently moved to Amesbury, the Bela plant in which the Temple Westcotts had been built was acquired by the Dennison Company.

TEMPLETON — John Templeton of Chicago, Illinois was among the hopefuls who entered the Chicago Times-Herald contest of 1895 with an automobile of his own design. He did not make it to the starting line, however, and whether he ever completed and successfully tested his vehicle is not known.

TEMPLETON-DuBRIE — Detroit, Michigan — (1910) — The Templeton-DuBrie Car Company was located at 687 Mack Avenue in Detroit. Its product was a combination delivery-pleasure car on a 124-inch wheelbase priced at $1250. The vehicle was fitted with a planetary transmission and shaft drive. Its most remarkable feature was the engine, a two-cylinder two-stroke 20 hp unit which was described in *The Motor World* as of "the differential piston order arranged in a manner at once suggestive to steam engineers of the Wolf type of compound engine." The Templeton-DuBrie's unit was valveless without crankcase compression. The car does not appear to have survived 1910, although there was some production. Designer of the Templeton-DuBrie was Stanley R. Du Brie, a mechanical engineer whose first car had been the Du Brie-Caille of 1904, also produced in Detroit.

TENNANT — Chicago, Illinois — (1915) — Tennant Motor, Limited was a Michigan Avenue automobile dealership established in Chicago in 1907 by W.G. Tennant. Peerless and Marmon were among the cars for which Tennant held agency. For the 1915 season, Tennant also offered a car under its own name: a 30/35 hp $875 four available with roadster or five-passenger touring bodies. Where the car was built for Tennant is not known, but after a single season the company discontinued it.

TERMAAT & MONAHAN — Although this 1914 cyclecar was built in the Termaat & Monahan shops in Oshkosh, Wisconsin, it is more correctly referred to by the name of the man who designed it. Refer to Ziebell.

TERRAPLANE

TERRAPLANE — Detroit, Michigan — (1932-1938) — The Terraplane began in 1932 as a model of the Essex built by the Hudson Motor Car Company. Considerable fanfare was expended upon its introduction that July with Orville Wright receiving the first car built, Amelia Earhart seeing to the Terraplane's christening and receiving car number two. With a top speed of 80 mph and price range of $425-$590, the Terraplane managed to create a stir in the industry that year exceeded only by Henry Ford's new V-8, with the logical result that within a year the Essex Terraplane had become simply the Terraplane. Its engine was a larger, more powerful version of the Essex six (193 cubic inches and 70 hp vis-a-vis 175 and 60) and, placed in a short wheelbase chassis, provided for a spirited performance which the company called "land-flying." A 94 hp Terraplane eight (with Hudson engine) joined the line in 1933. As with the Super Six of 1916, Hudson sent its Terraplane racing and by the end of 1933, the company held no fewer than fifty AAA hill climb records in addition to a flying mile of 85.8 mph and a standing mile of 68 mph at Daytona. In 1932 a Terraplane six had climbed Pikes Peak in record-breaking time, and in 1933 a Terraplane eight broke the Terraplane six's record there. Performances such as these naturally received a wide press, and resulted in the car being looked upon with favor by the British overseas and bootleggers and other nefarious fellows at home. Reid Railton used a Terraplane eight chassis for his first Railton sports cars in England (switching subsequently to a Hudson chassis). John Dillinger was a big fan of the Terraplane in the U.S. Like the Hudson, the Terraplane was provided "Axle-Flex" semi-independent front suspension in 1934, the Bendix "Electric Hand" gearshift as an option in 1935, and "Duo-Automatic" hydraulic brakes in '36. The industry's first all-steel turret top was introduced on the Terraplane in mid-November 1935, a month before Chevrolet and Pontiac. That the Terraplane was a popular car and contributing measurably to Hudson's financial well being during these mid-Depression years was undeniable. That Hudson believed the name might become even more popular than its own was among the reasons the car was referred to as the Hudson Terraplane in sales literature and on its hubcaps in 1938. The Terraplane had come full circle. By 1939 the name was dropped altogether.

Terraplane Data Compilation
by Robert C. Ackerson

1932

1932 Essex Terraplane, sedan, OCW

ESSEX TERRAPLANE — MODEL K — SIX: Prior to the introduction of the Essex-Terraplane in July, 1932 there was much consideration about what if any directions the automobile industry would take to reverse the downspiral of its sales charts. For Hudson's part, the mid-year introduction of the standard Essex series was seen as a step towards what was then described as the Model T market. Hudson denied that it had a new low-priced car in the works and just a few weeks before the Essex-Terraplane's arrival the biggest automotive news seemed to be the major price cuts made by Chevrolet, Ford, and Plymouth. The Essex-Terraplane changed all that in a hurry. Although its styling was decidedly conservative the Essex-Terraplane combined in one car the national preoccupation with economy via its low price with a much older interest in performance. With a $425 base price the least expensive Essex-Terraplane, the Roadster was $35 less than the Ford V-8 and $20 less than an equivalent Chevrolet model. Compared to the older Essex version the new Essex-Terraplane coach was $190 less expensive and weighed 485 pounds less. This light-

1409

1932 Essex Terraplane, coupe (with Orville Wright), WRG

weight was achieved by combining the body and frame into a single unit and utilizing virtually every part of the car as part of the body-chassis structure. For example the pressing that formed the web of the frame also served as the bottom of the body. The Essex-Terraplane engine was basically that used in the 1932 Essex models. However it had a lower, 5.5:1 compression ratio, a new 3-point mounting arrangement and a new down-draft induction system. The new result said Hudson, was that the Essex-Terraplane "has a higher propulsion effort per pound of car weight than any production car now on the market in this country or abroad."

I.D. DATA: Serial numbers on firewall, right side of frame, right front face of front axle and on rear axle housing. Starting: 350000. Ending: 364124. Engine numbers on left side of cylinder block near water inlet elbow. Starting engine no.: 5000.

1932 Essex Terraplane, coach, WRG

Model No.	Body Type & Seating	Price	Weight	Prod. Total
Series K	2-dr. Std. Rds.-2P	425	2010	NA
Series K	2-dr. Bus. Cpe.-2P	470	2135	NA
Series K	2-dr. C'ch.-5P	475	2205	NA
Series K	2-dr. Std. Cpe. R/S-4P	510	2490	NA
Series K	2-dr. Sp. Rds.-2P	525	2110	NA
Series K	4-dr. Std. Sed.-5P	550	2250	NA
Series K	Sp. C'ch.	515	2205	NA
Series K	4-dr. Sp. Sed.-5P	570	2250	NA
Series K	2-dr. Sp. Conv. Cpe.-2P	610	2145	NA
Series K	4-dr. Phae.-5P	495	2170	NA
Series K	2-dr. Sp. Bus. Cpe.-2P	510	235	NA
Series K	2-dr. Sp. Cpe. R/S-4P	550	2190	NA

ENGINE: Inline. Six. Cast iron block. B & S: 2-15/16 x 4-3/4 in. Disp.: 193.1 cu. in. C.R.: 5.8:1. Brake H.P. 70 @ 3200 R.P.M. Taxable H.P.: 20.7. Main bearings: 3. Valve lifters: mechanical. Carb.: Carter 243S downdraft.

CHASSIS: [Series K] W.B.: 106 in. Frt/Rear Tread: 51-1/2 x 54-1/2 in. Tires: 17 x 5.25.

1932 Essex Terraplane, roadster, OCW

TECHNICAL: Sliding gear transmission. Speeds: 3F/1R. Floor shift controls. Single plate controls clutch, cork inserts, running in oil. Shaft drive. Semi-floating rear axle. Overall ratio: 4.55:1 (sedans), 4.11:1 (all others). Bendix mechanical brakes on four wheels. Wire spoke wheels. (17").

OPTIONS: Interior visors. Passenger-side windshield wiper.

HISTORICAL: Introduced July 1932. The Essex-Terraplane soon became renown as the "Hill Buster." In nation-wide ads Hudson challenged every American marque to better Essex-Terraplane hill climbing or acceleration runs. At Pikes Peak an Essex-Terraplane won the Penrose Trophy. Innovations: light weight-body frame unit construction. Essex-Terraplane made 16,581 shipments to dealers during the 1932 calendar year. The president of Essex-Terraplane was William J. McAneeny.

1933

1933 Terraplane, Six, roadster, JAC

ESSEX TERRAPLANE SIX — SERIES K — SIX: The Series K Terraplane retained the 106" wheelbase of 1932 but the elimination of the exterior windshield visor gave them a fresh appearance. A revamped instrument panel placed all gauges directly in front of the driver.

1933 Terraplane, Six, coupe, OCW

TERRAPLANE DELUXE SIX — SERIES KU — SIX: In May the Terraplane Six line, which had consisted of both Standard and Special versions was revamped to make room for the 113" wheelbase Series KU Special Six models. The Special Six line was dropped and the Standard line was relabeled the Terraplane Standard Six. The Series KU line became the DeLuxe Six Terraplane in August. These were equipped with a walnut-finish dash panel, standard cigarette lighter and radio. External features included chrome grille bars, bright-finish dual horn, fender lights and twin taillamps.

1933 Terraplane, Eight, coach (OCW)

ESSEX TERRAPLANE EIGHT — SERIES KT — EIGHT: The eight cylinder Essex Terraplane was set apart from the six cylinder models by its hood doors and front fender mounted auxiliary lights. Corresponding to the mid-year DeLuxe Six Essex Terraplane were the DeLuxe Eight models identified by their chrome grille bars, twin horns mounted beneath the headlights.

I.D. DATA: Serial numbers on firewall, right side of frame, right front face on front axle and on rear axle housing. Starting: [Series K] 364125, [Series KU] 5001, [Series KU DeLuxe] 11865, [Series KT] 65001, [Series KT DeLuxe] 73463. Ending: [Series K] 372899, [Series KU] 11864, [Series KU DeLuxe] 21495, [Series KT] 73462, [Series KT DeLuxe] 78250. Engine numbers on left side of cylinder block near water inlet elbow. Starting [K/KU] 20501, [KT] 15001.

Model No.	Body Type & Seating	Price	Weight	Prod. Total
Series K	(standard) 2-dr. Rds.-2P	425	2135	NA
Series K	4-dr. Phae.-5P	515	2220	NA
Series K	2-dr. Bus. Cpe.-2P	485	2220	NA
Series K	2-dr. Cpe.-4P	535	2260	NA
Series K	2-dr. C'ch.-5P	505	2275	NA
Series K	4-dr. Sed.-5P	555	2345	NA
Series K	(Special) 2-dr. Cpe.-4P	555	2310	NA
Series K	2-dr. Rds. R/S-4P	505	2220	NA
Series K	2-dr. C'ch.-5P	525	2335	NA
Series K	4-dr. Sed.-5P	575	2415	NA
Series K	2-dr. Conv. Cpe. R/S-4P	575	2275	NA
Series K	4-dr. Sed.-5P	575	2420	NA
Series KU	2-dr. Cpe.-4P	555	2330	NA
Series KU	2-dr. Bus. Cpe.-2P	505	2320	NA
Series KU	2-dr. Spt. Rds. R/S-4P	505	2290	NA
Series KU	4-dr. Phae.-5P	535	—	NA
Series KU	2-dr. C'ch.-5P	525	2370	NA
Series KU	4-dr. Sed.-5P	575	2420	NA
Series KU	2-dr. Conv. Cpe.-2P	575	2315	NA
DeLuxe Six				
Series KU	4-dr. Sed.-5P	655	2500	NA
Series KU	2-dr. Bus. Cpe.-2P	585	2395	NA
Series KU	2-dr. Cpe. R/S-4P	635	2405	NA
Series KU	2-dr. Conv. Cpe. R/S-4P	655	2395	NA
Series KU	2-dr. C'ch.-5P	605	2450	NA
Series KU	2-dr. Spt. Rds. R/S-4P	585	2370	NA
Series KU	4-dr. Phae.-5P	615	—	NA
Std. Eight				
Series KT	2-dr. Bus. Cpe.-2P	615	2485	NA
Series KT	2-dr. Rds. R/S-4P	625	2455	NA
Series KT	2-dr. Rds.-2P	565	2410	NA
Series KT	2-dr. cpe. R/S-4P	655	2545	NA
Series KT	2-dr. C'ch.-5P	615	2565	NA
Series KT	4-dr. Sed.-5P	675	2640	NA
Series KT	2-dr. Conv. Cpe.-4P	695	2495	NA
DeLuxe Eight				
Series KT	2-dr. Bus. Cpe.-2P	685	2540	NA
Series KT	2-dr. Rds. R/S-4P	895	2510	NA
Series KT	2-dr. Rds.-2P	635	2465	NA
Series KT	2-dr. cpe. R/S-4P	725	2600	NA
Series KT	2-dr. C'ch.-5P	685	2625	NA
Series KT	4-dr. Sed.-5P	745	2700	NA
Series KT	2-dr. Conv. Cpe.-4P	765	2550	NA

ENGINE: [Series K, KU] Inline. Six. Cast iron block. B & S: 2-15/16 x 4-3/4 in. Disp.: 193.1 cu. in. C.R.: 5.8:1. Brake H.P.: 70 @ 3200 R.P.M. Taxable H.P.: 20-7. Main bearings: three. Valve lifters: mechanical. Carb.: Carter 267S. Optional Engine: Inline. Six cyl. Cast iron block. B & S: 2-15/16 x 4-3/4 in. Disp.: 193.1 cu. in. C.R.: 7.0:1. Brake H.P.: 80 @ 3200 R.P.M. Main bearings: three. Valve lifters: mechanical. Carb.: Carter 267S. [Essex Terraplane Eight] Inline. Eight cyl. Cast iron block. B & S: 2.94 x 4.50 in. Disp.: 243.9 cu. in. C.R.: 5.8:1. Brake H.P.: 94 @ 3600 R.P.M. Taxable H.P.: 27.6. Main bearings: five. Valve lifters: mechanical. Carb.: Carter 261S 1bbl downdraft.

CHASSIS: [Series K] W.B.: 106 in. Frt/Rear Tread: 56/56 in. Tires: 17 x 5.25, 16 x 6.00 — Series K Special. [Series KU] W.B.: 113 in. Frt/Rear Tread: 56/56 in. Tires: 17 x 5.25, 16 x 6.00 — Series KU DeLuxe. [Series KT] W.B.: 113 in. Frt/Rear Tread: 56/56 in. Tires: 16 x 6.00.

TECHNICAL: Sliding gear transmission. Speeds: 3F/1R. Floor shift controls. Single plate clutch, cork inserts, running in oil. Shaft drive. Semi-floating rear axle. Overall ratio: 4.11 (4.56, 3.8 opt). Bendix mechanical brakes on four wheels. Wire spoke wheels. Rim size: 17'' — Series K, 16'' — Series K Special. 17'' — Series KU, 16'' — Series KU DeLuxe, 16'' — Series KT and KT DeLuxe. Automatic clutch.

OPTIONS: Single or dual sidemounts. [Series KU, KT only], automatic clutch, trunk rack, Majestic radio, dual taillights (non-DeLuxe models), fender lamps (non-DeLuxe models), 16'' wheels [Series KU], two-tone paint.

HISTORICAL: Introduced Jan. 1933. Under AAA supervision, stock Terraplanes set 72 hillclimb and speed records in 1932 and 1933. Hudson touted the 8 cylinder model as the "only car that can beat the Terraplane 6" and at Daytona Beach a Terraplane 8 turned in an 85mph top speed run and a zero to 60mph time of under 15 seconds. At Pikes Peak Al Miller broke the 1932 Terraplane-set record and once again won the Penrose Trophy with a run of 19 minutes, 52.2 seconds. Second, third and fourth places in the stock class were also won by Terraplanes. Innovations: DeLuxe Six and Eight models had radios as std. equipment. Essex Terraplane made 38,150 shipments to dealers during the 1933 calendar year. The president of Essex-Terraplane was William J. McAneeny (Jan — May); after May — Roy D. Chapin.

1933
Six, 6-cyl., 106" wb

	FP	5	4	3	2	1
Rds	425	3150	6300	10,500	14,700	21,000
Phae	515	3300	6600	11,000	15,400	22,000
2P Cpe	485	850	1650	4200	5850	8400
RS Cpe	535	900	1800	4450	6250	8900
2 dr Sed	505	825	1600	3950	5500	7900
Sed	555	825	1600	4050	5650	8100

Special Six, 6-cyl., 113" wb

	FP	5	4	3	2	1
Spt Rds	505	3300	6600	11,000	15,400	22,000
Phae	535	3400	6900	11,500	16,100	23,000
Conv	575	3000	6000	10,000	14,000	20,000
Bus Cpe	505	900	1800	4400	6150	8800
RS Cpe	555	925	1900	4550	6350	9100
2 dr Sed	525	825	1600	4050	5650	8100
Sed	575	850	1650	4150	5800	8300
DeLuxe Six, 6-cyl., 113" wb						
Conv	655	3150	6300	10,500	14,700	21,000
2P Cpe	585	900	1900	4500	6300	9000
RS Cpe	635	950	2100	4700	6600	9400
2 dr Sed	605	850	1650	4100	5700	8200
Sed	655	850	1650	4200	5850	8400
Terraplane, 8-cyl.						
2P Rds	565	3300	6600	11,000	15,400	22,000
RS Rds	625	3400	6900	11,500	16,100	23,000
2P Cpe	615	925	2000	4650	6500	9300
RS Cpe	655	975	2300	4900	6850	9800
Conv	695	3000	6000	10,000	14,000	20,000
2 dr Sed	615	850	1650	4150	5800	8300
Sed	675	850	1650	4200	5850	8400
Terraplane DeLuxe Eight, 8-cyl.						
Conv	765	3150	6300	10,500	14,700	21,000
2P Cpe	725	950	2100	4700	6600	9400
RS Cpe	765	975	2300	4950	6900	9900
2 dr Sed	685	850	1650	4150	5800	8300
Sed	745	850	1650	4200	5850	8400

1934

1934 Terraplane, Series K, coach, WRG

TERRAPLANE — SERIES K — SIX: With the Essex name eliminated, Hudson's running mate was known just as the Terraplane for 1934. Its styling was also completely new, highlighted by a very broad grille with thin converging bars, flowing front and rear fender lines and seven tapered hood louvers. A built-in trunk was provided on Coach and Sedan models. Well equipped, the car had chrome windshield and vent window frames, chrome headlamps, front and rear ash trays, robe rail, foot rest rail, door sill plates, full walnut-finish dash with indicator lights for oil pressure and generator temperature gauge, ash receiver and rear arm rests. Became known as the "Terraplane Standard" after introduction of the "Challenger."

TERRAPLANE DELUXE — SERIES KU — SIX: Riding on a a 116-inch wheelbase, the DeLuxe added amenities such as twin chrome horns under the headlamps, twin taillamps, fender lamps, dual windshield wipers. For a brief time a three-door hood was factory installed in place of the seven-louver style. Promoted as the "Terraplane Major" after introduction of the "Challenger."

TERRAPLANE CHALLENGER — SERIES KS — SIX: A mid-year introduction, the Challenger series offered a lower price but carried painted headlamps and windshield frame, painted dash, modest interiors and deleted amenities.

I.D. DATA: Serial numbers on firewall, right side of frame, right front face on front axle and on rear axle housing. Starting: [Series K] 373000, [Series KU] 21500, [Series KS] 396727. Ending: [Series KU] 28593, [Series K/KS] 416991. Engine numbers on left side of cylinder block opposite number one cylinder. Starting: 48000. Ending: 102,999.

Model No.	Body Type & Seating	Price	Weight	Prod. Total
Series KS	2-dr. Cpe.-2P	565	2540	NA
Series KS	4-dr. Cpe. R/S-4P	610	2590	NA
Series KS	2-dr. C'ch.-5P	575	2600	NA
Series KS	4-dr. Sed.-5P	635	2670	NA
Series KS	4-dr. Sed. w/built-in trk.	635	NA	NA
Series KS	2-dr. C'ch. w/built-in trk.-5P	575	NA	NA
Series K	2-dr. Rds.-2P	NA	2465	NA
Series K	4-dr. Phae.-5P	NA	2615	NA
Series K	2-dr. Cpe.-2P	600	2600	NA
Series K	2-dr. Cpe.-4P	645	2605	NA
Series K	2-dr. Conv. Cpe. R/S-3P	695	2625	NA
Series K	2-dr. C'ch.-5P	615	2630	NA
Series K	2-dr. Compartment Vic.-5P	655	2655	NA
Series K	2-dr. C'ch. w/built-in trk.5P	615	2655	NA
Series K	4-dr. Sed.-5P	875	2710	NA

Model No.	Body Type & Seating	Price	Weight	Prod. Total
Series K	4-dr. Compartment Sed.-5P	715	2735	NA
Series K	4-dr. Sed. w/built-in trk.	675	NA	NA
Series KU	2-dr. Cpe.-4P	710	2700	NA
Series KU	2-dr. Cpe.-2P	665	NA	NA
Series KU	2-dr. Conv. Cpe. R/S-3P	750	2695	NA
Series KU	2-dr. C'ch.-5P	680	2730	NA
Series KU	2-dr. Compartment Vic.-5P	720	2755	NA
Series KU	4-dr. Sed.-5P	740	2780	NA
Series KU	4-dr. Compartment Sed.-5P	780	2805	NA
Series KU	4-dr. Sed. w/built-in trk.	740	NA	NA
Series KU	2-dr C'ch. w/built-in trk.	680	NA	NA

1934 Terraplane, convertible, OCW

ENGINE: [Series KS and K] L-head. Straight. Six. Chrome alloy block. B & S: 3 x 5 in. Disp.: 212 cu. in. C.R.: 5.75:1. Brake H.P.: 80 @ 3600 R.P.M. Taxable H.P.: 21.6. Main bearings: 3. Valve lifters: mechanical. Carb.: Carter downdraft. Optional Engine: L-head. Straight. Six cyl. Chrome alloy block. B & S: 3 x 5 in. Disp.: 212 cu. in. C.R.: 7.0:1. Brake H.P.: 89.5 @ 3600 R.P.M. Taxable H.P.: 21.6. Main bearings: three. Valve lifters: mechanical. Carb.: Carter downdraft. [Series KU] L-head. Straight. Six cyl. Chrome alloy block. B & S: 3 x 5 in. Disp.: 212 cu. in. C.R.: 6.25:1. Brake H.P.: 85 @ 3600 R.P.M. Main bearings: three. Valve lifters: mechanical. Carb.: Carter downdraft. Optional Engine: L-head. Straight. Six cyl. Chrome alloy block. B & S: 3 x 5 in. Disp.: 212 cu. in. C.R.: 7.0:1. Brake H.P.: 89.5 @ 3600 R.P.M. Taxable H.P.: 21.6. Main bearings: 3. Valve lifters: mechanical. Carb.: Carter downdraft. Carter numbers for K & KU, 281S; for KS, 295S.

CHASSIS: [Series K, KS] W.B.: 112 in. O.L.: 190 in. Frt/Rear Tread: 56/56 in. Tires: 17 x 5.50. [Series KU] W.B.: 116 in. O.L.: 194 in. Frt/Rear Tread: 56/56 in. Tires: 16 x 6.00.

TECHNICAL: Sliding gear transmission. Speeds: 3F/1R. Floor shift controls. Single plate clutch, cork inserts, running in oil. Shaft drive. Semi-floating rear axle. Overall Ratio: 4.1:1. Bendix mechanical brakes on four wheels. Pressed steel wheels (Series K,KU, rim size 16''). Wire spoke wheels (Series KS, rim size 17'').

OPTIONS: Single or dual sidemount. Sidemount covers. Radio. Heater. Dash, glove box or rear-view mirror-mounted clock. Cigar lighter. Bumper guards. Wheel trim rings. Turn signals. Wire spoke 16'' wheels (Series K, KU). Fender skirts. Fender lamps (Series K). Twin taillamps (Series K). Twin taillamps (Series K). Axleflex. High compression two-piece alloy cylinder head. Startix. Luggage rack. Two-tone paint.

HISTORICAL: Introduced Jan. 1934. Innovations: Axleflex front suspension — opt. at no extra cost. Two parallel bars replaced the front axle's mid-section to provide an independent front suspension system. Terraplane (and Hudson) first in industry to use pinned piston rings and direct-action (tube-type) shock absorbers this year. Terraplane made 56,804 shipments to dealers during the 1934 calendar year. The president of Terraplane was Roy D. Chapin.

1934
Terraplane Challenger KS, 6-cyl., 112" wb

	FP	5	4	3	2	1
2P Cpe	600	725	1400	3200	4850	6900
RS Cpe	645	825	1600	3950	5500	7900
2 dr Sed	615	675	1300	2500	4350	6200
Sed	675	700	1350	2700	4500	6400

Major Line KU, 6-cyl.

2P Cpe	665	750	1450	3300	4900	7000
RS Cpe	710	825	1600	4000	5600	8000
Conv	750	2800	5700	9500	13,300	19,000
Comp Vic	720	750	1450	3300	4900	7000
2 dr Sed	680	675	1300	2600	4400	6300
Sed	740	700	1350	2900	4600	6600
Comp Sed	780	725	1400	3100	4800	6800

Special Line K, 8-cyl.

2P Cpe	600	775	1500	3600	5100	7300
RS Cpe	645	850	1650	4150	5800	8300
Conv	695	2300	5400	9000	12,600	18,000
Comp Vic	655	750	1450	3400	5000	7100
2 dr Sed	615	700	1350	2700	4500	6400
Sed	675	700	1350	2900	4600	6600
Comp Sed	715	725	1400	3100	4800	6800

1935 Terraplane, 4-dr. sedan, OCW

TERRAPLANE DELUXE — SERIES GU — SIX: The 1935 Terraplanes were fitted with all steel bodies with styling that very closely approximated that of Hudson. After receiving an all-new appearance the previous year, changes were minor. A new grille design of stamped steel featured ten thin horizontal bars, stainless steel center spine and shell surround, and narrower vanes that angled outward from the grille base. The Terraplane's hood louvers were slightly tilted toward the rear of the car and were decorated with three horizontal stainless steel strips. Among the more significant changes to the Terraplane were new wider by 2 and 3 inches respectively, rear and front seats. In the Terraplane lineup only the DeLuxe Six models could be equipped with the Axleflex front suspension.

TERRAPLANE SPECIAL — SERIES G — SIX: The Special Six lacked the twin exterior horns that were mounted directly under the headlights on the GU models. In addition the Special Six was not fitted with the front window vent panes or two chrome taillamps that were standard on the DeLuxe Six.

I.D. DATA: Serial numbers on firewall, right side of frame. Starting: [Ser. GU] 52101, [Ser. G] 51101. Ending: [Ser. GU] 5213362, [Ser. G] 5137772. Engine numbers on left side of cylinder block opposite number one cylinder. Starting: 103,000. Ending: 154,813.

1935 Terraplane, Series GU, coach, WRG

Model No.	Body Type & Seating	Price	Weight	Prod. Total
Series G	2-dr. Tr. Brgh.-5P	625	2611	NA
Series G	2-dr. C'ch.-5P	595	2595	NA
Series G	4-dr. sed.-5P	655	2655	NA
Series G	4-dr. Sub. Sed.-5P	685	2670	NA
Series G	2-dr. Bus. Cpe.	585	2505	NA
Series G	2-dr. Cpe. R/S	625	NA	NA
Series GU	2-dr. Cpe. R/S-4P	675	2635	NA
Series GU	2-dr. Bus. Cpe.	635	2565	NA
Series GU	2-dr. Conv. Cpe.-3P	725	2590	NA
Series GU	4-dr. sed.-5P	705	2710	NA
Series GU	4-dr. Sub. Sed.	735	2425	NA
Series GU	2-dr. C'ch.-5P	645	2665	NA
Series GU	2-dr. Tr. Brgm.-5P	675	2680	NA

ENGINE: L-head. Inline. Six. Chrome alloy block. B & S: 3 x 5 in. Disp. 212 cu. in. C.R.: 6.0:1. Brake H.P.: 88 @ 3800 R.P.M. Taxable H.P.: 21.6. Main bearings: three. Valve lifters: mechanical. Carb.: Carter downdraft. Optional Engine: L-head Inline. Six cyl. Chrome alloy block. B & S: 3 x 5 in. Disp. 212 cu. in. C.R.: 7.0:1. Brake HP.: 100 @ 3800 R.P.M. Main bearings: three. Valve lifters: mechanical. Carb.: Carter downdraft. Carter carburetor numbers 311S for Series G, 209S for Series GU.

CHASSIS: [Series G] W.B.: 112 in. O.L.: 190 in. Frt/Rear Tread: 56/56 in. Tires: 16 x 6. [Series GU] W.B.: 112 in. O.L.: 190 in. Frt/Rear Tread: 56/56 in. Tires: 16 x 6.00.

1935 Terraplane, Series GU, coupe, WRG

TECHNICAL: Sliding gear transmission. Speeds: 3F/1R. Floor shift controls. Single plate clutch, cork inserts, running in oil. Shaft drive. Semi floating rear axle. Overall ratio: 4.11:1. Bendix mechanical brakes on four wheels. Pressed steel wheels. Rim size: 16 in. Axle flex (DeL Six only). Electric hand.

OPTIONS: Radio (51.81). Seat covers (7.50). High compression cylinder head (18.50). Startix (8.50). Luggage carrier (10.00). Zenith radio (44.00). Twin air horns (11.50). Leather upholstery (18.81). Dual tail-stop lights. Single or dual sidemount. Sidemount covers. Heater, Dash-or glove-box mounted clock. Cigar lighter. Bumper guard. Wheel trim rings. Turn singles. Fender skirts. Fender lamps (Series G). Twin taillamps (Series G). Two-tone paint not available.

HISTORICAL: Introduced Dec. 1934. Terraplanes participated in numerous economy and performance trials. At Bonneville Terraplanes averaged 24.24 mpg at a speed of 28 mph and 20.11 mpg at a speed of 50 mph. In an acceleration test the Terraplane needed 14.05 seconds to reach 50 mph from rest. In Brooklyn, NY the New York City Police conducted stopping ability tests that demonstrated the Terraplane could stop in less than 61 feet from a 39 mph speed which was approximately 30% better than the Department's requirement. Terraplane made 70,323 shipments to dealers during the 1935 calendar year. The president of Terraplane was Roy D. Chapin.

1935
Special G, 6-cyl.

	FP	5	4	3	2	1
2P Cpe	585	725	1400	3200	4850	6900
RS Cpe	625	750	1450	3500	5050	7200
Tr Brgm	625	725	1400	3000	4700	6700
2 dr Sed	595	700	1350	2900	4600	6600
Sed	655	725	1400	3000	4700	6700
Sub Sed	685	725	1400	3100	4800	6800

DeLuxe GU, 6-cyl., Big Six

2P Cpe	635	750	1450	3300	4900	7000
RS Cpe	675	775	1500	3700	5200	7400
Conv	725	3300	6600	11,000	15,400	22,000
Tr Brgm	675	725	1400	3000	4700	6700
2 dr Sed	645	700	1350	2700	4500	6400
Sed	705	700	1350	2900	4600	6600
Sub Sed	735	725	1400	3100	4800	6800

1936

1936 Terraplane, rumble-seat, coupe, OCW

TERRAPLANE CUSTOM — SERIES 62 — SIX: Terraplane shared Hudson's new bodies for 1936. Its primary identification feature was a large vertical grille with a thin center divider bisecting a large chromed V. The center bar also served as the focus point for a series of nine slanted V-lines that ran from the grille's top to bottom.

Early in May deliveries of the Terraplane station wagon which was the first such model offered by Hudson began.

1936 Terraplane, Series 61, coupe (with Amelia Earhart), WRG

TERRAPLANE DELUXE — SERIES 61 — SIX: The less costly DeLuxe Terraplanes lacked the externally mounted horns of the Custom models. In addition they were equipped with only a single taillight and their front door windows were not fitted with ventpanes. The wheelbase of all Terraplanes was increased to 115 inches.

I.D. DATA: Serial numbers on firewall, right side of frame right front door pillar post. Starting: [Ser. 61] 61101, [Ser. 62] 62101. Ending: [Ser. 61] 6169752, Ser. 62] 6217041. Engine numbers on left side of cylinder block opposite number one cylinder. Starting: 157000. Ending: 246326.

1936 Terraplane, Series 62, station wagon, WRG

Model No.	Body Type & Seating	Price	Weight	Prod. Total
Series 61	2-dr. Cpe.-3P	640	2695	NA
Series 61	2-dr. Bus. Cpe.-3P	595	2615	NA
Series 61	2-dr. Brgm.-6P	615	2715	NA
Series 61	2-dr. Tr. Brgm.-6P	NA	NA	NA
Series 61	2-dr. Conv. Cpe.-3/5P	715	2740	NA
Series 61	4-dr. Sed.-6P	670	2770	NA
Series 61	4-dr. Tr. Sed.-6P	690	2770	NA
Series 62	2-dr. Tr. Brgm.-6P	635	2715	NA
Series 62	2-dr. Bus. Cpe.-3P	650	2665	NA
Series 62	2-dr. Cpe.-3/5P	690	2750	NA
Series 62	2-dr. Conv. Cpe.-3/5P	760	2975	NA
Series 62	2-dr. Brgm.-6P	665	2755	NA
Series 62	4-dr. Sed.-6P	720	2810	NA
Series 62	4-dr. Tr. Sed.-6P	740	2810	NA
Series 62	4-dr. Sta. Wag.-6P*	750	2925	NA

Note: The Station Wagon was officially listed in Terraplane's Commercial line.

ENGINE: L-head. Inline. Six. Chrome alloy block. B & S: 3 x 5 in. Disp.: 212 cu. in. C.R.: 6.0:1. Brake H.P.: 88 @ 3800 R.P.M. Main bearings: three. Valve lifters: mechanical. Carb.: Carter 331S. Optional Engine: L-head. Inline Six. Chrome alloy block. B & S: 3 x 5 in. Disp.: 212 cu. in. C.R.: 7.0:1. Brake H.P.: 100 @ 3800 R.P.M. Taxable H.P.: 21.6. Main bearings: three. Valve lifters: mechanical. Carb.: Carter 329S.

CHASSIS: [Series 61] W.B.: 115 in. Tires: 16 x 6.00. [Series 62] W.B.: 115 in. Tires: 16 x 6.00.

1936 Terraplane, Series 62, sedan, WRG

TECHNICAL: Sliding gear transmission. Speeds: 3F/1R. Floor shift controls. Single plate clutch, cork inserts, running in oil. Shaft drive. Semi-floating rear axle. Bendix hydraulic brakes on four wheels. Pressed steel wheels. Rim size: 16 in.

OPTIONS: Dual sidemount. Fender skirts. Radio. Heater. Clock. Cigar lighter. Seat covers. Spotlight. Electric hand. Fog lights. Wheel trim rings. Sideview mirrors.

HISTORICAL: Introduced Nov. 1935. Terraplane first to offer all-steel turret top. Terraplane (and Hudson) had Bendix hydraulic brakes on four wheels with backup system in which foot pedal picked up rear wheel mechanicals in case of hydraulic failure. Terraplane made 93,309 shipments to dealers during the 1936 calendar year. The president of Terraplane was Abraham Edward Barit.

1936
DeLuxe 61, 6-cyl.

	FP	5	4	3	2	1
Conv	810	3750	7500	12,500	17,500	25,000
2P Cpe	710	650	1250	2400	4150	5900
RS Cpe	755	725	1400	3200	4850	6900
Brgm	730	600	1200	2200	3900	5600
Tr Brgm	755	650	1250	2400	4150	5900
Sed	785	600	1200	2300	4000	5700
Tr Sed	810	650	1200	2300	4100	5800

Custom 62, 6-cyl.

	FP	5	4	3	2	1
Conv	875	3800	7650	12,750	17,850	25,500
2P Cpe	760	675	1300	2500	4300	6100
RS Cpe	810	775	1500	3700	5200	7400
Brgm	875	650	1250	2400	4150	5900
Tr Brgm	790	675	1300	2500	4300	6100
Sed	815	650	1250	2400	4150	5900
Tr Sed	830	650	1250	2400	4150	5900

1937

1937 Terraplane, sedan, JAC

SUPER TERRAPLANE — SERIES 72 — SIX: With the exception of their hood length, wheelbase and grille design the 1937 Hudson and Terraplane were nearly identical. Key distinctions between the two makes included hubcaps, different shapes for the hood louver panel and domed taillight lenses for the Terraplane. Those used on the Hudson were cone shaped. The more costly Super Terraplanes carried front fender medallions, dual taillights and front window ventpanes.

TERRAPLANE DELUXE — SERIES 71 — SIX: The DeLuxe models had only a single taillight and did not have front window ventpanes.

I.D. DATA: Serial numbers on firewall, right side of frame right front door pillar post. Starting: [Ser. 71] 71101, [Ser. 72] 72101. Ending: [Ser. 71] 7170346, [Ser. 72] 7219907. Engine numbers on left side of cylinder block opposite number one cylinder. Starting: 250,000. Ending: 351,877.

Model No.	Body Type & Seating	Price	Weight	Prod. Total
Series 71	2-dr. Bus. Cpe.-3P	595	2370	NA
Series 71	2-dr. Cpe.-3P	605	2715	NA
Series 71	2-dr. Vic. Cpe.-4P	850	2765	NA
Series 71	2-dr. Conv. Cpe.-3P	725	2765	NA
Series 71	2-dr. Conv. Brgm.-6P	800	2780	NA
Series 71	2-dr. Brgm.-6P	825	2830	NA
Series 71	4-dr. Sed.-6P	675	2865	NA
Series 71	4-dr. Tr. Sed.-6P	695	2865	NA
Series 71	2-dr. Tr. Brgm.-6P	645	2830	NA
Series 72	2-dr. Cpe.-3P	880	2755	NA
Series 72	2-dr. Vic. Cpe.-4P	700	2795	NA
Series 72	4-dr. Tr. Sed.-6P	745	2905	NA
Series 72	2-dr. Conv. Cpe.-4P	770	2825	NA
Series 72	2-dr. Conv. Brgm.-6P	845	2915	NA
Series 72	2-dr. Brgm.-6P	680	2875	NA
Series 72	2-dr. Tr. Brgm.-6P	700	2875	NA
Series 72	4-dr. Sed.-6P	725	2905	NA

ENGINE: L-head. Inline. Six. Alloy block. B & S: 3 x 5 in. Disp. 212 cu. in. C.R.: 6.25:1. Brake H.P.: 96 @ 3900 R.P.M. Taxable H.P.: 21.6. Main bearings: three. Valve lifters: mechanical. Carb.: Carter WI-348S. Torque: 170. Optional Engine: L-head. Straight. Six cyl. Chrome alloy block. B & S: 3 x 5 in. Disp. 212 cu. in. C.R.: 7.0:1. Brake H.P.: 107 @ 4000 R.P.M. Taxable H.P.: 21.6. Main bearings: three. Valve lifters: mechanical. Carb.: Carter 329S. Torque: 170.

1937 Terraplane, coupe, WRG

CHASSIS: [Series 71] W.B.: 117 in. O.L.: 194 in. Tires: 16 x 6.00, 15 x 7.00 opt. [Series 72] W.B.: 117 in. O.L.: 194 in. Tires: 16 x 6.00, 15 x 7.00 opt.

TECHNICAL: Sliding gear transmission. Speeds: 3F/1R. Floor shift controls. Single disc clutch, cork inserts, running in oil. Shaft drive. Semi-floating rear axle. Overall ratio: 4.11:1 (4.54:1 opt). Bendix hydraulic brakes on four wheels. Steel artillery wheels - by Motor Wheel Corp. Rim size: 16 x 4.0 in. Hill-holder. Electric hand. 15'' wheels. 15 x 7.00 tires.

OPTIONS: Radio. Heater. Clock. Cigar lighter. Radio antenna. Seat covers. Rear fender skirts. White side walls. Mohair fabric (closed models). Lacquer finish.

HISTORICAL: Introduced Nov. 1936. Although it was soon broken by a Hudson 8, a Terraplane set a new 86.54 mph record for 24 hours at Bonneville in October, 1936. For its share of the Hudson company's efforts at speed runs, the Terraplane contributed 7 new Class C records. Terraplane (and Hudson) became first American automobile to have true three-passenger (a full 55'' wide) front seat. Terraplane made 83,436 shipments to dealers during the 1937 calendar year. The president of Terraplane was Abraham Edward Barit.

1937
DeLuxe 71, 6-cyl.

	FP	5	4	3	2	1
Bus Cpe	865	550	1150	2100	3800	5400
3P Cpe	905	600	1200	2200	3900	5600
Vic Cpe	950	650	1250	2400	4150	5900
Conv	1005	3600	7200	12,000	16,800	24,000
Brgm	930	600	1200	2200	3850	5500

1938

1938 Hudson Terraplane, Series 81, convertible, OCW

HUDSON TERRAPLANE DELUXE — SERIES 81 — SIX: Although there were two full series of Terraplanes offered, their days as a separate marque were limited. Sales literature and hubcaps indicated the cars as Hudson Terraplanes. The Hudson Terraplane had circular rather than oval-shaped headlights used on other Hudson series. The Terraplane grille featured a wide waterfall divider in addition to a horizontal bar pattern.

HUDSON SUPER TERRAPLANE — SERIES 82 — SIX: The Super Terraplane was powered by a 101 hp engine (compared to 91 hp in the DeLuxe versions). Both had identical exteriors without the front fender chevrons found on other Hudsons. Dual chrome exterial horns were fitted under the headlamps of the Series 82.

I.D. DATA: Hudson Terraplane DeLuxe: Car numbers on right front door post. Starting: 81119. Ending: 8156033. Hudson Super Terraplane: Car numbers on right front door post. Starting: 82153. Ending: 8256017. Engine numbers on top of cylinder block, right side, between numbers one and two exhaust flanges. Starting: 360000 all series. Engine number began matching serial number with car number 11630.

Hudson Terraplane DeLuxe — Series 81

Model No.	Body Type & Seating	Price	Weight	Prod. Total
Series 81	2-dr. Cpe.-3P	789	2725	NA
Series 81	2-dr. Vic. Cpe.-5P	835	2775	NA
Series 81	2-dr. Conv. Cpe.-3P	926	2780	NA
Series 81	2-dr. Brgm.-6P	822	2820	NA
Series 81	2-dr. Tr. Brgm.-6P	843	2825	NA
Series 81	2-dr. Conv. Brgm.-6P	990	2860	NA
Series 81	4-dr. Sed.-6P	864	2885	NA
Series 81	4-dr. Tr. Sed.	884	2890	NA

Hudson Super Terraplane — Series 82

Model No.	Body Type & Seating	Price	Weight	Prod. Total
Series 82	2-dr. Cpe.-3P	845	2755	NA
Series 82	2-dr. Vic. Cpe.-5P	886	2805	NA
Series 82	2-dr. Conv. Cpe.-3P	971	2835	NA
Series 82	2-dr. Brgm.-6P	878	2865	NA
Series 82	2-dr. Tr. Brgm.-6P	899	2870	NA
Series 82	2-dr. Conv. Brgm.-6P	1034	2880	NA
Series 82	4-dr. Sed.-6P	915	2925	NA
Series 82	4-dr. Tr. Sed.-6P	935	2930	NA

ENGINE: L-head. Six cyl. Chrome alloy block. B & S: 3 x 5 in. Disp.: 212 cu. in. C.R.: 6.25:1. Brake H.P.: 101 @ 4000 R.P.M. Taxable H.P.: 21:60. Main bearings: 3. Valve lifters: mechanical. Carb.: Dual Downdraft Carter WDO 397S.

CHASSIS: [Series 82] W.B.: 117 in. O.L.: 193-1/16 in. Frt/Rear Tread: 56/59 in. Tires: 16 x 6.00 (15 x 7.00 opt.). [Series 81] W.B.: 117 in. O.L.: 193-1/16 in. Frt/Rear Tread: 56/59 in. Tires: 16 x 6.00 (15 x 7.00 opt.).

TECHNICAL: Sliding gear, synchromesh transmission. Speeds: 3F/1R. Floor shift controls. Single disc cork inserts, running in oil. Shaft drive. Semi-floating rear axle. Overall Ratio: 4.11:1. Bendix Hydraulic on four wheels. Steel disc wheels. Drivetrain Options: Selective Automatic shift. Automatic clutch.

OPTIONS: DeLuxe heater. Custom radio (7 tubes) Hudson-RCA Victor DB-38. Custom hot water heater. Hydraulic hill-hold. Dual sidemounts (last year of availability). Fender skirts. Fog and spot lights. 15 x 7.00 tires.

1938
Terraplane Utility Series 80, 6-cyl., 117" wb

	FP	5	4	3	2	1
3P Cpe	789	500	1100	1850	3350	4900
2 dr Sed	779	450	1050	1700	3200	4600
Twn Sed	799	450	1050	1750	3250	4700
Sed	864	450	1050	1700	3200	4600
Tr Sed	884	450	1050	1750	3250	4700
Sta Wag	—	850	1650	4200	5850	8400

Terraplane Deluxe Series 81, 6-cyl., 117" wb

	FP	5	4	3	2	1
3P Conv	926	3600	7200	12,000	16,800	24,000
Conv Brgm	990	3750	7500	12,500	17,500	25,000
3P Cpe	879	500	1100	1950	3600	5100
Vic Cpe	835	550	1150	2100	3800	5400
Brgm	822	450	1050	1800	3300	4800
Tr Brgm	843	450	1050	1700	3200	4600
Sed	974	450	1050	1750	3250	4700
Tr Sed	995	450	1050	1800	3300	4800

Terraplane Super Series 82, 6-cyl., 117" wb

	FP	5	4	3	2	1
Conv	971	3750	7500	12,500	17,500	25,000
Conv Brgm	1034	3900	7800	13,000	18,200	26,000
Vic Cpe	886	600	1200	2200	3900	5600
Brgm	878	500	1100	1850	3350	4900
Tr Brgm	899	450	1050	1750	3250	4700
Sed	915	450	1050	1800	3300	4800
Tr Sed	935	500	1100	1850	3350	4900

TERRE HAUTE — The Terre Haute Carriage and Buggy Company of Terre Haute, Indiana was indicated as the manufacturer of an automobile in the Hiscox book *Horseless Vehicles, Automobiles, Motor Cycles* published in 1900. This has not been confirmed. According to the October 1899 issue of *The Carriage Monthly*, the firm was "preparing to enter upon the manufacture of automobiles on an extensive scale," but that this followed is very much to be doubted.

TERRY — The Terry Automobile Company was organized in Newark, New Jersey during the fall of 1909 with a capital stock of $25,000 to manufacture motor cars and carriages. Behind this venture were T.D. Vandervoort of Newark, R.M. Terry of Englewood and T.L. Terry of Glen Ridge. Manufacture is doubted.

TERWILLIGER STEAMER — In 1904 in Amsterdam, New York, the firm of William T. Terwilliger & Company produced a steam car which was marketed under the tradename of Empire. Refer to Empire Steamer.

TETFORD — During the summer of 1910, William L. Tetford of Little Rock, Arkansas announced his organization of the Tetford Auto Company "to manufacture automobiles and to conduct a wholesale accessory and supply business." That an automobile was subsequently manufactured is doubtful.

TEX — San Antonio, Texas — (1915) — The Texas Motor Car Company was organized in San Antonio by J.G. Hughes, George O. Pound and C.H. Dean. The Tex car was slated to be a 35 hp four offered as a five-passenger touring. In late November the company announced its ongoing search for a factory site, noting that the Tex prototype was being given "road tests for the benefit of prospective stockholders." The venture stalled soon thereafter.

1920 Texan, touring, WLB

TEXAN — Fort Worth, Texas — (1920-1922) — "In Texas Oil Fields, 'Where the goin' is rough,' " advertising headlines blared, "The Texan!" This car from Fort Worth was the idea of H.J. Wells of Detroit and F.E. Crotto of Dallas, who formed the Texas Motor Car Association in December of 1917, its unusual title because the firm was organized on a cooperative basis. No single stockholder could own over $500 worth of stock, Wells and Crotto said, and they expected to gather together about 5000 stockholders. The first car built was an altered Elcar, but with that experience behind them a proper Texan prototype followed, and announcement of an $850 price range was made. The war in Europe delayed the start of production, however, and when the Texan finally arrived in the marketplace in 1920, prices had risen over $1000. Except for its outsized tires — fitted for the "rough goin" — the Texan was a typical four-cylinder (Lycoming engine) assembled car of the period. At the helm of the Texas Motor Car Association now were J.C. Vernon as president, William Ginnuth as vice-president, C.F. Sanders as secretary-treasurer. J.T. Sandwich was factory and sales manager. Scarcely had production begun, when receivership arrived. The reason given in late October of 1920 for the company's financial crisis was its "inability to realize on assets and to borrow money." In April of 1921 Texan creditors indicated their wish that the plant be continued in operation in an effort "to realize something on their investment." At the time the factory had on hand one hundred unfinished cars, $500,000 worth of parts and $200,000 worth of tires. Presumably the cars were finished, and then so was the Texas Motor Car Association. Stockholders' meetings were held during the summer and fall of 1921 in an reorganization attempt, which failed. In April of 1922 the Fort Worth factory of the Texan was sold to the Moco Monkey Grip Rubber Company, boot and patch manufacturers from Oklahoma City.

1920-1922 TEXAN
Model A-38 — 4-cyl., 35 hp, 113" wb

	FP	5	4	3	2	1
Touring-5P	1195	3100	4200	6300	10,500	22,000
Roadster-2P	1195	3000	4000	6000	9500	21,000

Model B-38 — 4-cyl., 35 hp, 115" wb

	FP	5	4	3	2	1
Touring-5P	1495	3100	4200	6300	10,500	22,000
Roadster-2P	1495	3000	4000	5000	9500	21,000

TEXAS — The Texas Truck & Tractor Company purportedly built an assembled automobile in 1920 in Dallas, Texas. Documentation is lacking. Curiously, this firm is not known to have built either a truck or a tractor, despite its name.

TEXAS STEAM — (1902) — A steam car called the Texas was exhibited at Agricultural Hall during the Motor Show in London in 1902. It was claimed to be "self-adjusting for all roads, from a freshly ploughed field to glass-like asphalt," and it created a certain sensation. A shield mounted integrally with the front of the car formed the water tank and projected to a point in front in what was apparently an early try at aerodynamic styling. The vehicle was described in the British magazine *The Motor-Car Journal* that May: "A window at the top and an arrangement similar to a cow-catcher beneath are also conspicuous features, the latter being said to prevent a rush of wind beneath the car and thus obviate back wind, which is responsible for the dust so often associated with the pleasures of motoring. As a novelty it attracted notice; we should, however, like to see it actually on the road before passing final judgment on the idea." The builder of this car is not known, but it is possible that it was produced by the Grout brothers, who effected cow-catcher styling on one of their models and whose steamers were exported to England during the turn-of-the-century period. The Grouts built their cars in Orange, Massachusetts so selection of the name Texas is curious, unless it had been chosen by Van Toll and Company, the London agents exhibiting the car at the show.

TEXMOBILE — Grand Prairie, Texas — (1920-1921) — Grand Prairie was agog. "The Little Motor Kar Company is forging ahead by leaps and bounds," the local paper reported in March of 1920. "Mr. W.S. Livezey [is] just back from the north and east, where he placed orders for hundreds of thousands of dollars worth of raw material, which is being rushed to both the local factory and also the northern plant at Havre de Grace, Maryland." Livezey was president of the Little Motor Kar Company. It is known that he once worked in a canning plant in Maryland, but that was probably the extent of his factory involvement in the state. Grand Prairie did provide a fine factory for him, however, and in it the Texmobile was to be built. It looked like a smallish Stutz, a pleasantly styled four-cylinder tour-

1920 Texmobile, touring, KFG

ing car or roadster of 22.5 hp on a 109-inch wheelbase to sell for $750. The car debuted in roadster form at the Dallas Fair in mid-October 1919. Had this venture been a legitimate one, the Texmobile might have enjoyed a pleasant popularity in the Southwest. But this exercise was strictly flim-flam. In April of 1920, Livezey and four of his cohorts were arrested and charged with violation of postal laws with intent to defraud. The company went into receivership in Grand Prairie, and in February of 1921 Livezey and company went to trial in Dallas. The most interesting testimony came from C.E. Peters, a consulting engineer from Cleveland who had been brought to Texas early in 1920 to superintend the initial Texmobile operation. "There were six or seven cars on the floor," he testified, "and no two of them were alike." A good many component parts had been made by local blacksmiths; and, of the two brake drums on hand, one was a Ford, the other a homemade affair, and neither suitable to the brake design as blueprinted. In March of 1922, after his appeal was turned down, William S. Livezey began to serve his five-year sentence in Leavenworth. That December a board of trustees reopened the Little Motor Kar Company, though not for production of the Texmobile. Reportedly, a light truck was built, though the firm concentrated on road scrapers, road rollers and other highway construction machinery. Hopefully, the thousands of stockholders who had invested in the Texmobile did not lose everything.

1914 T & F Cyclecar, runabout, WLB

T & F — New Salem, Massachusetts — (1914) — The T & F Cycle Car Company was successor to the Climax Electric Works, builders of a gasoline car, ironically, in New Salem from 1906 to 1912. The business had begun in a henhouse on the homestead of Levi W. Flagg and around 1908 had proven successful enough to move into town. Though the T & F company did not market complete vehicles, it offered all components necessary for the dexterous do-it-yourselfer, and also for other cyclecar manufacturers. It is known, for example, that the Westfield cyclecar used T & F components.

THACHER — Albany, New York — (1902) — A gasoline automobile was built at the Thacher Car Wheel Works in Albany in 1902, but production was never contemplated, the vehicle being merely a pleasant diversion to test out some ideas of company president George H. Thacher.

THACKER-BRERETON — The Thacker-Brereton Company was organized in Peoria, Illinois early in 1908 with a capital stock of $5000 to manufacture and deal in automobiles. Incorporators were J.F. Thacker and J.T. Hunter. Manufacture is doubted.

THAYER — Marinette, Wisconsin — (1907-1908) — In 1907 Harry Thayer left his job in Oshkosh at Thomas Neville's carriage shop and moved to Marinette where he put himself into the accessory business as the Thayer Automobile Company. He also put together a four-cylinder runabout which he believed worthy of manufacture, convinced the Marinette Iron Manufacturing Company of the wisdom of his idea, and the result was the organization in November that year of the Marinette Automobile Company for the manufacture of Harry Thayer's car. Any production which resulted was short-lived, however, because on December 1st, 1908 Marinette was forced out of business by foreclosure of a chattel mortgage. Harry Thayer remained in Marinette long enough to open a dealership and garage which traded as the Thayer Isham Motor Car Company. But in

October of 1909 he disposed of his interest in that venture and went West, leaving partner Isham to continue selling Studebakers and Maxwells, and to operating what at the time was the only garage in Marinette.

THERMOBILE — The Thermobile Company of American was organized under the laws of New Jersey early in 1903 with a capital stock of $1 million for the manufacture of automobiles and "appliances to be used in the construction of automobiles." Incorporators were William H. Lake, Z. Wirt and B.M. Bell, all of Chicago. "If any deductions are to be drawn from the name and the amount of stock," The Automobile noted wryly, "it might be supposed that the vehicles will be run on hot air and water." Manufacture is doubted.

THIBERT — The Thibert Manufacturing Company was organized in Worcester, Massachusetts during the spring of 1917 with a capital stock of $50,000 for the manufacture of motor vehicles and accessories. N.R. Thibert and George E. Reed were the incorporators. Manufacture is doubted.

THIEM — St. Paul, Minnesota — (1901-1903) / Owatonna, Minnesota — (1903-1904) — The firm of Thiem & Company of 143-145 South Wabash Street in St. Paul began production of gasoline engines at the turn of the century. Most of these were single-cylinder units of modest horsepower, and the company fitted some of them into buggies for sale locally. In early 1903 Thiem sold the rights to and equipment for its 3 hp engine to Virtue & Pound Manufacturing Company of Owatonna (one reference indicates Rushford). Virtue & Pound commenced a short production run of buggies using that engine in September 1903. Meanwhile, Edward A. Thiem remained in Minnesota where he continued in the engine and motorcycle building field, and in 1910 joined with Fred Joerns in the manufacture of a new car called the Joerns-Thiem.

THIES — Chaffee, North Dakota — (1908) — In 1908 Frank Thies of Chaffee began building a 10/12 hp runabout for himself. Possibly he did not complete the car until 1910. He is not known to have built another.

THOMAS — The Thomas Manufacturing Company of Springfield, Ohio was the venue in which superintendent H.E. Owens built an automobile in 1900. Refer to Owens.
    The W.K. Thomas Company was organized in Baltimore, Maryland during the spring of 1905 with a capital stock of $5000 for the manufacture of engines and automobiles. Incorporators were Walter K. Thomas, Edwin D. Loane, Jr., William W. Varney, Thomas Benning and Samuel A. Van Trump. Manufacture is doubted.

THOMAS STEAM — Boston, Massachusetts — (1900) — D.W. Thomas of 23 Court Street in Boston completed the building of an experimental steam car in January 1900. By February he had decided to build more in all sizes and shapes, which he prematurely announced he was already doing. Apparently some correspondence ensued, because in March Thomas advised the trade press that he was not at present ready for market but that when he was he proposed "to sell vehicles and not stock." It does not appear he ultimately did either.

1904 Thomas, runabout, LC

THOMAS — Ann Arbor, Michigan — (1904 et seq.) — Charles C. Thomas built two automobiles in Michigan, the first a runabout powered by a single-cylinder horizontal gasoline engine, with frame and body, including dash, made of wood. Thomas designed and machined the engine himself, and all other components of the car, save for its chain drive, springs and steering wheel. His second car, built while he was a student at the University of Michigan, had a two-cylinder four-stroke engine, again designed and machined entirely by Thomas. This car's axle, springs and wheels were courtesy of an abandoned electric. The frame was angle iron this time, and a friction transmission was fitted, whereas the first car featured a single spur gear train later revised to vee-belt. Charles Thomas wanted to proceed into commercial manufacture of his car, but the wherewithal to do so was beyond his means.

1903 Thomas, model 18, touring, HAC

THOMAS — Buffalo, New York — (1903-1918) — In September of 1902 announcement was made that the E.R. Thomas Motor Company of Buffalo would take over the Buffalo Automobile & Auto-Bi Company on October 1st. Since both firms were owned by Erwin Ross Thomas, this was not earth-shaking news, and the move seems to have been made merely so Thomas could put his own name on the cars he had previously been selling as Buffalos. (Only engines had thus far been produced by the E.R. Thomas Motor Company.) The first Thomas cars were designated Models 17 and 18, and were slightly larger versions of the Model 16 which had been marketed as the Buffalo Senior in 1902. The three-speed sliding gear transmissions, chain drive and roller bearing axles of the Buffalo were continued, and the Thomas hood sloped a la Renault with a gilled-tube radiator underneath. This Thomas was produced only for a single season. In 1904 the Thomas became a three-cylinder car, acquired its famous Flyer designation, was fitted with a conventional hood and radiator, as well as a price tag twice as high as the first car ($2500 vis-a-vis $1250). Again, this car was built but a single season. For 1905 Thomas burst forth into the $3000+ range with a pair of fours of 40 and 50 hp and a 60 hp six which, though catalogued, was probably built only for the company itself or on special order from wealthy, sporting clients. There is no doubt that Thomas produced the car at this time simply because the company wanted to go racing. A six built in 1905 had finished fifth in the Vanderbilt Cup eliminating trials, but did not qualify for the event itself. In 1906 a Thomas did contest the Vanderbilt; although its eighth-place was unspectacular, the car put up the fastest lap (67.6 mph) and was the highest American car to finish. In 1908 a Thomas six tried the French Grand Prix but retired there; its best placing in the Vanderbilt Cup that year was the fifth of chief engineer George Salzman. It scarcely mattered, however, because several months earlier — in July 1908 — a specially-prepared but stock four-cylinder Thomas had won the most formidable sporting contest of all, the epic New York to Paris race of 1908, with George Schus-

1904 Thomas Flyer, touring, HAC

ter and Montague Roberts driving 'round the world in 169 days. Thomas sales, which had always been fine for such a high-priced car — 1000 units in 1905-1906 and 700 in 1907 — increased handsomely now: 817 cars in 1908, 1036 in 1909. A six (K-6-70) was a firm entry in the company lineup by 1908, followed later that year by another six (the L-6-40) which was the first shaft-drive Thomas. Apparently, laurels-resting became the Thomas frailty. The new Model L was, according to George Schuster, "noisy, underpowered, and leaked oil." The expensive K and the subsequent M were not much better. Basking in the success of the New York to Paris could only remain a viable marketing factor so long as the Thomas Flyers sold proved themselves worthy on ordinary roads. From such a splendid beginning — which had also included production in Detroit through an offshoot Thomas-Detroit during 1906-1908 and a lucrative entry into the taxicab market during the same period — the Thomas Company moved quickly into disarray. By 1911, with sales falling and squabbling in the management team becoming bitter, Erwin Ross Thomas elected to get out, turning over the firm to the New York banking house of Eugene Meyer and Company, and retaining only the taxicab business, which he continued for several years. Meyer installed former Packard sales manager E.P. Chalfant

as the new Thomas president, Chalfant bringing in a number of other former Packard men with him. Quality control was returned to the Thomas in 1912, when all cars were sixes and, alas, sales fell to 350 units. By now the company was in receivership. Early in 1913 the E.R. Thomas Motor Company went to the auction block, where its good will, patents, patterns and stock were purchased for $51,000 by C.A. Finnegan of the Empire Smelting Company in Depew (New York). Finnegan, who remained enamoured of the New York to Paris winner, indicated initially that he might move operations to his native Louisville, Kentucky though he instead set up shop elsewhere in Buffalo. Thomas production now was paltry, though it continued for a surprising number of years, the cars being catalogued until 1916, and built on order as late as 1918, and possibly into 1919.

1903 THOMAS
Model 17 — 1-cyl., 8 hp, 78" wb

	FP	5	4	3	2	1
Tonneau	1250	3900	4800	7700	14,300	27,000

Model 18 — 1-cyl., 8 hp, 78" wb

Tonneau	1400	4000	5000	8000	15,000	28,000

1904 THOMAS
Flyer — 3-cyl., 24 hp, 84" wb

No. 22 Tonneau-5P	2500	4200	5200	8400	15,700	29,000

Flyer — 3-cyl., 24 hp, 92" wb

No. 23 Limo.-6P	3000	3700	4700	7300	13,700	26,000

1905 Thomas Flyer, touring, WLB

1905 THOMAS
Flyer — 4-cyl., 40 hp, 106" wb

	FP	5	4	3	2	1
No. 25 Tour.-5/7P	3000	4900	6300	10,300	21,000	39,000

Flyer — 4-cyl., 50 hp, 110" wb

No. 26 Victoria	3500	5400	7300	11,800	25,000	38,000

Flyer — 4-cyl., 50 hp, 114" wb

No. 29 Limousine	4500	4200	5200	8400	15,700	29,000

Flyer — 6-cyl., 60 hp, 124" wb

No. 27 Tour. Phae.-3P	6000	7600	12,500	19,400	42,400	55,000
No. 30 Limousine	7000	5000	6500	11,000	22,000	35,000
Racer	6000	18,500	32,000	51,000	88,000	110,000

1906 Thomas Flyer, touring, HAC

1906 THOMAS
Flyer — 4-cyl., 50 hp, 118" wb

	FP	5	4	3	2	1
No. 31 Tour.-7P	3500	7200	11,300	17,700	38,700	50,000
No. 32 Limo.-7P	4500	4300	5400	8700	16,500	30,000
No. 33 Landaulet-7P	4600	4500	5800	9500	18,000	32,000
No. 34 Semi-Limo.-7P	4000	4300	5400	8700	16,500	30,000

1907 THOMAS
Thomas 40-Horse — 4-cyl., 35/40 hp, 112-1/2" wb

Runabout-2P	2750	7800	13,300	20,300	44,000	60,000
Touring-5P	2750	7900	13,700	20,700	44,500	62,000
Limousine-5P	2750	5400	7300	11,800	25,000	38,000

Flyer — 4-cyl., 60 hp, 118" wb

Touring-7P	4000	9400	18,800	26,500	53,800	75,000
Runabout-3P	4000	9300	18,500	26,000	52,500	74,000
Landaulet-7P	5200	6400	9300	14,500	33,000	45,000
Demi-Limousine	4500	5800	8000	12,500	28,000	40,000
Limousine	5000	6000	8500	13,000	30,000	42,000
Drop Window Limo.	5200	6200	8800	13,500	31,000	43,000

1417

1907 Thomas Flyer, "New York-to-Paris" car, HAC

1908 Thomas, model DX, Flyer touring, HAC

1908 THOMAS
Model G — 4-cyl., 18.2 hp, 103" wb

	FP	5	4	3	2	1
Cabriolet	3000	6700	9900	15,500	34,800	47,000
Limousine	3250	5400	7300	11,800	25,000	38,000
Taxicab	—	4500	5800	9500	18,000	32,000
Town Car	3000	5500	7500	12,000	26,000	39,000
Brougham		5400	7300	11,800	25,000	38,000
Landaulette		5800	8000	12,500	28,000	40,000

Model DX — 4-cyl., 48.4 hp, 115" wb

Touring-7P	4000	7600	12,500	19,400	42,400	55,000
Runabout	—	7300	11,800	18,400	40,400	52,000
Tourabout	—	7300	11,800	18,400	40,400	52,000
Limousine	—	5800	8000	12,500	28,000	40,000
Landaulette	—	6000	8500	13,000	30,000	42,000

Model F — 4-cyl., 48.4 hp, 127" wb

Touring-7P	4500	7800	13,200	20,200	43,800	59,000
Limousine	5700	6000	8500	13,000	30,000	42,000
Landaulette	—	6400	9300	14,500	33,000	45,000
Runabout	4500	7700	12,700	19,700	43,000	56,000
Tourabout	—	7800	12,900	19,900	43,300	57,000

Model K — 6-cyl., 72.6 hp, 140" wb

Touring-7P	6000	8700	16,500	23,500	48,500	69,000
Limousine	—	7200	11,300	17,700	38,700	50,000
Landaulet	—	7300	11,800	18,400	40,400	52,000
Runabout	6000	8400	15,500	22,500	47,300	67,000
Tourabout	—	8500	16,000	23,000	48,000	68,000

1909 Thomas, model G, town car, HAC

1909 THOMAS
Model G — 4-cyl., 18 hp, 103" wb

	FP	5	4	3	2	1
Town Car	3000	7000	10,800	16,900	37,100	49,000

Model L — 6-cyl., 31 hp, 122" wb

Touring-6P	3000	7800	13,000	20,000	43,500	58,000
Flyabout-4P	3000	7800	13,000	20,000	43,500	58,000
Tourabout	3000	7800	13,000	20,000	43,500	58,000
Limousine-6P	4500	7600	12,500	19,400	42,400	55,000

Model F — 4-cyl., 53 hp, 127" wb

Touring-7P	4500	7900	13,700	20,700	44,500	62,000
Flyabout	4400	7900	13,500	20,500	44,300	61,000
Tourabout	4500	7900	13,900	20,900	44,800	62,000
Limousine-7P	6000	7800	13,000	20,000	43,500	58,000
Landaulet	6000	7800	13,200	20,200	43,800	59,000

Model K — 6-cyl., 72 hp, 140" wb

Touring-7P	6000	11,300	21,300	32,500	65,000	85,000
Flyabout	6000	11,300	21,300	32,500	65,000	85,000
Tourabout	6000	11,300	21,300	32,500	65,000	85,000
Limousine	7500	7800	12,900	19,900	43,300	57,000
Landaulet	7500	7800	13,000	20,000	43,500	58,000

1910 Thomas, model R, ladies' special town car, HAC

1910 THOMAS
Model R-4-28 — 4-cyl., 28 hp, 123" wb

Limousine	4100	7600	12,500	19,400	42,400	55,000
Brougham	4250	7500	12,300	19,100	41,700	54,000
Town Car	4000	7800	12,900	19,900	43,300	57,000

Model M-6-40 — 6-cyl., 40 hp, 125" wb

Touring-5P	3500	7800	13,200	20,200	43,800	59,000
Tourabout	3400	7800	13,200	20,200	43,800	59,000
Limousine	5000	7800	12,900	19,900	43,300	57,000
Landaulet	5500	7800	13,200	20,200	43,800	58,000

Model F-4-60 — 4-cyl., 60 hp, 127" wb

Touring-7P	4500	8200	14,500	21,500	45,800	65,000
Tourabout	4500	8200	14,500	21,500	45,800	65,000
Flyabout	4500	8200	14,500	21,500	45,800	65,000
Limousine	6000	7800	13,200	20,200	43,800	59,000
Landaulet	6000	7800	13,300	20,300	44,000	60,000

Model K-6-70 — 6-cyl., 70 hp, 140" wb

Touring-7P	6000	10,000	20,000	30,000	60,000	80,000
Flyabout	6000	10,000	20,000	30,000	60,000	80,000
Tourabout	6000	10,000	20,000	30,000	60,000	80,000
Limousine	7500	7800	13,300	20,300	44,000	60,000
Landaulet	7500	7900	13,700	20,700	44,500	62,000

1911 Thomas, model M, touring, OCW

1911 THOMAS
Model E-4-30 — 4-cyl., 28.9 hp, 123" wb

Brougham	4000	6500	9500	15,000	34,000	46,000

Model M-6-40 — 6-cyl., 43 hp, 125" wb

Touring-5P	4000	7600	12,500	19,400	42,400	55,000
Flyabout	3750	7600	12,500	19,400	42,400	55,000
Torpedo	—	7600	12,500	19,400	42,400	55,000
Gunboat	—	7600	12,500	19,400	42,400	55,000
Limousine	5000	6700	9900	15,500	34,800	47,000
Landaulet	5100	6800	10,300	16,000	35,500	48,000

Model K-6-70 — 6-cyl., 72 hp, 140" wb

Touring	6000	11,300	21,300	32,500	65,000	85,000
Flyabout	6000	11,300	21,300	32,500	65,000	85,000
Runabout	6000	11,300	21,300	32,500	65,000	85,000
Landaulet	7600	7800	12,900	19,900	43,300	57,000
Limousine	7500	7600	12,500	19,400	42,400	55,000

1912 Thomas, model MC, touring, HAC

1912 THOMAS
Model MC-6-40 — 6-cyl., 40 hp, 126" wb

	FP	5	4	3	2	1
Runabout-2P	4000	7800	13,300	20,300	44,000	60,000
Surrey-4P	4000	7800	13,300	20,300	44,000	60,000
Coupe	4350	5800	8000	12,500	28,000	40,000
Phaeton-5P	4000	7800	13,300	20,300	44,000	60,000
Limousine-7P	5000	7600	12,500	19,400	42,400	55,000
Landaulet-7P	5000	7800	12,900	19,900	43,300	57,000
Inside Drive Brgm.-7P	4950	7200	11,300	17,700	38,700	50,000

Model KC-6-70 — 70 hp, 140" wb

Touring-7P	6000	11,800	21,800	33,500	67,000	87,000
Flyabout-4P	6000	11,300	21,300	32,500	65,000	85,000
Runabout-2P	6000	11,300	21,300	32,500	65,000	85,000
Tour. Limo.	7200	7800	12,900	19,900	43,300	57,000
Tour. Landaulet	7200	7800	13,000	20,000	43,500	58,000
Vestibuled Limo.	7350	7800	13,000	20,000	43,500	58,000
Vestibuled Landaulet	7350	7800	13,200	20,200	43,800	59,000

1913 Thomas, model 6-46, touring, HAC

1913 THOMAS
Model 6-46 — 6-cyl., 46 hp, 134" wb

Touring-7P	4800	9800	19,500	28,500	57,500	78,000
Touring-6P	4800	9400	18,800	26,500	53,800	75,000
Phaeton-5P	4750	9300	18,500	26,000	52,500	74,000
Surrey-4P	4700	9000	18,000	25,000	50,000	72,000
Runabout-2P	4600	9200	18,300	25,500	51,300	73,000

1914 Thomas, model MCX, roadster, HAC

1914-1915 THOMAS
Model MCX — 6-cyl., 43 hp, 134" wb

Touring-5P	3250	9500	19,000	27,000	55,000	76,000
Touring-7P	3250	9800	19,400	28,500	57,500	78,000

1916 Thomas, model MF, touring, HAC

1916-1917 THOMAS
Model MF — 6-cyl., 43 hp, 136" wb

	FP	5	4	3	2	1
Touring	4000	9800	19,400	28,500	57,500	78,000
Roadster	3600	9700	19,300	27,800	56,300	77,000
Limousine	4800	7600	12,500	19,400	42,400	55,000
Berline	5000	7800	12,900	19,900	43,300	57,000
Coupe	4500	6800	10,300	16,000	35,500	48,000
Sedan	4800	6000	8500	13,000	30,000	42,000

THOMAS — Saginaw, Michigan — (1914) — The Thomas of Saginaw was built in Lansing by the Acme Engine Company. That is, the prototype was which more than likely was the only car built. This Thomas venture was promoted by Saginaw businessmen — among them W.H. Porter and L.E. Rowley — who spent the prototype's incubation period looking for a suitable factory in town and trying to stir up local interest. The Thomas had the makings of an interesting small car. It was powered by a four-cylinder 18 hp water-cooled engine, and its chassis featured a gearless differential on the rear axle, a three-speed sliding gear transmission, and shaft drive. The body was streamlined, with a pointed radiator in front, and electric lights, left-hand steering and center controls fitted. But something went awry somewhere. The prototype was completed by late summer of 1914. Production did not follow.

1939 Thomas, streamlined coupe, MVMA

THOMAS — Batavia, New York — (1939) — Charles D. Thomas was a thirty-year-old Batavia mechanic when he built his dream car in 1939. Among other features, it sported a one-piece unit body, independent front suspension, a padded safety interior, suspended control pedals, and a streamlined periscope on the roof providing vision to the rear. The car was pictured in the August 1940 issue of *Motor* magazine, and although Thomas attempted to find backing to go into production, he was unsuccessful. After the Second World War, Charles Thomas tried again, however, with a new car called the Playboy. One of the most promising postwar sports cars, the Playboy was put into manufacture, though a few less than a hundred were built before the company went under in the early Fifties.

1908 Thomas-Detroit, roadster, JAC

THOMAS-DETROIT — Detroit, Michigan — (1906-1908) — In 1906 Erwin Ross Thomas.whose big 50 hp four-cylinder Thomas cars were being produced successfully in Buffalo (New York), was persuaded to help finance two Olds Motor Works veterans — engineer Howard E. Coffin and super salesman Roy Chapin — in a new company to produce a smaller 40 hp four in Detroit. Though built in Michigan, the product of the E.R. Thomas-Detroit Company was bought and marketed by Thomas in New York. By July of 1907 a total of 503 units had been shipped East, and Erwin Thomas asked for 750 more. This cross-country arrangement and control by Thomas soon lost its appeal for Chapin and Coffin, however. Consequently they talked Hugh Chalmers of Detroit into buying out Erwin Thomas — and the Thomas-Detroit became the Chalmers-Detroit in 1908.

1906-1908 THOMAS-DETROIT
Four — 40 hp, 112 1/2" wb

	FP	5	4	3	2	1
Runabout	2750	4000	5000	8000	15,000	28,000
Touring	2750	4200	5200	8400	15,700	29,000
Limousine	3750	2700	3600	5300	8800	19,000
Landaulette	3750	2900	3700	5600	9100	20,000

THOMPSON — The Thompson Automobile Company was organized in Camden, New Jersey late in 1899 with a capital stock of $60,000 of which $3400 was paid in. Involved in this venture were John K. Knox and W.F. Thompson of Philadelphia, and Theodore Leas of Camden. Manufacture is doubted.

Another Thompson Automobile Company was organized in Camden, New Jersey late in 1900 with a capital stock of $250,000. Offices were secured at 810 Broad Street in Newark. Involved in this venture were C.F. McGuire and J.C. Blevney of Newark and J.S.W. Thompson of Morristown. Manufacture is doubted. John C. Blevney went on to build an automobile on his own the year following.

The J.L. Thompson Manufacturing Company of Waltham, Massachusetts announced during the spring of 1907 its plans to manufacture a kerosene-engined automobile and "to have a machine on the market next year." That manufacture followed is doubted.

The Thompson-Schoeffel Company of Rochester, New York was organized during the spring of 1905 with a capital stock of $40,000 for the manufacture of automobiles. Involved in this venture were F.H. and G.B. Schoeffel and T.G. Thompson. Manufacture is doubted.

THOMPSON STEAM — Portland, Maine — (1901-1902) — After serving as the local agency for the Mobile steamer for awhile, Zenas Thompson & Brothers of Portland decided they could do at least as well themselves and commenced into manufacture of their own cars. "The vehicles are propelled by steam but are longer and larger generally than the carriages the firm has been handling," reported *The Motor Age* in August 1901. "The firm employs a superintendent, W.C. Buckman, who was for some years with the Stanleys." Except for the boiler, all parts of the Thompson were made in the Portland shop. The brothers' car-building venture is not believed to have survived more than a year.

THOMPSON — Olneyville, Rhode Island — (1901-1907) — The Thompson Automobile Company was organized in 1901 by J.P. Thompson, a prominent Providence businessman, and K.A. Juthe, formerly the superintendent for Steamobile in Keene, New Hampshire. A factory was secured in Olneyville at the corner of Stokes and Westminster streets, and in 1903 Arthur A. Morin was brought in as a part owner. The company's stated purpose was the manufacture of "delivery wagons, trucks and buses," and most of the production which followed was of commercial vehicles. All Thompsons were steam powered, usually featuring an 8/10 hp Fitzheney engine and Tonkin dry plate boiler. The Thompson Steam Wagonette — a solid-tired, canopy-topped surrey — was a popular model. Although the standard version sat eight to ten passengers, a few smaller seven-passenger cars were produced on special order. At least four Thompsons — a delivery wagon and three sixteen-passenger buses — are known to have been exported to Puerto Rico.

1901 Thompson Electric, runabout, NAHC

1420

THOMPSON ELECTRIC — Plainfield, New Jersey — (1901) — Andrew C. Thompson was a mechanic doing business at 313 West Front Street in Plainfield who built an electric in 1901 which he claimed would need "no more repairs than the ordinary horse vehicle." Though he did not incorporate a company for manufacture, he did produce his car for sale as a 1-1/4 hp $800 runabout with a maximum speed of 12 mph and a 20-mile run between battery charges, and as a 2 1/2 hp $1600 stanhope good for 18 mph and 40 miles per charge. The Thompson Electric was equipped, so Andrew Thompson said, "with both electric and foot brakes, electric headlight and electric gong." His automotive venture does not seem to have survived 1901, though he was back in the car-building business in 1904 in Elizabeth with the Mackle-Thompson.

1901 THOMPSON ELECTRIC

	FP	5	4	3	2	1
Electric Runabout	800	2300	3300	4600	7500	16,000
Electric Stanhope	1600	2500	3500	5000	8500	18,000

THOMPSON — Beverly Farms, Massachusetts — (1909) — The roadster built in 1909 by Newton Thompson of Beverly Farms was powered by a two-cylinder water-cooled engine and rode on pneumatic tires, Thompson also building himself a motorcycle during this same period.

1901 Thompson-Kanter, gasoline runabout, LC

THOMPSON-KANTER — Meadville, Pennsylvania — (1901) — The first automobile in Meadville was a big Haynes-Apperson surrey purchased in 1898 by Lew Quay for the purpose of transporting guests from his Thurston House to Conneaut Lake, an activity at which it was reportedly unsuccessful because it "was never able to get around the turn outside Kerrtown." Meadville's second car was built right in town in 1901, and was a success, though its purpose and configuration were considerably less lofty. William M. Thompson and Harold B. Kanter were students, short on money but long on ingenuity. For their car, they purchased only a single-cylinder gasoline engine and wheels; the rest they fashioned themselves. The Thompson-Kanter was a three-wheeler (single wheel at the rear), which cut the cost of buying another wheel and did away with the necessity for a pricey differential gear. The two-seater runabout was used frequently by the boys, and not only could negotiate the turn outside Kerrtown, but it also managed to climb College Hill.

1900 Thomson, steam surrey, FR

1897 Thomson, steam wagonette, HS

1900 Thomson, twin engine steamer, HS

THOMSON STEAM — Lynn, Massachusetts — (1898-1903) — In addition to the electrics he designed for the General Electric Company, Prof. Elihu Thomson experimented with steam and developed a twin-cylinder uniflow engine, followed by a four-cylinder engine of the same concept. Vehicles built at General Electric using the Thomson engines included a victoria in 1898, a runabout in 1900 and a surrey later that year. The Thomson steamers were, like all the General Electric-built cars, produced for experimental purposes only. The Thomson steam surrey remains extant in Australia. For how long this experimentation continued is not known. As late as June of 1903 one A.A. Ball of the "Thomson-Houston Company" of Lynn was reported to be testing a new design of steam carriage.

1900 Thomson, model A, gasoline runabout, NAHC

THOMSON — Philadelphia, Pennsylvania — (1900-1903) — Reason No. 6 of the seven offered by the Thomson Automobile Company of Philadelphia for purchase of its product was: "Moderate price, just what the general public has been waiting for, built on a fair business profit without having a large amount tacked on cost for expensive experiments, shows, runs, etc." The Thomson was a cute and ingenuous little gasoline runabout which sold for as low as $500. Its engine was a 5 hp one-lunger which the company offered to sell separately for $150. The company was a family affair with William Thomson as president, William J. Thomson as secretary and treasurer. Their little car's hickory wheels, which they had previously used in their horseless carriages, were a particular point of pride for the Thomsons, "more lively and elastic than a wire wheel," and easy to clean too. Production of the Thomson car began in 1900 at Seventeenth and Washington Avenue, with the company moving later that year to a new five-story factory at 2132 Market Street which was the tallest building on the block. Production was two cars a week by early 1901, and a *Motor Age* reporter who visited the factory that May was impressed both by the operation and the congenial candor of the Thomsons. The reason there was no plan to change their car's engine in the foreseeable future was that, as William Thomson explained, "a single cylinder can give sufficient trouble without having a pair of them." A subsequent move took the firm to 22nd and Market streets. "Things are coming (our) way," William J. Thomson said in January 1903 in announcing that every machine thus far built had been sold and though some mistakes had been made, the Thomson Automobile Company would "come on the stage for 1903 with one of the best and simplest machines for the price." Unfortunately, the Thomson Automobile Company was out of business later that year.

1900-1901 THOMSON

	FP	5	4	3	2	1
Model A Gasoline Rbt.	500	2000	3000	4200	6500	14,000
Model B Gasoline Rbt.	550	2000	3000	4200	6500	14,000
Model C Physician's Phae.	650	2200	3200	4400	7000	15,000
Model D Surrey	800	2300	3300	4600	7500	16,000
Model E Delivery	800	2000	3000	4200	6500	14,000

1902 Thomson, model BB, gasoline runabout, NAHC

1902-1903 THOMSON

Model A Gasoline Rbt.	500	2000	3000	4200	6500	14,000
Model B Gasoline Rbt.	550	2000	3000	4200	6500	14,000
Model BB Gasoline Rbt.	600	2100	3100	4300	6800	14,500
Model C Physician's Phae.	650	2300	3300	4600	7500	16,000

1912 Thomson, roadster, HS

THOMSON — Lynn, Massachusetts — (1911-1913) — Malcolm Thomson was a son of Prof. Elihu Thomson and, like his father, enjoyed experimenting with cars. He built a total of three, each of them for his own enjoyment. The first, completed in early 1911, might be described as a "gas-electric," since he used numerous parts from his father's electric in which to build it, though he also added a two-cylinder air-cooled Logan truck engine. His second car, completed in the fall of 1911, was fitted with a two-cylinder, two-stroke Willett engine, subsequently replaced with a four-stroke Pullman four. Car number three used a four-cylinder 40 hp Wisconsin engine and included a number of parts to his own design (among them the muffler, which he patented) which were fabricated in his father's shop. This final car was completed in 1913 and was driven by Malcolm Thomson until 1923, when he sold it.

1909 Thor, touring, LC

THOR — Aurora, Illinois — (1907-1909) — In the years before World War I, the Aurora Automatic Machinery Company (later renamed the Thor Power Tool Company) produced thousands of high-quality Thor motorcycles. The name became nationally famous. What is not so well known is that a Thor automobile was produced too. It was a large six-cylinder touring car that was an exact copy of the French Hotchkiss. Only four of these automobiles were built before the company decided to discontinue this side of its business. Probably none of them exists today, although the fate of one is known. It was driven for a number of years by Axel Levedahl, an Aurora resident. Apparently so much aluminum was used in the makeup of the Thor that when World War I arrived, and aluminum was placed on the critical materials list, the junk value of the Levedahl Thor exceeded its market value, and the automobile was surrendered to the war effort. Possibly the other three Thors suffered similarly.

THORP-ALLEN — The Thorp-Allen Motor Company was organized in Kansas City, Missouri during the fall of 1913 with a capital stock of $10,000 for the manufacture of automobiles. The partners in this venture were W.R. Thorp, H.B. Thorp and H.L. Allen. Manufacture is doubted.

THREE FIELD'S — The Three Field's Garage was organized in Portland, Maine during the summer of 1914 with a capital stock of $5000 to manufacture automobiles and conduct a garage. M.A. Thurston was the man behind this venture. Manufacture is doubted.

1900 Thresher Electric, dos-a-dos, NAHC

THRESHER ELECTRIC — Dayton, Ohio — (1900) — In 1900 the Thresher Electric Company of Dayton, which supplied motors to the general trade, entered the automobile industry with an electric car of its own. The body style was a brake, with room for four passengers sitting dos-a-dos. Coachwork was provided by Morris Woodhull, also of Dayton, and was praised in *The Motor Vehicle Review* as "having the appearance of being constructed especially as a motor vehicle." At the turn of the century, most automobiles betrayed their horsedrawn carriage antecedents. In addition to the brake, the Thresher Electric Company announced its plans to manufacture runabouts, stanhopes, broughams and both light and heavy delivery wagons. Probably only the brake was built, however, and production had ended before 1901.

T.H.T. — Detroit, Michigan — (1910) — The people behind the T.H.T. Motor Company of Detroit, which was incorporated for $100,000 in February 1910, were J.H. Taylor, C. Taylor and W.P. Barker, which makes curious the reason behind the initialed name of the company. Their plan was

the manufacture of a four-cylinder car, a prototype of which had been built and which was included among the assets of the firm. Probably the remaining assets were few, because this venture does not appear to have proceeded beyond the building of the single car.

THURSTON — Sunbury, Pennsylvania — (1903) — In 1903, in Sunbury, Silas Thurston built himself a three-wheeled gasoline car, its single wheel in front, its engine a small water-cooled one-lunger of Thurston's own devising. The wheelbase was 72 inches, the tread 36 inches, and final drive was by belt.

TIERNEY — Saginaw, Michigan — (1902) — The Tierney Brothers operated a bicycle store at 217 Genesee Avenue in Saginaw and in the 1902 city directory advertised themselves as automobile manufacturers. Their car doubtless was a primeval one, largely bicycle based, and actual production cannot be confirmed. The Tierneys obviously believed in diversification, advertising sporting goods and ammunition as well as "money to loan" among the other products and services of their shop.

1914 Tiffany Electric, NAHC

TIFFANY ELECTRIC — Flint, Michigan — (1913-1914) — The Tiffany Electric Car Company of Flint came into being in October of 1913 and went out in March of 1914. Its car was the successor to the Flanders Electric and the brainchild of LeRoy Pelletier. Available in De Luxe ($2750) and Mignon ($2500) versions, it was advertised with the phrase, "Of all things She'd like, She'd like a Tiffany best." In December 1913 an open two-passenger Bijou roadster was announced to sell for $750, a startlingly low price for an electric. "It is my ambition to become the Henry Ford of the electric automobile industry," LeRoy Pelletier was quoted as saying. By the following spring, however, he had decided to return to the Flanders Electric name. How many cars were produced as the Tiffany Electric is unknown.

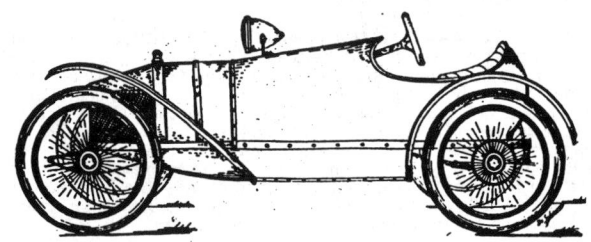

1914 Tiger, cyclecar, LC

TIGER — Detroit, Michigan — (1914-1915) — The Tiger was the last car in the checkered career of William Andrew de Schaum, whose earlier efforts had included the Schaum, the de Schaum and the Suburban. This time his venture was called the Automobile Cycle Car Company, and the preliminary announcement in December 1913 indicated that the product was to be a single-passenger roadster to carry the name Auto-Cyclecar. When the car arrived in June 1914, however, it afforded room for more than a driver and had been renamed the Tiger. Its engine was a four-cylinder water-cooled Farmer; its wheelbase was 90 inches, its tread 48. Model W was a two-passenger sociable, Model A a four-passenger de luxe, Model D a parcel light delivery. Prices were in the $300 range. A three-speed sliding gear transmission and shaft drive were featured. During the fall of 1914 de Schaum drove a Tiger cyclecar to victory in the 50-kilometer free-for-all race for cyclecars at Combination Park in Detroit. Because the scandal of his Suburban venture remained fresh in mind, de Schaum initially had problems selling stock in his new company, and indeed in February 1914 had to return all money collected following another de Schaum day in court. For a while, apparently, he had contemplated calling his car the Tigers after the local baseball team, but perhaps the management of the Detroit Tigers objected because the idea was quickly dropped. Although production figures are not known, there definitely was production. What killed the Tiger cyclecar was the death of William Andrew de Schaum in February 1915.

TILDEN — According to *The Motor Age* in August of 1901, N.F. Tilden of York, Nebraska built an automobile. Details are lacking.

TILESTON-PICKARD — The Tileston-Pickard Company was organized in Chicago, Illinois during the spring of 1906 with a capital stock of $30,000 for the manufacture of automobiles. Incorporators were Charles F. Tehune, Jeremiah B. O'Connell and William C. Asay. Manufacture is doubted.

1905 Tiley, roadster chassis, NAHC

TILEY — Essex, Connecticut — (1904-1913) — The Tiley-Pratt Company of Essex manufactured bicycle parts and, when customers asked, automobiles as well. About twenty-four people asked, and that represented the Tiley production during its nine years in the automobile business. The cars were built by Charles B. Tiley with the help of his two brothers. Most of them were fitted with Rutenber four-cylinder engines, though the Tileys would oblige with a six if requested. Sliding gear transmissions and shaft drive were generally featured. A fire at the plant in 1907 slowed down the company's pace, but the factory was rebuilt in 1908 and continued in business until about 1914.

TILIKUM — Seattle, Washington — (1914) — The Tilikum Cyclecar Company grew out of a garage in Seattle which traded under the name of Yukon Auto Shop. N.J. Veline, Ivan D.H. Adams and C.G. Benson were the men in charge. The Tilikum cyclecar was designed by Henry Hueber, who claimed extensive automotive experience in Germany and France. It was a side-by-side two-passenger roadster on an 84-inch wheelbase, with 42-inch tread. The engine was an air-cooled vee twin of 10/14 hp. Most unusual about the car was its transmission, a variable pulley set-up providing twelve speeds and a belt tightener. This latter, which moved the entire rear axle forward or backward about three inches, was operated by a lever at the driver's side and supposedly could be engaged while the car was in motion. Patents were said to be pending. The word Tilikum translated to friend in the Chinook language, but the reception accorded the car in Seattle was anything but friendly. One Tilikum is known to have been built, but whether the Tilikum Cyclecar Company ever moved out of its temporary quarters at 922 Howell Street and into its brand-new and hoped-for factory is not known.

TILLOTSON — Toledo, Ohio — (1912) — Harry Tillotson jumped on the sleeve-valve-engine bandwagon following the successful introduction of the Knight in this country, and jumped off after building just one car in 1912. Very little is known about it, except for the fact of its having been a prototype for possible production, this remembered by B.C. Phillips, who later was Tillotson's chief engineer, and confirmed by a report appearing in a 1912 trade publication. That his car did not see production did not alter Harry Tillotson's future good fortune. He had begun in the automobile business in 1905 as sales manager for the Kirk Manufacturing Company, producers of the Yale car built in Toledo, and now he continued his career as secretary of the carburetor-making Stromberg company in Chicago. By 1915 his experience with Stromberg parlayed him into establishment of his own Tillotson Carburetor Company back home in Toledo, which, thanks to John North Willys and the Willys-Overland Company, enjoyed a rapid growth.

TIME — Oostburg, Wisconsin — (1916) — Early in 1916, L.P. Timmer announced to the automotive trade press his plans to manufacture a six-cylinder five-passenger touring car to sell for $795. The Time Manufacturing Company was being organized in Oostburg, with a capital stock of $150,000, for that purpose. Joining Timmer, who was from Schleisengerville and who said he had "large business interests" in Milwaukee, was F.A. Tuschen, who was said to have been "connected with the automobile industry in Wisconsin," and A.A. Grau, who was a director of the Mutual Fire Insurance Company of Milwaukee. A fellow from Sheboygan named Mark Anthony Giblin was to handle the sale of stock. "The Time company expects to show its first car about April 1 and then begin a production of twelve cars a month," reported *Automobile Topics* in late March 1916. Possibly that first car was completed, but production never began. Oostburg, Wisconsin has a complete history of its businesses since the village's founding during the 1880's, and the Time Manufacturing Company is not among them.

TIMES — The Times Auto Supply Company was organized in New York City during the spring of 1909 with a capital stock of $20,000 for the manufacture of automobiles, engines and motor boats. Involved in this venture were C.O. Jones, B.H. Ellis and H.T. Johnson. Manufacture of a car is doubted.

The Times Square Automobile Company of New York City was organized early in 1905 with a capital stock of $10,000 for the manufacture of automobiles. The firm functioned largely as an agency dealing in rebuilt and used cars for the decade following, but in 1915 entered the ranks of automobile producers with a car called the Mecca. Refer to Mecca.

1903 Tincher, runabout, NAHC

TINCHER — Chicago, Illinois — (1903-1906) / South Bend, Indiana — (1907-1909) — At the Chicago Automobile Show in February 1903, Thomas L. Tincher showed his new car for the first time. What attracted attention there was its braking system. A small air pump was used to compress the air which not only stopped the car, but could be used to pump up the tires and toot the Tincher's whistle. Thomas Tincher became known thereafter as the builder of some of the biggest and most expensive cars in America. These were fours usually (a six was offered in 1908) with double side chain drive and four-speed selective transmissions. Wheelbases stretched up to 127 inches, and horsepower up to 90. A race car at $12,000 was one of two models offered in 1904; Tincher's prices generally started at $5000, and went on from there. While in Chicago, Tincher, whose previous work had been as vice-president of a local printing company, did not incorporate. The Tinchers were built for him by Chicago Coach & Carriage Company. Upon his move to South Bend in January 1907, however, Tincher organized as the Tincher Motor Car Company. Its capital stock was $200,000, and the majority stockholders were the wagon-building Studebaker brothers. No more than a half-dozen Tinchers were ever made in a single year, and the car was discontinued simply because the company could not make a profit on such a small production. During the summer of 1909, Thomas Tincher filed personal bankruptcy. The following January he joined the Economy Motor Buggy Company and moved to Joliet, Illinois where he superintended the manufacture of an automobile as unakin the Tincher as might possibly be imagined.

1903 TINCHER
Four — 18 hp, 90" wb

	FP	5	4	3	2	1
Touring-5P	—	2300	3300	4600	7500	16,000

1904 Tincher, touring, NAHC

1904 TINCHER
Four — 45 hp, 90" wb

Touring-5P	5000	4400	5600	9200	17,300	31,000

Four — 90 hp, 90" wb

Race Car	12,000	11,300	21,300	32,500	65,000	85,000

1905 TINCHER
Four — 60 hp, 125" wb

Touring-7P	5000	9400	18,800	26,500	53,800	75,000

1906-1907 TINCHER
Four — 50 hp, 120" wb

Touring-7P	6000	8200	14,500	21,500	45,800	65,000

1908 Tincher, roadster, WLB

1908 TINCHER
Four — 50 hp, 127" wb

	FP	5	4	3	2	1
Touring-7P	6500	8200	14,500	21,500	45,800	65,000
Four — 50 hp, 110" wb						
Roadster-3P	5500	8000	14,000	21,000	45,000	64,000
Six — 90 hp, 127" wb						
Roadster-3P	7500	9000	18,000	25,000	50,000	72,000
1909 TINCHER						
Four — 50/60 hp, 127" wb						
Touring-7P	6500	9400	18,800	26,500	53,800	75,000

TINKER — George M. Tinker was one-half of the Piper and Tinker partnership which produced the Waltham steam car in Waltham, Massachusetts from 1898-1902. Refer to Waltham Steam.

TINKHAM — New Haven, Connecticut — (1898-1899) — The Tinkham was a tricycle marketed by Julian R. Tinkham of the Tinkham Cycle Company at 310 West 59th Street in New York City and produced by J.F. Denison alongside the cars he manufactured under his own name in New Haven, Connecticut. Its engine was a two-cylinder two-stroke which was fitted into a 54-inch wheelbase chassis that featured chain drive. The prototype was completed in 1898 and was introduced by Tinkham at the cycle show in Madison Square Garden in January 1899. Production does not appear to have survived that year. Earlier, in 1895 and in association with Ernest F. Walton, Tinkham had formed a subsidiary Walton-Tinkham Manufacturing Company for the manufacture of electric and gasoline delivery tricycles.

1914 Tischer, tri-cycle, runabout, OCW

TISCHER — Peoria, Illinois — (1914) — Linton Tischer called his vehicle a tri-cycle car — part trike, part cyclecar. A three-wheeler with friction transmission in front of the dash and a long belt drive, the Tischer was powered by an air-cooled vee-twin mounted just aft of the front axle. The wheelbase was 86 inches, the tread 48 inches, and the body styling most peculiar. During the summer of 1914, Tischer said he would sell the car for $425; that fall, he lowered the price to $350. The few cars Linton Tischer sold were marketed from his bicycle shop at the back of 912 North Jefferson Street. The front of the street was occupied by a drugstore owned by William C. Tischer, who was most likely young Linton's father.

TITAN — The Titan Engine Company of America was organized in New York City during the summer of 1909 with a capital stock of $3000 to manufacture engines, automobiles and boats. Incorporators were N. Doyle, G.W. Garland and J.J. Hogan. Manufacture of a car is doubted.

TITAN — Detroit, Michigan — (1911-1913) — The Titan was produced by the United States Motor Company, the General-Motors-type conglomerate established by Benjamin Briscoe. A pretty little taxicab, it was built on the single-cylinder Brush chassis in the Brush factory in Detroit and was destined for service principally in New York City, which was the U.S. Motor headquarters. A short turning radius (the wheelbase was lengthened just eight inches from the Brush Runabout's eighty), a low price (only $850), and operating economy were the Titan's most widely touted features. "The makers claim that it can be run three miles at the usual cost of one mile," *Automobile Topics* reported, "with the result that the operator can accept a much lower rate than is charged at the present time, and still

make more money than his handicapped competitor." The Titan was an altogether admirable taxicab idea, but unfortunately the United States Motor Company was not. When Briscoe's conglomerate crashed, the Titan went down with it.

TITUS — The Fred J. Titus Company of Newark, New Jersey was organized during the spring of 1909 with a capital stock of $100,000 to manufacture and deal in automobiles. Joining Fred Titus in this venture was John N. Hance. Manufacture is doubted.

1901 Tivy, steam runabout, MVMA

TIVY STEAM — Williamsport, Pennsylvania — (1901-1903) — "The great cloud of steam that pours out of many machines is in this one diminished to a minimum and with the usual rattle of loosened joints and the loud thumping of the engine altogether eliminated, it is a pleasure to ride in a Tivy." That was the enthusiastic reaction of a reporter for the Williamsport *Gazette and Bulletin* following a test drive in a Tivy in 1902. The car was designed by Harry Rantz and was built by the Tivy Cycle Manufacturing Company, of which Lafayette Maxwell was head. Its price was $800. Although the first example was completed in 1901, production did not begin until the following year. In May of 1903, Lafayette Maxwell announced that the Tivy bicycle was being phased out of production and that henceforth all efforts would be directed to automobile manufacture. The firm's name was changed to L. Maxwell Company. It does not appear that the Tivy steam car — which was a typical tiller-steered runabout of the period — was built beyond 1903, however.

TJAARDA — During the mid-Thirties, John Tjaarda was in the employ of the Briggs Manufacturing Company of Detroit. Several of the advanced cars he designed were built as prototypes by the Briggs Company. Refer to Briggs.

T.J.K. SPECIAL — Ft. Wayne, Indiana — (1909) — In 1909 T.J. Kehoe, who worked for the Dayton Automobile Supply Company in Dayton, Ohio, built a car during his off hours. Details are lacking, but it is known that Kehoe christened it the T.J.K. Special, and that he returned to his native Ft. Wayne, Indiana later that year with hopes of organizing a company for its manufacture. Ft. Wayne didn't greet this returning son with open arms, and wallets, obviously, because the T.J.K. Special ended with the single car built.

T.M. — Oshkosh, Wisconsin — (1906)/T.M.F. — (1909) — The initials represent J.D. Termaat, a portrait photographer; Louis J. Monahan, a machinist; and H. Homer Fahrney, the wealthy son of a Chicago patent medicine man. All were residents of Oshkosh. Monahan and Termaat were the first to get together, at the turn of the century, to establish a small company on River Street for the manufacture of gasoline engines. Around 1906 this duo built an automobile designed by Alton Ripley, a mechanic in the company's shop. It was a typical air-cooled motor buggy, though its mounting of a steering wheel on the left side was avant-garde for a highwheeler in 1906. Serious manufacture of the T.M. was not embarked upon, but examples might have been built for local customers during the next two years. In 1909, Fahrney, who had financed other manufacturing efforts in Oshkosh, was persuaded to invest in the T.M. effort which resulted in the T.M.F. It was a highwheeler as well. A new organization — the Badger Manufacturing Company — was created to produce it, but the venture does not seem to have survived more than a year. A cyclecar called the Ziebell was built in the company shops in 1914, however. In 1916 Monahon and Termaat formed the Universal Motor Company for the manufacture of engines and other auto-related products. It survived three years.

TODD — H.C. Todd of the Chicago Fireproof Covering Company of Chicago, Illinois was among the hopefuls who entered the Chicago Times-Herald Contest with an automobile of his own design. He did not make it to the starting line, however, and whether he completed and successfully tested his car has not been documented.

The Todd Automobile Supply Company was organized in St. Louis, Missouri late in 1910 with a capital stock of $30,000 to manufacture and deal in cars and accessories. Incorporators were J.V. Todd, Charles Peters and E.F. Gee. Manufacture of a car is doubted.

TODD — Toledo, Ohio — (1903) — The Todd Manufacturing Company of Toledo was a gasoline-engine producer which announced its intention to build complete cars during the early summer of 1903. The firm secured quarters from the Standard Wire and Iron Works in town for that purpose, though any production which followed was minimal.

TODD ELECTRIC — Hartford, Connecticut — (1902) — In April of 1902 the Todd Electric Manufacturing Company was organized with a capital stock of $30,000 in Hartford, its incorporators including prominent businessmen of that city. ''Mr. Todd has his machine in first-class shape,'' *The Motor Review* commented, ''and it is said to be a wonder.'' Whether the magazine editor's tongue was lodged firmly in cheek is not known. But there is no evidence that the Todd Electric proceeded into sustained manufacture.

TOLEDO — The Toledo Steam and Air Motor Company of Toledo, Ohio was indicated as an automobile manufacturer in the Hiscox book *Horseless Vehicles, Automobiles, Motor Cycles* published in 1900. Documentation is lacking. Turn-of-the-century Toledo city directories do not reveal the existence of such a company in town.

The Toledo Motor Car Company was organized in Toledo, Ohio early in 1904 with a capital stock of $20,000 for the manufacture of automobiles. Incorporators were Harry E. King, Harry W. Lloyd, Charles F. Chapman, Jr. and Frank W. Caughlin. Manufacture is douted.

1901 Toledo, steam runabout, HAC

TOLEDO — Toledo, Ohio — (1901-1903) — In September of 1900 the American Bicycle Company announced that it would henceforth devote its entire plant in Toledo, Ohio to the manufacture of steam automobiles. The steam car to be manufactured was introduced that November on the American Bicycle Company stand at the New York Automobile show. The name it bore then was Billings, after its designer Frederick Billings who immediately surrendered all rights to its manufacture to American Bicycle. The American Bicycle operation in Toledo was reorganized as the International Motor Car Company, and its product was introduced early in 1901 as the International steam car in two models, the Toledo and the Westchester. By year's end, the marque name was changed to Toledo. In addition to an expanded line of steamers for 1902, International also introduced a three-cylinder 16 hp gasoline car under the Toledo name. Fifty gasoline Toledos were built that year. The line for 1903 dropped one of the steamers and added two more gasoline models. This was the last year for both the steam cars and the Toledo marque name. On May 27th, 1903 the Pope Motor Car Company succeeded the International Motor Car Company in Toledo, and all subsequent cars were called Pope-Toledos. The Waverley electric previously produced by International became the Pope-Waverley.

1901 TOLEDO

	FP	5	4	3	2	1
Int'l Toledo Steam Rbt.	1200	2700	3600	5300	8800	19,000
Int'l Westchester Steam Rbt.	1200	2700	3600	5300	8800	19,000

1902 TOLEDO
Toledo Steam

	FP	5	4	3	2	1
Model A Rbt.	900	2300	3300	4600	7500	16,000
Model B Carriage	1000	2400	3400	4800	8000	17,000
Model C Surrey	1600	2500	3500	5000	8500	18,000
Junior Rbt.	800	2200	3200	4400	7000	15,000
Tour. Car	1250	2500	3500	5000	8500	18,000

Toledo Gasoline — 3-cyl., 16 hp, 84''wb

	FP	5	4	3	2	1
Touring-5P	1800	2500	3500	5000	8500	18,000

1902 Toledo, model A, steam runabout, HAC

1903 Toledo, gasoline, touring, NAHC

1903 TOLEDO
Toledo Steam

	FP	5	4	3	2	1
Stnd. Rbt.	900	2500	3500	5000	8500	18,000
Model A Steam Car	1000	2700	3600	5300	8800	19,000
Dos-a-Dos Steam Car	1000	2700	3600	5300	8800	19,000
Junior Steam Rbt.	600	2400	3400	4800	8000	17,000
Toledo Gasoline						
Tr. (2-cyl., 12 hp, 76'' wb)	2000	2700	3600	5300	8800	19,000
Tr. (3-cyl., 18 hp, 84'' wb)	3000	2900	3700	5600	9100	20,000
Tr. (3-cyl., 24 hp, 94'' wb)	4000	3000	4000	6000	9500	21,000

1909 Toledo, type XXIII 50 h.p., limousine, WLB

TOLEDO — Toledo, Ohio — (1909) — By 1909 the automotive empire founded by Albert Pope was in disarray, though production of the star of that empire, the Pope-Toledo, was ongoing under receivership. In January that year Richard D. Apperson of Lynchburg, Virginia announced his plans to acquire the Pope-Toledo factory and to continue the car in production as the Apperson-Toledo. Apperson was the vice-president of the American National Bank in Lynchburg and was described as ''a prominent street railway man not heretofore connected with the automobile business.'' He was no relation either to the automobile-building Apperson brothers of Kokomo, Indiana — and among his first decisions regarding his new venture was to change the name of his product from Apperson-Toledo to simply Toledo to avoid confusion with the Indiana car. Apperson proceeded sufficiently further to run up an ''Advance Catalogue'' for 1909 and to display one of the Pope-cum-Toledos at the Chicago Automobile Show that January. A few more cars with Toledo emblems may have left the factory thereafter but by April Apperson's negotiations with the Pope-Toledo receivers fell apart and the factory was acquired instead by John North Willys for his Overland company that month.

1425

TOLEDO — Toledo, Ohio — (1913-1914) — The Toledo Auto-Cycle Car Company was established at 629 Erie Street in Toledo in late 1913 for the manufacture of a typical friction-transmission, belt-drive, tandem two-seater cyclecar designed by C.W. Carlisle, who also doubled as the firm's secretary-treasurer. E.P. Severcool was president, W.L. Vail vice-president. In December Carlisle announced that the new Toledo would be a "surprise to the public" and that deliveries would begin in February. There was no surprise, and there were no deliveries. Though the Toledo people had made arrangements for the marketing of their car through the National United Service Company of Detroit, evidence is lacking that this venture proceeded beyond the prototype stage.

TOLEDO ELECTRIC — The Toledo Auto and Garage Company was organized in Toledo, Ohio early in 1910 to take over the business of the Twenty-First Street Garage Company. H.L. Arnold and A.A. Campbell were the partners behind this venture. They secured agencies for the Stearns, Franklin and Jackson cars and announced in late January their plans to produce an electric car of their own. This does not appear to have followed.

The Toledo Electric Vehicle Company of 1909 was an outgrowth of the Allen & Clark Company of Toledo which had been organized to continue the electric car experimentation of Albert F. Clark. The car which was produced of this venture was called the Clark Electric. Refer to Clark Electric.

TOMLINSON — Batavia, New York — (1900) — At the turn of the century in Batavia, Daniel W. Tomlinson built two steam cars in collaboration with Robert L. Cooley. Manufacture was not embarked upon, however, and Tomlinson soon returned to his principal activity as a banker in Batavia, and as manager of the Baker Gun Company. Refer to Cooley.

TOM THUMB — The Detroit Boat Company manufactured launches and canoes at its works at 1252-1270 Jefferson Avenue in Detroit, Michigan. Hugo Scherer and Frederick E. Wadsworth headed this firm. In 1910, purportedly, a car called the Tom Thumb was built at the Detroit Boat Company. Documentation is lacking.

TONAWANDA — The Tonawanda Motor Vehicle Company has appeared on various car rosters as an automobile manufacturer in Tonawanda, New York at the turn of the century. This is in error, the result of careless editing in some trade periodicals of the period. Instead of Tonawanda, New York the car in question was built in Towanda, Pennsylvania by the Towanda Motor Vehicle Company.

TONE — Indianapolis, Indiana — (1913) — Fred I. Tone was the man behind the Tone Car Corporation which was organized to build a moderately-priced (under $1000) car using a single 110-inch chassis for roadster, touring, coupe and light delivery bodies. Joining him were Mark Miller and W.P. Kirk of Indianapolis. The prototype stage appears to be as far as this venture proceeded. In January 1913 Fred Tone submitted a bid of $100,000 for the Indianapolis plant of the defunct T.B. Laycock Manufacturing Company. He was anxious to move in somewhere "so that active operations may be started." It would not be Laycock, however, since there followed a court order to that company's receiver to reject the Tone bid as too low. Apparently, the Tone shoestring ran out before a factory for manufacture was ever found. Tone's greatest automotive success, undoubtedly, had occurred earlier, as the designer of the American Underslung.

TOOMEY — The S. Toomey Company was organized in Canal Dover, Ohio during the fall of 1912 with a capital stock of $60,000 for the manufacture and sale of automobiles. Incorporators were R.I. Toomey, S.J. Brister, Theodore Williams, M.C. Toomey and Oliver Toomey. Manufacture is doubted.

TOOT & VAN DERVOORT — The Toot & Van Dervoort Corporation was organized in Dover, Delaware during the summer of 1917 with a $4 million capital stock, according to trade publications of the period. This was a typographical error for Root & Vandervoort. Refer to R&V Knight.

TOPP — Manlius, New York — (1904) — "W.H. Topp of Manlius...is engaged in constructing an automobile which will be something of a novelty in the way of a horseless carriage," reported *The Motor Age* in March 1904. "It will consist of two tandems with a seat between and will be propelled by an air-cooled motor." Further details are lacking.

1905 Toquet, touring, NAHC

1426

TOQUET — Saugatuck, Connecticut — (1905) — B.L. Toquet of New York City designed a most interesting engine featuring a detachable head with copper gaskets and fitted with a flyball governor connected so clutch and brake operated the accelerator. The four-cylinder T-head developed 45 hp. Only a five-seater touring was planned, and it was a heavy car, at 3200 pounds. The Toquet Motor Car & Construction Company was organized for manufacture, with factory in Saugatuck, Connecticut. Very few cars were made, however.

1902 Torbensen, runabout, NAHC

TORBENSEN — Bloomfield, New Jersey — (1902-1906) — Viggo V. Torbensen emigrated to the United States from Denmark shortly before the Civil War. His early career was in the electric and steam fields, but with the advent of the gasoline engine, he immediately switched allegiance. After serving as superintending engineer for the American De Dion and consulting engineer for the Searchmont, he set himself up in business in Newark, New Jersey in 1901 as V.V. Torbensen Company, maker of automotive specialties. Later that year, after deciding upon the specialty he wished to focus upon, he changed his firm's name to Torbensen Gear, Inc. and relocated in Bloomfield. He built his first car in 1902, a small runabout which he took to the sporting events sponsored that spring by the Long Island Automobile Club. The Torbensen performed well in all contests except hill climbing, and that was due to improper gearing. It was back to the drawing

1906 Torbensen, touring, NAHC

board. Torbensen built a few cars in the years following which he sold locally. In 1905 he reorganized as the Torbensen Motor Car Company, with a capital stock of $500,000. The firm's name was deceptive, however. Although Torbensen did build a touring car that year equipped with an air-cooled 28 hp six-cylinder engine of his own design, this was largely for demonstration purposes. He also built a three-cylinder 14 hp delivery wagon for the same reason. Running gear and engines were the principal product of the Torbensen Motor Car Company, though an occasional complete car was probably built to specific customer request. The indications are that Torbensen remained in the vehicle-building business at least into 1911, though by then only commercial vehicles were being built. Torbenson subsequently went on to become a major supplier of axles to the truck industry, adding passenger-car axles to its product line in 1923.

1903 Torrence, runabout, NAHC

TORRENCE — Montrose, Colorado — (1903) — The Torrence was described in the trade press as "a home-made automobile that will not only run, but run well." It weighed but 280 pounds, was powered by a 2-1/2 hp air-cooled engine, and William W. Torrence claimed the vehicle capable of about 20 mph. He also claimed the Torrence took first prize at a local fair near Montrose in 1903, but did not indicate in what category it was exhibited. Conceivably, it was the only horseless carriage in attendance.

TOTEM — Seattle, Washington — (1921-1922) — In September of 1921, the Davis Car Company of Seattle announced that it had received adequate financing from sources in the East to begin manufacture of its new Totem car. The first announcement of this venture had arrived in 1917, but no doubt the First World War delayed things. The man behind the Totem was L.W. Davis. The president of the company bearing his name was J.M. Finley who had formerly headed the Finley Advertising Agency in Seattle; vice-president was Harry T. Hanover, who was also currently president of the Apex Motor Corporation which was building the Ace car in Ypsilanti, Michigan. The new Totem was a 38 hp four (Herschell-Spillman engine) mounted on a 117-inch wheelbase and selling in five-passenger touring guise for $1695. Light delivery cars, however, were slated to be the main focus of Totem production. The main feature of the Totem was its transmission, designed by Davis, and described as "a radical departure from standard drive designs." Its operation was described in *Automobile Topics* in 1921: "There is nothing behind the engine flywheel but two Davis universals on the driveshaft, and a light housing on the rear axle for beveled drive wheels. The drive consists of four beveled wheels or cones, these being flat-faced and not cut with teeth. The two larger ones are of cast iron and are keyed to the drive axles. On the end of the driveshaft are two smaller cones made of special composition. All four are set in place so that all point inward. Control levers are so arranged that one forms the forward and reverse shift, while the other determines the gear ratio." All this represented a variation on the theme of friction transmission, which had gone out of style years before. Most probably this was among the reasons the Totem car was not long in the marketplace, though at least ten were produced before the company went under. Published references to a production total of sixty cars seem quite inflated, however.

TOURAINE — Chicago, Illinois — (1907) — The Touraine was a two-cylinder water-cooled 22 hp five-passenger touring car fitted with a two-speed planetary transmission and shaft drive on a 100-inch wheelbase chassis and marketed in 1907 for $1500. The car represented one of the early manufacturing efforts of the Automobile Parts & Equipment Company of Chicago which produced cars into 1914, sometimes under the Auto Parts name, and often under a variety of other designations.

1913 Touraine, touring, WLB

TOURAINE — Philadelphia, Pennsylvania — (1912-1916) — The new Touraine of 1912 was the old Nance of 1911 with a fresh infusion of capital from an investor named Touraine, and the concomitant name change. The car remained a largish six in the medium-price range, and Harold B. Larzelere remained on as president. In 1914 the Touraine Motor Company also

built a cyclecar called the Vim, the same name which had been applied to the first truck produced the year previous. The company was sufficiently satisfied with its foray into the commercial vehicle field to decide to concentrate exclusively in that area after 1915. In November of that year Touraine announced that its name would be changed to Vim Motor Truck Company, and that trucks only would be produced in the future. The Touraine automobile for 1916 was simply a phasing out, the assembly of cars from parts previously on hand. Vim trucks continued in manufacture into 1923.

1912 TOURAINE
Six — 35/40 hp, 124'' wb

	FP	5	4	3	2	1
Touring-5P	2250	4000	5000	8000	15,000	28,000
Runabout-2P	2250	3700	4700	7300	13,700	26,000

1913 TOURAINE
Six — 45/50 hp, 134'' wb

Touring-7P	2950	4200	5200	8400	15,700	29,000
Phaeton-5P	2950	4000	5000	8000	15,000	28,000

Six — 40/50 hp, 124'' wb

Touring-5P	2250	3900	4800	7700	14,300	27,000
Roadster-3P	2250	3700	4700	7300	13,700	26,000
Victoria	2350	2300	3300	4600	7500	16,000
Limousine	3750	2700	3600	5300	8800	19,000

1914 TOURAINE
Six — 40/50 hp, 124'' wb

Raceabout-2P	3150	4000	5000	8000	15,000	28,000
Runabout-2P	3150	3900	4800	7700	14,300	27,000
Coupe-2P	4050	2500	3500	5000	8500	18,000

Six — 40/50 hp, 134'' wb

Limousine	4550	4000	5000	8000	15,000	28,000
Touring-7P	3250	4400	5600	9200	17,300	31,000
Victoria-7P	3400	3500	4500	7000	13,000	25,000
Touring-4/5P	3150	4200	5200	8400	15,700	29,000
Brougham	4250	3300	4400	6700	12,000	24,000
Town Landaulet	4350	3500	4500	7000	13,000	25,000

1915 TOURAINE
Six — 40/50 hp, 124'' wb

Runabout-2P	3150	3300	4400	6700	12,000	24,000

Six — 45/50 hp, 134'' wb

Touring-7P	3250	4500	5800	9500	18,000	32,000
Limousine-7P	4550	3700	4700	7300	13,700	26,000
Toy Tonneau-5P	3150	4400	5600	9200	17,300	31,000

1916 TOURAINE
Six — 45/50 hp, 134'' wb

Touring	3250	4500	5800	9500	18,000	32,000
Roadster	3150	4400	5600	9200	17,300	31,000

1903 Tourist, runabout, NAHC

TOURIST — Los Angeles, California — (1902-1910) — The Tourist was California's most popular car of the pre-World War I period. It was built by the Auto Vehicle Company which was organized in May of 1902 by William H. Burnham of Orange, Carroll S. Hartman of Pasadena, and Willis D. Longyear, who worked for the Security Savings Bank in Ocean Park. The company established its factory at 943 North Main Street in Los Angeles, and Ralph B. Hain left his machine shop nearby to superintend production. Hain designed the single-cylinder 6 hp Tourist prototype but it was a failure. Waldemar Hansen of Pasadena was called in and designed the two-cylinder car that was put into production. Twelve were built in 1902. Hain was not pleased and left the company by the end of the year. In 1903 Watt Moreland, who had built the Magnolia in Riverside the year previous, arrived. He remained with the company into 1906, when he left to produce the Durocar. By then Volney S. Beardsley, who had formerly built the Darling in Ohio, was sales manager of Auto Vehicle. Tourist production had steadily increased through the years: 17 cars in 1903, 75 cars in 1904, 150 cars in 1905. With Beardsley at the helm, sales zoomed to about 500 cars yearly. By 1905 the Auto Vehicle Company had moved into larger quarters at Tenth Street and South Main. Trucks had been produced from the beginning as well, and in 1908 the Auto Vehicle Company delivered a hose cart and chemical wagon to the fire department in Hollywood. The first press mention of any problems in the company came in November 1909 when the non-Selden-licensed Auto Vehicle Company complained of trouble in securing parts. Later that month the firm sold out to the newly-formed California Automobile Company, with Beardsley taking on its presidency. Both Tourist and California models were produced for the 1910 model year. That September, however, with securing parts remaining a problem, California elected to continue in business only as a dealership, taking on the Firestone Columbus, Warren-Detroit and Columbus Electric cars. Its factory, parts and equipment were sold to William James Burt, who announced that he would continue service for all Tourist and California cars on the road. Burt had formerly been superintendent of the Auto Vehicle factory, which bode well for owners in the area. As for the California Automobile Company, it returned to the manufacturing field for the 1914 model year, with a new electric car called the Beardsley.

1902 TOURIST
One-Cylinder — 7 hp, 72" wb

	FP	5	4	3	2	1
Touring 2/4P	1000	—	—	—	—	—

1903 TOURIST
Two-Cylinder — 8 hp, 72" wb

Touring-4P	1000	2400	3400	4800	8000	17,000
Touring-2P	1000	2300	3300	4600	7500	16,000

1904 Tourist, touring, NAHC

1904 TOURIST
Two-Cylinder — 12 hp, 72" wb

Touring-4P	1000	2000	3000	4200	6500	14,000
Touring-2P	1000	1800	2800	4000	6200	13,000

1905 TOURIST
Model K — 2-cyl., 20 hp, 90" wb

Touring-5P	1250	2200	3200	4400	7000	15,000

1906 Tourist, touring, NAHC

1906 TOURIST
Model K — 2-cyl., 20 hp, 88" wb

Touring-5P	1250	2200	3200	4400	7000	15,000

Model M — 4-cyl., 35 hp, 100" wb

Touring-5P	2500	3900	4800	7700	14,300	27,000

1907 Tourist, touring, HAC

1907-1908 TOURIST
Model K-7 — 2-cyl., 20 hp, 90" wb

Touring-5P	1250	2200	3200	4400	7000	15,000

Model N-7 — 4-cyl., 35/40 hp, 108" wb

Runabout-2P	2500	3700	4700	7300	13,700	26,000
Touring-7P	2600	3900	4800	7700	14,300	27,000

Model G-7 — 4-cyl., 35/40 hp, 108" wb

Limousine-7P	4500	3700	4700	7300	13,700	26,000

1908 Tourist, touring, OCW

1909 Tourist, touring, NAHC

1909-1910 TOURIST
Type B — 2-cyl., 22/24 hp, 102" wb

	FP	5	4	3	2	1
Touring-5P	1300	3100	4200	6300	10,500	22,000

Type O — 2-cyl., 22/24 hp, 102" wb

Roadster-4P	1300	3000	4000	6000	9500	21,000

Type G — 4-cyl., 25/30 hp, 106" wb

Touring-3/4/5P	1650	3500	4500	7000	13,000	25,000

Type H — 4-cyl., 35/40 hp, 118" wb

Roadster-4P	2250	3500	4500	7000	13,000	25,000
Touring-5P	2250	3700	4700	7300	13,700	26,000

Type L — 4-cyl., 35/40 hp, 118" wb

Limousine	3800	2700	3600	5300	8800	19,000

Type H — 4-cyl., 45/50 hp, 118" wb

Roadster-4P	2500	3900	4800	7700	14,300	27,000
Touring-5P	2500	4000	5000	8000	15,000	28,000

1904 Towanda Electric, runabout, MVMA

TOWANDA ELECTRIC — Towanda, Pennsylvania — (1902-1904) — By the summer of 1902, Charles Lindstrom was well aware that the Niagara Electric he was building in Buffalo, New York was going nowhere, and consequently he sought greener pastures. He thought he found them in

Towanda, Pennsylvania. There the Towanda Motor Vehicle Company was organized with a capital stock of $25,000 for production of his electric car. Company president was George W. Kipp of Punxsutawney, the town famous for its groundhog's prediction each year. Company superintendent was Edward Winckes, whom Lindstrom brought with him from Buffalo. Production of the Towanda Electric began in July of 1902 with a workforce of twenty men. At least seven cars were built before the Towanda people decided to give up that November. Among the reasons for the car's discontinuation undoubtedly was the infeasibility of any electric being marketed in this Pennsylvania mountain region. The Towanda factory on Plank Road remained idle for a year. Then, in 1904, the Towanda Motor Vehicle company was revived for manufacture of running gear, including a complete runabout outfit, with wheels and seats, but no engine.

TOWER — Syracuse, New York — (1899) — In 1899, in Syracuse, C.E. Tower built a gasoline trap fitted with a two-cylinder 4 hp engine with final drive by bevel gear and chain. He is not known to have built another car.

TOWER GROVE — The Tower Grove Motor Car Company was organized in St. Louis, Missouri early in 1910 with a capital stock of $5600 to manufacture and deal in automobiles. Incorporators were Thomas and H.B. Wiley and F.L. Schleicher. Manufacture is doubted.

TOWN — Town and Country was the name to be given to the car built by Frederick C. Billings which a number of businessmen in Hartford, Connecticut had notions of manufacturing. Attempts to establish the Town and Country Automobile Company in Hartford in 1905 came to naught, however, which apparently didn't bother Frederick Billings much. Refer to Billings.

The Town Taxi Company was organized in New York City late in 1913 with a capital stock of $5000 for the manufacture of taxicabs. Incorporators were Joseph F. Dempsey, John N. Scelsa and Eugene A. Donahue. Manufacture is doubted.

TOWNSEND — The Townsend Automobile & Piano Works of New York City has been indicated as the manufacturer of an automobile in 1903 on various car rosters. Documentation is lacking. A company of that name is not listed in Trow's Business Directory for New York from the years 1900-1905.

TOWNSLEY-COMSTOCK — The Townsley-Comstock Company was organized in Chicago, Illinois late in 1910 with a capital stock of $25,000 for the manufacture of automobiles and other motor vehicles. The partners in this venture were L.E. Townsley, S.E. Comstock and Edward F. Comstock. Manufacture is doubted, but the firm is known to have taken on the agency for the American Motor Car Company of Indianapolis.

TRABOLD — Johnstown, Pennsylvania — (1898, 1905) — Two cars were built by Adam G. Trabold of Johnstown, the first a simple gasoline motor buggy in 1898, the second a more sophisticated automobile in 1905. Both were experimental vehicles. Meanwhile Trabold was operating an automobile dealership. In 1911; when he did enter manufacturing ranks, it was with a four-cylinder Buda-engined truck. Trabold trucks were manufactured by Trabold Motors Compay until 1932, with the firm continuing in the truck-body-building field until 1960.

TRACTION — The Traction Motors Corporation was organized in Kalamazoo, Michigan during the spring of 1918 with a capital stock of $200,000 for the manufacture of tractors and automobiles. Incorporators were George Erwin, Edmund Hans and William Munroe. Manufacture of a car is doubted.

1901 Tractobile, runabout, NAHC

TRACTOBILE — Carlisle, Pennsylvania — (1900-1902) — The Tractobile was a device to convert a horsedrawn carriage into one requiring no horses. The attachment, which consisted of forked bicycle wheels fitted

with small steam engines, and a tie rod for single-lever control, saw to the conversion. The Tractobile attachment was priced at $450, and its manufacturer — the Pennsylvania Steam Vehicle Company of Carlisle — also provided complete vehicles equipped with the Tractobile outfit, viz., a stanhope for two at $500, a surrey for four at $650, and a depot wagon for six at $850. How many Tractobiles were sold is not known, but a safe guess would be not many, because the Pennsylvania Steam Vehicle Company had been organized by that master confidence man of the period, Edward Joel Pennington. At least a few Tractobiles were built, however, because years later a barber in Carlisle named Robert Day recalled their being tested on a "man-made incline" near the factory.

TRAFFIC — The Traffic Cycle Company of 944 Eighth Avenue in New York City was indicated as an automobile manufacturer in the Hiscox book *Horseless Vehicles, Automobiles, Motor Cycles* published in 1900. Documentation is lacking. A company of that name is not listed in turn-of-the-century New York City directories.

TRANSIT STEAMER — The Transit was a model of the Steamobile produced in Keene, New Hampshire from 1901-1902. Refer to Steamobile.

1922 Trask-Detroit, 5-pass. touring, WLB

TRASK STEAM — Detroit, Michigan — (1922-1923) — O.C. Trask was the Michigan distributor for the Stanley steam car, and in 1921 became a steam car builder himself. On the first of December that year, he announced his new Detroit Steam Motor Corporation, which would soon be on the market with a $1000 two-cylinder steam car built in four body styles on a 110-inch wheelbase chassis. A prototype phaeton was produced and exhibited as the Trask or Trask-Detroit, and perhaps a few

1923 Trask, Detroit Steam Car, touring, WLB

more followed. All of these cars were built at the plant of the Schlieder Manufacturing Company, which made valves in Detroit. By mid-1922 Trask had negotiated for manufacture in Canada with the establishment of Windsor Steam Motors, and by early 1923 he had changed the name of the U.S. product to Detroit Steam Car. Now it was on a 115-inch wheelbase, and its price had been raised to $1585. The entire venture fizzled soon after that.

TRAVELER — The Traveler was a kit car produced by the Neustadt Automobile & Supply Company of St. Louis, Missouri. Refer to Neustadt.

1907 Traveler, model A, touring, NAHC

1429

TRAVELER — Bellefontaine, Ohio — (1907-1908) — Early in 1907 the Bellefontaine Automobile Company superseded the Zent Automobile Manufacturing Company — and the former Zent four was revised into a new car called the Traveler. Its four-cylinder engine was rated at 24/32 hp, and its wheelbase was 104 inches. Shaft drive and a three-speed sliding gear transmission were fitted. Model A was air-cooled; Model B water-cooled. The price tag was $2200. In 1908 the car became slightly larger and more expensive — and was renamed the Bellefontaine.

1907-1908 TRAVELER
Model A — 4-cyl., 24/32 hp, 104" wb

	FP	5	4	3	2	1
Touring-5P	2200	3700	4700	7300	13,700	26,000

Model B — 4-cyl., 24/32 hp, 104" wb

	FP	5	4	3	2	1
Touring-5P	2200	3700	4700	7300	13,700	26,000

1910 Traveler, model D, runabout, NAHC

TRAVELER — Evansville, Indiana — (1910-1911) — In 1910 Willis Copeland organized the Traveler Automobile Company in Evansville for the production of a car to be known as the Traveler. Copeland was already manufacturing the Simplicity, and the Traveler was precisely the same car. The reason for the name change was to undo the damage done to the Simplicity reputation following Copeland's realization that he had previously been building a fair-weather car, literally, because rain-soaked friction gears meant the Simplicity wouldn't run when the weather turned foul. Enclosing the gears solved that. And changing the car's name from Simplicity to Traveler, Copeland figured, was a good public relations move. Curiously, he continued to build a car called the Simplicity too. His business failed in 1911. Subsequently Copeland became Evansville's first Chevrolet dealer.

1910 TRAVELER
Model D — 4-cyl., 30 hp, 105" wb

Runabout-4P	1350	3000	4000	6000	9500	21,000

Model E — 4-cyl., 30 hp, 105" wb

Touring-5P	1350	3100	4200	6300	10,500	22,000

1911 TRAVELER
Model D — 4-cyl., 30 hp, 105" wb

Runabout-4P	1300	3000	4000	6000	9500	21,000

Model E — 4-cyl., 30 hp, 105" wb

Touring-5P	1300	3100	4200	6300	10,500	22,000

1913 Traveler, model 36, touring, WLB

TRAVELER — Detroit, Michigan — (1913-1914) — This Traveler was the idea of J.P. La Vigne and was produced in Detroit alongside a cyclecar he had designed and named for himself. The cyclecar was a venture separate from the Traveler Motor Car Company, however, which was backed by W.K. McIntyre and F.W. Barstow. The Traveler was a four (Beaver engine) of 36 and 48 hp, and 120- and 130-inch wheelbase. Both touring and roadster body styles were offered, with $1295 the price tag for the smaller model, $2000 for the larger. In March of 1913 the Traveler Motor Car Company moved into the two-story factory it had purchased for $15,000 at 1146 Grand River Avenue, and late the following year the company moved out when the business failed.

1913-1914 TRAVELER
Model 36 — 4-cyl., 36 hp, 120" wb

Touring-5P	1295	2900	3700	5600	9100	20,000
Roadster-2P	1295	2700	3600	5300	8800	19,000

Model 48 — 4-cyl., 48 hp, 130" wb

Touring-5P	2000	3900	4800	7700	14,300	27,000
Roadster-2P	2000	3700	4700	7300	13,700	26,000

1430

TRAVERSE CITY — Although the Napoleon Motor Car Company of Napoleon, Ohio changed its name to the Traverse City Motor Car Company upon moving to that Michigan town in mid-1917, the name of the car produced remained Napoleon. Refer to Napoleon.

1924 Traveler, taxicab, MVMA

TRAVELER — New York, New York — (1924-1925) — The taxi that was a Traveler was built by the Taxicab Manufacturing Company of New York City. Mounted on a 108-1/2-inch wheelbase, it was powered by a four-cylinder Buda engine built in unit with a Brown-Lipe transmission. Its five-passenger body, provided by the Blue Ribbon Company, featured coach lamps mounted on the forward posts of the passenger compartment and a spotlight on the left side of the windshield. Introduced in March of 1924, the Traveler was built through 1925.

1907 Trebert, touring, NAHC

TREBERT — Rochester, New York — (1907-1908) — In 1902 Henry L. Trebert left his job as superintendent of the Stearns Steam Carriage Company in Syracuse to go into business for himself in Rochester as a gasoline engine builder. Although Stearns had begun development of a gasoline motor in 1898, this work had not proceeded beyond the experimental stage, and Trebert had in the meantime become convinced of the superiority of the internal combusion engine over steam power. Later in 1902 his new Trebert Gas Engine Company placed a two-cylinder 10 hp engine on the market; the year following the line was expanded to include units of 2 to 40 hp. Not until 1907 was an automobile built carrying the Trebert name — and, ironically, by that time Trebert had left the company he had founded to join forces with another Rochester engine builder named F.A. Brownell. The few Trebert automobiles that were produced by his old company seem all to have been medium-priced 30 hp machines. This was a low-key operation, the ads stressing the manufacturer-to-consumer aspect of the business. Interestingly, there was also a car built for a short while bearing the Brownell name. But both partners recognized that their most profitable course was engine building. The Brownell-Trebert Company was the linear descendent of the Rochester Motors Company, producer of the famous Rochester-Duesenberg engine of the post-World War I era.

1907-1908 TREBERT
Model A — 4-cyl., 30 hp, 103" wb

	FP	5	4	3	2	1
Touring-5P	1850	3000	4000	6000	9500	21,000

TRENTON — The Trenton Automobile Company at Eighth Avenue and 49th Street in New York City was indicated as an automobile manufacturer in the Hiscox book *Horseless Vehicles, Automobiles, Motor Cycles* published in 1900. Documentation is lacking. Turn-of-the-century New York City directories reveal no such company in town.

The Trenton Iron Works in Trenton, New Jersey produced several cars designed by Peter Cooper Hewitt in 1903-1904. Refer to Cooper Hewitt.

TREY — The Trey Air Cooled Motors Corporation was organized in New York City during the early Twenties with offices taken at 226 West 47th Street. Serge Trey was the man behind this venture which produced a brochure extolling the new air-cooled Trey with its gearless hydraulic drive as "A Car Years Ahead of Others." That even a prototype of the Trey was

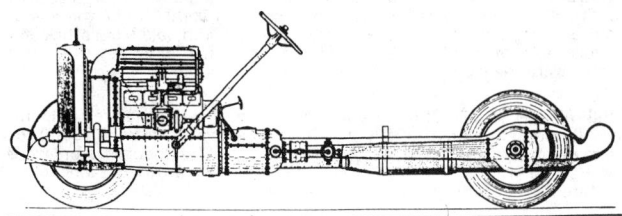

c.1923 Trey Air-Cooled Chassis, HAC

built has not been documented. In 1925 the Trey Air-Cooled Motors Corporation was disposed of at a bankruptcy sale, with Serge Trey arranging for his stockholders to exchange their stock for that of the Regent Engineering Company on West 38th Street.

TRIBUNE — The Tribune Engineering Company has been indicated as the producer of an automobile in Owego, New York circa 1916 on various car rosters. So far as is known this firm's sole product was a four-cylinder 15 hp delivery van featuring a friction transmission and a $365 price tag. No cars were built by the company.

1913 Tribune, touring, WLB

TRIBUNE — Detroit, Michigan — (1913) — In Detroit in early 1913 two brothers were busy trying to organize automobile companies. Louis G. Hupp's was called the Tribune Motor Company, which he capitalized in March at $10,000. H.C. Lueback was chief engineer, and assisted Hupp in the design of a small touring car on a 116-inch wheelbase powered by a four-cylinder Buda engine. The Tribune had its first test run in May, and was set to go to market with a $1250 price tag. But the car never made it, and undercapitalization was undoubtedly the reason. By November the factory in which the Tribune was to have been built was leased to the Mercury Cyclecar Company. In December Louis G. Hupp joined Briggs-Detroiter. Meanwhile, across town, brother Robert C. Hupp was trying to make a go with his Monarch.

TRI-CITY — The Tri-City Carriage Company of Davenport, Iowa reportedly was building two automobiles in 1899. "The company will engage extensively in the manufacture of the horseless vehicle," *The Autobain* reported that December. There is no evidence this ever happened.

The Tri-City Auto Supply Company was organized in Rock Island, Illinois early in 1912 with a capital stock of $2500 for the manufacture of automobiles. Incorporators were C.P. Sala, Jr., E.M. Sala and Frank Sala. Manufacture is doubted.

1904 Tricolet, three-wheeler, NAHC

TRICOLET — Indianapolis & Guthrie, Indiana — (1904-1906) — The first Tricolet was built by H. Pokorney while he was serving as chief mechanic for a local Indianapolis dealership called the Elston Automobile Company. He had been building a few gasoline engines in the back of his home at 1704 Bellefontaine Street, and he put one of them into a little three-wheeler which he immediately dubbed the Tricolet. So pleased was he

with the results that he decided to go into manufacture — of both engines and automobiles. He found a man named Richards who was willing to help financially, and the H. Pokorney & Richards Automobile & Gas Engine Company was born in nearby Guthrie. Though Pokorney had very definite ideas about what his car should be, he was willing to be flexible if a client wished. For example, the two-speed planetary transmission of the Tricolet had no reverse; because the car turned in a fourteen-foot circle, he didn't think one necessary, but he was willing to make one available as an option. Likewise, he really preferred his vehicle as a three-wheeler, but would add an extra wheel for an extra twenty-five dollars. The Tricolet three-wheeler was priced at $425. Regardless of the number of wheels, and the presence or absence of a reverse, all Tricolets were powered by a two-cylinder 6 hp engine mounted in the rear of a 66-inch wheelbase chassis and were provided with tiller steering. The Tricolet was discontinued in 1906, but Pokorney continued to build his engines for a while longer.

1904-1906 TRICOLET

	FP	5	4	3	2	1
Three-Wheeler	425	1600	2700	3800	5800	12,000
Four-Wheeler	450	1800	2800	4000	6200	13,000

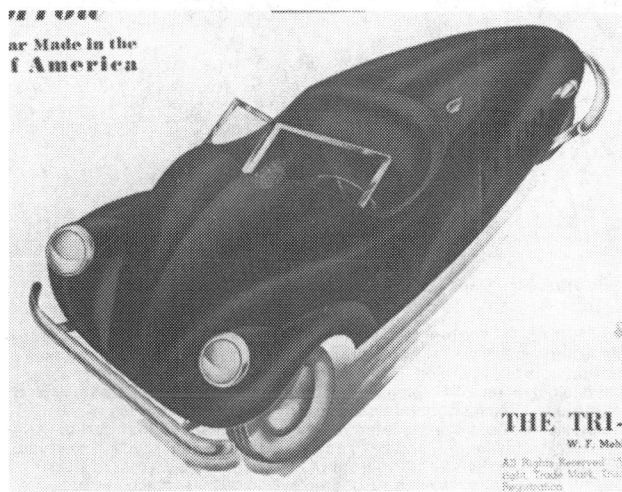

1938 Tri-Mobile, roadster, RNT

TRI-MOBILE — Kansas City, Missouri — (1938) — "The Car of Tomorrow," the brochure headlined. "The Only Car Made in the Heart of America." The place was 1006 East 21st Street, at the corner of Harrison, in Kansas City. W.F. Mehl designed the Tri-Mobile. And it was advertised as "an individual car for every member of the family who's old enough to drive." Alas, the "show me" state does not appear to have responded favorably to Mehl's all-encompassing automotive idea. No sustained manufacture has been documented.

1901 Trimoto, three-wheeler, HAC

TRIMOTO — Chicago, Illinois — (1900-1901) — The Trimoto was designed by Harry John Lawson and sponsored by the American Bicycle Company, with its manufacture seen to by the Western Wheel Works and its marketing by the Crescent organization, both divisions of A.B.C. A three-wheeler with the single front wheel carrying a 2-1/4 hp air-cooled gasoline engine together with all other mechanical bits and pieces, the car was also occasionally referred to as the Gyroscope, although brochures indicate it was never marketed as other than the Trimoto. Maximum speed was 12 mph, and the price was $425. Lawson, who referred to himself as "Sir Harry," was an Englishman and a promoter, and he allied himself with America's master promoter of the period, Edward Joel Pennington. Despite the nefarious taint that suggests, there is no doubt there was significant production of the Trimoto. One of these cars was bought and used by a Mrs. John Howell Phillips, who claimed a few years later to have received the first driver's license issued to a woman (No. 24 in the State of Illinois) in the United States.

TRINITY STEAMER — From 1900-1901 in Keene, New Hampshire, the Trinity Cycle Manufacturing Company produced a steam car which was marketed under the tradename of Keene Steamobile. Refer to Keene Steamobile.

1935 Tri-Phibian, land-sea-air car, SIA

TRI-PHIBIAN — Washington, D.C. — (1935) — In the course of automobile history, there have been a number of attempts to build and market a car that could navigate on both land and water, as well as attempts at cars that could fly. The Tri-Phibian was an effort at all three, and it was built and patented in 1935 by Constantios H. Vlachos, a Greek immigrant residing in the District of Columbia. In later years, Vlachos insisted that during early tests his Tri-Phibian ran and flew, and even took to the waves. Unfortunately, during a demonstration in front of the Library of Congress in Washington, it blew up. Vlachos, who suspected evil-doing by someone putting gasoline into an oxygen line, was seriously hurt in the explosion, but recovered. That was his first and last Tri-Phibian, however. After the Second World War, Vlachos built a Phibian, but it was designed for land use only.

1901 Tripler Liquid Air, runabout, WLB

TRIPLER — New York, New York — (1900-1901) — When it was announced that the car would be exhibited in New York City in the fall of 1900, considerable curiosity resulted. "It is probable that those who examined the machine were a trifle disappointed to find it such an ordinary looking carriage," *The Motor Age* reported thereafter. And ordinary looking the Tripler was, except for its copper boiler under the rear deck. The car was one of two announced during this period that was powered by liquid air. The man behind this one was G.A. Bolrich, the chief chemical engineer of the Tripler Liquid Air Company of New York City. The advantages claimed for liquid air were its economy (two cents a mile), its lack of complication, and the fact that it was as clean as electric power and with a greater radius of operation. "The company states that it has overcome many of the difficulties met in attempts to control the evaporation of liquid air," *The Motor Age* explained, "and that now the liquid may be retained in perfect condition in the automobile boiler for a period of from eight to ten days with but extremely slight loss through evaporation." Whether liquid air was viable or not remains moot, but the Tripler was doomed probably anyway because of the scandal surrounding the other liquid air car introduced by the Liquid Air Power and Automobile Company of Boston.

TRI-RICKSHA — The International Tri-Ricksha Company was organized in New York City late in 1914 with a capital stock of $500,000 for the manufacture of three-wheeled taxis and delivery cars. Archibald McClintock and Francis Kaley of New York City, and John P. Mahan of Jersey City, New Jersey, were the incorporators. Manufacture is doubted.

TRI-STATE — The Tri-State Automobile Company was organized in Memphis, Tennessee during the fall of 1903 with a capital stock of $3000 for the manufacture and sale of automobiles and supplies. Incorporators were L.M. Hall, F.F. Hill, W.T. Arrington, G.W. Browne and Caruthers Ewing. Manufacture of a car is doubted.

TRITT ELECTRIC — South Bend, Indiana — (1905) — Probably few complete cars were built by the Tritt Electrical Company of South Bend, which was organized with a capital stock of $100,000 in January 1905 by Burleigh E. Tritt, Daniel M. Calvert, Walter B. Pershing, Edgar R. Miller and Charles H. Kreighbaum. Electrical specialties and supplies were the firm's principal focus, though electric cars were stated to be a sideline.

1900 Triumph Electric, stanhope, LC

TRIUMPH ELECTRIC — Chicago, Illinois — (1900-1901) — "Triumph Automobiles," the company ballyhooed. "All Their Name Implies." The Triumph Motor Vehicle Company had been incorporated in Chicago in June of 1900 with a capital stock of $300,000. Very few dollars, however, appear to have been paid in. The company's product was a very pretty little electric stanhope, which was sometimes marketed under the name of Ellis, "a swell carriage for professional men, ladies, or family use." The Triumph people also were willing to build steam or gasoline cars, provided a customer give them ninety days notice. Prices ranged from $750 to $2000. The company was located at 1012-1013 Monadnock Block in Chicago, and in February of 1901 indicated that a new factory in Kankakee was planned. The Triumph Motor Vehicle Company was out of business before those plans were realized.

1907 Triumph, model A, runabout, HAC

TRIUMPH — Chicago, Illinois — (1907-1912) — The Triumph Motor Car Company was organized in Chicago in 1907 by John H. Behrens, and its marketing during the early years was handled by Eric B. Christopher, a former automobile repairman turned automobile dealer who brought his brothers R.B. and M.E. into the venture. What Christopher Brothers sold was the Triumph "Self-Starting Car." A compressed air device, designed by Triumph superintendent C.L. Halladay, was operated by a switch and a foot button in the driver's compartment. "A car to direct — not to labor with" was the Triumph slogan. A four-speed sliding gear transmission and shaft drive were featured. In August of 1907 the Triumph Motor Car Company was bought by two former Holsman employees: Vincent Bendix and O.M. Delauney. Though Bendix refined the Triumph's compressed-air starter, he seems to have interested himself thereafter more in the two new cars he would be building — the Duplex and the Bendix. Charge of the Triumph operation was largely left to Delauney. Under the new Triumph regime, the price of the car was gradually lowered from the high of $3500 in 1907 to $2250 in 1912, the final year of Triumph production.

1907 TRIUMPH
Model A — 4-cyl., 30 hp, 108" wb

	FP	5	4	3	2	1
Runabout-2/3P	2800	3700	4700	7300	13,700	26,000

Model B — 4-cyl., 45 hp, 113" wb

Touring-5P	3500	4200	5200	8400	15,700	29,000

1908 TRIUMPH
Model A — 4-cyl., 30 hp, 113 1/2" wb

Roadster-2/3P	2250	3700	4700	7300	13,700	26,000

Model B — 4-cyl., 30 hp, 113 1/2" wb

Touring-5P	3000	3900	4800	7700	14,300	27,000

1909 TRIUMPH
Model A — 4-cyl., 35 hp, 109" wb

Roadster-2/3P	2250	3700	4700	7300	13,700	26,000

Model B — 4-cyl., 35 hp, 113" wb

Touring-5P	2500	3900	4800	7700	14,300	27,000
Limousine	2500	2700	3600	5300	8800	19,000

1910-1911 TRIUMPH
Model A — 4-cyl., 40 hp, 109" wb

Roadster-4P	2250	4000	5000	8000	15,000	28,000

Model A — 4-cyl., 40 hp, 114" wb

Touring-5P	2500	4200	5200	8400	15,700	29,000

1912 TRIUMPH
Model A — 4-cyl., 35 hp, 114" wb

Roadster-4P	2250	3700	4700	7300	13,700	26,000

Model B — 4-cyl., 35 hp, 118" wb

Touring-5P	2250	3900	4800	7700	14,300	27,000

TROJAN — Troy, New York — (1903) — The Trojan was one of two cars built by William S. Howard during his short sojourn with the Trojan Launch and Automobile Works in Troy. The other was named for himself, and it was initially a small single-cylinder gasoline runabout which was produced there from 1901. For the 1903 model year, by which time the Howard had grown up into a two (or more) cylindered car and was being offered with a tonneau, William Howard elected to market another runabout under the Trojan name. The Trojan had a twin-cylinder engine and sliding gear transmission — and was built for only a few months. Later in 1903 Howard moved his operation to Yonkers, where all cars produced bore his name.

TROTT — The Trott Automobile Company was organized twice, and that a single automobile resulted from either venture has not been documented. Rolland S. Trott was the man involved in each case. During the summer of 1909 he was in Denver, Colorado where the Trott Automobile Company was incorporated with a capital stock of $100,000. James R. Killiam and Harry M. Ruby were his partners. Doubtless they had been left behind, however, by 1917 when Rolland Trott showed up in Detroit as the vice-president and general manager of the Trott Automobile Company which was headquartered at 723 Chamber of Commerce Building. No doubt the new Trott venture never left that room to enter a factory. By 1918 Rolland S. Trott had left Detroit. His further adventures are unknown.

TROTT & STUBBLEFIELD — The Trott & Stubblefield Company was organized in Bloomington, Illinois early in 1915 with a capital stock of $20,000 for the manufacture of automobiles and trucks. The partners involved were E.C. Trott and L.W. Stubblefield. Manufacture is doubted. Bloomington city directories for the period indicate the firm served as a dealership for both automobiles and auto supplies.

TROXEL — Elyria, Ohio — (1902) — In October of 1902 the Troxel Manufacturing Company of Elyria announced the completion of its experimental gasoline carriage which now was undergoing "severe road tests." The Troxel people declared their intention to organize a company "for the express purpose of building automobiles" and expected to have their car on the market by New Year's Day. The Troxel never made it.

TROY — In the late fall of 1908 James Stanley, producer of the Stanley car of Mooreland, Indiana, announced his company's merger with the Troy Buggy Company of Troy, Ohio. All operations moved to Troy, Ohio but the car continued to be marketed as a Stanley. Refer to Stanley.

TROY — Troy, New York — (1905) — During the spring of 1905, the Troy Carriage Works announced that it was "contemplating engaging in the manufacture of automobiles" and was now "putting through four cars, one a large touring car with three seats for seven persons." So far as is known, that represented the entire extent of the Troy automobile production. Apparently the firm tried again, however, in early 1907 with the organization of the Troy Motor Carriage Company by Myron J. Adams, Warren A. Pine and Charles L. Pine. Its capital stock was a mere $1000, and it went nowhere.

TRUE — Kenosha, Wisconsin — (1913) — The True cyclecar was the second automobile effort of the Badger Brass Manufacturing Company of Kenosha. The first was a steam car in 1901 which carried the company's own name and was built to demonstrate the superiority of its automobile lamps. The True, however, was planned to be marketed. The prototype arrived during the fall of 1913, a two-passenger tandem roadster on a 104-inch wheelbase chassis, powered by a two-cylinder 10 hp Spacke engine. The company announced its price tag was $400 at that time, then got cold feet. In January 1914, L.F. Keck said that "it would be some time

1913 True, cyclecar, JAC

before the company reached any decision" regarding manufacture. When the decision was reached, it was not to. Interestingly, the car had been designed by Badger Brass secretary Richard Welles, father of Orson Welles).

1913 TRUE
Cyclecar — 2-cyl., 10 hp, 104" wb

	FP	5	4	3	2	1
Tandem Rdstr.	400	2300	3300	4600	7500	16,000

TRUE BLUE — Detroit, Michigan — (1910) — The True Blue was a $1300 gasoline car built as a prototype only. The venture was begun in February of 1910 by Wallace E. Brown and Maurice Wolf of the Michigan Gas Mantle Company and Edmund H. Coombs of the Coombs-Gilmore Company, the distributors of the Mitchell car in Detroit. The first car built by their True Blue Motor Company was tested in the spring of 1910. It was also the last.

TRUMBULL — Seven cars were built from 1899-1905 in the shops of the Trumbull Manufacturing Company of Warren, Ohio. Some were called Trumbulls, others Pendleton. Refer to Pendleton.

1914 Trumbull, cyclecar, NAHC

TRUMBULL — Bridgeport, Connecticut — (1914-1915) — The Trumbull was a honey of a cyclecar. Had more cyclecars been as well made, this type of vehicle might have enjoyed more success in America. Powered by a water-cooled 14/18 hp four-cylinder engine, the Trumbull featured shaft drive and (in 1915) a three-speed selective sliding gear transmission. It was set on a 80-inch wheelbase chassis, with a tread of 44 inches, a ground clearance of nine inches, and a total weight of 950 pounds. A maximum speed of 50 mph was claimed; prices were $425 for roadster, $600 for coupe. The overall concept of the Trumbull was the work of Harry J. Stoops; its engine was designed by K.L. Hermann of the Hermann Engineering Company. And the whole project had the enthusiastic backing of the Trumbull brothers, Alexander H. and Isaac B., of Bridgeport. (There were seven Trumbull brothers, the eldest, John H., serving as governor of Connecticut during the mid-Twenties.) The car had been developed in Detroit by Stoops under the aegis of the American Cyclecar Company, with the presumption being that it would be introduced under his name. By January of 1914, however, the Trumbulls had bought the Stoops design as well as the American Cyclecar Company, and organized the Trumbull Motor Car Company as an outgrowth of their Connecticut Electric Manufacturing Company of Bridgeport. Production of the new Trumbull began in Bridgeport shortly thereafter, with the cars for 1914 being fitted with a friction transmission. Because the cyclecar so quickly earned a dreadful reputation in the United States, most Trumbulls were exported. In 1915 half of the cars were left-hand drive, half right-hand. Of the total production of 2000, 1500 were sold in Europe and Australia. There were twenty Trumbulls aboard the *Lusitania* on May 7th, 1915 when it was torpedoed by the German Navy. On board too was Isaac Trumbull who was en route to England to close a deal for 300 orders. With his death, the Trumbull Motor Car Company died too.

1914-1915 TRUMBULL
Cyclecar — 4-cyl., 14/18 hp, 80" wb

	FP	5	4	3	2	1
Roadster	425	2500	3500	5000	8500	18,000
Coupe	600	2000	3000	4200	6500	14,000

TRUXTON — The Truxton Motor Sales Company, Inc. was organized in Syracuse, New York during the fall of 1917 with a capital stock of $10,000 for the manufacture of automobiles, trucks and trailers. Incorporators were G.M. Wilson, O.H. Greene and J.H. O'Brien. Manufacture is doubted.

T.S. — The T.S. Wheel & Manufacturing Company was organized in Chicago, Illinois during the summer of 1913 with a $2000 capital stock for the manufacture of automobiles and accessories. Incorporators were S. Fred Schulz, Theodore J. Smulski and Stanley Zukowski. Manufacture of a car is doubted.

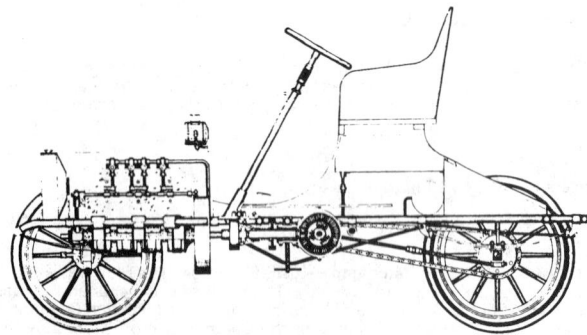

1904 Tuck, Kerosene, runabout, WLB

TUCK — Brooklyn, New York — (1904) — Probably only one Tuck was built at the company's shops at 58 Schermerhorn Street in Brooklyn, but if it had been successful, that would have been quite enough. The car was produced by the Tuck Petroleum Motor Company to demonstrate a new idea. Its 12 hp four-cylinder water-cooled engine was in general appearance similar to many of its type, but this one was designed to be powered by kerosene oil. Unlike other experimental cars of this period, there was no attempt made to vaporize the oil before it was admitted to the cylinders. There was no explosion in the Tuck. According to the company, this resulted in a relatively high torque being developed at low speed. Thus, there was no need for a low or starting speed — and so there wasn't one. Drive was through a friction clutch via bevel gears directly to a countershaft, with side driving chains running to sprockets attached to the rear wheels. Neither was there a reverse gear. As in steam-driven cars, the Tuck was backed up by reversing the engine. In this car, that meant stopping the motor and pulling a lever which shifted the valve-lifting cams in such a manner that the direction of rotation was changed. A chore. Since little was heard thereafter about the Tuck car, it would appear that the "very novel ideas . . . of which much is expected" just didn't work out as expected.

1936 Tucker, three-wheeler, MVMA

1936 Tucker, streamliner, SIA

TUCKER — Los Angeles, California — (1936) — The Tucker was yet another of the mid-Thirties exercises in modish streamlining. This one was built by G.S. Tucker, chief machinist at Grant Piston Rings in Los Angeles, for his bandleader son Tommy Tucker. Its flathead Ford engine was mounted just in front of the rear wheel which was held by modified front motorcycle forks. The rear axle was inverted and placed up front. This front-wheel-drive three-wheeler was dressed, spats and all, quasi-aircraft style with tubing and angle iron.

TUCKERMOBILE — Santa Clara, California — (1900-1903) — John O. Tucker purportedly built more than a dozen cars he called Tuckermobiles in Santa Clara at the turn of the century, with even earlier dates of 1894 and 1899 also being claimed. None of these vehicles were reported upon in the local Santa Clara newspaper, and official Santa Clara histories have ignored the Tuckermobile totally. It is known that by 1912 John Tucker had abandoned all automotive ambitions and was pursuing a career as a photographer instead.

TULSA — Tulsa, Oklahoma — (1912-1913) — The Tulsa Automobile & Manufacturing Company was organized in 1911 by F.L. Middleton, J.E. Crosbie and Schuyler C. French, who headquartered themselves at 210 Bank of Commerce Building and their factory at Wheeling avenue and the Frisco Railway. Manufacture does not seem to have begun until 1912, however, the firm buying out the Pioneer Car Company of Oklahoma, City that February. That the Tulsa product was a "light delivery wagon for oil-field work" was announced to the press. Interestingly, Chilton directories of the period indicate the Tulsa company as producing two separate makes, the Tulsa and the Oilflyer. Most probably, in buying the Pioneer assets the Tulsa people had found themselves with a number of unfinished cars and parts for the making of others which were badge-engineered for sale under the Tulsa banner. But there was no question as the primary focus of the company's efforts. "Manufacturers of good commercial motor trucks, that's all," read the firm's city directory listing. The Tulsa Automobile & Manufacturing Company did not survive 1913. Among the reasons may have been management shakeups. Musical chairs appears to have been the game played in the executive suite, and during its brief life the factory may have seen as many as three different general managers.

TULSA — Tulsa, Oklahoma — (1913) — In 1913 a racing special financed by Oklahoma oilman J.B. Levy was built by Cardin Green of Broken Arrow and driven by George Clark to a ninth-place finish in the Indianapolis 500 that year. After the event, announcement was made that race driver Hughie Hughes had been hired by Levy and Green to refine the car into a sporting production version. That August Hughes was reported "working on the design" in Indianapolis, and further plans for manufacturing the car in Tulsa were made. Manufacture never followed, however.

1918 Tulsa, touring, NAHC

TULSA — Tulsa, Oklahoma — (1917-1922) — The Tulsa Automobile Corporation was organized in February of 1917 by T.J. Hartman, J.O. Mitchell, Mark E. Carr and G.E. Darland who took general offices at Brady and North Boulder and took over the factory at Wheeling and the Frisco Railway which had formerly been the home of the Tulsa Automobile & Manufacturing Company. Because the 1913 Indianapolis race car called the Tulsa still retained considerable celebrity in Oklahoma, initial plans called for adapting it for the Tulsa production automobile. That idea ended quickly, however, and for probably the same reason it had in 1913: the cost would have been astronomical. So the Tulsa became a typical assembled car of the period instead. It was introduced with a Lycoming four-cylinder engine, Delco electrics, Borg & Beck clutch and Grant-Lee transmission. The prototype was christened with a bottle of Tulsa-made gasoline (and dubious wisdom) in February 1917. Production began for the 1918 model year, with the car called the Tulsa Four. Three models on a 117 1/2-inch wheelbase were offered: roadster, touring and "Oil Field Runabout," with prices under a thousand dollars. "The Peer of the West" was the company's slogan. Perhaps several hundred cars were produced each year. A factory fire in 1919 retarded the company's pace. Models from 1920 carried Herschell-Spillman engines (with a six added to the line), Dyneto electrics, Muncie transmission, with the Borg & Beck clutch being retained. Prices were upped to the $1500 range. During the summer of 1920 the firm was reorganized with an entirely new executive team (R.M. McFarlin, R.O. Holleron, H.H. Rogers and O.T. Hewlett) taking over. Floyd Thompson, former Ford distributor in the Southwest, was brought in as sales manager. This regime survived until the summer of 1921 when McFarlin and associates sold out the entire business to D.M. Witt of Oklahoma City. Witt allied himself with Floyd Thompson as the Witt-Thompson Motor Company. They finished up the last Tulsa cars on hand and continued in business as auto parts makers and distributors.

1918-1919 TULSA
Model D — 4-cyl., 37 hp, 117 1/2" wb

	FP	5	4	3	2	1
Touring-5P	985	3100	4200	6300	10,500	22,000
Roadster-4P	985	3000	4000	6000	9500	21,000
Oil Field Runabout	985	2900	3700	5600	9100	20,000

1920 Tulsa, oil field runabout, NAHC

1920-1922 TULSA
Model E — 4-cyl., 37 hp, 117 1/2" wb

Touring-5P	1550	3200	4300	6500	11,000	23,000
Roadster-4P	1550	3100	4200	6300	10,500	22,000
Oil Field Runabout	1335	3000	4000	6000	9500	21,000

Note: All models were priced at $1175 in 1922. Cars with the six-cylinder engine option were priced several hundred dollars more than their four-cylinder counterparts.

1921 Tunison, speedster, WLB

TUNISON — Oakland, California — (1921) — This speedster from Oakland had a V-8 engine, a frame of laminated spruce, and weighed 1600 pounds complete. Its inventor, M.C. Tunison, claimed speeds of up to 70 mph and fuel economy in the 30 mpg range. During the spring of 1921 he organized Tunison Motors Company with a grand capital stock of $2.5 million. The factory he was planning to build in Oakland, he said, would be capable of producing 250 cars a month, with later additions to bring output capacity to an even thousand. Probably no more than the prototype was built, before Tunison's grand plans fell apart. But Murray Tunison was back in the news two years later. His car this time was the Paramount of Azusa.

TURBINE — The Turbine Locomotive & Car Company was organized in Newark, New Jersey late in 1905 with a capital stock of $500,000 for the manufacture of "all kinds of motor vehicles for land and water." Incorporators were Stacey Wilson and Robert J. Keith of New York City and Albert G. Mahon of Newark. Manufacture of a car is doubted.

The Turbine Motor and Carriage Company at 7 Exchange Place in Boston, Massachusetts was indicated as an automobile manufacturer in the Hiscox book *Horseless Vehicles, Automobiles, Motor Cycles* published in 1900. Documentation is lacking. Turn-of-the-century Boston city directories do confirm the existence of this company, however.

The Turbine Motor Company was organized in Babylon, New York early in 1908 with a capital stock of $12,000 for the manufacture of automobiles, engines and motor boats. Incorporators were Paul Krause, Joseph Covert and David Sandman. Manufacture of a car is doubted.

TURBINE ELECTRIC — New York, New York — (1904) — Although mentioned in trade directories as having produced an automobile in 1904, the Turbine Electric Truck Company of 135 Broadway in New York City did not do so, except possibly as a prototype. As its title indicates, the company focus was on the commercial vehicle field, though even truck production was limited and of short duration. The Turbine electric motive power system was described in 1904 as being composed of a steam boiler of the Roberts marine water-tube type, a turbine electric generating set, and a pair of electric motors providing drive to the rear wheels.

TURK & BROWN — Turk & Brown, Inc. was organized in Rochester, New York late in 1911 with a capital stock of $10,000 for the manufacture of motor vehicles. Incorporators were indicated as Sophie H. Brown and Alfred H. Brown. Manufacture is doubted.

TURNER — "J.C. Turner, an architect of Augusta, Georgia has constructed a gasolene carriage weighing 800 pounds," reported *The Horseless Age* in June 1899. Further details are lacking.

The Turner-Hose Automobile and Launch Company was organized in Rochester, New York during the spring of 1909 with a capital stock of $5000 for the manufacture of motor boats and motor cars. Incorporators were F. Turner and R.H. Hose. Manufacture of a car is doubted.

1900 Turner, touring, LC

TURNER — Marysville, Ohio — (1900) — Richard S. Turner was the fire chief of Marysville in 1885. In 1892 he went into business for himself making a variety of products in his ever-expanding machine shop: iron gratings for sewers, cast iron ornamental parts for store fronts, iron furniture and toys, metal parts for school desk chairs. He also built and patented a gasoline engine, and in 1900 produced the first automobile in Union County. It sported a two-cylinder water-cooled engine, planetary transmission, and wood wheels with solid rubber tires. Turner drove the car on the streets of Marysville for about a decade, but he never embarked upon manufacture. Among his subsequent inventive endeavors was the first motion picture projection machine in Marysville and an ornamental wire fence-making machine which wove fences on location. He was also responsible for the building of a good many iron bridges in the area. He died in Marysville in 1936. His automobile was later presented by the Turner family to the Union County Historical Society.

TURNER — Philadelphia, Pennsylvania — (1901-1903) — The only really clever decisions that George T. Turner made regarding the cars he built in Philadelphia at the turn of the century were the names he used in designating them. Liliputian was a wonderful choice for a little three-wheeler. The car was otherwise undistinguished and unsophisticated, with a light tubular frame, wire wheels, a double fork at the front end, a small single-cylinder 1 1/4 hp engine mounted under the seat, and a tiller for steering. Its wheelbase was 51 inches, its track 36 inches, and its transmission had one speed forward and reverse. Turner did garner some press attention for his little car in 1902, including mention in the British magazine *Motorcycling*, but the Liliputian could not have been swift enough to have traveled as far as Gulliver. Turner's other car was called the Gadabout, and it had four wheels, a 3 hp engine, 90-inch wheelbase and 40-inch tread. Both the Liliputian and the Gadabout were built by the Turner Automobile Company, Ltd., which was located at 304 North Broad Street in Philadelphia. Production began during the summer of 1901 and ended during the summer of 1903 when George Turner filed voluntary bankruptcy papers.

1902 Turner Liliputian, three-wheeler, MVMA

TURNER — Chicago, Illinois — (1904) — The Turner Brass Works at Franklin and Michigan streets in Chicago manufactured the Turner carburetor, foot pedals and varying other automotive accoutrements — and in 1904 marketed an automobile of its own design. The Turner was a large touring car, powered by a two-cylinder 12 hp opposed engine and fitted with a three-speed sliding gear transmission and shaft drive. A special feature was the location of the starting crank on the dashboard so that a Turner owner could have the convenience of starting his car from the driver's seat. The Turner was produced for a single season only.

TURNER — Indianapolis, Indiana — (1910) — In 1910 George Turner of Indianapolis invented a motor sleigh which he said resembled an automobile in many respects "except that it is built close to the ground." A 2 hp air-cooled motor propelled it, and the final drive was by chain. The vehicle was mounted on a beech plank and a propeller was attached to the rear where two-pointed wheels resembling a saw were fitted, these set in motion by the chain drive. According to George Turner, the only place where his vehicle would be practical was "in the countries of the frozen north, where it will be of benefit in carrying mail." Alas, no one from the frozen north apparently wanted to produce the Turner.

TUTTLE — The D.M. Tuttle Company was organized in Canastota, New York during the fall of 1903 with a capital stock of $60,000 for the manufacture of engines, boats and automobiles. Joining Daniel M. Tuttle in this venture were William H. Lindley, Frank G. Bell, Otis M. Bigelow and James F. Williams. In 1910 the firm was reorganized as the Tuttle Motor Company with a capital stock of $150,000. S.E. Brown and J.S. Munroe joined Daniel Tuttle in this venture. That an automobile was ever manufactured has not been documented.

TWEED—THOMAS — The Tweed-Thomas Company has been indicated on various car rosters as the manufacturer of an automobile in Wheatley, Minnesota in 1906. There is no evidence of such a company in Wheatley.

TWENTIETH CENTURY — The Twentieth Century Auto Company of Cleveland, Ohio was indicated as the manufacturer of an automobile in the Hiscox book *Horseless Vehicles, Automobiles, Motor Cycles* published in 1900. Documentation is lacking. Turn-of-the-century Cleveland city directories do not reveal a company of that name in town.

The Twentieth Century Garage was organized in Springfield, Illinois during the fall of 1907 with a capital stock of $2500 for the manufacture and repair of automobiles. Incorporators were E.J. Nowak and Otto Kerner (who doubtless was the namesake for the later Illinois governor). Manufacture is doubted.

The Twentieth Century Manufacturing Company of New York City has been indicated as the producer of an automobile in 1900 on various car rosters. This is unlikely. The firm was well known as an accessory manufacturer, however, specializing in automobile lamps.

The Twentieth Century Motor Car Company was organized in Chicago, Illinois early in 1906 for the manufacture of motor vehicles. Incorporators were Lewis F. Haupt, George C. Marsh and Edward F. Heywood, Jr. Manufacture of a car is doubted.

The Twentieth Century Motor Car and Supply Company was organized in South Bend, Indiana during the summer of 1909 with a capital stock of $60,000 for the manufacture of automobiles and accessories. Incorporators were M.L. Williams, H.E. Keyer and H.L. Wolverton. Manufacture of a car is doubted.

TWENTIETH CENTURY — Hagerstown, Maryland — (1925-c.1927) — The Twentieth Century was an Astor with a choice of radiator (straight or vee) and a more subdued paint scheme. It was a taxicab built by the Moller factory in Hagerstown, which produced the Aristocrat, the Blue Light, the Five-Boro, the Luxor, the Paramount and the Super Paramount as well. Like the Astor, the Twentieth Century saw service principally in the city of Philadelphia.

TWIN CITY — The Twin City Auto-Car Company was organized in Minneapolis, Minnesota early in 1905 with a capital stock of $25,000 for the manufacture of automobiles and engines. Incorporators were N.L. Hills, F.W. Couse and F.B. Hills. Manufacture of a car is doubted.

Although the initial announcement of the new Twin City Four-Wheel Drive Company from September 1915 indicated that the firm would produce both trucks and "chassis for automobiles on the four-wheel-drive principle," it appears the latter were never manufactured. Four wheel drive Twin City trucks were produced in St. Paul and Minneapolis, Minnesota from 1917-1922.

1914 Twin City, cyclecar roadster, WLB

TWIN CITY — Minneapolis, Minnesota — (1914) — The Twin City appeared rather as if it had been designed for a comic book; Batman would have been comfortable in this car. Actually, the car's extraordinary fenderline had a practical purpose. The wide and substantial fenders which lifted upward in front were meant to deflect mud and dust; at mid-point, the fender served as an armrest; the flat line to the rear warded against mud and dust in that area and assisted in wind resistance. The car's designer was C.H. Scholer, and his ingenuity didn't end with coachwork. The Twin City's engine was air-cooled piston valve 20 hp four, the piston valves actuated by a mechanism which Scholer patented. The suspension system consisted of two double coil springs of vanadium steel set crosswise of the frame in front and lengthwise of the frame in the rear. A friction transmission was fitted, and final drive from the jackshaft to the rear axle was via a single chain inside of the frame. The car's wheelbase was 101 inches, its tread 36 inches, which provided for snug side-by-side seating for two passengers. The Twin City was claimed good for 50 mph, and its price of $425 included electric lights and horn. Scholer located his Twin City Cyclecar Company at 804 South Ninth Street in Minneapolis. The prototype had been built for him by R.R. Griffith. Whether any production followed has not been documented.

1914 TWIN CITY
Cyclecar — 4-cyl., 20 hp, 101" wb

	FP	5	4	3	2	1
Roadster	425	2200	3200	4400	7000	15,000

1904 Twombly, steam touring, MVMA

TWOMBLY — New York, New York — (1904) — Willard Irving Twombly had three tries at the American automobile industry. The first was in 1904 when he organized the Twombly Motor Carriage Company at 52 Broadway in Manhattan. There he built a large steam car on a 92-inch wheelbase which he offered at $2500 in touring guise, $3000 with a limousine top. Its four-cylinder engine was mounted up front under the hood, and could be changed from a 28 hp single-acting unit to a 12 hp compound. A flash boiler and kerosene burner were fitted. "This car is fireproof throughout," his brochure italicized for emphasis. And the Twombly was simple to

1436

operate, with all controls on the steering wheel. A top speed of 50 mph was claimed. Most likely the car was too expensive to produce, however, because by year's end Twombly had given up the idea of manufacture. He was heard from again in 1905, though, when he built a 30 hp gasoline car in order to experiment with a kerosene carburetor and pneumatic suspension system he had devised. Thereafter he retired to his Twombly Power Corporation at 12th and 51st Street in Manhattan to see to the business of making a living. But in 1910 he announced another idea for an automobile.

1910 Twombly "Quick Detachable" car, HAC

TWOMBLY — New York, New York — (1910) — The Twombly of 1910 was six years in development, W. Irving Twombly said when he let the world know about his new automobile idea. It was a quickly removable engine and a quickly convertible body. And it was a steamer too. Two cylinders were directly opposed on the same center, with a single piston used for both. The engine was a double-acting, with no stuffing box, piston rods, cross heads or packing of any kind. And it was removable from the car, Twombly said, in a mere five minutes. Converting the body took only two or three. It was a series of pressed steel sills and cast aluminum panels and glass windows which, if taken apart or put together correctly, made for an open torpedo-type touring car or completely closed limousine. When he demonstrated the speedy removability and convertibility of his prototype to newsmen in late 1910, he indicated that he had spent over $250,000 in experimental work on the design in the past half-dozen years. Now he stood ready for manufacture and had leased a big factory in Long Island City. Although Twombly planned to build for the passenger car market, he envisioned taxicab, livery and delivery operators as his most lucrative potential clients. "Suppose a machine has started out with a load and something goes wrong with the power plant," he said, "another car is sent for to which the load is transferred, and still another machine is required to tow in the disabled car...under the Twombly system this same company would purchase...one light emergency wagon with a complete power plant on board kept ready for call at any time, and a telephone call of a mishap...would rush the emergency wagon to the spot, the injured part could be removed and replaced by a new one in five or ten minutes, and the original car would go about its business without transferring its load. The broken part could then be returned to the repair shop on the emergency wagon, put in running order and held for the next call." Actually, W. Irving Twombly had a pretty good idea. Adequate financing never arrived, however, so neither did this Twombly. Its builder was next heard from two years later.

1914 Twombly, tandem, roadster, WLB

TWOMBLY — New York, New York — (1913-1915) — W. Irving Twombly's last automotive effort was also his best. This Twombly was a cyclecar that grew up. In 1913 it was a typical spindly tandem two-seater with 38-inch tread and 98-inch wheelbase which sold for $350. It was underslung, had a friction transmission and double chain drive. Its engine was a 7 hp vee-twin. For 1914, a 10 hp water-cooled piston-valve four-cylinder engine was substituted, the wheelbase was lengthened to 100 inches, and the price raised to $395. "I cannot understand it," Twombly was quoted as saying that year, "but I have come across those in the auto world who have expressed sentiments adverse to the cyclecar." When he did under-

stand it, he redesigned his cyclecar into a very fine light car with worm drive and three-speed sliding gear transmission. He thought awhile about using a Knight sleeve-valve engine, but ultimately decided on a water-cooled poppet valve 16 hp four. He had to raise his prices to the $600-$750 range for all this, but now he offered three models: a side-by-side two-passenger runabout, a four-passenger touring, and a taxicab. The latter he produced himself in the former plant of New York Motor Works which he leased in Nutley, New Jersey. Although the pilot models of his roadster and touring cars were built in a rented factory in Avondale, New Jersey, for production Twombly turned to Driggs-Seabury in Sharon, Pennsylvania. The order Twombly placed with Driggs was for 3000 cars. It appeared that W. Irving Twombly was going to make it this time. Alas, he did not. His chief financial backer in the Twombly Car Corporation was a retired Presbyterian minister named Reverend Dr. D. Stuart Dodge, who was not blessed with sainted patience. When salutary sales did not arrive, Dr. Dodge petitioned Twombly into bankruptcy in February of 1915.

1913 TWOMBLY
Cyclecar — 2-cyl., 7 hp, 98" wb

	FP	5	4	3	2	1
Tandem Rdstr.	350	1600	2700	3800	5800	12,000

1914 TWOMBLY
Cyclecar — 4-cyl., 10 hp, 100" wb

Tandem Rdstr.	395	1800	2800	4000	6200	13,000

1915 TWOMBLY
Light Car — 4-cyl., 16 hp, 100" wb

Touring-4P	750	2000	3000	4200	6500	14,000
Runabout-2P	650	1800	2800	4000	6200	13,000
Taxicab-4P	600	2200	3200	4400	7000	15,000

1906 Twyford, type B, tonneau, WLB

TWYFORD — Pittsburgh, Pennsylvania — (1899-1902)/Brookville, Pennsylvania — (1904-1907) — Among America's earliest proponents of four-wheel-drive was a general contractor from Pittsburgh named Robert E. Twyford. His first car was completed in 1899, though what its motive force was is not known. Twyford's patent, for which he had applied in 1898 and which was granted in 1900, showed an electric motor. All known Twyford cars were gasoline powered. Twyford's four-wheel-drive was something of a maze. The engine was mounted at the rear and drove a long shaft extending nearly the entire length of the chassis. Axles both front and rear were solid one-piece, with the front axle swinging to steer as in a horse-drawn wagon. Two pairs of friction clutches within the shaft combined with a welter of gears meshing with gears to provide a very crude drive for all four wheels. Another group of bevel gears provided an equally crude

1907 Twyford, roadster, MVMA

1437

form of power steering. Most probably, the Twyford also provided devilish problems in construction with frequent returns to the drawing board. Although the Twyford Motor Vehicle Company had been organized in the spring of 1899, the only Twyford news in 1900 was a report in November that two four-passenger cars had been built. By January of 1901, a full line of Twyfords was said to be in production, including both passenger cars and commercial vehicles, though only a $1200 stanhope is believed to have been built, and perhaps only one example of it. The Twyford venture in Pittsburgh was abandoned by the end of 1902, and Robert Twyford presumably spent the following year either at the drawing board or on the road attempting to secure the capital necessary to continue. By July of 1904 the town of Brookville, about 55 miles northeast of Pittsburgh, came through with an attractive offer, and Twyford moved there. Involved in the organization of the new Twyford Motorcar Company were William N. and J.M. Humphrey (local brick manufacturers), Walter Richards (a hardware dealer), and W.I. Burton and L.A. Leathers (dry goods merchants). A two-story brick factory was built next to Alexander D. Deemer's furniture factory in town, and the first two cars to be completed there were shown at the Buffalo Automobile Show in March 1905. Three Twyfords were exhibited at the Brookville Fair in September. All of these cars carried two-cylinder two-stroke 20 hp gasoline engines. Sales were few. In March of 1906 there was a management shakeup which saw Alexander Deemer installed as president, and by that summer Robert Twyford had resigned as factory superintendent. Although 1907 models were announced, and probably a few built, the Twyford venture in Brookville was dead before the end of 1906. The factory was later turned over to a company that made windshields. As for Robert Twyford, he was not about to say die. He continued to try to sell his four-wheel-drive idea, allying himself with Z.Z. and L.J. Brandon. In 1911 this trio sold Houston, Texas on the idea. There the Commercial Motor Car Company was established for the manufacture of automobiles and trucks using the Twyford patents and Brandon as a tra-

dename. The company proceeded into receivership in June of 1912, before this venture reached the manufacturing stage. Robert Twyford is not believed to have tried again.

1901-1902 TWYFORD

	FP	5	4	3	2	1
Stanhope	1200	1600	2700	3800	5800	12,000

1905 TWYFORD
Type B — 2-cyl., 20 hp, 87" wb

	FP	5	4	3	2	1
Tonneau	1800	1600	2700	3800	5800	12,000

Type A — 2-cyl., 20 hp, 87" wb

	FP	5	4	3	2	1
Tonneau	2700	1600	2700	3800	5800	12,000

Type F — 2-cyl., 16 hp, 104" wb

	FP	5	4	3	2	1
Delivery	—	1500	2500	3600	5500	11,000

1906-1907 TWYFORD
Type C — 2-cyl., 15 hp, 70" wb

	FP	5	4	3	2	1
Roadster-4P	1400	1500	2500	3600	5500	11,000

Type B — 2-cyl., 20 hp, 87" wb

	FP	5	4	3	2	1
Tonneau-5P	1800	1600	2700	3800	5800	12,000

TWYMAN — The Twyman Motor Car Company was organized in Columbus, Ohio during the summer of 1911 with a capital stock of $20,000 for the manufacture and sale of automobiles and accessories. Incorporators included B.W. Twyman, Lulu Lepold, Eugene Morgan and Henry O'Kane. Manufacture of a car is doubted.

TYRO — The Tyro Manufacturing Company was organized in Detroit, Michigan during the fall of 1912 with a capital stock of $5000 for the manufacture of automobiles. Incorporators were Roy I. Wellington, William C. Stuart and F.J.B. Gerald. Manufacture is doubted.

ULTIMATE — The Ultimate Car Company was organized in Chicago, Illinois during the spring of 1914 with a capital stock of $5000 for the manufacture and sale of motor vehicles. Incorporators were Maurice Alschuler, N.A. Stern and Charles C. Pickett. Manufacture of a car is doubted.

ULTIMOTOR — **Franklin, Indiana** — **(1915)** — The Ultimotor was Frank N. Martindale's next try at success following the failure of the Continental he had produced in association with Frank Millikan in Franklin. Unlike the Continental which was a car, the Ultimotor was an attachment which he said was adjustable to any horsedrawn vehicle for presto-chango conversion into an automobile. He converted one wagon himself as a demonstrator, and the device worked — but by 1915 the conversion idea was no longer a viable business proposition, and the Ultimotor failed even more quickly than had the Continental.

ULTRA — The Ultra Motor Company was organized in New Haven, Connecticut during the spring of 1906 with a capital stock of $25,000 for the manufacture of automobiles, engines and motor boats. Behind this venture were Joseph Schaeffers and John H. Connell of New Haven, and John K. Brachvogel and Otto S. Jung of New York City. Manufacture of a car is doubted.

ULTRA — **Amesbury, Massachusetts** — **(1912-1914)** — The Ultra Motor Car Company was established in Amesbury in 1912 and a prototype of its new car was completed in the shops of Howarth & Rogers Company that October. Designed by R.H. Randall, the Ultra was a 38 hp six, fitted with a four-speed selective transmission, and set into a 128-inch wheelbase chassis. "The first body which has been built is entirely an Amesbury production and gives promise that the new cars will be handsome ones," *Automobile Topics* reported. "The radiator is of the pointed type, aiding materially the sweeping lines in securing a low and speedy appearance." Sporty wire wheels were fitted. The Ultraline was to include touring cars for five ($3000) and seven ($3200) passengers, and a roadster at $2800. In the month following, the first car built was used as a demonstrator in and around Boston in an attempt to raise financing. In late November 1912, the Ultra Motor Car Company announced plans to relocate in Taunton where the firm would lease quarters in a building then occupied by the Interchangeable Rubber Heel Company and a tire manufacturer. Whether relocation followed is not known, nor is the quantity of cars built. Massachusetts registrations for 1914 include three Ultras, however, bearing serial numbers 010, 053 and 101.

UNCAS — The Uncas Manufacturing Company was organized in Norwich, Connecticut during the spring of 1914 with a capital stock of $5000 for the manufacture of automobiles. D.F. Leavitt was the principal involved. Shortly thereafter the firm announced that it would not build cars after all, but the "Leavitt ball contact ignition timer" and other automobile accessories instead.

UNDERWOOD — **Bucyrus, Ohio** — **(1896-1899)** — Frank M. Underwood was the manager of the gas engine department of the Frey-Sheckler Company of Bucyrus and the inventor of a new motor in 1896 which had one cylinder, two pistons and a double crank. "The two pistons will move in opposite directions," reported *The Horseless Age*, "making a balance so perfect that the inventor claims the motor can be suspended on wires from any point without causing more vibration than a sewing machine." Although the Frey-Sheckler Company built motors for stationary and marine purposes, this new unit was intended expressly for carriages. A buggy was so motorized by the firm in order to demonstrate the Underwood-designed engine, but automobile manufacture was not launched. The engine was marketed, however, as the American Vehicle Motor.

UNDERWOOD — **Sandusky, Ohio** — **(1900)** — The men behind the Underwood Motor Company of Sandusky were H.C. Strong, R.E. Schuck, George A. Schwehr and C. Faber Donahue. The firm specialized in gasoline engines for the trade, and built an occasional car for a local customer. The first car ever to run on the streets of Sandusky was built by the Underwood Motor Company. It was bought by George J. Schade and given its maiden test on July 8th, 1900.

UNION — The Union Automobile Company of Albany, Indiana promoted a car called the Coyote in 1909. Refer to Coyote.

The Union Automobile Company of Baltimore, Maryland was organized early in 1900 with a capital stock of $50,000 for the manufacture of vehicles "to use any of the motive powers and to operate in any county or city of the State." Incorporators were George Waters, Spencer C. Watkins, Le Page Cronmiller, Louis C. Barley and Julian O. Ellinger. Manufacture of a car is doubted.

The Union Automobile Company of Wheeling, West Virginia was organized during the summer of 1913 with a capital stock of $25,000 to manufacture and deal in motor cars. Incorporators were W.T. Shaffer, A.C. Shaffer, Albert M. Schenk, George F. Fahnar and B.J. Smith, all of Wheeling. Manufacture is doubted.

The Union Car Company of Los Angeles, California produced two cars in 1914 and 1915. Although Union was occasionally used as a designation, the cars were more frequently called by the tradenames of Gage and Per-

max. Refer to Gage and Permax.

The Union Electric Car Company of Rochester, New York was organized during the spring of 1912 with a capital stock of $5000 for the manufacture of motor vehicles. Incorporators were A. McNall, H.J. Schneider and H.E. Pramer. Manufacture is doubted.

The Union Iron Works of Oshkosh, Wisconsin produced an automobile in 1899. Refer to Doman.

The Union League Automobile Company of Brooklyn, New York was organized during the spring of 1905 with a capital stock of $50,000 to manufacture and deal in motor cars. Incorporators were Charles E. Togethoff, Raine Ewell and H. Milton Kennedy. Manufacture is doubted.

The Union Machine Works of St. Louis, Missouri advertised itself as providing "special machines built to order" in 1908. Automobile repair seems to have been its main activity, however.

The Union Motor Car Company of Eaton, Ohio was a reincorporation of the venture which was producing the Washington car. The Union designation was used to incorporate the firm in the state of Delaware during the spring of 1920 as a million-dollar company.

The Union Motor Car Company of Newark, New Jersey was organized during the summer of 1909 with a capital stock of $125,000 for the manufacture of automobiles and locomotives. Incorporators were P. Broderson, A. Broderson and F.C. Stowers, all of East Orange. Manufacture is doubted.

The Union Motor Car Company of Rochester, New York was organized late in 1907 with a capital stock of $15,000 for the manufacture of automobiles and parts. Incorporators were Edward C. White, Victor L. Kraft and A. Vernon Hart. Manufacture of a car is doubted.

The Union Motor Sales Company of Augusta, Georgia was organized early in 1912 with a capital stock of $200,000 to manufacture and deal in automobiles. E.M. Leavitt was backing this venture. Manufacture is doubted.

The Union Steel Manufacturing Company of Brazil, Indiana promoted an automobile called the Vanderbilt in 1920. Refer to Vanderbilt.

The Union Taxicab Auto Service Company of New York City was organized during the spring of 1908 with a capital stock of $150,000 to "manufacture, deal in, operate and hire motor cars." Incorporators were F.A. Phillips, William J. Duane and C.C. Bailey. Manufacture is doubted.

The Union Transit Company of Paterson, New Jersey was organized early in 1900 with a capital stock of $200,000 for the manufacture and operation of motor vehicles. Incorporators were Isaac A. Hall, George Longbottom, John W. Sturr and John Mallon (all of Paterson), and George White of New York City. Manufacture is doubted.

UNION — **Portland, Maine** — **(1899)** — During the early fall of 1899, the Union Electric Company of Portland announced its forthcoming manufacture of automobiles. Engines powered by compressed air, gasoline, electricity, naphtha or steam would be made available at the customer's choice, though the Union standard model would be a compressed air. Prices of these vehicles began at $200. Although Union Electric built a few cars, its ambitious manufacturing program was never put into effect. Most probably, the cars were not very good, and the company seems not to have survived the turn of the century.

1904 Union, runabout, WLB

UNION — **Union City, Indiana/Anderson, Indiana** — **(1902-1904/1905)** — The Union Automobile Company cribbed from several sources — including Longfellow in *Song of Hiawatha* — to come up with the slogan,

"In Union There Is Strength." Everything else about the car was quite original, however. Both its engine and its friction drive transmission were the invention of John W. Lambert, whose Buckeye Manufacturing Company in Anderson produced those and most other parts of the new Union. Favorable overtures from the Union City chamber of commerce had resulted in the company being organized there in December of 1901. The Union engine was available either air- or water-cooled, but it was the friction transmission feature — "no gears to grind or strip... no clutches to slip" — which was more widely touted. A two-seater runabout with a fold-down seat in the dash for two more passengers was the only model offered, at $1250, for 1902 to 1903. The line was augmented with larger tonneau models in 1904 and 1905, with prices dropped overall. All Unions were powered by two-cylinder engines with final drive by chain. By late 1904 the wisdom of manufacturing the Union's component parts in one town and assembling the car in another came to be regarded as dubious, and by early 1905 all operations were moved to Anderson. The Union was succeeded by a new car called the Lambert later that year. Total production had been approximately 300 units.

1905 Union, tonneau, NAHC

1902-1903 UNION
Two Cylinder — 8 hp, 72" wb

	FP	5	4	3	2	1
Runabout-2/4P	1250	1800	2800	4000	6200	13,000

1904 UNION
Two Cylinder — 12 hp, 72" wb

Runabout-2/4P	1000	2000	3000	4200	6500	14,000

Two Cylinder — 10 hp, 78" wb

Tonneau-5P	900	1800	2800	4000	6200	13,000

1905 UNION
Model D — 2-cyl., 12 hp, 81" wb

Detachable Tonneau	1000	2000	3000	4200	6500	14,000

Model E — 2-cyl., 16 hp, 94" wb

Runabout	925	2400	3400	4800	8000	17,000
Detachable Tonneau	1200	2450	3500	4900	8300	17,500

UNION — St. Louis, Missouri — (1905) — "You Auto Take This Home With You" advertised the Union Automobile Manufacturing Company of St. Louis. The firm had been organized in late November of 1904 with a capital stock of $12,000 and began production of its friction-drive motor buggy in 1905. The Union Automobile Manufacturing Company was in actuality the Missouri branch of the Union Automobile Company of Indiana. Two models were produced in St. Louis: a 12 hp twin on an 81-inch wheelbase with passenger accommodations for four at $1000 and a 16 hp twin on a 94-inch wheelbase that sat five and was priced at $1125. The demand for automobiles "is not a craze," the company said, "as the

1909 Union, runabout, WLB

experimental stages are past: a practical commercial value has been justly bestowed upon the horseless vehicle in this, the horseless age." When the Union company in Indiana began building the Lambert, it is believed the St. Louis venture metamorphosed into an agency dealing in that car. Benjamin Hulbert, George H. Martin and George B. Louderback had headed the Union operation in St. Louis.

1905 UNION
Model 2 D — 2-cyl., 12 hp, 81" wb

	FP	5	4	3	2	1
Touring-4P	1000	2200	3200	4400	7000	15,000

Model E — 2-cyl., 16 hp, 94" wb

Touring-5P	1125	2400	3400	4800	8000	17,000

UNION — St. Louis, Missouri — (1908-1909) — The Union Carriage Company of St. Louis had been building horsedrawn vehicles since 1891 and began automobile production during the fall of 1908. A $650 high-wheeled victoria buggy on a 70-inch wheelbase powered by an air-cooled two-cylinder 12 hp engine was the firm's only initial offering. In November of 1908, Union manager C.L. Fleming announced that a runabout and touring with motor mounted up front under a hood would be added, and that further additions would be made to the factory in order to increase output to 1000 cars for 1909. Twenty-five cars had thus far been produced. Perhaps as many as several hundred more were built before the company decided to confine its trade to vehicles with horses late in 1909.

1908-1909 UNION
Model A — 2-cyl., 12 hp, 70" wb

Victoria	650	1500	2500	3600	5500	11,000
Touring	—	1800	2800	4000	6200	13,000
Runabout	—	1600	2700	3800	5900	12,000

UNION — Auburn, Indiana — (1916) — This Union was an Auburn with a different nameplate and two fewer cylinders. It was built by the Union Automobile Company, which was organized late in 1915 for that purpose, though the firm's literature clearly indicated that the venture had not been incorporated. Obviously some business advantage must have accrued from doing things this way, though what it was remains a mystery. Instrumental in organizing this subsidiary for Auburn was John Zimmerman, and the new Union was built in the factory which had formerly seen production of the Zimmerman car. All cars with an Auburn nameplate in 1916 were sixes. The Union was a 24 hp four with an $895 price tag. It was produced for a single season only.

1916 UNION
Four — 24 hp, 120" wb

Touring-5P	895	3200	4300	6500	11,000	23,000
Roadster-2P	895	3100	4200	6300	10,500	22,000

1916 Union, 5-pass. touring, WLB

UNION CITY SIX — Union City, Indiana — (1916) — The Union City Carriage Manufacturing Company had been in business since the turn of the century and built a complete automobile only in 1916. It was a 48/52 hp six which promised 55 mph and was mounted on a 120-inch wheelbase chassis. A five-passenger touring car was the only model offered. This firm subsequently became famous when, allied with the Auburn Automobile Company, it became a coachbuilding arm of Errett Lobban Cord's empire and as the Union City Body Company produced coachwork under the name of Le Grande.

1916 Union City Six, touring, LC

UNION 25 — Columbus, Ohio — (1911-1912) — In late 1911, shortly after being organized as the Eagle Motor Car Company of Columbus for production of a car to be called the Eagle Roadster, this venture was renamed the Union Sales Company for production of the Union 25. The name change was made to avoid confusion with all of the other Eagles

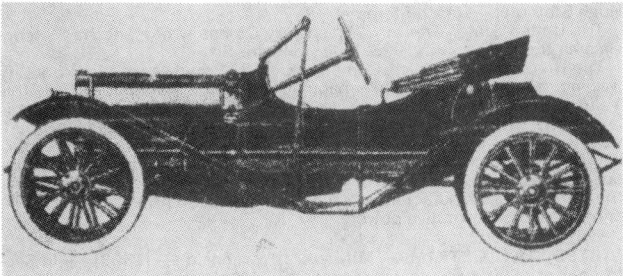

1912 Union 25, 2-pass. roadster, WLB

which had preceded this one into the marketplace. The Union 25 was a neat little roadster on a 100-inch wheelbase, powered by a four-cylinder 25 hp engine. It featured a three-speed sliding gear transmission, an oval gas tank on the rear deck, and was given a price tag of $650. J.W. O'Brian was the promoter of this venture, and he entrusted the building of the prototype to the Dunlap Engineering Company in Columbus. "It is known that he secured deposits totaling between $1500 and $2000, which he is supposed to have taken with him as he did not settle any bills while in Columbus," reported *The Automobile* in February 1912 when J.W. O'Brian disappeared from town. He was thought to have taken off for Omaha, and he was rumored to have been involved in the Primo venture in Atlanta previously. Undeniable was that Dunlap Engineering was left holding the uncompleted Union 25, which the firm attached and completed. Dunlap's general manager was quoted as saying that "the car as specified by O'Brian can be built for $650 and that there is every reason to believe that it will be moved to another town and a factory established." This does not appear to have happened, however; most likely Dunlap ultimately tossed the Union 25 off as a bad experience.

UNIQUE — Although late in 1906, Charles B. Hatfield announced that he would build a car alternately called a Buggyabout or a Unique in Cortland, New York, by the time the car arrived on the market in 1907 it had been renamed a Hatfield, and Hatfield himself had moved to Miamisburg, Ohio. Refer to Hatfield.

1903 Unique, runabout, WLB

UNIQUE — **Detroit, Michigan** — **(1903-1904)** — Philip Bingman called the car he built in Detroit in 1903-1904 a Unique — and it was that. It was the only one he built. Its engine was a single-cylinder water-cooled four-stroke, its transmission was planetary, its body was plywood, and wire wheels were fitted. Because Bingman made extra parts for the car, he may have envisioned building others but he does not seem to have done so. Possibly the extra parts were for the purpose of eventual replacement, Bingman wisely thinking ahead.

UNITED — The United Auto Company of Newark, New Jersey was organized during the spring of 1910 with a capital stock of $100,000 to manufacture and deal in automobiles. Incorporators were Samuel H. Levy, Joseph Sonnabend and Philip J. Schotland. Manufacture is doubted.

The United Horse Subduer Company of New York City was organized early in 1910 with a capital stock of $50,000 to manufacture and deal in electric vehicles. Incorporators were P.J. Minck of Brooklyn, J.A. Marin of Manhattan and W.A. Cooper of Jersey City, New Jersey. Manufacture, alas, is doubted.

The United Motor Company of New York City was organized during the summer of 1908 with a capital stock of $100,000 for the manufacture of engines, cars and carriages. Incorporators were H.E. Tobey and C.W. Cuthell. Manufacture is doubted.

The United Motor Corporation of Pawtucket, Rhode Island marketed the automobiles built in the James W. Brown Company factory in that same city from 1903-1904. The cars were sold, however, under the trade-

name of Cameron. This was the famous air-cooled car which was built in divers locations from 1903 into 1920. Refer to Cameron.

The United Motor & Vehicle Company of Boston, Massachusetts produced a steam car called the Ormond Steamer from 1904-1905. Refer to Ormond Steamer.

The United Motors Company of Camden, New Jersey was organized early in 1912 with a capital stock of $125,000 for the manufacture of motor cars. Incorporators were M.N. Carroll, W.B. MacDonald and H. Berger. Manufacture is doubted.

The United Motors Company of Chicago, Illinois was organized during the fall of 1909 with a capital stock of $5000 for the manufacture of automobiles. Incorporators were William F. Gray, George I. Derr and D.B. Cole. Manufacture is doubted.

The United Owners' Supply Company of Philadelphia, Pennsylvania was organized early in 1918 with a capital stock of $200,000 for the manufacture of automobiles and motor vehicles of all kinds. Incorporators were J. Berliner, P. Zak and B.F. Cowan. Manufacture is doubted.

The United Products Corporation of Grand Rapids, Michigan was organized late in 1919 with a capital stock of $1000 to manufacture and deal in automobiles and trucks. Incorporators were R.A. Bowman, Walter F. Whitman and N. Beal Kelly. Manufacture is doubted.

1914 United, model A, 2-pass. roadster, WLB

UNITED — **Detroit, Michigan** — **(1914)** — In 1914 the National United Service Company of Detroit produced a cyclecar which it marketed under the name of United. The United was powered by a four-cylinder 12 hp engine fitted into a 96-inch wheelbase chassis, with friction transmission and final drive by chain. The tread was 40 inches. Both a $395 roadster and a $425 light delivery were offered. In addition to producing the United and another cyclecar called the Arrow, the National United Service Company also served as the marketing agency for the Beisel manufactured in Monroe (Michigan) and the Arrow manufactured in Dayton (Ohio).

1901 United Power, victoria top phaeton, HAC

UNITED POWER — **New York, New York** — **(1901)** — The United Power Vehicle Company was a million-dollar incorporation succeeding the American Automobile Company. W. Myron Reynolds was president, Louie J. Harris general manager and mechanical engineer, and James McNab treasurer of this new venture which was announced early in 1901. The company produced a large catalog which indicated its forthcoming production of runabouts, dos-a-dos, surreys and victorias to be provided with the customer's choice of steam, gasoline or electric power. Typical prices were $650 for runabout, $900 for dos-a-dos. Delivery wagons and trucks at $1500-$2000 were also promised, as was a "Palatial Coach" — and it was ornately that — to seat sixty passengers. An example of the latter, Reynolds said, was being built for the Pan-American Exposition. How many United Power vehicles were ultimately produced remains a mystery, but there was some production. The general offices of the company were at 35 Nassau Street in the Financial District of New York City, with the firm's "warerooms" at the corner of Fifth Avenue and 17th Street. The United

Power steam cars were built in the former Klock factory in Stamford, Connecticut, its gasoline cars were put together in an unnamed Springfield, Massachusetts plant, and a factory leased by United Power in Rutland, Vermont was used for electric car assembly. The United Power venture was short-lived. Most probably, the International Power Vehicle Company which was subsequently organized during 1903 in Stamford, Connecticut and used the Klock factory address was an attempt to revive the original venture. No production at all seems to have come of it.

1914 UNITED
Model A — 4-cyl., 12 hp, 96" wb

	FP	5	4	3	2	1
Roadster-2P	395	1800	2800	4000	6200	13,000
Light Delivery	425	1500	2500	3600	5500	11,000

UNITED — Greensburg, Indiana — (1919-1920) — The United Engineering Company was organized in Greensburg during the summer of 1919 to manufacture and assemble chassis for automobiles. Incorporators were W.S. Reed, Frank Hamilton and Will G. Smiley. United Engineering did not market complete cars but sold its chassis to any automotive entrepreneur whose idea of an assembled car was one that someone else had assembled. The United chassis, which carried the designation Model G-58, featured a four-cylinder Herschell-Spillman engine, Carter carburetor, Berling magneto, Dyneto electrics, Bendix starter drive, Prest-O-Lite battery, Borg & Beck clutch, Muncie transmission, Peru rear axle and Stewart speedometer. United is not believed to have put all these parts together for more than a year. W.S. Reed's earlier automotive adventure (the Massillon in 1909) had been equally short-lived.

UNITED STATES — The United States Automotor Company of Jersey City, New Jersey was organized late in 1899 with a $1 million capital stock for the manufacture of automobiles. Charles O. Troll, Louis J. Frey and Frederick W. Hotchkiss were the incorporators. Manufacture is doubted.

The United States Carriage Company of Columbus, Ohio built an automobile marketed under the tradename of Great Eagle from 1910-1915. Refer to Great Eagle.

The United States Carriage Company of Andover, Maine was one of two ventures organized at the turn of the century to produce the car designed by Tom French. Refer to French Steamer.

The United States Mobile and Power Company was organized in 1901 for manufacture of a steam carriage designed by William E. Taft. Refer to Taft.

The United States Motor Company of Pittsburgh, Pennsylvania was indicated as an automobile manufacture in the Hiscox book *Horseless Vehicles, Automobiles, Motor Cycles* published in 1900. Documentation is lacking. The firm, which Pittsburgh city directories of the period list at 5917 Penn Avenue, was headed by Daniel McConvill and Thomas Cochran.

The United States Motor Company of New York City was born in 1910 and was an attempt by Benjamin Briscoe to produce an automobile conglomerate similar to General Motors, which had been founded two years before. Amongst other ancillary companies bought or acquired by Briscoe for his new empire were the Alden-Sampsen Manufacturing Company of Detroit, the Brush Runabout Company of Detroit, the Columbia Motor Car Company of Hartford (Connecticut), the Dayton Motor Car Company (producers of the Stoddard-Dayton in Dayton, Ohio), and the Maxwell-Briscoe Motor Company of Tarrytown, New York. The Titan taxicab was also produced by U.S. Motor itself. The United States Motor Company was placed in the hands of receivers on September 12th, 1912.

The United States Motor Carriage Company of Cleveland, Ohio was organized during the spring of 1898 with a capital stock of $25,000. That fall the firm was reported to be undergoing a reorganization. Manufacture is doubted.

1899 United States, gasoline motor carriage, WLB

The United States Motor Carriage Company of Rumford, Maine was one of two ventures organized at the turn of the century to produce the car designed by Tom French. Refer to French Steamer.

The United States Rapid Vehicle Company of New York City was an attempt in 1903 to organize the automobile-building efforts of Charles E. Duryea on a grand scale. Refer to Duryea.

The United States Standard Motor Vehicle Company at 22 Clinton Street in Newark, New Jersey was indicated as an automobile manufacturer in the Hiscox book *Horseless Vehicles. Automobiles, Motor Cycles* published in 1900. This was the company organized the year previous by

Hugh Stommel. Refer to Stommel.

The United States Tractor & Machinery Company of Menasha, Wisconsin built the Harris Six in 1923. Refer to Harris Six.

The United States Vehicle Company at 1123 Broadway in New York City was indicated as an automobile manufacturer in the Hiscox book *Horseless Vehicles, Automobiles, Motor Cycles* published in 1900. Documentation is lacking. The New York City directory for 1911 lists the firm at 52 Broadway. It had been incorporated during the summer of 1899 with a $25 million Delaware incorporation which, *The Hub* revealed, was "for the purpose of developing the Stackpole and Francesco inventions, and also for the purpose of manufacturing a full line of medium-priced vehicles with compressed air as motive power."

UNITED STATES STEAM — Milwaukee, Wisconsin — (1899) — In September of 1899 it was revealed that C.B. Thompson & Company, Charles Scholl and other local Milwaukee capitalists had incorporated the United States Automobile Company with a capital stock of $500,000. Although initially the plan was manufacture of both gasoline and steam motors and vehicles, this new venture quickly decided to concentrate on steam power. A small road buggy fitted with a condenser patented by E. Detweiler was assembled, and this probably was the only vehicle built. By November of 1899 the firm changed its name to the Wisconsin Automobile & Machinery Company, which built a single steam car too, but thereafter produced engines only. The patent rights to its car were sold to the United States Motor Vehicle Company of New York City.

UNITED STATES — Attleboro, Massachusetts — (1899-1903) — The United States Automobile Company was organized during the spring of 1899 to manufacture an electric car invented by Frank Mossberg. Mossberg owned a big bicycle bell factory in Attleboro, and it was largely his money which financed the venture. The car, which carried the tradename of United States, was a perky little $1000 electric with its motor mounted on the rear axle shaft. "No compensating gear is used," *Cycle and Automobile Trade Journal* reported. "The motor is of a new construction, in which both the field and armature revolve, one of the driving wheels being fastened to the field and the other to the armature, giving the necessary flexibility in rotation of the wheels." Production began in a building near the bell factory, but within a couple of years Mossberg soured on the venture because, as he later lamented, he had put $40,000 of his own money into the company and had been promised more by several Attleboro businessmen who simply reneged. Apparently, when Mossberg pulled out, these businessmen moved to acquire the rights to a gasoline car built by James E. Blake of Attleboro. Now the United States company began producing these cars, though not many nor for long before bankruptcy arrived. This brought Frank Mossberg back. In the meantime he had produced a few cars for the Webster Automobile Company of New York City and now, in 1903, he organized the United States Auto-Motor Company which absorbed Webster and the defunct United States Automobile Company — and into which was brought a new group of Attleboro businessmen. Among them was Homer M. Daggett, Jr., who had bought the parts of four Webster gasoline automobiles which were uncompleted when Webster went to the wall. Manufacture of both the Mossberg-designed electric and the Blake-designed gasoline car moved in the Mossberg bicycle bell factory. Again, Frank Mossberg seems to have involved himself with businessmen loath to deliver on their promises because by year's end he decided to get irrevocably out of the automobile business. Both of these United States companies were incorporated in Pawtucket, Rhode Island, incidentally, though the few cars built in each case were put together in Attleboro.

UNITED STATES — New York, New York — (1899-1900) — The United States Motor Vehicle Company opened offices at 25th Street and Broadway in Manhattan in September of 1899, and spent the next few months buying patents rights to vehicles which had seen little or no production by their inventors. Included among these was the gasoline car designed by W.T. McCullough, the electric of Harry E. Dey, and the steam car developed by the United States Automobile Company of Milwaukee. When production finally began in early 1900, however, only the McCullough gasoline car was produced in both passenger and commercial versions, and very few of either. The United States Motor Vehicle Company focused its manufacture on the McCullough motor principally, which it sold to the trade as a 2 hp one-lunger at $200 and a 4 hp twin at $400.

UNITED STATES — Chicago, Illinois — (1900) — The United States Construction Company of 475 Bowen Avenue in Chicago produced a gasoline engine which was claimed to be without noise or vibration, and which boasted bearings that never needed oiling. Since the company was not in business long, one imagines this wonder engine wasn't much good. However, before exiting the industry, United States Construction built at least several pleasure cars, a few delivery wagons and a 44-passenger "carette" bus.

UNITO — Cleveland, Ohio — (1909) — Sherwood Anderson was the president of the United Factories Company of Cleveland which manufactured buggy tops. For a short period in 1909, the firm also built a high-wheeler called the Unito. The Cleveland city directory for 1910 indicates that the company had by that year elected to remain in the buggy top business and to confine its activity in the automobile field to the selling of other manufacturer's cars.

UNIVERSAL — The Universal Auto Company of East Orange, New Jersey was organized during the summer of 1909 with a capital stock of $50,000 for the manufacture of motor cars and taxicabs. Incorporators were P. Osborne, H.B. Ludlum and W.H. Brearley. Manufacture is doubted.

The Universal Auto Bureau and Supply Company of Pittsburgh, Pennsylvania was organized during the summer of 1910 with a capital stock of $100,000 to manufacture, sell and deal in motor cars and supplies. Incorporators were L.G. Justin, W.G. Crawford and A.M. Binsley. Manufacture is doubted.

The Universal Auto and Motor Boat Supply Company of New York City

1909 Unito, auto buggy, WLB

was organized early in 1908 with a capital stock of $10,000 for the manufacture of motor cars and supplies. Incorporators were W.H. Orth and J.J. Kennedy. Manufacture is doubted.

The Universal Automobile Appliance Company of Chicago, Illinois was organized during the summer of 1908 with a capital stock of $20,000 to manufacture and deal in automobiles and appliances. Incorporators were C. Anred, R.P. Bates and William H. Enrich. Manufacture of a car is doubted.

The Universal Automobile Company of San Francisco was among the ventures with which William J. Woosley tried to launch himself into the automobile business in California at the turn of the century. Refer to Woosley.

The Universal Car Equipment Company of Detroit, Michigan built a car called the Beau Brummel in 1917. Refer to Beau Brummel.

The Universal Manufacturing Company of Martinsburg, West Virginia was organized during the spring of 1914 with a capital stock of $10,000 for the manufacture of automobiles. Incorporators were C.T. Custer, J.B. Carr and G.W. Dixon. Maufacture is doubted.

The Universal Manufacturing and Carbonating Corporation of Buffalo, New York was organized early in 1913 with a $1 million capital stock for the manufacture of automobiles. Henry J. Rosche headed this venture. Manufacture is doubted.

The Universal Products Company of Madison, Wisconsin was organized late in 1918 with a capital stock of $50,000 to "engage in the manufacture and sale of motor cars, trucks, tractors, machinery and other equipment, and the installation of lighting and heating plants." Incorporators were John L. Newman, John L. Bourke and Ethel Lee, all of Madison. Manufacture of a car is doubted.

The Universal Power & Promotion Company of Wilmington, Delaware was organized during the fall of 1905 with a capital stock of $100,000 for the manufacture of automobiles under patents held by C.A.A. Taylor and E.O. Brown, both Wilmington inventors. "The company proposes to manufacture cars in Wilmington," The Automobile reported, "and the company has secured two cars on which the new device is to be tried." In addition to Taylor and Brown, the others involved in this venture were General John P. Donohue, John H. Sehl, A.B. Vernon, Clarence Machlin and H.M. Trysinger, all of Wilmington. Manufacture is doubted.

The Universal Service Company of Detroit, Michigan has been indicated on various rosters as the producer of an automobile in 1917. This seems unlikely. The firm, which was located at 1120 Grand River at Stanton, indicated itself in the 1917 Detroit city directory only as the "builders of Universal motor trucks." Universal trucks were built from 1911-1918.

The Universal Steam Power Company of New York City was organized late in 1901 with a capital stock of $100,000 for the manufacture of automobiles. Directors of the firm were W. Foster, Melvin Seabury and W.B. Overt. Manufacture is doubted.

UNIVERSAL — Denver, Colorado & New Castle, Indiana — (1910) — The Universal Motor Company was originally promoted in Denver although almost immediately announcement was made that the factory would be relocated to New Castle. The man behind the Universal was W.S. Hostetter, who sold $30,000 worth of stock in his company to New Castle residents under contract that the factory would be moved within ninety days. It never was. "Just one day before the statute of limitations expired," as The Automobile later reported, Hostetter was arrested in Indianapolis on charges of "embezzlement, grand larceny and obtaining money under false pretenses."

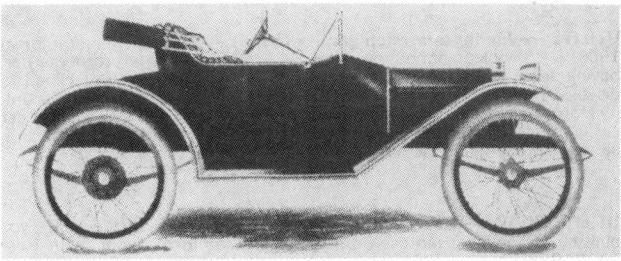

1914 Universal, roadster, WLB

UNIVERSAL — Washington, Pennsylvania — (1914) — Scarcely had the last Croxton left the assembly line of its Washington factory than the first Universal followed. The Universal Motor Car Company was a wholly new venture, with none of the former Croxton people involved. R.M. Patton was president, J.H. Donnan vice-president and J.B. Allison treasurer. The Universal was a light car with a four-cylinder water-cooled 18 hp engine, three-speed selective transmission and cone clutch. It was offered in one body style only, a two-passenger roadster at $475. It did not survive the year. In February of 1915 the Washington factory was sold at sheriff's auction for $25,500.

UNIVERSITY — The University Automobile Company of New Haven, Connecticut produced a small four-cylinder runabout in 1907 which was marketed under the tradename of Continental. The firm's name was changed to Continental as well in 1908. Refer to Continental.

The University Automobile and Boiler Company was organized in Augusta, Maine early in 1902 with a capital stock of $100,000 for the manufacture of "self-propelling vehicles." Charles H. Cobb of Brookline (Massachusetts) and Horace M. Oliver of Newton (Massachusetts) were the men behind this venture. Manufacture is doubted.

The University Motor Car Company of Detroit, Michigan was organized in 1909 for the manufacture of a car to be marketed under the tradename of Varsity. Refer to Varsity.

UNWIN — New York, New York — (1921-1922) — Gabriel Unwin of 305 Broadway in New York City was the man behind the Unwin Motor Car Company. His car was a 22.5 hp L-head four (Unwin's own design) set into a 100-inch wheelbase chassis. Although the Unwin was included in automobile trade journal listings, with complete specs, for both 1921 and 1922, it would seem likely that the car was built only in pilot models. Certainly substantial manufacture never occurred.

UPTON — The Upton Machine Company of 17 State Street in New York City was indicated as a manufacturer of automobiles in a 1904 "Buyer's Guide" section of Cycle and Automobile Trade Journal. This was in error. That address was merely the New York City sales agency for the Massachusetts Upton Company.

The Upton Pump Company of New Castle, Indiana has been indicated as an automobile manufacturer in 1903 on various car rosters. Documentation is lacking.

1903 Upton, Gasoline, touring, NAHC

UPTON — Beverly, Massachusetts — (1902-1903) — The Upton Machine Company in Beverly was organized in 1900 by Colcord Upton, a former merchant seaman, for the manufacture of a planetary transmission he had invented in the late 1890's. A small 3 1/2 hp single-cylinder (De Dion engine) runabout was built that year to demonstrate the Upton transmission and it was exhibited at the first New York Automobile Show in November. In 1901 two more of these cars were built, but for demonstration purposes only. It was not until the summer of 1902 that commercial manufacture of an Upton car began. Joining the one-lunger was a much larger touring car on a 90-inch wheelbase, powered by a four-cylinder 16 hp engine of the company's own design and priced at $3500. But only one such car seems to have been built. In July that year, Colcord Upton left the company. Although the reason is not known for certain, disagreement with his associates is a safe guess, because he took his name with him. In 1904 the Upton Machine Company in Massachusetts revised the Upton car and renamed it the Beverly, which survived for a single year. Meanwhile, Colcord Upton took himself to New York City and subsequently Lebanon, Pennsylvania where he was in production with another car bearing his name in 1905.

1902-1903 UPTON
Four — 16 hp, 90" wb

	FP	5	4	3	2	1
Touring-5P	3500	3700	4700	7300	13,700	26,000

UPTON — Lebanon, Pennsylvania — (1905-1907) — Following his departure during the summer of 1903 from the Beverly, Massachusetts company bearing his name, Colcord Upton initially set up shop in New York City as the Upton Gear Company for manufacture of a new sliding-gear transmission he had designed. At the same time, he came up with a water pump for automobiles which attracted the attention of Milton H. Schnader, who owned the Keystone Manufacturing Company in Lebanon, Pennsylvania and who contracted with Upton to produce the device in his factory. Schnader and Upton quickly decided to build an automobile too, and Upton promptly moved to Lebanon. There the Upton Motor Company was organized on December 30th, 1904, its factory facilities being shared with Schnader's Keystone operation. The Lebanon Upton was a bigger, but less expensive car than the Beverly Upton had been. Its engine was a

Continental four, its wheelbase was 100 inches, and its price $2500. ...ugust of 1906 seven Uptons had been produced in seven months. ...king capital was a problem — it had been a mere $5000 — and con...equently the firm was reorganized that summer into the Lebanon Motor Works with a capital stock of $200,000. Some stock was sold, but not enough to help much. About eight more cars were assembled during the remainder of 1905. The 1906 model was bigger yet, a 40 hp four on a 109-inch wheelbase, with an increase in price to $3000. But the company's problems were bigger too. In January of 1906 the factory was closed for a few days to satisfy a creditor's claim, but it was promptly reopened when a wealthy New York stockholder provided needed funds. Thirty-three Uptons were sold in 1906, one of them a custom-built runabout with two four-cylinder engines mounted back to back for a Rhode Island customer. Another car called the Riviera and designed by Milton Schnader was also built in the factory in early 1907. By the spring of that year, however, both the Upton and the Riviera were no more. A hoped-for contract for the production of 700 taxicabs for New York City had fallen through, and with it all chances of saving the company. Reportedly, the factory was taken over by the Hershey company, and chocolate kisses were made there for a few years thereafter.

1905 UPTON
Four — 30 hp, 100"wb

	FP	5	4	3	2	1
Touring-5P	2500	4400	5600	9200	17,300	31,000

1906-1907 UPTON
Four — 40 hp, 109"wb

Touring-5P	3000	4700	6100	9900	19,000	33,000

UPTON — Bristol, Indiana & Constantine, Michigan — (1914) — This Upton was a light car named for L.H. and J.C. Upton, who perhaps built no more than two demonstrators, though apparently they promoted their venture in two places. The Uptons collected approximately $25,000 from the citizens of Bristol and Constantine for the formation of their Upton Automobile Company, and announced a new one-story factory of 45-by-150 feet was being constructed in the former city. "The general plans of the company are at present being kept under cover," *The American Cyclecar* reported in May 1914. They remained there. Available references from the period reveal the Upton carried a four-cylinder Farmer engine. The wheelbase was 112 inches, overall weight 1200 pounds. The car was to sell for approximately $600.

USBORNE — Detroit, Michigan — (1914) — C.O. Usborne was an automobile salesman who was said to have been traveling for several years in Asia and Australia spreading the "motor gospel" before finally returning to Detroit in 1913 and settling down as a dealer for the Keeton car. With the onset of the cyclecar craze, Usborne decided he wanted in on the action and hastily put together a prototype. As *The American Cyclecar* explained, "He made a cyclecar for a test and used a rope instead of a belt, used pie plates fastened together to provide guides on the wheels around which the rope ran, covered his engine with canvas and did other things so crude that they were laughable." Usborne saw nothing wrong with his cyclecar, though he did admit an error in calling it the Comet since there was already another car of that name in Indianapolis. His plans to establish a factory in St. Louis for manufacture of his Usborne cyclecar quickly came to naught. And, to make matters worse, Keeton was already heading toward the wall in Detroit.

U.S. LONG DISTANCE — Although the firm referred to itself as the U.S. Long Distance Automobile Company in brochures and the United States Long Distance Automobile Company in advertisements, the car it built was always designated the Long Distance. Refer to Long Distance.

1905 UPTON
Four — 30 hp, 100" wb

Touring-5P	2500	4400	5600	9200	17,300	31,000

1906-1907 UPTON
Four — 40 hp, 109" wb

Touring-5P	3000	4700	6100	9900	19,000	33,000

UPTON — Bristol, Indiana & Constantine, Michigan — (1914) — This Upton was a light car named for L.H. and J.C. Upton, who perhaps built no more than two demonstrators, though apparently they promoted their venture in two places. The Uptons collected approximately $25,000 from the citizens of Bristol and Constantine for the formation of their Upton Automobile Company, and announced a new one-story factory of 45-by-150 feet was being constructed in the former city. "The general plans of the company are at present being kept under cover," *The American Cyclecar* reported in May 1914. They remained there. Available references from the period reveal the Upton carried a four-cylinder Farmer engine. The wheelbase was 112 inches, overall weight 1200 pounds. The car was to sell for approximately $600.

USBORNE — Detroit, Michigan — (1914) — C.O. Usborne was an automobile salesman who was said to have been traveling for several years in Asia and Australia spreading the "motor gospel" before finally returning to Detroit in 1913 and settling down as a dealer for the Keeton car. With the onset of the cyclecar craze, Usborne decided he wanted in on the action and hastily put together a prototype. As *The American Cyclecar* explained, "He made a cyclecar for a test and used a rope instead of a belt, used pie plates fastened together to provide guides on the wheels around which the rope ran, covered his engine with canvas and did other things so crude that they were laughable." Usborne saw nothing wrong with his cyclecar, though he did admit an error in calling it the Comet since there was already another car of that name in Indianapolis. His plans to establish a factory in St. Louis for manufacture of his Usborne cyclecar quickly came to naught. And, to make matters worse, Keeton was already heading toward the wall in Detroit.

U.S. MOBILE — In 1901 William E. Taft organized the U.S. Mobile and Power Company in Worcester, Massachusetts for the manufacture of a steam carriage he had designed. Refer to Taft.

1908 U.S. Runabout, WLB

U.S. RUNABOUT — Upper Sandusky, Ohio — (1907-1908) — During the summer of 1907 the U.S. Motor Car Company of Upper Sandusky announced its new car. It was a runabout powered by a four-cylinder 12 hp air-cooled engine, with a three-speed sliding gear transmission and shaft drive featured in a 90-inch wheelbase chassis. The car's frame was hickory, and its price was $750. That fall the company revised its specs to a 96-inch wheelbase, and its price tag up to $900. The U.S Runabout was produced thusly for about six months. Then the U.S. Motor Car Company of Upper Sandusky was no more.

1907-1908 U.S. RUNABOUT
Model A — 4-cyl., 12 hp, 96" wb

	FP	5	4	3	2	1
Runabout	900	2000	3000	4200	6500	14,000

UTICA — The Utica Gas Engine Company of Utica, New York has been indicated on various car rosters as the manufacturer of an automobile in 1900. The firm was in business during this period, but evidence of an automobile being built is lacking.

The Utica Motor Car Company of Utica, New York was organized late in 1905 with a capital stock of $15,000 for the manufacture of automobiles. Incorporators were F.P. Mills and H.H. Mundy of Utica, and G.H. Harris of Chadwicks. Manufacture is doubted.

UTILIS — Rockdale, Illinois — (1907) — During the spring of 1907 the Buckeye Foundry Company of Rockdale announced its forthcoming manufacture of automobiles to be sold under the name of Utilis. Both 12 hp gasoline runabouts and delivery wagons were to be built, with a hoped-for production of four cars a day. Certainly that schedule was never reached, but possibly a few Utilis vehicles were produced.

UTILITY — A car called the Utility has been indicated on various rosters as having been built by the Stephenson Motor Car Company of Milwaukee, Wisconsin in 1910. Documentation is lacking. The firm did build Stephenson trucks from 1910 to 1913 as well as a truck under the Utility name in 1911-1912.

The Utility Car Company of New York City has been indicated on various rosters as the manufacturers of a three-wheeler in 1913. Documentation is lacking. The firm was located at 106 West 30th Street in Manhattan, and it appears that commercial vehicles were its sole product.

The Utility Car Company of Richmond, Indiana has been indicated on various rosters as the manufacturer of an automobile in 1918. Documentation is lacking.

The Utility Motor Car Service Company was organized in Albany, New York during the fall of 1914 with a $3 million capital stock for the manufacture of automobiles. Incorporators were F.R. Hansell, G.H.B. Martin and S.C. Seymour, this trio having incorporated a number of ventures which seemingly produced no automobiles during this period.

UTILITY — Ludington, Michigan — (1909) — During the summer of 1909, A.H. Hopkins announced that he was in work on a prototype car, having secured control of "some new inventions" which he declined to discuss. That fall, in association with Walter Knight, he organized the Utility Motor Car Company and made plans to manufacture his new Utility car in Ludington. His plans appear to be the extent of actual manufacture, although presumably the prototype was completed.

UTILITY FOUR — This was to be a companion model to the Aero-Type built by Victor Page Motors Corporation in Stamford, Connecticut from 1921-1923. Four examples were assembled before the decision against its marketing was made. Refer to Victor Page.

1912 VELIE

Model H — 4-cyl., 40 hp, 115" wb

	FP	5	4	3	2	1
Torpedo Rdstr.	1900	4000	5000	8000	15,000	28,000
Racy Type Rdstr.	2000	4200	5200	8400	15,700	29,000

Model O — 4-cyl., 40 hp, 115" wb

	FP	5	4	3	2	1
Detachable Four-Dr. Rds.	2200	4300	5400	8700	16,500	30,000

Model M — 4-cyl., 40 hp, 118" wb

	FP	5	4	3	2	1
Touring-5P	2200	4300	5400	8700	16,500	30,000

Model N — 4-cyl., 40 hp, 118" wb

	FP	5	4	3	2	1
Torpedo-4P	2200	4200	5200	8400	15,700	29,000

Model L — 4-cyl., 40 hp, 121" wb

	FP	5	4	3	2	1
Torpedo-6P	2750	4400	5600	9200	17,300	31,000

1913 Velie, model 40, touring, HAC

1913 VELIE

Model 40 — 4-cyl., 40 hp, 118"wb

Touring-5P	2000	4200	5200	8400	15,700	29,000
Torpedo-4P	2000	4000	5000	8000	15,000	28,000
Limousine	3000	2700	3600	5300	8800	19,000

Model 32 — 4-cyl., 32 hp, 113" wb

Touring-5P	1350	3900	4800	7700	14,300	27,000

Dispatch — 4-cyl., 32 hp, 113" wb

Roadster-3P	1450	3700	4700	7300	13,700	26,000
Touring-5P	1500	4000	5000	8000	15,000	28,000

1914 Velie, series 9, touring, HAC

1914 VELIE

Series 5 — 4-cyl., 26 hp, 113" wb

Touring-5P	1500	3200	4300	6500	11,000	23,000

Series 9 — 4-cyl., 34 hp, 121" wb

Touring-5P	2000	3500	4500	7000	13,000	25,000
Roadster-4P	2000	3300	4400	6700	12,000	24,000
Torpedo-4P	2000	3500	4500	7000	13,000	25,000

Series 10 — 6-cyl., 34 hp, 126" wb

Touring-5P	2350	3700	4700	7300	13,700	26,000
Torpedo-4P	2350	3700	4700	7300	13,700	26,000
Roadster-2P	2350	3500	4500	7000	13,000	25,000

1915 Velie, town car, Seaman, JAC

1915 VELIE

Biltwel — 6-cyl., 29 hp, 124" wb

	FP	5	4	3	2	1
Touring-5P	1595	3500	4500	7000	13,000	25,
Touring-6P	1645	3500	4500	7000	13,000	25,
Roadster-2P	1595	3300	4400	6700	12,000	24,
Coupe-3P	—	2500	3500	5000	8500	1

Big Four — 4-cyl., 34 hp, 124" wb

Touring-5P	1750	3700	4700	7300	13,700	26,000
Roadster-2P	1750	3500	4500	7000	13,000	26,000
Toy Tonneau-4P	1750	3700	4700	7300	13,700	26,000

Big Six — 6-cyl., 34 hp, 128" wb

Touring-5P	2015	3900	4800	7700	14,300	27,000
Roadster-2P	2015	3700	4700	7300	13,700	26,000
Toy Tonneau-4P	2015	3700	4700	7300	13,700	26,000

1916 Velie, model 22, touring, HAC

1916 VELIE

Biltwel Model 22 — 6-cyl., 25 hp, 115" wb

Touring-5P	1065	3100	4200	6300	10,500	22,000
Roadster-2P	1045	3000	4000	6000	9500	21,000
Coupe	1750	2300	3300	4600	7500	16,000

Biltwel Model 15 — 6-cyl., 29 hp, 124" wb

Touring-5P	1400	3500	4500	7000	13,000	25,000
Touring-6P	1400	3700	4700	7300	13,700	26,000

1917 Velie, touring, OCW

1917 VELIE

"Biltwel" Six-28 — 25.35 hp, 115" wb

Touring-5P	1135	3300	4400	6700	12,000	24,000
Roadster-2P	1115	3200	4300	6500	11,000	23,000
Roadster-4P	1135	3200	4300	6500	11,000	23,000
Coupe-4P	1750	2500	3500	5000	8500	18,000
Town Car-5P	2200	3000	4000	6000	9500	21,000
Tour. Sed.-5P	1685	2400	3400	4800	8000	17,000
Cabriolet-3P	1485	3100	4200	6300	10,500	22,000

"Biltwel" Six-27 — 29.4 hp, 124" wb

Touring-5P	1600	3500	4500	7000	13,000	25,000

1918 VELIE

Model 38 — 6-cyl., 25.35 hp, 115" wb

Touring-5P	1340	3500	4500	7000	13,000	25,000
Roadster-4P	1340	3300	4400	6700	12,000	24,000
Roadster-2P	1340	3300	4400	6700	12,000	24,000
Sedan	1885	2000	3000	4200	6500	14,000
Coupe	1990	2400	3400	4800	8000	17,000
Cabriolet	1800	3200	4300	6500	11,000	23,000
Town Car	2450	3000	4000	6000	9500	21,000

Model 39 — 6-cyl., 29.4 hp, 124" wb

Sport Car-4P	1850	3700	4700	7300	13,700	26,000
Touring-7P	1595	3900	4800	7700	14,300	27,000

1918 Velie, roadster, OCW

1919 Velie, model 39, sport car, HAC

1919 VELIE
Model 39 — 6-cyl., 29.4 hp, 124" wb

	FP	5	4	3	2	1
Sport Car-4P	1975	3700	4700	7300	13,700	26,000
Touring-7P	1825	3900	4800	7700	14,300	27,000

Model 38 — 6-cyl., 25.35 hp, 115" wb

	FP	5	4	3	2	1
Touring-5P	1465	3500	4500	7000	13,000	25,000
Roadster-4P	1465	3300	4400	6700	12,000	24,000
Roadster-2P	1465	3300	4400	6700	12,000	24,000
Sedan	2025	2000	3000	4200	6500	14,000
Coupe	2025	2400	3400	4800	8000	17,000
Cabriolet	1925	3200	4300	6500	11,000	23,000
Town Car	2500	3000	4000	6000	9500	21,000

1920 Velie, model 48, touring, HAC

1920 VELIE
Model 48 — 6-cyl., 55 hp, 115" wb

	FP	5	4	3	2	1
Touring-5P	1885	4400	5600	9200	17,300	31,000
Roadster-2P	1885	4300	5400	8700	16,500	30,000
Speedster-4P	2100	5200	6800	11,300	23,000	36,000
Sedan-6P	2650	2200	3200	4400	7000	15,000
Coupe-4P	2650	2400	3400	4800	8000	17,000

Model 34 — 6-cyl., 37 hp, 112" wb

	FP	5	4	3	2	1
Touring-5P	1585	4000	5000	8000	15,00	28,000

1921 VELIE
Model 34 — 6-cyl., 37 hp, 112" wb

	FP	5	4	3	2	1
Touring-5P	1385	4000	5000	8000	15,000	28,000
Roadster-2P	1385	3900	4800	7700	14,300	27,000
Coupe-4P	2485	2200	3200	4400	7000	15,000
Sedan-5P	2485	1800	2800	4000	6200	13,000

1921 Velie, coupe, JAC

Model 48 — 6-cyl., 55 hp, 115" wb

	FP	5	4	3	2	1
Touring-5P	1885	4400	5600	9200	17,300	31,000
Sport-4P	2200	4700	6100	9900	19,000	33,000
Coupe-4P	2650	2400	3400	4800	8000	17,000
Sedan-6P	2650	2200	3200	4400	7000	15,000
Roadster-2P	1885	4300	5400	8700	16,500	30,000
Touring-7P	—	4700	6100	9900	19,000	33,000

1922 Velie, model 58, touring, HAC

1922 VELIE
Model 58 — 6-cyl., 45 hp, 115" wb

	FP	5	4	3	2	1
Touring-5P	1395	4200	5200	8400	15,700	29,000
Roadster-2P	1395	4000	5000	8000	15,000	28,000
Coupe-4P	2195	2300	3300	4600	7500	16,000
Sedan-5P	2195	2000	3000	4200	6500	14,000

NOTE: Models 34 and 48 were continued with price tags lowered an average of $200.

1923 Velie, model 58, brougham, JAC

1923 VELIE
Model 58 — 6-cyl., 45 hp, 115" wb

	FP	5	4	3	2	1
Touring-5P	1275	4200	5200	8400	15,700	29,000
Roadster-3P	1275	4000	5000	8000	15,000	28,000
Sport-5P	1305	4200	5200	8400	15,700	29,000
Sedan-5P	1795	2000	3000	4200	6500	14,000
Brougham-5P	1795	2200	3200	4400	7000	15,000

1924 VELIE
Model 58 — 6-cyl., 47 hp, 118" wb

	FP	5	4	3	2	1
Phaeton-5P	1275	4700	6100	9900	19,000	33,000
Roadster-3P	1275	4500	5800	9500	18,000	32,000
Sport-5P	1565	4700	6100	9900	19,000	33,000
Silver Swallow Sport	1645	5000	6500	11,000	22,000	35,000
Coupe-4P	1845	2700	3600	5300	8800	19,000
Sedan-5P	1895	2300	3300	4600	7500	16,000
Brougham-5P	1945	2400	3400	4800	8000	17,000
Tour. Sed.-5P	2095	2500	3500	5000	8500	18,000

1924 Velie, model 58, touring, HAC

1925 Velie, model 60, Royal sedan, HAC

1925 VELIE
Model 60 — 6-cyl., 48 hp, 118" wb

	FP	5	4	3	2	1
Phaeton-5P	1225	4900	6300	10,300	21,000	34,000
Club Phaeton-5P	1425	5000	6500	11,000	22,000	35,000
Coach Sedan-4P	1440	2200	3200	4400	7000	15,000
Standard Sedan-5P	1700	2300	3300	4600	7500	16,000
Royal Sedan-5P	1925	2400	3400	4800	8000	17,000

1926 Velie, model 60, club roadster, HAC

1926 VELIE
Model 60 — 6-cyl., 48 hp, 118" wb

Club Phaeton-5P	1450	5000	6500	11,000	22,000	35,000
Club Rdstr.-5P	1650	4700	6100	9900	19,000	33,000
Brougham-5P	1495	2300	3300	4600	7500	16,000
Royal Sedan-5P	1825	2400	3400	4800	8000	17,000
Coupe-3P	1425	2500	3500	5000	8500	18,000

1927 Velie, model 60, Royal sedan, JAC

1928 Velie, model 88, Royal sedan, HAC

1928 VELIE
Model 66 — 6-cyl., 50 hp, 112" wb

	FP	5	4	3	2	1
Touring-5P	—	5000	6500	11,000	22,000	35,000
Roadster-5P	—	4700	6100	9900	19,000	33,000
Standard Sed.-5P	1195	2000	3000	4200	6500	14,000
Metropolitan Sed.-5P	1325	2200	3200	4400	7000	15,000
Coupe-5P	1195	2500	3500	5000	8500	18,000
Two-Door Sed.-5P	1145	2800	4000	6200	13,000	
Model 77 — 6-cyl., 60 hp, 118" wb						
Club Phaeton-5P	—	5300	7000	11,500	24,000	37,000
Special Tour.-5P	—	5000	6500	11,000	22,000	35,000
Special Sed.-5P	1585	2300	3300	4600	7500	16,000
Royal Sed.-5P	1635	2500	3500	5000	8500	18,000
Model 88 — 8-cyl., 90 hp, 125" wb						
Club Phaeton-5P	—	6000	8500	13,000	30,000	42,000
Special Sed.-5P	2095	3100	4200	6300	10,500	22,000
Royal Sed.-5P	2095	3300	4400	6700	12,000	24,000

1929 Velie, model 77, Royal sedan, HAC

1929 VELIE
Model 66 — 6-cyl., 50 hp, 112" wb

Standard Sed.-5P	1165	5000	6500	11,000	22,000	35,000
Metropolitan Sed.-5P	1325	2200	3200	4400	7000	15,000
Coupe-5P	1165	2500	3500	5000	8500	18,000
Two-Door Sed.-5P	1115	1800	2800	4000	6200	13,000
Model 77 — 6-cyl., 60 hp, 118" wb						
Special Sed.-5P	1585	2300	3300	4600	7500	16,000
Royal Sed.-5P	1635	2400	3400	4800	8000	17,000
Model 88 — 8-cyl., 90 hp, 125" wb						
Special Sed.-5P	2095	3100	4200	6300	10,500	22,000
Royal Sed.-5P	2095	3300	4400	6700	12,000	24,000

1912 Vera Six, touring, MVMA

VERA — Providence, Rhode Island — (1912) — Lack of automotive and business experience was certainly not the downfall of the Vera Motor Car Company of Providence, and one is hard put to understand what was. The car was a big 50 hp six offered as a touring and roadster — and jointly designed by H.J. Willard, who was a veteran of Alco, and F.V. Cooke, whose former allegiance had been Packard. President of the company was Johns H. Congdon of the Congdon & Carpenter Company of Providence; vice-president and general manager was S.J. Greene, the treasurer of the Eastern Coal Company of Providence; secretary and treasurer was F.D.

immons, who was Eastern Coal's president. Production and testing of the
era was in the charge of William J. Harris, who had been the man in
arge of Alco's formidable race cars. The Vera was an altogether admira-
 automobile, and very pleasing of line. "It is well nigh noiseless, being
enced admirably," *The Automobile Journal* reported in March 1912. "It
ay be driven on second speed without evidence of the operation of the
gearset, so quiet are the gears." Equally as quietly, the Vera Motor Car
Company faded from the scene later in 1912.

VERACITY — From 1903 to 1905 the cars produced by the Smith Automobile Company of Topeka, Kansas were marketed under the name of
Veracity. Thereafter, the cars became known simply as the Smith into
1907, and as the Great Smith from 1907-1911. Refer to Smith.

VER LINDEN — Detroit, Michigan — (1922-1923) — In December of
1922, when he made his initial announcement, Edward Ver Linden was a
former president of Olds Motor Works and had just recently come from a
short sojourn with Billy Durant who was busily engaged in creating his
post-General Motors empire. Now, Ver Linden, he was preparing to
reenter the automobile industry with a light six-cylinder car of his own to
be priced below $1000. "The car has been fully developed," a release to
the trade press read, "and production on it will be started soon after the
first of the year if Ver Linden is successful in buying out the business of a
company now established." Ver Linden preferred that approach to organizing his own firm mainly to obtain a readymade dealer organization.
Whether he was unable to find an established company amenable to his
plan is not known. The Ver Linden was not produced in any case. In February of 1925, Ver Linden received a very attractive offer which he
accepted. He became the president of Pierce-Arrow.

VERNON — The Vernon Motor Company was organized in Newton, New
Jersey early in 1909 with a capital stock of $25,000 for the manufacture
and sale of motor vehicles of all kinds. Incorporators were R.D. Wallace,
W.H. Carey and J.H. Patterson. Manufacture is doubted.

VERNON — Mt. Vernon, New York — (1918-1921) — The Vernon Automobile Corporation came into being in Mt. Vernon in 1918, as an auxiliary
firm to the Able Engine Company, Inc. which had been established in late
1915 for manufacture of four-cylinder and V-8 engines. The Able venture
had been founded by F.D. Dorman, a Maxwell-Briscoe veteran, and George
T. Hanchett, who had been a consulting engineer in Benjamin Briscoe's
ill-fated United States Motor Company. The Vernon car, which would be
powered by Able engines, was the idea of Norton L. Dods. M.E. Cheney
was his chief engineer. The Vernon was introduced in 1919 as both a four
and a V-8, and in a variety of open body styles distinguished by their sporting flavor. Though his company seems to have gone under in 1920, Dods
apparently continued to sell vehicles on hand into 1921. Thereafter he
busied himself in the automobile insurance and financing business until
1926 when he returned to the manufacturing field with his next new idea,
a car called the Cavalier.

1919 VERNON
Model 419 — 4-cyl., 15.6 hp, 103" wb

	FP	5	4	3	2	1
Clubster-4P	675	2400	3400	4800	8000	17,000
Phaeton-5P	695	2500	3500	5000	8500	18,000
Roadster-2/3P	655	2400	3400	4800	8000	17,000
Raceabout-2P	625	2300	3300	4600	7500	16,000

Model 819 — 8-cyl., 22 hp, 115" wb

Phaeton-5P	1250	2900	3700	5600	9100	20,000
Clubster-4P	1250	2700	3600	5300	8800	19,000
Roadster-2/3P	1200	2700	3600	5300	8800	19,000

1920-1921 VERNON
Model 420 — 4-cyl., 15.6 hp, 103" wb

Tourabout-5P	845	2400	3400	4800	8000	17,000
Chumabout-4P	845	2500	3500	5000	8500	18,000
Runabout-3P	845	2500	3500	5000	8500	18,000
Raceabout-2P	845	2700	3600	5300	8800	19,000

Model 820 — 8-cyl., 22 hp, 115" wb

Tourster-7P	1695	3100	4200	6300	10,500	22,000
Clubster-4P	1695	2900	3700	5600	9100	20,000
Sportster-5P	1695	3200	4300	6500	11,000	23,000
Roadster-3P	1695	3100	4200	6300	10,500	22,000
Speedster-2P	1695	4200	5200	8400	15,700	29,000

1911 Vernon 30, touring, MVMA

VERNON 30 — Detroit, Michigan — (1911) — The Vernon 30 was born of
the Detroit-Dearborn. As the latter company was proceeding to the wall in
1910, its assets were purchased by Vernon C. Fry, who believed he had
the answer to the Detroit-Dearborn's problem. The Vernon 30 offered
practically the same specifications, but it was priced $400 less. Its four-
cylinder engine gave away just five horsepower to the former 35 hp Dear-

born-Detroit, the wheelbase was the same 112 inches, and the chassis
was provided a wider range of bodies — touring, demi-tonneau, roadster,
torpedo and coupe. At $1250, the Vernon 30 was a fine car. But the Ver-
non Motor Car Company survived no longer than had Detroit-Dearborn.
By March 1911 Fry had sold out to the Huron Motor Company. Vernon C.
Fry's further adventures in other aspects of the industry were also ill-
starred. Probably the potentially luckiest move he had ever made
occurred in 1903, when he became one of the twelve original stockholders
in the Ford Motor Company.

VERRETT — Pine Bluff, Arkansas — (1895) — N.J. Verrett was a
mechanic from Pine Bluff who entered the Chicago Times-Herald Contest
of 1895. Although he didn't make it to the starting line of that event, he is
believed to have finished and tested his car. Few details survive about the
car itself. it was described in *The Horseless Age* as "a general utility wagon
on the bicycle plan, weighing about 500 pounds, and costing about $500."
Although N.J. Verrett didn't follow through with manufacture of his automobile, he did remain in the business, subsequently establishing the Verrett Engine Company in Little Rock. In 1901 *The Horseless Age* noted its
receipt of "a circular calling attention to the Verrett 'shaft engine,' a
rotary recommended for automobiles."

VIALL — The Viall Motor Car Company of 19-21 East 111th Street in Chicago, Illinois was headed by Clarence S. Viall and Roswall A. Viall and produced trucks from approximately 1913 to 1919. That some passenger
cars were also manufactured has been reported, but documentation is
lacking.

VICKERS — Coshocton, Ohio — (1910-1911) — Carl Vickers, the proprietor of the Vickers Repair Shop in Coshocton, completed his first automobile in March of 1910. It was fitted with a four-cylinder two-stroke air-
cooled engine of his own design, and featured a sliding gear transmission
and shaft drive. Its wheelbase was 96 inches — and as a light runabout,
Vickers believed he could manufacture the car to sell at a profit with an
attractive price tag of $650. He convinced E.H. McMasters of nearby Bel-
laire of this, McMasters put up the money, and the Vickers Auto Car Company was organized that May. The factory at the corner of Chestnut and
Second streets in Coshocton, which had formerly been occupied by the
Atlantic Cigar Company, was leased for manufacture. Precisely one year
later, after a small production, the Vickers company was in receivership,
with the court appointing Sheriff McDonald as receiver, this step being
necessary, as *Motor Age* explained, "to prevent the machinery being
thrown into the street by the owners of the building." Apparently they had
threatened to.

1910-1911 VICKERS
Four — 20/24 hp, 96" wb

	FP	5	4	3	2	1
Roadster	650	2300	3300	4600	7500	16,000

VICTOR — The Victor Automobile Company was organized in Ridgefield,
Indiana in November 1906 for the manufacture of automobiles to be marketed under the tradename of Senator. Production continued through
1910. Refer to Senator.

The Victor Engine & Motor Carriage Company was organized in San
Francisco, California during the summer of 1902 with a capital stock of
$100,000 for the manufacture of automobiles. Incorporators were George
E. Hoyt, Charles N. Champion, Charles F. Thompson, Adolph Lorsbach and
Walter Rosie. In 1903 the company address was 305 Market Street, in
1904 the firm moved to 252 Spear Street and indicated itself as producing
engines only. Manufacture of an automobile is doubted. The firm survived
the earthquake, advertising in May 1906 that its doors remained open for
auto repair work and engine sales.

The Victor Motor Car Company was organized in Camden, New Jersey
during the summer of 1910 with a capital stock of $150,000 to manufac-
ture and deal in automobiles. Julia H. Harrington, J.T. Harrington, H.C.
Ochtiebeed, Dr. J.L. Boogher and Herman Boedecker were the incorporators. Manufacture is doubted.

1900 Victor Steamer, runabout, NAHC

VICTOR STEAM — Chicopee Falls, Massachusetts — (1899-1903) — The Overman Wheel Company of Chicopee Falls spent three years experimenting with gasoline engines and finally in 1899 moved into commercial manufacture of an automobile . . . powered by steam. The reason for A.H. Overman's change of mind was never elucidated, except by his comment in 1899 that "steam is by far the best power for motor vehicles." He had become convinced of this by James H. Bullard, who built his first steam car in 1888 in Springfield and obviously was quite persuasive. Harry A. Knox had been the young man in charge of Overman's gasoline car experimentation and had produced three gasoline wagons for him from 1895 to 1898. When Overman made his decision for steam, Harry Knox left to build a gasoline car named for himself. Ironically, this was in Springfield, the town from which Bullard now moved to take charge of Overman's steam automobile department. The new car would carry the same name as the bicycle that Overman had been successfully producing for some years — Victor — and would be offered as a $1000 runabout, a $1085 victoria and a $1500 surrey. Although the Victor was claimed to be the only automatic steam vehicle in the world, it was actually quite similar to many steamers then on the market. Its engine was a vertical 4 hp twin-cylinder; final drive was by single chain. In 1900 Overman sold his Victor bicycle business to the Stevens Arms & Tool Company. Although for a few months he leased the top floor for Victor steam car production, he soon moved out — and J. Frank Duryea moved in to build the Stevens-Duryea. By the summer of 1900 Overman had reorganized his firm as the Overman Automobile Company and leased the Ames Foundry Company plant elsewhere in Chicopee Falls. By November of 1901 about fifty Victor steam cars had been sold. In January of 1902 Overman began building steam water pumps for the Locomobile company of Bridgeport, Connecticut — and this contact led to a close relationship. The first Locomobile gasoline car was designed that year in the Overman plant by A.L. Riker. But it would not be put into manufacture there. Instead, in October of 1902, the Overman Automobile Company merged with Locomobile, and all of its machinery was moved to Bridgeport. The Victor steam car was discontinued early in 1903.

1902 Victor Steamer, runabout, HAC

VICTOR — Dayton, Ohio — (1903) — "The Victor automobile, which is being built by E.E. Euchenhoffer at Dayton, Ohio is made to order only," reported *The Motor Age* in April 1903. "The second lot is now being put through the shops." Details are lacking.

1907 Victor, model A, highwheeler, NAHC

VICTOR — St. Louis, Missouri — (1905-1911) — The Victor Automobile Manufacturing Company of 3936-3940 Laclede Avenue in St. Louis said its highwheeler was "Hand Forged" which made it quite a bargain at $450. Otherwise it was a typical highwheeler with a two-stroke single-cylinder water-cooled engine and friction transmission. "The planetary and other transmissions would be preferable to the friction transmission, but for one very serious drawback," the company advised. "It is impossible to change the speed of the machine from low to high or from high to low, without sharp, sudden jerks that are very annoying to the occupants, and constantly suggesting the motion of a freight train." In 1909 the Victor was given a 14/20 hp air-cooled two-cylinder engine, and the option of solid or pneumatic tires. Prices rose several hundred dollars. In 1911 the Victor became bigger yet, and considerably more expensive, with a four-cylinder 40 hp engine and body styling which had lost the buggy look. The firm — by now renamed the Victor Motor Car Company — failed that year, following the death of its founder and president, Joseph F. Harrington, in May.

1905-1908 VICTOR
Model A — 1-cyl., 6 hp

	FP	5	4	3	2	1
Motor Buggy	450	2000	3000	4200	6500	14,000

This model was renamed the Junior in 1908.

1909 Victor, model C, runabout, WLB

1908-1910 VICTOR
Model C — 2-cyl., 14/20 hp, 84" wb

	FP	5	4	3	2	1
Runabout, solid tire	650	2000	3000	4200	6500	14,000

Model D — 2-cyl., 14/20 hp, 84" wb

Runabout, pneumatic	720	2100	3100	4300	6800	14,500

Model E — 2-cyl., 14/20 hp, 94" wb

Touring, solid tire	750	2200	3200	4400	7000	15,000

Model H — 2-cyl., 14/20 hp, 94" wb

Light Delivery, solid tire	750	2300	3300	4600	7500	16,000

Model G — 2-cyl., 14/20 hp, 94" wb

Touring, pneumatic	800	2300	3300	4600	7500	16,000
Pullman, pneumatic	850	2400	3400	4800	8000	17,000

1911 Victor, model 4-40, touring, NAHC

1911 VICTOR
Model 4-40 — 4-cyl., 40 hp, 112" wb

Vestibule Touring	2000	3500	4500	7000	13,000	25,000
Runabout	1250	3300	4400	6700	12,000	24,000
Touring	1750	3300	4400	6700	12,000	24,000

The Models C/D were continued but on wheelbases increased to 103 inches.

VICTOR — Philadelphia, Pennsylvania — (1913) / South Carolina, Delaware & Pennsylvania — (1914-1917) — No matter where he went, C.V. Stahl didn't seem to have any better luck in getting his car venture going. Perpetual disappointment and the fact that he never changed his car's name from Victor seem to have been the two constants in his star-crossed career. Stahl began at 271 Diamond Street in Philadelphia as the Victor

Motor Car Company in 1913. His car was described in the press at that time as being on "the borderline between a cyclecar and a standard runabout." If it veered from that line, it was toward standard runabout. The Victor was a side-by-side two-seater powered by a four-cylinder 16.9 hp water-cooled engine, with three-speed selective sliding gear transmission and a bevel-driven rear axle. The wheelbase was 90 inches, the tread 52, the price $475, these figures changing to 98, 54 and $500 respectively by January 1914. The added length didn't help the look of the car much, however; it remained rather squatty and bulbous. And the move C.V. Stahl made early in 1914 to Greenville, South Carolina didn't help the fortunes of the car any either. There, Greenville businessmen A.G. Dale and O.K. Mauldin promised financial support and a factory for production of the $500 runabout as well as a $550 touring car. Minimal, if any, production

1913 Victor, 2-pass. runabout, WLB

resulted. Next, in September 1916, Stahl was in Grubbs Landing, north of Wilmington, Delaware, and the new Victor Motor Company was backed with $2 million in capital stock, very little of which apparently was sold. C.P. Grandfield, H.H. Skerrett, Regnault Johnson and W.H. Bischoff were backing Stahl now, but not for long. Later that year Stahl announced that he would try Jenkintown, Pennsylvania next, but he seems never to have made it there at all. His last stop in 1917 was York, Pennsylvania. By now the Victor's engine was up to 32 bhp and its price $795. And C.V. Stahl had to be fed up. Whether any production resulted in York is problematical. *Scientific American* included the Victor Motor Company in York in its list of active manufacturers published in January 1918, but C.V. Stahl had irrevocably called it quits by then certainly.

1914 Victor Cyclecar, roadster, WLB

VICTOR CYCLECAR — Richmond, Virginia — (1914-1915) — Unlike many cyclecars which had a peculiar look all their own, the Victor from Richmond appeared to be simply a large car on a reduced scale. Its wheelbase was 88 inches, and it weighed 600 pounds complete. Friction transmission, vee-belt drive, and a Spacke air-cooled vee-twin were typical cyclecar specifications. The price — $285 — was low, even for a cyclecar. H.F. Bernhard and E.J. Bernhard were the men behind the Richmond Cyclecar Manufacturing Company. Their Victor cyclecar was produced in very small numbers in 1914, and in early 1915 was discounted further. "Owing to change of model 'The Victor' at a sacrifice $245," a *Carette* advertisement read. The new model never arrived.

1915 Victor Cyclecar, roadster, WLB

VICTORIA — The Victoria Motor Vehicle Company was organized in Indianapolis, Indiana during the spring of 1900 with a capital stock of $25,000 for the manufacture of electric cars of all kinds. Incorporators were John H. Murphy, Victor Carman and O.M. Carman. Manufacture is doubted.

The Victoria Motor Car Company of Philadelphia, Pennsylvania announced its purchase for $300,000 of the "old Patterson Mill property in Chester" during the fall of 1914. The mill was to be remodeled into an automobile factory. This venture fell through before that happened, however.

1921 Victor Page, Utility Four prototypes, KM

VICTOR PAGE — Farmingdale, New York — (1921-1922) / Stamford, Connecticut — (1922-1923) — Major Victor Wilfred Page was an inventor, engineer, designer, writer and all-round authority on matters mechanical. His textbooks were used in technical schools throughout the world, and he broadened his automotive experience with work in the aviation field during the First World War. Immediately after the Armistice, he decided to produce an automobile. It would be his second. His first had been built in Providence, Rhode Island in 1906-1907 and it was called simply the Page. This time Major Page returned with his full name, including accent mark. With the first roar of the Twenties, he established the Victor Page' Motors Corporation with engineering and sales office in New York City, factory in Farmingdale, New York, and himself as president and chief engineer. Initially his plans included manufacture of a model to be called the Utility Four, a less expensive version of the Aero-Type, and with a flat-front radiator instead of the Aero-Type's vee. Only four of these cars were built before Page decided to forget about the Utility altogether and concentrate all efforts on the Aero-Type. It had but one chassis of 117-inch

1922 Victor Page, touring, WLB

wheelbase, and one engine, an air-cooled overhead valve four developing 30 bhp. Performance was meritorious, and 30 mpg was guaranteed. Disc wheels were standard equipment, and 6000 to 8000 miles per set of tires was promised. The price range was $1100 to $1750. The car was advertised with a vengeance, usually under the cumbersome title of Victor Page Aero-Type Four. What went wrong? Probably several things. First, trading on the celebrity of the Page name was a principal marketing ploy, but it was done with the subtlety of an avalanche — and must have been offputting to some potential purchasers. Second, the car was advertised as "What Practical Motorists Have Long Been Waiting For," and practicality

1923 Victor Page, coupe sedan, HAC

during the Twenties wasn't overly in demand. Third, and perhaps most important, Page apparently hadn't consulted a textbook regarding the proper running of a business. In October of 1923 some of his stockholders organized a committee to find out what was going on, claiming that although $1.5 million worth of stock had been sold in the three years past, they'd never received a dividend. Allegedly, only a few "sample" cars had been produced. It is known that four Aero-Types and a chassis had been exhibited at the New York Automobile Show in January 1922. Photographs from both the Farmingdale and Stamford plants show production in progress. During the court litigation, Victor Page — who was the innocent victim of his stock seller's shenanigans — testified that fifteen cars had been completed before the trouble began.

1921-1923 VICTOR PAGE
Aero-Type Four — 30 hp, 117" wb

	FP	5	4	3	2	1
Sedan	1750	2000	3000	4200	6500	14,000
Speedster	1250	4200	5200	8400	15,700	29,000
Touring	1300	3900	4800	7700	14,300	27,000
Taxicab	1650	2300	3300	4600	7500	16,000
Depot Wagon	1150	1800	2800	4000	6200	13,000
Light Delivery	1100	1800	2800	4000	6200	13,000

VICTORMOBILE STEAM — Omaha, Nebraska — (1900-1901) — The Victormobile Company was organized in Omaha with a capital stock of $50,000 during the early fall of 1900 by Dr. F.E. Coulter, Dr. W.O. Henry, Gustav Anderson and H.K. Clover. The first Victormobile was completed by year's end. A steamer fitted with a 5½ hp motor and an automatic boiler feed, the car was good for 25 mph, H.K. Clover noting that he had averaged that in three trips from Omaha, one to North Platte, one to Fremont, one to Lincoln. "We will, when we have gotten under fairly good headway, be able to turn out about three Victormobiles a week," he told *The Motor Vehicle Review* in January 1901. If that production was ever reached, it undoubtedly outstripped the demand in Omaha then because the Victormobile Company was out of business by the end of 1901.

VICTORY — Following the San Francisco earthquake and the destruction of its plant in 1906, the Sunset Automobile Company continued production of the Sunset car in a new plant in San Jose under the aegis of the Victory Motor Car Company. Refer to Sunset.

The Victory of 1916 which was marketed by Keep Brothers & Wood of Melbourne, Australia has been presumed an American export car. This may not have been the case. The car was born early in 1916 as the Anzac, that word an acronym for the Australian & New Zealand Army Corps which had covered itself in glory at Gallipoli in France. The Australian government prohibited the Keep Brothers using the name, however, and thus the car was renamed Victory in June. There is no question that its coachwork was entirely of Australian manufacture, and that its engine and chassis components were virtually entirely American. But whether the Victory was an American chassis exported intact to Australia is questionable. An October 1916 issue of *The Australasian Coachbuilder and Wheelwright* indicates that the components for the Victory were imported in unassembled form.

1920 Victory, roadster, WLB

VICTORY — Boston, Massachusetts — (1920-1921) — The 1920 Victory from Boston was a pepped-up and gussied-up Model T Ford. A Rajo head turned the T engine into an ohv four delivering 40 hp, and the wheelbase was extended to either 115 or 120 inches (sources vary) and provided a three-speed sliding gear transmission. Two-passenger roadster and four-passenger brougham body styles were featured, each with disc wheels. The cars were produced by the Victory Motor Company of Boston which introduced its new product at the Boston Automobile Show early in 1920. Production ceased sometime during 1921.

VIDEX — Early in 1903 the Marlboro Automobile & Carriage Company which had been producing a steam car in Marlboro, Massachusetts since 1900, sold out to the Videx Automobile & Carriage Company. Refer to Marlboro.

VIKING — The Viking Corporation was organized in Fulton, New York during the fall of 1917 with a capital stock of $60,000 "to make automobiles, airplanes and conduct a general engineering business." Incorporators

were H.H. Hunter, R.H. Allen and C.M. Allen. Manufacture of a car is doubted.

VIKING — Boston, Massachusetts — (1907-1908) — Arthur R. Bangs was the New England representative located in Boston for the H.H. Franklin Company of Syracuse, New York. In 1907 he decided to get in the automobile manufacturing business himself with a car he called the Viking. It carried a four-cylinder 40 hp Rutenber engine, mounted in a shaft-drive 126-inch wheelbase. A seven-passenger touring car was the only model available, priced at $2500. After establishing his Viking Company during the summer of 1907, he introduced his new car at the Boston Automobile Show early in 1908. Some production followed, but not for long — by the end of 1908 Arthur Bangs had returned to his old job of selling Franklins. In 1912 he attempted to enter producing ranks again with a $25,000 organization of the Viking Manufacturing Company, but this venture seems to have produced no cars at all.

1929 Viking, 4-dr. sedan, OCW

VIKING — Lansing, Michigan — (1929-1930) — The Viking was one of several "in-between" cars introduced by General Motors while the Twenties still roared and the stock market hadn't crashed. It rather resembled, but was cheaper than, the LaSalle, which was the less expensive companion car produced by Cadillac. It was more expensive than the Oldsmobile and was produced by the Olds Motor Works as the new upmarket companion car to the Olds F-28. It was an altogether fine car. Unlike the Olds which was a six, the Viking was powered by an 81 bhp V-8, a 90° unit in which the chain-driven camshaft operated horizontal valves between the cylinder banks, rendering the valves accessible by the simple removal of a cover plate. Although announced in March of 1929 at $1595, the price tag had risen to $1695 by year's end. A convertible coupe, sedan and a close-coupled sedan — all on 125-inch wheelbase — were offered, with deluxe variations available for a few more dollars. The car's emblem was a stylized "V" — to denote both V-8 and Viking. Doubtless had the Wall Street collapse not happened, the Viking would have longer survived. But with the onset of the Great Depression, Olds Motor Works was hard pressed to find sales enough for its Oldsmobile, which was priced at less than a thousand dollars. Continuing to market a $1700 car was no longer logical, and the Viking was discontinued at the end of 1930.

1929 VIKING
Eight — 81 hp, 125" wb

	FP	5	4	3	2	1
Convertible Coupe	1595	3500	4500	7000	13,000	25,000
Sedan	1595	1800	2800	4000	6200	13,000
Close-Coupled Sedan	1595	2000	3000	4200	6500	14,000

1930 Viking, convertible coupe, JAC

1930 VIKING
Eight — 81 hp, 125" wb

	FP	5	4	3	2	1
Convertible Coupe	1695	3700	4700	7300	13,700	26,000
Sedan	1695	2000	3000	4200	6500	14,000
Close-Coupled Sedan	1695	2200	3200	4400	7000	15,000

VIM — Philadelphia, Pennsylvania — (1914) — Vim was the tradename given in 1913 to the commercial vehicles built by the Touraine Motor Company of Philadelphia. In 1914 the firm also built a cyclecar which was given that name, most probably in order to distinguish it from the large six-cylinder Touraine automobiles. Production of the Vim cyclecar has not been documented; possibly it never proceeded beyond a prototype. The Touraine automobile itself was phased out in 1916; the company continued building Vim trucks into 1923.

VINCENNES — The Vincennes Motor Manufacturing Company was organized early in 1910 with a capital stock of $5000 for the manufacture of gasoline engines and motor vehicles in Vincennes, Indiana. Incorporators were W.T. Havill, M.E. Hunter and C.H. Huston. Manufacture of a car is doubted.

1905 Viqueot, touring, WLB

VIQUEOT — Long Island City, New York — (1905-1906) — The Viqueot Company of Long Island City was a subsidiary of the Vehicle Equipment Company, producer of electric V.E. passenger cars and commercial vehicles. The Viqueot was a gasoline car, however, and a very interesting one. Viqueot's president was a man with the delicious name of Hector H. Havemeyer; he was a director of Vehicle Equipment and he also happened to own the factory in Puteaux, France in which the Viqueot chassis would be built. Coachwork only would be added at Long Island City. Four-cylinder engines of 28/32 and 40/45 hp were used in the Viqueot, and the 112-inch wheelbase car featured a three-speed transmission, double chain drive, and cable-operated rear brakes. The Viqueot seems to have been a thoroughly admirable vehicle; its untimely demise was due to the 1906 bankruptcy of the parent Vehicle Equipment Company.

VIRGINIA — The Virginia Automobile Company was organized in Alexandria, Virginia during the spring of 1900 with a capital stock of $100,000 for the manufacture of motor cars. Incorporators were C.A. Lieb, J.B. Lackey, G.H. Harris, C.C. Carlin and L.C. Barley. Manufacture is doubted.

The Virginia Automobile Company of Norfolk, Virginia was organized late in 1904 with a capital stock of $25,000 to buy, sell, manufacture and lease automobiles. Officers were Moses Nushbaum, J. Roy Collins and J.J. Hellelly. Manufacture is doubted.

The Virginia Motor and Machine Company was organized in Petersburg, Virginia early in 1913 with a capital stock of $10,000 for the manufacture of automobiles and parts. Incorporators were W.E. Wells, D.F. Denton and J.B. Andrews. Manufacture is doubted.

Virginia Motors, Inc., which was organized in Lynchburg, Virginia in January 1923, was an attempt to revive the defunct Piedmont Motor Car Company. James T. Driver, formerly of Preston Motors Corporation, was the man who tried to get Virginia Motors moving. But he failed almost immediately, and not a single Virginia car resulted.

1911 Virginian, model A-50, torpedo touring, NAHC

VIRGINIAN — Richmond, Virginia — (1911-1912) — The Richmond Iron Works was a conglomerate of many years standing — an amalgamation of numerous small iron foundries in the area — when in 1910 the firm decided to enter the automotive field with a car called the Virginian. The prototype — a 40 hp four — was on the road in the early fall of 1910, but when the car arrived on the market early the year following, it had been pepped up to 50 hp. The Virginian was a big car, on a 130-inch wheelbase, with three-speed sliding gear transmission, cone clutch and shaft drive. Both a seven-passenger torpedo touring and a four-passenger torpedo roadster were offered, each carrying a $3000 price tag. The Richmond men behind the Virginian were M.A. Finn, H.H. McCurdy, M.J. Francis, W.P. Sessaussure, R. Massie Nolting, W.H. Woody and H.G. Wagner. Their automotive venture went into receivership quite quickly, in February of 1912.

1911-1912 VIRGINIAN
Model A-50 — 4-cyl., 50 hp, 130" wb

	FP	5	4	3	2	1
Torpedo Touring-7P	3000	6000	8500	13,000	30,000	42,000

Model AR-50 — 4-cyl., 50 hp, 130" wb

	FP	5	4	3	2	1
Torpedo Roadster-4P	3000	6000	8500	13,000	30,000	42,000

VIXEN — The Vixen Motor Company was organized in Indianapolis, Indiana during the spring of 1912 with a capital stock of $12,000 for the manufacture of automobiles. Incorporators were F.C. Schmid, W.J. Harris, C.O. Van Horn, S.B. Lindley and D.K. Lindley. Manufacture is doubted.

1915 Vixen, 3-pass. tandem touring, WLB

VIXEN — Milwaukee, Wisconsin — (1914-1916) — The Vixen survived longer than most cyclecars undoubtedly because it was better put together. It was built by the Davis Manufacturing Company of Milwaukee, which had been producing automobile, locomotive and tractor engines for years. A four-cylinder 16 hp water-cooled unit of the firm's own manufacture was used in the Vixen. The car was fitted with a friction transmission and shaft drive; its frame was reinforced ash suspended in front by double semi-elliptic springs, with coiled-radius cantilever springs in the rear. The wheelbase was a long 106 inches, with 36-inch tread, and four models were offered, all priced at $395: a three-passenger roadster, a merchants' light delivery, a two-passenger roadster and a racing monocar. The racing monocar was indeed that, as Vixen proved by dominating the International Cyclecar & Light Car Races held at the State Fair Grounds in Detroit on the Fourth of July, 1914. Harry Davidson triumphed in the 25-mile Free-For-All at an average speed of 51.2 mph. The Vixen was designed by Frank Davis, the head of Davis Manufacturing Company, and was distributed by him in Milwaukee. A Vixen salesroom was also opened at 2007 Michigan Avenue in Chicago, and a good many Vixens were sold there, one to a prominent tailoring establishment for use in a Chicago-to-Los Angeles cross-country trek. That was a lot further than most cyclecars traveled before falling apart. In 1915-1916 the Davis Manufacturing Company preferred to call its product a light car rather than cyclecar. Manufacture was discontinued by January 1917, and Davis returned to its engine producing business entirely.

1914-1916 VIXEN
Cyclecar — 4-cyl., 16 hp, 106" wb

	FP	5	4	3	2	1
Roadster-3P	395	2200	3200	4400	7000	15,000
Roadster-2P	395	2200	3200	4400	7000	15,000
Racing Monocar	395	2300	3300	4600	7500	16,000
Merchants' Light Delivery	395	2000	3000	4200	6500	14,000

VOGEL — The Vogel Car Manufacturing Company was organized in St. Louis, Missouri during the fall of 1909 with a capital stock of $75,000. H.L. Vogel, formerly vice-president of the St. Louis Car Company, was joined in this venture by Charles A. Gutke. The Palace Livery Stable at Garrison Avenue and Olive Street was leased for manufacture, but it appears the Vogel project failed before production began.

VOGT ELECTRIC — Newark, New Jersey — (1900) — More than likely, but a single car resulted from this venture which was organized as the Vogt Automobile Company at 105 Plain Street in Newark in 1900. The partners involved were a businessman named A.G. Vogt and an engineer named F.K. Irving, and the plan was to produce electric cars using Irving's patented system of batteries. Manufacture has not been documented.

VOGUE — The Vogue built in Tiffin, Ohio from 1921-1922 was the linear descendant of the Economy-Vogue of 1920 and the Economy of 1916-1919. Refer to Economy.

VOLOMOBILE STEAM — Brooklyn, New York — (1902) — The New York Motor Vehicle Company was incorporated during the summer of 1900 in Jersey City, New Jersey with a grand capital stock of $500,000 and plans for manufacture in the Worcester Cycle Company plant in Middletown, Connecticut. The company's executive roster included P.H. Flynn as president, Frederick C. Cochen as vice-president, P. Sherwood Dunn as secretary-treasurer, and Thomas F. Flynn as general manager. They didn't get around to doing much of anything until early in 1902 when announcement was made of the forthcoming manufacture of a 1200-pound steam carriage on a 66-inch wheelbase to be known as the Volomobile. The vehicle's double-acting compound engine had been invented by Thomas Flynn and was designed so that it could be run as a single-acting unit as well. Water consumption of only 2/3-gallon per mile was claimed. The carriage was a neat tiller-steering two-seater, although set rather high on flimsy bicycle-type wheels. No meaningful production of the Volomobile was ever embarked upon by New York Motor Vehicle Company. The few cars produced were put together at Thomas Flynn's machine shop in Brooklyn.

1902 Volomobile, steam carriage, NAHC

VOLTA-CAR — New York, New York — (1915-1916) — The Volta-Car was an electric cyclecar produced by the Cyco Letric Car Company of 1790 Broadway in New York City. Its price was $585, which bought a two-passenger roadster or a 500-pound light delivery. The Volta-Car was powered by a 12-cell lead battery and General Electric motor and featured shaft drive. Its top speed was 15 mph, and from 35 to 50 miles could be had on a single charge. Although some roadsters were sold, the Cyco Letric Car Company marketed many more of the light deliveries to small businesses in the Metropolitan New York area. Production was discontinued sometime during 1916.

VOLTZ — The Voltz Brothers — Daniel W. and Edward C. — built carriages at their shop at 814 South Halsted in Chicago, Illinois and operated a garage at 818 Forquer. That they also built automobiles during 1912-1913 was indicated in trade directory references of the period. Documentation is lacking.

VOLUNTEER — The Volunteer Carriage Company was organized in Nashville, Tennessee during the summer of 1905 with a capital stock of $25,000 for the manufacture and sale of automobiles. Incorporators were W.E. Metzger, Eugene Smith, J.D. Blaunton, W.M. Hunt and N.P. Leseuer. Manufacture is doubted.

VROOM — Vroom & Company was organized in Newark, New Jersey during the fall of 1910 with a capital stock of $25,000 to manufacture and deal in wagons and automobiles. Incorporators were Peter Vroom, C.W. Smalley and William Ward. Manufacture is doubted.

VULCAN — The Vulcan Motor Car Company of Detroit, Michigan has been indicated on various car rosters as the producer of an automobile in 1911. Documentation is lacking. No company of that name is listed in Detroit city directories of the period. There was a Vulcan Gear Works in Detroit in 1910. And in 1912 a Vulcan Motor Truck Company was organized in the city for manufacture of commercial vehicles, though it did not pass the prototype stage.

The Vulcan Motor Vehicle Company was organized in Pittsburgh, Pennsylvania during the summer of 1909 for the "manufacture, sale, renting and operation of motor vehicles, and also to deal in motor supplies and accessories of all kinds." Manufacture of a car is doubted.

VULCAN — Painesville, Ohio — (1913-1915) — "Like a thunder bolt from a clear sky, the Vulcan comes as a surprise." That bit of advertising was overdoing it, but the Vulcan from Painesville was a fine automobile. A trim little light car, it arrived in the midst of the American cyclecar debacle, and probably suffered unfairly through guilt by association. The Vulcan was powered by a four-cylinder 27 hp Buda engine and was offered in two wheelbase sizes (105 and 115 inches), with three-speed sliding gear transmission and shaft drive featured in both. Since price tags were under a thousand dollars, and included complete electrics, the cars were fine bargains. But there were financial problems from the beginning. Organized in Painesville as the Vulcan Motor Car Company early in 1913, the firm was reorganized later that year as the Vulcan Manufacturing Company. The car was never built in Painesville, however, but instead in the Sharon (Pennsylvania) factory of Driggs-Seabury, the ordnance company manufacturing a number of cars for other makers in addition to its own during these years. In July of 1914, Alonzo R. Marsh, whose idea the Vulcan was, left the company in a fit of pique and announced that he planned to build another light car called the Caesar. (This car never arrived on the marketplace, and Marsh thereon returned to his native Brockton, Massachusetts where he joined his brothers in another new car venture called the Sterling.) The Vulcan was finished shortly after that. Receivership arrived early in 1915. It was announced later that year that the Vulcan truck would continue to be manufactured, but by October of 1916 it was finished too, as M.E. Crowe moved into the Painesville plant with his Collier Motor Truck Company.

1913-1914 VULCAN
Model 27 — 4-cyl., 27 hp, 115" wb

	FP	5	4	3	2	1
Touring-5P	850	2500	3500	5000	8500	18,000

Model 27 — 4-cyl., 27 hp, 105" wb

Roadster-2P	750	2400	3400	4800	8000	17,000

1915 VULCAN
Model 27 — 4-cyl., 27 hp, 105" wb

Roadster-2P	975	2400	3400	4800	8000	17,000

Model 27 — 4 cyl., 27 hp, 115" wb

Touring-5P	975	2500	3500	5000	8500	18,000

W.A.C. — During the early years of this century the Woodburn Auto Company built cars in Woodburn, Indiana. Although occasionally they were referred to by the company initials, the company name is the more appropriate. Refer to Woodburn.

WACHMAN — The Wachman Auto Manufacturing & Supply Company has been indicated on various car rosters as the producer of an automobile in Detroit, Michigan in 1908. Documentation is lacking. Detroit city directories of the period do not reveal the existence of such a company. There was a Robert Wachman in town, however, who operated a machine shop at 78 Forest Avenue East. Conceivably, he could have built a few cars there. By 1910 he had changed jobs, and was the general manager of the U.S. Auto Supply & Manufacturing Company in Detroit.

WACO-SCHAFFER — During the spring of 1914 *The American Cyclecar* reported that William A. Schaffer of the Waco-Schaffer Motor Company had opened an office in Detroit and was "securing material for the manufacture of a large number of cars for Texas." During the spring of 1915 the Waco-Schaffer Motor Company was formally organized in Detroit with a capital stock of $200,000 to manufacture and deal in automobiles and to produce an automobile engine invented by Schaffer. "Prominent Waco bankers are included among the stockholders," *The Automobile* reported. Manufacture of a car or the Schaffer engine is doubted, however.

1917 Waco, touring, MVMA

WACO — Seattle, Washington — (1915-1917) — The Waco was built in a factory at the corner of Rainier Avenue and Lane Street in Seattle by the Western Automobile Company. Backing this venture were C.A. Cawley, G.L. Grant and S.W. North. The firm was incorporated in September 1915, by which time a prototype car had already been given a test run of 2000 miles. Deliveries began March 1st, 1916. "Washington Metropolis Enters a $950 Proposition in the Fight for Pacific Coast Trade," headlined *Motor West*. The Waco was attractively priced. It was an assembled car powered by a four-cylinder 37 hp engine set in a 112-inch wheelbase chassis. A touring car and roadster were the only models offered, and came equipped with windshield and one-man folding top. Although *The Automobile Journal* carried the Western Automobile Company in its annual listing of manufacturers through 1921, that appears to have simply been a pick-up of data from years previous. Most likely, the Waco venture died sometime in 1917. It is definitely known that C.A. Cawley left the company then, because he turned up later that year in Salt Lake City with another automobile named for himself.

1915-1917 WACO
Four — 37-hp, 112" wb

	FP	5	4	3	2	1
Touring-5P	950	3700	4700	7300	13,700	26,000
Roadster-3P	950	3500	4500	7000	13,000	25,000

WADDINGTON — The Waddington was a British-built gasoline car which was imported into this country, but not manufactured, by the Locke Regulator Company of Salem, Massachusetts. Locke exhibited the Waddington at the Boston Automobile Show in March 1904, and continued importation through year's end. During this period the Locke company did manufacture a car itself, however. Refer to Puritan Steam.

WAGENER — The Wagener Brothers Automobile Exchange of Penn Yan, New York was organized during the summer of 1911 with a capital stock of $10,000 to manufacture and deal in automobiles and other motor vehicles. Incorporators were H. Allen Wagener, John A. Underwood and McClellan Townsend, all of Penn Yan. Manufacture is doubted.

WAGENHAL — The news carried a Cincinnatti, Ohio dateline of August 10th, 1900. "Manager W.G. Wagenhal of the Mill Creek Valley Railway," *The Motor Vehicle Review* reported, "is building a motor vehicle which he expects will attain a speed of 30 miles an hour." Details are lacking.

1913 Wagenhals, runabout, NAHC

WAGENHALS — St. Louis, Missouri — (1910) / Detroit, Michigan — (1911-1915) — In 1910 W.G. Wagenhals was a mechanical engineer already well known for his design of the first successful arc headlight for electric cars and for his invention of the third-rail system then in use by the New York Central Railroad. His idea now was a three-wheeled gasoline car, and he organized the Wagenhals Manufacturing Company in St. Louis for its production in late summer of 1910. A small two-cylinder 14 hp motor was placed crosswise between the two front wheels of the Wagenhals, with the single driving wheel in the rear. Transmission was planetary, final drive by single chain. Wheelbase was 80 inches, tread a standard 56, and the price with open or closed body $690. Although an occasional runabout or taxi would be produced, Wagenhals envisioned his vehicle more marketable as a light delivery car. The first two Wagenhals sold went to a tailor and a florist in Detroit, and Wagenhals himself moved there late in 1910 where he reorganized as the Wagenhals Motor Company in 1911. Sales that year were twenty cars; in 1912 he sold forty Wagenhals, and in 1913 eighty. In the latter year his vehicle attracted the attention of the Parcel Post contractor for Detroit, who purchased five of them. Of the cars built in Wagenhals' factory at 668 Grand River Avenue in 1914, twenty-five were destined for the U.S. Post Office which dispatched them to a variety of cities east of the Mississippi. A $790 electric delivery car was added to the line for 1915, and the gasoline version was uprated to a four-cylinder engine. By now a smaller version was listing at $350. Precisely why the Wagenhals Motor Company moved into receivership in August of 1915 is not known. Its liabilities were indicated as $13,673.

WAGNER — B.T. Wagner of Columbus, Texas built the Zip cyclecar in 1914. Refer to Zip.

The Wagner Cycle Company of St. Paul, Minnesota was listed in the "Buyer's Guide Index" of automobile manufacturers published in the January 1902 issue of *Cycle and Automobile Trade Journal*. There is no evidence that Wagner ever built a car, however. The firm produced bicycles and motorcycles only.

The Wagner Electric Manufacturing Company of St. Louis, Missouri was indicated as an automobile manufacturer in the Hiscox book *Horseless, Vehicles, Automobiles, Motor Cycles* published in 1900. Documentation is lacking. The firm was in existence during the turn-of-the-century period, however, at 2017-2023 Locust.

The Wagner Motor Car Company, Inc. of Rochester, New York was organized during the fall of 1917 with a capital stock of $25,000 for the manufacture of automobiles, supplies and accessories. Incorporators were G.J. Wagner, G.Y. Webster and E.V. Scheely. Manufacture is doubted.

WAGNER — Rochester, New York — (1900-1901) — The Wagner Manufacturing Company was incorporated with a capital stock of $15,000 in the fall of 1900 for the manufacture of bicycles, tricycles and automobiles. The firm moved into the old Punnett bicycle factory at the corner of Prospect Street and West Avenue in Rochester, its initial activity consisting of the production of running gear for other autombile manufacturers and the revision of the Punnett companion two-seater bicycles into single-horse-power motor tricycles which were sold for $300 apiece. By early 1901 the Wagner company was building complete vehicles, finishing a run of twenty steam runabouts in March. The firm indicated that month that two delivery wagons ordered for a local business were in the works, and that gasoline-powered machines would follow by April. Most of the Wagner automobile production was by custom order — and does not appear to have survived 1901.

1913 Wahl, touring, NAHC

WAHL — Detroit, Michigan — (1913-1914) — The Wahl Motor Company was organized in Detroit during the late spring of 1913 by a group of entrepreneurs including George Wahl, Alvan M. Dodge and Joseph Hofweber. Back home in LaCrosse (Wisconsin), Hofweber was also trying to launch a car under his own name during this period, and in fact had made arrangements for its production in the Wahl factory at 3089 East Grand Boulevard. What Wahl itself would be producing there remained unsettled for a short while, as an earlier incorporation had indicated commercial vehicles and subsequent announcements a light car. When the Wahl arrived late that summer, however, it was a medium-sized automobile carrying a 23 hp four-cylinder Hazard engine and offered as a touring and roadster on a 108-inch wheelbase. Shaft drive and a four-speed selective transmission were featured. "Attention, Automobile Dealers, Sell This Car with Your Own Trademark on the Radiator," the company advertised, Wahl congenially willing to sacrifice its ego in supplying dealers desiring to satisfy theirs. The Wahl Motor Company really had no choice. Its capital stock was only $85,000, its cash on hand was dissipated soon. By early fall creditors began complaining. On October 6th, in his garage at the rear of his home in Detroit, George Wahl drank a bottle of carbolic acid. He was thirty-five years old. "Wahl had thrown extraordinary energy into the company . . . ," *Motor World* commented in its report of his suicide. "The only possible cause that can be ascribed for his rash act is that he suffered a temporary mental aberration because of his close application to business." In December, under receivership, the Wahl Motor Company reached a settlement for payment of creditors; in January 1914 the firm proved its solvency, and production resumed. The Wahl price tag had now risen a hundred dollars, to $890. But the business worries that had plagued George Wahl continued to harass Hofweber and Dodge. In February, Alvan Dodge departed to promote his own automobile company. Wahl was declared bankrupt that October. In December its assets were purchased by Albert C. Barley who earlier that year had bought out Halladay and who subsequently would build the Roamer. In 1915 Massnick-Phipps took over the factory.

1914 Wahl, roadster, WLB

1913 WAHL
Four — 25 hp, 108" wb

	FP	5	4	3	2	1
Touring-5P	790	3300	4400	6700	12,000	24,000
Roadster-2P	750	3200	4300	6500	11,000	23,000

1914 WAHL
Four — 25 hp, 108" wb

Touring-5P	890	3300	4400	6700	12,000	24,000
Roadster-2P	890	3200	4300	6500	11,000	23,000

WAITE — Milwaukee, Wisconsin — (1907-1908) — Harry Waite was a field service representative for a Milwaukee farm machinery company when, in 1907, he decided to build an automobile and rented a small store in Milwaukee's south side in which to do it. He was joined in this endeavor by his younger brother John. A two-passenger runabout with a boattail rear deck was their first effort, and it was fitted with a four-cylinder Beaver engine and Harry Waite's own patented version of a friction transmission. After building a couple of more cars in the small store, the Waites decided they were ready for manufacture. Finding the financing to do so proved

relatively easy. The brothers simply approached Samuel Watkins whose Beaver Manufacturing Company has provided the engines for the few Waites thus far built, and the partnership which resulted became the Petrel Motor Car Company. The Petrel was introduced for the 1909 model year and continued in production into 1912.

WALDON — Detroit, Michigan — (1920) — In 1920 Sidney D. Waldon briefly considered entering the automobile field with a car of his own. Already his name had been associated with two of the biggest manufacturers in the field: Packard, for whom he had worked since 1902 and gained considerable renown as a super salesman and energy-charged executive, and the Cadillac Motor Car Company, which had managed to lure him away from Packard in February 1915. Waldon's Cadillac tenure was short, however; with the inevitability of America's entrance into World War I, he joined the Liberty aero engine group and became a supervisor of government aircraft production. When peace came, Colonel Waldon returned to Detroit and designed an automobile. A single prototype was built. The engine was a cast aluminum V-8 with the base of the block flared to the sides of the frame and thus eliminating the need for a sod pan. Its body style was a cabriolet. Several Detroit people were sufficiently interested in the venture to join with Waldon in financing the building of the prototype, but the project was abandoned soon after that. Apparently, the capital for manufacture just wasn't there. There had been no publicity at all about either the car or the venture, which was probably at Colonel Waldon's insistence. He spent the remainder of his life pursuing aviation and philanthropic interests. He died in 1945. The single Waldon automobile built was acquired by the late Barney Pollard during the mid-Sixties.

WALDORF — The Waldorf Automobile Company of New York City was organized late in 1903 for the manufacture of automobiles. F.W. Chapman, L.O. Weilbacher and H.R. Weilbacher were the principals involved. Manufacture is doubted.

1909 Waldron, runabout, NAHC

WALDRON — Waldron, Illinois — (1908) / Kankakee, Illinois — (1909-1911) — Several hundred Waldrons were produced in three years in two factories. The venture began as the Waldron Runabout Manufacturing Company during the summer of 1908 in Waldron, Illinois. It continued in 1909 in Kankakee when Charles Keagle of that city invested in a reorganization of the firm to the Waldron Automobile Manufacturing Company. The product remained the same, a highwheeler offered in several body styles and wheelbase sizes, all powered by air-cooled two-cylinder engines and fitted with friction transmission and double chain drive. The reason for the car's demise according to residents of Waldron, where about fifty of the cars were built, was simply that it was noisy and underpowered and "no good." In November of 1911, the company was reported to be negotiating with Beaver Dam, Wisconsin for removal of its factory to that city. The Waldron died in Kankakee before that happened, however. One E.O. Parker seems to have remained as Waldron's president and treasurer in both Waldron and Kankakee.

1908-1909 WALDRON
Model A — 2 cyl., 14 hp, 69" wb

	FP	5	4	3	2	1
Runabout	500	2400	3400	4800	8000	17,000

Model B — 2 cyl., 14 hp, 80" wb

Surrey	600	2450	3500	4900	8300	17,500

Model C — 2 cyl., 14 hp, 80" wb

Runabout	500	2500	3500	5200	8500	18,000

1910-1911 WALDRON
Model E — 2 cyl., 18/20 hp, 82" wb

Roadster	650	2450	3500	4900	8300	17,500

Model F — 2 cyl., 18/20 hp, 94" wb

Surrey	750	2600	3600	5200	8700	18,500

Model G — 2 cyl., 18/20 hp, 94" wb

Touring	650	2700	3600	5300	8800	19,000

WALKER — "The first automobile built by J. Frank Walker and D.R. Thomas of Joplin, Missouri was recently completed," *The Motor Way* noted in May 1906, "and it is now reported that a company will be organized to build these cars regularly." Manufacture is doubted, however.

The Alfred J. Walker Company of New York City was organized during the summer of 1908 with a capital stock of $4000 to manufacture and repair wagons, carriages and automobiles. Joining Walker in this venture were W.J. Fickling and N.F. Lemmon. Manufacture of a car is doubted. During the spring of 1910 the A.J. Walker-Stoopes Company followed as a $15,000 incorporation to manufacture and deal in carriages, automobiles and bicycles. Stoopes was James C., who earlier had tried without success to build a car called the Crescent in New York City. Again, manufacture is doubted.

1906 Walker, runabout, NAHC

WALKER — Detroit, Michigan — (1905-1906) — The Walker Motor Car Company was organized in October of 1905 in Detroit with a capital stock of $300,000. Charles L. Walker headed the company, and his product was a tidy little runabout on a 78-inch wheelbase powered by a two-cylinder 10 hp engine, with shaft drive and a two-speed planetary transmission. Speeds of up to 25 mph were promised, and the price was $550. "The Walker Runabout is the Candy," ads said. But Charlie Walker was in financial trouble almost immediately. In the late spring of 1906, authorities arrived to close his factory at 109 Fort Street in Detroit, and to remove and sell his machinery. Judgments amounting to $34,915 had been entered against him.

1905-1906 WALKER
Model B — 2 cyl., 10 hp, 78" wb

	FP	5	4	3	2	1
Runabout-2P	550	2200	3200	4400	7000	15,000

1910 Walker Six, chassis, NAHC

WALKER SIX — Detroit, Michigan — (1910) — The car was designed by G.S. Greenlund, who was backed financially by C.M. Walker, an official with the Canadian Club Distillery in Ontario. The pilot model of the Walker Six was shown in Detroit during the late summer of 1910, at which time the Walker Motor Car Company was organized. Production in both Detroit and Ontario was planned. The Walker Six was a T-head which featured thermo-syphon cooling, high-tension magneto and a combination splash/force-feed lubrication. A multiple disc clutch and full-floating rear axle were fitted in the 127-inch wheelbase chassis. The Walker Six seemed a well-put-together automobile, but obviously the plans for its manufacture were not. The car did not proceed beyond the prototype.

WALKER STEAMER — Although initially in March of 1900, Orrin P. Walker named the steam car he built in Marlboro, Massachusetts after himself, he subsequently marketed the car as a Marlboro. It continued in production into early 1903. Refer to Marlboro.

Although occasionally referred to by the name of the man who built it — John Brisben Walker — the steam car produced in Tarrytown, New York from 1900-1903 by the Mobile Company of America was marketed as a Mobile. Refer to Mobile.

WALKER STEAMER — New Albany, Indiana — (1890 et seq.) — In 1890, as a teenager in New Albany, Earl C. Walker built a buckboard on which he mounted a steam engine of his own design. The vehicle scared New Albany residents sufficiently for the town's mayor to ban it from the road, unless a flagman preceded it to give warning. Walker's first steam car went into storage soon after. He built another in 1901, and possibly yet another in 1904, but he never became a steam car builder. Instead he went into the steam-car components business, the Walker Burner he invented being manufactured and sold nationally.

1895 Walker Steamer, runabout, LC

WALKER STEAMER — Bridgton, Maine — (1895) — The Walker Steamer was built by two brothers: Asaph J. Walker, a dentist, and Warren W. Walker, a furniture maker, both residents of Bridgton. It was the latter brother who was the more mechanically inclined, and an article in *The Horseless Age* about a two-cylinder steam engine which inclined him to build an automobile. The plans were sent for, and the brothers built their car. Much redesigning was done. Finally the Walker Steamer, with chain drive to the rear axle and a tiller for steering, was completed; its top speed was 12-15 mph, and the Walker brothers drove their little two-seater carriage for some time thereafter. The car remains in the Walker family to this day.

1896 Walkins Electric, runabout, NAHC

WALKINS — Springfield, Massachusetts — (1896) — L.E. Walkins was a civil engineer from Boston who designed both an electric and a gasoline car in early 1896 for the Self-Contained Equipment Motor Vehicle Company of Dorchester, Massachusetts. Although entered in the Cosmopolitan Race, the cars did not compete there. They were shown at the Franklin Park Exhibition in Boston on the 4th of July, however, and attracted the attention of several capitalists from Springfield. The Bay State Motive Power Company was organized later that summer, with Charles N. King, E. Abbot Todd, George N. Morton and C.W. Mansfield as executive officers. L.E. Walkins was made managing director, and the company revealed that fifty cars would be built to Walkins designs, ten of which would be electrics, ten powered by a compressed air motor, the remainder by gasoline. Both passenger and commercial vehicles were planned. Undoubtedly, considerably less than the fifty cars envisioned were ultimately produced, but it is known that a few of the Walkins vehicles were built.

WALL — Ernest Wall of Chicago, Illinois designed a gasoline runabout in 1903 for which Clyde P. Warner, according to *The Motor Age* that July, was "endeavoring to organize a company for manufacture." There were indications the car might be built in the plant of the Oak Cycle Company in Chicago, but it appears the car was never manufactured at all.

"W.S. Wall of Richmond, Virginia is building a gasoline motor vehicle in which great local hopes are centered," reported *The Motor Age* in October 1899. Subsequently *The Motor Vehicle Review* indicated that the car might be manufactured at the Smith-Courtney Company in Richmond. Manufacture is doubted, however.

WALL — Philadelphia, Pennsylvania — (1900-1903) — The R.C. Wall Manufacturing Company produced gasoline engines, running gear and complete cars at 1334 Race Street in Philadelphia. A small two-cylinder 4 hp, two-passenger runabout was the sole offering initially, which sold for $750 initially, $800 in 1902. In 1903 a three-cylinder 9 hp tonneau & delivery was added to the line, the price tag $1200 each. Both Mr. and Mrs. Wall were involved in the promotion of this Philadelphia company. Scarcely had production begun in 1900 when a fire forced the Walls to seek temporary quarters while rebuilding their factory. *The Motor Age*

1901 Wall, runabout, NAHC

remarked in February 1901 that although "temporarily crippled," the firm was "now on the broad road to prosperity." The company made it to the Philadelphia Automobile Show that year, although not on time. "Despite the hardest kind of work . . . the show was half over before its first vehicle was finished and placed on exhibition," the magazine said. "It is a remark-

1903 Wall, tonneau, NAHC

ably handsome and light runabout." Production continued into 1903, then the Walls turned their talents to the customizing field. Son Alfred Sinclair Wall continued this activity through the World War II. He became famous for his sporty "undercover" work (lowered chassis for boattail Auburns, jutting grilles for Hupmobiles, etc.), and many of his creations bore only scant resemblance to what they had been before Wall got to work. A racing enthusiast, Al Wall was an early member of SCCA. He died, at the age of eighty-four, in 1987.

WALLACE — "It is reported from Rantoul, Illinois that Joseph Wallace, Seeley Gulick and George Brown of that locality are now finishing an automobile of their own design," *The Motor Age* reported in January 1905, "and if it proves satisfactory will try to interest capitalists in the matter of forming a company." Manufacture is doubted.

The Wallace Automobile Company of New York City was organized during the summer of 1912 with a capital stock of $300,000 for the manufacture of automobiles. Incorporators were S.E. Robertson and H.W. Davis. Manufacture is doubted.

The Wallace Brothers Company of New Rochelle, New York was organized early in 1906 with a capital stock of $25,000 for the manufacture of carriages and automobiles. Incorporators were James A. Wallace, W.R. Wallace and Charles E. Malby. Manufacture is doubted.

The Wallace-DeWilde Company of Newark, New Jersey was organized during the fall of 1910 with a capital stock of $10,000 for the manufacture of automobiles. Incorporators were Henry A. O'Brien, John Beekman Wallace and Herbert DeWilde. Manufacture is doubted.

WALLER — The Waller Motor Company of Rutherford, New Jersey was organized early in 1906 with a capital stock of $5000 for the manufacture of automobiles. Incorporators were William E. Waller, Elwood F. Waller and John M. Bell, all of Rutherford. Manufacture is doubted.

WALLOF — That a steam car was built by the E.G. Wallof Machine Works of Minneapolis, Minnesota in 1902 has been indicated on various automobile rosters. Documentation is lacking. That a Wallof Motor Truck Company was organized in 1910 in Minneapolis has been documented, but its total production seems to have been limited to a single truck with an air-cooled two-cylinder engine.

WALSHE — Syracuse, New York — (1899-1900) — The firm of M.E. Walshe & Sons of 117 North Warren Street in Syracuse manufactured electrical appliances — and in 1899 one of the sons, John M., sought to move the company into the automobile field. The Walshe was a small electric runabout, the motor and battery for which were made in the Walshe factory and then shipped to the Cortland Wagon Company in nearby Cortland for attachment to one of that firm's standard horsedrawn wagons. The resulting electric car sold for $500. John Walshe claimed a run of up to eighty miles between charges, which probably was an exaggeration for this early period. "Any person of ordinary common sense will be able to charge it from any place where there is an electric light or arc light," he said. Although gasoline vehicles were promised as well for the near future, these seems not to have arrived. The Walshe automobile adventure did not long survive the turn of the century.

1898 Walter, runabout, HAC

WALTER — New York, New York — (1902-1906) / Trenton, New Jersey — (1906-1909) — William Walter was a Swiss immigrant and a successful manufacturer of candy-making machinery in New York City. In 1898 he became the owner of the first automobile on Staten Island, where he made his home, a three-wheeled voiturette imported from his native Switzerland which didn't satisfy him, so later that year he built his first car, a four-wheeler powered by a two-cylinder gasoline engine, which he put together in the shops of his American Chocolate Machinery Company at 49-51 West 66th Street in Manhattan. He experimented with the car for the four years following, and during the summer of 1902 introduced it on the market as the Waltomobile. In 1903 a 24 hp four — a car of twice the

1901 Walter, touring, HAC

cylinders and twice the horsepower as the original — was added to the line, and the name was changed to Walter, Waltomobile serving only as the company's cable address on stationery thereafter. These cars were made in small numbers through 1903; then William Walter hit the New York Automobile Show in January 1904 with a new car that was a sensation. It was a large and lavish touring car boasting such advanced features as a three-speed sliding gear transmission, shaft drive, wheel steering, steel frame, aluminum body, and a spring clutch which permitted starting the car in high gear. Its engine was a 30 hp four with overhead inlet valves. Its price was $4000. The Walter quickly attracted an elite clientele, "The Aristocrat of American Motordom" became a company slogan, more powerful 40 and 50 hp models followed in 1906. Interestingly, William Walter did not immediately set up a separate producing organization for his Walter car; it was manufactured during these years under the aegis of his American

1902 Walter, touring, HAC

Chocolate Machinery Company in the six-story American Chocolate factory on West 66th, to which the building next door at No. 53 had by now been added. In 1905 Walter finally incorporated the Walter Automobile Company with a capital stock of $250,000. Trade press references from 1906 indicate that approximately fifty Walter cars had been produced annually in New York City. By then a French automobile engineer named Etienne Planche had joined the Walter company. Early in 1906 manufacture of the Walter car was relocated to the former factory of the Consumers Brewing Company in Trenton, New Jersey — and it was revealed that the famed Roebling family had become interested in the Walter car. In 1909 there was a pell-mell rush of events. First, a new car was introduced which was initially announced as a Walter, but its name was quickly changed to Roebling-Planche, and in March it was revealed that only the Roebling-Planche would be built in the Walter factory. During the third week in May came word that foreclosure proceedings had been instituted against the Walter Automobile Company which had defaulted interest on its bonds amounting to $24,000. The week following the Walter Automobile Company became the Mercer Automobile Company. Meanwhile, William Walter returned to his American Chocolate factory in Manhattan where he entered the commercial vehicle field, Walter trucks and fire engines subsequently being built in New York and elsewhere in New York State until 1981. The new Mercer's life in the automobile industry would be considerably shorter, of course, though rather spectacular.

1902 WALTER
2-cyl., 12 hp

	FP	5	4	3	2	1
Touring	3000	2000	3000	4200	6500	14,000

1903 WALTER
2-cyl., 12 hp

Touring	3000	2000	3000	4200	6500	14,000

4-cyl., 24 hp

Touring	—	2300	3300	4600	7500	16,000

1905 Walter, touring, HAC

1904-1905 WALTER
Four — 30 hp, 96" wb

King of Belgium Tonneau	4000	2900	3700	5500	9100	20,000

1906 Walter, touring, NAHC

1906 WALTER
Four — 30 hp, 110" wb

	FP	5	4	3	2	1
Touring	3500	3000	4000	6000	9500	21,000

Four — 40 hp, 110" wb

Touring	4000	3300	4400	6700	12,000	24,000

Four — 50 hp, 122" wb

Touring	4750	4900	6300	10,300	21,000	34,000
Limousine	5500	4000	5000	8000	15,000	28,000

1907 WALTER
Four — 40 hp, 120" wb

Touring-7P	5000	4200	5200	8400	15,700	29,000
Limousine-7P	5800	2900	3700	5600	9100	20,000

Four — 50 hp, 122" wb

Touring-7P	5500	5000	6500	11,000	22,000	35,000
Limousine-7P	6300	4000	5000	8000	15,000	28,000

1908 Walter, touring, HAC

1908 WALTER
Four — 44 hp, 120" wb

Touring-7P	5000	4400	5600	9200	17,300	31,000

1909 WALTER
Model M — 4-cyl., 50 hp, 122" wb

Touring-7P	5000	5000	6500	11,000	22,000	35,000
Cape Top Touring-7P	5175	5200	6800	11,300	23,000	36,000

NOTE: Although introduced as the Walter, the car's name was soon changed to Roebling-Planche.

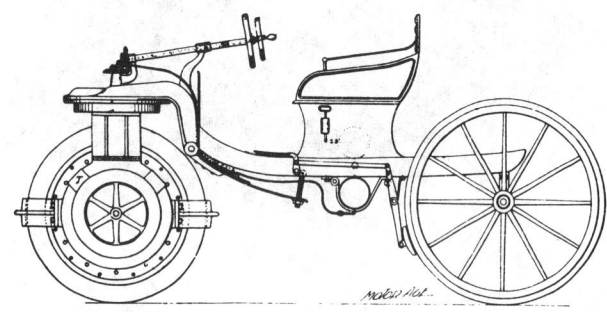

1899 Walters, detachable tractor, NAHC

WALTERS — New York, New York — (1899-1900) — During the late summer of 1899, Julius M. Walters of New York City was granted a patent on what he called a "detachable-tractor." This was simply a single wheel with a self-contained two-stroke gasoline engine. The device was attached to an ordinary delivery wagon and exhibited at the National Carriage and Harness Makers' Convention at Grand Central Palace in New York City that fall. Walters indicated that he was organizing the International Motor Wheel Company to exploit his invention, though he admitted that his idea could not be "considered as final in all its details." By 1900 he had established his International Motor Wheel Company at 302 West 53rd Street in Manhattan, next door to the shop in which G. Edgar Allen was pursuing his automotive venture. There Walters continued development, but most probably no viable production of his "detachable-tractor" resulted. Some years later the same basic idea was perfected by A.O. Smith of Milwaukee, Wisconsin and powered the Smith Flyer, and later the Briggs & Stratton and the Red Bug.

WALTERS — Austin, Minnesota — (1901) — Walters Brothers of Austin was a cycle dealership which announced during the spring of 1901 that it had begun the manufacture of automobiles "in a small way." The manufacture of engines for bicycles was also planned. This activity seems to have been of short duration.

WALTERSCHEID STEAM — Wichita, Kansas — (1902-1903) — In January 1902, C.H. and W. Walterscheid and Alexander Glass, makers of pumps in Wichita, organized the Walterscheid Automobile Company and began building their first steam car. When completed that spring, it was proudly proclaimed by the partners to be the first automobile in Wichita. Now the Walterscheids and Glass stood ready to build lots more. "They are not attempting to make anything revolutionary, having obtained most of their ideas from the machines at present in use," *The Motor Age* reported.

"They simply state their belief that the automobile has come to stay, that they can build as cheaply as anyone else, and that they want to get a share of the profits." The fact that it was often difficult for the owner of a car built in the East to find anyone in Wichita able to repair it was another reason the partners believed their venture would be a success. And it was for a short while, and on a small scale, the Walterscheid Automobile Company building steam cars to order for anyone in the area requesting them.

1898 Waltham, steam runabout, WJL

WALTHAM STEAM — Waltham, Massachusetts — (1898-1902) — John W. Piper and George M. Tinker built their first steam car in 1898. Their employer, Charles Herman Metz, gave them permission to do so and a small corner of the factory in which to do it. The car was a simple buggy with a double reversible engine developing 3 hp. The engine weighed 50 pounds, the copper boiler 110 pounds, the whole package but 600. The car was displayed at the Boston Automobile Show in 1898. Piper and Tinker built two more steamers in the Waltham shops, (which carried the Piper & Tinker name), as well as an Orient Electric which was shown at Madison Square Garden in February 1899. Shortly thereafter the two men left Waltham Manufacturing — with Metz's blessing and encouragement — and struck out on their own, forming the Waltham Auomobile Company. Their new factory was on Newton Street, and they marketed their small steam stanhope at $750. Production was discontinued in 1902.

1898-1902 WALTHAM STEAM

	FP	5	4	3	2	1
Waltham Steam Stanhope	750	2200	3200	4400	7000	15,000

1905 Waltham-Orient, touring, WLB

WALTHAM — Waltham, Massachusetts — (1905-1908, 1922) — The Waltham Manufacturing Company had been organized in 1893 for the production of Orient bicycles, and it was the Orient name that was given to the first automobiles built by the company beginning at the turn of the century. All Orients were small single-cylinder machines, the most famous of which was the Orient Buckboard. The company seemed to be in something of a quandary in 1905 when larger models were added to the line. The cars were referred to as both Orients and Walthams that year, but

doubtless it was felt that the former was well established in the public mind as a buckboard type, and so the name was dropped in 1906. The Buckboard was continued into 1907, but now Orient was merely its model name. Occasionally, the new cars were called Waltham-Orients, which further tended to confuse. There was nothing confusing about the new Walthams, however. Although not as primeval as the Orients, the cars were quite simple, with engines mounted up front, chain drive, friction transmission, and standard runabout or tonneau bodies. From being in quandary, the Waltham company moved to being in disarray. When Leo Melanowski left for Dragon, William Little took over his job as Waltham manager, but he would soon return to his native Detroit to join forces with William C. Durant in building the Little and the Chevrolet. There seemed to be no one heading Waltham now who knew much about cars. The company's founder, Charles Herman Metz, had left years before after disagreeing with his board of directors. During the summer of 1908 he got his old company back, the Watham board having wearied of its continuing financial problems. Metz took the parts on hand, produced the Metz Plan car, and got the company out of debt. By late summer of 1909 he reincorporated as the Metz Company, and all succeeding cars were called the Metzes — until 1921. By that year Metz was in trouble himself. In a desperate effort to save his company, he reorganized in December as Waltham Motor Manufacturers, Inc. The Master 6 that had been sold as a Metz in 1921 was sold as a Waltham in 1922. In August that year it was all over. Charles Herman Metz was in bankruptcy.

1905 WALTHAM
Single — 4 hp, 80" wb

	FP	5	4	3	2	1
Orient Buckboard-2P	375	2300	3300	4600	7500	16,000
Four — 16 hp, 82" wb						
Model E Tr. Runabout-2P	1500	2500	3500	5000	8500	18,000
Orient Light Touring-4/5P	1650	2600	3600	5200	8700	18,500
Four — 20 hp, 96" wb						
Deluxe Touring-5P	2250	2700	3600	5300	8800	19,000
Four — 20 hp, 110" wb						
Orient Limousine	3200	2500	3500	5000	8500	18,000

1906 Waltham-Orient, Buckboard, WLB

1906 WALTHAM
Single — 4 hp, 80" wb

	FP	5	4	3	2	1
Orient Buckboard	400	2300	3300	4600	7500	16,000
Four — 16 hp, 82" wb						
Model K Runabout-2P	1600	2400	3400	4800	8000	17,000
Model L Touring-5P	1750	2500	3500	5000	8500	18,000
Model M Tonneau-4P	1750	2500	3500	5000	8500	18,000
Four — 20 hp, 96" wb						
Model N Touring-5P	2000	2700	3600	5300	8800	19,000
Model R Touring-5P	2250	2800	3700	5500	9000	19,500
1907 WALTHAM						
Model B.R. — 1-cyl., 4 hp, 80" wb						
Orient Buckboard-2P	400	2300	3300	4600	7500	16,000
Model D.C. — 1-cyl, 4 hp, 89" wb						
Waltham Delivery Car-2P	450	2400	3400	4700	7800	16,500
Model E.R. — 1-cyl., 4 hp, 73" wb						
Orient Runabout	475	2200	3200	4400	7000	15,000
Model T.R. — 4-cyl., 16 hp, 82" wb						
Waltham-Orient Rbt.-2P	1250	2500	3500	5000	8500	18,000
Model T.T. — 4-cyl., 20 hp, 96" wb						
Waltham-Orient Touring-5P	1750	2700	3600	5300	8800	19,000
Model D.L. — 4-cyl., 20 hp, 96" wb						
Waltham-Orient Touring-5P	2000	2700	3600	5300	8800	19,000

1922 Waltham, touring, WLB

1908 WALTHAM
Model D — 4-cyl., 20 hp, 96" wb

	FP	5	4	3	2	1
Touring-5P	1800	2500	3500	5000	8500	18,000
Runabout	1750	2400	3400	4800	8000	17,000

Model 17 — 1-cyl., 4 hp, 84" wb

	FP	5	4	3	2	1
Runabout	350	2300	3300	4600	7500	16,000
Rbt. (Model 18, w/rear trunk)	400	2400	3400	4700	7800	16,500

Model 27 — 2-cyl., 8 hp, 84" wb

	FP	5	4	3	2	1
Runabout	525	2400	3400	4800	8000	17,000
Rbt. (Model 28, wheel steering)	600	2450	3500	4900	8300	17,500

Model E — 2-cyl., 8 hp, 84" wb

	FP	5	4	3	2	1
Tonneau-4P	650	2450	3500	4900	8300	17,500

1922 WALTHAM
Six — 45hp, 120" wb

	FP	5	4	3	2	1
Touring-5P	2450	4000	5000	8000	15,000	28,000
Roadster-2P	2450	3900	4800	7700	14,300	27,000

WALTOMOBILE — The first car placed on the market by William Walter of New York City was announced as the Waltomobile in 1902. The tradename was changed to Walter, in 1903, however. Refer to Walter.

WALTON — The Walton Motor Company was organized in Lynbrook, New York during the spring of 1908 with a capital stock of $10,000 for the manufacture of cars and carriages. Incorporators were J.N. Walton, E.N. Smith and G.F. Hickey. Manufacture is doubted.

1902 Walton, runabout, NAHC

WALTON — Neche, North Dakota — (1902-1908) — During the summer of 1902, W.L. Walton built an automobile. It was simply a buggy which he purchased from the J.L. Clark Carriage Company and motorized with a small 4½ hp gasoline engine. According to a report in the *Neche Chronotype* that August, the car was a success. Walton never considered manu-

c.1908 Walton, runabout, JB

facture, though he wrote *The Automobile Review* in 1903 that he had driven his car about 1000 miles in the past year and it "gives very fair satisfaction." Walton built two more cars, each time using the engine that had powered his first. By 1909 W.L. Walton was the owner of a Model T Ford. His last car remains extant in the Reynolds Museum in Alberta, Canada.

1917 Walton Special, roadster, DJK

WALTON SPECIAL — New York, New York — (1917) — The Walton Special began life as a Hudson. It was the idea of Wirt M. Walton, who patented this "ornamental design for an automobile body" in 1917. The Walton Special was advertised in the trade press in January 1918: "Progressive dealers will sell distinctive body styles this spring," the ad read. So far as is known, however, just the one Walton Special was built. The Walton Body Company, which was located at 155 Avenue D in Manhattan, became bona fide automobile manufacturers with another car called the Noma, which was produced from 1919 through 1923. The firm remained in the coachbuilding business until shortly after the Wall Street crash.

1905 Walworth, tonneau, MVMA

WALWORTH — Chicago, Illinois — (1904-1905) — The prototype of the Walworth was on a 76-inch wheelbase chassis, but the car put on the market was stretched to 80 inches. Powered by a two-cylinder 14 hp engine, the Walworth was fitted with a two-speed planetary transmission and shaft drive — and was offered as a rear entrance tonneau at $1500. Aso L. Walworth located his factory at 5110 Calumet Street in Chicago where early in 1905 he suffered a calamitous fire. By early spring the stock and machinery that was salvageable was purchased by George E. Bignall who was said to be "disposing of engines, running gears and other parts at very low prices." The firm of A.O. Walworth & Company quietly faded, and Aso Walworth found work elsewhere in Chicago as a machinist.

1904-1905 WALWORTH
Model A — 2-cyl., 14 hp, 80" wb

	FP	5	4	3	2	1
Rear Entrance Tonneau	1500	2300	3300	4600	7500	16,000

WANAMAKER — At the turn of the century, the Wanamaker department stores in Philadelphia and New York City served as agencies for such divers cars as the Searchmont, Studebaker, Cadillac and De Dion-Bouton. Wanamaker did not, however, ever produce an automobile itself.

1914 Ward, model A-2, roadster, WLB

WARD — Chicago, Illinois — (1913)/Milwaukee, Wisconsin — (1914) —
Since the summer of 1913, Ward Butler of 646 Fullerton Avenue in Chicago had been supplying component parts to do-it-yourself cyclecar builders. At the same time he was completing a prototype for production, which he tested in Chicago late that year. For manufacture he moved north. Early in 1914 he organized as the Ward Cyclecar Company and secured a plant in Milwaukee near the factory where Mack engines were built. The Ward cyclecar was offered as a 9 hp twin and a 12 hp four, both Mack engines, and both mounted in an underslung 100-inch wheelbase chassis with friction transmission and vee belt drive. Though his car's ground clearance was only 7½ inches, Ward Butler declared that this "has not hampered the splendid performance of the car when travelling rough and rutty roads." The Ward's tread was 42 inches, which provided for reasonably commodious side-by-side seating, and the body was well finished. Prices ranged from $375 to $500. Ten cars had been built by late summer of 1914, with a run of a further 100 planned next. The Ward Cyclecar Company failed later that year.

1913-1914 WARD
Model A - 2 cyl., 9 hp, 100" wb

	FP	5	4	3	2	1
Roadster-2P	400	2300	3300	4600	7500	16,000

Model A-2 — 2-cyl., 9 hp, 100" wb

	FP	5	4	3	2	1
Roadster-2P	375	2200	3200	4400	7000	15,000

Model B — 4-cyl., 12 hp, 100" wb

	FP	5	4	3	2	1
Roadster-2P	500	2400	3400	4800	8000	17,000

1914 Ward Electric, coupe, WLB

WARD ELECTRIC — Bronx, New York — (1914)/Mt. Vernon, New York — (1915-1916) — In 1902 Charles A. Ward received an engineering degree from Cornell and returned to Pittsburgh to join his family's baking business. In 1905 he organized the Pittsburgh Motor Vehicle Company for the production of small electric vans that were used largely for the local delivery of Ward bread. The Ward business prospered, and in 1910 the family moved to New York, establishing big baking factories in both Brooklyn and the Bronx. In the latter borough, at Concord Avenue and 143rd Street, Charles A. Ward established a new factory and reorganized as the Ward Motor Vehicle Company. For the first few years most of the vehicles built continued to be employed delivering Ward's "Tip-Top" bread, although there were sales to other New York City businesses. In October of 1913 Charles Ward began offering an electric passenger car too, a four-passenger coupe with a $2100 price tag. Trade press reporters were agreeably surprised by the low dropped frame of this Ward, "only 18 inches from the ground," which was low for an electric, though the result remained boxy looking. The car was shaft drive, and 100 miles between charges was claimed. In 1915 Charles Ward moved the company to 718 South Fulton Avenue in Mt. Vernon, and continued the coupe in production there until the end of 1916, reducing its price for the final model year to $1295, which was very low for an electric. Most likely, this discounting was to finish up cars for which parts remained on hand. From 1917 forward, commercial vehicles were the firm's only product. The company's tradename was changed to Ward-Electric in 1918. Charles Ward died in 1930. Commercial vehicle manufacture ceased in 1937, though the Ward Motor Vehicle Company remained in the truck-body-building business until 1965.

1914-1915 WARD ELECTRIC

	FP	5	4	3	2	1
Coupe-4P	2100	2500	3500	5000	8500	18,000

1916 WARD ELECTRIC

	FP	5	4	3	2	1
Coupe-4P	1295	2500	3500	5000	8500	18,000

WARD LEONARD — Bronxville, New York — (1903) — Harry Ward Leonard was an M.I.T. graduate and a member of the four-man team working with Thomas Alva Edison during his early electric experiments. Moving out on his own in 1892, Ward Leonard, as he preferred being called (he was descended from Artemus Ward, the American Army's first major general, second in command in Washington during the Revolution), established the Ward Leonard Electric Company in Bronxville which prospered in the manufacture of electrical equipment. In 1895 he returned from a trip to Europe filled with automobile enthusiasm. His earliest experimentation, in fact, was with a steamer, in association with steam engineer H.J. Westover. Together they developed a four-cylinder, single-acting steam engine in

1903 Ward-Leonard, tonneau, NAHC

1903 Ward Leonard, roadster, NAHC

1899, but by 1900 Ward Leonard was convinced that the gasoline car held more promise. Together with Westover, he designed a De Dion-engined runabout which was introduced in 1901 as the Century Tourist, joined a few months later by a larger car called the Knickerbocker, which performed very well in the 1902 Long Island Endurance Contest. Only in 1903 did Ward Leonard produce a car bearing his own name, a 30 hp four offered as a roadster and tonneau. The Ward Leonard was the largest of all the cars he produced, and was also the last. By the end of 1903 the Ward Leonard Electric Company abandoned the automobile manufacturing field, citing difficulty in obtaining materials as the reason. Probably H. Ward Leonard was anxious to get on with his other inventions too, most of which would be in the electrical field, including an electric lighting system for automobiles. On February 18th, 1915, while attending a dinner dance at the Hotel Astor in New York City, H. Ward Leonard died suddenly. His death, at the age of fifty-four, was said to have been the result of apoplexy. Obituaries indicated that over 100 of his patents were then in commercial use; he left an estate valued at a million dollars. The company founded by H. Ward Leonard remains in business today in Mount Vernon, New York, the firm having moved there from Bronxville in 1916.

1866 Ware Steam Wagon, JMP

WARE STEAM — Bayonne, New Jersey — (1861 et seq) — The precise number of steam vehicles produced by Elijah Ware of Bayonne has not been determined. "The inventor is confident that his machine can be made a success, as all those he has yet built perform their work admirably," *The Scientific American* reported in 1867. Eighteen sixty-one is believed to be the year in which he built his first steam car, and obviously

1465

at least a couple of others had followed by 1867. "It presents a graceful appearance," *The Scientific American* said of the Ware machine. "The boiler is hung between the forks of a frame of steel which meet on the forward axle and thence backward diverge, holding the boiler suspended in the triangle thus formed . . . The engines work on an incline and drive a shaft with a chain wheel, which by a machine chain, rotates the driving shaft and wheels. The engine is intended to give three revolutions to the first shaft to one revolution of the driving wheels." Of the steam vehicles built by Elijah Ware, one was sold for $300 in 1866 to a Roman Catholic priest in Charlottetown on Prince Edward Island. History does not record an earlier export sale of an automobile in the United States. Father Belcourt displayed the vehicle at a garden party on July 5th, 1866 — and, according to *Knight's Mechanical Dictionary* published in 1877, used the vehicle for some years thereafter.

WARNER — The Warner Automobile Company of Watertown, New York was organized early in 1908 with a capital stock of $10,000 for the manufacture of motor cars and accessories. Incorporators were Charles D. Warner, Albert F. Warner and Lynn M. Thomas, all of Watertown. Manufacture is doubted.

The Warner Manufacturing Company of Dayton, Ohio announced in the early spring of 1900 the completion of drawings of a double-cylinder steam engine of "most improved design" which was soon to be manufactured, in addition to boilers, running gear and complete vehicles. In November the Warner company was taken over by a new venture styled the Dayton Motor Vehicle Company. Refer to Dayton.

1898 Warner Electric, runabout, LC

WARNER ELECTRIC — **Northampton, Massachusetts** — **(1898)** — Lewis E. Warner was the son of the president of the Hampshire County Bank in Northampton and the inventor of an electric carriage in 1898. A small two-seater weighing 650 pounds, its motor was encased in a small box placed just in front of the rear axle with current supplied by a storage battery placed under the seat. "The carriage runs with very little noise," the *Springfield Republican* reported. "There is a soft humming sound which is inoffensive and of which animals are not afraid . . . there is no danger of an explosion." Although manufacture of the car was considered, with price tags in the $800 range, it does not appear this ever followed.

1902 Warner, touring, HAC

WARNER — **Muncie, Indiana** — **(1902)** — In 1902 Thomas W. Warner of Muncie built a gasoline touring car which featured a two-cylinder engine and a side-entrance tonneau body (which was very early for the latter). Manufacture of the vehicle apparently was not considered. Instead its inventor organized the Warner Gear Company, which produced transmission gears, differential gears, steering gears, rear axle parts and the like — and which ultimately became part of Borg-Warner Corporation. Among other companies organized by Thomas W. Warner were the T.W. Warner Company of Muncie, and the Warner Manufacturing Company (of both Muncie and Toledo, Ohio) — all of these firms being merged into General Motors during the Billy Durant era. Subsequently, Thomas Warner organized the Warner Corporation of Muncie, which became part of Durant Motors. His later efforts were in the aircraft industries.

WARNER — **Muncie, Indiana** — **(1903-1906)** — A steering column which performed a dual function was among the innovative features of the Warner. With the column bolt upright, a turn of the wheel started the engine; at an incline, it served to turn the wheels. The emergency brake was so located at the side of the car that, as *The Automobile* said, "when the brakes are off it stands in the way of the operator leaving his place, thereby reminding him to set the brakes, so that inquisitive boys, manipulating the governing mechanism, cannot start the machine should the motor be running." The Warner was a two-passenger runabout with its body bolted in just three places for easy removal and substitution of a light delivery box. It was powered by a single-cylinder rear-mounted engine with planetary transmission and center chain drive. The car was announced in 1903 by the Muncie Wheel & Jobbing Company, and was called the Warner after its designer, and factory superintendent, Hugh L. Warner. Apparently some of the car's innovative features posed problems, because the Warner was not immediately put on the market. Indeed it was not until October of 1905, according to the *Muncie Morning Star*, that the firm really got into gear. Organized now as the Muncie Auto Parts Company, with a capital stock of $15,000, the newspaper reported the plans for manufacture "of automobiles and all parts of automobile machinery." H.F. Quayle, Harvey L. Hooke, Roy Hathaway and Hugh L. Warner were the men involved. Although a few Warner cars were built into 1906, they still caused problems, and in the meantime the partners had a falling out. Early on Hugh L. Warner had left to join the Warner Gear Company elsewhere in Muncie, and Muncie Auto Parts thereafter went on to market a selective gearshift combined with emergency brake that had been invented by Harvey L. Hooke.

WARREN — The electric car built in 1892 for Fiske Warren is more properly designated by the name of its builders. Refer to Holtzer-Cabot.

Although the Warren Electric & Machine Company of Indianapolis built this cyclecar in 1914, it was marketed under the name of Hoosier Scout. Refer to Hoosier Scout.

WARREN — **Providence, Rhode Island** — **(1900)** — Probably the contretemps it caused persuaded Edward C. Warren never to try again. In 1900 he was the inventor of an automobile which one Joseph Leiter agreed to pay him to build: $2000 for the machine itself plus Warren's living expenses while he was perfecting it. The matter ended up in court when Leiter instituted a replevin suit against one Louis Lyons. How Lyons happened to come into possession of the Warren car was not indicated in the press story about the incident, but Leiter clearly wanted it back, claiming that his total payment had been over $4000 and he considered the machine his. Lyons' argument was that Leiter had violated his contract with Warren because he had formed no corporation for manufacture as agreed. The jury agreed with Leiter. He got the Warren car. And Edward C. Warren never built another.

WARREN — **Paterson, New Jersey** — **(1903)** — George I. Warren was a retired machinist from Paterson who built himself a car in 1903 out of two ladies' bicycles and a single-cylinder gasoline engine. "It is not a thing of beauty, but it is said to mote," *The Horseless Age* commented, adding very kindly, "Mr. Warren is an invalid and we hope that in addition to the satisfaction of seeing the product of his handicraft operate as intended he may have the pleasure of enjoying many a refreshing ride in it."

WARREN — **Warren, Pennsylvania** — **(1905)** — H.F. Barnhart was a dentist in Warren who had built his first gasoline car in 1897 in association with his father-in-law C.D. Betts. His dental practice occupied most of his time thereafter, but he continued to dabble in cars, coming up with one in 1905 which he considered worthy of manufacture. He organized the Warren Automobile Company for that purpose. The Warren was a big car with a formidably-sized hood under which was a four-cylinder engine that developed 44 hp routinely, and 49 during some of the company tests. A double side-entrance tonneau was the body style, and $3500 the price. Barnhart provided his car what he thought was a very practical device: an automatic control which was operated via the emergency brake lever and which cut out one, two or three cylinders, as desired. He claimed a fifty percent saving in gasoline consumption could result. But fuel efficiency was not a particularly marketable factor in those days. Dr. Barnhart returned to his dental practice exclusively in 1906.

1905 WARREN
Four — 44-hp, 110" wb

	FP	5	4	3	2	1
Double Side Ent. Tonn.	3500	5200	6800	11,300	23,000	36,000

WARREN — **Detroit, Michigan** — **(1910-1913)** — Homer Warren was a real estate tycoon and the postmaster of the city of Detroit. With John G. Bayerline (former purchasing agent for Olds Motor Works) as general manager, and W.H. Radford (former assistant engineer for Hudson) as chief engineer, he organized the Warren Motor Car Company during the fall of 1909 for manufacture of a medium-priced 30 hp four known alternately as the Warren and Warren-Detroit. Sporting roadsters with round gas tanks on their rear decks were the company's particular pride in 1911, and

1911 Warren, touring, OCW

1912 Warren, model 12-40G, touring, HAC

these cars were raced with an admirable success. Among other events, a Warren 30 won the National Beach Championship in Jacksonville, Florida in March, and in Mexico that April Raul Cueva drove a Warren to Victory in the Monterey Road Race. The flurry of 30 hp models on a 110-inch wheelbase offered in 1911 was revised in 1912 to three different fours on three different wheelbases, and with less emphasis on sporting models. That the company wasn't sure what its manufacturing program should be was reinforced in 1913 when the model lineup was revised yet again, with a new six called the Resolute, the names Pilgrim and Wolverine being given to the two four-cylinder models. Warren prices, which had begun in the $1100-$1250 range, had now risen to $1500-$2600. Warren's financial problems were first disclosed in November of 1912, when the firm was reorganized and given an extension of credit. The Warren company represents an example of a phenomenon peculiar to the industry during its formative years. Early in 1910 John Bayerline had announced the closing of a deal with the Taylor Distributing Company of Philadelphia for the purchase of the entire Warren output in 1910 and for 500 cars in 1911. That an automobile might be manufactured in one part of the country by one company, and distributed hundreds of miles away by an entirely different, and entirely independent, company was not unusual. What happened in Warren's case, probably, was that this lucrative contract was not renewed (possibly the Philadelphia distributing company went out of business), and with no distribution facilities of its own, the Warren company quickly went under. In August of 1913 the Warren factory at Isabella and Michigan avenues in Detroit was sold to the Rands Manufacturing Company to be used for the production of automobile accessories

1912 Warren, touring, JAC

1910 WARREN
Model 10 — 4-cyl., 30 hp, 110" wb

	FP	5	4	3	2	1
Runabout	1100	3100	4200	6300	10,500	22,000
Demi-Tonneau	1250	3200	4300	6500	11,000	23,000

1913 Warren, "Resolute", touring, HAC

1913 WARREN
Resolute Model — 6-cyl., 58 hp, 130" wb

	FP	5	4	3	2	1
Touring-7P	2600	5300	7000	11,500	24,000	37,000
Pilgrim Model — 4-cyl., 40 hp, 116" wb						
Touring-5P	1850	4300	5400	8700	16,500	30,000
Wolverine — 4-cyl., 35 hp, 112" wb						
Touring-5P	1500	4000	5000	8000	15,000	28,000
Roadster-2P	1500	3900	4800	7700	14,300	27,000

1911 Warren, roadster, WLB

1911 WARREN
Model 11 — 4-cyl., 30 hp, 110" wb

	FP	5	4	3	2	1
Touring-5P	1325	3100	4200	6300	10,500	22,000
Dickey Roadster-3P	1200	3000	4000	6000	9500	21,000
Demi Tonneau-4P	1300	3100	4200	6300	10,500	22,000
Round Tank Roadster-2P	1200	3700	4700	7300	13,700	26,000
Inside Side Coupe-2P	1750	2700	3600	5300	8800	19,000
Torpedo-4P	1500	3000	4000	6000	9500	21,000
Fore-Dr. Rd. Tank Rds.-5P	1500	3900	4800	7700	14,300	27,000
Fore-Dr. Rd. TankRds.-2P	1300	4000	5000	8000	15,000	28,000

1912 WARREN
Model 12-30K — 4-cyl., 30 hp, 110" wb

	FP	5	4	3	2	1
Fore-Door Touring	1300	3100	4200	6300	10,500	22,000
Model 12-35 — 4-cyl., 35 hp, 112" wb						
Roadster	1415	3300	4400	6700	12,000	24,000
Fore-Door Touring	1500	3500	4500	7000	13,000	25,000
Model 12-40G — 4-cyl., 40 hp, 116" wb						
Fore-Door Touring	1700	3900	4800	7700	14,300	27,000

1881 Warrington, gas carriage, LC

1467

WARRINGTON — West Chester, Pennsylvania — (1881) — The first horseless carriage in West Chester was built in 1881 by Curtis H. Warrington. It was a three-wheeler powered by common illuminating gas which mixed with air and exploded in the cylinder. The two passengers sat above a weighted bellows filled with the gas, which was admitted to the cylinder through a valve at the forward end. The bellows held from 80 to 100 cubic feet of gas, which Warrington said was good for two hours or more of running at speeds from 10 to 18 mph. "The two-horse engine, with carriage complete will cost $650," he reported in the West Chester *Daily Local News*. "This is no more than the cost of a good pair of horses, and will travel faster and more steady in the hottest weather, at a cost of only 10 to 12 cents per hour. It costs nothing when standing, and is ready for use upon applying a match. It needs no oats, no groom harnessing, no attention, except when in motion." Warrington had every intention of manufacturing his carriage, the prototype of which was completed, patented and operated successfully. Unfortunately, ill health squelched his plans. Only the one car was built.

1901 Warwick, stanhope, NAHC

WARWICK — Springfield, Massachusetts — (1901-1905) — That the Warwick Cycle Company did not enter the automobile industry from a position of strength might be indicated by the fact that this Springfield bicycle manufactory barely escaped insolvency in 1897. Perhaps president A.O. Very saw the coming automotive age as his salvation. The first Warwick runabout was completed in 1900, and its production was launched in early 1901. "Built on Honor" was the new Warwick Cycle & Automobile Company's slogan. Warwicks were fitted with single-cylinder De Dion engines and were priced in the $850-$1000 range. A Warwick was the only car to go the distance in the Labor Day parade in Springfield in 1902. In 1903 Warwick began producing its own 6 hp one-lunger, and its single $1150 model that year was called the Folding Front Seat Car. "The front seat is provided with a rail which not only supports the back and footboard when open," the brochure explained, "but also provides convenient handles to assist in getting in and out of both seats." Warwick models for 1904 were considerably larger: a two-cylinder 14 hp tonneau at $1250 and a three-cylinder 18 hp version at $1750. Trade press references confirm that the Warwick company continued to be plagued by creditors during its automotive period. In the early spring of 1905, A.O. Very announced his retirement from business.

1901 Warwick, stanhope, HAC

1901 WARWICK
One Cylinder

	FP	5	4	3	2	1
Stanhope 3½ hp	850	2000	3000	4200	6500	14,000
Stanhope 5 hp	950	2100	3100	4300	6800	14,500

1902 Warwick, stanhope, HAC

1902 WARWICK
One Cylinder

Stanhope 3½ hp	850	2000	3000	4200	6500	14,000
Stanhope 5 hp	950	2100	3100	4300	6800	14,500
Motor Car 5 hp	1000	2200	3200	4400	7000	15,000

1904 Warwick, tonneau, HAC

1903 WARWICK
Folding Front Seat — 1-cyl., 6 hp, 70" wb

Stanhope	1150	2000	3000	4200	6500	14,000

1905 WARWICK
Two Cylinder — 14 hp, 88" wb

Tonneau-5P	1250	2200	3200	4400	7000	15,000

Three Cylinder — 18 hp, 92" wb

Tonneau-5P	1750	2250	3300	4500	7300	15,500

WASATCH — The Wasatch Manufacturing Company was organized in Salt Lake City, Utah early in 1914 with a capital stock of $100,000 for the manufacture of pleasure cars and trucks. A.E. Young was president of the venture, John A. Maxwell and C.M. Fallas were vice-presidents, J.B. Hamby was secretary, R.E. Montrose was treasurer, and George T. Smith was chief engineer. "The company expects to devote its energies during the first twelve months to turning out trucks," *Motor Field* reported in February. That Wasatch turned out anything at all has not been documented.

WASHBURN — Cleveland, Ohio — (1896-1902) — In 1896 George A. Washburn of 12 Cedar Place in Cleveland told *The Horseless Age* that his automotive idea seemed "to be closer to a solution of a self-contained motor car than any thus far devised." It was a combination of gasoline engine, dynamo, electric motor and storage battery. Up hills, all systems were go; on level stretches, only the engine or electric motor needed to be used; down hills, all systems were disengaged and the car coasted — recharging the battery at the same time. Washburn was building a vehicle to demonstrate this new automotive idea, but whether it was ever completed is not known. Early in 1902 *The Automobile & Motor Review* reported his experimentation with a new car, but provided no particulars regarding it.

WASHBURNE — The firm of C.H. Washburne of Rochester, New York was organized late in 1914 with a capital stock of $25,000 for the manufacture of automobiles. E.P. Washburne and Edward H. Lamb were the incorporators. Manufacture is doubted.

WASHINGTON — The Washington of 1923 from Washington, Pennsylvania never was. Curiously the car was to have been built by the Detroit Motor Company, which was headed by a John A. Barr. But this venture never left the planning stage.

The Washington Auto Company of Indianapolis, Indiana was organized during the summer of 1910 with a capital stock of $10,000 to manufacture, repair, rent and deal in automobiles. Incorporators were A.M. New, F.H. Bruhn, J.N. Contler and F.J. Wallace. Manufacture is doubted.

The Washington Automobile Company of the District of Columbia was organized early in the 1900s with a capital stock of $50,000. Despite this firm's inclusion as an automobile manufacturer in the Hiscox book *Horseless Vehicles, Automobiles, Motor Cycles* published in 1900, it is doubtful that production ever began.

The Washington Automobile Company of Chicago, Illinois was organized during the spring of 1906 with a capital stock of $10,000 for the manufacture and repair of automobiles. Incorporators were Albert J. Brockman, Wilbur J. Wilkins and Leona Barth. Manufacture is doubted.

The Washington Automobile Company of Tacoma, Washington was organized during the fall of 1904 with a capital stock of $10,000 to manufacture, sell and rent automobiles and motor boats. Incorporators were F.L. Stiles, D.A. Young and Harry Hurley. Manufacture is doubted.

The Washington Automobile Company of Washington, Pennsylvania was organized during the spring of 1902 with a capital stock of $100,000 for the manufacture of a car invented by Louis Langan. Joining Langan in this venture were Charles A. Wales, James E. Duncan, C.A. Braden, John A. Howden and C.E. Shutters. Manufacture is doubted. Langan, incidentally, had built his first car prior to the turn of the century in his native St. Louis, Missouri.

The Washington Motor Car Company of Washington, Indiana was organized during the fall of 1906 with a capital stock of $150,000 for the manufacture of automobiles. Frank W. Fowler, Edward W. Strack and J.R. Fowler were the incorporators. Manufacture is doubted.

WASHINGTON — Washington, D.C. — (1901) — J. Sprigg Beale, J.B. Chamberlain and T. Janney Brown were the men behind the million-dollar incorporation of the Washington Auto-Vehicle Company which was organized in 1901 for the manufacture of automobiles and commercial vehicles, in addition to a variety of other self-propelled machines running the gamut from streetsweepers to ordnance tractors. The company's automobiles were to be fitted with Chamberlain's patented variable speed-gearing device, which was described as serving the ''same purpose in the carriages as the feathering propeller blades in a boat.'' The gear lever was also used to apply the brake. Prices were to begin at $350, and all vehicles were to be gasoline-powered. The company took temporary quarters at 511 Ninth Street in Washington, D.C. — but never left there. A few prototypes are known to have been built, but the venture failed soon thereafter.

WASHINGTON — Chicago, Illinois — (1902) — George Washington of Chicago built a turn-of-the-century equivalent of an R.V. His automobile weighed eight tons, required two gasoline engines to propel it at a cruising speed of about one mile per hour — and he used the car as his residence. In January 1902 he reported that he was embarking upon a trip from Chicago to Portland, Maine. It is not known whether he made it.

1909 Washington, touring, HAC

WASHINGTON — Hyattsville, Maryland — (1909-1912) — The Washington was the second car produced by the Carter Motor Car Corporation of Hyattsville. The first was called the Carter, and it had two engines and was the idea of Howard O. Carter. Though providing an automobile with a spare tire was by then not unusual in the industry, providing an automobile with a spare engine was — and obviously it wasn't a particularly viable marketing notion because the Carter two-engine car quickly failed. The Washington, which had only one engine, was the idea of Howard O. Carter's brother, A. Gary Carter. It moved into the Hyattsville factory as the Carter moved out. Many of the workers assembling the new Washington were students at the nearby Automobile College of Washington, D.C., who labored for the Carter brothers in exchange for tuition. The Washington was a typical medium-priced four of the period with shaft drive and three-speed sliding gear transmission. It did not prosper any better than had the atypical two-engined Carter. In early 1912 A. Gary Carter declared the company bankrupt, which led to something of a family spat. Another brother — Frank L., who was company treasurer — announced that the firm was not insolvent and that he had not been consulted prior to A. Gary

Carter's signing of the bankruptcy papers. A family reconciliation had been realized by June, however, when Howard O. Carter announced the formation of the Washington Motor Car Company to take over the Carter Motor Car Corporation. A. Gary Carter was president of that venture, with Frank L. as general manager and Howard O. as advertising manager. Almost immediately its name was changed to Independence Motor Company, and a new line of Independence cars was announced, which did not survive the year's end. In 1913 there was an aborted attempt to revive the venture as the Washington Motor Car Company again. The Carter brothers subsequently became involved in a number of further automotive adventures, including the Harvard (which originated in Upstate New York), the Monarch (which originated in Detroit), and the C.B. and Cartermobile which originated in the ever-optimistic minds of the Carter brothers.

1909 WASHINGTON
Model A-1 — 4 cyl., 30 hp, 112'' wb

	FP	5	4	3	2	1
Roadster-3P	1750	3100	4200	6300	10,500	22,000
Touring-5P	1750	3200	4300	6500	11,000	23,000

1910 Washington, touring, WLB

1910 WASHINGTON
Model A-2 — 4 cyl., 35 hp, 112'' wb

Roadster-3P	1750	4400	5600	9200	17,300	31,000
Tourabout-4P	1750	4500	5800	9500	18,000	32,000
Baby Tonneau-4P	1750	4500	5800	9500	18,000	32,000
Touring-5P	1750	4700	6100	9900	19,000	33,000

Model B-1 — 4 cyl., 45 hp, 112'' wb

Touring-5P	2250	5000	6500	11,000	22,000	35,000
Tourabout-4P	2250	5000	6500	11,000	22,000	35,000
Baby Tonneau-4P	2250	5000	6500	11,000	22,000	35,000
Roadster-3P	2250	4900	6300	10,300	21,000	34,000

1911 Washington, torpedo roadster, NAHC

1911 WASHINGTON
Model D-40 — 4 cyl., 40 hp, 118'' wb

Touring-5P	2250	4700	6100	9900	19,000	33,000
Torpedo Roadster	2250	4500	5800	9500	18,000	32,000
Baby Tonneau-4P	2250	4700	6100	9900	19,000	33,000
Limousine-6P	3250	4000	5000	8000	15,000	28,000

1912 WASHINGTON
Model E-40 — 4 cyl., 40 hp, 118'' wb

Roadster-2P	1750	4400	5600	9200	17,300	31,000
Roadster-4P	1775	4500	5800	9500	18,000	32,000
Touring-5P	1800	4700	6100	9900	19,000	33,000
Touring-7P	1850	4900	6300	10,300	21,600	34,000

WASHINGTON — Eaton Ohio, — (1921-1924) / Middletown, Ohio — (1924) — ''Washington — A Name That Stands for Character and Strength'' was the slogan — and a representation of the first American President (not quite as flattering as the one on the dollar bill) was used in the company's trademark. ''The Ideal of a Nation,'' as the Washington was also known, was not really that, but it was a thoroughly fine assembled car of the period. Its production was the idea of Otto M. Shipley (described in a prospectus as the former manager of Shipley Investment Company) who talked a number of merchants in Eaton into starting an automobile company, including Albert H. Christman, a hardware dealer who became president, and Edward C. Wysong, a mechanic who took the vice-presidency. Benjamin Hagedorn, who was president of the White Star Oil Company of Eaton, was on the board of directors. The Washington Motor Company

1921 Washington, touring, WLB

was incorporated in April 1920, had two Falls-engined test cars on the road that December, and introduced its new product on Washington's Birthday in February 1921, the inaugural car being driven by the local Methodist minister and his wife, dressed as George and Martha. Nine months after that festive opening ceremony, the first Washington was delivered. Its price tag was $1785. Now the engine was a Continental 7-R six (apparently oil consumption with the Falls had been excessive) — and Washington was already in financial distress. Early in 1922 the company announced that it was working up a $1275 economy six, but what the company was really doing was working to stay in business. A weekly output of four to five cars was necessary for profitability — and plans were made for the plant expansion necessary to step up production. The model lineup for 1922 was composed of four open and closed cars priced from $1785 to $2305, all powered by the Continental 8-R six, and all on a 119-inch wheelbase chassis featuring Alemite lubrication, wood artillery wheels, and the fine universal joints made by the Blood Brothers in Kalamazoo. Beveled plate glass was used in all windows. In February 1923 the company announced its purchase of ten acres of land in Middletown for a new factory. More capital was available there. Very few cars were made in Eaton during 1923; indeed the only new Washington built that year may have been the prototype of the Washington Steam Car, which the company planned to add to its product line. "Think of the possibilities of the Washington Motor Company building Gas Cars and also manufacturing a Steam Car, the car that the entire world has been asking for," the prospectus for potential investors pleaded. The steam car was similarly styled, but rather more attractive with disc wheels. Its wheelbase was 117 inches, and its slated touring car price was $1785, the same as the Washington gasoline touring. The steamer's engine was a four-cylinder single-acting semi-uniflow unit, the patents for which had been bought by the company from its inventor, Arnold Larsen. Washington moved into its new Middletown factory in February of 1924; the first car built there, a gasoline model, arrived in June; in September the company began advertising its steam car. Reportedly, three of them were built. Then the Washington Motor Company fell apart, its working capital consumed in the building of its new factory. Bankruptcy was declared late in 1924. Most of the money realized in the sale of the new plant was earmarked for payment of taxes due the federal and state governments. Total Washington production has been an estimated 25-35 gasoline cars and the three pilot steamers.

1921 WASHINGTON
Model B — 6 cyl., 55 hp, 116" wb

	FP	5	4	3	2	1
Touring-5P	1785	5400	7300	11,800	25,000	38,000

1923 Washington, steam car, NAHC

1922-1924 WASHINGTON
Model C — 6 cyl., 58 hp, 119" wb

Touring-5P	1785	5500	7500	12,000	26,000	39,000
Sport	1895	5800	8000	12,500	28,000	40,000
Sedan-5P	2385	2400	3400	4800	8000	17,000
California Top. Tour.	1985	5400	7300	11,800	25,000	38,000

Steam Car — 4 cyl., 70 hp, 117" wb

Touring-5P	1785	6400	9300	14,500	33,000	45,000

Note: Three steam cars built 1923-1924.

WASHINGTON ELECTRIC — The Washington Motor Vehicle Company was organized in the District of Columbia in 1909. Production centered on commercial vehicles carrying the Washington name through 1910. The tradename changed to Capitol in 1911 when a passenger car was added. Refer to Capitol Electric.

WASHINGTON SIX — Cleveland, Ohio — (1921) — The Washington Automobile Company of Cleveland announced its plans six months after the organization of the Washington Motor Company of Eaton, but two months before the other Ohio company's car was introduced, so most likely the Washington of Cleveland backers weren't even aware of it. Had their car made it into the marketplace, doubtless its name would have been changed. The Cleveland people were not confronted with that problem. The Washington Six was to be an assembled car (Timken axles, Delco electrics, Borg & Beck clutch, Grant-Lees transmission) set into a 120-inch wheelbase chassis. Its single point of departure from the horde of other assembled cars of the period was its overhead valve six-cylinder air-cooled engine. Walter R. Horning, whose former business had been electrical equipment, was the designer of the Washington Six. The car never went into production.

WASP — Bennington, Vermont — (1919-1924) — His first work had been in the oil fields of the Melrose and North Lima districts of Ohio, where he drilled a couple of wells and found the experience not at all aesthetically satisfying. Next he moved to New York where he entered the coachbuilding trade, specializing in artful bodies on European chassis, a task much more to his liking. By 1919, when he settled in Bennington to establish his Martin Wasp Corporation, Karl H. Martin had already designed the Roamer and Deering Magnetic and was working on the Kenworthy. He was ready for a car of his own. He was just thirty-two years old. The Wasp was introduced in the lobby of the Hotel Commodore during New York Automobile Show week in January 1920. Its chassis was nothing extraordinary, a 72 hp Wisconsin T-head four-cylinder engine was fitted; everything else underneath came from varying component suppliers in the field. But the look of the car was spectacular. Its wheelbase was a long 136 inches, and its body styling was aptly described by Martin as "rickshaw phaeton." The word flamboyance found all-new meaning in the Wasp, with its sharply pointed, stylized fenders, its fully-nickeled German radiator, its large stepplates, the natural wood bows on its top of many curves, the bullet lights in the windshield, the sheen of its black lacquer body contrasting with the high polish of its natural aluminum hood. And yet there was nothing gaudy about a Wasp, no striping, no excess ornamentation. The interior was tastefully furnished, with a handsome engine-turned dashboard complete with St. Christopher's medal, the only car in America (and possibly the world) to carry one as standard equipment. The price was $5000 f.o.b. Bennington. Douglas Fairbanks happened to stroll through the lobby of the Commodore, and he bought the Wasp on the spot, purportedly as a present for his bride, Mary Pickford. Five more cars were built through 1921. Late in 1922 Karl Martin announced his intention to go bigger and longer with his Wasp: a 70 hp Continental six-cylinder engine and a 144-inch wheelbase chassis. The price of the earlier model was now $5500, and he offered the new six-cylinder "rickshaw phaeton" at a hefty $10,000. But by now the money was running out; just three Wasp sixes were built, total production of the fours was fourteen cars. "I don't believe we really failed at all . . . ," Karl Martin reminisced in later years. "We were impractical, it is true . . . but the point is that we did build cars and we did sell them." The last Wasp automobile was built in 1924. Karl Martin's later work included the design and building of furniture, metal work and intricate inlaid cabinets. He died in 1954.

1920-1922 WASP
Model 211 — 4 cyl., 72 hp, 136" wb

	FP	5	4	3	2	1
Touring-4P	5000	6000	8500	13,000	30,000	42,000

1924 Wasp, rickshaw phaeton, KM

1923-1924 WASP
Model 211 — 4 cyl., 72 hp, 136" wb

Touring-4P	5500	6000	8500	13,000	30,000	42,000

Model 221 — 6 cyl., 70 hp, 144" wb

Touring-4P	—	6300	9000	14,000	32,000	44,000

WATCH CITY STEAM — Waltham, Massachusetts — (1900-1904) — The Watch City Automobile Company at 582 Main Street in Waltham began building steam carriages to customer order at the turn of the century. In 1903 one of Watch City's customers was race driver Louis S. Ross for whom the company built the steam race car called "Wogglebug" with which Ross competed successfully in 1904 at Ormond-Daytona Beach. Most Watch City cars were more sedate, and better looking. F.P. Worcester was the manager of the Watch City Automobile Company, and he indicated in 1904 that cars would continue to be built to customer order. His firm never offered a standard production line.

WATERLOO — Waterloo, Iowa — (1903-1905) — In November of 1902 the Waterloo Gas Engine Company and the Davis engine department of the Cascade Manufacturing Company combined into the Waterloo Motor Works. The reason for the merger of these two stationary engine producers was that Charles E. Duryea had come to town and convinced everyone to get into the automobile field producing cars under his patents. The resulting Waterloo was simply a Duryea under another name. In December of 1903 a fire at the factory resulted in $25,000 in damages, though production continued. The Waterloo was not offered in the wide variety of body styles available for the Duryea then being built in Reading (Pennsylvania), though for 1905, the four-passenger folding-seat phaeton was added to the two-passenger Anvil phaeton which had been the company's sole model for the two previous seasons. Production was discontinued later in 1905. The Waterloo company subsequently turned to manufacture of the Waterloo Boy tractor, and ultimately became part of the John Deere empire.

1903-1904 WATERLOO
Anvil — 3 cyl., 12 hp, 72" wb

	FP	5	4	3	2	1
Phaeton-2P	1350	2300	3300	4600	7500	16,000

1905 WATERLOO
Anvil — 3 cyl., 10/12 hp, 72" wb

	FP	5	4	3	2	1
Phaeton-2P	1350	2300	3300	4600	7500	16,000

Folding Seat — 3 cyl., 12/15 hp, 84" wb

	FP	5	4	3	2	1
Tonneau-4P	1750	2400	3400	4800	8000	17,000

WATERLOO — Waterloo, Iowa — (1908) — In the early spring of 1908 the Waterloo Car and Engine Company was organized by W.M. Law, E.P. Caldwell and H.B. White, who took the executive offices of president, secretary and treasurer respectively. Their plan was to produce both automobiles and street cars powered by a "new and improved means for cooling the cylinders," the method being described as "simply a combination of air and water — very much less of water than now is usually used." If a prototype was completed, the trade press was not made aware of it. This venture disappeared quickly.

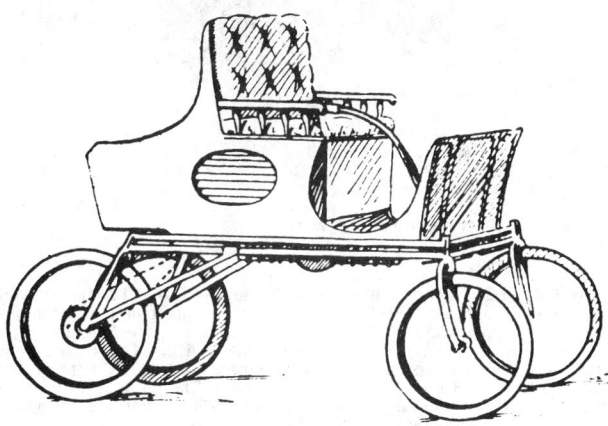

1900 Waterman & Chamberlain, gasoline runabout, NAHC

WATERMAN & CHAMBERLAIN — Medford, Massachusetts — (1900) — The firm of Waterman & Chamberlain of 26 High Street in Medford produced a small gasoline runabout powered by a Crest Duplex motor mounted under the seat. Everything about the car was typical of ingenuous automobile construction of the day, with one exception. "The power is transmitted to the rear wheels through a special gear of their own construction," explained *Cycle and Automobile Trade Journal*, "allowing running the engine free or the vehicle backward and forward." Production does not seem to have survived 1900.

1900 Waters, Buggymobile, OCW

WATERS — New Bern, North Carolina — (1900-1903) — G.S. Waters & Sons manufactured buggies and carriages in New Bern, advertising itself as "The Old Reliable Factory near Railroad, 78 Broad Street." Following a visit to Baltimore in 1899 where he saw his first automobile, Gilbert Waters returned to New Bern to build one himself. It was completed in 1900. In 1903 he took the small gasoline engine he had built for his first car and installed it in an improved second car. Its body, like the first, was a buggy of his own manufacture. Gilbert Waters was anxious to get into production of his vehicle, but was unable to convince anyone in New Bern of the viability of the horseless carriage idea. He reluctantly returned to his buggy business, though he used his Waters "Buggymobile," as he called it, for decades thereafter — always with the whip in the socket and the bicycle bell on the steering lever as installed at the turn of the century. In the late Thirties, Gilbert Waters drove his car in New York City and appeared on the "We, The People" radio show. The Waters car remains extant, on display at the North Carolina Museum of History in Raleigh.

1903 Waters, Buggymobile, OCW

WATERTOWN — The Watertown Automobile & Supply Company was organized early in 1906 with a capital stock of $5000 to manufacture and deal in automobiles and automobile supplies in Watertown, New York. Incorporators were Joseph A. McConnell, Lincoln G. De Cant and Perley A. Pitcher. Manufacture is doubted.

1905 Watrous, touring, NAHC

WATROUS — Elmira, New York — (1905) — Thomas S. Watrous thought he could realize success as the "Pioneer of Low Prices." Five hundred dollars for a two-cylinder air-cooled 12 hp, friction-transmission, short-wheelbase touring car ($400 for roadster) would have been an enticing proposition if the car had been any good. The Watrous Automobile Company was organized in the spring of 1905 and failed that fall when the sheriff arrived to close the doors of the small shop on Main Street. The Watrous had rather quickly earned a reputation as being a noisy car, and a pretty awful one. Local wags dubbed it the waterless, gearless, powerless, useless Watrous.

1905 WATROUS
Model B — 2 cyl., 12 hp, 85" wb

	FP	5	4	3	2	1
Detachable Tonneau	500	2300	3300	4600	7500	16,000

Model C — 2 cyl., 12 hp, 80" wb

	FP	5	4	3	2	1
Runabout	400	2200	3200	4400	7000	15,000

WATSON ELECTRIC — Calumet, Michigan — (1901) — The Watson was an electric built in Calumet in 1901 by Ralph Watson, who was the grandson of the superintendent at the Osceola mine and a student in the manual training school. According to the local papers, the vehicle "attracted a great deal of attention about the city." Its electrical apparatus, built entirely by young Watson, had been tested at the substation of the Peninsula Electric Light & Power Company and found to work very nicely. Except for the body which had been fashioned by local carpenters, the remainder of the Watson was the student's doing as well.

WATSON — New York, New York — (1912) — In March of 1912 the Watson Engineering Company of 38 West 32nd Street in Manhattan announced that it had leased part of the old Bogart factory on Lawrence Street in Flushing for the purpose of manufacturing a taxicab of the firm's own design. Production details are lacking, but any Watson taxi output to follow was minimal.

WATSON-CONOVER — The Watson Machine Company of Paterson, New Jersey produced an automobile from 1907-1912 which was marketed under the tradename of Conover. Refer to Conover.

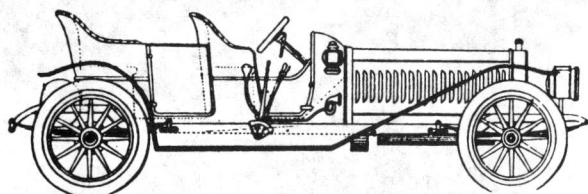

1910 Watt, model A, touring, NAHC

WATT — Detroit, Michigan — (1910) — The Watt Motor Car Company was organized in December of 1909 by Frank J. Watt and his brother George H., both of the Watt-Detroit Carburetor Company. James E. Delaney was president and chief promoter of this new venture. Temporary quarters were taken on Porter Street in Detroit. The Watt was to be powered by a six-cylinder "reversible" engine, and to be built in an extensive line of runabouts, touring cars and light delivery wagons. Only an $1850 touring model was produced, however, and only two of them. By early spring of 1910, the Watt Company was reported to be "skirmishing for money," and in early May six creditors petitioned the firm into bankruptcy. "The petition alleges that the company has committed acts of bankruptcy in that some of its property has been concealed and some has been transferred to the president of the company . . .," reported *The Motor World* on May 5th. "It also is said certain creditors have been favored." One of them was not George H. Watt. His claim of $1800 was the largest among the suing half-dozen creditors.

1910 WATT
Model A — 6-cyl., 45 hp, 132" wb

	FP	5	4	3	2	1
Touring-4P	1850	4700	6100	9900	19,000	33,000

WAUKEGAN APOLLO — This car built by the Chicago Recording Scale Company of Waukegan, Illinois was more usually known during 1906-1907 as the Apollo. Refer to Apollo.

1908 Waukesha, touring, LC

WAUKESHA — Waukesha, Wisconsin — (1906-1910) — The Blue Front Garage was established in Waukesha in 1906 by Harry L. Horning and Fred Ahrens, who formerly had been chief engineer and master mechanic respectively for the Modern Steel Structural Company of Milwaukee. A few

years previous the president of that firm had given Horning and Ahrens the job of trying to fix his balky boat engine, and that after-hours task had given them the idea to build a better engine of their own. Initially, they made ends meet by washing, storing and repairing cars in their Blue Front Garage, but when their new engine was ready, Horning and Ahrens secured fresh financing from a farmer in Wales named Allan Stebbins and reorganized as the Waukesha Motor Company. The firm's boat engines found a ready acceptance among resort owners on Lake Geneva and around Madison, and the city of Chicago bought a Waukesha in 1908 for one of its fire department trucks. Waukesha engines were purchased by a number of automobile manufacturers as well, and from 1906 to 1910 Harry L. Horning designed a few automobiles himself which carried his company's engines. These were strictly on a custom-order basis and included a snappy roadster for Ralph Simpson (secretary of the Modern Steel Structural Company) and a touring car for Theodore Axelsen (owner of a pattern works near Milwaukee). This sideline activity ceased, however, when the pressure of the firm's engine-building business began to consume all of Harry Horning's time. In 1911 the company moved from its original North Street shop to a big 55-acre site on West St. Paul Avenue. The Waukesha Motor Company was heavily involved in engine production for both World War I and World War II. By 1959 the firm was producing more than 3.5 million horsepower a year and powerplants, largely for industrial use, using diesel, gas, gasoline, kerosene and alcohol fuels.

1899 Waverley Electric, runabout, WLB

WAVERLEY ELECTRIC — Indianapolis, Indiana — (1898-1903) — (1909-1916) — The Waverley Electric had a tripartite existence in Indianapolis. The car was introduced in 1898 following a merger of the American Electric Vehicle Company of Chicago and the Indiana Bicycle Company of Indianapolis; in 1900 its sponsorship was the American Bicycle Company, and from 1901 to 1903 the International Motor Car Company. Each of these incarnations was simply the Pope empire operating under another name. For 1904 — during which year the Pope-Hartford, the Pope-Toledo and the Pope-Tribune were introduced — there was a certain logic to the Pope empire's electric car being a hyphenate too — and thus it was renamed the Pope-Waverley. It remained as such into 1908, by which time the Pope organization was in a financial panic and was retrenching as quickly as it could. The Indianapolis factory, now in receivership, was sold in September of 1908 by Pope to a group of local businessmen several of whom — H.H. Rice, W.B. Cooley and W.C. Johnson among them — had been executives with the company for years. They promptly reorganized as the Waverley Company, dropped Pope and the hyphen — and the car became simply the Waverley again. This new group apparently made money for awhile, which is something the car as the Pope-Waverley never had, according to newspaper reports of the period. Like many latterday electrics, the Waverley was given a pronounced hood and the look of a gasoline car by 1912. A particularly appealing model was a landaulet that carried the delightful designation of "Sheltered Roadster" in 1912. From 1913, the company's slogan was "The Silent Waverley," and it was rather silently too that the Waverley faded from the scene after the 1916 model year. Probably the most celebrated of all Waverley Electric purchasers was General Lew Wallace, the author of *Ben Hur*, who bought a Model 20a Surrey in 1902.

1898-1901 WAVERLEY ELECTRIC

	FP	5	4	3	2	1
Model 18 Piano-Box Rbt.	1000	3300	4400	6700	12,000	24,000

1902-1903 WAVERLEY ELECTRIC

Model 21 Road Wagon	850	2300	3300	4600	7500	16,000
Model 22 Road Wagon	925	2300	3300	4600	7500	16,000
Model 20a Surrey	1400	2400	3400	4800	8000	17,000

1909 WAVERLEY ELECTRIC

Model 74 Sthp. (73½" wb)	1500	2300	3300	4600	7500	16,000
Model 75C Coupe (79" wb)	2150	2200	3200	4400	7000	15,000
Model 67 Vic.-Phae. (68" wb)	1525	2400	3400	4800	8000	17,000
Model 69 Rbt. (72" wb)	1150	2000	3000	4200	6500	14,000
Model 71 Rbt. (69" wb)	1425	2000	3000	4200	6500	14,000
Model 53 Vic. (76" wb)	1800	2200	3200	4400	7000	15,000
Model 53 Coupe (76" wb)	2300	2000	3000	4200	6500	14,000
Model 70 Coupe (68" wb)	1900	1800	2800	4000	6200	13,000

1900 Waverley Electric, runabout, HAC

1902 Waverley Electric, model 21, road wagon, HAC

1903 Waverley Electric, model 20a, surrey, HAC

1909 Waverley Electric, model 74, stanhope, HAC

1910 Waverley Electric, model 75, brougham, HAC

	FP	5	4	3	2	1
Model 69 Rbt. (73-1/2'' wb)	1225	2200	3200	4400	7000	15,000
Model 60 Surrey (91'' wb)	1900	2500	3500	5000	8500	18,000

1911 Waverley Electric, model 81, brougham, HAC

1910 WAVERLEY ELECTRIC

	FP	5	4	3	2	1
Model 78 Rds. (94'' wb)	1700	2500	3500	5000	8500	18,000
Model 75 Brgm. (79'' wb)	2250	2400	3400	4800	8000	17,000
Model 76 Vic. Phae. (79'' wb)	1750	2500	3500	5000	8500	18,000
Model 74 Sthp. (73-1/2'' wb)	1600	2300	3300	4600	7500	16,000

1911 WAVERLEY ELECTRIC

	FP	5	4	3	2	1
Model 81 Brgm. (80'' wb)	2600	2400	3400	4800	8000	17,000
Model 75-C Brgm. (79'' wb)	2400	2350	3400	4700	7800	16,500
Model 70-C Cpe. (79'' wb)	2150	2000	3000	4200	6500	14,000
Model 78 Rds. (96'' wb)	1700	2400	3400	4800	8000	17,000
Model 76 Vic. (79'' wb)	1850	2450	3500	4900	8300	17,500
Model 74 Sthp. (80'' wb)	1600	2350	3400	4700	7800	16,500

1473

	FP	5	4	3	2	1
Ambulance (97-1/2" wb)	3250	2300	3300	460000	7500	16,000
Model 53 Sthp. (76" wb)	1800	2300	3300	4600	7500	16,000
Model 69 Rbt. (72" wb)	1150	2200	3200	4400	7000	15,000
Model 60 Sur. (91" wb)	1750	2400	3400	4800	8000	17,000

1912 Waverley Electric, model 90, sheltered roadster, HAC

1912 WAVERLEY ELECTRIC

	FP	5	4	3	2	1
Model 96 Vic.-Phae.(89" wb)	1850	2700	3600	5300	8800	19,000
Model 90 Sheltered Rds.(104" wb)	2000	3000	4000	6000	9500	21,000
Model 91 Brougham (89" wb)	2800	2500	3500	5000	8500	18,000
Model 88 Inside Drive Limo. (104" wb)	3500	2700	3600	5300	8800	19,000

1913 Waverley Electric, model 90, roadster, NAHC

1913 WAVERLEY ELECTRIC

	FP	5	4	3	2	1
Model 98 Limo.-5P (109" wb)	3500	2700	3600	5300	8800	19,000
Model 100 Limo.-4P (106" wb)	2900	2500	3500	5000	8500	18,000
Model 99 Georgian Brgm.-5P (109" wb)	3250	2400	3400	4800	8000	17,000
Model 101 Brgm.-4P (106" wb)	2800	2400	3400	4800	8000	17,000
Model 97 Colonial Brgm.-4P (104" wb)	2375	2500	3500	5000	8500	18,000
Model 90 Rds.-3P (104" wb)	2250	2700	3600	5300	8800	19,000

1914 WAVERLY ELECTRIC

	FP	5	4	3	2	1
Model 104 Front-Drive Four (106" wb)	2900	2700	3600	5300	8800	19,000
Model 108 Limo. (106" wb)	3500	2800	3700	5500	9000	19,500
Model 107 Four-Chair Brgm. (106" wb)	3150	3000	4000	6000	9500	21,000
Model 106 Front/Rear Drive Brgm. (106" wb)	3000	3200	4300	6500	11,000	23,000
Model 106 Rear-Drive Brgm. (106" wb)	2800	3100	4200	6300	10,500	22,000

1915 Waverley Electric, model 107, four-chair brougham, NAHC

1474

1915 WAVERLY ELECTRIC

	FP	5	4	3	2	1
Model 107 Four-Chair Brgm. (106" wb)	2750	3100	4200	6300	10,500	22,000
Model 108 Limo. (106" wb)	3000	3200	4300	6500	11,000	23,000
Model 104 Front-Drive Four (106" wb)	2400	3300	4400	6700	12,000	24,000
Model 109 Rear-Drive Four (106" wb)	2300	3500	4500	7000	13,000	25,000
Model 106 Dual-Drive Four (106" wb)	2600	3700	4700	7300	13,700	26,000
Model 90 Rds.-Cpe. (106" wb)	2000	3200	4300	6500	11,000	23,000

1916 Waverley Electric, roadster-coupe, HAC

1916 WAVERLY ELECTRIC

	FP	5	4	3	2	1
Roadster-Coupe (95" wb)	2150	3200	4300	6500	11,000	23,000
Four-Chair Brgm. (95" wb)	2200	3100	4200	6300	10,500	22,000

WAYMAN & MURPHY — Chicago, Illinois — (1903-1904) — The Wayman & Murphy Company of Chicago was a small carriage-making concern with a short history in the automobile field. At the Chicago Automobile Show in February 1903 the company exhibited a small 4-1/2 hp runabout on the stand of the Lindsay-Russell company of Indianapolis. Its running gear was from Lindsay, its transmission from Champion, the coachwork by Wayman & Murphy. All parts had been put together at the carriagemaker's shops at Randolph and Sangamon streets. The Wayman & Murphy was produced in small numbers into 1904.

WAYNE — The Wayne Motor Car Company of New York City was organized early in 1908 with a capital stock of $10,000 for the manufacture of engines, automobiles, boats and machinery. Incorporators were F.A. Sanford, A.C. Knoeller, and J.R. Beaty. Manufacture is doubted.

The Wayne Sulkyette & Road Cart Company of Decatur, Illinois was among the hopefuls which entered the Chicago Times-Herald Contest of 1895 with an automobile of its own design. Wayne never made it to the starting line, however, and whether its car was ever completed has not been documented.

Although in 1904-1905 the car produced by the Wayne Works of Richmond, Indiana was referred to as a Wayne, the car was in actuality marketed as a Richmond from the beginning. Richmond cars were built from 1904 to 1907. Refer to Richmond.

1904 Wayne, model A, touring, NAHC

WAYNE — Detroit, Michigan — (1904-1908) — The factory of the Wayne Automobile Company was at Dubois and Franklin streets in Detroit, and the men behind this venture were Charles L. Palms, E.A. Skae, Roger J. Sullivan, J.B. Brook and William E. Kelly. The Wayne was designed by Kelly, and was a refinement of the experimental car he had built in Detroit in 1901. Initially offered only as a two-cylinder 16 hp touring car priced at $1200, succeeding years saw a flurry of two- and four-cylinder models with horsepower up to 50 and prices up to $3500. The car was named for General Anthony Wayne, whose military achievements in the Revolutionary War and later in subduing the Indian uprisings in the Northwest Territory must have been known to the Wayne company founders, though perhaps they were unaware of Wayne's sobriquet of "Mad Anthony." A portrait of General Wayne appeared on the Wayne car emblem, and ''History repeats itself'' was the curious company slogan. Wayne cars were widely regarded as well-built and solid automobiles, the smaller models with chain drive and planetary transmissions, the larger cars with shaft drive and selective gearsets. Nearly 600 Wayne cars were built in 1907. In June of 1908, Wayne merged with the Northern Manufacturing Company of Detroit, and a managing interest in the firm was acquired by Barney F. Everitt and Walter E. Flanders, who allied themselves with William Metzger with plans to produce another car. Production of the Wayne ended during the summer of 1908; the new E-M-F followed. It too was designed by William Kelly.

1904 WAYNE
Model A — 2-cyl., 16 hp, 80'' wb

	FP	5	4	3	2	1
Touring-5P	1200	2500	3500	5000	8500	18,000

1905 Wayne, model C, touring, HAC

1905 WAYNE
Model A — 2-cyl., 16 hp, 80'' wb

Touring-5P	1200	2500	3500	5000	8500	18,000

Model B — 2-cyl., 16 hp, 90'' wb

Side Entrance Tonneau	1250	2600	3600	5200	8700	18,500

Model C — 4-cyl., 24 hp, 102'' wb

Touring-5P	2000	3000	4000	6000	9500	21,000

1906 Wayne, model H, runabout, NAHC

1906 WAYNE
Model C — 2-cyl., 20 hp, 90'' wb

Touring-5P	1250	2500	3500	5000	8500	18,000

Model F — 4-cyl., 50 hp, 117'' wb

Touring-5P	3500	4500	5800	9500	18,000	32,000

Model B — 4-cyl., 24/28 hp, 102'' wb

Touring-5P	2000	3100	4200	6300	10,500	22,000

Model K — 4-cyl., 35 hp, 100'' wb

Touring-5P	2500	3300	4400	6700	12,000	24,000

Model G — 2-cyl., 14 hp, 82'' wb

Touring-4P	1000	2300	3300	4600	7500	16,000

Model H — 2-cyl., 14 hp, 82'' wb

Runabout-2P	800	2200	3200	4400	7000	15,000

1907 WAYNE
Model K — 4-cyl., 35 hp, 102'' wb

Touring-5P	2500	3200	4300	6500	11,000	23,000

Model N — 4-cyl., 35 hp, 107'' wb

Touring-5P	2500	3300	4400	6700	12,000	24,000

Model R — 4-cyl., 50 hp, 120'' wb

Touring-7P	3500	4500	5800	9500	18,000	32,000

1907 Wayne, touring runabout, NAHC

1908 Wayne, model 30, touring, NAHC

1908 WAYNE
Model 30 — 4-cyl., 35 hp, 106'' wb

	FP	5	4	3	2	1
Touring-5P	2500	3300	4400	6700	12,000	24,000
Roadster-2P	2500	3200	4300	6500	11,000	23,000
Tourabout-4P	2500	3300	4400	6700	12,000	24,000

1921 W.B.C., taxicab, WLB

W.B.C. — Greenville, South Carolina — (1921) — The initials represented Well Built Cab, this taxi built by the Cyclone Motors Corporation of Greenville. Its chassis was a Ford extended fifteen inches and its price was $1600. Two cents per cab mile was said to be the vehicle's operating expense. A fleet of these cars was sold to the Black and White Cab Company of New York City, whose president enthusiastically informed Cyclone that ''you have solved our problems.'' Cyclone could not solve its own problems, however, and went into receivership during the fall of 1922.

W.C.D. — The W.C.D. Motor Car Company was organized in Westfield, New Jersey during the fall of 1912 with a capital stock of $50,000 for the manufacture of automobiles. The initials translated to Peter C. Wall, Walter E. Camping and W.J. Druppleman. Manufacture is doubted.

W.C.P. — New York, New York — (1909-1912) — The W.C.P. Taxicab Company was organized early in 1909 by C.F. Wyckoff and E.S. Partridge of the firm of Wyckoff, Church & Partridge, Inc., the importers of the Decauville and agents in New York City for the Stearns and, later, producers of the Vaughan. Like the Rockwell taxi, the W.C.P. metered cars were built by the Bristol Engineering Company in Bristol, Connecticut. Landaulet coachwork was used, with the chassis and lower body painted a bright orange yellow striped with black, the hood and upper body black. The driver sat on the left-hand side of the car, with the controlling levers to his right, and the taximeters were driven from the front wheels ''so that their measurements may be as accurate as possible, especially in slippery weather.'' The W.C.P. taxis were put into service on New York City streets in June 1909, and that October were paraded in the Mardi Gras celebration at Coney Island. Production continued until the bankruptcy of Wyckoff, Church & Partridge in 1912.

WEAVER — Although it cannot be documented with certainty, it is probably that George Briggs Weaver, Sr. built at least a few automobiles in Newport, Massachusetts. He apparently said he did in any case, and, given his subsequent career, truth rings clear. Certainly there were enough wealthy people in Newport who might have wished to have special cars built, and certainly Weaver could have built them. The conundrum is precisely when. George Briggs Weaver was born in Newport in 1884. His family owned a hardware store in town. Following study at the Rhode Island School of Design, he became a jewelery designer for Gorham in New York City. His father's death brought him back to Newport, and it was during this period that he presumably produced automobiles until a fire wiped out his business. Thereafter he worked as a tool designer for Gorham and as an automatic-machinery designer until the late Twenties when he joined the coachbuilding firm of Waterhouse. His body designs, especially for duPont, became famous during the pre-World War II era. After the war Weaver became famous all over again when he served as designer for the sports car produced by Briggs Cunningham.

WEAVER-EBLING — The Weaver-Ebling Automobile Company of New York City was organized early in 1909 with a capital stock of $25,000 to manufacture and deal in motor cars and to operate a garage. Incorporators were Raymond H. Weaver, Robert W. Ebling and H. Hardcastle Pennock. Manufacture is doubted.

WEBB — "W.H. Webb, Conneaut, Ohio, is putting the finishing touches on a steam carriage of his own design," reported *The Horseless Age* in February 1902. Details are lacking.

The Webb Company of Newark, New Jersey was organized during the fall of 1904 with a capital stock of $50,000 for the manufacture of motor vehicles and machinery. Incorporators were Walter H. Bond, Paul Munter and Joseph Gerrardt. Manufacture of a car is doubted, but the firm did enter the accessory field, exhibiting its speedometers at both the New York and Chicago automobile shows in 1905.

The Webb & Pine Automobile Company of Chicago, Illinois was organized during the spring of 1906 with a capital stock of $2500 for the manufacture of automobiles and accessories. Incorporators were William Friedman, Harry A. Riley and Morris Friedman. Manufacture of a car is doubted.

The Webb-Veitch Company of Jersey City, New Jersey was organized early in 1912 with a capital stock of $25,000 for the manufacture of automobiles, motorcycles and aeroplanes. Incorporators were C.N. King, Jr., G.H. Russell and E.H. Geran. Manufacture did not follow, this venture evolving into the Veitch Motor Manufacturing Company that summer, which presumably went nowhere as well.

WEBB STEAM — St. Louis, Missouri — (1903) — Albert C. Webb of St. Louis began experimenting with automobiles soon after the turn of the century, steamers particularly, including a special racing version in 1903. In 1906 he attempted the organization of a manufacturing company in Joplin, Missouri but it apparently went nowhere, so Webb went to Vincennes, Indiana where he organized the Webb Motor Fire Apparatus Company in 1908. In 1910 he returned with that company to his native St. Louis.

WEBBER — C.F. Webber, a bicycle man from Albany, New York, announced his intention to begin the manufacture of automobiles there late in 1900. It is doubtful he ever followed through on this, however.

Whether W.M. Webber of Parkersburg, West Virginia ever completed a car is not known, but he was experimenting around the time of the Cosmopolitan Race in 1896. "The prevailing method of applying the power through the wheels he criticizes as defective for sandy, muddy or frozen roads," *The Horseless Age* reported. "His idea is to transmit the power directly from the machinery to the ground, which, in his opinion, will make the motor vehicle capable of any road that is passable by horses."

1908 Webb Jay, steam touring, NAHC

WEBB JAY STEAM — Chicago, Illinois — (1908) — Webb Jay's racing career came to an end in 1906 when the White Steamer he was driving plunged into a pond in the infield of the Buffalo (New York) track where he was competing, and he came close to drowning. After months in the hospital, he decided to take up safer pursuits. Initially, this resulted in his becoming the White dealer in Chicago, the city where his brother Frank was selling Stanleys. In 1908 Webb and Frank Jay decided to build a steamer of their own. At $4000, it was an expensive car, powered by a two-cylinder 30 hp compound engine, and available as a five-passenger touring. The Webb Jay Motor Company offered the car only in 1908, and thereafter the brothers returned to dealing in automobiles of other manufacturers. Subsequently, Frank Jay became vice-president of the Stanley Motor Carriage Company, and Webb Jay devised a vacuum tank concept which was purchased by Stewart Warner and which, as was said at the time, "brought him sufficient of the world's goods to enable him to retire from the industry."

1908 WEBB JAY
Model A — 2-cyl., 30 hp

	FP	5	4	3	2	1
Touring	4000	3000	4000	6000	9500	21,000

WEBER — Orlando F. Weber had been an automobile dealer in Milwaukee, Wisconsin since 1903, handling the National (Oshkosh and Milwaukee) and General (Cleveland, Ohio) cars among others. In 1905 he organized the Orlando F. Weber Company with a capital stock of $80,000 for the manufacture of his own cars in Milwaukee. There is no evidence that production ever began, though Weber himself remained in the automobile field for a considerable period. In 1907 he took on the Milwaukee shop agency for the Pope lines. In 1913 he was vice-president and general manager of the Vaughan Car Company, Incorporated in Kingston, New York, and in 1915 Walter E. Flanders chose him as assistant manager for Maxwell.

The Weber Gas & Gasoline Engine Company was organized early in 1900 with a capital stock of $150,000 for the manufacture of motors and motor vehicles in Kansas City, Missouri. Manufacture of a car is doubted.

1925 Weber, miniature replica, NAHC

WEBER — Hoopeston, Illinois — (1925) — The Weber was an exquisite miniature replica of the Moon that was built in 1925 by R.S. Weber of the P.H. Weber Company, manufacturers of time-saving shop equipment in Hoopestown. Its engine was a small Continental four, its wheels were purchased from an airplane supply house, with most of the remaining parts cut, shortened and welded from components secured in an automobile graveyard. The Weber was used for advertising purposes in Hoopeston for approximately a year, then sold to the Ernest J. Krause Company of St. Louis, subsequently sold again, and shown at the Indiana State Fair. In 1927 R.S. Weber, who had since moved to Racine, Wisconsin, wrote *Motor Age* requesting help in locating the car. Whether he was ultimately lucky in this is not known.

1903 Webster, touring, NAHC

WEBSTER — New York, New York — (1902-1903) — The Webster Automobile Company was a New York City firm with offices on West 6th Street in Greenwich Village. The Webster car was introduced during the early fall of 1902. A four-cylinder 16 hp runabout on a 78-inch wheelbase, it featured a three-speed sliding gear transmission and shaft drive. Because Webster had no facilities for manufacture in Manhattan, the car was built for the firm by Frank Mossberg in his bicycle bell factory in Attleboro, Massachusetts. In December 1902 the company announced that it was seeking production facilities closer to New York City. Three months later, Webster chose to sell out instead, to Frank Mossberg and his new United States Auto-Car Company of Attleboro. Total Webster production had been five cars.

WEEBER — Albany, New York — (1898-1905) — Christian F. Weeber, a bicycle builder from Albany, began putting together his first automobile in

1903 Weeber, roadster, KM

1903 Welch, runabout, show car, NAHC

1903 Welch, Tourist, runabout, NAHC

1898. It was powered by a single-cylinder, four-stroke, air-cooled engine which was mounted under the floorboard, with a hood up front shrouding the gasoline tank and storage battery, and fitted with a sliding gear transmission and chain drive to the rear axle. Although initially suffering overheating problems, Weeber was able to put the machine right, and drove his "Weebermobile" for over 50,000 miles. He built a few more cars for a local clientele, *Automobile Review* noting in August 1904 that he had switched from a 4½ to an 8 hp air-cooled engine, and that the Weeber car "is strongly built and makes a neat appearance." By about 1905 Weeber decided to confine his efforts to the manufacture of varying automobile components which he designed. Among these was a gasoline engine muffler, a combination brake and steering tiller and a device for removing engine valves. His C.F. Weeber Manufacturing Works at 170-172 Central Avenue in Albany also served as a dealership for Ford, later Haynes, E-M-F and Studebaker. Following the First World War, he patented a wide variety of other devices, including a tire chain, tire carrier and fuel induction system. Christian Weeber died in 1932. His "Weebermobile" remains extant in the New York State Museum, together with portions of two other Weeber-built automobiles.

WEEDEN — The C.P. Weeden Motor Company was organized in Trenton, New Jersey early in 1910 with a capital stock of $100,000 for the manufacture of automobiles, motorcycles and other vehicles. Joining Claudius P. Weeden in this venture was Jacob S. Valentine. Manufacture is doubted, but Weeden is known to have operated a garage and dealership, buying out the former Valentine agency.

WEINERT — **Detroit, Michigan** — **(1914)** — R.H. Weinert of Detroit showed up at the International Cyclecar Races and Exposition held in that city on the Fourth of July, 1914 with a light car he had designed and built himself. Powered by a four-cylinder water-cooled engine fitted into a 79-inch wheelbase chassis with 44-inch tread, the Weinert featured a selective transmission, semi-elliptic springs in front, three-quarter elliptics in the rear, and rode on wire wheels. Weinert indicated at that time that he was at work on another car "equipped with a heavier motor." Obviously, too, he was scouting for potential investment capital to proceed into manufacture. Apparently, he was luckless in that regard.

WELBON — The Welbon Motor Car Company was organized in Cincinnati, Ohio during the summer of 1912 with a capital stock of $25,000 for the manufacture of automobiles. Incorporators were W.E. Welbon, H.S. Leymann, C.D. Wilson, C.W. Shepler and H.A. Welbon. Manufacture is doubted.

WELCH — The Welch-Estberg Company was organized in Milwaukee, Wisconsin late in 1904 with a capital stock of $50,000 for the manufacture of motor cars. The partners involved were William O. and Charles Gale Welch and Emil Estberg. Manufacture is doubted, but a dealership was established. Late in 1906 the firm's name was changed to Welch Brothers Motor Car Company following the withdrawal from the venture of Emil Estberg. The new firm retained the agencies for the Pope, Northern and Packard lines.

The Welch & Suthergreen Company was organized in Fitchburg, Massachusetts early in 1913 with a capital stock of $30,000 to manufacture and deal in automobiles. H.C. Mayo, E.J. Welch and F.S Suthergreen were the incorporators. Manufacture is doubted.

WELCH — **Chelsea, Michigan** — **(1903-1904)** / **Pontiac, Michigan** — **(1904-1911)** — Just before the turn of the century, A.R. Welch organized the Chelsea Manufacturing Company for the production of small metal novelties. With his younger brother Fred, he built his first automobile in 1901. It was powered by a two-cylinder 20 hp engine of the brothers' own design which featured overhead valves and hemispherical combustion chambers, a remarkably advanced construction at the time. The car was shown at the Chicago Automobile Show in early 1903, and production began in Chelsea soon after with the organization of the Chelsea Manufacturing Company. Ltd. Some financing was provided by J.D. Watson, but obviously not enough. Manufacture of about fifteen Welch Tourist cars a month commenced, but by early 1904 the firm was petitioned into bankruptcy. "The lack of the capital has not been occasioned by lack of business," *The Automobile* reported, "but through the inability of one

party to live up to his agreements with the company." With what could be salvaged from the operation, A.R. Welch moved to Pontiac where he reorganized as the Welch Motor Car Company, a $50,000 incorporation which was increased to $100,000 by year's end. Now, in addition to a healthy capital stock, the venture was also provided needed working capital and really got going. The Welch Tourist, which had been a small $2000 20 hp car on a 78-inch wheelbase, metamorphosed into the Welch, which became one of the largest cars of the period with four (and later six) cylinder engines up to 75 hp, wheelbases stretching to 138 inches, and prices which began at $4000. The advanced features of overhead valves and hemispherical combustion chambers were continued, now operated by a single overhead camshaft which Welch claimed late in 1905 to be an American industry first. (The Finch Limited of 1906 was also single overhead cam, so the Welch distinction was not long-lived.) In June of 1909 a separate company was set up in Detroit for the production of a smaller, less-expensive car to be known as the Welch-Detroit. Various references indicate the Pontiac-built car to have been referred to as the Welch-Pontiac thereafter, but more often simply Welch was used. These cars were among the best built and most luxurious of the period. During the summer of 1909 the Welch Motor Car Company became affiliated with General Motors, and formal takeover followed in 1910. The final Welch cars were produced by GM in 1911. During the fall of 1913 A.R. Welch announced that he was nearing completion on his next automotive effort, a cyclecar with a 110-inch wheelbase, 36-inch tread and a body as roomy as a touring car. "Mr. Welch will make all probability the highest-priced cyclecar on the market," *The American Cyclecar* predicted. But fate intervened. On November 8th, 1913 A.R. Welch went on a duck-hunting trip, a terrible storm ensued, and although the canoe in which he was hunting was subsequently discovered, the body of A.R. Welch never was.

1904 Welch, Tourist, tonneau limousine, HAC

1903-1904 WELCH
Tourist — 2-cyl., 20 hp, 78" wb

	FP	5	4	3	2	1
Runabout	2000	2000	3000	4200	6500	14,000
Tonneau	2185	2100	3100	4300	6800	14,500

1905 Welch, landaulette, JAC

1905 WELCH
Four — 30/36 hp, 114" wb

Side Entrance Tonneau	4000	3100	4200	6300	10,500	22,000
Limousine	—	2700	3600	5300	8800	19,000
Canopy Top Touring	—	3000	4000	6000	9500	21,000
Victoria	—	2300	3300	4600	7500	16,000
Landaulette	—	2900	3700	5600	9100	20,000

1906 Welch, touring, JAC

1906 WELCH
Model D — 4-cyl., 50 hp, 118" wb

Touring-5P	4250	5000	6500	11,000	22,000	35,000
Limousine-5P	5000	3100	4200	6300	10,500	22,000

Model F — 4-cyl., 50 hp, 118" wb

Touring-5P	4000	4900	6300	10,300	21,000	34,000

1907 Welch, touring, HAC

1907 WELCH
Model H — 6-cyl., 70 hp, 138" wb

Touring-7P	6000	7600	12,500	19,400	42,400	55,000

Model I — 4-cyl., 50 hp, 129" wb

Limousine-7P	5500	4400	5600	9200	17,300	31,000

Model G — 4-cyl., 50 hp, 129" wb

Touring-7P	4200	5300	7000	11,500	24,000	37,000

Model F — 4-cyl., 50 hp, 124" wb

	FP	5	4	3	2	1
Touring-7P	4000	5000	6500	11,000	22,000	35,000

Model D — 4-cyl., 50 hp, 118" wb

Touring-5P	4250	4500	5800	9500	18,000	32,000
Limousine-5P	5000	3000	4000	6000	9500	21,000

Model E — 4-cyl., 50 hp, 112" wb

Runabout-2/4P	5000	4300	5400	8700	16,500	30,000

1908 Welch, touring, WLB

1908 WELCH
Model 6-L — 6-cyl., 70 hp, 138" wb

Touring-7P	6000	7600	12,500	19,400	42,400	55,000

Model 6-I — 6-cyl., 70 hp, 138" wb

Limousine-7P	7000	4700	6100	9900	19,000	33,000

Model 4-L — 4-cyl., 50 hp, 129" wb

Touring-7P	4500	5300	7000	11,500	24,000	37,000

Model 4-I — 4-cyl., 50 hp, 129" wb

Limousine-7P	5500	4000	5000	8000	15,000	28,000

1909 Welch, model 6-L, touring, JAC

1909 WELCH
Model 4-L — 4-cyl., 50 hp, 125" wb

Touring-7P	4500	5000	6500	11,000	22,000	35,000

Model 4-I — 4-cyl., 50 hp, 125" wb

Limousine-7P	5500	4000	5000	8000	15,000	28,000
Landaulet-7P	5500	4200	5200	8400	15,700	29,000
Town Car-6P	5500	4200	5200	8400	15,700	29,000

Model 4-M — 4-cyl., 50 hp, 120" wb

Baby Tonneau	4500	4500	5800	9500	18,000	32,000

Model 6-L — 6-cyl., 75 hp, 138" wb

Touring-7P	6000	7600	12,500	19,400	42,400	55,000

Model 6-I — 6-cyl., 75 hp, 138" wb

Limousine-7P	7000	4700	6100	9900	19,000	33,000
Landaulet-7P	7000	4900	6300	10,300	21,000	34,000
Town Car-6P	7000	4900	6300	10,300	21,000	34,000

Model 6-M — 6-cyl., 75 hp, 138" wb

Baby Tonneau	6000	7400	12,100	18,800	41,100	53,000

1910 Welch, model 4-N, touring, HAC

1910 WELCH
Model 4-L — 4-cyl., 50 hp, 125" wb

Limousine-7P	5500	3300	4400	6700	12,000	24,000

Model 4-N — 4-cyl., 50 hp, 125" wb

Touring-7P	4500	5000	6500	11,000	22,000	35,000

Model 4-R — 4-cyl., 70 hp, 130" wb						
	FP	5	4	3	2	1
Touring-7P	6000	7800	12,900	19,900	43,300	57,000
Model 6-N — 6-cyl., 75 hp, 138" wb						
Touring-7P	6000	7800	13,200	20,200	43,800	59,000

1911 Welch, model 4-R, limousine, JAC

1911 WELCH
Model 4-R — 4-cyl., 70 hp, 130" wb

Touring-7P	6000	7800	12,900	19,900	43,300	57,000

1910 Welch-Detroit, model S, 7-pass. touring, SKY

WELCH-DETROIT — Detroit, Michigan — (1910-1911) — The Welch-Detroit was designed by A.B.C. Hardy, who earlier had built the Flint Roadster and who was a colleague of William C. Durant's both before and during his General Motors' adventures. The Welch Company of Detroit was an entity separate from the Welch Motor Car Company of Pontiac, and the Welch-Detroit was a smaller and less expensive companion to the large and costly Welch produced in Pontiac. Even so, the Welch-Detroit was a hefty motorcar, a 40 hp (45/50 in 1911) four on a 122-inch wheelbase with prices in the $3000 range. In 1909 the Welch companies became affiliated with General Motors, and in 1910 were taken over formally by GM. Both the Welch and the Welch-Detroit were discontinued in 1911. Durant-man Hardy saw to the removal of the Welch machinery from both the Pontiac and Detroit factories and its reinstallation in Saginaw in the factory formerly occupied by the Rainier company. Rainier was by now yet another company owned by Billy Durant's General Motors. The new car produced there was described as a composite of both the Rainier and the Welch-Detroit — and was marketed as the Marquette in 1912.

1910 WELCH-DETROIT
Model S — 4-cyl., 40 hp, 122" wb

Touring-7P	3200	4000	5000	8000	15,000	28,000

1911 WELCH-DETROIT
Model S — 4-cyl., 45/50 hp, 122" wb

Touring-7P	3000	4400	5600	9200	17,300	31,000
Limousine-7P	4000	3700	4700	7300	13,700	26,000
Landaulet-7P	4250	3900	4800	7700	14,300	27,000

WELCH & LAWSON — New York, New York — (1895) — Probably only one vehicle by this name was built. The firm of Welch & Lawson was located at 203-205 Centre Street in New York City and advertised itself as providing "Kerosene Motors for Wagons and Carriages." Samuel Lawson was the designer of these units, which were single cylinders available in two-, three- and four-horsepower sizes. A 2 hp engine was fitted into the Welch & Lawson car, which was built for the company by F. Bolten, a wagonmaker at 144 West 39th Street. Bolten indicated he planned to build another car for himself, but motor vehicle manufacture was apparently not contemplated by either company. Welch & Lawson used its car — which was fitted with a friction transmission and provided speeds up to 15 mph — principally for advertising and demonstrator purposes.

1895 Welch & Lawson, motor road wagon, WLB

WELCH TOURIST — The Welch Tourist was a 20 hp two-cylinder car produced in Chelsea, Michigan from 1903-1904. When the company moved to Pontiac that year, the name of its car was changed to Welch. Refer to Welch.

WELDON — Charles J. Weldon was a carriage builder from Rockford, Illinois who announced his plans to manufacture electric automobiles during the summer of 1903. Whether he ever followed through on this has not been documented.

The Weldon & Bauer Company was organized in Newark, New Jersey during the fall of 1908 with a capital stock of $15,000 for the manufacture of motor cars, trucks and wagons. Manufacture is doubted.

WELL — The H.C. Well Perfect Motor Company was organized during the summer of 1913 with a capital stock of $25,000 to manufacture and deal in automobiles in New York City. Joining H.C. Well in this venture were M.M. Well and F.B. Knowlton. Manufacture is doubted.

WELLER — Elyria, Ohio — (1902) — The Weller Engineering Company of Elyria built two experimental automobiles in 1902. "Thus far the machines have given good satisfaction," *The Motor Review* reported that May, "and the company is preparing to embark in their manufacture." Although purportedly the Weller company had received several orders already, the evidence is that manufacture was not long sustained.

WELLS — The R.C. Wells Manufacturing Company was organized in Fond du Lac, Wisconsin during the fall of 1912 with a capital stock of $200,000 for the manufacture of automobiles and accessories. Manufacture of a car is doubted.

WELLS — Des Moines, Iowa — (1904-1910) — Jesse O. Wells was probably Des Moines' most avid automobile enthusiast. His interest dated from 1890 when he saw the electric car built by William Morrison coursing the streets of town. But his first automobile purchase was a Locomobile steamer, and shortly after acquiring it, he also acquired the Locomobile agency for Des Moines. His garage and salesroom at Seventh and Grand Avenue was the first in the city. Jesse Wells also became president of the Iowa Automobile Club, the first such organization in the state. In 1904 he built a steam car, followed that year by a gasoline car. Several more Wells cars ensued, mostly for his own use and that of neighbors. In 1907 he did try organizing the Iowa Motor Car Company in nearby Kellogg, but it never did get off the ground. He tried again — and failed — in Des Moines in 1910. According to the *Midwestern* magazine of March 1910, Jesse Wells was responsible for the first electric elevator in Des Moines as well as "the first horse cleaning machine." The Wells cars that he did build were entirely satisfactory, one of them having accomplished a trip to Chicago and back. It appears he built his last car in 1910. In 1916 Jesse Wells was living in Los Angeles — and still driving one of his cars.

1914 Wells, touring, NAHC

WELLS — Des Moines, Iowa — (1914) — The Wells was powered by a four-cylinder L-head engine and was fitted with a Hele-Shaw clutch, Warner four-speed transmission and Timken axles. Its most unusual feature was its coachwork. The five-passenger touring body had its greatest width in the center of the car, a single cyclops headlight mounted in the center of the radiator, with two sidelights mounted on the inside guard of the front fenders. The recessing of all lights was regarded as a safety feature by the car's builder, Hal R. Wells, of Des Moines, who was described as director of the River-to-River Road and the holder of the "cross-Iowa speed record." The latter achievement he did not realize in the Wells, however, but in a Spaulding. The Wells was built for his personal motoring pleasure. Whether Hal R. Wells was any relation to Jesse O. Wells is not known, but would appear likely.

WELLS-MEEKER ELECTRIC — Columbus, Ohio — (1900) — The Wells-Meeker Motor Vehicle Company was incorporated in Columbus with a capital stock of $20,000 during the summer of 1900. The Wells brothers — W.C. and Frank E. — were mechanical engineers. Garry W. and Claude Meeker were stockbrokers and investment capitalists, and Claude Meeker was into politics too, having served as counsel to Great Britain under President Cleveland. The Wells-Meeker idea was an electric motor system which the Wells brothers had patented and which was tested in at least one experimental car that was constructed for that purpose. Automobile manufacture per se was not envisioned, however, but rather the use of the Wells-Meeker system for streetcar transit.

WENGER — Lancaster, Pennsylvania — (1907-1908) — "Auto's Built to Order and Repairing a Specialty" read the 1907 Lancaster city directory listing for L.S. Wenger & Company of 41-45 North Christian Street. In addition to Wenger's electrical contracting company, a blacksmith named John H. Kauffman and a carriage builder named John J.A. Hoover also operated their businesses at that same address. Obviously, among his trio, putting cars together would have posed no insuperable problem. That L.S. Wenger considered doing so on a more formal basis was indicated the following year when he incorporated the Wenger Simplified Motor Car Manufacturing Company. By 1909, however, he had changed his mind, moved to another building in Lancaster and advertised himself only as an electrical engineer and contractor.

WENTWORTH — Springvale, Maine — (1915) — Elmer E. Wentworth was the dealer for Overland cars, having secured a contract for the entire state of Maine. He advertised widely in the local Springvale press during the World War I years, but as a dealer only. Any cars built bearing his name would have been simply Overland chassis with custom coachwork to specific customer orders. Reportedly, Wentworth was later involved with Casco Motors, Incorporated, a company organized in Portland in 1921 to build trucks. That venture did proceed into manufacture, was reorganized as the Sanford Automotive Corporation in 1927, and continued with truck production until approximately 1930.

WENZELMANN — Galesburg, Illinois — (1907) — The Wenzelmann Manufacturing Company, makers of farm machinery and equipment in Galesburg, built the prototype of its two-stroke air-cooled friction-drive car during the fall of 1907 and announced at that time its ongoing negotiations with the Chamber of Commerce of Monmouth, Illinois regarding the "necessary concessions" for the company to locate its automobile factory there. The negotiations did not conclude favorably, and the Wenzelman car was not put into production. The following year Wenzelmann secretary-treasurer Ed Overholt left the firm to build his own car, the Illinois. Most probably he had been the man attempting to launch the Wenzelmann automotive venture.

WEST — William S. West built a steam automobile in Middleburgh, New York in 1899 in association with C. Edward Burgett. Refer to Burgett & West.

The West Coast Automobile Manufacturing Company promoted the Mission Car in Los Angeles in 1921. Refer to Mission.

The West 87th Street Garage of New York City was organized during the fall of 1906 with a capital stock of $5000 to manufacture, repair and store automobiles. Incorporators were B.C. Bell, J.B. Billinger and E.F. Riske. Manufacture is doubted.

The West Hudson Motor Company was organized in Trenton, New Jersey early in 1911 with a capital stock of $35,000 for the manufacture of automobiles. Incorporators were Arthur J. Stumpf, S.H. Crossman and Francis Stumpf. Manufacture is doubted.

The West Side Motor Company was organized in Hamilton, Ohio early in 1906 with a capital stock of $10,000 to manufacture, repair, rent and deal in automobiles. Incorporators included John E. Schmitt, Charles E. Schmitt and Clarence Murphy. Manufacture is doubted.

WEST STEAM — Rochester, New York — (1895) — John B. West of Rochester was several decades ahead of his time. The steam car he built in 1895 had disc wheels and balloon tires at the rear. The front wheels of his vehicle he purloined from a bicycle, which wasn't nearly so progressive. West's efforts earned a rave review in *The Carriage Monthly:* "Many of those who . . . started to make a vehicle discovered when the parts were put together and power applied that there was something wanting. The something wanting was in the brain of the inventor. Not so with the Rochester mechanic . . . What he knows he knows. He simply put two and two together, and the result was four wheels that are moved by an invisible power that does its work with the precision of clockwork and the force of a giant equal to six horses, nicely hidden where they do not interfere with the comfortable use of the vehicle." Unfortunately, John West wasn't able to persuade anyone to give him the money for manufacture of his car. In 1897, after a few investor nibbles, he told a reporter for *The Horseless Age* that he was just about ready to go into production. In 1899, when some capitalists from nearby Geneva expressed a mild interest, he told another *Horseless Age* reporter the same thing. He never did succeed. In 1899 a Rochester laundry owner sued the inventor after the West steamer frightened his horse and resulted in the turning over of a wagon of soiled linen. The suit was successful, and West was forced to pay damages of $53.40. Later that year West built another steam carriage for himself which presumably was less fearsome to the local equine population.

1895 West, steam runabout, NAHC

WESTBROOK — The Westbrook Garage & Machine Company was organized during the summer of 1910 with a capital stock of $10,000 to manufacture, repair and deal in automobiles in Westbrook, Maine. Incorporators were John T. Skill, Alexander Spiers and William Lyons. Manufacture is doubted.

1910 Westcott, touring, HAC

WESTCOTT — Richmond, Indiana — (1909-1916)/Springfield, Ohio — (1916-1925) — From the beginning, the Westcott had a good reputation. Though an assembled car, it was thoroughly well built and survived longer than most of its genre. The Westcott Carriage Company had been founded in 1896 in Richmond. In 1909 Burton J. Westcott moved his company into the automotive field, gingerly at first, producing only a motor buggy that year. In 1910 he switched manufacture to a standard four-cylinder 40 hp touring car, and changed his firm's name to Westcott Motor Car Company. According to the March 13th edition of the Richmond *Palladium and Sun-Telegraph* that year, Westcott was building three complete cars a day, and was six months behind on orders. In 1911 a Westcott was entered in the Indianapolis 500, driven by Harry Knight. At half distance it was "running like a watch and well up with the leaders," as reported by *The Automobile*, when, in front of the grandstand, Knight saw the Case car ahead careen into the retaining wall, its mechanic thrown directly into his path. Knight purposely crashed his car to avoid hitting him, and became the hero of the day. In 1913 the Westcott itself was lauded for heroism, following a disastrous flood in nearby Dayton, when the cars were used extensively for relief work and to bring supplies into the stricken area. The first Westcott six was introduced in 1913, and from 1916 on only sixes (Continental engines) were produced. In 1916 the company moved from Richmond to Springfield, Ohio, and the former factory there of the American Seeding Machine Company. Springfield was obviously quite pleased to have the automobile company in town, because in 1921 Burton Westcott was elected mayor. The peak production year for the Westcott was 1920, with 1850 cars built; in 1922 the company emphasized particulary its "Closure" (sedan) model with "Guest Room" — a large car that, Westcott hoped, would not be confused "with the old-fashioned, heavy cumbersome, seven-passenger 'road locomotive'." In 1924 Westcott introduced four-wheel brakes and balloon tires among available options, making these standard for 1925. But by January of 1925 the company was in receivership. Though its assets outweighed its liabilities, Westcott did not have and could not procure the funds necessary to meet debts of assorted supplier firms totaling $825,000. In March chief engineer J.H. Tuttle left Springfield for Kalamazoo to take on that same post for Checker. In April the Westcott real estate was sold at auction, though the new owners were not allowed possession until September because Westcott had orders on hand and a couple of dozen cars in the process of construction. On January 11th, 1926 Burton J. Westcott died in Springfield at the age of fifty-seven.

1910 WESTCOTT
Model F — 4-cyl., 40 hp, 112" wb

	FP	5	4	3	2	1
Touring-5P	2000	4200	5200	8400	15,700	29,000
Roadster-2P	1900	4000	5000	8000	15,000	28,000

1911 Westcott, touring, HAC

1911 WESTCOTT
Model S — 4-cyl., 45 hp, 122" wb

Fore-Door Touring	2100	4700	6100	9900	19,000	33,000
Model R — 4-cyl., 45 hp, 122" wb						
Touring-7P	2250	5000	6500	11,000	22,000	35,000
Model U — 4-cyl., 45 hp, 122" wb						
Roadster-2P	2000	4900	6300	10,300	21,000	34,000

1912 Westcott, touring, WLB

1912 WESTCOTT
Model K — 4-cyl., 40 hp, 120" wb

Fore-Door Touring	1800	4700	6100	9900	19,000	33,000
Model L — 4-cyl., 40 hp, 120" wb						
Fore-Door Torpedo	1800	4900	6300	10,300	21,000	34,000
Model M — 4-cyl., 40 hp, 120" wb						
Speedster	1800	7600	12,500	19,400	42,400	55,000
Model R — 4-cyl., 50 hp, 120" wb						
Fore-Door Touring-7P	2250	5400	7300	11,800	25,000	38,000

1913 Westcott, model 4-40, touring, HAC

1913 WESTCOTT
Model 4-40 — 4-cyl., 40 hp, 120" wb

Roadster-2P	1975	4000	5000	8000	15,000	28,000
Touring-4/5P	1975	4200	5200	8400	15,700	29,000
Model 6-50 — 6-cyl., 50 hp, 128" wb						
Touring-5P	2475	4900	6300	10,300	21,000	34,000

1914 WESTCOTT
Model 4-40 — 4-cyl., 40 hp, 120" wb

Roadster-2P	1975	4500	5800	9500	18,000	32,000
Touring-5P	1975	4700	6100	9900	19,000	33,000

1914 Westcott, model 6-50, touring, HAC

	FP	5	4	3	2	1
Torpedo-4P	1975	4700	6100	9900	19,000	33,000
Model 6-50 — 6-cyl., 50 hp, 128" wb						
Touring-5P	2485	5300	7000	11,500	24,000	37,000
Roadster-2P	2485	5200	6800	11,300	23,000	36,000
Touring-7P	2535	5400	7300	11,800	25,000	38,000

1915 WESTCOTT
Model O — 4-cyl., 35 hp, 113" wb

Touring-5P	1185	4300	5400	8700	16,500	30,000
Runabout-2P	1185	4200	5200	8400	15,700	29,000
Roadster-3P	1185	4300	5300	8600	16,100	29,500
Model U — 6-cyl., 50 hp, 125" wb						
Touring-6P	1585	5300	7000	11,500	24,000	37,000
Roadster-2P	1585	5200	6800	11,300	23,000	36,000

1916 Westcott, touring, HAC

1916 WESTCOTT
Model 41 — 6-cyl., 40 hp, 121" wb

Touring-5P	1295	4500	5800	9500	18,000	32,000
Cloverleaf Roaster-3P	1295	4400	5600	9200	17,300	31,000
Cloverleaf Cabriolet-3P	1595	4300	5400	8700	16,500	30,000
Model 42 — 6-cyl., 42 hp, 121" wb						
Touring-5P	1445	4900	6300	10,300	21,000	34,000
Cloverleaf Roadster-3P	1445	4700	6100	9900	19,000	33,000
Cloverleaf Cabriolet-3P	1745	4400	5600	9200	17,300	31,000
Model 51 — 6-cyl., 50 hp, 126" wb						
Touring-7P	1595	5400	7300	11,800	25,000	38,000
Cloverleaf Roadster-3P	1595	5200	6800	11,300	23,000	36,000
Sedan-7P	1945	3100	4200	6300	10,500	22,000

1917 Westcott, touring, JAC

1917 WESTCOTT
Series 17 — 6-cyl., 50 hp, 125" wb

	FP	5	4	3	2	1
Touring-7P	1690	5300	7000	11,500	24,000	37,000
Touring-5P	1590	5200	6800	11,300	23,000	36,000
Roadster-4P	1590	5000	6500	11,000	22,000	35,000
Touring Sedan-5P	2090	2900	3700	5600	9100	20,000
Sedan-7P	2190	3000	3900	5800	9300	20,500

1918 Westcott, coupe, HAC

1918 WESTCOTT
Series 18 — 16-cyl., 50 hp, 125" wb

Touring-7P	1940	5300	7000	11,500	24,000	37,000
Touring-5P	1940	5200	6800	11,300	23,000	36,000
Cloverleaf Roadster-4P	1890	5000	6500	11,000	22,000	35,000
Sportster	2290	5200	6800	11,300	23,000	36,000
Convertible Sedan-7P	2790	5000	6500	11,000	22,000	35,000
Convertible Sedan-5P	2790	4900	6300	10,300	21,000	34,000
Coupe-4P	2790	3000	4000	6000	9500	21,000

1919 Westcott, touring, HAC

1919 WESTCOTT
Series 19 — 6-cyl., 50 hp, 125" wb

Touring-7P	2590	5300	7000	11,500	24,000	37,000
Roadster-4P	2190	5200	6800	11,300	23,000	36,000
Convertible Sedan-7P	3190	5000	6500	11,000	22,000	35,000
Convertible Sedan-5P	3190	4900	6300	10,300	21,000	34,000
Convertible Coupe-4P	3190	5000	6500	11,000	22,000	35,000

1920 Westcott, model C-48, touring, HAC

1920 WESTCOTT
Model C-38 — 6-cyl., 55 hp, 118" wb

Touring-5P	2390	5300	7000	11,500	24,000	37,000
Roadster-2P	2390	5200	6800	11,300	23,000	36,000
Sedan-5P	3490	2700	3600	5300	8800	19,000
Coupe-3P	3190	3000	4000	6000	9500	21,000

Model C-48 — 6-cyl., 51 hp, 125" wb

Touring-7P	2890	5400	7300	11,800	25,000	38,000
Sedan-Limousine-7P	4490	3900	4800	7700	14,300	27,000
Sedan-7P	4390	2900	3700	5600	9100	20,000

1482

1921 Westcott, model C-48, touring, HAC

1921 WESTCOTT
Model C-38 — 6-cyl., 55 hp, 118" wb

	FP	5	4	3	2	1
Touring-5P	2290	5200	6800	11,300	23,000	36,000
Roadster-2P	2290	5000	6500	11,000	22,000	35,000
Coupe-4P	3390	2700	3600	5300	8800	19,000
Sedan-5P	3390	2400	3400	4800	8000	17,000

Model C-48 — 6-cyl., 51 hp, 125" wb

Touring-5P	2990	5200	6800	11,300	23,000	36,000
Touring-7P	2990	5300	7000	11,500	24,000	37,000
Sedan-7P	4590	2500	3500	5000	8500	18,000
Limousine-Sedan-7P	4690	2700	3600	5300	8800	19,000

1922 Westcott, model D-48, sedan, HAC

1922 WESTCOTT
Model A-44 — 6-cyl., 48 hp, 120" wb

Sedan-5P	2890	2400	3400	4800	8000	17,000
Touring-5P	—	3100	4200	6300	10,500	22,000
Roadster	—	3000	4000	6000	9500	21,000
Coupe	—	2700	3600	5300	8800	19,000
Special Touring	1990	3200	4300	6500	11,000	23,000

Model D-48 — 6-cyl., 51 hp, 125" wb

Touring-7P	2090	5200	6800	11,300	23,000	36,000
Sedan-7P	3490	2500	3500	5000	8500	18,000

1923 Westcott, model B-44, special touring, HAC

1923 WESTCOTT
Model B-44 — 6-cyl., 56 hp, 120" wb

Standard Touring-5P	1690	4900	6300	10,300	21,000	34,000
Special Touring-5P	1890	5200	6800	11,300	23,000	36,000
Brougham-4P	2490	2500	3500	5000	8500	18,000
Standard Sedan-5P	2690	2000	3000	4200	6500	14,000
Special Sedan-5P	2890	2200	3200	4400	7000	15,000

Model D-48 — 6-cyl., 52 hp, 125" wb

Touring-7P	1990	5000	6500	11,000	22,000	35,000
Special touring-7P	2190	5300	7000	11,500	24,000	37,000

1924 WESTCOTT
Model B-44 — 6-cyl., 56 hp, 120" wb

Touring-5P	1590	4500	5800	9500	18,000	32,000

	FP	5	4	3	2	1
Sport Touring-5P	1690	4700	6100	9900	19,000	33,000
Brougham-4P	2090	2700	3600	5300	8800	19,000
Sedan-5P	2490	2000	3000	4200	6500	14,000
Model D-48 — 6-cyl., 52 hp, 125" wb						
Touring-7P	1990	4900	6300	10,300	21,000	34,000
Special Touring-7P	2190	5000	6500	11,000	22,000	35,000

1924 Westcott, model B-44, sedan, JAC

1925 Westcott, model H-60, sedan, HAC

1925 WESTCOTT

Model H-44 — 6-cyl., 56 hp, 120" wb						
Touring-5P	1895	4500	5800	9500	18,000	32,000
Special Touring-5P	2045	4700	6100	9900	19,000	33,000
Four-Door Sedan-5P	2325	2000	3000	4200	6500	14,000
Brougham-5P	2395	2200	3200	4400	7000	15,000
Model H-60 — 6-cyl., 56 hp, 118" wb						
Sedan-5P	2325	1800	2800	4000	6200	13,000

WESTERN — The Western Automobile Company of Chicago, Illinois was organized during the fall of 1904 with a capital stock of $5000 to manufacture and repair motor cars. Incorporators were John E. Bensley, Neville McKeever and Harry J. Dunbaugh. Manufacture is doubted.

The Western Automobile Company of St. Louis, Missouri was organized during the fall of 1903 with a capital stock of $10,000 for the manufacture of motor cars. Incorporators were Marion L.J. Lambert, Samuel Brendon and Samuel B. McPheeters. Manufacture is doubted.

The Western Automobile Company of Seattle, Washington produced a car called the Waco from 1915-1917. Refer to Waco.

The Western Automobile Company of Trenton, New Jersey was organized with a capital stock of $6 million late in 1899 for the manufacture of "automobiles and electric motor vehicles." Incorporators were H.M. Martin, A.H. Chetselain, John R. Curtis and David H. Roolin, all of Camden. Manufacture is doubted.

The Western Automobile and Industrial Company of Chicago, Illinois was organized during the summer of 1904 with a capital stock of $25,000 for the manufacture of automobiles and engines. Incorporators were Michael Koener, John L. Biehl and Michael Heisser. Manufacture is doubted.

The Western Gas Engine Company of Mishawaka, Indiana provided the venue in which R.B. Hayn built a car in 1901. Refer to Hayn.

The Western Imperial Electric Company at 605 South Hill Street in Long Beach, California advertised itself as an automobile manufacturer in 1915. Dr. George Putenney was president. It would appear that the vehicles built by this firm were light delivery trucks only — and only for a short time.

The Western Motor Company of National City, California was organized during the fall of 1907 with a capital stock of $200,000 for the manufacture of engines and motor cars. Incorporators were W.H. and C.E. Hunt and C.L. Brimhall. Manufacture is doubted.

The Western Motor Car Manufacturing Company of Denver, Colorado was organized during the spring of 1917 with a capital stock of $700,000 for the manufacture of automobiles. Walter Scott Campbell headed this venture. "A factory site has been purchased," *Automobile Topics* reported that April. "The machines are to be assembled of standard components." Manufacture is doubted.

The Western Motor Truck & Vehicle Company of Chicago, Illinois, which had been experimenting in the automotive field since the turn of the century, proceeded into manufacture of a car in 1905 that was marketed under the tradename of Beebe. Refer to Beebe.

The Western Tool Works of Galesburg, Illinois built the Gale car from 1905-1907. Refer to Gale.

The Western Vehicle Company of New York City was organized early in 1913 with a capital stock of $1000 for the manufacture of motor vehicles. Incorporators were H. Davis, W.R. Williams and C.M. Frost. Manufacture is doubted.

WESTERN — Chicago, Illinois — (1900) — Included among the people behind the Western Automobile Company of Chicago were J.H. Curtis, Carl L. Jones, John Trier and Mr. and Mrs. M.M. Chessown. There may have been others, but the foregoing represented the quintet which descended upon Stevens Point, Wisconsin in mid-January 1900. "The representatives have one of their motor vehicles with them and considerable interest has been aroused," a dispatch from Milwaukee revealed. "The suggested proposition is a rather large one and the business men do not know whether to undertake it or not." The proposition was for the Stevens Point citizenry to subscribe $200,000 worth of stock and to help the Western folks in securing the old Wisconsin Central Railway shops to build a factory. Stevens Point did not remain interested long.

WESTERN — Los Angeles, California — (1900-1902) — The Western Iron Works, Inc. of 115 Bruno Street in Los Angeles was headed by William C. Woodward, William W. Wood and Cassius M. Smith. The firm, which manufactured gasoline engines and machinery, first announced its availability as an automobile builder in late 1900. In 1901 a move around the corner to 908 North Main Street put the company into larger quarters which now included a foundry. Automobiles continued to be advertised, although undoubtedly any produced were on a custom order basis. By 1903 Western Iron Works advertising ceased mention of the availability of Western-built automobiles. The company had taken on an agency for the Winton instead.

WESTERN — Denver, Colorado — (1907) — O.M. Davis was president of the Western Automobile Company which was located at 38 South Broadway in Denver. J.O. Breckenridge was manager. The Western's model lineup was a two-cylinder 16 hp runabout with a price tag of $850 and a 40/50 hp six to sell as a runabout at $1850 and a touring car at $2000. How many of any of these models the company sold is not known, but the firm assuredly did not long survive as a manufacturer.

WESTERN — Chicago, Illinois — (1908) — The Western Automobile Company was organized in Chicago during the late summer of 1907 by W.P Hall and J. Sidney. The capital stock was $25,000, and the company was ready with a car for the Chicago Automobile Show in early 1908. The Western was an 18/20 hp roadster with a neat body for two passengers and allowing for the addition of two more via a rear deck folding bench seat. A three-speed selective transmission was fitted. "The Western is a new car, never before exhibited," reported *The Automobile*, "and in fact, is only just ready for the market, its appearance at the show coming practically unheralded." Unheralded, too, was the exit of the Western Automobile Company later that year. The number of cars produced is not known.

WESTERN — Chicago, Illinois — (1908) — The Western Auto Parts Company of 107 Dearborn Street in Chicago offered a kit that would allow anyone to become an automobile builder: all parts, full-sized blueprints, even photographs of what the finished car should look like. "Others have done it, why not you?," the firm advertised. Actually, given the primeval look of the Western product, probably anybody could. How many did is not known.

WESTERN — Butte, Montana — (1910) — That the Western Carriage Works of 416 South Main Street in Butte produced automobiles in 1910 was indicated in several trade publications that year. Details regarding the cars built are lacking, however. J.A. Poitros was the general manager of the company, E.D. Souve was the purchasing agent.

WESTERNER — Topeka, Kansas — (1912) — In April of 1912, Charles and George Southwick, who had taken over the Smith Automobile Company factory in Topeka the year previous, announced that a workforce of sixteen men were busy at the plant assembling the Great Smith touring car, "a number of which will be ready to market by the time the roads are in condition for traveling." By that time, too, the new Westerner would be all set. Details regarding the Westerner are scant because the car did not survive the prototype stage. That it was to be offered as a roadster is known, and would have been a logical step since the Great Smith was a touring car only. A Westerner truck was also to be introduced. This venture was quickly over. In July of 1912 the Smith Automobile Company factory was sold to a Kansas City manufacturer of silos. "In connection with the assembling and manufacturing of silos," reported *Automobile Topics*, "the new owners intend to operate a general automobile repair shop and garage in the factory, as there is abundant 'elbow room' for all three enterprises." But no room for either the Great Smith or the Westerner.

WESTERN RESERVE — Warren, Ohio — (1921) — R.K. Johnson, S.T. Balltrip, K.B. Lyder and L.C. Heckel were the people behind the Western Reserve Motor Car Company, with headquarters in downtown Warren, factory in nearby Leavittsburg. The firm was incorporated for $300,000 in early 1921 for the purpose of manufacturing a six-cylinder 55 hp touring car on a 121-inch wheelbase. The car's engine was to be built by Western Reserve, with the rest of its component parts arriving from varied automotive supply companies in northeastern Ohio. This venture does not appear to have progressed beyond the prototype stage.

1902 Westfield, runabout, WLB

WESTFIELD STEAM — Westfield, Massachusetts — (1901-1903) — At the turn of the century, while working for the Lozier branch of the American Bicycle Company, Charles J. Moore built his first steam automobile. He proceeded into manufacture in November 1901, when he organized the C.J. Moore Manufacturing Company in Westfield with a capital stock of $35,000. The Westfield steam car — a small runabout powered by a two-cylinder 6 hp engine — was formally introduced in 1902, and early in 1903 the firm also exhibited a gasoline car equipped with a four-cylinder 16 hp engine. But complete cars were not Charles J. Moore's specialty. Brochures indicate he preferred providing his product "ready for power" — with its engine to be the customer's choice and responsibility. By late 1902 his advertising focused on running gear, either chain or shaft drive and with a wide variety of runabout, touring and delivery bodies. He continued to offer his $1000 and $1400 steam runabouts in 1903, but it appears the gasoline car he built was for demonstration purposes only and was not marketed. C.J. Moore achieved greater fame after he left Westfield to join the engineering department of the Packard Motor Car Company.

1901-1903 WESTFIELD STEAM
Model A Steam — 2-cyl., 6 hp

	FP	5	4	3	2	1
Runabout-2P	1000	2200	3200	4400	7000	15,000
Model B Steam — 2-cyl., 6 hp						
Runabout-4P	1400	2200	3200	4400	7000	15,000

WESTFIELD — Westfield, Massachusetts — (1915) — In August of 1915 a new organization styling itself the Westfield Manufacturing Company bought the former Pope plant at public auction for $725,000. The firm was subsequently capitalized at $1.2 million with the announced intention of producing motorcars. This did not happen. At least one prototype of a light car to be called the Westfield was built, however, because its components are known to have been supplied by the T & F Cycle Car Company of New Salem. Shortly thereafter Westfield turned to other manufacturing pursuits.

1906 Westinghouse, touring, NAHC

WESTINGHOUSE — Pittsburgh, Pennsylvania — (1901) / (1905-1907) — In 1901 the Westinghouse Electric & Manufacturing Company of Pittsburgh bought out the patents of Hub Motors Company of Chicago. Hub had built a number of small electric passenger carriages at the turn of the century, and Westinghouse may have subsequently built a few more of these cars. The Hub patents had been acquired, however, specifically to enable the firm to build forty electric buses, with bodies by American Carriage Company. In 1905 Westinghouse made a further foray into the automobile field, with a gasoline car this time. A water-cooled 40 hp four on a 122-inch wheelbase, this Westinghouse sold in chassis form for $7500, and with limousine body for $10,000. The car was designed in Pittsburgh, but was built in Le Havre, France by Societe Anonyme Westinghouse. "The owner of a Westinghouse car . . . can doubtless follow his own inclinations as to whether he calls his car an American or a French machine," *The Automobile* said in 1906. "However that may be, the car shows itself, in actual operation, to be one that neither American nor Frenchman need be ashamed of." Manufacture and importation of the Westinghouse seems to have ceased by the fall of 1907 when the company entered a short receivership.

WESTMAN — Minneapolis, Minnesota — (c. 1900) — That E. Westman of Minneapolis built an automobile in Minneapolis has been documented, but whether it was completed in 1897 or about 1900 is open to conjecture. Westman was an employee of the Enterprise Machine Company in town.

1899 Weston, steam runabout, MVMA

WESTON STEAM — Orange, Massachusetts — (1899-1903) — Weston was the name given to the steam car produced by the Grout Brothers of Orange when it was sent overseas to be marketed in England. It was handled there by the Weston Motor Syndicate on Regent Street in London. Five varied models were offered including a "Touring Weston" which *The Autocar* described as a "really handsome and serviceable carriage . . . with smart leather hood and imitation cane panelled body." The Weston was available in England from 1899 to 1903.

WESTON STEAM — Passaic, New Jersey — (1901) — How many of his new steam carriages he built is not known but in May of 1901 Frank H. Weston of Passaic indicated that he had secured a factory there and expected to have fifty cars completed before September. Further details are lacking.

WESTWICK — Galena, Illinois — (1901) — Although others like it may have been produced to specific customer order, only one car is documented to have been built at the Westwick Foundry in Galena. It was ordered by and destined for William Harris of Chicago.

WESTMINSTER — During the summer of 1904, Amandee V. Reyburn, Jr., James W. Bemis, Henry W. Blodgett and William W. Gardiner organized the Westminster Automobile Company in St. Louis for the manufacture of motor cars. Capital stock was a mere $5000 of which only half was paid in. Manufacture did not follow.

WETHERBEE — The Wetherbee Brothers Company was organized in Arlington, Massachusetts during the spring of 1912 with a capital stock of $20,000 for the manufacture of automobiles. The brothers were Ivers L. and Clarence A. Wetherbee. Manufacture is doubted.

1911 W.F.S., 5-pass. touring, NAHC

W.F.S. — Philadelphia, Pennsylvania — (1911-1912) — W.F. Shetzline was a Philadelphia electrical contractor who put himself into the automobile business in 1911 as the W.F.S. Motor Car Company for the manufacture of a car he had designed. In 1911 the W.F.S. was a 25 hp four on a 112-inch wheelbase; in 1912 it grew to 40 hp and a 118-inch wheelbase. Shaft drive, a three-speed sliding gear transmission located on the rear axle and a multiple-disc clutch were featured, as was right-hand steering, this last a curiosity since most American cars were left-steering by now. The price range was $2150-$3200. Shetzline's automotive venture survived two years only.

1911 W.F.S.
Four — 25 hp, 112" wb

	FP	5	4	3	2	1
Touring-5P	2250	3300	4400	6700	12,000	24,000
Runabout-4P	2300	3200	4300	6500	11,000	23,000
Roadster-2P	2150	3000	4000	6000	9500	21,000
Limousine	3200	2700	3600	5300	8800	19,000

1912 W.F.S
Four — 40 hp, 118" wb

Model A Roadster	2450	3200	4300	6500	11,000	23,000
Model B Gunboat-4P	2500	3300	4400	6700	12,000	24,000
Model C Touring-5P	2450	3500	4500	7000	13,000	25,000
Model D Raceabout	2400	3300	4400	6700	12,000	24,000
Model E Limousine	3200	2900	3700	5600	9100	20,000

1914 W-G, cyclecar roadster, LC

W-G — Waterloo, Iowa & Pottstown, Pennsylvania — (1914) — A veteran of the Chadwick works in Pottstown, Pennsylvania, N.H. White traveled to Waterloo, Iowa to begin his automotive venture. There he established the White Manufacturing Company, and there he designed a quite typical cyclecar: two-cylinder air-cooled vee engine, friction transmission, chain drive, 96-inch wheelbase, 40-inch tread, side-by-side two-seater. Within months, however, he decided to return home to Pottstown where he set himself up in a small factory and said quantity deliveries of his new car, now designated the W-G, would begin July 1914. The W-G's price was $375. Very few were built before White's venture ended. Whether he got his old job back at Chadwick is not known.

WHALEY-HENRIETTE — St. Paul, Minnesota — (1898-1900) — When he first completed his car in 1898, Charles F. Whaley frankly admitted that his chances of returning home from any outing under power were just fifty-fifty. But he continued tinkering with the automotive idea, and by the turn of the century had a vehicle that was more reliable although contemporary newspaper reports stated that it "vibrated violently when idling." The Whaley-Henriette, as he called his car, was powered by a single-cylinder 3 hp gasoline engine, was fitted with gear and chain drive, weighed a total of 800 pounds and was good for up to 25 mph. Although *The Automobile* in July 1900 reported that Whaley was building other automobiles, having "taken up this work with a great deal of enthusiasm," indications are that his enthusiasm soon waned, or harsh reality set in. During this period, Whaley was manufacturing bicycle specialities and hardware in association with John J. Dywer. The Whaley-Dwyer Company had ceased to exist by 1902, by which time Dwyer had opened his own plumbing company, and Whaley had become a travel agent.

1922 Wharton, roadster, WLB

WHARTON — Dallas, Texas — (1922-1923) — Although the Wharton Motors Company was organized in Dallas in 1920, it does not appear that anything other than stock in the company was sold until 1922. Thomas B. Wharton was the man behind the venture, and he was allied with John R. Pratt of Daytona (Florida) and a group of Dallas businessmen and bankers including William E. Grigsby, J. William Johnson and Matthew Troy. The company's product line was to include trucks and tractors, in addition to a variety of models of motorcar powered by the Curtiss-OX-5 aero engine. An elaborate brochure was produced claiming 104 hp for the Curtiss-engined Wharton, with seven body types available on a 136-inch wheelbase chassis: a touring at $3450, a victoria and sport at $3750, a sport roadster at $4000, a sedan at $4350, a town car at $4650, a Continental landaulet at $4800. In March of 1922 Wharton Motors Company announced that it was set for production in its Dallas factory, and had optioned a further plant site in Johnstown, Pennsylvania. Such manufacture as did follow took place wholly in Texas, however. Although a line of cheaper four-cylinder ($1450-$2450) and six-cylinder ($1750-$2750) cars was announced, none were built. Indeed, total Wharton automobile production may have been but a single OX-5-engined roadster. In March of

1924 several stockholders in the Wharton Motors Company brought suit against the firm requesting receivership and an injunction to restrain management from disposing of any of the Wharton property. The suit also asked damages of $200,000, alleging that Thomas Wharton had spent that amount of money without his board of directors' approval. The Wharton was no more.

1902 Wheeler, tonneau, GR

WHEELER — Marlboro, Massachusetts — (1900-1902) — Three Wheelers were built, and but for a bad bit of luck there might have been more. The cars were the idea of E.O. Wheeler, a graduate of Worcester Polytechnical Institute, and he talked his father, O.D. Wheeler, who owned a machine shop in Marlboro into helping him build them. Runabouts all, the first was powered by an air-cooled single-cylinder engine and was sold in 1900 for $900. A similar car was built and sold the year following. The third car arrived in 1902, powered by a water-cooled 4 1/2 hp De Dion this time. Its transmission was a two-speed planetary, final drive was by shaft, the engine was up front under a Renault-type hood, and an auxiliary seat was added at the rear. Now, the Wheelers thought, they had come up with an admirable car for quantity production. They proceeded far enough to decide upon $1200 as a price tag, the Wheeler Automobile Manufacturing Company as the designation for their venture, and they approached a bank in Boston for the necessary loan to gear up for manufacture. The bank was amenable — until it discovered that another financial institution in Boston had been bilked by a flim-flam artist promoting a steam car venture elsewhere in New England. The loan was off. The Wheelers preserved the last car, which had been their production dream. It remains extant. In 1911 E.O. Wheeler organized the Acme Motor Car Company in Worchester, though it served principally as a dealership.

WHEEL — The Wheel of Fortune Corporation was organized in Jersey City, New Jersey late in 1912 with a capital stock of $600,000 for the manufacture of automobiles. Incorporators were L.H. Gunther, H.A. Black and J.R. Turner. Why they chose that extraordinary name is not known. Manufacture is doubted.

The Wheel Within A Wheel Corporation of New York City was organized late in 1901 with Colonel George Pope as president. This venture is not believed to have proceeded any further than the mounting of the hub-motor-type device on a Gasmobile for experimental purposes.

WHEELING — "The Wheeling Novelty Company, Wheeling, West Virginia is building an experimental gasoline carriage," *The Horseless Age* reported in December 1899. Details are lacking.

WHIFFLER — Detroit, Michigan — (1903-1904) — At the corner of Sherman and Hastings streets in Detroit, Charles Whiffler set up his automobile company during the summer of 1903. His product was a touring car powered by a two-cylinder horizontal opposed engine and virtually every part of which he made himself. The price was $1000. Whiffler was a typical mechanic of the period, starting his automobile business on a shoestring, and surviving but a short time. The Charles Whiffler Automobile Company ceased building cars at the corner of Sherman and Hastings late in 1904.

1927 Whippet, coach, HAC

WHIPPET — Toledo, Ohio — (1927-1931) — The Whippet was wonderfully named. It was small and it was swift, and it was both those things in the superlative. At its introduction in the fall of 1926, the Whippet was America's smallest car, its wheelbase 100¼ inches, its engine a 134-cubic-inch 30 hp four, with a 40 hp six on a 109¼-inch wheelbase following in January 1927. That the Whippet was swift was effectively demonstrated when one of the sixes was taken to the Indianapolis Motor Speedway for a 24-hour endurance run which was completed at an average 56.52 mph to establish a new American record for stock cars priced under $1000. And the Whippet was priced well under a thousand, with a four-cylinder cabriolet at only $545 in 1928 (five dollars less than a comparable Ford), and the six's price range that year reduced to $615-$745 ("the world's lowest priced six" was an advertising slogan). The Whippet was produced by the Willys-Overland Company of Toledo, and superseded the Overland. Among the reasons for its carrying its own identity (complete with stylized Whippet typescript and Whippet emblem of the namesake dog jumping through a hoop) was probably the misfortunes having greeted earlier Overland attempts to market a contender in the lowest-priced field. The Whippet had its own distinctive personality, and a European look. The latter was largely the result of its development by Willys-Overland-Crossley Ltd., a subsidiary which John North Willys had set up in England in 1920. (Moreso than any other manufacturer, Willys had recognized the potential importance of export and had committed considerable effort to it; by 1913 no fewer than 37 countries, from Java to Bulgaria, had Willys-Overland dealerships; the first automobile agency in Iceland was the Overland dealership established in Reykjavic in 1914.) The European light car look of the Whippet was enhanced by a specification — four wheel mechanical brakes, seven-bearing crankshaft, full pressure lubrication to all bearings except piston pins, Nelson Bohnalite invar strut pistons — that was extraordinary given the car's low price. Both open and closed cars were produced, the Collegiate roadster becoming a particularly popular car on campuses throughout the country. Whippet sales for its first year in production totaled a healthy 110,000 units, and helped propel the Willys-Overland company into third place in the industry behind Chevrolet and Ford in 1928. In 1928 and 1929 the Whippet contributed handsomely to overall Willys-Overland sales of 315,000 and 242,000 cars respectively. But with the Wall Street crash and the aftermath of the Depression, the Willys company directed all efforts toward a single new model (the Willys 77) which, it was hoped, would carry the company through the hard times. The Whippet was discontinued in early 1931.

1926
Model 96, 4-cyl.

	FP	5	4	3	2	1
2P Cpe	—	800	1550	3800	5300	7600
5P Tr	—	2800	5700	9500	13,300	19,000
5P Sed	—	800	1550	3800	5300	7600

1927
Model 96, 4-cyl., 30 hp, 104-1/4" wb

	FP	5	4	3	2	1
5P Tr	—	2800	5700	9500	13,300	19,000
5P Coach	—	775	1500	3750	5250	7500
5P Rds	—	2300	5400	9000	12,600	18,000
2P Cpe	—	875	1700	4250	5900	8500
5P Sed	—	800	1550	3800	5300	7600
Cabr	—	1400	4200	7000	9800	14,000
5P Lan Sed	—	775	1500	3700	5200	7400

Model 93A, 6-cyl., 40 hp, 109-1/4" wb

	FP	5	4	3	2	1
5P Tr	—	3000	6000	10,000	14,000	20,000
2/4P Rds	—	2800	5700	9500	13,300	19,000
2P Cpe	—	900	1900	4500	6300	9000
5P Cpe	—	825	1600	4000	5600	8000
5P Sed	—	850	1650	4100	5700	8200
Cabr	—	1400	4200	7000	9800	14,000
5P Lan Sed	—	775	1500	3700	5200	7400

1928 Whippet, roadster, WLB

1928
Model 96, 4-cyl., 32 hp, 100-1/4" wb

	FP	5	4	3	2	1
2/4P Spt Rds	525	2300	5400	9000	12,600	18,000
5P Tr	—	2800	5700	9500	13,300	19,000
5P Coach	—	750	1450	3300	4900	7000
2P Cpe	525	825	1600	4000	5600	8000
2/4P Cabr	—	1400	4200	7000	9800	14,000
5P Sed	610	750	1450	3500	5050	7200

Model 98, 6-cyl.

	FP	5	4	3	2	1
2/4P Rds	685	2800	5700	9500	13,300	19,000
5P Tr	—	3000	6000	10,000	14,000	20,000
2P Cpe	695	900	1900	4500	6300	9000
5P Coach	—	825	1600	4000	5600	8000
5P Sed	770	850	1650	4100	5700	8200

1929
Model 96A, 4-cyl., 103-1/2" wb

	FP	5	4	3	2	1
2P Rds	—	2300	5400	9000	12,600	18,000
2/4P Rds	—	2800	5700	9500	13,300	19,000
2/4P Rds College	555	2800	5700	9500	13,300	19,000
5P Tr	—	2800	5700	9500	13,300	19,000
2P Cpe	575	825	1600	4000	5600	8000
Cabr	—	1400	4200	7000	9800	14,000
2/4P Cpe	—	1400	4200	7000	9800	14,000

1928 Whippet, touring, OCW

	FP	5	4	3	2	1
5P Coach	—	750	1450	3300	4900	7000
5P Sed	—	750	1450	3500	5050	7200
DeL Sed	630	775	1500	3750	5250	7500

Model 98A, 6-cyl.

	FP	5	4	3	2	1
2/4P Spt Rds	850	3150	6300	10,500	14,700	21,000
5P Tr	—	3300	6600	11,000	15,400	22,000
2P Cpe	695	875	1700	4250	5900	8500
2/4P Cpe	—	900	1800	4450	6250	8900
5P Coach	—	750	1450	3500	5050	7200
5P Sed	—	775	1500	3750	5250	7500
5P DeL Sed	785	775	1500	3750	5250	7500

1930 Whippet, six coach, JAC

1930
Model 96A, 4-cyl.

	FP	5	4	3	2	1
2P Rds	—	3150	6300	10,500	14,700	21,000
2/4P Rds	505	3300	6600	11,000	15,400	22,000
2/4P Rds College	—	3600	7200	12,000	16,800	24,000
5P Tr	—	3300	6600	11,000	15,400	22,000
2P Cpe	525	825	1600	4000	5600	8000
2/4P Cpe	—	875	1700	4250	5900	8500
5P Coach	—	750	1450	3300	4900	7000
5P Sed	—	750	1450	3500	5050	7200
5P DeL Sed	585	775	1500	3750	5250	7500

Model 98A, 6-cyl.

	FP	5	4	3	2	1
5P Tr	—	3400	6900	11,500	16,100	23,000
2/4P Spt Rds	850	3150	6300	10,500	14,700	21,000
2P Cpe	—	850	1650	4100	5700	8200
2/4P Cpe	695	875	1700	4300	6000	8600
5P Coach	—	750	1450	3500	5050	7200
5P Sed	—	775	1500	3600	5100	7300
5P DeL Sed	785	800	1550	3900	5450	7800

Model 96A, 4-cyl.

	FP	5	4	3	2	1
2P Cpe	—	825	1600	4000	5600	8000
2/4P Cpe	—	875	1700	4250	5900	8500
5P Sed	—	750	1450	3500	5050	7200

Model 98A, 6-cyl.

	FP	5	4	3	2	1
5P Coach	—	750	1450	3500	5050	7200
5P Sed	—	775	1500	3600	5100	7300
5P DeL Sed	—	800	1550	3900	5450	7800

WHIPPLE STEAM — Locke, New York — (1899) — Light weight and economy of running were the guiding principles used by William N. Whipple of Locke in the building of his steam carriage. Its 2½ hp engine and boiler were largely built of aluminum; soft coal or kerosene oil could be used as fuel, at a cost of about twelve cents a day. The engine and boiler were under the rear seat of the carriage, connected by tubes to the boiler in front of the driver's seat. Smoke from the firebox was carried directly under the bottom of the carriage and discharged through a pipe at the rear. The Whipple carriage sat four and had a canopy top. Though William Whipple was an engineer, and his shops in Union Springs could have been outfitted for production it does not appear he proceeded into manufacture.

WHIPPLE — Chicago, Illinois — (1902-1903) — Ira H. Whipple of the Whipple Cycle Company went automotive in 1902 simply by adding a small gasoline engine to his usual product. The Whipple motorcycle was a good-looking machine, and he added runners to the front of another bicycle in his shop to make a motor sleigh which was displayed at the Chicago Automobile Show that year. Apparently, he attempted four wheels in an experimental runabout but ultimately decided to confine his manufacturing efforts to two wheels — and took on an agency for the curved dash Oldsmobile instead.

WHITCOMB — G.A. Whitcomb of Natick, Massachusetts was indicated as an automobile manufacturer in the Hiscox book *Horseless Vehicles, Automobiles, Motor Cycles* published in 1900. Documentation is lacking. The Natick city directory listed his activity only as "bicycle repairer." Conceivably he may have been the George A. Whitcomb who is known to have invented a "valveless petroleum motor" which was described in *Modern Machinery* in October 1899. That Whitcomb was noted as hailing from Framingham, however, and there is no mention of the motor being tested in an experimental vehicle.

WHITE — The George White Buggy Company of Rock Island, Illinois built a two-cylinder shaft-drive highwheeler in 1909 which was marketed under the full company name. Refer to George White.

The White, Binford & Robenson Motor Company of Boston, Massachusetts was organized during the fall of 1911 with a capital stock of $20,000 for the manufacture of automobiles. Incorporators were Albert C. White, Jr., Cecil P. Robenson and Henry O. Cushman. Manufacture is doubted.

The White Manufacturing Company of Pottstown, Pennsylvania promoted a car called the W-G in 1914. Refer to W-G.

The White Manufacturing Company of Waterloo, Iowa purportedly built a cyclecar in 1914. Documentation is lacking.

The White Motor Company of Camden, New Jersey was organized during the spring of 1906 with a capital stock of $150,000 to manufacture and deal in automobiles. Incorporators were James A. White, Charles F. Woodhull and Charles S. King. Manufacture is doubted.

The White Motor Car Company of Cleveland, Ohio has been indicated on various rosters as an automobile manufacturer in 1909 unrelated to the famous White Company which had been producing its steamers in town since 1909. That no relationship existed is true, that this other White company manufactured a car is not. Will B. White was the man involved, and he had been the leading figure in the French-American Motor Company which had a brief fling in the automotive arena beginning in 1907. By the end of 1908, the French-American adventure was over and Will B. White and friends contented themselves thereafter in the auto-parts field. The White Motor Car Company was merely another name under which that business was continued a short while in 1909, probably until the White Company objected.

The White Motor Wagon Company organized in 1899 in the Greater New York area was the third attempt of Lewis B. White to get his New Power automotive idea into production. Refer to New Power.

The White Safety Firearms Company of Newport, Rhode Island was organized early in 1904 with a capital stock of $100,000 to manufacture and deal in "firearms, ammunition, general sporting goods, bicycles, automobiles, machinery and to buy and sell real estate and stocks." Incorporators in this ambitious venture were Norman Whitney, Henry B. Whitney, John D. Johnson, Allan Woodruff, Michael H. Sullivan, Thomas P. Griffith and Rufus E. Darrah. Manufacture of a car is doubted.

The White Steam Wagon Company of Indianapolis, Indiana was listed as the manufacture of a steam automobile in the "Buyer's Guide" section of *Cycle and Automobile Trade Journal* in 1903. The firm built trucks in Indianapolis from 1900 through 1903, but documentation regarding a passenger car is lacking.

WHITE — Cleveland, Ohio — (1900-1918) — Thomas H. White had begun the manufacture of sewing machines in Massachusetts in partnership with William L. Grout. Following the Civil War he moved to Cleveland where he established the White Sewing Machine Company and where at the turn of the century his sons (like the Grout brothers in Massachusetts) moved the company into the manufacture of steam cars. A semi-flash boiler invented by Rollin White in the late 1890's provided the impetus, though brothers Windsor and Walter were involved in the auto-making venture from the beginning. By the spring of 1900, four White steam cars had been built, and the company's first truck followed that year; production in 1901 climbed to 193 units. In the New York to Buffalo Endurance Run of 1901 four Whites were entered, each of them being awarded a first-class certificate. The first Whites were chain-drive, tiller-steered, wire-wheeled stanhopes, with their two-cylinder engines mounted under the floorboards. A condenser to recycle exhaust steam was added in 1902, and 1903 saw the White lose its buggy look with the engine now mounted up front under a hood in a touring model, and the substitution of wooden artillery wheels and shaft drive. A total of 502 cars was produced in 1903. Nineteen five saw introduction of the hood design known as the "White curve" which remained a distinguishing feature of White cars to the end — and White trucks into the Thirties. A special racing White nicknamed Whistling Billy and driven by Webb Jay set a world's mile record of 73.75 mph at Morris Park Track in July of 1905, catapulted the White steamer into national prominence, and was a principal factor in the healthy increase in White sales: 1015 cars in 1905, 1534 in 1906. The latter represented the White steamer's peak annual production, and was about twice the number of cars produced by its principal rival, Stanley, in any single calendar year. A White had been the only car in the 1905 inaugural parade of President Theodore Roosevelt, who became the first U.S. chief executive to drive an automobile when he took the wheel of a White in Puerto Rico the year following. His successor, President William Howard Taft, established the first official White House automobile fleet in 1909, and a White steamer was included in the Presidential garage. Other prominent White steam car owners included John D. Rockefeller and Buffalo Bill Cody. Until 1906 White's automobile business was simply part of the White Sewing Machine Company; in November that year it was given its own producing organization, the White Company, capitalized at $2.5 million. Unlike rival Stanley which remained with steam cars exclusively to the end, the White Company added a gasoline car to the line in 1910. Shaft drive and a four-speed transmission were standard. That year 1208 White steam cars and 1200 White gasoline cars were produced. In a clever piece of promotion, one of the former was used to pace James J. Jeffries, one of the latter Jack Johnson, in road work training prior to their world's heavyweight championship fight that year. In January 1911 the last White steam car was built; a big 60 hp six joined the four-cylinder White gasoline car for the 1912 model year. Only 432 sixes would be built through 1915, however, the company focusing efforts on the four. Taxicab production had commenced in 1911, White beginning its collaboration with Riddle in the funeral car business the year following. Meanwhile White trucks were finding their way into all corners of the world (including North China and Imperial Russia), the White Company enjoying extremely lucrative contracts with the U.S. military. Although White cars had always been upper echelon, these years saw them priced higher still, and with the addition of such ultra-luxury equipment as a two-way radio in the Berline Limousine. Family patriarch Thomas White died in June 1914, followed by the resignation of Rollin White later that year. (Subsequently he would build the Rollin car.) In 1916 the firm was reorganized as the White Motor Company (capitalized at $16 million) with Windsor White retaining the presidency and Walter White becoming vice-president. Two years later the White Motor Company formally ended the manufacture of passenger cars to concentrate on the commercial vehicle field. A total of 9122 White steam and 8927 White gasoline cars had been built. During 1921 the company built a few pilot models of a special salesman's coupe, which never proceeded into manufacture, and in the early Thirties the firm produced a few passenger cars to special order and developed a military scout car which ultimately was manufactured during World War II. White trucks, of course, continue in production, the White company through the years having absorbed such other car and truck producing firms as Autocar, Sterling, Reo and Diamond T.

1901 White, model A, steam stanhope, HAC

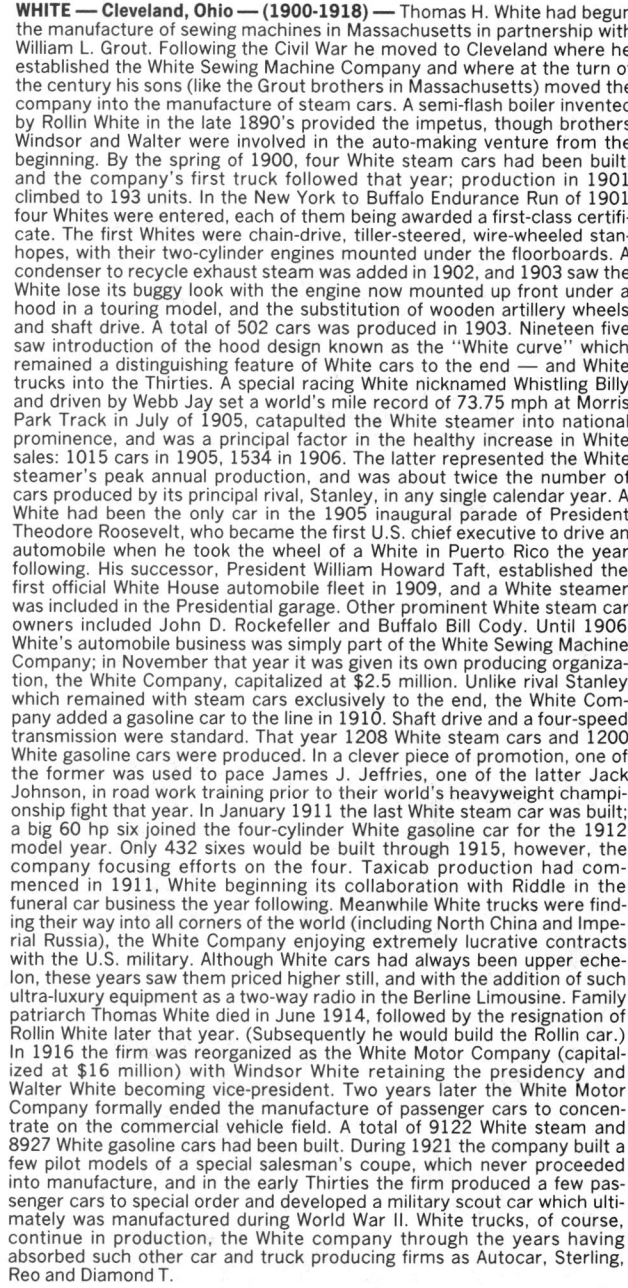

1902 White, model B, steam stanhope, JAC

1900-1901 WHITE
Model A Steam

	FP	5	4	3	2	1
Stanhope	—	6500	9500	15,000	34,000	46,000

1902 WHITE
Model B Steam

	FP	5	4	3	2	1
Stanhope	1200	6500	9500	15,000	34,000	46,000

"Next to Flying"

1903 White, model C, steam tonneau, OCW

1903 WHITE
Model B Steam

	FP	5	4	3	2	1
Stanhope	1200	6500	9500	15,000	34,000	46,000

Model C Steam

	FP	5	4	3	2	1
Tonneau	2000	6700	9900	15,500	34,800	47,000

1904 White, model D, steam canopy top touring, JDE

1904 WHITE
Model D Steam — 10 hp, 80" wb

	FP	5	4	3	2	1
Tonneau	2000	6700	9900	15,500	34,800	47,000
Canopy Top Touring	2275	6800	10,300	16,000	35,500	48,000

1905 White, model E, steam touring, OCW

1905 WHITE
Model E Steam — 15 hp, 93" wb

	FP	5	4	3	2	1
Standard Touring	2500	6500	9500	15,000	34,000	46,000
Limousine	2500	5800	8000	12,500	28,000	40,000
Canopy Top Touring	2700	6700	9900	15,500	34,800	47,000
Touring Runabout-2P	—	6700	9900	15,500	34,800	47,000

1906 White, model F, steam side-entrance touring, HAC

1906 White, model F, steam landaulette, JDE

1906 WHITE
Model F Steam — 18 hp, 114" wb

	FP	5	4	3	2	1
Touring	2800	6400	9300	14,500	33,000	45,000
Demi-Limousine-5P	3250	5800	8000	12,500	28,000	40,000
Landaulette Straight Front	3700	6000	8500	13,000	30,000	42,000
Imperial Victoria	3300	5800	8000	12,500	28,000	40,000
Extension Landaulet	3800	6200	8800	13,500	31,000	43,000
Runabout-2P	2500	6200	8800	13,500	31,000	43,000
Limousine-7P	3600	5900	8300	12,800	29,000	41,000

1907 White, model G, victoria touring, JDE

1907 WHITE
Model H Steam — 20 hp, 102" wb

	FP	5	4	3	2	1
Touring	2500	5800	8000	12,500	28,000	40,000

Model G Steam — 30 hp, 115" wb

	FP	5	4	3	2	1
Touring	3500	6000	8500	13,000	30,000	42,000
Pullman	3700	5800	8000	12,500	28,000	40,000
Limousine	4500	5500	7500	12,000	26,000	39,000

1907 White, model H, steam touring, HAC

1908 White, model K, steam limousine, OCW

1908 White, model L, steam touring, JAC

1909 White, model O, steam touring, JDE

	FP	5	4	3	2	1
1908 WHITE						
Model L Steam — 20 hp						
Touring	2500	5800	8000	12,500	28,000	40,000
Limousine	3200	5300	7000	11,500	24,000	37,000
Model K Steam — 30 hp						
Pullman	3700	6000	8500	13,000	30,000	42,000
Limousine	4500	5900	8300	12,800	29,000	41,000
1909 WHITE						
Model O Steam — 20 hp						
Touring-5P	2000	6200	8800	13,500	31,000	43,000
Runabout-2P	2000	6000	8500	13,000	3000	42,000
Limousine	2800	5300	7000	11,500	24,000	37,000
Model M Steam — 40 hp						
Touring-7P	4000	6400	9300	14,500	33,000	45,000
Runabout-2P	4000	6300	9000	14,000	32,000	44,000
Limousine	5000	5500	7500	12,000	26,000	39,000

1910 White, model G-A, gasoline opera coupe, HAC

1910 White, model M-M, steam toy tonneau, JDE

	FP	5	4	3	2	1
1910 WHITE						
Model O-O Steam — 20 hp, 110" wb						
Touring-5P	2000	6000	8500	13,000	30,000	42,000
Runabout	2000	5800	8000	12,500	28,000	40,000
Limousine	2800	5400	7300	11,800	25,000	38,000
Landaulet	3300	5500	7500	12,000	26,000	39,000
Model M-M Steam — 40 hp, 122" wb						
Touring-7P	4000	6400	9300	14,500	33,000	45,000
Roadster	4000	6200	8800	13,500	31,000	43,000
Toy Tonneau-5P	4000	6200	8800	13,500	31,000	43,000
Limousine-7P	5000	5800	8000	12,500	28,000	40,000
Landaulet-7P	5000	6000	8500	13,000	30,000	42,000
Pullman-5P	4800	5900	8300	12,800	29,000	41,000
Model G-A Gasoline — 4-cyl., 20/30 hp, 110" wb						
Touring-5P	2000	4300	5400	8700	16,500	30,000
Tonneau-5P	2000	4300	5400	8700	16,500	30,000
Model G-B Gasoline — 4-cyl., 20/30 hp, 120" wb						
Landaulette	3800	4000	5000	8000	15,000	28,000
Limousine	3600	3900	4800	7700	14,300	27,000
Touring-7P	2500	4500	5800	9500	18,000	32,000
1911 WHITE						
Model O-O Steam — 20 hp, 110" wb						
Touring-5P	2000	6000	8500	13,000	30,000	42,000
Runabout	2000	5900	8300	12,800	29,000	41,000
Limousine	2800	5300	7000	11,500	24,000	37,000
Landaulet	3300	5400	7300	11,800	25,000	38,000
Model M-M Steam — 40 hp, 122" wb						
Touring-5P	4000	6400	9300	14,500	33,000	45,000
Pullman	4000	6300	9000	14,000	32,000	44,000
Runabout	4000	6200	8800	13,500	31,000	43,000
Toy Tonneau	4000	6200	8800	13,500	31,000	43,000
Limousine-7P	5000	5800	8000	11,800	25,000	38,000
Limousine-5P	4800	5300	7000	11,500	24,000	37,000
Landaulet	3300	5500	7500	12,000	26,000	39,000
Model G-A Gasoline — 4-cyl., 30 hp, 110" wb						
Coupe-3P	3200	2700	3600	5300	8800	19,000
Touring	2000	3100	4200	6300	10,500	22,000
Toy Tonneau	2000	3000	4000	6000	9500	21,000
Torpedo	2250	3100	4200	6300	10,500	22,000

1911 White, model G-B, gasoline limousine, HAC

Model G-B Gasoline — 4-cyl.. 30 hp, 120" wb

	FP	5	4	3	2	1
Landaulette	3800	2900	3700	5600	9100	20,000
Touring	2500	3300	4400	6700	12,000	24,000
Torpedo	2750	3500	4500	7000	13,000	25,000
Limousine	3600	2700	3600	5300	8800	19,000

Model G-E Gasoline — 4-cyl., 40 hp, 120" wb

Touring-5P	3000	3500	4500	7000	13,000	25,000
Touring-7P	3000	3700	4700	7300	13,700	26,000

1912 White, roadster, HFM

1912 WHITE
Model Thirty — 4-cyl., 30 hp, 110" wb

G.A.D. Torpedo Touring	2250	4200	5200	8400	15,700	29,000
G.A.D. Roadster	2250	4000	5000	8000	15,000	28,000

Model Thirty — 4-cyl., 30 hp, 120" wb

G.B. Limousine	3800	2700	3600	5300	8800	19,000
G.B. Landaulet	3800	2900	3700	5600	9100	20,000

Model Forty — 4-cyl., 40 hp, 120" wb

G.E. Touring-5P	3300	4500	5800	9500	18,000	32,000
G.E. Roadster	3300	4400	5600	9200	17,300	31,000
G.E. Touring-7P	3500	5000	6500	11,000	22,000	35,000
G.E. Limousine	4700	3000	4000	6000	9500	21,000
G.E. Landaulet	4700	3100	4200	6300	10,500	22,000
G.E. Berline Limousine	5000	3300	4400	6700	12,000	24,000

Model Sixty — 6-cyl., 60 hp, 132" wb

G.F. Touring-7P	5000	6400	9300	14,500	33,000	45,000
G.F. Limousine	6200	4300	5400	8700	16,500	30,000
G.F. Landaulet	6200	4500	5800	9500	18,000	32,000
G.F. Berline Limousine	6500	4900	6300	10,300	21,000	34,000

1913 White, touring, JAC

1913 WHITE
Model Thirty — 4-cyl., 30 hp. 110" wb

	FP	5	4	3	2	1
G.A.F. Touring-5P	2500	4000	5000	8000	15,000	28,000
G.A.F. Roadster	2500	3900	4800	7700	14,300	27,000
G.A.F. Coupe	3250	2700	3600	5300	8800	19,000

Model Forty — 4-cyl., 40 hp, 120" wb

G.E.B. Touring-7P	3500	5000	6500	11,000	22,000	35,000
G.E.B. Touring-5P	3300	4500	5800	9500	18,000	32,000
G.E.B. Berline Limousine-7P	5000	2700	3600	5300	8800	19,000
G.E.B. Coupe	4100	2900	3700	5600	9100	20,000
G.E.B. Roadster	3300	4200	5200	8400	15,700	29,000

Model Sixty — 6-cyl., 60 hp, 132" wb

G.F. Touring-7P	5000	5500	7500	12,000	26,000	39,000
G.F. Touring-5P	5000	5300	7000	11,500	24,000	37,000
G.F. Roadster	4800	5200	6800	11,300	23,000	36,000
G.F. Berline Limousine-7P	6300	3300	4400	6700	12,000	24,000
G.F. Coupe	5400	3300	4400	6700	12,000	24,000

1914 White, model Thirty, roadster, HAC

1914 WHITE
Model Thirty — 4-cyl., 30 hp, 110" wb

G.A.F. Touring-5P	2500	4000	5000	8000	15,000	28,000
G.A.F. Roadster	2500	3900	4800	7700	14,300	27,000
G.A.F. Coupe	3250	2700	3600	5300	8800	19,000

Model Forty — 4-cyl., 40 hp, 120" wb

G.E.B. Touring-7P	3500	5000	6500	11,000	22,000	35,000
G.E.B. Touring-5P	3500	4500	5800	9500	18,000	32,000
G.E.B. Roadster	3300	4200	5200	8400	15,700	29,000
G.E.B. Berline Limousine	5000	2700	3600	5300	8800	19,000
G.E.B. Coupe	4100	2900	3700	5600	9100	20,000

Model Sixty — 6-cyl., 60 hp, 132" wb

G.F. Touring-7P	5000	5500	7500	12,000	26,000	39,000
G.F. Touring-5P	5000	5300	7000	11,500	24,000	37,000
G.F. Roadster	4800	5200	6800	11,300	23,000	36,000
G.F. Berline Limousine	6300	3300	4400	6700	12,000	24,000
G.F. Coupe	5400	3300	4400	6700	12,000	24,000

1915 WHITE
Model Thirty — 4-cyl., 30 hp, 115" wb

G.A.G. Touring-5P	2700	4000	5000	8000	15,000	28,000
G.A.G. Roadster	2650	3900	4800	7700	14,300	27,000
G.A.G. Town Car	4000	2900	3700	5600	9100	20,000
G.A.G. Sedan	4000	2000	3000	4200	6500	14,000

Model Forty-Five — 4-cyl., 45 hp, 133½" wb

G.E.C. Touring-7P	3800	4400	5600	9200	17,300	31,000
G.E.C. Semi-Touring	5300	4200	5200	8400	15,700	29,000
G.E.C. Landaulet-Limousine	5200	3100	4200	6300	10,500	22,000
G.E.C. Limousine	5200	3000	4000	6000	9500	21,000

Model Sixty — 6-cyl., 60 hp, 140-3/4" wb

G.F. Touring-7P	5500	5500	6500	11,000	22,000	35,000
G.F. Limousine-7P	—	3500	4500	7000	13,000	25,000

1916 White, model Forty-Five, touring, HAC

1916 WHITE
Model Thirty — 4-cyl., 30 hp, 115" wb

G.A.H. Touring-5P	2700	4000	5000	8000	15,000	28,000
G.A.H. Roadster	2650	3900	4800	7700	14,300	27,000
G.A.H. Town Car	4000	3100	4200	6300	10,500	22,000
G.A.H. Town Car Landaulet	4000	3200	4300	6500	11,000	23,000
G.A.H. Sedan	4000	1800	2800	4000	6200	13,000

Model Forty-Five — 4-cyl., 45 hp, 133½" wb

G.E.D. Touring-7P	3800	4400	5600	11,000	22,000	35,000
G.E.D. Limousine	5200	4200	5200	8400	15,700	29,000
G.E.D. Landaulet-Limousine	5200	4300	5400	8700	16,500	30,000
G.E.D. Semi-Touring	5300	4700	6100	9900	19,000	33,000
G.E.D. Roadster-3P	3750	4500	5800	9500	18,000	32,000

1917 White, 16-valve-"4" limousine, HAC

1917 WHITE
16-Valve-"4" — 4-cyl., 28.9 hp, 137½" wb

	FP	5	4	3	2	1
Touring-7P	4600	4000	5000	8000	15,000	28,000
Runabout	4600	3900	4800	7700	14,300	27,000
Limousine	5800	2500	3500	5000	8500	18,000
Landaulet	5800	2700	3600	5300	8800	19,000
Cabriolet	6000	3100	4200	6300	10,500	22,000
Town Car	5650	3000	4000	6000	9500	21,000
Sedan	5650	2000	3000	4200	6500	14,000
Coupe	5650	2400	3400	4800	8000	17,000

1918 White, 16-valve-"4" touring, HAC

1918 WHITE
16-Valve-"4" — 4-cyl., 28.9 hp, 124½" wb

	FP	5	4	3	2	1
Coupe-3P	6050	2700	3600	5300	8800	19,000
Runabout	5000	3900	4800	7700	14,300	27,000
Sedan	6050	2000	3000	4200	6500	14,000
Town Car	6050	3200	4300	6500	11,000	23,000
Town Car Landaulet	6050	3100	4200	6300	10,500	22,000

16-Valve-"4" — 4-cyl., 28.9 hp, 137½" wb

	FP	5	4	3	2	1
Touring-7P	5000	4300	5400	8700	16,500	30,000
Limousine	6200	3100	4200	6300	10,500	22,000
Cabriolet	6400	3700	4700	7300	13,700	26,000
Landaulet	6200	2900	3700	5600	9100	20,000

WHITEFIELD — The Whitefield Motor Car Company was organized in New York City during the summer of 1914 with a capital stock of $175,000 for the manufacture of automobiles. Incorporators were Morgan J. O'Brien, Alan J. Corey and Dewees Dilworth. Manufacture is doubted.

WHITE PRINCE — Until Buckingham Palace objected, the new car introduced by the Moon Motor Car Company in January of 1929 was known as the White Prince of Windsor. Thereafter it was called just the Windsor. Refer to Windsor.

WHITESIDE — Whiteside & Company was organized in Albany, New York during the spring of 1916 with a capital stock of $50,000 for the manufacture of automobiles and engines. Incorporators were R.W. Schuette, C.F. Novotney and A.A. Meschutt. Manufacture is doubted.

The Whiteside Wheel Company of Indianapolis, Indiana produced the Vaughn in 1909. Refer to Vaughn.

WHITE STAR — "Presumably unaware that already there is a White Star Automobile Company in Atlanta," wrote *The Motor World* in October 1909, "a group of enterprising citizens in Pleasanton, Kansas, have organized the White Star Automobile & Truck Manufacturing Company, which in addition to making runabouts and touring cars will produce motor trucks having four-wheel drive and steering." L.A. Hilks was indicated as manager of this enterprise, which seems to have gone precisely nowhere.

1910 White Star, touring, WLB

WHITE STAR — Atlanta, Georgia — (1909-1911) — Clarence Huston was president, N.P. Moss treasurer, William P. Milles secretary and Fred L. Sawyer general manager of the White Star Automobile Company which was organized in Atlanta in 1909 with a capital stock of $150,000 and the stated purpose of building highwheelers in the plant of the Atlanta Buggy Company. The two-cylinder 20 hp highwheeler was manufactured for only a few months, however. By August that year, the firm announced a name change to Atlanta Motor Car Company and that hereafter its White Star automobiles would be "standard and worth just what we ask for them." The asking price was $800 for a four-cylinder 22 hp roadster and $1600 for a four-cylinder 35 hp touring car. Further tourers were available at $1700 and $1750. Whereas the quickly discarded highwheeler had featured a planetary transmission and double chain drive, the new White Stars were shaft drive and with selective transmissions. One of these cars won the climb up Turkey Creek (described as "one of the hardest" hills in Laurens County, Georgia) in May of 1910. Its competition had included a Buick, White, Ohio and E-M-F. Unfortunately, the Atlanta Motor Car Company found competition in the automobile industry dismaying, and in 1912 effected a reversal of its business which saw the factory turned over for the manufacture of horsedrawn buggies carrying the tradenames of Golden Eagle and White Star. Golden Eagle buggies were built as late as 1918. The two-story building in Atlanta in which both the cars and the buggies were built remains extant, and is in use today as a warehouse.

1909 WHITE STAR
Highwheeler — 2-cyl., 20 hp

	FP	5	4	3	2	1
Motor Buggy	—	2000	3000	4200	6500	14,000

1909-1911 WHITE STAR
Four — 22 hp

	FP	5	4	3	2	1
Roadster	800	3700	4700	7300	13,700	26,000

Four — 35 hp

	FP	5	4	3	2	1
Touring	1600	4500	5800	9500	18,000	32,000
Touring	1700	4600	6000	9700	18,500	32,500
Touring	1750	4700	6100	9900	19,000	33,000

WHITE SWAN — Los Angeles, California — (1914) — Whether this West Coast cyclecar ever saw quantity production is unlikely, but at least pilot models were built. Its name derived from its graceful body lines, designed to resemble a cutter or sleigh, and painted white for a swan-like look. Front wheel drive was another unusual feature of the White Swan, its air-cooled engine coupled to a two-speed transmission driving the front axle. The side-by-side two seater had a wheelbase of 90 inches, and a standard tread of 56 inches, also unusual. George W. Tibbits was the man behind the White Swan Cyclecar Company which was incorporated "under the nonassessable laws of the state of Nevada" with a capital stock of $150,000 early in 1914. The first cars were slated to be built in Detroit, to take advantage of the availability of materials there, with a factory site later to be chosen in California. Tibbitts had his office at 215 West 7th Street in Los Angeles, and ultimately decided on Marysville for his White Swan plant — but, alas, his money ran out before he moved in.

WHITFORD — The Whitford Corporation was organized in Weedsport, New York early in 1914 with a capital stock of $25,000 for the manufacture of motor trucks and motor cars. Charles E. Whitford spearheaded this venture. Manufacture is doubted.

WHITING — Flint, Michigan — (1910-1912) — The Whiting Motor Car Company was the automobile department of the Flint Wagon Works. The Whiting car was a medium-sized and medium-priced four named for James H. Whiting, a longtime colleague of William C. Durant's who had served awhile as president of Buick. A well-built car with shaft drive and selective sliding gear transmission, the Whiting seems to have been produced as Whiting's final blaze of glory before retiring from the business world. The car was built for three seasons only. During the fall of 1911, shortly after the announcement of the new Whiting models for 1912, the rumor spread that Billy Durant had bought the Flint Wagon Works. The rumor was correct. Having been recently ousted from the driver's seat of General Motors, Durant was already at work on his plan to regain control. The Whiting car was discontinued, and James Whiting went off to a pleasant retirement. Durant commanded associate A.B.C. Hardy to the Flint Wagon Works to get a new automobile called the Little into production there, and dispatched William Little (for whom the Little was named) to Detroit to urge Louis Chevrolet into production on the Chevrolet there.

1910 Whiting, model A, roadster, WLB

1910 WHITING
Model A — 4-cyl., 20 hp, 90'' wb

	FP	5	4	3	2	1
Roadster	950	2500	3500	5000	8500	18,000
Model C — 4-cyl., 40 hp, 110'' wb						
Touring	1600	3300	4400	6700	12,000	24,000

1911 Whiting, model A, roadster, HAC

1911 WHITING
Model A — 4-cyl., 30 hp, 90'' wb

Roadster		750	3100	4200	6300	10,500	22,000
Model E — 4-cyl., 20 hp, 90'' wb						
Coupe		1050	2700	3600	5300	8800	19,000
Model C — 4-cyl., 40 hp, 116'' wb						
Touring		1600	3300	4400	6700	12,000	24,000
Model G — 4-cyl., 40 hp, 116'' wb						
Four-Door Tour.		1700	3300	4400	6700	12,000	24,000
1912 WHITING						
Model 22 — 4-cyl., 22 hp, 90'' wb						
Roadster		775	3000	4000	6000	9500	21,000

WHITMORE — In 1914 the M.C. Whitmore Company of Dayton, Ohio produced a cyclecar which was marketed under the tradename of Arrow. Refer to Arrow.

WHITNEY — George F. Whitney of Boston, Massachusetts was experimenting with a gasoline automobile, according to *Cycle Age* in November 1898. The magazine made careful reference that he was no relation to the George F. Whitney who was building steam cars in Boston, but provided no details on the other Whitney's efforts.

That an E.F. Whitney of Manchester, New Hampshire built an automobile in 1900 has been indicated on various car rosters. Documentation is lacking.

WHITNEY STEAM — Boston, Massachusetts — (1896-1900) — George Eli Whitney was the grand-nephew of the inventor of the cotton gin and a machinist in Boston. In 1883 he began his steam car development, completing his first car in October of 1896. The following year the Whitney Motor Wagon Company was organized for its manufacture. By the summer of 1898, George Whitney had built seven steam cars, virtually every one of them different. He was continually experimenting, and applying for patents. Most Whitneys had vertical engines, although at least one horizontal unit was built. In 1897 Whitney had boasted of his run from Boston to Hartford, a distance of over 130 miles, in 10-1/2 hours, and he subsequently advertised a ''start from cold water in six minutes,'' with his car running equally as well in soft sand or mud as a horsedrawn carriage. Most Whitney engines developed 4 to 6 hp, with gasoline used as fuel. George Whitney discontinued production of his steam car at the turn of the century, and seems to have spent a good deal of time thereafter suing people. The Whitney had been built under license during this period by Frank Stanley in Newton (Massachusetts) as the McKay, but other steam car builders had not approached Whitney first before getting into their ventures, which irked him mightily. In 1902 he brought suit for patent infringement against Grout, Prescott, the Milwaukee Automobile Company and the Stanley

1897 Whitney, steam wagon, NAHC

brothers (no relation to Newton's Frank Stanley). No doubt he was encouraged in initiating these lawsuits by the Locomobile Company for whom he was now working as chief engineer. Around 1905, when Locomobile discontinued steam-car manufacture for the gasoline-car field, Whitney departed. His further career found him designing equipment for the asphalt industry and serving as a consulting engineer fo the International Paving Company. George Eli Whitney died in 1963, at the age of 101, in Manchester, New Hampshire.

1902 Whitney, steam touring, HAC

WHITNEY STEAM — Brunswick, Maine — (1899-1905) — R.S. Whitney had his finger in a good many pies. He was a jeweler, he sold sporting goods, and he also dealt in guns and ammunition. In addition to this, he ran a small machine shop. All this he did in Lisbon Falls, where he began the construction of his first steam automobile in 1898. The following year, upon moving to Brunswick, he completed the vehicle which was sold to a resident of Greenville. Thereafter he devoted most of his time to his new

1905 Whitney, steam runabout, NAHC

Whitney Machine Company in Brunswick. In 1900 he began a second steam car, which he completed and sold in 1902 to a Brunswick resident. His first car had been a two-passenger runabout, his second a four-passenger touring. His third steamer, which he began in 1903 and completed in 1905, showed a number of progressive ideas including a front-mounted boiler and an all-steel chassis/body unit. This car was sold to Jay Potter of Camden, who resold it some time later in order to purchase a Model A Cadillac. Although Whitney's total automobile production was small, his cars were all very well built. Subsequently, Whitney moved to Lewiston, where he established an automotive repair shop, in the years thereafter patenting a number of his designs for automotive repair equipment.

1902 Whitney, runabout, HAC

WHITNEY — Whitney Point, New York — (1902-1903) — During the spring of 1902, the trade press reported rumors that an automobile factory was to be established in Whitney Point to manufacture cars the bodies for which would be made in the Birdsall-Waite-Perry carriage works nearby. The rumors were correct because the Whitney Automobile Company followed that summer, with its first car undergoing tests in the early fall. This Whitney was powered by a single-cylinder water-cooled four-stroke 6 hp engine and was available as a runabout with a two-speed planetary transmission and tiller steering. The price was $850 for the standard model, with fenders offered optionally for $30, a top for $40. The first brochure for the company must have been put together with a sense of urgency, because the headline on the cover page, in blaring 24-point type, reads "Whitney Aotomobile (sic) Company." If the same care in proofreading was exercised in the building of the Whitney itself, one might have the reason the car survived but a year in the marketplace.

WHITNEY — Detroit, Michigan — (1910) — This Whitney was a friction-drive roadster which was proposed to be sold in the $400 range but which never passed the prototype stage. Brock C. Eby, J.C. Hudson, H.C. Whitney and George O. Taeckels were the people behind the $150,000 incorporation of the Whitney Motor Car Company in Detroit which announced its presence on the automotive scene during the summer of 1910 and disappeared shortly thereafter.

WHYLAND-NELSON — Buffalo, New York — (1912-1913) / WHYLAND CYCLECAR — (1914) — Few cars resulted from either of the incarnations of this Buffalo venture which began late in 1911 with the establishment of the Whyland-Nelson Motor Car Company at 49-53 Illinois Street. Frank V. Whyland, formerly of the Berkshire Auto-Car Company, spearheaded its organization, Joel Nelson was his general manager, and the idea was manufacture of a light gasoline touring car with convertible delivery box attachment. By the end of 1913, however, Whyland had a better idea, shed himself of Nelson and latched on to the ubiquitous E.T. Birdsall. For Whyland's new F.V. Whyland & Company, Birdsall designed a cyclecar with four-cylinder four-stroke air-cooled engine, 100-inch wheelbase chassis and standard 56-inch tread. Whyland announced a $450 price tag and production of a thousand cars for 1914. Conceivably, however, he may never have proceeded into production at all. Meanwhile, he was also involved with the Buffalo automotive venture that was producing the Comet, another ill-starred enterprise.

WICHITA — Wichita was the name chosen for the car which was to be produced by the Solid Axle Automobile Company of Wichita, Kansas. During the summer of 1907, L.M. Osborn and J.E. Mannis advised that "sufficient capital" had been secured, part of the old Burton car works had been leased, the necessary machinery had been ordered and was due "to reach Kansas in 60 days," William H. Stanley had been hired to manage the factory — and they were all set to go. They were not heard from again.

The Wichita Motor Car Company of Wichita, Kansas was organized early in 1910 to produce a car designed by an engineer in town named D.N. Baxter. A.N. Jones and Rudolph Hatfield were joining him in this venture. Manufacture is doubted.

WICHITA — Wichita Falls, Texas — (1920-1921) — In November of 1920 the Wichita Motor Company of Wichita Falls announced its forthcoming production of a four-cylinder 50 hp, 127-inch wheelbase, $2150 utility car which the firm liked to call "the oil field tool pusher." It would accommodate three passengers and 1000 pounds of equipment. Apparently, this car to "take 'em to the gushers" was built for one season only. Trucks were produced by this company from 1911 to 1932.

1920-1921 WICHITA
Four — 50 hp, 127" wb

	FP	5	4	3	2	1
Utility	2150	3300	4400	6700	12,000	24,000

WICHITA FALLS — Wichita Falls, Kansas — (1914) — The Wichita Falls of 1914 was a cyclecar designed by Enio Salminen, Theodore T. Lane and Walter H. Ilg. Its engine was a Spacke vee-twin, its wheelbase was 105 inches, its tread 36, with tandem two-seating provided. The engine was visible through an opening in the hood, with a planetary transmission placed aft of it, and a long chain carrying drive to the rear axle. In the spring of 1914, the Wichita Falls Motor Company announced that this vehicle had been on the road since Thanksgiving of the year past, and had attained 55 mph in prototype testing. One might question this. In addition to the precariously long chain drive, the Wichita Falls — which initially was to have been called the Rival — was distinguished by a peculiar steering arrangement. "Steering is accomplished by means of a drum at the forward end of the steering post," *Carette* explained, "over which a cable is wound and passes through pulleys at right angles to the front axle, to which it is fastened on either side. No steering knuckles are thus employed, the hand wheel describes a semi-circle only." No more than a few of these cars could have been built. They all probably fell apart quite quickly. Late in 1914, Theodore T. Lane decided to try again with a car slightly more sophisticated and substantial which he named for himself.

1903 Wick, touring, NAHC

WICK — Youngstown, Ohio — (1902-1903) — Henry B. Wick was a Youngstown millionaire and the president of the Republic Rubber Company of that city. In 1902 he had an automobile built for himself that was widely touted as the largest and most expensive in America. Designed and produced by L.B. Smyser & Company of New York City, it was powered by a four-cylinder 30 hp engine, and featured chain drive and a three-speed sliding gear transmission in a 90-inch wheelbase chassis. The four-seater tonneau coachwork was provided by J.N. Quinby. The car's total weight, including canopy top and plate-glass windows, was 3100 pounds. It had cost $8000 to build. H.B. Wick & Company exhibited the car at the New York, Chicago and Cleveland automobile shows in 1903 and indicated at that time that manufacture would follow. It never did, however. En route to Chicago for further exhibition, the Wick collided with a streetcar and was damaged. Wick apparently lost interest. At an auction on October 31st, 1904, the car was bought for $765 by Roy York who worked for the F.B. Stearns Company. York had no intention of manufacture; he simply recognized a bargain when he saw it.

WIDMAYER — The Frank B. Widmayer Company of New York City was organized early in 1909 with a capital stock of $10,000 for the manufacture, sale and repair of automobiles, motorcycles, bicycles "and electrical and mechanical devices of all kinds." Joining Frank Widmayer in this venture were W.F. Widmayer, Jr. and H.C. Napp. Frank Widmayer had formerly been associated with the P.T. Motor Company which had produced gasoline engines and also the P.T. car at the turn of the century in New York. Subsequently he had become a motorcycle dealer at 2312 Broadway, which was the headquarters also of this new venture. Manufacture of a car is doubted.

Widmayer & Company of Atchison, Kansas was reported by *The Motor Age* during the spring of 1902 as being engaged in the manufacture of automobiles. "They have recently been figuring with New Yorkers for their machines," the magazine said. "They have one in their shop almost completed for an Atchison physician." Further details are lacking.

WIEMEYER — St. Louis, Missouri — (1900) — In his small machine shop at 1546 Ohio Avenue in St. Louis, J.L. Wiemeyer built a total of six cars beginning in 1900. The first was buggy type with a two-cylinder opposed engine, two-speed planetary transmission and single chain drive. Next he went to a three-cylinder two-stroke and a car outfitted for four passengers. A quartet of four-cylinder cars followed in varying body styles. Wiemeyer is believed to have built all parts of his cars himself, but he never considered formal manufacture. Subsequently he became a de[...] Apperson, Ford and Ames cars, among others.

WILCOX — The Wilcox Auto Company was organiz[...] Jersey late in 1910 with a capital stock of $25,000 fo[...] automobiles. Incorporators were A.R. Wilcox, A.S. Log[...] Manufacture is doubted.

The Wilcox Motor Car Company was organized in Chicago, Illinois during the spring of 1910 with a capital stock of $12,000 for the manufacture of engines and automobiles. Incorporators were A.L. Ballas, F.J. Wegg and George J. Meier. Manufacture is doubted.

1910 Wilcox, 5-pass. touring, NAHC

WILCOX — Minneapolis, Minnesota — (1910-1913) — The Wilcox was a continuation of the Wolfe and was produced by the H.E. Wilcox Motor Car Company of Minneapolis which had been incorporated in November 1906 by the brothers H.E. and John F. Wilcox, and Maurice Wolfe. Although the Wolfe had been available with either a water-cooled or Carrico air-cooled four-cylinder engine, it would appear that the subsequent Wilcox was fitted with a water-cooled unit only. Truck production, which had been embarked upon during this period, supplanted passenger car production entirely by the end of 1913. For a thankfully short while, the commercial vehicles of the company were referred to as Wilcox Trux. Wilcox survived in the truck industry until about 1928.

1910-1913 WILCOX
Model 36 — 4-cyl., 30/40 hp, 115" wb

	FP	5	4	3	2	1
Touring Tonneau-5P	1500	4200	5200	8400	15,700	29,000
Baby Tonneau-5P	1500	4000	5000	8000	15,000	28,000
Roadster-2P	1500	4000	5000	8000	15,000	28,000

1905 Wilcox-Bachle, touring, NAHC

WILCOX-BACHLE — Adrian, Michigan — (1905) — The Wilcox-Bachle was built in the factory of the Church Manufacturing Company of Adrian, which had previously seen production of the Murray from 1902-1903 and the Lenawee in 1904. This new car was an attempt to revive the flagging fortunes of the firm, but it appears just one was built. Andrew Bachle, designer of the Lenawee, collaborated with a Mr. Wilcox on its design. The car was begun in January 1905 and received its first road test on April 15th. The Wilcox-Bachle was a large touring car on a 102-inch wheelbase with a 19-gallon fuel tank located under the floorboard. Its principle novelty was its engine, which was a two-cylinder two-stroke. Although two-cycle motors were not uncommon during this period, their previous applications had generally been in runabouts weighing 1000 pounds or less. The Wilcox-Bachle was a 2500-pound bolide. Road testing indicated, as Hugh Dolnar reported in *Cycle and Automobile Trade Journal*, that the car "wastes no more fuel than the best of the four-cycle four-cylinder machines." Nonetheless, the Wilcox-Bachle was never produced, most likely because it was the last-gasp effort of a company which in reality had already breathed its last.

WILDAM CRON — The Wildam Cron Sons Company was organized in ⸏lina, Ohio during the fall of 1910 with a capital stock of $35,000 for the ⸏ufacture of wagons and automobiles. The Cron sons involved were ⸏., F.J. and A.W. Manufacture of a car is doubted.

1902 Wildman, runabout, NAHC

WILDMAN — Morrisville, Pennsylvania — (1902) — Alfred J. Wildman was one of five sons of a Morrisville wheelwright and the only one, it seems, who was enthusiastic about the automotive age. In 1902 he built a small and very attractive runabout powered by a two-cylinder Grant-Ferris engine which he offered for sale at $1000. It featured chain drive and a two-speed transmission, with low and reverse operated by foot and "fast speed" by lever. Wildman dubbed his car the Prince Henry. There is no evidence that he built very many of them. In 1904 he apparently put together two large twenty-passenger buses for use by a Philadelphia firm on its suburban lines. His further activities in the automotive field are not known.

WILKENS — V.C. Wilkens of Evanston, Illinois was among the hopefuls who entered the Chicago Times-Herald Contest of 1895 with an automobile of his own design. He did not make it to the starting line, however, and whether he ever completed his car is not known.

WILKES BARRE — The Wilkes Barre was to be a four-cylinder 40 hp touring car to be sold for $1000. Although the names of its promoters were not mentioned, *The Horseless Age* reported in January 1909 that efforts were being made to interest the good people of Wilkes Barre in its manufacture. Wilkes Barre wasn't interested.

1899 Wilkins, touring, NAHC

WILKINS — San Francisco, California — (1877/1899) — Although the full story on the vehicles built by J.W. Wilkins of San Francisco cannot be stated with assurance, certain aspects can be surmised. Apparently, Wilkins' first automotive vehicle was a steamer he built in 1877 which he called the Argonaut. His next known car was powered by gasoline, and it arrived in 1899. In late October that year, the vehicle was described in *The Horseless Age* as being powered by a three-cylinder 12 hp engine and sporting a wagon-type body with three bench seats for the transporting of up to twelve passengers. J.W. Wilkins was to have "the car on the road in a few days," and his Wilkins Automobile Company had "already secured orders for several vehicles, one of which is to be used on the sand deserts of Nevada." J.W. Wilkins disappeared from public print soon thereafter. His car resurfaced in 1909, however, at the New York Automobile Show. There it was displayed at the Maxwell-Briscoe stand, and carried a sign reading: "This car was built in San Francisco by J.W. Wilkins in 1877. It is believed to be the first gasoline propelled vehicle ever built." Pictures indicate it to be the car Wilkins announced in 1899. Conceivably, its body and frame may have been the 1877 vehicle which had been updated twenty-two years later with the gasoline engine. This is mentioned merely to give Benjamin Briscoe the benefit of doubt. The Wilkins car, which he had bought from the inventor, was on display at the Maxwell-Briscoe stand for a single purpose: to demonstrate that the gasoline-car idea in America did not begin with George B. Selden's patent of 1879. Whether Briscoe sincerely believed the Wilkins gasoline vehicle dated from 1877 is not known. Conceivably Wilkins could have deluded him into so thinking, or Briscoe could have paid off Wilkins for so stating. In any case, this attempt to invalidate the Selden patent did not work.

WILKIE-GROETSCH — The Wilkie-Groetsch Company of Pittsburgh, Pennsylvania was organized during the fall of 1913 with a capital stock of $10,000 to "build, alter, repair and deal in automobiles." The partners involved were F.M. Wilkie and John Groetsch. Manufacture is doubted.

WILKINSON — **Syracuse, New York** — **(1898/1925)** — John Wilkinson built his first experimental gasoline car in 1898; it was air cooled and was a pioneer in the valve-in-head configuration. The initial attempt to produce the car under the banner of the New York Automobile Company failed, though ultimately Wilkinson's car saw manufacture and fame as the air-cooled Franklin, which would be produced in Syracuse for three decades. In 1924 Wilkinson left the company, however, over vociferous objections to Herbert Franklin's decision to provide the unconventional Franklin with a conventional hood and radiator design. Ironically, in 1925, John Wilkinson proceeded to do the quite conventional himself. He designed a water-cooled car in both four- and six-cylinder versions. A prototype of the four was built, and the six was begun — but the Wilkinson car (which he planned to sell as a four at less than a thousand dollars and as a six for a few hundred dollars more) did not proceed beyond the prototype stage.

1904 Wilkinson, runabout, JHV

WILKINSON — **Los Angeles, California** — **(1904)** — At the turn of the century, whenever the pace slackened at the Johnson Machine Works where he was employed, William J. Wilkinson worked on the car he was building for himself. Its engine was a four, its body a two-passenger, its tread was narrower than the norm, its steering gear was especially designed by Wilkinson, and its inventor planned to both race the car and use it for commuting to work. Wilkinson later reported the successful completion of the vehicle, and a good speed of 40 mph.

WILLARD — **Cleveland, Ohio** — **(1903-1905)** — The first electric car designed by I. Willard was built for him in 1900 by Sipe & Sigler, the firm which manufactured his Willard storage battery. It was a small stanhope, and looked very much like an electric. The second car Willard designed, in 1903, was built to resemble a large gasoline touring car, complete with hood up front and generous tonneau in the rear. Seventy-five miles on a single charge was the claimed range of the Willard. With the exception of motor, controller and battery, which Willard built himself, this car was constructed in the shops of the Jacob Hoffman Wagon Company in Cleveland. The Hoffman firm was so pleased with the results that a deal was made whereby Hoffman produced the car in small numbers on custom order for two years thereafter.

WILLARD STEAM — **Rutland, Vermont** — **(1905)** — H.L. Willard of Rutland built a steam car in 1905. The body style was a runabout, with the boiler located up front, the horizontal engine to the rear and driving the rear wheels.

WILLIAMS — W.A. Williams of Lima, Ohio announced his entry into automobile-producing ranks in late 1914 with a car he planned to call the Independence. Refer to Independence.

The D.T. Williams Valve Company was organized in Cincinnati, Ohio late in 1904 for the manufacture of automobiles and automobile valves. "The concern will be located in a three-story building at Broadway and Eggleston avenues," The Motor Age reported that December. Manufacture of a car is doubted.

The Williams Air Compressor Company was organized in Indianapolis, Indiana early in 1904 with a capital stock of $40,000 for the manufacture of automobiles, automatic air brakes, air compressors and engines. Incorporators were John W. Williams, Alpheus G. Schomacher and John M. Tietuch, all of Indianapolis. Manufacture of a car is doubted.

WILLIAMS — **Montpelier, Vermont** — **(1901-1902)** — J.J. Williams was a machinist in Montpelier who built himself a car in 1901. "He has constructed nearly the whole of it in his own shop, including the gasoline motor," reported The Motor Age in May that year. By December of 1902 he had built a second car, again gasoline-powered and weighing 1750 pounds. The Horseless Age reported, regarding this second Williams, that it "has run as high as 30 miles per hour, taking all ordinary grades on high gear." J.J. Williams is not known to have built any further cars.

1905 Williams, tonneau, NAHC

WILLIAMS — **South Bend, Indiana** — **(1905)** — In November of 1904 the W.S. Casaday Manufacturing Company which produced agricultural implements in South Bend announced its forthcoming manufacture of commercial vehicles to be produced under the Cassaday name and a new car to be called the Williams. A 25 hp air-cooled four, the Williams — named for its inventor M.L. Williams — was set in a 96-inch wheelbase chassis, fitted with a three-speed sliding gear transmission. A $2500 touring car was the only model offered, and one of these was sold to the local South Bend police for use as a patrol car. Casaday built its Williams for only a single season. In November of 1905 the company announced that henceforth it would confine activity to the manufacture of stationary gasoline engines. M.L. Williams subsequently turned his attention to sleeve-valve-engine design. His resulting Wilmo engine was produced in 1916 in Mishawaka by the Gillette Motor Company.

1904-1905 WILLIAMS
Four — 25 hp, 96" wb

	FP	5	4	3	2	1
Touring	2500	4200	5200	8400	15,700	29,000

WILLIAMS — **Akron & Cleveland, Ohio** — **(1906)** — "An Akron man has devised and patented an automobile that is radically different in many respects from all others, and promises to revolutionize the pleasure and commercial car industry," the Akron Beacon Journal enthusiastically reported on March 7th, 1906. The Akron man was Harry A. Williams, and his revolutionary features included three-point body suspension, solid cast iron body, and an engine mounted parallel to the body. Of these, the solid cast iron body might have been revolutionary; it must also have been rather heavy. Nonetheless J.F. Townsend and a number of other prominent Akron residents backed Williams in the formation of the Williams Motor Carriage Company. Production did not begin in Akron, however. Instead, the Williams people moved to Cleveland that summer and took over the plant of the Blakeslee Electric Automobile Company which had been producing an electric victoria designed by William DeMars. The Williams gasoline car did make it into production there, marketed as a $760 runabout and $3500-$5000 touring car, but it quickly proved an abysmal failure and was promptly discontinued. Thereafter Williams' backers decided to produce the DeMars-designed electric instead, which left H.A. Williams rather put out. Literally. In 1907, when Williams removed itself from the electric car business too, Harry Williams complained that the company was still indebted to him for his gasoline car patents.

1916 Williams, roadster, NAHC

WILLIAMS — **Chicago, Illinois** — **(1916)** — This Williams wasn't pretty, but the reason for its building had been political anyway, so perhaps looks were secondary. ''As a dealer in tires he wanted to please the companies who make the cars whose owners buy tires from him,'' *Motor Age* reported regarding the automotive effort of Charles H. Williams, the Chicago branch manager for Goodyear. ''He would have liked to buy a machine from each of the different manufacturers, but this being impossible he did the next best thing and bought some one part of the new car from several.'' The result was part Ford, part Mercer, part Buick, part Overland, part Stutz, part Hupmobile, part Franklin — and very good publicity.

WILLIAMSON — The Williamson Motor Company was organized in Camden, New Jersey early in 1907 with a capital stock of $100,000 for the manufacture of engines and cars. Incorporators were J.C. Williamson, W.M. Swain and B.L. Johnson. Manufacture of a car is doubted.

WILLIAMSPORT — The Williamsport Engineering Company was organized in 1907 in Williamsport, Pennsylvania for the purpose of building a prototype car which ultimately was marketed as the Imperial. Refer to Imperial.

WILLIS — The Ernest J. Willis Company of New York City was organized during the fall of 1903 with a capital stock of $75,000 for the manufacture of automobiles and motorcycles. Joining Willis in this venture were Raymond Cole of Manhattan and William W. Myers of Brooklyn. Manufacture is doubted.

The Willis Garage was organized in Newark, New Jersey during the fall of 1914 with a capital stock of $10,000 for the manufacture of motorcars. Incorporators were J.H. Willis, J.J. Willis and G.F. Braidenbugh. Manufacture is doubted.

1928 Willis, 4-dr. sedan, WLB

WILLIS — **Maywood, Illinois** — **(1927-1928)** — The Willis was America's first, and undoubtedly only, straight-nine. This unusual car was the idea of a New York City inventor named Durward E. Willis who traveled to the Midwest and convinced a group of politicians and businessmen from the Chicago suburb of Maywood in the efficacy of his idea. The nine cylinders of the Willis were cast in blocks of three, and provided for an independent firing order much like a radial engine. In February of 1927 the Willis engine was bench-tested in a laboratory in Chicago, and presumably came through with flying colors. Both a commercial vehicle and an automobile were fitted with a Willis nine for further testing. The latter was a contemporary Gardner brougham with a revised radiator shell. In June 1928 the Willis Motors Corporation was chartered, and in September the offices of the company were opened in Maywood for the public to come and see this remarkable new car. Quite a few people apparently did. A full line of nine-cylinder Willis cars was projected, with the price of the seven-passenger sedan to be $5400. A three-cylinder export version to be called the Dew (Durward E. Willis' initials) was also planned, as was a Willis five. The venture died aborning, however. Probably the only Willis automobile ever made was the reconverted Gardner that a good many people in suburban Chicago saw during the fall of 1928. Following the Second World War, Durward Willis had another idea, a three-cylinder rotary valve engine (updated from the Dew) which he attempted to promote in 1963 for use in a small sporty-type car he planned to call the Cub. Cougar Motors was the name of this new venture, with Rockmart, Georgia chosen as the site of manufacture. A brochure resulted from all this, but probably nothing more.

WILLOUGHBY ELECTRIC — **Utica, New York** — **(1901-1902)** — Edward A. Willoughby was a carriage maker in Rome, New York whose factory was destroyed by fire in 1897. Thereafter he traveled to nearby Utica where he became the manager of the Utica Carriage Company, which firm he took over the year following in partnership with William H. Owen. In 1899 Willoughby, Owen & Company received contracts from the Columbia Automobile Company of Hartford, Connecticut for the building of 135 bodies for Columbia Electric cars. When this contract was completed, Willoughby, Owen produced an electric of its own for a short time beginning in 1901, but subsequently returned to the business of body building exclusively. The company is best remembered today for its town car and limousine coachwork on Lincolns of the mid to late Twenties. The firm survived until felled by the Depression in 1933.

1921 Wills Sainte Claire, model A-68, roadster, HAC

WILLS SAINTE CLAIRE — **Marysville, Michigan** — **(1921-1927)** — C. Harold Wills (his first name was Childe, his mother having been an admirer of Byron, though her son hated the name and never used it) left the Ford Motor Company in mid-1919 a very wealthy man. Via a previous verbal agreement with Henry Ford for a percentage of profits, he walked away from his old employer with a check for $1,592,128. He had earned it. Among other contributions to Ford, Wills had promoted the development of vanadium steel in this country which was vital to the Model T's design, had assisted in the engineering of the Model T (including its planetary transmission) and had even designed the famous Ford script. Now he was ready to strike out on his own, in partnership with another former Ford man, John R. Lee, to produce an eight-cylinder car ''ten years ahead of its time'' in a model industrial community to be built on the banks of the St. Clair River in the small town of Marysville, Michigan. The cornerstone for the new plant was laid in an elaborate ceremony in mid-November 1919. The first Wills Sainte Claire (the added ''e'' because it looked classier) was not delivered until March 1921. Therein was one of the Wills Sainte Claire problems. Wills was too much of a perfectionist for his car's own good, at least in the commercial sense. Molybdenum, a metal even stronger than vanadium, was the heart of the car, and C. Harold Wills was the first in the automobile industry to use it. The Wills' V-8 engine had its inspiration in the Hispano-Suiza aero engine which had won fame during World War I. Like the H-S unit, it had a twin overhead camshaft and one-piece cylinder head and block construction, though Wills fitted spiral bevel gears instead of the chatty straight-bevels of the aero engine. The car's emblem was the Gray Goose, Wills having watched the ''wisest, freest traveler of the skies'' in admiration for years as wedges of Canadian geese flew overhead to and from their winter home in the South. After interminable delays in getting the car ready, C.H. Wills & Company was finally in business by early spring of 1921 — and was out of it by the end of 1922. Total production by then was 1532 cars in 1921 and 2840 in 1922. Doubtless there would have been more than that save for Wills' penchant of shutting down the assembly line whenever he believed the slightest improvement might be made to the car. By December of 1922, all of the officers in the company, including John Lee, had deserted him. He got his company back in 1923 with the help of a Boston bank, however, and reorganized as the Wills Sainte Claire Motor Company. In addition to resuming production of the V-8, he began development of a new six. This was partly a cost-cutting measure, the V-8 being extremely expensive to build, and partly an answer to complaints that it was too complicated for the average garageman to fathom. The inline six arrived with overhead camshaft but detachable cylinder head for the 1925 model year. The year previous had seen introduction of four-wheel hydraulic brakes and balloon tires. Production these years was 1659 cars in 1923, 2162 in 1924, 1829 in 1925, 2085 in 1926 —never enough to make a profit. In November of 1926 Wills announced that the V-8 would henceforth be built on special order only, with the company now to concentrate solely on the six. The Wills Sainte Claire Motor Company simply faded away in 1927. In 1929 Wills was among the small coterie of engineers who developed the Ruxton car, and in the early Thirties he served Chrysler Corporation as a consulting metallurgist. His beloved Wills Sainte Claire factory was purchased by Chrysler in 1935. C. Harold Wills died following a stroke, at age sixty-two, on December 30th, 1940.

1922 Wills Sainte Claire, sport touring, OCW

1922 WILLS SAINTE CLAIRE
Model A-68 — 8-cyl., 67 hp, 121" wb

	FP	5	4	3	2	1
Tour.-5P	2875	5200	6800	11,300	23,000	36,000
Rdst.-4P	2875	4900	6300	10,300	21,000	34,000
Cpe.-4P	3750	2900	3700	5600	9100	20,000
Sed.-7P	4100	2300	3300	4600	7500	16,000
Limo.-7P	4775	3100	4200	6300	10,500	22,000
Twn. Car-7P	4775	3300	4400	6700	12,000	24,000

1923 Wills Sainte Claire, touring, JAC

1923 WILLS SAINTE CLAIRE
Model A-68 — 8-cyl., 67 hp, 121" wb

Tour.-5P	2475	5300	7000	11,500	24,000	37,000
Rdst.-2+2P	2575	5000	6500	11,000	22,000	35,000
Cpe.-2P & 4P	3275	2900	3700	5600	9100	20,000
Brgm.-5P	3375	2500	3500	5000	8500	18,000
Sed.-7P	3475	2300	3300	4600	7500	16,000
Limo.-7P	3850	3100	4200	6300	10,500	22,000
Twn. Car-7P	3850	3300	4400	6700	12,000	24,000

1924 Wills Sainte Claire, touring, JAC

1924 WILLS SAINTE CLAIRE
Model A-68 & B-68 — 8-cyl., 67 hp, 121" & 127" wb

Tour.-5P	2700	5200	6800	11,300	23,000	36,000
Rdst.-4P	2800	5000	6500	11,000	22,000	35,000
Tour.-7P	3100	5400	7300	11,800	25,000	38,000
Gray Goose Special	3100	5400	7300	11,800	25,000	38,000
Cpe.-4P	3550	2900	3700	5600	9100	20,000
Brgm.-5P	3650	2300	3300	4600	7500	16,000
Sed.-5P	3750	2400	3400	4800	8000	17,000
Imperial Sed.-5P	3850	2500	3500	5000	8000	18,000
Limo.-7P	4135	3100	4200	6300	10,500	22,000
Twn. Car	4134	3300	4400	6700	12,000	24,000

1925 Wills Sainte Claire, town car, AA

1925 Wills Sainte Claire, roadster, WLB

1925 WILLS SAINTE CLAIRE
Model B-68 — 8-cyl., 67 hp, 121" & 127" wb

	FP	5	4	3	2	1
Rdst.-4P	2885	5200	6800	11,300	23,000	36,000
Gray Goose Traveler	2885	5400	7300	11,800	25,000	38,000
Phae.-7P	2885	5400	7300	11,800	25,000	38,000
Cpe.-4P	3685	3900	4800	7700	14,300	27,000
Brgm.-4P	3810	2900	3700	5600	9100	20,000
Sed.-5P	3785	3100	4200	6300	10,500	22,000
Sed.-7P	3810	3200	4300	6500	11,000	23,000

Model W-6 — 6-cyl., 66 hp, 127" wb

Phae.-7P	—	5500	7500	12,000	26,000	39,000
Gray Goose Traveler-5P	—	5500	7500	12,000	26,000	39,000
Rdst.-4P	—	5300	7000	11,500	24,000	37,000
Four-Door Brgm.-5P	—	4200	5200	8400	15,700	29,000
Cabr. Rdst.-4P	—	5200	6800	11,300	23,000	36,000
Sed.-5P	—	2900	3700	5600	9100	20,000
Sed.-7P	—	3000	4000	6000	9500	21,000
Enclosed Limo.-7P	—	4500	5800	9500	18,000	32,000

1926 Wills Sainte Claire, roadster, AA

1926 WILLS SAINTE CLAIRE
Model C-68 — 8 cyl., 65 hp, 127" wb

Rdst.-4P	2985	5500	7500	12,000	26,000	39,000
Traveler-5P	3085	5800	8000	12,500	28,000	40,000
Phae.-7P	2885	6000	8500	13,000	30,000	42,000
Cpe.-4P	3765	4200	5200	8400	15,700	29,000
Brgm.-5P	3900	3900	4800	7700	14,300	27,000
Sed.-5P	3885	4000	5000	8000	15,000	28,000
Sed.-7P	3900	4200	5200	8400	15,700	29,000
Enclosed Drive Limo.-7P	4085	4700	6100	9900	19,000	23,000

Model W-6 — 6-cyl., 66 hp, 127" wb
Note: same models as year previous

1927 Wills Sainte Claire, sedan, HAC

1927 WILLS SAINTE CLAIRE
Model W-6 — 6-cyl., 66 hp, 127" wb

Rdst.	2700	6000	8500	13,000	30,000	42,000
Gray Goose Traveler	2700	6200	8800	13,500	31,000	43,000
Cabr. Rdst.	3350	5800	8000	12,500	28,000	40,000
Sed.-5P	3150	4000	5000	8000	15,000	28,000
Sed.-7P	3250	4200	5200	8400	15,700	29,000
Enclosed Drive Limo.	3350	4900	6300	10,300	21,000	34,000

1914 Willys-Knight, touring, HAC

WILLYS-KNIGHT — Toledo, Ohio — (1914-1933) / **WILLYS** — (1916-1918, 1930-1942 et. seq.) — Although John North Willys had been guiding the fortunes of the Overland company since 1907 (it was renamed Willys-Overland in 1909), it was not until 1914 that a car carried his name. Joining the Overland that year was the Willys-Knight, the sleeve-valve-engined car which was to endure longer than any other, with Willys-Overland ultimately producing more Knight-engined cars than virtually all other manufacturers in the world combined. Super salesman that he had been since his sporting goods store days in Elmira, New York at the turn of the century, Willys doubtlessly was drawn to the Knight engine because of its novelty and the promotional advantages it promised, rather than any engineering features in its favor. John North Willys didn't know a great deal about what made cars go, but he assuredly knew how to sell them. Already he had demonstrated that with the Overland; now he would become an unrelentingly ardent champion of the Knight. His first move had been made in this direction in 1913 with his outright purchase of the Edwards Motor Car Company, the drawings and factory equipment of which he moved from Long Island City (New York), together with H.J. Edwards himself, to Elyria (Ohio) and the former Garford plant which he owned. There the four-cylinder Willys-Knight was put into production as a relatively expensive $2500-range car, which it remained for only a single year. By 1915 quantity production of a car in the $1000 range was decided upon, with sleeve-valve engine manufacture only in Elyria thereafter, and Willys-Knight assembly integrated into the company's huge Toledo factory complex. A poppet-valve Willys Six (Continental engine) in the $1300 range was introduced in late 1916 and remained for three seasons, and a $1950 V-8 version of the Willys-Knight arrived in 1917 for a two-year stay. The flurry of Overland, Willy and Willys-Knight models now being offered by the company was bewildering, however, and not very practical in view of the wartime shortages of material which would continue to plague manufacturers for some time after the Armistice. Thus, by 1919, the Willys-Overland Company decided to focus emphasis on but three cars: a low-priced Overland to compete with the Model T (which alas it would not), a Willys-Knight four in the $2000 range (which, given the spiralling inflation of the period, would represent a fine buy, and by 1922 was down to $1375), and a new Willys six which was then undergoing development in the former Duesenberg plant in Elizabeth, New Jersey (which would ultimately arrive on the marketplace but not as a Willys). Rather like William C. Durant with General Motors, John North Willys had overextended himself. Buying the former Duesenberg plant had been but one of many company/factory purchases he made for his burgeoning empire, this one the most potentially interesting because of the six-cylinder car he ordered to be developed there for Willys Corporation (the holding company for all Willys' enterprises) by three former Studebaker engineers named Zeder, Skelton and Breer. In financial backwater in 1919, however, John North Willys was forced by Chase National Bank to accept outside management of his automobile business — and that management was in the person of former Buick president Walter Percy Chrysler. Chrysler remained in charge at Willys for just two years, ultimately leaving to perform a similar salvage operation at Maxwell-Chalmers. Thereafter John North Willys regained control of his Willys-Overland Company by a deft maneuvering of stock, and by moving the holding company of Willys Corporation into receivership. William C. Durant, now beginning his second empire, was high bidder for the former Duesenberg plant at the auction sale, but the Willys Six that had been developed there was not of particular interest to him. It most certainly was, however, to Walter Chrysler; he had eyed the design covetously during his Willys days, and now that concept would be evolved into the first Chrysler. Meanwhile, never one to cry over spilled milk, John North Willys was back heartily on the job in Toledo directing production of two cars he still had: the Overland and the Willys-Knight, neither of which Chrysler had particularly cared for. But Chrysler had been wrong obviously, for what John North Willys accomplished now was nothing short of phenomenal. From less than 50,000 cars in 1921, Willys worked sales up to over 200,000 in 1925. From an indebtedness of $20 million, he worked up to a profit almost equalling that figure, also in 1925. Although the lower-priced Overlands accounted for the vast majority of the cars he sold, the Willys-Knight proved an immensely popular contender in the medium-priced field, 50,000 or more of them being sold annually. For the 1925 model year the Lanchester vibration damper was introduced, as well as a new six-cylinder line of Willys-Knights. That year Willys bought out the Stearns-Knight of Cleveland, and continued that higher-priced Knight-engined car in production until well after the stock market crash. From 1926 forward, all Knights from Willys were sixes, including a brand-new lower-priced car called the Falcon-Knight which was built for him by a friend in Elyria (and which would be absorbed into the Willys-Knight line in 1929). In the fall of 1926, he introduced another new car called the Whippet, which took off like a rocket. In the fall of 1929, believing all was well with his company, John North Willys relinquished his firm's presidency to former first vice-president Linwood A. Miller; in March 1930 he became this nation's first ambassador to Poland. Two years later, with the Great Depression raging and at the request of President Hoover, he

returned to manage his now-troubled company in Toledo. In his absence a poppet-valve Willys Six good for 65 hp and 72 mph had been introduced for 1930 in the $695-$850 range, followed later that year by an 80 hp Continental-engined eight at $1245-$1395. Free-wheeling came in, and the Whippet went out for '31; a synchronized transmission from Warner Gear arrived for '32. Willys-Overland sales that year totaled just 26,444 cars. But already in development at the company was a new car which John North Willys believed would provide salvation. It was the Willys 77, in essence a developed version of the Whippet, a small 145.7-cubic-inch four on a 100-inch wheelbase which the company could sell for under $500, the cheapest of any car in the United States except for the American Austin. All other model lines were dropped in 1933, as Willys-Overland moved into receivership that February; John North Willys believed his company could survive only in the lowest-priced field. Though its Willys 77's horsepower was only 48, its top speed was an impressive 75.1 mph, and the car became a favorite for Automobile Racing Club of America events where tweaked racing versions performed handsomely amidst fields of Bugattis, Amilcars and M.G.'s. A stock sedan ran twenty-four hours at Muroc's dry lake for a 65.5 mph average. Stressed in advertising during the Depression, of course, was the car's economy: as much as 30 mpg. Production continued under receivership, and finally a viable reorganization plan seemed to be coming together. But John North Willys was a spent man. In January 1935 he was elected Willys-Overland president; in May he suffered a heart attack; in August he was working from his bed when he died; in December the Willys reorganization was completed. Receivership ended in February 1936. In 1939, when the new model 77 was given hydraulic brakes, it was given a new designation — or, rather, an old one; it was called an Overland. In 1941 the addition of hypoid final drive brought another new designation: Americar. The Americar was produced until shortly after Pearl Harbor. During World War II, together with the Ford Motor Company, Willys-Overland moved into manufacture of the Jeep which had been originated by American Bantam. Today the company that John North Willys built survives as Jeep Corporation, subsidiary of Chrysler Corporation.

1915 Willys-Knight, model K-19, touring, HAC

1915 WILLYS
Knight, Model K-19 — 4-cyl., 45 hp, 120" wb

	FP	5	4	3	2	1
Rds.	2475	2300	3300	4600	7500	16,000
Tr.	2475	2200	3200	4400	7000	15,000

Knight, Model K-17 — 4-cyl., 45 hp

	FP	5	4	3	2	1
Rds.	2750	2400	3400	4800	8000	17,000
Tr.	2750	2300	3300	4600	7500	16,000

1916 Willys-Knight, coupe, JAC

1916 WILLYS
Knight — 4-cyl., 40 hp, 114" wb

	FP	5	4	3	2	1
Rds.	1095	2300	3300	4600	7500	16,000
Tr.	1125	2250	3300	4500	7300	15,500
Cpe.	1500	1200	2300	3300	5100	9500
Limo.	1750	1400	2400	3500	5300	10,000

Knight — 6-cyl., 45 hp

	FP	5	4	3	2	1
Tr.-7P	1145	2400	3400	4800	8000	17,000

1917 WILLYS
Knight, Model 88-4 — 4-cyl., 40 hp, 114" wb

	FP	5	4	3	2	1
Tr.-7P	1285	2000	3000	4200	6500	14,000
Cpe.-4P	1875	1200	2300	3300	4100	9500
Tr. Sed.-7P	1950	1100	2200	3200	4900	9000
Limo.-7P	1950	1400	2400	3500	5300	10,000

Knight, Model 88-6 — 6-cyl.. 45 hp, 125" wb

	FP	5	4	3	2	1
Tr.-7P	1325	2500	3500	5000	8500	18,000

Knight, Model 88-8 — 8-cyl., 65 hp, 125" wb

Tr.-7P	2100	3300	4400	6700	12,000	24,000
Sed.-7P	2800	1400	2400	3500	5300	10,000
Limo.-7P	2900	1600	2700	3800	5800	12,000
Twn. Car-7P	2900	2200	3200	4400	7000	15,000

1917 Willys-Knight, model 88-8, Victoria, JAC

1918 Willys-Knight, model 88-8, touring, JAC

1918 WILLYS

Willys 89 — 6-cyl., 45 hp, 120" wb

	FP	5	4	3	2	1
Tr.-7P	1625	2500	3500	5000	8500	18,000
Clb. Rds.-4P	1450	2500	3500	5000	8500	18,000
Sed.-6P	2045	1100	2200	3200	4900	9000

Knight, Model 88-4 — 4-cyl., 40 hp, 121" wb

Tr.-7P	1625	2000	3000	4200	6500	14,000
Cpe.-4P	2275	1200	2300	3300	5100	9500
Tr. Sed.-7P	2225	1100	2200	3200	4900	9000
Limo.-7P	2325	1400	2400	3500	5300	10,000

Knight, Model 88-8 — 8-cyl., 65 hp, 125" wb

Tr.-7P	2100	3300	4400	6700	12,000	24,000
Sed.-7P	2800	1400	2400	3500	5300	10,000
Limo.-7P	2900	1600	2700	3800	5800	12,000
Twn. Car-7P	2900	2200	3200	4400	7000	15,000

1919 Willys-Knight, taxi cab, JAC

1919 WILLYS

Willys 89 — 6-cyl., 45 hp, 120" wb

		5	4	3	2	1
Tr.-7P	—	1500	2500	3600	5500	11,000
Clb. Rds.-4P	—	1600	2700	3800	5800	12,000
Sed.-6P	—	1200	2300	3300	5100	9500

Knight, Model 88-4 — 4-cyl., 40 hp, 121" wb

	FP	5	4	3	2	1
Tr.-7P	—	1600	2700	3800	5800	12,000
Cpe.-4P	—	1000	2100	3100	4800	8500
Sed.-7P	—	1000	2100	3100	4800	8500
Limo.-7P	—	1050	2150	3200	4900	8800

Knight, Model 88-8 — 8-cyl., 65 hp, 125" wb

Tr.-7P	—	2200	3200	4400	7000	15,000
Cpe.-4P	—	1000	2100	3100	4800	8500
Tr. Sed.-7P	—	1050	2150	3200	4900	8800
Limo.-7P	—	1400	2400	3500	5300	10,000

1920 Willys-Knight, coupe, OCW

1920 WILLYS

Willys 89 — 6-cyl., 45 hp, 120" wb

		5	4	3	2	1
Clb. Rds.	—	2200	3200	4400	7000	15,000
Tr.-7P	—	1800	2800	4000	6200	13,000
Sed.-6P	--	1000	1800	2800	4200	7000

Knight, Model 20 — 4-cyl., 48 hp, 118" wb

Rds.-3P	1750	2100	3100	4300	6800	14,500
Tr.-5P	1750	2000	3000	4200	6500	14,000
Cpe.-4P	265-	1000	2100	3100	4800	8500
Sed.-7P	2750	1000	2000	3000	4600	8000
Limo.-7P	2750	1000	2100	3100	4800	8500

Knight, Model 88-8 — 8-cyl., 65 hp, 125" wb

Tr.-7P	2750	3100	4200	6300	10,500	22,000
Limo.-7P	3500	2500	3500	5000	8500	18,000
Sed.-7P	3475	1600	2700	3800	5800	12,000
Cpe.	3425	2200	3200	4400	7000	15,000

1921 Willys-Knight, model 20, touring, JAC

1921 WILLYS

Knight, Model 20 — 4-cyl., 40 hp, 118" wb

		5	4	3	2	1
Rds.-3P	2195	1800	2800	4000	6200	13,000
Tr.-5P	2195	1700	2800	3900	6000	12,500
Cpe.-3P	2845	1000	2100	3100	4800	8500
Sed.-5P	2945	1000	2000	3000	4600	8000

1922 Willys-Knight, coupe, JAC

1922 WILLYS
Knight, Model 20 — 4-cyl., 40 hp, 118" wb

	FP	5	4	3	2	1
Rds.-3P	1475	2000	3000	4200	6500	14,000
Tr.-5P	1525	1800	2800	4000	6200	13,000
Sed.-5P	2395	1000	2100	3100	4800	8500
Cpe.-4P	2195	1100	2200	3200	4900	9000

Knight, Model 27 — 4-cyl.

	FP	5	4	3	2	1
Tr.-7P	—	2000	3000	4200	6500	14,000
Sed.-7P	—	1000	2100	3100	4800	8500

1923 Willys-Knight, taxi cab, JAC

1923 WILLYS
Knight, Model 64 — 4-cyl., 40 hp, 118" wb

Rds.-3P	1235	1800	2800	4000	6200	13,000
Tr.-5P	1235	1700	2800	3900	6000	12,500
Cty. Clb.	—	1500	2500	3600	5500	11,000
Cpe.-4P	1795	1000	1900	2900	4400	7500
Sed.-5P	1950	1000	1800	2800	4200	7000

Knight, Model 67 — 4-cyl., 40 hp, 124" wb

Tr.-7P	1435	2000	3000	4200	6500	14,000
Sed.-7P	2195	1000	1600	2700	4000	6500

1924 Willys-Knight, sport touring, OCW

1924 WILLYS
Knight, Model 64 — 4-cyl., 40 hp, 118" wb

Tr.-5P	1175	1700	2800	3900	6000	12,500
Cpe. Sed.-5P	1450	1000	1900	2900	4400	7200
Sed.-5P	1795	1000	1800	2800	4200	7000

Knight, Model 67 — 4-cyl., 40 hp, 124" wb

Tr.-7P	1435	2000	3000	4200	6500	14,000
Sed.-7P	2195	1000	1600	2700	4000	6500

1925 Willys-Knight, sedan, OCW

1925 Willys-Knight, model 66, roadster, JAC

1925 WILLYS
Knight, Model 65 — 4-cyl., 40 hp, 124" wb

	FP	5	4	3	2	1
Tr.-5P	1195	2000	3000	4200	6500	14,000
Cpe.-2P	1395	1100	2200	3200	4900	9000
Cpe. Sed.	1395	1000	2100	3100	4800	8500
Sed.	1450	1000	1800	2800	4200	7000
Brgm.	1595	1000	2000	3000	4600	8000

Knight, Model 66 — 6-cyl., 60 hp, 126" wb

Rds.	1750	2200	3200	4400	7000	15,000
Tr.-5P	1750	1800	2800	4000	6200	13,000
Cpe. Sed.	2095	1200	2300	3300	5100	9500
Brgm.	2095	1400	2400	3500	5300	10,000
Cpe.	2195	1200	2300	3300	5100	9500
Sed.	2295	1100	2200	3200	4900	9000

1926 WILLYS
Knight, Model 70 — 6-cyl., 53 hp, 113" wb

Tr.-5P	1295	2300	3300	4600	7500	16,000
Sed.	1495	1000	1900	2900	4400	7500
2-dr. Sed.	1395	1000	1800	2800	4200	7000
Cpe.	1395	1000	1900	2900	4400	7500
Rds.	1525	2300	3300	4600	7500	16,000

Knight, Model 66 — 6-cyl., 60 hp, 126" wb

Rds.	1850	2700	3600	5300	8800	19,000
Tr.-7P	1750	2400	3400	4800	8000	17,000
Tr.-5P	1750	2500	3500	5000	8500	18,000
Cpe.-4P	2195	1000	2100	3100	4800	8500
Sed.	2295	1000	2000	3000	4600	8000

1927 Willys-Knight, cabriolet, OCW

1928 Willys-Knight, sedan, OCW

1936 Willys, model 77, coupe, JAC

1937 Willys, coupe, JAC

1938 Willys, sedan, JAC

1940 Willys, sedan, JAC

1941 Willys, sedan, JAC

1941 WILLYS
Americar — 4-cyl., 63 hp, 104" wb

	FP	5	4	3	2	1
Spdwy. Cpe.	634	1000	2000	3000	4500	7800
Spdwy. Sed.	674	1000	1700	2800	4100	6800
Spdwy. DeL. Cpe.	689	1000	2000	3000	4600	8000
Spdwy. DeL. Sed.	720	1000	1800	2800	4200	7000
Spdwy. DeL. Sta. Wag.	916	1400	2400	3500	5300	10,000
Plainsman Cpe.	740	1000	2050	3100	4700	8300
Plainsman Sed.	771	1100	2000	3700	5200	7200

1942 Willys, coupe, JAC

1942 WILLYS
Americar — 4-cyl., 63 hp, 104" wb

Spdwy. Cpe.	737	1000	2000	3000	4500	7800
Spdwy. Sed.	788	1000	1700	2800	4100	6800
Spdwy. DeL. Cpe.	812	1000	2000	3000	4600	8000
Spdwy. DeL. Sed.	720	1000	1800	2800	4200	7000
Spdwy. DeL. Sta. Wag.	1027	1400	2400	3500	5300	10,000
Plainsman Cpe.	863	1000	2050	3100	4700	8300
Plainsman Sed.	890	1100	2000	3700	5200	7200

1938 WILLYS
Willys 38 — 4-cyl., 48 hp, 100" wb

	FP	5	4	3	2	1
Std. Cpe.	499	1000	1600	2700	4000	6500
DeL. Cpe.	574	1000	1800	2800	4200	7000
2-dr. Sed.	539	950	1400	2500	3700	6000
Sed.	563	950	1400	2400	3500	5800
DeL. 2-dr. Sed.	575	950	1500	2600	3800	6200
DeL. Sed.	614	950	1400	2600	3700	6000
Cus. Sed.	700	950	1500	2600	3800	6200

1939 WILLYS
Willys 48 — 4-cyl., 48 hp, 100" wb

Cpe.	495	1000	1900	2900	4400	7500
2-dr. Sed.	535	1000	1600	2700	4000	6500
Sed.	555	1000	1600	2700	4000	6000
Spdwy. Cpe.	596	1000	2000	3000	4600	8000
Spdwy. 2-dr. Sed.	616	1000	1800	2800	4200	7000
Spdwy. Sed.	631	1000	1600	2700	4000	6500
Spl. Spdwy. Cpe.	610	1000	2100	3100	4800	8500
Spl. Spdwy. 2-dr. Sed.	631	1000	1900	2900	4400	7500
Spl. Spdwy. Sed.	646	1000	1800	2800	4200	7000
DeL. Cpe.	646	1100	2200	3200	4900	9000
DeL. 2-dr. Sed.	667	1000	2000	3000	4600	8000
DeL. Sed.	689	1000	1900	2900	4400	7500

1940 WILLYS
Willys Speedway — 4-cyl., 48 hp, 102" wb

Cpe.	529	1000	1900	2900	4400	7500
Sed.	596	1000	1600	2700	3900	6500
DeL. Cpe.	641	1000	1950	2900	4500	7700
DeL. Sed.	672	1000	1650	2700	4100	6700
DeL. Sta. Wag.	830	1300	2350	3400	5200	9700

WILMOT — The Wilmot Motor and Cycle Manufacturing Company of Philadelphia, Pennsylvania was organized during the fall of 1906 with a capital stock of $125,000 for the manufacture of automobiles and bicycles. Incorporators were Charles M. Buckman, William Davis, Melvin M. Garrison, Amos S. Flowers and Robert K. Dix. F.A. Wilmot, the owner of a large steel rolling mill, is believed to have been behind the venture. Manufacture is doubted.

WILSON — David H. Wilson of Chicago, Illinois entered the Chicago Times-Herald Contest of 1895 with an electric car of his own design. He did not make it to the finish line, however, and whether he ever completed the vehicle has not been documented.

Captain Edward Wilson was the prime mover in a venture to manufacture automobiles and operate a taxicab service in Savannah, Georgia in 1909. In March that year he reported that a $350,000 company was being organized for this effort. Manufacture is doubted, however.

Harry Wilson of Doniphan, Nebraska completed his automobile early in 1901 and challenged Charles Jacobs of Hastings, who had just completed his as well, to a race "as soon as the roads are in a condition to permit it."

The Wilson Automobile Manufacturing Company of Wilson, New York produced a small single-cylinder runabout from 1903-1904 that was usually marketed under the tradename of Niagara. Refer to Niagara.

The Wilson & Greene Motor Company, Inc. of Syracuse, New York was organized early in 1918 with a capital stock of $50,000 to manufacture automobiles. The partners involved were G.M. Wilson and O.H. Greene. Manufacture is doubted.

The Wilson & Hayes Manufacturing Company was organized in Detroit, Michigan during the fall of 1904 for the manufacture of automobiles and automobile machinery and supplies. Thomas H. Wilson and H. Jay Hayes were behind this venture, together with Edwin A. Stevens, Jr. of Cleveland, Ohio. While in Cleveland, Wilson & Hayes had built its first all-steel body for an automobile (the Eastman) prior to the turn of the century. In Detroit, body building was continued, and by the Twenties the company was one of the principal producers of all-steel bodies in America. The company did not move into automobile manufacture, however.

The Wilson Motor Company was organized in Salt Lake City, Utah during the fall of 1917 with a capital stock of $300,000 for the manufacture of cars, trucks, farm machinery and water supply systems. This venture was a merger of the Wilson Brothers' Garage and Machine Works (headed by George S. Wilson) and the Aero Water Supply Company, both of Paxico, Kansas. Utah capital was said to be backing this venture, with both firms to be moved into a factory in Salt Lake City. The project appears to have died aborning.

The Wilson Motor Car Company of St. Louis, Missouri was organized during the summer of 1917 with a capital stock of $15,000 to manufacture, repair, sell and deal in automobiles. Albert C. Wilson, George A. Krause and Louis W. Jacobs were the incorporators. Manufacture is doubted.

Wilson, Roberts & Monroe, Inc. of New York City was organized during the fall of 1917 with a capital stock of $100,000 for the manufacture of automobiles, motors and hardware. Incorporators were A.G. Thaanum, A. Skillman and A. Foshay. Manufacture is doubted.

1906 Wilson, steamer, NAHC

WILSON STEAM — Minneapolis, Minnesota — (1906) — A steam car, said to be the first racing machine of its kind built in Minneapolis, was produced by the Wilson Brothers Automobile Company in early 1906. Its top speed was a claimed, and undoubtedly exaggerated, 90 mph, and the car was raced at local meets and exhibited at county fairs that summer. The Wilson company purportedly built at least one more sporting competition machine, but is not believed to have manufactured a production passenger car.

WINCHESTER — Rumors that the Winchester Repeating Arms Company of New Haven, Connecticut was about to enter the automobile industry were rampant during the summer of 1909. "Work is in progress on the erection of two concrete buildings . . . ," *The Motor Age* reported in August. "The Winchester company has a capital stock of $1,000,000, and a short time ago the legislature enlarged the charter of the company, and it is said that this will permit the concern to go into the manufacture of motor cars." The rumors, however, were false. Winchester did not enter the automobile industry.

WINDER STEAM — Cincinnati, Ohio — (1904) — John E. Winder of Cincinnati built himself a steam car in 1904 principally to allow himself increased mobility because an accident had deprived him of the use of his legs. The vehicle was operated by a pair of handles geared to the rear wheels, with the 3 hp steam engine located under the seat. As described in *The Motor Age*, "There is a small gasoline tank fitted in front of the seat [which] supplies fuel for a burner carrying 1800 jets, located under a small upright tubular boiler. The jets are surrounded by a hood to prevent the flame from blowing out or igniting the body of the machine when going at full speed....Instead of a horn a small steam whistle is used for tooting purposes." John Winder claimed his car was good for 12 mph.

WINDSOR — The Windsor was the proposed Canadian version of the steam car promoted by O.C. Trask in Detroit from 1922-1923. Refer to Trask.

1906 Windsor, touring, NAHC

WINDSOR — Evansville, Indiana — (1906) — During the late fall of 1905, J.A. Windsor incorporated the Windsor Automobile Company in his native Chicago. Unsure initially about precisely the car he wanted to build, and unable to get into production anyway in the Windy City (which he blamed on "Chicago labor trouble"), he traveled to Evansville, Indiana to talk to Willis Copeland of the Single Center Buggy Company, who agreed to build the car for him. The Windsor was a four-cylinder 30 hp touring with shaft drive and a friction-type transmission that Windsor preferred calling a "rolling traction drive." (It had been designed by Copeland's factory superintendent William O. Worth.) Although Copeland had no problem in building the car, J.A. Windsor found plenty in trying to sell it at his $2500 asking price. He was able to establish no viable sales organization and was out of business within the year. Copeland meantime went on to build his own car called the Simplicity.

1906 WINDSOR
Four — 30 hp, 105" wb

	FP	5	4	3	2	1
Touring-5P	2500	3100	4200	6300	10,500	22,000

1929 Windsor, White Prince, roadster, OCW

WINDSOR — St. Louis, Missouri — (1929-1930) — "Cementing the Bonds of Friendship and Good-will between the English-Speaking Peoples" was the way the Moon Motor Car Company introduced its brand-new car called the White Prince of Windsor in January of 1929. In early advertising, the illustration of H.R.H. the Prince of Wales was even larger than the car, and the Royal three-feathered crest appeared as well. Buckingham Palace objected, however, and the Moon Company, to preserve friendship bonds and good will (and also probably to avoid possible litigation or a nasty letter from the State Department), changed the car's name to just Windsor by year's end. And it received its own crest, complete with knight's helmet, flying horse and shield. The Windsor was a most interesting car in Moon's history. Quite stylishly turned out — "America's Smartest Motor Car" was a slogan — the Windsor was powered by an 88 hp Continental straight-eight engine fitted into a low slung chassis ("Dreadnaught Double-Drop Frame") with four wheel hydraulic brakes and automatic chassis lubrication. It was planned most probably to take the place of Moon's departed Diana, an earlier chic and upmarket car produced by the company. What happened in this case was that the Windsor took over the Moon. Although introduced as a companion to the six-cylinder line of Moons in January 1929, the Windsor name was given to all cars from the company that April, and subsequent brochures always indicated the producing organization as "Windsor Corporation, Saint Louis, U.S.A." All this was a thinly disguised attempt to provide a spurt to the flagging fortunes of the Moon Company, and alas it did not work. The Windsor was offered in

1929 Windsor, White Prince, roadster, JAC

two variations: Models 6-77 and 8-92 with four-speed Warner transmissions, Models 6-72, 8-82 and 6-69 with three-speed Warner units. Production was discontinued in 1930. Surviving a bit longer was the Moon venture with another car: the front-wheel-drive Ruxton.

1930 Windsor, model 6-69, White Prince, roadster, HAC

1929-1930 WINDSOR
Model 8-82 — 8-cyl., 88 hp, 125-1/2" wb

	FP	5	4	3	2	1
Royal Cabriolet	1845	4400	5600	9200	17,300	31,000
Victoria Coupe	1845	4000	5000	8000	15,000	28,000
Petite Sedan-5P	1845	3900	4800	7700	14,300	27,000
Full Sedan-5P	1845	3700	4700	7300	13,700	26,000
Sedan-7P	2195	4000	5000	8000	15,000	28,000

Model 8-92 — 8-cyl., 88 hp, 125-1/2" wb

	FP	5	4	3	2	1
Royal Cabriolet	1995	4700	6100	9900	19,000	33,000
Victoria Coupe	1995	4300	5400	8700	16,500	30,000
Petite Sedan-5P	1995	4200	5200	8400	15,700	29,000
Full Sedan-5P	1995	4000	5000	8000	15,000	28,000
Sedan-7P	2345	4300	5400	8700	16,500	30,000
Roadster-5P	1945	5400	7300	11,800	25,000	38,000

Model 6-72 — 6-cyl., 66 hp, 120" wb
Same body styles as 8-82 above, price range of $1545-$1895

Model 6-79 — 6-cyl., 66 hp, 120" wb
Same body styles as 8-92 above, price range of $1645-$1995.

Model 6-69 — 6-cyl., 66 hp, 120" wb

	FP	5	4	3	2	1
Stnd. Rdstr.	1145	5300	10,650	17,750	24,850	35,000
Stnd. Cabriolet	—	4200	5200	8400	15,700	29,000
Royal DeLuxe Four-Door Sed.	1345	3100	4200	6300	10,500	22,000
Royal DeLuxe Four-Door Brgm.	—	3000	4000	6000	9500	21,000

Note: In June 1929 the seven-passenger sedan 8-92 was put on a 140-inch wheelbase chassis, the seven-passenger sedan 6-72 on a 137-inch wheelbase chassis.

WINFIELD — In 1920 in Philadelphia the Winfield Barnes Company produced an export car which carried the name Adelphia. Refer to Adelphia.

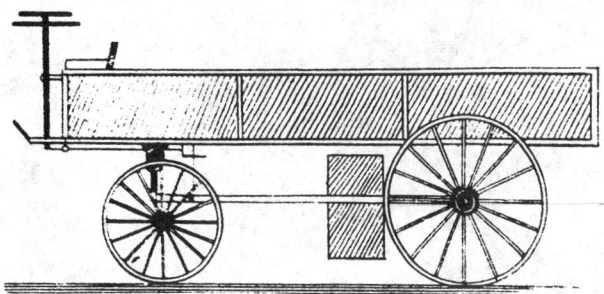

1896 Wing, gasoline wagon, LC

WING — **New York, New York** — **(1896)** — In 1896 L.J. Wing & Company was described as the "old-established gas-engine house" at 109 Liberty Street in New York City. Its business heretofore had principally been the marine engine field, but now Levi J. Wing stood prepared to enter the automobile industry. Although the firm outfitted a wagon with one of its engines, this was for demonstration purposes only. "They do not intend to manufacture wagons themselves," reported *The Horseless Age*, "but to furnish motors and connections to wagon manufacturers to apply to wagons." Fifteen miles an hour was the top speed of the vehicle, and naptha was the fuel used in the Wing engine.

WING — References indicating a Wing from Enid, Oklahoma as being in production from 1917-1920 are partially right. The car was a Geronimo, "Wing" the designation for those which were exported. Refer to Geronimo.

1922 Wing, Midget runabout, NAHC

WING — **Binghamton, New York** — **(1922)** — The principal difference of the Wing from Binghamton was its front suspension, two springs being placed between the two forward wheels in line with the axle instead of in line with the chassis. Otherwise, the Wing was a conventional assembled car of the period, with 55 hp Continental six-cylinder engine and five-passenger touring car coachwork on a 116-inch wheelbase. A price tag of $1800 was planned. The Wing was designed by former Packard chief engineer Earl G. Gunn, and Wing Motors Corporation was organized to manufacture it. Capital stock was indicated to be $10 million, although in May of 1922 announcement was made that no stock had yet been issued. Neither had a factory in Binghamton been selected, although negotiations were ongoing for the Hires tin can plant owned by the Nestles Food Company. Negotiations were still ongoing when this venture collapsed. Most probably, no more than pilot models were ever built.

1922 WING
Six — 55 hp, 116" wb

	FP	5	4	3	2	1
Touring-5P	1800	3500	4500	7000	13,000	25,000

WING MIDGET — **Greenfield, Massachusetts** — **(1922)** — Chauncey Wing's Sons of 78 Pierce Street in Greenfield was an establishment with roots tracing back to the Nineteenth Century. In 1892 the firm began manufacture of a mailing machine for addressing and wrapping newspapers and magazines, and soon after the turn of the century Chauncey Wing built an automobile for himself. Not until 1922 did his company build a car for sale. It was called the Wing Midget (or Special), and it looked like a miniaturization of the sort of race car that had competed in the Vanderbilts and Grand Prizes a number of years before. Its engine was an air-cooled four, its transmission a three-speed selective with final drive by chain; its wheelbase was 60 inches, its tread 40 — and there was room only for a driver. "The Wing is being manufactured as a sport, performance vehicle," reported *MoToR*, "though its utility value is higher than one might imagine at first." Maneuverability in crowded city traffic was considered a plausible marketing factor for the car. But undoubtedly it was as a tiny little sports car that the Wing Midget held its greatest appeal. Top speed was a claimed 80 mph, and the price was $380. Production appears to have been just one year only. Thereafter, Chauncey Wing's sons shifted manufacturing emphasis to the electronics field, producing two-way radio transmitters for use by police and reporters during the Depression and radar equipment for the Army during World War II. After the war the firm was among the first to enter the field of reproduction parts for antique automobiles.

WINNE — The Winne Manufacturing Company of Oneonta, New York was organized during the fall of 1899 with a capital stock of $1000 for the manufacture and sale of motor vehicles. Incorporations were H.C. Winne, W.R. Bell and J. Kirby. Manufacture is doubted.

1900 Winner, runabout, NAHC

WINNER — Elgin, Illinois — (1899-1901) — Following the demise of the Elgin Electric in 1899, several Chicago businessmen headed by Howard H. Brown moved into its Wright Avenue factory. Styling themselves as the Elgin Automobile Company, they produced a 3 hp single-cylinder $675 gasoline wagon they called "The Winner," which could carry sufficient oil for a run of 100 miles and which was guaranteed to be "perfectly safe." Fifteen of these vehicles — some of the last with two-cylinder engines — were built before the company went out of business in 1901. Immediately moving in thereafter was the Hartley Motor Company, with plans to build a steam automobile, but this enterprise produced no cars at all. In August 1901 the Fauber Manufacturing Company took possession of the factory and secured a contract the following year for the building of 100 cars for Walter L. Marr. Fauber was in the process of completing that contract when the factory burned to the ground in August 1904.

1907 Winner, motor buggy, WLB

WINNER — St. Louis, Missouri — (1907-1909) — The Winner Motor Buggy Company of St. Louis was but one of hundreds of Midwest carriage-makers which entered the automotive age by simply motorizing its traditional product. Details regarding the gasoline-powered highwheeler produced by the Winner company are lacking, but at least one of the cars remains extant.

WINONA — Winona, Minnesota — (1901-1903) — A May 1901 edition of *The Motor Age* revealed that H.S. Youmans was "operating with success" a vehicle that had been built in his New Winona Manufacturing Company. The following year, in October 1902, *The Horseless Age* announced that "the Winona (Minnesota) automobile factory has turned out a 12 hp gasoline automobile and is at work on a 20 hp machine." Apparently the second one was finished too, although the Minnesota facility was not exactly an automobile factory. New Winona produced farm implements, and these turn-of-the-century cars represented probably the firm's total automobile production. Later Minnesota motor vehicle registrations indicate two cars registered in the state as "Winona" or "New Winona." A single truck appears to have been produced by the company as well.

WINSHIP — During the fall of 1899, E.N. Winship of Napa, California announced his organization of a company to produce vehicles under the patents of Charles E. Duryea. It is believed this venture failed before any cars were produced, however.

WINSLOW — Doylestown, Pennsylvania — (1900) — Precisely what was built by the Winslow Motor Carriage Company of Doylestown is not known, though probably a car or two saw construction before this venture went asunder. The company was incorporated early in 1900 by three Philadelphians named A.S. Winslow, H.F. Ambler and J.G. Crasswell. They secured a factory in Doylestown from local banker William S. Hulshizer, and moved in. Soon, they moved out. "The Winslow Motor Carriage Company of Doylestown has joined the rapidly lengthening list of the missing ones," reported *The Motor World* that November, "and has been declared bankrupt." Prior to the sheriff's sale in early April of 1901, the Doylestown *Intelligencer* advised potential purchasers that "the factory is equipped with machinery essential in the manufacture of automobiles, bicycles and agricultural implements, and is operated by a 35-horsepower engine and 40-horsepower boiler." The purchaser of the property was Joseph A. Ruos, and the plant continued in business thereafter only in the agricultural field.

WINTERS — The Winters Automobile Company was organized in Scranton, Pennsylvania during the fall of 1909 with a capital stock of $25,000 for the manufacture of automobiles. Ralph Winters, Ara Adair and John R. Wilson were the incorporators. Manufacture is doubted.

WINTERTON — The Winterton Manufacturing Company was organized in Pittsburgh, Pennsylvania late in 1910 with a capital stock of $5000 to manufacture and deal in automobiles and other motor vehicles. Incorporators were E.Z. Wainwright, Jr., Willard G. Bratton, J.C. McQuillan and A.D. Griffith, all of Pittsburgh. Manufacture is doubted.

1921 Winther, Six, 5-pass. touring, WLB

WINTHER — Kenosha, Wisconsin — (1921-1923) — Winther trucks were produced for a full decade — 1917-1927 — in Kenosha. In November of 1919, Martin P. Winther announced that a car also would be made. "The announcement that the Winther company was to widen the scope of their truck manufacturing activities by entering the passenger car field caused no small sensation when made at a convention of distributors at the factory," *Motor World* reported that month. The Winther car wasn't much of a sensation, however. It was a well-built but pedestrian 60 hp six (Herschell-Spillman engine) on a 120-inch wheelbase offered as a five-passenger touring car only. The first example rolled out of the Kenosha plant in May of 1920, though it was not given its public debut until the Chicago Automobile Show early in 1921 when it was exhibited at the Sherman Hotel. Initially carrying a price tag of $2890, the Winther was reduced to $2250 in 1922. In 1923 production was discontinued, after approximately 500 cars in all had been built. The Winther patterns were immediately sold to G.D. Harris of Menasha, Wisconsin who resurrected the car as the Harris Six.

1921 WINTHER
Six-61 — 6-cyl., 60 hp, 120" wb

	FP	5	4	3	2	1
Touring-5P	2890	4900	6300	10,300	21,000	34,000

1922-1923 WINTHER
Six-61 — 6-cyl., 60 bhp, 120" wb

	FP	5	4	3	2	1
Touring-5P	2250	4900	6300	10,300	21,000	34,000

1896 Winton (first experimental car), HAC

1897 Winton (second experimental car), HAC

WINTON — Cleveland, Ohio — (1896-1924) — If any single individual can be credited with lighting the spark which set the automobile industry going in America, it would be Alexander Winton. A feisty Scotsman who emigrated to the United States in 1884, settling in Cleveland where he established the Winton Bicycle Company in 1891, he built his first experimental single-cylinder automobile there five years later. The year following — March 1st, 1897 — he organized the Winton Motor Carriage Company and by spring had his second car — a 10 hp twin — completed. On Memorial Day he drove it at the astonishing speed of 33.64 mph 'round Cleveland's famed horse-racing Glenville Track. That summer, in another two-cylinder Winton, he and his shop superintendent William A. Hatcher drove from Cleveland to New York City, an equally astonishing feat. Already Winton had begun laying plans for regular production. On March 24th, 1898 he sold his first car to a Pennsylvania mining engineer named Robert Allison; that afternoon he sold his second, his third followed two days later. By the end of 1898 Alexander Winton had sold twenty-two cars, the most celebrated historically of that first batch being car number twelve, bought by James Ward Packard. Although Winton did not sell the first gasoline automobile in America, he was the first to set up the orderly production schedule that was requisite for moving the automobile from machine or bicycle shop into a proper industry. One hundred Wintons were sold in 1899. Winton's vice-president was Thomas W. Henderson, his secretary-treasurer was George H. Brown; his first chief engineer was Leo Melanowski, who was European born and trained and who would enjoy a varied career in the American industry. Alexander Winton decided against hiring a mechanic suggested by Melanowski, believing Henry Ford not much of a prospect. Winton's second trip by automobile to New York in the spring of 1899 was with Cleveland *Plain Dealer* reporter Charles Shanks, later Winton's advertising manager. This widely-reported trek both spurred Winton sales and was said to have popularized the word "automobile" for the horseless carriage in which the pair were riding, since Shanks always referred to the Winton as such in his dispatches. Previously, "autobain" and "motocycle" were the more frequent designations for this new mode of transportation. In 1900, in what was described in the press as the "first gun of the Selden Patent War," the Electric Vehicle Company brought suit against Winton — although Winton elected not to fight and joined with other similarly-minded producers in the Association of Licensed Automobile Manufacturers. Ironically, the mechanic he had not hired a few years earlier did fight and ultimately won — and in a race against a Winton in 1901, Henry Ford won too, which gave his career a healthy leg up. Winton came back with his famous Bullet racers, however, in the first of which he competed himself. In Bullet No. 2, Barney Oldfield put up 83.7 mph at Daytona Beach for a mile record in January 1904. The latter car was a goliath, two horizontal four-cylinder engines bolted together for America's first eight-cylinder car, although its first competitive foray had ended early and dismally with an overheated engine. (This was the 1903 Gordon Ben-

1898 Winton, motor carriage, HAC

nett in Ireland; in 1900 Alexander Winton had been the first American to compete in a European race, the Gordon Bennett that year in France. He hadn't fared well there either.) A spectacular Winton triumph in 1903 was the crossing of the continent — San Francisco to New York — by Dr. H. Nelson Jackson and his chauffeur Sewell H. Croker. Alexander Winton, who was very good at making headlines for himself and his car, rather enjoyed having someone else do the honors for him. Winton sales steadily increased: 700 cars in 1901, 850 in 1903, 1100 in 1907. New in 1905 had been Winton's Model C, with shaft drive and its four-cylinder engine mounted up front under a hood shaped like the letter "D" which would remain a distinguishing feature of Wintons thereafter. (Earlier hoods had housed water and fuel tanks.) Since 1901 Wintons had featured wheel steering, a progressive feature, and two-speed planetary transmission, which had become rather retrograde for a car of Winton's class by 1905. From the beginning, Wintons had been on the uppermost rungs of the industry ladder. Nineteen seven brought the first Winton six, and all Wintons carried six-cylinder engines from that year forward. Sliding gear transmissions of three and four speeds arrived in 1907. But compressed air remained a Winton penchant for a considerable period. Early on Alexander Winton had favored compressed-air actuation of a variable-lift inlet valve. In 1909 he offered a compressed air starter, which could also pump up the tires. Not until 1915 did a Winton feature electric starting as an option, and then only because Alexander Winton's dealers had clamoured for it. In 1915, too, the Winton Motor Carriage Company was reorganized as the Winton Motor Car Company, and a smaller and less expensive six was announced (128-inch wheelbase, $2285-$3200 vis-a-vis 138-inch wheelbase, $3500-$4750). This was acknowledging a profitable trend the rest of the industry had recognized several years before. Winton production in 1916 was 2458 cars, one of the company's best years ever. The firm moved into heavy military production during World War I, and entered the postwar era in good position. An unusual feature of Wintons of the early Twenties was a four-speed transmission with a quasi-overdrive fourth. In February 1924, however, the trade press informed readers that

1899 Winton, motor carriage, OCW

1900 Winton, motor carriage, OCW

"the end of the long honorable career of Winton as a manufacturer is to come soon." What had happened? Several things, all of them perhaps linked to the character of Alexander Winton. The management team of Winton-Henderson-Brown which had guided the company since its first sale of a car in 1898 had remained intact throughout, a phenomenal testament to the solidity of the company, but one which perhaps also reflected its intransigence. Following the Armistice, two models of sixes were offered, but both were now high priced. Probably Alexander Winton abhorred the idea of a cheap Winton. Sales plummeted. In 1922 the company admitted to being "financially embarrassed." In 1923 there was a try at consolidation with Haynes and Dorris, but Alexander Winton scotched it. Feisty Scotsman to the end, he preferred to liquidate, though it cost him a good deal to do it. (During the glory years, his fortune was estimated at $5 million; when he died in 1932 he left an estate of less than $50,000.) Only twelve new Wintons remained unsold at the factory when the car's death notice came February 11th, 1924. The Winton organization continued in business as a maker of diesel engines. But a very important part of American automobile history died on the day the Winton did.

1898-1900 WINTON

	FP	5	4	3	2	1
Motor Carriage						

1901 Winton, runabout, HAC

1901 WINTON

	FP	5	4	3	2	1
One Cylinder — 8 hp						
Runabout-2P	1200	3100	4200	6300	10,500	22,000
One Cylinder — 9 hp						
Touring-4P	1500	3300	4400	6700	12,000	24,000
Mail Delivery	1200	3100	4200	6300	10,500	22,000

1902 Winton, runabout, HAC

1903 Winton, touring, OCW

1508

1902 WINTON

	FP	5	4	3	2	1
One Cylinder — 8½ hp						
Standard Runabout	1200	3100	4200	6300	10,500	22,000
Two Cylinder — 15 hp						
Detachable Tonneau	2000	3300	4400	6700	12,000	24,000

1903 WINTON

	FP	5	4	3	2	1
Two Cylinder — 20 hp						
Detachable Tonneau-5P	2500	3300	4400	6700	12,000	24,000

1904 Winton, two-cylinder roadster, HAC

1904 WINTON

	FP	5	4	3	2	1
Two Cylinder — 20 hp, 94½" wb						
Touring-5P	2300	3300	4400	6700	12,000	24,000
Quad — 4-cyl., 24 hp, 104" wb						
Touring-5P	3000	3700	4700	7300	13,700	26,000

1905 Winton, four-cylinder touring, HAC

1905 WINTON

	FP	5	4	3	2	1
Model C — 4-cyl., 16/20 hp, 88" wb						
Touring-5P	1800	3300	4400	6700	12,000	24,000
Model B — 4-cyl., 24/30 hp, 102" wb						
Touring-6P	2500	4000	5000	8000	15,000	28,000
Limousine-5/8P	3500	3100	4200	6300	10,500	22,000
Model A — 4-cyl., 40/50 hp, 106" wb						
Touring-6P	3500	5600	11,250	18,750	26,250	37,500

1906 Winton, model K, touring, HAC

1906 WINTON

	FP	5	4	3	2	1
Model K — 4-cyl., 30 hp, 102" wb						
Touring-5P	2500	4400	5600	9200	17,300	31,000
Limousine-7P	3500	3200	4300	6500	11,000	23,000

1907 Winton, type XIV, touring, HAC

1907 WINTON
Type XIV — 4-cyl., 30 hp, 104'' wb

	FP	5	4	3	2	1
Touring-5P	2500	4500	5800	9500	18,000	32,000
Runabout-2/4P	2500	4400	5600	9200	17,300	31,000
Limousine	3500	3300	4400	6700	12,000	24,000

Model M — 4-cyl., 40 hp, 112'' wb

	FP	5	4	3	2	1
Touring-7P	3500	5500	7500	12,000	26,000	39,000
Runabout-2/4P	3500	5400	7300	11,800	25,000	38,000
Limousine	4500	3700	4700	7300	13,700	26,000

1908 Winton, Six-Teen-Six touring, HAC

1908 WINTON
Six-Teen-Six — 6-cyl., 48.6 hp, 120'' wb

Touring-7P	4500	5400	7300	11,800	25,000	38,000
Runabout-3P	4500	5300	7000	11,500	24,000	37,000
Limousine-7P	5500	3500	4500	7000	13,000	25,000
Landaulet-7P	5750	3700	4700	7300	13,700	26,000

1909 Winton Six, landaulet, HAC

1909 WINTON
Model 17 — 6-cyl., 48 hp, 120'' wb

Touring-5P	3000	5400	7300	11,800	25,000	38,000
Cape Top Touring-5P	3150	5500	7500	12,000	26,000	39,000
Touring-4P	3000	5300	7000	11,500	24,000	37,000
Cape Top Touring-4P	3125	5400	7300	11,800	25,000	38,000
Limousine-5P	4250	3500	4500	7000	13,000	25,000
Touring-7P	4500	5500	7500	12,000	26,000	39,000
Cape Top Touring-7P	4650	5800	8000	12,500	28,000	40,000

Model 18 — 6-cyl., 60 hp, 130'' wb

Runabout-2/3/4P	4500	6400	9300	14,500	33,000	45,000
Limousine-2/3/4P	4500	4200	5200	8400	15,700	29,000
Landaulet-7P	6000	4300	5400	8700	16,500	30,000
Touring-7P	4500	6700	9900	15,500	34,800	47,000

1910 Winton Six, touring, HAC

1910 WINTON
Model 17 — 6-cyl., 48 hp, 124'' wb

	FP	5	4	3	2	1
Touring-7P	3000	5400	7300	11,800	25,000	38,000
Runabout	3000	5200	6800	11,300	23,000	36,000
Toy Tonneau	3000	5200	6800	11,300	23,000	36,000
Limousine	4250	3500	4500	7000	13,000	25,000
Landaulet	4500	3700	4700	7300	13,700	26,000

Model 18 — 6-cyl., 40 hp, 130'' wb

Touring-7P	4500	5500	7500	12,000	26,000	39,000
Runabout	4500	5400	7300	11,800	25,000	38,000
Toy Tonneau	4500	5400	7300	11,800	25,000	38,000
Limousine	5750	3700	4700	7300	13,700	26,000
Landaulet	6000	3900	4800	7700	14,300	27,000

1911 Winton Six, touring, HAC

1911 WINTON
Model 17-B — 6-cyl., 48 hp, 124'' wb

Touring-5P	3000	5400	7300	11,800	25,000	38,000
Roadster	3000	5200	6800	11,300	23,000	36,000
Toy Tonneau	3000	5200	6800	11,300	23,000	36,000
Torpedo	3250	5300	7000	11,500	24,000	37,000
Touring-7P	3250	5500	7500	12,000	26,000	39,000
Limousine-7P	4250	4000	5000	8000	15,000	28,000
Landaulet-7P	4500	4300	5400	8700	16,500	30,000

1912 Winton Six, touring, HAC

1912 WINTON
Model 17-C — 6-cyl., 48 hp, 130'' wb

Touring-5P	3000	6000	8500	13,000	30,000	42,000
Roadster-2P	3000	5800	8000	12,500	28,000	40,000
Touring-7P	3250	6400	9300	14,500	33,000	45,000
Toy Tonneau	3000	5900	8300	12,800	29,000	41,000
Torpedo	3250	6300	9000	14,000	32,000	44,000
Close-Coupled-4P	3000	4000	5000	8000	15,000	28,000
Close-Coupled-5P	3000	5200	8400	15,700	29,000	
Colonial Coupe	4200	3100	4200	6300	10,500	22,000
Limousine-7P	4250	4400	5600	9200	17,300	31,000
Town Car	4250	4500	5800	9500	18,000	32,000
Landaulet	4500	4700	6100	9900	19,000	33,000
Full Fore-Door Limousine	4500	4700	6100	9900	19,000	33,000

1913 Winton Six, touring, HAC

1913 WINTON
Model 17-D — 6-cyl., 48.6 hp, 130" wb

	FP	5	4	3	2	1
Touring-5P	3000	6200	8800	13,500	31,000	43,000
Touring-4P	3000	6000	8500	13,000	30,000	42,000
Touring-6P	3250	6300	9000	14,000	32,000	44,000
Touring-7P	3250	6400	9300	14,500	33,000	45,000
Roadster-2P	3000	6300	9000	14,000	32,000	44,000
Roadster-3P	3000	6300	9000	14,000	32,000	44,000
Limousine-7P	4500	4400	5600	9200	17,300	31,000
Landaulet	4500	4500	5800	9500	18,000	32,000
Three-Quarter Limousine	4250	4300	5400	8700	16,500	30,000
Colonial Coupe	4200	4200	5200	8400	15,700	29,000

1914 Winton Six, touring, FR

1914 WINTON
Model 20 — 6-cyl., 48.6 hp, 130" wb

	FP	5	4	3	2	1
Touring-5P	3250	6200	8800	13,500	31,000	43,000
Touring-4P	3250	6000	8500	13,000	30,000	42,000
Touring-6P	3500	6300	9000	14,000	32,000	44,000
Touring-7P	3500	6400	9300	14,500	33,000	45,000
Roadster-2P	3250	6300	9000	14,000	32,000	44,000
Roadster-3P	3250	6300	9000	14,000	32,000	44,000
Limousine-7P	4600	4400	5600	9200	17,300	31,000
Landaulet-7P	4600	4500	5800	9500	18,000	32,000
Sedan-7P	4600	2700	3600	5300	8800	19,000
Three-Quarter Limousine	4350	4300	5400	8700	16,500	30,000
Colonial Coupe	4350	4200	5200	8400	15,700	29,000

1915 Winton, model 21, center entrance sedan, HAC

1915 WINTON
Model 21 — 6-cyl., 48.6 hp, 136" wb

	FP	5	4	3	2	1
Touring-5P	3250	6400	9300	14,500	33,000	45,000
Touring-4P	3250	6300	9000	14,000	32,000	44,000
Touring-6P	3500	6500	9500	15,000	34,000	46,000
Touring-7P	3500	6800	10,300	16,000	35,500	48,000
Roadster-2P	3250	6500	9500	15,000	34,000	46,000
Roadster-3P	3250	6500	9500	15,000	34,000	46,000
Limousine-7P	4600	4500	5800	9500	18,000	32,000
Landaulet-7P	4600	4700	6100	9900	19,000	33,000
Sedan-7P	4600	3100	4200	6300	10,500	22,000
Three-Quarter Limousine	4350	4400	5600	9200	17,300	31,000

1916 WINTON
Six-33 — 6-cyl., 33.75 hp, 128" wb

	FP	5	4	3	2	1
Touring-5P	2285	4500	5800	9500	18,000	32,000
Touring-4P	2285	4400	5600	9200	17,300	31,000
Touring-6P	2435	4700	6100	9900	19,000	33,000
Touring-7P	2335	5000	6500	11,000	22,000	35,000
Runabout	2285	4900	6300	10,300	21,000	34,000
Three-Quarter Limousine	3250	4300	5400	8700	16,500	30,000
Full Four-Door Limousine	3500	4500	5800	9500	18,000	32,000
Sedan	3500	3100	4200	6300	10,500	22,000
Limousine Landaulet	3500	4700	6100	9900	19,000	33,000
Coupe	3200	4200	5200	8400	15,700	29,000

Six-48 — 6-cyl., 48.6 hp, 138" wb

	FP	5	4	3	2	1
Touring-7P	3500	6700	9900	15,500	34,800	47,000
Touring-4P	3500	6300	9000	14,000	32,000	44,000
Touring-5P	3500	6400	9300	14,500	33,000	45,000
Touring-6P	3500	6500	9500	15,000	34,000	46,000
Roadster-2P	3500	6400	9300	14,500	33,000	45,000
Runabout	3500	6400	9300	14,500	33,000	45,000
Three-Quarter Limousine	4500	4500	5800	9500	18,000	32,000
Full Four-Door Limousine	4750	5000	6500	11,000	22,000	35,000
Sedan	4750	3300	4400	6700	12,000	24,000
Limousine Landaulet	4750	5200	6800	11,300	23,000	36,000
Coupe	4500	4400	5600	9200	17,300	31,000

1917 Winton, Six-48, limousine, HAC

1917 WINTON
Model 33 — 6-cyl., 33.75 hp, 128" wb

	FP	5	4	3	2	1
Touring-5P	2685	4400	5600	9200	17,300	31,000
Touring-4P	2685	4300	5400	8700	16,500	30,000
Touring-6P	2735	4500	5800	9500	18,000	32,000
Touring-7P	2735	5000	6500	11,000	22,000	35,000
Runabout	2685	4700	6100	9900	19,000	33,000
Three-Quarter Limousine	3650	4000	5000	8000	15,000	28,000
Full Four-Door Limousine	3900	4400	5600	9200	17,300	31,000
Sedan	3900	3300	4400	6700	12,000	24,000
Limousine Landaulet	3900	4300	5400	8700	16,500	30,000
Coupe	3600	4000	5000	8000	15,000	28,000
Coupelet	3000	3900	4800	7700	14,300	27,000

Model 48 — 6-cyl., 48.6 hp, 138" wb

	FP	5	4	3	2	1
Touring-4P	3500	6300	9000	14,000	32,000	44,000
Touring-5P	3500	6400	9300	14,500	33,000	45,000
Touring-6P	3500	6500	9500	15,000	34,000	46,000
Touring-7P	3500	6700	9900	15,500	34,800	47,000
Runabout	3500	6500	9500	15,000	34,000	46,000
Full Four-Door Limousine	4750	4700	6100	9900	19,000	33,000
Three-Quarter Limousine	4500	4300	5400	8700	16,500	30,000
Sedan	4750	3700	4700	7300	13,700	26,000
Limousine Landaulet	4750	4500	5800	9500	18,000	32,000
Coupe	4500	4400	5600	9200	17,300	31,000
Coupelet	3750	4200	5200	8400	15,700	29,000

1918 Winton, Six-48, limousine, HAC

1918 WINTON
Model 33 — 6-cyl., 33.75 hp, 128" wb

	FP	5	4	3	2	1
Touring-5P	2950	4400	5600	9200	17,300	31,000
Touring-4P	2950	4300	5400	8700	16,500	30,000
Touring-6P	3000	4500	5800	9500	18,000	32,000
Touring-7P	3000	5000	6500	11,000	22,000	35,000
Runabout	2950	4700	6100	9900	19,000	33,000
Three-Quarter Limousine	3950	4000	5000	8000	15,000	28,000
Full Four-Door Limousine	4200	4400	5600	9200	17,300	31,000
Sedan	4200	3300	4400	6700	12,000	24,000
Limousine Coupe	4200	4300	5400	8700	16,500	30,000
Limousine-Landaulet	3950	4000	5000	8000	15,000	28,000
Coupelet	3265	3900	4800	7700	14,300	27,000

Model 48 — 6-cyl., 48.6 hp, 138" wb

	FP	5	4	3	2	1
Touring-4P	3500	6300	9000	14,000	32,000	44,000
Touring-5P	3500	6400	9300	14,500	33,000	45,000
Touring-6P	3500	6500	9500	15,000	34,000	46,000
Touring-7P	3500	6700	9900	15,500	34,800	47,000
Runabout	3500	6500	9500	15,000	34,000	46,000
Sedan	4750	3700	4700	7300	13,700	26,000
Full Four-Door Limousine	4750	4900	6300	10,300	21,000	34,000
Limousine Landaulet	4500	4700	6100	9900	19,000	33,000
Limousine	4500	4500	5800	9500	18,000	32,000
Coupe	4500	4400	5600	9200	17,300	31,000
Coupelet	3750	4200	5200	8400	15,700	29,000

1919 Winton, Six-33, touring, HAC

1919 WINTON
Model 33 — 6-cyl., 33.75 hp, 128" wb

Touring-5P	3150	4700	6100	9900	19,000	33,000
Touring-4P	3150	4500	5800	9500	18,000	32,000
Touring-6P	3200	4900	6300	10,300	21,000	34,000
Touring-7P	3200	5200	6800	11,300	23,000	36,000
Runabout	3150	4900	6300	10,300	21,000	34,000
Three-Quarter Limousine	4150	4200	5200	8400	15,700	29,000
Full Four-Door Limousine	4400	4500	5800	9500	18,000	32,000
Sedan	4400	3500	4500	7000	13,000	25,000
Limousine-Landaulet	4400	4500	5800	9500	18,000	32,000
Coupe	4150	4200	5200	8400	15,700	29,000
Coupelet	3465	4000	5000	8000	15,000	28,000

Model 48 — 6-cyl., 48.6 hp, 138" wb

Limousine-7P	4850	4900	6300	10,300	21,000	34,000
Touring-4P	3850	6300	9000	14,000	32,000	44,000
Touring-5P	3850	6400	9300	14,500	33,000	45,000
Touring-6P	3850	6500	9500	15,000	34,000	46,000
Touring-7P	3850	6700	9900	15,500	34,800	47,000
Runabout	3850	6500	9500	15,000	34,000	46,000
Full Four-Door Limousine	5100	5000	6500	11,000	22,000	35,000
Sedan	5100	4000	5000	8000	15,000	28,000
Coupe	4850	4300	5400	8700	16,500	30,000
Coupelet	4100	4200	5200	8400	15,700	29,000

1920 Winton, Six-24, touring, HAC

1920 WINTON
Model 25 — 6-cyl., 70 hp, 132" wb

Sport Touring-4P	3950	6800	10,300	16,000	35,500	48,000
Touring-5P	3950	6400	9300	14,500	33,000	45,000
Touring-6P	3959	6500	9500	15,000	34,000	46,000
Touring-7P	3950	6700	9900	15,500	34,800	47,000
Roadster-2P	3950	6500	9500	15,000	34,000	46,000
Roadster-3P	3950	6600	9700	15,300	34,400	46,500
Victoria-4P	4850	5400	7300	11,800	25,000	38,000
Sport Sedan-4P	5050	3300	4400	6700	12,000	24,000
Sedan-7P	5450	3100	4200	6300	10,500	32,000
French Limousine	5200	4000	5000	8000	15,000	28,000
Three-Quarter Limousine	5200	4400	5600	9200	17,300	31,000
Four-Door Limousine	5450	4500	5800	9500	18,000	32,000
Limousine-Landaulet	5450	4900	6300	10,300	21,000	34,000

Model 24 — 6-cyl., 85 hp, 138" wb

Sport Touring-4P	4350	7200	11,300	17,700	38,700	50,000
Touring-5P	4350	6700	9900	15,500	34,800	47,000
Touring-6P	4350	6800	10,300	16,000	35,500	48,000
Touring-7P	4350	7000	10,800	16,900	37,100	49,000
Roadster-2P	4350	6800	10,300	16,000	35,500	48,000
Roadster-3P	4350	6900	10,600	16,500	36,300	48,500
Sedan-7P	5600	4200	5200	8400	15,700	29,000
French Limousine-7P	5350	4700	6100	9900	19,000	33,000
Three-Quarter Limousine	5350	5000	6500	11,000	22,000	35,000
Four-Door Limousine	5600	5300	7000	11,500	24,000	37,000

1921 Winton, Six, limousine-sedan, HAC

1921 WINTON
Model 25 — 6-cyl., 70 hp, 132" wb

	FP	5	4	3	2	1
Touring-7P	4600	6700	9900	15,500	34,800	47,000
Roadster-2P	4600	6500	9500	15,000	34,000	46,000
Sport Touring-4P	4975	7200	11,300	17,700	38,700	50,000
Victoria-4P	5950	5400	7300	11,800	25,000	38,000
Sport Sedan-4P	5950	4500	5800	9500	18,000	32,000
Town Car-7P	5950	5400	7300	11,800	25,000	38,000
Limousine-7P	5950	5200	6800	11,300	23,000	36,000
Sedan-7P	6200	4900	6300	10,300	21,000	34,000
Limousine-7P	6200	5000	6500	11,000	22,000	35,000
Limousine Landaulet-7P	6350	5300	7000	11,500	24,000	37,000

1922 Winton, Six, roadster, JAC

1922 WINTON
Model 25 — 6-cyl., 70 bhp, 132" wb

Touring-7P	4600	7200	11,300	17,700	38,700	50,000
Roadster-2P	4600	7000	10,800	16,900	37,100	49,000
Sport Touring-4P	4975	7300	11,600	18,100	39,600	51,000
Victoria-4P	5950	5800	8000	12,500	28,000	40,000
Sport Sedan-4P	5950	5000	6500	11,000	22,000	35,000
Town Car-7P	5950	5800	8000	12,500	28,000	40,000
Sedan-7P	6200	5200	6800	11,300	23,000	36,000
Limousine-7P	6200	5300	7000	11,500	24,000	37,000
Limousine Landaulet-7P	6350	5800	8000	12,500	28,000	40,000

1923 Winton, Six, sedan, HAC

1923 WINTON
Model 40 — 6-cyl., 72 hp, 132" wb

Touring-7P	3400	6800	10,300	16,000	35,500	48,000
Roadster-2P	3400	6700	9900	15,500	34,800	47,000
Sport Phaeton-5P	3600	7200	11,300	17,700	38,700	50,000
Victoria-4P	4000	5000	6500	11,000	22,000	35,000
Sport Sedan-5P	4450	5200	6800	11,300	23,000	36,000
Sedan-7P	4550	4900	6300	10,300	21,000	34,000
Limousine-7P	4550	5300	7000	11,500	24,000	37,000
Limousine Sedan-7P	4700	5400	7300	11,800	25,000	38,000

1924 WINTON
Model 40 — 6-cyl., 78 hp, 132" wb

	FP	5	4	3	2	1
Touring-7P	3400	6800	10,300	16,000	35,500	48,000
Roadster-2P	3450	6700	9900	15,500	34,800	47,000
Sport Phaeton-5P	3600	7200	11,300	17,700	38,700	50,000
Coupe-5P	4250	5000	6500	11,000	22,000	35,000
Sedan-5P	4450	4700	6100	9900	19,000	33,000
Sedan-7P	4550	4900	6300	10,300	21,000	34,000
Limousine-7P	4450	5300	7000	11,500	24,000	37,000
Limousine Sedan-7P	4700	5400	7300	11,800	25,000	38,000

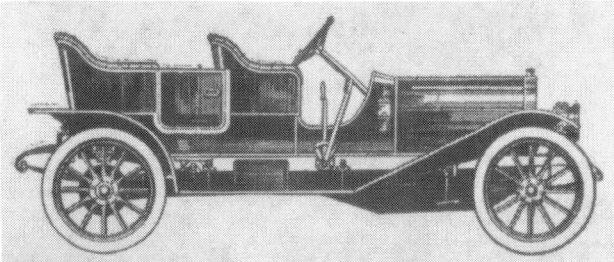

1910 Wisco, model A-5, touring, NAHC

WISCO — Janesville, Wisconsin — (1910) — The origins of the Wisconsin Carriage Company dated back to 1885 in Janesville, and the turn of the century found its factory at 600 West Milwaukee Street booming. William Morris, R.E. Wisner, Arthur P. Aller and Walter R. Kohler were the men in charge, and in 1909 they imported engineer T.E. Warnock from Detroit to design a car for them to be known as the Wisco. The Wisco was a 30 hp four on a 118-inch wheelbase featuring shaft drive, a three-speed selective transmission, cone clutch, semi-elliptic front springs, and three-quarter elliptics in the rear. Both a baby tonneau and a touring were offered at $1750, and a portion of the carriage factory was converted to automobile manufacture. In December of 1909 the company indicated to the trade press its intention to manufacture 100 Wiscos for the 1910 model year. Many fewer than that were built, however, when the Wisconsin Carriage Company people decided that carriage and cars couldn't congenially be produced together. Since their horsedrawn business was thriving, they discontinued the Wisco. All indications are that it had been a finely built car. Around 1915 the Wisconsin Carriage Company evolved into the Janesville Products Company and its manufacturing emphasis changed to coaster wagons, "skudder" cars and sidewalk toys. The firm remained in business until 1940.

1910 WISCO
Model A-4 — 4-cyl., 30.5 hp, 118" wb

Baby Tonneau-4P	1750	3000	4000	6000	9500	21,000

Model A-5 — 4-cyl., 30.5 hp, 118" wb

Touring-5P	1750	3100	4200	6300	10,500	22,000

WISCONSIN — The Wisconsin Cyclecar Company was organized in Milwaukee, Wisconsin during the spring of 1914 with a capital stock of $25,000 for the manufacture of automobiles. Incorporators were W.B. Christie, W.H. Schuab and Walter Fernekes. Manufacture is doubted.

WISCONSIN STEAM — Milwaukee, Wisconsin — (1899) — In November of 1899 the Wisconsin Automobile & Machinery Company superseded the United States Automobile Company which had been incorporated in September that year in Milwaukee. A single United States steam car had previously been built, and the Wisconsin firm built one too, apparently for demonstration purposes. Thereafter the firm produced engines only.

WISE — S.J. Wise & Company of New York City was organized during the fall of 1909 with a capital stock of $15,000 for the manufacture of motor cars and parts. Joining Wise in this venture were H. Greenberg and A. Kipp. Manufacture is doubted.

The Wise-Green Motor Car Company of Canton, Ohio was organized during the fall of 1911 with a capital stock of $25,000 to assemble and deal in automobiles and to conduct a garage. The principals involved were Richard S. Wise, George M. Green, Howard B. Fawcett, Joseph M. Blake and Charles T. Carlson. Manufacture is doubted.

WISNER — Flint, Michigan — (1900-1903) — The first automobile built in Flint had no brakes. In order to stop it, so an eyewitness later said, its inventor would run it into the side of the machine shop in which it had been built. Flint's first automobile was built by Charles H. Wisner, who was a Genesee County circuit judge, the son of a Michigan governor, and a very respected citizen in town. The car was powered by an air-cooled engine of Wisner's own design, which its inventor admitted was not wholly successful, especially when the weather turned warm. Although it may have been tested earlier, Wisner's car was given its public debut in the Labor Day parade in Flint on September 3rd, 1900. After completing his first vehicle, Judge Wisner began his second — and may have built one or two more as well. The second Wisner was reported favorably upon in *The Automobile Review* of January 1st, 1903. It featured a left-hand steering wheel, which was a rather avant-garde proposition at the time. It also had brakes. Apparently Wisner was interested in producing this vehicle and, as legend has it, among the Flint citizens he approached with the idea was one William Crapo Durant. When the Wisner stalled during a demonstration ride, Durant became disenchanted. Charles Wisner soon gave up on the manufacturing idea. Ironically, a few years later, Wisner became the purchaser of the automobile that Durant was by then producing. It was a Buick.

1512

WISNER — Grand Forks, North Dakota — (1907) — In 1907 Charles Wisner of Grand Forks built himself a two-passenger 12 hp automobile. So far as is known, this was the first and last automobile of his own design.

WISSMAN — The Wissman Auto Repair Company was organized in Cleveland, Ohio early in 1911 with a capital stock of $5000 to manufacture, repair and deal in motor vehicles. Among the incorporators were Joseph H. Wissman, William J. Cermak and Joseph C. Kocian. Manufacture is doubted.

WITHERS — Garden City, Kansas — (1908) — The Withers was built on a bet. When his cronies in Garden City expressed skepticism that he could do it, Charles Withers wagered that he could — and he did. The car he built in 1908 was cumbersome, but it ran. Its engine was a Monitor one-lunger. Its frame was scrap iron bolted together. Curiously, the front wheels were used for driving, the rear wheels for steering. A tiller was provided. So far as is known, Charles Withers never built another car.

WITT SPECIAL — Detroit, Michigan — (1912) — The Witt Special was a model of the Flanders 20 that was marketed following the string of class records put up by race driver Frank Witt at Indianapolis Motor Speedway late in 1911. Its body styling, higher gearing and other engine tweaks were the only differences from the standard Flanders 20. In addition to designing the Witt Special, Frank Witt took it racing (winning his class at the Dead Horse Hill Climb) and completing the Glidden Tour with but one penalty point.

WITTER — Granville, Ohio — (1900) — E.E. Witter of Granville built himself a car in 1900 of which he was inordinately proud. A trap carrying six passengers, it was powered by a four-cylinder engine developing a meager 7 hp, though Witter claimed that his specially-devised gearing on the engine shaft permitted speeds of up to 30 mph. He is not believed to have built another car.

WITTMANN — Lincoln, Nebraska — (1900) — The Wittmann Automobile Company was organized with a capital stock of $25,000 during the summer of 1900 for the manufacture and sale of automobiles. The people involved were J.H. Wittmann, O. Wittmann and O.J. Junge, and they set themselves up in business at 1612 Farnam Street. Unsatisfied with experimental attempts which produced a car that ran but not very well, the Wittmann people ultimately decided to sell the efforts of other manufacturers. In the early fall of 1900, O. Wittmann traveled East to check out the automotive scene there and returned to Lincoln with agencies for the Mobile and the Locomobile.

WIZARD — Indianapolis, Indiana — (1914) — In October of 1913 the Wizard Motor Company of Indianapolis — which was headed by P.S. Florea, O.C. Forbes and E.H. Habig — announced the addition to its product line of a small two-cylinder air-cooled engine specifically designed for cyclecar use. The price was $160, which was rather expensive for a cyclecar powerplant. In January 1914 the firm announced its intention to enter the cyclecar field itself, the Wizard Motor Company being reorganized with a capital stock of $50,000 for that purpose. Manufacture of a Wizard cyclecar did not follow, however; probably only a prototype was built.

WIZARD — Charlotte, North Carolina — (1920-1921) — The Wizard Junior was a two-passenger 800-pound roadster powered by a two-cylinder air cooled 15 hp engine and featuring a planetary transmission, artillery wheels, a 35 mph top speed and a $395 price tag. A Wizard Senior was promised but never arrived. The car was promoted in Charlotte by F.W. Edwardy, Sr. and F.W. Edwardy, Jr., and well as Charles Hamel, the president of the Cyclornobile Company of Toledo, Ohio. These people seem to have engaged in more wizardry selling stock in the venture than in producing automobiles. The Wizard Automobile Company was organized in Charlotte in late 1920 and was vigorously promoted. A factory was built on the southwest side of town, and so were a couple of Junior cars, these to induce the local citizenry to invest in the venture, which a good many of them did. In January of 1921, Wizard's advertising was branded as a "flagrant offense against truth" by the national vigilance committee of the Associated Advertising Clubs of the World. It was also revealed that F.W. Edwardy, Sr. was a "professional promoter," and that his son who had claimed previous automotive experience with Packard and White was unknown at either of those companies. Charles Hamel came under similar fire. Charlotte residents, at least those who did not lose a great deal of money in the venture, recall the Wizard as a "pretty car." In April of 1922 the factory of the Wizard Automobile Company was sold for $105,000 to the Automatic Car Step Company which used it for the manufacture of safety steps for railroad cars. Some years later the building became the home of the Morris Livestock Company.

1920-1921 WIZARD
Junior — 2-cyl., 15 hp, 100" wb

	FP	5	4	3	2	1
Roadster-2P	395	2200	3200	4400	7000	15,000
6617 W & L						

W & L — The W & L Manufacturing Company, Inc. of Buffalo, New York was organized during the fall of 1914 with a capital stock of $30,000 to manufacture, deal in and repair automobiles. The initials translated to H.Z. White and Benjamin C. Lee. Manufacture is doubted.

WOGGLEBUG — Wogglebug was the nickname given to a special race car built in 1903 by the Watch City Automobile Company for race driver Louis S. Ross. Refer to Ross Steamer.

1907 Wolfe, touring, NAHC

WOLFE — Minneapolis, Minnesota — (1907-1909) — Maurice Wolfe first made a name for himself in 1903 when, as a car salesman in Minneapolis, he sold a Cadillac to Chief Big Mouth of the Crow tribe in Billings, Montana. This was widely reported in the press as the first sale of an automobile to a "wild Indian." Three years later Wolfe joined with the Wilcox brothers — John F. and H.E. — in Minneapolis to form the H.E. Wilcox Motor Car Company for production of the Wolfe. Wolfe cars featured either water-cooled or Carrico air-cooled four-cylinder engines and had selective sliding gear transmissions and double chain drive. Prices were in the $2000 range. Approximately 200 cars had been produced by April of 1909 when the marque name was changed to Wilcox. The Wilcox was built into 1911. Maurice Wolfe turned up next in Shelbyville, Indiana with the Clark and the Meteor.

1907 WOLFE
Four — 24 hp, 108" wb

	FP	5	4	3	2	1
Touring-5P	1800	2500	3500	5000	8500	18,000

1908 WOLFE
Four — 24 hp, 108" wb

Touring	1800	2500	3500	5000	8500	18,000

1909 WOLFE
Four — 30 hp, 126" wb

Touring-5P	2250	2700	3600	5300	8800	19,000
Roadster-4P	2250	2500	3500	5000	8500	18,000

WOLVERINE — Wolverine was the model designation of the Jackson in 1917 and 1918, Jackson cars being built in Jackson, Michigan from 1903 to 1923. Refer to Jackson.

The Wolverine-Detroit built in 1912-1913 by the Pratt-Carter-Sigsbee Company of Detroit, Michigan has appeared on various car rosters. The only vehicles built by this company, however, were trucks.

The Wolverine Automobile & Commercial Vehicle Company of Dundee, Michigan was organized during the fall of 1905 with a capital stock of $28,000 to manufacture and sell automobiles, supplies, accessories and gasoline engines. H.J. Hunt was behind this venture. Manufacture of a car is doubted.

The Wolverine Car & Tractor Company of Wayne, Michigan was organized during the spring of 1916 by William J. and T.J. McNamara and William J. Wagenhals. By 1917, however, as the Wayne city directory reveals, the firm is simply the Wolverine Tractor Company. An automobile was not manufactured; the firm had gone under by 1918.

The Wolverine Motor Works of Grand Rapids, Michigan was headed by Clark Sintz, who reported his building of an automobile in 1895. Refer to Sintz.

1904 Wolverine, touring, WLB

WOLVERINE — Detroit, Michigan — (1904-1905) / Dundee, Michigan — (1906) — The Reid Manufacturing Company of Detroit was organized to produce sectional bookcases, display showcases, refrigerators, store furnishings and automobiles. The last named would be called Wolverine, "The Cleverest Automobile Built," according to the ads. The prototype was designed late in 1903 by Walter L. Marr, though by January 1904 he had been given a check for sixty dollars and a note saying his services were no longer needed — which left him free to join his old employer, David Dunbar Buick. Subsequently, Gilbert R. Albaugh — an automobile engineer who had already bounced from Olds in Lansing, to Rambler in Kenosha, to Peerless and Star in Cleveland — was brought in as chief engineer.

Albaugh seems to have revised the Wolverine considerably from Marr's prototype. As produced, the car was a shaft-drive two- or four-cylinder with selective sliding gear transmission. Why the name Wolverine was chosen for it when one of the slogans was "like the deer: swift, graceful and beautiful" is something of a mystery. A test drive reported in *Cycle and Automobile Trade Journal* indicates that the car was a fine product. Backstage, however, the affairs of the Reid Manufacturing Company were a tangle. During the fall of 1905, Reid was succeeded by the Wolverine Automobile Company in Detroit, which almost immediately metamorphosed into the Wolverine Auto & Commercial Vehicle Company of Dundee. Production in Dundee began in 1906 and almost immediately ended there. Later that year the factory was taken over for the building of a prototype car known as the Maumee which was subsequently produced in Toledo (Ohio) as the Craig-Toledo.

1904-1905 WOLVERINE
Model C — 4-cyl., 15 hp, 82" wb

	FP	5	4	3	2	1
Touring-5P	1750	2500	3500	5000	8500	18,000

Model D — 2-cyl., 16/20 hp, 88" wb

Touring-5P	1600	2900	3700	5600	9100	20,000

1906 Wolverine, runabout, WLB

1906 WOLVERINE
Model G — 2-cyl., 10 hp, 72" wb

Runabout	650	2700	3600	5300	8800	19,000

Model F — 2-cyl., 18 hp, 88" wb

Touring	1200	2900	3700	5600	9100	20,000

Model E — 4-cyl., 40 hp, 88" wb

Touring	2000	4200	5200	8400	15,700	29,000

WOLVERINE — Mt. Clemens, Michigan — (1910) — The Wolverine Motor Car Company of Mt. Clemens was born early in 1910 and died that summer before manufacture began. Apparently, a prototype of its car had been completed; that it was a 30 hp four-cylinder gasoline car represents the extent of details provided, however. In July, Thomas F. Ahern purchased the Wolverine machinery and equipment, which he moved to Alpena, Michigan. Production of the Alpena Flyer followed there from 1911 into 1914.

1917 Wolverine, speedster, OCW

WOLVERINE — Kalamazoo, Michigan — (1917-1919) — Although the original announcement came from Toledo in 1916, and the second from Battle Creek, this venture didn't come together until its arrival in Kalamazoo in 1917. Spearheading the Wolverine Motor Car Company was Albert H. Collins, formerly of Staver, Locomobile and R.C.H. Joining him was Harry A. Scott, a Kalamazoo garage owner. Their idea was a very nice one: a high-performance and rakish speedster to rival the Stutz Bearcat. Its price tag was to be $3500. One car was built, fitted with a four-cylinder Wisconsin engine set into a 125-inch wheelbase chassis and advertised as the Speedway Special. But material shortages and other exigencies concomitant to the First World War stopped the Speedway Special in its tracks. Not until early 1919 was the idea revived, and another car assembled, this one with a four-cylinder Duesenberg engine. Purportedly, a touring car prototype was also built, this model to sell for $3250, and a sample of a sedan version may have been put together too, these latter cars carrying Wisconsin engines. Undoubtedly, only pilot models were produced in this revival of the Wolverine which proved as short-lived as its original incarnation. Later in 1919 Albert H. Collins showed up in Huntington, New York with another car venture called the Collins. Meanwhile, Harry-Scott remained behind in Kalamazoo where he opened a car dealership in the building which had formerly housed the Wolverine Motor Car Company.

1928 Wolverine, 2-dr. sedan, WLB

WOLVERINE — Lansing, Michigan — (1927-1928) — This Wolverine was a product of the Reo Motor Car Company, introduced during the late spring of 1927 as a smaller and less expensive companion car to the Reo Flying Cloud. Unlike the Reo, the Wolverine was an assembled automobile: 199-cubic-inch 50 hp six-cylinder engine by Continental, clutch by Borg & Beck, transmission by Warner, axles by Salisbury. It did share the Reo's Lockheed hydraulic brakes, and look-alike styling from the cowl back. Its radiator and hood louver design was its own, however, as was the hubcab insignia. A five-passenger brougham was the only body style offered initially, at $1195; a $1295 sedan was announced in July of 1928. A coupe had been promised as well, but before it reached the marketing stage, Reo had second thoughts about the Wolverine idea itself. In December 1928 the company introduced a 215-cubic-inch 60 hp Continental-engined version of the Flying Cloud called the Mate (the larger Cloud became the Master) — and the Wolverine was summarily forgotten thereafter.

1927 WOLVERINE
Six — 50 hp, 114" wb

	FP	5	4	3	2	1
Brougham	1195	3700	4700	7300	13,700	26,000

1928 Wolverine, brougham, OCW

1928 WOLVERINE
Six — 50 hp, 114" wb

Brougham	1195	3700	4700	7300	13,700	26,000
Sedan	1295	3900	4800	7700	14,300	27,000

WONDER — The Wonder Manufacturing Company of Syracuse, New York had been in the gasoline-engine building business since 1907 and early in 1909 announced its plans to add automobiles to its product line. Ray M. Cornwell, the company's manager, was joined in this effort by W.D. Boyle and G.T. Hurd. Manufacture of a car does not seem to have followed, however. The company remained in the engine-building business in Syracuse through the First World War.

The Wonder Motor Company of Chicago, Illinois was organized during the spring of 1904 with a capital stock of $25,000 for the manufacture of engines and automobiles. Incorporators were Albert N. Eastman, W.C. McHenry and Harold F. White. Manufacture of a car is doubted.

The Wonder Motor Car Company of Kansas City, Missouri evolved from the Kansas City Motor Car Company in 1909. The automobile introduced by this new venture was sometimes called the Kansas City Wonder and sometimes simply the Wonder. Refer to Kansas City.

The Wonder Truck Company of Chicago, Illinois has been indicated on various rosters as the manufacturer of an automobile in 1917. Documentation is lacking. The firm's only known product during its short year in the industry was a truck.

WOOD — The W.A. Wood Manufacturing Company of Kingston, New York was organized during the spring of 1910 with a capital stock of $2 million for the manufacture of the British Commer truck and the automobile designed by race driver Guy Vaughan. Refer to Vaughan.

The Wood-Knight-Hawk Manufacturing Company was organized in Oklahoma City, Oklahoma during the spring of 1911 with a capital stock of $200,000 for the manufacture of automobiles and motor plows. The partners involved were J.W. Wood, H.D. Knight and J.W. Hawk. Manufacture of a car is doubted.

WOOD ELECTRIC — New York, New York — (1900-1902) — Although an occasional electric carriage was produced by Frederick R. Wood & Son of 219 West 19th Street in New York City, the firm's major emphasis was electric ambulances, the first of which was delivered to St. Vincent's Hospital in 1900, with several more delivered to the Roosevelt and Presbyterian hospitals in 1902. "When New York was in the throes of the deadly heated spell," *The Motor Review* editorialized that summer, "the undoubted superiority of the auto over the horse was made most convincingly apparent. When man and beast fell beneath the heat of the sun, the ambulances had their inning." Alas, however, the inning of the Wood Company was shortly over. The firm built a number of further vehicles for B. Altman's department store, but early in 1902 Frederick Wood announced that he had entered automobile manufacturing to make a profit, but had lost money instead. Although he insisted at the time he was abandoning the automobile field, he did not. A carriage maker since the 1880's, he transferred his efforts to the coachbuilding business, and produced bodies for passenger cars through 1926 and for trucks and buses into 1939.

1910 Woodburn, runabout, LC

WOODBURN — Woodburn, Indiana — (1905-1912) — In a small machine shop on Front Street, between Park and Center in Woodburn, the Woodburn Auto Company built cars, trucks and tractors from 1905 to 1912. William Keller and Herman Messman were the partners involved; Claude Spreuer was plant manager, and local townspeople were stockholders. The operation was a small one, and the vehicles were marketed in the local area. Most of the cars were high-wheeled buggy types with right-hand steering wheels and two-cylinder air-cooled engines, though the last car built carried a water-cooled four mounted up front under a hood. About a dozen cars had been built when production was discontinued in 1912. Although a specific reason for the company's demise cannot be recalled in Woodburn, more than likely it was simply the Model T Ford, which tolled the death knell for thousands of small machine-shop operations throughout the country.

WOODLAND — Worcester, Massachusetts — (1913) — That plans were afoot for the building of a cyclecar in Worcester was revealed to the trade press in early November of 1913. Frank O. Woodland broke the news, noting that he had interested some Worcester men in joining him in the enterprise. Recently he had received patents on a two-stroke engine, a rolling clutch transmission and a shock absorber, all of these components to be included in the new car, as well as the spring wheels on which he was then working. Whether Woodland completed an example of his proposed cyclecar cannot be stated with certainty, but quite possibly the prototype which is known to have been built during this period by the Morgan Motor Truck Company in Worcester was Frank Woodland's design.

WOODLAND — Cleveland, Ohio — (1909) — Although just four cars were built by the Woodland Motor Car Company of 2552 East 55th Street in Cleveland, one of them had four doors, a decided novelty for this early period, since even front doors (or fore-doors, as they were called then) only became popular after 1911. Woodlands were powered by three-cylinder, two-stroke engines, with coachwork provided by the Patterson Body Company of Cleveland. The cars were alternately called the Woodland 30 or Woodland Special, and all four cars were sold to Cleveland residents, at a price of $2300 apiece. Following this modest production, Woodland added "& Repair" to its company name and continued in that activity for a number of years thereafter.

1901 Wood-Loco, runabout, NAHC

1903 Wood Steamer, NAHC

1902 Woodruff, runabout, NAHC

WOOD-LOCO STEAM — Cohoes, New York — (1901-1902) / WOOD — Brooklyn, New York — (1903) — In 1900 J.C. Wood was engaged with his brothers in the new and second-hand furniture business in Worcester, Massachusetts. That October he sold out his interest. "J.C. Wood has built a number of motor vehicles," reported *The Motor Vehicle Review*, "and has found that his motor vehicle business has so increased that it was desirable that he withdraw from the furniture business." That Wood was exaggerating the extent of his automobile activity seems certain; most probably the cars built in Worcester were experimental. He did move into manufacture, in 1901, however, when he traveled to Cohoes and convinced local businessmen to back him in the establishment of a factory. There, as the Wood-Loco Vehicle Company, he built two steamer models: a delivery wagon and a runabout providing vis-a-vis seating for five passengers. The Wood-Loco's horizontal engine developed 8 hp, the boiler and fuel tank were under the seat, and either gasoline or kerosene could be used as fuel. Despite a New Jersey incorporation later in 1901 of the Wood Vehicle Company to "acquire land, buildings and water power in New Jersey and elsewhere for the manufacture of automobiles," production remained confined to Cohoes and continued through 1902. Early in 1903, and probably because more investment capital beckoned, Joseph C. Wood moved to Brooklyn where, with C.T. Sauer and E.S. Wood, he organized the Wood Vapor Vehicle Company with a capital stock of $50,000. His new factory was at 811 Union Street, and his new steam runabout was rather more refined than the Wood-Loco had been. Its steam generator hung under the carriage, with all other machinery mounted up front under the hood. The car had 36-inch wood wheels with solid tires. Weight and price of the vehicle were the same: 450 pounds, 450 dollars. J.C. Wood produced this steam runabout in 1903 only. Thereafter he elected to confine his production to delivery wagons, in which field he remained through 1905.

WOOD & MEAGHER — Richmond, Virginia — (1896) — James N. Wood, in partnership with a man named Meagher, ran a machine shop in Richmond, Virginia. In 1896 they submitted entries for two gasoline-propelled vehicles of their own design to the promoters of the Cosmopolitan Race: a motorcycle and a motor carriage. In April they reported to *The Horseless Age* that "on account of delay in the shipment of tubing and other important parts...being made in the North," the motor carriage wouldn't be completed on time. Wood and Meagher did plan to travel North with their motorcycle, however, until they were informed that a two-wheeler was ineligible for the Cosmopolitan event, so they stayed home instead. The Wood & Meagher gasoline carriage was ultimately finished and successfully tested, though manufacture of neither it nor the motorcycle was embarked upon. References from 1898 indicate that Wood, Meagher & Company would concentrate further efforts to the engine-building field.

WOODRUFF — The Woodruff Garage Company of Watertown, New York was organized late in 1908 with a capital stock of $1000 for the manufacture of engines, automobiles and machines. Incorporators wre H.G. Kubel and T.A. Mathews of Watertown and J.E. De Friend of Black River. Manufacture of a car is doubted.

WOODRUFF — Akron, Ohio — (1902-1904) — Both Cleveland and Akron money backed the Woodruff built by Albert M. and George E. Woodruff, who were brothers and machinists from Cleveland who worked for the Akron Motor Carriage Company at the turn of the century. That firm pro-

duced several prototypes, as well as an aborted attempt to organize a Woodruff Company but by July 1901 the Akron facilities and equipment had been taken over by the S.M. York Machinery Company of Cleveland. A fresh infusion of capital arrived for the Woodruffs in 1902, however, which resulted in the $50,000 incorporation of the Woodruff Automobile Company. Sales offices were in Cleveland, and the former Akron Bicycle Company plant in Akron was secured for manufacture. The first Woodruffs were offered as single-cylinder runabouts or stanhopes. The runabout featured a body mounted on long semi-elliptic leaf springs connecting front and rear axle on each side, a la curved dash Oldsmobile, a configuration which the Woodruffs said enhanced cushioning and provided for a lower center of gravity. The stanhope was conventionally suspended. Maximum speed of both cars was 25 mph. The runabout was lever steered, the stanhope had a wheel. Press reports late in 1902 that Woodruff would be moving into the former plant of the Aultman and Miller Company (agricultural machinery producers) which lay vacant next door were premature. Those negotiations broke down; International Harvester later moved in to manufacture its I.H.C. cars and trucks. The Woodruffs seemed to be doing well otherwise, however. Production during 1903 totaled 24 automobiles, and among these were several touring cars built to custom order. One of the customers was Goodyear Tire & Rubber Company which used its Woodruff for tire testing. Tragically, in March of 1903, George E. Woodruff died following an appendectomy at the age of thirty-two. Apparently, he had been the man most responsible for the Woodruff, but his brother Albert soldiered on without him. For 1904 a new larger three-cylinder 30 hp 45 mph Woodruff touring car was introduced. In February that year another merger was rumored which would have relocated the factory in Ashland (Ohio), but again negotiations fell through. Perhaps a half-dozen Woodruffs were built in 1904. Production ended that year. In 1905 Albert Woodruff organized another company for manufacture of a car called the Akron. He built only four of them before deciding to concentrate manufacture on gas engines only.

1902-1903 WOODRUFF

	FP	5	4	3	2	1
Runabout (1-cyl., 4-1/2 hp)	775	2000	3000	4200	6500	14,000
Stanhope (1-cyl., 6 hp)	900	2100	3100	4300	6800	14,500
Dos-a-Dos Sthp. (1-cyl., 6 hp)	925	2200	3300	4500	7300	15,000
Light Delivery Stanhope	1050	2300	3400	4700	7800	16,000

1904 Woodruff, touring, NAHC

1904 WOODRUFF

Tr. (3-cyl., 30 hp, 96" wb)	—	2500	3500	5000	8500	18,000

WOODS ELECTRIC — Chicago, Illinois — (1899-1916) / WOODS DUAL-POWER — (1917-1918) — The Woods Motor Vehicle Company was organized with a whopping capital stock of $10 million in early 1899 in Chicago. Among its prominent backers were Samuel Insull of Chicago, August Belmont of New York, a number of Standard Oil magnates, and a passel of big men from Toronto. The idea was to challenge the prominent East Coast-based Electric Vehicle Company with a massive Chicago-based operation. To get into business this venture bought up the patents of an

1899 Woods Electric, hansom, WLB

inventor who had been designing electrics under his own name of Clinton E. Woods since 1897. Clinton E. Woods himself was hired as superintendent of the new company but was soon eased out and returned to building cars under his own name by 1901. Understandably, there was some confusion in the trade press during this period regarding which cars were Woods and which were Clinton E. Woods, but this was resolved when Woods went into receivership in Chicago during the fall of 1901 and Clinton E. Woods quit the electric car manufacturing business soon after and became an automobile dealer. The number of cars produced by the Woods Motor Vehicle Company prior to the 1901 receivership is not known, but the firm seems to have been more promotion than production. An early electric carriage is known to have been ordered by the manager of the Honolulu Iron Works and was one of the first automobiles in Hawaii. Though a number of Chicago businesses had bought delivery wagons from Woods, and the company also operated a hansom cab fleet, at the time of receivership it was revealed that the vehicles in the factory totaled just one car completed and two in the process of construction. The Woods Motor Vehicle Company only really got moving after reorganization was completed late in 1902. In 1905, when Louis Burr (formerly of Kimball) was brought in as president, the company began construction of a vast new factory on 25th Street at Calumet and Cottage Grove avenues in Chicago where output would be tripled to 500 cars annually. Prior to 1903 the Woods looked typically electric, with small motors mounted on the rear axle, and coachwork that was largely a variation on the hansom cab theme. During the summer of that year, however, the company intro-

duced a larger rear-entrance tonneau model which closely resembled a gasoline car; its batteries were mounted up front under a hood, and its two individually connected 2 1/2 hp motors drove through a four-speed transmission. For three seasons — 1905-1907 — Woods offered a gasoline or gas-electric car as well, but thereafter returned to the building of electrics exclusively. Woods were expensive cars, hovering around the $3000 range. In 1915, with the waning popularity of electrics in the marketplace, the company began experiments with another gas-electric. Its prototype had a wheelbase of 105 inches (five inches longer than the electric), but it was introduced during the summer of 1916 with a longer 110-inch wheelbase. The car was called the Woods Dual Power, and initially used a four-cylinder gasoline engine built by Woods and fitted as an auxiliary to the usual Woods electric motor. At speeds below 15 mph, the gasoline engine idled, and the car was driven entirely by the electric motor. The gasoline auxiliary provided for increased speeds up to 35 mph. The Woods organization obviously was inexperienced at trying to beat the gasoline car makers at their own game, because the Dual Power was revised within a year. In June 1917 announcement was made that the car for the new season would be powered by a four-cylinder Continental engine and would be fitted into a much longer 124-inch wheelbase. The price was increased from $2650 to $2950. It was too late. By the early fall of 1918, the Woods Motor Vehicle Company disappeared from the automotive scene. During 1924 reportedly the Woods Dual Power was to be revived half a continent away in Pomona, California by the makers of the Balboa and apparently some prototypes were built, but the venture proceeded no further than that.

1903 Woods Electric, style no. 11, hansom cab, HAC

1901 Woods Electric, mail phaeton, HAC

1903 Woods Electric, tonneau, WLB

1903 WOODS ELECTRIC
Style 1/2A

	FP	5	4	3	2	1
Road Wagon	925	2000	3000	4200	6500	14,000
Style 1/2A						
Road Wagon	1000	2000	3000	4200	6500	14,000
Style 2						
Park Buggy	1400	2000	3000	4200	6500	14,000
Style 3						
Park Trap	1950	2200	3200	4400	7000	15,000

	FP	5	4	3	2	1
Style 4						
Brake	2000	2200	3200	4400	7000	15,000
Style 5						
Surrey	2000	2400	3400	4800	8000	17,000
Style 6-2						
Stanhope	2000	2300	3300	4600	7500	16,000
Style 7						
Phaeton	2000	2400	3400	4800	8000	17,000
Style 8						
Spider	2250	2000	3000	4200	6500	14,000
Style 9A						
Full Mail Phaeton	2900	2200	3200	4400	7000	15,000
Style 9B						
Demi Mail Phaeton	2600	2200	3200	4400	7000	15,000
Style 10						
Physician's Coupe	2200	2000	3000	4200	6500	14,000
Style 11						
Hansom Cab	3050	2200	3200	4400	7000	15,000
Style 12						
Victoria Hansom Cab	3110	2300	3300	4600	7500	16,000
Style 13						
Brougham	2800	2200	3200	4400	7000	15,000
Style 14						
Victoria	2000	2000	3000	4200	6500	14,000

1904 Woods Electric, style 115, landaulet, HAC

1904 WOODS ELECTRIC

	FP	5	4	3	2	1
Style 101 — 64" wb						
Runabout	1000	2000	3000	4200	6500	14,000
Style 102 — 69" wb						
Stanhope	1850	2200	3200	4400	7000	15,000
Style 114 — 73" wb						
Queen Victoria	1900	2300	3300	4600	7500	16,000
Style 103 — 74" wb						
Victoria	2400	2300	3300	4600	7500	16,000
Style 119 — 76" wb						
Surrey	1950	2400	3400	4800	8000	17,000
Style 105 — 68" wb						
Round Front Brougham	2500	2500	3500	5000	8500	18,000
Style 112 — 72" wb						
Delivery	2350	2200	3200	4400	7000	15,000
Style 120 — 73" wb						
Inside Operated Brougham	2800	2200	3200	4400	7000	15,000
Style 107 — 70" wb						
Straight Front Brougham	2800	2300	3300	4600	7500	16,000
Style 117 — 73" wb						
Rear Operated Extension Front Brougham	3000	2400	3400	4800	8000	17,000
Style 116 — 88" wb						
Front Operated Extension Front Brougham	3000	2500	3500	5000	8500	18,000
Style 118 — 86" wb						
Station Wagon	2800	2500	3500	5000	8500	18,000
Style 104 — 88" wb						
Tonneau	2500	2400	3400	4800	8000	17,000
Style 115 — 83" wb						
Landaulette	3000	2700	3600	5300	8800	19,000

1905 Woods Electric, style 201, runabout, HAC

1905 WOODS ELECTRIC

	FP	5	4	3	2	1
Style 201 — 64" wb						
Runabout	1000	2000	3000	4200	6500	14,000
Style 102 — 69" wb						
Stanhope	1850	2200	3200	4400	7000	15,000
Style 114 — 73" wb						
Queen Victoria	1900	2300	3300	4600	7500	16,000
Style 103 — 74" wb						
Victoria	2400	2300	3300	4600	7500	16,000
Style 119 — 76" wb						
Surrey	1850	2400	3400	4800	8000	17,000
Style 105 — 68" wb						
Round Front Brougham	2500	2500	3500	5000	8500	18,000
Style 120 — 73" wb						
Inside Operated Brougham	2500	2500	3500	5000	8500	18,000
Style 118 — 86" wb						
Station Wagon	2800	2400	3400	4800	8000	17,000
Style 107 — 70" wb						
Straight Front Brougham	2800	2500	3500	5000	8500	18,000
Style 116 — 88" wb						
Front Operated Extension Brougham	3000	2700	3600	5300	8800	19,000
Style 117 — 75" wb						
Rear Operated Extension Brougham	3000	2700	3600	5300	8800	19,000
Style 115 — 83" wb						
Open Landaulette	3000	2700	3600	5300	8800	19,000
Style 121 — 82" wb						
Canopy Top Bus	3000	2500	3500	5000	8500	18,000
Gasoline Car — 4-cyl., 40 hp, 108" wb						
Side Entrance Tonneau	4250	3900	4800	7700	14,300	27,000
Limousine	5000	3900	4800	7700	14,300	27,000

1906 Woods, model 40, gasoline touring, HAC

1906 WOODS ELECTRIC

	FP	5	4	3	2	1
Style 103 — 74" wb						
Victoria	2400	2400	3400	4800	8000	17,000
Style 214A — 73" wb						
Queen Victoria	1900	2300	3300	4600	7500	16,000
Style 119 — 76" wb						
Surrey	1850	2200	3200	4400	7000	15,000
Style 105 — 68" wb						
Round Front Brougham	2500	2500	3500	5000	8500	18,000
Style 118 — 86" wb						
Station Wagon	2800	2400	3400	4800	8000	17,000
Style 107 — 70" wb						
Straight Front Brougham	2800	2500	3500	5000	8500	18,000
Style 115 — 83" wb						
Landaulette	3000	2700	3600	5300	8800	19,000
Style 202 — 96" wb						
Extension Front Brougham	3500	2700	3600	5300	8800	19,000
Style 201 — 73" wb						
Runabout	1900	2400	3400	4800	8000	17,000
Style 120 — 73" wb						
Inside Drive Brougham	2800	2700	3600	5300	8800	19,000
Style 116 — 88" wb						
Front Drive Extension Brougham	3000	3000	4000	6000	9500	21,000
Style 117 — 75" wb						
Rear Drive Extension Brougham	3000	2900	3700	5600	9100	20,000
Gasoline Car — 4-cyl., 40 hp, 120" wb						
Tonneau	4500	3100	4200	6300	10,500	22,000
Touring	4750	3900	4800	7700	14,300	27,000
Limousine	5250	3300	4400	6700	12,000	24,000
Pullman	5500	4200	5200	8400	15,700	29,000

1907 WOODS ELECTRIC

	FP	5	4	3	2	1
Style 214B — 73" wb						
Queen Victoria	2150	2400	3400	4800	8000	17,000
Style 214A — 73" wb						
Queen Victoria Brougham	2700	2700	3600	5300	8800	19,000
Style 216 — 88" wb						
Extension Brougham	4000	2900	3700	5600	9100	20,000
Style 217 — 75" wb						
Special Landaulet	4500	3100	4200	6300	10,500	22,000
Style 215 — 83" wb						
Extension Landaulet	4000	3300	4400	6700	12,000	24,000
Gasoline Car — 4-cyl., 40/45 hp, 120" wb						
Touring-7P	4750	3900	4800	7700	14,300	27,000
Limousine-7P	5500	3500	4500	7000	13,000	25,000

1907 Woods Electric, style 214B, victoria, WLB

1909 Woods Electric, roadster, HAC

1907 Woods, 40/45 h.p., gasoline limousine, HAC

1910 Woods Electric, brougham, HAC

1910 WOODS ELECTRIC
Style 214 — 74" wb

	FP	5	4	3	2	1
Victoria	2100	2400	3400	4800	8000	17,000
Style 214C — 74" wb						
Brougham	2650	2500	3500	5000	8500	18,000
Style 1012 — 86" wb						
Coupe	2900	2700	3600	5300	8800	19,000
1911 WOODS ELECTRIC						
Model 1014C — 74" wb						
Brougham	2100	2400	3400	4800	8000	17,000
Model 1012 — 86" wb						
Coupe	2900	2900	3700	5600	9100	20,000
Model 1014 — 74" wb						
Coupe	2650	2700	3600	5300	8800	19,000

1908 Woods Electric, brougham, HAC

1908 WOODS ELECTRIC
Queen Victoria — 73" wb

	FP	5	4	3	2	1
Brougham	2700	2300	3300	4600	7500	16,000
Roadster	2100	2500	3500	5000	8500	18,000

1909 WOODS ELECTRIC
Queen Victoria — 73" wb

	FP	5	4	3	2	1
Brougham	2650	2300	3300	4600	7500	16,000
Roadster	2100	2500	3500	5000	8500	18,000

1912 Woods Electric, brougham, HAC

1912 WOODS ELECTRIC
Model 1316 — 90" wb

	FP	5	4	3	2	1
Extension Brougham	3000	2500	3500	5000	8500	18,000
Model 1317 — 92" wb						
Extension Brougham	2500	2700	3600	5300	8800	19,000
Model 1318 — 108" wb						
Limousine	4000	3100	4200	6300	10,500	22,000
1913 WOODS ELECTRIC						
Model 1319 — 92" wb						
Victoria	2500	2500	3500	5000	8500	18,000
Model 1320 — 92" wb						
Roadster	2400	3100	4200	6300	10,500	22,000
Model 1321 — 92" wb						
Brougham	2700	2400	3400	4800	8000	17,000
Model 1323 — 92" wb						
Front Drive Pony Limousine	3100	3000	4000	6000	9500	21,000
Model 1324 — 92" wb						
Rear Drive Pony Limousine	3000	2900	3700	5600	9100	20,000
Model 1325 — 92" wb						
Vis-a-Vis Brougham	2900	2700	3600	5300	8800	19,000
Model 1322 — 102" wb						
Brougham	3600	2900	3700	5600	9100	20,000

1916 Woods, Dual Power coupe, JAC

1914 Woods Electric, model 1334, brougham, HAC

1914 WOODS ELECTRIC

	FP	5	4	3	2	1
Model 1332 — 102" wb						
Brougham-5P	3600	2900	3700	5600	9100	20,000
Model 1333 — 92" wb						
Brougham-5P	3200	2700	3600	5300	8800	19,000
Model 1334 — 92" wb						
Brougham-4P	3100	2700	3600	5300	8800	19,000
Model 1335 — 92" wb						
Brougham	3000	2700	3600	5300	8800	19,000

1917 Woods, Dual Power coupe, NAHC

1917 WOODS DUAL POWER
Dual Power — 110" wb

	FP	5	4	3	2	1
Coupe Coach	2650	2900	3700	5600	9100	20,000
1918 WOODS DUAL POWER						
Dual Power — 124" wb						
Coupe Coach	2950	3300	4400	6700	12,000	24,000

1915 Woods Electric, model 1501, brougham, HAC

1915 WOODS ELECTRIC

	FP	5	4	3	2	1
Model 1501 — 100" wb						
Dual Control Brougham-5P	3250	3100	4200	6300	10,500	22,000
Model 1503 — 100" wb						
Front Control Brougham	3000	3000	4000	6000	9500	21,000
Model 1504 — 100" wb						
Rear Control Brougham-5P	3000	2900	3700	5600	9100	20,000
Model 1522 — 100" wb						
Rear Control Brougham-4P	2850	2900	3700	5600	9100	20,000

1916 WOODS ELECTRIC
Model 1600 — 100" wb

	FP	5	4	3	2	1
Front Control Brougham-4P	2850	3000	4000	6000	9500	21,000

WOODS ELECTRIC — New York, New York — (1901) — For a single season a range of cars produced by the Woods organization in Chicago was marketed in New York City by a firm designated as the Woods Motor Company, and located at Vanderbilt Avenue and 44th Street in Manhattan. Models included a road wagon at $1000, a stanhope phaeton at $2000 and two delivery cars. This venture was one of the prongs in the Woods' concerted attack on the prominence enjoyed at the turn of the century by the Electric Vehicle Company, which was headquartered on the East Coast. The attack failed later in 1901 when Woods went into receivership in Chicago. The New York Company was immediately disbanded, though the Chicago operation was reorganized and went on to a long and healthy career in the electric car field.

1915 Woods Mobilette, roadster, HAC

1519

WOODS MOBILETTE — Harvey, Illinois — (1913-1916) — "Built like a watch, and ownership will not cause Tuberculosis of one's wallet" read one rather ill-advised advertisement. "Here is the car that gives gasoline a new value, a new worth, new distances, new mileages." The car was the Woods Mobilette, and it was widely touted as America's first cyclecar. It was that, at least in prototype, Mobilette No. 1 having been built by Chicago inventor Francis A. Woods in 1910. He tinkered with it for eighteen months thereafter, before building No. 2, which like the first was powered by a four-cylinder 12 hp air-cooled engine. Mobilette No. 3, with a water-cooled 12 hp four, was the first Woods produced. It arrived in the fall of 1913, following financial help from Chicago investment banker W.M. Sheridan and incorporation of the Woods Mobilette Company on July 8th that year. The firm's offices were at 1509 Michigan Boulevard in Chicago; the factory was on 147th Street in nearby Harvey. Initially the Woods Mobilette was distributed by the International Cyclecar and Accessories Company in Chicago, though by October of 1915, Woods had bought out the International business and moved it to Harvey too. Mobilette No. 3 featured shaft drive and a selective sliding gear transmission. Its wheelbase was 102 inches, its tread 36, with two passengers sitting tandem. Mobilette No. 4 was much the same. In 1916 No. 5 arrived, with wheelbase lengthened to 104 inches, staggered seating, and electric lights and starting available as an option. The price tag throughout remained at $380, with Mobilette mph and mpg both in the 35-40 range. According to the Harvey *Tribune* of August 21st, 1914, production then stood at a thousand cars a month. It decreased steadily thereafter. Although 1917 models were announced, they were never produced. The Woods Mobilette Company had faded from the scene by the end of 1916. The Mobilette had survived far longer, however, than Francis A. Woods' first effort, a front-drive electric he had built in 1905 called the Interurban.

1913-1915 WOODS MOBILETTE
No. 3/4 — 4-cyl., 12 hp, 102" wb

	FP	5	4	3	2	1
Tandem Rdstr.	380	2400	3400	4800	8000	17,000

1916 Woods Mobilette, roadster, HAC

1916 WOODS MOBILETTE
No. 5 — 4-cyl., 12 hp, 104" wb

Staggered Rdstr.	380	2450	3500	4900	8300	17,500

WOODSMOBILE — Milwaukee, Wisconsin — (1908) — During the summer of 1908, from his temporary office in New York City, Walter A. Woods announced that he had resigned as general manager and treasurer of the Cleveland Motor Car Company in order to become the manufacturer of an automobile called the Woodsmobile. A factory in Milwaukee had already been secured. The Woodsmobile was to be powered by a Continental four and to feature a multiple disc clutch of Woods' own design. Two wheelbases were to be offered — 112 inches and 122 inches — with prices for all models to be a uniform $3500. Runabout, toy tonneau and town car were planned for the smaller wheelbase, touring, limousine and landaulet for the longer. Deliveries Walter Woods promised for October 1st, but he never delivered. The Woodsmobile venture did not proceed beyond the building of a few pilot cars.

WOODS & PHILBRICK STEAM — Beverly, Massachusetts — (1887) / **WOODS** — Worcester, Massachusetts — (1899) — Two bicycle makers, J. Elmer Woods from Beverly and Andrew J. Philbrick from Salem, built a three-wheeled steamer in 1887. With its big boiler up front and its two single-cylinder engines alongside, the vehicle resembled a steam fire-engine. Two wheels of forty inches in diameter were in the back, with the single twenty-two-inch steering wheel forward. The driver sat on a single seat to the rear of the boiler, with the throttle and steering lever close to his hand, and the exhaust pipe stuck up behind his back. Oil and water tanks were under his feet. The car was first publicly shown at the LaFavor Opera House. The Woods and Philbrick steamer did run, though not very well. "They had a hard job," an eyewitness reported in *The Horseless Age* shortly after the turn of the century, "but I guess no worse than does a beginner with an automobile...the steam dome was not big enough to hold the necessary steam to keep the carriage going for a long ride...The carriage incorporated a number of good ideas, but like many other good things, it was ahead of its day and it was discarded and went to pieces waiting for its day to come." Andrew Philbrick is not known to have built another car. In 1899 J. Elmer Woods, who had since moved his bicycle shop to Worcester, reportedly built three more cars.

1887 Woods & Philbrick Steamer, runabout, NAHC

WOODWARD — San Francisco, California — (1907-1908) — Just how far George H. Woodward of San Francisco proceeded with his plan is not known, but he was earnest about it. Following the city's disastrous earthquake, he decided to manufacture an automobile. In December 1906 the *Oakland Tribune* reported him about to leave for New York to make arrangements for the acquisition of necessary materials and parts to be shipped from East to West where Woodward would assemble them into automobiles in his own shops at 448 Fulton Street. A "high-class touring car type" and possibly a line of delivery trucks was on his agenda. For two years Woodward indicated himself as an automobile producer, but the extent of his activity cannot be determined.

WOOLSTON & BREW — New York, New York — (1904) — George F. Woolston, his brother Lee W., and William P. Brew had established engineering offices at 39 Cortlandt Street in New York City prior to the turn of the century. In December of 1903 they incorporated as Woolston & Brew with a capital stock of $25,000 for the manufacture of automobiles. Whether any Woolston & Brew cars followed is problematical; certainly formal manufacture did not. The company equipped a salesroom and garage at 152 West 56th Street and took on the agency for Thomas and Stevens-Duryea cars.

WOOLVERTON — G.C. Woolverton of Buffalo, New York was among the hopefuls who entered the Chicago Times-Herald Contest of 1895 with an automobile of his own design. He did not make it to the starting line, however, and whether he ever completed his vehicle has not been documented.

WOONSOCKET — Woonsocket, Rhode Island — (1907-1908) — Educated conjecture would be that the Woonsocket Napping Machinery Company played at being an automobile manufacturer. Certainly its efforts do not seem to have been concerted. The initial mention of the firm's activities, in January 1907, noted the completion of "the first of a number of autos which have been in process of construction at its factory, and the preliminary test have shown it up as being very satisfactory." The next word from Woonsocket did not arrive until June 1908 and advised that the company had "recently completed another model." In 1911 there was a formal incorporation, with a capital stock of $5000, of The Woonsocket Company for the manufacture of "automobile trucks and carriages." The people involved were L.V. Hubbard, N.J. Gordon, R.E. Ballou and Frederick S. Blackall. No cars at all arrived thereafter.

WOOSLEY — San Francisco, California — (1900-1903) — Although he apparently promoted a number of companies for automobile manufacture, William J. Woosley was never able to hit the big time. Indeed, even the small time seemed to have been something of a vexation. His first effort presumably was the Boston Automobile Company at 157 New Montgomery Street, which was grandiosely indicated to be "manufacturers of automobiles of every description." The Boston Automobile Company was gone by 1901, but Woosley continued to include himself among manufacturing ranks. His next venture was the Universal Automobile Company, located in 1902 at 129-135 First Street, which was even more adventurous: "manufacturers automobiles, machinery, engines, boilers, elevators and machinery repairing" read the city directory listing not very grammatically. Woosley was vice-president of Universal; William H. Hart was president. Conceivably, the Universal Automobile Company was an offshoot of the California Machine Works in which Woosley and Hart held the same positions and which was quartered at the same 137-51 First Street address. By 1904, of all this, only the California Machine Works remained, and its activity was modestly indicated to be confined to the machining field.

WORLD — An automobile called the World has appeared on various car rosters as being manufactured by Arnold, Schwinn & Company of Chicago, Illinois in 1902. Refer to Schwinn.

1928 Worldmobile, sedan, KM

WORLDMOBILE — Lima, Ohio — (1927-1928) — The initial announcement came from Cleveland in 1926, and indicated only that a new firm called the Worldmobile Company would soon be producing an eight-cylinder car (65 hp Lycoming engine) in a full line of sport and closed bodies on a single chassis (133 inches) with price tags in the $1700 range. Purportedly, seven prototypes were built, though that seems highly doubtful. A single car is known to have been put together, literally, its louverless hood appearing to have been formed with a sledgehammer. A six-passenger sedan, the body styling was unrelievedly ordinary and several years behind the times. The prettiest thing about the Worldmobile, which probably was built in 1927 or 1928, was its radiator badge. Aside from the unworthiness of the car itself, probably among the reasons it never came to be were the administrative changes being wrought during this period in the company that was backing the car. And that was Relay Motors Corporation, a conglomerate brought into being in early 1927 by Eastern banking money which brought out the truck-producing companies of Commerce (Ypsilanti, Michigan), Service (Wabash, Indiana) and Garford (Lima, Ohio). The Worldmobile probably just got lost in the shuffle. The six-passenger Worldmobile sedan remains extant.

1902 Worth, gasoline touring, OCW

WORTH — Chicago, Illinois — (1902) — The J.M. Worth Gas Engine Manufacturing Company was located at 2833 Cottage Grove Avenue in Chicago, and in 1902 produced a very interesting automobile alongside its usual product line. It was a touring-car/delivery-wagon combination, which was not unusual, though this one was considerably more refined than the norm. The vehicle's engine was a two-cylinder 12 hp that Worth mounted under the seat with final drive by chain to the rear axle. It was the coachwork which distinguished this car. Its sloping front hood was attractive — and, whether it was in four-seater touring trim or with canopy attached for delivery, it looked right. Most combination cars of the day looked wrong in one application, or both.

1910 Worth, model A, roadster, NAHC

WORTH — Evansville, Indiana — (1906-1907) / Kankakee, Illinois — (1908-1910) — In 1906 a New York consulting engineer named William O. Worth was brought to Evansville by Willis Copeland, the president of the Single Center Buggy Company. Copeland had agreed to manufacture an automobile designed by J.A. Windsor of Chicago, and he thought he could use some fresh production expertise to do it. Purportedly, Worth had that. Worth was also apparently a stubborn man. After the Windsor venture quickly failed, he designed a highwheeler which he talked Copeland into building. It had an air-cooled two-cylinder engine, double chain drive, tiller steering, and the friction transmission which he had previously run up for the Windsor, and which he had originally devised for the Chicago built in the late 1890's in Harvey, Illinois. And that was the car he insisted be built. When Copeland suggested changes to it, Worth abruptly departed and formed the Worth Motor Car Manufacturing Company. After only a few cars were produced in Evansville, Worth moved to Kankakee and after being evicted from the first factory he leased for failing to pay the rent, he found another — a former cattle pavilion — in the same city, and struggled on a while longer. In October of 1910 he finally declared bankruptcy. Reportedly, his vice-president disappeared with the last car in the factory and as many leftover parts as could be fit into the back seat.

1906-1910 WORTH
Model A — 2-cyl., 22.5 hp, 98" wb

	FP	5	4	3	2	1
Surrey-4P	600	—	—	—	—	—

WORTHINGTON — The Worthington Manufacturing Company was organized in Elyria, Ohio during the summer of 1902 to take over the businesses of the Fay Tricycle & Invalid Chair Company of Elyria and the leather bag and golf goods department of the Automobile & Cycle Parts Company of Westboro, Massachusetts. George C. Worthington was the man behind this venture, which now was to be centered in Elyria. Manufacture has not been documented.

"J.B. Worthington & Company has purchased machinery to be used in an automobile factory in Oklahoma City, Oklahoma," *The Automobile* reported in May 1909. "It has already been shipped to the Southwest and as soon as it can be installed it will turn out complete cars." Manufacture is doubted.

1904 Worthington-Bollee, gasoline touring, NAHC

WORTHINGTON-BOLLEE — New York, New York — (1904-1905) — C.C. Worthington, who described himself in his company's brochure as "so well known as the inventor of the Worthington Pump," bought out the Berg Automobile Company of Cleveland in 1904. He continued production of the Berg, introduced another car called the Meteor which was built for him by the Federal Manufacturing Company in Cleveland, and announced that he had also acquired the exclusive license to build in America the automobiles produced in Le Mans, France by Leon Bollee. His ambitions obviously were grand. Indeed, his brochure produced in January of 1904 indicated that he would be manufacturing steam, gasoline and electric vehicles, though the brochure following in October mentioned only steam and gasoline — and the steamer never did arrive. Possibly neither did the Worthington-Bollee, as a "made in America" car anyway. "Pending the completion of the works, arrangements have been made for importing these cars during 1904," C.C. Worthington said. His Meteor did go into production in Cleveland, but the Worthington-Bollee was not built there, and no mention in the automotive press was forthcoming regarding just where it might have been. Most likely, all Worthington-Bollees were imported. C.C. Worthington's tenure as an automobile producer ended in 1905, though possibly he had another business to fall back upon. His offices in New York City were initially at the corner of Broadway and 23rd Street, but he moved uptown later during 1904 to the corner of 45th Street and Fifth Avenue. He remarked at that time that he proposed "to erect and maintain in New York City, a large and ABSOLUTELY FIRE-PROOF GARAGE for the storage of automobiles." C.C. Worthington surfaced again in the trade press in 1909 when he reported his plans to build steam automobiles in Trenton, but nothing at all apparently came of that.

WORTHLEY STEAM — Boston, Massachusetts — (1897-1898) — In 1897 at his home at 111 Milk Street in Boston, C.A. Worthley began building a steam carriage for himself. Its tubular steel frame and wire wheels (34 inches in front, 36 inches in the rear) came from Weston-Mott, but the rest of the vehicle was of Worthley's own devising. The engine was placed under the seat, and the boiler was hidden from view. Chain drive was employed, and Worthley incorporated an air brake and air alarm (actuated, he said, by an automatic pump) in the car. There were two levers, one for steering and speedchanging, the other to operate the alarm and brake. Worthley completed the car in 1898. There is no evidence he ever built another.

1898 Worthley Steamer, HS

WOTTRING — The Wottrings were a carriage-building family from Prospect, Ohio. In 1902 and again in 1907-1908, they also built automobiles. Refer to Prospect.

W.R.C. — In 1907 in El Reno, Oklahoma a company called the W.R.C. Auto Works began in the automobile business with manufacture of a high-wheeler called the Pioneer. Refer to Pioneer.

1904 Wreisner, gasoline runabout, WLB

WREISNER — Dassel, Minnesota — (1901-1904) — This car was three years in the building by the Wreisner brothers — Peter and Nels — who were blacksmiths in Dassel. Every part of the vehicle was made in the Wreisners' shop, a six-inch pipe being used for the engine's single cylinder. Both chain and rope drive were fitted, the former from the engine to the jackshaft, the latter thence to the rear wheels. A tiller saw to the steering, and the vehicle could be operated from either of the front two seats. The Wreisners began their car in 1901 and completed it in 1904. Its engine, which was used to pump water after the vehicle was discarded, remains extant, and is on display at the American Swedish Institute in Minneapolis.

WRIGHT — "C.E. Wright & Company are preparing to build a plant in Norfolk, Virginia to manufacture automobiles," *The Automobile* reported in October 1912. Manufacture is doubted.

"C.F. Wright, Richmond, Indiana is seeking to establish an automobile factory at Muncie, Indiana," *The Horseless Age* reported in October 1902. It does not appear he managed to do it.

Frederick C. Wright & Company of Springfield, Massachusetts was indicated as an automobile manufacturer in the Hiscox book *Horseless Vehicle, Automobiles, Motor Cycles* published in 1900. Documentation is lacking.

The Wright-Lawes Motor Corporation was organized in Albany, New York during the spring of 1918 with a capital stock of $30,000 for the manufacture of automobiles and trucks. F.A. Wright and C.A.E. Lawes were the partners involved. Manufacture is doubted.

The Wright Manufacturing Company of Springfield, Massachusetts was

organized during the summer of 1915 with a capital stock of $100,000 for the manufacture of automobiles and airships. Incorporators were Charles H. Wright, Nelson E. Wright and W.S. Thompson. Manufacture is doubted.

The Wright Motor Car Company of Harrisburg, Pennsylvania was organized during the spring of 1910 with a capital stock of $5000 to manufacture and sell automobiles and motorcycles. Incorporators were George H. Reiff, George F. Bobb, Samuel Prowell, E.M. Brennan, Thomas F. Rogers and John J. Rogers. Manufacture is doubted.

The Wright-Rye Motor Company of Troy, New York was organized during the summer of 1909 with a capital stock of $40,000 for the manufacture of automobiles and other vehicles. William D.K. Wright and William H. Rye were joined in this venture by Elbert F. Grant, also of Troy, and George A. Hubbard of Loudonville. Manufacture is doubted.

1904 Wright, touring, WLB

WRIGHT — Dayton, Ohio — (1904) — The Wright was built in Dayton in 1904 by Fred and Ralph Wright. Its engine was a Herschell-Spillman, reportedly one of that company's first sixes; its round radiator was courtesy of Ferrette. The car, presumably the only example built by the Wrights, featured a sliding-gear transmission and right-hand drive.

1911 Wright, touring, NAHC

WRIGHT — New Cumberland, Pennsylvania — (1910-1911) — Upon hearing that New Cumberland was anxious to attract new industry to town, Thomas F. Rodgers and Ernest M. Brennan of Corning, New York left for Pennsylvania with a proposition and persuaded local businessmen to take them up on it. Of the New Cumberland automobile capitalists interested in the venture, probably the most significant was J.W. Wright, because the new Wright Motor Car Company would carry his surname. It has also been suggested that the celebrity of the name Wright — as in Orville and Wilbur — was another reason for the selection. Most likely, Rodgers and Brennan couldn't have cared less what their car was called, only that the money and a factory was provided for its building. The latter was the former Weatherby Electric Company at Second and Locust streets. Though Thomas Rodgers took the presidency of the new firm, and Ernest Brennan the vice-presidency, it seems Rodgers didn't tarry long in New Cumberland, returning to Corning soon after operations began. The man in charge of supervising the building of the Wright was Ansel Stryker, whom Rodgers and Brennan had known from his work with Pierce-Arrow in Buffalo, New York. He would have his hands full. Most of the parts of the new Wright — including its four-cylinder 20 hp Waukesha engine — were purchased outside. The problems arose when the parts arrived, literally, because they were late — and then they didn't fit. Assembly of the first Wright was a matter of cut-and-weld and, when finished, the car was discovered to be grossly underpowered, which shouldn't have been too much of a surprise since the wheelbase was a lengthy 130 inches. According to Paul E. Reiff who drove it at the time, the Wright cornered "like a four-masted sailing ship in a storm." Obviously the problems thus far had occasioned requests for further money from the New Cumberland backers, who were understandably loath to provide same. Ultimately, Ernest Brennan — and probably Stryker too — returned to Upstate New York, and a

1522

New Cumberland electrical contractor named J. Frank Bobb took over as factory manager. A grand total of six cars were built — and then the good people of New Cumberland decided that, though they might want new industry in town, they never again wanted it to be an automobile.

WRIGHT — Buffalo, New York — (1920) — Fred Wright of Buffalo had spent two decades in the marine and aviation engine field and was a foreman for the Curtiss Airplane and Motors Corporation in 1920 when he built an automobile for ten times less what a new Model T Ford would have cost him. Junkyards supplied his parts, with the chassis costing $22.50, the largest single expense a set of discarded tires and inner tubes for five bucks, and the total car coming in at less than $50.

1931 Wright Electric, NAHC

WRIGHT ELECTRIC — Hysham, Montana — (1931) — This miniature car was built by C.L. Wright at his Hysham Garage and Machine Shop in 1931. It was battery powered, weighed 300 pounds and featured ball and roller bearings throughout.

W.S. — The W.S. Motor Company of Newark, New Jersey was organized during the summer of 1912 with a capital stock of $300,000 for the manufacture of automobiles. Incorporators were J.M. Woods, C.H. Tebbets and L.F. Fester. Manufacture of a car is doubted. C.S. Tebbets is known to have been associated with the Standard Auto Coach Burial Company during this period.

WYATT & LISTMAN — The firm of Wyatt & Listman of New York City was organized early in 1908 with a capital stock of $4000 for the manufacture of automobiles. The partners involved were J.M. Wyatt and H.E. Listman. Manufacture is doubted.

1904 Wyckoff Steamer, NAHC

WYCKOFF STEAM — Newark, New Jersey — (1904) — The Wyckoff was a light steam runabout built by a teenager who worked in an automobile repair shop in Newark. L.J. Wyckoff introduced his car at the Eagle Rock hill climb on Thanksgiving Day in 1904 where, according to *The Automobile*, "his production attracted considerable attention."

WYETH — Waltham, Massachusetts — (1912-1913) — The Wyeth was the idea of C.E. Clemence and, like the Only of this period, featured a single-cylinder long-stroke engine which Clemence liked to call the "French type." Its bore/stroke dimensions were 4-1/2 by 6, and it developed 13 hp at 1200 rpm on brake test. Although the Wyeth Motor Car Company was incorporated during the summer of 1911, its first car was not on the road until August of 1912. There were no universal joints in the Wyeth. The engine, transmission (a two-speed planetary) and rear axle a single unit. The wheelbase was 90 inches, and the body hung between side members and was hinged at the front end and independently supported on full elliptic springs in the rear. "This construction makes possible the Wyeth original straight line drive," a company brochure said, "and produces an easy riding effect entirely new to motor vehicles." Both runabout and delivery models were available, with prices in the $500 range. Company headquarters were in Boston, with the factory in Waltham. The Wyeth did not survive 1913.

1912-1913 WYETH
Model B — 1-cyl., 13 hp, 90" wb

	FP	5	4	3	2	1
Runabout	450	2300	3300	4600	7500	16,000
Model C — 1-cyl., 13 hp, 90" wb						
Open Delivery	500	2200	3200	4400	7000	15,000
Model C — 1-cyl., 13 hp, 90" wb						
Closed Delivery	550	2400	3400	4800	8000	17,000

WYKOFF, CHURCH & PARTRIDGE — This was the New York City firm which imported the Decauville, was an agency for the Stearns, and was involved in the production of the Commer truck and the Vaughan car. No automobile was ever built under the company name, however. Refer to Vaughan.

WYLIE ELECTRIC — Ottawa, Illinois — (1894) — W.W. Wylie built the first car in Ottawa in 1894. It had an electric motor underneath the single seat, which perched high over four heavy solid wheels. The car's first outing occasioned "much interest and amusement," it was later reported; "pedestrians...watched the rather uncertain movements with some misgiving." This is the only passenger car believed to have been built by W.W. Wylie. Thereafter he worked as manager of the Ottawa Car Company for twenty years, but that firm manufactured streetcars and snow plows. W.W. Wylie died in 1921.

1901 Wyman, touring, OCW

WYMAN — Scottsburg, Indiana — (1901) — In 1901 W.A. Wyman was in partnership with his father, D.W. Wyman, in a small brick and tile factory in Scottsburg. Earlier that year the father bought an Oldsmobile, which was the first automobile in Scott County. Later that year the son, perhaps deciding he could do better, built his own car. Family members believe he may have used an Oldsmobile engine. W.A. Wyman had no intention of manufacture, however, and never built another car — though he drove his 1901 machine for years. Thereafter it was stored. Following the Second World War, the Wyman was sold to a collector in Louisville, Kentucky. It remains extant.

XANDER — Reading, Pennsylvania — (1901-1902) — Disappointed that the Keystone Match and Machine Company for which he worked in Lebanon had decided to give up the automobile business at the turn of the century, John G. Xander left for Reading where late in 1900 he opened an automobile repair and supply store, made himself available to give driving instructions to new automobilists, and assisted William Grubb in the building of the Light Steamer. By 1901 he had branched into the manufacture of steam engines, and gasoline units quickly followed. From there it was but a single step to producing a complete car, though Xander proceeded cautiously in that regard and built vehicles only to custom order and, apparently, only through 1902. His Xander Machine & Supply Company, however, remained in business for some time thereafter.

1914 Xenia, cyclecar, (Hawkins), WLB

XENIA — Xenia, Ohio — (1914) — The Xenia was a sporty little cyclecar designed by Paul Hawkins of Cleveland and built in Fred Baldner's machine shop in Xenia where the Baldner had been produced from 1900 to 1903. Its specifications were typically cyclecar: two-cylinder air-cooled 9/13 hp DeLuxe engine, planetary transmission, belt drive, 102-inch wheelbase, 36-inch tread, tandem two-seater, $385. But the Xenia was a heartier and sturdier version than most on the market. One of the cars was driven from Ohio all the way to San Francisco without mishap, and another triumphed over an O-We-Go and a Scripps-Booth in the championship cyclecar races held at Driving Park in Columbus in August of 1914. That month the *Xenia Daily Gazette* reported that twenty-five units were in the course of construction. Although the car was marketed as the Xenia, the firm producing it was named for its designer: the Hawkins Cyclecar Company. It appeared to be a solidly based operation, with George Little, a local paper manufacturer and banker, as its president, and a board of directors composed of prominent members of the business and banking community. The Xenia's problem was that it was a cyclecar, and even a well-built version couldn't long endure the pounding of American roads. Too, the outbreak of the war in Europe put an effective end to any hopes of export. Probably few more than the twenty-five cars under construction in August were built by October. That month the Hawkins Cyclecar Company announced its dissolution.

1914 Xenia, model 14A, 2-pass. tandem cyclecar, WLB

1914 XENIA
Cyclecar — 2-cyl., 9/13 hp, 102" wb

	FP	5	4	3	2	1
Tandem Rdstr.	385	2400	3400	4800	8000	17,000

YACHT • YORKVILLE

YACHT — The Yacht Gas Engine and Launch Company was organized in Camden, New Jersey in early 1906 with a capital stock of $100,000. F.A. Van Bayneburgh, H.H. Dantzebecker and G.H.B. Martin, all of Camden, were the principals involved — and the plan was the manufacture of automobiles and launches. No automobiles are believed to have followed.

YALE — Yale was the name used beginning in 1900 for the vehicles which J.F. Denison of New Haven, Connecticut had previously built under his own. Refer to Denison.

Yale Flyer or Featherweight Flyer was a model designation initiated about 1909 for a racy roadster produced by the Cameron Company. The Cameron was built in divers locations from 1903 to 1920. Refer to Cameron.

Yale Cycle and Supply Company was organized in Cleveland in 1911 "to manufacture, sell and repair motor vehicles of all kinds and to handle parts and accessories." Among the incorporators were C.H. Ferguson, Edward E. Thompkins, H.S. Jackson and H.E. Tiggle. Capital stock was $10,000. There is no indication an automobile was ever built.

1904 Yale, model C, touring, HAC

YALE — Toledo, Ohio — (1902-1905) — The Kirk Manufacturing Company was a bicycle builder in Toledo which announced its forthcoming production of automobiles to the trade press in the fall of 1899. Either the announcement was premature or initial plans went awry, however, because the car from Kirk did not arrive until the summer of 1902. It was a two-cylinder water-cooled 10 hp runabout with detachable tonneau that was priced at $1500 and featured planetary transmission and chain drive. And it was called the Yale. "The car with the doubt and the jar left out" was a slogan, and the company boasted that it made all mechanical parts of the Yale save for the oiling device and the differential. An order for fifty cars was shipped to a distributor in Chicago in December of 1902. Matters seemed well in hand, and in October of 1903 grand plans were laid for a bright new future as three Toledo firms (Kirk, the Snell Cycle Fittings Company and the Toledo Manufacturing Company, another bicycle producer) merged into the Consolidated Manufacturing Company. Consolidated was capitalized at $600,000 and soon executed a $200,000 mortgage in order to expand. The Yale was extended into three two-cylinder models for 1904, and a larger $2500 four-cylinder car was added in 1905. The Consolidated officers were E.T. Breckenridge as president, Ezra E. Kirk as vice-

1905 Yale, model G, side entrance tonneau, WLB

president, A.W. Coulter as secretary, J.B.R. Ransom as treasurer. In September 1905 the company announced that a single 35 hp four listing at $2000 would be the Yale offering for 1906, but three months later came the announcement there would be no Yale at all. "Too Busy to Make Cars" was the headline which provided the news that Consolidated would henceforth manufacture only Yale and Snell bicycles, Yale-California motorcycles, drop forgings, brazed tubing, sheet metal, stove trimmings and various fittings. Consolidated had hoped to sell its automobile department, but when there were no buyers, it was simply closed down instead. According to press reports, the Yale had become a popular car in Toledo and northwestern Ohio, and the reason for its discontinuation is curious. Possibly Consolidated had expanded too far and too fast. Less than a year later — in May of 1906 — the company proceeded into bankruptcy.

1902 YALE
Model A — 2-cyl., 10 hp

	FP	5	4	3	2	1
Detachable Tonneau-4P	1500	2400	3400	4800	8000	17,000

1903 YALE
Model A — 2-cyl., 12 hp

Detachable Tonneau-4P	1750	2500	3500	5000	8500	18,000

1904 YALE
Model B — 2-cyl., 16 hp, 84" wb

Touring-4P	1500	2700	3600	5300	8800	19,000

Model C — 2-cyl., 16 hp, 84" wb

Touring-5P	1600	2700	3600	5300	8800	19,000

Model D — 2-cyl., 16 hp, 84" wb

Canopy Top Tonneau	1800	2900	3700	5600	9100	20,000

1905 YALE
Model E — 2-cyl., 14/16 hp, 83" wb

Rear Entrance Tonneau-5P	1000	2500	3500	5000	8500	18,000

Model G — 2-cyl., 14/16 hp, 85" wb

Side Entrance Tonneau-5P	1100	2700	3600	5300	8800	19,000

Model F — 4-cyl., 24/28 hp, 104" wb

Touring-5P	2500	2900	3700	5600	9100	20,000

1916 Yale, touring, WLB

YALE — Saginaw, Michigan — (1916-1918) — Louis J. Lampke was an engineer from New Jersey who had plied his trade at Palmer-Singer in New York and Lion in Michigan before finally, he thought, finding the backing to manufacture a car of his own design. This was the M.P.M. whose woefully short life began and ended in Mount Pleasant, Michigan in 1915. Earlier that year Lampke had journeyed to Saginaw with hopes of moving his company there. Saginaw was disinterested in the M.P.M. but rather interested in Lampke, so he remained in town and kept talking. The result was the organization of the Saginaw Motor Company in June of 1916, with J.A. Cimmerer, J.W. Grant, W.C. Wiechmann and H.E. Oppenheimer — all Saginaw businessmen — dividing the executive responsibilities, and Lampke taking charge of the product and its production. Originally, Saginaw was to be the car's name, but the Lehr Motor Company across town was calling its new automobile that and objected. Consequently, the Saginaw people got together and decided on Yale. Unlike Lampke's M.P.M. which was offered as both a four and an eight, the new Yale would be a V-8 only, and both bigger and more expensive. The factory at Jefferson and Atwater which had formerly been used for manufacture of the Argo electric was purchased, and production began there in July of 1916. A $1350 seven-passenger touring car was the only model built that year, the line being expanded in 1917 to include a roadster and a sporty rumbleseat speedster. All cars were on the same 126-inch wheelbase chassis, with the price tag now raised to $1550. Though closed cars were announced, it is doubtful whether any were produced. The price of the Yale 8 was further increased to $1885 in January of 1918, and it was obvious by then that the company was not going to make it. In March the car was discontinued, with its parts and service taken over by Puritan of Detroit. The month following the Yale factory was acquired by Nelson Brothers for the manufacture of Jumbo trucks.

1916 YALE
Eight — 31 hp, 126" wb

	FP	5	4	3	2	1
Touring-7P	1350	3000	4000	6000	9500	21,000

1917 Yale, speedster

1917-1918 YALE
Eight — 31 hp, 126" wb

Touring-7P	1550	3100	4200	6300	10,500	22,000
Roadster-2P	1550	3000	4000	6000	9500	21,000
Speedster-3P	1550	4300	5400	8700	16,500	30,000

Note: prices raised to $1885 in January 1918

YANKEE — The 1914 Yankee was a $275 four-cylinder 18 hp cyclecar kit on a 102-inch wheelbase. It was one of a number of cars marketed by the Automobile Parts & Equipment Company of Chicago. Refer to Auto Parts.

1910 Yankee, roadster, NAHC

YANKEE — Chicago, Illinois — (1910) — The Yankee Motor Car Company of Chicago built an air-cooled two-cylinder $500 highwheeler with a two-speed planetary transmission and a long 100-inch wheelbase. Solid rubber tires were standard, though pneumatics were provided on a model that the company called its Racy Roadster. That designation was a contradiction in terms for any highwheeler. According to a city of Chicago directory for 1910, Vincent Bendix was manager of this operation. Undoubtedly the Yankee was discontinued because he had so many other irons in the fire during this period. Already he had decided against further production of his Duplex and Bendix highwheelers — and was launching himself into the automobile components field.

1910 YANKEE
Model MB — 2-cyl., 16 hp, 100" wb

High Wheel Buggy	500	2200	3200	4400	7000	15,000

Model RR — 2-cyl., 16 hp, 100" wb

Racy Roadster	500	2300	3300	4600	7500	16,000

YAPLE — Luther P. Yaple of Chillicothe, Ohio announced in the late summer of 1906 the impending organization of a company, capitalized at $250,000, for the manufacture of a four-cylinder car. Manufacture is doubted.

1925 Yarian, 4-dr. sedan, WLB

1526

YARIAN — Syracuse, New York — (1925) — In essence, the Yarian was a Franklin that had been rejected. Developed during the early Twenties as the Model Z, a four-cylinder air-cooled sedan to sell in the $1000 price range, the project had been ill-starred from the beginning. "Cooling troubles, cracked cylinders, valve and valve seat troubles, camshaft troubles, valve spring surge, timing chain stretch and wear, and, yes, bearing troubles" were among the ailments during early experimentation, as remembered later by Carl Doman, who had recently joined H.H. Franklin at the time and was a member of the design group headed by James L. Yarian that was working up the new Model Z. Once the engine problems were solved, arriving at a chassis that could be profitably built for the price tag became the bugaboo. The wood frames, full elliptic springs, tubular axles, aluminum shell and hood on a wooden body which were used in the first Model Z prototypes proved too costly; a steel frame, forged front axle, stamped rear axle housing, semi-elliptic springs and steel bodies were tried next. Then H.H. Franklin decided to scrap the entire project — and to fire James Yarian. Yarian immediately took the car as finally developed and organized Yarian Motors Corporation (capitalized at a grand $33 million) elsewhere in Syracuse. A handsome Yarian brochure was printed indicating specs (four-cylinder ohv 37-1/2 hp engine, 113-inch wheelbase and chassis details) that were a carbon copy of the Franklin Model Z. But Yarian couldn't bring the car in at the $1000 price tag either; $1350 was indicated for the standard five-passenger sedan, with only a touring car at $975. Yarian also planned a 52 hp six on a 118-inch wheelbase with $1250-$1650 price tags, which would have nicely undercut the Franklin Series 10 six then in production. Testimonial comments published in his brochure reveal that those people who took a test ride in a Yarian were most favorably impressed. But that didn't make up for the necessary capital to get the car into production. And Yarian never could come up with that.

YARLOTT — Ft. Wayne, Indiana — (1919-1920) — A patented rotary valve claimed to "eliminate valve disturbances" was the *raison d'etre* behind the organization of the Yarlott Brothers Motor & Car Company of Fort Wayne. The Yarlott was planned to be offered as both a six- and eight-cylinder car, to sell for $1000 and $1400 respectively. Economy of operation was a touted feature, the six having been tested to provide over 24 mpg. "The company has been waiting four years to bring this car out," *The Automobile* announced in December 1919. The company never stopped waiting. The Yarlott did not pass the prototype stage.

1915 Yellow, model H, taxicab, MVMA

YELLOW — Chicago, Illinois — (1915-1928)/Pontiac, Michigan — (1928-1930) — The idea of a yellow taxicab belonged to John Hertz, who had joined the Walden W. Shaw Livery Company of Chicago in 1905 as a salesman and who had become a partner by the close of 1908. Initially buying second-hand cars to be turned into taxis, Hertz brought the Shaw bank balance up sufficiently enough by 1910 to allow him the purchase of nine Thomas cars from Buffalo, which he painted yellow to attract attention. Several years later the Shaw Company began making its own chassis, and in 1915 the Yellow Taxicab Manufacturing Company was born. The

1925 Yellow, model O-4, brougham taxicab, HAC

first Yellow cabs were fitted with four-cylinder 24 hp Continental engines, Brown-Lipe transmissions, Timken axles and Hotchkiss drive. The cars were assembled completely in the Walden Shaw shops. In addition to the Yellow taxis, a fleet operator also received a manual of instructions on how to most effectively conduct his business (i.e., by using bonded and married men only). Yellow taxis were often sold on credit or a share of the profits from operating companies, and Yellow taxis were not always that color, the choice being up to the operator. A total of 150 Yellow taxis were built in 1915; they were widely successful, and thousands flowed out of the Walden Shaw factory annually thereafter. In 1923 Yellow purchased the rights to the R & V four-cylinder Knight engine built by Root & Vandervoort in Moline, Illinois — and some Yellow-Knights followed. During the early Twenties, too, Shaw marketed production cars under the tradenames of Shaw (Colonial) and Ambassador. By now John Hertz was in complete control of the Walden W. Shaw Livery Company, and in 1923 had launched into the bus business as well. In 1925 Yellow merged with the truck division of General Motors Corporation, John Hertz remaining on awhile as president, though by now he was already hatching his next idea in motoring for hire: a car for those people who might prefer to rent one than hail one. In 1928 Yellow operations were moved to a new GM plant in Pontiac, and in 1930 the Yellow name was discontinued, replaced by General Motors Cab.

1915 YELLOW CAB
Model H, 4-cyl.

	FP	5	4	3	2	1
Limo. Taxi-4P	—	3150	6300	10,500	14,700	21,000

Note: Continental engine; Racine body.

1916 YELLOW CAB
Model J, 4-cyl.

		5	4	3	2	1
Limo. Taxi-4P	—	3100	6150	10,250	14,350	20,500

1917 YELLOW CAB
Model K, 4-cyl.

		5	4	3	2	1
Limo. Taxi-4P	—	3100	6150	10,250	14,350	20,500

1918 YELLOW CAB
Model K, 4-cyl.

		5	4	3	2	1
Limo. Taxi-4P	—	3100	6150	10,250	14,350	20,500

1919 YELLOW CAB
Model L, 4-cyl.

		5	4	3	2	1
Limo. Taxi-4P	—	3100	6150	10,250	14,350	20,500

1920 YELLOW CAB
Model M, 4-cyl.

		5	4	3	2	1
Limo. Taxi-4P	—	3100	6150	10,250	14,350	20,500

1921 YELLOW CAB
Model O, 4-cyl., 19.6-22.5 hp (NACC), 109" wb

		5	4	3	2	1
Taxi Chassis-6P	1800	2500	3500	6500	9000	12,000
Brgm. Taxi-4P	2340	3100	6150	10,250	14,350	20,500

Note: Quantity discounts were available, as follows: (1-10) $2340; (11-25) $2290; (26-50) $2240; (51 or more) $2200. Serial nos. 8001 to 9470.

1922 YELLOW CAB
Model 02, 4-cyl. 22.5 hp (NACC), 109" wb

		5	4	3	2	1
Taxi Chassis-6P	1440	2500	3500	6500	9000	12,000

Model 03, 4-cyl., 19.6-22.5 hp (NACC), 109" wb

		5	4	3	2	1
Limo. Brgm. Taxi-4P	2340	2700	4500	7500	10,000	13,500

YELLOW-KNIGHT PASSENGER CARS
Ambassador Sport, 6-cyl., 31.5 hp (NACC), 136" wb

		5	4	3	2	1
Spt.-4P	4500	5000	8000	11,000	18,000	30,000
Tr.-7P	4500	7000	10,000	15,000	22,000	32,000
Berl. Limo.	6500	4000	7500	10,000	16,000	28,000
Berl. Sed.	6500	4000	6500	9500	15,000	25,000

Note: Quantity discounts available on taxicabs, as follows: (1-10) $2340; (11-25) $2290; (26-50) $2240; (51 or more) $2200. Quantity discounts available on taxicab chassis, as follows: (1-10) $1440; (11-25) $1390; (26-50) $1340; (51 or more) $1300. Serial nos. for Model 02 taxis 9471 & up. Serial nos. for Model 03 taxis 12001 & up. The Yellow-Knight was a large, powerful car built as part of a new passenger car line and used a Knight sleeve-valve engine built under license.

1923 YELLOW CAB
Model A2, 4-cyl., 18.23 hp (NACC), 109" wb

		5	4	3	2	1
Brgm. Taxi-4P	1975	3100	6150	10,250	14,350	20,500

Model 03, 4-cyl., 19.6-22.5 hp (NACC), 109" wb

		5	4	3	2	1
Brgm. Taxi-4P	2340	3100	6150	10,250	14,350	20,500

Note: Quantity discounts upon application. Serial nos. for Model A2 20001 & up. Serial nos. for Model 03 15620 & up.

1924 YELLOW CAB
Model A2, 4-cyl., 19.6 hp (NACC), 109" wb

		5	4	3	2	1
Brgm. Taxi-4P	1975	2500	3500	6500	9000	12,000

Model 04, 4-cyl., 22.5 hp (NACC), 109" wb

		5	4	3	2	1
Brgm. Taxi-5P	2340	2700	4500	7500	10,000	13,500

Note: Quantity discounts upon application. Serial nos. for Model A2 continued from 1923. Serial nos. for Model 04 18000 & up Company changed from Yellow Cab Manufacturing Co. of Chicago to Yellow Truck & Coach Co. of Chicago.

1925 YELLOW CAB
Model D, 6-cyl., 25.3 hp (NACC), 114" wb

		5	4	3	2	1
Limo. Taxi-5P	1795	3000	5000	8000	11,000	15,000

Model O-4, 4-cyl., 22.5 hp (NACC), 109" wb

		5	4	3	2	1
Brgm. Taxi-4P	2340	2700	4500	7500	10,000	13,500

Model O-5, 4-cyl., 18.99 hp (NACC), 114" wb

		5	4	3	2	1
Limo. Taxi-5P	2340	2800	4600	7600	10,300	14,000

Note: Quantity discounts upon application. Model D serial nos. unknown. Model O-4 serial nos. continued from 1924. Model O-5 serial nos. 4000 & up. Firm became part of GM with John Hertz remaining as president and headquarters remaining in Chicago.

1926 Yellow, model O-5, taxicab, MVMA

1926 YELLOW CAB
Model D, 6-cyl., 25.3 hp (NACC), 114" wb

	FP	5	4	3	2	1
Limo. Taxi-5P	1795	3000	5000	8000	11,000	15,000

Model O-5, 4-cyl., 18.99 hp (NACC), 114" wb

		5	4	3	2	1
Taxi-5P	2600	2800	4600	7600	10,300	14,000

Note: Quantity discounts available upon application. Serial nos. continued from 1925.

1927 YELLOW CAB
HERTZ (Yellow Truck & Coach Mfg. Co.)
Series Drive-It-Yourself, 6-cyl., 23.40 hp (NACC), 122" wb

		5	4	3	2	1
Tr.-5P	1495	5000	8000	12,000	15,000	18,000
Sed.-5P	1795	3000	5000	8000	11,000	15,000

Model O-5, 4-cyl., 18.9 hp (NACC), 114" wb

		5	4	3	2	1
Limo. Taxi-5P	2600	2800	4600	7600	10,300	14,000

Model D-10, 6-cyl., 25.3 hp (NACC), 114" wb

		5	4	3	2	1
Limo. Taxi-5P	1795	2900	4700	7700	10,500	14,400

Model O-6, 6-cyl., 23.4 hp (NACC), 122" wb

		5	4	3	2	1
Limo. Taxi-5P	2150	3000	5000	8000	11,000	15,000

Note: Quantity discounts available upon application. The passenger cars and the D-10 taxi were marketed under the Hertz trade name. The Models O-5 and O-6 were marketed under the Yellow Coach trade name. All of the cars were manufactured by Yellow Truck & Coach Manufacturing Co., of Chicago, Ill. Serial nos. for the Model O-6 were 4000 & up. Other serial nos. are not available.

1928 Yellow, model O-6, taxicab, HAC

1928 YELLOW CAB
HERTZ (Yellow Truck & Coach Mfg. Co.)
Series D-1, 6-cyl., 23.40 hp (NACC), 122" wb

		5	4	3	2	1
Sed.-5P	1745	3000	5000	8000	11,000	15,000
Taxi-5P	1795	3500	5500	9000	12,000	17,000

Model O-6, 6-cyl., 23.4 hp (NACC), 122" wb

		5	4	3	2	1
Limo. Taxi-5P	2200	3000	5000	8000	11,000	15,000

Note: Quantity discounts available upon application. First year for conventional headlights on taxicabs. Overhead valve Buick engine.

1929 Yellow, model O-10D (last model named Yellow)

1929 YELLOW CAB
Model O-6, 6-cyl., 26.3 hp (NACC), 122" wb

Limo. Taxi-5P		1995	3000	5000	8000	11,000	15,000

Note: Company name was changed to General Motors Truck Co. and production moved to Pontiac, Mich. Buick ohv engine used again. Serial nos. 92251 & up. The Yellow cab became known as the General Motors taxicab after 1929.

1930 General Motors Cab, model O-10

1930 GENERAL MOTORS CAB
Type O-10, 6-cyl., 28.33 hp (NACC), 122" wb

	FP	5	4	3	2	1
(A) Taxi Sed.-6P	1800	3600	7200	12,000	16,800	24,000
(D) Taxi Sed.-6P	1800	3600	7200	12,000	16,800	24,000
(E) Taxi Twn. Car-6P	2295	3600	7200	12,000	16,800	24,000
(F) Taxi Twn. Car.-6P	2295	3600	7200	12,000	16,800	24,000

Note: Model nos. were (A) 385, (D) 386, (E) 388 and (F) 384. Serial nos. were 385-101 & up; 386-101 & up; etc.

1931 General Motors Cab, model O-12

1931 GENERAL MOTORS CAB
Type O-10, 6-cyl., 28.33 hp (NACC), 122" wb

(I) Taxi Sed.-6P	1800	3600	7200	12,000	16,800	24,000
(J) Taxi Sed.-6P	1800	3600	7200	12,000	16,800	24,000
(L) Taxi Twn. Car-6P	2295	3600	7200	12,000	16,800	24,000
(M) Taxi Twn. Car-6P	2295	3600	7200	12,000	16,800	24,000

Note: Serial nos. 385001 & up; 388001 & up; etc.

1932 GENERAL MOTORS CAB
Model O-12, 6-cyl.

Taxi-6P	—	3600	7200	12,000	16,800	24,000

1933 General Motors Cab, model O-14

1933 GENERAL MOTORS CAB
Model O-13, 6-cyl.

	FP	5	4	3	2	1
Taxi-6P	—	3350	6750	11,250	15,750	22,500

Note: Pontiac-like appearance, during 1933 and 1934.

1934 GENERAL MOTORS CAB
Model O-14, 6-cyl.

Taxi-6P	—	3350	6750	11,250	15,750	22,500

Model O-15, 6-cyl.

Taxi-6P	—	3350	6750	11,250	15,750	22,500

1935 GENERAL MOTORS CAB

Note: According to Krause Publication's *Encyclopedia of Commercial Vehicles* there was no production during 1935.

1936 General Motors Cab, model O-16

1936 GENERAL MOTORS CAB
Model O-16, 6-cyl., 26.33 hp (NACC), 124.5" wb

Taxi-6P	—	2500	4300	7200	9500	12,000

Note: 1936-1938 General taxicabs used modified Chevy bodies on an extended chassis with Chevrolet truck rear axles. The engine was the overhead valve Chevrolet 6-cylinder.

1938 General Motors Cab, model O-18

1937 GENERAL MOTORS CAB
Model O-17, 6-cyl., 29.4 hp (NACC), 127" wb

Taxi-6P	—	3350	6750	11,250	15,750	22,500

1938 GENERAL MOTORS CAB
Model O-18, 6-cyl., 29.4 hp (NACC), 127" wb

Taxi-6P	—	3350	6750	11,250	15,750	22,500

YOCUM — The A.H. Yokum Company, Inc. was organized late in 1907 with a capital stock of $50,000 for the manufacture of motors, cars and parts. This was merely a formal incorporation of the small business in Reading, Pennsylvania which produced the Speed-Well car from 1904-1909. Refer to Speed-Well.

YONKERS — The Yonkers Auto Service Company, Inc. was organized early in 1912 with a capital stock of $2000 for the manufacture of automobiles in Yonkers, New York. Incorporators were George G. Frey of Mamaroneck, Frank P. Hoffman of Manhattan and Edward Keale of Brooklyn. Manufacture is doubted.

YORK — York, Pennsylvania — (1905) — The York was a trial balloon. In 1903 Albert P. Broomell — a partner in the steam apparatus manufacturing company of Broomell, Schmidt and Steacy — had built a two-cylinder six-wheeled automobile called the Pullman which was a failure. He concluded that with two more cylinders and two less wheels, it might be a success, and redesigned the car accordingly. Samuel E. Baily, president of the York Carriage Company, was impressed, but cautious. The two men formed the York Automobile Company, but on paper only. It existed solely for the purpose of printing up a brochure to test the marketing possibilities

1905 York, surrey, HAC

of the new car. Doubtless the name York was selected to eliminate any possible guilt by association with the six-wheeled fiasco. An advertisement for the 1905 York invited prospects to come to Pennsylvania to try out the car and "if you buy we will pay your expenses." Sufficient inquiries were received to convince the men to proceed into manufacture. Master mechanic James A. Kline was brought in from Harrisburg to assist in refinements to the car; official incorporation of the York Motor Car Company followed. By now Baily and Broomell had decided, the six-wheeler notwithstanding, that they preferred the sound and sales appeal of the Pullman name. Broomell had originally liked it because it connoted the luxurious ride of the railway car. Only the pilot models were called York. The car was put on the market as the Pullman.

YORKVILLE — The Yorkville Automobile & Garage Company of New York City was organized early in 1910 with a capital stock of $3000 for the manufacture and sale of automobiles and engines. Incorporators were Adolph Miller, Philips Freed and Armin H. Mittlemann. Manufacture is doubted.

YOUNG — Young & Company of Newburgh, New York was organized early in 1905 with a capital stock of $5000 for the manufacture of automobiles. Incorporators were Arthur Young, Walter H. Whitehall and Ralph W. Whitehall. Manufacture is doubted.

YUKON — The Yukon Automobile Company of Seattle, Washington has been indicated on various rosters as producing a cyclecar in 1914. Documentation is lacking.

ZACHARIAS — The Zacharias Garage Company of Asbury Park, New Jersey was organized during the spring of 1908 with a capital stock of $100,000 for the manufacture of "automobile vehicles and electric and other motors." C.R. Zacharias of Asbury Park and F.L.C. Martin of Plainfield were among the incorporators. Manufacture of an automobile is doubted.

ZACHOW & BESSERDICH — Otto Zachow and his brother-in-law William Besserdich were the partners behind the four-wheel-drive vehicle built in Clintonville, Wisconsin which became known as the F.W.D. Refer to F.W.D.

ZEDER — A car called the Zeder was the initial plan, but when that project fell through in 1922, the venture was carried on and ultimately resulted in the Rollin automobile of 1923-1925. Refer to Rollin.

1905 Zent, touring, WLB

ZENT — Marion, Ohio — (1900-1902)/Bellefontaine, Ohio — (1904-1906) — In 1900 at his machine shop at 213 South State Street in Marion, Schuyler W. Zent built his first automobile. It was a simple little gasoline runabout with single-cylinder engine and single chain drive — and in the two years following, he built and sold four more. He also came up with a model a little more sophisticated. In July of 1902 he announced his plans to manufacture commercially, and because he couldn't find the financing necessary to do that in Marion, he journeyed to Evansville, Indiana where his car was put into production as the Zentmobile in 1903. Nineteen four found him back in Ohio, where he secured sufficient capital to organize the Zent Automobile Manufacturing Company in Bellefontaine. This new venture, a $25,000 incorporation, was announced in late October, and the new Zent was in production early the following year. By now Schuyler Zent had progressed beyond the motorized buggy concept. His new Zent was powered by a three-cylinder 18 hp engine mounted under the hood, and featured shaft drive. A twin and a four joined the line in 1906. Early in 1907 the Zent company was superseded by the Bellefontaine Automobile Company, and the car's name was changed to Traveler.

	FP	5	4	3	2	1
1905 ZENT						
Three Cylinder — 18 hp, 90" wb						
Tour.-5P	1350	2300	3300	4600	7500	16,000
1906 ZENT						
Two Cylinder — 14 hp, 80" wb						
Rbt.-2P	1000	2000	3000	4200	6500	14,000
Three Cylinder — 18 hp, 90" wb						
Tour.-5P	1350	2400	3400	4800	8000	17,000
Four Cylinder — 35 hp, 100" wb						
Tour.-5P	2000	2500	3500	5000	8500	18,000

ZENTMOBILE — Evansville, Indiana — (1903) — In 1902 Schuyler W. Zent of Marion, Ohio built a single-cylinder 8 hp water-cooled two-seater buggy with planetary transmission, wire wheels and right-hand wheel steering which he thought would be a smash best-seller. Since he didn't have the facilities to produce it himself, he traveled to Evansville, Indiana where he approached Willis M. Copeland, president of the Single Center Buggy Company. Together they worked out an agreement whereby Copeland would manufacture the car, and all Zent had to worry about was selling it. This proved more difficult than Zent had envisioned, and within the year the partnership had broken up. Though not many cars had been produced, the Zentmobile does have the distinction of being the first automobile in Evansville to carry a tradename. Subsequently, Willis Copeland, whose Single Center Buggy Company had already built a few horseless carriages for anyone in town who wanted them, went into more serious automobile manufacture with the Simplicity. And Schuyler Zent returned to Ohio to build a new Zent in Bellefontaine.

1903 Zentmobile, touring, NAHC

1915 Ziebell, cyclecar, LC

ZIEBELL — Oshkosh, Wisconsin — (1914) — Arthur C. Ziebell was a draftsman at the Termaat & Monahan Company, makers of marine and stationary gasoline engines in Oshkosh and the builders earlier of a high-wheeler called the T.M.F. In 1914 he designed a nifty little cyclecar which he put together in the company's shops. It featured an underslung frame with a four-cylinder engine built in unit with a two-speed planetary transmission, the final drive by shaft to a bevel-driven rear axle. Two sets of brakes were provided, one on the rear wheels, the other on the transmission. The wheelbase was 98 inches, the tread 38 — and two passengers sat side-by-side in Ziebell's nicely styled roadster body. "No company has been organized as yet," *Carette* magazine reported in 1914, "nor has the name of the car been decided upon." Unfortunately, that decision would never have to be made, because although Arthur Ziebell very much wanted to manufacture the car, he could not find the financial backing to do so. Instead, in 1916 he left his job at Termaat & Monahan to join with H. Homer Fahrney (the wealthy son of a Chicago patent medicine man and the "F" in the former T.M.F.) to establish the Universal Motor Company and Universal Foundry Company, which built gasoline engines and an occasional motorboat and power lawnmower thereafter. The Universal companies remain in existence. Blindness forced Arthur Ziebell's retirement as president of the foundry in the mid-Fifties.

ZIM-KEL — Camden, New Jersey — (1907) — With a capital stock of $25,000, the Zim-Kel Motor Car Company was organized early in 1907 for the manufacture of motor vehicles. F.C. Zimmerman of Philadelphia, Y.F. Kelly of Cape May and W.G. Houck of New York City were the incorporators. Manufacture is doubted.

ZIMMERMAN — St. Louis, Missouri — (1901) — With help from William Jud, Charles Zimmerman of St. Louis built a gasoline automobile in 1901. The engine, a two-cylinder four-stroke horizontal unit, was built by the partners and was mounted in unit with the transmission. The float-feed carburetor was from Dyke; the axles, steering, wheels, solid rubber tires and stanhope body were purchased from H.F. Borbein. At the time Zimmerman was employed at the Scott Hydrocarbon Motor Works and he used the new car for commuting, though often, as he admitted later, he had to push it partway. Ultimately he traded the car for a Chase piano.

1909 Zimmerman, runabout, OCW

ZIMMERMAN — Auburn, Indiana — (1908-1915) —
The Zimmerman Manufacturing Company of Auburn was a buggy-building enterprise that announced its entrance into the automotive field in 1907 and proceeded into production early the following year. One of the more piquant examples of a motorized buggy, the Zimmerman placed its two-cylinder air-cooled engine under a gracefully curved hood and was offered in three variations of runabout and surrey. The Zimmerman company was strictly a family affair. Elias Zimmerman was president; Franklin T. and John were vice-president and secretary-treasurer respectively. As buggy builders, the Zimmermans were among the few to recognize early on the fate to which the highwheeler was headed and in 1910 added a standard four-cylinder car to their line, which was built for them by the Auburn Automobile Company across town. A Zimmerman six was added in 1913, as was a subsidiary enterprise which produced the de Soto. But already tragedy had struck this tradition-laden family operation. In 1910 Franklin Zimmerman had died, after thirty-seven years with the company. In 1914 he was followed in death by Elias Zimmerman, at the age of eighty-five. John Zimmerman continued on alone for a year — and then simply closed up shop. Late in 1915, following his joining forces with Auburn, John Zimmerman was instrumental in establishing the Union Automobile Company, an Auburn subsidiary which produced the Union car in the former Zimmerman plant in 1916.

1910 Zimmerman, surrey, WLB

1908-1909 ZIMMERMAN
Model G — 2-cyl., 14 hp, 80" wb

	FP	5	4	3	2	1
Rbt.-2P	650	1800	2800	4000	6200	13,000

Model H — 2-cyl., 14 hp, 80" wb

	FP	5	4	3	2	1
Rbt.-2P	650	1800	2800	4000	6200	13,000

Model I — 2-cyl., 16/18 hp, 95" wb

	FP	5	4	3	2	1
Surrey-4P	750	2000	3000	4200	6500	14,000

1910 ZIMMERMAN
Model H — 2-cyl., 16 hp, 80" wb

	FP	5	4	3	2	1
Rbt.-2P	650	2000	3000	4200	6500	14,000

Model I — 2-cyl., 16 hp, 95" wb

	FP	5	4	3	2	1
Surrey-4P	750	2200	3200	4400	7000	15,000

Model 35 — 4-cyl., 35 hp, 115" wb

	FP	5	4	3	2	1
Tour.-5P	1500	2900	3700	5600	9100	20,000

1911 ZIMMERMAN
Model E — 2-cyl., 16 hp, 80" wb

	FP	5	4	3	2	1
Rdst.-2P	675	2000	3000	4200	6500	14,000

Model L — 2-cyl., 20 hp, 95" wb

	FP	5	4	3	2	1
Surrey-4P	775	2200	3200	4400	7000	15,000

Model Z — 4-cyl., 35 hp, 115" wb

	FP	5	4	3	2	1
Tonneau	1600	2900	3700	5600	9100	20,000
Fore-Door Tour.	1650	2900	3700	5600	9100	20,000
Torpedo	1700	2900	3700	5600	9100	20,000
Rdst.	1500	2700	3600	5300	8800	19,000

1912 ZIMMERMAN
Model E — 2-cyl., 16 hp, 80" wb

	FP	5	4	3	2	1
Rdst.-2P	675	2000	3000	4200	6500	14,000

Model L — 2-cyl., 20 hp, 95" wb

	FP	5	4	3	2	1
Surrey-4P	775	2200	3200	4400	7000	15,000

Model Z — 4-cyl., 40 hp, 116" wb

	FP	5	4	3	2	1
Fore-Door Tour.	1600	3100	4200	6300	10,500	22,000
Rdst.	1485	3000	4000	6000	9500	21,000

1913-1914 ZIMMERMAN
Model D — 2-cyl., 16 hp, 80" wb

	FP	5	4	3	2	1
Rdst.-2P	450	2500	3500	5000	8500	18,000

Model Z-40 — 4-cyl., 40 hp, 116" wb

	FP	5	4	3	2	1
Tour.-5P	1600	3300	4400	6700	12,000	24,000

Model 6-46 — 6-cyl., 44 hp, 128" wb

	FP	5	4	3	2	1
Tour.-5P	1950	4200	5200	8400	15,700	29,000
Rdst.-2P	1950	4000	5000	8000	15,000	28,000

1915 ZIMMERMAN
Model Z-6 — 6-cyl., 38 hp, 132" wb

	FP	5	4	3	2	1
Tour.-5P	1750	4500	5800	9500	18,000	32,000

ZIMMERMANN — Waupun, Wisconsin — (1908) —
F.F. Zimmermann & Sons of Waupun provided coachwork to Bendix and Holsman and, as the company liked to brag in 1908, "have been supplying the Kissel Motor Car Company . . . with every body used since the establishment of the motor works." That year too, F.F. Zimmermann announced his plans to enter the car-making field. He quickly changed his mind. Whether a prototype was completed before his decision is not known.

1914 Zip, cyclecar, LC

ZIP — Davenport, Iowa — (1913-1914) —
The Zip Cyclecar Company of Davenport was among the early entries in the American cyclecar field. The company was announced in October of 1913 and was headed by R.W. Phelps (formerly advertising manager of the Moline Automobile Company), S. Decker French and Frank W. Skinner. The first Zip cyclecar was being tested by November. Powered by an air-cooled two-cylinder Mack motor, the Zip featured friction transmission, belt drive, and full elliptic springs both front and rear. Its wheelbase was 92 inches, its tread 40, with side-by-side seating. "The seat is wide enough to give comfort to good-sized men," *The American Cyclecar* reported, "and without in the least crowding the driver; besides, there is ample leg room for even a person having a height of six feet." The price was $395. Production began before year's end, 1913. During the summer of the following year, Zip announced experimentation with a commercial model, and the substitution of a four-cylinder water-cooled engine in its roadster. The last announcement from Zip arrived that November, and was short and to the point. The company was bankrupt.

ZIP — Columbus, Texas — (1914) —
The Zip from Texas was built by B.T. Wagner in the backyard of his home in Columbus. It had an air-cooled 16 hp four-cylinder engine, 102-inch wheelbase and 42-inch tread. The frame was ash, and there was no body per se, just a long sheet metal hood, shrouding the engine and transmission. Both the round gasoline tank and the two bucket seats were positioned over the rear axle, with the latter fastened directly to the frame for what must have been a bumpy ride. Wagner said the vehicle cost him $300 to build, and claimed a 60 mph top speed. He never planned to manufacture the vehicle.

ACKNOWLEDGMENTS

Acknowledgments to the First Edition

Just as the first, preparation of this second edition has been made both easier and more fun because of the help of friends, both new and old. Because this help extended over a long period, in both correspondence and telephone calls, I am certain I will inadvertently leave someone out. I apologize for that already.

First, thanks go to Chet Krause, whose support throughout has been wonderful, and to Henry Austin Clark, Jr. who, when I mentioned that a second edition was in the offing, responded, "great, when can you come out?"

My postman insists that the mail to my home has quadrupled over the past four years — and he's doubtlessly right. Scarcely a day has gone by when I didn't receive at least one letter from someone with new information or a fresh lead on one or more of the thousands of cars in the first edition. Almost weekly I heard from special consultants Ralph Dunwoodie or Keith Marvin with their latest finds.

On the East Coast, Fred Roe provided a wealth of material and opened many doors previously ajar. Kit Foster, Hayden Shepley and Walt MacIlvain offered important additions and corrections, as did Phil Dumka who also gave me a marvelous "drive report" on the Dudgeon steamer of the Civil War period.

My West Coast connections were solid too. First to be mentioned is Kevin Scott Tikker of San Francisco, whom I accidentally left out of the first edition and who is thus thanked double this time. In southern California, Jim Valentine continued with generous advice and counsel on the cars of that region. And, for this edition, I had a brand-new colleague, John Perala of Richmond, who shared with me the results of his formidable research into the early cars of the San Francisco Bay area.

From Texas, Roy Ames and D.J. Kava helped a lot; from Wisconsin, Bill Cameron did likewise. Counsel arrived often from John Conde in Michigan. Jim Benjaminson told me about many rare North Dakota automobiles, in addition to providing fascinating data on the export cars of Chrysler Corporation.

Valuable data on the cars built by the Hudson Motor Car Company was painstakingly (and that is the precise word) detailed by Wayne Graefen. Other historians who contributed handsomely to the information on various cars for which they had conducted specific research were Joe Ersland (White), Howard L. Miller (Lende), Stan Smith (Mercer and duPont), Fred Usher (Fageol and Comet), Gene Hustin (Kissel), Karl Zahm (Elcar and Graham-Paige), Pinky Randall (Chevrolet), Arch Brown (Nash), Warren Seely (Regal), Doris Whithorn (DeVault), Tom Mercer (Willys), Bob Du Bois (Chalmers), Steven Richmond (Columbia and Long Distance), Ken Ennis (R&V Knight), W.B. Newmiller (Rotary), Lee Beck (Black), Charles Bishop (Frisbie), George De Angelis (Ford), D. Krohne (Haase).

On cyclecars I had the estimable assistance of Joseph Hruska, who has spent decades studying the genre, and Dick Rash, who provided me the comprehensive roster prepared by the late Don Howland. Bill Lewis, my bi-coastal colleague (California his home now, the Eastern seaboard a while back), provided me enthralling tales and super data on a whole variety of cars. So did Dick Brigham, who's been

around a lot too and who cheerfully is always there when help is needed. From Marshall Naul, I received much, including documentation of healthy production for some cars which I had been loath to suggest went beyond the prototype stage in the first edition. Similarly, Robert Tuthill had something interestingly to report in every letter, including news of the Tri-Mobile and the Atkins Airmobile, two of the many "new" cars to be included in this edition. From Bern, Robert Braunschweig offered tantalizing details on American cars with a Swiss connection — and, as always, Nick Georgano was ever helpful with details from Great Britain.

For what can only be described as an assiduous reading of the first edition, I am indebted to Don Roetman of Beavercreek, Ohio. His pages-long notes, especially of cars the computer had failed to include in the geographical index the first time around, were extremely valuable in making corrections.

Space does not permit detailing all contributions, alas, but simply "paragraphing" them should not imply that my appreciation is anything but full measure. For their help, I am most grateful to Terry Boyce, Stephen M. Shine, Jim Forman, Robert E. Smith, Bob Hannaford, Tommy Protsman, William E. Swigart, Jr., Helen Earley, Rick Lenz, Elliott Kahn, John Utz, W.O. Frick, Jim Crank, R.H. McLaughlin, Jim Sturgis, Geoffrey Stein, Jim Cox, Jeff Gillis, Bill West, Julia Page, Dick Lee, William W. Guthbert, Peter Hupp, Henry F. Scannell of the Boston Public Library, Connie Rawson of the Stoneham (Massachusetts) Public Library, and the people of the Woburn National Bank in Woburn, Massachusetts.

As mentioned earlier, I'm sure I've left some people out — only because correspondence and telecon notes were too quickly filed under the car to which they referred — and my memory isn't as good as it used to be. I would be happy to learn any of these errors of omission so that they can be corrected next time.

Meanwhile, my gratitude to all. Do keep in touch. Automobile history is all the richer for the continuing inquiry into it. And it's such fun, isn't it?

-- Beverly Rae Kimes
October, 1988

One of the real joys and wonderful satisfactions of automobile history is its camaraderie, the spirited exchange of knowledge, wisdom and lore that has characterized its pursuit for decades now. Quite obviously, a book of this scope could not have been completed without a lot of help. And I have been very lucky to have it.

My partner in this project from the beginning has been Henry Austin Clark, Jr., who is both a legend in the hobby and a personification of the good fellowship in automobile history. It was in Austie's massive library that the preponderance of both documentary and illustrative research was undertaken. From the cracking of the first bound volume and the opening of the first brochure file to the last click of the shutter on the last picture for the book, Austie has been with me as mentor and guide. My debt to him is enormous.

Massive, too, is my gratitude to Keith Marvin and Ralph Dunwoodie, two more comrades in this adventure from the early days. Ralph and Keith have been renowned in automobile history circles for ages for their dedicated pursuit

1532

particularly of those cars that just about everybody else has forgotten — or never knew about in the first place. I spent a fascinating and fruitful week researching in Ralph's estimable archives in Sun Valley, Nevada; in Menands, New York, Keith read my first drafts of everything; and both provided counsel throughout whenever asked, which was often.

Sadly, another friend who had enthusiastically joined the cause early on is with us no longer. George Risley of Detroit died midway through the project. One of the most poignant tasks of my career was returning to Michigan to pick up the notes he had made on the last batch of material I had sent for his perusal and comment. His contribution was a wonderful one; decades ago George had visited many of the small Midwest towns which had seen automobile manufacturing at the dawn of the industry, making a careful record of what he had found there, information which he shared with me. I shall be eternally grateful to George both for his help and the pleasure of his company and his wry wit during our history sessions together in Detroit.

A number of research trips to Detroit were involved in this project. For years treks to the National Automotive History Collection of the Detroit Public Library and to the archives of the Motor Vehicle Manufacturers Association have been treasure hunts for me, and the search this time being of broader scope than ever before, the enjoyment was multiplied and so were the rewards. To Gloria Francis and Peggy Butzu Peters of the NAHC, and Jim Wren and friends at MVMA, my gratitude, with a special toast to Bill Bailey who was my "Detroit connection" in the photographic pursuit.

And to my friend Lou Helverson a note of appreciation, too, for making my research in the Automobile Reference Collection of the Free Library of Philadelphia both so diverting and so productive.

Two further automobile history collections should be singled out as proving valuable in this project. One is in the New York Public Library, its Annex on the west side of Manhattan housing an impressive number of rare automobile periodicals. The second is the Library of Congress in Washington, D.C. where I found some early publications in the field of which I had not been cognizant before. Both these collections seem to have been little used by automobile historians in the past, and are recommended.

Now comes the hard part: remembering with gratitude all those individuals who helped during varying stages of this project without leaving anyone out and without arriving at an acknowledgments section equally as lengthy as this book. Alas, it cannot be done. Human frailty dictates that I'm bound to forget someone (for which I apologize most heartily), and pragmatism dictates that the acknowledging cannot go on forever.

Finitely, then, it remains to be said that a good many automobile historians made my job considerably easier because a good many of them had long ago carved out areas of special interest. The cars on the East Coast attracted Charles Bishop's careful researching eye, Fred Roe staked out his native New England, Hayden Shepley has been pursuing Massachusetts and eastern Pennsylvania for a long time. The state of Indiana absorbs the focus and a good deal of the time of Wallace Spencer Huffman of Kokomo, and Southern California does the same for Jim Valentine of Culver City. All of these people shared their wisdom and their finds with me. And certainly too the studies that Don Summar has made of Pennsylvania cars, Willard J. Prentice of Maryland and District of Columbia cars, D.J. Kava of Texas cars provided invaluable guiding lights. Up in Minnesota Alan Ominsky focused on his state's automotive heritage, and was very helpful — and out in Kansas, Larry Jochims assisted in ferreting out the material gathered in a project of the Kansas State Historical Society.

Sometimes one just lucks out. Early on in this project I happened upon Jim Bellamy of Red Creek, New York who was immersed in a detailed study of the cars of New York State exclusive of Westchester County, New York City and Long Island. We immediately became frequent correspondents. A little later I chanced upon Ken Mains of Armonk who had just completed a study of the cars of Westchester County, still later I was put in touch with Robert McMulkin whose special interest is Long Island cars — and both of them helped. That meant that in the entire Empire State I was on my own only for New York City which happens to be where I live. Finding out about cars in one's own backyard — so to speak, since there are no backyards on the Upper East Side of Manhattan where, incidentally, the mighty Simplex was built awhile just four blocks from my home — is my idea of a super good time.

It is also fun for Ron Putz whose backyard is the Saginaw-Bay City (Michigan) area, and who amiably shared his researches with me. The cars of his native Connersville, Indiana have been Henry Blommel's special ardor for ages, and Gregg Buttermore helped with the cars built in neighboring Auburn which were not quite as well known as those for which the Auburn-Cord-Duesenberg Museum is named. Warren, Ohio has always been of absorbing interest for Terry Martin, while York County, Pennsylvania has been fortunate to have Theodore F. Freed and Fred Rosenmiller look into its automotive past, and Cleveland, Ohio has benefited handsomely from the scholarship of Richard Wager. I also figuratively shuffled off to Buffalo for help with the cars of that Upstate New York city from Tom Huestis and Herman Sass..

Many automobile historians, of course, are drawn to the field by particular marques, and their expertise was equally important to me on clarifying details. Jeff Gillis was marvelously helpful on all the cars in Billy Durant's second empire, as was Denney Freeston on the cars that John North Willys built, and Arch Brown on Charles Nash's efforts. Advice was sought and generously provided by William T. Cameron on his beloved Cameron automobiles, Jeff Godshall on Graham and Hupmobile, Walt Gosden on Franklin, Dick Greene on the L-29 Cord, Gene Husting on Kissel, Ledyard Pfund on Scripps-Booth, Jerry Riegel on du Pont, Fred Roe on Duesenberg and the cars designed by Henry Crane. In England the late and much-missed Michael Sedgwick provided a wealth of information on European cars that were built over here, and Nick Georgano offered interesting details on American cars that went over there. Bill Lewis had super information on obscure American front-drive cars, Bill Locke assisted admirably in sorting out the taxis from Elkhart, and Michael Lamm's researches through the years into some of the more unusual vehicles built in this country were just great.

Then there were all the folks I queried on occasions too numerous to mention and on matters too lengthy to detail. Leading this roster was Dick Brigham whose every letter ended with "did I tell you about . . ." Marshall Naul and Walter MacIlvain told me a lot as well, as did John Conde (who helped terrifically with pictures too). And they were joined by so many others that the resulting list would read rather like the membership directory of the Society of Automotive Historians. Sincere appreciation to Charlie Betts, Dave Brownell, Don Butler, Jerry Gebby, Dave Lewis, John Peckham, Dick Scharchburg and Karl Zahm.

Most rewarding too — in every sense of the word — was the response received from the hundreds of libraries and historical societies consulted throughout the country. Frequently arising from this were contacts with the sons or grandsons of early automobile builders, like Jim Leicher, Thorn Pendleton and John Ziebell — or Joe Perricone and Harold Mermel, the owners of rare early automobiles. The list of institutions and individuals which follows is as long as my appreciation to them is formidable.

Without Chet Krause, of course, none of the foregoing acknowledging would have been necessary. This project was

Chet's idea, and his support and enthusiasm throughout was more important than ever I could say. To John "Gunner" Gunnell, editor and liaison in Iola, multitudinous thanks for what obviously was one very difficult assignment. Finally, two personal acknowledgments: boundless appreciation to Wally Clark for her wonderful hospitality during the past three years when my visits to the Clark home were so frequent that I practically became a member of the family, and to Jim Cox for three years of alphabetizing, filing and editorial assistance above and beyond the call of the duty that became his when he cheerfully asked if he could help.

In any project of this magnitude, there are inevitably times when your energy flags, your spirits ebb or you just plain begin to question your own sanity. Many hands helped pick me up during the low spots, and are the reason this project will always remain a high for me. Looking back, it's really been fun.

--Beverly Rae Kimes

ARCHIVES, HISTORICAL SOCIETIES, LIBRARIES AND MUSEUMS

Abbott (Edith) Memorial Library, Grand Island, Nebraska
Adrian Public Library, Adrian, Michigan
Adriance Memorial Library, Poughkeepsie, New York
Akron-Summit County Public Library, Akron, Ohio
Alaska (University) Archives & Manuscript Collections, Fairbanks, Alaska
Albany County Public Library, Laramie, Wyoming
Albion Public Library, Albion, Michigan
Albright Memorial Library, Scranton, Pennsylvania
Alexandria Library, Alexandria, Virginia
Allen County Public Library, Fort Wayne, Indiana
Allentown Public Library, Allentown, Pennsylvania
Amador-Livermore Valley Historical Society, Hayward, California
Ames Free Library of Easton, North Easton, Massachusetts
Amesbury Public Library, Amesbury, Massachusetts
Andover Public Library, Andover, Maine
Andover Public Library, Andover, Massachusetts
Ann Arbor Public Library, Ann Arbor, Michigan
Appleton Public Library, Appleton, Wisconsin
Arkansas Historical Association, Fayetteville, Arkansas
Arlington County Department of Libraries, Arlington, Virginia
Arlington Public Library, Arlington, Texas
Artz (C. Burr) Library, Frederick, Maryland
Athol Public Library, Athol, Massachusetts
Atlanta Department of Archives and History, Atlanta, Georgia
Atlanta Historical Society, Atlanta, Georgia
Atlanta Public Library, Atlanta, Georgia
Atlantic City Public Library, Atlantic City, New Jersey
Attleboro Public Library, Attleboro, Massachusetts
Augusta College, Augusta, Georgia
Augusta-Richmond County Public Library, Augusta, Georgia
Aurora Public Library, Aurora, Illinois
Aurora Public Library, Aurora, Nebraska
Bacon Memorial Public Library, Wyandotte, Michigan
Bancroft Memorial Library, Hopedale, Massachusetts
Bangor Public Library, Bangor, Maine
Baraboo Public Library, Baraboo, Wisconsin
Barberton Public Library, Barberton, Ohio
Bar Harbor Historical Society, Bar Harbor, Maine
Bartholomew County Library, Columbus, Indiana
Batavia Public Library, Batavia, Illinois
Bayonne Free Public Library, Bayonne, New Jersey
Beacon Historical Society, Beacon, New York
Beaman Memorial Public Library, West Boylston, Massachusetts

Beaver Falls Public Library, Beaver Falls, Pennsylvania
Belding (Alvah N.) Library, Belding, Michigan
Belleville Public Library, Belleville, Illinois
Beloit Public Library, Beloit, Wisconsin
Benton Public Library, Benton, Illinois
Berkshire Athenaeum, Pittsfield, Massachusetts
Berlin Public Library, Berlin, Wisconsin
Bethlehem Public Library, Bethlehem, Pennsylvania
Bettendorf Public Library, Bettendorf, Iowa
Beverly Historical Society, Beverly, Massachusetts
Beverly Public Library, Beverly, Massachusetts
Billerica Public Library, Billerica, Massachusetts
Binghamton Public Library, Binghamton, New York
Birmingham Public Library, Birmingham, Alabama
Bloomfield Public Library, Bloomfield, New Jersey
Bloomington Public Library, Bloomington, Illinois
Bluffton-Wells County Public Library, Bluffton, Indiana
Boone County Historical Society Museum, Belvidere, Illinois
Borden (Gail) Public Library District, Elgin, Illinois
Braddock's Field Historical Society, Braddock, Pennsylvania
Bridgeport Public Library, Bridgeport, Connecticut
Bristol Public Library, Bristol, Connecticut
Brook-Iroquois Township Public Library, Brook, Indiana
Brookline Public Library, Brookline, Massachusetts
Brown County Library, Green Bay, Wisconsin
Brydges (Earl W.) Public Library, Niagara Falls, New York
Bucks County Free Library, Quakertown, Pennsylvania
Bucks County Historical Society, Doylestown, Pennsylvania
Buffalo & Erie County Public Library, Buffalo, New York
Butler Public Library, Butler, Pennsylvania
Butterfield Library, Westminster, Vermont
California Historical Society, San Francisco, California
Calumet Public Library, Calumet, Michigan
Cambria County Library System, Johnstown, Pennsylvania
Cambridge Historical Commission, Cambridge, Massachusetts
Cambridge Public Library, Cambridge, Massachusetts
Carnegie Free Library, Connellsville, Pennsylvania
Carnegie Free Library, McKeesport, Pennsylvania
Carnegie Library of Homestead, Munhall, Pennsylvania
Cascade County Historical Society, Great Falls, Montana
Catskill Public Library, Catskill, New York
Cedar Grove Public Library, Cedar Grove, Louisiana
Cedar Rapids Public Library, Cedar Rapids, Iowa
Centre County Library & Historical Museum, Bellefonte, Pennsylvania
Charlevoix Public Library, Charlevoix, Michigan

Charlotte Public Library, Charlotte, Michigan
Charlotte & Mecklenburg County Public Library, Charlotte, North Carolina
Chemung County Historical Society, Elmira, New York
Chester County Historical Society, West Chester, Pennsylvania
Chillicothe and Ross County Public Library, Chillicothe, Ohio
Chrisman Public Library, Chrisman, Illinois
Cincinnati Public Library, Cincinnati, Ohio
Citizens Library, Washington, Pennsylvania
Clarke Historical Library, Mount Pleasant, Michigan
Cleburne City Library, Cleburne, Texas
Cleveland Public Library, Cleveland, Ohio
Clyde Public Library, Clyde, Ohio
Colorado Historical Society, Denver, Colorado
Columbia Public Library, Columbia, South Carolina
Columbus Public Library, Columbus, Ohio
Comanche Public Library, Comanche, Texas
Concord Free Public Library, Concord, Massachusetts
Concord (City of) Library Department, Concord, New Hampshire
Connecticut Historical Society, Hartford, Connecticut
Connecticut State Library, Hartford, Connecticut
Coshocton Public Library, Coshocton, Ohio
Covington Public Library, Covington, Georgia
Crane (Thomas) Public Library, Quincy, Massachusetts
Craven-Pamlico-Cartaret Regional Library, New Bern, North Carolina
Crawford County Historical Society, Meadville, Pennsylvania
Cromwell Public Library, Cromwell, Connecticut
Culver City Library, Culver City, California
Cumberland Public Library, Cumberland, Maryland
Curtis Memorial Library, Brunswick, Maine
Dallas Public Library, Dallas, Texas
Danbury Public Library, Danbury, Connecticut
Danbury Scott-Fanton Museum & Historical Society, Danbury, Connecticut
Dansville Public Library, Dansville, New York
Danvers Archival Center, Danvers, Massachusetts
Danville Public Library, Danville, Illinois
Dauphin County Library System, Harrisburg, Pennsylvania
Davenport Public Library, Davenport, Iowa
Decatur Public Library, Decatur, Illinois
Decatur Public Library, Decatur, Indiana
Dedham Public Library, Dedham, Massachusetts
Defiance Public Library, Defiance, Ohio
Delaware County Historical Society, Chester, Pennsylvania
Delaware (State of) Division of Historical & Cultural Affairs, Dover, Delaware
Delaware Free Library, Callicoon, New York
Delaware Historical Society, Wilmington, Delaware
Derry Public Library, Derry, New Hampshire
Des Moines Public Library, Des Moines, Iowa
Dewitt Historical Society of Tompkins County, Ithaca, New York
Dixon Public Library, Dixon, Illinois
Dover Public Library, Dover, Delaware
Dover Free Public Library, Dover, New Jersey
Downers Grove Public Library, Downers Grove, Illinois
Easton Historical Society, North Easton, Massachusetts
East Orange Public Library, East Orange, New Jersey
Eleutherian Mills Historical Library, Wilmington, Delaware
Elizabeth Free Public Library, Elizabeth, New Jersey
Elkhart Public Library, Elkhart, Indiana
Ellsworth City Library, Ellsworth, Maine
El Reno Carnegie Library, El Reno, Oklahoma
Enid and Garfield County Public Library, Enid, Oklahoma
Erie County Library System, Erie, Pennsylvania

Essex Library Association, Essex, Connecticut
Eureka-Humboldt Library, Eureka, California
Evanston Public Library, Evanston, Illinois
Evansville & Vanderburgh County Public Library, Evansville, Indiana
Everett Public Library, Everett, Massachusetts
Fairmount Public Library, Fairmount, Indiana
Falconer Public Library, Falconer, New York
Fenton Historical Society, Jamestown, New York
Filson Club, Louisville, Kentucky
Findlay-Hancock County Public Library, Findlay, Ohio
Finney Public Library, Clintonville, Wisconsin
Fitchburg Historical Society, Fitchburg, Massachusetts
Fitchburg Public Library, Fitchburg, Massachusetts
Flagg Township Library, Rochelle, Illinois
Flint Public Library, Flint, Michigan
Florida Historical Society, Gainesville, Florida
Fond du Lac Public Library, Fond du Lac, Wisconsin
Forbes Library, Northampton, Massachusetts
Fowlerville Public Library, Fowlerville, Michigan
Framingham Public Library, Framingham, Massachusetts
Franklin Public Library, Franklin, Massachusetts
Frederick Public Library, Frederick, Oklahoma
Freedom Public Library, Freedom, Pennsylvania
Freeport Public Library, Freeport, Illinois
Galesburg Public Library, Galesburg, Illinois
Gary Public Library, Gary, Indiana
Geneva Free Library, Geneva, New York
Geneva Historical Society, Geneva, New York
Geneva Public Library, Geneva, Ohio
Georgia Historical Society, Savannah, Georgia
Gladbrook Public Library, Gladbrook, Iowa
Glendale (City) Library Division, Glendale, California
Glendale Public Library, Glendale, California
Gloucester City Public Library, Gloucester City, New Jersey
Gloucester Lyceum & Sawyer Free Library, Gloucester, Massachusetts
Goshen Public Library, Goshen, Indiana
Grand Prairie Historical Organization, Grand Prairie, Texas
Grand Prairie Historical Preservation Commission, Grand Prairie, Texas
Grand Prairie Memorial Library, Grand Prairie, Texas
Granite Falls Public Library, Granite Falls, Minnesota
Great Falls Public Library, Great Falls, Montana
Greeley Public Library, Greeley, Colorado
Green County District Library, Xenia, Ohio
Greene County Historical Society, Coxsackie, New York
Greenfield Daily Times Archives, Greenfield, Ohio
Greenfield Public Library, Greenfield, Massachusetts
Greenfield Public Library, Greenfield, Ohio
Greensburg Public Library, Greensburg, Indiana
Greenville County Library, Greenville, South Carolina
Harlan Community Library, Harlan, Iowa
Hartford Public Library, Hartford, Connecticut
Harvey Public Library, Harvey, Illinois
Haverhill Public Library, Haverhill, Massachusetts
Hazleton Area Public Library, Hazleton, Pennsylvania
Hayes (Rutherford B.) Presidential Center, Fremont, Ohio
Herkimer County Historical Society, Herkimer, New York
Herrick Public Library, Holland, Michigan
Heywood (Levi) Memorial Library, Gardner, Massachusetts
Hoboken Public Library, Hoboken, New Jersey
Holmes County Public Library, Millersburg, Ohio
Holyoke Public Library, Holyoke, Massachusetts
Houston Public Library, Houston, Texas
Hudson Historical Society, Hudson, Massachusetts
Hudson Public Library, Hudson, Michigan
Huntingburg Public Library, Huntingburg, Indiana
Ilion Free Public Library, Ilion, New York

Iowa State Historical Department, Des Moines, Iowa
Ipswich Public Library, Ipswich, Massachusetts
Jacksonville Public Library, Jacksonville, Florida
Jenkintown Library, Jenkintown, Pennsylvania
Jersey City Public Library, Jersey City, New Jersey
Jervis Public Library, Rome, New York
Joliet Public Library, Joliet, Illinois
Jones Memorial Library, Lynchburg, Virginia
Joplin Public Library, Joplin, Missouri
Juneau Public Library, Juneau, Wisconsin
Kalamazoo Public Library, Kalamazoo, Michigan
Kanawka County Public Library, Charleston, West
    Virginia
Kaubisch Memorial Public Library, Fostoria, Ohio
Keene Public Library, Keene, New Hampshire
Kendall Young Library, Webster City, Iowa
Kenosha Public Library, Kenosha, Wisconsin
Kent Free Library, Kent, Ohio
Kenton County Public Library, Covington, Kentucky
Kentucky Historical Society, Frankfort, Kentucky
Knightstown Public Library, Knightstown, Indiana
Knoxville-Knox County Public Library, Knoxville,
    Tennessee
Kokomo Public Library, Kokomo, Indiana
Laconia Public Library, Laconia, New Hampshire
La Crosse Public Library, La Crosse, Wisconsin
Lake Geneva Public Library, Lake Geneva, Wisconsin
Lancaster County Library, Lancaster, Pennsylvania
Lane Public Library, Hamilton, Ohio
Lansing Public Library, Lansing, Michigan
La Porte County Historical Society, La Porte, Indiana
La Porte County Museum, La Porte, Indiana
La Porte County Public Library, La Porte, Indiana
Lebanon Community Library, Lebanon, Pennsylvania
Lebanon County Historical Society, Lebanon,
    Pennsylvania
Lenox Library Association, Lenox, Massachusetts
Lewiston Public Library, Lewiston, Maine
Lexington Public Library, Lexington, Kentucky
Lima Public Library, Lima, Ohio
Lincoln City Libraries, Lincoln, Nebraska
Lincoln Library, Springfield, Illinois
Lincoln Public Library, Lincoln, Massachusetts
Logan County District Library, Bellefontaine, Ohio
Los Angeles Public Library, Los Angeles, California
Luke (Town of), Luke, Maryland
Luverne Public Library, Luverne, Minnesota
Macon Public Library, Macon, Missouri
Madera County Library, Madera, California
Madison Public Library, Madison, Wisconsin
Maine State Library, Augusta, Maine
Manchester City Library, Manchester, New Hampshire
Manitowoc Public Library, Manitowoc, Wisconsin
Mansfield-Richland County Library, Mansfield, Ohio
Margolies (Dr. Michael) Coatesville Area Public Library,
    Coatesville, Pennsylvania
Marion Public Library, Marion, Indiana
Marion Public Library, Marion, Ohio
Marlborough Historical Society, Marlborough,
    Massachusetts
Marshall Historical Society, Marshall, Michigan
Marshfield Public Library, Marshfield, Wisconsin
Martinsburg-Berkeley County Public Library,
    Martinsburg, West Virginia
Mason County Historical Society, Ludington, Michigan
Massillon Public Library, Massillon, Ohio
McKune Memorial Library, Chelsea, Michigan
McLean County Historical Society, Bloomington, Illinois
Mechanic Falls Public Library, Mechanic Falls, Maine
Memphis Public Library, Memphis, Michigan
Mentone Public Library, Mentone, Illinois
Meriden Public Library, Meriden, Connecticut

Metropolitan Library System, Oklahoma City, Oklahoma
Meyersdale Public Library, Meyersdale, Pennsylvania
Miami County Historical Museum, Peru, Indiana
Michigan City Public Library, Michigan City, Indiana
Michigan Technological University, Houghton, Michigan
Middletown Public Library, Middletown, California
Middletown Public Library, Middletown, Ohio
Mifflin County Historical Society, Lewistown,
    Pennsylvania
Milton Public Library, Milton, Massachusetts
Minnesota Historical Society, St. Paul, Minnesota
Mishawaka-Penn Public Library, Mishawaka, Indiana
Missouri Historical Society, St. Louis, Missouri
Missouri, State Historical Society of, Columbia, Missouri
Mitchell Public Library, Hillsdale, Michigan
Moline Public Library, Moline, Illinois
Momence Public Library, Momence, Illinois
Monroe County Library System, Monroe, Michigan
Montana Historical Society Library, Helena, Montana
Montrose Public Library, Montrose, Colorado
Mooresville Public Library, Mooresville, Indiana
Morley Library, Painesville, Ohio
Morrison-Reeves Library, Richmond, Indiana
Morristown and Morris Township Joint Free Library,
    Morristown, New Jersey
Morse Institute, Natick, Massachusetts
Mount Clemens Public Library, Mount Clemens, Michigan
Mount Vernon Public Library, Mount Vernon, New York
Muncie Public Library, Muncie, Indiana
Muskogee Public Library, Muskogee, Oklahoma
Napa City-County Library, Napa, California
Napa County Historical Society, Napa, California
Napoleon Public Library, Napoleon, Ohio
Nebraska State Historical Society, Lincoln, Nebraska
Nevada Historical Society, Reno, Nevada
Nevada State Library, Carson City, Nevada
New Albany Floyd County Public Library, New Albany,
    Indiana
Newark Free Library, Newark, Delaware
New Brighton Public Library, New Brighton, Pennsylvania
New Brunswick Free Public Library, New Brunswick, New
    Jersey
New Castle-Henry County Public Library, New Castle,
    Indiana
New Hampshire Historical Society, Concord, New
    Hampshire
New Haven Public Library, New Haven, Connecticut
New Jersey Historical Society, Newark, New Jersey
New London County Historical Society, New London,
    Connecticut
New Mexico Historical Review, Albuquerque, New Mexico
New Orleans Public Library, New Orleans, Pennsylvania
Newport Historical Society, Newport, Rhode Island
Newport Public Library, Newport, Rhode Island
New Rochelle Public Library, New Rochelle, New York
New Salem Office of Historical Commission, New Salem,
    Massachusetts
Newton Free Library, Newton, Massachusetts
Newton Public Library, Newton, Iowa
New York Society Library, New York, New York
New York State Historical Association, Cooperstown, New
    York
Niles Public Library, Niles, Michigan
Nodaway County Genealogical Society, Maryville, Missouri
North Carolina Museum of History, Raleigh, North
    Carolina
North Carolina State Archives, Raleigh, North Carolina
Northeast Oakland Historical Society, Oxford, Michigan
North Manchester Public Library, North Manchester,
    Indiana
North Tonawanda Public Library, North Tonawanda, New
    York

North Webster/Tippecanoe Township Library, North Webster, Indiana
North Wood County Historical Society, Marshfield, Wisconsin
Nutley Free Public Library, Nutley, New Jersey
Oakland Main Library, Oakland, California
Oceanside Public Library, Oceanside, California
Ogdensburg Public Library, Ogdensburg, New York
Ohio Historical Society, Columbus, Ohio
Ohio State Library, Winchester, Ohio
Oklahoma Historical Society, Oklahoma City, Oklahoma
Olean Public Library, Olean, New York
Onondaga County Public Library, Syracuse, New York
Orange County Historical Society, Orange, Texas
Orange Public Library, Orange, New Jersey
Orange Public Library, Orange, Texas
Oregon Historical Society, Portland, Oregon
Oshkosh Public Library, Oshkosh, Wisconsin
Ossining Historical Society, Ossining, New York
Oswego City Library, Oswego, New York
Otis Library, Norwich, Connecticut
Owatonna Public Library, Owatonna, Minnesota
Owensboro-Daviess County Public Library, Owensboro, Kentucky
Owosso Public Library, Owosso, Michigan
Packard (John) Library, Marysville, California
Parkersburg and Wood County Public Library, Parkersburg, West Virginia
Parlin Memorial Library, Everett, Massachusetts
Parlin Public Library, Canton, Illinois
Paterson Free Library, Paterson, New Jersey
Patten Free Library in the Park, Bath, Maine
Peabody Institute Library, Peabody, Massachusetts
Peoples Library, New Kensington, Pennsylvania
Peoria Public Library, Peoria, Illinois
Perry (H. Leslie) Memorial Library, Henderson, North Carolina
Phillipps (L.E.) Memorial Public Library, Eau Claire, Wisconsin
Phillip's (A.J.) Public Library, Fenton, Michigan
Plainfield Public Library, Plainfield, New Jersey
Plainsman Museum, Aurora, Nebraska
Pleasanton Library, Hayward, California
Pollard Memorial Library, Lowell, Massachusetts
Pontiac Public Library, Pontiac, Illinois
Port Jefferson Free Library, Port Jefferson, New York
Portland Public Library, Portland, Maine
Pottstown Public Library, Pottstown, Pennsylvania
Prince George's County Memorial Library, Hyattsville, Maryland
Providence Public Library, Providence, Rhode Island
Pueblo Library District, Pueblo, Colorado
Quincy Public Library, Quincy, Illinois
Racine Public Library, Racine, Wisconsin
Rawlins Municipal Library, Pierre, North Dakota
Red Bank Public Library, Red Bank, New Jersey
Red Wing Public Library, Red Wing, Minnesota
Rice Lake Public Library, Rice Lake, Wisconsin
Richland County Public Library, Columbia, South Carolina
Richmond County Historical Society, Augusta, Georgia
Richmond Memorial Library, Batavia, New York
Ripon Public Library, Ripon, Wisconsin
Riverside Public Library, Riverside, California
Riverton Public Library, Riverton, New Jersey
Rochester Public Library, Rochester, New York
Rock County Historical Society, Janesville, Wisconsin
Rockford Public Library, Rockford, Illinois
Rock Island Public Library, Rock Island, Illinois
Rosler Free Library, Carlisle, Pennsylvania
Ross (Annie Halenbake) Library, Lock Haven, Pennsylvania
Rushville Public Library, Rushville, Pennsylvania

Rutland Free Library, Rutland, Vermont
Sacramento City-County Library System, Sacramento, California
Sage Public Library, Osage, Iowa
St. Clair County Library, Port Huron, Michigan
St. Johnsbury Athenaeum, St. Johnsbury, Vermont
St. Joseph Public Library, St. Joseph, Missouri
St. Paul Public Library, St. Paul, Minnesota
Salem Public Library, Salem, Massachusetts
San Antonio Public Library, San Antonio, Texas
Sandusky County Historical Society, Fremont, Ohio
Sandusky Public Library, Sandusky, Ohio
Santa Clara Public Library, Santa Clara, California
Santa Maria Valley Historical Society, Santa Maria, California
Saratoga Springs Historical Society, Saratoga Springs, New York
Saratoga Springs Public Library, Saratoga Springs, New York
Saugus Public Library, Saugus, Massachusetts
Scott County Public Library, Scottsburg, Indiana
Scranton Public Library, Scranton, Pennsylvania
Seattle Public Library, Seattle, Washington
Sebring Public Library, Sebring, Ohio
Seneca Falls Historical Society, Seneca Falls, New York
Seneca Public Library, Attica, Ohio
Seymour Library, Auburn, New York
Shawnee County Historical Society, Topeka, Kansas
Sheboygan Falls Memorial Library, Sheboygan Falls, Wisconsin
Shelby Public Library, Shelby, Ohio
Shreveport-Bossier, the Times of, Shreveport, Louisiana
Simsbury Public Library, Simsbury, Connecticut
Sioux City Public Library, Sioux City, Iowa
Sioux Falls Historical Society, Sioux Falls, South Dakota
Sioux Falls Public Library, Sioux Falls, South Dakota
Smith (Edwin) Historical Museum, Westfield, Massachusetts
Somerville Public Library, Somerville, Massachusetts
South Bend Public Library, South Bend, Indiana
South Berwick Public Library, South Berwick, Maine
South Carolina Historical Society, Charleston, South Carolina
Spencer (Frances B.) Library, Middleburgh, New York
Spies Public Library, Menominee, Michigan
Springfield Town Library, Springfield, Vermont
Springvale Public Library, Springvale, Maine
Spruance Library, Doylestown, Pennsylvania
Stamford Public Library, Stamford, Connecticut
Stark County District Library, Canton, Ohio
Stephenson County Historical Society, Freeport, Illinois
Sterling Public Library, Sterling, Illinois
Stewart Library, Grinnell, Iowa
Stoneham Public Library, Stoneham, Massachusetts
Stonington Free Library Association, Stonington, Connecticut
Stoughton Public Library, Stoughton, Massachusetts
Streator Public Library, Streator, Illinois
Sun Prairie Public Library, Sun Prairie, Wisconsin
Superior Public Library, Superior, Wisconsin
Taunton Public Library, Taunton, Massachusetts
Taylor Memorial Public Library, Cuyahoga Falls, Ohio
Teaneck Public Library, Teaneck, New Jersey
Tell City Public Library, Tell City, Indiana
Tennessee State Library and Archives, Nashville, Tennessee
Texas State Historical Association, Austin, Texas
Tiffin-Seneca Public Library, Tiffin, Ohio
Toledo Public Library, Toledo, Ohio
Tompkins County Public Library, Ithaca, New York
Torrington Historical Society, Torrington, Connecticut
Trails Regional Library, Warrensburg, Missouri

Traverse City Public Library, Traverse City, Michigan
Trenton Free Public Library, Trenton, New Jersey
Troy Historical Society, Troy, Ohio
Tuck Memorial Museum, Hampton, New Hampshire
Tucson Public Library, Tucson, Arizona
Tullahoma Public Library, Tullahoma, Tennessee
Tulsa City-County Library, Tulsa, Oklahoma
Union City Public Library, Union City, Indiana
Union County Chapter of Ohio Genealogical Society, Marysville, Ohio
Utica Public Library, Utica, New York
Vermont (State) Department of Libraries, Montpelier, Vermont
Vermont Historical Society, Montpelier, Vermont
Waco-McLennan County Library, Waco, Texas
Wakeman Community Library, Wakeman, Ohio
Walker Memorial Library, Westbrook, Maine
Ware Public Library, Ware, Massachusetts
Warner Library, Tarrytown, New York
Warren Public Library, Warren, Michigan
Warren Public Library, Warren, Pennsylvania
Warren-Trumbull County Public Library, Warren, Ohio
Warrensville Community Library, Warrensville Heights, Ohio
Washington (University) Libraries, Seattle, Washington
Washington Memorial Library, Macon, Georgia
Waterloo Public Library, Waterloo, Iowa
Waterville Public Library, Waterville, Maine
Waukesha County Museum, Waukesha, Wisconsin
Waverly Free Library, Waverly, New York
Wayne Historical Museum, Wayne, Michigan
Wayne-Westland Library, Wayne, Michigan
Wells Memorial Library, Lafayette, Indiana
West Alexandria Archives, West Alexandria, Ohio
Westborough Public Library, Westborough, Massachusetts
Western Brown Local Schools, Hamersville, Ohio
Westfield Athenaeum, Westfield, Massachusetts
West Virginia Department of Culture and History, Charleston, West Virginia
Wheeler Memorial Library, Orange, Massachusetts
White (Peter) Public Library, Marquette, Michigan
White Pigeon Township Library, White Pigeon, Michigan
Wilkes Barre Public Library, Wilkes Barre, Pennsylvania
Willard Library, Battle Creek, Michigan
Williamsport Public Library, Williamsport, Pennsylvania
Wilmington Library, Wilmington, Delaware
Winchester Public Library, Winchester, Massachusetts
Windsor Historical Society, Windsor, Connecticut
Windsor Public Library, Windsor, Connecticut
Wisconsin State Historical Society, Madison, Wisconsin
Woburn Public Library, Woburn, Massachusetts
Worcester Public Library, Worcester, Massachusetts
Wyoming (University) American Heritage Center, Laramie, Wyoming
Yakima Valley Museum & Historical Association, Yakima, Washington
Yakima Valley Regional Library, Yakima, Washington

With special thanks to the following archivists, curators, librarians and local historians:

Elizabeth Abbe, Elizabeth W. Abbott, Deborah Abraham, Boyd Addlesperger, Mrs. J.W. Albsmeyer, George S. Aldrich, Mary Allegrini, Gwen Allen, James K. Allen, Julia Allen, Theda Alper, Donna B. Amberman, Frances Ambrose, Nancy S. Anderson, Susan Anderson, Toni Anderson, Roberta Y. Arminio, Gary J. Arnold, Sally D. Arrivee, Marie Ashley, Eldora Auch, Betty Babicz, Mrs. Jackie Badersnider, Elizabeth Bailey, Linda Bailey, Nancy Gwaltney Bales, W. Whitman Ball, Joan Banks, C.G. Barber, Martin Barlag, Wilda J. Baroody, Paula Colby Barrett, Julie B. Barrows, Annette Bartholomae, Choice Bartlett,

Sally Bast, Peggy Batten, Linda Beebe, Raymond Beecher, Linda Beeler, Barbara Bennett, Margaret Bentley, Norma Jean Bishop, Hazel C. Blackstone, Marilyn Blackwell, Renee Blahuta, Marilyn Boardman, Victoria Bolemian, Charles K. Boll, Fred Bomberger, Audrey Miller Bongar, Rich Bowra, Barbara R. Boyd, Persis E. Boyesen, Lucile Boykin, Susan B. Braunstein, Glenda Bremer, Patricia E. Brewer, Beverly Briese, Richard Bright, Nancy M. Brown, Sarah B. Brown, Diane Browne, Gerald G. Bruce, Vivian Bryan, Eva Bryson, Trenna J. Buchter, Doris Bunn, Lee Burbridge, Jeanette Burke, Maxine Burlile, Alice Burling, Karen M. Burns, Craig Buthod, Rebecca H. Byrum, Alice C. Caggiano, Robert Calder, Catherine C. Calhoun, Paul Eugen Camp, Teresa Canuti, Mrs. R.L. Caldwell, Carol B. Caro, Frederick A. Casey, Edward J. Cashin, Lorna Caulkins, Pamela Cawley, R. Lance Chaffee, Wynagene Cherry, Jeanne Chickering, Carolyn H. Chouinard, James Christman, Janie Clarke, Sebrena Cline, Mrs. Robert Clise, June Stevens Clyde, Marguerite L. Cockley, Ron Coffey, Ann E. Cohen, Marie Ann Coil, Sara Collins, Cheryl Conover, Kay Conrad, Dorothy Constance, Mrs. Horace D. Cook, Vesper Cook, Shelby Cook-Dorough, Constance J. Cooper, William Copeley, Doris Corrado, Dianne Costin, Kay Courtnage, Carol Coverly, Louise L. Cowling, Ann E. Coyne, George C. Crout, Nan Crowder, Karen A. Culp, Lawrence B. Davenport, Kitty Davis, A. Day, B. Day, David W. Deakle, Virginia Deffner, Ray Dickinson, Marcia Dievendorf, Donald N. Dimmitt, Christina M. DiNapoli, Joan F. Doherty, Greta Don, Vince Dornan, Ann Doss, Jess Doud, June Dougherty, Rondi Downs, Alden O. Droivold, Grinnell Dunham, Claire Dunne, Roger Dutcher, Phil Earl, Joan Eby, Jane Eigenrauch, Eric Eisney, Joan S. Eitel, Barbara J. Elliott, Catherine T. Engel, Stephen C. Erskine, Kathleen M. Facer, Patricia E. Fallon, Linda Fanselau, Kevin Feeney, C.B. Ferguson, Carol Ferlito, Mary L. Finken, Donald W. Fisher, Jr., Madeline Fisher, James G. Fitzgerald, Cathy Fitzpatrick, Gina Flannery, Jackie Flotow, Virginia P. Follstad, Maurice J. Forrestier III, Mrs. Raymond Fraley, Audrey Francis, Carol June Frisby, Charyl Frounfelter, Heidi Fuge, Virginia Gaines, Kevin J. Gallagher, Nandy E. Gaudette, Elmer A. Gerber, Audrey Gilbert, Jane Gill, J. Gillis, Diana Gin, Margean Gladysz, Patricia Golgart, Lola L. Gould, Norma Graim, Alison Graves, Joan Greenberg, Stanley Greenberg, Lisa L. Gregory, Carolyn Greufe, Margaret Grier, Mirrian Griffith, Paula Porter Griffith, Jean Grohman, Susan Grotyohann, Carolyn Gruber, Janice L. Haas, Shari Haber, Alice Hackett, Louis R. Hall, Patricia A. Hamilton, Mildred Hanchett, Enid Hanks, Frances A. Hare, Frederick W. Harnett, Mary Harper, C.H. Harris, Ann P. Hart, Paul Hass, Lois R. Hastings, Marjorie E. Hattersley, Linda Hay, Kathleen Hepker, Mary Jane Herber, Edwina Hewey, Virginia M. Hiatt, Walter V. Hickey, Alfred G. Hilbert, Edurnna C. Hillemeier, George K. Holland, P. Hollander, John M. Holman, Judy Holman, Marie Hoscheid, Barbara Hoskins, Cheryl Hughes, Mary Ann Hunsberger, Mildred E. Hurley, Lawrence R. Huss, Sibyle Hutchings, Janet Hutchins, Cheryl Jackson, Kenneth R. Jackson, Ruthe Jackson, Susan Jamieson, Hans W. Jensen, Marcia Jensen, Virginia Jobe, Andrew F. Johnson, Joyce Johnson, Susan Johnson, William M. Johnson, Janet R. Johnston, Alan Jorgenson, Laura Kahkonen, Mary E. Kates, Helen A. Kehoe, Ruth Kelsey, Margarett M. Kennard, Kathy Kennedy, Bettie Kepple, Mary S. Kern, Denyse Killgore, M. Hope Killinger, Barbara A. Kipplin, Kathryn D. Kistler, Jeanne Klein, Elizabeth B. Knox, Judith L. Koch, Robert Kolbe, Greg Koos, Dorothy Korth, Allan Kovan, Beth Kowaleski, Sharon M. Krawiecki, John M. Krivak, Virginia L. Krueger, Ann K. Kuftel, Martha Ladd, Gregory H. Laing, Clara Lalu, Janice Lanou, Roberta Lawrey, Dianne LeConte, Beth Lee, Charleen A. Lehnert, Charles W. Lenz, Denis J. Lesieur, Lizette R. Leveille, Pamela J. Lieser, Hilda Lipkin, Marie N. Liska, Mary Ann

List, Pat Little, Judith A. Lofaso, Nart Loften, M.E. Lohr, Donald E. Loker, Sonia K. Long, Mary Lontz, Ann R. Lorentz, Carol B. Lovett, Betty-Bright P. Low, Patricia T. Lull, Ruth N. Lunde, Doris Z. Luneau, Jack MacLean, Larry Manuel, Dorothy Mapes, Mildred F. March, Verna Mae Marks, Bonita C. Marley, June R. Martin, Harold F. Maschin, Stan Matli, Joanne A. Mattern, Charles D. Maurer, Marilynn E. McBeth, Carol McCafferty, Edith H. McCauley, Harriet McCauley, Jane McClary, Patricia J. McDougal, Ruth McEvoy, Dean E. McFadden, Daniel McGinnis, Shirley H. McGrath, Sherry L. McIntyre, Jeannette McKee, Dessie V. McKinney, Joyce McKnight, Terry A. McNealy, Philip E. McNulty, Margaret Meade, Betty C. Menges, Jerald Merrick, Rebecca Meta, Hazel Mikel, Emily J. Miles, William Miles, Helen Miller, Lydia Miller, Roger L. Miller, Virginia Miller, Ann Vanriette Mills, Richard Mobley, Rita M. Moore, Cindy Morgan, Dorothy Morgan, Joan Morgan, Jocelyn A. Moss, Marcia E. Moss, Martha Mulanox, Ted R. Mundt, Mara B. Munroe, Gladys C. Murray, J. Myler, Carl T. Narvestad, Bill Naughton, Lawrence Naukam, Olga Nazaroff, Dolly Newport, Carol J. Nicholas, Kathryn D. Nicholas, Margaret Nystrom, Wilma Obenauer, Renata Ochsner, Tom O'Connell, Jr., A.E. Olsen, Lynne Olsen, Cynthia O'Neil, Gladys O'Neil, Julia M. Overton, Susan Pallone, David W. Palmquist, George E. Parks, Gerald J. Parsons, Elizabeth Pattengill, Mrs. Roy Patterson, Andrea I. Paul, Everette J. Payette, Anne W. Penniman, Sara Peth, Mary L. Phillips, Eileen C. Piazza, Elise Pinckney, Mary Ann Pirone, Melinda J. Place, Gail Plattner, John M. Player, Rodney J. Poitier, Janet W. Postler, David R. Proper, Ruth Prostor, Virginia Putnam, Cole Puvogel, Martha Quinn, Wilfred J. Rauber, Greg L. Reese, Richard W. Reeves, Margaret Renwick, Ruth Rhinehart, Jeanine Rhodes, Rosemarie Rice, Mary Elizabeth Richardson, Sally Ripatti, Allan W. Robbins, Celia Ann Roberts, Ted Robertson, Dorothy Rock, Willard L. Rocker, William Rohlfs, Elizabeth A. Roland, Dorothy M. Rollins, Joanne P. Roukens, Virginia Rowden, Ray Rowland, Robert Royce, Edward J. Russo, Elaine J. Rutherford,

Bette Savage, Martin F. Schmidt, Mildred Schmidt, Maxine G. Schultz, Virginia K. Scott, Virginia G. Seitz, Victor A. Selby, Lois E. Severns, Sarah J. Shaw, A. Sheck, Anna R. Sherk, Nancy Shiflet, N. Shoots, Truman Short, Saundra Shuler, Richard P. Sibley, Jr., Shirley Mendel Simon, Susan M. Simpson, Sandra Smagala, Mrs. Irwin Smith, Judie Smith, William Smith, Bertha Snell, Geoff Socha, Shirley Soenksen, Dave Solomon, Nancy Solomon, Barbara Soper, Robert W. Spahr, Rita Specht, Jane P. Spellman, Theresa Sanderson Spence, J. Robert Starkey, Audrey E. Stedman, Patricia M. Steele, Lois Stephens, Ruth Stetter, Anne W. Stewart, Beverly J. Stewart, Muriel H. Stiles, J.P. Stokes, Keith D. Strawn, Noreen Stringfellow, Gordon Struble, Goodloe Stuck, William W. Sturm, Charles M. Sullivan, Jean A. Suloff, Dolores Swanson, Edna S. Sweely, Mrs. Michael Sweeney, Ruth Tallant, Donna Tarkington, Sonia Taub, Phyllis Taylor, William Te Ronde, Jack G. Thomas, John E. Thorau, Nancy Thorson, Georgie Throckmorton, Katherine A. Thurner, Jacqueline C. Tidman, Joe Tierney, Henry R. Timman, Vera Tobin, Anne Toll, Richard B. Trask, Tom Trice, Wendell Tripp, Ruth Trower, Mrs. Juel Troy, Maryjane Turbett, Frances L. Turner, Dorothea Tutwiler, Nellie Twbaugh, John Underwood, Louise Vajk, Richard J. Van Etten, Harold E. Van Huffel, Donald Vanreken, Joan K. VanVoorhis, Vicki Victoria, Arthur J. Voelliger, Katie Voss, Andrea Vossenberg, Mrs. C.W. Wadsworth, Dietman U. Wagner, George L. Wagner, Marybeth Wallick, Dave Walter, Martha Warden, Margaret Waring, Lyle W. Warrick, Mildred Watkins, George E. Wausnock, Eve Weinberg, G. Weiss, Nancy A. Welter, Eleanora F. West, Harry West, Carol Westphal, Pearl Wheeler, Ruth Widdicombe, Nancy E. Wight, Susan B. Wight, Mary Wilkins, Marjorie Wilkinson, Craig S. Williams, Cecilia Wiltzius, Darlene Winter, Rev. Robert C. Withington, Allan J. Woeckel, Theodore O. Wohlsen, Jr., Beverly Womach, Marlene Womack, Frances Woodhouse, Leslie Woods, Mrs. Edmund Wordell, Naomi Yeats, Virginia Zoch, Josie Zoretich

American Automobile, The. New York, New York. Volume I, Number 1, September 1899 through Volume II, Number 12, September 1901 (called *The Automobile* September and October 1899).

American Cyclecar, The. Chicago, Illinois. November 1913 through July 1914 (succeeded by *Carette*).

American Electrician. New York, New York, Volume XI, 1899 and Volume XII, 1900.

Automobile, The. New York, New York. Volume VIII, Number 1, January 3rd, 1903 through Volume XXXVII, Number 1, July 5th, 1917 (successor to *Automobile & Motor Review,* succeeded by *The Automobile and Automotive Industries*).

Automobile and Automotive Industries, The. New York, New York. Volume XXXVII, Number 2, July 12th, 1917 through Volume XXXVII, Number 17, October 25th, 1917 (successor to *The Automobile,* succeeded by *Automotive Industries*).

Automobile Dealer and Repairer. New York, New York. Volume I, Number 1, March 1906 through Volume XXIV, Number 6, February 1918.

Automobile Journal. Pawtucket, Rhode Island. Volume XXXI, Number 1, January 1911 through Volume LI, Number 9, September 1922 (successor to *New England Automobile Journal*).

Automobile Magazine, The. New York, New York. October 1899 through June 1907.

Automobile & Motor Review. New York, New York. Volume VII, June 7th, 1902 through December 27th, 1902 (successor to *Motor Review,* succeeded by *The Automobile*).

Automobile Review, The. Chicago, Illinois. Volume I, Number 1, August 1899 through Volume XII, Number 25, June 22nd, 1905 (successor to *Cycling Gazette,* succeeded by *The Motor Way*).

Automobile Topics. New York, New York. Volume I, Number 1, October 1900 through Volume CXLIV, Number 12, December 1942.

Automobile Trade Journal. Philadelphia, Chicago and New York City. Volume XVI, February 1912 through Volume VLX, Number 8, July 1940 (successor to *Cycle and Automobile Trade Journal*).

Automotive Exporter, The. New York, New York, Volume I, Number 1, July 1919 through Volume VI, Number 1, January 1922.

Automotive Industries. New York, New York. Volume XXXVII, Number 18, November 1st, 1917 through Volume LXXVII, December 1942 (successor to *The Automobile and Automotive Industries,* became *Automotive & Aviation Industries* Volumes LXXXVI and LXXXVI of 1942).

Automotive Manufacturer, The. New York, New York. Volume LXI, Number 6, September 1919 through Volume LXIX, Number 7, October 1927 (consolidated *The Hub* and *Automotive Engineering*).

Carette. Chicago, Illinois. August 1914 through August 1915 (successor to *The American Cyclecar*).

Carriage Monthly, The. Philadelphia, Pennsylvania. Volume XXX, Number 10, January 1895 through Volume XLI, Number 9, December 1905.

Cycle and Automobile Trade Journal. Philadelphia, Chicago and New York City. Volume III, 1899 through Volume XVI, January 1912 (successor to *Cycle Trade Journal,* succeeded by *Automobile Trade Journal*).

Cycle Age and Trade Review, The. Chicago, Illinois. Volume I, Number 1, November 1897 through Volume XXVIII, Number 9, December 26th, 1901.

Cycle Trade Journal. Philadelphia, Chicago and New York City. Volume I, 1896 through Volume III, 1899 (succeeded by *Cycle and Automobile Trade Journal*).

Cyclecar Age. New York, New York. November 1913 through September 1914 (successor to *Bicycle News,* succeeded by *Light Car Age*).

Dealer and Repairman, The. New York, New York. Volume I, Number 1, April 1902 through Volume II, Number 10, January 1904.

Electrical Engineer, The. New York, New York. Volume XXI, 1896 through Volume XXVII, 1899.

Electrical Review. New York, New York. Volume XXXVI, 1900.

Electrical World. New York, New York. Volume XXXIII, 1899 and Volume XXXIV, 1900.

Electrical World and Engineer. New York, New York. Volume XXXIV, 1899.

Gas Engine. Cincinnati, Ohio. Volume I, Number 1, May 1898 through Volume VI, Number 12, December 1904.

Hiscox, Gardner D., *Horseless Vehicles, Automobiles, Motor Cycles.* New York: Munn & Company, 1900.

Hobbs, George W. and Elliott, Ben. G., *The Gasoline Automobile.* New York: McGraw-Hill Book Company, Inc., 1915.

Horseless Age, The. New York, New York. Volume I, Number 1, November 1895 through Volume XLIV, Number 3, May 1st, 1918.

Hub, The. New York, New York. Volume XXXVII, Number 1, April 1895 through Volume XLVIII, Number 9, December 1906.

Light Car Age. New York, New York. October 1914 through March 1915 (successor to *Cyclecar Age,* succeeded by *Bicycle News*).

Motocycle, The. Chicago, Illinois. October 1895 through October 1897.

Motocycle Illustrated, The. New York, New York. Volume I, Number 1, January 1906 through Volume XIII, Number 17, April 26th, 1917.

Motocycle Maker & Dealer. New York, New York. 1895.

MoToR. New York, New York. Volume I, Number 1, October 1903 through Volume LXXVIII, Number 6, December 1942.

Motor Age. Chicago, Illinois. Volume 1, Number 1, September 12th, 1899 through Volume LXII, Number 1, December 1942.

Motor Car. Kansas City, Missouri, January 1908 through December 1912. Garden City, New York, January 1913 through March 1913 (succeeded by *Motor Life*).

Motor Field. Denver, Colorado and San Francisco, California. Volume XVII, Number 1, June 1903 through Volume XXIX, Number 2, November 1914 (succeeded *Cycle West*).

Motor Land. San Francisco, California. Volume VIII, Number 1, January 1921 through Volume XX, Number 1, January 1927.

Motor Life. Garden City, New York. April 1913 through October 1914 (merged with *Motor Print,* resumed *Motor*

Life name January 1917 through December 1927).

Motor Print. Philadelphia, Pennsylvania. Volume I, Number 1, March 1906 through October 1915. New York, New York. November 1915 through December 1916 (succeeded by *Motor Life*).

Motor Record. New York, New York. Volume I, Number 1, March 1917 through Volume XXII, Number 6, December 1927.

Motor Review. New York, New York. Volume IV, Number 18, July 4th, 1901 through Volume VI, Number 13, May 29th, 1902 (successor to *Motor Vehicle Review,* succeeded by *Automobile & Motor Review*).

Motor Traffic. New York, New York. April 16th, 1906 through January 15th, 1907.

Motor Vehicle Review. New York, New York. Volume I, Number 1, September 19th, 1899 through Volume IV, Number 17, June 27th, 1901 (succeeded by *Motor Review).*

Motor Way, The. Chicago, Illinois, Volume XIII, Number 1, July 6th, 1905 through Volume XVII, Number 11, December 1911 (succeeded *Automobile Review*).

Motor West. Los Angeles and San Francisco, California. February 1914 through December 1940.

Motor World. New York, New York and Philadelphia, Pennsylvania. Volume I, Number 1, October 4th, 1900 through Volume 101, Number 3, July 1940.

New England Automobile Journal. Pawtucket, Rhode Island. Volume I, Number 1, March 1906 through Volume XXX, Number 2, December 31st, 1910 (succeeded by *Automobile Journal*).

Northwestern Motorist. Seattle, Washington. Volume I, June 1916 through Volume III, June 1918.

In addition to those noted above, selected references were culled from such other periodicals in the field as *The Autobain, Automotive Abstracts, The Auto* (St. Louis) and *American Automobile Digest.* Various Nineteenth Century issues of *Scientific American* as well as the annual automobile editions from 1899 to 1918 (variously titled "Bicycle and Automobile," "Automobile and Outing," "Automobile and Yachting," "Automobile and Motoring," "Automobile" and "Motor") were researched. *MoToR's* annual *Motor Car Directory* published during the pre-World War I years was consulted as were the Ware and Chilton industry yearbooks and almanacs, and the National Blue Books, for the period covered by this volume. Manuals published for use by insurance companies handling automobiles were perused, as were state motor vehicle registration lists where available. *Branham's* was a frequently valuable source as were the handbooks published by the American Motor Car Manufacturers Association, the Association of Licensed Automobile Manufacturers and the National Automobile Chamber of Commerce. Useful too was the *Marvyn Scudder Manual of Extinct or Obsolete Companies,* first published in New York City in 1926 and thereafter sporadically into the World War II era. Frequently, too, city directories in the various locations where automobiles were built provided significant data and documentation.

INDEX: ALTERNATE-POWER CARS

COMPRESSED-AIR CARS

American Pneumatic
Autocrat
Automatic Air
Mac Kenzie & Mc Arthur
Meyers
Muir
Pneumatic

ELECTRIC CARS

A

Ajax
Altha Electric
American Beauty
American Borland/Broc
American Electric
American Electro-Mobile
American Juvenile
Amesbury
Amper
Anderson Electric
Andover
Anheuser-Busch
Annesley
Anthony
Argo Electric
Armstrong Electric
Arnold
Aspinwall Electric
Asprooth-Leoni Electric
Atlantic
Auto-Dynamic
Autocarette
Automatic Electric
Automobile Battery

B

Babcock Electirc
Bachelle Electric
Bailey Electric
Baker & Elberg Electric
Baker Electric
Baltimore
Bardwell
Barrett & Perret
Barrows Electric
Bartlett
Beardsley
Belknap
Berg Electric
Berwick
Bissell
Blake
Blakeslee Electric
Borbein
Borland Electric
Boston Electric
Brecht
Brenning
Broc Electric
Brower
Brunn
Brush
Buffalo Electric
Buffalo-Rochester Electric
Byrider Electric

C

Caffrey Electric
Campbell Electric
Cantono Electric
Capitol Electric
Carl Electric
Carpenter
Casler
Centaur
Century
Century Electric
Champion Electric
Chapman Electric
Chautauqua Electric
Chicago Electric
ch-Field Electric

Clark Electric
Cleveland Electric
Clinton E. Woods
Coey
Coleman Electric
Collins Electric
Colonial Electric
Columbia
Columbia Electric
Columbian Electric
Columbus Electric
Commercial Electric
Conklin Electric
Cooney
Copeland Electric
Crompton
Crowdus Electric
Cummings Electric
Cunard
Custer Electric
Cuyahoga Electirc
Cyco Lectric

D

D-S
Dayton Electric
Demars Electric
Detroit Electric
Dey
Dey-Griswold
Dolan
Douglas Electric
Dual
Dyke-Britton
Dyke/St. Louis

E

Eagle Electric
Eaton Electric
Eddy Electric
Edison Electric
Ehrlich Electric
Electrette
Electric
Electric Carriage
Electric Vehicle
Electrical
Electriquette
Electro
Electrobat
Electrobile
Electrocar
Electromobile
Elgin Electric
Ellis
Elwell-Parker Electric
Everett

F

Fanning
Fischer
Flanders Electric
Foster
Fritchle Electric
Fulton & Walker

G

G.V.
Gallia Electric
General Electric
Gibbs
Gilmore Electric
Graham Electric
Grinnell Electric
Grube
Guenther

H

H & F Electric
Hafer Electric
Haschke Electric
Healey
Henry Electric
Hercules Electric
Hewitt-Lindstrom
Hollis Electric
Holson
Holtzer-Cabot
Hopewell
Houghton
Hub Electric
Huebner
Hunter Electric
Hupp-Yeats

I

Ideal Electric
Illinois Electric
Imperial Electric
Interurban
Ithaca

J

Jack Frost Electric
Judd
Juvenile Electric

K

Kammann
Keating
Keller
Keller Electric
Kennedy Electric
Kensington
Kimball Electric
Kingsbury
Knudsen Electric
Koehler Electric
Kosmos Electric
Krotz Electric
Krotz Gas-Electric
Kuqua

L

Lakewood
Lamb Electric
Lansden Electric
Le Jeal
Lemp Electric
Lenox Electric
Levy
Lewis Electric
Lincoln Electric
Los Angeles Electric
Lugo Electric

M

M & C Electric
Mac Naughton
Macinnis Electric
Manhattan
Marion
Mark
Maryland Electric
Mason-Seaman
Maxen Electric
Maxim Motor Tricycle
Maxim-Goodridge Electric
Mc Can
Media
Menominee Electric
Milburn Electric
Miller Electric
Mills Electric
Montgomery Ward
Morris & Salom Electric
Morrison Electric
Munson
Murray Electric
Mystery Car Electric

N

National
Neftel
Nelson Electric
New Columbus
New England Electric
New Parry
Niagara Electric

O

O'Brien Electric
Ohio Electric
Orient
Osterberg & Sutton
Owatonna

P

Packard
Parry
Parsons Electric
Pawtucket Electric
Perret Electric
Perry Lewis

Philbrick
Phipps Electric
Phipps-Grinnell
Pierce Electric
Pittsburgh Electric
Pocock
Pope-Waverley Electric
Pratt

Q

Quinby

R

Rae Electric
Rauch & Lang Electric
Red Bug
Reid Electric
Republic Electric
Reuter Electric
Riker
Roberts Electric
Royal Electric
Russell-Springfield

S

Samuels Electric
Scholze
Schwinn
Scott
Specialty Electric
Speirs
Sperry Electric
Springfield Electric
Standard Electric
Standard G.E.
Stattery Electric
Stearns Electric
Steinmetz Electric
Sterrett
Storms Electric
Stringer
Strong & Rogers Electric
Sturges Electric
Sturgis
Synnestvedt Electric

T

Thompson Electric
Thresher Electric
Tiffany Electric
Todd Electric
Toledo Electric
Towanda Electric
Tritt Electric
Triumph Electric
Turbine Electric

U

Union
United Power
United States

V

V.E. (V.E.C.) Electric
Van Etten
Van Wagoner
Vogt Electric
Volta-Car

W

Walkins
Walshe
Ward Electric
Warner Electric
Warren
Washington Electric
Watson Electric
Waverley Electric
Wells-Meeker Electric
Willard
Williams Electric
Willoughby Electric
Wood Electric
Woods Dual Power
Woods Electric
Wright Electric
Wylie Electric

SPRING-POWERED CARS

Andrews
Burdick

STEAM CARS

A

A.B.C.
Abel
Aiken
Alena Steam
Alma Steam
Amalgamated Steam
American Steam
American Steam Car
American Steamer
American Waltham
Ames
Anderson Steam Carriage
Anderson Steamer
Artzberger
Atlantic Steamer
Augusta
Aultman Steam
Austen/Austenius
Auto Supply
Autocrat Steam
Automobile

B

Badger Steam
Baker Steam
Baldwin Steam
Ball Steam
Banks
Bar Harbor
Barlow Steam
Barnes Steam Trap
Batchelder & Writner Steam
Battey & Crickler Steam
Battin Steam
Bauer Steam
Bean-Chamberlain
Belger & Bowker
Bentel
Billings
Binney & Burnham Steam
Black Steam
Blair Steamer
Blaisdell
Blanchard
Blevney Steamer
Bliss
Bluff Climber
Bobcat
Bohnet
Boss Steam Car
Boston Steamer
Bosworth
Boulding Steam
Brecht
Breer
Briner
Brooks
Brown Steam
Brown Touring Cart
Buel Steamer
Bullard Steam
Bundy
Burdette
Burgett & West Steam

C

Caffrey Steam
Calimobile
Cannon Steam Racer
Capitol Steam
Cardon
Carey
Carhart Steam
Carqueville
Carter Steam
Caswell
Central Steam
Century Steamer
Chandler Steam
Chapman

Mierley
Pugh
Reuter Steam
Skinner
Stoltenburg & Reimers
Zip
Des Moines
Cannon
Criterion
Des Moines
Des Moines Dazzler
Fageol
Iowa
Lagerquist
Marvel
Mason
Monarch
Morrison Electric
Road King
Sturges Electric
Wells
Dubuque
Adams-Farwell
Ft. Madison
De Loura
Gladbrook
Mann
Grinnell
Spaulding
Hampton
Accessible
Hobbie Accessible
Harlan
Nelson
Jessup
Richmond
Keokuk
Gate City
Le Mars
Crawford
Lu Verne
Leicher
Marathon
Swanson
Marshalltown
Marshalltown
Mason City
Colby
Muscatine
Littlemac
Newton
Foster
Osage
Frazee
Oskaloosa
States
Redfield
Nelson Electric
Sidney
Lybe
Sioux City
Sioux City
Villisca
Brelsford
Walcott
Blank & Schreiber
Waterloo
Arabian
Asquith
Caldwell
Dartmobile
Davis
Duryea
Farmer-Mobile
Fishback
Galloway
L.C.E.
Mason
Mason-Mohler
Maytag
Summit
W-G
Waterloo
Webster City
Smisor

KANSAS

Cherryvale
Cloughley
Columbus
Filby
Elmo
Klingberg
Fort Scott
Kite
Fredonia
Belt
Griffin
Galesburg
Shaw
Garden City
Withers
Hays
Bissing
Hiawatha
Adams
Average Man's Runabout
Cash
Hiawatha
Hutchinson
Brown Steam
Rexroad
Sellers
Kansas City
Kansas City Hummer
Stafford
Leavenworth
Bayer
Beyer

Mc Cracken
Half Breed
Mc Pherson
Temple
Miltondale
Shroyer
Moundridge
Krehbiel
Newton
Lester
Parson
Cloughley
Pleasanton
White Star
Randall
Brough
Topeka
Cole & Lang
Cotton
Great Smith
Mitchell
Smith
Stafford
Veracity
Westerner
Westport
Buening
Wichita
Jones
Preston
Walterscheid Steam
Wichita
Wichita Falls
Wichita Falls

KENTUCKY

Covington
Bowman
Hambrick
Henderson
Park
Hopkinsville
Caye-Jones
Lexington
Bayless
Dewabout
Louisville
Cold Air
Crown
Dixie Flyer
Edwards
Falls
Haller
Huddleston
Kentucky
Longest
Louisville
Preferred
Rommel
Rubel
Marysville
Brown
Newport
Miller-Peters
Owensboro
Ames
Owensboro
Southland

LOUISIANA

Cedar Grove
Bour-Davis
Donaldsonville
Donaldsonville
New Orleans
A.C.
Autocycle
Fairchild
Gardner
Judson
Landry
Mackenzie
Mino
Mohawk
New Orleans
Peteler
Rex
Simplicia

MAINE

Andover
French Steam
Auburn
Rowell
Augusta
Atlantic
Bangor
Automosled
Mc Laughlin
Bar Harbor
Bar Harbor
Boston Steamer
Standard Steam
Bath
Bath
Biddeford
Rylander
Bridgton
Walker Steam
Brunswick
Whitney Steam
Ellsworth
Parker
Hallowell
Rice Steam
Hollis
Fletcher Steam

Lewiston
Field Steam
Manning
Rand & Harvey Steam
Skene Steam
Mechanic Falls
Penney
Portland
Allyn
Auto King
Belknap
Bond
Bowker
Brackett
Burrowes
Chapman Electric
Choate
Davis
Fairfield
Gray
Morrell & Higgins
Stickney Steam
Suburban
Thompson Steam
Three Field's
Union
Rumford Falls
Bouton
Sanford
American Populaire
Rawnsley
South Berwick
Ideal Steamer
Springvale
Wentworth
Waterville
Lombard
Westbrook
Foster Steam
Westbrook

MARYLAND

Baltimore
Aiken
Ariel
Automobile
Baltimore
Calvert
Columbia Steam
Crouch
Equipose
Fisher
Harris
Lazenby
Lehnert
Lord Baltimore
Maryland
Maryland Electric
Schanken
Schaum
Shaffer
Sinclair
Snodeal
Spoerer
Steinmetz Electric
Thomas
Chestertown
Chestertown
Cumberland
Paragon
Stegmaier
Frederick
Maryland
Hagerstown
Aristocrat
Astor
Blue Light
Crawford
Dagmar
Five-Boro
Luxor
Paramount
Pope-Tribune
Twentieth Century
Havre De Grace
Burns
Hyattsville
C.B.
Carter Two-Engine
Cartermobile
Harvard
Hyattsville
Independence
Washington
Luke
Maryland Steam
Rockville
Cissel

MASSACHUSETTS

Abington
Buffum
Central Greyhound
Greyhound
Hall
Adams
Allen
Allston
Porter Steam
Amesbury
Amesbury
Bailey Electric
Boston-Amesbury
Carriage
Crown
England
Graves & Congdon
Little

Miller
Ultra
Andover
Andover
Arlington
Wetherbee
Athol
Benton
Richardson
Atlantic
Murray-Mac
Attleboro
Blake
Bliss
Buurrassa
Mossberg
United States
Beverly
Beverly
Cameron
Johnson
Upton
Woods & Philbrick Steam
Beverly Farms
Thompson
Billerica
Casey
Boston
Ajax
American Motor Sleigh
American Napier
American Power
American Rotary
Ariel
Austin
Autocraft
Automatic
Autowa
Back Bay
Bantam
Bay State
Beacon
Bean
Berlo
Binney & Burnham Steam
Boston Electric
Boston High Wheel
Bostonia
Butler
Clark Steam Car
Colonial
Commonwealth
Compressed Air
Cooley Steam
Country Club
Cricket
Cummings
Defiance
Duo
Eaton Electric
Equitable
Essex Steam
Forest
Gilmore Electric
Graham Steam
Grant
Griffiths
Hale
Hammett Steam
Henshaw
Holden
Intrepid
Kent's Pacemaker
Kimball
Leighton
Linscott
Lowe-Howard
Lugo Electric
Lyman
Lyman & Burnham
Maddocks
Mason
Mayfair
Mc Cullough
Mc Phail Steam
Mc Question Steam
Mohawk
Murray Electric
Murray Mac
New England
New England Electric
New England Steam
Nichols
Norcross
Norman Lionel
Ormond Steamer
Oxford
Panther
Perry
Pickard
Pixley
Quinsler
Radford
Razoux
Republican
Richmobile
Rogers
Rotary
S-J-R
Salvador
Salzman
Shaw
Shaw Steam
Sigma
Stranahan-Eldridge
Strathmore
Sturtevant
Suburban Steam
Suffolk
Thomas Steam

Victory
Viking
Whitney Steam
Worthley Steam
Brockton
Atlantic Steamer
Cameron
Leighton
Marsh
Pickard
Roader
Sterling
Brookline
Holtzer-Cabot
K-D
Knight
Quinlan
Cambridge
Berkshire
Cambridge
Cannon Steam Racer
Clark Steam
Crest
Crestmobile
Guaranty
Kennedy Steam
Norris
Chicopee Falls
Lamb
Overman
R & L
Rauch & Lang Electric
Stevens-Duryea
Victor Steam
Clinton
French
Concord
Boston Electric
Concord
Hancock
Danvers
Electronomic
Hood Steamer
Read
Romer
Simplex
Dedham
Shatswell Steam
Dorchester
Crestmobile
Dorchester
Hub
Mason Steam
Self-Contained
East Boston
Carroll
Easton
Eclipse Steam
Everett
Bangs & Butler
Everett Steam
Leach Steam
Lynn
Milne Steamer
Oxford
Fall River
Altham
Fitchburg
Stratton
Taylor
Framingham
Bay State
Luxor
Puritan
Standish
Temple-Westcott
Franklin
Darling Steam
Gloucester
Hodgkins Steamer
Proctor
Greenfield
Hertel
Oakman
Wing Midget
Haverhill
Essex
Foster
Hill
Improved
Hingham
Gardner Steam
Holliston
Cricket
Holyoke
Bassett
Burrington
Desmarais
Greuter
Holyoke
Matheson
Hopedale
Draper
Hudson
Knight Steam
Raymond
Hyde Park
Bramwell-Robinson
Lenox
Pope-Robinson
Robinson
Ipswich
Safety Steam
Jamaica Plain
Lenox
Martell
Napier
Lawrence
Hamblet
Kress

Lenox
  Mc Kay Steam
  O'Neil
  Stanley Steam
  Stanley-Whitney
Lenox
  Bradford
Lowell
  Automotor
  Lowell Automotor
  Lowell-American
  Norton
  Shaw
Lynn
  Essex
  General Electric
  Lemp Electric
  Lynn
  Malden Steamer
  Massachusetts
  Simonds Steam
  Stanley Steam Car
  Thomson
  Thomson Steam
Malden
  Malden Steam
Marlboro
  Marlboro
  Videx
  Wheeler
Medford
  Teel
  Waterman & Chamberlain
Melrose
  Heymann
Middleboro
  Maxim
Millville
  Aldrich
Natick
  Belger & Bowker
  Goodnow
  Northway
  Whitcomb
New Bedford
  Allen
  Jenney
  New Bedford
New Salem
  Climax
  T & F
Newburyport
  Curtis Steam
Newport
  Weaver
Newton
  Alma Steam
  Derr Steam
  Hopewell
  Morse
  Stanley Steam
Newtonville
  Ross Steamer
Northampton
  Englehart
  Warner Electric
Northboro
  Blair Steamer
Orange
  Grout
  New Home
  Red Arrow
  Weston Steam
Peabody
  Corwin
  Gas-Au-Lec
  Strout
Pittsfield
  Alden-Simpson
  Berkshire
  Cunningham
  Massachusetts Steam
  Moyea
  Sisson
  Stilson
Plymouth
  Rounds
Quincy
  Badger Steam
  Fore-River
  Griswold
  Kemp
  Lynn & Burman
  Peter Pan
Roxbury
  Austen/Austenius
  Roper Steam
Salem
  Cook
  Little Steamer
  Locke
  Packard
  Puritan Steam
  Waddington
Saugus
  Bosworth
Somerville
  Orcutt
  Pilgrim Steam
South Boston
  Anderson Steamer
South Easton
  Easton
  Morse
Southbridge
  Baker
Springfield
  Atkins Airmobile
  Atlas
  Atlas Knight

Automotor
Bailey
Barrett
Battey & Crickler Steam
Blanchard
Brewster
Bullard Steam
Duryea
E.L.M.
Hampden
Hendee
Indian
Knox
Martin
Med-Bow
Meteor
Midget
Morse Steam
Morse-Readio
Navarre
Orson
Riga
Rolls-Royce
Scoutomobile
Smith
Springfield
Springfield Steam
Sultan
Walkins
Warwick
Stoneham
  Courier
  Crouch
  Phelps
  Shawmut
Taunton
  Taunton
Waltham
  American Steam
  American Waltham
  Doble
  Metz
  New England Steam
  Nichols
  Orient
  Piper & Tinker
  Stanton Steam
  Tinker
  Waltham
  Waltham Steam
  Watch City Steam
  Wyeth
Ware
  Ruggles
Waterloo
  Menus-Van Horn
Watertown
  Locomobile
  Stanley
Wellington
  Hopkins
West Boylston
  Ovenden
West Gardner
  Gage Steam
West Newton
  American Steam Car
  Houghton
West Roxbury
  Flinn Steam
Westborough
  Macker
  Taft Steam
Westfield
  Loomis
  Moore Steamer
  Westfield
  Westfield Steam
Winchendon
  Fell
Winchester
  Goddu
Woburn
  Buel Steamer
Woodville
  Barnhard-Briggs
  Farrar
Worcester
  Acme
  Baker
  Burlingame
  Chase Steam
  Crompton
  Friction Drive
  Morgan
  Morgan Steam
  Pneumatic
  Pond
  R.L. Morgan
  Speirs
  Steele
  Taft Steam
  Thibert
  U.S. Mobile
  Woodland
  Woods

MICHIGAN

Adrian
  Adrian
  Hagaman
  Lamb & Vedder
  Lenawee
  Lion
  Lyon
  Murray
  Page
  Wilcox-Bachle

Albion
  Gale Steam
Allegan
  Cornelian
Alma
  Cameron
Alpena
  Alpena
Ann Arbor
  Ann Arbor
  Coffin Steamer
  Ferguson
  Koch
  Thomas
Battle Creek
  Bollstrom
  Horsey Horseless
  Nichols & Shepard
Bay City
  Oswald
Belding
  Jacquet Flyer
Belleville
  Jaeger
Benton Harbor
  Bendix
  Benton Harbor
Birmingham
  Oriental-Detroit
Buchanan
  Lee & Porter
  Morrison
Calumet
  Ingot
  Watson Electric
Charlevoix
  Elston
Charlotte
  Dolson
  E & T
  Evans
Chelsea
  Chelsea
  Flanders Electric
  Hollier
  Welch
  Welch Tourist
Cheyboygan
  Flagler
Coldwater
  Phoenix
  Shugers
Constantine
  Constantine
  Hawley
  Upton
Dearborn
  D-D
  Detroit-Dearborn
  Ford
  Graham
  Graham-Paige
  Mercury
  Nike
Detroit
  Abbott-Detroit
  Ackerman
  Aerocar
  Aetna
  Aland
  Alger
  American Benham
  American Electro-Mobile
  American Motorete
  Anderson Electric
  Anhut
  Annesley
  Arrow
  Auto-Cyclecar
  B.O.S.S.
  Barlow Steam
  Barnes
  Barthel
  Beau Brummel
  Belmobile
  Benham
  Beyster-Detroit
  Bi-Autogo
  Bi-Car
  Bingman
  Blodgett
  Blomstrom
  Blue
  Bour-Davis
  Breed
  Briggs
  Briggs-Detroiter
  Brooks
  Brotherton
  Brush
  Buick
  Cadillac
  Caille
  Car De Luxe
  Car-Nation
  Carhartt
  Carson
  Cartercar
  Cavac
  Central
  Century
  Century Electric
  Chalmers-Detroit/Chalmers
  Chevrolet
  Chief
  Chrysler
  Clark
  Collins Six
  Colonial Electric
  Columbia Six

Columbian Electric
Commerce
Commercial Electric
Corrick
Cox
Crescent
Cricket
Crowe Thirty
Crown
Cygnet
D.A.C.
D.H.K.
Da Vinci
Davis
Davis Steam
Day Utility
De Palma
De Soto
Dealers
Demot
Demotcar
Detroit
Detroit Electric
Detroit Speedster
Detroit Taxi
Detroiter
Diamond
Dingfelder
Doble
Dodge
Dodgeson
Dodo
Downing
Downing-Detroit
Dragon
Du Brie-Caille
  STIT
Eagle
Eagle Electric
Eclipse
Eco
Edison Electric
Electromobile
Engler
Essex
Eureka
Evans
Everett
Excel
Fanvien
Fargo
Faulkner-Blanchard
Fee-American
Finch Limited
Fischer-Detroit
Flanders Six
Flanders 20
Fuller
Gadabout
Gates
Gilmore
Globe
Goodspeed-Detroit
Gove
Grant
Gray
Gremel
Grinnell Electric
Griswold
Gyroscope
H & F Electric
H-C
Hamlin-Holmes
Hammer
Hammer-Sommer
Hart
Hastings
Hawk
Herreshoff
Herrman
Hilsendegen
Hoffman
Hooper
Horton Autoette
House
Howard
Huber
Hudson
Hupmobile
Hupp-Yeats
Huron
Hussey
Imperial Electric
Independence
J P L
Jewett
Keeton
Kelly
Kermath
Kerston
Kess-Line
Kessler
King
King-Remick
Kinsey
Kirby
Knapp
Koehler Electric
Kosmath
Krass
Krit
Kull
L'Esperance
La Petite
La Salle
La Vigne
Lauer
Lee
Leslie
Liberty

Liberty Brush
Light Six
Lincoln
Lincoln Highway
Little Detroit
Little Four Steam
Little Mystery
Little Princess
Lotz
Lozier
M.C.C. Six
Mahs
Malcolm
Malcomson
Marr
Marsh
Marvel
Massnick-Phipps
Masterbilt Six
Maxwell
Mc Crary
Mc Hardy
Mercury
Meredith
Metzger
Michigan Six
Miller
Monarch
Morse
Nash
National Cyclecar
Nelson
Nielson
Noble
Northern
Oldsmobile
Owen
P.E.T.
Packard
Paige
Paige-Detroit
Palmer
Paragon
Peck
Pennsy
Perkins
Phipps Electric
Phipps-Grinnell
Pilgrim
Pioneer
Plymouth
Princess
Pungs-Finch
Queen
R.C.H.
R.M.C.
R-O
Racine
Radford Light Car
Rands
Read
Red Shield
Regal
Reliance
Rex
Rickenbacker
Rockne
Ross
Russel
S & M
S.E.M.
S.R.K.
Saginaw Speedster
Sampson
Savage
Saxon
Schneider
Scripps-Booth
Seabrook-R.M.C.
Sharp
Shaw Brothers
Sibley
Silent Northern
Simon
Simpson
Small
Snoburner
Sommer
Spider
Squires
Stanley
States
Steely
Still
Stoops
Storms Electric
Stout Scarab
Strouse
Suburban
T.H.T.
Templeton-Dubrie
Terraplane
Thomas-Detroit
Tiger
Titan
Tom Thumb
Trask Steam
Traveler
Tribune
True Blue
Trumbull
Tyro
Unique
United
Usborne
Varsity
Ver Linden
Vernon 30
Wachman
Waco-Schaffer

Custer Electric
Darling
Dayton
Dayton Electric
Dayton Steam
Elliot
Garrison
Geyer
Heatherman
J.L.B.
Kepler-Beery
Kero-Car
Lang
Mc Duffee
Mead
Meeker
Speedwell
Spencer
Stoddard-Dayton
Stutz
Thresher Electric
Victor
Whitmore
Wright
Defiance
Defiance
Highway
Krotz Gas-Electric
Delaware
Cook
Eaton
Cyriacks
Washington
Elyria
Elyria
Falcon-Knight
Garford
Troxel
Weller
Findlay
Adams
Bennett
Differential
Findlay
Grant
Gulliford
Fostoria
Allen
Fostoria
Seneca
Fremont
Fremont
Lehr
Galion
Ditwiler
Fetzger
Howard
Garfield
Bobcat
Mac Donald Steam
Geneva
Ewbank
Ewing
Geneva
Geneva Steam
Heifner
Granville
Witter
Greenfield
Patterson-Greenfield
Greenville
Dunkle
Hamilton
Advance
Columbia Motor Buggy
Hamilton
Republic
Ritchie
Kenton
Miller Electric
Lancaster
Dum
Leipsig
Koeb-Thompson
Lima
Coe
Independence
Leach
Lima
Lima Roadster
Worldmobile
Lorain
Carroll Six
Lorain
Mansfield
Darling
Forth
Richland
Marietta
Kent
Marion
Marion
Stringer
Sweney
Zent
Marysville
Marysville
Tarkington
Turner
Massillon
Boss
Croxton-Keeton
Jewell
Kessell
Massillon
Reed
Schworm Steam
Miamisburg
Buggyabout
Catrow

Hatfield
Kauffman
Middletown
Mc Adams
Merkel
Miami
Middletown
Moyea
Ramapaugh Steamer
Washington
Millersburg
Spahr
Millersville
Millersville
Mount Gilead
Cook
Mount Healthy
Markert
Napoleon
Napoleon
Ragan
Reya
New Athens
Burdette
New Bremen
Case
New Carlisle
Credlebaugh
New Concord
Steel-Mobile
New London
Healy Steam
New London
Post
Newark
Falcon
Halladay
Norwalk
Auto-Bug
Norwalk
Sly Steam
Ottawa
Krebs
Painesville
Erie
Vulcan
Piqua
Meteor
Mort
Plymouth
Plymouth
Portsmouth
Robe
Prospect
Prospect
Wottring
Ravenna
Byers
Riddle
Saint Paris
Brockshire & Robinson
Sandusky
Barnes
Caswell
Courier
Eagle-Macomber
Maibohm
Ogontz
Roberts
Sandusky
Servitor
Underwood
Sebring
Sebring
Shelby
Darling
Mansfield
Shelby
Sidney
Bimel
Bremac
Elco
Elwood
Springfield
Bramwell
Brenning
Foos
Frayer-Miller
Kelly Steam
Koeb-Thompson
Krotz Electric
Kuqua
Kuqua
Mc Nutt
Owens Steam
Russell-Springfield
Springfield
Westcott
Tiffin
Economy
Economy-Vogue
Hollis Electric
Vogue
Toledo
Allen & Clark
American Juvenile
Apperson-Toledo
Belmont Six
Bissell
Burwell
Car Deluxe
Carl Electric
Clark Electric
Consolidated
Cooney
Craig-Toledo
Cyclomobile
De Luxe
Dennis
Dusseau

Greyhound
Harruff
Hyslop
International
Interstate
Juvenile Electric
Kirk
Kirk-Snell
Lawrence
Lecklider
Macinnis Electric
Milburn Electric
National Juvenile
Odelot
Ohio Electric
Overland
Pilliod
Pope-Toledo
Rossel
Sun
Sypher
Tillotson
Todd
Toledo
Toledo Electric
Whippet
Willys
Willys-Knight
Yale
Trail
Miller
Trotwood
Niswender
Troy
Stanley
Upper Sandusky
U.S. Runabout
Wakeman
Brenenstul & Carpenter
Warren
Colonial Six
Hitchcock
Packard
Pendleton
Sterling Knight
Supreme
Valley
Western Reserve
Warrensville
Brice
Wash. Court House
Swope
Westerville
Paine
Scharf Gearless
Willoughby
Ben Hur
Winchester
Hydromobile
Xenia
Baldner
Jones
Xenia
Youngstown
Drury-Wells
Falcon
Flynn
Fredonia
Glenwood
Mahoning
Wick

OKLAHOMA

El Reno
Bonebrake-Roberts
Pioneer
W.R.C.
Enid
Geronimo
Manchester
Buckles
Muskogee
Midland
Scout
Oklahoma City
Mc Coole-Mercer
Midland
Nation
Northwest
Oklahoma Six
Pioneer
Tulsa
Tulsa

OREGON

Hillsboro
Menkenns
Portland
Beaver
Diehl
Gill
Portland
Redmond
Sheldon

PENNSYLVANIA

Allegheny
Artzberger
Pittsburgh Steamer
Allentown
Havana
Ideal
Nadig

Ambridge
Ardmore
Autocar
Krupp
Avonia
Stone & Maynard
Beaver Falls
Bauer Steam
Beavertown
Eureka
Kearns
Lulu
Bellefonte
Bellefonte
Berwick
Multiplex
Myers
Bethlehem
Bethlehem
Ideal
Peters
Bradford
Holley
Brookville
Twyford
Bryn Mawr
Pennsylvania
Butler
American Austin
American Bantam
Butler
Huselton
Standard
Carlisle
Bridges
Tractobile
Catawissa
Schmick
Cherryville
Frantz Steam
Chester
Mc Murtry
Pennsylvania
Connellsville
American Locomotor
Baldwin Steam
Locomotor
Paragon
Dillsburg
Bauman
Doylestown
Winslow
Du Bois
Keystone Six
East Pittsburgh
Auto-Bob
Erie
Hagenlocher
Le Jeal
Le Jeal
Payne-Modern
Everett
Karns
Fleetwood
Hill Steam
Flourtown
Jennis
Freedom
Headland
Greensburg
Airland
Greenville
Empire
Fay
Greenville
Hamburg
Tampsen
Hanover
Hanover
Harrisburg
Herman
Hunter
Kline
Hazleton
Deemster
Johnstown
Johnstown
Trabold
Kline
B.C.K.
Lancaster
K & M
Keystone
Kramer
Kreider
Safety
Wenger
Lebanon
Keystone Steamer
Lebanon
New Willar
Riviera
Upton
Lenover
Chalfant
Lewistown
Belmont
Falcon
Moller
Spangler
Lock Haven
Feerrar
Mahony City
Berwick
Manheim
Bailey Electric
Manheim
Manyunck
General Electric

Mc Keesport
Oberlin
Meadville
Randall Steam
Thompson-Kanter
Mechanicsburg
Madden
Media
Media
Meyersdale
Gurley
Miller Steam
Milton
Ritter
Moore
Du Pont
Morrisville
Wildman
New Brighton
Brighton
Crouch
New Castle
Bacon
Courtney
New Castle
New Cumberland
Wright
New Kensington
Fort Pitt
Pittsburgh Six
Silent
Vanderbilt
Newtown
Doan
Randall Three-Wheeler
Oakland
Speed-Well
Oil City
Reynolds
Oxford
Murdaugh
Oxford
Parkin
Palmerton
Pickford
Philadelphia
Adelphia
Albertson
Allen
Asprooth-Leoni Electric
Autocycle
Automobile Construction
Automotive
Baker-Bell
Barlow
Bartlett
Bergdoll
Biddle
Bigelow
Brazier
Carlson-Wenstrom
Carroll
Chadwick
Clark Electric
Corinthian
Devon
Diebel
Dolan
Dragon
Duryea
Electrobat
Erwin
Evans Steam Amphibian
Fortman
Foss-Hughes
Fournier-Searchmont
Fox
Frankford
Fulton & Walker
Gas-Electric
Gilmore
Godshall
Gregg
Halsey
Hess
Hummingbird
Hunter Electric
Imperial
Johnson Steam
Jones
Jones-Corbin
Kelsey
Kendel
Kennedy Electric
Keystone
Konollman
La Roche
Land Yacht
Lengert
Lewis
Liliputian
Louis
Mecky
Mercury
Meteor
Morris & Salom Electric
Muller
Nance
Otto
Ottomobile
Peters Tricar
Peters-Walton
Pitcairn
Pocock
Praul
Pyott Steam
Quaker City
Rech
Rech-Marbaker
Remington Dart

Renno-Leslie
Roach
Rudolph
Rush
S.S.E.
Schwarz
Searchmont
Sproehle
Standard
Standard G.E.
Standard Steam
Static
Thompson
Touraine
Turner
Vandegrift
Victor
Vim
W.F.S.
Wall
Wilmot
Pittsburgh
Aero Auto Bob
Alpine
Atlas
Banker Juvenile
Belden
Bentel
Co-Operative
Dixon
Duquesne
Ehrentraut
Empire
Gearless Steam
Geber
Hipwell
Iron City
Iverson
Keystone
Lancaster
Mills Steam
Morse
Murray
New Pittsburgh
Penn
Pennsy
Pittsburgh
Pittsburgh Six
Rex Buckboard
Seely
Senator
Standard
Synnestvedt Electric
Twyford
Westinghouse
Wilkie-Groetsch
Winterton
Plymouth
Reese
Pottstown
Chadwick
Champion
Direct Drive
Grubb
Light Steamer
Mel Special
W-G
Quakertown
Quakertown
Reading
Acme
Bertolet
Boss Steam Car
Daniels
Dile
Duryea
Eck
Edie Mac
Fries
Meteor Steam
Middleby
Raleigh
Reading
Reading Steamer
Reber
Relay
S.G.V.
Schnader
Speed-Well
Xander
Yocum
Scranton
Collins Electric
Scranton
Winters
Sharon
Driggs-Seabury
Ritz
Sharon
Sinking Spring
Blimline
Strasburg
Carroll
Sunbury
Thurston
Tarentum
Baker
Towanda
Towanda Electric
Tyrone
Neil
Uniontown
Johnston
Valley Forge
De Motte
Warren
Allegheny
Barnhart & Betts
Jamieson
Warren

Washington
Croxton
Universal
West Chester
Black Steam
Warrington
West Homestead
Doyle
Homestead
West Salisbury
Knecht
Wilkes-Barre
C.R.G.
Matheson
Owen Magnetic
Palmer Singer
Sheldon
Williamsport
Harris
Imperial
Luxor
Stutzman
Tivy Steam
Williamsport
York
Bell
Broomell
Hamilton
Hardinge
Kline Kar
Martin
Meisenhelder
Mount Wolf
Pullman
Pullman Six-Wheeler
Riess Royal
Sphinx
Victor
York

RHODE ISLAND

Bristol
Novara
Cranston
Maxwell
East Warren
Greyhound
Knightsville
Hughes & Atkin
Newport
Newport
Olneyville
Atkin
Hughes & Atkin
Thompson
Pawtucket
Maxwell
Moncrief Steam
Pawtucket Electric
Pawtucket Steam
Scholze
Providence
Alco
American Berliet
American Locomotive
Baldwin Steam
Cameron
Campbell Electric
Central Steam
Cross Steam
Cruickshank
Economycar
Hughes & Atkin
King Steamer
Manton Steam
Max
Page
Roberts Steam
Vera
Warren
Stonington
Brown Steam
Westerly
Cycleplane
Woonsocket
Dylande
Woonsocket

SOUTH CAROLINA

Aiken
Hofmann
Chester
Hough
Clemson
Barnes
Columbia
South Carolina
Greenville
Cyclone
Mountain City
Victor
W.B.C.
Rock Hill
Anderson
Mc Fadden
Rock Hill
Spartanburg
Long
Winston-Salem
H.E.

SOUTH DAKOTA

Aberdeen
Garicar

Huron
Reese Aero-Car
Pierre
Pierre
Sioux Falls
Fawick Flyer
Silent Sioux
Woonsocket
Callihan

TENNESSEE

Chattanooga
Chattanooga
Nyberg
Jackson
Marathon
Knoxville
Biddle
Blevins
Drake
Memphis
Falcon
Memphis
Southern Six
Tri-State
Nashville
Cloyd
Cyclette
Harding
Hermitage
Marathon
Mc Ewen
Volunteer
Tullahoma
Sherrill & Smith

TEXAS

Cleburne
Chaparral
Cleburne
Luck Utility
Columbus
Zip
Comanche
Holden
Dallas
Texas
Wharton
Fort Worth
Fort Worth
Mc Gill
Texan
Grand Prairie
Little Kar
Texmobile
Houston
Blackburn
Brandon
Dixie
Gearhart
Hawkins
Imperial
Magnolia
Model
Mosehart & Keller
Ranger
Lockhart
Seeliger
Orange
Blumberg
San Antonio
Lone Star
Lutz
Reuter Electric
Robertson
San Antonio
Stroud
Tex
Waco
Hall
Wichita Falls
Lane
Wichita

UTAH

Ogden
Ogden
Salt Lake City
Autocrat Steam
Cawley
Clover
Royalmobile
Wasatch

VERMONT

Barre
Lane & Daley Steam
Bellows Falls
Gregory
Bennington
Martin Wasp
Wasp
Brattleboro
Gore
Montpelier
Williams
Poultney
Mahana
Rutland
Archer
Frenier
Willard Steam

Springfield
Rae Electric
St Johnsbury
Ranlet
Westminster Station
Abenaque

VIRGINIA

Alexandria
American
Basic City
Dawson Auto-Mobile
Mc Nabb & Chapman
Hampton Roads
Gumher
Lynchburg
Piedmont
Nansemond
Robe
Norfolk
Coburn
Godwin & Wrenn
Richmond
Alsop
Binate
Coffee
Cub
Grasberger
Henrico
Kline Kar
Victor
Virginian
Wood & Meagher
South Boston
Barbour
Staunton
Falcon

WASHINGTON

Chehalis
Farnsworth
Colfax
Carley
Harrington
Inland
Renton
Pacific
Seattle
Seattle
Ajax
Articmobile
Beattie
Columbia
Elbert
Eureka
Hawkins
Hydromobile
Northwestern
Pacific
Schram
Shamrock Junior
Simplicity Six
Tilikum
Totem
Waco
Yukon
Spokane
Acme
Churchill
Olive
Spokane
Spokane Steam
Tacoma
Carr
Friddle
Gersix
Walla Walla
Guichard & Peck
Moore
Yakima
Flying Dutchman
Gauntt

WEST VIRGINIA

Charleston
Remington
Clarksburg
Osborn
Huntington
Enslow
Hambrick
Jarvis-Huntington
Keystone
Mc Dowell
Martinsburg
Norwalk
Stork-Kar
Morgantown
Chaplin
Humbert
Sistersville
Pierce Steamer
Wheeling
Hearne
Sheets

WISCONSIN

Appleton
Brill
Eagle
Kunz

Baraboo
Farnum
Lanich
Beloit
E.Z. Go-Cart
Lipman
Rocoit
Berlin
Brewer
Deibler
Schaefer
Brodhead
Brodhead
Chippewa Falls
Chippewa
Clintonville
Badger
Battleship
Besserdich & Zachow
F.W.D.
Four Wheel Drive
Zachow & Besserdich
Columbus
Badger
Eau Claire
Burdick
Darwin
Fond Du Lac
Abel
Cleaver
Hibbard & Bush
Nachtwey
Oriole
Green Bay
Anheuser
Hartford
Kissel
Lever
Ruxton
Janesville
Monitor
Owen-Thomas
Samson
Wisco
Juneau
Juno
Kenosha
Badger Steam
Earl
Harding
Jeffery
Nash
Petrel
Rambler
Sieg
True
Winther
Kiel
Kiel
Kilbourn
Kilbourn
Marshall
Kohler
Brotz Special
La Crosse
Hofweber
James
Lake Geneva
Classic
Logansville
Klondike
Madison
Cruiser
Keen
Ritter
Manitowoc
Beutel
Richards
Sooner
Marinette
Marinette
Thayer
Marshfield
Lang & Scharmann
Marshfield
Menasha
Harris Six
Milwaukee
A.E.C.
Abresch
Albrecht
Anger
Auto-Carriage
Automobile Construction
B. & P.
Beaver
Billiken
Brenkel-Anger
Briggs & Stratton
Cheney
Christensen
Eagle
Earl
Eclipse
Elite
Empress
Evinrude
F.S.
Fast
Four Wheel Drive
Francke
Haase
Haushalter
Hay-Berg
Hyde
Ideal
Iverson
Johnson
Jonas
Krueger

1556

Kunz
La Fayette
Leader
Mack
Majestic
Merkel
Middleton
Milwaukee
Milwaukee Star
Milwaukee Steam
Moehn
Monarch
Mueller
National
Neldner
Odenbrett
Ogren
Petrel
Reinertson
Rosenbauer

Schloemer
Schuel
Schuler
Shaver Steam
Smith Flyer
Speedwell
Splitt
Superior
United States Steam
Vixen
Waite
Ward
Wisconsin
Wisconsin Steam
Woodsmobile
Monroe
  E-Z Go-Cart
North Milwaukee
  Mc Kaig
  Meiselbach

Oostburg
  Time
Oshkosh
  Ballard
  Clark-Hatfield
  Doman
  National
  Neville
  Oshkosh Steam
  Radford
  T.M.
  T.M.F.
  Termaat & Monahan
  Ziebell
Racine
  Ajax
  Brietzke
  Carhart Steam
  Case
  Holbrook-Armstrong

Howell
Imhof
L.P.C.
Lewis
Maibohm
Mitchell
Pennington
Pierce-Racine
Piggins
Racine-Sattley

Rice Lake
  Field
Ripon
  Russell-Deibler
Sheboygan
  Falls
  Optenberg
Sun Prairie
  Milwaukee Steamer

Superior
  Superior
Watertown
  Hafemeister
Waukesha
  Hodgson
  Waukesha
Waupun
  Zimmermann
Wequiock
  Green Bay
West Superior
  Superior

WYOMING

Cheyenne
  House
Laramie
  Lovejoy

1557

BEVERLY RAE KIMES
HISTORIAN & AUTHOR

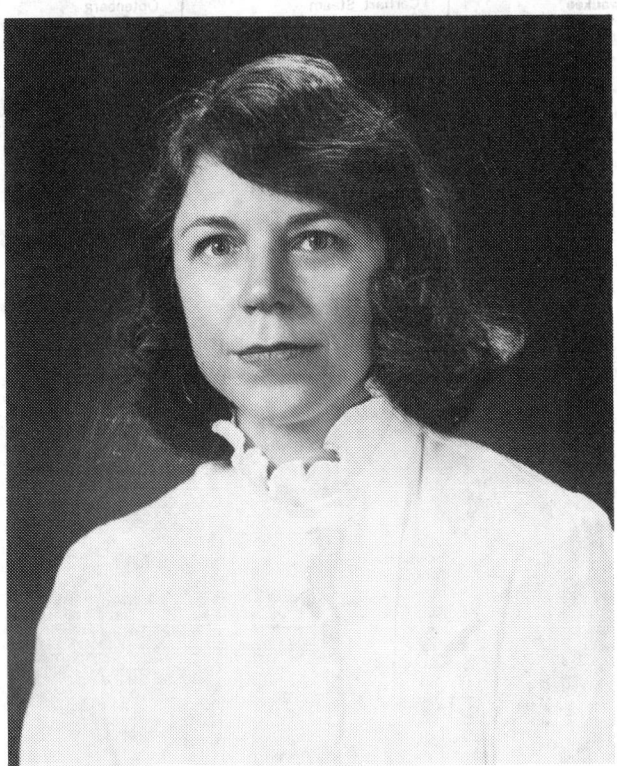

Beverly Rae Kimes

Following graduation from Pennsylvania State University in 1963, Beverly Rae Kimes joined *Automobile Quarterly* and wrote her first story about the Curved Dash Oldsmobile. She has been hooked on old cars ever since, with an especial interest in American automobiles of the pre-World War II era.

During her 18 years with *AQ*, Beverly authored or edited over 20 books, including works on Ford, Chevrolet, Lincoln, Oldsmobile, Packard and Buick. Her articles ranged from high wheelers to boattail speedsters and marques, literally, from A to Z (the Adams-Farwell of Dubuque to the Zip cyclecar of Davenport). Currently editor for the Classic Car Club of America, Beverly continues to write articles and books in the field of automotive history. The book you are holding has been the biggest challenge of her career.

A five-time winner of the Cugnot Award of the Society of Automotive Historians, Beverly has also won the Thomas McKean Trophy of the Antique Automobile Club of America three times and has been a three-time Moto Award winner of the National Association of Automotive Journalism. In 1986 she received the Friend of Automotive History Award of the Society of Automotive Historians; in 1988 she was elected its president. Her board memberships include the Milestone Car Society, the Auburn-Cord-Duesenberg Museum and the International Coordinating Committee for the National Automotive History Collection of the Detroit Public Library.

MUSEUMS IN AMERICA

ALABAMA

The Vintage Motor Museum
850 Government
Mobile, AL 36602

ALASKA

Alaska Historical & Transportation
Museum
Box 920
Palmer, AL 99645

ARIZONA

Hall of Fame Museum
6101 E. Van Buren
Phoenix, AZ 85008

ARKANSAS

The Museum of Automobiles
Petit Jean Mountain
Morrilton, AK 72110

CALIFORNIA

Concours Motorcars
619 E. Fourth St.
Santa Ana, CA 92703

Firehouse Museum
1972 Columbia Street
San Diego, CA 92117

Los Angeles Museum of
Natural History - Exposition Park
900 Exposition Blvd.
Los Angeles, CA 90007

Merle Norman Classic Beauty Collection
15180 Bledsoe Street
San Sylmar, CA 91342

Movieland Wax Museum
P.O. Box 5130
7711 Beach Boulevard
Buena Park, CA 90602

Millers Horse & Buggy Ranch
9425 Yosemite Blvd.
Modesto, CA 95351

National Maritime Museum
Hyde Street Pier
San Francisco, CA 94100

Metropolitan Historical Collection
5330 Laurel Canyon Boulevard
North Hollywood, CA 91607

Wagons to Wings Museum
15060 Foothill Road
Morgan Hill, CA 95037

Toyota Museum
1901 South Western Avenue
Torrance, CA 90509

Blackhawk Auto Collection
1975 San Ramon Valley Boulevard
San Ramon, CA 94583

COLORADO

Dougherty Museum Collection
8382 1075h Street
Longmont, CO 80501

Forney Transportation Museum
1416 Platte
Denver, CO 80200

Front Wheel Drive Auto Museum
250 North Main Street
Brighton, CO 80601

Ghost Town
Corner of Highway 24 West & 21st Street
Colorado Springs, CO 80907

CONNECTICUT

Hartford Automobile Club
815 Farmington Avenue
West Hartford, CT 06119

Museum of Connecticut History
231 Capitol Avenue
Hartford, CT 06115

DELAWARE

Delaware Agricultural Museum
866 North Dupont Highway
Dover, DE 19901

Memours Mansion & Gardens
P.O. Box 109
Rockland Road
Wilmington, DE 19899

DISTRICT OF COLUMBIA

Smithsonian Institution
14th & Constitution
Washington, D.C. 20560

FLORIDA

Bellm Cars & Music of Yesterday
5500 North Tamiami Trail
Sarasota, FL 33577

Elliott Museum
Hutchinson Island
Stuart, FL 33494

Silver Springs Antique Car Collection
State Road 40
Ocala, FL 32670

The Birthplace of Speed Museum
160 East Franada Boulevard
Ormond Beach, FL 32074

GEORGIA

Antique Auto & Music Museum
Stone Mountain Memorial Park
Sonte Mountain, GA 30088

IDAHO

Grant's Antique Cars & Museum
5603 Franklin Road
Boise, ID 83705

Idaho State Historical Society
Transportation Museum
Boise, ID 83705

Vintage Wheel Museum
218 Cedar Street
Sandpoint, ID 83864

ILLINOIS

Gasoline Alley
c/o Hitchin-Post Inn
1765 N. Milwaukee
Libertyville, IL 60048

Fagan's Antique & Classic Automobile
Museum
162nd Street & Clairmont Avenue
Markham, IL 60426

Grant Hills Antique Auto Museum
U.S. Highway 20
Galena, IL 61036

Hartung's Automotive Museum
3623 West Lake Street
Glenview, IL 60025

Lazarus Motor Museum
Box 368
211 Walnut St.
Forreston, IL 61030

Martin's Antique Automobile Museum
R.R. 1
Route 16
Metamora, IL 61548

Museum of Science & Industry
57th & Lakeshore Drive
Chicago, IL 60637

The Time Was Village Museum
U.S. Highway 51-52
Mendota, IL 61342

Volo Antique Auto Museum & Village
Route 120
Volo, IL 60073

Quinsippi Auto Museum
All America City Park
Quincy, IL 62301

INDIANA

Auburn - Cord - Duesenberg Museum
1600 South Wayne Street
Auburn, IN 46706

Early Wheels Museum
817 Wabash Avenue
Terre Haute, IN 47801

Elwood Haynes Museum
1915 South Webster Street
Kokomo, IN 46902

Indianapolis Motor Speedway & Hall of
Fame Museum
4790 West 16th Street
Speedway, IN 46224

Museum of Transportation &
Communication
P.O. Box 83
Forest Park
Noblesville, IN 46060

Plew's Indy 500 Museum, Inc.
9648 West Morris Street
Indianapolis, IN 46231

Bill Goodwin Museum
757 South Harrison St.
Frankfort, IN 46041

Studebaker National Museum
TWO LOCATIONS:
520 S. Lafayette St.

120 South St. Joseph St.
South Bend, IN 46600

IOWA

Auto Museum
Sioux Center, IA 51250

Don Jensen Museum
411 4th Ave.
N. Humbolt, IA 50548
1562

Iowa State Historical Museum
East 12th & Grand Avenue
Des Moines, IA 50319

Van Horn's Truck Museum
Highway 65
Mason City, IA 50401

KANSAS

Kansas State Historical Society Museum
120 West Tenth Street
Topeka, KS 66612

Van Arnsdale Antique
Highway 50
Macksville, KS 67557

LOUISIANA

Cars of Yesteryear Museum
P.O. Box 15080
12137 Airline Highway
Baton Rouge, LA 70801

Firefighters Museum
427 Laurel St.
Baton Rouge, LA 70801

MAINE

Boothbay Auto Museum
Box 123
Route 27
Boothbay, ME 04537

The Owls Head Transportation Museum
Box 277
Knox County Airport
Owls Head, ME 04854

Stanley Museum
PO Box 280
Kingfield, ME 04947

Wells Auto Museum
Route 1
Wells, ME 04090

MARYLAND

Fire Museum of Maryland
1301 York Road
Lutherville, MD 21093

U.S. Army Ordnance Museum
Aberdeen Proving Ground, MD 21005

MASSACHUSETTS

Heritage Plantation Auto Museum
Grove & Pine Streets
Sandwich, MA 02563

Sturbridge Auto Museum
P.O. Box 486
Sturbridge, MA 01566

Museum of Transportation
Larz Anderson Park
15 Newton St.
Brookline, MA 02146

MICHIGAN

Alfred P. Sloan Museum
1221 E. Kearsley Street
Flint, MI 48500

Automotive Hall of Fame, Inc.
P.O. Box 1742
Northwood Institute
Midland, MI 48640

Detroit Historical Museum
5401 Woodward
Detroit, MI 48202

Gilmore/CCCA Car Museum
6865 Hickory Road
Hickory Corners, MI 49060

Henry Ford Museum & Greenfield Village
P.O. Box 1970
20900 Oakwood Boulevard
Dearborn, MI 48120

Poll Museum of Transportation
353 East Sixth Street
Holland, MI 49423

R.E. Olds Museum
240 Museum Drive
Lansing, MI 48933

Domino's Rearview Mirror
3815 Plaza Drive
Ann Arbor, MI 48108

Pontiac Museum
c/o John Sawruk
One Pontiac Plaza
Pontiac, MI 48053

MINNESOTA

Roaring 20's Auto Museum
Highway 55
Brooten, MN 56316

MISSISSIPPI

Frank's Museum and Antiques
Highway 45 South
Booneville, MS 38829